THE COMPLETE WORKS OF SHAKESPEARE

Editorial Advisory Board

THE COMPLETE WORKS OF SHAKESPEARE

THIRD EDITION

EDITED BY

DAVID BEVINGTON

THE UNIVERSITY OF CHICAGO

SCOTT, FORESMAN AND COMPANY GLENVIEW, ILLINOIS

LONDON, ENGLAND

For Steve, Kate, and Sarah, and in memory of Philip.

Library of Congress Cataloging in Publication Data

Shakespeare, William, 1564–1616.
The complete works of Shakespeare.

Bibliography: p. 1676
Includes index.
I. Bevington, David M.
PR2754.B4 822.3'3 79-22390
ISBN 0-673-15193-X

Printed in the United States of America.
5678910-VHJ-8584

Cover: Engraving by Martin Droeshout from the First Folio, 1623.
Courtesy of the Trustees, The British Museum.

Endsheets: Map of London attributed to Georg Höfnagel, in *Civitates Orbis Terrarum,* 1572.
Guildhall Library, London.

Preface

A new edition of Shakespeare requires justification, if only because many people, including some teachers, suppose that the text of Shakespeare was established many years ago and that one edition differs from another merely in unimportant details. In fact, the preparation of texts is a constantly evolving art, and for no author is this more true than for Shakespeare. The sheer volume of criticism on his work, some of it repetitive and bad but much of it significant, continues to alter our view of what he wrote, both in the sense of how his words are to be interpreted, and in the literal sense of what words he committed to paper. In my 1973 revision of this volume, I was able to do much that was needed in the way of reediting play texts and incorporating recent scholarship. Since the text was not entirely reset, however, I was unable to make some of the changes that I wanted to make. Both the publisher and I have felt the need for a completely new resetting; hence this Third Edition. The following details about the revision in this edition should be of interest to those using this book for the first time as well as to the many users of the previous edition.

Organization of the Volume. After long consideration, I have abandoned the earlier ordering of the plays into various chronological periods in favor of a grouping by comedies, histories, tragedies, and romances. The present organization is close to that of the First Folio, and is also to be found in a number of modern editions. Within each genre, the plays are arranged in approximate chronological order. Shakespeare's non-dramatic writing is gathered in one poetry section that follows at the end of the plays. The poetry includes both major and minor poems as well as the *Sonnets.*

I have not included *The Two Noble Kinsmen,* though it very probably contains some scenes by Shakespeare among others by John Fletcher, and offers some useful insight into Shakespeare's latest work. In my judgment the play is not predominantly Shakespearean as all the rest (including *Pericles*) appear to be. For the same reason I have not included the fragment of *Sir Thomas More* which Shakespeare probably wrote; the fragment appears to be his, but the play as a whole is not. Such works deserve to be read and studied, but not necessarily to be included in a complete edition.

Text. Hardin Craig's text of the first edition of *The Complete Works of Shakespeare* was based on the Globe edition of 1864, though a considerable number of readings had been altered throughout. In my 1973 revision, I preserved some accidental features of the Globe text such as its English spellings *(labour, judgement)* and its style of punctuation, but I reedited the play texts conservatively on the basis of the preferred copy texts for each work. The changes were extensive although the physical appearance of the page remained much the same; many individual lines and passages were reset, and in some instances entire plays, although the book as a whole was not reset and the typeface remained the same.

The present edition has been reset throughout, enabling me and a panel of editorial advisors to reconsider every aspect of editing in fundamental terms. Some of the most visible changes have to do with style and format; as I have indicated, many substantive changes, "unediting" the Globe text by a return to the readings of the original, were introduced in 1973. This present edition features expanded speech prefixes to avoid confusion of such abbreviations as *Cas., Casca,* and *Caes.* (Cassius, Casca, and Caesar) in *Julius Caesar* or *Lucul.* (Lucullus) and *Luc.* (either Lucius or Lucilius) in *Timon of Athens.* The column of text is designed to be open and to afford room for notetaking. I have lightened the punctuation throughout in accordance with modern practice, always, to be sure with an eye on the copy text. Capitalization follows normal usage. In these matters, and in spelling, my hope has been to make the text seem as available and unmysterious as possible for the modern reader. Although poetic contractions such as *lov'd, rend'red, fall'n, t' account, y' are, th' art, spak'st,* and *'a* (for *he*) are necessary to indicate scansion of the verse (or at least seem less intrusive to me than the alternative system of marking sounded vowels, as in *condemnèd),* I have tried generally to present Shakespeare's language in a familiar modern form. In prose I have used contractions like *lov'd* and *turn'd* as the normal form, except for certain "humorous" characters like Don Armado or Fluellen whose idiosyncratic speech may have preferred the lengthened form; in poetry I have followed the copy text except where it appears to be in error.

Spelling has been modernized in accord with American practice. It seems to me that little is gained from spelling *murder* as *murther, struck* as *strook, fifth* as *fift, shrew* as *shrow, Bolingbroke* as *Bullingbrook;* a recovery of Shakespeare's pronunciation from a largely modernized text is impossible in any case, and where occasionally a pun or rhyme is obscured by modern spelling, an explanatory note is preferable to the sometimes aribtrary introduction of archaic forms. It is difficult to maintain precisely a dividing line in any system of modernization, but I have tried to keep such inconsistencies to a minimum, and have preferred modern spellings where I could.

Speech prefixes are normalized as well as expanded. Normalization in some instances deprives the reader of colorful variation and insight into the personality of a dramatic character like Capulet's Wife in *Romeo and Juliet,* who is variously referred to as Wife, Mother, Old Lady, and Lady, but normalization surely reduces confusion. In *Romeo and Juliet* I have chosen "Capulet's Wife" as the normalized form, since Capulet is not aristocrat and his wife is addressed as "lady" only in the polite sense of "my lady mother." To our ears, "Lady Capulet" suggests a higher rank than she can claim. I have differentiated supernumeraries by calling various servants "First Servant," "Second Servant," and the like. All such changes, made without indication by square brackets, are recorded in the textual notes. I have tried to rethink the *dramatis personae* placed at the head of each play, following the style of those that survive from our early texts even though they may not be Shakespeare's own.

Indications of place for each scene, previously located in the column of text, are now to be found in the interpretive notes at the foot of the page. The consultants have helped me to rethink these indications in theatrical terms, and to avoid overly specific or nontheatrical assertions based on sources or editorial tradition. Where the scene is fluid, continuous, or ambiguous, or where the implied location shifts in mid scene, I have tried to indicate as much in the notes. Providing indication of place is potentially restrictive and misleading, for "the forest of Arden" invites the reader to imagine a real forest rather than a stage, and so the editor's temptation to remain silent is strong. On the other hand, many readers can be helped by knowing that the scene in much of *King Lear* moves between Albany's palace in the north of Great Britain to Gloucester's house in the southwest, and eventually to Dover. Perhaps our concept of place should be guided by Shakespeare's own suggestions, in which he makes use of the theatre to invite us on an imaginative journey to battlefields, distant lands, ships at sea, palaces, and banqueting halls. His scene is both fluid and imaginatively particular.

A similar problem concerns act and scene division. The indications in this edition, like those of the First Folio, are boldly visible. As such they facilitate location of a place in the text, something that is indispensable for classroom use and play rehearsal as well as for reading. This convenience seems to me an overriding consideration, even though the divisions do not appear in most quarto texts, are probably not Shakespearean, at times do not reflect even a plausible structuring of the play into five acts (the length of acts in *Love's Labor's Lost*, for example, is very uneven), and at times interrupt the flow from one continuous scene to another (as in *Romeo and Juliet*, Act II scenes 1 and 2). The scene divisions are often simply those of editorial tradition. Until some international Shakespeare congress legislates a new standard, however, the traditional scene division of the Globe text represents a standard for reference, and I have retained it as the most universal available. I have tried in the notes to indicate where it is theatrically misleading, and have provided through line numbers (TLN) at the top of each page to give the reader a more reliable and truly universal key, though not yet widely in use except by textual scholars. These through line numbers, inclusive for each column of text, are keyed to Charlton Hinman's facsimile edition of the First Folio (New York, Norton, 1968). Where the text is based on a quarto edition, the equivalent line numbers in the First Folio are provided.

With the advice of the editorial advisers, I have made an effort to regularize the use of added stage directions. (All editorially added stage directions are in square brackets.) In my view the cumulative editorial tradition providing our heretofore "received" text of Shakespeare has been haphazard in the use of added stage directions; sometimes a kiss, or the giving of a letter or money, or kneeling, are indicated, and sometimes not. The early texts themselves differ widely in thoroughness of providing stage directions, owing in part to the different sorts of copy lying behind those texts. I have tried to indicate in added stage directions when significant action occurs on stage, to enable the reader to keep track of exchanged letters and the like. At times an experienced reader may find an added stage direction obvious because the action is indicated in the dialogue, but I would prefer to regularize such matters and to remind the reader that the script is intended to be acted on stage. Because at times careful readers may disagree as to whether an action mentioned in the dialogue actually occurs or not, or disagree as to how it is performed, an editor must proceed with caution; but if he can arrive at a reasonably certain conclusion to such a disputed point, he provides a useful editorial service.

Another matter in which I have found the "received" editorial tradition excessively timid is in the handling of short lines of verse. In the early texts, both First Folio and quarto, short lines of verse are almost universally run from the left-hand margin, following the speech prefix. Although Shakespeare clearly intended that many such short lines be linked in such a way as to make up full verses (usually of iambic pentameter), the decision to arrange short lines in verse patterns by the indentation of one or more short lines after the first short line is essentially an editorial decision. As Fredson Bowers has argued, the Globe text was inconsistent in its handling of short lines. It often linked two short lines in such a way as to produce a hexameter or a tetrameter rather than a pentameter line; at other times it left such lines unlinked. It was inconsistent as to whether a short line should be allowed to end one speech or begin the next speech in cases where a sequence of short lines divided among speakers provides the editor with an option. Recent editors, as Bowers has demonstrated, have bowed to the weight of editorial tradition, as though it were part of the original text, which it is not. Following Bowers' principles, I have reviewed lineation throughout, and among other matters have "unedited" a great many dubiously constructed lines of verse—especially in the later plays. As a result, my lineation of poetry often does not agree with that of most recent editions.

Although most substantive restorations of wording in the copy text were introduced into the 1973 edition, I have of course used the occasion of a complete resetting of this text to read against copy text repeatedly, and to reconsider anew the necessity of every emendation. In this review the editorial advisers have been enormously helpful, though I did not impose on them the task of systematically examining the whole text, and I must bear responsibility for errors or misjudgments. As in the 1973 edition, nearly all of the changes are in the direction of restoring original readings; I have not, of course, used the Globe text as a basis for this present edition. Like other recent editors I do not agree with the Globe's regularizing of Shakespeare's usage of such terms as *further* and *farther*, *show'd* and *shown*, *does* and *doth*, *seemeth* and *seems*, *mine* and *my*, and the like. I have avoided the Globe's tendency to "correct" agreement between a seemingly singular noun and a plural verb form. More importantly, I have tried to get away from the eclectic practice of choosing readings unsystematically from First Folio or quarto text (where both exist) according to which sounds most "Shakespearean." The texts here are edited conservatively on the basis of what appears to be the single preferred copy text at any given point. In the special case of *King Lear*, I have, like other recent editors, conservatively followed the First Folio text as my basic authority, but have also included in square brackets those parts of *King Lear* not found in the First Folio. Similarly I have bracketed First Folio passages incorporated into the quarto text of *Hamlet*, the First Folio deposition scene added to the quarto text of *Richard II*, the First Folio passages added to the quarto text of *2 Henry IV*, and the like. That is, I have used square brackets to alert the reader to conflation of this sort between two substantive texts; we cannot afford to eliminate these Shakespearean passages, or bury them in the notes, and yet in a real sense the quarto passages don't "belong" in a First Folio text of *King Lear* which is a complete play in its own right. Other than these instances of conflation, I have not used square brackets to indicate emended or added single words or short phrases, for brackets are potentially distracting and can easily become too numerous. Corrections to the text in the normal editorial process of emendation are recorded instead in the textual notes. These are to be found in the back of the volume, available but unobtrusively so; this is not a critical edition with full apparatus, but a readers' edition.

The General Introduction. I recast the introductory material in 1973. In the present edition I have continued the process of updating this material, with the able advice of David Kastan as general consultant. I have extensively rewritten the section on "London Theatres and Dramatic Companies," assisted by the criticisms of Ejner Jensen. D. F. Rowan has similarly offered suggestions on the section on "Shakespeare Criticism," and Barry Gaines has reviewed the section on "Editions and Editors of Shakespeare."

The Play Introductions. I first wrote these introductions for the 1973 edition, to provide an interpretive essay on each work incorporating recent criticism and identifying issues of critical debate. For this present edition I asked the editorial advisers for each individual work to criticize the existing introduction unsparingly as though it were a first draft. I was both sobered and gratified by the seriousness with which these dear people undertook the assignment. Galled and exhilarated by their penetrating observations, I have read much criticism and have rewritten many of the introductions extensively, wishing only that I had done more.

The Notes. Most of the time and effort spent on this edition has gone into a new set of interpretive notes. They are more extensive than in the earlier edition, and are now keyed to the text by means of line numbers; wherever a line number appears, a word or phrase is glossed. Where no glossing occurs, decimal line numbers in italic have been provided to facilitate locating a particular line. I cannot easily acknowledge the extent of the help I received from the editorial advisers on the individual works. Let me only assure the reader that any gloss in this edition that seems helpful may well owe its wording or entire inspiration to the editorial adviser rather than to myself; or perhaps it would be more accurate to say that the glosses arise out of a prolonged wrestling with the text by the editorial advisers and myself. In addition, my wife Peggy examined all the interpretive notes and made invaluable suggestions throughout; some of the readings I like best owe their existence to her. I must also thank my colleague Wayne Booth, who has pointedly remarked more than once that when he has consulted a Shakespeare edition to help him with a particularly thorny passage, he has often found the glosses to be discreetly and unhelpfully silent. I have kept his observation in mind as a criterion, and have tried to wrestle hardest with those passages where one is tempted to give up.

Appendices. I wrote these for the 1973 edition and have gone over them carefully with the help of the consultants. Barry Gaines reviewed the material in Appendix 1 on "Canon, Dates, and Early Texts." The consultants for the various individual works commented individually on the survey of sources in Appendix 2, and Michael Mullin offered many insights on the history of Shakespearean production in Appendix 3. At his suggestion I have added some paragraphs on Shakespeare on film.

Suggestions for Reading and Research. With the help of the editorial advisers, I have brought these bibliographies up to date. Almost half the items are new for many of the bibliographies on the individual works. I am indebted to the consultants for many choices that I would not have had the wisdom to make. I have been impressed, in working on these bibliographies, with how much important criticism has been written in the 1970s.

My first acknowledgment must be to Hardin Craig. An early version of his edition of Shakespeare was first published by Scott, Foresman and Company in 1931. For years afterwards, his Shakespeare was widely used as a teaching text and set a standard for many later editions. When I had the good fortune to be asked to revise Craig's edition in 1973, I retained many of his contributions. The notes were largely his, though with substantial supplements; the introductory material made use of historical information on text, dating, sources, and stage history gathered by him; and the organization of the volume by chronological periods bore his imprint. This Third Edition, as I have indicated, goes in a new direction. It departs sufficiently from Craig's edition so that he should no longer be held accountable for my choices, and so his name has been withdrawn from the title page. The occasion should not pass, however, without my expressing my deepest thanks for his inspiration and my acknowledgment that he is the "onlie begetter" of the commentary in this volume.

My other debts are many. Among members of my department, I have asked Raven McDavid, Joseph Williams, and Richard Payne about Shakespeare's language. Mark Ashin has called my attention to errors in the 1973 edition, and I have received much insight on Shakespearean interpretation from Richard Strier and William Ringler. Among students, present and former, I have learned much from Jeffrey Stern, Joseph Johnston, Gerald Kowarsky, Stuart Kurland, Kevin Hochberg, James Shapiro, and Kenneth Brown. Colleagues at other institutions who have been particularly helpful include Charles Lower, who has advised me on indications of place for the scenes; R. R. McLeod, whose ideas on "unediting" the work of earlier editors has forced me to reexamine a number of assumptions; Fredson Bowers, who, in addition to sending me a copy of his paper on short lines, has provided information on the speech prefixes in *All's Well* and on related matters; and many others.

During 1978–1979 I had the good fortune to work with a year-long residential seminar for college teachers, consisting of Thomas Berger, Huston Diehl, Richard Emmerson, Michael Hall, Ronald Herzman, Robert Knapp, Joan Marx, Pamela Sheingorn, and John Wyatt. With this remarkable group of teachers and scholars I shared ideas on editing Shakespeare and received much encouragement. My family, both nuclear and extended, has provided every sustenance and understanding during prolonged periods of intensive work. My mother Helen Bevington has helped with proofreading and invaluable suggestions on writing, as has my wife Peggy. And I have relied gratefully on John Nolan and William Graves of Scott, Foresman and Company for editorial assistance.

David Bevington

Contents

General Introduction

The Comedies

The Histories

The Tragedies

The Romances

The Poems

General Introduction

Life in Shakespeare's England

The Drama Before Shakespeare

London Theatres and Dramatic Companies

Shakespeare's Life and Work

Shakespeare's Language

Editions and Editors of Shakespeare

Shakespeare Criticism

General Introduction

Life in Shakespeare's England

England during Shakespeare's lifetime (1564–1616) was a proud nation with a strong sense of national identity, but was also a small nation by modern standards. Probably not more than five million people lived in the whole of England, considerably fewer than now live in London. England's territories in France were no longer extensive, as they had been during the fourteenth century and earlier; in fact, by the end of Queen Elizabeth's reign (1558–1603), England had virtually retired from her once-great empire on the Continent. Her overseas empire in America had scarcely begun. Scotland was not yet a part of Great Britain; union with Scotland would not take place until 1707, despite the fact that King James VI of Scotland assumed the English throne in 1603 as James I of England. Ireland, although declared a kingdom under English rule in 1541, was more a source of trouble than of economic strength. The last years of Elizabeth's reign, especially from 1597 to 1601, were plagued by the rebellion of the Irish under Hugh O'Neill, Earl of Tyrone. Thus, England of the sixteenth and early seventeenth centuries was both small and isolated.

The Social and Economic Background

By and large, England was a rural land. Much of the kingdom was still wooded, though timber was being used increasingly in manufacturing and shipbuilding. The area of the midlands, today heavily industrialized, was still at that time a region of great trees, green fields, and clear streams. England's chief means of livelihood was agriculture. This part of the economy was generally in a bad way, however, and Englishmen who lived off the land did not share in the prosperity of many Londoners. A problem throughout the sixteenth century was that of "enclosure": the conversion by rich landowners of crop lands into pasturage. Farmers and peasants complained bitterly that they were being dispossessed and starved for the benefit of livestock. Rural uprisings and food riots were common, to the dismay of the authorities. The agrarian poor of Oxfordshire arose in 1596, threatening to massacre the gentry and march on London; other riots had occurred in 1586 and 1591, provoking memories of the infamous May Day riots of 1517. Although the government did what it could to inhibit enclosure, the economic forces at work were too massive and too inadequately understood to be curbed by governmental fiat. Pasture used large areas with greater efficiency than in crop farming, and required far less labor. The wool produced by the pasturing of sheep was needed in ever-increasing amounts for the manufacture of cloth.

The wool industry also experienced occasional economic difficulties, to be sure; overexpansion in the early years of the sixteenth century created a glutted market that

THE FOLGER SHAKESPEARE LIBRARY

"Enclosure" was a problem throughout the sixteenth century in England. Crop lands were converted into pasturage. The livelihood of the plowman was threatened by the pasturing of sheep and the growing production of wool.

Sixteenth-century London was a city teeming with activity. Pedestrians were often forced to make way for the livestock that were driven through the streets.

had collapsed disastrously in 1551, producing widespread unemployment. Despite such fluctuations and reversals, however, the wool industry at least provided handsome profits for some landowners and middlemen. Mining and manufacture in coal, iron, tin, copper, and lead, although insignificant by modern standards, were also expanding at a significant rate. Trading companies exploited the rich new resources of the Americas, as well as of Eastern Europe and the Orient. Queen Elizabeth aided economic development by keeping England out of war with her continental enemies as long as possible, despite provocations from those powers and despite the eagerness of some of her advisers to retaliate.

Certainly England's economic condition was better than the economic condition of the rest of the Continent; an Italian called England "the land of comforts." Yet although some prosperity did exist, it was not evenly distributed. Especially during Shakespeare's first years in London, in the late 1580's and the 1590's, the gap between rich and poor grew more and more extreme. Elizabeth's efforts at peacemaking were no longer able to prevent years of war with the Catholic powers of the Continent. Taxation grew heavier, and inflation proceeded at an unusually rapid rate during this period. A succession of bad harvests compounded the miseries of those who dwelled on the land. When the hostilities on the Continent ceased for a time in about 1597, a wave of returning veterans added to unemployment and crime. The rising prosperity experienced by Shakespeare and other fortunate Londoners was undeniably real, but it was not universal. Nowhere was the contrast between rich and poor more visible than in London.

London

Sixteenth-century London was at once more attractive and less attractive than twentieth-century London. It was full of trees and gardens; meadows and cultivated lands reached in some places to its very walls. Today we can perhaps imagine the way in which it bordered clear streams and green fields, when we approach from a distance some noncommercial provincial city such as Lincoln, York, or Hereford. Surrounded by its ancient wall, London was by no means a large metropolis. It was nonetheless the largest city of Europe, and its dominance among English cities was even more striking; in 1543–1544, London paid thirty times the subsidy of Norwich, then the second largest city in the kingdom. Although London's population had expanded into the surrounding area in all directions, the city proper stretched along the north bank of the Thames River from the old Tower of London on the east to St. Paul's Cathedral and the Fleet Ditch on the west—a distance of little more than a mile. A visitor approaching London from the south bank of the Thames (the Bankside), and crossing London Bridge, could see virtually all of this exciting city lying before him. London Bridge itself was one of the major attractions of the city, lined with shops and richly decorated on occasion for the triumphal entry of a king or queen.

Yet London had its grim and ugly side as well. On London Bridge could sometimes be seen the heads of executed traitors. The city's houses were generally small and crowded; its streets were often narrow and filthy. In the absence of sewers, open ditches in the streets served to collect and carry off refuse. Frequent epidemics of the bu-

London Bridge, lined with shops, houses, and severed heads on poles, provided a grisly route for those traveling between the north and south banks of the Thames. A number of Elizabethan theatres were located on the south bank including the Globe.

bonic plague were the inevitable result of unsanitary conditions and medical ignorance. Lighting of the streets at night was generally nonexistent, and the constabulary was notoriously unreliable. Shakespeare gives us unforgettable satires of night watchmen and bumbling police officials in *Much Ado about Nothing* (Dogberry and the night watch) and *Measure for Measure* (Constable Elbow). Prostitution thrived in the suburbs, conveniently located although beyond the reach of the London authorities. Again, we are indebted to Shakespeare for a memorable portrayal in *Measure for Measure* of just such a demimonde (Mistress Overdone the bawd, Pompey her pimp, and various customers). Houses of prostitution were often to be found in the vicinity of the public theatres, since the theatres also took advantage of suburban locations to escape the stringent regulations imposed by London's Lord Mayor and Council of Aldermen. The famous Globe Theatre, for example, was on the south bank of the Thames, a short distance west of London Bridge. Another theatrical building (called simply "The Theatre") used earlier by Shakespeare and the Lord Chamberlain's players was located in Finsbury Fields, a short distance across Moorfields from London's northeast corner. The suburbs also housed various con games and illegal operations, some of them brilliantly illustrated (and no doubt exaggerated) in Ben Jonson's *The Alchemist* (1610).

London's population stood at perhaps one hundred thousand people within the walls and as many more in the suburbs. The royal palace of Whitehall, Westminster Abbey (then known as the Abbey Church of St. Peter), the Parliament House, and Westminster Hall were well outside London, two miles or so to the west on the Thames River. They remain today in the same location, in Westminster, although the metropolis of London has long since surrounded these official buildings.

Travel

Travel was still extremely painful and slow because of the poor condition of the roads. Highway robbers were a constant threat. (The celebrated highway robbery in Shakespeare's *1 Henry IV* takes place at Gads Hill, on the main road between London and Canterbury.) English inns seem to have been good, however, certainly much better than the inns of the Continent. Travel on horseback was the most common method of transportation, and probably the most comfortable, since coachbuilding was a new and imperfect art. Coaches of state, some of which we see in prints and pictures of the era, were lumbering affairs, no doubt handsome enough in processions, but springless, unwieldly, and hard to transport. Carts and wagons were used for carrying merchandise, but packsaddles were safer and quicker. Under such difficulties, no metropolitan area such as London could possibly have thrived in the interior. London depended for its commercial greatness upon the Thames River and its access to the North Sea.

Commerce

When Elizabeth came to the English throne in 1558, England's chief foreign trade was with Antwerp, Bruges, and other Belgian cities. Antwerp was an especially important market for England's export of wool cloth. This market was seriously threatened, however, since the Low Countries were under the domination of the Catholic King of Spain, Philip II. When Philip shortsightedly undertook to punish his Protestant subjects in the Low Countries for their religious heresy, many of Elizabeth's counselors and subjects urged her to come to the defense of England's Protestant neighbors and trading allies. Elizabeth prudently held back. Philip's armies attacked Antwerp in 1576 and again in 1585, putting to an end the commercial ascendancy of that great northern European metropolis. Perhaps as many as one third of Antwerp's merchants and artisans settled in London, bringing with them their expert knowledge of commerce and manufacture. The influx of so many skilled workmen and merchants into London produced problems

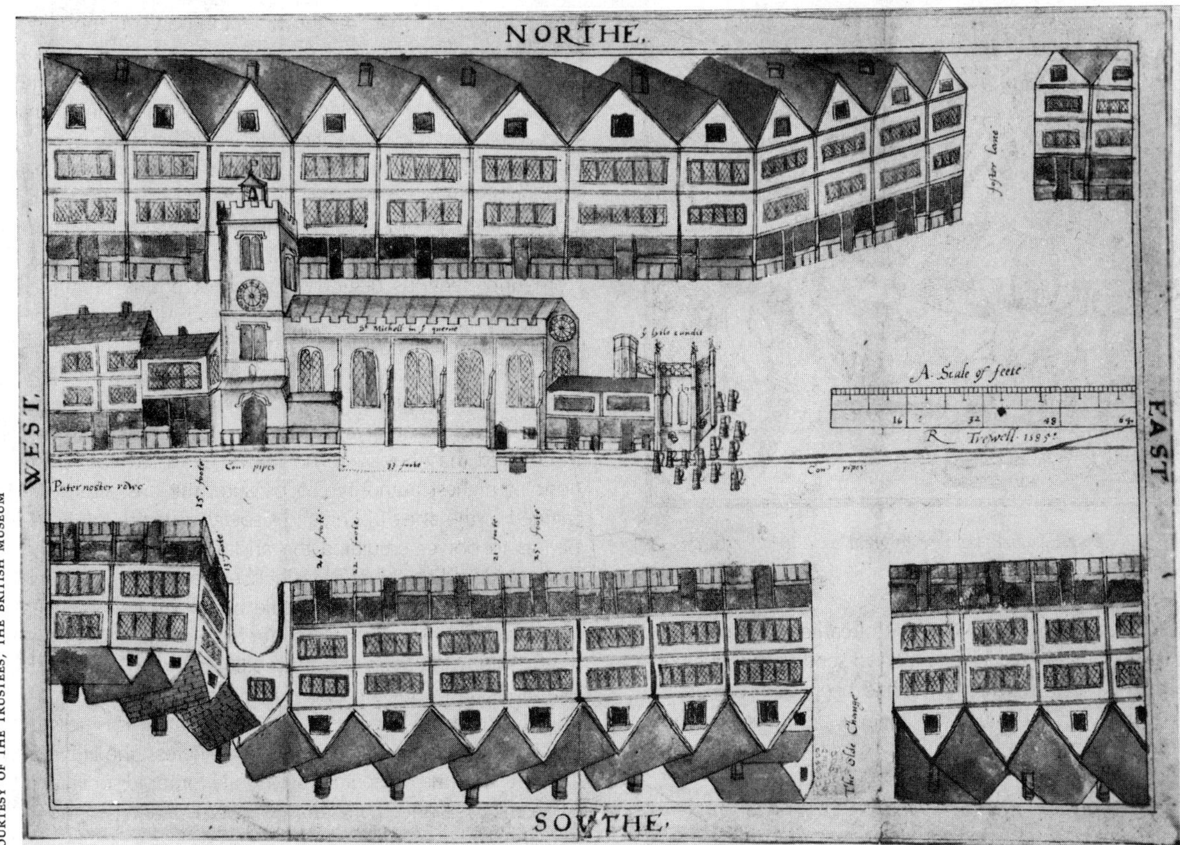

The taverns of Cheapside were the most popular and fashionable in London.

of unemployment and overcrowding, but contributed nevertheless to London's emergence as a leading port of trade.

English ships assumed a dominant position in Mediterranean trade, formerly carried on mainly by the Venetians. In the Baltic Sea, England captured trade that had previously been controlled by the Hanseatic League. Bristol thrived on commerce with Ireland and subsequently on trade with the Western Hemisphere. Boston and Hull increased their business with Scandinavian ports. The Russia Company was founded in 1555; the Levant Company became the famous East India Company in 1600; and the Virginia Company opened up trade with the New World in the Western Hemisphere. Fisheries were developed in the North Sea, in the waters north of Ireland, and off the banks of Newfoundland. Elizabeth and her ministers wisely encouraged this commercial expansion.

The Poor Laws and Apprenticeship

Despite the new prosperity experienced by many Elizabethans, especially in London, unemployment remained a serious problem. The suppresssion of the monasteries in 1536–1539, as part of Henry VIII's reformation of the Catholic Church, had dispossessed a large class of persons who were not easily reemployed. Other causes of unemployment, such as the periodic collapse of the wool trade, dispossession of farm workers by enclosure of land, the sudden influx of skilled artisans from Antwerp, and the return of army veterans, have already been mentioned. Elizabethan Parliaments attempted to cope with the problem of unemployment, but did so in ways that seem unduly harsh today. Several laws were passed between 1531, when the distinction between those poor needing charity and those unwilling to work first became law, and 1597–1598. The harshest of the laws was that of 1547, providing that vagabonds be branded and enslaved for two years; escape was punishable by death or life enslavement. This act was repealed in 1550, but subsequent acts of 1572 and 1576 designated ten classes of vagrants and required municipal authorities to provide work for the healthy unemployed of each town or parish. This localization of responsibility laid the basis for what has been known historically as the "poor rate" (a local tax levied for the support of the poor) and for that sinister institution, the workhouse. The provisions of this act remained in force for centuries. The most comprehensive laws were those of the Parliament of 1597–1598,

COURTESY OF THE TRUSTEES, THE BRITISH MUSEUM

Although some Elizabethans rose to great wealth, poverty and unemployment were widespread.

which repeated many provisions of earlier acts and added harsh punitive penalties intended to send vagabonds back to the parishes in which they had been born or had last worked. After 1597, no begging was permitted; the poor were supposed to be provided for by the "poor rate" already established.

Regulations for apprentices were no less strict. An act of Parliament of 1563, known as the Statute of Artificers, gave the craft trades of England—still organized as medieval guilds—virtually complete authority over the young persons apprenticed to a trade. Apprenticeship usually began at the age of fourteen to seventeen, and lasted for a period of not less than seven years. During this time the young worker lived with the family of his master. Without such an extensive apprenticeship, entry into the skilled crafts was virtually impossible. Apprenticeships were not open, however, in all guilds, and the law courts subsequently ruled that apprenticeship rules did not apply to crafts developed after 1563, so that exceptions did exist. All able-bodied workers not bound to crafts were supposed to work in agriculture. Acting companies, such as the company Shakespeare joined, were organized as guilds and took on boy actors in an apprenticeship role. We do not know, however, whether Shakespeare actually served such an indenture before becoming a full member of his acting company.

Social Change

The opportunities for rapid economic advance in Elizabethan England, though by no means available to all, did produce social change and a quality of restlessness in English society. "New men" at court were an increasing phenomenon under the Tudor monarchs, especially Henry VII and Henry VIII, who tended to rely on loyal counselors of humble origin rather than on the once-too-powerful nobility. Cardinal Wolsey, for example, rose from obscurity to become the most mighty subject of Henry VIII's realm, with a newly built residence (Hampton Court) rivaling the splendor of the King's own palaces. He was detested as an upstart by old aristocrats such as the Duke of Norfolk, and his sudden fall was as spectacular as had been his rise to power. The Earl of Leicester, Queen Elizabeth's first favorite, was a descendant of the Edmund Dudley who had risen from unpretentious beginnings to great eminence under Henry VII, Queen Elizabeth's grandfather. Although Queen Elizabeth did not contribute substantially to the new aristocracy—she created only three peers from 1573 onward—new and influential families were numerous throughout the century. Conversely, the ancient families discovered that they were no longer entrusted with positions of highest authority. To be sure, the aristocracy remained at the apex of England's social structure. New aspirants to power emulated the aristocracy by purchasing land and building splendid residences, rather than defining themselves as a rich new "middle class." Bourgeois status was something the new men put behind them as quickly as they could. Moreover, social mobility could work in both directions, both upward and downward. Many men were quickly ruined by the costly and competitive business of seeking favor at the Tudor court. Nonetheless, the Elizabethan era was one of greater opportunity for rapid social and economic advancement than England had heretofore known.

Increased economic contacts with the outside world inevitably led to the importation of new styles of living. Such new fashions, together with the rapid changes now possible in social position, produced a reaction of dismay from those who feared the destruction of traditional English values. Italy was particularly reviled, both as the home of the Catholic Church and as the originator of many supposedly decadent fashions. The word "Italianate" connoted a whole range of villainous practices, including diabolical methods of torture and revenge: poisoned books of devotion which would kill the unsuspecting victims who kissed them, ingeniously contrived chairs that would close upon the person who sat in them, and the like. The revenge plays of Shakespeare's contemporaries, such as *Antonio's Revenge* by John Marston, *The Revenger's Tragedy* perhaps by Cyril Tourneur or Thomas Middleton, and *The White Devil* by John Webster, offer spectacular caricatures of the so-called Italianate style in murder. The name of Italy was also associated with licentiousness, immorality, and outlandish fashions in clothes. France, too, was accused of encouraging such extravagances in dress as ornamented headdresses, stiffly pleated ruffs, padded doublets, puffed or double sleeves, and richly decorated hose. Rapid changes in fashion added to the costliness of being up to date, and thereby increased the outcry against vanity in dress. Fencing, dicing, the use of cosmetics, the smoking of

This brothel scene, featuring gambling or dicing, illustrates some of the vices that were attributed to the corrupting influence from abroad.

tobacco, the drinking of imported wines, and almost every vice known to man were attributed by angry moralists to the corrupting influence from abroad.

Not all Englishmen deplored continental fashion, of course. Persons of advanced taste saw the importation of European styles as a culturally liberating process. Fashion thus became a subject of debate between moral traditionalists and those who welcomed the new styles. The controversy was a bitter one, with religious overtones, in which the reformers' angry accusations became increasingly extreme. This attack on changing fashion was in fact an integral part of the Puritan movement. It therefore stressed the sinfulness not only of extravagance in clothing but of the costliness in building great houses and other such worldly pursuits. Those whose sympathies were Puritan became more and more disaffected with the cultural values represented by the court, and thus English society drifted further and further toward irreconcilable conflict.

Shakespeare's personal views on this controversy are hard to determine and do not bear importantly on his achievement as an artist. Generally, however, we can observe that his many references to changes in fashion cater neither to the avant-garde nor to reactionary traditionalists. Shakespeare's audience was after all a broadly national one. It included many well-informed Londoners who viewed "Italianate" fashion neither with enthusiasm nor with alarm, but with satiric laughter. Such spectators would certainly have seen the point, for example, in Mercutio's witty diatribe at the expense of the new French style in fencing. The object of his scorn is Tybalt, who, according to Mercutio, "fights as you sing prick-song" and fancies himself to be "the very butcher of a silk button." "Is not this a lamentable thing," asks Mercutio rhetorically, "that we should be thus afflicted with these strange flies, these fashion-mongers, these pardon-me's, who stand so much on the new form that they cannot sit at ease on the old bench?" (*Romeo and Juliet,* II,iv). In a similar vein, Shakespeare's audience would have appreciated the joking in *The Merchant of Venice* about England's servile imitation of continental styles in clothes. "What say you, then, to Falconbridge, the young baron of England?" asks Nerissa of her mistress Portia concerning one of Portia's many suitors. Portia replies, "How oddly he is suited! I think he bought his doublet in Italy, his round hose in France, his bonnet in Germany and his behavior everywhere" (I,ii). Court butterflies in Shakespeare's plays who bow and scrape and fondle their plumed headgear, like Le Beau in *As You Like It* and Osric in *Hamlet,* are the objects of ridicule. Hotspur in *1 Henry IV,* though flawed by aristocratic pride, contrasts favorably with the effeminate courtier, "perfumed like a milliner," who has come from King Henry to discuss the question of prisoners (I,iii). Throughout Shakespeare's plays, the use of cosmetics generally has the negative connotation of artificial beauty used to conceal inward corruption, as in Claudius' reference to "the harlot's cheek, beautied with plast'ring art" (*Hamlet,* III,i). Yet Shakespeare's treatment of newness in fashion is never shrill in tone. Nor does he fail in his dramas to give an honorable place to the ceremonial use of wealth and splendid costuming. His plays thus avoid both extremes in the controversy over changing fashions, though they give plentiful evidence as to the liveliness and currency of the topic.

Shakespeare also reflects a contemporary interest in the problem of usury, especially in *The Merchant of Venice.* Although usury was becoming more and more of a necessity, emotional attitudes toward it changed only slowly. The traditional moral view condemned usury as forbidden by Christian teaching; on the other hand, European governments of the sixteenth century found themselves increasingly obliged to borrow large sums of money. The laws against usury were alternatively relaxed and enforced, according to the economic exigencies of the moment. Shakespeare's plays capture the Elizabethan ambivalence of attitude toward this feared but necessary practice (see

Introduction to *The Merchant of Venice*). Similarly, most Englishmen had contradictory attitudes toward what we today would call the law of supply and demand in the marketplace. Conservative moralists complained bitterly when merchants exploited the scarcity of some commodity by forcing up prices; the practice was denounced as excessive profit-taking and declared to be sinful, like usury. In economic policy, then, as in matters of changing fashion or increased social mobility, many Englishmen were ambivalent about the perennial conflict between the old order and the new.

Elizabethan Houses

Those fortunate Englishmen who grew wealthy in the reign of Elizabeth took special pleasure in building themselves fine new houses with furnishings to match. Chimneys were increasingly common, so that smoke no longer had to escape through a hole in the roof. Pewter, or even silver dishes, took the place of the wooden spoon and trencher. Beds and even pillows became common. Carpets were replacing rushes as covering for the floors; wainscoting, tapestries or hangings, and pictures appeared on the walls; and glass began to be used extensively for windows.

Despite the warnings of those moralists who preached against the vanity of worldly acquisition, domestic comfort made considerable progress in Elizabethan England. Many splendid Tudor mansions stand today, testifying to the important social changes that had taken place between the strife-torn fifteenth century and the era of relative peace under Elizabeth. The battlement, the moat, the fortified gate, and the narrow window used for archery or firearms generally disappeared in favor of handsome gardens and terraces. On a lower social scale, the peasant enjoyed greater physical security, and no longer needed to bring his cows, pigs, and poultry into his house at night in order to protect them from thieves. City houses, of which many exist today, were often large and imposing structures, three or four stories in height, and framed usually of strong oak with the walls filled in with brick and plaster. Although the frontage on the streets of London was usually narrow, many houses had trees and handsome gardens at the rear.

With these finer houses, too, came features of privacy that had been virtually unknown to previous generations. Life in the household of a medieval lord had generally focused on the great hall, which could serve variously as the kitchen, dining hall, and sitting room for the entire family and its retainers. The men drank in the hall in the evenings

PHOTOGRAPH BY HERSCHEL LEVIT

In contrast to the fortresslike structures of an earlier, more tumultuous era, the Tudor house was usually a comfortable plaster–and–timber dwelling—evidence of the relative peace and prosperity of the times.

and slept there at night. The new dwellings of prosperous Elizabethans, on the other hand, featured private chambers into which the family and the chief guests could retire.

The Elizabethans built well. Not only do we still admire their houses, but we can see from their oriel windows and stained glass, their broad staircases, their jewels, and their costumes, that they treasured the new beauty of their lives made possible by the culture of the Renaissance. Although the graphic and plastic arts did not thrive in England to the same extent as in Italy, France, and the Low Countries, England made lasting achievements in architecture as well as in music, drama, and all forms of literature.

The Political and Religious Background

England under the Tudor kings suffered from almost unceasing religious conflict. The battle over religion affected every aspect of life, none more so than politics. At the very beginning of the Tudor reign, to be sure, England's problem was not religious but dynastic. Henry VII, the first of the Tudor kings, brought an end to the devastating civil wars of the fifteenth century by his overthrow of Richard III at the battle of Bosworth Field in 1485. The civil wars thus ended were the so-called Wars of the Roses, between the Lancastrian House of Henry VI (symbolized by the red rose) and the Yorkist House of Edward IV (symbolized by the white rose). Shakespeare chose these eventful struggles as the subject for his first series of English history plays, from *Henry VI* in three parts to *Richard III*. The House of Lancaster drew its title from John of Gaunt, Duke of Lancaster, father of Henry IV and great-grandfather of Henry VI; the House of York drew its title from Edmund Langley, Duke of York, great-grandfather of Edward IV and Richard III. Because John of Gaunt and Edmund Langley had been brothers, virtually all the noble contestants in this War of the Roses were cousins of one another, caught in a remorseless dynastic struggle for control of the English crown. Many of them lost their lives in the fighting. By 1485, England was exhausted from civil conflict. Although Henry VII's own dynastic claim to the throne was weak, he managed to suppress factional opposition and to give England the respite from war so desperately needed. His son, Henry VIII, inherited a throne in 1509 that was more secure than it had been in nearly a century.

Henry VIII's notorious marital difficulties, however, soon brought an end to dynastic security and civil accord. Moreover, religious conflict within the Catholic Church was growing to the extent that a break sooner or later with Rome appeared inevitable. Henry's marriage troubles precipitated that momentous event. Because he divorced his first wife, Katharine of Aragon, in 1530 without the consent of Rome, he was excommunicated from the Catholic Church; his response in 1534 was to have himself proclaimed "Protector and only Supreme Head of the Church and Clergy of England." This decisive act signaled the beginning of the Reformation in England, not many years after Martin Luther's momentous break with the Papacy in 1517 and the consequent beginning of Lutheran Protestantism on the Continent. In England, Henry's act of defiance split the church and the nation. Many men chose Sir Thomas More's path of martyrdom rather than submit to Henry's new title as supreme head of the English church. Henry's later years did witness a period of retrenchment in religion, after the downfall of Thomas Cromwell in 1540, and indeed Henry's break with Rome had had its origin in political and marital strife rather than in matters of dogma and liturgy. Nevertheless, the establishment of an Anglican church was now an accomplished fact. The accession of Henry's ten-year-old son Edward VI, in 1547, gave reformers an opportunity to bring about rapid changes in English Protestantism. Archbishop Cranmer's forty-two articles of religion (1551), and his prayer book, laid the basis for the Anglican church of the sixteenth century.

The death of the sickly Edward VI in 1553 brought with it an intense crisis in religious politics, and a temporary reversal of England's religious direction. For five years England returned to Catholicism under the rule of Edward's elder sister Mary, daughter of the Catholic Queen Katharine of Aragon. The crisis accompanying such changes of government during this midcentury period was greatly exacerbated by the fact that all three of Henry VIII's living children were considered illegitimate by one faction or another of the English people. In Protestant eyes, Mary was the daughter of the divorced Queen Katharine, whose marriage to Henry had never been valid because she had previously been the spouse of Henry VIII's older brother Arthur. This Arthur had died at a young age, in 1502, shortly after his state marriage to the Spanish princess. If, as the Protestants insisted, Arthur had consummated the marriage, then Katharine's subsequent union with her deceased husband's brother was invalid, and Henry was free instead to marry Anne Boleyn—the mother-to-be of Elizabeth. In Catholic eyes, however, both Elizabeth and her brother Edward VI (son of Jane Seymour, Henry VIII's third wife) were the bastard issue of Henry's bigamous marriages; Henry's one and only true marriage in the Catholic faith was that to Katharine of Aragon. Edward and Elizabeth were regarded by many Catholics, at home and abroad, not only as illegitimate children but as illegitimate rulers, to be disobeyed and even overthrown by force. Thus, dynastic and marital conflicts became matters of grave political consequence.

Because of these struggles, Elizabeth's accession to the throne in 1558 remained an uncertainty until the last moment. Once she actually became ruler, however, England returned once more to the Protestant faith. Even then, tact and moderation were required to prevent open religious war. Elizabeth's genius at compromise prompted her to seek a middle position for her church, one that combined an episcopal form of church government (owing no alle-

The Knights of the Garter belonged to the highest order of knighthood; many were influential courtiers and favorites of Queen Elizabeth. A marriage would have upset the political balance and would have committed her to one foreign nation or to one constituency at home. A masterful politician, Elizabeth remained unmarried throughout her life.

COURTESY OF THE TRUSTEES, THE BRITISH MUSEUM

giance to the Pope) with an essentially traditional form of liturgy and dogma. As much as was practicable, she left matters up to individual conscience; she drew the line, however, where matters of conscience tended to "exceed their bounds and grow to be matter of faction." In practice this meant that she did not tolerate avowed Catholics on the religious right, or Brownists and Unitarians (who denied the doctrine of the Trinity) on the religious left. The foundation for this so-called Elizabethan compromise was the thirty-nine articles, adopted in 1563 and based in many respects upon Cranmer's forty-two articles of 1551. The compromise did not please everyone, of course, but it did achieve a remarkable degree of consensus during Elizabeth's long reign.

Queen Elizabeth and Tudor Absolutism

Elizabeth had to cope with a religiously divided nation and with extremists of both right and left who wished her downfall. She was a woman, in an age openly skeptical of women's ability or right to rule. Her success in dealing with such formidable odds was in large measure the result of her personal style as a monarch. Her combination of imperious will and femininity and her brilliant handling of her many contending male admirers have become legendary. She remained unmarried throughout her life, in part at least because marriage would have upset the delicate balance she maintained among rival groups, both foreign and domestic. Marriage would have committed her irretrievably to either one foreign nation or to one constituency at home. She chose instead to bestow her favor on certain courtiers, notably Robert Dudley (whom she elevated to be the Earl of Leicester) and, after Leicester's death in 1588, Robert Devereux, second Earl of Essex. Her relationship with these men, despite her partiality to them, was marked by her outbursts of tempestuous jealousy. In addition, she relied on the staid counsel of her hard-working ministers: Lord Burghley, Sir Francis Walsingham, Burghley's son Robert Cecil, and a few others.

In her personal style as monarch, Elizabeth availed herself of the theory of absolute supremacy. Under all the Tudors, England was nominally at least an absolute monarchy in an age when many of England's greatest rivals—France, Spain, the Holy Roman Empire—were also under absolutist rule. The rise of absolutism throughout Renaissance Europe was the result of an increase of centralized national power and a corresponding decrease in autonomous baronial influence. Henry VII's strong assertion of his royal authority at the expense of the feudal lords corresponded roughly in time with the ascendancy of Francis I of France (1515) and Charles V of the Holy Roman Empire (1519). Yet England had long enjoyed a tradition of rule by consensus. When Elizabeth came to the throne, England was already in some ways a "limited" monarchy. Parliament, and

especially the members of the House of Commons, claimed prerogatives of their own and were steadily gaining in both experience and power. In the mid-1560's, for example, the Commons made repeated attempts to use parliamentary tax-levying authority as a means of obliging Elizabeth to name a Protestant successor to the throne. The attempt, despite its failure to achieve its immediate goal, was significant; the Commons had shown that they were a force to be reckoned with. Even though Elizabeth made skillful rhetorical use of the theory of absolutism, portraying herself as God's appointed deputy on earth, her idea of absolutism should not be confused with despotism. She never claimed or exercised the right to establish law; that was Parliament's prerogative. She needed all her considerable diplomatic skills in dealing with her Parliaments and with the English people, self-reliant and proud of their reputation for independence. Elizabeth had more direct authority over her Privy Council, since she could appoint its members herself; still, she consulted faithfully with them on virtually everything she did. Nor were her closest advisers reluctant to offer her advice. Many vocal leaders in her government, including Walsingham and Leicester, urged the Queen during the 1570's and 1580's to undertake a more active military role on the Continent against the Catholic powers. So did her later favorite, the Earl of Essex. With remarkable tact, she managed to retain the loyalty of her militant and sometimes exasperated counselors, and yet to keep England out of war with Spain until that country actually launched an invasion attempt in 1588 (the Great Armada).

Catholic Opposition

During her early years, Elizabeth sought through her religious compromise to ease the divisions of her kingdom, and attempted to placate her enemies abroad (notably Philip of Spain) rather than involve England in a costly war. For about twelve years, while England's economy gained much-needed strength, this policy of temporizing succeeded. Yet Elizabeth's more extreme Catholic opponents at home and abroad could never be reconciled to the daughter of that Protestant "whore," Anne Boleyn. England's period of relative accommodation came to an end in 1569 and 1570, with Catholic uprisings in the north and with Papal excommunication of the English queen. As a declared heretic, Elizabeth's very life was in danger; her Catholic subjects were enjoined by Rome to disobey her and to seek means for her violent overthrow.

Conspirators did in fact make attempts on the Queen's life, notably in the so-called Babington conspiracy of 1586. This plot, brought to light by Secretary of State Walsingham, sought to place Mary Queen of Scots on the English throne in Elizabeth's stead. Mary was Elizabeth's kinswoman; Mary's grandmother, sister to Henry VIII, had been married to James IV of Scotland. So long as Elizabeth remained childless, Mary was a prominent heir to the English throne. Catholics pinned their hopes on her succession, by force if necessary; Protestant leaders urged Elizabeth to marry and give birth to a Protestant heir, or at least name a Protestant successor. Mary had abdicated the Scottish throne in 1567, after the sensational murder of her Catholic counselor David Rizzio, the murder of Mary's husband the Earl of Darnley (in which Mary was widely suspected to have taken part), and her subsequent marriage to Darnley's slayer, the Earl of Bothwell. Taking refuge in England, Mary remained a political prisoner and the inevitable focus of Catholic plotting against Elizabeth for approximately two decades. She in fact assented in writing to Babington's plot against Elizabeth. All that long while Elizabeth resisted demands from her Protestant advisers that she execute her kinswoman and thereby end a constant threat to the throne; Elizabeth was reluctant to kill a fellow-monarch, and agreed fully with Mary's son James that "anointing by God cannot be defiled by man." Nonetheless, Mary's clear involvement in the Babington conspiracy led to the so-called Bond of Association, in which thousands of Englishmen pledged to prevent the succession of any person plotting Elizabeth's death, and then at last to Mary's execution in 1587. By that time, Spain was mounting an invasion against England, the Great Armada of 1588, and Elizabeth's temporizing tactics were no longer feasible. The long years of peace had done their work, however, and England was considerably stronger and more resolute than thirty years before. With Elizabeth's tacit approval, Sir Francis Drake and other naval commanders carried the fighting to Spain's very shore and to her American colonies. In 1585, Elizabeth had permitted troops under the command of the Earl of Leicester to aid the Dutch against Spain. The war with Spain continued from 1588 until about 1597.

Elizabeth's great compromise dealt not only with the political dangers of opposition but also with the more central religious issues as well. England was sorely divided, as was much of Europe, on such matters as whether Christ's body was transubstantially present in the Mass, as Catholic faith maintained; whether good works were efficacious in salvation or whether man could be saved by God's grace alone, as the Reformers insisted; whether a portion of mankind was predeterminately damned, as the Calvinists believed; and the like. During the turbulent years of the Reformation, many people died for their faith. In general, the

NATIONAL GALLERY OF SCOTLAND, SCOTTISH NATIONAL PORTRAIT GALLERY OF SCOTTISH NATIONAL GALLERY OF MODERN ART

The 1587 beheading of Mary, Queen of Scots, shown holding a crucifix and surrounded by official witnesses in this contemporary illustration, virtually ended any serious Catholic challenge to Elizabeth's throne.

Elizabethan compromise insisted on allegiance to the English throne, church, and ecclesiastical hierarchy, but allowed some latitude in matters of faith. The degree of elaboration in vestments and ritual was also an explosive issue on which the English church attempted to steer a central and pragmatic course, although conflicts inevitably arose within the church itself.

Protestant Opposition

The threat from the religious left was no less worrisome than that from the right. Protestant reformers had experienced their first taste of power at the time of Henry VIII's break with Rome in 1534. Under Thomas Cromwell, Cardinal Wolsey's successor as the King's chief minister, the monasteries were suppressed and William Tyndale's English Bible was authorized. The execution of Cromwell introduced a period of conservative retrenchment, but the accession of Edward VI in 1547 brought reform once more into prominence. Thereafter Mary's Catholic reign drove most of the reformers into exile on the Continent. When they returned after 1558, many had been made more radical by their continental experience.

To be sure, reform covered a wide spectrum from moderation to radicalism. Some preferred to work within the existing hierarchical structure of church and state, whereas others were religious separatists. Only the more radical groups, such as the Brownists and Anabaptists, endorsed ideas of equality and communal living. The abusive epithet "Puritan," applied indiscriminately to all reformers, tended to obscure the wide range of difference in the reform movement. The reformers were to some extent united by a dislike for formal ritual and ecclesiastical garments, by a preference for a simple and pious manner of living, and by a belief in the literal word of the Bible rather than the patristic teachings of the church. They stressed personal responsibility in religion and were Calvinist in their emphasis on human depravity and the need for grace through election. Yet at first only the more radical were involved in a movement to establish an entirely separate church.

The radicals on the religious left, even if they represented at first only a minority of the reformers, posed a serious threat to Elizabeth's government. Their program bore an ironic resemblance to that of the Catholic opposition on the religious right. In their theoretical writings, the extreme reformers justified overthrow of what they considered to be tyrannical rule, just as Catholic spokesmen had absolved Elizabeth's subjects of obedience to her on the grounds that she was illegitimate. Both extremes appealed to disobedience in the name of a higher religious law. Among the reforming theoreticians was John Ponet, whose *Shorte Treatise of Politike Power* (1556) argued that a monarch is subject to a social contract and must rule according to laws that are equally subscribed to by Parliament, the clergy, and the people.

The Doctrine of Passive Obedience

Elizabeth's government countered such assaults on its authority, from both the right and the left, with many arguments, of which perhaps the most central was that of passive obedience. This doctrine condemned rebellion under virtually all circumstances. Its basic assumption was that the king is God's appointed deputy on earth. To depose such a monarch must therefore be an act of disobedience against God's will. Since God is all-wise and all-powerful, his placing of an evil ruler in power must proceed from some divine intention such as the punishment of a wayward people. Rebellion against God's "scourge" merely displays further disobedience to God's will. A people suffering under a tyrant must wait patiently for God to remove the burden, which he will surely do when the proper time arrives.

This doctrine was included in the official book of homilies of the Church of England, and was read from the pulpit at regular intervals. The best-known such homily, entitled *Against Disobedience and Wilful Rebellion,* had been preceded by such tracts as William Tyndale's *Obedience of a Christian Man* (1528), a 1547 book of homilies including an "Exhortation Concerning Good Order and Obedience," Thomas Cranmer's *Notes for a Sermon on the Rebellion of 1549,* and Hugh Latimer's *Sermon on the Lord's Prayer* (1552). Shakespeare heard such homilies often, and he expresses their ideas through several of his characters such as John of Gaunt in *Richard II* (I,ii). This is not to say that he endorses such ideas, however, for he sets them in dramatic opposition to other and more heterodox concepts. We can say, nevertheless, that Shakespeare's audience would have recognized in Gaunt's speeches a clear expression of a familiar and officially correct position.

The Political Ideas of Machiavelli

The orthodoxies of the Elizabethan establishment were under attack not only from the Catholic right and the Protestant left, but also from a new and revolutionary point of view that set aside all criteria of religious morality. Tudor defense of order was based, as we have seen, on the assumption that the monarch rules in accord with a divine plan, a higher Law of Nature to which every just ruler is attuned. Political morality must be at one with religious morality. Catholic and Protestant critiques of the Tudor establishment made similar assumptions, even though they appealed to revolution in the name of that religious morality. To Niccolò Machiavelli, however, politics was a manipulative science best governed by the dictates of social expediency. His philosophy did not, as many accusingly charged, lead necessarily to the cynical promotion of mere self-interest. Nevertheless, he did argue, in his *Discourses* and *The Prince,* that survival and political stability are the first obligations of any ruler. Machiavelli regarded religion as a tool of the enlightened ruler rather than as a morally absolute guide. He extolled in his ideal leader the quality of *virtù*—a mixture of cunning and forcefulness. He saw history as a subject offering practical lessons in the kind of pragmatic statecraft he proposed.

Machiavelli was a hated name in England, and most of his works were never available in an English printed edition during Shakespeare's lifetime. (The *Florentine History* was translated in 1595.) Nevertheless, his writings were available in Italian, French, and Latin editions, and in manuscript English translations. His ideas certainly had a profound impact on the England of the 1590's. Marlowe caricatures the Italian writer in his *The Jew of Malta,* but he clearly was fascinated by what Machiavelli had to say. Shakespeare too reveals a complex awareness. However much he may lampoon the type of conscienceless villain in *Richard III,* he shows us more plausible pragmatists in *Richard II* and *1 Henry IV.* Conservative theories of the divine right of kings are set in debate with the more heterodox ambitions of Henry Bolingbroke and his associates. Bolingbroke is not a very attractive figure, but he does succeed politically where Richard has failed.

Shakespeare thus reveals himself as less a defender of the established order than as a great dramatist able to give sympathetic expression to the aspirations of all sides in a tense political struggle. His history plays have been variously interpreted as defenses of monarchy and as subtle pleas for rebellion, but the consensus today is that the plays use political conflict as a way of probing the motivations of our social behavior. To be sure, the plays do stress the painful consequences of disorder, and present on the whole an admiring view of monarchy (especially in *Henry V*) despite the manifest limitations of that institution. Certainly we can sense that Shakespeare's history plays were written for a generation of Englishmen who had experienced political crisis, and who could perceive issues of statecraft in Shakespeare's plays that were relevant to England's struggles in the 1580's and the 1590's. The play of *King John,* for example, deals with a king whose uncertain claim to the throne is challenged by France and the Papacy in the name of John's nephew, Arthur; Elizabeth faced a similar situation in her dilemma over her kinswoman, Mary Queen of Scots. Elizabeth also bitterly acknowledged the cogency of a popular analogy comparing her reign with that of King Richard II; and when Shakespeare's play about Henry IV's overthrow of Richard was apparently revived for political purposes shortly before the Earl of Essex' abortive rebellion against Elizabeth, Shakespeare's acting company had some explaining to do to the authorities (see Introduction to *Richard II*). Nevertheless, Shakespeare's attitudes toward the issues of his own day are ultimately unknowable and unimportant, since his main concern seems to have been with the dramatization of political conflict rather than with the urging of a controversial position.

Shakespeare on Religion

Our impressions of Shakespeare's personal sympathies in religion are similarly obscured by his refusal to use his art for polemical purposes. Although various attempts have been made to prove him a Catholic sympathizer or a loyal moderate Anglican, we see in his plays a spectrum of religious attitudes portrayed with an extraordinary range of insight. In matters of doctrine, his characters are at various times acquainted with Catholic theology (like the Ghost of Hamlet's father) or with the controversy concerning salvation by faith or good works (see *Measure for Measure,* I,ii), but a consistent polemical bias is absent. Some Catholic prelates are schemers, like Pandulph in *King John.* Ordinarily, however, Shakespeare's satirical digs at ecclesiastical pomposity and hypocrisy have little to do with the Catholic question. Cardinal Beaufort in *1 Henry VI* is a political maneuverer, but so are many of his secular rivals. Cardinal Wolsey in *Henry VIII* is motivated by personal ambition rather than by any sinister conspiracy of the international church. Many of Shakespeare's nominally Catholic clerics, such as Friar Laurence in *Romeo and Juliet* or Friar Francis in *Much Ado about Nothing,* are gentle and well-intentioned people even if occasionally bumbling. We can certainly say that Shakespeare consistently avoids the chauvinistic anti-Catholic baiting so often found in the plays of his contemporaries.

The same avoidance of extremes can be seen in his portrayal of Protestant reformers, though the instances in this case are few. Malvolio in *Twelfth Night* is fleetingly compared with a "Puritan," although Shakespeare insists that no extensive analogy can be made. Angelo in *Measure for Measure* is sometimes thought to be a critical portrait of the Puritan temperament. Even if so, Shakespeare's satire is extremely indirect compared with the lampoons written by his contemporaries Ben Jonson and Thomas Dekker.

Stuart Absolutism

Queen Elizabeth's successor, James I of the Scottish house of Stuarts, reigned from 1603 to 1625. Like Elizabeth, he was a strong believer in the divine right of kings. He did not possess Elizabeth's tact, however, in dealing with the heterogeneous and antagonistic forces that she had kept in precarious balance. At the Hampton Court Conference of 1604, James totally alienated the Puritan wing of the church and drove even its more moderate members into the arms of the separatists. He similarly antagonized an increasingly radical group in the House of Commons. In the widening rift between the absolutists and those who defended the supremacy of Parliament, James' court moved toward the right. Catholic sympathies at court became common. Open civil war and the beheading of King Charles I (James' son) would not occur until the 1640's, but throughout James' reign the estrangement between the right and the left was becoming more and more extreme. The infamous Gunpowder Plot of 1605, in which Guy Fawkes and other Catholic conspirators were accused of having plotted to blow up the houses of Parliament, raised hysteria to a new intensity. Penal laws against papists were harshly enforced. The Parliament of 1614 included in its membership John Pym, Thomas Wentworth, and John Eliot, men who were to become turbulent spokesmen against taxes imposed without parliamentary grant, imprisonment without the stating of specific criminal charges, and other abuses of royal power. The polarization of English society naturally affected the London theatres. Popular London audiences (often Puritan in sympathy) eventually grew disaffected with the stage, while even the popular acting companies came under the increasing domination of the court. Shakespeare's late plays reflect the increasing influence of a courtly audience.

THE HUNTINGTON LIBRARY, SAN MARINO, CALIFORNIA

COURTESY OF THE TRUSTEES, THE BRITISH MUSEUM

Ptolemy's earth-centered system of the universe (top) *was challenged by the sun-centered system of Copernicus* (bottom) *with the publishing of* De revolutionibus orbium coelestium *in 1543. Shakespeare, like other major poets of the English Renaissance, poetically represents the universe in cosmic terms as described by Ptolemy, but also reflects uncertainties generated by the new cosmology.*

The Intellectual Background

Renaissance Cosmology

In learning, as in politics and religion, Shakespeare's England was a time of conflict and excitement. Medieval ideas of a hierarchical and ordered creation were under attack but were still widely prevalent, and were used to justify a hierarchical order in society itself. According to the so-called Ptolemaic system of the universe, formulated by Ptolemy of Alexandria in the second century A.D., the earth stood at the center of creation. Around it moved in nine concentric spheres the heavenly bodies of the visible universe, in order as follows (from the earth outward): the moon, Mercury, Venus, the sun, Mars, Jupiter, Saturn, the fixed stars on a single plane, and lastly the *primum mobile* imparting motion to the whole system. Some medieval commentators proposed alternate arrangements or speculated as to the existence of one or two additional spheres, in particular a "crystalline sphere" between the fixed stars and the *primum mobile,* but they did not challenge the concept of an earth-centered cosmos.

The *primum mobile* was thought to turn the entire universe around the earth once every twenty-four hours. Simultaneously, the individual heavenly bodies moved more slowly around the earth on their individual spheres, constantly changing position with respect to the fixed stars. The moon, being the only heavenly body that seemed subject to change in its monthly waxing and waning, was thought to represent the boundary between the unchanging universe and the incessantly changing world. Beneath the moon, in the "sublunary" sphere, all creation was subject to death as a result of Adam's fall from grace; beyond the moon lay perfection. Hell was imagined to exist deep within the earth, as in Dante's *Inferno,* or else outside the *primum mobile* and far below the created universe in the realm of chaos, as in Milton's *Paradise Lost*.

Heaven or the Empyrean stood, according to most Ptolemaic systems, at the top of the universe. Between heaven and earth dwelled the nine angelic orders, each associated with one of the nine concentric spheres. According to a work attributed to Dionysius the Areopagite, *On the Heavenly Hierarchy* (fifth century A.D.), the nine angelic orders consisted of three hierarchies. Closest to God were the contemplative orders of Seraphim, Cherubim, and Thrones; next, the intermediate orders of Dominations, Powers, and Virtues; and finally the active orders of Principalities, Archangels, and Angels. These last served as God's messengers and intervened from time to time in the affairs of mortals. Ordered life among men, although manifestly imperfect when compared with the eternal bliss of the angelic orders, still modeled itself on that Platonic idea of perfect harmony. Thus the state, the church, and the family all resembled one another because they resembled (however distantly) the kingdom of God. An eloquent expression of the order of creation is to be found in Richard Hooker's *Of the Laws of Ecclesiastical Polity* (1594–1597).

The devils of hell were fallen angels, with Satan as their leader. Such evil spirits might assume any number of shapes as demons, goblins, wizards, or witches. Believers in evil spirits generally made no distinction between orthodox Christian explanations of evil and the more primitive folklore of witchcraft. Belief in witchcraft was widespread indeed; King James I took the matter very seriously. On the other hand, a book like Reginald Scot's *Discoverie of Witchcraft* (1584) attempted to confute what the author regarded as ignorant superstition. Throughout Shakespeare's lifetime, belief and skepticism about such matters existed side by side.

A similar ambiguity pertained to belief in the Ptolemaic universe itself. All major poets of the Renaissance, including Shakespeare, Spenser, and Milton (who completed *Paradise Lost* after 1660), represented the universe in cosmic terms essentially as described by Ptolemy. Yet Nicolaus Copernicus' *De revolutionibus orbium coelestium* had been published in 1543, the discovery of a new star in Cassiopeia in 1572 stimulated much new thought, and Galileo Galilei (who adopted the Copernican theory of a sun-centered system, though he was reluctant to speak out), published the results of his telescopic examinations of the moon in 1610. Even for such early reformers as Melanchthon (1497–1560) and Martin Luther (1483–1546), the new science posed significant problems in explaining the cohesiveness and harmony of God's creation, the universe. John Donne lamented in 1611–1612 that the "new philosophy" (i.e., the new science) "calls all in doubt." Skeptical uncertainty about the cosmos was on the rise. The poetic affirmations in Renaissance art of traditional ideas of the cosmos can best be understood as a response to uncertainty, a statement of faith in an age of increasing doubt.

Alchemy and Medicine

In all areas of Renaissance learning, the new and the old science were confusedly juxtaposed. Alchemy, for example, made important contributions to learning despite its superstitious character. Its chief goal was the transformation of base metals into gold, on the assumption that all metals were ranked on a hierarchical scale and could be raised from lower to higher positions on that scale by means of certain alchemical techniques. Other aims of alchemy included the discovery of a universal cure for diseases, and of a means for preserving life indefinitely. Such aims encouraged quackery and prompted various exposés, such as Chaucer's "The Canon's Yeoman's Tale" (late fourteenth century) and Jonson's *The Alchemist* (1610). Yet many of the procedures used in alchemy were essentially chemical procedures, and the science of chemistry received a valuable impetus from constant experimentation.

In physics, medicine, and psychology, as well, older concepts vied with new. Traditional learning apportioned all physical matter into four elements, earth, air, fire, and water. Each of these was thought to be a different combination of the four "qualities" of the universe, hot, cold, moist, and dry. Earth combined cold and dry, air hot and moist, fire hot and dry, water cold and moist. Earth and water were the baser or lower elements, confined to the physical world; fire and air were aspiring elements, tending upward. Man, as a microcosm of the larger universe, contained in himself the four elements. The individual man's temperament, or "humor" or "complexion," depended on which "humor" predominated in him. The four humors in man corresponded to the four elements of physical matter. The blood was hot and moist, like air; yellow bile or choler was hot and dry, like fire; phlegm was cold and moist, like water; and black bile was cold and dry, like earth. A predominance of blood in an individual created a sanguine or cheerful temperament (or humor), yellow bile produced a choleric or irascible temperament, phlegm a phlegmatic or stolid temperament, and black bile a melancholic temperament. Diet could affect the balance among these humors, since an excess of a particular food would stimulate overproduction of one humor. The stomach and the liver, which converted food into humors, were regarded as the seat of human passions. A common remedy for illness was to let blood and thereby purge the body of unwanted humors.

The name traditionally associated with such theories was that of Galen, the most celebrated of ancient writers on medicine (c. 130 A.D.). A more revolutionary name was that of Paracelsus, a famous German physician (c. 1493–1541), who attacked the Aristotelianism of his time and urged a more unfettered pragmatic research into pharmacy and medicine. Such experimentalism bore fruit in the anatomical research of Vesalius and in William Harvey's investigations of the circulation of the blood (c. 1616). Nev-

Alchemists employed relatively sophisticated equipment in their futile search for the "philosopher's stone," a reputed substance supposed to possess the property of changing other metals into gold and silver.

ertheless, the practice of medicine in Renaissance times remained under the influence of the "humors" theory until quite late, and its ideas are to be found throughout Shakespeare's plays.

Learning

In learning generally, and in theories of education, new ideas conflicted with old. The curriculum of schools and colleges in the Renaissance was inherited largely from the Middle Ages and displayed many traditional characteristics. The curriculum consisted of the seven Liberal Arts: a lower division called the trivium, comprised of grammar, rhetoric, and logic, and an upper division called the quadrivium, comprised of arithmetic, geometry, astronomy, and music. In addition there were the philosophical studies, associated chiefly with Aristotle: natural philosophy, ethics, and metaphysics.

Aristotle's name had a towering influence in medieval times, and remained important to the Renaissance as well. Even among his Renaissance admirers, however, Aristotle proved more compelling in practical matters than in the abstract scholastic reasoning associated with his name in the Middle Ages. The Italian Aristotelians whose work made its way into England were interested primarily in the science of human behavior. Aristotelian ethics was for them a practical subject, telling men how to live usefully and well and how to govern themselves politically. Rhetoric was the science of persuasion, enabling men to use eloquence for socially useful goals. Poetry was a kind of rhetoric, a language of persuasion which dramatists too might use for morally pragmatic ends.

At the same time, new thinkers were daring to attack Aristotle by name as a symbol of traditional medieval thought. The attack was not always fair to Aristotle himself, whose work had been bent to the *a priori* purposes of much medieval scholasticism. Nevertheless, his name had assumed such symbolic importance that he had to be confronted directly. The Huguenot logician Petrus Ramus (1515–1572), defiantly proclaiming that "everything that Aristotle taught is false," argued for rules of logic as derived from observation. He urged, for example, that his students learn about rhetoric from observing in detail Cicero's effect on his listeners, rather than by the rote practice of syllogism. Actually, Ramus' thought was less revolutionary in its concepts of logic than in the tremendous ferment of opinion caused by his iconoclastic teaching.

A basic issue at stake in the anti-Aristotelian movement was that of traditional authority versus independent observation. How does man best acquire true knowledge, through the teachings of his predecessors or through his own discovery? The issue had profound implications for religious truth as well: should the individual heed the collective wisdom of the earthly church, or read the Bible with his individual perceptions as his guide? Is "reason" an accretive wisdom handed down by authority or a quality of the individual soul? Obviously a middle ground exists between the two extremes, and no new thinker of the Renaissance professed to abandon entirely the use of ancient authority. For men like Henricus Agrippa (1486–1535) and Sir Francis Bacon (1561–1626), however, scholastic tradition had exerted its oppressive influence far too long. Authority needed to be examined critically and scientifically. Bacon, in his *The Advancement of Learning* (1605), fought against the blind acceptance of ancient wisdom, and argued that "knowledge derived from Aristotle, and exempted from liberty of examination, will not rise again higher than the knowledge of Aristotle." Sir Walter Ralegh and others joined in the excited new search for what human "reason" could discover when set free from scholastic restraint. The new learning did not seem to trouble these men in their religious faith, although a tension between scientific observation and faith in miracles was to become plentifully evident in the seventeenth century.

The Nature of Man

Another challenge to established concepts of thought came from Michel de Montaigne, Shakespeare's great French contemporary. In his "Apology for Raymond Sebond" and other of his essays, Montaigne questioned the assumption of man's superiority to the rest of the animal kingdom. That assumption rested on biblical and patristic teachings about the hierarchy of creation, in which man stood at the apex of physical creation nearest God and the angels. Man was thus supreme on earth in the so-called chain of being. His human reason, though subject to error because of his sinfulness, enabled man to aspire toward divinity. Man was, in the view of medieval philosophers, the great amphibian as well as the microcosm of the universe, part bestial and part immortal, doomed by Adam's fall to misery and death in this life but promised eternal salvation through Christ's atonement. Right reason, properly employed, could lead man to the truths of revealed Christianity and thus give him a glimpse of the heavenly perfection one day to be his. Renaissance neo-Platonism, as expounded, for example, in Castiglione's *The Courtier* (translated by Sir Thomas Hoby, 1561), offered man a vision of a Platonic ladder extending from the perception of a woman's beauty to the experiencing of God's transcendent love.

Montaigne, on the other hand, gave Shakespeare a fundamentally different way to consider the nature of man—a way that reflects itself, for example, in Hamlet's observations on man as a "quintessence of dust." Montaigne stressed man's arrogance, vanity, and frailty. He was unconvinced of man's purported moral superiority to the animals, and argued that animals are no less endowed with a soul. Montaigne destroyed, in other words, the hierarchy in which man was the unquestioned master of the physical world, just as Copernican science overturned the earth-centered cosmos and Machiavelli's political system dismissed as an improbable fiction the divinely constituted hierarchy of the state. Montaigne was not alone in his skepticism about man's nature; his ideas had much in common with Bernardino Telesio's *De Rerum Natura* and with the writings of the Italian Giordano Bruno. Montaigne was followed in the seventeenth century by that overpowering iconoclast, Thomas Hobbes, who extended the concept of mechanical laws governing human society and human psychology. Hobbes postdates Shakespeare, to be sure, but one has only to consider Iago's philosophy of the assertive individual will (in *Othello*), or Edmund's contempt for his father Gloucester's astrological pieties (in *King Lear*), to see the enormous impact on Shakespeare of the new heterodoxies of his age. Shakespeare customarily puts such insidious philosophies in the mouths of his villains, and affirms more traditional values through contrastingly virtuous characters; nevertheless, the challenge to the older cosmos in a play like *King Lear* is profound.

RADIO TIMES HULTON PICTURE LIBRARY

This guide graphically setting forth the ideals to which every English gentlewoman and gentleman should aspire illustrates the Renaissance concept that outward deportment and accomplishments should correctly and invariably mirror a person's inner nature.

The Drama Before Shakespeare

When William Shakespeare left Stratford-upon-Avon for London some time in the late 1580's, and made his first acquaintance with the professions of acting and playwriting, the English theatre was already a flourishing institution with a long and complex history. In order to understand what opportunities it offered Shakespeare, we need to look briefly at that history. We must consider the origin of the Elizabethan drama as an artistic form, the gradual provision of adequate physical equipment for the theatre and the stage, and the assemblage and organization of the personnel, under proper leadership, into licensed companies of players with effective business management.

The Liturgical Drama

The sixth-century Catholic Church had been largely responsible for closing down the late Roman theatre, with its bloody gladiatorial contests and its pervasive moral decadence. Thereafter, for about four centuries the theatre officially did not exist in Western Europe. Paradoxically, it was the church in the tenth century that sponsored the beginnings of a new dramatic form within the liturgy (the prescribed form of worship) of the church itself. This dramatic activity perhaps began as an insertion into the regular service of a "trope" or musical composition designed to be sung antiphonally by members of a monastic community. The earliest of these may have been composed for Easter morning, at the supremely important moment of Christ's resurrection. The Mass itself had long displayed semidramatic characteristics, and the first Easter expansions must not have seemed particularly revolutionary to anyone involved. The simplest of the early tropes (though perhaps not the first), composed at St. Gall in Switzerland some time early in the tenth century, consists merely of a chanted interrogation, *Quem quaeritis in sepulchro, Christicolae?* ("Whom do you seek in the sepulcher, O followers of Christ?"), and a chanted response, *Jesum Nazarenum crucifixum, o caelicolae* ("Jesus of Nazareth who was crucified, O heaven-dwellers"), followed by an announcement that Christ is risen as he had predicted. From other early texts of this sort, we can guess that this simple antiphon was accompanied by some stylized semidramatic assignment of roles to members of the religious community as the three Marys visiting Christ's tomb, and as the angels guarding the tomb. At any rate, tenth-century tropes of Easter soon included use of simple costume, physical movement toward the tomb, and appropriate gestures.

Other actions were appropriate to such a dramatic representation of the resurrection: the visit of the disciples to the sepulcher, the appearance of Christ as a gardener to Mary Magdalene, and his appearance to the disciples on the road to Emmaus. Moreover, other seasons of the year afforded similar opportunities, especially Christmas; the crèche was already a venerable custom, and Christmas tropes may have originated as early as Easter tropes or possibly even earlier.

In any event, Christmas liturgical dramatic activity grew apace, perhaps more rapidly than at Easter because of the sacred inhibitions associated with the resurrection. By the twelfth century, Christmas liturgical drama had become lengthy and complex, including not only the visit of the shepherds and the Magi but also the slaughter of the innocents and the flight into Egypt. Simultaneously, liturgical plays were developed for other festivals in the liturgical calendar. Some were in the vernacular: by the end of the twelfth century, an Anglo-Norman poet had written a play of Adam featuring the creation of man, the expulsion from the garden of Eden, the slaughter of Abel by Cain, and a lengthy procession of prophets announcing the advent of Christ. Such early vernacular plays may well have influenced the development of Latin liturgical drama. The twelfth century also saw a play about Daniel in the lions' den, various Saint Nicholas plays in which that popular saint performed miracles, a play at Tegernsee about the Antichrist, a play about the conversion of Saint Paul, and many others. In other words, by 1200 or thereabouts the liturgical drama had produced plays of considerable length and complexity for numerous religious festivals throughout the year. Montecassino in Italy had a complex passion play by this date. The late twelfth or early thirteenth century saw the performance at Benedicktbauern in Germany of the impressive "Carmina Burana" plays for Easter and Christmas.

The Corpus Christi Play

Although one might suppose that these liturgical plays would be gathered together into larger cycles of the divine history of the world, compilations of this sort do not seem generally to have taken place. Liturgical plays continued to be performed individually at appropriate times in the church calendar. Most religious communities owned and produced one or two such plays year after year, but no communities owned or produced very many such plays. The plays were numerous but scattered throughout Western Europe.

What appears to have happened instead of the forming of liturgical plays into a cycle is that the various craft guilds of certain towns, especially in England, banded together with the ecclesiastical authorities to produce a summer festival that would be both civic and religious in nature. One impetus was the institution of the feast of Corpus Christi in the early fourteenth century. The feast was designed to honor the Eucharist (the sacrament of the Lord's Supper) in a joyous mood, uninhibited by the somber reflections on

Christ's crucifixion that are appropriate to Passion Week. The date chosen, the Thursday after Trinity Sunday, came during a slack period in the liturgical calendar in very late spring. In May or June the days of the year are longest, and the English weather generally cooperative. The cycles that thus originated were performed on other festivals of the early summer season besides Corpus Christi day, but that festival has given its name to the genre.

The feast of Corpus Christi regularly featured elaborate processions through town, and indeed these processions may have preceded the plays themselves. Various guilds were usually assigned events in the divine history of the world for which they undertook to present dramatized renditions. The plays written for such guilds had to be numerous in most towns, since there were many guilds: the York cycle, for example, had forty-eight plays, the Towneley cycle (probably acted at Wakefield) thirty-two, the so-called N-Town or *Ludus Coventriae* cycle (perhaps acted in the vicinity of Lincoln) forty-three. The texts were evidently not translations from the Latin liturgical drama but were English compositions often based on medieval narrative accounts of the divine history of the world. Such versions contained much patristic and legendary material as well as straightforward biblical narrative: for example, the account of Christ's harrowing of hell had become an accepted part of the story, even though the Bible does not specifically mention it; the account is prominently mentioned in the apocryphal Gospel of Saint Thomas. More noncanonical still are accounts of Mary's childhood and of her marriage to Joseph. The cycles varied somewhat as to contents, but they tended to choose many of the same traditional stories embodied in church liturgy. The main figures in these favorite stories—Abel, Noah, Abraham and Isaac—were often seen as "typological," that is, prefiguring by their piety and suffering the advent of Christ himself.

The common core of most cycles included the following: the creation, the fall of Adam and expulsion from Paradise, Cain's slaying of Abel, Noah's flood, Abraham and Isaac, Moses, the prophets, the annunciation, the visit of the shepherds and the Magi, the flight into Egypt, the slaughter of the innocents, the baptism, the temptation in the wilderness, the raising of Lazarus, the entry into Jerusalem and the entire passion sequence, the burial, the harrowing of hell, the resurrection, Christ's appearances to the disciples, his ascension, and the day of doom. Other subjects were often added, such as the story of Pentecost, the assumption of the blessed Virgin Mary, and the coming of Antichrist.

Sometimes these medieval "pageants" were acted on pageant wagons before a series of audiences gathered at fixed locales throughout the town. Recent investigations have shown, however, the formidable difficulties involved in performing a complete cycle of plays in narrow streets, with each pageant having to wait in line until the preceding pageant had finished. Street processions remained common but may in some cases have involved displays in *tableau vivant* rather than full performance of each play. Certainly in some towns the plays themselves were acted not on pageant wagons but in the round, in arena theatres with several scaffolds on the periphery or even in the center of the acting area. Scaffolds variously represented Heaven and hell, Pilate's judgment hall, the house of the Last Supper, and the like. In the market place or in the cathedral close, the pageants may have been ranged in order about the open space so that the spectators themselves could move from scene to scene. Multiple-place staging certainly existed in London and in the south of England, and was the regular form of the mystery-play stage on the Continent. (The Corpus Christi plays are sometimes called "mystery" plays since they were acted by the "mystery" or trade guilds.)

Each subject or group of subjects in the Corpus Christi play was assigned to a particular company of artisans or to certain associated companies, who had their own playbook and pageant, and even pageant house in which to store the pageant wagon. For example, at Coventry the shearmen and tailors for a long time acted the scenes of the nativity, the shepherds, the visit of the Magi, the flight into Egypt, and the slaughter of the innocents. The weavers acted the story of the presentation of Jesus in the temple and the disputation of Jesus with the Jewish doctors. The texts of both these plays are preserved. In the former, the *Shearmen and Taylors Pageant,* Herod is a comic character who acts what Bottom in *A Midsummer Night's Dream* calls "a part to tear a cat in." At the point where the Magi, warned by an angel to depart into their own country by another way, escape Herod's clutches, a stage direction in the play specifies, "Here Erode ragis in the pagond and in the strete also." From such details we can perhaps understand what Hamlet means when he deplores an inflated or bombastic style of acting: "it out-herods Herod" (III,ii). The rich mercers' company of Coventry, able to supply clothes and hangings in abundance, acted the magnificent pageant of the assumption of the blessed Virgin Mary. In some other places we find the goldsmiths' company presenting the play of the Magi or "The Three Kings of Cologne," apparently because they were able to supply the necessary crowns and jewels. At Coventry the drapers' company presented the play of the Last Judgment and each year made provision for three "worlds" to be burnt. They had also an earthquake "with a barrel for the same." Among their characters were God, two demons, three white souls, three black souls, two spirits, four angels, three patriarchs, two worms of conscience, a prologue, two "clarks" for singing (one to sing bass), and a Pharisee. Unfortunately the text of this pageant, as well as that of the mercers, has been lost.

The annual Corpus Christi play was a source of municipal pride at Coventry and elsewhere, and of profit also, since it drew crowds of spectators. Royal persons and great noblemen frequently attended. King Richard III, for example, being at Kenilworth in 1484, came to Coventry at Cor-

Corpus Christi plays were performed both in procession on moving pageant wagons and in arena theatres with scaffolds located around the acting area. This is a reconstruction, executed in 1825 by Thomas Sharp, of a medieval performance of Christ's appearance before Pilate, a part of the Corpus Christi cycle at Coventry.

pus Christi-tide to see the pageants. As many as twenty full-scope plays, mostly of the Corpus Christi type, may have existed at one time in England, though the complete texts of only four have been preserved. The York, Towneley, and N-Town cycles have already been mentioned; a fourth extant cycle was acted at Chester. In addition, two fragments exist of a cycle acted at Coventry, one each from Norwich and Newcastle-on-Tyne, and several other single scenes from places not located. A Cornish cycle written in Celtic presents some Old Testament episodes and a passion sequence more like certain continental religious dramas than the English plays we have been discussing.

The Saints' Plays

Saints' plays were also widely current in England, although few examples survive today. These dramas resembled the Corpus Christi cycles in their staging and their panoramic religious spectacle, but differed from the cycles in that they told about the lives and miracles of individual saints and martyrs rather than, as in the cycles, telling the entire divine history of the human race as incorporated chiefly in the Old and New Testament. Some particular cases, to be sure, incorporated features of both saints' lives and Corpus Christi drama. The story of Mary Magdalene, for example, was derived in part from the biblical accounts of her meetings with Christ, but the narrative had been enormously expanded to include legendary reports of her travels and miraculous deeds as a saint. St. Paul was another biblical figure whose sudden conversion and subsequent travels gave to his story the characteristics of a typical saint's life. As a group, however, saints' plays offered more emphasis on miraculous conversion from sin to grace, and on the wondrous intervention of saints in the lives of ordinary men, than did the Corpus Christi cycles.

According to English historical records, a considerable number of plays dealing with St. Katharine, St. Laurence, St. Nicholas, and other saints existed at one time. As it happens, however, the only three surviving texts in English are not representative. The Croxton *Play of the Sacrament* (1461–1500) tells of five Jews who desecrate the Holy Sacrament and discover that Christ is truly present in it. Although no saint's life is told, the story is one of conversion by the greatest of all miracles. The Digby *Mary Magdalene* (c. 1480–1520) is a composite saint's life and biblical drama bringing together scenes from the life of Christ, moral allegory, and a romantic narrative of travel drawn from the *Legenda Aurea* or Golden Legend of the lives of the saints. The Digby *Conversion of St. Paul* (c. 1480–1520) centers on the conversion of Saul or Paul from sinfulness to a life of faith in Christ. These plays are especially interesting for their staging; *Mary Magdalene,* for example, seems to have been staged in the round, like some of the Corpus Christi cycles, with acting scaffolds on the periphery of a *platea* or open acting area. Despite their importance to later English drama, however, these few surviving English saints' plays are not really typical. To know what went on dramatically in honor of the saints one must study the many saints' plays preserved in French, including the *Miracles de Nôtre Dame.*

Shakespeare's debt to saints' plays may have been extensive if indirect. Some of his history plays reveal a pattern of conversion followed by glorious acts, as in the saga of Henry V. Comedies of repentance such as *Measure for Measure* and *The Winter's Tale* show us a pattern of redemptive sorrow and renewal in which the protagonist is given an almost miraculous second chance. Shakespeare's late romances are especially illuminated by this tradition that is both dramatic and nondramatic.

The Morality Play

Still another important genre in the religious drama of the late Middle Ages was the morality play. Its distinctive mode was the allegorical rendition of man's spiritual journey through life, his preparation for death, and his standing in judgment before God. Allegory was certainly not unknown in the cycles or in the saints' plays, but the morality play made extensive use of it. A number of fifteenth-century morality plays, such as *The Castle of Perseverance, Mankind,* and *Everyman,* are still in existence. The morality play survived late into the sixteenth century, late enough indeed to have made a significant impact on late Elizabethan drama—including that of Shakespeare and Ben Jonson. The morality told a story of spiritual struggle and eventual triumph over sin not unlike that of the cycles and saints' plays, but it did so in a way that could be adapted to the religious and social controversies of the era. The Corpus Christi cycles and saints' plays were, after all, tied to biblical or legendary event; when Reformation authorities sought to suppress the "idolatrous" representation of God on stage, or banned worship of the Virgin Mary and the saints, the cycles and saints' plays were doomed. Even though they were occasionally staged late enough in the sixteenth century for Shakespeare to have seen performances, they belonged chiefly to an earlier, pre-Reformation era. The morality play, on the other hand, thrived on controversy. Its simple plot of soul struggle between the forces of good and evil for the allegiance of Mankind or Everyman, and his wavering progress toward eventual salvation, could and did frequently serve as a vehicle for portraying many social phenomena of the sixteenth century.

In John Skelton's political morality play called *Magnificence* (1515–1518), for example, the protagonist is a representative king-figure who must choose between evil counselors urging fiscal extravagance on the one hand, and wise counselors urging fiscal prudence on the other hand. The plot, telling of the King's temptation and his choosing of the wrong path before he is finally awakened to his folly, is essentially that of nonpolitical morality plays such as *Hickescorner* or *Youth* (c. 1513–1520), in which the mankind figure inevitably succumbs to temptation but is eventually rescued through divine guidance. The issues in Skelton's play have embraced secular as well as spiritual concerns, while the simple story line and the dramatic structure have remained virtually unchanged. The study of a "historical" type, in this case a king, enables such a play to comment on contemporary history and yet appeal simultaneously to a universal moral pattern. Skelton's play may allude indirectly to the fiscal recklessness of Henry VIII under Cardinal Wolsey's persuasive tutelage, but it discusses fiscal responsibility in general terms that also apply

Four allegorical players in the morality play Hickescorner *were Contemplation, Perseverance, Imagination, and Free Will.*

NATIONAL PORTRAIT GALLERY, LONDON

Previous page *The Chandos Portrait of Shakespeare, the only painting done in the poet's lifetime.*

This engraving (above) *by Claes Janszoon de Visscher in the year of Shakespeare's death shows the London of 1616 as a thriving metropolis. The many boats on the Thames are evidence of the vital role the river played in the city's emergence as a center for international as well as national trade.*

THE FOLGER SHAKESPEARE LIBRARY

COURTESY OF THE TRUSTEES, THE BRITISH MUSEUM

A sketch (c. 1602) of the coat of arms (top) *granted to "Shakespeare the player" in 1596 by William Dethick, Garter King of Arms. A seventeenth-century watercolor based on de Visscher's* View of London (bottom) *shows the Globe theatre on the south bank of the Thames, a short distance west of London Bridge. In the vicinity were the competing Rose and Swan, making this area the leading theatre district of London.*

THE FOLGER SHAKESPEARE LIBRARY

Social classes and fashions in Shakespeare's England were clearly defined. People were required by law to dress according to their station. Shown here are an artisan (left), *carrying a tool; a gaudily dressed woman* (center), *attired beyond her appointed station; and a "gentleman"* (right), *privileged to wear his apparel.*

HATFIELD HOUSE, HERTFORDSHIRE. BY PERMISSION OF THE MARQUESS OF SALISBURY

A watercolor (below) *of the rural district of Buckinghamshire in about 1575, with neatly arranged villages and well-tended fields, reflects a bucolic serenity that sharply contrasts with the political and religious turmoil of the times.*

THE HUNTINGTON LIBRARY, SAN MARINO, CALIFORNIA

With London providing the background in this painting (opposite) *from about 1590, an elaborate Elizabethan wedding feast, complete with bakers, musicians, and elegantly attired guests, is about to begin.*

G. TYRWHITT-DRAKE, BERELEIGH, PETERSFIELD

Few monarchs have ever influenced an age so pervasively and left their stamp on it so permanently as did Elizabeth I during her reign from 1558 to 1603. Elizabeth is celebrated in this portrait that commemorates the defeat of the Spanish Armada in 1588.

THE NATIONAL MARITIME MUSEUM, LONDON

James I (left) *who reigned in England from 1603 until 1625 gave his name to one of the most creative periods in the history of all theatre—Jacobean drama. The word "Jacobean" is derived from* Jacobus, *the Latin word for* James.

DULWICH COLLEGE PICTURE GALLERY

NATIONAL PORTRAIT GALLERY, LONDON

Chief dramatic rival for public acclaim during Shakespeare's later years was Ben Jonson (above), *poet, playwright, critic, and literary high priest. The First Folio of 1623 contains a poetic eulogy of Shakespeare written by Jonson.*

Edward Alleyn (left) *was a leading Elizabethan actor who was famous in the roles of Tamburlaine and Faustus. A rival of Shakespeare, he was active in the Admiral's men and Lord Strange's men. Alleyn was also the founder of Dulwich College.*

Anne Hathaway's Cottage, also known as Hewland Farm, did not belong to Anne. The house was owned by Richard Hathaway, believed to be Anne's father. The house is located and can be viewed today in the hamlet of Shottery, a short distance from Stratford.

to any king—or to any man. Shakespeare's English history plays, especially the early plays about Henry VI and Richard III, owe an important debt to the tradition of the political morality as exemplified by *Magnificence.* (Shakespeare's histories also reflect traditions of the saints' plays, in their emphasis on conversion and on the glorious deeds of a king like *Henry V,* as we have seen.)

Shakespeare's history play of *King John* studies a king who had actually been the subject of one of the most important of political moralities, *King Johan* by John Bale (1538, later revised). Although Shakespeare may not have consulted Bale's play directly, Bale had still made an impressive contribution to the English history play by demonstrating how the morality structure could be used in the analysis of political crises. His play is an avowedly Protestant tract in the guise of a morality play, depicting its historical protagonist as a victim of Catholic duplicity and hence an example of what sixteenth-century England had to fear from its Catholic enemies. Later popular plays combining a morality structure with a passionate interest in history and contemporary political theory include Thomas Preston's *Cambises* (1560–1561) and John Pickering's *Horestes* (1567).

During the Reformation, the morality play was used polemically by both the Protestant and Catholic sides. Dramatists were often commissioned by governmental authorities to write plays for public performance by touring actors, as weapons of ideological persuasion. In Protestant plays such as *Lusty Juventus* (c. 1547–1553) or *New Custom* (c. 1570), the villainous Vices were depicted as Catholic tempters; in Catholic plays such as *Respublica* (1553, during the reign of Queen Mary), the Vices were Protestant. The protean flexibility of the morality formula enabled it to adapt itself to many different situations in this way. Polemical drama put ideology ahead of artistic concern, to be sure, but constant experimentation with new forms provided the popular drama of mid-century England with much-needed practical experience. One permutation of the Reformation morality play, for example, proved of considerable importance to the development of English tragedy. In some Protestant morality plays that Calvinistically stress man's innate depravity, such as William Wager's *Enough Is as Good as a Feast* (c. 1559–1570) and Nathaniel Woodes' *The Conflict of Conscience* (1570–1581), spiritual struggle ends in failure rather than in triumph for the mankind protagonist. Among the great English tragedies of the late sixteenth century, Marlowe's *Doctor Faustus* (c. 1588) is most obviously indebted to such dramatic renditions of spiritual despair, but Shakespeare's *Macbeth* and other plays may also have learned something from a native homiletic tradition in tragedy.

In staging and acting, as well, the morality play served as an important transition from late medieval religious drama to the drama of the late sixteenth century. In its origins, as seen, for example, in *The Castle of Perseverance* (early fif-

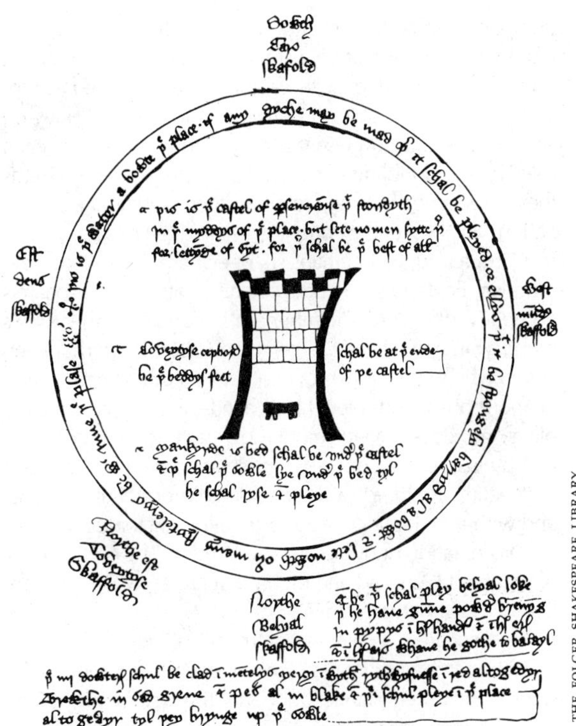

A fifteenth-century diagram for the presentation of The Castle of Perseverance *shows the scaffolds surrounding the open acting area with the castle in the center.*

teenth century), the morality play had been staged like many of the cycles or saints' plays such as *Mary Magdalene:* that is, in the round, with an open acting area surrounded by acting scaffolds on the periphery. The morality play developed great flexibility in its staging, however, just as it had developed flexibility in its approach to contemporary political or social issues. *Mankind* (c. 1471) required only an acting platform, raised probably on trestles to a height of four or five feet, and a curtain backdrop through which the actors could enter and exit. A stage of this simplicity could be carried anywhere in England and set up at a moment's notice—on a village green, in town hall, or in the banqueting hall of a lord's manor. The troupe acting *Mankind* was vastly more efficient and transportable than the company of twenty-two or more actors required for *The Castle of Perseverance; Mankind* required only six actors.

Troupes of four or five men and one boy apprentice (for women's roles) were quite standard in early Tudor England. Similar or even smaller troupes enacted folk plays and miracle plays, the texts of which are regrettably not as extensively preserved as those of morality plays. Such troupes traveled the length and breadth of the country, and dominated the field of popular entertainment from the late fifteenth century until Shakespeare's day. They were, in fact, the professional ancestors of the Shakespearean acting company. Under the direction of their leading player, who often acted the part of Vice since it was usually the choice role of the morality play, the actors were organized as repertory companies able to perform a number of plays on short notice and to present a remarkably large number of roles by the doubling of parts. They grew slowly in size as they prospered, but they retained their traditional organization. The best of the troupes gravitated to London, where, in 1576, a troupe of perhaps six or eight men and two boys founded England's first permanent theatre. Shakespeare's company, the Lord Chamberlain's men (later the King's men), was only slightly larger than this, with perhaps ten actors who were partners or "sharers" in the company, two or more boys, and a few hired hands. Shakespeare's early plays, moreover, were sometimes structured for presentation by just such a company, much as earlier popular plays had been structured, with considerable doubling of parts, and with a multiplicity of episodes allowing for the sequential presentation of numerous minor roles. The early history plays about Henry VI and Richard III are especially illustrative of this structural tradition.

Shakespeare's awareness of medieval religious drama, including the morality play, can be seen in his many allusions to it. When Hamlet addresses the visiting players on the subject of correct and incorrect styles of acting, for example, he cites ranting Herod and Termagent as illustrations of the worst kind of histrionic exaggeration (*Hamlet,* III,ii,12–14). Herod was the familiar tyrant of the Corpus Christi cycle, raging because he had failed to destroy Christ along with the slaughtered innocents; Termagent was a Saracen deity of ferocious mien who appeared in medieval drama and romance. Although these allusions may at first sound uncomplimentary to the older drama, the cycle plays themselves invite laughter at the expense of Herod's bombastic style; Shakespeare's reference is both friendly and familiar. In a similar vein, Prince Hal jestingly caricatures Falstaff as "that roasted Manningtree ox with the pudding in his belly, that reverend Vice, that grey iniquity, that father ruffian, that vanity in years . . . that old white-bearded Satan" (*1 Henry IV,* II,iv,447–458). Manningtree in Essex appears to have been renowned for its annual fair at which plays were acted and great-sized oxen were roasted; the Vice, as we have seen, was the chief comic tempter of most morality plays. Falstaff himself refers to the Vice's traditional dagger of lath in his contemptuous remarks about Justice Shallow: "And now is this Vice's dagger become a squire" (*2 Henry IV,* III,ii, 317–318). The Porter scene in *Macbeth* (II,iii) contains several allusions to the harrowing of hell, which Shakespeare's audience would have easily recognized, owing to their familiarity with dramatic representations of the harrowing of hell in the Corpus Christi cycles.

Shakespeare's specific references to late medieval drama are less important, however, than his larger indebtedness to it. His use of a structural tradition of episodic multiplicity, especially in the early history plays, has already been suggested. Of equal significance is his indebtedness to the Vice, the comic tempter of the morality play whose sinister but fascinating techniques of evil persuasion had become an enduring part of Tudor popular drama. The Vice's boastful and chortling brand of villainy is still clearly recognizable, though transmuted into superb poetry, in the insinuations of Richard III, Aaron the Moor (in *Titus Andronicus*), Iago (in *Othello*), and Edmund (in *King Lear*). As Bernard Spivack has argued, in his *Shakespeare and the Allegory of Evil,* Shakespeare's poetic vision of the contest between good and evil for men's souls owes much to the morality tradition and to other forms of medieval drama.

Early Tudor Humanist Drama

The development of the morality play and of other medieval drama, briefly sketched in the preceding section, tells only one part of the story of sixteenth-century drama. The trend we have observed in morality drama, toward the depiction of contemporary English life, manifested itself also in other kinds of plays that were not so plainly derived from the religious drama of the Middle Ages. A relatively new influence was that of classical and neoclassical drama, from the ancient classical world and from Renaissance Europe. Important too were the secular kinds of dramatic entertainment that had flourished in the English court even before the advent of neoclassicism. Early Tudor drama for courtly and well-educated audiences was heterogeneous because it reflected so many diverse impulses: the intensified renewal of classical learning that had come about through the activities of the new humanists, the ferment of ideologies introduced by the Reformation, the increase in social mobility in the Tudor court, and the like. In varying proportions, the courtly and intellectual drama of the period borrowed from the English morality play, from courtly pastimes such as the "disguising" (a kind of masque) and the dialogue or *débat,* from secular farce and romance, from classical and neoclassical literature, and even from the Corpus Christi cycles and saints' plays. The mixture, experimental and often uneven, was nonetheless stimulating because it attempted to fuse English culture with that of neoclassical Europe.

The dramatists who associated themselves with the great humanist Sir Thomas More and with his patron Cardinal Morton shared many humanist ideals that can be seen in their plays. Henry Medwall, chaplain to Cardinal Morton, wrote a morality play called *Nature* (c. 1490–1501) that reveals an interest in Aristotelian ethics as well as in traditional Christian ideas of salvation. Medwall also wrote *Fulgens and Lucrece* (c. 1490–1500), the earliest extant play in England to use an ancient Roman setting and a secular romantic love plot. The heroine, Lucrece, chooses the love of a virtuous but untitled "new" man at court, in preference to a haughty and degenerate aristocrat. This *débat* was derived from *De Vera Nobilitate* by Buonaccorso of Pistoia, an ardent Italian humanist. Despite its ancient setting and romantic plot it is also unmistakably relevant to the struggle between "new" men and old aristocrats in the court of Henry VII. Both of Medwall's plays were printed by John Rastell, another humanist in the service of Cardinal Morton. Rastell, who married More's sister, wrote a humanist interlude called *The Nature of the Four Elements* (c. 1517–1518), in which he excitedly discussed the latest scientific theories concerning the roundness of the world and other such new ideas. He is probably the author of *Of Gentleness and Nobility* (c. 1527–1530) as well, a play that iconoclastically asks whether monarchy and the inheritance of property are not social evils that ideally ought to be abolished. The influence of Thomas More's *Utopia* on this play is unmistakable.

John Heywood, son-in-law of John Rastell, was the most important and versatile dramatist of the humanist group. All his plays except *Witty and Witless,* which has been preserved in manuscript, were printed by John Rastell or his son William Rastell. Heywood's plays fall into two groups: the courtly disputations such as *The Play of Love, The Play of the Weather,* and *Witty and Witless* (c. 1525–1533), and the more popular farces that may have been intended for popular audiences as well, such as *The Pardoner and the Friar, The Four PP,* and *John John the Husband* (c. 1513–1533). In the first group, *Weather* reveals a characteristic attention to humanist and courtly themes. In an obvious analogy to the Tudor concept of an absolutist yet benevolent monarchy, the various petitioners of the play complain to Jupiter about the weather but are finally persuaded to be grateful for the mixed weather that is provided them. Heywood is suggesting, in other words, that the English monarchy must bestow its favors impartially on all classes of men, and that all subjects ought to recognize the essential soundness of the social order as it presently exists.

Heywood's second group of plays, however, eschews such courtly and political themes for a broader slapstick comedy in the vein of Chaucerian fabliau and French farce.

In addition to these humanist plays written by members of the Sir Thomas More circle, the learned drama of early Tudor England included many plays written for schoolboys or for the choristers attached to royal and noble households. The plays written under such auspices tended to reveal a much stronger interest in classical and neoclassical drama than did the plays written for popular audiences. Schoolmasters wrote dramatic texts derived from the classics for educational purposes; at court, sophisticated audiences were interested in the latest dramatic fashions from Italy or France. Ancient Greek drama did not receive nearly so much attention, however, as the Latin drama of Terence, Plautus, and Seneca. These Latin authors had long been used as schoolboys' texts, though they were frequently expurgated or allegorized into the terms of Christian morality in order to render them suitable for schoolboys' sensibilities. This academic tradition, on the Continent and in England, produced a number of imitative plays that could be acted by boys as part of their training in classical languages. Some plays, such as Palsgrave's *Acolastus* (1540), were intended to be read rather than acted. Many others were Latin biblical plays in classical guise, such as Thomas Watson's *Absalom* (c. 1535–1544) and George Buchanan's *Jephthes* (1540–1545).

At court and in noble households, choristers were becoming noted for their acting ability. They performed chiefly during seasons of revels, such as in the Christmas season. They did not appear commercially before public audiences during the early Tudor period, as did the players of moralities and popular interludes. The Children of the Royal Chapel are known to have presented plays as early as 1506. The boys of St. Paul's School acted before King Henry VIII in 1528. Later, in the 1570's and 1580's, these children's groups were organized into professional acting companies. Children's plays were generally written by

COURTESY OF THE TRUSTEES, THE BRITISH MUSEUM

Early Tudor drama employed the talents of boy actors on stage such as this company, the Children of the Royal Chapel.

schoolmasters or choirmasters. The plays were heavily influenced by continental traditions, and often depicted themes—such as that of the Prodigal Son—that were congenial to boys of school age. *Nice Wanton* (1547–1553) offers an instance of this sort. Biblical themes were common, and were sometimes used to urge a political lesson in the presence of a courtly audience. *Godly Queen Hester* (1525–1529), for example, seems to defend the cause of Katharine of Aragon and denounce the machinations of Cardinal Wolsey. *Jacob and Esau* (1547–1553) draws an unflattering comparison between the unregenerate Esau and those who refuse to abandon the Catholic faith. Classical subjects were of course much in demand as a way of educating youth, as in *Appius and Virginia* (1559–1567) and in Richard Edwards' *Damon and Pythias* (c. 1565).

Early Comedy

Schoolboys' drama was also vitally important in the development of classical or "regular" comedy on the English stage. Native morality drama was often highly comic, to be sure, especially in its depiction of the resourceful and scheming Vice; but English drama still had much to learn from classical example about play construction and about the presentation of various types of characters. Perhaps the two most famous early English "regular" comedies were *Ralph Roister Doister* and *Gammer Gurton's Needle.*

Ralph Roister Doister, by Nicholas Udall, at one time headmaster of Eton, was acted probably between 1552 and 1554 by boy actors. Its staging is essentially that of Latin comedy, with two houses facing onto a street. The play employs a classical five-act structure and preserves the unities of time and place. (According to classical and neoclassical theory, a play's action should be limited to one location—a city, for example—and to a single day.) Stock comic types include the *miles gloriosus* or braggart soldier, and the parasite. At the same time, Udall has transformed his heroine, usually a courtesan in Plautus' racy comedies, into a winsomely pious Englishwoman named Christian Custance. Ralph Roister Doister, the braggardly type for whom the play is named, is foiled in his mean-spirited determination to win Christian Custance away from her true love, Gawin Goodluck. Almost all the characters virtuously conspire to expose Ralph for his effrontery and pretended bravery; even Matthew Merrygreek, the fun-loving parasite, proves ultimately to be on the side of decency and fair play. Throughout, Udall has adapted Roman comedy to English customs and mores.

Gammer Gurton's Needle, written by William Stevenson, fellow of Christ's College, Cambridge, at about the same time as *Roister Doister,* is similarly designed for student acting. Stock Roman characters are transformed into hearty English types. Diccon the Bedlam, who engineers the farcical action of the lost needle, resembles not only the Roman parasite but also the English natural fool or zany. To some extent he also reminds us of the mischievous and inventive Vice of the morality play. Other characters are even less purely Roman in their origin: Hodge, the clownish servant, Dame Chat, the shrewish neighbor, and Dr. Rat, the impoverished and ill-trained clergyman who spends most of his time drinking and complaining about his wretched lot. The play is an educated college man's indulgent laugh at his country neighbors. Yet the play is, like *Ralph Roister Doister,* classically structured into five acts with a single stage setting that preserves the unities of time and place.

In 1566, the members of Gray's Inn saw a production of George Gascoigne's *Supposes,* translated from the Italian of Ariosto (1509). Because it was a translation and not an English adaptation, this play preserves essentially in their original form the stock character types of neoclassical comedy: the parasite, the pantaloon or miserly aged rival in love, the overly watchful father, the clever servant, the bawdy nurse, and so on. The heroine, though no longer a Roman courtesan as in Plautus, is nonetheless a self-possessed and sophisticated young woman who conducts a secret affair for some time without being detected by her father. The mores of this continental play must have seemed challengingly cosmopolitan to its fashionable courtly and intellectual audience. Just as importantly, the play offered graceful prose language as its medium, rather than the homely English verse of *Ralph Roister Doister* and *Gammer Gurton's Needle. Supposes* provided a new model for neoclassical comedy, and was to become (with some of its continental morality anglicized) a source for Shakespeare's *The Taming of the Shrew.* Indeed, Shakespeare learned much about play construction, dialogue, and characterization from neoclassical comedies of this sort; perhaps his earliest comedy, *The Comedy of Errors,* owes a great deal to Plautus and to neoclassical imitators of that Latin comic writer. Another early Italian comedy in English, *The Bugbears,* was adapted from Grazzini's *La Spiritata* and acted in about 1563–1565 by boy actors.

Early Tragedy

In early English tragedy, as in early comedy, native and neoclassical traditions coalesced and sometimes clashed. Native traditions of tragedy had partly originated in two great medieval commonplaces, the "wheel of fortune" and the "fall of princes." Both were incorporated in Chaucer's "The Monk's Tale" and its source, Boccaccio's *De Casibus Virorum Illustrium,* which presented moral examples from the lives of famous men. Chaucer had defined tragedy as the story of a great person "that stood in greet prosperitee, And is yfallen out of heigh degree Into myserie, and endeth wrecchedly." His examples, taken from Boccaccio, included Lucifer, Adam, Samson, Hercules, Julius Caesar, and others. These were men or evil beings who had either

The Tragicall Hiſtory of the Life and Death of Doctor FAVSTVS.

With new Additions.

Written by *Ch. Mar.*

Printed at London for *Iohn Wright*, and are to be ſold at his ſhop without Newgate, 1624.

COURTESY OF THE TRUSTEES, THE BRITISH MUSEUM

The title page of the 1624 edition of Christopher Marlowe's Doctor Faustus *shows Faustus' temptation by the devil. The play illustrates nature rather than classical traditions of tragedy in its disregard of the unities and its free use of comedy.*

fallen through sinful pride or had been brought low through the inevitable turn of fortune's wheel. Both types of tragedy illustrated to the medieval mind the folly of trusting to worldly expectations. The "fall of princes" tradition was extended into Elizabethan times through Lydgate's Chaucerian imitation, *The Fall of Princes,* and its Tudor sequel in *A Myrroure for Magistrates* (1559, with many subsequent revisions and enlargements). The morality play contributed a pattern similar to that of Satan's tragic fall through pride; and, although the mankind figure of early morality plays invariably was recovered to God's grace by the end of the play, some early Elizabethan Calvinistic moralities (such as *Enough Is as Good as a Feast* or *The Longer Thou Livest the More Fool Thou Art*) featured human protagonists who were eternally damned. As we have already seen, Elizabethan moralities of this sort anticipated the tragic pattern of Marlowe's *Doctor Faustus.*

Native traditions of tragedy evolved quite independent of classical tragic drama, and were in some ways strikingly different from it. Christian morality often served as a major explanation of the cause of tragic fall in medieval tragedy. Moreover, the focus was broad and cosmic, often embracing the protagonist's whole life (as in *Doctor Faustus*). Comedy was often made an integral part of stories ending tragically, especially in the morality plays. Classical tragedy, on the other hand, usually focused on a moment of crisis in the protagonist's life, and presented this crisis in its full tragic intensity without the undercutting of comic effect. In classical tragedy generally, narrative interest was subordinated to dramatic or lyrical interest. Unity of action, as understood by Renaissance theorists of drama, necessarily included unity of time and place. Thus the gap between native and classical tragedy was potentially vast.

Perhaps the earliest classical tragedy in England was Thomas Norton and Thomas Sackville's *Gorboduc,* presented before Queen Elizabeth at Whitehall on January 18, 1562. Although Sir Philip Sidney later complained about the play's violation of the unities in the fifth act, he praised it otherwise as "an exact model of all tragedies." To be sure, native concepts of tragedy are observable in *Gorboduc,* especially in its use of an ancient British setting and in its moral and Christian explanations of the causes of tragedy. Nevertheless, the classical element predominates.

This classical element is basically Senecan. Ancient Greek tragedy was relatively unknown to Elizabethan England except through Seneca's Roman adaptations. Seneca's ten plays were all translated into English by 1581, and had long been read in the schools as models of rhetoric (just as Terence and Plautus were also read). Seneca's plays were in fact closet dramas, intended to be recited rather than acted. Seneca provided *Gorboduc* with a model for its long declamatory speeches, its occasional passages of stichomythia (rapid one-line exchange of dialogue), its five-act structure punctuated by dumb shows, and its supernatural agents prognosticating doom. Moreover, *Gorboduc's* blank verse, created to approximate the Latin meters of Seneca, set a style for blank verse tragedy that dominated the English stage throughout Shakespeare's career. (Blank verse had been used shortly before *Gorboduc* by the Earl of Surrey in his translations from *The Aeneid,* but never before in drama.) *Gorboduc* also made an important contribution to the English history play by its use of chronicle materials in a tragic setting.

Other Senecan plays followed, written at first for gentlemanly audiences of the universities and the Inns of Court rather than for the popular stage. One such was George Gascoigne's *Jocasta* (1566). In 1588 eight gentlemen of Gray's Inn, including Thomas Hughes and Francis Bacon, presented before the Queen a drama similar in form to *Gorboduc* called *The Misfortunes of Arthur.* This tragedy borrows from Seneca not only chorus, messengers, and machinery, but ideas, sentiments, and words. Like *Gorboduc, The Misfortunes of Arthur* is somewhat free with the classical unities. Also, it is based upon the chronicle history of Britain, which was to become one of the chief sources of subject matter for English tragedy.

Another principal source for tragic writers was the Italian short story, which, because it was also impassioned and serious, offered to writers of tragedy many themes. *Gismond of Salerne* dramatizes a well-known Italian tale, and, like *Gorboduc* and *The Misfortunes of Arthur,* is Senecan in form and nature. It was acted before the Queen in 1566 or 1568. In the same storehouse of narrative, Shakespeare was later to find his sources for *Romeo and Juliet* and *Othello* as well as for such comedies as *The Merchant of Venice* and *Measure for Measure.*

Sir Philip Sidney as Dramatic Critic

The kind of tragedy that Shakespeare and other popular dramatists wrote in the late sixteenth and early seventeenth centuries is not rigorously classical. It preserves many of the elements of English tragedy already enumerated: a broad narrative focus, frequent violations or total ignoring of the classical unities of time and place, the inclusion of comedy, and the like. Tragedy of this sort might never have developed in England to so high a point or been accepted as the prevailing form of tragedy but for two things: in the first place, few Elizabethan dramatists learned their craft by studying the classical rules; and, in the second, the Elizabethan audience, with a taste for native English drama, demanded new, varied, and sensational plots accompanied by vaudeville clownage and songs. Such popular drama was often condemned by those critics who were familiar with classical literature, but to have made English tragedy conform with classical rules would have meant changing its nature. In France, where in Shakespeare's time the drama came under the control of the court and the learned classes, tragedy developed according to classical rules into the drama of Corneille and Racine; but in England, Shakespeare and his contemporaries created a kind of tragedy particularly their own.

The most famous classical critic of the age, Sir Philip Sidney, took vigorous exception to the kind of tragedy in vogue during the 1580's. His views are set forth in *The Defence of Poesie,* written in 1581 or slightly later:

> Our tragedies and comedies not without cause cried out against, observing rules neither of honest civility nor skillful poetry, excepting *Gorboduc*—again I say of those that I have seen. Which not withstanding as it is full of stately speeches and well-sounding phrases, climbing to the height of Seneca his style, and as full of notable morality, which it doth most delightfully teach, and so obtain the very end of poesy; yet in truth it is very defectious in the circumstances, which grieves me, because it might not remain as an exact model of all tragedies. For it is faulty both in place and time, the two necessary companions of all corporal actions. For where the stage should alway represent but one place, and the uttermost time presupposed in it should be, both by Aristotle's precept and common reason, but one day; there is both many days and many places inartificially imagined.
>
> But if it be so in *Gorboduc,* how much more in all the rest? where you shall have Asia of the one side and Afric of the other, and so many other under-kingdoms, that the player, when he comes in, must ever begin with telling where he is, or else the tale will not be conceived. Now you shall have three ladies walk to gather flowers, and then we must believe the stage to be a garden. By and by we hear news of shipwrack in the same place; then we are to blame if we accept it not for a rock. Upon the back of that comes out a hideous monster with fire and smoke, and then the miserable beholders are bound to take it for a cave. While in the meantime two armies fly in, represented with four swords and bucklers, and then what hard heart will not receive it for a pitched field?
>
> Now of time they are much more liberal. For ordinary it is that two young princes fall in love; after many traverses she is got with child, delivered of a fair boy; he is lost, groweth a man, falleth in love, and is ready to get another child,—and all this in two hours space; which how absurd it is in sense even sense may imagine, and art hath taught, and all ancient examples justified, and at this day the ordinary players in Italy will not err in. . . .

Later he tells us that English plays are "neither right tragedies nor right comedies," but that they mingle clowns and kings with "neither decency nor discretion."

To be sure, Sidney's criticism is never narrowly classical; in the essay as a whole, he affirms the power of the artist to range freely in the world of wit and imagination and to create artifacts that are more universally "true" than either philosophy or history. As a classical critic, Sidney is as much a Platonist as an Aristotelian. At the same time, his strictures against the contemporary English stage do invoke classical ideals of unity that many dramatists and audiences seem to have ignored. Popular audiences of the time seem to have had no more difficulty imagining the lapse of twenty years than the lapse of two hours. Nor were they troubled by scenic shifts from one continent to another, or by shifts in tone from the comic to the pathetic, the grotesque, or the tragic. Because native English drama had never paid much attention to classical precept, it worked out its own sense of cohesion according to different criteria of multiplicity, alternating effects, sudden juxtapositions, typological recurrence, and the like.

John Lyly

In facing the problem of understanding just what Elizabethan drama was and how it became what it was, we must recognize that the classification of drama into comedy and tragedy by the ancients does not tell the whole story. Even when we add the history or chronicle play to these two divisions of drama, we have at best a rough classification that leaves out a great deal and implies that these three forms were sharply discriminated. In fact Elizabethan drama is, generally speaking, a blend of many elements. Nearly all Elizabethan tragedies have in them comic scenes and by-plots; most comedies have in them serious issues, which might conceivably result in disaster; and history plays are often capable of being classified as comedies or as tragedies. To appreciate further this protean quality of genre in early Elizabethan drama, we might consider the varied works of a number of dramatists whose practice was successful on the stage and who influenced Shakespeare and his immediate contemporaries. Of these, John Lyly is one of the most important.

John Lyly (1554?–1606), son of the grammarian William Lyly or Lilly, educated at Oxford and Cambridge, first acquired fame not as a dramatist but as a writer of prose. His *Euphues, The Anatomy of Wit,* published in 1578, stands as the most sensational and brilliant effort in the struggle of English Renaissance prose to acquire a conscious artistic manner. The style is to a remarkable extent composed of rhetorical devices: antithesis, personification, rhetorical question, metaphor, simile, and above all of balance reinforced by alliteration. *Euphues, The Anatomy of Wit* and its sequel, *Euphues and his England,* published in 1580, were imitated by dozens of writers, including Robert Greene and Thomas Lodge, and seem to have set a new fashion of smart speech in the court of Queen Elizabeth. "Euphuism" itself had a vast influence on the style of the drama and other literature both in poetry and in prose.

Euphues and its sequel are made up of the slight adventures and the interminable discussions and letters of a seeker after true education and culture. They borrow facts, illustrations, and ideas from Plutarch, Pliny, Guevera, and many other writers, and may be said to embody the materials of Renaissance culture in the form of a handbook for the courtier, the lover, the traveler, and the statesman. They served to make the favorite ideas of the Renaissance current among ordinary educated men and women, and the expression of those ideas conscious and adequate. As for the actual fad of euphuistic speech, Shakespeare joins with those who ridiculed it; but, nonetheless, there are qualities in *Love's Labor's Lost, A Midsummer Night's Dream, As You Like It,* and elsewhere which could not have been as they are but for Lyly. (For amusing examples of Shakespeare's parodying of the euphuistic style, see Falstaff's speech in *1 Henry IV,* II,iv,397 f., beginning "for though the camomile, the more it is trodden on the faster it grows, yet youth, the more it is wasted the sooner it wears"; or Don Armado's love letter in *Love's Labor's Lost,* IV,i,61 f.: "Shall I command thy love? I may. Shall I enforce thy love? I could. Shall I entreat thy love? I will," and so on.)

Lyly was also the author of at least eight comedies, written to suit the taste of the court and possibly all acted before the Queen by the children of the Chapel Royal or of St. Paul's School. The plays are often courtly debates in the tradition of Medwall's *Fulgens and Lucrece,* with much wit combat and philosophical argument. These comedies are also sufficiently modeled on Plautus or Terence to indicate that the characteristic features of Latin comedy had by this time (1580–1590) become naturalized on the English stage. *Mother Bombie,* for example, is an adaptation of Latin comedy, containing stock figures such as the pedant, the rascally servant, the duped parent, the parasite, and the aged lover, although as usual in Lyly the clownage has an English flavor as well.

Indeed, however much Lyly may recall classical Latin comedy, he is most important as the inventor of a gay and fanciful type of comedy to which Shakespeare was significantly indebted in several of his plays. Lyly's *Sapho and Phao, Endymion,* and *Midas* have romantic plots derived from Ovidian mythology. Their use of topical allegory directed at a courtly audience is, to be sure, a mode that Shakespeare does not generally adopt. *Campaspe* plays fancifully with themes of love and friendship, art and nature, philosophy and politics in a context of classical history. Three others, *Gallathea, Love's Metamorphosis,* and *The Woman in the Moon,* are pastoral comedies—that is, comedies whose characters are shepherds and shepherdesses after the tradition of the ancient Arcadia. *Gallathea*'s scene is laid in Lincolnshire, just as the scene of *As You Like It* owes something to Shakespeare's boyhood acquaintance with Warwickshire. Two maidens are disguised as boys, and a good deal of the mythology, like that in *A Midsummer Night's Dream,* is manufactured for the occasion.

The Woman in the Moon is written in verse; all the rest of Lyly's plays are in prose, which is, of course, euphuistic. Yet this euphuistic style is turned to a purpose; it brightens the plays. The style is suited to dialogue and gives it a pungency and even a naturalness as dramatic conversation which the drama had hitherto lacked. Lyly may have learned something about the true sound of dialogue from the *Colloquies* of Erasmus, a much-used schoolbook for Latin classes; he may also have learned a great deal of the new comic method he followed from the *Dialogues* of Lucian. In any case, Lyly's followers in the drama discovered much from him about the writing of dialogue.

George Peele

Another author who contributed to the romantic and poetic tone of Shakespearean comedy was George Peele (1558?–1597), whose *Arraignment of Paris,* written about 1581 in varied and brilliant blank verse, is one of the most delightful things of its time. Peele follows Virgil, as Lyly followed Ovid, and connects himself with the spirit of Spenser's *Shepheardes Calendar.* He shows knowledge of the famous French group of poets headed by Clement Marot and known as the Pléiade. Fortunately Shakespeare, as the immediate follower of Lyly and Peele, and subjected to the same influences as they, began his work early enough to catch the fine imaginative fervor of the poets and dramatists of the decade from 1580 to 1590.

Peele was one of those "University Wits" who had to live by writing, and he turned to many styles of drama. *The Arraignment of Paris* was a courtly entertainment for Elizabeth, but his other plays were designed for the rapidly burgeoning popular stage. *Edward I* (1590–1593) is typical of the new genre of English history plays; it is jingoistically anti-Spanish, and features a popular folk-hero king who understands and respects the proud local customs of his people. *The Battle of Alcazar* (1588–1589) revels in the exotic world of Africa and the Middle East, in the vaunting heroic vein of Marlowe's *Tamburlaine*. *David and Bethsabe* (c. 1581–1594), perhaps his best play, is on a biblical topic dealing with erotic love and kingly power. *The Old Wives' Tale* (c. 1588–1594) is a seemingly naive but actually skillful medley of folk legends in the spirit of popular romance. Peele also devised two London civic pageants.

Robert Greene

Another of the striking figures of this decade is Robert Greene (1558–1592), a man whose dissolute and yet romantic impatience with the ways of the world became his own destruction. His undoubted talent and immense energy expressed themselves in a dozen love stories in euphuistic prose, largely based on Greek romantic fiction. (Shakespeare too was influenced by this genre, especially in his late "romances" such as *Pericles, The Winter's Tale,* and *Cymbeline;* the plot of *The Winter's Tale* came to Shakespeare by way of Greene's *Pandosto.*) Greek romantic fiction was written not during the great era of the Greek drama and Greek philosophy, but mainly during the second, third, and fourth centuries A.D., when the Greeks had been long under Roman rule and were scattered round the shores of the Mediterranean. The Greeks were the merchants, traders, sailors, and schoolmasters of the Roman Empire, and this earliest form of the prose romance reflects the adventurous life they lived. Such romances, as written by Heliodorus, Achilles Tatius, and others, are made up of a succession of strange and often improbable adventures, chance meetings, piracies, children exposed in infancy and restored grown and beautiful to their parents, families separated and reunited, indistinguishable twins, and many of the plot devices rendered familiar to us in the literature of the Renaissance; for the Renaissance, in its thirst for antiquity, did not distinguish between this kind of sensationalism and the real classics.

From Greek romantic fiction, and also no doubt from his own experience in life, Greene devised a type of plucky romantic heroine for his plays and novels that Shakespeare was to develop further in his comedies. The society depicted by Greek romance gave women great liberty, and like them Greene's heroines are independent, witty, and resourceful, though at the same time feminine. Greene's dramas are almost the first modern productions in which woman is in any degree represented as assuming a relatively dignified station as the friend and companion of man.

Greene also borrowed from Greek romantic fiction, and from other sources, an important element of pastoral. His plays, particularly *James IV* and *Friar Bacon and Friar Bungay* (c. 1589–1592), give us that blend of the pastoral and the romantic which the world has enjoyed in *As You Like It* and *Love's Labor's Lost. Friar Bacon* is particularly noteworthy for its multiple plot, its resourceful heroine, and its embracing of serious issues in a comic world. Greene must be regarded as the first great master of plot in English comedy.

Greene may also have written *George a Greene, the Pinner of Wakefield* (1587–1593), a play that exalts the virtues of England's yeoman class in defiance of the aristocracy and all foreign foes. The hero, George, is a patriot, a scorner of hereditary titles, and a representative of the common people against vested interests. As a new breed of English folk-hero, he is so invincible that even Robin Hood must yield to his authority. The appeal of this dream of power to the artisans and yeomen in Greene's popular audiences must have been heady indeed.

Shortly before he fell victim to the notorious debaucheries of his bohemian existence (he was reported to have died from a surfeit of pickled herring and Rhenish wine), Greene wrote many pamphlets, some about London roguery, some about his own hard usage at the hands of the world. In one of the latter, *Groats-worth of Wit Bought with a Million of Repentance* (1592), he gave us our first personal reference to Shakespeare. (See "The Onely Shake-scene in a Country" in the biographical account of Shakespeare's life and work, below.) Shakespeare was of course not the only dramatist to be influenced by Greene; Munday, Dekker, and most of the popular dramatists of the next decade were similarly indebted to Greene's example.

Thomas Kyd

While romantic comedy was being shaped and developed in the hands of Lyly, Peele, and Greene, the Senecan tradition was also finding its proponents on the English stage. The greatest genius in adapting Senecan action to the English theatre was Thomas Kyd (1558–1594). His influence on his contemporaries and on later dramatists was immense; *The Spanish Tragedy* (c. 1583–1587) was probably acted more times during the sixteenth century than any other English play, and became a pattern for subsequent revenge drama. Although Senecan tradition by no means accounts for all of the play's successful qualities, it remains a central part. Kyd catches the unabashed brutality and horror of the Senecan story and reveals it openly. Instead of having the action reported as taking place off the stage, as in Seneca and in most classical tragedy, he presents it directly. For tales of Greek mythology he substitutes a modern story of love, conspiracy, murder, and political intrigue. He retains the Senecan ghost, the revenge motive, the spirit of stoicism, and a modified form of the chorus. The play deals both seriously and sensationally with the conflicting

The Spanish Tragedie:
OR,
Hieronimo is mad againe.

Containing the lamentable end of *Don Horatio*, and *Belimperia*; with the pittifull death of *Hieronimo*.

Newly corrected, amended, and enlarged with new Additions of the *Painters* part, and others, as it hath of late been diuers times acted.

LONDON,
Printed by W. White, for I. White and T. Langley, and are to be sold at their Shop ouer against the Sarazens head without New-gate. 1615.

Thomas Kyd's The Spanish Tragedy *was perhaps the most popular play of the sixteenth century; it was performed more than any other English drama of the time.* The Spanish Tragedy *served as a pattern and influenced subsequent revenge drama—including Shakespeare's* Hamlet.

codes of revenge and Christian faith in God's providence. The protagonist Hieronimo, confronted with his son's murder and seemingly unable to obtain justice through the state, finds his pleas to the heavens unanswered and turns instead to a revenge that hardens his spirit and requires his own violent death as payment. The action is presided over by the spirit of Revenge, a chorus-like figure whose aims share nothing in common with Christian views of justice and mercy. *The Spanish Tragedy* is also noteworthy for its rhetorical style, an achievement both imitated and mocked by later dramatists. Probably Kyd is also the author of the first dramatic version of the story of Hamlet.

Christopher Marlowe

Kyd's work gave rise to a series of revenge plays not only in his own time, but later, in 1600 and the years following, when the revenge tragedy again became fashionable. Moreover, Kyd seems to have had a shaping influence on Greene and on Christopher Marlowe. *The Spanish Tragedy* probably preceded Marlowe's *Tamburlaine,* which is conjecturally dated 1587. In blank-verse style Kyd was, therefore, the forerunner of Marlowe, whose *Jew of Malta* (c. 1589) in its extravagance and sensational intrigue seems to follow *The Spanish Tragedy*.

Nevertheless, however much Kyd may have contributed in matters of style and form, Marlowe remains the leader in the great English type of Elizabethan tragedy. He shaped the genre subsequently perfected by Shakespeare. His achievement is all the more remarkable when we consider that he was born in the same year as Shakespeare (1564) and died in 1593 when Shakespeare had written no more than six or seven of his earliest plays. Marlowe's great contribution to English drama was a type of protagonist expressing something of the aspiration of the very Renaissance itself. Tamburlaine thirsts for world conquest; Dr. Faustus would go to the utmost bounds of knowledge and the power which knowledge gives; and Barabas in *The Jew of Malta* sets no limit to his longing for wealth.

Structurally, *Tamburlaine* is a good deal closer to the English popular morality play than to classical drama. Each of the play's two parts consists of a linear sequence of conquests by the humbly born but seemingly invincible Tamburlaine, until at last death ends his glory. Because many characters appear in one episode only, the cast is large and yet within the capacities of an Elizabethan acting company. Doubling of parts, as in Shakespeare's early history plays, is both common and necessary. Structural unity is achieved through thematic repetition rather than through a narrowing of the narrative focus. At the same time, the language of *Tamburlaine* is rich and new in its vibrant appeal to limitless human aspiration. The Elizabethan playgoer is invited to forget moral considerations in evaluating the play's ruthless hero, and to revel instead in the intoxicating spectacle of a baseborn shepherd "threat'ning the world with high astounding terms."

A profound ambivalence permeates all of Marlowe's plays, and gives them a restless brilliant energy that is characteristic of the times for which they were written. Tamburlaine is both a remorseless butcher of his enemies and a superhuman quester. He is fierce, mysterious, oriental, exotic, unknowable; as the projection of a universal human dream of aspiration, he is to be both admired and feared. Barabas in *The Jew of Malta* is at once colossally rich and colossally evil. Similarly, the protagonist of *Doctor Faustus* (c. 1588) is both a sinner who falls from grace and a noble but doomed Overreacher (as Harry Levin describes him) daring like Icarus to fly toward the sun. In medieval and Christian orthodox terms, Faustus is guilty of pride, the deadliest of the Deadly Sins; but in Renaissance terms he at least fleetingly resembles Prometheus, challenging the hierarchy of an oppressive and outmoded universe. In its free mixture of comedy and tragedy, and its wholesale disregard of the classical unities, *Doctor Faustus* brilliantly demonstrates what the native and homiletic tradition of tragedy had to offer Shakespeare.

Edward II, perhaps Marlowe's last play (1591–1593), is ambivalent toward its paired central figures, Edward and Mortimer Junior. At first the effeminate King seems chiefly in the wrong, while his baronial opponents lament England's decline. Toward the end of the play, however, the King becomes the sympathetic victim of a power-mad and Machiavellian Mortimer. Queen Isabella also changes radically from a long-suffering neglected wife into a scheming adultress. This shift in sympathy from the barons to King Edward is structurally much like that of Shakespeare's *Richard II,* and unquestionably Marlowe's history play had a profound effect on Shakespeare. Yet Marlowe's tone, as in his other plays, remains one of naturalistic amorality. He wryly regards England's political struggles as one more manifestation of the restlessness and ambition afflicting all mortal endeavors. His world is one of constant turmoil in which men of insatiable will must assert themselves and rise to the top, at whatever cost to themselves and to society. Shakespeare's world is basically different, even though he learned a great deal from Marlowe's tragic vision.

Marlowe first gave to English tragedy its realization of character and still more its dignity and seriousness. He endowed English drama with a spirit of aspiration. His enthusiasm for beauty of language, shared by Spenser, Greene, Peele, and others, provided a rich heritage for the young Shakespeare. Not the least among Marlowe's gifts to English drama was a new and more flexible blank-verse style. In the following prologue to *Tamburlaine the Great,* Part I, Marlowe does not treat each blank-verse line as a separate unit, but runs the sense on from line to line in order to produce what might be described as a blank-verse paragraph, a thing most necessary to drama if it was to represent widely varying emotions, thoughts, and characters:

From jigging veins of rhyming mother wits,
And such conceits as clownage keeps in pay,
We'll lead you to the stately tent of war,
Where you shall hear the Scythian Tamburlaine
Threat'ning the world with high astounding terms,
And scourging kingdoms with his conquering sword.
View but his picture in this tragic glass,
And then applaud his fortunes as you please.

This is not only a manifesto of tragic seriousness; it is also, in spite of its elevated style, one of the first examples in English tragedy of vigorous, natural, straightforward expression. Tamburlaine in his utterances is a typical Renaissance poet on the themes of both love and war, as can be seen in the following evocation of the aspiring mind:

If all the pens that ever poets held
Had fed the feeling of their masters' thoughts,
And every sweetness that inspir'd their hearts,
Their minds, and muses on admired themes;
If all the heavenly quintessence they still
From their immortal flowers of poesy,
Wherein, as in a mirror, we perceive
The highest reaches of a human wit;
If these had made one poem's period,
And all combin'd in beauty's worthiness,
Yet should there hover in their restless heads
One thought, one grace, one wonder, at the least,
Which into words no virtue can digest.
—*Tamburlaine,* Pt. I, V,ii,98–110

Shakespeare's Dramatic Heritage

Shakespearean tragedy began, roughly speaking, with marked indebtedness to the tragic writing of Marlowe and Kyd: poetry, character, and style from Marlowe; motive, plot, and tragic intensity from Kyd. No evidence suggests that Shakespeare was ever particularly aware of, or influenced by, Aristotelian theories of tragedy. His wish was to hold "the mirror up to nature" and show "virtue her feature, scorn her own image, and the very age and body of the time his form and pressure" (*Hamlet,* III,ii,22–24). Sometimes he approximated Aristotelian ideals in his plays (most nearly, perhaps, in *Othello, Macbeth,* and *Coriolanus*), but not by conscious design. Nor was he a slavish borrower from Marlowe and Kyd, even in his early tragedies such as *Titus Andronicus.* Greene and many others sought to imitate Marlowe in tragedy with but indifferent success. Shakespeare, Marlowe's only successful imitator, soon outdistanced Marlowe in those very qualities for which he was indebted to him.

Similarly, the elements of Shakespearean comedy are in part derived from Lyly, Peele, and Greene. The contributions of Lyly and Peele were those of style, setting, and movement. Greene, primarily a writer of romance, an adapter of Greek romantic fiction, furnished the element of love and adventure which makes so many Elizabethan plays delightful merely as stories. He also put upon the stage the witty, independent-minded woman, usually in boy's clothes, who gives point and naturalness to love intrigue whether in serious drama or in comedy. Not only did Shakespeare, who was a far greater genius than any of them, combine the elements of the comedies of these men and better the instruction, but, as his career went on, he realized on a broad scale the possibilities of the comic point of view in the representation of human life and character.

In the English history play, though he may have learned much from Marlowe, Peele, and others, Shakespeare was clearly an innovator as well. His early history plays on the reigns of Henry VI and Richard III were among the earliest such plays seen in London, and were (at least some of them) enormous stage successes. Even here, however, we can see how much Shakespeare learned from such earlier plays as *Gorboduc* and *The Troublesome Reign of King John.*

London Theatres and Dramatic Companies

Throughout Shakespeare's life the propriety of acting any plays at all was a matter of bitter controversy. Indeed, when one considers the power and earnestness of the opposition, one is surprised that such a wealth of dramatic excellence could come into being, and that Shakespeare's plays should reflect so little the anger and hostility generated by this continuing conflict.

Religious and Moral Opposition to the Theatre

From the 1570's onward, and even earlier, the city fathers of London revealed an ever-increasing distrust of the public performance of plays. They fretted about the dangers of plague and of riotous assembly. They objected to the fact that apprentices idly wasted their time instead of working in their shops. And always the municipal authorities suspected immorality. Thus, by an order of the Common Council of London, dated December 6, 1574, the players were put under severe restrictions.

Traveling players, shown foreground arriving at an inn, often played on bare platform stages, shown in background. Unruly crowds worried the authorities who enacted restrictive laws.

The order cites the reasons. The players, it was charged, had been acting in the innyards of the city, which in consequence were haunted by great multitudes of people, especially youths. These gatherings had been the occasions of frays and quarrels, "evil practices of incontinency in great inns"; the players published "uncomely and unshamefast speeches and doings," withdrew the Queen's subjects from divine service on Sundays and holidays, wasted the money of "poor and fond persons," gave opportunity to pick pockets, uttered "busy and seditious matters," and injured and maimed people by engines, by the falling of their scaffolds, and by weapons and powder used in plays. The order goes on to state the Common Council's fear that if the plays, which had been forbidden on account of the plague, should be resumed, God's wrath would manifest itself by an increase of the infection. Therefore, no innkeeper, tavernkeeper, or other person, might cause or suffer to be openly played "any play, interlude, comedy, tragedy, matter, or show" which had not been first licensed by the Mayor and the Court of Aldermen.

The Mayor and aldermen did not always state their case plainly, because Queen Elizabeth was a patron of the players, and because the players had friends and patrons in the Privy Council and among the nobility; sometimes, however, they did so quite boldly. One sees the case against plays stated syllogistically in the following words of Thomas White, a preacher at Paul's Cross in 1577:

> Looke but vppon the common playes of London, and see the multitude that flocketh to them and followeth them: beholde the sumptuous Theater houses, a continuall monument of London prodigalitie and folly. But I understand they are now forbidden bycause of the plague. I like the pollicye well if it hold still, for a disease is but bodged or patched vp that is not cured in the cause, and the cause of plagues is sinne, if you looke to it well: and the cause of sinne are playes: therefore the cause of plagues are playes. (From *A Sermon preached at Paules Cross . . . in the time of the Plague,* 1578.)

Moved, no doubt, by the prohibition of the Common Council, James Burbage, with a company of actors under the patronage of the Earl of Leicester, leased a site in Shoreditch, a London suburb in Middlesex, beyond the immediate jurisdiction of the official enemies in the Common Council, whose authority extended only to the city limits. By 1576 he had completed the Theatre. Perhaps he called it "the Theatre" because there was no other; Burbage erected what may have been England's first permanent commercial theatrical building. In general, the building combined features of the innyard and the animal-baiting house, having a central and probably paved courtyard open to the sky (like an innyard) and surrounding galleries on all sides (like an animal-baiting house). Burbage erected a stage at one side of the circular arena, and put dressing rooms behind it to form the "tiring house" or backstage area for the actors; the façade of this "tiring house" served as a visible backdrop to the stage itself. Burbage's Theatre became the model for other public playhouses such as the Curtain, the Swan, and the Globe which were constructed later.

By building his playhouse in Shoreditch, Burbage gained immunity from the London authorities. The city fathers could not suppress plays or control them with perfect success if they were performed in Middlesex or (in the case of later playhouses) on the Bankside across the Thames in Surrey. In order to get at them in these suburban regions, the city authorities had to petition the Queen's Privy Council to give orders to the magistrates and officers of the law in these counties. The Queen's Privy Council, although always on the most polite terms with the Lord Mayor and his brethren of the city and always open to the argument that the assemblage of crowds caused the spread of the plague, were to a much less degree in sympathy with the moral scruples of the city. Current arguments for the plays, derived from the works of scholars, poets, and playwrights were numerous and often heard: namely, that classical antiquity gave precedent for dramatic spectacles; that by drawing a true picture of both the bad and the good in life, plays enabled men to choose the good; that the people should have wholesome amusement; and that plays provided livelihood for loyal subjects of the Queen.

Of these arguments, to be sure, the Privy Council made little use, resting the case for plays instead on what was no doubt an unanswerable argument: that, since the players were to appear before Her Majesty, the players needed practice in order to prepare themselves to please the royal taste. A good deal of politic fencing ensued, and, so far as orders, complaints, and denunciations were concerned, the reforming opposition had much the better of it. The preachers thundered against plays. Pamphleteers denounced all matters pertaining to the stage: Stephen Gosson in *The Schoole of Abuse, Containing a pleasaunt invective against Poets, Pipers, Plaiers, Iesters and such like Caterpillers of a Commonwelth* (1579) and other works; Philip Stubbes in *The Anatomie of Abuses* (1583); and finally and most furiously of all, William Prynne in *Histrio-Mastix: the Players Scourge or Actors Tragedy* (1633). Gosson spoke of plays as "the inventions of the devil, the offerings of idolatry, the pomp of worldlings, the blossoms of vanity, the root of apostacy, food of iniquity, riot and adultery." "Detest them," he warned. "Players are masters of vice, teachers of wantonness, spurs to impurity, the sons of idleness."

At first, such diatribes represented an extreme reforming opinion obviously not shared by a majority of London viewers. They kept coming to plays, and the flourishing public theatres attracted the talents of the age's leading dramatists. An ominous note of polarization was sounded, however, early in the reign of James I (1603–1625) when the rift between the Puritans and the court broke into irreconcilable antagonism. After about 1604, when James openly alienated the Puritans at the Hampton Court Conference, the split between popular audiences and the best drama of the age became increasingly evident. Shakespeare's company, now the King's men, moved whether through choice or necessity toward the precinct of the court. Although the public theatre, with its capacity for large audiences, continued to serve as a lively center of theatrical activity, Puritan opposition to the stage gathered momentum. Many dramatists, in turn, grew more satirical of London customs and more attuned to courtly tastes. Eventually, in 1642, Puritan hostility forced the total closing of the theatres.

The Public Theatres

A year or more after Burbage built the Theatre in 1576, the Curtain was put up near it by Philip Henslowe, or possibly by Henry Laneman, or Lanman. About ten years later Henslowe built the Rose, the first playhouse on the Bankside (the southern bank of the Thames River). In 1599 James Burbage's sons Richard and Cuthbert dismantled the Theatre because of trouble about the lease of the land, and rebuilt it as the Globe on the Bankside. This Globe theatre burned on June 29, 1613, from the discharge of cannon backstage during a performance of *All is True,* a play thought to be identical with Shakespeare's *Henry VIII.* The

UTRECHT UNIVERSITY LIBRARY

This diagram of the Swan Theatre by Van Buchell (c. 1596), based on the observations of Johannes De Witt, shows features of the public playhouse shared by James Burbage's Theatre and the Globe.

Globe was rebuilt, probably in its original polygonal form—that is, essentially round with a large number of sides. In 1600 Henslowe built the Fortune as a theatre for the Lord Admiral's men, who were chief rivals to the Lord Chamberlain's men. The companies were differently organized, in that the Lord Chamberlain's men were joint sharers in their own enterprise and owners of their own theatrical building, whereas Henslowe owned the Fortune (and the Rose before it) and served as landlord to the Admiral's men—no doubt profiting handsomely from their activities.

Various records of these theatrical buildings have survived. One such record is the Fortune contract, preserved at Dulwich College among other invaluable papers of Edward Alleyn's father-in-law, Philip Henslowe. The contract for building the Fortune was let to the same contractor who had built the new Globe, and, since the specifications required that the Fortune should be like the Globe in all its main features, except that it was to be square instead of polygonal, we may gain from these specifications an idea of the Globe. A second documentary record is a drawing of the Swan, a Bankside theatre, accompanying a description of the playhouse by Johannes De Witt, who visited London in 1596. The drawing, which was discovered in the University Library at Utrecht, is the work of one Van Buchell and may be based on drawings by De Witt himself. Besides the Fortune contract and the Swan drawing, we have two or three little pictures of the Elizabethan public stage on the title pages of published plays, the most important being that on the title page of William Alabaster's *Roxana* (1632).

Elizabethan dancers, shown above, perform on a stage below a gallery of musicians. Imported stage designs from Italy made more use of perspective scenery than did the commercial theatres.

The Public Stage

From these documents and pictures and from scattered references to the theatres, as well as from extended studies of stage directions and scenic conditions in plays themselves, we have a fairly clear idea of the public stage. Its features are these: a pit about 70 feet in diameter, usually circular and open to the sky; surrounding this, galleries in three tiers, containing the most expensive seats; and a rectangular stage, about 43 by 27 feet, wider than it was deep, raised about 5½ feet above the surface of the yard, sometimes built on trestles so that it could be removed if the house was also customarily used for bearbaiting and bull-baiting. The flat open stage usually contained one trap door. Part of the stage was afforded some protection from the weather by a brightly decorated wooden roof supported by posts, constituting the "heavens." Above this roof was a "hut" perhaps containing suspension gear for ascents and descents.

At the back of the stage was a partition wall, the "tiring-house façade," with at least two doors in it connecting the stage with the actors' dressing rooms or "tiring house." Some theatres appear to have had no more than two doors, left and right, as shown in the Swan drawing; other theatres may have had a third door in the center. The arrangement of the Globe Theatre in this important matter cannot be finally determined, although some particular scenes from Shakespeare's plays seem to demand a third door. In any case, the so-called inner stage, long supposed to have stood at the rear of the Elizabethan stage, almost certainly did not exist. A more modest "discovery space" could be provided at one of the curtained doors when needed, as for example in *The Tempest* when Ferdinand and Miranda are suddenly "discovered" at their game of chess by Prospero. Such scenes never called for extensive action within the discovery space, however, and indeed the number of such discoveries in Elizabethan plays is very few. Well-to-do spectators who may have been seated in the gallery above the rear of the stage could not see into the discovery space. Accordingly it was used sparingly for brief visual effects. Otherwise, the actors performed virtually all their scenes on the open stage. Sometimes curtains were hung over the tiring-house façade between the doors to facilitate scenes of concealment, as when Polonius and Claudius eavesdrop on Hamlet and Ophelia.

An upper station was sometimes used as an acting space, but not nearly so often as was once supposed. The gallery seats above the stage, sometimes known as the "Lord's room," were normally sold to well-to-do spectators. (We can see such spectators in the Swan drawing and in the Alabaster's *Roxana*.) Occasionally these box seats could be used by the actors, as when Juliet appears at her window (it is never called a balcony). In military sequences, as in the *Henry VI* plays, the tiring-house façade could represent the walls of a besieged city, with the city's defenders appearing "on the walls" (i.e., in the gallery above the stage) in order to parley with the besieging enemy standing below on the main stage. Such scenes were relatively infrequent, however, and usually required only a small number of persons to be aloft. A music room, when needed, could be located in one of the gallery boxes over the stage; but public theatres did not emulate the private stages with music rooms and entr' act music until some time around 1609.

The use of scenery was almost wholly unknown on the Elizabethan public stage, although we do find occasional hints of the use of labels to designate a certain door or area as a fixed location (as, perhaps, in *The Comedy of Errors*). For the most part, the scene was unlimited and the concept of space fluid. No proscenium arch or curtain stood between the actors and audience, and so the action could not be easily interrupted. Only belatedly did the public companies adopt the private-theatre practice of entr' act music, as we have seen. Most popular Elizabethan plays were written to be performed nonstop. Five-act structure had little currency, especially at first, and the divisions in Shakespeare's text of this kind are nonauthorial. Acting tempo was brisk. The Prologue of *Romeo and Juliet* speaks of "the two hours' traffic of our stage." Plays were performed in the afternoons, and had to be completed by dark in order to allow the audience to return safely to London. During the winter season playing time was severely restricted. Outbreaks of plague often occasioned the closing of the theatres, especially in warm weather.

A capacity audience for the popular theatres came to about 3000 persons. For the most part, the audience was affluent, consisting chiefly of the gentry and of London's substantial mercantile citizenry who paid two to three pence or more for gallery seats or the "Lord's room"; but the ample pit or yard also provided room for small shopkeepers and artisans who stood for a penny. The spectators were lively, demanding, and intelligent. Although Shakespeare does allow Hamlet to refer disparagingly on one occasion to the "groundlings" who "for the most part are capable of nothing but inexplicable dumbshows and noise" (*Hamlet,* III,ii), Shakespeare appealed to the keenest understanding of his whole audience, thereby achieving a breadth of vision seldom found in continental courtly drama of the same period. The vitality and financial success of the Elizabethan public theatre is without parallel in English history. The city of London itself had only about 100,000 inhabitants, yet throughout Shakespeare's career several companies were competing simultaneously for this audience and constantly producing new plays. Most new plays ran for only a few performances, so that the acting companies were always in rehearsal with new shows. The actors needed phenomenal memories and a gift of improvisation as well. Their acting seems to have been of a high caliber despite the speed with which they worked. Among other things, many of them were expert fencers and singers.

The London public stage inherited many of its practices from native and medieval traditions. The fluid, open stage with spectators on four sides recalled the arena staging of many early Corpus Christi cycles, saints' plays, and moralities. The adult professional companies were, as we have seen, descended from the itinerant troupes who had taken their portable booth stages to every part of England, setting up in innyards, street corners, noble houses, and palaces. The Elizabethan tiring-house façade and platform stage owed much to the simple curtained booth stage and trestle platform of the itinerant troupes, set up against one wall of an innyard or animal-baiting house. Yet when those same

Elizabethan drama made frequent use of music performed by minstrels on various instruments, including drum, tabor (small drum), "hoboy" or oboe, and viol.

MANSELL COLLECTION

The Tudor banqueting hall provided a place to "stage" much early Tudor drama. The actors performed on the floor among the tables of the guests.

itinerant actors had set up their plays in noblemen's banqueting halls or at court, they encountered another structure that had an important influence on their concept of a stage: the Tudor hall screen. We must next examine the significance of this indoor theatrical setting.

The Tudor Hall

According to Richard Hosley, Richard Southern, and others, the Tudor banqueting hall and its hall screen played a major part in the staging of much early Tudor drama. Medwall's *Fulgens and Lucrece,* one of the earliest such plays, was written to be performed during the intervals of a state banquet. The patrician guests were seated at tables, while servingmen bustled to and fro or stood crowded together at the doors in the hall "screen." This screen or partition traversed the lower end of the rectangular hall, providing a passageway to the kitchens and to the outside. Its doors—often two, sometimes three—were normally curtained to prevent drafts. This arrangement of the doors anticipated that of many playhouses in late Elizabethan England, both public and private. Moreover, hall screens and passageways were normally surmounted by a gallery where musicians could play—an architectural feature markedly resembling the upper galleries of late Elizabethan theatres. The Tudor hall screen, then, provided a natural façade for dramatic action, with curtained doorways for entrances and exits. The actors of *Fulgens and Lucrece* clearly made use of those doorways, sometimes joking with the serving men as the actors pushed their way into the hall. Heywood's *Play of the Weather* calls for a similar *mise en scène.* The actors normally performed on the floor in front of the screen, among the spectators' tables. Although this ready-made "stage" sufficed for most Tudor plays, the actors sometimes provided additional stage structures; *Weather,* for example, calls for a throne-room into which Jupiter can retire without leaving the hall. Similar structures could represent a shop, an orchard, a mountain, or what have you.

Although both medieval and continental drama offered traditions of multiple staging, in which a series of simultaneously visible and adjacent structures would represent as fixed locations all the playing areas needed for the performance of a play, Tudor indoor staging seems to have made less use of this method than was once supposed. Nor did the various indoor theatres of Tudor England make extensive use of neoclassical staging from Italy, with its street scene in perspective created by means of lath-and-canvas stage "houses." Italian scenery of this sort came into use sooner in the court masque than in regular drama. Nevertheless, we do find in the Tudor indoor theatre a neoclassical tendency toward a fixed locale in preference to the unlimited open stage. *Gammer Gurton's Needle,* for example, acted probably in a university hall, seems to have used one stage structure, or possibly one door, to represent Gammer's house throughout the action, and another to represent Dame Chat's house. Shakespeare may well have been influenced by this kind of fixed-locale staging in his early neoclassical plays, especially *The Comedy of Errors.*

The Private Stage

Despite such influences on the public stage, the most significant contribution of the Tudor hall and its hall screen was to the so-called private stage of the late Elizabethan period. In the 1570's, choir boys began performing professionally to courtly and intellectual audiences in London. The choir boys had long performed plays for the royal and noble households to which they were attached, but in the 1570's they were in effect organized into professional acting companies. Sebastian Westcote and the Children of Paul's may have originated this enterprise. Their theatre was apparently some indoor hall in the vicinity of St. Paul's in London, outfitted much like the typical domestic Tudor hall to which the boys had grown accustomed. Comparable indoor "private" theatres soon followed at Blackfriars and Whitefriars.

At some point a low stage was constructed in front of the hall screen, and seats were provided for all the spectators. Many of these seats were in the "pit," or what we would call the "orchestra," facing toward the stage at one end of the rectangular room. Other seats were in galleries along both sides of the room; these were quite elaborate in the so-called Second Blackfriars of 1596, and provided two or three tiers of seats. Elegant box seats stood at either side of the stage itself. The Second Blackfriars had a permanently built tiring house to the rear of the stage, modeled on the Tudor hall screen with probably three doors. Above it was a gallery used variously as a lord's room, a music room, and an upper station for occasional acting.

The private theatre flourished during the 1580's and again after 1598–1599, having been closed down during most of the 1590's because of its satirical activities. Although a commercial theatre, it was "private" in its clientele because its high price of admission (sixpence) excluded those who could stand in the yards of the "public" theatres for a penny (roughly the equivalent of an hour's wage for a skilled worker). Plays written for the more select audiences of the "private" theatres tended to be more satirical and oriented to courtly values than those written for the "public" theatres, although the distinction is not absolute.

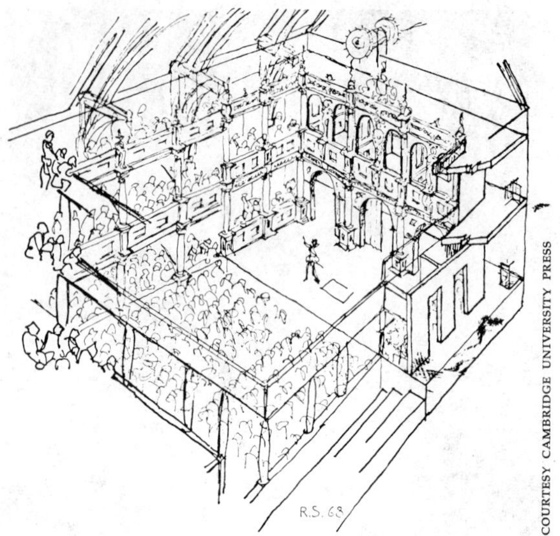

COURTESY CAMBRIDGE UNIVERSITY PRESS

A reconstruction of the Second Blackfriars, featuring a rectangular stage, a tiring house with three doors, and a gallery.

London Private Theatres

The important private theatres of Shakespeare's London were two in the precinct, or "liberty," of Blackfriars, an early one in Whitefriars about which little is known, a later one there, and a theatre at Paul's, the exact location and nature of which is not known. In the thirteenth century, the mother house of the Dominican friars, or Blackfriars, was established on the sloping ground between St. Paul's Cathedral and the river. It was a sizable institution, ultimately covering about five acres of ground. It stood on the very border of the city, and, after the custom of the time, was made a liberty; that is to say, it had its own local government and was removed from the immediate jurisdiction of the city of London. After the suppression of the friary and the confiscation of its lands, the jealousy existing between the Privy Council, representing the crown, and the Mayor and aldermen, representing the city and probably also the rights of property holders, prevented the district of the Blackfriars from losing its political independence of the municipality. It was still a liberty and therefore attractive to players and other persons wishing to avoid the London authorities. At the same time, aristocrats residing in the area required protection, and the crown had certain rights still in its control.

From 1576 to 1584 the Children of the Queen's Chapel, one of the two most important companies of boy actors, had used a hall in the precinct of Blackfriars in which to act their plays. Here were acted at least some of John Lyly's plays. In 1596 James Burbage purchased property in this precinct and seems to have spent a good deal of money in its adaptation for use as an indoor theatre (the so-called Second Blackfriars). He probably appreciated its advantages over Cripplegate or the Bankside, particularly for use in winter. But the aristocratic residents of the Blackfriars by petition to the Privy Council prevented him from making use of his theatre. Plays within the city proper had only recently been finally and successfully prohibited, and the petitioners no doubt objected to their intrusion into Blackfriars on the grounds that they and their crowds were a nuisance.

Burbage's new indoor theatre may have lain idle from the time of its preparation until 1600; but, in any case, in that year it became the scene of many plays. It was let by lease for the use of the Children of the Chapel, who in 1604 became the Children of the Queen's Revels. These theatre managers brought into their service a number of new dramatists, Ben Jonson, John Marston, George Chapman, and later John Webster; the vogue of the plays acted by the Children of the Chapel was so great as to damage the patronage of the established companies and to compel them to go on the road. Out of this rivalry between the children and the adult actors arose that open competition alluded to in *Hamlet* (II,ii) and sometimes referred to today as the "War of the Theatres." In 1608 the Burbage interests secured the evacuation of the lease, so that the theatre in Blackfriars became the winter playhouse of Shakespeare's company from that time forward.

System of Patronage

In 1572 common players of interludes, along with minstrels, bearwards, and fencers, were included within the hard terms of the act for the punishment of vagabonds, provided that such common players were not enrolled as the servants of a baron of the realm or of some honorable person of greater degree. The result was the system of patronage of theatrical companies in Elizabethan and Jacobean times, according to which players became the "servants" of some nobleman or of some member of the royal family.

By the time Shakespeare came to London in the late 1580's, more than a dozen of these companies were already in existence, some of them long antedating the passage of the act of 1572. Provincial records of the visits of players, to be sure, sometimes fail to distinguish actors from acrobats or other public performers who were similarly organized. Nonetheless, we have evidence that various companies of players performed in London and elsewhere in the late 1580's under the patronage of the Queen, the Earl of Worcester, the Earl of Leicester, the Earl of Oxford, the Earl of Sussex, the Lord Admiral, and Charles, Lord Howard of Effingham. These companies were eventually much reduced in number; usually only three adult companies acted at any given time in London during Shakespeare's prime. In addition, the children's companies, privately controlled, acted intermittently but at times very successfully. The most important of these were the Children of the Chapel and Queen's Revels and the Children of Paul's; but there were also boy players of Windsor, Eton College, the Merchant Taylors, Westminster, and other schools.

Shakespeare and the London Theatrical Companies

We know that by 1592 Shakespeare had arrived in London and had achieved sufficient notice as a young playwright to arouse the resentment of a rival dramatist, Robert Greene. In that year, shortly before he died, Greene—or possibly his editor after Greene's death—lashed out at an "vpstart Crow, beautified with our feathers," who had had the audacity to fancy himself "the onely Shake-scene in a countrey" (*Groats-worth of Wit*). This petulant outburst was plainly directed at Shakespeare, since Greene included in his remarks a parody of some lines from *3 Henry VI*. As a university man and an established dramatist, Greene seems to have resented the intrusion into his profession of a mere player who was not university trained. This "vpstart Crow" was achieving a very real success on the London stage. Shakespeare had probably already written *The Comedy of Errors, Love's Labor's Lost, The Two Gentlemen of Verona,* the *Henry VI* plays, and *Titus Andronicus,* and perhaps also *Richard III* and *The Taming of the Shrew*.

For what acting company or companies had he written these plays, however? By 1594 we know that Shakespeare was an established member of the Lord Chamberlain's company, important enough in fact to have been named along with Will Kempe and Richard Burbage as payee for court performances on December 26 and 28 of 1594. But when had he joined the Chamberlain's men, and for whom had he written and acted previously? These are the problems of the so-called dark years during which Shakespeare came to London (perhaps around 1587) and got started on his career.

One prestigious acting company he could have joined was the Earl of Leicester's company, led by James Burbage, father of Shakespeare's later colleague Richard Burbage. Leicester was a favorite minister of Queen Elizabeth until his death in 1588, and his company of actors received from the Queen in 1574 an extraordinary patent to perform plays anywhere in England despite all local prohibitions, provided that the plays were approved beforehand by the master of the Queen's Revels. Since an act of 1572 had outlawed all unlicensed troupes, Leicester's men and a few similar companies attached to important noblemen were given a virtual monopoly over public acting. In 1576 Burbage built the Theatre for his company in the northeast suburbs of London. This group also toured the provinces. Conceivably Shakespeare served an apprenticeship in this company, though no evidence exists to prove a connection. Leicester's company had lost some of its prominence in 1583, when several of its best men joined the newly formed Queen's men with Richard Tarleton as its most famous actor. The remaining members of Leicester's company disbanded in 1588 upon the death of the Earl, and many of its principal actors ultimately became part of Lord Strange's company. These probably included George Bryan, Will Kempe, and Thomas Pope, all of whom subsequently went on to become Lord Chamberlain's men.

Lord Strange's (The Earl of Derby's) Men

Besides Leicester's men and the Queen's men, other prominent companies of the 1580's and early 1590's included Lord Strange's men, the Lord Admiral's men, the Earl of Pembroke's men, and the Earl of Sussex' men. Scholars have long speculated that Shakespeare may have joined the company of Ferdinando Stanley, Lord Strange (who in 1593 became the Earl of Derby). The names of George Bryan, Will Kempe, and Thomas Pope appear on a roster of Strange's company in 1593, along with those of John Heminges and Augustine Phillips. All these men later became part of the Lord Chamberlain's company, most of them when it was first formed in 1594. Shakespeare's name does not appear on the 1593 Lord Strange's list (which was a license for touring in the provinces), but he may possibly have stayed in London to attend to his writing while the company toured. Certainly an important number of his later associates belonged to this group.

From about 1590 to 1594, Lord Strange's men formed an amalgamation with the Admiral's men, including the famous Edward Alleyn. This impressive combination of talents enjoyed a successful season in 1591–1592, with six performances at court. Alleyn's father-in-law, Philip Henslowe, recorded in his *Diary* the performances of the combined players in early 1592, probably at the Rose Theatre. Their repertory included a *Harey the vj* and a *Titus & Vespacia*. The latter play is, however, no longer thought to have any connection with Shakespeare's *Titus Andronicus;* and the *Harey the vj* may or may not have been Shakespeare's, since *3 Henry VI* was (according to its 1595 title page) acted by Pembroke's men rather than Lord Strange's men. If Shakespeare was a member of the Strange-Admiral's combination in 1591–1592, we are at a loss to explain why Henslowe's 1592 list records so many performances of plays by Marlowe, Greene, Kyd, and others, and none that are certainly by Shakespeare. On the other hand, the *Harey the vj* may be his, and the title page of the 1594 quarto of *Titus Andronicus* does list the Earl of Derby's men as performers of the play in addition to the Earl of Pembroke's and the Earl of Sussex' men. (Lord Strange's men became officially known as the Earl of Derby's men when Lord Strange was made an earl in September of 1593.) At any rate, the company disbanded when the Earl died in April of 1594, leaving them without a patron. The connection with the Admiral's men was discontinued, with Alleyn returning to the Admiral's and the rest of the group forming a new company under the patronage of Henry Carey, first Lord Hunsdon, the Lord Chamberlain.

The Earl of Pembroke's Men

The other company to which Shakespeare is most likely to have belonged prior to 1594 is the Earl of Pembroke's company. This group came to grief in 1593–1594, evidently as a result of virulent outbursts of the plague which had kept the theatres closed during most of 1592 and 1593. Pembroke's men were forced to tour the provinces and then to sell a number of their best plays to the booksellers. Henslowe wrote to Alleyn in September of 1593 of the extreme financial plight of Pembroke's company: "As for my lorde a Penbrockes [men], which you desier to knowe wheare they be, they ar all at home and hausse ben this v or sixe weackes, for they cane not saue ther carges [charges, expenses] with trauell, as I heare, & weare fayne to pane ther parell [pawn their apparel] for ther carge." Soon thereafter this company disbanded.

Pembroke's men were associated with a significant number of Shakespeare's early plays. Among the playbooks they evidently sold in 1593–1594 were *The Taming of A Shrew* and *The True Tragedy of Richard Duke of York*. The first of these was published in 1594 with the assertion that it had been "sundry times acted by the Right honorable the Earle of Pembrook his seruants." Although the text of this quarto is not Shakespeare's play as we know it but instead an anonymous version, most scholars now feel certain that it was an imitation of Shakespeare's play and that the work performed by Pembroke's men was in fact Shakespeare's. The same conclusion pertains to a performance in 1594 of *"the Tamynge of A Shrowe"* at Newington Butts, a playhouse south of London Bridge. Henslowe's *Diary* informs us that the actors on this occasion were either the Lord Chamberlain's or the Lord Admiral's men. The probability, then, is that Shakespeare's *The Taming of the Shrew* passed from Pembroke's men to the Chamberlain's men when Pembroke's company collapsed in 1593–1594.

The True Tragedy of Richard Duke of York, published in 1595, was a "bad" quarto of Shakespeare's *3 Henry VI*. Its title page declared that it had been "sundrie times acted by the Right Honourable the Earle of Pembrooke his seruants." Probably they acted *2 Henry VI* as well, to which part three was a sequel. In addition, the 1594 quarto of *Titus Andronicus* mentions on its title page the Earl of Pembroke's servants, although the Earl of Derby's and the Earl of Sussex' men are named there as well. Thus, Pembroke's men performed as many as four of Shakespeare's early plays, more than we can assign to any other known company. Nevertheless, their claim to Shakespeare remains uncertain. We simply do not know who acted several of Shakespeare's earliest plays, such as *The Comedy of Errors, Love's Labor's Lost,* and *The Two Gentlemen of Verona*. Lord Strange's (Derby's) men did act something called *Harey the vj,* and are named on the 1594 title page of *Titus Andronicus*. Sussex' men may conceivably have owned for a time some early Shakespearean plays that later went to the Lord Chamberlain's, such as *Titus Andronicus*. The Queen's men, although associated with no known Shakespeare play, other than the old *King Lear* (acted jointly with Sussex' men in 1593), were a leading company during the years in question. All we can say for sure is that the plague difficulties of 1592–1593, and the death of the Earl of Derby in 1594, led to a major reshuffling of the London acting companies. From this reshuffling emerged in 1594 the Lord Chamberlain's company, with Shakespeare and Richard Burbage (whose earlier history is also difficult to trace) as two of its earliest and most prominent members.

Shakespeare's Life and Work

Sources

The sources for a biography of Shakespeare fall into two large classes: documents and traditions. Formal written documents are impersonal, often official, and usually reliable. Yet such records, because they often give us only the insignificant and routine features of Shakespeare's life, are tantalizingly uncommunicative. Tradition, on the other hand, is likely to be fanciful, even false, arising as it does, for the most part, from posterity's craving for personal detail and anecdote.

Documents

Manuscripts of some of Shakespeare's plays and many documents containing personal information about him must have perished in the great fire of London in 1666. The records of Stratford, however, where he spent his first and his last years, still remain to give us many vital biographical statistics. Dates for his baptism and death are determined from the baptismal and burial registers of Stratford-upon-Avon. The *Episcopal Register* of the Diocese of Worcester records the issuing of his marriage license and of the marriage bond. Somerset House in London, a depository of legal documents, preserves Shakespeare's will, dated March 25, 1616. Other records, such as those of the land that he bought and sold, the lawsuits to which he was a party, and the tax returns which listed his property for taxation, indicate his financial resources and his activities as a man of the world. From these purely official documents one can usually learn where Shakespeare happened to be living at a particular time of his life, and often something about his activities at such times.

Documentary information about Shakespeare still continues to gather slowly, even after some three hundred years of collecting and setting down facts about his life. In 1910, for example, C. W. Wallace discovered in the Public Record Office in London a legal document pertaining to a suit in Chancery from the year 1612, in which Shakespeare was called as a witness. Shakespeare's signature to his deposition in this case added a sixth authentic signature to those previously known. His testimony in the lawsuit showed that he had been, possibly for some years after 1602, a lodger in the house of a Huguenot tire-maker (i.e., a maker of women's ornamental headdresses) named Mountjoy, at the corner of Muggle and Silver streets in London. He thus may have been for a considerable time in contact with a French-speaking household.

No letter written by Shakespeare exists today, and only one short letter addressed to him has been preserved. In it a Stratford neighbor, Richard Quiney, asked Shakespeare for the loan of thirty pounds. Other letters do exist that mention Shakespeare's name, mainly in connection with his activities as a citizen of Stratford. In addition to correspondence of this sort, a few diaries of the time have been discovered to contain personal anecdotes about him. Because he acted with his company at court, his name frequently appears in the official records of court performances, that is, in the accounts of the Office of Revels. He is several times mentioned as one of the principal members of his company to whom payment was made.

First publications of Shakespeare's works furnish a great deal of information about him. The famous First Folio of 1623 was edited by his fellow actors, John Heminges and Henry Condell, whose names are signed to a dedicatory epistle and to an epistle "To the great Variety of Readers." The book contains, besides other laudatory verses, a poetic eulogy of Shakespeare by his celebrated contemporary Ben Jonson. The title pages and dedicatory epistles of the two poems *Venus and Adonis* (1593) and *The Rape of Lucrece* (1594), the title pages of various plays issued singly

SHAKESPEARE BIRTHPLACE TRUST

The earliest written reference to William Shakespeare is this record of his christening in the register of Holy Trinity Church at Stratford, April 26, 1564. The entry reads, "Gulielmus filius Johannes Shakspere."

before the collected edition of 1623, and the entries of plays in the register of the Stationers' Company of London furnish information as to Shakespeare's claims to courtly patronage, his association with printers and dramatic companies, and approximate dates of composition of some of his works.

Quotations from Shakespeare and allusions to his work are an important source of biographical information. Some references of this sort have been found in commonplace books and poems even from his earliest years as a dramatist. Of the many allusions that have been found, the most valuable are those that are chronologically close to his time and unmistakably clear in their referring to Shakespeare. Probably the best known source of allusions is Francis Meres' *Palladis Tamia,* or *Wit's Treasury,* a slender volume on contemporary literature and art which would never be remembered today except for its valuable listing of most of Shakespeare's works prior to 1598.

Traditions

Although documentary information about Shakespeare is more extensive than for any other Elizabethan playwright except Ben Jonson, this information is still austerely statistical and tantalizing in its lack of personal details. Posterity has had to satisfy its craving for a more intimate knowledge of Shakespeare by turning instead to various traditions about him. Such traditions, usually written down fairly late, are often inconsistent with one another and with knowledge we have from documentary sources. Although they may in some instances contain important elements of truth and are certainly appealing, these traditions must be approached with caution.

The seventeenth century provides most of our ancedotes about Shakespeare's life. Although he was not yet regarded as deserving a full-scale biography, various men of letters jotted down what they had heard about him. Thomas Fuller wrote a not very informative sketch in his *Lives of the Worthies* (1662). John Aubrey includes Shakespeare in his *Lives of Eminent Men* (compiled between 1669 and 1696, though not published until 1813), where he records matters derived from the actor and theatre manager, William Beeston, whose father had almost certainly been an associate of Shakespeare's. The Reverend John Ward, vicar of Stratford, the Reverend William Fulman, the Reverend Richard Davies, and other persons collected local traditions and examined some records. All of these accounts, except Aubrey's, were gathered up and used by the first modern editor of Shakespeare, Nicholas Rowe, who prefixed a life of the dramatist to his edition of the plays in 1709.

Unfortunately, the collecting of information about Shakespeare had begun rather late—not until the end of the seventeenth century. Too many generations had passed since Shakespeare had lived, and the fire of London in 1666 had done its work. Those who had seen his plays were virtually all dead, and so were his direct descendants. Biographers in quest of personal details about Shakespeare had therefore to rely on oral traditions, handed down as stories from those who had claimed to know something about Shakespeare. Oral traditions of this sort were still widely in circulation in the second half of the eighteenth century, at the time of the great Shakespeare editors Samuel Johnson and Edmond Malone.

Late traditions sometimes seem implausible because they do not fit into what is known from more reliable sources; others, though questionable or even false in some details, seem authentically to confirm what we know or would expect. Consider, for example, the two following popular traditions. The first is set down in the *Lives of the Poets* attributed to Theophilus Cibber (1753). According to this report, Shakespeare's first employment in the theatre after he came to London was as a holder of horses for the gentlemen who rode to the playhouse to see the plays. Shakespeare is also supposed to have organized the boys of the neighborhood into a company of horseholders known as "Will's Boys." William Davenant and Thomas Betterton, both important persons in the Restoration theatre, are cited as authorities for this story. Such men would have been in a position to have learned a great deal of lore about the theatre in Shakespeare's time. Nevertheless, this particular story does not jibe with what we know about the actual conditions of entry into the acting profession in the 1580's and 1590's.

The second tradition comes through William Oldys, who, in about 1750–1760, wrote that one of Shakespeare's younger brothers, "who lived to a good old age, even some years, as I compute, after the restoration of *King Charles II,*" came, on more than one occasion, to London to see his brother act in plays. When he was asked at a later time what parts his brother played, he "was so stricken in years, and possibly his memory so weakened with infirmities (which might make him the easier pass for a man of weak intellects) that he could give them but little light into their enquiries; and all that could be recollected from him of his brother *Will,* in that station was, the faint, general, and almost lost ideas he had of having once seen him act a part in one of his own comedies, wherein being to personate a decrepit old man, he wore a long beard, and appeared so weak and drooping and unable to walk, that he was forced to be supported and carried by another person to a table, at which he was seated among some company, who were eating, and one of them sung a song." Actually, none of Shakespeare's brothers lived past Shakespeare's own death in 1616, so that the ascription of this later anecdote to a brother is impossible. Yet the recollection here by some aged person of the part of Adam in *As You Like It* does sound authentic. It lends some strength perhaps to other uncertain hints that Shakespeare may have acted old men's parts, including that of Adam. The tradition remains doubtful and yet fascinating, like so many late stories about him.

The Early Years, 1564–c. 1594

Stratford-upon-Avon

About Shakespeare's place of birth, Stratford-upon-Avon, there is no doubt. He spent his childhood there and returned periodically throughout his life. During most or all of his long professional career in London, his wife and children lived in Stratford. He acquired property and took some interest in local affairs. He retired to Stratford and chose to be buried there. Its Warwickshire surroundings lived in his poetic imagination.

The Stratford of Shakespeare's day was a "handsome small market town" (as described by William Camden), of perhaps 1,500 inhabitants, with fairly broad streets and half-timbered houses roofed with thatch. It could boast of a long history and an attractive setting on the river Avon. A bridge of fourteen arches, built in 1496 by Sir Hugh Clopton, Lord Mayor of London, spanned the river. Beside the Avon stood Trinity Church, built on the site of a Saxon monastery. The chapel of the Guild of the Holy Trinity, dating from the thirteenth century, and an old King Edward VI grammar school, were buildings of note. Stratford had maintained a grammar school at least since 1424 and probably long before that. It was a town without the domination of clergy, aristocracy, or great wealth, where simple, honest people plied their trades and occupied their own positions of honor in the local society.

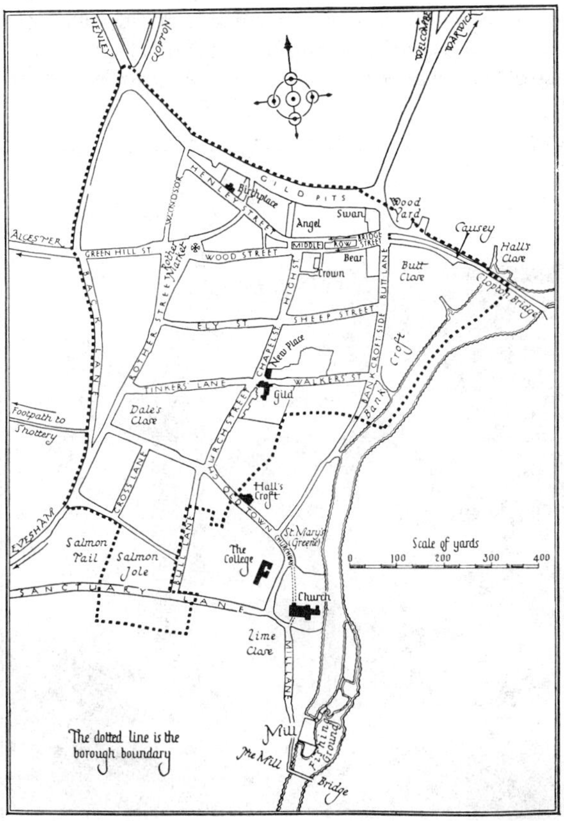

The town of Stratford-upon-Avon as Shakespeare knew it. From Henley Street, Shakespeare's writing career took him not only across Clopton Bridge to London but also across town to a residence on the corner of Chapel and Walkers Streets.

Warwickshire

Warwickshire, in which Stratford lies, is a midland county just south of the center of England and almost as far inland as one can get in that country. On the north side is Staffordshire, on the south Gloucestershire and Oxfordshire, on the east Leicestershire and Northampton, and on the west Worcestershire. It is an agricultural region broken by rich valleys of the Avon, the Stour, and the Thames. The northern part of the county was once occupied by the Forest of Arden, but even in Shakespeare's day almost the whole county was under cultivation. In his time the modern industrial city of Birmingham was inconspicuous. Coventry, today a manufacturing center, was a neat, clean, progressive borough devoted to varied cottage industries and noted for its active community life.

Warwick, the county seat, where the great Warwick Castle still stands, and Kenilworth, whose royal castle was destroyed by Oliver Cromwell, are on the road between Stratford and Coventry, the total distance between these places being about fourteen miles. Warwickshire, in the reign of Queen Elizabeth, was a rich county in which the standard of living was relatively high. Families and towns were more or less independent and self-supporting units, and agriculture was the basic occupation.

The Shakespeares

The family which bore the name of Shakespeare was well distributed throughout England, but was especially numerous in Warwickshire. A name "Saquespee," in various spellings, is found in Normandy at an early date. It means, according to J. Q. Adams, "to draw out the sword quickly." That name, in the form "Sakspee," with many variants, is found in England; also the name "Saksper," varying gradually to the form "Shakespeare." It may have been wrought into that form by the obvious military meaning of "one who shakes the spear."

Our first substantial records of the family begin with Richard Shakespeare, who was in all probability Shakespeare's grandfather, a farmer living in the village of Snitterfield four miles from Stratford. He was a tenant on the property of Robert Arden of Wilmcote, a wealthy man with the social status of gentleman. Richard Shakespeare died about 1561 possessed of an estate valued at the very respectable sum of £38 17s.

John Shakespeare

No doubt the prosperity of Richard laid the basis for the fortunes of John, the poet's father. About John Shakespeare, the first of the family to become in any way conspicuous, considerable information has been collected. He made a great step forward in the world by his marriage with Mary Arden, daughter of his father's landlord. John Shakespeare had some property of his own and through his wife acquired a good deal more. He moved from Snitterfield to Stratford at some date before 1552. He rose to great local importance in Stratford and bought several houses, among them the one on Henley Street traditionally identified as Shakespeare's birthplace. William Shakespeare was born in 1564 and was baptized on April 26. The exact date of his birth is not known, but traditionally we celebrate it on April 23, the feast day of St. George, England's patron saint. (The date is at least plausible in view of the practice of baptizing infants shortly after birth.) The house in which Shakespeare was probably born, though changed in various and unknown ways during the years which have intervened since Shakespeare's birth, still stands. It is of considerable size, having four rooms on the ground floor, and must, therefore, have been an important business house in the Stratford of those days. John Shakespeare's occupation seems to have been that of a tanner and glover—that is, he cured skins, made gloves and some other leather goods, and sold them in his shop. He was also a dealer in wool, grain, malt, and other farm produce.

The long story, beginning in 1552, of John Shakespeare's success and misfortunes in Stratford is attested by many borough records. He held various city offices. He was ale taster (inspector of bread and malt), burgess (petty constable), affeeror (assessor of fines), city chamberlain (treasurer), alderman, and high bailiff of the town—the highest municipal office in Stratford. At some time around 1576 he applied to the Herald's office for the right to bear arms and style himself a gentleman. This petition was later to be renewed and successfully carried through to completion by his famous son. In 1577 or 1578, however, when William was as yet only thirteen or fourteen years old, John Shakespeare's fortunes began a sudden and mysterious decline. He absented himself from council meetings. He had to mortgage his wife's property and showed other signs of being in financial difficulty. He became involved in serious litigation and was assessed heavy fines. Although he kept his position on the corporation council until 1586 or 1587, he was finally replaced as alderman because of his failure to attend. Conceivably John Shakespeare's sudden difficulties were the result of persecution for Catholic faith, since John's wife's family had remained loyal to Catholicism, and the old faith was being attacked with new vigor in the War-

SHAKESPEARE BIRTHPLACE TRUST

This house on Henley Street in Stratford is considered to have been the birthplace of Shakespeare. Its great size shows what must have been an important house of business. Shakespeare's father dealt chiefly in leather goods, though he also traded in wool, grain, and other farm produce.

wickshire region in 1577 and afterwards. This hypothesis is unsubstantial, however, especially in view of the fact that some Catholics and Puritans seemed to have held posts of trust and remained prosperous in Stratford during this period. In the last analysis, we have little evidence as to John Shakespeare's religious faith or as to the reasons for his sudden reversal of fortune.

Our only tentative personal glimpse of John Shakespeare comes from a note in the Memoranda of Archdeacon Plume of Rochester, written about 1656. This note purports to describe John Shakespeare in his later years as one who thought well of his own wit and was willing to match it at any time against that of his famous son:

> He [Shakespeare] was a glovers son. Sir John Mennis saw once his old Father in his shop—a merry Cheekd old man that said, "Will was a good Honest Fellow, but he [John Shakespeare] durst have crackt a jeast with him at any time."

This tradition may contain some element of truth, even though the name of Sir John Mennes cannot be accurate; Mennes was not born until 1599, two years before the death of Shakespeare's father.

The family of Shakespeare's mother could trace its ancestry back to the time of William the Conqueror; and Shakespeare's father, in spite of his troubles, was a citizen of importance. John Shakespeare made his mark instead of writing his name, but so did other men of the time who we know could read and write. His offices, particularly that of chamberlain, and the various public functions he discharged, indicate that he must have had some education.

Shakespeare in School

Nicholas Rowe, who published in 1709 the first extensive biographical account of Shakespeare, reports the tradition that Shakespeare studied "for some time at a Free-School." Although the list of students who actually attended the King's New School at Stratford-upon-Avon in the late sixteenth century has not survived, we cannot doubt that Rowe is reporting accurately. Shakespeare's father, as a leading citizen of Stratford, would scarcely have spurned the benefits of one of Stratford's most prized institutions. The town had had a free school since the thirteenth century, at first under the auspices of the church. During the reign of King Edward VI (1547–1553), the church lands were expropriated by the crown and the town of Stratford was granted a corporate charter. At this time the school was reorganized as the King's New School, named in honor of the reigning monarch. It prospered. Its teachers or "masters" regularly held degrees from Oxford during Shakespeare's childhood and received salaries that were superior to those of most comparable schools.

Much has been learned about the curriculum of such a school. A child would first learn the rudiments of reading and writing English by spending two or three years in a "petty" or elementary school. The child learned to read from his "hornbook," a single sheet of paper mounted on a board and protected by a thin transparent layer of horn, on which was usually printed the alphabet in small and capital letters and the Lord's Prayer. The child would also practice his ABC book with catechism. When he had demonstrated the ability to read satisfactorily, he was admitted, at about the age of seven, to the grammar school proper. Here the day was a rigorous one, usually extending from 6 A.M. in the summer or 7 A.M. in the winter until 5 P.M. Intervals for food or brief recreation came in midmorning, noon, and midafternoon. Holidays occurred at Christmas,

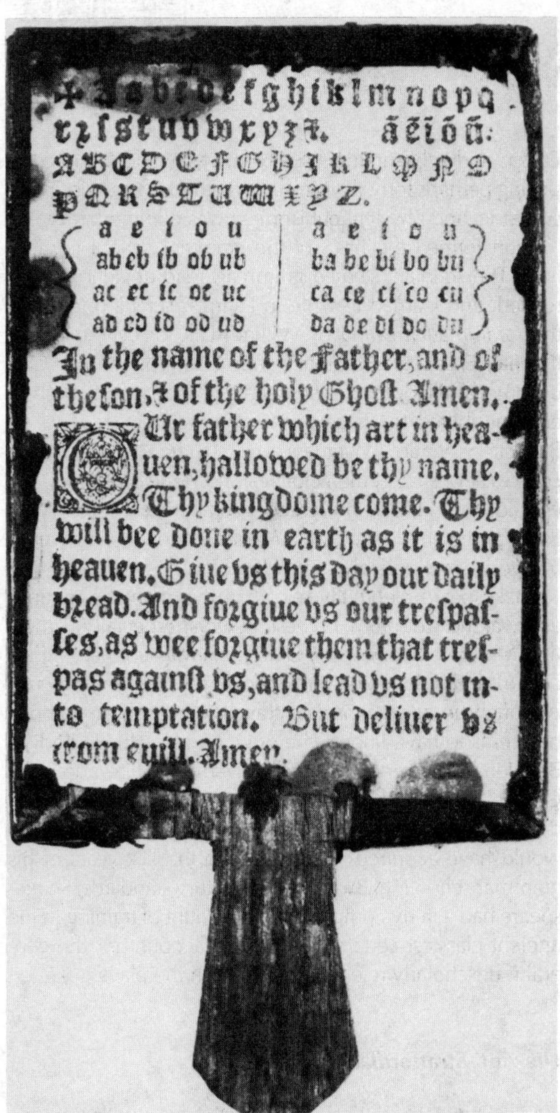

THE FOLGER SHAKESPEARE LIBRARY

The hornbook pictured here—showing the alphabet and the Lord's Prayer—was a part of every child's education in Shakespeare's time.

A schoolroom in Tudor England.

J. KOMENSKY: ORBIS SENSUALIUM PICTUS, 1659

Easter, and Whitsuntide (usually late May and June), comprising perhaps forty days in all through the year. Discipline was strict and physical punishment was common.

Latin formed the basis of the grammar school curriculum. The scholars studied grammar, read ancient writers, recited, and learned to write in Latin. A standard text was the *Grammatica Latina* by William Lilly or Lyly, father of the later Elizabethan dramatist John Lyly. The scholars also became familiar with the *Disticha de Moribus* (moral proverbs) attributed to Cato, *Aesop's Fables*, the *Eclogues* of Baptista Spagnuoli Mantuanus or Mantuan (alluded to in *Love's Labor's Lost*), the *Eclogues* and *Aeneid* of Virgil, the comedies of Plautus or Terence (sometimes performed in Latin by the children), Ovid's *Metamorphoses* and other of his works, and possibly some Horace and Seneca.

Shakespeare plentifully reveals in his dramatic writings an awareness of many of these authors, especially Plautus (in *The Comedy of Errors*), Ovid (in *A Midsummer Night's Dream* and elsewhere), and Seneca (in *Titus Andronicus*). Although he often consulted translations of these authors, he seems to have known the originals as well. He had, in Ben Jonson's learned estimation, "small Latine and lesse Greeke"; the tone is condescending, but the statement does concede that Shakespeare had some of both. He would have acquired some Greek in the last years of his grammar schooling. By twentieth-century standards, Shakespeare had a fairly comprehensive amount of training in the ancient classics, certainly enough to account for the general if unscholarly references we find in the plays.

The Anti-Stratfordian Movement

What we know of Shakespeare's life so far is really quite considerable. The information we have is just the kind one would expect. It hangs together and refers to one man and one career. Though lacking in the personal details we should like to have, it is both adequate and plausible. Yet the past hundred years or so have seen the growth of a tendency to doubt Shakespeare's authorship of the plays and poems ascribed to him. The phenomenon is sometimes called the "anti-Stratfordian" movement, since its attack is leveled at the literary credentials of the man who was born in Stratford and later became an actor in London. Although based on no reliable evidence, the movement has persisted long enough to become a kind of myth. It also has the appeal of a mystery thriller: who really wrote Shakespeare's plays? A brief account must be made here of the origins of the anti-Stratfordian movement.

Beginning in the late eighteenth century, and especially in the mid-nineteenth century, a few admirers of Shakespeare began to be troubled by the scantiness of information about England's greatest author. As we have already seen, good reasons exist for that scarcity: the great London fire of 1666 that destroyed many records, the relatively low social esteem accorded to popular dramatists during the Elizabethan period, and the like. Also, we do actually know more about Shakespeare than about most of his contemporaries in the theatre, despite the difficulties imposed by the passage of time. Still, some nineteenth-century readers saw only that they knew far less about Shakespeare than about many authors of more recent date.

Moreover, the impressions of the man did not seem to square with his unparalleled literary greatness. William Shakespeare had been brought up in a small country town; were his parents cultured folk, or even literate? No record of his schooling has been preserved; was Shakespeare himself able to read and write, much less write immortal plays and poems? The anti-Stratfordians did not deny the existence of a man called Shakespeare from Stratford-upon-Avon, but they found it incredible that such a person should be connected with the works ascribed to him. Mark Twain, himself an anti-Stratfordian, was fond of joking that the plays were not by Shakespeare but by another person of the same name. Beneath the humor in this remark lies a deep-seated mistrust: how could a country boy have written so knowledgeably and eloquently about the lives of kings and queens? Where could such a person have learned so much about the law, about medicine, about the art of war, about heraldry? The puzzle seemed a genuine one, even though no one until the late eighteenth century had thought to question Shakespeare's authorship of the plays—least of all his colleagues and friends, such as Ben Jonson, who admitted that Shakespeare's classical learning was "small," but insisted that Shakespeare was an incomparable genius.

The first candidate put forward in the anti-Stratfordian cause as the "real" author of the plays was Sir Francis Bacon, a reputable Elizabethan writer with connections at court and considerable cultural attainments. Yet the ascription of the plays to Bacon was based on no documentary evidence. It relied instead on the essentially snobbish argument that Bacon was better born and purportedly better educated than Shakespeare—an argument that appealed strongly to the nineteenth century in which a university education was becoming more and more a distinctive mark of the cultivated person. The assertion of Bacon's authorship was also based on a conspiratorial theory of history. That is, its believers had to assume the existence of a mammoth conspiracy in Elizabethan times in which Shakespeare would allow his name to be used by Bacon as a *nom de plume,* and in which Shakespeare's friends such as Ben Jonson would take part. (Jonson knew Shakespeare too well, after all, to have been duped for a period of almost twenty years.) The motive for such an arrangement, presumably, was that Bacon did not deign to lend his dignified name to the writing of popular plays (since they were considered subliterary) and so chose a common actor named Shakespeare to serve as his alter ego. This theory of an elaborate hoax involving England's greatest literary giant has proved powerfully attractive to modern writers like Mark Twain, who sometimes refer to themselves as rebels against the cultural "Establishment" of their own times.

The claim that Bacon wrote Shakespeare's works was soon challenged in the name of other prominent Elizabethans: the Earl of Oxford, the Earl of Southampton, Anthony Bacon, the Earl of Rutland, the Earl of Devonshire, Christopher Marlowe, and others. Since documentary claims as to Bacon's authorship of the Shakespearean canon were nonexistent, other Elizabethans could be proposed to fill his role just as satisfactorily as Bacon himself. The anti-Stratfordian movement gained momentum and came to include several prominent persons including Delia Bacon and Sigmund Freud as well as Mark Twain. One of the appeals of the anti-Stratfordian movement in recent years has proved to be a kind of amateur sleuthing or scholarship carried on by professional lawyers, doctors, and the like, who have explored Shakespeare's interest in law and medicine as a hobby and have convinced themselves that Shakespeare's wisdom in these subjects entitles him to claim a better birth than that of a glover's son from Stratford. Absurdly ingenious efforts at "deciphering" hidden meanings in the works have been adduced to prove some authorship claim or other. The academic "Establishments" of modern universities have been accused of perpetuating Shakespeare's name out of mere vested self-interest: Shakespeare scholarship is an industry, and its busy workers need to preserve their source of income.

We must ask in all seriousness, however, whether such assertions are not offering answers to nonexistent questions. Responsible scholarship has admirably dispelled the seeming mystery of Shakespeare's humble beginnings. T. W. Baldwin, for example, in *William Shakspere's Petty School* (1943) and *William Shakspere's Small Latine and Lesse Greeke* (1944) has shown just what sort of classical training Shakespeare almost surely received in the free grammar school of Stratford. It is precisely the sort of training that would have enabled him to use classical authors as he does, with the familiarity of one who likes to read. His Latin and Greek were passable but not strong; he often consulted modern translations as well as classical originals. Just as importantly, Shakespeare's social background was in fact typical of many of the greatest writers of the English Renaissance. He earned his living by his writing, and thus had one of the strongest of motives for success. So did his contemporaries Marlowe (who came from a shoemakers' family) and Jonson (whose stepfather was a brickmason). Greene, Peele, Nashe, and many others sold plays and other writings for a livelihood. Although a few well-born persons such as Bacon and Sir Philip Sidney also made exceptional contributions to literature, and although a number of courtiers emulated Henry VIII and Elizabeth as gifted amateurs in the arts, the court was not the direct or major source of England's literary greatness. Most courtiers were not, like Shakespeare, professional writers. A man like Bacon lacked Shakespeare's connection with a commercial acting company. Surely the theatre was a more relevant "university" for Shakespeare than Oxford or Cambridge, where most of his studies would have been in ancient languages and in divinity.

Shakespeare's Marriage

When Shakespeare was eighteen years old, he married Anne Hathaway, a woman eight years his senior. (The inscription on her grave states that she was sixty-seven when she died in August of 1623.) The bishop's register of Worcester, the central city of the diocese, shows for November 27, 1582, the issue of a bishop's license for the marriage of William Shakespeare and Anne Hathaway. She has been identified with all reasonable probability as Agnes (or Anne) Hathaway, daughter of the then recently deceased Richard Hathaway of the hamlet of Shottery, a short distance from Stratford.

The obtaining of a license was not normally required for

a marriage. William Shakespeare and Anne Hathaway seem to have applied for a license on this occasion because they wished to be married after only one reading of the banns rather than the usual three. (The reading of the banns, or announcement in church of a forthcoming marriage, usually on three successive Sundays, enabled any party to object to the marriage if he knew of any legal impediment.) Since the reading of all banns was suspended for long periods during Advent (before Christmas) and Lent (before Easter), a couple intending to marry shortly before Christmas might have had to wait until April before the banns could be read thrice. Accordingly, the bishop not uncommonly granted a license permitting couples to marry during the winter season with only one reading of the banns. To obtain such a license, two friends of the bride's family had to sign a bond obligating themselves to pay the bishop up to forty pounds, should any impediment to the marriage result in a legal action against the bishop for having issued the license.

The actual record of the marriage in a parish register has not survived, but presumably the couple were married shortly after obtaining the license. They may have been married in Temple Grafton, where Anne had relatives. The couple took up residence in Stratford. Anne was already pregnant at the time of the marriage, for she gave birth to a daughter, Susanna, on May 26, 1583. The birth of a child six months after the wedding may explain the need for haste the previous November. These circumstances, and Anne's considerable seniority in age to William, have given rise to much speculation about matters that can never be satisfactorily resolved. We do know that a formal betrothal in the presence of witnesses could legally validate a binding realtionship, enabling a couple to consummate their love without social stigma. We know also that Shakespeare dramatized the issue of premarital contract and pregnancy in *Measure for Measure.* Whether Shakespeare entered into such a formal relationship with Anne is, however, undiscoverable.

On February 2, 1585, Shakespeare's only other children, the twins Hamnet and Judith, were baptized in Stratford Church. The twins seem to have been named after Shakespeare's friends and neighbors, Hamnet Sadler, a baker, and his wife, Judith.

The Seven "Dark" Years

From 1585, the year in which his twins were baptized until 1592, when he is first referred to as an actor and dramatist of growing importance in London, Shakespeare's activities are wholly unknown. Presumably at some time during this period he made his way to London and entered its theatrical world, but otherwise we can only record traditions and guesses as to what he did between the ages of 21 and 28.

One of the oldest and most intriguing suggestions comes from John Aubrey, who, in collecting information about actors and dramatists for his "Minutes of Lives," sought the help of one William Beeston. John Dryden believed Beeston to be "the chronicle of the stage," and Aubrey seems also to have had a high opinion of Beeston's theatrical knowledge. In his manuscript, Aubrey made a note to himself: "W. Shakespeare—quaere [i.e., inquire of] Mr. Beeston, who knows most of him." Aubrey then cites Beeston as his authority for this tradition about Shakespeare:

> Though, as Ben: Johnson sayes of him, that he had but little Latine and lesse Greek, He understood Latine pretty well: for he had been in his younger yeares a Schoolmaster in the Countrey.

Beeston had been a theatrical manager all his life. He was the son of the actor Christopher Beeston, who had been a member of Shakespeare's company probably from 1596 until 1602 and who therefore had occasion to know Shakespeare well.

Shakespeare's own grammar school education would not have qualified him to be the master of a school, but he could have served as "usher" or assistant to the master. The idea that Shakespeare may have taught in this way is not unattractive. Although, as we have seen, he had some acquaintance with Plautus, Ovid, and other classical writers through his own grammar school reading, a stint as schoolmaster would have made these authors more familiar and readily accessible to him when he began writing his plays and nondramatic poems. His earliest works—*The Comedy of Errors, Love's Labor's Lost, Titus Andronicus, Venus and Adonis, the Rape of Lucrece*—show most steadily and directly the effect of his classical reading. Schoolteaching experience might have encouraged his ambitions to be a writer, like Marlowe or Greene, who went to London not to be actors but to try their hands at poetry and playwriting. All in all, however, it seems more probable that Shakespeare became a young actor rather than a schoolteacher.

Another tradition about the years from 1585 to 1592 asserts that Shakespeare served part of an apprenticeship in Stratford. This suggestion comes to us from one John Dowdall who, traveling through Warwickshire in 1693, heard the story from an old parish clerk who was showing him around the town of Stratford. According to this parish clerk, Shakespeare had been bound as apprentice to a butcher, but ran away from his master to London where he was received into a playhouse as "serviture." John Aubrey records a similar tradition: "when he [Shakespeare] was a boy he exercised his father's Trade." Aubrey believed this trade to have been that of a butcher. Moreover, says Aubrey, "when he kill'd a Calfe, he would doe it in a *high style,* & make a Speech." No other evidence confirms, however, that Shakespeare was a runaway apprentice. The allusion to "killing a calf" may instead refer to an ancient rural amusement in which the slaughter of a calf was staged behind a curtain for the entertainment of visitors at county fairs. Conceivably Shakespeare's participation in such a game during his youth may have given rise to the tradition that he had been a butcher's apprentice.

Deerstealing a Doubtful Tradition

Another legend, that of Shakespeare's deerstealing, has enjoyed wide currency. We are indebted for this story to the Reverend Richard Davies who, some time between 1688 and 1709, jotted down some gossipy interpolations in the manuscripts of the Reverend William Fulman. (Fulman himself was an antiquarian who had collected a number of notes about Shakespeare and Stratford.) According to Davies, Shakespeare was "much given to all unluckinesse in stealing venison & Rabbits, particularly from Sir ——— Lucy, who had him oft whipt & sometimes Imprisoned & at last made Him fly his Native Country, to his great Advancement."

This tradition was seized upon and augmented in 1709 by Nicholas Rowe, who saw a possible connection between Sir Thomas Lucy of Charlecote Hall, near Stratford, and Justice Shallow of *2 Henry IV* and *The Merry Wives of Windsor*. Shallow, observed Rowe, is a caricature of the rural magistrate and country squire. The dozen white "luces" in Justice Shallow's coat of arms may therefore, Rowe speculated, be intended as a slurring reference to the three white luces in the Lucy family's coat of arms. Rowe attempted to bolster his case by noting that Shallow in *The Merry Wives* is irate at Falstaff for the very offense that Sir Thomas Lucy is supposed to have charged against the young Shakespeare: deerstealing (I,i,105). Rowe even went so far as to suppose that Shakespeare composed a satirical ballad—his first poetic composition—for the occasion:

> He had, by a Misfortune common enough to young Fellows, fallen into ill Company; and amongst them, some that made a frequent practice of Deer-stealing, engag'd him with them more than once in robbing a Park that belong'd to Sir *Thomas Lucy* of *Cherlecot,* near *Stratford.* For this he was prosecuted by that Gentleman, as he thought, somewhat too severely; and in order to revenge that ill Usage, he made a Ballad upon him. And tho' this, probably the first Essay of his Poetry, be lost, yet it is said to have been so very bitter, that it redoubled the Prosecution against him to that degree, that he was oblig'd to leave his Business and Family in *Warwickshire,* for some time, and shelter himself in *London.*

In fact, however, the ballad is not lost, and it proves to have been written considerably later than Rowe supposed. Recent evidence suggests that deer were not introduced at Charlecote until the eighteenth century, and that Sir Thomas Lucy did not even have a "park" on the estate. Leslie Hotson has argued that Shallow is a hit not at Thomas Lucy at all but at Justice William Gardiner of Surrey (see Play Introduction to *The Merry Wives*). Neither explanation of Shakespeare's satiric treatment of Justice Shallow has received unanimous critical endorsement. We have no sure way of knowing whether Shakespeare's personal experience had anything whatsoever to do with his artistic creation in this instance, or even whether the purported incident actually took place. The deerstealing episode makes interesting fiction but unreliable biography.

Shakespeare's Arrival in London

Because of the total absence of reliable information concerning the seven years from 1585 to 1592, we do not know how Shakespeare got his start in the theatrical world. He may have joined one of the touring companies that came to Stratford, and then accompanied the players to London. Edmond Malone offered the unsupported statement (in 1780) that Shakespeare's "first office in the theatre was that of prompter's attendant." Presumably a young man from the country would have had to begin at the bottom. Shakespeare's later work certainly reveals an intimate and practical acquaintance with technical matters of stagecraft. In any case, his rise to eminence as an actor and writer seems to have been rapid. He was fortunate also in having at least one prosperous acquaintance in London, Richard Field, formerly of Stratford and the son of an associate of Shakespeare's father. Field was a printer, and in 1593 and 1594 he published two handsome editions of Shakespeare's first serious poems, *Venus and Adonis* and *The Rape of Lucrece.*

"The Onely Shake-scene in a Countrey"

The first allusion to Shakespeare after his Stratford days is a vitriolic attack on him. It occurs in *Greene's Groats-worth of Wit Bought with a Million of Repentance,* written by Robert Greene during the last months of his wretched existence (he died in poverty in September of 1592). A famous passage in this work lashes out at the actors of the public theatres for having deserted Greene and for bestowing their favor instead on a certain upstart dramatist. The passage warns three fellow dramatists and University Wits, Christopher Marlowe, Thomas Nashe, and George Peele, to abandon the writing of plays before they fall prey to a similar ingratitude. The diatribe runs as follows:

> . . . Base minded men all three of you, if by my miserie you be not warnd: for vnto none of you (like mee) sought those burres to cleaue: those Puppets (I meane) that spake from our mouths, those Anticks garnisht in our colours. Is it not strange, that I, to whom they all haue beene beholding: is it not like that you, to whome they all have beene beholding, shall (were yee in that case as I am now) bee both at once of them forsaken? Yes trust them not: for there is an vpstart Crow, beautified with our feathers, that with his *Tygers hart wrapt in a Players hyde,* supposes he is as well able to bombast out a blanke verse as the best of you: and beeing an absolute *Iohannes fac totum,* is in his owne conceit the onely Shake-scene in a countrey.

The "burres" here referred to are the actors who have forsaken Greene in his poverty for the rival playwright "Shake-scene"—an obvious hit at Shakespeare. The sneer at a "Johannes fac totum" suggests another dig at Shakespeare for being a Jack-of-all-trades—actor, playwright, poet, and theatrical handyman in the directing and producing of plays. The most unmistakable reference to Shakespeare, however, is to be found in the burlesque line, "Tygers hart wrapt in a Players hyde," modeled after "O tiger's heart wrapt in a woman's hide!" from *3 Henry VI* (I,iv,137). Shakespeare's success as a dramatist has led to an envious outburst from an older, disappointed rival.

Chettle's Apology

Shakespeare may understandably have resented this attack on his professional reputation. Marlowe, too, had cause for grievance, since Greene had accused him in the same pamphlet of atheism. Greene died soon after he had written *Groats-worth of Wit,* but some of his fellow dramatists were suspected of having had a hand in the libel. Thomas Nashe vigorously denied any responsibility. So did Henry Chettle, the man who saw Greene's manuscript through the press, although Chettle is even today under suspicion for having written the attack on Shakespeare and Marlowe himself. Whether or not Chettle was guilty, he quickly protected himself by denying in his *Kind-Harts Dreame* that he had done anything more than act as Greene's literary executor:

> . . . I had onely in the copy this share: it was il written, as sometime *Greenes* hand was none of the best; licensd it must be, ere it could bee printed, which could neuer be if it might not be read. To be breife, *I* writ it ouer; and as neare as *I* could, followed the copy; onely in that letter *I* put something out, but in the whole booke not a worde in: for I protest it was all *Greenes,* not mine nor Maister Nashes, as some vniustly haue affirmed.

Chettle professes not to have known Marlowe personally, and insists he has no desire to make the acquaintance of so notorious a person; but toward Shakespeare he expresses genuine concern and regret that the publishing incident took place:

> The other, whome at that time I did not so much spare, as since I wish I had, for that as I haue moderated the heate of liuing writers, and might have vsde my owne discretion (especially in such a case) the Author beeing dead, that I did not, I am as sory as if the originall fault had beene my fault, because my selfe haue seene his demeanor no lesse ciuill than he exelent in the qualitie he professes: Besides, diuers of worship haue reported his uprightnes of dealing, which argues his honesty, and his facetious grace in writting, that approoues his Art.

This handsome apology reveals the young Shakespeare in a most attractive light. It suggests that Chettle, though not having known Shakespeare previously, has been impressed by Shakespeare's civility. Chettle also praises the young dramatist as "exelent in the qualitie he professes," that is, excellent as an actor. Chettle notes with approval that Shakespeare enjoys the favor of certain persons of importance, some of whom have borne witness to his uprightness in dealing. By "diuers of worship" Chettle does not mean actors or theatrical people, but persons of gentle blood. *Groats-worth of Wit,* then, with its rancorous attack on Shakespeare, has served paradoxically to reveal the fact that in 1592 Shakespeare was regarded as a man of pleasant demeanor, honest reputation, and acknowledged skill as an actor and writer.

Dramatic Apprenticeship

By the end of the year 1594, when after the long plague the theatrical companies were again permitted to act before London audiences, we find Shakespeare a member of the Lord Chamberlain's company. He had already written *The Comedy of Errors, Love's Labor's Lost, The Two Gentlemen of Verona,* the *Henry VI* plays, and *Titus Andronicus.* (*A Love's Labor's Won,* mentioned by Francis Meres in 1598, is possibly either a lost play or an alternate title for one of the extant comedies.) He may also have completed *The Taming of the Shrew, A Midsummer Night's Dream, Richard III, King John,* and *Romeo and Juliet.* Although a few scholars still question his authorship in part or all of *Titus* and the *Henry VI* plays, no one questions that they are from the period around 1590.

Shakespeare's early development is hard to follow because of difficulties in exact dating of the early plays and because some of the texts (such as *Love's Labor's Lost*) may have been later revised. As a learner making rapid progress in the skill of his art, Shakespeare was also subjected to outside influences which can only partly be determined. Among these influences, we may be sure, were the plays of his contemporary dramatists. If we could define these influences and form an idea of the kinds of plays acceptable on the stage during Shakespeare's early period, we could better understand the milieu in which he began his work.

Fortunately, we know a fair amount concerning the dramatic repertory in London during Shakespeare's early years. Henslowe's *Diary,* for example, records the daily performances of plays by the Lord Strange's men, in conjunction with the Admiral's men, from 19 February to 22 June 1592. Many of their plays unfortunately are lost, but enough of them are preserved to indicate the sorts of drama then in vogue. The Strange-Admiral's repertory included Christopher Marlowe's *The Jew of Malta,* Robert Greene's *Orlando Furioso* and *Friar Bacon and Friar Bungay, A Looking Glass for London and England* by Greene and Thomas Lodge, Thomas Kyd's *The Spanish Tragedy,* the anonymous *A Knack to Know a Knave,* and possibly George Peele's *The Battle of Alcazar* and Shakespeare's *1 Henry VI.* We find, in other words, a tragedy with a villain hero, a romantic comedy masquerading as a heroic play, a love comedy featuring a lot of magic, a biblical moral, England's first great revenge tragedy, a popular satiric comedy aimed at dissolute courtiers and usurers, a history play about Portugal's African empire, and an English history play. The titles of other works now lost suggest a similar amalgam of widely differing genres.

Comparatively few plays may have been written during the period when plays were forbidden because of the long plague of 1592–1594. When the Lord Chamberlain's men and the Lord Admiral's men acted under Henslowe's management at the suburban theatre of Newington Butts from June 3 to 13, 1594, their repertories seem to have consisted largely of old plays. In this brief period, they are thought to have acted *Titus Andronicus, Hamlet* (the pre-Shakespearean version), *The Taming of A Shrew* (quite possibly Shakespeare's version), *The Jew of Malta,* a lost play called *Hester and Ahasuerus,* and others.

The Lord Admiral's men probably moved soon afterwards in 1594 to the Rose on the Bankside, across the river Thames from the city of London, where they continued to play under Henslowe's management until 1603. During the years 1594–1597 Henslowe kept in his *Diary* a careful record of their plays and of the sums of money taken. This circumstance enables us to know a great deal more about the repertory of Shakespeare's rival company than we can ever know about his own. When the Lord Admiral's men began again in 1594, they had five of Marlowe's plays. They seem also to have had Peele's *Edward I,* Kyd's *The Spanish Tragedy,* and a Henry V play. They may also have had plays by both Greene and Peele (Henslowe's chaotic spelling makes it hard to determine), although some of the principal dramas of these two authors had probably ceased to be acted.

We do not know the repertory of the Lord Chamberlain's company as a whole as we do that of the Lord Admiral's. We know enough of it, however, to be sure that in 1594, both companies were acting the same sorts of plays that had been on the boards in 1592. We have, therefore, grounds for assuming that, in spite of the loss of many plays (some of which may have been important), the chief contemporary influences upon Shakespeare during his early period were those of Marlowe, Greene, Peele, and Kyd. As an actor possibly in Lord Strange's company or the Earl of Pembroke's company, he would have been familiar with their plays.

Shakespeare learned also from Lyly, though perhaps more from reading than from actually seeing or performing in Lyly's plays. The boy actors for whom Lyly wrote were forced by the authorities to suspend acting in about 1591 because of their tendency toward controversial satire, and a number of Lyly's plays were printed at that time. As a theatrical figure, therefore, Lyly belonged really to the previous decade.

The Early Plays

Although Shakespeare's genius manifests itself in his early work, his indebtedness to contemporary dramatists and to classical writers is also more plainly evident than in his later writings. His first tragedy, *Titus Andronicus* (c. 1589–1591), is more laden with quotations and classical references than any other tragedy he wrote. Its genre owes much to the revenge play that had been made so popular by Thomas Kyd. Like Kyd, Shakespeare turns to Seneca but also reveals on stage a considerable amount of sensational violence in a manner that is distinctly not classical. For his first villain, Aaron the Moor, Shakespeare borrows some motifs from the morality play and its gleefully sinister tempter, the Vice. Shakespeare may also have had in mind the boastful antics of Marlowe's Vicelike Barabas, in *The Jew of Malta.* Certainly Shakespeare reveals an extensive debt in his early works to Ovid and to the vogue of Ovidian narrative poetry in the early 1590's, as for example in his repeated allusions to the story of Philomela and Tereus (in *Titus Andronicus*) and in his Ovidian poems, *Venus and Adonis* and *The Rape of Lucrece* (1593, 1594).

Shakespeare was still questing for a suitable mode in

A contemporary illustration from Titus Andronicus, *the earliest of Shakespeare's tragedies. Shakespeare's early plays demonstated that he was more than a slavish imitator of his predecessors, Kyd and Marlowe.*

LONGLEAT, WILTSHIRE. BY PERMISSION OF THE MARQUESS OF BATH
PHOTOGRAPH: COURTAULD INSTITUTE

tragedy, and was discovering that the English drama of the 1590's offered no single clear model. His only other early tragedy, *Romeo and Juliet* (c. 1594–1596), proved to be as different a tragedy from *Titus Andronicus* as could be imagined. Revenge is still prominent in *Romeo and Juliet,* but is ultimately far less compelling a theme than the brevity of love and the sacrifice the lovers make of themselves to one another. Shakespeare's source is not the revenge drama of Seneca or Kyd, but a romantic love narrative derived from the fiction of Renaissance Italy. Elements of comedy so predominate in the play's first half that one senses a closer affinity to *A Midsummer Night's Dream* than to *The Spanish Tragedy.*

Shakespeare discovered his true bent more quickly in comedy than in tragedy. Again, however, he experimented with a wide range of models and genres. *The Comedy of Errors* (c. 1589–1593) brings together elements of two plots from the Latin drama of Plautus. The character types and situation are partly derivative, but Shakespeare still reveals an impressive skill in plot construction. The characters too are given a human warmth and decency not often found in the original. *Love's Labor's Lost* (c. 1588–1589, perhaps later revised) is Shakespeare's most Lylyan early comedy, with its witty debates and its amicable war between the sexes. The play also features an array of humorous characters including a clownish bumpkin, a country slut, a fantastic courtier, a pedant, a country curate, and the like, whose mannerisms and word-play add to the rich feast of language in a play that centers its attention on proper and improper styles. *The Two Gentlemen of Verona* (c. 1590–1594) and *The Taming of the Shrew* (c. 1592–1594) are derived from Italianate romantic comedy. In both, Shakespeare skillfully combines simultaneous plots that offer contrasting views on love and friendship. (*The Taming of the Shrew* makes effective use of a "frame" plot involving a group of characters who serve as audience for the rest of the play.) *A Midsummer Night's Dream* (c. 1594–1595), with its four brilliantly interwoven actions involving court figures, lovers, fairies, and Athenian tradesmen, shows us Shakespeare already at the height of his powers in play construction, even though the comic emphasis on love's irrationality in this play is still in keeping with Shakespeare's early style. The early comedies are all "happy" comedies, almost untouched as yet by the social dilemmas of *The Merchant of Venice,* the narrowly averted catastrophe of *Much Ado about Nothing,* or the melancholy vein of *As You Like It* and *Twelfth Night.* On stage, early comedies such as *The Comedy of Errors* and *The Taming of the*

COURTESY OF THE NEWBERRY LIBRARY, CHICAGO

An engraving from about 1800 shows a scene from Act III of A Midsummer Night's Dream. *The Athenian tradesmen rehearse "Pyramus and Thisbe."*

This nineteenth-century rendition of a scene in Romeo and Juliet *by Ford Madox Brown shows the passionate parting of the two lovers after Romeo's banishment.*

Shrew are as hilariously funny as anything Shakespeare ever wrote.

Shakespeare's early history plays show a marked affinity to those of Marlowe, Peele, and Greene. Yet today Shakespeare is given more credit for pioneering in the genre of the English history play than he once was. If all the *Henry VI* plays (c. 1589–1592) are basically his, as scholars now generally allow, he had more imitators in this genre than predecessors. He scored a huge early success with the heroic character of Lord Talbot in *1 Henry VI;* and, by the time Richard Duke of Gloucester had emerged from the *Henry VI* plays to become King Richard III, Shakespeare's fame as a dramatist was assured. He had, of course, learned much from Marlowe's "mighty line" in *Tamburlaine* (1587–1588) and perhaps from Peele's *The Battle of Alcazar* (1588–1589). The anonymous *Famous Victories of Henry V* (1583–1588) must have preceded and influenced his work. Even so, Shakespeare had done much more than simply "beautify" himself with the "feathers" of earlier dramatists, as Greene (or Chettle) enviously charged. Even in his earliest work, Shakespeare already displayed an extraordinary ability to transcend the models from which he learned.

Shakespeare at the Theatre; The Lord Chamberlain's Men, c. 1594–1603

By the year 1594, Shakespeare had already achieved a considerable reputation as a poet and as a dramatist. We should not be surprised that many of his contemporaries thought of his nondramatic writing as his most significant literary achievement. Throughout his lifetime, in fact, his contemporary fame rested to a remarkable degree on his nondramatic poems, *Venus and Adonis, The Rape of Lucrece,* and the *Sonnets* (which were circulated in manuscript prior to their unauthorized publication in 1609). One of the earliest tributes suggesting the importance of the poems is to be found in an anonymous commendatory verse prefixed to Henry Willobie's *Willobie His Avisa* (1594):

> Though *Collatine* haue deerely bought,
> To high renowne, a lasting life,
> And found, that most in vaine haue sought,
> To haue a *Faire,* and *Constant* wife,
> Yet *Tarquyne* pluckt his glistering grape,
> And *Shake-speare,* paints poore Lucrece rape.

Richard Barnfield, in his *Poems in Divers Humors* (1598), praised the "hony-flowing Vaine" of Shakespeare's *Venus and Adonis* and *The Rape of Lucrece.* The poet Edmund Spenser may also have had Shakespeare's nondramatic poetry in mind when, in *Colin Clout's Come Home Again* (in a passage probably composed in 1594–1595) he listed twelve contemporary poets, most of them by fictional names, and included that of Aetion, "though last not least." Aetion has been identified by many scholars as Shakespeare, though other candidates have been proposed as well. Spenser wrote of Aetion:

> A gentler shepheard may no where be found:
> Whose *Muse* full of high thoughts inuention
> Doth like himselfe Heroically sound.

Yet Shakespeare's plays were also highly regarded by his contemporaries, even if those plays were accorded a literary status below that given to the narrative and lyrical poems. Francis Meres insisted, in 1598, that Shakespeare deserved to be compared not only with Ovid for his verse, but with Plautus and Seneca for his comedies and tragedies:

> As the soule of *Euphorbus* was thought to liue in *Pythagoras:* so the sweete wittie soule of *Ouid* liues in mellifluous & hony-tongued *Shakespeare,* witnes his *Venus* and *Adonis,* his *Lucrece,* his sugred Sonnets among his priuate friends, &c.
>
> As *Plautus* and *Seneca* are accounted the best for Comedy and Tragedy among the Latines: so *Shakespeare* among the English is the most excellent in both kinds for the stage; for Comedy, witnes his *Gentlemen of Verona,* his *Errors,* his *Loue labors lost,* his *Loue labours wonne,* his *Midsummers night dreame* & his *Merchant of Venice:* for Tragedy his *Richard the 2. Richard the 3. Henry the 4. King Iohn, Titus Andronicus* and his *Romeo* and *Iuliet.*

Comedy and tragedy were, after all, literary forms sanctioned by classical precept. By calling Shakespeare's English history plays "tragedies," Meres endowed them with the respectability of an ancient literary tradition.

John Weever too, in his epigram *Ad Gulielmum Shakespeare* in *Epigrammes in the oldest Cut, and newest Fashion* (1599), mentioned not only the ever-popular narrative poems but also *Romeo and Juliet* and a history play about one of the Richards:

> Honie-tong'd *Shakespeare* when I saw thine issue
> I swore *Apollo* got them and none other,
> Their rosie-tainted features cloth'd in tissue,
> Some heauen born goddesse said to be their mother:
> Rose-checkt *Adonis* with his amber tresses,
> Faire fire-hot *Venus* charming him to loue her,
> Chaste *Lucretia* virgine-like her dresses,
> Prowd lust-stung *Tarquine* seeking still to proue her:
> *Romea Richard;* more whose names I know not,
> Their sugred tongues, and power attractiue beuty
> Say they are Saints, althogh that Sts they shew not
> For thousands vowes to them subiectiue dutie:
> They burn in loue thy children *Shakespear* het them,
> Go, wo thy Muse more Nymphish brood beget them.

Even Gabriel Harvey, an esteemed classical scholar and friend of Edmund Spenser, considered Shakespeare's play of *Hamlet* to be worthy of no less praise than the best of the Ovidian poems. Harvey's comments are to be found in a marginal note to a copy of Speght's *Chaucer,* written down some time between 1598 and 1601:

> The younger sort takes much delight in Shakespeares Venus, & Adonis: but his Lucrece, & his tragedie of Hamlet, Prince of Denmarke, haue it in them, to please the wiser sort.

Shakespeare's growing fame was even such that his dramatic characters began to enter into the intellectual life of the time. The name of Falstaff became a by-word almost as soon as he made his appearance on the stage. The references were not always friendly. A play written to be performed by the rival Admiral's company in answer to *1 Henry IV,* called *Sir John Oldcastle* (1599), took Falstaff to task for being a "pamper'd glutton" and an "aged Counsellor to youthfull sinne." Evidently the authors of this attack were offended by the fact that Falstaff had been named "Oldcastle" in an early version of *1 Henry IV,* thereby dishonoring the name of one whom many Puritans regarded as a martyr to their cause (see Play Introduction). Generally, however, the references during this period to Falstaff and his cronies were fond. In a letter to a friend in London, for example, Sir Charles Percy fretted jocosely that his pro-

RADIO TIMES HULTON PICTURE LIBRARY

Falstaff plays the role of the King in The First Part of King Henry the Fourth. *This scene from Act II of the play was etched by the nineteenth-century illustrator, George Cruikshank.*

THE TATE GALLERY, LONDON

The many conceptions of A Midsummer Night's Dream *through the years attest to the play's continual popularity. William Blake, the famous Romantic poet and artist, catches the fanciful and dreamlike flavor of the play in his engraving of the meeting of Oberon, Titania, Puck, and attendant fairies.*

Entangled in spiraling wire, the angry lovers (above) *pursue each other in Peter Brook's production of* A Midsummer Night's Dream. *Under the spell of a love potion* (right), *the fairy queen Titania embraces the weaver, Bottom, whom Puck has mischievously given an ass's ears and a clown's nose. This modern British production reflects a distinctly contemporary interpretation of the play.*

TRUSTEES OF THE NATIONAL MARITIME MUSEUM, GREENWICH

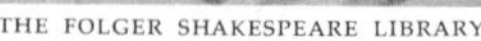

THE FOLGER SHAKESPEARE LIBRARY

BY COURTESY OF BIRMINGHAM MUSEUMS AND ART GALLERY

The English history play owed much to the excitement of the Armada Era. The English defeat of the Spanish Armada in 1588 (top left) *came about two years before Shakespeare began writing his* Henry VI *plays. The* Henry VI *plays helped to establish the vogue of the English history play, which was to flourish throughout the decade to follow. Shakespeare dramatized the historic struggles of the Plantagenet, Lancastrian, and Yorkish families and showed the eventual triumph of the Tudors.*

Certainly one of the greatest characters in Shakespeare's history plays is Sir John Falstaff. The nineteenth-century painting (above) *by Sir John Gilbert shows Falstaff reviewing his ragged troops from Act III of* 2 Henry IV. *Elizabeth I was so taken by the comic character of Falstaff that she is believed to have ordered to see him in love. Falstaff is hidden in a clothes basket by Mrs. Ford and Mrs. Page* (below left) *in* The Merry Wives of Windsor, *a comedy written for the Queen.*

REG WILSON, LONDON

In these three pictures from the Royal Shakespeare Company's 1968 production of King Lear, *Eric Porter as Lear displays a range and progression of suffering emotion.*

REG WILSON, LONDON

Juliet played by Olivia Hussey and Romeo played by Leonard Whiting (below and left) *are the star-crossed lovers in the 1968 film version of* Romeo and Juliet *directed by Franco Zeffirelli. This very popular film production was also the object of serious critical attention.*

HOLTE PHOTOGRAPHICS, LTD.

Modern staging of Shakespeare's plays has created new and imaginative sets. Shown above is the 1958 set design for the Duke's palace by Lila de Nobili for Peter Hall's Twelfth Night, *a Royal Shakespeare Theatre production performed at Stratford.*

HOLTE PHOTOGRAPHICS, LTD.

Prospero commands Ariel (left) *in Peter Brook's production of* The Tempest. *This production was the second attempt by Brook to stage this difficult romance and was performed by the Royal Shakespeare Company at Stratford in 1963.*

longed stay in the country among his rustic neighbors might cause him to "be taken for Justice Silence or Justice Shallow" (1600). In another letter, from the Countess of Southampton to her husband (written seemingly in 1599), Falstaff's name has become so familiar that it is used apparently as a privately understood substitute for the name of some real person in an item of court gossip:

> Al the nues I can send you that I thinke wil make you mery is that I reade in a letter from London that Sir John Falstaf is by his Mrs Dame Pintpot made father of a godly milers [miller's] thum, a boye thats all heade and veri litel body; but this is a secrit.

The Parnassus Trilogy

Shakespeare's immense popularity as a dramatist did not please everyone. One interesting example of a hostile reaction comes from the so-called *Parnassus* trilogy (1598–1603). The three plays in this series consist of *The Pilgrimage to Parnassus* and *The Return from Parnassus* in two parts, all acted by the students of St. John's College, Cambridge. The third play was published in 1606, the other two not until recently.

These *Parnassus* plays take a mordantly satirical view of English life around 1600, from the point of view of university graduates attempting to find gainful employment. The graduates discover to their vocal dismay that they must seek the patronage of fashionmongering courtiers, complacent justices of the peace, professional acting companies who offer them pitifully small wages, and the like. One especially foolish patron, to whom the witty Ingenioso applies for a position, is a poetaster named Gullio. This courtly fop aspires to be a fashionable poet himself, and agrees to hire Ingenioso if the latter will help him with his verse-writing. In fact, however, as Ingenioso scornfully observes in a series of asides, Gullio's verses are "nothinge but pure Shakespeare and shreds of poetrie that he hath gathered at the theators." Most of all, Gullio loves to plagiarize from *Venus and Adonis* and *Romeo and Juliet.* With unparalleled presumption, he actually requests Ingenioso to compose poems "in two or three divers vayns, in Chaucer's, Gower's and Spencer's and Mr. Shakespeare's," which Gullio will then pass off as his own inspiration. When Ingenioso does so extempore, producing among other things a fine parody of *Venus and Adonis,* Gullio is as delighted as a child. Although he admires Spenser, Chaucer, and Gower, Gullio confesses that Shakespeare is his favorite; he longs to hang Shakespeare's portrait "in my study at the courte," and vows he will sleep with *Venus and Adonis* under his pillow (*The Return from Parnassus,* Part I, 1009–1217).

Elsewhere in the same play (ll. 1875–1880), some university graduates trying out as actors in Shakespeare's company are requested to recite a few famous lines from the beginning of *Richard III*—lines that in the satirical context of this play sound both stereotyped and bombastic. From such passages in the *Parnassus* plays, we can see that Shakespeare had become not only famous but notorious among some Cambridge intellectuals. The dramatist of the *Parnassus* series treats Shakespeare satirically, and regards those who worship him as lowbrows. Still, Shakespeare's immense popularity is undeniable.

Shakespeare's Career and Private Life

During the years from 1594 to 1603, Shakespeare seems to have prospered as an actor and writer for the Lord Chamberlain's men. Whether he had previously belonged to Lord Strange's company or to the Earl of Pembroke's company, or possibly to some other group, is uncertain; but we know that he took part in 1594 in the general reorganization of the companies out of which emerged the Lord Chamberlain's company. In 1595 his name appeared for the first time in the accounts of the Treasurer of the Royal Chamber, as a member of the Chamberlain's company of players who had presented two comedies before Queen Elizabeth at Greenwich in the Christmas season of 1594. This company usually performed at the Theatre, northeast of London, from 1594 until 1599, when they moved to the Globe theatre south of the Thames. They seem to have been the victors in the intense economic rivalry between themselves and the Lord Admiral's company at the Rose theatre under Philip Henslowe's management. Fortunately for all the adult companies, the boys' private theatrical companies were shut down during most of the 1590's. Shakespeare's company enjoyed a phenomenal success, and in short time became the most successful theatrical organization in England.

The nucleus of the Chamberlain's company in 1594 was the family of Burbage. James Burbage, the father, was owner of the Theatre, Cuthbert Burbage was a manager, and Richard Burbage became the principal actor of the troupe. Together the Burbages owned five "shares" in the company, entitling them to half the profits. Shakespeare and four other principal actors—John Heminges, Thomas

DULWICH COLLEGE PICTURE GALLERY

First among the actors in Shakespeare's company was Richard Burbage (1567–1619). He became the chief tragedian of the Lord Chamberlain's men.

Pope, Augustine Phillips, and Will Kempe—owned one share each. Not only was Shakespeare a full sharing actor, but he was also the principal playwright of the company. He was named as a chief actor in the 1616 edition of Ben Jonson's *Every Man in His Humor,* performed by the Chamberlain's company in 1598. Later tradition reports, with questionable reliability, that Shakespeare specialized in "kingly parts" or in the roles of older men, such as Adam in *As You Like It* and the Ghost in *Hamlet.* Shakespeare was more celebrated as a playwright than as an actor, and his acting responsibilities may well have diminished as his writing reputation grew. The last occasion on which he is known to have acted was in Jonson's *Sejanus* in 1603.

His prosperity appears in the first record of his residence in London. The tax returns, or Subsidy Rolls, of a parliamentary subsidy granted to Queen Elizabeth for the year 1596, show Shakespeare resident in the parish of St. Helen's, Bishopsgate, near the Theatre, and assessed at the respectable sum of £5. By the next year Shakespeare had evidently moved to Southwark near the Bear Garden, for the returns from Bishopsgate show his taxes delinquent. He was later located and the taxes paid.

In 1596 Shakespeare suffered a serious personal loss: the death of his only son Hamnet, at the age of eleven. Hamnet was buried at Stratford in August.

Shakespeare acquired property in Stratford during these years as well as in London. In 1597 he purchased New Place, a house of importance and one of the two largest in the town. Shakespeare's family entered the house as residents shortly after the purchase and continued there until long after Shakespeare's death. The last of his family, his granddaughter, Lady Bernard, died in 1670, and New Place was sold.

Shakespeare was also interested in the purchase of land at Shottery in 1598. He was listed among the chief holders of corn and malt in Stratford that same year, and sold a load of stone to the Stratford corporation in 1599.

No less suggestive of Shakespeare's rapid rise in the world is his acquisition of the right to bear arms, or, in other words, his establishment in the rank and title of gentleman. The Herald's College in London preserves two drafts of a grant of arms to Shakespeare's father devised by one William Dethick and dated October 20, 1596. Although we may certainly believe that the application was put forward by William Shakespeare, John Shakespeare was still living, and the grant was drawn up in the father's name. The device for Shakespeare's coat-of-arms makes a somewhat easy use of the meaning of his name:

> Gould, on a Bend Sables, a Speare of the first steeled argent. And for his creast or cognizaunce a falcon his winges displayed Argent standing on a wrethe of his coullers: supporting a Speare Gould steeled as aforesaid sett vppon a helmett with mantelles & tasselles as hath ben accustomed and doth more playnely appeare depicted on this margent.

According to one of the documents in the grant, John Shakespeare, at the height of his prosperity as a Stratford burgher, had applied twenty years before to the Herald's College for authority to bear arms. The family may not have been able to meet the expense of seeing the application through, however, until William Shakespeare had made his fortune. The grant of heraldic honors to John Shakespeare was confirmed in 1599.

A lawsuit during this period gives us a rather baffling glimpse into Shakespeare's life in the theatre. From a writ discovered by Leslie Hotson (*Shakespeare Versus Shallow,*

This recreation of what New Place purportedly looked like during Shakespeare's ownership suggests that it must have indeed been an imposing structure. It was warmed by ten fireplaces and had surrounding grounds that included two gardens and two barns.

1931) in the records of the Court of the Queen's Bench, Michaelmas term 1596, we learn that a person named William Wayte sought "for fear of death" to have William Shakespeare, Francis Langley, and two unknown women bound over to keep the peace. Earlier in the same term, moreover, Francis Langley had sworn out a similar writ against this same William Wayte and his stepfather William Gardiner, a justice of the peace in Surrey. Langley was owner of the Swan theatre on the bankside, near the later-built Globe. His quarrel with Gardiner and Wayte appears to have jeopardized all the acting companies who performed plays south of the Thames, for William Gardiner's jurisdiction included the Bankside theatre district. Gardiner and Wayte vengefully tried to drive the theatres out of the area.

We do not know why Shakespeare is named in Wayte's writ; conceivably his company was acting at the Swan in 1596. At any rate, Leslie Hotson has argued that Shakespeare took occasion to punish Gardiner and Wayte by satirizing them in his plays. According to this theory, the greedy and meddlesome Justice Shallow of *2 Henry IV* and *The Merry Wives of Windsor* represents Gardiner, whereas Shallow's dim-witted cousin Slender in *The Merry Wives* represents Wayte. The joke about the "white luces" in Shallow's coat of arms (*Merry Wives,* I,i,14) is a dig not at Sir Thomas Lucy of Stratford, argues Hotson, but at Justice Gardiner who did in fact wear three white luces in his coat of arms by right of his wife (*née* Lucy). This theory has not won universal acceptance, however, in part because it requires such an early date for *The Merry Wives.*

During this period Shakespeare's plays began to appear occasionally in print, attesting to his popularity as a dramatist. His name was becoming such a drawing card that it appeared on the title pages of the second and third quartos of *Richard II* (1598), the second quarto of *Richard III* (1598), *Love's Labor's Lost* (1598), and the second quarto of *1 Henry IV* (1599).

In 1599 the printer William Jaggard sought to capitalize unscrupulously on Shakespeare's growing reputation by bringing out a slender volume of twenty or twenty-one poems called *The Passionate Pilgrim,* attributed to Shakespeare. In fact, only five of the poems were assuredly his, and none of them was newly composed for the occasion. Three came from *Love's Labor's Lost* (published 1598) and two from Shakespeare's as yet unpublished sonnet sequence.

Contemporary Drama

Shakespeare was without doubt the leading dramatist of the period from 1594 to 1601, not only in our view but in that of his contemporaries. The earlier group of dramatists from whom he had learned so much—Lyly, Greene, Marlowe, Peele, Kyd, Nashe—were either dead or no longer writing plays. The group of dramatists who were to rival him in the 1600's, and eventually surpass him in contemporary popularity, had not yet become well known.

Ben Jonson's early career is obscure. He may have written an early version of his *A Tale of a Tub* in 1596 and *The Case Is Altered* in 1597, though both were later revised. Unquestionably his first major play was *Every Man in His Humor* (1598), in which Shakespeare acted. This comedy did much to establish the new vogue of comedy of humors, a realistic and satirical kind of drama featuring "humors" characters whose personalities are dominated by some exaggerated trait. We are invited to laugh at the country simpleton, the jealous husband, the overly careful father, the cowardly braggart soldier, the poetaster, and the like. Shakespeare responded to the vogue of humors comedy in his *Henry IV* plays and *The Merry Wives.* Jonson followed his great success with *Every Man Out of His Humor* (1599), an even more biting vision of human folly. George Chapman also deserves important credit for the establishment of humors comedy, with his *The Blind Beggar of Alexandria* (1596) and *An Humorous Day's Mirth* (1597).

Despite the emergence of humors comedy, however, with its important anticipations of Jacobean and even Restoration comedy of manners, the prevailing comedy to be seen on the London stage between 1595 and 1601 was romantic comedy. William Haughton wrote *Englishmen for My Money* in 1598. Thomas Dekker's *Old Fortunatus,* the dramatization of a German folk tale, appeared in 1599. Dekker's *Shoemakers' Holiday* (1599), despite its seemingly realistic touches of life among the apprentices of London, is a thoroughly romanticized saga of rags to riches. A young aristocrat disguises himself as a shoemaker to woo a mayor's daughter; love conquers social rank, and the King himself sentimentally blesses the union. Thomas Heywood wrote heroical romances and comedies perhaps including *Godfrey of Boulogne,* (1594), although most of his early works have disappeared. The boys' private theatres were closed during most of the 1590's, until 1598–1599, and thus could not perform the satirical comedies at which they were so adept.

Patriotic history drama also continued to flourish on the public stage during these years when Shakespeare wrote his best history plays. Heywood wrote the two parts of *Edward IV* between 1592 and 1599. The anonymous *Edward III* appeared in 1595 or earlier, written with such poetic force that it still is a serious contender to join the Shakespeare canon. *Sir Thomas More,* by Munday, Dekker, Chettle, and perhaps Heywood, was written some time in the later 1590's and very probably revised by Shakespeare himself. Chettle and Munday wrote a trilogy of plays about *Robert, Earl of Huntingdon,* or Robin Hood (1598–1599), on themes that remind us of Shakespeare's *As You Like It.* These plays were performed by the Admiral's men, who also produced the two parts of *Sir John Oldcastle* (1599–1600) by Drayton, Hathway, Munday, and others, in rivalry with Shakespeare's *Henry IV* plays.

Shakespeare's Work

Shakespeare thus wrote his greatest history plays for an audience that knew the genre well. The history play had first become popular just at the start of Shakespeare's career, during the patriotic aftermath of the defeat of the Spanish Armada (1588). Shakespeare himself did much to establish the genre. He wrote first his tetralogy or four-play series dealing with the Lancastrian wars of the fifteenth century, and then went backwards in historical time to King John's reign and to the famous reigns of Henry IV and V.

His romantic comedies were also written for audiences that knew what to expect from the genre. From the comedies of Greene, Peele, Munday, and the rest, as well as Shakespeare himself, Elizabethan audiences were thoroughly familiar with such conventions as fairy charms, improbable adventures in forests, heroines disguised as young men, shipwrecks, love overcoming differences in social rank, and the like. Yet the convention also demanded more than mere horseplay or foolish antics. Plays of this sort customarily affirmed "wholesome" moral values and appealed to generosity and decency. They were written, like the history plays, for a socially diversified though generally intelligent and well-to-do audience.

Several critical terms have been used to suggest the special quality of Shakespeare's comedies during this period of the later 1590's. "Romantic comedy" implies first of all a story in which the main action is about love, but it can also imply elements of the improbable and the miraculous. (The difference between the "romantic comedies" of the later 1590's and the "romances" of Shakespeare's last years, 1606–1613, is that in part at least, romantic comedy seeks to "make wonder familiar," whereas the romances seek to make the familiar wonderful.) "Philosophical comedy" emphasizes the moral and sometimes Christian idealism underlying many of these comedies of the 1590's: the quest for deep and honest understanding between men and women in *Much Ado about Nothing,* the awareness of an eternal and spiritual dimension to love in *The Merchant of Venice,* the theme of love as a mysterious force able to regenerate a corrupted social world from which it has been banished in *As You Like It.* "Love-game comedy" pays particular attention to the witty battle of the sexes we find in several of these plays. "Festive comedy" urges the celebratory nature of comedy, especially in *Twelfth Night* and the *Henry IV* plays, in which Saturnalian revelry must contend against grim and disapproving forces of sobriety. "Comedy of forgiveness," although applicable to only a limited number of plays of this period (especially *Much Ado*), stresses the unexpected second chance that the world of comedy extends to even the most undeserving of heroes; Claudio is forgiven his ill treatment of Hero, although the play's villain, Don John, is not.

Shakespeare at the Globe; His Majesty's Servants, c.1601–1608

When the Globe, the most famous of the London public playhouses, was built in 1599, one-half interest in the property was assigned the Burbage family, especially to the brothers Cuthbert and Richard Burbage. The other half was divided among five actor-sharers: Shakespeare, Will Kempe, Thomas Pope, Augustine Phillips, and John Heminges. Kempe left the company, however, in 1599, and subsequently became a member of the Earl of Worcester's men. His place as leading comic actor was taken by Robert

ASHMOLEAN MUSEUM, OXFORD

DULWICH COLLEGE PICTURE GALLERY

DULWICH COLLEGE PICTURE GALLERY

Among the members of Shakespeare's acting company were John Lowin, William Sly, and Nathaniel Field.

THE FOLGER SHAKESPEARE LIBRARY

THE HUNTINGTON LIBRARY, SAN MARINO, CALIFORNIA

Will Kempe (above), *for whom Shakespeare created several clownish roles, was a member of the Lord Chamberlain's men and a noted Elizabethan comic. Kempe left the company in 1599 and was replaced by Robert Armin* (right), *an accomplished actor who specialized in fool's roles.*

Armin, an experienced man of the theatre and occasional author whose comic specialty was the role of the wise fool. We can observe in Shakespeare's plays the effects of Kempe's departure and of Armin's arrival. Kempe had apparently specialized in clownish and rustic parts, such as those of Dogberry in *Much Ado,* Launcelot Gobbo in *The Merchant of Venice,* and Bottom in *A Midsummer Night's Dream.* (We know that he played Dogberry because his name appears in the early quarto, derived from the play manuscript; similar evidence links his name to the role of Peter in *Romeo and Juliet.*) For Armin, on the other hand, Shakespeare evidently created such roles as Touchstone in *As You Like It,* Feste in *Twelfth Night,* Lavatch in *All's Well that Ends Well,* and the Fool in *King Lear.*

Other shifts in personnel can sometimes be traced in Shakespeare's plays, especially changes in the number and ability of the boy actors (whose voices would suddenly start to crack at puberty). Shakespeare makes an amusing point about the relative size of two boy actors, for example, in *A Midsummer Night's Dream* and in *As You Like It;* this option may have been available to him only at certain times. On the other hand, not all changes in the company roster can be related meaningfully to Shakespeare's dramatic development. Augustine Phillips, who died in 1605, was a full actor-sharer of long standing in the company, but his "type" of role was probably not sharply differentiated from that of several of his associates. Shakespeare's plays, after all, involve many important supporting roles, and versatility in the undertaking of such parts must have been more common than specialization. (Phillips is remembered, however, for his last will and testament: he left a bequest of "a thirty shillings peece in gould" to "my Fellowe, William Shakespeare," and similar bequests to other members of the troupe.)

With the reopening of the boys' acting companies in 1598–1599, a serious economic rivalry sprang up between them and the adult companies. The Children of the Chapel Royal occupied the theatre in Blackfriars, and the Children of Paul's probably acted in their own singing school in St. Paul's churchyard. Their plays exploited a new vogue for satire. The satiric laughter was often directed at the city of London and its bourgeois inhabitants: socially ambitious tradesmen's wives, Puritan zealots, and the like. Other favorite targets included parvenu knights at court, would-be poets, and hysterical governmental officials. The price of admission at the private theatres was considerably higher than at the Globe or Rose, so that the clientele tended to be more fashionable. Sophisticated authors like Ben Jonson, George Chapman, and John Marston tended to find writing for the boy actors more literarily rewarding than writing for the adult players.

One manifestation of the rivalry between public and private theatres was the so-called War of the Theatres, or Poetomachia. In part this was a personal quarrel between Jonson on one side and Marston and Thomas Dekker on the other. Underlying this quarrel, however, was a serious hostility between a public theatre and one that catered more to the elite. Dekker, with Marston's encouragement, attacked Jonson as a literary dictator and snob, one who subverted public decency. Jonson replied with a fervent defense of the artist's right to criticize everything he sees wrong. The major plays in the exchange (1600–1601) were Jonson's

Cynthia's Revels, Dekker's and Marston's *Satiromastix,* and Jonson's *The Poetaster.*

Shakespeare allows Hamlet to comment on the theatrical rivalry (II,ii), with seeming regret for the fact that the boys have been overly successful and that many adult troupes have been obliged to tour the provinces. Most of all, though, Hamlet's remarks deplore the needless bitterness on both sides. The tone of kindly remonstrance makes it seem unlikely that Shakespeare took an active part in the fracas. To be sure, in the Cambridge play *2 Return from Parnassus* (1601–1603) the character called Will Kempe does assert that his fellow actor Shakespeare had put down the famous Ben Jonson:

> Why, heres our fellow *Shakespeare* puts them all downe, I, and *Ben Ionson* too. O that *Ben Ionson* is a pestilent fellow, and he brought vp *Horace* giuing the Poets a pill, but our fellow *Shakespeare* hath giuen him a purge that made him bewray his credit.
>
> (ll. 1809–1813)

Nevertheless, no play exists in which Shakespeare did put down Jonson, and the reference may be instead to *Satiromastix* which was performed by Shakespeare's company. In fact, Shakespeare and Jonson remained on cordial terms despite their differences in artistic outlook.

Upon the death of Queen Elizabeth in 1603 and the accession to the throne of King James I, Shakespeare's company added an important new success to their already great prosperity. According to a document of instruction from King James to his Keeper of the Privy Seal, dated May 19, 1603, and endorsed as "The Players' Privilege," the acting company that had formerly been the Lord Chamberlain's men now became the King's servants. The document names Shakespeare, Richard Burbage, Augustine Phillips, John Heminges, Henry Condell, Will Sly, Robert Armin, Richard Cowley, and Lawrence Fletcher—the last an actor who had played before the King and the Scottish court in 1599 and 1601. These players are accorded the usual privileges of exercising their art anywhere within the kingdom and are henceforth to be known as the King's company. As the King's servants, the principal members of the troupe were also appointed to the honorary rank of Grooms of the Royal Chamber. We therefore find them duly recorded in the Accounts of the Master of the Wardrobe on March 15, 1604, as recipients of the customary grants of red cloth, so that they, dressed in the royal livery, might take part in the approaching coronation procession of King James. The same men are mentioned in these grants as in the Players' Privilege. Shakespeare's name stands second in the former document and first in the latter. In a somewhat similar manner the King's players, as Grooms of the Royal Chamber, were called in attendance on the Spanish ambassador at Somerset House in August 1604.

The Revels Accounts of performances at court during the winter season of 1604–1605 contain an unusually full entry listing several of Shakespeare's plays. The list includes *Othello, The Merry Wives of Windsor, Measure for Measure, "The plaie of Errors," Love's Labor's Lost, Henry V,* and *The Merchant of Venice.* The last play was "Againe Commanded By the Kings Maiestie," and so was performed a second time. This list also sporadically notes the names of "the poets which mayd the plaies," ascribing three of these works to "Shaxberd." (Probably the final "d" is an error for "e," since the two characters are easily confused in Elizabethan handwriting; the word represents "Shaxbere" or "Shaxpere.") The entire entry was once called into question as a possible forgery, but is now generally regarded as authentic.

Business and Family Affairs

A number of records during this period show us glimpses of Shakespeare as a man of property. On May 1, 1602, John and William Combe conveyed to Shakespeare one hundred and seven acres of arable land plus twenty acres of pasture in the parish of Old Stratford, for the sizable payment of three hundred and twenty pounds. The deed was delivered to Shakespeare's brother Gilbert and not to the poet, who was probably at that time occupied in London. On September 28th of the same year Shakespeare acquired the title to "one cottage and one garden by estimation a quarter of an acre," located opposite his home (New Place) in Stratford.

Shakespeare made still other real-estate investments in his home town. In 1605 he purchased an interest in the tithes of Stratford and adjacent villages from one Ralph Hubaud for the considerable sum of four hundred and forty pounds. The purchasing of tithes was a common financial transaction in Shakespeare's time, though unknown today. Tithes were originally intended for the support of the church, but had in many cases become privately owned and hence negotiable. The owners of tithes paid a fixed rental sum for the right to collect as many of these taxes as they could, up to the total amount due under the law. Shakespeare seems, on this occasion in 1605, to have bought from Ralph Hubaud a one-half interest, or "moiety," in certain tithes of Stratford and vicinity. Later, probably in 1609, Shakespeare was one of those who brought a bill of complaint before the Lord Chancellor, requesting that certain other titheholders be required to come into the High Court of Chancery and make answer to the complaints alleged, namely, that they had not paid their proportional part of an annual rental of £27 13s. 4d. on the whole property in the tithes to one Henry Barker. This Barker had the theoretical right to foreclose on the entire property if any one of the forty-two titheholders failed to contribute his share of the annual fee. The suit was in effect a friendly one, designed to ensure that all those who were supposed to contribute did so on an equitable and businesslike basis.

We learn from the Stratford Registers of baptism, marriage, and burial, of the changes in Shakespeare's family during this period. His father died in 1601, his brother Edmund in 1607, and his mother in 1608. On June 5, 1607, his daughter Susanna was married to Dr. John Hall in Holy Trinity Church, Stratford. Their first child and Shakespeare's first grandchild, Elizabeth, was christened in the same church on February 21, 1608.

Shakespeare's Reputation, 1601–1608

Allusions to Shakespeare are frequent during this period of his life. One amusing reference is not literary, but professes to tell about Shakespeare's prowess as a lover and rival of his good friend and theatrical colleague, Richard Burbage. Perhaps the joke was just a good bawdy story and should not be taken too seriously, but it is nonetheless one of the few anecdotes that date from Shakespeare's lifetime. Our informant is John Manningham, a young law student, who notes in his commonplace book in 1602 the following:

> 13 March 1601 [1602] . . . Vpon a tyme when Burbidge played Rich. 3. there was a citizen greue [grew] soe farr in liking with him, that before shee went from the play shee appointed him to come that night vnto hir by the name of Ri: the 3. Shakespeare overhearing their conclusion went before, was intertained, and at his game ere Burbidge came. Then message being brought that Rich. the 3.ᵈ was at the dore, Shakespeare caused returne to be made that William the Conqueror was before Rich. the 3. Shakespeare's name William.

Other allusions of the time are more literary. Shakespeare's greatness is by this time taken for granted. Anthony Scoloker, for example, in his epistle prefatory to *Diaphantus, or the Passions of Love* (1604), attempts to describe an excellent literary work in this way:

> It should be like the *Neuer-too-well read Arcadia,* . . . or to come home to the vulgars *Element,* like *Friendly Shakespeare's Tragedies,* where the *Commedian* rides, when the *Tragedian* stands on Tip-toe: Faith it should please all, like Prince *Hamlet.*

The antiquarian William Camden includes Shakespeare's name among his list of England's greatest writers in his *Remaines of a greater Worke concerning Britaine* (1605):

> These may suffice for some Poeticall descriptions of our auncient Poets, if I would come to our time, what a world could I present to you out of *Sir Philipp Sidney, Ed. Spencer, Samuel Daniel, Hugh Holland, Ben: Johnson, Th. Campion, Mich. Drayton, George Chapman, Iohn Marston, William Shakespeare,* & other most pregnant witts of these our times, whom succeeding ages may iustly admire.

A striking attempt to use Shakespeare's growing reputation and dramatic skill for political effect had some potentially serious repercussions. Two days before the abortive rebellion of the Earl of Essex on February 7, 1601, Shakespeare's company was commissioned to perform a well-known play in its repertory about King Richard II. This play must almost surely have been Shakespeare's. Evidently the purpose of this extraordinary performance was to awaken public sympathy for Essex by suggesting that Queen Elizabeth was another Richard II, surrounded by corrupt favorites and deaf to the pleas of her subjects. Essex' avowed intention was to remove from positions of influence those men whom he considered his political enemies. Fortunately Shakespeare's company was later exonerated of any blame in the affair (see Play Introduction to *Richard II*).

Perhaps no other allusion to Shakespeare during this period, however, can suggest so well as the following quotation the extent to which Shakespeare's plays had become familiar to Englishmen everywhere. The quotation is taken from the notes of a certain Captain Keeling, commander of the East India Company's ship *Dragon,* off Sierra Leone, in the years 1607 and 1608:

> 1607, Sept. 5. I sent the interpreter, according to his deseir, abord the Hector whear he brooke fast, and after came abord mee, wher we gaue the tragedie of Hamlett.
>
> 30. Captain Hawkins dinned with me, wher my companions acted Kinge Richard the Second.
>
> [March 31.] I envited Captain Hawkins to a ffishe dinner, and had Hamlet acted abord me; which I permitt to keepe my people from idlenes and unlawful games, or sleepe.

Other Drama of the Period

Even without Shakespeare, the early Jacobean drama in England would rank as one of the most creative periods in the history of all theatre. (The word "Jacobean" is derived from *Jacobus,* the Latin form of the name of King James I.) Shakespeare's earlier contemporaries—Lyly, Greene, Marlowe, Peele, Kyd—were dead or silent, but another generation of playwrights was at hand. George Chapman, John Marston, and Ben Jonson all began writing plays shortly before 1600. The names of Thomas Dekker and Thomas Heywood are perhaps to be associated with various lost plays as early as 1594, but these men are known today for the plays they wrote after 1599. Francis Beaumont, John Fletcher, Cyril Tourneur, and Thomas Middleton emerged into prominence in about 1606 or 1607. John Webster collaborated with Dekker and others in such plays as *Westward Ho* and *Sir Thomas Wyatt* around 1604, although he did not write his great tragedies until 1609–1614. Lesser talents such as Henry Chettle, Anthony Munday, Henry Porter, John Day, and William Haughton continued to pour forth an abundant supply of workmanlike plays. As Shakespeare's career developed, therefore, he enjoyed the fellowship and no doubt the rivalry of a remarkably gifted and diverse group of practicing dramatists.

Early Jacobean drama is, on the whole, characteristically different from the late Elizabethan drama that had preceded it. Other dramatists besides Shakespeare mirror his shift of focus from romantic comedies and patriotic histories to "problem" plays and tragedies. The boys' companies, reopening in 1598–1599 after virtually a decade of silence, did much to set the new tone. They avoided almost entirely the English history play with its muscularly heroic style, so unsuited for the acting capabilities of boys. Besides, sophisticated audiences were sated with jingoistic fare, and even in the public theatres the genre had pretty well run its course. The fashion of the moment turned instead to revenge tragedy and satiric comedy.

The Jacobean revenge play owed much of its original inspiration to Thomas Kyd's *The Spanish Tragedy* (c. 1587), with its pace-setting conventions: the intervention of supernatural forces, the feigned madness of the avenger, his difficulty in ascertaining the true facts of the murder, his morbid awareness of the conflict between human injustice and divine justice, his devising of a play within the play, and his invention of ingenious methods of slaughter in the play's gory ending. Kyd may also have written an early version of *Hamlet* featuring similar motifs. Shakespeare elevated the revenge play to sublimest tragedy in his *Hamlet* (c. 1599–1601), but most followers of Kyd preferred to revel in the sensationalism of the genre. Some private-theatre dramatists, such as Marston, even subjected the conventions of the genre to caricature. Marston's revenge plays, written chiefly for Paul's boys and (after 1604) for the Children of the Queen's Revels, include *Antonio's Revenge* (1599–1601), and *The Malcontent* (1600–1604). These dramas are marked by flamboyantly overstated cynicism, and are in many ways as close to satire as to tragedy. Marston had in fact made his first reputation as a nondramatic satirist, with *The Metamorphosis of Pygmalions Image* and *The Scourge of Villanie* in 1598. His plays represent a continuation in dramatic form of the techniques of the Roman satirist. The typical Marstonian avenger, such as Malevole in *The Malcontent,* is an exaggeratedly unattractive authorial spokesman, pouring forth venomous hatred upon the loathsome and degenerate court in which he finds himself.

Similar in their exaggerated pursuit of the grotesque and the morbid are Cyril Tourneur's *The Atheist's Tragedy* (1607–1611), and a play often attributed to Tourneur, *The Revenger's Tragedy* (1606–1607). These plays are brilliant in the plotting of impossible situations and in the invention of cunning Italianate forms of torture and murder. Any sympathetic identification with the characters of these plays is sacrificed in the interests of technical virtuosity. As a result, the plays are more ironic than cathartic in their effect; we are overwhelmed by life's dark absurdities rather than ennobled by a vision of man's tragic grandeur. *The Tragedy of Hoffman, or A Revenge for a Father* by Henry Chettle (Admiral's men, 1602) is similarly grotesque and lacking in sympathy for its revenger hero. To be sure, George Chapman's *Bussy D'Ambois* (1600–1604) and its sequel *The Revenge of Bussy D'Ambois* (1607–1612) are thoughtful plays about human aspiration, in the vein of Marlowe's *Tamburlaine,* but even these plays employ a good deal of Senecan melodrama of blood.

The revenge play enjoyed a great popularity on the public stage and (in a caricatured form) on the private stage. The public theatre did, however, cater also to its Puritan-leaning audiences with more pious and moral tragedy. *Arden of Feversham* (c. 1591) is a good early example of what has come to be called domestic or homiletic tragedy. In the studiously plain style of a broadside ballad, it sets forth the facts of an actual murder that had occurred in 1551 and had been reported in Holinshed's *Chronicles*. The play interprets those events earnestly and providentially. The most famous play in the genre of domestic tragedy is Thomas Heywood's *A Woman Killed with Kindness* (1603). It tells not of a murder but of an adultery, for which the good-hearted but offending wife must be perpetually banished by her grieving husband. The play succeeds in elevating the private sorrows of its ordinary characters to universally tragic stature. The moral stances are unambiguous: adultery is a heinous offense but can be transcended by Christian forgiveness; dueling is evil. Other plays in the vein of domestic tragedy include *A Yorkshire Tragedy* (1605–1608), *The Miseries of Enforced Marriage* (1605–1606), and *Two Lamentable Tragedies* (c. 1594–1598).

In comedy, the greatest writer of the period besides Shakespeare was Ben Jonson. His predilection was toward the private theatre, though he continued to write occasionally for the public stage as well. To an ever-increasing extent, he fixed his satirical gaze on those values and institutions which Thomas Heywood cherished: the city of London, its bourgeois citizens, its traditional approach to morality, its religious zeal. *Every Man Out of His Humor* (1599), written for the Chamberlain's men, features a foolish uxorious citizen, his socially aspiring wife, and her fashionmongering lover—humors types that were to appear again and again in the genre of satirical comedy known as "city comedy." (See Brian Gibbons, *Jacobean City Comedy,* 1968). *Volpone* (1605–1606), though technically not a London city comedy since it purportedly takes place in Venice, castigates greed among lawyers, businessmen, and other professional types. *The Alchemist* (1610) ridicules the affectations of petty shopkeepers, lawyers' clerks, Puritan divines, and others. *Bartholomew Fair* (1614) gives us Jonson's most memorable indictment of the Puritans.

Numerous other writers contributed to humors comedy and city comedy. George Chapman probably deserves more credit than he usually receives for having helped determine the shape of humors comedy in his *The Blind Beggar of Alexandria* (1596), *An Humorous Day's Mirth* (1597), *All Fools* (1599–1604), *May-Day* (1601–1609), *The Gentleman Usher* (1602–1604), and others. Francis Beaumont, assisted perhaps by John Fletcher, ridicules London grocers and apprentices for their naive tastes in romantic chivalry in *The Knight of the Burning Pestle* (1607–1610). Some satire in this vein, to be sure, is reasonably good-humored. *Eastward Ho* (1605), by Chapman, Jonson, and Marston, is genially sympathetic toward the

COURTESY OF THE TRUSTEES, THE BRITISH MUSEUM

Raphael Holinshed's Chronicles of England, Scotland, and Ireland, *which was published (1577) before Shakespeare's career began, served as principal historic source for many plays, including* Macbeth, King Lear, *and* Cymbeline, *as well as the history plays. Here, in a woodcut from the* Chronicles, *Macbeth and Banquo are shown encountering the three witches.*

life-style of the small shopkeeper, even though the play contains a good deal of satire directed at social climbing and sharp business practices. Thomas Dekker's collaboration with Thomas Middleton on *The Honest Whore* (Part I, 1604) gives us an amused and yet warm portrayal of a linen draper who succeeds in business by insisting that the customer is always right. Dekker often shows a wry but generous appreciation of bourgeois ethics, as in *The Shoemakers' Holiday* (1599). Yet even he turns against the Puritans in *If This Be Not a Good Play, the Devil Is in It* (1611–1612).

Marston shows his talent for city comedy in *The Dutch Courtesan* (1603–1605). Perhaps the most ingratiating and truly funny of the writers of city comedy, however, is Middleton. His *A Trick to Catch the Old One* (1604–1607) illustrates the tendency of Jacobean comedy to move away both from Shakespeare's romantic vein and Jonson's morally satirical vein towards a more lighthearted comedy of manners anticipating the style of Restoration comedy. One of Middleton's most hilarious and philosophically unpretentious plays, though plotted with great ingenuity of situation, is *A Mad World, My Masters* (1604–1607). *Michaelmas Term,* written about the same time, exposes the sharp practices of usurers and lawyers. All these Middleton plays were written for Paul's boys.

Romantic comedy, though overshadowed by humors and city comedy during the 1600's, still held forth at the public theatres. A leading exponent was Thomas Heywood, in such plays as *The Fair Maid of the West,* or *A Girl Worth Gold* (1597–1610). Heywood also wrote English history plays designed to prove the sturdiness and historical importance of the London citizenry he so loved, as in *Edward IV* (1597–1599), *The Four Prentices of London* (c. 1600), and *If You Know Not Me You Know Nobody* (1605). Classical tragedy also continued to be written, despite the vogue of revenge tragedy. Ben Jonson rather dogmatically illustrated his classical theories of tragedy in *Sejanus* (1603) and *Catiline* (1611). Samuel Daniel wrote *Philotas* in 1604 and a revision of his *Cleopatra* in 1607. Heywood's *The Rape of Lucrece* appeared in 1606–1608. These are not, however, the immortal tragedies for which the Jacobean period is remembered.

Shakespeare's Work, 1601–1608

Shakespeare's plays of this period reveal many Jacobean characteristics. The comedies are few in number and lack the joyous affirmation we associate with *Twelfth Night* and earlier plays. *Measure for Measure,* for example, is not about young men and women happily in love, but about premarital sex and the insoluble problems that arise when vice-prone men attempt to legislate morality for their fellow men. Angelo, self-hating and out of emotional control, is a tragic hero providentially rescued from his own worst self. The Duke and Isabella must use ethically dubious means—the bed trick—to effect their virtuous aims. Comedy in the play deals darkly in terms of prostitution, slander, and police inefficiency.

All's Well that Ends Well, though less grim than *Measure for Measure* in its confrontation of man's degeneracy, does apply a similar bed trick as its central plot device. Just as important, the obstacles to love are internal and psychological rather than external. That is, the happy union of Bertram and Helena is delayed not by parental objections or by accident (as in *Romeo and Juliet* and *A Midsummer Night's Dream*) but by Bertram's snobbish refusal to see Helena's true worth. *Troilus and Cressida* is a play in which love is paralyzed by a combination of external and internal forces. Troilus must hand Cressida over to the Greeks because his code of honor bids him put his country's cause before his own, and yet that code of "honor" is based on Paris' rape of Helen. Cressida simply gives herself up to Diomedes, knowing she is not strong enough to stand alone in a moral wilderness. The combatants in the greatest war in all history turn out to be petty bickerers, who play nasty games on one another and sulk when their reputations are impugned. The cause for which both sides fight is squalid and senseless.

In *Hamlet,* Shakespeare explores similar dilemmas posed by man's carnality. Women are too often frail, men are too often importunate and brutal. How is a thoughtful person to justify his own existence? Should he struggle actively against injustice and personal wrong? How can he know what is really true, or foresee the complex results of action? How, in *Othello,* can man resist diabolical evil prompting him to destroy the very thing on which his happiness depends? Is Macbeth tempted to sin by the weird sisters and his wife, or is the choice to murder Duncan ultimately his? To what extent is man responsible for his tragic fate? Most of all, in *King Lear,* are the heavens themselves indifferent to man's bestiality? Must Cordelia die? Yet despite these overwhelmingly pessimistic questions, and the tragic consequences they imply for all human life, Shakespeare's "great" tragedies affirm at least the nobility of man's striving to know himself, and the redeeming fact that human goodness does exist (in Desdemona, Duncan, Cordelia) even if those who practice goodness are often slaughtered.

The Roman or classical tragedies are something apart from the "great" tragedies. They are more ironic in tone, more dispiriting, though they too affirm an essential nobility in man. Brutus misguidedly leads a revolution against Caesar, but dies loyal to his great principles. Timon of Athens proves the appalling ingratitude of his fellow man and resolutely cuts himself off from all human contact. Coriolanus proclaims himself an enemy of the Roman people and seeks to destroy them for their ingratitude, though he is compromised and destroyed at last by his promptings of human feeling. Antony too is pulled apart by an irreconcilable conflict. Yet in this play at least Shakespeare achieves a triumph over defeat that seems to offer a new resolution of man's tragic dilemma.

The Late Years: 1608–1616

In the summer of 1608, Shakespeare's acting company signed a twenty-one-year lease for the use of the Blackfriars playhouse, an indoor and rather intimate, artificially lighted theatre inside the city of London, close to the site of St. Paul's cathedral. A private theatre had existed on this spot since 1576, when the Children of the Chapel and then Paul's boys began acting their courtly plays for paying spectators in a building that had once belonged to the Dominicans, or Black Friars. James Burbage had begun construction in 1596 of the so-called Second Blackfriars theatre in the same building. Although James encountered opposition from the residents of the area and died before he could complete the work, James' son Richard did suceed in opening the new theatre in 1600. At first he leased it (for twenty-one years) to a children's company; but when that company was suppressed in 1608 for offending the French ambassador in a play by George Chapman, Burbage seized the opportunity to take back the unexpired lease and set up Blackfriars as the winter playhouse for his adult company, the King's men. By this time the adult troupes could plainly see that they needed to cater more directly to courtly audiences than they once had done. Their popular audiences were becoming increasingly disenchanted with the drama. Puritan fulminations against the stage gained in effect, especially when many playwrights refused to disguise their satirical hostility toward Puritans and the London bourgeoisie.

Several of Shakespeare's late plays may have been acted both at the Globe and at Blackfriars. The plays he wrote after 1608–1609, *Cymbeline, The Winter's Tale,* and *The Tempest,* all show the distinct influence of the dramaturgy of the private theatres. Also, we know that an increasing number of Shakespeare's plays were acted at the court of King James. *Othello, King Lear,* and *The Tempest* are named in court revels accounts, and *Macbeth* attentively flatters the Scottish royal ancestry of King James as though for a court performance. On the other hand, Shakespeare's plays certainly continued to be acted at the Globe to the very end of his career. The 1609 quarto of *Pericles* advertises that it was acted "by his Maiesties Seruants, at the Globe on the Banck-side." The 1608 quarto of *King Lear* mentions a performance at court and assigns the play to "his Maiesties seruants playing vsually at the Gloabe on the Bancke-side." Simon Forman saw *Macbeth, Cymbeline,* and *The Winter's Tale* at the Globe. Finally, a performance of *Henry VIII* on June 29, 1613, resulted in the burning of the Globe to the ground, though afterwards it soon was rebuilt.

Shakespeare's last plays, written with a view to Blackfriars and the court as well as to the Globe, are usually called "romances" or "tragicomedies" or sometimes both. The term romance suggests a return to the kind of story Robert Greene had derived from Greek romance: tales of adventure, long separation, and tearful reunion, involving shipwreck, capture by pirates, riddling prophecies, children set adrift in boats or abandoned on foreign shores, the illusion of death and subsequent restoration to life, the revelation of the identity of long-lost children by birthmarks, and the like. The term tragicomedy suggests a play in which the protagonist commits a seemingly fatal error or crime, or (as in *Pericles*) suffers an extraordinarily adverse fortune to test his patience; in either event he must experience agonies of contrition and bereavement until he is providentially delivered from his tribulations. The tone is deeply melancholic and resigned, although suffused also with a sense of gratitude for the harmonies that are mysteriously restored.

The appropriateness of such plays to the elegant atmosphere of Blackfriars and the court is subtle but real. Although one might suppose at first that oldfashioned naiveté would seem out of place in a sophisticated milieu, the naiveté is only superficial. Tragicomedy and pastoral romance were, in the period from 1606 to 1610, beginning to enjoy a fashionable courtly revival. The leading practitioners of the new genre were Beaumont and Fletcher, though Shakespeare made a highly significant contribution. Perhaps sophisticated audiences responded to pastoral and romantic drama as the nostalgic evocation of an idealized past, a chivalric "golden world" fleetingly recovered through an artistic journey back to naiveté and innocence. The evocation of such a world demands the kind of studied but informal artifice we find in many tragicomic plays of the period: the elaborate masques and allegorical shows, the descents of enthroned gods from the heavens (as in *Cymbeline*), the use of quaint Chorus figures like Old Gower or Time (in *Pericles* and *The Winter's Tale*), the quasi-operatic blend of music and spectacle. At their best, such plays powerfully compel belief in the artistic world thus artificially created. The very improbability of the story becomes, paradoxically, part of the means by which an audience must "awake its faith" in a mysterious truth.

Shakespeare did not merely ape the new fashion in tragicomedy and romance. In fact, he may have done much to establish it. His *Pericles,* written seemingly in about 1606–1608 for the public stage before Shakespeare's company acquired Blackfriars, anticipated many important features not only of Shakespeare's own later romances but of Beaumont and Fletcher's *The Maid's Tragedy* and *Philaster* (c. 1608–1611). Still, Shakespeare was on the verge of retirement, and the future belonged to Beaumont and Fletcher. Gradually Shakespeare disengaged himself,

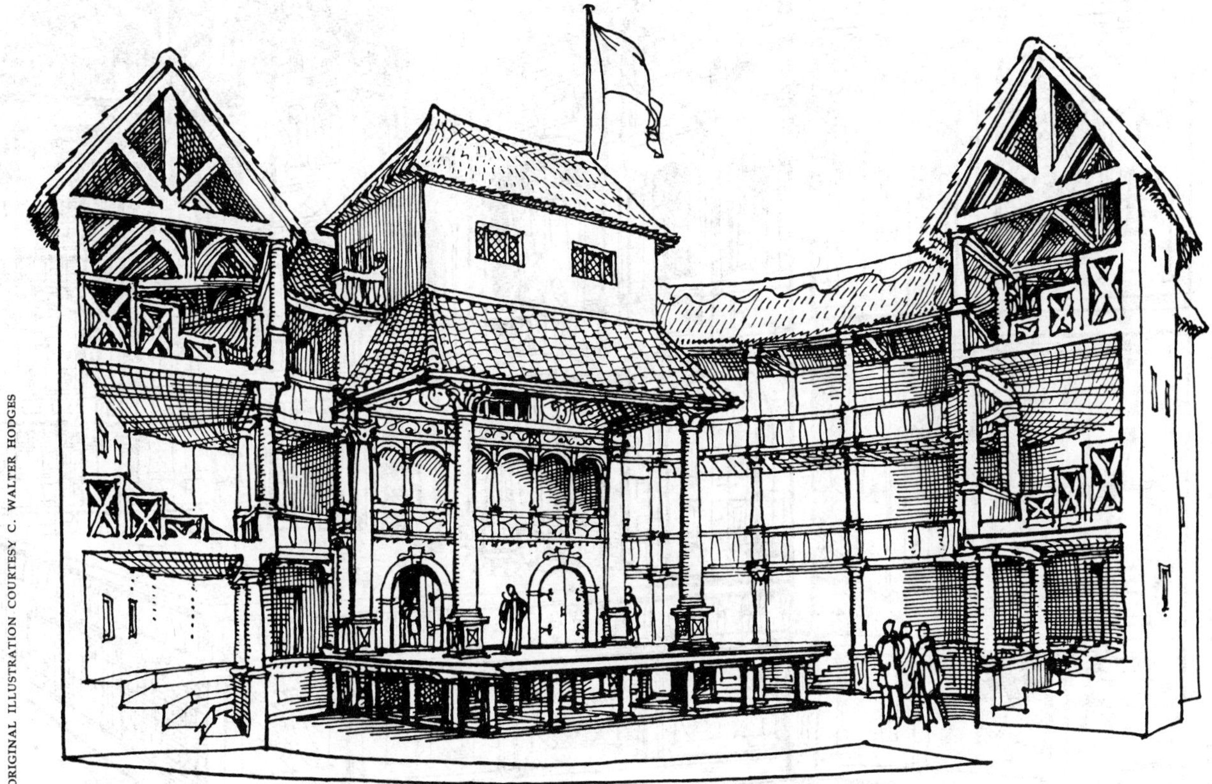

ORIGINAL ILLUSTRATION COURTESY C. WALTER HODGES

A modern sketch of the Swan Theatre shows the open, encircling roof and a full view of the tiring-house. Like the Globe and other open theatres, the design of the Swan seems to resemble the Elizabethan innyard with an added stage.

O
O
N
L
K
M
Q
J
E
E
H
G
F
A
C. WALTER
HODGES

The (Second) Globe Playhouse, 1614–1644.

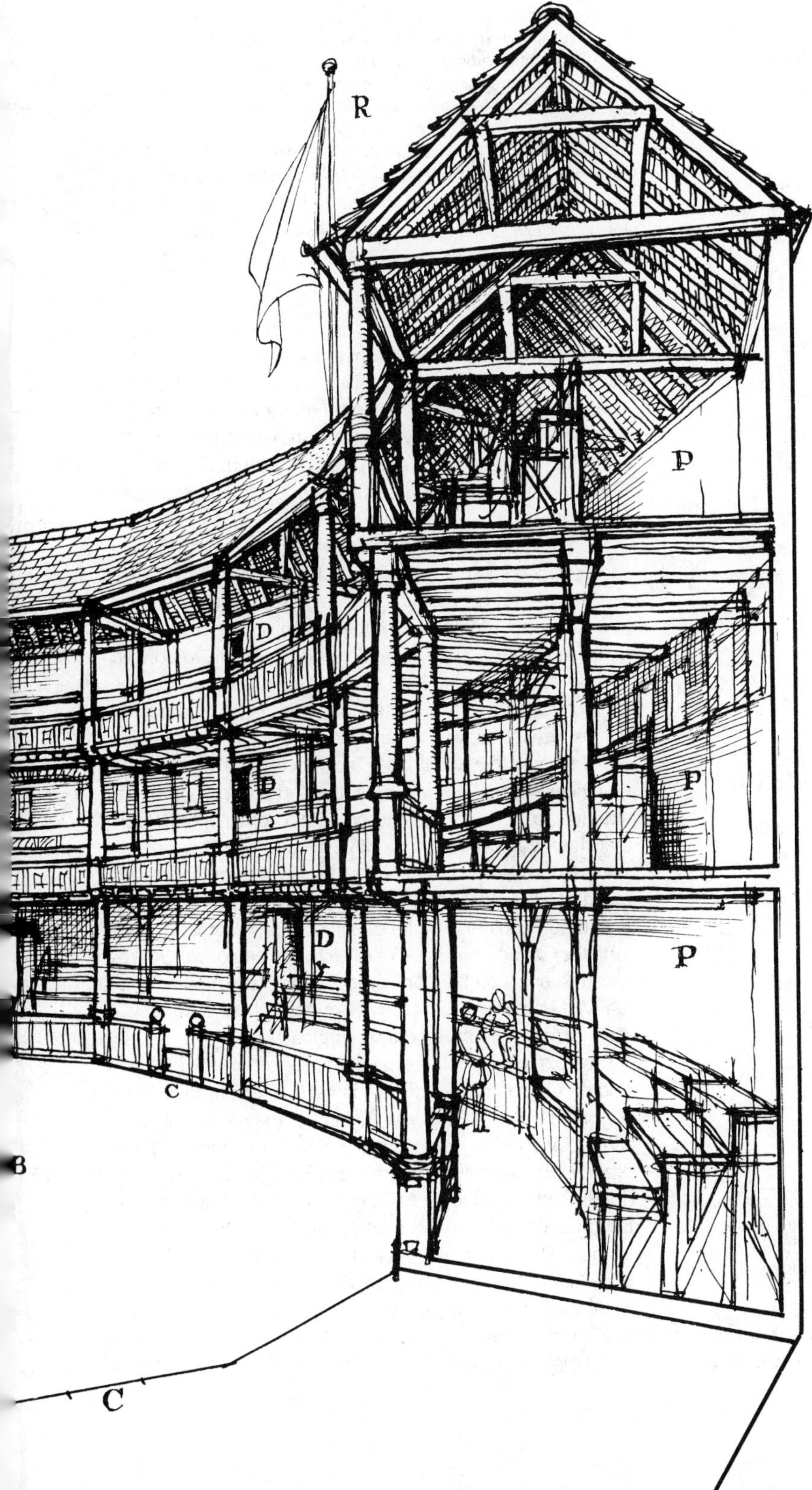

The second Globe Theatre, built in 1613 after a fire had destroyed the first Globe during a performance of Shakespeare's Henry VIII. *This building generally resembled its predecessor in the size of the stage and the "yard" for the spectators, the location of the stage doors and of a curtained area backstage for discovery scenes, etc. The upper acting station in this second Globe Theatre may, however, have been somewhat more elaborate than in the first Globe where spectators often sat above the stage. In neither theatre was the upper acting station used extensively for dramatic presentation.*

Key.

- *AA.* *Main entrances to auditorium.*
- *B.* *Yard for standing spectators.*
- *CC.* *Entrances to lowest gallery.*
- *DD.* *Entrances to staircase leading to upper galleries.*
- *EE.* *"Gentlemen's Rooms."*
- *F.* *The stage.*
- *G.* *The stage trap (leading from the "Hell" beneath the stage).*
- *H.* *Curtained space for "discovery" scenes.*
- *J.* *Upper stage.*
- *K.* *The "Heavens." (This area probably often covered across with a stretched canopy painted to represent sky.)*
- *L.* *Backing painted with clouds. A shutter is here shown open to allow a god's throne to travel forward. (c.f. "Cymbeline," Act V sc. IV)*
- *M.* *The throne about to descend to the stage.*
- *N.* *Backstage area (or "Tiring-house").*
- *O.* *Wardrobe and dressing-rooms.*
- *P.* *Spectator galleries.*
- *Q.* *"Fly" gallery in the Heavens.*
- *R.* *Playhouse flag (reached from top landing of staircase, and raised to denote performance days).*

spending more and more time in Stratford. His last-known stint as an actor was in Jonson's *Sejanus* in 1603. Some time in 1611 or 1612 he probably gave up his lodgings in London, though he still may have returned for such occasions as the opening performance of *Henry VIII* in 1613. He continued to be one of the proprietors of the newly rebuilt Globe, but his involvement in its day-to-day operations dwindled.

Shakespeare's Reputation

Shakespeare's reputation among his contemporaries was undiminished in his late years, even though Beaumont and Fletcher were the new rage at the Globe and Blackfriars. Among those who apostrophized Shakespeare was John Davies of Hereford in *The Scourge of Folly* (S.R. 1610):

To our English Terence, Mr. Will. Shake-speare.

Some say (good *Will*) which I, in sport, do sing,
Had'st thou not plaid some Kingly parts in sport,
Thou hadst bin a companion for a *King;*
And, beene a King among the meaner sort.
Some others raile; but, raile as they thinke fit,
Thou hast no rayling, but, a raigning Wit:
And honesty *thou sow'st, which they do reape;*
So, to increase their Stocke *which they do keepe.*

The following sonnet is from *Runne and a Great Cast* (1614) by Thomas Freeman:

To Master W. Shakespeare.

Shakespeare, that nimble *Mercury* thy braine,
Lulls many hundred *Argus*-eyes asleepe,
So fit, for all thou fashionest thy vaine,
At th' *horse-foote* fountaine thou hast drunk full deepe,
Vertues or vices theame to thee all one is:
Who loues chaste life, there's *Lucrece* for a Teacher:
Who list read lust there's *Venus* and *Adonis,*
True modell of a most lasciuious leatcher.
Besides in plaies thy wit windes like *Meander:*
Whence needy new-composers borrow more
Then *Terence* doth from *Plautus* or *Menander.*
But to praise thee aright I want thy store:
Then let thine owne works thine owne worth upraise,
And help t' adorne thee with deserued Baies.

Ben Jonson took a more critical view, though he also admired Shakespeare greatly. In the Induction to his *Bartholomew Fair* (1631 edition), Jonson compared the imaginary world he presented in his play with the more improbable fantasies of romantic drama:

If there bee neuer a *Seruant-monster* i' the Fayre; who can helpe it? he [the author, Jonson] sayes; nor a nest of *Antiques?* Hee is loth to make Nature afraid in his *Playes,* like those that beget *Tales, Tempests,* and such like *Drolleries,* to mixe his head with other mens heeles.

From this, one judges that Jonson had in mind not only *The Tempest* but Shakespeare's other late romances. He similarly protested in the Prologue to his 1616 edition of *Every Man in His Humor* that his own playwriting was free of the usual romantic claptrap:

Where neither *Chorus* wafts you ore the seas;
Nor creaking throne comes downe, the boys to please;
Nor nimble squibbe [fireworks] is seene, to make afear'd
The gentlewomen; nor roul'd bullet heard
To say, it thunders; nor tempestuous drumme
Rumbles, to tell you when the storme doth come.

Still, Shakespeare's reputation was assured. John Webster paid due homage, in his note To the Reader accompanying *The White Devil* (1612), to "the right happy and copious industry of M. *Shake-speare, M. Decker, & M. Heywood,*" along with Chapman, Jonson, Beaumont, and Fletcher.

Latest Records

Shakespeare's last recorded investment in real estate was the purchase of a house in Blackfriars, London, in 1613. There is no indication he lived there, for he had retired to Stratford. He did not pay the full purchase price of £140, and the mortgage deed executed for the unpaid balance furnishes one of the six absolutely unquestioned examples of his signature.

John Combe, a wealthy bachelor of Stratford and Shakespeare's friend, left him a legacy of five pounds in his will at the time of Combe's death in 1613. At about the same time, John's kinsman William Combe began a controversial attempt to enclose Welcombe Common—that is, to convert narrow strips of arable land to pasture. Presumably Combe was interested in a more efficient means of using the land. Enclosure was, however, an explosive issue, since many people feared they would lose the right to farm the land and be evicted to make room for cattle and sheep. Combe attempted to guarantee Shakespeare and other titheholders that they would lose no money. He offered similar assurances to the Stratford Council, but the townspeople were adamantly opposed. Shakespeare was consulted by letter as a leading titheholder. The letter is lost, but presumably it set forth the Council's reasons for objecting to enclosure. Shakespeare's views on the controversy remain unknown. Eventually the case went to the Privy Council, where Combe was ordered to restore the land to its original use.

One of the most interesting documents from the later period consists of the records of a lawsuit entered into in 1612 by Stephen Belott against his father-in-law Christopher Mountjoy, a Huguenot maker of woman's ornamental headdresses who resided on Silver Street, St. Olave's parish, London. Belott sought to secure the payment of a dower promised him at the time of his marriage to Mountjoy's daughter. In this suit Shakespeare was summoned as a witness and made deposition on five interrogatories. From this document we learn that Shakespeare was a lodger in Mountjoy's house at the time of the marriage in 1604 and probably for some time before that, since he states in his testimony that he had known Mountjoy for more than ten years. Shakespeare admitted that, at the solicitation of Mountjoy's wife, he had acted as an intermediary in the arrangement of the marriage between Belott and Mountjoy's daughter. Shakespeare declared himself unable, however, to recall the exact amount of the portion or the date on which it was to have been paid. Shakespeare's signature to his deposition is undoubtedly authentic, and one of the best samples of his handwriting that we have.

In January of 1615 or 1616, Shakespeare drew up his last will and testament with the assistance of his lawyer Francis Collins, who had aided him earlier in some of his transactions in real estate. On March 25, 1616, Shakespeare revised his will in order to provide for the marriage of his daughter Judith and Thomas Quiney in that same year. Shakespeare's three quavering signatures, one on each page of this document, suggest that he was in failing health. The cause of his death on April 23 is not known. An intriguing bit of Stratford gossip is reported by John Ward, vicar of Holy Trinity in Stratford from 1662 to 1689, in his diary: "Shakespear, Drayton, and Ben Jhonson, had a merry meeting, and itt seems drank too hard, for Shakespear died of a feavour there contracted." The report comes fifty years after Shakespeare's death, however, and is hardly an expert medical opinion.

The will disposes of all the property of which Shakespeare is known to have died possessed, the greater share of it going to his daughter Susanna. His recently married daughter Judith received a dowry, a provision for any children that might be born of her marriage, and other gifts. Ten pounds went to the poor of Stratford, Shakespeare's sword to Mr. Thomas Combe, 26s. 8d. apiece to Shakespeare's fellow actors Heminges, Burbage, and Condell to buy them mourning rings, and other small bequests to various other friends and relatives.

An interlineation contains the bequest of Shakespeare's "second best bed with the furniture," that is, the hangings, to his wife. Anne's name appears nowhere else in the will. Some scholars, beginning with Edmund Malone, have taken this reference as proof of an unhappy marriage, confirming earlier indications such as the hasty wedding to a woman who was William's senior by eight years, and his prolonged residence in London for twenty years or more seemingly without his family. The evidence is inconclusive, however. Shakespeare certainly supported his family handsomely, acquired much property in Stratford, and retired there when he might have remained still in London. Although he showed no great solicitude for Anne's well-being in the will, her rights were protected by law; a third of her husband's estate went to her without having to be mentioned in the will. New Place was to be the home of Shakespeare's favorite daughter Susanna, wife of the distinguished Dr. John Hall. Anne Shakespeare would make her home with her daughter, and with her dower rights secured by law would be quite as wealthy as she would need to be.

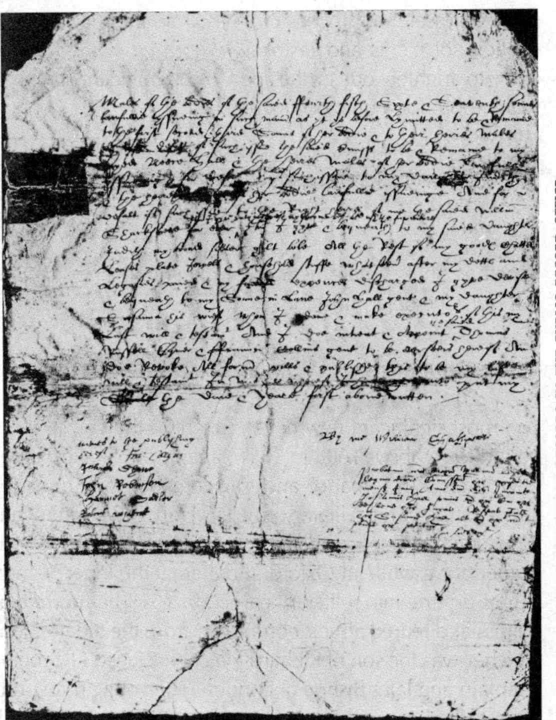

As with so many other things in his life, the curious terms of Shakespeare's will have led to endless and provocative conjecture.

The date of Shakespeare's death, April 23, 1616, is inscribed on his monument. This elaborate structure, still standing in the chancel of Trinity Church, Stratford, was erected some time before 1623 by the London stonecutting firm of Gheerart Janssen and his sons. Janssen's shop was in Southwark, near the Globe, and may have been familiar to the actors. The bust of Shakespeare is a conventional sort of statuary for its time. Still, it is one of the only two contemporary likenesses we have. The other is the Droeshout engraving of Shakespeare in the Folio of 1623.

The epitaph on the monument reads as follows:

> Ivdicio Pylivm, genio Socratem, arte Maronem:
> Terra tegit, popvlvs maeret, Olympvs habet.
> Stay Passenger, why goest thov by so fast?
> Read if thov canst, whom enviovs Death hath plast,
> With in this monvment Shakespeare: with whome,
> Quick natvre dide: whose name doth deck y^s^ Tombe,
> Far more then cost: sieh all, y^t^ He hath writt,
> Leaves living art, bvt page, to serve his witt.
>
> Obiit anno domini 1616
> Aetatis—53 die 23 April.

These lines, which seem to indicate, as well as anything could, the high reputation in which Shakespeare was held as a poet at the time of his death, are not so well known as those inscribed over Shakespeare's grave near the north wall of the chancel. A local tradition assigns them to Shakespeare himself and implies that he wrote them "to suit the capacity of clerks and sextons," whom he wished apparently to frighten out of the idea of opening the grave to make room for a new occupant:

> Good frend for Iesvs sake forbeare,
> To digg the dvst encloased heare.
> Bleste be ye man y^t spares thes stones,
> And cvrst be he y^t moves my bones.

Whether Shakespeare actually wrote these lines cannot, however, be determined.

Other Dramatists

The most significant new development in the drama of the period from about 1608 to 1616, apart from Shakespeare's new interest in romance and tragicomedy, was the emergence of the famous literary partners Francis Beaumont and John Fletcher. Beaumont, the son of a distinguished lawyer, studied for a while at Oxford and then at the Inner Temple before drifting into a literary career. In 1613 he married an heiress and retired almost completely from the theatre. John Fletcher was the son of Richard Fletcher, Queen Elizabeth's chaplain and later Bishop of London. The young man probably studied at Cambridge. The father died in 1596 heavily in debt, leaving the young Fletcher to support a family of eight children. Fletcher became a professional writer, earning his living as chief dramatist for the King's men. He was Shakespeare's successor. Fletcher's cousins Giles and Phineas Fletcher gained some reputation as poets. Beaumont and Fletcher, who were close friends, regarded themselves also as poets and as members of the "tribe of Ben"—the disciples of the great Ben Jonson who often gathered together at the Mermaid Tavern for an evening of witty literary conversation.

> What things have we seen
> Done at the Mermaid! heard words that have been
> So nimble, and so full of subtle flame,
> As if that every one from whence they came
> Had meant to put his whole wit in a jest,
> And had resolv'd to live a fool the rest
> Of his dull life!
>
> *(Master Francis Beaumont's Letter to Ben Jonson)*

Beaumont and Fletcher actually collaborated on only about seven plays: *The Woman Hater,* a comedy (1606), *The Maid's Tragedy,* a tragedy (1608–1611), *Philaster,* a tragicomedy (1608–1610), *Cupid's Revenge,* a tragedy (c. 1607–1612), *The Coxcomb,* a comedy (1608–1610), *A King and No King,* a tragicomedy (1611), *The Scornful Lady,* a tragicomedy (1613–1616), and perhaps one or two others. They may have collaborated on *The Knight of the Burning Pestle* (c. 1607–1610), though it was chiefly Beaumont's. Beaumont also wrote *Mask of the Inner Temple and Gray's Inn* (1613). Fletcher unassisted wrote *The Faithful Shepherdess* (1608–1609), *The Night Walker* (c. 1611), *Bonduca* (1611–1614), *Valentinian* (1610–1614), and others. He also collaborated with several other writers, including Massinger, Middleton, Field, and Rowley. Importantly, he may have collaborated with Shakespeare on *The Two Noble Kinsmen* (1613–1616), and conceivably *Henry VIII.* Eventually, most of these various dramatic enterprises were gathered together in 1647 as the works of Beaumont and Fletcher. They have remained known as such ever since, partly because the original collaboration of these two men did so much to set a new style in coterie drama.

The plays they wrote together, such as *The Maid's Tragedy* and *Philaster,* offer an interesting comparison with Shakespeare's contemporary writing in a similar genre. Beaumont and Fletcher often employ exotic settings, like Rhodes or Sicily. In such an environment, refined aristocratic characters are caught in dynastic struggles or in a rarified conflict between love and honor. They must cope with stereotyped villains such as tyrants or shamelessly lustful courtiers. The sentiments are lofty, the rhetoric is mannered; elaborately contrived situations are offered with no pretense of versimilitude. The characters live according to lofty chivalric codes, and despise ill breeding above all else. In the plotting of the tragicomic reversal, the audience is sometimes deliberately deceived into believing something that is not true, so that the sudden happy outcome arrives as a theatrically contrived surprise. Disguising and masking are common motifs. The audience is deliberately made aware throughout of the play's theatrical artifice, statuesque scene-building, and titillating sensationalism.

Although Shakespeare wrote no tragedies during his last years, great tragedy did continue to appear on the Jacobean stage. John Webster wrote his two most splendid plays, *The White Devil* and *The Duchess of Malfi,* between 1609 and 1614. Both contain elements of the still-popular revenge tradition. They also manage to achieve a vision of triumphant human dignity in defeat that merits comparison with Shakespeare's greatest tragic achievement. Still to come were *The Changeling* (1622) by Middleton and Rowley, *Women Beware Women* (c. 1620–1627) by Middleton, *'Tis Pity She's a Whore* (1629?–1633) by John Ford, and others. Although these tragedies are more concerned with the grotesque than Shakespeare's great tragedies, more obsessed with abnormal human psychology (incest, werewolfism, and the like), they are nonetheless sublime achievements in art. The genius of the age for tragedy did not die with Shakespeare. During Shakespeare's last years Chapman was also writing his best tragedies, including *Charles Duke of Byron* in 1608, *The Revenge of Bussy D'Ambois* in about 1610, and *Chabot, Admiral of France* between 1611 and 1622. Jonson's *Catiline His Conspiracy,* a classical tragedy, appeared in 1611, Marston's *The Insatiate Countess* in about 1610.

Shakespeare's Language: His Development as Poet and Dramatist

Language and Artistic Development

The study of Shakespeare's language affords many insights into his art, one of which concerns his development as a poet and dramatist. The style of the early Shakespeare is so markedly different from that of the late Shakespeare that scholars have been able to quantify various verse tests and the like, and use them to confirm or supplement the objective or "external" information we have about the order in which Shakespeare wrote his plays and poems. Shakespeare's artistic development is moreover a matter of interest in its own right, as a glimpse into the creative process by which he matured in his craft.

Our understanding of the order of composition of Shakespeare's works relies not at all on the First Folio, published in 1623. There, the plays are arranged in three groups—comedies, histories, and tragedies—without regard for dates for composition. The first comedy in the Folio is *The Tempest,* known to be one of Shakespeare's latest plays; the second is *The Two Gentlemen of Verona,* one of the earliest. The histories are arranged in order of the English kings whose reigns they treat, although Shakespeare clearly did not write them in that order. The tragedies show no discernible arrangement by date. We do have dating information, however, about eighteen of the thirty-six plays in the First Folio that had previously been published in single quarto volumes at various times, and about *Pericles,* which was not included in the First Folio but existed as a quarto only until its inclusion in the Third Folio of 1663–1664. All the quarto editions except *Romeo and Juliet* and *Love's Labor's Lost* were entered in the Register of the Stationers' Company of London; and two other plays, *As You Like It* (S.R. 1600) and *Antony and Cleopatra* (S.R. 1608), although not printed in quarto, were entered in the Stationers' Register possibly in order to forestall publication by printers who had no right to them. The date of entry of a play in the register indicates that at least by that time the play was in existence. The quarto editions have also certain information on their title pages regarding date, author, and publisher, and sometimes tell what theatrical company had acted the play. Other kinds of external evidence of date include references to Shakespeare's plays in diaries, journals, or accounts of the period, and quotations from his plays in the literary works of Elizabethan and Jacobean writers. Allusions in Shakespeare's plays themselves to contemporary events, although difficult to prove beyond dispute, can sometimes be helpful. See Appendix I, at the end of this volume, for a detailed discussion on "Canon, Dates, and Early Texts" of each of Shakespeare's plays.

Once Shakespeare's plays have been arranged in approximate chronological order on the basis of the kinds of external evidence already described, we can perceive that his style underwent a continuous development from his earliest work to the end of his career as a dramatist. This development can be seen in his use of certain types of images, of rhymes, of run-on lines, of weak or feminine endings, and the like, and is so remarkably consistent that various verse "tests" can actually be employed.

Certain difficulties are inevitable in the use of verse tests, and limit the extent to which we may rely on them for precise dating. In some instances, Shakespeare may have revised his own work, imposing a relatively late style on an early style. Theories of revision are not argued as extensively as they once were; but *Love's Labor's Lost,* for example, is still thought by some scholars to have been written as early as 1588–1589 and revised some eight years later. Again, Shakespeare may have collaborated with other writers, or rewritten the work of earlier dramatists. Although collaboration theories are also generally out of favor today, multiple authorship cannot be entirely ruled out as a possibility in the case of a play like *Henry VIII.* The texts of some plays, notably that of *Pericles,* are corrupt and may not represent exactly what Shakespeare wrote. Shakespeare may well have chosen on certain occasions to write in a deliberately "old-fashioned" style, as in the First Player's recitation about the slaying of Priam (*Hamlet,* II,ii) or in "The Murder of Gonzago" performed before King Claudius (*Hamlet,* III,ii). Conversely, Shakespeare may at times have anticipated his later style. If we make sufficient allowance for certain variations in detail, however, we can still discover a consistency in the overall pattern that is surprisingly clear. The very fact of this consistency lends support to one's impression of Shakespeare's extraordinary artistic growth.

The specific kinds of verse tests that can be applied to the dating of Shakespeare's plays are discussed in the following sections. Taken as a whole, they reveal a movement toward ever greater freedom in the use of both verse and prose. Shakespeare increasingly abandons rhyme for prose, and formal end-stopped blank verse for a fluid and often conversational style. He introduces more and more pauses in the middle of lines, and uses hypermetric lines containing more or less than the ten syllables of the conventional iambic pattern. Speeches end in the middle of lines with greater frequency. Shakespeare uses feminine, light, and weak endings in ever-increasing numbers. By the end of his career, his style has virtually been transformed from one of formal and rhetorical regularity to one of vast flexibility and range.

Table of Metrical Tests Applied to Shakespeare's Plays

*Name of Play**	*No. of Lines*	*Prose*	*Blank Verse*	*5-Foot Rhymes*	*Run-on Lines %*	*Double Endings*	*Speech Ending %*	*No. Light Weak End.*	*Probable Dates*
Com. Er.	1778	240	1150	380	12.9	137	0.6	0	c. 1589–1593
L. L. L.	2789	1086	579	1028	18.4	9	10.0	3	c. 1588–1589 rev. 1596–97(?)
Two Gent.	2294	409	1510	116	12.4	203	5.8	0	c. 1590–1594
Tit. And.	2523	43	2338	144	9.5	154	2.5	5	c. 1589–1591
1 Hen. VI	2677	0	2379	314	10.4	140	0.5	4	c. 1589–1592
2 Hen. VI	3162	448	2562	122	11.4	255	1.1	3	c. 1589–1592
3 Hen. VI	2904	0	2749	155	9.5	346	0.9	3	c. 1589–1592
Rich. III	3619	55(?)	3374	170	13.1	570	2.9	4	c. 1591–1594
Tam. Shrew	2649	516	1971	169	8.1	260	3.6	14(?)	c. 1592–1594
Mids. Dream	2174	441	878	731	13.2	29	17.3	1	c. 1594–1595
R. & J.	3052	405	2111	486	14.2	118	14.9	7	c. 1594–1596
K. John	2570	0	2403	150	17.7	54	12.7	7	c. 1594–1595
Rich. II	2756	0	2107	537	19.9	148	7.3	4	c. 1595–1596
Mer. Ven.	2660	673	1896	93	21.5	297	22.2	7	c. 1594–1598
1 Hen. IV	3176	1464	1622	84	22.8	60	14.2	7	c. 1596–1598
2 Hen. IV	3446	1860	1417	74	21.4	203	16.8	1	c. 1596–1598
Much Ado	2826	2106	643	40	19.3	129	20.7	2	c. 1598–1599
A. Y. L. I.	2857	1681	925	71	17.1	211	21.6	2	c. 1598–1600
Henry V	3380	1531	1678	101	21.8	291	18.3	2	c. 1599
J. C.	2478	165	2241	34	19.3	369	20.3	10	c. 1599
Merry Wives	3018	2703	227	69	20.1	32	20.5	1	c. 1597–1601
12th Night	2690	1741	763	120	14.7	152	36.3	4	c. 1600–1602
Hamlet	3931	1208	2490	81	23.1	508	51.6	8	c. 1599–1601
T. & C.	3496	1186	2025	196	27.4	441	31.3	6	c. 1601–1602
All's Well	2966	1453	1234	280	28.4	223	74.4	13	c. 1601–1604
Meas. Meas.	2821	1134	1574	73	23.0	338	51.4	7	c. 1603–1604
Othello	3316	541	2672	86	19.5	646	41.4	2	c. 1603–1604
K. Lear	3334	903	2238	74	29.3	567	60.9	6	c. 1605
Tim. of Ath.	2373	596	1560	184	32.5	257	62.8	30	c. 1605–1608
Macbeth	2108	158	1588	118	36.6	399	77.2	23	c. 1606–1607
A. & . C.	3063	255	2761	42	43.3	613	77.5	99	c. 1606–1607
Pericles	2389	418	1436	225	18.2	120	71.0	82	c. 1606–1608
Coriolanus	3410	829	2521	42	45.9	708	79.0	104	c. 1608
Cymbeline	3339	638	2585	107	46.0	726	85.0	130	c. 1608–1610
Wint. Tale	3075	844	1825	0	37.5	639	87.6	100	c. 1610–1611
Tempest	2064	458	1458	2	41.5	476	84.5	67	c. 1610–1611
Henry VIII	2822	67(?)	2613	16	46.3	1195	72.4	82	c. 1613

Mixture of Prose and Blank Verse

Statistically, not much can be determined as to the date of a play merely on the basis of its percentage of lines in prose or in blank verse; at best, these tests give only an approximation of date. Nevertheless, we can make several observations about Shakespeare's characteristic use of prose and blank verse. In his early plays he seldom uses prose except in the speeches of clowns, servants, and rustics. On the other hand, he uses blank verse often in his early plays, more so than in his later career. Blank verse is his common vehicle of expression in speeches of heightened oratory or dramatic seriousness, as in the early history plays. Blank verse remains of course important throughout Shakespeare's poetic career, but in terms of percentages it is especially prominent during his early years. Marlowe, the originator of the "mighty line" in blank verse, was an important influence, and a rival until his death in 1593. During the plays of Shakespeare's so-called lyric period, c. 1594–1596, rhymed verse often takes the place of blank verse; see, for example, *Romeo and Juliet, A Midsummer Night's Dream,* and *Richard II.*

The use of prose is striking in several mature comedies of the later 1590's, especially *Much Ado about Nothing* and *The Merry Wives of Windsor.* Thereafter, prose is always essential to Shakespeare's comic world, and is no longer limited to buffoonish types as in some early comedies. Prose also comprises a large percentage of lines in *Hamlet* and other great tragedies; and, as the verse grows more free, the alternations between verse and prose are no longer so formally distinguished as they were in the writings of the early Shakespeare.

Rhyme

The percentage of rhyme changes in a statistically significant way over the course of Shakespeare's career. Early plays and those of the lyric period, such as *A Midsummer Night's Dream* and *Romeo and Juliet,* use a great deal of rhyme, whereas late plays such as *The Tempest* use practically none. The commonest form of rhyme is the iambic pentameter measure rhymed in couplet, as when Phebe, quoting Marlowe's *Hero and Leander,* says in *As You Like It* (III,v,81–82):

> Dead shepherd, now I find thy saw of might,
> "Who ever lov'd that lov'd not at first sight?"

Shakespeare does not limit his use of rhyme to the couplet, however. *Romeo and Juliet* and *Love's Labor's Lost* each contains a number of complete sonnets, as well as rhymed sequences made up of a quatrain followed by a couplet, and a good deal of alternate rhyme. Doggerel lines of verse appear in some of the early plays.

One quite formal use of the rhymed couplet does not conform to the statistical pattern that we observe generally in the use of rhyme. Because the Elizabethan theatre lacked a front curtain to mark a pause between scenes in a play, Elizabethan dramatists often gave emphasis to a scene ending by means of a rhymed couplet. Possibly the device served also as a cue to those actors backstage who were waiting to begin the next scene. At any rate, the use of scene-ending couplets is common in some plays that otherwise make little use of rhyme. For example, Act I, scene v of *Hamlet* virtually ends with the following concluding statement by the protagonist:

> The time is out of joint. O cursed spite,
> That ever I was born to set it right!

Apart from this convention, however, use of rhyme in Shakespeare is normally indicative of early style. His lovers in the early plays often speak in rhyme; later, they tend to use prose.

Blank Verse Tests

Although the actual percentage of blank verse in Shakespeare's plays is not always statistically revealing, a number of tests can be applied to the blank verse that are meaningfully consistent. Throughout his career, Shakespeare's blank verse moves gradually but steadily toward greater freedom. Completely regular blank verse, invariably consisting of ten syllables to each unrhymed line with an accent falling on every other syllable, soon becomes monotonous. This iambic pattern can, however, be varied by a number of subtle changes. Extra syllables, accented or unaccented, can be added to the line, or a line may occasionally be short by one or more syllables. The regular alternation of accented and unaccented syllables, which produces the effect of five iambic "feet" in each line (each foot consisting of an unaccented and an accented syllable), can be interrupted by the occasional inversion of a foot. Pauses, or caesuras, may occur at several points in the line. Most importantly, the line can be "end-stopped"—with a strong pause at the end of the line—or "run on" without interruption into the next line. Variations of this sort can transform blank verse from a formal and rhetorical vehicle into one that is highly conversational, almost proselike.

Blank verse before Marlowe's time was usually quite formal, regular, and end-stopped. One of Marlowe's contributions was to provide for greater continuity in thought and style, by means of what has been called the "verse paragraph." His verses, though prevailingly end-stopped, are so constructed that they flow into each other. They have, in other words, somewhat the effect of run-on lines. Marlowe also varied the measure by breaking up the regularity in the forms of the individual feet within the line, sometimes substituting for the regular iambic a trochaic foot (consisting of a stressed followed by an unstressed syllable). The shifting of the medial pause, or caesura, was his chief means of rendering the verse sufficiently flexible to be used in dialogue.

After Marlowe's death in 1593, Shakespeare carried the movement toward stylistic freedom a great distance further. The "Marlovian" Shakespeare, as in *Richard III,* is still insistent upon metrical regularity. By means of rhetorical devices, such as parallelism or antithesis, he often groups his lines of blank verse into pairs or four-line units as though they were parts of a formal sonnet. He runs on past the ends of lines with relative infrequency. In his late years, on the other hand, perhaps influenced by the new styles in blank verse of John Fletcher and other Jacobean dramatists, Shakespeare employs far greater flexibility. We find many more hypermetric lines containing more or fewer than ten syllables. And, as the accompanying chart reveals, the percentage of run-on lines in his plays increases more or less steadily from the early to the late period.

The following passage from Clarence's description of his

dream in *Richard III* (I,iv,21–33) may serve as an example of Shakespeare's earlier blank verse style. Note the pause at the end of every line except the ninth:

O Lord, methought what pain it was to drown!
What dreadful noise of water in mine ears!
What sights of ugly death within mine eyes!
Methoughts I saw a thousand fearful wracks;
A thousand men that fishes gnaw'd upon;
Wedges of gold, great anchors, heaps of pearl,
Inestimable stones, unvalued jewels,
All scatt'red in the bottom of the sea.
Some lay in dead men's skulls; and, in the holes
Where eyes did once inhabit, there were crept,
As 'twere in scorn of eyes, reflecting gems,
That woo'd the slimy bottom of the deep,
And mock'd the dead bones that lay scatt'red by.

As an example of Shakespeare's late style, consider Prospero's description of his magic in *The Tempest* (V,i,33–50) where only the first, fifth, eighth, and tenth lines are end-stopped:

Ye elves of hills, brooks, standing lakes, and groves,
And ye that on the sands with printless foot
Do chase the ebbing Neptune, and do fly him
When he comes back; you demi-puppets that
By moonshine do the green sour ringlets make,
Whereof the ewe not bites; and you whose pastime
Is to make midnight mushrooms, that rejoice
To hear the solemn curfew; by whose aid,
Weak masters though ye be, I have bedimm'd
The noontide sun, call'd forth the mutinous winds,
And 'twixt the green sea and the azur'd vault
Set roaring war; to the dread rattling thunder
Have I given fire, and rifted Jove's stout oak
With his own bolt; the strong-bas'd promontory
Have I made shake, and by the spurs pluck'd up
The pine and cedar; graves at my command
Have wak'd their sleepers, op'd, and let 'em forth
By my so potent art.

These two passages have been chosen for comparison in part because they are both set speeches, rich in formal characteristics. Yet a comparison of more informal speeches from early and late plays ought to reveal no less clearly the shift in Shakespeare's style away from rhetorical balance toward a freedom from verse restraint, a deliberate syncopation of blank verse rhythms, and a complication of syntax.

The Speech-Ending Test

A verse freedom somewhat akin to Shakespeare's use of run-on rather than end-stopped lines is his growing tendency to divide a line between two speakers, or even among several speakers. The practice of dividing a line of verse in this fashion increases steadily from *The Comedy of Errors,* where there are almost none, to *The Winter's Tale,* where eighty-seven percent of the speeches end in the middle of a line. The speech-ending test might be even more impressive in its consistency were it not for the likelihood that some texts have been cut for acting (*Macbeth,* for instance) or otherwise tampered with in such a way as to alter the author's intention.

"Double" Endings

Another variation in the composition of blank verse has to do with the fifth foot at the end of the line. In early Shakespearean end-stopped blank verse, with its emphasis on the completion of each line of verse, the final syllable naturally tends to be stressed with great regularity. In the passage from *Richard III* quoted above, for example, every line except possibly the seventh ends in an accented syllable. As a means of breaking away from this regular and monotonous partition of the sense, Shakespeare introduces more and more frequently an extra unaccented syllable at the ends of lines, thus making the line consist of eleven instead of ten syllables. Even in the blank verse of *Richard III* and other early plays of Shakespeare, we find a good many more extra-syllable or "double" endings than in the blank verse of Marlowe.

To some Elizabethans this stylistic variation seemed sweeter and less abrupt than the regular pattern; for that reason, the extra unaccented syllable was called a "feminine" ending in contrast to the accented or "masculine" ending. The relative number of masculine and feminine endings forms another test of the time of composition, since feminine endings increase as Shakespeare's development progresses. A similar tendency also causes the introduction, more and more, of extra syllables before the pauses within the lines.

Light and Weak Endings

One other among the various tests is of major importance. Early in his career Shakespeare almost never ended lines with conjunctions, prepositions, auxiliary verbs, possessive pronouns, and other lightly stressed words. After 1600, however, he used such endings with increasing freedom. We find more than a hundred such lines each in *Coriolanus* and *Cymbeline,* whereas *The Comedy of Errors* and *The Two Gentlemen of Verona* contain none at all. These considerations form the basis for a light- and weak-ending test. A line ending in an unstressed word, such as a pronoun or an auxiliary verb, is said to have a light ending. A weak ending carries the process still further and seems to forbid any vocal stress at all. Prepositions and conjunctions, such as *in, to, and, if, or,* produce this effect.

Imagery

A highly useful study that reveals another chronological pattern in the evolution of Shakespeare's style, although not tabulated in the accompanying chart, is Wolfgang

Clemen's *The Development of Shakespeare's Imagery* (1951). As Clemen convincingly demonstrates, Shakespeare uses figures of speech for decoration and amplification in his early style, and learns only gradually to integrate these figures into a presentation of theme, subject, and individual character. In Shakespeare's later work, simile is often transformed into metaphor, and assumes an organic function in relation to the entire play.

For a study of Shakespeare's imagery not in a chronological framework but as a key to the dominant images of his poetic imagination, see for example Caroline Spurgeon, *Shakespeare's Imagery and What It Tells Us* (1935), and also a number of studies of imagery in individual plays or groups of plays such as Maurice Charney, *Shakespeare's Roman Plays: The Function of Imagery in the Drama* (1961).

Shakespeare's English

Pronunciation

Turning now from matters of Shakespeare's stylistic development to other more unchanging aspects of his language, let us consider first how Shakespeare's plays would have sounded to our ears. The distance between Shakespearean and modern English is clearly not as great as in the case of Chaucer, and yet significant differences remain. Spoken English, especially in the pronunciation of vowel sounds, has undergone many striking changes since the early seventeenth century. We can assume that however much Shakespeare's own speech may have been colored by his Warwickshire boyhood, his acting company as a whole was most heavily influenced by London dialect. This form of English had become notably more dominant than in Chaucer's day, though it also included an admixture of northern, eastern, and southern forms because of the cosmopolitan character of the city. Shakespeare often pokes fun at regional dialects in his plays, especially at Welsh, Scottish, and Irish, and at the accents of Frenchmen or other foreigners attempting to speak English (see, for example, *Henry V* and *The Merry Wives of Windsor*).

Here, in summary form, are some approximate suggestions for pronouncing words in Shakespeare that are not similarly pronounced today. These examples can be applied to similar words: for example, *way* and *say* have the same vowel sound as *day, night* the same vowel sound as *wide.*

folk (sound the *l*)
gnaw (sound the *g*)
knife (sound the *k; i* as in *wide,* below)
brush (rhymes with *push; r* somewhat trilled)
dull (rhymes with *pull*)
seam (pronounced *same,* with open *a*)
old (pronounced *auld*)
now (pronounced *noo*)
house (pronounced *hoos*)
soul (pronounced *saul*)
know (pronounced *knaw,* with sounded *k*)
own (pronounced *awn*)
tune (pronounced *tiwn*)
rule (pronounced *riwl; r* somewhat trilled)
day (pronounced *die*)
time (pronounced *toime*)
wide (pronounced *woide*)
join (rhymes with *line*)
creeping (pronounced *craypin,* with open *a*)
dissention (in four syllables, without *sh* sound)
persuasion (in four syllables, without *zh* sound)

A matter of more practical importance than phonetic changes is that of differences in Shakespeare's English and ours in the accentuation of syllables. Many cases of variable stress can be found in which he seems to have been at liberty to accent the word in two different ways; in other cases words were customarily accented on a different syllable from that in current speech. For example, the following accentuations are either usual or frequent: *aspect', charac'ter, com'mendable, com'plete, con'ceal'd, con'fessor, consort'* (as a noun), *contract'* (noun), *de'testable, dis'tinct, envy', for'lorn, hu'mane, instinct', ob'scure, persev'er, pi'oner, ple'beians, portents', pur'sue, record'* (noun), *reven'ue, se'cure, sinis'ter, welcome'.*

Not only are *-tion* and *-sion* regularly pronounced as two syllables, but the same situation causes other words in which *e* or *i* stand before vowels to be uttered in Shakespeare's language with one more syllable than in ours; for example, *oce-an, courti-er, marri-age.* We may even have *cre-ature, tre-asure,* and *venge-ance.* Nasals and liquids are frequently pronounced as if an extra vowel were introduced between them and a preceding letter. We accordingly have *wrest(e)ler, Eng(e)land, assemb(e)ly,* and *ent(e)rance,* as well as *de-ar, you(e)r,* and *mo-re.* Final *-er* often has a greater syllabic importance than it has in later poetry. Final *-(e)s* in the genitive singular and the plural of nouns not ending in an *s-* sound may constitute a separate syllable; for example, "To show his teeth as white as whale's bone" (*Love's Labor's Lost,* V,ii,333).

The scanning of Shakespeare's verse requires knowing how many syllables he intended a given word to have, for, as compared to current English, (a) a Shakespearean word may have an additional syllable, or (b) it may have one fewer syllables, or (c) two adjoining syllables in different words may coalesce or elide. Spelling may not always indicate these differences to a modern reader.

(a) The following lines give us extra-syllable words in *moon's, juggler, entrance,* and *complexion:*

I do wander everywhere,
Swifter than the *moon's* sphere.
(*A Midsummer Night's Dream,* II,i,6–7)

O me! You *juggler!* You cankerblossom!
(*A Midsummer Night's Dream,* III,ii,282)
After the prompter, for our *entrance.*
(*Romeo and Juliet,* I,iv,8)
Mislike me not for my *complexion.*
(*The Merchant of Venice,* II,i,1)

Similarly the words *captain, monstrous, esperance, this (this is), George (Richard III,*V,v,9*), valiant, villain,* and *jealous,* sometimes have extra syllables in pronunciation.

(b) In the following line, *marry* is elided into one syllable:

Good mother, do not *marry* me to yond fool.
(*The Merry Wives of Windsor,* III,iv,82)

Similarly, the words *lineal, journeying, carrion, celestial, herald, royal, malice, absolute, perjury, madame, needle, taken, heaven, spirit, devil, gentleman, unpeople, forward, gather, innocent, violet, Africa, eagle, listen, venomous* have usually one fewer syllables than in current English.

(c) The following examples are of elision between the syllables of adjoining words:

Why should I joy in *any abortive* birth?
(*Love's Labor's Lost,* I,i,104)
The *lover, all* as frantic,
(*A Midsummer Night's Dream,* V,i,10)
Romans, *do me* right. (*Titus Andronicus,* I,i,207)

Differences in accentuation and lengthening or shortening of words thus have great importance in the reading and scanning of Shakespeare's verse. Shortening of words by elision or by slurring is common in Shakespeare, but at least in this matter modern practice forms a good guide. Syllables ending in vowels are not infrequently elided before words beginning with a vowel, as in "How cáme / *we* ashóre" (*The Tempest,* I,ii,159) and "too hárd / a knót / for mé / *t' un*tie" (*Twelfth Night,* II,ii,41). Syncopation, or the omission of a syllable, often occurs in words with *r,* as "I wár-*r'nt* / it wíll" (*Hamlet,* I,ii,242); and in final *-er, -el,* and *-le,* as "Trá*vel* you / far ón" (*The Taming of the Shrew,* IV,ii,73). The following words and other similar ones may be treated as monosyllabic in Shakespeare's verse: *whether, ever, hither, other, father, evil, having.* Almost any unaccented syllable of a polysyllabic word (especially if it contains an *i*) may be softened and ignored; this syncopation is frequent in polysyllabic words and proper names; as "Thoughts spécu / latíve" (*Macbeth,* V,iv,19) and "Did sláy / this Fór*tinbras;* / who, bý / a seál'd / compáct" (*Hamlet,* I,i,86). Other occasions for slurring, as listed by Abbott in his *Shakespearian Grammar,* are light vowels preceded by heavy vowels, as *pow*er, *dy*ing, etc.; plurals and possessives of nouns ending in an *s*-sound, final *-ed* following *d* or *t,* as "you háve / exceéd*ed* / all prómise" (*As You Like It,* I,ii,234); and the *-est* of superlatives (pronounced *-st*) after dentals and liquids, as "the stérn'st / good-níght" (*Macbeth,* II,ii,4) and "thy éldest / son's són" (*King John,* II,i,177).

Grammar and Rhetoric

Shakespeare's grammar presents but few differences in forms from the grammar of current modern English. The *-eth* ending in the third person singular of the present tense, indicative mood, was very commonly used, especially in serious prose. Shakespeare frequently uses this older form, especially *hath, doth,* and *saith,* but seems to prefer the form in *-s* or *-es*. In a few cases he also seems to use the old northern plural in *-s* or *-es* in the third person of the present indicative; as ". . . at those springs On chalic'd flow'rs that *lies*" (*Cymbeline,* II,iii,22–23). He does not always agree with modern usage in the forms of the past tenses and the perfect participles of the verbs that he employs. He retains some lost forms of the strong verbs, sometimes confuses the past tense with the perfect participle, or vice versa, and treats some verbs as weak (or regular) which are now strong (or irregular). For example, he uses *arose* for *arisen, swam* for *swum, foughten* for *fought, gave* for *given, took* for *taken, sprung* for *sprang, writ* for *wrote.* He has *blowed* for *blew, weaved* for *wove, shaked* for *shaken.* Forms like *degenerate* for *degenerated* and *exhaust* for *exhausted* are especially common. A few instances are to be found of the archaic *y-* with the past participle, as in *yclad.* For the possessive case of the neuter personal pronoun *it,* Shakespeare normally uses the regular form at that time, *his*; but he also uses the possessive form *it*, and, in his plays first published in the First Folio in 1623, we find several occurrences of the new form *its.* Shakespeare uses the old form *moe* as well as *many*, and the form *enow* as the plural of *enough.* He uses *near* and *next* along with *nearer* and *nearest,* as the comparative and superlative of *nigh*. These are the most obvious of the formal differences between Shakespeare's grammar and our own.

The functional differences are more considerable. Elizabethan language exercised an extraordinary freedom, even for English, in the use of one part of speech for another. Shakespeare uses verbs, adjectives, adverbs, and pronouns as nouns. He makes verbs out of nouns and adjectives, and, of course, uses nouns as adjectives, for this is a distinguishing characteristic of English speech; but he uses also adverbs, verbs, and prepositional phrases as adjectives. Almost any adjective may be freely used as an adverb. He makes active words, both adjectives and adverbs, discharge a passive function; as "the sightless [invisible] couriers of the air" (*Macbeth,* I,vii,23) and "this aspect of mine Hath fear'd the valiant," i.e., caused the valiant to be afraid (*The Merchant of Venice,* II,i,8–9). He makes wider use of the infinitive as a verbal noun or as a gerundive participle than do we; as "This to be true, I do engage my life" (*As You Like It,* V,iv,164–165), "My operant powers their functions leave to do" (*Hamlet,* III,ii,172), "Nor do I now make moan to be abridg'd" (*The Merchant of Venice,* I,i,126), and "you might have sav'd me my pains, to have taken [by having taken] it away yourself" (*Twelfth Night,* II,ii,5–7). The functions of prepositions in Elizabethan English were so various that one can only refer the student to the notes to the text or to a dictionary.

In certain other features, however, as for example in the use of modal auxiliaries, Shakespeare's language is as restricted and conventional as ours is at formal levels, or even more so. *Shall* is regularly used in Shakespeare to express something inevitable in future time, and is, therefore, the usual future tense for all persons. *Will,* which originally expressed intention, determination, or willingness, was, to be sure, beginning to encroach on *shall* for the expression of futurity in the second and third persons; but its use usually still retains in Shakespeare a consciousness of its original meaning. *Should* and *would* had their original senses of obligation and volition, respectively, and had other peculiarities, then as now, of considerable difficulty. The subjunctive mood was vital to Shakespeare as a means of expressing condition, doubt, concession, and command, or to express wish or desire, and in dependent clauses to express indefinitiveness, purpose, or sometimes simple futurity. Note the following examples:

> But if my father *had* not scanted me . . .
> Yourself, renowned Prince, then *stood* as fair.
> (*The Merchant of Venice,* II,i,17,20)
> *Live* a thousand years,
> I *shall* not find myself so apt to die.
> (*Julius Caesar,* III,i,160–161)
> Lest your retirement *do amaze* your friends.
> (*1 Henry IV,* V,iv,6)
> *'Twere* best he speak no harm of Brutus here.
> (*Julius Caesar,* III,ii,70)
> *Melt* Egypt into Nile! And kindly creatures
> *Turn* all to serpents! (*Antony and Cleopatra,* II,v,78–79)
> Yet were it true
> To say this boy *were* like me.
> (*The Winter's Tale,* I,ii,134–135)
> And may direct his course as *please* himself.
> (*Richard III,* II,ii,129)

Some other features of Shakespeare's grammar are as follows: he often omits the relative pronoun; often uses the nominative case of the pronoun for the accusative case, and vice versa; uses *him, her, me,* and *them* as true reflexives to mean *himself, herself, myself,* and *themselves;* employs double negatives and double comparatives and superlatives; shows a consciousness in the use of *thee* and *thou* of their application to intimates and inferiors and of their insulting quality when addressed to strangers (e.g., "If thou thou'st him some thrice, it shall not be amiss," *Twelfth Night,* III,ii,43–44); employs *which* to refer to both persons and things; and does not discriminate closely between *ye,* nominative, and *you,* objective. He makes frequent use of the dative constructions, i.e., the objective forms of the pronouns, *me, thee, you, him, her,* etc., without prepositions where the meaning is "by me," "for me," "with me," "to me," "of me," etc. For example:

> I am appointed *him* [by him] to murder you.
> (*The Winter's Tale,* I,ii,411)
> She looks *us* [to us] like
> A thing made more of malice than of duty.
> (*Cymbeline,* III,v,32–33)

One prominent feature of Shakespeare's grammar is his use of the ethical dative, a construction in which the pronoun is generally used to indicate the person interested in the statement. In *King John* (III,iv,146), the phrase "John lays *you* plots," means something like "John lays plots which you may profit by." In the following, *me* means "to my detriment" or "to my disadvantage":

> See how this river comes *me* cranking in,
> And cuts *me* from the best of all my land
> A huge half-moon. (*1 Henry IV,* III,i,95–97)

"Whip *me* such honest knaves" (*Othello,* I,i,50) means "In my judgment such knaves should be whipped." In Quickly's description of Mistress Page, the dative *you* is equivalent to "mark you," "take notice":

> . . . a civil modest wife, and one, I tell you, that will not miss *you* morning nor evening prayer, as any is in Windsor.
> (*The Merry Wives of Windsor,* II,ii,92–94)

At times, however, the ethical dative is idiomatic and virtually without equivalent meaning in modern English; the sense of the passage is best obtained by omitting the pronoun.

Of the forms and figures of rhetoric, Shakespeare, like other Renaissance poets, makes extensive use. He is fond, for example, of using the abstract for the concrete, as in the words addressed by Surrey to Cardinal Wolsey, "Thou scarlet sin" (*Henry VIII,* III,ii,255). Transpositions are numerous, as are inversions, ellipses, and broken or confused constructions, as in the following examples:

> That thing you speak of,
> I took it for a man. (Absolute construction.)
> (*King Lear,* IV,vi,77–78)
> Souls and bodies hath he divorc'd three. (Transposition of adjective.) (*Twelfth Night,* III,iv,238–239)
> A happy gentleman in blood and lineaments. (Transposition of adjectival phrase.) (*Richard II,* III,i,9)
> Your state of fortune and your due of birth. (Transposition of pronoun.) (*Richard III,* III,vii,120)
> She calls me proud, and [says] that she could not love me. (Ellipsis.) (*As You Like It,* IV,iii,17)
> Returning were as tedious as [to] go o'er. (Ellipsis.)
> (*Macbeth,* III,iv,138)
> They call him Doricles; and boasts himself
> To have a worthy feeding. (Ellipsis of nominative.)
> (*The Winter's Tale,* IV,iv,168–169)
> Of all men else I have avoided thee. (Confusion of two constructions.) (*Macbeth,* V,viii,4)

The venom of such looks, we fairly hope,
Have lost their quality. (Confusion of number arising from proximity.) (*Henry V,* V, ii, 18–19)
Rather proclaim it, Westmorland, through my host,
That he which hath no stomach to this fight,
Let him depart. (Construction changed by change of thought.) (*Henry V,* IV,iii,34–36)
For always I am Caesar. (Inversion of adverb.) (*Julius Caesar,* I,ii,212)

Shakespeare often uses rhetorical figures for symmetrical effects, especially in the early, ornamental style of *Richard III* and the nondramatic poems. Following are definitions of some of the most popular figures he uses, with illustrations from *Venus and Adonis:*

(1) *Parison,* the symmetrical repetition of words in grammatically parallel phrases: "How love makes young men thrall, and old men dote" (l. 837).

(2) *Isocolon,* the symmetrical repetition of sounds and words in phrases of equal length, as in the previous example, and in this: "Or as the wolf doth grin before he barketh, Or as the berry breaks before it staineth" (ll. 459–460). Parison and isocolon are frequently combined.

(3) *Anaphora,* the symmetrical repetition of a word at the beginning of a sequence of clauses or sentences, often at the beginning of lines. Anaphora is frequently combined with parison and isocolon, as in the second example already given, and in this: " 'Give me my hand,' saith he. 'Why dost thou feel it?' 'Give me my heart,' saith she, 'and thou shalt have it' " (ll. 373–374).

(4) *Antimetabole,* the symmetrical repetition of words in inverted order: "She clepes him king of graves, and grave for kings" (l. 995).

(5) *Anadiplosis,* the beginning of a phrase with the final words of the previous phrase: "O, thou didst kill me, kill me once again!" (l. 499).

(6) *Epanalepsis,* the symmetrical repetition of a word or words at the beginning and ending of a line: "He sees his love, and nothing else he sees" (l. 287).

(7) *Ploce,* the insistent repetition of a word within the same line or phrase: "Then why not lips on lips, since eyes in eyes?" (l. 120).

(8) *Epizeuxis,* an intensified form of ploce, repeating the word without another intervening word: " 'Ay me!' she cries, and twenty times, 'Woe, woe!' And twenty echoes twenty times cry so" (ll. 833–834).

(9) *Antanaclasis,* the shifting of a repeated word from one meaning to another: "My love to love is love but to disprove it," or " 'Where did I leave?' 'No matter where,' quoth he, 'Leave me' " (ll. 715–716).

For other figures and illustrations, see Sister Miriam Joseph, *Shakespeare's Use of the Arts of Language* (1947) and Brian Vickers, "Shakespeare's Use of Rhetoric," in *A New Companion to Shakespeare Studies,* ed. Kenneth Muir and S. Schoenbaum (1971).

Vocabulary

Renaissance English was hospitable to foreign importation. Many words taken directly from Latin became a permanent part of the language, serving to enrich its power to express thought and its rhythmical capabilities; others were ultimately discarded. The principal borrowings were in the realm of learning and culture. Such words usually retained a vital sense of their original Latin meaning. Sometimes such words have not replaced native words of the same meaning, so that we have such pairs of synonyms as *acknowledge* and *confess,* just as Shakespeare had *wonder* and *admiration.* Because of this Latin heritage, even a slight knowledge of Latin is a great advantage in the correct understanding of Elizabethan writers, since many Latin borrowings have taken on since the sixteenth century a different shade of meaning from that in which they were borrowed. The Latin sense of *aggravate* still struggles for recognition; but *apparent* no longer means primarily *visible to sight,* and *intention* does not convey the idea of *intentness.*

Latin words were often taken over in their Latin forms, as *objectum* and *subjectum, statua* and *aristocratia,* and later were made to conform to English spelling and stress, though a few, such as *decorum*, still have a Latin form. French continued to be drawn upon and sometimes caused a new Latin borrowing to be adoped in a French form; just as, on the other hand, such words as *adventure* were supplied with a *d* to make them conform to Latin spelling. This principle is illustrated in the pedantry of Holofernes when he objects (*Love's Labor's Lost,* V,i,20) to "det" as the pronunciation of "debt." Spanish, Italian, and Dutch also supplied many terms. Spanish gave words having to do with commerce, religion, and the New World, such as *mosquito, alligator, ambuscado,* and *grandee.* From Italian came terms of art, learning, and dueling: *bandetto, portico, canto, stoccato.* The Dutch contributed many nautical and oriental words.

These foreign borrowings were a part of what might be called the linguistic ambition of the age, a desire for forcible expression. Language was in a plastic state, so that it had an unparalleled freedom in both vocabulary and form. With this freedom, to be sure, came some confusion, since the Elizabethan era saw few efforts at grammatical precision. Such efforts were later to be made by the age of Dryden and the Royal Society, and by learned men ever since, prompted by an awareness that English was too vague and irregular for use as a means of scientific expression. Still, we readily perceive that English profited from its Renaissance expansion and its subsequent absorption with Shakespeare and the English Bible. It gained, for example, an increased facility in making compounds. Shakespeare, with his *cloud-capp'd towers* and his *home-keeping wits,* was a genius at this. Also from Shakespeare's time came the English adaptability in the use of prefixes, such as *dis-, re-, en-,* and of suffixes, such as *-ful, -less, -ness, -hood.*

Obsolete words, or words employed by Shakespeare in entirely unfamiliar meanings, give us relatively little trouble today. We recognize the unfamiliarity, and consult a dictionary or a footnote. Difficulty arises from cases in which we are able to get without effort an idea fairly close to Shakespeare's meaning, so that we understand him only imperfectly, missing the exact shade of meaning and tone. Take, for example, Othello's account to the Venetian senators of the circumstances of his courtship of Desdemona (*Othello,* I,iii,160–168):

My story being done,
She gave me for my pains a world of sighs. . . .
She wish'd she had not heard it, yet she wish'd
That heaven had made her such a man. She thank'd
me,
And bade me, if I had a friend that lov'd her,
I should but teach him how to tell my story,
And that would woo her. Upon this *hint* I spake.

The word *hint* means *occasion* or *opportunity*; it does not mean *invitation* or *suggestion by covert allusion.* To understand the word in the contemporary sense changes subtly the meaning of the passage.

A key to understanding Shakespeare's language is to appreciate the attitude toward speech accepted by him and his contemporaries. Speech was traditionally and piously regarded as God's final and consummate gift to man. Speech was thus to Elizabethans a source of enormous power for good or ill. Truth, if truly uttered, was bound to prevail. To have heard truth and to have rejected it was an unnatural thing, a sign that Satan had entered the obdurate heart and had caused it to reject God's truth. Christians were bound to preach the Word, and to destroy that heretic who persisted in rejecting it. Hence the struggle to excel in eloquent utterance.

Editions and Editors of Shakespeare

The earliest complete edition of Shakespeare's plays was the so-called First Folio of 1623, sponsored by Shakespeare's theatrical colleagues John Heminges and Henry Condell. (A "folio" book was one in which the printing sheets were folded only once, each producing two "leaves" or four rather large printed pages of about 13½ × 8¼ inches. In a "quarto" book the sheets were folded twice, producing eight pages on four leaves half the folio size.) The First Folio brought together eighteen plays that had previously been published individually in quarto volumes, and eighteen plays that had never before been published. It did not include Shakespeare's nondramatic poetry, of which *Venus and Adonis* and *The Rape of Lucrece* had been published in 1593–1594 and the sonnets in 1609. Nor did it include *Pericles.*

The nature of the early printed texts, and their relationship to what Shakespeare actually wrote, is a complex subject requiring some understanding of the physical process by which Elizabethan plays were written, prepared for staging, licensed, and printed. What sorts of manuscripts lie behind the various printed early editions we have, and how were those manuscripts modified successively by scribes, governmental officials, theatrical producers, actors, editors, compositors, proofreaders, and editors of subsequent editions? Let us start at the beginning, with the manuscripts themselves.

Manuscripts: "Foul Papers"

Most often, Elizabethan dramatic companies obtained a play by commissioning a known professional dramatist to write a new play, to revise an old one, or to collaborate with another author. Usually the company paid the dramatist a flat fee. Shakespeare, on the other hand, was a "sharer" in the Chamberlain's (later the King's) company—that is, he was part owner and took a share of the profits. He seems to have written plays not for a fee but as his chief contribution to the company's activities. Whatever the financial arrangement between author and company, in any case, the play became the property of the acting company and the author gave up his individual right to sell it elsewhere. Moreover, he ordinarily wrote the play with a view not to publication but to performance. Occasionally, a literary-minded author like Ben Jonson would see his plays through the press (and be scoffed at for his pretentiousness). Shakespeare, however, almost certainly did not do this. The quarto texts of his plays that appeared during his lifetime show no trace of having been prepared for the reader. They are playhouse documents.

When Shakespeare had finished writing a play, he presumably submitted a readable manuscript to his acting company. This draft in his handwriting, or any earlier draft, went by the name of "foul papers," as distinguished from "fair papers" or a clean copy that might be prepared by the author or a playhouse scribe. Actually, the foul papers need not have been especially messy, although a certain amount of deletion, interlineation, inconsistency, and illegibility was inevitable. These foul papers were usually preserved by the acting company and were often turned over to the printer when the company decided to sell its rights in a play. The company usually preferred to hold on to its prompt-book copy of the play (see below), and to dispose of the foul papers as of little further value if they chose to have a play printed. A manuscript of this sort naturally posed some difficulties for the compositor.

Among the Shakespearean quarto texts thought to have

A CATALOGVE

of the ſeuerall Comedies, Hiſtories, and Tragedies contained in this Volume.

COMEDIES.

HISTORIES.

TRAGEDIES.

John Heminges and Henry Condell, Shakespeare's fellow actors, organized the original table of contents for the First Folio published in 1623. They collected thirty-six plays in the volume omitting Pericles. Troilus and Cressida *is included in the First Folio but not listed here in the contents.*

THE FOLGER SHAKESPEARE LIBRARY

been based on foul papers are the first quartos of *Titus Andronicus, Love's Labor's Lost, A Midsummer Night's Dream, Richard II, The Merchant of Venice, Much Ado about Nothing,* and *1* and *2 Henry IV,* and the second quartos of *Romeo and Juliet* and *Hamlet*. Three more first quartos—*Troilus and Cressida, Othello,* and *King Lear*—were also based apparently on foul papers, although each is an anomalous case. In addition, the First Folio contains several newly printed plays based on foul papers or a transcript thereof, including *The Comedy of Errors, The Taming of the Shrew, All's Well that Ends Well, Timon of Athens, Coriolanus,* and *Henry VIII*. Two more Folio plays are based on transcripts of foul papers by the scrivener Ralph Crane: *Measure for Measure* and *The Winter's Tale*. The text of *King John* seems to have been based on foul papers also, but with some reference to a prompt-book in the final two acts.

At their best, foul papers are close to what Shakespeare wrote, but they are also potentially laden with error. Some foul-paper texts preserve Shakespeare's work in an early state of composition: *Timon of Athens,* for example, seems never to have been finished by Shakespeare, since the text we have retains glaring inconsistencies and redundancies that he presumably would have straightened out in a final version. *Love's Labor's Lost* and *Romeo and Juliet* contain uncanceled duplicatory passages. On the other hand, *The Merchant of Venice, Richard II,* and the *Henry IV* plays are very good texts, and *Much Ado* is almost ready for stage production; the names of two actors appear among the speech-prefixes, although other irregularities suggest that the manuscript was in the last stages of authorial revision. Foul papers therefore represent a whole spectrum of states from unrevised manuscript to a text that has been thoroughly worked over.

Unfortunately, no manuscript of a regular Shakespearean play has survived today. Moreover, the distinction between foul papers and a prompt copy used in the theatre is not always as easily made as some scholars would like to assume; authors' papers were often used by the acting company without recopying and without extensive annotation. Nonetheless, we can perhaps identify an author's manuscript behind the printed text when we find some of the following characteristics: vagueness in specifying the number of supernumeraries needed for a scene, lack of precision in the marking of entrances and especially exits, authorial stage directions that tend to describe stage business or the emotional states of the characters, speech prefixes that inconsistently refer to a character both by his personal name and his generic title, and so on. Thus, in *Love's Labor's Lost,* Navarre, Armado, and Holofernes are at times referred to as King, Braggart, and Pedant; Navarre is also called Ferdinand. See Appendix I at the end of this volume for a play-by-play summary of the kind of manuscript thought to lie behind each of Shakespeare's plays and poems.

Licensing for Performance

Before a Shakespearean play could go into production, it had to be licensed by the Master of the Revels, an officer of the royal household responsible for supervising court entertainments. Since the beginning of Elizabeth's reign, and even earlier, dramatic performances throughout England had been made subject to governmental control. Elizabeth had authorized municipal and other local governments to scrutinize plays performed within their jurisdictions. In the vicinity of London, however, where municipal hostility toward the theatre was particularly strong, she took the unusual step in 1581 of transferring licensing power to her own Master of the Revels. Since many public plays came to court, as we have seen, Elizabeth was inclined to protect the players against the city authorities in this way, and to adopt the useful fiction that public performances were rehearsals of plays intended for her ultimate benefit.

The Master of the Revels did occasionally censor Shakespeare's plays. For example, the scene of Richard II's deposition, omitted from the three earliest quarto editions of the play, seems to have been disallowed for acting during Elizabeth's lifetime. (She was sensitive to a widespread and libelous analogy comparing her with Richard.) More often, one suspects, the mere threat of censorship was sufficient to keep the London dramatic companies in line. The Tudor establishment had no intention of tolerating openly seditious criticism in the drama. Generally, the Master of the Revels was more concerned with questions of religion and politics than with morals. Edmund Tilney served as Master of the Revels from 1579 to 1610, when he was succeeded by his deputy, Sir George Buc. In 1622 the office passed to Sir Henry Herbert.

The Prompt-Book

The document on which the Master of the Revels affixed his seal of approval was the prompt-book or prompt-copy or playbook—that is, the version prepared by the acting company for use in actual production. Sometimes this version was a fair copy of the manuscript, readied for stage performance—that is, with the technical inconsistencies weeded out and with more businesslike stage directions added. Often the author's last draft might be converted into a prompt-book, if it was legible enough. Whatever manuscript was thus used, the prompt-copy might undertake to normalize any inconsistent speech prefixes (such as those already noted in *Love's Labor's Lost*), in order to avoid confusion for actors and stage managers. Some stage directions might be added, concentrating on technical matters such as entrances, exits, and occasional specific effects. In *Julius Caesar*, for example, we find such stage directions as "Enter Brutus in his orchard," "Thunder and lightning. Enter Julius Caesar in his nightgown," and "Brutus goes into the pulpit." We cannot be sure, however, that these are not authorial stage directions, and indeed recent evidence suggests that the acting company often did rather little to an authorial manuscript to ready it for production. Shakespeare was an acting member of his own company, and must have known what his colleagues wanted, so that revision of his final draft need not have been extensive.

Comparatively few of Shakespeare's printed texts are derived from prompt-books, actually, since the prompt-book, bearing the official license of the Master of the Revels, was an invaluable document if the play was ever to be revived. Of the nineteen Shakespearean plays published in quarto prior to 1623, not one was printed from a prompt-book. The author's foul papers were far more expendable once the prompt-book had been prepared. Nevertheless, the First Folio does contain a few plays printed from prompt-books or transcripts of prompt-books, including *As You Like It, Twelfth Night, Julius Caesar,* and *Macbeth* (in a cut version). Two more plays, *The Two Gentlemen of Verona* and *The Merry Wives of Windsor,* were printed from transcriptions by Ralph Crane of prompt-books. Four additional plays seem to have been set from Shakespeare's drafts (or transcriptions of the drafts) that had already been annotated by the stage adapter, although not yet actually made into prompt-books: *1 Henry VI, Antony and Cleopatra,* perhaps, *Cymbeline,* and *The Tempest* (in a transcription by Crane).

Prompt-books are in some cases not as likely to correspond with the author's intentions as his own papers, and indeed some prompt-books probably reflect changes occurring in the theatre over a period of years. A prompt-book might be altered for the revival of an old favorite, or might even represent a cut performance intended to be taken on tour—as perhaps in the case of *Macbeth.* Such a text might incorporate non-Shakespearean material; *Macbeth* seems to contain songs and lines attributed to Thomas Middleton.

Prompt-books were also used to copy out individual parts for each actor. Although such actors' "rolls," as they were called, could conceivably have been used to assemble a printed text, no Shakespearean play is known to have been printed in this fashion. A few plays, such as *The Two Gentlemen of Verona* and *The Winter's Tale,* were once thought to have been made up out of actors' rolls, since the texts of these plays generally omit stage directions and group characters' names at the head of each scene; but these traits are now known to be the identifying characteristics of the professional scrivener named Ralph Crane. Apparently, Crane was employed to prepare copies (also including *The Tempest, The Merry Wives of Windsor,* and *Measure for Measure*) for the printers of the First Folio.

The Bad Quartos

An acting company did not normally like to see its plays in print. On occasion, to be sure, a company might disband and sell its plays, or experience financial difficulties and sell some older plays for ready money, but ordinarily the company regarded its plays as the very key to its economic prosperity. Popular plays that enjoyed long runs, and could later be revived, were especially valuable. Hence the company guarded carefully its authorial manuscripts and prompt-books, and did not usually permit other copies to be made or circulated.

By the same token, however, the temptation for some unscrupulous bookseller to pirate an edition of a popular play was obviously great. And, unfortunately, no copyright law protected the acting companies from such piracy. If a bookseller could obtain a dramatic text in any way, all he had to do was to present his book at Stationers' Hall and enter it in the Stationers' Register, or official record book of the London Company of Stationers (i.e., booksellers). By paying a fee, usually sixpence, he reserved the right to pubish the work he had thus entered. Indeed, even if a book was printed without having been entered in the Stationers' Register, it evidently received the protection of copyright by the very act of printing. Copyright had considerable legal force. Although authors and acting companies could not copyright their plays, the stationers or booksellers enjoyed a tight monopoly. Their London Company of Stationers had a patent from the crown to restrict the number of presses operating in London, the number of books that could be printed, and so on. Legal safeguards were all on the side of the booksellers.

To protect themselves, the acting companies sometimes formed friendly relationships with cooperative booksellers and entered agreements with them designed to forestall the piratical activities of less scrupulous publishers. The acting company might allow a friendly bookseller or printer to register a play for later publication. For example, on July 22, 1598, the printer James Roberts entered in the Stationers' Register "a booke of the Marchaunt of Venyce, or otherwise called the Jewe Of Venyce, Prouided, that yt bee not prynted by the said James Robertes or anye other whatsoeuer without lycence first had from the Right honorable the lord Chamberlen." This is what is generally known as a "staying entry," since Roberts agrees to "stay" or withhold publication pending further authorization from the acting company's patron. Such an entry would have prevented publication of *The Merchant of Venice* by an unauthorized publisher. Similar entries occur in August of 1600 for *Much Ado about Nothing, As You Like It,* and *Henry V.* The stratagem did not always work—an unauthorized quarto of *Henry V* appeared in August of 1600—but it did sometimes achieve its purpose.

Despite all precautions, unauthorized or "bad" quartos were fairly common. After all, the plays were publicly performed; a would-be pirate had easy access to repeated performances. Heminges and Condell, in their prefatory letter "To the great Variety of Readers" of the First Folio, complain about "diuerse stolne and surreptitious copies, maimed, and deformed by the frauds and stealthes of iniurious imposters." Thomas Heywood similarly protests against pirated editions of his plays, which "haue (vnknowen to me, and without any of my direction) accidentally come into the Printers handes, and therefore so corrupt and mangled, (coppied onely by the eare) that I haue bene vnable to know them" (Preface to *The Rape of Lucrece,* 1608).

How were such pirated texts obtained? Heywood says they were "coppied onely by the eare." Elsewhere, in *Pleasant Dialogues and Dramas* (1637), he complains about the pirating of one of his plays "by Stenography." The stenographic hypothesis is not now widely accepted, however, chiefly because the systems of shorthand available in Shakespeare's day were inadequate and because attempts at shorthand reporting might well have been detected by an alert acting company. Besides, the pirated texts we have seem to rely heavily on the use of memory.

Textual scholarship now generally supports the findings of W. W. Greg that most pirated texts were put together by "memorial reconstruction." The usual culprits seem to have been one or more actors, in league with an unscrupulous printer. Most pirates were temporary actors hired to perform minor roles, rather than actor-sharers having a vested interest in the acting company and its stock of plays. Possibly one or more such minor actors got together and slowly recited what they could remember of a play, while a scribe took down what they recited. The reporter or reporters of a pirated text can sometimes tentatively be identified by the relative accuracy of certain roles. For example, the actor who perhaps doubled the minor parts of Marcellus and Lucianus in *Hamlet* may have helped in the memorial reconstruction of the bad quarto of that play.

A bad quarto put together by memorial reconstruction can be identified with some accuracy by modern textual methods. Such a text tends to give a fairly accurate rendition of the overall plot, but garbles some speeches, transfers or misplaces lines of dialogue or even whole scenes, borrows scraps of phrases from other plays in which the actor-reporters may have acted, mislineates blank verse or crudely versifies passages of prose, ad-libs freely in half-remembered parts of the play, and so on. A bad quarto is always shorter than the regular version. Visual impressions are often vivid, since the actor-reporters are remembering things they have seen on stage. The stage directions tend to be more frequent and more detailed than in either an author's manuscript or a prompt-book.

Seven bad quartos have been identified. An unregistered and memorially reconstructed quarto of *Romeo and Juliet,* published in 1597, was answered two years later by an authorized second quarto, "Newly corrected, augmented, and amended." (A similar phrase, "Newly corrected and augmented," appears in the title of the 1598 quarto of *Love's Labor's Lost,* suggesting that a now-lost bad quarto of that play had appeared prior to 1598.) The famous bad quarto of *Hamlet* appeared in 1603, containing apparently some echoes of the lost pre-Shakespearean *Hamlet* known to have been in existence by 1589. Other bad quartos include *Henry V* (1600), *The Merry Wives of Windsor* (1602), and *Pericles* (1609—the only substantive text we have of this play). In addition, the quartos published in 1594 and 1595 as *The First part of the Contention betwixt the two famous Houses of Yorke and Lancaster* and *The true Tragedie of Richard Duke of Yorke* are now generally recognized to have been the memorially reconstructed bad quartos of *2* and *3 Henry VI.*

A few texts seem to have been put together by unusual circumstances that somewhat resemble memorial reconstruction. *The Taming of the Shrew* was not printed until the Folio of 1623, but a quarto did appear in 1594 of a very similar play called *The Taming of A Shrew.* Its place names and characters' names are different from those of the Folio version, and the language differs throughout. Some scholars still regard the play as a source for Shakespeare. Nevertheless, the generally held view today is that *A Shrew* is a special kind of pirated text, one in which a rival dramatist has changed the language and the names of the characters to make the work seem his own. A different sort of anomaly is seen in *Richard III.* The 1597 quarto shows many unmistakable signs of memorial reconstruction, and yet the text is much more accurate and full than in most bad quartos. Shakespeare's own company may have collaborated on this memorial reconstruction, perhaps while they were on tour and had no prompt-book with them. A somewhat similar circumstance occurs in the case of *King Lear*: the quarto of 1608 seems to have been based on a draft to which Shakespeare's company somehow contributed.

The Good Quartos

Despite their general unwillingness to see their plays in print, acting companies did sometimes sell texts to the printers for ready cash or to correct bad quartos that had already appeared (as in the case of the good quartos of *Romeo and Juliet,* 1599, *Hamlet,* 1604–1605, and probably *Love's Labor's Lost,* 1598). The good quartos were based generally on Shakespeare's own drafts, or transcripts of them. Good first quartos include *Titus Andronicus* (1594), *Richard II* (1597), *1 Henry IV* (1598), *2 Henry IV* (1600), *A Midsummer Night's Dream* (1600), *The Merchant of Venice* (1600), *Much Ado about Nothing* (1600), *Troilus and Cressida* (1609, printed seemingly without permission of Shakespeare's company), and the late first quarto of *Othello* (1622). This is a short list and is sporadic in its time schedule; Shakespeare's company did not regularly dispose of its plays to the printers. Once a play had appeared in print, however, it was apt to be reprinted. *Richard III* went through six quartos before the Folio of 1623. At the other extreme we have *2 Henry IV,* issued in only one quarto prior to 1623; possibly the printers ran off a large number of copies in anticipation of heavy sales. Some quarto texts continued to appear after the Folio of 1623.

Licensing for Printing

Before a play could be printed, it had to be licensed. The licensing agency responsible for printed matter was a panel of London clergymen known as the "correctors of the press," operating under the authority of the Privy Council, the Bishop of London, the Archbishop of Canterbury, and the Lord Chamberlain. In 1606, Parliament passed a law forbidding references to the Deity in the texts of plays.

The Pavier Collection of 1619

A few years before the Shakespearean First Folio appeared in 1623, a bookseller named Thomas Pavier and a printer named William Jaggard made an apparent attempt to collect Shakespeare's plays. Pavier already owned the publishing rights to *Henry V,* for in August of 1600 he had received assignment of rights to the bad quarto of the play published in that year. He brought out a second quarto of *Henry V* in 1602, and a third (printed by Jaggard) in 1619 as part of his anthologizing project. In 1602 Pavier had also obtained the rights to *The First part of the Contention* and *The true Tragedie of Richard Duke of Yorke,* now generally regarded as the bad quartos of *2* and *3 Henry VI.* Pavier issued them in 1619 under the combined title *The Whole Contention betweene the two Famous Houses, Lancaster and Yorke,* printed by Jaggard. Pavier also included in his collection two pseudo-Shakespearean plays to which he owned the rights, *A Yorkshire Tragedy* and *Sir John Oldcastle,* and five Shakespearean plays to which he may have obtained rights or which he considered to be unowned: *A Midsummer Night's Dream, The Merchant of Venice, The Merry Wives of Windsor, King Lear,* and *Pericles.*

Pavier's evident intention was to publish these ten plays in a single volume, and indeed two such copies exist today, one in the Folger Library and one in the Lewis Collection at Texas Christian University. Pavier's scheme was frustrated, however, seemingly by the Lord Chamberlain at the instigation of Shakespeare's company. Pavier chose the expedient of publishing his plays separately, some with fraudulently early dates and names of publishers on their title pages in an apparent attempt to obscure the fact of new publication. None of Pavier's texts provides any independent textual authority, for all were copied from earlier quartos.

Publishing Rights for the 1623 Folio

Pavier's dubious and abortive undertaking may possibly have given impetus to a more legitimate edition of Shakespeare's collected plays, some seven years after the author's death, although Shakespeare's company may already have been contemplating such an honor to its famous playwright. Ben Jonson's folio collection of plays in 1616 had established a major precedent for such a volume, despite the scorn of those who regarded all plays as subliterary. The large and tomelike folio format, normally reserved for edifying religious tracts, the "works" of classical authorities, and the like, might now be used also for a collection of plays.

The first task facing the supervisors of the Folio collection, Heminges and Condell, was the assembling of publishing rights to those eighteen Shakespearean plays that had already appeared in print. The most efficient means of doing so was to form a syndicate of publishers who already owned the rights to a large number of the plays. The colophon at the very end of the First Folio names those who took part: "Printed at the Charges of W. Jaggard, Ed. Blount, I. Smithweeke, and W. Aspley, 1623." William Jaggard had succeeded to the printing business of James Roberts in 1608. Despite Jaggard's part in the printing of the Pavier quartos of 1619, he evidently remained on good terms with

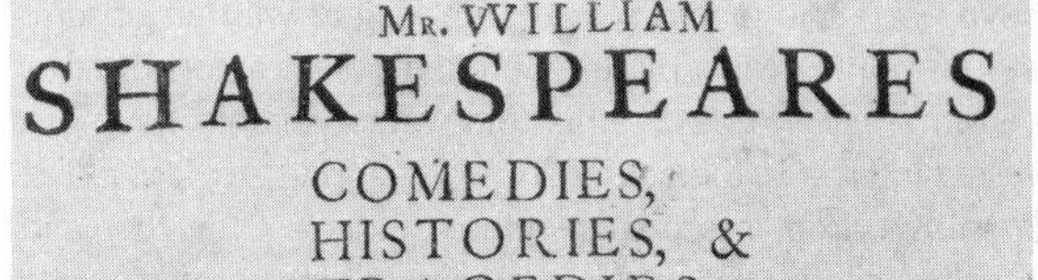
MR. WILLIAM
SHAKESPEARES
COMEDIES,
HISTORIES, &
TRAGEDIES.
Publiſhed according to the True Originall Copies.

LONDON
Printed by Iſaac Iaggard, and Ed. Blount. 1623.

Martin Droeshout's engraving on the title page of the First Folio is one of only two authenic likenesses of Shakespeare in existence.

Shakespeare's company and became (together with his son Isaac) the printer of the 1623 Folio. (William Jaggard died in November of 1623, but his son carried on the business.) Edward Blount had registered *Antony and Cleopatra* and *Pericles* in 1608, though he seems to have overlooked the fact, for *Antony* was re-registered in 1623, and *Pericles* never appeared in the Folio. John Smethwick had received from Nicholas Ling the rights to *Love's Labor's Lost, Romeo and Juliet,* and *Hamlet* in 1607. William Aspley owned the rights to *Much Ado about Nothing* and *2 Henry IV.* One other previously published play, *A Midsummer Night's Dream,* was "derelict" or no longer assigned to a publisher.

Some further negotiations must still have been necessary, with Richard Bonian and Henry Walley for *Troilus and Cressida,* with Nathaniel Butter for *King Lear,* with Thomas Pavier for *2* and *3 Henry VI, Titus Andronicus,* and *Henry V,* perhaps also with Edward White for *Titus Andronicus,* with Matthew Law for *Richard III, Richard II,* and *1 Henry IV,* with Thomas Heyes for *The Merchant of Venice,* with Arthur Johnson for *The Merry Wives of Windsor,* and with Thomas Walkley for *Othello.* The last-minute inclusion of *Troilus and Cressida* between the histories and the tragedies with incomplete pagination may suggest that Bonian and Walley held out for a long time.

Eighteen plays had never before been printed. To secure rights to these plays, Messrs. Blount and Isaac Jaggard caused the following entry to be made in the Stationers' Register on November 8, 1623:

> Mr Blounte Isaak Jaggard. Entred for their Copie vnder the hands of Mr Doctor Worrall and Mr Cole, warden, Mr William Shakespeers Comedyes Histories, and Tragedyes soe manie of the said Copies as are not formerly entred to other men. vizt. Comedyes. The Tempest. The two gentlemen of Verona. Measure for Measure. The Comedy of Errors. As you Like it. All's well that ends well. Twelfe night. The winters tale. Histories. The thirde parte of Henry the sixt. Henry the eight. Tragedies. Coriolanus. Timon of Athens. Julius Caesar. Mackbeth. Anthonie and Cleopatra. Cymbeline.

The Stationers' Register list includes only sixteen names, since *The Taming of the Shrew* and *King John* were considered to have been published previously: *The Taming of A Shrew* and *The Troublesome Reign of King John,* now generally regarded as a bad quarto and a source respectively, had appeared in print in 1594 and 1591. Two plays on the list had actually been registered previously, *As You Like It* and *Antony and Cleopatra.* "The thirde parte of Henry the sixt" refers to *1 Henry VI,* since the other two *Henry VI* plays had already been published as bad quartos.

The Texts Used for the 1623 Folio

In addition to securing publishing rights, Heminges and Condell and their associates had the further task of selecting copy from which the printers were to set up their work. In the case of the eighteen as yet unpublished plays, the editors selected the best manuscripts they could find: author's drafts for *The Comedy of Errors, All's Well,* and others, prompt-books for *As You Like It, Twelfth Night,* and so on. Perhaps the editors planned at first to give the printers clean new transcriptions of such plays, for the first four plays in the Folio—*The Tempest, The Two Gentlemen of Verona, The Merry Wives of Windsor,* and *Measure for Measure*—were all printed from copies made by the professional scribe Ralph Crane. If the editors had planned to continue this practice throughout the volume, however, they abandoned it after the fourth play and turned instead to a variety of sorts of copy. An alternative explanation is that the editors had these four clean copies on hand, and chose to begin the volume with them simply because they were available and ready for the printer.

The complicated choices involved plays that had already been published. Printers, then as now, preferred to work from printed copy because of its legibility. Yet some published Shakespearean plays were bad quartos, the "stolne and surreptitious copies" that Heminges and Condell had vowed to replace with more perfect copies. Although one might suppose that Heminges and Condell would have set aside bad quartos entirely, they did not always do so, perhaps because the manuscript alternatives were illegible or defective. In other cases, the editors had to make a more subtle choice between a "good" quarto and a still better manuscript. What the editors sometimes did in such cases was to use the inferior printed text but to annotate it by reference to a superior manuscript. This process of annotation might vary widely in its degree of thoroughness.

The use of bad quartos as copy was, to be sure, unusual. Yet it did sometimes happen. The Folio text of *Henry V* seems to have been set from pages of the second and third quartos, which were derived from the pirated quarto of 1600; fortunately, those pages had been conscientiously corrected by reference to a manuscript source—probably Shakespeare's own papers—and hence provided a fairly reliable text. The Folio texts of *2* and *3 Henry VI* may similarly have been set from pages of the second and third quartos of the pirated texts of those plays, as corrected by reference to independent manuscript sources. Even in these questionable cases, an attempt seems to have been made to overcome the limitations of the bad quarto copy.

More often, one of the good quartos was corrected by checking it against a manuscript source. The Folio text of *Titus Andronicus,* for example, was evidently derived from a copy of the third quarto, but that copy may have been corrected by reference to an annotated copy of the second quarto which had been used as a prompt-book. In any case, a portion of Act III that is missing from all the early quartos must have been derived from some manuscript source. Other texts of this kind include *Richard III, Richard II, Troilus and Cressida, Othello,* and *King Lear;* disputed cases include *Hamlet* and *2 Henry IV.* See Appendix I for statements on the texts of each play.

The Printing of the 1623 Folio

The printing of the 1623 Folio continued from April of 1621 to December of 1623 in the printing shop of William and Isaac Jaggard. The compositors who actually set the type were, according to Charlton Hinman (*The Printing and Proof-Reading of the First Folio of Shakespeare,* 2 vols., 1963), five in number. For convenient reference they are designated as compositors A through E. A and B were the principal workmen. E was evidently an inept apprentice, unfortunately brought into the project just in time to work on several of the tragedies.

Compositors had to rely on their ability to memorize large segments of their copy—perhaps whole lines of verse—at a time, since they needed to look at the type they were setting manually. Hence, they were apt to make mistakes based on imperfect remembering. Less skillful compositors not infrequently introduced errors by transposing words in a line, substituting a new word for what was in the copy, or maiming the scansion of a line of verse by adding or subtracting syllables.

Compositors were largely responsible for the "pointing" or punctuation of the text. They also usually imposed their own spelling practices on their copy. No copy editor went over the materials first to normalize spelling, and the compositors were free to normalize as they chose. They occasionally used variant spellings to "justify" prose lines. Elizabethan spelling was in any case chaotic by our standards. The modern textual business of identifying compositors relies mainly on discovering the characteristic spelling habits of each.

Rather than setting their pages in numbered sequence right through an entire play, as we would assume, the compositors of the Folio used a system known as "casting off": that is, they estimated the amount of copy needed to fill a page of type, and divided the whole text up into portions of the estimated correct length. They could then begin by setting pages six and seven, and would immediately start printing these two pages side by side on the same "forme" or side of a sheet. (When three large sheets are folded once and gathered together, the result is a "quire" of twelve pages with pages one and twelve printed on the outer side or "forme" of the outermost sheet, pages two and eleven on the inner forme of that same sheet, pages three and ten on the outer forme of the middle sheet, and so on.) Since type was expensive and in limited supply in a printing shop, the type had to be redistributed into the fonts as soon as the requisite number of copies of any forme had been run off. Casting off enabled the printers to print and redistribute the type of pages six and seven without having to wait for all the intervening pages to be set up also. (The reappearance of distributed type is in fact one clue by which Hinman was able to discover that the Folio had been set up throughout by casting off rather than by printing in sequence.)

Despite the advantages of flexibility, casting off had its disadvantages. If a compositor discovered he had been given too little copy for a page of text, he had to stretch his material by heavy "leading" or spacing. If, on the other hand, he discovered he had been given too much copy for a page, he had to crowd his lines, print verse as prose, or even eliminate words and lines. Knowledge of this sort of printing information is useful to a modern editor, since it enables him to determine when the compositors may have interfered with the text that Shakespeare wrote.

When a compositor had completed one entire forme, consisting of two pages of text to be printed on one side of a large printing sheet, the forme went into the press and the requisite number of copies was run off by hand. One side of the sheet, either the inner or outer forme, was printed at a time. Proofreading, or "press correction," took place while the printing continued. At first, a number of sides of the sheet would be printed in their "uncorrected," or hastily proofread, state. When the press corrector found more errors, the presses would be stopped so that the errors might be corrected, after which printing would continue. Such interruptions might occur several times. Uncorrected or partially corrected sheets were not destroyed, however; paper was too costly for that. Later, when the stacks of sheets printed on one side were printed on the other side, errors would again be corrected as printing continued. Ultimately, when the sheets were gathered by three's into a quire of twelve pages and then sewn into a complete volume, no single copy of the Folio was apt to be exactly like another. In fact, the many copies of the First Folio extant today differ from one another in their press variants. Even though we might regard this as evidence of carelessness, Jaggard's work on the First Folio seems to have been scrupulous when judged by the standards of the day.

About 1200 copies of the First Folio were printed and sold for twenty shillings. Approximately 230 copies survive today, of which 80 are to be found in the collection of the Folger Library, Washington, D.C.

The Later Folios

When after nine years the first edition of the Folio had been sold out, a second edition was printed in 1632 by Thomas Cotes. He had succeeded to the Jaggards' business after the death of Isaac in 1627. The Second Folio merely reprinted the text of the First Folio together with a considerable number of editorial emendations. These have no independent textual authority, although some of the more commonsense suggestions have since been adopted by modern editors. A third edition appeared in 1663, based on the second. A second issue of this same third edition in 1664 included seven new plays: *Pericles, The London Prodigal, Thomas Lord Cromwell, Sir John Oldcastle, The Puritan, A Yorkshire Tragedy,* and *Locrine.* Of these, only *Pericles* has gained general acceptance in the Shakespeare canon (see Appendix I and the play introduction). A fourth edition of the Folio in 1685, based on the third, also included the seven new plays. Like the second and third editions, this fourth edition offered many emendations or new errors not based on any textual authority.

Later Editions

The first editor of Shakespeare in the modern sense of the term was Nicholas Rowe. His seven-volume edition of 1709 (reissued in nine volumes in 1714) was based on the Fourth Folio, to which the publisher Jacob Tonson had acquired the rights. Rowe began many practices we now regard as standard for a reader's edition. He provided a complete list of *dramatis personae* for each play, whereas the earlier folios had done so only sporadically. He similarly extended the practice of announcing the locale at the beginning of a scene. He marked entrances and exits with more care than in the folios, and provided more extensive division of the plays into acts and scenes. Although he did not consult Shakespeare's early texts, Rowe did offer a number of textual emendations. He also modernized spelling and punctuation.

Alexander Pope was Shakespeare's next editor. Pope's text, completed in 1725 in six volumes (reissued in 1728), was printed from a copy of Rowe's edition with Pope's annotations. Pope excluded *Pericles* and the spurious plays that had been added to the Third Folio, although a companion volume containing these plays appeared with the reprint of Pope's edition in 1728, lacking his name and perhaps not authorized by him. He completed Rowe's task of indicating locale for each of the scenes, and also completed the division of the text into acts and scenes. In fact, Pope used the "continental" system of marking a new scene whenever a major character comes on stage, so that his text contained many more scenes than did other editions. Most importantly, Pope extensively rewrote Shakespeare. Although he claimed to have consulted the early quartos, Pope regarded Shakespeare's text as something to be "improved" because it had been written in a barbaric age for ignorant spectators. He excised parts of Shakespeare's text that he considered vulgar, regularized lines that struck him as defective, eliminated anachronisms he regarded as indecorous, and the like. Pope's edition reflected the "refined" eighteenth-century view of Shakespeare as a very rough diamond in need of polishing. As a result, Pope removed Shakespearean editing far indeed from any serious attempt to recover what Shakespeare had actually written.

A corrective was in order. Lewis Theobald took up the challenge, though he was to be rewarded for his pains by being crowned the King of Dullness in Pope's *The Dunciad* (1728 version). Theobald's edition appeared in 1733 and was later reissued several times. He was the first editor to consult the folios and quartos. He did not, however, wholly recognize the textual value of those quartos. He also failed to base his text directly on the earliest substantive texts; instead, he annotated a copy of Pope's edition, just as Pope had annotated Rowe and Rowe had annotated the Fourth Folio. Despite his consultation of the early texts and his occasional brilliance as an emender, therefore, Theobald inevitably perpetuated more errors than he eliminated from the Rowe-Pope tradition.

The convention of relying on one's predecessor's edition continued to afflict eighteenth-century editing of Shakespeare. Robert Walker (whose edition appeared in 1734–1735), Sir Thomas Hanmer (1744), and William Warburton (1751) contributed little that was new. (This Warburton is not, however, the John Warburton whose cook is said to have burned a number of now-lost early editions of plays by using them to line pie-plates.) Even Dr. Johnson (1765), who set a standard of conservatism in admitting emendations to the Shakespearean text, based his edition on an annotated copy of Warburton's edition.

Only with Edward Capell (1768) did an eighteenth-century editor finally base his text on the original Folio and quartos. Capell amassed an admirable collection of quartos and was the first to recognize that they might sometimes be preferred as copy text to the Folio itself. Unlike his eighteenth-century predecessors, who generally dismissed the quartos as based on prompt-books and hence contaminated by theatrical revision, Capell saw that they usually represented Shakespeare's own drafts. Capell's work heavily influenced George Steevens' 1773 revision of Dr. Johnson's text.

Edmond Malone, at first a collaborator with Steevens and later his rival, issued an eleven-volume edition in 1790. Malone reintroduced *Pericles,* which Pope and subsequent editors had eliminated along with the spurious plays of the Third Folio. Malone brought to his editing an extensive knowledge of Elizabethan documents such as the Stationers' Register, Henslowe's *Diary,* and the records of the Master of the Revels. He left uncompleted a variorum edition recording all textual variants; this edition was finished in 1821 by James Boswell, son of Dr. Johnson's biographer, and became known as the Third Variorum because Isaac Reed's earlier editions (1803, 1813) had called themselves the First and Second Variorums. The so-called New Variorum Shakespeare continued this tradition under Henry Howard Furness, beginning in 1871.

Nineteenth-century editions were numerous. One of the most famous and influential was the "bowdlerized" or expurgated *Family Shakespeare* of the Rev. Thomas Bowdler, first appearing in 1804 and 1818 and soon extending throughout the English-speaking world. Other editions included those of William Harness (1825), S. W. Singer (1826, 1856), John Payne Collier (1841–1844), Charles Knight (1838–1842), Alexander Dyce (1857), Howard Staunton (1858–1860), Nikolaus Delius (1854–1861), H. N. Hudson (1851–1856), and J. O. Halliwell-Phillips (1853–1861).

The outstanding scholarly edition of the nineteenth century was the so-called Cambridge Shakespeare of William George Clark and William Aldis Wright, 1863–1866, issued in 1864 in a single volume known as the Globe text. Although its choice of copy texts has been challenged in two or three instances by twentieth-century bibliographical research, the Globe text was soundly edited for its day and soon established itself as definitive. Its act and scene divisions and its line numbering became standards of reference for concordances, works of literary criticism, and the like.

Later nineteenth- and early twentieth-century editions included those of W. J. Rolfe (1871–1896), Appleton Morgan (1888), F. A. Marshall and others (The Henry Irving Shakespeare, 1888–1890), Sir Israel Gollancz (The Temple Shakespeare, 1894–1895), W. J. Craig (1892), C. H. Herford (1899), and Helen Porter and Charlotte Clarke (1903–1914). Influential American editions included those of W. A. Neilson (1906) and George Lyman Kittredge (1936).

The twentieth century has seen an enormous increase in the information available on bibliographical matters: memorial reconstruction of texts, printing-house procedures, the mechanics of book production, watermarks, printer's ornaments, Elizabethan handwriting, spelling, punctuation, and the like. Some pioneering studies include A. W. Pollard's *Shakespeare's Folios and Quartos* (1909) and *Shakespeare's Hand in the Play of Sir Thomas More* (1923), R. B. McKerrow's *An Introduction to Bibliography for Literary Students* (1927) and *Prolegomena for the Oxford Shakespeare* (1939), W. W. Greg's *Principles of Emendation in Shakespeare* (1928) and *The Editorial Problem in Shakespeare* (third edition, 1954), and E. K. Chambers' *William Shakespeare: A Study of Facts and Problems* (1930). No less important are Alice Walker's *Textual Problems of the First Folio* (1953) and Fredson Bowers' *Bibliography and Textual Criticism* (1964). An updated survey of problems and methods is to be found in Philip Gaskell's *A New Introduction to Bibliography* (1972). Significant studies have also appeared on individual plays, such as that of Peter Alexander on the *Henry VI* plays and *Richard III,* Madeleine Doran also on *Henry VI,* J. Dover Wilson on *Hamlet,* George Williams on *Romeo and Juliet,* and G. I. Duthie on *King Lear.*

These bibliographical studies have led to new twentieth-century editions of Shakespeare in which the textual method has been measurably advanced. Among the most significant are the New Cambridge Shakespeare of Sir Arthur Quiller-Couch and J. Dover Wilson, and the still-continuing Arden Shakespeare under a succession of general editors including W. J. Craig, R. H. Case, Una Ellis-Fermor, and Harold Jenkins and Harold Brooks. An old-spelling critical edition is in progress under the direction of J. Leeds Barroll. College editions reedited from original texts include the Pelican Shakespeare under the general editorship of Alfred Harbage (1956–1969), the revision of Kittredge's edition by Irving Ribner (1971), the Signet Classic Shakespeare under the general editorship of Sylvan Barnet (1972), the Riverside Shakespeare (1974) of which G. Blakemore Evans is the textual editor, and this present edition. Other new texts are forthcoming from the Oxford and Cambridge University Presses and from W. W. Norton.

Norton has also issued its Norton *Facsimile of The First Folio of Shakespeare,* prepared by Charlton Hinman from the Folios of the Folger Library (1968). Older facsimiles of the Folio are available in libraries, such as that prepared by Sidney Lee (1902) and J. Dover Wilson (in separate plays), but the Norton facsimile unquestionably sets a new standard of excellence. Facsimiles of the quartos are also available. Xerox copies of early printed books such as Shakespearean quartos are to be found in many libraries through the S.T.C. (Short Title Catalogue) series of University Microfilms. Photographic copies of early texts are also frequently available on microfilm.

Shakespeare Criticism

In his own time, Shakespeare achieved a reputation for immortal greatness that is astonishing when we consider the low regard in which playwrights were then generally held. Francis Meres compared him to Ovid, Plautus, and Seneca, and proclaimed Shakespeare to be England's most excellent writer in both comedy and tragedy. John Weever spoke of "Honie-tong'd *Shakespeare.*" The number of such praising allusions is high. Even Ben Jonson, a learned writer strongly influenced by the classical tradition, lauded Shakespeare as "a Moniment without a tombe," England's best poet exceeding Chaucer, Spenser, Beaumont, Kyd, and Marlowe. In tragedy, Jonson compared Shakespeare with Aeschylus, Euripides, and Sophocles; in comedy he insisted Shakespeare had no rival even in "insolent *Greece* or haughtie *Rome.*" This tribute appeared in Jonson's commendatory poem written for the Shakespearean Folio of 1623.

To be sure, Jonson had more critical things to say about Shakespeare. Even in the Folio commendatory poem, Jonson could not resist a dig at Shakespeare's "small *Latine,* and lesse *Greeke.*" To William Drummond of Hawthornden he objected that Shakespeare "wanted Arte" because in a play *(The Winter's Tale)* he "brought in a number of men saying they had suffered Shipwrack in Bohemia, wher ther is no Sea neer by some 100 Miles." In *Timber, or Discoveries,* Jonson chided Shakespeare for his unrestrained facility in writing. "The Players have often mentioned it as an honour to *Shakespeare,* that in his writing, (whatsoever he penn'd) hee never blotted out [a] line. My answer hath beene, would he had blotted a thousand." In a preface to his own play, *Every Man in His Humor* (1616 edition), Jonson satirized English history plays (such as Shakespeare's) that "with three rustie swords, And helpe of some few foot-and-halfe-foote words, Fight ouer *Yorke,* and *Lancasters* long iarres: And in the tyring-house bring wounds, to scarres." He also jeered at plays lacking unity of time in which children grow to the age of sixty or older, and at nonsensical romantic plays featuring fireworks, thunder, and a chorus that "wafts you ore the seas."

These criticisms are all of a piece. As a classicist himself, Jonson held in high regard the classical unities. He deplored much English popular drama, including some of Shakespeare's plays, for their undisciplined mixture of comedy and tragedy. Measured against his cherished ideals of classical decorum and refinement of language, Shakespeare's histories and the late romances — *Pericles, Cymbeline, The Winter's Tale,* and *The Tempest*—seemed irritatingly naive and loose-jointed. Yet Jonson knew that Shakespeare had an incomparable genius, superior even to Jonson's own. Jonson's affection and respect for Shakespeare seem to have been quite unforced. In the midst of his critical remarks in *Timber,* he freely conceded that "I lov'd the man, and doe honour his memory (on this side Idolatry) as much as any. Hee was (indeed) honest, and of an open, and free nature: had an excellent *Phantsie;* brave notions, and gentle expressions."

The Age of Dryden and Pope

Jonson's attitude toward Shakespeare lived on into the Restoration period of the late seventeenth century. A commonplace of that age held it proper to "admire" Ben Jonson but to "love" Shakespeare. Jonson was the more correct poet, the better model for imitation. Shakespeare often had to be rewritten according to the sophisticated tastes of the Restoration (see Appendix III for an account of Restoration stage adaptations of Shakespeare), but he was also regarded as a natural genius. Dryden reflected this view in his *Essay of Dramatic Poesy* (1668) and his *Essay on the Dramatic Poetry of the Last Age* (1672). Dryden condemned *The Winter's Tale, Pericles,* and several other late romances for "the lameness of their plots" and for their "ridiculous incoherent story" which is usually "grounded on impossibilities." Not only Shakespeare, he charged, but several of his contemporaries "neither understood correct plotting, nor that which they call *the decorum of the stage.*" Had Shakespeare lived in the Restoration, Dryden believed, he would doubtless have written "more correctly" under the influence of a language that had become more "courtly" and a wit that had grown more "refined." Shakespeare, he thought, had limitless "fancy" but sometimes lacked "judgment." Dryden regretted that Shakespeare had been forced to write in "ignorant" times and for audiences who "knew no better." Like Jonson, nevertheless, Dryden had the magnanimity to perceive that Shakespeare transcended his limitations. Shakespeare, said Dryden, was "the Man who of all Modern, and perhaps Ancient Poets, had the largest and most comprehensive soul." From a classical writer, this was high praise indeed.

Alexander Pope's edition of Shakespeare (1725) was based upon a similar estimate of Shakespeare as an untutored genius. Pope freely "improved" Shakespeare's language, rewriting lines and excising those parts he considered vulgar, in order to rescue Shakespeare from the barbaric circumstances of his Elizabethan milieu. Other critics of the Restoration and early eighteenth century who stressed Shakespeare's "natural" genius and imaginative powers were John Dennis, Joseph Addison, and the editors Nicholas Rowe and Lewis Theobald.

The Age of Johnson

Shakespeare was not without his detractors during the late seventeenth and early eighteenth centuries; after all, classical criticism tended to distrust imagination and fancy. Notable among the harsher critics of the Restoration period was Thomas Rymer, whose *Short View of Tragedy* (1692) included a famous attack on *Othello* for making too much out of Desdemona's handkerchief. In the eighteenth century, Voltaire spoke out sharply against Shakespeare's violation of the classical unities, though Voltaire also had some admiring things to say.

The most considered answer to such criticism in the later eighteenth century was that of Dr. Samuel Johnson, in his edition of Shakespeare's plays and its great preface (1765). Shakespeare, said Johnson, is the poet of nature who "holds up to his readers a faithful mirror of manners and of life. His characters are not modified by the customs of particular places, unpracticed by the rest of the world. . . . In the writings of other poets a character is too often an individual; in those of Shakespeare it is commonly a species." Johnson's attitudes were essentially classical in that he praised Shakespeare for being universal, for having provided a "just representation of general nature," for having stood the test of time. Yet Johnson also magnanimously praised Shakespeare for having transcended the classical rules. Johnson triumphantly vindicated the mixture of comedy and tragedy in Shakespeare's plays and the supposed indecorum of his characters.

Of course Johnson did not praise everything he saw. He objected to Shakespeare's loose construction of plot, careless huddling together of the ends of his plays, licentious humor, and above all the punning wordplay. He deplored Shakespeare's failure to satisfy the demands of poetic justice, especially in *King Lear,* and he regretted that Shakespeare seemed more anxious to please than to instruct. Still, Johnson did much to free Shakespeare from the constraint of an overly restrictive classical approach to criticism.

The Age of Coleridge

With the beginning of the Romantic period, in England and on the Continent, Shakespeare criticism increasingly turned away from classical precept in favor of a more spontaneous and enthusiastic approach to Shakespeare's creative genius. The new Shakespeare became indeed a rallying cry for those who now deplored such "regular" dramatic poets as Racine and Corneille. Shakespeare became a seer, a bard with mystic powers of insight into the human condition. Goethe, in *Wilhelm Meister* (1796), conceived of Hamlet as the archetypal "Romantic" poet, melancholic, delicate, unable to act.

Critical trends in England moved toward similar conclusions. Maurice Morgann, in his *Essay on the Dramatic Character of Sir John Falstaff* (1777), glorified Falstaff into a rare individual of courage, dignity, and—yes—honor. To do so, Morgann had to suppress much evidence as to Falstaff's overall function in the *Henry IV* plays. Dramatic structure in fact did not interest him; his passion was "character," and his study of Falstaff reflected a new Romantic preoccupation with character analysis. Like other character critics who followed him, Morgann tended to move away from the play itself and into a world where the dramatic personage being considered might lead an independent existence. What would it have been like to know Falstaff as a real person? How would he have behaved on occasions other than those reported by Shakespeare? Such questions fascinated Morgann and others because they led into grand speculations about human psychology and philosophy. Shakespeare's incomparably penetrating insights into character prompted further investigations of the human psyche.

Other late eighteenth-century works devoted to the study of character included Lord Kames' *Elements of Criticism* (1762), Thomas Whately's *Remarks on Some of the Characters of Shakespeare* (published 1785), William Richardson's *Philosophical Analysis and Illustration of Some of Shakespeare's Remarkable Characters* (1774), and William Jackson's *Thirty Letters on Various Subjects* (1782). Morgann spoke for this school of critics when he insisted, "it may be fit to consider them [Shakespeare's characters] rather as Historic than Dramatic beings; and, when occasion requires, to account for their conduct from the *whole* of character, from general principles, from latent motives, and from policies not avowed."

Samuel Taylor Coleridge, the greatest of the English Romantic critics, was profoundly influenced by character criticism, both English and continental. He himself made important contributions to the study of character. His conception of Hamlet, derived in part from Goethe and Hegel, as one who "vacillates from sensibility, and procrastinates from thought, and loses the power of action in the energy of resolve," was to dominate nineteenth-century interpretations of Hamlet. His insight into Iago's evil nature—"the motive-hunting of a motiveless malignity"—was also influential.

Nevertheless, Coleridge did not succumb to the temptation, as did so many character critics, of ignoring the unity of an entire play. Quite to the contrary, he affirmed in Shakespeare an "organic form" or "innate" sense of shape, developed from within, that gave new meaning to Shakespeare's fusion of comedy and tragedy, his seeming anachronisms, his improbable fictions, and his supposedly rambling plots. Coleridge heaped scorn on the eighteenth-century idea of Shakespeare as a "natural" but untaught genius. He praised Shakespeare not for having mirrored life, as Dr. Johnson had said, but for having created an imaginative world attuned to its own internal harmonies. He saw Shakespeare as an inspired but deliberate artist who fitted together the parts of his imaginative world with consummate skill. "The judgement of Shakespeare is commensurate with his genius."

In all this Coleridge was remarkably close to his German contemporary and rival, August Wilhelm Schlegel, who insisted that Shakespeare was "a profound artist, and not a blind and wildly luxuriant genius." In Shakespeare's plays, said Schlegel, "the Fancy lays claim to be considered as an independent mental power governed according to its own laws." Between them, Coleridge and Schlegel utterly inverted the critical values of the previous age, substituting "sublimity" and "imagination" for universality and trueness to nature.

Other Romantic critics included William Hazlitt *(Characters of Shakespear's Plays,* 1817), Charles Lamb (*On the Tragedies of Shakespeare,* 1811), and Thomas De Quincey (*On the Knocking at the Gate in Macbeth,* 1823). Keats also had some penetrating things to say in his letters. As a whole the Romantics were enthusiasts for Shakespeare, sometimes even idolaters. Yet they consistently refused to recognize him as a man of the theatre. Lamb wrote, "It may seem a paradox, but I cannot help being of opinion that the plays of Shakespeare are less calculated for performance on a stage, than those of almost any other dramatist whatever." Hazlitt similarly observed, "We do not like to see our author's plays acted, and least of all, *Hamlet.* There is no play that suffers so much in being transferred to the stage." These hostile attitudes toward the theatre reflected in part the condition of the stage in nineteenth-century England. In part, however, these attitudes were the inevitable result of character criticism, or what Lamb called the desire "to know the internal workings and movements of a great mind, of an Othello or a Hamlet for instance, the *when* and the *why* and the *how far* they should be moved." This fascination with character swept everything before it during the Romantic period.

A. C. Bradley

The tendency of nineteenth-century criticism, as we have seen, was to exalt Shakespeare as a poet and philosopher rather than playwright, and as a creator of immortal characters whose "lives" might be studied as though existing independent of a dramatic text. Not infrequently, this critical approach led to a biographical interpretation of Shakespeare through his plays, on the assumption that what he wrote was his own spiritual autobiography and a key to his own fascinating character. Perhaps the most famous critical studies in this line were Edward Dowden's *Shakspere: A Critical Study of His Mind and Art* (1875) and his *Shakespeare Primer* (1877), in which he traced a progression from Shakespeare's early exuberance and passionate involvement through brooding pessimism to a final philosophical calm.

At the same time, the nineteenth century also saw the rise of a more factual and methodological scholarship, especially in the German universities. Dowden in fact reflected this trend as well, for one of the achievements of philological study was to establish with some accuracy the dating of Shakespeare's plays and thus make possible an analysis of his artistic development. Hermann Ulrici's *Über Shakespeares dramatische Kunst* (1839) and Gottfried Gervinus' edition of 1849 were among the earliest studies to interest themselves in Shakespeare's chronological development.

The man who best summed up the achievement of nineteenth-century Shakespeare criticism was A. C. Bradley, in his *Shakespearean Tragedy* (1904) and other studies. *Shakespearean Tragedy* dealt with the four "great" tragedies, *Hamlet, Othello, King Lear,* and *Macbeth*. Bradley revealed his Romantic tendencies in his focus on psychological analysis of character, but he also brought to his work a scholarly awareness of the text that had been missing in some earlier character critics. His work continues to have considerable influence today, despite modern tendencies to rebel against nineteenth-century idealism. To Bradley, Shakespeare's tragic world was ultimately explicable and profoundly moral. Despite the overwhelming impression of tragic waste in *King Lear,* he argued, we as audience experience a sense of compensation and completion that implies an ultimate pattern in human life. "Good, in the widest sense, seems thus to be the principle of life and health in the world; evil, at least in these worst forms, to be a poison. The world reacts against it violently, and, in the struggle to expel it, is driven to devastate itself." Man must suffer because of his fatal tendency to pursue some extreme passion, but man learns through suffering about himself and the nature of his world. We as audience are reconciled to our existence through purgative release; we smile through our tears. Cordelia is wantonly destroyed, but the fact of her transcendent goodness is eternal. Although in one sense she fails, said Bradley, she is "in another sense superior to the world in which [she] appears; is, in some way which we do not seek to define, untouched by the doom that overtakes [her]; and is rather set free from life than deprived of it."

Historical Criticism

The first major twentieth-century reaction against character criticism was that of the so-called historical critics. These critics insisted on a more hardheaded and skeptical appraisal of Shakespeare through better understanding of his historical milieu: his theatre, his audience, his political and social environment. In good part, this movement was the result of a new professionalism of Shakespearean studies in the twentieth century. Whereas earlier critics—Dryden, Pope, Johnson, Coleridge—had generally been literary amateurs in the best sense, early twentieth-century criticism became increasingly the province of those who taught in universities. Historical research became a professional activity. Bradley himself was Professor of English Literature at Liverpool and Oxford, and did much to legitimize the incorporation of Shakespeare into the humanities curriculum. German scholarship produced the first regular periodical devoted to Shakespeare studies, *Shakespeare-Jahrbuch,* to be followed in due course in England and America by *Shakespeare Survey* (beginning in 1948), *Shakespeare Quarterly* (1950), and *Shakespeare Studies* (1965).

From the start, historical criticism took a new look at Shakespeare as a man of the theatre. Sir Walter Raleigh (Professor of English Literature at Oxford, not to be confused with his Elizabethan namesake) rejected the Romantic absorption in psychology and turned his attention instead to the artistic methods by which plays affect theatregoing spectators. The poet Robert Bridges insisted that Shakespeare had often sacrificed consistency and logic for primitive theatrical effects designed to please his vulgar audience. Bridges' objections were often based on serious lack of information about Shakespeare's stage, but they had a healthy iconoclastic effect nonetheless on the scholarship of his time. In Germany, Levin Schücking pursued a similar line of reasoning in his *Character Problems in Shakespeare's Plays* (1917, translated into English in 1922). Schücking argued that Shakespeare had disregarded coherent structure and had striven instead for vivid dramatic effect ("episodic intensification") in his particular scenes. Schücking's *The Meaning of Hamlet* (1937) explained the strange contradictions of that play as resulting from primitive and brutal Germanic source materials which Shakespeare had not fully assimilated.

A keynote for historical critics of the early twentieth century was the concept of artifice or convention in the construction of a play. Perhaps the leading spokesman for this approach was E. E. Stoll, a student of G. L. Kittredge of Harvard University, himself a leading force in historical scholarship in America. Stoll vigorously insisted, in such works as *Othello: An Historical and Comparative Study* (1915), *Hamlet: An Historical and Comparative Study* (1919), and *Art and Artifice in Shakespeare* (1933), that a critic must never be sidetracked by moral, psychological, or biographical interpretations. A play, he argued, is an artifice arising out of its historical milieu. Its conventions are implicit agreements between playwright and spectator. They alter with time, and a modern reader who is ignorant of Elizabethan conventions is all too apt to be misled by his own post-Romantic preconceptions. For example, a calumniator like Iago in *Othello* is conventionally supposed to be believed by the other characters on stage. We do not need to speculate about the "realities" of Othello's being duped, and in fact we are likely to be led astray by such Romantic speculations. Stoll went so far as to affirm, in fact, that Shakespearean drama intentionally distorts reality through its theatrical conventions in order to fulfill its own existence as artifice. *Hamlet* is not a play about delay but a revenge story of a certain length, containing many conventional revenge motifs such as the ghost and the "mousetrap" scheme used to test the villain, and deriving many of its circumstances from Shakespeare's sources; delay is a conventional device needed to continue the story to its conclusion.

Stoll's zeal led to excessive claims for historical criticism, as one might expect in the early years of a pioneering movement. At its extreme, historical criticism came close to implying that Shakespeare was a mere product of his environment. Indeed, the movement owed many of its evolutionist assumptions to the supposedly scientific "social Darwinism" of Thomas Huxley and other late nineteenth-century social philosophers. In more recent years, however, the crusading spirit has given way to a more moderate historical criticism that continues to be an important part of Shakespearean scholarship.

Alfred Harbage, for example, in *As They Liked It* (1947) and *Shakespeare and the Rival Traditions* (1952), has analyzed the audience for which Shakespeare wrote, and the rivalry between popular and elite theatres in the London of his day. Harbage sees Shakespeare as a popular dramatist writing for a highly intelligent, enthusiastic, and socially diversified audience. More recently, in *Shakespeare Studies* (1974), Ann Jennalie Cook has qualified Harbage's view, arguing that Shakespeare's audience was for the most part affluent and well-connected. G. E. Bentley has amassed an invaluable storehouse of information about *The Jacobean and Caroline Stage* (1941–1968), just as E. K. Chambers had earlier collected documents and data on *The Elizabethan Stage* (1923). Other studies by these historical scholars include Chambers' *William Shakespeare: A Study of Facts and Problems* (1930), and Bentley's *Shakespeare and His Theatre* (1964) and *The Profession of Dramatist in Shakespeare's Time* (1971). T. W. Baldwin exemplifies the historical scholar who like Stoll claims too much for the method; nevertheless, much information on Shakespeare's schooling, reading, and professional theatrical life is available in such works as *William Shakspere's Small Latine and Lesse Greeke* (1944) and *The Organization and Personnel of the Shakespearean Company* (1927). Hardin Craig uses historical method in *An Interpretation of Shakespeare* (1948).

Historical criticism has contributed greatly to our knowledge of the staging of Shakespeare's plays. George Pierce Baker, in *The Development of Shakespeare as a Dramatist* (1907), continued the line of investigation begun by Walter Raleigh. Harley Granville-Barker brought to his *Prefaces to Shakespeare* (1930, 1946) a wealth of professional theatrical experience of his own. Ever since his time, the new theatrical method of interpreting Shakespeare has been based to an ever-increasing extent on a genuine revival of interest in Shakespearean production. John Dover Wilson shows an awareness of the stage in *What Happens in Hamlet* (1935) and *The Fortunes of Falstaff* (1943). At its best, as in John Russell Brown's *Shakespeare's Plays in Performance* (1966), in John Styan's *Shakespeare's Stagecraft* (1967), in Michael Goldman's *Shakespeare and the Energies of Drama* (1972), and in Alan Dessen's *Elizabethan Drama and the Viewer's Eye* (1977), this critical method reveals many insights into the text that are hard to obtain without an awareness of theatrical technique.

Supporting this theatrical criticism, historical research has learned a great deal about the physical nature of Shakespeare's stage. J. C. Adams' well-known model of the Globe Playhouse, as presented in Irwin Smith's *Shakespeare's Globe Playhouse: A Modern Reconstruction* (1956), is now generally discredited in favor of a simpler building as reconstructed by C. Walter Hodges (*The Globe Restored,* 1953), Bernard Beckerman (*Shakespeare at the Globe,* 1962), Richard Hosley ("The Playhouses and the Stage" in *A New Companion to Shakespeare Studies,* ed. K. Muir and S. Schoenbaum, 1971, and several other good essays), T. J. King (*Shakespearean Staging, 1599–1642,* 1971), and others. Information on the private theatres such as the Blackfriars, where Shakespeare's plays were also performed, appears in William Armstrong, *The Elizabethan Private Theatres* (1958), Richard Hosley, "A Reconstruction of the Second Blackfriars" (*The Elizabethan Theatre,* 1969), Glynne Wickham, *Early English Stages* (1959–1972), and others. For further information on inn-yard theatres and on courtly or private theatres, see the contributions of Herbert Berry, D. F. Rowan, and others cited in the bibliography at the back of this volume.

A related pursuit of historical criticism has been the better understanding of Shakespeare through his dramatic predecessors and contemporaries. Willard Farnham, in *The Medieval Heritage of Elizabethan Tragedy* (1936), traces the evolution of native English tragedy through the morality plays of the early Tudor period. J. M. R. Margeson's *The Origins of English Tragedy* (1967) broadens the pattern to include still other sources for Elizabethan ideas on dramatic tragedy. Bernard Spivack, in *Shakespeare and the Allegory of Evil* (1958), sees Iago, Edmund, Richard III, and other boasting villains in Shakespeare as descendants of the morality Vice. In *Shakespeare and the Idea of the Play* (1962), Anne Righter traces the device of the play-within-the-play and the metaphor of the world as a stage back to medieval and classical ideas of dramatic illusion. Irving Ribner's *The English History Play in the Age of Shakespeare* (1959, rev. 1965) examines Shakespeare's plays on English history in the context of the popular Elizabethan genre to which they belonged. Robert Weimann's *Shakespeare and the Popular Tradition in the Theatre* (translated from the German in 1978) is a Marxist study in the social dimension of dramatic form and function. Many other studies of this sort could be cited, including Glynne Wickham's *Shakespeare's Dramatic Heritage* (1969), Oscar J. Campbell's *Shakespeare's Satire* (1943), M. C. Bradbrook's *Themes and Conventions of Elizabethan Tragedy* (1935), and S. L. Bethell's *Shakespeare and the Popular Dramatic Tradition* (1944).

Another important concern of historical criticism has been the relationship between Shakespeare and the ideas of his age—cosmological, philosophical, political. Among the first scholars to study Elizabethan cosmology were Hardin Craig, in *The Enchanted Glass* (1936), and A. O. Lovejoy in *The Great Chain of Being* (1936). As their successor, E. M. W. Tillyard provided in *The Elizabethan World Picture* (1943) a definitive view of the conservative and hierarchical values which Elizabethans were supposed to have espoused. In *Shakespeare's History Plays* (1944), Tillyard extended his essentially conservative view of Shakespeare's philosophical outlook to the histories, arguing that they embody a "Tudor myth" and thereby lend support to the Tudor state. Increasingly, however, critics have disputed the extent to which Shakespeare in fact endorsed the "establishment" values of the Elizabethan world picture. Theodore Spencer, in *Shakespeare and the Nature of Man* (1942), discusses the impact on Shakespeare of radical new thinkers like Machiavelli, Montaigne, and Copernicus. In political matters, Henry A. Kelly's *Divine Providence in the England of Shakespeare's Histories* (1970) has challenged the existence of a single "Tudor myth" and has argued that Shakespeare's history plays reflect contrasting political philosophies set dramatically in conflict with one another. M. M. Reese's *The Cease of Majesty* (1961) also offers a graceful corrective to Tillyard's lucid but occasionally one-sided interpretations.

Historical criticism has also yielded many profitable specialized studies, in which Shakespeare is illuminated by a better understanding of various sciences of his day. Lily Bess Campbell approaches Shakespearean tragedy through Renaissance psychology in *Shakespeare's Tragic Heroes: Slaves of Passion* (1930). Paul Jorgensen uses Elizabethan documents on the arts of war and generalship in his study of *Shakespeare's Military World* (1956). Many similar studies examine Shakespeare in relation to law, medicine, and other professions. For a summary of historical scholarship having to do with Shakespeare's texts, see "Editions and Editors of Shakespeare," above.

"New" Criticism

As we have seen, historical criticism is still an important part of Shakespeare criticism; for better and for worse, it is the stuff of many research-oriented universities and their Ph.D. programs. Since its beginning, however, historical criticism has had to face a critical reaction generated in part by its own utilitarian and fact-gathering tendencies. The suggestions urged by Stoll and others, that Shakespeare was the product of his cultural and theatrical environment, tended to obscure his achievement as a poet. Amassing of information about Shakespeare's reading or his theatrical company often seemed to inhibit the scholar from responding to the power of words and images.

Such at any rate was the rallying cry of the *Scrutiny* group in England, centered around F. R. Leavis, L. C. Knights, and Derek Traversi, and the "new" critics in America such as Cleanth Brooks. The new critics demanded close attention to the poetry without the encumbrance of historical research. Especially at first, the new critics were openly hostile to any criticism distracting readers from the text. The satirical force of the movement can perhaps best be savored in L. C. Knights' "How Many Children Had Lady Macbeth?" (1933), prompted by the learned appendices in Bradley's *Shakespearean Tragedy*: "When was the murder of Duncan first plotted? Did Lady Macbeth really faint? Duration of the action in *Macbeth*. Macbeth's age. 'He has no children.' "

In part, the new critical movement was (and still is) a pedagogical movement, a protest against the potential dryness of historical footnoting and an insistence that classroom study of Shakespeare ought to focus on a response to his language. Cleanth Brooks' "The Naked Babe and the Cloak of Manliness" (in *The Well Wrought Urn,* 1947), offers to the teacher a model of close reading that focuses on imagery and yet attempts to see a whole vision of the play through its language. G. Wilson Knight concentrates on imagery and verbal texture, sometimes to the exclusion of the play as a whole, in his *The Wheel of Fire* (1930), *The Imperial Theme* (1931), *The Shakespearian Tempest* (1932), *The Crown of Life* (1947), and others. William Empson is best known for his *Seven Types of Ambiguity* (1930) and *Some Versions of Pastoral* (1935). Derek Traversi's works include *An Approach to Shakespeare* (1938), *Shakespeare: The Last Phase* (1954), *Shakespeare: From Richard II to Henry V* (1957), and *Shakespeare: The Roman Plays* (1963). Perhaps the greatest critic of this school has been L. C. Knights, whose books include *Explorations* (1946), *Some Shakespearean Themes* (1959), *An Approach to Hamlet* (1960), and *Further Explorations* (1965). T. S. Eliot's perceptive and controversial observations have also had an important influence on critics of this school. Other studies making good use of the new critical method include Robert Heilman's *This Great Stage* (1948) and *Magic in the Web* (1956). Many of these critics are concerned not only with language but with the larger moral and structural implications of Shakespeare's plays as discovered through a sensitive reading of the text.

More specialized studies of Shakespearean imagery and language include Caroline Spurgeon's *Shakespeare's Imagery and What It Tells Us* (1935). Its classifications are now recognized to be overly statistical and restricted in definition, but the work has nonetheless prompted valuable further study. Among later works are Sister Miriam Joseph's *Shakespeare's Use of the Arts of Language* (1947, partly reprinted in *Rhetoric in Shakespeare's Time,* 1962), Wolfgang Clemen's *The Development of Shakespeare's Imagery* (1951), Maurice Charney's *Style in Hamlet* (1969) and *Shakespeare's Roman Plays* (1961), and M. M. Mahood's *Shakespeare's Wordplay* (1957). The study of prose has not received as much attention as that of poetry, although Brian Vickers' *The Artistry of Shakespeare's Prose* (1968) and Milton Crane's *Shakespeare's Prose* (1951) make significant contributions. See also Edward Armstrong's *Shakespeare's Imagination* (1963) and Kirby Farrell's *Shakespeare's Creation: The Language of Magic and Play* (1975).

Psychological Criticism

In a sense, Freudian and other psychological criticism continues the "character" criticism of the nineteenth century. Freudian critics sometimes follow a character into a world outside the text, analyzing Hamlet (for instance) as though he were a real person whose childhood traumas can be inferred from the symptoms he displays. The most famous work in this vein is *Hamlet and Oedipus* (1910, revised 1949), by Freud's disciple Ernest Jones. According to Jones, Hamlet's delay is caused by an oedipal trauma. Hamlet's uncle, Claudius, has done exactly what Hamlet himself incestuously and subconsciously wished to do: kill his father and marry his mother. Because he cannot articulate these forbidden impulses to himself, Hamlet is paralyzed into inactivity. Jones' critical analysis thus assumes, as did Romantic critics such as Coleridge, that the central problem of *Hamlet* is one of character and motivation: why does Hamlet delay? (Many modern critics would deny that this is a problem, or would insist at least that by setting such a problem Jones has limited the number of possible answers. Avi Erlich proposes an entirely different psychological reading of the play in *Hamlet's Absent Father,* 1977). Psychological criticism sometimes also reveals its affinities with nineteenth-century character criticism in its attempt to analyze Shakespeare's personality through his plays, as though the works constituted a spiritual autobiography. The terminology of psychological criticism is suspect to some readers because it is at least superficially anachronistic when dealing with a Renaissance writer. The terminology is also sometimes overburdened with technical jargon.

Nonetheless, psychological criticism has afforded many insights into Shakespeare not readily available through other modes of perception. Jones' book makes clear the intensity of Hamlet's revulsion toward women as a result of his mother's inconstancy. At a mythic level, Hamlet's story certainly resembles that of Oedipus, and Freudian criticism is often at its best when it shows us this universal aspect of the human psyche. Freudian terminology need not be anachronistic when it deals with timeless truths. Psychological criticism can reveal to us Shakespeare's preoccupation with certain types of women in his plays, such as the domineering and threatening masculine type (Joan of Arc, Margaret of Anjou) or conversely the long-suffering and patient heroine (Helena in *All's Well,* Hermione in *The Winter's Tale*). Psychological criticism is perhaps most useful in studying family relationships in Shakespeare. It also has much to say about the psychic or sexual connotations of symbol. Influential books include Norman O. Brown's *Life Against Death: The Psychoanalytical Meaning of History* (1959), and Norman Holland's *Psychoanalysis and Shakespeare* (1966) and *The Shakespearean Imagination* (1964).

Mythological Criticism

Related to psychological criticism is the search for archetypal myth in literature, as an expression of the "collective unconscious" of the human race. Behind such an approach lie the anthropological and psychological assumptions of Jung and his followers. One of the earliest studies of this sort was Gilbert Murray's *Hamlet and Orestes* (1914), analyzing the archetype of revenge for a murdered father. Clearly this custom goes far back into tribal prehistory, and emerges in varying but interrelated forms in many different societies. This anthropological universality enables us to look at *Hamlet* as the heightened manifestation of an incredibly basic story. *Hamlet* gives shape to urgings that are a part of our innermost social being. The struggle between the civilized and the primitive goes on in us as in the play *Hamlet*.

The vast interdisciplinary character of myth criticism leaves it vulnerable to charges of speculativeness and glib theorizing. At its best, however, myth criticism can illuminate the nature of our responses as audience to a work of art. Northrop Frye argues, in *A Natural Perspective* (1965), that we respond to mythic patterns by imagining ourselves participating in them communally. The Greek drama emerged, after all, from Dionysiac ritual. All drama celebrates in one form or another the primal myths of vegetation, from the death of the year to the renewal or resurrection of life. In his most influential book, *Anatomy of Criticism* (1957), Frye argues that mythic criticism presents a universal scheme for the investigation of all literature, or all art, since art is itself the ordering of our most primal stirrings. Frye sees in drama (as in other literature) a fourfold correspondence to the cyclical pattern of the year: comedy is associated with spring, romance with summer, tragedy with autumn, and satire with winter. Historically, civilization moves through a recurrent cycle from newness and flourishing to decadence and decay; this cycle expresses itself culturally in a progression from epic and romance to tragedy, to social realism, and finally to irony and satire before the cycle renews itself. Thus, according to Frye, the genres of dramatic literature (and of other literary forms as well) have an absolute and timeless relationship to myth and cultural history. That is why we as audience respond so deeply to form and meaning as contained in genre. C. L. Barber, in *Shakespeare's Festive Comedy* (1959), makes a similar argument: our enjoyment of comedy arises from our intuitive appreciation for such "primitive" social customs as Saturnalian revels, May games, and fertility rites. John Holloway offers an anthropological study of Shakespeare's tragedies in *The Story of the Night* (1961).

Frye's critical system has not been without its detractors. For example, Frederick Crews (*Psychoanalysis and Literary Process,* 1970), argues that Frye's system is too self-contained in its ivory tower, too much an abstract artifact of the critical mind, to be "relevant" to the social purposes of art. Nevertheless, Frye continues to be one of the most influential critics of the late twentieth century.

Typological Criticism

Another controversy of the later twentieth century has to do with the Christian interpretation of Shakespeare. Do the images and allusions of Shakespeare's plays show him to be deeply immersed in a Christian culture inherited from the Middle Ages? Does he reveal a typological cast of mind, so common in medieval literature, whereby a story can suggest through analogy a universal religious archetype? For example, does the mysterious Duke in *Measure for Measure* suggest to us a God-figure, hovering unseen throughout the play to test men's wills and then to present them with an omniscient but merciful judgment? Is the wanton slaughter of the good Cordelia in *King Lear* reminiscent of the Passion of Christ? Can Portia in *The Merchant of Venice* be seen as an angelic figure descending from Belmont into the fallen human world of Venice? Often the operative question we must ask is, how far should such analogy be pursued? Richard II unquestionably likens himself to Christ betrayed by the disciples, and at times the play evokes images of Adam banished from Paradise; but do these allusions coalesce into a sustained analogy?

Among the most enthusiastic searchers after Christian meaning are J. A. Bryant in *Hippolyta's View* (1961) and Roy Battenhouse in *Shakespearean Tragedy: Its Art and Christian Premises* (1969). Their efforts have encountered stern opposition, however. One notable dissenter is Roland M. Frye, whose *Shakespeare and Christian Doctrine* (1963) argues that Shakespeare cannot be shown to have known much Renaissance theology, and that in any case his plays are concerned wtih human drama rather than with otherworldly questions of damnation or salvation. Frye's argument stresses the incompatibility of Christianity and tragedy, as does also D. G. James' *The Dream of Learning* (1951) and Clifford Leech's *Shakespeare's Tragedies and Other Studies in Seventeenth-Century Drama* (1950). Virgil Whitaker's *The Mirror Up to Nature* (1965) sees religion as an essential element in Shakespeare's plays, but argues that Shakespeare uses the religious knowledge of his audience as a shortcut to characterization and meaning rather than as an ideological weapon. The controversy will doubtless long continue, even though the typological critics have had to assume a defensive posture.

Pluralism

In the increasingly diverse world of Shakespeare criticism, several other "schools" certainly ought to be mentioned. A group of critics at the University of Chicago, including R. S. Crane, Richard McKeon, Elder Olson, and Norman Maclean, has espoused a formal or structural approach to criticism using Aristotle as its point of departure. Crane is reacting to the "new" critics who, in his view, have restricted the kinds of answers they could obtain by limiting themselves to one methodology. Critics hostile to the "Chicago" school have responded, however, that Crane's own approach has tended to produce its own dogmatism. Another controversial brand of criticism is the existentialist approach of Jan Kott, whose *Shakespeare: Our Contemporary* (1964, translated from the Polish) sees Shakespeare as a dramatist of the absurd and the grotesque. In this view, Shakespearean plays are often close to "black" comedy or comedy of the absurd. Indeed, Kott has inspired productions that expose traditional values to skepticism and ridicule. Portia and Bassanio in *The Merchant of Venice* become scheming adventurers; Henry V becomes a priggish warmonger. This sardonic undercutting brings Shakespeare closer to modern theatre, but often at the expense of the language and the "meaning" of Shakespeare's plays.

At its best, however, late twentieth-century criticism transcends the splintering effect of a heterogeneous critical tradition to achieve a synthesis that is at once unified and multiform in its vision. The pluralistic approach aims at overall balance and a reinforcement of one critical approach through the methodology of another. Many of the works already cited in this introduction refuse to be constricted by methodological boundaries. The best historical criticism makes use of close explication of the text where appropriate; image patterns can certainly reinforce mythological patterns; typological interpretation, when sensibly applied, serves the cause of image study. Some fine books are so eclectic in their method that one hesitates to apply the label of any one critical school. Among such works are Maynard Mack's *King Lear in Our Time* (1965), David Young's *Something of Great Constancy: The Art of A Midsummer Night's Dream* (1966), R. G. Hunter's *Shakespeare and the Comedy of Forgiveness* (1965), Janet Adelman's *The Common Liar: An Essay on "Antony and Cleopatra"* (1973), Stanley Cavell's "The Avoidance of Love: A Reading of *King Lear*," in *Must We Mean What We Say?* (1969), and Paul Jorgensen's *Our Naked Frailties: Sensational Art and Meaning in Macbeth* (1971).

Whitaker's The Mirror up to Nature (1965) has offered an especially elegant defense of Shakespeare's [illegible] that Shakespeare uses the religious knowledge of his audience as a component to characterization, the dramatic rather than for ideological reasons. This controversy will doubtless continue, even though the [illegible] have had to assume a special position.

Pluralism

To the increasingly diverse world of Shakespeare criticism, several other schools of criticism ought to be mentioned. A group of critics at the University of Chicago, including R. S. Crane, Richard McKeon, Elder Olson, and Norman Maclean, [illegible] the Aristotelian method of studying the structure of art, emphasizing Aristotle's concept of definition. Crane, according to the "neo-Aristotelians" in this view, [illegible] the kinds of answers they could obtain by limiting themselves to one methodology. Critics hostile to the Chicago school have responded, however, that Crane's own approach has tended to produce its own dogmatism. Another controversial brand of criticism is the existentialist approach of Jan Kott, whose Shakespeare Our Contemporary (1964, translated from the Polish) sees Shakespeare as a dramatist of the absurd and the grotesque. In this view, Shakespeare's plays are often seen as "black" comedy or nightmares of the absurd. Indeed Kott has inspired productions that explore traditions of existential skepticism and nihilism [illegible] and Pirandello. [illegible] comes a [illegible] sceptical [illegible] Shakespeare closer to modern themes, but often at the expense of the original meaning of Shakespeare's plays.

A. P. Rossiter, in Angel with Horns (1961), [illegible] reads the splintering [illegible] of an age [illegible] to achieve a synthesis that is at once unified and [illegible] in its vision. The pluralistic approach aims at overall balance and a reinforcement of one critical approach through the methodology of another. Many of the works already cited in this introduction prove to be constructed by methodological compromise. The best historical critics make use of close explication of the text where appropriate; image patterns can certainly reinforce mythological patterns; typological interpretation, when sensitively applied, can enrich our understanding [illegible] are so eclectic in their method that one hesitates to assign the label of any one critical method. Such eclectic works are [illegible] Mack [illegible] (1960), David [illegible] Dream (1966), Cleanth Brooks's [illegible] and the Comedy of Forgiveness [illegible] The Common Liar: An Essay on Antony and Cleopatra (1973), Stanley Cavell's "The Avoidance of Love: A Reading of King Lear," in Must We Mean What We Say? (1969), and Paul Jorgensen's Our Naked Frailties: Sensational Art and Meaning in Macbeth (1971).

tragedy to social realism, and finally to irony and satire before the cycle renews itself. Thus, according to Frye, the heroic, pastoral, romance, and other literary forms as we have them are [illegible] and timeless relationship to myth and cultural history. That is why we as audience respond so deeply to form and structure as contained in genre. C. L. Barber, in Shakespeare's Festive Comedy (1959), makes a similar argument that the rhythm of comedy arises from our intuitive appreciation for such communal social customs as saturnalian revels, May games, and courtship rites. John Holloway offers an anthropological study of Shakespeare's tragedies in The Story of the Night (1961).

Archetypal criticism has not been without its detractors. For example, Frederick Crews [illegible] argues that Frye's system is [illegible] in any way [illegible] to the social purposes of art. Nevertheless, Frye continues to be one of the most influential critics of the late twentieth century.

Theological Criticism

Another controversy of the last twenty years or so has to do with the Christian interpretation of Shakespeare. Do the images and allusions of Shakespeare's plays show him to be deeply immersed in a Christian culture inherited from the Middle Ages? Does he reveal a typological cast of mind, as common in medieval literature, whereby a story can suggest through analogy a universal religious archetype? For example, does the mysterious Duke in Measure for Measure suggest to us a God-figure, beyond our reason, who tests the play to test men's wills and then to present them with an undeserved but needed judgment? Is the Edmund slaughter of the good Cordelia in King Lear reminiscent of the Passion of Christ? Can Portia in The Merchant of Venice be seen as an angelic figure descending from a dimension into the talent-hungry world of Venice? Often the important question we must ask is how far should such analogy be pushed? King Lear unquestionably means himself to be betrayed by the daughter, and at times the play evokes images of what is banished from Paradise, but do these allusions coalesce into a sustained analogy?

Among the most enthusiastic searchers after Christian meaning are Roy Battenhouse in [illegible] (1969), Bryan [illegible] [illegible] and Roy Battenhouse in Shakespearean Tragedy: Its Art and Christian Premises (1969). Their efforts have encountered stern opposition, however. One notable dissenter is Roland M. Frye, whose Shakespeare and Christian Doctrine (1963) argues that Shakespeare cannot be shown to have shown much Renaissance theology, and that in any case the plays are concerned with human drama rather than with otherworldly questions of damnation or salvation. Frye also emphasizes the incompatibility of theology and tragedy, as does [illegible] (1951) and Clifford Leech's Shakespeare's Tragedies and Other Studies in Seventeenth Century Drama (1950). Virgil

The Comedies

The Comedy of Errors

Love's Labor's Lost

The Two Gentlemen of Verona

The Taming of the Shrew

A Midsummer Night's Dream

The Merchant of Venice

Much Ado about Nothing

The Merry Wives of Windsor

As You Like It

Twelfth Night; or, What You Will

All's Well that Ends Well

Measure for Measure

Troilus and Cressida

The Comedy of Errors

The Comedy of Errors is a superb illustration of Shakespeare's "apprenticeship" in comedy. It is more imitative of classical comedy, especially of Plautus, than is Shakespeare's mature work. Its verbal humor, including the scatological jokes about breaking wind, the bawdy jests about cuckold's horns, and the overly ingenious chop-logic banter (as in II,ii) is at times adolescent. The play abounds in the farcical humor of physical abuse, so endearing to children of all ages. It is perhaps the most uncomplicatedly funny of all Shakespeare's plays. Yet the softening touches of Shakespeare's maturity are unmistakably present as well. Shakespeare frames his farce of mistaken identity with old Egeon's tragicomic story of separation, threatened death, and eventual reunion. He adds characters to the Plautine original in order to enhance the love interest and to reconcile Plautus with English moral conventions. He touches upon themes of illusion, madness, and Saturnalian inversion that are to figure prominently in *A Midsummer Night's Dream* and in *Twelfth Night,* a later comedy of mistaken identity. In these respects, *The Comedy of Errors* is both a fascinating prelude to Shakespeare's later development and a rich achievement in its own right. On stage, it has not attracted the greatest Shakespearean actors since it offers no complex or dominating roles, but it has seldom failed to delight audiences.

We cannot be sure precisely how early the play was written. A performance took place on December 28, 1594, at Gray's Inn, before an unruly assembly of lawyers, law students, and their guests. This was probably not the first performance, however. Topical allusions offer hints of an earlier date. When Dromio of Syracuse speaks of France as "arm'd and reverted, making war against her heir" (III,ii), Dromio clearly refers to the Catholic League's opposition to Henry of Navarre, who was the apparent heir to the French throne until 1593, when he became king. Another allusion, to Spain's sending "whole armadoes of carracks," would possibly have lost its comic point soon after the Invincible Armada of 1588. The play's style, characterization, and imitative construction are all consistent with a date between 1589 and 1593.

Whatever the exact date, Shakespeare's youthful fascination with Plautus is manifest. Shakespeare's command of Latin, though sneered at by Ben Jonson, was undoubtedly good enough to have let him read Plautus with pleasure. He must have been drilled in Latin for years as a student in the town of Stratford-upon-Avon, and, if John Aubrey is right, went on to teach Latin as a country schoolmaster before becoming an actor. Indeed, the influence not only of Plautus but of Ovid and Seneca (together with touches of Horace, Catullus, etc.) is a prominent feature of Shakespeare's early work, dramatic and nondramatic. Shakespeare may have consulted Plautus both in the original and in a contemporary translation, as was frequently his custom with non-English sources. From Renaissance Latin editions of Plautus he apparently took the odd designation "Antipholis Sereptus" (i.e., "surreptus," snatched away), which appears in the Folio text in a stage direction at II,i to indicate the twin who was separated from his father. On the other hand, a translation by "W. W."(? William Warner), published in 1595, was registered in 1594 and might have been available earlier to Shakespeare in manuscript.

Plautus had much to offer Shakespeare and his fellow dramatists, especially in the way of tightly organized and complex plot construction. Native English drama of the sixteenth century tended to be episodic and panoramic in its design. Shakespeare's apprenticeship in neoclassical form can be seen in his precise observation of the unities of time and place—those unities which he openly disregarded in most of his later plays. At the play's beginning, Egeon is informed that he has until sundown to raise his ransom money, and the play then moves toward that point in time with periodic observations that it is now noon, now 2 o'clock, and so on. (At one point time even seems to go backwards, but that is part of the illusion of madness.) The action is restricted to the city of Ephesus; events that have happened elsewhere, at an earlier time (such as the separation of the Antipholus family), are told to us by persons in the play such as old Egeon. Although Shakespeare's company did not employ the sort of painted scenery drawn in perspective used by continental neoclassicists, with fixed locations for houses facing on a street, the original production of this play may nonetheless have used one stage "house" or door to represent the dwelling of Antipholus of Ephesus (the Phoenix) throughout the drama. The entire play can be staged as if all the action occurs in the vicinity of this single "house," with the Abbey near at hand. Never again does Shakespeare utilize such a neoclassical stage.

These unities of time and place are mechanical matters, but they do also harmonize with a more essential unity of action. The story moves, as though in perfect accord with neoclassical five-act theory, from exposition and complication to climax, anagnorisis (discovery), and peripeteia (reversal of fortune). The brilliance of the plotting is decidedly Plautine. Shakespeare pushes to its limit the interweaving of comic misunderstandings only to unravel all these seemingly tightly woven knots with ease. Yet the imitation of Plautus, even in matters of construction, is by no means slavish, for Shakespeare borrows both from Plautus' farce on the mistaken identity of twins *(The Menaechmi)* and from Plautus' best-known comedy *(Amphitruo),* in which a husband and his servant are excluded from their own house while a disguised visitor usurps the master's role within. Such ingenious adaptations and rearrangements were common among neoclassical dramatists like Ariosto; and, although Shakespeare seems not to have used any of the sixteenth-century analogues to this play, he does reveal an acquaintance with neoclassical comedy and an ability to compete with the best that Europe had to offer in this vein. Such versatility is astonishing in a young dramatist who was to reveal himself in time as far less of a neoclassicist than a native English writer. Moreover, even if his self-imposed neoclassical training was only an apprenticeship, it was to prove invaluable to Shakespeare. Despite his later tendency toward "romantic" plotting—toward the depiction of multiple actions extending over widely separated spaces and extended periods of time—Shakespeare's greatest comedies continue to point toward the same gratifying resolution of dramatic conflict in a single and well-structured denouement.

For all its Plautine skill of design, however, *The Comedy of Errors* is quite far removed from *The Menaechmi* in tone and spirit. Gone are the cynicism, the satirical hardness, and the amoral tone of the Roman original. The characters, though still recognizable as types, are humanized. The familiar Plautine parasite is excluded entirely. The usual clever servant happily becomes the Dromio Twins. Plautus' quack Doctor, Medicus, is hilariously transmuted into Dr. Pinch, a pedantic schoolmaster. The Courtezan's role is no longer prominent. Instead Shakespeare creates Luciana, the virtuous sister of Adriana, who pleads the cause of forbearance in marriage and who eventually becomes the bride of Antipholus of Syracuse. *The Comedy of Errors* does not end, as do most of Shakespeare's later comedies, with a parade of couples to the altar, but the marriage of Antipholus and Luciana is at least one important step in that direction. Besides, we are told of yet another marriage still to come—that of Dromio of Ephesus to Luce, the fat kitchen wench. This belowstairs parody of wedded affection is thoroughly English in character, and recalls a similar mirroring of courtship among the comic servants of Medwall's *Fulgens and Lucrece* (c. 1497). The motif is not sufficiently stressed to threaten the unity of the main plot, but the potentiality for double plotting is unmistakable.

An even more significant contrast to Plautine farce is to be found in the romantic saga of old Egeon and his long-lost wife, the Abbess. Their story is one not of mistaken identity (though that contributes to the denouement) but of painful separation, wandering, and reunion. Indeed, the note struck at the beginning of the play might seem tragic, were we not already attuned to the conventional romantic expectation that separated members of a family are likely to be restored to one another again. Egeon, threatened with immediate execution, unfolds to us a narrative of wedded bliss interrupted by the malignancy of Fortune. In contrast to the tightly controlled unity of time of the farcical action, the romantic narrative extends (by recollection) over many years of error and suffering. Egeon's tragicomic story of testing and of patient endurance is very much like that of *Apollonius of Tyre,* a popular tale used by Shakespeare in his late romance *Pericles* (c. 1606–1608). The conventions of this sort of romance, ultimately Greek in origin, stress improbability: identical twins who can be told apart only by birthmarks, a storm at sea splitting a vessel in half and neatly dividing the family, and so on. The sea is emblematic of unpredictable Fortune, taking away with one hand and restoring with the other. The wife who is lost at sea, like her counterpart in *Apollonius* or *Pericles,* takes to a life of cloistered devotion, suggesting a pattern of symbolic death, healing, and ultimate rebirth. The ending of *The Comedy of Errors* has just a hint of death restored mysteriously to life: "After so long grief, such Nativity!"

Egeon's story of endurance counterpoints the farce in yet another way. His arraignment before the Duke of Ephesus introduces into the play a "tragic" world of law, punishment, and death. Egeon's date with the executioner is not illusory. His predicament is the result of the bitter "mortal and intestine jars" between two cities caught in a frenzy of economic reprisals. The law cannot be mericful, even though the unfairness of Egeon's plight is manifest to everyone, including the Duke. These potentially tragic factors must not be overstressed, for the first scene is brief and we are reassured by the play's hilarious tone (and by our surmising that Egeon is father of the Antipholus twins) that all will be well. Still, Shakespeare's addition of this romance plot suggests his restlessness with pure farce. As in his later comedies, which are virtually all threatened by catastrophes, the denouement of *The Comedy of Errors* is deepened into something approaching miraculous recovery. Moreover, the backdrop of a near-tragic world of genuine suffering heightens our appreciation of comic unreality in the self-contained world of Plautine farce, and stresses the illusory nature of the dilemmas arising out of purely mistaken identity. Such delusions are all the more comic because they are the delusions that supposedly sane people suffer: contentiousness and jealousy in marriage, concern for respectable appearances among one's neighbors, and the suspicion that one is always being cheated in money matters. These are the chimeras which, by being made to look so plausible and yet so patently insane, are farcically exploited in Shakespeare's comic device: the inversion of madness and sanity, dreaming and waking, illusion and reality.

What happens when the behavior of one twin is mistaken for that of the other? The situation is of course amusing in itself, but it also serves as a test of the other characters, to discover what mad hypotheses they will construct. Adriana, faced with her husband's seeming refusal to come home to dinner, launches into a jealous tirade against husbands who neglect their wives for courtesans. The illusory situation, in other words, brings out her latent fears. We understand better now why she acts shrewishly: she fears rejection and the fading of her beauty, and imagines that her fading beauty may be the cause of her husband's neglect. Actually, even as she speaks, her dutiful husband is busy making arrangements about a chain he means to give Adriana; but, when subsequently he is locked out of his own house, and jumps to the conclusion that Adriana is being faithless, he resolves in his fury to bestow the chain on a courtesan in order to "spite my wife." He would actually do so, were he not saved from this destructively revengeful impulse by the beneficently comic action of the farcical plot: through mistaken identity, the chain is delivered into the hands of his twin. Once again, illusion has prompted a character to assume the worst, to reveal his suspicions of a plot against him. And so it goes when Antipholus of Ephesus is arrested for nonpayment of the chain (he assumes that all merchants are thieves) or is denied his bail money by the servant he thinks he sent to fetch it (he assumes that all servants are thieves). We laugh at the endless capacity of the human mind for distortions of this self-punishing sort.

The metaphor used most often to convey this sense of bewilderment, even a confusion about one's own identity, is that of metamorphosis. All have drunk of Circe's cup (V,i) and have been transformed into animals—most of them into asses. All have hearkened to the mermaid's song, and are enchanted. Ephesus, they conclude, must be haunted by sorcerers, witches, goblins, and spirits (IV,iii). In such a mad world the characters assume a license to embark on Saturnalian holiday. The experience of transformation thus leads to various forms of "release" from ordinary social behavior, but the experience is also disturbing, and continually reminds the characters of exorcism, hell, and devils. The characters can explain their inverted world only by assuming that all men are lunatic, all honest women whores, and all true men thieves. "Do you know me, sir? . . . Am I myself?" "Am I in earth, or heaven, or in hell? Sleeping or waking' mad or well advis'd?" It is both reassuring and hilariously anticlimactic that these questionings can finally be dispelled by the most mundane of explanations: there are two Antipholuses and two Dromios.

This playfulness about illusion should not be overemphasized, for the play expends most of its energies in farce. The Dromios, with their incessant drubbings, are often the center of interest in performance, and rightly so. Shakespeare employs no behind-the-scenes manipulator of illusion, such as Puck in *A Midsummer Night's Dream* or the Duke in *Measure for Measure*. His interest in the metaphor of the world as a stage is discernible only as the foreshadowing of greatness to come. Nevertheless, Shakespeare's alterations of Plautus amply reveal the philosophic and idealistic direction that his subsequent comedy is to take.

The Comedy of Errors

[*Dramatis Personae*

SOLINUS, *Duke of Ephesus.*
EGEON, *a merchant of Syracuse.*

ANTIPHOLUS OF EPHESUS, ANTIPHOLUS OF SYRACUSE, } *twin brothers, and sons to Egeon and Emilia.*

DROMIO OF EPHESUS, DROMIO OF SYRACUSE, } *twin brothers, and attendants on the two Antipholuses.*

BALTHAZAR, *a merchant.*
ANGELO, *a goldsmith.*
FIRST MERCHANT, *friend to Antipholus of Syracuse.*
SECOND MERCHANT, *to whom Angelo is a debtor.*
PINCH, *a schoolmaster.*

EMILIA, *wife to Egeon, an abbess at Ephesus.*
ADRIANA, *wife to Antipholus of Ephesus.*
LUCIANA, *her sister.*
LUCE, *servant to Adriana, (also known as* NELL*).*
A COURTEZAN.

JAILER, OFFICERS, *and other* ATTENDANTS.

SCENE: *Ephesus.*]

ACT I • SCENE I

Enter the Duke of Ephesus, with [*Egeon*] *the Merchant of Syracusa, Jailer, and other Attendants.*

EGEON
Proceed, Solinus, to procure my fall,
And by the doom of death end woes and all. 2
DUKE
Merchant of Syracusa, plead no more.
I am not partial to infringe our laws. 4
The enmity and discord which of late
Sprung from the rancorous outrage of your Duke
To merchants, our well-dealing countrymen,
Who, wanting guilders to redeem their lives, 8
Have seal'd his rigorous statutes with their bloods, 9
Excludes all pity from our threat'ning looks.
For since the mortal and intestine jars 11
'Twixt thy seditious countrymen and us,
It hath in solemn synods been decreed,
Both by the Syracusians and ourselves,
To admit no traffic to our adverse towns. 15
Nay, more, if any born at Ephesus be seen 16
At any Syracusian marts and fairs;
Again, if any Syracusian born
Come to the bay of Ephesus, he dies,
His goods confiscate to the Duke's dispose, 20
Unless a thousand marks be levied 21
To quit the penalty and to ransom him. 22
Thy substance, valued at the highest rate, 23
Cannot amount unto a hundred marks;
Therefore by law thou art condemn'd to die.
EGEON
Yet this my comfort: when your words are done,
My woes end likewise with the evening sun.
DUKE
Well, Syracusian, say in brief the cause
Why thou departed'st from thy native home,
And for what cause thou cam'st to Ephesus.
EGEON
A heavier task could not have been impos'd
Than I to speak my griefs unspeakable.
Yet, that the world may witness that my end
Was wrought by nature, not by vile offense, 34
I'll utter what my sorrow gives me leave.
In Syracusa was I born, and wed
Unto a woman, happy but for me,
And by me, had not our hap been bad. 38
With her I liv'd in joy; our wealth increas'd
By prosperous voyages I often made
To Epidamium, till my factor's death 41
And the great care of goods at random left
Drew me from kind embracements of my spouse;
From whom my absence was not six months old
Before herself, almost at fainting under
The pleasing punishment that women bear,
Had made provision for her following me
And soon and safe arrived where I was.
There had she not been long but she became
A joyful mother of two goodly sons,
And, which was strange, the one so like the other
As could not be distinguish'd but by names. 52
That very hour and in the self-same inn
A mean woman was delivered 54
Of such a burden, male twins, both alike.

I.i. Location: In Ephesus, either in a public place or at the palace of Duke Solinus. The play may have been staged according to classical practice with three visible doors backstage representing the "houses" of Antipholus of Ephesus (in the center), the Courtezan, and the Priory, with the stage itself representing a street or public place. Alternatively, the stage may have been open and unlocalized.
s.d. Syracusa Syracuse, in Sicily **2 doom** judgment **4 partial** predisposed, biased

8 wanting lacking. **guilders** money; the guilder was a Dutch coin worth about 1 shilling 8 pence. **9 seal'd** ratified. **bloods** i.e., lives **11 mortal** deadly. **intestine** (The usual meaning, "civil" or "internal," may be used here with *mortal* as an intensifier.) **jars** quarrels **15 adverse** hostile **16 Ephesus** a port on the Aegean coast of modern Turkey **20 confiscate** confiscated. **dispose** disposal **21 marks** money worth 13 shillings 4 pence **22 quit** pay **23 Thy substance** the sum total of your wealth **34 nature** i.e., by natural affection, here, a father's love **38 hap** fortune **41 Epidamium** a port on the coast of modern Albania. **factor's** agent's **52 As** that they **54 mean** of low birth

Those, for their parents were exceeding poor,
I bought and brought up to attend my sons.
My wife, not meanly proud of two such boys,
Made daily motions for our home return;
Unwilling I agreed. Alas, too soon
We came aboard.
A league from Epidamium had we sail'd,
Before the always wind-obeying deep
Gave any tragic instance of our harm.
But longer did we not retain much hope;
For what obscured light the heavens did grant
Did but convey unto our fearful minds
A doubtful warrant of immediate death,
Which, though myself would gladly have embrac'd,
Yet the incessant weepings of my wife,
Weeping before for what she saw must come,
And piteous plainings of the pretty babes,
That mourn'd for fashion, ignorant what to fear,
Forc'd me to seek delays for them and me.
And this it was, for other means was none:
The sailors sought for safety by our boat,
And left the ship, then sinking-ripe, to us.
My wife, more careful for the latter-born,
Had fast'ned him unto a small spare mast,
Such as seafaring men provide for storms;
To him one of the other twins was bound,
Whilst I had been like heedful of the other.
The children thus dispos'd, my wife and I,
Fixing our eyes on whom our care was fix'd,
Fast'ned ourselves at either end the mast,
And, floating straight, obedient to the stream,
Was carried towards Corinth, as we thought.
At length the sun, gazing upon the earth,
Dispers'd those vapors that offended us;
And by the benefit of his wished light
The seas wax'd calm, and we discovered
Two ships from far, making amain to us,
Of Corinth that, of Epidaurus this.
But ere they came—O, let me say no more!
Gather the sequel by that went before.

DUKE

Nay, forward, old man. Do not break off so,
For we may pity, though not pardon thee.

EGEON

O, had the gods done so, I had not now
Worthily term'd them merciless to us!
For, ere the ships could meet by twice five leagues,
We were encount'red by a mighty rock,
Which being violently borne upon,
Our helpful ship was splitted in the midst;
So that, in this unjust divorce of us,
Fortune had left to both of us alike
What to delight in, what to sorrow for.
Her part, poor soul, seeming as burdened
With lesser weight, but not with lesser woe,
Was carried with more speed before the wind,
And in our sight they three were taken up
By fishermen of Corinth, as we thought.
At length, another ship had seiz'd on us,
And, knowing whom it was their hap to save,
Gave healthful welcome to their shipwrack'd guests,
And would have reft the fishers of their prey
Had not their bark been very slow of sail;
And therefore homeward did they bend their
course.
Thus have you heard me sever'd from my bliss,
That by misfortunes was my life prolong'd,
To tell sad stories of my own mishaps.

DUKE

And, for the sake of them thou sorrowest for,
Do me the favor to dilate at full
What hath befall'n of them and thee till now.

EGEON

My youngest boy, and yet my eldest care,
At eighteen years became inquisitive
After his brother, and importun'd me
That his attendant—so his case was like,
Reft of his brother, but retain'd his name—
Might bear him company in the quest of him,
Whom whilst I labored of a love to see,
I hazarded the loss of whom I lov'd.
Five summers have I spent in farthest Greece,
Roaming clean through the bounds of Asia,
And, coasting homeward, came to Ephesus—
Hopeless to find, yet loath to leave unsought
Or that or any place that harbors men.
But here must end the story of my life;
And happy were I in my timely death,
Could all my travels warrant me they live.

DUKE

Hapless Egeon, whom the fates have mark'd
To bear the extremity of dire mishap!
Now, trust me, were it not against our laws,
Against my crown, my oath, my dignity,
Which princes, would they, may not disannul,
My soul should sue as advocate for thee.
But, though thou art adjudged to the death
And passed sentence may not be recall'd
But to our honor's great disparagement,
Yet will I favor thee in what I can.
Therefore, merchant, I'll limit thee this day
To seek thy life by beneficial help.
Try all the friends thou hast in Ephesus;
Beg thou, or borrow, to make up the sum,
And live; if no, then thou art doom'd to die.
Jailer, take him to thy custody.

JAILER

I will, my lord.

58 not meanly to no small degree **59 motions** proposals **64 instance** proof, sign **68 doubtful** ominous **72 plainings** wailings **73 for fashion** in imitation **77 sinking-ripe** ready to sink **78 careful** anxious. **latter-born** (Cf. I. 124, however, from which we learn that the younger or "latter-born" was saved with the father.) **84 whom** him on whom **86 straight** at once **89 vapors** clouds. **offended** troubled **92 making amain** proceeding at full speed **93 Epidaurus** a Greek town southwest of Athens and Corinth; or possibly Dubrovnik, on the Adriatic coast **95 that** that which **103 helpful ship** i.e., the mast **106 What** something

107 as as if **114 healthful** saving **115 reft** bereft **122 dilate at full** relate at length **127 so . . . like** in a similar situation **128 Reft . . . name** (Evidently Egeon, presuming that the lost son and servant are dead, has given their names to the surviving twin brothers.) **130 labored of a love** i.e., longed greatly **133 clean** entirely **136 Or** either **138 timely** speedy; opportune **139 travels** "travails" or hardships as well as *travels*. **warrant** assure **144 would they** even if they wished. **disannul** annul, cancel **146 the death** i.e., death by judicial sentence

EGEON
Hopeless and helpless doth Egeon wend,
But to procrastinate his lifeless end. *Exeunt.*

[SCENE II]

Enter Antipholus [of Syracuse], [the First] Merchant, and Dromio [of Syracuse].

FIRST MERCHANT
Therefore give out you are of Epidamium,
Lest that your goods too soon be confiscate.
This very day a Syracusian merchant
Is apprehended for arrival here,
And, not being able to buy out his life
According to the statute of the town,
Dies ere the weary sun set in the west.
There is your money that I had to keep.
[Gives money.]

ANTIPHOLUS S.
Go bear it to the Centaur, where we host,
And stay there, Dromio, till I come to thee.
[Gives money.]
Within this hour it will be dinner-time.
Till that, I'll view the manners of the town,
Peruse the traders, gaze upon the buildings,
And then return and sleep within mine inn,
For with long travel I am stiff and weary.
Get thee away.

DROMIO S.
Many a man would take you at your word,
And go indeed, having so good a mean.
Exit Dromio [of Syracuse]

ANTIPHOLUS S.
A trusty villain, sir, that very oft,
When I am dull with care and melancholy,
Lightens my humor with his merry jests.
What, will you walk with me about the town,
And then go to my inn and dine with me?

FIRST MERCHANT
I am invited, sir, to certain merchants,
Of whom I hope to make much benefit;
I crave your pardon. Soon at five o'clock,
Please you, I'll meet with you upon the mart
And afterward consort you till bed-time;
My present business calls me from you now.

ANTIPHOLUS S.
Farewell till then. I will go lose myself
And wander up and down to view the city.

FIRST MERCHANT
Sir, I commend you to your own content. *Exit.*

ANTIPHOLUS S.
He that commends me to mine own content
Commends me to the thing I cannot get.
I to the world am like a drop of water
That in the ocean seeks another drop,
Who, falling there to find his fellow forth,
Unseen, inquisitive, confounds himself;
So I, to find a mother and a brother,
In quest of them, unhappy, lose myself.

Enter Dromio of Ephesus.

Here comes the almanac of my true date.
What now? How chance thou art return'd so soon?

DROMIO E.
Return'd so soon! Rather approach'd too late:
The capon burns, the pig falls from the spit,
The clock hath strucken twelve upon the bell;
My mistress made it one upon my cheek.
She is so hot because the meat is cold;
The meat is cold because you come not home;
You come not home because you have no stomach;
You have no stomach having broke your fast.
But we that know what 'tis to fast and pray
Are penitent for your default today.

ANTIPHOLUS S.
Stop in your wind, sir. Tell me this, I pray:
Where have you left the money that I gave you?

DROMIO E.
O—sixpence that I had a Wednesday last
To pay the saddler for my mistress' crupper?
The saddler had it, sir; I kept it not.

ANTIPHOLUS S.
I am not in a sportive humor now.
Tell me, and dally not, where is the money?
We being strangers here, how dar'st thou trust
So great a charge from thine own custody?

DROMIO E.
I pray you, jest, sir, as you sit at dinner.
I from my mistress come to you in post;
If I return, I shall be post indeed,
For she will score your fault upon my pate.
Methinks your maw, like mine, should be your
clock
And strike you home without a messenger.

ANTIPHOLUS S.
Come, Dromio, come, these jests are out of season;
Reserve them till a merrier hour than this.
Where is the gold I gave in charge to thee?

DROMIO E.
To me, sir? Why, you gave no gold to me.

ANTIPHOLUS S.
Come on, sir knave, have done your foolishness
And tell me how thou hast dispos'd thy charge.

DROMIO E.
My charge was but to fetch you from the mart
Home to your house, the Phoenix, sir, to dinner;

I.ii. Location: The Mart.
8 keep safeguard **9 Centaur** the name of an inn, identified by its sign over the door. **host** lodge **11 dinner-time** i.e., noon **18 mean** means, i.e., the money **19 villain** servant. (Said good-humoredly.) **21 humor** mood, disposition **26 Soon at** about **28 consort** accompany **30 lose myself** roam freely

35 to in relation to **37 forth** out **38 confounds himself** mingles indistinguishably **40 unhappy** unlucky **41 almanac . . . date** (I.e., being born in the same hour, Dromio serves as an almanac by which Antipholus can see his age.) **42 How chance** how comes it **46 made it one** i.e., struck (as a clock would strike one o'clock) **49 stomach** appetite **52 penitent** doing penance (i.e., suffering hunger). **default** fault **53 wind** i.e., words **56 crupper** leather strap on a saddle that is passed under the horse's tail in order to keep the saddle from riding forward **61 from** out of **63 post** haste **64 post** doorpost of a tavern used for keeping reckonings **66 maw** stomach. (Applied usually to animals.) **75 Phoenix** the sign of Antipholus of Ephesus' shop. (He lives and carries on his business in the same dwelling.)

My mistress and her sister stays for you.

ANTIPHOLUS S.
Now, as I am a Christian, answer me
In what safe place you have bestow'd my money,
Or I shall break that merry sconce of yours
That stands on tricks when I am undispos'd.
Where is the thousand marks thou hadst of me?

DROMIO E.
I have some marks of yours upon my pate,
Some of my mistress' marks upon my shoulders,
But not a thousand marks between you both.
If I should pay your worship those again,
Perchance you will not bear them patiently.

ANTIPHOLUS S.
Thy mistress' marks? What mistress, slave, hast thou?

DROMIO E.
Your worship's wife, my mistress at the Phoenix,
She that doth fast till you come home to dinner
And prays that you will hie you home to dinner.

ANTIPHOLUS S.
What, wilt thou flout me thus unto my face,
Being forbid? There, take you that, sir knave.
[*Beats him.*]

DROMIO E.
What mean you, sir? For God sake, hold your hands!
Nay, an you will not, sir, I'll take my heels.
Exit Dromio [*of*] *Ephesus.*

ANTIPHOLUS S.
Upon my life, by some device or other
The villain is o'erraught of all my money.
They say this town is full of cozenage,
As, nimble jugglers that deceive the eye,
Dark-working sorcerers that change the mind,
Soul-killing witches that deform the body,
Disguised cheaters, prating mountebanks,
And many such-like liberties of sin.
If it prove so, I will be gone the sooner.
I'll to the Centaur to go seek this slave;
I greatly fear my money is not safe. *Exit.*

ACT II • [SCENE I]

Enter Adriana, Wife to Antipholus [*of Ephesus*], *with Luciana, her Sister.*

ADRIANA
Neither my husband nor the slave return'd,
That in such haste I sent to seek his master!
Sure, Luciana, it is two o'clock.

LUCIANA
Perhaps some merchant hath invited him,
And from the mart he's somewhere gone to dinner.
Good sister, let us dine and never fret.
A man is master of his liberty;
Time is their master, and when they see time
They'll go or come. If so, be patient, sister.

ADRIANA
Why should their liberty than ours be more?

LUCIANA
Because their business still lies out o' door.

ADRIANA
Look when I serve him so, he takes it ill.

LUCIANA
O, know he is the bridle of your will.

ADRIANA
There's none but asses will be bridled so.

LUCIANA
Why, headstrong liberty is lash'd with woe.
There's nothing situate under heaven's eye
But hath his bound, in earth, in sea, in sky.
The beasts, the fishes, and the winged fowls
Are their males' subjects and at their controls.
Man, more divine, the master of all these,
Lord of the wide world and wild wat'ry seas,
Indued with intellectual sense and souls,
Of more preeminence than fish and fowls,
Are masters to their females, and their lords.
Then let your will attend on their accords.

ADRIANA
This servitude makes you to keep unwed.

LUCIANA
Not this, but troubles of the marriage-bed.

ADRIANA
But, were you wedded, you would bear some sway.

LUCIANA
Ere I learn love, I'll practice to obey.

ADRIANA
How if your husband start some other where?

LUCIANA
Till he come home again, I would forbear.

ADRIANA
Patience unmov'd! No marvel though she pause;
They can be meek that have no other cause.
A wretched soul, bruis'd with adversity,
We bid be quiet when we hear it cry;
But were we burd'ned with like weight of pain,
As much or more we should ourselves complain.
So thou, that hast no unkind mate to grieve thee,
With urging helpless patience would relieve me;
But, if thou live to see like right bereft,
This fool-begg'd patience in thee will be left.

LUCIANA
Well, I will marry one day, but to try.
Here comes your man; now is your husband nigh.

Enter Dromio of Ephesus.

ADRIANA
Say, is your tardy master now at hand?

DROMIO E. Nay, he's at two hands with me, and that my two ears can witness.

78 bestow'd deposited **79 sconce** head **80 stands on** insists on, engages in **94 an** if **96 o'erraught** overreached, cheated **97 cozenage** cheating **101 mountebanks** charlatans **102 liberties of sin** persons allowed improper freedom to sin

II.i. Location: Before the Phoenix, the house and shop of Antipholus of Ephesus. **11 still** always **12 Look when** whenever **15 lash'd** scourged, castigated; also, bound **17 his** its **22 intellectual sense** reason **25 accords** wishes **30 start . . . where** i.e., go off elsewhere, after other women **33 other cause** cause to be otherwise **39 helpless** unavailing, unprofitable **40 see . . . bereft** see your rights similarly taken away **41 This . . . left** you will abandon this foolishly-urged patience **45 at two hands** i.e., he boxed my ears

ADRIANA
Say, didst thou speak with him? Know'st thou his mind?
DROMIO E.
Ay, ay, he told his mind upon mine ear.
Beshrew his hand, I scarce could understand it.
LUCIANA
Spake he so doubtfully, thou couldst not feel his meaning?
DROMIO E. Nay, he struck so plainly, I could too well feel his blows; and withal so doubtfully that I could scarce understand them.
ADRIANA
But say, I prithee, is he coming home?
It seems he hath great care to please his wife.
DROMIO E.
Why, mistress, sure my master is horn-mad.
ADRIANA
Horn-mad, thou villain?
DROMIO E. I mean not cuckold-mad;
But, sure, he is stark mad.
When I desir'd him to come home to dinner,
He ask'd me for a thousand marks in gold.
" 'Tis dinner-time," quoth I; "My gold!" quoth he.
"Your meat doth burn," quoth I; "My gold!" quoth he.
"Will you come?" quoth I; "My gold!" quoth he,
"Where is the thousand marks I gave thee, villain?"
"The pig," quoth I, "is burn'd"; "My gold!" quoth he.
"My mistress, sir," quoth I; "Hang up thy mistress!
I know not thy mistress; out on thy mistress!"
LUCIANA Quoth who?
DROMIO E. Quoth my master.
"I know," quoth he, "no house, no wife, no mistress."
So that my errand, due unto my tongue,
I thank him, I bare home upon my shoulders;
For, in conclusion, he did beat me there.
ADRIANA
Go back again, thou slave, and fetch him home.
DROMIO E.
Go back again, and be new beaten home?
For God's sake, send some other messenger.
ADRIANA
Back, slave, or I will break thy pate across.
DROMIO E.
And he will bless that cross with other beating.
Between you I shall have a holy head.
ADRIANA
Hence, prating peasant! Fetch thy master home.
DROMIO E.
Am I so round with you as you with me,
That like a football you do spurn me thus?
You spurn me hence, and he will spurn me hither.
If I last in this service, you must case me in leather.
[*Exit.*]
LUCIANA
Fie, how impatience loureth in your face!
ADRIANA
His company must do his minions grace,
Whilst I at home starve for a merry look.
Hath homely age th' alluring beauty took
From my poor cheek? Then he hath wasted it.
Are my discourses dull? Barren my wit?
If voluble and sharp discourse be marr'd,
Unkindness blunts it more than marble hard.
Do their gay vestments his affections bait?
That's not my fault; he's master of my state.
What ruins are in me that can be found,
By him not ruin'd? Then is he the ground
Of my defeatures. My decayed fair
A sunny look of his would soon repair.
But, too unruly deer, he breaks the pale
And feeds from home; poor I am but his stale.
LUCIANA
Self-harming jealousy! Fie, beat it hence!
ADRIANA
Unfeeling fools can with such wrongs dispense.
I know his eye doth homage otherwhere,
Or else what lets it but he would be here?
Sister, you know he promis'd me a chain;
Would that alone, alone he would detain,
So he would keep fair quarter with his bed!
I see the jewel best enameled
Will lose his beauty; yet the gold bides still
That others touch, and often touching will
Wear gold; and no man that hath a name,
By falsehood and corruption doth it shame.
Since that my beauty cannot please his eye,
I'll weep what 's left away, and weeping die.
LUCIANA
How many fond fools serve mad jealousy!
Exit [*with Adriana*].

[SCENE II]

Enter Antipholus [*of Syracuse*].

ANTIPHOLUS S.
The gold I gave to Dromio is laid up
Safe at the Centaur, and the heedful slave
Is wand'red forth, in care to seek me out
By computation and mine host's report.

48 told (punning on *tolled*) **49 Beshrew** "bad luck to." **understand** (with pun on *stand under;* also in l. 53) **56 horn-mad** mad as a horned beast (with a quibble on the sense of *rage at being made a cuckold*) **71 due . . . tongue** which I should have delivered by my tongue **72 I bare . . . shoulders** I took in the form of a beating **78 he . . . cross** i.e., he will add further devotion in the form of a beating. (There is a pun on *to bless,* to wound, from the French *blesser. Cross* is a quibble on *across* of the previous line.) **79 holy** (punning on the sense *full of holes*) **81 round** plain-spoken (with pun on the sense of *spherical*)

85 loureth frowns, scowls **86 minions** paramours, darlings. **grace** honor, favor **90 discourses** conversations **93 affections** passions. **bait** entice **94 state** outward estate, condition, i.e., clothes **96 ground** cause **97 defeatures** disfigurements. **decayed fair** impaired or perished beauty **99 pale** enclosure **100 from** away from. **stale** dupe, laughingstock (with a pun on *stale,* tiresomely lacking in freshness; she is stale to him, he dear [*deer*] to her) **102 dispense** pardon, condone by dispensation **104 lets** hinders **106 Would . . . detain** would that he would withhold only that token of his affection (?) **107 So . . . bed** provided he would remain faithful to his marriage bed **108–111 I see . . . name** (A difficult passage, evidently corrupt. Adriana seemingly compares her beauty to that of a well-enameled jewel that tarnishes in time through neglect, whereas some beauty, like gold, is often touched and hence retains its luster through use; this latter kind of beauty is not shamed through falsehood and corruption by men of "name" or reputation like Antipholus of Ephesus, as Adriana feels she is being shamed.) **115 fond** doting

I could not speak with Dromio since at first
I sent him from the mart. See, here he comes.

Enter Dromio of Syracusa.

How now, sir, is your merry humor alter'd?
As you love strokes, so jest with me again.
You know no Centaur? You receiv'd no gold?
Your mistress sent to have me home to dinner?
My house was at the Phoenix? Wast thou mad,
That thus so madly thou didst answer me?

DROMIO S.
What answer, sir? When spake I such a word?

ANTIPHOLUS S.
Even now, even here, not half an hour since.

DROMIO S.
I did not see you since you sent me hence,
Home to the Centaur, with the gold you gave me.

ANTIPHOLUS S.
Villain, thou didst deny the gold's receipt
And told'st me of a mistress and a dinner;
For which, I hope, thou felt'st I was displeas'd.

DROMIO S.
I am glad to see you in this merry vein.
What means this jest? I pray you, master, tell me.

ANTIPHOLUS S.
Yea, dost thou jeer and flout me in the teeth?
Think'st thou I jest? Hold, take thou that, and that.
Beats Dromio.

DROMIO S.
Hold, sir, for God's sake! Now your jest is earnest.
Upon what bargain do you give it me?

ANTIPHOLUS S.
Because that I familiarly sometimes
Do use you for my fool and chat with you,
Your sauciness will jest upon my love
And make a common of my serious hours.
When the sun shines let foolish gnats make sport,
But creep in crannies when he hides his beams.
If you will jest with me, know my aspect
And fashion your demeanor to my looks,
Or I will beat this method in your sconce.

DROMIO S. Sconce call you it? So you would leave battering, I had rather have it a head. An you use these blows long, I must get a sconce for my head and insconce it too, or else I shall seek my wit in my shoulders. But, I pray, sir, why am I beaten?

ANTIPHOLUS S. Dost thou not know?

DROMIO S. Nothing, sir, but that I am beaten.

ANTIPHOLUS S. Shall I tell you why?

DROMIO S. Ay, sir, and wherefore; for they say every why hath a wherefore.

ANTIPHOLUS S. Why, first—for flouting me; and then, wherefore—for urging it the second time to me.

DROMIO S.
Was there ever any man thus beaten out of season,
When in the why and the wherefore is neither
rhyme nor reason?
Well, sir, I thank you.

ANTIPHOLUS S. Thank me, sir, for what?

DROMIO S. Marry, sir, for this something that you gave me for nothing.

ANTIPHOLUS S. I'll make you amends next, to give you nothing for something. But say, sir, is it dinner-time?

DROMIO S. No, sir, I think the meat wants that I have.

ANTIPHOLUS S. In good time, sir, what's that?

DROMIO S. Basting.

ANTIPHOLUS S. Well, sir, then 'twill be dry.

DROMIO S. If it be, sir, I pray you, eat none of it.

ANTIPHOLUS S. Your reason?

DROMIO S. Lest it make you choleric and purchase me another dry basting.

ANTIPHOLUS S. Well, sir, learn to jest in good time. There's a time for all things.

DROMIO S. I durst have denied that, before you were so choleric.

ANTIPHOLUS S. By what rule, sir?

DROMIO S. Marry, sir, by a rule as plain as the plain bald pate of father Time himself.

ANTIPHOLUS S. Let's hear it.

DROMIO S. There's no time for a man to recover his hair that grows bald by nature.

ANTIPHOLUS S. May he not do it by fine and recovery?

DROMIO S. Yes, to pay a fine for a periwig and recover the lost hair of another man.

ANTIPHOLUS S. Why is Time such a niggard of hair, being, as it is, so plentiful an excrement?

DROMIO S. Because it is a blessing that he bestows on beasts; and what he hath scanted men in hair he hath given them in wit.

ANTIPHOLUS S. Why, but there's many a man hath more hair than wit.

DROMIO S. Not a man of those but he hath the wit to lose his hair.

ANTIPHOLUS S. Why, thou didst conclude hairy men plain dealers without wit.

DROMIO S. The plainer dealer, the sooner lost; yet he loseth it in a kind of jollity.

ANTIPHOLUS S. For what reason?

DROMIO S. For two; and sound ones too.

ANTIPHOLUS S. Nay, not sound, I pray you.

DROMIO S. Sure ones then.

ANTIPHOLUS S. Nay, not sure, in a thing falsing.

DROMIO S. Certain ones then.

ANTIPHOLUS S. Name them.

DROMIO S. The one, to save the money that he spends

II.ii. Location: A public place; the Mart, or a street.
22 in the teeth to my face **24 earnest** money paid as an installment to secure a bargain (with a pun on *serious*) **28 jest upon** trifle with **29 common** public playground **32 aspect** look, expression; also, astrological favor or disfavor of a planet **34 sconce** head (with pun on the meaning *fort* in l. 35 and *helmet* or *protective covering* in l. 37; the *battering*, ll. 35–36, is both a beating and assault by a battering ram) **36 An** if **37–38 insconce** shelter within a sconce or fortification **38–39 I shall . . . shoulders** i.e., my head will be beaten into my shoulders

51 Marry i.e., truly. (A shortened form of the oath, *by the Virgin Mary*.) **55 wants that** lacks that which **56 In good time** indeed **61 choleric** (Hot or dry food was thought to produce or aggravate the choleric or irascible humor.) **62 dry basting** hard beating **73 fine and recovery** a legal procedure for converting an entailed estate, one in which the property is limited to specified heirs, into a fee-simple, one in which the owner has unqualified ownership **77 excrement** outgrowth (of hair) **83–84 he . . . hair** (A reference to the venereal diseases in which loss of hair was a symptom.) **87 dealer** i.e., dealer with women **88 a kind of jollity** i.e., sexual pleasure **91 not sound** invalid (with a pun on *venereally diseased*) **93 falsing** deceptive (continuing the joke on venereal disease)

in tiring; the other, that at dinner they should not drop 97
in his porridge.

ANTIPHOLUS S. You would all this time have prov'd there is no time for all things.

DROMIO S. Marry, and did, sir; namely, e'en no time to recover hair lost by nature.

ANTIPHOLUS S. But your reason was not substantial, why there is no time to recover.

DROMIO S. Thus I mend it: Time himself is bald and therefore to the world's end will have bald followers.

ANTIPHOLUS S. I knew 'twould be a bald conclusion. 107
But soft, who wafts us yonder? 108

Enter Adriana [beckoning them], and Luciana.

ADRIANA

Ay, ay, Antipholus, look strange and frown. 109
Some other mistress hath thy sweet aspects;
I am not Adriana nor thy wife.
The time was once when thou unurg'd wouldst vow
That never words were music to thine ear,
That never object pleasing in thine eye,
That never touch well welcome to thy hand,
That never meat sweet-savor'd in thy taste,
Unless I spake, or look'd, or touch'd, or carv'd to thee.
How comes it now, my husband, O, how comes it,
That thou art thus estranged from thyself?
Thyself I call it, being strange to me,
That, undividable, incorporate,
Am better than thy dear self's better part.
Ah, do not tear away thyself from me!
For know, my love, as easy mayst thou fall 124
A drop of water in the breaking gulf
And take unmingled thence that drop again,
Without addition or diminishing,
As take from me thyself and not me too. 128
How dearly would it touch thee to the quick,
Shouldst thou but hear I were licentious
And that this body, consecrate to thee,
By ruffian lust should be contaminate!
Wouldst thou not spit at me, and spurn at me,
And hurl the name of husband in my face,
And tear the stain'd skin off my harlot-brow,
And from my false hand cut the wedding-ring,
And break it with a deep-divorcing vow?
I know thou canst, and therefore see thou do it.
I am possess'd with an adulterate blot;
My blood is mingled with the crime of lust;
For if we two be one and thou play false,
I do digest the poison of thy flesh,
Being strumpeted by thy contagion. 143
Keep then fair league and truce with thy true bed;
I live distain'd, thou undishonored. 145

ANTIPHOLUS S.

Plead you to me, fair dame? I know you not.
In Ephesus I am but two hours old,
As strange unto your town as to your talk;
Who, every word by all my wit being scann'd,
Wants wit in all one word to understand. 150

LUCIANA

Fie, brother, how the world is chang'd with you!
When were you wont to use my sister thus? 152
She sent for you by Dromio home to dinner.

ANTIPHOLUS S. By Dromio?

DROMIO S. By me?

ADRIANA

By thee; and this thou didst return from him,
That he did buffet thee and in his blows
Denied my house for his, me for his wife.

ANTIPHOLUS S.

Did you converse, sir, with this gentlewoman?
What is the course and drift of your compact? 160

DROMIO S.

I, sir? I never saw her till this time.

ANTIPHOLUS S.

Villain, thou liest, for even her very words
Didst thou deliver to me on the mart.

DROMIO S.

I never spake with her in all my life.

ANTIPHOLUS S.

How can she thus then call us by our names,
Unless it be by inspiration?

ADRIANA

How ill agrees it with your gravity
To counterfeit thus grossly with your slave, 168
Abetting him to thwart me in my mood! 169
Be it my wrong you are from me exempt, 170
But wrong not that wrong with a more contempt. 171
Come, I will fasten on this sleeve of thine.
[*She clings to him.*]
Thou art an elm, my husband, I a vine,
Whose weakness, married to thy stronger state,
Makes me with thy strength to communicate.
If aught possess thee from me, it is dross, 176
Usurping ivy, brier, or idle moss, 177
Who, all for want of pruning, with intrusion 178
Infect thy sap and live on thy confusion. 179

ANTIPHOLUS S. [*Aside*]

To me she speaks; she moves me for her theme. 180
What, was I married to her in my dream?
Or sleep I now and think I hear all this?
What error drives our eyes and ears amiss?
Until I know this sure uncertainty, 184
I'll entertain the offer'd fallacy. 185

LUCIANA

Dromio, go bid the servants spread for dinner.

DROMIO S.

O, for my beads! I cross me for a sinner. 187
[*He crosses himself.*]

97 tiring dressing the hair **107 bald** i.e., senseless, stupid **108 soft** gently, wait a minute. **wafts** beckons **109 strange** estranged, distant **124 fall** let fall **128 and not me too** i.e., even when we are separated we are indivisible **143 strumpeted** made a strumpet **145 distain'd** unstained (by contagion)

150 all all you have said **152 use** treat **160 compact** plot **168 grossly** obviously **169 mood** anger **170 exempt** separated **171 more** greater **176 If . . . dross** If anything usurps my possession of you, it is an impure substance **177 idle** unprofitable **178 Who** which. **want** lack **179 confusion** ruin **180 moves . . . theme** appeals to me as her subject of discourse **184 sure uncertainty** (to be) undoubted illusion **185 entertain** accept. **fallacy** delusive notion, error **187 beads** rosary

This is the fairy land. O spite of spites,
We talk with goblins, owls, and sprites!
If we obey them not, this will ensue:
They'll suck our breath, or pinch us black and blue.

LUCIANA
Why prat'st thou to thyself and answer'st not?
Dromio, thou drone, thou snail, thou slug, thou sot!

DROMIO S.
I am transformed, master, am not I?

ANTIPHOLUS S.
I think thou art in mind, and so am I.

DROMIO S.
Nay, master, both in mind and in my shape.

ANTIPHOLUS S.
Thou hast thine own form.

DROMIO S. No, I am an ape.

LUCIANA
If thou art chang'd to aught, 'tis to an ass.

DROMIO S.
'Tis true; she rides me and I long for grass.
'Tis so, I am an ass; else it could never be
But I should know her as well as she knows me.

ADRIANA
Come, come, no longer will I be a fool,
To put the finger in the eye and weep,
Whilst man and master laughs my woes to scorn.
Come, sir, to dinner. Dromio, keep the gate.
Husband, I'll dine above with you today
And shrive you of a thousand idle pranks.
Sirrah, if any ask you for your master,
Say he dines forth and let no creature enter.
Come, sister. Dromio, play the porter well.

ANTIPHOLUS S.
Am I in earth, in heaven, or in hell?
Sleeping or waking, mad or well-advis'd?
Known unto these, and to myself disguis'd?
I'll say as they say, and persever so,
And in this mist at all adventures go.

DROMIO S.
Master, shall I be porter at the gate?

ADRIANA
Ay, and let none enter, lest I break your pate.

LUCIANA
Come, come, Antipholus, we dine too late.

[*Exeunt.*]

ACT III • SCENE I

Enter Antipholus of Ephesus, his Man Dromio, Angelo the Goldsmith, and Balthazar the Merchant.

ANTIPHOLUS E.
Good Signior Angelo, you must excuse us all;
My wife is shrewish when I keep not hours.
Say that I linger'd with you at your shop
To see the making of her carcanet,
And that tomorrow you will bring it home.
But here's a villain that would face me down
He met me on the mart, and that I beat him
And charg'd him with a thousand marks in gold,
And that I did deny my wife and house.
Thou drunkard, thou, what didst thou mean by this?

DROMIO E.
Say what you will, sir, but I know what I know.
That you beat me at the mart, I have your hand to show;
If the skin were parchment and the blows you gave were ink,
Your own handwriting would tell you what I think.

ANTIPHOLUS E.
I think thou art an ass.

DROMIO E. Marry, so it doth appear
By the wrongs I suffer and the blows I bear.
I should kick, being kick'd; and, being at that pass,
You would keep from my heels and beware of an ass.

ANTIPHOLUS E.
Y' are sad, Signior Balthazar. Pray God our cheer
May answer my good will and your good welcome here.

BALTHAZAR
I hold your dainties cheap, sir, and your welcome dear.

ANTIPHOLUS E.
O, Signior Balthazar, either at flesh or fish,
A table full of welcome makes scarce one dainty dish.

BALTHAZAR
Good meat, sir, is common; that every churl affords.

ANTIPHOLUS E.
And welcome more common, for that's nothing but words.

BALTHAZAR
Small cheer and great welcome makes a merry feast.

ANTIPHOLUS E.
Ay, to a niggardly host and more sparing guest.
But though my cates be mean, take them in good part;
Better cheer may you have, but not with better heart.
But, soft! My door is lock'd. Go bid them let us in.

DROMIO E.
Maud, Bridget, Marian, Cic'ly, Gillian, Ginn!

DROMIO S. [*Within*]
Mome, malt-horse, capon, coxcomb, idiot, patch!
Either get thee from the door or sit down at the hatch.

191 suck our breath (This piece of folklore was perhaps connected with the old idea that the breath of man was his soul.) **193 sot** fool **197 ape** i.e., counterfeit **206 above** i.e., on the second floor, above Antipholus' shop **207 shrive** hear confession and give absolution **208 Sirrah** (Customary form of address to servants.) **209 forth** away from home **212 well-advis'd** in my right mind **215 at all adventures** whatever may happen

III.i. Location: Before the house of Antipholus of Ephesus.
4 carcanet necklace of jewels **6 face me down** maintain to my face that **8 with** i.e., with possession of **9 deny** disown **12 hand** i.e., handiwork on my body (with a pun on *handwriting*) **17 at that pass** in that situation **19 sad** serious. **cheer** entertainment **20 answer** agree with, match **21 dainties** delicacies. **cheap** of minor importance. **dear** of primary importance **23 makes scarce** scarcely equals **24 churl** one of mean station **27 sparing** frugal **28 cates** provisions, dainties. **mean** plain, simple **32 Mome** dolt, blockhead. **malt-horse** brewer's horse; stupid person. **patch** fool, clown **33 hatch** a half-door that can be kept closed while the upper half is opened

Dost thou conjure for wenches, that thou call'st for such store,
When one is one too many? Go get thee from the door.

DROMIO E.
What patch is made our porter? My master stays in the street.

DROMIO S. [*Within*]
Let him walk from whence he came, lest he catch cold on 's feet.

ANTIPHOLUS E.
Who talks within there? Ho, open the door!

DROMIO S. [*Within*]
Right, sir; I'll tell you when, an you'll tell me wherefore.

ANTIPHOLUS E.
Wherefore? For my dinner. I have not din'd today.

DROMIO S. [*Within*]
Nor today here you must not; come again when you may.

ANTIPHOLUS E.
What art thou that keep'st me out from the house I owe?

DROMIO S. [*Within*]
The porter for this time, sir, and my name is Dromio.

DROMIO E.
O villain! Thou hast stol'n both mine office and my name.
The one ne'er got me credit, the other mickle blame.
If thou hadst been Dromio today in my place,
Thou wouldst have chang'd thy face for a name, or thy name for an ass.

Enter Luce [*Within*].

LUCE [*Within*]
What a coil is there, Dromio? Who are those at the gate?

DROMIO E.
Let my master in, Luce.

LUCE [*Within*]
Faith, no; he comes too late;
And so tell your master.

DROMIO E.
O Lord, I must laugh!
Have at you with a proverb: Shall I set in my staff?

LUCE [*Within*]
Have at you with another: that 's—When, can you tell?

DROMIO S. [*Within*]
If thy name be call'd Luce—Luce, thou hast answer'd him well.

ANTIPHOLUS E.
Do you hear, you minion? You'll let us in, I hope?

LUCE [*Within*]
I thought to have ask'd you.

DROMIO S. [*Within*]
And you said no.

DROMIO E.
So, come help. Well struck! There was blow for blow.

ANTIPHOLUS E.
Thou baggage, let me in.

LUCE [*Within*]
Can you tell for whose sake?

DROMIO E.
Master, knock the door hard.

LUCE [*Within*]
Let him knock till it ache.

ANTIPHOLUS E.
You'll cry for this, minion, if I beat the door down.
[*Knocks.*]

LUCE [*Within*]
What needs all that, and a pair of stocks in the town?

Enter Adriana [*Within*].

ADRIANA [*Within*]
Who is that at the door that keeps all this noise?

DROMIO S. [*Within*]
By my troth, your town is troubled with unruly boys.

ANTIPHOLUS E.
Are you there, wife? You might have come before.

ADRIANA [*Within*]
Your wife, sir knave? Go get you from the door.

DROMIO E.
If you went in pain, master, this "knave" would go sore.

ANGELO
Here is neither cheer, sir, nor welcome; we would fain have either.

BALTHAZAR
In debating which was best, we shall part with neither.

DROMIO E.
They stand at the door, master; bid them welcome hither.

ANTIPHOLUS E.
There is something in the wind, that we cannot get in.

DROMIO E.
You would say so, master, if your garments were thin.
Your cake there is warm within; you stand here in the cold.
It would make a man mad as a buck, to be so bought and sold.

ANTIPHOLUS E.
Go fetch me something. I'll break ope the gate.

34 conjure for summon by magic. **store** quantity (of wenches) **37 on 's** in his **42 owe** own **45 mickle** much **47 thy face for a name** (Perhaps this should read "thy office for an aim," i.e., for a blow, as various editors have suggested.) **47 s.d. Enter Luce** [**Within**] (Here and at l. 60, Luce and then Adriana may enter in such a way as to be seen by the audience but not by those who are calling at the door. Possibly Dromio of Syracuse is similarly visible.) **48 coil** noise, disturbance **51 Have . . . staff** let me come at you with a proverb: Shall I take up my abode here? (With a bawdy double meaning.) **52 When . . . tell** i.e., never. (Another proverbial expression, used derisively to turn aside a question.) **54 minion** hussy. **hope** (A line following with an answering rhyme may be missing; perhaps it would have cleared up the present obscurity of ll. 55 and 56.)

60 What . . . town i.e., why do we need to put up with this disturbance, when the town provides stocks for punishment? **61 keeps** keeps up **65 If . . . sore** i.e., yourself and this "knave" she mentions are the same person. **went** i.e., were **67 debating** discussing. **part** depart **72 as a buck** i.e., as a male deer in rutting season. (Cf. *horn-mad*, II.i.57.) **bought and sold** i.e., imposed upon

DROMIO S. [*Within*]
Break any breaking here, and I'll break your knave's pate.

DROMIO E.
A man may break a word with you, sir, and words are but wind, 75
Ay, and break it in your face, so he break it not behind. 76

DROMIO S. [*Within*]
It seems thou want'st breaking. Out upon thee, hind! 77

DROMIO E.
Here's too much "out upon thee!" I pray thee, let me in.

DROMIO S. [*Within*]
Ay, when fowls have no feathers and fish have no fin.

ANTIPHOLUS E.
Well, I'll break in. Go borrow me a crow. 80

DROMIO E.
A crow without feather? Master, mean you so?
For a fish without a fin, there's a fowl without a feather.
If a crow help us in, sirrah, we'll pluck a crow together. 83

ANTIPHOLUS E.
Go get thee gone; fetch me an iron crow.

BALTHAZAR
Have patience, sir; O, let it not be so!
Herein you war against your reputation,
And draw within the compass of suspect 87
Th' unviolated honor of your wife.
Once this—your long experience of her wisdom, 89
Her sober virtue, years, and modesty, 90
Plead on her part some cause to you unknown;
And doubt not, sir, but she will well excuse 92
Why at this time the doors are made against you. 93
Be rul'd by me. Depart in patience,
And let us to the Tiger all to dinner,
And about evening come yourself alone
To know the reason of this strange restraint.
If by strong hand you offer to break in 98
Now in the stirring passage of the day, 99
A vulgar comment will be made of it, 100
And that supposed by the common rout 101
Against your yet ungalled estimation, 102
That may with foul intrusion enter in
And dwell upon your grave when you are dead;
For slander lives upon succession, 105
For ever hous'd where it gets possession.

ANTIPHOLUS E.
You have prevail'd. I will depart in quiet,
And, in despite of mirth, mean to be merry. 108
I know a wench of excellent discourse,
Pretty and witty, wild and yet, too, gentle.
There will we dine. This woman that I mean,
My wife—but, I protest, without desert— 112
Hath oftentimes upbraided me withal.
To her will we to dinner. [*To Angelo.*] Get you home
And fetch the chain; by this I know 'tis made. 115
Bring it, I pray you, to the Porpentine, 116
For there's the house. That chain will I bestow—
Be it for nothing but to spite my wife—
Upon mine hostess there. Good sir, make haste.
Since mine own doors refuse to entertain me,
I'll knock elsewhere, to see if they'll disdain me.

ANGELO
I'll meet you at that place some hour hence.

ANTIPHOLUS E.
Do so. This jest shall cost me some expense. *Exeunt.*

[SCENE II]

Enter Luciana with Antipholus of Syracusa.

LUCIANA
And may it be that you have quite forgot 1
A husband's office? Shall, Antipholus,
Even in the spring of love, thy love-springs rot? 3
Shall love, in building, grow so ruinous?
If you did wed my sister for her wealth,
Then for her wealth's sake use her with more kindness;
Or if you like elsewhere, do it by stealth;
Muffle your false love with some show of blindness. 8
Let not my sister read it in your eye;
Be not thy tongue thy own shame's orator;
Look sweet, speak fair, become disloyalty; 11
Apparel vice like virtue's harbinger. 12
Bear a fair presence, though your heart be tainted;
Teach sin the carriage of a holy saint; 14
Be secret-false. What need she be acquainted?
What simple thief brags of his own attaint? 16
'Tis double wrong, to truant with your bed 17
And let her read it in thy looks at board; 18
Shame hath a bastard fame, well managed; 19
Ill deeds is doubled with an evil word.
Alas, poor women! Make us but believe,
Being compact of credit, that you love us; 22
Though others have the arm, show us the sleeve;
We in your motion turn, and you may move us. 24

75 break a word exchange words **76 behind** i.e., in farting **77 thou . . . breaking** you need to be beaten. **hind** slave **80 crow** crowbar (introducing a quibble by Dromio of Ephesus) **83 pluck . . . together** pick a bone together, settle accounts **87 draw . . . suspect** bring under suspicion **89 Once this** to be brief, in short **90 virtue** merit, general excellence **92 excuse** justify **93 made** fastened **98 offer** venture **99 stirring passage** bustle **100 vulgar** public **101 And . . . rout** And a rumor (will be) conjectured by the mob **102 yet . . . estimation** still unsullied reputation **105 slander . . . succession** i.e., one slander grows out of another **108 in . . . mirth** despite my not feeling mirthful

112 desert my deserving it **115 this** this time **116 Porpentine** Porcupine. (Here, the name of an inn.)

III.ii Location: The same.
1 may can **3 love-springs** tender shoots of love **8 show of blindness** deceptive appearance **11 fair** courteously. **become disloyalty** carry infidelity gracefully **12 harbinger** messenger **14 carriage** demeanor **16 simple** simple-minded. **attaint** stain, dishonor; or possibly, conviction of crime **17 truant with** be faithless to **18 board** table **19 bastard fame** sham reputation **22 Being . . . credit** being as we are entirely made up of credulity **24 We . . . turn** we are governed by your motion, orbit (referring to the motion of the heavenly spheres)

Then, gentle brother, get you in again.
Comfort my sister, cheer her, call her wife.
'Tis holy sport to be a little vain, 27
When the sweet breath of flattery conquers strife.

ANTIPHOLUS S.
Sweet mistress—what your name is else, I know not,
Nor by what wonder you do hit of mine— 30
Less in your knowledge and your grace you show not
Than our earth's wonder, more than earth divine. 32
Teach me, dear creature, how to think and speak;
Lay open to my earthy-gross conceit, 34
Smoth'red in errors, feeble, shallow, weak,
The folded meaning of your words' deceit. 36
Against my soul's pure truth why labor you
To make it wander in an unknown field?
Are you a god? Would you create me new?
Transform me then, and to your pow'r I'll yield.
But if that I am I, then well I know
Your weeping sister is no wife of mine,
Nor to her bed no homage do I owe.
Far more, far more to you do I decline. 44
O, train me not, sweet mermaid, with thy note, 45
To drown me in thy sister's flood of tears!
Sing, siren, for thyself and I will dote.
Spread o'er the silver waves thy golden hairs,
And as a bed I'll take them and there lie,
And in that glorious supposition think
He gains by death that hath such means to die.
Let Love, being light, be drowned if she sink! 52

LUCIANA
What, are you mad, that you do reason so? 53

ANTIPHOLUS S.
Not mad, but mated—how, I do not know. 54

LUCIANA
It is a fault that springeth from your eye.

ANTIPHOLUS S.
For gazing on your beams, fair sun, being by. 56

LUCIANA
Gaze where you should, and that will clear your sight.

ANTIPHOLUS S.
As good to wink, sweet love, as look on night. 58

LUCIANA
Why call you me love? Call my sister so.

ANTIPHOLUS S.
Thy sister's sister.

LUCIANA That's my sister.

ANTIPHOLUS S. No;
It is thyself, mine own self's better part,
Mine eye's clear eye, my dear heart's dearer heart,
My food, my fortune, and my sweet hope's aim,
My sole earth's heaven, and my heaven's claim. 64

LUCIANA
All this my sister is, or else should be.

ANTIPHOLUS S.
Call thyself sister, sweet, for I am thee.
Thee will I love and with thee lead my life;
Thou hast no husband yet nor I no wife.
Give me thy hand.

LUCIANA O, soft, sir! Hold you still.
I'll fetch my sister, to get her good will. *Exit.*

Enter Dromio [of] Syracusa, [running].

ANTIPHOLUS S. Why, how now, Dromio, where runn'st thou so fast?

DROMIO S. Do you know me, sir? Am I Dromio? Am I your man? Am I myself?

ANTIPHOLUS S. Thou art Dromio, thou art my man, thou art thyself.

DROMIO S. I am an ass, I am a woman's man, and be- 77
sides myself. 78

ANTIPHOLUS S. What woman's man? And how besides thyself?

DROMIO S. Marry, sir, besides myself, I am due to a woman: one that claims me, one that haunts me, one that will have me.

ANTIPHOLUS S. What claim lays she to thee?

DROMIO S. Marry, sir, such claim as you would lay to
your horse; and she would have me as a beast—not 86
that, I being a beast, she would have me, but that she,
being a very beastly creature, lays claim to me.

ANTIPHOLUS S. What is she?

DROMIO S. A very reverent body; ay, such a one as a
man may not speak of without he say "Sir-reverence." 91
I have but lean luck in the match, and yet is she a 92
wondrous fat marriage.

ANTIPHOLUS S. How dost thou mean a fat marriage?

DROMIO S. Marry, sir, she's the kitchen wench and all
grease; and I know not what use to put her to but to 96
make a lamp of her and run from her by her own light.
I warrant, her rags and the tallow in them will burn a
Poland winter. If she lives till doomsday, she'll burn a
week longer than the whole world.

ANTIPHOLUS S. What complexion is she of?

DROMIO S. Swart, like my shoe, but her face nothing 102
like so clean kept, for why, she sweats; a man may go 103
over shoes in the grime of it.

ANTIPHOLUS S. That's a fault that water will mend.

DROMIO S. No, sir, 'tis in grain; Noah's flood could not 106
do it.

ANTIPHOLUS S. What's her name?

DROMIO S. Nell, sir; but her name and three quarters, 109

27 vain false **30 wonder** miracle. **hit of** hit upon, guess **32 earth's wonder** (Perhaps a reference to Queen Elizabeth.) **34 earthy-gross conceit** understanding gross as earth **36 folded** concealed **44 decline** incline **45 train** entice. **note** music **52 light** buoyant (with a pun on the sense of *wanton,* perhaps carrying forward a common sexual pun in which *to die,* l. 51, is to have sexual climax. The idea in l. 52 is that Love cannot possibly sink.) **53 reason** talk, argue **54 mated** amazed, confounded (with quibble on the sense of *matched with a wife*) **56 by** near **58 wink** close the eyes

64 My sole . . . claim my sole heaven on earth and my claim on heaven hereafter **77–78 besides myself** also myself (with a pun on the sense of *out of my mind*) **86 a beast** (with a pun on *abased,* reflecting Elizabethan pronunciation of *beast* as "baste") **91 without** unless. **"Sir-reverence"** i.e., save your reverence, an expression used in apology for the remark that follows it **92 lean** poor, meager **96 grease** (with a pun on *grace,* reflecting Elizabethan pronunciation) **102 Swart** swarthy, dark **103 for why** because **106 in grain** indelible, fast dyed **109 Nell** (The maidservant appearing in III.i is named *Luce;* usually the two are assumed to be one person.)

that's an ell and three quarters, will not measure her from hip to hip.

ANTIPHOLUS S. Then she bears some breadth?

DROMIO S. No longer from head to foot than from hip to hip; she is spherical, like a globe. I could find out countries in her.

ANTIPHOLUS S. In what part of her body stands Ireland?

DROMIO S. Marry, sir, in her buttocks. I found it out by the bogs.

ANTIPHOLUS S. Where Scotland?

DROMIO S. I found it by the barrenness, hard in the palm of the hand.

ANTIPHOLUS S. Where France?

DROMIO S. In her forehead, arm'd and reverted, making war against her heir.

ANTIPHOLUS S. Where England?

DROMIO S. I look'd for the chalky cliffs, but I could find no whiteness in them. But I guess it stood in her chin, by the salt rheum that ran between France and it.

ANTIPHOLUS S. Where Spain?

DROMIO S. Faith, I saw it not, but I felt it hot in her breath.

ANTIPHOLUS S. Where America, the Indies?

DROMIO S. Oh, sir, upon her nose, all o'er embellish'd with rubies, carbuncles, sapphires, declining their rich aspect to the hot breath of Spain, who sent whole armadoes of carracks to be ballast at her nose.

ANTIPHOLUS S. Where stood Belgia, the Netherlands?

DROMIO S. Oh, sir, I did not look so low. To conclude, this drudge, or diviner, laid claim to me; call'd me Dromio; swore I was assur'd to her; told me what privy marks I had about me, as, the mark of my shoulder, the mole in my neck, the great wart on my left arm, that I amaz'd ran from her as a witch.

And, I think, if my breast had not been made of faith and my heart of steel,
She had transform'd me to a curtal dog and made me turn i' th' wheel.

ANTIPHOLUS S.
Go hie thee presently, post to the road.
An if the wind blow any way from shore,
I will not harbor in this town tonight.
If any bark put forth, come to the mart,
Where I will walk till thou return to me.
If everyone knows us and we know none,
'Tis time, I think, to trudge, pack, and be gone.

DROMIO S.
As from a bear a man would run for life,
So fly I from her that would be my wife. *Exit.*

ANTIPHOLUS S.
There's none but witches do inhabit here,
And therefore 'tis high time that I were hence.
She that doth call me husband, even my soul
Doth for a wife abhor. But her fair sister,
Possess'd with such a gentle sovereign grace,
Of such enchanting presence and discourse,
Hath almost made me traitor to myself.
But, lest myself be guilty to self-wrong,
I'll stop mine ears against the mermaid's song.

Enter Angelo with the chain.

ANGELO
Master Antipholus—

ANTIPHOLUS S. Ay, that's my name.

ANGELO
I know it well, sir. Lo, here's the chain.
I thought to have ta'en you at the Porpentine;
The chain unfinish'd made me stay thus long.
[*Presents the chain.*]

ANTIPHOLUS S.
What is your will that I shall do with this?

ANGELO
What please yourself, sir; I have made it for you.

ANTIPHOLUS S.
Made it for me, sir? I bespoke it not.

ANGELO
Not once, nor twice, but twenty times you have.
Go home with it and please your wife withal,
And soon at supper-time I'll visit you
And then receive my money for the chain.

ANTIPHOLUS S.
I pray you, sir, receive the money now,
For fear you ne'er see chain nor money more.

ANGELO
You are a merry man, sir. Fare you well. *Exit.*

ANTIPHOLUS S.
What I should think of this, I cannot tell.
But this I think, there's no man is so vain
That would refuse so fair an offer'd chain.
I see a man here needs not live by shifts,
When in the streets he meets such golden gifts.
I'll to the mart and there for Dromio stay;
If any ship put out, then straight away. *Exit.*

ACT IV • SCENE I

Enter a [Second] Merchant, Goldsmith [Angelo], and an Officer.

SECOND MERCHANT
You know since Pentecost the sum is due,
And since I have not much importun'd you,

110 an ell forty-five inches (with a pun on *a Nell*) **120 barrenness** callused hardness and dryness (perhaps with a pun on *barren-ness,* a barren promontory) **123 arm'd and reverted** (See Introduction for explanation of reference to the French war.) **124 heir** (with pun on *hair,* and a joke about syphilis as causing baldness) **127 them** i.e., her teeth **128 rheum** snot running from her nose **134–135 declining . . . aspect** looking or bending downward **135–136 armadoes of carracks** fleets of galleons **136 ballast** ballasted, loaded **139 diviner** sorceress **140 assur'd** affianced **145 curtal dog** dog with a docked tail (and hence not used in hunting). **turn i' th' wheel** run in a wheel to turn the spit **146 hie** hasten. **presently** at once. **post** hasten. **road** harbor, roadstead **147 An if** if **152 pack** depart

159 Possess'd with having possession of **162 to** of **170 bespoke** requested **179 vain** foolish **181 shifts** stratagems, tricks **184 straight** at once

Nor now I had not, but that I am bound
To Persia and want guilders for my voyage.
Therefore make present satisfaction,
Or I'll attach you by this officer. 6

ANGELO
Even just the sum that I do owe to you
Is growing to me by Antipholus, 8
And in the instant that I met with you
He had of me a chain. At five o'clock
I shall receive the money for the same.
Pleaseth you walk with me down to his house, 12
I will discharge my bond and thank you too.

Enter Antipholus [*of*] *Ephesus* [*and*] *Dromio* [*of Ephesus*] *from the Courtezan's.*

OFFICER
That labor may you save; see where he comes.

ANTIPHOLUS E.
While I go to the goldsmith's house, go thou
And buy a rope's end; that will I bestow 16
Among my wife and her confederates,
For locking me out of my doors by day.
But, soft! I see the goldsmith. Get thee gone;
Buy thou a rope and bring it home to me.

DROMIO E.
I buy a thousand pound a year! I buy a rope! 21
Exit Dromio.

ANTIPHOLUS E.
A man is well holp up that trusts to you. 22
I promised your presence and the chain, 23
But neither chain nor goldsmith came to me.
Belike you thought our love would last too long 25
If it were chain'd together, and therefore came not.

ANGELO [*Showing a paper*]
Saving your merry humor, here's the note
How much your chain weighs to the utmost carat,
The fineness of the gold and chargeful fashion, 29
Which doth amount to three odd ducats more
Than I stand debted to this gentleman.
I pray you, see him presently discharg'd,
For he is bound to sea and stays but for it.

ANTIPHOLUS E.
I am not furnish'd with the present money;
Besides, I have some business in the town.
Good signior, take the stranger to my house,
And with you take the chain, and bid my wife
Disburse the sum on the receipt thereof.
Perchance I will be there as soon as you.

ANGELO
Then you will bring the chain to her yourself?

ANTIPHOLUS E.
No, bear it with you, lest I come not time enough. 41

ANGELO
Well, sir, I will. Have you the chain about you?

ANTIPHOLUS E.
An if I have not, sir, I hope you have,
Or else you may return without your money.

ANGELO
Nay, come, I pray you, sir, give me the chain.
Both wind and tide stays for this gentleman,
And I, to blame, have held him here too long.

ANTIPHOLUS E.
Good Lord! You use this dalliance to excuse 48
Your breach of promise to the Porpentine.
I should have chid you for not bringing it,
But, like a shrew, you first begin to brawl.

SECOND MERCHANT
The hour steals on; I pray you, sir, dispatch.

ANGELO
You hear how he importunes me. The chain!

ANTIPHOLUS E.
Why, give it to my wife and fetch your money.

ANGELO
Come, come, you know I gave it you even now.
Either send the chain or send me by some token. 56

ANTIPHOLUS E.
Fie, now you run this humor out of breath.
Come, where's the chain? I pray you, let me see it.

SECOND MERCHANT
My business cannot brook this dalliance. 59
Good sir, say whe'er you'll answer me or no. 60
If not, I'll leave him to the officer.

ANTIPHOLUS E.
I answer you? What should I answer you?

ANGELO
The money that you owe me for the chain.

ANTIPHOLUS E.
I owe you none till I receive the chain.

ANGELO
You know I gave it you half an hour since.

ANTIPHOLUS E.
You gave me none; you wrong me much to say so.

ANGELO
You wrong me more, sir, in denying it.
Consider how it stands upon my credit. 68

SECOND MERCHANT
Well, officer, arrest him at my suit.

OFFICER
I do; and charge you in the Duke's name to obey me.

ANGELO
This touches me in reputation.
Either consent to pay this sum for me
Or I attach you by this officer.

ANTIPHOLUS E.
Consent to pay thee that I never had?
Arrest me, foolish fellow, if thou dar'st.

IV.i. Location: A public place; the Mart, or a street.
6 attach arrest, seize **8 growing** due, accruing **12 Pleaseth** may it please **16 bestow** employ **21 I . . . rope** (An obscure line. Dromio may mean that in buying a rope as he is bidden, he is purchasing for himself a thousand poundings or beatings a year.) **22 holp** helped **23 promised** was promised **25 Belike** perhaps **29 chargeful fashion** expensive workmanship **41 time enough** in time

48 dalliance idle delay **56 send me . . . token** send me with some object of yours authorizing me to receive payment **59 brook** endure **60 whe'er** whether **68 how . . . credit** how it concerns my reputation for honesty

ANGELO
Here is thy fee; arrest him, officer. [*Gives money.*]
I would not spare my brother in this case,
If he should scorn me so apparently. 78
OFFICER
I do arrest you, sir; you hear the suit.
ANTIPHOLUS E.
I do obey thee till I give thee bail.
But, sirrah, you shall buy this sport as dear
As all the metal in your shop will answer.
ANGELO
Sir, sir, I shall have law in Ephesus,
To your notorious shame, I doubt it not.

Enter Dromio [of] Syracusa, from the bay.

DROMIO S.
Master, there's a bark of Epidamium
That stays but till her owner comes aboard
And then, sir, she bears away. Our fraughtage, sir, 87
I have convey'd aboard, and I have bought
The oil, the balsamum, and aqua-vitae. 89
The ship is in her trim; the merry wind 90
Blows fair from land; they stay for nought at all
But for their owner, master, and yourself.
ANTIPHOLUS E.
How now? A madman? Why, thou peevish sheep, 93
What ship of Epidamium stays for me?
DROMIO S.
A ship you sent me to, to hire waftage. 95
ANTIPHOLUS E.
Thou drunken slave, I sent thee for a rope,
And told thee to what purpose and what end.
DROMIO S.
You sent me for a rope's end as soon. 98
You sent me to the bay, sir, for a bark.
ANTIPHOLUS E.
I will debate this matter at more leisure,
And teach your ears to list me with more heed. 101
To Adriana, villain, hie thee straight. [*Gives key.*]
Give her this key, and tell her, in the desk
That's cover'd o'er with Turkish tapestry
There is a purse of ducats; let her send it.
Tell her I am arrested in the street,
And that shall bail me. Hie thee, slave, be gone!
On, officer, to prison till it come.
Exeunt [*all but Dromio S.*].
DROMIO S.
To Adriana! That is where we din'd,
Where Dowsabel did claim me for her husband. 110
She is too big, I hope, for me to compass. 111
Thither I must, although against my will,
For servants must their masters' minds fulfill. *Exit.*

78 apparently openly **87 fraughtage** freight, cargo **89 balsamum** balm. **aqua-vitae** strong liquor **90 in her trim** rigged and ready to sail **93 peevish** silly. **sheep** (with play on *ship* of next line) **95 waftage** conveyance by ship **98 rope's end** hangman's noose **101 list** listen to **110 Dowsabel** (Used ironically for Nell or Luce; derived from the French *douce et belle,* gentle and beautiful.) **111 compass** achieve (with added meaning of *put my arms around*)

[SCENE II]

Enter Adriana and Luciana.

ADRIANA
Ah, Luciana, did he tempt thee so?
Mightst thou perceive austerely in his eye 2
That he did plead in earnest, yea or no?
Look'd he or red or pale, or sad or merrily?
What observation mad'st thou in this case
Of his heart's meteors tilting in his face? 6
LUCIANA
First he denied you had in him no right. 7
ADRIANA
He meant he did me none; the more my spite. 8
LUCIANA
Then swore he that he was a stranger here.
ADRIANA
And true he swore, though yet forsworn he were.
LUCIANA
Then pleaded I for you.
ADRIANA And what said he?
LUCIANA
That love I begg'd for you he begg'd of me.
ADRIANA
With what persuasion did he tempt thy love?
LUCIANA
With words that in an honest suit might move. 14
First he did praise my beauty, then my speech.
ADRIANA
Didst speak him fair?
LUCIANA Have patience, I beseech. 16
ADRIANA
I cannot, nor I will not, hold me still;
My tongue, though not my heart, shall have his
will. 18
He is deformed, crooked, old, and sere, 19
Ill-fac'd, worse bodied, shapeless everywhere; 20
Vicious, ungentle, foolish, blunt, unkind,
Stigmatical in making, worse in mind. 22
LUCIANA
Who would be jealous then of such a one?
No evil lost is wail'd when it is gone.
ADRIANA
Ah, but I think him better than I say,
And yet would herein others' eyes were worse. 26
Far from her nest the lapwing cries away; 27
My heart prays for him, though my tongue do
curse.

IV.ii. Location: Before the house of Antipholus of Ephesus.
2 austerely plainly, seriously **6 meteors tilting** passions warring. (The next line begins a passage of stichomythia, dialogue in which each speech consists of a single line, much used in classical drama.) **7 no** i.e., any **8 spite** vexation, grief **14 honest** honorable **16 speak him fair** speak engagingly to him **18 his** its **19 sere** wrinkled **20 shapeless** misshapen **22 Stigmatical in making** deformed in body **26 And . . . worse** i.e., and yet I wish other women found him in a less favorable light **27 lapwing** a bird that flies away from its nest to divert attention from its young

Enter Dromio of Syracusa.

DROMIO S.
Here, go—the desk, the purse! Sweet, now, make haste.

LUCIANA
How hast thou lost thy breath?

DROMIO S.
By running fast.

ADRIANA
Where is thy master, Dromio? Is he well?

DROMIO S.
No, he's in Tartar limbo, worse than hell.
A devil in an everlasting garment hath him,
One whose hard heart is button'd up with steel;
A fiend, a fairy, pitiless and rough;
A wolf, nay, worse, a fellow all in buff;
A back-friend, a shoulder-clapper, one that countermands
The passages of alleys, creeks, and narrow lands;
A hound that runs counter and yet draws dry-foot well;
One that before the judgment carries poor souls to hell.

ADRIANA
Why, man, what is the matter?

DROMIO S.
I do not know the matter. He is 'rested on the case.

ADRIANA
What, is he arrested? Tell me at whose suit.

DROMIO S.
I know not at whose suit he is arrested well;
But he's in a suit of buff which 'rested him, that can I tell.
Will you send him, mistress, redemption, the money in his desk?

ADRIANA
Go fetch it, sister. *(Exit Luciana.)* This I wonder at,
That he, unknown to me, should be in debt.
Tell me, was he arrested on a band?

DROMIO S.
Not on a band, but on a stronger thing:
A chain, a chain! Do you not hear it ring?

ADRIANA
What, the chain?

DROMIO S.
No, no, the bell; 'tis time that I were gone.
It was two ere I left him, and now the clock strikes one.

ADRIANA
The hours come back! That did I never hear.

DROMIO S.
O, yes; if any hour meet a sergeant, 'a turns back for very fear.

ADRIANA
As if Time were in debt! How fondly dost thou reason!

DROMIO S.
Time is a very bankrupt and owes more than he's worth to season.
Nay, he's a thief too. Have you not heard men say
That Time comes stealing on by night and day?
If 'a be in debt and theft, and a sergeant in the way,
Hath he not reason to turn back an hour in a day?

Enter Luciana [with a purse].

ADRIANA
Go, Dromio; there's the money, bear it straight, *[Gives the purse.]*
And bring thy master home immediately.
Come, sister. I am press'd down with conceit—
Conceit, my comfort and my injury. *Exeunt.*

[SCENE III]

Enter Antipholus [of] Syracusa.

ANTIPHOLUS S.
There's not a man I meet but doth salute me
As if I were their well-acquainted friend,
And every one doth call me by my name.
Some tender money to me; some invite me;
Some other give me thanks for kindnesses;
Some offer me commodities to buy.
Even now a tailor call'd me in his shop
And show'd me silks that he had bought for me
And therewithal took measure of my body.
Sure, these are but imaginary wiles
And Lapland sorcerers inhabit here.

Enter Dromio [of] Syracusa.

DROMIO S. Master, here's the gold you sent me for. What, have you got the picture of old Adam new-apparel'd?

ANTIPHOLUS S.
What gold is this? What Adam dost thou mean?

DROMIO S. Not that Adam that kept the Paradise, but that Adam that keeps the prison; he that goes in the calf's skin that was kill'd for the Prodigal; he that came

32 Tartar limbo Tartarus or pagan hell, worse than Christian hell **33 everlasting garment** i.e., buff-leather attire of the police officer, everlasting because of the joke about perpetual durance in limbo or jail **37 back-friend** i.e., a false friend; here the police officer who comes up behind and claps his victim on the back to signify arrest. **countermands** prohibits **38 creeks** narrow or winding passages **39 runs counter** follows a trail in the direction opposite to that which the game has taken (with a quibble on *counter,* a prison). **draws dry-foot** follows game by mere scent of the foot **40 judgment** legal decision (with a pun on *Judgment Day,* continuing the joke about jail as Tartar limbo) **42 'rested on the case** arrested in a lawsuit (with a pun on *case* meaning "the container" as distinguished from the *matter* contained in it. Dromio means that his master has been arrested in his suit of clothes.) **49 band** bond. (But Dromio puns on the sense *neck-band* in the next line.)

56 hour (with a pun on *whore,* similarly pronounced). **sergeant** arresting officer. **'a** it, she, he **57 fondly** foolishly **58 to season** at any given time or opportunity **65 conceit** thought

IV.iii. Location: A public place; the Mart, or a street.
10 imaginary wiles tricks of the imagination **11 Lapland sorcerers** (Lapland was said to surpass all nations in the practice of witchcraft and sorcery.) **13–14 have . . . apparel'd** (Dromio, noting the absence of the arresting officer, asks if his master has obtained for that officer a new apparel or "suit"—with a pun on lawsuit. The officer is likened to old Adam in that his buff-leather jerkin resembles Adam's garments of beasts' skins; see Genesis 3:21.) **18 calf's . . . Prodigal** (An allusion to the fatted calf killed for the Prodigal Son's return; see Luke 15:23.)

behind you, sir, like an evil angel, and bid you forsake
your liberty.

ANTIPHOLUS S. I understand thee not.

DROMIO S. No? Why, 'tis a plain case: he that went, like
a bass-viol, in a case of leather; the man, sir, that,
when gentlemen are tir'd, gives them a sob and 'rests 25
them; he, sir, that takes pity on decay'd men and gives
them suits of durance; he that sets up his rest to do 27
more exploits with his mace than a morris-pike. 28

ANTIPHOLUS S. What, thou mean'st an officer?

DROMIO S. Ay, sir, the sergeant of the band; he that
brings any man to answer it that breaks his band; one
that thinks a man always going to bed and says, "God
give you good rest!" 33

ANTIPHOLUS S. Well, sir, there rest in your foolery. Is
there any ships puts forth tonight? May we be gone?

DROMIO S. Why, sir, I brought you word an hour since
that the bark Expedition put forth tonight, and then 37
were you hind'red by the sergeant to tarry for the hoy 38
Delay. Here are the angels that you sent for to de- 39
liver you. [*Gives money.*]

ANTIPHOLUS S.
The fellow is distract, and so am I, 41
And here we wander in illusions.
Some blessed power deliver us from hence!

Enter a Courtezan.

COURTEZAN
Well met, well met, Master Antipholus.
I see, sir, you have found the goldsmith now.
Is that the chain you promis'd me today?

ANTIPHOLUS S.
Satan, avoid! I charge thee, tempt me not. 47

DROMIO S. Master, is this Mistress Satan?

ANTIPHOLUS S. It is the devil.

DROMIO S. Nay, she is worse, she is the devil's dam, 50
and here she comes in the habit of a light wench; and 51
thereof comes that the wenches say, "God damn me,"
that's as much to say, "God make me a light wench."
It is written, they appear to men like angels of light; 54
light is an effect of fire, and fire will burn; ergo, light 55
wenches will burn. Come not near her. 56

COURTEZAN
Your man and you are marvelous merry, sir.
Will you go with me? We'll mend our dinner here. 58

DROMIO S. Master, if you do, expect spoon-meat, or 59
bespeak a long spoon.

ANTIPHOLUS S. Why, Dromio?

DROMIO S. Marry, he must have a long spoon that must
eat with the devil.

ANTIPHOLUS S.
Avoid then, fiend! What tell'st thou me of supping?
Thou art, as you are all, a sorceress.
I conjure thee to leave me and be gone.

COURTEZAN
Give me the ring of mine you had at dinner
Or, for my diamond, the chain you promis'd,
And I'll be gone, sir, and not trouble you.

DROMIO S.
Some devils ask but the parings of one's nail, 70
A rush, a hair, a drop of blood, a pin,
A nut, a cherry-stone;
But she, more covetous, would have a chain.
Master, be wise; an if you give it her,
The devil will shake her chain and fright us with it.

COURTEZAN
I pray you, sir, my ring, or else the chain.
I hope you do not mean to cheat me so?

ANTIPHOLUS S.
Avaunt, thou witch! Come, Dromio, let us go.

DROMIO S.
"Fly pride," says the peacock. Mistress, that you
know. *Exit* [*with Antipholus*]. 79

COURTEZAN
Now, out of doubt Antipholus is mad,
Else would he never so demean himself. 81
A ring he hath of mine worth forty ducats,
And for the same he promis'd me a chain;
Both one and other he denies me now.
The reason that I gather he is mad,
Besides this present instance of his rage,
Is a mad tale he told today at dinner
Of his own doors being shut against his entrance.
Belike his wife, acquainted with his fits,
On purpose shut the doors against his way.
My way is now to hie home to his house
And tell his wife that, being lunatic,
He rush'd into my house and took perforce 93
My ring away. This course I fittest choose,
For forty ducats is too much to lose. [*Exit.*]

[SCENE IV]

Enter Antipholus [*of*] *Ephesus with a Jailer* [*or Officer*].

ANTIPHOLUS E.
Fear me not, man, I will not break away.
I'll give thee, ere I leave thee, so much money,
To warrant thee, as I am 'rested for. 3
My wife is in a wayward mood today,
And will not lightly trust the messenger.

25 sob i.e., breathing space (followed by a pun on *'rests,* meaning "arrests" and "gives a rest to") **27 durance** a kind of long-wearing cloth like buff (with a pun on *imprisonment*). **sets . . . rest** stakes his all (with a continuing pun on *'rest;* the metaphor of staking all one's venture is from the game of primero) **28 mace** staff of office carried by a constable. **morris-pike** a weapon supposedly of Moorish origin **33 rest** (continuing the pun on *arrest*) **37 bark** seagoing vessel **38 hoy** a small coasting vessel **39 angels** gold coins worth about 10 shillings **41 distract** distracted **47 avoid** be gone. (See Matthew 4:10.) **50 dam** mother **51 habit** demeanor, manner; also, dress. **light** wanton **54 angels of light** (See 2 Corinthians 11:14, where Satan is referred to as transformed into an angel of light.) **55 ergo** therefore **56 will burn** i.e., will transmit venereal disease **58 mend** supplement, complete

59 spoon-meat food for infants, hence delicacies **79 Fly . . . peacock** (I.e., the accusation of dishonesty coming from this woman, whom Dromio takes to be dishonest, seems to him as out of place as a warning against pride given by the peacock.) **81 demean** conduct **93 perforce** forcibly

IV.iv. Location: The same.
3 warrant give security to

That I should be attach'd in Ephesus, 6
I tell you, 'twill sound harshly in her ears.

Enter Dromio [*of*] *Ephesus with a rope's end.*

Here comes my man; I think he brings the money.
How now, sir? Have you that I sent you for?

DROMIO E.
Here's that, I warrant you, will pay them all.
[*Gives the rope.*]

ANTIPHOLUS E.
But where's the money?

DROMIO E.
Why, sir, I gave the money for the rope.

ANTIPHOLUS E.
Five hundred ducats, villain, for a rope?

DROMIO E.
I'll serve you, sir, five hundred at the rate. 14

ANTIPHOLUS E.
To what end did I bid thee hie thee home?

DROMIO E. To a rope's end, sir; and to that end am I return'd.

ANTIPHOLUS E. And to that end, sir, I will welcome you.
[*Starts to beat him.*]

OFFICER Good sir, be patient.

DROMIO E. Nay, 'tis for me to be patient; I am in adversity.

OFFICER Good now, hold thy tongue. 22

DROMIO E. Nay, rather persuade him to hold his hands.

ANTIPHOLUS E. Thou whoreson, senseless villain!

DROMIO E. I would I were senseless, sir, that I might not feel your blows.

ANTIPHOLUS E. Thou art sensible in nothing but blows, 27
and so is an ass.

DROMIO E. I am an ass, indeed; you may prove it by my long ears. I have serv'd him from the hour of my 30
nativity to this instant, and have nothing at his hands for my service but blows. When I am cold, he heats me with beating; when I am warm, he cools me with beating. I am wak'd with it when I sleep, rais'd with it when I sit, driven out of doors with it when I go from home, welcom'd home with it when I return. Nay, I bear it on my shoulders, as a beggar wont her 37
brat; and I think when he hath lam'd me, I shall beg with it from door to door.

Enter Adriana, Luciana, Courtezan, and a Schoolmaster call'd Pinch.

ANTIPHOLUS E.
Come, go along; my wife is coming yonder.

DROMIO E. Mistress, "respice finem," respect your end; 41
or rather, the prophecy like the parrot, "beware the rope's end."

ANTIPHOLUS E. Wilt thou still talk? *Beats Dromio.*

COURTEZAN
How say you now? Is not your husband mad?

ADRIANA
His incivility confirms no less.
Good Doctor Pinch, you are a conjurer; 47
Establish him in his true sense again,
And I will please you what you will demand. 49

LUCIANA
Alas, how fiery and how sharp he looks! 50

COURTEZAN
Mark how he trembles in his ecstasy! 51

PINCH
Give me your hand and let me feel your pulse.

ANTIPHOLUS E.
There is my hand, and let it feel your ear.
[*Striking him.*]

PINCH
I charge thee, Satan, hous'd within this man,
To yield possession to my holy prayers
And to thy state of darkness hie thee straight!
I conjure thee by all the saints in heaven!

ANTIPHOLUS E.
Peace, doting wizard, peace! I am not mad.

ADRIANA
O, that thou wert not, poor distressed soul!

ANTIPHOLUS E.
You minion, you, are these your customers? 60
Did this companion with the saffron face 61
Revel and feast it at my house today,
Whilst upon me the guilty doors were shut
And I denied to enter in my house?

ADRIANA
O husband, God doth know you din'd at home,
Where would you had remain'd until this time,
Free from these slanders and this open shame!

ANTIPHOLUS E.
Din'd at home? [*To Dromio E.*] Thou villain, what sayest thou?

DROMIO E.
Sir, sooth to say, you did not dine at home.

ANTIPHOLUS E.
Were not my doors lock'd up and I shut out?

DROMIO E.
Perdie, your doors were lock'd and you shut out. 71

ANTIPHOLUS E.
And did not she herself revile me there?

DROMIO E.
Sans fable, she herself revil'd you there. 73

ANTIPHOLUS E.
Did not her kitchen maid rail, taunt, and scorn me?

DROMIO E.
Certes, she did; the kitchen vestal scorn'd you. 75

ANTIPHOLUS E.
And did not I in rage depart from thence?

DROMIO E.
In verity you did; my bones bear witness,
That since have felt the vigor of his rage.

6 attach'd arrested **14 at the rate** for that amount **22 Good now** pray you **27 sensible in** sensitive to; also, made sensible by **30 ears** (with a pun on *years;* Dromio says he is an ass for having served his master so long) **37 wont** is accustomed to (bear) **41 respice finem** consider your end. (A pious sentiment on the brevity of life and the approach of death; with a play on *respice funem,* "consider the hangman's rope." A parrot might be taught to say "respice finem," or perhaps "rope.")

47 conjurer (Being able to speak Latin, Pinch could conjure spirits.) **49 please** pay **50 sharp** angry **51 ecstasy** madness **60 minion** hussy, i.e., Adriana **61 companion** fellow, i.e., Pinch. **saffron** yellow **71 Perdie** (An oath, from the French *par Dieu,* by God.) **73 Sans** without **75 Certes** certainly. **kitchen vestal** (Ironically, her task was like that of the vestal virgins of ancient Rome, to keep the fire burning.)

ADRIANA
Is 't good to soothe him in these contraries? 79

PINCH
It is no shame; the fellow finds his vein,
And yielding to him humors well his frenzy.

ANTIPHOLUS E.
Thou hast suborn'd the goldsmith to arrest me. 82

ADRIANA
Alas, I sent you money to redeem you,
By Dromio here, who came in haste for it.

DROMIO E.
Money by me? Heart and good will you might,
But surely, master, not a rag of money. 86

ANTIPHOLUS E.
Went'st not thou to her for a purse of ducats?

ADRIANA
He came to me and I deliver'd it.

LUCIANA
And I am witness with her that she did.

DROMIO E.
God and the rope-maker bear me witness
That I was sent for nothing but a rope!

PINCH
Mistress, both man and master is possess'd;
I know it by their pale and deadly looks. 93
They must be bound and laid in some dark room. 94

ANTIPHOLUS E.
Say wherefore didst thou lock me forth today?
And why dost thou deny the bag of gold?

ADRIANA
I did not, gentle husband, lock thee forth.

DROMIO E.
And, gentle master, I receiv'd no gold;
But I confess, sir, that we were lock'd out.

ADRIANA
Dissembling villain, thou speak'st false in both.

ANTIPHOLUS E.
Dissembling harlot, thou art false in all,
And art confederate with a damned pack
To make a loathsome abject scorn of me;
But with these nails I'll pluck out these false eyes
That would behold in me this shameful sport. 105

Enter three or four, and offer to bind him. He strives.

ADRIANA
O, bind him, bind him! Let him not come near me.

PINCH
More company! The fiend is strong within him.

LUCIANA
Ay me, poor man, how pale and wan he looks!

ANTIPHOLUS E.
What, will you murder me? Thou jailer, thou,
I am thy prisoner. Wilt thou suffer them
To make a rescue?

OFFICER Masters, let him go. 111
He is my prisoner, and you shall not have him.

PINCH
Go bind this man, for he is frantic too.
[*They offer to bind Dromio E.*]

ADRIANA
What wilt thou do, thou peevish officer?
Hast thou delight to see a wretched man
Do outrage and displeasure to himself?

OFFICER
He is my prisoner; if I let him go,
The debt he owes will be requir'd of me.

ADRIANA
I will discharge thee ere I go from thee. 119
Bear me forthwith unto his creditor
And, knowing how the debt grows, I will pay it. 121
Good Master Doctor, see him safe convey'd
Home to my house. O most unhappy day! 123

ANTIPHOLUS E.
O most unhappy strumpet!

DROMIO E.
Master, I am here ent'red in bond for you.

ANTIPHOLUS E.
Out on thee, villain! Wherefore dost thou mad me? 126

DROMIO E. Will you be bound for nothing? Be mad, good master; cry "The devil!"

LUCIANA
God help, poor souls, how idly do they talk! 129

ADRIANA
Go bear him hence. Sister, go you with me.
Exeunt. Mane[n]t Officer, Adriana, Luciana, Courtezan.
Say now, whose suit is he arrested at?

OFFICER
One Angelo, a goldsmith. Do you know him?

ADRIANA
I know the man. What is the sum he owes?

OFFICER
Two hundred ducats.

ADRIANA Say, how grows it due?

OFFICER
Due for a chain your husband had of him.

ADRIANA
He did bespeak a chain for me, but had it not. 136

COURTEZAN
When as your husband all in rage today 137
Came to my house and took away my ring—
The ring I saw upon his finger now—
Straight after did I meet him with a chain.

ADRIANA
It may be so, but I did never see it.
Come, jailer, bring me where the goldsmith is;
I long to know the truth hereof at large. 143

Enter Antipholus [of] Syracusa with his rapier drawn, and Dromio [of] Syracusa.

79 soothe encourage, humor **82 suborn'd** induced **86 rag** scrap **93 deadly** death-like **94 bound . . . room** (The regular treatment for lunacy in Shakespeare's day.) **105 s.d. offer** attempt **111 make a rescue** take a prisoner by force from legal custody

119 discharge pay **121 knowing . . . grows** when I know how the debt accrued **123 unhappy** fatal, miserable **126 mad** madden **129 idly** senselessly **136 bespeak** order **137 When as** when **143 at large** in full, in detail

LUCIANA
God, for thy mercy! They are loose again.
ADRIANA
And come with naked swords. Let's call more help
To have them bound again.
OFFICER Away! They'll kill us.
Run all out. Exeunt omnes, as fast as may be, frighted. [*Antipholus and Dromio of Syracuse remain.*]
ANTIPHOLUS S.
I see these witches are afraid of swords.
DROMIO S.
She that would be your wife now ran from you.
ANTIPHOLUS S.
Come to the Centaur; fetch our stuff from thence.
I long that we were safe and sound aboard.
DROMIO S. Faith, stay here this night; they will surely do us no harm. You saw they speak us fair, give us gold. Methinks they are such a gentle nation that, but for the mountain of mad flesh that claims marriage of me, I could find in my heart to stay here still and turn witch.
ANTIPHOLUS S.
I will not stay tonight for all the town;
Therefore away, to get our stuff aboard. *Exeunt.*

ACT V • SCENE I

Enter the [*Second*] *Merchant and* [*Angelo*] *the Goldsmith.*

ANGELO
I am sorry, sir, that I have hind'red you;
But, I protest, he had the chain of me,
Though most dishonestly he doth deny it.
SECOND MERCHANT
How is the man esteem'd here in the city?
ANGELO
Of very reverend reputation, sir,
Of credit infinite, highly belov'd,
Second to none that lives here in the city.
His word might bear my wealth at any time.
SECOND MERCHANT
Speak softly; yonder, as I think, he walks.

Enter Antipholus [*of Syracuse*] *and Dromio* [*of Syracuse*] *again.*

ANGELO
'Tis so; and that self chain about his neck
Which he forswore most monstrously to have.
Good sir, draw near to me, I'll speak to him.—
Signior Antipholus, I wonder much
That you would put me to this shame and trouble;
And, not without some scandal to yourself,
With circumstance and oaths so to deny
This chain which now you wear so openly.
Beside the charge, the shame, imprisonment,
You have done wrong to this my honest friend,
Who, but for staying on our controversy,
Had hoisted sail and put to sea today.
This chain you had of me; can you deny it?
ANTIPHOLUS S.
I think I had; I never did deny it.
SECOND MERCHANT
Yes, that you did, sir, and forswore it too.
ANTIPHOLUS S.
Who heard me to deny it or forswear it?
SECOND MERCHANT
These ears of mine, thou know'st, did hear thee.
Fie on thee, wretch! 'Tis pity that thou liv'st
To walk where any honest men resort.
ANTIPHOLUS S.
Thou art a villain to impeach me thus.
I'll prove mine honor and mine honesty
Against thee presently, if thou dar'st stand.
SECOND MERCHANT
I dare, and do defy thee for a villain. *They draw.*

Enter Adriana, Luciana, [*the*] *Courtezan, and others.*

ADRIANA
Hold, hurt him not, for God sake! He is mad.
Some get within him, take his sword away.
Bind Dromio too, and bear them to my house.
DROMIO S.
Run, master, run; for God's sake, take a house!
This is some priory. In, or we are spoil'd!
Exeunt [*Antipholus S. and Dromio S.*] *to the Priory.*

Enter [*the*] *Lady Abbess.*

ABBESS
Be quiet, people. Wherefore throng you hither?
ADRIANA
To fetch my poor distracted husband hence.
Let us come in, that we may bind him fast
And bear him home for his recovery.
ANGELO
I knew he was not in his perfect wits.
SECOND MERCHANT
I am sorry now that I did draw on him.
ABBESS
How long hath this possession held the man?
ADRIANA
This week he hath been heavy, sour, sad,
And much different from the man he was;
But till this afternoon his passion
Ne'er brake into extremity of rage.

145 naked drawn **149 stuff** goods, baggage **155 still** always

V.i. Location: Before a priory.
8 might bear is worth **10 self** same **11 forswore** repudiated on oath

16 circumstance details, particulars **18 charge** cost **19 honest** honorable **20 on** as a result of **31 presently** at once. **stand** take a fighting stance **32 defy** challenge. **villain** base person **34 within him** under his guard **36 take** take refuge in

ABBESS
Hath he not lost much wealth by wrack of sea? 49
Buried some dear friend? Hath not else his eye
Stray'd his affection in unlawful love— 51
A sin prevailing much in youthful men,
Who give their eyes the liberty of gazing?
Which of these sorrows is he subject to?

ADRIANA
To none of these, except it be the last,
Namely, some love that drew him oft from home.

ABBESS
You should for that have reprehended him.

ADRIANA
Why, so I did.

ABBESS Ay, but not rough enough.

ADRIANA
As roughly as my modesty would let me.

ABBESS
Haply, in private.

ADRIANA And in assemblies too.

ABBESS
Ay, but not enough.

ADRIANA
It was the copy of our conference. 62
In bed he slept not for my urging it; 63
At board he fed not for my urging it;
Alone, it was the subject of my theme;
In company I often glanced it; 66
Still did I tell him it was vile and bad. 67

ABBESS
And thereof came it that the man was mad.
The venom clamors of a jealous woman 69
Poisons more deadly than a mad dog's tooth.
It seems his sleeps were hind'red by thy railing,
And thereof comes it that his head is light.
Thou say'st his meat was sauc'd with thy
  upbraidings.
Unquiet meals make ill digestions;
Thereof the raging fire of fever bred,
And what's a fever but a fit of madness?
Thou sayest his sports were hind'red by thy brawls.
Sweet recreation barr'd, what doth ensue
But moody and dull melancholy,
Kinsman to grim and comfortless despair,
And at her heels a huge infectious troop
Of pale distemperatures and foes to life? 82
In food, in sport, and life-preserving rest
To be disturb'd, would mad or man or beast. 84
The consequence is then thy jealous fits
Have scar'd thy husband from the use of wits.

LUCIANA
She never reprehended him but mildly,
When he demean'd himself rough, rude, and wildly.
Why bear you these rebukes and answer not?

ADRIANA
She did betray me to my own reproof.
Good people, enter and lay hold on him.

ABBESS
No, not a creature enters in my house.

ADRIANA
Then let your servants bring my husband forth.

ABBESS
Neither. He took this place for sanctuary,
And it shall privilege him from your hands
Till I have brought him to his wits again,
Or lose my labor in assaying it.

ADRIANA
I will attend my husband, be his nurse,
Diet his sickness, for it is my office, 99
And will have no attorney but myself; 100
And therefore let me have him home with me.

ABBESS
Be patient, for I will not let him stir
Till I have us'd the approved means I have, 103
With wholesome syrups, drugs, and holy prayers,
To make of him a formal man again. 105
It is a branch and parcel of mine oath, 106
A charitable duty of my order.
Therefore depart and leave him here with me.

ADRIANA
I will not hence and leave my husband here;
And ill it doth beseem your holiness
To separate the husband and the wife.

ABBESS
Be quiet and depart. Thou shalt not have him. [*Exit.*]

LUCIANA
Complain unto the Duke of this indignity.

ADRIANA
Come, go. I will fall prostrate at his feet,
And never rise until my tears and prayers
Have won his Grace to come in person hither
And take perforce my husband from the Abbess.

SECOND MERCHANT
By this, I think, the dial points at five.
Anon, I'm sure, the Duke himself in person
Comes this way to the melancholy vale,
The place of death and sorry execution, 121
Behind the ditches of the abbey here.

ANGELO
Upon what cause?

SECOND MERCHANT
To see a reverend Syracusian merchant,
Who put unluckily into this bay
Against the laws and statutes of this town,
Beheaded publicly for his offense.

ANGELO
See where they come. We will behold his death.

LUCIANA
Kneel to the Duke before he pass the abbey.

Enter the Duke of Ephesus and [Egeon] the Merchant of Syracuse, barehead [and bound], with the Headsman and other Officers.

49 wrack of shipwreck at **51 Stray'd** led astray **62 copy** topic, theme **63 for** because of **66 glanced** alluded to **67 Still** continually **69 venom** venomous **82 distemperatures** physical disorder, illness **84 mad or** madden either

99 office duty **100 attorney** agent, deputy **103 approved** proved **105 formal** normal **106 parcel** part, portion **121 sorry** sad

DUKE
Yet once again proclaim it publicly,
If any friend will pay the sum for him,
He shall not die; so much we tender him. 132

ADRIANA
Justice, most sacred Duke, against the Abbess!

DUKE
She is a virtuous and a reverend lady.
It cannot be that she hath done thee wrong.

ADRIANA
May it please your Grace, Antipholus my husband,
Whom I made lord of me and all I had,
At your important letters, this ill day 138
A most outrageous fit of madness took him,
That desp'rately he hurried through the street—
With him his bondman, all as mad as he—
Doing displeasure to the citizens
By rushing in their houses, bearing thence
Rings, jewels, anything his rage did like. 144
Once did I get him bound and sent him home,
Whilst to take order for the wrongs I went 146
That here and there his fury had committed.
Anon, I wot not by what strong escape, 148
He broke from those that had the guard of him,
And with his mad attendant and himself,
Each one with ireful passion, with drawn swords,
Met us again and madly bent on us
Chas'd us away, till raising of more aid
We came again to bind them. Then they fled
Into this abbey, whither we pursu'd them;
And here the Abbess shuts the gates on us
And will not suffer us to fetch him out,
Nor send him forth that we may bear him hence.
Therefore, most gracious Duke, with thy command
Let him be brought forth and borne hence for help. 160

DUKE
Long since thy husband serv'd me in my wars,
And I to thee engag'd a prince's word, 162
When thou didst make him master of thy bed,
To do him all the grace and good I could.
Go, some of you, knock at the abbey gate
And bid the Lady Abbess come to me.
I will determine this before I stir.

Enter a [Servant as] Messenger.

SERVANT
O mistress, mistress, shift and save yourself!
My master and his man are both broke loose,
Beaten the maids a-row, and bound the doctor, 170
Whose beard they have sing'd off with brands of fire;
And ever, as it blaz'd, they threw on him
Great pails of puddled mire to quench the hair. 173
My master preaches patience to him, and the while
His man with scissors nicks him like a fool; 175
And sure, unless you send some present help,
Between them they will kill the conjurer.

ADRIANA
Peace, fool! Thy master and his man are here,
And that is false thou dost report to us.

SERVANT
Mistress, upon my life, I tell you true;
I have not breath'd almost since I did see it.
He cries for you and vows, if he can take you,
To scorch your face and to disfigure you.
Cry within.
Hark, hark! I hear him, mistress; fly, be gone!

DUKE
Come, stand by me; fear nothing. Guard with halberds! 185

ADRIANA
Ay me, it is my husband! Witness you,
That he is borne about invisible.
Even now we hous'd him in the abbey here,
And now he's there, past thought of human reason.

Enter Antipholus [of Ephesus] and Dromio of Ephesus.

ANTIPHOLUS E.
Justice, most gracious Duke, O, grant me justice!
Even for the service that long since I did thee,
When I bestrid thee in the wars and took 192
Deep scars to save thy life; even for the blood
That then I lost for thee, now grant me justice.

EGEON
Unless the fear of death doth make me dote,
I see my son Antipholus and Dromio.

ANTIPHOLUS E.
Justice, sweet prince, against that woman there!
She whom thou gav'st to me to be my wife,
That hath abused and dishonored me 199
Even in the strength and height of injury!
Beyond imagination is the wrong
That she this day hath shameless thrown on me.

DUKE
Discover how, and thou shalt find me just. 203

ANTIPHOLUS E.
This day, great Duke, she shut the doors upon me,
While she with harlots feasted in my house. 205

DUKE
A grievous fault! Say, woman, didst thou so?

ADRIANA
No, my good lord. Myself, he, and my sister,
Today did dine together. So befall my soul 208
As this is false he burdens me withal! 209

LUCIANA
Ne'er may I look on day, nor sleep on night,
But she tells to your Highness simple truth!

ANGELO
O perjur'd woman! They are both forsworn.
In this the madman justly chargeth them.

132 so . . . him so much consideration we grant him **138 important** importunate, pressing. **letters** (Adriana would seem to have been ward to the Duke and married at his urging.) **144 rage** madness, insanity **146 take order** settle, make reparation **148 wot** know. **strong** violent **160 help** cure **162 engag'd** pledged **170 a-row** one after another **173 puddled** from filthy puddles **175 nicks . . . fool** gives him a fantastic haircut in the short fashion of the court fool

185 halberds long-handled spears with blades **192 bestrid** stood over (to defend when fallen in battle) **199 abused** maltreated **203 Discover** reveal **205 harlots** rascals, vile companions **208 So . . . soul** i.e., as I hope to be saved **209 he . . . withal** he charges me with

ANTIPHOLUS E.
My liege, I am advised what I say,
Neither disturbed with the effect of wine,
Nor heady-rash, provok'd with raging ire,
Albeit my wrongs might make one wiser mad.
This woman lock'd me out this day from dinner.
That goldsmith there, were he not pack'd with her,
Could witness it, for he was with me then;
Who parted with me to go fetch a chain,
Promising to bring it to the Porpentine,
Where Balthazar and I did dine together.
Our dinner done, and he not coming thither,
I went to seek him. In the street I met him,
And in his company that gentleman.
There did this perjur'd goldsmith swear me down
That I this day of him receiv'd the chain,
Which, God he knows, I saw not; for the which
He did arrest me with an officer.
I did obey, and sent my peasant home
For certain ducats; he with none return'd.
Then fairly I bespoke the officer
To go in person with me to my house.
By th' way we met
My wife, her sister, and a rabble more
Of vile confederates. Along with them
They brought one Pinch, a hungry lean-fac'd villain,
A mere anatomy, a mountebank,
A threadbare juggler and a fortune-teller,
A needy, hollow-ey'd, sharp-looking wretch,
A living dead man. This pernicious slave,
Forsooth, took on him as a conjurer,
And, gazing in mine eyes, feeling my pulse,
And with no face, as 'twere, outfacing me,
Cries out, I was possess'd. Then all together
They fell upon me, bound me, bore me thence
And in a dark and dankish vault at home
There left me and my man, both bound together,
Till, gnawing with my teeth my bonds in sunder,
I gain'd my freedom, and immediately
Ran hither to your Grace; whom I beseech
To give me ample satisfaction
For these deep shames and great indignities.

ANGELO
My lord, in truth, thus far I witness with him,
That he din'd not at home, but was lock'd out.

DUKE
But had he such a chain of thee, or no?

ANGELO
He had, my lord, and when he ran in here,
These people saw the chain about his neck.

SECOND MERCHANT
Besides, I will be sworn these ears of mine
Heard you confess you had the chain of him
After you first forswore it on the mart,
And thereupon I drew my sword on you;
And then you fled into this abbey here,
From whence, I think, you are come by miracle.

ANTIPHOLUS E.
I never came within these abbey walls,
Nor ever didst thou draw thy sword on me.
I never saw the chain, so help me Heaven!
And this is false you burden me withal.

DUKE
Why, what an intricate impeach is this!
I think you all have drunk of Circe's cup.
If here you hous'd him, here he would have been.
If he were mad, he would not plead so coldly.
You say he din'd at home; the goldsmith here
Denies that saying. Sirrah, what say you?

DROMIO E.
Sir, he din'd with her there, at the Porpentine.

COURTEZAN
He did, and from my finger snatch'd that ring.

ANTIPHOLUS E.
'Tis true, my liege; this ring I had of her.

DUKE
Saw'st thou him enter at the abbey here?

COURTEZAN
As sure, my liege, as I do see your Grace.

DUKE
Why, this is strange. Go call the Abbess hither.
I think you are all mated or stark mad.
Exit one to the Abbess.

EGEON
Most mighty Duke, vouchsafe me speak a word.
Haply I see a friend will save my life
And pay the sum that may deliver me.

DUKE
Speak freely, Syracusian, what thou wilt.

EGEON
Is not your name, sir, call'd Antipholus?
And is not that your bondman, Dromio?

DROMIO E.
Within this hour I was his bondman, sir,
But he, I thank him, gnaw'd in two my cords.
Now am I Dromio, and his man, unbound.

EGEON
I am sure you both of you remember me.

DROMIO E.
Ourselves we do remember, sir, by you;
For lately we were bound, as you are now.
You are not Pinch's patient, are you, sir?

EGEON
Why look you strange on me? You know me well.

ANTIPHOLUS E.
I never saw you in my life till now.

EGEON
O, grief hath chang'd me since you saw me last,
And careful hours with time's deformed hand
Have written strange defeatures in my face.
But tell me yet, dost thou not know my voice?

ANTIPHOLUS E. Neither.

EGEON
Dromio, nor thou?

214 am advised know very well **219 pack'd** in conspiracy **233 fairly** civilly. **bespoke** requested **239 mere anatomy** absolute skeleton. **mountebank** quack, charlatan **240 juggler** sorcerer **243 took . . . as** pretended to be

270 intricate impeach involved accusation **271 Circe's cup** the charmed cup, a draft of which turned men into beasts **273 coldly** calmly, rationally **282 mated** stupified **299 careful** full of care. **deformed** deforming **300 defeatures** worsening of feature

DROMIO E. No, trust me, sir, nor I.

EGEON
I am sure thou dost.

DROMIO E. Ay, sir, but I am sure I do not; and whatsoever a man denies, you are now bound to believe him.

EGEON
Not know my voice! O time's extremity,
Hast thou so crack'd and splitted my poor tongue
In seven short years, that here my only son
Knows not my feeble key of untun'd cares?
Though now this grained face of mine be hid
In sap-consuming winter's drizzled snow,
And all the conduits of my blood froze up,
Yet hath my night of life some memory,
My wasting lamps some fading glimmer left,
My dull deaf ears a little use to hear.
All these old witnesses—I cannot err—
Tell me thou art my son Antipholus.

ANTIPHOLUS E.
I never saw my father in my life.

EGEON
But seven years since, in Syracusa, boy,
Thou know'st we parted; but perhaps, my son,
Thou sham'st to acknowledge me in misery.

ANTIPHOLUS E.
The Duke and all that know me in the city
Can witness with me that it is not so.
I ne'er saw Syracusa in my life.

DUKE
I tell thee, Syracusian, twenty years
Have I been patron to Antipholus,
During which time he ne'er saw Syracusa.
I see thy age and dangers make thee dote.

Enter the Abbess, with Antipholus [of] Syracusa and Dromio [of] Syracusa.

ABBESS
Most mighty Duke, behold a man much wrong'd.
All gather to see them.

ADRIANA
I see two husbands, or mine eyes deceive me.

DUKE
One of these men is genius to the other;
And so of these, which is the natural man,
And which the spirit? Who deciphers them?

DROMIO S.
I, sir, am Dromio; command him away.

DROMIO E.
I, sir, am Dromio; pray, let me stay.

ANTIPHOLUS S.
Egeon art thou not? Or else his ghost?

DROMIO S.
O, my old master! Who hath bound him here?

ABBESS
Whoever bound him, I will loose his bonds
And gain a husband by his liberty.
Speak, old Egeon, if thou be'st the man
That hadst a wife once call'd Emilia
That bore thee at a burden two fair sons.
O, if thou be'st the same Egeon, speak,
And speak unto the same Emilia!

EGEON
If I dream not, thou art Emilia.
If thou art she, tell me where is that son
That floated with thee on the fatal raft?

ABBESS
By men of Epidamium he and I
And the twin Dromio all were taken up;
But by and by rude fishermen of Corinth
By force took Dromio and my son from them,
And me they left with those of Epidamium.
What then became of them I cannot tell;
I to this fortune that you see me in.

DUKE
Why, here begins his morning story right:
These two Antipholuses, these two so like,
And these two Dromios, one in semblance—
Besides her urging of her wrack at sea—
These are the parents to these children,
Which accidentally are met together.
Antipholus, thou cam'st from Corinth first?

ANTIPHOLUS S.
No, sir, not I; I came from Syracuse.

DUKE
Stay, stand apart; I know not which is which.

ANTIPHOLUS E.
I came from Corinth, my most gracious lord—

DROMIO E.
And I with him.

ANTIPHOLUS E.
Brought to this town by that most famous warrior,
Duke Menaphon, your most renowned uncle.

ADRIANA
Which of you two did dine with me today?

ANTIPHOLUS S.
I, gentle mistress.

ADRIANA And are not you my husband?

ANTIPHOLUS E.
No; I say nay to that.

ANTIPHOLUS S.
And so do I; yet did she call me so;
And this fair gentlewoman, her sister here,
Did call me brother. [*To Luciana.*] What I told you then,
I hope I shall have leisure to make good,
If this be not a dream I see and hear.

ANGELO
That is the chain, sir, which you had of me.

ANTIPHOLUS S.
I think it be, sir; I deny it not.

ANTIPHOLUS E.
And you, sir, for this chain arrested me.

ANGELO
I think I did, sir; I deny it not.

ADRIANA
I sent you money, sir, to be your bail,
By Dromio; but I think he brought it not.

310 my . . . cares my voice enfeebled by discordant cares **311 grained** lined, furrowed **315 wasting lamps** i.e., dimming eyes **332 genius** attendant spirit

343 burden birth **359 urging** urgent account

DROMIO E.
No, none by me.

ANTIPHOLUS S.
This purse of ducats I receiv'd from you,
And Dromio my man did bring them me.
I see we still did meet each other's man,
And I was ta'en for him, and he for me,
And thereupon these errors are arose.

ANTIPHOLUS E.
These ducats pawn I for my father here.
[*Offers money.*]

DUKE
It shall not need; thy father hath his life.

COURTEZAN
Sir, I must have that diamond from you.

ANTIPHOLUS E.
There, take it, and much thanks for my good cheer.
[*Gives jewel.*]

ABBESS
Renowned Duke, vouchsafe to take the pains
To go with us into the abbey here,
And hear at large discoursed all our fortunes;
And all that are assembled in this place,
That by this sympathized one day's error
Have suffer'd wrong, go keep us company,
And we shall make full satisfaction.
Thirty-three years have I but gone in travail
Of you, my sons, and till this present hour
My heavy burden ne'er delivered.
The Duke, my husband, and my children both,
And you the calendars of their nativity,
Go to a gossips' feast, and go with me;
After so long grief, such nativity!

DUKE
With all my heart, I'll gossip at this feast.
Exeunt omnes. Mane[n]t the two Dromios and two Brothers.

DROMIO S.
Master, shall I fetch your stuff from shipboard?

ANTIPHOLUS E.
Dromio, what stuff of mine hast thou embark'd?

DROMIO S.
Your goods that lay at host, sir, in the Centaur.

ANTIPHOLUS S.
He speaks to me. I am your master, Dromio.
Come, go with us, we'll look to that anon.
Embrace thy brother there, rejoice with him.
Exit [with Antipholus of Ephesus].

DROMIO S.
There is a fat friend at your master's house,
That kitchen'd me for you today at dinner.
She now shall be my sister, not my wife.

DROMIO E.
Methinks you are my glass, and not my brother.
I see by you I am a sweet-fac'd youth.
Will you walk in to see their gossiping?

DROMIO S. Not I, sir; you are my elder.

DROMIO E. That's a question. How shall we try it?

DROMIO S. We'll draw cuts for the senior; till then lead thou first.

DROMIO E. Nay, then, thus:
We came into the world like brother and brother,
And now let's go hand in hand, not one before another.
Exeunt.

386 still continually **395 at large** at length **397 sympathized** shared in by all equally **404 calendars . . . nativity** i.e., the Dromios, since the servants were born at the same time as their masters **405 gossips' feast** feast of the godparents, christening feast **407 gossip** i.e., be a hearty companion, take part **410 lay at host** were put up **415 kitchen'd** entertained in the kitchen **417 glass** mirror

419 gossiping merrymaking **422 cuts** lots

Love's Labor's Lost

In much the same way that *The Comedy of Errors* is Shakespeare's apprenticeship to Plautus and neoclassical comedy, *Love's Labor's Lost* is his apprenticeship to John Lyly's courtly drama of the 1580's, to the court masque, and to conventions of Petrarchan lyric poetry. The play is word-conscious and stylistically mannered to an extent that is unusual even for the pun-loving Shakespeare. The humor abounds in the pert repartee for which juvenile actors were especially fitted, and an extraordinarily high percentage of roles are assigned to boys: four women and a diminutive page (Moth) among seventeen named roles. The social setting is patrician and the entertainments aristocratic. In some ways, little seems to happen in *Love's Labor's Lost.* Fast-moving plot is replaced by a structure that includes a series of debates on courtly topics reminiscent of John Lyly: love versus honor, the flesh versus the spirit, pleasure versus instruction, art versus nature. The songs and sonnets composed by the courtiers for the ladies (IV,iii) gracefully caricature the excesses of the Petrarchan love-convention: the lovers are "sick to death" with unrequited passion, they catalogue the charms of their proud mistresses, they express their exquisitely tortured emotions through elaborate poetical metaphors, and so on. Stage movements are often masquelike; characters group themselves and then pair off two by two as in a formal dance. Actual masques and pageants, presented by the courtiers or devised for their amusement, are essential ingredients of the spectacle.

Yet beneath the brightly polished surfaces of this sophisticated comedy, we often catch glimpses of a candor and a simplicity that offset the tinsel and glitter. The wits ultimately disclaim (with some qualification) their wittiness, and the ladies confess they have tried too zealously to put down the men; both sides disavow the excessive postures they have striven so to maintain. The clowns, though deflated by mocking laughter for their naiveté and pomposity, deflate the courtiers in turn for lack of compassion. From this interplay among various forms of courtly wit, Petrarchism, pedantry, and rustic speech emerges a "recommended style" that is witty but not irresponsibly so, courtly yet sincere, polished and yet free of affectation or empty verbal ornament. This new harmony is aptly expressed by Berowne and Rosaline, whose witty quest for self-understanding in love foreshadows that of Benedick and Beatrice in *Much Ado about Nothing.* The perfect expression of the true style is found in the song at the end of the play; taking the form of a medieval literary debate between Spring and Winter, it beautifully fuses the natural and the artificial into a concordant vision transcending the mundane.

Like *The Comedy of Errors, Love's Labor's Lost* may either be a very early play or just an early play. It was published in quarto in 1598 "as it was presented before her Highnes this last Christmas" (1597). The text also purports to be "newly corrected and augmented," though we know of no earlier published version. Perhaps a play that was already several years old may have seemed in need of stylistic revision. Act IV does in fact contain two long duplicatory passages, suggesting that a certain amount of rewriting did take place. (See Appendix I.) The revisions alter the meaning only slightly, however, and give little support to the widely held notion that Shakespeare must have reworked the ending of his play. The abrupt ending, in which no marriages take place and in which the Princess' territorial claims to Aquitaine are left unresolved, should be regarded not as unfinished but as highly imaginative and indeed indispensable. The title after all assures us that "love's labors" will be lost and the Princess affirms the principle of "form confounded."

Equally inconclusive are theories that the play was a topical satire written for a special audience, or that it was a comparatively late play of Shakespeare's "lyric" period, 1594–1595. Topical hypotheses arise from the quest for sources. Since the plot of *Love's Labor's Lost* is derived from no known literary source, may it have been drawn instead from the Elizabethan contemporary scene, poking fun at the pretentiousness of literary figures and intellectuals such as John Florio, Thomas Nashe, Gabriel Harvey, Sir Walter Ralegh, and George Chapman? Or should we seek topical meaning in the undoubted currency of such names as Navarre (Henry of Navarre, King Henry IV of France), Berowne (Biron, Henry IV's general), Dumaine (De Mayenne, brother of the Catholic Guise), and others? From the point of view of dating the play, however, such names would have been distastefully controversial in a courtly comedy after 1589. That date saw the beginning in France of a bitter civil conflict between the Catholic Guise and Protestant Navarre, continuing until Henry abjured Protestantism in 1593 and assumed the French throne. In the 1580's, on the other hand, the tiny kingdom of Navarre would have seemed charmingly appropriate as a setting for Shakespeare's play. Such an early date, although by no means certain, would also help explain the Lylyan tone of the comedy and its early techniques of versification: the high percentage of rhymed lines in couplets and quatrains, the end-stopped blank verse, the use of various sonnet forms and of seven-stress (septenary) couplets, and the like. Possibly, then, the play was first written in about 1588–1589 for a boys' company, and revised for Shakespeare's company in about 1596–1597.

The world of *Love's Labor's Lost,* as compared with that of most of Shakespeare's comedies, is not only uneventful but is remarkably unthreatened by danger or evil. The characters are menaced by nothing worse than themselves, and stand to lose nothing more serious than their dignity. In such an artificial world, however, the preservation of one's self-esteem assumes undue importance. Using the criteria of wit and self-awareness, Moth and Boyet, as manipulators and choric figures, show us how to laugh at folly in love and pomposity in language. They present to us variations on a theme of courtly behavior, creating in effect a scale of manners ranging from the most aristocratic (the King and the Princess, Berowne and Rosaline) to the most absurdly pretentious (Armado, Holofernes). Nearly all the characters are mocked, but those at the lower end of the scale are especially vulnerable because they are grossly unself-aware and hence unteachable.

The King and his companions deserve to be mocked because of the transparent hypocrisy and futility of their vows against love. As Berowne concedes from the start, such defiance of love is at odds with a fundamental natural rhythm that cannot ultimately be thwarted—a rhythm that provides a counterpoint and corrective to the frequently artificial rhythms of courtly life. This natural rhythm asserts itself throughout the play until it becomes starkly insistent in the death of the Princess' royal father and in the resulting twelve-month delay of all marriages.

Hypocritical defiance of love is doomed to comic failure and satirical punishment. The basic devices used to expose this hypocrisy are misdirected love letters and overhearings, both devices of unmasking. Appropriately the young ladies administer their most amusing comeuppance to the men by seeing through their Muscovite masks. The code governing this merry conflict is one of "mock for mock," and "sport by sport o'erthrown" (V,ii). Love is metaphorically a war, a siege, a battle of the sexes in which the women come off virtually unscathed. The language of love is that of parry and thrust (with occasional bawdy overtones). The men naturally are chagrined to be put down by the ladies, but are on their way to a cure: they laugh at their own pretentiousness and, even if hyperbolically, vow to cast aside all "affectation" and "maggot ostentation" in favor of "russet yeas and honest kersey noes."

The clownish types are generally more victimized by their affectations. The fantastical Don Armado, as lover of Jaquenetta the country wench, apes the courtly conventions of the aristocrats to whose company he aspires. Enervated by base passion, penning wretched love letters, and worshiping a dairy-maid as though she were an unapproachable goddess, he is a caricature of the Petrarchan lover. Generally, however, the affectations of the comic characters have to do with language rather than love. Armado himself is known as a phrase-maker, "a plume of feathers," a "weathercock": "Did you ever hear better?" (IV,i). His letter to Jaquenetta, read aloud for the Princess' amusement, is an exquisite spoof of John Lyly's exaggeratedly mannered style called Euphuism: "Shall I command thy love? I may. Shall I enforce thy love? I could. Shall I entreat thy love? I will. What shalt thou exchange for rags? Robes. For tittles? Titles. For thyself? Me." Here we see the repeated antitheses, the balanced structure (reflected also in the structure of the play), and the alliterative effects that so intoxicated literary sophisticates of the 1580's. In a similar spirit, other comic types are distinguished by their verbal habits: Constable Dull by his malapropisms (anticipating Dogberry and Elbow), Holofernes by his Latinisms, his philological definitions, and his varied epithets, Nathaniel by his deference to Holofernes as a fellow "book-man," Costard by his amiable but unlettered confusion over such grandiose terms as "remuneration" and "guerdon." The word-conscious humor of the play gives us parodies of excruciatingly bad verse (as in Holofernes' "extemporal epitaph on the death of the deer"), teeth-grating puns (enfranchise, en-Frances), and the longest Latin word in existence *(honorificabilitudinitatibus).*

A little of this sort of thing goes a long way, and occasional scenes of verbal sparring are as tedious as anything Shakespeare ever wrote. He tries to have it both ways, reveling in linguistic self-consciousness while laughing at its excesses. Yet the self-possessed characters do at least come to a realization that verbal overkill, like Petrarchan posturing, must be cast aside in favor of decorum and frankness in speech. There will always be "style," but it must be an appropriate style. The comic characters at their best help emphasize this same point. Costard especially is blessed with a pragmatic folk wisdom and simplicity that enable him to stand up unflinchingly to the ladies and gentlemen. He does not hesitate to tell the Princess that she is the "thickest and the tallest" of the ladies, for "Truth is truth." His forebearing description of Nathaniel as "a little o'erparted" in the role of Alexander serves as a gentle rebuke to the wits, whose caustic observations on "The Nine Worthies" have gotten out of hand. Even Holofernes justly chides, before retiring in confusion as Judas Maccabaeus, that "This is not generous, not gentle, not humble" (V,ii).

Above all, however, it is the play's unexpected ending that introduces an invaluable new insight on the courtiers' brittle war of wits. The death of the Princess' father brings everyone back to reality, to sober responsibility, to an awareness that marriage requires thoughtful decision. Devouring Time has entered the never-never land of Navarre's park. The song at the end, appropriately cast in the form of a dialogue or debate, gives us the two voices of Spring and Winter, love and death, Carnival and Lent, to remind us that human happiness and self-understanding are complex and perishable. And the song reminds us as well, in its "living art," of that subtle power of the imagination which transforms time, love, and death into artistic creation.

Love's Labor's Lost

[*Dramatis Personae*

FERDINAND, *King of Navarre.*
BEROWNE, LONGAVILLE, DUMAINE, } *lords attending on the King.*
BOYET, MARCADE, } *lords attending on the Princess of France.*

DON ADRIANO DE ARMADO, *a fantastical Spaniard.*
SIR NATHANIEL, *a curate.*
HOLOFERNES, *a schoolmaster.*
DULL, *a constable.*
COSTARD, *a clown.*
MOTH, *page to Armado.*
A FORESTER.

THE PRINCESS OF FRANCE.
ROSALINE, MARIA, KATHARINE, } *ladies attending on the Princess.*
JAQUENETTA, *a country wench.*

LORDS, ATTENDANTS, *&c.*

SCENE: *Navarre.*]

[ACT I • SCENE I]

Enter Ferdinand, King of Navarre, Berowne, Longaville, and Dumaine.

KING
Let fame, that all hunt after in their lives,
Live regist'red upon our brazen tombs 2
And then grace us in the disgrace of death; 3
When, spite of cormorant devouring Time, 4
Th' endeavor of this present breath may buy 5
That honor which shall bate his scythe's keen edge 6
And make us heirs of all eternity.
Therefore, brave conquerors—for so you are,
That war against your own affections 9
And the huge army of the world's desires—
Our late edict shall strongly stand in force:
Navarre shall be the wonder of the world;
Our court shall be a little Academe, 13
Still and contemplative in living art. 14
You three, Berowne, Dumaine, and Longaville,
Have sworn for three years' term to live with me
My fellow-scholars and to keep those statutes
That are recorded in this schedule here. 18
[*Shows document.*]
Your oaths are pass'd; and now subscribe your names, 19
That his own hand may strike his honor down 20
That violates the smallest branch herein.
If you are arm'd to do as sworn to do,
Subscribe to your deep oaths, and keep it too.

LONGAVILLE [*Signing*]
I am resolved. 'Tis but a three years' fast.
The mind shall banquet, though the body pine.
Fat paunches have lean pates, and dainty bits
Make rich the ribs, but bankrupt quite the wits.

DUMAINE [*Signing*]
My loving lord, Dumaine is mortified. 28
The grosser manner of these world's delights
He throws upon the gross world's baser slaves.
To love, to wealth, to pomp, I pine and die,
With all these living in philosophy. 32

BEROWNE
I can but say their protestation over.
So much, dear liege, I have already sworn,
That is, to live and study here three years.
But there are other strict observances:
As, not to see a woman in that term,
Which I hope well is not enrolled there;
And one day in a week to touch no food,
And but one meal on every day beside,
The which I hope is not enrolled there;
And then, to sleep but three hours in the night,
And not be seen to wink of all the day— 43
When I was wont to think no harm all night, 44
And make a dark night too of half the day—
Which I hope well is not enrolled there.
O, these are barren tasks, too hard to keep,
Not to see ladies, study, fast, not sleep!

KING
Your oath is pass'd to pass away from these.

BEROWNE
Let me say no, my liege, an if you please; 50
I only swore to study with your Grace
And stay here in your court for three years' space.

LONGAVILLE
You swore to that, Berowne, and to the rest.

BEROWNE
By yea and nay, sir, then I swore in jest. 54
What is the end of study, let me know?

KING
Why, that to know which else we should not know.

I.i. Location: The King of Navarre's park. (The locale remains the same throughout the play, sometimes immediately outside the gates of Navarre's court.)
2 brazen brass **3 grace** honor. **disgrace** disfigurement and dishonor **4 spite** in spite. **cormorant** ravenous, rapacious **5 breath** breathing time, i.e., life itself **6 bate** abate, blunt **9 affections** emotions, passions

13 Academe academy. (From the name of the grove near Athens where Plato and his followers gathered.) **14 Still** constant. **living art** the art of living. (An idea probably derived from the *ars vivendi* of the Roman Stoics.) **18 schedule** document **19 pass'd** pledged **20 hand** handwriting **28 mortified** i.e., dead to worldly desire **32 With . . . philosophy** i.e., the pleasure afforded by these (love, wealth, pomp) I find in philosophy **43 wink of** close the eyes during **44 think no harm** i.e., sleep well **50 an if** if **54 By . . . nay** earnestly. (A meaning derived from Matthew 5:33–37; Berowne is using a pious equivocation frequently invoked by those not having a proper answer.)

BEROWNE
Things hid and barr'd, you mean, from common sense?
KING
Ay, that is study's god-like recompense.
BEROWNE
Come on, then, I will swear to study so,
To know the thing I am forbid to know:
As thus—to study where I well may dine,
When I to feast expressly am forbid;
Or study where to meet some mistress fine,
When mistresses from common sense are hid;
Or, having sworn too hard a keeping oath,
Study to break it and not break my troth.
If study's gain be thus and this be so,
Study knows that which yet it doth not know.
Swear me to this, and I will ne'er say no.
KING
These be the stops that hinder study quite,
And train our intellects to vain delight.
BEROWNE
Why, all delights are vain, but that most vain,
Which, with pain purchas'd, doth inherit pain:
As, painfully to pore upon a book
To seek the light of truth, while truth the while
Doth falsely blind the eyesight of his look.
Light seeking light doth light of light beguile;
So, ere you find where light in darkness lies,
Your light grows dark by losing of your eyes.
Study me how to please the eye indeed
By fixing it upon a fairer eye,
Who dazzling so, that eye shall be his heed
And give him light that it was blinded by.
Study is like the heaven's glorious sun,
That will not be deep-search'd with saucy looks;
Small have continual plodders ever won
Save base authority from others' books.
These earthly godfathers of heaven's lights,
That give a name to every fixed star,
Have no more profit of their shining nights
Than those that walk and wot not what they are.
Too much to know is to know nought but fame;
And every godfather can give a name.
KING
How well he's read, to reason against reading!
DUMAINE
Proceeded well, to stop all good proceeding!
LONGAVILLE
He weeds the corn and still lets grow the weeding.
BEROWNE
The spring is near when green geese are a-breeding.
DUMAINE
How follows that?
BEROWNE
Fit in his place and time.
DUMAINE
In reason nothing.
BEROWNE
Something then in rhyme.
KING
Berowne is like an envious sneaping frost
That bites the first-born infants of the spring.
BEROWNE
Well, say I am; why should proud summer boast
Before the birds have any cause to sing?
Why should I joy in any abortive birth?
At Christmas I no more desire a rose
Than wish a snow in May's new-fangled shows,
But like of each thing that in season grows.
So you, to study now it is too late,
Climb o'er the house to unlock the little gate.
KING
Well, sit you out. Go home, Berowne; adieu.
BEROWNE
No, my good lord, I have sworn to stay with you;
And though I have for barbarism spoke more
Than for that angel knowledge you can say,
Yet confident I'll keep what I have sworn
And bide the penance of each three years' day.
Give me the paper, let me read the same,
And to the strictest decrees I'll write my name.
[*Takes the paper.*]
KING
How well this yielding rescues thee from shame!

BEROWNE [*Reads*] "Item, That no woman shall come within a mile of my court—" Hath this been proclaim'd?

LONGAVILLE Four days ago.

BEROWNE Let's see the penalty. [*Reads.*] "on pain of losing her tongue." Who devis'd this penalty?

LONGAVILLE
Marry, that did I.
BEROWNE
Sweet lord, and why?
LONGAVILLE
To fright them hence with that dread penalty.
BEROWNE
A dangerous law against gentility!

[*Reads.*] "Item, If any man be seen to talk with a woman within the term of three years, he shall endure such public shame as the rest of the court can possibly devise."

This article, my liege, yourself must break;
For well you know here comes in embassy

57 common sense ordinary observation or intelligence **65 too . . . oath** an oath too hard to keep **70 stops** obstacles **71 train** allure, entice **73 pain** labor, effort (with pun on *suffering*). **purchas'd** acquired. **inherit** take possession of **76 falsely** treacherously. **his look** its power to see **77 Light . . . beguile** i.e., searching for truth by excessive study paradoxically takes from the eyes their ability to see at all, just as staring at a bright light causes blindness **80 Study me** i.e., for my part, study instead. (*Me* is a so-called ethical dative.) **81 fairer** i.e., of a fair lady **82 Who dazzling so** i.e., the man who has fixed his eye on a fair lady being thus dazzled. **heed** guard, means of safety **83 it** i.e., his own eye **85 deep-search'd** scrutinized **86 Small** little **87 base** commonplace, lower **88 earthly godfathers** astronomers (who name stars just as godparents pronounce the name of the child at a christening) **90 shining** i.e., starlit **91 wot** know **92 fame** report, secondhand information **93 every . . . name** i.e., anyone, acting as godparent, can do as much as astronomers **95 Proceeded** advanced (in the academic sense of taking a degree) **96 He . . . weeding** He pulls out the wheat and allows the weeds to grow

97 green geese i.e., young geese born the previous autumn and sold at green-goose fair, a season of merriment, held on Whitmonday; here, young simpletons **98 Fit in his** exactly in its **99 In reason nothing** i.e., it doesn't follow at all logically **100 envious** malignant, malicious. **sneaping** biting, nipping **101 infants** buds **102 proud** glorious **107 like of** approve of **108 too late** i.e., too late in our lives to be students **109 Climb . . . gate** i.e., you begin at the wrong end **110 sit you out** don't take part. (A term from card playing.) **112 barbarism** ignorance **114 confident** confidently **115 bide** endure. **each . . . day** every day of the three years **127 gentility** civilized custom **133 in embassy** as an ambassador

The French King's daughter with yourself to speak—
A maid of grace and complete majesty—
About surrender up of Aquitaine
To her decrepit, sick, and bedrid father.
Therefore this article is made in vain,
Or vainly comes th' admired Princess hither.

KING
What say you, lords? Why, this was quite forgot.

BEROWNE
So study evermore is overshot.
While it doth study to have what it would
It doth forget to do the thing it should,
And when it hath the thing it hunteth most,
'Tis won as towns with fire—so won, so lost.

KING
We must of force dispense with this decree;
She must lie here on mere necessity.

BEROWNE
Necessity will make us all forsworn
Three thousand times within this three years' space;
For every man with his affects is born,
Not by might mast'red, but by special grace.
If I break faith, this word shall speak for me:
I am forsworn on "mere necessity."
So to the laws at large I write my name, [*He signs.*]
And he that breaks them in the least degree
Stands in attainder of eternal shame.
Suggestions are to other as to me;
But I believe, although I seem so loath,
I am the last that will last keep his oath.
But is there no quick recreation granted?

KING
Ay, that there is. Our court, you know, is haunted
With a refined traveler of Spain,
A man in all the world's new fashion planted,
That hath a mint of phrases in his brain;
One who the music of his own vain tongue
Doth ravish like enchanting harmony;
A man of compliments, whom right and wrong
Have chose as umpire of their mutiny.
This child of fancy, that Armado hight,
For interim to our studies shall relate
In high-born words the worth of many a knight
From tawny Spain, lost in the world's debate.
How you delight, my lords, I know not, I;
But I protest I love to hear him lie
And I will use him for my minstrelsy.

BEROWNE
Armado is a most illustrious wight,
A man of fire-new words, fashion's own knight.

LONGAVILLE
Costard the swain and he shall be our sport;
And so to study three years is but short.

Enter [*Dull,*] *a Constable, with Costard, with a letter.*

DULL Which is the Duke's own person?

BEROWNE This, fellow. What wouldst?

DULL I myself reprehend his own person, for I am his Grace's farborough, but I would see his own person in flesh and blood.

BEROWNE This is he.

DULL Signior Arme–Arme–commends you. There's villainy abroad. This letter will tell you more. [*Gives letter to King.*]

COSTARD Sir, the contempts thereof are as touching me.

KING A letter from the magnificent Armado.

BEROWNE How low soever the matter, I hope in God for high words.

LONGAVILLE A high hope for a low heaven. God grant us patience!

BEROWNE To hear, or forbear hearing?

LONGAVILLE To hear meekly, sir, and to laugh moderately, or to forbear both.

BEROWNE Well, sir, be it as the style shall give us cause to climb in the merriness.

COSTARD The matter is to me, sir, as concerning Jaquenetta. The matter of it is, I was taken with the manner.

BEROWNE In what manner?

COSTARD In manner and form following, sir, all those three: I was seen with her in the manor-house, sitting with her upon the form, and taken following her into the park; which, put together, is in manner and form following. Now, sir, for the manner—it is the manner of a man to speak to a woman; for the form—in some form.

BEROWNE For the following, sir?

COSTARD As it shall follow in my correction, and God defend the right!

KING Will you hear this letter with attention?

BEROWNE As we would hear an oracle.

COSTARD Such is the sinplicity of man to hearken after the flesh.

KING [*Reads*] "Great deputy, the welkin's vicegerent, and sole dominator of Navarre, my soul's earth's god, and body's fost'ring patron"—

COSTARD Not a word of Costard yet.

KING [*Reads*] "So it is"—

COSTARD It may be so, but if he say it is so, he is, in telling true, but so.

145 with fire by being burned down (continuing the metaphor of siege in *overshot,* l. 141) **146 of force** necessarily **147 lie** lodge. **mere** absolute **150 affects** natural passions **151 might** i.e., his own strength. **special grace** divine intervention **152 word** motto **154 at large** as a whole, in general **156 in attainder** under penalty, accused **157 Suggestions** temptations **160 quick** lively **161–162 haunted With** frequented by **165 who** whom **167 compliments** those formal manners that go to complete a gentleman **168 mutiny** discord **169 child of fancy** fantastic or grotesque creature. **hight** is called. (An archaic, affected term.) **170 interim** interlude **171 high-born** elegantly lofty **172 tawny** sunburned. **debate** warfare **173 How you delight** what delights you **176 wight** person **177 fire-new** newly coined

178 Costard (The name means a large apple; the term is frequently applied humorously or derisively to the head.) **swain** rustic young fellow **180 Duke's** i.e., King's **181 fellow** (Customary form of address to a servant.) **182 reprehend** (Malapropism for *represent.*) **183 farborough** (Malapropism for *tharborough* or *thirdborough,* a petty constable.) **188 contempts** (Malapropism for *contents.*) **189 magnificent Armado** boastful or grandiose Armado (with an allusion to the great Armada of Spain) **192 low heaven** i.e., small blessing **197 be it** so be it. **style** (with a pun on *stile,* giving point to *climb* in the next line) **199 is to** applies to **200 with the manner** with the stolen goods. (An Anglo-French law term *mainoure,* from *manoeuvre.*) **202 In manner and form** (A familiar empty cliché of the time.) **204 form** bench **210 correction** punishment **210–211 God defend the right** (Prayer before mortal combat.) **214 sinplicity** (Costard's appropriate malapropism for *simplicity.*) **216 welkin's vicegerent** heaven's deputy. (A pompous phrase, as most in the letter are.) **222 but so** i.e., not saying much

KING Peace!

COSTARD Be to me and every man that dares not fight!

KING No words!

COSTARD Of other men's secrets, I beseech you.

KING [*Reads*] "So it is, besieged with sable-colored melancholy, I did commend the black-oppressing humor to the most wholesome physic of thy health-giving air; and, as I am a gentleman, betook myself to walk. The time when? About the sixth hour, when beasts most graze, birds best peck, and men sit down to that nourishment which is called supper. So much for the time when. Now for the ground which; which, I mean, I walk'd upon: it is ycleped thy park. Then for the place where; where, I mean, I did encounter that obscene and most prepost'rous event that draweth from my snow-white pen the ebon-colored ink which here thou viewest, beholdest, surveyest, or seest. But to the place where; it standeth north-north-east and by east from the west corner of thy curious-knotted garden. There did I see that low-spirited swain, that base minnow of thy mirth"—

COSTARD Me?

KING [*Reads*] "that unlettered small-knowing soul"—

COSTARD Me?

KING [*Reads*] "that shallow vassal"—

COSTARD Still me?

KING [*Reads*] "which, as I remember, hight Costard,"—

COSTARD O! Me.

KING [*Reads*] "sorted and consorted, contrary to thy established proclaimed edict and continent canon, which with—O, with—but with this I passion to say wherewith"—

COSTARD With a wench.

KING [*Reads*] "with a child of our grandmother Eve, a female; or, for thy more sweet understanding, a woman. Him I, as my ever-esteemed duty pricks me on, have sent to thee, to receive the meed of punishment, by thy sweet Grace's officer, Anthony Dull, a man of good repute, carriage, bearing, and estimation."

DULL Me, an 't shall please you; I am Anthony Dull.

KING [*Reads*] "For Jaquenetta—so is the weaker vessel called which I apprehended with the aforesaid swain—I keep her as a vessel of thy law's fury; and shall, at the least of thy sweet notice, bring her to trial. Thine, in all compliments of devoted and heart-burning heat of duty, Don Adriano de Armado."

BEROWNE This is not so well as I look'd for, but the best that ever I heard.

KING Ay, the best for the worst. But, sirrah, what say you to this?

COSTARD Sir, I confess the wench.

KING Did you hear the proclamation?

COSTARD I do confess much of the hearing it, but little of the marking of it.

KING It was proclaim'd a year's imprisonment to be taken with a wench.

COSTARD I was taken with none, sir; I was taken with a damsel.

KING Well, it was proclaim'd "damsel."

COSTARD This was no damsel neither, sir; she was a virgin.

KING It is so varied too, for it was proclaim'd "virgin."

COSTARD If it were, I deny her virginity; I was taken with a maid.

KING This maid will not serve your turn, sir.

COSTARD This maid will serve my turn, sir.

KING Sir, I will pronounce your sentence: you shall fast a week with bran and water.

COSTARD I had rather pray a month with mutton and porridge.

KING

And Don Armado shall be your keeper.
My Lord Berowne, see him delivered o'er.
And go we, lords, to put in practice that
Which each to other hath so strongly sworn.
[*Exeunt King, Longaville, and Dumaine.*]

BEROWNE

I'll lay my head to any good man's hat,
These oaths and laws will prove an idle scorn.
Sirrah, come on.

COSTARD I suffer for the truth, sir; for true it is, I was taken with Jaquenetta, and Jaquenetta is a true girl; and therefore welcome the sour cup of prosperity! Affliction may one day smile again; and till then, sit thee down, sorrow! *Exeunt.*

[SCENE II]

Enter Armado and Moth, his Page.

ARMADO Boy, what sign is it when a man of great spirit grows melancholy?

MOTH A great sign, sir, that he will look sad.

ARMADO Why, sadness is one and the self-same thing, dear imp.

MOTH No, no; O Lord, sir, no.

ARMADO How canst thou part sadness and melancholy, my tender juvenal?

MOTH By a familiar demonstration of the working, my tough signor.

228–229 black-oppressing humor black bile or melancholy **229 physic** medicine **235 ycleped** called. (Archaic usage.) **238 snow-white pen** i.e., white goose quill **241 curious-knotted** delicately or intricately designed **243 minnow** contemptible little creature **245 unlettered** illiterate **247 vassal** base slave **249 hight** is called. (Archaic usage.) **252 sorted and consorted** associated **253 continent canon** restraint enforced by law **254 passion** grieve **259 pricks** spurs **260 meed** reward **265 weaker vessel** i.e., woman **267–268 at . . . notice** i.e., at your first hint **273 best . . . worst** i.e., best example of the worst. **sirrah** (Ordinary form of address to inferiors.)

286 so varied alternatively phrased (in typical legal jargon) **289 serve your turn** i.e., get you out of your difficulty. (But Costard, in the next line, interprets the phrase in a ribald sense.) **293–294 mutton and porridge** mutton broth (with a pun on *mutton,* whore) **299 lay** wager **304 prosperity** (Malapropism for *austerity?*) **305 Affliction** (Costard mixes this up with *prosperity.*) **305–306 sit thee down** i.e., abide with me

I.ii. Location: The same. Navarre's park.
s.d. Moth (with a play on *mote* or dust speck; Elizabethan pronunciation was *mote.* There may possibly be a play also on *mot,* French for "word.")
5 imp young shoot, child **7 part** distinguish between **8 juvenal** youth; satirist (after Juvenal, the Roman satirist) **9 familiar** plain, easily understood. **working** operation **10 signor** sir (with pun on *senior*)

ARMADO Why tough signor? Why tough signor?

MOTH Why tender juvenal? Why tender juvenal?

ARMADO I spoke it, tender juvenal, as a congruent epitheton appertaining to thy young days, which we may nominate tender.

MOTH And I, tough senior, as an appertinent title to your old time, which we may name tough.

ARMADO Pretty and apt.

MOTH How mean you, sir? I pretty, and my saying apt? Or I apt, and my saying pretty?

ARMADO Thou pretty, because little.

MOTH Little pretty, because little. Wherefore apt?

ARMADO And therefore apt, because quick.

MOTH Speak you this in my praise, master?

ARMADO In thy condign praise.

MOTH I will praise an eel with the same praise.

ARMADO What, that an eel is ingenious?

MOTH That an eel is quick.

ARMADO I do say thou art quick in answers. Thou heat'st my blood.

MOTH I am answer'd, sir.

ARMADO I love not to be cross'd.

MOTH [*Aside*] He speaks the mere contrary; crosses love not him.

ARMADO I have promised to study three years with the Duke.

MOTH You may do it in an hour, sir.

ARMADO Impossible.

MOTH How many is one thrice told?

ARMADO I am ill at reck'ning; it fitteth the spirit of a tapster.

MOTH You are a gentleman and a gamester, sir.

ARMADO I confess both. They are both the varnish of a complete man.

MOTH Then I am sure you know how much the gross sum of deuce-ace amounts to.

ARMADO It doth amount to one more than two.

MOTH Which the base vulgar do call three.

ARMADO True.

MOTH Why, sir, is this such a piece of study? Now here is three studied, ere ye'll thrice wink; and how easy it is to put "years" to the word "three," and study three years in two words, the dancing horse will tell you.

ARMADO A most fine figure!

MOTH [*Aside*] To prove you a cipher.

ARMADO I will hereupon confess I am in love; and as it is base for a soldier to love, so am I in love with a base wench. If drawing my sword against the humor of affection would deliver me from the reprobate thought of it, I would take Desire prisoner, and ransom him to any French courtier for a new-devis'd cur'sy. I think scorn to sigh; methinks I should outswear Cupid. Comfort me, boy. What great men have been in love?

MOTH Hercules, master.

ARMADO Most sweet Hercules! More authority, dear boy, name more; and, sweet my child, let them be men of good repute and carriage.

MOTH Samson, master; he was a man of good carriage, great carriage, for he carried the town gates on his back like a porter; and he was in love.

ARMADO O well-knit Samson! Strong-jointed Samson! I do excel thee in my rapier as much as thou didst me in carrying gates. I am in love too. Who was Samson's love, my dear Moth?

MOTH A woman, master.

ARMADO Of what complexion?

MOTH Of all the four, or the three, or the two, or one of the four.

ARMADO Tell me precisely of what complexion.

MOTH Of the sea-water green, sir.

ARMADO Is that one of the four complexions?

MOTH As I have read, sir, and the best of them too.

ARMADO Green indeed is the color of lovers; but to have a love of that color, methinks Samson had small reason for it. He surely affected her for her wit.

MOTH It was so, sir, for she had a green wit.

ARMADO My love is most immaculate white and red.

MOTH Most maculate thoughts, master, are mask'd under such colors.

ARMADO Define, define, well-educated infant.

MOTH My father's wit and my mother's tongue, assist me!

ARMADO Sweet invocation of a child; most pretty and pathetical!

MOTH

If she be made of white and red,
  Her faults will ne'er be known,
For blushing cheeks by faults are bred,
  And fears by pale white shown;
Then if she fear, or be to blame,
  By this you shall not know,
For still her cheeks possess the same
  Which native she doth owe.

A dangerous rhyme, master, against the reason of white and red.

ARMADO Is there not a ballad, boy, of the King and the Beggar?

MOTH The world was very guilty of such a ballad some three ages since, but I think now 'tis not to be found; or, if it were, it would neither serve for the writing nor the tune.

ARMADO I will have that subject newly writ o'er, that I may example my digression by some mighty precedent. Boy, I do love that country girl that I took in the

13–14 congruent epitheton appropriate epithet **15 nominate** call **16 appertinent** appertaining **25 condign** worthily deserved **29–30 Thou . . . blood** you make me angry **33 crosses** coins. (So called because many of them were impressed with crosses.) **36 Duke** i.e., King **39 told** counted **42 gamester** gambler **43 varnish** finish, ornament **48 vulgar** common people **53 dancing horse** a famous trained horse named Morocco, who could count by tapping with his hoof **54 figure** metaphor. (But Moth plays on the sense *numeral*.) **58–59 humor of affection** inclination to passion **61 new-devis'd cur'sy** newfangled manner of bowing; any new fashion **61–62 think scorn** disdain **62 outswear** overcome by swearing

67 carriage bearing (with pun on *ability to carry* in the following speech; see Judges 16:3 for the account of Samson's deed) **76 complexion** skin color; also temperament. (The four complexions were sanguine, choleric, phlegmatic, and melancholic, and were supposedly determined by the relative proportions of the four humors.) **83 Green** (A reference to lovers' "green-sickness," an anemic condition of puberty.) **85 affected** loved. **wit** intelligence **86 green** immature (with a punning reference perhaps to the seven green *withes* with which Samson was bound, Judges 16:7-9) **88 maculate** stained, polluted **89 colors** (with a pun on *pretexts*) **94 pathetical** moving **102 native** naturally. **owe** own **105–106 ballad . . . Beggar** ballad of King Cophetua and the beggar maid. (Cf. IV.i.66–67.) **109 serve** suffice **112 example** give an example of. **digression** lapse, waywardness

park with the rational hind Costard. She deserves 114
well.

MOTH *[Aside]* To be whipp'd; and yet a better love than 116
my master.

ARMADO Sing, boy; my spirit grows heavy in love.

MOTH And that's great marvel, loving a light wench. 119

ARMADO I say, sing.

MOTH Forbear till this company be past.

Enter [Costard the] Clown, [Dull the] Constable, and [Jaquenetta, a] Wench.

DULL Sir, the Duke's pleasure is that you keep Costard
safe, and you must suffer him to take no delight nor
no penance, but 'a must fast three days a week. For 124
this damsel, I must keep her at the park; she is allow'd 125
for the day-woman. Fare you well. 126

ARMADO I do betray myself with blushing. Maid!

JAQUENETTA Man?

ARMADO I will visit thee at the lodge.

JAQUENETTA That's hereby.

ARMADO I know where it is situate.

JAQUENETTA Lord, how wise you are!

ARMADO I will tell thee wonders.

JAQUENETTA With that face? 134

ARMADO I love thee.

JAQUENETTA So I heard you say.

ARMADO And so, farewell.

JAQUENETTA Fair weather after you!

DULL Come, Jaquenetta, away!

Exeunt [Dull and Jaquenetta].

ARMADO Villain, thou shalt fast for thy offenses ere 140
thou be pardoned.

COSTARD Well, sir, I hope when I do it I shall do it on a 142
full stomach. 143

ARMADO Thou shalt be heavily punished.

COSTARD I am more bound to you than your fellows, 145
for they are but lightly rewarded. 146

ARMADO Take away this villain. Shut him up.

MOTH Come, you transgressing slave, away!

COSTARD Let me not be pent up, sir. I will fast, being
loose.

MOTH No, sir, that were fast and loose. Thou shalt to 151
prison.

COSTARD Well, if ever I do see the merry days of deso- 153
lation that I have seen, some shall see. 154

MOTH What shall some see?

COSTARD Nay, nothing, Master Moth, but what they
look upon. It is not for prisoners to be too silent in
their words, and therefore I will say nothing. I thank
God I have as little patience as another man, and 159
therefore I can be quiet. *Exit [with Moth].*

ARMADO I do affect the very ground, which is base, 161
where her shoe, which is baser, guided by her foot,
which is basest, doth tread. I shall be forsworn, which
is a great argument of falsehood, if I love. And how 164
can that be true love which is falsely attempted? Love
is a familiar; Love is a devil. There is no evil angel but 166
Love. Yet was Samson so tempted, and he had an ex-
cellent strength; yet was Solomon so seduced, and he
had a very good wit. Cupid's butt-shaft is too hard for 169
Hercules' club, and therefore too much odds for a
Spaniard's rapier. The first and second cause will not 171
serve my turn; the passado he respects not, the duello 172
he regards not. His disgrace is to be called boy, but his
glory is to subdue men. Adieu, valor! Rust, rapier! Be
still, drum! For your manager is in love; yea, he loveth. 175
Assist me, some extemporal god of rhyme, for I am
sure I shall turn sonnet. Devise, wit; write, pen; for I 177
am for whole volumes in folio. *Exit.*

[ACT II • SCENE I]

Enter the Princess of France, with three attending Ladies [Rosaline, Maria, Katharine] and three Lords [one being Boyet].

BOYET

Now, madam, summon up your dearest spirits. 1
Consider who the King your father sends,
To whom he sends, and what's his embassy:
Yourself, held precious in the world's esteem,
To parley with the sole inheritor
Of all perfections that a man may owe, 6
Matchless Navarre; the plea of no less weight 7
Than Aquitaine, a dowry for a queen.
Be now as prodigal of all dear grace
As Nature was in making graces dear, 10
When she did starve the general world beside 11
And prodigally gave them all to you.

PRINCESS

Good Lord Boyet, my beauty, though but mean, 13
Needs not the painted flourish of your praise. 14
Beauty is bought by judgment of the eye,
Not utt'red by base sale of chapmen's tongues. 16
I am less proud to hear you tell my worth 17
Than you much willing to be counted wise
In spending your wit in the praise of mine.
But now to task the tasker: good Boyet, 20
You are not ignorant, all-telling fame 21
Doth noise abroad, Navarre hath made a vow,
Till painful study shall outwear three years, 23
No woman may approach his silent court.

114 rational capable of reason. (Said patronizingly.) **hind** rustic or clown **116 love** partner, mate **119 light** wanton (with a play on the opposite of *heavy,* l. 118) **124 penance** (Malapropism for *pleasance*?) **125–126 allow'd . . . day-woman** approved to act as dairy-maid **134 With that face** i.e., you don't mean it? (Slang, like most of Jaquenetta's expressions.) **140 Villain** (1) servant (2) rascal **142–143 on . . . stomach** (with a pun on *full-stomached,* with good courage) **145 fellows** servants **146 but lightly** only slightly **151 fast and loose** a cheating trick **153–154 desolation** (Malapropism for *consolation*?) **159 patience** (Costard means the opposite of what he says.) **161 affect** love

164 argument proof **166 familiar** attendant evil spirit **169 butt-shaft** unbarbed arrow, used in archery practice **171 first . . . cause** (An allusion to certain situations that necessitated a duel according to the code of honor. Armado complains that Cupid will not follow this code of honor.) **172 passado** forward thrust with the sword, one foot being advanced at the same time. **duello** established code of duelists **175 manager** skilled practitioner **177 sonnet** i.e., sonneteer

II.i. Location: The same. Outside the gates of Navarre's court.
1 dearest spirits best wits **6 owe** own **7 plea** suit, claim **10 dear** bearing a high price (playing on *dear,* "beloved," of the previous line) **11 beside** i.e., excepting yourself **13 mean** average, moderate **14 flourish** adornment **16 utt'red** offered for sale. **chapmen's** merchants' **17 tell** (1) speak of (2) reckon **20 task** lay a task upon **21 fame** rumor **23 painful** strenuous

Therefore to 's seemeth it a needful course, 25
Before we enter his forbidden gates,
To know his pleasure; and in that behalf,
Bold of your worthiness, we single you 28
As our best-moving fair solicitor. 29
Tell him, the daughter of the King of France,
On serious business, craving quick dispatch,
Importunes personal conference with his Grace.
Haste, signify so much, while we attend,
Like humble-visag'd suitors, his high will.

BOYET
Proud of employment, willingly I go.

PRINCESS
All pride is willing pride, and yours is so.
Exit Boyet.
Who are the votaries, my loving lords, 37
That are vow-fellows with this virtuous Duke?

FIRST LORD
Lord Longaville is one.

PRINCESS
Know you the man?

MARIA
I know him, madam. At a marriage-feast,
Between Lord Perigort and the beauteous heir
Of Jaques Falconbridge, solemnized
In Normandy, saw I this Longaville.
A man of sovereign parts he is esteem'd, 44
Well fitted in arts, glorious in arms; 45
Nothing becomes him ill that he would well. 46
The only soil of his fair virtue's gloss, 47
If virtue's gloss will stain with any soil,
Is a sharp wit match'd with too blunt a will, 49
Whose edge hath power to cut, whose will still wills 50
It should none spare that come within his power.

PRINCESS
Some merry mocking lord, belike; is 't so?

MARIA
They say so most that most his humors know.

PRINCESS
Such short-liv'd wits do wither as they grow.
Who are the rest?

KATHARINE
The young Dumaine, a well-accomplish'd youth,
Of all that virtue love for virtue loved; 57
Most power to do most harm, least knowing ill, 58
For he hath wit to make an ill shape good, 59
And shape to win grace though he had no wit. 60
I saw him at the Duke Alençon's once,
And much too little of that good I saw 62
Is my report to his great worthiness. 63

ROSALINE
Another of these students at that time
Was there with him, if I have heard a truth.
Berowne they call him; but a merrier man,
Within the limit of becoming mirth, 67
I never spent an hour's talk withal. 68
His eye begets occasion for his wit;
For every object that the one doth catch
The other turns to a mirth-moving jest,
Which his fair tongue, conceit's expositor, 72
Delivers in such apt and gracious words
That aged ears play truant at his tales 74
And younger hearings are quite ravished,
So sweet and voluble is his discourse.

PRINCESS
God bless my ladies! Are they all in love,
That every one her own hath garnished
With such bedecking ornaments of praise?

FIRST LORD
Here comes Boyet.

Enter Boyet.

PRINCESS
Now, what admittance, lord?

BOYET
Navarre had notice of your fair approach,
And he and his competitors in oath 82
Were all address'd to meet you, gentle lady, 83
Before I came. Marry, thus much I have learn'd:
He rather means to lodge you in the field,
Like one that comes here to besiege his court,
Than seek a dispensation for his oath
To let you enter his unpeopled house. 88

Enter [King of] Navarre, Longaville, Dumaine, and Berowne, [with Attendants].

Here comes Navarre. [*The Ladies-in-waiting mask.*]

KING Fair Princess, welcome to the court of Navarre.

PRINCESS "Fair" I give you back again, and "welcome" I have not yet. The roof of this court is too high to be 92 yours, and welcome to the wide fields too base to be mine.

KING
You shall be welcome, madam, to my court.

PRINCESS
I will be welcome, then. Conduct me thither.

KING
Hear me, dear lady: I have sworn an oath.

PRINCESS
Our Lady help my lord! He'll be forsworn.

KING
Not for the world, fair madam, by my will. 99

PRINCESS
Why, will shall break it, will, and nothing else.

KING
Your ladyship is ignorant what it is.

PRINCESS
Were my lord so, his ignorance were wise,

25 to 's to us. (The royal "we.") **28 Bold of** confident of **29 best-moving** most eloquent. **fair** just **37 votaries** those who have taken vows **44 sovereign parts** excellent qualities **45 in arts** with learning **46 would well** wants to do well **47 soil . . . gloss** blot on the appearance of his general excellence **49 too . . . will** i.e., an insensitivity to the feelings of others **50 Whose** i.e., the wit's. **still** continually **57 Of . . . loved** esteemed for his virtue by all who love virtue **58 Most . . . ill** i.e., Dumaine, as a talented and graceful person, has the utmost power of doing the greatest harm by the ill employment of those qualities, yet he is ignorant of ill **59–60 For . . . no wit** he has intelligence enough to compensate for a poor physique, if he had one, and conversely a physique shapely enough to compensate for lack of intelligence **62 little** short, inadequate **63 to** compared with

67 becoming suitable **68 withal** with **72 conceit's expositor** fancy's interpreter **74 play truant** i.e., neglect important business **82 competitors** associates **83 address'd** prepared **88 unpeopled** inadequately staffed with servants **92 roof of this court** i.e., heavens **99 by my will** willingly

Where now his knowledge must prove ignorance.
I hear your Grace hath sworn out house-keeping.
'Tis deadly sin to keep that oath, my lord,
And sin to break it.
But pardon me, I am too sudden-bold;
To teach a teacher ill beseemeth me.
Vouchsafe to read the purpose of my coming,
And suddenly resolve me in my suit.
[*Gives a paper.*]

KING
Madam, I will, if suddenly I may.

PRINCESS
You will the sooner, that I were away,
For you'll prove perjur'd if you make me stay.
[*The King reads silently.*]

BEROWNE [*To Rosaline*]
Did not I dance with you in Brabant once?

ROSALINE
Did not I dance with you in Brabant once?

BEROWNE
I know you did.

ROSALINE How needless was it then
To ask the question?

BEROWNE You must not be so quick.

ROSALINE
'Tis 'long of you that spur me with such questions.

BEROWNE
Your wit's too hot, it speeds too fast, 'twill tire.

ROSALINE
Not till it leave the rider in the mire.

BEROWNE
What time o' day?

ROSALINE
The hour that fools should ask.

BEROWNE
Now fair befall your mask!

ROSALINE
Fair fall the face it covers!

BEROWNE
And send you many lovers!

ROSALINE
Amen, so you be none.

BEROWNE
Nay, then will I be gone. [*Stands aside.*]

KING
Madam, your father here doth intimate
The payment of a hundred thousand crowns,
Being but the one half of an entire sum
Disbursed by my father in his wars.
But say that he or we, as neither have,
Receiv'd that sum, yet there remains unpaid
A hundred thousand more, in surety of the which
One part of Aquitaine is bound to us,
Although not valued to the money's worth.
If then the King your father will restore
But that one half which is unsatisfied,
We will give up our right in Aquitaine,
And hold fair friendship with his Majesty.
But that, it seems, he little purposeth,
For here he doth demand to have repaid
A hundred thousand crowns; and not demands,
On payment of a hundred thousand crowns,
To have his title live in Aquitaine;
Which we much rather had depart withal,
And have the money by our father lent,
Than Aquitaine so gelded as it is.
Dear Princess, were not his requests so far
From reason's yielding, your fair self should make
A yielding 'gainst some reason in my breast
And go well satisfied to France again.

PRINCESS
You do the King my father too much wrong,
And wrong the reputation of your name,
In so unseeming to confess receipt
Of that which hath so faithfully been paid.

KING
I do protest I never heard of it;
And, if you prove it, I'll repay it back
Or yield up Aquitaine.

PRINCESS We arrest your word.
Boyet, you can produce acquittances
For such a sum from special officers
Of Charles his father.

KING Satisfy me so.

BOYET
So please your Grace, the packet is not come
Where that and other specialties are bound.
Tomorrow you shall have a sight of them.

KING
It shall suffice me; at which interview
All liberal reason I will yield unto.
Meantime, receive such welcome at my hand
As honor without breach of honor may
Make tender of to thy true worthiness.
You may not come, fair Princess, within my gates;
But here without you shall be so receiv'd
As you shall deem yourself lodg'd in my heart,
Though so denied fair harbor in my house.
Your own good thoughts excuse me, and farewell.
Tomorrow shall we visit you again.

PRINCESS
Sweet health and fair desires consort your Grace!

KING
Thy own wish wish I thee in every place.
Exit [*with Longaville, Dumaine, and Attendants*].

BEROWNE Lady, I will commend you to mine own heart.

ROSALINE Pray you, do my commendations; I would be glad to see it.

BEROWNE I would you heard it groan.

ROSALINE Is the fool sick?

BEROWNE Sick at the heart.

104 sworn out house-keeping renounced hospitality **110 suddenly resolve** quickly answer **112 that . . . away** to procure my departure **117 quick** sharp **118 'long of** on account of **123 fair befall** good luck to **124 fall** befall **128 intimate** suggest, discuss, imply **129 The payment** i.e., that he has already paid **132 he** i.e., my father **136 valued** equal in value

141 little purposeth scarcely intends **142 demand . . . repaid** insists he has already repaid **143 and not demands** i.e., instead of proposing or stipulating **146 depart withal** part with **148 gelded** i.e., weakened in value **151 A yielding . . . breast** i.e., a willingness on my part to compromise, despite the fact that right is on my side **155 unseeming** being apparently unwilling **159 arrest** take as security **164 specialties** special documents **167 liberal** gentlemanlike **170 tender** offer **172 without** outside **173 As** that **177 consort** attend **184 the fool** (A term of endearment or gentle raillery.)

ROSALINE
Alack, let it blood. 186

BEROWNE
Would that do it good?

ROSALINE
My physic says "ay." 188

BEROWNE
Will you prick 't with your eye?

ROSALINE
No point, with my knife. 190

BEROWNE
Now, God save thy life!

ROSALINE
And yours from long living!

BEROWNE
I cannot stay thanksgiving. *Exit.* 193

Enter Dumaine.

DUMAINE
Sir, I pray you, a word. What lady is that same?

BOYET
The heir of Alençon, Katharine her name.

DUMAINE
A gallant lady. Monsieur, fare you well. *Exit.*

[*Enter Longaville.*]

LONGAVILLE
I beseech you a word. What is she in the white?

BOYET
A woman sometimes, an you saw her in the light.

LONGAVILLE
Perchance light in the light. I desire her name. 199

BOYET
She hath but one for herself; to desire that were a shame.

LONGAVILLE
Pray you, sir, whose daughter?

BOYET
Her mother's, I have heard.

LONGAVILLE
God's blessing on your beard! 203

BOYET
Good sir, be not offended.
She is an heir of Falconbridge.

LONGAVILLE
Nay, my choler is ended.
She is a most sweet lady.

BOYET
Not unlike, sir, that may be. *Exit Longaville.* 208

Enter Berowne.

BEROWNE
What's her name in the cap?

BOYET
Rosaline, by good hap.

BEROWNE
Is she wedded or no?

BOYET
To her will, sir, or so.

BEROWNE
Oh, you are welcome, sir. Adieu.

BOYET
Farewell to me, sir, and welcome to you. 214
Exit Berowne.

MARIA
That last is Berowne, the merry mad-cap lord.
Not a word with him but a jest.

BOYET
And every jest but a word.

PRINCESS
It was well done of you to take him at his word. 217

BOYET
I was as willing to grapple as he was to board. 218

MARIA
Two hot sheeps, marry.

BOYET
And wherefore not ships? 219
No sheep, sweet lamb, unless we feed on your lips.

MARIA
You sheep, and I pasture. Shall that finish the jest?

BOYET
So you grant pasture for me. [*Offering to kiss her.*]

MARIA
No so, gentle beast. 222
My lips are no common, though several they be. 223

BOYET
Belonging to whom?

MARIA
To my fortunes and me.

PRINCESS
Good wits will be jangling; but, gentles, agree.
This civil war of wits were much better used
On Navarre and his book-men, for here 'tis abused. 227

BOYET
If my observation, which very seldom lies,
By the heart's still rhetoric disclosed with eyes, 229
Deceive me not now, Navarre is infected.

PRINCESS
With what?

BOYET
With that which we lovers entitle "affected." 232

PRINCESS
Your reason?

BOYET
Why, all his behaviors did make their retire 234
To the court of his eye, peeping thorough desire. 235
His heart, like an agate, with your print impressed, 236
Proud with his form, in his eye pride expressed. 237
His tongue, all impatient to speak and not see, 238
Did stumble with haste in his eyesight to be; 239
All senses to that sense did make their repair, 240
To feel only looking on fairest of fair. 241
Methought all his senses were lock'd in his eye,

186 let it blood bleed it. (A reference to the medical practice of drawing blood.) **188 physic** medical knowledge **190 No point** (1) not at all (2) it is dull. (A play on the French *ne . . . point,* not at all.) **193 stay thanksgiving** stay long enough to thank you properly **199 light in the light** wanton when her conduct is known or brought to light **203 God's . . . beard** (Here, mildly insulting.) **208 unlike** unlikely

214 Farewell . . . you i.e., it's your cue to say "farewell," and mine to say "you're welcome" (?) **217 take . . . word** i.e., vie with him in word-play (with a pun on *take him seriously*) **218 grapple, board** (Tactics of sea warfare, here applied to word-play, with bawdy overtones.) **219 sheeps, ships** (Pronounced virtually alike by Elizabethans.) **222 So** provided. **pasture** (with a play on *pastor,* shepherd) **223 common** common land for pasturing. **several** private enclosed land (with pun on *more than one*) **227 abused** misapplied **229 still** silent **232 affected** being in love **234 retire** retirement **235 thorough** through **236 agate** (An allusion to small figures cut in agate stones.) **237 Proud . . . expressed** proud of the form (of the Princess) imprinted on it, expressed that pride through the look in his eye **238 to speak . . . see** to be able to speak only and not to see **239 in his . . . be** to take part in his seeing **240 that sense** i.e., the eyesight. **repair** resort **241 To . . . looking** to express themselves solely through looking

As jewels in crystal for some prince to buy,
Who, tend'ring their own worth from where they were glass'd,
Did point you to buy them, along as you pass'd.
His face's own margent did quote such amazes
That all eyes saw his eyes enchanted with gazes.
I'll give you Aquitaine and all that is his,
An you give him for my sake but one loving kiss.

PRINCESS
Come to our pavilion. Boyet is dispos'd.

BOYET
But to speak that in words which his eye hath disclos'd.
I only have made a mouth of his eye,
By adding a tongue which I know will not lie.

ROSALINE
Thou art an old love-monger and speakest skillfully.

MARIA
He is Cupid's grandfather, and learns news of him.

KATHARINE
Then was Venus like her mother, for her father is but grim.

BOYET
Do you hear, my mad wenches?

ROSALINE
No.

BOYET
What then, do you see?

ROSALINE
Ay, our way to be gone.

BOYET
You are too hard for me.
Exeunt omnes.

[ACT III • SCENE I]

Enter [Armado the] Braggart and [Moth,] his Boy.

ARMADO Warble, child; make passionate my sense of hearing.

MOTH Concolinel. [*Singing.*]

ARMADO Sweet air! Go, tenderness of years. [*Gives key.*] Take this key, give enlargement to the swain, bring him festinately hither. I must employ him in a letter to my love.

MOTH Master, will you win your love with a French brawl?

ARMADO How meanest thou? Brawling in French?

MOTH No, my complete master, but to jig off a tune at the tongue's end, canary to it with your feet, humor it with turning up your eyelids, sigh a note and sing a note, sometime through the throat, as if you swallow'd love with singing love, sometime through the nose, as if you snuff'd up love by smelling love; with your hat penthouse-like o'er the shop of your eyes; with your arms cross'd on your thin-bellied doublet like a rabbit on a spit; or your hands in your pocket like a man after the old painting; and keep not too long in one tune, but a snip and away. These are compliments, these are humors, these betray nice wenches that would be betray'd without these, and make them men of note—do you note? men that most are affected to these.

ARMADO How hast thou purchased this experience?

MOTH By my penny of observation.

ARMADO But O—but O—

MOTH "The hobby-horse is forgot."

ARMADO Call'st thou my love "hobby-horse"?

MOTH No, master; the hobby-horse is but a colt, and your love perhaps a hackney. But have you forgot your love?

ARMADO Almost I had.

MOTH Negligent student, learn her by heart.

ARMADO By heart and in heart, boy.

MOTH And out of heart, master. All those three I will prove.

ARMADO What wilt thou prove?

MOTH A man, if I live; and this, by, in, and without, upon the instant: by heart you love her, because your heart cannot come by her; in heart you love her, because your heart is in love with her; and out of heart you love her, being out of heart that you cannot enjoy her.

ARMADO I am all these three.

MOTH And three times as much more—[*Aside*] and yet nothing at all.

ARMADO Fetch hither the swain. He must carry me a letter.

MOTH A message well sympathiz'd—a horse to be ambassador for an ass.

ARMADO Ha, ha? What sayest thou?

MOTH Marry, sir, you must send the ass upon the horse, for he is very slow-gaited. But I go.

ARMADO The way is but short. Away!

MOTH As swift as lead, sir.

ARMADO
The meaning, pretty ingenious?
Is not lead a metal heavy, dull, and slow?

MOTH
Minimè, honest master; or rather, master, no.

ARMADO
I say lead is slow.

MOTH
You are too swift, sir, to say so.
Is that lead slow which is fir'd from a gun?

244 Who, tend'ring which, offering. **glass'd** encased in the glass (crystal) of his eyes **245 point** appoint, direct, invite **246 His . . . amazes** i.e., his expression of amazement offered such a visible commentary on what his eyes saw. (*Margents* or margins of books often bore commentary on the text proper.) **248 I'll give you** i.e., I warrant you can have **250 dispos'd** inclined (to be merry) **251 But** merely. **his** i.e., the King's

III.i. Location: Navarre's park.
1 passionate impassioned, responsive **3 Concolinel** (Unidentified; perhaps the name or refrain of a song.) **5 enlargement** release from confinement **6 festinately** hastily **9 brawl** a dance figure **12 canary** dance. (From the name of a lively dance; cf. *jig.*)

17 penthouse-like like the projecting second story of a house built out to shelter the shop on the ground floor **18 arms cross'd** (Betokening melancholy; cf. IV.iii.131.) **thin-bellied doublet** (1) man's jacket over his thin belly, thin because of love-sickness (2) a thinly-padded jacket **20 old painting** (Unidentified.) **21 a snip and away** a snippet or scrap of one song and then on to another. **compliments** gentlemanly accomplishments **22 nice** coy **24 affected** inclined, drawn **27–28 But O . . . forgot** (Probably the refrain of a popular song; it turns up again in *Hamlet,* III.ii. The hobbyhorse was the figure of a horse made of light material and fastened over the torso and head of a morris dancer.) **30–31 hobby-horse, colt, hackney** (Slang terms for prostitutes or wanton persons.) **48 me** for me **50 sympathiz'd** matched **59 Minimè** not at all

ARMADO
Sweet smoke of rhetoric!
He reputes me a cannon, and the bullet, that's he.
I shoot thee at the swain.

MOTH
Thump then and I flee. [*Exit.*]

ARMADO
A most acute juvenal, volable and free of grace!
By thy favor, sweet welkin, I must sigh in thy face,
Most rude melancholy, valor gives thee place.
My herald is return'd.

Enter [*Moth the*] *Page and* [*Costard the*] *Clown.*

MOTH
A wonder, master! Here's a costard broken in a shin.

ARMADO
Some enigma, some riddle. Come, thy l'envoy; begin.

COSTARD No egma, no riddle, no l'envoy, no salve in the mail, sir. O, sir, plantain, a plain plantain. No l'envoy, no l'envoy, no salve, sir, but a plantain!

ARMADO By virtue, thou enforcest laughter; thy silly thought, my spleen; the heaving of my lungs provokes me to ridiculous smiling. O, pardon me, my stars! Doth the inconsiderate take salve for l'envoy, and the word l'envoy for a salve?

MOTH
Do the wise think them other? Is not l'envoy a salve?

ARMADO
No, page, it is an epilogue or discourse, to make plain
Some obscure precedence that hath tofore been sain.
I will example it:
The fox, the ape, and the humble-bee
Were still at odds, being but three.
There's the moral. Now the l'envoy.

MOTH
I will add the l'envoy. Say the moral again.

ARMADO
The fox, the ape, and the humble-bee
Were still at odds, being but three.

MOTH
Until the goose came out of door,
And stay'd the odds by adding four.
Now will I begin your moral, and do you follow with my l'envoy.
The fox, the ape, and the humble-bee
Were still at odds, being but three.

ARMADO
Until the goose came out of door,
Staying the odds by adding four.

MOTH A good l'envoy, ending in the goose. Would you desire more?

COSTARD
The boy hath sold him a bargain, a goose, that's flat.
Sir, your pennyworth is good, an your goose be fat.
To sell a bargain well is as cunning as fast and loose.
Let me see: a fat l'envoy—ay, that's a fat goose.

ARMADO
Come hither, come hither. How did this argument begin?

MOTH
By saying that a costard was broken in a shin.
Then call'd you for the l'envoy.

COSTARD
True, and I for a plantain; thus came your argument in;
Then the boy's fat l'envoy, the goose that you bought;
And he ended the market.

ARMADO But tell me, how was there a costard broken in a shin?

MOTH I will tell you sensibly.

COSTARD Thou hast no feeling of it, Moth. I will speak that l'envoy:
I Costard, running out, that was safely within,
Fell over the threshold, and broke my shin.

ARMADO We will talk no more of this matter.

COSTARD Till there be more matter in the shin.

ARMADO Sirrah Costard, I will enfranchise thee.

COSTARD O, marry me to one Frances! I smell some l'envoy, some goose, in this.

ARMADO By my sweet soul, I mean setting thee at liberty, enfreedoming thy person. Thou wert immured, restrained, captivated, bound.

COSTARD True, true, and now you will be my purgation and let me loose.

ARMADO I give thee thy liberty, set thee from durance; and, in lieu thereof, impose on thee nothing but this: bear this significant [*Giving a letter*] to the country maid Jaquenetta. There is remuneration. [*Gives money.*] For the best ward of mine honor is rewarding my dependents. Moth, follow. [*Exit.*]

MOTH
Like the sequel, I. Signior Costard, adieu. *Exit.*

COSTARD
My sweet ounce of man's flesh, my incony Jew!

64 Thump (Representing the sound of cannon.) **65 volable** voluble, quick-witted **66 favor** good will, permission. **welkin** sky **67 gives thee place** gives way to you **69 costard . . . shin** an apple or a head with a bruised shin. (An *enigma,* as Armado points out, since apples and heads don't have shins.) **70 l'envoy** i.e., postscript or commendatory statement to the reader attached to a composition; here, an explanation **71 egma** (Costard's attempt at *enigma;* he evidently mistakes this strange name, along with *riddle* and *l'envoy,* as a kind of salve for his hurt shin.) **salve** (With a play seemingly on *salvé,* meaning "hail!" Armado points out in his next speech that Costard has mistaken *salvé,* a salutation, for *l'envoy,* a farewell.) **72 mail** pouch, bag (suggesting the bag of a mountebank or seller of cures). **plantain** an old-fashioned herbal remedy (which Costard prefers to the strangely sounding *egma,* etc.) **75 spleen** (The seat of emotions and passions; held to be the organ which controlled excessive mirth or anger.) **77 inconsiderate** mindless fellow **81 precedence** preceding discourse. **sain** said **82 example** give an example of **84 still** continually. **at odds** (1) at enmity (2) an odd number, i.e., three **90 stay'd the odds** (1) stopped the enmity (2) changed odd to even. **four** a fourth

97 the goose i.e., Armado has made himself the goose, by playing Moth's game **99 sold . . . goose** i.e., outwitted him. **flat** certain **100 your . . . good** i.e., you got your money's worth. **an** if **101 fast and loose** a cheating trick. (See I.ii.151.) **104 broken in a shin** with a broken shin **111 sensibly** feelingly. (But Costard protests that Moth cannot personally know what it *feels* like.) **117 matter** pun (playing on *matter,* business, in l. 116) **118 enfranchise** release from confinement. (Costard hears this as *en-Frances,* "provide with a Frances.") **120 goose** (Slang for *prostitute.*) **124 be my purgation** purge me of guilt (with pun on the sense of giving a purgative so that Costard's bowels will be *let loose*) **128 significant** sign, token **130 ward** guard **133 incony** fine, rare, delicate. **Jew** (Here a term of playful insult, possibly suggested by *juvenile.*)

Now will I look to his remuneration. [*Looks at his money.*] Remuneration! O, that's the Latin word for three farthings. Three farthings—remuneration. "What's the price of this inkle?"—"One penny."—"No, I'll give you a remuneration." Why, it carries it. Remuneration! Why, it is a fairer name than French crown. I will never buy and sell out of this word.

Enter Berowne.

BEROWNE O, my good knave Costard, exceedingly well met.

COSTARD Pray you, sir, how much carnation ribbon may a man buy for a remuneration?

BEROWNE O, what is a remuneration?

COSTARD Marry, sir, halfpenny farthing.

BEROWNE O, why then, three-farthing worth of silk.

COSTARD I thank your worship. God be wi' you!
[*Starts to leave.*]

BEROWNE O, stay, slave; I must employ thee.
As thou wilt win my favor, good my knave,
Do one thing for me that I shall entreat.

COSTARD When would you have it done, sir?

BEROWNE O, this afternoon.

COSTARD Well, I will do it, sir. Fare you well.

BEROWNE O, thou knowest not what it is.

COSTARD I shall know, sir, when I have done it.

BEROWNE Why, villain, thou must know first.

COSTARD I will come to your worship tomorrow morning.

BEROWNE It must be done this afternoon. Hark, slave, it is but this:
The Princess comes to hunt here in the park,
And in her train there is a gentle lady;
When tongues speak sweetly, then they name her name,
And Rosaline they call her. Ask for her,
And to her white hand see thou do commend
This seal'd-up counsel. There's thy guerdon; go.
[*Giving him a letter and a shilling.*]

COSTARD Gardon, O sweet gardon! Better than remuneration, a 'leven-pence farthing better. Most sweet gardon! I will do it, sir, in print. Gardon! Remuneration! *Exit.*

BEROWNE
O, and I, forsooth, in love! I, that have been love's whip,
A very beadle to a humorous sigh,
A critic, nay, a night-watch constable,
A domineering pedant o'er the boy,
Than whom no mortal so magnificent!
This wimpled, whining, purblind, wayward boy,
This senior-junior, giant-dwarf, Dan Cupid,
Regent of love-rhymes, lord of folded arms,
Th' anointed sovereign of sighs and groans,
Liege of all loiterers and malcontents,
Dread prince of plackets, king of codpieces,
Sole imperator and great general
Of trotting paritors—O my little heart!—
And I to be a corporal of his field,
And wear his colors like a tumbler's hoop!
What? I love, I sue, I seek a wife?
A woman, that is like a German clock,
Still a-repairing, ever out of frame,
And never going aright, being a watch,
But being watch'd that it may still go right?
Nay, to be perjur'd, which is worst of all;
And, among three, to love the worst of all,
A whitely wanton with a velvet brow,
With two pitch-balls stuck in her face for eyes;
Ay, and, by heaven, one that will do the deed
Though Argus were her eunuch and her guard.
And I to sigh for her, to watch for her,
To pray for her! Go to, it is a plague
That Cupid will impose for my neglect
Of his almighty dreadful little might.
Well, I will love, write, sigh, pray, sue, groan.
Some men must love my lady, and some Joan. [*Exit.*]

[ACT IV • SCENE I]

Enter the Princess, a Forester, her Ladies, and her Lords, [Boyet and others].

PRINCESS
Was that the King that spurr'd his horse so hard
Against the steep uprising of the hill?

BOYET
I know not, but I think it was not he.

PRINCESS
Whoe'er 'a was, 'a show'd a mounting mind.
Well, lords, today we shall have our dispatch;
On Saturday we will return to France.
Then, forester, my friend, where is the bush
That we must stand and play the murderer in?

FORESTER
Hereby, upon the edge of yonder coppice,
A stand where you may make the fairest shoot.

PRINCESS
I thank my beauty, I am fair that shoot,
And thereupon thou speak'st the fairest shoot.

FORESTER
Pardon me, madam, for I meant not so.

PRINCESS
What, what? First praise me and again say no?
O short-liv'd pride! Not fair? Alack for woe!

137 inkle a kind of linen tape **138 carries it** wins the day **139–140 French crown** (1) a coin (2) a bald head, the result of syphilis or "the French disease" **140 out of** i.e., without using **143 carnation** flesh-colored **166 commend** entrust **167 counsel** private or secret communication. **guerdon** reward **170 in print** i.e., most exactly **173 beadle** parish officer responsible for whipping minor offenders. **humorous** emotional **177 wimpled** blindfolded. **purblind** wholly blind **178 Dan** don, sir. (From the Latin *dominus.*) **179 folded arms** (Betokening melancholy; see III.i.18.)

182 plackets slits in petticoats (referring bawdily to women). **codpieces** flap or pouch concealing the opening in the front of men's breeches (referring bawdily to men) **184 paritors** apparitors, summoners of ecclesiastical courts (who could make a profit by spying out sexual offenders) **185 corporal of his field** his field officer **186 tumbler's hoop** (Such hoops were usually brightly decorated and highly visible.) **189 Still** always. **a-repairing** needing repair. **frame** order **191 But being watch'd** unless it is watched carefully (like a wandering wife) **194 whitely** pale, sallow **196 do the deed** engage in sex **197 Argus** a fabulous monster with a hundred eyes, some of which were always awake. **eunuch** guard in a seraglio **198 watch** lose sleep, stay awake **203 my lady, Joan** (Opposite types on the social scale, one a lady of quality and one a peasant woman.)

IV.i. Location: Navarre's park. A hunter's station at the edge of a coppice.
10 stand hunter's station, toward which the game was driven. **fairest** most favorable. (The Princess chooses to play on the word in a compliment to herself.)

FORESTER
Yes, madam, fair.
PRINCESS Nay, never paint me now;
Where fair is not, praise cannot mend the brow.
Here, good my glass, take this for telling true.
[*Gives him money.*]
Fair payment for foul words is more than due.
FORESTER
Nothing but fair is that which you inherit.
PRINCESS
See, see, my beauty will be sav'd by merit!
O heresy in fair, fit for these days!
A giving hand, though foul, shall have fair praise.
But come, the bow. Now mercy goes to kill,
And shooting well is then accounted ill.
[*Takes the bow.*]
Thus will I save my credit in the shoot:
Not wounding, pity would not let me do 't;
If wounding, then it was to show my skill,
That more for praise than purpose meant to kill.
And out of question so it is sometimes,
Glory grows guilty of detested crimes,
When, for fame's sake, for praise, an outward part,
We bend to that the working of the heart;
As I for praise alone now seek to spill
The poor deer's blood, that my heart means no ill.
BOYET
Do not curst wives hold that self-sovereignty
Only for praise' sake, when they strive to be
Lords o'er their lords?
PRINCESS
Only for praise; and praise we may afford
To any lady that subdues a lord.

Enter [*Costard the*] *Clown* [*with a letter*].

BOYET
Here comes a member of the commonwealth.
COSTARD God dig-you-den all! Pray you, which is the head lady?
PRINCESS Thou shalt know her, fellow, by the rest that have no heads.
COSTARD Which is the greatest lady, the highest?
PRINCESS The thickest and the tallest.
COSTARD
The thickest and the tallest! It is so; truth is truth.
An your waist, mistress, were as slender as my wit,
One o' these maids' girdles for your waist should
be fit.
Are not you the chief woman? You are the thickest
here.
PRINCESS What's your will, sir? What's your will?
COSTARD I have a letter from Monsieur Berowne to one Lady Rosaline.
PRINCESS
O, thy letter, thy letter! He's a good friend of mine.
Stand aside, good bearer. Boyet, you can carve;
Break up this capon. [*The letter is given to Boyet.*]
BOYET I am bound to serve.
This letter is mistook; it importeth none here.
It is writ to Jaquenetta.
PRINCESS We will read it, I swear.
Break the neck of the wax, and everyone give ear.
BOYET [*Reads*] "By heaven, that thou art fair is most infallible; true that thou art beauteous; truth itself that thou art lovely. More fairer than fair, beautiful than beauteous, truer than truth itself, have commiseration on thy heroical vassal! The magnanimous and most illustrate King Cophetua set eye upon the pernicious and indubitate beggar Zenelophon; and he it was that might rightly say, Veni, vidi, vici; which to annothanize in the vulgar—O base and obscure vulgar!—videlicet, He came, saw, and overcame. He came, one; saw, two; overcame, three. Who came? The King. Why did he come? To see. Why did he see? To overcome. To whom came he? To the beggar. What saw he? The beggar. Who overcame he? The beggar. The conclusion is victory. On whose side? The King's. The captive is enrich'd. On whose side? The beggar's. The catastrophe is a nuptial. On whose side? The King's—no, on both in one, or one in both. I am the King, for so stands the comparison; thou the beggar, for so witnesseth thy lowliness. Shall I command thy love? I may. Shall I enforce thy love? I could. Shall I entreat thy love? I will. What shalt thou exchange for rags? Robes. For tittles? Titles. For thyself? Me. Thus, expecting thy reply, I profane my lips on thy foot, my eyes on thy picture, and my heart on thy every part. Thine, in the dearest design of industry,
Don Adriano de Armado.
Thus dost thou hear the Nemean lion roar
'Gainst thee, thou lamb, that standest as his prey.
Submissive fall his princely feet before,
And he from forage will incline to play.
But if thou strive, poor soul, what art thou then?
Food for his rage, repasture for his den."
PRINCESS
What plume of feathers is he that indited this letter?
What vane? What weathercock? Did you ever hear
better?
BOYET
I am much deceived but I remember the style.
PRINCESS
Else your memory is bad, going o'er it erewhile.

16 paint flatter **17 fair** beauty. **brow** i.e., face **18 good my glass** my true mirror (i.e., a counselor who will not flatter. The Princess amuses herself with Renaissance commonplaces about the value of honest counselors to a true prince, much to the discomfort of the Forester.) **20 inherit** possess **21 my . . . merit** i.e., my beauty is complimented again in return for my giving a gratuity. (To be *saved by merit* was, however, a heresy according to orthodox Anglican doctrine, which taught salvation by faith rather than by merit or good works.) **22 in fair** regarding beauty **24 mercy** i.e., the Princess, who as a royal woman is an emblem of mercy **25 then** i.e., when a merciful person like the Princess goes hunting **26 credit** reputation **27 Not . . . do 't** i.e., I can claim, if I miss, that pity restrained me **29 That . . . kill** i.e., I shot accurately to earn praise for my skill rather than for the sake of killing **30 out of question** undoubtedly **31 Glory . . . crimes** i.e., an excessive desire for glory prompts us to commit detestable crimes **32 an outward part** a superficial thing **33 bend** force, adapt. **that** i.e., fame **36 curst** shrewish **41 commonwealth** ordinary citizenry **42 God dig-you-den** God give you good evening

57 Break up cut up (a technical term in carving), i.e., open. **capon** (Like the French *poulet, capon* designates figuratively a love-letter.) **58 mistook** mis-taken, misdirected. **importeth** concerns **60 wax** seal **66 illustrate** illustrious **67 indubitate** undoubted. **Zenelophon** Penelophon, the beggar-maid in the ballad about King Cophetua. (See I.ii. 105–106.) **68–69 annothanize** anatomize, explain, interpret **69 vulgar** vernacular **69–70 videlicet** namely **77 catastrophe** denouement **83 tittles** points or dots **84 profane** desecrate **86 dearest . . . industry** most excellent pattern of zealous gallantry **88 Nemean lion** lion slain by Hercules in the first of his twelve labors **91 forage** raging, ravening **93 repasture** food **94 What . . . feathers** what kind of bird, dandy **95 vane** weathervane (with play on *vain*) **96 but** unless **97 going o'er it** i.e., over a *stile,* playing on *style.* **erewhile** just now

BOYET
This Armado is a Spaniard, that keeps here in court, 98
A phantasime, a Monarcho, and one that makes
sport 99
To the Prince and his bookmates.

PRINCESS
Thou fellow, a word.
Who gave thee this letter?

COSTARD
I told you; my lord.

PRINCESS
To whom shouldst thou give it?

COSTARD
From my lord to my lady.

PRINCESS
From which lord to which lady?

COSTARD
From my lord Berowne, a good master of mine,
To a lady of France that he call'd Rosaline.

PRINCESS
Thou hast mistaken his letter. Come, lords, away.
[*To Rosaline.*] Here, sweet, put up this; 'twill be
thine another day. [*Exeunt Princess and train.*] 107

BOYET
Who is the shooter? Who is the shooter?

ROSALINE
Shall I teach you to know? 108

BOYET
Ay, my continent of beauty.

ROSALINE
Why, she that bears the bow. 109
Finely put off! 110

BOYET
My lady goes to kill horns, but, if thou marry, 111
Hang me by the neck if horns that year miscarry. 112
Finely put on! 113

ROSALINE
Well, then, I am the shooter.

BOYET
And who is your deer? 114

ROSALINE
If we choose by the horns, yourself come not near. 115
Finely put on, indeed!

MARIA
You still wrangle with her, Boyet, and she strikes at
the brow. 117

BOYET
But she herself is hit lower. Have I hit her now? 118

ROSALINE Shall I come upon thee with an old saying, 119
that was a man when King Pepin of France was a little 120
boy, as touching the hit it? 121

BOYET So I may answer thee with one as old, that was
a woman when Queen Guinover of Britain was a little 123
wench, as touching the hit it.

ROSALINE
"Thou canst not hit it, hit it, hit it,
Thou canst not hit it, my good man."

BOYET
"An I cannot, cannot, cannot,
An I cannot, another can."
Exit [*Rosaline with Katharine*].

COSTARD
By my troth, most pleasant. How both did fit it!

MARIA
A mark marvelous well shot, for they both did
hit it. 130

BOYET
A mark! O, mark but that mark! A mark, says my
lady!
Let the mark have a prick in 't, to mete at, if it
may be. 132

MARIA
Wide o' the bow hand! I' faith, your hand is out. 133

COSTARD
Indeed, 'a must shoot nearer, or he'll ne'er hit the
clout. 134

BOYET
An if my hand be out, then belike your hand is in.

COSTARD
Then will she get the upshoot by cleaving the pin. 136

MARIA
Come, come, you talk greasily, your lips grow foul. 137

COSTARD
She's too hard for you at pricks, sir. Challenge her to
bowl. 138

BOYET
I fear too much rubbing. Good night, my good owl. 139
[*Exeunt Boyet and Maria.*]

COSTARD
By my soul, a swain, a most simple clown!
Lord, Lord, how the ladies and I have put him
down!
O' my troth, most sweet jests, most incony
vulgar wit! 142
When it comes so smoothly off, so obscenely, as it
were, so fit. 143
Armado o' th' one side—O, a most dainty man! 144
To see him walk before a lady and to bear her fan!
To see him kiss his hand, and how most sweetly 'a
will swear!
And his page o' t'other side, that handful of wit!
Ah, heavens, it is a most pathetical nit! *Shout within.* 148
Sola, sola! *Exit* [*Costard, running*]. 149

98 keeps lives, dwells **99 phantasime** one who entertains fantastic notions. **Monarcho** (The nickname of an eccentric Italian who fancied himself the emperor of the world; hence, anyone who displays absurd pretentions.) **107 'twill be thine** i.e., it will be your turn. **s.d. train** (Perhaps the Forester exits here.) **108 shooter** archer. (With pun on *suitor.* Boyet may be asking who is to shoot, now that the Princess has left. Perhaps Rosaline has been given the bow.) **109 continent of** container of all **110 put off** answered evasively **111 horns** i.e., deer **112 horns** i.e., cuckold's horns. (Boyet saucily suggests that if Rosaline marries, cuckold's horns will not be in short supply.) **113 put on** urged, applied **114 deer** (with pun on *dear;* Rosaline is the natural target of all this double-entendre about the huntress who is hunting for a husband, since Berowne is known to have written her a love letter) **115 If . . . near** (Rosaline retorts to Boyet acerbically by intimating that he couldn't possibly be her choice.) **117 she . . . brow** i.e., she takes good aim at you (with pun on the idea that she has also put Boyet down with a joke about cuckoldry) **118 hit lower** i.e., in the heart. **hit her** scored on her in this game of wit, described her situation aright **119 come upon thee** answer or hit back (continuing the metaphor of hunting and marksmanship) **120 was a man** i.e., was already old. **King Pepin** Carolingian king (died 768) **121 as . . . hit it** concerning a catch or round, to be sung dancing. (The song itself is obviously bawdy.)

123 Guinover Guinevere, King Arthur's unfaithful queen **130 mark** target **132 prick** spot in the center of the target, the bull's eye (with sexual double meaning, as throughout this passage). **mete at** measure with the eye, aim at **133 Wide . . . hand** wide of the mark on the left side, too far to the left. **out** inaccurate **134 clout** mark at the center of the target **136 upshoot** leading or best shot. **cleaving the pin** splitting exactly the small nail holding the clout in place (with sexual suggestion, as Maria observes in the next line) **137 greasily** grossly (referring to sexual double entendre in *cleaving, hit it, prick, your hand is in,* etc.) **138 pricks** informal or illegal archery (with sexual pun) **139 rubbing** grazing or striking together of the bowling balls (with sexual pun) **142 incony** fine, rare **143 obscenely** (Perhaps a malapropism for *seemly,* with unintended appropriateness to the preceding passage.) **144 dainty** refined, elegant **148 pathetical nit** touching little mite. (A *nit* is the egg of a small insect.) **149 Sola** (A hunting cry.)

[SCENE II]

Enter Dull, Holofernes the Pedant, and Nathaniel.

NATHANIEL Very reverend sport, truly, and done in the testimony of a good conscience.

HOLOFERNES The deer was, as you know, sanguis, in blood, ripe as the pomewater, who now hangeth like a jewel in the ear of caelo, the sky, the welkin, the heaven, and anon falleth like a crab on the face of terra, the soil, the land, the earth.

NATHANIEL Truly, Master Holofernes, the epithets are sweetly varied, like a scholar at the least. But, sir, I assure ye, it was a buck of the first head.

HOLOFERNES Sir Nathaniel, haud credo.

DULL 'Twas not a haud credo, 'twas a pricket.

HOLOFERNES Most barbarous intimation! Yet a kind of insinuation, as it were, in via, in way, of explication; facere, as it were, replication, or rather, ostentare, to show, as it were, his inclination, after his undressed, unpolished, uneducated, unpruned, untrained, or rather, unlettered, or, ratherest, unconfirmed fashion, to insert again my haud credo for a deer.

DULL I said the deer was not a haud credo, 'twas a pricket.

HOLOFERNES Twice-sod simplicity, bis coctus!
O thou monster Ignorance, how deformed dost
thou look!

NATHANIEL
Sir, he hath never fed of the dainties that are bred
in a book;
He hath not eat paper, as it were; he hath not drunk ink. His intellect is not replenished; he is only an animal, only sensible in the duller parts;
And such barren plants are set before us, that we
thankful should be,
Which we of taste and feeling are, for those parts
that do fructify in us more than he.
For as it would ill become me to be vain, indiscreet,
or a fool,
So were there a patch set on learning, to see him in
a school.
But omne bene, say I, being of an old father's mind;
Many can brook the weather that love not the wind.

DULL
You two are book-men. Can you tell me by your wit
What was a month old at Cain's birth, that's not five
weeks old as yet?

HOLOFERNES
Dictynna, goodman Dull; Dictynna, goodman Dull.

DULL What is Dictynna?

NATHANIEL A title to Phoebe, to Luna, to the moon.

HOLOFERNES
The moon was a month old when Adam was no
more,
And raught not to five weeks when he came to five-
score.
Th' allusion holds in the exchange.

DULL 'Tis true indeed; the collusion holds in the exchange.

HOLOFERNES God comfort thy capacity! I say, th' allusion holds in the exchange.

DULL And I say, the pollusion holds in the exchange, for the moon is never but a month old; and I say beside that 'twas a pricket that the Princess kill'd.

HOLOFERNES Sir Nathaniel, will you hear an extemporal epitaph on the death of the deer? And, to humor the ignorant, call I the deer the Princess kill'd a pricket.

NATHANIEL Perge, good Master Holofernes, perge, so it shall please you to abrogate scurrility.

HOLOFERNES I will something affect the letter, for it argues facility.
The preyful Princess pierc'd and prick'd a pretty
pleasing pricket;
Some say a sore, but not a sore till now made sore
with shooting.
The dogs did yell. Put L to sore, then sorel jumps
from thicket,
Or pricket sore, or else sorel. The people fall a-
hooting.
If sore be sore, then L to sore makes fifty sores o'
sorel.
Of one sore I an hundred make by adding but one
more L.

NATHANIEL A rare talent!

DULL [*Aside*] If a talent be a claw, look how he claws him with a talent.

HOLOFERNES This is a gift that I have, simple, simple; a foolish extravagant spirit, full of forms, figures, shapes, objects, ideas, apprehensions, motions, revolutions. These are begot in the ventricle of memory, nourish'd in the womb of pia mater, and delivered upon the mellowing of occasion. But the gift is good in those in whom it is acute, and I am thankful for it.

NATHANIEL Sir, I praise the Lord for you, and so may my parishioners; for their sons are well tutor'd by you, and their daughters profit very greatly under you. You are a good member of the commonwealth.

HOLOFERNES Mehercle, if their sons be ingenuous, they shall want no instruction; if their daughters be capa-

IV.ii. Location: Navarre's park.
1–2 in the testimony with the warrant **3–4 in blood** in prime condition **4 pomewater** a kind of apple **6 crab** crab apple **9 at the least** to say the least **10 of . . . head** in its fifth year, hence with newly full antlers **11 Sir** (Term of address for ordinary clergymen.) **haud credo** I cannot believe it **12 haud credo** (Dull mistakes the Latin for something like "old grey doe.") **pricket** buck in its second year **13 intimation** intrusion **15 facere** to make. **replication** explanation **19 insert** put in, interpret. (Holofernes' point is that Dull is unwittingly taking Holofernes' side of the argument by interpreting "haud credo" as a doe rather than a buck.) **22 Twice-sod** twice sodden or cooked, boiled. **bis coctus,** twice cooked. (Holofernes is incensed at Dull's twice insisting on his error.) **25 eat** eaten. (Pronounced *et.*) **27 sensible** capable of perception **29 Which we** we who. **fructify** grow fruitful. **he** in him **31 were . . . learning** (1) it would be setting a fool or dolt to learn (2) it would be a disgrace to learning itself **32 omne bene** all is well. **old father's mind** opinion of an ancient sage **33 brook** put up with. (I.e., one must endure what one cannot change.)

36, 38 Dictynna, Phoebe, Luna (Classical names for the moon. The first is uncommon, and is appropriate to the pedant. It occurs in Golding's translation of Ovid, a book that Shakespeare knew.) **40 raught** reached, attained **41 allusion** riddle. **holds** remains valid. **exchange** substitution (of Adam's name for Cain's) **52 Perge** proceed **53 abrogate** refrain from **54 something . . . letter** somewhat make use of alliteration **56 preyful** intent upon prey **57 sore** deer in its fourth year **58 sorel** deer in its third year **59 Or** either **60 L** Roman numeral fifty **63 talent** i.e., talon. **claws** scratches, i.e., flatters **67 motions** impulses **68 ventricle of memory** one of the three sections of the brain, believed to contain the memory **69 pia mater** the membrane surrounding the brain; the brain itself **76 Mehercle** by Hercules **77 want** lack

ble, I will put it to them. But vir sapit qui pauca loqui- 78
tur. A soul feminine saluteth us. 79

Enter Jaquenetta and [Costard] the Clown.

JAQUENETTA God give you good morrow, master Person. 80
HOLOFERNES Master Person, quasi pers-one. And if one 81
should be pierc'd, which is the one? 82
COSTARD Marry, master schoolmaster, he that is
likel'est to a hogshead.
HOLOFERNES Of piercing a hogshead! A good luster of 85
conceit in a turf of earth; fire enough for a flint, pearl 86
enough for a swine. 'Tis pretty, it is well.
JAQUENETTA Good master Person, be so good as read
me this letter. It was given me by Costard, and sent
me from Don Armado. I beseech you, read it.
[Handing letter to Nathaniel.]
HOLOFERNES Facile, precor gelida quando pecus omne 91
sub umbra ruminat, and so forth. Ah, good old Man- 92
tuan! I may speak of thee as the traveler doth of Venice:
Venechia, Venechia, 94
Che non te vede, che non te prechia. 95
Old Mantuan, old Mantuan! Who understandeth thee
not, loves thee not. Ut, re, sol, la, mi, fa. [*Nathaniel is* 97
examining the letter.] Under pardon, sir, what are the
contents? Or rather, as Horace says in his—What, my
soul, verses?
NATHANIEL Ay, sir, and very learned.
HOLOFERNES Let me hear a staff, a stanze, a verse; lege, 102
domine. 103
NATHANIEL [*Reads*]
"If love make me forsworn, how shall I swear to
love? 104
Ah, never faith could hold, if not to beauty vowed!
Though to myself forsworn, to thee I'll faithful
prove;
Those thoughts to me were oaks, to thee like osiers
bowed.
Study his bias leaves and makes his book thine
eyes, 108
Where all those pleasures live that art would
comprehend.
If knowledge be the mark, to know thee shall
suffice;
Well learned is that tongue that well can thee
commend,
All ignorant that soul that sees thee without wonder;
Which is to me some praise that I thy parts admire.
Thy eye Jove's lightning bears, thy voice his
dreadful thunder,
Which, not to anger bent, is music and sweet fire.
Celestial as thou art, O, pardon love this wrong,
That sings heaven's praise with such an earthly
tongue."
HOLOFERNES You find not the apostraphas, and so miss 118
the accent. Let me supervise the canzonet. [*Takes the* 119
letter.] Here are only numbers ratified; but, for the ele- 120
gancy, facility, and golden cadence of poesy, caret. 121
Ovidius Naso was the man. And why, indeed, 122
"Naso," but for smelling out the odoriferous flowers
of fancy, the jerks of invention? Imitari is nothing. So 124
doth the hound his master, the ape his keeper, the
tired horse his rider. But, damosella virgin, was this
directed to you?
JAQUENETTA Ay, sir, from one Monsieur Berowne, one
of the strange queen's lords. 129
HOLOFERNES I will overglance the superscript: "To the 130
snow-white hand of the most beauteous Lady Rosa-
line." I will look again on the intellect of the letter, for 132
the nomination of the party writing to the person writ-
ten unto: "Your ladyship's in all desired employment,
Berowne." Sir Nathaniel, this Berowne is one of the
votaries with the King; and here he hath framed a let-
ter to a sequent of the stranger queen's, which acci- 137
dentally, or by the way of progression, hath miscar- 138
ried. Trip and go, my sweet; deliver this paper into
the royal hand of the King; it may concern much.
[*Gives her the letter.*] Stay not thy compliment; I forgive 141
thy duty. Adieu. 142
JAQUENETTA Good Costard, go with me. Sir, God save
your life!
COSTARD Have with thee, my girl. 145
Exit [with Jaquenetta].
NATHANIEL Sir, you have done this in the fear of God,
very religiously; and, as a certain father saith— 147
HOLOFERNES Sir, tell not me of the father; I do fear col- 148
orable colors. But to return to the verses: did they 149
please you, Sir Nathaniel?
NATHANIEL Marvelous well for the pen. 151
HOLOFERNES I do dine today at the father's of a certain
pupil of mine, where, if, before repast, it shall please
you to gratify the table with a grace, I will, on my priv-
ilege I have with the parents of the foresaid child or
pupil, undertake your bien venuto; where I will prove 156
those verses to be very unlearned, neither savoring of
poetry, wit, nor invention..I beseech your society.
NATHANIEL And thank you too; for society, saith the
text, is the happiness of life.

77–78 capable (1) apt as pupils (2) able to bear children (an unconscious sexual pun that goes back to *under you* in line 74) **78 put it to them** (with unintended sexual meaning) **78–79 vir . . . loquitur** he is a wise man who speaks little **80 Person** (Pronounced *parson.*) **81 quasi** that is **82 pierc'd** (Pronounced *persed;* playing on *pers-one,* pierce one. This is sometimes taken as an allusion to Nashe's *Pierce Penniless, His Supplication to the Devil,* a fantastic satire in which the author, in the character of Pierce, comments on the vices of the times; also to Harvey's answer, *Pierce's Supererogation,* in which Pierce is referred to as "the hogges-head of witt"; cf. l. 85.) **85 piercing a hogshead** i.e., getting drunk **85–86 luster of conceit** spark of fancy **91–92 Facile . . . ruminat** (The first line of the first eclogue of the Italian Renaissance poet, Mantuan. Although it was a well-known text in the schools, Holofernes mistakenly gives us *Facile* for *Fauste.* The passage means "Faustus, I beg, while all the cattle chew their cud in the cool shade.") **94–95 Venechia . . . prechia** Venice, Venice, he who sees you not loves you not **97 Ut** (Equivalent to the modern *do.* If Holofernes intends to sing the scale, *do, re, mi, fa, sol, la,* he displays his ignorance.) **102–103 lege, domine** read, master **104–117 If . . . tongue** (These lines were printed with minor changes in *The Passionate Pilgrim,* 1599; a collection of poems by various authors but attributed to Shakespeare. Two others of the volume are from this play, that read by Longaville, IV.iii.56–69, and that by Dumaine, IV.iii.97–116.) **108 Study . . . leaves** i.e., the student leaves his true inclination

118 find heed. **apostraphas** apostrophes, punctuation marks used to indicate omitted vowels and shortened pronunciation of a word **119 supervise** glance over, peruse. **canzonet** i.e., poem **120 only numbers ratified,** i.e., merely language made metrical **121 caret** it is lacking **122 Naso** (From Latin *nasus,* nose; the poet Ovid always referred to himself by this cognomen.) **124 jerks of invention** strokes of imagination. **Imitari** to imitate **129 strange** foreign. (Jaquenetta seems mistakenly to believe that Berowne is attached to the Princess' retinue.) **130 superscript** address **132 intellect** meaning, import, contents **137 sequent** follower, attendant **138 by . . . progression** in process of delivery **141 Stay . . . compliment** i.e., don't stand on ceremony **141–142 forgive thy duty** set aside the requirement of a curtsy **145 Have with thee** I'll go with you **147 father** church father **148–149 colorable colors** plausible pretexts **151 pen** penmanship, or style **156 bien venuto** welcome

HOLOFERNES And, certes, the text most infallibly con- 161
cludes it. [*To Dull.*] Sir, I do invite you too; you shall
not say me nay. Pauca verba. Away! The gentles are at 163
their game, and we will to our recreation. *Exeunt.*

[SCENE III]

Enter Berowne, with a paper in his hand, alone.

BEROWNE The King he is hunting the deer; I am cours- 1
ing myself. They have pitch'd a toil; I am toiling in a 2
pitch—pitch that defiles. Defile! A foul word. Well, 3
set thee down, sorrow! For so they say the fool said, 4
and so say I, and I the fool. Well prov'd, wit! By the
Lord, this love is as mad as Ajax. It kills sheep; it kills 6
me, I a sheep. Well prov'd again o' my side! I will not
love; if I do, hang me. I' faith, I will not. O, but her
eye! By this light, but for her eye, I would not love her;
yes, for her two eyes. Well, I do nothing in the world
but lie, and lie in my throat. By heaven, I do love, and 11
it hath taught me to rhyme and to be mallicholy; and 12
here is part of my rhyme, and here my mallicholy.
Well, she hath one o' my sonnets already. The clown
bore it, the fool sent it, and the lady hath it—sweet
clown, sweeter fool, sweetest lady! By the world, I
would not care a pin, if the other three were in. Here 17
comes one with a paper. God give him grace to groan! 18
He stands aside.

The King ent'reth [*with a paper*].

KING Ay me!

BEROWNE [*Aside*] Shot, by heaven! Proceed, sweet
Cupid. Thou hast thump'd him with thy bird-bolt un- 21
der the left pap. In faith, secrets! 22

KING [*Reads*]
"So sweet a kiss the golden sun gives not
To those fresh morning drops upon the rose,
As thy eye-beams, when their fresh rays have smote
The night of dew that on my cheeks down flows. 26
Nor shines the silver moon one half so bright
Through the transparent bosom of the deep,
As doth thy face, through tears of mine, give light;
Thou shin'st in every tear that I do weep.
No drop but as a coach doth carry thee;
So ridest thou triumphing in my woe.
Do but behold the tears that swell in me,
And they thy glory through my grief will show.
But do not love thyself; then thou wilt keep
My tears for glasses, and still make me weep. 36
O queen of queens! How far dost thou excel
No thought can think, nor tongue of mortal tell."
How shall she know my griefs? I'll drop the paper.
Sweet leaves, shade folly. Who is he comes here? 40

Enter Longaville [*with a paper*]. *The King steps aside.*

What, Longaville, and reading! Listen, ear.

BEROWNE [*Aside*]
Now, in thy likeness, one more fool appear!

LONGAVILLE
Ay me, I am forsworn!

BEROWNE [*Aside*]
Why, he comes in like a perjure, wearing papers. 44

KING [*Aside*]
In love, I hope. Sweet fellowship in shame!

BEROWNE [*Aside*]
One drunkard loves another of the name.

LONGAVILLE
Am I the first that have been purjur'd so?

BEROWNE [*Aside*]
I could put thee in comfort: not by two that I know.
Thou makest the triumviry, the corner-cap of
society, 49
The shape of Love's Tyburn that hangs up
simplicity. 50

LONGAVILLE
I fear these stubborn lines lack power to move.
O sweet Maria, empress of my love!
These numbers will I tear, and write in prose. 53

BEROWNE [*Aside*]
O, rhymes are guards on wanton Cupid's hose; 54
Disfigure not his shop.

LONGAVILLE This same shall go. 55
He reads the sonnet.
"Did not the heavenly rhetoric of thine eye, 56
'Gainst whom the world cannot hold argument,
Persuade my heart to this false perjury?
Vows for thee broke deserve not punishment.
A woman I forswore; but I will prove,
Thou being a goddess, I forswore not thee.
My vow was earthly, thou a heavenly love;
Thy grace being gain'd cures all disgrace in me. 63
Vows are but breath, and breath a vapor is.
Then thou, fair sun, which on my earth dost shine,
Exhal'st this vapor vow; in thee it is; 66
If broken then it is no fault of mine.
If by me broke, what fool is not so wise
To lose an oath to win a paradise?" 69

BEROWNE [*Aside*]
This is the liver-vein, which makes flesh a deity, 70
A green goose a goddess. Pure, pure idolatry. 71

161 certes surely **163 Pauca verba** few words. **gentles** gentlefolk

IV.iii. Location: Navarre's park.
1–2 coursing pursuing **2 pitch'd a toil** set a snare **2–3 toiling . . . pitch** (a quibbling reference to Rosaline's eyes, which he has earlier, III.i.195, called *two pitch-balls*) **4 set thee down** i.e., abide with me. (See I.i.305–306.) **6 mad as Ajax** (An allusion to the fable of Ajax, who, maddened by his failure in a contest for Achilles' armor, attacked a flock of sheep, supposing them to be a hostile army.) **11 in my throat** i.e., utterly **12 mallicholy** melancholy **17 in** involved **18 s.d. He stands aside** (Possibly Berowne hides in a tree or some elevated place; see IV.iii.75,161.) **21 bird-bolt** blunt arrow for shooting birds **22 left pap** left breast (where the heart is located) **26 night of dew** tears that flow nightly **36 glasses** mirrors

40 shade conceal **44 perjure** perjurer. **wearing papers** (An allusion to the custom of attaching to a convicted perjurer's breast the papers involved in and setting forth his offense; in this case, the poem, which is an open indication of Longaville's having forsworn his oath of celibacy.) **49 triumviry** triumvirate. **corner-cap** three-cornered cap **50 Tyburn** the site of a triangular gallows used in public executions **53 numbers** verses **54 guards** embroideries. **hose** breeches **55 shop** (Slang for *codpiece*, a baggy pouch at the fly of a man's hose.) **56–69 Did . . . paradise** (See note on IV.ii.104–117.) **63 grace** favor **66 Exhal'st** draws up **69 To** as to **70 liver-vein** i.e., the vein or style of a lover (since the liver was assumed to be the seat of the passions) **71 green goose** gosling, i.e., a young girl

God amend us, God amend! We are much out o'
th' way.

Enter Dumaine [with a paper].

LONGAVILLE
By whom shall I send this?—Company! Stay.
[*Steps aside.*]

BEROWNE [*Aside*]
All hid, all hid—an old infant play.
Like a demigod here sit I in the sky,
And wretched fools' secrets heedfully o'er-eye.
More sacks to the mill! O heavens, I have my wish!
Dumaine transformed! Four woodcocks in a dish!

DUMAINE
O most divine Kate!

BEROWNE [*Aside*]
O most profane coxcomb!

DUMAINE
By heaven, the wonder in a mortal eye!

BEROWNE [*Aside*]
By earth, she is not, corporal, there you lie.

DUMAINE
Her amber hairs for foul hath amber quoted.

BEROWNE [*Aside*]
An amber-color'd raven was well noted.

DUMAINE
As upright as the cedar.

BEROWNE [*Aside*] Stoop, I say;
Her shoulder is with child.

DUMAINE As fair as day.

BEROWNE [*Aside*]
Ay, as some days; but then no sun must shine.

DUMAINE
O that I had my wish!

LONGAVILLE [*Aside*] And I had mine!

KING [*Aside*]
And I mine too, good Lord!

BEROWNE [*Aside*]
Amen, so I had mine. Is not that a good word?

DUMAINE
I would forget her, but a fever she
Reigns in my blood and will remember'd be.

BEROWNE [*Aside*]
A fever in your blood! Why, then incision
Would let her out in saucers. Sweet misprision!

DUMAINE
Once more I'll read the ode that I have writ.

BEROWNE [*Aside*]
Once more I'll mark how love can vary wit.

DUMAINE (*Reads his sonnet*)
"On a day—alack the day!—
Love, whose month is ever May,
Spied a blossom passing fair
Playing in the wanton air.
Through the velvet leaves the wind,
All unseen, can passage find;
That the lover, sick to death,
Wish'd himself the heaven's breath.
'Air,' quoth he, 'thy cheeks may blow;
Air, would I might triumph so!
But, alack, my hand is sworn
Ne'er to pluck thee from thy thorn;
Vow, alack, for youth unmeet,
Youth so apt to pluck a sweet!
Do not call it sin in me,
That I am forsworn for thee;
Thou for whom Jove would swear
Juno but an Ethiope were,
And deny himself for Jove,
Turning mortal for thy love.' "
This will I send, and something else more plain,
That shall express my true love's fasting pain.
O, would the King, Berowne, and Longaville
Were lovers too! Ill, to example ill,
Would from my forehead wipe a perjur'd note,
For none offend where all alike do dote.

LONGAVILLE [*Advancing*]
Dumaine, thy love is far from charity,
That in love's grief desir'st society.
You may look pale, but I should blush, I know,
To be o'erheard and taken napping so.

KING [*Advancing*]
Come, sir, you blush! As his your case is such;
You chide at him, offending twice as much.
You do not love Maria! Longaville
Did never sonnet for her sake compile,
Nor never lay his wreathed arms athwart
His loving bosom to keep down his heart!
I have been closely shrouded in this bush
And mark'd you both, and for you both did blush.
I heard your guilty rhymes, observ'd your fashion,
Saw sighs reek from you, noted well your passion.
"Ay me!" says one. "O Jove!" the other cries;
One, her hairs were gold, crystal the other's eyes.
[*To Longaville.*]
You would for paradise break faith and troth;
[*To Dumaine.*]
And Jove, for your love, would infringe an oath.
What will Berowne say when that he shall hear
Faith infringed, which such zeal did swear?
How will he scorn! How will he spend his wit!
How will he triumph, leap, and laugh at it!
For all the wealth that ever I did see,
I would not have him know so much by me.

BEROWNE
Now step I forth to whip hypocrisy. [*Advances.*]
Ah, good my liege, I pray thee, pardon me.

72 much . . . way far gone **74 infant play** child's game (hide and seek) **75 in the sky** (Berowne speaks as though he were looking down on the others from some elevated position, possibly the gallery above the stage; see also IV.iii.161.) **77 More . . . mill** (A proverbial expression, "there's more to come.") **78 woodcocks** (Birds noted for stupidity.) **81 mortal** human **82 corporal** i.e., field officer for Cupid (See III.i.185.) **83 quoted** designated (Dumaine hyperbolically insists that her amber hair makes real amber seem foul, ugly, by comparison.) **84 An . . . noted** i.e., (ironically), Dumaine has aptly described a black fowl (with pun on *foul*) as amber-colored **85 Stoop** (1) stooped, stunted (2) Dumaine should avoid such lofty comparisons **86 is with child** i.e., is swollen, unshapely **90 Is . . . word** is that not kind of me **93 incision** letting blood **94 saucers** bowls to catch the blood. **misprision** mistake **97–116 On . . . love** (See note on IV.ii.104–117.)

102 can began to **103 That** so that **114 Ethiope** blackamoor **116 for** i.e., to be **118 fasting** hungering **120 example** serve as example for **121 note** mark, document (See IV.iii.44.) **123 charity** Christian love **131 lay . . . athwart** i.e., fold his arms in the conventional sign of melancholy; cf. III.i.18 **146 by** about

Good heart, what grace hast thou thus to reprove
These worms for loving, that art most in love?
Your eyes do make no coaches; in your tears
There is no certain princess that appears;
You'll not be perjur'd, 'tis a hateful thing—
Tush, none but minstrels like of sonneting!
But are you not asham'd? Nay, are you not,
All three of you, to be thus much o'ershot?
[*To Dumaine.*] You found his mote; [*To Longaville.*]
the King your mote did see;
But I a beam do find in each of three.
O, what a scene of fool'ry have I seen,
Of sighs, of groans, of sorrow, and of teen!
O me, with what strict patience have I sat,
To see a king transformed to a gnat!
To see great Hercules whipping a gig,
And profound Solomon to tune a jig,
And Nestor play at push-pin with the boys,
And critic Timon laugh at idle toys!
Where lies thy grief, O, tell me, good Dumaine?
And, gentle Longaville, where lies thy pain?
And where my liege's? All about the breast.
A caudle, ho!

KING Too bitter is thy jest.
Are we betrayed thus to thy overview?

BEROWNE
Not you by me, but I betrayed to you;
I, that am honest, I, that hold it sin
To break the vow I am engaged in,
I am betrayed by keeping company
With men like you, men of inconstancy.
When shall you see me write a thing in rhyme?
Or groan for love? Or spend a minute's time
In pruning me? When shall you hear that I
Will praise a hand, a foot, a face, an eye,
A gait, a state, a brow, a breast, a waist,
A leg, a limb— [*Starting to leave.*]

KING Soft! Whither away so fast?
A true man, or a thief, that gallops so?

BEROWNE
I post from love; good lover, let me go.

Enter Jaquenetta [*with letter*] *and* [*Costard the*] *Clown.*

JAQUENETTA
God bless the King!

KING What present hast thou there?

COSTARD
Some certain treason.

KING What makes treason here?

COSTARD
Nay, it makes nothing, sir.

KING If it mar nothing neither,
The treason and you go in peace away together.

JAQUENETTA
I beseech your Grace, let this letter be read.
Our person misdoubts it; 'twas treason, he said.
[*Gives letter.*]

KING
Berowne, read it over.
He [*Berowne*] *reads the letter* [*silently*].
[*To Jaquenetta.*] Where hadst thou it?

JAQUENETTA
Of Costard.

KING [*To Costard*]
Where hadst thou it?

COSTARD
Of Dun Adramadio, Dun Adramadio.
[*Berowne tears the letter.*]

KING
How now, what is in you? Why dost thou tear it?

BEROWNE
A toy, my liege, a toy. Your Grace needs not fear it.

LONGAVILLE
It did move him to passion, and therefore
let's hear it.

DUMAINE [*Gathering up the pieces*]
It is Berowne's writing, and here is his name.

BEROWNE [*To Costard*]
Ah, you whoreson loggerhead! You were born to do
me shame.—
Guilty, my lord, guilty! I confess, I confess.

KING What?

BEROWNE
That you three fools lack'd me fool to make up the
mess.
He, he, and you—and you, my liege!—and I,
Are pick-purses in love, and we deserve to die.
O, dismiss this audience, and I shall tell you more.

DUMAINE
Now the number is even.

BEROWNE True, true; we are four.
Will these turtles be gone?

KING Hence, sirs; away!

COSTARD
Walk aside the true folk, and let the traitors stay.
[*Exeunt Costard and Jaquenetta.*]

BEROWNE
Sweet lords, sweet lovers, O, let us embrace!
As true we are as flesh and blood can be.
The sea will ebb and flow, heaven show his face;
Young blood doth not obey an old decree.
We cannot cross the cause why we were born;
Therefore of all hands must we be forsworn.

KING
What, did these rent lines show some love of
thine?

151 Your . . . coaches (Alluding to the King's sonnet, IV.iii.32–33.) **156 o'ershot** wide of the mark; i.e., in error **157, 158 mote, beam** i.e., small speck, large defect. (See Matthew 7:3–5, Luke 6:41–42.) **160 teen** affliction, grief **162 gnat** i.e., a tiny creature (with a play perhaps on *mote*) **163 gig** top **164 tune** play **165 Nestor** wise old Greek chieftain in the Trojan war. **push-pin** a child's game **166 Timon** a fifth-century Athenian notorious for his misanthropy **laugh . . . toys** take delight in mindless entertainments **170 caudle** warm drink given to sick people **174 engaged in** sworn to **179 pruning** preening, i.e., trimming, dressing up **181 state** attitude, bearing **184 post** hasten **186 makes treason** has treason to do

190 person parson. **misdoubts** suspects **200 loggerhead** blockhead **203 mess** a group of four at table **208 turtles** turtledoves, lovers **214 cross . . . born** i.e., continue to defy love **215 of all hands** inevitably, in every way **216 rent lines** torn verses

BEROWNE
Did they, quoth you? Who sees the heavenly
Rosaline,
That, like a rude and savage man of Ind,
At the first op'ning of the gorgeous east,
Bows not his vassal head and, strucken blind,
Kisses the base ground with obedient breast?
What peremptory eagle-sighted eye
Dares look upon the heaven of her brow,
That is not blinded by her majesty?

KING
What zeal, what fury hath inspir'd thee now?
My love, her mistress, is a gracious moon,
She an attending star, scarce seen a light.

BEROWNE
My eyes are then no eyes, nor I Berowne.
O, but for my love, day would turn to night!
Of all complexions the cull'd sovereignty
Do meet, as at a fair, in her fair cheek,
Where several worthies make one dignity,
Where nothing wants that want itself doth seek.
Lend me the flourish of all gentle tongues—
Fie, painted rhetoric! O, she needs it not.
To things of sale a seller's praise belongs;
She passes praise, then praise too short doth blot.
A wither'd hermit, five-score winters worn,
Might shake off fifty, looking in her eye.
Beauty doth varnish age, as if new-born,
And gives the crutch the cradle's infancy.
O, 'tis the sun that maketh all things shine!

KING
By heaven, thy love is black as ebony.

BEROWNE
Is ebony like her? O wood divine!
A wife of such wood were felicity.
O, who can give an oath? Where is a book?
That I may swear Beauty doth beauty lack,
If that she learn not of her eye to look.
No face is fair that is not full so black.

KING
O paradox! Black is the badge of hell,
The hue of dungeons and the school of night;
And beauty's crest becomes the heavens well.

BEROWNE
Devils soonest tempt, resembling spirits of light.
O, if in black my lady's brows be deck'd,
It mourns that painting and usurping hair
Should ravish doters with a false aspect;
And therefore is she born to make black fair.
Her favor turns the fashion of the days,
For native blood is counted painting now;
And therefore red, that would avoid dispraise,
Paints itself black, to imitate her brow.

DUMAINE
To look like her are chimney-sweepers black.

LONGAVILLE
And since her time are colliers counted bright.

KING
And Ethiops of their sweet complexion crack.

DUMAINE
Dark needs no candles now, for dark is light.

BEROWNE
Your mistresses dare never come in rain,
For fear their colors should be wash'd away.

KING
'Twere good yours did; for, sir, to tell you plain,
I'll find a fairer face not wash'd today.

BEROWNE
I'll prove her fair, or talk till doomsday here.

KING
No devil will fright thee then so much as she.

DUMAINE
I never knew man hold vile stuff so dear.

LONGAVILLE [*Showing his shoe*]
Look, here's thy love; my foot and her face see.

BEROWNE
O, if the streets were paved with thine eyes,
Her feet were much too dainty for such tread!

DUMAINE
O vile! Then, as she goes, what upward lies
The street should see as she walk'd overhead.

KING
But what of this? Are we not all in love?

BEROWNE
O, nothing so sure, and thereby all forsworn.

KING
Then leave this chat; and, good Berowne, now prove
Our loving lawful, and our faith not torn.

DUMAINE
Ay, marry, there; some flattery for this evil.

LONGAVILLE
O, some authority how to proceed,
Some tricks, some quillets, how to cheat the devil.

DUMAINE
Some salve for perjury.

BEROWNE O, 'tis more than need.
Have at you, then, affection's men at arms.
Consider what you first did swear unto:
To fast, to study, and to see no woman—
Flat treason 'gainst the kingly state of youth.
Say, can you fast? Your stomachs are too young,
And abstinence engenders maladies.
[And where that you have vow'd to study, lords,
In that each of you have forsworn his book,
Can you still dream and pore and thereon look?

218 Ind India **219 op'ning** i.e., dawning **222 peremptory** bold **227 scarce . . . light** a light scarcely to be seen **230 the cull'd sovereignty** those chosen as most worthy **232 worthies** excellences. **dignity** i.e., supreme example of beauty **233 wants** lacks. **want** desire **234 flourish** adornment, eloquence. **gentle** noble **235 painted** artificial **236 of sale** for sale **237 then praise . . . blot** i.e., any praise of her is inadequate and hence must detract **246 book** i.e., Bible **248 If . . . look** unless Beauty herself learns from Rosaline's eyes how beauty should truly appear **251 school** master, model (?) **252 And . . . well** (ironically) and yet you assert that your dark-eyed beauty is suitable to adorn heaven (?) **253 Devils . . . light** (Berowne suggests that Rosaline's beauty is all the more dangerously deceptive because of its dark aspect.) **spirits of light** angels **255 usurping** i.e., false **258 favor** face. **turns** alters, inverts **259 native blood** natural ruddy complexion. **counted** accounted

264 crack boast **269 I'll . . . today** i.e., even unwashed faces are fairer than hers **271 then** i.e., on doomsday **274–275 O . . . tread** i.e., she walks so lightly that she would not even injure a street paved with your eyes **276 what upward lies** (Dumaine bawdily suggests that a street paved with his eyes would be able to look up constantly under her dress.) **284 quillets** verbal niceties, subtle distinctions **286 Have at you** I come at you, i.e., here it is. **affection's** love's **289 state** majesty **292–313** (These lines seem out of place and repetitive, and are regarded as a first draft of part of ll. 314–361.) **292 where that** whereas **293 In that** inasmuch as. **book** i.e., woman's face

For when would you, my lord, or you, or you,
Have found the ground of study's excellence
Without the beauty of a woman's face?
From women's eyes this doctrine I derive:
They are the ground, the books, the academes
From whence doth spring the true Promethean fire.
Why, universal plodding poisons up
The nimble spirits in the arteries,
As motion and long-during action tires
The sinewy vigor of the traveler.
Now, for not looking on a woman's face,
You have in that forsworn the use of eyes,
And study too, the causer of your vow.
For where is any author in the world
Teaches such beauty as a woman's eye?
Learning is but an adjunct to ourself,
And where we are our learning likewise is.
Then when ourselves we see in ladies' eyes,
Do we not likewise see our learning there?]
O, we have made a vow to study, lords,
And in that vow we have forsworn our books.
For when would you, my liege, or you, or you,
In leaden contemplation have found out
Such fiery numbers as the prompting eyes
Of beauty's tutors have enrich'd you with?
Other slow arts entirely keep the brain,
And therefore, finding barren practicers,
Scarce show a harvest of their heavy toil;
But love, first learned in a lady's eyes,
Lives not alone immured in the brain,
But, with the motion of all elements,
Courses as swift as thought in every power,
And gives to every power a double power,
Above their functions and their offices.
It adds a precious seeing to the eye:
A lover's eyes will gaze an eagle blind.
A lover's ear will hear the lowest sound,
When the suspicious head of theft is stopp'd.
Love's feeling is more soft and sensible
Than are the tender horns of cockled snails.
Love's tongue proves dainty Bacchus gross in taste.
For valor, is not Love a Hercules,
Still climbing trees in the Hesperides?
Subtle as Sphinx, as sweet and musical
As bright Apollo's lute, strung with his hair.
And when Love speaks, the voice of all the gods
Make heaven drowsy with the harmony.
Never durst poet touch a pen to write
Until his ink were temp'red with Love's sighs.
O, then his lines would ravish savage ears
And plant in tyrants mild humility.
From women's eyes this doctrine I derive:
They sparkle still the right Promethean fire;
They are the books, the arts, the academes,
That show, contain, and nourish all the world;
Else none at all in aught proves excellent.
Then fools you were these women to forswear,
Or, keeping what is sworn, you will prove fools.
For wisdom's sake, a word that all men love,
Or for love's sake, a word that loves all men,
Or for men's sake, the authors of these women,
Or women's sake, by whom we men are men,
Let us once lose our oaths to find ourselves,
Or else we lose ourselves to keep our oaths.
It is religion to be thus forsworn,
For charity itself fulfills the law,
And who can sever love from charity?

KING
Saint Cupid, then! And, soldiers, to the field!

BEROWNE
Advance your standards, and upon them, lords;
Pell-mell, down with them! But be first advis'd
In conflict that you get the sun of them.

LONGAVILLE
Now to plain-dealing. Lay these glozes by.
Shall we resolve to woo these girls of France?

KING
And win them too. Therefore let us devise
Some entertainment for them in their tents.

BEROWNE
First, from the park let us conduct them thither;
Then homeward every man attach the hand
Of his fair mistress. In the afternoon
We will with some strange pastime solace them,
Such as the shortness of the time can shape;
For revels, dances, masks, and merry hours
Forerun fair Love, strewing her way with flowers.

KING
Away, away! No time shall be omitted
That will be time, and may by us be fitted.

BEROWNE
Allons! Allons! Sow'd cockle reap'd no corn,
And justice always whirls in equal measure.
Light wenches may prove plagues to men forsworn;
If so, our copper buys no better treasure. *[Exeunt.]*

[ACT V • SCENE I]

Enter [Holofernes] the Pedant, [Nathaniel] the Curate, and Dull [the Constable].

HOLOFERNES Satis quid sufficit.

NATHANIEL I praise God for you, sir. Your reasons at dinner have been sharp and sententious, pleasant

296 ground basis **300 Promethean fire** divine fire. (From the legend that Prometheus stole fire from heaven and gave it to mankind.) **303 long-during** long-continuing **318 numbers** verses **320 arts** branches of knowledge. **keep** dwell within **325 elements** i.e., earth, air, fire, and water **328 Above . . . offices** above and beyond their ordinary functions **332 When . . . stopp'd** when even the most cautiously alert thief hears nothing **333 sensible** sensitive **334 cockled** having a shell **335 Bacchus** god of wine and revelry **337 Hesperides** where the golden apples grew (the gaining of which was the eleventh of Hercules' twelve labors)

354 loves is lovable to, inspires with love **357 once** for once, one time **360 For . . . law** (From Romans 13:8: "for he that loveth another hath fulfilled the law.") **365 get . . . them** i.e., take field position so that the sun is in their eyes (with a play on the idea of *begetting a son*) **366 glozes** sophistries **371 attach** seize **378 be time** betime, happen. **fitted** used. (I.e., we'll take advantage of every minute.) **379 Allons** come on, let's go. **cockle** a weed. **corn** wheat. (I.e., we won't get results without well-planned efforts.) **380 measure** proportion (again suggesting that reward comes only from effort) **381 Light** frivolous **382 copper** coin of little value. (I.e., as beggars and as men forsworn, we cannot afford to be choosers.)

V.i. Location: Navarre's park.
1 Satis quid sufficit (More faulty Latin. It should read *satis est quod sufficit,* "enough is as good as a feast.") **2 reasons** discourses

without scurrility, witty without affection, audacious without impudency, learned without opinion, and strange without heresy. I did converse this quondam day with a companion of the King's, who is intitled, nominated, or called, Don Adriano de Armado.

HOLOFERNES Novi hominem tanquam te. His humor is lofty, his discourse peremptory, his tongue filed, his eye ambitious, his gait majestical, and his general behavior vain, ridiculous, and thrasonical. He is too picked, too spruce, too affected, too odd, as it were, too peregrinate, as I may call it.

NATHANIEL A most singular and choice epithet.

Draw out his table-book.

HOLOFERNES He draweth out the thread of his verbosity finer than the staple of his argument. I abhor such fanatical phantasimes, such insociable and point-devise companions, such rackers of orthography, as to speak "dout," fine, when he should say "doubt"; "det," "debt"—when he should pronounce—d, e, b, t, not d, e, t. He clepeth a calf, "cauf"; half, "hauf"; neighbor vocatur "nebor"; neigh abbreviated "ne." This is abhominable—which he would call "abbominable"; it insinuateth me of insanie. Ne intelligis, domine? To make frantic, lunatic.

NATHANIEL Laus Deo, bone intelligo.

HOLOFERNES Bone? Bone for bene. Priscian a little scratch'd, 'twill serve.

Enter [Armado the] Braggart, [Moth, his] boy, [and Costard].

NATHANIEL Videsne quis venit?

HOLOFERNES Video, et gaudeo.

ARMADO [*To Moth*] Chirrah!

HOLOFERNES Quare chirrah, not sirrah?

ARMADO Men of peace, well encount'red.

HOLOFERNES Most military sir, salutation.

MOTH [*Aside to Costard*] They have been at a great feast of languages, and stol'n the scraps.

COSTARD O, they have liv'd long on the alms-basket of words. I marvel thy master hath not eaten thee for a word; for thou art not so long by the head as honorificabilitudinitatibus. Thou art easier swallow'd than a flap-dragon.

MOTH Peace! The peal begins.

ARMADO [*To Holofernes*] Monsieur, are you not lett'red?

MOTH Yes, yes; he teaches boys the horn-book. What is a, b, spell'd backward, with the horn on his head?

HOLOFERNES Ba, pueritia, with a horn added.

MOTH Ba, most silly sheep with a horn. You hear his learning.

HOLOFERNES Quis, quis, thou consonant?

MOTH The last of the five vowels, if you repeat them; or the fifth, if I.

HOLOFERNES I will repeat them: a, e, i—

MOTH The sheep. The other two concludes it—o, u.

ARMADO Now, by the salt wave of the Mediterraneum, a sweet touch, a quick venue of wit! Snip, snap, quick and home. It rejoiceth my intellect. True wit!

MOTH Offer'd by a child to an old man—which is wit-old.

HOLOFERNES What is the figure? What is the figure?

MOTH Horns.

HOLOFERNES Thou disputes like an infant. Go, whip thy gig.

MOTH Lend me your horn to make one, and I will whip about your infamy manu cita—a gig of a cuckold's horn.

COSTARD An I had but one penny in the world, thou shouldst have it to buy gingerbread. Hold, there is the very remuneration I had of thy master, thou halfpenny purse of wit, thou pigeon-egg of discretion. [*Gives money.*] O, an the heavens were so pleas'd that thou wert but my bastard, what a joyful father wouldst thou make me! Go to; thou hast it ad dunghill, at the fingers' ends, as they say.

HOLOFERNES O, I smell false Latin! "Dunghill" for unguem.

ARMADO Arts-man, preambulate, we will be singuled from the barbarous. Do you not educate youth at the charge-house on the top of the mountain?

HOLOFERNES Or mons, the hill.

ARMADO At your sweet pleasure, for the mountain.

HOLOFERNES I do, sans question.

ARMADO Sir, it is the King's most sweet pleasure and affection to congratulate the Princess at her pavilion in the posteriors of this day, which the rude multitude call the afternoon.

HOLOFERNES The posterior of the day, most generous sir, is liable, congruent, and measurable for the afternoon. The word is well cull'd, chose, sweet, and apt, I do assure you, sir, I do assure.

ARMADO Sir, the King is a noble gentleman, and my familiar, I do assure ye, very good friend. For what is inward between us, let it pass. I do beseech thee, remember thy courtesy; I beseech thee, apparel thy

5 opinion self-conceit, arrogance **6 strange** novel, new. **this quondam** the other **9 Novi . . . te** I know the man as well as I know you **10 peremptory** positive, overbearing. **filed** polished **12 thrasonical** boastful. (From Thraso, a braggart soldier in Terence's play *Eunuchus*.) **13 picked** fastidious **14 peregrinate** having the manner of one who has traveled **15 s.d. table-book** notebook **18 phantasimes** persons who entertain fantastic notions
18–19 point-devise companions extremely precise fellows **19 rackers of orthography** (Holofernes' tirade reflects a conscious attempt of some Renaissance educators to bring the English spelling and pronunciation of certain borrowed words more nearly to their Latin originals.) **20 fine** mincingly **22 clepeth** calls **23 vocatur** is called **25 it . . . insanie** (1) to me it savors of insanity (2) it drives me mad. **Ne intelligis, domine** do you understand, master **27 Laus . . . intelligo** praise be to God, I understand well **28 Bone for bene** i.e., the Latin should be *bene,* "well" **28–29 Priscian . . . scratch'd** i.e., your Latin is a little faulty. (Priscian was a grammarian of the fifth or sixth century whose textbooks were considered standard.) **30 Videsne quis venit** do you see who comes **31 Video, et gaudeo** I see and I rejoice. (This trivial Latin dialogue is after the manner of schoolboys' exercises.) **33 Quare** why **38 alms-basket** a basket used to gather scraps for the poor **40–41 honorificabilitudinitatibus** (Reputedly the longest word in existence. It is the dative plural of a Latin word meaning something like *honorableness.*) **42 flap-dragon** the raisin or plum in burning brandy to be snapped with the mouth in the game of snapdragon **43 peal** i.e., clatter of tongues, like a peal of bells **45 lett'red** i.e., educated

46 horn-book printed sheets of paper, covered by a protective thin layer of horn; used for teaching children their alphabet. (The *horn* sets up a joke on the sheep's or cuckold's horn.) **48 pueritia** childishness, child **51 Quis** who, what. **consonant** i.e., nonentity, since the consonants cannot be sounded without also sounding the vowels **55 The sheep** i.e., Holofernes, by saying "i," that is, "I," has labeled himself the sheep. **concludes it** (1) completes the list of the five vowels (2) proves my point. **o, u** i.e., oh you **57 venue** sally, thrust. (A fencing term, continued in *quick and home,* to the quick.) **60 wit-old** mentally feeble (with a pun on *wittol,* a contented cuckold) **61 figure** metaphor, figure of speech **63 Thou disputes** you reason **64 gig** top **66 manu cita** with ready hand **70–71 halfpenny purse** a tiny purse, just large enough to hold a halfpenny **76–77 unguem** i.e., *ad unguem,* to the nail, i.e., perfectly **78 Arts-man** scholar. **preambulate** walk (with me). **singuled** separated **80 chargehouse** some kind of school **83 sans** without **88 generous** cultivated, wellborn **89 liable** apt. **measurable** fitted **93 familiar** intimate acquaintance **94 inward** private **95 thy courtesy** i.e., that you've removed your hat

head. And among other importunate and most serious designs, and of great import indeed, too—but let that pass; for I must tell thee, it will please his Grace, by the world, sometime to lean upon my poor shoulder, and with his royal finger, thus, dally with my excrement, with my mustachio; but, sweet heart, let that pass. By the world, I recount no fable! Some certain special honors it pleaseth his greatness to impart to Armado, a soldier, a man of travel, that hath seen the world; but let that pass. The very all of all is—but, sweet heart, I do implore secrecy—that the King would have me present the Princess, sweet chuck, with some delightful ostentation, or show, or pageant, or antic, or firework. Now, understanding that the curate and your sweet self are good at such eruptions and sudden breaking out of mirth, as it were, I have acquainted you withal, to the end to crave your assistance.

HOLOFERNES Sir, you shall present before her the Nine Worthies. Sir Nathaniel, as concerning some entertainment of time, some show in the posterior of this day, to be rend'red by our assistance, the King's command, and this most gallant, illustrate, and learned gentleman, before the Princess—I say none so fit as to present the Nine Worthies.

NATHANIEL Where will you find men worthy enough to present them?

HOLOFERNES Joshua, yourself; myself; and this gallant gentleman, Judas Maccabaeus; this swain, because of his great limb or joint, shall pass Pompey the Great; the page, Hercules—

ARMADO Pardon, sir; error. He is not quantity enough for that Worthy's thumb; he is not so big as the end of his club.

HOLOFERNES Shall I have audience? He shall present Hercules in minority. His enter and exit shall be strangling a snake; and I will have an apology for that purpose.

MOTH An excellent device! So if any of the audience hiss, you may cry, "Well done, Hercules! Now thou crushest the snake!" That is the way to make an offense gracious, though few have the grace to do it.

ARMADO For the rest of the Worthies?

HOLOFERNES I will play three myself.

MOTH Thrice-worthy gentleman!

ARMADO Shall I tell you a thing?

HOLOFERNES We attend.

ARMADO We will have, if this fadge not, an antic. I beseech you, follow.

HOLOFERNES Via, goodman Dull! Thou hast spoken no word all this while.

DULL Nor understood none neither, sir.

HOLOFERNES Allons! We will employ thee.

DULL
I'll make one in a dance, or so; or I will play
On the tabor to the Worthies, and let them dance
the hay.

HOLOFERNES
Most dull, honest Dull! To our sport, away!
Exeunt.

[SCENE II]

Enter the Ladies [the Princess, Katharine, Rosaline, and Maria].

PRINCESS
Sweet hearts, we shall be rich ere we depart,
If fairings come thus plentifully in.
A lady wall'd about with diamonds!
Look you what I have from the loving King.
[*Shows jewel.*]

ROSALINE
Madam, came nothing else along with that?

PRINCESS
Nothing but this? Yes, as much love in rhyme
As would be cramm'd up in a sheet of paper,
Writ o' both sides the leaf, margent and all,
That he was fain to seal on Cupid's name.

ROSALINE
That was the way to make his godhead wax,
For he hath been five thousand years a boy.

KATHARINE
Ay, and a shrewd unhappy gallows too.

ROSALINE
You'll ne'er be friends with him; 'a kill'd your sister.

KATHARINE
He made her melancholy, sad, and heavy,
And so she died. Had she been light, like you,
Of such a merry, nimble, stirring spirit,
She might ha' been a grandam ere she died.
And so may you, for a light heart lives long.

ROSALINE
What's your dark meaning, mouse, of this light
word?

KATHARINE
A light condition in a beauty dark.

ROSALINE
We need more light to find your meaning out.

KATHARINE
You'll mar the light by taking it in snuff;
Therefore I'll darkly end the argument.

100–101 excrement outgrowth (of hair) **107 chuck** chick. (A term of endearment.) **109 antic** a pageant or entertainment using fantastic costumes **114–115 Nine Worthies** (A conventional subject familiar to Shakespeare's audience in poems, pageants, and tapestries. The nine were three pagans, Hector of Troy, Alexander the Great, and Julius Caesar; three Jews, Joshua, David, and Judas Maccabaeus; and three Christians, Arthur, Charlemagne, and Godfrey of Bouillon. The list varied, but Shakespeare makes an unusual departure when he introduces Pompey and Hercules.) **120 present** represent **123 myself** (Holofernes does not here assign a part to himself (see however l. 139), nor does he assign Nathaniel to Alexander or Armado to Hercules as in the actual production. Perhaps changes occur in rehearsal.) **125 pass** represent **130 audience** a hearing **131–132 strangling a snake** (According to legend, Hercules as an infant displayed his great strength by strangling two serpents sent by the envious Juno to destroy him in his cradle.) **132 apology** explanatory prologue **143 fadge** fit, be suitable **145 Via** on! (A cry of encouragement to troops.)

149 make one take part **150 tabor** small drum. **hay** country dance

V.ii. Location: Navarre's park. Near the ladies' tents.
2 fairings complimentary gifts **9 That . . . name** so that he was obliged to append Cupid's name by sealing a slip of paper to the letter itself, or, for lack of room, place the seal on top of Cupid's name. (Probably the Princess shows her letter, as do the other ladies in turn when they show their love tokens.) **10 wax** increase (with pun on the *wax* of the seal) **12 shrewd unhappy gallows** wicked mischievous knave, deserving to be hanged **19 mouse** (A term of endearment.) **20 light condition** wanton temperament **22 taking . . . snuff** taking offense (with pun on *snuff,* a burning candlewick)

ROSALINE
Look what you do, you do it still i' th' dark.
KATHARINE
So do not you, for you are a light wench.
ROSALINE
Indeed I weigh not you, and therefore light.
KATHARINE
You weigh me not? O, that's you care not for me.
ROSALINE
Great reason; for past cure is still past care.
PRINCESS
Well bandied both, a set of wit well played.
But, Rosaline, you have a favor too.
Who sent it? And what is it?
ROSALINE
I would you knew.
An if my face were but as fair as yours,
My favor were as great; be witness this.
[Shows love token.]
Nay, I have verses too, I thank Berowne;
The numbers true, and, were the numb'ring too,
I were the fairest goddess on the ground.
I am compar'd to twenty thousand fairs.
O, he hath drawn my picture in his letter!
PRINCESS
Anything like?
ROSALINE
Much in the letters, nothing in the praise.
PRINCESS
Beauteous as ink—a good conclusion.
KATHARINE
Fair as a text B in a copy-book.
ROSALINE
'Ware pencils, ho! Let me not die your debtor,
My red dominical, my golden letter.
O that your face were not so full of O's!
KATHARINE
A pox of that jest! And I beshrew all shrows.
PRINCESS
But, Katharine, what was sent to you from fair
Dumaine?
KATHARINE
Madam, this glove. *[Shows glove.]*
PRINCESS
Did he not send you twain?
KATHARINE
Yes, madam, and moreover
Some thousand verses of a faithful lover,
A huge translation of hypocrisy,
Vilely compil'd, profound simplicity.
MARIA
This, and these pearls, to me sent Longaville.
[Shows pearl necklace.]
The letter is too long by half a mile.
PRINCESS
I think no less. Dost thou not wish in heart
The chain were longer and the letter short?
MARIA
Ay, or I would these hands might never part.
PRINCESS
We are wise girls to mock our lovers so.
ROSALINE
They are worse fools to purchase mocking so.
That same Berowne I'll torture ere I go.
O that I knew he were but in by th' week!
How I would make him fawn, and beg, and seek,
And wait the season, and observe the times,
And spend his prodigal wits in bootless rhymes,
And shape his service wholly to my hests
And make him proud to make me proud that jests!
So perttaunt-like would I o'ersway his state
That he should be my fool and I his fate.
PRINCESS
None are so surely caught, when they are catch'd,
As wit turn'd fool. Folly, in wisdom hatch'd,
Hath wisdom's warrant and the help of school
And wit's own grace to grace a learned fool.
ROSALINE
The blood of youth burns not with such excess
As gravity's revolt to wantonness.
MARIA
Folly in fools bears not so strong a note
As fool'ry in the wise, when wit doth dote,
Since all the power thereof it doth apply
To prove, by wit, worth in simplicity.

Enter Boyet.

PRINCESS
Here comes Boyet, and mirth is in his face.
BOYET
O, I am stabb'd with laughter! Where's her Grace?
PRINCESS
Thy news, Boyet?
BOYET
Prepare, madam, prepare!
Arm, wenches, arm! Encounters mounted are
Against your peace. Love doth approach disguis'd,
Armed in arguments; you'll be surpris'd.
Muster your wits, stand in your own defense,
Or hide your heads like cowards, and fly hence.
PRINCESS
Saint Denis to Saint Cupid! What are they
That charge their breath against us? Say, scout, say.
BOYET
Under the cool shade of a sycamore
I thought to close mine eyes some half an hour,
When, lo, to interrupt my purpos'd rest,
Toward that shade I might behold address'd
The King and his companions. Warily
I stole into a neighbor thicket by,
And overheard what you shall overhear—
That, by and by, disguis'd they will be here.
Their herald is a pretty knavish page,

24 Look what whatever **26 weigh not you** don't weigh as much as you **27 weigh** regard seriously **28 past cure** i.e., Katharine is incurable **30 favor** love token **35 numbers** meter. **numb'ring** reckoning **37 fairs** fair women **40 letters** lettering **41 ink** (Referring to Rosaline's dark complexion.) **42 a text B** (Perhaps a heavily-ornamented capital B, boldly dark like Rosaline's complexion.) **43 'Ware pencils** i.e., have at you in this skirmish of satirical portraits **44 red dominical** red lettering used in calendars to mark Sundays and holy days. (From *dies dominica,* the Lord's day; here, a jesting reference to Katharine's fair complexion.) **45 O's** i.e., smallpox scars (to which Katharine replies in the next line) **46 beshrew all shrows** curse all shrews, scolds **52 simplicity** stupidity

61 in . . . week i.e., caught, trapped permanently **64 bootless** fruitless **65 hests** behests **66 And . . . jests** and make him take satisfaction in glorifying me, the one who mocks him **67 perttaunt-like** like one holding a winning hand (pair-taunt) in the card game of "post and pair" (with a pun on *taunt*) **74 As gravity's revolt** as a wise man's rebellion **75 note** stigma, notoriety **76 dote** grow foolish **77 thereof** i.e., of wit **78 simplicity** foolishness **84 surpris'd** overcome by surprise attack **87 Saint Denis** patron saint of France **92 might** could. **address'd** approaching **95 overhear** hear over again

That well by heart hath conn'd his embassage. 98
Action and accent did they teach him there; 99
"Thus must thou speak," and "thus thy body bear."
And ever and anon they made a doubt 101
Presence majestical would put him out;
"For," quoth the King, "an angel shalt thou see;
Yet fear not thou, but speak audaciously."
The boy replied, "An angel is not evil;
I should have fear'd her had she been a devil."
With that, all laugh'd and clapp'd him on the shoulder,
Making the bold wag by their praises bolder.
One rubb'd his elbow thus, and fleer'd, and swore 109
A better speech was never spoke before.
Another, with his finger and his thumb, 111
Cried, "Via! We will do 't, come what will come."
The third he caper'd, and cried, "All goes well."
The fourth turn'd on the toe, and down he fell.
With that, they all did tumble on the ground,
With such a zealous laughter, so profound,
That in this spleen ridiculous appears, 117
To check their folly, passion's solemn tears.

PRINCESS
But what, but what, come they to visit us?

BOYET
They do, they do; and are apparel'd thus,
Like Muscovites or Russians, as I guess. 121
Their purpose is to parle, to court, and dance; 122
And every one his love-feat will advance
Unto his several mistress, which they'll know 124
By favors several which they did bestow.

PRINCESS
And will they so? The gallants shall be task'd; 126
For, ladies, we will every one be mask'd,
And not a man of them shall have the grace,
Despite of suit, to see a lady's face. 129
Hold, Rosaline, this favor thou shalt wear,
And then the King will court thee for his dear.
Hold, take thou this, my sweet, and give me thine,
So shall Berowne take me for Rosaline.
[The Princess and Rosaline exchange favors; so do Katharine and Maria.]
And change you favors too; so shall your loves
Woo contrary, deceiv'd by these removes. 135

ROSALINE
Come on, then, wear the favors most in sight. 136

KATHARINE
But in this changing what is your intent?

PRINCESS
The effect of my intent is to cross theirs.
They do it but in mockery merriment, 139
And mock for mock is only my intent.
Their several counsels they unbosom shall 141
To loves mistook, and so be mock'd withal
Upon the next occasion that we meet,
With visages display'd, to talk and greet.

ROSALINE
But shall we dance, if they desire us to 't?

PRINCESS
No, to the death we will not move a foot, 146
Nor to their penn'd speech render we no grace,
But while 'tis spoke each turn away her face.

BOYET
Why, that contempt will kill the speaker's heart,
And quite divorce his memory from his part.

PRINCESS
Therefore I do it; and I make no doubt
The rest will ne'er come in, if he be out. 152
There's no such sport as sport by sport o'erthrown,
To make theirs ours and ours none but our own. 154
So shall we stay, mocking intended game,
And they, well mock'd, depart away with shame.
Sound trumpet [within].

BOYET
The trumpet sounds. Be mask'd; the maskers come.
[The Ladies mask.]

Enter Blackamoors with music; [Moth] the Boy, with a speech, and [the King, Berowne, and] the rest of the Lords disguised [in Russian habits].

MOTH
"All hail, the richest beauties on the earth!"—

BOYET
Beauties no richer than rich taffeta. 159

MOTH
"A holy parcel of the fairest dames 160
The Ladies turn their backs to him.
That ever turn'd their—backs—to mortal views!"

BEROWNE *[Aside to Moth]* "Their eyes," villain, "their eyes."

MOTH
"That ever turn'd their eyes to mortal views!
Out"—

BOYET True; out indeed.

MOTH
"Out of your favors, heavenly spirits, vouchsafe
Not to behold"—

BEROWNE *[Aside to Moth]* "Once to behold," rogue.

MOTH
"Once to behold with your sun-beamed eyes,
—with your sun-beamed eyes"—

BOYET
They will not answer to that epithet;
You were best call it "daughter-beamed eyes." 173

MOTH
They do not mark me, and that brings me out.

BEROWNE
Is this your perfectness? Be gone, you rogue!
[Exit Moth.]

ROSALINE *[Speaking as the Princess]*
What would these strangers? Know their minds, Boyet. 176
If they do speak our language, 'tis our will

98 conn'd memorized. **embassage** message **99 Action** gesture **101 made a doubt** expressed a fear **109 fleer'd** grinned **111 with . . . thumb** i.e., snapping his fingers **117 spleen ridiculous** excess of mirth **121 Muscovites or Russians** (Costumes not uncommon in court masquerades.) **122 parle** parley **124 which** whom **126 task'd** tried, tested **129 suit** petition, entreaty **135 removes** exchanges **136 most in sight** conspicuously **139 mockery** mocking **141 counsels** private intentions, secret purposes

146 to the death on pain of death **152 out** confused **154 theirs** i.e., their sport **159 taffeta** i.e., their masks of taffeta cloth **160 parcel** company **173 daughter-beamed** (substituting *daughter* for *sun*, i.e., son) **176 What would** (Rosaline, masquerading as the Princess, presides.)

That some plain man recount their purposes. 178
Know what they would.

BOYET
What would you with the Princess?

BEROWNE
Nothing but peace and gentle visitation.

ROSALINE
What would they, say they?

BOYET
Nothing but peace and gentle visitation.

ROSALINE
Why, that they have; and bid them so be gone.

BOYET
She says, you have it, and you may be gone.

KING
Say to her, we have measur'd many miles 185
To tread a measure with her on this grass. 186

BOYET
They say, that they have measur'd many a mile
To tread a measure with you on this grass.

ROSALINE
It is not so. Ask them how many inches
Is in one mile. If they have measur'd many,
The measure then of one is eas'ly told.

BOYET
If to come hither you have measur'd miles,
And many miles, the Princess bids you tell
How many inches doth fill up one mile.

BEROWNE
Tell her, we measure them by weary steps.

BOYET
She hears herself.

ROSALINE
How many weary steps,
Of many weary miles you have o'ergone,
Are numb'red in the travel of one mile?

BEROWNE
We number nothing that we spend for you.
Our duty is so rich, so infinite,
That we may do it still without account. 201
Vouchsafe to show the sunshine of your face,
That we, like savages, may worship it.

ROSALINE
My face is but a moon, and clouded too.

KING
Blessed are clouds, to do as such clouds do!
Vouchsafe, bright moon, and these thy stars, to shine,
Those clouds removed, upon our watery eyne. 207

ROSALINE
O vain petitioner! Beg a greater matter;
Thou now requests but moonshine in the water. 209

KING
Then, in our measure do but vouchsafe one change. 210
Thou bid'st me beg; this begging is not strange.

ROSALINE
Play, music, then! Nay, you must do it soon.
[*Music plays.*]
Not yet—no dance! Thus change I like the moon.

KING
Will you not dance? How come you thus estranged?

ROSALINE
You took the moon at full, but now she's changed.

KING
Yet still she is the moon, and I the man. 216
The music plays; vouchsafe some motion to it.

ROSALINE
Our ears vouchsafe it.

KING
But your legs should do it.

ROSALINE
Since you are strangers and come here by chance,
We'll not be nice; take hands. We will not dance. 220
[*She offers her hand.*]

KING
Why take we hands, then?

ROSALINE
Only to part friends.
Curtsy, sweet hearts; and so the measure ends.

KING
More measure of this measure; be not nice. 223

ROSALINE
We can afford no more at such a price.

KING
Price you yourselves. What buys your company?

ROSALINE
Your absence only.

KING
That can never be.

ROSALINE
Then cannot we be bought. And so, adieu—
Twice to your visor, and half once to you.

KING
If you deny to dance, let's hold more chat.

ROSALINE
In private, then.

KING
I am best pleas'd with that.
[*They converse apart.*]

BEROWNE
White-handed mistress, one sweet word with thee.

PRINCESS
Honey, and milk, and sugar; there is three.

BEROWNE
Nay then, two treys, an if you grow so nice, 233
Metheglin, wort, and malmsey; well run, dice! 234
There's half a dozen sweets.

PRINCESS
Seventh sweet, adieu.
Since you can cog, I'll play no more with you. 236

BEROWNE
One word in secret.

PRINCESS
Let it not be sweet.

BEROWNE
Thou grievest my gall.

PRINCESS
Gall! Bitter.

BEROWNE
Therefore meet.
[*They converse apart.*] 238

DUMAINE
Will you vouchsafe with me to change a word?

178 plain plainspoken **185 measur'd** traversed, paced **186 measure** dance **201 account** reckoning **207 clouds** i.e., the mask. **eyne** eyes **209 moonshine . . . water** (Proverbial expression meaning "nothing at all.") **210 change** a round in dancing (with a play on the idea of the moon's changing)

216 man i.e., man in the moon **220 nice** coy **223 More measure** i.e., (we wish) more quantity **233 treys** threes. **nice** subtle **234 Metheglin** a spiced drink made from herbs and honey. **wort,** sweet unfermented beer. **malmsey** a strong sweet wine **236 cog** cheat **238 meet** fitting

MARIA
Name it.
DUMAINE Fair lady—
MARIA Say you so? Fair lord—
Take that for your fair lady.
DUMAINE Please it you,
As much in private, and I'll bid adieu.
[*They converse apart.*]
KATHARINE
What, was your vizard made without a tongue?
LONGAVILLE
I know the reason, lady, why you ask.
KATHARINE
O for your reason! Quickly, sir, I long.
LONGAVILLE
You have a double tongue within your mask,
And would afford my speechless vizard half.
KATHARINE
"Veal," quoth the Dutchman. Is not "veal" a calf?
LONGAVILLE
A calf, fair lady!
KATHARINE No, a fair lord calf.
LONGAVILLE
Let's part the word.
KATHARINE No, I'll not be your half.
Take all, and wean it; it may prove an ox.
LONGAVILLE
Look how you butt yourself in these sharp mocks!
Will you give horns, chaste lady? Do not so.
KATHARINE
Then die a calf, before your horns do grow.
LONGAVILLE
One word in private with you, ere I die.
KATHARINE
Bleat softly then. The butcher hears you cry.
[*They converse apart.*]
BOYET
The tongues of mocking wenches are as keen
As is the razor's edge invisible,
Cutting a smaller hair than may be seen;
Above the sense of sense, so sensible
Seemeth their conference; their conceits have wings
Fleeter than arrows, bullets, wind, thought, swifter things.
ROSALINE
Not one word more, my maids; break off, break off.
[*The ladies break away from the gentlemen.*]
BEROWNE
By heaven, all dry-beaten with pure scoff!
KING
Farewell, mad wenches; you have simple wits.
Exeunt [*King, Lords, and Blackamoors*].
PRINCESS
Twenty adieus, my frozen Muscovits.
Are these the breed of wits so wondered at?
BOYET
Tapers they are, with your sweet breaths puff'd out.
ROSALINE
Well-liking wits they have; gross, gross; fat, fat.
PRINCESS
O poverty in wit, kingly-poor flout!
Will they not, think you, hang themselves tonight?
Or ever but in vizards show their faces?
This pert Berowne was out of count'nance quite.
ROSALINE
They were all in lamentable cases!
The King was weeping-ripe for a good word.
PRINCESS
Berowne did swear himself out of all suit.
MARIA
Dumaine was at my service, and his sword.
"No point," quoth I; my servant straight was mute.
KATHARINE
Lord Longaville said, I came o'er his heart;
And trow you what he call'd me?
PRINCESS Qualm, perhaps.
KATHARINE
Yes, in good faith.
PRINCESS Go, sickness as thou art!
ROSALINE
Well, better wits have worn plain statute-caps.
But will you hear? The King is my love sworn.
PRINCESS
And quick Berowne hath plighted faith to me.
KATHARINE
And Longaville was for my service born.
MARIA
Dumaine is mine, as sure as bark on tree.
BOYET
Madam, and pretty mistresses, give ear:
Immediately they will again be here
In their own shapes, for it can never be
They will digest this harsh indignity.
PRINCESS
Will they return?
BOYET They will, they will, God knows,
And leap for joy, though they are lame with blows.
Therefore change favors; and, when they repair,
Blow like sweet roses in this summer air.
PRINCESS
How blow? How blow? Speak to be understood.
BOYET
Fair ladies mask'd are roses in their bud;
Dismask'd, their damask sweet commixture shown,
Are angels vailing clouds, or roses blown.

243 vizard mask **247 And . . . half** i.e., you talk enough for the two of us **248 Veal** i.e., as a Dutchman would pronounce "well" (with a possible pun on *veil,* mask, as well as *veal,* calf; also, in ll. 245 and 248, Katharine completes Longaville's name: "long," "veal") **250 part** divide between us. **your half** (1) sharer with you of two halves (2) your partner in marriage **251 wean** i.e., raise. **ox** (A type of stupidity.) **252 butt** injure (with play on *giving horns* in the next line, meaning both to butt with horns and make a cuckold) **260 the sense of** the reach of. **sensible** quick-witted **261 conference** conversation. **conceits** fancies **264 dry-beaten** beaten soundly without blood drawn

269 Well-liking in good condition, plump (with a pun on *liking,* "like-king") **270 kingly-poor flout** poor mockery of a king (with a possible play on *kingly* as the syllabically reversed form of *liking,* "ly-king") **274 cases** (1) situations (2) visors **275 weeping-ripe** ready to weep **276 out of all suit** excessively and to no avail (with a play on the idea of *costume*) **278 No point** (See note on II.i.190.) **straight** immediately **280 trow you** would you believe. **Qualm** i.e., heartsickness (with a play perhaps on *came,* l. 279, as suggested by Elizabethan pronunciation) **282 better . . . statute-caps** i.e., one could find better wits even among London apprentices (who were required by statute to wear identifiable caps) **290 digest** stomach, put up with **293 change favors** exchange love tokens (giving them back to their original owners). **repair** return **294 Blow** bloom **297 damask** mingling red and white **298 vailing** letting fall, shedding. **blown** i.e., full-blown

PRINCESS
Avaunt, perplexity! What shall we do,
If they return in their own shapes to woo?

ROSALINE
Good madam, if by me you'll be advis'd,
Let's mock them still, as well known as disguis'd.
Let us complain to them what fools were here,
Disguis'd like Muscovites, in shapeless gear;
And wonder what they were, and to what end
Their shallow shows and prologue vilely penn'd,
And their rough carriage so ridiculous,
Should be presented at our tent to us.

BOYET
Ladies, withdraw. The gallants are at hand.

PRINCESS
Whip to our tents, as roes run o'er land.
Exeunt [Princess, Rosaline, Katharine, and Maria].

Enter the King and the rest [Berowne, Longaville, and Dumaine, in their proper habits].

KING
Fair sir, God save you! Where's the Princess?

BOYET
Gone to her tent. Please it your Majesty
Command me any service to her thither?

KING
That she vouchsafe me audience for one word.

BOYET
I will; and so will she, I know, my lord. *Exit.*

BEROWNE
This fellow pecks up wit as pigeons pease,
And utters it again when God doth please.
He is wit's pedler, and retails his wares
At wakes and wassails, meetings, markets, fairs;
And we that sell by gross, the Lord doth know,
Have not the grace to grace it with such show.
This gallant pins the wenches on his sleeve;
Had he been Adam, he had tempted Eve.
'A can carve too, and lisp. Why, this is he
That kiss'd his hand away in courtesy.
This is the ape of form, monsieur the nice,
That, when he plays at tables, chides the dice
In honorable terms. Nay, he can sing
A mean most meanly, and in ushering
Mend him who can. The ladies call him sweet.
The stairs, as he treads on them, kiss his feet.
This is the flow'r that smiles on every one,
To show his teeth as white as whale's bone;
And consciences that will not die in debt
Pay him the due of honey-tongued Boyet.

KING
A blister on his sweet tongue, with my heart,
That put Armado's page out of his part!

Enter the Ladies [wearing their original favors, with Boyet].

BEROWNE
See where it comes! Behavior, what wert thou
Till this madman show'd thee? And what art thou now?

KING
All hail, sweet madam, and fair time of day!

PRINCESS
"Fair" in "all hail" is foul, as I conceive.

KING
Construe my speeches better, if you may.

PRINCESS
Then wish me better, I will give you leave.

KING
We came to visit you, and purpose now
To lead you to our court. Vouchsafe it then.

PRINCESS
This field shall hold me, and so hold your vow.
Nor God, nor I, delights in perjur'd men.

KING
Rebuke me not for that which you provoke.
The virtue of your eye must break my oath.

PRINCESS
You nickname virtue. "Vice," you should have spoke,
For virtue's office never breaks men's troth.
Now by my maiden honor, yet as pure
As the unsullied lily, I protest,
A world of torments though I should endure,
I would not yield to be your house's guest,
So much I hate a breaking cause to be
Of heavenly oaths, vow'd with integrity.

KING
O, you have liv'd in desolation here,
Unseen, unvisited, much to our shame.

PRINCESS
Not so, my lord; it is not so, I swear.
We have had pastimes here and pleasant game:
A mess of Russians left us but of late.

KING
How, madam? Russians?

PRINCESS
Ay, in truth, my lord.
Trim gallants, full of courtship and of state.

ROSALINE
Madam, speak true.—It is not so, my lord.
My lady, to the manner of the days,
In courtesy gives undeserving praise.
We four indeed confronted were with four
In Russian habit. Here they stay'd an hour,
And talk'd apace; and in that hour, my lord,
They did not bless us with one happy word.
I dare not call them fools; but this I think,
When they are thirsty, fools would fain have drink.

299 Avaunt, perplexity i.e., away, riddler **302 as . . . disguis'd** in their familiar appearances just as previously in their disguises **304 shapeless gear** unshapely apparel **310 Whip** move quickly **316 pease** peas **319 wakes and wassails** revels **320 by gross** wholesale **322 pins . . . sleeve** i.e., flaunts his acquaintance with ladies as one might wear a love-token (?) **324 carve** i.e., woo with courtesy and affability **326 form** manners. **nice** fastidious **329 mean** middle voice. **meanly** moderately well. **ushering** serving in the role of gentleman-usher **330 Mend . . . can** i.e., let anyone who can improve on him try to do so

338 it i.e., Boyet. **Behavior** i.e., elegant manners **339 madman** madcap **341 all hail** (The Princess deliberately misconstrues the King to have referred to a hail storm, foul weather.) **346 so hold** so uphold **349 virtue** power. (But the Princess, in the next line, insists on interpreting the word as "moral goodness," the opposite of "vice.") **350 nickname** misname, mention in error **356 breaking cause** i.e., cause of breaking **362 mess** foursome **366 to** in **371 happy** felicitous

BEROWNE
This jest is dry to me. Gentle sweet,
Your wits makes wise things foolish. When we greet,
With eyes best seeing, heaven's fiery eye,
By light we lose light. Your capacity
Is of that nature that to your huge store
Wise things seem foolish and rich things but poor.

ROSALINE
This proves you wise and rich, for in my eye—

BEROWNE
I am a fool, and full of poverty.

ROSALINE
But that you take what doth to you belong,
It were a fault to snatch words from my tongue.

BEROWNE
O, I am yours, and all that I possess!

ROSALINE
All the fool mine?

BEROWNE
I cannot give you less.

ROSALINE
Which of the vizards was it that you wore?

BEROWNE
Where? When? What vizard? Why demand you this?

ROSALINE
There, then, that vizard; that superfluous case
That hid the worse and showed the better face.

KING [*To his Lords*]
We were descried; they'll mock us now downright.

DUMAINE [*To King*]
Let us confess and turn it to a jest.

PRINCESS
Amaz'd, my lord? Why looks your Highness sad?

ROSALINE
Help, hold his brows! He'll swoon! Why look you pale?
Sea-sick, I think, coming from Muscovy.

BEROWNE
Thus pour the stars down plagues for perjury.
Can any face of brass hold longer out?
Here stand I, lady, dart thy skill at me.
Bruise me with scorn, confound me with a flout,
Thrust thy sharp wit quite through my ignorance,
Cut me to pieces with thy keen conceit;
And I will wish thee never more to dance,
Nor never more in Russian habit wait.
O, never will I trust to speeches penn'd,
Nor to the motion of a schoolboy's tongue,
Nor never come in vizard to my friend,
Nor woo in rhyme, like a blind harper's song!
Taffeta phrases, silken terms precise,
Three-pil'd hyperboles, spruce affectation,
Figures pedantical—these summer-flies
Have blown me full of maggot ostentation.
I do forswear them; and I here protest
By this white glove—how white the hand, God knows!—
Henceforth my wooing mind shall be express'd
In russet yeas and honest kersey noes.
And, to begin, wench—so God help me, law!—
My love to thee is sound, sans crack or flaw.

ROSALINE
Sans "sans," I pray you.

BEROWNE
Yet I have a trick
Of the old rage. Bear with me, I am sick;
I'll leave it by degrees. Soft, let us see:
Write, "Lord have mercy on us" on those three.
They are infected, in their hearts it lies;
They have the plague, and caught it of your eyes.
These lords are visited; you are not free,
For the Lord's tokens on you do I see.

PRINCESS
No, they are free that gave these tokens to us.

BEROWNE
Our states are forfeit. Seek not to undo us.

ROSALINE
It is not so; for how can this be true,
That you stand forfeit, being those that sue?

BEROWNE
Peace! For I will not have to do with you.

ROSALINE
Nor shall not, if I do as I intend.

BEROWNE
Speak for yourselves. My wit is at an end.

KING
Teach us, sweet madam, for our rude transgression
Some fair excuse.

PRINCESS
The fairest is confession.
Were not you here but even now disguis'd?

KING
Madam, I was.

PRINCESS
And were you well advis'd?

KING
I was, fair madam.

PRINCESS
When you then were here,
What did you whisper in your lady's ear?

KING
That more than all the world I did respect her.

PRINCESS
When she shall challenge this, you will reject her.

KING
Upon mine honor, no.

PRINCESS
Peace, peace! Forbear.
Your oath once broke, you force not to forswear.

374 dry tart (playing on *thirsty* in l. 372) **375 foolish** i.e., seem foolish by comparison. **greet** regard, look at **377 By . . . light** i.e., the sun's powerful light overwhelms even our keenest vision **378 to** compared to **382–383 But . . . tongue** i.e., you took the words right out of my mouth **387 demand** inquire **388 case** covering, mask **396 face of brass** brazen manner **398 confound** destroy **401 wish** entreat **402 wait** be in attendance **405 friend** sweetheart **408 Three-pil'd** deep-piled, as in costly velvet **409 Figures** figures of speech

410 blown filled with maggot eggs, made foul **414 russet** simple homespun. **kersey** plain woolen cloth **415 law** la **416 sans** without. (But, as Rosaline points out in the next line, he is still using French expressions.) **417 Yet** still. **trick** trace **418 rage** fever **420 Lord . . . us** (Sign posted on houses containing the infectious plague within.) **those three** i.e., his companions **423 visited** infested by the plague **424 tokens** i.e., their love-tokens which they wear (punning still on the metaphor of plague, which leaves visible signs of infection) **425 free** (1) free of infection (2) generous with gifts **426 states** estates. **undo** absolve us from forfeiture (of ourselves) by declaring us *free* (l. 424) **428 being . . . sue** being the plaintiffs, not the defendants. (I.e., how can you bring legal action against yourselves?) **434 but even now** a short while ago **435 well advis'd** in your right mind **441 force not** have no hesitation

KING
Despise me when I break this oath of mine.
PRINCESS
I will, and therefore keep it. Rosaline,
What did the Russian whisper in your ear?
ROSALINE
Madam, he swore that he did hold me dear
As precious eyesight, and did value me
Above this world, adding thereto moreover
That he would wed me, or else die my lover.
PRINCESS
God give thee joy of him! The noble lord
Most honorably doth uphold his word.
KING
What mean you, madam? By my life, my troth,
I never swore this lady such an oath.
ROSALINE
By heaven, you did, and to confirm it plain,
You gave me this; but take it, sir, again.
[*She returns the favor.*]
KING
My faith and this the Princess I did give.
I knew her by this jewel on her sleeve.
PRINCESS
Pardon me, sir, this jewel did she wear;
And Lord Berowne, I thank him, is my dear.
What, will you have me, or your pearl again?
[*Offers favor.*]
BEROWNE
Neither of either; I remit both twain.
I see the trick on 't: here was a consent,
Knowing aforehand of our merriment,
To dash it like a Christmas comedy.
Some carry-tale, some please-man, some slight zany,
Some mumble-news, some trencher-knight, some Dick,
That smiles his cheek in years and knows the trick
To make my lady laugh when she's dispos'd,
Told our intents before; which once disclos'd,
The ladies did change favors, and then we,
Following the signs, woo'd but the sign of she.
Now, to our perjury to add more terror,
We are again forsworn, in will and error.
Much upon this 'tis. [*To Boyet.*] And might not you
Forestall our sport, to make us thus untrue?
Do not you know my lady's foot by th' squier,
And laugh upon the apple of her eye?
And stand between her back, sir, and the fire,
Holding a trencher, jesting merrily?
You put our page out. Go, you are allow'd;
Die when you will, a smock shall be your shroud.
You leer upon me, do you? There's an eye
Wounds like a leaden sword.
BOYET
Full merrily
Hath this brave manage, this career, been run.
BEROWNE
Lo, he is tilting straight! Peace, I have done.

Enter [*Costard the*] *Clown.*

Welcome, pure wit! Thou part'st a fair fray.
COSTARD
O Lord, sir, they would know
Whether the three Worthies shall come in or no.
BEROWNE
What, are there but three?
COSTARD
No, sir; but it is vara fine,
For every one pursents three.
BEROWNE
And three times thrice is nine.
COSTARD
Not so, sir, under correction, sir; I hope it is not so.
You cannot beg us, sir, I can assure you, sir; we know what we know.
I hope, sir, three times thrice, sir—
BEROWNE Is not nine.
COSTARD Under correction, sir, we know whereuntil it doth amount.
BEROWNE By Jove, I always took three threes for nine.
COSTARD O Lord, sir, it were pity you should get your living by reck'ning, sir.
BEROWNE How much is it?
COSTARD O Lord, sir, the parties themselves, the actors, sir, will show whereuntil it doth amount. For mine own part, I am, as they say, but to parfect one man in one poor man, Pompion the Great, sir.
BEROWNE Art thou one of the Worthies?
COSTARD It pleas'd them to think me worthy of Pompion the Great. For mine own part, I know not the degree of the Worthy, but I am to stand for him.
BEROWNE Go, bid them prepare.
COSTARD
We will turn it finely off, sir; we will take some care. *Exit.*
KING
Berowne, they will shame us. Let them not approach.
BEROWNE
We are shame-proof, my lord; and 'tis some policy
To have one show worse than the King's and his company.
KING
I say they shall not come.
PRINCESS
Nay, my good lord, let me o'errule you now.
That sport best pleases that doth least know how,
Where zeal strives to content, and the contents
Dies in the zeal of that which it presents.
Their form confounded makes most form in mirth,

461 consent agreement, plot **464 please-man** sycophant. **zany** stooge, clown **465 trencher-knight** i.e., parasite, one who feeds at his master's trencher or wooden dish. **Dick** (As in "Tom, Dick, and Harry.") **466 smiles . . . years** i.e., smiles flatteringly so hard that he wrinkles his face **470 sign of she** the outward appearance of one's sweetheart **473 Much . . . 'tis** i.e., it must have happened much this way **475 squier** square, rule. (I.e., know how to suit her fancy.) **476 apple** pupil. (I.e., know how to keep her eye amused.) **478 trencher** wooden dish (with which to offer her refreshment) **479 allow'd** treated like an allowed fool **480 smock** woman's undergarment (since Boyet is constantly in women's company)

482 leaden sword a mock weapon (no more threatening than Boyet's gaze) **483 brave manage** fine maneuver on horseback. **career** running, gallop **484 tilting straight** sparring with words immediately **488 vara** very **490 under** subject to **491 beg us** prove us fools **502 parfect** (He means *perform, present.*) **503 Pompion** pumpkin. (Malapropism for *Pompey.*) **511 policy** stratagem **516–517 and the . . . presents** and the (feeble) substance of what they perform is overwhelmed by the zeal of the presentation **518 Their . . . mirth** i.e., the artistic chaos of their performance has its own reward in mirth

When great things laboring perish in their birth.

BEROWNE
A right description of our sport, my lord.

Enter [Armado the] Braggart.

ARMADO Anointed, I implore so much expense of thy royal sweet breath as will utter a brace of words.

[Converses apart with the King, and delivers him a paper.]

PRINCESS Doth this man serve God?

BEROWNE Why ask you?

PRINCESS
'A speaks not like a man of God his making.

ARMADO That is all one, my fair, sweet, honey monarch; for, I protest, the schoolmaster is exceeding fantastical, too too vain, too too vain; but we will put it, as they say, to fortuna de la guerra. I wish you the peace of mind, most royal couplement! *Exit.*

KING Here is like to be a good presence of Worthies. He presents Hector of Troy; the swain, Pompey the Great; the parish curate, Alexander; Armado's page, Hercules; the pedant, Judas Maccabaeus;
And if these four Worthies in their first show thrive,
These four will change habits, and present the other five.

BEROWNE
There is five in the first show.

KING
You are deceived, 'tis not so.

BEROWNE
The pedant, the braggart, the hedge-priest, the fool, and the boy.
Abate throw at novum, and the whole world again
Cannot pick out five such, take each one in his vein.

KING
The ship is under sail, and here she comes amain.

Enter [Costard, for] Pompey.

COSTARD
"I Pompey am"—

BOYET
You lie, you are not he.

COSTARD
"I Pompey am"—

BOYET
With libbard's head on knee.

BEROWNE
Well said, old mocker. I must needs be friends with thee.

COSTARD
"I Pompey am, Pompey surnam'd the Big"—

DUMAINE "The Great."

COSTARD
It is "Great," sir. "Pompey surnam'd the Great,
That oft in field, with targe and shield, did make my foe to sweat.
And traveling along this coast, I here am come by chance,
And lay my arms before the legs of this sweet lass of France." *[Lays down his weapons.]*
If your ladyship would say, "Thanks, Pompey," I had done.

PRINCESS Great thanks, great Pompey.

COSTARD 'Tis not so much worth; but I hope I was perfect. I made a little fault in "Great."

BEROWNE My hat to a halfpenny, Pompey proves the best Worthy.

Enter [Nathaniel the] Curate, for Alexander.

NATHANIEL
"When in the world I liv'd, I was the world's commander;
By east, west, north, and south, I spread my conquering might.
My scutcheon plain declares that I am Alisander,"—

BOYET
Your nose says, no, you are not; for it stands too right.

BEROWNE
Your nose smells "no" in this, most tender-smelling knight.

PRINCESS
The conqueror is dismay'd. Proceed, good Alexander.

NATHANIEL
"When in the world I liv'd, I was the world's commander"—

BOYET
Most true, 'tis right; you were so, Alisander.

BEROWNE Pompey the Great—

COSTARD Your servant, and Costard.

BEROWNE Take away the conqueror, take away Alisander.

COSTARD *[To Nathaniel]* O, sir, you have overthrown Alisander the conqueror! You will be scrap'd out of the painted cloth for this. Your lion, that holds his poleax sitting on a close-stool, will be given to Ajax; he will be the ninth Worthy. A conqueror, and afeard to speak! Run away for shame, Alisander. *[Nathaniel retires.]* There, an 't shall please you, a foolish mild man, an honest man, look you, and soon dash'd. He is a marvelous good neighbor, faith, and a very good bowler. But, for Alisander—alas, you see how 'tis—a little o'erparted. But there are Worthies a-coming will speak their mind in some other sort.

PRINCESS Stand aside, good Pompey.

Enter [Holofernes the] Pedant, for Judas, and [Moth] the Boy, for Hercules.

520 right apt. **our sport** i.e., our appearance as Muscovites **525 God his** God's **529 fortuna . . . guerra** the fortune of war **530 couplement** couple **531 presence** assembly **539 hedge-priest** illiterate, rural priest **540 Abate** barring, setting aside. **throw at novum** a lucky throw of the dice in a game of *novum* or nines, having five and nine as its principal throws (joking on the business of offering nine characters with just five actors) **541 take . . . vein** i.e., they are each fantastical types **544 libbard's** leopard's (referring to his coat of arms, customarily on the shield rather than on the knee) **549 targe** shield

555–556 perfect accurate in memorizing **562 right** straight. (Alexander was supposed to have had a wry neck that twisted his head to one side.) **563 Your . . . this** (Berowne may be jibing again at Boyet's fastidiousness, as in ll. 464–482. Alexander was reputed to have a bodily odor of "marvellous good savor" according to North's translation of Plutarch.) **572–573 You will . . . this** (An allusion to the frequent representation of the Nine Worthies painted on an arras or tapestry.) **573–574 Your lion . . . close-stool** (A Renaissance memorial emblem of Alexander described a lion sitting in a chair, holding a battle-ax. A *close-stool* is a seat in a privy.) **574 Ajax** legendary Greek chieftain at the Trojan war who coveted the slain Achilles' armor (with a pun on *jakes,* privy) **581 o'erparted** having a part too difficult

HOLOFERNES
"Great Hercules is presented by this imp,
Whose club kill'd Cerberus, that three-headed canus;
And when he was a babe, a child, a shrimp,
Thus did he strangle serpents in his manus.
Quoniam he seemeth in minority,
Ergo I come with this apology."
Keep some state in thy exit, and vanish. *Exit Boy.*
"Judas I am"—
DUMAINE A Judas!
HOLOFERNES Not Iscariot, sir.
"Judas I am, ycliped Maccabaeus."
DUMAINE Judas Maccabaeus clipt is plain Judas.
BEROWNE A kissing traitor. How art thou prov'd Judas?
HOLOFERNES
"Judas I am"—
DUMAINE The more shame for you, Judas.
HOLOFERNES What mean you, sir?
BOYET To make Judas hang himself.
HOLOFERNES Begin, sir; you are my elder.
BEROWNE Well follow'd. Judas was hang'd on an elder.
HOLOFERNES I will not be put out of countenance.
BEROWNE Because thou hast no face.
HOLOFERNES What is this? [*Pointing to his face.*]
BOYET A cittern-head.
DUMAINE The head of a bodkin.
BEROWNE A death's face in a ring.
LONGAVILLE The face of an old Roman coin, scarce seen.
BOYET The pommel of Caesar's falchion.
DUMAINE The carv'd-bone face on a flask.
BEROWNE Saint George's half-cheek in a brooch.
DUMAINE Ay, and in a brooch of lead.
BEROWNE Ay, and worn in the cap of a tooth-drawer. And now forward; for we have put thee in countenance.
HOLOFERNES You have put me out of countenance.
BEROWNE False. We have given thee faces.
HOLOFERNES But you have out-fac'd them all.
BEROWNE
An thou wert a lion, we would do so.
BOYET
Therefore, as he is an ass, let him go.
And so adieu, sweet Jude! Nay, why dost thou stay?
DUMAINE
For the latter end of his name.
BEROWNE
For the ass to the Jude? Give it him. Jud-as, away!

585 Cerberus three-headed dog at the entrance to Hades, the capturing of which was one of Hercules' twelve labors. **canus** (More faulty Latin for *canis*, "dog.") **587 manus** hands **588 Quoniam** since **590 state** dignity **592 A Judas** i.e., a traitor. (The lords deliberately confuse the military hero Judas Maccabaeus with Judas Iscariot, who betrayed Christ.) **594 ycliped** called **595 clipt** shortened **596 kissing** (A reference to Judas' kiss of Jesus by which he betrayed his master; with a pun on *clipt,* embraced or kissed, in the preceding line.) **601 you . . . elder** i.e., you are my senior and so should take precedence. (But Berowne answers with a pun on *elder,* elder tree, traditionally the tree on which Judas hanged himself.) **606 cittern** cithern, guitar (the head of which was often grotesquely carved) **607 bodkin** a long, jeweled pin for a lady's hair, or a small dagger (similarly carved) **608 A death's . . . ring** i.e., a death's-head ring worn as a *memento mori* **609–610 scarce seen** worn almost smooth **611 falchion** curved sword. (The *pommel* or rounded knob on the hilt would be carved.) **612 flask** i.e., horn powder flask **613 half-cheek** profile **614 of lead** i.e., of inferior quality **615 tooth-drawer** (Tooth-extractors were not highly regarded; a brooch worn by such people in the cap might be of an inferior sort.) **616–617 we . . . countenance** i.e., we've drawn your portrait **620 out-fac'd** i.e., mocked them, put them down

HOLOFERNES
This is not generous, not gentle, not humble.
BOYET
A light for Monsieur Judas! It grows dark, he may stumble. [*Holofernes retires.*]
PRINCESS
Alas, poor Maccabaeus, how hath he been baited!

Enter [*Armado the*] *Braggart* [*for Hector*].

BEROWNE Hide thy head, Achilles! Here comes Hector in arms.
DUMAINE Though my mocks come home by me, I will now be merry.
KING Hector was but a Troyan in respect of this.
BOYET But is this Hector?
KING I think Hector was not so clean-timber'd.
LONGAVILLE His leg is too big for Hector's.
DUMAINE More calf, certain.
BOYET No; he is best indu'd in the small.
BEROWNE This cannot be Hector.
DUMAINE He's a god or a painter, for he makes faces.
ARMADO
"The armipotent Mars, of lances the almighty,
Gave Hector a gift"—
DUMAINE A gilt nutmeg.
BEROWNE A lemon.
LONGAVILLE Stuck with cloves.
DUMAINE No, cloven.
ARMADO
Peace!—
"The armipotent Mars, of lances the almighty,
Gave Hector a gift, the heir of Ilion;
A man so breathed, that certain he would fight, yea
From morn till night, out of his pavilion.
I am that flower"—
DUMAINE That mint.
LONGAVILLE That columbine.
ARMADO Sweet Lord Longaville, rein thy tongue.
LONGAVILLE I must rather give it the rein, for it runs against Hector.
DUMAINE Ay, and Hector's a greyhound.
ARMADO The sweet war-man is dead and rotten, sweet chucks, beat not the bones of the buried. When he breathed, he was a man. But I will forward with my device. [*To the Princess.*] Sweet royalty, bestow on me the sense of hearing.
Berowne steps forth [*to whisper to Costard, and then resumes his place*].
PRINCESS
Speak, brave Hector; we are much delighted.
ARMADO I do adore thy sweet Grace's slipper.
BOYET Loves her by the foot.
DUMAINE He may not by the yard.

631 by me to me, to my discomfiture **633 Troyan** (1) Trojan (2) a jolly companion, a roisterer. **in respect of** in comparison with **635 clean-timber'd** clean-limbed, well built **637 calf** (1) lower part of leg (2) dolt **638 best . . . small** well endowed in the part of the leg below the calf **641 armipotent** powerful in arms **643 gilt** glazed with egg yolk, saffron, etc. **649 Ilion** Troy **650 so breathed** i.e., in good condition, valiant **651 pavilion** tent or camp to which the combatant retired when not engaged in fight **667 yard** penis

ARMADO
"This Hector far surmounted Hannibal"—

COSTARD The party is gone. Fellow Hector, she is gone; she is two months on her way.

ARMADO What meanest thou?

COSTARD Faith, unless you play the honest Troyan, the poor wench is cast away. She's quick; the child brags in her belly already. 'Tis yours.

ARMADO Dost thou infamonize me among potentates? Thou shalt die.

COSTARD Then shall Hector be whipp'd for Jaquenetta that is quick by him and hang'd for Pompey that is dead by him.

DUMAINE Most rare Pompey!

BOYET Renowned Pompey!

BEROWNE Greater than great, great, great, great Pompey! Pompey the Huge!

DUMAINE Hector trembles.

BEROWNE Pompey is mov'd. More Ates, more Ates! Stir them on, stir them on!

DUMAINE Hector will challenge him.

BEROWNE Ay, if 'a have no more man's blood in his belly than will sup a flea.

ARMADO By the north pole, I do challenge thee.

COSTARD I will not fight with a pole, like a northren man. I'll slash; I'll do it by the sword. I bepray you, let me borrow my arms again.

DUMAINE Room for the incens'd Worthies!

COSTARD I'll do it in my shirt.

DUMAINE Most resolute Pompey!

MOTH Master, let me take you a button-hole lower. Do you not see Pompey is uncasing for the combat? What mean you? You will lose your reputation.

ARMADO Gentlemen and soldiers, pardon me, I will not combat in my shirt.

DUMAINE You may not deny it. Pompey hath made the challenge.

ARMADO Sweet bloods, I both may and will.

BEROWNE What reason have you for 't?

ARMADO The naked truth of it is, I have no shirt. I go woolward for penance.

BOYET True, and it was enjoin'd him in Rome for want of linen; since when, I'll be sworn, he wore none but a dishclout of Jaquenetta's, and that 'a wears next his heart for a favor.

Enter a Messenger, Monsieur Marcade.

MARCADE
God save you, madam!

PRINCESS
Welcome, Marcade,
But that thou interruptest our merriment.

MARCADE
I am sorry, madam, for the news I bring
Is heavy in my tongue. The King your father—

PRINCESS
Dead, for my life!

MARCADE
Even so. My tale is told.

BEROWNE
Worthies, away! The scene begins to cloud.

ARMADO For mine own part, I breathe free breath. I have seen the day of wrong through the little hole of discretion, and I will right myself like a soldier.

Exeunt Worthies.

KING
How fares your Majesty?

PRINCESS
Boyet, prepare. I will away tonight.

KING
Madam, not so. I do beseech you, stay.

PRINCESS
Prepare, I say. I thank you, gracious lords,
For all your fair endeavors, and entreat,
Out of a new-sad soul, that you vouchsafe
In your rich wisdom to excuse or hide
The liberal opposition of our spirits,
If overboldly we have borne ourselves
In the converse of breath; your gentleness
Was guilty of it. Farewell, worthy lord!
A heavy heart bears not a humble tongue.
Excuse me so, coming too short of thanks
For my great suit so easily obtain'd.

KING
The extreme parts of time extremely forms
All causes to the purpose of his speed,
And often, at his very loose, decides
That which long process could not arbitrate.
And though the mourning brow of progeny
Forbid the smiling courtesy of love
The holy suit which fain it would convince,
Yet, since love's argument was first on foot,
Let not the cloud of sorrow justle it
From what it purpos'd; since to wail friends lost
Is not by much so wholesome-profitable
As to rejoice at friends but newly found.

PRINCESS
I understand you not. My griefs are double.

BEROWNE
Honest plain words best pierce the ear of grief;
And by these badges understand the King.
For your fair sakes have we neglected time,
Play'd foul play with our oaths. Your beauty, ladies,
Hath much deform'd us, fashioning our humors
Even to the opposed end of our intents;
And what in us hath seem'd ridiculous—
As love is full of unbefitting strains,
All wanton as a child, skipping and vain,

669 The party i.e., Jaquenetta. (Costard may have received this news from Berowne when Berowne whispers to him.) **673 quick** pregnant **675 infamonize** slander **685 Ates** i.e., incitements to mischief. (Ate was the goddess of discord.) **691–692 northren man** a boorish ruffian from the north **697 take . . . lower** (1) help remove your doublet (2) "take you down a peg," humiliate you **706–707 go woolward for penance** i.e., with woolen clothing next to the skin and no linen underwear. (Armado's lame excuse is that he does so to punish the flesh.) **708–709 want of linen** lack of linen. (Boyet sees through the excuse.)

719–721 I have . . . discretion i.e., I now perceive my true situation, my wrong **728 hide** overlook **729 liberal opposition** too-free antagonism **731 converse of breath** conversation. **gentleness** courtesy **732 guilty of** responsible for **733 humble** i.e., suited to polite civilities **734 so** therefore **735 suit** i.e., the mission on which she came (which the King evidently has granted) **736–737 The . . . speed** i.e., a few last moments demand quick decisions **738 his** i.e., time's. **loose** release, discharge. (An archery term.) **740 progeny** i.e., the child of the dead king, the Princess **742 The . . . convince** the love-suit it would like to present **748 double** i.e., because of my father's death, and because I don't understand you **750 badges** i.e., my honest plain words **754 opposed** opposite **756 strains** impulses

Form'd by the eye and therefore, like the eye,
Full of straying shapes, of habits, and of forms,
Varying in subjects as the eye doth roll
To every varied object in his glance;
Which parti-coated presence of loose love
Put on by us, if, in your heavenly eyes,
Have misbecom'd our oaths and gravities,
Those heavenly eyes, that look into these faults,
Suggested us to make. Therefore, ladies,
Our love being yours, the error that love makes
Is likewise yours. We to ourselves prove false,
By being once false forever to be true
To those that make us both—fair ladies, you.
And even that falsehood, in itself a sin,
Thus purifies itself and turns to grace.

PRINCESS
We have receiv'd your letters full of love;
Your favors, the ambassadors of love;
And, in our maiden council, rated them
At courtship, pleasant jest, and courtesy,
As bombast and as lining to the time.
But more devout than this in our respects
Have we not been, and therefore met your loves
In their own fashion, like a merriment.

DUMAINE
Our letters, madam, show'd much more than jest.

LONGAVILLE
So did our looks.

ROSALINE We did not quote them so.

KING
Now, at the latest minute of the hour,
Grant us your loves.

PRINCESS A time, methinks, too short
To make a world-without-end bargain in.
No, no, my lord, your Grace is perjur'd much,
Full of dear guiltiness; and therefore this:
If for my love, as there is no such cause,
You will do aught, this shall you do for me:
Your oath I will not trust, but go with speed
To some forlorn and naked hermitage,
Remote from all the pleasures of the world;
There stay until the twelve celestial signs
Have brought about the annual reckoning.
If this austere insociable life
Change not your offer made in heat of blood;
If frosts and fasts, hard lodging, and thin weeds
Nip not the gaudy blossoms of your love,
But that it bear this trial, and last love;
Then, at the expiration of the year,
Come challenge me, challenge me by these deserts,
And, by this virgin palm now kissing thine,
[*Giving him her hand.*]
I will be thine; and till that instant shut
My woeful self up in a mourning house,
Raining the tears of lamentation
For the remembrance of my father's death.
If this thou do deny, let our hands part,
Neither intitled in the other's heart.

KING
If this, or more than this, I would deny,
To flatter up these powers of mine with rest,
The sudden hand of death close up mine eye!
Hence hermit then—my heart is in thy breast.

[BEROWNE
And what to me, my love? And what to me?

ROSALINE
You must be purged too, your sins are rack'd,
You are attaint with faults and perjury.
Therefore if you my favor mean to get,
A twelvemonth shall you spend, and never rest,
But seek the weary beds of people sick.]

DUMAINE
But what to me, my love? But what to me?
A wife?

KATHARINE A beard, fair health, and honesty;
With three-fold love I wish you all these three.

DUMAINE
O, shall I say "I thank you, gentle wife?"

KATHARINE
Not so, my lord; a twelvemonth and a day
I'll mark no words that smooth-fac'd wooers say.
Come when the King doth to my lady come;
Then, if I have much love, I'll give you some.

DUMAINE
I'll serve thee true and faithfully till then.

KATHARINE
Yet swear not, lest ye be forsworn again.

LONGAVILLE
What says Maria?

MARIA At the twelvemonth's end
I'll change my black gown for a faithful friend.

LONGAVILLE
I'll stay with patience, but the time is long.

MARIA
The liker you; few taller are so young.

BEROWNE
Studies my lady? Mistress, look on me;
Behold the window of my heart, mine eye,
What humble suit attends thy answer there.
Impose some service on me for thy love.

ROSALINE
Oft have I heard of you, my Lord Berowne,
Before I saw you; and the world's large tongue
Proclaims you for a man replete with mocks,
Full of comparisons and wounding flouts,
Which you on all estates will execute
That lie within the mercy of your wit.
To weed this wormwood from your fruitful brain,
And therewithal to win me, if you please,
Without the which I am not to be won,

762 parti-coated presence jesting or foolish appearance. **loose** unrestrained **764 misbecom'd** been unbecoming to **766 Suggested us to make** tempted us to commit all these follies of love **775 rated** evaluated **776 At** as merely **777 bombast** a loosely made fabric used for padding or stuffing garments **778 devout** serious. **respects** considerations **782 quote** interpret **787 dear** grievous **793 twelve celestial signs** signs of the zodiac (encompassing one year) **797 weeds** garments **799 last** remain, continue as **801 challenge** claim. **deserts** meritorious actions

810 flatter up pamper **813–818** (Evidently a first draft of ll. 833–850.) **814 rack'd** extended, stretched out **831 stay** wait **840 comparisons** i.e., witty, sarcastic similes **841 all estates** all classes of people

You shall this twelvemonth term from day to day
Visit the speechless sick and still converse
With groaning wretches; and your task shall be,
With all the fierce endeavor of your wit
To enforce the pained impotent to smile.

BEROWNE
To move wild laughter in the throat of death?
It cannot be; it is impossible.
Mirth cannot move a soul in agony.

ROSALINE
Why, that's the way to choke a gibing spirit,
Whose influence is begot of that loose grace
Which shallow laughing hearers give to fools.
A jest's prosperity lies in the ear
Of him that hears it, never in the tongue
Of him that makes it. Then, if sickly ears,
Deaf'd with the clamors of their own dear groans,
Will hear your idle scorns, continue then,
And I will have you and that fault withal;
But if they will not, throw away that spirit,
And I shall find you empty of that fault,
Right joyful of your reformation.

BEROWNE
A twelvemonth! Well, befall what will befall,
I'll jest a twelvemonth in an hospital.

PRINCESS [*To the King*]
Ay, sweet my lord, and so I take my leave.

KING
No, madam, we will bring you on your way.

BEROWNE
Our wooing doth not end like an old play;
Jack hath not Jill. These ladies' courtesy
Might well have made our sport a comedy.

KING
Come, sir, it wants a twelvemonth and a day,
And then 'twill end.

BEROWNE That's too long for a play.

Enter [*Armado the*] *Braggart.*

ARMADO Sweet Majesty, vouchsafe me—

PRINCESS Was not that Hector?

DUMAINE The worthy knight of Troy.

ARMADO I will kiss thy royal finger, and take leave. I am a votary; I have vow'd to Jaquenetta to hold the plough for her sweet love three year. But, most esteemed greatness, will you hear the dialogue that the two learned men have compiled in praise of the owl and the cuckoo? It should have followed in the end of our show.

KING Call them forth quickly; we will do so.

ARMADO Holla! Approach.

Enter all [*Holofernes, Nathaniel, Moth, Costard, and others*].

This side is Hiems, Winter, this Ver, the Spring; the one maintained by the owl, th' other by the cuckoo. Ver, begin.

The Song

[Spring.]

When daisies pied and violets blue
  And lady-smocks all silver-white
And cuckoo-buds of yellow hue
  Do paint the meadows with delight,
The cuckoo then, on every tree,
Mocks married men; for thus sings he,
        Cuckoo;
Cuckoo, cuckoo! O word of fear,
Unpleasing to a married ear!

When shepherds pipe on oaten straws
  And merry larks are ploughmen's clocks,
When turtles tread, and rooks, and daws,
  And maidens bleach their summer
    smocks,
The cuckoo then, on every tree,
Mocks married men; for thus sings he,
        Cuckoo;
Cuckoo, cuckoo! O word of fear,
Unpleasing to a married ear!

Winter.

When icicles hang by the wall
  And Dick the shepherd blows his nail
And Tom bears logs into the hall
  And milk comes frozen home in pail,
When blood is nipp'd and ways be foul,
Then nightly sings the staring owl,
        Tu-whit,
Tu-who! A merry note,
While greasy Joan doth keel the pot.

When all aloud the wind doth blow
  And coughing drowns the parson's saw
And birds sit brooding in the snow
  And Marian's nose looks red and raw,
When roasted crabs hiss in the bowl,
Then nightly sings the staring owl,
        Tu-whit,
Tu-who! A merry note,
While greasy Joan doth keel the pot.

[ARMADO] The words of Mercury are harsh after the songs of Apollo. [You that way; we this way.
Exeunt.]

847 still converse constantly associate **855 loose grace** carelessly given approval. (Rosaline is saying that Berowne's mocking manner has been nurtured by the fact that others have laughed shallowly and too easily at his foolish raillery.) **860 dear** grievous **862 withal** in addition **879–880 hold the plough** i.e., labor at farming **881 dialogue** debate

890 pied particolored **891 lady-smocks** cuckoo flowers **892 cuckoo-buds of yellow** buttercups (?) **898 Unpleasing** i.e., because the cuckoo suggests cuckoldry **900 clocks** (i.e., because ploughmen "rise with the lark") **901 turtles tread** turtledoves mate **909 nail** fingernails **916 keel** skim and stir **918 saw** maxim, moral observation **921 crabs** crab apples **926 Mercury** messenger of the gods and associated with eloquence or sophistry in antithesis to Apollo as the god of music **927 You . . . this way** (Armado may be directing those who have presented Winter to exit in one direction and those having presented Spring in another; and he may also be referring to the audience.)

The Two Gentlemen of Verona

If by "romantic comedy" we mean a love story in which the lovers overcome parental obstacles, jealousies, separations, and dangers to be united at last in married bliss, then *The Two Gentlemen of Verona* is perhaps Shakespeare's first. Although *The Comedy of Errors* may be an earlier play, it is a farce of mistaken identity with only a secondary interest in marriage, whereas *Love's Labor's Lost* is a courtly confection ending in the postponement of all marriages. No mention of *The Two Gentlemen of Verona* occurs until Francis Meres' list of 1598, but the play is often dated around 1590–1594 on the basis of style: rhymed couplets, end-stopped verse, passages of excessive wit-combat, and the like. *The Taming of the Shrew* (c. 1592–1594) is often dated a little later than *The Two Gentlemen,* although admittedly the two plays are much alike and perhaps ought to share the credit and the blame for Shakespeare's first experimentation with romantic comedy. In any event, this was to be the genre of Shakespeare's best-known "festive" comedies from *A Midsummer Night's Dream* to *Twelfth Night.*

The Two Gentlemen of Verona, then, is Shakespeare's apprenticeship to the romantic fiction of Italy and other southern European countries, whence he later derived so many plots of threatened love. He locates his story in Italy and gives his characters Italian names. He uses the conventional plot devices of romantic fiction: inconstancy in love and in friendship, the disguise of the heroine as a page, the overhearing of false vows, banishment, elopement, capture by outlaws, and so on. Virtually all the characters have a recognizable ancestry, not only in continental fiction but in neoclassical drama as well: Lucetta is the usual female confidante, Thurio is the rich but unwelcome rival wooer (the pantaloon), Antonio and the Duke are typically strong-willed fathers opposing the romantic marriages of their children, Speed and Launce are at least supposed to be the clever servants who deliver messages and arrange rendezvous, and the four young lovers are the romantic protagonists.

Even in this early apprenticeship, to be sure, Shakespeare departs from the neoclassical norm of his continental sources. The setting remains nominally Italian, but the tone is often heartily English and Shakespeare's attitude toward his romantic models borders occasionally on the irreverent. Lucetta is a true friend of Julia and a virtuous counselor in love; the jest about her being a "broker" or a go-between reminds us how unlike a bawdy duenna she really is. Thurio, Antonio, and the Duke are all portrayed with such amiable forbearance that they often seem inadequately motivated as the opponents of romantic happiness. Most of all, Speed and Launce have cast loose from their traditional roles as comic manipulators to become vaudeville jokesters.

Moreover, the very conventions of love and friendship are presented in such a way as to cast those conventions in an improbable light. What are we to make of the inconstant Proteus, who rejects his faithful Julia the moment he is away from her, tries instead to win the lady-fair of his dearest friend Valentine, informs the Duke of Valentine's plan to elope with Silvia, and then attempts a violent assault on Silvia's chastity? What sort of romantic hero is this, and why should he be rewarded by being forgiven and restored to his Julia? Most puzzling of all, is it credible that Valentine should respond to all this perfidy by offering to relinquish Silvia to Proteus? By the same token, isn't it absurd that the outlaws in the forest near Mantua should turn out to be gentlemen in exile, and that they should offer command of their group to Valentine, whom they have just captured? Isn't the Duke's forgiveness of his eloped daughter Silvia rather sudden and unconvincing? These problems, which have troubled many readers of the play (though they generally seem less formidable to spectators of an actual production), can perhaps best be analyzed in two ways: as a result of Shakespeare's having combined two sources with conflicting conventions, thereby subjecting those conventions to a playful perspective, and as a result of Shakespeare's conscious interest in the theme of unexpected forgiveness for his erring protagonist.

Using a device of plotting that was to become customary in his romantic comedies, Shakespeare combines two fictional sources and thereby sets up a dramatic tension between the two. His chief source appears to have been *Diana,* a popular pastoral romance in Spanish by the Portuguese Jorge de Montemayor (1520–1561). Its heroine, Felismena (corresponding to Julia), is wooed by Don Felix (Proteus), whose father (Antonio) disapproves of the match and sends Don Felix away to court. Felismena, following after him disguised as a page, stops at an inn and is invited by the host to listen to some music, whereupon she overhears Don Felix protesting his love to a new lady, Celia (Silvia). At this point the resemblance between *Diana* and Shakespeare's play breaks off. Even thus far, despite several striking resemblances, the story provides no counterpart for Valentine, Proteus' best friend and the faithful lover of Silvia. Montemayor's romance is solely concerned with inconstancy in love.

For the motif of true friendship, Shakespeare may have turned to the story of Titus and Gisippus, as told by Thomas Elyot in *The Governour* (1531). Here Gisippus, upon learning that his dear friend Titus has fallen in love with Gisippus' lady-love, not only relinquishes the lady to Titus but actually smuggles him into bed with her, all unbeknownst to the lady. The point of this story, as of other well-known treatises on friendship such as John Lyly's *Euphues* (1578) and *Endymion* (1588), or Richard Edwards' *Damon and Pythias* (1565), is that friendship is a higher form of human affection than erotic love since it is disinterested, Platonically pure, and capable of teaching selflessness to others. Such a tale of perfect friendship provides, however, no counterpart for Julia, the lady abandoned by Proteus. Shakespeare has neatly dovetailed the two stories, making a quartet of lovers out of two triangular situations. The false lover of the first story becomes also the false friend of the second—only to be overwhelmed at the end by the generosity of his true friend.

The dramatic problem created by combining these two stories is that they arouse different expectations. The one is dedicated to the virtue of constancy in love, the other to friendship. Valentine's ultimate function is to demonstrate the triumph of selfless friendship over love, and yet his function in the plot of love-rivalry is to demonstrate true loyalty to his Silvia. His relinquishing of her to Proteus seems inconsistent with his vows as a lover. Conversely, Proteus' double perfidy, toward his lover Julia and his friend Valentine, seems to render him unworthy of the generous action Valentine bestows on him. Proteus' very name is synonymous with inconstancy; his namesake in *The Odyssey* was infamous for his ability to change shapes at will. (Valentine's name, on the other hand, betokens constancy in love.) The coupling of the two plots simultaneously intensifies Proteus' guilt and Valentine's magnanimity.

Yet Shakespeare makes a virtue out of the seeming lack of credibility. First, the very implausibility of Valentine's selflessness in love and of Proteus' sudden conversion to virtue allows Shakespeare to mock gently the Petrarchan commonplaces of his sources. At the same time, Shakespeare finds serious value in his conventional topics of love and friendship, through the device of paradox. The more unlikely Valentine's actions seem, the more transcendent and wondrous they are bound to appear. Shakespeare prepares for his climactic scene of forgiveness in several ways. First, he presents Proteus as an essentially noble person who has fallen through a single fault. Proteus is well-born, accomplished, handsome. The worthy Julia loves him for his good qualities, and he responds with sincerity and passion. He is equally ardent as a friend to Valentine. Only when he sees Silvia does Proteus become helpless, "metamorphosed." He cannot completely be blamed for being overwhelmed by passion, for the other lovers are no less obedient to love's command. According to the Petrarchism that infuses this play, love cannot choose its object. Proteus' unhappy fate is to love Silvia. His self-hatred increases as he turns flatterer, liar, betrayer, and finally would-be rapist. Like Angelo in *Measure for Measure,* Proteus is compulsively driven to abhorrent sin. The psychological insight of that later dark comedy is lacking—the soliloquies do not create the suffocating atmosphere of a nightmare—but the pattern of a guilty fall is still manifest.

This pattern may in turn clarify Valentine's role as the selfless friend. He should not be taken too seriously as such; Shakespeare makes no attempt to conceal the absurd aspect of Valentine's self-righteous renunciation of the woman who has been unswervingly loyal to him, and who has no wish to be traded from one lover to another as though she were the object of some kind of moralistic barter. Nonetheless, the very implausibility of Valentine's offer to relinquish Silvia accentuates the noble intent behind the gesture. We are surprised, even comically surprised, because we don't expect such selflessness in human nature; but if friendship is to be seen as a supreme achievement of the human spirit, it must transcend man's all-too-common penchant for rivalry and ingratitude. Valentine's generosity is not achieved without inner struggle. In the climactic scene of attempted rape, his first natural reaction is angry denunciation. What changes his mind is the depth and earnestness of Proteus' confession and desire for forgiveness: "If hearty sorrow Be a sufficient ransom for offense, I tender 't here." Valentine responds in the name of mercy and at the prompting of divine example: "By penitence th' Eternal's wrath's appeas'd." The more undeserved the pardon, the more selfless the act of him who pardons. Only by conquering his desire for Silvia can Valentine teach his friend selflessness and thus reunite all four lovers in perfect joy. *The Two Gentlemen* is thus in part a comedy of forgiveness, anticipating later plays in which the romantic protagonist is equally culpable and yet equally forgiven: *Much Ado about Nothing, Measure for Measure, All's Well that Ends Well, Cymbeline,* and others (see R. G. Hunter's *Shakespeare and the Comedy of Forgiveness).*

Forgiveness of Proteus must proceed no less from Julia than from Valentine. She too has much to pardon; as Proteus contritely observes, "O heaven, were man But constant, he were perfect!" Julia initiates a line of Shakespearean heroines, including Hero, Isabella, Helena, and Imogen in the plays already named, who must similarly cure inconstancy by their constancy. Like many Shakespearean heroines Julia is plucky, resourceful, modest yet witty, patiently obedient in love and yet coyly flirtatious, a true friend of her confidante, and long-suffering. Disguised as a page, she overhears her lover's infidelity and yet never loses her faith in him. She patiently delivers Proteus' messages to her rival (like Viola in *Twelfth Night*) and gently acts as conscience to her erring master.

The repeated device of overhearing, as in later comedies, provides a test for the protagonists' intentions. Thinking themselves unobserved, they reveal their true natures for better or for worse. In the ingeniously devised if improbable climactic scene (V,iv), Proteus as would-be ravisher is overheard by both his rejected mistress and his betrayed friend. Conversely, Silvia proves loyal and chaste whenever she is silently observed by Julia (disguised as Sebastian) or by Valentine in the forest scenes. These overhearings suggest not only that men's good and evil deeds are witnessed, but that a beneficent providence will protect the virtuous. Valentine's unseen presence assures that Silvia will be saved from rape, and that Proteus will be prevented from committing an actual crime of violence. As in later comedies of this sort, forgiveness is possible because the guilt remains one of intent only.

These slightly absurd but happy resolutions of conflict take place in a forest near Mantua, the first of what Northrop Frye calls Shakespeare's "green worlds." Although sketchily presented, this forest does anticipate the forest of Arden and other sylvan restorative landscapes. Its inhabitants are banished men protesting the injustice of society at court, or fugitives from unkind love. Valentine learns to prefer "unfrequented woods" to "flourishing peopled towns." His "wild faction" of outlaws desist from attacking "silly women or poor passengers," and appropriately swear "By the bare scalp of Robin Hood's fat friar" (IV,i). They are charmingly suited to their role of threatening and then reuniting the lovers, providentially capturing Silvia just as she is on her way to find Valentine. Their actions are highly improbable, and poke fun at the very conventions they illustrate, but then the same can be said of Valentine's forgiveness of Proteus and the Duke's sudden reconciliation with his prospective son-in-law Valentine. Like Arden, this forest is a strange place in which such changes of heart are expected to occur. The aura of improbability may also explain the play's carelessness about social distinctions and the realities of geography: the Duke is sometimes called the Emperor, and at one point Valentine sets sail from Verona to Milan (both located inland).

The buffoonish comedy of Launce and Speed performs a function similar to that of romantic improbability by undercutting the Petrarchan seriousness of the love story. How can we worry long over Valentine's banishment when Launce bursts out, "Sir, there is a proclamation that you are vanish'd"? Or how can we fret about Proteus' courtship of Silvia when the love-token he sends her turns out to be Launce's odoriferous dog? This sort of absurd anticlimax occurs at every turn. Launce's first soliloquy, about the dog's refusal to mourn their departure from Verona (II,iii), is a brilliant example of what we would call vaudeville or "stand-up" comic joking, but it also comments on the immediately preceding scene of Proteus' tearful farewell to Julia. Launce's friendship for Speed, and especially his friendship for the dog, delightfully blaspheme the play's serious interest in true friendship. In Launce's funniest scene (IV,iv), he describes how he has selflessly taken on himself the punishment meted out to the dog for urinating on Silvia's farthingale. Similarly, the spectacle of Launce in love, cataloguing his mistress's virtues and vices, insures us against too deep an involvement in the hazards of Cupid. The play continually reminds us of the folly of love without denying its exquisite joys or its highest potential for selflessness.

The Two Gentlemen of Verona

The Names of All the Actors.

DUKE [OF MILAN], *father to Silvia.*
VALENTINE, PROTEUS, } *the two Gentlemen.*
ANTONIO, *father to Proteus.*
THURIO, *a foolish rival to Valentine.*
EGLAMOUR, *agent for Silvia in her escape.*
HOST, *where Julia lodges.*
OUTLAWS, *with Valentine.*
SPEED, *a clownish servant to Valentine.*
LAUNCE, *the like to Proteus.*
PANTHINO, *servant to Antonio.*

JULIA, *beloved of Proteus.*
SILVIA, *beloved of Valentine.*
LUCETTA, *waiting-woman to Julia.*

[SERVANTS, MUSICIANS.

SCENE: *Verona; Milan; the frontiers of Mantua.*]

ACT I • SCENE I

[*Enter*] *Valentine* [*and*] *Proteus.*

VALENTINE
Cease to persuade, my loving Proteus;
Home-keeping youth have ever homely wits.
Were 't not affection chains thy tender days
To the sweet glances of thy honor'd love,
I rather would entreat thy company
To see the wonders of the world abroad
Than, living dully sluggardiz'd at home,
Wear out thy youth with shapeless idleness.
But since thou lov'st, love still and thrive therein,
Even as I would when I to love begin.

PROTEUS
Wilt thou be gone? Sweet Valentine, adieu!
Think on thy Proteus, when thou hap'ly seest
Some rare noteworthy object in thy travel.
Wish me partaker in thy happiness
When thou dost meet good hap; and in thy danger,
If ever danger do environ thee,
Commend thy grievance to my holy prayers,
For I will be thy beadsman, Valentine.

VALENTINE
And on a love-book pray for my success?

PROTEUS
Upon some book I love I'll pray for thee.

VALENTINE
That's on some shallow story of deep love,
How young Leander cross'd the Hellespont.

PROTEUS
That's a deep story of a deeper love,
For he was more than over shoes in love.

VALENTINE
'Tis true; for you are over boots in love,
And yet you never swum the Hellespont.

PROTEUS
Over the boots? Nay, give me not the boots.

VALENTINE
No, I will not, for it boots thee not.

PROTEUS
What?

VALENTINE
To be in love, where scorn is bought with groans,
Coy looks with heart-sore sighs, one fading
moment's mirth
With twenty watchful, weary, tedious nights.
If hap'ly won, perhaps a hapless gain;
If lost, why then a grievous labor won;
However, but a folly bought with wit,
Or else a wit by folly vanquished.

PROTEUS
So, by your circumstance, you call me fool.

VALENTINE
So, by your circumstance, I fear you'll prove.

PROTEUS
'Tis love you cavil at; I am not Love.

VALENTINE
Love is your master, for he masters you;
And he that is so yoked by a fool,
Methinks should not be chronicled for wise.

PROTEUS
Yet writers say, as in the sweetest bud
The eating canker dwells, so eating love
Inhabits in the finest wits of all.

VALENTINE
And writers say, as the most forward bud
Is eaten by the canker ere it blow,
Even so by love the young and tender wit
Is turn'd to folly, blasting in the bud,
Losing his verdure even in the prime,
And all the fair effects of future hopes.
But wherefore waste I time to counsel thee
That art a votary to fond desire?
Once more adieu! My father at the road

I.i. Location: Verona. A street.
2 homely dull, simple **3 affection** passion, love **8 shapeless** aimless **9 still** always, constantly **12 hap'ly** by chance **15 hap** fortune

17 Commend thy grievance commit your distress **18 beadsman** one engaged to pray for others **22 Leander** famous lover of Greek legend who drowned as he swam the Hellespont to see his love Hero **27 give . . . boots** i.e., don't make fun of me, don't be so flippant **28 boots** profits, avails **32 watchful** wakeful **33 hapless** unlucky **35 However** either way. **but** nothing but **37 circumstance** detailed discourse **38 circumstance** situation, condition **44 canker** cankerworm **46 forward** early **47 blow** bloom **49 blasting** withering **50 his** its. **prime** spring **53 fond** foolish **54 road** roadstead, harbor

Expects my coming, there to see me shipp'd.

PROTEUS
And thither will I bring thee, Valentine.

VALENTINE
Sweet Proteus, no; now let us take our leave.
To Milan let me hear from thee by letters
Of thy success in love, and what news else
Betideth here in absence of thy friend;
And I likewise will visit thee with mine.

PROTEUS
All happiness bechance to thee in Milan!

VALENTINE
As much to you at home! And so, farewell. *Exit.*

PROTEUS
He after honor hunts, I after love.
He leaves his friends to dignify them more;
I leave myself, my friends, and all, for love.
Thou, Julia, thou hast metamorphis'd me,
Made me neglect my studies, lose my time,
War with good counsel, set the world at nought;
Made wit with musing weak, heart sick with
thought.

[*Enter*] *Speed.*

SPEED
Sir Proteus, save you! Saw you my master?

PROTEUS
But now he parted hence, to embark for Milan.

SPEED
Twenty to one then he is shipp'd already,
And I have play'd the sheep in losing him.

PROTEUS
Indeed, a sheep doth very often stray,
An if the shepherd be a while away.

SPEED You conclude that my master is a shepherd then and I a sheep?

PROTEUS I do.

SPEED Why then, my horns are his horns, whether I wake or sleep.

PROTEUS A silly answer and fitting well a sheep.

SPEED This proves me still a sheep.

PROTEUS True; and thy master a shepherd.

SPEED Nay, that I can deny by a circumstance.

PROTEUS It shall go hard but I'll prove it by another.

SPEED The shepherd seeks the sheep, and not the sheep the shepherd; but I seek my master, and my master seeks not me. Therefore I am no sheep.

PROTEUS The sheep for fodder follow the shepherd; the shepherd for food follows not the sheep. Thou for wages followest thy master; thy master for wages follows not thee. Therefore thou art a sheep.

SPEED Such another proof will make me cry "baa."

PROTEUS But, dost thou hear? Gav'st thou my letter to Julia?

SPEED Ay, sir. I, a lost mutton, gave your letter to her, a lac'd mutton, and she, a lac'd mutton, gave me, a lost mutton, nothing for my labor.

PROTEUS Here's too small a pasture for such store of muttons.

SPEED If the ground be overcharg'd, you were best stick her.

PROTEUS Nay, in that you are astray; 'twere best pound you.

SPEED Nay, sir, less than a pound shall serve me for carrying your letter.

PROTEUS You mistake; I mean the pound—a pinfold.

SPEED
From a pound to a pin? Fold it over and over,
'Tis threefold too little for carrying a letter to your
lover.

PROTEUS But what said she?

SPEED [*First nodding*] Ay.

PROTEUS Nod—Ay—why, that's "noddy."

SPEED You mistook, sir. I say, she did nod, and you ask me if she did nod, and I say, "Ay."

PROTEUS And that set together is "noddy."

SPEED Now you have taken the pains to set it together, take it for your pains.

PROTEUS No, no, you shall have it for bearing the letter.

SPEED Well, I perceive I must be fain to bear with you.

PROTEUS Why, sir, how do you bear with me?

SPEED Marry, sir, the letter, very orderly; having nothing but the word "noddy" for my pains.

PROTEUS Beshrew me, but you have a quick wit.

SPEED And yet it cannot overtake your slow purse.

PROTEUS Come, come, open the matter in brief. What said she?

SPEED Open your purse, that the money and the matter may be both at once deliver'd.

PROTEUS [*Giving him money*] Well, sir, here is for your pains. What said she?

SPEED Truly, sir, I think you'll hardly win her.

PROTEUS Why, couldst thou perceive so much from her?

SPEED Sir, I could perceive nothing at all from her, no, not so much as a ducat for delivering your letter. And being so hard to me that brought your mind, I fear she'll prove as hard to you in telling your mind. Give her no token but stones, for she's as hard as steel.

PROTEUS What said she? Nothing?

SPEED No, not so much as "Take this for thy pains." To testify your bounty, I thank you, you have testern'd me; in requital whereof, henceforth carry your letters yourself. And so, sir, I'll commend you to my master.

PROTEUS
Go, go, be gone, to save your ship from wrack,

59 success outcome **65 dignify** i.e., honor (by increasing his own fame) **66 leave** neglect **69 War . . . counsel** reject good advice **72 parted** departed **73, 74 shipp'd, sheep** (Elizabethan pronunciation doubtless made the pun obvious.) **76 An if** if **80 my horns . . . horns** i.e., presumably my master is a cuckold. (Traditionally, husbands whose wives deceived them were supposed to grow horns.) **85 circumstance** process of reasoning **94 baa** (with a pun on *bah,* humbug)

97, 98 lost, lac'd (As with *shipp'd, sheep,* above, the Elizabethan pronunciation of the two words was similar.) **98 lac'd mutton** i.e., whore **102 overcharg'd** overcrowded **103 stick** stab (with bawdy suggestion) **104 astray** (1) wandering like a lost sheep (2) going too far **105 pound** (1) impound, shut up in an animal pen (2) beat **106 pound** (1) 20 shillings (2) a beating **108 pinfold** a pen for stray animals **109 pin** i.e., an object worth very little **113 noddy** a simpleton **120 fain** content. **bear with** (1) put up with (2) carry for **124 Beshrew** curse **126 open** disclose **132 hardly** with difficulty **134 perceive** receive (punning on *perceive,* "understand," in the previous line) **135 ducat** (Here, a silver coin worth about 3 shillings 6 pence.) **136 mind** desires, intentions **137 in telling** when you tell her **138 stones** jewels **141-142 testern'd me** given me a testern, a sixpence

Which cannot perish having thee aboard, 145
Being destin'd to a drier death on shore. [*Exit Speed.*] 146
I must go send some better messenger.
I fear my Julia would not deign my lines,
Receiving them from such a worthless post. *Exit.* 149

SCENE II

Enter Julia and Lucetta.

JULIA
But say, Lucetta, now we are alone,
Wouldst thou then counsel me to fall in love?
LUCETTA
Ay, madam, so you stumble not unheedfully.
JULIA
Of all the fair resort of gentlemen 4
That every day with parle encounter me, 5
In thy opinion which is worthiest love?
LUCETTA
Please you repeat their names, I'll show my mind
According to my shallow simple skill.
JULIA
What think'st thou of the fair Sir Eglamour? 9
LUCETTA
As of a knight well-spoken, neat, and fine;
But, were I you, he never should be mine.
JULIA
What think'st thou of the rich Mercatio?
LUCETTA
Well of his wealth, but of himself, so so.
JULIA
What think'st thou of the gentle Proteus?
LUCETTA
Lord, Lord! To see what folly reigns in us!
JULIA
How now? What means this passion at his name? 16
LUCETTA
Pardon, dear madam, 'tis a passing shame 17
That I, unworthy body as I am,
Should censure thus on lovely gentlemen. 19
JULIA
Why not on Proteus, as of all the rest?
LUCETTA
Then thus: of many good I think him best.
JULIA
Your reason?
LUCETTA
I have no other but a woman's reason;
I think him so because I think him so.
JULIA
And wouldst thou have me cast my love on him?
LUCETTA
Ay, if you thought your love not cast away.
JULIA
Why he, of all the rest, hath never mov'd me. 27
LUCETTA
Yet he, of all the rest, I think best loves ye.
JULIA
His little speaking shows his love but small.
LUCETTA
Fire that's closest kept burns most of all.
JULIA
They do not love that do not show their love.
LUCETTA
O, they love least that let men know their love.
JULIA
I would I knew his mind.
LUCETTA
Peruse this paper, madam. [*Gives letter.*]
JULIA
"To Julia." Say, from whom?
LUCETTA
That the contents will show.
JULIA
Say, say, who gave it thee?
LUCETTA
Sir Valentine's page; and sent, I think, from Proteus.
He would have given it you, but I, being in the way, 39
Did in your name receive it. Pardon the fault, I pray.
JULIA
Now, by my modesty, a goodly broker! 41
Dare you presume to harbor wanton lines?
To whisper and conspire against my youth?
Now, trust me, 'tis an office of great worth,
And you an officer fit for the place.
There, take the paper. See it be return'd,
Or else return no more into my sight.
[*Gives the letter back.*]
LUCETTA
To plead for love deserves more fee than hate.
JULIA
Will ye be gone?
LUCETTA
That you may ruminate. *Exit.*
JULIA
And yet I would I had o'erlook'd the letter. 50
It were a shame to call her back again
And pray her to a fault for which I chid her. 52
What 'fool is she, that knows I am a maid,
And would not force the letter to my view!
Since maids, in modesty, say "no" to that
Which they would have the profferer construe "ay."
Fie, fie, how wayward is this foolish love
That, like a testy babe, will scratch the nurse
And presently, all humbled, kiss the rod! 59
How churlishly I chid Lucetta hence,

145-146 Which . . . shore (An allusion to the proverb, "He that is born to be hanged shall never be drowned.") **149 post** (1) messenger (2) blockhead

I.ii. Location: Verona. The garden of Julia's house.
4 resort assemblage, group **5 parle** talk **9 Eglamour** (Not to be identified with Silvia's friend of the same name.) **16 passion** passionate outburst **17 passing** surpassing **19 censure** pass judgment

27 mov'd urged (with a suit of love) **39 being . . . way** i.e., happening to encounter him **41 broker** intermediary **50 o'erlook'd** read **52 to a fault** to commit a fault **59 presently** immediately afterward. **rod** spanking rod

When willingly I would have had her here!
How angerly I taught my brow to frown,
When inward joy enforc'd my heart to smile!
My penance is to call Lucetta back
And ask remission for my folly past.
What ho! Lucetta!

[*Enter Lucetta.*]

LUCETTA
What would your ladyship?

JULIA
Is 't near dinner-time?

LUCETTA
I would it were,
That you might kill your stomach on your meat 68
And not upon your maid.
[*She drops the letter, and stoops to pick it up.*]

JULIA
What is 't that you took up so gingerly?

LUCETTA
Nothing.

JULIA
Why didst thou stoop, then?

LUCETTA
To take a paper up that I let fall.

JULIA
And is that paper nothing?

LUCETTA
Nothing concerning me.

JULIA
Then let it lie for those that it concerns.

LUCETTA
Madam, it will not lie where it concerns, 77
Unless it have a false interpreter.

JULIA
Some love of yours hath writ to you in rhyme.

LUCETTA
That I might sing it, madam, to a tune.
Give me a note; your ladyship can set. 81

JULIA
As little by such toys as may be possible. 82
Best sing it to the tune of "Light o' love." 83

LUCETTA
It is too heavy for so light a tune. 84

JULIA
Heavy! Belike it hath some burden then? 85

LUCETTA
Ay, and melodious were it, would you sing it.

JULIA
And why not you?

LUCETTA
I cannot reach so high. 87

JULIA
Let's see your song. [*Takes the letter.*] How now, minion? 88

LUCETTA
Keep tune there still, so you will sing it out. 89
And yet methinks I do not like this tune.

JULIA
You do not?

LUCETTA
No, madam, 'tis too sharp. 92

JULIA
You, minion, are too saucy.

LUCETTA
Nay, now you are too flat, 94
And mar the concord with too harsh a descant. 95
There wanteth but a mean to fill your song. 96

JULIA
The mean is drown'd with your unruly bass. 97

LUCETTA
Indeed, I bid the base for Proteus. 98

JULIA
This babble shall not henceforth trouble me.
Here is a coil with protestation! 100
[*Tears the letter and drops the pieces.*]
Go get you gone, and let the papers lie;
You would be fing'ring them, to anger me.

LUCETTA
She makes it strange; but she would be best pleas'd 103
To be so ang'red with another letter. [*Exit.*]

JULIA
Nay, would I were so ang'red with the same! 105
[*She picks up some fragments.*]
O hateful hands, to tear such loving words!
Injurious wasps, to feed on such sweet honey
And kill the bees that yield it with your stings!
I'll kiss each several paper for amends. 109
Look, here is writ "kind Julia." Unkind Julia! 110
As in revenge of thy ingratitude,
I throw thy name against the bruising stones,
Trampling contemptuously on thy disdain.
[*Throws down a fragment.*]
And here is writ "love-wounded Proteus."
Poor wounded name! My bosom as a bed
Shall lodge thee till thy wound be throughly heal'd;
And thus I search it with a sovereign kiss. 117
But twice or thrice was "Proteus" written down.
Be calm, good wind, blow not a word away
Till I have found each letter in the letter,
Except mine own name; that some whirlwind bear
Unto a ragged fearful-hanging rock
And throw it thence into the raging sea!
Lo, here in one line is his name twice writ,
"Poor forlorn Proteus, passionate Proteus,
To the sweet Julia." That I'll tear away;
And yet I will not, sith so prettily 127

68 kill your stomach (1) satisfy your appetite (2) appease your anger. **meat** (Pronounced *mate*, with a pun on *maid* in the next line.) **77 lie where it concerns** tell falsehoods in matters of importance (punning on the meaning *be left for those whose business it is* in the preceding line) **81 note** (with a punning reference to Proteus' letter). **set** (1) set to music (2) write a letter. (But Julia takes the word in the sense of setting store by something, regarding it of value.) **82 toys** trifles **83 "Light o' love"** (A familiar tune of the time.) **84 heavy** serious **85 burden** (1) bass accompaniment to a melody (2) heavy load **87 reach so high** (1) sing so high (2) aspire to a person of Proteus' rank **88 minion** hussy (with a pun on *minim*, half-note)

89 tune (1) pitch (2) temper, mood **92 sharp** (1) high in pitch (2) saucy, bitter. (Perhaps Julia pinches Lucetta here.) **94 flat** (1) low in pitch (2) blunt. (Perhaps Julia slaps Lucetta here.) **95 descant** improvised harmony accompanying a melody **96 wanteth but** is lacking only. **mean** (1) middle or tenor voice, i.e., Proteus (2) opportunity **97 unruly bass** (with pun on *base behavior*) **98 bid the base for** i.e., act in behalf of (referring to the game of "prisoner's base," and with a pun on *base*, "bass, low") **100 coil with protestation** commotion or fuss about protestations of love (i.e., about Proteus' letter) **103 makes it strange** pretends indifference **105 Nay . . . same** i.e., indeed, I wish I had this same letter intact to pretend to be angry about **109 several paper** separate piece of paper **110 Unkind** unnatural, cruel **117 search** probe, cleanse (as one would a wound). **sovereign** healing **127 sith** since

He couples it to his complaining names.
Thus will I fold them one upon another.
Now kiss, embrace, contend, do what you will.
[*Puts some folded papers in her bosom.*]

[*Enter Lucetta.*]

LUCETTA
Madam,
Dinner is ready, and your father stays.

JULIA
Well, let us go.

LUCETTA
What, shall these papers lie like telltales here?

JULIA
If you respect them, best to take them up.

LUCETTA
Nay, I was taken up for laying them down;
Yet here they shall not lie, for catching cold.
[*Gathers up the remaining fragments.*]

JULIA
I see you have a month's mind to them.

LUCETTA
Ay, madam, you may say what sights you see;
I see things too, although you judge I wink.

JULIA
Come, come, will 't please you go? *Exeunt.*

SCENE III

Enter Antonio and Panthino.

ANTONIO
Tell me, Panthino, what sad talk was that
Wherewith my brother held you in the cloister?

PANTHINO
'Twas of his nephew Proteus, your son.

ANTONIO
Why, what of him?

PANTHINO
He wond'red that your lordship
Would suffer him to spend his youth at home,
While other men, of slender reputation,
Put forth their sons to seek preferment out:
Some to the wars, to try their fortune there,
Some to discover islands far away,
Some to the studious universities.
For any or for all these exercises
He said that Proteus your son was meet,
And did request me to importune you
To let him spend his time no more at home,
Which would be great impeachment to his age,
In having known no travel in his youth.

ANTONIO
Nor need'st thou much importune me to that
Whereon this month I have been hammering.
I have consider'd well his loss of time
And how he cannot be a perfect man,
Not being tried and tutor'd in the world.
Experience is by industry achiev'd
And perfected by the swift course of time.
Then tell me, whither were I best to send him?

PANTHINO
I think your lordship is not ignorant
How his companion, youthful Valentine,
Attends the Emperor in his royal court.

ANTONIO
I know it well.

PANTHINO
'Twere good, I think, your lordship sent him thither.
There shall he practice tilts and tournaments,
Hear sweet discourse, converse with noblemen,
And be in eye of every exercise
Worthy his youth and nobleness of birth.

ANTONIO
I like thy counsel; well hast thou advis'd;
And that thou mayst perceive how well I like it,
The execution of it shall make known.
Even with the speediest expedition
I will dispatch him to the Emperor's court.

PANTHINO
Tomorrow, may it please you, Don Alphonso
With other gentlemen of good esteem
Are journeying to salute the Emperor
And to commend their service to his will.

ANTONIO
Good company. With them shall Proteus go.—

[*Enter*] *Proteus,* [*with a letter.*]

And, in good time! Now will we break with him.

PROTEUS
Sweet love, sweet lines, sweet life!
Here is her hand, the agent of her heart;
Here is her oath for love, her honor's pawn.
O, that our fathers would applaud our loves,
To seal our happiness with their consents!
O heavenly Julia!

ANTONIO
How now? What letter are you reading there?

PROTEUS
May 't please your lordship, 'tis a word or two
Of commendations sent from Valentine,
Deliver'd by a friend that came from him.
[*Attempts to conceal the letter.*]

ANTONIO
Lend me the letter; let me see what news.

PROTEUS
There is no news, my lord, but that he writes
How happily he lives, how well belov'd
And daily graced by the Emperor,

132 stays waits **135 respect** prize, esteem **136 taken up** scolded **137 for** for fear of **138 month's mind** inclination, liking **140 wink** close the eyes

I.iii. Location: Verona. Antonio's house.
1 sad serious **6 slender reputation** i.e., of lower station than yourself **7 Put . . . out** send their sons away from home to seek advancement **12 meet** fitted **15 impeachment to his age** detriment or cause for reproach to him in his mature years

18 hammering beating (an idea) into shape **20 perfect** i.e., educated, mature **27 Emperor** i.e., the Duke of Milan. (An apparent inconsistency.) **30 practice** perform, take part in **31 discourse** conversation. **converse** associate **32 in eye of** in a position to see **37 expedition** swiftness **44 in good time** i.e., just at the right time (here he comes). **break with** reveal, disclose the plan to **49 seal** ratify **58 graced** favored

Wishing me with him, partner of his fortune.

ANTONIO
And how stand you affected to his wish? 60

PROTEUS
As one relying on your lordship's will,
And not depending on his friendly wish.

ANTONIO
My will is something sorted with his wish. 63
Muse not that I thus suddenly proceed; 64
For what I will, I will, and there an end.
I am resolv'd that thou shalt spend some time
With Valentinus in the Emperor's court.
What maintenance he from his friends receives, 68
Like exhibition thou shalt have from me. 69
Tomorrow be in readiness to go.
Excuse it not, for I am peremptory. 71

PROTEUS
My lord, I cannot be so soon provided. 72
Please you, deliberate a day or two.

ANTONIO
Look what thou want'st shall be sent after thee. 74
No more of stay; tomorrow thou must go.
Come on, Panthino; you shall be employ'd
To hasten on his expedition.
[Exeunt Antonio and Panthino.]

PROTEUS
Thus have I shunn'd the fire for fear of burning,
And drench'd me in the sea, where I am drown'd.
I fear'd to show my father Julia's letter,
Lest he should take exceptions to my love;
And with the vantage of mine own excuse
Hath he excepted most against my love. 83
O, how this spring of love resembleth
The uncertain glory of an April day,
Which now shows all the beauty of the sun,
And by and by a cloud takes all away!

[Enter Panthino.]

PANTHINO
Sir Proteus, your father calls for you.
He is in haste; therefore, I pray you, go.

PROTEUS
Why, this it is: my heart accords thereto,
And yet a thousand times it answers "no." *Exeunt.*

ACT II • SCENE I

Enter Valentine [and] Speed.

SPEED
Sir, your glove. *[Offers glove.]*

VALENTINE Not mine; my gloves are on.

SPEED
Why, then, this may be yours, for this is but one. 2

VALENTINE
Ha! Let me see. Ay, give it me, it's mine.
Sweet ornament that decks a thing divine!
Ah, Silvia, Silvia!

SPEED *[Calling]* Madam Silvia! Madam Silvia!

VALENTINE How now, sirrah? 7

SPEED She is not within hearing, sir.

VALENTINE Why, sir, who bade you call her?

SPEED Your worship, sir, or else I mistook.

VALENTINE Well, you'll still be too forward.

SPEED And yet I was last chidden for being too slow.

VALENTINE Go to, sir. Tell me, do you know Madam 13
Silvia?

SPEED She that your worship loves?

VALENTINE Why, how know you that I am in love?

SPEED Marry, by these special marks: first, you have
learn'd, like Sir Proteus, to wreathe your arms, like a 18
malcontent; to relish a love-song, like a robin-red-
breast; to walk alone, like one that had the pestilence;
to sigh, like a schoolboy that had lost his A B C; to 21
weep, like a young wench that had buried her gran-
dam; to fast, like one that takes diet; to watch, like one 23
that fears robbing; to speak puling, like a beggar at Hal- 24
lowmas. You were wont, when you laugh'd, to crow 25
like a cock; when you walk'd, to walk like one of the
lions; when you fasted, it was presently after dinner; 27
when you look'd sadly, it was for want of money. And
now you are metamorphis'd with a mistress, that,
when I look on you, I can hardly think you my master.

VALENTINE Are all these things perceiv'd in me?

SPEED They are all perceiv'd without ye. 32

VALENTINE Without me? They cannot.

SPEED Without you? Nay, that's certain, for, without 34
you were so simple, none else would. But you are so 35
without these follies, that these follies are within you 36
and shine through you like the water in an urinal, that 37
not an eye that sees you but is a physician to comment
on your malady.

VALENTINE But tell me, dost thou know my lady Silvia?

SPEED She that you gaze on so as she sits at supper?

VALENTINE Hast thou observ'd that? Even she, I mean.

SPEED Why, sir, I know her not.

VALENTINE Dost thou know her by my gazing on her, and yet know'st her not?

SPEED Is she not hard-favor'd, sir? 46

VALENTINE Not so fair, boy, as well-favor'd. 47

SPEED Sir, I know that well enough.

VALENTINE What dost thou know?

SPEED That she is not so fair as, of you, well favor'd.

VALENTINE I mean that her beauty is exquisite, but her
favor infinite. 52

SPEED That 's because the one is painted and the other
out of all count. 54

VALENTINE How painted? And how out of count?

60 affected disposed, inclined **63 something sorted** rather in accordance **64 Muse** wonder **68 friends** i.e., relatives **69 exhibition** allowance of money **71 Excuse it not** offer no excuses. **peremptory** resolved **72 provided** equipped **74 Look what** whatever **83 excepted most against** most effectively hindered

II.i. Location: Milan. The Duke's palace.
2 one (Pronounced like *on*, thus providing a pun on the line above.)

7 sirrah fellow. (Form of address to inferiors.) **13 Go to** (An expression of remonstrance.) **18 wreathe** fold **21 ABC** primer **23 watch** lie awake, sit up at night **24 puling** whiningly **24–25 Hallowmas** All Saints' Day, November 1 (a day when beggars asked special alms) **27 presently** immediately **32 without ye** from your outside appearance **34 without** unless **35 would** i.e., would perceive them **35–36 you are . . . follies** i.e., you so surround and encompass these follies **37 urinal** glass container for medical examination of urine **46 hard-favor'd** ugly **47 fair** beautiful, blond-haired. **well-favor'd** gracious, charming; also, good-looking. (But Speed takes the word in the sense of *looked upon with approval*.) **52 favor** grace, charm **54 out of all count** incalculable

SPEED Marry, sir, so painted, to make her fair, that no man counts of her beauty.

VALENTINE How esteem'st thou me? I account of her beauty.

SPEED You never saw her since she was deform'd.

VALENTINE How long hath she been deform'd?

SPEED Ever since you lov'd her.

VALENTINE I have lov'd her ever since I saw her, and still I see her beautiful.

SPEED If you love her, you cannot see her.

VALENTINE Why?

SPEED Because Love is blind. O, that you had mine eyes, or your own eyes had the lights they were wont to have when you chid at Sir Proteus for going ungarter'd!

VALENTINE What should I see then?

SPEED Your own present folly and her passing deformity; for he, being in love, could not see to garter his hose, and you, being in love, cannot see to put on your hose.

VALENTINE Belike, boy, then, you are in love, for last morning you could not see to wipe my shoes.

SPEED True, sir, I was in love with my bed. I thank you, you swing'd me for my love, which makes me the bolder to chide you for yours.

VALENTINE In conclusion, I stand affected to her.

SPEED I would you were set, so your affection would cease.

VALENTINE Last night she enjoin'd me to write some lines to one she loves.

SPEED And have you?

VALENTINE I have.

SPEED Are they not lamely writ?

VALENTINE No, boy, but as well as I can do them. Peace, here she comes.

[Enter] Silvia.

SPEED *[Aside]* O excellent motion! O exceeding puppet! Now will he interpret to her.

VALENTINE Madam and mistress, a thousand good-morrows.

SPEED *[Aside]* O, give ye good ev'n! Here's a million of manners.

SILVIA Sir Valentine and servant, to you two thousand.

SPEED *[Aside]* He should give her interest, and she gives it him.

VALENTINE
As you enjoin'd me, I have writ your letter
Unto the secret nameless friend of yours,
Which I was much unwilling to proceed in
But for my duty to your ladyship. *[Gives letter.]*

SILVIA
I thank you, gentle servant. 'Tis very clerkly done.

VALENTINE
Now trust me, madam, it came hardly off,
For, being ignorant to whom it goes,
I writ at random, very doubtfully.

SILVIA
Perchance you think too much of so much pains?

VALENTINE
No, madam; so it stead you, I will write—
Please you command—a thousand times as much.
And yet—

SILVIA
A pretty period! Well, I guess the sequel;
And yet I will not name it—and yet I care not—
And yet take this again—and yet I thank you,
Meaning henceforth to trouble you no more.

SPEED *[Aside]*
And yet you will; and yet another "yet."

VALENTINE
What means your ladyship? Do you not like it?

SILVIA
Yes, yes. The lines are very quaintly writ,
But since unwillingly, take them again.
Nay, take them. *[Gives back the letter.]*

VALENTINE
Madam, they are for you.

SILVIA
Ay, ay, you writ them, sir, at my request,
But I will none of them. They are for you.
I would have had them writ more movingly.

VALENTINE
Please you, I'll write your ladyship another.

SILVIA
And when it's writ, for my sake read it over.
And if it please you, so; if not, why, so.

VALENTINE
If it please me, madam, what then?

SILVIA
Why, if it please you, take it for your labor.
And so, good morrow, servant. *Exit Silvia.*

SPEED
O jest unseen, inscrutable, invisible,
As a nose on a man's face, or a weathercock on a steeple!
My master sues to her, and she hath taught her suitor,
He being her pupil, to become her tutor.
O excellent device! Was there ever heard a better,
That my master, being scribe, to himself should write the letter?

VALENTINE How now, sir? What are you reasoning with yourself?

SPEED Nay, I was rhyming. 'Tis you that have the reason.

VALENTINE To do what?

SPEED To be a spokesman from Madam Silvia.

VALENTINE To whom?

SPEED To yourself. Why, she woos you by a figure.

VALENTINE What figure?

57 counts of her beauty esteems her beautiful **60 deform'd** i.e., transformed by the distorting perspective of Valentine's love for her **68 lights** sight **69–70 going ungarter'd** i.e., neglecting appearance in dress, a traditional sign of love melancholy **72 passing** very great **79 swing'd** thrashed **82 set** (1) seated, as distinguished from *stand* of the previous line (2) settled **91 motion** puppet show. **puppet** i.e., Silvia **92 interpret** i.e., supply dialogue or commentary as for a puppet show **95 give** i.e., God give. **million** i.e., an excessive amount **97 servant** i.e., a man devoted to serving a lady **103 duty** obedience, submission **104 clerkly** in a scholarly manner

105 hardly with difficulty **107 doubtfully** uncertainly **109 so** so long as. **stead** benefit **112 period** pause, stop **118 quaintly** ingeniously **137 reasoning** discussing **144 figure** device

SPEED By a letter, I should say.
VALENTINE Why, she hath not writ to me?
SPEED What need she, when she hath made you write to yourself? Why, do you not perceive the jest?
VALENTINE No, believe me.
SPEED No believing you, indeed, sir. But did you perceive her earnest? 152
VALENTINE She gave me none, except an angry word.
SPEED Why, she hath given you a letter.
VALENTINE That's the letter I writ to her friend.
SPEED And that letter hath she deliver'd, and there an end.
VALENTINE I would it were no worse.
SPEED I'll warrant you, 'tis as well.
For often have you writ to her, and she, in modesty,
Or else for want of idle time, could not again reply;
Or fearing else some messenger that might her mind discover,
Herself hath taught her love himself to write unto her lover.
All this I speak in print, for in print I found it. 164
Why muse you, sir? 'Tis dinnertime.
VALENTINE I have din'd. 166
SPEED Ay, but hearken, sir; though the chameleon Love 167
can feed on the air, I am one that am nourish'd by my
victuals and would fain have meat. O, be not like your 169
mistress; be mov'd, be mov'd. *Exeunt.*

SCENE II

Enter Proteus [and] Julia.

PROTEUS
Have patience, gentle Julia.
JULIA
I must, where is no remedy. 2
PROTEUS
When possibly I can, I will return.
JULIA
If you turn not, you will return the sooner. 4
Keep this remembrance for thy Julia's sake.
[Gives a ring.]
PROTEUS
Why, then, we'll make exchange; here, take you this. *[Gives her a favor.]*
JULIA
And seal the bargain with a holy kiss.
PROTEUS
Here is my hand for my true constancy;
And when that hour o'erslips me in the day
Wherein I sigh not, Julia, for thy sake,
The next ensuing hour some foul mischance
Torment me for my love's forgetfulness!
My father stays my coming; answer not. 13
The tide is now—nay, not thy tide of tears;
That tide will stay me longer than I should.
Julia, farewell! *[Exit Julia.]*
What, gone without a word?
Ay, so true love should do; it cannot speak,
For truth hath better deeds than words to grace it. 18
[Enter] Panthino.
PANTHINO
Sir Proteus, you are stay'd for.
PROTEUS
Go. I come, I come.
Alas! This parting strikes poor lovers dumb. *Exeunt.*

SCENE III

Enter Launce [leading a dog].

LAUNCE Nay, 'twill be this hour ere I have done weep-
ing. All the kind of the Launces have this very fault. I 2
have receiv'd my proportion, like the prodigious son, 3
and am going with Sir Proteus to the Imperial's court. 4
I think Crab my dog be the sourest-natur'd dog that
lives. My mother weeping, my father wailing, my sis-
ter crying, our maid howling, our cat wringing her
hands, and all our house in a great perplexity, yet did
not this cruel-hearted cur shed one tear. He is a stone,
a very pebblestone, and has no more pity in him than
a dog. A Jew would have wept to have seen our part-
ing. Why, my grandam, having no eyes, look you,
wept herself blind at my parting. Nay, I'll show you
the manner of it. This shoe is my father. No, this left 14
shoe is my father. No, no, this left shoe is my mother.
Nay, that cannot be so neither. Yes, it is so, it is so—
it hath the worser sole. This shoe, with the hole in it, 17
is my mother, and this my father. A vengeance on 't!
There 'tis. Now, sir, this staff is my sister, for, look
you, she is as white as a lily and as small as a wand.
This hat is Nan, our maid. I am the dog. No, the dog is
himself, and I am the dog—Oh!, the dog is me, and I
am myself. Ay, so, so. Now come I to my father: "Fa-
ther, your blessing." Now should not the shoe speak
a word for weeping. Now should I kiss my father;
well, he weeps on. Now come I to my mother. O, that
she could speak now like a wood woman! Well, I kiss 27
her; why, there 'tis; here's my mother's breath up and 28
down. Now come I to my sister; mark the moan she 29
makes. Now the dog all this while sheds not a tear nor
speaks a word; but see how I lay the dust with my
tears.

[Enter] Panthino.

PANTHINO Launce, away, away, aboard! Thy master is

152 earnest to be serious. (But Valentine takes the word as a noun meaning *money paid as an installment to secure a bargain.*) **164 speak in print** i.e., recite from memory, as though having read the speech somewhere (as a proof of how certain his information is) **166 din'd** i.e., feasted on the sight of Silvia **167 chameleon** an animal popularly thought to be able to live on air **169 fain** gladly

II.ii. Location: Verona. Julia's house.
2 where is where there is **4 turn** prove unfaithful

13 stays awaits **18 grace** adorn

II.iii. Location: Verona. A street.
2 kind kindred, race **3 proportion** (A malapropism for *portion, allotment.*) **prodigious** (A malapropism for *prodigal.*) **4 Imperial's** i.e., Emperor's **14 This shoe** (Launce demonstrates.) **17 sole** (with a pun on *soul*) **27 wood** mad, distraught (with punning allusion to a wooden shoe) **28–29 up and down** i.e., exactly

shipp'd and thou art to post after with oars. What's the matter? Why weep'st thou, man? Away, ass! You'll lose the tide if you tarry any longer.

LAUNCE It is no matter if the tied were lost, for it is the unkindest tied that ever any man tied.

PANTHINO What's the unkindest tide?

LAUNCE Why, he that's tied here, Crab, my dog.

PANTHINO Tut, man, I mean thou 'lt lose the flood, and, in losing the flood, lose thy voyage, and, in losing thy voyage, lose thy master, and, in losing thy master, lose thy service, and, in losing thy service—Why dost thou stop my mouth?

LAUNCE For fear thou shouldst lose thy tongue.

PANTHINO Where should I lose my tongue?

LAUNCE In thy tale.

PANTHINO In thy tail!

LAUNCE Lose the tide, and the voyage, and the master, and the service, and the tied! Why, man, if the river were dry, I am able to fill it with my tears; if the wind were down, I could drive the boat with my sighs.

PANTHINO Come, come away, man. I was sent to call thee.

LAUNCE Sir, call me what thou dar'st.

PANTHINO Wilt thou go?

LAUNCE Well, I will go. *Exeunt.*

SCENE IV

Enter Valentine, Silvia, Thurio, [and] Speed.

SILVIA Servant!

VALENTINE Mistress?

SPEED Master, Sir Thurio frowns on you.

VALENTINE Ay, boy, it's for love.

SPEED Not of you.

VALENTINE Of my mistress, then.

SPEED 'Twere good you knock'd him. *[Exit.]*

SILVIA Servant, you are sad.

VALENTINE Indeed, madam, I seem so.

THURIO Seem you that you are not?

VALENTINE Hap'ly I do.

THURIO So do counterfeits.

VALENTINE So do you.

THURIO What seem I that I am not?

VALENTINE Wise.

THURIO What instance of the contrary?

VALENTINE Your folly.

THURIO And how quote you my folly?

VALENTINE I quote it in your jerkin.

THURIO My jerkin is a doublet.

VALENTINE Well, then, I'll double your folly.

THURIO How?

SILVIA What, angry, Sir Thurio? Do you change color?

VALENTINE Give him leave, madam; he is a kind of chameleon.

THURIO That hath more mind to feed on your blood than live in your air.

VALENTINE You have said, sir.

THURIO Ay, sir, and done too, for this time.

VALENTINE I know it well, sir; you always end ere you begin.

SILVIA A fine volley of words, gentlemen, and quickly shot off.

VALENTINE 'Tis indeed, madam, we thank the giver.

SILVIA Who is that, servant?

VALENTINE Yourself, sweet lady, for you gave the fire. Sir Thurio borrows his wit from your ladyship's looks, and spends what he borrows kindly in your company.

THURIO Sir, if you spend word for word with me, I shall make your wit bankrupt.

VALENTINE I know it well, sir; you have an exchequer of words, and, I think, no other treasure to give your followers, for it appears, by their bare liveries, that they live by your bare words.

SILVIA No more, gentlemen, no more. Here comes my father.

[Enter] Duke.

DUKE
Now, daughter Silvia, you are hard beset.
Sir Valentine, your father is in good health.
What say you to a letter from your friends
Of much good news?

VALENTINE My lord, I will be thankful
To any happy messenger from thence.

DUKE
Know ye Don Antonio, your countryman?

VALENTINE
Ay, my good lord, I know the gentleman
To be of worth and worthy estimation
And not without desert so well reputed.

DUKE
Hath he not a son?

VALENTINE
Ay, my good lord, a son that well deserves
The honor and regard of such a father.

DUKE
You know him well?

VALENTINE
I know him as myself, for from our infancy
We have convers'd and spent our hours together.
And though myself have been an idle truant,
Omitting the sweet benefit of time
To clothe mine age with angel-like perfection,
Yet hath Sir Proteus, for that's his name,
Made use and fair advantage of his days;
His years but young, but his experience old;
His head unmellowed, but his judgment ripe;

34 post hasten. **with oars,** i.e., in a rowboat, in order to reach the sailing vessel at anchor **41 lose the flood** miss the tide

II.ii. Location: Milan. The Duke's palace.

11 Hap'ly perhaps **16 instance** proof **18 quote** notice, observe. (Pronounced *coat,* and punning on that idea.) **19 jerkin** close-fitting jacket worn over, or in place of, the doublet **20 doublet** a man's jacket (with play on *double* in the next line)

26 That i.e., one who **27 in your air** (1) in the air you breathe, i.e., near you (2) listening to your talk. (The phrase also plays on *chameleon* in the previous speech, since chameleons were supposed to be able to live on air alone.) **28 You have said** i.e., that's a lot of fine talk **29 done** (1) acted, in contrast to *said* (2) finished. (Thurio hints here that he's prepared to duel with Valentine at some future date.) **30–31 end . . . begin** i.e., stop before you come to actual blows **36 fire** i.e., spark to set off the volley **38 kindly** fittingly, naturally **41 exchequer** treasury **43 bare** threadbare **44 bare** mere **47 hard beset** strongly besieged (with two wooers at once) **51 happy messenger** bringer of good tidings **61 convers'd** associated **63 Omitting** neglecting **68 unmellowed** i.e., unmixed with grey hair

And, in a word, for far behind his worth
Comes all the praises that I now bestow,
He is complete in feature and in mind 71
With all good grace to grace a gentleman.

DUKE
Beshrew me, sir, but if he make this good, 73
He is as worthy for an empress' love
As meet to be an emperor's counselor. 75
Well, sir, this gentleman is come to me,
With commendation from great potentates,
And here he means to spend his time awhile.
I think 'tis no unwelcome news to you.

VALENTINE
Should I have wish'd a thing, it had been he.

DUKE
Welcome him then according to his worth.
Silvia, I speak to you, and you, Sir Thurio;
For Valentine, I need not cite him to it. 83
I will send him hither to you presently. [*Exit.*] 84

VALENTINE
This is the gentleman I told your ladyship
Had come along with me, but that his mistress
Did hold his eyes lock'd in her crystal looks.

SILVIA
Belike that now she hath enfranchis'd them 88
Upon some other pawn for fealty. 89

VALENTINE
Nay, sure, I think she holds them prisoners still.

SILVIA
Nay, then he should be blind; and, being blind,
How could he see his way to seek out you?

VALENTINE
Why, lady, Love hath twenty pair of eyes.

THURIO
They say that Love hath not an eye at all.

VALENTINE
To see such lovers, Thurio, as yourself.
Upon a homely object Love can wink. 96

SILVIA
Have done, have done. Here comes the gentleman.
[*Exit Thurio.*]

[*Enter*] *Proteus.*

VALENTINE
Welcome, dear Proteus! Mistress, I beseech you,
Confirm his welcome with some special favor.

SILVIA
His worth is warrant for his welcome hither,
If this be he you oft have wish'd to hear from.

VALENTINE
Mistress, it is. Sweet lady, entertain him 102
To be my fellow-servant to your ladyship.

SILVIA
Too low a mistress for so high a servant.

PROTEUS
Not so, sweet lady, but too mean a servant
To have a look of such a worthy mistress. 106

VALENTINE
Leave off discourse of disability. 107
Sweet lady, entertain him for your servant.

PROTEUS
My duty will I boast of, nothing else. 109

SILVIA
And duty never yet did want his meed. 110
Servant, you are welcome to a worthless mistress.

PROTEUS
I'll die on him that says so but yourself. 112

SILVIA
That you are welcome?

PROTEUS
That you are worthless.

[*Enter Thurio.*]

THURIO
Madam, my lord your father would speak with you.

SILVIA
I wait upon his pleasure. Come, Sir Thurio,
Go with me. Once more, new servant, welcome.
I'll leave you to confer of home affairs;
When you have done, we look to hear from you.

PROTEUS
We'll both attend upon your ladyship.
[*Exeunt Silvia and Thurio.*]

VALENTINE
Now, tell me, how do all from whence you came?

PROTEUS
Your friends are well and have them much
commended. 121

VALENTINE
And how do yours?

PROTEUS
I left them all in health.

VALENTINE
How does your lady, and how thrives your love?

PROTEUS
My tales of love were wont to weary you;
I know you joy not in a love discourse.

VALENTINE
Ay, Proteus, but that life is alter'd now.
I have done penance for contemning Love, 127
Whose high imperious thoughts have punish'd me
With bitter fasts, with penitential groans,
With nightly tears, and daily heart-sore sighs;
For, in revenge of my contempt of love,
Love hath chas'd sleep from my enthralled eyes
And made them watchers of mine own heart's
sorrow. 133
O gentle Proteus, Love's a mighty lord
And hath so humbled me as I confess 135
There is no woe to his correction 136
Nor to his service no such joy on earth. 137
Now no discourse, except it be of love;
Now can I break my fast, dine, sup, and sleep,

71 complete in feature perfect in shape of body and personal appearance **73 make this good** i.e., match your description **75 meet** suited **83 cite** urge **84 presently** at once **88 Belike that** perhaps. **enfranchis'd** freed **89 Upon . . . fealty** i.e., now that some other lover has pledged his service to her **96 wink** close the eyes **102 entertain** take into service

106 of from **107 Leave . . . disability** stop talking about your unworthiness **109 duty** i.e., to Silvia **110 want his meed** lack its reward **112 die on** die fighting with **121 them much commended** i.e., sent warm greetings **127 contemning** scorning **133 watchers of** those who stay awake with **135 as** that **136 to his correction** compared to the woe of his punishment **137 to his service** i.e., compared to serving Love

Upon the very naked name of love. 139
PROTEUS
Enough; I read your fortune in your eye.
Was this the idol that you worship so?
VALENTINE
Even she; and is she not a heavenly saint?
PROTEUS
No, but she is an earthly paragon.
VALENTINE
Call her divine.
PROTEUS I will not flatter her.
VALENTINE
O, flatter me, for love delights in praises.
PROTEUS
When I was sick, you gave me bitter pills,
And I must minister the like to you.
VALENTINE
Then speak the truth by her; if not divine, 148
Yet let her be a principality, 149
Sovereign to all the creatures on the earth.
PROTEUS
Except my mistress.
VALENTINE Sweet, except not any,
Except thou wilt except against my love. 152
PROTEUS
Have I not reason to prefer mine own? 153
VALENTINE
And I will help thee to prefer her too. 154
She shall be dignified with this high honor:
To bear my lady's train, lest the base earth
Should from her vesture chance to steal a kiss
And, of so great a favor growing proud,
Disdain to root the summer-swelling flow'r,
And make rough winter everlastingly.
PROTEUS
Why, Valentine, what braggardism is this?
VALENTINE
Pardon me, Proteus, all I can is nothing 162
To her whose worth makes other worthies nothing.
She is alone.
PROTEUS Then let her alone. 164
VALENTINE
Not for the world. Why, man, she is mine own,
And I as rich in having such a jewel
As twenty seas, if all their sand were pearl,
The water nectar, and the rocks pure gold.
Forgive me that I do not dream on thee, 169
Because thou see'st me dote upon my love.
My foolish rival, that her father likes
Only for his possessions are so huge, 172
Is gone with her along, and I must after,
For love, thou know'st, is full of jealousy.
PROTEUS
But she loves you?
VALENTINE
Ay, and we are betroth'd. Nay, more, our marriage hour,
With all the cunning manner of our flight,
Determin'd of—how I must climb her window,
The ladder made of cords, and all the means
Plotted and 'greed on for my happiness.
Good Proteus, go with me to my chamber,
In these affairs to aid me with thy counsel.
PROTEUS
Go on before; I shall inquire you forth. 183
I must unto the road, to disembark 184
Some necessaries that I needs must use,
And then I'll presently attend you. 186
VALENTINE
Will you make haste? *Exit.*
PROTEUS
I will.
Even as one heat another heat expels, 189
Or as one nail by strength drives out another,
So the remembrance of my former love
Is by a newer object quite forgotten.
Is it mine eye, or Valentine's praise,
Her true perfection, or my false transgression,
That makes me reasonless to reason thus? 195
She is fair; and so is Julia that I love—
That I did love, for now my love is thaw'd;
Which, like a waxen image 'gainst a fire,
Bears no impression of the thing it was.
Methinks my zeal to Valentine is cold,
And that I love him not as I was wont.
O, but I love his lady too too much,
And that's the reason I love him so little.
How shall I dote on her with more advice, 204
That thus without advice begin to love her!
'Tis but her picture I have yet beheld, 206
And that hath dazzled my reason's light;
But when I look on her perfections,
There is no reason but I shall be blind. 209
If I can check my erring love, I will; 210
If not, to compass her I'll use my skill. *Exit.* 211

SCENE V

Enter Speed and Launce [severally].

SPEED Launce! By mine honesty, welcome to Milan!
LAUNCE Forswear not thyself, sweet youth, for I am not welcome. I reckon this always, that a man is never un- 3
done till he be hang'd, nor never welcome to a place 4
till some certain shot be paid and the hostess say 5
"Welcome!"
SPEED Come on, you madcap, I'll to the alehouse with you presently, where, for one shot of five pence, thou

139 very naked mere **148 by** about **149 principality** a member of one of the nine orders of angels **152 Except . . . except** unless you want to cast aspersions **153 prefer** like better **154 prefer** advance **162 can** i.e., can say of her **164 is alone** is peerless **169 that . . . thee** i.e., that I seem neglectful of you **172 for** because

183 forth out **184 road** roadstead, harbor **186 presently** immediately **189 Even . . . expels** (It was a common saying that the application of heat would relieve the pain of a burn.) **195 reasonless** without justification, wrongly **204 advice** deliberation, reflection **206 picture** i.e., outer appearance **209 no reason but** no doubt but that **210 check** restrain **211 compass** obtain

II.v. Location: Milan. A street.
3–4 undone ruined **5 shot** fee, tavern reckoning

shalt have five thousand welcomes. But, sirrah, how
did thy master part with Madam Julia?

LAUNCE Marry, after they clos'd in earnest, they parted 11
very fairly in jest. 12

SPEED But shall she marry him?

LAUNCE No.

SPEED How then? Shall he marry her?

LAUNCE No, neither.

SPEED What, are they broken? 17

LAUNCE No, they are both as whole as a fish.

SPEED Why, then, how stands the matter with them?

LAUNCE Marry, thus: when it stands well with him, it 20
stands well with her.

SPEED What an ass art thou! I understand thee not.

LAUNCE What a block art thou, that thou canst not! My staff understands me.

SPEED What thou say'st?

LAUNCE Ay, and what I do too. Look thee, I'll but lean, and my staff understands me.

SPEED It stands under thee, indeed.

LAUNCE Why, stand-under and under-stand is all one.

SPEED But tell me true, will 't be a match?

LAUNCE Ask my dog. If he say ay, it will; if he say no, it will; if he shake his tail and say nothing, it will.

SPEED The conclusion is then that it will.

LAUNCE Thou shalt never get such a secret from me but
by a parable. 35

SPEED 'Tis well that I get it so. But, Launce, how say'st 36
thou, that my master is become a notable lover? 37

LAUNCE I never knew him otherwise.

SPEED Than how?

LAUNCE A notable lubber, as thou reportest him to be.

SPEED Why, thou whoreson ass, thou mistak'st me. 41

LAUNCE Why, fool, I meant not thee, I meant thy master.

SPEED I tell thee, my master is become a hot lover.

LAUNCE Why, I tell thee, I care not though he burn himself in love. If thou wilt, go with me to the alehouse; if not, thou art an Hebrew, a Jew, and not worth the name of a Christian.

SPEED Why?

LAUNCE Because thou hast not so much charity in thee
as to go to the ale with a Christian. Wilt thou go? 51

SPEED At thy service. *Exeunt.*

SCENE VI

Enter Proteus solus.

PROTEUS
To leave my Julia, shall I be forsworn;
To love fair Silvia, shall I be forsworn;
To wrong my friend, I shall be much forsworn.
And ev'n that pow'r which gave me first my oath
Provokes me to this threefold perjury.
Love bade me swear and Love bids me forswear.
O sweet-suggesting Love, if thou hast sinn'd, 7
Teach me, thy tempted subject, to excuse it! 8
At first I did adore a twinkling star,
But now I worship a celestial sun.
Unheedful vows may heedfully be broken, 11
And he wants wit that wants resolved will 12
To learn his wit t' exchange the bad for better. 13
Fie, fie, unreverend tongue! To call her bad,
Whose sovereignty so oft thou hast preferr'd 15
With twenty thousand soul-confirming oaths.
I cannot leave to love, and yet I do; 17
But there I leave to love where I should love.
Julia I lose and Valentine I lose.
If I keep them, I needs must lose myself;
If I lose them, thus find I by their loss
For Valentine myself, for Julia Silvia.
I to myself am dearer than a friend,
For love is still most precious in itself, 24
And Silvia—witness Heaven, that made her fair!—
Shows Julia but a swarthy Ethiope. 26
I will forget that Julia is alive,
Rememb'ring that my love to her is dead;
And Valentine I'll hold an enemy,
Aiming at Silvia as a sweeter friend.
I cannot now prove constant to myself,
Without some treachery us'd to Valentine.
This night he meaneth with a corded ladder
To climb celestial Silvia's chamber-window,
Myself in counsel, his competitor. 35
Now presently I'll give her father notice
Of their disguising and pretended flight, 37
Who, all enrag'd, will banish Valentine;
For Thurio, he intends, shall wed his daughter.
But, Valentine being gone, I'll quickly cross 40
By some sly trick blunt Thurio's dull proceeding.
Love, lend me wings to make my purpose swift,
As thou hast lent me wit to plot this drift! *Exit.* 43

SCENE VII

Enter Julia and Lucetta.

JULIA
Counsel, Lucetta; gentle girl, assist me;
And ev'n in kind love I do conjure thee,
Who art the table wherein all my thoughts 3
Are visibly character'd and engrav'd, 4
To lesson me and tell me some good mean
How, with my honor, I may undertake
A journey to my loving Proteus.

11 clos'd (1) embraced (2) came to terms **12 fairly** kindly, gently **17 broken** no longer engaged. (But Launce plays on the word in the sense of *smashed to pieces.*) **20 stands well** (with a bawdy pun) **35 parable** enigmatic talk **36–37 how say'st thou** what do you say to this **41 whoreson** (A friendly term of abuse.) **51 go . . . Christian** i.e., go to a church-ale, a village festival used to raise money for the church

II.vi. Location: Milan. The Duke's palace.

7 sweet-suggesting sweetly seductive **7–8 if thou . . . it** i.e., if even you, Love, have committed falsehoods or follies in love, teach frail me how to excuse myself by your example **11 Unheedful** ill considered. **heedfully** after careful consideration **12 wants** lacks **13 learn** teach **15 preferr'd** recommended **17 leave** cease **24 still** always **26 Shows Julia but** reveals Julia to be by comparison no more than **35 in counsel** taken into confidence. **competitor** associate, partner **37 pretended** intended **40 cross** thwart **43 drift** scheme

II.vii. Location: Verona. Julia's house.
3 table tablet **4 character'd** engraved, inscribed

LUCETTA
Alas, the way is wearisome and long!

JULIA
A true-devoted pilgrim is not weary
To measure kingdoms with his feeble steps;
Much less shall she that hath Love's wings to fly,
And when the flight is made to one so dear,
Of such divine perfection, as Sir Proteus.

LUCETTA
Better forbear till Proteus make return.

JULIA
O, know'st thou not his looks are my soul's food?
Pity the dearth that I have pined in,
By longing for that food so long a time.
Didst thou but know the inly touch of love,
Thou wouldst as soon go kindle fire with snow
As seek to quench the fire of love with words.

LUCETTA
I do not seek to quench your love's hot fire,
But qualify the fire's extreme rage,
Lest it should burn above the bounds of reason.

JULIA
The more thou damm'st it up, the more it burns.
The current that with gentle murmur glides,
Thou know'st, being stopp'd, impatiently doth rage;
But when his fair course is not hindered,
He makes sweet music with th' enamel'd stones,
Giving a gentle kiss to every sedge
He overtaketh in his pilgrimage,
And so by many winding nooks he strays
With willing sport to the wild ocean.
Then let me go, and hinder not my course.
I'll be as patient as a gentle stream
And make a pastime of each weary step,
Till the last step have brought me to my love,
And there I'll rest, as after much turmoil
A blessed soul doth in Elysium.

LUCETTA
But in what habit will you go along?

JULIA
Not like a woman; for I would prevent
The loose encounters of lascivious men.
Gentle Lucetta, fit me with such weeds
As may beseem some well-reputed page.

LUCETTA
Why, then, your ladyship must cut your hair.

JULIA
No, girl; I'll knit it up in silken strings
With twenty odd-conceited true-love knots.
To be fantastic may become a youth
Of greater time than I shall show to be.

LUCETTA
What fashion, madam, shall I make your breeches?

JULIA
That fits as well as "Tell me, good my lord,
What compass will you wear your farthingale?"
Why, ev'n what fashion thou best likes, Lucetta.

LUCETTA
You must needs have them with a codpiece,
madam.

JULIA
Out, out, Lucetta! That will be ill-favor'd.

LUCETTA
A round hose, madam, now 's not worth a pin,
Unless you have a codpiece to stick pins on.

JULIA
Lucetta, as thou lov'st me, let me have
What thou think'st meet and is most mannerly.
But tell me, wench, how will the world repute me
For undertaking so unstaid a journey?
I fear me, it will make me scandaliz'd.

LUCETTA
If you think so, then stay at home and go not.

JULIA
Nay, that I will not.

LUCETTA
Then never dream on infamy, but go.
If Proteus like your journey when you come,
No matter who's displeas'd when you are gone.
I fear me he will scarce be pleas'd withal.

JULIA
That is the least, Lucetta, of my fear.
A thousand oaths, an ocean of his tears,
And instances of infinite of love,
Warrant me welcome to my Proteus.

LUCETTA
All these are servants to deceitful men.

JULIA
Base men, that use them to so base effect!
But truer stars did govern Proteus' birth;
His words are bonds, his oaths are oracles,
His love sincere, his thoughts immaculate,
His tears pure messengers sent from his heart,
His heart as far from fraud as heaven from earth.

LUCETTA
Pray heav'n he prove so when you come to him!

JULIA
Now, as thou lov'st me, do him not that wrong
To bear a hard opinion of his truth.
Only deserve my love by loving him,
And presently go with me to my chamber
To take a note of what I stand in need of,
To furnish me upon my longing journey.
All that is mine I leave at thy dispose,
My goods, my lands, my reputation;
Only, in lieu thereof, dispatch me hence.
Come, answer not, but to it presently!
I am impatient of my tarriance. *Exeunt.*

10 measure traverse **18 inly** inward **22 qualify** control, regulate **39 habit** apparel **40 prevent** forestall **42 weeds** garments **43 beseem** suit **46 odd-conceited** strangely devised **47 fantastic** fanciful (in appearance) **48 Of greater time** of more years **51 compass** circumference, fullness. **farthingale** hooped petticoat

53 codpiece bagged appendage to the front of close-fitting hose or breeches, often conspicuous and ornamented **54 Out** (An expression of reproach or indignation.) **ill-favor'd** unsightly **55 round hose** short padded breeches **56 stick pins on** (One method used to decorate the codpiece.) **60 unstaid** reckless, unconventional **67 withal** with it **70 infinite** infinity **85 longing** prompted by longing **86 at thy dispose** in your charge **90 tarriance** delaying

ACT III • SCENE I

Enter Duke, Thurio, [and] Proteus.

DUKE
Sir Thurio, give us leave, I pray, awhile. 1
We have some secrets to confer about.
[Exit Thurio.]
Now, tell me, Proteus, what's your will with me?

PROTEUS
My gracious lord, that which I would discover 4
The law of friendship bids me to conceal;
But when I call to mind your gracious favors
Done to me, undeserving as I am,
My duty pricks me on to utter that
Which else no worldly good should draw from me.
Know, worthy prince, Sir Valentine, my friend,
This night intends to steal away your daughter.
Myself am one made privy to the plot.
I know you have determin'd to bestow her
On Thurio, whom your gentle daughter hates;
And should she thus be stol'n away from you,
It would be much vexation to your age.
Thus, for my duty's sake, I rather chose
To cross my friend in his intended drift 18
Than, by concealing it, heap on your head
A pack of sorrows which would press you down,
Being unprevented, to your timeless grave. 21

DUKE
Proteus, I thank thee for thine honest care,
Which to requite, command me while I live. 23
This love of theirs myself have often seen,
Haply when they have judg'd me fast asleep,
And oftentimes have purpos'd to forbid
Sir Valentine her company and my court.
But, fearing lest my jealous aim might err, 28
And so unworthily disgrace the man,
A rashness that I ever yet have shunn'd,
I gave him gentle looks, thereby to find
That which thyself hast now disclos'd to me.
And, that thou mayst perceive my fear of this,
Knowing that tender youth is soon suggested, 34
I nightly lodge her in an upper tow'r,
The key whereof myself have ever kept;
And thence she cannot be convey'd away.

PROTEUS
Know, noble lord, they have devis'd a mean
How he her chamber-window will ascend
And with a corded ladder fetch her down;
For which the youthful lover now is gone,
And this way comes he with it presently, 42
Where, if it please you, you may intercept him.
But, good my lord, do it so cunningly
That my discovery be not aimed at; 45
For love of you, not hate unto my friend,
Hath made me publisher of this pretense. 47

DUKE
Upon mine honor, he shall never know
That I had any light from thee of this.

PROTEUS
Adieu, my lord. Sir Valentine is coming. *[Exit.]*

[Enter] Valentine, [hurrying elsewhere, concealing a rope ladder beneath his cloak].

DUKE
Sir Valentine, whither away so fast?

VALENTINE
Please it your Grace, there is a messenger
That stays to bear my letters to my friends,
And I am going to deliver them.

DUKE
Be they of much import?

VALENTINE
The tenor of them doth but signify
My health and happy being at your court.

DUKE
Nay then, no matter; stay with me awhile.
I am to break with thee of some affairs 58
That touch me near, wherein thou must be secret.
'Tis not unknown to thee that I have sought
To match my friend Sir Thurio to my daughter.

VALENTINE
I know it well, my lord; and, sure, the match
Were rich and honorable. Besides, the gentleman 63
Is full of virtue, bounty, worth, and qualities 64
Beseeming such a wife as your fair daughter.
Cannot your Grace win her to fancy him?

DUKE
No, trust me; she is peevish, sullen, froward, 67
Proud, disobedient, stubborn, lacking duty,
Neither regarding that she is my child
Nor fearing me as if I were her father.
And, may I say to thee, this pride of hers,
Upon advice, hath drawn my love from her; 72
And, where I thought the remnant of mine age 73
Should have been cherish'd by her child-like duty,
I now am full resolv'd to take a wife,
And turn her out to who will take her in.
Then let her beauty be her wedding dow'r,
For me and my possessions she esteems not.

VALENTINE
What would your Grace have me to do in this?

DUKE
There is a lady in Verona here 80
Whom I affect, but she is nice and coy 81
And nought esteems my aged eloquence.
Now therefore would I have thee to my tutor—
For long agone I have forgot to court; 84
Besides, the fashion of the time is chang'd—
How and which way I may bestow myself 86
To be regarded in her sun-bright eye.

III.i. Location: Milan. The Duke's palace.
1 gives us leave (A polite form of dismissal.) **4 discover** reveal **18 cross** thwart. **drift** scheme **21 timeless** untimely **23 command me** ask any favor of me **28 jealous aim** suspicious conjecture **34 suggested** tempted **42 presently** now **45 discovery** disclosure. **aimed at** guessed

47 pretense intention **58 break** i.e., take up the subject **63 Were** would be **64 virtue** good accomplishments. **qualities** attainments **67 froward** perverse **72 Upon advice** after some careful consideration **73 where** whereas **80 Verona** (An error for Milan, seemingly, but *Verona* fits the line metrically.) **81 affect** am fond of. **nice** difficult to please. **coy** shy **84 forgot** forgotten how **86 bestow** behave

VALENTINE
Win her with gifts, if she respect not words. 88
Dumb jewels often in their silent kind 89
More than quick words do move a woman's mind.

DUKE
But she did scorn a present that I sent her.

VALENTINE
A woman sometime scorns what best contents her.
Send her another; never give her o'er,
For scorn at first makes after-love the more.
If she do frown, 'tis not in hate of you,
But rather to beget more love in you.
If she do chide, 'tis not to have you gone,
For why the fools are mad if left alone. 98
Take no repulse, whatever she doth say;
For "get you gone," she doth not mean "away!"
Flatter and praise, commend, extol their graces;
Though ne'er so black, say they have angels' faces. 102
That man that hath a tongue, I say, is no man,
If with his tongue he cannot win a woman.

DUKE
But she I mean is promis'd by her friends
Unto a youthful gentleman of worth,
And kept severely from resort of men,
That no man hath access by day to her.

VALENTINE
Why, then, I would resort to her by night.

DUKE
Ay, but the doors be lock'd and keys kept safe,
That no man hath recourse to her by night.

VALENTINE
What lets but one may enter at her window? 112

DUKE
Her chamber is aloft, far from the ground,
And built so shelving that one cannot climb it
Without apparent hazard of his life. 115

VALENTINE
Why then, a ladder quaintly made of cords, 116
To cast up, with a pair of anchoring hooks,
Would serve to scale another Hero's tow'r, 118
So bold Leander would adventure it. 119

DUKE
Now, as thou art a gentlemen of blood, 120
Advise me where I may have such a ladder.

VALENTINE
When would you use it? Pray, sir, tell me that.

DUKE
This very night; for Love is like a child,
That longs for every thing that he can come by.

VALENTINE
By seven o'clock I'll get you such a ladder.

DUKE
But, hark thee, I will go to her alone;
How shall I best convey the ladder thither?

VALENTINE
It will be light, my lord, that you may bear it
Under a cloak that is of any length.

DUKE
A cloak as long as thine will serve the turn? 130

VALENTINE
Ay, my good lord.

DUKE
Then let me see thy cloak.
I'll get me one of such another length. 132

VALENTINE
Why, any cloak will serve the turn, my lord.

DUKE
How shall I fashion me to wear a cloak?
I pray thee, let me feel thy cloak upon me.
[*Pulls open Valentine's cloak.*]
What letter is this same? What's here? "To Silvia"?
And here an engine fit for my proceeding. 137
I'll be so bold to break the seal for once. [*Reads.*]
"My thoughts do harbor with my Silvia nightly, 139
And slaves they are to me that send them flying.
O, could their master come and go as lightly, 141
Himself would lodge where senseless they are lying! 142
My herald thoughts in thy pure bosom rest them, 143
While I, their king, that thither them importune, 144
Do curse the grace that with such grace hath bless'd
them, 145
Because myself do want my servants' fortune. 146
I curse myself, for they are sent by me, 147
That they should harbor where their lord would be."
What's here?
"Silvia, this night I will enfranchise thee."
'Tis so; and here's the ladder for the purpose.
Why, Phaethon—for thou art Merops' son— 152
Wilt thou aspire to guide the heavenly car
And with thy daring folly burn the world?
Wilt thou reach stars, because they shine on thee?
Go, base intruder, overweening slave! 156
Bestow thy fawning smiles on equal mates, 157
And think my patience, more than thy desert,
Is privilege for thy departure hence. 159
Thank me for this more than for all the favors
Which all too much I have bestow'd on thee.
But if thou linger in my territories
Longer than swiftest expedition
Will give thee time to leave our royal court,
By heaven, my wrath shall far exceed the love
I ever bore my daughter or thyself.
Be gone! I will not hear thy vain excuse,
But, as thou lov'st thy life, make speed from hence.
[*Exit.*]

VALENTINE
And why not death rather than living torment?
To die is to be banish'd from myself,
And Silvia is myself; banish'd from her
Is self from self—a deadly banishment!

88 respect heed **89 kind** nature **98 For why** because **102 black** dark of complexion **112 lets** hinders **115 apparent** plain, evident **116 quaintly** skillfully **118, 119 Hero's, Leander** (See note to I.i.22.) **120 blood** good family

130 turn purpose **132 such another** the same **137 engine** contrivance, i.e., the rope ladder **139 harbor** reside **141 lightly** easily, quickly **142 senseless** lacking sensation. **lying** dwelling **143 them** themselves **144 importune** command **145 grace . . . grace** good fortune . . . charm, favor **146 want** lack **147 for** since **152 Phaethon, Merops** (Phaethon was the son of Helios, the sun god, and of Clymene, lawful wife of Merops. Phaethon aspired to guide the sun god's *car* (l. 153) or chariot and was slain by Zeus for his presumption after he had scorched a large portion of the earth.) **156 overweening** presumptuous **157 equal mates** i.e., women of equal social status **159 Is privilege for** authorizes, grants

What light is light, if Silvia be not seen?
What joy is joy, if Silvia be not by?
Unless it be to think that she is by
And feed upon the shadow of perfection. 176
Except I be by Silvia in the night, 177
There is no music in the nightingale;
Unless I look on Silvia in the day,
There is no day for me to look upon.
She is my essence, and I leave to be, 181
If I be not by her fair influence 182
Foster'd, illumin'd, cherish'd, kept alive.
I fly not death, to fly his deadly doom; 184
Tarry I here, I but attend on death, 185
But, fly I hence, I fly away from life.

[Enter Proteus and] *Launce.*

PROTEUS Run, boy, run, run, and seek him out.
LAUNCE Soho, soho! 188
PROTEUS What seest thou?
LAUNCE Him we go to find. There's not a hair on 's 190
head but 'tis a Valentine. 191
PROTEUS Valentine?
VALENTINE No.
PROTEUS Who then? His spirit?
VALENTINE Neither.
PROTEUS What then?
VALENTINE Nothing.
LAUNCE Can nothing speak? Master, shall I strike?
PROTEUS Who wouldst thou strike?
LAUNCE Nothing.
PROTEUS Villain, forbear.
LAUNCE Why, sir, I'll strike nothing. I pray you—
PROTEUS Sirrah, I say, forbear. Friend Valentine, a word.

VALENTINE
My ears are stopp'd and cannot hear good news,
So much of bad already hath possess'd them.

PROTEUS
Then in dumb silence will I bury mine, 207
For they are harsh, untuneable, and bad.

VALENTINE
Is Silvia dead?

PROTEUS
No, Valentine.

VALENTINE
No Valentine, indeed, for sacred Silvia.
Hath she forsworn me?

PROTEUS
No, Valentine.

VALENTINE
No Valentine, if Silvia have forsworn me.
What is your news?

LAUNCE
Sir, there is a proclamation that you are vanish'd.

PROTEUS
That thou art banish'd—O, that's the news!—
From hence, from Silvia and from me thy friend.

VALENTINE
O, I have fed upon this woe already,
And now excess of it will make me surfeit.
Doth Silvia know that I am banish'd?

PROTEUS
Ay, ay; and she hath offer'd to the doom— 222
Which, unrevers'd, stands in effectual force— 223
A sea of melting pearl, which some call tears.
Those at her father's churlish feet she tender'd;
With them, upon her knees, her humble self,
Wringing her hands, whose whiteness so became them
As if but now they waxed pale for woe.
But neither bended knees, pure hands held up,
Sad sighs, deep groans, nor silver-shedding tears,
Could penetrate her uncompassionate sire;
But Valentine, if he be ta'en, must die.
Besides, her intercession chaf'd him so,
When she for thy repeal was suppliant, 234
That to close prison he commanded her, 235
With many bitter threats of biding there. 236

VALENTINE
No more, unless the next word that thou speak'st
Have some malignant power upon my life;
If so, I pray thee, breathe it in mine ear,
As ending anthem of my endless dolor. 240

PROTEUS
Cease to lament for that thou canst not help, 241
And study help for that which thou lament'st. 242
Time is the nurse and breeder of all good.
Here if thou stay, thou canst not see thy love;
Besides, thy staying will abridge thy life.
Hope is a lover's staff; walk hence with that
And manage it against despairing thoughts. 247
Thy letters may be here, though thou art hence,
Which, being writ to me, shall be deliver'd
Even in the milk-white bosom of thy love.
The time now serves not to expostulate.
Come, I'll convey thee through the city gate;
And, ere I part with thee, confer at large 253
Of all that may concern thy love-affairs.
As thou lov'st Silvia, though not for thyself,
Regard thy danger, and along with me!

VALENTINE
I pray thee, Launce, an if thou seest my boy,
Bid him make haste and meet me at the North-gate.

PROTEUS
Go, sirrah, find him out. Come, Valentine.

VALENTINE
O my dear Silvia! Hapless Valentine!
[Exeunt Valentine and Proteus.]

LAUNCE I am but a fool, look you, and yet I have the
wit to think my master is a kind of a knave. But that's 262
all one, if he be but one knave. He lives not now that 263
knows me to be in love, yet I am in love. But a team of

176 shadow image **177 Except** unless **181 leave** cease **182 influence** (A metaphorical reference to an ethereal fluid supposed to flow from the stars and to have power over the destinies of men.) **184 I . . . doom** I shall not escape death by flying from the Duke's sentence of death **185 attend on** wait for **188 Soho** (Hunting cry used when the game is sighted.) **190 hair** (with pun on *hare*) **191 Valentine** (His name means "token of true love.") **207 mine** i.e., my news

222 to the doom i.e., to this news of the sentence **223 Which . . . force** which, if not reversed, must certainly take effect **234 repeal** recall from exile **235 close** tightly enclosed **236 biding** permanently dwelling **240 ending anthem** requiem **241 that** what **242 study** devise **247 manage** wield **253 confer at large** discuss at length **262–263 that's . . . knave** i.e., it's all right so long as he's knavish in one thing only (that is, in love)

horse shall not pluck that from me, nor who 'tis I love. And yet 'tis a woman, but what woman, I will not tell myself. And yet 'tis a milkmaid. Yet 'tis not a maid, for she hath had gossips. Yet 'tis a maid, for she is her master's maid, and serves for wages. She hath more qualities than a water-spaniel, which is much in a bare Christian. [*Pulling out a paper.*] Here is the cate-log of her condition. "Imprimis: She can fetch and carry." Why, a horse can do no more. Nay, a horse cannot fetch, but only carry; therefore is she better than a jade. "Item: She can milk." Look you, a sweet virtue in a maid with clean hands.

[*Enter*] *Speed.*

SPEED How now, Signior Launce, what news with your mastership?

LAUNCE With my master's ship? Why, it is at sea.

SPEED Well, your old vice still: mistake the word. What news, then, in your paper?

LAUNCE The black'st news that ever thou heardst.

SPEED Why, man, how black?

LAUNCE Why, as black as ink.

SPEED Let me read them.

LAUNCE Fie on thee, jolt-head! Thou canst not read.

SPEED Thou liest; I can.

LAUNCE I will try thee. Tell me this: who begot thee?

SPEED Marry, the son of my grandfather.

LAUNCE O illiterate loiterer! It was the son of thy grandmother. This proves that thou canst not read.

SPEED Come, fool, come; try me in thy paper.

LAUNCE There. [*Gives him the paper.*] And Saint Nicholas be thy speed!

SPEED [*Reads*] "Imprimis: She can milk."

LAUNCE Ay, that she can.

SPEED "Item: She brews good ale."

LAUNCE And thereof comes the proverb: "Blessing of your heart, you brew good ale."

SPEED "Item: She can sew."

LAUNCE That's as much as to say, "Can she so?"

SPEED "Item: She can knit."

LAUNCE What need a man care for a stock with a wench, when she can knit him a stock?

SPEED "Item: She can wash and scour."

LAUNCE A special virtue; for then she need not be wash'd and scour'd.

SPEED "Item: She can spin."

LAUNCE Then may I set the world on wheels, when she can spin for her living.

SPEED "Item: She hath many nameless virtues."

LAUNCE That's as much as to say, bastard virtues, that indeed know not their fathers and therefore have no names.

SPEED Here follow her vices.

LAUNCE Close at the heels of her virtues.

SPEED "Item: She is not to be kiss'd fasting, in respect of her breath."

LAUNCE Well, that fault may be mended with a breakfast. Read on.

SPEED "Item: She hath a sweet mouth."

LAUNCE That makes amends for her sour breath.

SPEED "Item: She doth talk in her sleep."

LAUNCE It's no matter for that, so she sleep not in her talk.

SPEED "Item: She is slow in words."

LAUNCE O villain, that set this down among her vices! To be slow in words is a woman's only virtue. I pray thee, out with 't, and place it for her chief virtue.

SPEED "Item: She is proud."

LAUNCE Out with that too; it was Eve's legacy, and cannot be ta'en from her.

SPEED "Item: She hath no teeth."

LAUNCE I care not for that neither, because I love crusts.

SPEED "Item: She is curst."

LAUNCE Well, the best is, she hath no teeth to bite.

SPEED "Item: She will often praise her liquor."

LAUNCE If her liquor be good, she shall. If she will not, I will, for good things should be prais'd.

SPEED "Item: She is too liberal."

LAUNCE Of her tongue she cannot, for that's writ down she is slow of; of her purse she shall not, for that I'll keep shut. Now, of another thing she may, and that cannot I help. Well, proceed.

SPEED "Item: She hath more hair than wit, and more faults than hairs, and more wealth than faults."

LAUNCE Stop there; I'll have her. She was mine and not mine twice or thrice in that last article. Rehearse that once more.

SPEED "Item: She hath more hair than wit"—

LAUNCE More hair than wit? It may be: I'll prove it. The cover of the salt hides the salt, and therefore it is more than the salt; the hair that covers the wit is more than the wit, for the greater hides the less. What's next?

SPEED "And more faults than hairs"—

LAUNCE That's monstrous. O, that that were out!

SPEED "And more wealth than faults."

LAUNCE Why, that word makes the faults gracious. Well, I'll have her; and if it be a match, as nothing is impossible—

SPEED What then?

LAUNCE Why, then will I tell thee—that thy master stays for thee at the North-gate.

SPEED For me?

LAUNCE For thee? Ay, who art thou? He hath stay'd for a better man than thee.

SPEED And must I go to him?

LAUNCE Thou must run to him, for thou hast stay'd so long that going will scarce serve the turn.

SPEED Why didst not tell me sooner? Pox of your love-letters! [*Exit.*]

268 gossips i.e., godparents to a child of hers **270 water-spaniel** (A fawning, subservient kind of dog.) **bare** mere **271 cate-log** (Launce's version of *catalogue*, but possibly a normal spelling.) **272 condition** qualities. **Imprimis** in the first place (to be followed, in a list, with each particular marked *Item*) **275 jade** (1) ill-conditioned horse (2) a loose woman **280 vice** (with added meaning of *Vice*, comic character in morality plays who speaks with double meaning) **286 jolt-head** blockhead **290 loiterer** idle person, lazy student **293–294 Saint Nicholas** patron saint of schoolboys **294 speed** protection **303 stock** dowry **304 stock** stocking **309 set . . . wheels** i.e., take life easy **311 nameless** inexpressible

321 sweet mouth sweet tooth (with a wanton sense) **324 sleep** (with a pun on *slip;* pronunciation was similar) **330 proud** (with additional meaning of *lascivious*) **335 curst** shrewish **337 praise** appraise, taste **340 liberal** free **343 another thing** (with bawdy suggestion, playing on *purse*) **352 cover of the salt** covered salt cellar **369 going** walking

LAUNCE Now will he be swing'd for reading my letter—an unmannerly slave, that will thrust himself into secrets! I'll after, to rejoice in the boy's correction. *Exit.*

SCENE II

Enter Duke [*and*] *Thurio.*

DUKE
Sir Thurio, fear not but that she will love you,
Now Valentine is banish'd from her sight.

THURIO
Since his exile she hath despis'd me most,
Forsworn my company and rail'd at me,
That I am desperate of obtaining her.

DUKE
This weak impress of love is as a figure
Trenched in ice, which with an hour's heat
Dissolves to water and doth lose his form.
A little time will melt her frozen thoughts,
And worthless Valentine shall be forgot.

[*Enter*] *Proteus.*

How now, Sir Proteus? Is your countryman,
According to our proclamation, gone?

PROTEUS
Gone, my good lord.

DUKE
My daughter takes his going grievously.

PROTEUS
A little time, my lord, will kill that grief.

DUKE
So I believe, but Thurio thinks not so.
Proteus, the good conceit I hold of thee—
For thou hast shown some sign of good desert—
Makes me the better to confer with thee.

PROTEUS
Longer than I prove loyal to your Grace
Let me not live to look upon your Grace.

DUKE
Thou know'st how willingly I would effect
The match between Sir Thurio and my daughter.

PROTEUS
I do, my lord.

DUKE
And also, I think, thou art not ignorant
How she opposes her against my will.

PROTEUS
She did, my lord, when Valentine was here.

DUKE
Ay, and perversely she persevers so.
What might we do to make the girl forget
The love of Valentine, and love Sir Thurio?

PROTEUS
The best way is to slander Valentine
With falsehood, cowardice, and poor descent,
Three things that women highly hold in hate.

DUKE
Ay, but she'll think that it is spoke in hate.

PROTEUS
Ay, if his enemy deliver it;
Therefore it must with circumstance be spoken
By one whom she esteemeth as his friend.

DUKE
Then you must undertake to slander him.

PROTEUS
And that, my lord, I shall be loath to do.
'Tis an ill office for a gentleman,
Especially against his very friend.

DUKE
Where your good word cannot advantage him,
Your slander never can endamage him;
Therefore the office is indifferent,
Being entreated to it by your friend.

PROTEUS
You have prevail'd, my lord. If I can do it
By aught that I can speak in his dispraise,
She shall not long continue love to him.
But say this weed her love from Valentine,
It follows not that she will love Sir Thurio.

THURIO
Therefore, as you unwind her love from him,
Lest it should ravel and be good to none,
You must provide to bottom it on me;
Which must be done by praising me as much
As you in worth dispraise Sir Valentine.

DUKE
And, Proteus, we dare trust you in this kind,
Because we know, on Valentine's report,
You are already Love's firm votary
And cannot soon revolt and change your mind.
Upon this warrant shall you have access
Where you with Silvia may confer at large—
For she is lumpish, heavy, melancholy,
And, for your friend's sake, will be glad of you—
Where you may temper her by your persuasion
To hate young Valentine and love my friend.

PROTEUS
As much as I can do, I will effect.
But you, Sir Thurio, are not sharp enough;
You must lay lime to tangle her desires
By wailful sonnets, whose composed rhymes
Should be full-fraught with serviceable vows.

DUKE
Ay, much is the force of heaven-bred poesy.

PROTEUS
Say that upon the altar of her beauty
You sacrifice your tears, your sighs, your heart.
Write till your ink be dry, and with your tears

372 swing'd thrashed

III.ii. Location: Milan. The Duke's palace.
5 That so that **6 impress** impression **7 Trenched** cut **8 his** its **17 conceit** opinion **19 the better** the rather, more willingly **26 opposes her** contends

35 deliver speak **36 circumstance** confirming detail **41 very** true **42 advantage** profit **44 indifferent** neither good nor bad **45 your friend** i.e., the Duke **53 bottom** wind, as a skein of thread **62 lumpish** dull, spiritless **68 lime** birdlime, a sticky substance smeared on twigs of trees to ensnare small birds

Moist it again, and frame some feeling line
That may discover such integrity.
For Orpheus' lute was strung with poets' sinews,
Whose golden touch could soften steel and stones,
Make tigers tame, and huge leviathans
Forsake unsounded deeps to dance on sands.
After your dire-lamenting elegies,
Visit by night your lady's chamber-window
With some sweet consort. To their instruments
Tune a deploring dump; the night's dead silence
Will well become such sweet-complaining grievance.
This, or else nothing, will inherit her.

DUKE
This discipline shows thou hast been in love.

THURIO
And thy advice this night I'll put in practice.
Therefore, sweet Proteus, my direction-giver,
Let us into the city presently
To sort some gentlemen well skill'd in music.
I have a sonnet that will serve the turn
To give the onset to thy good advice.

DUKE
About it, gentlemen!

PROTEUS
We'll wait upon your Grace till after supper,
And afterward determine our proceedings.

DUKE
Even now about it! I will pardon you. *Exeunt.*

ACT IV • SCENE I

Enter certain Outlaws.

FIRST OUTLAW
Fellows, stand fast; I see a passenger.

SECOND OUTLAW
If there be ten, shrink not, but down with 'em.

[*Enter*] *Valentine* [*and*] *Speed.*

THIRD OUTLAW
Stand, sir, and throw us that you have about ye.
If not, we'll make you sit, and rifle you.

SPEED
Sir, we are undone. These are the villains
That all the travelers do fear so much.

VALENTINE
My friends—

FIRST OUTLAW
That's not so, sir, we are your enemies.

SECOND OUTLAW
Peace! We'll hear him.

THIRD OUTLAW
Ay, by my beard, will we, for he is a proper man.

VALENTINE
Then know that I have little wealth to lose.
A man I am cross'd with adversity;
My riches are these poor habiliments,
Of which if you should here disfurnish me,
You take the sum and substance that I have.

SECOND OUTLAW
Whither travel you?

VALENTINE
To Verona.

FIRST OUTLAW
Whence came you?

VALENTINE
From Milan.

THIRD OUTLAW
Have you long sojourn'd there?

VALENTINE
Some sixteen months, and longer might have stay'd,
If crooked fortune had not thwarted me.

FIRST OUTLAW
What, were you banish'd thence?

VALENTINE
I was.

SECOND OUTLAW
For what offense?

VALENTINE
For that which now torments me to rehearse:
I kill'd a man, whose death I much repent,
But yet I slew him manfully in fight
Without false vantage or base treachery.

FIRST OUTLAW
Why, ne'er repent it, if it were done so.
But were you banish'd for so small a fault?

VALENTINE
I was, and held me glad of such a doom.

SECOND OUTLAW
Have you the tongues?

VALENTINE
My youthful travel therein made me happy,
Or else I often had been miserable.

THIRD OUTLAW
By the bare scalp of Robin Hood's fat friar,
This fellow were a king for our wild faction!

FIRST OUTLAW
We'll have him. Sirs, a word.
[*The Outlaws confer in whispers.*]

SPEED
Master, be one of them;
It's an honorable kind of thievery.

VALENTINE
Peace, villain!

SECOND OUTLAW
Tell us this: have you any thing to take to?

VALENTINE
Nothing but my fortune.

75 frame compose **76 discover** reveal. **integrity** true devotion **77 Orpheus** legendary musician whose music had the power to move inanimate objects as well as animals. **sinews** nerves **79 leviathans** whales **83 consort** a company of musicians **84 dump** mournful melody **86 inherit** put you in possession of **87 discipline** teaching **91 sort** choose **93 onset** beginning **97 pardon you** i.e., excuse you your *waiting upon* or attending upon me

IV.i. Location: The frontiers of Mantua. A forest.
1 passenger traveler **10 proper** good-looking

14 disfurnish deprive **22 crooked** perverse, malignant **27 I kill'd a man** (A lie presumably intended to impress the outlaws.) **32 held . . . doom** i.e., was pleased with such a light sentence **33 the tongues** ability in foreign languages **34 happy** fortunate **36 friar** i.e., Friar Tuck **37 were** would be suitable as. **faction** band, set of persons **42 any . . . take to** any means of subsistence

THIRD OUTLAW
Know, then, that some of us are gentlemen,
Such as the fury of ungovern'd youth
Thrust from the company of aweful men.
Myself was from Verona banished
For practicing to steal away a lady,
An heir, and near allied unto the Duke.

SECOND OUTLAW
And I from Mantua, for a gentleman,
Who, in my mood, I stabb'd unto the heart.

FIRST OUTLAW
And I for such like petty crimes as these.
But to the purpose—for we cite our faults
That they may hold excus'd our lawless lives;
And partly, seeing you are beautified
With goodly shape, and by your own report
A linguist, and a man of such perfection
As we do in our quality much want—

SECOND OUTLAW
Indeed, because you are a banish'd man,
Therefore, above the rest, we parley to you.
Are you content to be our general?
To make a virtue of necessity
And live, as we do, in this wilderness?

THIRD OUTLAW
What say'st thou? Wilt thou be of our consort?
Say ay, and be the captain of us all.
We'll do thee homage and be rul'd by thee,
Love thee as our commander and our king.

FIRST OUTLAW
But if thou scorn our courtesy, thou diest.

SECOND OUTLAW
Thou shalt not live to brag what we have offer'd.

VALENTINE
I take your offer and will live with you,
Provided that you do no outrages
On silly women or poor passengers.

THIRD OUTLAW
No, we detest such vile base practices.
Come, go with us, we'll bring thee to our crews,
And show thee all the treasure we have got,
Which, with ourselves, all rest at thy dispose. *Exeunt.*

SCENE II

Enter Proteus.

PROTEUS
Already have I been false to Valentine,
And now I must be as unjust to Thurio.
Under the color of commending him,
I have access my own love to prefer.
But Silvia is too fair, too true, too holy,
To be corrupted with my worthless gifts.
When I protest true loyalty to her,
She twits me with my falsehood to my friend.
When to her beauty I commend my vows,
She bids me think how I have been forsworn
In breaking faith with Julia whom I lov'd.
And notwithstanding all her sudden quips,
The least whereof would quell a lover's hope,
Yet, spaniel-like, the more she spurns my love,
The more it grows and fawneth on her still.
But here comes Thurio. Now must we to her window,
And give some evening music to her ear.

[*Enter*] *Thurio* [*and*] *Musicians.*

THURIO
How now, Sir Proteus, are you crept before us?

PROTEUS
Ay, gentle Thurio, for you know that love
Will creep in service where it cannot go.

THURIO
Ay, but I hope, sir, that you love not here.

PROTEUS
Sir, but I do, or else I would be hence.

THURIO
Who? Silvia?

PROTEUS Ay, Silvia—for your sake.

THURIO
I thank you for your own. Now, gentlemen,
Let's tune, and to it lustily awhile.

[*Enter, at a distance,*] *Host,* [*and*] *Julia* [*in boy's clothes*].

HOST Now, my young guest, methinks you're allycholly. I pray you, why is it?

JULIA Marry, mine host, because I cannot be merry.

HOST Come, we'll have you merry. I'll bring you where you shall hear music and see the gentleman that you ask'd for.

JULIA But shall I hear him speak?

HOST Ay, that you shall.

JULIA That will be music. [*Music plays.*]

HOST Hark, hark!

JULIA Is he among these?

HOST Ay, but peace! Let's hear 'em.

Song

Who is Silvia? What is she,
  That all our swains commend her?
Holy, fair, and wise is she;
  The heaven such grace did lend her,
That she might admired be.

Is she kind as she is fair?
  For beauty lives with kindness.
Love doth to her eyes repair,
  To help him of his blindness,
And, being help'd, inhabits there.

46 aweful law-abiding **48 practicing** plotting **51 mood** anger, displeasure **58 quality** profession. **want** lack **60 above the rest** for this reason chiefly **64 consort** company **72 silly** defenseless **74 crews** bands

IV.ii. Location: Milan. Outside the Duke's palace, under Silvia's window.
3 color pretext **4 prefer** urge

12 quips sharp, sarcastic remarks **20 go** walk at an ordinary pace **26–27 allycholly** (A form of *melancholy.*) **42 admired** wondered at **45 repair** visit

Then to Silvia let us sing,
  That Silvia is excelling.
She excels each mortal thing
  Upon the dull earth dwelling.
To her let us garlands bring.

HOST How now? Are you sadder than you were before? How do you, man? The music likes you not. 54
JULIA You mistake; the musician likes me not.
HOST Why, my pretty youth?
JULIA He plays false, father.
HOST How? Out of tune on the strings?
JULIA Not so, but yet so false that he grieves my very heart-strings.
HOST You have a quick ear.
JULIA Ay, I would I were deaf; it makes me have a slow 62
heart.
HOST I perceive you delight not in music.
JULIA Not a whit, when it jars so. 65
HOST Hark, what fine change is in the music! 66
JULIA Ay, that change is the spite.
HOST You would have them always play but one thing?
JULIA I would always have one play but one thing. But, host, doth this Sir Proteus that we talk on often resort unto this gentlewoman?
HOST I tell you what Launce, his man, told me: he lov'd
her out of all nick. 73
JULIA Where is Launce?
HOST Gone to seek his dog, which tomorrow, by his master's command, he must carry for a present to his lady.

JULIA
Peace! Stand aside; the company parts.
[*Julia and Host stand aside.*]

PROTEUS
Sir Thurio, fear not you. I will so plead
That you shall say my cunning drift excels. 80

THURIO
Where meet we?

PROTEUS At Saint Gregory's well.

THURIO Farewell.
[*Exeunt Thurio and Musicians.*]

[*Enter*] *Silvia* [*above, at her window*].

PROTEUS
Madam, good ev'n to your ladyship.

SILVIA
I thank you for your music, gentlemen.
Who is that that spake?

PROTEUS
One, lady, if you knew his pure heart's truth,
You would quickly learn to know him by his voice.

SILVIA
Sir Proteus, as I take it.

PROTEUS
Sir Proteus, gentle lady, and your servant.

SILVIA
What's your will?

PROTEUS That I may compass yours. 89

SILVIA
You have your wish. My will is even this:
That presently you hie you home to bed.
Thou subtle, perjur'd, false, disloyal man!
Think'st thou I am so shallow, so conceitless, 93
To be seduced by thy flattery,
That hast deceiv'd so many with thy vows?
Return, return, and make thy love amends.
For me, by this pale queen of night I swear, 97
I am so far from granting thy request
That I despise thee for thy wrongful suit,
And by and by intend to chide myself
Even for this time I spend in talking to thee.

PROTEUS
I grant, sweet love, that I did love a lady,
But she is dead.

JULIA [*Aside*] 'Twere false, if I should speak it,
For I am sure she is not buried.

SILVIA
Say that she be; yet Valentine thy friend
Survives, to whom—thyself art witness—
I am betroth'd. And art thou not asham'd
To wrong him with thy importunacy? 108

PROTEUS
I likewise hear that Valentine is dead.

SILVIA
And so suppose am I, for in his grave
Assure thyself my love is buried.

PROTEUS
Sweet lady, let me rake it from the earth.

SILVIA
Go to thy lady's grave and call hers thence.
Or, at the least, in hers sepulcher thine.

JULIA [*Aside*]
He heard not that.

PROTEUS
Madam, if your heart be so obdurate,
Vouchsafe me yet your picture for my love,
The picture that is hanging in your chamber.
To that I'll speak, to that I'll sigh and weep;
For since the substance of your perfect self
Is else devoted, I am but a shadow, 121
And to your shadow will I make true love. 122

JULIA [*Aside*]
If 'twere a substance, you would, sure, deceive it,
And make it but a shadow, as I am.

SILVIA
I am very loath to be your idol, sir.
But since your falsehood shall become you well 126
To worship shadows and adore false shapes,
Send to me in the morning, and I'll send it. 128
And so, good rest.

54 likes pleases **62 slow** heavy **65 jars** is discordant **66 change** modulation. (But Julia plays on the sense of *fickleness.*) **73 out of all nick** i.e., beyond all reckoning **80 drift** scheme

89 compass obtain **93 conceitless** witless **97 pale . . . night** i. e., the moon **108 importunacy** importunity **121 else** elsewhere. **shadow** i.e., shadow of myself, mere nothing **122 shadow** i.e., portrait **126 since . . . well** i.e., since it befits your false nature **128 Send** i.e., send a messenger

PROTEUS As wretches have o'ernight
That wait for execution in the morn.
[*Exeunt Proteus and Silvia severally.*]

JULIA Host, will you go?

HOST By my halidom, I was fast asleep.

JULIA Pray you, where lies Sir Proteus?

HOST Marry, at my house. Trust me, I think 'tis almost day.

JULIA
Not so; but it hath been the longest night
That e'er I watch'd, and the most heaviest. [*Exeunt.*]

SCENE III

Enter Eglamour.

EGLAMOUR
This is the hour that Madam Silvia
Entreated me to call and know her mind.
There's some great matter she 'd employ me in.
Madam, madam!

[*Enter*] *Silvia* [*above, at her window*].

SILVIA
Who calls?

EGLAMOUR
Your servant and your friend;
One that attends your ladyship's command.

SILVIA
Sir Eglamour, a thousand times good morrow.

EGLAMOUR
As many, worthy lady, to yourself.
According to your ladyship's impose,
I am thus early come to know what service
It is your pleasure to command me in.

SILVIA
O Eglamour, thou art a gentleman—
Think not I flatter, for I swear I do not—
Valiant, wise, remorseful, well accomplish'd.
Thou art not ignorant what dear good will
I bear unto the banish'd Valentine,
Nor how my father would enforce me marry
Vain Thurio, whom my very soul abhors.
Thyself hast lov'd, and I have heard thee say
No grief did ever come so near thy heart
As when thy lady and thy true love died,
Upon whose grave thou vow'dst pure chastity.
Sir Eglamour, I would to Valentine,
To Mantua, where I hear he makes abode;
And, for the ways are dangerous to pass,
I do desire thy worthy company,
Upon whose faith and honor I repose.
Urge not my father's anger, Eglamour,
But think upon my grief, a lady's grief,
And on the justice of my flying hence,
To keep me from a most unholy match,
Which heaven and fortune still rewards with
plagues.
I do desire thee, even from a heart
As full of sorrows as the sea of sands,
To bear me company and go with me;
If not, to hide what I have said to thee,
That I may venture to depart alone.

EGLAMOUR
Madam, I pity much your grievances,
Which, since I know they virtuously are plac'd,
I give consent to go along with you,
Recking as little what betideth me
As much I wish all good befortune you.
When will you go?

SILVIA
This evening coming.

EGLAMOUR
Where shall I meet you?

SILVIA
At Friar Patrick's cell,
Where I intend holy confession.

EGLAMOUR
I will not fail your ladyship.
Good morrow, gentle lady.

SILVIA
Good morrow, kind Sir Eglamour.
Exeunt [*severally*].

SCENE IV

Enter Launce [*with his Dog*].

LAUNCE When a man's servant shall play the cur with him, look you, it goes hard—one that I brought up of a puppy, one that I sav'd from drowning when three or four of his blind brothers and sisters went to it. I have taught him, even as one would say precisely, "Thus I would teach a dog." I was sent to deliver him as a present to Mistress Silvia from my master, and I came no sooner into the dining-chamber but he steps me to her trencher and steals her capon's leg. O, 'tis a foul thing when a cur cannot keep himself in all companies! I would have, as one should say, one that takes upon him to be a dog indeed, to be, as it were, a dog at all things. If I had not had more wit than he, to take a fault upon me that he did, I think verily he had been hang'd for 't; sure as I live, he had suffer'd for 't. You shall judge. He thrusts me himself into the company of three or four gentlemanlike dogs, under the Duke's table. He had not been there—bless the mark!—a pissing while, but all the chamber smelt him. "Out

132 halidom (Originally, a holy relic; here, a mild oath.) **133 lies** lodges **137 watch'd** stayed awake through

IV.iii. Location: The same.
10 impose command **15 remorseful** compassionate **24 would** wish to go **26 for** because

33 still always **42 Recking** heeding

IV.iv. Location: The same.
2 of from **4 to it** i.e., to drowning **8–9 steps me** i.e., to my injury, to my detriment. (Cf. *thrusts me*, l. 16.) **9 trencher** wooden dish or plate **10 keep** restrain **12–13 a dog at** (with a play on the meaning *adept at*) **18 bless the mark** (A phrase used to apologize for indecorous language.) **19 pissing while** (with a play on the meaning *short while*)

with the dog!" says one. "What cur is that?" says another. "Whip him out," says the third. "Hang him up," says the Duke. I, having been acquainted with the smell before, knew it was Crab, and goes me to the fellow that whips the dogs. "Friend," quoth I, "you mean to whip the dog?" "Ay, marry do I," quoth he. "You do him the more wrong," quoth I; " 'twas I did the thing you wot of." He makes me no more ado, but whips me out of the chamber. How many masters would do this for his servant? Nay, I'll be sworn, I have sat in the stocks for puddings he hath stol'n, otherwise he had been executed. I have stood on the pillory for geese he hath kill'd, otherwise he had suffer'd for 't.—Thou think'st not of this now. Nay, I remember the trick you serv'd me when I took my leave of Madam Silvia. Did not I bid thee still mark me and do as I do? When didst thou see me heave up my leg and make water against a gentlewoman's farthingale? Didst thou ever see me do such a trick?

[Enter] Proteus [and] Julia [in boy's clothes].

PROTEUS
Sebastian is thy name? I like thee well
And will employ thee in some service presently.

JULIA
In what you please; I'll do what I can.

PROTEUS
I hope thou wilt. [*To Launce.*] How now, you
whoreson peasant!
Where have you been these two days loitering?

LAUNCE Marry, sir, I carried Mistress Silvia the dog you bade me.

PROTEUS And what says she to my little jewel?

LAUNCE Marry, she says your dog was a cur, and tells you currish thanks is good enough for such a present.

PROTEUS But she receiv'd my dog?

LAUNCE No, indeed, did she not; here have I brought him back again. [*Points to his dog.*]

PROTEUS What, didst thou offer her this from me?

LAUNCE Ay, sir, the other squirrel was stol'n from me by the hangman's boys in the market-place; and then I offer'd her mine own, who is a dog as big as ten of yours, and therefore the gift the greater.

PROTEUS
Go get thee hence, and find my dog again,
Or ne'er return again into my sight.
Away, I say! Stayest thou to vex me here?
[*Exit Launce.*]
A slave, that still an end turns me to shame!—
Sebastian, I have entertained thee,
Partly that I have need of such a youth
That can with some discretion do my business,
For 'tis no trusting to yond foolish lout,
But chiefly for thy face and thy behavior,
Which, if my augury deceive me not,
Witness good bringing up, fortune, and truth.
Therefore know thou, for this I entertain thee.
Go presently and take this ring with thee.
[*Gives a ring.*]
Deliver it to Madam Silvia—
She lov'd me well deliver'd it to me.

JULIA
It seems you lov'd not her, to leave her token.
She is dead, belike?

PROTEUS Not so; I think she lives.

JULIA
Alas!

PROTEUS
Why dost thou cry "Alas"?

JULIA
I cannot choose but pity her.

PROTEUS
Wherefore shouldst thou pity her?

JULIA
Because methinks that she lov'd you as well
As you do love your lady Silvia.
She dreams on him that has forgot her love;
You dote on her that cares not for your love.
'Tis pity love should be so contrary;
And thinking on it makes me cry "Alas!"

PROTEUS
Well, give her that ring and therewithal
This letter. [*Gives a letter.*] That's her chamber. Tell
my lady
I claim the promise for her heavenly picture.
Your message done, hie home unto my chamber,
Where thou shalt find me, sad and solitary. [*Exit.*]

JULIA
How many women would do such a message?
Alas, poor Proteus! Thou hast entertain'd
A fox to be the shepherd of thy lambs.
Alas, poor fool, why do I pity him
That with his very heart despiseth me?
Because he loves her, he despiseth me;
Because I love him, I must pity him.
This ring I gave him when he parted from me,
To bind him to remember my good will;
And now am I, unhappy messenger,
To plead for that which I would not obtain,
To carry that which I would have refus'd,
To praise his faith which I would have disprais'd.
I am my master's true-confirmed love,
But cannot be true servant to my master
Unless I prove false traitor to myself.
Yet will I woo for him, but yet so coldly
As, heaven it knows, I would not have him speed.

[Enter] Silvia [attended].

Gentlewoman, good day! I pray you, be my mean
To bring me where to speak with Madam Silvia.

SILVIA
What would you with her, if that I be she?

27 wot of know about **37 farthingale** hooped petticoat **46 jewel** (Proteus is thinking of the small, elegant dog he intended as a present to Silvia.) **53 squirrel** i.e., the little dog **54 hangman's** i.e., fit for the hangman **60 still an end** continually **61 entertained** taken into service **67 Witness** bear witness to

71 deliver'd who gave **72 leave** part with **92 poor fool** i.e., Julia herself **106 speed** succeed **108 where to** where I may

JULIA
If you be she, I do entreat your patience
To hear me speak the message I am sent on.
SILVIA
From whom?
JULIA
From my master, Sir Proteus, madam.
SILVIA
O, he sends you for a picture?
JULIA
Ay, madam.
SILVIA
Ursula, bring my picture there.
[*A servant gives Silvia a picture, which she hands over to "Sebastian."*]
Go give your master this. Tell him from me,
One Julia, that his changing thoughts forget,
Would better fit his chamber than this shadow.
JULIA
Madam, please you peruse this letter.—
[*Gives a letter to Silvia, but takes it back and gives another letter instead.*]
Pardon me, madam; I have unadvis'd
Deliver'd you a paper that I should not.
This is the letter to your ladyship.
SILVIA
I pray thee, let me look on that again.
JULIA
It may not be; good madam, pardon me.
SILVIA
There, hold!
I will not look upon your master's lines.
I know they are stuff'd with protestations
And full of new-found oaths, which he will break
As easily as I do tear his paper. [*Tears letter.*]
JULIA
Madam, he sends your ladyship this ring.
[*Proffering ring.*]
SILVIA
The more shame for him that he sends it me,
For I have heard him say a thousand times
His Julia gave it him at his departure.
Though his false finger have profan'd the ring,
Mine shall not do his Julia so much wrong.
JULIA
She thanks you.
SILVIA
What say'st thou?
JULIA
I thank you, madam, that you tender her.
Poor gentlewoman! My master wrongs her much.
SILVIA
Dost thou know her?
JULIA
Almost as well as I do know myself.
To think upon her woes I do protest
That I have wept a hundred several times.
SILVIA
Belike she thinks that Proteus hath forsook her.
JULIA
I think she doth, and that's her cause of sorrow.
SILVIA
Is she not passing fair?
JULIA
She hath been fairer, madam, than she is.
When she did think my master lov'd her well,
She, in my judgment, was as fair as you;
But since she did neglect her looking-glass
And threw her sun-expelling mask away,
The air hath starv'd the roses in her cheeks
And pinch'd the lily-tincture of her face,
That now she is become as black as I.
SILVIA
How tall was she?
JULIA
About my stature; for at Pentecost,
When all our pageants of delight were play'd,
Our youth got me to play the woman's part,
And I was trimm'd in Madam Julia's gown,
Which served me as fit, by all men's judgments,
As if the garment had been made for me.
Therefore I know she is about my height.
And at that time I made her weep agood,
For I did play a lamentable part:
Madam, 'twas Ariadne passioning
For Theseus' perjury and unjust flight;
Which I so lively acted with my tears
That my poor mistress, moved therewithal,
Wept bitterly; and would I might be dead
If I in thought felt not her very sorrow!
SILVIA
She is beholding to thee, gentle youth.
Alas, poor lady, desolate and left!
I weep myself to think upon thy words.
Here, youth, there is my purse. [*Gives money.*] I give thee this
For thy sweet mistress' sake, because thou lov'st her.
Farewell. [*Exit Silvia, with attendants.*]
JULIA
And she shall thank you for 't, if e'er you know her.
A virtuous gentlewoman, mild and beautiful!
I hope my master's suit will be but cold,
Since she respects my mistress' love so much.
Alas, how love can trifle with itself!
Here is her picture. [*Looks at picture.*] Let me see; I think,
If I had such a tire, this face of mine
Were full as lovely as is this of hers;
And yet the painter flatter'd her a little,
Unless I flatter with myself too much.
Her hair is auburn, mine is perfect yellow;
If that be all the difference in his love,
I'll get me such a color'd periwig.

121 unadvis'd inadvertently **139 tender** feel sympathetically toward

147 passing surpassingly **152 sun-expelling mask** a mask to keep the complexion fair (considered more beautiful than a tan) **153 starv'd** caused to die **155 black** of a dark complexion, tanned **157 Pentecost** Whitsuntide (seven weeks after Easter) **158 pageants of delight** delightful entertainments **160 trimm'd** dressed up **164 agood** in earnest **166 Ariadne** daughter of Minos, King of Crete. (Ariadne, having fallen in love with one of her father's captives, Theseus, gave him a clue of thread by which he was able to find his way out of the labyrinth. He fled with her, but abandoned her on the island of Naxos.) **passioning** sorrowing **172 beholding** indebted, beholden **184 tire** headdress

Her eyes are grey as glass, and so are mine.
Ay, but her forehead's low, and mine's as high. 192
What should it be that he respects in her
But I can make respective in myself, 194
If this fond Love were not a blinded god? 195
Come, shadow, come, and take this shadow up, 196
For 'tis thy rival. O thou senseless form,
Thou shalt be worship'd, kiss'd, lov'd, and ador'd!
And, were there sense in his idolatry, 199
My substance should be statue in thy stead. 200
I'll use thee kindly for thy mistress' sake,
That us'd me so; or else, by Jove I vow,
I should have scratch'd out your unseeing eyes,
To make my master out of love with thee! *Exit.*

ACT V • SCENE I

Enter Eglamour.

EGLAMOUR
The sun begins to gild the western sky,
And now it is about the very hour
That Silvia at Friar Patrick's cell should meet me.
She will not fail, for lovers break not hours
Unless it be to come before their time,
So much they spur their expedition.
See where she comes.

[Enter] Silvia.

Lady, a happy evening!

SILVIA
Amen, amen! Go on, good Eglamour,
Out at the postern by the abbey wall. 9
I fear I am attended by some spies.

EGLAMOUR
Fear not. The forest is not three leagues off;
If we recover that, we are sure enough. *Exeunt.* 12

SCENE II

Enter Thurio, Proteus, [and] Julia.

THURIO
Sir Proteus, what says Silvia to my suit?

PROTEUS
O, sir, I find her milder than she was,
And yet she takes exceptions at your person. 3

THURIO
What, that my leg is too long?

PROTEUS
No; that it is too little.

THURIO
I'll wear a boot, to make it somewhat rounder.

JULIA *[Aside]*
But love will not be spurr'd to what it loathes. 7

THURIO
What says she to my face?

PROTEUS
She says it is a fair one.

THURIO
Nay then, the wanton lies; my face is black. 10

PROTEUS
But pearls are fair, and the old saying is,
Black men are pearls in beauteous ladies' eyes. 12

JULIA *[Aside]*
'Tis true, such pearls as put out ladies' eyes, 13
For I had rather wink than look on them. 14

THURIO
How likes she my discourse?

PROTEUS
Ill, when you talk of war.

THURIO
But well, when I discourse of love and peace?

JULIA *[Aside]*
But better, indeed, when you hold your peace. 18

THURIO
What says she to my valor?

PROTEUS
O, sir, she makes no doubt of that. 20

JULIA *[Aside]*
She needs not, when she knows it cowardice.

THURIO
What says she to my birth?

PROTEUS
That you are well deriv'd. 23

JULIA *[Aside]*
True; from a gentleman to a fool.

THURIO
Considers she my possessions?

PROTEUS
O, ay, and pities them. 26

THURIO
Wherefore?

JULIA *[Aside]*
That such an ass should owe them. 28

PROTEUS
That they are out by lease. 29

JULIA
Here comes the Duke.

[Enter] Duke.

DUKE
How now, Sir Proteus? How now, Thurio?
Which of you saw Sir Eglamour of late?

192 as high i.e., as high as hers is low **194 respective** worthy of regard **195 fond** foolish **196 shadow . . . shadow** i.e., (1) the mere shadow of myself (2) the picture of Silvia. (See also IV.ii.120–124.) **take . . . up** (1) pick up, carry (2) oppose, accept a challenge **199 sense** reason **200 My . . . stead** i.e., my real person would be the object of his veneration, his idol, instead of Silvia's mere picture

V.i. Location: Milan. An abbey.
9 postern small back or side door **12 recover** reach. **sure** safe

V.ii. Location: Milan. The Duke's palace.
3 takes exceptions at finds fault with

7 spurr'd incited (with a quibble on *boot*, i.e., "riding boot," in the preceding line) **10 black** dark, tanned (as contrasted with *fair*, light-skinned) **12 pearls** i.e., rare and beautiful objects **13 pearls** i. e., cataracts **14 wink** close the eyes **18 hold your peace** are silent (with quibble on *peace* in previous line) **20 makes . . . of** has no uncertainty about. (A deliberately ambiguous reply.) **23 deriv'd** descended **26 pities** (1) shows concern for (2) despises **28 owe** own **29 out by lease** rented out

THURIO
Not I.
PROTEUS Nor I.
DUKE Saw you my daughter?
PROTEUS Neither.
DUKE
Why then
She's fled unto that peasant Valentine,
And Eglamour is in her company.
'Tis true, for Friar Laurence met them both,
As he in penance wander'd through the forest.
Him he knew well, and guess'd that it was she,
But, being mask'd, he was not sure of it.
Besides, she did intend confession
At Patrick's cell this even, and there she was not.
These likelihoods confirm her flight from hence.
Therefore, I pray you, stand not to discourse,
But mount you presently and meet with me
Upon the rising of the mountain foot
That leads toward Mantua, whither they are fled.
Dispatch, sweet gentlemen, and follow me. *[Exit.]*
THURIO
Why, this it is to be a peevish girl,
That flies her fortune when it follows her.
I'll after, more to be reveng'd on Eglamour
Than for the love of reckless Silvia. *[Exit.]*
PROTEUS
And I will follow, more for Silvia's love
Than hate of Eglamour that goes with her. *[Exit.]*
JULIA
And I will follow, more to cross that love
Than hate for Silvia that is gone for love. *Exit.*

SCENE III

[Enter] Silvia, [led by] Outlaws.

FIRST OUTLAW
Come, come,
Be patient. We must bring you to our captain.
SILVIA
A thousand more mischances than this one
Have learn'd me how to brook this patiently.
SECOND OUTLAW
Come, bring her away.
FIRST OUTLAW
Where is the gentleman that was with her?
THIRD OUTLAW
Being nimble-footed, he hath outrun us,
But Moyses and Valerius follow him.
Go thou with her to the west end of the wood;
There is our captain. We'll follow him that's fled.
The thicket is beset; he cannot scape.
FIRST OUTLAW
Come, I must bring you to our captain's cave.
Fear not; he bears an honorable mind,
And will not use a woman lawlessly.
SILVIA
O Valentine, this I endure for thee! *Exeunt.*

SCENE IV

Enter Valentine.

VALENTINE
How use doth breed a habit in a man!
This shadowy desert, unfrequented woods,
I better brook than flourishing peopled towns.
Here can I sit alone, unseen of any,
And to the nightingale's complaining notes
Tune my distresses and record my woes.
O thou that dost inhabit in my breast,
Leave not the mansion so long tenantless,
Lest, growing ruinous, the building fall
And leave no memory of what it was!
Repair me with thy presence, Silvia;
Thou gentle nymph, cherish thy forlorn swain!
[Shouting within.]
What halloing and what stir is this today?
These are my mates, that make their wills their law,
Have some unhappy passenger in chase.
They love me well, yet I have much to do
To keep them from uncivil outrages.
Withdraw thee, Valentine. Who's this comes here?
[Withdraws.]

[Enter] Proteus, Silvia, [and] Julia [disguised as Sebastian].

PROTEUS
Madam, this service I have done for you,
Though you respect not aught your servant doth,
To hazard life and rescue you from him
That would have forc'd your honor and your love.
Vouchsafe me, for my meed, but one fair look;
A smaller boon than this I cannot beg,
And less than this, I am sure, you cannot give.
VALENTINE *[Aside]*
How like a dream is this I see and hear!
Love, lend me patience to forbear awhile.
SILVIA
O miserable, unhappy that I am!
PROTEUS
Unhappy were you, madam, ere I came;
But by my coming I have made you happy.
SILVIA
By thy approach thou mak'st me most unhappy.

48 Dispatch make haste

V.iii. Location: The frontiers of Mantua. The forest.
4 learn'd taught. **brook** endure **11 beset** surrounded

V.iv. Location: Another part of the forest.
1 use custom **2 desert** deserted region **3 brook** endure **6 record** sing
15 Have who have. **unhappy** unlucky **23 meed** reward. **fair** kind **31 approach** advances

JULIA [*Aside*]
And me, when he approacheth to your presence.

SILVIA
Had I been seized by a hungry lion,
I would have been a breakfast to the beast,
Rather than have false Proteus rescue me.
O, heaven be judge how I love Valentine,
Whose life's as tender to me as my soul!
And full as much—for more there cannot be—
I do detest false perjur'd Proteus.
Therefore be gone, solicit me no more.

PROTEUS
What dangerous action, stood it next to death,
Would I not undergó for one calm look?
O, 'tis the curse in love, and still approv'd,
When women cannot love where they're belov'd!

SILVIA
When Proteus cannot love where he's belov'd.
Read over Julia's heart, thy first best love,
For whose dear sake thou didst then rend thy faith
Into a thousand oaths, and all those oaths
Descended into perjury, to love me.
Thou hast no faith left now, unless thou 'dst two,
And that's far worse than none. Better have none
Than plural faith, which is too much by one.
Thou counterfeit to thy true friend!

PROTEUS
In love
Who respects friend?

SILVIA
All men but Proteus.

PROTEUS
Nay, if the gentle spirit of moving words
Can no way change you to a milder form,
I'll woo you like a soldier, at arms' end,
And love you 'gainst the nature of love—force ye.

SILVIA
O heaven!

PROTEUS I'll force thee yield to my desire.

VALENTINE [*Coming forward*]
Ruffian, let go that rude uncivil touch,
Thou friend of an ill fashion!

PROTEUS
Valentine!

VALENTINE
Thou common friend, that's without faith or love,
For such is a friend now! Treacherous man,
Thou hast beguil'd my hopes! Nought but mine eye
Could have persuaded me. Now I dare not say
I have one friend alive; thou wouldst disprove me.
Who should be trusted, when one's right hand
Is perjured to the bosom? Proteus,
I am sorry I must never trust thee more,
But count the world a stranger for thy sake.
The private wound is deepest. O time most accurst,
'Mongst all foes that a friend should be the worst!

PROTEUS
My shame and guilt confounds me.
Forgive me, Valentine. If hearty sorrow
Be a sufficient ransom for offense,
I tender 't here. I do as truly suffer
As e'er I did commit.

VALENTINE
Then I am paid,
And once again I do receive thee honest.
Who by repentance is not satisfied
Is nor of heaven nor earth, for these are pleas'd.
By penitence th' Eternal's wrath 's appeas'd;
And, that my love may appear plain and free,
All that was mine in Silvia I give thee.

JULIA
O me unhappy! [*Swoons.*]

PROTEUS Look to the boy.

VALENTINE Why, boy! Why, wag! How now? What's the matter? Look up; speak.

JULIA O good sir, my master charg'd me to deliver a ring to Madam Silvia, which, out of my neglect, was never done.

PROTEUS
Where is that ring, boy?

JULIA
Here 'tis; this is it. [*Gives ring.*]

PROTEUS
How? Let me see.
Why, this is the ring I gave to Julia.

JULIA
O, cry you mercy, sir, I have mistook.
This is the ring you sent to Silvia.
[*Shows another ring.*]

PROTEUS
But how cam'st thou by this ring? At my depart
I gave this unto Julia.

JULIA
And Julia herself did give it me;
And Julia herself hath brought it hither.
[*She reveals herself.*]

PROTEUS
How? Julia?

JULIA
Behold her that gave aim to all thy oaths,
And entertain'd 'em deeply in her heart.
How oft hast thou with perjury cleft the root!
O Proteus, let this habit make thee blush!
Be thou asham'd that I have took upon me
Such an immodest raiment, if shame live
In a disguise of love.
It is the lesser blot, modesty finds,
Women to change their shapes than men their minds.

PROTEUS
Than men their minds! 'Tis true. O heaven! Were man
But constant, he were perfect. That one error
Fills him with faults, makes him run through all th' sins;
Inconstancy falls off ere it begins.
What is in Silvia's face, but I may spy

37 tender dear **42 undergo** undertake. **calm** gentle, kind **43 still approv'd** continually reaffirmed by experience **57 arms' end** sword's point (with bawdy suggestion) **61 fashion** kind, sort **62 common** ordinary, superficial

77 commit sin **78 receive** acknowledge **82 love** friendship **86 wag** (A term of endearment for a youth.) **94 cry you mercy** I beg your pardon **101 gave aim to** was the object of **104 this habit** i.e., her page's costume **106–107 if shame . . . love** if a disguise undertaken for love can be thought shameful; or, if one who feigns love can feel shame **113 Inconstancy . . . begins** i.e., inconstant love falls away from loving almost before it has even begun

More fresh in Julia's with a constant eye?

VALENTINE
Come, come, a hand from either.
Let me be blest to make this happy close;
'Twere pity two such friends should be long foes.

PROTEUS
Bear witness, heaven, I have my wish forever.

JULIA
And I mine. [*They join hands.*]

[*Enter*] *Duke* [*and*] *Thurio,* [*led by*] *Outlaws.*

OUTLAWS
A prize, a prize, a prize!

VALENTINE
Forbear, forbear, I say! It is my lord the Duke.
Your Grace is welcome to a man disgrac'd,
Banished Valentine.

DUKE
Sir Valentine!

THURIO [*Advancing*]
Yonder is Silvia, and Silvia's mine.

VALENTINE [*Drawing sword*]
Thurio, give back, or else embrace thy death.
Come not within the measure of my wrath.
Do not name Silvia thine; if once again,
Verona shall not hold thee. Here she stands.
Take but possession of her with a touch;
I dare thee but to breathe upon my love.

THURIO
Sir Valentine, I care not for her, I.
I hold him but a fool that will endanger
His body for a girl that loves him not.
I claim her not, and therefore she is thine.

DUKE
The more degenerate and base art thou,
To make such means for her as thou hast done
And leave her on such slight conditions.
Now, by the honor of my ancestry,
I do applaud thy spirit, Valentine,
And think thee worthy of an empress' love.
Know then, I here forget all former griefs,
Cancel all grudge, repeal thee home again,
Plead a new state in thy unrival'd merit,
To which I thus subscribe: Sir Valentine,
Thou art a gentleman and well deriv'd.
Take thou thy Silvia, for thou hast deserv'd her.

VALENTINE
I thank your Grace; the gift hath made me happy.
I now beseech you, for your daughter's sake,
To grant one boon that I shall ask of you.

DUKE
I grant it, for thine own, whate'er it be.

VALENTINE
These banish'd men, that I have kept withal,
Are men endu'd with worthy qualities.
Forgive them what they have committed here,
And let them be recall'd from their exile.
They are reformed, civil, full of good,
And fit for great employment, worthy lord.

DUKE
Thou hast prevail'd; I pardon them and thee.
Dispose of them as thou know'st their deserts.
Come, let us go. We will include all jars
With triumphs, mirth, and rare solemnity.

VALENTINE
And, as we walk along, I dare be bold
With our discourse to make your Grace to smile.
What think you of this page, my lord?

DUKE
I think the boy hath grace in him; he blushes.

VALENTINE
I warrant you, my lord, more grace than boy.

DUKE
What mean you by that saying?

VALENTINE
Please you, I'll tell you as we pass along,
That you will wonder what hath fortuned.
Come, Proteus, 'tis your penance but to hear
The story of your loves discovered.
That done, our day of marriage shall be yours:
One feast, one house, one mutual happiness. *Exeunt.*

115 constant steady, loyal **117 close** union, conclusion **126 give back** stand back **127 measure** reach **129 Verona** (Again, probably an error for *Milan;* see III.i.80.) **137 means** exertions **138 on . . . conditions** for such a flimsy reason **142 griefs** grievances **143 repeal** recall **144 Plead . . . merit** i.e., I justify my abrupt reversal of my former judgment by noting your newly demonstrated superiority to Thurio **152 kept withal** lived with

160 include all jars conclude all discords **169 wonder** marvel. **fortuned** happened

The Taming of the Shrew

Like other early comedies, *The Taming of the Shrew* (c. 1592–1594) looks forward to Shakespeare's mature comic drama in several ways. By skillfully juxtaposing two plots and an "Induction," or framing plot, it offers contrasting views on the battle of the sexes. This debate on the nature of the love relationship continues through many later comedies, somewhat in the manner of Chaucer's "Marriage Group." Moreover, the play adroitly manipulates the device of mistaken identity, as in *The Comedy of Errors,* inverting appearance and reality, dream and awakening, and the master-servant relationship in order to create a transformed Saturnalian world anticipating that of *A Midsummer Night's Dream* and *Twelfth Night.*

The Induction sets up the theme of illusion, using an old motif known as "The Sleeper Awakened" (as found for example in *The Arabian Nights*). This device "frames" the main action of the play, giving to it an added perspective. *The Taming of the Shrew* purports in fact to be a play within a play, an entertainment devised by a witty nobleman as a practical joke on a drunken tinker, Christophero Sly. The jest is to convince Sly that he is not Sly at all, but an aristocrat suffering delusions. Outlandishly dressed in new finery, Sly is invited to witness a play from the gallery over the stage. In a version of the play called *The Taming of a Shrew,* printed in 1594 and now generally thought to be an imitation of Shakespeare's play by a rival dramatist (who relied chiefly on memory and who liberally changed the characters' names and setting), the framing plot concludes by actually putting Sly back out on the street in front of the alehouse where he was found. He awakes, recalls the play as a dream, and proposes to put the vision to good use by taming his own wife. Whether this ending reflects an epilogue now lost from the text of Shakespeare's play cannot be said, but it does reinforce the idea of the play as Sly's fantasy. Like Puck at the end of *A Midsummer Night's Dream,* urging us to dismiss what we have seen as the product of our own slumbering, Sly continually reminds us that the play is only an illusion or shadow.

With repeated daring, Shakespeare calls attention to the contrived nature of his artifact, the play. When, for example, Sly is finally convinced that he is in fact a noble lord recovering from madness, and lustily proposes to hasten off to bed with his long-neglected wife, we are comically aware that the wife or "lady" is an impostor, a young page in disguise. Yet this counterfeiting of roles is no more unreal than the employment of Elizabethan boy-actors for the parts of Katharina and Bianca in the "real" play. As we watch Sly watching a play, levels of meaning interplay in this evocative fashion. Again, the paintings offered to Sly by his new attendants call attention to art's ability to confound illusion and reality. In one painting, Cytherea is hidden by water-rushes "Which seem to move and wanton with her breath Even as the waving sedges play with wind," and in another painting Io appears "As lively painted as the deed was done." Sly's function, then, is that of the naive observer who inverts illusion and reality in his mind, concluding that his whole previous life of tinkers and alehouses and Cicely Hackets has been unreal. As his attendants explain to him, "These fifteen years you have been in a dream; Or when you wak'd, so wak'd as if you slept." We laugh at Sly's naiveté, and yet we too are moved and even transformed by an artistic vision that we know to be illusory.

Like Sly, many characters in the main action of the play are persuaded, or nearly persuaded, to be what they are not. Lucentio and Tranio exchange roles of master and servant. Bianca's supposed tutors are in fact her wooers, using their lessons to disguise messages of love. Katharina is prevailed upon by her husband, Petruchio, to declare that the sun is the moon and that an old gentleman (Vincentio) is a fair young maiden. Vincentio is publicly informed that he is an impostor, and that the "real" Vincentio (the Pedant) is at that very moment looking at him out of the window of his son Lucentio's house. This last ruse does not fool the real Vincentio, but it nearly succeeds in fooling everyone else. Baptista Minola is about to commit Vincentio to jail for the infamous slander of asserting that the supposed Lucentio is only a servant in disguise. Vincentio, as the newly arrived stranger, is able to see matters as they really are; but the dwellers of Padua have grown so accustomed to the mad and improbable fictions of their life that they are not easily awakened to reality.

Shakespeare multiplies these devices of illusion by combining two entirely distinct plots, each concerned at least in part with the comic inversion of appearance and reality: the shrew-taming plot involving Petruchio and Kate, and the more conventional romantic plot involving Lucentio and Bianca. The latter plot is derived from the *Supposes* of George Gascoigne, a play first presented at Gray's Inn in 1566 as translated from Ariosto's neoclassical comedy *I Suppositi,* 1509. (Ariosto's work was based in turn upon Terence's *Eunuchus* and Plautus' *Captivi.*) The "Supposes" are mistaken identities or misunderstandings, the kind of hilarious farcical mix-ups Shakespeare had already experimented with in *The Comedy of Errors.* Shakespeare has, as usual, both romanticized his source and moralized it in a characteristically English way. The heroine, who in classical "new" comedy would have been a courtesan, and who in *Supposes* is made pregnant by her clandestine lover, remains thoroughly chaste in Shakespeare's comedy. Consequently she has no need for a pander or go-between, such as the bawdy Duenna or Nurse of *Supposes.* The satire directed at the heroine's unwelcome old wooer is far less savage than in *Supposes,* where the "pantaloon," Dr. Cleander, is a villainously corrupt lawyer epitomizing the depravity of "respectable" society. Despite Shakespeare's modifications, however, the basic plot involves an effort to foil parental authority, using a "trick to catch the old one." The young lovers, choosing one another for romantic reasons, must fend off the materialistic calculations of their parents.

Because this comic situation is "stock" or conventional, the character types in this plot are also conventional. Gremio, the aged wealthy wooer, is actually labeled a "pantaloon" in the text (III,i) to stress his neoclassical ancestry. (Lean and foolish old wooers of this sort were customarily dressed in pantaloons, slippers, and spectacles on the Italian stage.) Gremio is typically "the greybeard," and Baptista Minola is "the narrow-prying father" (III,ii). Even though Shakespeare renders these "blocking" characters, or *alazons,* far less unattractive than in *Supposes,* their worldly behavior still invites reprisal from the young. Since Baptista Minola insists on selling his daughter Bianca to the highest bidder, it is fitting that her wealthiest suitor (the supposed Lucentio) should turn out in the end to be a penniless servant (Tranio) disguised as a man of affluence and position. In his traditional role as the clever servant of neoclassical comedy, Tranio skillfully apes the mannerisms of respectable society. He can deal in mere surfaces, or clothes, or reputation, out of which a man's social importance is created, and can even furnish himself with a rich father. Gremio and Baptista deserve to be foiled because they accept the illusion of respectability as real.

Even the romantic lovers of this borrowed plot are largely conventional. To be sure, Shakespeare emphasizes their virtuous qualities and their sincerity. He adds Hortensio (not in *Supposes*) to provide Lucentio with a genuine if foolish rival and Bianca with two wooers closer to her age than old Gremio. Lucentio and Bianca deserve their romantic triumph; they are self-possessed, witty, and steadfast to one another. Yet we know very little about them, nor have they seen deeply into one another. Lucentio's love-talk is laden with conventional Petrarchan images in praise of Bianca's dark eyes and scarlet lips. He discovers to his surprise, at the play's end, that she can be willful, even disobedient. Has her appearance of virtue concealed something from him and from us? Because the relationship between these lovers is superficial, they are appropriately destined to a superficial marriage as well. The passive Bianca becomes the proud and unmanageable wife.

By contrast, Petruchio and Kate are the more interesting lovers whose courtship involves mutual self-discovery. Admittedly, we must not overstate the case. Especially at first, these lovers are also stock types: the shrew-tamer and his proverbially shrewish wife. Although Shakespeare seems not to have used any single source for this plot, he was well acquainted with crude antifeminist stories demonstrating the need for putting women in their place. In a ballad called *A Merry Jest of a Shrewde and Curste Wyfe, Lapped in Morrelles Skin* (printed c. 1550), for example, the husband tames his shrewish spouse by flaying her bloody with birch rods and then wrapping her in the freshly salted skin of a plough-horse named Morel. (This shrewish wife, like Kate, has an obedient and gentle younger sister who is their father's favorite.) Other features of Shakespeare's plot can be found in similar tales: the tailor scolded for devising a gown of outlandish fashion (Gerard Legh's *Accidence of Armory,* 1562), the wife obliged to agree with her husband's assertion of some patent falsehood (Don Juan Manuel's *El Conde Lucanor,* 1335), and the three husbands' wager on their wives' obedience (*The Book of the Knight of La Tour-Landry,* printed 1484). In the raw spirit of this antifeminist tradition, so unlike the refined Italianate sentiment of his other plot, Shakespeare introduces Petruchio as a man of reckless bravado who is ready to marry the ugliest or sharpest-tongued woman alive so long as she is rich. However much he may be later attracted by Kate's fiery spirit, his first attraction to her is crassly financial. Kate is, moreover, a thoroughly disagreeable young woman at first, described by those who know her as "intolerable curst And shrewd and froward," aggressive in her bullying of Bianca. She and Petruchio meet as grotesque comic counterparts. Even at the play's end, the traditional pattern of male dominance and female acquiescence is still of course prominent. Kate achieves peace only by yielding to a divinely ordained hierarchical framework in which a husband is the princely ruler of his subservient wife.

Within this male-oriented frame of reference, however, Petruchio and Kate are surprisingly like Benedick and Beatrice of *Much Ado about Nothing*. Petruchio, for all his rant, is increasingly drawn to Kate by her spirit. As wit-combatants they are worthy of one another's enmity—or love. No one else in the play is a fit match for either of them. Kate too is attracted to Petruchio, despite her war of words. Her guise of hostility is part defensive protection, part testing of his sincerity. If she is contemptuous of the wooers she has seen till now, she has good reason to be so. We share her condescension toward the aged Gremio or the laughably inept Hortensio. She rightly fears that her father wishes to dispose of her so that he may auction off Bianca to the wealthiest competitor. Kate's jaded view of such marriage-broking is entirely defensible. Not surprisingly she first views Petruchio, whose professed intentions are far from reassuring, as another mere gamester in love. She is impressed by his "line" in wooing her, but needs to test his constancy and sincerity. Quite possibly, then, she is a woman who has always wanted to be possessed, but only by a man she can respect. She puts most men down with a shrewish manner that challenges their very masculinity; Petruchio is the first to be man enough to "board" her. He senses that she really longs to be mastered, even though she resists. His "schooling" is therefore curative. Having wooed and partly won her, he tests her with his late arrival at the marriage, his unconventional dress, and his crossing all her desires. In this display of willfulness, he shows her an ugly picture of what she herself is like. Most of all, however, he succeeds because he insists on what she too desires: subordination tempered by mutual respect and love. Kate is visibly a happier person at the play's end. Her closing speech, with its fine blend of irony and self-conscious hyperbole, together with its seriousness of concern, expresses beautifully the way in which Kate's independence of spirit and her newfound satisfaction in submissiveness are successfully fused.

The Taming of the Shrew

[*Dramatis Personae*

A LORD,
CHRISTOPHERO SLY, *a tinker*,
HOSTESS, PAGE, PLAYERS,
HUNTSMEN, *and* SERVANTS. } *Persons in the Induction.*

BAPTISTA, *a rich gentleman of Padua.*
VINCENTIO, *an old gentleman of Pisa.*
LUCENTIO, *son to Vincentio, in love with Bianca.*
PETRUCHIO, *a gentleman of Verona, a suitor to Katharina.*
GREMIO,
HORTENSIO, } *suitors to Bianca.*
TRANIO,
BIONDELLO, } *servants to Lucentio.*
GRUMIO,
CURTIS, } *servants to Petruchio.*
A PEDANT.

KATHARINA, *the shrew*,
BIANCA, } *daughters to Baptista.*
WIDOW.

TAILOR, HABERDASHER, *and* SERVANTS *attending on Baptista and Petruchio.*

SCENE: *Padua, and Petruchio's country house in Italy; the Induction is located in the countryside and at a Lord's house in England.*]

[INDUCTION] SCENE I

Enter Beggar (Christophero Sly) and Hostess.

SLY I'll pheeze you, in faith.

HOSTESS A pair of stocks, you rogue!

SLY Y' are a baggage, the Slys are no rogues. Look in the chronicles; we came in with Richard Conqueror. Therefore paucas pallabris, let the world slide. Sessa!

HOSTESS You will not pay for the glasses you have burst?

Induction i. Location: Before a country alehouse, and subsequently before the Lord's house nearby. (See ll.75,135.)

1 pheeze you i.e., settle your hash, get even with you **2 A . . . stocks** i.e., I'll have you put in the stocks **4 Richard** (Sly's mistake for *William.*) **5 paucas pallabris** i.e., *pocas palabras*, "few words." (Spanish.) **Sessa** (Of doubtful meaning; perhaps *be quiet, cease,* or *let it go.*)

SLY No, not a denier. Go by, Saint Jeronimy, go to thy cold bed, and warm thee.

HOSTESS I know my remedy: I must go fetch the thirdborough. *[Exit.]*

SLY Third, or fourth, or fifth borough, I'll answer him by law. I'll not budge an inch, boy; let him come, and kindly. *Falls asleep.*

Wind horns [within]. Enter a Lord from hunting, with his train.

LORD
Huntsman, I charge thee, tender well my hounds—
Brach Merriman, the poor cur, is emboss'd;
And couple Clowder with the deep-mouth'd brach.
Saw'st thou not, boy, how Silver made it good
At the hedge-corner, in the coldest fault?
I would not lose the dog for twenty pound.

FIRST HUNTSMAN
Why, Belman is as good as he, my lord.
He cried upon it at the merest loss
And twice today pick'd out the dullest scent.
Trust me, I take him for the better dog.

LORD
Thou art a fool. If Echo were as fleet,
I would esteem him worth a dozen such.
But sup them well and look unto them all.
Tomorrow I intend to hunt again.

FIRST HUNTSMAN
I will, my lord.

LORD *[Seeing Sly]*
What's here? One dead, or drunk? See, doth he breathe?

SECOND HUNTSMAN *[Examining Sly]*
He breathes, my lord. Were he not warm'd with ale,
This were a bed but cold to sleep so soundly.

LORD
O monstrous beast, how like a swine he lies!
Grim death, how foul and loathsome is thine image!
Sirs, I will practice on this drunken man.
What think you, if he were convey'd to bed,
Wrapp'd in sweet clothes, rings put upon his fingers,
A most delicious banquet by his bed,
And brave attendants near him when he wakes,
Would not the beggar then forget himself?

FIRST HUNTSMAN
Believe me, lord, I think he cannot choose.

SECOND HUNTSMAN
It would seem strange unto him when he wak'd.

LORD
Even as a flatt'ring dream or worthless fancy.
Then take him up and manage well the jest.
Carry him gently to my fairest chamber
And hang it round with all my wanton pictures.
Balm his foul head in warm distilled waters
And burn sweet wood to make the lodging sweet.
Procure me music ready when he wakes,
To make a dulcet and a heavenly sound.
And if he chance to speak, be ready straight
And with a low submissive reverence
Say "What is it your honor will command?"
Let one attend him with a silver basin
Full of rose-water and bestrew'd with flowers,
Another bear the ewer, the third a diaper,
And say "Will 't please your lordship cool your hands?"
Someone be ready with a costly suit
And ask him what apparel he will wear;
Another tell him of his hounds and horse,
And that his lady mourns at his disease.
Persuade him that he hath been lunatic,
And when he says he is, say that he dreams,
For he is nothing but a mighty lord.
This do and do it kindly, gentle sirs.
It will be pastime passing excellent,
If it be husbanded with modesty.

FIRST HUNTSMAN
My lord, I warrant you we will play our part
As he shall think by our true diligence
He is no less than what we say he is.

LORD
Take him up gently and to bed with him,
And each one to his office when he wakes.
[Some bear out Sly.] Sound trumpets [within].
Sirrah, go see what trumpet 'tis that sounds.
[Exit Servingman.]
Belike some noble gentleman that means,
Traveling some journey, to repose him here.

Enter Servingman.

How now? Who is it?

SERVINGMAN An 't please your honor, players
That offer service to your lordship.

Enter Players.

LORD
Bid them come near.—Now, fellows, you are welcome.

PLAYERS
We thank your honor.

LORD
Do you intend to stay with me tonight?

SECOND PLAYER
So please your lordship to accept our duty.

LORD
With all my heart. This fellow I remember
Since once he play'd a farmer's eldest son.
'Twas where you woo'd the gentlewoman so well.

8 denier copper coin of small value. **Go . . . Jeronimy** (Sly's variation of an often-quoted line from Kyd's *The Spanish Tragedy,* expressing impatience.) **8–9 go . . . thee** (Perhaps a proverb; see *King Lear* III.iv.47.) **10–11 thirdborough** constable **12 Third** (Sly shows his ignorance; the *third* in "thirdborough" derives from the Old English word *frith,* peace.) **14 kindly** welcome **14 s.d. Wind** blow **15 tender** care for **16 Brach** bitch hound. **emboss'd** foaming at the mouth from exhaustion **19 fault** loss of scent **22 cried . . . loss** bayed to signal recovery of the scent after it had been completely lost **34 image** likeness (since sleep was regarded as a likeness of death) **35 practice on** play a joke on **37 sweet** perfumed **38 banquet** light repast **39 brave** finely arrayed **43 fancy** flight of imagination

51 straight at once **56 diaper** towel **65 kindly** naturally (and thus persuasively) **66 passing** surpassingly **67 husbanded with modesty** managed with decorum **69 As** so that **72 office** duty **73 Sirrah** (Usual form of address to inferiors.) **74 Belike** perhaps **81 duty** expression of respect

I have forgot your name, but, sure, that part
Was aptly fitted and naturally perform'd.

FIRST PLAYER
I think 'twas Soto that your honor means.

LORD
'Tis very true. Thou didst it excellent.
Well, you are come to me in happy time,
The rather for I have some sport in hand
Wherein your cunning can assist me much.
There is a lord will hear you play tonight.
But I am doubtful of your modesties,
Lest, over-eyeing of his odd behavior—
For yet his honor never heard a play—
You break into some merry passion
And so offend him; for I tell you, sirs,
If you should smile he grows impatient.

FIRST PLAYER
Fear not, my lord, we can contain ourselves
Were he the veriest antic in the world.

LORD
Go, sirrah, take them to the buttery,
And give them friendly welcome every one.
Let them want nothing that my house affords.
Exit one with the Players.
Sirrah, go you to Barthol'mew my page,
And see him dress'd in all suits like a lady.
That done, conduct him to the drunkard's chamber,
And call him "madam," do him obeisance.
Tell him from me, as he will win my love,
He bear himself with honorable action,
Such as he hath observ'd in noble ladies
Unto their lords, by them accomplished.
Such duty to the drunkard let him do
With soft low tongue and lowly courtesy,
And say, "What is 't your honor will command,
Wherein your lady and your humble wife
May show her duty and make known her love?"
And then with kind embracements, tempting kisses,
And with declining head into his bosom,
Bid him shed tears, as being overjoyed
To see her noble lord restor'd to health,
Who for this seven years hath esteemed him
No better than a poor and loathsome beggar.
And if the boy have not a woman's gift
To rain a shower of commanded tears,
An onion will do well for such a shift,
Which in a napkin being close convey'd
Shall in despite enforce a watery eye.
See this dispatch'd with all the haste thou canst.
Anon I'll give thee more instructions.
Exit a Servingman.
I know the boy will well usurp the grace,
Voice, gait, and action of a gentlewoman.
I long to hear him call the drunkard husband,
And how my men will stay themselves from laughter
When they do homage to this simple peasant.
I'll in to counsel them. Haply my presence
May well abate the over-merry spleen
Which otherwise would grow into extremes.
[*Exeunt.*]

[SCENE II]

Enter aloft the Drunkard [*Sly*], *with Attendants; some with apparel, basin, and ewer and other appurtenances; and Lord.*

SLY For God's sake, a pot of small ale.

FIRST SERVANT
Will 't please your lordship drink a cup of sack?

SECOND SERVANT
Will 't please your honor taste of these conserves?

THIRD SERVANT
What raiment will your honor wear today?

SLY I am Christophero Sly, call not me "honor" nor "lordship." I ne'er drank sack in my life; and if you give me any conserves, give me conserves of beef. Ne'er ask me what raiment I'll wear, for I have no more doublets than backs, no more stockings than legs, nor no more shoes than feet—nay, sometime more feet than shoes, or such shoes as my toes look through the overleather.

LORD
Heaven cease this idle humor in your honor!
O, that a mighty man of such descent,
Of such possessions and so high esteem,
Should be infused with so foul a spirit!

SLY What, would you make me mad? Am not I Christopher Sly, old Sly's son of Burton-heath, by birth a pedlar, by education a card-maker, by transmutation a bear-herd, and now by present profession a tinker? Ask Marian Hacket, the fat alewife of Wincot, if she know me not. If she say I am not fourteen pence on the score for sheer ale, score me up for the lying'st knave in Christendom. What? I am not bestraught: here's—

THIRD SERVANT
O, this it is that makes your lady mourn!

SECOND SERVANT
O, this is it that makes your servants droop!

LORD
Hence comes it that your kindred shuns your house,

89 happy opportune **90 The rather for** the more so since **93 doubtful** apprehensive. **modesties** discretion, self-control **94 over-eying of** witnessing **96 merry passion** outburst of laughter **100 antic** grotesque figure **101 buttery** room for storing liquor (in butts) and other provisions **103 want** lack **105 in all suits** in every detail **108 him** i.e., the page Bartholomew **121 him** himself **125 shift** purpose **126 napkin** handkerchief. **close** secretly **129 Anon** soon **130 usurp** assume

136 spleen mood. (The spleen was the supposed seat of laughter and anger.)

Induction ii. Location: A bedchamber in the Lord's house.
s.d. aloft i.e., in the gallery over the rear façade of the stage **1 small** weak (and therefore cheap) **2 sack** sweet Spanish wine (suited for a gentleman to drink) **3 conserves** confections, preserves **7 conserves of beef** preserved (salted) beef **9 doublets** men's jackets **13 idle** vain, foolish. **humor** whim, fancy **18 Burton-heath** (Perhaps Barton-on-the-Heath, about sixteen miles from Stratford, the home of Shakespeare's aunt.) **19 card-maker** maker of cards or combs used to prepare wool for spinning **20 bear-herd** keeper of a tame bear. **tinker** pot-mender **21 Wincot** small village about four miles from Stratford. (The parish register shows that there were Hackets living there in 1591.) **22–23 on the score** in debt (since such reckonings were originally notched or scored on a stick) **23 sheer** nothing but. **score me up for** reckon me to be **24 bestraught** distracted

As beaten hence by your strange lunacy.
O noble lord, bethink thee of thy birth,
Call home thy ancient thoughts from banishment
And banish hence these abject lowly dreams.
Look how thy servants do attend on thee,
Each in his office ready at thy beck.
Wilt thou have music? Hark, Apollo plays *Music.*
And twenty caged nightingales do sing.
Or wilt thou sleep? We'll have thee to a couch
Softer and sweeter than the lustful bed
On purpose trimm'd up for Semiramis.
Say thou wilt walk; we will bestrew the ground.
Or wilt thou ride? Thy horses shall be trapp'd,
Their harness studded all with gold and pearl.
Dost thou love hawking? Thou hast hawks will soar
Above the morning lark. Or wilt thou hunt?
Thy hounds shall make the welkin answer them
And fetch shrill echoes from the hollow earth.

FIRST SERVANT
Say thou wilt course; thy greyhounds are as swift
As breathed stags, ay, fleeter than the roe.

SECOND SERVANT
Dost thou love pictures? We will fetch thee straight
Adonis painted by a running brook,
And Cytherea all in sedges hid,
Which seem to move and wanton with her breath,
Even as the waving sedges play with wind.

LORD
We'll show thee Io as she was a maid,
And how she was beguiled and surpris'd,
As lively painted as the deed was done.

THIRD SERVANT
Or Daphne roaming through a thorny wood,
Scratching her legs that one shall swear she bleeds,
And at that sight shall sad Apollo weep,
So workmanly the blood and tears are drawn.

LORD
Thou art a lord and nothing but a lord.
Thou hast a lady far more beautiful
Than any woman in this waning age.

FIRST SERVANT
And till the tears that she hath shed for thee
Like envious floods o'errun her lovely face,
She was the fairest creature in the world;
And yet she is inferior to none.

SLY
Am I a lord? And have I such a lady?
Or do I dream? Or have I dream'd till now?
I do not sleep: I see, I hear, I speak,
I smell sweet savors, and I feel soft things.
Upon my life, I am a lord indeed,
And not a tinker nor Christopher Sly.
Well, bring our lady hither to our sight;
And once again, a pot o' th' smallest ale.

SECOND SERVANT
Will 't please your mightiness to wash your hands?
O, how we joy to see your wit restor'd!
O, that once more you knew but what you are!
These fifteen years you have been in a dream,
Or when you wak'd, so wak'd as if you slept.

SLY
These fifteen years! By my fay, a goodly nap.
But did I never speak of all that time?

FIRST SERVANT
O, yes, my lord, but very idle words;
For though you lay here in this goodly chamber,
Yet would you say ye were beaten out of door,
And rail upon the hostess of the house,
And say you would present her at the leet,
Because she brought stone jugs and no seal'd quarts.
Sometimes you would call out for Cicely Hacket.

SLY
Ay, the woman's maid of the house.

THIRD SERVANT
Why, sir, you know no house nor no such maid,
Nor no such men as you have reckon'd up,
As Stephen Sly, and old John Naps of Greece,
And Peter Turph, and Henry Pimpernell,
And twenty more such names and men as these,
Which never were nor no man ever saw.

SLY
Now Lord be thanked for my good amends!

ALL
Amen.

Enter [the Page as a] lady, with Attendants.

SLY I thank thee. Thou shalt not lose by it.

PAGE
How fares my noble lord?

SLY
Marry, I fare well,
For here is cheer enough. Where is my wife?

PAGE
Here, noble lord. What is thy will with her?

SLY
Are you my wife and will not call me husband?
My men should call me "lord"; I am your goodman.

PAGE
My husband and my lord, my lord and husband,
I am your wife in all obedience.

SLY I know it well.—What must I call her?

LORD
Madam.

SLY Al'ce madam, or Joan madam?

LORD
Madam, and nothing else. So lords call ladies.

SLY
Madam wife, they say that I have dream'd
And slept above some fifteen year or more.

PAGE
Ay, and the time seems thirty unto me,

31 ancient former **35 Apollo** i.e., as god of music **39 Semiramis** legendary queen of Assyria famous for her voluptuousness **41 trapp'd** adorned **45 welkin** sky, heavens **47 course** hunt the hare **48 breathed** in good physical condition, with good wind. **roe** small, swift deer **50 Adonis** a young huntsman with whom Venus is vainly in love. (See Shakespeare's poem *Venus and Adonis*.) **51 Cytherea** one of the names for Venus (because of her association with the island of Cythera) **52 wanton** play seductively **54 Io** one of Jupiter's lovers, transformed by him into a heifer to conceal her from the envious Juno **57 Daphne** a wood nymph beloved by Apollo, changed by Diana into a laurel tree to preserve her from Apollo's assault **63 waning** degenerate **65 envious** spiteful **67 yet** even today

81 fay faith **86 house** tavern **87 present** bring accusation against. **leet** manorial court **88 seal'd quarts** quart containers officially stamped as a guarantee of that capacity **93 Stephen . . . Greece** (A Stephen Sly lived in Stratford during Shakespeare's day. *Greece* is an apparent error for *Greet*, a Gloucestershire hamlet not far from Stratford.) **97 amends** recovery **103 goodman** (A term appropriate to Sly's social class.)

Being all this time abandon'd from your bed.

SLY
'Tis much. Servants, leave me and her alone.
Madam, undress you and come now to bed.

PAGE
Thrice-noble lord, let me entreat of you
To pardon me yet for a night or two,
Or, if not so, until the sun be set.
For your physicians have expressly charg'd,
In peril to incur your former malady,
That I should yet absent me from your bed.
I hope this reason stands for my excuse.

SLY Ay, it stands so that I may hardly tarry so long. But I would be loath to fall into my dreams again. I will therefore tarry in despite of the flesh and the blood.

Enter a Messenger.

MESSENGER
Your honor's players, hearing your amendment,
Are come to play a pleasant comedy;
For so your doctors hold it very meet,
Seeing too much sadness hath congeal'd your blood,
And melancholy is the nurse of frenzy.
Therefore they thought it good you hear a play
And frame your mind to mirth and merriment,
Which bars a thousand harms and lengthens life.

SLY Marry, I will, let them play it. Is not a comonty a Christmas gambold or a tumbling-trick?

PAGE
No, my good lord, it is more pleasing stuff.

SLY What, household stuff?

PAGE It is a kind of history.

SLY Well, we'll see 't. Come, madam wife, sit by my side and let the world slip; we shall ne'er be younger.
[*They sit over the stage.*] *Flourish.*

[ACT I • SCENE I]

Enter Lucentio and his man Tranio.

LUCENTIO
Tranio, since for the great desire I had
To see fair Padua, nursery of arts,
I am arriv'd for fruitful Lombardy,
The pleasant garden of great Italy,
And by my father's love and leave am arm'd
With his good will and thy good company,
My trusty servant, well approv'd in all,
Here let us breathe and haply institute
A course of learning and ingenious studies.
Pisa, renowned for grave citizens,
Gave me my being and my father first,
A merchant of great traffic through the world,
Vincentio, come of the Bentivolii.
Vincentio's son, brought up in Florence,
It shall become to serve all hopes conceiv'd,
To deck his fortune with his virtuous deeds.
And therefore, Tranio, for the time I study,
Virtue and that part of philosophy
Will I apply that treats of happiness
By virtue specially to be achiev'd.
Tell me thy mind, for I have Pisa left
And am to Padua come, as he that leaves
A shallow plash to plunge him in the deep
And with satiety seeks to quench his thirst.

TRANIO
Mi perdonato, gentle master mine.
I am in all affected as yourself,
Glad that you thus continue your resolve
To suck the sweets of sweet philosophy.
Only, good master, while we do admire
This virtue and this moral discipline,
Let's be no stoics nor no stocks, I pray,
Or so devote to Aristotle's checks
As Ovid be an outcast quite abjur'd.
Balk logic with acquaintance that you have
And practice rhetoric in your common talk.
Music and poesy use to quicken you.
The mathematics and the metaphysics,
Fall to them as you find your stomach serves you.
No profit grows where is no pleasure ta'en.
In brief, sir, study what you most affect.

LUCENTIO
Gramercies, Tranio, well dost thou advise.
If, Biondello, thou wert come ashore,
We could at once put us in readiness,
And take a lodging fit to entertain
Such friends as time in Padua shall beget.
But stay a while; what company is this?

TRANIO
Master, some show to welcome us to town.

Enter Baptista with his two daughters Katharina and Bianca, Gremio a Pantaloon, [*and*] *Hortensio suitor to Bianca. Lucentio* [*and*] *Tranio stand by.*

BAPTISTA
Gentlemen, importune me no farther,
For how I firmly am resolv'd you know:
That is, not to bestow my youngest daughter
Before I have a husband for the elder.
If either of you both love Katharina,
Because I know you well and love you well,
Leave shall you have to court her at your pleasure.

GREMIO
To cart her rather; she's too rough for me.

122 stands is the case (with bawdy pun) **127 meet** suitable **133, 134 comonty, gambold** (Sly's blunders for *comedy* and *gambol*.) **137 history** story

I.i. Location: Padua. A street before Baptista's house.
2 Padua . . . arts (Padua's was one of the most renowned of universities during Shakespeare's time.) **3 for** in (?) on my way to (?) **7 approv'd** tested and proved trustworthy **8 breathe** pause, remain. **institute** begin **9 ingenious** intellectual **11 first** i.e., before me

15 It . . . conceiv'd i.e., it will befit me, Lucentio, to fulfill all the hopes entertained for me by my friends and relatives **16 deck** adorn **19 apply** study. **treats of** discusses, concerns **23 plash** pool **25 Mi perdonato** pardon me **26 affected** disposed **31 stocks** wooden posts, devoid of feeling (with a play on *stoics*) **32 devote** devoted. **checks** restraints **33 As** so that. **Ovid** Latin love poet (used here to typify amorous light entertainment as contrasted with the serious philosophic study of Aristotle) **34 Balk logic** argue, bandy words **36 quicken** stimulate **38 stomach** inclination, appetite **40 affect** find pleasant **41 Gramercies** many thanks **42 Biondello** (Lucentio apostrophizes his absent servant.) **come ashore** (Padua, though inland, is given a harbor by Shakespeare.) **47 s.d. Pantaloon** foolish old man, a stock character in Italian comedy **55 cart** carry in a cart through the streets by way of punishment or public exposure (with a play on *court*)

There, there, Hortensio, will you any wife?

KATHARINA [*To Baptista*]
I pray you, sir, is it your will
To make a stale of me amongst these mates?

HORTENSIO
Mates, maid? How mean you that? No mates for you,
Unless you were of gentler, milder mold.

KATHARINA
I' faith, sir, you shall never need to fear:
I wis it is not half way to her heart.
But if it were, doubt not her care should be
To comb your noddle with a three-legg'd stool
And paint your face and use you like a fool.

HORTENSIO
From all such devils, good Lord deliver us!

GREMIO
And me too, good Lord!

TRANIO
Husht, master! Here's some good pastime toward.
That wench is stark mad or wonderful froward.

LUCENTIO
But in other's silence do I see
Maid's mild behavior and sobriety.
Peace, Tranio!

TRANIO
Well said, master; mum, and gaze your fill.

BAPTISTA
Gentlemen, that I may soon make good
What I have said—Bianca, get you in,
And let it not displease thee, good Bianca,
For I will love thee ne'er the less, my girl.

KATHARINA
A pretty peat! It is best
Put finger in the eye, an she knew why.

BIANCA
Sister, content you in my discontent.
Sir, to your pleasure humbly I subscribe.
My books and instruments shall be my company,
On them to look and practice by myself.

LUCENTIO
Hark, Tranio, thou may'st hear Minerva speak.

HORTENSIO
Signior Baptista, will you be so strange?
Sorry am I that our good will effects
Bianca's grief.

GREMIO Why will you mew her up,
Signior Baptista, for this fiend of hell,
And make her bear the penance of her tongue?

BAPTISTA
Gentlemen, content ye; I am resolv'd.
Go in, Bianca. [*Exit Bianca.*]
And for I know she taketh most delight
In music, instruments, and poetry,
Schoolmasters will I keep within my house,
Fit to instruct her youth. If you, Hortensio,
Or Signior Gremio, you, know any such,
Prefer them hither; for to cunning men
I will be very kind, and liberal
To mine own children in good bringing up.
And so farewell. Katharina, you may stay;
For I have more to commune with Bianca. *Exit.*

KATHARINA
Why, and I trust I may go too, may I not?
What, shall I be appointed hours; as though, belike,
I knew not what to take, and what to leave? Ha! *Exit.*

GREMIO You may go to the devil's dam. Your gifts are so good, here's none will hold you. Their love is not so great, Hortensio, but we may blow our nails together, and fast it fairly out. Our cake 's dough on both sides. Farewell; yet, for the love I bear my sweet Bianca, if I can by any means light on a fit man to teach her that wherein she delights, I will wish him to her father.

HORTENSIO So will I, Signior Gremio. But a word, I pray. Though the nature of our quarrel yet never brook'd parle, know now, upon advice, it toucheth us both, that we may yet again have access to our fair mistress and be happy rivals in Bianca's love, to labor and effect one thing specially.

GREMIO What's that, I pray?

HORTENSIO Marry, sir, to get a husband for her sister.

GREMIO A husband? A devil.

HORTENSIO I say, a husband.

GREMIO I say, a devil. Think'st thou, Hortensio, though her father be very rich, any man is so very a fool to be married to hell?

HORTENSIO Tush, Gremio, though it pass your patience and mine to endure her loud alarums, why, man, there be good fellows in the world, an a man could light on them, would take her with all faults, and money enough.

GREMIO I cannot tell; but I had as lief take her dowry with this condition, to be whipp'd at the high cross every morning.

HORTENSIO Faith, as you say, there's small choice in rotten apples. But come, since this bar in law makes us friends, it shall be so far forth friendly maintain'd till by helping Baptista's eldest daughter to a husband we set his youngest free for a husband, and then have to 't afresh. Sweet Bianca! Happy man be his dole! He that runs fastest gets the ring. How say you, Signior Gremio?

GREMIO I am agreed, and would I had given him the best horse in Padua to begin his wooing that would thoroughly woo her, wed her, and bed her and rid the house of her! Come on. *Exeunt ambo. Mane[n]t Tranio and Lucentio.*

58 stale laughingstock (with a play on the meaning *harlot,* since a harlot might well be carted). **mates** rude fellows. (But Hortensio takes the word in the sense of *husband.*) **62 I wis** indeed. **it** i.e., marriage. **her** i.e., my, Kate's **65 paint** i.e., make red with scratches **68 toward** in prospect **69 froward** perverse **78 peat** darling, pet **79 Put . . . eye** i.e., weep. **an** if **84 Minerva** goddess of wisdom **85 strange** unnatural (as a father) **87 mew** coop (as one would a falcon) **89 her . . . her** i.e., Bianca . . . Katharina's **92 for** because

97 Prefer recommend. **cunning** skillful **105 dam** mother **106 Their love** i.e., men's love of women **107–108 blow . . . together** i.e., twiddle our thumbs, wait patiently **108 fast . . . out** abstain as best we can. **Our cake's dough** i.e., we're out of luck, getting nowhere **111 wish** commend **115 brook'd parle** tolerated conference. **advice** reflection. **toucheth** concerns **124 very** utterly **127 alarums** i.e., loud, startling noises. (A military metaphor.) **132 high cross** cross set on a pedestal in a market place or center of a town **135 bar in law** obstruction to our (legal) cause **139 Happy . . . dole** i.e., may happiness be the reward of him who wins. (Proverbial.) **140 the ring** (An allusion to the sport of riding at the ring, with quibble on *wedding ring.*) **145 s.d. ambo** both

TRANIO
I pray, sir, tell me, is it possible
That love should of a sudden take such hold?

LUCENTIO
O Tranio, till I found it to be true,
I never thought it possible or likely.
But see, while idly I stood looking on,
I found the effect of love in idleness,
And now in plainness do confess to thee,
That art to me as secret and as dear
As Anna to the Queen of Carthage was,
Tranio, I burn, I pine, I perish, Tranio,
If I achieve not this young modest girl.
Counsel me, Tranio, for I know thou canst;
Assist me, Tranio, for I know thou wilt.

TRANIO
Master, it is no time to chide you now.
Affection is not rated from the heart.
If love have touch'd you, nought remains but so,
"Redime te captum quam queas minimo."

LUCENTIO
Gramercies, lad. Go forward; this contents;
The rest will comfort, for thy counsel's sound.

TRANIO
Master, you look'd so longly on the maid,
Perhaps you mark'd not what's the pith of all.

LUCENTIO
O yes, I saw sweet beauty in her face,
Such as the daughter of Agenor had,
That made great Jove to humble him to her hand,
When with his knees he kiss'd the Cretan strand.

TRANIO
Saw you no more? Mark'd you not how her sister
Began to scold and raise up such a storm
That mortal ears might hardly endure the din?

LUCENTIO
Tranio, I saw her coral lips to move,
And with her breath she did perfume the air.
Sacred and sweet was all I saw in her.

TRANIO
Nay, then, 'tis time to stir him from his trance.—
I pray, awake, sir. If you love the maid,
Bend thoughts and wits to achieve her. Thus it stands:
Her elder sister is so curst and shrewd
That till the father rid his hands of her,
Master, your love must live a maid at home;
And therefore has he closely mew'd her up,
Because she will not be annoy'd with suitors.

LUCENTIO
Ah, Tranio, what a cruel father's he!
But art thou not advis'd, he took some care
To get her cunning schoolmasters to instruct her?

TRANIO
Ay, marry, am I, sir; and now 'tis plotted.

LUCENTIO
I have it, Tranio.

TRANIO
Master, for my hand,
Both our inventions meet and jump in one.

LUCENTIO
Tell me thine first.

TRANIO
You will be schoolmaster
And undertake the teaching of the maid:
That's your device.

LUCENTIO
It is. May it be done?

TRANIO
Not possible; for who shall bear your part,
And be in Padua here Vincentio's son,
Keep house and ply his book, welcome his friends,
Visit his countrymen, and banquet them?

LUCENTIO
Basta, content thee, for I have it full.
We have not yet been seen in any house,
Nor can we be distinguish'd by our faces
For man or master. Then it follows thus:
Thou shalt be master, Tranio, in my stead,
Keep house and port and servants, as I should.
I will some other be, some Florentine,
Some Neapolitan, or meaner man of Pisa.
'Tis hatch'd and shall be so. Tranio, at once
Uncase thee. Take my color'd hat and cloak.
When Biondello comes, he waits on thee;
But I will charm him first to keep his tongue.

TRANIO
So had you need.
In brief, sir, sith it your pleasure is,
And I am tied to be obedient—
For so your father charg'd me at our parting,
"Be serviceable to my son," quoth he,
Although I think 'twas in another sense—
I am content to be Lucentio,
Because so well I love Lucentio.

LUCENTIO
Tranio, be so, because Lucentio loves.
And let me be a slave, t' achieve that maid
Whose sudden sight hath thrall'd my wounded eye.

Enter Biondello.

Here comes the rogue. Sirrah, where have you been?

BIONDELLO
Where have I been? Nay, how now, where are you?
Master, has my fellow Tranio stol'n your clothes?
Or you stol'n his? Or both? Pray, what's the news?

LUCENTIO
Sirrah, come hither. 'Tis no time to jest,
And therefore frame your manners to the time.
Your fellow Tranio here, to save my life,
Puts my apparel and my count'nance on,

151 love in idleness the flower heartsease or pansy, to which was attributed magical power in love. (See *A Midsummer Night's Dream*, II.i.168.) **154 Anna** confidante of her sister Dido, Queen of Carthage, beloved of Aeneas **160 rated** driven away by chiding **162 Redime . . . minimo** buy yourself out of bondage for as little as you can. (From Terence's *Eunuchus* as quoted in Lily's *Latin Grammar*.) **165 longly** at length **168 daughter of Agenor** Europa, beloved of Jupiter, who took the form of a bull in order to abduct her **169 him** himself **170 kiss'd** i.e., knelt on **180 curst** shrewish. **shrewd** ill-natured **184 Because** so that **186 advis'd** aware

189 for by **190 inventions** plans. **jump** tally, agree **198 Basta** enough. **full** i.e., fully thought out **203 port** state, style of living **205 meaner** of a lower social class **207 Uncase** i.e., remove hat and cloak **209 charm** i.e., persuade **211 sith** since **220 Whose sudden sight** i.e., the sudden sight of whom

And I for my escape have put on his;
For in a quarrel since I came ashore
I kill'd a man and fear I was descried.
Wait you on him, I charge you, as becomes, 232
While I make way from hence to save my life.
You undestand me?

BIONDELLO Ay, sir.—[*Aside.*] Ne'er a whit.

LUCENTIO
And not a jot of Tranio in your mouth.
Tranio is chang'd into Lucentio.

BIONDELLO
The better for him. Would I were so too!

TRANIO
So could I, faith, boy, to have the next wish after,
That Lucentio indeed had Baptista's youngest daughter.
But, sirrah, not for my sake, but your master's, I advise 240
You use your manners discreetly in all kind of companies.
When I am alone, why, then I am Tranio,
But in all places else your master Lucentio.

LUCENTIO
Tranio, let's go.
One thing more rests, that thyself execute: 245
To make one among these wooers. If thou ask me why,
Sufficeth my reasons are both good and weighty. 247
Exeunt.

The presenters above speak.

FIRST SERVANT My lord, you nod; you do not mind the play. 248

SLY Yes, by Saint Anne, do I. A good matter, surely. Comes there any more of it?

PAGE My lord, 'tis but begun.

SLY 'Tis a very excellent piece of work, madam lady; would 'twere done! *They sit and mark.* 254

[SCENE II]

Enter Petruchio and his man Grumio.

PETRUCHIO
Verona, for a while I take my leave
To see my friends in Padua, but of all
My best beloved and approved friend,
Hortensio; and I trow this is his house. 4
Here, sirrah Grumio; knock, I say.

GRUMIO Knock, sir? Whom should I knock? Is there any man has rebus'd your worship? 7

PETRUCHIO Villain, I say, knock me here soundly. 8

GRUMIO Knock you here, sir? Why, sir, what am I, sir, that I should knock you here, sir?

PETRUCHIO
Villain, I say, knock me at this gate,
And rap me well, or I'll knock your knave's pate.

GRUMIO
My master is grown quarrelsome. I should knock you first,
And then I know after who comes by the worst.

PETRUCHIO
Will it not be?
Faith, sirrah, an you'll not knock, I'll ring it. 16
I'll try how you can sol, fa, and sing it. 17
He wrings him by the ears.

GRUMIO
Help, masters, help! My master is mad.

PETRUCHIO
Now, knock when I bid you, sirrah villain!

Enter Hortensio.

HORTENSIO How now, what's the matter? My old friend Grumio, and my good friend Petruchio! How do you all at Verona?

PETRUCHIO
Signior Hortensio, come you to part the fray?
Con tutto il cuore, ben trovato, may I say. 24

HORTENSIO
Alla nostra casa ben venuto, 25
Molto honorato signor mio Petruchio. 26
Rise, Grumio, rise. We will compound this quarrel. 27

GRUMIO Nay, 'tis no matter, sir, what he 'leges in Latin. 28
If this be not a lawful cause for me to leave his service,
look you, sir: he bid me knock him and rap him
soundly, sir. Well, was it fit for a servant to use his
master so, being perhaps, for aught I see, two and 32
thirty, a pip out? 33
Whom would to God I had well knock'd at first,
Then had not Grumio come by the worst.

PETRUCHIO
A senseless villain! Good Hortensio,
I bade the rascal knock upon your gate
And could not get him for my heart to do it.

GRUMIO Knock at the gate! O heavens! Spake you not these words plain, "Sirrah, knock me here, rap me here, knock me well, and knock me soundly"? And come you now with, "knocking at the gate"?

PETRUCHIO
Sirrah, be gone, or talk not, I advise you.

HORTENSIO
Petruchio, patience; I am Grumio's pledge. 44
Why, this' a heavy chance 'twixt him and you, 45
Your ancient, trusty, pleasant servant Grumio. 46
And tell me now, sweet friend, what happy gale
Blows you to Padua here from old Verona?

232 as becomes as is suitable **245 rests** remains to be done **247 Sufficeth** it suffices that **247 s.d. presenters** characters of the Induction, whose role it is to "present" the play proper **248 mind** attend to **254 s.d. mark** observe

I.ii. Location: Padua. Before Hortensio's house.
4 trow believe **7 rebus'd** (A blunder for *abused.*) **8 me** i.e., for me. (But Grumio, perhaps intentionally, misunderstands.)

16 ring (with a pun on *wring*) **17 I'll . . . sing it** i.e., I'll make you cry out, howl **24 Con . . . trovato** with all my heart, well met **25–26 Alla . . . Petruchio** welcome to our house, my much honored Petruchio. (Italian.) **27 compound** settle **28 'leges** alleges **32–33 two . . . out** i.e., drunk. (Derived from the card game called *one and thirty.*) **33 pip** a spot on a playing card. (Hence a *pip out* means "off by one," or "one in excess of thirty-one.") **44 pledge** surety **45 this'** this is. **heavy chance** sad occurrence **46 ancient** long-standing

PETRUCHIO

Such wind as scatters young men through the world
To seek their fortunes farther than at home,
Where small experience grows. But in a few, 51
Signior Hortensio, thus it stands with me:
Antonio, my father, is deceas'd,
And I have thrust myself into this maze,
Happily to wive and thrive as best I may. 55
Crowns in my purse I have and goods at home,
And so am come abroad to see the world.

HORTENSIO

Petruchio, shall I then come roundly to thee 58
And wish thee to a shrewd ill-favor'd wife?
Thou'dst thank me but a little for my counsel.
And yet I'll promise thee she shall be rich,
And very rich. But th' art too much my friend,
And I'll not wish thee to her.

PETRUCHIO

Signior Hortensio, 'twixt such friends as we
Few words suffice. And therefore, if thou know
One rich enough to be Petruchio's wife—
As wealth is burden of my wooing dance— 67
Be she as foul as was Florentius' love, 68
As old as Sibyl, and as curst and shrewd 69
As Socrates' Xanthippe, or a worse, 70
She moves me not, or not removes, at least,
Affection's edge in me, were she as rough
As are the swelling Adriatic seas.
I come to wive it wealthily in Padua;
If wealthily, then happily in Padua.

GRUMIO Nay, look you, sir, he tells you flatly what his
mind is. Why, give him gold enough and marry him 77
to a puppet or an aglet-baby, or an old trot with ne'er 78
a tooth in her head, though she have as many diseases
as two and fifty horses. Why, nothing comes amiss, so
money comes withal. 81

HORTENSIO

Petruchio, since we are stepp'd thus far in,
I will continue that I broach'd in jest. 83
I can, Petruchio, help thee to a wife
With wealth enough, and young and beauteous,
Brought up as best becomes a gentlewoman.
Her only fault, and that is faults enough,
Is that she is intolerable curst
And shrewd and froward, so beyond all measure
That, were my state far worser than it is, 90
I would not wed her for a mine of gold.

PETRUCHIO

Hortensio, peace! Thou know'st not gold's effect.
Tell me her father's name and 'tis enough;
For I will board her, though she chide as loud 94
As thunder when the clouds in autumn crack.

HORTENSIO

Her father is Baptista Minola,
An affable and courteous gentleman.
Her name is Katharina Minola,
Renown'd in Padua for her scolding tongue.

PETRUCHIO

I know her father, though I know not her;
And he knew my deceased father well.
I will not sleep, Hortensio, till I see her;
And therefore let me be thus bold with you
To give you over at this first encounter, 104
Unless you will accompany me thither.

GRUMIO I pray you, sir, let him go while the humor 106
lasts. A' my word, an she knew him as well as I do,
she would think scolding would do little good upon
him. She may perhaps call him half a score knaves or
so. Why, that's nothing; an he begin once, he'll rail in
his rope-tricks. I'll tell you what, sir, an she stand him 111
but a little, he will throw a figure in her face and so 112
disfigure her with it that she shall have no more eyes
to see withal than a cat. You know him not, sir.

HORTENSIO

Tarry, Petruchio, I must go with thee,
For in Baptista's keep my treasure is. 116
He hath the jewel of my life in hold, 117
His youngest daughter, beautiful Bianca,
And her withholds from me and other more,
Suitors to her and rivals in my love,
Supposing it a thing impossible,
For those defects I have before rehears'd,
That ever Katharina will be woo'd.
Therefore this order hath Baptista ta'en,
That none shall have access unto Bianca
Till Katharine the curst have got a husband.

GRUMIO

Katharine the curst!
A title for a maid of all titles the worst.

HORTENSIO

Now shall my friend Petruchio do me grace, 129
And offer me disguis'd in sober robes
To old Baptista as a schoolmaster
Well seen in music, to instruct Bianca, 132
That so I may by this device at least
Have leave and leisure to make love to her
And unsuspected court her by herself.

Enter Gremio [with a paper], and Lucentio disguised [as a schoolmaster].

GRUMIO Here's no knavery! See, to beguile the old folks, how the young folks lay their heads together! Master, master, look about you. Who goes there, ha?

HORTENSIO

Peace, Grumio, it is the rival of my love.
Petruchio, stand by a while. *[They stand aside.]*

51 in a few in short **55 Happily** haply, perchance **58 come roundly** speak plainly **67 burden** undersong, i.e., basis **68 foul** ugly. **Florentius' love** (An allusion to Gower's version in *Confessio Amantis* of the fairy tale of the knight who promised to marry an ugly old woman if she solved the riddle he must answer. After the fulfillment of all promises, she became young and beautiful. Another version of this story is Chaucer's "Tale of the Wife of Bath," from *The Canterbury Tales.*) **69 Sibyl** prophetess of Cumae to whom Apollo gave as many years of life as she held grains of sand in her hand **70 Xanthippe** the philosopher's notoriously shrewish wife **77 mind** intention **78 aglet-baby** small figure carved on the tag of a lace. **trot** old hag; also, prostitute **81 withal** with it **83 that** that which **90 state** estate **94 board** accost. (A metaphor from naval warfare.)

104 give you over leave you **106 humor** whim **111 rope-tricks** i.e., a blunder for rhetoric (?) or tricks worthy of hanging (?). **stand** withstand **112 figure** figure of speech **116 keep** keeping (with suggestion of *fortified place* where one would store a treasure) **117 hold** confinement (with a similar pun on *stronghold*) **129 grace** a favor **132 seen** skilled

GRUMIO [*Aside*]
A proper stripling and an amorous!
GREMIO [*To Lucentio*]
O, very well; I have perus'd the note.
Hark you, sir; I'll have them very fairly bound—
All books of love, see that at any hand—
And see you read no other lectures to her.
You understand me. Over and beside
Signior Baptista's liberality,
I'll mend it with a largess. Take your paper too,
[*Gives Lucentio the note.*]
And let me have them very well perfum'd,
For she is sweeter than perfume itself
To whom they go to. What will you read to her?
LUCENTIO
Whate'er I read to her, I'll plead for you
As for my patron, stand you so assur'd,
As firmly as yourself were still in place—
Yea, and perhaps with more successful words
Than you, unless you were a scholar, sir.
GREMIO
O this learning, what a thing it is!
GRUMIO [*Aside*]
O this woodcock, what an ass it is!
PETRUCHIO
Peace, sirrah!
HORTENSIO [*Coming forward*]
Grumio, mum!—God save you, Signior Gremio.
GREMIO
And you are well met, Signior Hortensio.
Trow you whither I am going? To Baptista Minola.
I promis'd to inquire carefully
About a schoolmaster for the fair Bianca,
And by good fortune I have lighted well
On this young man—for learning and behavior
Fit for her turn, well read in poetry
And other books, good ones, I warrant ye.
HORTENSIO
'Tis well. And I have met a gentleman
Hath promis'd me to help me to another,
A fine musician to instruct our mistress.
So shall I no whit be behind in duty
To fair Bianca, so beloved of me.
GREMIO
Beloved of me, and that my deeds shall prove.
GRUMIO [*Aside*]
And that his bags shall prove.
HORTENSIO
Gremio, 'tis now no time to vent our love.
Listen to me, and if you speak me fair,
I'll tell you news indifferent good for either.
Here is a gentleman whom by chance I met,
Upon agreement from us to his liking,
Will undertake to woo curst Katharine,
Yea, and to marry her, if her dowry please.
GREMIO
So said, so done, is well.
Hortensio, have you told him all her faults?
PETRUCHIO
I know she is an irksome brawling scold.
If that be all, masters, I hear no harm.
GREMIO
No, say'st me so, friend? What countryman?
PETRUCHIO
Born in Verona, old Antonio's son.
My father dead, my fortune lives for me,
And I do hope good days and long to see.
GREMIO
O sir, such a life, with such a wife, were strange.
But if you have a stomach, to 't a' God's name.
You shall have me assisting you in all.
But will you woo this wildcat?
PETRUCHIO Will I live?
GRUMIO [*Aside*]
Will he woo her? Ay, or I'll hang her.
PETRUCHIO
Why came I hither but to that intent?
Think you a little din can daunt mine ears?
Have I not in my time heard lions roar?
Have I not heard the sea, puff'd up with winds,
Rage like an angry boar chafed with sweat?
Have I not heard great ordnance in the field,
And heaven's artillery thunder in the skies?
Have I not in a pitched battle heard
Loud 'larums, neighing steeds, and trumpets' clang?
And do you tell me of a woman's tongue,
That gives not half so great a blow to hear
As will a chestnut in a farmer's fire?
Tush, tush! Fear boys with bugs.
GRUMIO [*Aside*] For he fears none.
GREMIO
Hortensio, hark.
This gentleman is happily arriv'd,
My mind presumes, for his own good and ours.
HORTENSIO
I promis'd we would be contributors
And bear his charge of wooing, whatsoe'er.
GREMIO
And so we will, provided that he win her.
GRUMIO [*Aside*]
I would I were as sure of a good dinner.

Enter Tranio brave, [*as Lucentio*], *and Biondello.*

TRANIO
Gentlemen, God save you. If I may be bold,
Tell me, I beseech you, which is the readiest way
To the house of Signior Baptista Minola?
BIONDELLO He that has the two fair daughters, is 't he you mean?
TRANIO Even he, Biondello.

141 proper stripling handsome young fellow. (Said ironically, in reference to Gremio.) **142 note** (Evidently, a list of books for Bianca's tutoring.) **144 at any hand** in any case **145 read . . . lectures** teach no other lessons **148 mend** improve, increase. **largess** gift of money **149 them** i.e., the books **154 as** as if. **in place** present **158 woodcock** (A bird easily caught; proverbially stupid.) **162 Trow** know **170 Hath** who has **175 bags** moneybags **176 vent** express **177 fair** civilly, courteously **178 indifferent** equally **180 Upon . . . liking** who, on terms agreeable to him. (In ll. 212–213 we learn that Bianca's suitors will *bear his charge of wooing.*)

204 'larums calls to arms **208 Fear . . . bugs** frighten children with bugbears, bogeymen **210 happily** fortunately, just when needed **213 charge** expense **215 s.d. brave** elegantly dressed

GREMIO
Hark you, sir, you mean not her to—

TRANIO
Perhaps him and her, sir. What have you to do?

PETRUCHIO
Not her that chides, sir, at any hand, I pray.

TRANIO
I love no chiders, sir. Biondello, let 's away.

LUCENTIO [*Aside*]
Well begun, Tranio.

HORTENSIO
Sir, a word ere you go.
Are you a suitor to the maid you talk of, yea or no?

TRANIO
An if I be, sir, is it any offense?

GREMIO
No, if without more words you will get you hence.

TRANIO
Why, sir, I pray, are not the streets as free
For me as for you?

GREMIO
But so is not she.

TRANIO
For what reason, I beseech you?

GREMIO
For this reason, if you'll know,
That she's the choice love of Signior Gremio.

HORTENSIO
That she's the chosen of Signior Hortensio.

TRANIO
Softly, my masters! If you be gentlemen,
Do me this right: hear me with patience.
Baptista is a noble gentleman,
To whom my father is not all unknown;
And were his daughter fairer than she is,
She may more suitors have, and me for one.
Fair Leda's daughter had a thousand wooers;
Then well one more may fair Bianca have,
And so she shall. Lucentio shall make one,
Though Paris came in hope to speed alone.

GREMIO
What, this gentleman will out-talk us all.

LUCENTIO
Sir, give him head. I know he'll prove a jade.

PETRUCHIO
Hortensio, to what end are all these words?

HORTENSIO
Sir, let me be so bold as ask you,
Did you yet ever see Baptista's daughter?

TRANIO
No, sir; but hear I do that he hath two,
The one as famous for a scolding tongue
As is the other for beauteous modesty.

PETRUCHIO
Sir, sir, the first 's for me; let her go by.

GREMIO
Yea, leave that labor to great Hercules,
And let it be more than Alcides' twelve.

PETRUCHIO
Sir, understand you this of me in sooth:
The youngest daughter, whom you hearken for,
Her father keeps from all access of suitors,
And will not promise her to any man
Until the elder sister first be wed.
The younger then is free and not before.

TRANIO
If it be so, sir, that you are the man
Must stead us all and me amongst the rest,
And if you break the ice and do this feat,
Achieve the elder, set the younger free
For our access, whose hap shall be to have her
Will not so graceless be to be ingrate.

HORTENSIO
Sir, you say well and well you do conceive.
And since you do profess to be a suitor,
You must, as we do, gratify this gentleman,
To whom we all rest generally beholding.

TRANIO
Sir, I shall not be slack, in sign whereof,
Please ye we may contrive this afternoon
And quaff carouses to our mistress' health,
And do as adversaries do in law,
Strive mightily, but eat and drink as friends.

GRUMIO, BIONDELLO
O excellent motion! Fellows, let's be gone.

HORTENSIO
The motion 's good indeed and be it so.
Petruchio, I shall be your ben venuto. *Exeunt.*

[ACT II • SCENE I]

Enter Katharina and Bianca [*with her hands tied*].

BIANCA
Good sister, wrong me not, nor wrong yourself,
To make a bondmaid and a slave of me.
That I disdain. But for these other gauds,
Unbind my hands, I'll pull them off myself,
Yea, all my raiment, to my petticoat,
Or what you will command me will I do,
So well I know my duty to my elders.

KATHARINA
Of all thy suitors, here I charge thee, tell
Whom thou lov'st best. See thou dissemble not.

BIANCA
Believe me, sister, of all the men alive
I never yet beheld that special face
Which I could fancy more than any other.

KATHARINA
Minion, thou liest. Is 't not Hortensio?

223 him and her i.e., both Baptista Minola and his daughter. **What . . . do** what's that to you **241 Leda's daughter** Helen of Troy **244 Paris** Trojan prince who abducted Helen from her husband Menelaus. **speed** succeed **246 prove a jade** tire like an ill-conditioned horse **255 Alcides'** descendant of Alcaeus. (I.e., Hercules, who, noted for the achievement of the twelve great labors, is the only one capable of conquering Katharina.)

256 sooth truth **263 Must stead** who must help **266 whose hap** he whose good fortune **268 conceive** understand **270 gratify** requite **273 contrive** spend, pass (time) **275 adversaries** opposing lawyers **277 motion** suggestion **279 ben venuto** welcome, i.e., host

II.i. Location: Padua. Baptista's house.
3 gauds ornaments **13 Minion** hussy

BIANCA
If you affect him, sister, here I swear
I'll plead for you myself, but you shall have him.

KATHARINA
O then, belike, you fancy riches more:
You will have Gremio to keep you fair.

BIANCA
Is it for him you do envy me so?
Nay then you jest, and now I well perceive
You have but jested with me all this while.
I prithee, sister Kate, untie my hands.

KATHARINA
If that be jest, then all the rest was so. *Strikes her.*

Enter Baptista.

BAPTISTA
Why, how now, dame, whence grows this insolence?—
Bianca, stand aside. Poor girl! She weeps.
Go ply thy needle, meddle not with her.—
For shame, thou hilding of a devilish spirit,
Why dost thou wrong her that did ne'er wrong thee?
When did she cross thee with a bitter word?

KATHARINA
Her silence flouts me, and I'll be reveng'd. *Flies after Bianca.*

BAPTISTA
What, in my sight? Bianca, get thee in. *Exit [Bianca].*

KATHARINA
What, will you not suffer me? Nay, now I see
She is your treasure, she must have a husband;
I must dance barefoot on her wedding day,
And for your love to her lead apes in hell.
Talk not to me. I will go sit and weep
Till I can find occasion of revenge. *[Exit.]*

BAPTISTA
Was ever gentleman thus griev'd as I?
But who comes here?

Enter Gremio, Lucentio [as a schoolmaster] in the habit of a mean man, Petruchio, with [Hortensio as a musician, and] Tranio [as Lucentio] with his Boy [Biondello] bearing a lute and books.

GREMIO Good morrow, neighbor Baptista.

BAPTISTA Good morrow, neighbor Gremio. God save you, gentlemen!

PETRUCHIO
And you, good sir! Pray, have you not a daughter
Call'd Katharina, fair and virtuous?

BAPTISTA
I have a daughter, sir, call'd Katharina.

GREMIO
You are too blunt. Go to it orderly.

PETRUCHIO
You wrong me, Signior Gremio; give me leave.
I am a gentleman of Verona, sir,
That, hearing of her beauty and her wit,
Her affability and bashful modesty,
Her wondrous qualities and mild behavior,
Am bold to show myself a forward guest
Within your house, to make mine eye the witness
Of that report which I so oft have heard.
And, for an entrance to my entertainment,
I do present you with a man of mine,
[Presenting Hortensio.]
Cunning in music and the mathematics,
To instruct her fully in those sciences,
Whereof I know she is not ignorant.
Accept of him, or else you do me wrong.
His name is Litio, born in Mantua.

BAPTISTA
Y' are welcome, sir, and he, for your good sake.
But for my daughter Katharine, this I know,
She is not for your turn, the more my grief.

PETRUCHIO
I see you do not mean to part with her,
Or else you like not of my company.

BAPTISTA
Mistake me not, I speak but as I find.
Whence are you, sir? What may I call your name?

PETRUCHIO
Petruchio is my name, Antonio's son,
A man well known throughout all Italy.

BAPTISTA
I know him well. You are welcome for his sake.

GREMIO
Saving your tale, Petruchio, I pray,
Let us, that are poor petitioners, speak too.
Backare! You are marvelous forward.

PETRUCHIO
O, pardon me, Signior Gremio, I would fain be doing.

GREMIO
I doubt it not, sir, but you will curse your wooing.
Neighbor, this is a gift very grateful, I am sure of it. To express the like kindness, myself, that have been more kindly beholding to you than any, freely give unto you this young scholar [*Presenting Lucentio*], that hath been long studying at Rheims, as cunning in Greek, Latin, and other languages, as the other in music and mathematics. His name is Cambio. Pray accept his service.

BAPTISTA A thousand thanks, Signior Gremio. Welcome, good Cambio. [*To Tranio.*] But, gentle sir, methinks you walk like a stranger. May I be so bold to know the cause of your coming?

TRANIO
Pardon me, sir, the boldness is mine own,
That, being a stranger in this city here,
Do make myself a suitor to your daughter,

14 affect love **17 fair** resplendent with finery **26 hilding** worthless baggage **33, 34 dance . . . day, lead . . . hell** (Popularly supposed to be the fate of old maids.) **38 s.d. mean** of low social station. (Said here of a schoolmaster.)

54 entrance entrance fee. **entertainment** reception **70 know him** i.e., know him by reputation **71 Saving** with all due respect for **73 Backare** stand back **74 fain** gladly. **doing** getting on with the business (with sexual suggestion)

Unto Bianca, fair and virtuous.
Nor is your firm resolve unknown to me,
In the preferment of the eldest sister.
This liberty is all that I request,
That, upon knowledge of my parentage,
I may have welcome 'mongst the rest that woo
And free access and favor as the rest.
And, toward the education of your daughters,
I here bestow a simple instrument,
And this small packet of Greek and Latin books.
If you accept them, then their worth is great.
[*Biondello brings forward the lute and books.*]

BAPTISTA
Lucentio is your name; of whence, I pray?

TRANIO
Of Pisa, sir, son to Vincentio.

BAPTISTA
A mighty man of Pisa. By report
I know him well. You are very welcome, sir.
[*To Hortensio.*] Take you the lute, [*To Lucentio.*] and you the set of books;
You shall go see your pupils presently.
Holla, within!

Enter a Servant.

Sirrah, lead these gentlemen
To my daughters, and tell them both
These are their tutors. Bid them use them well.
[*Exit Servant, with Lucentio and Hortensio, Biondello following.*]
We will go walk a little in the orchard,
And then to dinner. You are passing welcome,
And so I pray you all to think yourselves.

PETRUCHIO
Signior Baptista, my business asketh haste,
And every day I cannot come to woo.
You knew my father well, and in him me,
Left solely heir to all his lands and goods,
Which I have bettered rather than decreas'd.
Then tell me, if I get your daughter's love,
What dowry shall I have with her to wife?

BAPTISTA
After my death the one half of my lands,
And in possession twenty thousand crowns.

PETRUCHIO
And, for that dowry, I'll assure her of
Her widowhood, be it that she survive me,
In all my lands and leases whatsoever.
Let specialties be therefore drawn between us,
That covenants may be kept on either hand.

BAPTISTA
Ay, when the special thing is well obtain'd,
That is, her love; for that is all in all.

PETRUCHIO
Why, that is nothing, for I tell you, father,
I am as peremptory as she proud-minded;
And where two raging fires meet together
They do consume the thing that feeds their fury.
Though little fire grows great with little wind,
Yet extreme gusts will blow out fire and all.
So I to her and so she yields to me,
For I am rough and woo not like a babe.

BAPTISTA
Well mayst thou woo, and happy be thy speed!
But be thou arm'd for some unhappy words.

PETRUCHIO
Ay, to the proof, as mountains are for winds,
That shake not, though they blow perpetually.

Enter Hortensio [*as Litio*], *with his head broke.*

BAPTISTA
How now, my friend, why dost thou look so pale?

HORTENSIO
For fear, I promise you, if I look pale.

BAPTISTA
What, will my daughter prove a good musician?

HORTENSIO
I think she'll sooner prove a soldier.
Iron may hold with her, but never lutes.

BAPTISTA
Why, then thou canst not break her to the lute?

HORTENSIO
Why, no, for she hath broke the lute to me.
I did but tell her she mistook her frets,
And bow'd her hand to teach her fingering,
When, with a most impatient devilish spirit,
"Frets, call you these?" quoth she, "I'll fume with them."
And with that word she struck me on the head,
And through the instrument my pate made way;
And there I stood amazed for a while,
As on a pillory, looking through the lute,
While she did call me rascal fiddler
And twangling Jack, with twenty such vile terms,
As had she studied to misuse me so.

PETRUCHIO
Now, by the world, it is a lusty wench!
I love her ten times more than e'er I did.
O, how I long to have some chat with her!

BAPTISTA [*To Hortensio*]
Well, go with me and be not so discomfited.
Proceed in practice with my younger daughter;
She's apt to learn and thankful for good turns.
Signior Petruchio, will you go with us,
Or shall I send my daughter Kate to you?

PETRUCHIO
I pray you do. *Exeunt. Manet Petruchio.*
I'll attend her here,
And woo her with some spirit when she comes.
Say that she rail, why then I'll tell her plain

97 favor leave, permission **102 Lucentio . . . name** (Baptista may have learned this information from a note accompanying the books and lute.) **104 report** reputation **107 presently** immediately **111 orchard** garden **112 passing** exceedingly **122 in possession** i.e., in immediate possession **124 widowhood** i.e., widow's share of the estate **126 specialties** terms of contract

140 to the proof i.e., in armor, proof against her shrewishness **141 s.d. broke** i.e., with a bleeding cut. (Hortensio usually appears on stage with his head emerging through a broken lute.) **146 hold with** hold out against **147 break** train (with pun in the next line) **149 frets** ridges or bars on the finger board of the lute. (But Kate puns on the sense of *fume*, "be indignant.") **158 Jack** knave **160 lusty** lively

She sings as sweetly as a nightingale.
Say that she frown, I'll say she looks as clear
As morning roses newly wash'd with dew.
Say she be mute and will not speak a word,
Then I'll commend her volubility
And say she uttereth piercing eloquence.
If she do bid me pack, I'll give her thanks, 177
As though she bid me stay by her a week.
If she deny to wed, I'll crave the day 179
When I shall ask the banns and when be married. 180
But here she comes; and now, Petruchio, speak.

Enter Katharina.

Good morrow, Kate, for that's your name, I hear.

KATHARINA
Well have you heard, but something hard of
hearing. 183
They call me Katharine that do talk of me.

PETRUCHIO
You lie, in faith; for you are call'd plain Kate,
And bonny Kate and sometimes Kate the curst;
But Kate, the prettiest Kate in Christendom,
Kate of Kate Hall, my super-dainty Kate,
For dainties are all Kates, and therefore, Kate, 189
Take this of me, Kate of my consolation: 190
Hearing thy mildness prais'd in every town,
Thy virtues spoke of, and thy beauty sounded, 192
Yet not so deeply as to thee belongs,
Myself am mov'd to woo thee for my wife.

KATHARINA
Mov'd? In good time! Let him that mov'd you hither 195
Remove you hence. I knew you at the first
You were a moveable.

PETRUCHIO Why, what's a moveable? 197

KATHARINA
A join'd-stool.

PETRUCHIO Thou hast hit it. Come, sit on me. 198

KATHARINA
Asses are made to bear, and so are you. 199

PETRUCHIO
Women are made to bear, and so are you.

KATHARINA
No such jade as you, if me you mean. 201

PETRUCHIO
Alas, good Kate, I will not burden thee,
For knowing thee to be but young and light. 203

KATHARINA
Too light for such a swain as you to catch, 204
And yet as heavy as my weight should be.

PETRUCHIO
Should be! Should—buzz!

KATHARINA Well ta'en, and like a buzzard. 206

PETRUCHIO
O slow-wing'd turtle, shall a buzzard take thee?

KATHARINA
Ay, for a turtle, as he takes a buzzard.

PETRUCHIO
Come, come, you wasp, i' faith, you are too angry. 209

KATHARINA
If I be waspish, best beware my sting.

PETRUCHIO
My remedy is then to pluck it out.

KATHARINA
Ay, if the fool could find it where it lies.

PETRUCHIO
Who knows not where a wasp does wear his sting?
In his tail.

KATHARINA In his tongue.

PETRUCHIO Whose tongue?

KATHARINA
Yours, if you talk of tails, and so farewell. 217

PETRUCHIO
What, with my tongue in your tail? Nay, come
again,
Good Kate; I am a gentleman.

KATHARINA That I'll try. *She strikes him.*

PETRUCHIO
I swear I'll cuff you, if you strike again.

KATHARINA
So may you lose your arms.
If you strike me, you are no gentleman,
And if no gentleman, why then no arms. 223

PETRUCHIO
A herald, Kate? O, put me in thy books! 224

KATHARINA
What is your crest, a coxcomb? 225

PETRUCHIO
A combless cock, so Kate will be my hen.

KATHARINA
No cock of mine; you crow too like a craven. 227

PETRUCHIO
Nay, come, Kate, come, you must not look so sour.

KATHARINA
It is my fashion, when I see a crab. 229

PETRUCHIO
Why, here's no crab, and therefore look not sour.

KATHARINA
There is, there is.

PETRUCHIO
Then show it me.

KATHARINA Had I a glass, I would.

PETRUCHIO
What, you mean my face?

177 pack be gone **179 deny** refuse **180 ask the banns** have a reading of the required announcement in church of a forthcoming marriage **183 heard, hard** (Pronounced nearly alike.) **189 all Kates** (with a quibble on *cates*, confections, delicacies) **190 of me** from me **192 sounded** proclaimed (with a quibble on *plumbed*, as indicated by *deeply* in the next line) **195 In good time** forsooth, indeed **197 moveable** (1) one easily changed or dissuaded (2) an article of furniture **198 join'd-stool** a well-fitted stool made by an expert craftsman **199 bear** carry (with puns in the following lines suggesting *bear children* and *support a man during sexual intercourse*) **201 jade** an ill-conditioned horse **203 light** (1) of delicate stature (2) lascivious (3) lacking a *burden* (see previous line) in the musical sense of lacking a bass undersong or accompaniment (4) elusive (in the following line) **204 swain** young rustic in love

206 buzz i.e., a *bee* (punning on *be*) should make a buzzing sound; also, an interjection expressing impatience or contempt. **buzzard** (1) figuratively, a fool (2) in the next line, an inferior kind of hawk, fit only to overtake a slow-winged *turtle* or turtledove, as Petruchio might overtake Kate (3) a buzzing insect, caught by a turtle **209 wasp** i.e., waspish, scolding woman (but suggested by *buzzard*, buzzing insect) **217 talk of tails** i.e., idly tells stories (with pun on *tale, tail*) **223 no arms** no coat of arms (with pun on *arms* as limbs of the body) **224 books** (1) books of heraldry, heraldic registers (2) grace, favor **225 crest** (1) armorial device (2) a rooster's comb, setting up the joke on *coxcomb*, the cap of the court fool **227 craven** a cock that is not "game" or willing to fight **229 crab** crab apple

KATHARINA
Well aim'd of such a young one.

PETRUCHIO
Now, by Saint George, I am too young for you.

KATHARINA
Yet you are wither'd.

PETRUCHIO
'Tis with cares.

KATHARINA
I care not.

PETRUCHIO
Nay, hear you, Kate. In sooth you scape not so.

KATHARINA
I chafe you if I tarry. Let me go.

PETRUCHIO
No, not a whit. I find you passing gentle.
'Twas told me you were rough and coy and sullen,
And now I find report a very liar,
For thou art pleasant, gamesome, passing courteous,
But slow in speech, yet sweet as spring-time flowers.
Thou canst not frown, thou canst not look askance,
Nor bite the lip, as angry wenches will,
Nor hast thou pleasure to be cross in talk;
But thou with mildness entertain'st thy wooers,
With gentle conference, soft and affable.
Why does the world report that Kate doth limp?
O sland'rous world! Kate like the hazel-twig
Is straight and slender, and as brown in hue
As hazel nuts, and sweeter than the kernels.
O, let me see thee walk. Thou dost not halt.

KATHARINA
Go, fool, and whom thou keep'st command.

PETRUCHIO
Did ever Dian so become a grove
As Kate this chamber with her princely gait?
O, be thou Dian, and let her be Kate;
And then let Kate be chaste and Dian sportful!

KATHARINA
Where did you study all this goodly speech?

PETRUCHIO
It is extempore, from my mother-wit.

KATHARINA
A witty mother! Witless else her son.

PETRUCHIO
Am I not wise?

KATHARINA
Yes, keep you warm.

PETRUCHIO
Marry, so I mean, sweet Katharine, in thy bed.
And therefore, setting all this chat aside,
Thus in plain terms: your father hath consented
That you shall be my wife; your dowry 'greed on;
And, will you, nill you, I will marry you.
Now, Kate, I am a husband for your turn;
For, by this light, whereby I see thy beauty—
Thy beauty that doth make me like thee well—
Thou must be married to no man but me;

Enter Baptista, Gremio, [and] Tranio [as Lucentio].

For I am he am born to tame you, Kate,
And bring you from a wild Kate to a Kate
Conformable as other household Kates.
Here comes your father. Never make denial;
I must and will have Katharine to my wife.

BAPTISTA
Now, Signior Petruchio, how speed you with my daughter?

PETRUCHIO
How but well, sir, how but well?
It were impossible I should speed amiss.

BAPTISTA
Why, how now, daughter Katharine, in your dumps?

KATHARINA
Call you me daughter? Now, I promise you,
You have show'd a tender fatherly regard,
To wish me wed to one half lunatic,
A mad-cap ruffian and a swearing Jack,
That thinks with oaths to face the matter out.

PETRUCHIO
Father, 'tis thus: yourself and all the world,
That talk'd of her, have talk'd amiss of her.
If she be curst, it is for policy,
For she's not froward, but modest as the dove.
She is not hot, but temperate as the morn.
For patience she will prove a second Grissel,
And Roman Lucrece for her chastity.
And to conclude, we have 'greed so well together
That upon Sunday is the wedding-day.

KATHARINA
I'll see thee hang'd on Sunday first.

GREMIO
Hark, Petruchio, she says she'll see thee hang'd first.

TRANIO
Is this your speeding? Nay, then, good night our part!

PETRUCHIO
Be patient, gentlemen. I choose her for myself.
If she and I be pleas'd, what's that to you?
'Tis bargain'd 'twixt us twain, being alone,
That she shall still be curst in company.
I tell you, 'tis incredible to believe
How much she loves me. O, the kindest Kate!
She hung about my neck, and kiss on kiss
She vied so fast, protesting oath on oath,
That in a twink she won me to her love.

234 aim'd of guessed for. **young** i.e., inexperienced. (But Petruchio picks up the word in the sense of *strong*.) **240 coy** disdainful **243 But slow** never anything but slow **244 askance** scornfully **253 halt** limp **254 whom thou keep'st** i.e., those whom you employ, your servants **255 Dian** Diana, goddess of the hunt and of chastity. **become** adorn **258 sportful** amorous **260 mother-wit** native intelligence **261 Witless . . . son** i.e., without the intelligence inherited from her, he would have none at all **262–263 wise . . . warm** (An allusion to the proverbial phrase "enough wit to keep oneself warm.") **268 nill you** will you not

269 for your turn to suit you **274 wild Kate** (with a quibble on *wildcat*) **282 promise** assure **286 face** brazen **289 policy** cunning, ulterior motive **292 Grissel** patient Griselda, the epitome of wifely patience and devotion (whose story was told by Chaucer in "The Clerk's Tale" of *The Canterbury Tales* and earlier by Boccaccio and Petrarch) **293 Roman Lucrece** Lucretia, a Roman lady who took her own life after her chastity had been violated by the Tarquin prince, Sextus. (Shakespeare told the story in *The Rape of Lucrece*.) **306 vied** went me one better, kiss for kiss

O, you are novices! 'Tis a world to see 308
How tame, when men and women are alone,
A meacock wretch can make the curstest shrew. 310
Give me thy hand, Kate. I will unto Venice
To buy apparel 'gainst the wedding-day. 312
Provide the feast, father, and bid the guests;
I will be sure my Katharine shall be fine. 314

BAPTISTA
I know not what to say. But give me your hands.
God send you joy, Petruchio! 'Tis a match.

GREMIO, TRANIO
Amen, say we. We will be witnesses.

PETRUCHIO
Father, and wife, and gentlemen, adieu.
I will to Venice. Sunday comes apace.
We will have rings and things, and fine array;
And kiss me, Kate, we will be married a' Sunday. 321
Exeunt Petruchio and Katharine [*severally*].

GREMIO
Was ever match clapp'd up so suddenly? 322

BAPTISTA
Faith, gentlemen, now I play a merchant's part,
And venture madly on a desperate mart. 324

TRANIO
'Twas a commodity lay fretting by you; 325
'Twill bring you gain, or perish on the seas.

BAPTISTA
The gain I seek is quiet in the match.

GREMIO
No doubt but he hath got a quiet catch. 328
But now, Baptista, to your younger daughter.
Now is the day we long have looked for.
I am your neighbor, and was suitor first.

TRANIO
And I am one that love Bianca more
Than words can witness, or your thoughts can
guess.

GREMIO
Youngling, thou canst not love so dear as I.

TRANIO
Greybeard, thy love doth freeze.

GREMIO
But thine doth fry.
Skipper, stand back, 'tis age that nourisheth. 336

TRANIO
But youth in ladies' eyes that flourisheth.

BAPTISTA
Content you, gentlemen, I will compound this strife. 338
'Tis deeds must win the prize; and he of both 339
That can assure my daughter greatest dower
Shall have my Bianca's love.
Say, Signior Gremio, what can you assure her?

GREMIO
First, as you know, my house within the city
Is richly furnished with plate and gold,
Basins and ewers to lave her dainty hands; 345
My hangings all of Tyrian tapestry; 346
In ivory coffers I have stuff'd my crowns;
In cypress chests my arras counterpoints, 348
Costly apparel, tents, and canopies, 349
Fine linen, Turkey cushions boss'd with pearl, 350
Valance of Venice gold in needlework, 351
Pewter and brass, and all things that belongs
To house or housekeeping. Then at my farm
I have a hundred milch-kine to the pail, 354
Sixscore fat oxen standing in my stalls,
And all things answerable to this portion. 356
Myself am struck in years, I must confess; 357
And if I die tomorrow, this is hers,
If whilst I live she will be only mine.

TRANIO
That "only" came well in. Sir, list to me:
I am my father's heir and only son.
If I may have your daughter to my wife,
I'll leave her houses three or four as good,
Within rich Pisa walls, as any one
Old Signior Gremio has in Padua,
Besides two thousand ducats by the year 366
Of fruitful land, all which shall be her jointure. 367
What, have I pinch'd you, Signior Gremio?

GREMIO [*Aside*]
Two thousand ducats by the year of land!
My land amounts not to so much in all.—
That she shall have, besides an argosy 371
That now is lying in Marseilles' road. 372
What, have I chok'd you with an argosy?

TRANIO
Gremio, 'tis known my father hath no less
Than three great argosies, besides two galliases, 375
And twelve tight galleys. These I will assure her, 376
And twice as much, whate'er thou off'rest next.

GREMIO
Nay, I have off'red all, I have no more,
And she can have no more than all I have.
If you like me, she shall have me and mine.

TRANIO
Why, then the maid is mine from all the world,
By your firm promise. Gremio is out-vied.

BAPTISTA
I must confess your offer is the best;
And, let your father make her the assurance, 384
She is your own; else, you must pardon me.
If you should die before him, where's her dower?

TRANIO
That's but a cavil. He is old, I young.

GREMIO
And may not young men die, as well as old?

BAPTISTA
Well, gentlemen, I am thus resolv'd:

308 a world worth a whole world **310 meacock** cowardly **312 'gainst** in anticipation of **314 fine** elegantly dressed **321 kiss me** (Petruchio probably kisses her.) **322 clapp'd up** settled (by a shaking of hands) **324 mart** bargain **325 lay fretting** i.e., which lay in storage being destroyed by moths, weevils, or spoilage (with a pun on *chafing*) **328 quiet catch** i.e., acquisition (Kate) that others will yield him without dispute (?) **336 Skipper** flighty fellow **338 compound** settle **339 he of both** i.e., the one of you two

345 lave wash **346 Tyrian** dark red or purple **348 arras counterpoints** counterpanes of tapestry **349 tents** bed curtains **350 boss'd** embossed **351 Valance** drapery around the canopy or bed frame **354 milch-kine to the pail** dairy cattle **356 answerable to** on the same scale as **357 struck** advanced **366 ducats** gold coins **367 Of** from. **jointure** marriage settlement **371 argosy** merchant vessel of the largest size **372 road** roadstead, harbor **375 galliases** heavy, low-built vessels **376 tight** watertight **384 let** provided

On Sunday next, you know
My daughter Katharine is to be married.
Now, on the Sunday following, shall Bianca
Be bride to you, if you make this assurance;
If not, to Signior Gremio.
And so, I take my leave, and thank you both. *Exit.*

GREMIO
Adieu, good neighbor.—Now I fear thee not.
Sirrah young gamester, your father were a fool
To give thee all, and in his waning age
Set foot under thy table. Tut, a toy!
An old Italian fox is not so kind, my boy. *Exit.*

TRANIO
A vengeance on your crafty withered hide!
Yet I have fac'd it with a card of ten.
'Tis in my head to do my master good.
I see no reason but suppos'd Lucentio
Must get a father, call'd suppos'd Vincentio,
And that's a wonder. Fathers commonly
Do get their children; but in this case of wooing,
A child shall get a sire, if I fail not of my cunning.
Exit.

ACT III • [SCENE I]

Enter Lucentio [as Cambio], Hortensio [as Litio], and Bianca.

LUCENTIO
Fiddler, forbear. You grow too forward, sir.
Have you so soon forgot the entertainment
Her sister Katharine welcom'd you withal?

HORTENSIO
But, wrangling pedant, this is
The patroness of heavenly harmony.
Then give me leave to have prerogative,
And when in music we have spent an hour
Your lecture shall have leisure for as much.

LUCENTIO
Preposterous ass, that never read so far
To know the cause why music was ordain'd!
Was it not to refresh the mind of man
After his studies or his usual pain?
Then give me leave to read philosophy,
And, while I pause, serve in your harmony.

HORTENSIO
Sirrah, I will not bear these braves of thine.

BIANCA
Why, gentlemen, you do me double wrong,
To strive for that which resteth in my choice.
I am no breeching scholar in the schools;
I'll not be tied to hours nor 'pointed times,
But learn my lessons as I please myself.
And, to cut off all strife, here sit we down.
[*To Hortensio.*] Take you your instrument, play you the whiles;
His lecture will be done ere you have tun'd.

HORTENSIO
You'll leave his lecture when I am in tune?

LUCENTIO
That will be never. Tune your instrument.
[*Hortensio moves aside and tunes.*]

BIANCA Where left we last?

LUCENTIO Here, madam. [*Reads.*]
"Hic ibat Simois; hic est Sigeia tellus;
Hic steterat Priami regia celsa senis."

BIANCA Conster them.

LUCENTIO "Hic ibat," as I told you before, "Simois," I am Lucentio, "hic est," son unto Vincentio of Pisa, "Sigeia tellus," disguis'd thus to get your love; "Hic steterat," and that Lucentio that comes a-wooing, "Priami," is my man Tranio, "regia," bearing my port, "celsa senis," that we might beguile the old pantaloon.

HORTENSIO Madam, my instrument's in tune.

BIANCA Let's hear. [*He plays.*] O fie! The treble jars.

LUCENTIO Spit in the hole, man, and tune again.
[*Hortensio moves aside.*]

BIANCA Now let me see if I can conster it: "Hic ibat Simois," I know you not, "hic est Sigeia tellus," I trust you not; "Hic steterat Priami," take heed he hear us not, "regia," presume not, "celsa senis," despair not.

HORTENSIO
Madam, 'tis now in tune.

LUCENTIO All but the base.

HORTENSIO
The base is right, 'tis the base knave that jars.
[*Aside.*] How fiery and forward our pedant is!
Now, for my life, the knave doth court my love.
Pedascule, I'll watch you better yet.

BIANCA
In time I may believe, yet I mistrust.

LUCENTIO
Mistrust it not, for, sure, Aeacides
Was Ajax, call'd so from his grandfather.

BIANCA
I must believe my master; else, I promise you,
I should be arguing still upon that doubt.
But let it rest. Now, Litio, to you:
Good master, take it not unkindly, pray,
That I have been thus pleasant with you both.

HORTENSIO [*To Lucentio*]
You may go walk, and give me leave a while.
My lessons make no music in three parts.

LUCENTIO
Are you so formal, sir? Well, I must wait,

399 Set . . . table i.e., become a dependent in your household. **a toy** nonsense **402 fac'd . . . ten** brazened it out with only a ten-spot of cards **407 get** beget (with a play on *get,* obtain, in l. 405)

III.i. Location: The same.
6 prerogative precedence **8 lecture** lesson **9 Preposterous** inverting the natural order of things **12 pain** labor **15 braves** insults **18 breeching scholar** i.e., schoolboy liable to be whipped

28–29 Hic . . . senis here flowed the river Simois; here is the Sigeian land; here stood the lofty palace of old Priam. (Ovid, *Heroides,* I.33–34.) **30 Conster** construe **35 port** social position, style of living **36–37 pantaloon** foolish old man, i.e., Gremio **40 Spit in the hole** i.e., to make the peg stick **49 Pedascule** (A word contemptuously coined by Hortensio, the vocative of *pedasculus,* little pedant.) **51 Aeacides** (Aeacus, King of Aegina, was father of Telamon and grandfather of Ajax; Lucentio is pretending to go on with his lesson.) **60 formal** precise

[*Aside*] And watch withal; for, but I be deceiv'd,
Our fine musician groweth amorous.
[*He moves aside.*]

HORTENSIO
Madam, before you touch the instrument,
To learn the order of my fingering,
I must begin with rudiments of art,
To teach you gamut in a briefer sort,
More pleasant, pithy, and effectual
Than hath been taught by any of my trade.
And there it is in writing, fairly drawn.
[*Gives her a paper.*]

BIANCA
Why, I am past my gamut long ago.

HORTENSIO
Yet read the gamut of Hortensio.

BIANCA [*Reads*]
" 'Gamut' I am, the ground of all accord,
'A re,' to plead Hortensio's passion;
'B mi,' Bianca, take him for thy lord,
'C fa ut,' that loves with all affection.
'D sol re,' one clef, two notes have I;
'E la mi,' show pity, or I die."
Call you this gamut? Tut, I like it not.
Old fashions please me best; I am not so nice
To change true rules for odd inventions.

Enter a [*Servant as*] *Messenger.*

SERVANT
Mistress, your father prays you leave your books
And help to dress your sister's chamber up.
You know tomorrow is the wedding-day.

BIANCA
Farewell, sweet masters both, I must be gone.
[*Exeunt Bianca and Servant.*]

LUCENTIO
Faith, mistress, then I have no cause to stay. [*Exit.*]

HORTENSIO
But I have cause to pry into this pedant.
Methinks he looks as though he were in love.
Yet if thy thoughts, Bianca, be so humble
To cast thy wand'ring eyes on every stale,
Seize thee that list. If once I find thee ranging,
Hortensio will be quit with thee by changing. *Exit.*

[SCENE II]

Enter Baptista, Gremio, Tranio [*as Lucentio*], *Katharine, Bianca,* [*Lucentio as Cambio*], *and others, attendants.*

BAPTISTA [*To Tranio*]
Signior Lucentio, this is the 'pointed day
That Katharine and Petruchio should be married,
And yet we hear not of our son-in-law.
What will be said? What mockery will it be,
To want the bridegroom when the priest attends
To speak the ceremonial rites of marriage?
What says Lucentio to this shame of ours?

KATHARINA
No shame but mine. I must, forsooth, be forc'd
To give my hand oppos'd against my heart
Unto a mad-brain rudesby full of spleen,
Who woo'd in haste and means to wed at leisure.
I told you, I, he was a frantic fool,
Hiding his bitter jests in blunt behavior.
And, to be noted for a merry man,
He'll woo a thousand, 'point the day of marriage,
Make friends, invite, and proclaim the banns,
Yet never means to wed where he hath woo'd.
Now must the world point at poor Katharine,
And say, "Lo, there is mad Petruchio's wife,
If it would please him come and marry her!"

TRANIO
Patience, good Katharine, and Baptista too.
Upon my life, Petruchio means but well,
Whatever fortune stays him from his word.
Though he be blunt, I know him passing wise;
Though he be merry, yet withal he's honest.

KATHARINA
Would Katharine had never seen him though!
Exit weeping [*followed by Bianca and others*].

BAPTISTA
Go, girl. I cannot blame thee now to weep,
For such an injury would vex a very saint,
Much more a shrew of thy impatient humor.

Enter Biondello.

BIONDELLO Master, master! News, old news, and such news as you never heard of!

BAPTISTA Is it new and old too? How may that be?

BIONDELLO Why, is it not news, to hear of Petruchio's coming?

BAPTISTA Is he come?

BIONDELLO Why, no, sir.

BAPTISTA What then?

BIONDELLO He is coming.

BAPTISTA When will he be here?

BIONDELLO When he stands where I am and sees you there.

TRANIO But say, what to thine old news?

BIONDELLO Why, Petruchio is coming in a new hat and an old jerkin; a pair of old breeches thrice turn'd; a pair of boots that have been candle-cases, one buckled, another lac'd; an old rusty sword ta'en out of the town-armory, with a broken hilt, and chapeless; with two broken points; his horse hipp'd, with an old

61 but unless **66 gamut** the scale, from the alphabet name *(gamma)* of the first note plus *ut,* its syllable name, now commonly called *do.* (The *gamut* of Hortensio begins on G instead of on C.) **72 ground** base note, foundation. **accord** harmony **75 fa ut** (The note C is the fourth note, or *fa,* of a scale based on G, but is the first note, *ut,* or *do,* of the more universal major scale based on C. Similarly, D is fifth note or *sol* in the G scale but second or *re* in the C scale; similarly with E as sixth and third.) **79 nice** capricious **89 stale** decoy, bait **90 Seize . . . list** let him who wants you have you. **ranging** inconstant **91 quit** quits. **changing** i.e., loving another

III.ii. Location: Padua. Before Baptista's house.

10 rudesby unmannerly fellow. **spleen** i.e., changeable temper **30 old** rare; or perhaps referring to Petruchio's old clothes **42 to** about **44 jerkin** man's jacket **45 candle-cases** i.e., discarded boots, used only as a receptacle for candle ends **47 chapeless** without the chape, the metal plate or mounting of a scabbard, especially that which covers the point **48 points** tagged laces for attaching hose to doublet. **hipp'd** lamed in the hip. (Almost all the diseases here named are described in Gervase Markham's *How to chuse, ride, trayne, and dyet, both Hunting Horses and Running Horses . . . Also a Discourse of Horsemanship,* probably first published in 1593.)

mothy saddle and stirrups of no kindred; besides, possess'd with the glanders and like to mose in the chine, troubled with the lampass, infected with the fashions, full of windgalls, sped with spavins, ray'd with the yellows, past cure of the fives, stark spoil'd with the staggers, begnawn with the bots, sway'd in the back and shoulder-shotten; near-legg'd before, and with a half-cheek'd bit and a head-stall of sheep's leather which, being restrain'd to keep him from stumbling, hath been often burst and now repair'd with knots; one girth six times piec'd, and a woman's crupper of velure, which hath two letters for her name fairly set down in studs, and here and there piec'd with packthread.

BAPTISTA Who comes with him?

BIONDELLO O, sir, his lackey, for all the world caparison'd like the horse; with a linen stock on one leg and a kersey boot-hose on the other, gart'red with a red and blue list; an old hat and the humor of forty fancies prick'd in 't for a feather—a monster, a very monster in apparel, and not like a Christian footboy or a gentleman's lackey.

TRANIO
'Tis some odd humor pricks him to this fashion;
Yet oftentimes he goes but mean apparel'd.

BAPTISTA I am glad he's come, howsoe'er he comes.

BIONDELLO Why, sir, he comes not.

BAPTISTA Didst thou not say he comes?

BIONDELLO Who? That Petruchio came?

BAPTISTA Ay, that Petruchio came.

BIONDELLO No, sir, I say his horse comes, with him on his back.

BAPTISTA Why, that's all one.

BIONDELLO
Nay, by Saint Jamy,
I hold you a penny,
A horse and a man
Is more than one,
And yet not many.

Enter Petruchio and Grumio.

PETRUCHIO
Come, where be these gallants? Who's at home?

BAPTISTA
You are welcome, sir.

PETRUCHIO And yet I come not well.

BAPTISTA
And yet you halt not.

TRANIO Not so well apparel'd
As I wish you were.

PETRUCHIO
Were it better, I should rush in thus.
But where is Kate? Where is my lovely bride?
How does my father? Gentles, methinks you frown.
And wherefore gaze this goodly company,
As if they saw some wondrous monument,
Some comet, or unusual prodigy?

BAPTISTA
Why, sir, you know this is your wedding-day.
First were we sad, fearing you would not come,
Now sadder, that you come so unprovided.
Fie, doff this habit, shame to your estate,
An eye-sore to our solemn festival!

TRANIO
And tell us, what occasion of import
Hath all so long detain'd you from your wife,
And sent you hither so unlike yourself?

PETRUCHIO
Tedious it were to tell, and harsh to hear.
Sufficeth, I am come to keep my word,
Though in some part enforced to digress,
Which at more leisure I will so excuse
As you shall well be satisfied withal.
But where is Kate? I stay too long from her.
The morning wears, 'tis time we were at church.

TRANIO
See not your bride in these unreverent robes.
Go to my chamber, put on clothes of mine.

PETRUCHIO
Not I, believe me. Thus I'll visit her.

BAPTISTA
But thus, I trust, you will not marry her.

PETRUCHIO
Good sooth, even thus. Therefore ha' done with
words.
To me she's married, not unto my clothes.
Could I repair what she will wear in me
As I can change these poor accoutrements,
'Twere well for Kate and better for myself.
But what a fool am I to chat with you,
When I should bid good morrow to my bride,
And seal the title with a lovely kiss!
Exit [with Grumio].

TRANIO
He hath some meaning in his mad attire.
We will persuade him, be it possible,
To put on better ere he go to church.

BAPTISTA
I'll after him, and see the event of this.
Exit [with Gremio, and attendants].

TRANIO
But, sir, love concerneth us to add
Her father's liking, which to bring to pass,
As I before imparted to your worship,

50 glanders contagious disease in horses causing swelling beneath the jaw and mucous discharge from the nostrils **50–51 mose in the chine** suffer from glanders **51 lampass** a thick spongy flesh growing over a horse's upper teeth and hindering his eating **52 fashions** i.e., farcins, or farcy, a disease like glanders. **windgalls** soft tumors or swellings generally found on the fetlock joint, so called from having been supposed to contain air. **sped** far gone. **spavins** a disease of the hock, marked by a small bony enlargement inside the leg. **ray'd** defiled **53 yellows** jaundice. **fives** avives, a glandular disease causing swelling behind the ear **54 staggers** a disease causing palsy-like staggering. **bots** parasitic worms **55 shoulder-shotten** with sprained or dislocated shoulder. **near-legg'd before** with knock-kneed forelegs **56 half-cheek'd bit** one to which the bridle is attached halfway up the cheek or sidepiece and thus not giving sufficient control over the horse. **head-stall** part of the bridle over the head **56–57 sheep's leather** (I.e., of inferior quality; pigskin was used for strongest harness.) **57 restrain'd** drawn back **59 piec'd** mended **60 crupper** leather loop passing under the horse's tail and fastened to the saddle. **velure** velvet **65 stock** stocking **66 kersey boot-hose** overstocking of coarse material for wearing under boots **67 list** strip of cloth. **the humor . . . fancies** i.e., some ornament of fantastic appearance **68 prick'd** pinned **71 humor pricks** whim that spurs **80 all one** the same thing **82 hold** wager

88 halt limp, move slowly **90 Were it** even if it (my apparel) were. **rush** come quickly (referring to *halt not* in l. 88) **98 unprovided** ill-equipped **99 estate** position, station **106 digress** i.e., deviate from my promise **117 Could . . . me** if I could amend in my character what she'll have to put up with **122 lovely** loving **126 event** outcome **127–128 love . . . liking** i.e., our love-plot to secure Bianca makes it our business to secure Baptista's approval of the feigned "Lucentio" as wooer

I am to get a man—whate'er he be,
It skills not much, we'll fit him to our turn—
And he shall be Vincentio of Pisa,
And make assurance here in Padua
Of greater sums than I have promised.
So shall you quietly enjoy your hope,
And marry sweet Bianca with consent.

LUCENTIO
Were it not that my fellow schoolmaster
Doth watch Bianca's steps so narrowly,
'Twere good, methinks, to steal our marriage,
Which once perform'd, let all the world say no,
I'll keep mine own, despite of all the world.

TRANIO
That by degrees we mean to look into,
And watch our vantage in this business.
We'll overreach the greybeard, Gremio,
The narrow-prying father, Minola,
The quaint musician, amorous Litio,
All for my master's sake, Lucentio.

Enter Gremio.

Signior Gremio, came you from the church?

GREMIO
As willingly as e'er I came from school.

TRANIO
And is the bride and bridegroom coming home?

GREMIO
A bridegroom say you? 'Tis a groom indeed,
A grumbling groom, and that the girl shall find.

TRANIO
Curster than she? Why, 'tis impossible.

GREMIO
Why, he 's a devil, a devil, a very fiend.

TRANIO
Why, she's a devil, a devil, the devil's dam.

GREMIO
Tut, she 's a lamb, a dove, a fool to him!
I'll tell you, Sir Lucentio. When the priest
Should ask if Katharine should be his wife,
"Ay, by gogs-wouns," quoth he, and swore so loud
That, all amaz'd, the priest let fall the book,
And, as he stoop'd again to take it up,
This mad-brain'd bridegroom took him such a cuff
That down fell priest and book and book and priest.
"Now take them up," quoth he, "if any list."

TRANIO
What said the wench when he rose again?

GREMIO
Trembled and shook, for why he stamp'd and swore
As if the vicar meant to cozen him.
But after many ceremonies done,
He calls for wine. "A health!" quoth he, as if
He had been aboard, carousing to his mates
After a storm; quaff'd off the muscadel
And threw the sops all in the sexton's face,
Having no other reason
But that his beard grew thin and hungerly
And seem'd to ask him sops as he was drinking.
This done, he took the bride about the neck
And kiss'd her lips with such a clamorous smack
That at the parting all the church did echo.
And I seeing this came thence for very shame,
And after me, I know, the rout is coming.
Such a mad marriage never was before.
Hark, hark! I hear the minstrels play. *Music plays.*

Enter Petruchio, Kate, Bianca, Hortensio [as Litio], Baptista, [Grumio, and train].

PETRUCHIO
Gentlemen and friends, I thank you for your pains.
I know you think to dine with me today,
And have prepar'd great store of wedding cheer,
But so it is, my haste doth call me hence,
And therefore here I mean to take my leave.

BAPTISTA
Is 't possible you will away tonight?

PETRUCHIO
I must away today, before night come.
Make it no wonder. If you knew my business,
You would entreat me rather go than stay.
And, honest company, I thank you all
That have beheld me give away myself
To this most patient, sweet, and virtuous wife.
Dine with my father, drink a health to me,
For I must hence; and farewell to you all.

TRANIO
Let us entreat you stay till after dinner.

PETRUCHIO
It may not be.

GREMIO Let me entreat you.

PETRUCHIO
It cannot be.

KATHARINA Let me entreat you.

PETRUCHIO
I am content.

KATHARINA Are you content to stay?

PETRUCHIO
I am content you shall entreat me stay;
But yet not stay, entreat me how you can.

KATHARINA
Now, if you love me, stay.

PETRUCHIO Grumio, my horse.

GRUMIO Ay, sir, they be ready; the oats have eaten the horses.

KATHARINA Nay, then,
Do what thou canst, I will not go today,
No, nor tomorrow, not till I please myself.
The door is open, sir, there lies your way;
You may be jogging whiles your boots are green.

131 skills matters **139 steal our marriage** i.e., elope **143 vantage** opportunity, advantage **146 quaint** skillful **151 a groom indeed** i.e., a fine bridegroom he is. (Said ironically, with pun on the sense of *servant, rough fellow.*) **155 dam** mother **156 a fool to** i.e., a pitiable weak creature compared with **159 gogs-wouns** God's (Christ's) wounds **162 took** gave, struck **164 list** choose **166 for why** because **167 cozen** cheat **170 aboard** aboard ship

172 sops cakes or bread soaked in the wine **174 hungerly** i.e., sparsely **180 rout** crowd, wedding party **190 Make** consider **192 honest** worthy, kind **203 horse** horses **204–205 oats . . . horses** (A comic inversion.) **210 be . . . green** (Proverbial for "getting an early start," with a sarcastic allusion to his unseemly attire.) **green** fresh, new

For me, I'll not be gone till I please myself.
'Tis like you'll prove a jolly surly groom,
That take it on you at the first so roundly.

PETRUCHIO
O Kate, content thee; prithee, be not angry.

KATHARINA
I will be angry. What hast thou to do?
Father, be quiet. He shall stay my leisure.

GREMIO
Ay, marry, sir, now it begins to work.

KATHARINA
Gentlemen, forward to the bridal dinner.
I see a woman may be made a fool,
If she had not a spirit to resist.

PETRUCHIO
They shall go forward, Kate, at thy command.
Obey the bride, you that attend on her.
Go to the feast, revel and domineer,
Carouse full measure to her maidenhead,
Be mad and merry, or go hang yourselves.
But for my bonny Kate, she must with me.
Nay, look not big, nor stamp, nor stare, nor fret;
I will be master of what is mine own.
She is my goods, my chattels; she is my house,
My household stuff, my field, my barn,
My horse, my ox, my ass, my any thing;
And here she stands, touch her whoever dare.
I'll bring mine action on the proudest he
That stops my way in Padua. Grumio,
Draw forth thy weapon, we are beset with thieves.
Rescue thy mistress, if thou be a man.
Fear not, sweet wench, they shall not touch thee, Kate!
I'll buckler thee against a million.
Exeunt Petruchio, Katharina, [*and Grumio*].

BAPTISTA
Nay, let them go, a couple of quiet ones.

GREMIO
Went they not quickly, I should die with laughing.

TRANIO
Of all mad matches never was the like.

LUCENTIO
Mistress, what's your opinion of your sister?

BIANCA
That, being mad herself, she's madly mated.

GREMIO
I warrant him, Petruchio is Kated.

BAPTISTA
Neighbors and friends, though bride and bridegroom wants
For to supply the places at the table,
You know there wants no junkets at the feast.
Lucentio, you shall supply the bridegroom's place,
And let Bianca take her sister's room.

TRANIO
Shall sweet Bianca practice how to bride it?

BAPTISTA
She shall, Lucentio. Come, gentlemen, let's go.
Exeunt.

[ACT IV • SCENE I]

Enter Grumio.

GRUMIO Fie, fie on all tir'd jades, on all mad masters, and all foul ways! Was ever man so beaten? Was ever man so ray'd? Was ever man so weary? I am sent before to make a fire, and they are coming after to warm them. Now, were not I a little pot and soon hot, my very lips might freeze to my teeth, my tongue to the roof of my mouth, my heart in my belly, ere I should come by a fire to thaw me. But I, with blowing the fire, shall warm myself; for, considering the weather, a taller man than I will take cold. Holla, ho! Curtis!

Enter Curtis.

CURTIS Who is that calls so coldly?

GRUMIO A piece of ice. If thou doubt it, thou mayst slide from my shoulder to my heel with no greater a run but my head and my neck. A fire, good Curtis.

CURTIS Is my master and his wife coming, Grumio?

GRUMIO O, ay, Curtis, ay, and therefore fire, fire; cast on no water.

CURTIS Is she so hot a shrew as she's reported?

GRUMIO She was, good Curtis, before this frost. But, thou know'st, winter tames man, woman, and beast; for it hath tam'd my old master and my new mistress and myself, fellow Curtis.

CURTIS Away, you three-inch fool! I am no beast.

GRUMIO Am I but three inches? Why, thy horn is a foot, and so long am I at the least. But wilt thou make a fire, or shall I complain on thee to our mistress, whose hand, she being now at hand, thou shalt soon feel, to thy cold comfort, for being slow in thy hot office?

CURTIS I prithee, good Grumio, tell me, how goes the world?

GRUMIO A cold world, Curtis, in every office but thine, and therefore fire. Do thy duty, and have thy duty, for my master and mistress are almost frozen to death.

CURTIS There's fire ready, and therefore, good Grumio, the news.

GRUMIO Why, "Jack boy, ho, boy!" and as much news as wilt thou.

CURTIS Come, you are so full of cony-catching!

212 like likely. **jolly** arrogant, overbearing **213 take it on you** i.e., throw your weight around. **roundly** unceremoniously **215 What . . . do** i.e., what business is it of yours **216 stay** await **223 domineer** feast riotously **227 big** threatening **231 ox . . . any thing** (This catalogue of a man's possessions is from the Tenth Commandment.) **233 action** (1) lawsuit (2) attack **235 Draw** (Perhaps Petruchio and Grumio actually draw their swords.) **238 buckler** shield, defend **245 wants** are lacking **247 junkets** sweetmeats

IV.i. Location: Petruchio's country house. A table is set out, with seats.
1 jades ill-conditioned horses **2 ways** roads **3 ray'd** dirtied **5 a little . . . hot** (Proverbial expression for a person of small stature soon angered.) **10 taller** (with play on the meaning *better, finer*) **16–17 cast . . . water** (Alludes to the round, "Scotland's burning," in which the phrase "Fire, fire!" is followed by "Pour on water, pour on water.") **23 three-inch fool** (Another reference to Grumio's size.) **I am no beast** (Curtis protests being called *fellow* by Grumio, since Grumio in his previous speech has paralleled himself with *beast.*) **24 horn** i.e., cuckold's horn **28 hot office** i.e., duty of providing a fire **32 have thy duty** receive your reward **36 Jack . . . boy** (The first line of another round or catch.) **38 cony-catching** cheating, trickery (with a play on *catch,* round, in the previous line)

GRUMIO Why, therefore fire, for I have caught extreme cold. Where's the cook? Is supper ready, the house trimm'd, rushes strew'd, cobwebs swept, the servingmen in their new fustian, their white stockings, and every officer his wedding-garment on? Be the jacks fair within, the jills fair without, the carpets laid, and everything in order?

CURTIS All ready; and therefore, I pray thee, news.

GRUMIO First, know, my horse is tir'd, my master and mistress fall'n out.

CURTIS How?

GRUMIO Out of their saddles into the dirt—and thereby hangs a tale.

CURTIS Let's ha 't, good Grumio.

GRUMIO Lend thine ear.

CURTIS Here.

GRUMIO There. [*Strikes him.*]

CURTIS This 'tis to feel a tale, not to hear a tale.

GRUMIO And therefore 'tis call'd a sensible tale, and this cuff was but to knock at your ear, and beseech list'ning. Now I begin: Imprimis, we came down a foul hill, my master riding behind my mistress—

CURTIS Both of one horse?

GRUMIO What's that to thee?

CURTIS Why, a horse.

GRUMIO Tell thou the tale. But hadst thou not cross'd me, thou shouldst have heard how her horse fell and she under her horse; thou shouldst have heard in how miry a place, how she was bemoil'd, how he left her with the horse upon her, how he beat me because her horse stumbled, how she waded through the dirt to pluck him off me, how he swore, how she pray'd that never pray'd before, how I cried, how the horses ran away, how her bridle was burst, how I lost my crupper, with many things of worthy memory, which now shall die in oblivion and thou return unexperienc'd to thy grave.

CURTIS By this reck'ning he is more shrew than she.

GRUMIO Ay, and that thou and the proudest of you all shall find when he comes home. But what talk I of this? Call forth Nathaniel, Joseph, Nicholas, Philip, Walter, Sugarsop, and the rest. Let their heads be sleekly comb'd, their blue coats brush'd, and their garters of an indifferent knit; let them curtsy with their left legs, and not presume to touch a hair of my master's horse-tail till they kiss their hands. Are they all ready?

CURTIS They are.

GRUMIO Call them forth.

CURTIS Do you hear, ho? You must meet my master to countenance my mistress.

GRUMIO Why, she hath a face of her own.

CURTIS Who knows not that?

GRUMIO Thou, it seems, that calls for company to countenance her.

CURTIS I call them forth to credit her.

Enter four or five Servingmen.

GRUMIO Why, she comes to borrow nothing of them.

NATHANIEL Welcome home, Grumio!

PHILIP How now, Grumio!

JOSEPH What, Grumio!

NICHOLAS Fellow Grumio!

NATHANIEL How now, old lad?

GRUMIO Welcome, you; how now, you; what, you; fellow, you—and thus much for greeting. Now, my spruce companions, is all ready, and all things neat?

NATHANIEL All things is ready. How near is our master?

GRUMIO E'en at hand, alighted by this; and therefore be not—Cock's passion, silence! I hear my master.

Enter Petruchio and Kate.

PETRUCHIO
Where be these knaves? What, no man at door
To hold my stirrup nor to take my horse?
Where is Nathaniel, Gregory, Philip?

ALL SERVANTS Here, here, sir, here, sir.

PETRUCHIO
Here, sir! Here, sir! Here, sir! Here, sir!
You loggerheaded and unpolish'd grooms!
What, no attendance? No regard? No duty?
Where is the foolish knave I sent before?

GRUMIO
Here, sir, as foolish as I was before.

PETRUCHIO
You peasant swain, you whoreson malt-horse
drudge!
Did I not bid thee meet me in the park
And bring along these rascal knaves with thee?

GRUMIO
Nathaniel's coat, sir, was not fully made,
And Gabriel's pumps were all unpink'd i' th' heel.
There was no link to color Peter's hat,
And Walter's dagger was not come from sheathing.
There were none fine but Adam, Ralph, and
Gregory;
The rest were ragged, old, and beggarly.
Yet, as they are, here are they come to meet you.

PETRUCHIO
Go, rascals, go, and fetch my supper in.
Exeunt Servants.
[*Sings.*] "Where is the life that late I led?"
Where are those—Sit down, Kate, and welcome.—
[*They sit at table.*]
Soud, soud, soud, soud!

Enter Servants with supper.

Why, when, I say? —Nay, good sweet Kate, be
merry.—

41 rushes (Used to cover the floor.) **42 fustian** coarse cloth of cotton and flax **43 officer** household servant **43, 44 jacks, jills** drinking measures of one-half and one-fourth pints (with quibble on *servingmen* and *maidservants*) **44 carpets** table covers **57 sensible** (1) capable of being felt (2) showing good sense **59 Imprimis** in the first place **61 of** on **64 cross'd** thwarted, interrupted **67 bemoil'd** befouled with mire **78 what** why **81 blue coats** (Usual dress for servingmen.) **82 indifferent** i.e., well matched and not flamboyant **89 countenance** pay respects to (with a following pun on the meaning *face*)

94 credit pay respects to (with another pun following, on *extending financial credit*) **107 Cock's passion** by God's (Christ's) suffering **115 before** ahead (with pun in next line on *previously*) **117 swain** rustic. **whoreson . . . drudge** worthless plodding work animal, such as would be used on a treadmill to grind malt **121 pumps** lowcut shoes. **unpink'd** lacking in eyelets or in ornamental tracing in the leather **122 link** torch, the smoke or soot of which was used as blackening **123 sheathing** being fitted with a sheath **124 fine** well clothed **130 Soud** (A nonsense song, or expression of impatience, or perhaps "food!")

Off with my boots, you rogues! You villains, when?
[*A Servant takes off Petruchio's boots.*]
[*Sings.*] "It was the friar of orders grey,
As he forth walked on his way"—
Out, you rogue! You pluck my foot awry. 135
Take that, and mend the plucking off the other.
[*Strikes him.*]
Be merry, Kate.—Some water, here; what, ho!

Enter one with water.

Where's my spaniel Troilus? Sirrah, get you hence,
And bid my cousin Ferdinand come hither—
[*Exit Servant.*]
One, Kate, that you must kiss, and be acquainted with.
Where are my slippers? Shall I have some water?
Come, Kate, and wash, and welcome heartily.
[*Servant offers water, but spills some.*]
You whoreson villain, will you let it fall?
[*Strikes him.*]

KATHARINA
Patience, I pray you, 'twas a fault unwilling.

PETRUCHIO
A whoreson beetle-headed, flap-ear'd knave! 145
Come, Kate, sit down, I know you have a stomach. 146
Will you give thanks, sweet Kate, or else shall I? 147
What's this? Mutton?

FIRST SERVANT Ay.

PETRUCHIO Who brought it?

PETER I.

PETRUCHIO
'Tis burnt, and so is all the meat.
What dogs are these? Where is the rascal cook?
How durst you, villains, bring it from the dresser, 151
And serve it thus to me that love it not?
There, take it to you, trenchers, cups, and all. 153
[*Throws the meat, etc., at them. They run out.*]
You heedless joltheads and unmanner'd slaves! 154
What, do you grumble? I'll be with you straight. 155

KATHARINA
I pray you, husband, be not so disquiet.
The meat was well, if you were so contented.

PETRUCHIO
I tell thee, Kate, 'twas burnt and dried away,
And I expressly am forbid to touch it;
For it engenders choler, planteth anger, 160
And better 'twere that both of us did fast,
Since, of ourselves, ourselves are choleric,
Than feed it with such overroasted flesh.
Be patient. Tomorrow 't shall be mended,
And, for this night, we'll fast for company.
Come, I will bring thee to thy bridal chamber.
Exeunt.

Enter Servants severally.

NATHANIEL Peter, didst ever see the like?

PETER He kills her in her own humor. 168

Enter Curtis.

GRUMIO Where is he?

CURTIS In her chamber, making a sermon of continency to her,
And rails, and swears, and rates, that she, poor soul, 172
Knows not which way to stand, to look, to speak,
And sits as one new-risen from a dream.
Away, away! For he is coming hither. [*Exeunt.*]

Enter Petruchio.

PETRUCHIO
Thus have I politicly begun my reign,
And 'tis my hope to end successfully.
My falcon now is sharp and passing empty, 178
And till she stoop she must not be full-gorg'd, 179
For then she never looks upon her lure.
Another way I have to man my haggard, 181
To make her come and know her keeper's call:
That is, to watch her, as we watch these kites 183
That bate and beat and will not be obedient. 184
She eat no meat today, nor none shall eat. 185
Last night she slept not, nor tonight she shall not.
As with the meat, some undeserved fault
I'll find about the making of the bed,
And here I'll fling the pillow, there the bolster,
This way the coverlet, another way the sheets.
Ay, and amid this hurly I intend 191
That all is done in reverend care of her.
And in conclusion she shall watch all night,
And if she chance to nod I'll rail and brawl
And with the clamor keep her still awake.
This is a way to kill a wife with kindness;
And thus I'll curb her mad and headstrong humor.
He that knows better how to tame a shrew,
Now let him speak; 'tis charity to shew. *Exit.* 199

[SCENE II]

Enter Tranio [*as Lucentio*] *and Hortensio* [*as Litio*].

TRANIO
Is 't possible, friend Litio, that Mistress Bianca
Doth fancy any other but Lucentio?
I tell you, sir, she bears me fair in hand. 3

HORTENSIO
Sir, to satisfy you in what I have said,

135 Out (Exclamation of anger or reproach.) **145 beetle-headed** i.e., blockheaded (since a *beetle* is a pounding tool) **146 stomach** appetite (with a suggestion also of *temper*) **147 give thanks** say grace **151 dresser** sideboard **153 trenchers** wooden dishes or plates **154 joltheads** blockheads **155 with you straight** after you at once (to get even for this) **160 choler** the humor or bodily fluid, hot and dry in character, that supposedly produced ill temper and was thought to be aggravated by the eating of roast meat

168 kills . . . humor i.e., uses anger to subdue anger in her **172 rates** scolds **178 sharp** hungry **179 stoop** fly down to the lure **181 man** tame (with a pun on the sense of *assert masculine authority*). **haggard** wild female hawk; hence, an intractable woman **183 watch her** keep her watching, i.e., awake. **kites** a kind of hawk **184 bate and beat** beat the wings impatiently and flutter away from the hand or perch **185 She eat** she ate. (Pronounced *et.*) **191 intend** pretend **199 shew** show

IV.ii. Location: Padua. Before Baptista's house.
3 bears . . . hand gives me encouragement

Stand by and mark the manner of his teaching.
[They stand aside.]

Enter Bianca [and Lucentio as Cambio].

LUCENTIO
Now, mistress, profit you in what you read?
BIANCA
What, master, read you? First resolve me that.
LUCENTIO
I read that I profess, the Art to Love.
BIANCA
And may you prove, sir, master of your art!
LUCENTIO
While you, sweet dear, prove mistress of my heart!
[They stand aside.]
HORTENSIO *[To Tranio]*
Quick proceeders, marry! Now, tell me, I pray,
You that durst swear that your mistress Bianca
Lov'd none in the world so well as Lucentio.
TRANIO
O despiteful love! Unconstant womankind!
I tell thee, Litio, this is wonderful.
HORTENSIO
Mistake no more. I am not Litio,
Nor a musician, as I seem to be,
But one that scorn to live in this disguise
For such a one as leaves a gentleman
And makes a god of such a cullion.
Know, sir, that I am call'd Hortensio.
TRANIO
Signior Hortensio, I have often heard
Of your entire affection to Bianca;
And since mine eyes are witness of her lightness,
I will with you, if you be so contented,
Forswear Bianca and her love forever.
HORTENSIO
See, how they kiss and court! Signior Lucentio,
Here is my hand, and here I firmly vow
[Gives hand.]
Never to woo her more, but do forswear her,
As one unworthy all the former favors
That I have fondly flatter'd her withal.
TRANIO
And here I take the like unfeigned oath,
Never to marry with her though she would entreat.
Fie on her, see how beastly she doth court him!
HORTENSIO
Would all the world but he had quite forsworn!
For me, that I may surely keep mine oath,
I will be married to a wealthy widow,
Ere three days pass, which hath as long lov'd me
As I have lov'd this proud disdainful haggard.
And so farewell, Signior Lucentio.
Kindness in women, not their beauteous looks,
Shall win my love. And so I take my leave,
In resolution as I swore before. *[Exit.]*
TRANIO
Mistress Bianca, bless you with such grace
As 'longeth to a lover's blessed case!
Nay, I have ta'en you napping, gentle love,
And have forsworn you with Hortensio.
BIANCA *[Advancing]*
Tranio, you jest. But have you both forsworn me?
TRANIO
Mistress, we have.
LUCENTIO Then we are rid of Litio.
TRANIO
I' faith, he'll have a lusty widow now,
That shall be woo'd and wedded in a day.
BIANCA
God give him joy!
TRANIO
Ay, and he'll tame her.
BIANCA He says so, Tranio?
TRANIO
Faith, he is gone unto the taming-school.
BIANCA
The taming-school! What, is there such a place?
TRANIO
Ay, mistress, and Petruchio is the master,
That teacheth tricks eleven and twenty long,
To tame a shrew and charm her chattering tongue.

Enter Biondello.

BIONDELLO
O master, master, I have watch'd so long
That I am dog-weary, but at last I spied
An ancient angel coming down the hill
Will serve the turn.
TRANIO What is he, Biondello?
BIONDELLO
Master, a mercatante, or a pedant,
I know not what; but formal in apparel,
In gait and countenance surely like a father.
LUCENTIO
And what of him, Tranio?
TRANIO
If he be credulous and trust my tale,
I'll make him glad to seem Vincentio,
And give assurance to Baptista Minola,
As if he were the right Vincentio.
Take in your love, and then let me alone.
[Exeunt Lucentio and Bianca.]

Enter a Pedant.

PEDANT
God save you, sir!
TRANIO And you sir! You are welcome.
Travel you far on, or are you at the farthest?

6 read (Evidently, both Bianca and "Cambio" carry books.) **7 resolve** answer **8 that** that which. **Art to Love** Ovid's *Ars Amandi* **11 proceeders** (1) workers, doers (2) candidates for academic degrees (as suggested by the phrase *master of your art* in l. 9) **15 wonderful** cause for wonder **19 such a one** i.e., Bianca **20 cullion** base fellow (referring to "Cambio"; literally the word means *testicle*) **24 lightness** wantonness **31 fondly** foolishly **35 Would . . . forsworn** i.e., may everyone in the world forsake her except the penniless "Cambio," and may she thus get what she deserves

45 'longeth belongs **50 lusty** merry, lively **57 eleven . . . long** i.e., in sufficient number (alluding to the card game called "one and thirty") **61 ancient angel** i.e., fellow of the good old stamp. (Literally, an "angel" or gold coin bearing the stamp of the archangel Michael and thus distinguishable from more recent debased coinage.) **62 Will . . . turn** who will serve our purposes **63 mercatante** merchant. **pedant** schoolmaster

PEDANT
Sir, at the farthest for a week or two,
But then up farther, and as far as Rome,
And so to Tripoli, if God lend me life.

TRANIO
What countryman, I pray?

PEDANT
Of Mantua.

TRANIO
Of Mantua, sir? Marry, God forbid!
And come to Padua, careless of your life?

PEDANT
My life, sir! How, I pray? For that goes hard.

TRANIO
'Tis death for anyone in Mantua
To come to Padua. Know you not the cause?
Your ships are stay'd at Venice, and the Duke,
For private quarrel 'twixt your Duke and him,
Hath publish'd and proclaim'd it openly.
'Tis marvel, but that you are but newly come,
You might have heard it else proclaim'd about.

PEDANT
Alas, sir, it is worse for me than so,
For I have bills for money by exchange
From Florence and must here deliver them.

TRANIO
Well, sir, to do you courtesy,
This will I do, and this I will advise you—
First, tell me, have you ever been at Pisa?

PEDANT
Ay, sir, in Pisa have I often been,
Pisa renowned for grave citizens.

TRANIO
Among them know you one Vincentio?

PEDANT
I know him not, but I have heard of him;
A merchant of incomparable wealth.

TRANIO
He is my father, sir, and, sooth to say,
In count'nance somewhat doth resemble you.

BIONDELLO [*Aside*] As much as an apple doth an oyster,
and all one.

TRANIO
To save your life in this extremity,
This favor will I do you for his sake;
And think it not the worst of all your fortunes
That you are like to Sir Vincentio.
His name and credit shall you undertake,
And in my house you shall be friendly lodg'd.
Look that you take upon you as you should.
You understand me, sir? So shall you stay
Till you have done your business in the city.
If this be court'sy, sir, accept of it.

PEDANT
O sir, I do, and will repute you ever
The patron of my life and liberty.

TRANIO
Then go with me to make the matter good.
This, by the way, I let you understand:
My father is here look'd for every day,
To pass assurance of a dow'r in marriage
'Twixt me and one Baptista's daughter here.
In all these circumstances I'll instruct you.
Go with me to clothe you as becomes you.
Exeunt.

[SCENE III]

Enter Katharina and Grumio.

GRUMIO
No, no, forsooth, I dare not for my life.

KATHARINA
The more my wrong, the more his spite appears.
What, did he marry me to famish me?
Beggars, that come unto my father's door
Upon entreaty have a present alms;
If not, elsewhere they meet with charity.
But I, who never knew how to entreat,
Nor never needed that I should entreat,
Am starv'd for meat, giddy for lack of sleep,
With oaths kept waking, and with brawling fed.
And that which spites me more than all these wants,
He does it under name of perfect love;
As who should say, if I should sleep or eat,
'Twere deadly sickness or else present death.
I prithee go and get me some repast,
I care not what, so it be wholesome food.

GRUMIO
What say you to a neat's foot?

KATHARINA
'Tis passing good. I prithee let me have it.

GRUMIO
I fear it is too choleric a meat.
How say you to a fat tripe finely broil'd?

KATHARINA
I like it well, good Grumio, fetch it me.

GRUMIO
I cannot tell, I fear 'tis choleric.
What say you to a piece of beef and mustard?

KATHARINA
A dish that I do love to feed upon.

GRUMIO
Ay, but the mustard is too hot a little.

KATHARINA
Why then, the beef, and let the mustard rest.

GRUMIO
Nay then, I will not; you shall have the mustard,
Or else you get no beef of Grumio.

KATHARINA
Then both, or one, or anything thou wilt.

80 goes hard is serious indeed **102 all one** no matter **107 credit** reputation **109 take upon you** play your part

118 pass assurance convey a legal guarantee

IV.iii. Location: Petruchio's house. A table is set out, with seats.
2 my wrong the wrong done to me **5 present** immediate **13 As who** as if one **17 neat's** ox's

GRUMIO
Why then, the mustard without the beef. 30

KATHARINA
Go, get thee gone, thou false deluding slave,
Beats him.
That feed'st me with the very name of meat!
Sorrow on thee and all the pack of you,
That triumph thus upon my misery!
Go, get thee gone, I say.

Enter Petruchio and Hortensio with meat.

PETRUCHIO
How fares my Kate? What, sweeting, all amort? 36

HORTENSIO
Mistress, what cheer?

KATHARINA
Faith, as cold as can be.

PETRUCHIO
Pluck up thy spirits, look cheerfully upon me.
Here, love, thou see'st how diligent I am
To dress thy meat myself and bring it thee. 40
I am sure, sweet Kate, this kindness merits thanks.
What, not a word? Nay, then thou lov'st it not,
And all my pains is sorted to no proof. 43
Here, take away this dish.

KATHARINA
I pray you, let it stand.

PETRUCHIO
The poorest service is repaid with thanks,
And so shall mine before you touch the meat.

KATHARINA
I thank you, sir.

HORTENSIO
Signior Petruchio, fie! You are to blame.
Come, Mistress Kate, I'll bear you company.
[*They sit at table.*]

PETRUCHIO [*Aside to Hortensio*]
Eat it up all, Hortensio, if thou lovest me.—
Much good do it unto thy gentle heart!
Kate, eat apace. And now, my honey love,
Will we return unto thy father's house
And revel it as bravely as the best, 54
With silken coats and caps and golden rings,
With ruffs and cuffs and farthingales and things, 56
With scarfs and fans and double change of brav'ry, 57
With amber bracelets, beads, and all this knav'ry.
What, hast thou din'd? The tailor stays thy leisure,
To deck thy body with his ruffling treasure. 60

Enter Tailor [*with a gown*].

Come, tailor, let us see these ornaments.
Lay forth the gown.

Enter Haberdasher [*with a cap*].

What news with you, sir?

HABERDASHER
Here is the cap your worship did bespeak.

PETRUCHIO
Why, this was molded on a porringer— 64
A velvet dish. Fie, fie, 'tis lewd and filthy. 65
Why, 'tis a cockle or a walnut-shell, 66
A knack, a toy, a trick, a baby's cap. 67
Away with it! Come, let me have a bigger.

KATHARINA
I'll have no bigger. This doth fit the time, 69
And gentlewomen wear such caps as these.

PETRUCHIO
When you are gentle, you shall have one too,
And not till then.

HORTENSIO [*Aside*] That will not be in haste.

KATHARINA
Why, sir, I trust I may have leave to speak,
And speak I will. I am no child, no babe.
Your betters have endur'd me say my mind,
And if you cannot, best you stop your ears.
My tongue will tell the anger of my heart
Or else my heart, concealing it, will break,
And rather than it shall, I will be free
Even to the uttermost, as I please, in words.

PETRUCHIO
Why, thou say'st true. It is a paltry cap,
A custard-coffin, a bauble, a silken pie. 82
I love thee well in that thou lik'st it not.

KATHARINA
Love me or love me not, I like the cap,
And it I will have, or I will have none.
[*Exit Haberdasher.*]

PETRUCHIO
Thy gown? Why, ay. Come, tailor, let us see 't.
O mercy, God! What masquing stuff is here? 87
What's this, a sleeve? 'Tis like a demi-cannon. 88
What, up and down carv'd like an apple-tart? 89
Here's snip and nip and cut and slish and slash,
Like to a censer in a barber's shop. 91
Why, what a' devil's name, tailor, call'st thou this? 92

HORTENSIO [*Aside*]
I see she's like to have neither cap nor gown.

TAILOR
You bid me make it orderly and well,
According to the fashion and the time.

PETRUCHIO
Marry, and did. But if you be remember'd, 96
I did not bid you mar it to the time.
Go, hop me over every kennel home, 98
For you shall hop without my custom, sir.
I'll none of it. Hence, make your best of it.

KATHARINA
I never saw a better fashion'd gown,
More quaint, more pleasing, nor more
commendable. 102
Belike you mean to make a puppet of me.

PETRUCHIO
Why, true, he means to make a puppet of thee.

36 all amort dejected, dispirited **40 dress** prepare **43 sorted to no proof** proved to be to no purpose **54 bravely** splendidly dressed **56 farthingales** hooped petticoats **57 brav'ry** finery **60 ruffling treasure** finery trimmed with ruffles **64 porringer** porridge bowl

65 lewd vile **66 cockle** cockleshell **67 trick** trifle **69 fit the time** suit the current fashion **82 custard-coffin** crust over a custard **87 masquing** i.e., suited only for a masque **88 demi-cannon** large cannon **89 up and down** all over, exactly **91 censer** perfuming pan having an ornamental lid **92 a'** in (the) **96 be remember'd** recollect **98 hop . . . home** hop on home over every street gutter **102 quaint** elegant

TAILOR
She says your worship means to make a puppet of her.

PETRUCHIO
O monstrous arrogance! Thou liest, thou thread, thou thimble,
Thou yard, three-quarters, half-yard, quarter, nail!
Thou flea, thou nit, thou winter-cricket thou!
Brav'd in mine own house with a skein of thread?
Away, thou rag, thou quantity, thou remnant,
Or I shall so be-mete thee with thy yard
As thou shalt think on prating whilst thou liv'st!
I tell thee, I, that thou hast marr'd her gown.

TAILOR
Your worship is deceiv'd. The gown is made
Just as my master had direction.
Grumio gave order how it should be done.

GRUMIO I gave him no order. I gave him the stuff.

TAILOR
But how did you desire it should be made?

GRUMIO Marry, sir, with needle and thread.

TAILOR
But did you not request to have it cut?

GRUMIO Thou hast fac'd many things.

TAILOR I have.

GRUMIO Face not me. Thou hast brav'd many men; brave not me. I will neither be fac'd nor brav'd. I say unto thee, I bid thy master cut out the gown, but I did not bid him cut it to pieces. Ergo, thou liest.

TAILOR Why, here is the note of the fashion to testify.
[Displays his bill.]

PETRUCHIO Read it.

GRUMIO The note lies in 's throat, if he say I said so.

TAILOR *[Reads]* "Imprimis, a loose-bodied gown"—

GRUMIO Master, if ever I said loose-bodied gown, sew me in the skirts of it, and beat me to death with a bottom of brown thread. I said a gown.

PETRUCHIO Proceed.

TAILOR *[Reads]* "With a small compass'd cape"—

GRUMIO I confess the cape.

TAILOR *[Reads]* "With a trunk sleeve"—

GRUMIO I confess two sleeves.

TAILOR *[Reads]* "The sleeves curiously cut."

PETRUCHIO Ay, there's the villainy.

GRUMIO Error i' th' bill, sir, error i' th' bill. I commanded the sleeves should be cut out and sew'd up again, and that I'll prove upon thee, though thy little finger be arm'd in a thimble.

TAILOR This is true that I say. An I had thee in place where, thou shouldst know it.

GRUMIO I am for thee straight. Take thou the bill, give me thy mete-yard, and spare not me.

HORTENSIO God-a-mercy, Grumio, then he shall have no odds.

PETRUCHIO Well, sir, in brief, the gown is not for me.

GRUMIO You are i' th' right, sir, 'tis for my mistress.

PETRUCHIO Go, take it up unto thy master's use.

GRUMIO Villain, not for thy life! Take up my mistress' gown for thy master's use!

PETRUCHIO Why sir, what's your conceit in that?

GRUMIO
O, sir, the conceit is deeper than you think for:
Take up my mistress' gown to his master's use!
O, fie, fie, fie!

PETRUCHIO *[Aside to Hortensio]*
Hortensio, say thou wilt see the tailor paid.—
Go take it hence, be gone, and say no more.

HORTENSIO *[Aside to Tailor]*
Tailor, I'll pay thee for thy gown tomorrow.
Take no unkindness of his hasty words.
Away, I say. Commend me to thy master.
Exit Tailor.

PETRUCHIO
Well, come, my Kate. We will unto your father's
Even in these honest mean habiliments.
Our purses shall be proud, our garments poor,
For 'tis the mind that makes the body rich;
And as the sun breaks through the darkest clouds,
So honor peereth in the meanest habit.
What, is the jay more precious than the lark
Because his feathers are more beautiful?
Or is the adder better than the eel
Because his painted skin contents the eye?
O, no, good Kate; neither art thou the worse
For this poor furniture and mean array.
If thou account'st it shame, lay it on me.
And therefore frolic; we will hence forthwith,
To feast and sport us at thy father's house.
[To Grumio.] Go, call my men, and let us straight to him;
And bring our horses unto Long-lane end.
There will we mount, and thither walk on foot.
Let's see, I think 'tis now some seven o'clock,
And well we may come there by dinnertime.

KATHARINA
I dare assure you, sir, 'tis almost two,
And 'twill be suppertime ere you come there.

PETRUCHIO
It shall be seven ere I go to horse.
Look what I speak, or do, or think to do,
You are still crossing it.—Sirs, let 't alone.
I will not go today, and ere I do,
It shall be what o'clock I say it is.

HORTENSIO *[Aside]*
Why, so this gallant will command the sun.
[Exeunt.]

107 nail a measure of length for cloth: 2¼ inches **108 nit** louse egg **109 Brav'd** defied. **with** by **110 quantity** fragment **111 be-mete** measure, i.e., thrash. **yard** yardstick **112 think on prating** i.e., remember this thrashing and think twice before talking so again **121 fac'd** trimmed. (But Grumio puns on the meaning *bullied.*) **123 Face** bully. **brav'd** dressed finely **124 brave** defy **126 Ergo** therefore **131 loose-bodied gown** (Grumio plays on *loose,* wanton; a gown fit for a prostitute.) **133 bottom** ball wound from a skein. (A weaver's term.) **135 compass'd** with the edges forming a semicircle **137 trunk** full, wide **139 curiously** elaborately **145–146 in place where** in a suitable place **147 bill** (1) the note ordering the gown (2) a weapon, a halberd **148 mete-yard** measuring-stick

153 use i.e., whatever use he can make of it. (But Grumio deliberately misinterprets in a bawdy sense.) **156 conceit** idea **170 peereth** is seen. **habit** attire **176 furniture** furnishings of attire **184 dinnertime** i.e., about noon **188 Look what** whatever

[SCENE IV]

Enter Tranio [as Lucentio], and the Pedant dress'd like Vincentio, [booted and bare-headed].

TRANIO
Sir, this is the house. Please it you that I call?

PEDANT
Ay, what else? And but I be deceived,
Signior Baptista may remember me,
Near twenty years ago, in Genoa,
Where we were lodgers at the Pegasus.

TRANIO
'Tis well; and hold your own, in any case,
With such austerity as 'longeth to a father.

Enter Biondello.

PEDANT
I warrant you. But, sir, here comes your boy;
'Twere good he were school'd.

TRANIO
Fear you not him.—Sirrah Biondello,
Now do your duty throughly, I advise you.
Imagine 'twere the right Vincentio.

BIONDELLO
Tut, fear not me.

TRANIO
But hast thou done thy errand to Baptista?

BIONDELLO
I told him that your father was at Venice,
And that you look'd for him this day in Padua.

TRANIO
Th' art a tall fellow. Hold thee that to drink.
[Gives money.]
Here comes Baptista. Set your countenance, sir.

Enter Baptista and Lucentio [as Cambio].

Signior Baptista, you are happily met.
[*To the Pedant.*] Sir, this is the gentleman I told you of.
I pray you, stand good father to me now,
Give me Bianca for my patrimony.

PEDANT
Soft, son!
Sir, by your leave, having come to Padua
To gather in some debts, my son Lucentio
Made me acquainted with a weighty cause
Of love between your daughter and himself;
And, for the good report I hear of you
And for the love he beareth to your daughter
And she to him, to stay him not too long,
I am content, in a good father's care,
To have him match'd. And if you please to like
No worse than I, upon some agreement
Me shall you find ready and willing
With one consent to have her so bestowed;
For curious I cannot be with you,
Signior Baptista, of whom I hear so well.

BAPTISTA
Sir, pardon me in what I have to say;
Your plainness and your shortness please me well.
Right true it is, your son Lucentio here
Doth love my daughter, and she loveth him,
Or both dissemble deeply their affections.
And therefore, if you say no more than this,
That like a father you will deal with him
And pass my daughter a sufficient dower,
The match is made, and all is done.
Your son shall have my daughter with consent.

TRANIO
I thank you, sir. Where then do you know best
We be affied and such assurance ta'en
As shall with either part's agreement stand?

BAPTISTA
Not in my house, Lucentio; for, you know,
Pitchers have ears, and I have many servants.
Besides, old Gremio is heark'ning still,
And happily we might be interrupted.

TRANIO
Then at my lodging, an it like you.
There doth my father lie, and there, this night,
We'll pass the business privately and well.
Send for your daughter by your servant here;
My boy shall fetch the scrivener presently.
The worst is this, that at so slender warning
You are like to have a thin and slender pittance.

BAPTISTA
It likes me well. Cambio, hie you home,
And bid Bianca make her ready straight.
And, if you will, tell what hath happ'ned:
Lucentio's father is arriv'd in Padua,
And how she's like to be Lucentio's wife.
[Exit Lucentio.]

BIONDELLO
I pray the gods she may with all my heart!

TRANIO
Dally not with the gods, but get thee gone.
Exit [Biondello].
Signior Baptista, shall I lead the way?
Welcome! One mess is like to be your cheer.
Come, sir, we will better it in Pisa.

BAPTISTA
I follow you. *Exeunt [Tranio, Pedant, and Baptista].*

Enter Lucentio [as Cambio] and Biondello.

BIONDELLO Cambio!
LUCENTIO What say'st thou, Biondello?
BIONDELLO You saw my master wink and laugh upon you?

IV.iv. Location: Padua. Before Baptista's house.
s.d. booted (signifying travel) **2 but** unless **3 may remember** (The Pedant is rehearsing what he is to say.) **5 the Pegasus** i.e., an inn, so named after the famous winged horse of classical myth **9 school'd** i.e., rehearsed in his part **11 throughly** thoroughly **17 tall** fine

36 curious overly particular **45 pass** settle on **49 affied** betrothed **53 heark'ning still** continually listening **54 happily** haply, perhaps **55 an it like** if it please **56 lie** lodge **57 pass** transact **59 scrivener** notary, one to draw up contracts **61 like** likely. **slender pittance** i.e., scanty banquet **70 mess** dish. **cheer** entertainment

LUCENTIO Biondello, what of that?

BIONDELLO Faith, nothing; but h'as left me here behind to expound the meaning or moral of his signs and tokens.

LUCENTIO I pray thee, moralize them.

BIONDELLO Then thus. Baptista is safe, talking with the deceiving father of a deceitful son.

LUCENTIO And what of him?

BIONDELLO His daughter is to be brought by you to the supper.

LUCENTIO And then?

BIONDELLO The old priest at Saint Luke's church is at your command at all hours.

LUCENTIO And what of all this?

BIONDELLO I cannot tell, except they are busied about a counterfeit assurance. Take you assurance of her, "cum privilegio ad imprimendum solum." To th' church take the priest, clerk, and some sufficient honest witnesses.
If this be not that you look for, I have no more to
  say,
But bid Bianca farewell for ever and a day.
[Biondello starts to leave.]

LUCENTIO Hear'st thou, Biondello?

BIONDELLO I cannot tarry. I knew a wench married in an afternoon as she went to the garden for parsley to stuff a rabbit, and so may you, sir. And so, adieu, sir. My master hath appointed me to go to Saint Luke's, to bid the priest be ready to come against you come with your appendix. *Exit.*

LUCENTIO
I may, and will, if she be so contented.
She will be pleas'd; then wherefore should I doubt?
Hap what hap may, I'll roundly go about her.
It shall go hard if Cambio go without her. *Exit.*

[SCENE V]

Enter Petruchio, Kate, Hortensio, [and Servants].

PETRUCHIO
Come on, a' God's name, once more toward our
  father's.
Good Lord, how bright and goodly shines the
  moon!

KATHARINA
The moon? The sun. It is not moonlight now.

PETRUCHIO
I say it is the moon that shines so bright.

KATHARINA
I know it is the sun that shines so bright.

PETRUCHIO
Now, by my mother's son, and that's myself,
It shall be moon, or star, or what I list,
Or ere I journey to your father's house.—
Go on, and fetch our horses back again—
Evermore cross'd and cross'd, nothing but cross'd!

HORTENSIO
Say as he says, or we shall never go.

KATHARINA
Forward, I pray, since we have come so far,
And be it moon, or sun, or what you please;
An if you please to call it a rush-candle,
Henceforth I vow it shall be so for me.

PETRUCHIO
I say it is the moon.

KATHARINA I know it is the moon.

PETRUCHIO
Nay, then you lie. It is the blessed sun.

KATHARINA
Then, God be bless'd, it is the blessed sun.
But sun it is not, when you say it is not;
And the moon changes even as your mind.
What you will have it nam'd, even that it is,
And so it shall be so for Katharine.

HORTENSIO
Petruchio, go thy ways, the field is won.

PETRUCHIO
Well, forward, forward, thus the bowl should run,
And not unluckily against the bias.
But, soft! Company is coming here.

Enter Vincentio.

[To Vincentio.] Good morrow, gentle mistress.
  Where away?
Tell me, sweet Kate, and tell me truly too,
Hast thou beheld a fresher gentlewoman?
Such war of white and red within her cheeks!
What stars do spangle heaven with such beauty,
As those two eyes become that heavenly face?
Fair lovely maid, once more good day to thee.
Sweet Kate, embrace her for her beauty's sake.

HORTENSIO
'A will make the man mad, to make a woman of
  him.

KATHARINA *[Embracing Vincentio]*
Young budding virgin, fair and fresh and sweet,
Whither away, or where is thy abode?
Happy the parents of so fair a child!
Happier the man whom favorable stars
Allot thee for his lovely bedfellow!

PETRUCHIO
Why, how now, Kate? I hope thou art not mad.
This is a man, old, wrinkled, faded, withered,
And not a maiden, as thou say'st he is.

KATHARINA
Pardon, old father, my mistaking eyes,

78 h'as he has **79 moral** hidden meaning **81 moralize** elucidate **82 safe** i.e., safely deceived **91 except** unless **92 counterfeit assurance** pretended betrothal agreement. **Take . . . of her** make her sure to you **93 cum . . . solum** with exclusive printing rights. (A copyright formula often appearing on the title pages of books, here jokingly applied to the marriage.) **103 against you come** in anticipation of your arrival **104 appendix** something appended, i.e., the bride (continuing the metaphor of printing) **107 roundly . . . her** set about marrying her in no uncertain terms **108 go hard** be unfortunate (with bawdy pun)

IV.v. Location: A road on the way to Padua.

7 list please **8 Or ere** before **14 rush-candle** a rush dipped into tallow; hence a very feeble light **25 against the bias** off its proper course. (The *bias* is an off-center weight in a bowling ball enabling the bowler to roll the ball in an oblique or curving path; it runs *unluckily,* that is, unsuccessfully, *against the bias* when it encounters an obstacle.) **35 'A** he

That have been so bedazzled with the sun
That everything I look on seemeth green.
Now I perceive thou art a reverend father.
Pardon, I pray thee, for my mad mistaking.

PETRUCHIO
Do, good old grandsire, and withal make known
Which way thou travellest—if along with us,
We shall be joyful of thy company.

VINCENTIO
Fair sir, and you my merry mistress,
That with your strange encounter much amaz'd me,
My name is call'd Vincentio; my dwelling Pisa,
And bound I am to Padua, there to visit
A son of mine, which long I have not seen.

PETRUCHIO
What is his name?

VINCENTIO Lucentio, gentle sir.

PETRUCHIO
Happily met, the happier for thy son.
And now by law, as well as reverend age,
I may entitle thee my loving father.
The sister to my wife, this gentlewoman,
Thy son by this hath married. Wonder not,
Nor be not griev'd. She is of good esteem,
Her dowry wealthy, and of worthy birth;
Beside, so qualified as may beseem
The spouse of any noble gentleman.
Let me embrace with old Vincentio,
And wander we to see thy honest son,
Who will of thy arrival be full joyous.
[*Embraces him.*]

VINCENTIO
But is this true? Or is it else your pleasure,
Like pleasant travelers, to break a jest
Upon the company you overtake?

HORTENSIO
I do assure thee, father, so it is.

PETRUCHIO
Come, go along, and see the truth hereof,
For our first merriment hath made thee jealous.
Exeunt [*all but Hortensio*].

HORTENSIO
Well, Petruchio, this has put me in heart.
Have to my widow! And if she be froward,
Then hast thou taught Hortensio to be untoward.
Exit.

[ACT V • SCENE I]

Enter Biondello, Lucentio, and Bianca. Gremio is out before [*and stands aside*].

BIONDELLO Softly and swiftly, sir, for the priest is ready.

LUCENTIO I fly, Biondello. But they may chance to need thee at home; therefore leave us.

BIONDELLO Nay, faith, I'll see the church a' your back, and then come back to my master's as soon as I can.
[*Exeunt Lucentio, Bianca, and Biondello.*]

GREMIO
I marvel Cambio comes not all this while.

Enter Petruchio, Kate, Vincentio, Grumio, with Attendants.

PETRUCHIO
Sir, here's the door, this is Lucentio's house.
My father's bears more toward the marketplace;
Thither must I, and here I leave you, sir.

VINCENTIO
You shall not choose but drink before you go.
I think I shall command your welcome here,
And, by all likelihood, some cheer is toward.
Knock.

GREMIO [*Advancing*] They're busy within. You were best knock louder.

Pedant looks out of the window.

PEDANT What's he that knocks as he would beat down the gate?

VINCENTIO Is Signior Lucentio within, sir?

PEDANT He's within, sir, but not to be spoken withal.

VINCENTIO What if a man bring him a hundred pound or two, to make merry withal?

PEDANT Keep your hundred pounds to yourself. He shall need none, so long as I live.

PETRUCHIO Nay, I told you your son was well belov'd in Padua.—Do you hear, sir? To leave frivolous circumstances, I pray you, tell Signior Lucentio that his father is come from Pisa and is here at the door to speak with him.

PEDANT Thou liest. His father is come from Padua and here looking out at the window.

VINCENTIO Art thou his father?

PEDANT Ay, sir, so his mother says, if I may believe her.

PETRUCHIO [*To Vincentio*] Why, how now, gentleman! Why, this is flat knavery, to take upon you another man's name.

PEDANT Lay hands on the villain. I believe 'a means to cozen somebody in this city under my countenance.

Enter Biondello.

BIONDELLO [*To himself*] I have seen them in the church together, God send 'em good shipping! But who is here? Mine old master Vincentio! Now we are undone and brought to nothing.

VINCENTIO [*Seeing Biondello*] Come hither, crack-hemp.

BIONDELLO I hope I may choose, sir.

46 green young and fresh **62 by this** by this time **63 esteem** reputation **75 jealous** suspicious **77 froward** perverse **78 untoward** unmannerly

V.i. Location: Padua. Before Lucentio's house.
s.d. out before i.e., on stage first. (Gremio does not see Biondello, Lucentio, and Bianca as they steal to church.)

5 a' your back on your back, over you. (I.e., I'll see you in church.) **9 father's** i.e., father-in-law's, Baptista's. **bears** lies. (A nautical term.) **13 toward** in prospect **15 s.d. window** i.e., probably the gallery to the rear, over the stage **25–26 circumstances** matters **35 flat** downright **38 cozen** cheat. **countenance** i.e., alias **40 good shipping** bon voyage **43 crack-hemp** i.e., gallows bird **44 choose** do as I choose

VINCENTIO Come hither, you rogue. What, have you forgot me?

BIONDELLO Forgot you! No, sir. I could not forget you, for I never saw you before in all my life.

VINCENTIO What, you notorious villain, didst thou never see thy master's father, Vincentio?

BIONDELLO What, my old worshipful old master? Yes, marry, sir, see where he looks out of the window.

VINCENTIO Is 't so, indeed? *He beats Biondello.*

BIONDELLO Help, help, help! Here's a madman will murder me. [*Exit.*]

PEDANT Help, son! Help, Signior Baptista!
[*Exit from above.*]

PETRUCHIO Prithee, Kate, let's stand aside and see the end of this controversy. [*They stand aside.*]

Enter [*below*] *Pedant with Servants, Baptista,* [*and*] *Tranio* [*as Lucentio*].

TRANIO Sir, what are you that offer to beat my servant?

VINCENTIO What am I, sir? Nay, what are you, sir? O immortal gods! O fine villain! A silken doublet, a velvet hose, a scarlet cloak, and a copatain hat! O, I am undone, I am undone! While I play the good husband at home, my son and my servant spend all at the university.

TRANIO How now, what's the matter?

BAPTISTA What, is the man lunatic?

TRANIO Sir, you seem a sober ancient gentleman by your habit, but your words show you a madman. Why, sir, what 'cerns it you if I wear pearl and gold? I thank my good father, I am able to maintain it.

VINCENTIO Thy father! O villain, he is a sailmaker in Bergamo.

BAPTISTA You mistake, sir, you mistake, sir. Pray, what do you think is his name?

VINCENTIO His name! As if I knew not his name! I have brought him up ever since he was three years old, and his name is Tranio.

PEDANT Away, away, mad ass! His name is Lucentio, and he is mine only son, and heir to the lands of me, Signior Vincentio.

VINCENTIO Lucentio! O, he hath murd'red his master! Lay hold on him, I charge you, in the Duke's name. O, my son, my son! Tell me, thou villain, where is my son Lucentio?

TRANIO Call forth an officer.

[*A Servant summons an Officer.*]

Carry this mad knave to the jail. Father Baptista, I charge you see that he be forthcoming.

VINCENTIO Carry me to the jail?

GREMIO Stay, officer, he shall not go to prison.

BAPTISTA Talk not, Signior Gremio, I say he shall go to prison.

GREMIO Take heed, Signior Baptista, lest you be cony-catch'd in this business. I dare swear this is the right Vincentio.

PEDANT Swear, if thou dar'st.

GREMIO Nay, I dare not swear it.

TRANIO Then thou wert best say that I am not Lucentio.

GREMIO Yes, I know thee to be Signior Lucentio.

BAPTISTA Away with the dotard! To the jail with him!

Enter Biondello, Lucentio, and Bianca.

VINCENTIO Thus strangers may be hal'd and abus'd.
—O monstrous villain!

BIONDELLO O! We are spoil'd and—yonder he is. Deny him, forswear him, or else we are all undone.
Exeunt Biondello, Tranio, and Pedant, as fast as may be. Kneel.

LUCENTIO
Pardon, sweet father.

VINCENTIO Lives my sweet son?

BIANCA
Pardon, dear father.

BAPTISTA How hast thou offended?
Where is Lucentio?

LUCENTIO Here's Lucentio,
Right son to the right Vincentio,
That have by marriage made thy daughter mine,
While counterfeit supposes bleard thine eyne.

GREMIO
Here's packing, with a witness, to deceive us all!

VINCENTIO
Where is that damned villain Tranio,
That fac'd and braved me in this matter so?

BAPTISTA
Why, tell me, is not this my Cambio?

BIANCA
Cambio is chang'd into Lucentio.

LUCENTIO
Love wrought these miracles. Bianca's love
Made me exchange my state with Tranio,
While he did bear my countenance in the town,
And happily I have arrived at the last
Unto the wished haven of my bliss.
What Tranio did, myself enforc'd him to;
Then pardon him, sweet father, for my sake.

VINCENTIO I'll slit the villain's nose, that would have sent me to the jail.

BAPTISTA But do you hear, sir? Have you married my daughter without asking my good will?

VINCENTIO Fear not, Baptista, we will content you, go to. But I will in, to be reveng'd for this villainy. *Exit.*

BAPTISTA And I, to sound the depth of this knavery. *Exit.*

LUCENTIO Look not pale, Bianca; thy father will not frown. *Exeunt* [*Lucentio and Bianca*].

GREMIO
My cake is dough, but I'll in among the rest,
Out of hope of all but my share of the feast. [*Exit.*]

62 copatain high-crowned, sugar-loaf shape **63 good husband** careful provider, manager **70 'cerns** concerns **88 forthcoming** ready to stand trial when required **93–94 cony-catch'd** tricked

98 wert best might as well **101 hal'd** hauled about, maltreated **110 supposes** suppositions, false appearances (with an allusion to Gascoigne's *Supposes,* an adaptation of *I Suppositi* by Ariosto, from which Shakespeare took the Lucentio-Bianca plot of intrigue). **eyne** eyes **111 packing** conspiracy **113 fac'd and braved** bullied and defied **117 state** social station **118 countenance** appearance **132 My . . . dough** i.e., I'm out of luck **133 Out . . . but** having hope for nothing other than

KATHARINA Husband, let's follow, to see the end of this ado.
PETRUCHIO First kiss me, Kate, and we will.
KATHARINA What, in the midst of the street?
PETRUCHIO What, art thou asham'd of me?
KATHARINA No, sir, God forbid, but asham'd to kiss.
PETRUCHIO
Why, then let's home again. [*To Grumio.*] Come, sirrah, let's away.
KATHARINA
Nay, I will give thee a kiss. Now pray thee, love, stay. [*Kisses him.*]
PETRUCHIO
Is not this well? Come, my sweet Kate.
Better once than never, for never too late. *Exeunt.* 143

[SCENE II]

Enter Baptista, Vincentio, Gremio, the Pedant, Lucentio, and Bianca; [Petruchio, Kate, Hortensio,] Tranio, Biondello, Grumio, and Widow; the Servingmen with Tranio bringing in a banquet.

LUCENTIO
At last, though long, our jarring notes agree,
And time it is, when raging war is done,
To smile at scapes and perils overblown.
My fair Bianca, bid my father welcome,
While I with self-same kindness welcome thine.
Brother Petruchio, sister Katharina,
And thou, Hortensio, with thy loving widow,
Feast with the best, and welcome to my house.
My banquet is to close our stomachs up 9
After our great good cheer. Pray you, sit down,
For now we sit to chat as well as eat. [*They sit.*]
PETRUCHIO
Nothing but sit and sit, and eat and eat!
BAPTISTA
Padua affords this kindness, son Petruchio.
PETRUCHIO
Padua affords nothing but what is kind.
HORTENSIO
For both our sakes, I would that word were true.
PETRUCHIO
Now, for my life, Hortensio fears his widow. 16
WIDOW
Then never trust me, if I be afeard.
PETRUCHIO
You are very sensible, and yet you miss my sense:
I mean, Hortensio is afeard of you. 19
WIDOW
He that is giddy thinks the world turns round.
PETRUCHIO
Roundly replied.
KATHARINA Mistress, how mean you that? 21
WIDOW
Thus I conceive by him. 22
PETRUCHIO
Conceives by me! How likes Hortensio that?
HORTENSIO
My widow says, thus she conceives her tale. 24
PETRUCHIO
Very well mended. Kiss him for that, good widow.
KATHARINA
"He that is giddy thinks the world turns round":
I pray you, tell me what you meant by that.
WIDOW
Your husband, being troubled with a shrew,
Measures my husband's sorrow by his woe— 29
And now you know my meaning.
KATHARINA
A very mean meaning.
WIDOW Right, I mean you. 31
KATHARINA
And I am mean indeed, respecting you. 32
PETRUCHIO
To her, Kate!
HORTENSIO
To her, widow!
PETRUCHIO
A hundred marks, my Kate does put her down. 35
HORTENSIO
That's my office.
PETRUCHIO
Spoke like an officer. Ha' to thee, lad! 37
Drinks to Hortensio.
BAPTISTA
How likes Gremio these quick-witted folks?
GREMIO
Believe me, sir, they butt together well.
BIANCA
Head, and butt! An hasty-witted body
Would say your head and butt were head and horn. 41
VINCENTIO
Ay, mistress bride, hath that awakened you?
BIANCA
Ay, but not frighted me. Therefore I'll sleep again.
PETRUCHIO
Nay, that you shall not; since you have begun,
Have at you for a bitter jest or two! 45
BIANCA
Am I your bird? I mean to shift my bush; 46
And then pursue me as you draw your bow.
You are welcome all.
Exit Bianca [with Kate and Widow].

143 once at some time. (Cf. "better late than never.")

V.ii. Location: Padua. Lucentio's house.
s.d. banquet i.e., dessert **9 stomachs** (with pun on *quarrels*) **16 fears** is afraid of. (But the Widow takes the word in the sense of *frightens;* she protests she is not at all *afeard,* frightened by Hortensio.) **19 afeard** (Petruchio takes up the Widow's word and uses it in the sense of *suspicious,* fearful she will be untrue.)

21 Roundly frankly **22 Thus . . . him** i.e., that's what I think of him, Petruchio. (But Petruchio takes up *conceives* in the sense of *is made pregnant.*) **24 conceives** devises (with a possible pun on *tale, tail*) **29 Measures** judges **31 very mean** contemptible. (But the Widow takes up *mean* in the sense of *have in mind,* and Kate replies in the sense of *moderate in shrewishness.*) **32 respecting** compared to **35 marks** coins worth 13 shillings 4 pence. **put her down** overcome her. (But Hortensio takes up the phrase in a bawdy sense.) **37 officer** (playing on Hortensio's speaking of his *office* or function). **Ha'** have, i.e., here's **41 head and horn** (alluding to the familiar joke about cuckold's horns) **45 Have at** I shall come at. **bitter** sharp **46 Am . . . bush** i.e., if you mean to shoot your barbs at me, I intend to move out of the way, as a bird would fly to another bush

PETRUCHIO
She hath prevented me. Here, Signior Tranio,
This bird you aim'd at, though you hit her not.
Therefore a health to all that shot and miss'd.

TRANIO
O, sir, Lucentio slipp'd me like his greyhound,
Which runs himself and catches for his master.

PETRUCHIO
A good swift simile, but something currish.

TRANIO
'Tis well, sir, that you hunted for yourself;
'Tis thought your deer does hold you at a bay.

BAPTISTA
O ho, Petruchio! Tranio hits you now.

LUCENTIO
I thank thee for that gird, good Tranio.

HORTENSIO
Confess, confess, hath he not hit you here?

PETRUCHIO
'A has a little gall'd me, I confess;
And, as the jest did glance away from me,
'Tis ten to one it maim'd you two outright.

BAPTISTA
Now, in good sadness, son Petruchio,
I think thou hast the veriest shrew of all.

PETRUCHIO
Well, I say no. And therefore for assurance
Let's each one send unto his wife;
And he whose wife is most obedient
To come at first when he doth send for her,
Shall win the wager which we will propose.

HORTENSIO
Content. What is the wager?

LUCENTIO Twenty crowns.

PETRUCHIO
Twenty crowns!
I'll venture so much of my hawk or hound,
But twenty times so much upon my wife.

LUCENTIO
A hundred then.

HORTENSIO Content.

PETRUCHIO A match! 'Tis done.

HORTENSIO
Who shall begin?

LUCENTIO
That will I.
Go, Biondello, bid your mistress come to me.

BIONDELLO
I go. *Exit.*

BAPTISTA
Son, I'll be your half, Bianca comes.

LUCENTIO
I'll have no halves; I'll bear it all myself.

Enter Biondello.

How now, what news?

BIONDELLO
Sir, my mistress sends you word
That she is busy and she cannot come.

PETRUCHIO
How? She's busy and she cannot come!
Is that an answer?

GREMIO Ay, and a kind one too.
Pray God, sir, your wife send you not a worse.

PETRUCHIO
I hope, better.

HORTENSIO
Sirrah Biondello, go and entreat my wife
To come to me forthwith. *Exit Biondello.*

PETRUCHIO O, ho, entreat her!
Nay, then she must needs come.

HORTENSIO I am afraid, sir,
Do what you can, yours will not be entreated.

Enter Biondello.

Now, where's my wife?

BIONDELLO
She says you have some goodly jest in hand.
She will not come. She bids you come to her.

PETRUCHIO
Worse and worse; she will not come!
O vile, intolerable, not to be endur'd!
Sirrah Grumio, go to your mistress;
Say, I command her come to me. *Exit* [*Grumio*].

HORTENSIO
I know her answer.

PETRUCHIO What?

HORTENSIO She will not.

PETRUCHIO
The fouler fortune mine, and there an end.

Enter Katharina.

BAPTISTA
Now, by my holidame, here comes Katharina!

KATHARINA
What is your will, sir, that you send for me?

PETRUCHIO
Where is your sister, and Hortensio's wife?

KATHARINA
They sit conferring by the parlor fire.

PETRUCHIO
Go, fetch them hither. If they deny to come,
Swinge me them soundly forth unto their husbands.
Away, I say, and bring them hither straight.
[*Exit Katharina.*]

LUCENTIO
Here is a wonder, if you talk of a wonder.

HORTENSIO
And so it is. I wonder what it bodes.

PETRUCHIO
Marry, peace it bodes, and love, and quiet life,
An aweful rule, and right supremacy,
And, to be short, what not that's sweet and happy?

49 prevented forestalled **50 This bird** i.e., Bianca, whom Tranio courted *(aim'd at)* in his disguise as Lucentio **52 slipp'd** unleashed **54 swift** (1) quick-witted (2) concerning swiftness. **currish** (1) ignoble (2) concerning dogs **56 deer** (punning on *dear*). **does . . . bay** turns on you like a cornered animal and holds you at a distance **58 gird** sharp, biting jest **63 sadness** seriousness **65 assurance** proof **72 of** on **79 be your half** take half your bet

101 by my holidame (Originally an oath by the holy relics, but confused with an oath to the Virgin Mary.) **106 Swinge** thrash. **me** i.e., at my behest. (*Me* is the ethical dative.) **111 aweful rule** authority commanding awe or respect

BAPTISTA
Now, fair befall thee, good Petruchio!
The wager thou hast won, and I will add
Unto their losses twenty thousand crowns,
Another dowry to another daughter,
For she is chang'd, as she had never been.

PETRUCHIO
Nay, I will win my wager better yet
And show more sign of her obedience,
Her new-built virtue and obedience.

Enter Kate, Bianca, and Widow.

See where she comes and brings your froward wives
As prisoners to her womanly persuasion.
Katharina, that cap of yours becomes you not.
Off with that bauble, throw it under-foot.
[*She obeys.*]

WIDOW
Lord, let me never have a cause to sigh,
Till I be brought to such a silly pass!

BIANCA
Fie! What a foolish duty call you this?

LUCENTIO
I would your duty were as foolish too.
The wisdom of your duty, fair Bianca,
Hath cost me an hundred crowns since suppertime.

BIANCA
The more fool you, for laying on my duty.

PETRUCHIO
Katharina, I charge thee, tell these headstrong women
What duty they do owe their lords and husbands.

WIDOW
Come, come, you're mocking; we will have no telling.

PETRUCHIO
Come on, I say, and first begin with her.

WIDOW
She shall not.

PETRUCHIO
I say she shall—and first begin with her.

KATHARINA
Fie, fie! Unknit that threatening unkind brow,
And dart not scornful glances from those eyes,
To wound thy lord, thy king, thy governor.
It blots thy beauty as frosts do bite the meads,
Confounds thy fame as whirlwinds shake fair buds,
And in no sense is meet or amiable.
A woman mov'd is like a fountain troubled,
Muddy, ill-seeming, thick, bereft of beauty;
And while it is so, none so dry or thirsty
Will deign to sip or touch one drop of it.
Thy husband is thy lord, thy life, thy keeper,
Thy head, thy sovereign; one that cares for thee,
And for thy maintenance commits his body
To painful labor both by sea and land,
To watch the night in storms, the day in cold,
Whilst thou li'st warm at home, secure and safe;
And craves no other tribute at thy hands
But love, fair looks, and true obedience—
Too little payment for so great a debt.
Such duty as the subject owes the prince,
Even such a woman oweth to her husband;
And when she is froward, peevish, sullen, sour,
And not obedient to his honest will,
What is she but a foul contending rebel
And graceless traitor to her loving lord?
I am asham'd that women are so simple
To offer war where they should kneel for peace,
Or seek for rule, supremacy, and sway,
When they are bound to serve, love, and obey.
Why are our bodies soft and weak and smooth,
Unapt to toil and trouble in the world,
But that our soft conditions and our hearts
Should well agree with our external parts?
Come, come, you froward and unable worms!
My mind hath been as big as one of yours,
My heart as great, my reason haply more,
To bandy word for word and frown for frown;
But now I see our lances are but straws,
Our strength as weak, our weakness past compare,
That seeming to be most which we indeed least are.
Then vail your stomachs, for it is no boot,
And place your hands below your husband's foot,
In token of which duty, if he please,
My hand is ready; may it do him ease.

PETRUCHIO
Why, there's a wench! Come on, and kiss me, Kate.
[*They kiss.*]

LUCENTIO
Well, go thy ways, old lad; for thou shalt ha 't.

VINCENTIO
'Tis a good hearing when children are toward.

LUCENTIO
But a harsh hearing when women are froward.

PETRUCHIO
Come, Kate, we'll to bed.
We three are married, but you two are sped.
[*To Lucentio.*] 'Twas I won the wager, though you hit the white,
And, being a winner, God give you good night!
Exit Petruchio [*and Kate*].

HORTENSIO
Now, go thy ways, thou hast tam'd a curst shrow.

LUCENTIO
'Tis a wonder, by your leave, she will be tam'd so.
[*Exeunt.*]

126 pass state of affairs **131 laying** wagering **142 Confounds thy fame** ruins your reputation **144 mov'd** angry

159 peevish obstinate **163 simple** foolish **168 Unapt** unfit **169 conditions** qualities **171 unable worms** i.e., poor feeble creatures **172 big** haughty **178 vail your stomachs** lower your pride. **boot** profit, use **181 do him ease** give him pleasure **184 'Tis . . . toward** i.e., one likes to hear when children are obedient **187 We . . . sped** i.e., all we three men have taken wives, but you two are done for *(sped)* through disobedient wives **188 white** the center of the target (with quibble on the name of Bianca, which in Italian means "white") **190 shrow** shrew

A Midsummer Night's Dream

A Midsummer Night's Dream (c. 1594–1595) belongs to the period of transition from Shakespeare's experimental, imitative comedy to his mature, romantic, philosophical, "festive" vein. The play resembles Shakespeare's earlier attempts in its lighthearted presentation of love's tribulations. The two sets of lovers, scarcely distinguishable one from the other, are conventional figures. In them we find scarcely a hint of the profound self-discovery experienced by Beatrice and Benedick *(Much Ado about Nothing)* or Rosalind and Orlando *(As You Like It)*. At the same time, this play develops the motif of love as an imaginative journey from reality into a fantasy world created by the artist, ending in return to a reality that has itself been partly transformed by the experience of the journey. (Shakespeare gives us an earlier hint of such an imaginary silvan landscape in *The Two Gentlemen of Verona*.) This motif, with its contrasting worlds of social order and imaginative escape, remained an enduring vision for Shakespeare to the very last.

In construction, *A Midsummer Night's Dream* is a skillful interweaving of four plots involving four groups of characters: the court party of Duke Theseus, the four young lovers, the fairies, and the "rude mechanicals" or would-be actors. Mendelssohn's nineteenth-century incidental music evokes the contrasting textures of the various groups: Theseus' hunting horns and ceremonial wedding marches, the lovers' soaring and throbbing melodies, the fairies' pianissimo staccato, the tradesmen's clownish bassoon. Moreover, each plot is derived from its own set of source materials. The action involving Theseus and Hippolyta, for example, owes several details to Thomas North's translation (1579) of Plutarch's *Lives of the Noble Grecians and Romanes,* to Chaucer's *Knight's Tale* and perhaps his *Legend of Good Women,* and to Ovid's *Metamorphoses* (in the Latin text or in Golding's popular Elizabethan translation). The lovers' story, meanwhile, is Italianate and Ovidian in tone, and also in the broadest sense follows the conventions of plot in Plautus' and Terence's Roman comedies, although no particular source is known. Shakespeare's rich fairy lore, by contrast, is part folk tradition and part "learned." Although he certainly needed no books to tell him about mischievous spirits that could prevent churned milk from turning to butter, for instance, Shakespeare might have borrowed Oberon's name either from the French romance *Huon of Bordeaux* (translated into English by 1540), or from Greene's play *James IV* (c. 1591), or from Spenser's *The Faerie Queene,* II,i,8 (1590). Similarly, he may have taken Titania's name from the *Metamorphoses,* where it is used as an epithet for both Diana and Circe. Finally, for Bottom the Weaver and company, Shakespeare's primary inspiration was doubtless his own theatrical experience, although even here he is indebted to Ovid for the story of Pyramus and Thisbe, and probably to Apuleius' *Golden Ass* (translated by William Adlington, 1566) for Bottom's transformation.

Each of the four main plots in *A Midsummer Night's Dream* contains one or more pairs of lovers whose happiness has been frustrated by misunderstanding or parental opposition. Theseus and Hippolyta, once enemies in battle, become husband and wife; and their court marriage, constituting the "overplot" of the play, provides a framework for other dramatic actions that similarly oscillate between conflict and harmony. Theseus' actions are in fact instrumental in setting in motion and finally resolving the tribulations of the other characters. In the beginning of the play, for example, the lovers flee from Theseus' Athenian law; at the end, they are awakened by him from their dream. The king and queen of fairies come to Athens to celebrate Theseus' wedding, but quarrel with one another because Oberon has long been partial to Hippolyta, and Titania partial to Theseus. The Athenian tradesmen go off into the forest to rehearse their performance of "Pyramus and Thisbe" in anticipation of the wedding festivities.

The tragic love story of Pyramus and Thisbe, although it seems absurdly ill-suited for a wedding, simply reinforces by contrast the universal accord reuniting the other couples. Theseus, who originally won the Amazonian Hippolyta with his sword, doing her injuries, finally becomes the devoted husband. Hippolyta, legendary figure of woman's self-assertive longing to dominate the male, emerges as the happily submissive wife. The reconciliation of Oberon and Titania, meanwhile, reinforces this hierarchy of male over female. Having taught Titania a lesson concerning the changeling boy she tried to keep from him, Oberon relents and eventually frees Titania from her enchantment. Thus, the occasion of Theseus' wedding both initiates and brings to an end the difficulties that have beset the drama's various couples.

Despite Theseus' cheerful preoccupation with marriage, his court embodies at first a stern attitude toward young love. As administrator of the law, Theseus must accede to the remorseless demands of Hermia's father, Egeus. The inflexible Athenian law sides with parentage, age, wealth, and position against youth and romantic choice in love. The penalties are harsh: death, or perpetual virginity—and virginity is presented in this comedy (despite the nobly chaste examples of Christ, St. Paul, and Queen Elizabeth) as a fate worse than death. Egeus is a "blocking" or "heavy" character, the enemy of festival, the *alazon* of Plautus' or Terence's Latin versions of Grecian New Comedy. Indeed, the lovers' story is distantly derived from that New Comedy, which conventionally celebrated the triumph of young love over the machinations of age and wealth. Lysander reminds us that "the course of true love never did run smooth," and he sees its enemies as being chiefly external: the conflicting interests of parents or friends, or mismating in respect of years and blood, or war, or death, or sickness (I,i). This description clearly applies to "Pyramus and Thisbe," and it is tested by the action of *A Midsummer Night's Dream* as a whole (as well as by other early Shakespearean plays, such as *Romeo and Juliet*). The archetypal story, whether ending happily or sadly, is an evocation of love's difficulties in the face of social hostility and indifference.

While Shakespeare uses several "New Comedy" elements in setting up the basic conflicts of his drama, however, he also introduces important modifications from the very beginning. For example, he discards one conventional confrontation of classical and neoclassical comedy in which the heroine must choose between an old, wealthy suitor supported by her family, and the young but impecunious darling of her heart. Lysander is equal to his rival in social position, income, and attractiveness. Egeus' demand, therefore—that Hermia marry Demetrius rather than Lysander—seems simply arbitrary and unjust. Shakespeare emphasizes in this way the irrationality of Egeus' harsh insistence on being obeyed, and Theseus' rather complacent acceptance of the law's inequity. Spurned by an unfeeling social order, Lysander and Hermia are compelled to elope. To be sure, Egeus proves at the last to be no formidable threat; even he must admit the logic of permitting the lovers to couple as they ultimately desire. Thus, the obstacles to love are from the start seen as fundamentally superficial and indeed almost whimsical. Egeus is as "heavy" a villain as we are likely to find in this *jeu d'esprit*. Moreover, the very irrationality of his position paves the way for an ultimate resolution of the conflict. Nevertheless, by the end of Act I the supposedly rational world of conformity and duty has, by its customary insensitivity to youthful happiness, set in motion a temporary escape to a fantasy world where the law cannot reach.

In the forest, all the lovers—including Titania and Bottom—undergo a transforming experience engineered by the mischievous Puck. This experience demonstrates the universal power of love, which can overcome the queen of fairies as readily as the lowliest of men. It also suggests the irrational nature of love and its affinity to enchantment, witchcraft, and even madness. Love is seen as an affliction taken in through the frail senses, particularly the eyes. When it strikes, the victim cannot choose but to embrace the object of his dotage. By his amusing miscalculations, Puck shuffles the four interchangeable lovers through various permutations with mathematical predictability. First, two gentlemen compete for one lady, leaving the second lady sadly unrequited in love; then everything is at cross-purposes, with each gentleman pursuing the lady who is in love with the other man; then the two gentlemen compete for the lady they both previously ignored. Finally, of course, Jack shall have his Jill—whom else should he have? The couples are properly united, as they evidently were at some time prior to the commencement of the play when Demetrius had made love to Helena, and Lysander and Hermia had preferred one another.

We sense that Puck is by no means unhappy about his knavish errors. "Lord, what fools these mortals be!" Along with the other fairies in this play, Puck takes his being and his complex motivation from many denizens of the invisible world. As the agent of all-powerful love, Puck compares himself to Cupid. The love-juice he administers comes from Cupid's flower, "love-in-idleness." Like Cupid, Puck acts at the behest of the gods, and yet he wields a power that the chiefest gods themselves cannot resist. Essentially, however, Puck is less a classical love deity than a prankish folk spirit, such as we find in every folklore: gremlin, leprechaun, hobgoblin, and the like. Titania's fairies recognize Puck as one who, for example, can deprive a beer barrel of its yeast so that it spoils rather than ferments. Puck characterizes himself as a practical joker, pulling stools out from behind old ladies.

Folk wisdom imagines the inexplicable and unaccountable events in life to be caused by invisible forces who laugh at man's discomfiture and mock him for mere sport. Puck is related to such mysterious forces dwelling in nature, who must be placated with gifts and ceremonies. Although Shakespeare restricts Puck to a benign sportive role in dealing with the lovers or with Titania, the actual folk legends about Puck mentioned in this play are frequently disquieting. Puck is known to "mislead night-wanderers, laughing at their harm"; indeed, he demonstrates as much with Demetrius and Lysander, engineering a confrontation that greatly oppresses the lovers even though we perceive the sportful intent. At the play's end, Puck links himself and his fellows with the ghoulish apparitions of death and night: wolves howling at the moon, screech-owls, shrouds, gaping graves. Associations of this sort go beyond mere sportiveness to the witchcraft and demonology practiced by spirits rising from the dead. Even Oberon's assurance that the fairies will bless all the marriages of this play, shielding their progeny against mole, harelip, or other birth defects, carries the implication that such misfortunes can be caused by offended spirits. The magic of this play is thus explicitly related to deep irrational powers and forces capable of doing great harm, although of course the spirit of comedy keeps such veiled threats safely at a distance in *A Midsummer Night's Dream*.

Oberon and Titania, in their view of the relationship between gods and men, reflect yet another aspect of the fairies' spiritual ancestry—one more nearly related to the gods and goddesses of the world of Greek mythology. The king and queen of fairies assert that, because they are immortal, their regal quarrels in love must inevitably have dire consequences on earth, either in the love relationship of Theseus and Hippolyta or in the management of the weather. Floods, storms, diseases, and sterility abound, "And this same progeny of evils comes From our debate, from our dissension; We are their parents and original" (II,i). Even though this motif of the gods' quarreling over human affairs is Homeric or Virgilian in conception, however, the motif in this lighthearted play is more nearly mock-epic than truly epic. The consequences of the gods' anger are simply mirth-provoking, most of all in Titania's love affair with Bottom the Weaver.

The "Bottom" incident is recognizably a "metamorphosis" in a playfully classical mode, a love affair between a god and an earthly creature, underscoring man's dual nature. Bottom is himself half man and half beast, although he is ludicrously unlike the centaurs, mermaids, and other half-human beings of classical mythology. Whereas the head should be the aspiring part of him and his body the bestial part, Bottom wears an ass's knoll on his shoulders. His very name suggests the solid nature of his fleshly being ("bottom" is also appropriately a weaving term). He and Titania represent the opposites of flesh and spirit, miraculously yoked for a time in a twofold vision of man's absurd and ethereal nature.

A play bringing together fairies and mortals inevitably raises questions of illusion and reality. These questions reach their greatest intensity in the presentation of "Pyramus and Thisbe." This play within a play focuses our attention on the familiarly Shakespearean metaphor of art as illusion, and of the world itself as a stage on which men and women are merely players. As Theseus observes, apologizing for the ineptness of the tradesmen's performance, "the best in this kind are but shadows." That is, Shakespeare's own play is of the same order of reality as Bottom's play. Puck too, in his epilogue, enjoins any spectator offended by Shakespeare's play to dismiss it as a mere dream—as, indeed, the play's very title suggests. Theseus goes even further, linking dream to the essence of imaginative art, although he does so in a clearly critical and rather patronizing way. The artist, he says, is like the madman or the lover in his frenzy of inspiration, giving "to airy nothing A local habitation and a name" (V,i). Artistic achievements are too unsubstantial for Theseus; from his point of view they are the products of mere fantasy and irrationality, mere myths or fairy stories or old wives' tales. Behind this critical persona defending the "real" world of his court, however, we can hear Shakespeare's characteristically self-effacing defense of "dreaming."

"Pyramus and Thisbe," like the larger play surrounding it, attempts to body forth "the forms of things unknown." The play within the play gives us personified moonshine, a speaking wall, and an apologetic lion. Of course it is an absurdly bad play, full of lame epithets, bombastic alliteration, and bathos. In part Shakespeare is here satirizing the abuses of a theatre he had helped reform. The players' chosen method of portraying imaginative matters is ridiculous, and calls forth deliciously wry comments from the courtly spectators on stage: "Would you desire lime and hair to speak better?" At the same time, those spectators on stage are actors in our play. Their sarcasms render them less sympathetic in our eyes; we see that their kind of sophistication is as restrictive as it is illuminating. Bottom and his friends have conceived moonshine and lion as they did because these simple men are so responsive to the terrifying power of art. A lion might frighten the ladies and get the men all hanged. Theirs is a primitive faith, naive but strong, and in this sense it contrasts favorably with the jaded rationality of the court party. Theseus' valuable reminder, that all art is only "illusion," is thus juxtaposed with Bottom's insistence that imaginative art has a reality of its own.

Theseus above all embodies the sophistication of the court in his description of art as a frenzy of seething brains. Genially scoffing at "These antic fables" and "these fairy toys," he is unmoved by the lovers' account of their dreamlike experience. Limited by his own skepticism, Theseus has never experienced the enchantment of the forest. Even Bottom can claim more than that, for he has been lover of the queen of fairies; and, although his language cannot adequately describe the experience, Bottom will see it made into a ballad called "Bottom's Dream." Shakespeare leaves the status of his fantasy world deliberately complex; Theseus' lofty denial of dreaming is too abrupt. Even if the Athenian forest world can be made only momentarily substantial in the artifact of Shakespeare's play, we as audience respond to its tantalizing vision. We emerge back into our lives wondering if the fairies were "real," that is, puzzled by the relationship of these artistic symbols to the tangible concreteness of our daily existence. Unless our perceptions have been thus enlarged by sharing in the author's "dream," we have not surrendered to the imaginative experience.

A Midsummer Night's Dream is remarkable for its stylistic richness and theatrical versatility. It is often grouped with *Romeo and Juliet, Richard II,* and *The Merchant of Venice,* plays of Shakespeare's exuberantly lyrical period in the mid 1590's. Like these plays, *A Midsummer Night's Dream* is chiefly in verse, much of it rhymed, and gives us a variety of metrical effects, poetic set-pieces, and image patterns. The play is almost operatic in its symmetry and in its tendency to pause for "arias." Such poetic tours de force can be seen, for example, in Titania's description of meteorological catastrophes produced by the strife between herself and Oberon (II,i,82 ff.) or in Oberon's gracefully inventive account of the "little western flower" for which he sends Puck (II,i,155 ff.). One dominant image pattern concerns the moon: it is at times the old waning moon hindering the desires of lovers, at times the governess of floods and other natural disasters, and at times the benign provider of light to bumbling actors rehearsing or acting their play for the Duke. The forest is likewise a continual presence in the play, alternatively a refuge for young lovers and a place of darkness, confusion, and estrangement.

The variety of pacing in the language lends itself to theatrical richness, and the play has always proved a great favorite on the amateur and professional stages. As the 1970 production at Stratford-on-Avon by Peter Brook has shown, the play can be seen to alternate from wildly gymnastic actions to moments of stillness and concentration when actors and audience focus intently on what is being said, on the imagery and atmospherics. The play similarly shifts from poetic tenderness and delicacy to the hilarious lighthearted satire of bad theatre in the performance of "Pyramus and Thisbe." Few plays have fared better on the stage, and for good reason. The blend of entertainment and poetic illumination is hard to match anywhere.

A Midsummer Night's Dream

[*Dramatis Personae*

THESEUS, *Duke of Athens.*
EGEUS, *father to Hermia.*
LYSANDER, }
DEMETRIUS, } *in love with Hermia.*
PHILOSTRATE, *Master of the Revels to Theseus.*

QUINCE, *a carpenter.*
SNUG, *a joiner.*
BOTTOM, *a weaver.*
FLUTE, *a bellows-mender.*
SNOUT, *a tinker.*
STARVELING, *a tailor.*

HIPPOLYTA, *Queen of the Amazons, betrothed to Theseus.*
HERMIA, *daughter to Egeus, in love with Lysander.*
HELENA, *in love with Demetrius.*

OBERON, *King of the Fairies.*
TITANIA, *Queen of the Fairies.*
PUCK, *or Robin Goodfellow.*
PEASEBLOSSOM, }
COBWEB, }
MOTH, }
MUSTARDSEED, } *fairies.*
Other FAIRIES *attending their king and queen.*

ATTENDANTS *on Theseus and Hippolyta.*

SCENE: *Athens, and a wood near it.*]

[ACT I • SCENE I]

Enter Theseus, Hippolyta, [Philostrate,] with others.

THESEUS
Now, fair Hippolyta, our nuptial hour
Draws on apace. Four happy days bring in
Another moon; but, O, methinks, how slow
This old moon wanes! She lingers my desires, 4

I.i. Location: Athens. The palace of Theseus.
4 lingers lengthens, protracts

Like to a step-dame or a dowager
Long withering out a young man's revenue.

HIPPOLYTA

Four days will quickly steep themselves in night,
Four nights will quickly dream away the time;
And then the moon, like to a silver bow
New-bent in heaven, shall behold the night
Of our solemnities.

THESEUS Go, Philostrate,
Stir up the Athenian youth to merriments,
Awake the pert and nimble spirit of mirth,
Turn melancholy forth to funerals;
The pale companion is not for our pomp.
[*Exit Philostrate.*]
Hippolyta, I woo'd thee with my sword,
And won thy love doing thee injuries;
But I will wed thee in another key,
With pomp, with triumph, and with reveling.

Enter Egeus and his daughter Hermia, and Lysander, and Demetrius.

EGEUS

Happy be Theseus, our renowned Duke!

THESEUS

Thanks, good Egeus. What's the news with thee?

EGEUS

Full of vexation come I, with complaint
Against my child, my daughter Hermia.
Stand forth, Demetrius. My noble lord,
This man hath my consent to marry her.
Stand forth, Lysander. And, my gracious Duke,
This man hath bewitch'd the bosom of my child.
Thou, thou, Lysander, thou hast given her rhymes
And interchang'd love-tokens with my child.
Thou hast by moonlight at her window sung
With feigning voice verses of feigning love,
And stol'n the impression of her fantasy
With bracelets of thy hair, rings, gauds, conceits,
Knacks, trifles, nosegays, sweetmeats—messengers
Of strong prevailment in unhardened youth.
With cunning hast thou filch'd my daughter's heart,
Turn'd her obedience, which is due to me,
To stubborn harshness. And, my gracious Duke,
Be it so she will not here before your Grace
Consent to marry with Demetrius,
I beg the ancient privilege of Athens:
As she is mine, I may dispose of her,
Which shall be either to this gentleman
Or to her death, according to our law
Immediately provided in that case.

THESEUS

What say you, Hermia? Be advis'd, fair maid.
To you your father should be as a god—
One that compos'd your beauties, yea, and one
To whom you are but as a form in wax
By him imprinted and within his power
To leave the figure or disfigure it.
Demetrius is a worthy gentleman.

HERMIA

So is Lysander.

THESEUS In himself he is;
But in this kind, wanting your father's voice,
The other must be held the worthier.

HERMIA

I would my father look'd but with my eyes.

THESEUS

Rather your eyes must with his judgment look.

HERMIA

I do entreat your Grace to pardon me.
I know not by what power I am made bold,
Nor how it may concern my modesty,
In such a presence here to plead my thoughts;
But I beseech your Grace that I may know
The worst that may befall me in this case,
If I refuse to wed Demetrius.

THESEUS

Either to die the death, or to abjure
Forever the society of men.
Therefore, fair Hermia, question your desires,
Know of your youth, examine well your blood,
Whether, if you yield not to your father's choice,
You can endure the livery of a nun,
For aye to be in shady cloister mew'd,
To live a barren sister all your life,
Chanting faint hymns to the cold fruitless moon.
Thrice blessed they that master so their blood
To undergo such maiden pilgrimage;
But earthlier happy is the rose distill'd,
Than that which withering on the virgin thorn
Grows, lives, and dies in single blessedness.

HERMIA

So will I grow, so live, so die, my lord,
Ere I will yield my virgin patent up
Unto his lordship, whose unwished yoke
My soul consents not to give sovereignty.

THESEUS

Take time to pause; and, by the next new moon—
The sealing-day betwixt my love and me,
For everlasting bond of fellowship—
Upon that day either prepare to die
For disobedience to your father's will,
Or else to wed Demetrius, as he would,
Or on Diana's altar to protest
For aye austerity and single life.

DEMETRIUS

Relent, sweet Hermia, and, Lysander, yield
Thy crazed title to my certain right.

LYSANDER

You have her father's love, Demetrius;
Let me have Hermia's. Do you marry him.

5 step-dame stepmother. **dowager** widow with a jointure or dower **15 companion** fellow. **pomp** ceremonial magnificence **16 with my sword** i.e., in a military engagement against the Amazons, when Hippolyta was taken captive **19 triumph** public festivity **31 feigning** (1) counterfeiting (2) faining, desirous **32 And . . . fantasy** and made her fall in love with you (imprinting your image on her imagination) by stealthy and dishonest means **33 gauds** playthings. **conceits** fanciful trifles **34 Knacks** knickknacks **45 Immediately** expressly

51 leave i.e., leave unaltered. **disfigure** obliterate **54 kind** respect. **wanting** lacking. **voice** approval **60 concern** befit **68 blood** passions **70 livery** habit **71 aye** ever. **mew'd** shut in. (Said of a hawk, poultry, etc.) **76 earthlier happy** happier as respects this world **80 patent** privilege **88 Or** either **89 protest** vow **92 crazed** cracked, unsound

EGEUS
Scornful Lysander! True, he hath my love,
And what is mine my love shall render him.
And she is mine, and all my right of her
I do estate unto Demetrius.

LYSANDER
I am, my lord, as well deriv'd as he,
As well possess'd; my love is more than his;
My fortunes every way as fairly rank'd,
If not with vantage, as Demetrius';
And, which is more than all these boasts can be,
I am belov'd of beauteous Hermia.
Why should not I then prosecute my right?
Demetrius, I'll avouch it to his head,
Made love to Nedar's daughter, Helena,
And won her soul; and she, sweet lady, dotes,
Devoutly dotes, dotes in idolatry,
Upon this spotted and inconstant man.

THESEUS
I must confess that I have heard so much,
And with Demetrius thought to have spoke thereof;
But, being over-full of self-affairs,
My mind did lose it. But, Demetrius, come,
And come, Egeus, you shall go with me;
I have some private schooling for you both.
For you, fair Hermia, look you arm yourself
To fit your fancies to your father's will;
Or else the law of Athens yields you up—
Which by no means we may extenuate—
To death, or to a vow of single life.
Come, my Hippolyta. What cheer, my love?
Demetrius and Egeus, go along.
I must employ you in some business
Against our nuptial, and confer with you
Of something nearly that concerns yourselves.

EGEUS
With duty and desire we follow you.
Exeunt [*all but Lysander and Hermia*].

LYSANDER
How now, my love, why is your cheek so pale?
How chance the roses there do fade so fast?

HERMIA
Belike for want of rain, which I could well
Beteem them from the tempest of my eyes.

LYSANDER
Ay me! For aught that I could ever read,
Could ever hear by tale or history,
The course of true love never did run smooth;
But either it was different in blood—

HERMIA
O cross, too high to be enthrall'd to low!

LYSANDER
Or else misgraffed in respect of years—

HERMIA
O spite, too old to be engag'd to young!

LYSANDER
Or else it stood upon the choice of friends—

HERMIA
O hell, to choose love by another's eyes!

LYSANDER
Or, if there were a sympathy in choice,
War, death, or sickness did lay siege to it,
Making it momentany as a sound,
Swift as a shadow, short as any dream,
Brief as the lightning in the collied night,
That, in a spleen, unfolds both heaven and earth,
And ere a man hath power to say "Behold!"
The jaws of darkness do devour it up.
So quick bright things come to confusion.

HERMIA
If then true lovers have been ever cross'd,
It stands as an edict in destiny.
Then let us teach our trial patience,
Because it is a customary cross,
As due to love as thoughts and dreams and sighs,
Wishes and tears, poor fancy's followers.

LYSANDER
A good persuasion. Therefore, hear me, Hermia.
I have a widow aunt, a dowager
Of great revenue, and she hath no child.
From Athens is her house remote seven leagues;
And she respects me as her only son.
There, gentle Hermia, may I marry thee,
And to that place the sharp Athenian law
Cannot pursue us. If thou lovest me, then,
Steal forth thy father's house tomorrow night;
And in the wood, a league without the town,
Where I did meet thee once with Helena
To do observance to a morn of May,
There will I stay for thee.

HERMIA
My good Lysander!
I swear to thee, by Cupid's strongest bow,
By his best arrow with the golden head,
By the simplicity of Venus' doves,
By that which knitteth souls and prospers loves,
And by that fire which burn'd the Carthage queen,
When the false Troyan under sail was seen,
By all the vows that ever men have broke,
In number more than ever women spoke,
In that same place thou hast appointed me
Tomorrow truly will I meet with thee.

LYSANDER
Keep promise, love. Look, here comes Helena.

Enter Helena.

HERMIA
God speed fair Helena, whither away?

98 estate unto settle or bestow upon **99 deriv'd** descended, i.e., as well born **100 possess'd** endowed with wealth **101 fairly** handsomely **102 vantage** superiority **106 head** i.e., face **110 spotted** i.e., morally stained **117 look you arm** take care you prepare **118 fancies** likings, thoughts of love **120 extenuate** mitigate **123 go** i.e., come **125 Against** in preparation for **126 nearly that** that closely **130 Belike** very likely **131 Beteem** grant, afford **135 blood** hereditary station **136 cross** vexation **137 misgraffed** ill grafted, badly matched

139 friends relatives **143 momentany** lasting but a moment **145 collied** blackened (as with coal-dust), darkened **146 in a spleen** in a swift impulse, in a violent flash. **unfolds** discloses **149 quick** quickly; or, perhaps, living, alive. **confusion** ruin **150 ever cross'd** always thwarted **152 teach . . . patience** i.e., teach ourselves patience in this trial **155 fancy's** amorous passion's **160 respects** regards **167 do . . . May** perform the ceremonies of May Day **170 best arrow** (Cupid's best gold-pointed arrows were supposed to induce love, his blunt leaden arrows aversion.) **171 simplicity** innocence. **doves** i.e., those that drew Venus' chariot **173, 174 Carthage queen, false Troyan** (Dido, Queen of Carthage, immolated herself on a funeral pyre after having been deserted by the Trojan hero Aeneas.) **180 fair** fair-complexioned (generally regarded by the Elizabethans as more beautiful than dark complexion)

HELENA
Call you me fair? That fair again unsay.
Demetrius loves your fair. O happy fair! 182
Your eyes are lodestars, and your tongue's sweet air 183
More tuneable than lark to shepherd's ear 184
When wheat is green, when hawthorn buds appear.
Sickness is catching. O, were favor so, 186
Yours would I catch, fair Hermia, ere I go;
My ear should catch your voice, my eye your eye,
My tongue should catch your tongue's sweet melody.
Were the world mine, Demetrius being bated, 190
The rest I 'd give to be to you translated. 191
O, teach me how you look, and with what art
You sway the motion of Demetrius' heart. 193

HERMIA
I frown upon him, yet he loves me still.

HELENA
O that your frowns would teach my smiles such skill!

HERMIA
I give him curses, yet he gives me love.

HELENA
O that my prayers could such affection move! 197

HERMIA
The more I hate, the more he follows me.

HELENA
The more I love, the more he hateth me.

HERMIA
His folly, Helena, is no fault of mine.

HELENA
None, but your beauty. Would that fault were mine!

HERMIA
Take comfort. He no more shall see my face.
Lysander and myself will fly this place.
Before the time I did Lysander see,
Seem'd Athens as a paradise to me.
O, then, what graces in my love do dwell,
That he hath turn'd a heaven unto a hell!

LYSANDER
Helen, to you our minds we will unfold.
Tomorrow night, when Phoebe doth behold 209
Her silver visage in the wat'ry glass, 210
Decking with liquid pearl the bladed grass,
A time that lovers' flights doth still conceal, 212
Through Athens' gates have we devis'd to steal.

HERMIA
And in the wood, where often you and I
Upon faint primrose beds were wont to lie, 215
Emptying our bosoms of their counsel sweet, 216
There my Lysander and myself shall meet;
And thence from Athens turn away our eyes,
To seek new friends and stranger companies.
Farewell, sweet playfellow. Pray thou for us,
And good luck grant thee thy Demetrius!
Keep word, Lysander. We must starve our sight
From lovers' food till morrow deep midnight.

LYSANDER
I will, my Hermia. *Exit Hermia.*
Helena, adieu.
As you on him, Demetrius dote on you!
Exit Lysander.

HELENA
How happy some o'er other some can be! 226
Through Athens I am thought as fair as she.
But what of that? Demetrius thinks not so;
He will not know what all but he do know.
And as he errs, doting on Hermia's eyes,
So I, admiring of his qualities. 231
Things base and vile, holding no quantity, 232
Love can transpose to form and dignity.
Love looks not with the eyes, but with the mind,
And therefore is wing'd Cupid painted blind.
Nor hath Love's mind of any judgment taste; 236
Wings, and no eyes, figure unheedy haste. 237
And therefore is Love said to be a child,
Because in choice he is so oft beguil'd.
As waggish boys in game themselves forswear, 240
So the boy Love is perjur'd everywhere.
For ere Demetrius look'd on Hermia's eyne, 242
He hail'd down oaths that he was only mine;
And when this hail some heat from Hermia felt,
So he dissolv'd, and show'rs of oaths did melt.
I will go tell him of fair Hermia's flight.
Then to the wood will he tomorrow night
Pursue her; and for this intelligence 248
If I have thanks, it is a dear expense. 249
But herein mean I to enrich my pain,
To have his sight thither and back again. *Exit.*

[SCENE II]

Enter Quince the Carpenter, and Snug the Joiner, and Bottom the Weaver, and Flute the Bellows Mender, and Snout the Tinker, and Starveling the Tailor.

QUINCE Is all our company here?
BOTTOM You were best to call them generally, man by 2
man, according to the scrip. 3

QUINCE Here is the scroll of every man's name which is thought fit, through all Athens, to play in our interlude before the Duke and the Duchess on his wedding-day at night.

BOTTOM First, good Peter Quince, say what the play treats on, then read the names of the actors, and so
grow to a point. 10
QUINCE Marry, our play is "The most lamentable com- 11
edy and most cruel death of Pyramus and Thisby."

182 your fair your beauty (even though Hermia is dark-complexioned). **happy fair** lucky fair one **183 lodestars** guiding stars. **air** music **184 tuneable** tuneful, melodious **186 favor** appearance, looks **190 bated** excepted **191 translated** transformed **193 motion** impulse **197 affection** passion. **move** arouse **209 Phoebe** Diana, the moon **210 glass** mirror **212 still** always **215 faint** pale **216 counsel** secret thought

226 o'er . . . can be can be in comparison to some others **231 admiring of** wondering at **232 holding no quantity** i.e., unsubstantial, unshapely **236 Nor . . . taste** i.e., nor has Love, which dwells in the fancy or imagination, any *taste* or least bit of judgment or reason **237 figure** are a symbol of **240 game** sport, jest **242 eyne** eyes. (Old form of plural.) **248 intelligence** information **249 a dear expense** i.e., a trouble worth taking. **dear** costly

I.ii. Location: Athens. Quince's house (?)
2 generally (Bottom's blunder for *individually*.) **3 scrip** script, written list **10 grow to** come to **11 Marry** (A mild oath, originally the name of the Virgin Mary.)

BOTTOM A very good piece of work, I assure you, and a merry. Now, good Peter Quince, call forth your actors by the scroll. Masters, spread yourselves.

QUINCE Answer as I call you. Nick Bottom, the weaver.

BOTTOM Ready. Name what part I am for, and proceed.

QUINCE You, Nick Bottom, are set down for Pyramus.

BOTTOM What is Pyramus? A lover, or a tyrant?

QUINCE A lover, that kills himself most gallant for love.

BOTTOM That will ask some tears in the true performing
of it. If I do it, let the audience look to their eyes. I will
move storms; I will condole in some measure. To the 23
rest—yet my chief humor is for a tyrant. I could play 24
Ercles rarely, or a part to tear a cat in, to make all split. 25

"The raging rocks
And shivering shocks
Shall break the locks
Of prison gates;
And Phibbus' car 30
Shall shine from far
And make and mar
The foolish Fates."

This was lofty! Now name the rest of the players. This is Ercles' vein, a tyrant's vein. A lover is more condoling.

QUINCE Francis Flute, the bellows-mender.

FLUTE Here, Peter Quince.

QUINCE Flute, you must take Thisby on you.

FLUTE What is Thisby? A wand'ring knight?

QUINCE It is the lady that Pyramus must love.

FLUTE Nay, faith, let not me play a woman. I have a beard coming.

QUINCE That's all one. You shall play it in a mask, and 43
you may speak as small as you will. 44

BOTTOM An I may hide my face, let me play Thisby too. 45
I'll speak in a monstrous little voice, "Thisne, Thisne!" "Ah Pyramus, my lover dear! Thy Thisby dear, and lady dear!"

QUINCE No, no; you must play Pyramus; and, Flute, you Thisby.

BOTTOM Well, proceed.

QUINCE Robin Starveling, the tailor.

STARVELING Here, Peter Quince.

QUINCE Robin Starveling, you must play Thisby's mother. Tom Snout, the tinker.

SNOUT Here, Peter Quince.

QUINCE You, Pyramus' father; myself, Thisby's father; Snug, the joiner, you, the lion's part; and I hope here is a play fitted.

SNUG Have you the lion's part written? Pray you, if it 60
be, give it me, for I am slow of study.

QUINCE You may do it extempore, for it is nothing but roaring.

BOTTOM Let me play the lion too. I will roar that I will do any man's heart good to hear me. I will roar that I will make the Duke say, "Let him roar again, let him roar again."

QUINCE An you should do it too terribly, you would fright the Duchess and the ladies, that they would shriek; and that were enough to hang us all.

ALL That would hang us, every mother's son.

BOTTOM I grant you, friends, if you should fright the
ladies out of their wits, they would have no more dis-
cretion but to hang us; but I will aggravate my voice 74
so that I will roar you as gently as any sucking dove; I 75
will roar you an 'twere any nightingale.

QUINCE You can play no part but Pyramus; for Pyramus
is a sweet-fac'd man, a proper man as one shall see in 78
a summer's day, a most lovely gentleman-like man. Therefore you must needs play Pyramus.

BOTTOM Well, I will undertake it. What beard were I best to play it in?

QUINCE Why, what you will.

BOTTOM I will discharge it in either your straw-color 84
beard, your orange-tawny beard, your purple-in-grain 85
beard, or your French-crown-color beard, your perfect 86
yellow.

QUINCE Some of your French crowns have no hair at all, 88
and then you will play barefac'd. But, masters, here
are your parts. [*He distributes parts.*] And I am to en-
treat you, request you, and desire you, to con them by 91
tomorrow night; and meet me in the palace wood, a
mile without the town, by moonlight. There will we
rehearse; for if we meet in the city, we shall be dogg'd
with company, and our devices known. In the mean- 95
time I will draw a bill of properties, such as our play 96
wants. I pray you, fail me not.

BOTTOM We will meet, and there we may rehearse most
obscenely and courageously. Take pains, be perfect; 99
adieu.

QUINCE At the Duke's oak we meet.

BOTTOM Enough. Hold, or cut bow-strings. *Exeunt.* 102

[ACT II • SCENE I]

Enter a Fairy at one door, and Robin Goodfellow [Puck] at another.

PUCK
How now, spirit! Whither wander you?

FAIRY
Over hill, over dale,
Thorough bush, thorough brier, 3
Over park, over pale, 4
Thorough flood, thorough fire,
I do wander every where,
Swifter than the moon's sphere;

23 condole lament, arouse pity **24 humor** inclination, whim **25 Ercles** Hercules. (The tradition of ranting came from Seneca's *Hercules Furens.*) **tear a cat** i.e., rant. **make all split** i.e., cause a stir, bring the house down **30 Phibbus' car** Phoebus', the sun-god's, chariot **43 That's all one** it makes no difference **44 small** high-pitched **45 An** if

74 aggravate (Bottom's blunder for *diminish.*) **75 roar you** i.e., roar for you **78 proper** handsome **84 discharge** perform. **your** i.e., you know the kind I mean **85 purple-in-grain** dyed a very deep red. (From *grain,* the name applied to the dried insect used to make the dye.) **86 French-crown-color** i.e., color of a French crown, a gold coin **88 crowns** heads bald from syphilis, the "French disease" **91 con** learn by heart **95 devices** plans **96 bill** list **99 obscenely** (An unintentionally funny blunder, whatever Bottom meant to say.) **perfect** i.e., letter-perfect in memorizing your parts **102 Hold . . . bow-strings** (An archer's expression not definitely explained, but probably meaning here "keep your promises, or give up the play.")

II.i. Location: A wood near Athens.
3 Thorough through **4 pale** enclosure

And I serve the Fairy Queen,
To dew her orbs upon the green.
The cowslips tall her pensioners be.
In their gold coats spots you see;
Those be rubies, fairy favors,
In those freckles live their savors.
I must go seek some dewdrops here
And hang a pearl in every cowslip's ear.
Farewell, thou lob of spirits; I'll be gone.
Our Queen and all her elves come here anon.

PUCK
The King doth keep his revels here tonight.
Take heed the Queen come not within his sight.
For Oberon is passing fell and wrath,
Because that she as her attendant hath
A lovely boy, stolen from an Indian king;
She never had so sweet a changeling.
And jealous Oberon would have the child
Knight of his train, to trace the forests wild.
But she perforce withholds the loved boy,
Crowns him with flowers and makes him all her joy.
And now they never meet in grove or green,
By fountain clear, or spangled starlight sheen,
But they do square, that all their elves for fear
Creep into acorn-cups and hide them there.

FAIRY
Either I mistake your shape and making quite,
Or else you are that shrewd and knavish sprite
Call'd Robin Goodfellow. Are not you he
That frights the maidens of the villagery,
Skim milk, and sometimes labor in the quern,
And bootless make the breathless huswife churn,
And sometime make the drink to bear no barm,
Mislead night-wanderers, laughing at their harm?
Those that Hobgoblin call you and sweet Puck,
You do their work, and they shall have good luck.
Are you not he?

PUCK
Thou speakest aright;
I am that merry wanderer of the night.
I jest to Oberon and make him smile
When I a fat and bean-fed horse beguile,
Neighing in likeness of a filly foal;
And sometime lurk I in a gossip's bowl,
In very likeness of a roasted crab,
And when she drinks, against her lips I bob
And on her withered dewlap pour the ale.
The wisest aunt, telling the saddest tale,
Sometime for three-foot stool mistaketh me;
Then slip I from her bum, down topples she,
And "tailor" cries, and falls into a cough;
And then the whole quire hold their hips and laugh,
And waxen in their mirth and neeze and swear
A merrier hour was never wasted there.
But, room, fairy! Here comes Oberon.

FAIRY
And here my mistress. Would that he were gone!

Enter [Oberon] the King of Fairies at one door, with his train; and [Titania] the Queen at another, with hers.

OBERON
Ill met by moonlight, proud Titania.

TITANIA
What, jealous Oberon? Fairies, skip hence.
I have forsworn his bed and company.

OBERON
Tarry, rash wanton. Am not I thy lord?

TITANIA
Then I must be thy lady; but I know
When thou hast stolen away from fairy land,
And in the shape of Corin sat all day,
Playing on pipes of corn and versing love
To amorous Phillida. Why art thou here,
Come from the farthest steep of India,
But that, forsooth, the bouncing Amazon,
Your buskin'd mistress and your warrior love,
To Theseus must be wedded, and you come
To give their bed joy and prosperity.

OBERON
How canst thou thus for shame, Titania,
Glance at my credit with Hippolyta,
Knowing I know thy love to Theseus?
Didst not thou lead him through the glimmering night
From Perigenia, whom he ravished?
And make him with fair Aegles break his faith,
With Ariadne and Antiopa?

TITANIA
These are the forgeries of jealousy;
And never, since the middle summer's spring,
Met we on hill, in dale, forest, or mead,
By paved fountain or by rushy brook,
Or in the beached margent of the sea,
To dance our ringlets to the whistling wind,
But with thy brawls thou hast disturb'd our sport.
Therefore the winds, piping to us in vain,
As in revenge, have suck'd up from the sea
Contagious fogs; which falling in the land
Hath every pelting river made so proud
That they have overborne their continents.
The ox hath therefore stretch'd his yoke in vain,

9 orbs circles, i.e., fairy rings **10 pensioners** retainers, members of the royal bodyguard **12 favors** love tokens **13 savors** sweet smells **16 lob** country bumpkin **17 anon** at once **20 passing fell** exceedingly angry. **wrath** wrathful **23 changeling** child exchanged for another by the fairies **25 trace** range through **26 perforce** forcibly **29 fountain** spring **30 square** quarrel **33 shrewd** mischievous. **sprite** spirit **36 quern** handmill **37 bootless** in vain **38 barm** yeast, head on the ale **47 gossip's** old woman's **48 crab** crab apple **50 dewlap** loose skin on neck **51 aunt** old woman. **saddest** most serious **54 tailor** (Possibly because she ends up sitting cross-legged on the floor, looking like a tailor.) **55 quire** company

56 waxen increase. **neeze** sneeze **63 wanton** headstrong creature **66, 68 Corin, Phillida** (Conventional names of pastoral lovers.) **67 corn** (Here, oat stalks.) **69 steep** mountain range **71 buskin'd** wearing half-boots called buskins **75 Glance . . . Hippolyta** make insinuations about my favored relationship with Hippolyta **78 Perigenia** i.e., Perigouna, one of Theseus' conquests. (This and the following women are named in Thomas North's translation of Plutarch's *Life of Theseus*.) **79 Aegles** i.e., Aegle, for whom Theseus deserted Ariadne according to some accounts **80 Ariadne** the daughter of Minos, King of Crete, who helped Theseus to escape the labyrinth after killing the Minotaur; later she was abandoned by Theseus. **Antiopa** Queen of the Amazons and wife of Theseus; elsewhere identified with Hippolyta, but here thought of as a separate woman **82 middle summer's spring** beginning of midsummer **84 paved** with pebbled bottom. **rushy** bordered with rushes **85 in** on. **margent** edge, border **86 ringlets** dances in a ring. (See *orbs* in l. 9.) **90 Contagious** noxious **91 pelting** paltry; or, striking, moving forcefully **92 continents** banks that contain them

The ploughman lost his sweat, and the green corn
Hath rotted ere his youth attain'd a beard;
The fold stands empty in the drowned field,
And crows are fatted with the murrion flock;
The nine men's morris is fill'd up with mud,
And the quaint mazes in the wanton green
For lack of tread are undistinguishable.
The human mortals want their winter here;
No night is now with hymn or carol bless'd.
Therefore the moon, the governess of floods,
Pale in her anger, washes all the air,
That rheumatic diseases do abound.
And thorough this distemperature we see
The seasons alter: hoary-headed frosts
Fall in the fresh lap of the crimson rose,
And on old Hiems' thin and icy crown
An odorous chaplet of sweet summer buds
Is, as in mockery, set. The spring, the summer,
The childing autumn, angry winter, change
Their wonted liveries, and the mazed world,
By their increase, now knows not which is which.
And this same progeny of evils comes
From our debate, from our dissension;
We are their parents and original.

OBERON
Do you amend it then; it lies in you.
Why should Titania cross her Oberon?
I do but beg a little changeling boy,
To be my henchman.

TITANIA
Set your heart at rest.
The fairy land buys not the child of me.
His mother was a vot'ress of my order,
And, in the spiced Indian air, by night,
Full often hath she gossip'd by my side,
And sat with me on Neptune's yellow sands,
Marking th' embarked traders on the flood,
When we have laugh'd to see the sails conceive
And grow big-bellied with the wanton wind;
Which she, with pretty and with swimming gait,
Following—her womb then rich with my young
squire—
Would imitate, and sail upon the land
To fetch me trifles, and return again,
As from a voyage, rich with merchandise.
But she, being mortal, of that boy did die;
And for her sake do I rear up her boy,
And for her sake I will not part with him.

OBERON
How long within this wood intend you stay?

TITANIA
Perchance till after Theseus' wedding-day.
If you will patiently dance in our round
And see our moonlight revels, go with us;
If not, shun me, and I will spare your haunts.

OBERON
Give me that boy, and I will go with thee.

TITANIA
Not for thy fairy kingdom. Fairies, away!
We shall chide downright, if I longer stay.
Exeunt [*Titania with her train*].

OBERON
Well, go thy way. Thou shalt not from this grove
Till I torment thee for this injury.
My gentle Puck, come hither. Thou remember'st
Since once I sat upon a promontory,
And heard a mermaid on a dolphin's back
Uttering such dulcet and harmonious breath
That the rude sea grew civil at her song
And certain stars shot madly from their spheres,
To hear the sea-maid's music.

PUCK
I remember.

OBERON
That very time I saw, but thou couldst not,
Flying between the cold moon and the earth,
Cupid all arm'd. A certain aim he took
At a fair vestal throned by the west,
And loos'd his love-shaft smartly from his bow,
As it should pierce a hundred thousand hearts;
But I might see young Cupid's fiery shaft
Quench'd in the chaste beams of the wat'ry moon,
And the imperial vot'ress passed on,
In maiden meditation, fancy-free.
Yet mark'd I where the bolt of Cupid fell:
It fell upon a little western flower,
Before milk-white, now purple with love's wound,
And maidens call it love-in-idleness.
Fetch me that flow'r; the herb I showed thee once.
The juice of it on sleeping eyelids laid
Will make or man or woman madly dote
Upon the next live creature that it sees.
Fetch me this herb, and be thou here again
Ere the leviathan can swim a league.

PUCK
I'll put a girdle round about the earth
In forty minutes. [*Exit*.]

OBERON
Having once this juice,
I'll watch Titania when she is asleep,
And drop the liquor of it in her eyes.
The next thing then she waking looks upon,
Be it on lion, bear, or wolf, or bull,
On meddling monkey, or on busy ape,
She shall pursue it with the soul of love.
And ere I take this charm from off her sight,
As I can take it with another herb,
I'll make her render up her page to me.

94 corn grain of any kind **96 fold** pen for sheep or cattle **97 murrion** having died of the murrain, plague **98 nine men's morris** i.e., portion of the village green marked out in a square for a game played with nine pebbles or pegs **99 quaint mazes** i.e., intricate paths marked out on the village green to be followed rapidly on foot as a kind of contest. **wanton** luxuriant **101 want** lack. **winter** i.e., regular winter season; or, proper observances of winter, such as the *hymn or carol* in the next line (?) **103 Therefore** i.e., as a result of our quarrel **105 rheumatic diseases** colds, flu, and other respiratory infections **106 distemperature** disturbance in nature **109 Hiems'** the winter god's **112 childing** fruitful, pregnant **113 wonted liveries** usual apparel. **mazed** bewildered **114 their increase** their yield, what they produce **116 debate** quarrel **117 original** origin **121 henchman** attendant, page **127 traders** trading vessels. **flood** flood tide **129 wanton** sportive

140 round circular dance **142 spare** shun **146 from** go from **149 Since** when **151 breath** voice, song **157 all** fully **158 vestal** vestal virgin. (Contains a complimentary allusion to Queen Elizabeth as a votaress of Diana and probably refers to an actual entertainment in her honor at Elvetham in 1591.) **160 As** as if **161 might** could **164 fancy-free** free of love's spell **168 love-in-idleness** pansy, heartsease **171 or . . . or** either . . . or **174 leviathan** sea-monster, whale **176 forty** (Used indefinitely.)

But who comes here? I am invisible,
And I will overhear their conference.

Enter Demetrius, Helena following him.

DEMETRIUS
I love thee not, therefore pursue me not.
Where is Lysander and fair Hermia?
The one I'll slay, the other slayeth me.
Thou told'st me they were stol'n unto this wood;
And here am I, and wode within this wood,
Because I cannot meet my Hermia.
Hence, get thee gone, and follow me no more.

HELENA
You draw me, you hard-hearted adamant;
But yet you draw not iron, for my heart
Is true as steel. Leave you your power to draw,
And I shall have no power to follow you.

DEMETRIUS
Do I entice you? Do I speak you fair?
Or, rather, do I not in plainest truth
Tell you I do not nor I cannot love you?

HELENA
And even for that do I love you the more.
I am your spaniel; and, Demetrius,
The more you beat me, I will fawn on you.
Use me but as your spaniel, spurn me, strike me,
Neglect me, lose me; only give me leave,
Unworthy as I am, to follow you.
What worser place can I beg in your love—
And yet a place of high respect with me—
Than to be used as you use your dog?

DEMETRIUS
Tempt not too much the hatred of my spirit,
For I am sick when I do look on thee.

HELENA
And I am sick when I look not on you.

DEMETRIUS
You do impeach your modesty too much
To leave the city and commit yourself
Into the hands of one that loves you not,
To trust the opportunity of night
And the ill counsel of a desert place
With the rich worth of your virginity.

HELENA
Your virtue is my privilege. For that
It is not night when I do see your face,
Therefore I think I am not in the night;
Nor doth this wood lack worlds of company,
For you in my respect are all the world.
Then how can it be said I am alone,
When all the world is here to look on me?

DEMETRIUS
I'll run from thee and hide me in the brakes,
And leave thee to the mercy of wild beasts.

HELENA
The wildest hath not such a heart as you.
Run when you will, the story shall be chang'd:
Apollo flies and Daphne holds the chase,
The dove pursues the griffin, the mild hind
Makes speed to catch the tiger—bootless speed,
When cowardice pursues and valor flies.

DEMETRIUS
I will not stay thy questions. Let me go!
Or if thou follow me, do not believe
But I shall do thee mischief in the wood.

HELENA
Ay, in the temple, in the town, the field,
You do me mischief. Fie, Demetrius!
Your wrongs do set a scandal on my sex.
We cannot fight for love, as men may do;
We should be woo'd and were not made to woo.
[*Exit Demetrius.*]
I'll follow thee and make a heaven of hell,
To die upon the hand I love so well. [*Exit.*]

OBERON
Fare thee well, nymph. Ere he do leave this grove,
Thou shalt fly him and he shall seek thy love.

Enter Puck.

Hast thou the flower there? Welcome, wanderer.

PUCK
Ay, there it is. [*Offers the flower.*]

OBERON I pray thee, give it me.
I know a bank where the wild thyme blows,
Where oxlips and the nodding violet grows,
Quite over-canopied with luscious woodbine,
With sweet musk-roses and with eglantine.
There sleeps Titania sometime of the night,
Lull'd in these flowers with dances and delight;
And there the snake throws her enamel'd skin,
Weed wide enough to wrap a fairy in.
And with the juice of this I'll streak her eyes,
And make her full of hateful fantasies.
Take thou some of it, and seek through this grove.
[*Gives some love-juice.*]
A sweet Athenian lady is in love
With a disdainful youth. Anoint his eyes,
But do it when the next thing he espies
May be the lady. Thou shalt know the man
By the Athenian garments he hath on.
Effect it with some care, that he may prove
More fond on her than she upon her love;
And look thou meet me ere the first cock crow.

PUCK
Fear not, my lord, your servant shall do so.
Exeunt.

192 wode mad. (Pronounced *wood* and often spelled so.) **195 adamant** lodestone, magnet (with pun on *hard-hearted,* since adamant was also thought to be the hardest of all stones and was confused with the diamond) **197 Leave** give up **199 fair** courteously **214 impeach** call into question **218 desert** deserted **220 virtue** goodness or power to attract. **privilege** safeguard, warrant. **For that** because **224 in my respect** as far as I am concerned **227 brakes** thickets

231 Apollo . . . chase (In the ancient myth, Daphne fled from Apollo and was saved from rape by being transformed into a laurel tree; here it is the female who *holds the chase,* or pursues, instead of the male.) **232 griffin** a fabulous monster with the head of an eagle and the body of a lion. **hind** female deer **233 bootless** fruitless **235 stay** wait for. **questions** talk or argument **244 upon** by **249 blows** blooms **250 oxlips** flowers resembling cowslip and primrose **251 woodbine** honeysuckle **252 musk-roses** a kind of large, sweet-scented rose. **eglantine** sweetbriar, another kind of rose **255 throws** sloughs off, sheds **256 Weed** garment **257 streak** anoint, touch gently **266 fond on** doting on

[SCENE II]

Enter Titania, Queen of Fairies, with her train.

TITANIA
Come, now a roundel and a fairy song; 1
Then, for the third part of a minute, hence—
Some to kill cankers in the musk-rose buds, 3
Some war with rere-mice for their leathern wings, 4
To make my small elves coats, and some keep back
The clamorous owl, that nightly hoots and wonders
At our quaint spirits. Sing me now asleep. 7
Then to your offices and let me rest.

Fairies sing.

FIRST FAIRY
You spotted snakes with double tongue, 9
Thorny hedgehogs, be not seen;
Newts and blindworms, do no wrong, 11
Come not near our fairy queen.
[*Chorus.*] Philomel, with melody 13
Sing in our sweet lullaby;
Lulla, lulla, lullaby, lulla, lulla, lullaby.
Never harm,
Nor spell nor charm,
Come our lovely lady nigh.
So, good night, with lullaby.

FIRST FAIRY
Weaving spiders, come not here; 20
Hence, you long-legg'd spinners, hence!
Beetles black, approach not near;
Worm nor snail, do no offense.
[*Chorus.*] Philomel, with melody, etc.

SECOND FAIRY
Hence, away! Now all is well.
One aloof stand sentinel.
[*Exeunt Fairies. Titania sleeps.*]

Enter Oberon [and squeezes the flower on Titania's eyelids].

OBERON
What thou seest when thou dost wake,
Do it for thy true-love take;
Love and languish for his sake.
Be it ounce, or cat, or bear, 30
Pard, or boar with bristled hair, 31
In thy eye that shall appear
When thou wak'st, it is thy dear.
Wake when some vile thing is near. [*Exit.*]

Enter Lysander and Hermia.

LYSANDER
Fair love, you faint with wand'ring in the wood;
And to speak troth, I have forgot our way. 36
We'll rest us, Hermia, if you think it good,
And tarry for the comfort of the day.

HERMIA
Be 't so, Lysander. Find you out a bed,
For I upon this bank will rest my head.

LYSANDER
One turf shall serve as pillow for us both,
One heart, one bed, two bosoms, and one troth. 42

HERMIA
Nay, good Lysander; for my sake, my dear,
Lie further off yet, do not lie so near.

LYSANDER
O, take the sense, sweet, of my innocence! 45
Love takes the meaning in love's conference. 46
I mean, that my heart unto yours is knit
So that but one heart we can make of it;
Two bosoms interchained with an oath—
So then two bosoms and a single troth.
Then by your side no bed-room me deny,
For lying so, Hermia, I do not lie. 52

HERMIA
Lysander riddles very prettily.
Now much beshrew my manners and my pride 54
If Hermia meant to say Lysander lied.
But, gentle friend, for love and courtesy
Lie further off, in human modesty; 57
Such separation as may well be said
Becomes a virtuous bachelor and a maid,
So far be distant; and, good night, sweet friend.
Thy love ne'er alter till thy sweet life end!

LYSANDER
Amen, amen, to that fair prayer, say I,
And then end life when I end loyalty!
Here is my bed. Sleep give thee all his rest!

HERMIA
With half that wish the wisher's eyes be press'd! 65
[*They sleep, separated by a short distance.*]

Enter Puck.

PUCK
Through the forest have I gone,
But Athenian found I none
On whose eyes I might approve 68
This flower's force in stirring love.
Night and silence.—Who is here?
Weeds of Athens he doth wear.
This is he, my master said,
Despised the Athenian maid;
And here the maiden, sleeping sound,
On the dank and dirty ground.
Pretty soul! She durst not lie
Near this lack-love, this kill-courtesy.
Churl, upon thy eyes I throw

II.ii. Location: The wood.
1 roundel dance in a ring **3 cankers** cankerworms **4 rere-mice** bats **7 quaint** dainty **9 double** forked **11 Newts** water lizards (considered poisonous, as were *blindworms*—small snakes with tiny eyes—and spiders) **13 Philomel** the nightingale. (Philomela, daughter of King Pandion, was transformed into a nightingale, according to Ovid's *Metamorphoses* vi, after she had been raped by her sister Procne's husband, Tereus.) **30 ounce** lynx **31 Pard** leopard

36 troth truth **42 troth** faith, troth-plight **45 take . . . innocence** i.e., interpret my intention as innocent **46 Love . . . conference** i.e., when lovers confer, love teaches each lover to interpret the others' meaning lovingly **52 lie** tell a falsehood (with a riddling pun on *lie*, recline) **54 beshrew** curse. (But mildly meant.) **57 human** courteous **65 With . . . press'd** i.e., may we share your wish, so that your eyes too are *press'd*, closed, in sleep **68 approve** test

All the power this charm doth owe.
[*Applies the love-juice.*]
When thou wak'st, let love forbid
Sleep his seat on thy eyelid.
So awake when I am gone,
For I must now to Oberon. *Exit.*

Enter Demetrius and Helena, running.

HELENA
Stay, though thou kill me, sweet Demetrius.

DEMETRIUS
I charge thee, hence, and do not haunt me thus.

HELENA
O, wilt thou darkling leave me? Do not so.

DEMETRIUS
Stay, on thy peril! I alone will go. [*Exit.*]

HELENA
O, I am out of breath in this fond chase!
The more my prayer, the lesser is my grace.
Happy is Hermia, wheresoe'er she lies,
For she hath blessed and attractive eyes.
How came her eyes so bright? Not with salt tears;
If so, my eyes are oft'ner wash'd than hers.
No, no, I am as ugly as a bear;
For beasts that meet me run away for fear.
Therefore no marvel though Demetrius
Do, as a monster, fly my presence thus.
What wicked and dissembling glass of mine
Made me compare with Hermia's sphery eyne?
But who is here? Lysander, on the ground?
Dead, or asleep? I see no blood, no wound.
Lysander, if you live, good sir, awake.

LYSANDER [*Awaking*]
And run through fire I will for thy sweet sake.
Transparent Helena! Nature shows art,
That through thy bosom makes me see thy heart.
Where is Demetrius? O, how fit a word
Is that vile name to perish on my sword!

HELENA
Do not say so, Lysander, say not so.
What though he love your Hermia? Lord, what though?
Yet Hermia still loves you. Then be content.

LYSANDER
Content with Hermia? No! I do repent
The tedious minutes I with her have spent.
Not Hermia but Helena I love.
Who will not change a raven for a dove?
The will of man is by his reason sway'd,
And reason says you are the worthier maid.
Things growing are not ripe until their season;
So I, being young, till now ripe not to reason.
And touching now the point of human skill,
Reason becomes the marshal to my will
And leads me to your eyes, where I o'erlook
Love's stories written in love's richest book.

HELENA
Wherefore was I to this keen mockery born?
When at your hands did I deserve this scorn?
Is 't not enough, is 't not enough, young man,
That I did never, no, nor never can,
Deserve a sweet look from Demetrius' eye,
But you must flout my insufficiency?
Good troth, you do me wrong, good sooth, you do,
In such disdainful manner me to woo.
But fare you well. Perforce I must confess
I thought you lord of more true gentleness.
O, that a lady, of one man refus'd,
Should of another therefore be abus'd! *Exit.*

LYSANDER
She sees not Hermia. Hermia, sleep thou there,
And never mayst thou come Lysander near!
For as a surfeit of the sweetest things
The deepest loathing to the stomach brings,
Or as the heresies that men do leave
Are hated most of those they did deceive,
So thou, my surfeit and my heresy,
Of all be hated, but the most of me!
And, all my powers, address your love and might
To honor Helen and to be her knight! *Exit.*

HERMIA [*Awaking*]
Help me, Lysander, help me! Do thy best
To pluck this crawling serpent from my breast!
Ay me, for pity! What a dream was here!
Lysander, look how I do quake with fear.
Methought a serpent eat my heart away,
And you sat smiling at his cruel prey.
Lysander! What, remov'd? Lysander! Lord!
What, out of hearing? Gone? No sound, no word?
Alack, where are you? Speak, an if you hear.
Speak, of all loves! I swoon almost with fear.
No? Then I well perceive you are not nigh.
Either death, or you, I'll find immediately.
Exit. [*Manet Titania lying asleep.*]

[ACT III • SCENE I]

Enter the Clowns [*Quince, Snug, Bottom, Flute, Snout, and Starveling*].

BOTTOM Are we all met?

QUINCE Pat, pat; and here's a marvailes convenient place for our rehearsal. This green plot shall be our stage, this hawthorn brake our tiring-house, and we will do it in action as we will do it before the Duke.

BOTTOM Peter Quince?

QUINCE What sayest thou, bully Bottom?

79 owe own **86 darkling** in the dark **87 on thy peril** i.e., on pain of danger to you if you don't obey me and stay **88 fond** doting **89 my grace** the favor I obtain **90 lies** dwells **99 sphery eyne** eyes as bright as stars in their spheres **104 Transparent** (1) radiant (2) able to be seen through **118 ripe not** (am) not ripened **119 touching** reaching. **point** summit. **skill** judgment **121 o'erlook** read

129 Good troth, good sooth i.e., indeed, truly **132 lord of** i.e., possessor of. **gentleness** courtesy **133 of** by **134 abus'd** ill treated **149 eat** ate. (Pronounced et.) **150 prey** act of preying **154 of all loves** for all love's sake

III.i. Location: Scene continues.
4 brake thicket. **tiring-house** attiring area, hence back stage **7 bully** i.e., worthy, jolly, fine fellow

BOTTOM There are things in this comedy of Pyramus
and Thisby that will never please. First, Pyramus must
draw a sword to kill himself, which the ladies cannot
abide. How answer you that?
SNOUT By 'r lakin, a parlous fear. 12
STARVELING I believe we must leave the killing out,
when all is done. 14
BOTTOM Not a whit. I have a device to make all well.
Write me a prologue; and let the prologue seem to say, 16
we will do no harm with our swords and that Pyramus
is not kill'd indeed; and, for the more better assurance,
tell them that I Pyramus am not Pyramus, but Bottom
the weaver. This will put them out of fear.
QUINCE Well, we will have such a prologue, and it shall
be written in eight and six. 22
BOTTOM No, make it two more; let it be written in eight
and eight.
SNOUT Will not the ladies be afeard of the lion?
STARVELING I fear it, I promise you.
BOTTOM Masters, you ought to consider with your-
selves, to bring in—God shield us!—a lion among la- 28
dies, is a most dreadful thing. For there is not a more 29
fearful wild-fowl than your lion living; and we ought 30
to look to 't.
SNOUT Therefore another prologue must tell he is not a
lion.
BOTTOM Nay, you must name his name, and half his
face must be seen through the lion's neck, and he him-
self must speak through, saying thus, or to the same
defect: "Ladies"—or "Fair ladies—I would wish 37
you"—or "I would request you"—or "I would entreat
you—not to fear, not to tremble; my life for yours. If 39
you think I come hither as a lion, it were pity of my 40
life. No, I am no such thing; I am a man as other men 41
are." And there indeed let him name his name, and
tell them plainly he is Snug the joiner.
QUINCE Well, it shall be so. But there is two hard things:
that is, to bring the moonlight into a chamber; for, you
know, Pyramus and Thisby meet by moonlight.
SNOUT Doth the moon shine that night we play our
play?
BOTTOM A calendar, a calendar! Look in the almanac.
Find out moonshine, find out moonshine.
[*They consult an almanac.*]
QUINCE Yes, it doth shine that night.
BOTTOM Why then may you leave a casement of the
great chamber window, where we play, open, and the
moon may shine in at the casement.
QUINCE Ay; or else one must come in with a bush of 55
thorns and a lantern, and say he comes to disfigure, or 56
to present, the person of Moonshine. Then there is 57
another thing: we must have a wall in the great cham-
ber; for Pyramus and Thisby, says the story, did talk
through the chink of a wall.
SNOUT You can never bring in a wall. What say you,
Bottom?
BOTTOM Some man or other must present Wall. And let
him have some plaster, or some loam, or some rough- 64
cast about him, to signify wall; and let him hold his 65
fingers thus, and through that cranny shall Pyramus
and Thisby whisper.
QUINCE If that may be, then all is well. Come, sit down,
every mother's son, and rehearse your parts. Pyramus,
you begin. When you have spoken your speech, enter
into that brake, and so every one according to his cue.

Enter Robin [*Puck*].

PUCK
What hempen home-spuns have we swagg'ring
here,
So near the cradle of the Fairy Queen?
What, a play toward? I'll be an auditor; 74
An actor too perhaps, if I see cause.
QUINCE Speak, Pyramus. Thisby, stand forth.
BOTTOM
"Thisby, the flowers of odious savors sweet,"—
QUINCE Odors, odors.
BOTTOM
—"Odors savors sweet;
So hath thy breath, my dearest Thisby dear.
But hark, a voice! Stay thou but here awhile,
And by and by I will to thee appear." *Exit.*
PUCK
A stranger Pyramus than e'er played here. [*Exit.*] 83
FLUTE Must I speak now?
QUINCE Ay, marry, must you; for you must understand
he goes but to see a noise that he heard, and is to come
again.
FLUTE
"Most radiant Pyramus, most lily-white of hue,
Of color like the red rose on triumphant brier,
Most brisky juvenal and eke most lovely Jew, 90
As true as truest horse that yet would never tire.
I'll meet thee, Pyramus, at Ninny's tomb."
QUINCE "Ninus' tomb," man. Why, you must not 93
speak that yet. That you answer to Pyramus. You
speak all your part at once, cues and all. Pyramus en-
ter. Your cue is past; it is, "never tire."
FLUTE
O—"As true as truest horse, that yet would never
tire." 97

[*Enter Puck, and Bottom as Pyramus with the ass head.*]

BOTTOM
"If I were fair, Thisby, I were only thine." 98

12 By 'r lakin by our ladykin, i.e., the Virgin Mary. **parlous** perilous **14 when all is done** i.e., when all is said and done **16 Write me** i.e., write at my suggestion. (*Me* is the ethical dative.) **22 eight and six** alternate lines of eight and six syllables, a common ballad measure **28–29 lion among ladies** (A contemporary pamphlet tells how at the christening in 1594 of Prince Henry, eldest son of King James VI of Scotland, later James I of England, a "blackmoor" instead of a lion drew the triumphal chariot, since the lion's presence might have "brought some fear to the nearest.") **30 fearful** fear-inspiring **37 defect** (Bottom's blunder for *effect.*) **39 my life for yours** i.e., I pledge my life to make your lives safe **40–41 it were . . . life** my life would be endangered **55–56 bush of thorns** bundle of thornbush faggots (part of the accoutrements of the man in the moon, according to the popular notions of the time, along with his lantern and his dog) **56 disfigure** (Quince's blunder for *prefigure.*) **57 present** represent

64–65 rough-cast a mixture of lime and gravel used to plaster the outside of buildings **74 toward** about to take place **83 here** i.e., in this theatre (?) **90 brisky juvenal** brisk youth. **eke** also. **Jew** (Probably an absurd repetition of the first syllable of *juvenal.*) **93 Ninus** mythical founder of Nineveh (whose wife, Semiramis, was supposed to have built the walls of Babylon where the story of Pyramis and Thisbe takes place) **97 s.d. with the ass head** (This stage direction, taken from the Folio, presumably refers to a standard stage property.) **98 fair** handsome. **were** would be

QUINCE O monstrous! O strange! We are haunted.
Pray, masters! Fly, masters! Help!
[Exeunt Quince, Snug, Flute, Snout, and Starveling.]

PUCK
I'll follow you, I'll lead you about a round, 101
Through bog, through bush, through brake, through brier.
Sometime a horse I'll be, sometime a hound,
A hog, a headless bear, sometime a fire; 104
And neigh, and bark, and grunt, and roar, and burn,
Like horse, hound, hog, bear, fire, at every turn. *Exit.*

BOTTOM Why do they run away? This is a knavery of them to make me afeard.

Enter Snout.

SNOUT O Bottom, thou art chang'd! What do I see on thee?

BOTTOM What do you see? You see an ass-head of your own, do you? *[Exit Snout.]*

Enter Quince.

QUINCE Bless thee, Bottom, bless thee! Thou art trans- 113
lated. *Exit.* 114

BOTTOM I see their knavery. This is to make an ass of me, to fright me, if they could. But I will not stir from this place, do what they can. I will walk up and down here, and I will sing, that they shall hear I am not afraid. *[Sings.]*
The woosel cock so black of hue, 120
With orange-tawny bill,
The throstle with his note so true, 122
The wren with little quill— 123

TITANIA *[Awaking]*
What angel wakes me from my flow'ry bed?

BOTTOM *[Sings]*
The finch, the sparrow, and the lark,
The plain-song cuckoo grey, 126
Whose note full many a man doth mark,
And dares not answer nay— 128
For, indeed, who would set his wit to so foolish a
bird? Who would give a bird the lie, though he cry 130
"cuckoo" never so? 131

TITANIA
I pray thee, gentle mortal, sing again.
Mine ear is much enamored of thy note;
So is mine eye enthralled to thy shape;
And thy fair virtue's force perforce doth move me 135
On the first view to say, to swear, I love thee.

BOTTOM Methinks, mistress, you should have little reason for that. And yet, to say the truth, reason and love keep little company together nowadays. The more the pity that some honest neighbors will not make them
friends. Nay, I can gleek upon occasion. 141

TITANIA
Thou art as wise as thou art beautiful.

BOTTOM Not so, neither. But if I had wit enough to get
out of this wood, I have enough to serve mine own 144
turn. 145

TITANIA
Out of this wood do not desire to go.
Thou shalt remain here, whether thou wilt or no.
I am a spirit of no common rate. 148
The summer still doth tend upon my state; 149
And I do love thee. Therefore, go with me.
I'll give thee fairies to attend on thee,
And they shall fetch thee jewels from the deep,
And sing while thou on pressed flowers dost sleep.
And I will purge thy mortal grossness so
That thou shalt like an airy spirit go.
Peaseblossom, Cobweb, Moth, and Mustardseed! 156

Enter four Fairies [Peaseblossom, Cobweb, Moth, and Mustardseed].

PEASEBLOSSOM
Ready.

COBWEB
And I.

MOTH And I.

MUSTARDSEED And I.

ALL Where shall we go?

TITANIA
Be kind and courteous to this gentleman.
Hop in his walks and gambol in his eyes;
Feed him with apricocks and dewberries,
With purple grapes, green figs, and mulberries;
The honey-bags steal from the humble-bees,
And for night-tapers crop their waxen thighs
And light them at the fiery glow-worm's eyes,
To have my love to bed and to arise;
And pluck the wings from painted butterflies
To fan the moonbeams from his sleeping eyes.
Nod to him, elves, and do him courtesies.

PEASEBLOSSOM Hail, mortal! 170

COBWEB Hail!

MOTH Hail!

MUSTARDSEED Hail!

BOTTOM I cry your worships mercy, heartily. I beseech your worship's name.

COBWEB Cobweb.

BOTTOM I shall desire you of more acquaintance, good
Master Cobweb. If I cut my finger, I shall make bold 178
with you. Your name, honest gentleman? 179

PEASEBLOSSOM Peaseblossom.

BOTTOM I pray you, commend me to Mistress Squash, 181
your mother, and to Master Peascod, your father. 182
Good Master Peaseblossom, I shall desire you of more acquaintance too. Your name, I beseech you, sir?

MUSTARDSEED Mustardseed.

101 about a round roundabout **104 fire** will-o'-the-wisp **113–114 translated** transformed **120 woosel cock** male ousel or ouzel, blackbird **122 throstle** song thrush **123 quill** (Literally, a reed pipe; hence, the bird's piping song.) **126 plain-song** singing a melody without variations **128 dares . . . nay** i.e., cannot deny that he is a cuckold **130 give . . . lie** call the bird a liar **131 never so** ever so much **135 thy . . . force** the power of your beauty **141 gleek** scoff, jest

144–145 serve . . . turn answer my purpose **148 rate** rank, value **149 still** ever, always. **doth . . . state** waits upon me as a part of my royal retinue **156 Moth** i.e., mote, speck. (The two words *moth* and *mote* were pronounced alike.) **178–179 If . . . you** (Cobwebs were used to stanch bleeding.) **181 Squash** unripe pea pod **182 Peascod** ripe pea pod

BOTTOM Good Master Mustardseed, I know your patience well. That same cowardly, giant-like ox-beef hath devour'd many a gentleman of your house. I promise you your kindred hath made my eyes water ere now. I desire you of more acquaintance, good Master Mustardseed.

TITANIA
Come wait upon him; lead him to my bower.
The moon methinks looks with a wat'ry eye;
And when she weeps, weeps every little flower,
Lamenting some enforced chastity.
Tie up my lover's tongue, bring him silently.
Exeunt.

[SCENE II]

Enter [Oberon,] King of Fairies.

OBERON
I wonder if Titania be awak'd;
Then, what it was that next came in her eye,
Which she must dote on in extremity.

[Enter] Robin Goodfellow [Puck].

Here comes my messenger. How now, mad spirit?
What night-rule now about this haunted grove?

PUCK
My mistress with a monster is in love.
Near to her close and consecrated bower,
While she was in her dull and sleeping hour,
A crew of patches, rude mechanicals,
That work for bread upon Athenian stalls,
Were met together to rehearse a play
Intended for great Theseus' nuptial day.
The shallowest thick-skin of that barren sort,
Who Pyramus presented, in their sport
Forsook his scene and ent'red in a brake.
When I did him at this advantage take,
An ass's nole I fixed on his head.
Anon his Thisby must be answered,
And forth my mimic comes. When they him spy,
As wild geese that the creeping fowler eye,
Or russet-pated choughs, many in sort,
Rising and cawing at the gun's report,
Sever themselves and madly sweep the sky,
So, at his sight, away his fellows fly;
And, at our stamp, here o'er and o'er one falls;
He murder cries and help from Athens calls.
Their sense thus weak, lost with their fears thus strong,
Made senseless things begin to do them wrong,
For briers and thorns at their apparel snatch;
Some, sleeves—some, hats; from yielders all things catch.
I led them on in this distracted fear
And left sweet Pyramus translated there,
When in that moment, so it came to pass,
Titania wak'd and straightway lov'd an ass.

OBERON
This falls out better than I could devise.
But hast thou yet latch'd the Athenian's eyes
With the love-juice, as I did bid thee do?

PUCK
I took him sleeping—that is finish'd too—
And the Athenian woman by his side,
That, when he wak'd, of force she must be ey'd.

Enter Demetrius and Hermia.

OBERON
Stand close. This is the same Athenian.

PUCK
This is the woman, but not this the man.
[They stand aside.]

DEMETRIUS
O, why rebuke you him that loves you so?
Lay breath so bitter on your bitter foe.

HERMIA
Now I but chide; but I should use thee worse,
For thou, I fear, hast given me cause to curse.
If thou hast slain Lysander in his sleep,
Being o'er shoes in blood, plunge in the deep,
And kill me too.
The sun was not so true unto the day
As he to me. Would he have stolen away
From sleeping Hermia? I'll believe as soon
This whole earth may be bor'd and that the moon
May through the center creep and so displease
Her brother's noontide with th' Antipodes.
It cannot be but thou hast murd'red him;
So should a murderer look, so dead, so grim.

DEMETRIUS
So should the murdered look, and so should I,
Pierc'd through the heart with your stern cruelty.
Yet you, the murderer, look as bright, as clear,
As yonder Venus in her glimmering sphere.

HERMIA
What's this to my Lysander? Where is he?
Ah, good Demetrius, wilt thou give him me?

DEMETRIUS
I had rather give his carcass to my hounds.

HERMIA
Out, dog! Out, cur! Thou driv'st me past the bounds
Of maiden's patience. Hast thou slain him, then?
Henceforth be never numb'red among men!
O, once tell true, tell true, even for my sake!
Durst thou have look'd upon him being awake,
And hast thou kill'd him sleeping? O brave touch!
Could not a worm, an adder, do so much?

186–187 your patience what you have endured **194 she weeps** i.e., she causes dew **195 enforced** forced, violated; or, possibly, constrained (since Titania at this moment is hardly concerned about chastity)

III.ii. Location: The wood.
5 night-rule diversion for the night. **haunted** much frequented **7 close** secret, private **8 dull** drowsy **9 patches** clowns, fools. **rude mechanicals** ignorant artisans **13 barren sort** stupid company or crew **14 presented** acted **15 scene** playing area **17 nole** noddle, head **19 mimic** burlesque actor **21 russet-pated choughs** grey-headed jackdaws. **in sort** in a flock **23 Sever** i.e., scatter

36 latch'd moistened, anointed **40 of force** perforce **53 whole** solid **55 Her brother's** i.e., the sun's. **th' Antipodes** the people on the opposite side of the earth **57 dead** deadly, or deathly pale **70 brave touch** noble exploit. (Said ironically.) **71 worm** serpent

An adder did it; for with doubler tongue
Than thine, thou serpent, never adder stung.

DEMETRIUS
You spend your passion on a mispris'd mood. 74
I am not guilty of Lysander's blood,
Nor is he dead, for aught that I can tell.

HERMIA
I pray thee, tell me then that he is well.

DEMETRIUS
An if I could, what should I get therefore?

HERMIA
A privilege never to see me more.
And from thy hated presence part I so.
See me no more, whether he be dead or no. *Exit.*

DEMETRIUS
There is no following her in this fierce vein.
Here therefore for a while I will remain.
So sorrow's heaviness doth heavier grow 84
For debt that bankrupt sleep doth sorrow owe; 85
Which now in some slight measure it will pay, 86
If for his tender here I make some stay. 87
Lie down [*and sleep*].

OBERON
What hast thou done? Thou hast mistaken quite
And laid the love-juice on some true-love's sight.
Of thy misprision must perforce ensue 90
Some true love turn'd and not a false turn'd true.

PUCK
Then fate o'er-rules, that, one man holding troth, 92
A million fail, confounding oath on oath. 93

OBERON
About the wood go swifter than the wind,
And Helena of Athens look thou find.
All fancy-sick she is and pale of cheer 96
With sighs of love, that cost the fresh blood dear. 97
By some illusion see thou bring her here.
I'll charm his eyes against she do appear. 99

PUCK
I go, I go; look how I go,
Swifter than arrow from the Tartar's bow. 101
[*Exit.*]

OBERON
Flower of this purple dye,
Hit with Cupid's archery.
Sink in apple of his eye.
[*Applies love-juice to Demetrius' eyes.*]
When his love he doth espy,
Let her shine as gloriously
As the Venus of the sky.
When thou wak'st, if she be by,
Beg of her for remedy.

Enter Puck.

PUCK
Captain of our fairy band,
Helena is here at hand,
And the youth, mistook by me,
Pleading for a lover's fee. 113
Shall we their fond pageant see? 114
Lord, what fools these mortals be!

OBERON
Stand aside. The noise they make
Will cause Demetrius to awake.

PUCK
Then will two at once woo one;
That must needs be sport alone; 119
And those things do best please me
That befall prepost'rously. 121
[*They stand aside.*]

Enter Lysander and Helena.

LYSANDER
Why should you think that I should woo in scorn?
Scorn and derision never come in tears.
Look when I vow, I weep; and vows so born, 124
In their nativity all truth appears. 125
How can these things in me seem scorn to you,
Bearing the badge of faith, to prove them true? 127

HELENA
You do advance your cunning more and more. 128
When truth kills truth, O devilish-holy fray! 129
These vows are Hermia's. Will you give her o'er?
Weigh oath with oath, and you will nothing weigh.
Your vows to her and me, put in two scales,
Will even weigh, and both as light as tales. 133

LYSANDER
I had no judgment when to her I swore.

HELENA
Nor none, in my mind, now you give her o'er.

LYSANDER
Demetrius loves her, and he loves not you.

DEMETRIUS [*Awaking*]
O Helen, goddess, nymph, perfect, divine!
To what, my love, shall I compare thine eyne?
Crystal is muddy. O, how ripe in show 139
Thy lips, those kissing cherries, tempting grow!
That pure congealed white, high Taurus' snow, 141
Fann'd with the eastern wind, turns to a crow 142
When thou hold'st up thy hand. O, let me kiss
This princess of pure white, this seal of bliss! 144

HELENA
O spite! O hell! I see you all are bent
To set against me for your merriment.
If you were civil and knew courtesy,
You would not do me thus much injury.
Can you not hate me, as I know you do,
But you must join in souls to mock me too?

74 passion violent feelings. **mispris'd mood** anger based on misconception **84 heavier** (1) harder to bear (2) more drowsy **85 bankrupt** (Demetrius is saying that his sleepiness adds to the weariness caused by sorrow.) **86–87 Which . . . stay** i.e., to a small extent I will be able to "pay back" and hence find some relief from sorrow, if I pause here a while *(make some stay)* while sleep "tenders" or offers itself by way of paying the debt owed to sorrow **90 misprision** mistake **92 troth** faith **93 confounding . . . oath** i.e., invalidating one oath with another **96 fancy-sick** lovesick. **cheer** face **97 sighs . . . blood** (An allusion to the physiological theory that each sigh costs the heart a drop of blood.) **99 against . . . appear** in anticipation of her coming **101 Tartar's bow** (Tartars were famed for their skill with the bow.)

113 fee privilege, reward **114 fond pageant** foolish exhibition **119 alone** unequaled **121 prepost'rously** out of the natural order **124 Look when** whenever **124–125 vows . . . appears** i.e., vows made by one who is weeping give evidence thereby of their sincerity **127 badge** identifying device such as that worn on servants' livery **128 advance** carry forward, display **129 truth kills truth** i.e., one of Lysander's vows must invalidate the other **133 tales** lies **139 show** appearance **141 Taurus** a lofty mountain range in Asia Minor **142 turns to a crow** i.e., seems black by contrast **144 seal** pledge

If you were men, as men you are in show,
You would not use a gentle lady so—
To vow, and swear, and superpraise my parts, 153
When I am sure you hate me with your hearts.
You both are rivals, and love Hermia;
And now both rivals, to mock Helena.
A trim exploit, a manly enterprise, 157
To conjure tears up in a poor maid's eyes
With your derision! None of noble sort
Would so offend a virgin and extort 160
A poor soul's patience, all to make you sport.

LYSANDER

You are unkind, Demetrius. Be not so;
For you love Hermia; this you know I know.
And here, with all good will, with all my heart,
In Hermia's love I yield you up my part;
And yours of Helena to me bequeath,
Whom I do love and will do till my death.

HELENA

Never did mockers waste more idle breath.

DEMETRIUS

Lysander, keep thy Hermia; I will none. 169
If e'er I lov'd her, all that love is gone.
My heart to her but as guest-wise sojourn'd,
And now to Helen is it home return'd,
There to remain.

LYSANDER Helen, it is not so.

DEMETRIUS

Disparage not the faith thou dost not know,
Lest, to thy peril, thou aby it dear. 175
Look where thy love comes; yonder is thy dear.

Enter Hermia.

HERMIA

Dark night, that from the eye his function takes, 177
The ear more quick of apprehension makes;
Wherein it doth impair the seeing sense,
It pays the hearing double recompense.
Thou art not by mine eye, Lysander, found;
Mine ear, I thank it, brought me to thy sound.
But why unkindly didst thou leave me so?

LYSANDER

Why should he stay, whom love doth press to go?

HERMIA

What love could press Lysander from my side?

LYSANDER

Lysander's love, that would not let him bide,
Fair Helena, who more engilds the night
Than all yon fiery oes and eyes of light. 188
Why seek'st thou me? Could not this make thee know,
The hate I bear thee made me leave thee so?

HERMIA

You speak not as you think. It cannot be.

HELENA

Lo, she is one of this confederacy!
Now I perceive they have conjoin'd all three
To fashion this false sport, in spite of me. 194
Injurious Hermia, most ungrateful maid!
Have you conspir'd, have you with these contriv'd 196
To bait me with this foul derision? 197
Is all the counsel that we two have shar'd, 198
The sisters' vows, the hours that we have spent,
When we have chid the hasty-footed time
For parting us—O, is all forgot?
All school-days friendship, childhood innocence?
We, Hermia, like two artificial gods, 203
Have with our needles created both one flower,
Both on one sampler, sitting on one cushion,
Both warbling of one song, both in one key,
As if our hands, our sides, voices, and minds
Had been incorporate. So we grew together,
Like to a double cherry, seeming parted,
But yet an union in partition;
Two lovely berries molded on one stem; 211
So, with two seeming bodies, but one heart;
Two of the first, like coats in heraldry, 213
Due but to one and crowned with one crest. 214
And will you rent our ancient love asunder, 215
To join with men in scorning your poor friend?
It is not friendly, 'tis not maidenly.
Our sex, as well as I, may chide you for it,
Though I alone do feel the injury.

HERMIA

I am amazed at your passionate words.
I scorn you not. It seems that you scorn me.

HELENA

Have you not set Lysander, as in scorn,
To follow me and praise my eyes and face?
And made your other love, Demetrius,
Who even but now did spurn me with his foot,
To call me goddess, nymph, divine and rare,
Precious, celestial? Wherefore speaks he this
To her he hates? And wherefore doth Lysander
Deny your love, so rich within his soul,
And tender me, forsooth, affection, 230
But by your setting on, by your consent?
What though I be not so in grace as you, 232
So hung upon with love, so fortunate,
But miserable most, to love unlov'd?
This you should pity rather than despise.

HERMIA

I understand not what you mean by this.

HELENA

Ay, do! Persever, counterfeit sad looks, 237
Make mouths upon me when I turn my back, 238
Wink each at other, hold the sweet jest up.
This sport, well carried, shall be chronicled. 240
If you have any pity, grace, or manners,
You would not make me such an argument. 242
But fare ye well. 'Tis partly my own fault,
Which death, or absence, soon shall remedy.

153 superpraise overpraise. **parts** qualities **157 trim** pretty, fine. (Said ironically.) **160 extort** twist, torture **169 will none** i.e., wish none of her **175 aby** pay for **177 his** its **188 oes** i.e., circles, orbs, stars

194 in spite of me to vex me **196 contriv'd** plotted **197 bait** torment, as one sets on dogs to bait a bear **198 counsel** confidential talk **203 artificial** skilled in art or creation **211 lovely** loving **213–214 Two . . . crest** i.e., we have two separate bodies, just as a coat of arms in heraldry can be represented twice on a shield but surmounted by a single crest **215 rent** rend **230 tender** offer **232 grace** favor **237 sad** grave, serious **238 mouths** i.e., mows, faces, grimaces. **upon** at **240 carried** managed **242 argument** subject for a jest

LYSANDER
Stay, gentle Helena; hear my excuse,
My love, my life, my soul, fair Helena!

HELENA
O excellent!

HERMIA Sweet, do not scorn her so.

DEMETRIUS
If she cannot entreat, I can compel.

LYSANDER
Thou canst compel no more than she entreat.
Thy threats have no more strength than her weak
prayers.
Helen, I love thee, by my life, I do!
I swear by that which I will lose for thee,
To prove him false that says I love thee not.

DEMETRIUS
I say I love thee more than he can do.

LYSANDER
If thou say so, withdraw, and prove it too.

DEMETRIUS
Quick, come!

HERMIA Lysander, whereto tends all this?

LYSANDER
Away, you Ethiope!
[*He tries to break away from Hermia.*]

DEMETRIUS No, no; he'll
Seem to break loose; take on as you would follow,
But yet come not. You are a tame man, go!

LYSANDER
Hang off, thou cat, thou burr! Vile thing, let loose,
Or I will shake thee from me like a serpent!

HERMIA
Why are you grown so rude? What change is this,
Sweet love?

LYSANDER Thy love? Out, tawny Tartar, out!
Out, loathed med'cine! O hated potion, hence!

HERMIA
Do you not jest?

HELENA Yes, sooth, and so do you.

LYSANDER
Demetrius, I will keep my word with thee.

DEMETRIUS
I would I had your bond, for I perceive
A weak bond holds you. I'll not trust your word.

LYSANDER
What, should I hurt her, strike her, kill her dead?
Although I hate her, I'll not harm her so.

HERMIA
What, can you do me greater harm than hate?
Hate me? Wherefore? O me, what news, my love?
Am not I Hermia? Are not you Lysander?
I am as fair now as I was erewhile.
Since night you lov'd me; yet since night you left
me.
Why, then you left me—O, the gods forbid!—
In earnest, shall I say?

LYSANDER Ay, by my life!
And never did desire to see thee more.
Therefore be out of hope, of question, of doubt;
Be certain, nothing truer. 'Tis no jest
That I do hate thee and love Helena.

HERMIA
O me! You juggler! You cankerblossom!
You thief of love! What, have you come by night
And stol'n my love's heart from him?

HELENA Fine, i' faith!
Have you no modesty, no maiden shame,
No touch of bashfulness? What, will you tear
Impatient answers from my gentle tongue?
Fie, fie! You counterfeit, you puppet, you!

HERMIA
Puppet? Why so? Ay, that way goes the game.
Now I perceive that she hath made compare
Between our statures; she hath urg'd her height,
And with her personage, her tall personage,
Her height, forsooth, she hath prevail'd with him.
And are you grown so high in his esteem,
Because I am so dwarfish and so low?
How low am I, thou painted maypole? Speak!
How low am I? I am not yet so low
But that my nails can reach unto thine eyes.
[*She flails at Helena, but is restrained.*]

HELENA
I pray you, though you mock me, gentlemen,
Let her not hurt me. I was never curst;
I have no gift at all in shrewishness;
I am a right maid for my cowardice.
Let her not strike me. You perhaps may think,
Because she is something lower than myself,
That I can match her.

HERMIA Lower! Hark, again!

HELENA
Good Hermia, do not be so bitter with me.
I evermore did love you, Hermia,
Did ever keep your counsels, never wrong'd you;
Save that, in love unto Demetrius,
I told him of your stealth unto this wood.
He followed you; for love I followed him.
But he hath chid me hence and threat'ned me
To strike me, spurn me, nay, to kill me too.
And now, so you will let me quiet go,
To Athens will I bear my folly back
And follow you no further. Let me go.
You see how simple and how fond I am.

HERMIA
Why, get you gone. Who is 't that hinders you?

HELENA
A foolish heart, that I leave here behind.

HERMIA
What, with Lysander?

HELENA With Demetrius.

LYSANDER
Be not afraid; she shall not harm thee, Helena.

248 entreat i.e., succeed by entreaty **257 Ethiope** (Referring to Hermia's relatively dark hair and complexion; see also *tawny Tartar* six lines later.) **260 Hang off** let go **264 med'cine** i.e., poison **265 sooth** truly **268 weak bond** i.e., Hermia's arm (with a pun on *bond,* oath, in the previous line) **272 what news** what is the matter **274 erewhile** just now

282 cankerblossom worm that destroys the flower bud (?) **288 puppet** (1) counterfeit (2) dwarfish woman (in reference to Hermia's smaller stature) **300 curst** shrewish **302 right** true **304 something** somewhat **310 stealth** stealing away **314 so** if only **317 fond** foolish

DEMETRIUS
No, sir, she shall not, though you take her part.

HELENA
O, when she is angry, she is keen and shrewd!
She was a vixen when she went to school;
And though she be but little, she is fierce.

HERMIA
"Little" again! Nothing but "low" and "little"!
Why will you suffer her to flout me thus?
Let me come to her.

LYSANDER Get you gone, you dwarf!
You minimus, of hind'ring knot-grass made!
You bead, you acorn!

DEMETRIUS You are too officious
In her behalf that scorns your services.
Let her alone. Speak not of Helena;
Take not her part. For, if thou dost intend
Never so little show of love to her,
Thou shalt aby it.

LYSANDER Now she holds me not;
Now follow, if thou dar'st, to try whose right,
Of thine or mine, is most in Helena. [*Exit.*]

DEMETRIUS
Follow? Nay, I'll go with thee, cheek by jowl.
[*Exit, following Lysander.*]

HERMIA
You, mistress, all this coil is 'long of you.
Nay, go not back.

HELENA I will not trust you, I,
Nor longer stay in your curst company.
Your hands than mine are quicker for a fray;
My legs are longer, though, to run away. [*Exit.*]

HERMIA
I am amaz'd, and know not what to say. *Exit.*

OBERON
This is thy negligence. Still thou mistak'st,
Or else committ'st thy knaveries willfully.

PUCK
Believe me, king of shadows, I mistook.
Did not you tell me I should know the man
By the Athenian garments he had on?
And so far blameless proves my enterprise
That I have 'nointed an Athenian's eyes;
And so far am I glad it so did sort
As this their jangling I esteem a sport.

OBERON
Thou see'st these lovers seek a place to fight.
Hie therefore, Robin, overcast the night;
The starry welkin cover thou anon
With drooping fog as black as Acheron,
And lead these testy rivals so astray
As one come not within another's way.
Like to Lysander sometime frame thy tongue,
Then stir Demetrius up with bitter wrong;
And sometime rail thou like Demetrius.
And from each other look thou lead them thus,
Till o'er their brows death-counterfeiting sleep
With leaden legs and batty wings doth creep.
Then crush this herb into Lysander's eye,
[*Gives herb.*]
Whose liquor hath this virtuous property,
To take from thence all error with his might
And make his eyeballs roll with wonted sight.
When they next wake, all this derision
Shall seem a dream and fruitless vision,
And back to Athens shall the lovers wend
With league whose date till death shall never end.
Whiles I in this affair do thee employ,
I'll to my queen and beg her Indian boy;
And then I will her charmed eye release
From monster's view, and all things shall be peace.

PUCK
My fairy lord, this must be done with haste,
For night's swift dragons cut the clouds full fast,
And yonder shines Aurora's harbinger,
At whose approach, ghosts, wand'ring here and there,
Troop home to churchyards. Damned spirits all,
That in crossways and floods have burial,
Already to their wormy beds are gone.
For fear lest day should look their shames upon,
They willfully themselves exile from light
And must for aye consort with black-brow'd night.

OBERON
But we are spirits of another sort.
I with the Morning's love have oft made sport,
And, like a forester, the groves may tread
Even till the eastern gate, all fiery-red,
Opening on Neptune with fair blessed beams,
Turns into yellow gold his salt green streams.
But, notwithstanding, haste; make no delay.
We may effect this business yet ere day. [*Exit.*]

PUCK
Up and down, up and down,
I will lead them up and down.
I am fear'd in field and town.
Goblin, lead them up and down.
Here comes one.

Enter Lysander.

LYSANDER
Where art thou, proud Demetrius? Speak thou now.

PUCK [*Mimicking Demetrius*]
Here, villain, drawn and ready. Where art thou?

LYSANDER
I will be with thee straight.

PUCK Follow me, then,
To plainer ground.
[*Lysander wanders about, following the voice.*]

323 shrewd shrewish **329 minimus** diminutive creature. **knot-grass** a weed, an infusion of which was thought to stunt the growth **333 intend** give sign of **335 aby** pay for **338 cheek by jowl** i.e., side by side **339 coil** turmoil, dissension. **'long of** on account of **340 go not back** i.e., don't retreat. (Hermia is again proposing a fight.) **352 sort** turn out **356 welkin** sky **357 Acheron** river of Hades (here representing Hades itself) **359 As** that **361 wrong** insults

365 batty batlike **366 this herb** i.e., the antidote (mentioned in II.i.184) to love-in-idleness **367 virtuous** efficacious **368 his** its **369 wonted** accustomed **370 derision** laughable business **373 date** term of existence **379 dragons** (Supposed by Shakespeare to be yoked to the car of the goddess of night.) **380 Aurora's harbinger** the morning star, precursor of dawn **383 crossways . . . burial** (Those who had committed suicide were buried at crossways, with a stake driven through them; those drowned, i.e., buried in floods or great waters, would be condemned to wander disconsolate for want of burial rites.) **387 for aye** forever **389 Morning's love** Cephalus, a beautiful youth beloved by Aurora; or perhaps the goddess of the dawn herself **390 forester** keeper of a royal forest **402 drawn** with drawn sword **403 straight** immediately

Enter Demetrius.

DEMETRIUS Lysander! Speak again!
Thou runaway, thou coward, art thou fled?
Speak! In some bush? Where dost thou hide thy
head?

PUCK [*Mimicking Lysander*]
Thou coward, art thou bragging to the stars,
Telling the bushes that thou look'st for wars,
And wilt not come? Come, recreant; come, thou
child,
I'll whip thee with a rod. He is defil'd
That draws a sword on thee.

DEMETRIUS Yea, art thou there?

PUCK
Follow my voice. We'll try no manhood here.
Exeunt.

[*Lysander returns.*]

LYSANDER
He goes before me and still dares me on.
When I come where he calls, then he is gone.
The villain is much lighter-heel'd than I.
I followed fast, but faster he did fly,
That fallen am I in dark uneven way,
And here will rest me. [*Lies down.*] Come, thou
gentle day!
For if but once thou show me thy grey light,
I'll find Demetrius and revenge this spite. [*Sleeps.*]

[*Enter*] *Robin* [*Puck*] *and Demetrius.*

PUCK
Ho, ho, ho! Coward, why com'st thou not?

DEMETRIUS
Abide me, if thou dar'st; for well I wot
Thou runn'st before me, shifting every place,
And dar'st not stand nor look me in the face.
Where art thou now?

PUCK Come hither. I am here.

DEMETRIUS
Nay, then, thou mock'st me. Thou shalt buy this
dear,
If ever I thy face by daylight see.
Now, go thy way. Faintness constraineth me
To measure out my length on this cold bed.
By day's approach look to be visited.
[*Lies down and sleeps.*]

Enter Helena.

HELENA
O weary night, O long and tedious night,
Abate thy hours! Shine, comforts, from the east,
That I may back to Athens by daylight,
From these that my poor company detest;
And sleep, that sometimes shuts up sorrow's eye,
Steal me awhile from mine own company.
[*Lies down and*] *sleep*[*s*].

PUCK
Yet but three? Come one more;
Two of both kinds makes up four.
Here she comes, curst and sad.
Cupid is a knavish lad,
Thus to make poor females mad.

[*Enter Hermia.*]

HERMIA
Never so weary, never so in woe,
Bedabbled with the dew and torn with briers,
I can no further crawl, no further go;
My legs can keep no pace with my desires.
Here will I rest me till the break of day.
Heavens shield Lysander, if they mean a fray!
[*Lies down and sleeps.*]

PUCK
On the ground
Sleep sound.
I'll apply
To your eye,
Gentle lover, remedy.
[*Squeezing the juice on Lysander's eyes.*]
When thou wak'st,
Thou tak'st
True delight
In the sight
Of thy former lady's eye;
And the country proverb known,
That every man should take his own,
In your waking shall be shown:
Jack shall have Jill;
Nought shall go ill;
The man shall have his mare again, and all
shall be well. [*Exit. Manent the four lovers.*]

[ACT IV • SCENE I]

Enter [*Titania,*] *Queen of Fairies, and* [*Bottom the*] *Clown, and Fairies; and* [*Oberon,*] *the King, behind them.*

TITANIA
Come, sit thee down upon this flow'ry bed,
While I thy amiable cheeks do coy,
And stick musk-roses in thy sleek smooth head,
And kiss thy fair large ears, my gentle joy.
[*They recline.*]

BOTTOM Where's Peaseblossom?

PEASEBLOSSOM Ready.

BOTTOM Scratch my head, Peaseblossom. Where's Mounsieur Cobweb?

COBWEB Ready.

BOTTOM Mounsieur Cobweb, good mounsieur, get you your weapons in your hand, and kill me a red-hipp'd humble-bee on the top of a thistle; and, good moun-

404 plainer smoother **404 s.d. Lysander wanders about** (It is not clearly necessary that Lysander exit at this point; neither exit nor reentrance is indicated in the early texts.) **409 recreant** cowardly wretch **412 try** test **422 wot** know **426 buy** aby, pay for. **dear** dearly **432 Abate** lessen, shorten

IV.i. Location: Scene continues. The four lovers are still asleep on stage.
2 amiable lovely. **coy** caress

sieur, bring me the honey-bag. Do not fret yourself too much in the action, mounsieur; and, good mounsieur, have a care the honey-bag break not; I would be loath to have you overflown with a honey-bag, signior. Where's Mounsieur Mustardseed?

MUSTARDSEED Ready.

BOTTOM Give me your neaf, Mounsieur Mustardseed. Pray you, leave your curtsy, good mounsieur.

MUSTARDSEED What's your will?

BOTTOM Nothing, good mounsieur, but to help Cavalery Cobweb to scratch. I must to the barber's, mounsieur; for methinks I am marvailes hairy about the face; and I am such a tender ass, if my hair do but tickle me, I must scratch.

TITANIA
What, wilt thou hear some music, my sweet love?

BOTTOM I have a reasonable good ear in music. Let's have the tongs and the bones.

[*Music: tongs, rural music.*]

TITANIA
Or say, sweet love, what thou desirest to eat.

BOTTOM Truly, a peck of provender. I could munch your good dry oats. Methinks I have a great desire to a bottle of hay. Good hay, sweet hay, hath no fellow.

TITANIA
I have a venturous fairy that shall seek
The squirrel's hoard, and fetch thee new nuts.

BOTTOM I had rather have a handful or two of dried peas. But, I pray you, let none of your people stir me. I have an exposition of sleep come upon me.

TITANIA
Sleep thou, and I will wind thee in my arms.
Fairies, be gone, and be all ways away.

[*Exeunt fairies.*]

So doth the woodbine the sweet honeysuckle
Gently entwist; the female ivy so
Enrings the barky fingers of the elm.
Oh, how I love thee! How I dote on thee!

[*They sleep.*]

Enter Robin Goodfellow [*Puck*].

OBERON [*Advancing*]
Welcome, good Robin. See'st thou this sweet sight?
Her dotage now I do begin to pity.
For, meeting her of late behind the wood,
Seeking sweet favors for this hateful fool,
I did upbraid her and fall out with her.
For she his hairy temples then had rounded
With coronet of fresh and fragrant flowers;
And that same dew, which sometime on the buds
Was wont to swell like round and orient pearls,
Stood now within the pretty flouriets' eyes
Like tears that did their own disgrace bewail.
When I had at my pleasure taunted her,
And she in mild terms begg'd my patience,
I then did ask of her her changeling child;
Which straight she gave me, and her fairy sent
To bear him to my bower in fairy land.
And, now I have the boy, I will undo
This hateful imperfection of her eyes.
And, gentle Puck, take this transformed scalp
From off the head of this Athenian swain,
That, he awaking when the other do,
May all to Athens back again repair,
And think no more of this night's accidents
But as the fierce vexation of a dream.
But first I will release the Fairy Queen.

[*Squeezes juice in her eyes.*]

Be as thou wast wont to be;
See as thou wast wont to see.
Dian's bud o'er Cupid's flower
Hath such force and blessed power.
Now, my Titania, wake you, my sweet queen.

TITANIA [*Waking*]
My Oberon! What visions have I seen!
Methought I was enamor'd of an ass.

OBERON
There lies your love.

TITANIA How came these things to pass?
O, how mine eyes do loathe his visage now!

OBERON
Silence awhile. Robin, take off this head.
Titania, music call, and strike more dead
Than common sleep of all these five the sense.

TITANIA
Music, ho! Music, such as charmeth sleep!

[*Music.*]

PUCK [*Removing the ass's head*]
Now, when thou wak'st, with thine own fool's eyes peep.

OBERON
Sound, music! Come, my queen, take hands with me,
And rock the ground whereon these sleepers be.

[*Dance.*]

Now thou and I are new in amity,
And will tomorrow midnight solemnly
Dance in Duke Theseus' house triumphantly
And bless it to all fair prosperity.
There shall the pairs of faithful lovers be
Wedded, with Theseus, all in jollity.

PUCK
Fairy King, attend, and mark:
I do hear the morning lark.

OBERON
Then, my queen, in silence sad,
Trip we after night's shade.
We the globe can compass soon,
Swifter than the wand'ring moon.

19 neaf fist **20 leave your curtsy** i.e., put on your hat **22–23 Cavalery** cavalier. (Form of address for a gentleman.) **23 Cobweb** (Seemingly an error, since Cobweb has been sent to bring honey while Peaseblossom has been asked to scratch.) **29 tongs . . . bones** instruments for rustic music. (The tongs were played like a triangle, whereas the bones were held between the fingers and used as clappers.) **29 s.d. Music . . . music** (This stage direction is added from the Folio.) **33 bottle** bundle. **fellow** equal **38 exposition** (Bottom's word for *disposition*.) **40 all ways** in all directions **48 favors** i.e., gifts of flowers **52 sometime** formerly **53 orient pearls** i.e., the most beautiful of all pearls, those coming from the Orient **54 flouriets'** flowerets'

65 other others **72 Dian's bud** (Perhaps the flower of the *agnus castus* or chaste-tree, supposed to preserve chastity; or perhaps referring simply to Oberon's herb by which he can undo the effects of "Cupid's flower," the love-in-idleness of II.i.166 f.) **81 these five** i.e., the four lovers and Bottom **87 solemnly** ceremoniously **94 sad** sober

TITANIA
Come, my lord, and in our flight
Tell me how it came this night
That I sleeping here was found
With these mortals on the ground. *Exeunt.*
Wind horn [*within*].

Enter Theseus and all his train; [*Hippolyta, Egeus*].

THESEUS
Go, one of you, find out the forester,
For now our observation is perform'd;
And since we have the vaward of the day,
My love shall hear the music of my hounds.
Uncouple in the western valley; let them go.
Dispatch, I say, and find the forester.
[*Exit an Attendant.*]
We will, fair queen, up to the mountain's top
And mark the musical confusion
Of hounds and echo in conjunction.

HIPPOLYTA
I was with Hercules and Cadmus once,
When in a wood of Crete they bay'd the bear
With hounds of Sparta. Never did I hear
Such gallant chiding; for, besides the groves,
The skies, the fountains, every region near
Seem'd all one mutual cry. I never heard
So musical a discord, such sweet thunder.

THESEUS
My hounds are bred out of the Spartan kind,
So flew'd, so sanded; and their heads are hung
With ears that sweep away the morning dew;
Crook-knee'd, and dewlapp'd like Thessalian bulls;
Slow in pursuit, but match'd in mouth like bells,
Each under each. A cry more tuneable
Was never holla'd to, nor cheer'd with horn,
In Crete, in Sparta, nor in Thessaly.
Judge when you hear. [*Sees the sleepers.*] But, soft!
What nymphs are these?

EGEUS
My lord, this' my daughter here asleep;
And this, Lysander; this Demetrius is;
This Helena, old Nedar's Helena.
I wonder of their being here together.

THESEUS
No doubt they rose up early to observe
The rite of May, and, hearing our intent,
Came here in grace of our solemnity.
But speak, Egeus. Is not this the day
That Hermia should give answer of her choice?

EGEUS
It is, my lord.

THESEUS
Go, bid the huntsmen wake them with their horns.
[*Exit an Attendant.*]

Shout within. Wind horns. They all start up.

Good morrow, friends. Saint Valentine is past.
Begin these wood-birds but to couple now?

LYSANDER
Pardon, my lord. [*They kneel.*]

THESEUS
I pray you all, stand up.
I know you two are rival enemies;
How comes this gentle concord in the world,
That hatred is so far from jealousy
To sleep by hate and fear no enmity?

LYSANDER
My lord, I shall reply amazedly,
Half sleep, half waking; but as yet, I swear,
I cannot truly say how I came here.
But, as I think—for truly would I speak,
And now I do bethink me, so it is—
I came with Hermia hither. Our intent
Was to be gone from Athens, where we might,
Without the peril of the Athenian law—

EGEUS
Enough, enough, my lord; you have enough.
I beg the law, the law, upon his head.
They would have stol'n away; they would, Demetrius,
Thereby to have defeated you and me,
You of your wife and me of my consent,
Of my consent that she should be your wife.

DEMETRIUS
My lord, fair Helen told me of their stealth,
Of this their purpose hither to this wood,
And I in fury hither followed them,
Fair Helena in fancy following me.
But, my good lord, I wot not by what power—
But by some power it is—my love to Hermia,
Melted as the snow, seems to me now
As the remembrance of an idle gaud
Which in my childhood I did dote upon;
And all the faith, the virtue of my heart,
The object and the pleasure of mine eye,
Is only Helena. To her, my lord,
Was I betroth'd ere I saw Hermia,
But like a sickness did I loathe this food;
But, as in health, come to my natural taste,
Now I do wish it, love it, long for it,
And will for evermore be true to it.

THESEUS
Fair lovers, you are fortunately met.
Of this discourse we more will hear anon.
Egeus, I will overbear your will;
For in the temple, by and by, with us
These couples shall eternally be knit.
And, for the morning now is something worn,
Our purpos'd hunting shall be set aside.

103 observation i.e., observance to a morn of May (I.i.167) **104 vaward** vanguard, i.e., earliest part **111 Cadmus** mythical founder of Thebes. (This story about him is unknown.) **112 bay'd** brought to bay **113 hounds of Sparta** (A breed famous in antiquity for their hunting skill.) **119 So flew'd** similarly having large hanging chaps or fleshy covering of the jaw. **sanded** of sandy color **121 dewlapp'd** having pendulous folds of skin under the neck **122–123 match'd . . . each** i.e., harmoniously matched in their various cries like a set of bells, from treble down to bass **123 cry** pack of hounds. **tuneable** well tuned, melodious **133 solemnity** i.e., observance of these same rites of May

138 Saint Valentine (Birds were supposed to choose their mates on St. Valentine's Day.) **151 where** wherever; or, to where **152 Without** outside of, beyond **166 idle gaud** worthless trinket **181 for** since. **something** somewhat

Away with us to Athens. Three and three,
We'll hold a feast in great solemnity.
Come, Hippolyta.
[*Exeunt Theseus, Hippolyta, Egeus, and train.*]

DEMETRIUS
These things seem small and undistinguishable,
Like far-off mountains turnèd into clouds.

HERMIA
Methinks I see these things with parted eye,
When every thing seems double.

HELENA
So methinks;
And I have found Demetrius like a jewel,
Mine own, and not mine own.

DEMETRIUS
Are you sure
That we are awake? It seems to me
That yet we sleep, we dream. Do not you think
The Duke was here, and bid us follow him?

HERMIA
Yea, and my father.

HELENA
And Hippolyta.

LYSANDER
And he did bid us follow to the temple.

DEMETRIUS
Why, then, we are awake. Let's follow him,
And by the way let us recount our dreams. [*Exeunt.*]

BOTTOM [*Awaking*] When my cue comes, call me, and I will answer. My next is, "Most fair Pyramus." Heigh-ho! Peter Quince! Flute, the bellows-mender! Snout, the tinker! Starveling! God's my life, stol'n hence, and left me asleep! I have had a most rare vision. I have had a dream, past the wit of man to say what dream it was. Man is but an ass, if he go about to expound this dream. Methought I was—there is no man can tell what. Methought I was—and methought I had—but man is but a patch'd fool, if he will offer to say what methought I had. The eye of man hath not heard, the ear of man hath not seen, man's hand is not able to taste, his tongue to conceive, nor his heart to report, what my dream was. I will get Peter Quince to write a ballad of this dream. It shall be call'd "Bottom's Dream," because it hath no bottom; and I will sing it in the latter end of a play, before the Duke. Peradventure, to make it the more gracious, I shall sing it at her death. [*Exit.*]

[SCENE II]

Enter Quince, Flute, [Snout, and Starveling].

QUINCE Have you sent to Bottom's house? Is he come home yet?

STARVELING He cannot be heard of. Out of doubt he is transported.

FLUTE If he come not, then the play is marr'd. It goes not forward, doth it?

QUINCE It is not possible. You have not a man in all Athens able to discharge Pyramus but he.

FLUTE No, he hath simply the best wit of any handicraft man in Athens.

QUINCE Yea, and the best person too; and he is a very paramour for a sweet voice.

FLUTE You must say "paragon." A paramour is, God bless us, a thing of naught.

Enter Snug the Joiner.

SNUG Masters, the Duke is coming from the temple, and there is two or three lords and ladies more married. If our sport had gone forward, we had all been made men.

FLUTE O sweet bully Bottom! Thus hath he lost sixpence a day during his life; he could not have scap'd sixpence a day. An the Duke had not given him sixpence a day for playing Pyramus, I'll be hang'd. He would have deserv'd it. Sixpence a day in Pyramus, or nothing.

Enter Bottom.

BOTTOM Where are these lads? Where are these hearts?

QUINCE Bottom! O most courageous day! O most happy hour!

BOTTOM Masters, I am to discourse wonders. But ask me not what; for if I tell you, I am no true Athenian. I will tell you everything, right as it fell out.

QUINCE Let us hear, sweet Bottom.

BOTTOM Not a word of me. All that I will tell you is, that the Duke hath din'd. Get your apparel together, good strings to your beards, new ribands to your pumps; meet presently at the palace; every man look o'er his part; for the short and the long is, our play is preferr'd. In any case, let Thisby have clean linen; and let not him that plays the lion pare his nails, for they shall hang out for the lion's claws. And, most dear actors, eat no onions nor garlic, for we are to utter sweet breath; and I do not doubt but to hear them say, it is a sweet comedy. No more words. Away! Go, away! [*Exeunt.*]

[ACT V • SCENE I]

Enter Theseus, Hippolyta, and Philostrate, [Lords, and Attendants].

HIPPOLYTA
'Tis strange, my Theseus, that these lovers speak of.

THESEUS
More strange than true. I never may believe
These antic fables, nor these fairy toys.
Lovers and madmen have such seething brains,
Such shaping fantasies, that apprehend
More than cool reason ever comprehends.
The lunatic, the lover, and the poet

188 parted improperly focused **190–191 like . . . mine own** i.e., like a jewel that one finds by chance and therefore possesses but cannot certainly consider one's own property **205 go about** attempt **208 patch'd** wearing motley, i.e., a dress of various colors. **offer** venture **216 her** Thisby's (?)

IV.ii. Location: Athens. Quince's house (?)
4 transported carried off by fairies; or, possibly, transformed

8 discharge perform **19–20 sixpence a day** i.e., as a royal pension **25 hearts** good fellows **28 am . . . wonders** have wonders to relate **32 of** out of **34 strings** (to attach the beards). **ribands** ribbons **35 presently** immediately **37 preferr'd** selected for consideration

V.i. Location: Athens. The palace of Theseus.
1 that that which **2 may** can **3 antic** strange, grotesque (with additional punning sense of *antique*, ancient). **fairy toys** trifling stories about fairies **5 fantasies** imaginations

Are of imagination all compact. 8
One sees more devils than vast hell can hold;
That is the madman. The lover, all as frantic,
Sees Helen's beauty in a brow of Egypt. 11
The poet's eye, in a fine frenzy rolling,
Doth glance from heaven to earth, from earth to heaven;
And as imagination bodies forth
The forms of things unknown, the poet's pen
Turns them to shapes and gives to airy nothing
A local habitation and a name.
Such tricks hath strong imagination
That, if it would but apprehend some joy,
It comprehends some bringer of that joy; 20
Or in the night, imagining some fear, 21
How easy is a bush suppos'd a bear!

HIPPOLYTA

But all the story of the night told over,
And all their minds transfigur'd so together,
More witnesseth than fancy's images 25
And grows to something of great constancy; 26
But, howsoever, strange and admirable. 27

Enter lovers: Lysander, Demetrius, Hermia, and Helena.

THESEUS

Here come the lovers, full of joy and mirth.
Joy, gentle friends! Joy and fresh days of love
Accompany your hearts!

LYSANDER More than to us
Wait in your royal walks, your board, your bed!

THESEUS

Come now, what masques, what dances shall we have,
To wear away this long age of three hours
Between our after-supper and bed-time?
Where is our usual manager of mirth?
What revels are in hand? Is there no play,
To ease the anguish of a torturing hour?
Call Philostrate.

PHILOSTRATE Here, mighty Theseus.

THESEUS

Say, what abridgement have you for this evening? 39
What masque? What music? How shall we beguile
The lazy time, if not with some delight?

PHILOSTRATE

There is a brief how many sports are ripe. 42
Make choice of which your Highness will see first.
[*Giving a paper.*]

THESEUS [*Reads*]

"The battle with the Centaurs, to be sung 44
By an Athenian eunuch to the harp."
We'll none of that. That have I told my love,
In glory of my kinsman Hercules. 47
[*Reads.*] "The riot of the tipsy Bacchanals, 48
Tearing the Thracian singer in their rage." 49
That is an old device; and it was play'd
When I from Thebes came last a conqueror.
[*Reads.*] "The thrice three Muses mourning for the death 52
Of Learning, late deceas'd in beggary." 53
That is some satire, keen and critical,
Not sorting with a nuptial ceremony. 55
[*Reads.*] "A tedious brief scene of young Pyramus
And his love Thisby; very tragical mirth."
Merry and tragical? Tedious and brief?
That is, hot ice and wondrous strange snow. 59
How shall we find the concord of this discord?

PHILOSTRATE

A play there is, my lord, some ten words long,
Which is as brief as I have known a play;
But by ten words, my lord, it is too long,
Which makes it tedious. For in all the play
There is not one word apt, one player fitted.
And tragical, my noble lord, it is,
For Pyramus therein doth kill himself.
Which, when I saw rehears'd, I must confess,
Made mine eyes water; but more merry tears
The passion of loud laughter never shed.

THESEUS

What are they that do play it?

PHILOSTRATE

Hard-handed men that work in Athens here,
Which never labor'd in their minds till now,
And now have toil'd their unbreathed memories 74
With this same play, against your nuptial. 75

THESEUS

And we will hear it.

PHILOSTRATE No, my noble lord,
It is not for you. I have heard it over,
And it is nothing, nothing in the world;
Unless you can find sport in their intents,
Extremely stretch'd and conn'd with cruel pain, 80
To do you service.

THESEUS I will hear that play;
For never anything can be amiss
When simpleness and duty tender it.
Go, bring them in; and take your places, ladies.
[*Philostrate goes to summon the players.*]

HIPPOLYTA

I love not to see wretchedness o'ercharg'd 85
And duty in his service perishing. 86

THESEUS

Why, gentle sweet, you shall see no such thing.

HIPPOLYTA

He says they can do nothing in this kind. 88

8 compact formed, composed **11 Helen's** i.e., of Helen of Troy, pattern of beauty. **brow of Egypt** i.e., face of a gypsy **20 bringer** i.e., source **21 fear** object of fear **25 More . . . images** testifies to something more substantial than mere imaginings **26 constancy** certainty **27 howsoever** in any case. **admirable** a source of wonder **39 abridgement** pastime (to abridge or shorten the evening) **42 brief** short written statement, list **44 battle . . . Centaurs** (Probably refers to the battle of the Centaurs and the Lapithae, when the Centaurs attempted to carry off Hippodamia, bride of Theseus' friend Pirothous.)

47 kinsman (Plutarch's *Life of Theseus* states that Hercules and Theseus were near kinsmen. Theseus is referring to a version of the battle of the Centaurs in which Hercules was said to be present.) **48–49 The riot . . . rage** (This was the story of the death of Orpheus, as told in *Metamorphoses,* Bk. XI.) **52–53 The thrice . . . beggary** (Possibly an allusion to Spenser's *Teares of the Muses,* 1591, though "satires" deploring the neglect of learning and the creative arts were commonplace.) **55 sorting with** befitting **59 strange** (Seemingly an error for some adjective that would contrast with *snow,* just as *hot* contrasts with *ice.*) **74 toil'd** taxed. **unbreathed** unexercised **75 against** in preparation for **80 stretch'd** strained. **conn'd** memorized **85 wretchedness o'ercharg'd** incompetence overburdened **86 his service** its attempt to serve **88 kind** kind of thing

THESEUS
The kinder we, to give them thanks for nothing.
Our sport shall be to take what they mistake;
And what poor duty cannot do, noble respect
Takes it in might, not merit. 92
Where I have come, great clerks have purposed 93
To greet me with premeditated welcomes;
Where I have seen them shiver and look pale,
Make periods in the midst of sentences,
Throttle their practic'd accent in their fears, 97
And in conclusion dumbly have broke off,
Not paying me a welcome. Trust me, sweet,
Out of this silence yet I pick'd a welcome;
And in the modesty of fearful duty
I read as much as from the rattling tongue
Of saucy and audacious eloquence.
Love, therefore, and tongue-tied simplicity
In least speak most, to my capacity. 105

[*Philostrate returns.*]

PHILOSTRATE
So please your Grace, the Prologue is address'd. 106

THESEUS
Let him approach. [*Flourish of trumpets.*]

Enter the Prologue [*Quince*].

PROLOGUE
If we offend, it is with our good will.
That you should think, we come not to offend,
But with good will. To show our simple skill,
That is the true beginning of our end.
Consider, then, we come but in despite.
We do not come, as minding to content you, 113
Our true intent is. All for your delight
We are not here. That you should here repent you,
The actors are at hand; and, by their show,
You shall know all that you are like to know.

THESEUS This fellow doth not stand upon points. 118

LYSANDER He hath rid his prologue like a rough colt; 119
he knows not the stop. A good moral, my lord: it is not 120
enough to speak, but to speak true.

HIPPOLYTA Indeed he hath play'd on his prologue like
a child on a recorder; a sound, but not in government. 123

THESEUS His speech was like a tangled chain, nothing 124
impair'd, but all disorder'd. Who is next?

Enter Pyramus and Thisby, and Wall, and Moonshine, and Lion.

PROLOGUE
Gentles, perchance you wonder at this show;
But wonder on, till truth make all things plain.
This man is Pyramus, if you would know;
This beauteous lady Thisby is certain.
This man, with lime and rough-cast, doth present
Wall, that vile Wall which did these lovers sunder;
And through Wall's chink, poor souls, they are content
To whisper. At the which let no man wonder.
This man, with lantern, dog, and bush of thorn,
Presenteth Moonshine; for, if you will know,
By moonshine did these lovers think no scorn 136
To meet at Ninus' tomb, there, there to woo.
This grisly beast, which Lion hight by name, 138
The trusty Thisby, coming first by night,
Did scare away, or rather did affright;
And, as she fled, her mantle she did fall, 141
Which Lion vile with bloody mouth did stain.
Anon comes Pyramus, sweet youth and tall, 143
And finds his trusty Thisby's mantle slain;
Whereat, with blade, with bloody blameful blade,
He bravely broach'd his boiling bloody breast. 146
And Thisby, tarrying in mulberry shade,
His dagger drew, and died. For all the rest,
Let Lion, Moonshine, Wall, and lovers twain
At large discourse, while here they do remain. 150
Exeunt Lion, Thisby, and Moonshine.

THESEUS I wonder if the lion be to speak.

DEMETRIUS No wonder, my lord. One lion may, when many asses do.

WALL
In this same interlude it doth befall
That I, one Snout by name, present a wall;
And such a wall, as I would have you think,
That had in it a crannied hole or chink,
Through which the lovers, Pyramus and Thisby,
Did whisper often very secretly.
This loam, this rough-cast, and this stone doth show
That I am that same wall; the truth is so.
And this the cranny is, right and sinister, 162
Through which the fearful lovers are to whisper.

THESEUS Would you desire lime and hair to speak better?

DEMETRIUS It is the wittiest partition that ever I heard 166
discourse, my lord.

[*Pyramus comes forward.*]

THESEUS
Pyramus draws near the wall. Silence!

PYRAMUS
O grim-look'd night! O night with hue so black! 169
O night, which ever art when day is not!
O night, O night! Alack, alack, alack,
I fear my Thisby's promise is forgot.
And thou, O wall, O sweet, O lovely wall,
That stand'st between her father's ground and mine,
Thou wall, O wall, O sweet and lovely wall,
Show me thy chink, to blink through with mine eyne! [*Wall holds up his fingers.*]
Thanks, courteous wall. Jove shield thee well for this!
But what see I? No Thisby do I see.

92 Takes . . . merit values it for the effort made rather than for the excellence achieved **93 clerks** learned men **97 practic'd accent** i.e., rehearsed speech; or, usual way of speaking **105 least** i.e., saying least. **to my capacity** in my judgment and understanding **106 Prologue** speaker of the prologue. **address'd** ready **113 minding** intending **118 stand upon points** (1) heed niceties or small points (2) pay attention to punctuation in his reading. (The humor of Quince's speech is in the blunders of its punctuation.) **119 rough** unbroken **120 stop** (1) the stopping of a colt by reining it in (2) punctuation mark **123 recorder** a wind instrument like a flute or flageolet. **government** control **124 nothing** not at all

136 think no scorn think it no disgraceful matter **138 hight** is called **141 fall** let fall **143 tall** courageous **146 broach'd** stabbed **150 At large** in full, at length **162 right and sinister** i.e., the right side of it and the left; or, running from right to left, horizontally **166 partition** (1) wall (2) section of a learned treatise or oration **169 grim-look'd** grim-looking

O wicked wall, through whom I see no bliss!
Curs'd be thy stones for thus deceiving me!

THESEUS The wall, methinks, being sensible, should curse again. 181

PYRAMUS No, in truth, sir, he should not. "Deceiving me" is Thisby's cue: she is to enter now, and I am to spy her through the wall. You shall see, it will fall pat as I told you. Yonder she comes.

Enter Thisby.

THISBY
O wall, full often hast thou heard my moans,
For parting my fair Pyramus and me.
My cherry lips have often kiss'd thy stones,
Thy stones with lime and hair knit up in thee.

PYRAMUS
I see a voice. Now will I to the chink,
To spy an I can hear my Thisby's face. 192
Thisby!

THISBY My love! Thou art my love, I think.

PYRAMUS
Think what thou wilt, I am thy lover's grace; 194
And, like Limander, am I trusty still. 195

THISBY
And I like Helen, till the Fates me kill. 196

PYRAMUS
Not Shafalus to Procrus was so true. 197

THISBY
As Shafalus to Procrus, I to you.

PYRAMUS
O, kiss me through the hole of this vile wall!

THISBY
I kiss the wall's hole, not your lips at all.

PYRAMUS
Wilt thou at Ninny's tomb meet me straightway?

THISBY
'Tide life, 'tide death, I come without delay. 202
[*Exeunt Pyramus and Thisby.*]

WALL
Thus have I, Wall, my part discharged so;
And, being done, thus Wall away doth go. [*Exit.*]

THESEUS Now is the mural down between the two neighbors.

DEMETRIUS No remedy, my lord, when walls are so willful to hear without warning. 208

HIPPOLYTA This is the silliest stuff that ever I heard.

THESEUS The best in this kind are but shadows; and the 210 worst are no worse, if imagination amend them.

HIPPOLYTA It must be your imagination then, and not theirs.

THESEUS If we imagine no worse of them than they of themselves, they may pass for excellent men. Here come two noble beasts in, a man and a lion.

Enter Lion and Moonshine.

LION
You, ladies, you, whose gentle hearts do fear
The smallest monstrous mouse that creeps on floor,
May now perchance both quake and tremble here,
When lion rough in wildest rage doth roar.
Then know that I, as Snug the joiner, am
A lion fell, nor else no lion's dam; 222
For, if I should as lion come in strife
Into this place, 'twere pity on my life.

THESEUS A very gentle beast, and of a good conscience.

DEMETRIUS The very best at a beast, my lord, that e'er I saw.

LYSANDER This lion is a very fox for his valor. 228

THESEUS True; and a goose for his discretion. 229

DEMETRIUS Not so, my lord; for his valor cannot carry his discretion; and the fox carries the goose.

THESEUS His discretion, I am sure, cannot carry his valor; for the goose carries not the fox. It is well. Leave it to his discretion, and let us listen to the moon.

MOON
This lanthorn doth the horned moon present— 235

DEMETRIUS He should have worn the horns on his 236
head. 237

THESEUS He is no crescent, and his horns are invisible within the circumference.

MOON
This lanthorn doth the horned moon present;
Myself the man i' th' moon do seem to be.

THESEUS This is the greatest error of all the rest. The man should be put into the lanthorn. How is it else the man i' th' moon?

DEMETRIUS He dares not come there for the candle; for, 245
you see, it is already in snuff. 246

HIPPOLYTA I am aweary of this moon. Would he would change!

THESEUS It appears, by his small light of discretion, that he is in the wane; but yet, in courtesy, in all reason, we must stay the time.

LYSANDER Proceed, Moon.

MOON All that I have to say is to tell you that the lanthorn is the moon, I, the man in the moon, this thorn-bush my thorn-bush, and this dog my dog.

DEMETRIUS Why, all these should be in the lanthorn; for all these are in the moon. But silence! Here comes Thisby.

Enter Thisby.

THISBY
This is old Ninny's tomb. Where is my love?

LION [*Roaring*] Oh— [*Thisby runs off.*] 260

DEMETRIUS Well roar'd, Lion.

THESEUS Well run, Thisby.

HIPPOLYTA Well shone, Moon. Truly, the moon shines with a good grace.
[*The Lion shakes Thisby's mantle, and exit.*]

181 sensible capable of feeling **192 an** if **194 lover's grace** i.e., gracious lover **195, 196 Limander, Helen** (Blunders for "Leander" and "Hero.") **197 Shafalus, Procrus** (Blunders for "Cephalus" and "Procris," also famous lovers.) **202 'Tide** betide, come **208 to hear** as to hear. **without warning** i.e., without warning the parents **210 in this kind** of this sort. **shadows** likenesses, representations

222 lion fell fierce lion (with a play on the idea of *lion skin*) **228 is . . . valor** i.e., his valor consists of craftiness and discretion **229 goose . . . discretion** i.e., as discreet as a goose, that is, more foolish than discreet **235 lanthorn** (This original spelling, *lanthorn,* may suggest a play on the *horn* of which lanterns were made, and also on a cuckold's horns; but the spelling *lanthorn* is not used consistently for comic effect in this play or elsewhere. At V.i.134, for example, the word is *lantern* in the original.) **236–237 on his head** (as a sign of cuckoldry) **245 for the** because of the **246 in snuff** (1) offended (2) in need of snuffing

THESEUS Well mous'd, Lion.

DEMETRIUS And then came Pyramus.

LYSANDER And so the lion vanish'd.

Enter Pyramus.

PYRAMUS
Sweet Moon, I thank thee for thy sunny beams;
I thank thee, Moon, for shining now so bright;
For, by thy gracious, golden, glittering gleams,
I trust to take of truest Thisby sight.
But stay, O spite!
But mark, poor knight,
What dreadful dole is here!
Eyes, do you see?
How can it be?
O dainty duck! O dear!
Thy mantle good,
What, stain'd with blood!
Approach, ye Furies fell!
O Fates, come, come,
Cut thread and thrum;
Quail, crush, conclude, and quell!

THESEUS This passion, and the death of a dear friend, would go near to make a man look sad.

HIPPOLYTA Beshrew my heart, but I pity the man.

PYRAMUS
O wherefore, Nature, didst thou lions frame?
Since lion vile hath here deflow'r'd my dear,
Which is—no, no—which was the fairest dame
That liv'd, that lov'd, that lik'd, that look'd with cheer.
Come, tears, confound,
Out, sword, and wound
The pap of Pyramus;
Ay, that left pap,
Where heart doth hop. [*Stabs himself.*]
Thus die I, thus, thus, thus.
Now am I dead,
Now am I fled;
My soul is in the sky.
Tongue, lose thy light;
Moon, take thy flight. [*Exit Moonshine.*]
Now die, die, die, die, die. [*Dies.*]

DEMETRIUS No die, but an ace, for him; for he is but one.

LYSANDER Less than an ace, man; for he is dead, he is nothing.

THESEUS With the help of a surgeon he might yet recover, and yet prove an ass.

HIPPOLYTA How chance Moonshine is gone before Thisby comes back and finds her lover?

THESEUS She will find him by starlight. Here she comes; and her passion ends the play.

[*Enter Thisby.*]

HIPPOLYTA Methinks she should not use a long one for such a Pyramus. I hope she will be brief.

DEMETRIUS A mote will turn the balance, which Pyramus, which Thisby, is the better: he for a man, God warr'nt us; she for a woman, God bless us.

LYSANDER She hath spied him already with those sweet eyes.

DEMETRIUS And thus she means, videlicet:

THISBY
Asleep, my love?
What, dead, my dove?
O Pyramus, arise!
Speak, speak. Quite dumb?
Dead, dead? A tomb
Must cover thy sweet eyes.
These lily lips,
This cherry nose,
These yellow cowslip cheeks,
Are gone, are gone!
Lovers, make moan.
His eyes were green as leeks.
O Sisters Three,
Come, come to me,
With hands as pale as milk;
Lay them in gore,
Since you have shore
With shears his thread of silk.
Tongue, not a word.
Come, trusty sword,
Come, blade, my breast imbrue! [*Stabs herself.*]
And farewell, friends.
Thus Thisby ends.
Adieu, adieu, adieu. [*Dies.*]

THESEUS Moonshine and Lion are left to bury the dead.

DEMETRIUS Ay, and Wall too.

BOTTOM [*Starting up*] No, I assure you; the wall is down that parted their fathers. Will it please you to see the epilogue, or to hear a Bergomask dance between two of our company?

THESEUS No epilogue, I pray you; for your play needs no excuse. Never excuse; for when the players are all dead, there need none to be blam'd. Marry, if he that writ it had play'd Pyramus and hang'd himself in Thisby's garter, it would have been a fine tragedy; and so it is, truly, and very notably discharg'd. But, come, your Bergomask. Let your epilogue alone. [*A dance.*]
The iron tongue of midnight hath told twelve.
Lovers, to bed; 'tis almost fairy time.
I fear we shall outsleep the coming morn
As much as we this night have overwatch'd.
This palpable-gross play hath well beguil'd
The heavy gait of night. Sweet friends, to bed.
A fortnight hold we this solemnity,
In nightly revels and new jollity. *Exeunt.*

Enter Puck.

265 mous'd shaken **274 dole** grievous event **280 fell** fierce **282 thread and thrum** the warp in weaving and the loose end of the warp **283 Quail** overpower. **quell** kill, destroy **284–285 This . . . sad** i.e., if one had other reason to grieve, one might be sad, but not from this absurd portrayal of passion **290 cheer** countenance **303 ace** the side of the die featuring the single pip, or spot. (The pun is on *die* as a singular of *dice;* Bottom's performance is not worth a whole *die* but rather one single face of it, one small portion.) **304 one** (1) an individual person (2) unique **308 ass** (with a pun on ace)

315–316 which . . . which whether . . . or **320 means** moans, laments. **videlicet** to wit **333 Sisters Three** the Fates **337 shore** shorn **341 imbrue** stain with blood **349 Bergomask dance** a rustic dance named from Bergamo, a province in the state of Venice **358 told** counted, struck ("tolled") **361 overwatch'd** stayed up too late **362 palpable-gross** palpably gross, obviously crude **363 heavy** drowsy, dull

PUCK

Now the hungry lion roars,
  And the wolf behowls the moon;
Whilst the heavy ploughman snores,
  All with weary task fordone. 369
Now the wasted brands do glow, 370
  Whilst the screech-owl, screeching loud,
Puts the wretch that lies in woe
  In remembrance of a shroud.
Now it is the time of night
  That the graves, all gaping wide,
Every one lets forth his sprite, 376
  In the churchway paths to glide.
And we fairies, that do run
  By the triple Hecate's team 379
From the presence of the sun,
  Following darkness like a dream,
Now are frolic. Not a mouse 382
Shall disturb this hallowed house.
I am sent with broom before,
To sweep the dust behind the door. 386

Enter [*Oberon and Titania,*] *King and Queen of Fairies, with all their train.*

OBERON

Through the house give glimmering light,
  By the dead and drowsy fire;
Every elf and fairy sprite
  Hop as light as bird from brier;
And this ditty, after me,
Sing, and dance it trippingly.

TITANIA

First, rehearse your song by rote,
To each word a warbling note.
Hand in hand, with fairy grace,
Will we sing, and bless this place.

[*Song and dance.*]

OBERON

Now, until the break of day,
Through this house each fairy stray.
To the best bride-bed will we,
Which by us shall blessed be;
And the issue there create 401
Ever shall be fortunate.
So shall all the couples three
Ever true in loving be;
And the blots of Nature's hand
Shall not in their issue stand;
Never mole, hare lip, nor scar,
Nor mark prodigious, such as are 408
Despised in nativity,
Shall upon their children be.
With this field-dew consecrate, 411
Every fairy take his gait, 412
And each several chamber bless, 413

369 fordone exhausted **370 wasted brands** burned-out logs **376 Every . . . sprite** every grave lets forth its ghost **379 triple Hecate's** (Hecate ruled in three capacities: as Luna or Cynthia in heaven, as Diana on earth, and as Proserpina in hell.) **382 frolic** merry **386 behind** from behind. (Robin Goodfellow was a household spirit who helped good housemaids and punished lazy ones.) **401 create** created **408 prodigious** monstrous, unnatural **411 consecrate** consecrated **412 take his gait** go his way **413 several** separate

Through this palace, with sweet peace;
And the owner of it blest
Ever shall in safety rest.
Trip away; make no stay;
Meet me all by break of day.

Exeunt [*Oberon, Titania, and train*].

PUCK

If we shadows have offended,
Think but this, and all is mended,
That you have but slumb'red here 421
While these visions did appear.
And this weak and idle theme,
No more yielding but a dream, 424
Gentles, do not reprehend.
If you pardon, we will mend.
And, as I am an honest Puck,
If we have unearned luck
Now to scape the serpent's tongue, 429
We will make amends ere long;
Else the Puck a liar call.
So, good night unto you all.
Give me your hands, if we be friends, 433
And Robin shall restore amends. [*Exit.*]

421 That . . . here i.e., that it is a "midsummer night's dream" **424 No . . . but** yielding no more than **429 serpent's tongue** i.e., hissing **433 Give . . . hands** applaud

The Merchant of Venice

Although Shylock is the most prominent character in *The Merchant of Venice,* he takes part in neither the beginning nor the ending of the play. Nor is he the "merchant" of the title, but a moneylender whose usury is portrayed as the very opposite of true commerce. His revengeful struggle to obtain a pound of flesh from Antonio contrasts with the various romantic episodes woven together in this play: Bassanio's choosing of Portia by means of the caskets, Gratiano's wooing of Nerissa, Jessica's elopement with Lorenzo, Launcelot Gobbo's changing of masters, and the episode of the rings. In all these stories, friendship and love triumph over faithlessness and hatred. However much we may come to sympathize with Shylock's own misfortunes and question the motives of his enemies, however much we are made uncomfortable by the potential insularity of a Venetian ethic that has no genuine place for non-Christians or cultural outsiders, Shylock remains essentially as the villain of a love-comedy. Structurally he is the "blocking" character or "heavy" character. His remorseless pursuit of Antonio darkens the mood of the play, so that it becomes tragicomic. His overthrow signals the providential triumph of love and friendship, even though that triumph is not without its undercurrent of melancholy. Before we examine the undoubted ironies of his situation more closely, we need to establish the philosophical context of the love-comedy as a whole.

Like many of Shakespeare's philosophical and festive comedies, *The Merchant of Venice* presents two contrasting worlds, one idealized and the other more recognizably worldly. To an extent, these contrasting worlds can be identified with the locations of Belmont and Venice. Belmont, to which the various happy lovers and their friends eventually retire, is a place of magic and love. As its name implies it is on a mountain, reached by a journey across water. It is pure, serene, ethereal. As often happens in fairy stories, a princess dwells on this mountain who must be won by means of a riddling contest. We usually see Belmont at night. Music surrounds it, and women preside over it. Even its caskets, houses, and rings are essentially feminine symbols. Venice, on the other hand, is a place of bustle and economic competition, seen most characteristically in the heat of the day. It lies low and flat, at a point where rivers reach the sea. Men preside over its contentious marketplace and its haggling law courts. Actually, the apparent opposition of Venice and Belmont is not quite so clear-cut: Venice contains much compassionate friendship, whereas Belmont is subject to the arbitrary command of Portia's dead father. (Portia somewhat resembles Jessica in being "imprisoned" by her father's will.) Even though Portia descends to Venice in the angelic role of mercy-giver, she also remains very human: sharp-tongued and even venomous in caricaturing her unwelcome wooers, crafty in her legal maneuvering, saucily prankish in her torturing of Bassanio about the rings. Nevertheless the polarity of two contrasting localities and two groups of characters is vividly real in this play.

The play's opening scene, from which Shylock is excluded, sets forth the interrelated themes of friendship, romantic love, and risk or "hazard." The actual merchant of the title, Antonio, is the victim of a mysterious melancholy. He is wealthy enough and surrounded by friends, but something is missing from his life. He assures his solicitous companions that he has no financial worries, for he has been too careful to trust all his cargoes to one sea vessel. Antonio in fact has no idea why he is so sad. The question is haunting: what is the matter? Perhaps the answer is to be found in a paradox: those who strive to prosper in the world's terms are doomed to frustration, not because prosperity will necessarily elude them but because it will not satisfy the spirit. "You have too much respect upon the world," argues the carefree Gratiano. "They lose it that do buy it with much care." Portia and Jessica too are at first afflicted by a melancholy that stems from the incompleteness of living isolated lives, with insufficient opportunities for love and sacrifice. They must learn, as Antonio learns with the help of his dear friend Bassanio, to seek happiness by daring to risk everything for friendship. Antonio's risk is most extreme: only when he has thrown away concern for his very life can he discover what there is to live for.

At first, Bassanio's request for assistance seems just as materialistic as the worldliness from which Antonio suffers. Bassanio proposes to marry a rich young lady, Portia, in order to recoup his fortune lost through prodigality, and he needs money from Antonio so that he may woo Portia in proper fashion. She is "richly left," the heiress of a dead father, a golden fleece for whom this new Jason will make a "quest." Bassanio's adventure is partly commercial. Yet his "pilgrimage" for Portia is magnanimous as well. The modern tendency to play Bassanio and Portia as cynical antiheroes of a "black" comedy points up the problematic character of their materialism and calculation, but it inevitably distorts the play. Bassanio has lost his previous fortune through the amiable faults of reckless generosity and a lack of concern for financial prudence. The money he must now borrow, and the fortune he hopes to acquire, are to him no more than a means to carefree happiness. Although Portia's rich dowry is a strong consideration, he describes her also as "fair, and fairer than that word, Of wondrous virtues." Moreover, he enjoys the element of risk in wooing her. It is like shooting a second arrow in order to recover one that has been lost—double or nothing. This gamble, or "hazard," involves risk for Antonio as well as for Bassanio, and ultimately brings a double reward to them both, spiritual as well as financial. Unless one recognizes these aspects of Bassanio's quest, as well as the clear "fairy-tale" quality with which Shakespeare deliberately invests this part of the plot, one cannot properly assess Bassanio's role in this romantic comedy.

Bassanio's quest for Portia can in fact never succeed until he disavows the very financial considerations which brought him to Belmont in the first place. This is the lesson of the riddle of the three caskets, an ancient parable stressing the need for choosing by true substance rather than by outward show. To choose "what many men desire," as the Prince of Morocco does, is to pin one's hopes on worldly wealth; to believe that one "deserves" good fortune, as the Prince of Arragon does, is to reveal a fatal pride in one's own merit. Bassanio perceives that in order to win true love he must "give and hazard all he hath." He is not "deceiv'd with ornament." Just as Antonio must risk all for friendship, and just as Bassanio himself must later be willing to risk losing Portia for the higher cause of true friendship (in the episode of the rings), Bassanio must now renounce worldly ambition and beauty before he can be rewarded with success. Paradoxically, only those who learn to subdue such worldly desires may then legitimately enjoy the world's pleasures. Only they have acknowledged the hierarchical subservience of the flesh to the spirit. These are the philosophical truisms of Renaissance neo-Platonism, depicting love as a chain or ladder from the basest carnality to the supreme love of God for man. On this ladder, perfect friendship and spiritual union are more sublimely Godlike than sexual fulfillment. This idealism may seem a strange doctrine for Bassanio the fortune-hunter, but actually its conventional wisdom simply confirms his role as romantic hero. He and Portia are not denied worldly happiness or erotic pleasure; they are merely asked to give first thought to their Christian duty in marriage. The essentially Christian paradox of losing the world in order to gain the world lies at the center of their love relationship. This paradox illuminates not only the casket episode but the struggle for the pound of flesh, the elopement of Jessica, the ring episode, and even the comic foolery of Launcelot Gobbo.

Shylock, in his quest for the pound of flesh, represents a denial of all the paradoxical Christian truths just described. As a usurer he refuses to lend money interest free in the name of friendship. Instead of taking risks, he insists on his bond. He spurns mercy and demands strict justice. By calculating all his chances too craftily, he appears to win at first but must eventually lose all. He has "too much respect upon the world." His God is the Old-Testament God of Moses, the God of wrath, the God of the Ten Commandments with their forbidding emphasis on "Thou shalt not." (This oversimplified contrast between Judaism and Christianity was commonplace in Shakespeare's time.) Shylock abhors stealing but admires equivocation as a means of outmaneuvering a competitor; he cites approvingly Jacob's ruse to deprive Laban of his sheep (I,iii). Any tactic is permissible so long as it falls within the realm of legality and contract.

Shylock's ethical outlook, then, justifies both usury and the old dispensation of the Jewish law. The two are philosophically combined, just as usury and Judaism had become equated in the popular imagination of Renaissance Europe. Even though lending at interest was becoming increasingly necessary and common, old phobias against it still persisted. Angry moralists pointed out that the New Testament had condemned usury and that Aristotle had described money as barren. To breed money was therefore regarded as unnatural. Usury was sinful because, unlike commerce, it involved no risk; the usurer seemed to be getting something for nothing. Partly because usury was at times illegal, its practitioners were regarded as corrupt and grasping, hated as misers. In some European countries, Jews were permitted to practice this un-Christian living (and permitted to do very little else) and then were hypocritically detested for performing un-Christian deeds. Ironically, however, very few Jewish moneylenders were to be found in England. Nominally excluded since Edward I's reign, the Jews had returned in small numbers to London but did not practice their Judaism openly. They attended Anglican services as required by law and then worshiped in private, relatively undisturbed by the authorities. They followed ordinary trades and professions rather than usury. Shylock is not based on observation from London life. He is derived from continental tradition, and reflects a widespread conviction that Jews and usurers were alike in being non-Christian and sinister.

Shylock is unquestionably sinister. On the Elizabethan stage he apparently wore a red beard like Judas, and a hooked nose. He bears an "ancient grudge" against Antonio simply because Antonio is "a Christian." We recognize in Shylock the archetype of the Jew who wishes to kill a Christian and obtain his flesh. In early medieval anti-Semitic legends of this sort, the flesh thus obtained was imagined to be eaten ritually during Passover. The Jews who had once persecuted Christ were presumed to be implacable enemies of all Christians. These anti-Semitic superstitions were likely to erupt into hysteria at any time, as in 1594 when Dr. Roderigo Lopez, a Portuguese Jewish physician, was accused of having plotted against the life of Queen Elizabeth and of Don Antonio, pretender to the Portuguese throne. Marlowe's *The Jew of Malta* was revived for this occasion, enjoying an unusually successful run of fifteen performances, and scholars have often wondered if Shakespeare's play was not written under the same impetus. On this score the evidence is inconclusive, and the play might have been written any time between 1594 and 1598 (when it is mentioned by Francis Meres), but in any case Shakespeare has made no attempt to avoid the anti-Semitic nature of his story.

To offset the portrayal of Jewish villainy, however, the play also dramatizes the possibility of conversion to Christianity, suggesting that Judaism is more a matter of benighted faith than of ethnic origin. Converted Jews were not new on the stage: they had appeared in medieval cycle drama, in the Croxton *Play of the Sacrament* (late fifteenth century), and more recently in *The Jew of Malta,* in which Barabas' daughter Abigail falls in love with a Christian and eventually becomes a nun. Shylock's daughter Jessica similarly embraces Christianity as Lorenzo's wife and is received into the happy comradeship of Belmont. Shylock is forced to accept Christianity, presumably for the benefit of his eternal soul. Earlier in the play, Antonio repeatedly indicates his willingness to befriend Shylock if the latter will only give up usury, and is even cautiously hopeful when Shylock offers him an interest-free loan: "The Hebrew will turn Christian; he grows kind" (I,iii). To be sure, Antonio's denunciation of Shylock's usurious Judaism has been vehement and personal; we learn that he has spit on Shylock's gaberdine and kicked him as one would kick a dog. This violent disapproval offers no opportunity for the toleration of cultural and religious differences that we expect today from men of good will, but at least Antonio is prepared to accept Shylock if Shylock will embrace Christian faith and its ethical responsibilities. Whether the play itself endorses Antonio's Christian point of view as normative, or insists on a darker reading as well by making us uneasy with intolerance, is a matter of unceasing critical debate. Quite possibly, the play's power to disturb emanates at least in part from the dramatic conflict of irreconcilable sets of values.

To Antonio, then, as well as to other Venetians, true Christianity is both an absolute good from which no deviation is possible without evil, and a state of faith to which aliens may turn by abjuring the benighted creeds of their ancestors. By this token, the Prince of Morocco is condemned to failure in his quest for Portia not so much because he is black as because he is an infidel, one who worships "blind fortune" and therefore chooses a worldly rather than a spiritual reward. Although Portia pertly dismisses him with "Let all of his complexion choose me so" (II,vii), she professes earlier to find him handsome and agrees that he should not be judged by his complexion (II,i). Unless she is merely being hypocritical, she means by her later remark that black-skinned men are generally infidels, just as Jews are as a group non-Christian. Such pejorative thinking about persons as types is no doubt distressing, and suggests at least to a modern audience the cultural limitation of Portia's view, but in any case it shows her to be no less well-disposed toward black men than toward others who are also alien. She rejects the Prince of Arragon because he too lacks proper faith, though nominally a Christian. All men, therefore, may aspire to truly virtuous conduct, and those who choose virtue are equally blessed; but the terms of defining that ideal are essentially Christian. Jews and blacks may rise spiritually only by abandoning their pagan creeds for the new dispensation of charity and forgiveness.

The superiority of Christian teaching to the older Jewish dispensation was of course a widely accepted notion of Shakespeare's time. After all, these were the years when men fought and died to maintain their religious beliefs. Today we find the notion of a single true church intolerant, and we have difficulty understanding why anyone would wish to force conversion on Shylock. Modern productions find it tempting to portray Shylock as a victim of bigotry, and to put great stress on his heartrending assertions of his humanity: "Hath not a Jew eyes? . . . If you prick us, do we not bleed?" Shylock does indeed suffer from his enemies, and his sufferings add a tortured complexity to this play—even, one suspects, for an Elizabethan audience. Those who profess Christianity must surely examine their own motives and conduct. Is it fair to steal treasure from Shylock's house along with his eloped daughter? Is it thoughtful of Jessica and Lorenzo to squander Shylock's turquoise ring, the gift of his wife Leah, on a monkey? Does Shylock's vengeful insistence on law justify the quibbling countermeasures devised by Portia even as she piously declaims about mercy? Do Shylock's misfortunes deserve the mirthful parodies of Solanio ("My daughter! O my ducats!") or the hostile jeering of Gratiano at the conclusion of the trial? Because he stands outside Christian faith, Shylock can serve as a perspective whereby we see the hypocrisies of those who profess a higher ethical code. Nevertheless, Shylock's compulsive desire for vengeance according to an Old Testament code of an eye for an eye cannot be justified by the wrongdoings of any particular Christian. Such deeds condemn the doer rather than undermine the Christian standards of true virtue as ideally expressed. Shakespeare humanizes Shylock by portraying him as a believable and sensitive man, and shows much that is to be regretted in Shylock's Christian antagonists, but he also allows Shylock to place himself in the wrong by his refusal to forgive his enemies.

Shylock thus loses everything through his effort to win everything on his own terms. His daughter Jessica, by her elopement, follows an opposite course. She characterizes her father's home as "hell," and she resents being locked up behind closed windows. Shylock detests music and the sounds of merriment; Jessica's new life in Belmont is immersed in music. He is old, suspicious, miserly; she is young, loving, adventurous. Most important, she seems to be at least part Christian when we first see her. As Launcelot jests half in earnest, "if a Christian did not play the knave and get thee, I am much deceiv'd." Her removal from Shylock's house involves theft, and her running from Venice is, she confesses, an "unthrift love." Paradoxically, however, this recklessness is of more blessed effect than her father's legalistic caution. As she says, "I shall be sav'd by my husband. He hath made me a Christian."

Launcelot Gobbo's clowning offers a similarly paradoxical comment on the tragedy of Shylock. Launcelot debates whether or not to leave Shylock's service in terms of a soul-struggle between his conscience and the devil (II,ii). Conscience bids him stay, for service is a debt, a bond, an obligation, whereas abandonment of one's indenture is a kind of rebellion or stealing away. Yet Shylock's house is "hell" to Launcelot as to Jessica. Comparing his new master with his old, Launcelot observes to Bassanio, "You have the grace of God, sir, and he hath enough." Service with Bassanio involves imprudent risks, since Bassanio is a spendthrift. The miserly Shylock rejoices to see the ever hungry Launcelot, this "huge feeder," wasting the substance of a hated Christian. Once again, however, Shylock will lose everything in his grasping quest for security. Another spiritual renewal occurs when Launcelot encounters his old and nearly blind father (II,ii). In a scene echoing the biblical stories of the Prodigal Son and of Jacob and Esau, Launcelot teases the old man with false rumors of Launcelot's own death in order to make their reunion seem all the more unexpected and precious. The illusion of tragedy gives way to joy: Launcelot is, in language adapted from the liturgy, "your boy that was, your son that is, your child that shall be."

In the episode of the rings we encounter a final playful variation on the paradox of winning through losing. Portia and Nerissa cleverly present their new husbands with a cruel choice: disguised as a doctor of law and his clerk, who have just saved the life of Antonio from Shylock's wrath, the two wives ask nothing more for their services than the rings they see on the fingers of Bassanio and Gratiano. The two husbands, who have vowed never to part with these wedding rings, must therefore choose between love and friendship. The superior claim of friendship is clear, no matter what the cost, and Portia knows well enough that Bassanio's obedience to this neo-Platonic ideal is an essential part of his virtue. Just as he previously renounced beauty and riches before he could deserve Portia, he must now risk losing her for friendship's sake. The testing of the husbands' constancy poses no real threat to romantic happiness, for we know that the wives' little joke is farcically based on mistaken identity. The young men have accordingly been tricked into bestowing their rings on their wives for a second time in the name of perfect friendship, thereby confirming a relationship that is both Platonic and fleshly. As Gratiano bawdily points out in the play's last line, the ring is both a spiritual and a sexual symbol of marriage. The resolution of this illusory quarrel also brings to an end the merry battle of the sexes between wives and husbands. Having hinted at the sorts of misunderstandings that afflict even the best of human relationships, and having proved themselves wittily able to torture and deceive their husbands, Portia and Nerissa happily submit themselves to the authority of Bassanio and Gratiano.

All appears to be in harmony in Belmont. The disorders of Venice have been left far behind, however imperfectly they may have been resolved. Jessica and Lorenzo contrast their present happiness with the sufferings of less fortunate lovers of long ago: Troilus and Cressida, Pyramus and Thisbe, Aeneas and Dido, Jason and Medea. The tranquil joy found in Belmont is attuned to the music of the spheres, the singing of the "young-ey'd cherubin," although with a proper Christian humility the lovers also realize that the harmony of immortal souls is infinitely beyond their comprehension. Bound in by the grossness of the flesh, "this muddy vesture of decay," they can only reach toward the bliss of eternity through music and the perfect friendship of true love. Even in their final joy, accordingly, the lovers find an incompleteness that lends a wistful and slightly melancholy reflective tone to the play's ending; but this Christian sense of the unavoidable incompleteness of all human life is of a very different order from that earlier melancholy of isolation and lack of commitment experienced by Portia, Jessica, Antonio, and others.

The thematic linking of the numerous episodes of this play is perhaps Shakespeare's most important contribution to his sources. To be sure, in Ser Giovanni Fiorentino's *Il Pecarone* (written c. 1378, published in Italian in 1558), Shakespeare did find three plot lines already combined: Gianotto's wooing of the lady of Belmonte, the pawning of a pound of flesh to a Jewish moneylender by a Venetian merchant who is subsequently rescued by the lady disguised as a lawyer, and the exchanging of the rings. Nevertheless, Shakespeare's changes are extensive. In Fiorentino's *novella* the Jew is an underdeveloped character who makes no attempt to pass off his "merry bond" as a jest. The ring story is a comic afterthought. Most significantly, the casket-choosing story is missing. The mercenary lady of Belmonte has devised her own scheme for confiscating the fortunes of her hapless suitors: after setting them the task of staying awake all night to win her, she drugs them asleep and then confiscates all their worldly wealth as the penalty for failure. Shakespeare retains the folk-tale element of a contest, but substitutes a choice among three caskets. (See Appendix II on sources for numerous earlier instances of this ancient and widespread motif.) The plot of Jessica's elopement recalls not only Marlowe's *The Jew of Malta* but also Massucio of Salerno's *Novellino* and Anthony Munday's *Zelauto.* No source has been found for Launcelot Gobbo, but he contributes to a central thematic purpose as does every element of this masterfully constructed play.

Shylock has always been a towering dramatic presence on stage. The part has attracted many great actors, who understandably portray him as a complex, sensitive man.

In his moment of ruin, Shylock is usually seen on stage not as a comic villain brought down by his own overreaching but as one who deeply experiences humiliation, disappointment, and rejection. Laurence Olivier's portrayal of Shylock and his long cry of pain as he leaves the courtroom, for instance, is likely to reverberate in the spectator's memory long after other details of the National Theatre production (subsequently televised in 1970) have been forgotten. Actors and directors find themselves attracted to non-Shakespearean additions as a way of making the most of Shylock's fall, as for instance in the added business of Shylock's return after the trial to an empty house, or in the playing of Jewish sacred music during the final scene to remind us of his being excluded from the Christian feast of reconciliation at Belmont. The dangers of critical distortion in such sentimentalized presentations of Shylock are apparent, but the vitality of this stage tradition can help remind us that *The Merchant of Venice* does not seem content with easy answers.

The Merchant of Venice

[*Dramatis Personae*

THE DUKE OF VENICE.
THE PRINCE OF MOROCCO, } *suitors to Portia.*
THE PRINCE OF ARRAGON, }
ANTONIO, *a merchant of Venice.*
BASSANIO, *his friend, suitor likewise to Portia.*
SOLANIO, }
SALERIO, } *friends to Antonio and Bassanio.*
GRATIANO, }
LORENZO, *in love with Jessica.*
SHYLOCK, *a rich Jew.*
TUBAL, *a Jew, his friend.*
LAUNCELOT GOBBO, *the clown, servant to Shylock.*
OLD GOBBO, *father to Launcelot.*
LEONARDO, *servant to Bassanio.*
BALTHASAR, } *servants to Portia.*
STEPHANO, }

PORTIA, *a rich heiress.*
NERISSA, *her waiting-maid.*
JESSICA, *daughter to Shylock.*

MAGNIFICOES *of Venice,* OFFICERS *of the Court of Justice,* JAILER, SERVANTS *to Portia, and other* ATTENDANTS.

SCENE: *Partly at Venice, and partly at Belmont, the seat of Portia.*]

[ACT I • SCENE I]

Enter Antonio, Salerio, and Solanio.

ANTONIO
In sooth, I know not why I am so sad.
It wearies me, you say it wearies you;
But how I caught it, found it, or came by it,
What stuff 'tis made of, whereof it is born,
I am to learn;
And such a want-wit sadness makes of me,
That I have much ado to know myself.
SALERIO
Your mind is tossing on the ocean,
There where your argosies with portly sail, 9
Like signiors and rich burghers on the flood,

I.i. Location: A street in Venice.
5 am to learn have yet to learn **9 argosies** large merchant ships. (So named from *Ragusa,* an Italian seaport.) **portly** large and full **10 signiors** gentlemen

Or, as it were, the pageants of the sea, 11
Do overpeer the petty traffickers 12
That cur'sy to them, do them reverence, 13
As they fly by them with their woven wings.

SOLANIO
Believe me, sir, had I such venture forth, 15
The better part of my affections would
Be with my hopes abroad. I should be still 17
Plucking the grass, to know where sits the wind,
Peering in maps for ports and piers and roads; 19
And every object that might make me fear
Misfortune to my ventures, out of doubt
Would make me sad.

SALERIO My wind cooling my broth
Would blow me to an ague, when I thought
What harm a wind too great might do at sea.
I should not see the sandy hour-glass run
But I should think of shallows and of flats,
And see my wealthy Andrew dock'd in sand, 27
Vailing her high-top lower than her ribs 28
To kiss her burial. Should I go to church
And see the holy edifice of stone,
And not bethink me straight of dangerous rocks,
Which touching but my gentle vessel's side
Would scatter all her spices on the stream,
Enrobe the roaring waters with my silks,
And, in a word, but even now worth this,
And now worth nothing? Shall I have the thought
To think on this, and shall I lack the thought
That such a thing bechanc'd would make me sad? 38
But tell not me; I know, Antonio
Is sad to think upon his merchandise.

ANTONIO
Believe me, no. I thank my fortune for it,
My ventures are not in one bottom trusted, 42
Nor to one place; nor is my whole estate
Upon the fortune of this present year. 44
Therefore my merchandise makes me not sad.

SOLANIO
Why, then you are in love.

ANTONIO Fie, fie!

SOLANIO
Not in love neither? Then let us say you are sad
Because you are not merry; and 'twere as easy
For you to laugh and leap, and say you are merry
Because you are not sad. Now, by two-headed
Janus, 50
Nature hath fram'd strange fellows in her time:
Some that will evermore peep through their eyes
And laugh like parrots at a bagpiper, 53
And other of such vinegar aspect
That they'll not show their teeth in way of smile
Though Nestor swear the jest be laughable. 56

Enter Bassanio, Lorenzo, and Gratiano.

Here comes Bassanio, your most noble kinsman,
Gratiano, and Lorenzo. Fare ye well.
We leave you now with better company.

SALERIO
I would have stay'd till I had made you merry,
If worthier friends had not prevented me. 61

ANTONIO
Your worth is very dear in my regard.
I take it your own business calls on you,
And you embrace th' occasion to depart. 64

SALERIO
Good morrow, my good lords.

BASSANIO
Good signiors both, when shall we laugh? Say,
when? 66
You grow exceeding strange. Must it be so? 67

SALERIO
We'll make our leisures to attend on yours. 68
Exeunt Salerio and Solanio.

LORENZO
My Lord Bassanio, since you have found Antonio,
We two will leave you, but at dinner-time,
I pray you, have in mind where we must meet.

BASSANIO
I will not fail you.

GRATIANO
You look not well, Signior Antonio,
You have too much respect upon the world; 74
They lose it that do buy it with much care.
Believe me, you are marvelously chang'd.

ANTONIO
I hold the world but as the world, Gratiano,
A stage where every man must play a part,
And mine a sad one.

GRATIANO Let me play the fool!
With mirth and laughter let old wrinkles come,
And let my liver rather heat with wine 81
Than my heart cool with mortifying groans. 82
Why should a man, whose blood is warm within,
Sit like his grandsire cut in alabaster? 84
Sleep when he wakes and creep into the jaundice 85
By being peevish? I tell thee what, Antonio—
I love thee, and 'tis my love that speaks—
There are a sort of men whose visages
Do cream and mantle like a standing pond, 89
And do a willful stillness entertain, 90
With purpose to be dress'd in an opinion 91
Of wisdom, gravity, profound conceit, 92
As who should say "I am Sir Oracle,
And when I ope my lips let no dog bark!"

11 pageants mobile stages, like "floats," used in plays or processions **12 overpeer** look down upon **13 cur'sy** curtsy, i.e., bob up and down **15 venture forth** investment risked **17 still** continually **19 roads** roadsteads, anchorages **27 Andrew** name of a ship **28 Vailing** lowering. **high-top** topmast **38 bechanc'd** having happened **42 bottom** ship **44 Upon . . . year** i.e., risked upon the chance of the present **50 two-headed Janus** a Roman god of all beginnings, represented by a figure with two faces **53 at a bagpiper** i.e., even at a bagpiper, whose music was regarded as melancholic **56 Nestor** venerable senior officer in the *Iliad,* noted for gravity

61 prevented forestalled **64 occasion** opportunity **66 laugh** i.e., be merry together **67 strange** distant. **Must it be so** must you go; or, must you show reserve **68 attend on** wait upon, i.e., suit **74 respect . . . world** concern for worldly affairs of business **81 heat with wine** (The liver was regarded as the seat of the passions and wine as an agency for inflaming them.) **82 mortifying** deadly **84 in alabaster** i.e., in a stone effigy upon a tomb **85 jaundice** (Regarded as arising from the effects of too much choler or yellow bile, one of the four humors, in the blood.) **89 cream and mantle** become covered with scum, i.e., acquire a lifeless, stiff expression. **standing** stagnant **90 And . . . entertain** and who maintain or assume a self-imposed, obstinate silence **91 opinion** reputation **92 profound conceit** deep thought

O my Antonio, I do know of these
That therefore only are reputed wise
For saying nothing, when, I am very sure,
If they should speak, would almost damn those ears
Which, hearing them, would call their brothers
fools.
I'll tell thee more of this another time;
But fish not with this melancholy bait
For this fool gudgeon, this opinion.
Come, good Lorenzo. Fare ye well awhile;
I'll end my exhortation after dinner.

LORENZO
Well, we will leave you then till dinner-time.
I must be one of these same dumb wise men,
For Gratiano never lets me speak.

GRATIANO
Well, keep me company but two years moe,
Thou shalt not know the sound of thine own
tongue.

ANTONIO
Fare you well; I'll grow a talker for this gear.

GRATIANO
Thanks, i' faith, for silence is only commendable
In a neat's tongue dried and a maid not vendible.
Exeunt [*Gratiano and Lorenzo*].

ANTONIO Is it that—any thing now!

BASSANIO Gratiano speaks an infinite deal of nothing, more than any man in all Venice. His reasons are as two grains of wheat hid in two bushels of chaff; you shall seek all day ere you find them, and when you have them, they are not worth the search.

ANTONIO
Well, tell me now what lady is the same
To whom you swore a secret pilgrimage,
That you today promis'd to tell me of?

BASSANIO
'Tis not unknown to you, Antonio,
How much I have disabled mine estate,
By something showing a more swelling port
Than my faint means would grant continuance.
Nor do I now make moan to be abridg'd
From such a noble rate; but my chief care
Is to come fairly off from the great debts
Wherein my time something too prodigal
Hath left me gag'd. To you, Antonio,
I owe the most, in money and in love,
And from your love I have a warranty
To unburden all my plots and purposes
How to get clear of all the debts I owe.

ANTONIO
I pray you, good Bassanio, let me know it;
And if it stand, as you yourself still do,
Within the eye of honor, be assur'd,
My purse, my person, my extremest means,
Lie all unlock'd to your occasions.

BASSANIO
In my school-days, when I had lost one shaft,
I shot his fellow of the self-same flight
The self-same way with more advised watch
To find the other forth, and by adventuring both
I oft found both. I urge this childhood proof,
Because what follows is pure innocence.
I owe you much, and, like a willful youth,
That which I owe is lost; but if you please
To shoot another arrow that self way
Which you did shoot the first, I do not doubt,
As I will watch the aim, or to find both
Or bring your latter hazard back again
And thankfully rest debtor for the first.

ANTONIO
You know me well, and herein spend but time
To wind about my love with circumstance;
And out of doubt you do me now more wrong
In making question of my uttermost
Than if you had made waste of all I have.
Then do but say to me what I should do
That in your knowledge may by me be done,
And I am prest unto it. Therefore, speak.

BASSANIO
In Belmont is a lady richly left;
And she is fair and, fairer than that word,
Of wondrous virtues. Sometimes from her eyes
I did receive fair speechless messages.
Her name is Portia, nothing undervalu'd
To Cato's daughter, Brutus' Portia.
Nor is the wide world ignorant of her worth,
For the four winds blow in from every coast
Renowned suitors, and her sunny locks
Hang on her temples like a golden fleece,
Which makes her seat of Belmont Colchos' strond,
And many Jasons come in quest of her.
O my Antonio, had I but the means
To hold a rival place with one of them,
I have a mind presages me such thrift
That I should questionless be fortunate!

ANTONIO
Thou know'st that all my fortunes are at sea;
Neither have I money nor commodity
To raise a present sum. Therefore go forth.
Try what my credit can in Venice do;
That shall be rack'd, even to the uttermost,
To furnish thee to Belmont, to fair Portia.
Go, presently inquire, and so will I,
Where money is, and I no question make
To have it of my trust or for my sake. *Exeunt.*

99 fools (Cf. Matthew 5:22, in which anyone calling another fool is threatened with damnation.) **102 gudgeon** a small fish used for bait **108 moe** more **110 for this gear** as a result of this business, i.e., your talk **112 neat's** ox's. **vendible** salable, i.e., in the marriage market **124 By . . . port** by showing a somewhat more lavish style of living **125 grant continuance** allow to continue **126–127 make . . . rate** complain at being cut back from such a high style of living **130 gag'd** pledged

140 shaft arrow **141 his** its. **self-same flight** same kind and range **142 advised** considered **143 forth** out **145 innocence** ingenuousness, sincerity **148 self** same **150 or** either **153 spend but time** only waste time **154 To . . . circumstance** i.e., to approach my favor cautiously, as though stalking me, with all this fine reasoning **155 out of** beyond **156 In . . . uttermost** in showing any doubt of my intention to do all I can **160 prest** ready **161 richly left** left a large fortune (by her father's will) **165–166 nothing undervalu'd To** of no less worth than **166 Portia** (The same Portia as in Shakespeare's *Julius Caesar.*) **171 Colchos'** (Jason adventured for the golden fleece in the land of Colchis, on the Black Sea.) **strond** strand, shore **175 presages** i.e., which presages. **thrift** profit and good fortune **178 commodity** merchandise **181 rack'd** stretched **184 no question make** have no doubt **185 of my trust** on the basis of my credit as a merchant. **sake** i.e., personal sake

[SCENE II]

Enter Portia with her waiting woman, Nerissa.

PORTIA By my troth, Nerissa, my little body is aweary of this great world.

NERISSA You would be, sweet madam, if your miseries were in the same abundance as your good fortunes are; and yet, for aught I see, they are as sick that surfeit with too much as they that starve with nothing. It is no mean happiness, therefore, to be seated in the mean; superfluity comes sooner by white hairs, but competency lives longer.

PORTIA Good sentences and well pronounc'd.

NERISSA They would be better, if well follow'd.

PORTIA If to do were as easy as to know what were good to do, chapels had been churches and poor men's cottages princes' palaces. It is a good divine that follows his own instructions; I can easier teach twenty what were good to be done, than to be one of the twenty to follow mine own teaching. The brain may devise laws for the blood, but a hot temper leaps o'er a cold decree—such a hare is madness the youth, to skip o'er the meshes of good counsel the cripple. But this reasoning is not in the fashion to choose me a husband. O me, the word "choose!" I may neither choose who I would nor refuse who I dislike; so is the will of a living daughter curb'd by the will of a dead father. Is it not hard, Nerissa, that I cannot choose one nor refuse none?

NERISSA Your father was ever virtuous, and holy men at their death have good inspirations; therefore the lott'ry that he hath devis'd in these three chests of gold, silver, and lead, whereof who chooses his meaning chooses you, will, no doubt, never be chosen by any rightly but one who you shall rightly love. But what warmth is there in your affection towards any of these princely suitors that are already come?

PORTIA I pray thee, over-name them; and as thou namest them, I will describe them; and, according to my description, level at my affection.

NERISSA First, there is the Neapolitan prince.

PORTIA Ay, that's a colt indeed, for he doth nothing but talk of his horse; and he makes it a great appropriation to his own good parts that he can shoe him himself. I am much afeard my lady his mother play'd false with a smith.

NERISSA Then is there the County Palatine.

PORTIA He doth nothing but frown, as who should say "An you will not have me, choose." He hears merry tales and smiles not; I fear he will prove the weeping philosopher when he grows old, being so full of unmannerly sadness in his youth. I had rather be married to a death's-head with a bone in his mouth than to either of these. God defend me from these two!

NERISSA How say you by the French lord, Monsieur Le Bon?

PORTIA God made him, and therefore let him pass for a man. In truth, I know it is a sin to be a mocker, but he! Why, he hath a horse better than the Neapolitan's, a better bad habit of frowning than the Count Palatine; he is every man in no man. If a throstle sing, he falls straight a cap'ring. He will fence with his own shadow. If I should marry him, I should marry twenty husbands. If he would despise me, I would forgive him, for if he love me to madness, I shall never requite him.

NERISSA What say you, then, to Falconbridge, the young baron of England?

PORTIA You know I say nothing to him, for he understands not me, nor I him. He hath neither Latin, French, nor Italian, and you will come into the court and swear that I have a poor pennyworth in the English. He is a proper man's picture, but, alas, who can converse with a dumb-show? How oddly he is suited! I think he bought his doublet in Italy, his round hose in France, his bonnet in Germany, and his behavior everywhere.

NERISSA What think you of the Scottish lord, his neighbor?

PORTIA That he hath a neighborly charity in him, for he borrow'd a box of the ear of the Englishman and swore he would pay him again when he was able. I think the Frenchman became his surety and seal'd under for another.

NERISSA How like you the young German, the Duke of Saxony's nephew?

PORTIA Very vilely in the morning, when he is sober, and most vilely in the afternoon, when he is drunk. When he is best, he is a little worse than a man, and when he is worst, he is little better than a beast. An the worst fall that ever fell, I hope I shall make shift to go without him.

NERISSA If he should offer to choose, and choose the right casket, you should refuse to perform your father's will, if you should refuse to accept him.

PORTIA Therefore, for fear of the worst, I pray thee, set a deep glass of Rhenish wine on the contrary casket, for if the devil be within and that temptation without, I know he will choose it. I will do anything, Nerissa, ere I will be married to a sponge.

NERISSA You need not fear, lady, the having any of these lords. They have acquainted me with their de-

I.ii. Location: Belmont. Portia's house.
7–8 in the mean having neither too much nor too little **8 comes sooner by** acquires sooner **9 competency** modest means **10 sentences** maxims **14 divine** clergyman **18 blood** (Thought of as a chief agent of the passions, which in turn were regarded as the enemies of reason.) **20 meshes** nets (used here for hunting hares). **good counsel the cripple** (Wisdom is portrayed as old and no longer agile.) **20–22 But . . . husband** but this talk is not the way to help me choose a husband **24 will . . . will** volition . . . testament **30 who** whoever **his** i.e., the father's **35 over-name them** name them over **37 level** aim, guess **40 appropriation** addition **41 good parts** accomplishments **44 County** count. **Palatine** one possessing royal privileges **46 An** if. **choose** i.e., do as you please

47–48 weeping philosopher i.e., Heraclitus of Ephesus, a melancholic and retiring philosopher of about 500 B.C., often contrasted with Democritus, the "laughing philosopher" **58 throstle** thrush **70 He . . . picture** i.e., he looks handsome **71 suited** dressed **72 doublet** upper garment corresponding to a jacket. **hose** tight-fitting breeches **73 bonnet** hat **80–81 became . . . another** guaranteed the Scot's payment (of a box on the ear) and put himself under obligation to give the Englishman yet another on his own behalf. (An allusion to the age-old alliance of the French and the Scots against the English.) **88 fall** befall. **make shift** manage **94 Rhenish wine** a German white wine from the Rhine valley. **contrary** i.e., wrong

terminations, which is, indeed, to return to their home and to trouble you with no more suit, unless you may be won by some other sort than your father's imposition depending on the caskets.

PORTIA If I live to be as old as Sibylla, I will die as chaste as Diana, unless I be obtain'd by the manner of my father's will. I am glad this parcel of wooers are so reasonable, for there is not one among them but I dote on his very absence, and I pray God grant them a fair departure.

NERISSA Do you not remember, lady, in your father's time, a Venetian, a scholar and a soldier, that came hither in company of the Marquess of Montferrat?

PORTIA Yes, yes, it was Bassanio; as I think, so was he call'd.

NERISSA True, madam. He, of all the men that ever my foolish eyes look'd upon, was the best deserving a fair lady.

PORTIA I remember him well, and I remember him worthy of thy praise.

Enter a Servingman.

How now, what news?

SERVINGMAN The four strangers seek for you, madam, to take their leave; and there is a forerunner come from a fifth, the Prince of Morocco, who brings word the Prince his master will be here tonight.

PORTIA If I could bid the fifth welcome with so good heart as I can bid the other four farewell, I should be glad of his approach. If he have the condition of a saint and the complexion of a devil, I had rather he should shrive me than wive me.
Come, Nerissa. [*To Servingman.*] Sirrah, go before.
Whiles we shut the gate upon one wooer, another knocks at the door. *Exeunt.*

[SCENE III]

Enter Bassanio with Shylock the Jew.

SHYLOCK Three thousand ducats; well.

BASSANIO Ay, sir, for three months.

SHYLOCK For three months; well.

BASSANIO For the which, as I told you, Antonio shall be bound.

SHYLOCK Antonio shall become bound; well.

BASSANIO May you stead me? Will you pleasure me? Shall I know your answer?

SHYLOCK Three thousand ducats for three months and Antonio bound.

BASSANIO Your answer to that.

SHYLOCK Antonio is a good man.

BASSANIO Have you heard any imputation to the contrary?

SHYLOCK Ho, no, no, no, no. My meaning in saying he is a good man is to have you understand me that he is sufficient. Yet his means are in supposition: he hath an argosy bound to Tripolis, another to the Indies; I understand, moreover, upon the Rialto, he hath a third at Mexico, a fourth for England, and other ventures he hath, squand'red abroad. But ships are but boards, sailors but men; there be land-rats and water-rats, water-thieves and land-thieves, I mean pirates, and then there is the peril of waters, winds, and rocks. The man is, notwithstanding, sufficient. Three thousand ducats; I think I may take his bond.

BASSANIO Be assur'd you may.

SHYLOCK I will be assur'd I may; and, that I may be assur'd, I will bethink me. May I speak with Antonio?

BASSANIO If it please you to dine with us.

SHYLOCK Yes, to smell pork; to eat of the habitation which your prophet the Nazarite conjur'd the devil into. I will buy with you, sell with you, talk with you, walk with you, and so following, but I will not eat with you, drink with you, nor pray with you. What news on the Rialto? Who is he comes here?

Enter Antonio.

BASSANIO
This is Signior Antonio.

SHYLOCK [*Aside*]
How like a fawning publican he looks!
I hate him for he is a Christian,
But more for that in low simplicity
He lends out money gratis and brings down
The rate of usance here with us in Venice.
If I can catch him once upon the hip,
I will feed fat the ancient grudge I bear him.
He hates our sacred nation, and he rails,
Even there where merchants most do congregate,
On me, my bargains, and my well-won thrift,
Which he calls interest. Cursed be my tribe
If I forgive him!

BASSANIO Shylock, do you hear?

SHYLOCK
I am debating of my present store,
And, by the near guess of my memory,
I cannot instantly raise up the gross
Of full three thousand ducats. What of that?
Tubal, a wealthy Hebrew of my tribe,
Will furnish me. But soft! How many months
Do you desire? [*To Antonio.*] Rest you fair, good signior!

102 sort way, manner **102–103 imposition** conditions imposed **104 Sibylla** the Cumaean Sibyl, to whom Apollo gave as many years as there were grains in her handful of sand **121 four** (Nerissa actually names six suitors; possibly a sign of revision.) **127 condition** disposition, character **128 complexion of a devil** (Devils were thought to be black; but *complexion* can also mean "temperament," "disposition.") **129 shrive me** act as my confessor

I.iii. Location: Venice. A public place.
1 ducats gold coins **7 stead** help, supply a need

12 good (Shylock means *solvent,* a good credit risk; Bassanio interprets in the moral sense.) **17 sufficient** i.e., a good security. **in supposition** doubtful, uncertain **19 Rialto** the merchants' exchange in Venice and the center of commercial activity **27, 28 assur'd** (Bassanio means that Shylock may trust Antonio, whereas Shylock means that he will provide legal assurances.) **32 Nazarite** Nazarene. (For the reference to Christ's casting evil spirits into a herd of swine, see Luke 8:32–33 and Mark 5:1–13.) **38 publican** Roman tax-gatherer (a term of opprobrium); or, innkeeper **39 for** because **42 usance** usury, interest **43 upon the hip** i.e., at my mercy. (A figure of speech from wrestling; see Genesis 32:24–29.) **47 thrift** thriving **50 store** supply (of money) **52 gross** total

Your worship was the last man in our mouths.

ANTONIO

Shylock, albeit I neither lend nor borrow
By taking nor by giving of excess, 59
Yet, to supply the ripe wants of my friend,
I'll break a custom. [*To Bassanio.*] Is he yet possess'd 61
How much ye would?

SHYLOCK Ay, ay, three thousand ducats.

ANTONIO

And for three months.

SHYLOCK

I had forgot—three months, you told me so.
Well then, your bond. And let me see—but hear
you,
Methoughts you said you neither lend nor borrow
Upon advantage.

ANTONIO I do never use it. 67

SHYLOCK

When Jacob graz'd his uncle Laban's sheep— 68
This Jacob from our holy Abram was,
As his wise mother wrought in his behalf,
The third possessor; ay, he was the third— 71

ANTONIO

And what of him? Did he take interest?

SHYLOCK

No, not take interest, not, as you would say,
Directly int'rest. Mark what Jacob did.
When Laban and himself were compromis'd 75
That all the eanlings which were streak'd and pied 76
Should fall as Jacob's hire, the ewes, being rank, 77
In end of autumn turned to the rams,
And, when the work of generation was
Between these woolly breeders in the act,
The skillful shepherd pill'd me certain wands 81
And, in the doing of the deed of kind, 82
He stuck them up before the fulsome ewes,
Who then conceiving did in eaning time 84
Fall parti-color'd lambs, and those were Jacob's. 85
This was a way to thrive, and he was blest;
And thrift is blessing, if men steal it not.

ANTONIO

This was a venture, sir, that Jacob serv'd for, 88
A thing not in his power to bring to pass,
But sway'd and fashion'd by the hand of heaven.
Was this inserted to make interest good? 91
Or is your gold and silver ewes and rams?

SHYLOCK

I cannot tell; I make it breed as fast.
But note me, signior.

ANTONIO Mark you this, Bassanio,
The devil can cite Scripture for his purpose. 95
An evil soul producing holy witness
Is like a villain with a smiling cheek,
A goodly apple rotten at the heart.
O, what a goodly outside falsehood hath!

SHYLOCK

Three thousand ducats; 'tis a good round sum.
Three months from twelve; then, let me see; the
rate—

ANTONIO

Well, Shylock, shall we be beholding to you?

SHYLOCK

Signior Antonio, many a time and oft
In the Rialto you have rated me 104
About my moneys and my usances.
Still have I borne it with a patient shrug,
For suff'rance is the badge of all our tribe. 107
You call me misbeliever, cut-throat dog,
And spit upon my Jewish gaberdine, 109
And all for use of that which is mine own.
Well then, it now appears you need my help.
Go to, then. You come to me, and you say 112
"Shylock, we would have moneys"—you say so,
You, that did void your rheum upon my beard 114
And foot me as you spurn a stranger cur 115
Over your threshold! Moneys is your suit.
What should I say to you? Should I not say
"Hath a dog money? Is it possible
A cur can lend three thousand ducats?" Or
Shall I bend low and in a bondman's key,
With bated breath and whisp'ring humbleness,
Say this:
"Fair sir, you spit on me on Wednesday last,
You spurn'd me such a day, another time
You call'd me dog, and for these courtesies
I'll lend you thus much moneys"?

ANTONIO

I am as like to call thee so again,
To spit on thee again, to spurn thee too.
If thou wilt lend this money, lend it not
As to thy friends; for when did friendship take
A breed for barren metal of his friend? 131
But lend it rather to thine enemy,
Who, if he break, thou mayst with better face 133
Exact the penalty.

SHYLOCK Why, look you, how you storm!
I would be friends with you and have your love,
Forget the shames that you have stain'd me with,
Supply your present wants, and take no doit 137
Of usance for my moneys, and you'll not hear me.
This is kind I offer.

BASSANIO

This were kindness.

SHYLOCK This kindness will I show. 140
Go with me to a notary, seal me there
Your single bond; and, in a merry sport, 142
If you repay me not on such a day,

59 excess interest **61 possess'd** informed **67 advantage** interest **68 Jacob** (See Genesis 27, 30:25–43.) **71 possessor** i.e., of God's promise **75 compromis'd** agreed **76 eanlings** young lambs or kids. **pied** spotted **77 hire** wages, share. **rank** in heat **81 pill'd me** stripped, peeled. (*Me* is the so-called ethical dative, used colloquially.) **82 deed of kind** i.e., copulation **84 eaning** lambing **85 Fall** give birth to **88 venture . . . for** uncertain commercial venture on which Jacob risked his wages **91 inserted . . . good** brought in to justify the practice of usury **95 devil . . . Scripture** (See Matthew 4:6.)

104 rated berated, rebuked **107 suff'rance** endurance **109 gaberdine** loose upper garment like a cape or mantle **112 Go to** (An exclamation of impatience or annoyance.) **114 rheum** spittle **115 spurn** kick **131 breed . . . metal** offspring from money, which cannot naturally breed. (One of the oldest arguments against usury was that it was thereby "unnatural.") **133 Who** from whom. **break** fail to pay on time **137 doit** a Dutch coin of very small value **140 were** would be (if seriously offered) **142 single bond** bond signed alone without other security

In such a place, such sum or sums as are
Express'd in the condition, let the forfeit
Be nominated for an equal pound
Of your fair flesh, to be cut off and taken
In what part of your body pleaseth me.

ANTONIO
Content, in faith. I'll seal to such a bond
And say there is much kindness in the Jew.

BASSANIO
You shall not seal to such a bond for me!
I'll rather dwell in my necessity.

ANTONIO
Why, fear not, man; I will not forfeit it.
Within these two months, that's a month before
This bond expires, I do expect return
Of thrice three times the value of this bond.

SHYLOCK
O father Abram, what these Christians are,
Whose own hard dealings teaches them suspect
The thoughts of others! Pray you, tell me this:
If he should break his day, what should I gain
By the exaction of the forfeiture?
A pound of man's flesh taken from a man
Is not so estimable, profitable neither,
As flesh of muttons, beefs, or goats. I say
To buy his favor I extend this friendship.
If he will take it, so; if not, adieu.
And, for my love, I pray you wrong me not.

ANTONIO
Yes, Shylock, I will seal unto this bond.

SHYLOCK
Then meet me forthwith at the notary's;
Give him direction for this merry bond,
And I will go and purse the ducats straight,
See to my house, left in the fearful guard
Of an unthrifty knave, and presently
I'll be with you. *Exit.*

ANTONIO Hie thee, gentle Jew.
The Hebrew will turn Christian; he grows kind.

BASSANIO
I like not fair terms and a villain's mind.

ANTONIO
Come on. In this there can be no dismay;
My ships come home a month before the day.
Exeunt.

[ACT II • SCENE I]

[*Flourish of cornets.*] *Enter* [*the Prince of*] *Morocco, a tawny Moor all in white, and three or four followers accordingly, with Portia, Nerissa, and their train.*

MOROCCO
Mislike me not for my complexion,
The shadowed livery of the burnish'd sun,
To whom I am a neighbor and near bred.
Bring me the fairest creature northward born,
Where Phoebus' fire scarce thaws the icicles,
And let us make incision for your love,
To prove whose blood is reddest, his or mine.
I tell thee, lady, this aspect of mine
Hath fear'd the valiant. By my love, I swear
The best-regarded virgins of our clime
Have lov'd it too. I would not change this hue,
Except to steal your thoughts, my gentle queen.

PORTIA
In terms of choice I am not solely led
By nice direction of a maiden's eyes;
Besides, the lott'ry of my destiny
Bars me the right of voluntary choosing.
But if my father had not scanted me
And hedg'd me by his wit, to yield myself
His wife who wins me by that means I told you,
Yourself, renowned Prince, then stood as fair
As any comer I have look'd on yet
For my affection.

MOROCCO Even for that I thank you.
Therefore, I pray you, lead me to the caskets
To try my fortune. By this scimitar
That slew the Sophy and a Persian prince,
That won three fields of Sultan Solyman,
I would o'erstare the sternest eyes that look,
Outbrave the heart most daring on the earth,
Pluck the young sucking cubs from the she-bear,
Yea, mock the lion when 'a roars for prey,
To win thee, lady. But, alas the while!
If Hercules and Lichas play at dice
Which is the better man, the greater throw
May turn by fortune from the weaker hand.
So is Alcides beaten by his page,
And so may I, blind fortune leading me,
Miss that which one unworthier may attain,
And die with grieving.

PORTIA You must take your chance,
And either not attempt to choose at all
Or swear before you choose, if you choose wrong
Never to speak to lady afterward
In way of marriage. Therefore be advis'd.

MOROCCO
Nor will not. Come, bring me unto my chance.

PORTIA
First, forward to the temple. After dinner
Your hazard shall be made.

MOROCCO Good fortune then!
To make me blest or cursed'st among men.
[*Cornets, and*] *exeunt.*

146 nominated named, specified. **equal** exact **152 dwell** remain **167 wrong me not** do not think evil of me **172 fearful** to be mistrusted

II.i. Location: Belmont. Portia's house.

2 shadowed livery i.e., dark complexion, worn as though it were a costume of the sun's servants **3 near bred** closely related **5 Phoebus'** i.e., the sun's **7 reddest** (Red blood was regarded as a sign of courage.) **8 aspect** visage **9 fear'd** frightened **14 nice** dainty **17 scanted** limited **25 Sophy** Shah of Persia **26 fields** battles. **Solyman** a Turkish sultan ruling 1520–1566 **27 o'erstare** outstare **30 'a** he **32 Lichas** a page of Hercules (Alcides) **43 Nor will not** i.e., nor indeed will I violate the oath **44 to the temple** i.e., in order to take the oaths

[SCENE II]

Enter [Launcelot] the Clown, alone.

LAUNCELOT Certainly my conscience will serve me to run from this Jew my master. The fiend is at mine elbow and tempts me saying to me "Gobbo, Launcelot Gobbo, good Launcelot," or "good Gobbo," or "good Launcelot Gobbo, use your legs, take the start, run away." My conscience says, "No; take heed, honest Launcelot; take heed, honest Gobbo," or, as aforesaid, "honest Launcelot Gobbo; do not run; scorn running with thy heels." Well, the most courageous fiend bids me pack. "Fia!" says the fiend; "away!" says the fiend; "for the heavens, rouse up a brave mind," says the fiend, "and run." Well, my conscience, hanging about the neck of my heart, says very wisely to me, "My honest friend Launcelot, being an honest man's son," or rather an honest woman's son; for, indeed, my father did something smack, something grow to, he had a kind of taste; well, my conscience says, "Launcelot, budge not." "Budge," says the fiend. "Budge not," says my conscience. "Conscience," say I, "you counsel well." "Fiend," say I, "you counsel well." To be rul'd by my conscience, I should stay with the Jew my master, who, God bless the mark, is a kind of devil; and, to run away from the Jew, I should be rul'd by the fiend, who, saving your reverence, is the devil himself. Certainly the Jew is the very devil incarnation; and, in my conscience, my conscience is but a kind of hard conscience, to offer to counsel me to stay with the Jew. The fiend gives the more friendly counsel. I will run, fiend; my heels are at your commandment; I will run.

Enter Old Gobbo, with a basket.

GOBBO Master young man, you, I pray you, which is the way to master Jew's?

LAUNCELOT [*Aside*] O heavens, this is my true-begotten father, who, being more than sand-blind, high-gravel-blind, knows me not. I will try confusions with him.

GOBBO Master young gentleman, I pray you, which is the way to master Jew's?

LAUNCELOT Turn up on your right hand at the next turning, but, at the next turning of all, on your left; marry, at the very next turning, turn of no hand, but turn down indirectly to the Jew's house.

GOBBO By God's sonties, 'twill be a hard way to hit. Can you tell me whether one Launcelot, that dwells with him, dwell with him or no?

LAUNCELOT Talk you of young Master Launcelot? [*Aside.*] Mark me now; now will I raise the waters.— Talk you of young Master Launcelot?

GOBBO No master, sir, but a poor man's son. His father, though I say 't, is an honest exceeding poor man and, God be thank'd, well to live.

LAUNCELOT Well, let his father be what 'a will, we talk of young Master Launcelot.

GOBBO Your worship's friend and Launcelot, sir.

LAUNCELOT But I pray you, ergo, old man, ergo, I beseech you, talk you of young Master Launcelot?

GOBBO Of Launcelot, an 't please your mastership.

LAUNCELOT Ergo, Master Launcelot. Talk not of Master Launcelot, father; for the young gentleman, according to Fates and Destinies and such odd sayings, the Sisters Three and such branches of learning, is indeed deceas'd, or, as you would say in plain terms, gone to heaven.

GOBBO Marry, God forbid! The boy was the very staff of my age, my very prop.

LAUNCELOT Do I look like a cudgel or a hovel-post, a staff, or a prop? Do you know me, father?

GOBBO Alack the day, I know you not, young gentleman, but I pray you tell me, is my boy, God rest his soul, alive or dead?

LAUNCELOT Do you not know me, father?

GOBBO Alack, sir, I am sand-blind; I know you not.

LAUNCELOT Nay, indeed, if you had your eyes, you might fail of the knowing me; it is a wise father that knows his own child. Well, old man, I will tell you news of your son. [*Kneels.*] Give me your blessing; truth will come to light; murder cannot be hid long; a man's son may, but in the end truth will out.

GOBBO Pray you, sir, stand up. I am sure you are not Launcelot, my boy.

LAUNCELOT Pray you, let's have no more fooling about it, but give me your blessing. I am Launcelot, your boy that was, your son that is, your child that shall be.

GOBBO I cannot think you are my son.

LAUNCELOT I know not what I shall think of that; but I am Launcelot, the Jew's man, and I am sure Margery your wife is my mother.

GOBBO Her name is Margery, indeed! I'll be sworn, if thou be Launcelot, thou art mine own flesh and blood. Lord worship'd might he be, what a beard hast thou got! Thou hast got more hair on thy chin than Dobbin my fill-horse has on his tail.

LAUNCELOT [*Rising*] It should seem, then, that Dobbin's tail grows backward. I am sure he had more hair of his tail than I have of my face when I last saw him.

GOBBO Lord, how art thou chang'd! How dost thou and thy master agree? I have brought him a present. How 'gree you now?

II.ii. Location: Venice. A street.
9 with thy heels i.e., emphatically (with a pun on the literal sense) **10 pack** be gone. **Fia** i.e., Via, away **16–17 something . . . taste** i.e., had a tendency to lechery **22 God . . . mark** (An expression by way of apology for introducing something potentially offensive, as also in *saving your reverence.*) **25 incarnation** (Launcelot means "incarnate.") **33 sand-blind** dim-sighted **34 high-gravel-blind** blinder than sand-blind. (A term seemingly invented by Launcelot.) **40 marry** i.e., by the Virgin Mary, indeed. (A mild interjection.) **42 sonties** little saints (?)

46 raise the waters start tears (?) **48 master** (The title was applied to gentlefolk only.) **50 well to live** having a good livelihood (?) in good health (?) **53 Your . . . Launcelot** (Again, Old Gobbo denies that Launcelot is entitled to be called "Master.") **54 ergo** therefore (if it means anything) **58 father** i.e., old man **59–60 Sisters Three** the three Fates **65 hovel-post** support for a hovel or open shed **73–74 it is . . . child** (Reverses the proverb, "it is a wise child that knows his own father.") **81–82 your . . . shall be** (Echoes the *Gloria* from the Book of Common Prayer: "As it was in the beginning, is now, and ever shall be.") **89 beard** (Stage tradition has Old Gobbo mistake Launcelot's long hair for a beard.) **91 fill-horse** cart-horse **93 grows backward** (1) grows inward, shorter (2) grows at the wrong end **94 of** in

LAUNCELOT Well, well; but, for mine own part, as I have set up my rest to run away, so I will not rest till I have run some ground. My master's a very Jew. Give him a present! Give him a halter. I am famish'd in his service; you may tell every finger I have with my ribs. Father, I am glad you are come. Give me your present to one Master Bassanio, who, indeed, gives rare new liveries. If I serve not him, I will run as far as God has any ground. O rare fortune, here comes the man! To him, father, for I am a Jew if I serve the Jew any longer.

Enter Bassanio, with [*Leonardo and*] *a follower or two.*

BASSANIO You may do so; but let it be so hasted that supper be ready at the farthest by five of the clock. See these letters deliver'd, put the liveries to making, and desire Gratiano to come anon to my lodging. [*Exit a Servant.*]

LAUNCELOT To him, father.

GOBBO [*Advancing*] God bless your worship!

BASSANIO Gramercy. Wouldst thou aught with me?

GOBBO Here's my son, sir, a poor boy—

LAUNCELOT Not a poor boy, sir, but the rich Jew's man, that would, sir, as my father shall specify—

GOBBO He hath a great infection, sir, as one would say, to serve—

LAUNCELOT Indeed, the short and the long is, I serve the Jew, and have a desire, as my father shall specify—

GOBBO His master and he, saving your worship's reverence, are scarce cater-cousins—

LAUNCELOT To be brief, the very truth is that the Jew, having done me wrong, doth cause me, as my father, being, I hope, an old man, shall frutify unto you—

GOBBO I have here a dish of doves that I would bestow upon your worship, and my suit is—

LAUNCELOT In very brief, the suit is impertinent to myself, as your worship shall know by this honest old man; and, though I say it, though old man, yet poor man, my father.

BASSANIO One speak for both. What would you?

LAUNCELOT Serve you, sir.

GOBBO That is the very defect of the matter, sir.

BASSANIO
I know thee well; thou hast obtain'd thy suit.
Shylock thy master spoke with me this day,
And hath preferr'd thee, if it be preferment
To leave a rich Jew's service, to become
The follower of so poor a gentleman.

LAUNCELOT The old proverb is very well parted between my master Shylock and you, sir: you have the grace of God, sir, and he hath enough.

BASSANIO
Thou speak'st it well. Go, father, with thy son.
Take leave of thy old master and inquire
My lodging out. [*To a Servant.*] Give him a livery
More guarded than his fellows'. See it done.

LAUNCELOT Father, in. I cannot get a service, no; I have ne'er a tongue in my head, well! [*Looks at his palm.*] If any man in Italy have a fairer table which doth offer to swear upon a book, I shall have good fortune. Go to, here's a simple line of life. Here's a small trifle of wives! Alas, fifteen wives is nothing. Eleven widows and nine maids is a simple coming-in for one man. And then to scape drowning thrice, and to be in peril of my life with the edge of a feather-bed! Here are simple scapes. Well, if Fortune be a woman, she's a good wench for this gear. Father, come; I'll take my leave of the Jew in the twinkling.
Exit Clown [*with Old Gobbo*].

BASSANIO
I pray thee, good Leonardo, think on this:
[*Gives him a list.*]
These things being bought and orderly bestow'd,
Return in haste, for I do feast tonight
My best-esteem'd acquaintance. Hie thee, go.

LEONARDO
My best endeavors shall be done herein.

Enter Gratiano.

GRATIANO
Where's your master?

LEONARDO Yonder, sir, he walks.
Exit Leonardo.

GRATIANO
Signior Bassanio!

BASSANIO
Gratiano!

GRATIANO
I have a suit to you.

BASSANIO You have obtain'd it.

GRATIANO You must not deny me. I must go with you to Belmont.

BASSANIO
Why, then you must. But hear thee, Gratiano;
Thou art too wild, too rude and bold of voice—
Parts that become thee happily enough,
And in such eyes as ours appear not faults,
But where thou art not known, why, there they show
Something too liberal. Pray thee, take pain
To allay with some cold drops of modesty
Thy skipping spirit, lest through thy wild behavior
I be misconst'red in the place I go to
And lose my hopes.

GRATIANO Signior Bassanio, hear me:
If I do not put on a sober habit,
Talk with respect and swear but now and then,
Wear prayer-books in my pocket, look demurely,
Nay more, while grace is saying, hood mine eyes
Thus with my hat, and sigh and say "amen,"

99 set up my rest determined, risked all. (A metaphor from the card game *primero,* in which a final wager is made.) **100 very** veritable **101 halter** hangman's noose **102 tell** count. **tell . . . ribs** (Comically reverses the usual saying of counting one's ribs with one's fingers.) **103 Give me** give. (*Me* is an ethical dative.) **105 liveries** uniforms or costumes for servants **114 Gramercy** many thanks **118 infection** (Blunder for *affection* or *inclination.*) **123 cater-cousins** good friends **126 frutify** (Launcelot may be trying to say "fructify," but he means "certify" or "notify.") **129 impertinent** (Blunder for *pertinent.*) **135 defect** (Blunder for *effect,* i.e., "purport.") **138 preferr'd** recommended **141 proverb** i.e., "He who has the grace of God has enough"

147 guarded trimmed with braided ornament **150 table** palm of the hand. (Launcelot now reads the lines of his palm.) **154 simple coming-in** modest income (with sexual suggestion) **156 feather-bed** (suggesting marriage-bed or love-bed) **157 Fortune . . . woman** (Fortune was personified as a goddess.) **158 gear** matter **173 Parts** qualities **176 liberal** free of manner (often with sexual connotation)

Use all the observance of civility,
Like one well studied in a sad ostent
To please his grandam, never trust me more.

BASSANIO
Well, we shall see your bearing.

GRATIANO
Nay, but I bar tonight. You shall not gauge me
By what we do tonight.

BASSANIO
No, that were pity.
I would entreat you rather to put on
You boldest suit of mirth, for we have friends
That purpose merriment. But fare you well;
I have some business.

GRATIANO
And I must to Lorenzo and the rest,
But we will visit you at supper-time. *Exeunt.*

[SCENE III]

Enter Jessica and [Launcelot] the Clown.

JESSICA
I am sorry thou wilt leave my father so.
Our house is hell, and thou, a merry devil,
Didst rob it of some taste of tediousness.
But fare thee well; there is a ducat for thee.
[*Gives money.*]
And, Launcelot, soon at supper shalt thou see
Lorenzo, who is thy new master's guest.
Give him this letter; do it secretly. [*Gives letter.*]
And so farewell; I would not have my father
See me in talk with thee.

LAUNCELOT Adieu! Tears exhibit my tongue. Most beautiful pagan, most sweet Jew! If a Christian did not play the knave and get thee, I am much deceiv'd. But, adieu! These foolish drops do something drown my manly spirit. Adieu!

JESSICA
Farewell, good Launcelot. [*Exit Launcelot.*]
Alack, what heinous sin is it in me
To be asham'd to be my father's child!
But though I am a daughter to his blood,
I am not to his manners. O Lorenzo,
If thou keep promise, I shall end this strife,
Become a Christian and thy loving wife. *Exit.*

[SCENE IV]

Enter Gratiano, Lorenzo, Salerio, and Solanio.

LORENZO
Nay, we will slink away in supper-time,
Disguise us at my lodging and return

187 sad ostent grave appearance

II.iii. Location: Venice. Shylock's house.
10 exhibit (Blunder for *inhibit,* "restrain.") **12 get** beget

II.iv. Location: Venice. A street.

All in an hour.

GRATIANO
We have not made good preparation.

SALERIO
We have not spoke us yet of torch-bearers.

SOLANIO
'Tis vile, unless it may be quaintly ordered,
And better in my mind not undertook.

LORENZO
'Tis now but four o'clock. We have two hours
To furnish us.

Enter Launcelot [with a letter].

Friend Launcelot, what's the news?

LAUNCELOT An it shall please you to break up this, it shall seem to signify. [*Gives letter.*]

LORENZO
I know the hand. In faith, 'tis a fair hand,
And whiter than the paper it writ on
Is the fair hand that writ.

GRATIANO
Love-news, in faith.

LAUNCELOT By your leave, sir. [*Starts to leave.*]

LORENZO Whither goest thou?

LAUNCELOT Marry, sir, to bid my old master the Jew to sup tonight with my new master the Christian.

LORENZO
Hold here, take this. [*Gives money.*] Tell gentle
Jessica
I will not fail her; speak it privately.
Exit Clown [Launcelot].
Go, gentlemen,
Will you prepare you for this masque tonight?
I am provided of a torch-bearer.

SALERIO
Ay, marry, I'll be gone about it straight.

SOLANIO
And so will I.

LORENZO
Meet me and Gratiano
At Gratiano's lodging some hour hence.

SALERIO
'Tis good we do so. *Exit [with Solanio].*

GRATIANO
Was not that letter from fair Jessica?

LORENZO
I must needs tell thee all. She hath directed
How I shall take her from her father's house,
What gold and jewels she is furnish'd with,
What page's suit she hath in readiness.
If e'er the Jew her father come to heaven,
It will be for his gentle daughter's sake;
And never dare misfortune cross her foot,
Unless she do it under this excuse,
That she is issue to a faithless Jew.
Come, go with me; peruse this as thou goest.
[*Gives him the letter.*]
Fair Jessica shall be my torch-bearer. *Exeunt.*

5 spoke . . . of yet bespoken, ordered **6 quaintly ordered** skillfully and tastefully managed **10 break up** i.e., break open. (Literally, a term from carving.) **34 gentle** (with pun on *gentile?*) **35 foot** footpath **36 she** i.e., misfortune **37 she is issue** i.e., Jessica is child. **faithless** pagan

[SCENE V]

Enter [Shylock the] Jew and [Launcelot,] his man that was, the Clown.

SHYLOCK
Well, thou shalt see, thy eyes shall be thy judge,
The difference of old Shylock and Bassanio.—
What, Jessica!—Thou shalt not gormandize,
As thou hast done with me—What, Jessica!—
And sleep and snore, and rend apparel out—
Why, Jessica, I say!

LAUNCELOT Why, Jessica!

SHYLOCK
Who bids thee call? I do not bid thee call.

LAUNCELOT Your worship was wont to tell me I could do nothing without bidding.

Enter Jessica.

JESSICA
Call you? What is your will?

SHYLOCK
I am bid forth to supper, Jessica.
There are my keys. But wherefore should I go?
I am not bid for love—they flatter me—
But yet I'll go in hate, to feed upon
The prodigal Christian. Jessica, my girl,
Look to my house. I am right loath to go.
There is some ill a-brewing towards my rest,
For I did dream of money-bags tonight.

LAUNCELOT I beseech you, sir, go. My young master doth expect your reproach.

SHYLOCK
So do I his.

LAUNCELOT And they have conspir'd together. I will not say you shall see a masque, but if you do, then it was not for nothing that my nose fell a-bleeding on Black-Monday last at six o'clock i' th' morning, falling out that year on Ash-Wednesday was four year in th' afternoon.

SHYLOCK
What, are there masques? Hear you me, Jessica:
Lock up my doors; and when you hear the drum
And the vile squealing of the wry-neck'd fife,
Clamber not you up to the casements then,
Nor thrust your head into the public street
To gaze on Christian fools with varnish'd faces,
But stop my house's ears, I mean my casements.
Let not the sound of shallow fopp'ry enter
My sober house. By Jacob's staff, I swear,
I have no mind of feasting forth tonight.
But I will go. Go you before me, sirrah.
Say I will come.

LAUNCELOT I will go before, sir. [*To Jessica.*] Mistress, look out at window, for all this;
There will come a Christian by,
Will be worth a Jewess' eye. [*Exit.*]

SHYLOCK
What says that fool of Hagar's offspring, ha?

JESSICA
His words were "Farewell, mistress," nothing else.

SHYLOCK
The patch is kind enough, but a huge feeder,
Snail-slow in profit, and he sleeps by day
More than the wildcat. Drones hive not with me;
Therefore I part with him, and part with him
To one that I would have him help to waste
His borrowed purse. Well, Jessica, go in.
Perhaps I will return immediately.
Do as I bid you; shut doors after you.
Fast bind, fast find—
A proverb never stale in thrifty mind. *Exit.*

JESSICA
Farewell; and if my fortune be not cross'd,
I have a father, you a daughter, lost. *Exit.*

[SCENE VI]

Enter the masquers, Gratiano and Salerio.

GRATIANO
This is the penthouse under which Lorenzo
Desired us to make stand.

SALERIO
His hour is almost past.

GRATIANO
And it is marvel he out-dwells his hour,
For lovers ever run before the clock.

SALERIO
O, ten times faster Venus' pigeons fly
To seal love's bonds new-made, than they are wont
To keep obliged faith unforfeited!

GRATIANO
That ever holds. Who riseth from a feast
With that keen appetite that he sits down?
Where is the horse that doth untread again
His tedious measures with the unbated fire
That he did pace them first? All things that are,
Are with more spirit chased than enjoy'd.
How like a younger or a prodigal
The scarfed bark puts from her native bay,
Hugg'd and embraced by the strumpet wind!
How like the prodigal doth she return,
With over-weather'd ribs and ragged sails,

II.v. Location: Venice. Before Shylock's house.
2 of between **5 rend apparel out** i.e., wear out your clothes **19 tonight** last night **21 reproach** (Launcelot's blunder for *approach*. Shylock takes it in grim humor.) **26 Black-Monday** Easter Monday. (So called, according to Stow, because of a cold and stormy Easter Monday when Edward III was besieging Paris. Launcelot's talk of omens is perhaps intentional gibberish, a parody of Shylock's fears.)
31 wry-neck'd i.e., played with the musician's head awry; or, on an instrument with the head twisted awry **34 varnish'd faces** i.e., painted masks **37 Jacob's staff** (See Genesis 32:10 and Hebrews 11:21.)

45 Hagar's offspring (Hagar, a Gentile and Abraham's servant, gave birth to Ishmael; both mother and son were cast out after the birth of Isaac.) **47 patch** fool **48 profit** profitable labor

II.vi. Location: Before Shylock's house, as in scene v.
1 penthouse projecting roof from a house **6 Venus' pigeons** the doves that drew Venus' chariot **8 obliged** bound by marriage or engagement. **unforfeited** unbroken **11 untread** retrace **15 younger** i.e., younger son, as in the parable of the Prodigal Son (Luke 15). (Often emended to *younker*, youth.) **16 scarfed** decorated with flags or streamers **17 strumpet** (Refers metaphorically to the harlots with whom the Prodigal Son wasted his fortune.)

Lean, rent, and beggar'd by the strumpet wind!

Enter Lorenzo, [masqued].

SALERIO
Here comes Lorenzo. More of this hereafter.

LORENZO
Sweet friends, your patience for my long abode;
Not I, but my affairs, have made you wait.
When you shall please to play the thieves for wives,
I'll watch as long for you then. Approach;
Here dwells my father Jew. Ho! Who's within?

[Enter] Jessica, above [in boy's clothes].

JESSICA
Who are you? Tell me, for more certainty,
Albeit I'll swear that I do know your tongue.

LORENZO
Lorenzo, and thy love.

JESSICA
Lorenzo, certain, and my love indeed,
For who love I so much? And now who knows
But you, Lorenzo, whether I am yours?

LORENZO
Heaven and thy thoughts are witness that thou art.

JESSICA
Here, catch this casket; it is worth the pains.
[Throws down a casket.]
I am glad 'tis night, you do not look on me,
For I am much asham'd of my exchange.
But love is blind, and lovers cannot see
The pretty follies that themselves commit,
For if they could, Cupid himself would blush
To see me thus transformed to a boy.

LORENZO
Descend, for you must be my torch-bearer.

JESSICA
What, must I hold a candle to my shames?
They in themselves, good sooth, are too too light.
Why, 'tis an office of discovery, love,
And I should be obscur'd.

LORENZO
So are you, sweet,
Even in the lovely garnish of a boy.
But come at once,
For the close night doth play the runaway,
And we are stay'd for at Bassanio's feast.

JESSICA
I will make fast the doors, and gild myself
With some moe ducats, and be with you straight.
[Exit above.]

GRATIANO
Now, by my hood, a gentle and no Jew.

LORENZO
Beshrew me but I love her heartily,
For she is wise, if I can judge of her,
And fair she is, if that mine eyes be true,
And true she is, as she hath prov'd herself;
And therefore, like herself, wise, fair and true,
Shall she be placed in my constant soul.

Enter Jessica [below].

What, art thou come? On, gentlemen; away!
Our masquing mates by this time for us stay.
Exit [with Jessica and Salerio].

Enter Antonio.

ANTONIO Who's there?

GRATIANO Signior Antonio!

ANTONIO
Fie, fie, Gratiano! Where are all the rest?
'Tis nine o'clock; our friends all stay for you.
No masque tonight. The wind is come about;
Bassanio presently will go aboard.
I have sent twenty out to seek for you.

GRATIANO
I am glad on 't. I desire no more delight
Than to be under sail and gone tonight. *Exeunt.*

[SCENE VII]

[Flourish of cornets.] Enter Portia, with [the Prince of] Morocco, and both their trains.

PORTIA
Go draw aside the curtains and discover
The several caskets to this noble prince.
Now make your choice. *[Curtains are drawn.]*

MOROCCO
The first, of gold, who this inscription bears,
"Who chooseth me shall gain what many men
desire";
The second, silver, which this promise carries,
"Who chooseth me shall get as much as he
deserves";
This third, dull lead, with warning all as blunt,
"Who chooseth me must give and hazard all he
hath."
How shall I know if I do choose the right?

PORTIA
The one of them contains my picture, Prince.
If you choose that, then I am yours withal.

MOROCCO
Some god direct my judgment! Let me see;
I will survey th' inscriptions back again.
What says this leaden casket?
"Who chooseth me must give and hazard all he
hath."
Must give—for what? For lead? Hazard for lead?
This casket threatens. Men that hazard all
Do it in hope of fair advantages.
A golden mind stoops not to shows of dross;
I'll then nor give nor hazard aught for lead.
What says the silver with her virgin hue?

22 abode delay **26 father** i.e., father-in-law **36 exchange** change of clothes **43 light** immodest (with pun on literal meaning) **44 'tis . . . discovery** i.e., torch-bearing is intended to shed light on matters **46 garnish** outfit, trimmings **48 close** secret. **doth . . . runaway** i.e., is quickly passing **49 stay'd** waited **52 gentle** (with pun on *gentile,* as at II.iv.34) **53 Beshrew** i.e., a mischief on. (A mild oath.)

II.vii. Location: Belmont. Portia's house.
1 discover reveal **21 nor give** neither give

"Who chooseth me shall get as much as he deserves."
As much as he deserves! Pause there, Morocco,
And weigh thy value with an even hand.
If thou be'st rated by thy estimation,
Thou dost deserve enough; and yet enough
May not extend so far as to the lady;
And yet to be afeard of my deserving
Were but a weak disabling of myself.
As much as I deserve! Why, that's the lady.
I do in birth deserve her, and in fortunes,
In graces, and in qualities of breeding;
But more than these, in love I do deserve.
What if I stray'd no farther, but chose here?
Let's see once more this saying grav'd in gold:
"Who chooseth me shall gain what many men desire."
Why, that's the lady; all the world desires her.
From the four corners of the earth they come
To kiss this shrine, this mortal breathing saint.
The Hyrcanian deserts and the vasty wilds
Of wide Arabia are as throughfares now
For princes to come view fair Portia.
The watery kingdom, whose ambitious head
Spits in the face of heaven, is no bar
To stop the foreign spirits, but they come,
As o'er a brook, to see fair Portia.
One of these three contains her heavenly picture.
Is 't like that lead contains her? 'Twere damnation
To think so base a thought; it were too gross
To rib her cerecloth in the obscure grave.
Or shall I think in silver she's immur'd,
Being ten times undervalued to tried gold?
O sinful thought! Never so rich a gem
Was set in worse than gold. They have in England
A coin that bears the figure of an angel
Stamp'd in gold, but that's insculp'd upon;
But here an angel in a golden bed
Lies all within. Deliver me the key.
Here do I choose, and thrive I as I may!

PORTIA
There, take it, Prince; and if my form lie there,
Then I am yours. [*He unlocks the golden casket.*]

MOROCCO O hell! What have we here?
A carrion Death, within whose empty eye
There is a written scroll! I'll read the writing.
[*Reads.*] All that glisters is not gold;
Often have you heard that told.
Many a man his life hath sold
But my outside to behold.
Gilded tombs do worms infold.
Had you been as wise as bold,
Young in limbs, in judgment old,
Your answer had not been inscroll'd.
Fare you well, your suit is cold."
Cold, indeed; and labor lost.
Then, farewell, heat, and welcome, frost!
Portia, adieu. I have too griev'd a heart
To take a tedious leave. Thus losers part.
Exit [*with his train. Flourish of cornets*].

PORTIA
A gentle riddance. Draw the curtains, go.
Let all of his complexion choose me so.
[*Close curtain, and*] *Exeunt.*

26 estimation valuation **30 disabling** underrating **41 Hyrcanian** (Hyrcania was the country south of the Caspian Sea celebrated for its wildness.) **51 rib** i.e., enclose. **cerecloth** wax cloth used in wrapping for burial **53 Being . . . to** which has only one tenth of the value of **57 insculp'd upon** merely engraved upon the surface **63 carrion Death** death's-head **72 inscroll'd** i.e., written on this scroll

79 complexion temperament (not merely skin color)

[SCENE VIII]

Enter Salerio and Solanio.

SALERIO
Why, man, I saw Bassanio under sail.
With him is Gratiano gone along,
And in their ship I am sure Lorenzo is not.

SOLANIO
The villain Jew with outcries rais'd the Duke,
Who went with him to search Bassanio's ship.

SALERIO
He came too late, the ship was under sail;
But there the Duke was given to understand
That in a gondola were seen together
Lorenzo and his amorous Jessica.
Besides, Antonio certified the Duke
They were not with Bassanio in his ship.

SOLANIO
I never heard a passion so confus'd,
So strange, outrageous, and so variable
As the dog Jew did utter in the streets:
"My daughter! O my ducats! O my daughter!
Fled with a Christian! O my Christian ducats!
Justice! The law! My ducats, and my daughter!
A sealed bag, two sealed bags of ducats,
Of double ducats, stol'n from me by my daughter!
And jewels, two stones, two rich and precious stones,
Stol'n by my daughter! Justice! Find the girl!
She hath the stones upon her, and the ducats."

SALERIO
Why, all the boys in Venice follow him,
Crying, his stones, his daughter, and his ducats.

SOLANIO
Let good Antonio look he keep his day,
Or he shall pay for this.

SALERIO Marry, well rememb'red.
I reason'd with a Frenchman yesterday,
Who told me, in the narrow seas that part
The French and English, there miscarried
A vessel of our country richly fraught.
I thought upon Antonio when he told me,
And wish'd in silence that it were not his.

II.viii. Location: Venice. A street.
25 look . . . day see to it that he repays his loan on time **27 reason'd** talked **28 narrow seas** the English Channel **30 fraught** freighted

SOLANIO
You were best to tell Antonio what you hear.
Yet do not suddenly, for it may grieve him.

SALERIO
A kinder gentleman treads not the earth.
I saw Bassanio and Antonio part.
Bassanio told him he would make some speed
Of his return; he answered, "Do not so.
Slubber not business for my sake, Bassanio,
But stay the very riping of the time;
And for the Jew's bond which he hath of me,
Let it not enter in your mind of love.
Be merry, and employ your chiefest thoughts
To courtship and such fair ostents of love
As shall conveniently become you there."
And even there, his eye being big with tears,
Turning his face, he put his hand behind him,
And with affection wondrous sensible
He wrung Bassanio's hand; and so they parted.

SOLANIO
I think he only loves the world for him.
I pray thee let us go and find him out
And quicken his embraced heaviness
With some delight or other.

SALERIO
Do we so. *Exeunt.*

[SCENE IX]

Enter Nerissa and a Servitor.

NERISSA
Quick, quick, I pray thee, draw the curtain straight.
[*Curtains are drawn.*]
The Prince of Arragon hath ta'en his oath,
And comes to his election presently.

[*Flourish of cornets.*] *Enter* [*the Prince of*] *Arragon, his train, and Portia.*

PORTIA
Behold, there stand the caskets, noble Prince.
If you choose that wherein I am contain'd,
Straight shall our nuptial rites be solemniz'd;
But if you fail, without more speech, my lord,
You must be gone from hence immediately.

ARRAGON
I am enjoin'd by oath to observe three things:
First, never to unfold to anyone
Which casket 'twas I chose; next, if I fail
Of the right casket, never in my life
To woo a maid in way of marriage;
Lastly,
If I do fail in fortune of my choice,
Immediately to leave you and be gone.

PORTIA
To these injunctions everyone doth swear
That comes to hazard for my worthless self.

ARRAGON
And so have I address'd me. Fortune now
To my heart's hope! Gold, silver, and base lead.
"Who chooseth me must give and hazard all he
hath."
You shall look fairer ere I give or hazard.
What says the golden chest? Ha, let me see:
"Who chooseth me shall gain what many men
desire."
What many men desire! That "many" may be meant
By the fool multitude that choose by show,
Not learning more than the fond eye doth teach,
Which pries not to th' interior, but, like the martlet,
Builds in the weather on the outward wall,
Even in the force and road of casualty.
I will not choose what many men desire,
Because I will not jump with common spirits
And rank me with the barbarous multitudes.
Why, then to thee, thou silver treasure-house!
Tell me once more what title thou dost bear:
"Who chooseth me shall get as much as he
deserves."
And well said too; for who shall go about
To cozen fortune, and be honorable
Without the stamp of merit? Let none presume
To wear an undeserved dignity.
O, that estates, degrees, and offices
Were not deriv'd corruptly, and that clear honor
Were purchas'd by the merit of the wearer!
How many then should cover that stand bare?
How many be commanded that command?
How much low peasantry would then be gleaned
From the true seed of honor, and how much honor
Pick'd from the chaff and ruin of the times
To be new-varnish'd? Well, but to my choice:
"Who chooseth me shall get as much as he
deserves."
I will assume desert. Give me a key for this,
And instantly unlock my fortunes here.
[*He opens the silver casket.*]

PORTIA
Too long a pause for that which you find there.

ARRAGON
What's here? The portrait of a blinking idiot,
Presenting me a schedule! I will read it.
How much unlike art thou to Portia!
How much unlike my hopes and my deservings!
"Who chooseth me shall have as much as he
deserves."
Did I deserve no more than a fool's head?
Is that my prize? Are my deserts no better?

39 Slubber do hastily and badly **40 But . . . time** i.e., pursue your business at Belmont until it is brought to completion **41 for** as for **44 ostents** expressions, shows **48 sensible** strongly evident **52 quicken . . . heaviness** lighten the sorrow he has embraced

II.ix. Location: Belmont. Portia's house.
1 straight at once **3 election** choice **presently** immediately

19 address'd me prepared myself (by this swearing) **25 meant** interpreted **27 fond** foolish **28 martlet** martin **29 in** exposed to **30 force . . . casualty** power and path of mischance **32 jump** agree **38 cozen** cheat **39 stamp** seal of approval **41 estates, degrees** status, social rank **44 cover . . . bare** i.e., wear hats (of authority) who now stand bareheaded **45 How . . . command** how many then should be servants that are now masters **46 gleaned** culled out **47 the true seed of honor** i.e., persons of noble descent **49 new-varnish'd** i.e., having the luster of their true nobility restored to them **55 schedule** written paper

PORTIA
To offend, and judge, are distinct offices
And of opposed natures.

ARRAGON
What is here?
[*Reads.*] "The fire seven times tried this;
Seven times tried that judgment is,
That did never choose amiss.
Some there be that shadows kiss;
Such have but a shadow's bliss.
There be fools alive, iwis,
Silver'd o'er, and so was this.
Take what wife you will to bed,
I will ever be your head.
So be gone, you are sped."

Still more fool I shall appear
By the time I linger here.
With one fool's head I came to woo,
But I go away with two.
Sweet, adieu. I'll keep my oath,
Patiently to bear my wroth.
[*Exeunt Arragon and train.*]

PORTIA
Thus hath the candle sing'd the moth.
O, these deliberate fools! When they do choose,
They have the wisdom by their wit to lose.

NERISSA
The ancient saying is no heresy,
Hanging and wiving goes by destiny.

PORTIA
Come, draw the curtain, Nerissa.
[*The curtain is closed.*]

Enter Messenger.

MESSENGER
Where is my lady?

PORTIA
Here. What would my lord?

MESSENGER
Madam, there is alighted at your gate
A young Venetian, one that comes before
To signify th' approaching of his lord,
From whom he bringeth sensible regreets,
To wit, besides commends and courteous breath,
Gifts of rich value. Yet I have not seen
So likely an ambassador of love.
A day in April never came so sweet,
To show how costly summer was at hand,
As this fore-spurrer comes before his lord.

PORTIA
No more, I pray thee. I am half afeard
Thou wilt say anon he is some kin to thee,
Thou spend'st such high-day wit in praising him.
Come, come, Nerissa, for I long to see
Quick Cupid's post that comes so mannerly.

NERISSA
Bassanio, Lord Love, if thy will it be! *Exeunt.*

[ACT III • SCENE I]

[*Enter*] *Solanio and Salerio.*

SOLANIO Now, what news on the Rialto?

SALERIO Why, yet it lives there uncheck'd that Antonio hath a ship of rich lading wrack'd on the narrow seas—the Goodwins, I think they call the place, a very dangerous flat, and fatal, where the carcasses of many a tall ship lie buried, as they say, if my gossip Report be an honest woman of her word.

SOLANIO I would she were as lying a gossip in that as ever knapp'd ginger or made her neighbors believe she wept for the death of a third husband. But it is true, without any slips of prolixity or crossing the plain highway of talk, that the good Antonio, the honest Antonio—O that I had a title good enough to keep his name company!—

SALERIO Come, the full stop.

SOLANIO Ha, what sayest thou? Why, the end is, he hath lost a ship.

SALERIO I would it might prove the end of his losses.

SOLANIO Let me say "amen" betimes, lest the devil cross my prayer, for here he comes in the likeness of a Jew.

Enter Shylock.

How now, Shylock, what news among the merchants?

SHYLOCK You knew, none so well, none so well as you, of my daughter's flight.

SALERIO That's certain. I, for my part, knew the tailor that made the wings she flew withal.

SOLANIO And Shylock, for his own part, knew the bird was fledge; and then it is the complexion of them all to leave the dam.

SHYLOCK She is damn'd for it.

SALERIO That's certain, if the devil may be her judge.

SHYLOCK My own flesh and blood to rebel!

SOLANIO Out upon it, old carrion! Rebels it at these years?

SHYLOCK I say, my daughter is my flesh and my blood.

SALERIO There is more difference between thy flesh and hers than between jet and ivory, more between your bloods than there is between red wine and Rhenish. But tell us, do you hear whether Antonio have had any loss at sea or no?

61–62 To offend . . . natures i.e., you have no right, having submitted your case to judgment, to attempt to judge your own case **63 tried** tested, purified (?) **68 iwis** certainly **71 I . . . head** i.e., you will always have a fool's head **72 sped** done for **73–74 Still . . . here** i.e., I shall seem all the greater fool for wasting any more time here **78 wroth** sorrow, unhappy lot. (A variant of *ruth*.) **80 deliberate** reasoning, calculating **85 my lord** (A jesting response to "my lady.") **89 sensible regreets** heartfelt greeting; also, tangible greetings, gifts **90 commends** greetings **91 Yet** heretofore **92 likely** promising **94 costly** lavish, rich **98 high-day** holiday

100 post messenger

III.i. Location: Venice. A street.
2 uncheck'd undenied **4 Goodwins** Goodwin Sands, off the Kentish coast near the Thames estuary **6 gossip Report** i.e., Dame Rumor **9 knapp'd** chewed **11 slips of prolixity** lapses into longwindedness; or, longwinded lies **11–12 crossing . . . talk** deviating from honest plain speech **15 Come . . . stop** finish your story **20 cross** thwart **28 fledge** ready to fly. **complexion** natural disposition **29 dam** mother **33–34 Rebels . . . years** (Solanio pretends to interpret Shylock's cry about the rebellion of his own flesh and blood as referring to his own carnal desires.) **38 Rhenish** i.e., a German white wine from the Rhine valley

SHYLOCK There I have another bad match! A bankrupt, a prodigal, who dare scarce show his head on the Rialto; a beggar, that was us'd to come so smug upon the mart! Let him look to his bond. He was wont to call me usurer. Let him look to his bond. He was wont to lend money for a Christian cur'sy. Let him look to his bond.

SALERIO Why, I am sure, if he forfeit, thou wilt not take his flesh. What's that good for?

SHYLOCK To bait fish withal. If it will feed nothing else, it will feed my revenge. He hath disgrac'd me, and hind'red me half a million, laugh'd at my losses, mock'd at my gains, scorn'd my nation, thwarted my bargains, cool'd my friends, heated mine enemies; and what's his reason? I am a Jew. Hath not a Jew eyes? Hath not a Jew hands, organs, dimensions, senses, affections, passions? Fed with the same food, hurt with the same weapons, subject to the same diseases, heal'd by the same means, warm'd and cool'd by the same winter and summer, as a Christian is? If you prick us, do we not bleed? If you tickle us, do we not laugh? If you poison us, do we not die? And if you wrong us, shall we not revenge? If we are like you in the rest, we will resemble you in that. If a Jew wrong a Christian, what is his humility? Revenge. If a Christian wrong a Jew, what should his sufferance be by Christian example? Why, revenge. The villainy you teach me, I will execute, and it shall go hard but I will better the instruction.

Enter a Man from Antonio.

MAN Gentlemen, my master Antonio is at his house and desires to speak with you both.

SALERIO We have been up and down to seek him.

Enter Tubal.

SOLANIO Here comes another of the tribe. A third cannot be match'd, unless the devil himself turn Jew.

Exeunt gentlemen [Solanio, Salerio, with Man].

SHYLOCK How now, Tubal, what news from Genoa? Hast thou found my daughter?

TUBAL I often came where I did hear of her, but cannot find her.

SHYLOCK Why, there, there, there, there! A diamond gone, cost me two thousand ducats in Frankfort! The curse never fell upon our nation till now; I never felt it till now. Two thousand ducats in that, and other precious, precious jewels. I would my daughter were dead at my foot, and the jewels in her ear! Would she were hears'd at my foot, and the ducats in her coffin! No news of them? Why, so—and I know not what's spent in the search. Why, thou loss upon loss! The thief gone with so much, and so much to find the thief; and no satisfaction, no revenge! Nor no ill luck stirring but what lights o' my shoulders; no sighs but o' my breathing; no tears but o' my shedding.

TUBAL Yes, other men have ill luck too. Antonio, as I heard in Genoa—

SHYLOCK What, what, what? Ill luck, ill luck?

TUBAL Hath an argosy cast away, coming from Tripolis.

SHYLOCK I thank God, I thank God. Is it true, is it true?

TUBAL I spoke with some of the sailors that escap'd the wrack.

SHYLOCK I thank thee, good Tubal. Good news, good news! Ha, ha! Heard in Genoa?

TUBAL Your daughter spent in Genoa, as I heard, one night fourscore ducats.

SHYLOCK Thou stick'st a dagger in me. I shall never see my gold again. Fourscore ducats at a sitting, fourscore ducats!

TUBAL There came divers of Antonio's creditors in my company to Venice that swear he cannot choose but break.

SHYLOCK I am very glad of it. I'll plague him; I'll torture him. I am glad of it.

TUBAL One of them show'd me a ring that he had of your daughter for a monkey.

SHYLOCK Out upon her! Thou torturest me, Tubal. It was my turquoise; I had it of Leah when I was a bachelor. I would not have given it for a wilderness of monkeys.

TUBAL But Antonio is certainly undone.

SHYLOCK Nay, that's true, that's very true. Go, Tubal, fee me an officer; bespeak him a fortnight before. I will have the heart of him, if he forfeit; for, were he out of Venice, I can make what merchandise I will. Go, Tubal, and meet me at our synagogue; go, good Tubal; at our synagogue, Tubal. *Exeunt.*

[SCENE II]

Enter Bassanio, Portia, Gratiano, [Nerissa,] and all their trains.

PORTIA

I pray you, tarry. Pause a day or two
Before you hazard; for, in choosing wrong,
I lose your company. Therefore forbear awhile.
There's something tells me, but it is not love,
I would not lose you; and you know yourself,
Hate counsels not in such a quality.
But lest you should not understand me well—
And yet a maiden hath no tongue but thought—
I would detain you here some month or two
Before you venture for me. I could teach you
How to choose right, but then I am forsworn.
So will I never be. So may you miss me.
But if you do, you'll make me wish a sin,
That I had been forsworn. Beshrew your eyes,
They have o'erlook'd me and divided me!
One half of me is yours, the other half yours—

41 match bargain **46 for . . . cur'sy** as a Christian courtesy **65–66 his . . . his** the Christian's . . . the Jew's **74 match'd** i.e., found to match them

108 break go bankrupt **114 Leah** Shylock's wife **119 fee** hire. **officer** bailiff. **bespeak** engage **121 make . . . I will** drive whatever bargains I please

III.ii. Location: Belmont. Portia's house.
2 in choosing in your choosing **6 quality** way, manner **15 o'erlook'd** bewitched

Mine own, I would say; but if mine, then yours,
And so all yours. O, these naughty times 18
Puts bars between the owners and their rights!
And so, though yours, not yours. Prove it so, 20
Let fortune go to hell for it, not I.
I speak too long, but 'tis to peize the time, 22
To eche it and to draw it out in length, 23
To stay you from election.

BASSANIO
Let me choose,
For as I am, I live upon the rack.

PORTIA
Upon the rack, Bassanio? Then confess 26
What treason there is mingled with your love. 27

BASSANIO
None but that ugly treason of mistrust, 28
Which makes me fear th' enjoying of my love. 29
There may as well be amity and life
'Tween snow and fire, as treason and my love.

PORTIA
Ay, but I fear you speak upon the rack,
Where men enforced do speak anything.

BASSANIO
Promise me life, and I'll confess the truth.

PORTIA
Well then, confess and live.

BASSANIO
Confess and love
Had been the very sum of my confession.
O happy torment, when my torturer
Doth teach me answers for deliverance!
But let me to my fortune and the caskets. 39

PORTIA
Away, then! I am lock'd in one of them.
If you do love me, you will find me out.
Nerissa and the rest, stand all aloof.
Let music sound while he doth make his choice;
Then, if he lose, he makes a swan-like end, 44
Fading in music. That the comparison
May stand more proper, my eye shall be the stream
And wat'ry death-bed for him. He may win;
And what is music then? Then music is
Even as the flourish when true subjects bow 49
To a new-crowned monarch. Such it is
As are those dulcet sounds in break of day
That creep into the dreaming bridegroom's ear
And summon him to marriage. Now he goes,
With no less presence, but with much more love,
Than young Alcides, when he did redeem 55
The virgin tribute paid by howling Troy 56
To the sea-monster. I stand for sacrifice; 57
The rest aloof are the Dardanian wives, 58
With bleared visages, come forth to view 59
The issue of th' exploit. Go, Hercules! 60
Live thou, I live. With much, much more dismay 61
I view the fight than thou that mak'st the fray.

A song, the whilst Bassanio comments on the caskets to himself.

[Song.]

Tell me where is fancy bred, 63
Or in the heart or in the head? 64
How begot, how nourished?
Reply, reply.
It is engend'red in the eyes, 67
With gazing fed, and fancy dies
In the cradle where it lies. 69
Let us all ring fancy's knell.
I'll begin it—Ding, dong, bell.

ALL
Ding, dong, bell.

BASSANIO
So may the outward shows be least themselves; 73
The world is still deceiv'd with ornament. 74
In law, what plea so tainted and corrupt
But, being season'd with a gracious voice,
Obscures the show of evil? In religion,
What damned error but some sober brow
Will bless it and approve it with a text, 79
Hiding the grossness with fair ornament?
There is no vice so simple but assumes 81
Some mark of virtue on his outward parts.
How many cowards, whose hearts are all as false
As stairs of sand, wear yet upon their chins 84
The beards of Hercules and frowning Mars,
Who, inward search'd, have livers white as milk! 86
And these assume but valor's excrement 87
To render them redoubted. Look on beauty, 88
And you shall see 'tis purchas'd by the weight,
Which therein works a miracle in nature,
Making them lightest that wear most of it. 91
So are those crisped snaky golden locks, 92
Which maketh such wanton gambols with the wind
Upon supposed fairness, often known 94
To be the dowry of a second head, 95
The skull that bred them in the sepulcher. 96
Thus ornament is but the guiled shore 97
To a most dangerous sea, the beauteous scarf
Veiling an Indian beauty; in a word, 99
The seeming truth which cunning times put on
To entrap the wisest. Therefore, thou gaudy gold,
Hard food for Midas, I will none of thee; 102
Nor none of thee, thou pale and common drudge 103
'Tween man and man. But thou, thou meager lead, 104
Which rather threaten'st than dost promise aught,

18 naughty worthless, wicked **20 Prove it so** if it prove so **22 peize** retard (by hanging on of weights) **23 eche** eke out, augment **26–27 confess What treason** (The rack was used to force traitors to confess.) **28 mistrust** misapprehension **29 fear** fearful about **39 fortune . . . caskets** (Presumably the curtains are drawn at about this point, as in the previous "casket" scenes, revealing the three caskets.) **44 swan-like** (Swans were believed to sing when they came to die.) **49 flourish** sounding of trumpets **55 Alcides** (Hercules rescued Hesione, daughter of the Trojan king Laomedon, from a monster to which, by command of Neptune, she was about to be sacrificed. Hercules was rewarded, however, not with the lady's love, but with a famous pair of horses.) **56 howling** lamenting **57 stand for sacrifice** represent the sacrificial victim **58 Dardanian** Trojan **59 bleared** weeping **60 issue** outcome

61 Live thou if you live **63 fancy** love **64 Or** either **67 eyes** (Love entered the heart especially through the eyes.) **69 In the cradle** i.e., in its infancy, in the eyes **73 be least themselves** least represent the inner reality **74 still** ever **79 approve** confirm **81 simple** unadulterated **84 stairs** steps **86 livers** (The liver was thought to be the seat of courage; for it to be deserted by the blood would be the condition of cowardice.) **87 excrement** outgrowth, such as a beard (as in this case) or fingernails **88 redoubted** feared **91 lightest** most lascivious (with pun on the sense of *least heavy*) **92 crisped** curly **94 Upon supposed fairness** i.e., on a woman supposed beautiful and fairhaired **95–96 To . . . sepulcher** i.e., to be a wig of hair taken from a woman now dead **97 guiled** treacherous **99 Indian** i.e., swarthy, not fair **102 Midas** the Phrygian king whose touch turned everything to gold, including his food **103–104 pale . . . man** i.e., silver, used in commerce

Thy paleness moves me more than eloquence;
And here choose I. Joy be the consequence!

PORTIA [*Aside*]
How all the other passions fleet to air,
As doubtful thoughts, and rash-embrac'd despair,
And shudd'ring fear, and green-ey'd jealousy!
O love, be moderate; allay thy ecstasy,
In measure rain thy joy, scant this excess!
I feel too much thy blessing. Make it less,
For fear I surfeit.

BASSANIO What find I here?
[*Opening the leaden casket.*]
Fair Portia's counterfeit! What demi-god
Hath come so near creation? Move these eyes?
Or whether, riding on the balls of mine,
Seem they in motion? Here are sever'd lips,
Parted with sugar breath; so sweet a bar
Should sunder such sweet friends. Here in her hairs
The painter plays the spider, and hath woven
A golden mesh t' entrap the hearts of men
Faster than gnats in cobwebs. But her eyes—
How could he see to do them? Having made one,
Methinks it should have power to steal both his
And leave itself unfurnish'd. Yet look how far
The substance of my praise doth wrong this shadow
In underprizing it, so far this shadow
Doth limp behind the substance. Here's the scroll,
The continent and summary of my fortune.
[*Reads.*] "You that choose not by the view,
Chance as fair, and choose as true!
Since this fortune falls to you,
Be content and seek no new.
If you be well pleas'd with this
And hold your fortune for your bliss,
Turn you where your lady is
And claim her with a loving kiss."
A gentle scroll. Fair lady, by your leave; [*Kiss.*]
I come by note, to give and to receive.
Like one of two contending in a prize,
That thinks he hath done well in people's eyes,
Hearing applause and universal shout,
Giddy in spirit, still gazing in a doubt
Whether those peals of praise be his or no,
So, thrice-fair lady, stand I, even so,
As doubtful whether what I see be true,
Until confirm'd, sign'd, ratified by you.

PORTIA
You see me, Lord Bassanio, where I stand,
Such as I am. Though for myself alone
I would not be ambitious in my wish,
To wish myself much better, yet for you
I would be trebled twenty times myself,
A thousand times more fair, ten thousand times
More rich, that only to stand high in your account,
I might in virtues, beauties, livings, friends,
Exceed account. But the full sum of me
Is sum of something, which, to term in gross,
Is an unlesson'd girl, unschool'd, unpracticed;
Happy in this, she is not yet so old
But she may learn; happier than this,
She is not bred so dull but she can learn;
Happiest of all is that her gentle spirit
Commits itself to yours to be directed,
As from her lord, her governor, her king.
Myself and what is mine to you and yours
Is now converted. But now I was the lord
Of this fair mansion, master of my servants,
Queen o'er myself; and even now, but now,
This house, these servants, and this same myself
Are yours, my lord's. I give them with this ring,
Which when you part from, lose, or give away,
Let it presage the ruin of your love
And be my vantage to exclaim on you.
[*She puts a ring on his finger.*]

BASSANIO
Madam, you have bereft me of all words.
Only my blood speaks to you in my veins,
And there is such confusion in my powers
As, after some oration fairly spoke
By a beloved prince, there doth appear
Among the buzzing pleased multitude,
Where every something, being blent together,
Turns to a wild of nothing, save of joy
Express'd and not express'd. But when this ring
Parts from this finger, then parts life from hence.
O, then be bold to say Bassanio's dead!

NERISSA
My lord and lady, it is now our time,
That have stood by and seen our wishes prosper,
To cry, good joy. Good joy, my lord and lady!

GRATIANO
My lord Bassanio and my gentle lady,
I wish you all the joy that you can wish—
For I am sure you can wish none from me.
And when your honors mean to solemnize
The bargain of your faith, I do beseech you,
Even at that time I may be married too.

BASSANIO
With all my heart, so thou canst get a wife.

GRATIANO
I thank your lordship, you have got me one.
My eyes, my lord, can look as swift as yours.
You saw the mistress, I beheld the maid;
You lov'd, I lov'd; for intermission
No more pertains to me, my lord, than you.
Your fortune stood upon the caskets there,
And so did mine too, as the matter falls;
For wooing here until I sweat again,
And swearing till my very roof was dry
With oaths of love, at last, if promise last,
I got a promise of this fair one here

109 As such as **112 rain** rain down, pour forth. **scant** lessen **115 counterfeit** portrait. **demi-god** i.e., the painter as creator **119 so sweet a bar** i.e., Portia's breath **120 sweet friends** i.e., her lips **123 Faster** more tightly **126 unfurnish'd** i.e., without a companion. **look how far** however far **127 shadow** painting **129 the substance** the subject, i.e., Portia **130 continent** container **132 Chance as fair** hazard as fortunately **140 by note** i.e., as directed in writing **141 prize** competition **145 his** for him **155 account** estimation **156 livings** possessions

157 account calculation **158 something** i.e., at least something. **term in gross** relate in full **167 But now** only a short while ago **174 exclaim on** reproach **177 powers** faculties **187 That** we who **191 none from me** i.e., none more than you have already wished for yourselves **195 so** provided **199 intermission** delay (in loving) **203 sweat again** sweated repeatedly **204 roof** roof of my mouth **205 if promise last** i.e., if Nerissa's promise should last, hold out

To have her love, provided that your fortune
Achiev'd her mistress.

PORTIA
Is this true, Nerissa?

NERISSA
Madam, it is, so you stand pleas'd withal. 209

BASSANIO
And do you, Gratiano, mean good faith?

GRATIANO Yes, faith, my lord.

BASSANIO
Our feast shall be much honored in your marriage.

GRATIANO We'll play with them the first boy for a thousand ducats. 213

NERISSA What, and stake down? 215

GRATIANO No; we shall ne'er win at that sport, and stake down.
But who comes here? Lorenzo and his infidel?
What, and my old Venetian friend Salerio?

Enter Lorenzo, Jessica, and Salerio, a Messenger from Venice.

BASSANIO
Lorenzo and Salerio, welcome hither,
If that the youth of my new int'rest here 221
Have power to bid you welcome. By your leave,
I bid my very friends and countrymen, 223
Sweet Portia, welcome.

PORTIA
So do I, my lord.
They are entirely welcome.

LORENZO
I thank your honor. For my part, my lord,
My purpose was not to have seen you here,
But meeting with Salerio by the way,
He did intreat me, past all saying nay,
To come with him along.

SALERIO
I did, my lord,
And I have reason for it. Signor Antonio
Commends him to you. [*Gives Bassanio a letter.*]

BASSANIO
Ere I ope his letter, 232
I pray you tell me how my good friend doth.

SALERIO
Not sick, my lord, unless it be in mind,
Nor well, unless in mind. His letter there
Will show you his estate. *Open the letter.* 236

GRATIANO
Nerissa, cheer yond stranger; bid her welcome.
Your hand, Salerio. What's the news from Venice?
How doth that royal merchant, good Antonio? 239
I know he will be glad of our success;
We are the Jasons, we have won the fleece. 241

SALERIO
I would you had won the fleece that he hath lost.

PORTIA
There are some shrewd contents in yond same paper, 243
That steals the color from Bassanio's cheek—
Some dear friend dead, else nothing in the world
Could turn so much the constitution
Of any constant man. What, worse and worse! 247
With leave, Bassanio; I am half yourself,
And I must freely have the half of anything
That this same paper brings you.

BASSANIO
O sweet Portia,
Here are a few of the unpleasant'st words
That ever blotted paper! Gentle lady,
When I did first impart my love to you,
I freely told you all the wealth I had
Ran in my veins, I was a gentleman;
And then I told you true. And yet, dear lady,
Rating myself at nothing, you shall see
How much I was a braggart. When I told you
My state was nothing, I should then have told you 259
That I was worse than nothing; for, indeed,
I have engag'd myself to a dear friend,
Engag'd my friend to his mere enemy, 262
To feed my means. Here is a letter, lady,
The paper as the body of my friend,
And every word in it a gaping wound
Issuing life-blood. But is it true, Salerio?
Hath all his ventures fail'd? What, not one hit?
From Tripolis, from Mexico, and England,
From Lisbon, Barbary, and India?
And not one vessel scape the dreadful touch
Of merchant-marring rocks?

SALERIO
Not one, my lord. 271
Besides, it should appear, that if he had
The present money to discharge the Jew, 273
He would not take it. Never did I know 274
A creature that did bear the shape of man
So keen and greedy to confound a man.
He plies the Duke at morning and at night,
And doth impeach the freedom of the state 278
If they deny him justice. Twenty merchants,
The Duke himself, and the magnificoes 280
Of greatest port, have all persuaded with him, 281
But none can drive him from the envious plea
Of forfeiture, of justice, and his bond.

JESSICA
When I was with him I have heard him swear
To Tubal and to Chus, his countrymen,
That he would rather have Antonio's flesh
Than twenty times the value of the sum
That he did owe him; and I know, my lord,
If law, authority, and power deny not,
It will go hard with poor Antonio.

PORTIA
Is it your dear friend that is thus in trouble?

BASSANIO
The dearest friend to me, the kindest man,
The best-condition'd and unwearied spirit 293

209 so provided **213 play** wager **215 stake down** cash placed in advance. (But Gratiano, in his reply, turns the phrase into a bawdy joke; *stake down* to him suggests a nonerect phallus.) **221 youth . . . int'rest** i.e., newness of my household authority **223 very** true **232 Commends him** desires to be remembered **236 estate** condition **239 royal merchant** i.e., chief among merchants **241 Jasons . . . fleece** (Cf. I.i.170–72.) **243 shrewd** cursed, grievous

247 constant settled, not swayed by passion **259 state** estate **262 mere** absolute **271 merchant** merchant ship **273 present** ready. **discharge** pay off **274 He** i.e., Shylock **278 impeach . . . state** i.e., call in question the ability of Venice to defend legally the freedom of commerce of its citizens **280 magnificoes** chief men of Venice **281 port** dignity. **persuaded** argued **293 best-condition'd** best natured

In doing courtesies, and one in whom
The ancient Roman honor more appears
Than any that draws breath in Italy.

PORTIA
What sum owes he the Jew?

BASSANIO
For me, three thousand ducats.

PORTIA
What, no more?
Pay him six thousand, and deface the bond;
Double six thousand, and then treble that,
Before a friend of this description
Shall lose a hair through Bassanio's fault.
First go with me to church and call me wife,
And then away to Venice to your friend;
For never shall you lie by Portia's side
With an unquiet soul. You shall have gold
To pay the petty debt twenty times over.
When it is paid, bring your true friend along.
My maid Nerissa and myself meantime
Will live as maids and widows. Come, away!
For you shall hence upon your wedding-day.
Bid your friends welcome, show a merry cheer;
Since you are dear bought, I will love you dear.
But let me hear the letter of your friend.

BASSANIO [*Reads*] "Sweet Bassanio, my ships have all miscarried, my creditors grow cruel, my estate is very low, my bond to the Jew is forfeit; and since in paying it, it is impossible I should live, all debts are clear'd between you and I, if I might but see you at my death. Notwithstanding, use your pleasure; if your love do not persuade you to come, let not my letter."

PORTIA
O love, dispatch all business, and be gone!

BASSANIO
Since I have your good leave to go away,
I will make haste; but, till I come again,
No bed shall e'er be guilty of my stay,
Nor rest be interposer 'twixt us twain. *Exeunt.*

[SCENE III]

Enter [Shylock] the Jew and Solanio and Antonio and the Jailer.

SHYLOCK
Jailer, look to him. Tell not me of mercy.
This is the fool that lent out money gratis.
Jailer, look to him.

ANTONIO
Hear me yet, good Shylock.

SHYLOCK
I'll have my bond. Speak not against my bond!
I have sworn an oath that I will have my bond.
Thou call'dst me dog before thou hadst a cause;
But, since I am a dog, beware my fangs.
The Duke shall grant me justice. I do wonder,
Thou naughty jailer, that thou art so fond
To come abroad with him at his request.

ANTONIO
I pray thee, hear me speak.

SHYLOCK
I'll have my bond. I will not hear thee speak.
I'll have my bond, and therefore speak no more.
I'll not be made a soft and dull-ey'd fool,
To shake the head, relent, and sigh, and yield
To Christian intercessors. Follow not;
I'll have no speaking. I will have my bond. *Exit Jew.*

SOLANIO
It is the most impenetrable cur
That ever kept with men.

ANTONIO
Let him alone.
I'll follow him no more with bootless prayers.
He seeks my life. His reason well I know:
I oft deliver'd from his forfeitures
Many that have at times made moan to me;
Therefore he hates me.

SOLANIO
I am sure the Duke
Will never grant this forfeiture to hold.

ANTONIO
The Duke cannot deny the course of law;
For the commodity that strangers have
With us in Venice, if it be denied,
Will much impeach the justice of the state,
Since that the trade and profit of the city
Consisteth of all nations. Therefore, go.
These griefs and losses have so bated me,
That I shall hardly spare a pound of flesh
Tomorrow to my bloody creditor.
Well, jailer, on. Pray God Bassanio come
To see me pay his debt, and then I care not! *Exeunt.*

[SCENE IV]

Enter Portia, Nerissa, Lorenzo, Jessica, and [Balthasar,] a Man of Portia's.

LORENZO
Madam, although I speak it in your presence,
You have a noble and a true conceit
Of god-like amity, which appears most strongly
In bearing thus the absence of your lord.
But if you knew to whom you show this honor,
How true a gentleman you send relief,
How dear a lover of my lord your husband,
I know you would be prouder of the work
Than customary bounty can enforce you.

PORTIA
I never did repent for doing good,

312 cheer countenance
III.iii. Location: Venice. A street.

9 naughty worthless. **fond** foolish **19 kept** associated, dwelt **20 bootless** unavailing **27 commodity** facilities or privileges for trading. **strangers** noncitizens, including Jews **32 bated** reduced
III.iv. Location: Belmont. Portia's house.
2 conceit understanding **9 Than . . . you** than ordinary benevolence can make you

Nor shall not now; for in companions
That do converse and waste the time together,
Whose souls do bear an egall yoke of love,
There must be needs a like proportion
Of lineaments, of manners, and of spirit;
Which makes me think that this Antonio,
Being the bosom lover of my lord,
Must needs be like my lord. If it be so,
How little is the cost I have bestowed
In purchasing the semblance of my soul
From out the state of hellish cruelty!
This comes too near the praising of myself;
Therefore no more of it. Hear other things:
Lorenzo, I commit into your hands
The husbandry and manage of my house
Until my lord's return. For mine own part,
I have toward heaven breath'd a secret vow
To live in prayer and contemplation,
Only attended by Nerissa here,
Until her husband and my lord's return.
There is a monastery two miles off,
And there we will abide. I do desire you
Not to deny this imposition,
The which my love and some necessity
Now lays upon you.

LORENZO Madam, with all my heart;
I shall obey you in all fair commands.

PORTIA
My people do already know my mind,
And will acknowledge you and Jessica
In place of Lord Bassanio and myself.
So fare you well, till we shall meet again.

LORENZO
Fair thoughts and happy hours attend on you!

JESSICA
I wish your ladyship all heart's content.

PORTIA
I thank you for your wish, and am well pleas'd
To wish it back on you. Fare you well, Jessica.
Exeunt [*Jessica and Lorenzo*].
Now, Balthasar,
As I have ever found thee honest-true,
So let me find thee still. Take this same letter,
[*Gives a letter.*]
And use thou all th' endeavor of a man
In speed to Padua. See thou render this
Into my cousin's hands, Doctor Bellario;
And look what notes and garments he doth give
thee,
Bring them, I pray thee, with imagin'd speed
Unto the traject, to the common ferry
Which trades to Venice. Waste no time in words,
But get thee gone. I shall be there before thee.

BALTHASAR
Madam, I go with all convenient speed. [*Exit.*]

PORTIA
Come on, Nerissa, I have work in hand
That you yet know not of. We'll see our husbands
Before they think of us.

NERISSA Shall they see us?

PORTIA
They shall, Nerissa, but in such a habit
That they shall think we are accomplished
With that we lack. I'll hold thee any wager,
When we are both accoutred like young men,
I'll prove the prettier fellow of the two,
And wear my dagger with the braver grace,
And speak between the change of man and boy
With a reed voice, and turn two mincing steps
Into a manly stride, and speak of frays
Like a fine bragging youth, and tell quaint lies,
How honorable ladies sought my love,
Which, I denying, they fell sick and died—
I could not do withal! Then I'll repent,
And wish, for all that, that I had not kill'd them;
And twenty of these puny lies I'll tell,
That men shall swear I have discontinued school
Above a twelvemonth. I have within my mind
A thousand raw tricks of these bragging Jacks,
Which I will practice.

NERISSA Why, shall we turn to men?

PORTIA
Fie, what a question 's that,
If thou wert near a lewd interpreter!
But come, I'll tell thee all my whole device
When I am in my coach, which stays for us
At the park gate; and therefore haste away,
For we must measure twenty miles today. *Exeunt.*

[SCENE V]

Enter [*Launcelot the*] *Clown and Jessica.*

LAUNCELOT Yes, truly, for, look you, the sins of the father are to be laid upon the children; therefore, I promise you, I fear you. I was always plain with you, and so now I speak my agitation of the matter. Therefore be o' good cheer, for truly I think you are damn'd. There is but one hope in it that can do you any good, and that is but a kind of bastard hope neither.

JESSICA And what hope is that, I pray thee?

LAUNCELOT Marry, you may partly hope that your father got you not, that you are not the Jew's daughter.

JESSICA That were a kind of bastard hope, indeed! So the sins of my mother should be visited upon me.

LAUNCELOT Truly then I fear you are damn'd both by

12 waste spend **13 egall** equal **20 the semblance of my soul** i.e., Antonio, so like my Bassanio **25 husbandry and manage** care of the household **33 deny this imposition** refuse this charge imposed **51 look what** whatever **52 imagin'd speed** speed of imagination, as quick as thought **53 traject** ferry. (Italian *traghetto.*) **54 trades** plies back and forth

60 habit apparel, garb **61 accomplished** supplied **69 quaint** elaborate, clever **72 do withal** help it **76 Above** more than **77 Jacks** fellows **78 turn to** turn into. (But Portia sees the occasion for a bawdy quibble on the idea of *turning toward, lying next to.*)

III.v. Location: Belmont. A garden.
3 fear you fear for you **4 agitation** (Blunder for *cogitation?*) **7 neither** i.e., to be sure **10 got** begot

father and mother. Thus when I shun Scylla, your father, I fall into Charybdis, your mother. Well, you are gone both ways.

JESSICA I shall be sav'd by my husband. He hath made me a Christian.

LAUNCELOT Truly, the more to blame he! We were Christians enow before; e'en as many as could well live one by another. This making of Christians will raise the price of hogs. If we grow all to be pork-eaters, we shall not shortly have a rasher on the coals for money.

Enter Lorenzo.

JESSICA I'll tell my husband, Launcelot, what you say. Here he comes.

LORENZO I shall grow jealous of you shortly, Launcelot, if you thus get my wife into corners.

JESSICA Nay, you need not fear us, Lorenzo. Launcelot and I are out. He tells me flatly there's no mercy for me in heaven because I am a Jew's daughter; and he says you are no good member of the commonwealth, for in converting Jews to Christians you raise the price of pork.

LORENZO I shall answer that better to the commonwealth than you can the getting up of the Negro's belly. The Moor is with child by you, Launcelot.

LAUNCELOT It is much that the Moor should be more than reason; but if she be less than an honest woman, she is indeed more than I took her for.

LORENZO How every fool can play upon the word! I think the best grace of wit will shortly turn into silence, and discourse grow commendable in none only but parrots. Go in, sirrah; bid them prepare for dinner.

LAUNCELOT That is done, sir. They have all stomachs.

LORENZO Goodly Lord, what a wit-snapper are you! Then bid them prepare dinner.

LAUNCELOT That is done too, sir; only "cover" is the word.

LORENZO Will you cover then, sir?

LAUNCELOT Not so, sir, neither! I know my duty.

LORENZO Yet more quarreling with occasion! Wilt thou show the whole wealth of thy wit in an instant? I pray thee, understand a plain man in his plain meaning: go to thy fellows, bid them cover the table, serve in the meat, and we will come in to dinner.

LAUNCELOT For the table, sir, it shall be serv'd in; for the meat, sir, it shall be cover'd; for your coming in to dinner, sir, why, let it be as humors and conceits shall govern. *Exit Clown.*

LORENZO
O dear discretion, how his words are suited!
The fool hath planted in his memory
An army of good words; and I do know
A many fools, that stand in better place,
Garnish'd like him, that for a tricksy word
Defy the matter. How cheer'st thou, Jessica?
And now, good sweet, say thy opinion,
How dost thou like the Lord Bassanio's wife?

JESSICA
Past all expressing. It is very meet
The Lord Bassanio live an upright life,
For, having such a blessing in his lady,
He finds the joys of heaven here on earth;
And if on earth he do not merit it,
In reason he should never come to heaven.
Why, if two gods should play some heavenly match
And on the wager lay two earthly women,
And Portia one, there must be something else
Pawn'd with the other, for the poor rude world
Hath not her fellow.

LORENZO Even such a husband
Hast thou of me as she is for a wife.

JESSICA
Nay, but ask my opinion too of that!

LORENZO
I will anon. First let us go to dinner.

JESSICA
Nay, let me praise you while I have a stomach.

LORENZO
No, pray thee, let it serve for table-talk;
Then, howsome'er thou speak'st, 'mong other things
I shall digest it.

JESSICA Well, I'll set you forth. *Exeunt.*

[ACT IV • SCENE I]

Enter the Duke, the Magnificoes, Antonio, Bassanio, [Salerio,] and Gratiano [with others. The judges take their places.]

DUKE
What, is Antonio here?

ANTONIO
Ready, so please your Grace.

DUKE
I am sorry for thee. Thou art come to answer
A stony adversary, an inhuman wretch
Uncapable of pity, void and empty
From any dram of mercy.

14, 15 Scylla, Charybdis twin dangers of *The Odyssey,* xii.255, a monster and a whirlpool guarding the straits presumably between Italy and Sicily **16 gone** done for **20 enow** enough; i.e., there were enough of us **21 one by another** together **23 rasher** i.e., of bacon **23–24 for money** even for ready money, at any price **30 are out** have fallen out **38–39 more than reason** larger than is reasonable (with wordplay on *Moor,* more, continued in l. 40) **39 honest** chaste **42 best grace** highest quality **46 stomachs** appetites **49, 51 cover** spread the table for the meal. (But in his next speech Launcelot uses the word to mean *put on one's hat.*) **53 quarreling with occasion** i.e., quibbling at every word **57 meat** food **58 table** (Here Launcelot quibblingly uses the word to mean the food itself.) **59 cover'd** (Here used in the sense of providing a cover for each separate dish.) **60 humors and conceits** whims and fancies

62 discretion discrimination. **suited** suited to the occasion **65 A many** many. **better place** higher social station **66 Garnish'd** i.e., furnished with words **66–67 that . . . matter** who for the sake of ingenious wordplay do violence to common sense **67 How cheer'st thou** i.e., what cheer **77 lay** stake **78 else** more **79 Pawn'd** staked, wagered **84 stomach** (1) appetite (2) inclination **86 howsome'er** howsoever **87 set you forth** (1) serve you up, as at a feast (2) set forth your praises

IV.i. Location: Venice. A court of justice. Benches, etc., are provided for the justices.

ANTONIO I have heard
Your Grace hath ta'en great pains to qualify
His rigorous course; but since he stands obdurate
And that no lawful means can carry me
Out of his envy's reach, I do oppose
My patience to his fury, and am arm'd
To suffer, with a quietness of spirit,
The very tyranny and rage of his.

DUKE
Go one, and call the Jew into the court.

SALERIO
He is ready at the door; he comes, my lord.

Enter Shylock.

DUKE
Make room, and let him stand before our face.
Shylock, the world thinks, and I think so too,
That thou but leadest this fashion of thy malice
To the last hour of act, and then 'tis thought
Thou 'lt show thy mercy and remorse more strange
Than is thy strange apparent cruelty;
And where thou now exacts the penalty,
Which is a pound of this poor merchant's flesh,
Thou wilt not only loose the forfeiture,
But, touch'd with human gentleness and love,
Forgive a moi'ty of the principal,
Glancing an eye of pity on his losses
That have of late so huddled on his back—
Enow to press a royal merchant down
And pluck commiseration of his state
From brassy bosoms and rough hearts of flint,
From stubborn Turks and Tartars, never train'd
To offices of tender courtesy.
We all expect a gentle answer, Jew.

SHYLOCK
I have possess'd your Grace of what I purpose,
And by our holy Sabbath have I sworn
To have the due and forfeit of my bond.
If you deny it, let the danger light
Upon your charter and your city's freedom.
You'll ask me why I rather choose to have
A weight of carrion flesh than to receive
Three thousand ducats. I'll not answer that,
But, say, it is my humor. Is it answer'd?
What if my house be troubled with a rat
And I be pleas'd to give ten thousand ducats
To have it ban'd? What, are you answer'd yet?
Some men there are love not a gaping pig,
Some that are mad if they behold a cat,
And others, when the bagpipe sings i' th' nose,
Cannot contain their urine; for affection,
Mistress of passion, sways it to the mood
Of what it likes or loathes. Now, for your answer:
As there is no firm reason to be rend'red
Why he cannot abide a gaping pig,
Why he a harmless necessary cat,
Why he, a woolen bagpipe, but of force
Must yield to such inevitable shame
As to offend, himself being offended;
So can I give no reason, nor I will not,
More than a lodg'd hate and a certain loathing
I bear Antonio, that I follow thus
A losing suit against him. Are you answered?

BASSANIO
This is no answer, thou unfeeling man,
To excuse the current of thy cruelty.

SHYLOCK
I am not bound to please thee with my answers.

BASSANIO
Do all men kill the things they do not love?

SHYLOCK
Hates any man the thing he would not kill?

BASSANIO
Every offense is not a hate at first.

SHYLOCK
What, wouldst thou have a serpent sting thee twice?

ANTONIO
I pray you, think you question with the Jew.
You may as well go stand upon the beach
And bid the main flood bate his usual height;
You may as well use question with the wolf
Why he hath made the ewe bleat for the lamb;
You may as well forbid the mountain pines
To wag their high tops and to make no noise
When they are fretten with the gusts of heaven;
You may as well do any thing most hard
As seek to soften that—than which what's
  harder?—
His Jewish heart. Therefore, I do beseech you,
Make no moe offers, use no farther means,
But with all brief and plain conveniency
Let me have judgment and the Jew his will.

BASSANIO
For thy three thousand ducats here is six.

SHYLOCK
If every ducat in six thousand ducats
Were in six parts and every part a ducat
I would not draw them. I would have my bond.

DUKE
How shalt thou hope for mercy, rend'ring none?

SHYLOCK
What judgment shall I dread, doing no wrong?
You have among you many a purchas'd slave,
Which, like your asses and your dogs and mules,
You use in abject and in slavish parts,
Because you bought them. Shall I say to you,
"Let them be free, marry them to your heirs!
Why sweat they under burdens? Let their beds
Be made as soft as yours, and let their palates
Be season'd with such viands"? You will answer

6 dram 60 grains apothecaries' weight, a tiny quantity **7 qualify** moderate **13 tyranny** cruelty **16 our** (The royal plural.) **18 thou . . . fashion** you only maintain this pretense or form **19 act** action, performance **20 remorse** pity. **strange** remarkable **24 loose** release, waive **26 moi'ty** part, portion **29 Enow** enough **35 possess'd** informed **38 danger** injury **39 Upon . . . freedom** (See III.ii.278.) **43 humor** whim **46 ban'd** killed, especially by poison or *ratsbane* **47 gaping pig** pig roasted whole with its mouth open **50 affection** feeling, inclination

54, 55, 56 he, he, he one person, another, yet another **56 woolen** i.e., with flannel-covered bag **60 lodg'd** settled, steadfast **62 losing** unprofitable **70 think** bear in mind. **question** argue **72 main flood** sea at high tide. **bate** abate **77 fretten** fretted **87 draw** receive **92 parts** duties, capacities

"The slaves are ours." So do I answer you:
The pound of flesh, which I demand of him,
Is dearly bought as mine, and I will have it.
If you deny me, fie upon your law!
There is no force in the decrees of Venice.
I stand for judgment. Answer: shall I have it?

DUKE
Upon my power I may dismiss this court,
Unless Bellario, a learned doctor,
Whom I have sent for to determine this,
Come here today.

SALERIO My lord, here stays without
A messenger with letters from the doctor,
New come from Padua.

DUKE
Bring us the letters. Call the messenger.

BASSANIO
Good cheer, Antonio! What, man, courage yet!
The Jew shall have my flesh, blood, bones, and all,
Ere thou shalt lose for me one drop of blood.

ANTONIO
I am a tainted wether of the flock,
Meetest for death. The weakest kind of fruit
Drops earliest to the ground, and so let me.
You cannot better be employ'd, Bassanio,
Than to live still and write mine epitaph.

Enter Nerissa [dressed like a lawyer's clerk].

DUKE
Came you from Padua, from Bellario?

NERISSA
From both, my lord. Bellario greets your Grace.
[Presents a letter. Shylock whets his knife.]

BASSANIO
Why dost thou whet thy knife so earnestly?

SHYLOCK
To cut the forfeiture from that bankrupt there.

GRATIANO
Not on thy sole, but on thy soul, harsh Jew,
Thou mak'st thy knife keen; but no metal can,
No, not the hangman's axe, bear half the keenness
Of thy sharp envy. Can no prayers pierce thee?

SHYLOCK
No, none that thou hast wit enough to make.

GRATIANO
O, be thou damn'd, inexecrable dog!
And for thy life let justice be accus'd.
Thou almost mak'st me waver in my faith
To hold opinion with Pythagoras,
That souls of animals infuse themselves
Into the trunks of men. Thy currish spirit
Govern'd a wolf, who, hang'd for human slaughter,
Even from the gallows did his fell soul fleet,
And, whilst thou layest in thy unhallowed dam,
Infus'd itself in thee; for thy desires
Are wolvish, bloody, starv'd, and ravenous.

SHYLOCK
Till thou canst rail the seal from off my bond,
Thou but offend'st thy lungs to speak so loud.
Repair thy wit, good youth, or it will fall
To cureless ruin. I stand here for law.

DUKE
This letter from Bellario doth commend
A young and learned doctor to our court.
Where is he?

NERISSA He attendeth here hard by
To know your answer, whether you'll admit him.

DUKE
With all my heart. Some three or four of you
Go give him courteous conduct to this place.
[Exeunt some.]
Meantime the court shall hear Bellario's letter.

[Reads.] "Your Grace shall understand that at the receipt of your letter I am very sick; but in the instant that your messenger came, in loving visitation was with me a young doctor of Rome. His name is Balthasar. I acquainted him with the cause in controversy between the Jew and Antonio the merchant. We turned o'er many books together. He is furnish'd with my opinion, which, better'd with his own learning, the greatness whereof I cannot enough commend, comes with him, at my importunity, to fill up your Grace's request in my stead. I beseech you, let his lack of years be no impediment to let him lack a reverend estimation; for I never knew so young a body with so old a head. I leave him to your gracious acceptance, whose trial shall better publish his commendation."

Enter Portia for Balthasar [dressed like a doctor of laws, escorted].

You hear the learn'd Bellario, what he writes;
And here, I take it, is the doctor come.
Give me your hand. Come you from old Bellario?

PORTIA
I did, my lord.

DUKE You are welcome. Take your place.
[Portia takes her place.]
Are you acquainted with the difference
That holds this present question in the court?

PORTIA
I am informed throughly of the cause.
Which is the merchant here, and which the Jew?

DUKE
Antonio and old Shylock, both stand forth.

PORTIA
Is your name Shylock?

SHYLOCK Shylock is my name.

PORTIA
Of a strange nature is the suit you follow,

104 Upon in accordance with **107 stays without** waits outside **114 tainted wether** old and diseased ram **115 Meetest** fittest **125 hangman's** executioner's **128 inexecrable** that cannot be execrated too much **129 for thy life** i.e., because you are allowed to live **131 Pythagoras** ancient Greek philosopher who argued for the transmigration of souls **134 hang'd for human slaughter** (A possible allusion to the ancient practice of trying and punishing animals for various crimes.) **135 fell** fierce, cruel. **fleet** flit

140 offend'st injurest **142 cureless** incurable **150 [Reads.]** (In many modern editions, the reading of the letter is assigned to a clerk, but the original text gives no such indication.) **159 comes with him** i.e., my opinion is brought by him **161 to let him lack** such as would deprive him of **164 trial** testing, performance. **publish** make known. **s.d. for** i.e., disguised as **169 difference** argument **171 throughly** thoroughly. **cause** case

Yet in such rule that the Venetian law
Cannot impugn you as you do proceed.—
You stand within his danger, do you not?

ANTONIO
Ay, so he says.

PORTIA Do you confess the bond?

ANTONIO
I do.

PORTIA Then must the Jew be merciful.

SHYLOCK
On what compulsion must I? Tell me that.

PORTIA
The quality of mercy is not strain'd.
It droppeth as the gentle rain from heaven
Upon the place beneath. It is twice blest:
It blesseth him that gives and him that takes.
'Tis mightiest in the mightiest; it becomes
The throned monarch better than his crown.
His scepter shows the force of temporal power,
The attribute to awe and majesty,
Wherein doth sit the dread and fear of kings.
But mercy is above this sceptred sway;
It is enthroned in the hearts of kings;
It is an attribute to God himself;
And earthly power doth then show likest God's
When mercy seasons justice. Therefore, Jew,
Though justice be thy plea, consider this,
That, in the course of justice, none of us
Should see salvation. We do pray for mercy,
And that same prayer doth teach us all to render
The deeds of mercy. I have spoke thus much
To mitigate the justice of thy plea,
Which, if thou follow, this strict court of Venice
Must needs give sentence 'gainst the merchant there.

SHYLOCK
My deeds upon my head! I crave the law,
The penalty and forfeit of my bond.

PORTIA
Is he not able to discharge the money?

BASSANIO
Yes, here I tender it for him in the court,
Yea, twice the sum. If that will not suffice,
I will be bound to pay it ten times o'er,
On forfeit of my hands, my head, my heart.
If this will not suffice, it must appear
That malice bears down truth. And I beseech you,
Wrest once the law to your authority.
To do a great right, do a little wrong,
And curb this cruel devil of his will.

PORTIA
It must not be. There is no power in Venice
Can alter a decree established.
'Twill be recorded for a precedent,
And many an error by the same example
Will rush into the state. It cannot be.

SHYLOCK
A Daniel come to judgment! Yea, a Daniel!
O wise young judge, how I do honor thee!

PORTIA
I pray you, let me look upon the bond.

SHYLOCK
Here 'tis, most reverend doctor, here it is.
[*Gives the bond.*]

PORTIA
Shylock, there's thrice thy money off'red thee.

SHYLOCK
An oath, an oath, I have an oath in heaven!
Shall I lay perjury upon my soul?
No, not for Venice.

PORTIA Why, this bond is forfeit;
And lawfully by this the Jew may claim
A pound of flesh, to be by him cut off
Nearest the merchant's heart. Be merciful.
Take thrice thy money; bid me tear the bond.

SHYLOCK
When it is paid according to the tenure.
It doth appear you are a worthy judge;
You know the law, your exposition
Hath been most sound. I charge you by the law,
Whereof you are a well-deserving pillar,
Proceed to judgment. By my soul I swear
There is no power in the tongue of man
To alter me. I stay here on my bond.

ANTONIO
Most heartily I do beseech the court
To give the judgment.

PORTIA Why then, thus it is:
You must prepare your bosom for his knife—

SHYLOCK
O noble judge! O excellent young man!

PORTIA
For the intent and purpose of the law
Hath full relation to the penalty,
Which here appeareth due upon the bond.

SHYLOCK
'Tis very true. O wise and upright judge!
How much more elder art thou than thy looks!

PORTIA
Therefore lay bare your bosom.

SHYLOCK Ay, his breast;
So says the bond, doth it not, noble judge?
"Nearest his heart," those are the very words.

PORTIA
It is so. Are there balance here
To weigh the flesh?

SHYLOCK I have them ready.

PORTIA
Have by some surgeon, Shylock, on your charge,
To stop his wounds, lest he do bleed to death.

SHYLOCK
Is it so nominated in the bond?

176 rule order **177 impugn** find fault with **178 danger** power to do harm **182 strain'd** forced, constrained **201 To . . . plea** i.e., to show merciful reasons why you should not ask for strict justice **204 My . . . head** i.e., I am prepared to be judged, as well as live, by a code of strict justice **212 bears down truth** overwhelms righteousness **213 Wrest once** for once, forcibly subject

221 Daniel (In the Apocryphal book of *Susannah,* Daniel is the young judge who rescues Susannah from her false accusers.) **233 tenure** tenor, conditions **240 stay here on** take a stand upon (the fulfilling of) **246 Hath . . . to** is fully in accord with **253 balance** scales **255 on your charge** at your personal expense

PORTIA
It is not so express'd, but what of that?
'Twere good you do so much for charity.

SHYLOCK
I cannot find it; 'tis not in the bond.

PORTIA
You, merchant, have you anything to say?

ANTONIO
But little. I am arm'd and well prepar'd.
Give me your hand, Bassanio; fare you well!
Grieve not that I am fall'n to this for you,
For herein Fortune shows herself more kind
Than is her custom. It is still her use 266
To let the wretched man outlive his wealth,
To view with hollow eye and wrinkled brow
An age of poverty; from which ling'ring penance
Of such misery doth she cut me off.
Commend me to your honorable wife.
Tell her the process of Antonio's end, 272
Say how I lov'd you, speak me fair in death; 273
And, when the tale is told, bid her be judge
Whether Bassanio had not once a love. 275
Repent but you that you shall lose your friend, 276
And he repents not that he pays your debt;
For if the Jew do cut but deep enough,
I'll pay it instantly with all my heart.

BASSANIO
Antonio, I am married to a wife
Which is as dear to me as life itself;
But life itself, my wife, and all the world,
Are not with me esteem'd above thy life.
I would lose all, ay, sacrifice them all
Here to this devil, to deliver you.

PORTIA
Your wife would give you little thanks for that,
If she were by, to hear you make the offer.

GRATIANO
I have a wife, who, I protest, I love;
I would she were in heaven, so she could
Entreat some power to change this currish Jew.

NERISSA
'Tis well you offer it behind her back;
The wish would make else an unquiet house.

SHYLOCK [*Aside*]
These be the Christian husbands. I have a daughter;
Would any of the stock of Barrabas 294
Had been her husband rather than a Christian!—
We trifle time. I pray thee, pursue sentence.

PORTIA
A pound of that same merchant's flesh is thine.
The court awards it, and the law doth give it.

SHYLOCK
Most rightful judge!

PORTIA
And you must cut this flesh from off his breast.
The law allows it, and the court awards it.

SHYLOCK
Most learned judge! A sentence! Come, prepare!

PORTIA
Tarry a little; there is something else.
This bond doth give thee here no jot of blood;
The words expressly are "a pound of flesh."
Take then thy bond, take thou thy pound of flesh;
But, in the cutting it, if thou dost shed
One drop of Christian blood, thy lands and goods
Are, by the laws of Venice, confiscate
Unto the state of Venice.

GRATIANO
O upright judge! Mark, Jew. O learned judge!

SHYLOCK
Is that the law?

PORTIA
Thyself shalt see the act;
For, as thou urgest justice, be assur'd
Thou shalt have justice, more than thou desir'st.

GRATIANO
O learned judge! Mark, Jew, a learned judge!

SHYLOCK
I take this offer, then; pay the bond thrice
And let the Christian go.

BASSANIO
Here is the money.

PORTIA
Soft! 318
The Jew shall have all justice. Soft, no haste. 319
He shall have nothing but the penalty.

GRATIANO
O Jew! An upright judge, a learned judge!

PORTIA
Therefore prepare thee to cut off the flesh.
Shed thou no blood, nor cut thou less nor more
But just a pound of flesh. If thou tak'st more
Or less than a just pound, be it but so much
As makes it light or heavy in the substance 326
Or the division of the twentieth part 327
Of one poor scruple, nay, if the scale do turn 328
But in the estimation of a hair,
Thou diest, and all thy goods are confiscate.

GRATIANO
A second Daniel, a Daniel, Jew!
Now, infidel, I have you on the hip.

PORTIA
Why doth the Jew pause? Take thy forfeiture.

SHYLOCK
Give me my principal, and let me go.

BASSANIO
I have it ready for thee; here it is.

PORTIA
He hath refus'd it in the open court.
He shall have merely justice and his bond.

GRATIANO
A Daniel, still say I, a second Daniel!
I thank thee, Jew, for teaching me that word.

SHYLOCK
Shall I not have barely my principal?

266 still her use i.e., commonly Fortune's practice **272 process** story **273 speak me fair** speak well of me **275 a love** a friend's love **276 Repent but you** grieve only **294 Barrabas** a thief whom Pontius Pilate set free instead of Christ in response to the people's demand (see Mark 15); also, the villainous protagonist of Marlowe's *The Jew of Malta*

318 Soft i.e., not so fast **319 all** nothing but **326 substance** mass or gross weight **327 division** fraction **328 scruple** 20 grains apothecaries' weight, a small quantity

PORTIA
Thou shalt have nothing but the forfeiture,
To be so taken at thy peril, Jew.
SHYLOCK
Why, then the devil give him good of it!
I'll stay no longer question. [*Starts to go.*]
PORTIA Tarry, Jew! 344
The law hath yet another hold on you.
It is enacted in the laws of Venice,
If it be proved against an alien
That by direct or indirect attempts
He seek the life of any citizen,
The party 'gainst the which he doth contrive
Shall seize one half his goods; the other half
Comes to the privy coffer of the state, 352
And the offender's life lies in the mercy 353
Of the Duke only, 'gainst all other voice.
In which predicament, I say, thou stand'st;
For it appears, by manifest proceeding,
That indirectly and directly too
Thou hast contriv'd against the very life
Of the defendant; and thou hast incurr'd
The danger formerly by me rehears'd. 360
Down therefore and beg mercy of the Duke.
GRATIANO
Beg that thou mayst have leave to hang thyself!
And yet, thy wealth being forfeit to the state,
Thou hast not left the value of a cord;
Therefore thou must be hang'd at the state's charge. 365
DUKE
That thou shalt see the difference of our spirit,
I pardon thee thy life before thou ask it.
For half thy wealth, it is Antonio's; 368
The other half comes to the general state,
Which humbleness may drive unto a fine. 370
PORTIA
Ay, for the state, not for Antonio. 371
SHYLOCK
Nay, take my life and all! Pardon not that!
You take my house when you do take the prop
That doth sustain my house. You take my life
When you do take the means whereby I live.
PORTIA
What mercy can you render him, Antonio?
GRATIANO
A halter gratis; nothing else, for God sake. 377
ANTONIO
So please my lord the Duke and all the court
To quit the fine for one half of his goods, 379
I am content; so he will let me have
The other half in use, to render it, 381
Upon his death, unto the gentleman
That lately stole his daughter.
Two things provided more, that, for this favor,
He presently become a Christian; 385
The other, that he do record a gift,
Here in the court, of all he dies possess'd, 387
Unto his son Lorenzo and his daughter.
DUKE
He shall do this, or else I do recant
The pardon that I late pronounced here.
PORTIA
Art thou contented, Jew? What dost thou say?
SHYLOCK
I am content.
PORTIA Clerk, draw a deed of gift.
SHYLOCK
I pray you, give me leave to go from hence;
I am not well. Send the deed after me,
And I will sign it.
DUKE Get thee gone, but do it.
GRATIANO
In christ'ning shalt thou have two godfathers.
Had I been judge, thou shouldst have had ten more, 397
To bring thee to the gallows, not the font.
Exit [*Shylock*].
DUKE
Sir, I entreat you home with me to dinner.
PORTIA
I humbly do desire your Grace of pardon.
I must away this night toward Padua,
And it is meet I presently set forth.
DUKE
I am sorry that your leisure serves you not.
Antonio, gratify this gentleman, 404
For, in my mind, you are much bound to him.
Exeunt Duke and his train.
BASSANIO
Most worthy gentleman, I and my friend
Have by your wisdom been this day acquitted
Of grievous penalties, in lieu whereof, 408
Three thousand ducats, due unto the Jew,
We freely cope your courteous pains withal. 410
[*Offers money.*]
ANTONIO
And stand indebted, over and above,
In love and service to you evermore.
PORTIA
He is well paid that is well satisfied;
And I, delivering you, am satisfied
And therein do account myself well paid.
My mind was never yet more mercenary.
I pray you, know me when we meet again.
I wish you well, and so I take my leave.
[*Starts to leave.*]
BASSANIO
Dear sir, of force I must attempt you further. 419
Take some remembrance of us, as a tribute,
Not as fee. Grant me two things, I pray you,
Not to deny me, and to pardon me.

344 I'll . . . question I'll stay no further pursuing of the case **352 privy coffer** private treasury **353 lies in** lies at **360 danger . . . rehears'd** penalty already cited by me **365 charge** expense **368 For** as for **370 Which . . . fine** i.e., which penitence on your part may persuade me to reduce to a fine **371 Ay . . . Antonio** i.e., yes, the state's half may be reduced to a fine, but not Antonio's half **377 halter** hangman's noose **379 quit** remit, relinquish, or perhaps settle for. (That is, Antonio may ask the court to forgive even the fine imposed in lieu of a heavier penalty.) **381 in use** in trust, or possibly, to be used as a source of income

385 presently at once **387 of . . . possess'd** i.e., what remains of the portion not placed under Antonio's trust (which will also go to Lorenzo and Jessica) **397 ten more** i.e., to make up a jury of twelve **404 gratify** reward **408 in lieu whereof** in return for which **410 cope** requite **419 attempt** urge

PORTIA
You press me far, and therefore I will yield.
[*To Antonio.*] Give me your gloves, I'll wear them for your sake;
[*To Bassanio.*] And, for your love, I'll take this ring from you.
Do not draw back your hand; I'll take no more,
And you in love shall not deny me this.

BASSANIO
This ring, good sir, alas, it is a trifle!
I will not shame myself to give you this.

PORTIA
I will have nothing else but only this;
And now methinks I have a mind to it.

BASSANIO
There's more depends on this than on the value.
The dearest ring in Venice will I give you,
And find it out by proclamation;
Only for this, I pray you, pardon me.

PORTIA
I see, sir, you are liberal in offers.
You taught me first to beg, and now methinks
You teach me how a beggar should be answer'd.

BASSANIO
Good sir, this ring was given me by my wife,
And when she put it on, she made me vow
That I should neither sell nor give nor lose it.

PORTIA
That 'scuse serves many men to save their gifts.
An if your wife be not a madwoman,
And know how well I have deserv'd this ring,
She would not hold out enemy forever
For giving it to me. Well, peace be with you!
Exeunt [*Portia and Nerissa*].

ANTONIO
My Lord Bassanio, let him have the ring.
Let his deservings and my love withal
Be valued 'gainst your wife's commandement.

BASSANIO
Go, Gratiano, run and overtake him;
Give him the ring, and bring him, if thou canst,
Unto Antonio's house. Away, make haste!
Exit Gratiano [*with the ring*].
Come, you and I will thither presently,
And in the morning early will we both
Fly toward Belmont. Come, Antonio. *Exeunt.*

[SCENE II]

Enter [*Portia and*] *Nerissa* [*still disguised*].

PORTIA
Inquire the Jew's house out, give him this deed 1
And let him sign it. We'll away tonight
And be a day before our husbands home.
This deed will be well welcome to Lorenzo.
[*Gives deed.*]

Enter Gratiano.

GRATIANO
Fair sir, you are well o'erta'en.
My Lord Bassanio upon more advice 6
Hath sent you here this ring, and doth entreat
Your company at dinner. [*Gives ring.*]

PORTIA
That cannot be.
His ring I do accept most thankfully,
And so, I pray you, tell him. Furthermore,
I pray you, show my youth old Shylock's house.

GRATIANO
That will I do.

NERISSA
Sir, I would speak with you.
[*Aside to Portia.*] I'll see if I can get my husband's ring,
Which I did make him swear to keep for ever.

PORTIA [*Aside to Nerissa*]
Thou mayst, I warrant. We shall have old swearing 15
That they did give the rings away to men;
But we'll outface them, and outswear them too.—
Away, make haste! Thou know'st where I will tarry.

NERISSA
Come, good sir, will you show me to this house?
[*Exeunt severally.*]

IV.ii. Location: Venice. A street.
1 deed i.e., the deed of gift

6 advice consideration **15 old** plenty of

[ACT V • SCENE I]

Enter Lorenzo and Jessica.

LORENZO
The moon shines bright. In such a night as this,
When the sweet wind did gently kiss the trees
And they did make no noise, in such a night
Troilus methinks mounted the Troyan walls 4
And sigh'd his soul toward the Grecian tents,
Where Cressid lay that night.

JESSICA
In such a night
Did Thisbe fearfully o'ertrip the dew, 7
And saw the lion's shadow ere himself,
And ran dismay'd away.

LORENZO
In such a night
Stood Dido with a willow in her hand 10
Upon the wild sea banks, and waft her love 11
To come again to Carthage.

JESSICA
In such a night
Medea gathered the enchanted herbs 13
That did renew old Aeson.

V.i. Location: Belmont. The avenue to Portia's house.
4 Troilus Trojan prince deserted by Cressida after she had been transferred to the Greek camp **7 Thisbe** beloved of Pyramus who, arranging to meet him by night, was affrighted by a lion. (See *A Midsummer Night's Dream*, Act V.) **10 Dido** Queen of Carthage, deserted by Aeneas. **willow** (A symbol of forsaken love.) **11 waft** wafted, beckoned **13 Medea** famous sorceress of Colchis who, after falling in love with Jason and helping him to gain the Golden Fleece, used her magic to restore youth to Aeson, Jason's father

LORENZO In such a night
Did Jessica steal from the wealthy Jew,
And with an unthrift love did run from Venice
As far as Belmont.

JESSICA In such a night
Did young Lorenzo swear he lov'd her well,
Stealing her soul with many vows of faith,
And ne'er a true one.

LORENZO In such a night
Did pretty Jessica, like a little shrew,
Slander her love, and he forgave it her.

JESSICA
I would out-night you, did nobody come;
But, hark, I hear the footing of a man.

Enter [Stephano,] a Messenger.

LORENZO
Who comes so fast in silence of the night?

STEPHANO
A friend.

LORENZO
A friend? What friend? Your name, I pray you,
friend?

STEPHANO
Stephano is my name, and I bring word
My mistress will before the break of day
Be here at Belmont. She doth stray about
By holy crosses, where she kneels and prays
For happy wedlock hours.

LORENZO Who comes with her?

STEPHANO
None but a holy hermit and her maid.
I pray you, is my master yet return'd?

LORENZO
He is not, nor we have not heard from him.
But go we in, I pray thee, Jessica.
And ceremoniously let us prepare
Some welcome for the mistress of the house.

Enter [Launcelot, the] Clown.

LAUNCELOT Sola, sola! Wo ha, ho! Sola, sola!

LORENZO Who calls?

LAUNCELOT Sola! Did you see Master Lorenzo? Master Lorenzo, sola, sola!

LORENZO Leave hollaing, man! Here.

LAUNCELOT Sola! Where, where?

LORENZO Here.

LAUNCELOT Tell him there's a post come from my master, with his horn full of good news: my master will be here ere morning. *[Exit.]*

LORENZO
Sweet soul, let's in, and there expect their coming.
And yet no matter. Why should we go in?
My friend Stephano, signify, I pray you,
Within the house, your mistress is at hand;
And bring your music forth into the air.
[Exit Stephano.]
How sweet the moonlight sleeps upon this bank!
Here will we sit and let the sounds of music
Creep in our ears. Soft stillness and the night
Become the touches of sweet harmony.
Sit, Jessica. [*They sit.*] Look how the floor of heaven
Is thick inlaid with patens of bright gold.
There's not the smallest orb which thou behold'st
But in his motion like an angel sings,
Still quiring to the young-ey'd cherubins;
Such harmony is in immortal souls,
But whilst this muddy vesture of decay
Doth grossly close it in, we cannot hear it.

[Enter Musicians.]

Come, ho, and wake Diana with a hymn!
With sweetest touches pierce your mistress' ear
And draw her home with music. *Play music.*

JESSICA
I am never merry when I hear sweet music.

LORENZO
The reason is, your spirits are attentive.
For do but note a wild and wanton herd,
Or race of youthful and unhandled colts,
Fetching mad bounds, bellowing and neighing loud,
Which is the hot condition of their blood;
If they but hear perchance a trumpet sound,
Or any air of music touch their ears,
You shall perceive them make a mutual stand,
Their savage eyes turn'd to a modest gaze
By the sweet power of music. Therefore the poet
Did feign that Orpheus drew trees, stones, and
floods,
Since nought so stockish, hard, and full of rage,
But music for the time doth change his nature.
The man that hath no music in himself,
Nor is not mov'd with concord of sweet sounds,
Is fit for treasons, stratagems, and spoils;
The motions of his spirit are dull as night
And his affections dark as Erebus.
Let no such man be trusted. Mark the music.

Enter Portia and Nerissa.

PORTIA
That light we see is burning in my hall.
How far that little candle throws his beams!
So shines a good deed in a naughty world.

NERISSA
When the moon shone, we did not see the candle.

PORTIA
So doth the greater glory dim the less.
A substitute shines brightly as a king
Until a king be by, and then his state

16 unthrift prodigal **24 footing** footsteps **31 holy crosses** wayside shrines **39 Sola** (Imitation of a post horn.) **49 expect** await **51 signify** make known

57 Become suit. **touches** notes (produced by the fingering of an instrument) **59 patens** thin, circular plates of metal **62 quiring** singing. **young-ey'd** eternally clear-sighted **64 muddy . . . decay** i.e., mortal flesh **65 close it in** i.e., enclose the soul. **hear it** i.e., hear the music of the spheres **66 Diana** (Here, goddess of the moon; cf. I.ii.105.) **70 spirits are attentive** (The spirits would be in motion within the body in merriment, whereas in sadness they would be drawn to the heart and, as it were, busy listening.) **72 race** herd **77 mutual** common or simultaneous **79 poet** possibly Ovid, with whom the story of Orpheus was a favorite theme **80 Orpheus** legendary musician. **drew** attracted, charmed **81 stockish** unfeeling **85 spoils** acts of pillage **87 Erebus** primeval darkness

Empties itself, as doth an inland brook
Into the main of waters. Music! Hark! 97

NERISSA
It is your music, madam, of the house.

PORTIA
Nothing is good, I see, without respect. 99
Methinks it sounds much sweeter than by day.

NERISSA
Silence bestows that virtue on it, madam.

PORTIA
The crow doth sing as sweetly as the lark
When neither is attended; and I think
The nightingale, if she should sing by day,
When every goose is cackling, would be thought
No better a musician than the wren.
How many things by season season'd are
To their right praise and true perfection!
Peace, ho! The moon sleeps with Endymion 109
And would not be awak'd. [*Music ceases.*]

LORENZO
That is the voice,
Or I am much deceiv'd, of Portia.

PORTIA
He knows me as the blind man knows the cuckoo,
By the bad voice.

LORENZO
Dear lady, welcome home.

PORTIA
We have been praying for our husbands' welfare,
Which speed, we hope, the better for our words.
Are they return'd?

LORENZO
Madam, they are not yet;
But there is come a messenger before,
To signify their coming.

PORTIA
Go in, Nerissa.
Give order to my servants that they take
No note at all of our being absent hence; 120
Nor you, Lorenzo; Jessica, nor you. [*A tucket sounds.*] 121

LORENZO
Your husband is at hand; I hear his trumpet.
We are no tell-tales, madam; fear you not.

PORTIA
This night methinks is but the daylight sick;
It looks a little paler. 'Tis a day
Such as the day is when the sun is hid.

Enter Bassanio, Antonio, Gratiano, and their followers.

BASSANIO
We should hold day with the Antipodes, 127
If you would walk in absence of the sun. 128

PORTIA
Let me give light, but let me not be light; 129
For a light wife doth make a heavy husband, 130
And never be Bassanio so for me.
But God sort all! You are welcome home, my lord. 132

97 main of waters sea **99 respect** comparison, context **109 Endymion** a shepherd loved by the moon-goddess, who caused him to sleep a perennial sleep in a cave on Mount Latmos where she could visit him **121 s.d. tucket** flourish on a trumpet **127–128 We . . . sun** i.e., if you, Portia, like a second sun, would always walk about during the sun's absence, we should never have night, but would enjoy daylight even when the Antipodes, those who dwell on the opposite side of the globe, enjoy daylight **129 be light** be wanton, unchaste **130 heavy** sad **132 sort** decide, dispose

BASSANIO
I thank you, madam. Give welcome to my friend.
This is the man, this is Antonio,
To whom I am so infinitely bound.

PORTIA
You should in all sense be much bound to him, 136
For, as I hear, he was much bound for you.

ANTONIO
No more than I am well acquitted of.

PORTIA
Sir, you are very welcome to our house.
It must appear in other ways than words;
Therefore I scant this breathing courtesy. 141

GRATIANO [*To Nerissa*]
By yonder moon I swear you do me wrong!
In faith, I gave it to the judge's clerk.
Would he were gelt that had it, for my part, 144
Since you do take it, love, so much at heart.

PORTIA
A quarrel, ho, already? What's the matter?

GRATIANO
About a hoop of gold, a paltry ring
That she did give me, whose posy was 148
For all the world like cutler's poetry
Upon a knife, "Love me, and leave me not."

NERISSA
What talk you of the posy or the value?
You swore to me, when I did give it you,
That you would wear it till your hour of death
And that it should lie with you in your grave.
Though not for me, yet for your vehement oaths,
You should have been respective and have kept it. 156
Gave it a judge's clerk! No, God's my judge,
The clerk will ne'er wear hair on 's face that had it.

GRATIANO
He will, an if he live to be a man.

NERISSA
Ay, if a woman live to be a man.

GRATIANO
Now, by this hand, I gave it to a youth,
A kind of boy, a little scrubbed boy, 162
No higher than thyself, the judge's clerk,
A prating boy, that begg'd it as a fee.
I could not for my heart deny it him.

PORTIA
You were to blame—I must be plain with you—
To part so slightly with your wife's first gift,
A thing stuck on with oaths upon your finger,
And so riveted with faith unto your flesh.
I gave my love a ring, and made him swear
Never to part with it; and here he stands.
I dare be sworn for him he would not leave it
Nor pluck it from his finger, for the wealth
That the world masters. Now, in faith, Gratiano, 174
You give your wife too unkind a cause of grief.
An 'twere to me, I should be mad at it. 176

136 in all sense in every way, with every reason **141 scant . . . courtesy** make brief this courteous speaking **144 gelt** gelded. **for my part** as far as I'm concerned **148 posy** a motto on a ring **156 respective** mindful **162 scrubbed** stunted **174 masters** owns **176 mad** beside myself

BASSANIO [*Aside*]
Why, I were best to cut my left hand off
And swear I lost the ring defending it.

GRATIANO
My Lord Bassanio gave his ring away
Unto the judge that begg'd it and indeed
Deserv'd it too; and then the boy, his clerk,
That took some pains in writing, he begg'd mine;
And neither man nor master would take aught
But the two rings.

PORTIA What ring gave you, my lord?
Not that, I hope, which you receiv'd of me.

BASSANIO
If I could add a lie unto a fault,
I would deny it; but you see my finger
Hath not the ring upon it; it is gone.

PORTIA
Even so void is your false heart of truth.
By heaven, I will ne'er come in your bed
Until I see the ring!

NERISSA Nor I in yours
Till I again see mine.

BASSANIO Sweet Portia,
If you did know to whom I gave the ring,
If you did know for whom I gave the ring,
And would conceive for what I gave the ring,
And how unwillingly I left the ring,
When nought would be accepted but the ring,
You would abate the strength of your displeasure.

PORTIA
If you had known the virtue of the ring,
Or half her worthiness that gave the ring,
Or your own honor to contain the ring,
You would not then have parted with the ring.
What man is there so much unreasonable,
If you had pleas'd to have defended it
With any terms of zeal, wanted the modesty
To urge the thing held as a ceremony?
Nerissa teaches me what to believe:
I'll die for 't but some woman had the ring.

BASSANIO
No, by my honor, madam, by my soul,
No woman had it, but a civil doctor,
Which did refuse three thousand ducats of me
And begg'd the ring, the which I did deny him
And suffer'd him to go displeas'd away—
Even he that had held up the very life
Of my dear friend. What should I say, sweet lady?
I was enforc'd to send it after him.
I was beset with shame and courtesy.
My honor would not let ingratitude
So much besmear it. Pardon me, good lady!
For by these blessed candles of the night,
Had you been there, I think you would have begg'd
The ring of me to give the worthy doctor.

PORTIA
Let not that doctor e'er come near my house.
Since he hath got the jewel that I lov'd,
And that which you did swear to keep for me,
I will become as liberal as you;
I'll not deny him any thing I have,
No, not my body nor my husband's bed.
Know him I shall, I am well sure of it.
Lie not a night from home. Watch me like Argus;
If you do not, if I be left alone,
Now, by mine honor, which is yet mine own,
I'll have that doctor for my bedfellow.

NERISSA
And I his clerk; therefore be well advis'd
How you do leave me to mine own protection.

GRATIANO
Well, do you so. Let not me take him, then!
For if I do, I'll mar the young clerk's pen.

ANTONIO
I am th' unhappy subject of these quarrels.

PORTIA
Sir, grieve not you; you are welcome
notwithstanding.

BASSANIO
Portia, forgive me this enforced wrong,
And, in the hearing of these many friends,
I swear to thee, even by thine own fair eyes,
Wherein I see myself—

PORTIA Mark you but that!
In both my eyes he doubly sees himself,
In each eye, one. Swear by your double self,
And there's an oath of credit.

BASSANIO Nay, but hear me.
Pardon this fault, and by my soul I swear
I never more will break an oath with thee.

ANTONIO
I once did lend my body for his wealth,
Which, but for him that had your husband's ring,
Had quite miscarried. I dare be bound again,
My soul upon the forfeit, that your lord
Will never more break faith advisedly.

PORTIA
Then you shall be his surety. Give him this
And bid him keep it better than the other.
[*Gives ring to Antonio, who gives it to Bassanio.*]

ANTONIO
Here, Lord Bassanio. Swear to keep this ring.

BASSANIO
By heaven, it is the same I gave the doctor!

PORTIA
I had it of him. Pardon me. Bassanio,
For, by this ring, the doctor lay with me.

NERISSA
And pardon me, my gentle Gratiano;
For that same scrubbed boy, the doctor's clerk,
In lieu of this last night did lie with me.

GRATIANO
Why, this is like the mending of highways
In summer, where the ways are fair enough.

199 virtue power **201 contain** retain **205 wanted the modesty** who would have been so lacking in consideration as **206 urge** insist upon receiving. **ceremony** something sacred **210 civil doctor** i.e., doctor of civil law

226 liberal generous (sexually as well as otherwise) **230 from** away from. **Argus** mythological monster with a hundred eyes **236 take** apprehend **237 pen** (with sexual double meaning) **245 double** i.e., deceitful **246 of credit** worthy to be believed **249 wealth** welfare **253 advisedly** intentionally **262 In lieu of** in return for

What, are we cuckolds ere we have deserv'd it?

PORTIA
Speak not so grossly. You are all amaz'd.
Here is a letter; read it at your leisure.
[*Gives letter.*]
It comes from Padua, from Bellario.
There you shall find that Portia was the doctor,
Nerissa there her clerk. Lorenzo here
Shall witness I set forth as soon as you,
And even but now return'd; I have not yet
Enter'd my house. Antonio, you are welcome,
And I have better news in store for you
Than you expect. Unseal this letter soon;
[*Gives him another letter.*]
There you shall find three of your argosies
Are richly come to harbor suddenly.
You shall not know by what strange accident
I chanced on this letter.

ANTONIO
I am dumb.

BASSANIO
Were you the doctor and I knew you not?

GRATIANO
Were you the clerk that is to make me cuckold?

NERISSA
Ay, but the clerk that never means to do it,
Unless he live until he be a man.

BASSANIO
Sweet doctor, you shall be my bedfellow.
When I am absent, then lie with my wife.

ANTONIO
Sweet lady, you have given me life and living;
For here I read for certain that my ships
Are safely come to road.

PORTIA
How now, Lorenzo?
My clerk hath some good comforts too for you.

NERISSA
Ay, and I'll give them him without a fee.
There do I give to you and Jessica,
From the rich Jew, a special deed of gift,
After his death, of all he dies possess'd of.
[*Gives deed.*]

LORENZO
Fair ladies, you drop manna in the way
Of starved people.

PORTIA
It is almost morning,
And yet I am sure you are not satisfied
Of these events at full. Let us go in;
And charge us there upon inter'gatories,
And we will answer all things faithfully.

GRATIANO
Let it be so. The first inter'gatory
That my Nerissa shall be sworn on is,
Whether till the next night she had rather stay
Or go to bed now, being two hours to day.
But were the day come, I should wish it dark
Till I were couching with the doctor's clerk.
Well, while I live I'll fear no other thing
So sore as keeping safe Nerissa's ring. *Exeunt.*

265 cuckolds husbands whose wives are unfaithful **266 amaz'd** bewildered **288 road** anchorage **298 charge . . . inter'gatories** require ourselves to answer all things under oath **302 stay** wait **307 ring** (with sexual suggestion)

Much Ado about Nothing

Much Ado about Nothing belongs to a group of Shakespeare's most mature romantic comedies, linked by similar titles, that also includes *As You Like It* and *Twelfth Night.* All date from the period 1598 (the year of Francis Meres' *Palladis Tamia,* which mentions none of them) to 1600 (when *Much Ado* and *As You Like It* were entered in the Stationers' Register but briefly stayed from publication). These plays are the culmination of Shakespeare's exuberant, philosophical, and "festive" vein in comedy, with only an occasional anticipation of the darker "problem" comedies of the early 1600's. They also parallel the culmination of Shakespeare's writing of history plays, in *Henry IV* and *V.*

Much Ado excels in combative wit and in swift, colloquial prose. It differs too from several other comedies (including *A Midsummer Night's Dream* and *The Merchant of Venice*) in that it features no journey of the lovers, no heroine disguised as a man, no envious court or city contrasted with an idealized landscape of the artist's imagination. Instead, the prevailing motif is that of the mask. Prominent scenes include a masked ball (II,i), a charade offstage in which the villainous Borachio misrepresents himself as the lover of Hero (actually Margaret in disguise), and a marriage ceremony with the supposedly dead bride masking as her own cousin (V,iii). Overhearings are constant, and are essential to the process of both misunderstanding (as in the false rumor of Don Pedro's wooing Hero for himself) and eventual clarification (as in the discovery by the night watch of the slander done to Hero's reputation, or in the revelation to Beatrice and Benedick of each other's true state of mind). The masks, or roles, that the characters incessantly assume are for the most part defensive and inimical to mutual understanding. How can they be dispelled? It is the search for candor and self-awareness in relationships with others, the quest for honesty and respect beneath conventional outward appearances, that provides the "journey" in this play.

Structurally the play contrasts two pairs of lovers. The young ladies, Beatrice and Hero, are cousins and close friends. The gentlemen, Benedick and Claudio, Italian gentlemen and fellow-officers under the command of Don Pedro, have returned from the war in which they have fought bravely. These similarities only serve, however, to accentuate the differences between the two couples. Hero is modest, retiring, usually silent, and obedient to her father's will. Claudio appears ideally suited to her, since he is also respectful and decorous. They are conventional Petrarchan lovers in the roles of ingenue hero and heroine. Beatrice and Benedick, on the other hand, are renowned for "a kind of merry war" between them. Although obviously destined to come together, they are seemingly too independent and skeptical of convention to be tolerant and accepting in love. They scoff so at romantic sentimentality that they cannot permit themselves to drop their satirical masks. Yet paradoxically their relationship is the more surefooted because it is relentlessly probing and candid.

As in some of his other comic double plots (*The Taming of the Shrew,* for example), Shakespeare has linked together two stories of diverse origins and contrasting tones in order to set off one against the other. The Hero-Claudio plot is Italianate in flavor and origin, sensational, melodramatic, potentially tragic. In fact the often-told story of the maiden falsely slandered did frequently end in disaster—as, for example, in Spenser's *Faerie Queene,* II,iv (1590). Spenser was apparently indebted to Ariosto's *Orlando Furioso* (translated into English by Sir John Harington, 1591), as were Peter Beverly in *The Historie of Ariodanto and Ieneura* (1566) and Richard Mulcaster in his play *Ariodante and Genevora* (1583). Shakespeare seems to have relied more on the Italian version by Matteo Bandello (Lucca, 1554) and its French translation by Belleforest, *Histoires Tragiques* (1569). Still other versions have been discovered, both nondramatic and dramatic, although it cannot be established that Shakespeare was reworking an old play. Various factual inconsistencies in Shakespeare's text (such as Leonato's wife Imogen and a "kinsman" who are named briefly in both quarto and Folio but have no roles in the play) can perhaps be explained by Shakespeare's having worked quickly from more than one source.

Shakespeare's other plot, of Benedick and Beatrice, is much more English and his own. The battle of the sexes is a staple of English medieval humor (Chaucer's Wife of Bath, the Wakefield *Noah*) and of Shakespeare's own early comedy: Berowne and Rosaline in *Love's Labor's Lost,* Petruchio and Katharine in *The Taming of the Shrew.* The merry war of Benedick and Beatrice is Shakespeare's finest achievement in this vein, and was to become a rich legacy in the later English comedy of Congreve, Wilde, and Shaw. The tone is lighthearted, bantering, and reassuring, in contrast with the Italianate mood of vengeance and duplicity. No less English are the clownish antics of Dogberry and his crew, representing still another group of characters although not a separate plot. Like Constable Dull in *Love's Labor's Lost* or the tradesmen of *A Midsummer Night's Dream,* the buffoons of *Much Ado* function in a nominally

Mediterranean setting but are nonetheless recognizable London types. Their preposterous antics not only puncture the ominous mood threatening our enjoyment of the main plot, but absurdly enough even help to abort a potential crime. When Dogberry comes, laughter cannot be far behind.

The two plots provide contrasting perspectives on the nature of love. Because it is sensational and melodramatic, the Claudio-Hero plot stresses situation at the expense of character. The conspiracy that nearly overwhelms the lovers is an engrossing story, but they themselves remain one-dimensional. They interest us more as Petrarchan types, and hence as "foils" to Benedick and Beatrice, than as lovers in their own right. Benedick and Beatrice, on the other hand, are psychologically complex. Clearly they are fascinated with one another. Beatrice's questions in the first scene, although abusive in tone, betray her concern for Benedick's welfare. Has he safely returned from the wars? How did he bear himself in battle? Who are his companions? She tests his moral character by high standards, suspecting that he will fail because she demands so much. We are not surprised when she lectures her docile cousin, Hero, on the folly of submitting to parental choice in marriage: "It is my cousin's duty to make curtsy and say 'Father, as it please you.' But yet for all that, cousin, let him be a handsome fellow, or else make another curtsy and say 'Father, as it please me'" (II,i). Beatrice remains single not from love of spinsterhood but from insistence on a nearly perfect mate. Paradoxically, she who is the inveterate scoffer is the true idealist. And we know from her unceasing fascination with Benedick that he, of all the men in her acquaintance, comes closest to her mark. The only fear preventing the revelation of her love—a not unnatural fear, in view of the insults she and Benedick exchange—is that he will prove faithless and jest at her weakness.

Benedick is similarly hemmed in by his posturing as "a professed tyrant to their sex." Despite his reputation as a perennial bachelor, and his wry amusement at Claudio's new-found passion, Benedick confesses in soliloquy (II,iii) that he could be won to affection by the ideal woman. Again his criteria are chiefly those of temperament and moral character, although he by no means spurns wealth, beauty, and social position; the happiest couples are those well-matched in fortune's gifts. "Rich she shall be, that's certain; wise, or I'll none; virtuous, or I'll never cheapen her; fair, or I'll never look on her; mild, or come not near me; noble, or not I for an angel; of good discourse, an excellent musician, and her hair shall be of what color it please God." This last self-amused concession indicates that Benedick is aware how impossibly much he is asking. Still, there is one woman, Beatrice, who may well possess all of these qualities except mildness. Even her sharp wit is part of her admirable intelligence. She is a match for Benedick, and he is a man who would never tolerate the submissive conventionality of someone like Hero. All that appears to be lacking, in fact, is any sign of fondness on Beatrice's part. For him to make overtures would be to invite her withering scorn—not to mention the I-told-you-so mockery of his friends.

Benedick and Beatrice have been playing the game of verbal abuse so long they scarcely remember how it started—perhaps as a squaring-off between the only two intelligences worthy of contending with one another, perhaps as a more profoundly defensive reaction of two sensitive persons not willing to part lightly with their independence. They know that true involvement with others is a complex matter, one that can cause heartache. Yet the masks they wear to one another are scarcely satisfactory. At the masked ball (II,i), we see how hurtful the "merry war" has become. Benedick, attempting to pass himself off as a stranger in a mask, abuses Beatrice by telling her of her reputation for disdain; but she, perceiving who he is, retaliates by telling him as a purported stranger what she "really" thinks of Benedick. These devices cut deeply, and confirm the worst fears of each partner. Ironically, these fears can be dispelled only by the virtuous deceptions practiced on them by their friends. For, once Benedick is assured that Beatrice secretly loves him, masking her affection with scorn, he acquires the confidence he needs to make a commitment, and vice versa. The beauty of the virtuous deceptions, moreover, is that they are so plausible—because, indeed, they are essentially true. Benedick overhears himself described as a person so satirical that Beatrice dare not reveal her affection, for fear of being repulsed (II,iii). Beatrice learns that she is indeed called disdainful by her friends (III,i). Both lovers respond nobly to these revelations, accepting the accusations as richly deserved and placing no blame on the other. As Beatrice proclaims to herself, "Contempt, farewell, and maiden pride, adieu!" The relief afforded by this honesty is genuine and lasting.

Because Claudio knows so little about Hero, and is content with superficial expectations, he is vulnerable to a far more ugly sort of deception. Claudio's first questions about Hero betray his romantically stereotyped attitudes and his willingness to let Don Pedro and Hero's father, Leonato, arrange a financially advantageous match. Claudio treasures Hero's outward reputation for modesty, an appearance easily besmirched. When a false rumor suggests that Don Pedro is wooing the lady for himself, Claudio's response is predictably cliché-ridden: all's fair in love and war, you can't trust friends in an affair of the heart, and so farewell Hero. The rumor has a superficial plausibility about it, especially when the villainous Don John steps into the situation. Motivated in part by pure malice and the sport of ruining others' happiness, John speaks to the masked Claudio at the ball (II,i) as though he were speaking to Benedick, and in this guise pretends to reveal the secret "fact" of Don Pedro's duplicity in love. (The device is precisely that used by Beatrice to put down Benedick in the same scene.) With this specious confirmation, Claudio leaps to a wrong conclusion, thereby judging both his friend and mistress to be false. He gives them no chance to speak in their own defense. To be sure, Hero's father and uncle have also believed in the false report, and have welcomed the prospect of the wealthy Don Pedro as Hero's husband. The lady herself raises no objection to marriage with the older man. Still, Claudio has revealed a lack of faith resulting from his slender knowledge of Hero and of himself.

The nearly tragic "demonstration" of Hero's infidelity follows the same course, because Claudio has not learned from his first experience. Once again the diabolical Don John first implants the insidious suggestion in Claudio's mind, then creates an illusion entirely plausible to the senses, and finally confirms it with Borachio's testimony. What Claudio and Don Pedro have actually seen is Margaret wooed at Hero's window, shrouded in the dark of night and seen from "afar off in the orchard." The power of suggestion is enough to do the rest. John's method, and his pleasure in evil, are much like those of his later counterparts, Iago in *Othello* and Edmund in *King Lear*. Indeed, John is compared with the devil, who has power over men's frail senses but must rely on their complicity and acquiescence in evil. Claudio is once again led to denounce faithlessly the virtuous woman whose loyalty he no longer deserves. Yet his fault is very typically human, and is shared by Don Pedro. Providence gives him a second chance, through the ludicrous and bumbling intervention of Dogberry's night watch. These men overhear the plot of Don John as soon as it is announced to us, so that we know justice will eventually prevail even though it will also be farcically delayed. Once again, misunderstanding has become "much ado about nothing," an escalating of recriminations based on a purely chimerical assumption that must eventually be deflated. The painful experience is not without value, for it tests men's spiritual worth in a crisis. Beatrice, like Friar Francis, shows herself to be a person of unshakable faith in goodness. Benedick, though puzzled and torn in his loyalties, also passes the test and proves himself worthy of Beatrice. Claudio is found wanting, but Hero forgives and accepts him anyway. In her role as the granter of a merciful second chance, she foreshadows the beatifically symbolic nature of many of Shakespeare's later heroines.

Much Ado about Nothing comes perhaps closer to potentially tragic action than Shakespeare's other festive comedies. Virtually all the characters are affected by misunderstanding, resort to deception, or take refuge in protective masks. Candor and straightforwardness are ideals more easily praised than achieved. Even Benedick and Beatrice, marvelous though they may be, are far from perfect. Beatrice almost provokes Benedick into a vindictive and unnecessary murder. Despite their self-awareness, these lovers must be rescued from their isolation by a trick that ironically resembles the villainous practices of Don John. In this important sense, Benedick and Beatrice are not wholly unlike Claudio and Hero after all. Both pairs of lovers are saved from their own worst selves by a harmonizing force that works its will through strange and improbable means—even through Constable Dogberry and his watch.

Much Ado about Nothing

[*Dramatis Personae*

DON PEDRO, *Prince of Arragon.*
DON JOHN, *his bastard brother.*
CLAUDIO, *a young lord of Florence.*
BENEDICK, *a young lord of Padua.*
LEONATO, *governor of Messina.*
ANTONIO, *his brother.*
BALTHASAR, *attendant on Don Pedro.*
CONRADE, } *followers of Don John.*
BORACHIO, }
FRIAR FRANCIS.
DOGBERRY, *a constable.*
VERGES, *a headborough.*
A SEXTON.
A BOY.

HERO, *daughter to Leonato.*
BEATRICE, *niece to Leonato.*
MARGARET, } *gentlewomen attending on Hero.*
URSULA, }

MESSENGERS, WATCH, ATTENDANTS, *etc.*

SCENE: *Messina.*]

[ACT I • SCENE I]

Enter Leonato, Governor of Messina, Hero his daughter, and Beatrice his niece, with a Messenger.

LEONATO [*Holding a letter*] I learn in this letter that Don Pedro of Arragon comes this night to Messina.

MESSENGER He is very near by this. He was not three leagues off when I left him.

LEONATO How many gentlemen have you lost in this action?

MESSENGER But few of any sort, and none of name.

LEONATO A victory is twice itself when the achiever brings home full numbers. I find here that Don Pedro hath bestow'd much honor on a young Florentine call'd Claudio.

MESSENGER Much deserv'd on his part and equally remembr'red by Don Pedro. He hath borne himself beyond the promise of his age, doing, in the figure of a lamb, the feats of a lion. He hath indeed better bett'red expectation than you must expect of me to tell you how.

LEONATO He hath an uncle here in Messina will be very much glad of it.

MESSENGER I have already deliver'd him letters, and there appears much joy in him, even so much that joy could not show itself modest enough without a badge of bitterness.

LEONATO Did he break out into tears?

MESSENGER In great measure.

LEONATO A kind overflow of kindness. There are no faces truer than those that are so wash'd. How much better is it to weep at joy than to joy at weeping!

BEATRICE I pray you, is Signior Mountanto return'd from the wars or no?

MESSENGER I know none of that name, lady. There was none such in the army of any sort.

LEONATO What is he that you ask for, niece?

HERO My cousin means Signior Benedick of Padua.

MESSENGER O, he's return'd, and as pleasant as ever he was.

BEATRICE He set up his bills here in Messina and challeng'd Cupid at the flight; and my uncle's fool, reading the challenge, subscrib'd for Cupid, and challeng'd him at the burbolt. I pray you, how many hath he kill'd and eaten in these wars? But how many hath he kill'd? For indeed I promis'd to eat all of his killing.

LEONATO Faith, niece, you tax Signior Benedick too much; but he'll be meet with you, I doubt it not.

MESSENGER He hath done good service, lady, in these wars.

BEATRICE You had musty victual, and he hath holp to eat it. He is a very valiant trencher-man; he hath an excellent stomach.

MESSENGER And a good soldier too, lady.

BEATRICE And a good soldier to a lady; but what is he to a lord?

MESSENGER A lord to a lord, a man to a man; stuff'd with all honorable virtues.

BEATRICE It is so, indeed. He is no less than a stuff'd man. But for the stuffing—well, we are all mortal.

LEONATO You must not, sir, mistake my niece. There is a kind of merry war betwixt Signior Benedick and her. They never meet but there's a skirmish of wit between them.

BEATRICE Alas! He gets nothing by that. In our last conflict four of his five wits went halting off, and now is the whole man govern'd with one; so that if he have wit enough to keep himself warm, let him bear it for

I.i. Location: Messina. Before Leonato's house.
6 action battle **7 sort** rank. **name** reputation, or noble name

15 bett'red surpassed **18 will** who will **22 modest** moderate **22–23 badge of bitterness** sign of sorrow, i.e., tears **26 kind** natural **29 Mountanto** montanto, an upward blow or thrust in fencing **35 pleasant** jocular **37 bills** placards, advertisements **37–38 challeng'd . . . flight** undertook to rival Cupid as an archer **38 my uncle's fool** (Perhaps a professional fool in her uncle's service; possibly Beatrice means herself, recalling an earlier flirtation with Benedick.) **39 subscrib'd for** signed on behalf of **40 burbolt** birdbolt, a blunt-headed arrow used for fowling (sometimes used by children because of its relative harmlessness and thus conventionally appropriate to Cupid) **43 tax** blame **44 meet** even, quits **48 valiant trencher-man** great eater **49 stomach** appetite **52 to** compared to **55–56 stuff'd man** i.e., a figure stuffed to resemble a man **56 the stuffing** i.e., what he's truly made of. **well . . . mortal** i.e., well, we all have our faults **62 five wits** i.e., not the five senses, but the five faculties: memory, imagination, judgment, fantasy, common wit. **halting** limping

a difference between himself and his horse, for it is all the wealth that he hath left to be known a reasonable creature. Who is his companion now? He hath every month a new sworn brother.

MESSENGER Is 't possible?

BEATRICE Very easily possible. He wears his faith but as the fashion of his hat; it ever changes with the next block.

MESSENGER I see, lady, the gentleman is not in your books.

BEATRICE No; an he were, I would burn my study. But I pray you, who is his companion? Is there no young squarer now that will make a voyage with him to the devil?

MESSENGER He is most in the company of the right noble Claudio.

BEATRICE O Lord, he will hang upon him like a disease! He is sooner caught than the pestilence, and the taker runs presently mad. God help the noble Claudio! If he have caught the Benedick, it will cost him a thousand pound ere 'a be cur'd.

MESSENGER I will hold friends with you, lady.

BEATRICE Do, good friend.

LEONATO You will never run mad, niece.

BEATRICE No, not till a hot January.

MESSENGER Don Pedro is approach'd.

Enter Don Pedro, Claudio, Benedick, Balthasar, and [*Don*] *John the Bastard.*

DON PEDRO Good Signior Leonato, are you come to meet your trouble? The fashion of the world is to avoid cost, and you encounter it.

LEONATO Never came trouble to my house in the likeness of your Grace. For trouble being gone, comfort should remain; but when you depart from me, sorrow abides and happiness takes his leave.

DON PEDRO You embrace your charge too willingly.—I think this is your daughter.

[*Presenting himself to Hero.*]

LEONATO Her mother hath many times told me so.

BENEDICK Were you in doubt, sir, that you ask'd her?

LEONATO Signior Benedick, no; for then were you a child.

DON PEDRO You have it full, Benedick. We may guess by this what you are, being a man. Truly, the lady fathers herself. Be happy, lady, for you are like an honorable father.

BENEDICK If Signior Leonato be her father, she would not have his head on her shoulders for all Messina, as like him as she is.

BEATRICE I wonder that you will still be talking, Signior Benedick. Nobody marks you.

BENEDICK What, my dear Lady Disdain! Are you yet living?

BEATRICE Is it possible disdain should die while she hath such meet food to feed it as Signior Benedick? Courtesy itself must convert to disdain, if you come in her presence.

BENEDICK Then is courtesy a turncoat. But it is certain I am lov'd of all ladies, only you excepted; and I would I could find in my heart that I had not a hard heart, for truly I love none.

BEATRICE A dear happiness to women! They would else have been troubled with a pernicious suitor. I thank God and my cold blood, I am of your humor for that. I had rather hear my dog bark at a crow than a man swear he loves me.

BENEDICK God keep your ladyship still in that mind! So some gentleman or other shall scape a predestinate scratch'd face.

BEATRICE Scratching could not make it worse, an 'twere such a face as yours were.

BENEDICK Well, you are a rare parrot-teacher.

BEATRICE A bird of my tongue is better than a beast of yours.

BENEDICK I would my horse had the speed of your tongue, and so good a continuer. But keep your way, a God's name; I have done.

BEATRICE You always end with a jade's trick. I know you of old.

DON PEDRO That is the sum of all, Leonato. Signior Claudio and Signior Benedick, my dear friend Leonato hath invited you all. I tell him we shall stay here at the least a month, and he heartily prays some occasion may detain us longer. I dare swear he is no hypocrite, but prays from his heart.

LEONATO If you swear, my lord, you shall not be forsworn. [*To Don John.*] Let me bid you welcome, my lord, being reconcil'd to the Prince your brother. I owe you all duty.

DON JOHN I thank you. I am not of many words, but I thank you.

LEONATO Please it your Grace lead on?

DON PEDRO Your hand, Leonato. We will go together.

Exeunt. Manent Benedick and Claudio.

CLAUDIO Benedick, didst thou note the daughter of Signior Leonato?

BENEDICK I noted her not, but I look'd on her.

CLAUDIO Is she not a modest young lady?

BENEDICK Do you question me, as an honest man should do, for my simple true judgment? Or would

65 difference heraldic distinguishing feature (with a play on the usual sense) **66 to be known** i.e., in order that he may be recognized as **68 sworn brother** brother in arms. (*Frater juratus,* an allusion to the ancient practice of swearing brotherhood.) **70 faith** allegiance, or fidelity **72 block** mold for shaping hats **73–74 in your books** i.e., in favor with you, in your account books for credit **75 an** if **77 squarer** quarreler **81 he** i.e., Benedick **83 presently** immediately **84 the Benedick** i.e., as if he were a disease **85 'a** he **86 hold friends** keep on friendly terms (so as not to earn your enmity) **88 run mad** i.e., "catch the Benedick" **92 your trouble** i.e., the expense of entertaining me and my retinue **93 encounter** go to meet **98 embrace your charge** greet your burden **104 have it full** are fully answered, tit for tat **106 fathers herself** shows by appearance who her father is **109 his head** i.e., with Leonato's white beard and signs of age

117 convert change **123 dear happiness** precious good luck **125–126 I am . . . that** I am of the same disposition in that matter, i.e., of loving no one **129 predestinate** inevitable (for any man who should woo Beatrice) **132 were** i.e., is **133 rare** outstanding. **parrot-teacher** i.e., one who would teach a parrot well, because you say the same things over and over **134 of my tongue** taught to speak like me, i.e., incessantly **134–135 of yours** taught to speak like you **137 a continuer** i.e., in staying power **139 jade's trick** i.e., ill-conditioned horse's trick of dropping out of a race before it is over (as Benedick does in this race of wits) **141 sum of all** (Don Pedro and Leonato have been conversing apart on other matters.) **149 being** since you are **154 go together** i.e., arm in arm (thus avoiding the question of precedence in order of leaving) **157 noted her not** gave her no special attention

you have me speak after my custom, as being a profess'd tyrant to their sex?

CLAUDIO No, I pray thee speak in sober judgment.

BENEDICK Why, i' faith, methinks she's too low for a high praise, too brown for a fair praise, and too little for a great praise. Only this commendation I can afford her, that were she other than she is, she were unhandsome, and being no other but as she is, I do not like her.

CLAUDIO Thou thinkest I am in sport. I pray thee tell me truly how thou lik'st her.

BENEDICK Would you buy her, that you inquire after her?

CLAUDIO Can the world buy such a jewel?

BENEDICK Yea, and a case to put it into. But speak you this with a sad brow? Or do you play the flouting Jack, to tell us Cupid is a good hare-finder and Vulcan a rare carpenter? Come, in what key shall a man take you, to go in the song?

CLAUDIO In mine eye she is the sweetest lady that ever I look'd on.

BENEDICK I can see yet without spectacles and I see no such matter. There's her cousin, an she were not possess'd with a fury, exceeds her as much in beauty as the first of May doth the last of December. But I hope you have no intent to turn husband, have you?

CLAUDIO I would scarce trust myself, though I had sworn the contrary, if Hero would be my wife.

BENEDICK Is 't come to this? In faith, hath not the world one man but he will wear his cap with suspicion? Shall I never see a bachelor of threescore again? Go to, i' faith; an thou wilt needs thrust thy neck into a yoke, wear the print of it and sigh away Sundays. Look, Don Pedro is return'd to seek you.

Enter Don Pedro.

DON PEDRO What secret hath held you here, that you follow'd not to Leonato's?

BENEDICK I would your Grace would constrain me to tell.

DON PEDRO I charge thee on thy allegiance.

BENEDICK You hear, Count Claudio. I can be secret as a dumb man—I would have you think so—but, on my allegiance, mark you this, on my allegiance! He is in love. With who? Now that is your Grace's part. Mark how short his answer is: with Hero, Leonato's short daughter.

CLAUDIO If this were so, so were it utt'red.

BENEDICK Like the old tale, my lord: "It is not so, nor 'twas not so, but indeed, God forbid it should be so."

CLAUDIO If my passion change not shortly, God forbid it should be otherwise.

DON PEDRO Amen, if you love her; for the lady is very well worthy.

CLAUDIO You speak this to fetch me in, my lord.

DON PEDRO By my troth, I speak my thought.

CLAUDIO And, in faith, my lord, I spoke mine.

BENEDICK And, by my two faiths and troths, my lord, I spoke mine.

CLAUDIO That I love her, I feel.

DON PEDRO That she is worthy, I know.

BENEDICK That I neither feel how she should be lov'd, nor know how she should be worthy, is the opinion that fire cannot melt out of me. I will die in it at the stake.

DON PEDRO Thou wast ever an obstinate heretic in the despite of beauty.

CLAUDIO And never could maintain his part but in the force of his will.

BENEDICK That a woman conceiv'd me, I thank her; that she brought me up, I likewise give her most humble thanks. But that I will have a rechate winded in my forehead, or hang my bugle in an invisible baldrick, all women shall pardon me. Because I will not do them the wrong to mistrust any, I will do myself the right to trust none; and the fine is, for the which I may go the finer, I will live a bachelor.

DON PEDRO I shall see thee, ere I die, look pale with love.

BENEDICK With anger, with sickness, or with hunger, my lord, not with love. Prove that ever I lose more blood with love than I will get again with drinking, pick out mine eyes with a ballad-maker's pen and hang me up at the door of a brothel-house for the sign of blind Cupid.

DON PEDRO Well, if ever thou dost fall from this faith, thou wilt prove a notable argument.

BENEDICK If I do, hang me in a bottle like a cat and shoot at me; and he that hits me, let him be clapp'd on the shoulder and call'd Adam.

DON PEDRO Well, as time shall try:
"In time the savage bull doth bear the yoke."

BENEDICK The savage bull may; but if ever the sensible Benedick bear it, pluck off the bull's horns and set them in my forehead, and let me be vilely painted, and in such great letters as they write "Here is good horse to hire," let them signify under my sign "Here you may see Benedick the married man."

162 tyrant one cruel or pitiless in attitude **164 low** short **175 case** (1) jewel case (2) clothing, outer garments. (There is also a bawdy play on *female pudenda*.) **176 sad** serious. **flouting Jack** i.e., mocking rascal **177–178 to tell . . . carpenter** i.e., are you mocking us with nonsense? (Cupid was blind, not sharp-eyed like a hunter, and Vulcan was a blacksmith, not a carpenter.) **179 go in** join in, harmonize with **190 wear . . . suspicion** i.e., be suspected of wearing his cap to hide his cuckold's horns, signs of his wife's infidelity **193 Sundays** i.e., when, owing to the domesticity of the day, you cannot escape from your yoke-fellow **203 part** speaking part. (I.e., to say, "With who?") **206 If this . . . utt'red** i.e., if I really were in love with Hero, and told Benedick, he would blab the secret this way **207 old tale** (In the English fairy tale known as "Mr. Fox," a murderous wooer, discovered in his crimes by the lady he seeks to marry and victimize, repeatedly disclaims her recital of what she has seen by the refrain here set in quotations. The story is a variant of the theme known as "the Robber Bridegroom." Benedick uses it mockingly here to characterize Claudio's reluctance to admit his "crime" of falling in love.)

213 fetch me in get me to confess **225 despite** contempt **227 force of his will** i.e., refusing to be guided by reason (which, as defined by the Schoolmen, was the state of the heretic) **230–232 But that . . . me** i.e., women must pardon me for refusing to have my horn placed on my head (like a cuckold) **230 rechate** blast blown (winded) to recall the hounds **231 baldrick** strap that supports the horn (here invisible because the horn is the metaphorical one of cuckoldry) **234 fine** end **234–235 go the finer** have more to spend on fine clothes **239 Prove** if you can prove **239–240 lose . . . drinking** (According to Elizabethan theory, each sigh cost the heart a drop of blood, whereas blood was replenished by wine.) **241 ballad-maker's pen** i.e., such as would be used to write love ballads or satires **242 sign** a painted sign, such as hung over inns and shops **245 notable argument** notorious subject for conversation, example **246 bottle** wicker basket (to hold the cat used as target in archery matches) **248 Adam** (Probably refers to Adam Bell, archer outlaw of the ballads.) **250 In . . . yoke** (Proverbial; also appearing in a varied form in Kyd's *The Spanish Tragedy*, II.i.3.)

CLAUDIO If this should ever happen, thou wouldst be horn-mad.

DON PEDRO Nay, if Cupid have not spent all his quiver in Venice, thou wilt quake for this shortly.

BENEDICK I look for an earthquake too, then.

DON PEDRO Well, you will temporize with the hours. In the meantime, good Signior Benedick, repair to Leonato's. Commend me to him and tell him I will not fail him at supper, for indeed he hath made great preparation.

BENEDICK I have almost matter enough in me for such an embassage; and so I commit you—

CLAUDIO To the tuition of God. From my house, if I had it—

DON PEDRO The sixth of July. Your loving friend, Benedick.

BENEDICK Nay, mock not, mock not. The body of your discourse is sometime guarded with fragments, and the guards are but slightly basted on neither. Ere you flout old ends any further, examine your conscience. And so I leave you. *Exit.*

CLAUDIO
My liege, your Highness now may do me good.

DON PEDRO
My love is thine to teach. Teach it but how,
And thou shalt see how apt it is to learn
Any hard lesson that may do thee good.

CLAUDIO
Hath Leonato any son, my lord?

DON PEDRO
No child but Hero; she's his only heir.
Dost thou affect her, Claudio?

CLAUDIO O, my lord,
When you went onward on this ended action,
I look'd upon her with a soldier's eye,
That lik'd, but had a rougher task in hand
Than to drive liking to the name of love.
But now I am return'd and that war-thoughts
Have left their places vacant, in their rooms
Come thronging soft and delicate desires,
All prompting me how fair young Hero is,
Saying, I lik'd her ere I went to wars.

DON PEDRO
Thou wilt be like a lover presently
And tire the hearer with a book of words.
If thou dost love fair Hero, cherish it,
And I will break with her and with her father,
And thou shalt have her. Was 't not to this end
That thou began'st to twist so fine a story?

CLAUDIO
How sweetly you do minister to love,
That know love's grief by his complexion!
But lest my liking might too sudden seem,
I would have salv'd it with a longer treatise.

DON PEDRO
What need the bridge much broader than the flood?
The fairest grant is the necessity.
Look what will serve is fit. 'Tis once, thou lovest,
And I will fit thee with the remedy.
I know we shall have reveling tonight;
I will assume thy part in some disguise
And tell fair Hero I am Claudio,
And in her bosom I'll unclasp my heart
And take her hearing prisoner with the force
And strong encounter of my amorous tale.
Then after to her father will I break,
And the conclusion is, she shall be thine.
In practice let us put it presently. *Exeunt.*

[SCENE II]

Enter Leonato and an Old Man [*Antonio*], *brother to Leonato,* [*meeting*].

LEONATO How, now, brother! Where is my cousin, your son? Hath he provided this music?

ANTONIO He is very busy about it. But, brother, I can tell you strange news that you yet dreamt not of.

LEONATO Are they good?

ANTONIO As the event stamps them, but they have a good cover; they show well outward. The Prince and Count Claudio, walking in a thick-pleach'd alley in mine orchard, were thus much overheard by a man of mine. The Prince discover'd to Claudio that he lov'd my niece your daughter and meant to acknowledge it this night in a dance; and if he found her accordant, he meant to take the present time by the top and instantly break with you of it.

LEONATO Hath the fellow any wit that told you this?

ANTONIO A good sharp fellow. I will send for him, and question him yourself.

LEONATO No, no. We will hold it as a dream till it appear itself; but I will acquaint my daughter withal, that she may be the better prepar'd for an answer, if peradventure this be true. Go you and tell her of it. [*Enter some of Antonio's kinsmen with a Musician.*] Cousins, you know what you have to do.—O, I cry you mercy, friend; go you with me, and I will use your skill.—Good cousin, have a care this busy time. *Exeunt.*

258 horn-mad stark mad. (From the fury of horned beasts; with allusion to cuckoldry.) **260 Venice** (A city noted for licentiousness.) **quake** (with a pun on *quiver* in the previous line) **261 I . . . then** i.e., my falling in love will be at least as rare as an earthquake **262 temporize . . . hours** come to terms, or become milder, in time (with perhaps a bawdy pun on *hours, whores;* pronounced something like *hoors*) **267 matter** wit, intelligence **268 and so . . . you** (A conventional close, which Claudio and Don Pedro mockingly play with as though it were the complimentary close of a letter.) **269 tuition** protection **274 guarded** ornamented, trimmed **275 guards . . . neither** trimmings are tenuously stitched on at best, have only the flimsiest connection **276 flout old ends** quote or recite mockingly tag ends of wisdom. **examine your conscience** look to your own behavior or speech **284 affect** love **285 ended action** military action now ended **289 now** now that **297 break** open the subject **299 twist** draw out the thread of **301 his complexion** its outward appearance **303 salv'd** softened, smoothed **304 flood** river **305 The . . . necessity** the best gift is one that is really needed **306 Look what** whatever. **'Tis once** in short, the fact is. (This speech of Don Pedro's is overheard by a servant of Antonio's, as we learn in the next scene.)

I.ii. Location: Leonato's house.
1 cousin kinsman **6 event** outcome **6–7 stamps . . . cover.** (The image is of news that is printed and bound in a book; Antonio means that things look promising at the moment, and will be good indeed if they turn out so.) **8 thick-pleach'd alley** walk lined with dense hedges of intertwined shrubs **9 orchard** garden **10 discover'd** disclosed **12 accordant** agreeing, consenting **13 top** i.e., forelock **15 wit** sense, intelligence **18–19 till . . . itself** till it manifest itself **23 cry you mercy** beg your pardon

[SCENE III]

Enter Sir [Don] John the Bastard and Conrade, his companion.

CONRADE What the good-year, my lord! Why are you thus out of measure sad?

DON JOHN There is no measure in the occasion that breeds; therefore the sadness is without limit.

CONRADE You should hear reason.

DON JOHN And when I have heard it, what blessing brings it?

CONRADE If not a present remedy, at least a patient sufferance.

DON JOHN I wonder that thou, being, as thou say'st thou art, born under Saturn, goest about to apply a moral medicine to a mortifying mischief. I cannot hide what I am: I must be sad when I have cause and smile at no man's jests, eat when I have stomach and wait for no man's leisure, sleep when I am drowsy and tend on no man's business, laugh when I am merry and claw no man in his humor.

CONRADE Yea, but you must not make the full show of this till you may do it without controlment. You have of late stood out against your brother, and he hath ta'en you newly into his grace, where it is impossible you should take true root but by the fair weather that you make yourself. It is needful that you frame the season for your own harvest.

DON JOHN I had rather be a canker in a hedge than a rose in his grace, and it better fits my blood to be disdain'd of all than to fashion a carriage to rob love from any. In this, though I cannot be said to be a flattering honest man, it must not be denied but I am a plain-dealing villain. I am trusted with a muzzle and enfranchis'd with a clog; therefore I have decreed not to sing in my cage. If I had my mouth, I would bite; if I had my liberty, I would do my liking. In the meantime let me be that I am, and seek not to alter me.

CONRADE Can you make no use of your discontent?

DON JOHN I make all use of it, for I use it only. Who comes here?

Enter Borachio.

What news, Borachio?

BORACHIO I came yonder from a great supper. The Prince your brother is royally entertain'd by Leonato; and I can give you intelligence of an intended marriage.

DON JOHN Will it serve for any model to build mischief on? What is he for a fool that betroths himself to unquietness?

BORACHIO Marry, it is your brother's right hand.

DON JOHN Who, the most exquisite Claudio?

BORACHIO Even he.

DON JOHN A proper squire! And who, and who? Which way looks he?

BORACHIO Marry, one Hero, the daughter and heir of Leonato.

DON JOHN A very forward March-chick! How came you to this?

BORACHIO Being entertain'd for a perfumer, as I was smoking a musty room, comes me the Prince and Claudio, hand in hand, in sad conference. I whipp'd me behind the arras, and there heard it agreed upon that the Prince should woo Hero for himself, and having obtain'd her, give her to Count Claudio.

DON JOHN Come, come, let us thither. This may prove food to my displeasure. That young start-up hath all the glory of my overthrow. If I can cross him any way, I bless myself every way. You are both sure, and will assist me?

CONRADE To the death, my lord.

DON JOHN Let us to the great supper. Their cheer is the greater that I am subdu'd. Would the cook were o' my mind! Shall we go prove what's to be done?

BORACHIO We'll wait upon your lordship. *Exeunt.*

[ACT II • SCENE I]

Enter Leonato, his brother [Antonio], Hero his daughter, and Beatrice his niece [with Margaret and Ursula], and a kinsman.

LEONATO Was not Count John here at supper?

ANTONIO I saw him not.

BEATRICE How tartly that gentleman looks! I never can see him but I am heart-burn'd an hour after.

HERO He is of a very melancholy disposition.

BEATRICE He were an excellent man that were made just in the midway between him and Benedick. The one is too like an image and says nothing, and the other too like my lady's eldest son, evermore tattling.

LEONATO Then half Signior Benedick's tongue in Count John's mouth, and half Count John's melancholy in Signior Benedick's face—

BEATRICE With a good leg and a good foot, uncle, and money enough in his purse, such a man would win any woman in the world, if 'a could get her good will.

LEONATO By my troth, niece, thou wilt never get thee a husband, if thou be so shrewd of thy tongue.

ANTONIO In faith, she's too curst.

I.iii. Location: Leonato's house.
1 What the good-year (An unexplained expletive, perhaps suggesting disgust; cf. *Merry Wives*, I.iv.115.) **2 out of measure** immoderately **4 breeds** causes (it) **5 hear** listen to **8–9 sufferance** endurance **11 under Saturn** (hence, of a morose disposition) **11–12 goest . . . mischief** endeavor to cure with moral commonplaces a deadly disease **15–16 tend on** attend to **17 claw** flatter. **humor** whim **19 controlment** restraint **20 stood out** rebelled **21 grace** favor **23 frame** produce **25 canker** dog rose (considered a weed) **26 blood** mood, disposition **27 fashion a carriage** counterfeit a behavior. **rob love** gain undeserved affection **30 trusted . . . muzzle** i.e., trusted only as far as one trusts a muzzled animal **30–31 enfranchis'd . . . clog** allowed freedom only to the extent of being hampered by a heavy wooden block **31 decreed** determined

44 What . . . fool what kind of fool is he **46 Marry** by the Virgin Mary, i.e., indeed **49 proper squire** handsome young man. (Said contemptuously.) **53 forward March-chick** precocious young thing (like a chick hatched prematurely) **55 entertain'd for** hired as **56 smoking** sweetening the air of (with aromatic smoke) **57 sad** serious **58 arras** tapestry, hanging **62 start-up** upstart **63 cross** thwart (with allusion, in bless *myself*, to making the sign of the cross) **64 sure** trustworthy **68–69 Would . . . mind** i.e., would the cook were of a mind to poison the food **69 prove** try out

II.i. Location: Leonato's house.
4 heart-burn'd affected with heartburn or indigestion **6 He were** a man would be **8 image** statue **9 my . . . son** i.e., a spoiled child **17 shrewd** sharp **18 curst** shrewish

BEATRICE Too curst is more than curst. I shall lessen God's sending that way; for it is said "God sends a curst cow short horns," but to a cow too curst he sends none.

LEONATO So, by being too curst, God will send you no horns.

BEATRICE Just, if he send me no husband; for the which blessing I am at him upon my knees every morning and evening. Lord, I could not endure a husband with a beard on his face! I had rather lie in the woolen.

LEONATO You may light on a husband that hath no beard.

BEATRICE What should I do with him? Dress him in my apparel and make him my waiting-gentlewoman? He that hath a beard is more than a youth, and he that hath no beard is less than a man; and he that is more than a youth is not for me, and he that is less than a man, I am not for him. Therefore I will even take sixpence in earnest of the berrord, and lead his apes into hell.

LEONATO Well, then, go you into hell?

BEATRICE No, but to the gate; and there will the devil meet me, like an old cuckold, with horns on his head, and say, "Get you to heaven, Beatrice, get you to heaven, here's no place for you maids." So deliver I up my apes, and away to Saint Peter. For the heavens, he shows me where the bachelors sit, and there live we as merry as the day is long.

ANTONIO [*To Hero*] Well, niece, I trust you will be rul'd by your father.

BEATRICE Yes, faith, it is my cousin's duty to make cur'sy and say, "Father, as it please you." But yet for all that, cousin, let him be a handsome fellow, or else make another cur'sy and say "Father, as it please me."

LEONATO Well, niece, I hope to see you one day fitted with a husband.

BEATRICE Not till God make men of some other metal than earth. Would it not grieve a woman to be overmaster'd with a piece of valiant dust? To make an account of her life to a clod of wayward marl? No, uncle, I'll none. Adam's sons are my brethren, and truly I hold it a sin to match in my kindred.

LEONATO [*To Hero*] Daughter, remember what I told you. If the Prince do solicit you in that kind, you know your answer.

BEATRICE The fault will be in the music, cousin, if you be not woo'd in good time. If the Prince be too important, tell him there is measure in everything, and so dance out the answer. For, hear me, Hero: wooing, wedding, and repenting is as a Scotch jig, a measure, and a cinquepace. The first suit is hot and hasty, like a Scotch jig, and full as fantastical; the wedding, mannerly-modest, as a measure, full of state and ancientry; and then comes Repentance and, with his bad legs, falls into the cinquepace faster and faster, till he sink into his grave.

LEONATO Cousin, you apprehend passing shrewdly.

BEATRICE I have a good eye, uncle; I can see a church by daylight.

LEONATO The revelers are ent'ring, brother. Make good room. [*All put on their masks.*]

Enter [*as maskers*] *Prince* [*Don*] *Pedro, Claudio, and Benedick, and Balthasar,* [*Borachio,*] *and Don John.*

DON PEDRO Lady, will you walk about with your friend?

HERO So you walk softly and look sweetly and say nothing, I am yours for the walk; and especially when I walk away.

DON PEDRO With me in your company?

HERO I may say so, when I please.

DON PEDRO And when please you to say so?

HERO When I like your favor; for God defend the lute should be like the case!

DON PEDRO My visor is Philemon's roof; within the house is Jove.

HERO Why, then, your visor should be thatch'd.

DON PEDRO Speak low, if you speak love. [*They step aside.*]

BALTHASAR Well, I would you did like me.

MARGARET So would not I, for your own sake; for I have many ill qualities.

BALTHASAR Which is one?

MARGARET I say my prayers aloud.

BALTHASAR I love you the better. The hearers may cry Amen.

MARGARET God match me with a good dancer!

BALTHASAR Amen.

MARGARET And God keep him out of my sight when the dance is done! Answer, clerk.

BALTHASAR No more words. The clerk is answer'd. [*They step aside.*]

URSULA I know you well enough. You are Signior Antonio.

ANTONIO At a word, I am not.

URSULA I know you by the waggling of your head.

ANTONIO To tell you true, I counterfeit him.

URSULA You could never do him so ill-well, unless you were the very man. Here's his dry hand up and down. You are he, you are he.

ANTONIO At a word, I am not.

URSULA Come, come, do you think I do not know you by your excellent wit? Can virtue hide itself? Go to, mum, you are he. Graces will appear, and there 's an end. [*They step aside.*]

20 that way in that respect **21 curst** i.e., savage, vicious **25 Just** right, exactly so **28 in the woolen** between blankets, without sheets **37 in earnest** in advance payment for. **berrord** bear-ward or bear-herd, one who keeps and exhibits a bear (and sometimes apes) **37–38 lead . . . hell** (An ancient proverb says, "Such as die maids do all lead apes in hell.") **44 For the heavens** as far as heaven is concerned **45 bachelors** unmarried persons of either sex **50 cur'sy** curtsy **55 metal** substance **58 marl** clay, earth **60 match . . . kindred** i.e., marry incestuously **65–66 important** importunate, urgent **66 measure** moderation (with a pun on the musical idea of dance, l. 68; see also *in good time* in l. 65) **69 cinquepace** five-step lively dance, galliard **71 state and ancientry** dignity and traditional stateliness

75 apprehend passing shrewdly understand with unusual perspicacity **81 friend** lover of either sex **88 favor** face **88–89 God . . . case** i.e., God forbid the face within should be as unhandsome as its cover, your visor **90 Philemon's roof** i.e., the humble cottage in which the peasants Philemon and Baucis entertained Jove or Jupiter unawares. (See Ovid, *Metamorphoses*, viii.) **92 thatch'd** i.e., whiskered, to resemble the thatch of a humble cottage **94–105 Balthasar** (The speech-prefixes in Q for Balthasar's lines read *Bene.* and *Balth.*; some editors speculate that *Borachio* is intended.) **104 clerk** (So addressed because of Balthasar's repeatedly answering "Amen" like the parish clerk saying the responses.) **108 At a word** in short **111 do . . . ill-well** imitate his imperfections so perfectly **112 dry hand** (A sign of age.) **up and down** exactly **117 mum** be silent **117–118 an end** no more to be said

BEATRICE Will you not tell me who told you so?

BENEDICK No, you shall pardon me.

BEATRICE Nor will you not tell me who you are?

BENEDICK Not now.

BEATRICE That I was disdainful, and that I had my good wit out of the "Hundred Merry Tales"—well, this was Signior Benedick that said so.

BENEDICK What's he?

BEATRICE I am sure you know him well enough.

BENEDICK Not I, believe me.

BEATRICE Did he never make you laugh?

BENEDICK I pray you, what is he?

BEATRICE Why, he is the Prince's jester, a very dull fool. Only his gift is in devising impossible slanders. None but libertines delight in him; and the commendation is not in his wit, but in his villainy, for he both pleases men and angers them, and then they laugh at him and beat him. I am sure he is in the fleet. I would he had boarded me.

BENEDICK When I know the gentleman, I'll tell him what you say.

BEATRICE Do do. He'll but break a comparison or two on me which, peradventure not mark'd or not laugh'd at, strikes him into melancholy; and then there's a partridge wing sav'd, for the fool will eat no supper that night. [*Music.*] We must follow the leaders.

BENEDICK In every good thing.

BEATRICE Nay, if they lead to any ill, I will leave them at the next turning.

Dance. Exeunt [*all except Don John, Borachio, and Claudio. Don John and Borachio are unmasked.*]

DON JOHN [*To Borachio*] Sure my brother is amorous on Hero and hath withdrawn her father to break with him about it. The ladies follow her and but one visor remains.

BORACHIO And that is Claudio. I know him by his bearing.

DON JOHN [*Advancing to Claudio*] Are not you Signior Benedick?

CLAUDIO You know me well. I am he.

DON JOHN Signior, you are very near my brother in his love. He is enamor'd on Hero. I pray you, dissuade him from her; she is no equal for his birth. You may do the part of an honest man in it.

CLAUDIO How know you he loves her?

DON JOHN I heard him swear his affection.

BORACHIO So did I too; and he swore he would marry her tonight.

DON JOHN Come, let us to the banquet.

Exeunt. Manet Claudio.

CLAUDIO

Thus answer I in name of Benedick,
But hear these ill news with the ears of Claudio.
'Tis certain so. The Prince woos for himself.
Friendship is constant in all other things
Save in the office and affairs of love;
Therefore all hearts in love use their own tongues.
Let every eye negotiate for itself
And trust no agent; for beauty is a witch
Against whose charms faith melteth into blood.
This is an accident of hourly proof,
Which I mistrusted not. Farewell therefore Hero!

Enter Benedick.

BENEDICK Count Claudio?

CLAUDIO Yea, the same.

BENEDICK Come, will you go with me?

CLAUDIO Whither?

BENEDICK Even to the next willow, about your own business, County. What fashion will you wear the garland of? About your neck, like an usurer's chain? Or under your arm, like a lieutenant's scarf? You must wear it one way, for the Prince hath got your Hero.

CLAUDIO I wish him joy of her.

BENEDICK Why, that's spoken like an honest drovier; so they sell bullocks. But did you think the Prince would have serv'd you thus?

CLAUDIO I pray you, leave me.

BENEDICK Ho, now you strike like the blind man. 'Twas the boy that stole your meat, and you'll beat the post.

CLAUDIO If it will not be, I'll leave you. *Exit.*

BENEDICK Alas, poor hurt fowl! Now will he creep into sedges. But that my Lady Beatrice should know me, and not know me! The Prince's fool! Ha? It may be I go under that title because I am merry. Yea, but so I am apt to do myself wrong. I am not so reputed. It is the base, though bitter, disposition of Beatrice that puts the world into her person, and so gives me out. Well, I'll be reveng'd as I may.

Enter the Prince [*Don Pedro*].

DON PEDRO Now, signior, where 's the Count? Did you see him?

BENEDICK Troth, my lord, I have play'd the part of Lady Fame. I found him here as melancholy as a lodge in a warren. I told him, and I think I told him true, that your Grace had got the good will of this young lady, and I off'red him my company to a willow-tree, either to make him a garland, as being forsaken, or to bind him up a rod, as being worthy to be whipp'd.

DON PEDRO To be whipp'd! What's his fault?

BENEDICK The flat transgression of a schoolboy, who, being overjoy'd with finding a birds' nest, shows it his companion, and he steals it.

DON PEDRO Wilt thou make a trust a transgression? The transgression is in the stealer.

124 Hundred Merry Tales (A popular collection of anecdotes first published by Rastell in 1526.) **132 Only his gift** his only talent. **impossible** incredible **134 villainy** i.e., mocking, raillery; also, clownishness **136 fleet** i.e., crowd, company **137 boarded** i.e., accosted (continuing the nautical metaphor begun in *fleet*) **140 break a comparison** make a scornful simile or innuendo **144 leaders** i.e., of the dance **157–158 near . . . love** close to my brother **165 banquet** light repast of fruit, wine, and dessert

171 all i.e., let all **174 faith . . . blood** honor gives way to passion **175 accident** occurrence **176 mistrusted** suspected **181 willow** (An emblem of disappointed love.) **182 County** count **182–183 garland** i.e., of willow **184 lieutenant's scarf** sash worn as a badge of rank **185 one way** one way or the other **187 drovier** cattle dealer **191 like the blind man** (An unidentified allusion to some proverbial story. Cf. the romance of *Lazarillo de Tormes*, in which the hero steals his master's meat and revenges himself for the beating he receives by causing the blind man to jump against a stone pillar.) **192 post** (1) pillar (2) bearer of news **193 If . . . be** i.e., if you won't leave me as I asked **194–195 creep into sedges** i.e., hide himself away, as wounded fowl creep into rushes along the river **198–200 It is . . . out** it is Beatrice's low and harsh disposition that causes her to attribute to the world her own attitudes and to represent me accordingly **204 Troth** by my faith **204–205 Lady Fame** Dame Rumor **205–206 lodge in a warren** hutch in a rabbit warren. (Rabbits symbolized melancholy.) **209–210 bind . . . rod** tie several willow switches into a scourge **212 flat** plain **215 a trust** the act of trusting someone

BENEDICK Yet it had not been amiss the rod had been made, and the garland too; for the garland he might have worn himself, and the rod he might have bestow'd on you, who, as I take it, have stol'n his birds' nest.

DON PEDRO I will but teach them to sing, and restore them to the owner.

BENEDICK If their singing answer your saying, by my faith, you say honestly.

DON PEDRO The Lady Beatrice hath a quarrel to you. The gentleman that danc'd with her told her she is much wrong'd by you.

BENEDICK O, she misus'd me past the endurance of a block! An oak but with one green leaf on it would have answer'd her. My very visor began to assume life and scold with her. She told me, not thinking I had been myself, that I was the Prince's jester, that I was duller than a great thaw; huddling jest upon jest with such impossible conveyance upon me that I stood like a man at a mark, with a whole army shooting at me. She speaks poniards, and every word stabs. If her breath were as terrible as her terminations, there were no living near her; she would infect to the north star. I would not marry her, though she were endow'd with all that Adam had left him before he transgress'd. She would have made Hercules have turn'd spit, yea, and have cleft his club to make the fire too. Come, talk not of her. You shall find her the infernal Ate in good apparel. I would to God some scholar would conjure her, for certainly, while she is here, a man may live as quiet in hell as in a sanctuary, and people sin upon purpose because they would go thither; so indeed all disquiet, horror, and perturbation follows her.

Enter Claudio and Beatrice, [*Leonato, and Hero*].

DON PEDRO Look, here she comes.

BENEDICK Will your Grace command me any service to the world's end? I will go on the slightest errand now to the Antipodes that you can devise to send me on; I will fetch you a toothpicker now from the furthest inch of Asia, bring you the length of Prester John's foot, fetch you a hair off the great Cham's beard, do you any embassage to the Pigmies, rather than hold three words' conference with this harpy. You have no employment for me?

DON PEDRO None, but to desire your good company.

BENEDICK O God, sir, here's a dish I love not! I cannot endure my Lady Tongue. *Exit.*

DON PEDRO Come, lady, come; you have lost the heart of Signior Benedick.

BEATRICE Indeed, my lord, he lent it me awhile, and I gave him use for it, a double heart for his single one. Marry, once before he won it of me with false dice, therefore your Grace may well say I have lost it.

DON PEDRO You have put him down, lady, you have put him down.

BEATRICE So I would not he should do me, my lord, lest I should prove the mother of fools. I have brought Count Claudio, whom you sent me to seek.

DON PEDRO Why, how now, Count? Wherefore are you sad?

CLAUDIO Not sad, my lord.

DON PEDRO How then? Sick?

CLAUDIO Neither, my lord.

BEATRICE The Count is neither sad, nor sick, nor merry, nor well; but civil count, civil as an orange, and something of that jealous complexion.

DON PEDRO I' faith, lady, I think your blazon to be true; though, I'll be sworn, if he be so, his conceit is false. Here, Claudio, I have woo'd in thy name, and fair Hero is won. I have broke with her father, and his good will obtain'd. Name the day of marriage, and God give thee joy!

LEONATO Count, take of me my daughter, and with her my fortunes. His Grace hath made the match, and all grace say Amen to it.

BEATRICE Speak, Count, 'tis your cue.

CLAUDIO Silence is the perfectest herald of joy. I were but little happy, if I could say how much! Lady, as you are mine, I am yours. I give away myself for you and dote upon the exchange.

BEATRICE Speak, cousin; or, if you cannot, stop his mouth with a kiss, and let not him speak neither.

[*Claudio and Hero embrace.*]

DON PEDRO In faith, lady, you have a merry heart.

BEATRICE Yea, my lord; I thank it, poor fool, it keeps on the windy side of care. My cousin tells him in his ear that he is in her heart.

CLAUDIO And so she doth, cousin.

BEATRICE Good Lord, for alliance! Thus goes every one to the world but I, and I am sunburnt. I may sit in a corner and cry "Heigh-ho for a husband!"

DON PEDRO Lady Beatrice, I will get you one.

BEATRICE I would rather have one of your father's getting. Hath your Grace ne'er a brother like you? Your father got excellent husbands, if a maid could come by them.

DON PEDRO Will you have me, lady?

BEATRICE No, my lord, unless I might have another for working-days. Your Grace is too costly to wear every day. But I beseech your Grace, pardon me. I was born to speak all mirth and no matter.

222 them i.e., the young birds in the nest **224 answer your saying** correspond to what you say **226 to** with **229 misus'd** abused **234 great thaw** i.e., time when roads are muddy and impassable, obliging one to stay dully at home. **huddling** piling, heaping up **235 impossible conveyance** incredible dexterity **236 at a mark** at the focus of aim **238 terminations** terms, expressions **239 north star** (Supposed the most remote of stars.) **242 Hercules . . . spit** (The Amazon Omphale forced the captive Hercules to wear women's clothing and spin; turning the spit would be an even more menial kitchen duty.) **244 Ate** goddess of discord **245 scholar . . . conjure** (Scholars were supposed to have the power to control evil spirits, which had to be addressed in Latin.) **254 toothpicker** toothpick **255 Prester John** a legendary Christian king of the Far East **256 great Cham** the Khan of Tartary, ruler of the Mongols **257 Pigmies** legendary small race thought to live in India **258 harpy** legendary creature with a woman's face and body and a bird's wings and claws

266 use usury, interest. **double** deceitful (?) **269 put him down** got the better of him. (But Beatrice plays with the phrase in its literal sense.) **280 civil** serious, grave (punning on *Seville* in Spain whence came bitter-tasting oranges) **280–281 something** somewhat **281 jealous complexion** i.e., yellow, associated with melancholy and symbolic of jealousy **282 blazon** description. (A heraldic term.) **283 conceit** (1) notion, idea (2) heraldic device (continuing the metaphor of *blazon*) **289–290 all grace** i.e., the source of grace, God **300 windy** windward, safe **303 alliance** relationship by marriage (Claudio has just called her "cousin.") **303–304 goes . . . world** i.e., everyone gets married **304 sunburnt** (The Renaissance considered dark complexions unattractive.) **305 Heigh-ho . . . husband** (The title of a ballad.) **307–308 getting** begetting (playing on *get,* "procure," in the previous speech) **315 matter** substance

DON PEDRO Your silence most offends me, and to be
merry best becomes you; for, out o' question, you
were born in a merry hour.

BEATRICE No, sure, my lord, my mother cried; but then
there was a star danc'd, and under that was I born.
Cousins, God give you joy!

LEONATO Niece, will you look to those things I told
you of?

BEATRICE I cry you mercy, uncle. By your Grace's 324
pardon. *Exit Beatrice.*

DON PEDRO By my troth, a pleasant-spirited lady.

LEONATO There's little of the melancholy element in 327
her, my lord. She is never sad but when she sleeps,
and not ever sad then; for I have heard my daughter 329
say, she hath often dreamt of unhappiness and wak'd
herself with laughing.

DON PEDRO She cannot endure to hear tell of a husband.

LEONATO O, by no means. She mocks all her wooers
out of suit. 334

DON PEDRO She were an excellent wife for Benedick.

LEONATO O Lord, my lord, if they were but a week
married, they would talk themselves mad.

DON PEDRO County Claudio, when mean you to go to
church?

CLAUDIO Tomorrow, my lord. Time goes on crutches
till love have all his rites.

LEONATO Not till Monday, my dear son, which is hence
a just sevennight, and a time too brief, too, to have all 343
things answer my mind. 344

DON PEDRO Come, you shake the head at so long a
breathing; but, I warrant thee, Claudio, the time shall 346
not go dully by us. I will in the interim undertake one
of Hercules' labors, which is, to bring Signior Bene-
dick and the Lady Beatrice into a mountain of affection
th' one with th' other. I would fain have it a match,
and I doubt not but to fashion it, if you three will but
minister such assistance as I shall give you direction. 352

LEONATO My lord, I am for you, though it cost me ten
nights' watchings. 354

CLAUDIO And I, my lord.

DON PEDRO And you too, gentle Hero?

HERO I will do any modest office, my lord, to help my
cousin to a good husband.

DON PEDRO And Benedick is not the unhopefullest hus-
band that I know. Thus far can I praise him: he is of a
noble strain, of approv'd valor, and confirm'd honesty. 361
I will teach you how to humor your cousin, that she
shall fall in love with Benedick; and I, with your two
helps, will so practice on Benedick that, in despite of
his quick wit and his queasy stomach, he shall fall in 365
love with Beatrice. If we can do this, Cupid is no
longer an archer; his glory shall be ours, for we are the
only love-gods. Go in with me, and I will tell you my
drift. *Exeunt.* 369

324 cry you mercy beg your pardon (for not having obeyed earlier). **your Grace's** i.e., Don Pedro's, from whom Beatrice begs leave to depart **327 melancholy element** i.e., earth, associated with the humor of melancholy in the old physiology **329 ever** always **334 out of suit** out of being wooers to her **343 a just sevennight** exactly a week **344 answer my mind** suit my wishes **346 breathing** pause, interval **352 minister** furnish, supply **354 watchings** staying awake **361 strain** ancestry. **approv'd** tested. **honesty** honor **365 queasy** squeamish, delicate (about marriage) **369 drift** purpose

[SCENE II]

Enter [Don] John and Borachio.

DON JOHN It is so. The Count Claudio shall marry the 1
daughter of Leonato.

BORACHIO Yea, my lord; but I can cross it.

DON JOHN Any bar, any cross, any impediment will be
med'cinable to me. I am sick in displeasure to him, 5
and whatsoever comes athwart his affection ranges 6
evenly with mine. How canst thou cross this mar- 7
riage?

BORACHIO Not honestly, my lord, but so covertly that
no dishonesty shall appear in me.

DON JOHN Show me briefly how.

BORACHIO I think I told your lordship, a year since,
how much I am in the favor of Margaret, the waiting
gentlewoman to Hero.

DON JOHN I remember.

BORACHIO I can, at any unseasonable instant of the
night, appoint her to look out at her lady's chamber-
window.

DON JOHN What life is in that, to be the death of this
marriage?

BORACHIO The poison of that lies in you to temper. Go 21
you to the Prince your brother; spare not to tell him
that he hath wrong'd his honor in marrying the re-
nown'd Claudio—whose estimation do you mightily 24
hold up—to a contaminated stale, such a one as Hero. 25

DON JOHN What proof shall I make of that?

BORACHIO Proof enough to misuse the Prince, to vex 27
Claudio, to undo Hero, and kill Leonato. Look you for
any other issue?

DON JOHN Only to despite them, I will endeavor any
thing.

BORACHIO Go, then, find me a meet hour to draw Don 32
Pedro and the Count Claudio alone. Tell them that you
know that Hero loves me; intend a kind of zeal both 34
to the Prince and Claudio, as—in love of your 35
brother's honor, who hath made this match, and his
friend's reputation, who is thus like to be cozen'd with 37
the semblance of a maid—that you have discover'd 38
thus. They will scarcely believe this without trial. Offer
them instances, which shall bear no less likelihood 40
than to see me at her chamber-window, hear me call
Margaret Hero, hear Margaret term me Claudio; and 42
bring them to see this the very night before the in-
tended wedding—for in the meantime I will so fash-
ion the matter that Hero shall be absent—and there
shall appear such seeming truth of Hero's disloyalty

II.ii. Location: Leonato's house.
1 shall is going to **5 med'cinable** medicinal. **displeasure to** dislike of **6–7 whatsoever . . . mine** whatever crosses his inclination runs parallel with mine **21 lies in** rests with. **temper** mix, compound **24 estimation** worth **25 stale** prostitute **27 misuse** abuse, deceive **32 meet** suitable **34 intend** pretend **35 as** i.e., saying as follows. (The words between the dashes are to be understood as instructions to Don John as to what he is to say.) **37 like** likely. **cozen'd** deceived, cheated **38 semblance** semblance only, outward appearance. **discover'd** revealed **40 instances** proofs **42 hear . . . Claudio** (Many editors follow Theobald and read *Borachio* for *Claudio.* The present reading may be defended if one imagines that, by arrangement with Margaret, Borachio is playing the part of Claudio, but the reading may also be an inconsistency.)

that jealousy shall be call'd assurance and all the pre- 47
paration overthrown. 48

DON JOHN Grow this to what adverse issue it can, I will
put it in practice. Be cunning in the working this, and
thy fee is a thousand ducats. 51

BORACHIO Be you constant in the accusation, and my
cunning shall not shame me.

DON JOHN I will presently go learn their day of marriage. *Exit* [*with Borachio*].

[SCENE III]

Enter Benedick alone.

BENEDICK Boy!

[*Enter Boy.*]

BOY Signior?

BENEDICK In my chamber-window lies a book. Bring it
hither to me in the orchard. 4

BOY I am here already, sir. 5

BENEDICK I know that, but I would have thee hence,
and here again. *Exit* [*Boy*]. I do much wonder that one
man, seeing how much another man is a fool when he
dedicates his behaviors to love, will, after he hath
laugh'd at such shallow follies in others, become the
argument of his own scorn by falling in love; and such 11
a man is Claudio. I have known when there was no
music with him but the drum and the fife; and now
had he rather hear the tabor and the pipe. I have 14
known when he would have walk'd ten mile afoot to
see a good armor; and now will he lie ten nights 16
awake, carving the fashion of a new doublet. He was 17
wont to speak plain and to the purpose, like an honest
man and a soldier; and now is he turn'd orthogra- 19
phy—his words are a very fantastical banquet, just so 20
many strange dishes. May I be so converted and see
with these eyes? I cannot tell; I think not. I will not be
sworn but love may transform me to an oyster; but I'll
take my oath on it, till he have made an oyster of me,
he shall never make me such a fool. One woman is
fair, yet I am well; another is wise, yet I am well; another virtuous, yet I am well; but till all graces be in
one woman, one woman shall not come in my grace.
Rich she shall be, that's certain; wise, or I'll none; vir- 29
tuous, or I'll never cheapen her; fair, or I'll never look 30
on her; mild, or come not near me; noble, or not I for 31
an angel; of good discourse, an excellent musician, 32
and her hair shall be of what color it please God.
Ha! The Prince and Monsieur Love! I will hide me in
the arbor. [*Withdraws.*]

Enter Prince [*Don Pedro*], *Leonato, Claudio.*

DON PEDRO
Come, shall we hear this music?

CLAUDIO
Yea, my good lord. How still the evening is,
As hush'd on purpose to grace harmony! 38

DON PEDRO [*Aside to them*]
See you where Benedick hath hid himself?

CLAUDIO [*Aside*]
O, very well, my lord. The music ended, 40
We'll fit the kid-fox with a pennyworth. 41

Enter Balthasar with Music.

DON PEDRO
Come, Balthasar, we'll hear that song again.

BALTHASAR
O, good my lord, tax not so bad a voice
To slander music any more than once.

DON PEDRO
It is the witness still of excellency 45
To put a strange face on his own perfection. 46
I pray thee, sing, and let me woo no more. 47

BALTHASAR
Because you talk of wooing, I will sing,
Since many a wooer doth commence his suit
To her he thinks not worthy, yet he woos,
Yet will he swear he loves.

DON PEDRO Nay, pray thee, come;
Or, if thou wilt hold longer argument,
Do it in notes.

BALTHASAR Note this before my notes: 53
There's not a note of mine that's worth the noting.

DON PEDRO
Why, these are very crotchets that he speaks! 55
Note, notes, forsooth, and nothing. [*Air.*] 56

BENEDICK Now, divine air! Now is his soul ravish'd! Is
it not strange that sheeps' guts should hale souls out of 58
men's bodies? Well, a horn for my money, when all 's 59
done.

[BALTHASAR] The Song.

Sigh no more, ladies, sigh no more,
  Men were deceivers ever,
One foot in sea and one on shore,
  To one thing constant never.
Then sigh not so, but let them go,
  And be you blithe and bonny,
Converting all your sounds of woe
  Into Hey nonny, nonny.

47 jealousy suspicion. **assurance** certainty **47–48 preparation** i.e., for marriage **51 ducats** gold coins

II.iii. Location: Leonato's garden.
4 orchard garden **5 I . . . already** i.e., I will be so quick as to use no time at all. (But Benedick quibbles on the literal sense.) **11 argument** subject **14 tabor . . . pipe** (Symbols of peaceful merriment.) **16 armor** suit of armor **17 carving** planning. **doublet** jacket **19–20 turn'd orthography** become fastidious and fashionable in his choice of language **29 I'll none** I'll have none of her **30 cheapen** ask the price of, bid for **31, 32 noble, angel** (Each of these words involves a pun on the meaning "a coin," a *noble* being worth 6 shillings 8 pence and an *angel,* 10 shillings.)

38 grace harmony do honor to music **40 The music ended** when the music is over **41 We'll . . . pennyworth** i.e., we'll give our sly victim more than he bargained for. (Benedick is called *kid-fox,* a term from beast fable, because he is both sly like a fox and is being duped in their game like a kid.) **45–46 It . . . perfection** it is always characteristic of excellence to have the performer unwilling to admit his own skill **47 woo** entreat **53 notes** music **55 crotchets** (1) whim, fancy (2) musical notes of brief duration **56 nothing** (With a pun on *noting;* the two words were pronounced alike. Cf. the same pun in the title of the play, where *Nothing* suggests "noting," or eavesdropping.) **58 sheeps' guts** strings on musical instruments. **hale** draw **59 horn** a hunting horn, a more masculine instrument than a fiddle. (But with a perhaps unconscious allusion to cuckold's horns.)

Sing no more ditties, sing no moe,
  Of dumps so dull and heavy;
The fraud of men was ever so,
  Since summer first was leavy.
Then sigh not so, etc.

DON PEDRO By my troth, a good song.

BALTHASAR And an ill singer, my lord.

DON PEDRO Ha, no, no, faith, thou sing'st well enough for a shift.

BENEDICK [*Aside*] An he had been a dog that should have howl'd thus, they would have hang'd him; and I pray God his bad voice bode no mischief. I had as lief have heard the night-raven, come what plague could have come after it.

DON PEDRO Yea, marry, dost thou hear, Balthasar? I pray thee, get us some excellent music; for tomorrow night we would have it at the Lady Hero's chamber-window.

BALTHASAR The best I can, my lord.

DON PEDRO Do so. Farewell. (*Exit Balthasar.*) Come hither, Leonato. What was it you told me of today, that your niece Beatrice was in love with Signior Benedick?

CLAUDIO O, ay! [*Aside to Pedro*] Stalk on, stalk on; the fowl sits.—I did never think that lady would have lov'd any man.

LEONATO No, nor I neither; but most wonderful that she should so dote on Signior Benedick, whom she hath in all outward behaviors seem'd ever to abhor.

BENEDICK [*Aside*] Is 't possible? Sits the wind in that corner?

LEONATO By my troth, my lord, I cannot tell what to think of it but that she loves him with an enrag'd affection; it is past the infinite of thought.

DON PEDRO May be she doth but counterfeit.

CLAUDIO Faith, like enough.

LEONATO O God, counterfeit? There was never counterfeit of passion came so near the life of passion as she discovers it.

DON PEDRO Why, what effects of passion shows she?

CLAUDIO [*Aside*] Bait the hook well; this fish will bite.

LEONATO What effects, my lord? She will sit you—you heard my daughter tell you how.

CLAUDIO She did indeed.

DON PEDRO How, how, I pray you? You amaze me. I would have thought her spirit had been invincible against all assaults of affection.

LEONATO I would have sworn it had, my lord—especially against Benedick.

BENEDICK [*Aside*] I should think this a gull, but that the white-bearded fellow speaks it. Knavery cannot, sure, hide himself in such reverence.

CLAUDIO [*Aside*] He hath ta'en th' infection. Hold it up.

DON PEDRO Hath she made her affection known to Benedick?

LEONATO No, and swears she never will. That's her torment.

CLAUDIO 'Tis true, indeed. So your daughter says. "Shall I," says she, "that have so oft encount'red him with scorn, write to him that I love him?"

LEONATO This says she now when she is beginning to write to him; for she'll be up twenty times a night, and there will she sit in her smock till she have writ a sheet of paper. My daughter tells us all.

CLAUDIO Now you talk of a sheet of paper, I remember a pretty jest your daughter told us of.

LEONATO O, when she had writ it and was reading it over, she found "Benedick" and "Beatrice" between the sheet?

CLAUDIO That.

LEONATO O, she tore the letter into a thousand halfpence; rail'd at herself, that she should be so immodest to write to one that she knew would flout her. "I measure him," says she, "by my own spirit; for I should flout him, if he writ to me. Yea, though I love him, I should."

CLAUDIO Then down upon her knees she falls, weeps, sobs, beats her heart, tears her hair, prays, curses: "O sweet Benedick! God give me patience!"

LEONATO She doth indeed; my daughter says so. And the ecstasy hath so much overborne her that my daughter is sometime afeard she will do a desperate outrage to herself. It is very true.

DON PEDRO It were good that Benedick knew of it by some other, if she will not discover it.

CLAUDIO To what end? He would make but a sport of it and torment the poor lady worse.

DON PEDRO An he should, it were an alms to hang him. She's an excellent sweet lady, and, out of all suspicion, she is virtuous.

CLAUDIO And she is exceeding wise.

DON PEDRO In every thing but in loving Benedick.

LEONATO O, my lord, wisdom and blood combatting in so tender a body, we have ten proofs to one that blood hath the victory. I am sorry for her, as I have just cause, being her uncle and her guardian.

DON PEDRO I would she had bestow'd this dotage on me. I would have daff'd all other respects and made her half myself. I pray you, tell Benedick of it, and hear what 'a will say.

LEONATO Were it good, think you?

CLAUDIO Hero thinks surely she will die; for she says she will die if he love her not, and she will die ere she make her love known, and she will die if he woo her, rather than she will bate one breath of her accustom'd crossness.

DON PEDRO She doth well. If she should make tender of her love, 'tis very possible he'll scorn it; for the man, as you know all, hath a contemptible spirit.

69 moe more **70 dumps** mournful songs; also, dances **72 leavy** leafy **77 for a shift** in a pinch **81 night-raven** some bird of night, portending disaster **83 Yea, marry** (A continuation of Don Pedro's speech preceding Benedick's aside.) **92–93 Stalk . . . sits** i.e., proceed warily; the hunted bird is hiding in the bush **101 enrag'd** maddened with passion **102 infinite** furthest reach **107 discovers** betrays **110 sit you** i.e., sit. (*You* is the ethical dative.) **118 gull** trick, deception **121–122 Hold it up** keep up the jest

140–141 halfpence i.e., small pieces **157 alms** good deed **158 out of** beyond **162 blood** natural feeling **167 daff'd** doffed, put or turn aside. **respects** considerations **168 half myself** i.e., my wife **174 bate** abate **176 tender** offer **178 contemptible** contemptuous

CLAUDIO He is a very proper man.

DON PEDRO He hath indeed a good outward happiness.

CLAUDIO Before God, and, in my mind, very wise.

DON PEDRO He doth indeed show some sparks that are like wit.

CLAUDIO And I take him to be valiant.

DON PEDRO As Hector, I assure you; and in the managing of quarrels you may say he is wise, for either he avoids them with great discretion, or undertakes them with a most Christian-like fear.

LEONATO If he do fear God, 'a must necessarily keep peace. If he break the peace, he ought to enter into a quarrel with fear and trembling.

DON PEDRO And so will he do; for the man doth fear God, howsoever it seems not in him by some large jests he will make. Well, I am sorry for your niece. Shall we go seek Benedick, and tell him of her love?

CLAUDIO Never tell him, my lord. Let her wear it out with good counsel.

LEONATO Nay, that's impossible. She may wear her heart out first.

DON PEDRO Well, we will hear further of it by your daughter. Let it cool the while. I love Benedick well, and I could wish he would modestly examine himself, to see how much he is unworthy so good a lady.

LEONATO My lord, will you walk? Dinner is ready.

[*They walk aside.*]

CLAUDIO If he do not dote on her upon this, I will never trust my expectation.

DON PEDRO Let there be the same net spread for her; and that must your daughter and her gentlewomen carry. The sport will be, when they hold one an opinion of another's dotage, and no such matter; that 's the scene that I would see, which will be merely a dumb-show. Let us send her to call him in to dinner.

[*Exeunt Don Pedro, Claudio, and Leonato.*]

BENEDICK [*Coming forward*] This can be no trick. The conference was sadly borne. They have the truth of this from Hero. They seem to pity the lady. It seems her affections have their full bent. Love me? Why, it must be requited. I hear how I am censur'd. They say I will bear myself proudly, if I perceive the love come from her; they say too that she will rather die than give any sign of affection. I did never think to marry. I must not seem proud; happy are they that hear their detractions and can put them to mending. They say the lady is fair; 'tis a truth, I can bear them witness; and virtuous; 'tis so, I cannot reprove it; and wise, but for loving me; by my troth, it is no addition to her wit, nor no great argument of her folly, for I will be horribly in love with her. I may chance have some odd quirks and remnants of wit broken on me, because I have rail'd so long against marriage. But doth not the appetite alter? A man loves the meat in his youth that he cannot endure in his age. Shall quips and sentences and these paper bullets of the brain awe a man from the career of his humor? No, the world must be peopled. When I said I would die a bachelor, I did not think I should live till I were married. Here comes Beatrice. By this day, she's a fair lady! I do spy some marks of love in her.

Enter Beatrice.

BEATRICE Against my will I am sent to bid you come in to dinner.

BENEDICK Fair Beatrice, I thank you for your pains.

BEATRICE I took no more pains for those thanks than you take pains to thank me. If it had been painful, I would not have come.

BENEDICK You take pleasure then in the message?

BEATRICE Yea, just so much as you may take upon a knife's point and choke a daw withal. You have no stomach, signior. Fare you well. *Exit.*

BENEDICK Ha! "Against my will I am sent to bid you come in to dinner." There's a double meaning in that. "I took no more pains for those thanks than you took pains to thank me." That's as much as to say, "Any pains that I take for you is as easy as thanks." If I do not take pity of her, I am a villain; if I do not love her, I am a Jew. I will go get her picture. *Exit.*

[ACT III • SCENE I]

Enter Hero and two gentlewomen, Margaret and Ursula.

HERO

Good Margaret, run thee to the parlor.
There shalt thou find my cousin Beatrice
Proposing with the Prince and Claudio.
Whisper her ear, and tell her I and Ursula
Walk in the orchard, and our whole discourse
Is all of her. Say that thou overheard'st us;
And bid her steal into the pleached bower,
Where honeysuckles, ripened by the sun,
Forbid the sun to enter, like favorites,
Made proud by princes, that advance their pride
Against that power that bred it. There will she hide her,
To listen our propose. This is thy office.
Bear thee well in it and leave us alone.

MARGARET

I'll make her come, I warrant you, presently. [*Exit.*]

179 proper handsome **180 outward happiness** fortune in his good looks **185 Hector** the mightiest of the Trojans **193 by** to judge by. **large** broad, indelicate **197 counsel** reflection, deliberation **209–210 they . . . dotage** each believes the other to be in love **210 no such matter** the reality is quite otherwise **211–212 dumb-show** pantomime (lacking their usual banter) **214 sadly borne** soberly conducted **216 have . . . bent** are tightly stretched **221–222 their detractions** criticisms of themselves **222 put . . . mending** undertake to remedy the defect **224 reprove** refute **227 quirks** witty conceits or jokes

231 quips sharp or sarcastic remarks. **sentences** saws, maxims **232 paper bullets** i.e., words **233 career of his humor** pursuit of his inclination **246 choke . . . withal** i.e., make a mouthful for a jackdaw **247 stomach** appetite

III.i. Location: Leonato's garden.
3 Proposing conversing **7 pleached** formed by densely interwoven branches **10–11 that . . . it** i.e., who dare set themselves up against the very princes who advanced them **12 listen our propose** listen to our conversation **13 leave us alone** leave the rest to us

HERO
Now, Ursula, when Beatrice doth come,
As we do trace this alley up and down,
Our talk must only be of Benedick.
When I do name him, let it be thy part
To praise him more than ever man did merit.
My talk to thee must be how Benedick
Is sick in love with Beatrice. Of this matter
Is little Cupid's crafty arrow made,
That only wounds by hearsay.

Enter Beatrice [behind].

Now begin;
For look where Beatrice, like a lapwing, runs
Close by the ground, to hear our conference.

URSULA
The pleasant'st angling is to see the fish
Cut with her golden oars the silver stream,
And greedily devour the treacherous bait.
So angle we for Beatrice, who even now
Is couched in the woodbine coverture.
Fear you not my part of the dialogue.

HERO
Then go we near her, that her ear lose nothing
Of the false sweet bait that we lay for it.
[Approaching the bower.]
No, truly, Ursula, she is too disdainful;
I know her spirits are as coy and wild
As haggards of the rock.

URSULA
But are you sure
That Benedick loves Beatrice so entirely?

HERO
So says the Prince and my new-trothed lord.

URSULA
And did they bid you tell her of it, madam?

HERO
They did entreat me to acquaint her of it;
But I persuaded them, if they lov'd Benedick,
To wish him wrestle with affection,
And never to let Beatrice know of it.

URSULA
Why did you so? Doth not the gentleman
Deserve as full as fortunate a bed
As ever Beatrice shall couch upon?

HERO
O god of love! I know he doth deserve
As much as may be yielded to a man;
But Nature never fram'd a woman's heart
Of prouder stuff than that of Beatrice.
Disdain and scorn ride sparkling in her eyes,
Misprising what they look on, and her wit
Values itself so highly that to her
All matter else seems weak. She cannot love,
Nor take no shape nor project of affection,
She is so self-endeared.

URSULA
Sure, I think so;
And therefore certainly it were not good
She knew his love, lest she'll make sport at it.

HERO
Why, you speak truth. I never yet saw man,
How wise, how noble, young, how rarely featur'd,
But she would spell him backward. If fair-fac'd,
She would swear the gentleman should be her
sister;
If black, why, Nature, drawing of an antic,
Made a foul blot; if tall, a lance ill-headed;
If low, an agate very vilely cut;
If speaking, why, a vane blown with all winds;
If silent, why, a block moved with none.
So turns she every man the wrong side out,
And never gives to truth and virtue that
Which simpleness and merit purchaseth.

URSULA
Sure, sure, such carping is not commendable.

HERO
No, not to be so odd, and from all fashions,
As Beatrice is, cannot be commendable.
But who dare tell her so? If I should speak,
She would mock me into air; O, she would
laugh me
Out of myself, press me to death with wit.
Therefore let Benedick, like cover'd fire,
Consume away in sighs, waste inwardly.
It were a better death than die with mocks,
Which is as bad as die with tickling.

URSULA
Yet tell her of it. Hear what she will say.

HERO
No, rather I will go to Benedick
And counsel him to fight against his passion.
And truly, I'll devise some honest slanders
To stain my cousin with. One doth not know
How much an ill word may empoison liking.

URSULA
O, do not do your cousin such a wrong!
She cannot be so much without true judgment—
Having so swift and excellent a wit
As she is priz'd to have—as to refuse
So rare a gentleman as Signior Benedick.

HERO
He is the only man of Italy,
Always excepted my dear Claudio.

URSULA
I pray you, be not angry with me, madam,
Speaking my fancy: Signior Benedick,
For shape, for bearing, argument and valor,
Goes foremost in report through Italy.

HERO
Indeed, he hath an excellent good name.

16 trace walk **23 only . . . hearsay** wounds by mere report **24 lapwing** bird of the plover family **27 oars** i.e., fins **30 woodbine coverture** bower, or arbor, of honeysuckle **35 coy** disdainful **36 haggards** untamed female hawks. **rock** i.e., mountainous terrain **45 as full as** fully as **52 Misprising** undervaluing **55 project** conception, idea **56 self-endeared** full of self-love

60 How however. **rarely** excellently **61 spell him backward** i.e., speak contrarily of him by characterizing his virtues as vices **63 black** dark. **antic** buffoon, grotesque figure **65 agate** i.e., diminutive person (alluding to the small figures cut in agate for rings) **70 simpleness** integrity, plainness **72 from** contrary to **76 press me to death** (Pressing to death with weights was the usual punishment for those accused of crimes who refused to plead either guilty or not guilty.) **78 Consume . . . sighs** (An allusion to the belief that each sigh cost the heart a drop of blood.) **84 honest slanders** i.e., slanders which do not involve her virtue **90 priz'd** esteemed **96 argument** skill in discourse

URSULA
His excellence did earn it, ere he had it.
When are you married, madam?

HERO
Why, every day tomorrow. Come, go in. 101
I'll show thee some attires, and have thy counsel
Which is the best to furnish me tomorrow.
[*They walk away.*]

URSULA
She's lim'd, I warrant you. We have caught her,
madam. 104

HERO
If it prove so, then loving goes by haps; 105
Some Cupid kills with arrows, some with traps.
[*Exeunt Hero and Ursula.*]

BEATRICE [*Coming forward*]
What fire is in mine ears? Can this be true? 107
Stand I condemn'd for pride and scorn so much?
Contempt, farewell, and maiden pride, adieu!
No glory lives behind the back of such. 110
And, Benedick, love on; I will requite thee,
Taming my wild heart to thy loving hand. 112
If thou dost love, my kindness shall incite thee
To bind our loves up in a holy band;
For others say thou dost deserve, and I
Believe it better than reportingly. *Exit.* 116

[SCENE II]

Enter Prince [*Don Pedro*], *Claudio, Benedick, and Leonato.*

DON PEDRO I do but stay till your marriage be consum-
mate, and then go I toward Arragon.
CLAUDIO I'll bring you thither, my lord, if you'll vouch- 3
safe me.
DON PEDRO Nay, that would be as great a soil in the
new gloss of your marriage as to show a child his new
coat and forbid him to wear it. I will only be bold with 7
Benedick for his company; for, from the crown of his
head to the sole of his foot, he is all mirth. He hath
twice or thrice cut Cupid's bow-string, and the little
hangman dare not shoot at him. He hath a heart as 11
sound as a bell, and his tongue is the clapper, for what
his heart thinks his tongue speaks.
BENEDICK Gallants, I am not as I have been.
LEONATO So say I. Methinks you are sadder. 15
CLAUDIO I hope he be in love.
DON PEDRO Hang him, truant! There's no true drop of
blood in him, to be truly touch'd with love. If he be
sad, he wants money.
BENEDICK I have the toothache. 20
DON PEDRO Draw it. 21
BENEDICK Hang it! 22
CLAUDIO You must hang it first, and draw it after-
wards.
DON PEDRO What, sigh for the toothache?
LEONATO Where is but a humor or a worm. 26
BENEDICK Well, every one can master a grief but he that
has it.
CLAUDIO Yet say I, he is in love.
DON PEDRO There is no appearance of fancy in him, un- 30
less it be a fancy that he hath to strange disguises; as, 31
to be a Dutchman today, a Frenchman tomorrow, or
in the shape of two countries at once, as, a German
from the waist downward, all slops, and a Spaniard 34
from the hip upward, no doublet. Unless he have a 35
fancy to this foolery, as it appears he hath, he is no
fool for fancy, as you would have it appear he is. 37
CLAUDIO If he be not in love with some woman, there
is no believing old signs. 'A brushes his hat o' morn-
ings. What should that bode?
DON PEDRO Hath any man seen him at the barber's?
CLAUDIO No, but the barber's man hath been seen with
him, and the old ornament of his cheek hath already 43
stuff'd tennis-balls. 44
LEONATO Indeed he looks younger than he did, by the
loss of a beard.
DON PEDRO Nay, 'a rubs himself with civet. Can you 47
smell him out by that?
CLAUDIO That's as much as to say, the sweet youth's in
love.
DON PEDRO The greatest note of it is his melancholy. 51
CLAUDIO And when was he wont to wash his face? 52
DON PEDRO Yea, or to paint himself? For the which I
hear what they say of him.
CLAUDIO Nay, but his jesting spirit, which is now crept
into a lute-string, and now govern'd by stops. 56
DON PEDRO Indeed, that tells a heavy tale for him. Con-
clude, conclude he is in love.
CLAUDIO Nay, but I know who loves him.
DON PEDRO That would I know too. I warrant, one that
knows him not.
CLAUDIO Yes, and his ill conditions; and, in despite of 62
all, dies for him.
DON PEDRO She shall be buried with her face upwards. 64
BENEDICK Yet is this no charm for the toothache. Old
signior, walk aside with me. I have studied eight or

101 every day tomorrow every day after tomorrow **104 lim'd** caught, like a bird in birdlime, a sticky substance spread on branches to trap the birds that perch on them **105 by haps** by chance **107 What . . . ears** (An allusion to the old saying that a person's ears burn when one is being discussed in one's absence.) **110 No . . . such** no good is spoken of such persons when their backs are turned **112 Taming . . . hand** (A figure derived from the taming of the hawk by the hand of the falconer.) **116 better than reportingly** on better evidence than mere report

III.ii. Location: Leonato's house.
3 bring escort **7 be bold with** ask **11 hangman** executioner; rogue. (Playfully applied to Cupid.) **15 sadder** more serious

20 toothache (Thought to be a common ailment of lovers.) **21 Draw** extract. (But Claudio jokes on the method of executing traitors, who were hanged first and then cut down alive and drawn, i.e., disembowelled, and finally quartered.) **22 Hang it** confound it **26 Where . . . worm** (Toothache was ascribed to "humors" or unhealthy secretions and to actual worms in the teeth.) **30–31 fancy . . . fancy** love . . . whim, liking **34 slops** loose breeches **35 no doublet** i.e., covered with a Spanish cloak **37 fool for fancy** i.e., lover **43–44 old . . . tennis-balls** i.e., Benedick's beard has gone to stuff tennis balls. (He appears on stage beardless in this scene for the first time.) **47 civet** perfume derived from the civet cat **51 note** mark **52 wash** i.e., with cosmetics; similarly with *paint* in the next line **56 stops** (1) frets on the finger board (2) restraints **62 ill conditions** bad qualities **64 buried . . . upwards** i.e., as a Christian, not as a suicide, who were sometimes buried face downwards (?). (Probably there is also a ribald suggestion, continuing the joke on *dies for him* meaning to make love.)

nine wise words to speak to you, which these hobby-horses must not hear. [*Exeunt Benedick and Leonato.*]

DON PEDRO For my life, to break with him about Beatrice.

CLAUDIO 'Tis even so. Hero and Margaret have by this play'd their parts with Beatrice, and then the two bears will not bite one another when they meet.

Enter [Don] John the Bastard.

DON JOHN My lord and brother, God save you!

DON PEDRO Good den, brother.

DON JOHN If your leisure serv'd, I would speak with you.

DON PEDRO In private?

DON JOHN If it please you. Yet Count Claudio may hear, for what I would speak of concerns him.

DON PEDRO What's the matter?

DON JOHN [*To Claudio*] Means your lordship to be married tomorrow?

DON PEDRO You know he does.

DON JOHN I know not that, when he knows what I know.

CLAUDIO If there be any impediment, I pray you discover it.

DON JOHN You may think I love you not. Let that appear hereafter, and aim better at me by that I now will manifest. For my brother, I think he holds you well, and in dearness of heart hath holp to effect your ensuing marriage—surely suit ill spent and labor ill bestow'd.

DON PEDRO Why, what's the matter?

DON JOHN I came hither to tell you, and, circumstances short'ned, for she has been too long a-talking of, the lady is disloyal.

CLAUDIO Who, Hero?

DON JOHN Even she—Leonato's Hero, your Hero, every man's Hero.

CLAUDIO Disloyal?

DON JOHN The word is too good to paint out her wickedness. I could say she were worse; think you of a worse title, and I will fit her to it. Wonder not till further warrant. Go but with me tonight, you shall see her chamber-window ent'red, even the night before her wedding-day. If you love her then, tomorrow wed her; but it would better fit your honor to change your mind.

CLAUDIO May this be so?

DON PEDRO I will not think it.

DON JOHN If you dare not trust that you see, confess not that you know. If you will follow me, I will show you enough; and when you have seen more and heard more, proceed accordingly.

CLAUDIO If I see any thing tonight why I should not marry her tomorrow, in the congregation, where I should wed, there will I shame her.

DON PEDRO And, as I woo'd for thee to obtain her, I will join with thee to disgrace her.

DON JOHN I will disparage her no farther till you are my witnesses. Bear it coldly but till midnight, and let the issue show itself.

DON PEDRO O day untowardly turn'd!

CLAUDIO O mischief strangely thwarting!

DON JOHN O plague right well prevented! So will you say when you have seen the sequel. [*Exeunt.*]

[SCENE III]

Enter Dogberry and his compartner [Verges] with the Watch.

DOGBERRY Are you good men and true?

VERGES Yea, or else it were pity but they should suffer salvation, body and soul.

DOGBERRY Nay, that were a punishment too good for them, if they should have any allegiance in them, being chosen for the Prince's watch.

VERGES Well, give them their charge, neighbor Dogberry.

DOGBERRY First, who think you the most desartless man to be constable?

FIRST WATCH Hugh Oatcake, sir, or George Seacole, for they can write and read.

DOGBERRY Come hither, neighbor Seacole. [*Seacole, or Second Watch, steps forward.*] God hath bless'd you with a good name. To be a well-favor'd man is the gift of fortune, but to write and read comes by nature.

SECOND WATCH Both which, Master Constable—

DOGBERRY You have. I knew it would be your answer. Well, for your favor, sir, why, give God thanks, and make no boast of it; and for your writing and reading, let that appear when there is no need of such vanity. You are thought here to be the most senseless and fit man for the constable of the watch; therefore bear you the lantern. This is your charge: you shall comprehend all vagrom men; you are to bid any man stand, in the Prince's name.

SECOND WATCH. How if 'a will not stand?

DOGBERRY Why, then, take no note of him, but let him go, and presently call the rest of the watch together and thank God you are rid of a knave.

VERGES If he will not stand when he is bidden, he is none of the Prince's subjects.

DOGBERRY True, and they are to meddle with none but the Prince's subjects. You shall also make no noise in

67–68 hobby-horses i.e., buffoons. (Originally figures in a morris dance made to resemble a horse and rider.) **69 For** upon **71 Margaret** (Ursula joined Hero in playing the trick on Beatrice, but Margaret has been in on it.) **75 Good den** good evening **87–88 discover** reveal **90 aim better at** judge better of **91 holds you well** thinks well of you **96–97 circumstances short'ned** without unnecessary details **97 a-talking of** under discussion (by us) **103 paint out** portray in full **105–106 till further warrant** till further proof appears **113–114 If . . . know** i.e., when you have seen what I'll show you, either admit that what you know is true or admit that you're denying a certainty

123 coldly calmly **125 untowardly turn'd** perversely altered

III.iii. Location: A street.

3 salvation (A blunder for *damnation.*) **5 allegiance** (For *treachery.*) **7 charge** instructions **9 desartless** (For *deserving.*) **15 well-favor'd** good-looking **22 senseless** (For *sensible.*) **24 comprehend** (For *apprehend.*) **25 vagrom** vagrant. **stand** stand still, stop

the streets; for, for the watch to babble and to talk is most tolerable and not to be endur'd.

SECOND WATCH We will rather sleep than talk. We know what belongs to a watch.

DOGBERRY Why, you speak like an ancient and most quiet watchman; for I cannot see how sleeping should offend. Only have a care that your bills be not stol'n. Well, you are to call at all the alehouses, and bid those that are drunk get them to bed.

SECOND WATCH How if they will not?

DOGBERRY Why, then, let them alone till they are sober. If they make you not then the better answer, you may say they are not the men you took them for.

SECOND WATCH Well, sir.

DOGBERRY If you meet a thief, you may suspect him, by virtue of your office, to be no true man; and, for such kind of men, the less you meddle or make with them, why, the more is for your honesty.

SECOND WATCH If we know him to be a thief, shall we not lay hands on him?

DOGBERRY Truly, by your office you may; but I think they that touch pitch will be defil'd. The most peaceable way for you, if you do take a thief, is to let him show himself what he is and steal out of your company.

VERGES You have been always call'd a merciful man, partner.

DOGBERRY Truly, I would not hang a dog by my will, much more a man who hath any honesty in him.

VERGES If you hear a child cry in the night, you must call to the nurse and bid her still it.

SECOND WATCH How if the nurse be asleep and will not hear us?

DOGBERRY Why, then, depart in peace, and let the child wake her with crying; for the ewe that will not hear her lamb when it baes will never answer a calf when he bleats.

VERGES 'Tis very true.

DOGBERRY This is the end of the charge: you, constable, are to present the Prince's own person. If you meet the Prince in the night, you may stay him.

VERGES Nay, by 'r lady, that I think 'a cannot.

DOGBERRY Five shillings to one on 't, with any man that knows the statutes, he may stay him; marry, not without the Prince be willing, for, indeed, the watch ought to offend no man, and it is an offense to stay a man against his will.

VERGES By 'r lady, I think it be so.

DOGBERRY Ha, ah, ha! Well, masters, good night. An there be any matter of weight chances, call up me. Keep your fellows' counsels and your own, and good night. Come, neighbor. [*Starts to leave, with Verges.*]

SECOND WATCH Well, masters, we hear our charge. Let us go sit here upon the church-bench till two, and then all to bed.

DOGBERRY One word more, honest neighbors. I pray you, watch about Signior Leonato's door, for the wedding being there tomorrow, there is a great coil tonight. Adieu. Be vigitant, I beseech you.

Exeunt [Dogberry and Verges].

Enter Borachio and Conrade.

BORACHIO What, Conrade!

SECOND WATCH [*Aside*] Peace! Stir not.

BORACHIO Conrade, I say!

CONRADE Here, man. I am at thy elbow.

BORACHIO Mass, and my elbow itch'd; I thought there would a scab follow.

CONRADE I will owe thee an answer for that; and now forward with thy tale.

BORACHIO Stand thee close, then, under this penthouse, for it drizzles rain, and I will, like a true drunkard, utter all to thee.

SECOND WATCH [*Aside*] Some treason, masters. Yet stand close.

BORACHIO Therefore know I have earn'd of Don John a thousand ducats.

CONRADE Is it possible that any villainy should be so dear?

BORACHIO Thou shouldst rather ask if it were possible any villainy should be so rich; for when rich villains have need of poor ones, poor ones may make what price they will.

CONRADE I wonder at it.

BORACHIO That shows thou art unconfirm'd. Thou knowest that the fashion of a doublet, or a hat, or a cloak, is nothing to a man.

CONRADE Yes, it is apparel.

BORACHIO I mean, the fashion.

CONRADE Yes, the fashion is the fashion.

BORACHIO Tush! I may as well say the fool's the fool. But seest thou not what a deform'd thief this fashion is?

SECOND WATCH [*Aside*] I know that Deform'd. 'A has been a vile thief this seven year; 'a goes up and down like a gentleman. I remember his name.

BORACHIO Didst thou not hear somebody?

CONRADE No; 'twas the vane on the house.

BORACHIO Seest thou not, I say, what a deform'd thief this fashion is, how giddily 'a turns about all the hot bloods between fourteen and five-and-thirty, sometimes fashioning them like Pharaoh's soldiers in the reechy painting, sometime like god Bel's priests in the old church-window, sometime like the shaven Hercules in the smirch'd worm-eaten tapestry, where his codpiece seems as massy as his club?

36 tolerable (For *intolerable.*) **38 belongs to** are the duties of **41 bills** pikes, with axes fixed to long poles **50 true** honest **51 meddle or make** have to do **52 is** it is **56 they . . . defil'd** (A commonplace derived from Ecclesiasticus 13:1.) **74 present** represent **76 by 'r lady** i.e., by Our Lady. (A mild oath.)

92 coil to-do **93 vigitant** (For *vigilant.*) **98 Mass** i.e., by the Mass **99 scab** i.e., scoundrel (with play on literal meaning) **100 owe thee an answer** answer later **102–103 penthouse** overhanging structure **103–104 true drunkard** (Alludes to the commonplace that the drunkard tells all; Borachio's name in Spanish means "drunkard.") **106 stand close** stay hidden **110 dear** expensive **112 villainy** i.e., instigator of villainy **116 unconfirm'd** inexperienced **118 is . . . man** does not make the man. (But Conrade plays on the phrase in its usual sense.) **123 deform'd thief** i.e., so called because fashion takes such varied and extreme shapes, and because it impoverishes those who follow fashion **126 up and down** about, here and there **134 reechy** dirty, grimy. (Perhaps this painting is of the Israelites passing through the Red Sea.) **god Bel's priests** (Probably alludes to the story of Bel and the Dragon, from the Apocryphal book of *Daniel,* depicted in a stained-glass window.) **135–136 shaven Hercules** (A reference either to Hercules in the service of Omphale—see II.i.242, note—or, confusedly, to the story of Samson.) **137 codpiece** decorative pouch at the fly of a man's breeches (indelicately conspicuous in this tapestry)

CONRADE All this I see; and I see that the fashion wears out more apparel than the man. But art not thou thyself giddy with the fashion too, that thou hast shifted out of thy tale into telling me of the fashion?

BORACHIO Not so, neither. But know that I have tonight woo'd Margaret, the Lady Hero's gentlewoman, by the name of Hero. She leans me out at her mistress' chamber-window, bids me a thousand times good night—I tell this tale vilely; I should first tell thee how the Prince, Claudio, and my master, planted and plac'd and possess'd by my master Don John, saw afar off in the orchard this amiable encounter.

CONRADE And thought they Margaret was Hero?

BORACHIO Two of them did, the Prince and Claudio, but the devil my master knew she was Margaret; and partly by his oaths, which first possess'd them, partly by the dark night, which did deceive them, but chiefly by my villainy, which did confirm any slander that Don John had made, away went Claudio enrag'd; swore he would meet her, as he was appointed, next morning at the temple, and there, before the whole congregation, shame her with what he saw o'er night and send her home again without a husband.

SECOND WATCH We charge you, in the Prince's name, stand!

FIRST WATCH Call up the right Master Constable. We have here recover'd the most dangerous piece of lechery that ever was known in the commonwealth.

SECOND WATCH And one Deform'd is one of them. I know him; 'a wears a lock.

CONRADE Masters, masters—

SECOND WATCH You'll be made bring Deform'd forth, I warrant you.

CONRADE Masters—

SECOND WATCH Never speak, we charge you. Let us obey you to go with us.

BORACHIO We are like to prove a goodly commodity, being taken up of these men's bills.

CONRADE A commodity in question, I warrant you. Come, we'll obey you. *Exeunt.*

[SCENE IV]

Enter Hero, and Margaret and Ursula.

HERO Good Ursula, wake my cousin Beatrice, and desire her to rise.

URSULA I will, lady.

HERO And bid her come hither.

URSULA Well. *[Exit.]*

MARGARET Troth, I think your other rabato were better.

HERO No, pray thee, good Meg, I'll wear this.

MARGARET By my troth, 's not so good; and I warrant your cousin will say so.

HERO My cousin 's a fool, and thou art another. I'll wear none but this.

MARGARET I like the new tire within excellently, if the hair were a thought browner; and your gown 's a most rare fashion, i' faith. I saw the Duchess of Milan's gown that they praise so.

HERO O, that exceeds, they say.

MARGARET By my troth, 's but a night-gown in respect of yours: cloth o' gold, and cuts, and lac'd with silver, set with pearls, down sleeves, side sleeves, and skirts, round underborne with a bluish tinsel. But for a fine, quaint, graceful, and excellent fashion, yours is worth ten on 't.

HERO God give me joy to wear it! For my heart is exceeding heavy.

MARGARET 'Twill be heavier soon by the weight of a man.

HERO Fie upon thee! Art not asham'd?

MARGARET Of what, lady? Of speaking honorably? Is not marriage honorable in a beggar? Is not your lord honorable without marriage? I think you would have me say, "saving your reverence, a husband." An bad thinking do not wrest true speaking, I'll offend nobody. Is there any harm in "the heavier for a husband"? None, I think, an it be the right husband and the right wife; otherwise 'tis light, and not heavy. Ask my Lady Beatrice else. Here she comes.

Enter Beatrice.

HERO Good morrow, coz.

BEATRICE Good morrow, sweet Hero.

HERO Why, how now? Do you speak in the sick tune?

BEATRICE I am out of all other tune, methinks.

MARGARET Clap 's into "Light o' love." That goes without a burden; do you sing it, and I'll dance it.

BEATRICE Ye light o' love with your heels! Then, if your husband have stables enough, you'll see he shall lack no barns.

MARGARET O illegitimate construction! I scorn that with my heels.

BEATRICE 'Tis almost five o'clock, cousin; 'tis time you were ready. By my troth, I am exceeding ill. Heigh-ho!

MARGARET For a hawk, a horse, or a husband?

BEATRICE For the letter that begins them all, H.

MARGARET Well, an you be not turn'd Turk, there 's no more sailing by the star.

138–139 fashion . . . man i.e., fashion prompts the discarding of clothes faster than honest use **148 possess'd** (misleadingly) informed; also, perhaps, possessed as by the devil **149 amiable** amorous **163 right Master Constable** (A comic title on the pattern of "right worshipful," etc.) **164 recover'd** (For *discovered.*) **164–165 lechery** (For *treachery.*) **167 lock** lock of hair hanging down on the left shoulder; the lovelock **172–173 Let . . . to** (A blunder for *obey us and.*) **174 commodity** goods acquired **175 taken up** (1) obtained on credit (2) arrested. **bills** (1) bonds given as security (2) pikes **176 in question** (1) subject to judicial examination (2) of doubtful value

III.iv. Location: Hero's apartment in the house of Leonato.
5 Well very well, as you wish

6 rabato tall collar supporting a ruff, stiffened with wire or starch **8 troth, 's** faith, it is **12 tire within** headdress in the inner room **16 exceeds** i.e., exceeds comparison **17 night-gown** dressing gown **17–18 in respect of** compared to **18 cuts** slashes in a garment revealing the underlying fabric. **lac'd** trimmed. **silver** i.e., silver thread **19 down sleeves** tight-fitting sleeves to the wrist. **side sleeves** secondary ornamental sleeves hanging from the shoulder **20 round underborne** with a lining around the edge of the skirt **21 quaint** elegant **29 in** even in **31 saving . . . husband** (By this apologetic formula, Margaret suggests that Hero is too prudish even to hear the word "husband" mentioned.) **32 wrest** misinterpret **35 light** (with a pun on the meaning *wanton*) **41 Clap 's** let's shift. **Light o' love** (A popular song.) **42 burden** bass accompaniment (with pun on the idea of "a weight of a man") **43 Ye . . . heels** i.e., you're light-heeled, wanton **45 barns** (with pun on *bairns,* children) **46–47 with my heels** (A proverbial expression of scorn.) **51 H** (with a pun on *ache,* pronounced *aitch*) **52 turn'd Turk** i.e., turned apostate to the true faith (by violating your oath not to become a lover) **52–53 no . . . star** no more navigating by the north star, i.e., no certain truth in which to trust

BEATRICE What means the fool, trow?

MARGARET Nothing I; but God send every one their heart's desire!

HERO These gloves the Count sent me, they are an excellent perfume.

BEATRICE I am stuff'd cousin; I cannot smell.

MARGARET A maid, and stuff'd! There 's goodly catching of cold.

BEATRICE O, God help me! God help me! How long have you profess'd apprehension?

MARGARET Ever since you left it. Doth not my wit become me rarely?

BEATRICE It is not seen enough, you should wear it in your cap. By my troth, I am sick.

MARGARET Get you some of this distill'd Carduus Benedictus, and lay it to your heart. It is the only thing for a qualm.

HERO There thou prick'st her with a thistle.

BEATRICE Benedictus! Why Benedictus? You have some moral in this Benedictus.

MARGARET Moral? No, by my troth, I have no moral meaning, I meant plain holy-thistle. You may think perchance that I think you are in love. Nay, by 'r lady, I am not such a fool to think what I list, nor I list not to think what I can, nor indeed I cannot think, if I would think my heart out of thinking, that you are in love or that you will be in love or that you can be in love. Yet Benedick was such another, and now is he become a man. He swore he would never marry, and yet now, in despite of his heart, he eats his meat without grudging; and how you may be converted I know not, but methinks you look with your eyes as other women do.

BEATRICE What pace is this that thy tongue keeps?

MARGARET Not a false gallop.

Enter Ursula.

URSULA Madam, withdraw. The Prince, the Count, Signior Benedick, Don John, and all the gallants of the town are come to fetch you to church.

HERO Help to dress me, good coz, good Meg, good Ursula. [*Exeunt.*]

[SCENE V]

Enter Leonato and the Constable [*Dogberry*] *and the Headborough* [*Verges*].

LEONATO What would you with me, honest neighbor?

DOGBERRY Marry, sir, I would have some confidence with you that decerns you nearly.

LEONATO Brief, I pray you, for you see it is a busy time with me.

DOGBERRY Marry, this it is, sir.

VERGES Yes, in truth it is, sir.

LEONATO What is it, my good friends?

DOGBERRY Goodman Verges sir, speaks a little off the matter—an old man, sir, and his wits are not so blunt as, God help, I would desire they were, but, in faith, honest as the skin between his brows.

VERGES Yes, I thank God I am as honest as any man living that is an old man and no honester than I.

DOGBERRY Comparisons are odorous. Palabras, neighbor Verges.

LEONATO Neighbors, you are tedious.

DOGBERRY It pleases your worship to say so, but we are the poor Duke's officers; but truly, for mine own part, if I were as tedious as a king, I could find in my heart to bestow it all of your worship.

LEONATO All thy tediousness on me, ah?

DOGBERRY Yea, an 'twere a thousand pound more than 'tis; for I hear as good exclamation on your worship as of any man in the city, and though I be but a poor man, I am glad to hear it.

VERGES And so am I.

LEONATO I would fain know what you have to say.

VERGES Marry, sir, our watch tonight, excepting your worship's presence, ha' ta'en a couple of as arrant knaves as any in Messina.

DOGBERRY A good old man, sir; he will be talking. As they say, "When the age is in, the wit is out." God help us, it is a world to see! Well said, i' faith, neighbor Verges. Well, God 's a good man. An two men ride of a horse, one must ride behind. An honest soul, i' faith, sir, by my troth he is, as ever broke bread; but God is to be worship'd; all men are not alike, alas, good neighbor!

LEONATO Indeed, neighbor, he comes too short of you.

DOGBERRY Gifts that God gives.

LEONATO I must leave you.

DOGBERRY One word, sir. Our watch, sir, have indeed comprehended two aspicious persons, and we would have them this morning examin'd before your worship.

LEONATO Take their examination yourself and bring it me. I am now in great haste, as it may appear unto you.

DOGBERRY It shall be suffigance.

LEONATO Drink some wine ere you go. Fare you well.

[*Enter a Messenger.*]

MESSENGER My lord, they stay for you to give your daughter to her husband.

54 trow I wonder **58 perfume** (Gloves were often perfumed.) **59 stuff'd** i.e., stuffed up with a cold. (But Margaret plays on the sense of *pregnant.*) **63 profess'd apprehension** made claim to be witty **66–67 wear . . . cap** i.e., as a fool does his coxcomb **68–69 Carduus Benedictus** the blessed thistle, noted for medicinal properties (with a pun on *Benedick*) **73 moral** hidden meaning **81–82 a man** i.e., like other men **83–84 eats . . . grudging** has a normal appetite, like other men's (in love) **87 false gallop** canter

III.v. Location: Leonato's house.
s.d. Headborough local constable **2 confidence** (A blunder for *conference.*) **3 decerns** (For *concerns.*)

9 Goodman (Title of persons under the social rank of gentleman.) **10 blunt** (He means *sharp.*) **12 honest . . . brows** (Proverbial expression of honesty.) **15 odorous** (For *odious.*) **Palabras** (For *pocas palabras,* "few words" in Spanish.) **19 poor Duke's officers** (For *Duke's poor officers.*) **21 of** on **24 exclamation** (Possibly for *acclamation.*) **29 tonight** last night. **excepting** (For *respecting.*) **33 When . . . out** (An adaptation of the proverb: "When ale is in, wit is out.") **34 a world** i.e., wonderful. (Proverbial.) **35 God 's . . . man** i.e., God is good. (A proverbial saying.) **36 of** on **44 comprehended** (For *apprehended.*) **aspicious** (For *suspicious.*) **50 suffigance** (For *sufficient.*)

LEONATO I'll wait upon them. I am ready.
[*Exeunt Leonato and Messenger.*]

DOGBERRY Go, good partner, go, get you to Francis Seacole. Bid him bring his pen and inkhorn to the jail. We are now to examination these men.

VERGES And we must do it wisely.

DOGBERRY We will spare for no wit, I warrant you. Here 's that shall drive some of them to a noncome. Only get the learned writer to set down our excommunication and meet me at the jail. [*Exeunt.*]

[ACT IV • SCENE I]

Enter Prince [*Don Pedro*], [*Don John the*] *Bastard, Leonato, Friar* [*Francis*], *Claudio, Benedick, Hero, and Beatrice* [*with Attendants*].

LEONATO Come, Friar Francis, be brief—only to the plain form of marriage, and you shall recount their particular duties afterwards.

FRIAR You come hither, my lord, to marry this lady.

CLAUDIO No.

LEONATO To be married to her. Friar, you come to marry her.

FRIAR Lady, you come hither to be married to this Count.

HERO I do.

FRIAR If either of you know any inward impediment why you should not be conjoin'd, I charge you, on your souls, to utter it.

CLAUDIO Know you any, Hero?

HERO None, my lord.

FRIAR Know you any, Count?

LEONATO I dare make his answer, none.

CLAUDIO O, what men dare do! What men may do! What men daily do, not knowing what they do!

BENEDICK How now? Interjections? Why, then, some be of laughing, as ah, ha, he!

CLAUDIO Stand thee by, friar. Father, by your leave,
Will you with free and unconstrained soul
Give me this maid, your daughter?

LEONATO
As freely, son, as God did give her me.

CLAUDIO
And what have I to give you back, whose worth
May counterpoise this rich and precious gift?

DON PEDRO
Nothing, unless you render her again.

CLAUDIO
Sweet Prince, you learn me noble thankfulness.
[*Hands Hero to Leonato.*]
There, Leonato, take her back again.
Give not this rotten orange to your friend;
She 's but the sign and semblance of her honor.
Behold how like a maid she blushes here!
O, what authority and show of truth
Can cunning sin cover itself withal!
Comes not that blood as modest evidence
To witness simple virtue? Would you not swear,
All you that see her, that she were a maid,
By these exterior shows? But she is none:
She knows the heat of a luxurious bed;
Her blush is guiltiness, not modesty.

LEONATO
What do you mean, my lord?

CLAUDIO
Not to be married,
Not to knit my soul to an approved wanton.

LEONATO
Dear my lord, if you, in your own proof,
Have vanquish'd the resistance of her youth,
And made defeat of her virginity—

CLAUDIO
I know what you would say: if I have known her,
You will say she did embrace me as a husband,
And so extenuate the 'forehand sin.
No, Leonato,
I never tempted her with word too large,
But, as a brother to his sister, show'd
Bashful sincerity and comely love.

HERO
And seem'd I ever otherwise to you?

CLAUDIO
Out on thee seeming! I will write against it.
You seem to me as Dian in her orb,
As chaste as is the bud ere it be blown;
But you are more intemperate in your blood
Than Venus, or those pamp'red animals
That rage in savage sensuality.

HERO
Is my lord well, that he doth speak so wide?

LEONATO
Sweet Prince, why speak not you?

DON PEDRO
What should I speak?
I stand dishonor'd, that have gone about
To link my dear friend to a common stale.

LEONATO
Are these things spoken, or do I but dream?

DON JOHN
Sir, they are spoken, and these things are true.

BENEDICK
This looks not like a nuptial.

HERO
True! O God!

CLAUDIO
Leonato, stand I here?

54 wait upon attend **55–56 Francis Seacole** i.e., the Sexton of IV.ii, not the member of the watch in III.iii **57 examination** (For *examine.*) **60 noncome** (Probably a contraction for *non compos mentis,* "not of sound mind," but Dogberry may have intended *nonplus.*) **61–62 excommunication** (For *examination* or *communication.*)

IV.i. Location: A church.
20–21 some . . . he (Benedick quotes from Lilly's Latin Grammar on the subject of interjections; according to Lilly, these are to be classified as laughing interjections.) **27 counterpoise** balance, be equivalent to **29 learn** teach

34 authority assurance **36 modest evidence** evidence of modesty **37 witness** bear witness to **40 luxurious** lascivious, lustful **43 approved** proved **44 in . . . proof** in making trial of her yourself **49 extenuate** excuse, lessen. **'forehand sin** sin of anticipating (marriage) **51 large** broad, immodest **55 Out . . . seeming** i.e., shame on you, a mere semblance of good **56 Dian . . . orb** i.e., Diana, goddess of chastity, enthroned in the moon **57 be blown** open, flower **61 wide** wide of the mark **63 gone about** undertaken **64 stale** whore **68 True** (A reply to Don John's speech.)

Is this the Prince? Is this the Prince's brother?
Is this face Hero's? Are our eyes our own?

LEONATO
All this is so. But what of this, my lord?

CLAUDIO
Let me but move one question to your daughter;
And, by that fatherly and kindly power
That you have in her, bid her answer truly.

LEONATO
I charge thee do so, as thou art my child.

HERO
O, God defend me, how am I beset!
What kind of catechizing call you this?

CLAUDIO
To make you answer truly to your name.

HERO
Is it not Hero? Who can blot that name
With any just reproach?

CLAUDIO Marry, that can Hero!
Hero itself can blot out Hero's virtue.
What man was he talk'd with you yesternight
Out at your window betwixt twelve and one?
Now, if you are a maid, answer to this.

HERO
I talk'd with no man at that hour, my lord.

DON PEDRO
Why, then are you no maiden. Leonato,
I am sorry you must hear. Upon mine honor,
Myself, my brother, and this grieved Count
Did see her, hear her, at that hour last night
Talk with a ruffian at her chamber-window,
Who hath indeed, most like a liberal villain,
Confess'd the vile encounters they have had
A thousand times in secret.

DON JOHN
Fie, fie, they are not to be nam'd, my lord,
Not to be spoke of!
There is not chastity enough in language
Without offense to utter them. Thus, pretty lady,
I am sorry for thy much misgovernment.

CLAUDIO
O Hero, what a Hero hadst thou been,
If half thy outward graces had been plac'd
About thy thoughts and counsels of thy heart!
But fare thee well, most foul, most fair! Farewell,
Thou pure impiety and impious purity!
For thee I'll lock up all the gates of love,
And on my eyelids shall conjecture hang,
To turn all beauty into thoughts of harm,
And never shall it more be gracious.

LEONATO
Hath no man's dagger here a point for me?
[*Hero swoons.*]

BEATRICE
Why, how now, cousin, wherefore sink you down?

DON JOHN
Come, let us go. These things, come thus to light,
Smother her spirits up.
[*Exeunt Don Pedro, Don John, and Claudio.*]

BENEDICK
How doth the lady?

BEATRICE Dead, I think. Help, uncle!
Hero, why, Hero! Uncle! Signior Benedick! Friar!

LEONATO
O Fate, take not away thy heavy hand!
Death is the fairest cover for her shame
That may be wish'd for.

BEATRICE How now, cousin Hero!

FRIAR
Have comfort, lady.

LEONATO
Dost thou look up?

FRIAR Yea, wherefore should she not?

LEONATO
Wherefore? Why, doth not every earthly thing
Cry shame upon her? Could she here deny
The story that is printed in her blood?
Do not live, Hero, do not ope thine eyes;
For, did I think thou wouldst not quickly die,
Thought I thy spirits were stronger than thy shames,
Myself would, on the rearward of reproaches,
Strike at thy life. Griev'd I, I had but one?
Chid I for that at frugal nature's frame?
O, one too much by thee! Why had I one?
Why ever wast thou lovely in my eyes?
Why had I not with charitable hand
Took up a beggar's issue at my gates,
Who, smirched thus and mir'd with infamy,
I might have said "No part of it is mine;
This shame derives itself from unknown loins"?
But mine, and mine I lov'd, and mine I prais'd,
And mine that I was proud on, mine so much
That I myself was to myself not mine,
Valuing of her—why, she, O, she is fall'n
Into a pit of ink, that the wide sea
Hath drops too few to wash her clean again,
And salt too little which may season give
To her foul-tainted flesh!

BENEDICK Sir, sir, be patient.
For my part, I am so attir'd in wonder,
I know not what to say.

BEATRICE
O, on my soul, my cousin is belied!

BENEDICK
Lady, were you her bedfellow last night?

BEATRICE
No, truly, not; although, until last night,
I have this twelvemonth been her bedfellow.

LEONATO
Confirm'd, confirm'd! O, that is stronger made
Which was before barr'd up with ribs of iron!
Would the two princes lie, and Claudio lie,
Who lov'd her so, that, speaking of her foulness,

73 kindly natural **81 Hero itself** the name Hero **88 grieved** (1) aggrieved, wronged (2) struck with grief **91 liberal** licentious **98 much misgovernment** great misconduct **104 For thee** because of you **105 conjecture** evil suspicion **107 be gracious** seem attractive, graceful

121 blood i.e., blushes **125 on . . . reproaches** i.e., if the reproaches of Claudio and Don Pedro (and myself) don't finish you off **127 frame** plan, order **137 That . . . mine** i.e., she was so much a part of me that by comparison I was not myself **141 season** preservative

Wash'd it with tears? Hence from her! Let her die.

FRIAR

Hear me a little;
For I have only been silent so long,
And given way unto this course of fortune,
By noting of the lady. I have mark'd
A thousand blushing apparitions
To start into her face, a thousand innocent shames
In angel whiteness beat away those blushes,
And in her eye there hath appear'd a fire
To burn the errors that these princes hold
Against her maiden truth. Call me a fool;
Trust not my reading nor my observations,
Which with experimental seal doth warrant
The tenor of my book; trust not my age,
My reverence, calling, nor divinity,
If this sweet lady lie not guiltless here
Under some biting error.

LEONATO

Friar, it cannot be.
Thou seest that all the grace that she hath left
Is that she will not add to her damnation
A sin of perjury; she not denies it.
Why seek'st thou then to cover with excuse
That which appears in proper nakedness?

FRIAR

Lady, what man is he you are accus'd of?

HERO

They know that do accuse me; I know none.
If I know more of any man alive
Than that which maiden modesty doth warrant,
Let all my sins lack mercy! O my father,
Prove you that any man with me convers'd
At hours unmeet, or that I yesternight
Maintain'd the change of words with any creature,
Refuse me, hate me, torture me to death!

FRIAR

There is some strange misprision in the princes.

BENEDICK

Two of them have the very bent of honor;
And if their wisdoms be misled in this,
The practice of it lives in John the bastard,
Whose spirits toil in frame of villainies.

LEONATO

I know not. If they speak but truth of her,
These hands shall tear her; if they wrong her honor
The proudest of them shall well hear of it.
Time hath not yet so dried this blood of mine,
Nor age so eat up my invention,
Nor fortune made such havoc of my means,
Nor my bad life reft me so much of friends,
But they shall find, awak'd in such a kind,
Both strength of limb and policy of mind,
Ability in means, and choice of friends,
To quit me of them throughly.

FRIAR

Pause awhile,
And let my counsel sway you in this case.
Your daughter here the princes left for dead.
Let her awhile be secretly kept in,
And publish it that she is dead indeed;
Maintain a mourning ostentation,
And on your family's old monument
Hang mournful epitaphs, and do all rites
That appertain unto a burial.

LEONATO

What shall become of this? What will this do?

FRIAR

Marry, this well carried shall on her behalf
Change slander to remorse. That is some good.
But not for that dream I on this strange course,
But on this travail look for greater birth.
She dying, as it must be so maintain'd,
Upon the instant that she was accus'd,
Shall be lamented, pitied, and excus'd
Of every hearer, for it so falls out
That what we have we prize not to the worth
Whiles we enjoy it, but, being lack'd and lost,
Why then we rack the value, then we find
The virtue that possession would not show us
Whiles it was ours. So will it fare with Claudio.
When he shall hear she died upon his words,
Th' idea of her life shall sweetly creep
Into his study of imagination,
And every lovely organ of her life
Shall come apparel'd in more precious habit,
More moving, delicate, and full of life,
Into the eye and prospect of his soul,
Than when she liv'd indeed. Then shall he mourn,
If ever love had interest in his liver,
And wish he had not so accused her,
No, though he thought his accusation true.
Let this be so, and doubt not but success
Will fashion the event in better shape
Than I can lay it down in likelihood.
But if all aim but this be level'd false,
The supposition of the lady's death
Will quench the wonder of her infamy.
And if it sort not well, you may conceal her,
As best befits her wounded reputation,
In some reclusive and religious life,
Out of all eyes, tongues, minds, and injuries.

BENEDICK

Signior Leonato, let the friar advise you;
And though you know my inwardness and love
Is very much unto the Prince and Claudio,
Yet, by mine honor, I will deal in this
As secretly and justly as your soul

156 course of fortune turn of events **157 By . . . lady** i.e., so that I might observe Hero's reaction (?) **162 errors** (Personified as a heretic burned at the stake.) **165–166 Which . . . book** i.e., by means of which observations and experience I have confirmed what I learned from books **174 proper** its own **181 unmeet** improper **182 Maintain'd the change** held exchange **183 Refuse** disown **184 misprision** mistake, misunderstanding **185 the very bent of** an absolute inclination of the mind toward **187 practice** scheming **188 frame** contriving **193 eat** eaten. (Pronounced *et*.) **invention** power to plan (vengeance) **196 kind** manner **197 policy** shrewdness, contriving

199 quit . . . throughly settle my account with them thoroughly **204 Maintain . . . ostentation** perform all the resemblances of mourning **208 become of** result from **209 carried** managed **212 on this travail** (1) as a result of this effort (2) from this labor in childbirth **217 to the worth** as fully as it deserves **219 rack** stretch (as on a rack) **222 upon** in consequence of **224 study of imagination** musing, imaginative contemplation **225 organ . . . life** aspect of her when she was alive **226 habit** apparel **228 prospect** range of vision **230 interest in** claim upon. **liver** (The supposed seat of the passion of love.) **233 success** i.e., what succeeds or happens in time as my plan unfolds **234 event** outcome **235 lay . . . likelihood** anticipate its probable course **236 if . . . false** i.e., if every other aim miscarry **239 sort** turn out **241reclusive** cloistered **242 injuries** insults **244 inwardness and love** close friendship

Should with your body.

LEONATO Being that I flow in grief, 248
The smallest twine may lead me.

FRIAR
'Tis well consented. Presently away;
For to strange sores strangely they strain the cure. 251
Come, lady, die to live. This wedding-day
Perhaps is but prolong'd. Have patience and endure. 253
Exit [with all but Benedick and Beatrice].

BENEDICK Lady Beatrice, have you wept all this while?

BEATRICE Yea, and I will weep a while longer.

BENEDICK I will not desire that.

BEATRICE You have no reason; I do it freely.

BENEDICK Surely I do believe your fair cousin is wrong'd.

BEATRICE Ah, how much might the man deserve of me that would right her!

BENEDICK Is there any way to show such friendship?

BEATRICE A very even way, but no such friend. 263

BENEDICK May a man do it?

BEATRICE It is a man's office, but not yours.

BENEDICK I do love nothing in the world so well as you. Is not that strange?

BEATRICE As strange as the thing I know not. It were as possible for me to say I lov'd nothing so well as you. But believe me not; and yet I lie not. I confess nothing, nor I deny nothing. I am sorry for my cousin.

BENEDICK By my sword, Beatrice, thou lovest me.

BEATRICE Do not swear and eat it. 273

BENEDICK I will swear by it that you love me, and I will make him eat it that says I love not you.

BEATRICE Will you not eat your word?

BENEDICK With no sauce that can be devis'd to it. I pro- 277
test I love thee. 278

BEATRICE Why, then, God forgive me!

BENEDICK What offense, sweet Beatrice?

BEATRICE You have stay'd me in a happy hour. I was 281
about to protest I lov'd you.

BENEDICK And do it with all thy heart.

BEATRICE I love you with so much of my heart that none is left to protest.

BENEDICK Come, bid me do any thing for thee.

BEATRICE Kill Claudio.

BENEDICK Ha! Not for the wide world.

BEATRICE You kill me to deny it. Farewell. [*Going.*]

BENEDICK Tarry, sweet Beatrice.

BEATRICE I am gone, though I am here. There is no love 291
in you. Nay, I pray you, let me go.

BENEDICK Beatrice—

BEATRICE In faith, I will go.

BENEDICK We'll be friends first.

BEATRICE You dare easier be friends with me than fight with mine enemy.

BENEDICK Is Claudio thine enemy?

BEATRICE Is 'a not approv'd in the height a villain, that 299
hath slander'd, scorn'd, dishonor'd my kinswoman?
O that I were a man! What, bear her in hand until they 301
come to take hands, and then, with public accusation,
uncover'd slander, unmitigated rancor—O God, that 303
I were a man! I would eat his heart in the market-place.

BENEDICK Hear me, Beatrice—

BEATRICE Talk with a man out at a window! A proper saying!

BENEDICK Nay, but, Beatrice—

BEATRICE Sweet Hero! She is wrong'd, she is sland'red, she is undone.

BENEDICK Beat—

BEATRICE Princes and counties! Surely, a princely testi- 313
mony, a goodly count, Count Comfect; a sweet gallant, 314
surely! O that I were a man for his sake! Or that I had
any friend would be a man for my sake! But manhood
is melted into cur'sies, valor into compliment, and 317
men are only turn'd into tongue, and trim ones too. 318
He is now as valiant as Hercules that only tells a lie, and swears it. I cannot be a man with wishing, therefore I will die a woman with grieving.

BENEDICK Tarry, good Beatrice. By this hand, I love thee.

BEATRICE Use it for my love some other way than swearing by it.

BENEDICK Think you in your soul the Count Claudio hath wrong'd Hero?

BEATRICE Yea, as sure as I have a thought or a soul.

BENEDICK Enough, I am engag'd. I will challenge him. 329
I will kiss your hand, and so I leave you. By this hand,
Claudio shall render me a dear account. As you hear 331
of me, so think of me. Go, comfort your cousin. I must say she is dead; and so, farewell. [*Exeunt severally.*]

[SCENE II]

Enter the Constables [Dogberry and Verges] and the Town Clerk [Sexton] in gowns, Borachio, [Conrade, and Watch].

DOGBERRY Is our whole dissembly appear'd? 1

VERGES O, a stool and a cushion for the sexton.
[*Stool and cushion are brought. The Sexton sits.*]

SEXTON Which be the malefactors?

DOGBERRY Marry, that am I and my partner.

VERGES Nay, that's certain; we have the exhibition to 5
examine.

SEXTON But which are the offenders that are to be examin'd? Let them come before Master Constable.

DOGBERRY Yea, marry, let them come before me. [*The prisoners are brought forward.*] What is your name, friend?

BORACHIO Borachio.

248 Being that seeing that, since. **flow in** overflow with, or am afloat in **251 For . . . cure** strange diseases require strange and desperate cures **253 prolong'd** deferred, put off **263 even** without obstacles **273 eat it** i.e., eat your words **277–278 protest** affirm **281 stay'd** stopped. **in . . . hour** at an appropriate moment **291 gone** i.e., in spirit **299 approv'd** proved. **height** extreme

301 bear her in hand delude her with false hopes **303 uncover'd** open, unconcealed **313 counties** counts **314 count** (1) the title (2) declaration of complaint in an indictment **Comfect** candy or sweetmeat **317 cur'sies** curtsies **318 trim** nice. (Used ironically.) **329 I am engag'd** I pledge myself **331 dear** costly

IV.ii. Location: a prison.
1 dissembly (A blunder for *assembly.*) **5 exhibition** (Possibly for *commission.*)

DOGBERRY Pray, write down Borachio. Yours, sirrah? 13
CONRADE I am a gentleman, sir, and my name is Con-
rade.
DOGBERRY Write down, Master Gentleman Conrade.
Masters, do you serve God?
CONRADE, BORACHIO Yea, sir, we hope.
DOGBERRY Write down, that they hope they serve God;
and write God first, for God defend but God should 20
go before such villains! Masters, it is prov'd already
that you are little better than false knaves, and it will
go near to be thought so shortly. How answer you for
yourselves?
CONRADE Marry, sir, we say we are none.
DOGBERRY A marvelous witty fellow, I assure you; but 26
I will go about with him. [*To Borachio.*] Come you 27
hither, sirrah; a word in your ear. Sir, I say to you, it
is thought you are false knaves.
BORACHIO Sir, I say to you we are none.
DOGBERRY Well, stand aside. 'Fore God, they are both
in a tale. Have you writ down that they are none? 32
SEXTON Master Constable, you go not the way to ex-
amine. You must call forth the watch that are their ac-
cusers.
DOGBERRY Yea, marry, that's the eftest way. Let the 36
watch come forth. Masters, I charge you, in the
Prince's name, accuse these men.
FIRST WATCH This man said, sir, that Don John, the
Prince's brother, was a villain.
DOGBERRY Write down Prince John a villain. Why, this
is flat perjury, to call a prince's brother villain.
BORACHIO Master Constable—
DOGBERRY Pray thee, fellow, peace. I do not like thy
look, I promise thee.
SEXTON What heard you him say else?
SECOND WATCH Marry, that he had receiv'd a thousand
ducats of Don John for accusing the Lady Hero wrong-
fully.
DOGBERRY Flat burglary as ever was committed. 50
VERGES Yea, by mass, that it is.
SEXTON What else, fellow?
FIRST WATCH And that Count Claudio did mean, upon
his words, to disgrace Hero before the whole assem-
bly, and not marry her.
DOGBERRY O villain! Thou wilt be condemn'd into ev-
erlasting redemption for this. 57
SEXTON What else?
WATCHMEN This is all.
SEXTON And this is more, masters, than you can deny.
Prince John is this morning secretly stol'n away. Hero
was in this manner accus'd, in this very manner
refus'd, and upon the grief of this suddenly died. Mas-
ter Constable, let these men be bound, and brought to
Leonato's. I will go before and show him their exami-
nation. [*Exit.*]
DOGBERRY Come, let them be opinion'd. 67
VERGES Let them be in the hands—
CONRADE Off, coxcomb!
DOGBERRY God 's my life, where's the sexton? Let him 70
write down the Prince's officer coxcomb. Come, bind
them. Thou naughty varlet!
CONRADE Away! You are an ass, you are an ass.
DOGBERRY Dost thou not suspect my place? Dost thou 74
not suspect my years? O that he were here to write me
down an ass! But, masters, remember that I am an ass;
though it be not written down, yet forget not that I am
an ass. No, thou villain, thou art full of piety, as shall 78
be prov'd upon thee by good witness. I am a wise
fellow, and, which is more, an officer, and, which is
more, a householder, and, which is more, as pretty a
piece of flesh as any is in Messina, and one that knows
the law, go to; and a rich fellow enough, go to; and a
fellow that hath had losses, and one that hath two
gowns and every thing handsome about him. Bring
him away. O that I had been writ down an ass!
Exeunt.

[ACT V • SCENE I]

Enter Leonato and his Brother [*Antonio*].

ANTONIO
If you go on thus, you will kill yourself;
And 'tis not wisdom thus to second grief 2
Against yourself.
LEONATO I pray thee, cease thy counsel,
Which falls into mine ears as profitless
As water in a sieve. Give not me counsel,
Nor let no comforter delight mine ear
But such a one whose wrongs do suit with mine. 7
Bring me a father that so lov'd his child,
Whose joy of her is overwhelm'd like mine,
And bid him speak of patience;
Measure his woe the length and breadth of mine, 11
And let it answer every strain for strain, 12
As thus for thus, and such a grief for such,
In every lineament, branch, shape, and form;
If such a one will smile and stroke his beard,
Bid sorrow wag, cry "hem!" when he should groan, 16
Patch grief with proverbs, make misfortune drunk 17
With candle-wasters, bring him yet to me 18
And I of him will gather patience.
But there is no such man. For, brother, men
Can counsel and speak comfort to that grief
Which they themselves not feel; but, tasting it,
Their counsel turns to passion, which before
Would give preceptial med'cine to rage, 24
Fetter strong madness in a silken thread,
Charm ache with air and agony with words. 26
No, no! 'Tis all men's office to speak patience

13 sirrah (Used to address inferiors; Conrade objects.) **20 defend** forbid **26 witty** clever, cunning **27 go about with** get the better of **32 in a tale** in agreement **36 eftest** (Some sort of blunder for *easiest* or *deftest.*) **57 redemption** (Dogberry means *damnation.*) **67 opinion'd** (For *pinioned.*)

70 God 's God save **74 suspect** (For *respect.*) **78 piety** (For *impiety.*)

V.i. Location: Before Leonato's house.
2 second assist, encourage **7 suit with** match **11 Measure his woe** let his woe equal in scope **12 strain** strong impulse of the mind **16 wag** be off **17 drunk** i.e., insensible to pain **18 candle-wasters** those who waste candles by late study, bookworms, moral philosophers **24 preceptial** consisting of precepts **26 air** mere breath, words

To those that wring under the load of sorrow,
But no man's virtue nor sufficiency
To be so moral when he shall endure
The like himself. Therefore give me no counsel.
My griefs cry louder than advertisement.

ANTONIO
Therein do men from children nothing differ.

LEONATO
I pray thee, peace. I will be flesh and blood;
For there was never yet philosopher
That could endure the toothache patiently,
However they have writ the style of gods
And made a push at chance and sufferance.

ANTONIO
Yet bend not all the harm upon yourself.
Make those that do offend you suffer too.

LEONATO
There thou speak'st reason. Nay, I will do so.
My soul doth tell me Hero is belied,
And that shall Claudio know; so shall the Prince
And all of them that thus dishonor her.

Enter Prince [*Don Pedro*] *and Claudio.*

ANTONIO
Here comes the Prince and Claudio hastily.

DON PEDRO
Good den, good den.

CLAUDIO
Good day to both of you.

LEONATO
Hear you, my lords—

DON PEDRO
We have some haste, Leonato.

LEONATO
Some haste, my lord! Well, fare you well, my lord.
Are you so hasty now? Well, all is one.

DON PEDRO
Nay, do not quarrel with us, good old man.

ANTONIO
If he could right himself with quarreling,
Some of us would lie low.

CLAUDIO
Who wrongs him?

LEONATO
Marry, thou dost wrong me, thou dissembler, thou!
Nay, never lay thy hand upon thy sword;
I fear thee not.

CLAUDIO
Marry, beshrew my hand,
If it should give your age such cause of fear.
In faith, my hand meant nothing to my sword.

LEONATO
Tush, tush, man, never fleer and jest at me.
I speak not like a dotard nor a fool,
As under privilege of age to brag
What I have done being young, or what would do
Were I not old. Know, Claudio, to thy head,
Thou hast so wrong'd mine innocent child and me
That I am forc'd to lay my reverence by
And, with grey hairs and bruise of many days,
Do challenge thee to trial of a man.
I say thou hast belied mine innocent child.
Thy slander hath gone through and through her
heart,
And she lies buried with her ancestors—
O, in a tomb where never scandal slept,
Save this of hers, fram'd by thy villainy!

CLAUDIO
My villainy?

LEONATO
Thine, Claudio, thine, I say.

DON PEDRO
You say not right, old man.

LEONATO
My lord, my lord,
I'll prove it on his body, if he dare,
Despite his nice fence and his active practice,
His May of youth and bloom of lustihood.

CLAUDIO
Away! I will not have to do with you.

LEONATO
Canst thou so daff me? Thou hast kill'd my child.
If thou kill'st me, boy, thou shalt kill a man.

ANTONIO
He shall kill two of us, and men indeed.
But that's no matter; let him kill one first.
Win me and wear me! Let him answer me.
Come, follow me, boy. Come, sir boy, come,
follow me.
Sir boy, I'll whip you from your foining fence!
Nay, as I am a gentleman, I will.

LEONATO
Brother—

ANTONIO
Content yourself. God knows I lov'd my niece,
And she is dead, slander'd to death by villains,
That dare as well answer a man indeed
As I dare take a serpent by the tongue.
Boys, apes, braggarts, Jacks, milksops!

LEONATO
Brother Antony—

ANTONIO
Hold you content. What, man! I know them, yea,
And what they weigh, even to the utmost scruple—
Scambling, out-facing, fashion-monging boys,
That lie and cog and flout, deprave and slander,
Go anticly, show outward hideousness,
And speak off half a dozen dang'rous words,
How they might hurt their enemies, if they durst;
And this is all.

LEONATO
But, brother Antony—

ANTONIO
Come, 'tis no matter.

28 wring writhe **29 sufficiency** ability, power **30 moral** prone to moralizing **32 advertisement** advice, counsel **37 writ the style of** written in language worthy of **38 push at** defiance of. **sufferance** suffering **49 all is one** it makes no difference **52 Some of us** i.e., Don Pedro and Claudio **53 thou** (Used contemptuously instead of the more polite *you*.) **55 beshrew** curse **57 my . . . sword** I had no intention of using my sword **58 fleer** sneer, jeer **62 head** i.e., face

64 my reverence i.e., the reverence due old age **66 trial of a man** manly contest, i.e., duel **71 fram'd** devised **75 nice fence** dextrous swordsmanship. (Said contemptuously.) **76 lustihood** bodily vigor **78 daff** doff, put or turn aside **82 Win . . . me** (A proverbial expression, used as a challenge, meaning he'll have to overcome me before he can claim me as a prize.) **answer me** i.e., in a duel **84 foining** thrusting **87 Content yourself** i.e., don't try to stop me **94 scruple** small measure of weight **95 Scambling . . . boys** contentious, swaggering, dandified boys **96 cog** cheat. **deprave** defame, traduce **97 anticly** fantastically dressed. **hideousness** frightening appearance **98 dang'rous** threatening, haughty

Do not you meddle; let me deal in this.

DON PEDRO
Gentlemen both, we will not wake your patience.
My heart is sorry for your daughter's death;
But, on my honor, she was charg'd with nothing
But what was true and very full of proof.

LEONATO
My lord, my Lord—

DON PEDRO
I will not hear you.

LEONATO
No? Come, brother, away! I will be heard.

ANTONIO
And shall, or some of us will smart for it.

Exeunt ambo [*Leonato and Antonio*].

Enter Benedick.

DON PEDRO
See, see, here comes the man we went to seek.

CLAUDIO Now, signior, what news?

BENEDICK Good day, my lord.

DON PEDRO Welcome, signior. You are almost come to part almost a fray.

CLAUDIO We had lik'd to have had our two noses snapp'd off with two old men without teeth.

DON PEDRO Leonato and his brother. What think'st thou? Had we fought, I doubt we should have been too young for them.

BENEDICK In a false quarrel there is no true valor. I came to seek you both.

CLAUDIO We have been up and down to seek thee, for we are high-proof melancholy, and would fain have it beaten away. Wilt thou use thy wit?

BENEDICK It is in my scabbard. Shall I draw it?

DON PEDRO Dost thou wear thy wit by thy side?

CLAUDIO Never any did so, though very many have been beside their wit. I will bid thee draw, as we do the minstrels; draw, to pleasure us.

DON PEDRO As I am an honest man, he looks pale. Art thou sick, or angry?

CLAUDIO What, courage, man! What though care kill'd a cat, thou hast mettle enough in thee to kill care.

BENEDICK Sir, I shall meet your wit in the career, an you charge it against me. I pray you choose another subject.

CLAUDIO Nay, then, give him another staff. This last was broke cross.

DON PEDRO By this light, he changes more and more. I think he be angry indeed.

CLAUDIO If he be, he knows how to turn his girdle.

BENEDICK Shall I speak a word in your ear?

CLAUDIO God bless me from a challenge!

BENEDICK [*Aside to Claudio*] You are a villain. I jest not; I will make it good how you dare, with what you dare, and when you dare. Do me right, or I will protest your cowardice. You have kill'd a sweet lady, and her death shall fall heavy on you. Let me hear from you.

CLAUDIO Well, I will meet you, so I may have good cheer.

DON PEDRO What, a feast, a feast?

CLAUDIO I' faith, I thank him, he hath bid me to a calf's head and a capon, the which if I do not carve most curiously, say my knife's naught. Shall I not find a woodcock too?

BENEDICK Sir, your wit ambles well; it goes easily.

DON PEDRO I'll tell thee how Beatrice prais'd thy wit the other day. I said thou hadst a fine wit. "True," said she, "a fine little one." "No," said I, "a great wit." "Right," says she, "a great gross one." "Nay," said I, "a good wit." "Just," said she, "it hurts nobody." "Nay," said I, "the gentleman is wise." "Certain," said she, "a wise gentleman." "Nay," said I, "he hath the tongues." "That I believe," said she, "for he swore a thing to me on Monday night, which he forswore on Tuesday morning. There's a double tongue; there's two tongues." Thus did she, an hour together, transshape thy particular virtues. Yet at last she concluded with a sigh, thou wast the proper'st man in Italy.

CLAUDIO For the which she wept heartily and said she car'd not.

DON PEDRO Yea, that she did; but yet, for all that, an if she did not hate him deadly, she would love him dearly. The old man's daughter told us all.

CLAUDIO All, all. And, moreover, God saw him when he was hid in the garden.

DON PEDRO But when shall we set the savage bull's horns on the sensible Benedick's head?

CLAUDIO Yea, and text underneath, "Here dwells Benedick the married man"?

BENEDICK Fare you well, boy. You know my mind. I will leave you now to your gossip-like humor. You break jests as braggarts do their blades, which, God be thank'd, hurt not. My lord, for your many courtesies I thank you. I must discontinue your company. Your brother the bastard is fled from Messina. You have among you kill'd a sweet and innocent lady. For my Lord Lackbeard there, he and I shall meet; and, till then, peace be with him. [*Exit.*]

DON PEDRO He is in earnest.

CLAUDIO In most profound earnest; and, I'll warrant you, for the love of Beatrice.

DON PEDRO And hath challeng'd thee?

CLAUDIO Most sincerely.

DON PEDRO What a pretty thing man is when he goes in his doublet and hose and leaves off his wit!

103 wake your patience put your patience to any further test **110 s.d. ambo** both **116 We had . . . had** we almost had **119 doubt** fear, suspect **124 high-proof** to the highest degree. **fain** gladly **129 beside their wit** out of their wits (playing on *by thy side* in l. 127) **130 draw** (1) draw your weapon (2) draw a bow across a musical instrument **135 career** short gallop at full speed (as in a tourney) **136 charge** level (as a weapon) **138 staff** spear shaft **139 broke cross** i.e., broken by clumsily allowing the spear to break crosswise against his opponent's shield. (In other words, Claudio accuses Benedick of having failed in his sally of wit.) **142 turn his girdle** i.e., find harmless outlet for his anger (? A proverbial expression of uncertain meaning.)

147 Do me right give me satisfaction. **protest** proclaim before witnesses **153–156 calf's head, capon, woodcock** (Used as types of dullness.) **155 curiously** daintily. **naught** good for nothing **157 ambles** i.e., it does not gallop **164 wise gentleman** i.e., an old fool **164–165 hath the tongues** masters several languages **168–169 transshape** distort, turn the wrong side out **170 proper'st** handsomest **176–177 God . . . garden** (Alluding to the trick played on Benedick to love Beatrice, and also to Genesis 3:8.) **180 text** (In I.i.251–256, Benedick vowed that if he were ever to fall in love, his friends might set a bull's horns on his head and label him "Benedick the married man.") **184 as . . . blades** i.e., as braggarts furtively damage their blades to make it appear they have been fighting fiercely **196–197 goes . . . wit** goes about fully dressed but forgets to equip himself with good sense

CLAUDIO He is then a giant to an ape; but then is an ape a doctor to such a man.

DON PEDRO But, soft you, let me be. Pluck up, my heart, and be sad. Did he not say my brother was fled?

Enter Constables, [Dogberry and Verges, and the Watch, with] Conrade and Borachio.

DOGBERRY Come you, sir. If justice cannot tame you, she shall ne'er weigh more reasons in her balance. Nay, an you be a cursing hypocrite once, you must be look'd to.

DON PEDRO How now? Two of my brother's men bound? Borachio one!

CLAUDIO Hearken after their offense, my lord.

DON PEDRO Officers, what offense have these men done?

DOGBERRY Marry, sir, they have committed false report; moreover, they have spoken untruths; secondarily, they are slanders; sixth and lastly, they have belied a lady; thirdly, they have verified unjust things; and, to conclude, they are lying knaves.

DON PEDRO First, I ask thee what they have done; thirdly, I ask thee what's their offense; sixth and lastly, why they are committed; and, to conclude, what you lay to their charge.

CLAUDIO Rightly reason'd, and in his own division; and, by my troth, there's one meaning well suited.

DON PEDRO Who have you offended, masters, that you are thus bound to your answer? This learned constable is too cunning to be understood. What's your offense?

BORACHIO Sweet Prince, let me go no farther to mine answer. Do you hear me, and let this count kill me. I have deceiv'd even your very eyes. What your wisdoms could not discover, these shallow fools have brought to light, who in the night overheard me confessing to this man how Don John your brother incens'd me to slander the Lady Hero, how you were brought into the orchard and saw me court Margaret in Hero's garments, how you disgrac'd her when you should marry her. My villainy they have upon record, which I had rather seal with my death than repeat over to my shame. The lady is dead upon mine and my master's false accusation; and, briefly, I desire nothing but the reward of a villain.

DON PEDRO *[To Claudio]*
Runs not this speech like iron through your blood?

CLAUDIO
I have drunk poison whiles he utter'd it.

DON PEDRO
But did my brother set thee on to this?

BORACHIO Yea, and paid me richly for the practice of it.

DON PEDRO
He is compos'd and fram'd of treachery,
And fled he is upon this villainy.

CLAUDIO
Sweet Hero! Now thy image doth appear
In the rare semblance that I lov'd it first.

DOGBERRY Come, bring away the plaintiffs. By this time our sexton hath reform'd Signior Leonato of the matter. And, masters, do not forget to specify, when time and place shall serve, that I am an ass.

VERGES Here, here comes master Signior Leonato, and the sexton too.

Enter Leonato, his Brother [Antonio], and the Sexton.

LEONATO
Which is the villain? Let me see his eyes,
That, when I note another man like him,
I may avoid him. Which of these is he?

BORACHIO
If you would know your wronger, look on me.

LEONATO
Art thou the slave that with thy breath hast kill'd
Mine innocent child?

BORACHIO Yea, even I alone.

LEONATO
No, not so, villain, thou beliest thyself.
Here stand a pair of honorable men—
A third is fled—that had a hand in it.
I thank you, princes, for my daughter's death.
Record it with your high and worthy deeds.
'Twas bravely done, if you bethink you of it.

CLAUDIO
I know not how to pray your patience,
Yet I must speak. Choose your revenge yourself;
Impose me to what penance your invention
Can lay upon my sin. Yet sinn'd I not
But in mistaking.

DON PEDRO By my soul, nor I.
And yet, to satisfy this good old man,
I would bend under any heavy weight
That he'll enjoin me to.

LEONATO
I cannot bid you bid my daughter live—
That were impossible—but, I pray you both,
Possess the people in Messina here
How innocent she died; and if your love
Can labor aught in sad invention,
Hang her an epitaph upon her tomb,
And sing it to her bones—sing it tonight.
Tomorrow morning come you to my house,
And since you could not be my son-in-law,
Be yet my nephew. My brother hath a daughter,
Almost the copy of my child that's dead,
And she alone is heir to both of us.
Give her the right you should have giv'n her cousin,
And so dies my revenge.

CLAUDIO O noble sir,
Your over-kindness doth wring tears from me!

198–199 He . . . man he is superior to an ape in stature, but an ape is superior to him in wisdom. (A *doctor* is a scholar.) **200 soft you** wait a minute, not so fast **200–201 Pluck . . . sad** collect yourself, my mind, and be serious **203 balance** scales **208 Hearken after** inquire into **213 slanders** (For *slanderers.*) **221 well suited** put into many different dresses **223 bound** (playing on the meanings *pinioned* and *headed for a destination*). **answer** trial, account **230–231 incens'd** instigated, incited **236 upon** in consequence of **242 practice** execution

247 plaintiffs (For *defendants.*) **248 reform'd** (For *informed.*) **249 specify** (For *testify?*) **260 honorable** i.e., Don Pedro and Claudio, men of rank **267 Impose me to** impose on me **275 Possess** inform **284 heir to both** (He overlooks Antonio's son mentioned in I.ii.2.)

I do embrace your offer; and dispose
For henceforth of poor Claudio.

LEONATO
Tomorrow then I will expect your coming;
Tonight I take my leave. This naughty man
Shall face to face be brought to Margaret,
Who I believe was pack'd in all this wrong,
Hir'd to it by your brother.

BORACHIO
No, by my soul, she was not,
Nor knew not what she did when she spoke to me,
But always hath been just and virtuous
In any thing that I do know by her.

DOGBERRY Moreover, sir, which indeed is not under white and black, this plaintiff here, the offender, did call me ass. I beseech you, let it be rememb'red in his punishment. And also, the watch heard them talk of one Deform'd. They say he wears a key in his ear and a lock hanging by it, and borrows money in God's name, the which he hath us'd so long and never paid that now men grow hard-hearted and will lend nothing for God's sake. Pray you, examine him upon that point.

LEONATO I thank thee for thy care and honest pains.

DOGBERRY Your worship speaks like a most thankful and reverend youth; and I praise God for you.

LEONATO There's for thy pains. [*Gives money.*]

DOGBERRY God save the foundation!

LEONATO Go, I discharge thee of thy prisoner, and I thank thee.

DOGBERRY I leave an arrant knave with your worship, which I beseech your worship to correct yourself, for the example of others. God keep your worship! I wish your worship well. God restore you to health! I humbly give you leave to depart; and if a merry meeting may be wish'd, God prohibit it! Come, neighbor.

[*Exeunt Dogberry and Verges.*]

LEONATO
Until tomorrow morning, lords, farewell.

ANTONIO
Farewell, my lords. We look for you tomorrow.

DON PEDRO
We will not fail.

CLAUDIO Tonight I'll mourn with Hero.

LEONATO [*To the Watch*]
Bring you these fellows on.— We'll talk with Margaret,
How her acquaintance grew with this lewd fellow.

Exeunt [*severally*].

[SCENE II]

Enter Benedick and Margaret, [*meeting*].

BENEDICK Pray thee, sweet Mistress Margaret, deserve well at my hands by helping me to the speech of Beatrice.

MARGARET Will you then write me a sonnet in praise of my beauty?

BENEDICK In so high a style, Margaret, that no man living shall come over it; for, in most comely truth, thou deservest it.

MARGARET To have no man come over me! Why, shall I always keep below stairs?

BENEDICK Thy wit is as quick as the greyhound's mouth; it catches.

MARGARET And yours as blunt as the fencer's foils, which hit, but hurt not.

BENEDICK A most manly wit, Margaret; it will not hurt a woman. And so, I pray thee, call Beatrice. I give thee the bucklers.

MARGARET Give us the swords; we have bucklers of our own.

BENEDICK If you use them, Margaret, you must put in the pikes with a vice, and they are dangerous weapons for maids.

MARGARET Well, I will call Beatrice to you, who I think hath legs. *Exit Margaret.*

BENEDICK And therefore will come.
[*Sings.*] "The god of love,
That sits above,
And knows me, and knows me,
How pitiful I deserve"—

I mean in singing; but in loving, Leander the good swimmer, Troilus the first employer of pandars, and a whole bookful of these quondam carpet-mongers, whose names yet run smoothly in the even road of a blank verse, why, they were never so truly turn'd over and over as my poor self in love. Marry, I cannot show it in rhyme; I have tried. I can find out no rhyme to "lady" but "baby," an innocent rhyme; for "scorn," "horn," a hard rhyme; for "school," "fool," a babbling rhyme; very ominous endings. No, I was not born under a rhyming planet, nor I cannot woo in festival terms.

Enter Beatrice.

Sweet Beatrice, wouldst thou come when I call'd thee?

288 dispose you may dispose **291 naughty** wicked **293 pack'd** involved as an accomplice **298 by** concerning **299–300 under . . . black** written down in black and white **303–304 key . . . by it** (This is what Dogberry has made out of the lovelock mentioned in III.iii.167.) **304–305 in God's name** (A phrase of the professional beggar.) **313 God . . . foundation** (A formula of those who received alms at religious houses or charitable foundations.) **320 give you leave** (For *ask your leave.*) **321 prohibit** (For *permit.*) **326 lewd** wicked, worthless

V.ii. Location: Leonato's garden (?) (At the scene's end, Leonato's house is some distance away.)
6 style (1) poetic style (2) stile, stairs over a fence **7 come over** (1) excel beyond (2) traverse, as one would cross a stile (3) in Margaret's next speech, the phrase is taken to mean *mount sexually.* **comely** good (with an allusion to Margaret's beauty) **10 keep below stairs** dwell in the servants' quarters **16–17 I . . . bucklers** i.e., I acknowledge myself beaten (in repartee). (*Bucklers* are shields with spikes *(pikes)* in their centers; Margaret uses the word in a bawdy sense in her reply.) **21 pikes** spikes in the center of a shield. **vice** screw **26–29 The god . . . deserve** (The beginning of an old song by William Elderton.) **29 How . . . deserve** how I deserve pity. (But Benedick uses the phrase to mean *how little I deserve.*) **30 Leander** lover of Hero of Sestos; he swam the Hellespont nightly to see her until he drowned **31 Troilus** lover of Cressida, whose affair was assisted by her uncle Pandarus **32 quondam carpet-mongers** carpet-knights, i.e., ladies' men, stay-at-home soldiers, of former days **34–35 over and over** i.e., head over heels **37 innocent** childish **38 hard** (1) exact (2) unpleasant, because of the association with cuckold's horns

BEATRICE Yea, signior, and depart when you bid me.

BENEDICK O, stay but till then!

BEATRICE "Then" is spoken; fare you well now. And yet, ere I go, let me go with that I came; which is, with knowing what hath pass'd between you and Claudio.

BENEDICK Only foul words; and thereupon I will kiss thee.

BEATRICE Foul words is but foul wind, and foul wind is but foul breath, and foul breath is noisome; therefore I will depart unkiss'd.

BENEDICK Thou hast frighted the word out of his right sense, so forcible is thy wit. But I must tell thee plainly, Claudio undergoes my challenge; and either I must shortly hear from him, or I will subscribe him a coward. And, I pray thee now tell me, for which of my bad parts didst thou first fall in love with me?

BEATRICE For them all together, which maintain'd so politic a state of evil that they will not admit any good part to intermingle with them. But for which of my good parts did you first suffer love for me?

BENEDICK Suffer love! A good epithet! I do suffer love indeed, for I love thee against my will.

BEATRICE In spite of your heart, I think. Alas, poor heart, if you spite it for my sake, I will spite it for yours, for I will never love that which my friend hates.

BENEDICK Thou and I are too wise to woo peaceably.

BEATRICE It appears not in this confession. There's not one wise man among twenty that will praise himself.

BENEDICK An old, an old instance, Beatrice, that liv'd in the time of good neighbors. If a man do not erect in this age his own tomb ere he dies, he shall live no longer in monument than the bell rings and the widow weeps.

BEATRICE And how long is that, think you?

BENEDICK Question: why, an hour in clamor and a quarter in rheum. Therefore is it most expedient for the wise, if Don Worm, his conscience, find no impediment to the contrary, to be the trumpet of his own virtues, as I am to myself. So much for praising myself, who, I myself will bear witness, is praiseworthy. And now tell me, how doth your cousin?

BEATRICE Very ill.

BENEDICK And how do you?

BEATRICE Very ill too.

BENEDICK Serve God, love me, and mend. There will I leave you too, for here comes one in haste.

Enter Ursula.

URSULA Madam, you must come to your uncle. Yonder's old coil at home. It is prov'd my Lady Hero hath been falsely accus'd, the Prince and Claudio mightily abus'd, and Don John is the author of all, who is fled and gone. Will you come presently?

BEATRICE Will you go hear this news, signior?

BENEDICK I will live in thy heart, die in thy lap, and be buried in thy eyes; and moreover I will go with thee to thy uncle's. *Exeunt.*

[SCENE III]

Enter Claudio, Prince [Don Pedro, Lord], and three or four with tapers.

CLAUDIO Is this the monument of Leonato?

A LORD It is, my lord.

CLAUDIO [*Reading out of a scroll*]

Epitaph.

"Done to death by slanderous tongues
Was the Hero that here lies.
Death, in guerdon of her wrongs,
Gives her fame which never dies.
So the life that died with shame
Lives in death with glorious fame."

Hang thou there upon the tomb,
[*Hangs up the scroll.*]
Praising her when I am dumb.
Now, music, sound, and sing your solemn hymn.

Song.

Pardon, goddess of the night,
Those that slew thy virgin knight;
For the which, with songs of woe,
Round about her tomb they go.
Midnight, assist our moan;
Help us to sigh and groan,
Heavily, heavily.
Graves, yawn and yield your dead,
Till death be uttered,
Heavily, heavily.

CLAUDIO
Now, unto thy bones good night!
Yearly will I do this rite.

DON PEDRO
Good morrow, masters. Put your torches out.
The wolves have prey'd; and look, the gentle day,
Before the wheels of Phoebus, round about
Dapples the drowsy east with spots of grey.
Thanks to you all, and leave us. Fare you well.

CLAUDIO
Good morrow, masters. Each his several way.

DON PEDRO
Come, let us hence, and put on other weeds,
And then to Leonato's we will go.

46 that I came what I came for **51 noisome** noxious **53 his** its **55 undergoes** bears **56 subscribe** formally proclaim in writing **60 politic** prudently governed **62 suffer** (1) experience (2) feel the pain of **63 epithet** expression **69 It . . . confession** i.e., you don't show your wisdom in praising yourself for being wise **71 instance** proverb **72 time . . . neighbors** good old times (when one's neighbors spoke well of one) **77 Question** that is the question. **clamor** noise (of the bell) **78 rheum** tears (of the widow) **79 Don . . . conscience** (The action of the conscience was traditionally described as the gnawing of a worm; cf. Mark 9:48.) **90 old coil** great confusion **92 abus'd** deceived

95 die (with the common connotation of *experience sexual climax*)

V.iii. Location: A churchyard.
5 guerdon recompense **12 goddess of the night** i.e., Diana, moon goddess, patroness of chastity **20 uttered** fully expressed **25 have prey'd** i.e., have ceased preying **26 wheels of Phoebus** i.e., chariot of the sun god **30 weeds** garments

CLAUDIO
And Hymen now with luckier issue speed 's
Than this for whom we rend'red up this woe.
Exeunt.

[SCENE IV]

Enter Leonato, Benedick, [Beatrice,] Margaret, Ursula, Old Man [Antonio], Friar [Francis], Hero.

FRIAR
Did I not tell you she was innocent?

LEONATO
So are the Prince and Claudio, who accus'd her
Upon the error that you heard debated.
But Margaret was in some fault for this,
Although against her will, as it appears
In the true course of all the question.

ANTONIO
Well, I am glad that all things sorts so well.

BENEDICK
And so am I, being else by faith enforc'd
To call young Claudio to a reckoning for it.

LEONATO
Well, daughter, and you gentlewomen all,
Withdraw into a chamber by yourselves,
And, when I send for you, come hither mask'd.
The Prince and Claudio promis'd by this hour
To visit me. You know your office, brother:
You must be father to your brother's daughter,
And give her to young Claudio. *Exeunt Ladies.*

ANTONIO
Which I will do with confirm'd countenance.

BENEDICK
Friar, I must entreat your pains, I think.

FRIAR
To do what, signior?

BENEDICK
To bind me, or undo me—one of them.
Signior Leonato, truth it is, good signior,
Your niece regards me with an eye of favor.

LEONATO
That eye my daughter lent her. 'Tis most true.

BENEDICK
And I do with an eye of love requite her.

LEONATO
The sight whereof I think you had from me,
From Claudio, and the Prince. But what's your will?

BENEDICK
Your answer, sir, is enigmatical.
But, for my will, my will is your good will
May stand with ours, this day to be conjoin'd
In the state of honorable marriage,
In which, good friar, I shall desire your help.

LEONATO
My heart is with your liking.

FRIAR
And my help.
Here comes the Prince and Claudio.

Enter Prince [Don Pedro] and Claudio, and two or three other.

DON PEDRO
Good morrow to this fair assembly.

LEONATO
Good morrow, Prince; good morrow, Claudio.
We here attend you. Are you yet determin'd
Today to marry with my brother's daughter?

CLAUDIO
I'll hold my mind, were she an Ethiope.

LEONATO
Call her forth, brother. Here's the friar ready.
[Exit Antonio.]

DON PEDRO
Good morrow, Benedick. Why, what's the matter,
That you have such a February face,
So full of frost, of storm, and cloudiness?

CLAUDIO
I think he thinks upon the savage bull.
Tush, fear not, man! We'll tip thy horns with gold,
And all Europa shall rejoice at thee,
As once Europa did at lusty Jove
When he would play the noble beast in love.

BENEDICK
Bull Jove, sir, had an amiable low,
And some such strange bull leapt your father's cow
And got a calf in that same noble feat
Much like to you, for you have just his bleat.

Enter [Leonato's] Brother [Antonio], Hero, Beatrice, Margaret, Ursula [the ladies masked].

CLAUDIO
For this I owe you. Here comes other reck'nings.
Which is the lady I must seize upon?

ANTONIO
This same is she, and I do give you her.

CLAUDIO
Why, then she's mine. Sweet, let me see your face.

LEONATO
No, that you shall not, till you take her hand
Before this friar and swear to marry her.

CLAUDIO
Give me your hand before this holy friar.
I am your husband, if you like of me.

HERO
And when I liv'd, I was your other wife;
[Unmasking.]

32 Hymen god of marriage. **speed 's** favor or speed us

V.iv. Location: Leonato's house.
3 Upon because of **5 against her will** unintentionally **6 question** investigation **7 sorts** turn out **8 by faith** i.e., by my promise to Beatrice **17 confirm'd** grave, unmoved **20 undo** (1) ruin (2) untie, unbind **23 That . . . her** (Alludes to Hero's role in coaxing Beatrice to love Benedick.) **25–26 The sight . . . Prince** (Alludes to their role in coaxing Benedick to love Beatrice.) **28 is** is that

35 yet still **42 I . . . bull** (A jocular reminiscence of the conversation in I.i.250 ff.) **44 Europa** Europe **45 Europa** a princess whom Jove approached in the form of a white bull and bore on his back through the sea to Crete **51 I owe you** i.e., I'll pay you back later (for calling me a calf and a bastard child of Jove). **other reck'nings** i.e., other matters to be settled first **58 like of** care for

And when you lov'd, you were my other husband.

CLAUDIO
Another Hero!

HERO Nothing certainer.
One Hero died defil'd, but I do live,
And surely as I live, I am a maid.

DON PEDRO
The former Hero! Hero that is dead!

LEONATO
She died, my lord, but whiles her slander liv'd.

FRIAR
All this amazement can I qualify,
When, after that the holy rites are ended,
I'll tell you largely of fair Hero's death.
Meantime let wonder seem familiar,
And to the chapel let us presently.

BENEDICK
Soft and fair, friar. Which is Beatrice?

BEATRICE [*Unmasking*]
I answer to that name. What is your will?

BENEDICK
Do not you love me?

BEATRICE Why, no; no more than reason.

BENEDICK
Why, then your uncle and the Prince and Claudio
Have been deceiv'd. They swore you did.

BEATRICE
Do not you love me?

BENEDICK Troth, no; no more than reason.

BEATRICE
Why, then my cousin Margaret and Ursula
Are much deceiv'd, for they did swear you did.

BENEDICK
They swore that you were almost sick for me.

BEATRICE
They swore that you were well-nigh dead for me.

BENEDICK
'Tis no such matter. Then you do not love me?

BEATRICE
No, truly, but in friendly recompense.

LEONATO
Come, cousin, I am sure you love the gentleman.

CLAUDIO
And I'll be sworn upon 't that he loves her;
For here's a paper written in his hand,
A halting sonnet of his own pure brain,
Fashion'd to Beatrice. [*Shows a paper.*]

HERO And here's another
Writ in my cousin's hand, stol'n from her pocket,
Containing her affection unto Benedick.
[*Shows another paper.*]

BENEDICK A miracle! Here's our own hands against our hearts. Come, I will have thee; but, by this light, I take thee for pity.

BEATRICE I would not deny you; but, by this good day, I yield upon great persuasion, and partly to save your life, for I was told you were in a consumption.

66 qualify moderate **68 largely** at large, in full **69 let . . . familiar** treat these marvels as ordinary matters **86 his own pure** purely his own **90–91 against our hearts** i.e., to prove our hearts guilty as charged

BENEDICK Peace! I will stop your mouth. [*Kissing her.*]

DON PEDRO How dost thou, Benedick, the married man?

BENEDICK I'll tell thee what, Prince: a college of witcrackers cannot flout me out of my humor. Dost thou think I care for a satire or an epigram? No. If a man will be beaten with brains, 'a shall wear nothing handsome about him. In brief, since I do purpose to marry, I will think nothing to any purpose that the world can say against it; and therefore never flout at me for what I have said against it; for man is a giddy thing, and this is my conclusion. For thy part, Claudio, I did think to have beaten thee; but in that thou art like to be my kinsman, live unbruis'd, and love my cousin.

CLAUDIO I had well hop'd thou wouldst have denied Beatrice, that I might have cudgel'd thee out of thy single life, to make thee a double-dealer, which, out of question, thou wilt be, if my cousin do not look exceeding narrowly to thee.

BENEDICK Come, come, we are friends. Let's have a dance ere we are married, that we may lighten our own hearts and our wives' heels.

LEONATO We'll have dancing afterward.

BENEDICK First, of my word! Therefore play, music. Prince, thou art sad. Get thee a wife, get thee a wife. There is no staff more reverend than one tipp'd with horn.

Enter Messenger.

MESSENGER
My lord, your brother John is ta'en in flight,
And brought with armed men back to Messina.

BENEDICK Think not on him till tomorrow. I'll devise thee brave punishments for him. Strike up, pipers.
Dance. [*Exeunt.*]

99 college assembly **101–103 If . . . him** i.e., if a man allows himself to be cowed by ridicule, he'll never dare dress handsomely or do anything conspicuous that will draw attention **112 double-dealer** (1) a married man (2) a deceiver, adulterer **119 of** on **121–122 tipp'd with horn** (Alludes to the usual joke about cuckolds.) **126 brave** fine

The Merry Wives of Windsor

According to an early eighteenth-century tradition, Shakespeare composed *The Merry Wives of Windsor* at the behest of Queen Elizabeth. John Dennis asserted in 1702 that the Queen "was so eager to see it acted, that she commanded it to be finished in fourteen days." Nicholas Rowe added in 1709 that the Queen, having been so pleased with Falstaff in the *Henry IV* plays, wished to see him in love. Such legends, emerging more than a century after the event, must be regarded with caution. Whether true or not, however, they do point to a passage of courtly flattery in the play that strongly suggests the presence of the court at some performance.The fairy blessing bestowed on Windsor Castle in Act V is unquestionably intended to celebrate the famous Order of the Garter. Mistress Quickly, disguised as leader of the fairies, orders her charges to sing nightly "Like to the Garter's compass, in a ring," to write "Honi soit qui mal y pense," the motto of the Garter, and to tend carefully the "several chairs of order"—those decorated stalls in the Chapel of St. George belonging to the illustrious lords who made up the Order of the Garter. Every such "installment" receives her blessing, along with each knight's "coat," "crest," and "blazon." The topical nature of this passage is stressed by its apparent lack of relevance to the plot.

Other extraneous bits of action may allude to courtly matters or to Windsor gossip. The business about the three German horse thieves and their Duke (IV,iii–v), which makes little sense in the play as it stands, can perhaps be explained as an in-group joke on Frederick of Würtemburg, Count Mompelgard, a German nobleman obsessively intent on joining the Garter. He was the object of much anti-German scorn. His name, Mompelgard, is possibly scrambled into "garmombles" in the corrupt 1602 quarto text (IV,v,80). Also, the geography of Windsor is rendered with loving and accurate attention to detail, as though for an audience familiar with its environs.

Such topical flourishes do not rob the drama of its general appeal; it has had great success, both as a stage play and in Verdi's and Nicolai's operatic versions, and was presumably popular with Shakespeare's London audience. Shakespeare never composed exclusively for special audiences, so far as we know, and indeed the blessing of Windsor Castle could have been added to a commercial play in order to render it particularly suitable for royal performance. The allusion to "the fat woman of Brainford," a notorious tavern keeper of Brentford (halfway between London and Windsor) would have been as meaningful to Shakespeare's London audience as to the court. The same may be true of the "luces" in the coat of arms of Justice Shallow (I,i), sometimes thought to ridicule Shakespeare's Stratford neighbor Sir Thomas Lucy, but believed by Leslie Hotson to be a dig at William Gardiner, a Justice of the Peace in Surrey near London. Nevertheless, *The Merry Wives* could have been originally planned as entertainment to please Queen Elizabeth. A Feast of St. George in honor of the Garter was held at Westminster on April 23, 1597, in the Queen's presence. Among those elected to the Order was George Carey, Lord Hunsdon, the patron of Shakespeare's company and the new Lord Chamberlain. He was actually installed in the Order at Windsor in May. This date is early for a play that appears to borrow several comic figures from the *Henry IV* plays and perhaps from *Henry V* (usually dated 1599) as well. Recently, however, it has been argued persuasively that *The Merry Wives* may have been written while *2 Henry IV* was in the process of composition, making use of its comic types but before they had actually appeared on the London stage. According to this theory, Nym was created first for *The Merry Wives* and was then reintroduced into *Henry V*. The dating and order of composition of these plays is still controversial, however, so that the dating of *The Merry Wives* must remain uncertain from 1597 to 1601.

Despite this uncertainty, Shakespeare's comic strategy in *The Merry Wives* seems reasonably clear: to translate highly popular comic figures such as Falstaff, Bardolph, Pistol, and Slender from the history plays into a ludicrously different kind of situation. Falstaff, the once resourceful and self-aware companion of Prince Hal, becomes the buffoonish wooer of two virtuously married women who thoroughly best him and subject him to a series of amusingly humiliating punishments. Hal too, of course, treats Falstaff as a scapegoat in the *Henry IV* plays and ultimately rejects him, but the farcical nature of the action in *The Merry Wives* exposes Falstaff to more openly satirical laughter and discomfiture than in the history plays. Some admirers of Falstaff have been dismayed by the falling off, and dismiss the play as an insult to his greatness, but surely to view the play thus is to create false expectations and thereby miss the point of Shakespeare's comic intent. Falstaff and his companions should not be judged against their counterparts in the history plays, even though an awareness of their existence in that different context is an essential part of the jest. To see Falstaff in love! This tour de force required that Shakespeare devise a multiple plot as unlike that of the history plays as possible, in order to stress the comic discrepancy.

The result is a structurally complex comic plot that appropriately bears more resemblance to Shakespeare's other comedies than to the history plays. At the center of *The Merry Wives* is a familiar plot of romantic intrigue, featuring a young heroine (Anne Page) whose parents object to her attachment to young Fenton. They pester her with unwelcome rival wooers (Slender and Dr. Caius), obliging her finally to dupe her parents by a cleverly engineered elopement. This plot of "a trick to catch the old one" has an ancestry in Plautine and neoclassical comedy, though Shakespeare uses no particular recognizable source. To this plot he adds a second and parallel story of a lover (Falstaff) caught in the act of making love to two women. Italian *novelle* provide many situations of this sort, including that in which the husband is deceived by concealment of the lover in a clothes-basket; see especially "Of Two Brethren and Their Wives" from *Riche his Farewell to Militarie profession,* 1581, "Two Lovers of Pisa" from *Tarltons Newes Out of Purgatorie,* 1590, and the second story of the first day from Ser Giovanni Fiorentino's *Il Pecorone,* 1558. The effect of the combined plots is often farcelike, especially in the emphasis on swift, hilarious action and comic physical abuse at the expense of consistency in character. For example, we must accept as a "given" the preference of wise Master Page for Slender as his son-in-law, and the inexplicable preference of Mistress Page for the suit of Dr. Caius. Reasons are stated, but symmetry of the design is paramount.

In addition, Shakespeare enriches these two plot situations with minor characters, such as the rival wooers, go-betweens, and informers who inevitably come in conflict with one another and thereby reveal their "humors." Only tangentially connected with the plot, these characters are prized for their eccentricity. The Welsh Parson Evans and the French Dr. Caius nearly come to blows over Caius' courtship of Anne Page. They are safely kept apart by the genial Host of the Garter Inn, and are reconciled to the extent of plotting against the Host for having deceived them both. (Perhaps they carry out their threat as the mysterious Germans who steal the Host's horses, though the text is murky on this point.) Justice Shallow, a "humors" character in *2 Henry IV,* is given nominal justification in this play as cousin of Anne's second unwanted suitor, Slender; but Shallow's essential function is to quarrel with Falstaff about the latter's poaching and riotous behavior. This "plot" goes nowhere, and indeed is little more than a means for the revelation of humorous characters. Shallow's is a "cameo" role, like many others, enabling him to assume the fatuous postures we also encounter in *2 Henry IV.* Pistol and Nym, similarly requiring some pretext for being on hand, revenge their dismissal from Falstaff's service by informing the two husbands of Falstaff's designs on the two merry wives. Bardolph finds suitable employment as a bartender. Mistress Quickly's transformation is perhaps the most gloriously improbable of all: she becomes confidante of all three wooers of Anne Page (offering equal encouragement to each, and receiving payment from each), as well as go-between for Falstaff and the two wives. She is no longer a married and then widowed hostess of a London tavern, but an unmarried housekeeper of Windsor. She triumphs over Falstaff in a way not possible in the history plays, joining the entire cast as they jeer at the discomfited horn-browed knight.

By providing occasion for the exhibition of idiosyncratic character for its own sake, side by side with his fast-moving farcical action, Shakespeare seems to have been responding to the newest dramatic genre of the late 1590's: the "humors" comedy. Chapman's *The Blind Beggar of Alexandria* (1596) had done much to establish the new fashion. Ben Jonson's *Every Man in His Humor* (1598) either influenced Shakespeare or was influenced by him, depending upon the dates. Jonson's plot, like Shakespeare's, is chiefly a vehicle for displaying various "humors" or comically obsessed types: the overly watchful father, the jealous husband, the braggart soldier, the country simpleton intent on learning to quarrel like a gentleman, the waspishly impatient man. Similar types appear in *The Merry Wives,* although Shakespeare characteristically does not satirize affectation so much as cherish it.

Shakespeare's comic types endear themselves chiefly through their verbal traits: Nym with his use of the word "humor"; Pistol with his anachronistic terms, recondite allusions, stilted poetic inversions, and hyperboles ("O base Hungarian wight! Wilt thou the spigot wield?"); Mistress Quickly with her pungent homely metaphors (comparing a beard to "a glover's paring knife") and her pat phrases ("But let that pass"); Shallow with his legal jargon; and the French Caius and the Welsh Evans with their ability to "keep their limbs whole and hack our English." Shakespeare also caricatures these humorous types by distinctive physical traits, such as Bardolph's "tinderbox" nose, or Slender's unappealing face and little yellow beard that so aptly suit his passion for bearbaiting and his idiotic deference to his superiors. We laugh at these deformities, and yet see that no one is incorrigible. The characters amiably poke fun at one another, and every discomfiture leads ultimately to a reconciliation. Few escape laughter, even those we might regard as "normative" characters if this were a satire; the Host, for example, loses his horses, and Mistress Page is tricked at last by her daughter's elopement.

Nevertheless, the merry wives of the play's title come as close as any to representing the normative vision of the play, functioning as witty manipulators in a plot to expose hypocrisy and lechery. The devices they invent for Falstaff are rather like Maria's schemes for Malvolio in *Twelfth Night,* since all depend upon the complicity of the self-blinded victim. Falstaff is the dominant "humors" character of the play, obsessed both with lust and greed, amusing to us because the greed is predominant. His hypocritical reasons for lovemaking deserve comic reprisal, or "vengeance." His greed and his fatuous belief in his own charm overwhelm his natural sagacity and leave him vulnerable. He credulously accepts the bribes of the jealous Ford, disguised as Brook, and is deceived by the wives on no less than three occasions. For their part, the wives are delighted with their "sport," for they must devise increasingly clever schemes to offset Falstaff's growing suspicions. The more unlikely he is to return for more punishment, the greater must be their ingenuity in order to fool him once again. Mistress Ford enjoys the added pleasure of teaching her husband a lesson about jealousy. The cleverness of their sport is justified by its moral intent, and conversely the moral point is deprived of any tedious didacticism by the good humor of the jest. In his final humiliation, plagued by virtually all the play's characters, reduced to an absurd belief in fairies, Falstaff becomes a "scapegoat" in the truest sense of that term: a horned figure who embodies the faults of an entire society, and whose chastisement brings about purification. Yet as Mistress Quickly observes, "nobody but has his fault," and this comic rejection of Falstaff leads not to banishment but to a reconciling feast at the Pages' house. Without intending it, Falstaff has cured Ford's jealousy and has helped show that "Wives may be merry, and yet honest too."

The Merry Wives of Windsor

[*Dramatis Personae*

SIR JOHN FALSTAFF.
FENTON, *a gentleman.*
ROBERT SHALLOW, *a country justice.*
ABRAHAM SLENDER, *cousin to Shallow.*
FRANCIS FORD, } *two gentlemen dwelling at Windsor.*
GEORGE PAGE, }
WILLIAM PAGE, *a boy, son to Page.*
SIR HUGH EVANS, *a Welsh parson.*
DOCTOR CAIUS, *a French physician.*
HOST *of the Garter Inn.*
BARDOLPH, }
PISTOL, } *followers of Falstaff.*
NYM, }
ROBIN, *page to Falstaff.*
PETER SIMPLE, *servant to Slender.*
JOHN RUGBY, *servant to Doctor Caius.*

MISTRESS ALICE FORD.
MISTRESS MARGARET PAGE.
ANNE PAGE, *her daughter.*
MISTRESS QUICKLY, *servant to Doctor Caius.*

SERVANTS *to Page, Ford, etc.*

SCENE: *Windsor, and the neighborhood.*]

ACT I • SCENE I

Enter Justice Shallow, Slender, [and] Sir Hugh Evans.

SHALLOW Sir Hugh, persuade me not; I will make a Star-chamber matter of it. If he were twenty Sir John Falstaffs, he shall not abuse Robert Shallow, esquire.

SLENDER In the county of Gloucester, Justice of Peace and Coram.

SHALLOW Ay, cousin Slender, and Custalorum.

SLENDER Ay, and Ratolorum too; and a gentleman born, master parson, who writes himself Armigero, in

I.i. Location: Windsor. Before Page's house.
s.d. Sir (Courtesy title for a priest.) **2 Star-chamber matter** (The court of Star Chamber, composed chiefly of the King's Council, was the highest and most powerful court in the realm.) **5 Coram** i.e., quorum, a title of certain justices whose presence was necessary to constitute a bench **6 Custalorum** (A corruption of Latin *custos rotulorum,* keeper of the rolls.) **7 Ratolorum** (For *rotulorum.*) **8 Armigero** esquire, one entitled to bear arms. (A heraldic term.)

any bill, warrant, quittance, or obligation, Armigero.

SHALLOW Ay, that I do, and have done any time these three hundred years.

SLENDER All his successors gone before him hath done 't; and all his ancestors that come after him may. They may give the dozen white luces in their coat.

SHALLOW It is an old coat.

EVANS The dozen white louses do become an old coat well; it agrees well, passant. It is a familiar beast to man, and signifies love.

SHALLOW The luce is the fresh fish. The salt fish is an old coat.

SLENDER I may quarter, coz.

SHALLOW You may, by marrying.

EVANS It is marring indeed, if he quarter it.

SHALLOW Not a whit.

EVANS Yes, py'r lady. If he has a quarter of your coat, there is but three skirts for yourself, in my simple conjectures. But that is all one. If Sir John Falstaff have committed disparagements unto you, I am of the church, and will be glad to do my benevolence to make atonements and compremises between you.

SHALLOW The council shall hear it. It is a riot.

EVANS It is not meet the council hear a riot. There is no fear of Got in a riot. The council, look you, shall desire to hear the fear of Got, and not to hear a riot. Take your vizaments in that.

SHALLOW Ha! O' my life, if I were young again, the sword should end it.

EVANS It is petter that friends is the sword, and end it. And there is also another device in my prain, which peradventure prings goot discretions with it: there is Anne Page, which is daughter to Master George Page, which is pretty virginity.

SLENDER Mistress Anne Page? She has brown hair, and speaks small like a woman?

EVANS It is that fery person for all the 'orld, as just as you will desire; and seven hundred pounds of moneys, and gold and silver, is her grandsire upon his death's-bed—Got deliver to a joyful resurrections!—give, when she is able to overtake seventeen years old. It were a goot motion if we leave our pribbles and prabbles, and desire a marriage between Master Abraham and Mistress Anne Page.

SHALLOW Did her grandsire leave her seven hundred pound?

EVANS Ay, and her father is make her a petter penny.

SHALLOW I know the young gentlewoman. She has good gifts.

EVANS Seven hundred pounds and possibilities is goot gifts.

SHALLOW Well, let us see honest Master Page. Is Falstaff there?

EVANS Shall I tell you a lie? I do despise a liar as I do despise one that is false, or as I despise one that is not true. The knight, Sir John, is there; and, I beseech you, be rul'd by your well-willers. I will peat the door for Master Page. [*Knocks.*] What, hoa! Got pless your house here!

PAGE [*Within*] Who's there?

[*Enter*] *Master Page.*

EVANS Here is Got's plessing, and your friend, and Justice Shallow; and here young Master Slender, that peradventures shall tell you another tale, if matters grow to your likings.

PAGE I am glad to see your worships well. I thank you for my venison, Master Shallow.

SHALLOW Master Page, I am glad to see you. Much good do it your good heart! I wish'd your venison better; it was ill kill'd. How doth good Mistress Page?—and I thank you always with my heart, la, with my heart.

PAGE Sir, I thank you.

SHALLOW Sir, I thank you; by yea and no, I do.

PAGE I am glad to see you, good Master Slender.

SLENDER How does your fallow greyhound, sir? I heard say he was outrun on Cotsall.

PAGE It could not be judg'd, sir.

SLENDER You'll not confess, you'll not confess.

SHALLOW That he will not, 'Tis your fault, 'tis your fault; 'tis a good dog.

PAGE A cur, sir.

SHALLOW Sir, he's a good dog, and a fair dog. Can there be more said? He is good and fair. Is Sir John Falstaff here?

PAGE Sir, he is within; and I would I could do a good office between you.

EVANS It is spoke as a Christians ought to speak.

SHALLOW He hath wrong'd me, Master Page.

PAGE Sir, he doth in some sort confess it.

SHALLOW If it be confess'd, it is not redress'd. Is not that so, Master Page? He hath wrong'd me, indeed he hath; at a word, he hath. Believe me, Robert Shallow, esquire, saith he is wrong'd.

PAGE Here comes Sir John.

[*Enter Sir John*] *Falstaff, Bardolph, Nym,* [*and*] *Pistol.*

FALSTAFF Now, Master Shallow, you'll complain of me to the King?

SHALLOW Knight, you have beaten my men, kill'd my deer, and broke open my lodge.

FALSTAFF But not kiss'd your keeper's daughter?

SHALLOW Tut, a pin! This shall be answer'd.

FALSTAFF I will answer it straight: I have done all this. That is now answer'd.

9 bill bill of financial exchange. **quittance** discharge from legal agreement. **obligation** contract **14 give** display heraldically. **luce** a fresh-water fish **17 passant** (1) walking (in heraldic language) (2) passing, exceeding. **familiar** (1) domestic (2) overfamiliar **19–20 The luce . . . coat** (Meaning unclear.) **21 quarter** combine the arms of two families by adding to one's own coat the arms of another family in one quarter of the escutcheon. **coz** cousin **25 py'r lady** by our Lady. (Evans' Welsh dialect often substitutes "p" for "b" at the start of words, as in *petter, prain,* and *prings* ll. 38–40, and also leaves out initial "w" as in *'orld* and *'oman,* ll. 45, 210.) **26 skirts** the tails of a long doublet. (Evans is still thinking of a literal coat that would be marred by quartering, i.e., cutting into quarters.) **30 compremises** compromises, i.e., settlement by arbitration **31 The council . . . riot** (The King's Council, sitting in Star Chamber, frequently concerned itself with riots. Evans, however, understands *council* to refer to an ecclesiastical council.) **35 vizaments** (For *advisements,* deliberations.) **38 that friends is the sword** i.e., that the quarrel be ended by friendly motions **43 Mistress** (Used of married or unmarried women.) **44 small** with a gentle, high voice **50 motion** plan **50–51 pribbles and prabbles** i.e., petty disputes

58 possibilities pecuniary prospects **65 well-willers** well wishers. **peat** beat, knock **77 ill** i.e., illegally, by Falstaff. (See below, l. 105.) **83 fallow** fawn-colored **84 on Cotsall** in the Cotswold hills in Gloucestershire **87 fault** misfortune **108 pin** trifle. **answer'd** accounted for. (But Falstaff plays on the meaning *replied to.*) **109 straight** (1) at once (2) strictly

SHALLOW The council shall know this.

FALSTAFF 'Twere better for you if it were known in counsel. You'll be laugh'd at.

EVANS Pauca verba, Sir John; goot worts.

FALSTAFF Good worts! Good cabbage. Slender, I broke your head. What matter have you against me?

SLENDER Marry, sir, I have matter in my head against you, and against your cony-catching rascals, Bardolph, Nym, and Pistol.

BARDOLPH You Banbury cheese!

SLENDER Ay, it is no matter.

PISTOL How now, Mephostophilus!

SLENDER Ay, it is no matter.

NYM Slice, I say! Pauca, pauca. Slice, that's my humor.

SLENDER Where's Simple, my man? Can you tell, cousin?

EVANS Peace, I pray you. Now let us understand. There is three umpires in this matter, as I understand; that is, Master Page, fidelicet Master Page; and there is myself, fidelicet myself; and the three party is, lastly and finally, mine host of the Garter.

PAGE We three, to hear it and end it between them.

EVANS Fery goot. I will make a prief of it in my notebook, and we will afterwards ork upon the cause with as great discreetly as we can.

FALSTAFF Pistol!

PISTOL He hears with ears.

EVANS The tevil and his tam! What phrase is this, "He hears with ear"? Why, it is affectations.

FALSTAFF Pistol, did you pick Master Slender's purse?

SLENDER Ay, by these gloves, did he, or I would I might never come in mine own great chamber again else, of seven groats in mill-sixpences, and two Edward shovel-boards, that cost me two shilling and two pence apiece of Yead Miller, by these gloves.

FALSTAFF Is this true, Pistol?

EVANS No; it is false, if it is a pick-purse.

PISTOL

Ha, thou mountain-foreigner! Sir John and master mine,
I combat challenge of this latten bilbo.
Word of denial in thy labras here!
Word of denial! Froth and scum, thou liest!

SLENDER By these gloves, then, 'twas he.

NYM Be avis'd, sir, and pass good humors. I will say "marry trap" with you, if you run the nuthook's humor on me. That is the very note of it.

SLENDER By this hat, then, he in the red face had it; for though I cannot remember what I did when you made me drunk, yet I am not altogether an ass.

FALSTAFF What say you, Scarlet and John?

BARDOLPH Why, sir, for my part, I say the gentleman had drunk himself out of his five sentences.

EVANS It is his five senses. Fie, what the ignorance is!

BARDOLPH And being fap, sir, was, as they say, cashier'd; and so conclusions pass'd the careers.

SLENDER Ay, you spake in Latin then too; but 'tis no matter. I'll ne'er be drunk whilst I live again, but in honest, civil, godly company, for this trick. If I be drunk, I'll be drunk with those that have the fear of God, and not with drunken knaves.

EVANS So Got udge me, that is a virtuous mind.

FALSTAFF You hear all these matters denied, gentlemen; you hear it.

[Enter] Anne Page [with wine]; Mistress Ford [and] Mistress Page [following].

PAGE Nay, daughter, carry the wine in; we'll drink within. *[Exit Anne Page.]*

SLENDER O heaven! This is Mistress Anne Page.

PAGE How now, Mistress Ford?

FALSTAFF Mistress Ford, by my troth, you are very well met. By your leave, good mistress. *[Kisses her.]*

PAGE Wife, bid these gentlemen welcome. Come, we have a hot venison pasty to dinner. Come, gentlemen, I hope we shall drink down all unkindness.

[Exeunt all except Shallow, Slender, and Evans.]

SLENDER I had rather than forty shillings I had my Book of Songs and Sonnets here.

[Enter] Simple.

How now, Simple, where have you been? I must wait on myself, must I? You have not the Book of Riddles about you, have you?

SIMPLE Book of Riddles? Why, did you not lend it to Alice Shortcake upon All-hallowmas last, a fortnight afore Michaelmas?

SHALLOW Come, coz; come, coz, we stay for you. A word with you, coz—marry, this, coz—there is, as 'twere, a tender, a kind of tender, made afar off by Sir Hugh here. Do you understand me?

SLENDER Ay, sir, you shall find me reasonable. If it be so, I shall do that that is reason.

SHALLOW Nay, but understand me.

SLENDER So I do, sir.

EVANS Give ear to his motions. Master Slender, I will description the matter to you, if you be capacity of it.

SLENDER Nay, I will do as my cousin Shallow says. I pray you, pardon me; he's a Justice of Peace in his country, simple though I stand here.

112–113 in counsel secretly (playing on *King's Council*) **114 Pauca verba** few words **115 worts** vegetables. (A quibble on Sir Hugh's pronunciation of "words.") **118 cony-catching** cheating **120 Banbury cheese** (Banbury cheeses were noted for their thinness; a reference to Slender's name and physique.) **122 Mephostophilus** name of the devil in Marlowe's *Doctor Faustus* **124 Slice** (1) speak briefly (2) I will slice with my sword (3) a reference to Bardolph's calling Slender a cheese (?). **humor** mood **129 fidelicet** i.e., *videlicet,* namely **131 Garter** the name of an inn in Windsor **138 tam** dam, mother **143 groats** coins equal to four pence. **mill-sixpences** coins stamped by means of the mill and press **143–144 Edward shovel-boards** shillings coined in the reign of Edward VI (so called from their use in the gambling game of shovelboard) **145 Yead** Ed, Edward **148 mountain-foreigner** i.e., Welshman **149 latten** mixed metal of yellow color, resembling brass. **bilbo** finely tempered sword of Bilbao in Spain. (Here alludes to Slender's thinness.) **150 labras** lips, i.e., face **153 avis'd** advised, on your guard. **pass good humors** do nothing ill-natured **154 marry trap** (An insulting phrase meaning something like "run off," "beat it.") **154–155 run . . . me** threaten me with a constable, or behave like one. (A *nuthook* literally is a hooked stick used to pull nuts from trees; applied to a constable.) **155 very note** true observation **156 he . . . face** i.e., Bardolph

159 Scarlet and John (Names of Robin Hood's companions, Will Scarlet and Little John; *Scarlet* is humorously applied to Bardolph's color.) **163 fap** drunk **163–164 cashier'd** deprived (of his senses) **164 conclusion . . . careers** i.e., his conclusions about matters made a wild gallop, went wide of the mark. (*Careers:* a short gallop at full speed, a feat of horsemanship.) **170 udge** (For *judge.*) **180 to** for **182–183 Book of Songs and Sonnets** (Probably refers to Tottel's *Miscellany,* published 1557 and quite old-fashioned by the late 1590's.) **185 Book of Riddles** (Such a book is mentioned as in the library of Captain Cox in *Laneham's Letter,* 1575. No copy is extant earlier than 1629.) **188–189 All-hallowmas . . . Michaelmas** (Simple's blunder. Michaelmas occurs on September 29, All-hallowmas or All Saints' Day on November 1.) **192 tender** offer **202 simple . . . here** i.e., however humble I, his kinsman, may appear to be

EVANS But that is not the question. The question is concerning your marriage.

SHALLOW Ay, there's the point, sir.

EVANS Marry, is it, the very point of it; to Mistress Anne Page.

SLENDER Why, if it be so, I will marry her upon any reasonable demands.

EVANS But can you affection the 'oman? Let us command to know that of your mouth or of your lips; for divers philosophers hold that the lips is parcel of the mouth. Therefore, precisely, can you carry your good will to the maid?

SHALLOW Cousin Abraham Slender, can you love her?

SLENDER I hope, sir, I will do as it shall become one that would do reason.

EVANS Nay, Got's lords and his ladies! You must speak possitable, if you can carry her your desires towards her.

SHALLOW That you must. Will you, upon good dowry, marry her?

SLENDER I will do a greater thing than that, upon your request, cousin, in any reason.

SHALLOW Nay, conceive me, conceive me, sweet coz; what I do is to pleasure you, coz. Can you love the maid?

SLENDER I will marry her, sir, at your request; but if there be no great love in the beginning, yet heaven may decrease it upon better acquaintance, when we are married and have more occasion to know one another. I hope, upon familiarity will grow more content. But if you say, "Marry her," I will marry her; that I am freely dissolv'd, and dissolutely.

EVANS It is a fery discretion answer; save the fall is in the 'ort "dissolutely." The 'ort is, according to our meaning, "resolutely." His meaning is good.

SHALLOW Ay, I think my cousin meant well.

SLENDER Ay, or else I would I might be hang'd, la!

SHALLOW Here comes fair Mistress Anne.

[*Enter Anne Page.*]

Would I were young for your sake, Mistress Anne!

ANNE The dinner is on the table. My father desires your worships' company.

SHALLOW I will wait on him, fair Mistress Anne.

EVANS Od's plessed will! I will not be absence at the grace.

[*Exeunt Shallow and Evans.*]

ANNE Will 't please your worship to come in, sir?

SLENDER No, I thank you, forsooth, heartily; I am very well.

ANNE The dinner attends you, sir.

SLENDER I am not a-hungry, I thank you, forsooth.—Go, sirrah, for all you are my man, go wait upon my cousin Shallow. [*Exit Simple.*] A Justice of Peace sometime may be beholding to his friend for a man. I keep but three men and a boy yet, till my mother be dead. But what though? Yet I live like a poor gentleman born.

ANNE I may not go in without your worship. They will not sit till you come.

SLENDER I' faith, I'll eat nothing. I thank you as much as though I did.

ANNE I pray you, sir, walk in.

SLENDER I had rather walk here, I thank you. I bruis'd my shin th' other day with playing at sword and dagger with a master of fence—three veneys for a dish of stew'd prunes—and, by my troth, I cannot abide the smell of hot meat since. Why do your dogs bark so? Be there bears i' th' town?

ANNE I think there are, sir; I heard them talk'd of.

SLENDER I love the sport well, but I shall as soon quarrel at it as any man in England. You are afraid, if you see the bear loose, are you not?

ANNE Ay, indeed, sir.

SLENDER That's meat and drink to me, now. I have seen Sackerson loose twenty times, and have taken him by the chain; but I warrant you, the women have so cried and shriek'd at it, that it pass'd. But women, indeed, cannot abide 'em; they are very ill-favor'd rough things.

[*Enter Page.*]

PAGE Come, gentle Master Slender, come. We stay for you.

SLENDER I'll eat nothing, I thank you, sir.

PAGE By cock and pie, you shall not choose, sir! Come, come.

SLENDER Nay, pray you, lead the way.

PAGE Come on, sir.

SLENDER Mistress Anne, yourself shall go first.

ANNE Not I, sir; pray you, keep on.

SLENDER Truly, I will not go first; truly, la! I will not do you that wrong.

ANNE I pray you, sir.

SLENDER I'll rather be unmannerly than troublesome. You do yourself wrong, indeed, la! *Exeunt.*

SCENE II

Enter [*Sir Hugh*] *Evans and Simple* [*from dinner*].

EVANS Go your ways, and ask of Doctor Caius' house which is the way; and there dwells one Mistress Quickly, which is in the manner of his nurse, or his dry nurse, or his cook, or his laundry, his washer, and his wringer.

SIMPLE Well, sir.

EVANS Nay, it is petter yet. Give her this letter. [*Gives*

212 parcel part **219 possitable** (For *positively.*) **225 conceive** understand **230 decrease** (For *increase.*) **232 content** (Suggesting *contempt,* as in the proverb, "Familiarity breeds contempt.") **234 dissolv'd** (For *resolved.*) **dissolutely** (For *resolutely.*) **235 fall** i.e., fault **236 'ort** word **244 wait on him** keep him company **245 Od's** God's **250 attends** waits for

256 what though what of it **265 fence** fencing. **veneys** thrusts in fencing **266 stew'd prunes** (A favorite dish at the "stews" or brothel houses; hence an indelicate remark to address to Anne.) **270 the sport** i.e., bear-baiting **275 Sackerson** a famous bear at the Paris Garden near the theatres on the Bankside **277 pass'd** i.e., surpassed description **283 cock** (A perversion of *God.*) **pie** service book of the pre-Reformation church

I.ii. Location: The same scene, a short time later.
4 dry nurse i.e., attendant to an adult, not a child

letter.] For it is a 'oman that altogether's acquaintance
with Mistress Anne Page; and the letter is, to desire
and require her to solicit your master's desires to Mis-
tress Anne Page. I pray you, be gone. I will make an
end of my dinner; there's pippins and cheese to come. 12
Exeunt [*severally*].

SCENE III

Enter Falstaff, Host, Bardolph, Nym, Pistol, [*and Robin, Falstaff's*] *Page.*

FALSTAFF Mine host of the Garter!
HOST What says my bully-rook? Speak scholarly and 2
wisely.
FALSTAFF Truly, mine host, I must turn away some of
my followers.
HOST Discard, bully Hercules, cashier. Let them wag; 6
trot, trot.
FALSTAFF I sit at ten pounds a week. 8
HOST Thou 'rt an emperor, Caesar, Keiser, and Phea- 9
zar. I will entertain Bardolph; he shall draw, he shall 10
tap. Said I well, bully Hector? 11
FALSTAFF Do so, good mine host.
HOST I have spoke; let him follow. [*To Bardolph.*] Let
me see thee froth and lime. I am at a word; follow. 14
[*Exit.*]
FALSTAFF Bardolph, follow him. A tapster is a good
trade. An old cloak makes a new jerkin; a wither'd 16
servingman a fresh tapster. Go; adieu.
BARDOLPH It is a life that I have desir'd. I will thrive.
PISTOL O base Hungarian wight! Wilt thou the spigot 19
wield? [*Exit Bardolph.*]
NYM He was gotten in drink. Is not the humor con- 21
ceited? 22
FALSTAFF I am glad I am so acquit of this tinderbox. His 23
thefts were too open. His filching was like an unskill-
ful singer; he kept not time.
NYM The good humor is to steal at a minute's rest. 26
PISTOL "Convey," the wise it call. "Steal"? Foh! A fico 27
for the phrase!
FALSTAFF Well, sirs, I am almost out at heels. 29
PISTOL Why, then, let kibes ensue. 30
FALSTAFF There is no remedy; I must cony-catch, I must
shift. 32
PISTOL Young ravens must have food.
FALSTAFF Which of you know Ford of this town?
PISTOL I ken the wight. He is of substance good. 35
FALSTAFF My honest lads, I will tell you what I am 36
about. 37
PISTOL Two yards, and more.
FALSTAFF No quips now, Pistol! Indeed, I am in the
waist two yards about; but I am now about no waste;
I am about thrift. Briefly, I do mean to make love to
Ford's wife. I spy entertainment in her. She dis-
courses, she carves, she gives the leer of invitation. I 43
can construe the action of her familiar style; and the 44
hardest voice of her behavior, to be English'd rightly, 45
is, "I am Sir John Falstaff's."
PISTOL He hath studied her well, and translated her
will, out of honesty into English. 48
NYM The anchor is deep. Will that humor pass? 49
FALSTAFF Now, the report goes she has all the rule of
her husband's purse. He hath a legion of angels. 51
PISTOL As many devils entertain; and "To her, boy," 52
say I.
NYM The humor rises; it is good. Humor me the an-
gels.
FALSTAFF [*Showing letters*] I have writ me here a letter
to her; and here another to Page's wife, who even now
gave me good eyes too, examin'd my parts with most
judicious oeillades. Sometimes the beam of her view 59
gilded my foot, sometimes my portly belly.
PISTOL [*Aside*] Then did the sun on dunghill shine.
NYM [*Aside*] I thank thee for that humor.
FALSTAFF O, she did so course o'er my exteriors with
such a greedy intention, that the appetite of her eye
did seem to scorch me up like a burning-glass! Here's 65
another letter to her. She bears the purse too; she is a
region in Guiana, all gold and bounty. I will be cheat- 67
ers to them both, and they shall be exchequers to me. 68
They shall be my East and West Indies, and I will trade
to them both. [*To Pistol.*] Go bear thou this letter to
Mistress Page; [*To Nym*] and thou this to Mistress
Ford. We will thrive, lads, we will thrive.
PISTOL
Shall I Sir Pandarus of Troy become, 73
And by my side wear steel? Then Lucifer take all! 74
NYM I will run no base humor. Here, take the humor-
letter. [*Gives letter back.*] I will keep the havior of rep- 76
utation. 77
FALSTAFF [*To Robin*]
Hold, sirrah, bear you these letters tightly; 78
[*Gives letters.*]
Sail like my pinnace to these golden shores.
Rogues, hence, avaunt! Vanish like hailstones, go!
Trudge, plod away o' th' hoof! Seek shelter, pack! 81

12 pippins a kind of apple

I.iii. Location: The Garter Inn.
2 bully-rook fine fellow **6 wag** move on **8 I sit at** my expenses are **9 Keiser** Kaiser, emperor **9–10 Pheazar** i.e., Vizier (?) **10 entertain** employ. **draw** draw liquor **11 tap** serve as tapster **14 froth** draw liquor in such a way as to make it frothy, filling the glass with less beer. **lime** adulterate wine by putting lime into it to mask the sour taste. **at a word** a man of few words **16 jerkin** jacket **19 Hungarian wight** i.e., beggarly person **21 gotten** begotten **21–22 conceited** ingenious **23 acquit** rid. **tinderbox** (alluding to Bardolph's fiery complexion) **26 minute's rest** (Perhaps an error for *minim rest,* the shortest rest in music.) **27 fico** Italian for *fig* **29 out at heels** i.e., out of money. (Literally, with stocking or shoes worn through at the heel.) **30 kibes** chilblains. (Pistol interprets *out at heels* literally.) **32 shift** devise a stratagem **35 ken the wight** know the person

36–37 what I am about what I am up to. (But Pistol plays with the meaning *what I measure round about.*) **43 carves** shows courtesy and affability **44 construe** interpret (introducing an extended grammatical pun, continued in *style, voice,* and *English'd*) **45 English'd** expressed in English **48 honesty** chastity **49 The . . . deep** i.e., the plan is fixed firmly, or is a deep one (?). **Will . . . pass** i.e., will my expression pass muster **51 angels** coins stamped with the figure of the archangel Michael, worth about ten shillings **52 entertain** take into service **59 oeillades** amorous glances **65 burning-glass** magnifying glass to focus rays of the sun **67 region in Guiana** (A possible reference to Ralegh's *Discoverie of the Large, Rich, and Beautiful Empyre of Guiana,* published 1596.) **67–68 cheater** escheater, officer appointed to look after the King's escheats, i.e., land reverted to the crown (with a quibble on the ordinary sense of *those who cheat*) **68 exchequers** treasuries **73 Sir Pandarus** uncle of Cressida, and go-between in the story of Troilus and Cressida. (From his name originated the word "pandar.") **74 And . . . steel** i.e., even though I am a soldier **76–77 keep . . . reputation** keep up good appearances **78 tightly** deftly **81 pack** be off

Falstaff will learn the humor of the age:
French thrift, you rogues—myself and skirted page.
[Exeunt Falstaff and Robin severally.]

PISTOL
Let vultures gripe thy guts! For gourd and fullam holds,
And high and low beguiles the rich and poor.
Tester I'll have in pouch when thou shalt lack,
Base Phrygian Turk!

NYM I have operations which be humors of revenge.

PISTOL Wilt thou revenge?

NYM By welkin and her star!

PISTOL With wit or steel?

NYM
With both the humors, I.
I will discuss the humor of this love to Page.

PISTOL
And I to Ford shall eke unfold
How Falstaff, varlet vile,
His dove will prove, his gold will hold,
And his soft couch defile.

NYM My humor shall not cool. I will incense Page to deal with poison; I will possess him with yellowness, for the revolt of mine is dangerous. That is my true humor.

PISTOL Thou art the Mars of malecontents. I second thee; troop on. *Exeunt.*

SCENE IV

Enter Mistress Quickly, Simple, [and] John Rugby.

QUICKLY What, John Rugby! I pray thee, go to the casement, and see if you can see my master, Master Doctor Caius, coming. If he do, i' faith, and find anybody in the house, here will be an old abusing of God's patience and the King's English.

RUGBY I'll go watch.

QUICKLY Go; and we'll have a posset for 't soon at night, in faith, at the latter end of a sea-coal fire. *[Rugby goes to look out the window.]* An honest, willing, kind fellow, as ever servant shall come in house withal, and, I warrant you, no tell-tale nor no breedbate. His worst fault is, that he is given to prayer; he is something peevish that way, but nobody but has his fault; but let that pass. Peter Simple, you say your name is?

SIMPLE Ay, for fault of a better.

QUICKLY And Master Slender's your master?

SIMPLE Ay, forsooth.

QUICKLY Does he not wear a great round beard, like a glover's paring-knife?

SIMPLE No, forsooth. He hath but a little whey face, with a little yellow beard, a Cain-color'd beard.

QUICKLY A softly-sprighted man, is he not?

SIMPLE Ay, forsooth. But he is as tall a man of his hands as any is between this and his head. He hath fought with a warrener.

QUICKLY How say you? O, I should remember him. Does he not hold up his head, as it were, and strut in his gait?

SIMPLE Yes, indeed, does he.

QUICKLY Well, heaven send Anne Page no worse fortune! Tell Master Parson Evans I will do what I can for your master. Anne is a good girl, and I wish—

[Rugby returns.]

RUGBY Out, alas! Here comes my master.

QUICKLY We shall all be shent. Run in here, good young man; go into this closet. He will not stay long. *[Shuts Simple in the room.]* What, John Rugby! John! What, John, I say! Go, John, go inquire for my master; I doubt he be not well, that he comes not home. *[Exit Rugby.]*
[Singing] And down, down, adown-a, etc.

[Enter] Doctor Caius.

CAIUS Vat is you sing? I do not like des toys. Pray you, go and vetch me in my closet un boitier verd, a box, a green-a box. Do intend vat I speak? A green-a box.

QUICKLY Ay, forsooth; I'll fetch it you. *[Aside.]* I am glad he went not in himself. If he had found the young man, he would have been horn-mad. *[She goes to the room.]*

CAIUS Fe, fe, fe, fe! Ma foi, il fait fort chaud. Je m'en vais a la cour—la grande affaire.

QUICKLY Is it this, sir? *[Gives him a box.]*

CAIUS Oui; mette le au mon pocket. Dépêche, quickly. Vere is dat knave Rugby?

QUICKLY What, John Rugby! John!

[Enter Rugby.]

RUGBY Here, sir!

CAIUS You are John Rugby, and you are Jack Rugby. Come take-a your rapier, and come after my heel to the court.

RUGBY 'Tis ready, sir, here in the porch.

CAIUS By my trot, I tarry too long. Od's me! Qu'ai-j'oublié! Dere is some simples in my closet, dat I vill not for the varld I shall leave behind.

QUICKLY *[Aside]* Ay me, he'll find the young man there, and be mad!

83 French thrift (Alludes to the current practice in France of economizing with one page instead of a more numerous retinue.) **skirted** wearing a doublet with long skirts or tails **84 gourd and fullam** two kinds of false dice **85 high and low** i.e., dice numbers (?) **86 Tester** sixpence **87 Phrygian Turk** (A term of opprobrium.) **88 operations** plans **90 welkin** sky **91 wit or steel** i.e., cunning or violence **93 discuss** declare **94 eke** also **96 prove** test **99 yellowness** i.e., jealousy **100 revolt . . . dangerous** i.e., my turning against Falstaff will harm him **102 the Mars** i.e., the most warlike and mighty

I.iv. Location: Doctor Caius' house.
4 old plentiful, great **7 posset** a drink of hot milk curdled with ale or wine **8 sea-coal** mineral coal brought by sea (as distinguished from charcoal) **11–12 breed-bate** mischief maker **13 something peevish** somewhat foolish

21 whey i.e., pallid **22 Cain-color'd** (Cain is often pictured in old tapestries with a yellow or reddish beard.) **23 softly-sprighted** gentle **24 as tall . . . hands** as valiant a man, as stout of arms **25 between . . . head** (Meaning not clear.) **26 warrener** gamekeeper **35 shent** blamed, disgraced **36 closet** private room **39 doubt** fear **40 toys** trifles, i.e., songs **41 un boitier verd** a green box **42 Do intend** do you understand. (French *entendre*.) **45 horn-mad** (1) enraged, like a horned beast (2) enraged like a jealous cuckold **46–47 Ma foi . . . affaire** by my faith, it is very hot; I am going to court—the great affair **49 Oui . . . Dépêche** yes, put it in my pocket; be quick **54 your rapier** i.e., your master's rapier **57–58 Qu'ai-j'oublié** what have I forgotten **58 simples** medicinal herbs

CAIUS [*Going to the room*] O diable, diable! Vat is in my closet? Villainy! Larron! [*Pulling Simple out.*] Rugby, my rapier!

QUICKLY Good master, be content.

CAIUS Wherefore shall I be content-a?

QUICKLY The young man is an honest man.

CAIUS What shall de honest man do in my closet? Dere is no honest man dat shall come in my closet.

QUICKLY I beseech you, be not so phlegmatic. Hear the truth of it: he came of an errand to me from Parson Hugh.

CAIUS Vell?

SIMPLE Ay, forsooth, to desire her to—

QUICKLY Peace, I pray you.

CAIUS Peace-a your tongue.—Speak-a your tale.

SIMPLE To desire this honest gentlewoman, your maid, to speak a good word to Mistress Anne Page for my master in the way of marriage.

QUICKLY This is all, indeed, la! But I'll ne'er put my finger in the fire, and need not.

CAIUS Sir Hugh send-a you? Rugby, baille me some paper.—Tarry you a little-a while. [*Rugby fetches paper, and Dr. Caius writes.*]

QUICKLY [*Aside to Simple*] I am glad he is so quiet. If he had been throughly mov'd, you should have heard him so loud and so melancholy. But notwithstanding, man, I'll do you your master what good I can; and the very yea and the no is, the French doctor, my master—I may call him my master, look you, for I keep his house; and I wash, wring, brew, bake, scour, dress meat and drink, make the beds, and do all myself—

SIMPLE [*Aside to Quickly*] 'Tis a great charge to come under one body's hand.

QUICKLY [*Aside to Simple*] Are you avis'd o' that? You shall find it a great charge. And to be up early and down late; but notwithstanding—to tell you in your ear; I would have no words of it—my master himself is in love with Mistress Anne Page. But notwithstanding that, I know Anne's mind—that's neither here nor there.

CAIUS You jack'nape, give-a this letter to Sir Hugh. [*Gives letter.*] By gar, it is a shallenge. I will cut his troat in de park; and I will teach a scurvy jack-a-nape priest to meddle or make. You may be gone; it is not good you tarry here. By gar, I will cut all his two stones; by gar, he shall not have a stone to throw at his dog. [*Exit Simple.*]

QUICKLY Alas, he speaks but for his friend.

CAIUS It is no matter-a ver dat. Do not you tell-a me dat I shall have Anne Page for myself? By gar, I vill kill de Jack priest; and I have appointed mine host of de Jarteer to measure our weapon. By gar, I will myself have Anne Page.

QUICKLY Sir, the maid loves you, and all shall be well. We must give folks leave to prate; what the good-jer!

CAIUS Rugby, come to the court with me. By gar, if I have not Anne Page, I shall turn your head out of my door. Follow my heels, Rugby. [*Exeunt Caius and Rugby.*]

QUICKLY You shall have An fool's-head of your own. No, I know Anne's mind for that. Never a woman in Windsor knows more of Anne's mind than I do, nor can do more than I do with her, I thank heaven.

FENTON [Within] Who's within there, ho?

QUICKLY Who's there, I trow? Come near the house, I pray you.

[*Enter*] *Fenton.*

FENTON How now, good woman! How dost thou?

QUICKLY The better that it pleases your good worship to ask.

FENTON What news? How does pretty Mistress Anne?

QUICKLY In truth, sir, and she is pretty, and honest, and gentle; and one that is your friend, I can tell you that by the way, I praise heaven for it.

FENTON Shall I do any good, think'st thou? Shall I not lose my suit?

QUICKLY Troth, sir, all is in His hands above. But notwithstanding, Master Fenton, I'll be sworn on a book she loves you. Have not your worship a wart above your eye?

FENTON Yes, marry, have I. What of that?

QUICKLY Well, thereby hangs a tale. Good faith, it is such another Nan! But, I detest, an honest maid as ever broke bread. We had an hour's talk of that wart. I shall never laugh but in that maid's company! But indeed she is given too much to allicholy and musing. But for you—well, go to.

FENTON Well, I shall see her today. Hold, there's money for thee. [*Gives money.*] Let me have thy voice in my behalf. If thou seest her before me, commend me.

QUICKLY Will I? I' faith, that we will; and I will tell your worship more of the wart the next time we have confidence, and of other wooers.

FENTON Well, farewell. I am in great haste now.

QUICKLY Farewell to your worship. [*Exit Fenton.*] Truly, an honest gentleman. But Anne loves him not, for I know Anne's mind as well as another does.—Out upon 't! What have I forgot? *Exit.*

ACT II • SCENE I

Enter Mistress Page [*with a letter*].

MRS PAGE What, have I scap'd love-letters in the holiday-time of my beauty, and am I now a subject for them? Let me see. [*Reads.*]

"Ask me no reason why I love you; for though Love

62 diable devil **63 Larron** robber **70 phlegmatic** (Probably a blunder for *choleric,* hot-tempered; phlegmatic is the very opposite in the physiology of humors.) **81 and need not** if I don't need to **82 baille** fetch **86 melancholy** (Perhaps a blunder again, like *phlegmatic,* above.) **91–92 dress meat** prepare food **92 charge** responsibility **94 Are . . . that** i.e., you may well say so **101 jack'nape** ape, tame monkey; i.e., fop, worthless fellow **104 meddle or make** meddle **105–106 cut . . . stones** castrate him **109 ver** for **111 Jack** (A contemptuous epithet.) **111–112 Jarteer** Garter **112 measure our weapon** i.e., act as second. (Literally, to make sure that the swords are of equal length.)

115 what the good-jer what the good-year. (An expression of disgust? Cf. *Much Ado,* I.iii.1.) **119 An** (The Folio uses the same spelling, *An,* for *Anne,* in ll. 120 and 121, suggesting a pun on Anne Page; Caius is to have a fool's head for wooing Anne.) **124 trow** wonder. **Come near** enter **130 honest** chaste **131 gentle** well-bred **140–141 it . . . Nan** i.e., Anne is so remarkable a girl **141 detest** (For *protest.*) **144 allicholy** (For *melancholy.*) **145 go to** i.e., enough

II.i. Location: Before Page's house.

use Reason for his precisian, he admits him not for his counselor. You are not young, no more am I; go to then, there's sympathy. You are merry, so am I; ha, ha! Then there's more sympathy. You love sack, and so do I; would you desire better sympathy? Let it suffice thee, Mistress Page—at the least, if the love of soldier can suffice—that I love thee. I will not say, pity me—'tis not a soldier-like phrase—but I say, love me. By me,

Thine own true knight,
By day or night,
Or any kind of light,
With all his might
For thee to fight,
John Falstaff."

What a Herod of Jewry is this! O wicked, wicked world! One that is well-nigh worn to pieces with age to show himself a young gallant! What an unweigh'd behavior hath this Flemish drunkard pick'd—with the devil's name!—out of my conversation, that he dares in this manner assay me? Why, he hath not been thrice in my company! What should I say to him? I was then frugal of my mirth. Heaven forgive me! Why, I'll exhibit a bill in the parliament for the putting down of men. How shall I be reveng'd on him? For reveng'd I will be, as sure as his guts are made of puddings.

[Enter] Mistress Ford.

MRS FORD Mistress Page! Trust me, I was going to your house.

MRS PAGE And, trust me, I was coming to you. You look very ill.

MRS FORD Nay, I'll ne'er believe that; I have to show to the contrary.

MRS PAGE Faith, but you do, in my mind.

MRS FORD Well, I do then; yet I say I could show you to the contrary. O Mistress Page, give me some counsel!

MRS PAGE What's the matter, woman?

MRS FORD O woman, if it were not for one trifling respect, I could come to such honor!

MRS PAGE Hang the trifle, woman, take the honor. What is it? Dispense with trifles. What is it?

MRS FORD If I would but go to hell for an eternal moment or so, I could be knighted.

MRS PAGE What? Thou liest! Sir Alice Ford! These knights will hack; and so thou shouldst not alter the article of thy gentry.

MRS FORD We burn daylight. Here, read, read; perceive how I might be knighted. [*Gives letter.*] I shall think the worse of fat men, as long as I have an eye to make difference of men's liking. And yet he would not swear; prais'd women's modesty; and gave such orderly and well-behav'd reproof to all uncomeliness, that I would have sworn his disposition would have gone to the truth of his words; but they do no more adhere and keep place together than the Hundredth Psalm to the tune of "Greensleeves." What tempest, I trow, threw this whale, with so many tuns of oil in his belly, ashore at Windsor? How shall I be reveng'd on him? I think the best way were to entertain him with hope, till the wicked fire of lust have melted him in his own grease. Did you ever hear the like?

MRS PAGE Letter for letter, but that the name of Page and Ford differs! To thy great comfort in this mystery of ill opinions, here's the twin-brother of thy letter. [*Shows her letter.*] But let thine inherit first; for, I protest, mine never shall. I warrant he hath a thousand of these letters, writ with blank space for different names—sure, more—and these are of the second edition. He will print them, out of doubt; for he cares not what he puts into the press, when he would put us two. I had rather be a giantess, and lie under Mount Pelion. Well, I will find you twenty lascivious turtles ere one chaste man.

MRS FORD [*Comparing the letters*] Why, this is the very same; the very hand, the very words. What doth he think of us?

MRS PAGE Nay, I know not. It makes me almost ready to wrangle with mine own honesty. I'll entertain myself like one that I am not acquainted withal; for, sure, unless he know some strain in me that I know not myself, he would never have boarded me in this fury.

MRS FORD "Boarding," call you it? I'll be sure to keep him above deck.

MRS PAGE So will I. If he come under my hatches, I'll never to sea again. Let's be reveng'd on him. Let's appoint him a meeting, give him a show of comfort in his suit, and lead him on with a fine-baited delay, till he hath pawn'd his horses to mine host of the Garter.

MRS FORD Nay, I will consent to act any villainy against him that may not sully the chariness of our honesty. O, that my husband saw this letter! It would give eternal food to his jealousy.

MRS PAGE Why, look where he comes; and my good man too. He's as far from jealousy as I am from giving him cause; and that I hope is an unmeasurable distance.

MRS FORD You are the happier woman.

MRS PAGE Let's consult together against this greasy knight. Come hither. [*They retire.*]

[Enter] Master Page [with] Nym, Master Ford [with] Pistol.

FORD Well, I hope it be not so.

5 precisian strict adviser **6 counselor** practical guide **8 sack** a Spanish wine **20 Herod of Jewry** bombastic ranter, like the comic villain of the Corpus Christi plays **22 unweigh'd** ill-considered **23 Flemish drunkard** (The Flemish were proverbially heavy drinkers.) **with** in **24 conversation** conduct **25 assay** accost, address (with proposals of love) **26 should I say** could I have said **27 exhibit** introduce **30 puddings** mixture of meat, herbs, etc., stuffed into intestines of animals, as sausage **49 hack** (Of uncertain meaning; perhaps "fight with swords," together with a play on the idea of sexual intercourse; see also "to hick and to hack," IV.i.61) **50 article of thy gentry** character of your rank **51 burn daylight** i.e., waste time **53–54 make . . . liking** discriminate among men's looks and physiques

56 uncomeliness unseemly behavior **58 gone . . . of** supported **60 Greensleeves** (A popular tune to which many sets of words have been sung; cf. V.v.19.) **74 into the press** (1) into the printing press (2) under his weight **76 Pelion** mountain in Thessaly. (The giants, according to Greek mythology, heaped it on a neighboring mountain, Ossa, and Ossa on Olympus, in their attempts to overthrow the gods.) **turtles** turtledoves, proverbially chaste, i.e., faithful to their mates **82 wrangle** quarrel. **entertain** treat **84 strain** quality **85 boarded** accosted, made advances to. (A term of naval warfare.) **91 fine-baited** i.e., subtly alluring **94 chariness** scrupulous integrity

PISTOL
Hope is a curtal dog in some affairs.
Sir John affects thy wife.

FORD Why, sir, my wife is not young.

PISTOL
He woos both high and low, both rich and poor,
Both young and old, one with another, Ford.
He loves the gallimaufry. Ford, perpend.

FORD Love my wife?

PISTOL
With liver burning hot. Prevent, or go thou,
Like Sir Actaeon he, with Ringwood at thy heels.—
O, odious is the name!

FORD What name, sir?

PISTOL
The horn, I say. Farewell.
Take heed, have open eye, for thieves do foot by
night.
Take heed, ere summer comes or cuckoo-birds do
sing.
Away, Sir Corporal Nym!
Believe it, Page; he speaks sense. [*Exit.*]

FORD [*Aside*] I will be patient; I will find out this.

NYM [*To Page*] And this is true; I like not the humor of lying. He hath wrong'd me in some humors. I should have borne the humor'd letter to her; but I have a sword and it shall bite upon my necessity. He loves your wife; there's the short and the long. My name is Corporal Nym; I speak and I avouch; 'tis true. My name is Nym and Falstaff loves your wife. Adieu. I love not the humor of bread and cheese, and there's the humor of it. Adieu.

PAGE "The humor of it," quoth 'a! Here's a fellow frights English out of his wits.

FORD [*Aside*] I will seek out Falstaff.

PAGE [*Aside*] I never heard such a drawling, affecting rogue.

FORD [*Aside*] If I do find it—well.

PAGE [*Aside*] I will not believe such a Cataian, though the priest o' th' town commended him for a true man.

FORD [*Aside*] 'Twas a good sensible fellow—well.

PAGE How now, Meg?

[*Mrs Page and Mrs Ford come forward.*]

MRS PAGE Whither go you, George? Hark you.

MRS FORD How now, sweet Frank, why art thou melancholy?

FORD I melancholy? I am not melancholy. Get you home, go.

MRS FORD Faith, thou hast some crotchets in thy head now. Will you go, Mistress Page?

MRS PAGE Have with you. You'll come to dinner, George? [*Aside to Mrs Ford.*] Look who comes yonder. She shall be our messenger to this paltry knight.

MRS FORD [*Aside to Mrs Page*] Trust me, I thought on her. She'll fit it.

[*Enter Mistress*] *Quickly.*

MRS PAGE You are come to see my daughter Anne?

QUICKLY Ay, forsooth; and, I pray, how does good Mistress Anne?

MRS PAGE Go in with us and see. We have an hour's talk with you.

[*Exeunt Mrs Page, Mrs Ford, and Mrs Quickly.*]

PAGE How now, Master Ford?

FORD You heard what this knave told me, did you not?

PAGE Yes, and you heard what the other told me?

FORD Do you think there is truth in them?

PAGE Hang 'em, slaves! I do not think the knight would offer it. But these that accuse him in his intent towards our wives are a yoke of his discarded men—very rogues, now they be out of service.

FORD Were they his men?

PAGE Marry, were they.

FORD I like it never the better for that. Does he lie at the Garter?

PAGE Ay, marry, does he. If he should intend this voyage toward my wife, I would turn her loose to him; and what he gets more of her than sharp words, let it lie on my head.

FORD I do not misdoubt my wife; but I would be loath to turn them together. A man may be too confident. I would have nothing lie on my head. I cannot be thus satisfied.

PAGE Look where my ranting host of the Garter comes. There is either liquor in his pate or money in his purse when he looks so merrily.

[*Enter*] *Host.*

How now, mine host?

HOST How now, bully-rook? Thou 'rt a gentleman. Cavaleiro-justice, I say!

[*Enter*] *Shallow.*

SHALLOW I follow, mine host, I follow. Good even and twenty, good Master Page! Master Page, will you go with us? We have sport in hand.

HOST Tell him, cavaleiro-justice; tell him, bully-rook.

SHALLOW Sir, there is a fray to be fought between Sir Hugh the Welsh priest and Caius the French doctor.

FORD Good mine host o' th' Garter, a word with you.

[*Drawing him aside.*]

HOST What say'st thou, my bully-rook?

SHALLOW [*To Page*] Will you go with us to behold it? My merry host hath had the measuring of their weapons, and, I think, hath appointed them contrary places; for, believe me, I hear the parson is no jester.

105 curtal having the tail docked. (A term of opprobrium or condescension.) **106 affects** loves **110 gallimaufry** a dish of miscellaneous ingredients. **perpend** consider **112 burning hot** (Allusion to the liver as the seat of the passions.) **113 Actaeon** huntsman who was changed into a stag by Diana as punishment for watching her and her nymphs at their bath, and was torn to pieces by his own hounds. (The comparison here is to a horned beast, like a cuckold, being pursued.) **Ringwood** one of Actaeon's hounds (mentioned in Golding's translation of Ovid) **114 the name** i.e., the name of cuckold **118 cuckoo-birds** (Associated with cuckoldry because of their call, "cuckoo," and because they laid eggs in other birds' nests.) **123–124 I . . . borne** i.e., he wanted me to **125 upon my necessity** when I have need **129 humor . . . cheese** (Alludes to the scant rations Nym received as Falstaff's retainer.) **132 his** its **134 affecting** affected **137 Cataian** Cathaian, person from Cathay, i.e., China; hence, sharper, scoundrel **146 crotchets** whims, fancies **148 Have with you** I'll go along with you

163 offer venture **164 yoke** pair **168 lie** lodge **173 lie on my head** be my responsibility. (But Ford, in his reply, sees a joke on cuckold's horns.) **183 Cavaleiro** gentleman trained in arms, a gallant military man **184–185 Good . . . twenty** i.e., good evening, many times over **194–195 contrary places** different meeting places

Hark, I will tell you what our sport shall be.
[*They converse apart.*]

HOST Hast thou no suit against my knight, my guest-cavaleir?

FORD None, I protest. But I'll give you a pottle of burnt sack to give me recourse to him and tell him my name is Brook—only for a jest.

HOST My hand, bully. Thou shalt have egress and regress—said I well?—and thy name shall be Brook. It is a merry knight. Will you go, mynheers?

SHALLOW Have with you, mine host.

PAGE I have heard the Frenchman hath good skill in his rapier.

SHALLOW Tut, sir, I could have told you more. In these times you stand on distance, your passes, stoccadoes, and I know not what. 'Tis the heart, Master Page; 'tis here, 'tis here. I have seen the time, with my long sword I would have made you four tall fellows skip like rats.

HOST Here, boys, here, here! Shall we wag?

PAGE Have with you. I had rather hear them scold than fight. *Exeunt [Host, Shallow, and Page].*

FORD Though Page be a secure fool, and stands so firmly on his wife's frailty, yet I cannot put off my opinion so easily. She was in his company at Page's house; and what they made there, I know not. Well, I will look further into 't, and I have a disguise to sound Falstaff. If I find her honest, I lose not my labor; if she be otherwise, 'tis labor well bestow'd. [*Exit.*]

SCENE II

Enter Falstaff [and] Pistol.

FALSTAFF I will not lend thee a penny.

PISTOL
Why, then the world's mine oyster,
Which I with sword will open.
[I will retort the sum in equipage.]

FALSTAFF Not a penny. I have been content, sir, you should lay my countenance to pawn. I have grated upon my good friends for three reprieves for you and your coach-fellow Nym, or else you had look'd through the grate, like a geminy of baboons. I am damn'd in hell for swearing to gentlemen my friends, you were good soldiers and tall fellows; and when Mistress Bridget lost the handle of her fan, I took 't upon mine honor thou hadst it not.

PISTOL
Didst not thou share? Hadst thou not fifteen pence?

FALSTAFF Reason, you rogue, reason. Think'st thou I'll endanger my soul gratis? At a word, hang no more about me, I am no gibbet for you. Go. A short knife and a throng! To your manor of Pickt-hatch! Go. You'll not bear a letter for me, you rogue? You stand upon your honor! Why, thou unconfinable baseness, it is as much as I can do to keep the terms of my honor precise. I, I, I myself sometimes, leaving the fear of God on the left hand and hiding mine honor in my necessity, am fain to shuffle, to hedge, and to lurch; and yet you, you rogue, will ensconce your rags, your cat-a-mountain looks, your red-lattice phrases, and your bold-beating oaths, under the shelter of your honor! You will not do it, you!

PISTOL
I do relent. What would thou more of man?

[*Enter*] *Robin.*

ROBIN Sir, here's a woman would speak with you.

FALSTAFF Let her approach.

[*Enter Mistress*] *Quickly.*

QUICKLY Give your worship good morrow.

FALSTAFF Good morrow, good wife.

QUICKLY Not so, an 't please your worship.

FALSTAFF Good maid, then.

QUICKLY I'll be sworn, as my mother was, the first hour I was born.

FALSTAFF I do believe the swearer. What with me?

QUICKLY Shall I vouchsafe your worship a word or two?

FALSTAFF Two thousand, fair woman, and I'll vouchsafe thee the hearing.

QUICKLY There is one Mistress Ford, sir—I pray, come a little nearer this ways. I myself dwell with Master Doctor Caius—

FALSTAFF Well, on. Mistress Ford, you say—

QUICKLY Your worship says very true. I pray your worship, come a little nearer this ways.

FALSTAFF I warrant thee, nobody hears—mine own people, mine own people.

QUICKLY Are they so? God bless them and make them his servants!

FALSTAFF Well, Mistress Ford; what of her?

QUICKLY Why, sir, she's a good creature. Lord, Lord! Your worship's a wanton! Well, heaven forgive you and all of us, I pray!

FALSTAFF Mistress Ford; come, Mistress Ford—

QUICKLY Marry, this is the short and the long of it: you have brought her into such a canaries as 'tis wonderful. The best courtier of them all, when the court lay at Windsor, could never have brought her to such a canary. Yet there has been knights, and lords, and gen-

199 pottle two-quart measure. **burnt** heated **204 mynheers** gentlemen. (Dutch.) **209 stand on distance** rely on prescribed space between fencers. **passes** lunges. **stoccadoes** thrusts **212 tall** valiant **214 wag** go. (See I.iii.6.) **217 secure** overconfident **219 She** i.e., Mrs. Ford. **his** i.e., Falstaff's **221 sound** plumb

II.ii. Location: The Garter Inn.
4 retort . . . equipage i.e., pay back the whole amount in military equipment **6 lay . . . pawn** i.e., borrow money on the strength of my patronage **6–7 grated upon** i.e., persistently and irritatingly begged **8 coach-fellow** partner (like a fellow horse in harness) **9 grate** i.e., of a debtor's prison window. **geminy** pair **12–13 took 't upon** swore by

17–18 A short . . . throng i.e., with a short knife you might cut purses in a crowd **18 Pickt-hatch** (A quarter in London notorious in Elizabethan times for criminal types and prostitutes, the houses having hatches, or half doors, guarded with spikes.) **20 unconfinable** infinite **21 terms** condition **24 to shuffle . . . lurch** to practice trickery, to dodge, and to steal **25–26 cat-a-mountain** catamount, leopard or panther, hence, wild-man **26 red-lattice phrases** alehouse talk. (Lattices painted red identified an alehouse.) **27 bold-beating** (Perhaps a conflation of "bold-faced" and "brow-beating.") **36–37 as . . . born** (Mistress Quickly probably means "as much a maid as when I was born, just like my mother before me," but what she says is quite the opposite.) **39 vouchsafe** deign to grant. (Used with comical incorrectness here.) **58 canaries** state of excitement. (From the dance called the canary?) **59 lay** resided

tlemen, with their coaches, I warrant you, coach after coach, letter after letter, gift after gift; smelling so sweetly, all musk, and so rushling, I warrant you, in silk and gold; and in such alligant terms; and in such wine and sugar of the best and the fairest, that would have won any woman's heart; and, I warrant you, they could never get an eye-wink of her. I had myself twenty angels given me this morning; but I defy all angels, in any such sort, as they say, but in the way of honesty; and, I warrant you, they could never get her so much as sip on a cup with the proudest of them all. And yet there has been earls, nay, which is more, pensioners; but, I warrant you, all is one with her.

FALSTAFF But what says she to me? Be brief, my good she-Mercury.

QUICKLY Marry, she hath receiv'd your letter, for the which she thanks you a thousand times; and she gives you to notify that her husband will be absence from his house between ten and eleven.

FALSTAFF Ten and eleven?

QUICKLY Ay, forsooth; and then you may come and see the picture, she says, that you wot of. Master Ford, her husband, will be from home. Alas, the sweet woman leads an ill life with him. He's a very jealousy man. She leads a very frampold life with him, good heart.

FALSTAFF Ten and eleven. Woman, commend me to her; I will not fail her.

QUICKLY Why, you say well. But I have another messenger to your worship. Mistress Page hath her hearty commendations to you too; and let me tell you in your ear, she's as fartuous a civil modest wife, and one, I tell you, that will not miss you morning nor evening prayer, as any is in Windsor, whoe'er be the other. And she bade me tell your worship that her husband is seldom from home, but she hopes there will come a time. I never knew a woman so dote upon a man. Surely I think you have charms, la; yes, in truth.

FALSTAFF Not I, I assure thee. Setting the attraction of my good parts aside, I have no other charms.

QUICKLY Blessing on your heart for 't!

FALSTAFF But, I pray thee, tell me this: has Ford's wife and Page's wife acquainted each other how they love me?

QUICKLY That were a jest indeed! They have not so little grace, I hope. That were a trick indeed! But Mistress Page would desire you to send her your little page, of all loves. Her husband has a marvelous infection to the little page; and truly Master Page is an honest man. Never a wife in Windsor leads a better life than she does. Do what she will, say what she will, take all, pay all, go to bed when she list, rise when she list, all is as she will. And truly she deserves it; for if there be a kind woman in Windsor, she is one. You must send her your page, no remedy.

FALSTAFF Why, I will.

QUICKLY Nay, but do so, then. And, look you, he may come and go between you both; and in any case have a nay-word, that you may know one another's mind, and the boy never need to understand anything; for 'tis not good that children should know any wickedness. Old folks, you know, have discretion, as they say, and know the world.

FALSTAFF Fare thee well, commend me to them both. There's my purse; I am yet thy debtor. [*Gives money.*] Boy, go along with this woman. [*Exeunt Mistress Quickly and Robin.*] This news distracts me!

PISTOL [*Aside*]
This punk is one of Cupid's carriers.
Clap on more sails; pursue; up with your fights;
Give fire! She is my prize, or ocean whelm them all!
[*Exit.*]

FALSTAFF Say'st thou so, old Jack? Go thy ways; I'll make more of thy old body than I have done. Will they yet look after thee? Wilt thou, after the expense of so much money, be now a gainer? Good body, I thank thee. Let them say 'tis grossly done; so it be fairly done, no matter.

[*Enter*] *Bardolph.*

BARDOLPH Sir John, there's one Master Brook below would fain speak with you, and be acquainted with you; and hath sent your worship a morning's draught of sack.

FALSTAFF Brook is his name?

BARDOLPH Ay, sir.

FALSTAFF Call him in. [*Exit Bardolph.*] Such Brooks are welcome to me, that o'erflows such liquor. Ah, ha! Mistress Ford and Mistress Page, have I encompass'd you? Go to; via!

[*Enter Bardolph, with*] *Ford* [*disguised*].

FORD Bless you, sir!

FALSTAFF And you, sir! Would you speak with me?

FORD I make bold to press with so little preparation upon you.

FALSTAFF You're welcome. What's your will? Give us leave, drawer. [*Exit Bardolph.*]

FORD Sir, I am a gentleman that have spent much; my name is Brook.

FALSTAFF Good Master Brook, I desire more acquaintance of you.

FORD Good Sir John, I sue for yours—not to charge you, for I must let you understand I think myself in better plight for a lender than you are, the which hath something embold'ned me to this unseason'd intrusion; for they say, if money go before, all ways do lie open.

FALSTAFF Money is a good soldier, sir, and will on.

FORD Troth, and I have a bag of money here troubles

64 rushling i.e., rustling **65 alligant** i.e., elegant, or eloquent (?) **69 twenty angels** i.e., as a bribe to act as go-between **73–74 pensioners** gentlemen bodyguards to a sovereign in the royal palace **76 she-Mercury** woman messenger **86 frampold** disagreeable **92 fartuous** (For *virtuous.*) **modest** decent, proper **93 miss you** miss. (*You* is the ethical dative.) **98 have charms** use magic **100 parts** qualities **107–108 of all loves** for love's sake **108 infection to** i.e., affection for

119 nay-word watchword **127 distracts** bewilders (with ecstasy) **128 punk** whore. **carriers** messengers **129 fights** fighting sails, i.e., screens raised during naval engagements to conceal and protect the crew **130 prize** booty **135 grossly** badly (with pun on fat) **fairly** handsomely, fortunately **145–146 encompass'd you** taken you in **146 via** go on **151–152 Give us leave** i.e., leave us alone **152 drawer** tapster **157–158 charge you** put you to expense **160 unseason'd** unseasonable

me. If you will help to bear it, Sir John, take all, or half, for easing me of the carriage. [*Gives money.*]

FALSTAFF Sir, I know not how I may deserve to be your porter.

FORD I will tell you, sir, if you will give me the hearing.

FALSTAFF Speak, good Master Brook. I shall be glad to be your servant.

FORD Sir, I hear you are a scholar—I will be brief with you—and you have been a man long known to me, though I had never so good means, as desire, to make myself acquainted with you. I shall discover a thing to you, wherein I must very much lay open mine own imperfection. But, good Sir John, as you have one eye upon my follies, as you hear them unfolded, turn another into the register of your own, that I may pass with a reproof the easier, sith you yourself know how easy it is to be such an offender.

FALSTAFF Very well, sir; proceed.

FORD There is a gentlewoman in this town; her husband's name is Ford.

FALSTAFF Well, sir.

FORD I have long lov'd her, and, I protest to you, bestow'd much on her, follow'd her with a doting observance, engross'd opportunities to meet her, fee'd every slight occasion that could but niggardly give me sight of her, not only bought many presents to give her, but have given largely to many to know what she would have given. Briefly, I have pursu'd her as love hath pursu'd me, which hath been on the wing of all occasions. But whatsoever I have merited, either in my mind or in my means, meed, I am sure, I have receiv'd none, unless experience be a jewel. That I have purchas'd at an infinite rate, and that hath taught me to say this:

"Love like a shadow flies when substance love
pursues,
Pursuing that that flies, and flying what pursues."

FALSTAFF Have you receiv'd no promise of satisfaction at her hands?

FORD Never.

FALSTAFF Have you importun'd her to such a purpose?

FORD Never.

FALSTAFF Of what quality was your love, then?

FORD Like a fair house built on another man's ground; so that I have lost my edifice by mistaking the place where I erected it.

FALSTAFF To what purpose have you unfolded this to me?

FORD When I have told you that, I have told you all. Some say that, though she appear honest to me, yet in other places she enlargeth her mirth so far that there is shrewd construction made of her. Now, Sir John, here is the heart of my purpose. You are a gentleman of excellent breeding, admirable discourse, of great admittance, authentic in your place and person, generally allow'd for your many war-like, court-like, and learned preparations.

FALSTAFF O, sir!

FORD Believe it, for you know it. There is money; spend it, spend it; spend more; spend all I have. [*Offers money.*] Only give me so much of your time in exchange of it, as to lay an amiable siege to the honesty of this Ford's wife. Use your art of wooing; win her to consent to you. If any man may, you may as soon as any.

FALSTAFF Would it apply well to the vehemency of your affection, that I should win what you would enjoy? Methinks you prescribe to yourself very preposterously.

FORD O, understand my drift. She dwells so securely on the excellency of her honor, that the folly of my soul dares not present itself; she is too bright to be look'd against. Now, could I come to her with any detection in my hand, my desires had instance and argument to commend themselves. I could drive her then from the ward of her purity, her reputation, her marriage-vow, and a thousand other her defenses, which now are too too strongly embattled against me. What say you to 't, Sir John?

FALSTAFF Master Brook, I will first make bold with your money; next, give me your hand; and last, as I am a gentleman, you shall, if you will, enjoy Ford's wife.

FORD O good sir!

FALSTAFF I say you shall.

FORD Want no money, Sir John; you shall want none.

FALSTAFF Want no Mistress Ford, Master Brook; you shall want none. I shall be with her, I may tell you, by her own appointment; even as you came in to me, her assistant or go-between parted from me. I say I shall be with her between ten and eleven; for at that time the jealous rascally knave her husband will be forth. Come you to me at night; you shall know how I speed.

FORD I am blest in your acquaintance. Do you know Ford, sir?

FALSTAFF Hang him, poor cuckoldly knave! I know him not. Yet I wrong him to call him poor. They say the jealous wittolly knave hath masses of money; for the which his wife seems to me well-favor'd. I will use her as the key of the cuckoldly rogue's coffer, and there's my harvest-home.

FORD I would you knew Ford, sir, that you might avoid him if you saw him.

FALSTAFF Hang him, mechanical salt-butter rogue! I will stare him out of his wits. I will awe him with my cudgel; it shall hang like a meteor o'er the cuckold's horns. Master Brook, thou shalt know I will predominate over the peasant, and thou shalt lie with his wife. Come to me soon at night. Ford's a knave, and I will aggravate his style; thou, Master Brook, shalt know

175 discover reveal **179 register** record **180 sith** since **188 engross'd** devoted myself to. **fee'd** employed **191–192 what . . . given** what she would like to have given to her **195 meed** reward **215 enlargeth** gives free scope to **218–219 great admittance** i.e., readily received in society **219 authentic** recognized

220 allow'd acknowledged **221 preparations** accomplishments **226 amiable** amorous **240 ward** defensive posture in fencing **249 Want** lack **261 wittolly** one willingly cheated on by his wife, a complacent cuckold **261–262 for the which** for which reason **264 harvest-home** occasion for reaping a profit **267 mechanical** (Literally, one engaged in manual occupation, hence, base.) **salt-butter** i.e., smelly, or coarse of taste (?) **270–271 predominate** be in the ascendancy. (An astrological term.) **273 aggravate his style** increase or add to his title (by adding *cuckold*)

him for knave and cuckold. Come to me soon at night. [*Exit.*]

FORD What a damn'd Epicurean rascal is this! My heart is ready to crack with impatience. Who says this is improvident jealousy? My wife hath sent to him, the hour is fix'd, the match is made. Would any man have thought this? See the hell of having a false woman! My bed shall be abus'd, my coffers ransack'd, my reputation gnawn at; and I shall not only receive this villainous wrong, but stand under the adoption of abominable terms, and by him that does me this wrong. Terms! Names! Amaimon sounds well; Lucifer, well; Barbason, well; yet they are devils' additions, the names of fiends. But Cuckold! Wittol!—Cuckold! The devil himself hath not such a name. Page is an ass, a secure ass. He will trust his wife; he will not be jealous. I will rather trust a Fleming with my butter, Parson Hugh the Welshman with my cheese, an Irishman with my aqua-vitae bottle, or a thief to walk my ambling gelding, than my wife with herself. Then she plots, then she ruminates, then she devises; and what they think in their hearts they may effect, they will break their hearts but they will effect. God be prais'd for my jealousy! Eleven o'clock the hour. I will prevent this, detect my wife, be reveng'd on Falstaff, and laugh at Page. I will about it; better three hours too soon than a minute too late. Fie, fie, fie! Cuckold, cuckold, cuckold! *Exit.*

SCENE III

Enter Caius [*and*] *Rugby.*

CAIUS Jack Rugby!

RUGBY Sir?

CAIUS Vat is de clock, Jack?

RUGBY 'Tis past the hour, sir, that Sir Hugh promis'd to meet.

CAIUS By gar, he has save his soul, dat he is no come; he has pray his Pible well, dat he is no come. By gar, Jack Rugby, he is dead already, if he be come.

RUGBY He is wise, sir; he knew your worship would kill him, if he came.

CAIUS By gar, de herring is no dead so as I vill kill him. Take your rapier, Jack; I vill tell you how I vill kill him.

RUGBY Alas, sir, I cannot fence.

CAIUS Villainy, take your rapier.

RUGBY Forbear; here's company.

[*Enter*] *Page, Shallow, Slender,* [*and*] *Host.*

HOST Bless thee, bully doctor!

SHALLOW Save you, Master Doctor Caius!

PAGE Now, good master doctor!

275 Epicurean sensual **284, 285 Amaimon, Lucifer, Barbason** (Names of devils; they occur in Scot's *Discoverie of Witchcraft,* 1584.) **285 additions** titles **288 secure** overconfident **291 aqua-vitae** any strong spirit like brandy. (Irish were known for their drinking, just as Welshmen for eating of cheese and Flemish for love of butter.) **296 prevent** come there before

II.iii. Location: A field near Windsor.
11 no dead not so dead. (Cf. "dead as a herring.")

SLENDER Give you good morrow, sir.

CAIUS Vat be all you, one, two, tree, four, come for?

HOST To see thee fight, to see thee foin, to see thee traverse; to see thee here, to see thee there; to see thee pass thy punto, thy stock, thy reverse, thy distance, thy montant. Is he dead, my Ethiopian? Is he dead, my Francisco? Ha, bully? What says my Aesculapius? My Galen? My heart of elder? Ha? Is he dead, bully stale? Is he dead?

CAIUS By gar, he is de coward Jack priest of de vorld; he is not show his face.

HOST Thou art a Castalion-King-Urinal. Hector of Greece, my boy!

CAIUS I pray you, bear vitness that me have stay six or seven, two, tree hours for him, and he is no come.

SHALLOW He is the wiser man, master doctor. He is a curer of souls, and you a curer of bodies. If you should fight, you go against the hair of your professions. Is it not true, Master Page?

PAGE Master Shallow, you have yourself been a great fighter, though now a man of peace.

SHALLOW Bodykins, Master Page, though I now be old and of the peace, if I see a sword out, my finger itches to make one. Though we are justices and doctors and churchmen, Master Page, we have some salt of our youth in us; we are the sons of women, Master Page.

PAGE 'Tis true, Master Shallow.

SHALLOW It will be found so, Master Page. Master Doctor Caius, I am come to fetch you home. I am sworn of the peace. You have show'd yourself a wise physician, and Sir Hugh hath shown himself a wise and patient churchman. You must go with me, master doctor.

HOST Pardon, guest-justice. A word, Mounseur Mockwater.

CAIUS Mock-vater? Vat is dat?

HOST Mock-water, in our English tongue, is valor, bully.

CAIUS By gar, den, I have as mush mock-vater as de Englishman. Scurvy jack-dog priest! By gar, me vill cut his ears.

HOST He will clapper-claw thee tightly, bully.

CAIUS Clapper-de-claw? Vat is dat?

HOST That is, he will make thee amends.

CAIUS By gar, me do look he shall clapper-de-claw me; for, by gar, me vill have it.

HOST And I will provoke him to 't, or let him wag.

CAIUS Me tank you for dat.

HOST And, moreover, bully—but first, master guest, and Master Page, and eke Cavaleiro Slender, go you through the town to Frogmore. [*Aside to them.*]

21 foin thrust **21–22 traverse** march back and forth, or from side to side **23–24 thy punto . . . montant** your stroke or thrust with the point of the sword, your stoccado or thrust, your backhand stroke, your keeping of the prescribed distance between contestants, your upright thrust **24 Ethiopian** i.e., one of dark complexion (?) **25 Francisco** i.e., Frenchman. **Aesculapius** i.e., doctor. (Literally, Greek god of medicine.) **26 Galen** famous Greek physician. **heart of elder** i.e., opposite of "heart of oak"; the elder has no heart **27 stale** i.e., doctor. (Literally, *urine,* used as in medical diagnosis; see also *urinal* in Host's next speech, and *Mockwater,* ll. 51–52.) **30 Castalion** i.e., Castilian, Spanish. (Suggesting cowardice.) **Hector** chief warrior of ancient Troy (not Greece) **36 go . . . of** i.e., act contrary to. (Literally, rub hair the wrong way.) **40 Bodykins** i.e., by God's little body **42 make one** join in **43 salt** savor **51–52 Mockwater** (See note to l. 27, above.) **57 jack-dog** mongrel **59 clapper-claw** thrash. **tightly** soundly **68 Frogmore** small village near Windsor

PAGE Sir Hugh is there, is he?

HOST He is there. See what humor he is in; and I will bring the doctor about by the fields. Will it do well?

SHALLOW We will do it.

PAGE, SHALLOW, AND SLENDER Adieu, good master doctor. *[Exeunt Page, Shallow, and Slender.]*

CAIUS By gar, me vill kill de priest, for he speak for a jack-an-ape to Anne Page.

HOST Let him die. [But first,] sheathe thy impatience, throw cold water on thy choler. Go about the fields with me through Frogmore. I will bring thee where Mistress Anne Page is, at a farmhouse a-feasting; and thou shalt woo her. Cried game? Said I well?

CAIUS By gar, me dank you vor dat. By gar, I love you; and I shall procure-a you de good guest, de earl, de knight, de lords, de gentlemen, my patients.

HOST For the which I will be thy adversary toward Anne Page. Said I well?

CAIUS By gar, 'tis good; vell said.

HOST Let us wag, then.

CAIUS Come at my heels, Jack Rugby. *Exeunt.*

ACT III • SCENE I

Enter [Sir Hugh] Evans, [and] Simple.

EVANS I pray you now, good Master Slender's servingman, and friend Simple by your name, which way have you look'd for Master Caius, that calls himself doctor of physic?

SIMPLE Marry, sir, the pittie-ward, the park-ward, every way; old Windsor way, and every way but the town way.

EVANS I most fehemently desire you you will also look that way.

SIMPLE I will, sir. *[Exit.]*

EVANS Pless my soul, how full of chollors I am, and trempling of mind! I shall be glad if he have deceiv'd me. How melancholies I am! I will knog his urinals about his knave's costard when I have good opportunities for the ork. Pless my soul! *[Sings.]*

"To shallow rivers, to whose falls
Melodious birds sings madrigals;
There will we make our peds of roses,
And a thousand fragrant posies.
To shallow—"

Mercy on me! I have a great dispositions to cry. *[Sings.]*

"Melodious birds sing madrigals—
When as I sat in Pabylon—
And a thousand vagram posies.
To shallow," etc.

[Enter Simple.]

SIMPLE Yonder he is coming, this way, Sir Hugh.

EVANS He's welcome. *[Sings.]*

"To shallow rivers, to whose falls—"

Heaven prosper the right! What weapons is he?

SIMPLE No weapons, sir. There comes my master, Master Shallow, and another gentleman, from Frogmore, over the stile, this way.

EVANS Pray you, give me my gown; or else keep it in your arms. *[Reads in a book.]*

[Enter] Page, Shallow, [and] Slender.

SHALLOW How now, master parson? Good morrow, good Sir Hugh. Keep a gamester from the dice, and a good student from his book, and it is wonderful.

SLENDER *[Aside]* Ah, sweet Anne Page!

PAGE Save you, good Sir Hugh!

EVANS Pless you from his mercy sake, all of you!

SHALLOW What, the sword and the word? Do you study them both, master parson?

PAGE And youthful still, in your doublet and hose this raw rheumatic day?

EVANS There is reasons and causes for it.

PAGE We are come to you to do a good office, master parson.

EVANS Fery well; what is it?

PAGE Yonder is a most reverend gentleman, who, belike having receiv'd wrong by some person, is at most odds with his own gravity and patience that ever you saw.

SHALLOW I have liv'd fourscore years and upward; I never heard a man of his place, gravity, and learning, so wide of his own respect.

EVANS What is he?

PAGE I think you know him: Master Doctor Caius, the renown'd French physician.

EVANS Got's will, and his passion of my heart! I had as lief you would tell me of a mess of porridge.

PAGE Why?

EVANS He has no more knowledge in Hibocrates and Galen—and he is a knave besides, a cowardly knave as you would desires to be acquainted withal.

PAGE *[To Shallow]* I warrant you, he's the man should fight with him.

SLENDER *[Aside]* O sweet Anne Page!

SHALLOW It appears so by his weapons. Keep them asunder; here comes Doctor Caius.

[Enter] Host, Caius, [and] Rugby. [Evans and Caius offer to fight.]

PAGE Nay, good master parson, keep in your weapon.

SHALLOW So do you, good master doctor.

HOST Disarm them, and let them question. Let them keep their limbs whole and hack our English.

CAIUS I pray you, let-a me speak a word with your ear. Vherefore vill you not meet-a me?

---

81 Cried game have I announced good sport. (From bearbaiting.)

III.i. Location: A field near Frogmore.
5 the pittie-ward toward Windsor Petty (or Little) Park. **the park-ward** toward Windsor Great Park **13 knog** knock **14 costard** i.e., head. (Literally, apple.) **16 To shallow rivers,** etc. (Lines from Marlowe's "Come live with me and be my love.") **23 When . . . Pabylon** (An insertion of a line from the metrical Psalms, number 137.) **24 vagram** i.e., vagrant. (But Evans means *fragrant.*)

36–37 Keep . . . wonderful i.e., it's as hard to keep a true student from his book as to keep a gamester from dice **41 the word** i.e., the Bible **43 in . . . hose** i.e., without a cloak **51 gravity** dignity **55 wide . . . respect** at variance with his reputation **62 Hibocrates** Hippocrates, ancient Greek physician **65 he's** i.e., Evans is. **should** who is supposed to **72 question** talk, discuss

EVANS [*Aside to Caius*] Pray you, use your patience. [*Aloud.*] In good time.

CAIUS By gar, you are de coward, de Jack dog, John ape.

EVANS [*Aside to Caius*] Pray you, let us not be laughing-stocks to other men's humors; I desire you in friendship, and I will one way or other make you amends. [*Aloud.*] I will knog your urinals about your knave's cogscomb [for missing your meetings and appointments.]

CAIUS Diable! Jack Rugby—mine host de Jarteer—have I not stay for him to kill him? Have I not, at de place I did appoint?

EVANS As I am a Christians soul now, look you, this is the place appointed. I'll be judgment by mine host of the Garter.

HOST Peace, I say, Gallia and Gaul, French and Welsh, soul-curer and body-curer!

CAIUS Ay, dat is very good, excellent.

HOST Peace, I say! Hear mine host of the Garter. Am I politic? Am I subtle? Am I a Machiavel? Shall I lose my doctor? No, he gives me the potions and the motions. Shall I lose my parson, my priest, my Sir Hugh? No, he gives me the proverbs and the no-verbs. [Give me thy hand, terrestrial; so.] Give me thy hand, celestial; so. [*He joins their hands.*] Boys of art, I have deceiv'd you both; I have directed you to wrong places. Your hearts are mighty, your skins are whole, and let burnt sack be the issue. Come, lay their swords to pawn. Follow me, lads of peace; follow, follow, follow.

SHALLOW Trust me, a mad host. Follow, gentlemen, follow.

SLENDER [*Aside*] O sweet Anne Page!

[*Exeunt Shallow, Slender, Page, and Host.*]

CAIUS Ha, do I perceive dat? Have you make-a de sot of us, ha, ha?

EVANS This is well! He has made us his vlouting-stog. I desire you that we may be friends; and let us knog our prains together to be revenge on this same scall, scurvy, cogging companion, the host of the Garter.

CAIUS By gar, with all my heart. He promise to bring me where is Anne Page; by gar, he deceive me too.

EVANS Well, I will smite his noddles. Pray you, follow.

[*Exeunt.*]

SCENE II

[*Enter*] *Mistress Page,* [*and*] *Robin.*

MRS PAGE Nay, keep your way, little gallant; you were wont to be a follower, but now you are a leader. Whether had you rather lead mine eyes, or eye your master's heels?

ROBIN I had rather, forsooth, go before you like a man than follow him like a dwarf.

MRS PAGE O, you are a flattering boy. Now I see you'll be a courtier.

[*Enter*] *Ford.*

FORD Well met, Mistress Page. Whither go you?

MRS PAGE Truly, sir, to see your wife. Is she at home?

FORD Ay; and as idle as she may hang together, for want of company. I think, if your husbands were dead, you two would marry.

MRS PAGE Be sure of that—two other husbands.

FORD Where had you this pretty weathercock?

MRS PAGE I cannot tell what the dickens his name is my husband had him of. What do you call your knight's name, sirrah?

ROBIN Sir John Falstaff.

FORD Sir John Falstaff!

MRS PAGE He, he; I can never hit on 's name. There is such a league between my good man and he! Is your wife at home indeed?

FORD Indeed she is.

MRS PAGE By your leave, sir. I am sick till I see her.

[*Exeunt Mrs Page and Robin.*]

FORD Has Page any brains? Hath he any eyes? Hath he any thinking? Sure, they sleep; he hath no use of them. Why, this boy will carry a letter twenty mile, as easy as a cannon will shoot point-blank twelve score. He pieces out his wife's inclination; he gives her folly motion and advantage. And now she's going to my wife, and Falstaff's boy with her. A man may hear this show'r sing in the wind. And Falstaff's boy with her! Good plots, they are laid; and our revolted wives share damnation together. Well, I will take him, then torture my wife, pluck the borrow'd veil of modesty from the so-seeming Mistress Page, divulge Page himself for a secure and willful Actaeon; and to these violent proceedings all my neighbors shall cry aim. [*Clock heard.*] The clock gives me my cue, and my assurance bids me search. There I shall find Falstaff. I shall be rather prais'd for this than mock'd, for it is as positive as the earth is firm that Falstaff is there. I will go.

[*Enter*] *Page, Shallow, Slender, Host,* [*Sir Hugh*] *Evans, Caius,* [*and Rugby*].

SHALLOW, PAGE, ETC. Well met, Master Ford.

FORD Trust me, a good knot. I have good cheer at home, and I pray you all go with me.

SHALLOW I must excuse myself, Master Ford.

SLENDER And so must I, sir. We have appointed to dine with Mistress Anne, and I would not break with her for more money than I'll speak of.

SHALLOW We have linger'd about a match between

87 stay waited **92 Gallia and Gaul** Wales and France **96 Machiavel** Italian political philosopher who symbolized crafty and ruthless ambition to Elizabethans; an intriguer **97 motions** purges **99 proverbs . . . no-verbs** i.e., wisdom and some Welsh colorful speech **100 terrestrial** i.e., the doctor, who treats the body **101 art** learning **104 issue** outcome **109 sot** fool **111 vlouting-stog** flouting-stock, i.e., laughingstock **113 scall** scald, i.e., scurvy **114 cogging** cheating

III.ii. Location: A street in Windsor.
3 Whether had i.e., had

11 as idle . . . together i.e., as idle as she can be without going to pieces; or, persons as idle as she (and you) are may keep company **15 pretty weathercock** i.e., sprucely dressed little fellow. (A *weathercock* changes quickly, here in matters of fashion of dress.) **22 good man** husband **29 twelve score** i.e., 240 paces **30 pieces out** augments. **folly** wantonness **31 motion** instigation. **advantage** opportunity **32–33 hear . . . wind** tell from the rising wind that a storm is coming up, i.e., that trouble is brewing **38 Actaeon** i.e., horned man, cuckold. (See II.i.113, note.) **39 cry aim** applaud. (A term from archery.) **45 knot** group, company

Anne Page and my cousin Slender, and this day we shall have our answer.

SLENDER I hope I have your good will, father Page.

PAGE You have, Master Slender; I stand wholly for you. But my wife, master doctor, is for you altogether.

CAIUS Ay, be-gar; and de maid is love-a me. My nursh-a Quickly tell me so mush.

HOST What say you to young Master Fenton? He capers, he dances, he has eyes of youth, he writes verses, he speaks holiday, he smells April and May. He will carry 't, he will carry 't; 'tis in his buttons; he will carry 't.

PAGE Not by my consent, I promise you. The gentleman is of no having. He kept company with the wild Prince and Poins; he is of too high a region; he knows too much. No, he shall not knit a knot in his fortunes with the finger of my substance. If he take her, let him take her simply. The wealth I have waits on my consent, and my consent goes not that way.

FORD I beseech you heartily, some of you go home with me to dinner. Besides your cheer, you shall have sport; I will show you a monster. Master doctor, you shall go; so shall you, Master Page; and you, Sir Hugh.

SHALLOW Well, fare you well. We shall have the freer wooing at Master Page's.

[Exeunt Shallow and Slender.]

CAIUS Go home, John Rugby; I come anon.

[Exit Rugby.]

HOST Farewell, my hearts. I will to my honest knight Falstaff, and drink canary with him. *[Exit.]*

FORD *[Aside]* I think I shall drink in pipe-wine first with him; I'll make him dance.—Will you go, gentles?

ALL Have with you to see this monster. *Exeunt.*

SCENE III

Enter Mistress Ford, [and] Mistress Page.

MRS FORD What, John! What, Robert!

MRS PAGE Quickly, quickly! Is the buck-basket—

MRS FORD I warrant. What, Robin, I say!

[Enter] Servants [with a great basket, and set it down].

MRS PAGE Come, come, come.

MRS FORD Here, set it down.

MRS PAGE Give your men the charge. We must be brief.

MRS FORD Marry, as I told you before, John and Robert, be ready here hard by in the brew-house; and when I suddenly call you, come forth, and without any pause or staggering take this basket on your shoulders. That done, trudge with it in all haste, and carry it among the whitsters in Datchet Mead, and there empty it in the muddy ditch close by the Thames side.

MRS PAGE You will do it?

MRS FORD I ha' told them over and over; they lack no direction. Be gone, and come when you are call'd.

[Exeunt Servants.]

MRS PAGE Here comes little Robin.

[Enter] Robin.

MRS FORD How now, my eyas-musket, what news with you?

ROBIN My master, Sir John, is come in at your back door, Mistress Ford, and requests your company.

MRS PAGE You little Jack-a-Lent, have you been true to us?

ROBIN Ay, I'll be sworn. My master knows not of your being here, and hath threat'ned to put me into everlasting liberty if I tell you of it; for he swears he'll turn me away.

MRS PAGE Thou 'rt a good boy. This secrecy of thine shall be a tailor to thee and shall make thee a new doublet and hose. I'll go hide me.

MRS FORD Do so.—Go tell thy master I am alone. *[Exit Robin.]* Mistress Page, remember you your cue.

MRS PAGE I warrant thee. If I do not act it, hiss me.

[Exit.]

MRS FORD Go to, then. We'll use this unwholesome humidity, this gross wat'ry pumpion. We'll teach him to know turtles from jays.

[Enter] Falstaff.

FALSTAFF "Have I caught thee, my heavenly jewel?" Why, now let me die, for I have liv'd long enough. This is the period of my ambition. O this blessed hour!

MRS FORD O sweet Sir John!

FALSTAFF Mistress Ford, I cannot cog, I cannot prate, Mistress Ford. Now shall I sin in my wish: I would thy husband were dead. I'll speak it before the best lord; I would make thee my lady.

MRS FORD I your lady, Sir John? Alas, I should be a pitiful lady!

FALSTAFF Let the court of France show me such another. I see how thine eye would emulate the diamond. Thou hast the right arch'd beauty of the brow that becomes the ship-tire, the tire-valiant, or any tire of Venetian admittance.

MRS FORD A plain kerchief, Sir John; my brows become nothing else, nor that well neither.

FALSTAFF By the Lord, thou art a tyrant to say so. Thou wouldst make an absolute courtier; and the firm fix-

61 speaks holiday uses choice language **62 carry 't** win the day. **'tis in his buttons** i.e., he's sure to succeed **65 having** estate **65–66 wild . . . Poins** i.e., Prince Hal and Poins of *1* and *2 Henry IV* **66 region** social status **67 knit a knot in** mend **69 simply** i.e., by herself **79 canary** a sweet wine from the Canaries **80 pipe-wine** wine from the cask, or wood (with musical pun continuing the metaphor of *canary,* a lively dance)

III.iii. Location: Ford's house.
1 What i.e., move quickly **2 buck-basket** basket for soiled clothes. (*Bucking* means "washing.") **6 charge** instructions

12 whitsters bleachers of linen. **Datchet Mead** a meadow along the Thames, near Windsor Park **18 eyas-musket** young sparrow hawk **22 Jack-a-Lent** figure of a man set up to be pelted, a puppet **26 liberty** i.e., unemployment **35 pumpion** pumpkin **36 turtles** turtle doves, a type of constancy in love. **jays** i.e., loose women **37 Have . . . jewel.** (From Sidney's *Astrophel and Stella.*) **39 period** goal **41 cog** cheat, flatter **50 ship-tire** woman's headdress resembling a ship. **tire-valiant** fanciful headdress **51 admittance** fashion **55 absolute** perfect

ture of thy foot would give an excellent motion to thy gait in a semicircled farthingale. I see what thou wert, if Fortune thy foe were not, Nature thy friend. Come, thou canst not hide it.

MRS FORD Believe me, there's no such thing in me.

FALSTAFF What made me love thee? Let that persuade thee there's something extraordinary in thee. Come, I cannot cog and say thou art this and that, like a many of these lisping hawthorn buds, that come like women in men's apparel, and smell like Bucklersbury in simple time. I cannot. But I love thee, none but thee; and thou deserv'st it.

MRS FORD Do not betray me, sir. I fear you love Mistress Page.

FALSTAFF Thou mightst as well say I love to walk by the Counter-gate, which is as hateful to me as the reek of a lime-kiln.

MRS FORD Well, heaven knows how I love you, and you shall one day find it.

FALSTAFF Keep in that mind; I'll deserve it.

MRS FORD Nay, I must tell you, so you do, or else I could not be in that mind.

[Enter Robin.]

ROBIN Mistress Ford, Mistress Ford! Here's Mistress Page at the door, sweating and blowing and looking wildly, and would needs speak with you presently.

FALSTAFF She shall not see me. I will ensconce me behind the arras.

MRS FORD Pray you, do so; she's a very tattling woman. *[Falstaff hides himself behind the arras.]*

[Enter Mistress Page.]

What's the matter? How now?

MRS PAGE O Mistress Ford, what have you done? You're shamed, y' are overthrown, y' are undone forever!

MRS FORD What's the matter, good Mistress Page?

MRS PAGE O well-a-day, Mistress Ford, having an honest man to your husband, to give him such cause of suspicion!

MRS FORD What cause of suspicion?

MRS PAGE What cause of suspicion? Out upon you! How am I mistook in you!

MRS FORD Why, alas, what's the matter?

MRS PAGE Your husband's coming hither, woman, with all the officers in Windsor, to search for a gentleman that he says is here now in the house by your consent, to take an ill advantage of his absence. You are undone.

MRS FORD 'Tis not so, I hope.

MRS PAGE Pray heaven it be not so, that you have such a man here! But 'tis most certain your husband's coming, with half Windsor at his heels, to search for such a one. I come before to tell you. If you know yourself clear, why, I am glad of it; but if you have a friend here, convey, convey him out. Be not amaz'd; call all your senses to you; defend your reputation, or bid farewell to your good life forever.

MRS FORD What shall I do? There is a gentleman, my dear friend; and I fear not mine own shame so much as his peril. I had rather than a thousand pound he were out of the house.

MRS PAGE For shame! Never stand "you had rather" and "you had rather." Your husband's here at hand! Bethink you of some conveyance. In the house you cannot hide him. O, how have you deceiv'd me! Look, here is a basket. If he be of any reasonable stature, he may creep in here; and throw foul linen upon him, as if it were going to bucking. Or—it is whiting-time—send him by your two men to Datchet Mead.

MRS FORD He's too big to go in there. What shall I do?

FALSTAFF *[Coming forward]* Let me see 't, let me see 't, O, let me see 't! I'll in, I'll in. Follow your friend's counsel. I'll in.

MRS PAGE What, Sir John Falstaff? *[Aside.]* Are these your letters, knight?

FALSTAFF *[Aside]* I love thee. Help me away. Let me creep in here. I'll never—

[Gets into the basket; they cover him with foul linen.]

MRS PAGE Help to cover your master, boy. Call your men, Mistress Ford. You dissembling knight!

MRS FORD What, John! Robert! John! *[Exit Robin.]*

[Enter Servants.]

Go take up these clothes here quickly. Where's the cowl-staff? Look how you drumble! Carry them to the laundress in Datchet Mead; quickly, come.

[Enter] Ford, Page, Caius, [and Sir Hugh] Evans.

FORD Pray you, come near. If I suspect without cause, why then make sport at me. Then let me be your jest; I deserve it. How now? Whither bear you this?

SERVANT To the laundress, forsooth.

MRS FORD Why, what have you to do whither they bear it? You were best meddle with buck-washing.

FORD Buck? I would I could wash myself of the buck! Buck, buck, buck! Ay, buck; I warrant you, buck; and of the season too, it shall appear. *[Exeunt Servants with the basket.]* Gentlemen, I have dream'd tonight; I'll tell you my dream. Here, here, here be my keys. Ascend my chambers; search, seek, find out. I'll warrant we'll unkennel the fox. Let me stop this way first. *[Locking the door.]* So, now uncape.

PAGE Good Master Ford, be contented. You wrong yourself too much.

57 semicircled farthingale petticoat with hoops at the sides and back but not meeting in front **57–58 I see . . . friend** i.e., I can imagine how impressive you would be at court if Fortune had not cast you in a lowly lot with only your natural beauty to assist you. (*Fortune My Foe* is the name of a popular ballad tune.) **64 hawthorn buds** i.e., young fops **65 Bucklersbury** a London street inhabited by herbalists **65–66 simple time** midsummer, the time when apothecaries were supplied with simples or herbs **68 betray** deceive **71 Counter-gate** gate of the Counter or debtors' prison in London **82 arras** tapestry wall hanging **91 to** as

110 your good life your respectability **115 stand** lose time over **121 bucking** washing. **whiting-time** bleaching time **135 cowl-staff** pole on which a "cowl" or basket is carried between two persons. **drumble** are sluggish **142 buck-washing** washing clothes. (But Ford puns on the meaning of *horned male deer,* resembling the cuckold.) **145 of the season** in season **146 tonight** last night **149 unkennel** reveal, unearth **150 uncape** i.e., unleash, unloose (?) **151 be contented** be calm

FORD True, Master Page. Up, gentlemen, you shall see sport anon. Follow me, gentlemen. [*Exit.*]

EVANS This is fery fantastical humors and jealousies.

CAIUS By gar, 'tis no the fashion of France; it is not jealous in France.

PAGE Nay, follow him, gentlemen. See the issue of his search. [*Exeunt Page, Caius, and Evans.*]

MRS PAGE Is there not a double excellency in this?

MRS FORD I know not which pleases me better, that my husband is deceiv'd, or Sir John.

MRS PAGE What a taking was he in when your husband ask'd who was in the basket!

MRS FORD I am half afraid he will have need of washing; so throwing him into the water will do him a benefit.

MRS PAGE Hang him, dishonest rascal! I would all of the same strain were in the same distress.

MRS FORD I think my husband hath some special suspicion of Falstaff's being here, for I never saw him so gross in his jealousy till now.

MRS PAGE I will lay a plot to try that; and we will yet have more tricks with Falstaff. His dissolute disease will scarce obey this medicine.

MRS FORD Shall we send that foolish carrion, Mistress Quickly, to him, and excuse his throwing into the water, and give him another hope, to betray him to another punishment?

MRS PAGE We will do it. Let him be sent for tomorrow, eight o'clock, to have amends.

[*Enter Ford, Page, Caius, and Sir Hugh Evans.*]

FORD I cannot find him. May be the knave bragg'd of that he could not compass.

MRS PAGE [*Aside to Mrs Ford*] Heard you that?

MRS FORD You use me well, Master Ford, do you?

FORD Ay, I do so.

MRS FORD Heaven make you better than your thoughts!

FORD Amen!

MRS PAGE You do yourself mighty wrong, Master Ford.

FORD Ay, ay; I must bear it.

EVANS If there be any pody in the house, and in the chambers, and in the coffers, and in the presses, heaven forgive my sins at the day of judgment!

CAIUS By gar, nor I too; there is no bodies.

PAGE Fie, fie, Master Ford! Are you not asham'd? What spirit, what devil suggests this imagination? I would not ha' your distemper in this kind for the wealth of Windsor Castle.

FORD 'Tis my fault, Master Page. I suffer for it.

EVANS You suffer for a pad conscience. Your wife is as honest a 'omans as I will desires among five thousand, and five hundred too.

CAIUS By gar, I see 'tis an honest woman.

FORD Well, I promis'd you a dinner. Come, come, walk in the Park. I pray you, pardon me; I will hereafter make known to you why I have done this. Come, wife; come, Mistress Page. I pray you, pardon me; pray heartily, pardon me.

PAGE Let's go in, gentlemen; but, trust me, we'll mock him. I do invite you tomorrow morning to my house to breakfast. After, we'll a-birding together. I have a fine hawk for the bush. Shall it be so?

FORD Any thing.

EVANS If there is one, I shall make two in the company.

CAIUS If there be one or two, I shall make-a the turd.

FORD Pray you, go, Master Page.

EVANS [*To Caius*] I pray you now, remembrance tomorrow on the lousy knave, mine host.

CAIUS Dat is good; by gar, with all my heart!

EVANS A lousy knave, to have his gibes and his mockeries! *Exeunt.*

163 taking fright **169 strain** character, kind **175 obey this medicine** i.e., yield to this first dose **176 carrion** rotten old flesh, bawd (?) **177 excuse** make excuses for **192 presses** cupboards, clothes presses **204–205 walk . . . Park** i.e., stroll till dinnertime

209 go in i.e., go in to dinner at the proper time **211 a-birding** hunting small birds of the bush with a hawk **217–218 remembrance . . . host** (A seeming allusion to the conversation at the end of III.i and to the plot carried out in IV.v.)

SCENE IV

Enter Fenton, [and] Anne Page.

FENTON
I see I cannot get thy father's love;
Therefore no more turn me to him, sweet Nan.

ANNE
Alas, how then?

FENTON
Why, thou must be thyself.
He doth object I am too great of birth,
And that, my state being gall'd with my expense,
I seek to heal it only by his wealth.
Besides these, other bars he lays before me,
My riots past, my wild societies;
And tells me 'tis a thing impossible
I should love thee but as a property.

ANNE
May be he tells you true.

FENTON
No, heaven so speed me in my time to come!
Albeit I will confess thy father's wealth
Was the first motive that I woo'd thee, Anne.
Yet, wooing thee, I found thee of more value
Than stamps in gold or sums in sealed bags;
And 'tis the very riches of thyself
That now I aim at.

ANNE
Gentle Master Fenton,
Yet seek my father's love; still seek it, sir.
If opportunity and humblest suit
Cannot attain it, why, then—hark you hither!
[*They converse apart.*]

[*Enter*] *Shallow, Slender,* [*and Mistress*] *Quickly.*

SHALLOW Break their talk, Mistress Quickly. My kinsman shall speak for himself.

SLENDER I'll make a shaft or a bolt on 't. 'Slid, 'tis but venturing.

III.iv. Location: Before Page's house.
3 be thyself be your own mistress **5 state . . . expense** estate being hurt by my extravagance **12 speed** prosper **16 stamps in gold** gold coins **22 Break** interrupt **24 I'll . . . on 't** i.e., whether I make a good or bad job of it, I'll give it a try. (A *shaft* was a slender arrow, a *bolt* a thick and blunt one.) **'Slid** by his (God's) eyelid

SHALLOW Be not dismay'd.

SLENDER No, she shall not dismay me. I care not for that, but that I am afeard.

QUICKLY [*To Anne*] Hark ye, Master Slender would speak a word with you.

ANNE
I come to him. [*Aside.*] This is my father's choice.
O, what a world of vile ill-favor'd faults
Looks handsome in three hundred pounds a year!

QUICKLY And how does good Master Fenton? Pray you, a word with you. [*Draws him aside.*]

SHALLOW She 's coming; to her, coz. O boy, thou hadst a father!

SLENDER I had a father, Mistress Anne; my uncle can tell you good jests of him. Pray you, uncle, tell Mistress Anne the jest how my father stole two geese out of a pen, good uncle.

SHALLOW Mistress Anne, my cousin loves you.

SLENDER Ay, that I do, as well as I love any woman in Gloucestershire.

SHALLOW He will maintain you like a gentlewoman.

SLENDER Ay, that I will, come cut and long-tail, under the degree of a squire.

SHALLOW He will make you a hundred and fifty pounds jointure.

ANNE Good Master Shallow, let him woo for himself.

SHALLOW Marry, I thank you for it; I thank you for that good comfort. She calls you, coz. I'll leave you.

ANNE Now, Master Slender—

SLENDER Now, good Mistress Anne—

ANNE What is your will?

SLENDER My will? 'Od's heartlings, that's a pretty jest indeed! I ne'er made my will yet, I thank God; I am not such a sickly creature, I give heaven praise.

ANNE I mean, Master Slender, what would you with me?

SLENDER Truly, for mine own part, I would little or nothing with you. Your father and my uncle hath made motions. If it be my luck, so; if not, happy man be his dole! They can tell you how things go better than I can. You may ask your father; here he comes.

[Enter] Page, [and] Mistress Page.

PAGE
Now, Master Slender. Love him, daughter Anne.
Why, how now? What does Master Fenton here?
You wrong me, sir, thus still to haunt my house.
I told you, sir, my daughter is dispos'd of.

FENTON
Nay, Master Page, be not impatient.

MRS PAGE
Good Master Fenton, come not to my child.

PAGE
She is no match for you.

FENTON
Sir, will you hear me?

PAGE No, good Master Fenton.
Come, Master Shallow; come, son Slender, in.
Knowing my mind, you wrong me, Master Fenton.
[*Exeunt Page, Shallow, and Slender.*]

QUICKLY Speak to Mistress Page.

FENTON
Good Mistress Page, for that I love your daughter
In such a righteous fashion as I do,
Perforce, against all checks, rebukes, and manners,
I must advance the colors of my love
And not retire. Let me have your good will.

ANNE Good mother, do not marry me to yond fool.

MRS PAGE I mean it not; I seek you a better husband.

QUICKLY That's my master, master doctor.

ANNE
Alas, I had rather be set quick i' th' earth
And bowl'd to death with turnips!

MRS PAGE
Come, trouble not yourself. Good Master Fenton,
I will not be your friend nor enemy.
My daughter will I question how she loves you,
And, as I find her, so am I affected.
Till then farewell, sir. She must needs go in;
Her father will be angry.

FENTON
Farewell, gentle mistress: farewell, Nan.
[*Exeunt Mrs Page and Anne.*]

QUICKLY This is my doing, now. "Nay," said I, "will you cast away your child on a fool, and a physician? Look on Master Fenton." This is my doing.

FENTON
I thank thee; and I pray thee, once tonight
Give my sweet Nan this ring. There's for thy pains.
[*Gives ring, and money.*]

QUICKLY Now heaven send thee good fortune! [*Exit Fenton.*] A kind heart he hath. A woman would run through fire and water for such a kind heart. But yet I would my master had Mistress Anne; or I would Master Slender had her; or, in sooth, I would Master Fenton had her. I will do what I can for them all three; for so I have promis'd, and I'll be as good as my word, but speciously for Master Fenton. Well, I must of another errand to Sir John Falstaff from my two mistresses. What a beast am I to slack it! *Exit.*

SCENE V

Enter Falstaff.

FALSTAFF Bardolph, I say!

[Enter] Bardolph.

BARDOLPH Here, sir.

FALSTAFF Go fetch me a quart of sack; put a toast in 't. [*Exit Bardolph.*] Have I liv'd to be carried in a basket,

36–37 thou hadst a father i.e., remember that your father wooed a woman; be like him. (But Slender misses the point.) **42 cousin** i.e., kinsman **46 come . . . long-tail** i.e., come what may. (Literally, horses or dogs with docked and long tails, i.e., all sorts.) **56 'Od's heartlings** by God's little heart **63 motions** offers **63–64 happy . . . dole** i.e., may whoever succeeds with you be happy

79 checks reproofs **80 colors** banners **85 quick** alive **86 bowl'd** pelted **90 affected** inclined **97 once** sometime **106 speciously** (For *specially*.)

III.v. Location: The Garter Inn.
3 toast piece of toast

like a barrow of butcher's offal, and to be thrown in the Thames? Well, if I be serv'd such another trick, I'll have my brains ta'en out and butter'd, and give them to a dog for a new-year's gift. The rogues slighted me into the river with as little remorse as they would have drown'd a blind bitch's puppies, fifteen i' th' litter; and you may know by my size that I have a kind of alacrity in sinking; if the bottom were as deep as hell, I should down. I had been drown'd, but that the shore was shelvy and shallow—a death that I abhor; for the water swells a man; and what a thing should I have been when I had been swell'd! I should have been a mountain of mummy.

[*Enter Bardolph with sack.*]

BARDOLPH Here's Mistress Quickly, sir, to speak with you.

FALSTAFF Come, let me pour in some sack to the Thames water; for my belly's as cold as if I had swallow'd snowballs for pills to cool the reins. [*Drinks.*] Call her in.

BARDOLPH Come in, woman!

[*Enter Mistress*] *Quickly.*

QUICKLY By your leave; I cry you mercy. Give your worship good morrow.

FALSTAFF Take away these chalices. Go brew me a pottle of sack finely.

BARDOLPH With eggs, sir?

FALSTAFF Simple of itself; I'll no pullet-sperm in my brewage. [*Exit Bardolph.*] How now?

QUICKLY Marry, sir, I come to your worship from Mistress Ford.

FALSTAFF Mistress Ford? I have had ford enough. I was thrown into the ford; I have my belly full of ford.

QUICKLY Alas the day! Good heart, that was not her fault. She does so take on with her men; they mistook their erection.

FALSTAFF So did I mine, to build upon a foolish woman's promise.

QUICKLY Well, she laments, sir, for it, that it would yearn your heart to see it. Her husband goes this morning a-birding; she desires you once more to come to her between eight and nine. I must carry her word quickly. She'll make you amends, I warrant you.

FALSTAFF Well, I will visit her, tell her so. And bid her think what a man is: let her consider his frailty, and then judge of my merit.

QUICKLY I will tell her.

FALSTAFF Do so. Between nine and ten, say'st thou?

QUICKLY Eight and nine, sir.

FALSTAFF Well, be gone. I will not miss her.

QUICKLY Peace be with you, sir. [*Exit.*]

FALSTAFF I marvel I hear not of Master Brook; he sent me word to stay within. I like his money well. O, here he comes.

[*Enter*] *Ford* [*disguised*].

FORD Bless you, sir!

FALSTAFF Now, Master Brook, you come to know what hath pass'd between me and Ford's wife?

FORD That, indeed, Sir John, is my business.

FALSTAFF Master Brook, I will not lie to you. I was at her house the hour she appointed me.

FORD And sped you, sir?

FALSTAFF Very ill-favoredly, Master Brook.

FORD How so, sir? Did she change her determination?

FALSTAFF No, Master Brook, but the peaking cornuto her husband, Master Brook, dwelling in a continual 'larum of jealousy, comes me in the instant of our encounter, after we had embrac'd, kiss'd, protested, and, as it were, spoke the prologue of our comedy; and at his heels a rabble of his companions, thither provok'd and instigated by his distemper, and, forsooth, to search his house for his wife's love.

FORD What, while you were there?

FALSTAFF While I was there.

FORD And did he search for you, and could not find you?

FALSTAFF You shall hear. As good luck would have it, comes in one Mistress Page, gives intelligence of Ford's approach, and, in her invention, and Ford's wife's distraction, they convey'd me into a buck-basket.

FORD A buck-basket?

FALSTAFF By the Lord, a buck-basket! Ramm'd me in with foul shirts and smocks, socks, foul stockings, greasy napkins, that, Master Brook, there was the rankest compound of villainous smell that ever offended nostril.

FORD And how long lay you there?

FALSTAFF Nay, you shall hear, Master Brook, what I have suffer'd to bring this woman to evil for your good. Being thus cramm'd in the basket, a couple of Ford's knaves, his hinds, were call'd forth by their mistress to carry me in the name of foul clothes to Datchet Lane. They took me on their shoulders, met the jealous knave their master in the door, who ask'd them once or twice what they had in their basket. I quak'd for fear, lest the lunatic knave would have search'd it; but fate, ordaining he should be a cuckold, held his hand. Well, on went he for a search, and away went I for foul clothes. But mark the sequel, Master Brook. I suffer'd the pangs of three several deaths: first, an intolerable fright, to be detected with a jealous rotten bell-wether; next, to be compass'd, like a good bilbo, in the circumference of a peck, hilt to point, heel to head; and then, to be stopp'd in, like a strong distillation, with stinking clothes that fretted in their own grease. Think of that—a man of my kidney. Think of that—that am as subject to heat as butter; a man of

8 slighted me tossed me heedlessly **9 remorse** pity, compassion **17 mummy** dead flesh **22 reins** kidneys **25 cry you mercy** beg your pardon **27–28 pottle** two-quart measure **37 take on with** berate, scold **38 erection** (Blunder for *direction;* Falstaff plays bawdily on her malapropism.) **42 yearn** grieve **47 his** i.e., man's

66 peaking cornuto sneaking cuckold **91 hinds** servants **100 several** distinct **101 with** by **102 bell-wether** old ram, leader of a flock **103 bilbo** finely tempered sword of Bilbao in Spain. **peck** a quarter of a bushel; i.e., a very small space. **hilt to point** (Falstaff is bent over, head to toes, like a fine Spanish sword that could be bent thus without breaking.) **105 fretted** decayed **106 kidney** temperament, constitution

continual dissolution and thaw. It was a miracle to scape suffocation. And in the height of this bath, when I was more than half stew'd in grease, like a Dutch dish, to be thrown in the Thames, and cool'd, glowing hot, in that surge, like a horse-shoe! Think of that—hissing hot—think of that, Master Brook!

FORD In good sadness, sir, I am sorry that for my sake you have suffer'd all this. My suit then is desperate; you'll undertake her no more?

FALSTAFF Master Brook, I will be thrown into Etna, as I have been into Thames, ere I will leave her thus. Her husband is this morning gone a-birding. I have receiv'd from her another embassy of meeting. 'Twixt eight and nine is the hour, Master Brook.

FORD 'Tis past eight already, sir.

FALSTAFF Is it? I will then address me to my appointment. Come to me at your convenient leisure, and you shall know how I speed; and the conclusion shall be crown'd with your enjoying her. Adieu. You shall have her, Master Brook; Master Brook, you shall cuckold Ford. [*Exit.*]

FORD Hum, ha! Is this a vision? Is this a dream? Do I sleep? Master Ford, awake! Awake, Master Ford! There's a hole made in your best coat, Master Ford. This 'tis to be married! This 'tis to have linen and buck-baskets! Well, I will proclaim myself what I am. I will now take the lecher; he is at my house. He cannot scape me; 'tis impossible he should; he cannot creep into a halfpenny purse, nor into a pepper-box. But, lest the devil that guides him should aid him, I will search impossible places. Though what I am I cannot avoid, yet to be what I would not shall not make me tame. If I have horns to make one mad, let the proverb go with me: I'll be horn-mad. *Exit.*

ACT IV • SCENE I

Enter Mistress Page, [*Mistress*] *Quickly,* [*and*] *William.*

MRS PAGE Is he at Master Ford's already, think'st thou?

QUICKLY Sure he is by this, or will be presently. But, truly, he is very courageous mad about his throwing into the water. Mistress Ford desires you to come suddenly.

MRS PAGE I'll be with her by and by; I'll but bring my young man here to school. Look where his master comes; 'tis a playing-day, I see.

[*Enter Sir Hugh*] *Evans.*

How now, Sir Hugh, no school today?

EVANS No. Master Slender is let the boys leave to play.

QUICKLY Blessing of his heart!

MRS PAGE Sir Hugh, my husband says my son profits nothing in the world at his book. I pray you, ask him some questions in his accidence.

EVANS Come hither, William. Hold up your head; come.

MRS PAGE Come on, sirrah, hold up your head. Answer your master, be not afraid.

EVANS William, how many numbers is in nouns?

WILLIAM Two.

QUICKLY Truly, I thought there had been one number more, because they say, "'Od's nouns."

EVANS Peace your tattlings!—What is "fair," William?

WILLIAM "Pulcher."

QUICKLY Polecats? There are fairer things than polecats, sure.

EVANS You are a very simplicity 'oman. I pray you, peace. What is "lapis," William?

WILLIAM A stone.

EVANS And what is "a stone," William?

WILLIAM A pebble.

EVANS No, it is "lapis." I pray you, remember in your prain.

WILLIAM Lapis.

EVANS That is a good William. What is he, William, that does lend articles?

WILLIAM Articles are borrow'd of the pronoun, and be thus declin'd, "Singulariter, nominativo, hic, haec, hoc."

EVANS "Nominativo, hig, hag, hog." Pray you, mark: genitivo, hujus. Well, what is your accusative case?

WILLIAM "Accusativo, hinc."

EVANS I pray you, have your remembrance, child. "Accusativo, hung, hang, hog."

QUICKLY "Hang-hog" is Latin for bacon, I warrant you.

EVANS Leave your prabbles, 'oman.—What is the focative case, William?

WILLIAM O—"vocativo, O."

EVANS Remember, William; focative is "caret."

QUICKLY And that's a good root.

EVANS 'Oman, forbear.

MRS PAGE Peace!

EVANS What is your genitive case plural, William?

WILLIAM Genitive case?

EVANS Ay.

WILLIAM "Genitivo—horum, harum, horum."

QUICKLY Vengeance of Jenny's case! Fie on her! Never name her, child, if she be a whore.

EVANS For shame, 'oman.

QUICKLY You do ill to teach the child such words. He teaches him to hick and to hack, which they'll do fast enough of themselves, and to call "horum." Fie upon you!

EVANS 'Oman, art thou lunatics? Hast thou no understandings for thy cases and the numbers of the gen-

108 dissolution liquefaction **114 sadness** seriousness **117 Etna** volcano in Sicily **123 address me to** prepare myself for

IV.i. Location: A street in Windsor.
3 courageous (For *outrageous?*)

14 accidence rudiments of Latin grammar **19 numbers** i.e., singular and plural **22 'Od's nouns** by God's wounds (confused with *odd* numbers, i.e., three) **25 Polecats** (Many of Quickly's misconstruings are bawdy: *polecats* (prostitutes), *horum* (whores), *harum* (hare, prostitute), *Jenny's case* (a whore's pudendum), etc. **38 Singulariter** in the singular. **nominativo** in the nominative. (Similarly with *genitivo, accusativo,* and *vocativo.*) **45 Hang-hog** (Bacon is made by hanging up a hog.) **49 caret** is lacking. (But Quickly interprets it as *carrot.*) **61 to hick and to hack** i.e., to engage in sex; see II.i.49

ders? Thou art as foolish Christian creatures as I would desires.

MRS PAGE Prithee, hold thy peace.

EVANS Show me now, William, some declensions of your pronouns.

WILLIAM Forsooth, I have forgot.

EVANS It is "qui, quae, quod." If you forget your "qui's," your "quae's," and your "quod's," you must be preeches. Go your ways, and play, go.

MRS PAGE He is a better scholar than I thought he was.

EVANS He is a good sprag memory. Farewell, Mistress Page.

MRS PAGE Adieu, good Sir Hugh. [*Exit Sir Hugh.*] Get you home, boy. Come, we stay too long. *Exeunt.*

SCENE II

Enter Falstaff, [*and*] *Mistress Ford.*

FALSTAFF Mistress Ford, your sorrow hath eaten up my sufferance. I see you are obsequious in your love, and I profess requital to a hair's breadth, not only, Mistress Ford, in the simple office of love, but in all the accoutrement, compliment, and ceremony of it. But are you sure of your husband now?

MRS FORD He's a-birding, sweet Sir John.

MRS PAGE [*Within*] What ho, gossip Ford! What ho!

MRS FORD Step into th' chamber, Sir John. [*Exit Falstaff.*]

[*Enter*] *Mistress Page.*

MRS PAGE How now, sweetheart, who's at home besides yourself?

MRS FORD Why, none but mine own people.

MRS PAGE Indeed?

MRS FORD No, certainly. [*Aside to her.*] Speak louder.

MRS PAGE Truly, I am so glad you have nobody here.

MRS FORD Why?

MRS PAGE Why, woman, your husband is in his old lunes again. He so takes on yonder with my husband, so rails against all married mankind, so curses all Eve's daughters, of what complexion soever, and so buffets himself on the forehead, crying, "Peer out, peer out!" that any madness I ever yet beheld seem'd but tameness, civility, and patience to this his distemper he is in now. I am glad the fat knight is not here.

MRS FORD Why, does he talk of him?

MRS PAGE Of none but him, and swears he was carried out, the last time he search'd for him, in a basket; protests to my husband he is now here, and hath drawn him and the rest of their company from their sport, to make another experiment of his suspicion. But I am glad the knight is not here. Now he shall see his own foolery.

MRS FORD How near is he, Mistress Page?

MRS PAGE Hard by; at street end; he will be here anon.

MRS FORD I am undone! The knight is here.

MRS PAGE Why then you are utterly sham'd, and he's but a dead man. What a woman are you! Away with him, away with him! Better shame than murder.

MRS FORD Which way should he go? How should I bestow him? Shall I put him into the basket again?

[*Enter Falstaff.*]

FALSTAFF No, I'll come no more i' th' basket. May I not go out ere he come?

MRS PAGE Alas, three of Master Ford's brothers watch the door with pistols, that none shall issue out; otherwise you might slip away ere he came. But what make you here?

FALSTAFF What shall I do? I'll creep up into the chimney.

MRS FORD There they always use to discharge their birding-pieces.

MRS PAGE Creep into the kiln-hole.

FALSTAFF Where is it?

MRS FORD He will seek there, on my word. Neither press, coffer, chest, trunk, well, vault, but he hath an abstract for the remembrance of such places, and goes to them by his note. There is no hiding you in the house.

FALSTAFF I'll go out then.

MRS PAGE If you go out in your own semblance, you die, Sir John, unless you go out disguis'd.

MRS FORD How might we disguise him?

MRS PAGE Alas the day, I know not! There is no woman's gown big enough for him; otherwise he might put on a hat, a muffler, and a kerchief, and so escape.

FALSTAFF Good hearts, devise something. Any extremity rather than a mischief.

MRS FORD My maid's aunt, the fat woman of Brainford, has a gown above.

MRS PAGE On my word, it will serve him; she's as big as he is. And there's her thrumm'd hat and her muffler too. Run up, Sir John.

MRS FORD Go, go, sweet Sir John. Mistress Page and I will look some linen for your head.

MRS PAGE Quick, quick! We'll come dress you straight. Put on the gown the while. [*Exit Falstaff.*]

MRS FORD I would my husband would meet him in this shape. He cannot abide the old woman of Brainford. He swears she's a witch, forbade her my house, and hath threat'ned to beat her.

MRS PAGE Heaven guide him to thy husband's cudgel, and the devil guide his cudgel afterwards!

MRS FORD But is my husband coming?

MRS PAGE Ay, in good sadness, is he, and talks of the basket too, howsoever he hath had intelligence.

74 preeches breeched, i.e., whipped **76 sprag** sprack, lively, alert

IV.ii. Location: Ford's house.
2 sufferance suffering, pain. **obsequious** zealously devoted **8 gossip** i.e., friend, neighbor. (Literally, fellow godparent.) **18 lunes** lunacies **21 Peer out** i.e., let my cuckold's horns come forth and be visible

45 make do **51 kiln-hole** oven **55 abstract** inventory **68 Brainford** Brentford, a nearby village **69 above** upstairs **71 thrumm'd** made of coarse yarn **84 in good sadness** in all seriousness

MRS FORD We'll try that; for I'll appoint my men to carry the basket again, to meet him at the door with it, as they did last time.

MRS PAGE Nay, but he'll be here presently. Let's go dress him like the witch of Brainford.

MRS FORD I'll first direct my men what they shall do with the basket. Go up; I'll bring linen for him straight. [*Exit.*]

MRS PAGE Hang him, dishonest varlet! We cannot misuse him enough.
We'll leave a proof, by that which we will do,
Wives may be merry, and yet honest too.
We do not act that often jest and laugh;
'Tis old, but true, "Still swine eats all the draff."
[*Exit.*]

[*Enter Mistress Ford with two*] *Servants.*

MRS FORD Go, sirs, take the basket again on your shoulders. Your master is hard at door. If he bid you set it down, obey him. Quickly, dispatch. [*Exit.*]

FIRST SERVANT Come, come, take it up.

SECOND SERVANT Pray heaven it be not full of knight again.

FIRST SERVANT I hope not; I had as lief bear so much lead.

[*Enter*] *Ford, Page, Caius,* [*Sir Hugh*] *Evans,* [*and*] *Shallow.*

FORD Ay, but if it prove true, Master Page, have you any way then to unfool me again?—Set down the basket, villain! Somebody call my wife. Youth in a basket! O you pandarly rascals! There's a knot, a ging, a pack, a conspiracy against me. Now shall the devil be sham'd. What, wife, I say! Come, come forth! Behold what honest clothes you send forth to bleaching!

PAGE Why, this passes, Master Ford. You are not to go loose any longer; you must be pinion'd.

EVANS Why, this is lunatics! This is mad as a mad dog!

SHALLOW Indeed, Master Ford, this is not well, indeed.

FORD So say I too, sir.

[*Enter Mistress Ford.*]

Come hither, Mistress Ford—Mistress Ford, the honest woman, the modest wife, the virtuous creature, that hath the jealous fool to her husband! I suspect without cause, mistress, do I?

MRS FORD Heaven be my witness you do, if you suspect me in any dishonesty.

FORD Well said, brazen-face! Hold it out. Come forth, sirrah! [*Pulling clothes out of the basket.*]

PAGE This passes!

MRS FORD Are you not asham'd? Let the clothes alone.

FORD I shall find you anon.

EVANS 'Tis unreasonable! Will you take up your wife's clothes? Come, away.

FORD Empty the basket, I say!

MRS FORD Why, man, why?

FORD Master Page, as I am a man, there was one convey'd out of my house yesterday in this basket. Why may not he be there again? In my house I am sure he is. My intelligence is true; my jealousy is reasonable. Pluck me out all the linen.

MRS FORD If you find a man there, he shall die a flea's death.

PAGE Here's no man.

SHALLOW By my fidelity, this is not well, Master Ford; this wrongs you.

EVANS Master Ford, you must pray, and not follow the imaginations of your own heart. This is jealousies.

FORD Well, he's not here I seek for.

PAGE No, nor nowhere else but in your brain.

FORD Help to search my house this one time. If I find not what I seek, show no color for my extremity; let me for ever be your table-sport. Let them say of me, "As jealous as Ford, that search'd a hollow walnut for his wife's leman." Satisfy me once more; once more search with me.

MRS FORD [*Calling upstairs*] What ho, Mistress Page! Come you and the old woman down; my husband will come into the chamber.

FORD Old woman? What old woman's that?

MRS FORD Why, it is my maid's aunt of Brainford.

FORD A witch, a quean, an old cozening quean! Have I not forbid her my house? She comes of errands, does she? We are simple men; we do not know what's brought to pass under the profession of fortune-telling. She works by charms, by spells, by th' figure, and such daub'ry as this is, beyond our element; we know nothing. Come down, you witch, you hag, you; come down, I say!

MRS FORD Nay, good sweet husband! Good gentlemen, let him not strike the old woman.

[*Enter Falstaff in woman's clothes, and Mistress Page.*]

MRS PAGE Come, Mother Prat, come, give me your hand.

FORD I'll prat her. [*Beating him.*] Out of my door, you witch, you hag, you baggage, you polecat, you runnion! Out, out! I'll conjure you, I'll fortune-tell you.
[*Exit Falstaff.*]

MRS PAGE Are you not asham'd? I think you have kill'd the poor woman.

MRS FORD Nay, he will do it. 'Tis a goodly credit for you.

FORD Hang her, witch!

EVANS By yea and no, I think the 'oman is a witch indeed. I like not when a 'oman has a great peard. I spy a great peard under his muffler.

FORD Will you follow, gentlemen? I beseech you, fol-

99 Still quiet. **draff** pig-wash. (The proverb reinforces Mrs. Page's point that merry talk does not ensure wantonness; adulterous women are usually quiet about it.) **102 dispatch** hurry **111 a knot . . . pack** a company, a gang, a confederacy **112–113 Now . . . sham'd** i.e., now truth will out. (From the proverb, "Tell truth and shame the devil.") **115 passes** surpasses, goes beyond all bounds **126 Hold it out** i.e., continue to maintain your falsehood

138 intelligence information **150 show . . . extremity** make no attempt to excuse my extreme behavior **151 your table-sport** butt or laughingstock of the company **153 leman** paramour **160 quean** jade, hussy **161 of** on **164 by th' figure** i.e., by making wax figures and sticking pins in them, or, by astrological charts **165 daub'ry** false show **172 prat** strike (?) **173 baggage** hussy. **polecat** whore **173–174 runnion** ronyon, disreputable woman

low; see but the issue of my jealousy. If I cry out thus upon no trail, never trust me when I open again.

PAGE Let's obey his humor a little further. Come, gentlemen.

[*Exeunt Ford, Page, Shallow, Caius, and Evans.*]

MRS PAGE Trust me, he beat him most pitifully.

MRS FORD Nay, by th' mass, that he did not; he beat him most unpitifully, methought.

MRS PAGE I'll have the cudgel hallow'd and hung o'er the altar; it hath done meritorious service.

MRS FORD What think you? May we, with the warrant of womanhood and the witness of a good conscience, pursue him with any further revenge?

MRS PAGE The spirit of wantonness is, sure, scar'd out of him. If the devil have him not in fee-simple, with fine and recovery, he will never, I think, in the way of waste, attempt us again.

MRS FORD Shall we tell our husbands how we have serv'd him?

MRS PAGE Yes, by all means, if it be but to scrape the figures out of your husband's brains. If they can find in their hearts the poor unvirtuous fat knight shall be any further afflicted, we two will still be the ministers.

MRS FORD I'll warrant they'll have him publicly sham'd, and methinks there would be no period to the jest, should he not be publicly sham'd.

MRS PAGE Come, to the forge with it, then shape it. I would not have things cool. *Exeunt.*

SCENE III

Enter Host and Bardolph.

BARDOLPH Sir, the Germans desire to have three of your horses. The Duke himself will be tomorrow at court, and they are going to meet him.

HOST What duke should that be comes so secretly? I hear not of him in the court. Let me speak with the gentlemen. They speak English?

BARDOLPH Ay, sir; I'll call them to you.

HOST They shall have my horses, but I'll make them pay; I'll sauce them. They have had my house a week at command. I have turn'd away my other guests. They must come off; I'll sauce them. Come. *Exeunt.*

SCENE IV

Enter Page, Ford, Mistress Page, Mistress Ford, and [Sir Hugh] Evans.

EVANS 'Tis one of the best discretions of a 'oman as ever I did look upon.

PAGE And did he send you both these letters at an instant?

MRS PAGE Within a quarter of an hour.

FORD
Pardon me, wife. Henceforth do what thou wilt;
I rather will suspect the sun with cold
Than thee with wantonness. Now doth thy honor stand,
In him that was of late an heretic,
As firm as faith.

PAGE 'Tis well, 'tis well; no more.
Be not as extreme in submission as in offense.
But let our plot go forward. Let our wives
Yet once again, to make us public sport,
Appoint a meeting with this old fat fellow,
Where we may take him and disgrace him for it.

FORD
There is no better way than that they spoke of.

PAGE How? To send him word they'll meet him in the park at midnight? Fie, fie! He'll never come.

EVANS You say he has been thrown in the rivers and has been grievously peaten as an old 'oman. Methinks there should be terrors in him that he should not come; methinks his flesh is punish'd, he shall have no desires.

PAGE So think I too.

MRS FORD
Devise but how you'll use him when he comes,
And let us two devise to bring him thither.

MRS PAGE
There is an old tale goes that Herne the hunter,
Sometime a keeper here in Windsor forest,
Doth all the winter-time, at still midnight,
Walk round about an oak, with great ragg'd horns;
And there he blasts the tree, and takes the cattle,
And makes milch-kine yield blood, and shakes a chain
In a most hideous and dreadful manner.
You have heard of such a spirit, and well you know
The superstitious idle-headed eld
Receiv'd and did deliver to our age
This tale of Herne the hunter for a truth.

PAGE
Why, yet there want not many that do fear
In deep of night to walk by this Herne's oak.
But what of this?

MRS FORD Marry, this is our device:
That Falstaff at that oak shall meet with us,
[Disguis'd like Herne, with huge horns on his head.]

PAGE
Well, let it not be doubted but he'll come.
And in this shape when you have brought him thither,
What shall be done with him? What is your plot?

MRS PAGE
That likewise have we thought upon, and thus:

184–185 cry . . . trail bay like a hunting dog despite the absence of a scent **185 open** give voice (like a hunting dog) **197 fee-simple** estate belonging to an owner and his heirs forever; hence, absolute possession **198 fine and recovery** procedures by which an entailed state was converted into fee-simple **199 waste** spoliation, despoiling **203 figures** fantasies, conceits **205 ministers** agents **207 period** suitable conclusion

IV.iii. Location: The Garter Inn.
9 sauce them i.e., make them pay dearly **10 at command** retained for their use upon their expected arrival **11 come off** pay, disburse handsomely

IV.iv. Location: Ford's house.
1 best. . . 'oman i.e., most discreet woman

3–4 at an instant at the same time **28 Sometime** formerly **30 ragg'd** pronged **31 blasts** blights, or blasts with lightning. **takes** bewitches **35 eld** old age, i.e., elders, an earlier generation **38 want** lack

Nan Page my daughter, and my little son,
And three or four more of their growth, we'll dress
Like urchins, ouphes, and fairies, green and white, 49
With rounds of waxen tapers on their heads,
And rattles in their hands. Upon a sudden,
As Falstaff, she, and I, are newly met,
Let them from forth a sawpit rush at once 53
With some diffused song. Upon their sight, 54
We two in great amazedness will fly.
Then let them all encircle him about,
And, fairy-like, to pinch the unclean knight,
And ask him why, that hour of fairy revel,
In their so sacred paths he dares to tread
In shape profane.

MRS FORD And, till he tell the truth,
Let the supposed fairies pinch him sound 61
And burn him with their tapers.

MRS PAGE The truth being known,
We'll all present ourselves, dis-horn the spirit,
And mock him home to Windsor.

FORD The children must
Be practic'd well to this, or they'll nev'r do 't.

EVANS I will teach the children their behaviors; and I will be like a jack-an-apes also, to burn the knight with 67
my taber.

FORD
That will be excellent. I'll go buy them vizards. 69

MRS PAGE
My Nan shall be the queen of all the fairies,
Finely attired in a robe of white.

PAGE
That silk will I go buy. [*Aside.*] And in that tire
Shall Master Slender steal my Nan away
And marry her at Eton.—Go, send to Falstaff
straight. 74

FORD
Nay, I'll to him again in name of Brook.
He'll tell me all his purpose. Sure, he'll come.

MRS PAGE
Fear not you that. Go get us properties
And tricking for our fairies. 78

EVANS Let us about it. It is admirable pleasures and fery honest knaveries.

[*Exeunt Page, Ford, and Evans.*]

MRS PAGE
Go, Mistress Ford,
Send quickly to Sir John, to know his mind.

[*Exit Mrs Ford.*]

I'll to the doctor; he hath my good will,
And none but he, to marry with Nan Page.
That Slender, though well landed, is an idiot;
And he my husband best of all affects. 86
The doctor is well money'd, and his friends
Potent at court. He, none but he, shall have her,
Though twenty thousand worthier come to crave
her. [*Exit.*]

SCENE V

Enter Host, [*and*] *Simple.*

HOST What wouldst thou have, boor? What, thick-skin? 1
Speak, breathe, discuss; brief, short, quick, snap.

SIMPLE Marry, sir, I come to speak with Sir John Falstaff from Master Slender.

HOST There's his chamber, his house, his castle, his standing-bed and truckle-bed; 'tis painted about with 6
the story of the Prodigal, fresh and new. Go knock and 7
call; he'll speak like an Anthropophaginian unto thee. 8
Knock, I say.

SIMPLE There's an old woman, a fat woman, gone up into his chamber. I'll be so bold as stay, sir, till she come down; I come to speak with her, indeed.

HOST Ha, a fat woman? The knight may be robb'd. I'll call. Bully knight! Bully Sir John! Speak from thy lungs military. Art thou there? It is thine host, thine Ephe- 15
sian, calls. 16

FALSTAFF [*Within*] How now, mine host?

HOST Here's a Bohemian-Tartar tarries the coming 18
down of thy fat woman. Let her descend, bully, let her descend; my chambers are honorable. Fie, privacy? Fie!

[*Enter*] *Falstaff.*

FALSTAFF There was, mine host, an old fat woman even now with me, but she's gone.

SIMPLE Pray you, sir, was 't not the wise woman of Brainford?

FALSTAFF Ay, marry, was it, mussel-shell. What would 26
you with her?

SIMPLE My master, sir, Master Slender, sent to her, seeing her go thorough the streets, to know, sir, whether one Nym, sir, that beguil'd him of a chain, had the chain or no.

FALSTAFF I spake with the old woman about it.

SIMPLE And what says she, I pray, sir?

FALSTAFF Marry, she says that the very same man that beguil'd Master Slender of his chain cozen'd him of it.

SIMPLE I would I could have spoken with the woman herself. I had other things to have spoken with her too from him.

FALSTAFF What are they? Let us know.

HOST Ay, come; quick.

SIMPLE I may not conceal them, sir. 41

HOST Conceal them, or thou diest.

SIMPLE Why, sir, they were nothing but about Mistress Anne Page, to know if it were my master's fortune to have her or no.

FALSTAFF 'Tis, 'tis his fortune.

SIMPLE What, sir?

49 urchins, ouphes (Terms for goblins or elves.) **53 sawpit** a pit over which wood was sawed **54 diffused** confused, disorderly **61 sound** soundly **67 like a jack-an-apes** disguised as an ape or monkey **69 vizards** visors, masks **74 Eton** town across the Thames from Windsor **78 tricking** adornment, costumes **86 he** i.e., him. **affects** prefers

IV.v. Location: The Garter Inn.
1 thick-skin one slow or dull of feeling **6 truckle-bed** trundle-bed, low bed that was stored under the *standing-bed* orrregular bed **7 the Prodigal** (Cf. *2 Henry IV*, II.i.143, where this story from Luke 15:11-32 is again associated with Falstaff.) **8 Anthropophaginian** i.e., cannibal **15–16 Ephesian** i.e., boon companion **18 Bohemian-Tartar** i.e., barbarian, wild man **26 mussel-shell** i.e., one who gapes **41 conceal** (For *reveal.*)

FALSTAFF To have her, or no. Go; say the woman told me so.

SIMPLE May I be bold to say so, sir?

FALSTAFF Ay, sir; like who more bold.

SIMPLE I thank your worship. I shall make my master glad with these tidings. [*Exit.*]

HOST Thou art clerkly, thou art clerkly, Sir John. Was there a wise woman with thee?

FALSTAFF Ay, that there was, mine host, one that hath taught me more wit than ever I learn'd before in my life; and I paid nothing for it neither, but was paid for my learning.

[Enter] Bardolph.

BARDOLPH Out, alas, sir! Cozenage, mere cozenage!

HOST Where be my horses? Speak well of them, varletto.

BARDOLPH Run away with the cozeners; for so soon as I came beyond Eton, they threw me off from behind one of them, in a slough of mire; and set spurs and away, like three German devils, three Doctor Faustuses.

HOST They are gone but to meet the Duke, villain. Do not say they be fled; Germans are honest men.

[Enter Sir Hugh] Evans.

EVANS Where is mine host?

HOST What is the matter, sir?

EVANS Have a care of your entertainments. There is a friend of mine come to town, tells me there is three cozen-germans that has cozen'd all the hosts of Readins, of Maidenhead, of Colebrook, of horses and money. I tell you for good will, look you. You are wise and full of gibes and vlouting-stocks, and 'tis not convenient you should be cozen'd. Fare you well. [*Exit.*]

[Enter Doctor] Caius.

CAIUS Vere is mine host de Jarteer?

HOST Here, master doctor, in perplexity and doubtful dilemma.

CAIUS I cannot tell vat is dat; but it is tell-a me dat you make grand preparation for a duke de Jamany. By my trot, dere is no duke that the court is know to come. I tell you for good will; adieu. [*Exit.*]

HOST Hue and cry, villain, go! Assist me, knight. I am undone! Fly, run, hue and cry, villain! I am undone! [*Exeunt Host and Bardolph.*]

FALSTAFF I would all the world might be cozen'd, for I have been cozen'd and beaten too. If it should come to the ear of the court how I have been transform'd, and how my transformation hath been wash'd and cudgel'd, they would melt me out of my fat drop by drop and liquor fishermen's boots with me. I warrant they would whip me with their fine wits till I were as crest-fall'n as a dried pear. I never prosper'd since I forswore myself at primero. Well, if my wind were but long enough to say my prayers, I would repent.

[Enter Mistress] Quickly.

Now, whence come you?

QUICKLY From the two parties, forsooth.

FALSTAFF The devil take one party and his dam the other! And so they shall be both bestow'd. I have suffer'd more for their sakes, more than the villainous inconstancy of man's disposition is able to bear.

QUICKLY And have not they suffer'd? Yes, I warrant, speciously one of them. Mistress Ford, good heart, is beaten black and blue, that you cannot see a white spot about her.

FALSTAFF What tell'st thou me of black and blue? I was beaten myself into all the colors of the rainbow; and I was like to be apprehended for the witch of Brainford. But that my admirable dexterity of wit, my counterfeiting the action of an old woman, deliver'd me, the knave constable had set me i' th' stocks, i' th' common stocks, for a witch.

QUICKLY Sir, let me speak with you in your chamber. You shall hear how things go, and, I warrant, to your content. Here is a letter will say somewhat. [*Gives letter.*] Good hearts, what ado here is to bring you together! Sure, one of you does not serve heaven well, that you are so cross'd.

FALSTAFF Come up into my chamber. *Exeunt.*

SCENE VI

Enter Fenton, [and] Host.

HOST Master Fenton, talk not to me. My mind is heavy. I will give over all.

FENTON
Yet hear me speak. Assist me in my purpose,
And, as I am a gentleman, I'll give thee
A hundred pound in gold more than your loss.

HOST I will hear you, Master Fenton, and I will at the least keep your counsel.

FENTON
From time to time I have acquainted you
With the dear love I bear to fair Anne Page,
Who mutually hath answer'd my affection,
So far forth as herself might be her chooser,
Even to my wish. I have a letter from her
Of such contents as you will wonder at,
The mirth whereof so larded with my matter

51 like who more bold like the boldest **54 clerkly** scholarly, wise **58 was paid** (i.e., with a beating) **60 mere** absolute **61–62 varletto** varlet, rascal **66–67 Doctor Faustuses** (Named for the scholar-magician of Marlowe's play.) **72 your entertainments** i.e., your guests **74 cozen-germans** (1) cousin-germans, close relatives (2) cozening or cheating Germans **74–75 Readins** Reading, a town not far from Windsor. (Also true of *Maidenhead* and *Colebrook* or *Coinbrook.*) **77 vlouting-stocks** flouting-stock, i.e., laughingstock. (But Evans may mean *jibes* here.) **77–78 convenient** fitting **80 doubtful** full of doubts **83 Jamany** Germany **86 Hue and cry** (The shout raised for pursuit of a felon.)

93 liquor saturate with oil to make waterproof **94–95 crest-fall'n** i.e., shriveled **95–96 forswore . . . primero** cheated in a gambling card game **105 speciously** (For *specially.*) **120 cross'd** thwarted

IV.vi. Location: The Garter Inn.
2 give over abandon **14 larded . . . matter** intermingled with what concerns me

That neither singly can be manifested
Without the show of both. Fat Falstaff
Hath a great scene; the image of the jest 17
I'll show you here at large. [*Shows a letter.*] Hark,
good mine host. 18
Tonight at Herne's oak, just 'twixt twelve and one,
Must my sweet Nan present the Fairy Queen— 20
The purpose why, is here—in which disguise,
While other jests are something rank on foot, 22
Her father hath commanded her to slip
Away with Slender, and with him at Eton
Immediately to marry. She hath consented.
Now, sir,
Her mother, even strong against that match 27
And firm for Doctor Caius, hath appointed
That he shall likewise shuffle her away,
While other sports are tasking of their minds, 30
And at the dean'ry, where a priest attends,
Straight marry her. To this her mother's plot
She seemingly obedient likewise hath
Made promise to the doctor. Now, thus it rests:
Her father means she shall be all in white,
And in that habit, when Slender sees his time
To take her by the hand and bid her go,
She shall go with him. Her mother hath intended,
The better to denote her to the doctor—
For they must all be mask'd and vizarded—
That quaint in green she shall be loose enrob'd, 41
With ribands pendent, flaring 'bout her head; 42
And when the doctor spies his vantage ripe,
To pinch her by the hand, and, on that token
The maid hath given consent to go with him.

HOST
Which means she to deceive, father or mother?

FENTON
Both, my good host, to go along with me.
And here it rests, that you'll procure the vicar
To stay for me at church 'twixt twelve and one,
And, in the lawful name of marrying,
To give our hearts united ceremony.

HOST
Well, husband your device; I'll to the vicar. 52
Bring you the maid, you shall not lack a priest.

FENTON
So shall I evermore be bound to thee;
Besides, I'll make a present recompense. *Exeunt.* 55

ACT V • SCENE I

Enter Falstaff, [and Mistress] Quickly.

FALSTAFF Prithee, no more prattling; go. I'll hold. This 1
is the third time; I hope good luck lies in odd num-
bers. Away, go. They say there is divinity in odd 3
numbers, either in nativity, chance, or death. Away!

QUICKLY I'll provide you a chain, and I'll do what I can to get you a pair of horns.

FALSTAFF Away, I say, time wears. Hold up your head,
and mince. [*Exit Mrs Quickly.*] 8

[Enter] Ford [disguised].

How now, Master Brook? Master Brook, the matter will be known tonight, or never. Be you in the Park about midnight, at Herne's oak, and you shall see wonders.

FORD Went you not to her yesterday, sir, as you told 13
me you had appointed?

FALSTAFF I went to her, Master Brook, as you see, like a poor old man, but I came from her, Master Brook, like a poor old woman. That same knave Ford, her husband, hath the finest mad devil of jealousy in him, Master Brook, that ever govern'd frenzy. I will tell you: he beat me grievously, in the shape of a woman; for
in the shape of man, Master Brook, I fear not Goliath 21
with a weaver's beam, because I know also life is a 22
shuttle. I am in haste. Go along with me; I'll tell you 23
all, Master Brook. Since I pluck'd geese, play'd truant, 24
and whipp'd top, I knew not what 'twas to be beaten 25
till lately. Follow me. I'll tell you strange things of this knave Ford, on whom tonight I will be reveng'd, and I will deliver his wife into your hand. Follow. Strange things in hand, Master Brook! Follow. *Exeunt.*

SCENE II

Enter Page, Shallow, [and] Slender.

PAGE Come, come; we'll couch i' th' castle-ditch till we 1
see the light of our fairies. Remember, son Slender, my daughter.

SLENDER Ay, forsooth; I have spoke with her and we have a nay-word how to know one another. I come to
her in white, and cry "mum," she cries "budget," and 6
by that we know one another.

SHALLOW That's good too. But what needs either your "mum" or her "budget?" The white will decipher her well enough. It hath struck ten o'clock.

PAGE The night is dark; light and spirits will become it well. Heaven prosper our sport! No man means evil but the devil, and we shall know him by his horns. Let's away; follow me. *Exeunt.*

17 image form, idea **18 at large** at length **20 present** represent **22 something rank** rather abundantly **27 even** equally **30 tasking of** busily occupying **41 quaint** decorously **42 ribands** ribbons **52 husband** manage prudently **55 present** immediate

V.i. Location: The Garter Inn.
1 hold persevere

3 divinity mysterious power **8 mince** trip off **13 yesterday** (Actually, the meeting appears to have been earlier this same day.) **21–22 Goliath . . . beam** (See I Samuel 17:7: "The staff of his [Goliath's] spear was like a weaver's beam." See also II Samuel 21:19. A weaver's beam is a wooden cylinder in a loom.) **22–23 life is a shuttle** (See Job 7:6: "My days are swifter than a weaver's shuttle.") **24–25 pluck'd . . . top** i.e., committed various boyhood pranks

V.ii. Location: The outskirts of Windsor Park.
1 couch hide **6 mum, budget** (*Mumbudget* connotes silence, as in a children's game by that name.)

SCENE III

Enter Mistress Page, Mistress Ford, [*and Doctor*] *Caius.*

MRS PAGE Master doctor, my daughter is in green. When you see your time, take her by the hand, away with her to the deanery, and dispatch it quickly. Go before into the Park; we two must go together.

CAIUS I know vat I have to do. Adieu.

MRS PAGE Fare you well, sir. [*Exit Caius.*] My husband will not rejoice so much at the abuse of Falstaff as he will chafe at the doctor's marrying my daughter. But 'tis no matter; better a little chiding than a great deal of heartbreak.

MRS FORD Where is Nan now and her troop of fairies, and the Welsh devil Hugh?

MRS PAGE They are all couch'd in a pit hard by Herne's oak, with obscur'd lights; which, at the very instant of Falstaff's and our meeting, they will at once display to the night.

MRS FORD That cannot choose but amaze him.

MRS PAGE If he be not amaz'd, he will be mock'd; if he be amaz'd, he will every way be mock'd.

MRS FORD We'll betray him finely.

MRS PAGE
Against such lewdsters and their lechery,
Those that betray them do no treachery.

MRS FORD The hour draws on. To the oak, to the oak!
Exeunt.

SCENE IV

Enter [*Sir Hugh*] *Evans* [*as a satyr*] *and* [*others disguised as*] *Fairies.*

EVANS Trib, trib, fairies. Come, and remember your parts. Be pold, I pray you. Follow me into the pit, and when I give the watch-'ords, do as I pid you. Come, come; trib, trib. *Exeunt.*

SCENE V

Enter Falstaff [*disguised as Herne, wearing a buck's head*].

FALSTAFF The Windsor bell hath struck twelve; the minute draws on. Now, the hot-blooded gods assist me! Remember, Jove, thou wast a bull for thy Europa; love set on thy horns. O powerful love, that, in some respects, makes a beast a man, in some other, a man a beast. You were also, Jupiter, a swan for the love of Leda. O omnipotent Love, how near the god drew to the complexion of a goose! A fault done first in the form of a beast.—O Jove, a beastly fault!—and then another fault in the semblance of a fowl; think on 't, Jove, a foul fault! When gods have hot backs, what shall poor men do? For me, I am here a Windsor stag, and the fattest, I think, i' th' forest. Send me a cool rut-time, Jove, or who can blame me to piss my tallow? Who comes here? My doe?

[*Enter*] *Mistress Page* [*and*] *Mistress Ford.*

MRS FORD Sir John! Art thou there, my deer, my male deer?

FALSTAFF My doe with the black scut! Let the sky rain potatoes; let it thunder to the tune of "Greensleeves," hail kissing-comfits, and snow eringoes; let there come a tempest of provocation, I will shelter me here. [*Embraces her.*]

MRS FORD Mistress Page is come with me, sweetheart.

FALSTAFF Divide me like a brib'd buck, each a haunch. I will keep my sides to myself, my shoulders for the fellow of this walk, and my horns I bequeath your husbands. Am I a woodman, ha? Speak I like Herne the hunter? Why, now is Cupid a child of conscience; he makes restitution. As I am a true spirit, welcome! [*Noise within.*]

MRS PAGE Alas, what noise?

MRS FORD Heaven forgive our sins!

FALSTAFF What should this be?

MRS FORD, MRS PAGE Away, away! [*They run off.*]

FALSTAFF I think the devil will not have me damn'd, lest the oil that's in me should set hell on fire. He would never else cross me thus.

[*Enter Sir Hugh*] *Evans,* [*disguised as before, Mistress*] *Quickly, Anne Page,* [*and others as*] *Fairies,* [*with tapers, and*] *Pistol* [*as Hobgoblin*].

QUICKLY
Fairies, black, grey, green, and white,
You moonshine revelers, and shades of night,
You orphan heirs of fixed destiny,
Attend your office and your quality.
Crier Hobgoblin, make the fairy oyes.

PISTOL
Elves, list your names; silence, you airy toys!
Cricket, to Windsor chimneys shalt thou leap.
Where fires thou find'st unrak'd and hearths unswept,
There pinch the maids as blue as bilberry.
Our radiant Queen hates sluts and sluttery.

FALSTAFF
They are fairies. He that speaks to them shall die.

V.iii. Location: The outskirts of Windsor Park, as before.
17 amaze perplex

V.iv. Location: Windsor Park.
1 Trib trip, move nimbly

V.v. Location: Windsor Park, as before.
3, 6–7 bull . . . Europa, swan . . . Leda (References to legends of Jupiter's disguises when engaged in various amours.)

13–14 rut-time mating season **14 piss my tallow** i.e., sweat off and excrete excess fat during mating season, like a stag **18 scut** tail, pudend **19 potatoes** i.e., sweet potatoes. (Regarded by Elizabethans as aphrodisiac.) **19 Greensleeves** (A popular tune; see II.i.60, note.) **20 kissing-comfits** perfumed sweetmeats for sweetening the breath. **eringoes** candied root of a plant called sea-holly. (Regarded as aphrodisiac.) **21 provocation** i.e., sexual stimulation **23 brib'd** stolen (and then quickly cut up and divided by the poachers) **25 fellow of this walk** i.e., keeper of this forest **27 is Cupid . . . conscience** i.e., Cupid is keeping faith with me **38 orphan** i.e., fatherless. (Fairies were thought to be the result of spontaneous birth.) **heirs . . . destiny** i.e., those endowed with power to fulfill destiny (?) **39 office** duty. **quality** business, particular function **40 oyes** hear ye. (The call of the public crier.) **43 unrak'd** not raked together to last through the night **44 bilberry** a kind of blueberry **46 He . . . die** (A widespread tradition about fairies.)

I'll wink and couch; no man their works must eye.
[Lies down upon his face.]

EVANS
Where's Bede? Go you, and where you find a maid
That, ere she sleep, has thrice her prayers said,
Raise up the organs of her fantasy,
Sleep she as sound as careless infancy.
But those as sleep and think not on their sins,
Pinch them, arms, legs, backs, shoulders, sides, and shins.

QUICKLY
About, about!
Search Windsor Castle, elves, within and out.
Strew good luck, ouphes, on every sacred room,
That it may stand till the perpetual doom,
In state as wholesome as in state 'tis fit,
Worthy the owner, and the owner it.
The several chairs of order look you scour
With juice of balm and every precious flow'r.
Each fair installment, coat, and sev'ral crest,
With loyal blazon, evermore be blest!
And nightly, meadow-fairies, look you sing,
Like to the Garter's compass, in a ring.
Th' expressure that it bears, green let it be,
More fertile-fresh than all the field to see;
And "Honi soit qui mal y pense" write
In em'rald tufts, flow'rs purple, blue, and white,
Like sapphire, pearl, and rich embroidery,
Buckled below fair knighthood's bending knee;
Fairies use flow'rs for their charactery.
Away; disperse! But till 'tis one o'clock,
Our dance of custom round about the oak
Of Herne the hunter, let us not forget.

EVANS
Pray you,
Lock hand in hand. Yourselves in order set;
And twenty glow-worms shall our lanterns be,
To guide our measure round about the tree.
But, stay! I smell a man of middle-earth.

FALSTAFF Heavens defend me from that Welsh fairy, lest he transform me to a piece of cheese!
[They discover Falstaff, hiding.]

PISTOL
Vile worm, thou wast o'erlook'd even in thy birth.

QUICKLY
With trial-fire touch me his finger-end.
If he be chaste, the flame will back descend
And turn him to no pain; but if he start,
It is the flesh of a corrupted heart.

PISTOL
A trial, come.

EVANS Come, will this wood take fire?
[They touch his finger-ends with their tapers, and he starts.]

FALSTAFF Oh, Oh, Oh!

QUICKLY
Corrupt, corrupt, and tainted in desire!
About him, fairies, sing a scornful rhyme;
And, as you trip, still pinch him to your time.

The Song.

Fie on sinful fantasy!
Fie on lust and luxury!
Lust is but a bloody fire,
Kindled with unchaste desire,
Fed in heart, whose flames aspire
As thoughts do blow them, higher and higher.
Pinch him, fairies, mutually!
Pinch him for his villainy.
Pinch him, and burn him, and turn him about,
Till candles and starlight, and moonshine be out.

[During this song they pinch Falstaff. Doctor] Caius *[comes one way, and steals away a boy in green];* Slender, *[another way, and takes off a boy in white; and]* Fenton *[comes, and steals away Mistress Anne Page. A noise of hunting is heard within. All the Fairies run away. Falstaff pulls off his buck's head, and rises.]*

[Enter] Page, Ford, *[Mistress Page, and Mistress Ford].*

PAGE
Nay, do not fly; I think we have watch'd you now.
Will none but Herne the hunter serve your turn?

MRS PAGE
I pray you, come, hold up the jest no higher.
Now, good Sir John, how like you Windsor wives?
See you these, husband? Do not these fair yokes
Become the forest better than the town?

FORD Now, sir, who's a cuckold now? Master Brook, Falstaff's a knave, a cuckoldly knave; here are his horns, Master Brook. And, Master Brook, he hath enjoy'd nothing of Ford's but his buck-basket, his cudgel, and twenty pounds of money, which must be paid to Master Brook; his horses are arrested for it, Master Brook.

MRS FORD Sir John, we have had ill luck; we could never meet. I will never take you for my love again, but I will always count you my deer.

FALSTAFF I do begin to perceive that I am made an ass.

FORD Ay, and an ox too; both the proofs are extant.

FALSTAFF And these are not fairies? I was three or four times in the thought they were not fairies; and yet the guiltiness of my mind, the sudden surprise of my powers, drove the grossness of the foppery into a receiv'd belief, in despite of the teeth of all rhyme and reason, that they were fairies. See now how wit may be made a Jack-a-Lent, when 'tis upon ill employment!

47 wink close my eyes. **couch** lie hidden **50 Raise . . . fantasy** i.e., give her elevating and pleasant dreams **51 Sleep she** let her sleep. **careless** free of care **56 ouphes** auf, elf's child **60 several . . . order** i.e., the individual stalls of the Garter knights (in St. George's Chapel at Windsor) **62 installment** stall, place or seat in which a knight is installed **63 blazon** coat of arms, armorial bearings **65 compass** circle. (The garter was worn below the left knee by knights of the order.) **66 expressure** image, picture **68 Honi . . . pense** Evil to him who evil thinks. (The motto of the Order of the Garter.) **72 charactery** writing **79 measure** stately dance **80 middle-earth** i.e., the earth, the center of the universe, conceived of as between the heavens and the underworld **82 cheese** (The Welshman's favorite food; cf. II.ii.290.) **83 o'erlook'd** bewitched, looked on with an evil eye

92 still continually **94 luxury** lechery **95 bloody fire** fire in the blood **99 mutually** jointly, in common **103 watch'd you** caught you in the act **105 hold . . . higher** maintain the jest no longer **107 fair yokes** i.e., the horns **114 arrested** seized by warrant as a security for paying **120 ox** i.e., fool (with reference to the ox's horns, the *proofs* that are *extant*) **124 powers** faculties. **foppery** deceit **127 Jack-a-Lent** butt. (See III.iii.22, note.)

EVANS Sir John Falstaff, serve Got, and leave your desires, and fairies will not pinse you.

FORD Well said, fairy Hugh.

EVANS And leave you your jealousies too, I pray you.

FORD I will never mistrust my wife again, till thou art able to woo her in good English.

FALSTAFF Have I laid my brain in the sun and dried it, that it wants matter to prevent so gross o'erreaching as this? Am I ridden with a Welsh goat too? Shall I have a coxcomb of frize? 'Tis time I were chok'd with a piece of toasted cheese.

EVANS Seese is not good to give putter; your belly is all putter.

FALSTAFF "Seese" and "putter"! Have I liv'd to stand at the taunt of one that makes fritters of English? This is enough to be the decay of lust and late-walking through the realm.

MRS PAGE Why, Sir John, do you think, though we would have thrust virtue out of our hearts by the head and shoulders, and have given ourselves without scruple to hell, that ever the devil could have made you our delight?

FORD What, a hodge-pudding? A bag of flax?

MRS PAGE A puff'd man?

PAGE Old, cold, wither'd and of intolerable entrails?

FORD And one that is as slanderous as Satan?

PAGE And as poor as Job?

FORD And as wicked as his wife?

EVANS And given to fornications, and to taverns and sack and wine and metheglins, and to drinkings and swearings and starings, pribbles and prabbles?

FALSTAFF Well, I am your theme. You have the start of me; I am dejected; I am not able to answer the Welsh flannel. Ignorance itself is a plummet o'er me. Use me as you will.

FORD Marry, sir, we'll bring you to Windsor, to one Master Brook, that you have cozen'd of money, to whom you should have been a pandar. Over and above that you have suffer'd, I think to repay that money will be a biting affliction.

PAGE Yet be cheerful, knight. Thou shalt eat a posset tonight at my house, where I will desire thee to laugh at my wife, that now laughs at thee. Tell her Master Slender hath married her daughter.

MRS PAGE [*Aside*] Doctors doubt that. If Anne Page be my daughter, she is, by this, Doctor Caius' wife.

[*Enter Slender.*]

SLENDER Whoa, ho! Ho, father Page!

PAGE Son, how now? How now, son? Have you dispatch'd?

SLENDER Dispatch'd? I'll make the best in Gloucestershire know on 't. Would I were hang'd, la, else!

PAGE Of what, son?

SLENDER I came yonder at Eton to marry Mistress Anne Page, and she's a great lubberly boy. If it had not been i' th' church, I would have swing'd him, or he should have swing'd me. If I did not think it had been Anne Page, would I might never stir!—and 'tis a postmaster's boy.

PAGE Upon my life, then, you took the wrong.

SLENDER What need you tell me that? I think so, when I took a boy for a girl. If I had been married to him, for all he was in woman's apparel, I would not have had him.

PAGE Why, this is your own folly. Did not I tell you how you should know my daughter by her garments?

SLENDER I went to her in white, and cried "mum," and she cried "budget," as Anne and I had appointed; and yet it was not Anne, but a postmaster's boy.

MRS PAGE Good George, be not angry. I knew of your purpose; turn'd my daughter into green; and indeed, she is now with the doctor at the dean'ry, and there married.

[*Enter Caius.*]

CAIUS Vere is Mistress Page? By gar, I am cozen'd. I ha' married un garçon, a boy; un paysan, by gar, a boy. It is not Anne Page. By gar, I am cozen'd.

MRS PAGE Why, did you take her in green?

CAIUS Ay, by gar, and 'tis a boy. By gar, I'll raise all Windsor. [*Exit.*]

FORD This is strange. Who hath got the right Anne?

PAGE My heart misgives me. Here comes Master Fenton.

[*Enter Fenton and Anne Page.*]

How now, Master Fenton?

ANNE
Pardon, good father! Good my mother, pardon!

PAGE Now, mistress, how chance you went not with Master Slender?

MRS PAGE
Why went you not with master doctor, maid?

FENTON
You do amaze her. Hear the truth of it.
You would have married her most shamefully,
Where there was no proportion held in love.
The truth is, she and I, long since contracted,
Are now so sure that nothing can dissolve us.
Th' offense is holy that she hath committed,
And this deceit loses the name of craft,
Of disobedience, or unduteous title,
Since therein she doth evitate and shun
A thousand irreligious cursed hours
Which forced marriage would have brought upon her.

FORD
Stand not amaz'd; here is no remedy.
In love the heavens themselves do guide the state;
Money buys lands, and wives are sold by fate.

137 coxcomb fool's cap. **frize** kind of coarse woolen cloth, common in Wales **150 hodge-pudding** large "pudding" or sausage made with a medley of ingredients. **bag of flax** i.e., a large, shapeless bag **155 his wife** i.e., Job's wife, who advised him to curse God **157 metheglins** spiced drink made from wort and honey, Welsh in origin **158 starings** swaggering **159 theme** i.e., subject of mirth **160 dejected** cast down **161 flannel** a Welsh cloth. **plummet** (A quibble on *plumbet,* a woolen fabric, and *plummet,* a line for fathoming; Falstaff laments that he has been fathomed even by an ignorant Welshman.) **165 should have been** were to have been **166 that** that which **168 eat** imbibe. **posset** curdled ale or wine **172 Doctors doubt that** (Proverbial; i.e., the wise are skeptical.)

182 swing'd thrashed **184–185 postmaster** master of the post horses **201 paysan** peasant, i.e., yokel **214 amaze** bewilder **218 sure** fast knit **221 unduteous title** title of unduteousness **222 evitate** avoid

FALSTAFF I am glad, though you have ta'en a special
stand to strike at me, that your arrow hath glanc'd. 229

PAGE
Well, what remedy? Fenton, heaven give thee joy!
What cannot be eschew'd must be embrac'd.

FALSTAFF
When night-dogs run, all sorts of deer are chas'd.

MRS PAGE
Well, I will muse no further. Master Fenton, 233
Heaven give you many, many merry days!
Good husband, let us everyone go home,
And laugh this sport o'er by a country fire—
Sir John and all.

FORD Let it be so. Sir John,
To Master Brook you yet shall hold your word,
For he tonight shall lie with Mistress Ford. *Exeunt.*

229 stand concealed place for shooting **233 muse** grumble, complain

As You Like It

As You Like It represents, together with *Much Ado about Nothing* and *Twelfth Night,* the summation of Shakespeare's achievement in festive, happy comedy during the years 1598–1601. (This play, not appearing in Francis Meres' list of 1598, was entered in the Stationers' Register in 1600 although not actually published until the Folio of 1623.) *As You Like It* contains several motifs found in other Shakespearean comedies: the journey from a jaded court into a transforming silvan environment and back to a revitalized court (as in *A Midsummer Night's Dream*); hence, a contrasting of two "worlds" in the play, presided over by a virtuous but exiled older brother and a usurping younger brother (as in *The Tempest*); the heroine disguised as a man (as in *The Merchant of Venice, The Two Gentlemen of Verona, Cymbeline,* and *Twelfth Night*); and a structure of multiple plotting in which numerous groups of characters are thematically played off against one another (as in several of Shakespeare's comedies). What chiefly distinguishes this play from the others, however, is the nature and function of its pastoral setting—the Forest of Arden.

The Forest of Arden is seen in many perspectives. As a natural wilderness, it is probably most like the real forest Shakespeare knew near Stratford-upon-Avon in Warwickshire—a place capable of producing the vulgarity of an Audrey or the gentle simplicity of a Corin. As the abode of Robin Hood, it is a mythic folk world compensating for social injustice, offering an alternative way of life to those persons in retreat from a society seemingly beyond repair. As the "golden world," the forest evokes an even deeper longing for a mythological past age of innocence and plenty, when men shared some attributes of the giants and the gods. This myth has its parallel in the biblical Garden of Eden, before men learned to feel "the penalty of Adam" (II,i). Finally, in another of its aspects, the forest is Arcadia, a pastoral landscape embodied in an ancient and sophisticated literary tradition.

All but the first of these Ardens, compared and contrasted with one another, involve some idealization not only of "nature" and the natural landscape, but also of the human condition. These various Ardens place our real life in a complex perspective, and force us to a fresh appraisal of our own ordinary existence. Duke Senior, for example, describes the forest environment as a corrective for the evils of society. He addresses his followers in the forest as "my co-mates and brothers in exile" (II,i), suggesting a kind of social equality that he could never know in the cramped formality of his previous official existence. The banished Duke and his followers have perforce left behind their lands and revenues in the grip of the usurping Frederick. No longer rich though adequately provided with all of life's necessities, the Duke and his "merry men" live "like the old Robin Hood of England," and "fleet the time carelessly as they did in the golden world" (I,i). In this friendly society, a strong communal sense replaces the necessity for individual proprietorship. All comers are welcome, with food for all.

There are no luxuries in the forest, to be sure, but even this spare existence affords relief from the decadence of courtly life. "Sweet are the uses of adversity," insists the Duke. He welcomes the cold of winter because, instead of flattering him as courtiers do, it teaches him the true condition of mankind and of himself. The forest is serenely impartial, neither malicious nor compassionate. Death, and even killing for food, are an inevitable part of forest existence. The Duke concedes that his presence in the forest means the slaughter of deer, who were the original inhabitants; Orlando and Adam find that death through starvation in the forest is all too real a possibility. The forest never stoops to the degrading perversity of man at his worst, but it is equally incapable of charity and forgiveness.

Shakespeare's sources reflect the complexity of his vision of Arden. The original of the Orlando story, which Shakespeare may not have used directly, is *The Cokes Tale of Gamelyn,* found in a number of manuscripts of *The Canterbury Tales* and wrongly attributed to Chaucer. This hearty English romance glorifies the rebellious and even violent spirit of its Robin Hood hero, the neglected youngest son Gamelyn, who, aided by faithful old Adam the Spencer, evades his wicked eldest brother in a cunning and bloody escape. As king of the outlaws in Sherwood Forest, Gamelyn eventually triumphs over his eldest brother (now the sheriff) and sees him hanged. Here then originates the motif of refuge from social injustice in Arden, even though most of the actual violence has been omitted from Shakespeare's version. (A series of Robin Hood plays on a similar theme, beginning in 1598 with Anthony Munday's *The Downfall of Robert Earl of Huntingdon after called Robin Hood,* were being performed with great success by the Admiral's company, chief rivals of the Lord Chamberlain's company to which Shakespeare belonged.)

As You Like It is clearly indebted to Thomas Lodge's version of the Gamelyn story entitled *Rosalynde: Euphues*

Golden Legacie (published 1590), a prose narrative romance in the ornate Euphuistic style of the 1580's. (Lodge's Epistle to the Gentleman Readers, casually inviting them to be pleased with this story if they are so inclined—"*If you like it,* so"—probably gave Shakespeare a hint for the name of his own play.) Lodge accentuated the love story with its courtship in masquerade, provided some charming songs, and introduced the pastoral love motif involving Corin, Silvius, Phebe, and Ganymede. Shakespeare's ordering of episode is generally close to that of Lodge. "Pastoral" literature, which had become a literary rage in the 1580's and early 1590's owing particularly to Spenser's *Shepheardes Calendar* (1579) and Sidney's *Arcadia* (1590), traced its ancestry through such Renaissance continental writers as Montemayor, Sannazaro, and Guarini to the so-called Greek romances, and finally back to the *Eclogues* of Virgil, Theocritus, and Bion. A literary mode that had begun originally as a realistic evocation of difficult country life had become, by the Renaissance, an elegant vehicle for the loftiest and most patrician sentiments in love, for philosophic debate, and even for extensive political analysis.

Shakespeare's alterations and additions give us insight into his method of construction and his thematic focus. Whereas Lodge cheerfully accepts the pastoral conventions of his day, Shakespeare exposes those conventions to some criticism and considerable irony. Alongside the mannered and literary Silvius and Phebe, he places William and Audrey, as peasantlike a couple as ever drew milk from a cow's teat. They are Shakespeare's own creation, based presumably on observation and also on the dramatic convention of the rustic clown and wench as exemplified earlier in his Costard and Jaquenetta *(Love's Labor's Lost).* Equally original, and essential to the many-sided debate concerning the virtues of the court versus those of the country, are Touchstone and Jaques. Touchstone is a professional court fool, dressed in motley, a new comic type in Shakespeare, created apparently in response to the recent addition to the Lord Chamberlain's company of the brilliant actor Robert Armin. Jaques is also a new type, the malcontent satirist, reflecting the very latest literary vogue in the nondramatic poetry and drama for the private theatre of Chapman, Marston, and Jonson. (The private theatres, featuring boy actors, reopened in 1598–1599 after nearly a decade of enforced silence, and proceeded at once to specialize in satirical drama.) Once we have been exposed to this assortment of newly created characters, we can no longer view either pastoral life or pastoral love as simply as Lodge and other writers of the period portray them.

When *As You Like It* is compared with its chief source, Shakespeare can also be seen to have altered and softened considerably the characters of the wicked brothers Oliver and Frederick. Whereas Lodge's Saladyne is motivated by a greedy desire to seize his younger brother Rosader's property, Shakespeare's Oliver is envious of Orlando's natural goodness and popularity. As he confesses in soliloquy, Orlando is "so much in the heart of the world, and especially of my own people . . . that I am altogether mispris'd" (I,i). In his warped way Oliver desires to be more like Orlando, and in the enchanted forest of Arden he eventually becomes so. Duke Frederick too is plainly envious of goodness. Trying to persuade his daughter Celia of the need for banishing Rosalind, he argues, "thou wilt show more bright and seem more virtuous When she is gone" (I,iii). In a sense Frederick is ripe for conversion. Penitence and conciliation replace the vengeful conclusion of Lodge's novel, in which the nobles of France finally overthrow and execute the usurping king. Although Shakespeare's resolutions are sudden and inadequately explained, like all miracles they attest to the inexplicable power of goodness.

The court of Duke Frederick is "the envious court," identified by this fixed epithet. In it, brothers turn unnaturally against brothers: the younger Frederick usurps his older brother's throne, whereas the older Oliver denies the younger Orlando his birthright of education. In still another parallel, both Rosalind and Orlando find themselves mistrusted as the children of Frederick's political enemies, Duke Senior and Sir Rowland de Boys. A daughter and a son are held to be guilty by association. "Thou art thy father's daughter, there's enough" (I,iii), Frederick curtly retorts in explaining Rosalind's exile. And to Orlando, triumphant in wrestling with Charles, Frederick asserts, "I would thou hadst been son to some man else" (I,ii). Here again, Frederick plaintively reveals his attraction to goodness, even if at present this attraction is thwarted by tyrannous whim. Many of Frederick's entourage might also be better persons, if they only knew how to escape the insincerities of their courtly life. Charles the wrestler, for example, places himself at Oliver's service, and yet he would happily avoid breaking Orlando's neck if to do so were consistent with self-interest. Even Le Beau, the giddy fop so delighted at first with the cruel sport of wrestling, takes Orlando aside at some personal risk to warn him of Duke Frederick's foul humor. Ideally, Le Beau would prefer to be a companion of Orlando's "in a better world than this" (I,ii). The vision of a regenerative Utopia secretly abides in the heart of this courtly creature.

It is easier to anatomize the defects of a social order than to propound solutions. As have other Utopian visionaries (including Thomas More), Shakespeare uses playful debate to elicit complicated responses on the part of his audience. Which is preferable, the court or the country? Jaques and Touchstone are adept gadflies, incessantly pointing out contradictions and ironies. Jaques, the malcontent railer derived from literary satire, takes delight in being out of step with everyone. Seemingly his chief reason for having joined the others in the forest is to jibe at their motives for being there. To their song about the rejection of courtly ambition he mockingly supplies another verse, charging them with having left their wealth and ease out of mere willfulness (II,v). With ironic appropriateness, Jaques eventually decides to remain in the forest in the company of Frederick; Jaques cannot thrive on resolution and harmony. His humor is "melancholy," from which, as he observes, he draws consolation as a weasel sucks eggs. The others treat him as a sort of profane jester whose soured conceits add relish to their enjoyment of the forest life.

Despite his affectation, however, Jaques is serious and even excited in his defense of satire as a curative form of laughter (II,vii). The appearance of Touchstone in the forest has reaffirmed in Jaques his profound commitment to a view of life as a meaningless process of decay governed by inexorable time. His function in such a life is to be mordant, unsparing. As literary satirist he must be free to awaken men's minds to their own folly. To the Duke's protestation that the satirist is merely self-indulgent and licentious, Jaques counters with a thoughtful and classically Horatian defense of satire as an art form devoted not to libelous attacks on individuals but to exposing "types" of folly. Any observer who feels himself individually portrayed merely condemns himself by confessing his resemblance to the type. This particular debate between the Duke and Jaques ends, appropriately, in a draw. The Duke's point is well taken, for Jaques' famous "Seven Ages of Man" speech, so often read out of context, occurs in a scene that also witnesses the rescue of Orlando and Adam from the forest. As though in answer to Jaques' acid depiction of covetous old age, we see the self-sacrifice and trust in Providence of old Adam. Instead of "mere oblivion," we see charitable compassion prompting the Duke to aid Orlando and Orlando to aid Adam. Perhaps this vision seems of a higher spiritual order than that of Jaques. Nonetheless, without him the forest would be a dull and humorless place.

Touchstone's name suggests that he similarly offers a multiplicity of viewpoints. He shares with Jaques a skeptical view of life, but for Touchstone the inconsistency and absurdity of life are occasions for wit and humor rather than melancholy and cynicism. As a professional fool he observes that sane men are more foolish than he—as, for example, in their elaborate dueling code of the Retort Courteous and the Reply Churlish, leading finally to the Lie Circumstantial and the Lie Direct. He is fascinated by the games people make of their lives, and amused by their inability to be content with what they already have. Of the shepherd's life, he comments, "In respect that it is solitary, I like it very well; but in respect that it is private, it is a very vile life" (III,ii). This paradox, though nonsensical, captures the restlessness of human striving for a life that can somehow combine the peaceful solitude of nature with the convenience and excitement of city life. Although Touchstone marries, even his marriage is a spoof of the institution rather than a serious attempt at commitment. Like all fools, who in Renaissance times were regarded as a breed apart, Touchstone exists outside the realm of ordinary human responses. There he can comment disinterestedly on human folly. He is prevented, however, from sharing fully in the human love and conciliation with which the play ends. He and Jaques are not touched by the play's regenerative magic; Jaques will remain in the forest, Touchstone will remain forever a childlike entertainer.

The regenerative power of Arden, as we have seen, is not the forest's alone. What saves Orlando is the human charity practiced by himself and by the Duke who, for all his love of the forest, longs to rejoin that human society where he has "with holy bell been knoll'd to church" (II,vii). Civilization at its best is no less necessary to man's spirit than is the "natural" order of the forest. In love, also, perception and wisdom must be combined with nature's gifts. Orlando, when we first see him, is a young man of the finest natural qualities, but admittedly lacking experience in the nuances of complex human relationships. Nowhere does his lack of "breeding" betray him more unhappily than in his first encounter with Rosalind, following the wrestling match. In response to her unmistakable hints of favor he stands oxlike, tongue-tied. Later, however, in the forest, his first attempts at self-education in love lead him into an opposite danger: an excess of platitudinous "manners" parading in the guise of Petrarchism. Orlando's newfound self-abasement and idealization of his absent mistress are as unsatisfactory as his former naiveté. He must learn from Rosalind that a quest for true understanding in love avoids the extreme of pretentious mannerism as well as that of mere artlessness. Orlando as Petrarchan lover too much resembles Silvius, the greensick young man, cowering before the imperious will of his coy mistress Phebe. This stereotyped relationship, taken from the pages of fashionable pastoral romance, represents a posturing which Rosalind hopes to cure in Silvius and Phebe even as she will also cure Orlando.

Rosalind is above all the realistic one, the plucky Shakespearean heroine showing her mettle in the world of men, emotionally more mature than her lover. Her concern is with a working and clear-sighted relationship in love, and to that end she daringly insists that Orlando learn something of woman's changeable mood. Above all, she must disabuse him of the dangerously misleading clichés of the Petrarchan love myth. When he protests he would die for love of Rosalind, she lectures him mockingly: "No, faith, die by attorney. The poor world is almost six thousand years old, and in all this time there was not any man died in his own person, videlicet, in a love-cause." She debunks the legends of Troilus and Leander, youths supposed to have died for love who in fact met with more prosaic ends. "But these are all lies. Men have died from time to time, and worms have eaten them, but not for love" (IV,i). When Orlando has been sufficiently tested as to patience, loyalty, and understanding, she unmasks herself to him and simultaneously unravels the plot of Silvius and Phebe.

Rosalind's disguise name, Ganymede, taken from Jove's amorous cupbearer, has faintly homosexual connotations.

Shakespeare delicately exploits these overtones, both in Phebe's pursuit of a young lady (but really a boy actor) in male attire, and in Orlando's courtship of Ganymede as though addressed to Rosalind. In this innocent titillation, found also in Shakespeare's source, there is no suggestion of deviate sexual practice. On the contrary, the point is that Orlando can speak frankly and personally to "Ganymede" as to a perfect friend, one to whom he can relate in Platonically spiritual terms without the potentially distracting note of sexual attraction. Once this disinterested love has grown strong between them, the unmasking of Rosalind's sexual identity makes possible a physical union between them to confirm and express the spiritual. In these terms, the play's happy ending affirms marriage as an institution, not simply as the expected denouement. The procession to the altar is synchronous with the return to civilization's other institutions, made whole again not solely by the forest but by the power of goodness embodied in Rosalind, Orlando, Duke Senior, and the others who persevere.

As You Like It

[*Dramatis Personae*

DUKE SENIOR, *living in banishment.*
FREDERICK, *his brother, and usurper of his dominions.*
AMIENS, JAQUES, } *lords attending on the banished Duke.*
LE BEAU, *a courtier attending upon Frederick.*
CHARLES, *wrestler to Frederick.*
OLIVER, JAQUES, ORLANDO, } *sons of Sir Rowland de Boys.*
ADAM, DENNIS, } *servants to Oliver.*
TOUCHSTONE, *a clown.*
SIR OLIVER MARTEXT, *a vicar.*
CORIN, SILVIUS, } *shepherds.*
WILLIAM, *a country fellow, in love with Audrey.*
HYMEN, *god of marriage.*

ROSALIND, *daughter to the banished Duke.*
CELIA, *daughter to Frederick.*
PHEBE, *a shepherdess.*
AUDREY, *a country wench.*

LORDS, PAGES, *and* ATTENDANTS, *etc.*

SCENE: *Oliver's house; Duke Frederick's court; and the Forest of Arden.*]

ACT I • SCENE I

Enter Orlando and Adam.

ORLANDO As I remember, Adam, it was upon this fashion bequeath'd me by will but poor a thousand crowns, and, as thou say'st, charg'd my brother, on his blessing, to breed me well; and there begins my sadness. My brother Jaques he keeps at school, and report speaks goldenly of his profit. For my part, he

I.i. Location: The garden of Oliver's house.
2 bequeath'd i.e., he, my father, bequeathed. **but poor** merely **3–4 on his blessing** on pain of losing his blessing **5 keeps at school** maintains at the university **6 profit** i.e., progress

keeps me rustically at home, or, to speak more properly, stays me here at home unkept; for call you that keeping for a gentleman of my birth, that differs not from the stalling of an ox? His horses are bred better; for, besides that they are fair with their feeding, they are taught their manage, and to that end riders dearly hir'd. But I, his brother, gain nothing under him but growth, for the which his animals on his dunghills are as much bound to him as I. Besides this nothing that he so plentifully gives me, the something that nature gave me his countenance seems to take from me. He lets me feed with his hinds, bars me the place of a brother, and as much as in him lies, mines my gentility with my education. This is it, Adam, that grieves me; and the spirit of my father, which I think is within me, begins to mutiny against this servitude. I will no longer endure it, though yet I know no wise remedy how to avoid it.

Enter Oliver.

ADAM Yonder comes my master, your brother.

ORLANDO Go apart, Adam, and thou shalt hear how he will shake me up. [*Adam stands aside.*]

OLIVER Now, sir, what make you here?

ORLANDO Nothing. I am not taught to make anything.

OLIVER What mar you then, sir?

ORLANDO Marry, sir, I am helping you to mar that which God made, a poor unworthy brother of yours, with idleness.

OLIVER Marry, sir, be better employ'd, and be naught awhile.

ORLANDO Shall I keep your hogs and eat husks with them? What prodigal portion have I spent, that I should come to such penury?

OLIVER Know you where you are, sir?

ORLANDO O, sir, very well; here in your orchard.

OLIVER Know you before whom, sir?

ORLANDO Ay, better than him I am before knows me. I know you are my eldest brother; and, in the gentle condition of blood, you should so know me. The courtesy of nations allows you my better, in that you are the first-born; but the same tradition takes not away my blood, were there twenty brothers betwixt us. I have as much of my father in me as you, albeit I confess your coming before me is nearer to his reverence.

OLIVER What, boy! [*Strikes him.*]

ORLANDO Come, come, elder brother, you are too young in this. [*Seizes him.*]

OLIVER Wilt thou lay hands on me, villain?

ORLANDO I am no villain; I am the youngest son of Sir Rowland de Boys. He was my father, and he is thrice a villain that says such a father begot villains. Wert thou not my brother, I would not take this hand from thy throat till this other had pull'd out thy tongue for saying so. Thou hast rail'd on thyself.

ADAM Sweet masters, be patient! For your father's remembrance, be at accord.

OLIVER Let me go, I say.

ORLANDO I will not, till I please. You shall hear me. My father charg'd you in his will to give me good education. You have train'd me like a peasant, obscuring and hiding from me all gentleman-like qualities. The spirit of my father grows strong in me, and I will no longer endure it; therefore allow me such exercises as may become a gentleman, or give me the poor allottery my father left me by testament; with that I will go buy my fortunes. [*Releases him.*]

OLIVER And what wilt thou do? Beg, when that is spent? Well, sir, get you in. I will not long be troubled with you; you shall have some part of your will. I pray you, leave me.

ORLANDO I will no further offend you than becomes me for my good.

OLIVER Get you with him, you old dog.

ADAM Is "old dog" my reward? Most true, I have lost my teeth in your service. God be with my old master! He would not have spoke such a word.

Exeunt Orlando [and] Adam.

OLIVER Is it even so? Begin you to grow upon me? I will physic your rankness, and yet give no thousand crowns neither. Holla, Dennis!

Enter Dennis.

DENNIS Calls your worship?

OLIVER Was not Charles, the Duke's wrestler, here to speak with me?

DENNIS So please you, he is here at the door and importunes access to you.

OLIVER Call him in. [*Dennis goes to the door.*] 'Twill be a good way; and tomorrow the wrestling is.

Enter Charles.

CHARLES Good morrow to your worship.

OLIVER Good Monsieur Charles, what's the new news at the new court?

CHARLES There's no news at the court, sir, but the old news: that is, the old Duke is banish'd by his younger brother the new Duke, and three or four loving lords have put themselves into voluntary exile with him, whose lands and revenues enrich the new Duke; therefore he gives them good leave to wander.

OLIVER Can you tell if Rosalind, the Duke's daughter, be banish'd with her father?

CHARLES O, no; for the Duke's daughter, her cousin, so loves her, being ever from their cradles bred together,

8 stays detains. **unkept** not maintained properly **11 fair** in handsome shape **12 manage** paces and movements. **dearly** expensively **17 countenance** behavior, show of feeling **18 hinds** farm hands. **bars me** excludes me from **19 as in him lies** as he is able. **mines** undermines **20 education** i.e., lack of proper education **28 make** do. (But Orlando takes it in the more usual sense.) **31 Marry** i.e., indeed. (Originally an oath by the Virgin Mary.) **34–35 be naught awhile** (A mild malediction, like "go to the devil.") **36–38 Shall . . . penury** (Alluding to the story of the Prodigal Son, in Luke 15:11–32, who, having wasted his "portion" or inheritance, had to tend swine and eat with them.) **39 where** i.e., in whose presence. (But Orlando sarcastically takes the more literal meaning.) **40 orchard** garden **42 him** he whom **43–44 in . . . blood** i.e., acknowledging the bond of our being of gentle birth **44–45 courtesy of nations** recognized custom (of primogeniture, whereby the eldest son inherits all the land) **49 is nearer to his reverence** i.e., places you closer to the respect that was due him **52 young** raw, inexperienced (at fighting) **53 villain** i.e., worthless fellow. (But Orlando again plays on the literal meaning, *bondman, serf.*)

59 rail'd on thyself i.e., reviled your own blood **60–61 your father's remembrance** the memory of your father **65 obscuring** i.e., obscuring in me **66 qualities** accomplishments **69 allottery** share, portion **82 grow upon me** i.e., encroach on my place **83 physic** apply medicine to. **rankness** overgrowth, overweening

that she would have follow'd her exile, or have died to stay behind her. She is at the court, and no less belov'd of her uncle than his own daughter, and never two ladies lov'd as they do.

OLIVER Where will the old Duke live?

CHARLES They say he is already in the forest of Arden, and a many merry men with him; and there they live like the old Robin Hood of England. They say many young gentlemen flock to him every day, and fleet the time carelessly, as they did in the golden world.

OLIVER What, you wrestle tomorrow before the new Duke?

CHARLES Marry, do I, sir; and I came to acquaint you with a matter. I am given, sir, secretly to understand that your younger brother Orlando hath a disposition to come in disguis'd against me to try a fall. Tomorrow, sir, I wrestle for my credit, and he that escapes me without some broken limb shall acquit him well. Your brother is but young and tender, and, for your love, I would be loath to foil him, as I must for my own honor if he come in. Therefore, out of my love to you, I came hither to acquaint you withal, that either you might stay him from his intendment, or brook such disgrace well as he shall run into, in that it is a thing of his own search and altogether against my will.

OLIVER Charles, I thank thee for thy love to me, which thou shalt find I will most kindly requite. I had myself notice of my brother's purpose herein, and have by underhand means labor'd to dissuade him from it, but he is resolute. I'll tell thee, Charles, it is the stubbornest young fellow of France, full of ambition, an envious emulator of every man's good parts, a secret and villainous contriver against me his natural brother. Therefore use thy discretion. I had as lief thou didst break his neck as his finger. And thou wert best look to 't; for if thou dost him any slight disgrace, or if he do not mightily grace himself on thee, he will practice against thee by poison, entrap thee by some treacherous device, and never leave thee till he hath ta'en thy life by some indirect means or other; for I assure thee, and almost with tears I speak it, there is not one so young and so villainous this day living. I speak but brotherly of him; but should I anatomize him to thee as he is, I must blush and weep, and thou must look pale and wonder.

CHARLES I am heartily glad I came hither to you. If he come tomorrow, I'll give him his payment. If ever he go alone again, I'll never wrestle for prize more. And so God keep your worship!

OLIVER Farewell, good Charles. *Exit [Charles].* Now will I stir this gamester. I hope I shall see an end of him; for my soul, yet I know not why, hates nothing more than he. Yet he's gentle, never school'd and yet learned, full of noble device, of all sorts enchantingly belov'd, and indeed so much in the heart of the world, and especially of my own people, who best know him, that I am altogether mispris'd. But it shall not be so long; this wrestler shall clear all. Nothing remains but that I kindle the boy thither, which now I'll go about.

Exit.

SCENE II

Enter Rosalind and Celia.

CELIA I pray thee, Rosalind, sweet my coz, be merry.

ROSALIND Dear Celia, I show more mirth than I am mistress of; and would you yet I were merrier? Unless you could teach me to forget a banish'd father, you must not learn me how to remember any extraordinary pleasure.

CELIA Herein I see thou lov'st me not with the full weight that I love thee. If my uncle, thy banish'd father, had banish'd thy uncle, the Duke my father, so thou hadst been still with me, I could have taught my love to take thy father for mine. So wouldst thou, if the truth of thy love to me were so righteously temper'd as mine is to thee.

ROSALIND Well, I will forget the condition of my estate, to rejoice in yours.

CELIA You know my father hath no child but I, nor none is like to have. And, truly, when he dies, thou shalt be his heir, for, what he hath taken away from thy father perforce, I will render thee again in affection. By mine honor, I will, and when I break that oath, let me turn monster. Therefore, my sweet Rose, my dear Rose, be merry.

ROSALIND From henceforth I will, coz, and devise sports. Let me see; what think you of falling in love?

CELIA Marry, I prithee, do, to make sport withal. But love no man in good earnest; nor no further in sport neither than with safety of a pure blush thou mayst in honor come off again.

ROSALIND What shall be our sport, then?

CELIA Let us sit and mock the good huswife Fortune from her wheel, that her gifts may henceforth be bestow'd equally.

ROSALIND I would we could do so, for her benefits are mightily misplac'd, and the bountiful blind woman doth most mistake in her gifts to women.

CELIA 'Tis true, for those that she makes fair she scarce makes honest, and those that she makes honest she makes very ill-favoredly.

105–106 died to stay died from staying **113 fleet** pass **114 carelessly** free from care. **golden world** the primal age of innocence and ease from which man was thought to have degenerated. (See Ovid, *Metamorphoses,* Book I.) **120 fall** bout **121 credit** reputation **122 shall** must **124 foil** overthrow **127 intendment** purpose, intent. **brook** endure **129 search** seeking **133 underhand** indirect **136 emulator** rival. **parts** qualities **137 contriver** plotter. **natural** by blood, legitimate **141 grace . . . thee** distinguish himself at your expense. **practice** plot **147 brotherly** i.e., with a reserve proper to a brother. **anatomize** lay open in detail, analyze **152 go alone** walk unassisted **155 gamester** sportive fellow **157 gentle** gentlemanly

158 noble device lofty aspiration. **sorts** classes of people. **enchantingly** as if by the effect of enchantment **161 mispris'd** despised **163 kindle** incite (to go). **thither** i.e., to the wrestling match

I.ii. Location: Lawn before the Duke's palace.
1 sweet my coz my sweet cousin **5 learn** teach **9 so** provided that **12 righteously temper'd** properly compounded **19 perforce** by force **27 pure** innocent **28 come off** retire, escape **30 huswife** one who manages household affairs, partially by spinning at a spinning wheel. (Shakespeare conflates this wheel with the commonplace Wheel of Fortune.) **34 bountiful blind woman** i.e., Fortune **37 honest** chaste **38 ill-favoredly** ugly

ROSALIND Nay, now thou goest from Fortune's office to
Nature's. Fortune reigns in gifts of the world, not in
the lineaments of Nature. 41

Enter [Touchstone the] Clown.

CELIA No; when Nature hath made a fair creature, may
she not by Fortune fall into the fire? Though Nature
hath given us wit to flout at Fortune, hath not Fortune 44
sent in this fool to cut off the argument?

ROSALIND Indeed, there is Fortune too hard for Nature,
when Fortune makes Nature's natural the cutter-off of 47
Nature's wit.

CELIA Peradventure this is not Fortune's work neither,
but Nature's, who perceiveth our natural wits too dull
to reason of such goddesses and hath sent this natural
for our whetstone; for always the dullness of the fool
is the whetstone of the wits. How now, wit, whither 53
wander you? 54

TOUCHSTONE Mistress, you must come away to your father.

CELIA Were you made the messenger?

TOUCHSTONE No, by mine honor, but I was bid to come for you.

ROSALIND Where learn'd you that oath, fool?

TOUCHSTONE Of a certain knight, that swore by his
honor they were good pancakes and swore by his 62
honor the mustard was naught. Now I'll stand to it,
the pancakes were naught and the mustard was good,
and yet was not the knight forsworn. 65

CELIA How prove you that, in the great heap of your knowledge?

ROSALIND Ay, marry, now unmuzzle your wisdom.

TOUCHSTONE Stand you both forth now. Stroke your chins, and swear by your beards that I am a knave.

CELIA By our beards, if we had them, thou art.

TOUCHSTONE By my knavery, if I had it, then I were; but if you swear by that that is not, you are not forsworn. No more was this knight, swearing by his honor, for he never had any; or if he had, he had sworn it away before ever he saw those pancakes or that mustard.

CELIA Prithee, who is 't that thou mean'st?

TOUCHSTONE One that old Frederick, your father, loves.

CELIA My father's love is enough to honor him enough.
Speak no more of him; you'll be whipp'd for taxation 81
one of these days.

TOUCHSTONE The more pity that fools may not speak wisely what wise men do foolishly.

CELIA By my troth, thou sayest true; for since the little wit that fools have was silenc'd, the little foolery that wise men have makes a great show. Here comes Monsieur Le Beau.

Enter Le Beau.

ROSALIND With his mouth full of news.

CELIA Which he will put on us, as pigeons feed their 90
young.

ROSALIND Then shall we be news-cramm'd.

CELIA All the better; we shall be the more
marketable.—Bon jour, Monsieur Le Beau. What's the 94
news?

LE BEAU Fair princess, you have lost much good sport.

CELIA Sport? Of what color? 97

LE BEAU What color, madam? How shall I answer you?

ROSALIND As wit and fortune will.

TOUCHSTONE Or as the Destinies decrees.

CELIA Well said; that was laid on with a trowel. 101

TOUCHSTONE Nay, if I keep not my rank— 102

ROSALIND Thou losest thy old smell.

LE BEAU You amaze me, ladies. I would have told you 104
of good wrestling, which you have lost the sight of.

ROSALIND Yet tell us the manner of the wrestling.

LE BEAU I will tell you the beginning; and, if it please your ladyships, you may see the end, for the best is yet to do; and here, where you are, they are coming to perform it.

CELIA Well, the beginning, that is dead and buried.

LE BEAU There comes an old man and his three sons—

CELIA I could match this beginning with an old tale.

LE BEAU Three proper young men, of excellent growth 114
and presence.

ROSALIND With bills on their necks, "Be it known unto 116
all men by these presents." 117

LE BEAU The eldest of the three wrestled with Charles,
the Duke's wrestler; which Charles in a moment threw
him and broke three of his ribs, that there is little hope
of life in him. So he serv'd the second, and so the
third. Yonder they lie, the poor old man, their father,
making such pitiful dole over them that all the behold- 123
ers take his part with weeping.

ROSALIND Alas!

TOUCHSTONE But what is the sport, monsieur, that the ladies have lost?

LE BEAU Why, this that I speak of.

TOUCHSTONE Thus men may grow wiser every day. It is the first time that ever I heard breaking of ribs was sport for ladies.

CELIA Or I, I promise thee.

ROSALIND But is there any else longs to see this broken 133
music in his sides? Is there yet another dotes upon rib- 134
breaking? Shall we see this wrestling, cousin?

LE BEAU You must, if you stay here; for here is the place appointed for the wrestling, and they are ready to perform it.

CELIA Yonder, sure, they are coming. Let us now stay and see it.

Flourish. Enter Duke [Frederick], Lords, Orlando, Charles, and Attendants.

DUKE FREDERICK Come on. Since the youth will not be
entreated, his own peril on his forwardness. 142

ROSALIND Is yonder the man?

41 s.d. Touchstone a kind of stone used to test for gold and silver **44 flout** mock, scoff **47 natural** idiot, half-wit **53–54 whither wander you** (An allusion to the expression "wandering wits.") **62 pancakes** fritters (which might be made of meat and so require mustard) **65 forsworn** perjured **81 taxation** censure, slander **90 put on** force upon

94 marketable i.e., fattened by being crammed with food **97 color** kind **101 with a trowel** i.e., clumsily, bluntly **102 rank** i.e., status as a wit. (But Rosalind plays on the sense of *evil-smelling*.) **104 amaze** bewilder **114 proper** handsome **116 bills** advertisements, proclamations **117 these presents** this document presented (with pun on *presence*) **123 dole** grief, lamentation **133 any else** anyone else who **133–134 broken music** (Literally, music arranged in parts for different instruments; here applied to the breaking of ribs.) **142 entreated . . . forwardness** i.e., entreated to desist, let the risk be blamed upon his own rashness

LE BEAU Even he, madam.

CELIA Alas, he is too young! Yet he looks successfully.

DUKE FREDERICK How now, daughter and cousin? Are you crept hither to see the wrestling?

ROSALIND Ay, my liege, so please you give us leave.

DUKE FREDERICK You will take little delight in it, I can tell you, there is such odds in the man. In pity of the challenger's youth I would fain dissuade him, but he will not be entreated. Speak to him, ladies; see if you can move him.

CELIA Call him hither, good Monsieur Le Beau.

DUKE FREDERICK Do so. I'll not be by. [*Steps aside.*]

LE BEAU Monsieur the challenger, the princess calls for you.

ORLANDO [*Approaching the ladies*] I attend them with all respect and duty.

ROSALIND Young man, have you challeng'd Charles the wrestler?

ORLANDO No, fair princess; he is the general challenger. I come but in, as others do, to try with him the strength of my youth.

CELIA Young gentleman, your spirits are too bold for your years. You have seen cruel proof of this man's strength. If you saw yourself with your eyes or knew yourself with your judgment, the fear of your adventure would counsel you to a more equal enterprise. We pray you, for your own sake, to embrace your own safety and give over this attempt.

ROSALIND Do, young sir. Your reputation shall not therefore be mispris'd. We will make it our suit to the Duke that the wrestling might not go forward.

ORLANDO I beseech you, punish me not with your hard thoughts, wherein I confess me much guilty to deny so fair and excellent ladies anything. But let your fair eyes and gentle wishes go with me to my trial; wherein if I be foil'd, there is but one sham'd that was never gracious; if kill'd, but one dead that is willing to be so. I shall do my friends no wrong, for I have none to lament me; the world no injury, for in it I have nothing. Only in the world I fill up a place, which may be better supplied when I have made it empty.

ROSALIND The little strength that I have, I would it were with you.

CELIA And mine, to eke out hers.

ROSALIND Fare you well. Pray heaven I be deceiv'd in you!

CELIA Your heart's desires be with you!

CHARLES Come, where is this young gallant that is so desirous to lie with his mother earth?

ORLANDO Ready, sir, but his will hath in it a more modest working.

DUKE FREDERICK You shall try but one fall.

CHARLES No, I warrant your Grace, you shall not entreat him to a second, that have so mightily persuaded him from a first.

ORLANDO You mean to mock me after; you should not have mock'd me before. But come your ways.

ROSALIND Now Hercules be thy speed, young man!

CELIA I would I were invisible, to catch the strong fellow by the leg. [*They*] *wrestle.*

ROSALIND O excellent young man!

CELIA If I had a thunderbolt in mine eye, I can tell who should down. *Shout.* [*Charles is thrown.*]

DUKE FREDERICK No more, no more.

ORLANDO Yes, I beseech your Grace. I am not yet well breath'd.

DUKE FREDERICK
How dost thou, Charles?

LE BEAU
He cannot speak, my lord.

DUKE FREDERICK
Bear him away. What is thy name, young man?
[*Charles is borne out.*]

ORLANDO Orlando, my liege, the youngest son of Sir Rowland de Boys.

DUKE FREDERICK
I would thou hadst been son to some man else.
The world esteem'd thy father honorable,
But I did find him still mine enemy.
Thou shouldst have better pleas'd me with this deed
Hadst thou descended from another house.
But fare thee well; thou art a gallant youth.
I would thou hadst told me of another father.
Exit Duke [*with train*].

CELIA
Were I my father, coz, would I do this?

ORLANDO
I am more proud to be Sir Rowland's son,
His youngest son, and would not change that calling
To be adopted heir to Frederick.

ROSALIND [*To Celia*]
My father lov'd Sir Rowland as his soul,
And all the world was of my father's mind.
Had I before known this young man his son,
I should have given him tears unto entreaties,
Ere he should thus have ventur'd.

CELIA
Gentle cousin,
Let us go thank him and encourage him.
My father's rough and envious disposition
Sticks me at heart.—Sir, you have well deserv'd.
If you do keep your promises in love
But justly as you have exceeded all promise,
Your mistress shall be happy.

ROSALIND
Gentleman,
[*Giving him a chain from her neck.*]
Wear this for me, one out of suits with fortune,
That could give more, but that her hand lacks means.
Shall we go, coz?

CELIA
Ay. Fare you well, fair gentleman.
[*They start to leave.*]

145 successfully i.e., as if he would be successful **150 odds** advantage. **the man** i.e., Charles **167–168 If . . . judgment** i.e., if you saw yourself objectively, using your observation and your judgment **169 equal** i.e., where the odds are more equal **173 therefore** on that account. **mispris'd** despised **180 gracious** looked upon with favor **188–189 deceiv'd in you** i.e., mistaken in fearing you will lose **194 modest working** decorous endeavor (than to lie with one's mother earth—an endeavor, Orlando implies, with sexual overtones)

200 come your ways come on **201 Hercules be thy speed** may Hercules favor you **208–209 well breath'd** warmed up **216 still** continually **223 calling** name. (Orlando speaks here to no one in particular; Celia and Rosalind are conversing between themselves.) **228 unto** in addition to **232 Sticks** stabs **235 s.d. chain** (See III.ii.178, where Celia speaks of a *chain* given to Orlando by Rosalind.) **236 out . . . fortune** not wearing the livery of fortune, not in her service; or one whose suits to fortune are rejected **237 could** would be disposed to

ORLANDO
Can I not say, I thank you? My better parts
Are all thrown down, and that which here stands up
Is but a quintain, a mere lifeless block.

ROSALIND
He calls us back. My pride fell with my fortunes;
I'll ask him what he would.—Did you call, sir?
Sir, you have wrestled well, and overthrown
More than your enemies.

CELIA
Will you go, coz?

ROSALIND
Have with you.—Fare you well. *Exit* [*with Celia*].

ORLANDO
What passion hangs these weights upon my tongue?
I cannot speak to her, yet she urg'd conference.
O poor Orlando, thou art overthrown!
Or Charles or something weaker masters thee.

Enter Le Beau.

LE BEAU
Good sir, I do in friendship counsel you
To leave this place. Albeit you have deserv'd
High commendation, true applause, and love,
Yet such is now the Duke's condition
That he misconsters all that you have done.
The Duke is humorous. What he is indeed
More suits you to conceive than I to speak of.

ORLANDO
I thank you, sir. And, pray you, tell me this:
Which of the two was daughter of the Duke
That here was at the wrestling?

LE BEAU
Neither his daughter, if we judge by manners;
But yet indeed the taller is his daughter.
The other is daughter to the banish'd Duke,
And here detain'd by her usurping uncle
To keep his daughter company, whose loves
Are dearer than the natural bond of sisters.
But I can tell you that of late this Duke
Hath ta'en displeasure 'gainst his gentle niece,
Grounded upon no other argument
But that the people praise her for her virtues
And pity her for her good father's sake;
And, on my life, his malice 'gainst the lady
Will suddenly break forth. Sir, fare you well.
Hereafter, in a better world than this,
I shall desire more love and knowledge of you.

ORLANDO
I rest much bounden to you. Fare you well.
[*Exit Le Beau.*]
Thus must I from the smoke into the smother,
From tyrant Duke unto a tyrant brother.
But heavenly Rosalind! *Exit.*

241 **quintain** wooden figure used as a target in tilting 246 **Have with you** I'll go with you 250 **Or** either 254 **condition** state of mind, disposition 255 **misconsters** misconstrues 256 **humorous** given to whims, capricious, self-willed 262 **taller** (Possibly a textual error for "smaller" or "lesser," or else an inconsistency on Shakespeare's part; later on, Rosalind is shown to be the taller.) 274 **world** i.e., state of affairs 277 **smoke into the smother** i.e., frying-pan into the fire. (*Smother* means "suffocation.")

SCENE III

Enter Celia and Rosalind.

CELIA Why, cousin, why, Rosalind! Cupid have mercy! Not a word?

ROSALIND Not one to throw at a dog.

CELIA No, thy words are too precious to be cast away upon curs; throw some of them at me. Come, lame me with reasons.

ROSALIND Then there were two cousins laid up, when the one should be lam'd with reasons and the other mad without any.

CELIA But is all this for your father?

ROSALIND No, some of it is for my child's father. O, how full of briers is this working-day world!

CELIA They are but burrs, cousin, thrown upon thee in holiday foolery; if we walk not in the trodden paths, our very petticoats will catch them.

ROSALIND I could shake them off my coat; these burrs are in my heart.

CELIA Hem them away.

ROSALIND I would try, if I could cry "hem" and have him.

CELIA Come, come, wrestle with thy affections.

ROSALIND O, they take the part of a better wrestler than myself!

CELIA O, a good wish upon you! You will try in time, in despite of a fall. But, turning these jests out of service, let us talk in good earnest. Is it possible, on such a sudden, you should fall into so strong a liking with old Sir Rowland's youngest son?

ROSALIND The Duke my father lov'd his father dearly.

CELIA Doth it therefore ensue that you should love his son dearly? By this kind of chase, I should hate him, for my father hated his father dearly; yet I hate not Orlando.

ROSALIND No, faith, hate him not, for my sake.

CELIA Why should I not? Doth he not deserve well?

Enter Duke [*Frederick*], *with Lords.*

ROSALIND Let me love him for that, and do you love him because I do. Look, here comes the Duke.

CELIA With his eyes full of anger.

DUKE FREDERICK
Mistress, dispatch you with your safest haste
And get you from our court.

ROSALIND
Me, uncle?

DUKE FREDERICK
You, cousin.
Within these ten days if that thou beest found
So near our public court as twenty miles,
Thou diest for it.

I.iii. Location: Duke Frederick's palace.
5–6 lame . . . reasons i.e., throw some explanations (for your silence) at me 11 **my child's father** one who might sire my children, i.e., Orlando 18 **Hem** cough (since you say they are in the chest) 19 **cry "hem"** clear away with a "hem" or a cough (with a play on *him*) **24–25 You . . . fall** i.e., you'll undertake to wrestle with Orlando sooner or later, despite the danger of your being thrown down. (Contains sexual suggestion.) **25–26 turning . . . service** i.e., dismissing this banter 31 **chase** argument that is pursued 32 **dearly** intensely 35 **deserve well** i.e., well deserve to be hated. (But Rosalind interprets in the sense of *deserve favor.*) 39 **safest haste** speed, which is your best security 40 **cousin** i.e., kinsman

ROSALIND I do beseech your Grace
Let me the knowledge of my fault bear with me.
If with myself I hold intelligence
Or have acquaintance with mine own desires,
If that I do not dream or be not frantic—
As I do trust I am not—then, dear uncle,
Never so much as in a thought unborn
Did I offend your Highness.

DUKE FREDERICK Thus do all traitors.
If their purgation did consist in words,
They are as innocent as grace itself.
Let it suffice thee that I trust thee not.

ROSALIND
Yet your mistrust cannot make me a traitor.
Tell me whereon the likelihood depends.

DUKE FREDERICK
Thou art thy father's daughter, there's enough.

ROSALIND
So was I when your Highness took his dukedom;
So was I when your Highness banish'd him.
Treason is not inherited, my lord;
Or, if we did derive it from our friends,
What's that to me? My father was no traitor.
Then, good my liege, mistake me not so much
To think my poverty is treacherous.

CELIA
Dear sovereign, hear me speak.

DUKE FREDERICK
Ay, Celia, we stay'd her for your sake,
Else had she with her father rang'd along.

CELIA
I did not then entreat to have her stay;
It was your pleasure and your own remorse.
I was too young that time to value her,
But now I know her. If she be a traitor,
Why so am I. We still have slept together,
Rose at an instant, learn'd, play'd, eat together,
And wheresoe'er we went, like Juno's swans,
Still we went coupled and inseparable.

DUKE FREDERICK
She is too subtle for thee; and her smoothness,
Her very silence and her patience
Speak to the people, and they pity her.
Thou art a fool. She robs thee of thy name,
And thou wilt show more bright and seem more virtuous
When she is gone. Then open not thy lips.
Firm and irrevocable is my doom
Which I have pass'd upon her; she is banish'd.

CELIA
Pronounce that sentence then on me, my liege!
I cannot live out of her company.

DUKE FREDERICK
You are a fool. You, niece, provide yourself.
If you outstay the time, upon mine honor,
And in the greatness of my word, you die.
Exit Duke, etc.

CELIA
O my poor Rosalind, whither wilt thou go?
Wilt thou change fathers? I will give thee mine.
I charge thee, be not thou more griev'd than I am.

ROSALIND
I have more cause.

CELIA Thou hast not, cousin.
Prithee, be cheerful. Know'st thou not the Duke
Hath banish'd me, his daughter?

ROSALIND That he hath not.

CELIA
No, hath not? Rosalind lacks then the love
Which teacheth thee that thou and I am one.
Shall we be sund'red? Shall we part, sweet girl?
No, let my father seek another heir.
Therefore devise with me how we may fly,
Whither to go, and what to bear with us.
And do not seek to take your change upon you,
To bear your griefs yourself and leave me out;
For, by this heaven, now at our sorrows pale,
Say what thou canst, I'll go along with thee.

ROSALIND
Why, whither shall we go?

CELIA
To seek my uncle in the forest of Arden.

ROSALIND
Alas, what danger will it be to us,
Maids as we are, to travel forth so far!
Beauty provoketh thieves sooner than gold.

CELIA
I'll put myself in poor and mean attire
And with a kind of umber smirch my face;
The like do you. So shall we pass along
And never stir assailants.

ROSALIND Were it not better,
Because that I am more than common tall,
That I did suit me all points like a man?
A gallant curtle-axe upon my thigh,
A boar-spear in my hand; and—in my heart
Lie there what hidden woman's fear there will—
We'll have a swashing and a martial outside,
As many other mannish cowards have
That do outface it with their semblances.

CELIA
What shall I call thee when thou art a man?

ROSALIND
I'll have no worse a name than Jove's own page,
And therefore look you call me Ganymede.
But what will you be call'd?

CELIA
Something that hath a reference to my state:
No longer Celia, but Aliena.

ROSALIND
But, cousin, what if we assay'd to steal
The clownish fool out of your father's court?
Would he not be a comfort to our travel?

45 hold intelligence am in communication **47 If that** if. **frantic** insane **51 purgation** exculpation **60 friends** relatives, kinsfolk **66 rang'd** roamed **69 that time** then **71 still** continually **73 Juno's swans** (According to Ovid, it was Venus and not Juno who possessed swans.) **78 name** reputation, praise **81 doom** sentence **87 in . . . word** i.e., upon my authority as Duke

100 change change of fortune **109 mean** lowly **110 umber** brown pigment **114 suit** dress **115 curtle-axe** broad cutting sword **118 swashing** swaggering, blustering **120 outface . . . semblances** bluff their way through with mere appearances **123 Ganymede** Jupiter's cupbearer. (Used also in Lodge's *Rosalynde.*) **126 Aliena** the estranged one

CELIA
He'll go along o'er the wide world with me;
Leave me alone to woo him. Let's away, 131
And get our jewels and our wealth together,
Devise the fittest time and safest way
To hide us from pursuit that will be made
After my flight. Now go we in content 135
To liberty, and not to banishment. *Exeunt.*

ACT II • SCENE I

Enter Duke Senior, Amiens, and two or three Lords, like foresters.

DUKE SENIOR
Now, my co-mates and brothers in exile,
Hath not old custom made this life more sweet
Than that of painted pomp? Are not these woods
More free from peril than the envious court?
Here feel we not the penalty of Adam, 5
The seasons' difference, as the icy fang 6
And churlish chiding of the winter's wind, 7
Which, when it bites and blows upon my body,
Even till I shrink with cold, I smile and say
"This is no flattery; these are counselors
That feelingly persuade me what I am."
Sweet are the uses of adversity,
Which, like the toad, ugly and venomous, 13
Wears yet a precious jewel in his head; 14
And this our life, exempt from public haunt, 15
Finds tongues in trees, books in the running brooks,
Sermons in stones, and good in everything.

AMIENS
I would not change it. Happy is your Grace
That can translate the stubbornness of fortune
Into so quiet and so sweet a style.

DUKE SENIOR
Come, shall we go and kill us venison?
And yet it irks me the poor dappled fools, 22
Being native burghers of this desert city, 23
Should in their own confines with forked heads 24
Have their round haunches gor'd.

FIRST LORD
Indeed, my lord,
The melancholy Jaques grieves at that,
And, in that kind, swears you do more usurp
Than doth your brother that hath banish'd you.
Today my Lord of Amiens and myself
Did steal behind him as he lay along 30
Under an oak whose antique root peeps out 31
Upon the brook that brawls along this wood, 32
To the which place a poor sequest'red stag, 33
That from the hunter's aim had ta'en a hurt,
Did come to languish; and indeed, my lord,
The wretched animal heav'd forth such groans
That their discharge did stretch his leathern coat
Almost to bursting, and the big round tears
Cours'd one another down his innocent nose
In piteous chase; and thus the hairy fool,
Much marked of the melancholy Jaques, 41
Stood on th' extremest verge of the swift brook, 42
Augmenting it with tears.

DUKE SENIOR
But what said Jaques?
Did he not moralize this spectacle? 44

FIRST LORD
O, yes, into a thousand similes.
First, for his weeping into the needless stream: 46
"Poor deer," quoth he, "thou mak'st a testament
As worldings do, giving thy sum of more 48
To that which had too much." Then, being there alone,
Left and abandoned of his velvet friends: 50
"'Tis right," quoth he, "thus misery doth part 51
The flux of company." Anon a careless herd, 52
Full of the pasture, jumps along by him
And never stays to greet him. "Ay," quoth Jaques,
"Sweep on, you fat and greasy citizens;
'Tis just the fashion. Wherefore do you look
Upon that poor and broken bankrupt there?"
Thus most invectively he pierceth through
The body of the country, city, court,
Yea, and of this our life, swearing that we
Are mere usurpers, tyrants, and what's worse, 61
To fright the animals and to kill them up 62
In their assign'd and native dwelling-place.

DUKE SENIOR
And did you leave him in this contemplation?

SECOND LORD
We did, my lord, weeping and commenting
Upon the sobbing deer.

DUKE SENIOR
Show me the place.
I love to cope him in these sullen fits, 67
For then he's full of matter. 68

FIRST LORD
I'll bring you to him straight. *Exeunt.*

SCENE II

Enter Duke [*Frederick*], *with Lords.*

DUKE FREDERICK
Can it be possible that no man saw them?
It cannot be. Some villains of my court
Are of consent and sufferance in this. 3

131 woo persuade **135 content** contentment

II.i. Location: The Forest of Arden.
5 feel we not we do not seriously suffer from. (*Not* is often emended to *but.*) **penalty of Adam** expulsion from Eden, bringing with it loss of innocence and *the seasons' difference,* the change of seasons from summer to winter **6 as** such as **7 churlish** rough **13–14 like . . . head** (The widespread idea that the toad was venomous comes from Pliny's *Natural History.* The jewel referred to is the toadstone, which was thought to be in the head of the toad.) **15 exempt** cut off. **haunt** society **22 irks** grieves, vexes. **fools** innocent creatures **23 burghers** citizens. **desert** uninhabited **24 forked heads** i.e., barbed hunting arrows **30 along** stretched prone **31 antique** ancient **32 brawls** noisily makes its way **33 sequest'red** separated (from the herd)

41 marked of observed by **42 extremest verge** very edge **44 moralize** draw out the hidden meaning of **46 needless** having no need (of more water) **48 worldings** mortal men; worldly men. **sum of more** additional quantity **50 velvet** i.e., prosperous. (Velvet was an appropriately rich dress for a courtier; it also alludes here to the velvet of the deers' antlers during rapid growth.) **51 'Tis right** i.e., that's how it goes. **part** depart from **52 flux** flow, confluence. **careless** without cares **61 what's worse** anything worse **62 up** off **67 cope** deal with **68 matter** substance, sentiment

II.ii. Location: Duke Frederick's palace.
3 of . . . sufferance in connivance

FIRST LORD
I cannot hear of any that did see her.
The ladies, her attendants of her chamber,
Saw her a-bed, and in the morning early
They found the bed untreasur'd of their mistress.

SECOND LORD
My lord, the roynish clown, at whom so oft 8
Your Grace was wont to laugh, is also missing.
Hisperia, the princess' gentlewoman,
Confesses that she secretly o'erheard
Your daughter and her cousin much commend
The parts and graces of the wrestler 13
That did but lately foil the sinewy Charles;
And she believes, wherever they are gone,
That youth is surely in their company.

DUKE FREDERICK
Send to his brother; fetch that gallant hither. 17
If he be absent, bring his brother to me; 18
I'll make him find him. Do this suddenly, 19
And let not search and inquisition quail 20
To bring again these foolish runaways. *Exeunt.* 21

SCENE III

Enter Orlando and Adam, [*meeting*].

ORLANDO
Who's there?

ADAM
What, my young master? O my gentle master,
O my sweet master, O you memory 3
Of old Sir Rowland! Why, what make you here?
Why are you virtuous? Why do people love you?
And wherefore are you gentle, strong, and valiant?
Why would you be so fond to overcome 7
The bonny priser of the humorous Duke? 8
Your praise is come too swiftly home before you.
Know you not, master, to some kind of men
Their graces serve them but as enemies?
No more do yours. Your virtues, gentle master, 12
Are sanctified and holy traitors to you.
O, what a world is this, when what is comely
Envenoms him that bears it!

ORLANDO
Why, what's the matter?

ADAM
O unhappy youth,
Come not within these doors! Within this roof
The enemy of all your graces lives.
Your brother—no, no brother; yet the son—
Yet not the son, I will not call him son
Of him I was about to call his father—
Hath heard your praises, and this night he means
To burn the lodging where you use to lie 23
And you within it. If he fail of that,
He will have other means to cut you off.
I overheard him and his practices. 26
This is no place, this house is but a butchery; 27
Abhor it, fear it, do not enter it.

ORLANDO
Why, whither, Adam, wouldst thou have me go?

ADAM
No matter whither, so you come not here.

ORLANDO
What, wouldst thou have me go and beg my food?
Or with a base and boist'rous sword enforce
A thievish living on the common road?
This I must do, or know not what to do;
Yet this I will not do, do how I can.
I rather will subject me to the malice
Of a diverted blood and bloody brother. 37

ADAM
But do not so. I have five hundred crowns,
The thrifty hire I sav'd under your father, 39
Which I did store to be my foster-nurse
When service should in my old limbs lie lame, 41
And unregarded age in corners thrown. 42
Take that, and He that doth the ravens feed, 43
Yea, providently caters for the sparrow, 44
Be comfort to my age! Here is the gold; [*Gives gold.*]
All this I give you. Let me be your servant.
Though I look old, yet I am strong and lusty, 47
For in my youth I never did apply
Hot and rebellious liquors in my blood,
Nor did not with unbashful forehead woo 50
The means of weakness and debility;
Therefore my age is as a lusty winter,
Frosty, but kindly. Let me go with you.
I'll do the service of a younger man
In all your business and necessities.

ORLANDO
O good old man, how well in thee appears
The constant service of the antique world, 57
When service sweat for duty, not for meed! 58
Thou art not for the fashion of these times,
Where none will sweat but for promotion,
And having that do choke their service up 61
Even with the having. It is not so with thee. 62
But, poor old man, thou prun'st a rotten tree,
That cannot so much as a blossom yield
In lieu of all thy pains and husbandry. 65
But come thy ways; we'll go along together,
And, ere we have thy youthful wages spent,
We'll light upon some settled low content. 68

ADAM
Master, go on, and I will follow thee
To the last gasp, with truth and loyalty.
From seventeen years till now almost fourscore
Here lived I, but now live here no more.

8 roynish scurvy, coarse **13 parts** good qualities **17, 18 his brother** i.e., Oliver **18 he** i.e., Orlando **19 suddenly** speedily **20 inquisition** inquiry. **quail** fail, slacken **21 again** back

II.iii. Location: Before Oliver's house.
3 memory memorial **7 fond to** foolish as to **8 bonny priser** sturdy champion or prize fighter. **humorous** temperamental **12 No more** no better **23 use** are accustomed

26 practices plots **27 place** residence, dwelling. **butchery** slaughterhouse **37 diverted blood** kinship diverted from the natural source **39 thrifty . . . sav'd** wages I thriftily saved **41 lie lame** i.e., be performed only lamely **42 thrown** be thrown **43–44 He . . . sparrow** (See Luke 12:6, 22–24, Psalms 147:9, Job 38:41, etc.) **47 lusty** vigorous **50 unbashful forehead** shameless countenance **57 constant** faithful **58 sweat** sweated. **meed** reward **61–62 do choke . . . having** i.e., cease serving once they have gained promotion **65 lieu of** return for **68 low content** lowly contented state

At seventeen years many their fortunes seek,
But at fourscore it is too late a week; 74
Yet fortune cannot recompense me better
Than to die well and not my master's debtor.
Exeunt.

SCENE IV

Enter Rosalind for Ganymede, Celia for Aliena, and Clown, alias Touchstone.

ROSALIND O Jupiter, how weary are my spirits!

TOUCHSTONE I care not for my spirits, if my legs were not weary.

ROSALIND I could find in my heart to disgrace my man's
apparel and to cry like a woman; but I must comfort
the weaker vessel, as doublet and hose ought to show 6
itself courageous to petticoat. Therefore courage, good
Aliena!

CELIA I pray you, bear with me; I cannot go no further.

TOUCHSTONE For my part, I had rather bear with you
than bear you; yet I should bear no cross if I did bear 11
you, for I think you have no money in your purse.

ROSALIND Well, this is the forest of Arden.

TOUCHSTONE Ay, now am I in Arden, the more fool I. When I was at home, I was in a better place, but travelers must be content.

Enter Corin and Silvius.

ROSALIND Ay, be so, good Touchstone.—Look you who comes here, a young man and an old in solemn talk. [*They stand aside and listen.*]

CORIN
That is the way to make her scorn you still. 20

SILVIUS
O Corin, that thou knew'st how I do love her!

CORIN
I partly guess, for I have lov'd ere now.

SILVIUS
No, Corin, being old, thou canst not guess,
Though in thy youth thou wast as true a lover
As ever sigh'd upon a midnight pillow.
But if thy love were ever like to mine—
As sure I think did never man love so—
How many actions most ridiculous
Hast thou been drawn to by thy fantasy? 29

CORIN
Into a thousand that I have forgotten.

SILVIUS
O, thou didst then never love so heartily!
If thou remember'st not the slightest folly
That ever love did make thee run into,
Thou hast not lov'd.
Or if thou hast not sat as I do now,
Wearing thy hearer in thy mistress' praise, 36
Thou hast not lov'd.
Or if thou hast not broke from company
Abruptly, as my passion now makes me,
Thou has not lov'd.
O Phebe, Phebe, Phebe! *Exit.*

ROSALIND
Alas, poor shepherd! Searching of thy wound, 42
I have by hard adventure found mine own.

TOUCHSTONE And I mine. I remember, when I was in
love I broke my sword upon a stone and bid him take
that for coming a-night to Jane Smile; and I remember 46
the kissing of her batler and the cow's dugs that her 47
pretty chopt hands had milk'd; and I remember the 48
wooing of a peascod instead of her, from whom I took 49
two cods and, giving her them again, said with weep- 50
ing tears, "Wear these for my sake." We that are true
lovers run into strange capers; but as all is mortal in 52
nature, so is all nature in love mortal in folly. 53

ROSALIND Thou speak'st wiser than thou art ware of. 54

TOUCHSTONE Nay, I shall ne'er be ware of mine own wit till I break my shins against it.

ROSALIND
Jove, Jove! This shepherd's passion
Is much upon my fashion. 58

TOUCHSTONE
And mine; but it grows something stale with me. 59

CELIA
I pray you, one of you question yond man
If he for gold will give us any food.
I faint almost to death.

TOUCHSTONE Holla, you clown! 62

ROSALIND
Peace, fool! He's not thy kinsman.

CORIN Who calls?

TOUCHSTONE
Your betters, sir.

CORIN Else are they very wretched.

ROSALIND
Peace, I say.—Good even to you, friend.

CORIN
And to you, gentle sir, and to you all.

ROSALIND
I prithee, shepherd, if that love or gold
Can in this desert place buy entertainment, 68
Bring us where we may rest ourselves and feed.
Here's a young maid with travel much oppress'd,
And faints for succor.

CORIN Fair sir, I pity her 71
And wish, for her sake more than for mine own,
My fortunes were more able to relieve her;
But I am shepherd to another man
And do not shear the fleeces that I graze. 75

74 week i.e., time

II.iv. Location: The Forest of Arden.
6 weaker vessel i.e., woman. (See 1 Peter 3:7.) **doublet and hose** close-fitting jacket and breeches; typical male attire **11 cross** (1) burden (2) coin having on it a figure of a cross **29 fantasy** love-imaginings

36 Wearing wearying **42 Searching of** probing **46 a-night** by night **47 batler** club or bat for beating clothes in process of washing **48 chopt** chapped **49 peascod** pea pod. (Regarded as a lucky gift by rustic lovers.) **whom** i.e., which (referring to the whole pea plant) **50 her** i.e., the pea plant **52 mortal** subject to death **53 mortal** humanly frail **54 ware** aware **58 upon** after, according to **59 something** somewhat **62 clown** yokel. (But Rosalind uses the word as it applies to Touchstone.) **68 desert** uninhabited. **entertainment** accommodation **71 for succor** for lack of succor, i.e., food **75 do . . . fleeces** i.e., do not obtain the profits from the flock

My master is of churlish disposition,
And little recks to find the way to heaven
By doing deeds of hospitality.
Besides, his cote, his flocks, and bounds of feed
Are now on sale, and at our sheepcote now,
By reason of his absence, there is nothing
That you will feed on. But what is, come see,
And in my voice most welcome shall you be.

ROSALIND
What is he that shall buy his flock and pasture?

CORIN
That young swain that you saw here but erewhile,
That little cares for buying any thing.

ROSALIND
I pray thee, if it stand with honesty,
Buy thou the cottage, pasture, and the flock,
And thou shalt have to pay for it of us.

CELIA
And we will mend thy wages. I like this place,
And willingly could waste my time in it.

CORIN
Assuredly the thing is to be sold.
Go with me. If you like upon report
The soil, the profit, and this kind of life,
I will your very faithful feeder be
And buy it with your gold right suddenly. *Exeunt.*

SCENE V

Enter Amiens, Jaques, and others.

Song.

[AMIENS]
Under the greenwood tree
Who loves to lie with me,
And turn his merry note
Unto the sweet bird's throat,
Come hither, come hither, come hither.
Here shall he see
No enemy
But winter and rough weather.

JAQUES More, more, I prithee, more.

AMIENS It will make you melancholy, Monsieur Jaques.

JAQUES I thank it. More, I prithee, more. I can suck melancholy out of a song, as a weasel sucks eggs. More, I prithee, more.

AMIENS My voice is ragged. I know I cannot please you.

JAQUES I do not desire you to please me; I do desire you to sing. Come, more, another stanzo. Call you 'em stanzos?

AMIENS What you will, Monsieur Jaques.

JAQUES Nay, I care not for their names; they owe me nothing. Will you sing?

AMIENS More at your request than to please myself.

JAQUES Well then, if ever I thank any man, I'll thank you; but that they call compliment is like th' encounter of two dog-apes, and when a man thanks me heartily, methinks I have given him a penny and he renders me the beggarly thanks. Come, sing; and you that will not, hold your tongues.

AMIENS Well, I'll end the song. Sirs, cover the while; the Duke will drink under this tree. He hath been all this day to look you.

[*They start to set out a light repast at a table.*]

JAQUES And I have been all this day to avoid him. He is too disputable for my company. I think of as many matters as he, but I give heaven thanks and make no boast of them. Come, warble, come.

Song.

Who doth ambition shun *All together here.*
And loves to live i' th' sun,
Seeking the food he eats
And pleas'd with what he gets,
Come hither, come hither, come hither.
Here shall he see
No enemy
But winter and rough weather.

JAQUES I'll give you a verse to this note that I made yesterday in despite of my invention.

AMIENS And I'll sing it. [*Takes verse.*] Thus it goes:

If it do come to pass
That any man turn ass,
Leaving his wealth and ease,
A stubborn will to please,
Ducdame, ducdame, ducdame.
Here shall he see
Gross fools as he,
An if he will come to me.

What's that "ducdame"?

JAQUES 'Tis a Greek invocation, to call fools into a circle. I'll go sleep, if I can; if I cannot, I'll rail against all the first-born of Egypt.

AMIENS And I'll go seek the Duke. His banquet is prepar'd. *Exeunt* [*severally*].

76 churlish niggardly, miserly **77 recks** cares, reckons **79 cote** cottage. **bounds of feed** limits within which he has the right of pasturage **83 in my voice** insofar as I have authority to speak **85 erewhile** a short time since **87 stand** be consistent **89 have to pay** have the money **90 mend** improve **91 waste** spend **95 feeder** servant

II.v. Location: The forest.
3 turn attune, adopt

19–20 they owe me nothing (Jaques speaks of *names* as of something valuable only when written as signatures to a bond of indebtedness.) **23 compliment** formal politeness **24 dog-apes** dog-faced baboons **26 beggarly** effusive, like the thanks of a beggar **28 cover the while** spread the cloth for a meal meanwhile **30 to look** looking for **32 disputable** inclined to dispute **36 live i' th' sun** dwell in the open air **43 note** tune **44 in . . . invention** although I lack imagination; or, without even using my imagination **50 Ducdame** (Unexplained. One possible suggestion is that it is a corruption of the gypsy words dukrā mē, meaning "I foretell," "I tell fortunes or prophesy"; therefore, as the call of a gypsy fortuneteller at fairs, it is a "Greek" [or sharper's] invocation. This also renders the allusion to the *first-born of Egypt* intelligible, since the first-born Duke is banished and in the condition of a gypsy.) **58 banquet** wine and dessert after dinner. (This repast, now prepared on stage, seemingly is to remain there during the short following scene.)

SCENE VI

Enter Orlando and Adam.

ADAM Dear master, I can go no further. O, I die for food! Here lie I down, and measure out my grave. Farewell, kind master. [*Lies down.*]

ORLANDO Why, how now, Adam? No greater heart in thee? Live a little; comfort a little; cheer thyself a little. If this uncouth forest yield any thing savage, I will either be food for it or bring it for food to thee. Thy conceit is nearer death than thy powers. For my sake be comfortable; hold death awhile at the arm's end. I will here be with thee presently, and if I bring thee not something to eat, I will give thee leave to die; but if thou diest before I come, thou art a mocker of my labor. Well said! Thou look'st cheerly, and I'll be with thee quickly. Yet thou liest in the bleak air. Come, I will bear thee to some shelter; and thou shalt not die for lack of a dinner, if there live any thing in this desert. [*Picks up Adam.*] Cheerly, good Adam! *Exeunt.*

SCENE VII

Enter Duke Senior, and Lords, like outlaws.

DUKE SENIOR
I think he be transform'd into a beast,
For I can nowhere find him like a man.

FIRST LORD
My lord, he is but even now gone hence.
Here was he merry, hearing of a song.

DUKE SENIOR
If he, compact of jars, grow musical,
We shall have shortly discord in the spheres.
Go, seek him, tell him I would speak with him.

Enter Jaques.

FIRST LORD
He saves my labor by his own approach.

DUKE SENIOR
Why, how now, monsieur, what a life is this,
That your poor friends must woo your company?
What, you look merrily!

JAQUES
A fool, a fool! I met a fool i' th' forest,
A motley fool. A miserable world!
As I do live by food, I met a fool,
Who laid him down and bask'd him in the sun,
And rail'd on Lady Fortune in good terms,
In good set terms, and yet a motley fool.
"Good morrow, fool," quoth I. "No, sir," quoth he,
"Call me not fool till heaven hath sent me fortune."
And then he drew a dial from his poke,
And, looking on it with lack-luster eye,
Says very wisely, "It is ten o'clock.
Thus we may see," quoth he, "how the world wags.
'Tis but an hour ago since it was nine,
And after one hour more 'twill be eleven;
And so, from hour to hour, we ripe and ripe,
And then, from hour to hour, we rot and rot;
And thereby hangs a tale." When I did hear
The motley fool thus moral on the time,
My lungs began to crow like chanticleer,
That fools should be so deep-contemplative,
And I did laugh sans intermission
An hour by his dial. O noble fool!
A worthy fool! Motley's the only wear.

DUKE SENIOR
What fool is this?

JAQUES
O worthy fool! One that hath been a courtier,
And says, if ladies be but young and fair,
They have the gift to know it. And in his brain,
Which is as dry as the remainder biscuit
After a voyage, he hath strange places cramm'd
With observation, the which he vents
In mangled forms. O that I were a fool!
I am ambitious for a motley coat.

DUKE SENIOR
Thou shalt have one.

JAQUES It is my only suit,
Provided that you weed your better judgments
Of all opinion that grows rank in them
That I am wise. I must have liberty
Withal, as large a charter as the wind,
To blow on whom I please, for so fools have.
And they that are most galled with my folly,
They most must laugh. And why, sir, must they so?
The "why" is plain as way to parish church:
He that a fool doth very wisely hit
Doth very foolishly, although he smart,
Not to seem senseless of the bob. If not,
The wise man's folly is anatomiz'd
Even by the squand'ring glances of the fool.
Invest me in my motley; give me leave
To speak my mind, and I will through and through
Cleanse the foul body of th' infected world,
If they will patiently receive my medicine.

DUKE SENIOR
Fie on thee! I can tell what thou wouldst do.

JAQUES
What, for a counter, would I do but good?

II.vi. Location: The forest. The scene is continuous.
6 uncouth strange, wild **8 conceit** thought, imagination **9 comfortable** cheerful

II.vii. Location: The forest; the scene is continuous. (A light repast, set out for the Duke in II.v, seemingly has remained on stage during II.vi.)
5 compact of jars composed of discords **6 spheres** (Refers to the heavenly music supposed to be produced by the revolving concentric spheres of the Ptolemaic solar system.) **13 motley** wearing motley, the parti-colored dress of the clown or professional jester

19 Call . . . fortune (An allusion to the proverb, "Fortune favors fools.") **20 dial** portable sundial. **poke** pocket **29 moral** moralize **30 crow** i.e., laugh merrily. **chanticleer** a rooster **32 sans** without **34 only wear** only thing worth wearing **39 dry** (A quality that supposedly improved the memory.) **44 suit** (1) request (2) suit of clothes **48 charter** license, privilege **50 galled** chafed, rubbed on a sore spot **53 He . . . hit** he whom a fool wittily attacks **54 Doth** acts. **smart** feels the sting **55 senseless of the bob** unaware of the jibe, taunt. **If not** otherwise **56 anatomiz'd** dissected, revealed openly **57 squand'ring glances** random hits **63 counter** (Type of a thing of no intrinsic value, a metal disk used in counting.)

DUKE SENIOR
Most mischievous foul sin, in chiding sin.
For thou thyself hast been a libertine,
As sensual as the brutish sting itself;
And all th' embossed sores and headed evils,
That thou with license of free foot hast caught,
Wouldst thou disgorge into the general world.

JAQUES
Why, who cries out on pride
That can therein tax any private party?
Doth it not flow as hugely as the sea,
Till that the weary very means do ebb?
What woman in the city do I name,
When that I say the city-woman bears
The cost of princes on unworthy shoulders?
Who can come in and say that I mean her,
When such a one as she, such is her neighbor?
Or what is he of basest function
That says his bravery is not on my cost,
Thinking that I mean him, but therein suits
His folly to the mettle of my speech?
There then; how then? What then? Let me see wherein
My tongue hath wrong'd him. If it do him right,
Then he hath wrong'd himself. If he be free,
Why then my taxing like a wild goose flies,
Unclaim'd of any man.—But who comes here?

Enter Orlando [*with his sword drawn*].

ORLANDO
Forbear, and eat no more.

JAQUES
Why, I have eat none yet.

ORLANDO
Nor shalt not, till necessity be serv'd.

JAQUES
Of what kind should this cock come of?

DUKE SENIOR
Art thou thus bolden'd, man, by thy distress,
Or else a rude despiser of good manners,
That in civility thou seem'st so empty?

ORLANDO
You touch'd my vein at first. The thorny point
Of bare distress hath ta'en from me the show
Of smooth civility; yet am I inland bred,
And know some nurture. But forbear, I say.
He dies that touches any of this fruit
Till I and my affairs are answered.

JAQUES
An you will not be answer'd with reason, I must die.

DUKE SENIOR
What would you have? Your gentleness shall force
More than your force move us to gentleness.

ORLANDO
I almost die for food, and let me have it!

DUKE SENIOR
Sit down and feed, and welcome to our table.

ORLANDO
Speak you so gently? Pardon me, I pray you.
I thought that all things had been savage here,
And therefore put I on the countenance
Of stern commandment. But whate'er you are
That in this desert inaccessible,
Under the shade of melancholy boughs,
Lose and neglect the creeping hours of time;
If ever you have look'd on better days,
If ever been where bells have knoll'd to church,
If ever sat at any good man's feast,
If ever from your eyelids wip'd a tear
And know what 'tis to pity and be pitied,
Let gentleness my strong enforcement be,
In the which hope I blush, and hide my sword.
[*Puts up his sword.*]

DUKE SENIOR
True is it that we have seen better days,
And have with holy bell been knoll'd to church,
And sat at good men's feasts, and wip'd our eyes
Of drops that sacred pity hath engend'red;
And therefore sit you down in gentleness,
And take upon command what help we have
That to your wanting may be minist'red.

ORLANDO
Then but forbear your food a little while,
Whiles, like a doe, I go to find my fawn
And give it food. There is an old poor man,
Who after me hath many a weary step
Limp'd in pure love. Till he be first suffic'd,
Oppress'd with two weak evils, age and hunger,
I will not touch a bit.

DUKE SENIOR
Go find him out,
And we will nothing waste till you return.

ORLANDO
I thank ye; and be blest for your good comfort!
[*Exit.*]

DUKE SENIOR
Thou seest we are not all alone unhappy.
This wide and universal theatre
Presents more woeful pageants than the scene
Wherein we play in.

JAQUES
All the world's a stage,
And all the men and women merely players.
They have their exits and their entrances,
And one man in his time plays many parts,
His acts being seven ages. At first the infant,
Mewling and puking in the nurse's arms.
Then the whining school-boy, with his satchel
And shining morning face, creeping like snail

66 brutish sting carnal impulse, appetite **67 embossed** swollen, tumid. **headed evils** diseases and sores that have come to a head **68 license . . . foot** the licentious freedom of a libertine **70 pride** i.e., extravagance **71 tax** blame, accuse. **any private party** i.e., only some individual **73 Till . . . ebb** until the ostentation finally subsides, having exhausted what fed it (?). (There are many conjectures, such as *wearer's very means.*) **75 the city-woman** the typical citizen's wife **76 The cost of princes** i.e., clothes rich enough to adorn a prince **79 basest function** lowest position in society **80 bravery** splendor, finery. **on my cost** at my expense, i.e., guilty of what I am criticizing **81 suits** (1) fits (2) dresses **82 mettle** substance, contents **84 right** justice. (I.e., if I have described him accurately.) **85 wrong'd himself** (by calling attention to the accuracy of my description). **free** i.e., blameless **88 eat** eaten. (Pronounced *et.*) **94 vein** condition, situation. **at first** i.e., in what you first suggested **96 inland bred** i.e., raised in civilized society, in the center of civilization rather than on the outskirts **97 nurture** education, training **99 answered** satisfied

113 knoll'd rung **124 upon command** for the asking **131 weak** causing weakness **143 Mewling** crying

Unwillingly to school. And then the lover,
Sighing like furnace, with a woeful ballad
Made to his mistress' eyebrow. Then a soldier,
Full of strange oaths and bearded like the pard,
Jealous in honor, sudden and quick in quarrel,
Seeking the bubble reputation
Even in the cannon's mouth. And then the justice,
In fair round belly with good capon lin'd,
With eyes severe and beard of formal cut,
Full of wise saws and modern instances;
And so he plays his part. The sixth age shifts
Into the lean and slipper'd pantaloon,
With spectacles on nose and pouch on side,
His youthful hose, well sav'd, a world too wide
For his shrunk shank; and his big manly voice,
Turning again toward childish treble, pipes
And whistles in his sound. Last scene of all,
That ends this strange eventful history,
Is second childishness and mere oblivion,
Sans teeth, sans eyes, sans taste, sans everything.

Enter Orlando, with Adam.

DUKE SENIOR
Welcome. Set down your venerable burden
And let him feed.

ORLANDO
I thank you most for him. *[Sets down Adam.]*

ADAM
So had you need.
I scarce can speak to thank you for myself.

DUKE SENIOR
Welcome; fall to. I will not trouble you
As yet, to question you about your fortunes.
Give us some music; and, good cousin, sing.
[They eat, while Orlando and Duke Senior converse apart.]

Song.

[AMIENS]
Blow, blow, thou winter wind,
Thou art not so unkind
As man's ingratitude;
Thy tooth is not so keen,
Because thou art not seen,
Although thy breath be rude.
Heigh-ho, sing, heigh-ho, unto the green holly.
Most friendship is feigning, most loving mere folly.
Then, heigh-ho, the holly!
This life is most jolly.

Freeze, freeze, thou bitter sky,
That dost not bite so nigh
As benefits forgot;
Though thou the waters warp,
Thy sting is not so sharp
As friend rememb'red not.
Heigh-ho, sing, etc.

DUKE SENIOR
If that you were the good Sir Rowland's son,
As you have whisper'd faithfully you were,
And as mine eye doth his effigies witness
Most truly limn'd and living in your face,
Be truly welcome hither. I am the Duke
That lov'd your father. The residue of your fortune,
Go to my cave and tell me. Good old man,
Thou art right welcome as thy master is.
Support him by the arm. Give me your hand,
And let me all your fortunes understand. *Exeunt.*

ACT III • SCENE I

Enter Duke [Frederick], Lords, and Oliver.

DUKE FREDERICK
Not see him since? Sir, sir, that cannot be.
But were I not the better part made mercy,
I should not seek an absent argument
Of my revenge, thou present. But look to it:
Find out thy brother, wheresoe'er he is;
Seek him with candle; bring him dead or living
Within this twelvemonth, or turn thou no more
To seek a living in our territory.
Thy lands and all things that thou dost call thine
Worth seizure do we seize into our hands
Till thou canst quit thee by thy brother's mouth
Of what we think against thee.

OLIVER
O that your Highness knew my heart in this!
I never lov'd my brother in my life.

DUKE FREDERICK
More villain thou. Well, push him out of doors,
And let my officers of such a nature
Make an extent upon his house and lands.
Do this expediently and turn him going. *Exeunt.*

SCENE II

Enter Orlando [with a paper].

ORLANDO
Hang there, my verse, in witness of my love;
And thou, thrice-crownèd queen of night, survey

149 bearded . . . pard having bristling mustaches like the panther's or leopard's whiskers **150 Jealous in honor** full of emulation in matters of honor **153 capon** (Probably alludes to the widespread practice of bribing the judge with a capon.) **155 saws** sayings. **modern instances** commonplace illustrations **157 pantaloon** ridiculous, enfeebled old man. (A stock type in Italian comedy.) **162 his** its **179 holly** (An emblem of mirth.) **186 warp** freeze

192 effigies likeness, portrait **193 limn'd** painted, portrayed **199 s.d. Exeunt** (The table must be removed at this point.)

III.i. Location: Duke Frederick's palace.
2 better greater. **made** made of **3 argument** subject. (I.e., I would not seek revenge on Orlando.) **4 thou present** i.e., with you here to feed my revenge **6 Seek . . . candle** (See Luke 15:8.) **7 turn** return **11 quit** acquit. **by . . . mouth** i.e., by Orlando's direct testimony **16 of such a nature** i.e., who attend to such duties **17 extent** seizure of land in execution of a writ **18 expediently** expeditiously. **turn him going** send him packing

III.ii. Location: The forest.
2 thrice-crownèd queen i.e., Diana in the three aspects of her divinity: as Luna or Cynthia, goddess of the moon; as Diana, goddess on earth; and as Hecate or Proserpina, goddess in the lower world

With thy chaste eye, from thy pale sphere above,
Thy huntress' name that my full life doth sway.
O Rosalind! These trees shall be my books,
And in their barks my thoughts I'll character,
That every eye which in this forest looks
Shall see thy virtue witness'd everywhere.
Run, run, Orlando, carve on every tree
The fair, the chaste, and unexpressive she. *Exit.*

Enter Corin and [Touchstone the] Clown.

CORIN And how like you this shepherd's life, Master Touchstone?

TOUCHSTONE Truly, shepherd, in respect of itself, it is a good life; but in respect that it is a shepherd's life, it is naught. In respect that it is solitary, I like it very well; but in respect that it is private, it is a very vile life. Now, in respect it is in the fields, it pleaseth me well; but in respect it is not in the court, it is tedious. As it is a spare life, look you, it fits my humor well; but as there is no more plenty in it, it goes much against my stomach. Hast any philosophy in thee, shepherd?

CORIN No more but that I know the more one sickens the worse at ease he is; and that he that wants money, means, and content is without three good friends; that the property of rain is to wet and fire to burn; that good pasture makes fat sheep, and that a great cause of the night is lack of the sun; that he that hath learn'd no wit by nature nor art may complain of good breeding, or comes of a very dull kindred.

TOUCHSTONE Such a one is a natural philosopher. Wast ever in court, shepherd?

CORIN No, truly.

TOUCHSTONE Then thou art damn'd.

CORIN Nay, I hope.

TOUCHSTONE Truly, thou art damn'd, like an ill-roasted egg all on one side.

CORIN For not being at court? Your reason.

TOUCHSTONE Why, if thou never wast at court, thou never saw'st good manners; if thou never saw'st good manners, then thy manners must be wicked; and wickedness is sin, and sin is damnation. Thou art in a parlous state, shepherd.

CORIN Not a whit, Touchstone. Those that are good manners at the court are as ridiculous in the country as the behavior of the country is most mockable at the court. You told me you salute not at the court but you kiss your hands; that courtesy would be uncleanly, if courtiers were shepherds.

TOUCHSTONE Instance, briefly; come, instance.

CORIN Why, we are still handling our ewes, and their fells, you know, are greasy.

TOUCHSTONE Why, do not your courtier's hands sweat? And is not the grease of a mutton as wholesome as the sweat of a man? Shallow, shallow. A better instance, I say; come.

CORIN Besides, our hands are hard.

TOUCHSTONE Your lips will feel them the sooner. Shallow again. A more sounder instance, come.

CORIN And they are often tarr'd over with the surgery of our sheep; and would you have us kiss tar? The courtier's hands are perfum'd with civet.

TOUCHSTONE Most shallow man! Thou worms-meat, in respect of a good piece of flesh indeed! Learn of the wise, and perpend: civet is of a baser birth than tar, the very uncleanly flux of a cat. Mend the instance, shepherd.

CORIN You have too courtly a wit for me. I'll rest.

TOUCHSTONE Wilt thou rest damn'd? God help thee, shallow man! God make incision in thee! Thou art raw.

CORIN Sir, I am a true laborer: I earn that I eat, get that I wear, owe no man hate, envy no man's happiness, glad of other men's good, content with my harm, and the greatest of my pride is to see my ewes graze and my lambs suck.

TOUCHSTONE That is another simple sin in you, to bring the ewes and the rams together and to offer to get your living by the copulation of cattle; to be bawd to a bell-wether, and to betray a she-lamb of a twelve-month to a crooked-pated old cuckoldly ram, out of all reasonable match. If thou beest not damn'd for this, the devil himself will have no shepherds; I cannot see else how thou shouldst scape.

CORIN Here comes young Master Ganymede, my new mistress's brother.

Enter Rosalind [with a paper, reading].

ROSALIND

"From the east to western Ind,
No jewel is like Rosalind.
Her worth, being mounted on the wind,
Through all the world bears Rosalind.
All the pictures fairest lin'd
Are but black to Rosalind.
Let no face be kept in mind
But the fair of Rosalind."

TOUCHSTONE I'll rhyme you so eight years together, dinners and suppers and sleeping-hours excepted. It is the right butter-women's rank to market.

ROSALIND Out, fool!

TOUCHSTONE For a taste:

If a hart do lack a hind,
Let him seek out Rosalind.
If the cat will after kind,
So be sure will Rosalind.

4 Thy huntress' i.e., Rosalind's, who is here thought of as a chaste huntress accompanying Diana, patroness of the hunt **6 character** inscribe **10 unexpressive** inexpressible **13 in respect of itself** considered in and for itself **28 wit** wisdom. **art** study **28–29 complain . . . breeding** lament the lack of good breeding **39, 40 manners** (1) etiquette (2) morals **42 parlous** perilous **46–47 but you kiss** without kissing **49 Instance** proof **50 still** always **51 fells** skins with the wool, or fleeces

59 tarr'd over anointed with tar on their cuts and sores **61 civet** (A perfume derived from the civet cat, as Touchstone points out.) **62 worms-meat** food for worms, i.e., subject to decay of the flesh **63 respect of** comparison with **64 perpend** reflect, consider **65 flux** secretion. **Mend** improve **69 incision** cutting for the purpose of letting blood. (Here, to let out folly.) **70 raw** inexperienced (with a play on *sore,* requiring surgery) **71 that** what **73 content . . . harm** patient with my ill fortune **77 offer** undertake **78 cattle** livestock **80 crooked-pated** with crooked horns. **cuckoldly** i.e., horned like a cuckold. **out of** contrary to **90 lin'd** drawn **91 black** dark-complexioned. (Thought to be ugly.) **94 together** without stop **95–96 It is . . . market** i.e., the rhymes, all alike, follow each other precisely like a line of butter-women or dairy-women jogging along to market **101 after kind** follow its natural instinct

Wint'red garments must be lin'd, 103
So must slender Rosalind.
They that reap must sheaf and bind;
Then to cart with Rosalind. 106
Sweetest nut hath sourest rind,
Such a nut is Rosalind.
He that sweetest rose will find
Must find love's prick and Rosalind. 110

This is the very false gallop of verses. Why do you 111
infect yourself with them?

ROSALIND Peace, you dull fool! I found them on a tree.

TOUCHSTONE Truly, the tree yields bad fruit.

ROSALIND I'll graff it with you, and then I shall graff it 115
with a medlar. Then it will be the earliest fruit i' th' 116
country; for you'll be rotten ere you be half ripe, and
that's the right virtue of the medlar. 118

TOUCHSTONE You have said; but whether wisely or no, let the forest judge.

Enter Celia, with a writing.

ROSALIND Peace! Here comes my sister, reading. Stand aside.

CELIA [*Reads*]

"Why should this a desert be?
For it is unpeopled? No;
Tongues I'll hang on every tree,
That shall civil sayings show: 126
Some, how brief the life of man
Runs his erring pilgrimage, 128
That the stretching of a span 129
Buckles in his sum of age; 130
Some, of violated vows
'Twixt the souls of friend and friend;
But upon the fairest boughs,
Or at every sentence end,
Will I "Rosalinda" write,
Teaching all that read to know
The quintessence of every sprite 137
Heaven would in little show. 138
Therefore Heaven Nature charg'd
That one body should be fill'd
With all graces wide-enlarg'd. 141
Nature presently distill'd
Helen's cheek, but not her heart, 143
Cleopatra's majesty,
Atalanta's better part, 145
Sad Lucretia's modesty. 146
Thus Rosalind of many parts
By heavenly synod was devis'd, 148
Of many faces, eyes, and hearts,
To have the touches dearest priz'd. 150
Heaven would that she these gifts should have,
And I to live and die her slave."

ROSALIND O most gentle Jupiter, what tedious homily 153
of love have you wearied your parishioners withal,
and never cried "Have patience, good people!"

CELIA How now? Back, friends. Shepherd, go off a lit- 156
tle. Go with him, sirrah. 157

TOUCHSTONE Come, shepherd, let us make an honor-
able retreat; though not with bag and baggage, yet 159
with scrip and scrippage. *Exit* [*with Corin*]. 160

CELIA Didst thou hear these verses?

ROSALIND O, yes, I heard them all, and more too; for some of them had in them more feet than the verses would bear.

CELIA That's no matter. The feet might bear the verses.

ROSALIND Ay, but the feet were lame and could not
bear themselves without the verse, and therefore stood 167
lamely in the verse.

CELIA But didst thou hear without wondering how thy name should be hang'd and carv'd upon these trees?

ROSALIND I was seven of the nine days out of the won- 171
der before you came; for look here what I found on a 172
palm-tree. I was never so berhym'd since Pythagoras' 173
time, that I was an Irish rat, which I can hardly re- 174
member.

CELIA Trow you who hath done this? 176

ROSALIND Is it a man?

CELIA And a chain, that you once wore, about his neck. 178
Change you color?

ROSALIND I prithee, who?

CELIA O Lord, Lord, it is a hard matter for friends to 181
meet; but mountains may be remov'd with earth- 182
quakes, and so encounter. 183

ROSALIND Nay, but who is it?

CELIA Is it possible?

ROSALIND Nay, I prithee now with most petitionary vehemence, tell me who it is.

CELIA O wonderful, wonderful, and most wonderful
wonderful! And yet again wonderful, and after that,
out of all hooping! 190

ROSALIND Good my complexion! Dost thou think, 191
though I am caparison'd like a man, I have a doublet 192
and hose in my disposition? One inch of delay more

103 Wint'red prepared for winter **106 to cart** (1) onto the harvest cart (2) onto the cart used to carry delinquent women through the streets, exposing them to public ridicule **110 prick** thorn. (With bawdy suggestion, as elsewhere in Touchstone's verses: *will after kind*, etc.) **111 false gallop** canter **115 graff** graft. **you** (with pun on *yew*) **116 medlar** a fruit like a small brown-skinned apple which is eaten when it starts to decay (with a pun on *meddler*) **118 right virtue** true quality **126 civil sayings** maxims of civilized life **128 his erring** its wandering **129 That . . . span** so that the distance across an open-spread hand **130 Buckles in** encompasses **137 quintessence** highest perfection. (Literally, the fifth essence or element of the medieval alchemists, purer even than fire.) **sprite** spirit **138 in little** in small space, i.e., in one person, Rosalind. (Alludes probably to the idea of man as the microcosm; the heavenly bodies would be composed of quintessence, which is here thought of as the supreme quality of a person.) **141 wide-enlarg'd** i.e., spread through the world until they are concentrated in Rosalind **143 Helen's . . . heart** i.e., the beauty of Helen of Troy but not her false heart **145 Atalanta's better part** i.e., her fleetness of foot, not her scornfulness and greed. (She refused to marry any man who was unable to defeat her in a foot-race, and, when challenged by Hippomenes, lost to him because Hippomenes dropped in her way three apples of the Hesperides.)

146 Lucretia honorable Roman lady raped by Tarquin (whose story Shakespeare tells in *The Rape of Lucrece*) **148 synod** assembly **150 touches** traits **153 Jupiter** (Often emended to *pulpiter*.) **156 Back** i.e., move back, away. (Addressed to Corin and Touchstone.) **157 sirrah** (Form of address to inferiors; here, Touchstone.) **159 bag and baggage** i.e., equipment appropriate to a retreating army **160 scrip and scrippage** shepherd's pouch and its contents **167 without** (1) without the help of (2) outside **171–172 seven . . . wonder** (A reference to the common phrase "a nine days' wonder.") **173 Pythagoras** Greek philosopher credited with the doctrine of the transmigration of souls **174 that** when. **Irish rat** (Refers to a current belief that Irish enchanters could rhyme rats and other animals to death.) **176 Trow you** have you any idea **178 And a chain** i.e., and with a chain **181–183 friends . . . encounter** (A playful inversion of the proverb, "Friends may meet, but mountains never greet." Celia appears to be teasing Rosalind's eagerness to meet Orlando.) **remov'd with** moved by **190 out . . . hooping** beyond all whooping, i.e., power to utter **191 Good my complexion** O my (feminine) temperament, my woman's curiosity **192 caparison'd** bedecked. (Usually said of a horse.)

is a South-sea of discovery. I prithee, tell me who is it quickly, and speak apace. I would thou couldst stammer, that thou mightst pour this conceal'd man out of thy mouth, as wine comes out of a narrow-mouth'd bottle, either too much at once, or none at all. I prithee, take the cork out of thy mouth that I may drink thy tidings.

CELIA So you may put a man in your belly.

ROSALIND Is he of God's making? What manner of man? Is his head worth a hat, or his chin worth a beard?

CELIA Nay, he hath but a little beard.

ROSALIND Why, God will send more, if the man will be thankful. Let me stay the growth of his beard, if thou delay me not the knowledge of his chin.

CELIA It is young Orlando, that tripp'd up the wrestler's heels and your heart both in an instant.

ROSALIND Nay, but the devil take mocking. Speak sad brow and true maid.

CELIA I' faith, coz, 'tis he.

ROSALIND Orlando?

CELIA Orlando.

ROSALIND Alas the day, what shall I do with my doublet and hose? What did he when thou saw'st him? What said he? How look'd he? Wherein went he? What makes he here? Did he ask for me? Where remains he? How parted he with thee? And when shalt thou see him again? Answer me in one word.

CELIA You must borrow me Gargantua's mouth first; 'tis a word too great for any mouth of this age's size. To say ay and no to these particulars is more than to answer in a catechism.

ROSALIND But doth he know that I am in this forest and in man's apparel? Looks he as freshly as he did the day he wrestled?

CELIA It is as easy to count atomies as to resolve the propositions of a lover. But take a taste of my finding him, and relish it with good observance. I found him under a tree, like a dropp'd acorn.

ROSALIND It may well be call'd Jove's tree, when it drops forth such fruit.

CELIA Give me audience, good madam.

ROSALIND Proceed.

CELIA There lay he, stretch'd along, like a wounded knight.

ROSALIND Though it be pity to see such a sight, it well becomes the ground.

CELIA Cry "holla" to thy tongue, I prithee; it curvets unseasonably. He was furnish'd like a hunter.

ROSALIND O, ominous! He comes to kill my heart.

CELIA I would sing my song without a burden. Thou bring'st me out of tune.

ROSALIND Do you not know I am a woman? When I think, I must speak. Sweet, say on.

Enter Orlando and Jaques.

CELIA You bring me out.—Soft, comes he not here?

ROSALIND 'Tis he. Slink by, and note him.

[*They stand aside and listen.*]

JAQUES I thank you for your company; but, good faith, I had as lief have been myself alone.

ORLANDO And so had I; but yet, for fashion sake, I thank you too for your society.

JAQUES God buy you. Let's meet as little as we can.

ORLANDO I do desire we may be better strangers.

JAQUES I pray you, mar no more trees with writing love-songs in their barks.

ORLANDO I pray you, mar no moe of my verses with reading them ill-favoredly.

JAQUES Rosalind is your love's name?

ORLANDO Yes, just.

JAQUES I do not like her name.

ORLANDO There was no thought of pleasing you when she was christen'd.

JAQUES What stature is she of?

ORLANDO Just as high as my heart.

JAQUES You are full of pretty answers. Have you not been acquainted with goldsmiths' wives, and conn'd them out of rings?

ORLANDO Not so; but I answer you right painted cloth, from whence you have studied your questions.

JAQUES You have a nimble wit; I think 'twas made of Atalanta's heels. Will you sit down with me? And we two will rail against our mistress the world and all our misery.

ORLANDO I will chide no breather in the world but myself, against whom I know most faults.

JAQUES The worst fault you have is to be in love.

ORLANDO 'Tis a fault I will not change for your best virtue. I am weary of you.

JAQUES By my troth, I was seeking for a fool when I found you.

ORLANDO He is drown'd in the brook. Look but in, and you shall see him.

JAQUES There I shall see mine own figure.

ORLANDO Which I take to be either a fool or a cipher.

JAQUES I'll tarry no longer with you. Farewell, good Signior Love.

ORLANDO I am glad of your departure. Adieu, good Monsieur Melancholy. [*Exit Jaques.*]

ROSALIND [*Aside to Celia*] I will speak to him like a saucy lackey, and under that habit play the knave with him.—Do you hear, forester?

ORLANDO Very well. What would you?

ROSALIND I pray you, what is 't o'clock?

ORLANDO You should ask me what time o' day. There's no clock in the forest.

194 a South-sea of discovery i.e., as tedious as the long delays on exploratory voyages to the South Seas **201 belly** (1) stomach (2) womb **202 of God's making** i.e., a real man, not of his tailor's making **207 stay** wait for **211–212 sad . . . maid** seriously and truthfully **218 Wherein went he** in what clothes was he dressed **219 makes** does **222 Gargantua's mouth** (Gargantua is the giant in Rabelais who swallowed five pilgrims in a salad.) **225 catechism** catechizing **229 atomies** motes **230 propositions** questions **231 relish it** heighten its pleasant taste. **observance** attention **233 Jove's tree** the oak **240 becomes** adorns **241 holla** stop. **curvets** prances **242 furnish'd** equipped, dressed **243 heart** (with pun on *hart*) **244 burden** undersong, bass part **244–245 Thou bring'st** you put

254 God buy you God be with you, i.e., goodbye **258 moe** more **261 just** just so **268 conn'd** memorized **269 rings** (Verses or "posies" were often inscribed in rings.) **270 right** true, perfect. **painted cloth** canvas painted with pictures and mottoes (frequently scriptural), hence a ready source of commonplaces **273 Atalanta's heels** (See above, l. 145, note.) **276 breather** living being **286 cipher** (1) nonentity (2) figure **292 habit** guise

ROSALIND Then there is no true lover in the forest, else sighing every minute and groaning every hour would detect the lazy foot of Time as well as a clock.

ORLANDO And why not the swift foot of Time? Had not that been as proper?

ROSALIND By no means, sir. Time travels in divers paces with divers persons. I'll tell you who Time ambles withal, who Time trots withal, who Time gallops withal, and who he stands still withal.

ORLANDO I prithee, who doth he trot withal?

ROSALIND Marry, he trots hard with a young maid between the contract of her marriage and the day it is solemniz'd. If the interim be but a se'nnight, Time's pace is so hard that it seems the length of seven year.

ORLANDO Who ambles Time withal?

ROSALIND With a priest that lacks Latin and a rich man that hath not the gout, for the one sleeps easily because he cannot study and the other lives merrily because he feels no pain, the one lacking the burden of lean and wasteful learning, the other knowing no burden of heavy tedious penury. These Time ambles withal.

ORLANDO Who doth he gallop withal?

ROSALIND With a thief to the gallows, for though he go as softly as foot can fall, he thinks himself too soon there.

ORLANDO Who stays it still withal?

ROSALIND With lawyers in the vacation; for they sleep between term and term, and then they perceive not how Time moves.

ORLANDO Where dwell you, pretty youth?

ROSALIND With this shepherdess, my sister; here in the skirts of the forest, like fringe upon a petticoat.

ORLANDO Are you native of this place?

ROSALIND As the cony that you see dwell where she is kindled.

ORLANDO Your accent is something finer than you could purchase in so remov'd a dwelling.

ROSALIND I have been told so of many. But indeed an old religious uncle of mine taught me to speak, who was in his youth an inland man, one that knew courtship too well, for there he fell in love. I have heard him read many lectures against it, and I thank God I am not a woman, to be touch'd with so many giddy offences as he hath generally tax'd their whole sex withal.

ORLANDO Can you remember any of the principal evils that he laid to the charge of women?

ROSALIND There were none principal; they were all like one another as half-pence are, every one fault seeming monstrous till his fellow-fault came to match it.

ORLANDO I prithee, recount some of them.

ROSALIND No, I will not cast away my physic but on those that are sick. There is a man haunts the forest, that abuses our young plants with carving "Rosalind" on their barks, hangs odes upon hawthorns, and elegies on brambles, all, forsooth, deifying the name of Rosalind. If I could meet that fancy-monger, I would give him some good counsel, for he seems to have the quotidian of love upon him.

ORLANDO I am he that is so love-shak'd. I pray you, tell me your remedy.

ROSALIND There is none of my uncle's marks upon you. He taught me how to know a man in love, in which cage of rushes I am sure you are not prisoner.

ORLANDO What were his marks?

ROSALIND A lean cheek, which you have not; a blue eye and sunken, which you have not; an unquestionable spirit, which you have not; a beard neglected, which you have not—but I pardon you for that, for simply your having in beard is a younger brother's revenue. Then your hose should be ungarter'd, your bonnet unbanded, your sleeve unbutton'd, your shoe untied, and everything about you demonstrating a careless desolation. But you are no such man; you are rather point-device in your accoutrements, as loving yourself, than seeming the lover of any other.

ORLANDO Fair youth, I would I could make thee believe I love.

ROSALIND Me believe it? You may as soon make her that you love believe it, which, I warrant, she is apter to do than to confess she does. That is one of the points in the which women still give the lie to their consciences. But, in good sooth, are you he that hangs the verses on the trees, wherein Rosalind is so admir'd?

ORLANDO I swear to thee, youth, by the white hand of Rosalind, I am that he, that unfortunate he.

ROSALIND But are you so much in love as your rhymes speak?

ORLANDO Neither rhyme nor reason can express how much.

ROSALIND Love is merely a madness, and, I tell you, deserves as well a dark house and a whip as madmen do; and the reason why they are not so punish'd and cur'd is, that the lunacy is so ordinary that the whippers are in love too. Yet I profess curing it by counsel.

ORLANDO Did you ever cure any so?

ROSALIND Yes, one, and in this manner. He was to imagine me his love, his mistress; and I set him every day to woo me. At which time would I, being but a moonish youth, grieve, be effeminate, changeable, longing and liking, proud, fantastical, apish, shallow, inconstant, full of tears, full of smiles; for every passion something and for no passion truly anything, as boys and women are for the most part cattle of this color; would now like him, now loathe him; then entertain him, then forswear him; now weep for him, then spit

305 withal with **308 hard** slowly, with uneven pace **310 se'nnight** week **317 wasteful** making one waste away **321–322 go as softly** walk as slowly **326 term** court session **332 cony** rabbit **333 kindled** littered, born **335 purchase** acquire. **remov'd** remote **337 religious** i.e., member of a religious order **338 inland** from a center of civilization **338–339 courtship** (1) wooing (2) knowledge of courtly manners **341 touch'd** tainted

355 fancy-monger dealer or advertiser of love **357 quotidian** fever recurring daily. (See *love-shak'd*, l. 358). **362 cage of rushes** i.e., flimsy prison **364 blue eye** i.e., having dark circles **365 unquestionable** unwilling to converse **367–368 simply . . . revenue** i.e., truly what you have by way of a beard is small. (Younger brothers traditionally received small inheritances.) **369–370 bonnet unbanded** hat lacking a band around the crown **373 point-device** faultless, correct **380 still** continually **381 good sooth** honest truth **390 merely** utterly **391 dark . . . whip** (The common treatment of lunatics.) **399 moonish** changeable

at him; that I drave my suitor from his mad humor of love to a living humor of madness, which was, to forswear the full stream of the world and to live in a nook merely monastic. And thus I cur'd him; and this way will I take upon me to wash your liver as clean as a sound sheep's heart, that there shall not be one spot of love in 't.

ORLANDO I would not be cur'd, youth.

ROSALIND I would cure you, if you would but call me Rosalind and come every day to my cote and woo me.

ORLANDO Now, by the faith of my love, I will. Tell me where it is.

ROSALIND Go with me to it, and I'll show it you; and by the way you shall tell me where in the forest you live. Will you go?

ORLANDO With all my heart, good youth.

ROSALIND Nay, you must call me Rosalind. Come, sister, will you go? *Exeunt.*

SCENE III

Enter [*Touchstone the*] *Clown, Audrey; and Jaques* [*apart*].

TOUCHSTONE Come apace, good Audrey. I will fetch up your goats, Audrey. And how, Audrey? Am I the man yet? Doth my simple feature content you?

AUDREY Your features, Lord warrant us! What features?

TOUCHSTONE I am here with thee and thy goats, as the most capricious poet, honest Ovid, was among the Goths.

JAQUES [*Aside*] O knowledge ill-inhabited, worse than Jove in a thatch'd house!

TOUCHSTONE When a man's verses cannot be understood, nor a man's good wit seconded with the forward child, understanding, it strikes a man more dead than a great reckoning in a little room. Truly, I would the gods had made thee poetical.

AUDREY I do not know what "poetical" is. Is it honest in deed and word? Is it a true thing?

TOUCHSTONE No, truly; for the truest poetry is the most feigning, and lovers are given to poetry, and what they swear in poetry may be said as lovers they do feign.

AUDREY Do you wish then that the gods had made me poetical?

TOUCHSTONE I do, truly; for thou swear'st to me thou art honest. Now, if thou wert a poet, I might have some hope thou didst feign.

AUDREY Would you not have me honest?

TOUCHSTONE No, truly, unless thou wert hard-favor'd; for honesty coupled to beauty is to have honey a sauce to sugar.

JAQUES [*Aside*] A material fool!

AUDREY Well, I am not fair, and therefore I pray the gods make me honest.

TOUCHSTONE Truly, and to cast away honesty upon a foul slut were to put good meat into an unclean dish.

AUDREY I am not a slut, though I thank the gods I am foul.

TOUCHSTONE Well, prais'd be the gods for thy foulness! Sluttishness may come hereafter. But be it as it may be, I will marry thee, and to that end I have been with Sir Oliver Martext, the vicar of the next village, who hath promis'd to meet me in this place of the forest and to couple us.

JAQUES [*Aside*] I would fain see this meeting.

AUDREY Well, the gods give us joy!

TOUCHSTONE Amen. A man may, if he were of a fearful heart, stagger in this attempt; for here we have no temple but the wood, no assembly but horn-beasts. But what though? Courage! As horns are odious, they are necessary. It is said, "Many a man knows no end of his goods." Right! Many a man has good horns, and knows no end of them. Well, that is the dowry of his wife; 'tis none of his own getting. Horns? Even so. Poor men alone? No, no; the noblest deer hath them as huge as the rascal. Is the single man therefore bless'd? No; as a wall'd town is more worthier than a village, so is the forehead of a married man more honorable than the bare brow of a bachelor; and by how much defense is better than no skill, by so much is a horn more precious than to want.

Enter Sir Oliver Martext.

Here comes Sir Oliver. Sir Oliver Martext, you are well met. Will you dispatch us here under this tree, or shall we go with you to your chapel?

SIR OLIVER Is there none here to give the woman?

TOUCHSTONE I will not take her on gift of any man.

SIR OLIVER Truly, she must be given, or the marriage is not lawful.

JAQUES [*Advancing*] Proceed, proceed. I'll give her.

TOUCHSTONE Good even, good Master What-ye-call 't. How do you, sir? You are very well met. God 'ild you for your last company. I am very glad to see you. Even a toy in hand here, sir. Nay, pray be cover'd.

JAQUES Will you be married, motley?

406–407 mad . . . madness mad fancy of love to a real madness **409 merely** utterly **410 liver** (Supposed seat of the emotions, especially love.) **415 cote** cottage

III.iii. Location: The forest.

3 simple feature plain appearance. (But Audrey does not understand.) **6 capricious** witty, fanciful. (Derived from Latin *caper,* male goat; hence, *goatish, lascivious.*) **7 Goths** (with pun on *goats;* the two words were pronounced alike) **8 ill-inhabited** ill-lodged **9 Jove . . . house** (An allusion to Ovid's *Metamorphoses,* viii, containing the story of Jupiter and Mercury lodging disguised in the humble cottage of Baucis and Philemon.) **10–11 verses . . . understood** (Ovid's verses were misunderstood by the barbaric Goths among whom he lived in exile, just as Touchstone's wit is misunderstood by Audrey.) **11–12 forward** precocious **13 great . . . room** exorbitant charge for refreshment or lodging in a cramped tavern-room. (Some scholars see in this passage an allusion to the death of Christopher Marlowe, who was stabbed by Ingram Frysar at an inn in Deptford in a quarrel over a tavern reckoning, May 30, 1593.) **18 feigning** inventive, imaginative. (But Touchstone plays on the sense of *false, lying.*) **19 may be said** i.e., it may be said

24 honest chaste **25 feign** (1) pretend (2) desire **27 hard-favor'd** ugly **28 honesty** chastity **30 material** full of sense **34 foul** ugly **40 Sir** (Courtesy title for a clergyman.) **46 stagger** hesitate **47 horn-beasts** (Alludes to the joke about cuckolds or cheated husbands having horns.) **48 what though** what though it be so. **As** though **49 necessary** unavoidable **49–50 knows . . . goods** thinks there will be no end to his wealth **51 knows . . . them** i.e., doesn't realize he has pointed horns on his brow. **dowry** marriage gift **52 getting** (1) obtaining (2) begetting (since his wife's children will not be his) **54 rascal** deer that are lean and out of season **58 defense** the art of self-defense **59 than to want** i.e., than to be without a horn **61 dispatch us** finish off our business **69 'ild you** yield you, reward you **71 a toy in hand** a trifle to be attended to. **be cover'd** put on your hat, i.e., no need to show respect. (Perhaps said to Audrey.)

TOUCHSTONE As the ox hath his bow, sir, the horse his curb, and the falcon her bells, so man hath his desires; and as pigeons bill, so wedlock would be nibbling.

JAQUES And will you, being a man of your breeding, be married under a bush like a beggar? Get you to church, and have a good priest that can tell you what marriage is. This fellow will but join you together as they join wainscot; then one of you will prove a shrunk panel and, like green timber, warp, warp.

TOUCHSTONE [*Aside*] I am not in the mind but I were better to be married of him than of another, for he is not like to marry me well; and not being well married, it will be a good excuse for me hereafter to leave my wife.

JAQUES Go thou with me, and let me counsel thee.

TOUCHSTONE Come, sweet Audrey. We must be married, or we must live in bawdry. Farewell, good Master Oliver; not

"O sweet Oliver,
O brave Oliver,
Leave me not behind thee;"

but

"Wind away,
Begone, I say,
I will not to wedding with thee."

Exeunt [Jaques, Touchstone, and Audrey].

SIR OLIVER 'Tis no matter. Ne'er a fantastical knave of them all shall flout me out of my calling. [*Exit.*]

SCENE IV

Enter Rosalind and Celia.

ROSALIND Never talk to me; I will weep.

CELIA Do, I prithee; but yet have the grace to consider that tears do not become a man.

ROSALIND But have I not cause to weep?

CELIA As good cause as one would desire; therefore weep.

ROSALIND His very hair is of the dissembling color.

CELIA Something browner than Judas's. Marry, his kisses are Judas's own children.

ROSALIND I' faith, his hair is of a good color.

CELIA An excellent color. Your chestnut was ever the only color.

ROSALIND And his kissing is as full of sanctity as the touch of holy bread.

CELIA He hath bought a pair of cast lips of Diana. A nun of winter's sisterhood kisses not more religiously; the very ice of chastity is in them.

ROSALIND But why did he swear he would come this morning, and comes not?

CELIA Nay, certainly, there is no truth in him.

ROSALIND Do you think so?

CELIA Yes; I think he is not a pick-purse nor a horse-stealer, but for his verity in love, I do think him as concave as a cover'd goblet or a worm-eaten nut.

ROSALIND Not true in love?

CELIA Yes, when he is in; but I think he is not in.

ROSALIND You have heard him swear downright he was.

CELIA "Was" is not "is." Besides, the oath of a lover is no stronger than the word of a tapster; they are both the confirmer of false reckonings. He attends here in the forest on the Duke your father.

ROSALIND I met the Duke yesterday and had much question with him. He ask'd me of what parentage I was. I told him, of as good as he; so he laugh'd and let me go. But what talk we of fathers, when there is such a man as Orlando?

CELIA O, that's a brave man! He writes brave verses, speaks brave words, swears brave oaths, and breaks them bravely, quite traverse, athwart the heart of his lover, as a puisny tilter, that spurs his horse but on one side, breaks his staff like a noble goose. But all 's brave that youth mounts and folly guides. Who comes here?

Enter Corin.

CORIN
Mistress and master, you have oft inquir'd
After the shepherd that complain'd of love,
Who you saw sitting by me on the turf,
Praising the proud disdainful shepherdess
That was his mistress.

CELIA Well, and what of him?

CORIN
If you will see a pageant truly play'd
Between the pale complexion of true love
And the red glow of scorn and proud disdain,
Go hence a little, and I shall conduct you,
If you will mark it.

ROSALIND O, come, let us remove!
The sight of lovers feedeth those in love.
Bring us to this sight, and you shall say
I'll prove a busy actor in their play. *Exeunt.*

SCENE V

Enter Silvius and Phebe.

SILVIUS
Sweet Phebe, do not scorn me; do not, Phebe!
Say that you love me not, but say not so

73 bow yoke **74 curb** chain or strap under the horse's jaw used to control it **77 under a bush** i.e., by a "hedge-priest," an uneducated clergyman **78–79 tell . . . is** expound the obligations of marriage **82–83 I am . . . better** I do not know but that it would be better for me **91–97 O . . . thee** (Phrases from a current ballad.) **95 Wind** wander **98 fantastical** affected

III.iv. Location: The forest.
7 the dissembling color i.e., reddish, traditionally the color of Judas' hair **8 Something** somewhat **9 Judas' own children** i.e., false, betraying **11 Your chestnut** i.e., this chestnut color that people talk about **14 holy bread** ordinary leavened bread which was blessed after the Eucharist and distributed to those who had not communed **15 cast** cast off, discarded, once belonging to; or, cast, molded. **Diana** goddess of chastity **16 of winter's sisterhood** i.e., devoted to barrenness and cold

24 concave hollow. **cover'd goblet** i.e., an empty goblet. (The cover is on only when the goblet is empty.) **31 false reckonings** (Tapsters or barkeeps were notoriously poor at simple addition.) **34 question** conversation **36 what** why **38 brave** fine, excellent **40 traverse** across, awry. (A term from tilting.) **41 puisny** puny, inexperienced. (Literally, junior.) **42 noble goose** i.e., a goose-headed young nobleman **51 pale complexion** (Sighing was believed to draw the blood from the heart.)

III.v. Location: The forest.

In bitterness. The common executioner,
Whose heart th' accustom'd sight of death makes hard,
Falls not the axe upon the humbled neck
But first begs pardon. Will you sterner be
Than he that dies and lives by bloody drops?

Enter Rosalind, Celia, and Corin [*behind*].

PHEBE
I would not be thy executioner;
I fly thee, for I would not injure thee.
Thou tell'st me there is murder in mine eye.
'Tis pretty, sure, and very probable,
That eyes, that are the frail'st and softest things,
Who shut their coward gates on atomies,
Should be call'd tyrants, butchers, murderers!
Now I do frown on thee with all my heart,
And if mine eyes can wound, now let them kill thee.
Now counterfeit to swoon; why, now fall down,
Or if thou canst not, O, for shame, for shame,
Lie not, to say mine eyes are murderers!
Now show the wound mine eye hath made in thee.
Scratch thee but with a pin, and there remains
Some scar of it; lean but upon a rush,
The cicatrice and capable impressure
Thy palm some moment keeps; but now mine eyes,
Which I have darted at thee, hurt thee not,
Nor, I am sure, there is no force in eyes
That can do hurt.

SILVIUS
O dear Phebe,
If ever—as that ever may be near—
You meet in some fresh cheek the power of fancy,
Then shall you know the wounds invisible
That love's keen arrows make.

PHEBE
But till that time
Come not thou near me; and when that time comes,
Afflict me with thy mocks, pity me not,
As till that time I shall not pity thee.

ROSALIND [*Advancing*]
And why, I pray you? Who might be your mother,
That you insult, exult, and all at once,
Over the wretched? What though you have no beauty—
As, by faith, I see no more in you
Than without candle may go dark to bed—
Must you be therefore proud and pitiless?
Why, what means this? Why do you look on me?
I see no more in you than in the ordinary
Of nature's sale-work. 'Od 's my little life,
I think she means to tangle my eyes too!
No, faith, proud mistress, hope not after it.
'Tis not your inky brows, your black silk hair,
Your bugle eyeballs, nor your cheek of cream
That can entame my spirits to your worship.
You foolish shepherd, wherefore do you follow her,
Like foggy south, puffing with wind and rain?
You are a thousand times a properer man
Than she a woman. 'Tis such fools as you
That makes the world full of ill-favor'd children.
'Tis not her glass, but you, that flatters her,
And out of you she sees herself more proper
Than any of her lineaments can show her.
But, mistress, know yourself. Down on your knees,
And thank heaven, fasting, for a good man's love;
For I must tell you friendly in your ear,
Sell when you can, you are not for all markets.
Cry the man mercy; love him, take his offer.
Foul is most foul, being foul to be a scoffer.
So take her to thee, shepherd. Fare you well.

PHEBE
Sweet youth, I pray you, chide a year together.
I had rather hear you chide than this man woo.

ROSALIND [*To Phebe*] He 's fall'n in love with your foulness, [*To Silvius*] and she'll fall in love with my anger. If it be so, as fast as she answers thee with frowning looks, I'll sauce her with bitter words.—Why look you so upon me?

PHEBE
For no ill will I bear you.

ROSALIND
I pray you, do not fall in love with me,
For I am falser than vows made in wine.
Besides, I like you not. If you will know my house,
'Tis at the tuft of olives here hard by.
Will you go, sister? Shepherd, ply her hard.
Come, sister. Shepherdess, look on him better,
And be not proud. Though all the world could see,
None could be so abus'd in sight as he.
Come, to our flock. *Exit* [*with Celia and Corin*].

PHEBE
Dead shepherd, now I find thy saw of might,
"Who ever lov'd that lov'd not at first sight?"

SILVIUS
Sweet Phebe—

PHEBE
Ha, what say'st thou, Silvius?

SILVIUS
Sweet Phebe, pity me.

PHEBE
Why, I am sorry for thee, gentle Silvius.

SILVIUS
Wherever sorrow is, relief would be.
If you do sorrow at my grief in love,
By giving love, your sorrow and my grief
Were both extermin'd.

PHEBE
Thou hast my love. Is not that neighborly?

5 Falls lets fall **6 But first begs** without first begging **7 dies and lives** i.e., makes his living his life long **11 sure** surely **13 gates on atomies** i.e., eyelids to ward off motes **23 cicatrice** mark, impression. **capable impressure** perceptible impression **29 fancy** love **36 all at once** i.e., all in a breath **37 no** i.e., no more **38–39 I see . . . bed** i.e., your beauty is not so brilliant that it will suffice to light you to bed in the dark **42 ordinary** common run **43 sale-work** ready-made products, i.e., not of the best quality, not distinctive. **'Od's** God save **47 bugle** black and glassy **48 to your worship** to worship of you

50 south south wind (from which came fog and rain; i.e., Silvius' sighs and tears) **51 properer** handsomer **55 out of you** i.e., with you as her mirror **61 Cry . . . mercy** beg the man's pardon **62 Foul . . . scoffer** i.e., ugliness is most ugly when it is rough and abusive. (Plays on two meanings of *foul*.) **64 together** continuously **78 could see** i.e., could look at you **79 abus'd in sight** deceived through the eyes **81 Dead shepherd** i.e., Christopher Marlowe, who died in 1593. **saw** saying. **of might** forceful, convincing **82 Who . . . sight** (From Marlowe's *Hero and Leander,* Sestiad I, 176, first published in 1598.) **86 Wherever . . . be** i.e., whenever one experiences sorrow, one ought to wish to offer relief **89 Were both extermin'd** would both be banished, ended **90 Is . . . neighborly** i.e., I love you as one is supposed to love one's neighbor or fellow-Christian (as distinguished from conjugal love)

SILVIUS
I would have you.
PHEBE Why, that were covetousness.
Silvius, the time was that I hated thee;
And yet it is not that I bear thee love,
But since that thou canst talk of love so well,
Thy company, which erst was irksome to me,
I will endure, and I'll employ thee too.
But do not look for further recompense
Than thine own gladness that thou art employ'd.
SILVIUS
So holy and so perfect is my love,
And I in such a poverty of grace,
That I shall think it a most plenteous crop
To glean the broken ears after the man
That the main harvest reaps. Loose now and then
A scatt'red smile, and that I'll live upon.
PHEBE
Know'st thou the youth that spoke to me erewhile?
SILVIUS
Not very well, but I have met him oft;
And he hath bought the cottage and the bounds
That the old carlot once was master of.
PHEBE
Think not I love him, though I ask for him;
'Tis but a peevish boy; yet he talks well.
But what care I for words? Yet words do well
When he that speaks them pleases those that hear.
It is a pretty youth—not very pretty—
But, sure, he's proud, and yet his pride becomes him.
He'll make a proper man. The best thing in him
Is his complexion; and, faster than his tongue
Did make offense, his eye did heal it up.
He is not very tall; yet for his years he's tall.
His leg is but so so; and yet 'tis well.
There was a pretty redness in his lip,
A little riper and more lusty red
Than that mix'd in his cheek; 'twas just the difference
Betwixt the constant red and mingled damask.
There be some women, Silvius, had they mark'd him
In parcels as I did, would have gone near
To fall in love with him; but, for my part,
I love him not nor hate him not; and yet
I have more cause to hate him than to love him.
For what had he to do to chide at me?
He said mine eyes were black and my hair black;
And, now I am rememb'red, scorn'd at me.
I marvel why I answer'd not again.
But that's all one; omittance is no quittance.
I'll write to him a very taunting letter,
And thou shalt bear it. Wilt thou, Silvius?
SILVIUS
Phebe, with all my heart.
PHEBE I'll write it straight;
The matter 's in my head and in my heart.
I will be bitter with him and passing short.
Go with me, Silvius. *Exeunt.*

ACT IV • SCENE I

Enter Rosalind and Celia, and Jaques.

JAQUES I prithee, pretty youth, let me be better acquainted with thee.

ROSALIND They say you are a melancholy fellow.

JAQUES I am so; I do love it better than laughing.

ROSALIND Those that are in extremity of either are abominable fellows, and betray themselves to every modern censure worse than drunkards.

JAQUES Why, 'tis good to be sad and say nothing.

ROSALIND Why then, 'tis good to be a post.

JAQUES I have neither the scholar's melancholy, which is emulation, nor the musician's, which is fantastical, nor the courtier's, which is proud, nor the soldier's, which is ambitious, nor the lawyer's, which is politic, nor the lady's, which is nice, nor the lover's, which is all these; but it is a melancholy of mine own, compounded of many simples, extracted from many objects, and indeed the sundry contemplation of my travels, in which my often rumination wraps me in a most humorous sadness.

ROSALIND A traveler! By my faith, you have great reason to be sad. I fear you have sold your own lands to see other men's. Then to have seen much and to have nothing is to have rich eyes and poor hands.

JAQUES Yes, I have gain'd my experience.

Enter Orlando.

ROSALIND And your experience makes you sad. I had rather have a fool to make me merry than experience to make me sad—and to travel for it too!

ORLANDO Good day and happiness, dear Rosalind!

JAQUES Nay, then, God buy you, an you talk in blank verse.

ROSALIND Farewell, Monsieur Traveler. Look you lisp and wear strange suits, disable all the benefits of your own country, be out of love with your nativity, and almost chide God for making you that countenance you are, or I will scarce think you have swam in a gundello. *[Exit Jaques.]*

91 covetousness (The tenth commandment forbids coveting anything that is your neighbor's.) **93 yet it is not** it (the time) is not yet come **95 erst** formerly **100 poverty of grace** (I.e., love, his divinity, has been ungracious to him.) **107 bounds** i.e., bounds within which he can feed stock **108 carlot** churl, countryman **123 mingled damask** mingled red and white, i.e., the color of the damask rose **125 In parcels** piecemeal, in detail. **gone near** come close **126 fall** falling **129 what . . . do** what business had he **131 am remembʼred** remember, recollect **133 But . . . quittance** i.e., but just the same, my failure to answer him doesn't mean I won't do so later

136 straight immediately **138 passing short** exceedingly curt

IV.i. Location: The forest.
5 are . . . of go to extremes in **7 modern censure** common judgment **11 emulation** envy **13 politic** calculated **14 nice** fastidious **16 simples** ingredients (usually herbs) of a drug **16–17 objects** i.e., objects of my observation **17 sundry** various, collected **19 humorous** moody **27 travel** (with a pun on *travail*, labor) **29 God buy** God be with. **an** if **32 disable** depreciate, disparage **33 nativity** i.e., place of birth **35–36 swam . . . gundello** ridden in a gondola, i.e., been in Venice, where almost all travelers go

Why, how now, Orlando, where have you been all this while? You a lover? An you serve me such another trick, never come in my sight more.

ORLANDO My fair Rosalind, I come within an hour of my promise.

ROSALIND Break an hour's promise in love? He that will divide a minute into a thousand parts and break but a part of the thousandth part of a minute in the affairs of love, it may be said of him that Cupid hath clapp'd him o' th' shoulder, but I'll warrant him heart-whole.

ORLANDO Pardon me, dear Rosalind.

ROSALIND Nay, an you be so tardy, come no more in my sight. I had as lief be woo'd of a snail.

ORLANDO Of a snail?

ROSALIND Ay, of a snail; for though he comes slowly, he carries his house on his head—a better jointure, I think, than you make a woman. Besides, he brings his destiny with him.

ORLANDO What's that?

ROSALIND Why, horns, which such as you are fain to be beholding to your wives for. But he comes arm'd in his fortune and prevents the slander of his wife.

ORLANDO Virtue is no horn-maker, and my Rosalind is virtuous.

ROSALIND And I am your Rosalind.

CELIA It pleases him to call you so; but he hath a Rosalind of a better leer than you.

ROSALIND Come, woo me, woo me, for now I am in a holiday humor and like enough to consent. What would you say to me now, an I were your very very Rosalind?

ORLANDO I would kiss before I spoke.

ROSALIND Nay, you were better speak first, and when you were gravel'd for lack of matter, you might take occasion to kiss. Very good orators, when they are out, they will spit; and for lovers lacking—God warn us!—matter, the cleanliest shift is to kiss.

ORLANDO How if the kiss be denied?

ROSALIND Then she puts you to entreaty, and there begins new matter.

ORLANDO Who could be out, being before his belov'd mistress?

ROSALIND Marry, that should you, if I were your mistress, or I should think my honesty ranker than my wit.

ORLANDO What, of my suit?

ROSALIND Not out of your apparel, and yet out of your suit. Am not I your Rosalind?

ORLANDO I take some joy to say you are, because I would be talking of her.

ROSALIND Well, in her person I say I will not have you.

ORLANDO Then in mine own person I die.

ROSALIND No, faith, die by attorney. The poor world is almost six thousand years old, and in all this time there was not any man died in his own person, videlicet, in a love-cause. Troilus had his brains dash'd out with a Grecian club; yet he did what he could to die before, and he is one of the patterns of love. Leander, he would have liv'd many a fair year, though Hero had turn'd nun, if it had not been for a hot midsummer night; for, good youth, he went but forth to wash him in the Hellespont and being taken with the cramp was drown'd; and the foolish chroniclers of that age found it was "Hero of Sestos." But these are all lies. Men have died from time to time, and worms have eaten them, but not for love.

ORLANDO I would not have my right Rosalind of this mind, for, I protest, her frown might kill me.

ROSALIND By this hand, it will not kill a fly. But come, now I will be your Rosalind in a more coming-on disposition, and ask me what you will, I will grant it.

ORLANDO Then love me, Rosalind.

ROSALIND Yes, faith, will I, Fridays and Saturdays and all.

ORLANDO And wilt thou have me?

ROSALIND Ay, and twenty such.

ORLANDO What sayest thou?

ROSALIND Are you not good?

ORLANDO I hope so.

ROSALIND Why then, can one desire too much of a good thing? Come, sister, you shall be the priest and marry us. Give me your hand, Orlando. What do you say, sister?

ORLANDO Pray thee, marry us.

CELIA I cannot say the words.

ROSALIND You must begin, "Will you, Orlando"—

CELIA Go to. Will you, Orlando, have to wife this Rosalind?

ORLANDO I will.

ROSALIND Ay, but when?

ORLANDO Why now, as fast as she can marry us.

ROSALIND Then you must say, "I take thee, Rosalind, for wife."

ORLANDO I take thee, Rosalind, for wife.

ROSALIND I might ask you for your commission; but I do take thee, Orlando, for my husband. There's a girl goes before the priest, and certainly a woman's thought runs before her actions.

ORLANDO So do all thoughts; they are wing'd.

ROSALIND Now tell me how long you would have her after you have possess'd her.

ORLANDO For ever and a day.

ROSALIND Say "a day," without the "ever." No, no, Orlando; men are April when they woo, December when

45–46 clapp'd . . . shoulder i.e., accosted or arrested him **52 jointure** marriage settlement **56 horns** (1) snails' horns (2) cuckold's horns, signs of an unfaithful wife **57 beholding** beholden, indebted **57–58 arm'd . . . fortune** i.e., with the horns of a cuckold, which it was his fate to earn **58 prevents** forestalls, anticipates **63 of . . . leer** better-looking **70 gravel'd** stuck, at a standstill. (Literally, run aground on a shoal.) **71 out** i.e., at a loss through forgetfulness or confusion **72 warn** i.e., warrant, defend **73 shift** device **80 honesty** chastity. **ranker** even more corrupt. (Rosalind playfully interprets *being out before one's mistress,* l. 77–78, as *not being inside her,* not having sex with her; she says her lover will have to stay *out,* and thus will not obtain his *suit,* l. 84.) **82 of my suit** (Orlando means *out of my suit,* at a loss for words in my wooing; but Rosalind puns on the meaning *suit of clothes;* to be *out of apparel* would be to be undressed.)

89 attorney proxy **90 six . . . old** (A common figure in Biblical calculation.) **91–92 videlicet** namely **92 Troilus** hero of the story of Troilus and Cressida in which he remains faithful to her but she faithless in love **92–93 had . . . club** (Troilus was slain by Achilles; Rosalind's account of his death is calculatedly unromantic.) **94 Leander** hero of the story of Hero and Leander, who lost his life swimming the Hellespont to visit his sweetheart. (Rosalind's account of the cramp is more undercutting of romantic idealism.) **100 found it was** arrived at the verdict that the cause (of his death) was **103 right** real **131 ask . . . commission** ask you what authority you have for taking her (since no one is here to give the bride away) **133 goes before** (who) anticipates

they wed. Maids are May when they are maids, but the sky changes when they are wives. I will be more jealous of thee than a Barbary cock-pigeon over his hen, more clamorous than a parrot against rain, more new-fangled than an ape, more giddy in my desires than a monkey. I will weep for nothing, like Diana in the fountain, and I will do that when you are dispos'd to be merry; I will laugh like a hyen, and that when thou art inclin'd to sleep.

ORLANDO But will my Rosalind do so?

ROSALIND By my life, she will do as I do.

ORLANDO O, but she is wise.

ROSALIND Or else she could not have the wit to do this; the wiser, the waywarder. Make the doors upon a woman's wit, and it will out at the casement; shut that, and 'twill out at the key-hole; stop that, 'twill fly with the smoke out at the chimney.

ORLANDO A man that had a wife with such a wit, he might say "Wit, whither wilt?"

ROSALIND Nay, you might keep that check for it till you met your wife's wit going to your neighbor's bed.

ORLANDO And what wit could wit have to excuse that?

ROSALIND Marry, to say she came to seek you there. You shall never take her without her answer, unless you take her without her tongue. O, that woman that cannot make her fault her husband's occasion, let her never nurse her child herself, for she will breed it like a fool!

ORLANDO For these two hours, Rosalind, I will leave thee.

ROSALIND Alas, dear love, I cannot lack thee two hours!

ORLANDO I must attend the Duke at dinner. By two o'clock I will be with thee again.

ROSALIND Ay, go your ways, go your ways; I knew what you would prove. My friends told me as much, and I thought no less. That flattering tongue of yours won me. 'Tis but one cast away, and so, come, death! Two o'clock is your hour?

ORLANDO Ay, sweet Rosalind.

ROSALIND By my troth, and in good earnest, and so God mend me, and by all pretty oaths that are not dangerous, if you break one jot of your promise or come one minute behind your hour, I will think you the most pathetical break-promise, and the most hollow lover, and the most unworthy of her you call Rosalind, that may be chosen out of the gross band of the unfaithful. Therefore beware my censure and keep your promise.

ORLANDO With no less religion than if thou wert indeed my Rosalind. So adieu.

ROSALIND Well, Time is the old justice that examines all such offenders, and let Time try. Adieu.

Exit [*Orlando*].

CELIA You have simply misus'd our sex in your love prate. We must have your doublet and hose pluck'd over your head, and show the world what the bird hath done to her own nest.

ROSALIND O coz, coz, coz, my pretty little coz, that thou didst know how many fathom deep I am in love! But it cannot be sounded; my affection hath an unknown bottom, like the bay of Portugal.

CELIA Or rather, bottomless, that as fast as you pour affection in, it runs out.

ROSALIND No, that same wicked bastard of Venus that was begot of thought, conceiv'd of spleen, and born of madness, that blind rascally boy that abuses everyone's eyes because his own are out, let him be judge how deep I am in love. I'll tell thee, Aliena, I cannot be out of the sight of Orlando. I'll go find a shadow and sigh till he come.

CELIA And I'll sleep. *Exeunt.*

SCENE II

Enter Jaques, and Lords [*as*] *Foresters.*

JAQUES Which is he that kill'd the deer?

FIRST LORD Sir, it was I.

JAQUES Let's present him to the Duke, like a Roman conqueror; and it would do well to set the deer's horns upon his head, for a branch of victory. Have you no song, forester, for this purpose?

SECOND LORD Yes, sir.

JAQUES Sing it. 'Tis no matter how it be in tune, so it make noise enough. *Music.*

Song.

SECOND LORD

What shall he have that kill'd the deer?
His leather skin and horns to wear.
Then sing him home.
(The rest shall bear this burden.)
Take thou no scorn to wear the horn;
It was a crest ere thou wast born.
Thy father's father wore it,
And thy father bore it.
The horn, the horn, the lusty horn
Is not a thing to laugh to scorn. *Exeunt.*

SCENE III

Enter Rosalind and Celia.

ROSALIND How say you now? Is it not past two o'clock? And here much Orlando!

CELIA I warrant you, with pure love and troubled

143 Barbary cock-pigeon a pigeon originally from the Barbary (north) coast of Africa. (Hence, applicable to the mid East and suggestive of oriental jealousy.) **144 against** before, in expectation of **145 new-fangled** infatuated with novelty **146–147 Diana in the fountain** (Diana frequently appeared as the centerpiece of fountains. Stow's *Survey of London* describes the setting up of a fountain with a Diana in green marble in the year 1596.) **148 hyen** hyena **154 Make** make fast, shut **159 Wit, whither wilt** wit, where are you going. (A common Elizabethan expression implying that one is talking fantastically, with a wildly wandering wit.) **160 check** retort **166 make . . . occasion** i.e., turn a defense of her own conduct into an accusation against her husband **184 pathetical** pitiable, miserable **186 gross** whole **189 religion** strict fidelity **192 try** determine

193 simply misus'd absolutely slandered **194–196 We . . . nest** i.e., we must expose you for what you are, a woman, and show everyone how a woman has defamed her own kind just as a foul bird proverbially fouls its own nest **203 bastard of Venus** i.e., Cupid **204 thought** fancy. **spleen** i.e., impulse **208 shadow** shady spot

IV.ii. Location: The forest.
12 s.d. bear this burden sing this refrain ("Then sing him home") **13 Take . . . scorn** be not ashamed. (Alludes to joke about cuckold's horns.)

IV.iii. Location: The forest. (Two hours have passed since the end of IV.i.)

brain, he hath ta'en his bow and arrows and is gone forth—to sleep.

Enter Silvius.

Look who comes here.

SILVIUS
My errand is to you, fair youth.
My gentle Phebe bid me give you this.
[*Gives a letter.*]
I know not the contents; but, as I guess
By the stern brow and waspish action
Which she did use as she was writing of it,
It bears an angry tenor. Pardon me,
I am but as a guiltless messenger.

ROSALIND [*Examining the letter*]
Patience herself would startle at this letter
And play the swaggerer. Bear this, bear all!
She says I am not fair, that I lack manners;
She calls me proud, and that she could not love me
Were man as rare as phoenix. 'Od's my will!
Her love is not the hare that I do hunt.
Why writes she so to me? Well, shepherd, well,
This is a letter of your own device.

SILVIUS
No, I protest, I know not the contents.
Phebe did write it.

ROSALIND Come, come, you are a fool,
And turn'd into the extremity of love.
I saw her hand. She has a leathern hand,
A freestone-colored hand. I verily did think
That her old gloves were on, but 'twas her hands;
She has a huswife's hand—but that's no matter.
I say she never did invent this letter;
This is a man's invention and his hand.

SILVIUS
Sure, it is hers.

ROSALIND
Why, 'tis a boisterous and a cruel style,
A style for challengers. Why, she defies me,
Like Turk to Christian. Women's gentle brain
Could not drop forth such giant-rude invention,
Such Ethiop words, blacker in their effect
Than in their countenance. Will you hear the letter?

SILVIUS
So please you, for I never heard it yet;
Yet heard too much of Phebe's cruelty.

ROSALIND
She Phebes me. Mark how the tyrant writes. *Read.*
"Art thou god to shepherd turn'd,
That a maiden's heart hath burn'd?"
Can a woman rail thus?

SILVIUS
Call you this railing?

ROSALIND *Read.*
"Why, thy godhead laid apart,
Warr'st thou with a woman's heart?"
Did you ever hear such railing?
"Whiles the eye of man did woo me,
That could do no vengeance to me."
Meaning me a beast.
"If the scorn of your bright eyne
Have power to raise such love in mine,
Alack, in me what strange effect
Would they work in mild aspect!
Whiles you chid me, I did love;
How then might your prayers move!
He that brings this love to thee
Little knows this love in me;
And by him seal up thy mind,
Whether that thy youth and kind
Will the faithful offer take
Of me and all that I can make,
Or else by him my love deny,
And then I'll study how to die."

SILVIUS
Call you this chiding?

CELIA
Alas, poor shepherd!

ROSALIND Do you pity him? No, he deserves no pity. Wilt thou love such a woman? What, to make thee an instrument and play false strains upon thee? Not to be endur'd! Well, go your way to her, for I see love hath made thee a tame snake, and say this to her: that if she love me, I charge her to love thee; if she will not, I will never have her unless thou entreat for her. If you be a true lover, hence, and not a word; for here comes more company. *Exit Silvius.*

Enter Oliver.

OLIVER
Good morrow, fair ones. Pray you, if you know,
Where in the purlieus of this forest stands
A sheep-cote fenc'd about with olive trees?

CELIA
West of this place, down in the neighbor bottom;
The rank of osiers by the murmuring stream
Left on your right hand brings you to the place.
But at this hour the house doth keep itself;
There's none within.

OLIVER
If that an eye may profit by a tongue,
Then should I know you by description,
Such garments and such years: "The boy is fair,
Of female favor, and bestows himself
Like a ripe sister; the woman low,
And browner than her brother." Are not you
The owner of the house I did inquire for?

CELIA
It is no boast, being ask'd, to say we are.

OLIVER
Orlando doth commend him to you both,
And to that youth he calls his Rosalind

18 phoenix a fabulous bird of Arabia, the only one of its kind, which lived five hundred years, died in flames, and was reborn of its own ashes **24 turn'd** brought **26 freestone-colored** sandstone-colored, brownish-yellow **28 hand** handwriting (with play on the ordinary meaning) **36 Ethiop** i.e., black **40 Phebes** i.e., treats cruelly **45 thy . . . apart** having laid aside your godhead (for human shape)

49 vengeance mischief, harm **50 Meaning me** i.e., implying that I am **54 in mild aspect** i.e., if they looked on me mildly. (Suggests also astrological influence.) **59 by . . . mind** i.e., send your thoughts in a letter via Silvius **60 youth and kind** youthful nature **69 instrument** (1) tool (2) musical instrument **77 purlieus** tracts of land on the border of a forest **79 neighbor bottom** neighboring dell **80 rank of osiers** row of willows **87 favor** features. **bestows** behaves **88 ripe** mature or elder

He sends this bloody napkin. Are you he?
[*Produces a bloody handkerchief.*]

ROSALIND
I am. What must we understand by this?

OLIVER
Some of my shame, if you will know of me
What man I am, and how, and why, and where
This handkercher was stain'd.

CELIA
I pray you, tell it.

OLIVER
When last the young Orlando parted from you
He left a promise to return again
Within an hour, and, pacing through the forest,
Chewing the food of sweet and bitter fancy,
Lo, what befell! He threw his eye aside,
And mark what object did present itself
Under an old oak, whose boughs were moss'd with age
And high top bald with dry antiquity:
A wretched ragged man, o'ergrown with hair,
Lay sleeping on his back. About his neck
A green and gilded snake had wreath'd itself,
Who with her head nimble in threats approach'd
The opening of his mouth; but suddenly,
Seeing Orlando, it unlink'd itself,
And with indented glides did slip away
Into a bush, under which bush's shade
A lioness, with udders all drawn dry,
Lay couching, head on ground, with catlike watch,
When that the sleeping man should stir; for 'tis
The royal disposition of that beast
To prey on nothing that doth seem as dead.
This seen, Orlando did approach the man
And found it was his brother, his elder brother.

CELIA
O, I have heard him speak of that same brother,
And he did render him the most unnatural
That liv'd amongst men.

OLIVER
And well he might so do,
For well I know he was unnatural.

ROSALIND
But, to Orlando: did he leave him there,
Food to the suck'd and hungry lioness?

OLIVER
Twice did he turn his back and purpos'd so;
But kindness, nobler ever than revenge,
And nature, stronger than his just occasion,
Made him give battle to the lioness,
Who quickly fell before him; in which hurtling
From miserable slumber I awak'd.

CELIA
Are you his brother?

ROSALIND
Was 't you he rescu'd?

CELIA
Was 't you that did so oft contrive to kill him?

OLIVER
'Twas I; but 'tis not I. I do not shame
To tell you what I was, since my conversion
So sweetly tastes, being the thing I am.

ROSALIND
But, for the bloody napkin?

OLIVER
By and by.
When from the first to last betwixt us two
Tears our recountments had most kindly bath'd,
As how I came into that desert place,
In brief, he led me to the gentle Duke
Who gave me fresh array and entertainment,
Committing me unto my brother's love;
Who led me instantly unto his cave,
There stripp'd himself, and here upon his arm
The lioness had torn some flesh away,
Which all this while had bled; and now he fainted
And cried, in fainting, upon Rosalind.
Brief, I recover'd him, bound up his wound,
And, after some small space, being strong at heart,
He sent me hither, stranger as I am,
To tell this story, that you might excuse
His broken promise, and to give this napkin
Dyed in his blood unto the shepherd youth
That he in sport doth call his Rosalind.
[*Rosalind swoons.*]

CELIA
Why, how now, Ganymede, sweet Ganymede!

OLIVER
Many will swoon when they do look on blood.

CELIA
There is more in it. Cousin Ganymede!

OLIVER
Look, he recovers.

ROSALIND
I would I were at home.

CELIA
We'll lead you thither.
I pray you, will you take him by the arm?
[*They help Rosalind up.*]

OLIVER Be of good cheer, youth. You a man? You lack a man's heart.

ROSALIND I do so, I confess it. Ah, sirrah, a body would think this was well counterfeited! I pray you, tell your brother how well I counterfeited. Heigh-ho!

OLIVER This was not counterfeit. There is too great testimony in your complexion that it was a passion of earnest.

ROSALIND Counterfeit, I assure you.

OLIVER Well then, take a good heart and counterfeit to be a man.

ROSALIND So I do; but, i' faith, I should have been a woman by right.

CELIA Come, you look paler and paler. Pray you, draw homewards. Good sir, go with us.

OLIVER
That will I, for I must bear answer back
How you excuse my brother, Rosalind.

ROSALIND I shall devise something. But, I pray you, commend my counterfeiting to him. Will you go?
Exeunt.

113 indented sinuous **115 udders . . . dry** (It would therefore be fierce with hunger.) **123 render him** describe him as **130 just occasion** fair chance (of revenge) **132 hurtling** clatter, tumult **136 do not shame** am not ashamed

139 for as regards **141 recountments** relating of events (to one another) **151 Brief** in brief. **recover'd** revived

ACT V • SCENE I

Enter [Touchstone the] Clown and Audrey.

TOUCHSTONE We shall find a time, Audrey. Patience, gentle Audrey.

AUDREY Faith, the priest was good enough, for all the old gentleman's saying.

TOUCHSTONE A most wicked Sir Oliver, Audrey, a most vile Martext. But, Audrey, there is a youth here in the forest lays claim to you.

AUDREY Ay, I know who 'tis. He hath no interest in me in the world. Here comes the man you mean.

Enter William.

TOUCHSTONE It is meat and drink to me to see a clown. By my troth, we that have good wits have much to answer for. We shall be flouting; we cannot hold.

WILLIAM Good ev'n, Audrey.

AUDREY God ye good ev'n, William.

WILLIAM And good ev'n to you, sir. *[Removes hat.]*

TOUCHSTONE Good ev'n, gentle friend. Cover thy head, cover thy head; nay, prithee, be cover'd. How old are you, friend?

WILLIAM Five and twenty, sir.

TOUCHSTONE A ripe age. Is thy name William?

WILLIAM William, sir.

TOUCHSTONE A fair name. Wast born i' th' forest here?

WILLIAM Ay, sir, I thank God.

TOUCHSTONE "Thank God"—a good answer. Art rich?

WILLIAM Faith, sir, so so.

TOUCHSTONE "So so" is good, very good, very excellent good; and yet it is not, it is but so so. Art thou wise?

WILLIAM Ay, sir, I have a pretty wit.

TOUCHSTONE Why, thou say'st well. I do now remember a saying, "The fool doth think he is wise, but the wise man knows himself to be a fool." The heathen philosopher, when he had a desire to eat a grape, would open his lips when he put it into his mouth, meaning thereby that grapes were made to eat and lips to open. You do love this maid?

WILLIAM I do, sir.

TOUCHSTONE Give me your hand. Art thou learned?

WILLIAM No, sir.

TOUCHSTONE Then learn this of me: to have, is to have; for it is a figure in rhetoric that drink, being pour'd out of a cup into a glass, by filling the one doth empty the other; for all your writers do consent that ipse is he. Now, you are not ipse, for I am he.

WILLIAM Which he, sir?

TOUCHSTONE He, sir, that must marry this woman. Therefore, you clown, abandon—which is in the vulgar leave—the society—which in the boorish is company—of this female—which in the common is woman; which together is, abandon the society of this female, or, clown, thou perishest; or, to thy better understanding, diest; or, to wit, I kill thee, make thee away, translate thy life into death, thy liberty into bondage. I will deal in poison with thee, or in bastinado, or in steel; I will bandy with thee in faction; I will o'errun thee with policy; I will kill thee a hundred and fifty ways. Therefore tremble, and depart.

AUDREY Do, good William.

WILLIAM God rest you merry, sir. *Exit.*

Enter Corin.

CORIN Our master and mistress seeks you. Come, away, away!

TOUCHSTONE Trip, Audrey, trip, Audrey! I attend, I attend. *Exeunt.*

V.i. Location: The forest.
8 interest in claim to **10 clown** i.e., country yokel **12 shall** must. **flouting** scoffing, expressing contempt. **hold** i.e., hold back, hold our tongues **14 God ye good ev'n** God give you good evening **31–35 The heathen . . . open** (This is probably Touchstone's way of telling William, whose mouth is no doubt gaping like a rustic's, that the grape, i.e., Audrey, is not for his lips.) **40–42 drink . . . other** i.e., both Touchstone and William cannot possess Audrey **42 your writers** i.e., the authorities. **ipse** he himself. (Latin.)

53–54 bastinado beating with a cudgel **54 bandy** contend. **in faction** factiously **55 o'errun . . . policy** overwhelm you with craft, cunning **58 God . . . merry** (Common salutation at parting.)

SCENE II

Enter Orlando and Oliver.

ORLANDO Is 't possible that on so little acquaintance you should like her? That but seeing you should love her? And loving woo? And, wooing, she should grant? And will you persevere to enjoy her?

OLIVER Neither call the giddiness of it in question, the poverty of her, the small acquaintance, my sudden wooing, nor her sudden consenting; but say with me, I love Aliena; say with her that she loves me; consent with both that we may enjoy each other. It shall be to your good; for my father's house and all the revenue that was old Sir Rowland's will I estate upon you, and here live and die a shepherd.

Enter Rosalind.

ORLANDO You have my consent. Let your wedding be tomorrow. Thither will I invite the Duke and all 's contented followers. Go you and prepare Aliena; for look you, here comes my Rosalind.

ROSALIND God save you, brother.

OLIVER And you, fair sister. *[Exit.]*

ROSALIND O, my dear Orlando, how it grieves me to see thee wear thy heart in a scarf!

ORLANDO It is my arm.

ROSALIND I thought thy heart had been wounded with the claws of a lion.

V.ii. Location: The forest.
5 giddiness sudden speed **11 estate** settle as an estate, bestow **14 all 's** all his **17 brother** i.e., brother-in-law to be **18 sister** (Rosalind is still dressed as a man, but Oliver evidently adopts the fiction that "Ganymede" is Orlando's Rosalind.) **20 wear . . . scarf** (Perhaps she suggests that Orlando has been wearing his heart on his sleeve; literally, she refers to the sling for his wounded arm.)

ORLANDO Wounded it is, but with the eyes of a lady.

ROSALIND Did your brother tell you how I counterfeited to swoon when he show'd me your handkercher?

ORLANDO Ay, and greater wonders than that.

ROSALIND O, I know where you are. Nay, 'tis true. There was never anything so sudden but the fight of two rams and Caesar's thrasonical brag of "I came, saw, and overcame." For your brother and my sister no sooner met but they look'd, no sooner look'd but they lov'd, no sooner lov'd but they sigh'd, no sooner sigh'd but they ask'd one another the reason, no sooner knew the reason but they sought the remedy; and in these degrees have they made a pair of stairs to marriage which they will climb incontinent, or else be incontinent before marriage. They are in the very wrath of love, and they will together. Clubs cannot part them.

ORLANDO They shall be married tomorrow, and I will bid the Duke to the nuptial. But, O, how bitter a thing it is to look into happiness through another man's eyes! By so much the more shall I tomorrow be at the height of heart-heaviness, by how much I shall think my brother happy in having what he wishes for.

ROSALIND Why then, tomorrow I cannot serve your turn for Rosalind?

ORLANDO I can live no longer by thinking.

ROSALIND I will weary you then no longer with idle talking. Know of me then, for now I speak to some purpose, that I know you are a gentleman of good conceit. I speak not this that you should bear a good opinion of my knowledge, insomuch I say I know you are; neither do I labor for a greater esteem than may in some little measure draw a belief from you, to do yourself good and not to grace me. Believe then, if you please, that I can do strange things. I have, since I was three years old, convers'd with a magician, most profound in his art and yet not damnable. If you do love Rosalind so near the heart as your gesture cries it out, when your brother marries Aliena, shall you marry her. I know into what straits of fortune she is driven; and it is not impossible to me, if it appear not inconvenient to you, to set her before your eyes tomorrow, human as she is, and without any danger.

ORLANDO Speak'st thou in sober meanings?

ROSALIND By my life, I do; which I tender dearly, though I say I am a magician. Therefore, put you in your best array; bid your friends; for if you will be married tomorrow, you shall, and to Rosalind, if you will.

Enter Silvius and Phebe.

Look, here comes a lover of mine and a lover of hers.

PHEBE
Youth, you have done me much ungentleness,
To show the letter that I writ to you.

ROSALIND
I care not if I have. It is my study
To seem despiteful and ungentle to you.
You are there followed by a faithful shepherd;
Look upon him, love him; he worships you.

PHEBE
Good shepherd, tell this youth what 'tis to love.

SILVIUS
It is to be all made of sighs and tears;
And so am I for Phebe.

PHEBE And I for Ganymede.

ORLANDO And I for Rosalind.

ROSALIND And I for no woman.

SILVIUS
It is to be all made of faith and service;
And so am I for Phebe.

PHEBE And I for Ganymede.

ORLANDO And I for Rosalind.

ROSALIND And I for no woman.

SILVIUS
It is to be all made of fantasy,
All made of passion and all made of wishes,
All adoration, duty, and observance,
All humbleness, all patience, and impatience,
All purity, all trial, all observance;
And so am I for Phebe.

PHEBE And so am I for Ganymede.

ORLANDO And so am I for Rosalind.

ROSALIND And so am I for no woman.

PHEBE [*To Rosalind*]
If this be so, why blame you me to love you?

SILVIUS [*To Phebe*]
If this be so, why blame you me to love you?

ORLANDO
If this be so, why blame you me to love you?

ROSALIND Why do you speak too, "Why blame you me to love you?"

ORLANDO To her that is not here, nor doth not hear.

ROSALIND Pray you, no more of this; 'tis like the howling of Irish wolves against the moon. [*To Silvius.*] I will help you, if I can. [*To Phebe.*] I would love you, if I could. Tomorrow meet me all together. [*To Phebe.*] I will marry you, if ever I marry woman, and I'll be married tomorrow. [*To Orlando.*] I will satisfy you, if ever I satisfied man, and you shall be married tomorrow. [*To Silvius.*] I will content you, if what pleases you contents you, and you shall be married tomorrow. [*To Orlando.*] As you love Rosalind, meet. [*To Silvius.*] As you love Phebe, meet. And as I love no woman, I'll meet. So fare you well. I have left you commands.

SILVIUS I'll not fail, if I live.

PHEBE Nor I.

ORLANDO Nor I. *Exeunt.*

28 where you are i.e., what you mean **30 thrasonical** boastful (From Thraso, the boaster in Terence's *Eunuchus*.) **36 degrees** (Plays on the original meaning, *steps*.) **pair** flight **37 incontinent** immediately (followed by a pun on the meaning, *unchaste* or *sexually unrestrained*) **39 wrath** impetuosity, ardor **52–53 conceit** intelligence, understanding **54 insomuch** inasmuch as **56 belief** i.e., confidence in my ability **57 grace me** bring favor on myself **59 convers'd** associated **60 not damnable** not a practicer of forbidden or black magic, worthy of damnation **61 gesture** bearing. **cries it out** proclaims **64–65 inconvenient** inappropriate **66 human . . . danger** i.e., the real Rosalind, not a phantom such as might involve the danger attendant on rites of incantation **68 tender dearly** value highly **69 though . . . magician** (According to Elizabethan anti-witchcraft statutes, some forms of witchcraft were punishable by death; Rosalind thus endangers her life by what she has said.)

76 study conscious endeavor **93 observance** devotion, respect **95 observance** (Perhaps a compositor's error, repeated from two lines previous; many editors emend to *obedience*.)

SCENE III

Enter [Touchstone the] Clown and Audrey.

TOUCHSTONE Tomorrow is the joyful day, Audrey; tomorrow will we be married.

AUDREY I do desire it with all my heart; and I hope it is no dishonest desire to desire to be a woman of the world. Here come two of the banish'd Duke's pages.

Enter two Pages.

FIRST PAGE Well met, honest gentleman.

TOUCHSTONE By my troth, well met. Come, sit, sit, and a song. *[They sit.]*

SECOND PAGE We are for you. Sit i' th' middle.

FIRST PAGE Shall we clap into 't roundly, without hawking or spitting or saying we are hoarse, which are the only prologues to a bad voice?

SECOND PAGE I' faith, i' faith; and both in a tune, like two gipsies on a horse.

Song.

It was a lover and his lass,
With a hey, and a ho, and a hey nonino,
That o'er the green corn-field did pass
In the spring time, the only pretty ring time,
When birds do sing, hey ding a ding, ding.
Sweet lovers love the spring.

Between the acres of the rye,
With a hey, and a ho, and a hey nonino,
These pretty country folks would lie
In spring time, etc.

This carol they began that hour,
With a hey, and a ho, and hey nonino,
How that a life was but a flower
In spring time, etc.

And therefore take the present time,
With a hey, and a ho, and a hey nonino,
For love is crowned with the prime
In spring time, etc.

TOUCHSTONE Truly, young gentlemen, though there was no great matter in the ditty, yet the note was very untuneable.

FIRST PAGE You are deceiv'd, sir. We kept time, we lost not our time.

TOUCHSTONE By my troth, yes; I count it but time lost to hear such a foolish song. God buy you; and God mend your voices! Come, Audrey. *Exeunt.*

V.iii. Location: The forest.
4 dishonest immodest **4–5 woman of the world** married woman; also, one who advances herself socially **9 We are for you** i.e., fine, we're ready **10 clap . . . roundly** begin at once and with spirit **10–11 hawking** clearing the throat **12 only** common, customary **13 in a tune** (1) in unison (2) keeping time **14 on a** on one **17 corn-field** field of grain **18 ring time** time most apt for marriage **21 Between the acres** i.e., on unploughed strips between the fields **31 prime** spring **34 matter** sense, meaning. **note** music **35 untuneable** untuneful, discordant

SCENE IV

Enter Duke Senior, Amiens, Jaques, Orlando, Oliver, [and] Celia.

DUKE SENIOR
Dost thou believe, Orlando, that the boy
Can do all this that he hath promised?

ORLANDO
I sometimes do believe, and sometimes do not,
As those that fear they hope, and know they fear.

Enter Rosalind, Silvius, and Phebe.

ROSALIND
Patience once more, whiles our compact is urg'd.
You say, if I bring in your Rosalind,
You will bestow her on Orlando here?

DUKE SENIOR
That would I, had I kingdoms to give with her.

ROSALIND
And you say you will have her, when I bring her?

ORLANDO
That would I, were I of all kingdoms king.

ROSALIND
You say, you'll marry me, if I be willing?

PHEBE
That will I, should I die the hour after.

ROSALIND
But if you do refuse to marry me,
You'll give yourself to this most faithful shepherd?

PHEBE
So is the bargain.

ROSALIND
You say that you'll have Phebe, if she will?

SILVIUS
Though to have her and death were both one thing.

ROSALIND
I have promis'd to make all this matter even.
Keep you your word, O Duke, to give your daughter;
You yours, Orlando, to receive his daughter;
Keep you your word, Phebe, that you'll marry me,
Or else, refusing me, to wed this shepherd:
Keep your word, Silvius, that you'll marry her
If she refuse me; and from hence I go,
To make these doubts all even.
Exeunt Rosalind and Celia.

DUKE SENIOR
I do remember in this shepherd boy
Some lively touches of my daughter's favor.

ORLANDO
My lord, the first time that I ever saw him
Methought he was a brother to your daughter.
But, my good lord, this boy is forest-born,
And hath been tutor'd in the rudiments
Of many desperate studies by his uncle,

V.iv. Location: The forest.
4 they hope i.e., that they merely hope **5 urg'd** put forward **18 even** smooth **27 lively** lifelike. **favor** appearance **32 desperate** dangerous

Whom he reports to be a great magician,
Obscured in the circle of this forest.

Enter [*Touchstone the*] *Clown and Audrey.*

JAQUES There is, sure, another flood toward, and these couples are coming to the ark. Here comes a pair of very strange beasts, which in all tongues are call'd fools.

TOUCHSTONE Salutation and greeting to you all!

JAQUES Good my lord, bid him welcome. This is the motley-minded gentleman that I have so often met in the forest. He hath been a courtier, he swears.

TOUCHSTONE If any man doubt that, let him put me to my purgation. I have trod a measure; I have flatt'red a lady; I have been politic with my friend, smooth with mine enemy; I have undone three tailors; I have had four quarrels, and like to have fought one.

JAQUES And how was that ta'en up?

TOUCHSTONE Faith, we met, and found the quarrel was upon the seventh cause.

JAQUES How seventh cause? Good my lord, like this fellow.

DUKE SENIOR I like him very well.

TOUCHSTONE God 'ild you, sir; I desire you of the like. I press in here, sir, amongst the rest of the country copulatives, to swear and to forswear, according as marriage binds and blood breaks. A poor virgin, sir, an ill-favor'd thing, sir, but mine own; a poor humor of mine, sir, to take that that no man else will. Rich honesty dwells like a miser, sir, in a poor house, as your pearl in your foul oyster.

DUKE SENIOR By my faith, he is very swift and sententious.

TOUCHSTONE According to the fool's bolt, sir, and such dulcet diseases.

JAQUES But, for the seventh cause. How did you find the quarrel on the seventh cause?

TOUCHSTONE Upon a lie seven times remov'd—bear your body more seeming, Audrey—as thus, sir. I did dislike the cut of a certain courtier's beard. He sent me word, if I said his beard was not cut well, he was in the mind it was: this is call'd the Retort Courteous. If I sent him word again it was not well cut, he would send me word he cut it to please himself: this is call'd the Quip Modest. If again, it was not well cut, he disabled my judgment: this is call'd the Reply Churlish. If again, it was not well cut, he would answer I spake not true: this is call'd the Reproof Valiant. If again, it was not well cut, he would say I lie: this is call'd the Countercheck Quarrelsome. And so to the Lie Circumstantial and the Lie Direct.

JAQUES And how oft did you say his beard was not well cut?

TOUCHSTONE I durst go no further than the Lie Circumstantial, nor he durst not give me the Lie Direct; and so we measur'd swords and parted.

JAQUES Can you nominate in order now the degrees of the lie?

TOUCHSTONE O sir, we quarrel in print, by the book, as you have books for good manners. I will name you the degrees. The first, the Retort Courteous; the second, the Quip Modest; the third, the Reply Churlish; the fourth, the Reproof Valiant; the fifth, the Countercheck Quarrelsome; the sixth, the Lie with Circumstance; the seventh, the Lie Direct. All these you may avoid but the Lie Direct; and you may avoid that too, with an If. I knew when seven justices could not take up a quarrel, but when the parties were met themselves, one of them thought but of an If, as, "If you said so, then I said so;" and they shook hands and swore brothers. Your If is the only peacemaker; much virtue in If.

JAQUES Is not this a rare fellow, my lord? He's as good at anything and yet a fool.

DUKE SENIOR He uses his folly like a stalking-horse, and under the presentation of that he shoots his wit.

Enter Hymen, Rosalind, and Celia. Still Music.

HYMEN
Then is there mirth in heaven,
When earthly things made even
Atone together.
Good Duke, receive thy daughter;
Hymen from heaven brought her,
Yea, brought her hither,
That thou mightst join her hand with his
Whose heart within his bosom is.

ROSALIND [*To Duke*]
To you I give myself, for I am yours.
[*To Orlando.*] To you I give myself, for I am yours.

DUKE SENIOR
If there be truth in sight, you are my daughter.

ORLANDO
If there be truth in sight, you are my Rosalind.

PHEBE
If sight and shape be true,
Why then, my love adieu!

ROSALIND [*To Duke*]
I'll have no father, if you be not he.
[*To Orlando.*] I'll have no husband, if you be not he.
[*To Phebe.*] Nor ne'er wed woman, if you be
not she.

34 Obscured hidden (with a possible allusion to the magic circle which protected the magician from the devil during incantation) **35 toward** coming on **44 purgation** proof, trial. **measure** slow, stately dance **46 undone** ruined, bankrupted (by refusing to pay massive debts owed them) **47 like** been likely, came close **48 ta'en up** settled, made up **54 'ild** yield, reward. **I . . . like** I wish the same to you (A polite phrase used to reply to a compliment.) **56 copulatives** i.e., people about to copulate within marriage **57 blood breaks** passion violates one's vows (with a suggestion of breaking the maidenhead) **58 humor** whim **60 honesty** chastity **61 your pearl** i.e., the pearl that one hears about **62 swift** quick-witted. **62–63 sententious** pithy **64 fool's bolt** (Alluding to the proverb, "A fool's bolt [arrow] is soon shot.") **65 dulcet diseases** pleasant afflictions, entertaining yet sharp **69 seeming** seemly **70 dislike** express dislike of **75–76 disabled** disparaged **80 Countercheck** rebuff

86 measur'd swords (i.e., as in the mere preliminary to a duel) **89 quarrel . . . book** (Touchstone is travestying books on the general subject of honor and arms, which dealt with occasions and circumstances of the duel.) **97–98 take up** settle **101 swore brothers** (Alludes to the practice of swearing brotherhood.) **105 stalking-horse** a real or artificial horse under cover of which the hunter approached his game **106 presentation** semblance **106 s.d. Hymen** Roman god of faithful marriage. **Still** soft **109 Atone** are at one

HYMEN
Peace, ho! I bar confusion.
'Tis I must make conclusion
Of these most strange events.
Here's eight that must take hands
To join in Hymen's bands,
If truth holds true contents. 129
[To Orlando and Rosalind.]
You and you no cross shall part. 130
[To Oliver and Celia.]
You and you are heart in heart.
[To Phebe.]
You to his love must accord, 132
Or have a woman to your lord. 133
[To Touchstone and Audrey.]
You and you are sure together, 134
As the winter to foul weather.
[To All.]
Whiles a wedlock-hymn we sing,
Feed yourselves with questioning, 137
That reason wonder may diminish, 138
How thus we met, and these things finish.

Song.

Wedding is great Juno's crown, 140
O blessed bond of board and bed!
'Tis Hymen peoples every town;
High wedlock then be honored. 143
Honor, high honor, and renown,
To Hymen, god of every town!

DUKE SENIOR
O my dear niece, welcome thou art to me!
Even daughter, welcome, in no less degree. 147
PHEBE *[To Silvius]*
I will not eat my word, now thou art mine;
Thy faith my fancy to thee doth combine. 149

Enter Second Brother [Jaques de Boys].

JAQUES DE BOYS
Let me have audience for a word or two.
I am the second son of old Sir Rowland,
That bring these tidings to this fair assembly.
Duke Frederick, hearing how that every day
Men of great worth resorted to this forest,
Address'd a mighty power, which were on foot 155
In his own conduct, purposely to take 156
His brother here and put him to the sword;
And to the skirts of this wild wood he came,
Where, meeting with an old religious man,
After some question with him, was converted 160
Both from his enterprise and from the world,
His crown bequeathing to his banish'd brother,
And all their lands restor'd to them again
That were with him exil'd. This to be true,
I do engage my life.
DUKE SENIOR Welcome, young man. 165
Thou offer'st fairly to thy brothers' wedding: 166
To one his lands withheld, and to the other 167
A land itself at large, a potent dukedom. 168
First, in this forest let us do those ends 169
That here were well begun and well begot; 170
And after, every of this happy number
That have endur'd shrewd days and nights with us 172
Shall share the good of our returned fortune,
According to the measure of their states. 174
Meantime, forget this new-fall'n dignity
And fall into our rustic revelry.
Play, music! And you, brides and bridegrooms all,
With measure heap'd in joy, to th' measures fall.
JAQUES
Sir, by your patience. If I heard you rightly, 179
The Duke hath put on a religious life
And thrown into neglect the pompous court. 181
JAQUES DE BOYS
He hath.
JAQUES
To him will I. Out of these convertites 183
There is much matter to be heard and learn'd. 184
[To Duke.] You to your former honor I bequeath;
Your patience and your virtue well deserves it.
[To Orlando.] You to a love that your true faith doth merit;
[To Oliver.] You to your land and love and great allies;
[To Silvius.] You to a long and well-deserved bed;
[To Touchstone.] And you to wrangling, for thy loving voyage
Is but for two months victuall'd. So, to your pleasures.
I am for other than for dancing measures.
DUKE SENIOR
Stay, Jaques, stay.
JAQUES
To see no pastime I. What you would have
I'll stay to know at your abandon'd cave. *Exit.*
DUKE SENIOR
Proceed, proceed. We'll begin these rites,
As we do trust they'll end, in true delights.
Exeunt [in a dance].

[EPILOGUE]

ROSALIND It is not the fashion to see the lady the epi-
logue; but it is no more unhandsome than to see the 2
lord the prologue. If it be true that good wine needs 3
no bush, 'tis true that a good play needs no epilogue. 4

129 If . . . contents if truth be true **130 cross** disagreement **132 his** i.e., Silvius'. **accord** agree **133 to** for. **lord** i.e., husband **134 sure** closely united **137 Feed** satisfy **138 reason** understanding **140 Juno's** (Juno was Roman queen of the gods, presiding, in the Renaissance view, over faithful wedlock.) **143 High** solemn **147 Even . . . degree** i.e., you are no less welcome than my own daughter **149 combine** unite **155 Address'd** prepared. **power** army **156 In . . . conduct** under his own command **160 question** conversation

165 engage pledge **166 Thou offer'st fairly** you contribute handsomely **167 the other** i.e., Orlando **168 A land . . . large** i.e., an entire dukedom. (As husband of Rosalind, Orlando will eventually inherit as Duke.) **169 do those ends** accomplish those purposes **170 begot** conceived **172 shrewd** hard, trying **174 states** status, rank **179 by your patience** by your leave, i.e., let the music wait a moment **181 pompous** ceremonious **183 convertites** converts **184 matter** sound sense

Epilogue
2 unhandsome in bad taste **3–4 good . . . bush** (A proverb derived from the custom of displaying a piece of ivy or holly at the tavern door to denote that wine was for sale there.)

Yet to good wine they do use good bushes, and good
plays prove the better by the help of good epilogues.
What a case am I in then, that am neither a good epi-
logue nor cannot insinuate with you in the behalf of a 8
good play! I am not furnish'd like a beggar, therefore 9
to beg will not become me. My way is to conjure you, 10
and I'll begin with the women. I charge you, O
women, for the love you bear to men, to like as much
of this play as please you; and I charge you, O men,
for the love you bear to women—as I perceive by your
simp'ring, none of you hates them—that between you
and the women the play may please. If I were a 16
woman I would kiss as many of you as had beards 17
that pleas'd me, complexions that lik'd me, and 18
breaths that I defied not; and, I am sure, as many as 19
have good beards or good faces, or sweet breaths will,
for my kind offer, when I make curtsy, bid me fare- 21
well. 22

Exit.

8 insinuate ingratiate myself **9 furnish'd** equipped, decked out **10 conjure** adjure, earnestly charge **16–17 If . . . woman** (Women's parts on the Elizabethan stage were played by boys in feminine costume.) **18 lik'd** pleased **19 defied** disliked **21–22 bid me farewell** i.e., applaud me

Twelfth Night; or, What You Will

Twelfth Night is possibly the latest in the festive group of comedies, including *Much Ado about Nothing* and *As You Like It,* with which Shakespeare climaxed his distinctively philosophical and joyous vein of comic writing. Performed on February 2, 1602, at the Middle Temple and written possibly as early as 1599, *Twelfth Night* is usually dated 1600 or 1601. This play is indeed the most festive of the lot. Its keynote is Saturnalian release and the carnival pursuit of love and mirth. Along with such familiar motifs (found, for example, in *As You Like It* and *The Merchant of Venice*) as the plucky heroine disguised as a man, *Twelfth Night* also returns to the more farcical routines of mistaken identity found in Shakespeare's early comedy. As a witness of the 1602 performance, John Manningham, observes, the play is "much like the Commedy of Errores, or Menechmi in Plautus, but most like and neere to that in Italian called *Inganni.*" Manningham might have added Shakespeare's *Two Gentlemen of Verona* as another early instance, since it too employs the device of the heroine Julia disguised in the service of her unresponsive lover Proteus.

The carnival atmosphere is appropriate to the season designated in the play's title: the twelfth night of Christmas, January 6, the Feast of Epiphany. (The prologue to *Gl'Ingannati,* perhaps the Italian play referred to by Manningham, speaks of "La Notte di Beffania," Epiphany night.) Although Epiphany has of course a primary Christian significance as the Feast of the Magi, it was also in Renaissance times the last day of the Christmas revels. Over a twelve-day period, from Christmas until January 6, noble households sponsored numerous performances of plays, masks, banquets, and every kind of festivity. (Leslie Hotson argues, in fact, that *Twelfth Night* was first performed on twelfth night in early 1601, in the presence of Queen Elizabeth.) Students left schools for vacations, celebrating release from study with plays and revels of their own. The stern rigors of a rule-bound society gave way temporarily to playful inversions of authority. The reign of the Boy Bishop and the Feast of Fools, for example, gave choristers and minor church functionaries the cherished opportunity to boss the hierarchy around, mock the liturgy with outrageous lampooning, and generally let off steam. Although such customs occasionally got out of hand, the idea was to channel potentially destructive insubordination into playacting and thereby promote harmony. Behind these Elizabethan midwinter customs lies the Roman Saturnalia, with its pagan spirit of gift-giving, sensual indulgence, and satirical hostility to those who would curb merriment.

Shakespeare's choice of sources for *Twelfth Night* underscores his commitment to mirth. Renaissance literature offered numerous instances of mistaken identity among twins, and of the disguised heroine serving as page to her beloved. Among those in English were the anonymous play *Sir Clyomon and Sir Clamydes* (c. 1570–1583), Sidney's *Arcadia* (1590), and the prose romance *Parismus* by Emmanuel Forde (1598), featuring both a shipwreck and two characters with the names of Olivia and Violetta. Of particular significance, but largely for negative reasons, is Barnabe Riche's tale of "Apolonius and Silla" in *Riche his Farewell to Militarie profession,* 1581, based on Belleforest's 1571 French version of Bandello's *Novelle,* 1554. Here we find most of the requisite plot elements: the shipwreck, Silla's disguise as a page in Duke Apolonius' court, her office as ambassador of love from Apolonius to the Lady Julina who thereupon falls in love with Silla, the arrival of Silla's twin brother Silvio and his consequent success in winning Julina's affection. To Riche, however, this tale is merely a long warning against the enervating power of infatuation. Silvio gets Julina with child and disappears forthwith, making his belated reappearance almost too late to save the wrongly accused Silla (who is, of course, sexually incapable of fatherhood). Riche's moralizing, in the cautionary vein of Geoffrey Fenton's 1567 translation of Belleforest, puts the blame on the gross and drunken appetite of carnal love. The total mismatching of affection with which the story begins, and the sudden realignments of desire based on mere outward resemblances, are seen as proofs of love's unreasonableness. Shakespeare of course retains and capitalizes on the irrational quality of love, as in *A Midsummer Night's Dream,* but in doing so he minimizes the harm done (Olivia is not made pregnant) and repudiates any negative moral judgments. The added subplot, with its rebuking of Malvolio's censoriousness, may have been conceived as a further answer to Riche, Fenton, and their sober school.

Shakespeare's festive spirit owes much, as Manningham observed, to Plautus and the neoclassical Italian comic writers. At least three Italian comedies called *Gl'Inganni* ("The Frauds") employ the motif of mistaken identity, and one of them, by Curzio Gonzaga, 1592, supplies Viola's assumed name of "Cesare" or Cesario. Another play with the same title appeared in 1562. More useful is *Gl'Ingannati* ("The Deceived"), acted 1531, translated into French in 1543. Besides a plot line generally similar to *Twelfth Night*, and the reference to La Notte di Beffania (Epiphany), this play offers the suggestive name *Malevolti*, evil-faced, and *Fabio* (resembling "Fabian"). It also contains possible hints for Malvolio, Toby, and company, although the plot of the counterfeit letter is original with Shakespeare. Essentially, Shakespeare superimposes his own subplot on an Italianate novelle plot, as he did in *The Taming of the Shrew* and *Much Ado about Nothing*. And it is in the Malvolio story that Shakespeare most pointedly defends merriment. Feste the professional fool, an original stage type for Shakespeare in *Twelfth Night* and in *As You Like It,* also reinforces the theme of seizing the moment of mirth.

This great lesson, of savoring life's pleasures while one is still young, is something that Duke Orsino and the Countess Olivia have not yet learned when the play commences. Although suited to one another in rank, wealth, and attractiveness, they are unable to overcome their own willful posturing in the elaborate charade of courtship. Like Silvius in *As You Like It,* Orsino is the conventional Petrarchan wooer trapped in the courtly artifice of love's rules. He opens the play on a cloying note of self-pity. He is fascinated with his own degradation as a rejected suitor, and bores his listeners with his changeable moods and fondness for poetical "conceits." He sees himself as a hart pursued by his desires "like fell and cruel hounds," reminding us that enervating lovesickness has in fact robbed him of his manly occupation, hunting. He sends ornately contrived messages to Olivia but has not seen her in so long that his passion has become unreal and fantastical, feeding on itself.

Olivia plays the opposite role of chaste, denying womanhood. She explains her retirement from the world as mourning for a dead brother, but this brother (whose name we never learn) is another unreal vision. Olivia's practice of mourning, whereby she will "water once a day her chamber round With eye-offending brine" (I,i), is a lifeless ritual. As others view the matter, she is senselessly wasting her beauty and affection on the dead. "What a plague means my niece, to take the death of her brother thus?" Sir Toby expostulates (I,iii). Viola, though she too has seemingly lost a brother, is an important foil in this regard, for she continues to hope for her brother's safety, trusts his soul is in heaven if he is dead, and refuses to give up her commitment to life in any case. We suspect that Olivia takes a willful pleasure in self-denial not unlike Orsino's self-congratulatory suffering. She appears to derive satisfaction from the power she holds over Orsino, a power of refusal. And she must know that she looks stunning in black.

Olivia's household reflects in part her mood of self-denial. She keeps Malvolio as steward because he too dresses somberly, insists on quiet as befits a house in mourning, and maintains order. Yet Olivia also retains the fool, Feste, who is Malvolio's opposite in every way. Hard-pressed to defend his mirthful function in a household so given over to melancholy, Feste must find some way of persuading his mistress that her very gravity is itself the essence of folly. This is a paradox, because sobriety and order appeal to the conventional wisdom of the world. Malvolio, sensing that his devotion to propriety is being challenged by the fool's prating, chides Olivia for taking "delight in such a barren rascal" (I,v).

Feste must argue for an inversion of appearance and reality whereby many of the world's ordinary pursuits can be seen to be ridiculous. As he observes, in his habitually elliptical manner of speech, *"cucullus non facit monachum* [the cowl doesn't make the monk]; that's as much to say as I wear not motley in my brain." Feste wins his case by making Olivia laugh at her own illogic in grieving for a brother whose soul she assumes to be in heaven. By extension, Olivia has indeed been a fool for allowing herself to be deprived of happiness in love by her brother's death ("there is no true cuckold but calamity"), and for failing to consider the brevity of youth ("beauty's a flower"). Yet paradoxically only one who professes to be a fool can point this out, enabled by his detachment and innocence to perceive simple but profound truths denied to supposedly rational persons. This vision of the fool as naturally wise, and of society as self-indulgently insane, fascinated Renaissance writers, from Erasmus' *In Praise of Folly* and Cervantes' *Don Quixote* to Shakespeare's *King Lear.*

Viola, although not dressed in motley, aligns herself with Feste's rejection of self-denial. Refreshingly, even comically, she challenges the staid artifice of Orsino's and Olivia's lives. She is an ocean traveler, like many of Shakespeare's later heroines (Marina in *Pericles,* Perdita in *The Winter's Tale),* arriving on Illyria's shore plucky and determined. On her first embassy to Olivia from Orsino, she exposes with disarming candor the willfully ritualistic quality of Olivia's existence. Viola discards the flowery set speech she had prepared and memorized at Orsino's behest; despite her charmingly conceited assertion that the speech has been "excellently well penn'd," she senses that its elegant but empty rhetoric is all too familiar to the disdainful Olivia. Instead, Viola departs from her text to urge seizing the moment of happiness. "You do usurp yourself," she lectures Olivia, "for what is yours to bestow is not yours to reserve" (I,v). Beauty is a gift of nature, and failure to use it is a sin against nature. Or, again, "Lady, you are the cruell'st she alive If you will lead these graces [Olivia's beauty] to the grave And leave the world no copy." An essential argument in favor of love, as in Shakespeare's sonnets, is the necessity of marriage and childbearing in order to perpetuate beauty. This line is new to Olivia, and catches her wholly by surprise. In part she reacts, like Phebe in *As You Like It,* with perversely feminine logic, rejecting a too-willing wooer for one who is hard to get. Yet Olivia is also attracted by a new note of sincerity, prompting her to reenter life and accept maturely both the risks and rewards of romantic involvement. Her longing for "Cesario" is of course sexually misdirected, but the appearance of Viola's identical twin Sebastian soon puts all to rights.

The motifs of Olivia's attraction for another woman (both are really boy actors), and of Orsino's deep fondness for "Cesario" that matures into sexual love, evoke delicately homosexual suggestions as in *As You Like It.* Once again, however, we must approach the notion circumspectly, remembering that these elements are also found in Shakespeare's sources and reflect a convention wholly different from a modern psychological analysis of sexual aberration. Like Rosalind, Viola uses her male attire to win Orsino's pure affection, in a friendship devoid of sexual interest since both are seemingly men. Viola as Cesario can teach Orsino about the conventions of love, in relaxed and frank conversations that would not be possible if she were known to be a woman. She teaches him to avoid the beguiling but misleading myths of Petrarchan love, and so prepares him for the realities of marriage. Comparing men and women in love, she confides, "We men may say more, swear more, but indeed Our shows are more than will; for still we prove Much in our vows, but little in our love" (II,iv). Once she and Orsino have achieved an instinctive rapport all the more remarkable for their talking so often at cross-purposes, Viola's unmasking can make possible a physical communion as well. The friendship of Sebastian and Antonio, sorely tested by the mix-ups of the mistaken identity plot, presents further insight into the debate of love and friendship.

The below-stairs characters of the subplot, Sir Toby and the rest, share with Feste and Viola a commitment to joy. As Sir Toby proclaims in his first speech, "care's an enemy to life" (I,iii). Even the simpleton Sir Andrew, although gulled by Sir Toby into spending his money on a hopeless pursuit of Olivia, seems none the worse for his treatment; he loves to drink in Sir Toby's company, and can afford to pay for his entertainment. Sir Toby gives us some of the richly inventive humor of Falstaff, another lovable fat roguish knight. In this subplot, however, the confrontations between merriment and sobriety are more harshly drawn than in the main plot. Whereas the gracious Olivia is won away from her folly, the obdurate Malvolio can only be exposed to ridicule. He is chiefly to blame for the polarization of attitudes, for he insists on rebuking the mirth of others. His name, Mal-Volio, the ill-wisher, implies a self-satisfied determination to impose his rigid moral code on others. As Sir Toby taunts him, "Dost thou think, because thou art virtuous, there shall be no more cakes and ale?" (II,iii). Malvolio's inflexible hostility provokes a desire for comic vengeance. The method is satiric: the clever manipulators, Maria and Toby, invent a scheme to entrap Malvolio in his own self-deceit. The punishment fits the crime, for he has long dreamed of himself as Count Malvolio, rich, powerful, in a position to demolish Toby and the rest. Without Malvolio's infatuated predisposition to believe that Olivia could actually love him and write such a letter as he finds, Maria's scheme would have no hope of success. He tortures the text to make it yield a suitable meaning, much in the style of Puritan theologizing.

Indeed, Malvolio does in some ways resemble a Puritan, as Maria observes (II,iii), even though she qualifies the assertion by saying that he is not a religious fanatic but a "time-pleaser." She directs her observation not at a religious group but at all who would be killjoys; if the Puritans are like that, she intimates, so much the worse for them. This uncharacteristic lack of charity gives a sharp tone to the vengeance practiced on Malvolio, evoking from Olivia a protestation that "he hath been most notoriously abus'd" (V,i). The belated attempt to make a reconciliation with him seems, however, doomed to failure, in light of his grim resolve to "be reveng'd on the whole pack of you." At the height of his discomfiture he has been tricked into doing the one thing he hates most: smiling affably, and wearing sportive attire. The appearance of merriment is so grossly unsuited to him that he is declared mad and put into safekeeping. The apostle of sobriety in this play thus comes before us as a declared madman, while the fool Feste offers him sage comment in the guise of a priest. Wisdom and folly have changed places. The upside-down character of the play is epitomized in Malvolio's plaintive remark to Feste (no longer posing as the priest): "I am as well in my wits, fool, as thou art" (IV,ii). Malvolio's comeuppance is richly deserved, but the severity of vengeance and countervengeance suggests that the triumph of festival will not last long. This brevity is, of course, inherent in the nature of such holiday release from responsibility. As Feste sings, "What's to come is still unsure. In delay there lies no plenty."

Twelfth Night; or, What You Will

[*Dramatis Personae*

ORSINO, *Duke of Illyria.*
SEBASTIAN, *brother to Viola.*
ANTONIO, *a sea captain, friend to Sebastian.*
A SEA CAPTAIN, *friend to Viola.*
VALENTINE, } *gentlemen attending on the Duke.*
CURIO, }
SIR TOBY BELCH, *uncle to Olivia.*
SIR ANDREW AGUECHEEK.
MALVOLIO, *Steward to Olivia.*
FABIAN, } *servants to Olivia.*
FESTE, *a Clown,* }

OLIVIA, *a rich countess.*
VIOLA, *sister to Sebastian.*
MARIA, *Olivia's gentlewoman.*

LORDS, PRIESTS, SAILORS, OFFICERS, MUSICIANS, *and other* ATTENDANTS.

SCENE: *A city in Illyria, and the sea-coast near it.*]

ACT I • SCENE I

Enter Orsino Duke of Illyria, Curio, and other Lords [with Musicians].

DUKE
If music be the food of love, play on;
Give me excess of it, that, surfeiting,
The appetite may sicken, and so die.
That strain again! It had a dying fall;
O, it came o'er my ear like the sweet sound
That breathes upon a bank of violets,
Stealing and giving odor. Enough, no more.
'Tis not so sweet now as it was before.
O spirit of love, how quick and fresh art thou, 9
That, notwithstanding thy capacity
Receiveth as the sea, nought enters there,
Of what validity and pitch soe'er, 12
But falls into abatement and low price,
Even in a minute. So full of shapes is fancy 14
That it alone is high fantastical. 15

CURIO
Will you go hunt, my lord?

DUKE
What, Curio?

CURIO
The hart.

DUKE
Why, so I do, the noblest that I have. 17
O, when mine eyes did see Olivia first,
Methought she purg'd the air of pestilence!
That instant was I turn'd into a hart,
And my desires, like fell and cruel hounds, 21
E'er since pursue me.

Enter Valentine.

How now, what news from her? 22

VALENTINE
So please my lord, I might not be admitted,
But from her handmaid do return this answer:
The element itself, till seven years' heat, 25
Shall not behold her face at ample view;
But like a cloistress she will veiled walk,
And water once a day her chamber round
With eye-offending brine—all this to season 29
A brother's dead love, which she would keep fresh 30
And lasting in her sad remembrance.

DUKE
O, she that hath a heart of that fine frame
To pay this debt of love but to a brother,
How will she love, when the rich golden shaft 34
Hath kill'd the flock of all affections else
That live in her; when liver, brain, and heart, 36
These sovereign thrones, are all supplied, and fill'd 37
Her sweet perfections, with one self king! 38
Away before me to sweet beds of flow'rs.
Love-thoughts lie rich when canopied with bow'rs.
Exeunt.

I.i. Location: The Duke's palace.
s.d. Illyria country on the east coast of the Adriatic Sea **9 quick and fresh** keen and hungry

12 validity value. **pitch** superiority. (Literally, the highest point of a falcon's flight.) **14 shapes** imagined forms. **fancy** love **15 it . . . fantastical** it surpasses everything else in imaginative power **17 the noblest . . . have** i.e., my noblest part, my heart (punning on *hart*) **21 fell** fierce **22 pursue me** (Alludes to the story in Ovid of Actaeon, who, having seen Diana bathing, was transformed into a stag and killed by his own hounds.) **25 element** sky. **seven years' heat** seven summers **29 season** keep fresh (playing on the idea of the salt in her tears) **30 brother's dead** dead brother's **34 golden shaft** i.e., of Cupid **36 liver, brain, and heart** (In medieval and Elizabethan psychology these organs were the seats of the passions, of thought, and of feeling.) **37 supplied** filled **37–38 and . . . perfections** and her sweet perfections filled **38 self king** single lord (the object of her entire affection)

SCENE II

Enter Viola, a Captain, and Sailors.

VIOLA
What country, friends, is this?

CAPTAIN
This is Illyria, lady.

VIOLA
And what should I do in Illyria?
My brother he is in Elysium. 4

I.ii. Location: The sea-coast.
4 Elysium classical abode of the blessed dead

Perchance he is not drown'd. What think you, sailors?

CAPTAIN
It is perchance that you yourself were saved.

VIOLA
O my poor brother! And so perchance may he be.

CAPTAIN
True, madam; and, to comfort you with chance,
Assure yourself, after our ship did split,
When you and those poor number saved with you
Hung on our driving boat, I saw your brother,
Most provident in peril, bind himself,
Courage and hope both teaching him the practice,
To a strong mast that liv'd upon the sea;
Where, like Arion on the dolphin's back,
I saw him hold acquaintance with the waves
So long as I could see.

VIOLA
For saying so, there's gold. [*Gives money.*]
Mine own escape unfoldeth to my hope,
Whereto thy speech serves for authority,
The like of him. Know'st thou this country?

CAPTAIN
Ay, madam, well, for I was bred and born
Not three hours' travel from this very place.

VIOLA
Who governs here?

CAPTAIN
A noble duke, in nature as in name.

VIOLA
What is his name?

CAPTAIN
Orsino.

VIOLA
Orsino! I have heard my father name him.
He was a bachelor then.

CAPTAIN
And so is now, or was so very late;
For but a month ago I went from hence,
And then 'twas fresh in murmur—as, you know,
What great ones do the less will prattle of—
That he did seek the love of fair Olivia.

VIOLA
What's she?

CAPTAIN
A virtuous maid, the daughter of a count
That died some twelvemonth since, then leaving her
In the protection of his son, her brother,
Who shortly also died; for whose dear love,
They say, she hath abjur'd the sight
And company of men.

VIOLA
O that I serv'd that lady
And might not be delivered to the world
Till I had made mine own occasion mellow,
What my estate is!

CAPTAIN
That were hard to compass,
Because she will admit no kind of suit,
No, not the Duke's.

VIOLA
There is a fair behavior in thee, captain;
And, though that nature with a beauteous wall
Doth oft close in pollution, yet of thee
I will believe thou hast a mind that suits
With this thy fair and outward character.
I prithee, and I'll pay thee bounteously,
Conceal me what I am, and be my aid
For such disguise as haply shall become
The form of my intent. I'll serve this duke.
Thou shalt present me as an eunuch to him;
It may be worth thy pains. For I can sing
And speak to him in many sorts of music
That will allow me very worth his service.
What else may hap to time I will commit;
Only shape thou thy silence to my wit.

CAPTAIN
Be you his eunuch, and your mute I'll be;
When my tongue blabs, then let mine eyes not see.

VIOLA
I thank thee. Lead me on. *Exeunt.*

SCENE III

Enter Sir Toby [*Belch*] *and Maria.*

SIR TOBY What a plague means my niece to take the death of her brother thus? I am sure care's an enemy to life.

MARIA By my troth, Sir Toby, you must come in earlier o' nights. Your cousin, my lady, takes great exceptions to your ill hours.

SIR TOBY Why, let her except before excepted.

MARIA Ay, but you must confine yourself within the modest limits of order.

SIR TOBY Confine? I'll confine myself no finer than I am. These clothes are good enough to drink in, and so be these boots too. An they be not, let them hang themselves in their own straps.

MARIA That quaffing and drinking will undo you. I heard my lady talk of it yesterday; and of a foolish knight that you brought in one night here to be her wooer.

SIR TOBY Who, Sir Andrew Aguecheek?

MARIA Ay, he.

SIR TOBY He's as tall a man as any's in Illyria.

MARIA What's that to th' purpose?

SIR TOBY Why, he has three thousand ducats a year.

5–6 Perchance . . . perchance perhaps . . . by mere chance **8 chance** i.e., what one may hope that chance will bring about **11 driving** driven **14 liv'd** i.e., kept afloat **15 Arion** a Greek poet who so charmed the dolphins with his lyre that they saved him when he leaped into the sea to escape murderous sailors **19–21 unfoldeth . . . him** i.e., offers a hopeful example that he may have escaped similarly, to which hope your speech provides support **32 murmur** gossip **42 delivered** discovered, made known **43 mellow** ready or convenient (to be made known)

44 estate position in society. **compass** bring about, encompass **51 character** face or features as indicating moral qualities **54 become** suit **55 form of my intent** nature of my purpose (with suggestion of outward appearance in *form*) **56 eunuch** *castrato,* high-voiced singer **59 allow me** cause me to be acknowledged **61 wit** plan, invention

I.iii. Location: Olivia's house.
5 cousin i.e., kinswoman **7 except before excepted** (Plays on the legal phrase, *exceptis excipiendis,* "with the exceptions before named." Sir Toby means that enough exceptions to his behavior have already been taken.) **10 confine myself** dress myself (playing on Maria's use of *confine,* limit). **finer** (1) better (2) tighter **12 An** if **20 tall** brave

MARIA Ay, but he'll have but a year in all these ducats. He's a very fool and a prodigal.

SIR TOBY Fie, that you'll say so! He plays o' th' viol-de-gamboys, and speaks three or four languages word for word without book, and hath all the good gifts of nature.

MARIA He hath indeed, almost natural; for, besides that he's a fool, he's a great quarreler; and but that he hath the gift of a coward to allay the gust he hath in quarreling, 'tis thought among the prudent he would quickly have the gift of a grave.

SIR TOBY By this hand, they are scoundrels and substractors that say so of him. Who are they?

MARIA They that add, moreov'r, he's drunk nightly in your company.

SIR TOBY With drinking healths to my niece. I'll drink to her as long as there is a passage in my throat and drink in Illyria. He's a coward and a coistrel that will not drink to my niece till his brains turn o' th' toe like a parish-top. What, wench? Castiliano vulgo! For here comes Sir Andrew Agueface.

Enter Sir Andrew [Aguecheek].

SIR ANDREW Sir Toby Belch! How now, Sir Toby Belch?

SIR TOBY Sweet Sir Andrew!

SIR ANDREW Bless you, fair shrew.

MARIA And you too, sir.

SIR TOBY Accost, Sir Andrew, accost.

SIR ANDREW What's that?

SIR TOBY My niece's chambermaid.

SIR ANDREW Good Mistress Accost, I desire better acquaintance.

MARIA My name is Mary, sir.

SIR ANDREW Good Mistress Mary Accost—

SIR TOBY You mistake, knight. "Accost" is front her, board her, woo her, assail her.

SIR ANDREW By my troth, I would not undertake her in this company. Is that the meaning of "accost"?

MARIA Fare you well, gentlemen. *[Going.]*

SIR TOBY An thou let part so, Sir Andrew, would thou mightst never draw sword again.

SIR ANDREW An you part so, mistress, I would I might never draw sword again. Fair lady, do you think you have fools in hand?

MARIA Sir, I have not you by th' hand.

SIR ANDREW Marry, but you shall have; and here's my hand.

MARIA Now, sir, thought is free. I pray you, bring your hand to th' butt'ry-bar and let it drink.

SIR ANDREW Wherefore, sweetheart? What's your metaphor?

MARIA It's dry, sir.

SIR ANDREW Why, I think so. I am not such an ass but I can keep my hand dry. But what's your jest?

MARIA A dry jest, sir.

SIR ANDREW Are you full of them?

MARIA Ay, sir, I have them at my fingers' ends. Marry, now I let go your hand, I am barren. *Exit Maria.*

SIR TOBY O knight, thou lack'st a cup of canary! When did I see thee so put down?

SIR ANDREW Never in your life, I think, unless you see canary put me down. Methinks sometimes I have no more wit than a Christian or an ordinary man has. But I am a great eater of beef, and I believe that does harm to my wit.

SIR TOBY No question.

SIR ANDREW An I thought that, I 'd forswear it. I'll ride home tomorrow, Sir Toby.

SIR TOBY Pourquoi, my dear knight?

SIR ANDREW What is "pourquoi"? Do, or not do? I would I had bestow'd that time in the tongues that I have in fencing, dancing, and bear-baiting. O, had I but follow'd the arts!

SIR TOBY Then hadst thou had an excellent head of hair.

SIR ANDREW Why, would that have mended my hair?

SIR TOBY Past question, for thou seest it will not curl by nature.

SIR ANDREW But it becomes me well enough, does 't not?

SIR TOBY Excellent. It hangs like flax on a distaff; and I hope to see a huswife take thee between her legs and spin it off.

SIR ANDREW Faith, I'll home tomorrow, Sir Toby. Your niece will not be seen; or if she be, it's four to one she'll none of me. The Count himself here hard by woos her.

SIR TOBY She'll none o' th' Count. She'll not match above her degree, neither in estate, years, nor wit; I have heard her swear 't. Tut, there's life in 't, man.

SIR ANDREW I'll stay a month longer. I am a fellow o' th' strangest mind i' th' world; I delight in masques and revels sometimes altogether.

SIR TOBY Art thou good at these kickshawses, knight?

SIR ANDREW As any man in Illyria, whatsoever he be, under the degree of my betters; and yet I will not compare with an old man.

SIR TOBY What is thy excellence in a galliard, knight?

SIR ANDREW Faith, I can cut a caper.

SIR TOBY And I can cut the mutton to 't.

25–26 viol-de-gamboys viola da gamba, leg-viol, bass viol **27 without book** by heart **29 natural** (with a pun on the sense *born idiot*) **31 allay the gust** moderate the taste **34–35 substractors** i.e., detractors **40 coistrel** horse-groom, base fellow **42 parish-top** a large top provided by the parish to be spun by whipping, apparently for exercise in cold weather. **Castiliano vulgo** (Of uncertain meaning. Castilians were noted for their decorum, and possibly Sir Toby is urging Maria to behave politely to Sir Andrew.) **43 Agueface** (Like *Aguecheek,* this name betokens the thin, pale countenance of one suffering from an ague.) **48 Accost** make up to (Maria) **50 chambermaid** lady in waiting (a gentlewoman, not one who would do menial tasks) **56 board** greet, approach (as though preparing to board in a naval encounter) **64 have . . . hand** i.e., have to do with fools. (But Maria puns on the literal sense.) **66 Marry** i.e., indeed (Originally, "By the Virgin Mary.") **68 thought is free** i.e., I may think what I like. (Proverbial; replying to *do you think . . . in hand,* above.) **69 butt'ry-bar** door of the buttery or wine-cellar

72 dry thirsty; also dried up, a sign of age and debility **75 dry** (1) ironic (2) dull, barren (referring to Sir Andrew) **78 barren** i.e., barren of jests **79 canary** a sweet wine from the Canary Islands **89 Pourquoi** why **91 tongues** languages (Perhaps also suggests *tongs,* curling irons.) **93 the arts** the liberal arts, learning (But Sir Toby plays on the phrase as meaning *artifice,* the antithesis of *nature.*) **95 mended** improved **100 distaff** a staff for holding the flax, tow, or wool in spinning **102 spin it off** i.e., cause you to lose hair as a result of venereal disease, gotten from the *huswife* (suggesting *hussy, whore*) **108 degree** social position. **estate** fortune, social position **113 kickshawses** delicacies, fancy trifles (From the French, *quelque chose.*) **115 under . . . betters** excepting those who are above me **116 old man** experienced person (?) **117 galliard** lively dance in triple time **118 cut a caper** make a lively leap (But Sir Toby puns on the *caper* used to make a sauce served with mutton. *Mutton* in turn suggests *whore.*)

SIR ANDREW And I think I have the back-trick simply as strong as any man in Illyria.

SIR TOBY Wherefore are these things hid? Wherefore have these gifts a curtain before 'em? Are they like to take dust, like Mistress Mall's picture? Why dost thou not go to church in a galliard and come home in a coranto? My very walk should be a jig; I would not so much as make water but in a sink-a-pace. What dost thou mean? Is it a world to hide virtues in? I did think, by the excellent constitution of thy leg, it was form'd under the star of a galliard.

SIR ANDREW Ay, 'tis strong, and it does indifferent well in a flame-color'd stock. Shall we set about some revels?

SIR TOBY What shall we do else? Were we not born under Taurus?

SIR ANDREW Taurus? That's sides and heart.

SIR TOBY No, sir; it is legs and thighs. Let me see thee caper. Ha, higher! Ha, ha, excellent!

[Sir Andrew capers.] Exeunt.

SCENE IV

Enter Valentine, and Viola in man's attire.

VALENTINE If the Duke continue these favors towards you, Cesario, you are like to be much advanc'd. He hath known you but three days, and already you are no stranger.

VIOLA You either fear his humor or my negligence, that you call in question the continuance of his love. Is he inconstant, sir, in his favors?

VALENTINE No, believe me.

Enter Duke, Curio, and Attendants.

VIOLA I thank you. Here comes the Count.

DUKE Who saw Cesario, ho?

VIOLA On your attendance, my lord, here.

DUKE
Stand you a while aloof. [*The others stand aside.*]
Cesario,
Thou know'st no less but all. I have unclasp'd
To thee the book even of my secret soul.
Therefore, good youth, address thy gait unto her;
Be not denied access, stand at her doors,
And tell them, there thy fixed foot shall grow
Till thou have audience.

VIOLA
Sure, my noble lord,
If she be so abandon'd to her sorrow
As it is spoke, she never will admit me.

DUKE
Be clamorous and leap all civil bounds
Rather than make unprofited return.

VIOLA
Say I do speak with her, my lord, what then?

DUKE
O, then unfold the passion of my love;
Surprise her with discourse of my dear faith.
It shall become thee well to act my woes;
She will attend it better in thy youth
Than in a nuncio's of more grave aspect.

VIOLA
I think not so, my lord.

DUKE
Dear lad, believe it;
For they shall yet belie thy happy years
That say thou art a man. Diana's lip
Is not more smooth and rubious; thy small pipe
Is as the maiden's organ, shrill and sound,
And all is semblative a woman's part.
I know thy constellation is right apt
For this affair. Some four or five attend him—
All, if you will, for I myself am best
When least in company. Prosper well in this,
And thou shalt live as freely as thy lord,
To call his fortunes thine.

VIOLA
I'll do my best
To woo your lady. [*Aside.*] Yet a barful strife!
Whoe'er I woo, myself would be his wife. *Exeunt.*

SCENE V

Enter Maria and Clown.

MARIA Nay, either tell me where thou hast been, or I will not open my lips so wide as a bristle may enter in way of thy excuse. My lady will hang thee for thy absence.

CLOWN Let her hang me. He that is well hang'd in this world needs to fear no colors.

MARIA Make that good.

CLOWN He shall see none to fear.

MARIA A good lenten answer. I can tell thee where that saying was born, of "I fear no colors."

CLOWN Where, good Mistress Mary?

MARIA In the wars; and that may you be bold to say in your foolery.

CLOWN Well, God give them wisdom that have it; and those that are fools, let them use their talents.

MARIA Yet you will be hang'd for being so long absent; or to be turn'd away, is not that as good as a hanging to you?

120 back-trick backward step in the galliard **123–124 like to take** likely to collect **124 Mistress Mall's picture** i.e., perhaps the portrait of some woman protected from fading, as many pictures were, by curtains **126 coranto** lively running dance **127 sink-a-pace** dance like the galliard (From French, *cinque-pace.*) **128 virtues** talents **130 under . . . galliard** i.e., under a star favorable to dancing **131 indifferent** moderately **132 stock** stocking **135 Taurus** zodiacal sign (Sir Andrew is mistaken, since Leo governed *sides and hearts* in medical astrology. Taurus governed legs and thighs, or, more commonly, neck and throat.)

I.iv. Location: The Duke's palace.
5 humor changeableness **15 address thy gait** go

21 civil bounds bounds of civility **25 Surprise** take by storm (A military term.) **28 nuncio's** messenger's **32 rubious** ruby red. **pipe** voice, throat **33 shrill and sound** high and clear, uncracked **34 semblative** resembling, like **35 constellation** i.e., nature as determined by your horoscope **41 barful strife** endeavor full of impediments

I.v. Location: Olivia's house.
6 fear no colors i.e., fear no foe, fear nothing (with pun on *colors,* worldly deceptions, and *collars,* halters or nooses) **7 Make that good** explain that **9 lenten** meager, scanty (like lenten fare) **12 In the wars** (where *colors* would mean "military standards") **17 turn'd away** dismissed (possibly also meaning *turned off, hanged*)

CLOWN Many a good hanging prevents a bad marriage;
and, for turning away, let summer bear it out. 20
MARIA You are resolute, then?
CLOWN Not so, neither; but I am resolv'd on two
points. 23
MARIA That if one break, the other will hold; or, if both
break, your gaskins fall. 25
CLOWN Apt, in good faith, very apt. Well, go thy way;
if Sir Toby would leave drinking, thou wert as witty a 27
piece of Eve's flesh as any in Illyria. 28
MARIA Peace, you rogue, no more o' that. Here comes
my lady. Make your excuse wisely, you were best.
[*Exit.*]

Enter Lady Olivia with Malvolio, [and Attendants].

CLOWN Wit, an 't be thy will, put me into good fooling! 31
Those wits that think they have thee do very oft prove
fools, and I that am sure I lack thee may pass for a wise
man. For what says Quinapalus? "Better a witty fool 34
than a foolish wit."—God bless thee, lady!
OLIVIA Take the fool away.
CLOWN Do you not hear, fellows? Take away the lady.
OLIVIA Go to, y' are a dry fool. I'll no more of you. Be- 38
sides, you grow dishonest. 39
CLOWN Two faults, madonna, that drink and good 40
counsel will amend. For give the dry fool drink, then
is the fool not dry. Bid the dishonest man mend him-
self; if he mend, he is no longer dishonest; if he can-
not, let the botcher mend him. Anything that's 44
mended is but patch'd; virtue that transgresses is but
patch'd with sin, and sin that amends is but patch'd
with virtue. If that this simple syllogism will serve, so;
if it will not, what remedy? As there is no true cuckold 48
but calamity, so beauty's a flower. The lady bade take 49
away the fool; therefore, I say again, take her away.
OLIVIA Sir, I bade them take away you.
CLOWN Misprision in the highest degree! Lady, cucul- 52
lus non facit monachum; that's as much to say as I 53
wear not motley in my brain. Good madonna, give me 54
leave to prove you a fool.
OLIVIA Can you do it?
CLOWN Dexteriously, good madonna.
OLIVIA Make your proof.
CLOWN I must catechize you for it, madonna. Good my 59
mouse of virtue, answer me. 60
OLIVIA Well, sir, for want of other idleness, I'll bide 61
your proof.
CLOWN Good madonna, why mourn'st thou?
OLIVIA Good fool, for my brother's death.
CLOWN I think his soul is in hell, madonna.
OLIVIA I know his soul is in heaven, fool.
CLOWN The more fool, madonna, to mourn for your
brother's soul, being in heaven. Take away the fool,
gentlemen.
OLIVIA What think you of this fool, Malvolio? Doth he
not mend? 71
MALVOLIO Yes, and shall do till the pangs of death
shake him. Infirmity, that decays the wise, doth ever
make the better fool.
CLOWN God send you, sir, a speedy infirmity, for the
better increasing your folly! Sir Toby will be sworn
that I am no fox, but he will not pass his word for two
pence that you are no fool.
OLIVIA How say you to that, Malvolio?
MALVOLIO I marvel your ladyship takes delight in such
a barren rascal. I saw him put down the other day with 81
an ordinary fool that has no more brain than a stone.
Look you now, he's out of his guard already. Unless 83
you laugh and minister occasion to him, he is gagg'd. 84
I protest I take these wise men that crow so at these set 85
kind of fools no better than the fools' zanies. 86
OLIVIA O, you are sick of self-love, Malvolio, and taste
with a distemper'd appetite. To be generous, guiltless,
and of free disposition, is to take those things for bird- 89
bolts that you deem cannon-bullets. There is no slan- 90
der in an allow'd fool, though he do nothing but rail; 91
nor no railing in a known discreet man, though he do
nothing but reprove.
CLOWN Now Mercury endue thee with leasing, for 94
thou speak'st well of fools!

Enter Maria.

MARIA Madam, there is at the gate a young gentleman
much desires to speak with you.
OLIVIA From the Count Orsino, is it?
MARIA I know not, madam. 'Tis a fair young man, and
well attended.
OLIVIA Who of my people hold him in delay?
MARIA Sir Toby, madam, your kinsman.
OLIVIA Fetch him off, I pray you. He speaks nothing
but madman. Fie on him! [*Exit Maria.*] Go you, Mal- 104
volio. If it be a suit from the Count, I am sick, or not at
home; what you will, to dismiss it. (*Exit Malvolio.*)
Now you see, sir, how your fooling grows old, and 107
people dislike it.
CLOWN Thou hast spoke for us, madonna, as if thy eld-
est son should be a fool; whose skull Jove cram with
brains, for—here he comes—

Enter Sir Toby.

one of thy kin has a most weak pia mater. 112
OLIVIA By mine honor, half drunk. What is he at the
gate, cousin?

20 for as for. **let . . . out** i.e., let mild weather make dismissal endurable **23 points** (Maria puns on the meaning *laces used to hold up hose or breeches.*) **25 gaskins** hose, breeches **27–28 thou . . . Illyria** (The Clown may be observing ironically that Maria is as likely to prove witty as Sir Toby is to give up drinking; or he may hint at a match between the two.) **31 an 't** if it **34 Quinapalus** (The clown's invented authority.) **38 dry** dull **39 dishonest** unreliable; wicked **40 madonna** my lady **44 botcher** mender of old clothes and shoes **48–49 As . . . flower** i.e., Olivia has wedded calamity but will not be faithful to it, for the natural course is to seize the moment of youth and beauty before we lose it **52 Misprision** mistake, misunderstanding (with suggestion of the legal use meaning *the arrest or imprisonment of the wrong person*) **52–53 cucullus . . . monachum** the cowl does not make the monk **54 motley** the many-colored garment of jesters **59–60 Good . . . virtue** my good virtuous mouse (A term of endearment.) **61 idleness** pastime. **bide** endure

71 mend i.e., improve, grow more amusing (But Malvolio uses the word to mean "grow more like a fool.") **81 with** by **83 out of his guard** defenseless, unprovided with a witty answer **84 minister occasion** provide opportunity (for his fooling) **85 protest** avow, declare. **set** artificial, stereotyped **86 zanies** assistants, aping attendants **89 free** magnanimous **89–90 bird-bolts** blunt arrows for shooting small birds **91 allow'd** licensed (to speak freely) **94 Mercury** god of guile and trickery. **leasing** lying **104 madman** i.e., the words of madness **107 old** stale **112 pia mater** soft inner lining of the brain; i.e., brain

SIR TOBY A gentleman.

OLIVIA A gentleman? What gentleman?

SIR TOBY 'Tis a gentleman here—[*Belches.*] A plague o' these pickle-herring! How now, sot!

CLOWN Good Sir Toby.

OLIVIA Cousin, cousin, how have you come so early by this lethargy?

SIR TOBY Lechery? I defy lechery. There's one at the gate.

OLIVIA Ay, marry, what is he?

SIR TOBY Let him be the devil, an he will, I care not. Give me faith, say I. Well, it's all one. *Exit.*

OLIVIA What's a drunken man like, fool?

CLOWN Like a drown'd man, a fool, and a madman. One draught above heat makes him a fool, the second mads him, and a third drowns him.

OLIVIA Go thou and seek the crowner, and let him sit o' my coz; for he's in the third degree of drink, he's drown'd. Go, look after him.

CLOWN He is but mad yet, madonna; and the fool shall look to the madman. [*Exit.*]

Enter Malvolio.

MALVOLIO Madam, yond young fellow swears he will speak with you. I told him you were sick; he takes on him to understand so much, and therefore comes to speak with you. I told him you were asleep; he seems to have a foreknowledge of that too, and therefore comes to speak with you. What is to be said to him, lady? He's fortified against any denial.

OLIVIA Tell him he shall not speak with me.

MALVOLIO H' as been told so; and he says he'll stand at your door like a sheriff's post, and be the supporter to a bench, but he'll speak with you.

OLIVIA What kind o' man is he?

MALVOLIO Why, of mankind.

OLIVIA What manner of man?

MALVOLIO Of very ill manner. He'll speak with you, will you or no.

OLIVIA Of what personage and years is he?

MALVOLIO Not yet old enough for a man, nor young enough for a boy; as a squash is before 'tis a peascod, or a codling when 'tis almost an apple. 'Tis with him in standing water, between boy and man. He is very well-favor'd and he speaks very shrewishly. One would think his mother's milk were scarce out of him.

OLIVIA Let him approach. Call in my gentlewoman.

MALVOLIO Gentlewoman, my lady calls. *Exit.*

Enter Maria.

OLIVIA Give me my veil. Come, throw it o'er my face. We'll once more hear Orsino's embassy.

[*Olivia veils.*]

Enter Viola.

VIOLA The honorable lady of the house, which is she?

OLIVIA Speak to me; I shall answer for her. Your will?

VIOLA Most radiant, exquisite, and unmatchable beauty—I pray you, tell me if this be the lady of the house, for I never saw her. I would be loath to cast away my speech; for besides that it is excellently well penn'd, I have taken great pains to con it. Good beauties, let me sustain no scorn; I am very comptible, even to the least sinister usage.

OLIVIA Whence came you, sir?

VIOLA I can say little more than I have studied, and that question's out of my part. Good gentle one, give me modest assurance if you be the lady of the house, that I may proceed in my speech.

OLIVIA Are you a comedian?

VIOLA No, my profound heart; and yet, by the very fangs of malice I swear, I am not that I play. Are you the lady of the house?

OLIVIA If I do not usurp myself, I am.

VIOLA Most certain, if you are she, you do usurp yourself; for what is yours to bestow is not yours to reserve. But this is from my commission. I will on with my speech in your praise, and then show you the heart of my message.

OLIVIA Come to what is important in 't. I forgive you the praise.

VIOLA Alas, I took great pains to study it, and 'tis poetical.

OLIVIA It is the more like to be feign'd. I pray you, keep it in. I heard you were saucy at my gates, and allow'd your approach rather to wonder at you than to hear you. If you be not mad, be gone; if you have reason, be brief. 'Tis not that time of moon with me to make one in so skipping a dialogue.

MARIA Will you hoist sail, sir? Here lies your way.

VIOLA No, good swabber, I am to hull here a little longer. Some mollification for your giant, sweet lady. Tell me your mind. I am a messenger.

OLIVIA Sure you have some hideous matter to deliver, when the courtesy of it is so fearful. Speak your office.

VIOLA It alone concerns your ear. I bring no overture of war, no taxation of homage. I hold the olive in my hand; my words are as full of peace as matter.

OLIVIA Yet you began rudely. What are you? What would you?

VIOLA The rudeness that hath appear'd in me have I learn'd from my entertainment. What I am, and what I would, are as secret as maidenhead—to your ears, divinity, to any other's, profanation.

118 sot (1) fool (2) drunkard **126 Give me faith** i.e., to resist the devil. **it's all one** it doesn't matter **129 above heat** above the point needed to make him normally warm **131 crowner** coroner **131–132 sit o' my coz** hold an inquest on my kinsman (Sir Toby) **144 H' as** he has **145 sheriff's post** post before the sheriff's door on which proclamations and notices were fixed **154 squash** unripe pea pod. **peascod** pea pod **155 codling** unripe apple **156 in standing water** at the turn of the tide **157 well-favor'd** good-looking. **shrewishly** sharply

170 con learn by heart **171 comptible** susceptible, sensitive **172 least sinister** slightest discourteous **176 modest** reasonable **178 comedian** actor **179 profound** very wise, figuratively deep **182 do . . . myself** am not an impostor **183–184 usurp yourself** i.e., betray yourself, by withholding yourself from Orsino **185 from** outside of **188 forgive you** excuse you from repeating **195 If . . . mad** i.e., if you don't have madness to excuse your saucy behavior (?) Possibly an error for *If . . . but mad* (?) **reason** sanity **196 moon** (The moon was thought to affect lunatics according to its changing phases.) **196–197 make one** take part **199 swabber** one in charge of washing the decks. (A nautical retort to *hoist sail.*) **hull** stay with sails furled **200 Some . . . for** i.e., please mollify, pacify. **giant** i.e., the diminutive Maria who, like many giants in medieval romances, is guarding the lady **203 office** commission **205 taxation** demand for the payment **210 entertainment** reception

OLIVIA Give us the place alone. We will hear this divinity. [*Exeunt Maria and Attendants.*] Now, sir, what is your text?

VIOLA Most sweet lady—

OLIVIA A comfortable doctrine, and much may be said of it. Where lies your text?

VIOLA In Orsino's bosom.

OLIVIA In his bosom? In what chapter of his bosom?

VIOLA To answer by the method, in the first of his heart.

OLIVIA O, I have read it; it is heresy. Have you no more to say?

VIOLA Good madam, let me see your face.

OLIVIA Have you any commission from your lord to negotiate with my face? You are now out of your text. But we will draw the curtain and show you the picture. Look you, sir, such a one I was this present. Is 't not well done? [*Unveiling.*]

VIOLA Excellently done, if God did all.

OLIVIA 'Tis in grain, sir; 'twill endure wind and weather.

VIOLA
'Tis beauty truly blent, whose red and white
Nature's own sweet and cunning hand laid on.
Lady, you are the cruell'st she alive
If you will lead these graces to the grave
And leave the world no copy.

OLIVIA O, sir, I will not be so hard-hearted. I will give out divers schedules of my beauty. It shall be inventoried, and every particle and utensil label'd to my will: as, item, two lips, indifferent red; item, two grey eyes, with lids to them; item, one neck, one chin, and so forth. Were you sent hither to praise me?

VIOLA
I see you what you are, you are too proud;
But, if you were the devil, you are fair.
My lord and master loves you. O, such love
Could be but recompens'd, though you were
 crown'd
The nonpareil of beauty!

OLIVIA How does he love me?

VIOLA
With adorations, fertile tears,
With groans that thunder love, with sighs of fire.

OLIVIA
Your lord does know my mind; I cannot love him.
Yet I suppose him virtuous, know him noble,
Of great estate, of fresh and stainless youth;
In voices well divulg'd, free, learn'd, and valiant,
And in dimension and the shape of nature
A gracious person. But yet I cannot love him.
He might have took his answer long ago.

VIOLA
If I did love you in my master's flame,
With such a suff'ring, such a deadly life,
In your denial I would find no sense;
I would not understand it.

OLIVIA Why, what would you?

VIOLA
Make me a willow cabin at your gate,
And call upon my soul within the house;
Write loyal cantons of contemned love
And sing them loud even in the dead of night;
Halloo your name to the reverberate hills,
And make the babbling gossip of the air
Cry out "Olivia!" O, you should not rest
Between the elements of air and earth
But you should pity me!

OLIVIA You might do much.
What is your parentage?

VIOLA
Above my fortunes, yet my state is well.
I am a gentleman.

OLIVIA Get you to your lord.
I cannot love him. Let him send no more—
Unless, perchance, you come to me again
To tell me how he takes it. Fare you well.
I thank you for your pains. Spend this for me.
[*Offers a purse.*]

VIOLA
I am no fee'd post, lady; keep your purse.
My master, not myself, lacks recompense.
Love make his heart of flint that you shall love,
And let your fervor, like my master's, be
Plac'd in contempt! Farewell, fair cruelty. *Exit.*

OLIVIA
"What is your parentage?"
"Above my fortunes, yet my state is well.
I am a gentleman." I'll be sworn thou art!
Thy tongue, thy face, thy limbs, actions, and spirit
Do give thee five-fold blazon. Not too fast, soft, soft!
Unless the master were the man. How now?
Even so quickly may one catch the plague?
Methinks I feel this youth's perfections
With an invisible and subtle stealth
To creep in at mine eyes. Well, let it be.
What ho, Malvolio!

Enter Malvolio.

MALVOLIO Here, madam, at your service.

OLIVIA
Run after that same peevish messenger,
The County's man. He left this ring behind him,
[*Gives ring.*]
Would I or not. Tell him I'll none of it.
Desire him not to flatter with his lord,
Nor hold him up with hopes. I am not for him.
If that the youth will come this way tomorrow,
I'll give him reasons for 't. Hie thee, Malvolio.

MALVOLIO
Madam, I will. *Exit.*

217 comfortable comforting **221 To . . . method** i.e., to continue the metaphor (of delivering a sermon, begun with *divinity* and *what is your text* and continued in *doctrine, heresy,* etc.) **229 this present** at this present time. (Since it was customary to hang curtains in front of pictures, Olivia in unveiling speaks as if she were displaying a picture of herself.) **232 in grain** fast dyed **234 blent** blended **238 copy** i.e., a child. (But Olivia uses the word to mean *transcript.*) **240 schedules** inventories **241 utensil** article, item. **label'd** added as a codicil **246 if** even if **248 but . . . though** no more than evenly repaid even though **250 fertile** copious **255 In . . . divulg'd** well reported in public opinion **259 flame** passion

260 deadly deathlike **263 willow cabin** arbor. (Willow was a symbol of unrequited love.) **264 my soul** i.e., Olivia **265 cantons** songs. **contemned** rejected **268 babbling . . . air** echo **279 fee'd post** messenger to be tipped **281 Love . . . love** may Love make the heart of the man you love as hard as flint **288 blazon** heraldic description **296 County's** Count's, i.e., Duke's **298 flatter with** encourage

OLIVIA
I do I know not what, and fear to find
Mine eye too great a flatterer for my mind. 304
Fate, show thy force. Ourselves we do not owe; 305
What is decreed must be, and be this so. *[Exit.]*

ACT II • SCENE I

Enter Antonio and Sebastian.

ANTONIO Will you stay no longer? Nor will you not that
I go with you?
SEBASTIAN By your patience, no. My stars shine darkly 3
over me. The malignancy of my fate might perhaps 4
distemper yours; therefore I shall crave of you your
leave, that I may bear my evils alone. It were a bad
recompense for your love, to lay any of them on you.
ANTONIO Let me yet know of you whither you are
bound.
SEBASTIAN No, sooth, sir; my determinate voyage is 10
mere extravagancy. But I perceive in you so excellent 11
a touch of modesty, that you will not extort from me
what I am willing to keep in; therefore it charges me 13
in manners the rather to express myself. You must 14
know of me then, Antonio, my name is Sebastian,
which I call'd Roderigo. My father was that Sebastian
of Messaline whom I know you have heard of. He left 17
behind him myself and a sister, both born in an hour. 18
If the heavens had been pleas'd, would we had so
ended! But you, sir, alter'd that, for some hour before
you took me from the breach of the sea was my sister 21
drown'd.
ANTONIO Alas the day!
SEBASTIAN A lady, sir, though it was said she much re-
sembled me, was yet of many accounted beautiful. But
though I could not with such estimable wonder over- 26
far believe that, yet thus far I will boldly publish her:
she bore a mind that envy could not but call fair. She
is drown'd already, sir, with salt water, though I seem
to drown her remembrance again with more.
ANTONIO Pardon me, sir, your bad entertainment. 31
SEBASTIAN O good Antonio, forgive me your trouble. 32
ANTONIO If you will not murder me for my love, let me 33
be your servant.
SEBASTIAN If you will not undo what you have done,
that is, kill him whom you have recover'd, desire it
not. Fare ye well at once. My bosom is full of kindness, 37
and I am yet so near the manners of my mother, that 38
upon the least occasion more mine eyes will tell tales
of me. I am bound to the Count Orsino's court. Fare-
well. *Exit.*

ANTONIO
The gentleness of all the gods go with thee!
I have many enemies in Orsino's court,
Else would I very shortly see thee there.
But come what may, I do adore thee so
That danger shall seem sport, and I will go. *Exit.*

SCENE II

Enter Viola and Malvolio at several doors.

MALVOLIO Were not you ev'n now with the Countess
Olivia?
VIOLA Even now, sir. On a moderate pace I have since
arriv'd but hither.
MALVOLIO She returns this ring to you, sir. You might
have sav'd me my pains, to have taken it away your-
self. She adds, moreover, that you should put your
lord into a desperate assurance she will none of him. 8
And one thing more, that you be never so hardy to 9
come again in his affairs, unless it be to report your
lord's taking of this. Receive it so.
VIOLA She took the ring of me. I'll none of it. 12
MALVOLIO Come, sir, you peevishly threw it to her,
and her will is, it should be so return'd. *[Throws down
the ring.]* If it be worth stooping for, there it lies, in
your eye; if not, be it his that finds it. *Exit.*

VIOLA *[Picking up the ring]*
I left no ring with her. What means this lady?
Fortune forbid my outside have not charm'd her!
She made good view of me; indeed, so much, 19
That sure methought her eyes had lost her tongue, 20
For she did speak in starts distractedly.
She loves me, sure! The cunning of her passion
Invites me in this churlish messenger. 23
None of my lord's ring? Why, he sent her none.
I am the man. If it be so, as 'tis,
Poor lady, she were better love a dream.
Disguise, I see, thou art a wickedness
Wherein the pregnant enemy does much. 28
How easy is it for the proper-false 29
In women's waxen hearts to set their forms! 30
Alas, our frailty is the cause, not we,
For such as we are made of, such we be. 32
How will this fadge? My master loves her dearly; 33
And I, poor monster, fond as much on him; 34
And she, mistaken, seems to dote on me.
What will become of this? As I am man,
My state is desperate for my master's love;
As I am woman—now alas the day!—

304 Mine . . . mind i.e., that my eyes (through which love enters the soul) have betrayed my reason **305 owe** own, control

II.i. Location: Somewhere in Illyria.
3 patience leave **4 malignancy** malevolence (of the stars; also in a medical sense) **10 sooth** truly. **determinate** intended, determined upon **11 extravagancy** aimless wandering **13 am willing . . . in** wish to keep secret **13–14 it . . . manners** it is incumbent upon me in all courtesy **14 express** reveal **17 Messaline** (Not identified; possibly Mytilene or Messina.) **18 in an hour** in the same hour **21 breach of the sea** surf **26 estimable wonder** admiring judgment **31 entertainment** reception, hospitality **32 your trouble** the trouble I put you to **33 murder me for** i.e., be the cause of my death in return for **37 kindness** tenderness, natural emotion (of grief) **38 manners of my mother** womanish qualities

II.ii. Location: A street.
s.d. several different **8 desperate** without hope **9 hardy** bold **12 She . . . it** (Viola tells a quick and friendly lie to shield Olivia.) **19 made good view of** took a careful look at **20 lost** caused her to lose; or, ruined **23 Invites** tries to attract **28 pregnant** quick, resourceful. **enemy** i.e., Satan **29 proper-false** men who are handsome and deceitful **30 waxen** i.e., malleable, impressionable. **set their forms** stamp their images (as of a seal) **32 such as . . . of** i.e., feminine frailty **33 fadge** turn out **34 monster** i.e., being both man and woman. **fond** dote

What thriftless sighs shall poor Olivia breathe!
O time, thou must untangle this, not I;
It is too hard a knot for me t' untie. [*Exit.*]

SCENE III

Enter Sir Toby and Sir Andrew.

SIR TOBY Approach, Sir Andrew. Not to be abed after midnight is to be up betimes; and "diluculo surgere," thou know'st—

SIR ANDREW Nay, by my troth, I know not, but I know to be up late is to be up late.

SIR TOBY A false conclusion. I hate it as an unfill'd can. To be up after midnight and to go to bed then, is early; so that to go to bed after midnight is to go to bed betimes. Does not our lives consist of the four elements?

SIR ANDREW Faith, so they say, but I think it rather consists of eating and drinking.

SIR TOBY Th' art a scholar; let us therefore eat and drink. Marian, I say, a stoup of wine!

Enter Clown.

SIR ANDREW Here comes the fool, i' faith.

CLOWN How now, my hearts! Did you never see the picture of "we three"?

SIR TOBY Welcome, ass. Now let's have a catch.

SIR ANDREW By my troth, the fool has an excellent breast. I had rather than forty shillings I had such a leg, and so sweet a breath to sing, as the fool has. In sooth, thou wast in very gracious fooling last night, when thou spok'st of Pigrogromitus, of the Vapians passing the equinoctial of Queubus. 'Twas very good, i' faith. I sent thee sixpence for thy leman. Hadst it?

CLOWN I did impeticos thy gratillity; for Malvolio's nose is no whipstock. My lady has a white hand, and the Myrmidons are no bottle-ale houses.

SIR ANDREW Excellent! Why, this is the best fooling, when all is done. Now, a song.

SIR TOBY Come on; there is sixpence for you. [*Gives money.*] Let's have a song.

SIR ANDREW There's a testril of me too. [*Gives money.*] If one knight give a—

CLOWN Would you have a love-song, or a song of good life?

SIR TOBY A love-song, a love-song.

SIR ANDREW Ay, ay. I care not for good life.

CLOWN [*Sings*]

O mistress mine, where are you roaming?
O, stay and hear; your true love 's coming,
  That can sing both high and low.
Trip no further, pretty sweeting;
Journeys end in lovers meeting,
  Every wise man's son doth know.

SIR ANDREW Excellent good, i' faith.

SIR TOBY Good, good.

CLOWN [*Sings*]

What is love? 'tis not hereafter;
Present mirth hath present laughter;
  What's to come is still unsure.
In delay there lies no plenty;
Then come kiss me, sweet and twenty,
  Youth's a stuff will not endure.

SIR ANDREW A mellifluous voice, as I am true knight.

SIR TOBY A contagious breath.

SIR ANDREW Very sweet and contagious, i' faith.

SIR TOBY To hear by the nose, it is dulcet in contagion. But shall we make the welkin dance indeed? Shall we rouse the night-owl in a catch that will draw three souls out of one weaver? Shall we do that?

SIR ANDREW An you love me, let's do 't. I am dog at a catch.

CLOWN By 'r lady, sir, and some dogs will catch well.

SIR ANDREW Most certain. Let our catch be, "Thou knave."

CLOWN "Hold thy peace, thou knave," knight? I shall be constrain'd in 't to call thee knave, knight.

SIR ANDREW 'Tis not the first time I have constrain'd one to call me knave. Begin, fool. It begins "Hold thy peace."

CLOWN I shall never begin if I hold my peace.

SIR ANDREW Good, i' faith. Come, begin. *Catch sung.*

Enter Maria.

MARIA What a caterwauling do you keep here! If my lady have not call'd up her steward Malvolio and bid him turn you out of doors, never trust me.

SIR TOBY My lady's a Cataian, we are politicians, Malvolio's a Peg-a-Ramsey, and [*Sings.*] "Three merry men be we." Am not I consanguineous? Am I not of her blood? Tillyvally! Lady! [*Sings.*] "There dwelt a man in Babylon, lady, lady!"

CLOWN Beshrew me, the knight's in admirable fooling.

SIR ANDREW Ay, he does well enough if he be dispos'd, and so do I too. He does it with a better grace, but I do it more natural.

39 thriftless unprofitable

II.iii. Location: Olivia's house.
2 diluculo surgere [**saluberrimum est**] to rise early is most healthful. (A sentence from Lilly's *Latin Grammar.*) **6 can** tankard **14 stoup** drinking vessel **17 picture of "we three"** picture of two fools or asses inscribed "we three," the spectator being the third **18 catch** round **20 breast** voice **23–24 Pigrogromitus . . . Queubus** (Feste's mock erudition.) **25 leman** sweetheart **26 impeticos thy gratillity** (Suggests "impetticoat, or pocket up, thy gratuity.") **27 whipstock** whip handle. (Possibly suggests that Malvolio is not very formidable as overseer in Olivia's household; or, just nonsense.) **has a white hand** i.e., is ladylike. (But Feste's speech may be mere nonsense.) **28 Myrmidons** followers of Achilles. **bottle-ale houses** (Used contemptuously of taverns because they sold low-class drink.) **33 testril** i.e., tester, a coin worth sixpence **35–36 good life** virtuous living. (Or perhaps the Clown means simply *life's pleasures,* but is misunderstood by Sir Andrew to mean *virtuous living.*)

56 To . . . nose i.e., to describe hearing in olfactory terms. **dulcet in contagion** (Sir Toby may be mocking Sir Andrew's unfortunate choice of words.) **57 make . . . dance** i.e., drink till the sky seems to turn around **58–59 draw three souls** (Refers to the threefold nature of the soul, vegetal, sensible, and intellectual; or to the three singers; or, just a comic exaggeration.) **59 weaver** (Weavers were often associated with psalm-singing.) **60 dog at** very clever at (But Feste uses the word literally.) **61 catch** round. (But Feste uses it to mean *seize.*) **75 Cataian** Cathayan, i.e., Chinese, a trickster; or, just nonsense. **politicians** schemers, intriguers **76 Peg-a-Ramsey** character in a popular song. (Used here contemptuously.) **76–77 Three . . . we** (A snatch of an old song.) **78 Tillyvally** i.e., nonsense, fiddle-faddle **78–79 There . . . lady** (The first line of a ballad, "The Constancy of Susanna," together with the refrain, "Lady, lady.") **83 natural** naturally (but unconsciously suggesting idiocy)

SIR TOBY [*Sings*] "O' the twelfth day of December"— 84
MARIA For the love o' God, peace!

Enter Malvolio.

MALVOLIO My masters, are you mad? Or what are you?
Have you no wit, manners, nor honesty, but to gabble
like tinkers at this time of night? Do ye make an ale-
house of my lady's house, that ye squeak out your coz- 89
iers' catches without any mitigation or remorse of 90
voice? Is there no respect of place, persons, nor time in
you?
SIR TOBY We did keep time, sir, in our catches. Sneck 93
up! 94
MALVOLIO Sir Toby, I must be round with you. My 95
lady bade me tell you, that, though she harbors you as
her kinsman, she's nothing allied to your disorders. If
you can separate yourself and your misdemeanors,
you are welcome to the house; if not, an it would
please you to take leave of her, she is very willing to
bid you farewell.
SIR TOBY [*Sings*]
"Farewell, dear heart, since I must needs be gone." 102
MARIA Nay, good Sir Toby.
CLOWN [*Sings*]
"His eyes do show his days are almost done."
MALVOLIO Is 't even so?
SIR TOBY [*Sings*]
"But I will never die."
CLOWN
Sir Toby, there you lie.
MALVOLIO This is much credit to you.
SIR TOBY [*Sings*]
"Shall I bid him go?"
CLOWN [*Sings*]
"What an if you do?"
SIR TOBY [*Sings*]
"Shall I bid him go, and spare not?"
CLOWN [*Sings*]
"O no, no, no, no, you dare not."
SIR TOBY Out o' tune, sir? Ye lie. Art any more than a
steward? Dost thou think, because thou art virtuous,
there shall be no more cakes and ale?
CLOWN Yes, by Saint Anne, and ginger shall be hot i' 116
th' mouth too.
SIR TOBY Th' art i' th' right. Go, sir, rub your chain with 118
crumbs. A stoup of wine, Maria! 119
MALVOLIO Mistress Mary, if you priz'd my lady's favor
at anything more than contempt, you would not give 121
means for this uncivil rule. She shall know of it, by 122
this hand. *Exit.*
MARIA Go shake your ears. 124
SIR ANDREW 'Twere as good a deed as to drink when a
man's a-hungry, to challenge him the field, and then 126
to break promise with him and make a fool of him.
SIR TOBY Do 't, knight. I'll write thee a challenge; or I'll
deliver thy indignation to him by word of mouth.
MARIA Sweet Sir Toby, be patient for tonight. Since the
youth of the Count's was today with my lady, she is
much out of quiet. For Monsieur Malvolio, let me
alone with him. If I do not gull him into a nayword, 133
and make him a common recreation, do not think I 134
have wit enough to lie straight in my bed. I know I
can do it.
SIR TOBY Possess us, possess us. Tell us something of 137
him.
MARIA Marry, sir, sometimes he is a kind of puritan. 139
SIR ANDREW O, if I thought that, I 'd beat him like a
dog!
SIR TOBY What, for being a puritan? Thy exquisite rea-
son, dear knight?
SIR ANDREW I have no exquisite reason for 't, but I have
reason good enough.
MARIA The devil a puritan that he is, or anything con-
stantly, but a time-pleaser; an affection'd ass, that cons 147
state without book and utters it by great swarths; the 148
best persuaded of himself, so cramm'd, as he thinks, 149
with excellencies, that it is his grounds of faith that all
that look on him love him; and on that vice in him
will my revenge find notable cause to work.
SIR TOBY What wilt thou do?
MARIA I will drop in his way some obscure epistles of
love; wherein, by the color of his beard, the shape of
his leg, the manner of his gait, the expressure of his 156
eye, forehead, and complexion, he shall find himself 157
most feelingly personated. I can write very like my 158
lady your niece; on a forgotten matter we can hardly
make distinction of our hands.
SIR TOBY Excellent! I smell a device.
SIR ANDREW I have 't in my nose too.
SIR TOBY He shall think, by the letters that thou wilt
drop, that they come from my niece, and that she's in
love with him.
MARIA My purpose is, indeed, a horse of that color.
SIR ANDREW And your horse now would make him an
ass.
MARIA Ass, I doubt not.
SIR ANDREW O, 'twill be admirable!
MARIA Sport royal, I warrant you. I know my physic 171
will work with him. I will plant you two, and let the
fool make a third, where he shall find the letter. Ob-
serve his construction of it. For this night, to bed, and
dream on the event. Farewell. *Exit.* 175
SIR TOBY Good night, Penthesilea. 176
SIR ANDREW Before me, she's a good wench. 177
SIR TOBY She's a beagle, true-bred, and one that adores
me. What o' that?

84 O' . . . December (Part of a ballad.) **89–90 coziers'** cobblers' **90 mitigation or remorse** i.e., considerate lowering **93–94 Sneck up** go hang **95 round** plain **102 Farewell . . . gone** (From the ballad "Corydon's Farewell to Phyllis.") **116 ginger** (Commonly used to spice ale.) **118–119 Go . . . crumbs** i.e., scour or polish your steward's chain; attend to your own business and remember your station **121–122 give means** i.e., supply drink **122 rule** conduct **124 your ears** i.e., your ass's ears **126 the field** i.e., to a duel

133 gull trick. **nayword** byword **134 recreation** sport **137 Possess** inform **139 puritan** (Maria's point is that Malvolio is sometimes a *kind* of puritan, insofar as he is precise about moral conduct and censorious of others for immoral conduct, but that he is nothing consistently except a time-server. He is not then simply a satirical type of the Puritan sect. The extent of the resemblance is left unstated.) **147 time-pleaser** time-server, sycophant. **affection'd** affected **147–148 cons . . . book** learns by heart the phrases and mannerisms of the great **148 swarths** swaths, quantities **149 best persuaded** having the best opinion **156 expressure** expression **157 complexion** countenance **158 personated** represented **171 physic** medicine **175 event** outcome **176 Penthesilea** Queen of the Amazons. (Another ironical allusion to Maria's diminutive stature.) **177 Before me** i.e., on my soul

SIR ANDREW I was ador'd once too.

SIR TOBY Let's to bed, knight. Thou hadst need send for more money.

SIR ANDREW If I cannot recover your niece, I am a foul 183
way out. 184

SIR TOBY Send for money, knight. If thou hast her not
i' th' end, call me cut. 186

SIR ANDREW If I do not, never trust me, take it how you will.

SIR TOBY Come, come, I'll go burn some sack. 'Tis too 189
late to go to bed now. Come, knight; come, knight.
Exeunt.

SCENE IV

Enter Duke, Viola, Curio, and others.

DUKE
Give me some music. Now, good morrow, friends.
Now, good Cesario, but that piece of song, 2
That old and antique song we heard last night. 3
Methought it did relieve my passion much,
More than light airs and recollected terms 5
Of these most brisk and giddy-paced times.
Come, but one verse.

CURIO He is not here, so please your lordship, that should sing it.

DUKE Who was it?

CURIO Feste, the jester, my lord; a fool that the lady Olivia's father took much delight in. He is about the house.

DUKE
Seek him out, and play the tune the while.
[*Exit Curio.*] *Music plays.*
Come hither, boy. If ever thou shalt love,
In the sweet pangs of it remember me;
For such as I am all true lovers are,
Unstaid and skittish in all motions else, 18
Save in the constant image of the creature
That is belov'd. How dost thou like this tune?

VIOLA
It gives a very echo to the seat 21
Where Love is thron'd.

DUKE
Thou dost speak masterly.
My life upon 't, young though thou art, thine eye
Hath stay'd upon some favor that it loves. 24
Hath it not, boy?

VIOLA
A little, by your favor.

DUKE
What kind of woman is 't?

VIOLA
Of your complexion.

DUKE
She is not worth thee, then. What years, i' faith?

VIOLA
About your years, my lord.

DUKE
Too old, by heaven. Let still the woman take 29
An elder than herself; so wears she to him, 30
So sways she level in her husband's heart. 31
For, boy, however we do praise ourselves,
Our fancies are more giddy and unfirm,
More longing, wavering, sooner lost and worn,
Than women's are.

VIOLA
I think it well, my lord.

DUKE
Then let thy love be younger than thyself,
Or thy affection cannot hold the bent; 37
For women are as roses, whose fair flow'r
Being once display'd, doth fall that very hour.

VIOLA
And so they are. Alas, that they are so,
To die, even when they to perfection grow!

Enter Curio and Clown.

DUKE
O, fellow, come, the song we had last night.
Mark it, Cesario, it is old and plain;
The spinsters and the knitters in the sun, 44
And the free maids that weave their thread with bones, 45
Do use to chant it. It is silly sooth, 46
And dallies with the innocence of love,
Like the old age. 48

CLOWN Are you ready, sir?

DUKE Ay, prithee, sing. *Music.*

The Song.

[CLOWN]
Come away, come away, death,
And in sad cypress let me be laid. 52
Fly away, fly away, breath;
I am slain by a fair cruel maid.
My shroud of white, stuck all with yew, 55
O, prepare it!
My part of death, no one so true 57
Did share it. 58

Not a flower, not a flower sweet,
On my black coffin let there be strown;
Not a friend, not a friend greet
My poor corpse, where my bones shall be thrown.
A thousand thousand sighs to save,
Lay me, O, where
Sad true lover never find my grave,
To weep there!

183 recover win **183–184 foul way out** i.e., miserably out of pocket. (Literally, out of my way and in the mire.) **186 cut** a horse with a docked tail; also, a gelding, or the female genital organ **189 burn some sack** warm some Spanish wine

II.iv. Location: The Duke's palace.
2 but i.e., I ask only **3 antique** quaint **5 recollected terms** studied and artificial expressions (?) **18 motions else** other thoughts and emotions **21 seat** i.e., the heart **24 stay'd . . . favor** rested upon some face

29 still always **30 wears she** she adapts herself **31 sways she level** she keeps steady, constant **37 hold the bent** hold steady (like the tension of a bow) **44 spinsters** spinners **45 free** carefree, innocent. **bones** bobbins on which bone-lace was made **46 Do use** are accustomed. **silly sooth** simple truth **48 Like . . . age** as in the good old times **52 cypress** i.e., a coffin of cypress wood, or bier strewn with sprigs of cypress **55 yew** i.e., yew sprigs. (Emblematic of mourning, like cypress.) **57–58 My . . . it** i.e., no one died for love so true to love as I

DUKE There's for thy pains.
CLOWN No pains, sir; I take pleasure in singing, sir.
DUKE I'll pay thy pleasure then. [*Gives money.*]
CLOWN Truly, sir, and pleasure will be paid, one time 70
or another. 71
DUKE Give me now leave to leave thee. 72
CLOWN Now, the melancholy god protect thee, and the
tailor make thy doublet of changeable taffeta, for thy 74
mind is a very opal. I would have men of such con-
stancy put to sea, that their business might be every
thing and their intent every where, for that's it that 77
always makes a good voyage of nothing. Farewell. 78
Exit.
DUKE
Let all the rest give place.
[*Curio and Attendants retire.*]
Once more, Cesario, 79
Get thee to yond same sovereign cruelty.
Tell her, my love, more noble than the world,
Prizes not quantity of dirty lands;
The parts that fortune hath bestow'd upon her, 83
Tell her, I hold as giddily as fortune; 84
But 'tis that miracle and queen of gems 85
That nature pranks her in attracts my soul. 86
VIOLA
But if she cannot love you, sir?
DUKE
I cannot be so answer'd.
VIOLA Sooth, but you must.
Say that some lady, as perhaps there is,
Hath for your love as great a pang of heart
As you have for Olivia. You cannot love her;
You tell her so. Must she not then be answer'd?
DUKE
There is no woman's sides
Can bide the beating of so strong a passion 94
As love doth give my heart; no woman's heart
So big, to hold so much; they lack retention. 96
Alas, their love may be call'd appetite,
No motion of the liver, but the palate, 98
That suffer surfeit, cloyment, and revolt; 99
But mine is all as hungry as the sea,
And can digest as much. Make no compare
Between that love a woman can bear me
And that I owe Olivia.
VIOLA Ay, but I know— 103
DUKE
What dost thou know?
VIOLA
Too well what love women to men may owe.
In faith, they are as true of heart as we.
My father had a daughter lov'd a man,
As it might be, perhaps, were I a woman,
I should your lordship.
DUKE And what's her history?
VIOLA
A blank, my lord. She never told her love,
But let concealment, like a worm i' th' bud,
Feed on her damask cheek. She pin'd in thought, 112
And with a green and yellow melancholy
She sat like Patience on a monument, 114
Smiling at grief. Was not this love indeed?
We men may say more, swear more, but indeed
Our shows are more than will; for still we prove 117
Much in our vows, but little in our love.
DUKE
But died thy sister of her love, my boy?
VIOLA
I am all the daughters of my father's house,
And all the brothers too—and yet I know not.
Sir, shall I to this lady?
DUKE Ay, that's the theme.
To her in haste; give her this jewel. [*Gives jewel.*]
Say
My love can give no place, bide no denay. *Exeunt.* 124

SCENE V

Enter Sir Toby, Sir Andrew, and Fabian.

SIR TOBY Come thy ways, Signior Fabian.
FABIAN Nay, I'll come. If I lose a scruple of this sport, 2
let me be boil'd to death with melancholy. 3
SIR TOBY Wouldst thou not be glad to have the nig-
gardly rascally sheep-biter come by some notable 5
shame?
FABIAN I would exult, man. You know he brought me
out o' favor with my lady about a bear-baiting here.
SIR TOBY To anger him we'll have the bear again, and
we will fool him black and blue. Shall we not, Sir An- 10
drew?
SIR ANDREW An we do not, it is pity of our lives. 12

Enter Maria.

SIR TOBY Here comes the little villain. How now, my
metal of India? 14
MARIA Get ye all three into the box-tree. Malvolio's
coming down this walk. He has been yonder i' the sun
practicing behavior to his own shadow this half hour.
Observe him, for the love of mockery; for I know this
letter will make a contemplative idiot of him. Close, in 19

70–71 pleasure . . . another i.e., sooner or later one must pay for indulgence **72 leave to leave** permission to take leave of, dismiss **74 doublet** close-fitting jacket. **changeable taffeta** a silk so woven of various-colored threads that its color shifts with changing perspective **77–78 for . . . nothing** (Ironical, meaning that such changeable enterprise will make a good voyage come to nothing and would think a voyage that led anywhere a good one.) **79 give place** withdraw **83 parts** gifts such as wealth or rank **84 I . . . fortune** i.e., I esteem as carelessly as does fortune, that fickle goddess **85 miracle . . . gems** i.e., her beauty **86 pranks** adorns. **attracts** i.e., that attracts **94 bide** withstand **96 retention** constancy, power of retaining **98 motion** impulse. **liver . . . palate** (Real love is a passion of the liver, whereas fancy, light love, is born in the eye and nourished in the palate.) **99 cloyment** satiety. **revolt** sickness, revulsion **103 owe** have for

112 damask pink and white like the damask rose **114 on a monument** carved in statuary on a tomb **117 more than will** greater than our feelings **124 can . . . denay** cannot yield or endure denial

II.v. Location: Olivia's garden.
2 scruple bit **3 boil'd** (with a pun on *biled;* black bile was the "humor" of melancholy) **5 sheep-biter** a dog that bites sheep, i.e., a nuisance **10 fool . . . blue** mock him until he is figuratively black and blue **12 pity of our lives** a pity we should live **14 metal** gold, i.e., priceless one **19 contemplative** i.e., from his musings. **Close** i.e., keep close, stay hidden

the name of jesting! [*The others hide.*] Lie thou there
[*Throws down a letter.*]; for here comes the trout that
must be caught with tickling. *Exit.* 22

Enter Malvolio.

MALVOLIO 'Tis but fortune; all is fortune. Maria once
told me she did affect me; and I have heard herself 24
come thus near, that, should she fancy, it should be 25
one of my complexion. Besides, she uses me with a
more exalted respect than any one else that follows 27
her. What should I think on 't?

SIR TOBY Here's an overweening rogue!

FABIAN O, peace! Contemplation makes a rare turkey-
cock of him. How he jets under his advanc'd plumes! 31

SIR ANDREW 'Slight, I could so beat the rogue! 32

SIR TOBY Peace, I say.

MALVOLIO To be Count Malvolio.

SIR TOBY Ah, rogue!

SIR ANDREW Pistol him, pistol him.

SIR TOBY Peace, peace!

MALVOLIO There is example for 't. The lady of the Stra- 38
chy married the yeoman of the wardrobe. 39

SIR ANDREW Fie on him, Jezebel! 40

FABIAN O, peace! Now he's deeply in. Look how imag-
ination blows him. 42

MALVOLIO Having been three months married to her,
sitting in my state— 44

SIR TOBY O, for a stone-bow, to hit him in the eye! 45

MALVOLIO Calling my officers about me, in my
branch'd velvet gown; having come from a daybed, 47
where I have left Olivia sleeping—

SIR TOBY Fire and brimstone!

FABIAN O, peace, peace!

MALVOLIO And then to have the humor of state; and 51
after a demure travel of regard, telling them I know my 52
place as I would they should do theirs, to ask for my
kinsman, Toby— 54

SIR TOBY Bolts and shackles!

FABIAN O peace, peace, peace! Now, now.

MALVOLIO Seven of my people, with an obedient start,
make out for him. I frown the while; and perchance
wind up my watch, or play with my—some rich 59
jewel. Toby approaches; curtsies there to me—

SIR TOBY Shall this fellow live?

FABIAN Though our silence be drawn from us with 62
cars, yet peace. 63

MALVOLIO I extend my hand to him thus, quenching
my familiar smile with an austere regard of control— 65

SIR TOBY And does not Toby take you a blow o' the lips 66
then?

MALVOLIO Saying, "Cousin Toby, my fortunes having
cast me on your niece give me this prerogative of
speech,"—

SIR TOBY What, what?

MALVOLIO "You must amend your drunkenness."

SIR TOBY Out, scab! 73

FABIAN Nay, patience, or we break the sinews of our
plot.

MALVOLIO "Besides, you waste the treasure of your
time with a foolish knight"—

SIR ANDREW That's me, I warrant you.

MALVOLIO "One Sir Andrew"—

SIR ANDREW I knew 'twas I, for many do call me fool.

MALVOLIO What employment have we here? 81
[*Taking up the letter.*]

FABIAN Now is the woodcock near the gin. 82

SIR TOBY O, peace, and the spirit of humors intimate 83
reading aloud to him!

MALVOLIO By my life, this is my lady's hand. These be
her very c's, her u's and her t's; and thus makes she 86
her great P's. It is, in contempt of question, her hand. 87

SIR ANDREW Her c's, her u's and her t's. Why that?

MALVOLIO [*Reads*] "To the unknown belov'd, this, and
my good wishes."—Her very phrases! By your leave, 90
wax. Soft! And the impressure her Lucrece, with 91
which she uses to seal. 'Tis my lady. To whom should 92
this be? [*Opens the letter.*]

FABIAN This wins him, liver and all. 94

MALVOLIO [*Reads*]

"Jove knows I love,
But who?
Lips, do not move;
No man must know."

"No man must know." What follows? The numbers 99
alter'd! "No man must know." If this should be thee,
Malvolio?

SIR TOBY Marry, hang thee, brock! 102

MALVOLIO [*Reads*]

"I may command where I adore,
But silence, like a Lucrece knife,
With bloodless stroke my heart doth gore;
M.O.A.I. doth sway my life.

FABIAN A fustian riddle! 107

SIR TOBY Excellent wench, say I.

MALVOLIO "M.O.A.I. doth sway my life." Nay, but
first, let me see, let me see, let me see.

FABIAN What dish o' poison has she dress'd him! 111

SIR TOBY And with what wing the staniel checks 112
at it! 113

MALVOLIO "I may command where I adore." Why, she
may command me; I serve her, she is my lady. Why,
this is evident to any formal capacity; there is no ob- 116
struction in this. And the end—what should that al-

22 tickling (1) stroking gently about the gills—an actual method of fishing (2) flattery **24 she** i.e., Olivia. **affect** have fondness for **25 fancy** fall in love **27 follows** serves **31 jets** struts. **advanc'd** raised **32 'Slight** by His (God's) light **38 example** precedent **38–39 lady of the Strachy** (Apparently a lady who had married below her station; no certain identification.) **40 Jezebel** the proud queen of Ahab, King of Israel **42 blows** puffs up **44 state** chair of state **45 stone-bow** crossbow that shot stones **47 branch'd** adorned with a figured pattern suggesting branched leaves or flowers. **daybed** sofa, couch **51 have . . . state** adopt the imperious manner of authority **52 demure . . . regard** grave survey of the company. **telling** indicating to **54 Toby** (Malvolio omits the title *Sir.*) **59 play with my** (Malvolio perhaps means his steward's chain, but checks himself in time.) **62–63 with cars** i.e., by force, as by a team of horses **65 familiar** friendly. **regard of control** look of authority **66 take** deliver

73 scab scurvy fellow **81 employment** business **82 woodcock** (A bird proverbial for its stupidity.) **gin** snare **83 humors** whim, caprice **86 c's . . . t's** i.e., *cut,* slang for the female pudenda **87 great** capital **in contempt of** beyond **90–91 By . . . wax** (Addressed to the seal on the letter.) **91 Soft** softly, not so fast. **impressure** device imprinted on the seal. **Lucrece** Lucretia, chaste matron who, ravished by Tarquin, committed suicide **92 uses** is accustomed **94 liver** i.e., the seat of passion **99 numbers** meter **102 brock** badger. (Used contemptuously.) **107 fustian** bombastic, ridiculously pompous **111 dress'd** prepared for **112 staniel** an inferior kind of hawk **112–113 checks at it** turns to fly at it **116 formal capacity** normal mind

phabetical position portend? If I could make that resemble something in me! Softly! M.O.A.I.—

SIR TOBY O, ay, make up that. He is now at a cold scent.

FABIAN Sowter will cry upon 't for all this, though it be as rank as a fox.

MALVOLIO M—Malvolio; M—why, that begins my name.

FABIAN Did not I say he would work it out? The cur is excellent at faults.

MALVOLIO M—But then there is no consonancy in the sequel that suffers under probation: A should follow, but O does.

FABIAN And O shall end, I hope.

SIR TOBY Ay, or I'll cudgel him, and make him cry O!

MALVOLIO And then I comes behind.

FABIAN Ay, an you had any eye behind you, you might see more detraction at your heels than fortunes before you.

MALVOLIO M.O.A.I. This simulation is not as the former. And yet, to crush this a little, it would bow to me, for every one of these letters are in my name. Soft! Here follows prose.

[*Reads.*] "If this fall into thy hand, revolve. In my stars I am above thee, but be not afraid of greatness. Some are born great, some achieve greatness, and some have greatness thrust upon 'em. Thy Fates open their hands; let thy blood and spirit embrace them; and, to inure thyself to what thou art like to be, cast thy humble slough and appear fresh. Be opposite with a kinsman, surly with servants. Let thy tongue tang arguments of state; put thyself into the trick of singularity. She thus advises thee that sighs for thee. Remember who commended thy yellow stockings, and wish'd to see thee ever cross-garter'd. I say, remember. Go to, thou art made, if thou desir'st to be so. If not, let me see thee a steward still, the fellow of servants, and not worthy to touch Fortune's fingers. Farewell. She that would alter services with thee,

The Fortunate-Unhappy."

Daylight and champain discovers not more. This is open. I will be proud, I will read politic authors, I will baffle Sir Toby, I will wash off gross acquaintance, I will be point-devise the very man. I do not now fool myself, to let imagination jade me; for every reason excites to this, that my lady loves me. She did commend my yellow stockings of late, she did praise my leg being cross-garter'd; and in this she manifests herself to my love, and with a kind of injunction drives me to these habits of her liking. I thank my stars, I am happy. I will be strange, stout, in yellow stockings, and cross-garter'd, even with the swiftness of putting on. Jove and my stars be prais'd! Here is yet a postscript. [*Reads.*] "Thou canst not choose but know who I am. If thou entertain'st my love, let it appear in thy smiling; thy smiles become thee well. Therefore in my presence still smile, dear my sweet, I prithee."

Jove, I thank thee. I will smile; I will do everything that thou wilt have me. *Exit.*

FABIAN I will not give my part of this sport for a pension of thousands to be paid from the Sophy.

SIR TOBY I could marry this wench for this device.

SIR ANDREW So could I too.

SIR TOBY And ask no other dowry with her but such another jest.

Enter Maria.

SIR ANDREW Nor I neither.

FABIAN Here comes my noble gull-catcher.

SIR TOBY Wilt thou set thy foot o' my neck?

SIR ANDREW Or o' mine either?

SIR TOBY Shall I play my freedom at tray-trip, and become thy bond-slave?

SIR ANDREW I' faith, or I either?

SIR TOBY Why, thou hast put him in such a dream, that when the image of it leaves him he must run mad.

MARIA Nay, but say true, does it work upon him?

SIR TOBY Like aqua-vitae with a midwife.

MARIA If you will then see the fruits of the sport, mark his first approach before my lady. He will come to her in yellow stockings, and 'tis a color she abhors, and cross-garter'd, a fashion she detests; and he will smile upon her, which will now be so unsuitable to her disposition, being addicted to a melancholy as she is, that it cannot but turn him into a notable contempt. If you will see it, follow me.

SIR TOBY To the gates of Tartar, thou most excellent devil of wit!

SIR ANDREW I'll make one too. *Exeunt.*

ACT III • SCENE I

Enter Viola, and Clown [*with a tabor*].

VIOLA Save thee, friend, and thy music. Dost thou live by thy tabor?

CLOWN No, sir, I live by the church.

VIOLA Art thou a churchman?

CLOWN No such matter, sir. I do live by the church; for I do live at my house, and my house doth stand by the church.

120 O, ay (playing on *A.I.* of *M.O.A.I.*) **make up** work out **121 Sowter** cobbler. (Here, the name for a hound.) **cry upon 't** bay aloud (as though picking up the scent) **122 rank as a fox** (i.e., Malvolio is so crude a hunter that he will leave the trail of a hare and follow the rank scent of a fox.) **126 at faults** i.e., at maneuvering his way past breaks in the line of scent **127–128 consonancy in the sequel** pattern in the following letters. (In fact, the letters M.O.A.I. represent the first, last, second, and next to last letters of Malvolio's name.) **128 suffers under probation** stands up under examination **130 O shall end** (1) O ends Malvolio's name (2) a noose shall end his life (3) omega ends the Greek alphabet (4) his cry of pain will end the joke **134 detraction** defamation **136 simulation** disguised meaning **140 revolve** consider. **stars** fortune **145 inure** accustom. **cast** cast off **146 slough** skin of a snake; hence, former demeanor of humbleness. **opposite** contradictory **147 tang** sound loud with **148 state** politics, statecraft. **trick of singularity** eccentricity of manner **151 cross-garter'd** wearing garters above and below the knee so as to cross behind it **155 alter services** i.e., exchange place of mistress and servant **157 champain** open country **158 politic** dealing with state affairs **159 baffle** put down **160 point-devise** correct to the letter **161 jade** trick

166 these habits this attire **167 happy** fortunate. **strange** aloof. **stout** haughty **177 Sophy** Shah of Persia **186 play** gamble. **tray-trip** a game of dice, success in which depended on throwing a three *(tray)* **192 aqua-vitae** brandy or other distilled liquors **201 Tartar** Tartarus, the infernal regions

III.i. Location: Olivia's garden.

1 Save God save **1–2 live by** earn your living with. (But Feste uses the phrase to mean *dwell near.*) **2 tabor** small drum

VIOLA So thou mayst say, the king lies by a beggar, if a beggar dwell near him; or, the church stands by thy tabor, if thy tabor stand by the church.

CLOWN You have said, sir. To see this age! A sentence is but a chev'ril glove to a good wit. How quickly the wrong side may be turn'd outward!

VIOLA Nay, that's certain. They that dally nicely with words may quickly make them wanton.

CLOWN I would therefore my sister had had no name, sir.

VIOLA Why, man?

CLOWN Why, sir, her name's a word, and to dally with that word might make my sister wanton. But indeed words are very rascals since bonds disgrac'd them.

VIOLA Thy reason, man?

CLOWN Troth, sir, I can yield you none without words, and words are grown so false I am loath to prove reason with them.

VIOLA I warrant thou art a merry fellow and car'st for nothing.

CLOWN Not so, sir, I do care for something; but in my conscience, sir, I do not care for you. If that be to care for nothing, sir, I would it would make you invisible.

VIOLA Art not thou the Lady Olivia's fool?

CLOWN No, indeed, sir. The Lady Olivia has no folly. She will keep no fool, sir, till she be married; and fools are as like husbands as pilchers are to herrings, the husband's the bigger. I am indeed not her fool, but her corrupter of words.

VIOLA I saw thee late at the Count Orsino's.

CLOWN Foolery, sir, does walk about the orb like the sun, it shines everywhere. I would be sorry, sir, but the fool should be as oft with your master as with my mistress. I think I saw your wisdom there.

VIOLA Nay, an thou pass upon me, I'll no more with thee. Hold, there's expenses for thee.

[*Gives a coin.*]

CLOWN Now Jove, in his next commodity of hair, send thee a beard!

VIOLA By my troth, I'll tell thee, I am almost sick for one—[*Aside*] though I would not have it grow on my chin.—Is thy lady within?

CLOWN Would not a pair of these have bred, sir?

VIOLA Yes, being kept together and put to use.

CLOWN I would play Lord Pandarus of Phrygia, sir, to bring a Cressida to this Troilus.

VIOLA I understand you, sir; 'tis well begg'd.

[*Gives another coin.*]

CLOWN The matter, I hope, is not great, sir, begging but a beggar; Cressida was a beggar. My lady is within, sir. I will conster to them whence you come. Who you are and what you would are out of my welkin—I might say "element," but the word is overworn. *Exit.*

VIOLA

This fellow is wise enough to play the fool,
And to do that well craves a kind of wit.
He must observe their mood on whom he jests,
The quality of persons, and the time,
And, like the haggard, check at every feather
That comes before his eye. This is a practice
As full of labor as a wise man's art;
For folly that he wisely shows is fit,
But wise men, folly-fall'n, quite taint their wit.

Enter Sir Toby and [Sir] Andrew.

SIR TOBY Save you, gentleman.

VIOLA And you, sir.

SIR ANDREW Dieu vous garde, monsieur.

VIOLA Et vous aussi; votre serviteur.

SIR ANDREW I hope, sir, you are; and I am yours.

SIR TOBY Will you encounter the house? My niece is desirous you should enter, if your trade be to her.

VIOLA I am bound to your niece, sir; I mean, she is the list of my voyage.

SIR TOBY Taste your legs, sir; put them to motion.

VIOLA My legs do better understand me, sir, than I understand what you mean by bidding me taste my legs.

SIR TOBY I mean, to go, sir, to enter.

VIOLA I will answer you with gait and entrance.—But we are prevented.

Enter Olivia and Gentlewoman [Maria].

Most excellent accomplish'd lady, the heavens rain odors on you!

SIR ANDREW That youth's a rare courtier. "Rain odors," well.

VIOLA My matter hath no voice, lady, but to your own most pregnant and vouchsafed ear.

SIR ANDREW "Odors," "pregnant," and "vouchsafed." I'll get 'em all three all ready.

OLIVIA Let the garden door be shut, and leave me to my hearing. [*Exeunt Sir Toby, Sir Andrew, and Maria.*] Give me your hand, sir.

VIOLA

My duty, madam, and most humble service.

OLIVIA

What is your name?

VIOLA

Cesario is your servant's name, fair princess.

OLIVIA

My servant, sir? 'Twas never merry world
Since lowly feigning was call'd compliment.
Y' are servant to the Count Orsino, youth.

12 chev'ril kidskin **14 dally nicely** play subtly **15 wanton** i.e., unmanageable **20 wanton** unchaste **21 since . . . them** i.e., since sworn statements have been needed to make them good **30 invisible** i.e., nothing; absent **34 pilchers** pilchards, fish resembling herring **38 orb** earth **39 but** unless **41 your wisdom** i.e., you **42 pass upon me** fence (verbally) with me, joke at my expense **44 commodity** supply **50 put to use** put out at interest **51 Pandarus** the go-between in the love story of Troilus and Cressida; uncle to Cressida **54–55 begging . . . Cressida** (A reference to Henryson's *Testament of Cresseid* in which Cressida became a leper and a beggar. The Clown desires another coin to be the mate of the one he has, as Cressida, the beggar, was mate to Troilus.) **56 conster** construe, explain

58 welkin sky. **element** (The word can be synonymous with *welkin,* but the common phrase *out of my element* means "beyond my scope.") **63 quality** character **64 haggard** untrained adult hawk, hence unmanageable **64–65 check . . . eye** strike at every bird it sees, i.e., dart adroitly from subject to subject **65 practice** exercise of skill **67 folly . . . fit** the folly he displays is a proper skill **68 folly-fall'n** having fallen into folly. **taint** impair **71 Dieu . . . monsieur** God keep you, sir **72 Et . . . serviteur** and you, too; (I am) your servant. (Sir Andrew is not quite up to a reply in French.) **74 encounter** (High-sounding word to express "enter.") **76 I am bound** I am on a journey. (Continues Sir Toby's metaphor in *trade.*) **77 list** limit, destination **78 Taste** try **79 understand** stand under, support **82 gait and entrance** going and entering **83 prevented** anticipated **88 hath no voice** cannot be uttered **89 pregnant** receptive **99 lowly feigning** affected humility. **was call'd** began to be called

VIOLA
And he is yours, and his must needs be yours;
Your servant's servant is your servant, madam.

OLIVIA
For him, I think not on him. For his thoughts,
Would they were blanks, rather than fill'd with me!

VIOLA
Madam, I come to whet your gentle thoughts
On his behalf.

OLIVIA O, by your leave, I pray you,
I bade you never speak again of him.
But, would you undertake another suit,
I had rather hear you to solicit that
Than music from the spheres.

VIOLA Dear lady—

OLIVIA
Give me leave, beseech you. I did send,
After the last enchantment you did here,
A ring in chase of you; so did I abuse
Myself, my servant, and, I fear me, you.
Under your hard construction must I sit,
To force that on you, in a shameful cunning
Which you knew none of yours. What might you think?
Have you not set mine honor at the stake
And baited it with all th' unmuzzled thoughts
That tyrannous heart can think? To one of your receiving
Enough is shown; a cypress, not a bosom,
Hides my heart. So, let me hear you speak.

VIOLA
I pity you.

OLIVIA That's a degree to love.

VIOLA
No, not a grize; for 'tis a vulgar proof
That very oft we pity enemies.

OLIVIA
Why, then, methinks 'tis time to smile again.
O world, how apt the poor are to be proud!
If one should be a prey, how much the better
To fall before the lion than the wolf! *Clock strikes.*
The clock upbraids me with the waste of time.
Be not afraid, good youth, I will not have you;
And yet, when wit and youth is come to harvest,
Your wife is like to reap a proper man.
There lies your way, due west.

VIOLA Then westward ho!
Grace and good disposition attend your ladyship.
You'll nothing, madam, to my lord by me?

OLIVIA
Stay.
I prithee tell me what thou think'st of me.

VIOLA
That you do think you are not what you are.

OLIVIA
If I think so, I think the same of you.

VIOLA
Then think you right. I am not what I am.

OLIVIA
I would you were as I would have you be!

VIOLA
Would it be better, madam, than I am?
I wish it might, for now I am your fool.

OLIVIA
O, what a deal of scorn looks beautiful
In the contempt and anger of his lip!
A murd'rous guilt shows not itself more soon
Than love that would seem hid; love's night is noon.
Cesario, by the roses of the spring,
By maidhood, honor, truth, and every thing,
I love thee so, that maugre all thy pride,
Nor wit nor reason can my passion hide.
Do not extort thy reasons from this clause,
For that I woo, thou therefore hast no cause;
But rather reason thus with reason fetter,
Love sought is good, but given unsought is better.

VIOLA
By innocence I swear, and by my youth,
I have one heart, one bosom, and one truth,
And that no woman has; nor never none
Shall mistress be of it, save I alone.
And so adieu, good madam. Never more
Will I my master's tears to you deplore.

OLIVIA
Yet come again; for thou perhaps mayst move
That heart, which now abhors, to like his love.
Exeunt.

SCENE II

Enter Sir Toby, Sir Andrew, and Fabian.

SIR ANDREW No, faith, I'll not stay a jot longer.
SIR TOBY Thy reason, dear venom, give thy reason.
FABIAN You must needs yield your reason, Sir Andrew.
SIR ANDREW Marry, I saw your niece do more favors to the Count's servingman than ever she bestow'd upon me; I saw 't i' th' orchard.
SIR TOBY Did she see thee the while, old boy? Tell me that.
SIR ANDREW As plain as I see you now.
FABIAN This was a great argument of love in her toward you.

103 For as for **110 music from the spheres** (The heavenly bodies were thought to be fixed in hollow concentric spheres which revolved one about the other, producing a harmony too exquisite to be heard by human ears.) **115 hard construction** harsh interpretation **116 To force** for forcing **118 stake** (The figure is from bear-baiting.) **119 baited** harassed (as dogs *bait* a bear) **120 tyrannous** cruel. **receiving** capacity, intelligence **121 cypress** a thin, gauzelike, black material **124 grize** step. (Synonymous with *degree* in the preceding line.) **vulgar proof** common experience **126 smile** i.e., cast off love's melancholy **127 the poor** i.e., the unfortunate and rejected (like Olivia). **proud** i.e., of their distress **129 To fall . . . wolf** i.e., to fall before a noble adversary **133 proper** handsome, worthy **134 westward ho** (The cry of Thames watermen to attract westward-bound passengers.)

139 That . . . are i.e., that you think you are in love with a man, and you are mistaken **140 If . . . you** (Olivia may interpret Viola's cryptic statement as suggesting that Olivia "does not know herself," i.e., is distracted with passion; she may also hint at her suspicion that "Cesario" is higher born than he admits.) **144 fool** butt **148 love's . . . noon** i.e., love, despite its attempt to be secret, reveals itself as plain as day **151 maugre** in spite of **152 Nor** neither **153–154 Do . . . cause** i.e., do not rationalize your indifference along these lines, that because I am the wooer you have no cause to reciprocate **155 But . . . fetter** but instead take possession of your reasoning with the following reason **162 deplore** beweep

III.ii. Location: Olivia's house.
2 venom i.e., person filled with venom **6 orchard** garden **10 argument** proof

SIR ANDREW 'Slight, will you make an ass o' me?

FABIAN I will prove it legitimate, sir, upon the oaths of judgment and reason.

SIR TOBY And they have been grand-jurymen since before Noah was a sailor.

FABIAN She did show favor to the youth in your sight only to exasperate you, to awake your dormouse valor, to put fire in your heart, and brimstone in your liver. You should then have accosted her, and with some excellent jests, fire-new from the mint, you should have bang'd the youth into dumbness. This was look'd for at your hand, and this was balk'd. The double gilt of this opportunity you let time wash off, and you are now sail'd into the north of my lady's opinion, where you will hang like an icicle on a Dutchman's beard, unless you do redeem it by some laudable attempt either of valor or policy.

SIR ANDREW An 't be any way, it must be with valor; for policy I hate. I had as lief be a Brownist as a politician.

SIR TOBY Why, then, build me thy fortunes upon the basis of valor. Challenge me the Count's youth to fight with him; hurt him in eleven places. My niece shall take note of it; and assure thyself, there is no love-broker in the world can more prevail in man's commendation with woman than report of valor.

FABIAN There is no way but this, Sir Andrew.

SIR ANDREW Will either of you bear me a challenge to him?

SIR TOBY Go, write it in a martial hand. Be curst and brief; it is no matter how witty, so it be eloquent and full of invention. Taunt him with the license of ink. If thou thou'st him some thrice, it shall not be amiss; and as many lies as will lie in thy sheet of paper, although the sheet were big enough for the bed of Ware in England, set 'em down. Go, about it. Let there be gall enough in thy ink, though thou write with a goose-pen, no matter. About it.

SIR ANDREW Where shall I find you?

SIR TOBY We'll call thee at the cubiculo. Go.

Exit Sir Andrew.

FABIAN This is a dear manikin to you, Sir Toby.

SIR TOBY I have been dear to him, lad, some two thousand strong, or so.

FABIAN We shall have a rare letter from him; but you'll not deliver 't?

SIR TOBY Never trust me, then; and by all means stir on the youth to an answer. I think oxen and wainropes cannot hale them together. For Andrew, if he were open'd, and you find so much blood in his liver as will clog the foot of a flea, I'll eat the rest of th' anatomy.

FABIAN And his opposite, the youth, bears in his visage no great presage of cruelty.

Enter Maria.

SIR TOBY Look, where the youngest wren of nine comes.

MARIA If you desire the spleen, and will laugh yourselves into stitches, follow me. Yond gull Malvolio is turn'd heathen, a very renegado; for there is no Christian that means to be sav'd by believing rightly can ever believe such impossible passages of grossness. He's in yellow stockings.

SIR TOBY And cross-garter'd?

MARIA Most villainously; like a pedant that keeps a school i' th' church. I have dogg'd him like his murderer. He does obey every point of the letter that I dropp'd to betray him. He does smile his face into more lines than is in the new map with the augmentation of the Indies. You have not seen such a thing as 'tis. I can hardly forbear hurling things at him. I know my lady will strike him. If she do, he'll smile and take 't for a great favor.

SIR TOBY Come, bring us, bring us where he is.

Exeunt omnes.

SCENE III

Enter Sebastian and Antonio.

SEBASTIAN

I would not by my will have troubled you;
But, since you make your pleasure of your pains,
I will no further chide you.

ANTONIO

I could not stay behind you. My desire,
More sharp than filed steel, did spur me forth;
And not all love to see you, though so much
As might have drawn one to a longer voyage,
But jealousy what might befall your travel,
Being skilless in these parts; which to a stranger,
Unguided and unfriended, often prove
Rough and unhospitable. My willing love,
The rather by these arguments of fear,
Set forth in your pursuit.

SEBASTIAN My kind Antonio,
I can no other answer make but thanks,
And thanks; and ever oft good turns
Are shuffled off with such uncurrent pay.
But, were my worth as is my conscience firm,

12 'Slight by his (God's) light **13 oaths** i.e., testimony under oath **18 dormouse** i.e., sleepy **23 balk'd** missed, neglected **23–24 double gilt** thick layer of gold, i.e., rare worth **25 north** i.e., out of the warmth and sunshine of her favor **26–27 icicle . . . beard** (Alludes to the arctic voyage of William Barentz in 1596–1597.) **28 policy** stratagem **30 Brownist** (Early name of the Congregationalists, from the name of the founder, Robert Browne.) **30–31 politician** intriguer **32 build me** i.e., build **35–36 love-broker** agent between lovers **41 curst** fierce **43 with . . . ink** i.e., with the lack of restraint one enjoys in writing **44 thou'st** ("Thou" was used only between friends or to inferiors.) **46 bed of Ware** (A famous bedstead capable of holding twelve persons, about eleven feet square, said to have been at the Stag Inn in Ware, Hertfordshire.) **49 goose-pen** (1) goose quill (2) foolish style **51 call thee** call for you. **cubiculo** little chamber **52 manikin** puppet **53 dear** expensive (playing on *dear,* fond, in the previous speech) **58 wainropes** wagon ropes **59 hale** haul **60 liver** (Seat of the passions.)

64 youngest . . . nine i.e., the last hatched and smallest of a nest of wrens **66 the spleen** a laughing fit. (The spleen was thought to be the seat of immoderate laughter.) **68 renegado** renegade, deserter of his religion **70 passages of grossness** exaggerated statements (i.e., in the letter) **73 pedant** schoolmaster **77 new map** (Probably a reference to a map published in 1599 in an edition of Hakluyt's *Voyages,* showing more of the East Indies than had ever been mapped before.)

III.iii. Location: A street.
6 not all not only, not altogether **8 jealousy** anxiety **9 skilless in** unacquainted with **15 And . . . turns** (This probably corrupt line is usually made to read, "And thanks and ever thanks; and oft good turns.") **16 uncurrent** worthless (such as mere thanks) **17 worth** wealth. **conscience** i.e., moral inclination to assist

You should find better dealing. What's to do?
Shall we go see the reliques of this town? 19

ANTONIO
Tomorrow, sir. Best first go see your lodging.

SEBASTIAN
I am not weary, and 'tis long to night.
I pray you, let us satisfy our eyes
With the memorials and the things of fame
That do renown this city.

ANTONIO Would you'd pardon me. 24
I do not without danger walk these streets.
Once, in a sea-fight, 'gainst the Count his galleys 26
I did some service; of such note indeed
That were I ta'en here it would scarce be answer'd. 28

SEBASTIAN
Belike you slew great number of his people?

ANTONIO
Th' offense is not of such a bloody nature,
Albeit the quality of the time and quarrel
Might well have given us bloody argument. 32
It might have since been answer'd in repaying 33
What we took from them, which, for traffic's sake, 34
Most of our city did. Only myself stood out,
For which, if I be lapsed in this place, 36
I shall pay dear.

SEBASTIAN Do not then walk too open.

ANTONIO
It doth not fit me. Hold, sir, here's my purse.
[*Gives purse.*]
In the south suburbs, at the Elephant, 39
Is best to lodge. I will bespeak our diet, 40
Whiles you beguile the time and feed your
knowledge
With viewing of the town. There shall you have me.

SEBASTIAN
Why I your purse?

ANTONIO
Haply your eye shall light upon some toy 44
You have desire to purchase, and your store, 45
I think, is not for idle markets, sir. 46

SEBASTIAN
I'll be your purse-bearer and leave you
For an hour.

ANTONIO To th' Elephant.

SEBASTIAN I do remember. *Exeunt.*

SCENE IV

Enter Olivia and Maria.

OLIVIA [*Aside*]
I have sent after him; he says he'll come; 1
How shall I feast him? What bestow of him? 2
For youth is bought more oft than begg'd or
borrow'd.
I speak too loud.—
Where's Malvolio? He is sad and civil, 5
And suits well for a servant with my fortunes.
Where is Malvolio?

MARIA He's coming, madam, but in very strange man-
ner. He is, sure, possess'd, madam. 9

OLIVIA Why, what's the matter? Does he rave?

MARIA No, madam, he does nothing but smile. Your
ladyship were best to have some guard about you, if
he come, for sure the man is tainted in 's wits.

OLIVIA
Go call him hither. [*Malvolio is summoned.*] I am as
mad as he,
If sad and merry madness equal be.

Enter Malvolio.

How now, Malvolio?

MALVOLIO Sweet lady, ho, ho.

OLIVIA Smil'st thou? I sent for thee upon a sad occa-
sion.

MALVOLIO Sad, lady! I could be sad. This does make
some obstruction in the blood, this cross-gartering,
but what of that? If it please the eye of one, it is with
me as the very true sonnet is, "Please one, and please 23
all." 24

OLIVIA Why, how dost thou, man? What is the matter
with thee?

MALVOLIO Not black in my mind, though yellow in my 27
legs. It did come to his hands, and commands shall be
executed. I think we do know the sweet Roman hand. 29

OLIVIA Wilt thou go to bed, Malvolio?

MALVOLIO To bed? Ay, sweetheart, and I'll come to
thee.

OLIVIA God comfort thee! Why dost thou smile so and
kiss thy hand so oft?

MARIA How do you, Malvolio?

MALVOLIO At your request? Yes, nightingales answer 36
daws. 37

MARIA Why appear you with this ridiculous boldness
before my lady?

MALVOLIO "Be not afraid of greatness." 'Twas well writ.

OLIVIA What mean'st thou by that, Malvolio?

MALVOLIO "Some are born great,"—

OLIVIA Ha?

MALVOLIO "Some achieve greatness,"—

OLIVIA What say'st thou?

MALVOLIO "And some have greatness thrust upon
them."

OLIVIA Heaven restore thee!

MALVOLIO "Remember who commended thy yellow
stockings,"— 50

OLIVIA Thy yellow stockings?

MALVOLIO "And wish'd to see thee cross-garter'd."

19 reliques antiquities **24 renown** give renown to **26 Count his** Count's, i.e., Duke's **28 it . . . answer'd** i.e., I'd be hard put to offer a defense **32 bloody argument** cause for bloodshed **33 answer'd** compensated **34 traffic's** trade's **36 lapsed** i.e., caught **39 Elephant** (The name of an inn.) **40 diet** dinner, food **44 toy** trifle **45 store** store of money **46 idle markets** unnecessary purchases, luxuries

III.iv. Location: Olivia's garden.
1 he . . . come i.e., suppose he says he'll come **2 of** on

5 sad and civil sober and decorous **9 possess'd** i.e., possessed with an evil spirit **23 sonnet** song, ballad **23–24 Please . . . all** (The refrain of a ballad.) **27 black** i.e., melancholic **29 Roman hand** fashionable Italian style of handwriting **36–37 nightingales answer daws** i.e., (to Maria), do you suppose a fine fellow like me would answer a lowly creature (a *daw*, a crow) like you

OLIVIA Cross-garter'd?

MALVOLIO "Go to, thou art made, if thou desir'st to be so;"—

OLIVIA Am I made?

MALVOLIO "If not, let me see thee a servant still."

OLIVIA Why, this is very midsummer madness.

Enter Servant.

SERVANT Madam, the young gentleman of the Count Orsino's is return'd. I could hardly entreat him back. He attends your ladyship's pleasure.

OLIVIA I'll come to him. [*Exit Servant.*] Good Maria, let this fellow be look'd to. Where's my cousin Toby? Let some of my people have a special care of him. I would not have him miscarry for the half of my dowry. *Exit* [*with Maria*].

MALVOLIO O, ho, do you come near me now? No worse man than Sir Toby to look to me! This concurs directly with the letter. She sends him on purpose, that I may appear stubborn to him; for she incites me to that in the letter. "Cast thy humble slough," says she; "be opposite with a kinsman, surly with servants; let thy tongue tang with arguments of state; put thyself into the trick of singularity." And consequently sets down the manner how: as, a sad face, a reverend carriage, a slow tongue, in the habit of some sir of note, and so forth. I have lim'd her; but it is Jove's doing, and Jove make me thankful! And when she went away now, "Let this fellow be look'd to." "Fellow!" Not "Malvolio," nor after my degree, but "fellow." Why, every thing adheres together, that no dram of a scruple, no scruple of a scruple, no obstacle, no incredulous or unsafe circumstance—What can be said? Nothing that can be can come between me and the full prospect of my hopes. Well, Jove, not I, is the doer of this, and he is to be thank'd.

Enter [*Sir*] *Toby, Fabian, and Maria.*

SIR TOBY Which way is he, in the name of sanctity? If all the devils of hell be drawn in little, and Legion himself possess'd him, yet I'll speak to him.

FABIAN Here he is, here he is. How is 't with you, sir? How is 't with you, man?

MALVOLIO Go off; I discard you. Let me enjoy my private. Go off.

MARIA Lo, how hollow the fiend speaks within him! Did not I tell you? Sir Toby, my lady prays you to have a care of him.

MALVOLIO Ah, ha, does she so?

SIR TOBY Go to, go to; peace, peace; we must deal gently with him. Let me alone.—How do you, Malvolio? How is 't with you? What, man, defy the devil! Consider, he's an enemy to mankind.

MALVOLIO Do you know what you say?

MARIA La you, an you speak ill of the devil, how he takes it at heart! Pray God he be not bewitch'd!

FABIAN Carry his water to th' wise woman.

MARIA Marry, and it shall be done tomorrow morning, if I live. My lady would not lose him for more than I'll say.

MALVOLIO How now, mistress?

MARIA O Lord!

SIR TOBY Prithee, hold thy peace; this is not the way. Do you not see you move him? Let me alone with him.

FABIAN No way but gentleness; gently, gently. The fiend is rough, and will not be roughly us'd.

SIR TOBY Why, how now, my bawcock? How dost thou, chuck?

MALVOLIO Sir!

SIR TOBY Ay, biddy, come with me. What, man, 'tis not for gravity to play at cherry-pit with Satan. Hang him, foul collier!

MARIA Get him to say his prayers, good Sir Toby, get him to pray.

MALVOLIO My prayers, minx?

MARIA No, I warrant you, he will not hear of godliness.

MALVOLIO Go, hang yourselves all! You are idle shallow things; I am not of your element. You shall know more hereafter. *Exit.*

SIR TOBY Is 't possible?

FABIAN If this were play'd upon a stage now, I could condemn it as an improbable fiction.

SIR TOBY His very genius hath taken the infection of the device, man.

MARIA Nay, pursue him now, lest the device take air and taint.

FABIAN Why, we shall make him mad indeed.

MARIA The house will be the quieter.

SIR TOBY Come, we'll have him in a dark room and bound. My niece is already in the belief that he's mad. We may carry it thus, for our pleasure and his penance, till our very pastime, tir'd out of breath, prompt us to have mercy on him; at which time we will bring the device to the bar and crown thee for a finder of madmen. But see, but see.

Enter Sir Andrew [*with a letter*].

FABIAN More matter for a May morning.

SIR ANDREW Here's the challenge, read it. I warrant there's vinegar and pepper in 't.

FABIAN Is 't so saucy?

SIR ANDREW Ay, is 't, I warrant him. Do but read.

SIR TOBY Give me. [*Reads.*] "Youth, whatsoever thou art, thou art but a scurvy fellow."

FABIAN Good, and valiant.

58 midsummer madness (A proverbial phrase; the midsummer moon was supposed to cause madness.) **65 miscarry** come to harm **66 come near** understand **73 consequently** thereafter **74 sad** serious **75 habit . . . note** attire suited to a gentleman of distinction **76 lim'd** caught like a bird with birdlime (a sticky substance spread on branches) **78 Fellow** (Malvolio takes the original meaning, *companion.*) **79 after my degree** according to my position **80 dram** (Literally, one-eighth of a fluid ounce.) **scruple** (Literally, one-third of a dram.) **81 incredulous** incredible **81–82 unsafe** uncertain **87 drawn in little** gathered into a small space, i.e., in Malvolio's heart. **Legion** (Cf. "My name is Legion, for we are many," Mark 5:9.) **91–92 private** privacy **98 Let me alone** leave him to me

104 water urine (for medical analysis) **115 bawcock** fine fellow. (From French *beau-coq.*) **116 chuck** (A form of "chick," term of endearment.) **118 biddy** chicken **119 for gravity** suitable for a man of your dignity. **cherry-pit** a children's game consisting of throwing cherry stones into a hole **120 collier** i.e., Satan **126–127 know more** i.e., hear about this **131 genius** i.e., soul, spirit **133–134 take . . . taint** become exposed to air (i.e., become known) and thus spoil **142 bar** i.e., bar of judgment **144 matter . . . morning** sport for Mayday **147 saucy** (1) spicy (2) insolent

SIR TOBY [*Reads*] "Wonder not, nor admire not in thy 152
mind, why I do call thee so, for I will show thee no
reason for 't."

FABIAN A good note, that keeps you from the blow of 155
the law.

SIR TOBY [*Reads*] "Thou com'st to the lady Olivia, and
in my sight she uses thee kindly. But thou liest in thy
throat; that is not the matter I challenge thee for."

FABIAN Very brief, and to exceeding good sense—less.

SIR TOBY [*Reads*] "I will waylay thee going home;
where if it be thy chance to kill me,"—

FABIAN Good.

SIR TOBY [*Reads*] "Thou kill'st me like a rogue and a
villain."

FABIAN Still you keep o' th' windy side of the law. 166
Good.

SIR TOBY [*Reads*] "Fare thee well, and God have mercy
upon one of our souls! He may have mercy upon
mine, but my hope is better, and so look to thyself.
Thy friend, as thou usest him, and thy sworn enemy,
Andrew Aguecheek."

If this letter move him not, his legs cannot. I'll give 't
him.

MARIA You may have very fit occasion for 't. He is now
in some commerce with my lady, and will by and by
depart.

SIR TOBY Go, Sir Andrew. Scout me for him at the cor- 178
ner of the orchard like a bum-baily. So soon as ever 179
thou seest him, draw; and, as thou draw'st, swear hor-
rible; for it comes to pass oft that a terrible oath, with
a swaggering accent sharply twang'd off, gives man-
hood more approbation than ever proof itself would 183
have earn'd him. Away!

SIR ANDREW Nay, let me alone for swearing. *Exit.* 185

SIR TOBY Now will not I deliver his letter; for the behav-
ior of the young gentleman gives him out to be of
good capacity and breeding; his employment between
his lord and my niece confirms no less. Therefore this
letter, being so excellently ignorant, will breed no ter-
ror in the youth. He will find it comes from a clodpole. 191
But, sir, I will deliver his challenge by word of mouth,
set upon Aguecheek a notable report of valor, and
drive the gentleman, as I know his youth will aptly
receive it, into a most hideous opinion of his rage,
skill, fury, and impetuosity. This will so fright them
both that they will kill one another by the look, like
cockatrices. 198

Enter Olivia and Viola.

FABIAN Here he comes with your niece. Give them way
till he take leave, and presently after him.

SIR TOBY I will meditate the while upon some horrid
message for a challenge.
[*Exeunt Sir Toby, Fabian, and Maria.*]

OLIVIA
I have said too much unto a heart of stone
And laid mine honor too unchary on 't. 204
There's something in me that reproves my fault;
But such a headstrong potent fault it is,
That it but mocks reproof.

VIOLA
With the same havior that your passion bears
Goes on my master's griefs.

OLIVIA
Here, wear this jewel for me, 'tis my picture. 210
[*Gives locket.*]
Refuse it not; it hath no tongue to vex you.
And I beseech you come again tomorrow.
What shall you ask of me that I'll deny,
That honor, sav'd, may upon asking give?

VIOLA
Nothing but this: your true love for my master.

OLIVIA
How with mine honor may I give him that
Which I have given to you?

VIOLA
I will acquit you. 217

OLIVIA
Well, come again tomorrow. Fare thee well.
A fiend like thee might bear my soul to hell. [*Exit.*] 219

Enter [Sir] Toby and Fabian.

SIR TOBY Gentleman, God save thee.

VIOLA And you, sir.

SIR TOBY That defense thou hast, betake thee to 't. Of
what nature the wrongs are thou hast done him, I
know not; but thy intercepter, full of despite, bloody 224
as the hunter, attends thee at the orchard-end. Dis- 225
mount thy tuck, be yare in thy preparation, for thy 226
assailant is quick, skillful, and deadly.

VIOLA You mistake sir. I am sure no man hath any
quarrel to me. My remembrance is very free and clear
from any image of offense done to any man.

SIR TOBY You'll find it otherwise, I assure you. There-
fore, if you hold your life at any price, betake you to
your guard; for your opposite hath in him what youth,
strength, skill, and wrath can furnish man withal.

VIOLA I pray you sir, what is he?

SIR TOBY He is knight, dubb'd with unhatch'd rapier 236
and on carpet consideration, but he is a devil in 237
private brawl. Souls and bodies hath he divorc'd
three; and his incensement at this moment is so im-
placable, that satisfaction can be none but by pangs of
death and sepulcher. Hob, nob, is his word; give 't or 241
take 't.

VIOLA I will return again into the house and desire
some conduct of the lady. I am no fighter. I have heard 244
of some kind of men that put quarrels purposely on

152 admire marvel **155 note** observation, remark **166 windy** windward, i.e., safe, where the law may get no scent of you **178 Scout me** keep watch **179 bum-baily** minor sheriff's officer employed in making arrests **183 approbation** reputation (for courage). **proof** performance **185 let . . . swearing** don't worry about my ability in swearing **191 clodpole** blockhead **198 cockatrices** basilisks, fabulous serpents reputed to be able to kill by a mere look **199 Give them way** stay out of their way **200 presently** immediately

204 laid hazarded. **unchary on 't** recklessly on it **210 jewel** (Any piece of jewelry; here, seemingly, a locket.) **217 acquit you** release you of your promise **219 like** resembling **224 intercepter** i.e., he who lies in wait. **despite** defiance, malice **224–225 bloody as the hunter** bloodthirsty as a hunting dog **225–226 Dismount thy tuck** draw your rapier **226 yare** ready, nimble **236 unhatch'd** unhacked, unused in battle **237 carpet consideration** (A carpet knight was one whose title was obtained not in battle but through connections at court.) **241 Hob, nob** have or have not, i.e., give it or take it. **word** motto **244 conduct** escort

others, to taste their valor. Belike this is a man of that 246
quirk. 247

SIR TOBY Sir, no, his indignation derives itself out of a
very competent injury; therefore, get you on and give 249
him his desire. Back you shall not to the house, unless
you undertake that with me which with as much 251
safety you might answer him. Therefore, on, or strip
your sword stark naked; for meddle you must, that's 253
certain, or forswear to wear iron about you. 254

VIOLA This is as uncivil as strange. I beseech you, do me this courteous office, as to know of the knight what my offense to him is. It is something of my negligence, nothing of my purpose.

SIR TOBY I will do so. Signior Fabian, stay you by this gentleman till my return. *Exit Toby.*

VIOLA Pray you, sir, do you know of this matter?

FABIAN I know the knight is incens'd against you, even
to a mortal arbitrement, but nothing of the circum- 263
stance more.

VIOLA I beseech you, what manner of man is he?

FABIAN Nothing of that wonderful promise, to read 266
him by his form, as you are like to find him in the 267
proof of his valor. He is, indeed, sir, the most skillful,
bloody, and fatal opposite that you could possibly
have found in any part of Illyria. Will you walk to-
wards him? I will make your peace with him if I can.

VIOLA I shall be much bound to you for 't. I am one that
had rather go with sir priest than sir knight. I care not 273
who knows so much of my mettle. *Exeunt.*

Enter [Sir] Toby and [Sir] Andrew.

SIR TOBY Why, man, he's a very devil; I have not seen
such a firago. I had a pass with him, rapier, scabbard, 276
and all, and he gives me the stuck in with such a mor- 277
tal motion, that it is inevitable; and on the answer, he 278
pays you as surely as your feet hits the ground they
step on. They say he has been fencer to the Sophy.

SIR ANDREW Pox on 't, I'll not meddle with him.

SIR TOBY Ay, but he will not now be pacified. Fabian can scarce hold him yonder.

SIR ANDREW Plague on 't, an I thought he had been val-
iant and so cunning in fence, I'd have seen him
damn'd ere I'd have challeng'd him. Let him let the
matter slip, and I'll give him my horse, grey Capilet. 287

SIR TOBY I'll make the motion. Stand here, make a good 288
show on 't. This shall end without the perdition of 289
souls. [*Aside.*] Marry, I'll ride your horse as well as I 290
ride you.

Enter Fabian and Viola.

[*To Fabian.*] I have his horse to take up the quarrel. I 292
have persuaded him the youth's a devil.

FABIAN He is as horribly conceited of him; and pants 294
and looks pale, as if a bear were at his heels.

SIR TOBY [*To Viola*] There's no remedy, sir; he will fight with you for 's oath sake. Marry, he hath better bethought him of his quarrel, and he finds that now scarce to be worth talking of. Therefore draw, for the supportance of his vow. He protests he will not hurt you.

VIOLA [*Aside*] Pray God defend me! A little thing would make me tell them how much I lack of a man.

FABIAN Give ground, if you see him furious.

SIR TOBY Come, Sir Andrew, there's no remedy. The
gentleman will, for his honor's sake, have one bout
with you. He cannot by the duello avoid it. But he has 307
promis'd me, as he is a gentleman and a soldier, he
will not hurt you. Come on; to 't.

SIR ANDREW Pray God he keep his oath!

VIOLA I do assure you, 'tis against my will. [*They draw.*]

Enter Antonio.

ANTONIO
Put up your sword. If this young gentleman
Have done offense, I take the fault on me;
If you offend him, I for him defy you.

SIR TOBY
You, sir? Why, what are you?

ANTONIO
One, sir, that for his love dares yet do more
Than you have heard him brag to you he will.

SIR TOBY
Nay, if you be an undertaker, I am for you. 318
[*They draw.*]

Enter Officers.

FABIAN O good Sir Toby, hold! Here come the officers.

SIR TOBY [*To Antonio*] I'll be with you anon.

VIOLA [*To Sir Andrew*] Pray, sir, put your sword up, if you please.

SIR ANDREW Marry, will I, sir; and, for that I promis'd you, I'll be as good as my word. He will bear you easily, and reins well.

FIRST OFFICER This is the man; do thy office.

SECOND OFFICER Antonio, I arrest thee at the suit of Count Orsino.

ANTONIO
You do mistake me, sir.

FIRST OFFICER
No, sir, no jot. I know your favor well, 330
Though now you have no sea-cap on your head.
Take him away. He knows I know him well.

ANTONIO
I must obey. [*To Viola.*] This comes with seeking
you.
But there's no remedy; I shall answer it. 334
What will you do, now my necessity
Makes me to ask you for my purse? It grieves me
Much more for what I cannot do for you
Than what befalls myself. You stand amaz'd;
But be of comfort.

246 taste test **247 quirk** peculiar humor **249 competent** sufficient **251 that** i.e., to give satisfaction in a duel **253 meddle** engage (in conflict) **254 forswear . . . iron** give up your right to wear a sword **263 mortal arbitrement** trial to the death **266–267 read . . . form** judge him by his appearance **273 sir priest** (*Sir* was a courtesy title for priests.) **276 firago** virago. **pass** bout **277 stuck in** stoccado, a thrust in fencing **278 answer** return hit **287 Capilet** i.e., "little horse." (From "capel," a nag.) **288 motion** offer **289–290 perdition of souls** loss of lives **292 take up** settle, make up **294 He . . . him** i.e., Cesario has as horrible a conception of Sir Andrew

307 duello duelling code **318 undertaker** one who takes upon himself a task or business; here, a challenger **330 favor** face **334 answer it** suffer for it

SECOND OFFICER Come, sir, away.

ANTONIO
I must entreat of you some of that money.

VIOLA
What money, sir?
For the fair kindness you have show'd me here,
And part being prompted by your present trouble,
Out of my lean and low ability
I'll lend you something. My having is not much;
I'll make division of my present with you.
Hold, there's half my coffer. [*Offers money.*]

ANTONIO
Will you deny me now?
Is 't possible that my deserts to you
Can lack persuasion? Do not tempt my misery,
Lest that it make me so unsound a man
As to upbraid you with those kindnesses
That I have done for you.

VIOLA
I know of none,
Nor know I you by voice or any feature.
I hate ingratitude more in a man
Than lying, vainness, babbling, drunkenness,
Or any taint of vice whose strong corruption
Inhabits our frail blood.

ANTONIO
O heavens themselves!

SECOND OFFICER
Come, sir, I pray you, go.

ANTONIO
Let me speak a little. This youth that you see here
I snatch'd one half out of the jaws of death,
Reliev'd him with such sanctity of love,
And to his image, which methought did promise
Most venerable worth, did I devotion.

FIRST OFFICER
What's that to us? The time goes by. Away!

ANTONIO
But O how vile an idol proves this god!
Thou hast, Sebastian, done good feature shame.
In nature there's no blemish but the mind;
None can be call'd deform'd but the unkind.
Virtue is beauty, but the beauteous evil
Are empty trunks o'erflourish'd by the devil.

FIRST OFFICER
The man grows mad. Away with him! Come, come, sir.

ANTONIO Lead me on. *Exit* [*with Officers*].

VIOLA [*To herself*]
Methinks his words do from such passion fly
That he believes himself; so do not I.
Prove true, imagination, O, prove true,
That I, dear brother, be now ta'en for you!

SIR TOBY Come hither, knight; come hither, Fabian.
We'll whisper o'er a couplet or two of most sage saws.
[*They gather apart from Viola.*]

VIOLA
He nam'd Sebastian. I my brother know
Yet living in my glass; even such and so
In favor was my brother, and he went
Still in this fashion, color, ornament,
For him I imitate. O, if it prove,
Tempests are kind and salt waves fresh in love!
[*Exit.*]

SIR TOBY A very dishonest paltry boy, and more a coward than a hare. His dishonesty appears in leaving his friend here in necessity and denying him; and for his cowardship, ask Fabian.

FABIAN A coward, a most devout coward, religious in it.

SIR ANDREW 'Slid, I'll after him again and beat him.

SIR TOBY Do; cuff him soundly, but never draw thy sword.

SIR ANDREW An I do not— [*Exit.*]

FABIAN Come, let's see the event.

SIR TOBY I dare lay any money 'twill be nothing yet.
Exeunt.

ACT IV • SCENE I

Enter Sebastian and Clown.

CLOWN Will you make me believe that I am not sent for you?

SEBASTIAN Go to, go to, thou art a foolish fellow. Let me be clear of thee.

CLOWN Well held out, i' faith! No, I do not know you; nor I am not sent to you by my lady, to bid you come speak with her; nor your name is not Master Cesario; nor this is not my nose neither. Nothing that is so is so.

SEBASTIAN I prithee, vent thy folly somewhere else. Thou know'st not me.

CLOWN Vent my folly! He has heard that word of some great man and now applies it to a fool. Vent my folly! I am afraid this great lubber, the world, will prove a cockney. I prithee now, ungird thy strangeness and tell me what I shall vent to my lady. Shall I vent to her that thou art coming?

SEBASTIAN I prithee, foolish Greek, depart from me. There's money for thee. [*Gives money.*] If you tarry longer, I shall give worse payment.

CLOWN By my troth, thou hast an open hand. These wise men that give fools money get themselves a good report—after fourteen years' purchase.

Enter [*Sir*] *Andrew,* [*Sir*] *Toby, and Fabian.*

SIR ANDREW Now, sir, have I met you again? There 's for you. [*Strikes Sebastian.*]

343 part partly **345 having** wealth **346 present** present store **347 coffer** purse. (Literally, strong box.) **349–350 deserts . . . persuasion** claims on you can fail to persuade you to help me **351 unsound** weak **363 image** what he appeared to be (playing on the idea of a religious icon to be venerated) **364 venerable worth** worthiness of being venerated **367 Thou . . . shame** i.e., you have shamed physical beauty by showing that it does not always reflect inner beauty **369 unkind** unnatural **370 beauteous evil** those who are outwardly beautiful but evil within **371 trunks** (1) chests (2) bodies. **o'erflourish'd** (1) covered with ornamental carvings (2) made outwardly beautiful **375 so . . . I** i.e., I do not believe myself (in the hope that has arisen in me) **379 saws** sayings

380–381 I . . . glass i.e., I know my brother is virtually alive every time I look in a mirror, because we looked so much alike **384 prove** prove true **386 dishonest** dishonorable **391 'Slid** i.e., by his (God's) eyelid **395 event** outcome **396 yet** nevertheless, after all

IV.i. Location: Before Olivia's house.
5 held out kept up **9 vent** give vent to **13 lubber** lout **14 cockney** effeminate or foppish fellow. **ungird thy strangeness** put off your affectation of being a stranger **17 Greek** i.e., jester. (From "merry Greek.") **22 after . . . purchase** i.e., if they are sufficiently generous. (Land was ordinarily valued at the price of twelve years' rental; the Fool adds two years to this figure.)

SEBASTIAN Why, there's for thee, and there, and there.
[*Strikes Sir Andrew.*] Are all the people mad?
[*Draws his dagger.*]

SIR TOBY Hold, sir, or I'll throw your dagger o'er the house. [*Seizes Sebastian's arm.*]

CLOWN This will I tell my lady straight. I would not be in some of your coats for twopence. [*Exit.*]

SIR TOBY Come on, sir; hold.

SIR ANDREW Nay, let him alone. I'll go another way to work with him; I'll have an action of battery against 33
him, if there be any law in Illyria. Though I struck him first, yet it's no matter for that.

SEBASTIAN Let go thy hand.

SIR TOBY Come, sir, I will not let you go. Come, my young soldier, put up your iron. You are well flesh'd; 38
come on.

SEBASTIAN
I will be free from thee. [*Breaks free and draws his sword.*] What wouldst thou now?
If thou dar'st tempt me further, draw thy sword.

SIR TOBY What, what? Nay, then I must have an ounce or two of this malapert blood from you. [*Draws.*] 43

Enter Olivia.

OLIVIA
Hold, Toby! On thy life I charge thee, hold!

SIR TOBY Madam—

OLIVIA
Will it be ever thus? Ungracious wretch,
Fit for the mountains and the barbarous caves,
Where manners ne'er were preach'd! Out of my sight!
Be not offended, dear Cesario.
Rudesby, be gone!
[*Exeunt Sir Toby, Sir Andrew, and Fabian.*]
I prithee, gentle friend, 50
Let thy fair wisdom, not thy passion, sway
In this uncivil and unjust extent 52
Against thy peace. Go with me to my house,
And hear thou there how many fruitless pranks
This ruffian hath botch'd up, that thou thereby 55
Mayst smile at this. Thou shalt not choose but go.
Do not deny. Beshrew his soul for me, 57
He started one poor heart of mine, in thee. 58

SEBASTIAN
What relish is in this? How runs the stream?
Or I am mad, or else this is a dream. 60
Let fancy still my sense in Lethe steep; 61
If it be thus to dream, still let me sleep!

OLIVIA
Nay, come, I prithee. Would thou'dst be rul'd by me!

SEBASTIAN
Madam, I will.

OLIVIA O, say so, and so be! *Exeunt.*

33 action of battery lawsuit for beating (me) **38 are well flesh'd** i.e., have had enough fighting for now (?) **43 malapert** saucy, impudent **50 Rudesby** ruffian **52 extent** attack **55 botch'd up** clumsily contrived **57 Beshrew** curse **58 He . . . thee** i.e., he alarmed half of my heart, which lies in your bosom. (The word *started* also suggests a play on *heart, hart.*) **60 Or** either **61 fancy** imagination. **Lethe** the river of forgetfulness in the underworld; i.e., forgetfulness

SCENE II

Enter Maria [with garments] and Clown.

MARIA Nay, I prithee, put on this gown and this beard; make him believe thou art Sir Topas the curate. Do it 2
quickly; I'll call Sir Toby the whilst. [*Exit.*] 3

CLOWN Well, I'll put it on, and I will dissemble myself 4
in 't; and I would I were the first that ever dissembled in such a gown. [*He disguises himself in gown and beard.*] I am not tall enough to become the function 7
well, nor lean enough to be thought a good student; 8
but to be said an honest man and a good housekeeper 9
goes as fairly as to say a careful man and a great scholar. The competitors enter. 11

Enter [Sir] Toby [and Maria].

SIR TOBY Jove bless thee, master Parson.

CLOWN Bonos dies, Sir Toby. For, as the old hermit of 13
Prague, that never saw pen and ink, very wittily said 14
to a niece of King Gorboduc, "That that is is;" so I, 15
being master Parson, am master Parson; for, what is "that" but "that," and "is" but "is"?

SIR TOBY To him, Sir Topas.

CLOWN What, ho, I say! Peace in this prison!
[*He approaches the door behind which Malvolio is confined.*]

SIR TOBY The knave counterfeits well; a good knave.

MALVOLIO *(Within)* Who calls there?

CLOWN Sir Topas the curate, who comes to visit Malvolio the lunatic.

MALVOLIO Sir Topas, Sir Topas, good Sir Topas, go to my lady.

CLOWN Out, hyperbolical fiend! How vexest thou this 26
man! Talkest thou nothing but of ladies?

SIR TOBY Well said, master Parson.

MALVOLIO Sir Topas, never was man thus wrong'd. Good Sir Topas, do not think I am mad. They have laid me here in hideous darkness.

CLOWN Fie, thou dishonest Satan! I call thee by the most modest terms, for I am one of those gentle ones that will use the devil himself with courtesy. Say'st thou that house is dark? 35

MALVOLIO As hell, Sir Topas.

CLOWN Why, it hath bay windows transparent as bar- 37
ricadoes, and the clerestories toward the south north 38
are as lustrous as ebony; and yet complainest thou of obstruction?

MALVOLIO I am not mad, Sir Topas. I say to you, this house is dark.

IV.ii. Location: Olivia's house.
2 Sir (Honorific title for priests.) **Topas** (A name perhaps derived from Chaucer's comic knight in the "Rime of Sir Thopas" or from a similar character in Lyly's *Endymion.*) **3 the whilst** in the meantime **4 dissemble** disguise (with a pun on *feign*) **7 become** grace, adorn. **function** profession **8 student** scholar (in divinity) **9 said** called, known as. **housekeeper** household manager, hospitable person **11 competitors** associates, partners **13 Bonos dies** good day **13–14 hermit of Prague** (Probably another invented authority.) **15 King Gorboduc** a legendary king of ancient Britain, protagonist in the English tragedy *Gordobuc* (1562) **26 hyperbolical** vehement, boisterous. **fiend** i.e., the devil supposedly possessing Malvolio **35 house** i.e., room **37–38 barricadoes** barricades **38 clerestories** windows in an upper wall

CLOWN Madman, thou errest. I say, there is no darkness but ignorance, in which thou art more puzzled than the Egyptians in their fog.

MALVOLIO I say, this house is as dark as ignorance, though ignorance were as dark as hell; and I say there was never man thus abus'd. I am no more mad than you are. Make the trial of it in any constant question.

CLOWN What is the opinion of Pythagoras concerning wild fowl?

MALVOLIO That the soul of our grandam might happily inhabit a bird.

CLOWN What think'st thou of his opinion?

MALVOLIO I think nobly of the soul, and no way approve his opinion.

CLOWN Fare thee well. Remain thou still in darkness. Thou shalt hold th' opinion of Pythagoras ere I will allow of thy wits, and fear to kill a woodcock lest thou disposses the soul of thy grandam. Fare thee well.
[*Moves away from Malvolio's prison.*]

MALVOLIO Sir Topas, Sir Topas!

SIR TOBY My most exquisite Sir Topas!

CLOWN Nay, I am for all waters.

MARIA Thou mightst have done this without thy beard and gown. He sees thee not.

SIR TOBY To him in thine own voice, and bring me word how thou find'st him. I would we were well rid of this knavery. If he may be conveniently deliver'd, I would he were, for I am now so far in offense with my niece that I cannot pursue with any safety this sport to the upshot. Come by and by to my chamber.
Exit [*with Maria*].

CLOWN [*Sings as he approaches Malvolio's prison*]
"Hey, Robin, jolly Robin,
Tell me how thy lady does."

MALVOLIO Fool!

CLOWN "My lady is unkind, perdie."

MALVOLIO Fool!

CLOWN "Alas, why is she so?"

MALVOLIO Fool, I say!

CLOWN "She loves another"—Who calls, ha?

MALVOLIO Good fool, as ever thou wilt deserve well at my hand, help me to a candle, and pen, ink, and paper. As I am a gentleman, I will live to be thankful to thee for 't.

CLOWN Master Malvolio?

MALVOLIO Ay, good fool.

CLOWN Alas, sir, how fell you besides your five wits?

MALVOLIO Fool, there was never man so notoriously abus'd. I am as well in my wits, fool, as thou art.

CLOWN But as well? Then you are mad indeed, if you be no better in your wits than a fool.

MALVOLIO They have here propertied me, keep me in darkness, send ministers to me, asses, and do all they can to face me out of my wits.

CLOWN Advise you what you say. The minister is here. [*Speaks as Sir Topas.*]—Malvolio, Malvolio, thy wits the heavens restore! Endeavor thyself to sleep, and leave thy vain bibble babble.

MALVOLIO Sir Topas!

CLOWN Maintain no words with him, good fellow.—Who, I, sir? Not I, sir. God buy you, good Sir Topas.—Marry, amen.—I will, sir, I will.

MALVOLIO Fool, fool, fool, I say!

CLOWN Alas, sir, be patient. What say you, sir? I am shent for speaking to you.

MALVOLIO Good fool, help me to some light and some paper. I tell thee, I am as well in my wits as any man in Illyria.

CLOWN Well-a-day that you were, sir!

MALVOLIO By this hand, I am. Good fool, some ink, paper, and light; and convey what I will set down to my lady. It shall advantage thee more than ever the bearing of letter did.

CLOWN I will help you to 't. But tell me true, are you not mad indeed, or do you but counterfeit?

MALVOLIO Believe me, I am not. I tell thee true.

CLOWN Nay, I'll ne'er believe a madman till I see his brains. I will fetch you light and paper and ink.

MALVOLIO Fool, I'll requite it in the highest degree. I prithee, be gone.

CLOWN [*Sings*]
I am gone, sir,
And anon, sir,
I'll be with you again,
In a trice,
Like to the old Vice,
Your need to sustain;

Who, with dagger of lath,
In his rage and his wrath,
Cries, ah, ha! to the devil;
Like a mad lad,
Pare thy nails, dad.
Adieu, goodman devil. *Exit.*

SCENE III

Enter Sebastian [*with a pearl*].

SEBASTIAN
This is the air; that is the glorious sun;
This pearl she gave me, I do feel 't and see 't;
And though 'tis wonder that enwraps me thus,
Yet 'tis not madness. Where's Antonio, then?

45 Egyptians . . . fog (Alluding to the darkness brought upon Egypt by Moses; see Exodus 10:21, 22.) **49 constant question** set problem **50–51 Pythagoras . . . wild fowl** (An opening for the discussion of transmigration of souls, a doctrine held by Pythagoras.) **52 happily** haply, perhaps **59 allow of** acknowledge. **woodcock** (A proverbially stupid bird, easily caught.) **63 for all waters** i.e., ready for anything **68 deliver'd** i.e., delivered from prison **72–73 Hey, Robin . . . does** (Another fragment of an old song, a version of which is attributed to Sir Thomas Wyatt.) **75 perdie** i.e., by God, certainly **86 besides** out of. **five wits** (The intellectual faculties, usually listed as common wit, imagination, fantasy, judgment, and memory.) **91 propertied me** i.e., treated me as property and thrown me into the lumber-room

93 face . . . wits brazenly represent me as having lost my wits **94 Advise you** take care **100 God buy you** God be with you. (The Fool uses two voices in this passage to carry on a dialogue between himself and "Sir Topas.") **104 shent** scolded, rebuked **108 Well-a-day** alas, would that **124 Vice** comic tempter of the morality plays **126 dagger of lath** comic weapon of the Vice **131 goodman** title for a person of substance but not of gentle birth

IV.iii. Location: Olivia's garden.

I could not find him at the Elephant;
Yet there he was, and there I found this credit, 6
That he did range the town to seek me out.
His counsel now might do me golden service;
For though my soul disputes well with my sense 9
That this may be some error, but no madness,
Yet doth this accident and flood of fortune
So far exceed all instance, all discourse, 12
That I am ready to distrust mine eyes
And wrangle with my reason that persuades me
To any other trust but that I am mad, 15
Or else the lady's mad. Yet, if 'twere so,
She could not sway her house, command her followers, 17
Take and give back affairs and their dispatch 18
With such a smooth, discreet, and stable bearing
As I perceive she does. There's something in 't
That is deceivable. But here the lady comes. 21

Enter Olivia and Priest.

OLIVIA
Blame not this haste of mine. If you mean well,
Now go with me and with this holy man
Into the chantry by. There, before him, 24
And underneath that consecrated roof,
Plight me the full assurance of your faith,
That my most jealous and too doubtful soul 27
May live at peace. He shall conceal it
Whiles you are willing it shall come to note, 29
What time we will our celebration keep 30
According to my birth. What do you say? 31

SEBASTIAN
I'll follow this good man, and go with you;
And, having sworn truth, ever will be true.

OLIVIA
Then lead the way, good father; and heavens so shine
That they may fairly note this act of mine! *Exeunt.*

ACT V • SCENE I

Enter Clown and Fabian.

FABIAN Now, as thou lov'st me, let me see his letter.
CLOWN Good Master Fabian, grant me another request.
FABIAN Any thing.
CLOWN Do not desire to see this letter.
FABIAN This is to give a dog and in recompense desire my dog again.

Enter Duke, Viola, Curio, and Lords.

DUKE Belong you to the Lady Olivia, friends?
CLOWN Ay, sir; we are some of her trappings.
DUKE I know thee well. How dost thou, my good fellow?
CLOWN Truly, sir, the better for my foes and the worse 10
for my friends.
DUKE Just the contrary; the better for thy friends.
CLOWN No, sir, the worse.
DUKE How can that be?
CLOWN Marry, sir, they praise me and make an ass of
me. Now my foes tell me plainly I am an ass; so that
by my foes, sir, I profit in the knowledge of myself,
and by my friends I am abus'd; so that, conclusions to 18
be as kisses, if your four negatives make your two af- 19
firmatives, why then, the worse for my friends and the 20
better for my foes.
DUKE Why, this is excellent.
CLOWN By my troth, sir, no; though it please you to be
one of my friends. 24
DUKE Thou shalt not be the worse for me. There's gold. [*Gives a coin.*]
CLOWN But that it would be double-dealing, sir, I 26
would you could make it another.
DUKE O, you give me ill counsel.
CLOWN Put your grace in your pocket, sir, for this once, 29
and let your flesh and blood obey it.
DUKE Well, I will be so much a sinner to be a double-
dealer. There's another. [*Gives another coin.*]
CLOWN Primo, secundo, tertio, is a good play; and the 33
old saying is, the third pays for all. The triplex, sir, is 34
a good tripping measure; or the bells of Saint Bennet, 35
sir, may put you in mind—one, two, three.
DUKE You can fool no more money out of me at this
throw. If you will let your lady know I am here to 38
speak with her, and bring her along with you, it may
awake my bounty further.
CLOWN Marry, sir, lullaby to your bounty till I come again. I go, sir, but I would not have you to think that my desire of having is the sin of covetousness; but, as you say, sir, let your bounty take a nap, I will awake it anon. *Exit.*

Enter Antonio and Officers.

VIOLA
Here comes the man, sir, that did rescue me.

DUKE
That face of his I do remember well;
Yet, when I saw it last, it was besmear'd
As black as Vulcan in the smoke of war. 49
A baubling vessel was he captain of, 50
For shallow draught and bulk unprizable, 51
With which such scathful grapple did he make 52

6 was was previously. **credit** belief **9 my soul . . . sense** i.e., both my rational faculties and my physical senses come to the conclusion **12 instance** precedent. **discourse** reasoning **15 trust** belief **17 sway** rule **18 Take . . . dispatch** undertake matters of business and see to their execution **21 deceivable** deceptive **24 chantry by** privately endowed chapel near by **27 jealous** anxious, mistrustful **29 Whiles** until. **come to note** become known **30 our celebration** i.e., the actual marriage; what they are about to perform is a binding betrothal **31 birth** social position

V.i. Location: Before Olivia's house.

10 for because of **18 abus'd** flatteringly deceived **18–20 conclusions . . . affirmatives** i.e., as when a young lady, asked for a kiss, says "no, no" really meaning "yes, yes," showing that things are the opposite of what they seem (?); or, as the four lips of two contrary lovers come together to make one passionate kiss **24 friends** i.e., those who, according to the Clown's syllogism, flatter him **26 But** except for the fact. **double-dealing** (1) giving twice (2) deceit, duplicity **29 Put . . . pocket** (1) pocket up your virtue, your grace before God (2) reach in your pocket or purse and show your customary grace or munificence **33 play** (Perhaps a children's game or game of dice.) **34 triplex** triple time in music **35 Saint Bennet** church of St. Benedict **38 throw** (1) time (2) throw of the dice **49 Vulcan** Roman god of fire and smith to the other gods; his face was blackened by the fire **50 baubling** insignificant, trifling **51 For** because of. **unprizable** of value too slight to be estimated, not worth taking as a "prize" **52 scathful** destructive

With the most noble bottom of our fleet,
That very envy and the tongue of loss
Cried fame and honor on him. What's the matter?

FIRST OFFICER
Orsino, this is that Antonio
That took the Phoenix and her fraught from Candy;
And this is he that did the Tiger board,
When your young nephew Titus lost his leg.
Here in the streets, desperate of shame and state,
In private brabble did we apprehend him.

VIOLA
He did me kindness, sir, drew on my side;
But in conclusion put strange speech upon me.
I know not what 'twas but distraction.

DUKE
Notable pirate, thou salt-water thief!
What foolish boldness brought thee to their mercies
Whom thou, in terms so bloody and so dear,
Hast made thine enemies?

ANTONIO Orsino, noble sir,
Be pleas'd that I shake off these names you give me.
Antonio never yet was thief or pirate,
Though I confess, on base and ground enough,
Orsino's enemy. A witchcraft drew me hither.
That most ingrateful boy there by your side
From the rude sea's enrag'd and foamy mouth
Did I redeem; a wrack past hope he was.
His life I gave him, and did thereto add
My love, without retention or restraint,
All his in dedication. For his sake
Did I expose myself, pure for his love,
Into the danger of this adverse town,
Drew to defend him when he was beset;
Where being apprehended, his false cunning,
Not meaning to partake with me in danger,
Taught him to face me out of his acquaintance,
And grew a twenty years removed thing
While one would wink; denied me mine own purse,
Which I had recommended to his use
Not half an hour before.

VIOLA How can this be?

DUKE
When came he to this town?

ANTONIO
Today, my lord; and for three months before,
No int'rim, not a minute's vacancy,
Both day and night did we keep company.

Enter Olivia and Attendants.

DUKE
Here comes the Countess; now heaven walks on earth.
But for thee, fellow—fellow, thy words are madness.
Three months this youth hath tended upon me;
But more of that anon. Take him aside.

OLIVIA
What would my lord, but that he may not have,
Wherein Olivia may seem serviceable?
Cesario, you do not keep promise with me.

VIOLA
Madam?

DUKE
Gracious Olivia—

OLIVIA
What do you say, Cesario? Good my lord—

VIOLA
My lord would speak; my duty hushes me.

OLIVIA
If it be aught to the old tune, my lord,
It is as fat and fulsome to mine ear
As howling after music.

DUKE Still so cruel?

OLIVIA
Still so constant, lord.

DUKE
What, to perverseness? You uncivil lady,
To whose ingrate and unauspicious altars
My soul the faithfull'st off'rings have breath'd out
That e'er devotion tender'd! What shall I do?

OLIVIA
Even what it please my lord, that shall become him.

DUKE
Why should I not, had I the heart to do it,
Like to th' Egyptian thief at point of death,
Kill what I love?—a savage jealousy
That sometime savors nobly. But hear me this:
Since you to non-regardance cast my faith,
And that I partly know the instrument
That screws me from my true place in your favor,
Live you the marble-breasted tyrant still.
But this your minion, whom I know you love,
And whom, by heaven I swear, I tender dearly,
Him will I tear out of that cruel eye
Where he sits crowned in his master's spite.
Come, boy, with me. My thoughts are ripe in mischief.
I'll sacrifice the lamb that I do love,
To spite a raven's heart within a dove. [*Going.*]

VIOLA
And I, most jocund, apt, and willingly,
To do you rest, a thousand deaths would die. [*Going.*]

OLIVIA
Where goes Cesario?

VIOLA After him I love
More than I love these eyes, more than my life,
More, by all mores, than e'er I shall love wife.

53 bottom ship **54 very envy** i.e., even those who hated him, his enemies. **loss** i.e., the losers **57 fraught** freight, cargo. **from Candy** on her return from *Candia* or Crete **60 desperate . . . state** recklessly disregarding disgrace and his status as a wanted man **61 brabble** brawl **63 put . . . me** spoke to me strangely **64 but distraction** unless (it was) madness **67 dear** costly, grievous **69 Be pleas'd that** allow me to **71 base and ground** solid grounds **75 wrack** goods from a wrecked vessel **77 retention** reservation **79 pure** entirely, purely **80 Into** unto. **adverse** hostile **84 face . . . acquaintance** brazenly deny he knew me **85–86 grew . . . wink** in the twinkling of an eye acted as though we had been estranged for twenty years **87 recommended** consigned

97 but that except that which. **he . . . have** i.e., my love **105 fat and fulsome** gross and offensive **114 Egyptian thief** (An allusion to the story of Theagenes and Chariclea in the *Ethiopica*, a Greek romance by Heliodorus. The robber chief, Thyamis of Memphis, having captured Chariclea and fallen in love with her, is attacked by a larger band of robbers; threatened with death, he attempts to slay her first.) **116 savors nobly** is not without nobility **117 non-regardance** neglect **119 screws** pries, forces **121 minion** darling, favorite **122 tender** regard **124 in . . . spite** in defiance of his master **129 do you rest** give you ease **132 by all mores** by all such comparisons

If I do feign, you witnesses above
Punish my life for tainting of my love!

OLIVIA
Ay me, detested! How am I beguil'd!

VIOLA
Who does beguile you? Who does do you wrong?

OLIVIA
Hast thou forgot thyself? Is it so long?
Call forth the holy father. [*Exit an Attendant.*]

DUKE [*To Viola*] Come, away!

OLIVIA
Whither, my lord? Cesario, husband, stay.

DUKE
Husband?

OLIVIA Ay, husband. Can he that deny?

DUKE
Her husband, sirrah?

VIOLA No, my lord, not I.

OLIVIA
Alas, it is the baseness of thy fear
That makes thee strangle thy propriety. 143
Fear not, Cesario; take thy fortunes up;
Be that thou know'st thou art, and then thou art 145
As great as that thou fear'st.

Enter Priest.

O, welcome, father! 146
Father, I charge thee, by thy reverence,
Here to unfold, though lately we intended
To keep in darkness what occasion now
Reveals before 'tis ripe, what thou dost know
Hath newly pass'd between this youth and me.

PRIEST
A contract of eternal bond of love,
Confirm'd by mutual joinder of your hands, 153
Attested by the holy close of lips, 154
Strength'ned by interchangement of your rings,
And all the ceremony of this compact
Seal'd in my function, by my testimony; 157
Since when, my watch hath told me, toward my grave
I have travel'd but two hours.

DUKE
O thou dissembling cub! What wilt thou be
When time hath sow'd a grizzle on thy case? 161
Or will not else thy craft so quickly grow
That thine own trip shall be thine overthrow? 163
Farewell, and take her; but direct thy feet
Where thou and I henceforth may never meet.

VIOLA
My Lord, I do protest—

OLIVIA O, do not swear!
Hold little faith, though thou hast too much fear. 167

Enter Sir Andrew.

SIR ANDREW For the love of God, a surgeon! Send one presently to Sir Toby.

OLIVIA What's the matter?

SIR ANDREW H'as broke my head across and has given 171
Sir Toby a bloody coxcomb too. For the love of God, 172
your help! I had rather than forty pound I were at home.

OLIVIA Who has done this, Sir Andrew?

SIR ANDREW The Count's gentleman, one Cesario. We
took him for a coward, but he's the very devil incar- 177
dinate. 178

DUKE My gentleman, Cesario?

SIR ANDREW 'Od's lifelings, here he is! You broke my 180
head for nothing; and that that I did, I was set on to do 't by Sir Toby.

VIOLA
Why do you speak to me? I never hurt you.
You drew your sword upon me without cause,
But I bespake you fair, and hurt you not. 185

SIR ANDREW If a bloody coxcomb be a hurt, you have
hurt me. I think you set nothing by a bloody cox- 187
comb.

Enter [Sir] Toby and Clown.

Here comes Sir Toby halting; you shall hear more. But 189
if he had not been in drink, he would have tickled you
othergates than he did. 191

DUKE How now, gentleman? How is 't with you?

SIR TOBY That's all one. H'as hurt me, and there's th'
end on 't. Sot, didst see Dick surgeon, sot? 194

CLOWN O, he's drunk, Sir Toby, an hour agone; his
eyes were set at eight i' th' morning. 196

SIR TOBY Then he's a rogue, and a passy measures 197
pavin. I hate a drunken rogue. 198

OLIVIA Away with him! Who hath made this havoc with them?

SIR ANDREW I'll help you, Sir Toby, because we'll be 201
dress'd together. 202

SIR TOBY Will you help? An ass-head and a coxcomb and a knave, a thin-fac'd knave, a gull!

OLIVIA
Get him to bed, and let his hurt be look'd to.
[*Exeunt Clown, Fabian, Sir Toby, and Sir Andrew.*]

Enter Sebastian.

SEBASTIAN
I am sorry, madam, I have hurt your kinsman;
But, had it been the brother of my blood,
I must have done no less with wit and safety.— 208
You throw a strange regard upon me, and by that 209
I do perceive it hath offended you.
Pardon me, sweet one, even for the vows
We made each other but so late ago.

DUKE
One face, one voice, one habit, and two persons, 213

143 strangle thy propriety deny what you are **145 that** that which **146 that thou fear'st** him you fear, i.e., Orsino **153 joinder** joining **154 close** meeting **157 Seal'd** ratified **161 a grizzle** grey hair. **case** sheath, skin **163 trip** wrestling trick. (I.e., you'll get over-clever, and trip yourself up.) **167 little** i.e., a little

171 H'as he has. **broke** broken the skin, cut **172 coxcomb** fool's cap resembling the crest of a cock; here, head **177–178 incardinate** (For *incarnate.*) **180 'Od's lifelings** by God's little lives **185 fair** courteously **187 set nothing by** regard as insignificant **189 halting** limping **191 othergates** otherwise **194 Sot** (1) fool (2) drunkard **196 set** fixed or extinguished, closed **197–198 passy measures pavin** a slow-moving eight-bar grave and stately dance (suggesting Sir Toby's impatience to have his wounds dressed) **201–202 be dress'd** i.e., have our wounds surgically dressed **208 with wit and safety** with intelligent concern for my own safety **209 strange regard** look such as one directs at a stranger **213 habit** dress

A natural perspective, that is and is not!

SEBASTIAN
Antonio, O my dear Antonio!
How have the hours rack'd and tortur'd me,
Since I have lost thee!

ANTONIO
Sebastian are you?

SEBASTIAN
Fear'st thou that, Antonio?

ANTONIO
How have you made division of yourself?
An apple cleft in two is not more twin
Than these two creatures. Which is Sebastian?

OLIVIA
Most wonderful!

SEBASTIAN [*Seeing Viola*]
Do I stand there? I never had a brother;
Nor can there be that deity in my nature
Of here and every where. I had a sister,
Whom the blind waves and surges have devour'd.
Of charity, what kin are you to me?
What countryman? What name? What parentage?

VIOLA
Of Messaline; Sebastian was my father;
Such a Sebastian was my brother too,
So went he suited to his watery tomb.
If spirits can assume both form and suit,
You come to fright us.

SEBASTIAN
A spirit I am indeed,
But am in that dimension grossly clad
Which from the womb I did participate.
Were you a woman, as the rest goes even,
I should my tears let fall upon your cheek,
And say "Thrice welcome, drowned Viola!"

VIOLA
My father had a mole upon his brow.

SEBASTIAN
And so had mine.

VIOLA
And died that day when Viola from her birth
Had numb'red thirteen years.

SEBASTIAN
O, that record is lively in my soul!
He finished indeed his mortal act
That day that made my sister thirteen years.

VIOLA
If nothing lets to make us happy both
But this my masculine usurp'd attire,
Do not embrace me till each circumstance
Of place, time, fortune, do cohere and jump
That I am Viola—which to confirm,
I'll bring you to a captain in this town,
Where lie my maiden weeds; by whose gentle help
I was preserv'd to serve this noble count.
All the occurrence of my fortune since
Hath been between this lady and this lord.

SEBASTIAN [*To Olivia*]
So comes it, lady, you have been mistook.
But nature to her bias drew in that.
You would have been contracted to a maid;
Nor are you therein, by my life, deceiv'd,
You are betroth'd both to a maid and man.

DUKE
Be not amaz'd; right noble is his blood.
If this be so, as yet the glass seems true,
I shall have share in this most happy wrack.
[*To Viola.*] Boy, thou hast said to me a thousand times
Thou never shouldst love woman like to me.

VIOLA
And all those sayings will I over swear,
And all those swearings keep as true in soul
As doth that orbed continent the fire
That severs day from night.

DUKE
Give me thy hand,
And let me see thee in thy woman's weeds.

VIOLA
The captain that did bring me first on shore
Hath my maid's garments. He upon some action
Is now in durance, at Malvolio's suit,
A gentleman, and follower of my lady's.

OLIVIA
He shall enlarge him. Fetch Malvolio hither.
And yet, alas, now I remember me,
They say, poor gentleman, he's much distract.

Enter Clown with a letter, and Fabian.

A most extracting frenzy of mine own
From my remembrance clearly banish'd his.
How does he, sirrah?

CLOWN Truly, madam, he holds Belzebub at the stave's end as well as a man in his case may do. H'as here writ a letter to you; I should have given 't you today morning. But as a madman's epistles are no gospels, so it skills not much when they are deliver'd.

OLIVIA Open 't, and read it.

CLOWN Look then to be well edified when the fool delivers the madman. [*Reads loudly.*] "By the Lord, madam"—

OLIVIA How now, art thou mad?

CLOWN No, madam, I do but read madness. An your ladyship will have it as it ought to be, you must allow vox.

OLIVIA Prithee, read i' thy right wits.

CLOWN So I do, madonna; but to read his right wits is to read thus. Therefore perpend, my princess, and give ear.

OLIVIA Read it you, sirrah. [*To Fabian.*]

FABIAN [*Reads*] "By the Lord madam, you wrong me,

214 natural perspective an optical device or illusion created by nature **225 here and every where** omnipresence **226 blind** heedless, indiscriminating **227 Of charity** (tell me) in kindness **231 suited** dressed; clad in human form **234 in . . . clad** clothed in that fleshly shape **235 participate** possess **236 as . . . even** since everything else agrees **243 record** recollection **246 lets** hinders **249 jump** coincide, fit exactly **252 weeds** clothes

257 nature . . . that nature followed her bent in that **260 maid** i.e., a virgin man **262 glass** i.e., the *natural perspective* of l. 214 **263 wrack** goods from a wrecked vessel **266 over swear** swear again **268 As . . . fire** i.e., as the sphere of the sun keeps the fire **272 action** legal charge **273 durance** captivity **275 enlarge** release **278 extracting** i.e., that obsessed me and drew me away from all other thoughts **281–282 holds . . . end** i.e., holds off the devil **284 a madman's . . . gospels** i.e., there is no truth in a madman's letters. (An allusion to readings in the church service of selected passages from the epistles and the gospels.) **285 skills** matters **287–288 delivers** speaks the words of **293 vox** voice, i.e., an appropriately loud voice **296 perpend** consider, attend

and the world shall know it. Though you have put me
into darkness and given your drunken cousin rule
over me, yet have I the benefit of my senses as well as
your ladyship. I have your own letter that induc'd me
to the semblance I put on; with the which I doubt not 304
but to do myself much right, or you much shame.
Think of me as you please. I leave my duty a little
unthought of and speak out of my injury.

The madly-us'd Malvolio."

OLIVIA Did he write this?

CLOWN Ay, madam.

DUKE This savors not much of distraction.

OLIVIA
See him deliver'd, Fabian; bring him hither.
[*Exit Fabian.*]
My lord, so please you, these things further thought on, 313
To think me as well a sister as a wife, 314
One day shall crown th' alliance on 't, so please you, 315
Here at my house and at my proper cost. 316

DUKE
Madam, I am most apt t' embrace your offer.
[*To Viola.*] Your master quits you; and for your service done him, 318
So much against the mettle of your sex, 319
So far beneath your soft and tender breeding,
And since you call'd me master for so long,
Here is my hand. You shall from this time be
Your master's mistress.

OLIVIA A sister! You are she.

Enter [*Fabian, with*] *Malvolio.*

DUKE
Is this the madman?

OLIVIA Ay, my lord, this same.
How now, Malvolio?

MALVOLIO Madam, you have done me wrong,
Notorious wrong.

OLIVIA Have I, Malvolio? No.

MALVOLIO
Lady, you have. Pray you, peruse that letter.
[*Gives letter.*]
You must not now deny it is your hand.
Write from it, if you can, in hand or phrase, 329
Or say 'tis not your seal, not your invention. 330
You can say none of this. Well, grant it then,
And tell me, in the modesty of honor, 332
Why you have given me such clear lights of favor,
Bade me come smiling and cross-garter'd to you,
To put on yellow stockings, and to frown
Upon Sir Toby and the lighter people; 336
And, acting this in an obedient hope,
Why have you suffer'd me to be imprison'd,
Kept in a dark house, visited by the priest,
And made the most notorious geck and gull 340
That e'er invention play'd on? Tell me why? 341

OLIVIA
Alas, Malvolio, this is not my writing,
Though, I confess, much like the character;
But out of question 'tis Maria's hand. 344
And now I do bethink me, it was she
First told me thou wast mad; then cam'st in smiling, 346
And in such forms which here were presuppos'd 347
Upon thee in the letter. Prithee, be content.
This practice hath most shrewdly pass'd upon thee; 349
But when we know the grounds and authors of it,
Thou shalt be both the plaintiff and the judge
Of thine own cause.

FABIAN Good madam, hear me speak,
And let no quarrel nor no brawl to come
Taint the condition of this present hour,
Which I have wond'red at. In hope it shall not,
Most freely I confess, myself and Toby
Set this device against Malvolio here,
Upon some stubborn and uncourteous parts 358
We had conceiv'd against him. Maria writ 359
The letter at Sir Toby's great importance, 360
In recompense whereof he hath married her.
How with a sportful malice it was follow'd 362
May rather pluck on laughter than revenge,
If that the injuries be justly weigh'd
That have on both sides pass'd.

OLIVIA
Alas, poor fool, how have they baffled thee! 366

CLOWN Why, "some are born great, some achieve
greatness, and some have greatness thrown upon
them." I was one, sir, in this interlude, one Sir Topas, 369
sir, but that's all one. "By the Lord, fool, I am not
mad." But do you remember? "Madam, why laugh
you at such a barren rascal? An you smile not, he's
gagg'd." And thus the whirligig of time brings in his 373
revenges.

MALVOLIO I'll be reveng'd on the whole pack of you!
[*Exit.*]

OLIVIA
He hath been most notoriously abus'd.

DUKE
Pursue him, and entreat him to a peace.
He hath not told us of the captain yet.
When that is known, and golden time convents, 379
A solemn combination shall be made
Of our dear souls. Meantime, sweet sister,
We will not part from hence. Cesario, come—
For so you shall be, while you are a man;
But when in other habits you are seen,
Orsino's mistress and his fancy's queen.
Exeunt [*all, except Clown*].

CLOWN (*Sings*)
When that I was and a little tiny boy,

304 the which i.e., the letter **313 so . . . on** if you are pleased on further consideration **314 To . . . wife** to regard me as favorably as a sister-in-law as you had hoped to regard me as a wife **315 crown . . . on 't** i.e., serve as occasion for two marriages confirming our new relationship **316 proper** own **318 quits** releases **319 mettle** natural disposition **329 from it** differently **330 invention** composition **332 modesty of honor** sense of propriety belonging to honorable persons **336 lighter** lesser

340 geck dupe **341 invention** contrivance **344 out of** beyond **346 cam'st** you came **347 presuppos'd** specified beforehand **349 shrewdly** cruelly, grievously. **pass'd upon** imposed on **358 Upon** on account of. **parts** qualities, deeds **359 conceiv'd against him** seen and resented in him **360 importance** importunity **362 follow'd** carried out **366 baffled** disgraced, quelled **369 interlude** little play **373 whirligig** spinning top **379 convents** suits

With hey, ho, the wind and the rain,
A foolish thing was but a toy,
For the rain it raineth every day.

But when I came to man's estate,
With hey, ho, etc.
'Gainst knaves and thieves men shut their gate,
For the rain, etc.

But when I came, alas, to wive,
With hey, ho, etc.
By swaggering could I never thrive,
For the rain, etc.

But when I came unto my beds,
With hey, ho, etc.
With toss-pots still had drunken heads,
For the rain, etc.

A great while ago the world begun,
With hey, ho, etc.
But that's all one, our play is done,
And we'll strive to please you every day.
[*Exit.*]

400 toss-pots drunkards

All's Well that Ends Well

All's Well that Ends Well belongs to that period of Shakespeare's creative life when he concentrated on his great tragedies and wrote little comedy. The few apparent exceptions do not fit readily into conventional dramatic genres. *Measure for Measure* (1603–1604), usually called a "problem" play, is darkly preoccupied with human carnality and injustice. *Troilus and Cressida* (c. 1601–1602), printed between the histories and the tragedies in the Folio of 1623, is a disillusioning satire of love and war somewhat akin to the "black" comedy of our modern theatre. *All's Well* shares to an extent the satiric and brooding spirit of these two plays. Its "bed trick," resembling that of *Measure for Measure,* poses ethical problems for the audience, who accordingly may regard the heroine as too much of a schemer. The relations between the sexes are problematic in this play, written as it seemingly was amidst tragedies that are haunted by images of destructive femaleness and of debasing sexuality. The action of *All's Well* is to a large extent controlled by a good sexual woman, and yet the play dwells more than any previous comedy on the potential hazards of sexuality. For these and other reasons, *All's Well* is often grouped with the "problem" plays.

At the same time, the play also looks forward to Shakespeare's late romances, *Pericles, Cymbeline, The Winter's Tale,* and *The Tempest.* Here the mode of comedy turns toward the miraculous and tragicomic, with journeys of separation ending in tearful reunion, and sinful error ending in spiritual rebirth. This mode was not unknown in Shakespeare's comedies of the late 1590's: *As You Like It* ends with the sudden and implausible conversion of its villains, and *Much Ado about Nothing* offers forgiveness to the undeserving Claudio while restoring his traduced fiancée, Hero, to a new life. *Measure for Measure* follows a similar pattern of redemptive pardon for the corrupted Angelo and providential deliverance for Isabella. Both *All's Well* and *Measure for Measure* contain features of this "comedy of forgiveness," even if admittedly the ironies surrounding the gesture of forgiving are far less controlled than in the late romances.

Certainly, in any case, *All's Well* occupies a central position in the line of development from the early comedies to the late romances. Helena points back to earlier comic women in her role as engineer of the love plot, and forward to women of the late romances in her role as daughter, victim, and savior (though early comedy and late romance are, to be sure, not as neatly distinguishable as this antithesis suggests). Bertram, although virtually without precedent in earlier comedies, anticipates to a degree Posthumus, Florizel, and Ferdinand in that he takes part in a marriage sanctioned and defined largely by paternal intervention. *All's Well,* like the romances and unlike the earlier comedies, affords a remarkably prominent role to the older generation.

The probable date of *All's Well* is consistent with such a transitional function. Its dates are hard to fix by external evidence, for it was neither registered nor printed until 1623, and allusions to it are scarce. Some scholars would like to think that it is the *Love's Labor's Won* intriguingly mentioned by Francis Meres in 1598, which Shakespeare might then have revised some time around 1601–1604. Portions of the play do feature the rhymed couplets, letters in sonnet form, and witty conceits that we normally associate with Shakespeare's early style. These old-fashioned effects may have been deliberate on Shakespeare's part, however, not unlike the anachronisms he later introduces in *Pericles* and *Cymbeline.* Certainly a major portion of the play dates stylistically from 1601–1604 or even later. Here the language is elliptical and compact, the images complexly interwoven, the verse rhythms free.

In any event, with its two contrasting styles poised between romance and satire, *All's Well* plaintively seeks comic reassurance amid the pessimistic ironies of Shakespeare's tragic period. It lacks many of the felicities we associate with the festive comedies of the 1590's, the love songs, the innocently hedonistic joy, the well-mated young lovers escaping from stern parents or an envious court. *All's Well* has too often been judged negatively for its failure to achieve a festive mood that Shakespeare probably did not intend. The hero, Bertram, is undeniably a cad. As the undeserving hero forgiven in spite of his waywardness, however, he plays an essential role in the play's problematic resolution—or failure to achieve complete resolution. He is, like all mankind, unworthy of the forgiveness he receives, whereas Helena's generosity in forgiving him suggests at least a capability in mankind for decency and compassion. We are left, as in *Measure for Measure,* with a sense of the perennially unbridgeable gap between human ideals and their achievement, and yet we view this dilemma in a comic context where second chances and hope are bestowed even on those who appear to deserve them least.

The satiric mode in *All's Well* is conveyed chiefly through Lavatch the clown and through Parolles, the boastful cowardly knave who accompanies Bertram to the wars. Lavatch, with his bitter and riddling wit of the professional fool, gives expression to many of the satirical themes also illustrated by the exposure of Parolles. Lavatch jests about cuckoldry and the other marital difficulties that cause men to flee from women; he pokes fun at court manners, and apes the prodigal disobedience of his master Bertram. He is, like Parolles, called a "foul-mouthed and calumnious knave," although the inversion of appearance and reality is evident here as with all Shakespearean fools: Parolles is truly more fool and knave than his mocking counterpart. Parolles is all pretense. Full of sound, but hollow like the drum to which he is compared, he is a swaggerer and a fashion-monger whose clothes conceal his lack of inner substance. He is a recognizable satiric type going back to Plautus and Terence, the braggart soldier. He is, to be sure, endearing in his outrageousness; Shakespeare endows him with that vitality or "rarity" we find also in those earlier braggart soldiers, Falstaff and Pistol. Yet because Parolles lacks the self-awareness of Falstaff, we merely laugh at him rather than with him. To the impressionable young Bertram, hungry for fame, Parolles represents smartness and military style. Bertram rejects the true worth of Helena because she lacks family position, and ironically embraces the false worth of a parvenu. Parolles and Helena are foils from their first encounter, when the braggart sardonically derides virginity as unnatural and out of fashion. Parolles stands opposite also to Lafew, to the Countess, and to the King, those dignified embodiments of a traditional chivalrous order whose generous teachings Bertram rejects for the company of Parolles and of attractive young women. By offering Bertram the slick insolence of the new guise, Parolles wins for a time his friend's allegiance. Parolles is not really a tempter, for we never see him bending Bertram from his true inclination; rather, Bertram is himself too much in love with sham reputation, too rebellious against the civilized decencies of his elders. He is the Prodigal Son, or Youth in the old morality play, perversely eager to prove his own worst enemy.

Yet Bertram is not without a redeeming nobleness—he bears himself bravely in the Florentine wars—and cannot be fooled indefinitely by his roguish companion. The exposure of Parolles is one of satiric humiliation, like that of Malvolio in *Twelfth Night* or one of Ben Jonson's "humorous" gulls. The engineers of Parolles' exposure use the language of Jonsonian satire in their devices to outwit him: their game is a "sport" done "for the love of laughter," employing a snare whereby the "fox" or the "woodcock" will entrap himself. The device of public humiliation is particularly appropriate because Parolles is himself a railing slanderer, like Lucio in *Measure for Measure,* caustically brilliant in his invective but nonetheless a slayer of men's reputations. The punishment of ridicule fits his particular crime. His callous disregard for the good name of various French military commanders is parallel to Bertram's indifference to the public shame he has heaped upon his virtuous wife. Once Parolles' bluff has been called, Bertram is in part disabused of his folly; but other more wondrous and spiritual means are needed to convince him of the wrong he has done to Helena. Indeed, Bertram's very coldness in turning away from Parolles shows a lack of that humility which he must learn by being tricked, exposed, and humiliated himself.

The fabulous romancelike aspect of *All's Well* is conveyed chiefly through its folktale plot and through the character of Helena. The story is derived from the third "day" of Boccaccio's *Decameron,* a day devoted to tales of lovers obliged to overcome seemingly impossible obstacles in order to achieve love's happiness. The story was translated into English by William Painter in *The Palace of Pleasure* (1566). To win the nobly born Beltramo, Giletta of Narbona must cure the French King with her physician-father's secret remedy, and then must perform the riddling tasks assigned her by Beltramo as his means of being rid of her. Both these motifs have ancient antecedents in folklore, and, as in his late romances, Shakespeare puts great stress on the wondrous and improbable nature of these events.

All common sense warns against the likelihood of Helena's success. She is vastly below Bertram in social station or in "blood," even though she excels in "virtue." (This low station is unique among Shakespeare's comic heroines, and contributes to what is so unusual about this play.) Her only hope is a desperate gamble: to cure the ailing King and so win Bertram as her reward. No one supposes at first she will even be admitted to the King, who has given up all hope of living; his "congregated college" of learned doctors "have concluded That laboring art can never ransom nature From her inaidible estate" (II,i). Helena transcends these rational doubts through resourcefulness and above all through a faith in help from above. She is willing to "hazard" all for love. She senses that her father's legacy will "be sanctified by the luckiest stars in heaven," and she manages to convince not only the Countess and Lafew (persons who do not appear in Boccaccio) but also the King himself. Believing, like Shaw's Saint Joan, that God will perform his greatest works through the humblest of his creatures, Helena inspires her listeners with faith in the impossible. Lafew is so moved by her simple eloquence that he proclaims to the King, "I have seen a medicine That's able to breathe life into a stone." Soon the King too is persuaded that in Helena "some blessed spirit doth speak His powerful sound within an organ weak." Once the King's cure has been effected, even Parolles and Bertram must agree with Lafew that the age of miracles, long thought to have passed, is with them again. The King's cure by the "very hand of heaven," through the agency of a "weak and debile minister," is matter for a pious ballad or an old tale (II,iii).

The impossible tasks Helena must perform are stated as riddles, as usual in a folk tale, and must be solved by riddling or paradoxical means. Bertram writes that she must "get the ring upon my finger which never shall come off, and show me a child begotten of thy body that I am father to" (III,ii). Such a challenge invites ingenuity, as in Boccaccio, but in Shakespeare the solution also requires providential aid. Helena's first sad response is to set Bertram free and renounce her audacious pretentions. Her pilgrimage of grief takes her to Florence, where Bertram happens to be serving in the wars. Is this mere coincidence, or conscious scheming on her part? Throughout, her motives are at once virtuous and deceitful, lawful and sinful, just as her very sexuality, so unlike that of earlier Shakespearean heroines, is wholesome and yet is perceived by us in a context of debased human nature. Her acts are prompted at once by providence and by shrewd calculation. Even if providence must be credited with introducing her to Diana, the very lady whom Bertram is importuning in love, Helena makes the most of such opportunities afforded her, never doubting that "heaven" has "fated" her both to help Diana and simultaneously to serve her own turn (IV,iv). The bed trick is a "plot," but a virtuous one, a "deceit" that is "lawful," a deed that is "not sin, and yet a sinful fact" (III,vii). Diana repeatedly plays upon these same riddles in accusing Bertram before the King: he is "guilty, and he is not guilty" (V,iii).

The conundrums, although playful and entertaining in Shakespeare's highly complicated denouement (not found in Boccaccio), also hint at paradoxes in the nature of man. Bertram's typically human waywardness justifies a cunning response. "I think 't no sin," argues Diana, "To cozen him that would unjustly win" (IV,ii). Justice among men, as in *Measure for Measure,* must take forms only roughly approximating those of heavenly justice, for man's bestial nature sometimes requires an answer in kind. Yet by a providential paradox, man's thwarted nature, which seems his fatal enemy, contributes essentially to his regeneration: by being humbled, he is enabled to rise. "The web of our life is of a mingled yarn, good and ill together," says a sympathetic observer of Bertram. "Our virtues would be proud, if our faults whipp'd them not; and our crimes would despair, if they were not cherish'd by our virtues" (IV,iii). Man's perversity reminds him of his dependence on grace.

Helena is a romantic heroine, only metaphorically the "angel" who must "Bless this unworthy husband," reprieving him by her "prayers" from "the wrath Of greatest justice" (III,iv). Still, the spiritual overtones are not extraneous to this bittersweet comedy. Bertram typifies the "Natural rebellion" of all youth, Helena the "herb of grace" whom he has willfully rejected. However much we may sympathize with his desire to choose in love for himself, Bertram's revolt is incomprehensible to every witness except Parolles. Bertram himself confesses, too late it seems, that he has recognized Helena's precious worth. This note of "love that comes too late," wherein the penitent sinner confesses "That's good that's gone," hovers over the play with its tragicomic mood. Helena is a "jewel" thrown away and seemingly forever lost. The semblance of her death is in fact only another one of her inventive schemes, along with the bewildering contretemps of the final scene. Yet when she reappears, setting all to rights, she comes as "one that's dead" but is now "quick," alive again, merely a "shadow" of her former self. Bertram has not actually committed the evil he intended; by a providential sophistry he is innocent, like Claudio in *Much Ado* or Angelo in *Measure for Measure,* and so is reconciled to the goodness he has failed to merit. Even Parolles is given a second chance by the magnanimous Lafew. As the play's title implies, all might have miscarried through man's "rash faults" that "Make trivial price of serious things we have," were it not for a forgiving power that can make man's worst failings an instrument of his penitence and recovery. This resolution fleetingly comforts us in the final scene, even though it must do battle with such manifest imbalances as the prolonged shaming of Bertram and the scant attention paid to his reunion with Helena. The web of man's life remains a mingled yarn.

All's Well that Ends Well

[*Dramatis Personae*

KING OF FRANCE.
DUKE OF FLORENCE.
BERTRAM, *Count of Rossillion.*
LAFEW, *an old lord.*
PAROLLES, *a follower of Bertram.*
RINALDO, *a Steward,* } *servants to the Countess of Rossillion.*
LAVATCH, *a Clown,* }
TWO FRENCH LORDS *or Captains, the brothers Dumain.*
PAGE.
COUNTESS OF ROSSILLION, *mother to Bertram.*
HELENA, *a gentlewoman protected by the Countess.*
An old WIDOW *of Florence.*
DIANA, *daughter to the Widow.*
MARIANA, *neighbor and friend to the Widow.*

LORDS, OFFICERS, SOLDIERS, *etc., French and Florentine.*

SCENE: *Rossillion; Paris; Florence; Marseilles.*]

ACT I • SCENE I

Enter young Bertram, Count of Rossillion, his Mother [*the Countess*], *and Helena,* [*with*] *Lord Lafew, all in black.*

COUNTESS In delivering my son from me, I bury a second husband.

BERTRAM And I in going, madam, weep o'er my father's death anew. But I must attend his Majesty's command, to whom I am now in ward, evermore in subjection.

LAFEW You shall find of the King a husband, madam; you, sir, a father. He that so generally is at all times good must of necessity hold his virtue to you, whose worthiness would stir it up where it wanted rather than lack it where there is such abundance.

COUNTESS What hope is there of his Majesty's amendment?

LAFEW He hath abandon'd his physicians, madam, under whose practices he hath persecuted time with hope, and finds no other advantage in the process but only the losing of hope by time.

COUNTESS This young gentlewoman had a father—O, that "had," how sad a passage 'tis!—whose skill was almost as great as his honesty; had it stretch'd so far, would have made nature immortal, and death should have play for lack of work. Would, for the King's sake, he were living! I think it would be the death of the King's disease.

LAFEW How call'd you the man you speak of, madam?

COUNTESS He was famous, sir, in his profession, and it was his great right to be so: Gerard de Narbon.

LAFEW He was excellent indeed, madam. The King very lately spoke of him admiringly and mourningly. He was skillful enough to have liv'd still, if knowledge could be set up against mortality.

BERTRAM What is it, my good lord, the King languishes of?

LAFEW A fistula, my lord.

BERTRAM I heard not of it before.

LAFEW I would it were not notorious. Was this gentlewoman the daughter of Gerard de Narbon?

COUNTESS His sole child, my lord, and bequeath'd to my overlooking. I have those hopes of her good that her education promises her dispositions she inherits, which makes fair gifts fairer; for where an unclean mind carries virtuous qualities, there commendations go with pity—they are virtues and traitors too. In her they are the better for their simpleness; she derives her honesty, and achieves her goodness.

LAFEW Your commendations, madam, get from her tears.

COUNTESS 'Tis the best brine a maiden can season her praise in. The remembrance of her father never approaches her heart but the tyranny of her sorrows takes all livelihood from her cheek. No more of this, Helena. Go to, no more, lest it be rather thought you affect a sorrow than to have—

HELENA I do affect a sorrow indeed, but I have it too.

LAFEW Moderate lamentation is the right of the dead, excessive grief the enemy to the living.

COUNTESS If the living be enemy to the grief, the excess makes it soon mortal.

BERTRAM Madam, I desire your holy wishes.

LAFEW How understand we that?

COUNTESS
Be thou blest, Bertram, and succeed thy father
In manners, as in shape! Thy blood and virtue
Contend for empire in thee, and thy goodness

I.i. Location: Rossillion, i.e., Rousillon, in south-east France. The Count's palace.
1 delivering sending (with play on *giving birth to* and *freeing*) **5 in ward** (According to a feudal custom, the King became the guardian of orphaned heirs to estates, who remained "in ward" so long as they were minors. The King's jurisdiction extended even so far as the bestowal of his ward in marriage, but only to someone of equal rank.) **9 hold** continue to devote **10 wanted** is lacking **12–13 amendment** recovery

15 persecuted time i.e., continued to live in pain **19 passage** (1) phrase, expression (2) passing away **20 honesty** integrity of character **27 his great right** i.e., his right in proportion to his greatness **30 still** (1) now as before (2) forever **34 fistula** ulcerous sore **39–41 that . . . fairer** that her upbringing promises to the innate qualities she inherits, which upbringing makes even more attractive her natural gifts **41–43 where . . . pity** i.e., when an innately evil disposition is given the accomplishments of a good education, in that instance praises are mingled with regrets **43 virtues and traitors too** i.e., accomplishments which serve evil purposes. **In her** i.e., in Helena **44 simpleness** purity, being unmixed with vice. **derives** inherits **45 achieves** i.e., by her own efforts in response to her upbringing **48 season** preserve (as with salt) **55 right** rightful due **57–58 If . . . mortal** if those who live resist excessive grief, the excess will soon extinguish itself **60 How . . . that** i.e., what holy wishes do you desire (?) **62 blood** noble birth, inherited qualities; also passion

Share with thy birthright! Love all, trust a few,
Do wrong to none. Be able for thine enemy
Rather in power than use, and keep thy friend
Under thy own life's key. Be check'd for silence,
But never tax'd for speech. What heaven more will,
That thee may furnish, and my prayers pluck down,
Fall on thy head!—Farewell, my lord.
'Tis an unseason'd courtier; good my lord,
Advise him.

LAFEW He cannot want the best
That shall attend his love.

COUNTESS Heaven bless him! Farewell, Bertram. [*Exit.*]

BERTRAM The best wishes that can be forg'd in your thoughts be servants to you! [*To Helena.*] Be comfortable to my mother, your mistress, and make much of her.

LAFEW Farewell, pretty lady. You must hold the credit of your father. [*Exeunt Bertram and Lafew.*]

HELENA
O, were that all! I think not on my father,
And these great tears grace his remembrance more
Than those I shed for him. What was he like?
I have forgot him. My imagination
Carries no favor in 't but Bertram's.
I am undone; there is no living, none,
If Bertram be away. 'Twere all one
That I should love a bright particular star
And think to wed it, he is so above me.
In his bright radiance and collateral light
Must I be comforted, not in his sphere.
Th' ambition in my love thus plagues itself;
The hind that would be mated by the lion
Must die for love. 'Twas pretty, though a plague,
To see him every hour, to sit and draw
His arched brows, his hawking eye, his curls,
In our heart's table—heart too capable
Of every line and trick of his sweet favor.
But now he's gone, and my idolatrous fancy
Must sanctify his reliques. Who comes here?

Enter Parolles.

[*Aside.*] One that goes with him. I love him for his sake;
And yet I know him a notorious liar,
Think him a great way fool, solely a coward.
Yet these fix'd evils sit so fit in him
That they take place when virtue's steely bones
Looks bleak i' th' cold wind. Withal, full oft we see
Cold wisdom waiting on superfluous folly.

PAROLLES Save you, fair queen!

HELENA And you, monarch!

PAROLLES No.

HELENA And no.

PAROLLES Are you meditating on virginity?

HELENA Ay. You have some stain of soldier in you; let me ask you a question. Man is enemy to virginity; how may we barricado it against him?

PAROLLES Keep him out.

HELENA But he assails, and our virginity, though valiant, in the defense yet is weak. Unfold to us some warlike resistance.

PAROLLES There is none. Man, setting down before you, will undermine you and blow you up.

HELENA Bless our poor virginity from underminers and blowers up! Is there no military policy how virgins might blow up men?

PAROLLES Virginity being blown down, man will quicklier be blown up. Marry, in blowing him down again, with the breach yourselves made, you lose your city. It is not politic in the commonwealth of nature to preserve virginity. Loss of virginity is rational increase, and there was never virgin got till virginity was first lost. That you were made of is metal to make virgins. Virginity by being once lost may be ten times found; by being ever kept, it is ever lost. 'Tis too cold a companion; away with 't!

HELENA I will stand for 't a little, though therefore I die a virgin.

PAROLLES There's little can be said in 't; 'tis against the rule of nature. To speak on the part of virginity is to accuse your mothers, which is most infallible disobedience. He that hangs himself is a virgin; virginity murders itself, and should be buried in highways out of all sanctified limit, as a desperate offendress against nature. Virginity breeds mites, much like a cheese, consumes itself to the very paring, and so dies with feeding his own stomach. Besides, virginity is peevish, proud, idle, made of self-love, which is the most inhibited sin in the canon. Keep it not; you cannot choose but lose by 't. Out with 't! Within t' one year it will make itself two, which is a goodly increase, and the principal itself not much the worse. Away with 't!

HELENA How might one do, sir, to lose it to her own liking?

PAROLLES Let me see. Marry, ill, to like him that ne'er it likes. 'Tis a commodity will lose the gloss with lying; the longer kept, the less worth. Off with 't while 'tis vendible; answer the time of request. Virginity, like an old courtier, wears her cap out of fashion, richly

65–66 Be able . . . use i.e., be powerful enough to keep your enemies in awe without having to use that power **66–67 keep . . . key** protect your friend's life as you protect your own. **67 check'd** reproved **68 tax'd for speech** rebuked for idle talk. **will** may bestow **69 pluck** draw **72 want the best** lack the best advice **73 attend his love** accompany my love for him **76–77 comfortable** comforting, serviceable **79 hold** uphold. **credit** reputation **82 his** i.e., Bertram's (?) **83 for him** i.e., for my father when he died **85 favor** (1) face (2) love-token **90 collateral** distant, shed from a different sphere. (The different Ptolemaic spheres were said to move *collaterally*, the implication here being that the distance cannot be closed.) **93 hind** female deer **96 hawking** keen **97 table** drawing-board. **capable** susceptible **101 his** i.e., Bertram's **104 sit so fit** are so natural and plausible (in him) **105–106 take . . . wind** find acceptance, while virtue, in its uncompromising severity, looks coldly forbidding **107 Cold . . . folly** naked and unprovided wisdom being forced to defer to overdressed folly **108 Save** i.e., God save. **queen** (A hyperbolical compliment, which Helena answers in kind, whereupon they both deny their titles.)

113 stain tinge **120–121 setting . . . you** i.e., preparing to lay siege as though to a town. (But with bawdy double meaning of siege as sexual conquest, continued in *blow you up*, i.e., "explode with mines" and "impregnate.") **123 policy** stratagem **126 blown up** i.e., reinflated, given an erection **126–128 in blowing . . . city** i.e., in satisfying his desire by making a breach in your virginity, you will be forced to surrender entirely, paying the loss of your virginity for the subsiding of his erection **128 politic** expedient **129 rational** reasonable **130 got** begotten **131 That** that which. **metal** substance **132–133 may . . . found** i.e., may reproduce itself tenfold **135 stand** fight, stand up. **die** (with probable quibble on *experience sexual orgasm*) **137 in 't** in its behalf **138 on the part of** in behalf of **139 infallible** certain **140 is a virgin** i.e., is like a virgin, since virginity is a kind of suicide **141–142 buried . . . limit** (Suicides were customarily buried at crossroads of highways, not in consecrated ground.) **145 his** its. **stomach** (1) maw (2) pride **147 inhibited** prohibited. **canon** catalogue of sins. (Pride is the first of the Deadly Sins.) **Keep** hoard **148 Out with 't** put it out at interest **150 principal** original investment, i.e., the former virgin **153–154 ill . . . likes** i.e., one must do ill, by liking a man that dislikes virginity **154 will** that will. **gloss** gloss of newness. **with lying** with being unused (with quibble on *lying down*) **156 the time of request** when there is demand

suited, but unsuitable, just like the brooch and the toothpick, which wear not now. Your date is better in your pie and your porridge than in your cheek; and your virginity, your old virginity, is like one of our French wither'd pears, it looks ill, it eats drily. Marry, 'tis a wither'd pear; it was formerly better; marry, yet 'tis a wither'd pear. Will you anything with it?

HELENA
Not my virginity yet . . . . .
There shall your master have a thousand loves,
A mother, and a mistress, and a friend,
A phoenix, captain, and an enemy,
A guide, a goddess, and a sovereign,
A counselor, a traitress, and a dear;
His humble ambition, proud humility,
His jarring concord, and his discord dulcet,
His faith, his sweet disaster; with a world
Of pretty, fond, adoptious christendoms
That blinking Cupid gossips. Now shall he—
I know not what he shall. God send him well!
The court 's a learning place, and he is one—

PAROLLES
What one, i' faith?

HELENA
That I wish well. 'Tis pity—

PAROLLES
What's pity?

HELENA
That wishing well had not a body in 't,
Which might be felt, that we, the poorer born,
Whose baser stars do shut us up in wishes,
Might with effects of them follow our friends,
And show what we alone must think, which never
Returns us thanks.

Enter Page.

PAGE Monsieur Parolles, my lord calls for you. [*Exit.*]

PAROLLES Little Helen, farewell. If I can remember thee, I will think of thee at court.

HELENA Monsieur Parolles, you were born under a charitable star.

PAROLLES Under Mars, I.

HELENA I especially think, under Mars.

PAROLLES Why under Mars?

HELENA The wars have so kept you under that you must needs be born under Mars.

PAROLLES When he was predominant.

HELENA When he was retrograde, I think, rather.

PAROLLES Why think you so?

HELENA You go so much backward when you fight.

PAROLLES That's for advantage.

HELENA So is running away, when fear proposes the safety. But the composition that your valor and fear makes in you is a virtue of a good wing, and I like the wear well.

PAROLLES I am so full of businesses, I cannot answer thee acutely. I will return perfect courtier, in the which my instruction shall serve to naturalize thee, so thou wilt be capable of a courtier's counsel, and understand what advice shall thrust upon thee; else thou diest in thine unthankfulness, and thine ignorance makes thee away. Farewell. When thou hast leisure, say thy prayers; when thou hast none, remember thy friends. Get thee a good husband, and use him as he uses thee. So, farewell. [*Exit.*]

HELENA
Our remedies oft in ourselves do lie,
Which we ascribe to heaven. The fated sky
Gives us free scope, only doth backward pull
Our slow designs when we ourselves are dull.
What power is it which mounts my love so high,
That makes me see, and cannot feed mine eye?
The mightiest space in fortune nature brings
To join like likes, and kiss like native things.
Impossible be strange attempts to those
That weigh their pains in sense, and do suppose
What hath been cannot be. Who ever strove
To show her merit, that did miss her love?
The King's disease—my project may deceive me,
But my intents are fix'd and will not leave me. *Exit.*

[SCENE II]

Flourish cornets. Enter the King of France, with letters, and divers Attendants.

KING
The Florentines and Senoys are by th' ears,
Have fought with equal fortune and continue
A braving war.

FIRST LORD So 'tis reported, sir.

KING
Nay, 'tis most credible. We here receive it
A certainty, vouch'd from our cousin Austria,
With caution that the Florentine will move us
For speedy aid, wherein our dearest friend

158 unsuitable unfashionable **159 wear not** are not in fashion. (I.e., brooches in hats and the affectation of using toothpicks, once fashionable, are no longer so.) **159–160 Your . . . cheek** i.e., the date does better as an ingredient in cooking than as an emblem of withering in your cheek **162 wither'd pears** i.e., objects of (sexual) appetite that have become unappetizing through age and atrophy. **eats drily** tastes dry **165 Not . . . yet** the moment for surrendering my virginity has not yet arrived (?). (There may be a textual omission here.) **166 There** i.e., at court **167–173 A mother . . . disaster** (Helena here recites a series of epithets, like those used in Elizabethan love poetry to describe the beloved person, which may be used to characterize the ladies Bertram will meet at court.) **174 adoptious christendoms** pet names **175 blinking . . . gossips** blind Cupid is godfather to, sponsors **180–181 That . . . felt** i.e., that good wishing does not have a tangible body which could be perceived by the object (Bertram) of this wishing **182 Whose . . . wishes** whose lower births confine us to mere wishing **183 Might . . . them** i.e., might with the assistance of such perceivable wishes **184–185 show . . . thanks** make manifest what we can in fact only think, and for which we receive no thanks **194 under** down **196 predominant** in the ascendant, ruling **197 retrograde** moving apparently in a direction contrary to the order of the signs of the zodiac, from east to west

202 composition mixture **203 of a good wing** strong in flight (and hence useful in rapid retreat) **204 wear** fashion **206 perfect** complete. **in the which** i.e., in which courtly behavior **207 naturalize** familiarize; also, deflower. **so** provided that **208 capable** receptive (with bawdy double meaning, continued in *understand, thrust,* and *diest*) **210–211 makes thee away** destroys, puts an end to you **216 fated** invested with the power of destiny **218 dull** slow, sluggish **219 so high** to so exalted an object, i.e., Bertram **220 That . . . eye** i.e., that puts a desirable object in my mind but will not let me feed my longings in his presence **221–222 The . . . things** i.e., natural affection causes those separated by the widest diversity in social status to come together **223–225 Impossible . . . be** extraordinary attempts (at surmounting social barriers) seem impossible to those who too carefully calculate the extent and cost of their difficulties, and suppose something to be impossible which in fact has been done before (?) **226 miss** fail to achieve

I.ii. Location: Paris. The King's palace.

1 Senoys natives of Siena. **by th' ears** at variance, quarreling **3 braving war** a war of mutual defiance **5 our cousin** my fellow sovereign of **6 move** petition **7 friend** i.e., the Duke of Austria

Prejudicates the business, and would seem 8
To have us make denial.

FIRST LORD His love and wisdom,
Approv'd so to your Majesty, may plead 10
For amplest credence.

KING He hath arm'd our answer, 11
And Florence is denied before he comes.
Yet, for our gentlemen that mean to see 13
The Tuscan service, freely have they leave
To stand on either part.

SECOND LORD It well may serve 15
A nursery to our gentry, who are sick 16
For breathing and exploit.

KING What's he comes here? 17

Enter Bertram, Lafew, and Parolles.

FIRST LORD
It is the Count Rossillion, my good lord,
Young Bertram.

KING Youth, thou bear'st thy father's face.
Frank nature, rather curious than in haste, 20
Hath well compos'd thee. Thy father's moral parts
Mayst thou inherit too! Welcome to Paris.

BERTRAM
My thanks and duty are your Majesty's.

KING
I would I had that corporal soundness now
As when thy father and myself in friendship
First tried our soldiership! He did look far 26
Into the service of the time, and was 27
Discipled of the bravest. He lasted long, 28
But on us both did haggish age steal on, 29
And wore us out of act. It much repairs me 30
To talk of your good father. In his youth
He had the wit which I can well observe
Today in our young lords; but they may jest
Till their own scorn return to them unnoted 34
Ere they can hide their levity in honor. 35
So like a courtier, contempt nor bitterness 36
Were in his pride or sharpness; if they were, 37
His equal had awak'd them, and his honor, 38
Clock to itself, knew the true minute when 39
Exception bid him speak, and at this time 40
His tongue obey'd his hand. Who were below him 41
He us'd as creatures of another place, 42
And bow'd his eminent top to their low ranks, 43
Making them proud of his humility,
In their poor praise he humbled. Such a man 45
Might be a copy to these younger times, 46
Which, followed well, would demonstrate them now 47
But goers backward.

BERTRAM His good remembrance, sir, 48
Lies richer in your thoughts than on his tomb.
So in approof lives not his epitaph 50
As in your royal speech.

KING
Would I were with him! He would always say—
Methinks I hear him now; his plausive words 53
He scatter'd not in ears, but grafted them, 54
To grow there and to bear—"Let me not live"—
This his good melancholy oft began,
On the catastrophe and heel of pastime, 57
When it was out—"Let me not live," quoth he, 58
"After my flame lacks oil, to be the snuff 59
Of younger spirits, whose apprehensive senses 60
All but new things disdain; whose judgments are 61
Mere fathers of their garments; whose constancies 62
Expire before their fashions." This he wish'd.
I, after him, do after him wish too, 64
Since I nor wax nor honey can bring home, 65
I quickly were dissolved from my hive, 66
To give some laborers room.

SECOND LORD You're loved, sir.
They that least lend it you shall lack you first. 68

KING
I fill a place, I know 't. How long is 't, Count,
Since the physician at your father's died?
He was much fam'd.

BERTRAM Some six months since, my lord.

KING
If he were living, I would try him yet.—
Lend me an arm.—The rest have worn me out
With several applications. Nature and sickness 74
Debate it at their leisure. Welcome, Count; 75
My son 's no dearer.

BERTRAM Thank your Majesty.

Exeunt. Flourish.

[SCENE III]

Enter Countess, Steward, and Clown.

COUNTESS I will now hear. What say you of this gentle-
woman?

STEWARD Madam, the care I have had to even your con- 3
tent I wish might be found in the calendar of my past 4
endeavors; for then we wound our modesty, and

8 Prejudicates prejudges **10 Approv'd** demonstrated by proofs **11 arm'd** fortified (against denial) **13 for** as for **15 stand** serve, fight. **part** side. **serve** serve as **16 nursery** training school **17 For breathing** for want of vigorous exercise **20 Frank** free, bountiful. **curious** careful, solicitous **26–27 did look far Into** understood deeply, from experience **27 service** military affairs **28 Discipled of** followed by **29 haggish** like a hag, malevolent **30 wore . . . act** deprived us of ability to be active **34 unnoted** unnoticed **35 hide . . . honor** i.e., cover their frivolous jesting of youth with truly honorable action **36–37 So . . . sharpness** i.e., so like a true courtier as he was, he showed no contemptuousness in his proper self-esteem nor bitterness of tongue in his sharpness of wit **37 if they were** i.e., if he ever spoke sharply **38 equal** i.e., social equal, not an inferior **39 Clock to itself** i.e., self-governing. **true** exact **40 Exception** disapproval **41 obey'd his hand** i.e., said no more than the hand of his clock of honor indicated, or than his own hand was ready to maintain. **Who** those who **42 creatures . . . place** people of a different (i.e., more elevated) station **43 top** head **45 In . . . humbled** i.e., he humbling himself in the praise of them, poor though they were **46 copy** model

47–48 demonstrate . . . backward i.e., show most young men today as regressive and inferior by comparison with him **50 So . . . epitaph** i.e., the epitaph on his tomb is nowhere so amply confirmed **53 plausive** praiseworthy **54 scatter'd not** did not strew haphazardly **57 On . . . pastime** i.e., at the drawing to a close of some sport (such as hunting) **58 it was out** i.e., the sport was over **59 snuff** burned wick that interferes with proper burning of the candle, hence, hindrance **60 apprehensive** quick to perceive, keen but impatient **61–62 whose . . . garments** i.e., whose judgments are given over to designing new fashions **64 I . . . too** I, surviving him, wish as he did **65 nor . . . nor** neither . . . nor **66 dissolved** separated **68 lend it you** give love (or perhaps *room* of l. 67) to you **74 several applications** various medical treatments **75 Debate . . . leisure** i.e., contend over my condition at length

I.iii. Location: Rossillion. The Count's palace.
3–4 to . . . content to match my service with your wishes **4 calendar** record

make foul the clearness of our deservings, when of ourselves we publish them.

COUNTESS What does this knave here? Get you gone, sirrah. The complaints I have heard of you I do not all believe. 'Tis my slowness that I do not, for I know you lack not folly to commit them, and have ability enough to make such knaveries yours.

CLOWN 'Tis not unknown to you, madam, I am a poor fellow.

COUNTESS Well, sir.

CLOWN No, madam, 'tis not so well that I am poor, though many of the rich are damn'd; but, if I may have your ladyship's good will to go to the world, Isbel the woman and I will do as we may.

COUNTESS Wilt thou needs be a beggar?

CLOWN I do beg your good will in this case.

COUNTESS In what case?

CLOWN In Isbel's case and mine own. Service is no heritage, and I think I shall never have the blessing of God till I have issue o' my body; for they say barnes are blessings.

COUNTESS Tell me thy reason why thou wilt marry.

CLOWN My poor body, madam, requires it. I am driven on by the flesh; and he must needs go that the devil drives.

COUNTESS Is this all your worship's reason?

CLOWN Faith, madam, I have other holy reasons, such as they are.

COUNTESS May the world know them?

CLOWN I have been, madam, a wicked creature, as you and all flesh and blood are; and, indeed, I do marry that I may repent.

COUNTESS Thy marriage, sooner than thy wickedness.

CLOWN I am out o' friends, madam; and I hope to have friends for my wife's sake.

COUNTESS Such friends are thine enemies, knave.

CLOWN Y' are shallow, madam, in great friends; for the knaves come to do that for me which I am aweary of. He that ears my land spares my team and gives me leave to in the crop; if I be his cuckold, he's my drudge. He that comforts my wife is the cherisher of my flesh and blood; he that cherishes my flesh and blood loves my flesh and blood; he that loves my flesh and blood is my friend. Ergo, he that kisses my wife is my friend. If men could be contented to be what they are, there were no fear in marriage; for young Charbon the puritan and old Poysam the papist, howsome'er their hearts are sever'd in religion, their heads are both one—they may jowl horns together, like any deer i' th' herd.

COUNTESS Wilt thou ever be a foul-mouth'd and calumnious knave?

CLOWN A prophet I, madam, and I speak the truth the next way:

For I the ballad will repeat,
Which men full true shall find:
Your marriage comes by destiny,
Your cuckoo sings by kind.

COUNTESS Get you gone, sir. I'll talk with you more anon.

STEWARD May it please you, madam, that he bid Helen come to you. Of her I am to speak.

COUNTESS Sirrah, tell my gentlewoman I would speak with her—Helen, I mean.

CLOWN [*Sings*]

"Was this fair face the cause," quoth she,
"Why the Grecians sacked Troy?
Fond done, done fond,
Was this King Priam's joy?"
With that she sighed as she stood,
With that she sighed as she stood,
And gave this sentence then:
"Among nine bad if one be good,
Among nine bad if one be good,
There's yet one good in ten."

COUNTESS What, one good in ten? You corrupt the song, sirrah.

CLOWN One good woman in ten, madam, which is a purifying o' th' song. Would God would serve the world so all the year! We'd find no fault with the tithe-woman, if I were the parson. One in ten, quoth 'a? An we might have a good woman born but or every blazing star, or at an earthquake, 'twould mend the lottery well; a man may draw his heart out ere 'a pluck one.

COUNTESS You'll be gone, sir knave, and do as I command you?

CLOWN That man should be at woman's command, and yet no hurt done! Though honesty be no puritan, yet it will do no hurt; it will wear the surplice of humility over the black gown of a big heart. I am going, forsooth. The business is for Helen to come hither. *Exit.*

COUNTESS Well, now.

STEWARD I know, madam, you love your gentlewoman entirely.

COUNTESS Faith, I do. Her father bequeath'd her to me, and she herself, without other advantage, may lawfully make title to as much love as she finds. There is more owing her than is paid, and more shall be paid her than she'll demand.

STEWARD Madam, I was very late more near her than I

7 publish make known **18 go . . . world** i.e., marry **23 case** (with a bawdy pun on *female pudenda*) **23–24 Service is no heritage** i.e., being a servant gives me little to bequeath to my heirs **25 barnes** children **37 repent** i.e., (1) atone for my carnal ways by making them legitimate (2) regret marrying **38 Thy marriage** i.e., you'll repent your marriage (since proverbially hasty marriage leads to regret) **42 shallow . . . in** a superficial judge of **44–45 He . . . crop** i.e., he that plows (*ears*) my wife sexually takes the load off my *team,* my sexual organs, and provides me with a *crop* of children **45 in** get in, harvest. **cuckold** a man whose wife is unfaithful **50–51 what they are** i.e., cuckolds **52 Charbon, Poysam** (Corruptions of *chairbonne,* good meat, and *poisson,* fish, the fast-day diets of Puritans and Catholics respectively.) **54 both one** alike (in having cuckolds' horns). **jowl** dash, knock **56 ever** always

59 next nearest, most direct **63 kind** nature (I.e., cuckoldry is natural.) **72 Fond** foolishly **73 Priam** King of Troy **76 sentence** maxim **80–81 You . . . song** (The song must have had one *bad* in ten, referring probably to Paris as Priam's one bad son; but the clown indicates he is singing of women, for whom one *good* in ten is a "purifying" or improvement.) **84–85 tithe-woman** (An allusion to the practice of paying tithes, or a tenth part of one's farm produce, in kind rather than in money. The parson ought to be satisfied with one good woman in ten.) **85 quoth 'a** said he, i.e., forsooth **86–87 or . . . star** either on the occasion of every comet or new star **87 mend the lottery** improve the current odds **88 pluck one** i.e., draw one good woman **92–94 Though . . . heart** i.e., though my hearty good nature (*my honesty*) is manly and impulsive (*no puritan*), it will not offend authority; it will, like the puritan, hide its proud spirit (*big heart*) beneath the guise of humble obedience. (The metaphor concerns those Puritans who demurred at obedience to some of the rubrics and canons pertaining to public worship; some of them, to *do no hurt,* conformed in some respect by wearing the surplice; nevertheless they wore it over the black Genevan gown customarily worn by Calvinistic Protestants on the Continent.) **101 make title** lay claim **104 late** recently

think she wish'd me. Alone she was, and did communicate to herself her own words to her own ears; she thought, I dare vow for her, they touch'd not any stranger sense. Her matter was, she lov'd your son. Fortune, she said, was no goddess, that had put such difference betwixt their two estates; Love no god, that would not extend his might only where qualities were level; Dian no queen of virgins, that would suffer her poor knight surpris'd without rescue in the first assault or ransom afterward. This she deliver'd in the most bitter touch of sorrow that e'er I heard virgin exclaim in, which I held my duty speedily to acquaint you withal, sithence, in the loss that may happen, it concerns you something to know it.

COUNTESS You have discharg'd this honestly; keep it to yourself. Many likelihoods inform'd me of this before, which hung so tott'ring in the balance that I could neither believe nor misdoubt. Pray you, leave me. Stall this in your bosom; and I thank you for your honest care. I will speak with you further anon.

Exit Steward.

Enter Helena.

Even so it was with me when I was young.
If ever we are nature's, these are ours. This thorn
Doth to our rose of youth rightly belong;
Our blood to us, this to our blood is born.
It is the show and seal of nature's truth,
Where love's strong passion is impress'd in youth.
By our remembrances of days forgone,
Such were our faults, or then we thought them
none.
Her eye is sick on 't; I observe her now.

HELENA
What is your pleasure, madam?

COUNTESS
You know, Helen, I am a mother to you.

HELENA
Mine honorable mistress.

COUNTESS Nay, a mother.
Why not a mother? When I said "a mother,"
Methought you saw a serpent. What's in "mother,"
That you start at it? I say, I am your mother,
And put you in the catalogue of those
That were enwombed mine. 'Tis often seen
Adoption strives with nature, and choice breeds
A native slip to us from foreign seeds.
You ne'er oppress'd me with a mother's groan,
Yet I express to you a mother's care.
God's mercy, maiden! Does it curd thy blood
To say I am thy mother? What's the matter,
That this distempered messenger of wet,
The many-color'd Iris, rounds thine eye?
Why? That you are my daughter?

HELENA That I am not.

COUNTESS
I say, I am your mother.

HELENA Pardon, madam;
The Count Rossillion cannot be my brother.
I am from humble, he from honored name;
No note upon my parents, his all noble.
My master, my dear lord he is, and I
His servant live, and will his vassal die.
He must not be my brother.

COUNTESS Nor I your mother?

HELENA
You are my mother, madam; would you were—
So that my lord your son were not my brother—
Indeed my mother! Or were you both our mothers,
I care no more for than I do for heaven,
So I were not his sister. Can 't no other
But, I your daughter, he must be my brother?

COUNTESS
Yes, Helen, you might be my daughter-in-law.
God shield you mean it not! "Daughter" and
"mother"
So strive upon your pulse. What, pale again?
My fear hath catch'd your fondness! Now I see
The myst'ry of your loneliness, and find
Your salt tears' head. Now to all sense 'tis gross:
You love my son. Invention is asham'd,
Against the proclamation of thy passion,
To say thou dost not. Therefore tell me true,
But tell me then, 'tis so; for, look, thy cheeks
Confess it, th' one to th' other, and thine eyes
See it so grossly shown in thy behaviors
That in their kind they speak it. Only sin
And hellish obstinacy tie thy tongue
That truth should be suspected. Speak, is 't so?
If it be so, you have wound a goodly clew;
If it be not, forswear 't. Howe'er, I charge thee,
As heaven shall work in me for thine avail,
To tell me truly.

HELENA Good madam, pardon me!

COUNTESS
Do you love my son?

HELENA Your pardon, noble mistress!

COUNTESS
Love you my son?

HELENA Do not you love him, madam?

COUNTESS
Go not about; my love hath in 't a bond,

107–108 any stranger sense any other person's sense of hearing **108 matter** theme **111 extend his might only** exercise his (Love's) power except **111–112 qualities were level** social rank was equal **112 Dian** Diana, goddess of chastity **112–113 suffer . . . surpris'd** allow her hapless devotee to be captured **114 deliver'd** spoke **115 touch** note **117 sithence** since **118 something** somewhat **119 discharg'd** performed **122 misdoubt** doubt. **Stall** lodge **126 these** i.e., these pangs of love (signs of which the Countess sees manifested in Helena) **128 blood** natural feeling, especially *love's strong passion*, l. 130, and linked to the sexual suggestion of *thorn* and *rose* in ll. 126–127 **132 or . . . none** i.e., or perhaps they were not faults, since we didn't think them so then **133 on 't** of it **142 strives** vies (in strength of attachment) **142–143 choice . . . seeds** choice of a grafting or scion grown of an unrelated stock makes wholly ours what was originally foreign

148 distempered . . . wet disordered tear **149 Iris** Juno's messenger; also the rainbow (which appears refracted in Helena's tears). **rounds** encircles **150 not** i.e., not daughter-in-law **154 note** mark of distinction. **parents** ancestors **160 both our mothers** mother of us both **165 shield** forbid. (But the construction with *not* is ambiguous.) **167 fondness** love (of Bertram); or foolishness. (The Countess speaks ambiguously while she tests Helena.) **169 head** source. **sense** perception. **gross** palpable, apparent **170 Invention** i.e., of excuses **171 Against** in the face of **176 in their kind** in their natural way, i.e., by weeping **178 suspected** surmised (by me) rather than openly declared; or, rendered suspect **179 wound . . . clew** wound up a fine ball of thread, i.e., snarled things up beautifully **180 forswear 't** deny it under oath. **Howe'er** in any case **185 Go not about** don't evade me

Whereof the world takes note. Come, come, disclose 186
The state of your affection, for your passions
Have to the full appeach'd.

HELENA [*Kneeling*] Then I confess 188
Here on my knee, before high heaven and you,
That before you, and next unto high heaven, 190
I love your son.
My friends were poor but honest, so 's my love. 192
Be not offended, for it hurts not him
That he is lov'd of me. I follow him not
By any token of presumptuous suit,
Nor would I have him till I do deserve him,
Yet never know how that desert should be.
I know I love in vain, strive against hope;
Yet in this captious and intenible sieve 199
I still pour in the waters of my love
And lack not to lose still. Thus, Indian-like, 201
Religious in mine error, I adore
The sun, that looks upon his worshiper,
But knows of him no more. My dearest madam,
Let not your hate encounter with my love 205
For loving where you do; but if yourself,
Whose aged honor cites a virtuous youth, 207
Did ever in so true a flame of liking 208
Wish chastely and love dearly, that your Dian 209
Was both herself and Love, O, then, give pity 210
To her whose state is such that cannot choose
But lend and give where she is sure to lose;
That seeks not to find that her search implies, 213
But riddle-like lives sweetly where she dies! 214

COUNTESS
Had you not lately an intent—speak truly—
To go to Paris?

HELENA Madam, I had.

COUNTESS Wherefore?
Tell true.

HELENA
I will tell truth, by grace itself I swear.
You know my father left me some prescriptions
Of rare and prov'd effects, such as his reading
And manifest experience had collected 221
For general sovereignty; and that he will'd me 222
In heedfull'st reservation to bestow them, 223
As notes whose faculties inclusive were 224
More than they were in note. Amongst the rest 225
There is a remedy, approv'd, set down, 226
To cure the desperate languishings whereof
The King is render'd lost. 228

COUNTESS
This was your motive for Paris, was it? Speak.

HELENA
My lord your son made me to think of this;
Else Paris, and the medicine, and the King
Had from the conversation of my thoughts
Happily been absent then.

COUNTESS But think you, Helen, 233
If you should tender your supposed aid, 234
He would receive it? He and his physicians
Are of a mind; he, that they cannot help him,
They, that they cannot help. How shall they credit
A poor unlearned virgin, when the schools,
Embowel'd of their doctrine, have left off 239
The danger to itself?

HELENA There's something in 't,
More than my father's skill, which was the great'st
Of his profession, that his good receipt 242
Shall for my legacy be sanctified
By th' luckiest stars in heaven; and, would your honor
But give me leave to try success, I'd venture
The well-lost life of mine on his Grace's cure 246
By such a day and hour.

COUNTESS Dost thou believe 't?

HELENA
Ay, madam, knowingly. 248

COUNTESS
Why, Helen, thou shalt have my leave and love,
Means and attendants, and my loving greetings
To those of mine in court. I'll stay at home
And pray God's blessing into thy attempt.
Be gone tomorrow, and be sure of this,
What I can help thee to thou shalt not miss. *Exeunt.* 254

ACT II • [SCENE I]

Enter the King [in his chair] with divers young Lords taking leave for the Florentine war: [Bertram] Count Rossillion, and Parolles. Flourish cornets.

KING
Farewell, young lords. These warlike principles
Do not throw from you. And you, my lords, farewell.
Share the advice betwixt you; if both gain all, 3
The gift doth stretch itself as 'tis receiv'd, 4
And is enough for both.

FIRST LORD 'Tis our hope, sir,
After well ent'red soldiers, to return 6
And find your Grace in health.

KING
No, no, it cannot be; and yet my heart
Will not confess he owes the malady 9

186 Whereof . . . note which society acknowledges **188 appeach'd** informed against (you) **190 before you** more than (I love) you **192 friends** kinfolk **199 captious** deceptive; also, capacious. **intenible** incapable of holding **201 lack . . . still** still have enough to keep pouring without diminishing my supply; also, continually lose. **Indian-like** idolatrously, like the savage (who worships the sun) **205 encounter with** oppose **207 aged honor cites** honorable old age bespeaks, gives evidence of **208 liking** love **209 that** so that **210 both . . . Love** i.e., both Diana and Venus, chaste and passionate **213 that . . . implies** i.e., what her search is for **214 riddle-like** paradoxically, with an unguessed mystery **221 manifest experience** i.e., the practice, in antithesis to the theory (reading) **222 general sovereignty** general efficacy and use **223 In . . . them** to employ them only with the greatest care **224–225 As . . . note** i.e., as prescriptions whose power was greater than recognized **226 approv'd** tested **228 render'd lost** reckoned to be incurable

233 Happily haply, perhaps **234 tender** offer **239 Embowel'd** emptied **242 that** whereby. **receipt** prescription **246 well-lost** i.e., well lost in such a cause, worthless otherwise **248 knowingly** knowing what I'm about **254 miss** be lacking

II.i. Location: Paris. The King's palace.
3 if . . . all i.e., if both groups (one going to the aid of Florence, one of Siena) wish to follow all of my advice **4 as 'tis receiv'd** i.e., to accommodate the demand **6 After . . . soldiers** after having become seasoned soldiers; or, in the manner of experienced soldiers **9 owes** owns

That doth my life besiege. Farewell, young lords.
Whether I live or die, be you the sons
Of worthy Frenchmen. Let higher Italy— 12
Those bated that inherit but the fall 13
Of the last monarchy—see that you come 14
Not to woo honor, but to wed it, when 15
The bravest questant shrinks. Find what you seek, 16
That fame may cry you loud. I say, farewell. 17

SECOND LORD
Health, at your bidding, serve your Majesty!

KING
Those girls of Italy, take heed of them.
They say our French lack language to deny
If they demand. Beware of being captives 21
Before you serve.

BOTH Our hearts receive your warnings.

KING
Farewell.—Come hither to me. [*The King converses privately; Bertram and his companions move apart.*]

FIRST LORD
O my sweet lord, that you will stay behind us!

PAROLLES
'Tis not his fault, the spark.

SECOND LORD O, 'tis brave wars! 25

PAROLLES Most admirable. I have seen those wars.

BERTRAM I am commanded here, and kept a coil with 27
"Too young" and "the next year" and "'tis too early."

PAROLLES
An thy mind stand to 't, boy, steal away bravely.

BERTRAM
I shall stay here the forehorse to a smock, 30
Creaking my shoes on the plain masonry, 31
Till honor be bought up, and no sword worn 32
But one to dance with! By heaven, I'll steal away. 33

FIRST LORD
There's honor in the theft.

PAROLLES Commit it, Count.

SECOND LORD
I am your accessary; and so, farewell.

BERTRAM I grow to you, and our parting is a tortur'd 36
body. 37

FIRST LORD Farewell, captain.

SECOND LORD Sweet Monsieur Parolles!

PAROLLES Noble heroes, my sword and yours are kin.
Good sparks and lustrous, a word, good metals: you 41
shall find in the regiment of the Spinii one Captain
Spurio, with his cicatrice, an emblem of war, here on 43
his sinister cheek; it was this very sword entrench'd it. 44
Say to him I live, and observe his reports for me. 45

FIRST LORD We shall, noble captain.

PAROLLES Mars dote on you for his novices! 47
[*Exeunt Lords.*]
[*To Bertram.*] What will ye do?

BERTRAM Stay the King. 49

PAROLLES [*To Bertram*] Use a more spacious ceremony 50
to the noble lords; you have restrain'd yourself within
the list of too cold an adieu. Be more expressive to 52
them, for they wear themselves in the cap of the time, 53
there do muster true gait, eat, speak, and move under 54
the influence of the most receiv'd star; and, though the 55
devil lead the measure, such are to be follow'd. After 56
them, and take a more dilated farewell. 57

BERTRAM And I will do so.

PAROLLES Worthy fellows, and like to prove most sinewy swordmen. *Exeunt* [*Bertram and Parolles*].

Enter Lafew [*and approaches the King*].

LAFEW [*Kneeling*]
Pardon, my lord, for me and for my tidings.

KING
I'll fee thee to stand up. 62

LAFEW [*Rising*]
Then here's a man stands that has brought his pardon. 63
I would you had kneel'd, my lord, to ask me mercy,
And that at my bidding you could so stand up.

KING
I would I had, so I had broke thy pate, 66
And ask'd thee mercy for 't.

LAFEW Good faith, across! 67
But, my good lord, 'tis thus: will you be cur'd
Of your infirmity?

KING No.

LAFEW O, will you eat 69
No grapes, my royal fox? Yes, but you will 70
My noble grapes, an if my royal fox 71
Could reach them. I have seen a medicine 72
That's able to breathe life into a stone,
Quicken a rock, and make you dance canary 74
With spritely fire and motion, whose simple touch
Is powerful to araise King Pepin, nay, 76
To give great Charlemain a pen in 's hand
And write to her a love-line.

KING What "her" is this? 78

LAFEW
Why, Doctor She! My lord, there's one arriv'd,
If you will see her. Now by my faith and honor,
If seriously I may convey my thoughts
In this my light deliverance, I have spoke 82

12 higher Italy (1) the knightly class of Italy, corresponding to *worthy Frenchmen,* or (2) Tuscany, of which Florence and Siena are cities **13–14 Those . . . monarchy** i.e., except those who have merely profited as upstarts by recent engagements involving the fall of a monarchy (?) **15 woo** flirt with. **wed** possess as your own **16 questant** seeker **17 cry you loud** proclaim you loudly **21 captives** i.e., to love **25 spark** elegant young man. **brave** splendid **27 here** i.e., to remain here. **kept a coil** pestered, fussed over **30 forehorse . . . smock** the lead horse of a team, harnessed with a female; i.e., ushering in and squiring ladies **31 plain masonry** smooth masonry floor (instead of a battlefield) **32 Till . . . up** till opportunity for winning honor in the wars is past, all consumed **33 one . . . with** i.e., a light ornamental weapon **36 grow to** grow deeply attached to, become as one with **36–37 a tortur'd body** i.e., as painful as a body being torn apart by torture **41 metals** i.e., "blades"; spirits of mettle **43 Spurio** (This name suggests *spurious, counterfeit.*) **cicatrice** scar **44 sinister** left **45 reports** reply

47 novices devotees **49 Stay the King** support or wait on the King. (But also interpreted, with different punctuation, as "Stay; the King wills it," or "Stay; the King approaches.") **50 ceremony** courtesy **52 list** boundary **53 wear . . . time** stand out as ornaments of the fashionable world **54 muster true gait** set the right pace **55 receiv'd** fashionable **56 measure** dance **57 dilated** protracted; expansive **62 I'll . . . up** i.e., I bid you rise; or, I will rather reward you for rising **63 pardon** i.e., something to win the King's indulgence **66–67 so . . . for 't** i.e., that would be like wounding you on the head and begging your pardon for it **67 across** (A metaphor from tilting; to break a lance *across* one's opponent was to hold the lance awkwardly athwart.) **69–70 will . . . fox** i.e., will you be like the fox in Aesop's fable and call the grapes sour because they are beyond your reach **71 an if** if **72 medicine** i.e., physician **74 Quicken** bring to life. **canary** a lively Spanish dance **76 araise** raise from the dead. **King Pepin** French king of the eighth century, father of Charlemagne **78 love-line** (Some of Lafew's terms, such as *stone, quicken, fire and motion, touch, araise, pen in 's hand,* have possible erotic undertones that link recovery to restored potency.) **82 light deliverance** frivolous utterance

With one that, in her sex, her years, profession,
Wisdom, and constancy, hath amaz'd me more
Than I dare blame my weakness. Will you see her,
For that is her demand, and know her business?
That done, laugh well at me.

KING
Now, good Lafew,
Bring in the admiration, that we with thee
May spend our wonder too, or take off thine
By wond'ring how thou took'st it.

LAFEW
Nay, I'll fit you,
And not be all day neither. [*Goes to the door.*]

KING
Thus he his special nothing ever prologues.

LAFEW
Nay, come your ways.

Enter Helena.

KING
This haste hath wings indeed.

LAFEW
Nay, come your ways.
This is his Majesty; say your mind to him.
A traitor you do look like, but such traitors
His Majesty seldom fears. I am Cressid's uncle,
That dare leave two together. Fare you well. *Exit.*

KING
Now, fair one, does your business follow us?

HELENA
Ay, my good lord.
Gerard de Narbon was my father;
In what he did profess, well found.

KING
I knew him.

HELENA
The rather will I spare my praises towards him;
Knowing him is enough. On 's bed of death
Many receipts he gave me; chiefly one,
Which, as the dearest issue of his practice,
And of his old experience th' only darling,
He bade me store up, as a triple eye,
Safer than mine own two, more dear. I have so;
And, hearing your high Majesty is touch'd
With that malignant cause wherein the honor
Of my dear father's gift stands chief in power,
I come to tender it and my appliance
With all bound humbleness.

KING
We thank you, maiden;
But may not be so credulous of cure,
When our most learned doctors leave us, and
The congregated college have concluded
That laboring art can never ransom nature
From her inaidible estate. I say we must not
So stain our judgment, or corrupt our hope,
To prostitute our past-cure malady
To empirics, or to dissever so
Our great self and our credit, to esteem
A senseless help when help past sense we deem.

HELENA
My duty then shall pay me for my pains.
I will no more enforce mine office on you,
Humbly entreating from your royal thoughts
A modest one, to bear me back again.

KING
I cannot give thee less, to be call'd grateful.
Thou thought'st to help me; and such thanks I give
As one near death to those that wish him live.
But what at full I know, thou know'st no part,
I knowing all my peril, thou no art.

HELENA
What I can do can do no hurt to try,
Since you set up your rest 'gainst remedy.
He that of greatest works is finisher
Oft does them by the weakest minister.
So holy writ in babes hath judgment shown,
When judges have been babes; great floods have
flown
From simple sources, and great seas have dried
When miracles have by the great'st been denied.
Oft expectation fails, and most oft there
Where most it promises, and oft it hits
Where hope is coldest and despair most fits.

KING
I must not hear thee; fare thee well, kind maid.
Thy pains not us'd must by thyself be paid;
Proffers not took reap thanks for their reward.

HELENA
Inspired merit so by breath is barr'd.
It is not so with Him that all things knows
As 'tis with us that square our guess by shows;
But most it is presumption in us when
The help of heaven we count the act of men.
Dear sir, to my endeavors give consent;
Of heaven, not me, make an experiment.
I am not an impostor that proclaim
Myself against the level of mine aim;
But know I think, and think I know most sure,
My art is not past power, nor you past cure.

KING
Art thou so confident? Within what space
Hop'st thou my cure?

HELENA
The great'st grace lending grace,
Ere twice the horses of the sun shall bring
Their fiery torcher his diurnal ring,
Ere twice in murk and occidental damp
Moist Hesperus hath quench'd her sleepy lamp,
Or four and twenty times the pilot's glass

83 profession what she professes to be able to do **84–85 more . . . weakness** more than I can attribute to my feebleness or susceptibility as an old man **88 admiration** wonder **89 spend** expend. **take off** dispel **90 took'st** conceived (with a play on *take* in the previous line). **fit** satisfy **92 special nothing** particular trifles **93 come your ways** come along **97 Cressid's uncle** Pandarus, go-between for the lovers Troilus and Cressida **102 well found** i.e., to be good **106 issue** product **108 triple** third **109 Safer** more safely **111–112 cause . . . power** disease for which my father's remedy is most particularly effective **113 tender** offer. **appliance** treatment **114 bound** dutiful **117 congregated college** college of physicians **118 art** skill, i.e., medicine **120 stain** pervert **122 empirics** quack doctors **122–123 dissever . . . credit** divorce thus my kingly self from my reputation, or from my faith

123 esteem value, put faith in **124 A senseless help** irrational quackery. **past sense** beyond reason **125 My duty** i.e., having tried to do my duty **126 office** dutiful service **128 A modest one** i.e., a favorable regard commensurate with my humble station, and with my maidenly modesty **132 no part** not at all **135 set . . . rest** stake your all. (A figure from gambling.) **139 babes** i.e., babyish, foolish. (The inversion of babes and wise men appears several times in the New Testament.) **140 simple** small, insignificant **143 hits** succeeds, is confirmed **148 Inspired . . . barr'd** divinely inspired virtue is thus denied by mere spoken words **150 square . . . shows** support our conjectures on the basis of appearances **152 count** account **155–156 proclaim . . . aim** claim something other than what I aim to accomplish **158 My . . . power** my professed skill (as a doctor) is not beyond my range of ability **160 great'st grace** divine grace (I.e., with God's help.) **162 torcher** torchbearer. **diurnal ring** daily round **163 occidental** western, sunset **164 Hesperus** evening star (actually Venus) **165 glass** hourglass

Hath told the thievish minutes how they pass,
What is infirm from your sound parts shall fly,
Health shall live free, and sickness freely die.

KING
Upon thy certainty and confidence
What dar'st thou venture?

HELENA Tax of impudence,
A strumpet's boldness, a divulged shame
Traduc'd by odious ballads; my maiden's name
Sear'd otherwise; nay, worse of worst, extended
With vilest torture let my life be ended.

KING
Methinks in thee some blessed spirit doth speak
His powerful sound within an organ weak;
And what impossibility would slay
In common sense, sense saves another way.
Thy life is dear, for all that life can rate
Worth name of life in thee hath estimate:
Youth, beauty, wisdom, courage, all
That happiness and prime can happy call.
Thou this to hazard needs must intimate
Skill infinite, or monstrous desperate.
Sweet practicer, thy physic I will try,
That ministers thine own death if I die.

HELENA
If I break time, or flinch in property
Of what I spoke, unpitied let me die,
And well deserv'd. Not helping, death 's my fee;
But, if I help, what do you promise me?

KING
Make thy demand.

HELENA But will you make it even?

KING
Ay, by my scepter and my hopes of heaven.

HELENA
Then shalt thou give me with thy kingly hand
What husband in thy power I will command.
Exempted be from me the arrogance
To choose from forth the royal blood of France,
My low and humble name to propagate
With any branch or image of thy state;
But such a one, thy vassal, whom I know
Is free for me to ask, thee to bestow.

KING
Here is my hand. The premises observ'd,
Thy will by my performance shall be serv'd.
So make the choice of thy own time, for I,
Thy resolv'd patient, on thee still rely.
More should I question thee, and more I must—
Though more to know could not be more to trust—
From whence thou cam'st, how tended on, but rest
Unquestion'd welcome and undoubted blest.—
Give me some help here, ho!—If thou proceed
As high as word, my deed shall match thy meed.

Flourish. Exeunt, [*the King carried in*].

170 **Tax** accusation 173 **otherwise** in other ways as well. **extended** stretched out on the rack; or, drawn out in time 177–178 **what . . . way** what common sense would regard as impossible, a higher sense (faith) can regard as possible 180 **hath estimate** must be reckoned present 182 **happiness** good fortune. **prime** youth 183 **Thou . . . intimate** that you are prepared to hazard all this argues 185 **physic** medicine 187 **break** infringe, fail to keep. **flinch in property** fall short in any detail 191 **make it even** carry it out 204 **still** continually 207 **tended on** attended 210 **meed** merit

[SCENE II]

Enter Countess and Clown.

COUNTESS Come on, sir; I shall now put you to the height of your breeding.

CLOWN I will show myself highly fed and lowly taught. I know my business is but to the court.

COUNTESS To the court? Why, what place make you special, when you put off that with such contempt? But to the court!

CLOWN Truly, madam, if God have lent a man any manners, he may easily put if off at court. He that cannot make a leg, put off 's cap, kiss his hand, and say nothing, has neither leg, hands, lip, nor cap; and indeed such a fellow, to say precisely, were not for the court; but for me, I have an answer will serve all men.

COUNTESS Marry, that's a bountiful answer that fits all questions.

CLOWN It is like a barber's chair that fits all buttocks: the pin-buttock, the quatch-buttock, the brawn-buttock, or any buttock.

COUNTESS Will your answer serve fit to all questions?

CLOWN As fit as ten groats is for the hand of an attorney, as your French crown for your taffety punk, as Tib's rush for Tom's forefinger, as a pancake for Shrove Tuesday, a morris for May-day, as the nail to his hole, the cuckold to his horn, as a scolding quean to a wrangling knave, as the nun's lip to the friar's mouth, nay, as the pudding to his skin.

COUNTESS Have you, I say, an answer of such fitness for all questions?

CLOWN From below your duke to beneath your constable, it will fit any question.

COUNTESS It must be an answer of most monstrous size that must fit all demands.

CLOWN But a trifle neither, in good faith, if the learned should speak truth of it. Here it is, and all that belongs to 't. Ask me if I am a courtier; it shall do you no harm to learn.

COUNTESS To be young again, if we could! I will be a fool in question, hoping to be the wiser by your answer. I pray you, sir, are you a courtier?

CLOWN O Lord, sir!—There's a simple putting off. More, more, a hundred of them.

COUNTESS Sir, I am a poor friend of yours, that loves you.

CLOWN O Lord, sir!—Thick, thick, spare not me.

COUNTESS I think, sir, you can eat none of this homely meat.

II.ii. Location: Rossillion. The Count's palace.
1–2 put . . . breeding test your good manners 3 **highly . . . taught** overfed and underdisciplined 5–6 **make you special** do you consider special 6 **put off** dismiss 9 **put it off** carry it off 10 **leg** respectful bow 17 **pin** narrow, pointed. **quatch** fat, wide. **brawn** hefty, fleshy 20 **ten groats** forty pence 21 **French crown** (1) coin (2) *corona veneris,* a scab on the head symptomatic of syphilis, the "French disease." **taffety punk** prostitute finely dressed 22 **Tib's rush** (Refers to a folk custom of exchanging rings made of rushes in a marriage without benefit of clergy.) **pancake** (Traditionally eaten as a last feast on the final day before Lent, Shrove Tuesday.) 23 **morris** morris dance, country dance common at May Day celebrations 24 **his** its. **quean** wench 26 **pudding** sausage 33 **But . . . neither** on the contrary, it's only a trifle 40 **O Lord, sir** (A foppish phrase currently in vogue at court.) **putting off** evasion 44 **Thick** quickly 45–46 **homely meat** plain fare

CLOWN O Lord, sir!—Nay, put me to 't, I warrant you.
COUNTESS You were lately whipp'd, sir, as I think.
CLOWN O Lord, sir!—Spare not me.
COUNTESS Do you cry, "O Lord, sir!" at your whipping,
and "spare not me"? Indeed your "O Lord, sir!" is 51
very sequent to your whipping; you would answer 52
very well to a whipping, if you were but bound to 't. 53
CLOWN I ne'er had worse luck in my life in my "O
Lord, sir!" I see things may serve long, but not serve
ever.
COUNTESS
I play the noble huswife with the time,
To entertain it so merrily with a fool.
CLOWN O Lord, sir!—Why, there 't serves well again.
COUNTESS
An end, sir; to your business. Give Helen this, [*Gives letter.*]
And urge her to a present answer back.
Commend me to my kinsmen and my son.
This is not much.
CLOWN Not much commendation to them?
COUNTESS Not much employment for you. You under-
stand me?
CLOWN Most fruitfully. I am there before my legs.
COUNTESS Haste you again. *Exeunt* [*severally*]. 68

[SCENE III]

Enter Count [*Bertram*], *Lafew, and Parolles.*

LAFEW They say miracles are past, and we have our
philosophical persons, to make modern and familiar, 2
things supernatural and causeless. Hence is it that we 3
make trifles of terrors, ensconcing ourselves into seem- 4
ing knowledge, when we should submit ourselves to
an unknown fear. 6
PAROLLES Why, 'tis the rarest argument of wonder that 7
hath shot out in our latter times.
BERTRAM And so 'tis.
LAFEW To be relinquish'd of the artists— 10
PAROLLES So I say, both of Galen and Paracelsus. 11
LAFEW Of all the learned and authentic fellows— 12
PAROLLES Right, so I say.
LAFEW That gave him out incurable—
PAROLLES Why, there 'tis; so say I too.
LAFEW Not to be help'd—
PAROLLES Right! As 'twere a man assur'd of a—
LAFEW Uncertain life, and sure death.
PAROLLES Just, you say well; so would I have said.
LAFEW I may truly say it is a novelty to the world.
PAROLLES It is, indeed. If you will have it in showing, 21
you shall read it in—what-do-ye-call-there?
[*Points to a ballad in Lafew's hand.*]
LAFEW [*Reading*] "A showing of a heavenly effect in an
earthly actor."
PAROLLES That's it I would have said, the very same.
LAFEW Why, your dolphin is not lustier. 'Fore me, I 26
speak in respect— 27
PAROLLES Nay, 'tis strange, 'tis very strange, that is the 28
brief and the tedious of it; and he's of a most faciner- 29
ious spirit that will not acknowledge it to be the— 30
LAFEW Very hand of heaven.
PAROLLES Ay, so I say.
LAFEW In a most weak—
PAROLLES And debile minister; great power, great tran- 34
scendence, which should indeed give us a further use
to be made than alone the recov'ry of the King, as to
be—
LAFEW Generally thankful.

Enter King, Helena, and Attendants. [*The King sits.*]

PAROLLES I would have said it; you say well. Here
comes the King.
LAFEW Lustick, as the Dutchman says. I'll like a maid 41
the better whilst I have a tooth in my head. Why, he's 42
able to lead her a coranto. 43
PAROLLES Mort du vinaigre! Is not this Helen? 44
LAFEW 'Fore God, I think so.
KING
Go, call before me all the lords in court.
[*Exit an Attendant.*]
Sit, my preserver, by thy patient's side; [*She sits.*]
And with this healthful hand, whose banish'd sense
Thou hast repeal'd, a second time receive 49
The confirmation of my promis'd gift,
Which but attends thy naming. 51

Enter three or four Lords.

Fair maid, send forth thine eye. This youthful parcel
Of noble bachelors stand at my bestowing, 53
O'er whom both sovereign power and father's voice
I have to use. Thy frank election make; 55
Thou hast power to choose, and they none to
forsake.
HELENA
To each of you one fair and virtuous mistress
Fall, when Love please! Marry, to each but one!
LAFEW [*Aside*]
I'd give bay Curtal and his furniture 59
My mouth no more were broken than these boys', 60
And writ as little beard.
KING Peruse them well. 61
Not one of those but had a noble father.

51–52 is very sequent to is a pertinent response to (because it would be a plea for mercy) **52–53 answer . . . to** (1) reply cleverly to (2) repay, serve as a suitable subject for **53 bound to 't** (1) obliged to reply (2) tied up for it **68 again** back again

II.iii. Location: Paris. The King's palace.
2 modern commonplace **3 causeless** of unexplained cause **4 ensconcing** taking refuge, fortifying **6 unknown fear** awe of the unknown **7 argument** theme, proof **10 artists** i.e., physicians **11 Galen** Greek physician of the second century; the traditional authority. **Paracelsus** Swiss physician of the sixteenth century; the new and more radical authority **12 authentic fellows** those properly licensed to practice **21 showing** i.e., print

26 dolphin (A sportive and vigorous fish; with a pun perhaps on *dauphin,* French crown prince.) **'Fore me** i.e., on my soul **27 in respect** i.e., intending no disrespect **28–29 the brief . . . it** i.e., the short and the long of it **29–30 facinerious** infamous, wicked **34 debile minister** weak agent **41 Lustick** lusty **42 have a tooth** (with a play on the meaning *have a taste still for girls*) **43 coranto** lively dance **44 Mort du vinaigre** (Possibly an oath by the vinegar in Christ's wounds; literally, "death of the vinegar.") **49 repeal'd** recalled (from the banishment of illness) **51 attends** waits upon **53 stand . . . bestowing** i.e., are my wards, whom I may give in marriage **55 frank election** uninhibited choice **59 bay . . . furniture** i.e., my dock-tailed horse and his trappings **60 My . . . than** i.e., I had lost no more teeth than **61 writ** (if I) laid claim to

HELENA
Gentlemen,
Heaven hath through me restor'd the King to health.

ALL
We understand it, and thank heaven for you.

HELENA
I am a simple maid, and therein wealthiest
That I protest I simply am a maid.—
Please it your Majesty, I have done already.
The blushes in my cheeks thus whisper me,
"We blush that thou shouldst choose; but, be refused,
Let the white death sit on thy cheek forever, 71
We'll ne'er come there again."

KING Make choice and see;
Who shuns thy love shuns all his love in me.

HELENA
Now, Dian, from thy altar do I fly,
And to imperial Love, that god most high,
Do my sighs stream. *(She addresses her to a Lord.)* Sir, will you hear my suit?

FIRST LORD
And grant it.

HELENA Thanks, sir; all the rest is mute. 77

LAFEW [*Aside*] I had rather be in this choice than throw ames-ace for my life. 79

HELENA [*To another*]
The honor, sir, that flames in your fair eyes,
Before I speak, too threat'ningly replies.
Love make your fortunes twenty times above
Her that so wishes, and her humble love! 83

SECOND LORD
No better, if you please.

HELENA My wish receive, 84
Which great Love grant! And so I take my leave.

LAFEW [*Aside*] Do all they deny her? An they were sons 86
of mine, I'd have them whipp'd, or I would send them
to th' Turk, to make eunuchs of.

HELENA [*To a third*]
Be not afraid that I your hand should take;
I'll never do you wrong for your own sake.
Blessing upon your vows, and in your bed
Find fairer fortune, if you ever wed!

LAFEW [*Aside*] These boys are boys of ice, they'll none have her. Sure they are bastards to the English; the French ne'er got 'em. 95

HELENA [*To a fourth*]
You are too young, too happy, and too good,
To make yourself a son out of my blood.

FOURTH LORD
Fair one, I think not so.

LAFEW [*Aside*] There's one grape yet; I am sure thy fa- 99
ther drunk wine. But if thou be'st not an ass, I am a 100
youth of fourteen; I have known thee already. 101

HELENA [*To Bertram*]
I dare not say I take you, but I give
Me and my service, ever whilst I live,
Into your guiding power.—This is the man.

KING
Why, then, young Bertram, take her; she's thy wife.

BERTRAM
My wife, my liege? I shall beseech your Highness,
In such a business give me leave to use
The help of mine own eyes.

KING Know'st thou not, Bertram,
What she has done for me?

BERTRAM Yes, my good lord;
But never hope to know why I should marry her.

KING
Thou know'st she has rais'd me from my sickly bed.

BERTRAM
But follows it, my lord, to bring me down 112
Must answer for your raising? I know her well;
She had her breeding at my father's charge.
A poor physician's daughter my wife? Disdain 115
Rather corrupt me ever! 116

KING
'Tis only title thou disdain'st in her, the which
I can build up. Strange is it that our bloods,
Of color, weight, and heat, pour'd all together,
Would quite confound distinction, yet stands off 120
In differences so mighty. If she be 121
All that is virtuous—save what thou dislik'st,
A poor physician's daughter—thou dislik'st
Of virtue for the name. But do not so.
From lowest place when virtuous things proceed, 125
The place is dignified by th' doer's deed.
Where great additions swell 's, and virtue none, 127
It is a dropsied honor. Good alone 128
Is good without a name; vileness is so; 129
The property by what it is should go, 130
Not by the title. She is young, wise, fair;
In these to nature she's immediate heir, 132
And these breed honor. That is honor's scorn 133
Which challenges itself as honor's born 134
And is not like the sire. Honors thrive 135
When rather from our acts we them derive
Than our foregoers. The mere word's a slave
Debosh'd on every tomb, on every grave 138
A lying trophy, and as oft is dumb 139
Where dust and damn'd oblivion is the tomb
Of honor'd bones indeed. What should be said? 141
If thou canst like this creature as a maid,
I can create the rest. Virtue and she 143
Is her own dower; honor and wealth from me. 144

BERTRAM
I cannot love her, nor will strive to do 't.

71 the white death i.e., death in its pallor **77 all . . . mute** I have nothing more to say to you **79 ames-ace** two aces, the lowest possible throw in dice. (To throw ames-ace with one's life at stake is to risk all on a throw.) **83 Her . . . wishes** her that speaks this wish, i.e., Helena herself **84 No better** i.e., I wish for no one better than yourself. **My wish receive** i.e., take my wish for your fortunate marriage **86 Do . . . her** (Lafew, unable to hear, misinterprets her passing from one to another.) **95 got** begot **99 grape** i.e., scion of a good family. **thy** i.e., Bertram's **100 drunk wine** i.e., was red-blooded. **thou** i.e., the fourth lord **101 known** i.e., seen through

112 bring me down i.e., to a socially inferior wife, to the (marriage) bed **115–116 Disdain . . . ever** i.e., rather let my disdain for her ruin me forever in your favor **120 stands off** stand separated **121 differences** i.e., social differences **125 proceed** emanate **127 great . . . swell 's** pompous titles puff us up **128 dropsied** unhealthily swollen **129 is so** i.e., is vile without having to be named such **130 property** quality. **go** i.e., be known **132 In . . . heir** in these qualities she inherits directly from nature **133–135 That . . . sire** that person is contemptible from the vantage point of true honor who claims himself to be of honorable birth but does not show it in his behavior **138 Debosh'd** debauched, debased **139 trophy** memorial. **dumb** silent **141 honor'd bones indeed** i.e., the remains of those who were genuinely honorable **143–144 Virtue . . . dower** i.e., her marriage gift to you will be her virtue and her self

KING
Thou wrong'st thyself, if thou shouldst strive to
choose.

HELENA
That you are well restor'd, my lord, I'm glad.
Let the rest go.

KING
My honor's at the stake, which to defeat,
I must produce my power. Here, take her hand,
Proud scornful boy, unworthy this good gift,
That dost in vile misprision shackle up
My love and her desert; that canst not dream,
We, poising us in her defective scale,
Shall weigh thee to the beam; that wilt not know
It is in us to plant thine honor where
We please to have it grow. Check thy contempt;
Obey our will, which travails in thy good;
Believe not thy disdain, but presently
Do thine own fortunes that obedient right
Which both thy duty owes and our power claims,
Or I will throw thee from my care forever
Into the staggers and the careless lapse
Of youth and ignorance, both my revenge and hate
Loosing upon thee, in the name of justice,
Without all terms of pity. Speak; thine answer.

BERTRAM
Pardon, my gracious lord; for I submit
My fancy to your eyes. When I consider
What great creation and what dole of honor
Flies where you bid it, I find that she, which late
Was in my nobler thoughts most base, is now
The praised of the King, who, so ennobled,
Is as 'twere born so.

KING Take her by the hand,
And tell her she is thine, to whom I promise
A counterpoise, if not to thy estate
A balance more replete.

BERTRAM I take her hand.

KING
Good fortune and the favor of the King
Smile upon this contract, whose ceremony
Shall seem expedient on the now-born brief,
And be perform'd tonight. The solemn feast
Shall more attend upon the coming space,
Expecting absent friends. As thou lov'st her,
Thy love's to me religious; else, does err.

Exeunt. Parolles and Lafew stay behind, commenting of this wedding.

LAFEW Do you hear, monsieur? A word with you.

PAROLLES Your pleasure, sir?

LAFEW Your lord and master did well to make his recantation.

PAROLLES Recantation? My lord? My master?

LAFEW Ay; is it not a language I speak?

PAROLLES A most harsh one, and not to be understood without bloody succeeding. My master?

LAFEW Are you companion to the Count Rossillion?

PAROLLES To any count, to all counts, to what is man.

LAFEW To what is count's man. Count's master is of another style.

PAROLLES You are too old, sir; let it satisfy you, you are too old.

LAFEW I must tell thee, sirrah, I write man, to which title age cannot bring thee.

PAROLLES What I dare too well do, I dare not do.

LAFEW I did think thee, for two ordinaries, to be a pretty wise fellow; thou didst make tolerable vent of thy travel; it might pass. Yet the scarfs and the bannerets about thee did manifoldly dissuade me from believing thee a vessel of too great a burden. I have now found thee. When I lose thee again, I care not; yet art thou good for nothing but taking up, and that thou 'rt scarce worth.

PAROLLES Hadst thou not the privilege of antiquity upon thee—

LAFEW Do not plunge thyself too far in anger, lest thou hasten thy trial; which if—Lord have mercy on thee for a hen! So, my good window of lattice, fare thee well. Thy casement I need not open, for I look through thee. Give me thy hand.

PAROLLES My lord, you give me most egregious indignity.

LAFEW Ay, with all my heart, and thou art worthy of it.

PAROLLES I have not, my lord, deserv'd it.

LAFEW Yes, good faith, ev'ry dram of it, and I will not bate thee a scruple.

PAROLLES Well, I shall be wiser.

LAFEW Ev'n as soon as thou canst, for thou hast to pull at a smack o' th' contrary. If ever thou be'st bound in thy scarf and beaten, thou shall find what it is to be proud of thy bondage. I have a desire to hold my acquaintance with thee, or rather my knowledge, that I may say in the default, "He is a man I know."

PAROLLES My lord, you do me most insupportable vexation.

LAFEW I would it were hell-pains for thy sake, and my poor doing eternal; for doing I am past, as I will by

146 strive to choose try to assert your own choice **149 which** i.e., which threat to my honor **152 misprision** contempt and poor judgment (with a play on *undeserved imprisonment*) **153–155 that . . . beam** you who cannot imagine that I, weighing my royal self on her underweight (defective) side of the scales, will outweigh yours and pull it up to the cross-beam **156 in us** within my royal power **158 travails in** labors for **159 Believe not** do not place faith in or obey. **presently** at once **160 obedient right** right of obedience **163 staggers** giddy decline. **lapse** fall **166 all . . . pity** pity in any form **169 great creation** creating of greatness. **dole** share, doling out **170 which late** who lately **175–176 A counterpoise . . . replete** i.e., an equal weight of money as dowry, if not an amount even exceeding your estate **178–179 whose . . . brief** i.e., the consecration of which will serve as a fitting or rapid conclusion to the agreement just made (?) **180 solemn** ceremonial **181–182 more . . . friends** be delayed for a time until absent friends and relatives can arrive **183 to me religious** directed in my view toward a worthy object of worship

191 succeeding consequences; i.e., a fight **193 what is man** i.e., any true man; or, what is manly **194 count's man** i.e., servant. (Said belittlingly.) **196 too old** i.e., for me to duel with. **let . . . you** i.e., don't force me to fight you **198 write man** i.e., account myself a man, lay claim to that title **200 What . . . not do** i.e., what I could too easily accomplish—beat you—I must not do because of your age **201 for two ordinaries** during the space of two meals **202 didst . . . of** discoursed tolerably upon **203–204 scarfs, bannerets** i.e., soldier's scarfs, reminding Lafew of a ship's pennants **205 burden** cargo **206 found** found out **207 taking up** contradicting; arresting; picking up (as opposed to *losing*) **212 thy trial** i.e., the testing of your supposed valor **213 hen** i.e., cackling, cowardly female. **window of lattice** (Sign of an alehouse.) **221 bate** abate, remit. **scruple** smallest bit **222 wiser** i.e., wiser than to deal with such dotards in the future **223–224 pull . . . contrary** drink a taste of the very opposite of your folly, i.e., wisdom **226 bondage** i.e., the scarf, in which you would be bound and of which you are now vainly proud. **hold** continue **228 in the default** when you fail **231–232 my poor doing** i.e., my inadequate taking you to task **232 for doing** for energetic activity (with a sexual suggestion) **232–233 will by thee** i.e., will pass by you

thee, in what motion age will give me leave. *Exit.*

PAROLLES Well, thou hast a son shall take this disgrace off me—scurvy, old, filthy, scurvy lord! Well, I must be patient; there is no fettering of authority. I'll beat him, by my life, if I can meet him with any convenience, an he were double and double a lord. I'll have no more pity of his age than I would have of—I'll beat him, an if I could but meet him again.

Enter Lafew.

LAFEW Sirrah, your lord and master's married; there's news for you. You have a new mistress.

PAROLLES I most unfeignedly beseech your lordship to make some reservation of your wrongs. He is my good lord; whom I serve above is my master.

LAFEW Who? God?

PAROLLES Ay, sir.

LAFEW The devil it is that's thy master. Why dost thou garter up thy arms o' this fashion? Dost make hose of thy sleeves? Do other servants so? Thou wert best set thy lower part where thy nose stands. By mine honor, if I were but two hours younger, I'd beat thee. Methink'st thou art a general offense, and every man should beat thee. I think thou wast created for men to breathe themselves upon thee.

PAROLLES This is hard and undeserv'd measure, my lord.

LAFEW Go to, sir. You were beaten in Italy for picking a kernel out of a pomegranate. You are a vagabond and no true traveler. You are more saucy with lords and honorable personages than the commission of your birth and virtue gives you heraldry. You are not worth another word, else I'd call you knave. I leave you. *Exit.*

PAROLLES Good, very good! It is so then. Good, very good. Let it be conceal'd awhile.

Enter [Bertram] Count Rossillion.

BERTRAM
Undone, and forfeited to cares forever!

PAROLLES
What's the matter, sweetheart?

BERTRAM
Although before the solemn priest I have sworn,
I will not bed her.

PAROLLES
What, what, sweetheart?

BERTRAM
O my Parolles, they have married me!
I'll to the Tuscan wars, and never bed her.

PAROLLES
France is a dog-hole, and it no more merits
The tread of a man's foot. To th' wars!

BERTRAM
There's letters from my mother. What th' import is,
I know not yet.

PAROLLES
Ay, that would be known. To th' wars, my
boy, to th' wars!
He wears his honor in a box unseen,
That hugs his kicky-wicky here at home,
Spending his manly marrow in her arms,
Which should sustain the bound and high curvet
Of Mars's fiery steed. To other regions!
France is a stable, we that dwell in 't jades.
Therefore, to th' war!

BERTRAM
It shall be so. I'll send her to my house,
Acquaint my mother with my hate to her,
And wherefore I am fled; write to the King
That which I durst not speak. His present gift
Shall furnish me to those Italian fields
Where noble fellows strike. War is no strife
To the dark house and the detested wife.

PAROLLES
Will this capriccio hold in thee? Art sure?

BERTRAM
Go with me to my chamber, and advise me.
I'll send her straight away. Tomorrow
I'll to the wars, she to her single sorrow.

PAROLLES
Why, these balls bound; there's noise in it. 'Tis
hard!
A young man married is a man that's marr'd.
Therefore away, and leave her bravely; go.
The King has done you wrong, but hush, 'tis so.
Exit [with Bertram].

[SCENE IV]

Enter Helena [with a letter], and Clown.

HELENA
My mother greets me kindly. Is she well?

CLOWN She is not well, but yet she has her health. She's very merry, but yet she is not well. But thanks be given, she's very well and wants nothing i' th' world; but yet she is not well.

HELENA If she be very well, what does she ail that she's not very well?

CLOWN Truly, she's very well indeed, but for two things.

HELENA What two things?

CLOWN One, that she's not in heaven, whither God send her quickly! The other, that she's in earth, from whence God send her quickly!

Enter Parolles.

233 in . . . leave with whatever speed age will allow me **234–235 shall . . . me** i.e., on whom I will vindicate myself for these insults **244 make . . . wrongs** put some restraint upon your insults **244–245 good lord** i.e., patron (not master, as Lafew has insultingly said) **245 whom** i.e., God whom **255 breathe** exercise **258–259 for . . . pomegranate** i.e., for some petty offense, or on a slight pretext **262 heraldry** warrant **275 letters** i.e., a letter

279 kicky-wicky woman (with sexual suggestion, as also in *box* in the previous line and *Spending* and *marrow* in the following line) **281 curvet** leap **283 jades** worn-out horses **289 furnish me** (Knights customarily provided themselves with trappings and armed retainers when enlisting in warlike enterprises.) **291 To . . . house** i.e., compared to the madhouse (of marriage) **292 capriccio** caprice **294 straight** at once **296 balls** tennis balls

II.iv. Location: Paris. The King's palace.
2 not well (Referring to the Elizabethan euphemism by which the dead were spoken of as "well.")

PAROLLES Bless you, my fortunate lady!
HELENA I hope, sir, I have your good will to have mine
own good fortunes.
PAROLLES You had my prayers to lead them on, and to
keep them on, have them still. O, my knave, how does
my old lady?
CLOWN So that you had her wrinkles and I her money, 20
I would she did as you say.
PAROLLES Why, I say nothing.
CLOWN Marry, you are the wiser man; for many a
man's tongue shakes out his master's undoing. To say 24
nothing, to do nothing, to know nothing, and to have
nothing, is to be a great part of your title, which is 26
within a very little of nothing.
PAROLLES Away! Th' art a knave.
CLOWN You should have said, sir, "Before a knave th' 29
art a knave"; that's, "Before me th' art a knave." This 30
had been truth, sir.
PAROLLES Go to, thou art a witty fool; I have found 32
thee. 33
CLOWN Did you find me in yourself, sir? Or were you 34
taught to find me? The search, sir, was profitable; and
much fool may you find in you, even to the world's
pleasure and the increase of laughter.
PAROLLES
A good knave, i' faith, and well fed.
Madam, my lord will go away tonight;
A very serious business calls on him.
The great prerogative and rite of love,
Which, as your due, time claims, he does
acknowledge, 42
But puts it off to a compell'd restraint; 43
Whose want, and whose delay, is strew'd with
sweets, 44
Which they distill now in the curbed time, 45
To make the coming hour o'erflow with joy
And pleasure drown the brim.
HELENA What's his will else? 47
PAROLLES
That you will take your instant leave o' th' King,
And make this haste as your own good proceeding, 49
Strength'ned with what apology you think
May make it probable need.
HELENA What more commands he? 51
PAROLLES
That, having this obtain'd, you presently
Attend his further pleasure. 53
HELENA
In everything I wait upon his will.
PAROLLES
I shall report it so. *Exit Parolles.*
HELENA
I pray you. Come, sirrah. *Exit [with Clown].*

24 man's servant's. **shakes out** i.e., brings about by talking too freely **26 title** worth **29 Before** in presence of **30 Before me** i.e., upon my soul. (But by substituting "me" for "knave" the Clown suggests that Parolles call himself a knave.) **32–33 found thee** found you out **34 in yourself** (1) by your own efforts (2) in your reflection **42 time** i.e., the present time **43 to** owing to **44 Whose want** the lack of which (rite of love) **45 they** i.e., the lack and delay. **curbed time** period of restraint (and also of distillation, as in the making of perfume from *curbing* flowers or *sweets*, l. 44, in a still) **47 else** besides **49 make** represent **51 a probable need** plausibly appear to be necessary **53 Attend** await. **pleasure** command

[SCENE V]

Enter Lafew and Bertram.

LAFEW But I hope your lordship thinks not him a soldier.
BERTRAM Yes, my lord, and of very valiant approof. 3
LAFEW You have it from his own deliverance. 4
BERTRAM And by other warranted testimony.
LAFEW Then my dial goes not true. I took this lark for a 6
bunting. 7
BERTRAM I do assure you, my lord, he is very great in
knowledge and accordingly valiant. 9
LAFEW I have then sinn'd against his experience and
transgress'd against his valor; and my state that way is 11
dangerous, since I cannot yet find in my heart to repent. Here he comes. I pray you, make us friends; I
will pursue the amity.

Enter Parolles.

PAROLLES [*To Bertram*] These things shall be done, sir.
LAFEW Pray you, sir, who's his tailor? 16
PAROLLES Sir?
LAFEW O, I know him well, I, sir; he, sir, 's a good 18
workman, a very good tailor. 19
BERTRAM [*Aside to Parolles*] Is she gone to the King?
PAROLLES She is.
BERTRAM Will she away tonight?
PAROLLES As you'll have her.
BERTRAM
I have writ my letters, casketed my treasure,
Given order for our horses; and tonight,
When I should take possession of the bride,
End ere I do begin.
LAFEW A good traveler is something at the latter end of 28
a dinner; but one that lies three thirds, and uses a 29
known truth to pass a thousand nothings with, should
be once heard and thrice beaten. God save you, captain.
BERTRAM Is there any unkindness between my lord
and you, monsieur?
PAROLLES I know not how I have deserv'd to run into
my lord's displeasure.
LAFEW You have made shift to run into 't, boots and 37
spurs and all, like him that leapt into the custard; and 38
out of it you'll run again, rather than suffer question 39
for your residence. 40
BERTRAM It may be you have mistaken him, my lord. 41
LAFEW And shall do so ever, though I took him at 's
prayers. Fare you well, my lord, and believe this of

II.v. Location: Paris. The King's palace.
3 valiant approof proven valor **4 deliverance** testimony, word **6 dial** clock, compass, i.e., judgment **6–7 lark, bunting** (The two birds resemble one another, but the bunting lacks the lark's beautiful song.) **9 accordingly** correspondingly **11 my state** i.e., the state of my soul. (Lafew uses ironically an elaborate metaphor of religious penitence.) **16 who's his tailor** i.e., what tailor made this stuffed (bombast) figure **18–19 O . . . tailor** (Lafew continues as though Parolles had answered his previous question.) **28–29 A good . . . dinner** i.e., a person with many traveling experiences is an asset as a story-teller after dinner **37 made shift** contrived (at our previous meeting) **38 like . . . custard** i.e., like a clown at an annual city entertainment jumping into a large, deep custard **39–40 suffer . . . residence** undergo questioning about your being there, i.e., explain how your cowardice displeased me **41 mistaken him** misjudged or misidentified him. (But Lafew deliberately takes the phrase in the sense of *taken exception to his behavior.*)

me, there can be no kernel in this light nut; the soul of this man is his clothes. Trust him not in matter of heavy consequence; I have kept of them tame, and know their natures. Farewell, monsieur. I have spoken better of you than you have or will to deserve at my hand; but we must do good against evil. [*Exit.*]

PAROLLES An idle lord, I swear.

BERTRAM I think so.

PAROLLES Why, do you not know him?

BERTRAM
Yes, I do know him well, and common speech
Gives him a worthy pass. Here comes my clog.

Enter Helena.

HELENA
I have, sir, as I was commanded from you,
Spoke with the King, and have procur'd his leave
For present parting; only he desires
Some private speech with you.

BERTRAM I shall obey his will.
You must not marvel, Helen, at my course,
Which holds not color with the time, nor does
The ministration and required office
On my particular. Prepar'd I was not
For such a business; therefore am I found
So much unsettled. This drives me to entreat you
That presently you take your way for home;
And rather muse than ask why I entreat you,
For my respects are better than they seem,
And my appointments have in them a need
Greater than shows itself at the first view
To you that know them not. This to my mother.
[*Giving a letter.*]
'Twill be two days ere I shall see you, so
I leave you to your wisdom.

HELENA Sir, I can nothing say
But that I am your most obedient servant.

BERTRAM
Come, come, no more of that.

HELENA And ever shall
With true observance seek to eke out that
Wherein toward me my homely stars have fail'd
To equal my great fortune.

BERTRAM Let that go.
My haste is very great. Farewell; hie home.
[*He starts to go.*]

HELENA
Pray, sir, your pardon.

BERTRAM Well, what would you say?

HELENA
I am not worthy of the wealth I owe,
Nor dare I say 'tis mine, and yet it is;
But, like a timorous thief, most fain would steal
What law does vouch mine own.

BERTRAM What would you have?

HELENA
Something, and scarce so much; nothing, indeed.
I would not tell you what I would, my lord. Faith,
yes—
Strangers and foes do sunder, and not kiss.

BERTRAM
I pray you, stay not, but in haste to horse.

HELENA
I shall not break your bidding, good my lord.

BERTRAM
Where are my other men, monsieur?—Farewell.
Exit [*Helena*].
Go thou toward home, where I will never come
Whilst I can shake my sword or hear the drum.
Away, and for our flight.

PAROLLES Bravely, coragio! [*Exeunt.*]

ACT III • [SCENE I]

Flourish. Enter the Duke of Florence [*attended*]; *the two Frenchmen, with a troop of soldiers.*

DUKE
So that from point to point now have you heard
The fundamental reasons of this war,
Whose great decision hath much blood let forth
And more thirsts after.

FIRST LORD Holy seems the quarrel
Upon your Grace's part; black and fearful
On the opposer.

DUKE
Therefore we marvel much our cousin France
Would in so just a business shut his bosom
Against our borrowing prayers.

SECOND LORD Good my lord,
The reasons of our state I cannot yield
But like a common and an outward man
That the great figure of a council frames
By self-unable motion, therefore dare not
Say what I think of it, since I have found
Myself in my incertain grounds to fail
As often as I guess'd.

DUKE Be it his pleasure.

FIRST LORD
But I am sure the younger of our nature,
That surfeit on their ease, will day by day
Come here for physic.

DUKE Welcome shall they be;
And all the honors that can fly from us
Shall on them settle. You know your places well;

46 I . . . tame I have kept tame creatures of this kind (for the amusement they provide) **48 have . . . deserve** have deserved or are likely to deserve **54 pass** reputation. **clog** a heavy weight attached to the leg or neck of a man or animal to prevent freedom of movement **60–62 Which . . . particular** which does not appear to suit with the occasion (of our marriage), nor does it fulfill what is incumbent upon me as a husband **66 muse** wonder **67 respects** motives **68 appointments** purposes **75 observance** service. **eke out** add to **76 homely stars** i.e., lowly origin **80 owe** own **82 fain** gladly

92 coragio courage, bravo

III.i. Location: Florence. The Duke's palace.
3 decision combat to decide an issue **9 borrowing prayers** prayers for assistance **10 yield** communicate, produce **11 But** except. **outward** not having intimate knowledge of things **12 figure** scheme. **frames** constructs **13 self-unable motion** i.e., his own imperfect guess **16 Be . . . pleasure** i.e., be it as the King of France wishes **17 nature** outlook, disposition **19 physic** i.e., cure of their surfeit (through bloodletting)

When better fall, for your avails they fell. 22
Tomorrow to the field. *Flourish.* [*Exeunt.*]

[SCENE II]

Enter Countess and Clown.

COUNTESS It hath happen'd all as I would have had it,
save that he comes not along with her.
CLOWN By my troth, I take my young lord to be a very
melancholy man.
COUNTESS By what observance, I pray you? 5
CLOWN Why, he will look upon his boot and sing,
mend the ruff and sing, ask questions and sing, pick 7
his teeth and sing. I know a man that had this trick of 8
melancholy sold a goodly manor for a song.
COUNTESS Let me see what he writes, and when he
means to come. [*Opening a letter.*]
CLOWN I have no mind to Isbel since I was at court.
Our old ling and our Isbels o' th' country are nothing 13
like your old ling and your Isbels o' th' court. The
brains of my Cupid's knock'd out, and I begin to love,
as an old man loves money, with no stomach. 16
COUNTESS What have we here?
CLOWN E'en that you have there. *Exit.*
[COUNTESS *reads*] *a letter.* "I have sent you a daughter-
in-law. She hath recover'd the King, and undone me.
I have wedded her, not bedded her; and sworn to
make the 'not' eternal. You shall hear I am run away; 22
know it before the report come. If there be breadth
enough in the world, I will hold a long distance. My
duty to you.

Your unfortunate son,
Bertram."

This is not well, rash and unbridled boy,
To fly the favors of so good a king,
To pluck his indignation on thy head
By the misprising of a maid too virtuous
For the contempt of empire. 32

Enter Clown.

CLOWN O madam, yonder is heavy news within between two soldiers and my young lady!
COUNTESS What is the matter?
CLOWN Nay, there is some comfort in the news, some comfort. Your son will not be kill'd so soon as I thought he would.
COUNTESS Why should he be kill'd?
CLOWN So say I, madam, if he run away, as I hear he
does. The danger is in standing to 't; that's the loss of 41
men, though it be the getting of children. Here they 42
come will tell you more. For my part, I only hear your
son was run away. [*Exit.*]

Enter Helena and [*the*] *two* [*French*] *Gentlemen* [*or Lords*].

SECOND LORD
Save you, good madam.
HELENA
Madam, my lord is gone, forever gone!
FIRST LORD
Do not say so.
COUNTESS
Think upon patience. Pray you, gentlemen,
I have felt so many quirks of joy and grief 49
That the first face of neither, on the start, 50
Can woman me unto 't. Where is my son, I pray
you? 51
FIRST LORD
Madam, he's gone to serve the Duke of Florence.
We met him thitherward; for thence we came,
And, after some dispatch in hand at court,
Thither we bend again.
HELENA
Look on his letter, madam; here's my passport. 56
[*Reads.*] "When thou canst get the ring upon my finger, which never shall come off, and show me a child begotten of thy body that I am father to, then call me husband; but in such a 'then' I write a 'never.' " This is a dreadful sentence.
COUNTESS
Brought you this letter, gentlemen?
FIRST LORD Ay, madam;
And for the contents' sake are sorry for our pains.
COUNTESS
I prithee, lady, have a better cheer.
If thou engrossest all the griefs are thine, 65
Thou robb'st me of a moi'ty. He was my son, 66
But I do wash his name out of my blood,
And thou art all my child. Towards Florence is he? 68
FIRST LORD
Ay, madam.
COUNTESS And to be a soldier?
FIRST LORD
Such is his noble purpose; and, believe 't,
The Duke will lay upon him all the honor
That good convenience claims.
COUNTESS Return you thither? 72
SECOND LORD
Ay, madam, with the swiftest wing of speed.
HELENA [*Reads*]
"Till I have no wife, I have nothing in France."
'Tis bitter.
COUNTESS Find you that there?
HELENA Ay, madam.
SECOND LORD
'Tis but the boldness of his hand, haply, 76
Which his heart was not consenting to.
COUNTESS
Nothing in France, until he have no wife!

22 better fall i.e., better places fall vacant. **fell** will have fallen

III.ii. Location: Rossillion. The Count's palace.
5 observance observation **7 mend the ruff** adjust the loose turned-over flap at the top of his boot **7–8 pick his teeth.** (A fashionable mannerism.) **13 old ling** salted fish (also a vulgar way of referring to women by the pudenda) **16 stomach** appetite **22 not** (with a pun on *knot*) **32 of empire** of even an emperor **41 standing to 't** standing one's ground (with sexual pun) **42 getting** begetting

49 quirks sudden shifts **50 face** appearance. **on the start** appearing suddenly **51 woman me unto 't** i.e., make me respond emotionally **56 passport** license to wander as a beggar **65 thou engrossest** you monopolize. **are** that are **66 moi'ty** half **68 all my** my only **72 convenience** propriety **76 haply** perhaps

There's nothing here that is too good for him
But only she, and she deserves a lord
That twenty such rude boys might tend upon
And call her hourly mistress. Who was with him?

SECOND LORD
A servant only, and a gentleman
Which I have sometime known.

COUNTESS Parolles, was it not?

SECOND LORD
Ay, my good lady, he.

COUNTESS
A very tainted fellow, and full of wickedness.
My son corrupts a well-derived nature
With his inducement.

SECOND LORD Indeed, good lady,
The fellow has a deal of that too much
Which holds him much to have.

COUNTESS Y' are welcome, gentlemen.
I will entreat you, when you see my son,
To tell him that his sword can never win
The honor that he loses. More I'll entreat you
Written to bear along.

FIRST LORD We serve you, madam,
In that and all your worthiest affairs.

COUNTESS
Not so, but as we change our courtesies.
Will you draw near? *Exit [with Gentlemen].*

HELENA
"Till I have no wife, I have nothing in France."
Nothing in France, until he has no wife!
Thou shalt have none, Rossillion, none in France;
Then hast thou all again. Poor lord, is 't I
That chase thee from thy country, and expose
Those tender limbs of thine to the event
Of the none-sparing war? And is it I
That drive thee from the sportive court, where thou
Wast shot at with fair eyes, to be the mark
Of smoky muskets? O you leaden messengers,
That ride upon the violent speed of fire,
Fly with false aim; move the still-peering air,
That sings with piercing; do not touch my lord!
Whoever shoots at him, I set him there;
Whoever charges on his forward breast,
I am the caitiff that do hold him to 't;
And, though I kill him not, I am the cause
His death was so effected. Better 'twere
I met the ravin lion when he roar'd
With sharp constraint of hunger; better 'twere
That all the miseries which nature owes
Were mine at once. No, come thou home,
Rossillion,
Whence honor but of danger wins a scar,
As oft it loses all. I will be gone.
My being here it is that holds thee hence.
Shall I stay here to do 't? No, no, although
The air of paradise did fan the house
And angels offic'd all. I will be gone,
That pitiful rumor may report my flight
To consolate thine ear. Come, night; end, day!
For with the dark, poor thief, I'll steal away. *Exit.*

[SCENE III]

Flourish. Enter the Duke of Florence, [Bertram, Count] Rossillion, drum and trumpets, Soldiers, Parolles.

DUKE
The general of our horse thou art; and we,
Great in our hope, lay our best love and credence
Upon thy promising fortune.

BERTRAM Sir, it is
A charge too heavy for my strength, but yet
We'll strive to bear it for your worthy sake
To th' extreme edge of hazard.

DUKE Then go thou forth,
And fortune play upon thy prosperous helm,
As thy auspicious mistress!

BERTRAM This very day,
Great Mars, I put myself into thy file.
Make me but like my thoughts, and I shall prove
A lover of thy drum, hater of love. *Exeunt omnes.*

[SCENE IV]

Enter Countess and Steward.

COUNTESS
Alas! And would you take the letter of her?
Might you not know she would do as she has done,
By sending me a letter? Read it again.

[STEWARD *reads the*] *letter*
"I am Saint Jaques' pilgrim, thither gone.
Ambitious love hath so in me offended
That barefoot plod I the cold ground upon,
With sainted vow my faults to have amended.
Write, write, that from the bloody course of war
My dearest master, your dear son, may hie.
Bless him at home in peace, whilst I from far
His name with zealous fervor sanctify.
His taken labors bid him me forgive;
I, his despiteful Juno, sent him forth

88 With his inducement i.e., by Parolles' corrupt influence **89–90 has . . . have** i.e., has considerably too much of that ingratiating and persuasive quality which he uses to his advantage **96 Not so . . . courtesies** i.e., only as we serve each other—I by giving you entertainment. **(Change:** exchange.) **97 draw near** come with me **109 still-peering** always observing (?). (Frequently emended to *still-piercing*.) **110 sings with piercing** i.e., whistles when a bullet passes through it **113 caitiff** base wretch **116 ravin** ravenous **118 nature owes** human nature possesses, suffers **120–121 Whence . . . all** i.e., from war, in which honor is at best rewarded for danger with a scar, and often loses life itself

125 offic'd all performed all domestic duties **126 pitiful** compassionate

III.iii. Location: Florence. Before the Duke's palace.
2 Great pregnant, expectant **6 edge of hazard** limit of peril **9 file** battle line; ranks, catalogue **10 like my thoughts** i.e.. as valiant as I aspire to be

III.iv. Location: Rossillion. The Count's palace.
4 Saint Jaques' pilgrim i.e., a pilgrim to the shrine identified as that of St. James of Compostella in Spain **12 His taken labors** for the labors he has undertaken **13 despiteful Juno** (An allusion to Juno's persecution of Hercules by assigning him the twelve labors.)

From courtly friends, with camping foes to live,
Where death and danger dogs the heels of worth.
He is too good and fair for death and me;
Whom I myself embrace, to set him free."

COUNTESS
Ah, what sharp stings are in her mildest words!
Rinaldo, you did never lack advice so much
As letting her pass so. Had I spoke with her,
I could have well diverted her intents,
Which thus she hath prevented.

STEWARD
Pardon me, madam.
If I had given you this at overnight,
She might have been o'erta'en; and yet she writes
Pursuit would be but vain.

COUNTESS
What angel shall
Bless this unworthy husband? He cannot thrive,
Unless her prayers, whom heaven delights to hear
And loves to grant, reprieve him from the wrath
Of greatest justice. Write, write, Rinaldo,
To this unworthy husband of his wife.
Let every word weigh heavy of her worth
That he does weigh too light. My greatest grief,
Though little he do feel it, set down sharply.
Dispatch the most convenient messenger.
When haply he shall hear that she is gone,
He will return; and hope I may that she,
Hearing so much, will speed her foot again,
Led hither by pure love. Which of them both
Is dearest to me, I have no skill in sense
To make distinction. Provide this messenger.
My heart is heavy and mine age is weak;
Grief would have tears, and sorrow bids me speak.
Exeunt.

[SCENE V]

Enter old Widow of Florence, her Daughter [Diana], and Mariana, with other Citizens.

WIDOW Nay, come; for if they do approach the city, we shall lose all the sight.

DIANA They say the French count has done most honorable service.

WIDOW It is reported that he has taken their great'st commander, and that with his own hand he slew the Duke's brother. [*Tucket.*] We have lost our labor; they are gone a contrary way. Hark! You may know by their trumpets.

MARIANA Come, let's return again, and suffice ourselves with the report of it. Well, Diana, take heed of this French earl. The honor of a maid is her name, and no legacy is so rich as honesty.

WIDOW I have told my neighbor how you have been solicited by a gentleman his companion.

MARIANA I know that knave, hang him! One Parolles, a filthy officer he is in those suggestions for the young earl. Beware of them, Diana; their promises, enticements, oaths, tokens, and all these engines of lust, are not the things they go under. Many a maid hath been seduc'd by them; and the misery is, example, that so terrible shows in the wrack of maidenhood, cannot for all that dissuade succession, but that they are lim'd with the twigs that threatens them. I hope I need not to advise you further, but I hope your own grace will keep you where you are, though there were no further danger known but the modesty which is so lost.

DIANA You shall not need to fear me.

Enter Helena [disguised like a Pilgrim].

WIDOW I hope so.—Look, here comes a pilgrim. I know she will lie at my house; thither they send one another. I'll question her. God save you, pilgrim! Whither are bound?

HELENA
To Saint Jaques le Grand.
Where do the palmers lodge, I do beseech you?

WIDOW
At the Saint Francis here beside the port.

HELENA
Is this the way? *(A march afar.)*

WIDOW
Ay, marry, is 't. Hark you, they come this way.
If you will tarry, holy pilgrim,
But till the troops come by,
I will conduct you where you shall be lodg'd;
The rather, for I think I know your hostess
As ample as myself.

HELENA
Is it yourself?

WIDOW
If you shall please so, pilgrim.

HELENA
I thank you, and will stay upon your leisure.

WIDOW
You came, I think, from France?

HELENA
I did so.

WIDOW
Here you shall see a countryman of yours
That has done worthy service.

HELENA
His name, I pray you?

DIANA
The Count Rossillion. Know you such a one?

HELENA
But by the ear, that hears most nobly of him.
His face I know not.

DIANA
Whatsome'er he is,

17 Whom i.e., death **19 advice** judgment **22 prevented** forestalled **23 at overnight** last night **39 in sense** in what I feel

III.v. Location: Florence. Outside the walls.
12 earl i.e., Count Bertram. **her name** her reputation (for chastity) **13 honesty** chastity **14 my neighbor** i.e., Mariana

17 officer agent. **suggestions for** solicitings on behalf of **19 engines** artifices, devices **20 go under** pretend to be **21–23 example . . . succession** the dreadful example of what happens with the loss of virginity nonetheless cannot dissuade another from a similar course **23–24 they . . . twigs** i.e., other maidens are caught in the traps. (Birdlime was smeared on twigs to ensnare birds.) **26–27 further danger** i.e., pregnancy **28 fear** worry about **30 lie** lodge **34 palmers** pilgrims **35 port** city gate **42 ample** fully, completely **44 stay . . . leisure** await your convenience

He's bravely taken here. He stole from France,
As 'tis reported, for the King had married him
Against his liking. Think you it is so?

HELENA
Ay, surely, mere the truth. I know his lady.

DIANA
There is a gentleman that serves the Count
Reports but coarsely of her.

HELENA What's his name?

DIANA
Monsieur Parolles.

HELENA O, I believe with him.
In argument of praise, or to the worth
Of the great Count himself, she is too mean
To have her name repeated. All her deserving
Is a reserved honesty, and that
I have not heard examin'd.

DIANA Alas, poor lady!
'Tis a hard bondage to become the wife
Of a detesting lord.

WIDOW
I warrant, good creature, wheresoe'er she is,
Her heart weighs sadly. This young maid might do her
A shrewd turn, if she pleas'd.

HELENA How do you mean?
May be the amorous Count solicits her
In the unlawful purpose.

WIDOW He does indeed,
And brokes with all that can in such a suit
Corrupt the tender honor of a maid.
But she is arm'd for him, and keeps her guard
In honestest defense.

Drum and colors. Enter [Bertram] Count Rossillion, Parolles, and the whole army.

MARIANA The gods forbid else!

WIDOW
So, now they come.
That is Antonio, the Duke's eldest son;
That, Escalus.

HELENA Which is the Frenchman?

DIANA He,
That with the plume. 'Tis a most gallant fellow.
I would he lov'd his wife. If he were honester
He were much goodlier. Is 't not a handsome gentleman?

HELENA
I like him well.

DIANA
'Tis pity he is not honest. Yond 's that same knave
That leads him to these places. Were I his lady,
I would poison that vile rascal.

HELENA Which is he?

DIANA
That jackanapes with scarfs. Why is he melancholy?

HELENA
Perchance he's hurt i' th' battle.

PAROLLES Lose our drum? Well.

MARIANA He's shrewdly vex'd at something. Look, he has spied us.

WIDOW Marry, hang you!

MARIANA And your courtesy, for a ring-carrier!

Exeunt [Bertram, Parolles, and army].

WIDOW
The troop is past. Come, pilgrim, I will bring you
Where you shall host. Of enjoin'd penitents
There's four or five, to great Saint Jaques bound,
Already at my house.

HELENA I humbly thank you.
Please it this matron and this gentle maid
To eat with us tonight, the charge and thanking
Shall be for me; and, to requite you further,
I will bestow some precepts of this virgin
Worthy the note.

BOTH We'll take your offer kindly.

Exeunt.

[SCENE VI]

Enter [Bertram] Count Rossillion and the [two] Frenchmen, as at first.

FIRST LORD Nay, good my lord, put him to 't; let him have his way.

SECOND LORD If your lordship find him not a hilding, hold me no more in your respect.

FIRST LORD On my life, my lord, a bubble.

BERTRAM Do you think I am so far deceiv'd in him?

FIRST LORD Believe it, my lord, in mine own direct knowledge, without any malice, but to speak of him as my kinsman, he's a most notable coward, an infinite and endless liar, an hourly promise-breaker, the owner of no one good quality worthy your lordship's entertainment.

SECOND LORD It were fit you knew him, lest, reposing too far in his virtue, which he hath not, he might at some great and trusty business in a main danger fail you.

BERTRAM I would I knew in what particular action to try him.

SECOND LORD None better than to let him fetch off his drum, which you hear him so confidently undertake to do.

FIRST LORD I, with a troop of Florentines, will suddenly surprise him; such I will have whom I am sure he knows not from the enemy. We will bind and hoodwink him so, that he shall suppose no other but that he is carried into the leaguer of the adversaries, when we bring him to our own tents. Be but your

51 bravely taken highly regarded **52 for** because **54 mere** absolutely **57 believe** agree **58 In argument of** as a subject for. **to** compared to **60–61 All . . . honesty** her only merit is a well-preserved chastity **62 examin'd** doubted, questioned **67 shrewd** malicious, hurtful **70 brokes** bargains **84 jackanapes** monkey

87 shrewdly sorely **90 courtesy** ceremonious bow. **ring-carrier** go-between **92 host** lodge. **enjoin'd** obligated by oath (to a pilgrimage) **96 charge** expense. **thanking** my gratitude **98 of** on

III.vi. Location: Camp before Florence.
1 to 't i.e., to the test **3 hilding** good-for-nothing **9 as** as if he were **12 entertainment** patronage **13 reposing** trusting **19 fetch off** recapture **23 surprise** capture **25 hoodwink** blindfold **26 leaguer** camp

lordship present at his examination. If he do not, for the promise of his life and in the highest compulsion of base fear, offer to betray you and deliver all the intelligence in his power against you, and that with the divine forfeit of his soul upon oath, never trust my judgment in any thing.

SECOND LORD O, for the love of laughter, let him fetch his drum; he says he has a stratagem for 't. When your lordship sees the bottom of his success in 't, and to what metal this counterfeit lump of ore will be melted, if you give him not John Drum's entertainment, your inclining cannot be remov'd. Here he comes.

Enter Parolles.

FIRST LORD [*Aside to Bertram*] O, for the love of laughter, hinder not the honor of his design. Let him fetch off his drum in any hand.

BERTRAM How now, monsieur? This drum sticks sorely in your disposition.

SECOND LORD A pox on 't, let it go, 'tis but a drum.

PAROLLES But a drum! Is 't but a drum? A drum so lost! There was excellent command—to charge in with our horse upon our own wings, and to rend our own soldiers!

SECOND LORD That was not to be blam'd in the command of the service; it was a disaster of war that Caesar himself could not have prevented, if he had been there to command.

BERTRAM Well, we cannot greatly condemn our success. Some dishonor we had in the loss of that drum, but it is not to be recover'd.

PAROLLES It might have been recover'd.

BERTRAM It might, but it is not now.

PAROLLES It is to be recover'd. But that the merit of service is seldom attributed to the true and exact performer, I would have that drum or another, or "hic jacet."

BERTRAM Why, if you have a stomach, to 't, monsieur! If you think your mystery in stratagem can bring this instrument of honor again into his native quarter, be magnanimous in the enterprise and go on; I will grace the attempt for a worthy exploit. If you speed well in it, the Duke shall both speak of it, and extend to you what further becomes his greatness, even to the utmost syllable of your worthiness.

PAROLLES By the hand of a soldier, I will undertake it.

BERTRAM But you must not now slumber in it.

PAROLLES I'll about it this evening, and I will presently pen down my dilemmas, encourage myself in my certainty, put myself into my mortal preparation; and by midnight look to hear further from me.

BERTRAM May I be bold to acquaint his Grace you are gone about it?

PAROLLES I know not what the success will be, my lord, but the attempt I vow.

BERTRAM I know th' art valiant, and, to the possibility of thy soldiership, will subscribe for thee. Farewell.

PAROLLES I love not many words. *Exit.*

FIRST LORD No more than a fish loves water. Is not this a strange fellow, my lord, that so confidently seems to undertake this business, which he knows is not to be done, damns himself to do, and dares better be damn'd than to do 't?

SECOND LORD You do not know him, my lord, as we do. Certain it is that he will steal himself into a man's favor, and for a week escape a great deal of discoveries; but when you find him out, you have him ever after.

BERTRAM Why, do you think he will make no deed at all of this that so seriously he does address himself unto?

FIRST LORD None in the world, but return with an invention, and clap upon you two or three probable lies. But we have almost emboss'd him; you shall see his fall tonight; for indeed he is not for your lordship's respect.

SECOND LORD We'll make you some sport with the fox ere we case him. He was first smok'd by the old lord Lafew. When his disguise and he is parted, tell me what a sprat you shall find him, which you shall see this very night.

FIRST LORD
I must go look my twigs. He shall be caught.

BERTRAM
Your brother he shall go along with me.

FIRST LORD
As 't please your lordship. I'll leave you. [*Exit.*]

BERTRAM
Now will I lead you to the house, and show you
The lass I spoke of.

SECOND LORD But you say she's honest.

BERTRAM
That's all the fault. I spoke with her but once
And found her wondrous cold; but I sent to her,
By this same coxcomb that we have i' th' wind,
Tokens and letters which she did re-send,
And this is all I have done. She's a fair creature.
Will you go see her?

SECOND LORD With all my heart, my lord.

Exeunt.

[SCENE VII]

Enter Helena and Widow.

HELENA
If you misdoubt me that I am not she,
I know not how I shall assure you further

36 bottom extent **38 John Drum's entertainment** (Slang phrase for a thorough beating and unceremonious dismissal.) **39 inclining** partiality (for Parolles) **42 in any hand** in any case **48 wings** flanks. **rend** cut up, attack **50–51 in . . . service** i.e., upon the generalship **54–55 we . . . success** i.e., we were successful enough **59 But that** were it not that **61–62 hic jacet** here lies. (The beginning phrase of tomb inscriptions.) **64 mystery** skill **65 again . . . quarter** back home again **66 grace** honor **67 speed** succeed **69 becomes** suits, is worthy of **74 pen . . . dilemmas** examine my uncertainties **75 mortal preparation** extreme unction; or, death-dealing readiness

81 possibility capacity **82 subscribe** vouch **87 damns** condemns. **better** rather **92 have him** have a true knowledge of him **97 probable** plausible **98 emboss'd** driven to exhaustion, cornered. (A hunting term.) **102 case** skin, strip, unmask. **smok'd** smelled out; smoked out into the open **104 sprat** a small fish; a contemptible creature **106 look my twigs** i.e., see to my trap (as in catching birds with birdlime on twigs) **107 Your brother** i.e., the Second Lord **110 honest** chaste **113 have i' th' wind** have to our downwind side, whom we are tracking **114 re-send** send back

III.vii. Location: Florence. The Widow's house.

But I shall lose the grounds I work upon. 3
WIDOW
Though my estate be fall'n, I was well born, 4
Nothing acquainted with these businesses,
And would not put my reputation now
In any staining act.
HELENA Nor would I wish you.
First give me trust the Count he is my husband, 8
And what to your sworn counsel I have spoken 9
Is so from word to word; and then you cannot, 10
By the good aid that I of you shall borrow, 11
Err in bestowing it.
WIDOW I should believe you,
For you have show'd me that which well approves 13
Y' are great in fortune.
HELENA Take this purse of gold,
[Gives money.]
And let me buy your friendly help thus far,
Which I will over-pay and pay again
When I have found it. The Count he woos your daughter, 17
Lays down his wanton siege before her beauty,
Resolv'd to carry her. Let her in fine consent, 19
As we'll direct her how 'tis best to bear it. 20
Now his important blood will nought deny 21
That she'll demand. A ring the County wears, 22
That downward hath succeeded in his house
From son to son some four or five descents
Since the first father wore it. This ring he holds
In most rich choice; yet in his idle fire, 26
To buy his will, it would not seem too dear,
Howe'er repented after.
WIDOW
Now I see the bottom of your purpose.
HELENA
You see it lawful, then. It is no more
But that your daughter, ere she seems as won,
Desires this ring; appoints him an encounter;
In fine, delivers me to fill the time,
Herself most chastely absent. After,
To marry her, I'll add three thousand crowns 35
To what is past already.
WIDOW I have yielded.
Instruct my daughter how she shall persever,
That time and place with this deceit so lawful
May prove coherent. Every night he comes
With musics of all sorts and songs compos'd
To her unworthiness. It nothing steads us 41
To chide him from our eaves, for he persists
As if his life lay on 't.
HELENA Why then tonight
Let us assay our plot, which, if it speed, 44
Is wicked meaning in a lawful deed, 45
And lawful meaning in a lawful act,
Where both not sin, and yet a sinful fact. 47
But let's about it. *[Exeunt.]*

ACT IV • [SCENE I]

Enter one of the Frenchmen [the First Lord] with five or six other Soldiers, in ambush.

FIRST LORD He can come no other way but by this hedge-corner. When you sally upon him, speak what terrible language you will. Though you understand it not yourselves, no matter; for we must not seem to understand him, unless some one among us whom we must produce for an interpreter.
FIRST SOLDIER Good captain, let me be th' interpreter.
FIRST LORD Art not acquainted with him? Knows he not thy voice?
FIRST SOLDIER No, sir, I warrant you.
FIRST LORD But what linsey-woolsey hast thou to speak 11
to us again?
FIRST SOLDIER E'en such as you speak to me.
FIRST LORD He must think us some band of strangers 14
i' th' adversary's entertainment. Now he hath a smack 15
of all neighboring languages. Therefore we must every
one be a man of his own fancy, not to know what we
speak one to another; so we seem to know, is to know 18
straight our purpose: choughs' language, gabble 19
enough, and good enough. As for you, interpreter,
you must seem very politic. But couch, ho! Here he 21
comes, to beguile two hours in a sleep, and then to 22
return and swear the lies he forges. *[They hide.]*

Enter Parolles.

PAROLLES Ten o'clock. Within these three hours 'twill
be time enough to go home. What shall I say I have
done? It must be a very plausive invention that carries 26
it. They begin to smoke me; and disgraces have of late 27
knock'd too often at my door. I find my tongue is too
foolhardy; but my heart hath the fear of Mars before
it, and of his creatures, not daring the reports of my 30
tongue. 31
FIRST LORD *[Aside]* This is the first truth that e'er thine own tongue was guilty of.
PAROLLES What the devil should move me to undertake
the recovery of this drum, being not ignorant of the
impossibility, and knowing I had no such purpose? I
must give myself some hurts, and say I got them in
exploit. Yet slight ones will not carry it—they will say,
"Came you off with so little?"—and great ones I dare
not give. Wherefore, what's the instance? Tongue, I 40

3 But . . . upon i.e., unless I give up my basic plan (of concealing my identity from Bertram) **4 estate** worldly condition **8 give me trust** believe me **9 counsel** secrecy **10 so . . . word** true in every word **11 By** with regard to **13 approves** proves **17 found it** i.e., received your help with success **19 carry** win. **in fine** at length **20 bear** manage **21 important** importunate **22 County** Count **26 idle fire** reckless passion **35 To marry her** i.e., to give her a dowry **41 To her unworthiness** to her, his social inferior; or, to the end of persuading her to do an unworthy deed. **nothing steads** profits not at all **44 speed** succeed **45 meaning** intention (on Bertram's part)

47 fact deed (which is sinful because of Bertram's intention)

IV.i. Location: Outside the Florentine camp.
11 linsey-woolsey a fabric woven from wool and flax; figuratively, nonsense **14 strangers** foreigners **15 entertainment** service **18 so** provided that **19 choughs'** small, chattering species of the crow family, the jackdaw **21 politic** shrewd, cunning. **couch** take concealment **22 sleep** nap **26 plausive** plausible **27 smoke** detect **30 his creatures** i.e., soldiers **30–31 not . . . tongue** not daring to carry out my boasts **40 what's the instance** what is to be offered as evidence

must put you into a butter-woman's mouth and buy myself another of Bajazeth's mule, if you prattle me into these perils.

FIRST LORD [*Aside*] Is it possible he should know what he is, and be that he is?

PAROLLES I would the cutting of my garments would serve the turn, or the breaking of my Spanish sword.

FIRST LORD [*Aside*] We cannot afford you so.

PAROLLES Or the baring of my beard, and to say it was in stratagem.

FIRST LORD [*Aside*] 'Twould not do.

PAROLLES Or to drown my clothes, and say I was stripp'd.

FIRST LORD [*Aside*] Hardly serve.

PAROLLES Though I swore I leapt from the window of the citadel—

FIRST LORD [*Aside*] How deep?

PAROLLES Thirty fathom.

FIRST LORD [*Aside*] Three great oaths would scarce make that be believ'd.

PAROLLES I would I had any drum of the enemy's. I would swear I recover'd it.

FIRST LORD [*Aside*] You shall hear one anon.

PAROLLES A drum now of the enemy's—

Alarum within.

FIRST LORD [*Coming forward*] Throca movousus, cargo, cargo, cargo.

ALL Cargo, cargo, cargo, villianda par corbo, cargo.

PAROLLES
O, ransom, ransom! Do not hide mine eyes.

[*They seize and blindfold him.*]

FIRST SOLDIER Boskos thromuldo boskos.

PAROLLES
I know you are the Muskos' regiment,
And I shall lose my life for want of language.
If there be here German, or Dane, Low Dutch,
Italian, or French, let him speak to me;
I'll discover that which shall undo the Florentine.

FIRST SOLDIER Boskos vauvado. I understand thee, and can speak thy tongue. Kerelybonto, sir, betake thee to thy faith, for seventeen poniards are at thy bosom.

PAROLLES O!

FIRST SOLDIER O, pray, pray, pray! Manka revania dulche.

FIRST LORD Oscorbidulchos volivorco.

FIRST SOLDIER
The general is content to spare thee yet,
And, hoodwink'd as thou art, will lead thee on
To gather from thee. Haply thou mayst inform
Something to save thy life.

PAROLLES
O, let me live,
And all the secrets of our camp I'll show,
Their force, their purposes; nay, I'll speak that
Which you will wonder at.

FIRST SOLDIER
But wilt thou faithfully?

PAROLLES
If I do not, damn me.

FIRST SOLDIER
Acordo linta.
Come on; thou art granted space.

Exit [*with Parolles guarded*]. *A short alarum within.*

FIRST LORD
Go, tell the Count Rossillion, and my brother,
We have caught the woodcock, and will keep him muffled
Till we do hear from them.

SECOND SOLDIER
Captain, I will.

FIRST LORD
'A will betray us all unto ourselves;
Inform on that.

SECOND SOLDIER
So I will, sir.

FIRST LORD
Till then I'll keep him dark and safely lock'd. *Exeunt.*

[SCENE II]

Enter Bertram and the Maid called Diana.

BERTRAM
They told me that your name was Fontibell.

DIANA
No, my good lord, Diana.

BERTRAM
Titled goddess,
And worth it, with addition! But, fair soul,
In your fine frame hath love no quality?
If the quick fire of youth light not your mind,
You are no maiden, but a monument.
When you are dead, you should be such a one
As you are now, for you are cold and stern;
And now you should be as your mother was
When your sweet self was got.

DIANA
She then was honest.

BERTRAM
So should you be.

DIANA
No.
My mother did but duty—such, my lord,
As you owe to your wife.

BERTRAM
No more o' that.
I prithee, do not strive against my vows.
I was compell'd to her, but I love thee
By love's own sweet constraint, and will for ever
Do thee all rights of service.

DIANA
Ay, so you serve us
Till we serve you; but when you have our roses,
You barely leave our thorns to prick ourselves

41 butter-woman dairy-woman, i.e., a proverbial scold and garrulous talker **42 of Bajazeth's mule** i.e., from a Turkish mule, since mules are notoriously mute(?) (Many emendations have been proposed.) **48 afford you so** grant you (belief for) that **49 baring** shaving **74 discover** reveal **76–77 betake . . . faith** i.e., say your prayers **83 hoodwink'd** blindfolded. **on** onward, elsewhere **84 gather** get information. **Haply** perhaps

90 space time **92 woodcock** (A proverbially stupid bird.) **95 Inform on** report

IV.ii. Location: Florence. The Widow's house.
2–3 Titled . . . addition you who have the name of a goddess, and who deserve that and more **4 quality** position **10 got** begotten **11 honest** chaste, true to marriage vows. (But Bertram uses it to mean *frank*.) **14 vows** i.e., vows to live apart from Helena **18 serve you** i.e., sexually. (The sexual suggestion is continued in *roses* and in *prick*, l. 19.) **19 barely** bare

And mock us with our bareness.
BERTRAM How have I sworn!
DIANA
'Tis not the many oaths that makes the truth,
But the plain single vow that is vow'd true.
What is not holy, that we swear not by,
But take the High'st to witness. Then pray you
tell me,
If I should swear by Jove's great attributes
I lov'd you dearly, would you believe my oaths
When I did love you ill? This has no holding,
To swear by Him whom I protest to love,
That I will work against Him. Therefore your oaths
Are words and poor conditions, but unseal'd—
At least in my opinion.
BERTRAM Change it, change it!
Be not so holy-cruel. Love is holy,
And my integrity ne'er knew the crafts
That you do charge men with. Stand no more off,
But give thyself unto my sick desires,
Who then recovers. Say thou art mine, and ever
My love as it begins shall so persever.
DIANA
I see that men may rope 's in such a snare
That we'll forsake ourselves. Give me that ring.
BERTRAM
I'll lend it thee, my dear, but have no power
To give it from me.
DIANA Will you not, my lord?
BERTRAM
It is an honor 'longing to our house,
Bequeathed down from many ancestors,
Which were the greatest obloquy i' th' world
In me to lose.
DIANA Mine honor's such a ring.
My chastity's the jewel of our house,
Bequeathed down from many ancestors,
Which were the greatest obloquy i' th' world
In me to lose. Thus your own proper wisdom
Brings in the champion Honor on my part,
Against your vain assault.
BERTRAM Here, take my ring!
My house, mine honor, yea, my life, be thine,
And I'll be bid by thee. [*Gives the ring.*]
DIANA
When midnight comes, knock at my chamber-
window.
I'll order take my mother shall not hear.
Now will I charge you in the band of truth,
When you have conquer'd my yet maiden bed,
Remain there but an hour, nor speak to me.
My reasons are most strong, and you shall know
them
When back again this ring shall be deliver'd.
And on your finger in the night I'll put
Another ring, that what in time proceeds
May token to the future our past deeds.
Adieu, till then; then, fail not. You have won
A wife of me, though there my hope be done.
BERTRAM
A heaven on earth I have won by wooing thee.
[*Exit.*]
DIANA
For which live long to thank both heaven and me!
You may so in the end.
My mother told me just how he would woo,
As if she sat in 's heart; she says all men
Have the like oaths. He had sworn to marry me
When his wife's dead; therefore I'll lie with him
When I am buried. Since Frenchmen are so braid,
Marry that will, I live and die a maid.
Only in this disguise I think 't no sin
To cozen him that would unjustly win. *Exit.*

[SCENE III]

Enter the two French Captains and some two or three Soldiers.

FIRST LORD You have not given him his mother's letter?

SECOND LORD I have deliver'd it an hour since. There is something in 't that stings his nature; for on the reading it he chang'd almost into another man.

FIRST LORD He has much worthy blame laid upon him for shaking off so good a wife and so sweet a lady.

SECOND LORD Especially he hath incurr'd the everlasting displeasure of the King, who had even tun'd his bounty to sing happiness to him. I will tell you a thing, but you shall let it dwell darkly with you.

FIRST LORD When you have spoken it, 'tis dead, and I am the grave of it.

SECOND LORD He hath perverted a young gentlewoman here in Florence, of a most chaste renown, and this night he fleshes his will in the spoil of her honor. He hath given her his monumental ring, and thinks himself made in the unchaste composition.

FIRST LORD Now, God delay our rebellion! As we are ourselves, what things are we!

SECOND LORD Merely our own traitors. And as in the common course of all treasons we still see them reveal themselves, till they attain to their abhorr'd ends, so he that in this action contrives against his own nobility in his proper stream o'erflows himself.

20 our bareness i.e., the loss of our rose of virginity **27 ill** wickedly, and hence contrary to the purport of an oath sworn to God. **holding** power to bind; consistency **28 protest** profess **29 work against Him** i.e., defy God's injunction against carnal and illicit sex **30 words . . . unseal'd** mere words and invalid provisos, unsealed and hence lacking in legally binding force **36 Who** which. **recovers** recover **38 rope 's** rope us, entrap us. (F reads *make rope's in such a scarre.*) **49 proper** pertaining to yourself **50 part** side **53 bid** commanded **55 order take** make provision **56 band** bond

62 that . . . proceeds which, whatever may happen **63 token** betoken, indicate **65 though . . . done** although all hope (of marriage) is thereby destroyed for me **71 had** has (?) would have (?) **73 braid** i.e., deceitful. (A *braid* is a trick.) **74 Marry** let those marry **76 cozen** cheat

IV.iii. Location: The Florentine camp.
15 fleshes his will gratifies his lust (like a hunter giving some meat to his hounds from the hunted animal, the quarry or *spoil*) **16 monumental** i.e., serving as a token of his identity **17 made** a made man. **composition** bargain **18 delay our rebellion** assuage our lustful appetites **18–19 are ourselves** i.e., unaided by God **20 Merely** absolutely, entirely **21–22 still . . . themselves** always see traitors reveal themselves for what they are **22 attain . . . ends** achieve their abhorrent desires and the inevitable consequences of them **23–24 he . . . himself** i.e., Bertram, who thus seduces a woman, subverts his own nobility by abusing the qualities that should channel and perpetuate it

FIRST LORD Is it not meant damnable in us, to be trumpeters of our unlawful intents? We shall not then have his company tonight?

SECOND LORD Not till after midnight, for he is dieted to his hour.

FIRST LORD That approaches apace. I would gladly have him see his company anatomiz'd, that he might take a measure of his own judgments wherein so curiously he had set this counterfeit.

SECOND LORD We will not meddle with him till he come, for his presence must be the whip of the other.

FIRST LORD In the mean time, what hear you of these wars?

SECOND LORD I hear there is an overture of peace.

FIRST LORD Nay, I assure you, a peace concluded.

SECOND LORD What will Count Rossillion do then? Will he travel higher, or return again into France?

FIRST LORD I perceive, by this demand, you are not altogether of his council.

SECOND LORD Let it be forbid, sir! So should I be a great deal of his act.

FIRST LORD Sir, his wife some two months since fled from his house. Her pretense is a pilgrimage to Saint Jaques le Grand, which holy undertaking with most austere sanctimony she accomplish'd. And, there residing, the tenderness of her nature became as a prey to her grief; in fine, made a groan of her last breath, and now she sings in heaven.

SECOND LORD How is this justified?

FIRST LORD The stronger part of it by her own letters, which makes her story true, even to the point of her death. Her death itself, which could not be her office to say is come, was faithfully confirm'd by the rector of the place.

SECOND LORD Hath the Count all this intelligence?

FIRST LORD Ay, and the particular confirmations, point from point, to the full arming of the verity.

SECOND LORD I am heartily sorry that he'll be glad of this.

FIRST LORD How mightily sometimes we make us comforts of our losses!

SECOND LORD And how mightily some other times we drown our gain in tears! The great dignity that his valor hath here acquir'd for him shall at home be encount'red with a shame as ample.

FIRST LORD The web of our life is of a mingled yarn, good and ill together; our virtues would be proud if our faults whipp'd them not, and our crimes would despair if they were not cherish'd by our virtues.

Enter a [Servant as] Messenger.

How now? Where's your master?

SERVANT He met the Duke in the street, sir, of whom he hath taken a solemn leave. His lordship will next morning for France. The Duke hath offer'd him letters of commendations to the King.

SECOND LORD They shall be no more than needful there, if they were more than they can commend.

Enter [Bertram] Count Rossillion.

FIRST LORD They cannot be too sweet for the King's tartness.—Here's his lordship now. How now, my lord, is 't not after midnight?

BERTRAM I have tonight dispatch'd sixteen businesses, a month's length apiece, by an abstract of success: I have congied with the Duke, done my adieu with his nearest, buried a wife, mourn'd for her, writ to my lady mother I am returning, entertain'd my convoy, and between these main parcels of dispatch effected many nicer needs. The last was the greatest, but that I have not ended yet.

SECOND LORD If the business be of any difficulty, and this morning your departure hence, it requires haste of your lordship.

BERTRAM I mean, the business is not ended, as fearing to hear of it hereafter. But shall we have this dialogue between the fool and the soldier? Come, bring forth this counterfeit module; h'as deceiv'd me like a double-meaning prophesier.

SECOND LORD Bring him forth. [*Exeunt Soldiers.*] H'as sat i' th' stocks all night, poor gallant knave.

BERTRAM No matter, his heels have deserv'd it, in usurping his spurs so long. How does he carry himself?

SECOND LORD I have told your lordship already, the stocks carry him. But to answer you as you would be understood, he weeps like a wench that had shed her milk. He hath confess'd himself to Morgan, whom he supposes to be a friar, from the time of his remembrance to this very instant disaster of his setting i' th' stocks. And what think you he hath confess'd?

BERTRAM Nothing of me, has 'a?

SECOND LORD His confession is taken, and it shall be read to his face. If your lordship be in 't, as I believe you are, you must have the patience to hear it.

Enter Parolles [guarded] with [First Soldier as] his Interpreter.

BERTRAM A plague upon him! Muffled! He can say nothing of me.

FIRST LORD Hush, hush! Hoodman comes!—Portotartarosa.

FIRST SOLDIER He calls for the tortures. What will you say without 'em?

PAROLLES I will confess what I know without constraint. If ye pinch me like a pasty, I can say no more.

FIRST SOLDIER Bosko chimurcho.

25 meant damnable a revelation or confirmation of wickedness (?) **28 dieted** restricted **31 company** companion. **anatomiz'd** dissected, exposed **32 curiously** carefully, elaborately **33 counterfeit** false jewel, i.e., Parolles **34 him . . . he** i.e., Parolles . . . Bertram **35 his . . . the other** i.e., Bertram's . . . Parolles **41 higher** farther **42 demand** question **43 of his council** in his confidence **45 of his act** i.e., an accessory to his misdeeds **47 pretense** intent **49 sanctimony** holiness **51 in fine** at last **53 justified** made certain **55 point** time, moment **61 arming** corroboration, strengthening **64–65 make . . . losses** i.e., take as apparent benefits what actually are great deprivations

79 no . . . needful i.e., urgently needed **80 if . . . commend** even if they were stronger than any recommendation could be **85 by . . . success** i.e., by successfully condensing my affairs; or, by a series of successful moves, as follows **86 congied with** taken leave of **86–87 his nearest** those persons nearest him **88 entertain'd my convoy** arranged my transportation **90 nicer** more delicate. **The last** i.e., the affair with Diana **98 module** mere image. **h'as** he has **98–99 double-meaning** ambiguous, equivocating **107 shed** spilled **109–110 the time . . . remembrance** as far back as he can recall **110 instant** present **116 Muffled** blindfolded **118 Hoodman comes** (Customary call in the game of blindman's buff.) **123 pasty** meat pie

FIRST LORD Boblibindo chicurmurco.
FIRST SOLDIER You are a merciful general. Our general
bids you answer to what I shall ask you out of a note. 127
PAROLLES And truly, as I hope to live.
FIRST SOLDIER [*Reads*] "First demand of him how many
horse the Duke is strong." What say you to that?
PAROLLES Five or six thousand, but very weak and un-
serviceable. The troops are all scatter'd, and the com-
manders very poor rogues, upon my reputation and
credit and as I hope to live.
FIRST SOLDIER Shall I set down your answer so?
[*Writes.*]
PAROLLES Do. I'll take the sacrament on 't, how and
which way you will.
BERTRAM [*Aside to the Lords*] All's one to him. What a
past-saving slave is this!
FIRST LORD [*Aside to Bertram*] Y' are deceived, my lord.
This is Monsieur Parolles, the gallant militarist—that
was his own phrase—that had the whole theoric of
war in the knot of his scarf, and the practice in the
chape of his dagger. 144
SECOND LORD [*Aside*] I will never trust a man again for
keeping his sword clean, nor believe he can have 146
every thing in him by wearing his apparel neatly.
FIRST SOLDIER Well, that's set down.
PAROLLES "Five or six thousand horse," I said—I will
say true—"or thereabouts," set down, for I'll speak
truth.
FIRST LORD [*Aside*] He's very near the truth in this.
BERTRAM [*Aside*] But I con him no thanks for 't, in the 153
nature he delivers it. 154
PAROLLES "Poor rogues," I pray you, say.
FIRST SOLDIER Well, that's set down.
PAROLLES I humbly thank you, sir. A truth's a truth, the
rogues are marvelous poor.
FIRST SOLDIER [*Reads*] "Demand of him, of what
strength they are a-foot." What say you to that?
PAROLLES By my troth, sir, if I were to live this present 161
hour, I will tell true. Let me see: Spurio, a hundred and
fifty; Sebastian, so many; Corambus, so many; Jaques,
so many; Guiltian, Cosmo, Lodowick, and Gratii, two
hundred fifty each; mine own company, Chitopher,
Vaumond, Bentii, two hundred fifty each; so that the
muster-file, rotten and sound, upon my life, amounts 167
not to fifteen thousand poll, half of the which dare not 168
shake the snow from off their cassocks, lest they shake 169
themselves to pieces.
BERTRAM [*Aside to the Lords*] What shall be done to
him?
FIRST LORD [*Aside*] Nothing, but let him have thanks.—
Demand of him my condition, and what credit I have
with the Duke.
FIRST SOLDIER Well, that's set down. [*Reads.*] "You shall
demand of him, whether one Captain Dumain be i'
th' camp, a Frenchman; what his reputation is with
the Duke; what his valor, honesty, and expertness in
wars; or whether he thinks it were not possible, with
well-weighing sums of gold, to corrupt him to a 181
revolt." What say you to this? What do you know
of it?
PAROLLES I beseech you, let me answer to the particular
of the inter'gatories. Demand them singly.
FIRST SOLDIER Do you know this Captain Dumain?
PAROLLES I know him. 'A was a botcher's prentice in 187
Paris, from whence he was whipp'd for getting the
shrieve's fool with child—a dumb innocent, that 189
could not say him nay.
BERTRAM [*Aside to First Lord, who makes as if to strike
Parolles*] Nay, by your leave, hold your hands—
though I know his brains are forfeit to the next tile 193
that falls. 194
FIRST SOLDIER Well, is this captain in the Duke of Flor-
ence's camp?
PAROLLES Upon my knowledge, he is, and lousy.
FIRST LORD [*Aside to Bertram*] Nay, look not so upon
me; we shall hear of your lordship anon.
FIRST SOLDIER What is his reputation with the Duke?
PAROLLES The Duke knows him for no other but a poor
officer of mine, and writ to me this other day to turn
him out o' th' band. I think I have his letter in my
pocket.
FIRST SOLDIER Marry, we'll search.
[*They search his pockets.*]
PAROLLES In good sadness, I do not know; either it is 206
there, or it is upon a file with the Duke's other letters
in my tent.
FIRST SOLDIER Here 'tis; here's a paper. Shall I read it to
you?
PAROLLES I do not know if it be it or no.
BERTRAM [*Aside*] Our interpreter does it well.
FIRST LORD [*Aside*] Excellently.
FIRST SOLDIER [*Reads*] "Dian, the Count's a fool, and
full of gold"—
PAROLLES That is not the Duke's letter, sir; that is an
advertisement to a proper maid in Florence, one 217
Diana, to take heed of the allurement of one Count
Rossillion, a foolish idle boy, but for all that very rut- 219
tish. I pray you, sir, put it up again. 220
FIRST SOLDIER Nay, I'll read it first, by your favor.
PAROLLES My meaning in 't, I protest, was very honest
in the behalf of the maid; for I knew the young Count
to be a dangerous and lascivious boy, who is a whale
to virginity, and devours up all the fry it finds. 225
BERTRAM [*Aside*] Damnable both-sides rogue!
FIRST SOLDIER [*Reads the*] *letter*

"When he swears oaths, bid him drop gold, and
take it;
After he scores, he never pays the score. 228
Half won is match well made; match, and well make
it; 229

127 note memorandum or list **144 chape** scabbard-tip **146 clean** i.e., polished **153 con** offer. (Literally, "know.") **154 nature** manner **161 live** i.e., live only **167 file** roll **168 poll** heads **169 cassocks** cloaks

181 well-weighing heavy and persuasive **187 botcher's** mender's, especially a tailor or cobbler who makes repairs **189 shrieve's fool** feeble-minded girl in the sheriff's custody **193–194 his . . . falls** i.e., he is such a liar that he is bound to be in danger of death from some providential "accident" soon **206 sadness** seriousness **217 advertisement** warning. **proper** respectable **219–220 ruttish** lecherous **225 fry** small fish **228 scores** (1) buys on credit (2) hits the mark, scores sexually **229 Half . . . made** one is halfway to success if the *match* or bargain is well started with clearly defined agreements

He ne'er pays after-debts, take it before.
And say a soldier, Dian, told thee this:
Men are to mell with, boys are not to kiss.
For count of this, the Count's a fool, I know it,
Who pays before, but not when he does owe it.
Thine, as he vow'd to thee in thine ear,
Parolles."

BERTRAM [*Aside*] He shall be whipp'd through the army with this rhyme in 's forehead.

SECOND LORD [*Aside*] This is your devoted friend, sir, the manifold linguist and the armipotent soldier.

BERTRAM [*Aside*] I could endure any thing before but a cat, and now he's a cat to me.

FIRST SOLDIER I perceive, sir, by our general's looks, we shall be fain to hang you.

PAROLLES My life, sir, in any case! Not that I am afraid to die; but that, my offenses being many, I would repent out the remainder of nature. Let me live, sir, in a dungeon, i' th' stocks, or any where, so I may live.

FIRST SOLDIER We'll see what may be done, so you confess freely. Therefore, once more to this Captain Dumain. You have answer'd to his reputation with the Duke, and to his valor. What is his honesty?

PAROLLES He will steal, sir, an egg out of a cloister. For rapes and ravishments he parallels Nessus. He professes not keeping of oaths; in breaking 'em he is stronger than Hercules. He will lie, sir, with such volubility, that you would think truth were a fool. Drunkenness is his best virtue, for he will be swine-drunk, and in his sleep he does little harm, save to his bedclothes about him; but they know his conditions, and lay him in straw. I have but little more to say, sir, of his honesty. He has every thing that an honest man should not have; what an honest man should have, he has nothing.

FIRST LORD [*Aside*] I begin to love him for this.

BERTRAM [*Aside*] For this description of thine honesty? A pox upon him for me, he's more and more a cat.

FIRST SOLDIER What say you to his expertness in war?

PAROLLES Faith, sir, h'as led the drum before the English tragedians. To belie him I will not, and more of his soldiership I know not, except in that country he had the honor to be the officer at a place there call'd Mile-end, to instruct for the doubling of files. I would do the man what honor I can, but of this I am not certain.

FIRST LORD [*Aside*] He hath out-villain'd villainy so far that the rarity redeems him.

BERTRAM [*Aside*] A pox on him, he's a cat still.

FIRST SOLDIER His qualities being at this poor price, I need not to ask you if gold will corrupt him to revolt.

PAROLLES Sir, for a cardecue he will sell the fee-simple of his salvation, the inheritance of it; and cut th' entail from all remainders, and a perpetual succession for it perpetually.

FIRST SOLDIER What's his brother, the other Captain Dumain?

SECOND LORD [*Aside*] Why does he ask him of me?

FIRST SOLDIER What's he?

PAROLLES E'en a crow o' th' same nest; not altogether so great as the first in goodness, but greater a great deal in evil. He excels his brother for a coward, yet his brother is reputed one of the best that is. In a retreat he outruns any lackey; marry, in coming on he has the cramp.

FIRST SOLDIER If your life be sav'd, will you undertake to betray the Florentine?

PAROLLES Ay, and the captain of his horse, Count Rossillion.

FIRST SOLDIER I'll whisper with the general, and know his pleasure.

PAROLLES [*To himself*] I'll no more drumming; a plague of all drums! Only to seem to deserve well, and to beguile the supposition of that lascivious young boy the Count, have I run into this danger. Yet who would have suspected an ambush where I was taken?

FIRST SOLDIER There is no remedy, sir, but you must die. The general says, you that have so traitorously discover'd the secrets of your army and made such pestiferous reports of men very nobly held, can serve the world for no honest use; therefore you must die. Come, headsman, off with his head.

PAROLLES O Lord, sir, let me live, or let me see my death!

FIRST SOLDIER That shall you, and take your leave of all your friends. [*Unblinding him.*] So, look about you. Know you any here?

BERTRAM Good morrow, noble captain.

SECOND LORD God bless you, Captain Parolles.

FIRST LORD God save you, noble captain.

SECOND LORD Captain, what greeting will you to my Lord Lafew? I am for France.

FIRST LORD Good captain, will you give me a copy of the sonnet you writ to Diana in behalf of the Count Rossillion? An I were not a very coward, I'd compel it of you; but fare you well. *Exeunt* [*Bertram and Lords*].

FIRST SOLDIER You are undone, captain, all but your scarf; that has a knot on 't yet.

PAROLLES Who cannot be crush'd with a plot?

FIRST SOLDIER If you could find out a country where but women were that had receiv'd so much shame, you might begin an impudent nation. Fare ye well, sir; I am for France too. We shall speak of you there.

Exit [*with Soldiers*].

PAROLLES

Yet am I thankful. If my heart were great,
'Twould burst at this. Captain I'll be no more,
But I will eat and drink, and sleep as soft

230 after-debts debts payable after the goods are received. **it** i.e., payment **232 mell** meddle (sexually) **233 count of** take note of **234 before** in advance (when he is required to do so). **owe it** (1) owe payment for something already received (2) possess it, i.e., her maidenhood **240 armipotent** powerful in arms **244 fain** obliged **247 remainder of nature** i.e., what is left of my natural life **254 Nessus** a centaur who attempted to rape the wife of Hercules **254–255 professes** makes a practice of **260 they** i.e., his servants **269–270 led . . . tragedians** (It was a custom of actors entering a village or town to parade the street before the performance of a play.) **273 Mile-end** place near London where citizen militiamen were regularly exercised. **doubling of files** (Simple drill maneuvers.) **281 cardecue** quart d'écu, quarter of a French crown. **fee-simple** total and perpetual ownership

282–284 cut . . . perpetually prevent it from being passed on successively to a number of predetermined heirs **293 lackey** running footman. **coming on** moving forward **303 supposition** judgment **308 discover'd** revealed **309 held** regarded

As captain shall. Simply the thing I am
Shall make me live. Who knows himself a braggart,
Let him fear this, for it will come to pass
That every braggart shall be found an ass.
Rust, sword! Cool, blushes! And, Parolles, live
Safest in shame! Being fool'd, by fool'ry thrive!
There's place and means for every man alive.
I'll after them.
Exit.

[SCENE IV]

Enter Helena, Widow, and Diana.

HELENA
That you may well perceive I have not wrong'd you,
One of the greatest in the Christian world
Shall be my surety; 'fore whose throne 'tis needful,
Ere I can perfect mine intents, to kneel.
Time was, I did him a desired office,
Dear almost as his life, which gratitude
Through flinty Tartar's bosom would peep forth,
And answer thanks. I duly am inform'd
His Grace is at Marseilles; to which place
We have convenient convoy. You must know
I am supposed dead. The army breaking,
My husband hies him home, where, heaven aiding,
And by the leave of my good lord the King,
We'll be before our welcome.
WIDOW Gentle madam,
You never had a servant to whose trust
Your business was more welcome.
HELENA Nor you, mistress,
Ever a friend whose thoughts more truly labor
To recompense your love. Doubt not but heaven
Hath brought me up to be your daughter's dower,
As it hath fated her to be my motive
And helper to a husband. But, O strange men!
That can such sweet use make of what they hate,
When saucy trusting of the cozen'd thoughts
Defiles the pitchy night; so lust doth play
With what it loathes for that which is away.
But more of this hereafter. You, Diana,
Under my poor instructions yet must suffer
Something in my behalf.
DIANA Let death and honesty
Go with your impositions, I am yours
Upon your will to suffer.
HELENA Yet, I pray you;
But with the word the time will bring on summer,
When briers shall have leaves as well as thorns,
And be as sweet as sharp. We must away;
Our wagon is prepar'd, and time revives us.
All's well that ends well. Still the fine 's the crown;
Whate'er the course, the end is the renown. *Exeunt.*

[SCENE V]

Enter Clown, Old Lady [Countess], and Lafew.

LAFEW No, no, no, your son was misled with a snipt-taffeta fellow there, whose villainous saffron would have made all the unbak'd and doughy youth of a nation in his color. Your daughter-in-law had been alive at this hour, and your son here at home, more advanc'd by the King than by that red-tail'd humble-bee I speak of.

COUNTESS I would I had not known him! It was the death of the most virtuous gentlewoman that ever nature had praise for creating. If she had partaken of my flesh, and cost me the dearest groans of a mother, I could not have ow'd her a more rooted love.

LAFEW 'Twas a good lady, 'twas a good lady. We may pick a thousand sallets ere we light on such another herb.

CLOWN Indeed, sir, she was the sweet-marjoram of the sallet, or rather the herb of grace.

LAFEW They are not herbs, you knave, they are nose-herbs.

CLOWN I am no great Nebuchadnezzar, sir; I have not much skill in grass.

LAFEW Whether dost thou profess thyself, a knave or a fool?

CLOWN A fool, sir, at a woman's service, and a knave at a man's.

LAFEW Your distinction?

CLOWN I would cozen the man of his wife and do his service.

LAFEW So you were a knave at his service, indeed.

CLOWN And I would give his wife my bauble, sir, to do her service.

LAFEW I will subscribe for thee, thou art both knave and fool.

CLOWN At your service.

LAFEW No, no, no!

CLOWN Why, sir, if I cannot serve you, I can serve as great a prince as you are.

LAFEW Who's that? A Frenchman?

CLOWN Faith, sir, 'a has an English name, but his fisnomy is more hotter in France than there.

IV.iv. Location: Florence. The Widow's house.
6 which gratitude gratitude for which **11 breaking** disbanding **14 be . . . welcome** i.e., arrive before we are expected **20 motive** means **23–24 When . . . night** when lascivious yielding to the deceptions of lust makes blacker the already black night **25 for** i.e., believing it to be. **away** absent. (Helena describes how Bertram has lustfully enjoyed Helena, making *sweet use* of what he hates, believing her to be the absent Diana.) **27 yet** for a time yet. (Also at l. 30.) **28 Let death and honesty** i.e., even if death (provided my honor be maintained) **29 your impositions** what you impose or command **30 Upon . . . suffer** to suffer as you wish **31 with . . . summer** i.e., with the promise that the fullness of time will bring reward and happiness (?) **32 leaves** petals

34 revives will revive **35 the fine 's** the end is

IV.v. Location: Rossillion. The Count's palace.
1 with by **1–2 snipt-taffeta** wearing taffeta silk garments with slashes to allow the under material to be visible **2 saffron** bright yellow spice used in making pastry and also in dyeing starched ruffs and collars **6–7 humble-bee** bumblebee **14 sallets** salads **17 herb of grace** rue **18 not herbs** i.e., not edible salad herbs or greens **18–19 nose-herbs** fragrant herbs used for bouquets, not salads **20–21 Nebuchadnezzar . . . grass** (In Daniel 4:28–37, King Nebuchadnezzar is reported to have gone mad and eaten grass like an ox.) **21 grass** (with a pun on *grace;* the word in the Folio is *grace*) **22 Whether** which of the two **27–28 do his service** i.e., usurp his sexual role **30 bauble** stick carried by a court fool (with bawdy suggestion) **32 subscribe** vouch **35 No, no, no** i.e., not under the terms of service you have described **39 English name** i.e., the Black Prince, a widely known name for the eldest son of Edward III who defeated the French **39–40 fisnomy** physiognomy

LAFEW What prince is that?

CLOWN The black prince, sir, alias the prince of darkness, alias the devil.

LAFEW Hold thee, there's my purse. [*Gives money.*] I give thee not this to suggest thee from thy master thou talk'st of; serve him still.

CLOWN I am a woodland fellow, sir, that always lov'd a great fire, and the master I speak of ever keeps a good fire. But, sure, he is the prince of the world; let his nobility remain in 's court. I am for the house with the narrow gate, which I take to be too little for pomp to enter. Some that humble themselves may, but the many will be too chill and tender, and they'll be for the flow'ry way that leads to the broad gate and the great fire.

LAFEW Go thy ways, I begin to be aweary of thee; and I tell thee so before, because I would not fall out with thee. Go thy ways. Let my horses be well look'd to, without any tricks.

CLOWN If I put any tricks upon 'em, sir, they shall be jades' tricks, which are their own right by the law of nature. *Exit.*

LAFEW A shrewd knave and an unhappy.

COUNTESS So 'a is. My lord that's gone made himself much sport out of him. By his authority he remains here, which he thinks is a patent for his sauciness; and indeed he has no pace, but runs where he will.

LAFEW I like him well; 'tis not amiss. And I was about to tell you, since I heard of the good lady's death, and that my lord your son was upon his return home, I mov'd the King my master to speak in the behalf of my daughter, which, in the minority of them both, his Majesty, out of a self-gracious remembrance, did first propose. His Highness hath promis'd me to do it; and, to stop up the displeasure he hath conceiv'd against your son, there is no fitter matter. How does your ladyship like it?

COUNTESS With very much content, my lord, and I wish it happily effected.

LAFEW His Highness comes post from Marseilles, of as able body as when he number'd thirty. 'A will be here tomorrow, or I am deceiv'd by him that in such intelligence hath seldom fail'd.

COUNTESS It rejoices me, that I hope I shall see him ere I die. I have letters that my son will be here tonight. I shall beseech your lordship to remain with me till they meet together.

LAFEW Madam, I was thinking with what manners I might safely be admitted.

COUNTESS You need but plead your honorable privilege.

LAFEW Lady, of that I have made a bold charter, but I thank my God it holds yet.

Enter Clown.

CLOWN O madam, yonder's my lord your son with a patch of velvet on 's face. Whether there be a scar under 't or no, the velvet knows, but 'tis a goodly patch of velvet. His left cheek is a cheek of two pile and a half, but his right cheek is worn bare.

LAFEW A scar nobly got, or a noble scar, is a good liv'ry of honor; so belike is that.

CLOWN But it is your carbonado'd face.

LAFEW Let us go see your son, I pray you. I long to talk with the young noble soldier.

CLOWN Faith, there's a dozen of 'em, with delicate fine hats, and most courteous feathers, which bow the head and nod at every man. *Exeunt.*

ACT V • [SCENE I]

Enter Helena, Widow, and Diana, with two Attendants.

HELENA
But this exceeding posting day and night
Must wear your spirits low; we cannot help it.
But since you have made the days and nights as one
To wear your gentle limbs in my affairs,
Be bold you do so grow in my requital
As nothing can unroot you. In happy time;

Enter a Gentleman.

This man may help me to his Majesty's ear,
If he would spend his power. God save you, sir.

GENTLEMAN
And you.

HELENA
Sir, I have seen you in the court of France.

GENTLEMAN
I have been sometimes there.

HELENA
I do presume, sir, that you are not fall'n
From the report that goes upon your goodness;
And therefore, goaded with most sharp occasions,
Which lay nice manners by, I put you to
The use of your own virtues, for the which
I shall continue thankful.

GENTLEMAN What's your will?

HELENA
That it will please you
To give this poor petition to the King,
[*Shows petition.*]
And aid me with that store of power you have
To come into his presence.

45 suggest tempt **47 woodland** rustic **53 many** multitude. **chill and tender** sensitive to cold (and hence preferring the hotter place) **56 Go thy ways** get along with you **57 before** i.e., before I grow thoroughly weary **61 jades' tricks** (1) tricks played on jades or brokendown horses (2) mischievous, mean tricks **63 shrewd** sharp-tongued and witty. **unhappy** discontented **67 has no pace** observes no restraint **73 self-gracious remembrance** thoughtful recollection that came to him without prompting **80 post** posthaste **81 number'd thirty** was thirty years old **82 him** i.e., a messenger **84 that . . . shall** that I can hope to **89 admitted** i.e., allowed to stay on for that meeting **90–91 honorable privilege** privilege due your honor **92 made . . . charter** asserted my claim as far as I dare

97–98 two . . . half i.e., a thick velvet **98 worn bare** i.e., without a velvet patch **101 carbonado'd** slashed or scored across with gashes, as to broil meat (here suggesting a cut made to drain a venereal ulcer and covered with a velvet patch)

V.i. Location: Marseilles. A street.
1 posting riding in haste **4 wear** wear out **5 bold** sure. **requital** i.e., debt, thankfulness **6 happy** opportune **8 spend** expend **14 sharp occasions** urgent circumstances **15 nice** scrupulous

GENTLEMAN
The King's not here.
HELENA Not here, sir?
GENTLEMAN Not, indeed.
He hence remov'd last night, and with more haste
Than is his use.
WIDOW Lord, how we lose our pains!
HELENA
All's well that ends well yet,
Though time seem so adverse and means unfit.
I do beseech you, whither is he gone?
GENTLEMAN
Marry, as I take it, to Rossillion,
Whither I am going.
HELENA I do beseech you, sir,
Since you are like to see the King before me,
Commend the paper to his gracious hand,
[*Gives petition.*]
Which I presume shall render you no blame
But rather make you thank your pains for it.
I will come after you with what good speed
Our means will make us means.
GENTLEMAN This I'll do for you.
HELENA
And you shall find yourself to be well thank'd,
Whate'er falls more. We must to horse again.
Go, go, provide. [*Exeunt severally.*]

[SCENE II]

Enter Clown, and Parolles.

PAROLLES Good Monsieur Lavatch, give my Lord Lafew this letter. [*Offers letter.*] I have ere now, sir, been better known to you, when I have held familiarity with fresher clothes; but I am now, sir, muddied in fortune's mood, and smell somewhat strong of her strong displeasure.

CLOWN Truly, fortune's displeasure is but sluttish, if it smell so strongly as thou speak'st of. I will henceforth eat no fish of fortune's butt'ring. Prithee, allow the wind.

PAROLLES Nay, you need not to stop your nose, sir; I spake but by a metaphor.

CLOWN Indeed, sir, if your metaphor stink, I will stop my nose, or against any man's metaphor. Prithee, get thee further.

PAROLLES Pray you, sir, deliver me this paper.

CLOWN Foh! Prithee, stand away. A paper from fortune's close-stool to give to a nobleman! Look, here he comes himself.

Enter Lafew.

Here is a purr of fortune's, sir, or of fortune's cat—but not a musk-cat—that has fall'n into the unclean fishpond of her displeasure, and, as he says, is muddied withal. Pray you, sir, use the carp as you may, for he looks like a poor, decay'd, ingenious, foolish, rascally knave. I do pity his distress in my similes of comfort, and leave him to your lordship. [*Exit.*]

PAROLLES My lord, I am a man whom fortune hath cruelly scratch'd.

LAFEW And what would you have me to do? 'Tis too late to pare her nails now. Wherein have you play'd the knave with fortune that she should scratch you, who of herself is a good lady and would not have knaves thrive long under her? There's a cardecue for you. [*Gives money.*] Let the justices make you and fortune friends; I am for other business. [*Starts to leave.*]

PAROLLES I beseech your honor to hear me one single word.

LAFEW You beg a single penny more. Come, you shall ha 't; save your word.

PAROLLES My name, my good lord, is Parolles.

LAFEW You beg more than "word," then. Cox my passion! Give me your hand. How does your drum?

PAROLLES O my good lord, you were the first that found me!

LAFEW Was I, in sooth? And I was the first that lost thee.

PAROLLES It lies in you, my lord, to bring me in some grace, for you did bring me out.

LAFEW Out upon thee, knave! Dost thou put upon me at once both the office of God and the devil? One brings thee in grace and the other brings thee out. [*Trumpets sound.*] The King's coming; I know by his trumpets. Sirrah, inquire further after me. I had talk of you last night; though you are a fool and a knave, you shall eat. Go to, follow.

PAROLLES I praise God for you. [*Exeunt.*]

[SCENE III]

Flourish. Enter King, Old Lady [Countess], Lafew, the two French Lords, with Attendants.

KING
We lost a jewel of her, and our esteem
Was made much poorer by it; but your son,

24 use usual practice **35 Our . . . means** our resources will allow

V.ii. Location: Rossillion. Before the Count's palace.
9 of fortune's butt'ring i.e., prepared and served by fortune **9–10 allow the wind** let me have the windward side of you (since you have been befouled by evil-smelling fortune) **18 close-stool** privy

20 purr (The multiple pun here may include *male child, piece of dung, the purr of a cat,* and *the name given to the jack or knave in the card game "post and pair."*) **21 musk-cat** musk-deer, prized for its musk scent **23 carp** (1) a fish often bred in sewage-rich fishponds or moats (2) a chatterer **24 ingenious** stupid, lacking in genius or intellect (?) **25 similes of comfort** comforting similes **33 cardecue** quart d'écu, quarter of a French crown **34 justices** i.e., Justices of the Peace, responsible in Elizabethan England for tending to the deserving poor **41 more than "word"** i.e., many words; *Parolles* suggests a plural of the French *parole,* word **41–42 Cox my passion** i.e., by God's (Christ's) passion on the cross **44 found me** found me out **45 lost** abandoned **48 grace** favor. **out** out of favor

V.iii. Location: Rossillion. The Count's palace.
1 of in. **our esteem** my own value

As mad in folly, lack'd the sense to know
Her estimation home.

COUNTESS 'Tis past, my liege,
And I beseech your Majesty to make it
Natural rebellion, done i' th' blade of youth;
When oil and fire, too strong for reason's force,
O'erbears it and burns on.

KING My honor'd lady,
I have forgiven and forgotten all,
Though my revenges were high bent upon him,
And watch'd the time to shoot.

LAFEW This I must say—
But first I beg my pardon—the young lord
Did to his Majesty, his mother, and his lady
Offense of mighty note; but to himself
The greatest wrong of all. He lost a wife
Whose beauty did astonish the survey
Of richest eyes, whose words all ears took captive,
Whose dear perfection hearts that scorn'd to serve
Humbly call'd mistress.

KING Praising what is lost
Makes the remembrance dear. Well, call him hither;
We are reconcil'd, and the first view shall kill
All repetition. Let him not ask our pardon;
The nature of his great offense is dead,
And deeper than oblivion we do bury
Th' incensing relics of it. Let him approach,
A stranger, no offender; and inform him
So 'tis our will he should.

GENTLEMAN I shall, my liege. [*Exit.*]

KING
What says he to your daughter? Have you spoke?

LAFEW
All that he is hath reference to your Highness.

KING
Then shall we have a match. I have letters sent me
That sets him high in fame.

Enter Count Bertram.

LAFEW He looks well on 't.

KING
I am not a day of season,
For thou mayst see a sunshine and a hail
In me at once. But to the brightest beams
Distracted clouds give way; so stand thou forth,
The time is fair again.

BERTRAM My high-repented blames,
Dear sovereign, pardon to me.

KING All is whole;
Not one word more of the consumed time.
Let's take the instant by the forward top;
For we are old, and on our quick'st decrees
Th' inaudible and noiseless foot of Time
Steals ere we can effect them. You remember
The daughter of this lord?

BERTRAM
Admiringly, my liege. At first
I stuck my choice upon her, ere my heart
Durst make too bold a herald of my tongue;
Where the impression of mine eye infixing,
Contempt his scornful perspective did lend me,
Which warp'd the line of every other favor,
Scorn'd a fair color, or express'd it stol'n,
Extended or contracted all proportions
To a most hideous object. Thence it came
That she whom all men prais'd, and whom myself,
Since I have lost, have lov'd, was in mine eye
The dust that did offend it.

KING. Well excus'd.
That thou didst love her strikes some scores away
From the great compt. But love that comes too late,
Like a remorseful pardon slowly carried,
To the great sender turns a sour offense,
Crying, "That's good that's gone." Our rash faults
Make trivial price of serious things we have,
Not knowing them until we know their grave.
Oft our displeasures, to ourselves unjust,
Destroy our friends, and after weep their dust;
Our own love waking cries to see what's done,
While shameful hate sleeps out the afternoon.
Be this sweet Helen's knell, and now forget her.
Send forth your amorous token for fair Maudlin.
The main consents are had; and here we'll stay
To see our widower's second marriage-day.

COUNTESS
Which better than the first, O dear heaven, bless!
Or, ere they meet, in me, O nature, cesse!

LAFEW
Come on, my son, in whom my house's name
Must be digested, give a favor from you
To sparkle in the spirits of my daughter,
That she may quickly come. [*Bertram gives a ring.*]
By my old beard,
And ev'ry hair that's on 't, Helen, that's dead,
Was a sweet creature; such a ring as this,
The last that e'er I took her leave at court,
I saw upon her finger.

BERTRAM Hers it was not.

KING
Now, pray you, let me see it; for mine eye,
While I was speaking, oft was fasten'd to 't.
[*The ring is given to the King.*]
This ring was mine; and, when I gave it Helen,
I bade her, if her fortunes ever stood
Necessitied to help, that by this token

3–4 know . . . home appreciate her value fully **6 blade** greenness, freshness **10 high bent** i.e., as with a fully drawn bow **16 astonish the survey** dazzle the sight **17 richest** i.e., richest in experience **22 repetition** rehearsing what is past **25 relics** reminders **26 A stranger** i.e., as one whose story is unknown **29 hath reference to** defers to **32 of season** i.e., of one consistent kind of weather **35 Distracted . . . way** clouds disperse and give way **39 forward top** forelock

47 Where i.e., in my heart. **the impression . . . infixing** i.e., the image of her entering first at my eye and then fixing itself in my heart **48 perspective** an optical glass for producing distorted images **49 favor** face **50 express'd it stol'n** declared it to be counterfeit **51–52 Extended . . . object** elongated or compressed all other forms until they made a hideous sight **53 she** i.e., Helena **55 offend it** (1) give it offense (2) blur its vision **57 compt** account, reckoning **58 slowly carried** i.e., arriving too late **59 turns . . . offense** i.e., turns sour on him **62 knowing** i.e., appreciating. **know their grave** i.e., are aware of their irrevocable loss **63 displeasures** offenses **64 weep their dust** mourn their ashes **66 sleeps . . . afternoon** i.e., sleeps at ease having done its work **68 Maudlin** i.e., Magdalen, the daughter of Lafew **72 ere they meet** i.e., before the two marriages come to resemble one another in unhappiness. **cesse** cease **74 digested** assimilated. **favor** token **79 took her leave** took leave of her **85 Necessitied to** in need of

I would relieve her. Had you that craft to reave her
Of what should stead her most?

BERTRAM My gracious sovereign,
Howe'er it pleases you to take it so,
The ring was never hers.

COUNTESS Son, on my life,
I have seen her wear it, and she reckon'd it
At her life's rate.

LAFEW I am sure I saw her wear it.

BERTRAM
You are deceiv'd, my lord, she never saw it.
In Florence was it from a casement thrown me,
Wrapp'd in a paper, which contain'd the name
Of her that threw it. Noble she was, and thought
I stood engag'd; but when I had subscrib'd
To mine own fortune, and inform'd her fully
I could not answer in that course of honor
As she had made the overture, she ceas'd
In heavy satisfaction, and would never
Receive the ring again.

KING Plutus himself,
That knows the tinct and multiplying med'cine,
Hath not in nature's mystery more science
Than I have in this ring. 'Twas mine, 'twas Helen's,
Whoever gave it you. Then, if you know
That you are well acquainted with yourself,
Confess 'twas hers, and by what rough enforcement
You got it from her. She call'd the saints to surety
That she would never put it from her finger
Unless she gave it to yourself in bed,
Where you have never come, or sent it us
Upon her great disaster.

BERTRAM She never saw it.

KING
Thou speak'st it falsely, as I love mine honor,
And mak'st conjectural fears to come into me,
Which I would fain shut out. If it should prove
That thou art so inhuman—'twill not prove so,
And yet I know not—thou didst hate her deadly,
And she is dead, which nothing but to close
Her eyes myself could win me to believe,
More than to see this ring. Take him away.
[*Guards seize Bertram.*]
My fore-past proofs, howe'er the matter fall,
Shall tax my fears of little vanity,
Having vainly fear'd too little. Away with him!
We'll sift this matter further.

BERTRAM If you shall prove
This ring was ever hers, you shall as easy
Prove that I husbanded her bed in Florence,
Where yet she never was. [*Exit, guarded.*]

Enter a Gentleman.

KING
I am wrapp'd in dismal thinkings.

GENTLEMAN Gracious sovereign,
Whether I have been to blame or no, I know not.
Here's a petition from a Florentine, [*Gives petition.*]
Who hath for four or five removes come short
To tender it herself. I undertook it,
Vanquish'd thereto by the fair grace and speech
Of the poor suppliant, who by this I know
Is here attending. Her business looks in her
With an importing visage, and she told me,
In a sweet verbal brief, it did concern
Your Highness with herself.

[KING *reads*] *a letter.* "Upon his many protestations to marry me when his wife was dead, I blush to say it, he won me. Now is the Count Rossillion a widower, his vows are forfeited to me, and my honor's paid to him. He stole from Florence, taking no leave, and I follow him to his country for justice. Grant it me, O King! In you it best lies; otherwise a seducer flourishes, and a poor maid is undone. Diana Capilet"

LAFEW I will buy me a son-in-law in a fair, and toll for this. I'll none of him.

KING
The heavens have thought well on thee, Lafew,
To bring forth this discov'ry. Seek these suitors.
Go speedily and bring again the Count.
[*Exeunt some Attendants.*]
I am afeard the life of Helen, lady,
Was foully snatch'd.

COUNTESS Now, justice on the doers!

Enter Bertram [*guarded*].

KING
I wonder, sir, sith wives are monsters to you,
And that you fly them as you swear them lordship,
Yet you desire to marry.

Enter Widow [*and*] *Diana.*

What woman's that?

DIANA
I am, my lord, a wretched Florentine,
Derived from the ancient Capilet.
My suit, as I do understand, you know,
And therefore know how far I may be pitied.

WIDOW
I am her mother, sir, whose age and honor
Both suffer under this complaint we bring,
And both shall cease, without your remedy.

KING
Come hither, Count. Do you know these women?

BERTRAM
My lord, I neither can nor will deny

86 reave deprive, rob **87 stead** help **91 rate** value **96 engag'd** i.e., pledged to her; or, possibly, not pledged to another. (The F spelling, *ingag'd,* may suggest a negative prefix.) **96–97 subscrib'd . . . fortune** i.e., explained my true situation (of my marriage) **98–99 answer . . . overture** respond honorably to the proposal (of marriage) that she honorably made **100 heavy satisfaction** doleful resignation **101 Plutus** the god of wealth **102 tinct . . . med'cine** the alchemical elixir for transmuting base metals into gold **103 science** knowledge **105–106 if . . . yourself** i.e., you know the ring was hers as well as you know yourself (?) **108 to surety** to witness **112 Upon . . . disaster** on the occasion of a disaster to her **114 conjectural** suspicious **121 My fore-past proofs** the evidence I already have. **fall** turn out **122–123 Shall . . . little** will hardly censure my fears (concerning Helena) as inconsequential; indeed, I have foolishly been too little apprehensive

131 for . . . short on account of four or five shifts of residence of the court (as it moved from Marseilles to Rossillion) come too late **132 tender** offer **133 Vanquish'd** won **134 by this** by this time **135 looks** manifests itself **136 importing** urgent and full of import **137 brief** summary **142 are . . . me** i.e., are debts to which I am legally entitled **147 in a fair** i.e., where stolen and disreputable merchandise are common. (Lafew says he can do better at such a place than with Bertram.) **147–148 toll for this** i.e., put Bertram up for sale. (Merchants wishing to sell at market paid a toll or fee in order to enter their goods in a register.) **154 sith** since **155 swear them lordship** swear to be their lord and husband **158 Derived** descended

But that I know them. Do they charge me further?
DIANA
Why do you look so strange upon your wife?
BERTRAM
She's none of mine, my lord.
DIANA
If you shall marry,
You give away this hand, and that is mine; 169
You give away heaven's vows, and those are mine;
You give away myself, which is known mine;
For I by vow am so embodied yours
That she which marries you must marry me,
Either both or none.

LAFEW Your reputation comes too short for my daughter; you are no husband for her. 175

BERTRAM
My lord, this is a fond and desp'rate creature, 177
Whom sometime I have laugh'd with. Let your Highness
Lay a more noble thought upon mine honor
Than for to think that I would sink it here.
KING
Sir, for my thoughts, you have them ill to friend 181
Till your deeds gain them. Fairer prove your honor
Than in my thought it lies!
DIANA
Good my lord,
Ask him upon his oath if he does think
He had not my virginity.
KING
What say'st thou to her?
BERTRAM
She's impudent, my lord,
And was a common gamester to the camp. 187
DIANA
He does me wrong, my lord; if I were so,
He might have bought me at a common price.
Do not believe him. O, behold this ring,
[*Shows ring.*]
Whose high respect and rich validity 191
Did lack a parallel; yet for all that
He gave it to a commoner o' th' camp,
If I be one.
COUNTESS He blushes, and 'tis hit. 194
Of six preceding ancestors, that gem,
Conferr'd by testament to th' sequent issue, 196
Hath it been owed and worn. This is his wife; 197
That ring's a thousand proofs.
KING
Methought you said
You saw one here in court could witness it.
DIANA
I did, my lord, but loath am to produce
So bad an instrument. His name's Parolles.
LAFEW
I saw the man today, if man he be.
KING
Find him, and bring him hither. [*Exit an attendant.*]
BERTRAM
What of him?
He's quoted for a most perfidious slave, 204
With all the spots o' th' world tax'd and debosh'd, 205
Whose nature sickens but to speak a truth.
Am I or that or this for what he'll utter, 207
That will speak any thing?
KING
She hath that ring of yours.
BERTRAM
I think she has. Certain it is I lik'd her,
And boarded her i' th' wanton way of youth. 210
She knew her distance and did angle for me, 211
Madding my eagerness with her restraint, 212
As all impediments in fancy's course 213
Are motives of more fancy; and, in fine, 214
Her infinite cunning, with her modern grace, 215
Subdu'd me to her rate. She got the ring; 216
And I had that which any inferior might
At market-price have bought.
DIANA
I must be patient.
You that have turn'd off a first so noble wife
May justly diet me. I pray you yet— 220
Since you lack virtue, I will lose a husband—
Send for your ring, I will return it home,
And give me mine again.
BERTRAM
I have it not.
KING
What ring was yours, I pray you?
DIANA
Sir, much like the same upon your finger.
KING
Know you this ring? This ring was his of late.
DIANA
And this was it I gave him, being abed.
KING
The story then goes false, you threw it him
Out of a casement.
DIANA
I have spoke the truth.

Enter Parolles.

BERTRAM
My lord, I do confess the ring was hers.
KING
You boggle shrewdly, every feather starts you.— 231
Is this the man you speak of?
DIANA
Ay, my lord.
KING
Tell me, sirrah—but tell me true, I charge you,
Not fearing the displeasure of your master,
Which on your just proceeding I'll keep off— 235
By him and by this woman here what know you? 236

PAROLLES So please your Majesty, my master hath been an honorable gentleman. Tricks he hath had in him, which gentlemen have.

KING Come, come, to th' purpose. Did he love this woman?

PAROLLES Faith, sir, he did love her; but how?

KING How, I pray you?

PAROLLES He did love her, sir, as a gentleman loves a woman.

169 this hand i.e., Bertram's hand **175 Your** (Addressed to Bertram.) **177 fond** foolish **181 you . . . friend** they are not well disposed toward you **187 gamester** prostitute **191 validity** value **194 'tis hit** i.e., that point scored **196 sequent issue** next heir **197 owed** owned **204 quoted for** set down as **205 With . . . debosh'd** censured for being debauched with all the vices in the world

207 or . . . or either . . . or. **for** because of **210 boarded** accosted (with sexual meaning) **211 knew her distance** i.e., knew how to keep her distance, knew her value **212 Madding** making mad, exciting **213 fancy's** love's **214 motives** causes. **fine** conclusion **215 modern** commonplace **216 her rate** her terms **220 diet** restrain; provide for **231 boggle shrewdly** startle excessively. **starts** startles **235 on . . . proceeding** if you speak honestly **236 By** concerning

KING How is that?

PAROLLES He lov'd her, sir, and lov'd her not.

KING As thou art a knave, and no knave. What an equivocal companion is this!

PAROLLES I am a poor man, and at your Majesty's command.

LAFEW He's a good drum, my lord, but a naughty orator.

DIANA Do you know he promis'd me marriage?

PAROLLES Faith, I know more than I'll speak.

KING But wilt thou not speak all thou know'st?

PAROLLES Yes, so please your Majesty. I did go between them, as I said; but more than that, he lov'd her, for indeed he was mad for her, and talk'd of Satan and of Limbo and of Furies and I know not what. Yet I was in that credit with them at that time that I knew of their going to bed, and of other motions, as promising her marriage, and things which would derive me ill will to speak of; therefore I will not speak what I know.

KING Thou hast spoken all already, unless thou canst say they are married. But thou art too fine in thy evidence, therefore stand aside.
This ring, you say, was yours?

DIANA
Ay, my good lord.

KING
Where did you buy it? Or who gave it you?

DIANA
It was not given me, nor I did not buy it.

KING
Who lent it you?

DIANA
It was not lent me neither.

KING
Where did you find it, then?

DIANA
I found it not.

KING
If it were yours by none of all these ways,
How could you give it him?

DIANA
I never gave it him.

LAFEW This woman's an easy glove, my lord; she goes off and on at pleasure.

KING
This ring was mine; I gave it his first wife.

DIANA
It might be yours or hers, for aught I know.

KING
Take her away, I do not like her now.
To prison with her. And away with him.
Unless thou tell'st me where thou hadst this ring,
Thou diest within this hour.

DIANA
I'll never tell you.

KING
Take her away.

DIANA
I'll put in bail, my liege.

KING
I think thee now some common customer.

DIANA
By Jove, if ever I knew man, 'twas you.

KING
Wherefore hast thou accus'd him all this while?

DIANA
Because he's guilty, and he is not guilty.
He knows I am no maid, and he'll swear to 't;
I'll swear I am a maid, and he knows not.
Great King, I am no strumpet, by my life;
I am either maid, or else this old man's wife.
[*Pointing to Lafew.*]

KING
She does abuse our ears. To prison with her!

DIANA
Good mother, fetch my bail. Stay, royal sir.
[*Exit Widow.*]
The jeweler that owes the ring is sent for,
And he shall surety me. But for this lord,
Who hath abus'd me, as he knows himself,
Though yet he never harm'd me, here I quit him.
He knows himself my bed he hath defil'd,
And at that time he got his wife with child.
Dead though she be, she feels her young one kick.
So there's my riddle: one that's dead is quick—
And now behold the meaning.

Enter Helena and Widow. [*Diana returns Helena her ring.*]

KING
Is there no exorcist
Beguiles the truer office of mine eyes?
Is 't real that I see?

HELENA
No, my good lord,
'Tis but the shadow of a wife you see,
The name and not the thing.

BERTRAM
Both, both. O, pardon!

HELENA
O my good lord, when I was like this maid,
I found you wondrous kind. There is your ring,
And, look you, here's your letter. [*Produces letter.*]
This it says:
"When from my finger you can get this ring
And are by me with child," etc. This is done.
Will you be mine, now you are doubly won?

BERTRAM
If she, my liege, can make me know this clearly,
I'll love her dearly, ever, ever dearly.

HELENA
If it appear not plain and prove untrue,
Deadly divorce step between me and you!
O my dear mother, do I see you living?

LAFEW Mine eyes smell onions; I shall weep anon. [*To Parolles.*] Good Tom Drum, lend me a handkercher. So, I thank thee. Wait on me home, I'll make sport with thee. Let thy curtsies alone, they are scurvy ones.

KING
Let us from point to point this story know,
To make the even truth in pleasure flow.

247 lov'd her not i.e., desired her only sexually **249 companion** knave **252 drum** drummer. **naughty** worthless **263 derive** gain **266 fine** subtle **283 put in bail** make bail, i.e., produce evidence to assure my liberty **284 customer** i.e., prostitute

285 knew i.e., sexually **294 owes** owns **295 surety me** be my security **297 quit** (1) acquit (2) repay **301 quick** alive (and pregnant) **302 exorcist** one who conjures up spirits **307 like this maid** i.e., disguised like Diana **323 even** precise, plain

[*To Diana.*] If thou be'st yet a fresh uncropped
flower,
Choose thou thy husband, and I'll pay thy dower;
For I can guess that by thy honest aid
Thou kept'st a wife herself, thyself a maid.
Of that and all the progress, more and less,
Resolvedly more leisure shall express.
All yet seems well, and if it end so meet,
The bitter past, more welcome is the sweet. *Flourish.*

[EPILOGUE]

[KING, *advancing*]
The king's a beggar, now the play is done.
All is well ended, if this suit be won,
That you express content; which we will pay,
With strife to please you, day exceeding day.
Ours be your patience then, and yours our parts;
Your gentle hands lend us, and take our hearts.
Exeunt omnes.

329 Resolvedly so that all doubts are removed

Epilogue
3 express content i.e., applaud **4 strife** effort **5 Ours . . . parts** i.e., we will patiently attend, like an audience, while you undertake the active role by applauding

Measure for Measure

"A play Caled Mesur for Mesur" by "Shaxberd" was performed at court, for the new King James I, by "his Maiesties plaiers" on December 26, 1604. Probably it had been composed that same year, or in late 1603. The play dates from the very height of Shakespeare's tragic period, three years or so after *Hamlet,* contemporary with *Othello,* shortly before *King Lear* and *Macbeth*. This period includes very little comedy of any sort, and what there is differs markedly from the "festive" comedy of the 1590's. *Troilus and Cressida* (c. 1601–1602), hovering between satire and tragedy, bleakly portrays a hopeless love affair caught in the toils of a pointless and stalemated war. *All's Well that Ends Well* (c. 1601–1604) resembles *Measure for Measure* in its portrayal of an undeserving protagonist who must be deceived into marriage by an ethically ambiguous bed trick. *Measure for Measure,* the last such unfestive comedy from the tragic period, illustrates most clearly of all what critics usually mean by "problem comedy" or "problem play."

Its chief concern is not with the triumphs of love, as in the happy comedies, but with moral and social problems: "filthy vices" arising from sexual desire, and the abuses of judicial authority. Images of disease abound in this play. We see corruption in Vienna "boil and bubble Till it o'errun the stew." Angelo is for most of the play a deeply torn protagonist, abhorring his own perverse sinfulness, compulsively driven to an attempted murder in order to cover up his lust for Isabella. His soliloquies are introspective, tortured, focused on the psychological horror of an intelligent mind succumbing to criminal desire. The disguised Duke, witnessing this fall into depravity and despair, can offer Angelo's intended victims no better philosophical counsel than Christian renunciation of the world and all its vain hopes. Tragedy is averted only by providential intervention and by the harsh trickery of "Craft against vice," in which the Duke becomes involved as chief manipulator and stage manager. Of the concluding marriages, two are foisted on the bridegrooms (Angelo and Lucio) against their wills, whereas that of the Duke and Isabella jars oddly with his stoical teachings and with her previous determination to be a nun. The ending thus seems arbitrary; both justice and romantic happiness are so perilously achieved in this play that they seem inconsistent with the injustice and lechery that have prevailed until the last.

Yet the very improbability of the ending, and the sense of tragedy narrowly averted, are perhaps intentional. These features are appropriate not only for "problem" comedy but for "tragicomedy" or "comedy of forgiveness," overlapping genres toward which Shakespeare gravitated in his late romances. Angelo is, like Leontes in *The Winter's Tale* (or, earlier, like Bertram in *All's Well* or Claudio in *Much Ado about Nothing*), an erring protagonist forgiven in excess of his deserving, spared by a benign overseeing providence from destroying that which is most precious to him.

The play's title, *Measure for Measure,* introduces a paradox of human justice which this "problem" play cannot wholly resolve. How is fallible man to judge the sins of his fellow mortals and still obey Christ's injunction of the Sermon on the Mount, "Judge not that ye be not judged"? Three positions emerge from the debate: absolute justice at one extreme, mercy at the other, and equity as a middle ground. Isabella speaks for mercy, and her words ring with biblical authority. Since all men would be condemned to eternal darkness were God not merciful as well as just, should not men also be merciful? The difficulty, however, is that Vienna shows all too clearly the effects of leniency under the kindly Duke. Vice is rampant; stern measures are needed. Though he has not wished to crack the whip himself, the Duke firmly endorses "strict statutes and most biting laws, The needful bits and curbs to headstrong weeds" (I,iii). To carry out necessary reform, the Duke has chosen Lord Angelo, spokesman for absolute justice, to represent him. Angelo's position is cold but consistent. Only by a literal and impartial administering of the statutes, he maintains, can the law deter potential offenders. If the judge is found guilty, he must pay the penalty as well. One difficulty here, however, is that literal enforcement of the statute on fornication seems ironically to catch the wrong culprits. Claudio and Juliet, who are about to be married and are already joined by a "true contract" of betrothal, are sentenced to the severest limit of the law, whereas the pimps and whores of Vienna's suburbs manage at first to evade punishment entirely. Angelo's deputy, Escalus, can only shake his head in dismay at this unjust result of strict justice. Angelo has not remembered fully the terms of his commission from the Duke: he was enjoined to practice both "Mortality and mercy" in Vienna, to "enforce or qualify the laws As to your soul seem good." The attributes of a ruler, like those of God, must include "terror" but also "love" (I,i).

Escalus' compassionate and pragmatic approach to law illustrates equity, or the flexible application of the law to particular cases. Because Claudio is only technically guilty (though still guilty), Escalus would pronounce for him a light sentence. Pompey and Mistress Overdone, on the other hand, require vigorous and unceasing prosecution.

The problem of policing vice is compounded by the law's inefficiency as well as by man's own bestial nature, which will never be wholly tamed. Constable Elbow, like Dogberry in *Much Ado,* is a pompous user of malapropisms, less clever by far than the criminals he would arrest. His evidence against Pompey is so absurdly circumstantial that Escalus is first obliged to let off this engaging pimp with a stern warning. Yet Escalus patiently and tenaciously attends to such proceedings, unlike Angelo, whose interest in the law is too theoretical. Escalus deals with day-to-day problems effectively. He orders reforms of the system by which constables are selected, instructs Elbow in the rudiments of his office, and so proceeds ultimately to an effective arrest. Vice is not eliminated; as Pompey defiantly points out, unless someone plans to "geld and splay all the youth of the city," they "will to 't then" (II,i). Still, vice is held in check. Law can shape the outer man and hope for some inner reform. Even Pompey is taught a trade, albeit a grisly one, as an apprentice hangman. The law must use both "correction" and "instruction."

The solutions arrived at in the comic subplot do not fit the case of Angelo, for he is powerful enough to be above the Viennese law. Indeed, he tries finally to brazen it out, pitting his authority against that of the seemingly friendless Isabella, much like the biblical Elders when justly accused of immorality by the innocent Susannah. Society is on Angelo's side—even the well-meaning Escalus; only providence can rescue the defenseless. The Duke of Vienna, hovering in the background and seeing all that happens, intervenes just at those points when tragedy threatens to become irreversible. Moreover, the Duke is testing those he observes. As he says to Friar Thomas, explaining why he has delegated his power to Angelo: "Hence shall we see, If power change purpose, what our seemers be" (I,iii). The Duke obviously expects Angelo to fall. Indeed, he has known all along how Angelo has dishonorably repudiated his solemn contract to Mariana when her marriage dowry disappeared at sea (III,i). Like an all-seeing deity who keeps a reckoning of men's good and evil deeds, the Duke has found out Angelo's great weakness. As Angelo confesses, "I perceive your grace, like pow'r divine, Hath look'd upon my passes" (V,i). Paradoxically, however, this seemingly tragic story of temptation and fall yields precious benefits of remorse and humility. Angelo is rescued from his self-made nightmare of seduction, murder, and tyranny. Knowing now that he is prone like other men to fleshly weakness, he knows also that he needs spiritual assistance and that as judge he ought to use mercy. Seen in restrospect, his panic, despair, and humiliation are curative.

The disguised Duke tests the other characters as well, intentionally misleading them to expect the worst in order to try their resolve. On a comic level, he exposes the amiable but loose-tongued Lucio as a slanderer against the Duke himself, and devises for Lucio a suitably satirical exposure and witty punishment. More seriously, as confessor to Juliet he assures her that her beloved Claudio must die on the morrow. As she ought, she penitentially accepts "shame with joy," and so is cleansed (II,iii). To Claudio, the Duke offers the counsel of Christian renunciation. In a poignantly melancholy reflection on the vanity of human striving, the Duke characterizes life as a breath, a dreamlike "after-dinner's sleep," a fever of inconstancy in which timorous man longs fretfully for what he does not have and spurns those things he has (III,i). Claudio responds as he ought, resolving to "find life" by "seeking death." He achieves this calm, however, in the face of certain execution; ironically, what he must then learn to overmaster is the desperate hope of living by means of his sister's dishonor. Claudio is broken by this test, and perversely begs for a few years of guilty life at the cost of eternal shame for himself and Isabella. The searing encounter between Claudio and Isabella puts her to the test as well, and her response seems hysterical and no doubt prudish to modern audiences. She has much to learn about the complexities of human behavior. Although she is sincere in protesting that she would lay down her life for her brother, and is correct in the play's terms to prefer virtue to mere existence, her tone is too strident. Like other major characters, she must be humbled before she can rise. She and Claudio must heed the Duke's essential admonition: "Do not satisfy your resolution with hopes that are fallible." Only then, paradoxically, can Isabella and Claudio go on to achieve earthly happiness.

In her final testing, Isabella shows greatness of spirit. Here Shakespeare significantly alters his chief source, George Whetstone's *Promos and Cassandra* (1578), and the other versions of the story which Shakespeare probably also consulted—Cinthio's *Hecatommithi* and Whetstone's *Heptameron of Civill Discourses.* In all these versions, the character corresponding to Angelo does actually ravish the heroine, and in Cinthio he also murders her brother. Shakespeare, by withholding these irreversible acts, not only gives to Angelo a technical innocence, but allows the Duke as *deus ex machina* to practice virtuous deception on Isabella one more time. Can she forgive the supposed murderer of her brother? Her affirmative answer confutes the Old Testament ethic of "An Angelo for Claudio, death for death" whereby "Like doth quit like, and Measure still for Measure" (V,i). Although Angelo concedes that he deserves to die for what he intended, the forfeit need not be paid so long as humanity can reveal itself capable of Isabella's godlike mercy.

With its apparently unsuitable marriages and its improbable plotting, *Measure for Measure* does end by dealing directly with the problems of human nature confronted in the earlier scenes. The bed trick may seem a legalistic and contrived way to bring Angelo to terms with his own carnality, but it is instructive, not only to him but to Isabella; she, like Angelo, must learn to accept the realities of the human condition. By helping Mariana to achieve a legitimate desire to couple and marry, Isabella sees into her own need. Her begging for Angelo's life is not merely an act of forgiveness to an enemy; it is a gift of continued marriage to Mariana. This realization helps to prepare Isabella herself for a marriage that, although dramatically surprising on stage (and even rejected by her in some modern productions), is clearly intended to demonstrate her having given up the cloistered life for all that marriage signifies. *Measure for Measure* is thus essentially comic (unlike *Troilus and Cressida*), despite its harrowing scenes of conflict and its awareness of vice everywhere in man. The play celebrates the *felix culpa* of human nature, the fall from grace that is an integral part of man's rise to happiness and self knowledge. Throughout, in the play's finest scenes, poignancy is tempered by a wit and humor that are ultimately gracious. The formal and substantive emphasis on marriage stresses not just the benefits of remorse and humility but also the real possibility of psychic and spiritual growth: Isabella can acknowledge that she is a woman, Angelo can be genuinely freed from repression, and Claudio can value life more intensely because he has confronted death. All these recognitions affirm the acceptance and proper use of man's physical nature, and yet they derive from charity and forgiveness. Man can learn, however slowly and painfully, that the talents entrusted to him by providence are to be used wisely. (See Arthur C. Kirsch, "The Integrity of Measure for Measure," *Shakespeare Survey*, 1975.)

Measure for Measure

The Names of All the Actors

VINCENTIO, *the Duke.*
ANGELO, *the Deputy.*
ESCALUS, *an ancient Lord.*
CLAUDIO, *a young gentleman.*
LUCIO, *a fantastic.*
Two other like GENTLEMEN.
PROVOST.
THOMAS, PETER, } *two friars.*
[A JUSTICE.]
[VARRIUS.]
ELBOW, *a simple constable.*
FROTH, *a foolish gentleman.*
CLOWN [POMPEY, *a servant to Mistress Overdone*].
ABHORSON, *an executioner.*
BARNARDINE, *a dissolute prisoner.*

ISABELLA, *sister to Claudio.*
MARIANA, *betrothed to Angelo.*
JULIET, *beloved of Claudio.*
FRANCISCA, *a nun.*
MISTRESS OVERDONE, *a bawd.*

[LORDS, OFFICERS, CITIZENS, BOY, *and* ATTENDANTS.]

THE SCENE: *Vienna.*

ACT I • SCENE I

Enter Duke, Escalus, Lords, [and Attendants].

DUKE
Escalus.
ESCALUS
My lord.
DUKE
Of government the properties to unfold
Would seem in me t' affect speech and discourse,
Since I am put to know that your own science
Exceeds, in that, the lists of all advice
My strength can give you. Then no more remains

Names of all the Actors. **fantastic** one given to dandified dress (?)

I.i. Location: Vienna. The Duke's Palace.

3 Of . . . unfold to explain the qualities needed in governing well **4 seem . . . discourse** i.e., make me seem enamored of the sound of my own voice **5 put to know** obliged to admit. **science** knowledge **6 that** i.e., *properties of government* (l. 3). **lists** limits

But that to your sufficiency 8
. . . . as your worth is able, 9
And let them work. The nature of our people,
Our city's institutions, and the terms 11
For common justice, y' are as pregnant in
As art and practice hath enriched any
That we remember. There is our commission,
[*Gives paper.*]
From which we would not have you warp. Call hither,
I say, bid come before us Angelo. [*Exit an Attendant.*]
What figure of us think you he will bear? 17
For you must know, we have with special soul 18
Elected him our absence to supply,
Lent him our terror, dress'd him with our love,
And given his deputation all the organs 21
Of our own pow'r. What think you of it?

ESCALUS
If any in Vienna be of worth
To undergo such ample grace and honor, 24
It is Lord Angelo.

Enter Angelo.

DUKE Look where he comes.

ANGELO
Always obedient to your Grace's will,
I come to know your pleasure.

DUKE Angelo,
There is a kind of character in thy life, 28
That to th' observer doth thy history
Fully unfold. Thyself and thy belongings 30
Are not thine own so proper as to waste 31
Thyself upon thy virtues, they on thee.
Heaven doth with us as we with torches do,
Not light them for themselves; for if our virtues
Did not go forth of us, 'twere all alike
As if we had them not. Spirits are not finely touch'd 36
But to fine issues, nor Nature never lends 37
The smallest scruple of her excellence
But, like a thrifty goddess, she determines 39
Herself the glory of a creditor, 40
Both thanks and use. But I do bend my speech 41
To one that can my part in him advertise. 42
Hold therefore, Angelo:
In our remove be thou at full ourself. 44
Mortality and mercy in Vienna 45
Live in thy tongue and heart. Old Escalus,
Though first in question, is thy secondary. 47
Take thy commission. [*Gives paper.*]

ANGELO Now, good my lord,
Let there be some more test made of my mettle 49
Before so noble and so great a figure
Be stamp'd upon it.

DUKE No more evasion.
We have with a leaven'd and prepared choice 52
Proceeded to you; therefore take your honors.
Our haste from hence is of so quick condition 54
That it prefers itself, and leaves unquestion'd 55
Matters of needful value. We shall write to you,
As time and our concernings shall importune, 57
How it goes with us, and do look to know 58
What doth befall you here. So, fare you well.
To th' hopeful execution do I leave you 60
Of your commissions.

ANGELO Yet give leave, my lord,
That we may bring you something on the way. 62

DUKE
My haste may not admit it;
Nor need you, on mine honor, have to do
With any scruple. Your scope is as mine own, 65
So to enforce or qualify the laws
As to your soul seems good. Give me your hand.
I'll privily away. I love the people,
But do not like to stage me to their eyes; 69
Though it do well, I do not relish well
Their loud applause and aves vehement, 71
Nor do I think the man of safe discretion 72
That does affect it. Once more, fare you well. 73

ANGELO
The heavens give safety to your purposes!

ESCALUS
Lead forth and bring you back in happiness!

DUKE
I thank you. Fare you well. *Exit.*

ESCALUS
I shall desire you, sir, to give me leave
To have free speech with you; and it concerns me
To look into the bottom of my place. 79
A pow'r I have, but of what strength and nature
I am not yet instructed.

ANGELO
'Tis so with me. Let us withdraw together,
And we may soon our satisfaction have
Touching that point.

ESCALUS I'll wait upon your honor.
Exeunt.

SCENE II

Enter Lucio and two other Gentlemen.

LUCIO If the Duke with the other dukes come not to
composition with the King of Hungary, why then all 2
the dukes fall upon the King.

8–9 But . . . able (The passage appears in F as a single line. Several attempts at emendation have been made, but the most plausible explanation is that something has been deleted or inadvertently omitted.) **11 terms** terms of court; or, methods of procedure **17 figure** representation **18 special soul** all the powers of the mind; whole heart **21 his deputation** him as deputy. **organs** instruments **24 undergo** bear the weight of **28 character** charactery, written sign **30 belongings** attributes, endowments **31 proper** exclusively **36 touch'd** endowed **37 issues** purposes **39 determines** assumes **40 Herself** for herself. **glory** privileges **41 use** interest **42 my . . . advertise** instruct that part of me now vested in him, i.e., knows more already than I know **44 remove** absence. **at full** in every respect. **ourself** i.e., myself. (The royal plural.) **45 Mortality** the full rigor of the law, the death sentence **47 first in question** senior and first appointed **49 mettle** temper, quality (with play on *metal,* a common variant spelling)

52 leaven'd i.e., carefully considered (just as yeast leavens dough) **54–55 Our . . . itself** the cause for my hasty departure is so urgent *(quick)* that it takes precedence over all other matters **55 unquestion'd** not yet considered **57 importune** urge **58 look to know** expect to be informed **60 hopeful execution** (A transferred modifier; i.e., I hopefully leave you.) **62 bring you something** accompany you for a short distance **65 scruple** misgiving. (Literally, a small weight.) **69 stage me** make a show of myself **71 aves** hails of acclamation **72 safe** sound **73 affect** desire, court **79 the bottom of my place** the extent of my commission and authority

I.ii. Location: A street.
2 composition agreement

FIRST GENTLEMAN Heaven grant us its peace, but not the King of Hungary's!

SECOND GENTLEMAN Amen.

LUCIO Thou conclud'st like the sanctimonious pirate, that went to sea with the Ten Commandments, but scrap'd one out of the table.

SECOND GENTLEMAN "Thou shalt not steal"?

LUCIO Ay, that he raz'd.

FIRST GENTLEMAN Why, 'twas a commandment to command the captain and all the rest from their functions; they put forth to steal. There's not a soldier of us all that, in the thanksgiving before meat, do relish the petition well that prays for peace.

SECOND GENTLEMAN I never heard any soldier dislike it.

LUCIO I believe thee; for I think thou never wast where grace was said.

SECOND GENTLEMAN No? A dozen times at least.

FIRST GENTLEMAN What, in meter?

LUCIO In any proportion or in any language.

FIRST GENTLEMAN I think, or in any religion.

LUCIO Ay, why not? Grace is grace, despite of all controversy; as, for example, thou thyself art a wicked villain, despite of all grace.

FIRST GENTLEMAN Well, there went but a pair of shears between us.

LUCIO I grant; as there may between the lists and the velvet. Thou art the list.

FIRST GENTLEMAN And thou the velvet. Thou art good velvet; thou 'rt a three-pil'd piece, I warrant thee. I had as lief be a list of an English kersey as be pil'd, as thou art pil'd, for a French velvet. Do I speak feelingly now?

LUCIO I think thou dost; and indeed with most painful feeling of thy speech. I will, out of thine own confession, learn to begin thy health; but, whilst I live, forget to drink after thee.

FIRST GENTLEMAN I think I have done myself wrong, have I not?

SECOND GENTLEMAN Yes, that thou hast, whether thou art tainted or free.

Enter Bawd [*Mistress Overdone*].

LUCIO Behold, behold, where Madam Mitigation comes! I have purchas'd as many diseases under her roof as come to—

SECOND GENTLEMAN To what, I pray?

LUCIO Judge.

SECOND GENTLEMAN To three thousand dolors a year.

FIRST GENTLEMAN Ay, and more.

LUCIO A French crown more.

FIRST GENTLEMAN Thou art always figuring diseases in me; but thou art full of error, I am sound.

LUCIO Nay, not as one would say, healthy; but so sound as things that are hollow. Thy bones are hollow; impiety has made a feast of thee.

FIRST GENTLEMAN [*To the Bawd*] How now, which of your hips has the most profound sciatica?

MISTRESS OVERDONE Well, well; there's one yonder arrested and carried to prison was worth five thousand of you all.

SECOND GENTLEMAN Who's that, I pray thee?

MISTRESS OVERDONE Marry, sir, that's Claudio, Signior Claudio.

FIRST GENTLEMAN Claudio to prison? 'Tis not so.

MISTRESS OVERDONE Nay, but I know 'tis so. I saw him arrested, saw him carried away; and, which is more, within these three days his head to be chopp'd off.

LUCIO But, after all this fooling, I would not have it so. Art thou sure of this?

MISTRESS OVERDONE I am too sure of it; and it is for getting Madam Julietta with child.

LUCIO Believe me, this may be. He promis'd to meet me two hours since, and he was ever precise in promise-keeping.

SECOND GENTLEMAN Besides, you know, it draws something near to the speech we had to such a purpose.

FIRST GENTLEMAN But most of all agreeing with the proclamation.

LUCIO Away! Let's go learn the truth of it.

Exit [*Lucio with the Gentlemen*].

MISTRESS OVERDONE Thus, what with the war, what with the sweat, what with the gallows, and what with poverty, I am custom-shrunk.

Enter Clown [*Pompey*].

How now, what's the news with you?

POMPEY Yonder man is carried to prison.

MISTRESS OVERDONE Well, what has he done?

POMPEY A woman.

MISTRESS OVERDONE But what's his offense?

POMPEY Groping for trouts in a peculiar river.

MISTRESS OVERDONE What, is there a maid with child by him?

POMPEY No, but there's a woman with maid by him. You have not heard of the proclamation, have you?

MISTRESS OVERDONE What proclamation, man?

POMPEY All houses in the suburbs of Vienna must be pluck'd down.

MISTRESS OVERDONE And what shall become of those in the city?

POMPEY They shall stand for seed. They had gone down too, but that a wise burgher put in for them.

MISTRESS OVERDONE But shall all our houses of resort in the suburbs be pull'd down?

POMPEY To the ground, mistress.

9 table tablet **11 raz'd** erased, scraped out **22 proportion** form **24 Grace is grace** (Refers to the Catholic–Protestant *controversy,* ll. 24–25, as to whether man can be saved by works or by grace alone; with punning on *grace* as *thanks for a meal,* l. 19, and *gracefulness* or *becomingness,* l. 26.) **27–28 there . . . between us** i.e., we're cut from the same cloth **29 lists** selvages, edges of a woven fabric **32 three-pil'd** having a threefold pile or nap **33 kersey** a coarse woolen fabric. **be pil'd** (1) have a nap (2) be pilled or peeled, i.e., hairless, bald, as a result of venereal disease (known as the French disease; see *French velvet* in the next line and *French crown,* l. 50) **34 feelingly** to the purpose. (But Lucio's reply quibbles on *painfully,* meaning the Gentleman's mouth is affected by the French disease; hence Lucio will not drink from the same cup after him.) **37 begin thy health** begin drinking to your health **37–38 forget . . . thee** take care not to drink from your cup **39 done myself wrong** i.e., asked for that **42 tainted** infected **43 Mitigation** (So called because her function is to relieve desire.) **48 dolors** (quibbling on *dollars;* spelled *Dollours* in F) **50 French crown** (1) gold coin (2) bald head incurred through syphilis, the French disease

54 sound resounding (with hollow bones caused by syphilis) **82 sweat** sweating sickness; a form of the plague **83 custom-shrunk** having fewer customers **89 peculiar** privately owned (with bawdy suggestion) **95 houses** i.e., brothels. **suburbs** (Location of the brothels in Shakespeare's London.) **99 for seed** to preserve the species (with ribald pun) **100 put . . . them** interceded on their behalf

MISTRESS OVERDONE Why, here's a change indeed in the commonwealth! What shall become of me?

POMPEY Come; fear not you. Good counselors lack no clients. Though you change your place, you need not change your trade; I'll be your tapster still. Courage! There will be pity taken on you. You that have worn your eyes almost out in the service, you will be consider'd.

MISTRESS OVERDONE What's to do here, Thomas tapster? Let's withdraw.

POMPEY Here comes Signior Claudio, led by the Provost to prison; and there's Madam Juliet. *Exeunt.*

Enter Provost, Claudio, Juliet, Officers; Lucio and two Gentlemen [*follow*].

CLAUDIO
Fellow, why dost thou show me thus to th' world?
Bear me to prison, where I am committed.

PROVOST
I do it not in evil disposition,
But from Lord Angelo by special charge.

CLAUDIO
Thus can the demigod Authority
Make us pay down for our offense by weight
The words of heaven; on whom it will, it will;
On whom it will not, so; yet still 'tis just.

LUCIO Why, how now, Claudio? Whence comes this restraint?

CLAUDIO
From too much liberty, my Lucio, liberty.
As surfeit is the father of much fast,
So every scope by the immoderate use
Turns to restraint. Our natures do pursue,
Like rats that ravin down their proper bane,
A thirsty evil, and when we drink we die.

LUCIO If I could speak so wisely under an arrest, I would send for certain of my creditors. And yet, to say the truth, I had as lief have the foppery of freedom as the morality of imprisonment. What's thy offense, Claudio?

CLAUDIO
What but to speak of would offend again.

LUCIO What, is 't murder?

CLAUDIO
No.

LUCIO Lechery?

CLAUDIO
Call it so.

PROVOST Away, sir, you must go.

CLAUDIO
One word, good friend. Lucio, a word with you.

LUCIO A hundred, if they'll do you any good. Is lechery so look'd after?

CLAUDIO
Thus stands it with me: upon a true contract
I got possession of Julietta's bed.
You know the lady; she is fast my wife,
Save that we do the denunciation lack
Of outward order. This we came not to,
Only for propagation of a dow'r
Remaining in the coffer of her friends,
From whom we thought it meet to hide our love
Till time had made them for us. But it chances
The stealth of our most mutual entertainment
With character too gross is writ on Juliet.

LUCIO With child, perhaps?

CLAUDIO
Unhappily, even so.
And the new deputy now for the Duke—
Whether it be the fault and glimpse of newness,
Or whether that the body public be
A horse whereon the governor doth ride,
Who, newly in the seat, that it may know
He can command, lets it straight feel the spur;
Whether the tyranny be in his place,
Or in his eminence that fills it up,
I stagger in—but this new governor
Awakes me all the enrolled penalties
Which have, like unscour'd armor, hung by th' wall
So long that nineteen zodiacs have gone round
And none of them been worn; and, for a name,
Now puts the drowsy and neglected act
Freshly on me. 'Tis surely for a name.

LUCIO I warrant it is, and thy head stands so tickle on thy shoulders that a milkmaid, if she be in love, may sigh it off. Send after the Duke and appeal to him.

CLAUDIO
I have done so, but he's not to be found.
I prithee, Lucio, do me this kind service:
This day my sister should the cloister enter
And there receive her approbation.
Acquaint her with the danger of my state;
Implore her, in my voice, that she make friends
To the strict deputy; bid herself assay him.
I have great hope in that, for in her youth
There is a prone and speechless dialect,
Such as move men; beside, she hath prosperous art
When she will play with reason and discourse,
And well she can persuade.

LUCIO I pray she may, as well for the encouragement of the like, which else would stand under grievous imposition, as for the enjoying of thy life, who I would be sorry should be thus foolishly lost at a game of tick-tack. I'll to her.

CLAUDIO
I thank you, good friend Lucio.

LUCIO Within two hours.

115 s.d. Provost officer charged with apprehension, custody, and punishment of offenders **121–123 pay . . . so** pay the exact amount due for our offense, thus confirming the biblical observation (Romans 9:15-18): ". . . Therefore hath he (God) mercy on whom he will have mercy, and whom he will he hardeneth" **128 scope** freedom **130 ravin . . . bane** greedily devour what is poisonous to them **133 creditors** (who would arrest me for debt) **134 foppery** foolishness **144 so look'd after** taken so seriously **145 true contract** i.e., in the presence of witnesses

147 fast my wife i.e., firmly bound by precontract and hence almost married **148 denunciation** formal declaration **150 propagation** increase, begetting **151 friends** relatives **153 made . . . us** disposed them in our favor **155 character too gross** letters too large **159 the fault . . . newness** imperfection accompanying the sudden and unaccustomed brightness or flash of novelty **163 straight** at once **164 in his place** inherent in the office **165 his eminence** the eminence of him **166 I stagger in** I am uncertain **167 Awakes me** i.e., awakes. (*Me* is the ethical dative.) **169 zodiacs** i.e., years **170 for a name** for reputation's sake **171 puts** i.e., like a rusty suit of armor **173 tickle** uncertain, unstable **179 approbation** novitiate **184 prone** eager. **dialect** language **185 prosperous art** skill or ability to gain favorable results **186 play with** use **189–190 imposition** accusation **191–192 tick-tack** a form of backgammon in which pegs were driven into holes (here applied bawdily)

CLAUDIO
Come, officer, away! *Exeunt.*

SCENE [III]

Enter Duke and Friar Thomas.

DUKE
No, holy father, throw away that thought;
Believe not that the dribbling dart of love
Can pierce a complete bosom. Why I desire thee
To give me secret harbor hath a purpose
More grave and wrinkled than the aims and ends
Of burning youth.
FRIAR THOMAS May your Grace speak of it?
DUKE
My holy sir, none better knows than you
How I have ever lov'd the life removed,
And held in idle price to haunt assemblies
Where youth and cost witless bravery keeps.
I have deliver'd to Lord Angelo,
A man of stricture and firm abstinence,
My absolute power and place here in Vienna,
And he supposes me travel'd to Poland;
For so I have strew'd it in the common ear,
And so it is receiv'd. Now, pious sir,
You will demand of me why I do this?
FRIAR THOMAS
Gladly, my lord.
DUKE
We have strict statutes and most biting laws,
The needful bits and curbs to headstrong weeds,
Which for this fourteen years we have let slip,
Even like an o'ergrown lion in a cave
That goes not out to prey. Now, as fond fathers,
Having bound up the threat'ning twigs of birch,
Only to stick it in their children's sight
For terror, not to use, in time the rod
Becomes more mock'd than fear'd; so our decrees,
Dead to infliction, to themselves are dead,
And liberty plucks justice by the nose;
The baby beats the nurse, and quite athwart
Goes all decorum.
FRIAR THOMAS It rested in your Grace
To unloose this tied-up justice when you pleas'd;
And it in you more dreadful would have seem'd
Than in Lord Angelo.
DUKE I do fear, too dreadful.
Sith 'twas my fault to give the people scope,
'Twould be my tyranny to strike and gall them
For what I bid them do; for we bid this be done
When evil deeds have their permissive pass
And not the punishment. Therefore indeed, my father,
I have on Angelo impos'd the office,
Who may, in th' ambush of my name, strike home,
And yet my nature never in the fight
To do in slander. And to behold his sway
I will, as 'twere a brother of your order,
Visit both prince and people. Therefore, I prithee,
Supply me with the habit, and instruct me
How I may formally in person bear
Like a true friar. Moe reasons for this action
At our more leisure shall I render you.
Only, this one: Lord Angelo is precise;
Stands at a guard with envy; scarce confesses
That his blood flows, or that his appetite
Is more to bread than stone. Hence shall we see,
If power change purpose, what our seemers be.
Exeunt.

SCENE [IV]

Enter Isabella and Francisca, a Nun.

ISABELLA
And have you nuns no farther privileges?
FRANCISCA
Are not these large enough?
ISABELLA
Yes, truly. I speak not as desiring more,
But rather wishing a more strict restraint
Upon the sisterhood, the votarists of Saint Clare.
LUCIO *(Within)*
Ho! Peace be in this place!
ISABELLA Who's that which calls?
FRANCISCA
It is a man's voice. Gentle Isabella,
Turn you the key, and know his business of him.
You may, I may not; you are yet unsworn.
When you have vow'd; you must not speak with men
But in the presence of the prioress;
Then, if you speak, you must not show your face,
Or, if you show your face, you must not speak.
He calls again. I pray you, answer him. *[Exit.]*
ISABELLA
Peace and prosperity! Who is 't that calls?

[She opens the door. Enter Lucio.]

LUCIO
Hail, virgin, if you be, as those cheek-roses

I.iii. Location: A friary.
2 dribbling falling short or wide of the mark **3 complete** perfect, whole, strong **9 idle** unprofitable **10 cost** costly expenditure. **witless . . . keeps** maintain a foolish display **12 stricture** strictness **20 weeds** i.e., lawless and uncontrolled impulses. (But often emended to *jades, steeds, wills,* etc.) **21 fourteen** (Claudio mentions nineteen years at I.ii.169; probably the compositor confused *xiv* and *xix*.) **23 fond** doting **28 Dead to infliction** dead in that they are not executed **29 liberty** license **35 Sith** since

37 we . . . done i.e., we virtually order a crime to be committed **38 pass** sanction **41 in th' ambush** under cover **42 nature** i.e., true nature (as distinguished from name or appearance) **43 do in slander** put in disrepute **47 bear** i.e., bear myself **48 Moe** more **49 more** greater **50 precise** strict, puritanical **51 at . . . envy** in a defensive posture against malice **52–53 his appetite . . . stone** i.e., he has any normal human appetites

I.iv. Location: A nunnery.

Proclaim you are no less. Can you so stead me 17
As bring me to the sight of Isabella,
A novice of this place, and the fair sister
To her unhappy brother Claudio?

ISABELLA
Why "her unhappy brother"? Let me ask,
The rather for I now must make you know
I am that Isabella and his sister.

LUCIO
Gentle and fair, your brother kindly greets you.
Not to be weary with you, he's in prison. 25

ISABELLA
Woe me! For what?

LUCIO
For that which, if myself might be his judge,
He should receive his punishment in thanks:
He hath got his friend with child.

ISABELLA
Sir, make me not your story.

LUCIO 'Tis true. 30
I would not—though 'tis my familiar sin
With maids to seem the lapwing, and to jest, 32
Tongue far from heart—play with all virgins so.
I hold you as a thing enskied and sainted,
By your renouncement an immortal spirit,
And to be talk'd with in sincerity,
As with a saint.

ISABELLA
You do blaspheme the good in mocking me.

LUCIO
Do not believe it. Fewness and truth, 'tis thus: 39
Your brother and his lover have embrac'd.
As those that feed grow full, as blossoming time
That from the seedness the bare fallow brings 42
To teeming foison, even so her plenteous womb 43
Expresseth his full tilth and husbandry. 44

ISABELLA
Some one with child by him? My cousin Juliet?

LUCIO
Is she your cousin?

ISABELLA
Adoptedly, as school-maids change their names 47
By vain though apt affection.

LUCIO She it is. 48

ISABELLA
O, let him marry her.

LUCIO This is the point.
The Duke is very strangely gone from hence;
Bore many gentlemen, myself being one, 51
In hand and hope of action; but we do learn 52
By those that know the very nerves of state,
His givings-out were of an infinite distance
From his true-meant design. Upon his place,
And with full line of his authority,
Governs Lord Angelo, a man whose blood
Is very snow-broth; one who never feels
The wanton stings and motions of the sense, 59
But doth rebate and blunt his natural edge 60
With profits of the mind, study, and fast.
He—to give fear to use and liberty, 62
Which have for long run by the hideous law,
As mice by lions—hath pick'd out an act,
Under whose heavy sense your brother's life
Falls into forfeit. He arrests him on it,
And follows close the rigor of the statute
To make him an example. All hope is gone,
Unless you have the grace by your fair prayer
To soften Angelo. And that's my pith of business
'Twixt you and your poor brother.

ISABELLA Doth he so
Seek his life?

LUCIO H'as censur'd him already, 72
And, as I hear, the Provost hath a warrant
For 's execution.

ISABELLA Alas, what poor
Ability 's in me to do him good?

LUCIO
Assay the pow'r you have.

ISABELLA
My power? Alas, I doubt—

LUCIO Our doubts are traitors,
And makes us lose the good we oft might win,
By fearing to attempt. Go to Lord Angelo,
And let him learn to know, when maidens sue,
Men give like gods; but when they weep and kneel,
All their petitions are as freely theirs 82
As they themselves would owe them. 83

ISABELLA
I'll see what I can do.

LUCIO
But speedily.

ISABELLA I will about it straight,
No longer staying but to give the Mother
Notice of my affair. I humbly thank you.
Commend me to my brother. Soon at night
I'll send him certain word of my success. 89

LUCIO
I take my leave of you.

ISABELLA Good sir, adieu.
Exeunt [severally].

ACT II • SCENE I

Enter Angelo, Escalus, and Servants, [a] Justice.

ANGELO
We must not make a scarecrow of the law,
Setting it up to fear the birds of prey, 2

17 stead help **25 weary** wearisome **30 story** subject for mirth **32 lapwing** peewit or plover (with reference to its habit of running away from its nest in order to draw away enemies from its young) **39 Fewness and truth** in few words and truly **42 seedness** sowing **43 foison** plentiful harvest **44 his** its. **tilth** tillage **47 change** exchange **48 vain though apt** foolish though natural **51–52 Bore . . . action** i.e., misleadingly kept us in expectation of some military action

59 motions promptings **60 rebate** dull, abate. **his** its. **edge** sharpness of desire **62 use and liberty** habitual licentiousness **72 H'as censur'd** he has passed sentence on **82 their petitions** i.e., the things the maidens ask for **83 As** as if. **they** i.e., the maidens. **owe** possess **89 my success** how I have succeeded

II.i. Location: A courtroom.
2 fear frighten

And let it keep one shape, till custom make it
Their perch and not their terror.

ESCALUS Ay, but yet
Let us be keen and rather cut a little,
Than fall and bruise to death. Alas, this gentleman, 6
Whom I would save, had a most noble father!
Let but your honor know, 8
Whom I believe to be most strait in virtue,
That, in the working of your own affections, 10
Had time coher'd with place, or place with wishing,
Or that the resolute acting of your blood 12
Could have attain'd th' effect of your own purpose,
Whether you had not sometime in your life
Err'd in this point which now you censure him,
And pull'd the law upon you.

ANGELO
'Tis one thing to be tempted, Escalus,
Another thing to fall. I not deny
The jury, passing on the prisoner's life,
May in the sworn twelve have a thief or two
Guiltier than him they try. What's open made to
justice,
That justice seizes. What knows the laws 22
That thieves do pass on thieves? 'Tis very pregnant, 23
The jewel that we find, we stoop and take 't
Because we see it; but what we do not see
We tread upon, and never think of it.
You may not so extenuate his offense
For I have had such faults; but rather tell me, 28
When I, that censure him, do so offend,
Let mine own judgment pattern out my death, 30
And nothing come in partial. Sir, he must die. 31

Enter Provost.

ESCALUS
Be it as your wisdom will.

ANGELO Where is the Provost?

PROVOST
Here, if it like your honor.

ANGELO See that Claudio 33
Be executed by nine tomorrow morning.
Bring him his confessor, let him be prepar'd,
For that's the utmost of his pilgrimage. 36
[*Exit Provost.*]

ESCALUS
Well, heaven forgive him, and forgive us all!
Some rise by sin, and some by virtue fall;
Some run from breaks of ice and answer none, 39
And some condemned for a fault alone.

Enter Elbow, Froth, Clown [Pompey], Officers.

ELBOW Come, bring them away. If these be good peo-
ple in a commonweal that do nothing but use their 42
abuses in common houses, I know no law. Bring them 43
away.

ANGELO How now, sir, what's your name? And what's
the matter?

ELBOW If it please your honor, I am the poor Duke's 47
constable, and my name is Elbow. I do lean upon jus-
tice, sir, and do bring in here before your good honor
two notorious benefactors.

ANGELO Benefactors? Well, what benefactors are they?
Are they not malefactors?

ELBOW If it please your honor, I know not well what
they are; but precise villains they are, that I am sure
of, and void of all profanation in the world that good 55
Christians ought to have.

ESCALUS [*Aside to Angelo*] This comes off well. Here's a
wise officer.

ANGELO Go to. What quality are they of? Elbow is your 59
name? Why dost thou not speak, Elbow?

POMPEY He cannot, sir; he's out at elbow. 61

ANGELO What are you, sir?

ELBOW He, sir? A tapster, sir, parcel-bawd, one that 63
serves a bad woman, whose house, sir, was, as they
say, pluck'd down in the suburbs; and now she pro- 65
fesses a hot-house, which, I think, is a very ill house 66
too.

ESCALUS How know you that?

ELBOW My wife, sir, whom I detest before heaven and 69
your honor—

ESCALUS How? Thy wife?

ELBOW Ay, sir; whom, I thank heaven, is an honest
woman—

ESCALUS Dost thou detest her therefore?

ELBOW I say, sir, I will detest myself also, as well as she,
that this house, if it be not a bawd's house, it is pity 76
of her life, for it is a naughty house. 77

ESCALUS How dost thou know that, constable?

ELBOW Marry, sir, by my wife, who, if she had been a
woman cardinally given, might have been accus'd in 80
fornication, adultery, and all uncleanliness there.

ESCALUS By the woman's means?

ELBOW Ay, sir, by Mistress Overdone's means; but as
she spit in his face, so she defied him. 84

POMPEY Sir, if it please your honor, this is not so.

ELBOW Prove it before these varlets here, thou honor- 86
able man, prove it. 87

ESCALUS Do you hear how he misplaces?

POMPEY Sir, she came in great with child, and longing,
saving your honor's reverence, for stew'd prunes. Sir, 90
we had but two in the house, which at that very dis- 91
tant time stood, as it were, in a fruit-dish, a dish of 92

6 fall let fall heavily **8 know** consider **10 affections** desires **12 blood** passion **22–23 What . . . on thieves** i.e., what cognizance can the laws take of the possibility that thieves may pass sentence upon thieves **23 pregnant** clear **28 For** because **30 judgment pattern out** sentence (imposed in this and similar cases) serve as a model for **31 nothing . . . partial** let there be no mitigation **33 like** please **36 utmost** furthest point **39 Some . . . none** i.e., some commit sin (grossly violate chastity) and escape the consequences (?). (A famous crux; F reads *brakes of ice.*)

42–43 use . . . houses practice their vices in bawdy houses **47 poor Duke's** i.e., Duke's poor **55 profanation** (A blunder for *profession*? Elbow already has used several seeming malapropisms, including *lean upon, benefactors,* and *precise.*) **59 quality** occupation **61 out at elbow** (1) impoverished—in intellect (2) having missed his cue **63 parcel-bawd** part-time bawd (and part-time tapster) **65–66 professes a hot-house** professes to run a bath-house **69 detest** (For *protest.*) **76–77 pity of her life** i.e., a sad state of affairs for her **77 naughty** wicked **80 cardinally** (For *carnally.*) **84 his** i.e., Pompey's, who was carrying out Mistress Overdone's wishes and was therefore her *means* **86–87 varlets . . . honorable** (Elbow reverses or *misplaces* these epithets.) **90 saving . . . reverence** i.e., begging your pardon for what I'm about to say. **stew'd prunes** (Commonly served in houses of prostitution, or *stews,* and therefore suggesting *prostitutes.* The pronunciation is suggested by the F spelling *prewyns.*) **91–92 distant** (Blunder for *instant?*)

some three-pence—your honors have seen such dishes; they are not China dishes, but very good dishes—

ESCALUS Go to, go to. No matter for the dish, sir.

POMPEY No, indeed, sir, not of a pin; you are therein in the right. But to the point. As I say, this Mistress Elbow, being, as I say, with child, and being great-bellied, and longing, as I said, for prunes; and having but two in the dish, as I said, Master Froth here, this very man, having eaten the rest, as I said, and, as I say, paying for them very honestly—for, as you know, Master Froth, I could not give you three-pence again.

FROTH No, indeed.

POMPEY Very well; you being then, if you be rememb'red, cracking the stones of the foresaid prunes—

FROTH Ay, so I did indeed.

POMPEY Why, very well; I telling you then, if you be rememb'red, that such a one and such a one were past cure of the thing you wot of, unless they kept very good diet, as I told you—

FROTH All this is true.

POMPEY Why, very well, then—

ESCALUS Come, you are a tedious fool. To the purpose. What was done to Elbow's wife, that he hath cause to complain of? Come me to what was done to her.

POMPEY Sir, your honor cannot come to that yet.

ESCALUS No, sir, nor I mean it not.

POMPEY Sir, but you shall come to it, by your honor's leave. And, I beseech you, look into Master Froth here, sir; a man of fourscore pound a year, whose father died at Hallowmas. Was 't not at Hallowmas, Master Froth?

FROTH All-hallond eve.

POMPEY Why, very well; I hope here be truths. He, sir, sitting, as I say, in a lower chair, sir—'twas in the Bunch of Grapes, where indeed you have a delight to sit, have you not?

FROTH I have so, because it is an open room and good for winter.

POMPEY Why, very well, then; I hope here be truths.

ANGELO

This will last out a night in Russia,
When nights are longest there. I'll take my leave,
And leave you to the hearing of the cause;
Hoping you'll find good cause to whip them all.

ESCALUS

I think no less. Good morrow to your lordship.

Exit [*Angelo*].

Now, sir, come on. What was done to Elbow's wife, once more?

POMPEY Once, sir? There was nothing done to her once.

ELBOW I beseech you, sir, ask him what this man did to my wife.

POMPEY I beseech your honor, ask me.

ESCALUS Well, sir, what did this gentleman to her?

POMPEY I beseech you, sir, look in this gentleman's face. Good Master Froth, look upon his honor; 'tis for a good purpose. Doth your honor mark his face?

ESCALUS Ay, sir, very well.

POMPEY Nay, I beseech you, mark it well.

ESCALUS Well, I do so.

POMPEY Doth your honor see any harm in his face?

ESCALUS Why, no.

POMPEY I'll be suppos'd upon a book, his face is the worst thing about him. Good, then; if his face be the worst thing about him, how could Master Froth do the constable's wife any harm? I would know that of your honor.

ESCALUS He's in the right, constable, what say you to it?

ELBOW First, an it like you, the house is a respected house; next, this is a respected fellow; and his mistress is a respected woman.

POMPEY By this hand, sir, his wife is a more respected person than any of us all.

ELBOW Varlet, thou liest! Thou liest, wicked varlet! The time is yet to come that she was ever respected with man, woman, or child.

POMPEY Sir, she was respected with him before he married with her.

ESCALUS Which is the wiser here, Justice or Iniquity? Is this true?

ELBOW O thou caitiff! O thou varlet! O thou wicked Hannibal! I respected with her before I was married to her? If ever I was respected with her, or she with me, let not your worship think me the poor Duke's officer. Prove this, thou wicked Hannibal, or I'll have mine action of batt'ry on thee.

ESCALUS If he took you a box o' th' ear, you might have your action of slander too.

ELBOW Marry, I thank your good worship for it. What is 't your worship's pleasure I shall do with this wicked caitiff?

ESCALUS Truly, officer, because he hath some offenses in him that thou wouldst discover if thou couldst, let him continue in his courses till thou know'st what they are.

ELBOW Marry, I thank your worship for it. Thou seest, thou wicked varlet, now, what's come upon thee: thou art to continue now, thou varlet, thou art to continue.

ESCALUS [*To Froth*] Where were you born, friend?

FROTH Here in Vienna, sir.

ESCALUS Are you of fourscore pounds a year?

FROTH Yes, an 't please you, sir.

ESCALUS So. [*To Pompey*.] What trade are you of, sir?

POMPEY A tapster, a poor widow's tapster.

ESCALUS Your mistress' name?

POMPEY Mistress Overdone.

ESCALUS Hath she had any more than one husband?

POMPEY Nine, sir; Overdone by the last.

97 pin i.e., an insignificant trifle **113 the thing . . . of** you know what I mean (i.e., venereal disease) **119 Come me** i.e., come. (*Me* is the ethical dative. Pompey makes a vulgar joke on the word *come*.) **125 Hallowmas** All Saints' Day, November 1 **127 All-hallond eve** Hallowe'en, October 31 **130 Bunch of Grapes** (It was not uncommon to designate particular rooms in inns by such names.) **132 open** public **140 done** (Pompey, in his answer, uses *done* in a sexual sense.)

156 suppos'd (A malapropism for *deposed*, i.e., sworn.) **book** i.e., Bible **163 an it like** if it please. **respected** (For *suspected*.) **173 Justice or Iniquity** (Personified characters in a morality play.) **176 Hannibal** (For *cannibal*.) **180 batt'ry** (An error for *slander*, as Escalus amusedly points out.) **181 took** gave **187 discover** reveal **195 of** possessed of

ESCALUS Nine? Come hither to me, Master Froth. Master Froth, I would not have you acquainted with tapsters. They will draw you, Master Froth, and you will hang them. Get you gone, and let me hear no more of you.

FROTH I thank your worship. For mine own part, I never come into any room in a taphouse, but I am drawn in.

ESCALUS Well, no more of it, Master Froth. Farewell. [*Exit Froth.*] Come you hither to me, Master tapster. What's your name, Master tapster?

POMPEY Pompey.

ESCALUS What else?

POMPEY Bum, sir.

ESCALUS Troth, and your bum is the greatest thing about you, so that in the beastliest sense you are Pompey the Great. Pompey, you are partly a bawd, Pompey, howsoever you color it in being a tapster, are you not? Come, tell me true. It shall be the better for you.

POMPEY Truly, sir, I am a poor fellow that would live.

ESCALUS How would you live, Pompey? By being a bawd? What do you think of the trade, Pompey? Is it a lawful trade?

POMPEY If the law would allow it, sir.

ESCALUS But the law will not allow it, Pompey; nor it shall not be allow'd in Vienna.

POMPEY Does your worship mean to geld and splay all the youth of the city?

ESCALUS No, Pompey.

POMPEY Truly, sir, in my poor opinion, they will to 't then. If your worship will take order for the drabs and the knaves, you need not to fear the bawds.

ESCALUS There is pretty orders beginning, I can tell you. It is but heading and hanging.

POMPEY If you head and hang all that offend that way but for ten year together, you'll be glad to give out a commission for more heads. If this law hold in Vienna ten year, I'll rent the fairest house in it after threepence a bay. If you live to see this come to pass, say Pompey told you so.

ESCALUS Thank you, good Pompey. And, in requital of your prophecy, hark you, I advise you, let me not find you before me again upon any complaint whatsoever; no, not for dwelling where you do. If I do, Pompey, I shall beat you to your tent, and prove a shrewd Caesar to you; in plain dealing, Pompey, I shall have you whipp'd. So, for this time, Pompey, fare you well.

POMPEY I thank your worship for your good counsel. [*Aside.*] But I shall follow it as the flesh and fortune shall better determine.
Whip me? No, no; let carman whip his jade:
The valiant heart's not whipp'd out of his trade.
Exit.

ESCALUS Come hither to me, Master Elbow; come hither, Master Constable. How long have you been in this place of constable?

ELBOW Seven year and a half, sir.

ESCALUS I thought, by your readiness in the office, you had continued in it some time. You say, seven years together?

ELBOW And a half, sir.

ESCALUS Alas, it hath been great pains to you. They do you wrong to put you so oft upon 't. Are there not men in your ward sufficient to serve it?

ELBOW Faith, sir, few of any wit in such matters. As they are chosen, they are glad to choose me for them. I do it for some piece of money, and go through with all.

ESCALUS Look you bring me in the names of some six or seven, the most sufficient of your parish.

ELBOW To your worship's house, sir?

ESCALUS To my house. Fare you well. [*Exit Elbow.*] What's o'clock, think you?

JUSTICE Eleven, sir.

ESCALUS I pray you home to dinner with me.

JUSTICE I humbly thank you.

ESCALUS
It grieves me for the death of Claudio;
But there's no remedy.

JUSTICE
Lord Angelo is severe.

ESCALUS It is but needful.
Mercy is not itself, that oft looks so;
Pardon is still the nurse of second woe.
But yet—poor Claudio! There is no remedy.
Come, sir. *Exeunt.*

SCENE II

Enter Provost [*and a*] *Servant.*

SERVANT
He's hearing of a cause; he will come straight.
I'll tell him of you.

PROVOST Pray you, do. [*Exit Servant.*] I'll know
His pleasure; may be he will relent. Alas,
He hath but as offended in a dream!
All sects, all ages smack of this vice—and he
To die for 't!

Enter Angelo.

ANGELO Now, what's the matter, Provost?

PROVOST
Is it your will Claudio shall die tomorrow?

ANGELO
Did not I tell thee yea? Hadst thou not order?
Why dost thou ask again?

205 draw (1) cheat, take in (2) empty, deplete (with a pun on the tapster's trade of drawing liquor from a barrel, and on Froth's name) (3) disembowel, or drag to execution **205–206 will hang them** will be the cause of their hanging **220 color** disguise **229 splay** spay **233 take order for** attend to **236 heading** beheading **240 after** at the rate of **241 bay** division of a house included under one gable **247 Caesar** (Escalus refers to Caesar's defeat of Pompey at Pharsalus in 48 B.C.) **253 carman** carter. **jade** broken-down horse

267 for them i.e., to take their place **281 Mercy . . . so** i.e., excessive leniency encourages crime and thus eventually leads to more punishment

II.ii. Location: Angelo's house.
4 He i.e., Claudio **5 sects** classes of people, ranks

PROVOST
Lest I might be too rash.
Under your good correction, I have seen 11
When, after execution, judgment hath
Repented o'er his doom. 13
ANGELO
Go to; let that be mine.
Do you your office, or give up your place,
And you shall well be spar'd.
PROVOST
I crave your honor's pardon.
What shall be done, sir, with the groaning Juliet?
She's very near her hour.
ANGELO Dispose of her
To some more fitter place, and that with speed.

[*Enter Servant.*]

SERVANT
Here is the sister of the man condemn'd
Desires access to you.
ANGELO Hath he a sister?
PROVOST
Ay, my good lord; a very virtuous maid,
And to be shortly of a sisterhood,
If not already.
ANGELO Well, let her be admitted.
[*Exit Servant.*]
See you the fornicatress be remov'd.
Let her have needful, but not lavish, means;
There shall be order for 't.

Enter Lucio and Isabella.

PROVOST Save your honor! 28
ANGELO
Stay a little while. [*To Isabella.*] Y' are welcome.
What's your will?
ISABELLA
I am a woeful suitor to your honor,
Please but your honor hear me.
ANGELO Well; what's your suit?
ISABELLA
There is a vice that most I do abhor,
And most desire should meet the blow of justice,
For which I would not plead, but that I must;
For which I must not plead, but that I am
At war 'twixt will and will not.
ANGELO Well; the matter?
ISABELLA
I have a brother is condemn'd to die.
I do beseech you, let it be his fault, 38
And not my brother.
PROVOST [*Aside*] Heaven give thee moving graces!
ANGELO
Condemn the fault, and not the actor of it?
Why, every fault's condemn'd ere it be done.
Mine were the very cipher of a function,
To fine the faults whose fine stands in record, 43
And let go by the actor.
ISABELLA
O just but severe law!
I had a brother, then. Heaven keep your honor!
LUCIO [*Aside to Isabella*]
Give 't not o'er so. To him again, entreat him! 47
Kneel down before him, hang upon his gown.
You are too cold. If you should need a pin, 49
You could not with more tame a tongue desire it.
To him, I say!
ISABELLA
Must he needs die?
ANGELO Maiden, no remedy.
ISABELLA
Yes; I do think that you might pardon him,
And neither heaven nor man grieve at the mercy.
ANGELO
I will not do 't.
ISABELLA But can you, if you would?
ANGELO
Look what I will not, that I cannot do. 56
ISABELLA
But might you do 't, and do the world no wrong,
If so your heart were touch'd with that remorse 58
As mine is to him?
ANGELO He's sentenc'd; 'tis too late.
LUCIO [*Aside to Isabella*]
You are too cold.
ISABELLA
Too late? Why, no; I, that do speak a word,
May call it back again. Well, believe this,
No ceremony that to great ones 'longs,
Not the king's crown, nor the deputed sword, 64
The marshal's truncheon, nor the judge's robe, 65
Become them with one half so good a grace
As mercy does.
If he had been as you and you as he,
You would have slipp'd like him; but he, like you,
Would not have been so stern.
ANGELO Pray you be gone.
ISABELLA
I would to heaven I had your potency,
And you were Isabel! Should it then be thus?
No; I would tell what 'twere to be a judge,
And what a prisoner.
LUCIO [*Aside to Isabella*]
Ay, touch him; there's the vein.
ANGELO
Your brother is a forfeit of the law,
And you but waste your words.
ISABELLA Alas, alas!
Why, all the souls that were were forfeit once, 77
And He that might the vantage best have took 78
Found out the remedy. How would you be, 79
If He, which is the top of judgment, should 80

11 Under . . . correction i.e., allow me to say **13 doom** sentence **28 Save** God save **38 let . . . fault** i.e., let the fault die

43 fine . . . fine punish . . . penalty **47 Give 't . . . so** don't give up so soon **49 need a pin** i.e., ask for the smallest trifle **56 Look what** whatever **58 remorse** pity **64 deputed sword** sword of justice entrusted by God to his deputy **65 truncheon** staff borne by military officers **77–79 Why . . . remedy** (A reference to the Redemption, despite man's sinfulness which would have justified God's destruction of humankind.) **80 top of judgment** supreme judge

But judge you as you are? O, think on that,
And mercy then will breathe within your lips,
Like man new made.

ANGELO
Be you content, fair maid. 83
It is the law, not I, condemn your brother.
Were he my kinsman, brother, or my son,
It should be thus with him. He must die tomorrow.

ISABELLA
Tomorrow! O, that's sudden! Spare him, spare him!
He's not prepar'd for death. Even for our kitchens
We kill the fowl of season. Shall we serve heaven 89
With less respect than we do minister
To our gross selves? Good, good my lord, bethink
you:
Who is it that hath died for this offense?
There's many have committed it.

LUCIO [*Aside to Isabella*] Ay, well said.

ANGELO
The law hath not been dead, though it hath slept.
Those many had not dar'd to do that evil
If the first that did th' edict infringe
Had answer'd for his deed. Now 'tis awake,
Takes note of what is done, and like a prophet
Looks in a glass that shows what future evils, 99
Either now, or by remissness new-conceiv'd, 100
And so in progress to be hatch'd and born, 101
Are now to have no successive degrees, 102
But here they live, to end.

ISABELLA
Yet show some pity. 103

ANGELO
I show it most of all when I show justice;
For then I pity those I do not know,
Which a dismiss'd offense would after gall, 106
And do him right that, answering one foul wrong, 107
Lives not to act another. Be satisfied;
Your brother dies tomorrow. Be content.

ISABELLA
So you must be the first that gives this sentence,
And he, that suffers. O, it is excellent
To have a giant's strength, but it is tyrannous
To use it like a giant.

LUCIO [*Aside to Isabella*] That's well said.

ISABELLA
Could great men thunder
As Jove himself does, Jove would never be quiet, 115
For every pelting, petty officer 116
Would use his heaven for thunder,
Nothing but thunder! Merciful Heaven,
Thou rather with thy sharp and sulphurous bolt
Splits the unwedgeable and gnarled oak
Than the soft myrtle; but man, proud man,
Dress'd in a little brief authority,
Most ignorant of what he's most assur'd, 123
His glassy essence, like an angry ape, 124
Plays such fantastic tricks before high heaven
As makes the angels weep; who, with our spleens, 126
Would all themselves laugh mortal. 127

LUCIO [*Aside to Isabella*]
O, to him, to him, wench! He will relent.
He's coming, I perceive 't.

PROVOST [*Aside*] Pray heaven she win him!

ISABELLA
We cannot weigh our brother with ourself. 130
Great men may jest with saints; 'tis wit in them,
But in the less foul profanation. 132

LUCIO [*Aside to Isabella*]
Thou 'rt i' th' right, girl; more o' that.

ISABELLA
That in the captain's but a choleric word, 134
Which in the soldier is flat blasphemy. 135

LUCIO [*Aside to Isabella*]
Art avis'd o' that? More on 't. 136

ANGELO
Why do you put these sayings upon me? 137

ISABELLA
Because authority, though it err like others,
Hath yet a kind of medicine in itself,
That skins the vice o' th' top. Go to your bosom; 140
Knock there, and ask your heart what it doth know
That's like my brother's fault. If it confess
A natural guiltiness such as is his,
Let it not sound a thought upon your tongue
Against my brother's life.

ANGELO [*Aside*]
She speaks, and 'tis such sense 146
That my sense breeds with it.—Fare you well. 147
[*He starts to go.*]

ISABELLA
Gentle my lord, turn back. 148

ANGELO
I will bethink me. Come again tomorrow.

ISABELLA
Hark how I'll bribe you. Good my lord, turn back.

ANGELO
How? Bribe me?

ISABELLA
Ay, with such gifts that heaven shall share with
you. 152

LUCIO [*Aside to Isabella*]
You had marr'd all else. 153

ISABELLA
Not with fond sicles of the tested gold, 154
Or stones whose rate are either rich or poor 155
As fancy values them, but with true prayers
That shall be up at heaven and enter there
Ere sunrise—prayers from preserved souls, 158
From fasting maids whose minds are dedicate

83 new made i.e., new created by salvation, born again **89 of season** that is in season and properly mature **99 glass** magic crystal **100 Either . . . new-conceiv'd** i.e., both evils already hatched and those that would be encouraged by continued laxity of enforcement **101 in progress** in the course of time **102 successive degrees** successors **103 here** i.e., in potential offenders **106 dismiss'd** forgiven. **gall** irritate, injure **107 right** justice **115 be quiet** have any quiet **116 pelting** paltry **123 assur'd** assured of (by God's merciful promises) **124 glassy essence** i.e., his soul, which is reflected from God; "glassy" refers to a mirror. **angry ape** i.e., ludicrous buffoon

126 with our spleens i.e., if they laughed at folly as we do **127 themselves laugh mortal** i.e., laugh as though they were mortal **130 cannot . . . ourself** cannot judge our fellow men by the same standards we use in judging ourselves (because we are so blinded to justice) **132 in the less** in men of lesser rank (it is) **134 That . . . word** i.e., we treat the abusive language a general uses in anger merely as an outburst; we are indulgent toward the failings of *great men* **135 blasphemy** defamation **136 avis'd** informed, aware **137 put . . . me** apply these sayings to me **140 skins . . . top** covers over the sore with skin, leaving it unhealed. (The *medicine* of l. 139 is thus only a palliative.) **146–147 sense . . . sense** import . . . sensuality **148 Gentle my lord** my noble lord **152 that** as **153 else** otherwise **154 fond** i.e., foolishly valued. **sicles** shekels. **tested** purest, tested by the touchstone **155 rate** values **158 preserved** protected (from the world)

To nothing temporal.

ANGELO Well, come to me tomorrow.

LUCIO [*Aside to Isabella*]
Go to; 'tis well. Away!

ISABELLA
Heaven keep your honor safe!

ANGELO [*Aside*] Amen!
For I am that way going to temptation,
Where prayers cross.

ISABELLA At what hour tomorrow 164
Shall I attend your lordship?

ANGELO
At any time 'fore noon.

ISABELLA
Save your honor!

[*Exeunt Isabella, Lucio, and Provost.*]

ANGELO From thee, even from thy virtue!
What's this, what's this? Is this her fault or mine?
The tempter or the tempted, who sins most, ha?
Not she, nor doth she tempt; but it is I
That, lying by the violet in the sun,
Do as the carrion does, not as the flow'r,
Corrupt with virtuous season. Can it be 173
That modesty may more betray our sense 174
Than woman's lightness? Having waste ground enough,
Shall we desire to raze the sanctuary
And pitch our evils there? O, fie, fie, fie! 177
What dost thou, or what art thou, Angelo?
Dost thou desire her foully for those things
That make her good? O, let her brother live!
Thieves for their robbery have authority
When judges steal themselves. What, do I love her,
That I desire to hear her speak again,
And feast upon her eyes? What is 't I dream on?
O cunning enemy that, to catch a saint,
With saints dost bait thy hook! Most dangerous
Is that temptation that doth goad us on
To sin in loving virtue. Never could the strumpet,
With all her double vigor, art, and nature, 189
Once stir my temper; but this virtuous maid 190
Subdues me quite. Ever till now,
When men were fond, I smil'd and wond'red how. 192

Exit.

SCENE III

Enter, [meeting,] Duke [disguised as a friar] and Provost.

DUKE
Hail to you, Provost—so I think you are.

PROVOST
I am the Provost. What's your will, good friar?

DUKE
Bound by my charity and my blest order,
I come to visit the afflicted spirits
Here in the prison. Do me the common right
To let me see them, and to make me know
The nature of their crimes, that I may minister
To them accordingly.

PROVOST
I would do more than that, if more were needful.

Enter Juliet.

Look, here comes one: a gentlewoman of mine,
Who, falling in the flaws of her own youth, 11
Hath blister'd her report. She is with child, 12
And he that got it, sentenc'd; a young man 13
More fit to do another such offense
Than die for this.

DUKE
When must he die?

PROVOST As I do think, tomorrow.
[*To Juliet.*] I have provided for you. Stay awhile,
And you shall be conducted.

DUKE
Repent you, fair one, of the sin you carry?

JULIET
I do; and bear the shame most patiently.

DUKE
I'll teach you how you shall arraign your conscience,
And try your penitence, if it be sound,
Or hollowly put on.

JULIET I'll gladly learn.

DUKE
Love you the man that wrong'd you?

JULIET
Yes, as I love the woman that wrong'd him.

DUKE
So then it seems your most offenseful act
Was mutually committed?

JULIET Mutually.

DUKE
Then was your sin of heavier kind than his.

JULIET
I do confess it, and repent it, father.

DUKE
'Tis meet so, daughter. But lest you do repent
As that the sin hath brought you to this shame, 31
Which sorrow is always toward ourselves, not heaven,
Showing we would not spare heaven as we love it, 33
But as we stand in fear—

JULIET
I do repent me as it is an evil,
And take the shame with joy.

DUKE There rest. 36
Your partner, as I hear, must die tomorrow,
And I am going with instruction to him.
Grace go with you, Benedicite! *Exit.* 39

164 cross are at cross purposes **173 Corrupt . . . season** i.e., putrify while all else flourishes **174 sense** sensual nature **177 pitch our evils there** i.e., erect a privy not on *waste ground* (l. 175) but on sanctified ground **189 art** artifice. **nature** sensual nature **190 temper** mental balance, temperament **192 fond** foolishly in love

II.iii. Location: A prison.

11 flaws sudden gusts (of passion) **12 report** reputation **13 got** begot **31 As that** because **33 spare heaven** i.e., spare heaven the sorrow felt there for unconfessed sins. **as** because (also in ll. 34 and 35) **36 There rest** hold fast to that truth **39 Benedicite** blessings on you

JULIET

Must die tomorrow? O injurious love,
That respites me a life, whose very comfort 41
Is still a dying horror!

PROVOST 'Tis pity of him. *Exeunt.* 42

SCENE IV

Enter Angelo.

ANGELO

When I would pray and think, I think and pray
To several subjects. Heaven hath my empty words, 2
Whilst my invention, hearing not my tongue, 3
Anchors on Isabel; Heaven in my mouth,
As if I did but only chew his name, 5
And in my heart the strong and swelling evil
Of my conception. The state, whereon I studied, 7
Is like a good thing, being often read,
Grown sere and tedious; yea, my gravity, 9
Wherein—let no man hear me—I take pride,
Could I with boot change for an idle plume, 11
Which the air beats for vain. O place, O form, 12
How often dost thou with thy case, thy habit, 13
Wrench awe from fools, and tie the wiser souls
To thy false seeming! Blood, thou art blood. 15
Let's write "good angel" on the devil's horn, 16
'Tis not the devil's crest.

Enter Servant.

How now, who's there? 17

SERVANT

One Isabel, a sister, desires access to you.

ANGELO

Teach her the way. [*Exit Servant.*] O heavens!
Why does my blood thus muster to my heart,
Making both it unable for itself,
And dispossessing all my other parts
Of necessary fitness?
So play the foolish throngs with one that swoons;
Come all to help him, and so stop the air
By which he should revive; and even so
The general subject to a well-wish'd king 27
Quit their own part, and in obsequious fondness 28
Crowd to his presence, where their untaught love
Must needs appear offense.

Enter Isabella.

How now, fair maid?

ISABELLA

I am come to know your pleasure.

ANGELO

That you might know it would much better
please me 32
Than to demand what 'tis. Your brother cannot live.

ISABELLA

Even so. Heaven keep your honor!

ANGELO

Yet may he live awhile; and, it may be,
As long as you or I. Yet he must die.

ISABELLA

Under your sentence?

ANGELO

Yea.

ISABELLA

When, I beseech you? That in his reprieve,
Longer or shorter, he may be so fitted 40
That his soul sicken not.

ANGELO

Ha? Fie, these filthy vices! It were as good
To pardon him that hath from nature stol'n 43
A man already made, as to remit 44
Their saucy sweetness that do coin heaven's image 45
In stamps that are forbid. 'Tis all as easy 46
Falsely to take away a life true made
As to put metal in restrained means 48
To make a false one.

ISABELLA

'Tis set down so in heaven, but not in earth. 50

ANGELO

Say you so? Then I shall pose you quickly. 51
Which had you rather, that the most just law
Now took your brother's life, or, to redeem him,
Give up your body to such sweet uncleanness
As she that he hath stain'd?

ISABELLA Sir, believe this,
I had rather give my body than my soul.

ANGELO

I talk not of your soul. Our compell'd sins 57
Stand more for number than for account.

ISABELLA How say you? 58

ANGELO

Nay, I'll not warrant that; for I can speak 59
Against the thing I say. Answer to this:
I, now the voice of the recorded law,
Pronounce a sentence on your brother's life;
Might there not be a charity in sin
To save this brother's life?

41 respites prolongs, does not forfeit. (Her life is spared because she is pregnant.) **41–42 whose . . . horror** i.e., whose best of comfort will be an unending horror

II.iv. Location: Angelo's house.
2 several separate **3 invention** imagination **5 his** i.e., God's **7 conception** thought. **The state** statecraft **9 sere** withered, old **11 Could . . . boot** I could advantageously **12 vain** vanity. **place** official position, rank. **form** dignity of office **13 case** outward appearance. **habit** garb **15 Blood . . . blood** i.e., passions are inherent in human nature, under all these outward appearances **16–17 Let's write . . . crest** i.e., in our secret viciousness we may give an outwardly virtuous appearance to the devil himself, but that is not his true nature. (Angelo is punning on his own name.) **Let's write** i.e., even if we were to write. **crest** heraldic device indicating true identity **27 general subject** i.e., commoners, subjects **28 Quit . . . part** abandon their proper function and (politely distant) place

32 know it i.e., know my pleasure, my desire. (Angelo is thinking of his desire for Isabella.) **40 fitted** prepared **43–44 To . . . made** i.e., to pardon a murderer **44 remit** pardon **45 Their . . . sweetness** the wanton pleasures of those persons **45–46 coin . . . forbid** i.e., produce illegitimate offspring, like counterfeit coiners **48 metal** (with a play on *mettle*, a variant spelling, and as it is spelled in F; i.e., substance). **restrained** prohibited, illicit **50 'Tis . . . earth** i.e., equating murder and bastardizing accords with divine law but not with human law, to which murder is more heinous **51 pose** put a question to **57–58 compell'd . . . account** sins committed under compulsion are recorded but not charged to our spiritual account **59 I'll . . . that** i.e., I'm not necessarily endorsing the view I just expressed

ISABELLA Please you to do 't,
I'll take it as a peril to my soul,
It is no sin at all, but charity.

ANGELO
Pleas'd you to do 't at peril of your soul, 67
Were equal poise of sin and charity. 68

ISABELLA
That I do beg his life, if it be sin,
Heaven let me bear it! You granting of my suit,
If that be sin, I'll make it my morn prayer
To have it added to the faults of mine,
And nothing of your answer.

ANGELO Nay, but hear me. 73
Your sense pursues not mine. Either you are ignorant,
Or seem so craftily; and that's not good.

ISABELLA
Let me be ignorant, and in nothing good,
But graciously to know I am no better. 77

ANGELO
Thus wisdom wishes to appear most bright
When it doth tax itself, as these black masks 79
Proclaim an enshield beauty ten times louder 80
Than beauty could, display'd. But mark me.
To be received plain, I'll speak more gross: 82
Your brother is to die.

ISABELLA
So.

ANGELO
And his offense is so, as it appears,
Accountant to the law upon that pain. 86

ISABELLA
True.

ANGELO
Admit no other way to save his life—
As I subscribe not that, nor any other, 89
But in the loss of question—that you, his sister, 90
Finding yourself desir'd of such a person,
Whose credit with the judge, or own great place,
Could fetch your brother from the manacles
Of the all-binding law; and that there were
No earthly mean to save him, but that either
You must lay down the treasures of your body
To this suppos'd, or else to let him suffer. 97
What would you do?

ISABELLA
As much for my poor brother as myself:
That is, were I under the terms of death,
Th' impression of keen whips I 'd wear as rubies,
And strip myself to death, as to a bed
That longing have been sick for, ere I 'd yield 103
My body up to shame.

ANGELO Then must your brother die.

ISABELLA
And 'twere the cheaper way.
Better it were a brother died at once 106
Than that a sister, by redeeming him,
Should die for ever.

ANGELO
Were not you then as cruel as the sentence
That you have slander'd so?

ISABELLA
Ignomy in ransom and free pardon 111
Are of two houses. Lawful mercy 112
Is nothing kin to foul redemption. 113

ANGELO
You seem'd of late to make the law a tyrant,
And rather prov'd the sliding of your brother 115
A merriment than a vice.

ISABELLA
O, pardon me, my lord. It oft falls out,
To have what we would have, we speak not what we mean.
I something do excuse the thing I hate 119
For his advantage that I dearly love.

ANGELO
We are all frail.

ISABELLA Else let my brother die,
If not a fedary, but only he 122
Owe and succeed thy weakness. 123

ANGELO
Nay, women are frail too.

ISABELLA
Ay, as the glasses where they view themselves,
Which are as easy broke as they make forms. 126
Women? Help Heaven! Men their creation mar 127
In profiting by them. Nay, call us ten times frail,
For we are soft as our complexions are, 129
And credulous to false prints.

ANGELO I think it well. 130
And from this testimony of your own sex—
Since I suppose we are made to be no stronger
Than faults may shake our frames—let me be bold. 133
I do arrest your words. Be that you are, 134
That is, a woman; if you be more, you're none. 135
If you be one, as you are well express'd 136
By all external warrants, show it now
By putting on the destin'd livery. 138

ISABELLA
I have no tongue but one. Gentle my lord, 139
Let me entreat you speak the former language. 140

ANGELO
Plainly conceive, I love you.

67 Pleas'd if it pleased **68 Were equal poise** there would be equal balance **73 of your answer** to which you will have to answer **77 graciously** through divine grace **79 tax itself** accuse itself (of ignorance). **these** (Generically referring to any.) **80 enshield** enshielded, protected from view behind the black masks **82 received plain** plainly understood. **gross** openly **86 Accountant** accountable. **pain** penalty **89 subscribe** assent to **90 But . . . question** i.e., provided nothing more can be said to defend Claudio's case. (*Loss* means *default.*) **97 suppos'd** hypothetical person. **him** i.e., Claudio **103 longing . . . for** i.e., that I have been sick with longing for

106 died at once i.e., should experience physical death (as contrasted to the death of the soul through sin, to *die for ever,* l. 108) **111 Ignomy** ignominy **112 of two houses** i.e., utterly different, of different kinds **113 nothing** not at all **115 prov'd** argued, condoned **119 something** to some extent **122 fedary** associate, i.e., one of the whole group of mankind **123 Owe . . . weakness** possess and own through succession or inheritance the weakness you speak of, or the weakness to which all men as a class are prone **126 forms** (1) images (2) copies of themselves, i.e., children **127 their . . . mar** debase their nature **129 complexions** constitutions **130 credulous . . . prints** susceptible to false impressions. (The metaphor is from the stamping of metal.) **133 Than** than that **134 arrest your words** take what you have said and hold you to it. **that** what **135 if . . . none** i.e., if you strive for the perfection of chastity, you are no longer a woman as we have defined that term **136 express'd** shown to be **138 putting . . . livery** i.e., assuming the characteristic frailty which all women possess **139 tongue** language **140 former** i.e., customary

ISABELLA
My brother did love Juliet,
And you tell me that he shall die for 't.

ANGELO
He shall not, Isabel, if you give me love.

ISABELLA
I know your virtue hath a license in 't,
Which seems a little fouler than it is,
To pluck on others.

ANGELO Believe me, on mine honor,
My words express my purpose.

ISABELLA
Ha! Little honor to be much believ'd,
And most pernicious purpose! Seeming, seeming!
I will proclaim thee, Angelo, look for 't!
Sign me a present pardon for my brother,
Or with an outstretch'd throat I'll tell the world
aloud
What man thou art.

ANGELO Who will believe thee, Isabel?
My unsoil'd name, th' austereness of my life,
My vouch against you, and my place i' th' state
Will so your accusation overweigh
That you shall stifle in your own report
And smell of calumny. I have begun,
And now I give my sensual race the rein.
Fit thy consent to my sharp appetite,
Lay by all nicety and prolixious blushes
That banish what they sue for. Redeem thy brother
By yielding up thy body to my will,
Or else he must not only die the death,
But thy unkindness shall his death draw out
To ling'ring sufferance. Answer me tomorrow,
Or, by the affection that now guides me most,
I'll prove a tyrant to him. As for you,
Say what you can, my false o'erweighs your true.
Exit.

ISABELLA
To whom should I complain? Did I tell this,
Who would believe me? O perilous mouths,
That bear in them one and the self-same tongue,
Either of condemnation or approof,
Bidding the law make curtsy to their will,
Hooking both right and wrong to th' appetite,
To follow as it draws! I'll to my brother.
Though he hath fall'n by prompture of the blood,
Yet hath he in him such a mind of honor
That, had he twenty heads to tender down
On twenty bloody blocks, he 'd yield them up
Before his sister should her body stoop
To such abhorr'd pollution.
Then, Isabel, live chaste, and, brother, die;
More than our brother is our chastity.
I'll tell him yet of Angelo's request,
And fit his mind to death, for his soul's rest. *Exit.*

145–147 your . . . others i.e., you, although virtuous, are pretending foul purposes in order to mislead *(pluck on)* me **156 vouch** testimony **160 race** natural or inherited disposition **162 prolixious** tedious **163 banish** i.e., seem to thrust away **167 sufferance** torture **168 affection** passion **174 approof** approval, sanction **177 as it draws** wherever it drags

ACT III • SCENE I

Enter Duke [disguised as before], Claudio, and Provost.

DUKE
So then you hope of pardon from Lord Angelo?

CLAUDIO
The miserable have no other medicine
But only hope.
I have hope to live, and am prepar'd to die.

DUKE
Be absolute for death. Either death or life
Shall thereby be the sweeter. Reason thus with life:
If I do lose thee, I do lose a thing
That none but fools would keep. A breath thou art,
Servile to all the skyey influences
That dost this habitation where thou keep'st
Hourly afflict. Merely, thou art death's fool,
For him thou labor'st by thy flight to shun,
And yet runn'st toward him still. Thou art not
noble,
For all th' accommodations that thou bear'st
Are nurs'd by baseness. Thou 'rt by no means
valiant,
For thou dost fear the soft and tender fork
Of a poor worm. Thy best of rest is sleep,
And that thou oft provok'st, yet grossly fear'st
Thy death, which is no more. Thou art not thyself,
For thou exists on many a thousand grains
That issue out of dust. Happy thou art not,
For what thou hast not, still thou striv'st to get,
And what thou hast, forget'st. Thou art not certain,
For thy complexion shifts to strange effects,
After the moon. If thou art rich, thou 'rt poor,
For, like an ass whose back with ingots bows,
Thou bear'st thy heavy riches but a journey,
And death unloads thee. Friend hast thou none,
For thine own bowels, which do call thee sire,
The mere effusion of thy proper loins,
Do curse the gout, serpigo, and the rheum
For ending thee no sooner. Thou hast nor youth
nor age,
But as it were an after-dinner's sleep,
Dreaming on both, for all thy blessed youth
Becomes as aged, and doth beg the alms
Of palsied eld; and, when thou art old and rich,
Thou hast neither heat, affection, limb, nor beauty,
To make thy riches pleasant. What's yet in this
That bears the name of life? Yet in this life
Lie hid moe thousand deaths; yet death we fear,

III.i. Location: The prison.
9 skyey influences influence of the stars **10 keep'st** dwell **11 Merely** utterly, only **14 accommodations** conveniences, civilized comforts **15 nurs'd by baseness** nurtured by ignoble means **17 worm** snake **18 thou oft provok'st** you often invoke, summon **23 certain** steadfast **24 complexion** constitution. **effects** appearances, manifestations **25 After the moon** as changeably as the moon **29 bowels** i.e., offspring **30 mere** very. **proper** own **31 serpigo** a skin eruption. **rheum** catarrh **32 nor youth** neither youth **33 after-dinner's** i.e., afternoon's **35 as aged** like old age, having to depend on it. (Youth is penniless and dependent on the aged, whereas the old lack the physical capacity of youth.) **36 eld** old age **37 heat** vigor. **affection** passion **40 moe** more

That makes these odds all even.

CLAUDIO I humbly thank you.
To sue to live, I find I seek to die,
And, seeking death, find life. Let it come on.

Enter Isabella.

ISABELLA
What, ho! Peace here; grace and good company!

PROVOST
Who's there? Come in. The wish deserves a
welcome. [*He goes to greet her.*]

DUKE [*To Claudio*]
Dear sir, ere long I'll visit you again.

CLAUDIO
Most holy sir, I thank you.

ISABELLA
My business is a word or two with Claudio.

PROVOST
And very welcome. Look, signior, here's your sister.

DUKE [*Aside to Provost*]
Provost, a word with you.

PROVOST
As many as you please.

DUKE
Bring me to hear them speak, where I may be
Conceal'd. [*Duke and Provost withdraw.*]

CLAUDIO Now, sister, what's the comfort?

ISABELLA Why,
As all comforts are; most good, most good indeed.
Lord Angelo, having affairs to heaven,
Intends you for his swift ambassador,
Where you shall be an everlasting leiger.
Therefore your best appointment make with speed;
Tomorrow you set on.

CLAUDIO Is there no remedy?

ISABELLA
None but such remedy as, to save a head,
To cleave a heart in twain.

CLAUDIO
But is there any?

ISABELLA Yes, brother, you may live.
There is a devilish mercy in the judge,
If you'll implore it, that will free your life,
But fetter you till death.

CLAUDIO Perpetual durance?

ISABELLA
Ay, just; perpetual durance, a restraint,
Though all the world's vastidity you had,
To a determin'd scope.

CLAUDIO But in what nature?

ISABELLA
In such a one as, you consenting to 't,
Would bark your honor from that trunk you bear,
And leave you naked.

CLAUDIO Let me know the point.

ISABELLA
O, I do fear thee, Claudio, and I quake,
Lest thou a feverous life shouldst entertain,
And six or seven winters more respect
Than a perpetual honor. Dar'st thou die?
The sense of death is most in apprehension,
And the poor beetle that we tread upon
In corporal sufferance finds a pang as great
As when a giant dies.

CLAUDIO
Why give you me this shame?
Think you I can a resolution fetch
From flow'ry tenderness? If I must die,
I will encounter darkness as a bride,
And hug it in mine arms.

ISABELLA
There spake my brother! There my father's grave
Did utter forth a voice. Yes, thou must die.
Thou art too noble to conserve a life
In base appliances. This outward-sainted deputy,
Whose settled visage and deliberate word
Nips youth i' th' head, and follies doth enew
As falcon doth the fowl, is yet a devil;
His filth within being cast, he would appear
A pond as deep as hell.

CLAUDIO The prenzie Angelo?

ISABELLA
O, 'tis the cunning livery of hell,
The damned'st body to invest and cover
In prenzie guards! Dost thou think, Claudio,
If I would yield him my virginity,
Thou mightst be freed!

CLAUDIO O heavens, it cannot be.

ISABELLA
Yes, he would give 't thee, from this rank offense,
So to offend him still. This night's the time
That I should do what I abhor to name,
Or else thou diest tomorrow.

CLAUDIO
Thou shalt not do 't.

ISABELLA O, were it but my life,
I 'd throw it down for your deliverance
As frankly as a pin.

CLAUDIO Thanks, dear Isabel.

ISABELLA
Be ready, Claudio, for your death tomorrow.

CLAUDIO
Yes. Has he affections in him,
That thus can make him bite the law by th' nose,
When he would force it? Sure, it is no sin,
Or of the deadly seven it is the least.

ISABELLA
Which is the least?

42 To sue suing **57 leiger** resident ambassador **58 appointment** preparation **65 durance** imprisonment **66 just** just so **66–68 restraint . . . scope** a confinement to fixed limits or bounds (i.e., to certain damnation and perpetual remorse for the sinful bargain you had struck), even if you had the entire vastness of the world to wander in **70 bark** strip off (as one strips bark from a tree *trunk*)

72 fear fear for **73 entertain** maintain, desire **74 respect** value **76 apprehension** anticipation **81 fetch** derive **82 flow'ry tenderness** i.e., comforting figures of speech **88 In base appliances** by means of ignoble devices, remedies **89 settled visage** composed features **90 Nips . . . head** strikes from on high, like a falcon swooping upon its prey. **enew** drive prey down into the water or into covert **92 cast** vomited; cleared out; reckoned up (?) **93, 96 prenzie** (A word unknown elsewhere, perhaps meaning *princely* or *precise*.) **95 invest** clothe **96 guards** trimmings **99 give 't thee** i.e., grant you license. **from** in return for **100 So . . . still** i.e., to continue with your fornication **105 frankly** freely **107 affections** passions **108 bite . . . nose** i.e., flout the law **109 force** enforce

CLAUDIO
If it were damnable, he being so wise,
Why would he for the momentary trick
Be perdurably fin'd? O Isabel!

ISABELLA
What says my brother?

CLAUDIO Death is a fearful thing.

ISABELLA
And shamed life a hateful.

CLAUDIO
Ay, but to die, and go we know not where,
To lie in cold obstruction and to rot,
This sensible warm motion to become
A kneaded clod; and the delighted spirit
To bathe in fiery floods, or to reside
In thrilling region of thick-ribbed ice,
To be imprison'd in the viewless winds
And blown with restless violence round about
The pendent world; or to be worse than worst
Of those that lawless and incertain thought
Imagine howling—'tis too horrible!
The weariest and most loathed worldly life
That age, ache, penury, and imprisonment
Can lay on nature is a paradise
To what we fear of death.

ISABELLA
Alas, alas!

CLAUDIO Sweet sister, let me live.
What sin you do to save a brother's life,
Nature dispenses with the deed so far
That it becomes a virtue.

ISABELLA O you beast!
O faithless coward! O dishonest wretch!
Wilt thou be made a man out of my vice?
Is 't not a kind of incest, to take life
From thine own sister's shame? What should I think?
Heaven shield my mother play'd my father fair!
For such a warped slip of wilderness
Ne'er issu'd from his blood. Take my defiance!
Die, perish! Might but my bending down
Reprieve thee from thy fate, it should proceed.
I'll pray a thousand prayers for thy death,
No word to save thee.

CLAUDIO
Nay, hear me, Isabel.

ISABELLA O, fie, fie, fie!
Thy sin's not accidental, but a trade.
Mercy to thee would prove itself a bawd;
'Tis best that thou diest quickly.

CLAUDIO O hear me, Isabella!
[*Duke comes forward.*]

DUKE
Vouchsafe a word, young sister, but one word.

ISABELLA What is your will?

DUKE Might you dispense with your leisure, I would by and by have some speech with you. The satisfaction I would require is likewise your own benefit.

ISABELLA I have no superfluous leisure—my stay must be stolen out of other affairs—but I will attend you awhile. [*Walks apart.*]

DUKE Son, I have overheard what hath pass'd between you and your sister. Angelo had never the purpose to corrupt her; only he hath made an assay of her virtue to practice his judgment with the disposition of natures. She, having the truth of honor in her, hath made him that gracious denial which he is most glad to receive. I am confessor to Angelo, and I know this to be true; therefore prepare yourself to death. Do not satisfy your resolution with hopes that are fallible. Tomorrow you must die. Go to your knees and make ready.

CLAUDIO Let me ask my sister pardon. I am so out of love with life that I will sue to be rid of it.

DUKE Hold you there. Farewell. [*Claudio retires.*] Provost, a word with you!
[*Provost comes forward.*]

PROVOST What's your will, father?

DUKE That now you are come, you will be gone. Leave me awhile with the maid. My mind promises with my habit no loss shall touch her by my company.

PROVOST In good time.
Exit [*Provost with Claudio. Isabella comes forward*].

DUKE The hand that hath made you fair hath made you good. The goodness that is cheap in beauty makes beauty brief in goodness; but grace, being the soul of your complexion, shall keep the body of it ever fair. The assault that Angelo hath made to you, fortune hath convey'd to my understanding; and, but that frailty hath examples for his falling, I should wonder at Angelo. How will you do to content this substitute, and to save your brother?

ISABELLA I am now going to resolve him. I had rather my brother die by the law than my son should be unlawfully born. But, O, how much is the good Duke deceiv'd in Angelo! If ever he return and I can speak to him, I will open my lips in vain, or discover his government.

DUKE That shall not be much amiss. Yet, as the matter now stands, he will avoid your accusation; he made trial of you only. Therefore fasten your ear on my advisings: to the love I have in doing good a remedy presents itself. I do make myself believe that you may most uprighteously do a poor wrong'd lady a merited benefit, redeem your brother from the angry law, do no stain to your own gracious person, and much please the absent Duke, if peradventure he shall ever return to have hearing of this business.

113 trick trifle **114 perdurably fin'd** everlastingly punished **118 obstruction** cessation of vital functions **119 sensible** endowed with feeling. **motion** organism **120 kneaded** i.e., reduced to shapelessness. **delighted spirit** spirit attended with delight; or, beloved spirit **122 thrilling** causing one to shiver **123 viewless** invisible **125 pendent** hanging in space. (A Ptolemaic concept.) **126 lawless . . . thought** i.e., wild conjecture **134 dispenses with** grants a dispensation for, excuses **140 shield** defend **141 warped . . . wilderness** perverse scion of a wild stock **149 prove . . . bawd** provide opportunity for sexual license

157 attend await **162–163 to practice . . . natures** to test his ability to judge people's characters **171 Hold you there** hold fast to that resolution **175–176 with my habit** as well as my priestly garb (that) **177 In good time** i.e., very well **179–180 The goodness . . . in goodness** i.e., the physical graces that come easily with beauty make beauty soon cease to be morally good **181 complexion** character and appearance **183 but that** were it not that **185 this substitute** i.e., the deputy, Angelo **187 resolve** answer **191–192 discover his government** i.e., expose Angelo's misconduct

ISABELLA Let me hear you speak farther. I have spirit to do anything that appears not foul in the truth of my spirit.

DUKE Virtue is bold, and goodness never fearful. Have you not heard speak of Mariana, the sister of Frederick the great soldier who miscarried at sea?

ISABELLA I have heard of the lady, and good words went with her name.

DUKE She should this Angelo have married, was affianced to her by oath, and the nuptial appointed; between which time of the contract and limit of the solemnity, her brother Frederick was wrack'd at sea, having in that perish'd vessel the dowry of his sister. But mark how heavily this befell to the poor gentlewoman. There she lost a noble and renown'd brother, in his love toward her ever most kind and natural; with him, the portion and sinew of her fortune, her marriage-dowry; with both, her combinate husband, this well-seeming Angelo.

ISABELLA Can this be so? Did Angelo so leave her?

DUKE Left her in her tears, and dried not one of them with his comfort; swallow'd his vows whole, pretending in her discoveries of dishonor; in few, bestow'd her on her own lamentation, which she yet wears for his sake; and he, a marble to her tears, is wash'd with them, but relents not.

ISABELLA What a merit were it in death to take this poor maid from the world! What corruption in this life, that it will let this man live! But how out of this can she avail?

DUKE It is a rupture that you may easily heal; and the cure of it not only saves your brother, but keeps you from dishonor in doing it.

ISABELLA Show me how, good father.

DUKE This forenam'd maid hath yet in her the continuance of her first affection; his unjust unkindness, that in all reason should have quench'd her love, hath, like an impediment in the current, made it more violent and unruly. Go you to Angelo; answer his requiring with a plausible obedience; agree with his demands to the point. Only refer yourself to this advantage, first, that your stay with him may not be long; that the time may have all shadow and silence in it; and the place answer to convenience. This being granted in course—and now follows all—we shall advise this wrong'd maid to stead up your appointment, go in your place. If the encounter acknowledge itself hereafter, it may compel him to her recompense. And here, by this, is your brother sav'd, your honor untainted, the poor Mariana advantag'd, and the corrupt deputy scal'd. The maid will I frame and make fit for his attempt. If you think well to carry this as you may, the doubleness of the benefit defends the deceit from reproof. What think you of it?

ISABELLA The image of it gives me content already, and I trust it will grow to a most prosperous perfection.

DUKE It lies much in your holding up. Haste you speedily to Angelo. If for this night he entreat you to his bed, give him promise of satisfaction. I will presently to Saint Luke's; there, at the moated grange, resides this dejected Mariana. At that place call upon me, and dispatch with Angelo, that it may be quickly.

ISABELLA I thank you for this comfort. Fare you well, good father. *Exit.* [*Manet Duke.*]

[SCENE II]

Enter [*to the Duke*] *Elbow, Clown* [*Pompey, and*] *Officers.*

ELBOW Nay, if there be no remedy for it, but that you will needs buy and sell men and women like beasts, we shall have all the world drink brown and white bastard.

DUKE O heavens, what stuff is here?

POMPEY 'Twas never merry world since, of two usuries, the merriest was put down, and the worser allow'd by order of law; a furr'd gown to keep him warm; and furr'd with fox on lamb-skins too, to signify that craft, being richer than innocency, stands for the facing.

ELBOW Come your way, sir. Bless you, good father friar.

DUKE And you, good brother father. What offense hath this man made you, sir?

ELBOW Marry, sir, he hath offended the law; and, sir, we take him to be a thief too, sir, for we have found upon him, sir, a strange picklock, which we have sent to the deputy.

DUKE

Fie, sirrah, a bawd, a wicked bawd!
The evil that thou causest to be done,
That is thy means to live. Do thou but think
What 'tis to cram a maw or clothe a back
From such a filthy vice; say to thyself,
From their abominable and beastly touches
I drink, I eat, array myself, and live.
Canst thou believe thy living is a life,
So stinkingly depending? Go mend, go mend.

POMPEY Indeed, it does stink in some sort, sir; but yet, sir, I would prove—

DUKE

Nay, if the devil have given thee proofs for sin,
Thou wilt prove his. Take him to prison, officer.
Correction and instruction must both work
Ere this rude beast will profit.

213–214 limit . . . solemnity date set for the ceremony **220 combinate husband** i.e., betrothed **224–225 pretending** alleging **225 in her** i.e., to have found in her. **in few** in short **225–226 bestow'd . . . lamentation** left her to her grief (with quibble on *bestow'd* meaning "gave in marriage") **232 avail** benefit **242–243 to the point** precisely **243 refer . . . advantage** i.e., obtain as a proviso the following favorable condition **245 shadow** darkness, secrecy **248 stead . . . appointment** go in your stead **249–250 If the . . . hereafter** i.e., if she should become pregnant **253 scal'd** weighed (and found wanting). **frame** prepare

259 holding up ability to carry it off **262 moated grange** country house surrounded by a ditch **264 dispatch** settle, conclude (business)

III.ii. Location: Scene continues. The Duke remains on stage.
4 bastard sweet Spanish wine (used quibblingly) **6–7 two usuries** i.e., money-lending (the *worser*) and procuring for fornication (the *merriest*), both of which yield increase **8 furr'd gown** (Characteristic attire of usurers.) **10–11 stands . . . facing** represents the outer covering. (Fox symbolizes *craft* or craftiness, lamb-skin *innocency.*) **14 brother father** (The Duke's retort to Elbow's *father friar,* i.e., father brother.) **18 strange picklock** (referring to a chastity belt) **23 cram a maw** fill a stomach **30 prove** i.e., argue **31 proofs for** arguments in defense of **32 prove** turn out to be

ELBOW He must before the deputy, sir; he has given him warning. The deputy cannot abide a whoremaster. If he be a whoremonger, and comes before him, he were as good go a mile on his errand.

DUKE
That we were all, as some would seem to be,
From our faults, as faults from seeming, free!

Enter Lucio.

ELBOW His neck will come to your waist—a cord, sir.

POMPEY I spy comfort, I cry bail. Here's a gentleman and a friend of mine.

LUCIO How now, noble Pompey? What, at the wheels of Caesar? Art thou led in triumph? What, is there none of Pygmalion's images, newly made woman, to be had now, for putting the hand in the pocket and extracting it clutch'd? What reply, ha? What say'st thou to this tune, matter, and method? Is 't not drown'd i' th' last rain, ha? What say'st thou, Trot? Is the world as it was, man? Which is the way? Is it sad, and few words? Or how? The trick of it?

DUKE Still thus, and thus; still worse!

LUCIO How doth my dear morsel, thy mistress? Procures she still, ha?

POMPEY Troth, sir, she hath eaten up all her beef, and she is herself in the tub.

LUCIO Why, 'tis good. It is the right of it, it must be so. Ever your fresh whore and your powder'd bawd; an unshunn'd consequence, it must be so. Art going to prison, Pompey?

POMPEY Yes, faith, sir.

LUCIO Why, 'tis not amiss, Pompey. Farewell. Go say I sent thee thither. For debt, Pompey? Or how?

ELBOW For being a bawd, for being a bawd.

LUCIO Well, then, imprison him. If imprisonment be the due of a bawd, why, 'tis his right. Bawd is he doubtless, and of antiquity too; bawd-born. Farewell, good Pompey. Commend me to the prison, Pompey. You will turn good husband now, Pompey, you will keep the house.

POMPEY I hope, sir, your good worship will be my bail.

LUCIO No, indeed, will I not, Pompey, it is not the wear. I will pray, Pompey, to increase your bondage. If you take it not patiently, why, your mettle is the more. Adieu, trusty Pompey.—Bless you, friar.

DUKE And you.

LUCIO Does Bridget paint still, Pompey, ha?

ELBOW Come your ways, sir, come.

POMPEY You will not bail me, then, sir?

35 deputy i.e., Angelo, though Escalus gave Pompey the warning **38 he . . . errand** i.e., he will have a hard road to travel **39 That** would that **40 From . . . free** i.e., free from faults, and our faults free from dissembling **41 His . . . cord** i.e., he is likely to hang by a cord like that around your waist. (The Duke is habited like a friar.) **45 Caesar** (who defeated Pompey at Pharsalia, and led his sons in triumph) **46 Pygmalion's images** i.e., prostitutes, so called because they "painted" with cosmetics like a painted statue. (Pygmalion was a sculptor, according to legend, whose female statue came to life.) **48 clutch'd** i.e., with money in it **49–50 drown'd . . . rain** i.e., out of fashion (?) **50 Trot** old bawd **51 Which . . . way** i.e., how goes the world **56 eaten . . . beef** i.e., run through all her prostitutes **57 in the tub** (1) being pickled, as in preserving beef (2) being treated for venereal disease by the sweating-tub treatment **59 Ever . . . bawd** i.e., it always happens that young whores turn into old bawds, preserved as in salt pickling brine and caked with cosmetics **60 unshunn'd** unshunnable, unavoidable **68 antiquity** long continuance **70 good husband** thrifty manager **71 keep the house** stay indoors (with pun on the pimp's function as doorkeeper) **74 wear** fashion **75 mettle** spirit (with quibble on *metal,* i.e., the irons with which he will be shackled) **78 paint** use cosmetics **79 your ways** i.e., along

LUCIO Then, Pompey, nor now. What news abroad, friar? What news?

ELBOW Come your ways, sir, come.

LUCIO Go to kennel, Pompey, go. [*Exeunt Elbow, Pompey, and Officers.*] What news, friar, of the Duke?

DUKE I know none. Can you tell me of any?

LUCIO Some say he is with the Emperor of Russia; other some, he is in Rome. But where is he, think you?

DUKE I know not where; but wheresoever, I wish him well.

LUCIO It was a mad fantastical trick of him to steal from the state, and usurp the beggary he was never born to. Lord Angelo dukes it well in his absence; he puts transgression to 't.

DUKE He does well in 't.

LUCIO A little more lenity to lechery would do no harm in him. Something too crabbed that way, friar.

DUKE It is too general a vice, and severity must cure it.

LUCIO Yes, in good sooth, the vice is of a great kindred; it is well allied. But it is impossible to extirp it quite, friar, till eating and drinking be put down. They say this Angelo was not made by man and woman after this downright way of creation. Is it true, think you?

DUKE How should he be made, then?

LUCIO Some report a sea-maid spawn'd him; some, that he was begot between two stock-fishes. But it is certain that when he makes water his urine is congeal'd ice; that I know to be true. And he is a motion generative, that's infallible.

DUKE You are pleasant, sir, and speak apace.

LUCIO Why, what a ruthless thing is this in him, for the rebellion of a codpiece to take away the life of a man! Would the Duke that is absent have done this? Ere he would have hang'd a man for the getting a hundred bastards, he would have paid for the nursing a thousand. He had some feeling of the sport; he knew the service, and that instructed him to mercy.

DUKE I never heard the absent Duke much detected for women. He was not inclin'd that way.

LUCIO O, sir, you are deceiv'd.

DUKE 'Tis not possible.

LUCIO Who, not the Duke? Yes, your beggar of fifty; and his use was to put a ducat in her clack-dish. The Duke had crotchets in him. He would be drunk too, that let me inform you.

DUKE You do him wrong, surely.

LUCIO Sir, I was an inward of his. A shy fellow was the Duke, and I believe I know the cause of his withdrawing.

DUKE What, I prithee, might be the cause?

LUCIO No, pardon. 'Tis a secret must be lock'd within the teeth and the lips. But this I can let you understand, the greater file of the subject held the Duke to be wise.

DUKE Wise? Why, no question but he was.

81 Then neither then **93–94 puts . . . to 't** puts lawbreaking under severe restraint **100 extirp** eradicate **105 sea-maid** mermaid **106 stock-fishes** dried codfish **108–109 motion generative** masculine puppet, without power of generation **110 pleasant** jocose **112 codpiece** an appendage to the front of close-fitting hose or breeches worn by men, often ornamented and indelicately conspicuous; hence, slang for "penis" **123 clack-dish** beggar's wooden dish with a lid, which was "clacked" to attract attention; probably used metaphorically here for the female pudenda **124 crotchets** whims **127 inward** intimate acquaintance **133 the greater . . . subject** the majority of his subjects

LUCIO A very superficial, ignorant, unweighing fellow.

DUKE Either this is envy in you, folly, or mistaking. The very stream of his life and the business he hath helm'd must, upon a warranted need, give him a better proclamation. Let him be but testimonied in his own bringings-forth, and he shall appear to the envious a scholar, a statesman, and a soldier. Therefore you speak unskillfully; or, if your knowledge be more, it is much dark'ned in your malice.

LUCIO Sir, I know him, and I love him.

DUKE Love talks with better knowledge, and knowledge with dearer love.

LUCIO Come, sir, I know what I know.

DUKE I can hardly believe that, since you know not what you speak. But if ever the Duke return, as our prayers are he may, let me desire you to make your answer before him. If it be honest you have spoke, you have courage to maintain it. I am bound to call upon you; and, I pray you, your name?

LUCIO Sir, my name is Lucio, well known to the Duke.

DUKE He shall know you better, sir, if I may live to report you.

LUCIO I fear you not.

DUKE O, you hope the Duke will return no more, or you imagine me too unhurtful an opposite. But indeed I can do you little harm; you'll forswear this again.

LUCIO I'll be hang'd first. Thou art deceiv'd in me, friar. But no more of this. Canst thou tell if Claudio die tomorrow or no?

DUKE Why should he die, sir?

LUCIO Why? For filling a bottle with a tun-dish. I would the Duke we talk of were return'd again. This ungenitur'd agent will unpeople the province with continency. Sparrows must not build in his house-eaves, because they are lecherous. The Duke yet would have dark deeds darkly answer'd; he would never bring them to light. Would he were return'd! Marry, this Claudio is condemn'd for untrussing. Farewell, good friar. I prithee, pray for me. The Duke, I say to thee again, would eat mutton on Fridays. He's now past it, yet, and I say to thee, he would mouth with a beggar, though she smelt brown bread and garlic. Say that I said so. Farewell. *Exit.*

DUKE
No might nor greatness in mortality
Can censure scape; back-wounding calumny
The whitest virtue strikes. What king so strong
Can tie the gall up in the slanderous tongue?
But who comes here?

Enter Escalus, Provost, and [*Officers with*] *Bawd* [*Mistress Overdone*].

ESCALUS Go, away with her to prison.

MISTRESS OVERDONE Good my lord, be good to me. Your honor is accounted a merciful man. Good my lord.

ESCALUS Double and treble admonition, and still forfeit in the same kind! This would make mercy swear and play the tyrant.

PROVOST A bawd of eleven years' continuance, may it please your honor.

MISTRESS OVERDONE My lord, this is one Lucio's information against me. Mistress Kate Keepdown was with child by him in the Duke's time; he promis'd her marriage. His child is a year and a quarter old, come Philip and Jacob. I have kept it myself; and see how he goes about to abuse me!

ESCALUS That fellow is a fellow of much licence. Let him be call'd before us. Away with her to prison! Go to; no more words. [*Exeunt Officers with Mistress Overdone.*] Provost, my brother Angelo will not be alter'd. Claudio must die tomorrow. Let him be furnish'd with divines, and have all charitable preparation. If my brother wrought by my pity, it should not be so with him.

PROVOST So please you, this friar hath been with him, and advis'd him for th' entertainment of death.

ESCALUS Good even, good father.

DUKE Bliss and goodness on you!

ESCALUS Of whence are you?

DUKE
Not of this country, though my chance is now
To use it for my time. I am a brother
Of gracious order, late come from the See
In special business from his Holiness.

ESCALUS What news abroad i' th' world?

DUKE None, but that there is so great a fever on goodness that the dissolution of it must cure it. Novelty is only in request, and, as it is, as dangerous to be aged in any kind of course, as it is virtuous to be constant in any undertaking. There is scarce truth enough alive to make societies secure, but security enough to make fellowships accurs'd. Much upon this riddle runs the wisdom of the world. This news is old enough, yet it is every day's news. I pray you, sir, of what disposition was the Duke?

ESCALUS One that, above all other strifes, contended especially to know himself.

DUKE What pleasure was he given to?

ESCALUS Rather rejoicing to see another merry, than merry at any thing which profess'd to make him rejoice; a gentleman of all temperance. But leave we him to his events, with a prayer they may prove prosperous, and let me desire to know how you find Claudio prepar'd. I am made to understand that you have lent him visitation.

136 unweighing not considering carefully **137 envy** malice **138 helm'd** steered **139 upon . . . need** if a warrant were needed **139–140 give . . . proclamation** proclaim him better (than you assert) **140–141 in . . . bringings-forth** by his own public actions **141 to the envious** even to the malicious **160 too . . . opposite** too harmless an adversary **161 forswear this** deny under oath what you've said **166 tun-dish** funnel (here representing the penis) **167–168 ungenitur'd agent** sexless deputy **169 Sparrows** (Proverbially lecherous birds.) **171 darkly answer'd** not made public **173 untrussing** undressing. (Specifically, untying the points used to fasten hose to doublet.) **175 mutton** i.e., prostitute. (To *eat mutton on Fridays* is to violate religious observance by eating meat on fast-days, i.e., to frequent prostitutes.) **177 smelt brown bread** smelled of coarse bran bread **179 mortality** humankind **180 back-wounding** backbiting

188–189 forfeit . . . kind guilty of the same offense **189 mercy** i.e., even mercy **196–197 Philip and Jacob** the Feast of St. Philip and St. James (*Jacobus* in Latin), May 1 **202 brother** i.e., fellow officer of state **205 wrought . . . pity** acted in accord with my impulses of pity **208 entertainment** reception, acceptance **214 the See** Rome **218 the dissolution . . . cure it** i.e., only by dying can goodness be rid of the disease **218–219 is only in request** is the only thing people desire **219–221 as it . . . undertaking** as things currently stand, (it is) as dangerous to be constant in any undertaking as it is virtuous to be thus constant **221–223 There . . . accurs'd** i.e., there is hardly enough integrity and trust extant to bind men in sincere affection, but binding contractual obligations enough to make ordinary transactions intolerable **223 upon this riddle** in this riddling fashion **227 strifes** endeavors **233 his events** the outcome of his affairs

DUKE He professes to have receiv'd no sinister measure from his judge, but most willingly humbles himself to the determination of justice; yet had he fram'd to himself, by the instruction of his frailty, many deceiving promises of life, which I, by my good leisure, have discredited to him, and now is he resolv'd to die.

ESCALUS You have paid the heavens your function, and the prisoner the very debt of your calling. I have labor'd for the poor gentleman to the extremest shore of my modesty, but my brother justice have I found so severe, that he hath forc'd me to tell him he is indeed Justice.

DUKE If his own life answer the straitness of his proceeding, it shall become him well; wherein if he chance to fail, he hath sentenc'd himself.

ESCALUS I am going to visit the prisoner. Fare you well.

DUKE
Peace be with you! [*Exeunt Escalus and Provost.*]
He who the sword of heaven will bear
Should be as holy as severe;
Pattern in himself to know,
Grace to stand, and virtue go;
More nor less to others paying
Than by self-offenses weighing.
Shame to him whose cruel striking
Kills for faults of his own liking!
Twice treble shame on Angelo,
To weed my vice and let his grow!
O, what may man within him hide,
Though angel on the outward side!
How may likeness made in crimes,
Making practice on the times,
To draw with idle spiders' strings
Most ponderous and substantial things!
Craft against vice I must apply.
With Angelo tonight shall lie
His old betrothed but despised;
So disguise shall, by th' disguised,
Pay with falsehood false exacting,
And perform an old contracting. *Exit.*

ACT IV • SCENE I

Enter Mariana, and Boy singing.

Song.

Take, O, take those lips away,
  That so sweetly were forsworn;
And those eyes, the break of day,
  Lights that do mislead the morn.
But my kisses bring again, bring again,
Seals of love, but seal'd in vain, seal'd in vain.

Enter Duke [*disguised as before*].

MARIANA
Break off thy song, and haste thee quick away.
Here comes a man of comfort, whose advice
Hath often still'd my brawling discontent. [*Exit Boy.*]
I cry you mercy, sir, and well could wish
You had not found me here so musical.
Let me excuse me, and believe me so,
My mirth it much displeas'd, but pleas'd my woe.

DUKE
'Tis good; though music oft hath such a charm
To make bad good, and good provoke to harm.
I pray you, tell me, hath any body inquir'd for me here today? Much upon this time have I promis'd here to meet.

MARIANA You have not been inquir'd after. I have sat here all day.

Enter Isabella.

DUKE I do constantly believe you. The time is come even now. I shall crave your forbearance a little. May be I will call upon you anon, for some advantage to yourself.

MARIANA I am always bound to you. *Exit.*

DUKE
Very well met, and well come.
What is the news from this good deputy?

ISABELLA
He hath a garden circummur'd with brick,
Whose western side is with a vineyard back'd;
And to that vineyard is a planched gate,
That makes his opening with this bigger key.
[*Shows keys.*]
This other doth command a little door
Which from the vineyard to the garden leads;
There have I made my promise, upon the
Heavy middle of the night, to call upon him.

DUKE
But shall you on your knowledge find this way?

ISABELLA
I have ta'en a due and wary note upon 't.
With whispering and most guilty diligence,
In action all of precept, he did show me
The way twice o'er.

DUKE Are there no other tokens
Between you 'greed concerning her observance?

ISABELLA
No, none, but only a repair i' th' dark,
And that I have possess'd him my most stay
Can be but brief; for I have made him know
I have a servant comes with me along,
That stays upon me, whose persuasion is

237 sinister unfair, unjust **239–240 fram'd to himself** formulated in his mind **240 by . . . frailty** at the prompting of his natural human weakness **245–246 shore . . . modesty** limit of propriety **249 straitness** strictness **256 Pattern . . . know** to find an example or *pattern* in himself by which to judge others (?) **257 Grace . . . go** (to find in himself) grace to keep him upright and virtue to guide him forward (?) **258–259 More . . . weighing** inflicting no more and no less punishment on others than he would inflict upon himself for his own offenses **263 my vice** i.e., someone else's sin **266–269 How . . . things** (Seemingly a corrupt passage, perhaps missing two lines.) **267 Making . . . times** practicing deception on the world **274 falsehood** illusion, i.e., Mariana's disguise. **false exacting** extortion, bribery (by Angelo)

IV.i. Location: The moated grange at St. Luke's.
4 mislead the morn i.e., into thinking the sun has risen

9 brawling clamorous **10 cry you mercy** beg your pardon **13 My . . . woe** i.e., it suited not a merry but a melancholy mood **15 bad good** i.e., bad seem good, attractive. (The Duke, echoing Renaissance conceptions of the psychological effects of music, warns that music may soothe melancholy at times but may also produce distressing effects on the mind.) **17 upon** about **21 constantly** confidently **22 crave . . . little** i.e., ask you to withdraw briefly **28 circummur'd** walled about **30 planched** made of boards, planks **39 In action . . . precept** i.e., teaching by demonstration **41 her observance** what she is supposed to do **42 repair** act of going or coming to a place **43 possess'd** informed. **my most stay** my stay at the longest **46 stays upon** waits for

I come about my brother.
DUKE 'Tis well borne up.
I have not yet made known to Mariana
A word of this. What, ho, within! Come forth!

Enter Mariana.

I pray you, be acquainted with this maid;
She comes to do you good.
ISABELLA I do desire the like.
DUKE
Do you persuade yourself that I respect you?
MARIANA
Good friar, I know you do, and have found it.
DUKE
Take, then, this your companion by the hand,
Who hath a story ready for your ear.
I shall attend your leisure. But make haste;
The vaporous night approaches.
MARIANA
Will 't please you walk aside? *Exit [with Isabella].*
DUKE
O place and greatness! Millions of false eyes
Are stuck upon thee. Volumes of report
Run with these false, and most contrarious quest
Upon thy doings; thousand escapes of wit
Make thee the father of their idle dream,
And rack thee in their fancies.

Enter Mariana and Isabella.

Welcome, how agreed?
ISABELLA
She'll take the enterprise upon her, father,
If you advise it.
DUKE It is not my consent,
But my entreaty too.
ISABELLA Little have you to say
When you depart from him, but, soft and low,
"Remember now my brother."
MARIANA Fear me not.
DUKE
Nor, gentle daughter, fear you not at all.
He is your husband on a pre-contract;
To bring you thus together, 'tis no sin,
Sith that the justice of your title to him
Doth flourish the deceit. Come, let us go.
Our corn's to reap, for yet our tithe's to sow. *Exeunt.*

SCENE II

Enter Provost and Clown [Pompey].

PROVOST Come hither, sirrah. Can you cut off a man's head?

POMPEY If the man be a bachelor, sir, I can; but if he be a married man, he's his wife's head, and I can never cut off a woman's head.

PROVOST Come, sir, leave me your snatches, and yield me a direct answer. Tomorrow morning are to die Claudio and Barnardine. Here is in our prison a common executioner, who in his office lacks a helper. If you will take it on you to assist him, it shall redeem you from your gyves; if not, you shall have your full time of imprisonment and your deliverance with an unpitied whipping, for you have been a notorious bawd.

POMPEY Sir, I have been an unlawful bawd time out of mind, but yet I will be content to be a lawful hangman. I would be glad to receive some instruction from my fellow partner.

PROVOST What, ho, Abhorson! Where's Abhorson, there?

Enter Abhorson.

ABHORSON Do you call, sir?

PROVOST Sirrah, here's a fellow will help you tomorrow in your execution. If you think it meet, compound with him by the year, and let him abide here with you; if not, use him for the present and dismiss him. He cannot plead his estimation with you; he hath been a bawd.

ABHORSON A bawd, sir? Fie upon him! He will discredit our mystery.

PROVOST Go to, sir, you weigh equally; a feather will turn the scale. *Exit.*

POMPEY Pray, sir, by your good favor—for surely, sir, a good favor you have, but that you have a hanging look—do you call, sir, your occupation a mystery?

ABHORSON Ay, sir, a mystery.

POMPEY Painting, sir, I have heard say, is a mystery, and your whores, sir, being members of my occupation, using painting, do prove my occupation a mystery. But what mystery there should be in hanging, if I should be hang'd, I cannot imagine.

ABHORSON Sir, it is a mystery.

POMPEY Proof?

ABHORSON Every true man's apparel fits your thief. If it be too little for your thief, your true man thinks it big enough; if it be too big for your thief, your thief thinks it little enough. So every true man's apparel fits your thief.

Enter Provost.

PROVOST Are you agreed?

POMPEY Sir, I will serve him, for I do find your hangman is a more penitent trade than your bawd; he doth oft'ner ask forgiveness.

52 respect you are concerned for your welfare **53 found it** i.e., found it to be true **60 stuck** fastened. **report** rumor **61 these false** i.e., these false eyes. **contrarious** perversely. **quest** give tongue, like hunting dogs in sight of their prey (continuing the hunting metaphor begun in *Run with*) **62 escapes** sallies **64 rack** stretch as on the rack, distort **66 not** not only **67 Little . . . say** say little **69 Fear me not** i.e., don't worry about my carrying out my part **71 pre-contract** legally binding agreement **74 flourish** embellish, make fair **75 Our corn's . . . sow** we must first sow grain before we can expect to reap a harvest; i.e., we must get started. **tithe** grain sown for tithe dues

IV.ii. Location: The prison.

5 head i.e., maidenhead **6 leave . . . snatches** leave off your quips **8–9 common** public **11 gyves** fetters, shackles **23 compound** make an agreement **26 plead his estimation** claim any respect on account of his reputation **29 mystery** craft, occupation **32–33 favor . . . favor** leave . . . face **33–34 hanging look** (1) downcast look (2) look of a hangman **36 Painting** (1) painting of pictures (2) applying cosmetics **43–46 Every . . . enough** (Just as Pompey argues that whores belong to a skilled craft because they are like painters, Abhorson implies that hangmen are skilled craftsmen because they are like thieves who in turn are like tailors; both thieves and tailors "fit" honest men's apparel, by stealing or adjusting it. Hangmen in turn are like thieves because they receive the garments of the men they execute.) **44–45 big enough** i.e., enough of a loss **46 little enough** i.e., because it can be cut down to fit (?) **50–51 he doth . . . forgiveness** (The executioner perfunctorily asked forgiveness of those whose lives he was about to take.)

PROVOST You, sirrah, provide your block and your axe tomorrow four o'clock.

ABHORSON Come on, bawd. I will instruct thee in my trade; follow.

POMPEY I do desire to learn, sir; and I hope, if you have occasion to use me for your own turn, you shall find me yare. For truly, sir, for your kindness I owe you a good turn.

PROVOST
Call hither Barnardine and Claudio.
Exit [Pompey, with Abhorson].
Th' one has my pity; not a jot the other,
Being a murderer, though he were my brother.

Enter Claudio.

Look, here's the warrant, Claudio, for thy death.
'Tis now dead midnight, and by eight tomorrow
Thou must be made immortal. Where's Barnardine?

CLAUDIO
As fast lock'd up in sleep as guiltless labor
When it lies starkly in the traveler's bones.
He will not wake.

PROVOST Who can do good on him?
Well, go, prepare yourself. [*Knocking within.*] But, hark, what noise?
Heaven give your spirits comfort! [*Exit Claudio.*] By and by.—
I hope it is some pardon or reprieve
For the most gentle Claudio.

Enter Duke [disguised as before].

DUKE Welcome, father.
The best and wholesom'st spirits of the night
Envelop you, good Provost! Who call'd here of late?

PROVOST
None, since the curfew rung.

DUKE
Not Isabel?

PROVOST No.

DUKE They will, then, ere 't be long.

PROVOST
What comfort is for Claudio?

DUKE
There's some in hope.

PROVOST It is a bitter deputy.

DUKE
Not so, not so. His life is parallel'd
Even with the stroke and line of his great justice.
He doth with holy abstinence subdue
That in himself which he spurs on his pow'r
To qualify in others. Were he meal'd with that
Which he corrects, then were he tyrannous;
But this being so, he's just. [*Knocking within.*]
Now are they come.
[*Provost goes to the door.*]
This is a gentle Provost; seldom when
The steeled jailer is the friend of men.
[*Knocking within.*]
How now, what noise? That spirit's possess'd with haste
That wounds th' unsisting postern with these strokes.

PROVOST [*Speaking at the door*]
There he must stay until the officer
Arise to let him in; he is call'd up.
[*He returns to the Duke.*]

DUKE
Have you no countermand for Claudio yet,
But he must die tomorrow?

PROVOST None, sir, none.

DUKE
As near the dawning, Provost, as it is,
You shall hear more ere morning.

PROVOST Happily
You something know, yet I believe there comes
No countermand; no such example have we.
Besides, upon the very siege of justice
Lord Angelo hath to the public ear
Profess'd the contrary.

Enter a Messenger.

This is his lordship's man.

DUKE
And here comes Claudio's pardon.

MESSENGER [*Giving a paper*] My lord hath sent you this note, and by me this further charge, that you swerve not from the smallest article of it, neither in time, matter, or other circumstance. Good morrow; for, as I take it, it is almost day.

PROVOST I shall obey him. [*Exit Messenger.*]

DUKE [*Aside*]
This is his pardon, purchas'd by such sin
For which the pardoner himself is in.
Hence hath offense his quick celerity,
When it is borne in high authority.
When vice makes mercy, mercy's so extended
That for the fault's love is th' offender friended.—
Now, sir, what news?

PROVOST I told you. Lord Angelo, belike thinking me remiss in mine office, awakens me with this unwonted putting-on—methinks strangely, for he hath not us'd it before.

DUKE Pray you, let's hear.

[PROVOST *reads*] *the letter*
"Whatsoever you may hear to the contrary, let Claudio be executed by four of the clock, and in the afternoon Barnardine. For my better satisfaction, let me have Claudio's head sent me by five. Let this be duly perform'd, with a thought that more depends on it than we must yet deliver. Thus fail not to do your office, as you will answer it at your peril."
What say you to this, sir?

DUKE What is that Barnardine who is to be executed in th' afternoon?

PROVOST A Bohemian born, but here nurs'd up and bred, one that is a prisoner nine years old.

57 for . . . turn (1) in seeking sexual consolation, using me as a pimp (2) for your own hanging or "turning off" **58 yare** ready, alacritous **67 starkly** stiffly. **traveler's** laborer's, of one who travails **83 qualify** mitigate. **meal'd** spotted, stained **86 seldom when** i.e., it is seldom that **87 steeled** hardened

89 unsisting unassisting, or unresisting (?). **postern** small door **95 Happily** haply, perhaps **97 example** precedent **98 siege** seat **110 his** its **115 belike** perchance **117 putting-on** urging **123 better satisfaction** greater assurance **126 deliver** make known **131 here** i.e., in Vienna **132 a prisoner . . . old** nine years a prisoner

DUKE How came it that the absent Duke had not either
deliver'd him to his liberty or executed him? I have
heard it was ever his manner to do so.
PROVOST His friends still wrought reprieves for him;
and indeed his fact, till now in the government of Lord 137
Angelo, came not to an undoubtful proof.
DUKE It is now apparent?
PROVOST Most manifest, and not denied by himself.
DUKE Hath he borne himself penitently in prison? How
seems he to be touch'd?
PROVOST A man that apprehends death no more dread-
fully but as a drunken sleep—careless, reckless, and
fearless of what's past, present, or to come; insensible 145
of mortality, and desperately mortal. 146
DUKE He wants advice. 147
PROVOST He will hear none. He hath evermore had the
liberty of the prison; give him leave to escape hence,
he would not. Drunk many times a day, if not many
days entirely drunk. We have very oft awak'd him, as
if to carry him to execution, and show'd him a seem-
ing warrant for it; it hath not mov'd him at all.
DUKE More of him anon. There is written in your brow,
Provost, honesty and constancy; if I read it not truly,
my ancient skill beguiles me, but, in the boldness of 156
my cunning, I will lay my self in hazard. Claudio, 157
whom here you have warrant to execute, is no greater
forfeit to the law than Angelo who hath sentenc'd him.
To make you understand this in a manifested effect, I 160
crave but four days' respite, for the which you are to
do me both a present and a dangerous courtesy. 162
PROVOST Pray, sir, in what?
DUKE In the delaying death.
PROVOST Alack, how may I do it, having the hour lim- 165
ited, and an express command, under penalty, to de- 166
liver his head in the view of Angelo? I may make my
case as Claudio's, to cross this in the smallest.
DUKE By the vow of mine order I warrant you, if my
instructions may be your guide. Let this Barnardine
be this morning executed, and his head borne to An-
gelo.
PROVOST Angelo hath seen them both, and will dis- 173
cover the favor. 174
DUKE O, death's a great disguiser, and you may add to
it. Shave the head, and tie the beard, and say it was 176
the desire of the penitent to be so bar'd before his
death. You know the course is common. If any thing
fall to you upon this, more than thanks and good for- 179
tune, by the saint whom I profess, I will plead against
it with my life.
PROVOST Pardon me, good father, it is against my oath.
DUKE Were you sworn to the Duke, or to the deputy?
PROVOST To him, and to his substitutes.
DUKE You will think you have made no offense, if the
Duke avouch the justice of your dealing? 186
PROVOST But what likelihood is in that?
DUKE Not a resemblance, but a certainty. Yet since I see
you fearful, that neither my coat, integrity, nor persua-
sion can with ease attempt you, I will go further than 190
I meant, to pluck all fears out of you. Look you, sir,
here is the hand and seal of the Duke. [*Shows letter.*]
You know the character, I doubt not, and the signet is 193
not strange to you.
PROVOST I know them both.
DUKE The contents of this is the return of the Duke.
You shall anon over-read it at your pleasure, where
you shall find, within these two days he will be here.
This is a thing that Angelo knows not, for he this very
day receives letters of strange tenor, perchance of the
Duke's death, perchance entering into some monas-
tery, but by chance nothing of what is writ. Look, th' 202
unfolding star calls up the shepherd. Put not yourself 203
into amazement how these things should be; all diffi-
culties are but easy when they are known. Call your
executioner, and off with Barnardine's head. I will give
him a present shrift and advise him for a better place. 207
Yet you are amaz'd, but this shall absolutely resolve 208
you. Come away; it is almost clear dawn. 209
Exit [*with Provost*].

SCENE III

Enter Clown [*Pompey*].

POMPEY I am as well acquainted here as I was in our 1
house of profession. One would think it were Mistress
Overdone's own house, for here be many of her old
customers. First, here's young Master Rash; he's in for
a commodity of brown paper and old ginger, nine- 5
score and seventeen pounds, of which he made five
marks, ready money. Marry, then ginger was not
much in request, for the old women were all dead. 8
Then is there here one Master Caper, at the suit of
Master Three-pile the mercer, for some four suits of
peach-color'd satin, which now peaches him a beggar. 11
Then have we here young Dizzy, and young Master
Deep-vow, and Master Copper-spur, and Master
Starve-lackey the rapier and dagger man, and young
Drop-heir that kill'd lusty Pudding, and Master Forth-
light the tilter, and brave Master Shoe-tie the great 16
traveler, and wild Half-can that stabb'd Pots, and, I
think, forty more, all great doers in our trade, and are
now "for the Lord's sake." 19

Enter Abhorson.

ABHORSON Sirrah, bring Barnardine hither.
POMPEY Master Barnardine! You must rise and be
hang'd, Master Barnardine!

137 fact crime **145–146 insensible . . . mortal** incapable of comprehending the meaning of death, and without hope of immortality or of escaping execution **147 wants** needs **156–157 boldness . . . hazard** confident in my knowledge (of human character), I will risk my life **160 in . . . effect** by means of concrete proof **162 present** immediate **165–166 limited** fixed, set **173–174 discover the favor** recognize the face **176 tie** trim, dress (?) **179 fall to** befall **186 avouch** confirm

190 attempt win, influence **193 character** handwriting **202 writ** i.e., written here (?) **203 unfolding star** i.e., morning star, which bids the shepherd lead his sheep from the fold **207 present shrift** immediate absolution for sins (after confession) **208–209 resolve you** dispel your uncertainties

IV.iii. Location: The prison.
1 well widely **5 a commodity . . . ginger** (To circumvent the laws against excessive rates of interest, moneylenders often advanced cheap commodities such as brown paper to gullible borrowers in lieu of cash at a high rate of interest. Master Rash, having agreed to a valuation of 197 pounds for such merchandise, has been able to resell it for five marks, each mark worth about two thirds of a pound, and has been thrown into prison for debt.) **8 old women** (Proverbially fond of ginger.) **11 peaches him** denounces him as **16 tilter** jouster **19 for . . . sake** (The cry of prisoners from jail windows to passers-by to give them food or alms.)

ABHORSON What, ho, Barnardine!

BARNARDINE *(Within)* A pox o' your throats! Who makes that noise there? What are you?

POMPEY Your friends, sir, the hangman. You must be so good, sir, to rise and be put to death.

BARNARDINE [*Within*] Away, you rogue, away! I am sleepy.

ABHORSON Tell him he must awake, and that quickly too.

POMPEY Pray, Master Barnardine, awake till you are executed, and sleep afterwards.

ABHORSON Go in to him, and fetch him out.

POMPEY He is coming, sir, he is coming. I hear his straw rustle.

Enter Barnardine.

ABHORSON Is the axe upon the block, sirrah?

POMPEY Very ready, sir.

BARNARDINE How now, Abhorson? What's the news with you?

ABHORSON Truly, sir, I would desire you to clap into your prayers; for, look you, the warrant's come.

BARNARDINE You rogue, I have been drinking all night. I am not fitted for 't.

POMPEY O, the better, sir; for he that drinks all night, and is hang'd betimes in the morning, may sleep the sounder all the next day.

Enter Duke [*disguised as before*].

ABHORSON Look you, sir, here comes your ghostly father. Do we jest now, think you?

DUKE Sir, induc'd by my charity, and hearing how hastily you are to depart, I am come to advise you, comfort you, and pray with you.

BARNARDINE Friar, not I. I have been drinking hard all night, and I will have more time to prepare me, or they shall beat out my brains with billets. I will not consent to die this day, that's certain.

DUKE
O, sir, you must, and therefore I beseech you
Look forward on the journey you shall go.

BARNARDINE I swear I will not die today for any man's persuasion.

DUKE But hear you—

BARNARDINE Not a word. If you have any thing to say to me, come to my ward, for thence will not I today. *Exit.*

Enter Provost.

DUKE
Unfit to live or die. O gravel heart!
After him, fellows; bring him to the block.
[*Exeunt Abhorson and Pompey.*]

PROVOST
Now, sir, how do you find the prisoner?

DUKE
A creature unprepar'd, unmeet for death;
And to transport him in the mind he is
Were damnable.

PROVOST Here in the prison, father,
There died this morning of a cruel fever
One Ragozine, a most notorious pirate,
A man of Claudio's years; his beard and head
Just of his color. What if we do omit
This reprobate till he were well inclin'd,
And satisfy the deputy with the visage
Of Ragozine, more like to Claudio?

DUKE
O, 'tis an accident that heaven provides!
Dispatch it presently; the hour draws on
Prefix'd by Angelo. See this be done,
And sent according to command, whiles I
Persuade this rude wretch willingly to die.

PROVOST
This shall be done, good father, presently.
But Barnardine must die this afternoon.
And how shall we continue Claudio,
To save me from the danger that might come
If he were known alive?

DUKE Let this be done.
Put them in secret holds, both Barnardine and
Claudio.
Ere twice the sun hath made his journal greeting
To th' under generation, you shall find
Your safety manifested.

PROVOST
I am your free dependent.

DUKE
Quick, dispatch, and send the head to Angelo.
Exit [*Provost*].
Now will I write letters to Angelo—
The Provost, he shall bear them—whose contents
Shall witness to him I am near at home,
And that, by great injunctions, I am bound
To enter publicly. Him I'll desire
To meet me at the consecrated fount
A league below the city; and from thence,
By cold gradation and well-balanc'd form,
We shall proceed with Angelo.

Enter Provost [*with Ragozine's head*].

PROVOST
Here is the head; I'll carry it myself.

DUKE
Convenient is it. Make a swift return,
For I would commune with you of such things
That want no ear but yours.

PROVOST I'll make all speed. *Exit.*

ISABELLA *(Within)*
Peace, ho, be here!

DUKE
The tongue of Isabel. She's come to know
If yet her brother's pardon be come hither.
But I will keep her ignorant of her good,

46 betimes early **48 ghostly** spiritual **55 billets** cudgels, blocks of wood **63 ward** cell **64 gravel** stony

84 continue retain **87 holds** cells, dungeons **88 journal** daily **89 th' under generation** i.e., people in the Antipodes, on the opposite side of the earth, or, people under the sun, the human race **91 free dependent** willing servant **93 to Angelo** (Perhaps an error for *to Varrius,* picked up from the end of the preceding line. Angelo is not to meet the Duke *at the consecrated fount a league below the city,* but at the city gates.) **96 by great injunctions** by powerful precedent, or for compelling reasons **98 fount** spring **100 cold . . . form** i.e., moving deliberately and with proper observance of all formalities **103 Convenient** timely, fitting

To make her heavenly comforts of despair
When it is least expected.

Enter Isabella.

ISABELLA Ho, by your leave!

DUKE
Good morning to you, fair and gracious daughter.

ISABELLA
The better, given me by so holy a man.
Hath yet the deputy sent my brother's pardon?

DUKE
He hath releas'd him, Isabel, from the world.
His head is off and sent to Angelo.

ISABELLA
Nay, but it is not so!

DUKE It is no other.
Show your wisdom, daughter, in your close patience.

ISABELLA
O, I will to him and pluck out his eyes!

DUKE
You shall not be admitted to his sight.

ISABELLA
Unhappy Claudio! Wretched Isabel!
Injurious world! Most damned Angelo!

DUKE
This nor hurts him nor profits you a jot.
Forbear it therefore; give your cause to heaven.
Mark what I say, which you shall find
By every syllable a faithful verity.
The Duke comes home tomorrow—nay, dry your eyes—
One of our covent, and his confessor,
Gives me this instance. Already he hath carried
Notice to Escalus and Angelo,
Who do prepare to meet him at the gates,
There to give up their pow'r. If you can, pace your wisdom
In that good path that I would wish it go,
And you shall have your bosom on this wretch,
Grace of the Duke, revenges to your heart,
And general honor.

ISABELLA I am directed by you.

DUKE
This letter, then, to Friar Peter give;
[*Gives her letter.*]
'Tis that he sent me of the Duke's return.
Say, by this token, I desire his company
At Mariana's house tonight. Her cause and yours
I'll perfect him withal, and he shall bring you
Before the Duke, and to the head of Angelo
Accuse him home and home. For my poor self,
I am combined by a sacred vow
And shall be absent. Wend you with this letter.
Command these fretting waters from your eyes
With a light heart; trust not my holy order
If I pervert your course. Who's here?

Enter Lucio.

LUCIO Good even. Friar, where's the Provost?

DUKE Not within, sir.

LUCIO O pretty Isabella, I am pale at mine heart to see thine eyes so red; thou must be patient. I am fain to dine and sup with water and bran; I dare not for my head fill my belly; one fruitful meal would set me to 't. But they say the Duke will be here tomorrow. By my troth, Isabel, I lov'd thy brother. If the old fantastical Duke of dark corners had been at home, he had liv'd. [*Exit Isabella.*]

DUKE Sir, the Duke is marvelous little beholding to your reports; but the best is, he lives not in them.

LUCIO Friar, thou knowest not the Duke so well as I do. He's a better woodman than thou tak'st him for.

DUKE Well, you'll answer this one day. Fare ye well. [*Starts to go.*]

LUCIO Nay, tarry, I'll go along with thee. I can tell thee pretty tales of the Duke.

DUKE You have told me too many of him already, sir, if they be true; if not true, none were enough.

LUCIO I was once before him for getting a wench with child.

DUKE Did you such a thing?

LUCIO Yes, marry, did I, but I was fain to forswear it. They would else have married me to the rotten medlar.

DUKE Sir, your company is fairer than honest. Rest you well.

LUCIO By my troth, I'll go with thee to the lane's end. If bawdy talk offend you, we'll have very little of it. Nay, friar, I am a kind of burr; I shall stick. *Exeunt.*

SCENE IV

Enter Angelo and Escalus, [*reading letters*].

ESCALUS Every letter he hath writ hath disvouch'd other.

ANGELO In most uneven and distracted manner. His actions show much like to madness. Pray heaven his wisdom be not tainted! And why meet him at the gates, and redeliver our authorities there?

ESCALUS I guess not.

ANGELO And why should we proclaim it in an hour before his ent'ring that, if any crave redress of injustice, they should exhibit their petitions in the street?

ESCALUS He shows his reason for that: to have a dispatch of complaints, and to deliver us from devices hereafter, which shall then have no power to stand against us.

ANGELO Well, I beseech you, let it be proclaim'd betimes i' th' morn. I'll call you at your house. Give notice to such men of sort and suit as are to meet him.

118 close patience silent enduring **123 nor hurts** neither hurts **128 covent** convent **129 instance** proof **132 pace** teach to move in response to your will, as with a horse **134 bosom** desire **141 perfect** acquaint completely **142 head** i.e., face **143 home and home** thoroughly **144 combined** bound **146 fretting** corroding

151 I am . . . heart i.e., from sighing, since sighs cost the heart loss of blood **152 fain** compelled **153–154 for my head** i.e., on my life **154–155 set me to 't** i.e., awaken my lust and thus place me in danger of Angelo's edict **159 beholding** beholden **160 he . . . them** i.e., he is not accurately described by them **162 woodman** i.e., woman hunter **172 medlar** a fruit that was eaten after it had begun to rot; here, signifying a prostitute

IV.iv. Location: Angelo's house.
1 disvouch'd contradicted **8 in an hour** i.e., a full hour **12 devices** contrived complaints **15–16 betimes** early **17 sort** rank. **suit** such as owe attendance

ESCALUS I shall, sir. Fare you well.
ANGELO Good night. *Exit* [*Escalus*].
This deed unshapes me quite, makes me unpregnant 20
And dull to all proceedings. A deflow'red maid:
And by an eminent body that enforc'd 22
The law against it! But that her tender shame 23
Will not proclaim against her maiden loss,
How might she tongue me! Yet reason dares her no, 25
For my authority bears of a credent bulk, 26
That no particular scandal once can touch
But it confounds the breather. He should have liv'd, 28
Save that his riotous youth, with dangerous sense, 29
Might in the times to come have ta'en revenge,
By so receiving a dishonor'd life
With ransom of such shame. Would yet he had liv'd!
Alack, when once our grace we have forgot,
Nothing goes right; we would, and we would not.
Exit.

SCENE V

Enter Duke [*in his own habit*] *and Friar Peter.*

DUKE
These letters at fit time deliver me. 1
[*Giving letters.*]
The Provost knows our purpose and our plot.
The matter being afoot, keep your instruction, 3
And hold you ever to our special drift, 4
Though sometimes you do blench from this to that, 5
As cause doth minister. Go call at Flavius' house, 6
And tell him where I stay. Give the like notice
To Valencius, Rowland, and to Crassus,
And bid them bring the trumpets to the gate; 9
But send me Flavius first.
FRIAR PETER
It shall be speeded well. [*Exit.*]

Enter Varrius.

DUKE
I thank thee, Varrius; thou hast made good haste.
Come, we will walk. There's other of our friends
Will greet us here anon. My gentle Varrius! *Exeunt.*

SCENE VI

Enter Isabella and Mariana.

ISABELLA
To speak so indirectly I am loath.
I would say the truth, but to accuse him so,
That is your part. Yet I am advis'd to do it,
He says, to veil full purpose.
MARIANA Be rul'd by him.
ISABELLA
Besides, he tells me that, if peradventure
He speak against me on the adverse side,
I should not think it strange, for 'tis a physic
That's bitter to sweet end.

Enter [*Friar*] *Peter.*

MARIANA
I would Friar Peter—
ISABELLA O, peace! The friar is come.
FRIAR PETER
Come, I have found you out a stand most fit,
Where you may have such vantage on the Duke,
He shall not pass you. Twice have the trumpets sounded;
The generous and gravest citizens 13
Have hent the gates, and very near upon 14
The Duke is ent'ring. Therefore, hence, away!
Exeunt.

ACT V • SCENE I

Enter Duke, Varrius, Lords, Angelo, Escalus, Lucio, [*Provost, Officers, and*] *Citizens at several doors.*

DUKE
My very worthy cousin, fairly met! 1
Our old and faithful friend, we are glad to see you.
ANGELO, ESCALUS
Happy return be to your royal Grace!
DUKE
Many and hearty thankings to you both.
We have made inquiry of you, and we hear
Such goodness of your justice that our soul
Cannot but yield you forth to public thanks, 7
Forerunning more requital. 8
ANGELO
You make my bonds still greater.
DUKE
O, your desert speaks loud, and I should wrong it,
To lock it in the wards of covert bosom, 11
When it deserves, with characters of brass, 12
A forted residence 'gainst the tooth of time 13
And razure of oblivion. Give me your hand, 14
And let the subject see, to make them know 15
That outward courtesies would fain proclaim
Favors that keep within. Come, Escalus, 17
You must walk by us on our other hand;
And good supporters are you.

Enter [*Friar*] *Peter and Isabella.*

20 unpregnant unapt **22 body** person **23 But that** were it not that **25 dares her no** i.e., frightens her to do nothing **26 bears . . . bulk** bears a huge credibility **28 But . . . breather** without confounding the person who speaks **29 sense** passion (?)

IV.v. Location: Outside the city.
1 me for me **3 keep** keep to **4 drift** plot **5 blench** deviate **6 minister** provide occasion **9 trumpets** trumpeters

IV.vi. Location: Street near the city gate.

13 generous highborn **14 hent** reached, occupied. **very near upon** almost immediately now

V.i. Location: The city gate.
1 cousin fellow nobleman. (Addressed to Angelo.) **7 yield . . . to** i.e., present you with **8 more requital** further reward **11 To lock . . . bosom** i.e., to keep it locked up in my heart **12 characters** writing, letters **13 forted** fortified **14 razure** effacement **15 the subject** those who are subjects **17 keep** reside. **within** i.e., in the heart

FRIAR PETER
Now is your time. Speak loud and kneel before him.
ISABELLA [*Kneeling*]
Justice, O royal Duke! Vail your regard
Upon a wrong'd—I would fain have said a maid!
O worthy Prince, dishonor not your eye
By throwing it on any other object
Till you have heard me in my true complaint
And given me justice, justice, justice, justice!
DUKE
Relate your wrongs. In what? By whom? Be brief.
Here is Lord Angelo shall give you justice.
Reveal yourself to him.
ISABELLA O worthy Duke,
You bid me seek redemption of the devil.
Hear me yourself; for that which I must speak
Must either punish me, not being believ'd,
Or wring redress from you.
Hear me, O hear me, here!
ANGELO
My lord, her wits, I fear me, are not firm.
She hath been a suitor to me for her brother
Cut off by course of justice—
ISABELLA By course of justice!
ANGELO
And she will speak most bitterly and strange.
ISABELLA
Most strange, but yet most truly, will I speak.
That Angelo's forsworn, is it not strange?
That Angelo's a murderer, is 't not strange?
That Angelo is an adulterous thief,
An hypocrite, a virgin-violator,
Is it not strange, and strange?
DUKE
Nay, it is ten times strange.
ISABELLA
It is not truer he is Angelo
Than this is all as true as it is strange.
Nay, it is ten times true, for truth is truth
To th' end of reck'ning.
DUKE Away with her! Poor soul,
She speaks this in th' infirmity of sense.
ISABELLA
O Prince, I conjure thee, as thou believ'st
There is another comfort than this world,
That thou neglect me not with that opinion
That I am touch'd with madness! Make not
impossible
That which but seems unlike. 'Tis not impossible
But one the wicked'st caitiff on the ground
May seem as shy, as grave, as just, as absolute
As Angelo; even so may Angelo,
In all his dressings, caracts, titles, forms,
Be an arch-villain. Believe it, royal prince,
If he be less, he's nothing; but he's more,
Had I more name for badness.
DUKE By mine honesty,
If she be mad—as I believe no other—
Her madness hath the oddest frame of sense,
Such a dependency of thing on thing,
As e'er I heard in madness.
ISABELLA O gracious Duke,
Harp not on that, nor do not banish reason
For inequality, but let your reason serve
To make the truth appear where it seems hid,
And hide the false seems true.
DUKE
Many that are not mad
Have, sure, more lack of reason. What would
you say?
ISABELLA
I am the sister of one Claudio,
Condemn'd upon the act of fornication
To lose his head; condemn'd by Angelo.
I, in probation of a sisterhood,
Was sent to by my brother, one Lucio
As then the messenger—
LUCIO That's I, an 't like your Grace.
I came to her from Claudio, and desir'd her
To try her gracious fortune with Lord Angelo
For her poor brother's pardon.
ISABELLA That's he indeed.
DUKE
You were not bid to speak.
LUCIO No, my good lord,
Nor wish'd to hold my peace.
DUKE I wish you now, then.
Pray you, take note of it. And when you have
A business for yourself, pray heaven you then
Be perfect.
LUCIO
I warrant your honor.
DUKE
The warrant's for yourself; take heed to 't.
ISABELLA
This gentleman told somewhat of my tale—
LUCIO
Right.
DUKE
It may be right, but you are i' the wrong
To speak before your time.—Proceed.
ISABELLA I went
To this pernicious caitiff deputy—
DUKE
That's somewhat madly spoken.
ISABELLA Pardon it;
The phrase is to the matter.
DUKE
Mended again. The matter; proceed.
ISABELLA
In brief, to set the needless process by,
How I persuaded, how I pray'd, and kneel'd,

21 Vail your regard look down **50 in . . . sense** out of a sick mind, out of the weakness of passion **55 unlike** unlikely **56 But one the wicked'st** but that the most wicked **57 absolute** flawless **59 dressings** ceremonial robes. **caracts** insignia, symbols of office **61 If . . . nothing** i.e., even if he were less than an arch-villain he would be worthless

64 frame of sense form of reason **65 dependency . . . thing** coherence **67–68 do . . . inequality** i.e., do not assume lack of reason on my part because of the inconsistency between my story and Angelo's refutation, or because of the inequality in our reputations **70 hide** remove from consideration. **seems** that seems **76 in probation** i.e., a novice **86 perfect** prepared **95 to the matter** to the purpose **96 Mended again** i.e., again you have explained seemingly mad speech. **The matter** i.e., proceed to the main point **97 to set . . . by** not to dwell on unnecessary details in the story

How he refell'd me, and how I replied—
For this was of much length—the vile conclusion
I now begin with grief and shame to utter.
He would not, but by gift of my chaste body
To his concupiscible intemperate lust,
Release my brother; and, after much debatement,
My sisterly remorse confutes mine honor,
And I did yield to him. But the next morn betimes,
His purpose surfeiting, he sends a warrant
For my poor brother's head.

DUKE
This is most likely!

ISABELLA
O, that it were as like as it is true!

DUKE
By heaven, fond wretch, thou know'st not what thou speak'st,
Or else thou art suborn'd against his honor
In hateful practice. First, his integrity
Stands without blemish. Next, it imports no reason
That with such vehemency he should pursue
Faults proper to himself. If he had so offended,
He would have weigh'd thy brother by himself
And not have cut him off. Some one hath set you on.
Confess the truth, and say by whose advice
Thou cam'st here to complain.

ISABELLA
And is this all?
Then, O you blessed ministers above,
Keep me in patience, and with ripened time
Unfold the evil which is here wrapp'd up
In countenance! Heaven shield your Grace from woe,
As I, thus wrong'd, hence unbelieved go!
[*Starts to leave.*]

DUKE
I know you 'd fain be gone. An officer!
To prison with her! Shall we thus permit
A blasting and a scandalous breath to fall
On him so near us? This needs must be a practice.
Who knew of your intent and coming hither?

ISABELLA
One that I would were here, Friar Lodowick.

DUKE
A ghostly father, belike. Who knows that Lodowick?

LUCIO
My lord, I know him; 'tis a meddling friar.
I do not like the man. Had he been lay, my lord,
For certain words he spake against your Grace
In your retirement, I had swing'd him soundly.

DUKE
Words against me? This' a good friar, belike!
And to set on this wretched woman here
Against our substitute! Let this friar be found.

LUCIO
But yesternight, my lord, she and that friar,
I saw them at the prison. A saucy friar,
A very scurvy fellow.

FRIAR PETER
Blessed be your royal Grace!
I have stood by, my lord, and I have heard
Your royal ear abus'd. First, hath this woman
Most wrongfully accus'd your substitute,
Who is as free from touch or soil with her
As she from one ungot.

DUKE
We did believe no less.
Know you that Friar Lodowick that she speaks of?

FRIAR PETER
I know him for a man divine and holy,
Not scurvy, nor a temporary meddler,
As he's reported by this gentleman;
And, on my trust, a man that never yet
Did, as he vouches, misreport your Grace.

LUCIO
My lord, most villainously, believe it.

FRIAR PETER
Well, he in time may come to clear himself;
But at this instant he is sick, my lord,
Of a strange fever. Upon his mere request,
Being come to knowledge that there was complaint
Intended 'gainst Lord Angelo, came I hither,
To speak, as from his mouth, what he doth know
Is true and false; and what he with his oath
And all probation will make up full clear,
Whensoever he's convented. First, for this woman,
To justify this worthy nobleman,
So vulgarly and personally accus'd,
Her shall you hear disproved to her eyes,
Till she herself confess it.

DUKE
Good friar, let's hear it.
[*Isabella is carried off guarded.*]
Do you not smile at this, Lord Angelo?
O heaven, the vanity of wretched fools!
Give us some seats. [*They sit.*] Come, cousin Angelo,
In this I'll be impartial. Be you judge
Of your own cause.

Enter Mariana, [*veiled*].

Is this the witness, friar?
First, let her show her face, and after speak.

MARIANA
Pardon, my lord; I will not show my face
Until my husband bid me.

DUKE What, are you married?

MARIANA No, my lord.

DUKE Are you a maid?

MARIANA No, my lord.

DUKE A widow, then?

MARIANA Neither, my lord.

DUKE Why, you are nothing then, neither maid, widow, nor wife?

LUCIO My lord, she may be a punk, for many of them are neither maid, widow, nor wife.

99 refell'd refuted **103 concupiscible** lustful **105 remorse** pity **110 fond** foolish **112 practice** machination, conspiracy **113 imports no reason** i.e., makes no sense **115 proper to himself** of which he himself is guilty **116 weigh'd** judged **122 Unfold** disclose **122–123 wrapp'd . . . countenance** concealed by means of authority **127 blasting** blighting **133 lay** not a cleric **135 swing'd** beaten **136 This'** this is

147 ungot unbegotten **151 temporary meddler** meddler in temporal affairs **158 Upon . . . request** solely at his request **159 Being . . . knowledge** he having learned **163 probation** proof **164 convented** summoned **166 vulgarly** publicly **170 vanity** folly **185 punk** harlot

DUKE
Silence that fellow. I would he had some cause
To prattle for himself.
LUCIO Well, my lord.
MARIANA
My lord, I do confess I ne'er was married,
And I confess besides I am no maid.
I have known my husband, yet my husband
Knows not that ever he knew me.
LUCIO He was drunk then, my lord; it can be no better.
DUKE For the benefit of silence, would thou wert so too!
LUCIO Well, my lord.
DUKE
This is no witness for Lord Angelo.
MARIANA
Now I come to 't, my lord.
She that accuses him of fornication,
In self-same manner doth accuse my husband,
And charges him, my lord, with such a time
When I'll depose I had him in mine arms
With all th' effect of love.
ANGELO
Charges she moe than me?
MARIANA Not that I know.
DUKE
No? You say your husband.
MARIANA
Why, just, my lord, and that is Angelo,
Who thinks he knows that he ne'er knew my body,
But knows he thinks that he knows Isabel's.
ANGELO
This is a strange abuse. Let's see thy face.
MARIANA
My husband bids me; now I will unmask.
[*Unveiling.*]
This is that face, thou cruel Angelo,
Which once thou swor'st was worth the looking on;
This is the hand which, with a vow'd contract,
Was fast belock'd in thine; this is the body
That took away the match from Isabel,
And did supply thee at thy garden-house
In her imagin'd person.
DUKE Know you this woman?
LUCIO Carnally, she says.
DUKE Sirrah, no more!
LUCIO Enough, my lord.
ANGELO
My lord, I must confess I know this woman,
And five years since there was some speech of marriage
Betwixt myself and her; which was broke off,
Partly for that her promised proportions
Came short of composition, but in chief
For that her reputation was disvalued
In levity. Since which time of five years
I never spake with her, saw her, nor heard from her,
Upon my faith and honor.
MARIANA Noble Prince,
As there comes light from heaven and words from breath,
As there is sense in truth and truth in virtue,
I am affianc'd this man's wife as strongly
As words could make up vows; and, my good lord,
But Tuesday night last gone in 's garden-house
He knew me as a wife. As this is true,
Let me in safety raise me from my knees,
Or else for ever be confixed here,
A marble monument!
ANGELO I did but smile till now.
Now, good my lord, give me the scope of justice;
My patience here is touch'd. I do perceive
These poor informal women are no more
But instruments of some more mightier member
That sets them on. Let me have way, my lord,
To find this practice out.
DUKE Ay, with my heart;
And punish them to your height of pleasure.
Thou foolish friar, and thou pernicious woman,
Compact with her that's gone, think'st thou thy oaths,
Though they would swear down each particular saint,
Were testimonies against his worth and credit
That's seal'd in approbation? You, Lord Escalus,
Sit with my cousin; lend him your kind pains
To find out this abuse, whence 'tis deriv'd.
There is another friar that set them on;
Let him be sent for.
[*The Duke rises; Escalus takes his chair.*]
FRIAR PETER
Would he were here, my lord! For he indeed
Hath set the women on to this complaint.
Your Provost knows the place where he abides
And he may fetch him.
DUKE Go do it instantly.
[*Exit Provost.*]
And you, my noble and well-warranted cousin,
Whom it concerns to hear this matter forth,
Do with your injuries as seems you best,
In any chastisement. I for a while will leave you;
But stir not you till you have well determin'd
Upon these slanderers.
ESCALUS
My lord, we'll do it throughly. *Exit* [*Duke*].
Signior Lucio, did not you say you knew that Friar Lodowick to be a dishonest person?
LUCIO "Cucullus non facit monachum"; honest in nothing but in his clothes, and one that hath spoke most villainous speeches of the Duke.
ESCALUS We shall entreat you to abide here till he come and enforce them against him. We shall find this friar a notable fellow.
LUCIO As any in Vienna, on my word.

192 known had intercourse with **201 with . . . time** with doing the deed at just the same time **202 depose** testify under oath **203 effect** manifestations **204 Charges . . . me** does she (Isabella) bring charges against persons besides myself **209 abuse** deception **215 match** meeting **224 proportions** dowry **225 composition** agreement **226–227 disvalued In levity** discredited for lightness

237 confixed firmly fixed **241 informal** rash, distracted **247 Compact** in collusion **248 swear . . . saint** call down to witness every single saint **250 seal'd in approbation** ratified by proof **263 determin'd** reached judgment **265 throughly** thoroughly **268 Cucullus . . . monachum** a cowl doesn't make a monk **272 enforce them** forcefully charge them **273 notable** notorious

ESCALUS Call that same Isabel here once again. I would speak with her. [*Exit an Attendant.*] Pray you, my lord, give me leave to question; you shall see how I'll handle her.

LUCIO Not better than he, by her own report.

ESCALUS Say you?

LUCIO Marry, sir, I think, if you handled her privately, she would sooner confess; perchance publicly she'll be asham'd.

ESCALUS I will go darkly to work with her. 284

LUCIO That's the way; for women are light at midnight. 285

Enter Duke [*disguised as a friar*], *Provost, Isabella,* [*and Officers*].

ESCALUS Come on, mistress. Here's a gentlewoman denies all that you have said.

LUCIO My lord, here comes the rascal I spoke of, here with the Provost.

ESCALUS In very good time. Speak not you to him till we call upon you.

LUCIO Mum.

ESCALUS Come, sir, did you set these women on to slander Lord Angelo? They have confess'd you did.

DUKE 'Tis false.

ESCALUS How? Know you where you are?

DUKE
Respect to your great place! And let the devil 297
Be sometime honor'd for his burning throne! 298
Where is the Duke? 'Tis he should hear me speak.

ESCALUS
The Duke 's in us, and we will hear you speak.
Look you speak justly.

DUKE
Boldly, at least. But, O, poor souls,
Come you to seek the lamb here of the fox?
Good night to your redress! Is the Duke gone?
Then is your cause gone too. The Duke 's unjust,
Thus to retort your manifest appeal, 306
And put your trial in the villain's mouth
Which here you come to accuse.

LUCIO This is the rascal; this is he I spoke of.

ESCALUS
Why, thou unreverend and unhallowed friar,
Is 't not enough thou hast suborn'd these women
To accuse this worthy man, but, in foul mouth
And in the witness of his proper ear, 313
To call him villain? And then to glance from him
To th' Duke himself, to tax him with injustice?
Take him hence; to th' rack with him! We'll
touse you 316
Joint by joint, but we will know his purpose.
What, "unjust"?

DUKE Be not so hot. The Duke
Dare no more stretch this finger of mine than he
Dare rack his own. His subject am I not,
Nor here provincial. My business in this state 321
Made me a looker on here in Vienna,
Where I have seen corruption boil and bubble
Till it o'er-run the stew; laws for all faults, 324
But faults so countenanc'd, that the strong statutes 325
Stand like the forfeits in a barber's shop, 326
As much in mock as mark.

ESCALUS Slander to th' state! 327
Away with him to prison.

ANGELO
What can you vouch against him, Signior Lucio?
Is this the man that you did tell us of?

LUCIO 'Tis he, my lord. Come hither, goodman baldpate. Do you know me?

DUKE I remember you, sir, by the sound of your voice. I met you at the prison, in the absence of the Duke.

LUCIO O, did you so? And do you remember what you said of the Duke?

DUKE Most notedly, sir.

LUCIO Do you so, sir? And was the Duke a flesh-
monger, a fool, and a coward, as you then re-
ported him to be? 340

DUKE You must, sir, change persons with me, ere you make that my report. You indeed spoke so of him, and much more, much worse.

LUCIO O thou damnable fellow! Did not I pluck thee by the nose for thy speeches?

DUKE I protest I love the Duke as I love myself.

ANGELO Hark how the villain would close now, after his 347
treasonable abuses!

ESCALUS Such a fellow is not to be talk'd withal. Away
with him to prison! Where is the Provost? Away with
him to prison! Lay bolts enough upon him. Let him
speak no more. Away with those giglots too, and with 352
the other confederate companion! 353

[*The Provost lays hands on the Duke.*]

DUKE [*To Provost*] Stay, sir, stay awhile.

ANGELO What, resists he? Help him, Lucio.

LUCIO Come, sir, come, sir, come, sir; foh, sir! Why, you bald-pated, lying rascal, you must be hooded, must you? Show your knave's visage, with a pox to you! Show your sheep-biting face, and be hang'd an hour! Will 't not off?

[*Pulls off the friar's hood, and discovers the Duke. Escalus rises.*]

DUKE
Thou art the first knave that e'er mad'st a duke.
First, Provost, let me bail these gentle three. 362
[*To Lucio.*] Sneak not away, sir, for the friar
and you
Must have a word anon.—Lay hold on him.

LUCIO This may prove worse than hanging.

DUKE [*To Escalus*]
What you have spoke I pardon. Sit you down.
We'll borrow place of him. [*To Angelo.*] Sir, by your
leave. [*Takes Angelo's seat. Escalus also sits.*]
Hast thou or word, or wit, or impudence,

284 darkly subtly, slyly **285 light** wanton, unchaste **297–298 let . . . throne** i.e., may all authority be respected, even the devil's. (Said sardonically.) **306 retort** turn back **313 in . . . ear** within his own hearing **316 touse** tear **321 provincial** subject to the religious authority of this province or state

324 stew (1) stew-pot (2) brothel **325 countenanc'd** allowed **326 forfeits** i.e., the extracted teeth of patients (barbers were also tooth-drawers) strung and hung on the walls **327 As . . . mark** i.e., as often flouted as observed **347 close** come to terms **352 giglots** wanton women **353 confederate companion** i.e., Friar Peter **362 gentle three** i.e., Mariana, Isabella, and Friar Peter

That yet can do thee office? If thou hast,
Rely upon it till my tale be heard,
And hold no longer out.

ANGELO [*Kneeling*] O my dread lord,
I should be guiltier than my guiltiness,
To think I can be undiscernible,
When I perceive your Grace, like pow'r divine,
Hath look'd upon my passes. Then, good prince,
No longer session hold upon my shame,
But let my trial be mine own confession.
Immediate sentence then and sequent death
Is all the grace I beg.

DUKE Come hither, Mariana.
Say, wast thou e'er contracted to this woman?

ANGELO
I was, my lord.

DUKE
Go take her hence, and marry her instantly.
Do you the office, friar; which consummate,
Return him here again. Go with him, Provost.
Exit [Angelo, with Mariana, Friar Peter, and Provost].

ESCALUS
My Lord, I am more amaz'd at his dishonor
Than at the strangeness of it.

DUKE Come hither, Isabel.
Your friar is now your prince. As I was then
Advertising and holy to your business,
Not changing heart with habit, I am still
Attorney'd at your service.

ISABELLA O, give me pardon,
That I, your vassal, have employ'd and pain'd
Your unknown sovereignty!

DUKE You are pardon'd, Isabel.
And now, dear maid, be you as free to us.
Your brother's death, I know, sits at your heart;
And you may marvel why I obscur'd myself,
Laboring to save his life, and would not rather
Make rash remonstrance of my hidden pow'r
Than let him so be lost. O most kind maid,
It was the swift celerity of his death,
Which I did think with slower foot came on,
That brain'd my purpose. But, peace be with him!
That life is better life, past fearing death,
Than that which lives to fear. Make it your comfort,
So happy is your brother.

Enter Angelo, Mariana, [Friar] Peter, [and] Provost.

ISABELLA I do, my lord.

DUKE
For this new-married man approaching here,
Whose salt imagination yet hath wrong'd
Your well defended honor, you must pardon
For Mariana's sake. But as he adjudg'd your
brother—
Being criminal, in double violation
Of sacred chastity and of promise-breach
Thereon dependent, for your brother's life—
The very mercy of the law cries out
Most audible, even from his proper tongue,
"An Angelo for Claudio, death for death!"
Haste still pays haste, and leisure answers leisure;
Like doth quit like, and measure still for measure.
Then, Angelo, thy fault 's thus manifested,
Which, though thou wouldst deny, denies thee
vantage.
We do condemn thee to the very block
Where Claudio stoop'd to death, and with like
haste.
Away with him!

MARIANA O my most gracious lord,
I hope you will not mock me with a husband!

DUKE
It is your husband mock'd you with a husband.
Consenting to the safeguard of your honor,
I thought your marriage fit; else imputation,
For that he knew you, might reproach your life
And choke your good to come. For his possessions,
Although by confiscation they are ours,
We do instate and widow you withal,
To buy you a better husband.

MARIANA O my dear lord,
I crave no other, nor no better man.

DUKE
Never crave him; we are definitive.

MARIANA [*Kneeling*]
Gentle my liege—

DUKE You do but lose your labor.
Away with him to death! [*To Lucio.*] Now, sir,
to you.

MARIANA
O my good lord! Sweet Isabel, take my part!
Lend me your knees, and all my life to come
I'll lend you all my life to do you service.

DUKE
Against all sense you do importune her.
Should she kneel down in mercy of this fact,
Her brother's ghost his paved bed would break,
And take her hence in horror.

MARIANA Isabel,
Sweet Isabel, do yet but kneel by me!
Hold up your hands, say nothing; I'll speak all.
They say best men are molded out of faults,
And, for the most, become much more the better
For being a little bad; so may my husband.
O Isabel, will you not lend a knee?

DUKE
He dies for Claudio's death.

ISABELLA [*Kneeling*] Most bounteous sir,
Look, if it please you, on this man condemn'd

375 passes trespasses **388 Advertising** attentive **390 Attorney'd at** serving as agent in **391 pain'd** put to trouble **393 free to us** i.e., generous in pardoning me **397 rash remonstrance** sudden manifestation **401 brain'd** dashed, defeated **404 So** thus **406 salt** lecherous

410–411 promise-breach . . . dependent i.e., breaking his promise made in return for the yielding up of chastity **412 The very . . . law** i.e., even mercy itself **413 his proper** its own **415 still** always **416 quit** requite **425 imputation** accusation, slander **426 For that** because **427 For** as for **429 widow** settle a jointure upon **432 definitive** firmly resolved **439 in . . . fact** pleading mercy for this crime **440 paved bed** grave covered with a stone slab **444 best men** even the best of men **445 most** most part

As if my brother liv'd. I partly think
A due sincerity govern'd his deeds,
Till he did look on me. Since it is so,
Let him not die. My brother had but justice,
In that he did the thing for which he died.
For Angelo,
His act did not o'ertake his bad intent,
And must be buried but as an intent
That perish'd by the way. Thoughts are no subjects,
Intents but merely thoughts.

MARIANA
Merely, my lord.

DUKE
Your suit 's unprofitable; stand up, I say.
[*They stand.*]
I have bethought me of another fault.
Provost, how came it Claudio was beheaded
At an unusual hour?

PROVOST
It was commanded so.

DUKE
Had you a special warrant for the deed?

PROVOST
No, my good lord, it was by private message.

DUKE
For which I do discharge you of your office.
Give up your keys.

PROVOST
Pardon me, noble lord.
I thought it was a fault, but knew it not,
Yet did repent me, after more advice;
For testimony whereof, one in the prison,
That should by private order else have died,
I have reserv'd alive.

DUKE
What's he?

PROVOST
His name is Barnardine.

DUKE
I would thou hadst done so by Claudio.
Go fetch him hither; let me look upon him.
[*Exit Provost.*]

ESCALUS
I am sorry one so learned and so wise
As you, Lord Angelo, have still appear'd,
Should slip so grossly, both in the heat of blood,
And lack of temper'd judgment afterward.

ANGELO
I am sorry that such sorrow I procure,
And so deep sticks it in my penitent heart
That I crave death more willingly than mercy;
'Tis my deserving, and I do entreat it.

Enter Barnardine and Provost, Claudio [*muffled*], [*and*] *Juliet.*

DUKE
Which is that Barnardine?

PROVOST
This, my lord.

DUKE
There was a friar told me of this man.
Sirrah, thou art said to have a stubborn soul
That apprehends no further than this world,
And squar'st thy life according. Thou 'rt condemn'd;
But, for those earthly faults, I quit them all,
And pray thee take this mercy to provide
For better times to come. Friar, advise him;
I leave him to your hand. What muffled fellow 's that?

PROVOST
This is another prisoner that I sav'd,
Who should have died when Claudio lost his head,
As like almost to Claudio as himself.
[*Unmuffles Claudio.*]

DUKE [*To Isabella*]
If he be like your brother, for his sake
Is he pardon'd; and, for your lovely sake,
Give me your hand and say you will be mine,
He is my brother too. But fitter time for that.
By this Lord Angelo perceives he's safe;
Methinks I see a quick'ning in his eye.
Well, Angelo, your evil quits you well.
Look that you love your wife; her worth worth yours.
I find an apt remission in myself;
And yet here's one in place I cannot pardon.
[*To Lucio.*] You, sirrah, that knew me for a fool, a coward,
One all of luxury, an ass, a madman—
Wherein have I so deserv'd of you
That you extol me thus?

LUCIO Faith, my lord, I spoke it but according to the trick. If you will hang me for it, you may; but I had rather it would please you I might be whipp'd.

DUKE
Whipp'd first, sir, and hang'd after.
Proclaim it, Provost, round about the city,
If any woman wrong'd by this lewd fellow,
As I have heard him swear himself there's one
Whom he begot with child, let her appear,
And he shall marry her. The nuptial finish'd,
Let him be whipp'd and hang'd.

LUCIO I beseech your Highness, do not marry me to a whore. Your Highness said even now I made you a duke; good my lord, do not recompense me in making me a cuckold.

DUKE
Upon mine honor, thou shalt marry her.
Thy slanders I forgive, and therewithal
Remit thy other forfeits. Take him to prison,
And see our pleasure herein executed.

LUCIO Marrying a punk, my lord, is pressing to death, whipping, and hanging.

DUKE
Slandering a prince deserves it.
[*Exeunt Officers with Lucio.*]
She, Claudio, that you wrong'd, look you restore.
Joy to you, Mariana! Love her, Angelo.
I have confess'd her and I know her virtue.

458 no subjects i.e., not subject to the state's authority **468 knew it not** was not sure **469 advice** consideration **476 still** always

487 squar'st regulates **488 for** as for. **quit** pardon **501 quits** rewards, requites **503 remission** readiness to show mercy **506 luxury** lechery **510 trick** fashion **527 pressing to death** i.e., by having heavy weights placed on the chest. (A standard form of executing those who refused to plead to a felony charge.)

Thanks, good friend Escalus, for thy much goodness;
There's more behind that is more gratulate.
Thanks, Provost, for thy care and secrecy.
We shall employ thee in a worthier place.
Forgive him, Angelo, that brought you home
The head of Ragozine for Claudio's;
Th' offense pardons itself. Dear Isabel,
I have a motion much imports your good,
Whereto if you'll a willing ear incline,
What's mine is yours and what is yours is mine.
So, bring us to our palace, where we'll show
What's yet behind, that's meet you all should know.
[*Exeunt.*]

534 behind in store, to come. **gratulate** gratifying **540 motion** proposal (which) **543 bring** escort **544 What's yet behind** what is still to be told

Troilus and Cressida

Troilus and Cressida has long proved a puzzling play. Its early printing history contains a number of obscurities. On February 7, 1603, the printer James Roberts entered his name on the Stationers' Register to print, "when he hath gotten sufficient aucthority for yt, The booke of Troilus and Cresseda as yt is acted by my lord Chamberlens Men." Evidently the authority was not forthcoming, for in 1609 the play was re-registered to R. Bonian and H. Walley and published by them that year in quarto as "The Historie of Troylus and Cresseida. *As it was acted by the Kings Maiesties* seruants at the Globe. *Written by* William Shakespeare." Immediately afterwards, and well before this first printing had sold out, a new title page was substituted as follows: "The Famous Historie of Troylus *and* Cresseid. *Excellently expressing the beginning* of their loues, with the conceited wooing of *Pandarus* Prince of *Licia. Written by* William Shakespeare." This second version had, moreover, a preface to the reader (something found in no other Shakespearean quarto) declaring *Troilus and Cressida* to be *"a new play, neuer stal'd with the Stage, neuer clapper-clawd with the palmes of the vulger,"* nor *"sullied, with the smoaky breath of the multitude."* The preface goes on to imply that the play's *"grand possessors"* (i.e., Shakespeare's company) had not wished to see the play released at all. What this substituted title page and added preface may suggest is that Bonian and Walley felt constrained to present their text as a new one, a literary rather than a theatrical text, and hence different from the version entered in the Stationers' Register "as yt is acted by my lord Chamberlens Men." Because that version had been legally registered in the name of James Roberts, the new publishers made their case for legal possession by offering a "new" play.

Later, the editors of the First Folio in 1623 seem to have had difficulty in obtaining permission to print *Troilus and Cressida.* Three pages of the play were actually printed to follow *Romeo and Juliet,* among the tragedies, but were then withdrawn to be replaced by *Timon of Athens.* Ultimately the play appeared in the Folio almost without pagination, unlisted in the table of contents, and placed with fitting ambiguity between the histories and tragedies.

This unusual printing history offers conflicting information about original stage performance. Against the evidence of the second version of the 1609 quarto with its preface proclaiming a play "neuer stal'd with the Stage," we have the evidence of the first title page mentioning the King's Majesty's servants at the Globe and of the Stationers' Register entry in 1603 referring to the play "as yt is acted." Since the 1609 preface may be part of a legal maneuver designed to represent the play as "new," the case in favor of actual performance has some weight. We cannot be sure, however, that performance was successful, or that it reached a very large audience. Some scholars have hypothesized that Shakespeare's company mounted a special production of the play for a private audience, such as the Inns of Court, even though an arrangement of this sort would have been most unusual if not unique; Shakespeare's company often took its regular plays to court or other special audiences, but no instance is positively known in which Shakespeare wrote on commission for a private showing. More likely, *Troilus and Cressida* was performed publicly without great success. A sequel, promised in the closing lines of the play by Pandarus to be presented some "two months hence," evidently did not materialize, perhaps because public demand was insufficient. The 1609 quarto, with its revised title page and added preface, may have attempted to capitalize on the play's public failure by touting it as caviare to the general and hence to be appreciated only by discerning readers. Possibly Shakespeare and his company took another look at *Troilus and Cressida* in 1608, after they had acquired the right to perform in their indoor private theatre at Blackfriars, only to discover anew that the play did not draw large audiences. Its subsequent stage history, in any case, is largely a blank until the twentieth century, except for a much-changed Restoration adaptation by Dryden in which Cressida remains true to Troilus and slays herself when accused of infidelity.

Shakespeare must have had some relative failures in the theatre as well as enormous successes. Even if *Troilus and Cressida* was such a practical failure in its time, however, it today enjoys high critical esteem and has shown itself to be theatrically powerful. What we perceive is that its mordant wit, its satirical depiction of war, and its dispiriting portrayal of sexual infidelity call for a very different sort of response from that required for an appreciation of Shakespeare's romantic comedies and history plays of the 1590's. Were some of Shakespeare's audience put off at first by this difference? Certainly *Troilus and Cressida* is less "popular" in a sense than *As You Like It* or *A Midsummer Night's Dream. Troilus and Cressida,* written probably in 1601–1602 shortly before the S. R. entry of 1603, is attuned to a new and darker mood emerging during this period in Shakespeare's work and that of his contemporaries.

In the early 1600's, dramatic satire enjoyed a sudden and highly visible notoriety. Catering in large part to select and courtly audiences, and given new impetus with the reopening of the boys' companies at the private theatres in 1599, satirical drama quickly employed the talents of Ben Jonson, John Marston, and George Chapman as well as other sophisticated dramatists. Jonson launched a series of plays he called "comicall satyres," in which he rebuked the London citizenry and presumed to teach manners to the court as well. The so-called War of the Theatres among Jonson, Marston, and Dekker, although partly a personality clash of no consequence, was also a serious debate between public and private stages on the proper uses of satire. Public dramatists complained about the libelous boldness of the new satire and were galled by the preference of some audiences for this new theatrical phenomenon; even Shakespeare fretted in *Hamlet* (II,ii,353–379) about the rivalry. Yet as an artist in search of new forms, he also responded with positive interest. He experimented with a Jonsonian type of satirical plot in the exposure of Malvolio, in *Twelfth Night* (1600–1602). *Troilus and Cressida* seems to have been another and more ambitious experiment embracing a different kind of satire, not of witty exposure but of disillusionment.

This satiric genre is hard to classify according to the conventional definitions of tragedy, comedy, or history, but does have its own clearly defined rationale that makes special sense in terms of our modern theatre. The play is nominally tragic in that it presents the fall of great Hector and adumbrates the fall of Troy, yet its love story merely dwindles into frustrated estrangement without the death of either lover. The play is comic only as what we might call "black" comedy or comedy of the absurd. Its leering sexual titillation and its mood of spiritual paralysis link *Troilus and Cressida* to the "problem" comedies *All's Well that Ends Well* (c. 1601–1604) and *Measure for Measure* (1603–1604). The play is called a "Historie" on both its early title pages, and assuredly deals with the great events of history's most famous war, but history has become essentially ironic. In this, *Troilus and Cressida* represents a culmination of Shakespeare's ironic exploration of history as begun in the impasses of *Richard II* or *Henry IV* and portrayed more fully in the sustained ambiguities of *Julius Caesar* (1599). However much Shakespeare may have been influenced by the contemporary vogue of satire in the boys' theatre, his own satire of disillusion is integral to his development as an artist. *Troilus and Cressida* is a fitting companion and contemporary for *Hamlet* (c. 1599–1601). Like that play it evokes a universal disorder that may well reflect Jacobean loss of an assured sense of philosophical reliance on the medieval hierarchies of the old Ptolemaic earth-centered cosmos.

Troilus and Cressida achieves its disillusioning effect through repeated ironic juxtaposition of heroic ideals and tarnished realities. Although it deals with the greatest war in history and a renowned love affair, we as audience know that Troy and the lovers will be overthrown by cunning and infidelity. Shakespeare partly inherited from his sources this duality of epic grandness and dispiriting conclusion. To learn of the war itself, he must have known Chapman's translation of the *Iliad* (of which seven books were published in 1598), and of course Virgil's account of the destruction of Troy, but he relied more particularly on medieval romances: Raoul Lefevre's *Receuil des Histoires de Troyes* as translated and published by William Caxton, and perhaps Lydgate's *Troy Book,* derived in part from Guido delle Colonne's *Historia Trojana.* These romances were Trojan in point of view and hence concerned with the fall of that city. For the bitter love story, Shakespeare went to Chaucer's *Troilus and Criseyde* (c. 1385–1386), which had been derived from the twelfth-century medieval romance of Benoit de Sainte-Maure, *Le Roman de Troie,* as amplified and retold in Boccaccio's *Il Filostrato.* Chaucer's Criseyde is an admirably self-possessed young woman, and her love for Troilus captures the spirit of the courtly love tradition upon which the story was based. After the late fourteenth century, however, Chaucer's heroine suffered a drastic decline in esteem. In Robert Henryson's *Testament of Cresseid,* for example, Cressida becomes a leper and beggar, the "lazar kite of Cressid's kind" to whom Pistol alludes in *Henry V.* Her name has become synonymous with womanly infidelity, as Shakespeare wryly points out in *Troilus and Cressida:* "Let all constant men be Troiluses, all false women Cressids, and all brokers-between Pandars" (III,ii). Shakespeare is fascinated by this phenomenon of declining reputations. Just as the illustrious warrior Achilles must learn that envious time detracts from our best achievements and stigmatizes us for our worst failings, Troilus, Cressida, and Pandarus all anticipate the lasting consequences to their reputations of a failed love relationship. The passion to which they commit themselves eternally becomes not only an emblem of lost hopes and promises but a caricature to later generations of enervating and frustrated desire, promiscuity, and pandering. Thus Shakespeare finds in his materials both chivalric splendor and a deflation of it.

Stylistically, Shakespeare exploits this juxtaposition. He employs epic conventions more than is his custom. The narrative commences, as the chorus informs us, *in medias res,* "Beginning in the middle." Epic similes adorn the formal speeches of Ulysses, Agamemnon, and Nestor. The rhetoric of persuasion plays an important role, as in *Julius Caesar* and other Roman plays. The great names of antiquity are paraded past us in a roll call of heroes. Hector above all is an epic hero, although in the fashion of medieval romance he is also the prince of chivalry. He longs to resolve the war by a challenge to single combat, in tournament, with the breaking of lances and with each warrior defending the honor of his lady fair (I,iii). The Greeks respond for a time to this stirring call to arms. Yet in the broader context of the war itself, with its unworthy causes, its frustrating irresolution, and its enervating effect on the morale of both sides, Hector's idealism cannot prevail. On the Greek side, Ulysses' ennobling vision of "degree, priority, and place" by which the heavens show man the value of harmonious order serves more to criticize and mock the present disorder of the Greek army than to offer guidance toward a restoration of that order. Epic convention becomes hollow travesty, as man's chivalric aspirations repeatedly dissolve into the sordid insinuations of Thersites or Pandarus. Despite the play's epic machinery, the gods are nowhere to be found.

A prevailing metaphor is that of disease (as also in *Hamlet*). Insubordinate conduct "infects" the body politic. The Greek commanders hope to "physic" Achilles lest his virtues, "like fair fruit in an unwholesome dish," rot untasted (II,iii). Hector deplores the way his fellow-Trojans "infectiously" enslave themselves to willful appetite (II,ii). Elsewhere, love is described as an open ulcer and as an itch that must be scratched; Helen is "contaminated carrion." Thersites most of all teaches us to regard both love and war as disease-ridden, afflicted by boils, plagues, scabs, the Neapolitan "bone-ache" (syphilis), "lethargies, cold palsies, raw eyes, dirt-rotten livers, wheezing lungs, bladders full of imposthume [abscess], sciaticas," and still more (II,iii and V,i). Pandarus ends the play on a similarly tawdry note by jesting about prostitutes (Winchester geese, he calls them) and the "sweating" or venereal diseases.

The war is both glorious and absurd. It calls forth brave deeds and heroic sacrifices. Yet it is correctly labeled by the chorus a "quarrel," begun over an "old aunt" whom the Greeks have held captive and Helen, whom the Trojans abducted in reprisal. No one believes the original cause to justify the bloodletting that has ensued. Menelaus' cuckoldry is the subject of obscene mirth in the Greek camp. Among the Trojans, Troilus can argue only that one doesn't return soiled goods; since all Troy consented to Helen's abduction, Troy must continue the war to maintain its honor. The war thus assumes a grim momentum of its own. The combatants repeatedly discover that they are trapped in the ironies of a situation they helped make but can no longer unmake. Hector's challenge to single combat falls upon Ajax, his "father's sister's son." Achilles too has allegiances in the enemy's camp, since he is enamored of Priam's daughter Polyxena. In the parleys between the two sides, the warriors greet one another as long-lost brothers, though they vow to slaughter one another on the morrow. With fitting oxymoron, Paris comments on the paradox of this "most despiteful gentle greeting," this "noblest hateful love" (IV,i). Only a barbarian could be free of regret for a peace that seems so near and is yet so far. The war offers insidious temptations to potentially worthy men, perverting Achilles' once-honorable quest for fame into maniacal ambition and an irresistible impulse to murder Hector. History and tradition, we know, will mock Achilles for this craven deed. It will put him down as a bully rather than a brave soldier, just as Troilus, Cressida, and Pandarus will come to be regarded in time as stereotypes of the cheated man, the whore, and the procurer. Even before the murder of Hector, Achilles sees his reputation for bravery tarnished by his inaction while Ajax is hoisted into prominence by the machinations of Ulysses and the other generals.

Hector's tragedy is in its own way no less ironic. Even though he emerges as the most thoughtful and courageous man on either side, and advises his fellow-Trojans to let Helen go in response to the "moral laws Of nature and of nations," he nonetheless ends the Trojan council of war by resolving to fight on with them (II,ii). This conclusion may represent in part a realization that the others will fight on in any case, and that he must therefore be loyal to them, but the choice also reflects *hubris*. Hector is not unlike Julius Caesar in the proud repudiation of his wife Andromache's ominous dreams, his sister Cassandra's mad but oracular prophecies, and his own conviction that Troy's pursuit of honor stems from a sickened appetite. He goes to his death because "the gods have heard me swear" (V,iii). His character is his fate. Even his humane compunctions, like Brutus', hold against him; he spares the life of Achilles, and is murdered as his reward. War is no place for men of scruple, as Troilus reminds his older brother. Yet by dying as a victim rather than allowing himself to become corrupted by war's savage ethic, Hector morally transcends the conflict from which, as a warrior, he could find no escape.

The lovers as well are caught in war's trap, not only Troilus and Cressida but Paris and Helen, Achilles and Polyxena. Achilles vows to Polyxena not to fight and thereby misses his cherished opportunity for fame; ironically he is aroused to vengeful action only by the death of a male friend, Patroclus, who is whispered to be his "male varlet" or "masculine whore." Paris is obliged to ask his brother Troilus to return Cressida to the Greeks, so that Paris may continue to enjoy Helen. What else can Paris do? "There is no help," he complains. "The bitter disposition of the time Will have it so" (IV,i). Troilus prepares his own undoing when he argues in the Trojan council of war that Helen must be kept at all cost; the cost, it turns out, is his own Cressida. He sees this irony at once: "How my achievements mock me!" (IV,ii). That is, he has no sooner achieved her sexually than he must give her up so that the war may go on with Trojan honor intact and Helen still in Paris' bed. The love of Troilus and Cressida is dwarfed by the war, which impersonally has no regard for their private concerns. Troilus wins Cressida after many months of wooing, only to lose her the next day. Yet how could Cressida's father Calchas know of her personal situation? He wishes only to have his daughter back. And although the Trojan leaders do know of Troilus' affair, they must pay heed first to matters of state such as the exchange of prisoners.

So too must Troilus. Perhaps the greatest irony is that he must himself choose to send Cressida to the Greeks, placing duty above personal longing. He appears to have no real choice, but the result is surrounded by absurdities, and it is something that Cressida cannot comprehend. She has determined to stay no matter what the world may think;

passionate love is more important to her. Although Cressida was first introduced to us as a sardonic and worldly young woman, urbane, mocking, self-possessed, witty, anti-sentimental, even scheming and opportunistic, above all wary of emotional commitment, her brief involvement with Troilus does touch deep emotion. For a moment she catches a glimpse of something precious to which she would cling, something genuine in her unstable world. Yet Troilus, caught between love and duty, consents to her departure to the Greek camp. There she reverts to her former disillusioned self, behaving as is expected of her. Who has deserted whom? Cressida gives up, hating herself for doing so. She knows she cannot be true because, like too many women in her experience, she is led by "the error of our eye" and is thus a prey to male importunity (V,ii). She is, as Ulysses acidly depicts her, one of those "sluttish spoils of opportunity And daughters of the game" (IV,v). Still, this surrender to will and appetite in her is not unsympathetic, and does not happen without inner struggle. Her weakness is emblematic of a universal disorder, and is partly caused by it. In the grim interplay of war and love, both men and women are powerless to assert their true selves. As the malcontent Thersites concludes, "Lechery, lechery, still wars and lechery; nothing else holds fashion."

The following is a complete text of the preface to the reader from the 1609 quarto:

A Never Writer, to an Ever Reader. News.

Eternal reader, you have here a new play, never stal'd with the stage, never clapper-claw'd with the palms of the vulgar, and yet passing full of the palm comical; for it is a birth of your brain that never undertook anything comical vainly. And were but the vain names of comedies chang'd for the titles of commodities, or of plays for pleas, you should see all those grand censors, that now style them such vanities, flock to them for the main grace of their gravities, especially this author's comedies, that are so fram'd to the life that they serve for the most common commentaries of all the actions of our lives, showing such a dexterity and power of wit that the most displeas'd with plays are pleas'd with his comedies. And all such dull and heavy-witted worldlings as were never capable of the wit of a comedy, coming by report of them to his representations, have found that wit there that they never found in themselves and have parted better witted than they came, feeling an edge of wit set upon them more than ever they dream'd they had brain to grind it on. So much and such savor'd salt of wit is in his comedies that they seem, for their height of pleasure, to be born in that sea that brought forth Venus. Amongst all there is none more witty than this; and had I time I would comment upon it, though I know it needs not, for so much as will make you think your testern well bestow'd, but for so much worth as even poor I know to be stuff'd in it. It deserves such a labor as well as the best comedy in Terence or Plautus. And believe this, that when he is gone and his comedies out of sale, you will scramble for them and set up a new English Inquisition. Take this for a warning, and at the peril of your pleasure's loss, and judgment's, refuse not, nor like this the less for not being sullied with the smoky breath of the multitude; but thank fortune for the 'scape it hath made amongst you, since by the grand possessors' wills I believe you should have pray'd for them rather than been pray'd. And so I leave all such to be pray'd for, for the states of their wits' healths, that will not praise it. Vale.

Troilus and Cressida

[*Dramatis Personae*

PRIAM, *King of Troy.*
HECTOR,
TROILUS,
PARIS,
DEIPHOBUS,
HELENUS, } *his sons.*
MARGARELON, *a bastard son of Priam.*
AENEAS,
ANTENOR, } *Trojan commanders.*
CALCHAS, *a Trojan priest, taking part with the Greeks.*
PANDARUS, *uncle to Cressida.*
AGAMEMNON, *the Greek general.*
MENELAUS, *his brother.*
ACHILLES,
AJAX,
ULYSSES,
NESTOR,
DIOMEDES,
PATROCLUS, } *Greek commanders.*
THERSITES, *a deformed and scurrilous Greek.*
ALEXANDER, *servant to Cressida.*
SERVANT *to Troilus.*
SERVANT *to Paris.*
SERVANT *to Diomedes.*

HELEN, *wife to Menelaus.*
ANDROMACHE, *wife to Hector.*
CASSANDRA, *daughter to Priam, a prophetess.*
CRESSIDA, *daughter to Calchas.*

TROJAN *and* GREEK SOLDIERS, *and* ATTENDANTS.

SCENE: *Troy, and the Greek camp before it.*]

PROLOGUE

In Troy, there lies the scene. From isles of Greece
The princes orgulous, their high blood chaf'd, 2
Have to the port of Athens sent their ships,
Fraught with the ministers and instruments 4
Of cruel war. Sixty and nine, that wore
Their crownets regal, from th' Athenian bay 6
Put forth toward Phrygia, and their vow is made 7
To ransack Troy, within whose strong immures 8
The ravish'd Helen, Menelaus' queen,
With wanton Paris sleeps; and that's the quarrel.
To Tenedos they come, 11
And the deep-drawing barks do there disgorge 12
Their warlike fraughtage. Now on Dardan plains 13
The fresh and yet unbruised Greeks do pitch
Their brave pavilions. Priam's six-gated city, 15
Dardan, and Tymbria, Helias, Chetas, Troien, 16
And Antenorides, with massy staples 17
And corresponsive and fulfilling bolts, 18
Sperr up the sons of Troy. 19
Now expectation, tickling skittish spirits,
On one and other side, Troyan and Greek,
Sets all on hazard. And hither am I come,
A prologue arm'd, but not in confidence 23
Of author's pen or actor's voice, but suited 24
In like conditions as our argument, 25
To tell you, fair beholders, that our play
Leaps o'er the vaunt and firstlings of those broils, 27
Beginning in the middle, starting thence away
To what may be digested in a play.
Like or find fault, do as your pleasures are;
Now good or bad, 'tis but the chance of war.

Prologue
2 orgulous proud **4 ministers** agents, i.e., soldiers **6 crownets** coronets **7 Phrygia** district in Western Asia Minor, identified as Troy by the Roman poets, and hence in Renaissance poetry

[ACT I • SCENE I]

Enter Pandarus and Troilus.

TROILUS
Call here my varlet; I'll unarm again. 1
Why should I war without the walls of Troy,
That find such cruel battle here within?
Each Troyan that is master of his heart,
Let him to field; Troilus, alas, hath none. 5
PANDARUS Will this gear ne'er be mended? 6
TROILUS
The Greeks are strong and skillful to their strength, 7
Fierce to their skill, and to their fierceness valiant; 8
But I am weaker than a woman's tear,
Tamer than sleep, fonder than ignorance, 10
Less valiant than the virgin in the night,
And skilless as unpractic'd infancy.

PANDARUS Well, I have told you enough of this. For my part, I'll not meddle nor make no farther. He that will 14
have a cake out of the wheat must needs tarry the 15
grinding.

TROILUS Have I not tarried?

PANDARUS Ay, the grinding, but you must tarry the bolting. 19

8 immures walls **11 Tenedos** small island in the Aegean Sea off the coast of Asia Minor **12 deep-drawing** deep in draught, low in the water with cargo **13 fraughtage** freight, cargo. **Dardan** Trojan. (From *Dardanus,* son of Zeus and Electra, daughter of Atlas. According to legend, Dardanus was the ancestor of the Trojan race.) **15 brave** splendid **16–17 Dardan . . . Antenorides** (The names of Troy's six gates.) **17–18 massy . . . bolts** i.e., massive posts fitted with sockets to receive matching and well-fitted bolts **19 Sperr** close **23 arm'd** in armor **23–24 not . . . voice** i.e., not to display arrogance on the part of author or actor **25 argument** plot (of the play) **27 vaunt** van, beginning. **firstlings** first-fruits, beginning

I.i. Location: Troy. Before Priam's palace.
1 varlet page or servant of a knight **5 none** i.e., no heart to fight **6 gear** business **7,8 to** in addition to, in proportion to **10 fonder** more foolish **14 make** act, be involved **15 tarry** wait for **19 bolting** sifting

TROILUS Have I not tarried?

PANDARUS Ay, the bolting, but you must tarry the leavening.

TROILUS Still have I tarried.

PANDARUS Ay, to the leavening, but here's yet in the word "hereafter" the kneading, the making of the cake, the heating the oven, and the baking; nay, you must stay the cooling too, or you may chance burn your lips.

TROILUS

Patience herself, what goddess e'er she be,
Doth lesser blench at suff'rance than I do.
At Priam's royal table do I sit,
And when fair Cressid comes into my thoughts—
So, traitor, then she comes when she is thence.

PANDARUS Well, she look'd yesternight fairer than ever I saw her look, or any woman else.

TROILUS

I was about to tell thee—when my heart,
As wedged with a sigh, would rive in twain,
Lest Hector or my father should perceive me,
I have, as when the sun doth light a-scorn,
Buried this sigh in wrinkle of a smile;
But sorrow that is couch'd in seeming gladness
Is like that mirth fate turns to sudden sadness.

PANDARUS An her hair were not somewhat darker than Helen's—well, go to—there were no more comparison between the women. But, for my part, she is my kinswoman; I would not, as they term it, praise her. But I would somebody had heard her talk yesterday, as I did. I will not dispraise your sister Cassandra's wit, but—

TROILUS

O Pandarus! I tell thee, Pandarus—
When I do tell thee, there my hopes lie drown'd,
Reply not in how many fathoms deep
They lie indrench'd. I tell thee I am mad
In Cressid's love. Thou answer'st she is fair;
Pour'st in the open ulcer of my heart
Her eyes, her hair, her cheek, her gait, her voice;
Handlest in thy discourse, O, that her hand,
In whose comparison all whites are ink,
Writing their own reproach, to whose soft seizure
The cygnet's down is harsh, and spirit of sense
Hard as the palm of ploughman. This thou tell'st me,
As true thou tell'st me, when I say I love her;
But, saying thus, instead of oil and balm,
Thou lay'st in every gash that love hath given me
The knife that made it.

PANDARUS I speak no more than truth.

TROILUS Thou dost not speak so much.

PANDARUS Faith, I'll not meddle in it. Let her be as she is. If she be fair, 'tis the better for her; an she be not, she has the mends in her own hands.

TROILUS Good Pandarus, how now, Pandarus!

PANDARUS I have had my labor for my travail; ill thought on of her and ill thought on of you; gone between and between, but small thanks for my labor.

TROILUS What, art thou angry, Pandarus? What, with me?

PANDARUS Because she's kin to me, therefore she's not so fair as Helen. An she were not kin to me, she would be as fair o' Friday as Helen is on Sunday. But what care I? I care not an she were a blackamoor; 'tis all one to me.

TROILUS Say I she is not fair?

PANDARUS I do not care whether you do or no. She's a fool to stay behind her father. Let her to the Greeks, and so I'll tell her the next time I see her. For my part, I'll meddle nor make no more i' th' matter.

TROILUS Pandarus—

PANDARUS Not I.

TROILUS Sweet Pandarus—

PANDARUS Pray you, speak no more to me. I will leave all as I found it, and there an end.

Exit. Sound alarum.

TROILUS

Peace, you ungracious clamors! Peace, rude sounds!
Fools on both sides! Helen must needs be fair,
When with your blood you daily paint her thus.
I cannot fight upon this argument;
It is too starv'd a subject for my sword.
But Pandarus—O gods, how do you plague me!
I cannot come to Cressid but by Pandar;
And he's as tetchy to be woo'd to woo
As she is stubborn-chaste against all suit.
Tell me, Apollo, for thy Daphne's love,
What Cressid is, what Pandar, and what we?
Her bed is India, there she lies, a pearl;
Between our Ilium and where she resides,
Let it be call'd the wild and wand'ring flood,
Ourself the merchant, and this sailing Pandar
Our doubtful hope, our convoy, and our bark.

Alarum. Enter Aeneas.

AENEAS

How now, Prince Troilus, wherefore not afield?

TROILUS

Because not there. This woman's answer sorts,
For womanish it is to be from thence.
What news, Aeneas, from the field today?

AENEAS

That Paris is returned home and hurt.

TROILUS

By whom, Aeneas?

AENEAS Troilus, by Menelaus.

29 what goddess e'er however much a goddess; or, if she is a goddess **30 Doth . . . suff'rance** flinches under suffering with less fortitude; or, sits less statuelike in patience, with face blanched or pale **33 So . . . thence** (Troilus rebukes himself as a traitor to Love for implying that Cressida is ever out of his thoughts, as she would have to be before she could come into them.) **37 As wedged** as if cleft by a wedge. **rive** split **39 a-scorn** scorningly, mockingly (?) (Troilus compares his face to that of the sun, putting on a false look of joviality.) **41 couch'd** hidden **43 An** if **57 that her hand** that hand of hers **58 In whose comparison** in comparison with which **59 to** in comparison with. **seizure** clasp **60 cygnet's** young swan's. **spirit of sense** (Spirits were thin vaporous substances believed to transmit sense impressions to the soul via hollow, tubelike nerves.) **67 so much** i.e., the whole truth about Cressida (since she is indescribable)

70 has . . . hands i.e., can apply remedy, such as cosmetics **73 of** by **79 as fair . . . Sunday** i.e., as attractive in her plainest attire as Helen in her Sunday best **84 her father** i.e., Calchas, a Trojan priest, who, advised by the oracle of Apollo that Troy would fall, fled to the Greeks **91 s.d. alarum** trumpet signal to arms **95 upon this argument** for this cause, theme **99 tetchy** fretful, peevish **101 Apollo** (I.e., in his role of god of music and poetry; the nymph Daphne was changed into a bay tree to elude his pursuit.) **102 we** i.e., I **104 Ilium** i.e., Troy generally, but here Priam's palace **109 sorts** is appropriate

TROILUS
Let Paris bleed. 'Tis but a scar to scorn;
Paris is gor'd with Menelaus' horn. *Alarum.*

AENEAS
Hark, what good sport is out of town today!

TROILUS
Better at home, if "would I might" were "may."
But to the sport abroad. Are you bound thither?

AENEAS
In all swift haste.

TROILUS Come, go we then together. *Exeunt.*

[SCENE II]

Enter Cressida and her man [*Alexander*].

CRESSIDA
Who were those went by?

ALEXANDER Queen Hecuba and Helen.

CRESSIDA
And whither go they?

ALEXANDER Up to the eastern tower,
Whose height commands as subject all the vale,
To see the battle. Hector, whose patience
Is as a virtue fix'd, today was mov'd.
He chid Andromache and struck his armorer,
And, like as there were husbandry in war,
Before the sun rose he was harness'd light,
And to the field goes he, where every flower
Did, as a prophet, weep what it foresaw
In Hector's wrath.

CRESSIDA What was his cause of anger?

ALEXANDER
The noise goes, this: there is among the Greeks
A lord of Troyan blood, nephew to Hector;
They call him Ajax.

CRESSIDA Good; and what of him?

ALEXANDER
They say he is a very man per se,
And stands alone.

CRESSIDA So do all men, unless they are drunk, sick, or have no legs.

ALEXANDER This man, lady, hath robb'd many beasts of their particular additions. He is as valiant as the lion, churlish as the bear, slow as the elephant; a man into whom nature hath so crowded humors that his valor is crush'd into folly, his folly sauc'd with discretion. There is no man hath a virtue that he hath not a glimpse of, nor any man an attaint but he carries some stain of it. He is melancholy without cause, and merry against the hair. He hath the joints of every thing, but every thing so out of joint that he is a gouty Briareus, many hands and no use, or purblind Argus, all eyes and no sight.

CRESSIDA But how should this man, that makes me smile, make Hector angry?

ALEXANDER They say he yesterday cop'd Hector in the battle and struck him down, the disdain and shame whereof hath ever since kept Hector fasting and waking.

[*Enter Pandarus.*]

CRESSIDA Who comes here?

ALEXANDER Madam, your uncle Pandarus.

CRESSIDA Hector's a gallant man.

ALEXANDER As may be in the world, lady.

PANDARUS What's that? What's that?

CRESSIDA Good morrow, uncle Pandarus.

PANDARUS Good morrow, cousin Cressid. What do you talk of? Good morrow, Alexander. How do you, cousin? When were you at Ilium?

CRESSIDA This morning, uncle.

PANDARUS What were you talking of when I came? Was Hector arm'd and gone ere ye came to Ilium? Helen was not up, was she?

CRESSIDA Hector was gone, but Helen was not up.

PANDARUS E'en so; Hector was stirring early.

CRESSIDA That were we talking of, and of his anger.

PANDARUS Was he angry?

CRESSIDA So he says here.

PANDARUS True, he was so. I know the cause too. He'll lay about him today, I can tell them that; and there's Troilus will not come far behind him. Let them take heed of Troilus, I can tell them that too.

CRESSIDA What, is he angry too?

PANDARUS Who, Troilus? Troilus is the better man of the two.

CRESSIDA O Jupiter! There's no comparison.

PANDARUS What, not between Troilus and Hector? Do you know a man if you see him?

CRESSIDA Ay, if I ever saw him before and knew him.

PANDARUS Well, I say Troilus is Troilus.

CRESSIDA Then you say as I say; for, I am sure, he is not Hector.

PANDARUS No, nor Hector is not Troilus in some degrees.

CRESSIDA 'Tis just to each of them; he is himself.

PANDARUS Himself? Alas, poor Troilus! I would he were.

CRESSIDA So he is.

PANDARUS Condition, I had gone barefoot to India.

CRESSIDA He is not Hector.

PANDARUS Himself? No, he's not himself. Would 'a were himself! Well, the gods are above; time must friend or end. Well, Troilus, well, I would my heart

114 a scar to scorn (1) a wound not sufficiently serious to be regarded (2) a scar in return for Paris' scorn of Menelaus **115 horn** i.e., cuckold's horn, since Paris had stolen Helen from Menelaus **116 out of town** outside the walls **117 Better . . . may** i.e., if I had my wish, I'd have better entertainment at home with Cressida

I.ii. Location: Troy. A street, or perhaps at Calchas' house, where Cressida lives; at l. 179 Pandarus urges her to "stand up here" and see the returning army, as though from a balcony or point of vantage.
5 fix'd steadfast **7 husbandry** thrift, good management **8 harness'd** dressed in armor **15 per se** i.e., unique, in the absolute sense **20 additions** qualities bestowing special distinction **22 humors** temperamental characteristics **25 glimpse** trace. **attaint** defect, stain

27 against the hair contrary to natural tendency **28 Briareus** Greek mythological monster with fifty heads and one hundred hands; here, all those hands are gouty **29 Argus** a monster with one hundred eyes; here, all are blind **33 cop'd** encountered, came to blows with **43 cousin** kinswoman, i.e., niece **45 Ilium** the palace **69 in some** by several **71 he** each **75 Condition . . . India** i.e., if it could help to make Troilus himself again, I would walk barefoot to India

were in her body. No, Hector is not a better man than Troilus.

CRESSIDA Excuse me.

PANDARUS He is elder.

CRESSIDA Pardon me, pardon me.

PANDARUS Th' other's not come to 't. You shall tell me another tale, when th' other's come to 't. Hector shall not have his wit this year.

CRESSIDA He shall not need it, if he have his own.

PANDARUS Nor his qualities.

CRESSIDA No matter.

PANDARUS Nor his beauty.

CRESSIDA 'Twould not become him; his own's better.

PANDARUS You have no judgment, niece. Helen herself swore th' other day that Troilus, for a brown favor—for so 'tis, I must confess—not brown neither—

CRESSIDA No, but brown.

PANDARUS Faith, to say truth, brown and not brown.

CRESSIDA To say the truth, true and not true.

PANDARUS She prais'd his complexion above Paris.

CRESSIDA Why, Paris hath color enough.

PANDARUS So he has.

CRESSIDA Then Troilus should have too much. If she prais'd him above, his complexion is higher than his. He having color enough, and the other higher, is too flaming a praise for a good complexion. I had as lief Helen's golden tongue had commended Troilus for a copper nose.

PANDARUS I swear to you, I think Helen loves him better than Paris.

CRESSIDA Then she's a merry Greek indeed.

PANDARUS Nay, I am sure she does. She came to him th' other day into the compass'd window—and, you know, he has not past three or four hairs on his chin—

CRESSIDA Indeed, a tapster's arithmetic may soon bring his particulars therein to a total.

PANDARUS Why, he is very young; and yet will he, within three pound, lift as much as his brother Hector.

CRESSIDA Is he so young a man and so old a lifter?

PANDARUS But to prove to you that Helen loves him: she came and puts me her white hand to his cloven chin—

CRESSIDA Juno have mercy! How came it cloven?

PANDARUS Why, you know, 'tis dimpled. I think his smiling becomes him better than any man in all Phrygia.

CRESSIDA O, he smiles valiantly.

PANDARUS Does he not?

CRESSIDA O yes, an 'twere a cloud in autumn.

PANDARUS Why, go to, then. But to prove to you that Helen loves Troilus—

CRESSIDA Troilus will stand to the proof, if you'll prove it so.

PANDARUS Troilus! Why, he esteems her no more than I esteem an addle egg.

CRESSIDA If you love an addle egg as well as you love an idle head, you would eat chickens i' th' shell.

PANDARUS I cannot choose but laugh to think how she tickled his chin. Indeed, she has a marvel's white hand, I must needs confess—

CRESSIDA Without the rack.

PANDARUS And she takes upon her to spy a white hair on his chin.

CRESSIDA Alas, poor chin! Many a wart is richer.

PANDARUS But there was such laughing! Queen Hecuba laugh'd that her eyes ran o'er.

CRESSIDA With millstones.

PANDARUS And Cassandra laugh'd.

CRESSIDA But there was a more temperate fire under the pot of her eyes. Did her eyes run o'er too?

PANDARUS And Hector laugh'd.

CRESSIDA At what was all this laughing?

PANDARUS Marry, at the white hair that Helen spied on Troilus' chin.

CRESSIDA An 't had been a green hair, I should have laugh'd too.

PANDARUS They laugh'd not so much at the hair as at his pretty answer.

CRESSIDA What was his answer?

PANDARUS Quoth she, "Here's but two and fifty hairs on your chin, and one of them is white."

CRESSIDA This is her question.

PANDARUS That's true; make no question of that. "Two and fifty hairs," quoth he, "and one white. That white hair is my father, and all the rest are his sons." "Jupiter!" quoth she, "which of these hairs is Paris my husband?" "The fork'd one," quoth he, "pluck 't out, and give it him." But there was such laughing! And Helen so blush'd, and Paris so chaf'd, and all the rest so laugh'd, that it pass'd.

CRESSIDA So let it now, for it has been a great while going by.

PANDARUS Well, cousin, I told you a thing yesterday; think on 't.

CRESSIDA So I do.

PANDARUS I'll be sworn 'tis true; he will weep you, an 'twere a man born in April.

CRESSIDA And I'll spring up in his tears, an 'twere a nettle against May. *Sound a retreat.*

PANDARUS Hark, they are coming from the field. Shall we stand up here, and see them as they pass toward Ilium? Good niece, do, sweet niece Cressida.

CRESSIDA At your pleasure.

PANDARUS Here, here, here's an excellent place; here we may see most bravely. I'll tell you them all by their names as they pass by; but mark Troilus above the rest.

CRESSIDA Speak not so loud.

Enter Aeneas [and passes across the stage].

85 to 't i.e., to Hector's age **94 for a brown favor** considering he has a dark complexion **103 higher than his** i.e., ruddier than Paris' **107 copper** red **110 merry Greek** (Slang for a frivolous person, loose in morals.) **112 compass'd** bay **114 tapster** barkeep. (Proverbially slow at simple addition.) **118 lifter** (with a quibble on the meaning *thief*) **120 puts me** i.e., puts. (*Me* is the ethical dative.) **130 stand . . . proof** i.e., not shrink from the test (with bawdy pun on *stand*, be erect) **133 addle** spoiled

137 marvel's marvelously **139 rack** i.e., torture device **145 With millstones** i.e., mirthlessly, since nothing has been said funny enough to make the eyes weep tears of laughter **158 two and fifty** (Priam had fifty sons. Some commentators assume that the bastard Margarelon is to be included.) **165 fork'd** i.e., bearing a cuckold's horns. (The suggestion is that Helen will cheat Paris in love as she has done Menelaus.) **168 it pass'd** it exceeded all description. (But Cressida puns on the sense of *passed by*.) **174–175 an 'twere** as if he were **175 April** i.e., the season of showers **176–177 an 'twere . . . May** as if I were a nettle in anticipation of May **177 s.d. retreat** trumpet signal for withdrawal **183 bravely** excellently

PANDARUS That's Aeneas. Is not that a brave man? He's
one of the flowers of Troy, I can tell you. But mark
Troilus; you shall see anon.

Enter Antenor [and passes across the stage].

CRESSIDA Who's that?

PANDARUS That's Antenor. He has a shrewd wit, I can
tell you, and he's man good enough. He's one o' th'
soundest judgments in Troy, whosoever, and a proper 193
man of person. When comes Troilus? I'll show you
Troilus anon. If he see me, you shall see him nod
at me.

CRESSIDA Will he give you the nod? 197

PANDARUS You shall see.

CRESSIDA If he do, the rich shall have more. 199

Enter Hector [and passes across the stage].

PANDARUS That's Hector, that, that, look you, that;
there's a fellow! Go thy way, Hector! There's a brave
man, niece. O brave Hector! Look how he looks!
There's a countenance! Is 't not a brave man?

CRESSIDA O, a brave man!

PANDARUS Is 'a not? It does a man's heart good. Look
you what hacks are on his helmet! Look you yonder,
do you see? Look you there. There's no jesting; there's
laying on, take 't off who will, as they say. There be 208
hacks!

CRESSIDA Be those with swords?

PANDARUS Swords, anything, he cares not; an the
devil come to him, it's all one. By God's lid, it does 212
one's heart good. Yonder comes Paris, yonder comes
Paris.

Enter Paris [and passes across the stage].

Look ye yonder, niece; is 't not a gallant man too, is 't
not? Why, this is brave now. Who said he came hurt
home today? He's not hurt. Why, this will do Helen's
heart good now, ha! Would I could see Troilus now!
You shall see Troilus anon.

CRESSIDA Who's that?

Enter Helenus [and passes across the stage].

PANDARUS That's Helenus. I marvel where Troilus is.
That's Helenus. I think he went not forth today. That's 222
Helenus.

CRESSIDA Can Helenus fight, uncle?

PANDARUS Helenus? No. Yes, he'll fight indifferent
well. I marvel where Troilus is. Hark, do you not hear
the people cry "Troilus"? Helenus is a priest.

CRESSIDA What sneaking fellow comes yonder?

Enter Troilus [and passes across the stage].

PANDARUS Where? Yonder? That's Deiphobus. 'Tis
Troilus! There's a man, niece! Hem! Brave Troilus! The
prince of chivalry!

CRESSIDA Peace, for shame, peace!

PANDARUS Mark him, note him. O brave Troilus! Look
well upon him, niece. Look you how his sword is
bloodied, and his helm more hack'd than Hector's,
and how he looks, and how he goes! O admirable
youth! He ne'er saw three and twenty. Go thy way,
Troilus, go thy way! Had I a sister were a grace, or a 238
daughter a goddess, he should take his choice. O
admirable man! Paris? Paris is dirt to him; and I warrant
Helen, to change, would give an eye to boot.

CRESSIDA Here comes more.

[Forces pass across the stage.]

PANDARUS Asses, fools, dolts! Chaff and bran, chaff
and bran! Porridge after meat! I could live and die in
the eyes of Troilus. Ne'er look, ne'er look. The eagles
are gone; crows and daws, crows and daws! I had
rather be such a man as Troilus than Agamemnon and
all Greece.

CRESSIDA There is amongst the Greeks Achilles, a better
man than Troilus.

PANDARUS Achilles? A drayman, a porter, a very camel. 251

CRESSIDA Well, well.

PANDARUS "Well, well!" Why, have you any discretion?
Have you any eyes? Do you know what a man is? Is
not birth, beauty, good shape, discourse, manhood,
learning, gentleness, virtue, youth, liberality, and such
like, the spice and salt that season a man?

CRESSIDA Ay, a minc'd man; and then to be bak'd with 258
no date in the pie, for then the man's date is out. 259

PANDARUS You are such a woman, a man knows not at
what ward you lie. 261

CRESSIDA Upon my back, to defend my belly, upon my
wit, to defend my wiles, upon my secrecy, to defend
mine honesty, my mask, to defend my beauty, and 264
you, to defend all these, and at all these wards I lie, at 265
a thousand watches. 266

PANDARUS Say one of your watches.

CRESSIDA Nay, I'll watch you for that; and that's one of
the chiefest of them too. If I cannot ward what I would
not have hit, I can watch you for telling how I took the
blow—unless it swell past hiding, and then it's past 271
watching. 272

PANDARUS You are such another!

Enter [Troilus'] Boy.

BOY Sir, my lord would instantly speak with you.

PANDARUS Where?

BOY At your own house; there he unarms him.

PANDARUS Good boy, tell him I come. *[Exit Boy.]*
I doubt he be hurt. Fare ye well, good niece. 278

CRESSIDA Adieu, uncle.

PANDARUS I will be with you, niece, by and by.

193 proper handsome **197 nod** (with a pun on *noddy,* fool, simpleton) **199 the rich . . . more** i.e., the fool will become more foolish (since foolish Pandarus will receive a nod or *noddy*) **208 laying on** i.e., evidence of blows exchanged. **take 't off who will** whatever anyone may say to the contrary (with a pun on *taking off* as contrasted with *laying on*) **212 By God's lid** by God's eyelid. (An oath.) **222 he** i.e., Troilus

238 a grace one of the three Graces, handmaidens of Venus **251 drayman** one who draws a cart **258 minc'd** (1) simpering (2) made up of many diced ingredients, like a meat pie, and spiced for preservation **259 date is** time is (playing on the fruit, the date, a common ingredient of such pies) **261 ward, lie** (Technical terms in fencing; a *ward* is a posture of defense.) **264 honesty** i.e., reputation for chastity **265–266 at a thousand watches** i.e., guarding myself in a thousand ways. (Subsequently, in the word play, *watch* means *night watch,* l. 267, *keep under observation,* l. 268, and *watch out lest you tell,* l. 270.) **271 swell** i.e., in pregnancy **271–272 past watching** too late to be concerned about **278 doubt** fear

CRESSIDA To bring, uncle?
PANDARUS Ay, a token from Troilus.
CRESSIDA By the same token, you are a bawd.
[*Exit Pandarus.*]
Words, vows, gifts, tears, and love's full sacrifice
He offers in another's enterprise;
But more in Troilus thousand fold I see
Than in the glass of Pandar's praise may be.
Yet hold I off. Women are angels, wooing; 288
Things won are done, joy's soul lies in the doing.
That she belov'd knows nought that knows not this: 290
Men prize the thing ungain'd more than it is. 291
That she was never yet that ever knew
Love got so sweet as when desire did sue. 293
Therefore this maxim out of love I teach: 294
Achievement is command; ungain'd, beseech. 295
Then though my heart's content firm love doth bear, 296
Nothing of that shall from mine eyes appear.
Exit [*with Alexander*].

[SCENE III]

[*Sennet.*] *Enter Agamemnon, Nestor, Ulysses, Diomedes, Menelaus, with others.*

AGAMEMNON
Princes,
What grief hath set the jaundice on your cheeks?
The ample proposition that hope makes 3
In all designs begun on earth below
Fails in the promis'd largeness. Checks and disasters 5
Grow in the veins of actions highest rear'd, 6
As knots, by the conflux of meeting sap, 7
Infects the sound pine and diverts his grain 8
Tortive and errant from his course of growth. 9
Nor, princes, is it matter new to us
That we come short of our suppose so far 11
That after seven years' siege yet Troy walls stand,
Sith every action that hath gone before, 13
Whereof we have record, trial did draw 14
Bias and thwart, not answering the aim, 15
And that unbodied figure of the thought 16
That gave 't surmised shape. Why then, you princes, 17
Do you with cheeks abash'd behold our works,
And call them shames, which are indeed nought else
But the protractive trials of great Jove
To find persistive constancy in men? 21
The fineness of which metal is not found
In fortune's love; for then the bold and coward, 23
The wise and fool, the artist and unread, 24
The hard and soft, seem all affin'd and kin. 25
But in the wind and tempest of her frown, 26
Distinction, with a broad and powerful fan, 27
Puffing at all, winnows the light away, 28
And what hath mass or matter, by itself
Lies rich in virtue and unmingled. 30
NESTOR
With due observance of thy godlike seat, 31
Great Agamemnon, Nestor shall apply
Thy latest words. In the reproof of chance
Lies the true proof of men. The sea being smooth,
How many shallow bauble boats dare sail 35
Upon her patient breast, making their way
With those of nobler bulk!
But let the ruffian Boreas once enrage 38
The gentle Thetis, and anon behold 39
The strong-ribb'd bark through liquid mountains cut,
Bounding between the two moist elements, 41
Like Perseus' horse. Where's then the saucy boat 42
Whose weak untimber'd sides but even now
Corival'd greatness? Either to harbor fled,
Or made a toast for Neptune. Even so 45
Doth valor's show and valor's worth divide 46
In storms of fortune. For in her ray and brightness 47
The herd hath more annoyance by the breese 48
Than by the tiger; but when the splitting wind
Makes flexible the knees of knotted oaks,
And flies fled under shade, why, then the thing of courage, 51
As rous'd with rage, with rage doth sympathize,
And with an accent tun'd in selfsame key
Retorts to chiding fortune.
ULYSSES Agamemnon,
Thou great commander, nerves and bone of Greece, 55
Heart of our numbers, soul and only spright, 56
In whom the tempers and the minds of all
Should be shut up, hear what Ulysses speaks. 58
Besides th' applause and approbation
The which, [*To Agamemnon*] most mighty for thy place and sway,
[*To Nestor*] And thou most reverend for thy stretch'd-out life,
I give to both your speeches, which were such
As Agamemnon and the hand of Greece

288 wooing i.e., being wooed **290 That she** that woman. (Also in l. 292.) **291 than it is** i.e., than it is worth in essence, in objective reality **293 got** obtained (by the man) **294 out of** derived from **295 Achievement . . . beseech** i.e., to achieve (to win a woman) is to command her; unwon, she must be besought **296 content** i.e., essence, body. **bear** bear the impress (of love; or, the line may mean, "though I carry firm love as the content of my heart")

I.iii. Location: The Greek camp. Before Agamemnon's tent.
s.d. Sennet trumpet call signaling a processional entrance or exit **3 proposition** offer **5–6 Checks . . . rear'd** i.e., hindrances and disaster attend great enterprises **7 conflux** flowing together **8,9 his** its **9 Tortive and errant** distorted and wandering **11 suppose** expectation **13–17 Sith . . . shape** i.e., since an attempt at performance *(trial)* has drawn awry and crosswise every previous action of which we have record, so that it has not corresponded to the aim of its originator nor to the impalpable shape which it assumed in thought

21 persistive enduring **23 In fortune's love** i.e., when fortune smiles **24 artist** scholar **25 affin'd** related **26 her** i.e., fortune's **27 Distinction** the making of distinctions (between those who persevere and those who do not) **28 the light** i.e., the chaff, the inconstant **30 unmingled** unalloyed, uncontaminated **31 observance** respect. **seat** throne, i.e., position as king **35 bauble** toy **38 Boreas** north wind **39 Thetis** a sea deity, mother of Achilles; here used for the sea itself. (Probably confused with Tethys, the wife of Oceanus.) **41 moist elements** air and water **42 Perseus' horse** Pegasus, a winged horse which sprang from the blood of Medusa when Perseus cut off her head. (The horse was given to Bellerophon by the gods. It is associated, however, with Perseus, probably because Ovid relates that the latter hero was mounted on Pegasus when he rescued Andromeda from the sea monster.) **45 toast** rich morsel to be swallowed, like toasted bread floating in liquor **46 show** mere appearance **47 storms of fortune** trials and tests visited by misfortune **48 breese** gadfly **51 fled** are fled. **the thing of courage** any brave heart **55 nerves** sinews **56 numbers** armies **58 shut up** gathered in, embodied

Should hold up high in brass, and such again
As venerable Nestor, hatch'd in silver,
Should with a bond of air, strong as the axle-tree
On which heaven rides, knit all the Greekish ears
To his experienc'd tongue, yet let it please both,
Thou great, and wise, to hear Ulysses speak.

[AGAMEMNON

Speak, Prince of Ithaca; and be 't of less expect
That matter needless, of importless burden,
Divide thy lips, than we are confident,
When rank Thersites opes his mastic jaws,
We shall hear music, wit, and oracle.]

ULYSSES

Troy, yet upon his basis, had been down,
And the great Hector's sword had lack'd a master,
But for these instances.
The specialty of rule hath been neglected;
And look how many Grecian tents do stand
Hollow upon this plain, so many hollow factions.
When that the general is not like the hive
To whom the foragers shall all repair,
What honey is expected? Degree being vizarded,
Th' unworthiest shows as fairly in the mask.
The heavens themselves, the planets, and this center
Observe degree, priority, and place,
Insisture, course, proportion, season, form,
Office, and custom, in all line of order.
And therefore is the glorious planet Sol
In noble eminence enthron'd and spher'd
Amidst the other; whose med'cinable eye
Corrects the ill aspects of planets evil,
And posts, like the commandment of a king,
Sans check, to good and bad. But when the planets
In evil mixture to disorder wander,
What plagues and what portents, what mutiny,
What raging of the sea, shaking of earth,
Commotion in the winds, frights, changes, horrors,
Divert and crack, rend and deracinate
The unity and married calm of states
Quite from their fixure! O, when degree is shak'd,
Which is the ladder of all high designs,
The enterprise is sick. How could communities,
Degrees in schools, and brotherhoods in cities,
Peaceful commerce from dividable shores,
The primogenity and due of birth,
Prerogative of age, crowns, scepters, laurels,
But by degree stand in authentic place?
Take but degree away, untune that string,
And hark what discord follows. Each thing meets
In mere oppugnancy. The bounded waters
Should lift their bosoms higher than the shores
And make a sop of all this solid globe;
Strength should be lord of imbecility,
And the rude son should strike his father dead;
Force should be right, or rather, right and wrong,
Between whose endless jar justice resides,
Should lose their names, and so should justice too.
Then every thing includes itself in power,
Power into will, will into appetite;
And appetite, an universal wolf,
So doubly seconded with will and power,
Must make perforce an universal prey,
And last eat up himself. Great Agamemnon,
This chaos, when degree is suffocate,
Follows the choking.
And this neglection of degree it is
That by a pace goes backward with a purpose
It hath to climb. The general's disdain'd
By him one step below, he by the next,
That next by him beneath; so every step,
Exampled by the first pace that is sick
Of his superior, grows to an envious fever
Of pale and bloodless emulation.
And 'tis this fever that keeps Troy on foot,
Not her own sinews. To end a tale of length,
Troy in our weakness stands, not in her strength.

NESTOR

Most wisely hath Ulysses here discover'd
The fever whereof all our power is sick.

AGAMEMNON

The nature of the sickness found, Ulysses,
What is the remedy?

ULYSSES

The great Achilles, whom opinion crowns
The sinew and the forehand of our host,
Having his ear full of his airy fame,
Grows dainty of his worth, and in his tent
Lies mocking our designs. With him Patroclus
Upon a lazy bed the livelong day
Breaks scurril jests,
And with ridiculous and awkward action,
Which, slanderer, he imitation calls,
He pageants us. Sometime, great Agamemnon,
Thy topless deputation he puts on,
And, like a strutting player, whose conceit
Lies in his hamstring, and doth think it rich
To hear the wooden dialogue and sound
'Twixt his stretch'd footing and the scaffoldage,
Such to-be-pitied and o'er-wrested seeming

65 hatch'd in silver (1) adorned with silver hair, a sign of age and wisdom (2) born wise **66 bond of air** i.e., his breath or words as speech, powerful oration **70–74 be 't . . . oracle** i.e., we should expect unimportant matter from you even less than we should expect music, wit, and truth from Thersites **70 expect** expectation **73 mastic** abusive, scouring **78 specialty of rule** particular rights and responsibilities of supreme authority **79 look how many** however many, just as many **80 Hollow** (1) empty, because of the present assembly (2) symbolizing faction **81 like the hive** i.e., serving as the focus of activity, the command center **83 Degree being vizarded** when the hierarchical function of authority is masked **84 shows as fairly** appears as attractive (as the most noble) **85 this center** the earth, center of the Ptolemaic universe **87 Insisture** steady continuance in their path **89 Sol** sun **91 other** others. **med'cinable** healing **92 aspects** relative positions of the heavenly bodies as they appear to an observer on the earth's surface at a given time, and the influence attributed thereto **93 posts** speeds **94 Sans** without **95 mixture** conjunction **99 deracinate** uproot **101 fixure** stability **104 Degrees in schools** academic rank. **brotherhoods** corporations, guilds **105 dividable** separated, which divide **106 primogenity** right of the eldest son to succeed to his father's estate

111 mere oppugnancy total strife **113 sop** piece of bread or cake floating in liquor; pulp **114 imbecility** weakness **117 jar** collision **119 includes** subsumes **126 choking** act of suffocation **128 by a pace** step by step **128–129 with . . . climb** when it intends to climb **132 Exampled** shown a precedent. **first pace** i.e., he who is in second place, just below the general. **sick** envious **138 discover'd** revealed **139 power** army **143 forehand** first in might **144 airy** unsubstantial, spoken by rumor **145 dainty . . . worth** i.e., overprizing his presumed worth **151 pageants** dramatizes, mimics **152 topless deputation** supreme power **153 conceit** understanding, intelligence **154 hamstring** tendon behind the knee **155–156 To hear . . . scaffoldage** i.e., to hear the echoing sound of his marching to and fro on the stage or scaffolding **157 to-be-pitied . . . seeming** pitiful and exaggerated acting

He acts thy greatness in; and when he speaks,
'Tis like a chime a-mending, with terms unsquar'd,
Which, from the tongue of roaring Typhon dropp'd,
Would seem hyperboles. At this fusty stuff
The large Achilles, on his press'd bed lolling,
From his deep chest laughs out a loud applause,
Cries "Excellent! 'Tis Agamemnon right.
Now play me Nestor; hem, and stroke thy beard,
As he being dress'd to some oration."
That's done, as near as the extremest ends
Of parallels, as like as Vulcan and his wife,
Yet god Achilles still cries "Excellent!
'Tis Nestor right. Now play him me, Patroclus,
Arming to answer in a night alarm."
And then, forsooth, the faint defects of age
Must be the scene of mirth; to cough and spit,
And, with a palsy fumbling on his gorget,
Shake in and out the rivet. And at this sport
Sir Valor dies; cries "O, enough, Patroclus,
Or give me ribs of steel! I shall split all
In pleasure of my spleen." And in this fashion,
All our abilities, gifts, natures, shapes,
Severals and generals of grace exact,
Achievements, plots, orders, preventions,
Excitements to the field, or speech for truce,
Success or loss, what is or is not, serves
As stuff for these two to make paradoxes.

NESTOR
And in the imitation of these twain—
Who, as Ulysses says, opinion crowns
With an imperial voice—many are infect.
Ajax is grown self-will'd, and bears his head
In such a rein, in full as proud a place
As broad Achilles; keeps his tent like him;
Makes factious feasts; rails on our state of war,
Bold as an oracle, and sets Thersites,
A slave whose gall coins slanders like a mint,
To match us in comparisons with dirt,
To weaken and discredit our exposure,
How rank soever rounded in with danger.

ULYSSES
They tax our policy, and call it cowardice,
Count wisdom as no member of the war,
Forestall prescience, and esteem no act
But that of hand. The still and mental parts,
That do contrive how many hands shall strike
When fitness calls them on, and know by measure
Of their observant toil the enemies' weight—
Why, this hath not a finger's dignity.
They call this bed-work, mapp'ry, closet-war;
So that the ram that batters down the wall,
For the great swing and rudeness of his poise,
They place before his hand that made the engine,
Or those that with the fineness of their souls
By reason guide his execution.

NESTOR
Let this be granted, and Achilles' horse
Makes many Thetis' sons. [*A tucket.*]

AGAMEMNON
What trumpet? Look, Menelaus.

MENELAUS
From Troy.

[*Enter Aeneas, accompanied.*]

AGAMEMNON
What would you 'fore our tent?

AENEAS
Is this great Agamemnon's tent, I pray you?

AGAMEMNON
Even this.

AENEAS
May one, that is a herald and a prince,
Do a fair message to his kingly eyes?

AGAMEMNON
With surety stronger than Achilles' arm
'Fore all the Greekish heads, which with one voice
Call Agamemnon head and general.

AENEAS
Fair leave and large security. How may
A stranger to those most imperial looks
Know them from eyes of other mortals?

AGAMEMNON
How?

AENEAS
Ay.
I ask, that I might waken reverence,
And bid the cheek be ready with a blush
Modest as morning when she coldly eyes
The youthful Phoebus.
Which is that god in office, guiding men?
Which is the high and mighty Agamemnon?

AGAMEMNON
This Troyan scorns us, or the men of Troy
Are ceremonious courtiers.

AENEAS
Courtiers as free, as debonair, unarm'd,
As bending angels; that's their fame in peace.
But when they would seem soldiers, they have galls,
Good arms, strong joints, true swords; and, great
Jove's accord,
Nothing so full of heart. But peace, Aeneas,

159 a-mending being repaired or retuned. **terms unsquar'd** expressions unadapted to their subject, ill-fitted (like unsquared stones in architecture) **160 from** even if from. **Typhon** Greek mythological monster with a hundred heads which breathed fire; he made war against the gods and was destroyed by one of Zeus' thunderbolts **161 fusty** (1) stale (2) fustian, bombastic **162 press'd** weighed down (by its occupant) **168 Vulcan . . . wife** i.e., the ugliest god, and Venus, the most beautiful goddess **172 faint** weak **174 palsy** tremulous, quivering. **gorget** piece of armor for the throat **178 spleen** (Regarded as the seat of laughter.) **180 Severals . . . exact** well-ordered gifts, individual and general **182 Excitements** exhortations **184 paradoxes** absurdities **186–187 crowns . . . voice** i.e., regards most highly, adulates **189 In . . . rein** i.e., so haughtily **190 keeps** keeps to **191 state** council **193 gall** the seat of bile and rancor **195 our exposure** the danger to which we are exposed **196 rank** thickly. **rounded in with** surrounded by **197 tax our policy** censure our prudent management **199 Forestall prescience** condemn beforehand any attempts at foresight **200 that of hand** i.e., an act involving physical combat **202 fitness** suitability of occasion **202–203 by measure . . . weight** the enemy's strength by the reckoning up of laborious observation on the part of our mental faculties

204 hath . . . dignity is not worth a mere finger's measure **205 bed-work** i.e., armchair strategy. **mapp'ry** mere making of maps. **closet** the study **207 swing** impetus. **rudeness** roughness. **his poise** its weight **208 place before** give precedence to **209 fineness . . . souls** i.e., subtle skill of their intelligence **210 his execution** i.e., the use of the battering ram **211–212 Let . . . sons** i.e., if this is granted, then Achilles' horse in its brute strength outvalues many an Achilles (the son of Thetis) **s.d. tucket** signal given on a trumpet **219 to . . . eyes** i.e., in his presence **220 surety** security **221 'Fore** i.e., leading into battle **229 she** i.e., Aurora, the dawn goddess **230 Phoebus** Apollo, here referred to as the sun god **235 debonair** gentle, meek **237 galls** i.e., spirit to resent injury. (See l. 193.) **238 great Jove's accord** Jove being in full accord **239 Nothing . . . heart** nothing is so full of heart (courage) as they

Peace, Troyan; lay thy finger on thy lips!
The worthiness of praise distains his worth,
If that the prais'd himself bring the praise forth.
But what the repining enemy commends,
That breath fame blows; that praise, sole pure,
transcends.

AGAMEMNON
Sir, you of Troy, call you yourself Aeneas?

AENEAS
Ay, Greek, that is my name.

AGAMEMNON
What's your affair, I pray you?

AENEAS
Sir, pardon; 'tis for Agamemnon's ears.

AGAMEMNON
He hears nought privately that comes from Troy.

AENEAS
Nor I from Troy come not to whisper him.
I bring a trumpet to awake his ear,
To set his sense on the attentive bent,
And then to speak.

AGAMEMNON Speak frankly as the wind;
It is not Agamemnon's sleeping hour.
That thou shalt know, Troyan, he is awake,
He tells thee so himself.

AENEAS Trumpet, blow loud,
Send thy brass voice through all these lazy tents;
And every Greek of mettle, let him know,
What Troy means fairly shall be spoke aloud.
Sound trumpet.
We have, great Agamemnon, here in Troy
A prince call'd Hector—Priam is his father—
Who in this dull and long-continued truce
Is resty grown. He bade me take a trumpet,
And to this purpose speak. Kings, princes, lords!
If there be one among the fair'st of Greece
That holds his honor higher than his ease
And feeds his praise more than he fears his peril,
That knows his valor, and knows not his fear,
That loves his mistress more than in confession
With truant vows to her own lips he loves,
And dare avow her beauty and her worth
In other arms than hers—to him this challenge.
Hector, in view of Troyans and of Greeks,
Shall make it good, or do his best to do it,
He hath a lady, wiser, fairer, truer,
Than ever Greek did couple in his arms,
And will tomorrow with his trumpet call
Midway between your tents and walls of Troy,
To rouse a Grecian that is true in love.
If any come, Hector shall honor him;
If none, he'll say in Troy when he retires,
The Grecian dames are sunburnt and not worth
The splinter of a lance. Even so much.

AGAMEMNON
This shall be told our lovers, Lord Aeneas.
If none of them have soul in such a kind,
We left them all at home. But we are soldiers;
And may that soldier a mere recreant prove,
That means not, hath not, or is not in love!
If then one is, or hath, or means to be,
That one meets Hector; if none else, I am he.

NESTOR
Tell him of Nestor, one that was a man
When Hector's grandsire suck'd. He is old now,
But if there be not in our Grecian host
A noble man that hath no spark of fire
To answer for his love, tell him from me
I'll hide my silver beard in a gold beaver,
And in my vantbrace put my withered brawns,
And meeting him will tell him that my lady
Was fairer than his grandam, and as chaste
As may be in the world. His youth in flood,
I'll prove this troth with my three drops of blood.

AENEAS
Now heavens forfend such scarcity of youth!

ULYSSES
Amen.

AGAMEMNON
Fair Lord Aeneas, let me touch your hand;
To our pavilion shall I lead you, sir.
Achilles shall have word of this intent;
So shall each lord of Greece, from tent to tent.
Yourself shall feast with us before you go,
And find the welcome of a noble foe.
[*Exeunt all but Ulysses and Nestor.*]

ULYSSES
Nestor!

NESTOR
What says Ulysses?

ULYSSES
I have a young conception in my brain,
Be you my time to bring it to some shape.

NESTOR
What is 't?

ULYSSES
[This 'tis:]
Blunt wedges rive hard knots; the seeded pride
That hath to this maturity blown up
In rank Achilles must or now be cropp'd,
Or, shedding, breed a nursery of like evil,
To overbulk us all.

NESTOR Well, and how?

ULYSSES
This challenge that the gallant Hector sends,
However it is spread in general name,
Relates in purpose only to Achilles.

NESTOR
True, the purpose is perspicuous as substance,
Whose grossness little characters sum up;

241 distains his sullies its **243 repining** begrudging **244 That . . . blows** fame proclaims abroad that speech. **sole** utterly **252 set . . . bent** i.e., bend his sense of hearing attentively toward me **263 resty** sluggish, unused **269–270 more . . . loves** more than in protestation made with false vows to the lips of her whom he loves **272 In . . . hers** i.e., in the arms of warfare rather than those of his mistress **276 couple** embrace **282 sunburnt** i.e., unattractive, according to Elizabethan tastes in beauty

288 means not intends not to be **296 beaver** face guard of a helmet **297 vantbrace** armor for the front part of the arm **300 His . . . flood** i.e., though his manhood and vigor be at their height **301 troth** truth **302 forfend** forbid **313 Be . . . time** i.e., act as midwife to my newly-conceived plan **316 seeded pride** pride that is gone to seed, overblown **318 rank** overripe, swollen. **or** either **319 shedding** i.e., if it scatters its seeds **320 overbulk** overwhelm **324–325 perspicuous . . . up** as perceivable as great wealth, the size of which can be rendered in little figures

And, in the publication, make no strain
But that Achilles, were his brain as barren
As banks of Libya—though, Apollo knows,
'Tis dry enough—will, with great speed of
 judgment,
Ay, with celerity, find Hector's purpose
Pointing on him.

ULYSSES
And wake him to the answer, think you?

NESTOR
Why, 'tis most meet. Who may you else oppose,
That can from Hector bring those honors off,
If not Achilles? Though 't be a sportful combat,
Yet in the trial much opinion dwells,
For here the Troyans taste our dear'st repute
With their fin'st palate. And trust to me, Ulysses,
Our imputation shall be oddly pois'd
In this vild action. For the success,
Although particular, shall give a scantling
Of good or bad unto the general;
And in such indexes, although small pricks
To their subsequent volumes, there is seen
The baby figure of the giant mass
Of things to come at large. It is suppos'd
He that meets Hector issues from our choice;
And choice, being mutual act of all our souls,
Makes merit her election, and doth boil,
As 'twere from forth us all, a man distill'd
Out of our virtues; who miscarrying,
What heart receives from hence the conquering part,
To steel a strong opinion to themselves?
[Which entertain'd, limbs are his instruments,
In no less working than are swords and bows
Directive by the limbs.]

ULYSSES
 Give pardon to my speech:
Therefore 'tis meet Achilles meet not Hector.
Let us, like merchants, first show foul wares,
And think, perchance, they'll sell; if not,
The luster of the better shall exceed
By showing the worst first. Do not consent
That ever Hector and Achilles meet;
For both our honor and our shame in this
Are dogg'd with two strange followers.

NESTOR
I see them not with my old eyes. What are they?

ULYSSES
What glory our Achilles shares from Hector,
Were he not proud, we all should share with him.
But he already is too insolent,
And it were better parch in Afric sun
Than in the pride and salt scorn of his eyes,
Should he scape Hector fair. If he were foil'd,
Why then, we do our main opinion crush
In taint of our best man. No, make a lott'ry,
And, by device, let blockish Ajax draw
The sort to fight with Hector. Among ourselves
Give him allowance for the better man;
For that will physic the great Myrmidon
Who broils in loud applause, and make him fall
His crest that prouder than blue Iris bends.
If the dull brainless Ajax come safe off,
We'll dress him up in voices; if he fail,
Yet go we under our opinion still
That we have better men. But, hit or miss,
Our project's life this shape of sense assumes:
Ajax employ'd plucks down Achilles' plumes.

NESTOR
Now, Ulysses, I begin to relish thy advice;
And I will give a taste thereof forthwith
To Agamemnon. Go we to him straight.
Two curs shall tame each other; pride alone
Must tarre the mastiffs on, as 'twere a bone. *Exeunt.*

[ACT II • SCENE I]

Enter Ajax and Thersites.

AJAX Thersites!

THERSITES Agamemnon, how if he had boils—full, all over, generally?

AJAX Thersites!

THERSITES And those boils did run? Say so. Did not the general run then? Were not that a botchy core?

AJAX Dog!

THERSITES Then would come some matter from him; I see none now.

AJAX Thou bitch-wolf's son, canst thou not hear? [*Beating him.*] Feel, then.

THERSITES The plague of Greece upon thee, thou mongrel beef-witted lord!

AJAX Speak then, thou vinewedst leaven, speak. I will beat thee into handsomeness.

THERSITES I shall sooner rail thee into wit and holiness; but I think thy horse will sooner con an oration than thou learn a prayer without book. Thou canst strike, canst thou? A red murrain o' thy jade's tricks!

AJAX Toadstool, learn me the proclamation.

THERSITES Dost thou think I have no sense, thou strikest me thus?

AJAX The proclamation!

THERSITES Thou art proclaim'd fool, I think.

326 in . . . strain when it is publicly announced have no doubt **328 banks** sandbanks **329 dry** i.e., dull **336 opinion** reputation **337 taste our dear'st repute** i.e., put to the test Achilles, our warrior of greatest reputation **338 their fin'st palate** i.e., Hector **339 imputation** reputation. **pois'd** balanced **340 vild** trivial, paltry. **success** outcome **341 particular** relating to (two) particular men. **scantling** specimen, sample **342 general** army at large **343 indexes** indications, table of contents **343–344 small . . . volumes** small indicators in comparison with the volumes that follow **349 election** basis of choice **351 miscarrying** i.e., if he should fail **352 conquering part** share of victory **353 steel** strengthen **354–356 Which . . . limbs** i.e., if one does entertain a strong opinion of oneself, one's limbs become the instruments of that strong opinion, no less efficacious and responsive than swords and bows are subject to the direction of the limbs

372 main opinion crush destroy our general reputation **373 In taint** in the dishonor **375 sort** lot **376 allowance for** acknowledgment as **377 physic** purge medically. **Myrmidon** i.e., Achilles. (So called here because accompanied by a band of Myrmidon warriors, from a tribe living in Thessaly.) **378 broils in** basks in. **fall** let fall, bow **379 crest** plumes on helmet. **Iris** the messenger of Juno, i.e., the rainbow. **bends** arches **381 voices** applause **384 life** success **390 tarre** provoke, incite

II.i. Location: The Greek camp.
6 botchy core central hard mass of a boil or tumor **8 matter** (1) sense (2) pus **12–13 mongrel** (Ajax's mother was a Trojan, the sister of Priam; cf. II.ii.77, note, IV.v.83, and IV.v.120.) **14 vinewedst** most moldy. **leaven** dough **17 con** memorize **18 without book** by heart **19 murrain** plague. **jade's tricks** i.e., ill-tempered kicking and rearing, as of a worthless horse **20 learn me** find out for me **21 sense** feeling

AJAX Do not, porpentine, do not. My fingers itch.

THERSITES I would thou didst itch from head to foot; an I had the scratching of thee, I would make thee the loathsomest scab in Greece. When thou art forth in the incursions, thou strikest as slow as another.

AJAX I say, the proclamation!

THERSITES Thou grumblest and railest every hour on Achilles, and thou art as full of envy at his greatness as Cerberus is at Proserpina's beauty, ay, that thou bark'st at him.

AJAX Mistress Thersites!

THERSITES Thou shouldst strike him.

AJAX Cobloaf!

THERSITES He would pun thee into shivers with his fist, as a sailor breaks a biscuit.

AJAX [*Beating him*] You whoreson cur!

THERSITES Do, do.

AJAX Thou stool for a witch!

THERSITES Ay, do, do, thou sodden-witted lord! Thou hast no more brain than I have in mine elbows; an asinico may tutor thee. Thou scurvy-valiant ass! Thou art here but to thrash Troyans; and thou art bought and sold among those of any wit, like a barbarian slave. If thou use to beat me, I will begin at thy heel, and tell what thou art by inches, thou thing of no bowels, thou!

AJAX You dog!

THERSITES You scurvy lord!

AJAX [*Beating him*] You cur!

THERSITES Mars his idiot! Do, rudeness, do, camel, do, do.

[*Enter Achilles and Patroclus.*]

ACHILLES Why, how now, Ajax, wherefore do ye thus?
How now, Thersites, what's the matter, man?

THERSITES You see him there, do you?

ACHILLES Ay; what's the matter?

THERSITES Nay, look upon him.

ACHILLES So I do. What's the matter?

THERSITES Nay, but regard him well.

ACHILLES Well, why, so I do.

THERSITES But yet you look not well upon him; for, whosomever you take him to be, he is Ajax.

ACHILLES I know that, fool.

THERSITES Ay, but that fool knows not himself.

AJAX Therefore I beat thee.

THERSITES Lo, lo, lo, lo, what modicums of wit he utters! His evasions have ears thus long. I have bobb'd his brain more than he has beat my bones. I will buy nine sparrows for a penny, and his pia mater is not worth the ninth part of a sparrow. This lord, Achilles, Ajax, who wears his wit in his belly and his guts in his head, I'll tell you what I say of him.

ACHILLES What?

THERSITES I say, this Ajax— [*Ajax offers to beat him.*]

ACHILLES Nay, good Ajax.

THERSITES Has not so much wit—

ACHILLES Nay, I must hold you.

THERSITES As will stop the eye of Helen's needle, for whom he comes to fight.

ACHILLES Peace, fool!

THERSITES I would have peace and quietness, but the fool will not—he there, that he. Look you there.

AJAX O thou damn'd cur! I shall—

ACHILLES Will you set your wit to a fool's?

THERSITES No, I warrant you; the fool's will shame it.

PATROCLUS Good words, Thersites.

ACHILLES What's the quarrel?

AJAX I bade the vile owl go learn me the tenor of the proclamation, and he rails upon me.

THERSITES I serve thee not.

AJAX Well, go to, go to.

THERSITES I serve here voluntary.

ACHILLES Your last service was suff'rance, 'twas not voluntary; no man is beaten voluntary. Ajax was here the voluntary, and you as under an impress.

THERSITES E'en so; a great deal of your wit, too, lies in your sinews, or else there be liars. Hector shall have a great catch, an 'a knock out either of your brains; 'a were as good crack a fusty nut with no kernel.

ACHILLES What, with me too, Thersites?

THERSITES There's Ulysses and old Nestor, whose wit was moldy ere your grandsires had nails on their toes, yoke you like draught-oxen and make you plough up the wars.

ACHILLES What, what?

THERSITES Yes, good sooth. To, Achilles! To, Ajax! To!

AJAX I shall cut out your tongue.

THERSITES 'Tis no matter; I shall speak as much as thou afterwards.

PATROCLUS No more words, Thersites. Peace!

THERSITES I will hold my peace when Achilles' brooch bids me, shall I?

ACHILLES There's for you, Patroclus.

THERSITES I will see you hang'd, like clotpoles, ere I come any more to your tents. I will keep where there is wit stirring and leave the faction of fools. *Exit.*

PATROCLUS A good riddance.

ACHILLES
Marry, this, sir, is proclaim'd through all our host:
That Hector, by the fifth hour of the sun,
Will with a trumpet 'twixt our tents and Troy
Tomorrow morning call some knight to arms
That hath a stomach, and such a one that dare
Maintain—I know not what, 'tis trash. Farewell.

AJAX
Farewell. Who shall answer him?

25 porpentine porcupine **29 incursions** i.e., attacks upon the Trojan forces **33 Cerberus** three-headed dog which guarded the entrance to Hades. **Proserpina** Queen of Hades **37 Cobloaf** small round loaf; a bun **38 pun** pound **42 stool** privy **43 sodden-witted** boiled-brained **45 asinico** little ass **46–47 bought and sold** i.e., treated like merchandise **48 use** continue **49–50 bowels** sensitivity, human feeling **54 Mars his** Mars' **65 whosomever** whosoever. **Ajax** (with probable pun on a *jakes,* a latrine) **67 that fool . . . himself** (Thersites answers as though Achilles had said, "I know that fool.") **70 have . . . long** i.e., are those of an ass, are asinine. **bobb'd** thumped **72 pia mater** (Literally, membrane cover of the brain; used here for the brain.)

87 set your wit to match wits with **89 Good words** i.e., speak gently **98 impress** (1) impressment, military draft (2) imprint (of blows) **99 E'en so** exactly **102 fusty** moldy **109 To . . . To** (Thersites impersonates Nestor and Ulysses as drivers of a team, urging Achilles and Ajax to plow.) **114 brooch** bauble, plaything (i.e., Patroclus; often emended to *brach,* bitch-hound) **117 clotpoles** blockheads **122 fifth hour** i.e., eleven o'clock **125 stomach** appetite (for fighting)

ACHILLES
I know not. 'Tis put to lott'ry. Otherwise,
He knew his man. 129

AJAX
O, meaning you? I will go learn more of it.
[*Exeunt severally.*]

[SCENE II]

Enter Priam, Hector, Troilus, Paris, and Helenus.

PRIAM
After so many hours, lives, speeches spent,
Thus once again says Nestor from the Greeks:
"Deliver Helen, and all damage else—
As honor, loss of time, travail, expense,
Wounds, friends, and what else dear that is
consum'd
In hot digestion of this cormorant war— 6
Shall be struck off." Hector, what say you to 't?

HECTOR
Though no man lesser fears the Greeks than I
As far as toucheth my particular, 9
Yet, dread Priam,
There is no lady of more softer bowels, 11
More spongy to suck in the sense of fear,
More ready to cry out, "Who knows what follows?"
Than Hector is. The wound of peace is surety, 14
Surety secure; but modest doubt is call'd 15
The beacon of the wise, the tent that searches 16
To th' bottom of the worst. Let Helen go.
Since the first sword was drawn about this question,
Every tithe soul, 'mongst many thousand dismes, 19
Hath been as dear as Helen; I mean, of ours.
If we have lost so many tenths of ours
To guard a thing not ours nor worth to us,
Had it our name, the value of one ten, 23
What merit's in that reason which denies
The yielding of her up?

TROILUS
Fie, fie, my brother!
Weigh you the worth and honor of a king
So great as our dread father's in a scale
Of common ounces? Will you with counters sum 28
The past proportion of his infinite, 29
And buckle in a waist most fathomless
With spans and inches so diminutive 31
As fears and reasons? Fie, for godly shame!

HELENUS [*To Troilus*]
No marvel, though you bite so sharp at reasons, 33
You are so empty of them. Should not our father 34
Bear the great sway of his affairs with reasons,
Because your speech hath none that tell him so?

TROILUS
You are for dreams and slumbers, brother priest;
You fur your gloves with reason. Here are your
reasons: 38
You know an enemy intends you harm;
You know a sword employ'd is perilous,
And reason flies the object of all harm.
Who marvels then, when Helenus beholds
A Grecian and his sword, if he do set
The very wings of reason to his heels
And fly like chidden Mercury from Jove, 45
Or like a star disorb'd? Nay, if we talk of reason, 46
Let's shut our gates and sleep. Manhood and honor
Should have hare-hearts, would they but fat their
thoughts
With this cramm'd reason. Reason and respect 49
Make livers pale and lustihood deject. 50

HECTOR
Brother, she is not worth what she doth cost
The keeping.

TROILUS
What's aught but as 'tis valued?

HECTOR
But value dwells not in particular will; 53
It holds his estimate and dignity 54
As well wherein 'tis precious of itself 55
As in the prizer. 'Tis mad idolatry 56
To make the service greater than the god;
And the will dotes that is attributive 58
To what infectiously itself affects, 59
Without some image of th' affected merit. 60

TROILUS
I take today a wife, and my election 61
Is led on in the conduct of my will—
My will enkindled by mine eyes and ears,
Two traded pilots 'twixt the dangerous shores 64
Of will and judgment. How may I avoid, 65
Although my will distaste what it elected, 66
The wife I chose? There can be no evasion
To blench from this and to stand firm by honor. 68
We turn not back the silks upon the merchant
When we have soil'd them, nor the remainder
viands
We do not throw in unrespective sieve, 71
Because we now are full. It was thought meet
Paris should do some vengeance on the Greeks. 73
Your breath with full consent bellied his sails;
The seas and winds, old wranglers, took a truce 75

129 knew would know

II.ii. Location: Troy. Priam's palace.
6 cormorant gluttonous **9 my particular** me personally **11 bowels** mercy, pity **14 The . . . surety** i.e., the danger of peace is in the sense of security it breeds **15 secure** overconfident. **modest doubt** a reasonable estimate of danger **16 beacon** warning signal. **tent** probe **19 Every tithe soul** every soul exacted by the war as a tithe. **dismes** tenths (of men sacrificed) **23 Had . . . name** i.e., even if Helen were a Trojan. **one ten** i.e., one tithe exacted by the war, one Trojan life **28 counters** pieces of coin-shaped metal used in calculation. **sum** total up **29 The past . . . infinite** his infinitude past all comparison **31 spans** measures of nine inches spanning the hand from thumb to little finger **33 reasons** (Pronounced like *raisins,* with pun.) **34 not our father** our father not

38 fur line with soft fur. (Troilus accuses Helenus of using reason as a justification for personal comfort, explaining cowardly flight as prudence.) **45 chidden Mercury** (Mercury as Jove's errand boy was subject to his chiding or impatient bidding.) **46 disorb'd** removed from its sphere (like a shooting star) **49 cramm'd reason** i.e., thoughts fattened or crammed with this reason. **respect** caution **50 livers pale** (A bloodless liver was thought to be a sign of cowardice.) **lustihood** bodily vigor **53 particular will** i.e., one person's preference merely **54 his** its. **dignity** worth **55 of itself** intrinsically **56 the prizer** i.e., the opinion of him who prizes it **58–60 the will . . . merit** i.e., that will is mad which subserviently pays tribute to what the will itself prefers in a diseased way, without some appearance in the desired object of intrinsic merit **61 I take today a wife** (Troilus, in setting up a hypothetical case that applies to Paris, is also stating his own credo about love.) **election** choice **64 traded** skillful in their trade; trafficing back and forth **65 avoid** rid myself of **66 distaste** dislike (in time) **68 blench** shrink. **and** and simultaneously **71 unrespective sieve** worthless receptacle, i.e., garbage can **73 vengeance** i.e., in return for Hesione's abduction; see l. 77 and note **75 old wranglers** traditional enemies

And did him service. He touch'd the ports desir'd,
And for an old aunt whom the Greeks held captive, 77
He brought a Grecian queen, whose youth and freshness
Wrinkles Apollo's, and makes pale the morning. 79
Why keep we her? The Grecians keep our aunt.
Is she worth keeping? Why, she is a pearl
Whose price hath launch'd above a thousand ships, 82
And turn'd crown'd kings to merchants. 83
If you'll avouch 'twas wisdom Paris went—
As you must needs, for you all cried "Go, go"—
If you'll confess he brought home worthy prize—
As you must needs, for you all clapp'd your hands,
And cried "Inestimable!"—why do you now
The issue of your proper wisdoms rate, 89
And do a deed that never Fortune did,
Beggar the estimation which you priz'd 91
Richer than sea and land? O, theft most base,
That we have stol'n what we do fear to keep!
But thieves unworthy of a thing so stol'n,
That in their country did them that disgrace 95
We fear to warrant in our native place! 96

CASSANDRA [*Within*]
Cry, Troyans, cry!

PRIAM
What noise? What shriek is this?

TROILUS
'Tis our mad sister, I do know her voice.

CASSANDRA [*Within*]
Cry, Troyans!

HECTOR
It is Cassandra.

Enter Cassandra, raving, [*with her hair about her ears*].

CASSANDRA
Cry, Troyans, cry! Lend me ten thousand eyes,
And I will fill them with prophetic tears.

HECTOR
Peace, sister, peace!

CASSANDRA
Virgins and boys, mid-age and wrinkled eld, 104
Soft infancy, that nothing canst but cry, 105
Add to my clamors! Let us pay betimes 106
A moi'ty of that mass of moan to come. 107
Cry, Troyans, cry! Practice your eyes with tears!
Troy must not be, nor goodly Ilion stand;
Our firebrand brother, Paris, burns us all. 110
Cry, Troyans, cry! A Helen and a woe!
Cry, cry! Troy burns, or else let Helen go. *Exit.*

HECTOR
Now, youthful Troilus, do not these high strains
Of divination in our sister work
Some touches of remorse? Or is your blood
So madly hot that no discourse of reason,
Nor fear of bad success in a bad cause,
Can qualify the same?

TROILUS
Why, brother Hector,
We may not think the justness of each act
Such and no other than event doth form it, 120
Nor once deject the courage of our minds 121
Because Cassandra's mad. Her brain-sick raptures
Cannot distaste the goodness of a quarrel 123
Which hath our several honors all engag'd
To make it gracious. For my private part, 125
I am no more touch'd than all Priam's sons,
And Jove forbid there should be done amongst us
Such things as might offend the weakest spleen 128
To fight for and maintain!

PARIS
Else might the world convince of levity 130
As well my undertakings as your counsels.
But I attest the gods, your full consent 132
Gave wings to my propension, and cut off 133
All fears attending on so dire a project.
For what, alas, can these my single arms?
What propugnation is in one man's valor, 136
To stand the push and enmity of those
This quarrel would excite? Yet, I protest,
Were I alone to pass the difficulties, 139
And had as ample power as I have will,
Paris should ne'er retract what he hath done,
Nor faint in the pursuit.

PRIAM
Paris, you speak
Like one besotted on your sweet delights.
You have the honey still, but these the gall;
So to be valiant is no praise at all.

PARIS
Sir, I propose not merely to myself
The pleasures such a beauty brings with it;
But I would have the soil of her fair rape 148
Wip'd off, in honorable keeping her.
What treason were it to the ransack'd queen, 150
Disgrace to your great worths, and shame to me,
Now to deliver her possession up
On terms of base compulsion! Can it be
That so degenerate a strain as this
Should once set footing in your generous bosoms? 155
There's not the meanest spirit on our party 156
Without a heart to dare or sword to draw
When Helen is defended, nor none so noble
Whose life were ill bestow'd or death unfam'd
Where Helen is the subject. Then I say,
Well may we fight for her whom we know well
The world's large spaces cannot parallel.

77 an old aunt i.e., Hesione, Priam's sister, rescued from the wrath of Poseidon by Hercules and bestowed by him on the Greek, Telamon, father of Ajax; we learn in IV.v.83 and 120 that she was Ajax's mother **79 Wrinkles Apollo's** i.e., makes Apollo's youthful countenance look old and ugly by comparison **82 Whose . . . ships** (Perhaps echoes the famous line from Marlowe's *Doctor Faustus:* "Was this the face that launched a thousand ships?") **83 turn'd . . . merchants** i.e., made kings like merchants seeking a rare pearl. (Cf. Matthew 13:45.) **89 The issue . . . rate** condemn the results of your own wise deliberation **91 Beggar . . . which** consider valueless the once-esteemed object which **95–96 That . . . place** i.e., we who in Greece itself visited a disgrace upon the Greeks (by abducting Helen) which we are now afraid to justify through defending her right here in our own native land **104 eld** old age **105 nothing canst** can do nothing **106 betimes** in advance **107 moi'ty** part **110 firebrand** (Paris' mother, Hecuba, dreamed when pregnant with Paris that she would be delivered of a firebrand destined to burn down Troy.)

120 event outcome **121 once deject** ever abate **123 distaste** render distasteful **125 gracious** righteous, dignified (because our honorable selves "grace" the enterprise) **128 spleen** i.e., temper **130 convince** convict **132 attest** call to witness **133 propension** propensity, inclination **136 propugnation** defense, might **139 pass** experience, undergo **148 rape** abduction **150 ransack'd** carried off **155 generous** noble **156 party** part, side

HECTOR
Paris and Troilus, you have both said well,
And on the cause and question now in hand
Have gloz'd, but superficially; not much 165
Unlike young men, whom Aristotle thought
Unfit to hear moral philosophy. 167
The reasons you allege do more conduce
To the hot passion of distemp'red blood
Than to make up a free determination
'Twixt right and wrong, for pleasure and revenge
Have ears more deaf than adders to the voice 172
Of any true decision. Nature craves
All dues be rend'red to their owners. Now,
What nearer debt in all humanity
Than wife is to the husband? If this law
Of nature be corrupted through affection, 177
And that great minds, of partial indulgence 178
To their benumbed wills, resist the same,
There is a law in each well-order'd nation
To curb those raging appetites that are
Most disobedient and refractory.
If Helen then be wife to Sparta's king,
As it is known she is, these moral laws
Of nature and of nations speak aloud
To have her back return'd. Thus to persist
In doing wrong extenuates not wrong,
But makes it much more heavy. Hector's opinion
Is this in way of truth; yet ne'ertheless,
My spritely brethren, I propend to you 190
In resolution to keep Helen still,
For 'tis a cause that hath no mean dependence 192
Upon our joint and several dignities. 193

TROILUS
Why, there you touch'd the life of our design!
Were it not glory that we more affected
Than the performance of our heaving spleens, 196
I would not wish a drop of Troyan blood
Spent more in her defense. But, worthy Hector,
She is a theme of honor and renown,
A spur to valiant and magnanimous deeds,
Whose present courage may beat down our foes, 201
And fame in time to come canonize us; 202
For I presume brave Hector would not lose
So rich advantage of a promis'd glory
As smiles upon the forehead of this action
For the wide world's revenue.

HECTOR
I am yours,
You valiant offspring of great Priamus.
I have a roisting challenge sent amongst 208
The dull and factious nobles of the Greeks
Will strike amazement to their drowsy spirits. 210
I was advertis'd their great general slept, 211
Whilst emulation in the army crept. 212
This, I presume, will wake him. *Exeunt.*

165 gloz'd commented on **167 moral philosophy** (Aristotle says this of political philosophy in the *Nichomachean Ethics.*) **172 adders** (Cf. Psalms 58:4-5.) **177 affection** passion **178 that** i.e., if that, if. **of partial** out of self-interested **190 spritely** full of spirit. **propend** incline **192–193 'tis . . . dignities** i.e., it is a cause upon which depend to no small degree our collective and individual honors **196 heaving spleens** aroused anger **201 Whose** of which **202 canonize** enroll among famous persons **208 roisting** roistering, clamorous **210 Will** which will **211 advertis'd** informed. **their great general** i.e., Achilles; or possibly Agamemnon **212 emulation** ambitious or jealous rivalry

[SCENE III]

Enter Thersites, solus.

THERSITES How now, Thersites? What, lost in the lab-
yrinth of thy fury? Shall the elephant Ajax carry it 2
thus? He beats me, and I rail at him. O, worthy satis-
faction! Would it were otherwise, that I could beat
him, whilst he rail'd at me. 'Sfoot, I'll learn to conjure 5
and raise devils, but I'll see some issue of my spiteful 6
execrations. Then there's Achilles, a rare enginer! If 7
Troy be not taken till these two undermine it, the walls
will stand till they fall of themselves. O thou great
thunder-darter of Olympus, forget that thou art Jove,
the king of gods, and, Mercury, lose all the serpentine 11
craft of thy caduceus, if ye take not that little little less 12
than little wit from them that they have, which short- 13
arm'd ignorance itself knows is so abundant scarce, it 14
will not in circumvention deliver a fly from a spider,
without drawing their massy irons and cutting the 16
web! After this, the vengeance on the whole camp! Or
rather, the Neapolitan bone-ache! For that, methinks, 18
is the curse depending on those that war for a placket. 19
I have said my prayers, and devil Envy say Amen.
What ho! My Lord Achilles!

[*Enter Patroclus.*]

PATROCLUS Who's there? Thersites? Good Thersites, come in and rail.

THERSITES If I could 'a remembr'red a gilt counterfeit, 24
thou wouldst not have slipp'd out of my contempla- 25
tion. But it is no matter; thyself upon thyself! The com- 26
mon curse of mankind, folly and ignorance, be thine
in great revenue! Heaven bless thee from a tutor, and 28
discipline come not near thee! Let thy blood be thy 29
direction till thy death; then if she that lays thee out
says thou art a fair corse, I'll be sworn and sworn
upon 't she never shrouded any but lazars. Amen. 32
Where's Achilles?

PATROCLUS What, art thou devout? Wast thou in prayer?

THERSITES Ay; the heavens hear me!

PATROCLUS Amen.

Enter Achilles.

ACHILLES Who's there?

PATROCLUS Thersites, my lord.

ACHILLES Where, where? O where? Art thou come?
Why, my cheese, my digestion, why hast thou not 40

II.iii. Location: The Greek camp. Before Achilles' tent.
2 carry it carry off the honors **5 'Sfoot** by His (God's) foot **6 but I'll see** rather than not see **7 enginer** one who digs countermines or tunnels underneath the enemy's battlements **11–12 serpentine . . . caduceus** (Alludes to Mercury's wand, having two serpents twined round it.) **13–14 short-arm'd** inadequate in its reach, finding everything beyond its grasp **16 massy irons** massive swords (used with overkill on a mere spider's web) **18 Neapolitan bone-ache** i.e., venereal disease **19 depending on** hanging over. **placket** slit in a petticoat; hence (indecently) a woman **24 'a** have **25 slipp'd** (with a quibble on *slip,* counterfeit coin) **26 thyself upon thyself** (Thersites, after alleging that he would have cursed Patroclus along with Ajax and Achilles if he were not counterfeit and hence so easily overlooked, now undertakes to curse Patroclus with the most dire curse imaginable: may Patroclus be plagued by himself.) **28 great revenue** generous amounts. **bless thee from** bless you by protecting you from (so as to preserve your native ignorance) **29 blood** violent passion **32 lazars** lepers **40 cheese** (Supposed, proverbially, to aid digestion.)

serv'd thyself in to my table so many meals? Come, what's Agamemnon?

THERSITES Thy commander, Achilles. Then tell me, Patroclus, what's Achilles?

PATROCLUS Thy lord, Thersites. Then tell me, I pray thee, what's thyself?

THERSITES Thy knower, Patroclus. Then tell me, Patroclus, what art thou?

PATROCLUS Thou mayst tell that knowest.

ACHILLES O, tell, tell.

THERSITES I'll decline the whole question. Agamemnon commands Achilles, Achilles is my lord, I am Patroclus' knower, and Patroclus is a fool.

[PATROCLUS You rascal!

THERSITES Peace, fool! I have not done.

ACHILLES He is a privileg'd man. Proceed, Thersites.

THERSITES Agamemnon is a fool, Achilles is a fool, Thersites is a fool, and, as aforesaid, Patroclus is a fool.]

ACHILLES Derive this; come.

THERSITES Agamemnon is a fool to offer to command Achilles, Achilles is a fool to be commanded of Agamemnon, Thersites is a fool to serve such a fool, and Patroclus is a fool positive.

PATROCLUS Why am I a fool?

THERSITES Make that demand of the prover. It suffices me thou art. Look you, who comes here?

Enter [*at a distance*] *Agamemnon, Ulysses, Nestor, Diomedes, Ajax, and Calchas.*

ACHILLES Patroclus, I'll speak with nobody. Come in with me, Thersites. [*Exit.*]

THERSITES Here is such patchery, such juggling, and such knavery! All the argument is a whore and a cuckold, a good quarrel to draw emulous factions and bleed to death upon. [Now, the dry serpigo on the subject, and war and lechery confound all!] [*Exit.*]

AGAMEMNON Where is Achilles?

PATROCLUS
Within his tent, but ill dispos'd, my lord.

AGAMEMNON
Let it be known to him that we are here.
He shent our messengers, and we lay by
Our appertainings, visiting of him.
Let him be told so, lest perchance he think
We dare not move the question of our place,
Or know not what we are.

PATROCLUS I shall say so to him. [*Exit.*]

ULYSSES We saw him at the opening of his tent. He is not sick.

AJAX Yes, lion-sick, sick of proud heart. You may call it melancholy, if you will favor the man; but, by my head, 'tis pride. But why, why? Let him show us the cause. [A word, my lord.] [*Takes Agamemnon aside.*]

NESTOR What moves Ajax thus to bay at him?

ULYSSES Achilles hath inveigled his fool from him.

NESTOR Who, Thersites?

ULYSSES He.

NESTOR Then will Ajax lack matter, if he have lost his argument.

ULYSSES No, you see, he is his argument that has his argument, Achilles.

NESTOR All the better; their fraction is more our wish than their faction. But it was a strong composure a fool could disunite.

ULYSSES The amity that wisdom knits not, folly may easily untie.

[*Enter Patroclus.*]

Here comes Patroclus.

NESTOR No Achilles with him.

ULYSSES The elephant hath joints, but none for courtesy. His legs are legs for necessity, not for flexure.

PATROCLUS
Achilles bids me say, he is much sorry
If any thing more than your sport and pleasure
Did move your greatness and this noble state
To call upon him. He hopes it is no other
But for your health and your digestion sake,
An after-dinner's breath.

AGAMEMNON Hear you, Patroclus:
We are too well acquainted with these answers;
But his evasion, wing'd thus swift with scorn,
Cannot outfly our apprehensions.
Much attribute he hath, and much the reason
Why we ascribe it to him; yet all his virtues,
Not virtuously on his own part beheld,
Do in our eyes begin to lose their gloss,
Yea, like fair fruit in an unwholesome dish,
Are like to rot untasted. Go and tell him
We come to speak with him. And you shall not sin
If you do say we think him over-proud
And under-honest, in self-assumption greater
Than in the note of judgment; and worthier than himself
Here tend the savage strangeness he puts on,
Disguise the holy strength of their command,
And underwrite in an observing kind
His humorous predominance—yea, watch
His pettish lunes, his ebbs, his flows, as if
The passage and whole carriage of this action
Rode on his tide. Go tell him this, and add
That if he overhold his price so much,
We'll none of him, but let him, like an engine

51 decline go through in order from beginning to end (as when declining a noun) **56 privileg'd man** (Fools were permitted to speak without restraint.) **60 Derive** give the origin of. (The grammatical metaphor is continued here and also in l. 64). **64 positive** i.e., absolute **70 patchery** knavery **71 All the argument** i.e., the issue of the war **72 draw** (1) attract (2) draw blood; see l. 73. **emulous** envious **73 serpigo** skin eruption **78 shent** sent back insultingly **79 appertainings** rights, prerogatives **81 move the question** insist upon the prerogatives **85 lion-sick** i.e., sick with pride

93 matter subject matter (to rail upon) **93–94 his argument** i.e., the subject of his railing, Thersites **95–96 he . . . Achilles** i.e., Achilles, who now has Ajax' former subject of railing, Thersites, has himself become Ajax' new target of raillery **97 fraction** discord **98 faction** i.e., union, alliance. **composure** union. (Said contemptuously.) **104 elephant hath joints** (Refers to a common belief that elephants' joints did not enable them to lie down.) **108 this noble state** i.e., the distinguished men accompanying Agamemnon **114 apprehensions** understanding **115 attribute** credit, reputation **117 Not . . . beheld** not modestly borne **124 Than . . . judgment** than men of true judgment know him to be; or, than in qualities of wise judgment **125 tend** wait upon. **savage strangeness** uncivil aloofness **127 underwrite** i.e., submit to (as observers), subscribe to. **in . . . kind** deferentially **128 humorous predominance** the currently dominant humor in him, i.e., blood, leading to pride **129 lunes** lunacies **132 overhold** overvalue **133 engine** military machine

Not portable, lie under this report:
"Bring action hither, this cannot go to war."
A stirring dwarf we do allowance give
Before a sleeping giant. Tell him so.

PATROCLUS
I shall, and bring his answer presently. [*Exit.*]

AGAMEMNON
In second voice we'll not be satisfied.
We come to speak with him. Ulysses, enter you.
[*Exit Ulysses.*]

AJAX What is he more than another?

AGAMEMNON No more than what he thinks he is.

AJAX Is he so much? Do you not think he thinks himself a better man than I am?

AGAMEMNON No question.

AJAX Will you subscribe his thought, and say he is?

AGAMEMNON No, noble Ajax; you are as strong, as valiant, as wise, no less noble, much more gentle, and altogether more tractable.

AJAX Why should a man be proud? How doth pride grow? I know not what pride is.

AGAMEMNON Your mind is the clearer, Ajax, and your virtues the fairer. He that is proud eats up himself. Pride is his own glass, his own trumpet, his own chronicle; and whatever praises itself but in the deed, devours the deed in the praise.

Enter Ulysses.

AJAX I do hate a proud man, as I do hate the engend'ring of toads.

NESTOR [*Aside*] And yet he loves himself. Is 't not strange?

ULYSSES
Achilles will not to the field tomorrow.

AGAMEMNON
What's his excuse?

ULYSSES He doth rely on none,
But carries on the stream of his dispose
Without observance or respect of any,
In will peculiar and in self-admission.

AGAMEMNON
Why will he not upon our fair request
Untent his person and share th' air with us?

ULYSSES
Things small as nothing, for request's sake only,
He makes important. Possess'd he is with greatness,
And speaks not to himself but with a pride
That quarrels at self-breath. Imagin'd worth
Holds in his blood such swoll'n and hot discourse
That 'twixt his mental and his active parts
Kingdom'd Achilles in commotion rages
And batters down himself. What should I say?
He is so plaguy proud that the death-tokens of it
Cry "No recovery."

AGAMEMNON Let Ajax go to him.
Dear lord, go you and greet him in his tent.
'Tis said he holds you well, and will be led
At your request a little from himself.

ULYSSES
O Agamemnon, let it not be so!
We'll consecrate the steps that Ajax makes
When they go from Achilles. Shall the proud lord
That bastes his arrogance with his own seam
And never suffers matter of the world
Enter his thoughts, save such as doth revolve
And ruminate himself, shall he be worship'd
Of that we hold an idol more than he?
No, this thrice worthy and right valiant lord
Shall not so stale his palm, nobly acquir'd,
Nor, by my will, assubjugate his merit,
As amply titled as Achilles' is,
By going to Achilles.
That were to enlard his fat-already pride
And add more coals to Cancer when he burns
With entertaining great Hyperion.
This lord go to him? Jupiter forbid,
And say in thunder, "Achilles go to him."

NESTOR [*Aside to Diomedes*]
O, this is well. He rubs the vein of him.

DIOMEDES [*Aside to Nestor*]
And how his silence drinks up this applause!

AJAX
If I go to him, with my armed fist
I'll pash him o'er the face.

AGAMEMNON
O, no, you shall not go.

AJAX
An he be proud with me, I'll pheeze his pride.
Let me go to him.

ULYSSES Not for the worth that hangs upon our quarrel.

AJAX A paltry, insolent fellow!

NESTOR [*Aside*] How he describes himself!

AJAX Can he not be sociable?

ULYSSES [*Aside*] The raven chides blackness.

AJAX I'll let his humors blood.

AGAMEMNON [*Aside*] He will be the physician that should be the patient.

AJAX An all men were of my mind—

ULYSSES [*Aside*] Wit would be out of fashion.

AJAX 'A should not bear it so, 'a should eat swords first. Shall pride carry it?

NESTOR [*Aside*] An 'twould, you'd carry half.

ULYSSES [*Aside*] 'A would have ten shares.

AJAX I will knead him; I'll make him supple.

NESTOR [*Aside*] He's not yet through warm. Force him with praises. Pour in, pour in; his ambition is dry.

134 lie under suffer under **136 allowance** approbation **146 subscribe** concur in **154 glass** mirror **155 but in the deed** in any way other than doing (praiseworthy) deeds **163 dispose** bent of mind **165 will peculiar** i.e., his own independent will. **self-admission** self-approbation **168 for . . . only** only because they are requested **171 quarrels at self-breath** i.e., finds inadequate even the praise he speaks of himself **174 Kingdom'd** i.e., like a microcosm of a state **176 death-tokens** symptoms of impending death

180 from himself i.e., from his usual arrogant behavior **184 seam** fat, grease. (I.e., Achilles feeds his own pride.) **186–187 doth . . . himself** i.e., serves for endless self-contemplation **188 Of that** by one whom (i.e., Ajax). **idol** thing worthy of worship **190 stale . . . acquir'd** sully his nobly won honor **191 assubjugate** debase **192 As . . . is** being as he is as well reputed as Achilles **195–196 add . . . Hyperion** i.e., add a fire to the heat of summer. (Cancer is the sign of the zodiac into which the sun [Hyperion] enters at the beginning of summer.) **199 vein** humor, disposition **202 pash** smash **204 pheeze** settle the matter of **206 our quarrel** i.e., with the Trojans **211 let . . . blood** bleed him (as a physician) to cure his excessive humors **219 ten shares** i.e., the whole without sharing **221 through** thoroughly

ULYSSES [*To Agamemnon*]
My lord, you feed too much on this dislike.
NESTOR
Our noble general, do not do so.
DIOMEDES
You must prepare to fight without Achilles.
ULYSSES
Why, 'tis this naming of him does him harm.
Here is a man—but 'tis before his face;
I will be silent.
NESTOR Wherefore should you so?
He is not emulous, as Achilles is.
ULYSSES
Know the whole world, he is as valiant.
AJAX A whoreson dog, that shall palter with us thus!
Would he were a Troyan!
NESTOR What a vice were it in Ajax now—
ULYSSES If he were proud—
DIOMEDES Or covetous of praise—
ULYSSES Ay, or surly borne—
DIOMEDES Or strange, or self-affected!
ULYSSES
Thank the heavens, lord, thou art of sweet composure.
Praise him that gat thee, she that gave thee suck;
Fam'd be thy tutor, and thy parts of nature
Thrice fam'd, beyond all erudition;
But he that disciplin'd thine arms to fight,
Let Mars divide eternity in twain,
And give him half; and, for thy vigor,
Bull-bearing Milo his addition yield
To sinewy Ajax. I will not praise thy wisdom,
Which, like a bourn, a pale, a shore, confines
Thy spacious and dilated parts. Here's Nestor,
Instructed by the antiquary times;
He must, he is, he cannot but be wise.
But pardon, father Nestor, were your days
As green as Ajax' and your brain so temper'd,
You should not have the eminence of him,
But be as Ajax.
AJAX Shall I call you father?
NESTOR
Ay, my good son.
DIOMEDES Be rul'd by him, Lord Ajax.
ULYSSES
There is no tarrying here; the hart Achilles
Keeps thicket. Please it our great general
To call together all his state of war;
Fresh kings are come to Troy. Tomorrow
We must with all our main of power stand fast.
And here's a lord—come knights from east to west,
And cull their flower, Ajax shall cope the best.
AGAMEMNON
Go we to council. Let Achilles sleep.
Light boats sail swift, though greater hulks draw deep. *Exeunt.*

223 this dislike i.e., Achilles' truculence **226 this . . . harm** this continual citing of him as our chief hero that creates the difficulty **229 emulous** envious, eager for glory **231 palter** trifle, dodge **237 strange** distant. **self-affected** in love with himself **239 gat** begot **240–241 thy parts . . . erudition** i.e., your natural gifts thrice exceeding what erudition can add thereto (with an ironic double meaning, suggesting that erudition can add little) **242 But he** but as for him **245 Bull-bearing . . . yield** let bull-bearing Milo yield up his title. (Milo, a celebrated athlete of phenomenal strength, was able to carry a bull on his shoulders.) **246 I will not** (1) I will forbear to (2) I won't **247 bourn** boundary. **pale** fence **248 dilated parts** extensive qualities **258 state** council **260 main** full force **262 cull their flower** choose their flower of chivalry

[ACT III • SCENE I]

[*Music within*]. *Enter* [*a Servant and*] *Pandarus.*

PANDARUS Friend, you, pray you, a word. Do you not follow the young Lord Paris?
SERVANT Ay, sir, when he goes before me.
PANDARUS You depend upon him, I mean?
SERVANT Sir, I do depend upon the lord.
PANDARUS You depend upon a noble gentleman; I must needs praise him.
SERVANT The lord be prais'd!
PANDARUS You know me, do you not?
SERVANT Faith, sir, superficially.
PANDARUS Friend, know me better. I am the Lord Pandarus.
SERVANT I hope I shall know your honor better.
PANDARUS I do desire it.
SERVANT You are in the state of grace.
PANDARUS Grace? Not so, friend. Honor and lordship are my titles. What music is this?
SERVANT I do but partly know, sir. It is music in parts.
PANDARUS Know you the musicians?
SERVANT Wholly, sir.
PANDARUS Who play they to?
SERVANT To the hearers, sir.
PANDARUS At whose pleasure, friend?
SERVANT At mine, sir, and theirs that love music.
PANDARUS Command, I mean, friend.
SERVANT Who shall I command, sir?
PANDARUS Friend, we understand not one another; I am too courtly and thou too cunning. At whose request do these men play?
SERVANT That's to 't indeed, sir. Marry, sir, at the request of Paris my lord, who is there in person; with him, the mortal Venus, the heart-blood of beauty, love's invisible soul—
PANDARUS Who, my cousin Cressida?
SERVANT No, sir, Helen. Could not you find out that by her attributes?
PANDARUS It should seem, fellow, thou hast not seen the Lady Cressid. I come to speak with Paris from the Prince Troilus. I will make a complimental assault upon him, for my business seethes.
SERVANT Sodden business! There's a stew'd phrase indeed!

III.i. Location: Troy. Priam's palace.
2 follow serve. (But the servant takes it in the sense of *follow after.*) **15 in . . . grace** i.e., in the way of salvation because of desiring to be better. (Pandarus answers as though *grace* referred to the courtly title applicable to a duke.) **30 to 't** to the point **33 love's invisible soul** the very essence or spirit of love, personified in Helen **39 complimental** courteous **40 seethes** boils, requires haste **41 Sodden, stew'd** (A play on *seethes* and with quibbling reference to stews or brothels and to the sweating treatment for venereal disease.)

Enter Paris and Helen [*attended*].

PANDARUS Fair be to you, my lord, and to all this fair company! Fair desires, in all fair measure, fairly guide them! Especially to you, fair queen, fair thoughts be your fair pillow!

HELEN Dear lord, you are full of fair words.

PANDARUS You speak your fair pleasure, sweet queen. Fair prince, here is good broken music.

PARIS You have broke it, cousin, and, by my life, you shall make it whole again; you shall piece it out with a piece of your performance. Nell, he is full of harmony.

PANDARUS Truly, lady, no.

HELEN O, sir—

PANDARUS Rude, in sooth; in good sooth, very rude.

PARIS Well said, my lord. Well, you say so in fits.

PANDARUS I have business to my lord, dear queen. My lord, will you vouchsafe me a word?

HELEN Nay, this shall not hedge us out. We'll hear you sing, certainly.

PANDARUS Well, sweet queen, you are pleasant with me. But, marry, thus, my lord: my dear lord and most esteem'd friend, your brother Troilus—

HELEN My Lord Pandarus, honey-sweet lord—

PANDARUS Go to, sweet queen, go to—commends himself most affectionately to you—

HELEN You shall not bob us out of our melody. If you do, our melancholy upon your head!

PANDARUS Sweet queen, sweet queen, that's a sweet queen, i' faith.

HELEN And to make a sweet lady sad is a sour offense.

PANDARUS Nay, that shall not serve your turn, that shall it not, in truth, la. Nay, I care not for such words, no, no. And, my lord, he desires you, that if the King call for him at supper, you will make his excuse.

HELEN My Lord Pandarus—

PANDARUS What says my sweet queen, my very very sweet queen?

PARIS What exploit's in hand? Where sups he tonight?

HELEN Nay, but, my lord—

PANDARUS What says my sweet queen? My cousin will fall out with you.

HELEN You must not know where he sups.

PARIS I'll lay my life, with my disposer Cressida.

PANDARUS No, no, no such matter; you are wide. Come, your disposer is sick.

PARIS Well, I'll make 's excuse.

PANDARUS Ay, good my lord. Why should you say Cressida? No, your poor disposer's sick.

PARIS I spy.

PANDARUS You spy? What do you spy?—Come, give me an instrument. [*He is handed a musical instrument.*] Now, sweet queen.

HELEN Why, this is kindly done.

PANDARUS My niece is horribly in love with a thing you have, sweet queen.

HELEN She shall have it, my lord, if it be not my lord Paris.

PANDARUS He? No, she'll none of him. They two are twain.

HELEN Falling in, after falling out, may make them three.

PANDARUS Come, come, I'll hear no more of this; I'll sing you a song now.

HELEN Ay, ay, prithee now. By my troth, sweet lord, thou hast a fine forehead.

PANDARUS Ay, you may, you may.

HELEN Let thy song be love. This love will undo us all. O Cupid, Cupid, Cupid!

PANDARUS Love? Ay, that it shall, i' faith.

PARIS Ay, good now, love, love, nothing but love.

PANDARUS [In good troth, it begins so:] [*Sings.*]

"Love, love, nothing but love, still love, still more!
For, O, love's bow
Shoots buck and doe.
The shaft confounds
Not that it wounds,
But tickles still the sore.
These lovers cry O ho, they die!
Yet that which seems the wound to kill,
Doth turn O ho! to ha, ha, he!
So dying love lives still.
O ho! a while, but ha, ha, ha!
O ho! groans out for ha! ha! ha!
Heigh-ho!"

HELEN In love, i' faith, to the very tip of the nose.

PARIS He eats nothing but doves, love, and that breeds hot blood, and hot blood begets hot thoughts, and hot thoughts beget hot deeds, and hot deeds is love.

PANDARUS Is this the generation of love? Hot blood, hot thoughts, and hot deeds? Why, they are vipers. Is love a generation of vipers? Sweet lord, who's a-field today?

PARIS Hector, Deiphobus, Helenus, Antenor, and all the gallantry of Troy. I would fain have arm'd today, but my Nell would not have it so. How chance my brother Troilus went not?

HELEN He hangs the lip at something. You know all, Lord Pandarus.

PANDARUS Not I, honey-sweet queen. I long to hear how they sped today. You'll remember your brother's excuse?

PARIS To a hair.

PANDARUS Farewell, sweet queen.

HELEN Commend me to your niece.

PANDARUS I will, sweet queen. [*Exit.*]

Sound a retreat.

PARIS
They're come from the field. Let us to Priam's hall,
To greet the warriors. Sweet Helen, I must woo you

49 broken music music arranged for various instruments **50 broke** interrupted **56 Rude** unpolished **57 in fits** (1) by fits and starts (2) in divisions of a song, in stanzas **60 hedge** shut **62 pleasant** jocular **68 bob** cheat **82–83 My . . . you** i.e., Paris (called *cousin* as a social equal) will be angry with you for interrupting so **84 You must not** i.e., Pandarus does not want you to. (Addressed to Paris.) **he** i.e., Troilus **85 lay** wager. **my disposer** i.e., one who may dispose of me or order me as she wishes (?) **86 wide** wide of the mark **88 make 's excuse** make his (Troilus') excuse (to Priam)

101 twain not in accord **102–103 Falling . . . three** (Helen bawdily jokes that Cressida's game will result in the birth of a child, a third person.) **108 you may** i.e., go on, have your joke **119 sore** (1) wound (2) buck in its fourth year **120,123 die, dying** (with quibble on the idea of experiencing orgasm) **133 generation of vipers** (See Matthew 3:7, 12:34, and 23:33.) **142 sped** succeeded

To help unarm our Hector. His stubborn buckles,
With these your white enchanting fingers touch'd,
Shall more obey than to the edge of steel
Or force of Greekish sinews. You shall do more
Than all the island kings—disarm great Hector. 154

HELEN
'Twill make us proud to be his servant, Paris.
Yea, what he shall receive of us in duty
Gives us more palm in beauty than we have, 157
Yea, overshines ourself.

PARIS
Sweet, above thought I love thee. *Exeunt.*

[SCENE II]

Enter Pandarus [*and*] *Troilus' Man,* [*meeting*].

PANDARUS How now, where's thy master? At my cousin Cressida's?

MAN No, sir; he stays for you to conduct him thither.

[*Enter Troilus.*]

PANDARUS O, here he comes.—How now, how now?

TROILUS Sirrah, walk off. [*Exit Man.*]

PANDARUS Have you seen my cousin?

TROILUS
No, Pandarus. I stalk about her door,
Like a strange soul upon the Stygian banks 8
Staying for waftage. O, be thou my Charon, 9
And give me swift transportance to those fields 10
Where I may wallow in the lily-beds
Propos'd for the deserver! O gentle Pandar, 12
From Cupid's shoulder pluck his painted wings,
And fly with me to Cressid!

PANDARUS Walk here i' th' orchard, I'll bring her 15
straight. [*Exit.*]

TROILUS
I am giddy; expectation whirls me round.
Th' imaginary relish is so sweet
That it enchants my sense. What will it be,
When that the wat'ry palates taste indeed 20
Love's thrice repured nectar? Death, I fear me,
Swooning destruction, or some joy too fine,
Too subtle, potent, tun'd too sharp in sweetness
For the capacity of my ruder powers.
I fear it much; and I do fear besides
That I shall lose distinction in my joys, 26
As doth a battle, when they charge on heaps 27
The enemy flying.

[*Enter Pandarus.*]

PANDARUS She's making her ready, she'll come
straight. You must be witty now. She does so blush, 30
and fetches her wind so short, as if she were fray'd 31
with a spirit. I'll fetch her. It is the prettiest villain! She 32
fetches her breath as short as a new-ta'en sparrow.
[*Exit.*]

TROILUS
Even such a passion doth embrace my bosom.
My heart beats thicker than a feverous pulse, 35
And all my powers do their bestowing lose, 36
Like vassalage at unawares encount'ring 37
The eye of majesty.

Enter Pandarus and Cressida, [*veiled*].

PANDARUS Come, come, what need you blush?
Shame's a baby. Here she is now. Swear the oaths
now to her that you have sworn to me. [*Cressida draws
back.*] What, are you gone again? You must be watch'd 42
ere you be made tame, must you? Come your ways,
come your ways; an you draw backward, we'll put you
i' th' fills. Why do you not speak to her? Come, draw 45
this curtain, and let's see your picture. [*He draws back* 46
her veil.] Alas the day, how loath you are to offend
daylight! An 'twere dark, you'd close sooner. So, so; 48
rub on, and kiss the mistress. [*They kiss.*] How now, 49
a kiss in fee-farm? Build there, carpenter; the air is 50
sweet. Nay, you shall fight your hearts out ere I part
you—the falcon as the tercel, for all the ducks i' th' 52
river. Go to, go to.

TROILUS You have bereft me of all words, lady.

PANDARUS Words pay no debts, give her deeds; but
she'll bereave you o' th' deeds too, if she call your ac- 56
tivity in question. What, billing again? Here's "In wit- 57
ness whereof the parties interchangeably"—Come in, 58
come in. I'll go get a fire. [*Exit.*]

CRESSIDA Will you walk in, my lord?

TROILUS O Cressid, how often have I wish'd me thus!

CRESSIDA Wish'd, my lord! The gods grant—O my lord!

TROILUS What should they grant? What makes this
pretty abruption? What too curious dreg espies my 65
sweet lady in the fountain of our love?

CRESSIDA More dregs than water, if my fears have eyes.

TROILUS Fears make devils of cherubins; they never see truly.

CRESSIDA Blind fear that seeing reason leads finds safer footing than blind reason stumbling without fear. To fear the worst oft cures the worse.

TROILUS O, let my lady apprehend no fear. In all Cupid's pageant there is presented no monster.

CRESSIDA Nor nothing monstrous neither?

TROILUS Nothing but our undertakings, when we vow 76
to weep seas, live in fire, eat rocks, tame tigers, think-

154 island kings i.e., Greek chieftains **157 more palm** i.e., more honor

III.ii. Location: Troy. Calchas' garden.
s.d. Man servant. (Probably the *varlet* referred to in I.i.1.) **8–9 a strange . . . Charon** (Refers to the Greek mythological conception of the fate of departed souls who had to wait on the banks of the Styx or the Acheron until the boatman Charon ferried them across to the infernal region.) **10 fields** i.e., the Elysian fields **12 Propos'd for** promised to **15 orchard** garden **20 wat'ry palates** i.e., sense of taste watering with anticipation **26 lose . . . joys** be unable to distinguish one delight from another **27 battle** army **30 witty** alert, resourceful in easy conversation

31–32 fray'd . . . spirit frightened by a ghost **32 villain** (Used endearingly.) **35 thicker** faster **36 bestowing** proper use **37 vassalage** vassals **42 watch'd** kept awake (like a hawk that is being tamed through sleeplessness) **45 fills** shafts of a cart or wagon **46 curtain** veil. (Curtains were hung in front of pictures.) **48 close** (1) encounter (2) come to terms **49 kiss the mistress** (In bowls, to touch the central target; to *rub* is to maneuver obstacles as the ball rolls; *mistress* is analogous to "master," short for "master bowl," a small bowl placed as a mark for players to aim at.) **50 fee-farm** grant of lands in fee, that is, forever; i.e., a kiss of endless duration **52 the falcon . . . tercel** the female hawk as well as the male **56–57 bereave . . . question** i.e., wear you down in lovemaking **57–58 In . . . interchangeably** (A legal formula used for contracts, ending "have set their hand and seals.") **65 abruption** breaking off. **curious** causing anxiety **76 undertakings** vows

ing it harder for our mistress to devise imposition enough than for us to undergo any difficulty impos'd. This is the monstrosity in love, lady, that the will is infinite and the execution confin'd, that the desire is boundless and the act a slave to limit.

CRESSIDA They say all lovers swear more performance than they are able, and yet reserve an ability that they never perform, vowing more than the perfection of ten and discharging less than the tenth part of one. They that have the voice of lions and the act of hares, are they not monsters?

TROILUS Are there such? Such are not we. Praise us as we are tasted, allow us as we prove; our head shall go bare till merit crown it. No perfection in reversion shall have a praise in present; we will not name desert before his birth, and, being born, his addition shall be humble. Few words to fair faith. Troilus shall be such to Cressid as what envy can say worst shall be a mock for his truth, and what truth can speak truest not truer than Troilus.

CRESSIDA Will you walk in, my lord?

[*Enter Pandarus.*]

PANDARUS What, blushing still? Have you not done talking yet?

CRESSIDA Well, uncle, what folly I commit, I dedicate to you.

PANDARUS I thank you for that. If my lord get a boy of you, you'll give him me. Be true to my lord; if he flinch, chide me for it.

TROILUS You know now your hostages, your uncle's word and my firm faith.

PANDARUS Nay, I'll give my word for her too. Our kindred, though they be long ere they be woo'd, they are constant being won. They are burrs, I can tell you; they'll stick where they are thrown.

CRESSIDA
Boldness comes to me now, and brings me heart.
Prince Troilus, I have lov'd you night and day
For many weary months.

TROILUS
Why was my Cressid then so hard to win?

CRESSIDA
Hard to seem won; but I was won, my lord,
With the first glance that ever—pardon me—
If I confess much, you will play the tyrant.
I love you now, but till now not so much
But I might master it. In faith, I lie;
My thoughts were like unbridled children, grown
Too headstrong for their mother. See, we fools!
Why have I blabb'd? Who shall be true to us,
When we are so unsecret to ourselves?
But, though I lov'd you well, I woo'd you not;
And yet, good faith, I wish'd myself a man,
Or that we women had men's privilege
Of speaking first. Sweet, bid me hold my tongue,
For in this rapture I shall surely speak
The thing I shall repent. See, see, your silence,
Cunning in dumbness, from my weakness draws
My very soul of counsel! Stop my mouth.

TROILUS
And shall, albeit sweet music issues thence.
[*Kisses her.*]

PANDARUS Pretty, i' faith.

CRESSIDA
My lord, I do beseech you, pardon me;
'Twas not my purpose, thus to beg a kiss.
I am asham'd. O heavens, what have I done?
For this time will I take my leave, my lord.

TROILUS
Your leave, sweet Cressid!

PANDARUS Leave! An you take leave till tomorrow morning—

CRESSIDA
Pray you, content you.

TROILUS
What offends you, lady?

CRESSIDA
Sir, mine own company.

TROILUS
You cannot shun yourself.

CRESSIDA
Let me go and try.
I have a kind of self resides with you;
But an unkind self, that itself will leave,
To be another's fool. I would be gone.
Where is my wit? I know not what I speak.

TROILUS
Well know they what they speak that speak so wisely.

CRESSIDA
Perchance, my lord, I show more craft than love,
And fell so roundly to a large confession
To angle for your thoughts. But you are wise,
Or else you love not, for to be wise and love
Exceeds man's might; that dwells with gods above.

TROILUS
O that I thought it could be in a woman—
As, if it can, I will presume in you—
To feed for aye her lamp and flames of love,
To keep her constancy in plight and youth,
Outliving beauty's outward, with a mind
That doth renew swifter than blood decays!
Or that persuasion could but thus convince me
That my integrity and truth to you
Might be affronted with the match and weight
Of such a winnowed purity in love;
How were I then uplifted! But, alas,
I am as true as truth's simplicity,
And simpler than the infancy of truth.

CRESSIDA
In that I'll war with you.

TROILUS
O virtuous fight,
When right with right wars who shall be most right!
True swains in love shall in the world to come

85 perfection of ten performance of ten perfect lovers **90 tasted** tried, proved. **allow** acknowledge, approve **91 No . . . reversion** no promise of perfection to come **93 addition** title **95–96 as what . . . truth** that the worst envy can do is to mock Troilus' loyalty

132 soul of counsel my inmost thoughts **147–148 that . . . fool** i.e., that will desert its true nature to be your dupe or plaything **152 roundly** outspokenly **159 To . . . youth** to keep her pledged constancy fresh **161 blood decays** passions wane **164 affronted** equaled, matched

Approve their truth by Troilus. When their rhymes,
Full of protest, of oath and big compare,
Wants similes, truth tir'd with iteration,
As true as steel, as plantage to the moon,
As sun to day, as turtle to her mate,
As iron to adamant, as earth to th' center,
Yet, after all comparisons of truth,
As truth's authentic author to be cited,
"As true as Troilus" shall crown up the verse,
And sanctify the numbers.

CRESSIDA Prophet may you be!
If I be false, or swerve a hair from truth,
When time is old and hath forgot itself,
When waterdrops have worn the stones of Troy,
And blind oblivion swallow'd cities up,
And mighty states characterless are grated
To dusty nothing, yet let memory,
From false to false, among false maids in love,
Upbraid my falsehood! When th' have said "as false
As air, as water, wind, or sandy earth,
As fox to lamb, or wolf to heifer's calf,
Pard to the hind, or stepdame to her son,"
Yea, let them say, to stick the heart of falsehood,
"As false as Cressid."

PANDARUS Go to, a bargain made. Seal it, seal it; I'll be the witness. Here I hold your hand, here my cousin's. If ever you prove false one to another, since I have taken such pain to bring you together, let all pitiful goers-between be call'd to the world's end after my name; call them all Pandars. Let all constant men be Troiluses, all false women Cressids, and all brokers-between Pandars! Say, amen.

TROILUS Amen.

CRESSIDA Amen.

PANDARUS Amen. Whereupon I will show you a chamber, which bed, because it shall not speak of your pretty encounters, press it to death. Away!

Exeunt [Troilus and Cressida].

And Cupid grant all tongue-tied maidens here
Bed, chamber, Pandar to provide this gear! *Exit.*

[SCENE III]

Enter Ulysses, Diomedes, Nestor, Agamemnon, [Ajax, Menelaus, and] Calchas. [Flourish.]

CALCHAS
Now, princes, for the service I have done,
Th' advantage of the time prompts me aloud
To call for recompense. Appear it to your mind
That, through the sight I bear in things to come,

172 Approve attest. **by Troilus** i.e., using Troilus as an ideal comparison **173 protest** protestation (of love). **big compare** extravagant comparisons **175 plantage** vegetation (waxing in growth by the moon's influence) **176 turtle** turtledove **177 adamant** loadstone (magnetic) **181 numbers** verses **186 characterless** unrecorded, without a mark left **192 Pard** leopard or panther. **hind** doe **193 stick** pierce **206 which bed** (Pandarus speaks of the bed and chamber as though synonymous.) **207 press . . . death** (Alludes to the usual punishment by weights for accused persons refusing to plead or "speak.")

III.iii. Location: The Greek camp. Before Achilles' tent.

I have abandon'd Troy, left my possession,
Incurr'd a traitor's name, expos'd myself
From certain and possess'd conveniences
To doubtful fortunes, sequest'ring from me all
That time, acquaintance, custom, and condition
Made tame and most familiar to my nature;
And here, to do you service, am become
As new into the world, strange, unacquainted.
I do beseech you, as in way of taste,
To give me now a little benefit
Out of those many regist'red in promise,
Which, you say, live to come in my behalf.

AGAMEMNON
What wouldst thou of us, Troyan? Make demand.

CALCHAS
You have a Troyan prisoner, call'd Antenor,
Yesterday took; Troy holds him very dear.
Oft have you—often have you thanks therefore—
Desir'd my Cressid in right great exchange,
Whom Troy hath still denied; but this Antenor,
I know, is such a wrest in their affairs
That their negotiations all must slack,
Wanting his manage, and they will almost
Give us a prince of blood, a son of Priam,
In change of him. Let him be sent, great princes,
And he shall buy my daughter; and her presence
Shall quite strike off all service I have done,
In most accepted pain.

AGAMEMNON Let Diomedes bear him,
And bring us Cressid hither. Calchas shall have
What he requests of us. Good Diomed,
Furnish you fairly for this interchange.
Withal bring word if Hector will tomorrow
Be answered in his challenge. Ajax is ready.

DIOMEDES
This shall I undertake, and 'tis a burden
Which I am proud to bear. *Exit [with Calchas].*

Achilles and Patroclus stand in their tent.

ULYSSES
Achilles stands i' th' entrance of his tent.
Please it our general pass strangely by him,
As if he were forgot; and, princes all,
Lay negligent and loose regard upon him.
I will come last. 'Tis like he'll question me
Why such unplausive eyes are bent on him.
If so, I have derision medicinable
To use between your strangeness and his pride,
Which his own will shall have desire to drink.
It may do good. Pride hath no other glass
To show itself but pride, for supple knees
Feed arrogance and are the proud man's fees.

7 From turning from **8 sequest'ring** separating, removing **10 tame** familiar, domestic **13 taste** foretaste **21 right great exchange** i.e., exchange for distinguished captives **23 wrest** tuning key, i.e., one producing harmony and order **25 Wanting** lacking. **manage** management **27 change of** exchange for **30 In . . . pain** in pains (troubles, hardships) which I have endured most willingly **39 strangely** i.e., as one who pretends to be a stranger **43 unplausive** disapproving **44–45 I . . . pride** i.e., I can make use of your aloofness to cure his pride, to deflate it through the mockery of your proud behavior **48 To show . . . pride** i.e., in which to see its image except the pride of others **48–49 for supple . . . fees** i.e., obsequiousness merely encourages arrogance by rewarding pride with the adulation it expects

AGAMEMNON
We'll execute your purpose, and put on
A form of strangeness as we pass along.
So do each lord, and either greet him not,
Or else disdainfully, which shall shake him more
Than if not look'd on. I will lead the way.
[*They move in procession past Achilles' tent.*]

ACHILLES
What comes the general to speak with me?
You know my mind, I'll fight no more 'gainst Troy.

AGAMEMNON
What says Achilles? Would he aught with us?

NESTOR
Would you, my lord, aught with the general?

ACHILLES No.

NESTOR Nothing, my lord.

AGAMEMNON The better.
[*Exeunt Agamemnon and Nestor.*]

ACHILLES Good day, good day.

MENELAUS How do you? How do you? [*Exit.*]

ACHILLES What, does the cuckold scorn me?

AJAX How now, Patroclus?

ACHILLES Good morrow, Ajax.

AJAX Ha?

ACHILLES Good morrow.

AJAX Ay, and good next day too.
Exit. [*Ulysses remains behind, reading.*]

ACHILLES
What mean these fellows? Know they not Achilles?

PATROCLUS
They pass by strangely. They were us'd to bend,
To send their smiles before them to Achilles,
To come as humbly as they us'd to creep
To holy altars.

ACHILLES What, am I poor of late?
'Tis certain, greatness, once fall'n out with fortune,
Must fall out with men too. What the declin'd is
He shall as soon read in the eyes of others
As feel in his own fall; for men, like butterflies,
Show not their mealy wings but to the summer,
And not a man, for being simply man,
Hath any honor, but honor for those honors
That are without him, as place, riches, and favor—
Prizes of accident as oft as merit,
Which when they fall, as being slippery standers,
The love that lean'd on them as slippery too,
Doth one pluck down another, and together
Die in the fall. But 'tis not so with me;
Fortune and I are friends. I do enjoy
At ample point all that I did possess,
Save these men's looks, who do, methinks, find out
Something not worth in me such rich beholding
As they have often given. Here is Ulysses;
I'll interrupt his reading.—How now, Ulysses?

ULYSSES
Now, great Thetis' son!

ACHILLES
What are you reading?

ULYSSES A strange fellow here
Writes me that man, how dearly ever parted,
How much in having, or without or in,
Cannot make boast to have that which he hath,
Nor feels not what he owes, but by reflection;
As when his virtues, aiming upon others,
Heat them, and they retort that heat again
To the first giver.

ACHILLES This is not strange, Ulysses.
The beauty that is borne here in the face
The bearer knows not, but commends itself
To others' eyes; nor doth the eye itself,
That most pure spirit of sense, behold itself,
Not going from itself, but eye to eye oppos'd
Salutes each other with each other's form.
For speculation turns not to itself
Till it hath travel'd and is mirror'd there
Where it may see itself. This is not strange at all.

ULYSSES
I do not strain at the position—
It is familiar—but at the author's drift,
Who, in his circumstance, expressly proves
That no man is the lord of anything,
Though in and of him there be much consisting,
Till he communicate his parts to others;
Nor doth he of himself know them for aught
Till he behold them formed in the applause
Where th' are extended; who, like an arch,
reverb'rate
The voice again, or, like a gate of steel
Fronting the sun, receives and renders back
His figure and his heat. I was much rapt in this,
And apprehended here immediately
Th' unknown Ajax. Heavens, what a man is there!
A very horse, that has he knows not what.
Nature, what things there are
Most abject in regard and dear in use!
What things again most dear in the esteem
And poor in worth! Now shall we see tomorrow—
An act that very chance doth throw upon him—
Ajax renown'd. O heavens, what some men do,
While some men leave to do!
How some men creep in skittish fortune's hall,
Whiles others play the idiots in her eyes!
How one man eats into another's pride,
While pride is fasting in his wantonness!
To see these Grecian lords—why, even already

55 What why **79 mealy** powdery **82 without** external to **84 being . . . standers** i.e., standing on uncertain foundation **89 At ample point** to the full **91 Something . . . beholding** something in me not worthy of such high respect

96 Writes me writes. (*Me* is the ethical dative.) **how . . . parted** however richly endowed with natural good qualities **97 having** possession. **or . . . in** whether with external or internal qualities **99 owes** owns. **by reflection** i.e., as reflected in others' opinions **101 retort** reflect **106 most . . . sense** most exquisite of the five senses. (Cf. I.i.60.) **107 Not . . . itself** unless it could go out from itself. **eye to eye oppos'd** i.e., two men's eyes gazing on one another **109 speculation** power of sight **112 strain at** find difficulty in. **position** i.e., general stance of the writer **113 drift** i.e., particular application **114 circumstance** detailed argument **116 Though . . . consisting** although in him there are qualities from which much may be expected **120 Where th' are extended** of those persons on whom they are bestowed **123 His** its, the sun's **125 unknown Ajax** i.e., the Ajax whose true worth is not yet generally known **128 abject . . . use** lowly esteemed and yet valuable, of practical value **129 again** on the other hand **133 to do** undone **134 in** into **136–137 How . . . wantonness** i.e., how one man, like Ajax, encroaches on another's glory, while that other man, like Achilles, starves his own glory through self-indulgence

They clap the lubber Ajax on the shoulder,
As if his foot were on brave Hector's breast
And great Troy shrieking.

ACHILLES I do believe it,
For they pass'd by me as misers do by beggars,
Neither gave to me good word nor look.
What, are my deeds forgot?

ULYSSES
Time hath, my lord, a wallet at his back,
Wherein he puts alms for oblivion, 146
A great-siz'd monster of ingratitudes.
Those scraps are good deeds past, which are devour'd
As fast as they are made, forgot as soon
As done. Perseverance, dear my lord,
Keeps honor bright; to have done is to hang
Quite out of fashion, like a rusty mail 152
In monumental mock'ry. Take the instant way, 153
For honor travels in a strait so narrow,
Where one but goes abreast. Keep then the path,
For emulation hath a thousand sons
That one by one pursue. If you give way, 157
Or hedge aside from the direct forthright, 158
Like to an ent'red tide, they all rush by
And leave you hindmost;
[Or, like a gallant horse fall'n in first rank,
Lie there for pavement to the abject rear, 162
O'er-run and trampled on.] Then what they do in present,
Though less than yours in past, must o'ertop yours;
For Time is like a fashionable host
That slightly shakes his parting guest by th' hand, 166
And with his arms outstretch'd, as he would fly,
Grasps in the comer. The welcome ever smiles,
And farewell goes out sighing. Let not virtue seek
Remuneration for the thing it was;
For beauty, wit,
High birth, vigor of bone, desert in service,
Love, friendship, charity, are subjects all
To envious and calumniating Time.
One touch of nature makes the whole world kin, 175
That all with one consent praise new-born gauds,
Though they are made and molded of things past,
And give to dust that is a little gilt 178
More laud than gilt o'er-dusted. 179
The present eye praises the present object.
Then marvel not, thou great and complete man,
That all the Greeks begin to worship Ajax,
Since things in motion sooner catch the eye
Than what stirs not. The cry went once on thee, 184
And still it might, and yet it may again,
If thou wouldst not entomb thyself alive
And case thy reputation in thy tent, 187
Whose glorious deeds but in these fields of late
Made emulous missions 'mongst the gods themselves, 189
And drave great Mars to faction.

ACHILLES Of this my privacy 190
I have strong reasons.

ULYSSES But 'gainst your privacy
The reasons are more potent and heroical.
'Tis known, Achilles, that you are in love
With one of Priam's daughters.

ACHILLES Ha! Known? 194

ULYSSES
Is that a wonder?
The providence that's in a watchful state 196
Knows almost every grain of Pluto's gold, 197
Finds bottom in th' uncomprehensive deeps, 198
Keeps place with thought and almost, like the gods, 199
Do thoughts unveil in their dumb cradles. 200
There is a mystery—with whom relation 201
Durst never meddle—in the soul of state, 202
Which hath an operation more divine
Than breath or pen can give expressure to.
All the commerce that you have had with Troy 205
As perfectly is ours as yours, my lord; 206
And better would it fit Achilles much
To throw down Hector than Polyxena.
But it must grieve young Pyrrhus now at home, 209
When fame shall in our islands sound her trump,
And all the Greekish girls shall tripping sing,
"Great Hector's sister did Achilles win,
But our great Ajax bravely beat down him."
Farewell, my lord. I as your lover speak; 214
The fool slides o'er the ice that you should break. 215
[*Exit.*]

PATROCLUS
To this effect, Achilles, have I mov'd you.
A woman impudent and mannish grown
Is not more loath'd than an effeminate man
In time of action. I stand condemn'd for this;
They think my little stomach to the war 220
And your great love to me restrains you thus.
Sweet, rouse yourself, and the weak wanton Cupid
Shall from your neck unloose his amorous fold, 223
And, like a dewdrop from the lion's mane,
Be shook to air.

ACHILLES Shall Ajax fight with Hector?

PATROCLUS
Ay, and perhaps receive much honor by him.

ACHILLES
I see my reputation is at stake;
My fame is shrewdly gor'd.

146 alms for oblivion i.e., noble deeds to be forgotten **152 mail** suit of armor **153 In . . . mock'ry** i.e., serving as a mocking trophy of forgotten noble deeds. **instant way** way that lies immediately before you now **157 one by one pursue** follow one another in single file **158 forthright** straight path **162 abject rear** inferior specimens in the rear **166 slightly** carelessly **175 nature** i.e., natural human weakness; here, the propensity of men to praise frivolous novelty (*new-born gauds)* **178 dust** i.e., trivial things. **a little gilt** slightly gilded over **179 More . . . o'er-dusted** more praise than they give to gold, i.e., objects worthy of praise, that are covered by dust (of oblivion) **184 cry** acclaim **187 case** box up, enclose

189–190 Made . . . faction i.e., caused the gods themselves to join in the fighting on opposing sides, emulously, and even drove the god of war to be partisan **194 one . . . daughters** i.e., Polyxena **196 providence** foresight **197 Pluto's** (Pluto, god of the underworld, was often confused with Plutus, god of riches.) **198 uncomprehensive** unfathomable **199 Keeps . . . thought** keeps up with what is being thought **200 Do . . . cradles** discovers thought before it is conceived (in the mind) **201–202 with . . . meddle** that can never be talked about **205 commerce** dealings (i.e., with Polyxena) **206 is ours** i.e., is known to us of the Greek council **209 Pyrrhus** Achilles' son, also called Neoptolemus **214 lover** friend **215 The fool . . . break** i.e., the fool easily escapes dangers that to a man of your dignity would be fatal **220 little stomach to** lack of enthusiasm for **223 fold** embrace

PATROCLUS O, then, beware!
Those wounds heal ill that men do give themselves.
Omission to do what is necessary
Seals a commission to a blank of danger;
And danger, like an ague, subtly taints
Even then when they sit idly in the sun.

ACHILLES
Go call Thersites hither, sweet Patroclus.
I'll send the fool to Ajax and desire him
T' invite the Troyan lords after the combat
To see us here unarm'd. I have a woman's longing,
An appetite that I am sick withal,
To see great Hector in his weeds of peace,
To talk with him and to behold his visage,
Even to my full of view.

Enter Thersites.

A labor sav'd!

THERSITES A wonder!

ACHILLES What?

THERSITES Ajax goes up and down the field, asking for himself.

ACHILLES How so?

THERSITES He must fight singly tomorrow with Hector, and is so prophetically proud of an heroical cudgeling that he raves in saying nothing.

ACHILLES How can that be?

THERSITES Why, 'a stalks up and down like a peacock—a stride and a stand; ruminates like an hostess that hath no arithmetic but her brain to set down her reckoning; bites his lip with a politic regard, as who should say "There were wit in this head, an 'twould out"—and so there is, but it lies as coldly in him as fire in a flint, which will not show without knocking. The man's undone forever, for if Hector break not his neck i' th' combat, he'll break 't himself in vainglory. He knows not me. I said "Good morrow, Ajax," and he replies "Thanks, Agamemnon." What think you of this man that takes me for the general? He's grown a very land-fish, languageless, a monster. A plague of opinion! A man may wear it on both sides, like a leather jerkin.

ACHILLES Thou must be my ambassador to him, Thersites.

THERSITES Who, I? Why, he'll answer nobody; he professes not answering. Speaking is for beggars; he wears his tongue in 's arms. I will put on his presence; let Patroclus make demands to me, you shall see the pageant of Ajax.

ACHILLES To him, Patroclus. Tell him I humbly desire the valiant Ajax to invite the most valorous Hector to come unarm'd to my tent, and to procure safe-conduct for his person of the magnanimous and most illustrious six-or-seven-times-honor'd captain-general of the army, Agamemnon, et cetera. Do this.

PATROCLUS Jove bless great Ajax!

THERSITES Hum!

PATROCLUS I come from the worthy Achilles—

THERSITES Ha?

PATROCLUS Who most humbly desires you to invite Hector to his tent—

THERSITES Hum!

PATROCLUS And to procure safe-conduct from Agamemnon.

THERSITES Agamemnon?

PATROCLUS Ay, my lord.

THERSITES Ha!

PATROCLUS What say you to 't?

THERSITES God buy you, with all my heart.

PATROCLUS Your answer, sir.

THERSITES If tomorrow be a fair day, by eleven of the clock it will go one way or other. Howsoever, he shall pay for me ere he has me.

PATROCLUS Your answer, sir.

THERSITES Fare you well, with all my heart.

ACHILLES Why, but he is not in this tune, is he?

THERSITES No, but he's out of tune thus. What music will be in him when Hector has knock'd out his brains, I know not; but, I am sure, none, unless the fiddler Apollo get his sinews to make catlings on.

ACHILLES Come, thou shalt bear a letter to him straight.

THERSITES Let me bear another to his horse, for that's the more capable creature.

ACHILLES
My mind is troubled, like a fountain stirr'd;
And I myself see not the bottom of it.
[*Exeunt Achilles and Patroclus.*]

THERSITES Would the fountain of your mind were clear again, that I might water an ass at it! I had rather be a tick in a sheep than such a valiant ignorance. [*Exit.*]

[ACT IV • SCENE I]

Enter, at one door, Aeneas, [*and Servant with a torch;*] *at another, Paris, Deiphobus, Antenor, Diomedes the Grecian* [*and others*], *with torches.*

PARIS
See, ho! Who is that there?

DEIPHOBUS
It is the Lord Aeneas.

AENEAS
Is the Prince there in person?
Had I so good occasion to lie long
As you, Prince Paris, nothing but heavenly business
Should rob my bed-mate of my company.

DIOMEDES
That's my mind too. Good morrow, Lord Aeneas.

PARIS
A valiant Greek, Aeneas; take his hand.

231 Seals . . . danger i.e., gives danger unlimited license, a blank check. (Literally, a warrant with blank spaces.) **239 weeds** garments **245 himself** i.e., "Ajax" (with a quibble on a *jakes* or latrine) **252–253 hostess . . . arithmetic** (Tavern keepers were proverbially poor at addition; cf. I.ii.114.) **254 politic regard** assumption of a knowing manner **263 land-fish** i.e., monstrous creature **264 opinion** reputation **265 jerkin** close-fitting jacket **268–269 professes** i.e., makes a point of **270 put . . . presence** assume his demeanor

292 buy be with **295 Howsoever** in either case **302–303 the fiddler Apollo** i.e., Apollo as god of music **303 catlings** catgut, of which strings for instruments were made

IV.i. Location: Troy. A street.

Witness the process of your speech, wherein
You told how Diomed, a whole week by days,
Did haunt you in the field.

AENEAS
Health to you, valiant sir,
During all question of the gentle truce;
But when I meet you arm'd, as black defiance
As heart can think or courage execute.

DIOMEDES
The one and other Diomed embraces.
Our bloods are now in calm; and, so long, health!
But when contention and occasion meet,
By Jove, I'll play the hunter for thy life
With all my force, pursuit, and policy.

AENEAS
And thou shalt hunt a lion that will fly
With his face backward. In humane gentleness,
Welcome to Troy! Now, by Anchises' life,
Welcome, indeed! By Venus' hand I swear,
No man alive can love in such a sort
The thing he means to kill more excellently.

DIOMEDES
We sympathize. Jove, let Aeneas live,
If to my sword his fate be not the glory,
A thousand complete courses of the sun!
But, in mine emulous honor, let him die,
With every joint a wound, and that tomorrow!

AENEAS
We know each other well.

DIOMEDES
We do; and long to know each other worse.

PARIS
This is the most despiteful gentle greeting,
The noblest hateful love, that e'er I heard of.
What business, lord, so early?

AENEAS
I was sent for to the King; but why, I know not.

PARIS
His purpose meets you. 'Twas to bring this Greek
To Calchas' house, and there to render him,
For the enfreed Antenor, the fair Cressid.
Let's have your company, or, if you please,
Haste there before us. I constantly do think—
Or rather, call my thought a certain knowledge—
My brother Troilus lodges there tonight.
Rouse him and give him note of our approach,
With the whole quality wherefore. I fear
We shall be much unwelcome.

AENEAS
That I assure you.
Troilus had rather Troy were borne to Greece
Than Cressid borne from Troy.

PARIS
There is no help.
The bitter disposition of the time
Will have it so. On, lord; we'll follow you.

AENEAS
Good morrow, all. *[Exit with Servant.]*

PARIS
And tell me, noble Diomed, faith, tell me true,
Even in soul of sound good-fellowship,
Who, in your thoughts, deserves fair Helen best,
Myself or Menelaus?

DIOMEDES
Both alike.
He merits well to have her that doth seek her,
Not making any scruple of her soilure,
With such a hell of pain and world of charge;
And you as well to keep her, that defend her,
Not palating the taste of her dishonor,
With such a costly loss of wealth and friends.
He, like a puling cuckold, would drink up
The lees and dregs of a flat tamed piece;
You, like a lecher, out of whorish loins
Are pleas'd to breed out your inheritors.
Both merits pois'd, each weighs nor less nor more;
But he as he, the heavier for a whore.

PARIS
You are too bitter to your countrywoman.

DIOMEDES
She's bitter to her country. Hear me, Paris:
For every false drop in her bawdy veins
A Grecian's life hath sunk; for every scruple
Of her contaminated carrion weight,
A Troyan hath been slain. Since she could speak,
She hath not given so many good words breath
As for her Greeks and Troyans suff'red death.

PARIS
Fair Diomed, you do as chapmen do,
Dispraise the thing that you desire to buy.
But we in silence hold this virtue well,
We'll not commend what we intend to sell.
Here lies our way. *Exeunt.*

[SCENE II]

Enter Troilus and Cressida.

TROILUS
Dear, trouble not yourself. The morn is cold.

CRESSIDA
Then, sweet my lord, I'll call mine uncle down;
He shall unbolt the gates.

TROILUS
Trouble him not;
To bed, to bed. Sleep kill those pretty eyes,
And give as soft attachment to thy senses
As infants' empty of all thought!

CRESSIDA
Good morrow, then.

TROILUS
I prithee now, to bed.

CRESSIDA
Are you a-weary of me?

9 process drift **10 a whole . . . days** every day for a week **13 question** discussion, parley (allowed by the truce) **17 so long** i.e., for as long as this truce lasts **18 when . . . meet** i.e., when the battle gives us opportunity **22 face backward** i.e., bravely facing the enemy **23,24 Anchises, Venus** (Aeneas' parents) **25 in . . . sort** to such a degree **27 sympathize** share your feeling **42 constantly** confirmedly **46 quality wherefore** reasons and circumstances

59 charge cost **61 Not palating** not tasting, being insensible of **64 flat tamed piece** wine cask so long opened that the wine is flat; hence, a used woman **66 breed out** breed, sire. **inheritors** descendants **67 pois'd** weighed. **nor less** neither less **68 he as he** i.e., the one like the other **72 scruple** smallest unit of weight **77 chapmen** traders, merchants

IV.ii. Location: Troy. Calchas' house.
5 attachment arrest, confinement

TROILUS
O Cressida! But that the busy day,
Wak'd by the lark, hath rous'd the ribald crows,
And dreaming night will hide our joys no longer,
I would not from thee.

CRESSIDA Night hath been too brief.

TROILUS
Beshrew the witch! With venomous wights she stays
As tediously as hell, but flies the grasps of love
With wings more momentary-swift than thought.
You will catch cold, and curse me.

CRESSIDA
Prithee, tarry. You men will never tarry.
O foolish Cressid! I might have still held off,
And then you would have tarried. Hark, there's one up.

PANDARUS [*Within*] What's all the doors open here?

TROILUS
It is your uncle.

[*Enter Pandarus.*]

CRESSIDA
A pestilence on him! Now will he be mocking.
I shall have such a life!

PANDARUS How now, how now, how go maidenheads? Here, you maid! Where's my cousin Cressid?

CRESSIDA
Go hang yourself, you naughty mocking uncle!
You bring me to do—and then you flout me too.

PANDARUS To do what, to do what? Let her say what. What have I brought you to do?

CRESSIDA
Come, come, beshrew your heart! You'll ne'er be good,
Nor suffer others.

PANDARUS Ha, ha! Alas, poor wretch! Ah, poor capocchia! Hast not slept tonight? Would he not, a naughty man, let it sleep? A bugbear take him!

CRESSIDA
Did not I tell you? Would he were knock'd i' th' head! *One knocks.*
Who's that at door? Good uncle, go and see.
My lord, come you again into my chamber.
You smile and mock me, as if I meant naughtily.

TROILUS Ha, ha!

CRESSIDA
Come, you are deceiv'd, I think of no such thing. *Knock.*
How earnestly they knock! Pray you, come in.
I would not for half Troy have you seen here.
Exeunt [*Troilus and Cressida*].

PANDARUS Who's there? What's the matter? Will you beat down the door? [*Opens the door.*] How now, what's the matter?

[*Enter Aeneas.*]

AENEAS
Good morrow, lord, good morrow.

PANDARUS Who's there? My Lord Aeneas! By my troth, I knew you not. What news with you so early?

AENEAS
Is not Prince Troilus here?

PANDARUS Here? What should he do here?

AENEAS
Come, he is here, my lord. Do not deny him.
It doth import him much to speak with me.

PANDARUS Is he here, say you? It's more than I know, I'll be sworn. For my own part, I came in late. What should he do here?

AENEAS Who!—Nay, then. Come, come, you'll do him wrong ere you are ware. You'll be so true to him, to be false to him. Do not you know of him, but yet go fetch him hither; go.

[*Enter Troilus.*]

TROILUS
How now, what's the matter?

AENEAS
My lord, I scarce have leisure to salute you,
My matter is so rash. There is at hand
Paris your brother, and Deiphobus,
The Grecian Diomed, and our Antenor
Deliver'd to us; and for him forthwith,
Ere the first sacrifice, within this hour,
We must give up to Diomedes' hand
The Lady Cressida.

TROILUS Is it so concluded?

AENEAS
By Priam and the general state of Troy.
They are at hand and ready to effect it.

TROILUS
How my achievements mock me!
I will go meet them. And, my Lord Aeneas,
We met by chance; you did not find me here.

AENEAS
Good, good, my lord; the secrets of neighbor Pandar
Have not more gift in taciturnity.
Exeunt [*Troilus and Aeneas*].

PANDARUS Is 't possible? No sooner got but lost? The devil take Antenor! The young prince will go mad. A plague upon Antenor! I would they had broke 's neck!

Enter Cressida.

CRESSIDA
How now, what's the matter? Who was here?

PANDARUS Ah, ah!

CRESSIDA
Why sigh you so profoundly? Where's my lord?
Gone? Tell me, sweet uncle, what's the matter?

PANDARUS Would I were as deep under the earth as I am above!

CRESSIDA
O the gods! What's the matter?

PANDARUS Pray thee, get thee in. Would thou hadst ne'er been born! I knew thou wouldst be his death. O, poor gentleman! A plague upon Antenor!

10 ribald offensively noisy, irreverent **13 venomous wights** malignant beings **32–33 capocchia** dolt, simpleton. (Italian.) **34 bugbear** hobgoblin

52 import concern **57–58 You'll . . . of him** i.e., in seeking to guard Troilus' secret, you'll protect him from knowing of a matter that concerns him. Go ahead and pretend you don't know he is here **62 rash** urgent, pressing **69 state** council

CRESSIDA *[Kneeling]*
Good uncle, I beseech you, on my knees,
What's the matter?

PANDARUS Thou must be gone, wench, thou must be gone; thou art chang'd for Antenor. Thou must to thy father, and be gone from Troilus. 'Twill be his death, 'twill be his bane; he cannot bear it.

CRESSIDA
O you immortal gods! I will not go.

PANDARUS Thou must.

CRESSIDA
I will not, uncle. I have forgot my father.
I know no touch of consanguinity;
No kin, no love, no blood, no soul so near me
As the sweet Troilus. O you gods divine!
Make Cressid's name the very crown of falsehood,
If ever she leave Troilus! Time, force, and death,
Do to this body what extremes you can;
But the strong base and building of my love
Is as the very center of the earth,
Drawing all things to it. I'll go in and weep—

PANDARUS Do, do.

CRESSIDA
Tear my bright hair and scratch my praised cheeks,
Crack my clear voice with sobs, and break my heart
With sounding Troilus. I will not go from Troy.
[Exeunt.]

[SCENE III]

Enter Paris, Troilus, Aeneas, Deiphobus, Antenor, [and] Diomedes.

PARIS
It is great morning, and the hour prefix'd
For her delivery to this valiant Greek
Comes fast upon. Good my brother Troilus,
Tell you the lady what she is to do,
And haste her to the purpose.

TROILUS Walk into her house.
I'll bring her to the Grecian presently.
And to his hand when I deliver her,
Think it an altar, and thy brother Troilus
A priest there off'ring to it his own heart. *[Exit.]*

PARIS
I know what 'tis to love;
And would, as I shall pity, I could help!
Please you walk in, my lords. *Exeunt.*

[SCENE IV]

Enter Pandarus and Cressida.

PANDARUS Be moderate, be moderate.

CRESSIDA
Why tell you me of moderation?
The grief is fine, full, perfect, that I taste,
And violenteth in a sense as strong
As that which causeth it. How can I moderate it?
If I could temporize with my affections,
Or brew it to a weak and colder palate,
The like allayment could I give my grief.
My love admits no qualifying dross;
No more my grief, in such a precious loss.
Enter Troilus.

PANDARUS Here, here, here he comes. Ah, sweet ducks!

CRESSIDA
O Troilus! Troilus! *[Embracing him.]*

PANDARUS What a pair of spectacles is here! Let me embrace too. "O heart," as the goodly saying is,
"——O heart, heavy heart,
Why sigh'st thou without breaking?"
where he answers again,
"Because thou canst not ease thy smart
By friendship nor by speaking."
There was never a truer rhyme. Let us cast away nothing, for we may live to have need of such a verse. We see it, we see it. How now, lambs?

TROILUS
Cressid, I love thee in so strain'd a purity
That the blest gods, as angry with my fancy,
More bright in zeal than the devotion which
Cold lips blow to their deities, take thee from me.

CRESSIDA
Have the gods envy?

PANDARUS Ay, ay, ay, ay; 'tis too plain a case.

CRESSIDA
And is it true that I must go from Troy?

TROILUS
A hateful truth.

CRESSIDA What, and from Troilus too?

TROILUS
From Troy and Troilus.

CRESSIDA Is 't possible?

TROILUS
And suddenly, where injury of chance
Puts back leave-taking, justles roughly by
All time of pause, rudely beguiles our lips
Of all rejoindure, forcibly prevents
Our lock'd embrasures, strangles our dear vows
Even in the birth of our own laboring breath.
We two, that with so many thousand sighs
Did buy each other, must poorly sell ourselves
With the rude brevity and discharge of one.
Injurious Time now with a robber's haste
Crams his rich thiev'ry up, he knows not how.
As many farewells as be stars in heaven,
With distinct breath and consign'd kisses to them,
He fumbles up into a loose adieu,
And scants us with a single famish'd kiss,
Distasted with the salt of broken tears.

AENEAS *(Within)*
My lord, is the lady ready?

94 bane death **110 sounding** uttering

IV.iii. Location: Troy. Before Calchas' house.
1 great morning broad day

IV.iv. Location: Troy. Calchas' house.

4 violenteth is violent **7 palate** taste **14 spectacles** sights (with pun on eye-*glasses*) **24 strain'd** purified as by filtering **25 as** as if. **fancy** love **33 injury of chance** injurious Fortune **34 Puts back** forestalls, prevents **36 rejoindure** reunion (in a farewell kiss) **43 he . . . how** every which way, distractedly **45 With . . . them** with the words of farewell and the kisses with which those words are ratified **48 Distasted** rendered distasteful

TROILUS
Hark! You are call'd. Some say the Genius
Cries so to him that instantly must die.—
Bid them have patience; she shall come anon.

PANDARUS Where are my tears? Rain, to lay this wind, or my heart will be blown up by the root. [*Exit.*]

CRESSIDA
I must then to the Grecians?

TROILUS No remedy.

CRESSIDA
A woeful Cressid 'mongst the merry Greeks!
When shall we see again?

TROILUS
Hear me, love. Be thou but true of heart—

CRESSIDA
I true? How now? What wicked deem is this?

TROILUS
Nay, we must use expostulation kindly,
For it is parting from us.
I speak not "be thou true" as fearing thee,
For I will throw my glove to Death himself
That there is no maculation in thy heart;
But "be thou true," say I, to fashion in
My sequent protestation; be thou true,
And I will see thee.

CRESSIDA
O, you shall be expos'd, my lord, to dangers
As infinite as imminent! But I'll be true.

TROILUS
And I'll grow friend with danger. Wear this sleeve.
[*They exchange favors.*]

CRESSIDA
And you this glove. When shall I see you?

TROILUS
I will corrupt the Grecian sentinels,
To give thee nightly visitation.
But yet be true.

CRESSIDA O heavens, "be true" again!

TROILUS
Hear why I speak it, love.
The Grecian youths are full of quality;
[Their loving well compos'd with gifts of nature,]
And swelling o'er with arts and exercise.
How novelty may move, and parts with person,
Alas, a kind of godly jealousy—
Which, I beseech you, call a virtuous sin—
Makes me afeard.

CRESSIDA O heavens! You love me not.

TROILUS
Die I a villain, then!
In this I do not call your faith in question
So mainly as my merit. I cannot sing,
Nor heel the high lavolt, nor sweeten talk,
Nor play at subtle games—fair virtues all,
To which the Grecians are most prompt and pregnant—
But I can tell that in each grace of these
There lurks a still and dumb-discoursive devil
That tempts most cunningly. But be not tempted.

CRESSIDA
Do you think I will?

TROILUS
No.
But something may be done that we will not;
And sometimes we are devils to ourselves,
When we will tempt the frailty of our powers,
Presuming on their changeful potency.

AENEAS (*Within*)
Nay, good my lord—

TROILUS Come, kiss, and let us part.

PARIS (*Within*)
Brother Troilus!

TROILUS Good brother, come you hither,
And bring Aeneas and the Grecian with you.

CRESSIDA
My lord, will you be true?

TROILUS
Who, I? Alas, it is my vice, my fault.
Whiles others fish with craft for great opinion,
I with great truth catch mere simplicity;
Whilst some with cunning gild their copper crowns,
With truth and plainness I do wear mine bare.
Fear not my truth. The moral of my wit
Is "plain and true"; there's all the reach of it.

[*Enter Aeneas, Paris, Antenor, Deiphobus, and Diomedes.*]

Welcome, Sir Diomed. Here is the lady
Which for Antenor we deliver you.
At the port, lord, I'll give her to thy hand,
And by the way possess thee what she is.
Entreat her fair; and, by my soul, fair Greek,
If e'er thou stand at mercy of my sword,
Name Cressid, and thy life shall be as safe
As Priam is in Ilion.

DIOMEDES Fair Lady Cressid,
So please you, save the thanks this prince expects.
The luster in your eye, heaven in your cheek,
Pleads your fair usage; and to Diomed
You shall be mistress, and command him wholly.

TROILUS
Grecian, thou dost not use me courteously,
To shame the seal of my petition to thee
In praising her. I tell thee, lord of Greece,
She is as far high-soaring o'er thy praises
As thou unworthy to be call'd her servant.
I charge thee use her well, even for my charge;
For, by the dreadful Pluto, if thou dost not,

50 Genius attendant spirit supposed to be allotted to a person at birth **53 Rain . . . wind** i.e., tears, to allay my sighs **54 by the root** i.e., as though the heart were a tree in a storm of sighs. (Sighs were thought to deprive the heart of its blood.) **59 deem** thought **60 expostulation** opportunity for discourse **62 as fearing thee** i.e., as if not trusting your constancy **63 throw . . . to** i.e., challenge **64 maculation** stain of impurity **65 fashion in** serve as introduction for **76 quality** good qualities **77 Their . . . compos'd** i.e., their skill in lovemaking is well endowed **78 arts and exercise** skills sharpened by practice **79 parts with person** accomplishments with personal charm **80,81 godly jealousy, virtuous sin** (Instances of oxymoron.) **86 lavolt** lavolta, a lively dance for two

88 pregnant ready **90 dumb-discoursive** eloquently silent **94 will not** do not desire **96 will tempt** deliberately tempt **97 changeful potency** power which may change to failure **103 craft** cunning. **opinion** reputation (for wisdom) **104 I . . . simplicity** I, in my use of simple truth, earn a reputation for being simple and plain **107 moral** maxim **108 reach** sphere to which an agency or power is limited **111 port** gate of the city **112 possess** inform **113 Entreat** treat **117 So please** if it please **122–123 To . . . her** i.e., to praise her as though you were her lover and thus scornfully refuse to consent to my petition that you treat her courteously **126 even . . . charge** simply because I demand that you do so

Though the great bulk Achilles be thy guard,
I'll cut thy throat.

DIOMEDES O, be not mov'd, Prince Troilus.
Let me be privileg'd by my place and message
To be a speaker free. When I am hence,
I'll answer to my lust. And know you, lord,
I'll nothing do on charge. To her own worth
She shall be priz'd; but that you say "be 't so,"
I speak it in my spirit and honor, "no."

TROILUS
Come, to the port. I'll tell thee, Diomed,
This brave shall oft make thee to hide thy head.
Lady, give me your hand, and, as we walk,
To our own selves bend we our needful talk.
[Exeunt Troilus, Cressida, and Diomedes. Trumpet within.]

PARIS
Hark! Hector's trumpet.

AENEAS How have we spent this morning!
The Prince must think me tardy and remiss,
That swore to ride before him to the field.

PARIS
'Tis Troilus' fault. Come, come, to field with him.

[DEIPHOBUS
Let us make ready straight.

AENEAS
Yea, with a bridegroom's fresh alacrity,
Let us address to tend on Hector's heels.
The glory of our Troy doth this day lie
On his fair worth and single chivalry.] *Exeunt.*

[SCENE V]

Enter Ajax, armed, Achilles, Patroclus, Agamemnon, Menelaus, Ulysses, Nestor, etc.

AGAMEMNON
Here art thou in appointment fresh and fair,
Anticipating time. With starting courage,
Give with thy trumpet a loud note to Troy,
Thou dreadful Ajax, that the appalled air
May pierce the head of the great combatant
And hale him hither.

AJAX Thou, trumpet, there's my purse.
[Throws money to his trumpeter.]
Now crack thy lungs, and split thy brazen pipe.
Blow, villain, till thy sphered bias cheek
Outswell the colic of puff'd Aquilon.
Come, stretch thy chest, and let thy eyes spout blood;
Thou blowest for Hector. *[Trumpet sounds.]*

ULYSSES
No trumpet answers.

ACHILLES 'Tis but early days.

[Enter Diomedes, with Cressida.]

AGAMEMNON
Is not yond Diomed, with Calchas' daughter?

ULYSSES
'Tis he, I ken the manner of his gait;
He rises on the toe. That spirit of his
In aspiration lifts him from the earth.

AGAMEMNON
Is this the Lady Cressid?

DIOMEDES Even she.

AGAMEMNON
Most dearly welcome to the Greeks, sweet lady.
[Kisses her.]

NESTOR
Our general doth salute you with a kiss.

ULYSSES
Yet is the kindness but particular;
'Twere better she were kiss'd in general.

NESTOR
And very courtly counsel. I'll begin. *[Kisses her.]*
So much for Nestor.

ACHILLES
I'll take that winter from your lips, fair lady.
Achilles bids you welcome. *[Kisses her.]*

MENELAUS
I had good argument for kissing once.

PATROCLUS
But that's no argument for kissing now;
For thus popp'd Paris in his hardiment,
And parted thus you and your argument.
[Kisses her.]

ULYSSES
O deadly gall, and theme of all our scorns,
For which we lose our heads to gild his horns!

PATROCLUS
The first was Menelaus' kiss; this, mine;
Patroclus kisses you. *[Kisses her again.]*

MENELAUS O, this is trim!

PATROCLUS
Paris and I kiss evermore for him.

MENELAUS
I'll have my kiss, sir. Lady, by your leave.

CRESSIDA
In kissing, do you render or receive?

PATROCLUS
Both take and give.

CRESSIDA I'll make my match to live,
The kiss you take is better than you give;
Therefore no kiss.

MENELAUS
I'll give you boot, I'll give you three for one.

CRESSIDA
You are an odd man; give even, or give none.

132 my lust my pleasures, desires **133 on charge** i.e., because you command it **137 brave** boast, defiance **140 spent** consumed by using **146 address** get ready

IV.v. Location: The Greek camp. Lists set out.
1 appointment equipment, accouterment **2 starting courage** bold, active defiance **6 trumpet** trumpeter **8 bias** puffed out (and shaped like a weighted bowling ball used in bowls) **9 Aquilon** the north wind (here personified as distended by colic)

12 days in the day **20 particular** single, limited to one **21 in general** by everyone (with a play on *by the general*) **24 that winter** (Alludes to Nestor's old age.) **26 argument** i.e., Helen **28 hardiment** bold exploits, boldness (with bawdy double meaning of *hardness*) **37 I'll . . . to live** I'll wager my life **40 boot** odds, something in addition **41 odd** (1) strange (2) single, no longer having a wife

MENELAUS
An odd man, lady? Every man is odd.
CRESSIDA
No, Paris is not, for you know 'tis true,
That you are odd, and he is even with you.
MENELAUS
You fillip me o' th' head.
CRESSIDA No, I'll be sworn.
ULYSSES
It were no match, your nail against his horn.
May I, sweet lady, beg a kiss of you?
CRESSIDA
You may.
ULYSSES I do desire it.
CRESSIDA Why, beg, then.
ULYSSES
Why then for Venus' sake, give me a kiss
When Helen is a maid again, and his.
CRESSIDA
I am your debtor, claim it when 'tis due.
ULYSSES
Never's my day, and then a kiss of you.
DIOMEDES
Lady, a word. I'll bring you to your father.
[*Exit with Cressida.*]
NESTOR
A woman of quick sense.
ULYSSES Fie, fie upon her!
There's language in her eye, her cheek, her lip,
Nay, her foot speaks; her wanton spirits look out
At every joint and motive of her body.
O, these encounterers, so glib of tongue,
That give a coasting welcome ere it comes,
And wide unclasp the tables of their thoughts
To every ticklish reader! Set them down
For sluttish spoils of opportunity
And daughters of the game.

Flourish. Enter all of Troy [*Hector, Paris, Aeneas, Helenus, Troilus, and Attendants*].

ALL
The Troyans' trumpet.
AGAMEMNON Yonder comes the troop.
AENEAS
Hail, all you state of Greece! What shall be done
To him that victory commands? Or do you purpose
A victor shall be known? Will you the knights
Shall to the edge of all extremity
Pursue each other, or shall they be divided
By any voice or order of the field?
Hector bade ask.
AGAMEMNON Which way would Hector have it?
AENEAS
He cares not; he'll obey conditions.
ACHILLES
'Tis done like Hector; but securely done,
A little proudly, and great deal misprizing
The knight oppos'd.
AENEAS If not Achilles, sir,
What is your name?
ACHILLES If not Achilles, nothing.
AENEAS
Therefore Achilles. But, whate'er, know this:
In the extremity of great and little,
Valor and pride excel themselves in Hector,
The one almost as infinite as all,
The other blank as nothing. Weigh him well,
And that which looks like pride is courtesy.
This Ajax is half made of Hector's blood,
In love whereof, half Hector stays at home;
Half heart, half hand, half Hector comes to seek
This blended knight, half Troyan and half Greek.
ACHILLES
A maiden battle, then? O, I perceive you.

[*Enter Diomedes.*]

AGAMEMNON
Here is Sir Diomed. Go, gentle knight,
Stand by our Ajax. As you and Lord Aeneas
Consent upon the order of their fight,
So be it, either to the uttermost,
Or else a breath. The combatants being kin
Half stints their strife before their strokes begin.
[*Ajax and Hector enter the lists.*]
[ULYSSES
They are oppos'd already.]
AGAMEMNON [*To Ulysses*]
What Troyan is that same that looks so heavy?
ULYSSES
The youngest son of Priam, a true knight,
Not yet mature, yet matchless, firm of word,
Speaking in deeds and deedless in his tongue,
Not soon provok'd, nor being provok'd soon calm'd;
His heart and hand both open and both free,
For what he has he gives, what thinks he shows,
Yet gives he not till judgment guide his bounty,
Nor dignifies an impare thought with breath;
Manly as Hector, but more dangerous,
For Hector in his blaze of wrath subscribes
To tender objects, but he in heat of action
Is more vindicative than jealous love.
They call him Troilus, and on him erect
A second hope, as fairly built as Hector.
Thus says Aeneas, one that knows the youth
Even to his inches, and with private soul
Did in great Ilion thus translate him to me.
Alarum. [*Hector and Ajax fight.*]
AGAMEMNON
They are in action.

45 fillip . . . head tap me on the head. (Suggesting the presence of cuckold's horns.) **46 It . . . horn** i.e., the fingernail with which you tap his head would be no match for Menelaus' cuckold's horn **50 his** i.e., Menelaus' wife **52 and . . . you** i.e., I'll never claim that kiss **57 motive** moving limb or organ **59 a coasting welcome** an (inviting) approach **60 tables** tablets **61 ticklish** wanton **62 sluttish . . . opportunity** "corrupt wenches, of whose chastity every opportunity may make a prey" (Johnson) **63 daughters of the game** i.e., prostitutes **65 state** noble lords. **What . . . done** i.e., what honors shall be afforded **66 that . . . commands** that wins the victory **67 Will you** do you desire

73 securely overconfidently **74 misprizing** disdaining, underrating **78–79 In . . . Hector** i.e., Hector's valor excels in the extreme of greatness, his pride in the extreme of littleness **83 Ajax . . . blood** (Cf. II.ii.77, note, and IV.v.120.) **87 maiden battle** one without bloodshed **90 Consent** agree. **order** procedure, rules **92 a breath** mere exercise **95 heavy** sad **98 deedless in his tongue** i.e., never boastful **100 free** open, generous **103 impare** unconsidered. (Or perhaps *impair*, unsuitable.) **105–106 subscribes . . . objects** i.e., yields mercy to those who awaken his pity **107 vindicative** vindictive **111 Even . . . inches** i.e., every inch of him. **with private soul** in private confidence

NESTOR
Now, Ajax, hold thine own!
TROILUS
Hector, thou sleep'st. Awake thee!
AGAMEMNON
His blows are well dispos'd. There, Ajax!
DIOMEDES
You must no more. *Trumpets cease.*
AENEAS Princes, enough, so please you.
AJAX
I am not warm yet; let us fight again.
DIOMEDES
As Hector pleases.
HECTOR Why, then will I no more.
Thou art, great lord, my father's sister's son,
A cousin-german to great Priam's seed; 121
The obligation of our blood forbids
A gory emulation 'twixt us twain.
Were thy commixtion Greek and Troyan so
That thou couldst say "This hand is Grecian all,
And this is Troyan; the sinews of this leg
All Greek, and this all Troy; my mother's blood
Runs on the dexter cheek, and this sinister 128
Bounds in my father's," by Jove multipotent,
Thou shouldst not bear from me a Greekish member
Wherein my sword had not impressure made
[Of our rank feud.] But the just gods gainsay
That any drop thou borrow'dst from thy mother,
My sacred aunt, should by my mortal sword
Be drained! Let me embrace thee, Ajax.
By him that thunders, thou hast lusty arms!
Hector would have them fall upon him thus.
Cousin, all honor to thee! [*They embrace.*]
AJAX I thank thee, Hector.
Thou art too gentle and too free a man.
I came to kill thee, cousin, and bear hence
A great addition earned in thy death. 141
HECTOR
Not Neoptolemus so mirable, 142
On whose bright crest Fame with her loud'st Oyes 143
Cries "This is he," could promise to himself
A thought of added honor torn from Hector.
AENEAS
There is expectance here from both the sides,
What further you will do.
HECTOR We'll answer it;
The issue is embracement. Ajax, farewell. 148
AJAX
If I might in entreaties find success—
As seld I have the chance—I would desire 150
My famous cousin to our Grecian tents.
DIOMEDES
'Tis Agamemnon's wish, and great Achilles
Doth long to see unarm'd the valiant Hector.
HECTOR
Aeneas, call my brother Troilus to me,
And signify this loving interview
To the expecters of our Troyan part; 156
Desire them home. Give me thy hand, my cousin. 157
I will go eat with thee and see your knights.
[*Agamemnon and the rest approach them.*]
AJAX
Great Agamemnon comes to meet us here.
HECTOR
The worthiest of them tell me name by name;
But for Achilles, my own searching eyes
Shall find him by his large and portly size. 162
AGAMEMNON [*Embraces him.*]
Worthy all arms! As welcome as to one 163
That would be of such an enemy—
[But that's no welcome. Understand more clear,
What's past and what's to come is strew'd with husks
And formless ruin of oblivion;
But in this extant moment, faith and troth,
Strain'd purely from all hollow bias-drawing, 169
Bids thee, with most divine integrity,]
From heart of very heart, great Hector, welcome.
HECTOR
I thank thee, most imperious Agamemnon.
AGAMEMNON [*To Troilus*]
My well-fam'd lord of Troy, no less to you.
MENELAUS
Let me confirm my princely brother's greeting.
You brace of warlike brothers, welcome hither.
HECTOR
Who must we answer?
AENEAS The noble Menelaus.
HECTOR
O, you, my lord? By Mars his gauntlet, thanks!
Mock not that I affect th' untraded oath; 178
Your quondam wife swears still by Venus' glove.
She's well, but bade me not commend her to you.
MENELAUS
Name her not now, sir; she's a deadly theme.
HECTOR
O, pardon! I offend.
NESTOR
I have, thou gallant Troyan, seen thee oft,
Laboring for destiny, make cruel way 184
Through ranks of Greekish youth, and I have seen thee,
As hot as Perseus, spur thy Phrygian steed, 186
Despising many forfeits and subduements, 187
When thou hast hung thy advanced sword i' th' air, 188
Not letting it decline on the declined,
That I have said to some my standers by
"Lo, Jupiter is yonder, dealing life!"
And I have seen thee pause and take thy breath,
When that a ring of Greeks have hemm'd thee in,

121 cousin-german first cousin **128 dexter** right. **sinister** left **141 addition** honorable title **142 Neoptolemus** (Evidently intended for Achilles; this is the name of Achilles' son.) **mirable** to be marveled at **143 Oyes** hear ye (call of the public crier) **148 issue** outcome **150 seld** seldom

156 expecters . . . part i.e., those waiting the outcome on our Trojan side **157 home** to go home **162 portly** stately, dignified **163 as to one** as it is possible to one **169 Strain'd** refined, purged. **hollow bias-drawing** i.e., insincerities, obliquities, such as the bias gives the bowling ball in the game of bowls **178 untraded** unhackneyed. (Hector insists that his use of a new oath, "by Mars' gauntlet," is not an affectation.) **184 Laboring for destiny** employed in the service of fate, putting people to death **186 Perseus** (See I.iii.42, note.) **187 Despising . . . subduements** i.e., ignoring those already vanquished, whose lives were forfeit; refusing easy prey **188 advanced** raised aloft

Like an Olympian wrestling. This have I seen;
But this thy countenance, still lock'd in steel,
I never saw till now. I knew thy grandsire,
And once fought with him. He was a soldier good;
But, by great Mars, the captain of us all,
Never like thee. O, let an old man embrace thee;
And, worthy warrior, welcome to our tents.
[*They embrace.*]

AENEAS
'Tis the old Nestor.

HECTOR
Let me embrace thee, good old chronicle,
That hast so long walk'd hand in hand with time.
Most reverend Nestor, I am glad to clasp thee.

NESTOR
I would my arms could match thee in contention,
[As they contend with thee in courtesy.]

HECTOR
I would they could.

NESTOR
Ha!
By this white beard, I'd fight with thee tomorrow.
Well, welcome, welcome!—I have seen the time.

ULYSSES
I wonder now how yonder city stands
When we have here her base and pillar by us.

HECTOR
I know your favor, Lord Ulysses, well.
Ah, sir, there's many a Greek and Troyan dead
Since first I saw yourself and Diomed
In Ilion, on your Greekish embassy.

ULYSSES
Sir, I foretold you then what would ensue.
My prophecy is but half his journey yet,
For yonder walls, that pertly front your town,
Yon towers, whose wanton tops do buss the clouds,
Must kiss their own feet.

HECTOR I must not believe you.
There they stand yet, and modestly I think
The fall of every Phrygian stone will cost
A drop of Grecian blood. The end crowns all,
And that old common arbitrator, Time,
Will one day end it.

ULYSSES So to him we leave it.
Most gentle and most valiant Hector, welcome!
After the general, I beseech you next
To feast with me and see me at my tent.

ACHILLES
I shall forestall thee, Lord Ulysses, thou!
Now, Hector, I have fed mine eyes on thee;
I have with exact view perus'd thee, Hector,
And quoted joint by joint.

HECTOR Is this Achilles?

ACHILLES
I am Achilles.

HECTOR
Stand fair, I pray thee. Let me look on thee.

ACHILLES
Behold thy fill.

HECTOR Nay, I have done already.

ACHILLES
Thou art too brief. I will the second time,
As I would buy thee, view thee limb by limb.

HECTOR
O, like a book of sport thou 'lt read me o'er;
But there's more in me than thou understand'st.
Why dost thou so oppress me with thine eye?

ACHILLES
Tell me, you heavens, in which part of his body
Shall I destroy him? Whether there, or there, or
there?
That I may give the local wound a name
And make distinct the very breach whereout
Hector's great spirit flew. Answer me, heavens!

HECTOR
It would discredit the blest gods, proud man,
To answer such a question. Stand again.
Think'st thou to catch my life so pleasantly
As to prenominate in nice conjecture
Where thou wilt hit me dead?

ACHILLES I tell thee, yea.

HECTOR
Wert thou an oracle to tell me so,
I 'd not believe thee. Henceforth guard thee well;
For I'll not kill thee there, nor there, nor there,
But, by the forge that stithied Mars his helm,
I'll kill thee everywhere, yea, o'er and o'er.
You wisest Grecians, pardon me this brag;
His insolence draws folly from my lips.
But I'll endeavor deeds to match these words,
Or may I never—

AJAX Do not chafe thee, cousin.
And you, Achilles, let these threats alone,
Till accident or purpose bring you to 't.
You may have every day enough of Hector,
If you have stomach. The general state, I fear,
Can scarce entreat you to be odd with him.

HECTOR
I pray you, let us see you in the field.
We have had pelting wars, since you refus'd
The Grecians' cause.

ACHILLES Dost thou entreat me, Hector?
Tomorrow do I meet thee, fell as death;
Tonight all friends.

HECTOR Thy hand upon that match.
[*They grasp hands.*]

AGAMEMNON
First, all you peers of Greece, go to my tent;
There in the full convive we. Afterwards,
As Hector's leisure and your bounties shall
Concur together, severally entreat him.
Beat loud the taborines, let the trumpets blow,
That this great soldier may his welcome know.
Exeunt [*all except Troilus and Ulysses*].

194 Olympian i.e., Olympian god **195 still** always **196 grandsire** i.e., Laomedon, builder of the walls of Troy and defender of the city against an earlier Greek army under Hercules **213 favor** face **219 front** i.e., are the front of **233 quoted** noted, marked **235 fair** i.e., still

249 pleasantly easily **250 prenominate** name beforehand. **nice** precise **255 stithied** forged **264 stomach** appetite (for fight). **general state** i.e., Greek commanders in council **265 be odd** be at odds, undertake to fight **267 pelting** paltry **269 fell** fierce **272 convive** feast together **274 severally** individually. **entreat** invite

TROILUS
My Lord Ulysses, tell me, I beseech you,
In what place of the field doth Calchas keep?

ULYSSES
At Menelaus' tent, most princely Troilus.
There Diomed doth feast with him tonight,
Who neither looks upon the heaven nor earth,
But gives all gaze and bent of amorous view
On the fair Cressid.

TROILUS
Shall I, sweet lord, be bound to you so much,
After we part from Agamemnon's tent,
To bring me thither?

ULYSSES
You shall command me, sir.
But gentle tell me, of what honor was
This Cressida in Troy? Had she no lover there
That wails her absence?

TROILUS
O, sir, to such as boasting show their scars
A mock is due. Will you walk on, my lord?
She was belov'd, she lov'd; she is, and doth.
But still sweet love is food for fortune's tooth. *Exeunt.*

[ACT V • SCENE I]

Enter Achilles and Patroclus.

ACHILLES
I'll heat his blood with Greekish wine tonight,
Which with my scimitar I'll cool tomorrow.
Patroclus, let us feast him to the height.

PATROCLUS
Here comes Thersites.

Enter Thersites.

ACHILLES
How now, thou core of envy!
Thou crusty batch of nature, what's the news?

THERSITES Why, thou picture of what thou seemest, and idol of idiot-worshipers, here's a letter for thee.

ACHILLES From whence, fragment?

THERSITES Why, thou full dish of fool, from Troy.
[*Gives letter. Achilles reads it.*]

PATROCLUS Who keeps the tent now?

THERSITES The surgeon's box, or the patient's wound.

PATROCLUS Well said, adversity! And what needs these tricks?

THERSITES Prithee, be silent, boy; I profit not by thy talk. Thou art said to be Achilles' male varlet.

PATROCLUS Male varlet, you rogue? What's that?

THERSITES Why, his masculine whore. Now, the rotten diseases of the south, the guts-griping, ruptures, catarrhs, loads o' gravel i' the back, lethargies, cold palsies, raw eyes, dirt-rotten livers, wheezing lungs, bladders full of imposthume, sciaticas, limekilns i' th' palm, incurable bone-ache, and the rivell'd fee-simple of the tetter, take and take again such preposterous discoveries!

PATROCLUS Why, thou damnable box of envy, thou, what means thou to curse thus?

THERSITES Do I curse thee?

PATROCLUS Why, no, you ruinous butt, you whoreson indistinguishable cur, no.

THERSITES No? Why art thou then exasperate, thou idle immaterial skein of sleave-silk, thou green sarcenet flap for a sore eye, thou tassel of a prodigal's purse, thou? Ah, how the poor world is pest'red with such waterflies, diminutives of nature!

PATROCLUS Out, gall!

THERSITES Finch-egg!

ACHILLES
My sweet Patroclus, I am thwarted quite
From my great purpose in tomorrow's battle.
Here is a letter from Queen Hecuba,
A token from her daughter, my fair love,
Both taxing me and gaging me to keep
An oath that I have sworn. I will not break it.
Fall Greeks, fail fame, honor or go or stay;
My major vow lies here, this I'll obey.
Come, come, Thersites, help to trim my tent.
This night in banqueting must all be spent.
Away, Patroclus! [*Exeunt Achilles and Patroclus.*]

THERSITES With too much blood and too little brain, these two may run mad; but, if with too much brain and too little blood they do, I'll be a curer of madmen. Here's Agamemnon, an honest fellow enough, and one that loves quails, but he has not so much brain as ear-wax: and the goodly transformation of Jupiter there, his brother, the bull—the primitive statue and oblique memorial of cuckolds, a thrifty shoeing-horn in a chain, hanging at his brother's leg—to what form but that he is, should wit larded with malice and malice forc'd with wit turn him to? To an ass, were nothing; he is both ass and ox; to an ox, were nothing; he's both ox and ass. To be a dog, a mule, a cat, a fitchew, a toad, a lizard, an owl, a puttock, or a herring without a roe, I would not care; but to be Menelaus! I would conspire against destiny. Ask me not what I would be, if I were not Thersites; for I care not to be the louse of a lazar, so I were not Menelaus. Hey-day! Sprites and fires!

278 keep dwell **287 gentle** in courtesy

V.i. Location: The Greek camp. Before Achilles' tent.
4 core central hard mass of a boil or tumor **5 crusty . . . nature** i.e., scabbed like a batch of overbaked bread **6 picture** i.e., mere image **8 fragment** i.e., crust of bread **10 Who . . . now** (Patroclus may be pointing out that Achilles no longer keeps to his tent, thus depriving Thersites of an object of satirical humor.) **11 surgeon's box** (Thersites puns on *tent* in the previous line, i.e., a probe for cleaning a wound.) **19 gravel** i.e., stones. **back** kidney

21 imposthume abscesses. **limekilns** burning sensations **22 rivell'd** wrinkled. **fee-simple** absolute possession, i.e., incurable disease **23 tetter** skin disease. **take** afflict with disease **23–24 preposterous discoveries** i.e., the revelation of such relationships as exist between Patroclus and Achilles **28 ruinous butt** dilapidated cask **29 indistinguishable** shapeless **31 sleave-silk** floss silk, i.e., unwoven and hence worthless *(immaterial).* **sarcenet** fine, soft silk **36 Finch-egg** (The finch is a small bird.) **41 taxing . . . gaging** i.e., urging . . . binding, pledging **50 I'll . . . madmen** i.e., a most unlikely circumstance **52 quails** i.e., prostitutes. (Cant term.) **53–54 transformation . . . bull** (Alludes ironically to the myth of Jupiter's rape of Europa, whom he encountered in a meadow after changing himself into a bull. Thersites has in mind the bull's horns, which are like Menelaus' cuckold's horns.) **54–55 primitive . . . cuckolds** i.e., the prototype and indirect reminder of cuckolds in having horns **55–56 thrifty . . . leg** i.e., a convenient tool, always available to do Agamemnon's will (with another joke on the cuckold's horn) **58 forc'd** stuffed **60–61 fitchew** polecat **61 puttock** bird of prey of the kite kind **61–62 herring . . . roe** i.e., least valuable kind of herring **64 I care not to be** I wouldn't mind being **65 lazar** leper **66 Sprites and fires** (Thersites sees those who are entering with lights, reminding him of will-o'-the-wisps and other spirits.)

Enter [Hector, Troilus, Ajax,] Agamemnon, Ulysses, Nestor, [Menelaus,] and Diomedes, with lights.

AGAMEMNON
We go wrong, we go wrong.
AJAX No, yonder 'tis,
There, where we see the lights.
HECTOR I trouble you.
AJAX
No, not a whit.
ULYSSES Here comes himself to guide you.

[Enter Achilles.]

ACHILLES
Welcome, brave Hector; welcome, princes all.
AGAMEMNON
So now, fair Prince of Troy, I bid good night.
Ajax commands the guard to tend on you.
HECTOR
Thanks and good night to the Greeks' general.
MENELAUS
Good night, my lord.
HECTOR
Good night, sweet Lord Menelaus.
THERSITES Sweet draught. "Sweet," quoth 'a! Sweet sink, sweet sewer.
ACHILLES
Good night and welcome, both at once, to those
That go or tarry.
AGAMEMNON
Good night. *Exeunt Agamemnon [and] Menelaus.*
ACHILLES
Old Nestor tarries; and you too, Diomed,
Keep Hector company an hour or two.
DIOMEDES
I cannot, lord; I have important business,
The tide whereof is now. Good night, great Hector.
HECTOR
Give me your hand.
ULYSSES *[Aside to Troilus]*
Follow his torch; he goes to Calchas' tent.
I'll keep you company.
TROILUS Sweet sir, you honor me.
HECTOR
And so, good night.
[Exit Diomedes; Ulysses and Troilus following.]
ACHILLES Come, come, enter my tent.
Exeunt [Achilles, Hector, Ajax, and Nestor].
THERSITES That same Diomed's a false-hearted rogue, a most unjust knave. I will no more trust him when he leers than I will a serpent when he hisses. He will spend his mouth and promise, like Brabbler the hound; but when he performs, astronomers foretell it, it is prodigious, there will come some change. The sun borrows of the moon, when Diomed keeps his word. I will rather leave to see Hector than not to dog him. They say he keeps a Troyan drab, and uses the traitor Calchas' tent. I'll after. Nothing but lechery! All incontinent varlets! *[Exit.]*

[SCENE II]

Enter Diomedes.

DIOMEDES
What, are you up here, ho? Speak.
CALCHAS *[Within]*
Who calls?
DIOMEDES
Diomed. Calchas, I think. Where's your daughter?
CALCHAS *[Within]*
She comes to you.

[Enter Troilus and Ulysses, at a distance; after them, Thersites.]

ULYSSES *[To Troilus]*
Stand where the torch may not discover us.
[He and Troilus conceal themselves in one place, Thersites in another.]

Enter Cressida.

TROILUS
Cressid comes forth to him.
DIOMEDES
How now, my charge?
CRESSIDA
Now, my sweet guardian! Hark, a word with you.
[Whispers.]
TROILUS
Yea, so familiar?
ULYSSES
She will sing any man at first sight.
THERSITES *[Aside]* And any man may sing her, if he can take her cliff; she's noted.
DIOMEDES
Will you remember?
CRESSIDA
Remember? Yes.
DIOMEDES
Nay, but do, then,
And let your mind be coupled with your words.
TROILUS
What should she remember?
ULYSSES
List.
CRESSIDA
Sweet honey Greek, tempt me no more to folly.
THERSITES *[Aside]* Roguery!
DIOMEDES
Nay, then—

76 draught privy **77 sink** cesspool **84 tide** time **92 spend his mouth** bay without scenting the game **95 borrows of** i.e., borrows reflected light from (reversing the natural superiority of the sun) **96 leave to see** cease looking upon. **him** i.e., Diomedes

V.ii. Location: The Greek camp. Before Calchas' tent.
10 sing i.e., make music with, play upon **12 cliff** clef, key (with obscene pun on *cleft*). **noted** set to music (with quibble on the meaning *stigmatized,* i.e., in bad repute)

CRESSIDA
I'll tell you what—

DIOMEDES
Foh, foh! Come, tell a pin. You are forsworn.

CRESSIDA
In faith, I cannot. What would you have me do?

THERSITES [*Aside*] A juggling trick—to be secretly open.

DIOMEDES
What did you swear you would bestow on me?

CRESSIDA
I prithee, do not hold me to mine oath;
Bid me do any thing but that, sweet Greek.

DIOMEDES
Good night. [*Starts to go.*]

TROILUS
Hold, patience!

ULYSSES
How now, Troyan!

CRESSIDA
Diomed—

DIOMEDES
No, no, good night. I'll be your fool no more.

TROILUS
Thy better must.

CRESSIDA
Hark, a word in your ear.

TROILUS
O plague and madness!

ULYSSES
You are moved, Prince; let us depart, I pray,
Lest your displeasure should enlarge itself
To wrathful terms. This place is dangerous,
The time right deadly. I beseech you, go.
[*Tries to lead him away.*]

TROILUS
Behold, I pray you!

ULYSSES Now, good my lord, go off.
You flow to great distraction. Come, my lord.

TROILUS
I prithee, stay.

ULYSSES You have not patience; come.

TROILUS
I pray you, stay. By hell and all hell's torments,
I will not speak a word!

DIOMEDES
And so, good night.

CRESSIDA Nay, but you part in anger.

TROILUS
Doth that grieve thee? O withered truth!

ULYSSES
How now, my lord!

TROILUS By Jove, I will be patient.

CRESSIDA
Guardian!—Why, Greek!

DIOMEDES Foh, foh! Adieu, you palter.

CRESSIDA
In faith, I do not. Come hither once again.

ULYSSES
You shake, my lord, at something. Will you go?
You will break out.

TROILUS She strokes his cheek!

ULYSSES Come, Come.

TROILUS
Nay, stay. By Jove, I will not speak a word.
There is between my will and all offenses
A guard of patience. Stay a little while.

THERSITES [*Aside*] How the devil Luxury, with his fat rump and potato-finger, tickles these together! Fry, lechery, fry!

DIOMEDES
But will you, then?

CRESSIDA
In faith, I will, la; never trust me else.

DIOMEDES
Give me some token for the surety of it.

CRESSIDA
I'll fetch you one. *Exit.*

ULYSSES
You have sworn patience.

TROILUS Fear me not, my lord.
I will not be myself, nor have cognition
Of what I feel. I am all patience.

Enter Cressida, [*with Troilus' sleeve*].

THERSITES [*Aside*] Now the pledge; now, now, now!

CRESSIDA
Here, Diomed, keep this sleeve. [*Gives it to him.*]

TROILUS
O beauty! Where is thy faith?

ULYSSES My lord—

[TROILUS
I will be patient; outwardly I will.]

CRESSIDA
You look upon that sleeve; behold it well.
He lov'd me—O false wench!—Give 't me again.
[*She takes it back again.*]

DIOMEDES
Whose was 't?

CRESSIDA
It is no matter, now I ha 't again.
I will not meet with you tomorrow night.
I prithee, Diomed, visit me no more.

THERSITES [*Aside*] Now she sharpens. Well said, whetstone!

DIOMEDES
I shall have it.

CRESSIDA What, this?

DIOMEDES Ay, that.

CRESSIDA
O, all you gods! O pretty, pretty pledge!
Thy master now lies thinking on his bed
Of thee and me, and sighs, and takes my glove,
And gives memorial dainty kisses to it,
As I kiss thee. Nay, do not snatch it from me;
He that takes that doth take my heart withal.

23 tell a pin i.e., tell me no trifles **26 open** (1) frank (2) sexually available **50 palter** use trickery

57 Luxury lechery **58 potato-finger** (Potatoes were accounted stimulants to lechery.) **77 sharpens** i.e., whets his appetite

DIOMEDES
I had your heart before, this follows it.

TROILUS
I did swear patience.

CRESSIDA
You shall not have it, Diomed; faith, you shall not.
I'll give you something else.

DIOMEDES
I will have this. Whose was it? [*He takes it.*]

CRESSIDA
It is no matter.

DIOMEDES
Come, tell me whose it was.

CRESSIDA
'Twas one's that lov'd me better than you will.
But, now you have it, take it.

DIOMEDES
Whose was it?

CRESSIDA
By all Diana's waiting-women yond,
And by herself, I will not tell you whose.

DIOMEDES
Tomorrow will I wear it on my helm,
And grieve his spirit that dares not challenge it.

TROILUS
Wert thou the devil, and wor'st it on thy horn,
It should be challeng'd.

CRESSIDA
Well, well, 'tis done, 'tis past. And yet it is not;
I will not keep my word.

DIOMEDES
Why, then, farewell.
Thou never shalt mock Diomed again. [*Starts to go.*]

CRESSIDA
You shall not go. One cannot speak a word,
But it straight starts you.

DIOMEDES
I do not like this fooling.

THERSITES [*Aside*] Nor I, by Pluto; but that that likes not you pleases me best.

DIOMEDES
What, shall I come? The hour?

CRESSIDA
Ay, come—O Jove!—do come—I shall be plagu'd.

DIOMEDES
Farewell till then.

CRESSIDA
Good night. I prithee, come.
[*Exit Diomedes.*]
Troilus, farewell! One eye yet looks on thee;
But with my heart the other eye doth see.
Ah, poor our sex! This fault in us I find,
The error of our eye directs our mind.
What error leads must err; O, then conclude
Minds sway'd by eyes are full of turpitude. *Exit.*

THERSITES [*Aside*]
A proof of strength she could not publish more,
Unless she said "My mind is now turn'd whore."

ULYSSES
All's done, my lord.

TROILUS
It is.

ULYSSES
Why stay we, then?

TROILUS
To make a recordation to my soul
Of every syllable that here was spoke.
But if I tell how these two did co-act,
Shall I not lie in publishing a truth?
Sith yet there is a credence in my heart,
An esperance so obstinately strong,
That doth invert th' attest of eyes and ears,
As if those organs had deceptious functions,
Created only to calumniate.
Was Cressid here?

ULYSSES
I cannot conjure, Troyan.

TROILUS
She was not, sure.

ULYSSES
Most sure she was.

TROILUS
Why, my negation hath no taste of madness.

ULYSSES
Nor mine, my lord. Cressid was here but now.

TROILUS
Let it not be believ'd for womanhood!
Think, we had mothers. Do not give advantage
To stubborn critics, apt, without a theme
For depravation, to square the general sex
By Cressid's rule. Rather think this not Cressid.

ULYSSES
What hath she done, Prince, that can soil our mothers?

TROILUS
Nothing at all, unless that this were she.

THERSITES [*Aside*] Will 'a swagger himself out on 's own eyes?

TROILUS
This she? No, this is Diomed's Cressida.
If beauty have a soul, this is not she;
If souls guide vows, if vows be sanctimonies,
If sanctimony be the gods' delight,
If there be rule in unity itself,
This was not she. O madness of discourse,
That cause sets up with and against itself!
Bi-fold authority, where reason can revolt
Without perdition, and loss assume all reason
Without revolt! This is, and is not, Cressid.
Within my soul there doth conduce a fight
Of this strange nature, that a thing inseparate
Divides more wider than the sky and earth,
And yet the spacious breadth of this division
Admits no orifex for a point as subtle
As Ariachne's broken woof to enter.
Instance, O instance, strong as Pluto's gates,
Cressid is mine, tied with the bonds of heaven;

94 Diana's . . . yond i.e., yonder stars. (Diana is the moon goddess and, ironically, the goddess of chastity.) **104 straight starts you** immediately starts you off on some abrupt action **105 likes** pleases **116 A proof . . . more** she could not state a stronger proof

124 esperance hope **125 attest** witness **126 deceptious** deceiving **132 for** for the sake of **134–136 apt . . . rule** apt enough, even when they lack grounds for negative comment, to make Cressida the standard by which all womankind is measured **139–140 Will . . . eyes** i.e., will he succeed in deceiving his own eyes **143 sanctimonies** sacred things **145 If . . . itself** i.e., if an entity (like Cressida) can only be itself and not two entities **146 discourse** reason **147 That . . . up** that sets up a debate or argument **148–150 where . . . Without revolt** where reason can revolt against itself (by denying the testimony of the senses that this is indeed Cressida) without becoming madness, and where loss of reason can put on the appearance of reason without actually revolting against it **151 conduce** take place **152 a thing inseparate** i.e., Cressida, an indivisible entity **155 orifex** orifice **156 Ariachne's broken woof** i.e., a thread of a spider's web. (Arachne [the correct spelling] challenged Minerva to a weaving contest; the goddess became angered, tore up Arachne's work, and turned her into a spider.) **157 Instance** proof, evidence

Instance, O instance, strong as heaven itself,
The bonds of heaven are slipp'd, dissolv'd, and loos'd,
And with another knot, five-finger-tied,
The fractions of her faith, orts of her love,
The fragments, scraps, the bits and greasy relics
Of her o'er-eaten faith, are bound to Diomed.

ULYSSES
May worthy Troilus be half attach'd
With that which here his passion doth express?

TROILUS
Ay, Greek; and that shall be divulged well
In characters as red as Mars his heart
Inflam'd with Venus. Never did young man fancy
With so eternal and so fix'd a soul.
Hark, Greek: as much as I do Cressid love,
So much by weight hate I her Diomed.
That sleeve is mine that he'll bear on his helm.
Were it a casque compos'd by Vulcan's skill,
My sword should bite it. Not the dreadful spout
Which shipmen do the hurricano call,
Constring'd in mass by the almighty sun,
Shall dizzy with more clamor Neptune's ear
In his descent than shall my prompted sword
Falling on Diomed.

THERSITES [*Aside*] He'll tickle it for his concupy.

TROILUS
O Cressid! O false Cressid! False, false, false!
Let all untruths stand by thy stained name,
And they'll seem glorious.

ULYSSES O, contain yourself;
Your passion draws ears hither.

Enter Aeneas.

AENEAS
I have been seeking you this hour, my lord.
Hector, by this, is arming him in Troy;
Ajax, your guard, stays to conduct you home.

TROILUS
Have with you, Prince. My courteous lord, adieu.
Farewell, revolted fair! And, Diomed,
Stand fast, and wear a castle on thy head!

ULYSSES
I'll bring you to the gates.

TROILUS
Accept distracted thanks.

Exeunt Troilus, Aeneas, and Ulysses.

THERSITES Would I could meet that rogue Diomed! I would croak like a raven; I would bode, I would bode. Patroclus will give me any thing for the intelligence of this whore. The parrot will not do more for an almond than he for a commodious drab. Lechery, lechery, still wars and lechery; nothing else holds fashion. A burning devil take them! *Exit.*

161 five-finger-tied i.e., tied by giving her hand to Diomedes **162 orts** refuse, fragments **164 o'er-eaten** i.e., surfeiting through overfeeding **165 half attach'd** half as much affected (as it appears) **172 So . . . weight** to the same extent **174 casque** headpiece, helmet **175 spout** waterspout **177 Constring'd** compressed **181 concupy** (1) concupiscence, lust; or (2) concubine, i.e., Cressida **189 Have with you** let us go together **191 castle** fortress, i.e., strong helmet **195 bode** warn, prognosticate **196 intelligence** news **198 commodious** accommodating **199–200 A burning devil** i.e., venereal disease

[SCENE III]

Enter Hector, [armed,] and Andromache.

ANDROMACHE
When was my lord so much ungently temper'd
To stop his ears against admonishment?
Unarm, unarm, and do not fight today.

HECTOR
You train me to offend you. Get you in.
By all the everlasting gods, I'll go!

ANDROMACHE
My dreams will, sure, prove ominous to the day.

HECTOR
No more, I say.

Enter Cassandra.

CASSANDRA Where is my brother Hector?

ANDROMACHE
Here, sister, arm'd, and bloody in intent.
Consort with me in loud and dear petition,
Pursue we him on knees; for I have dreamt
Of bloody turbulence, and this whole night
Hath nothing been but shapes and forms of slaughter.

CASSANDRA
O, 'tis true.

HECTOR Ho! Bid my trumpet sound.

CASSANDRA
No notes of sally, for the heavens, sweet brother.

HECTOR
Be gone, I say. The gods have heard me swear.

CASSANDRA
The gods are deaf to hot and peevish vows.
They are polluted off'rings, more abhorr'd
Than spotted livers in the sacrifice.

ANDROMACHE
O, be persuaded! Do not count it holy
[To hurt by being just. It is as lawful,
For we would give much, to use violent thefts,
And rob in the behalf of charity.

CASSANDRA]
It is the purpose that makes strong the vow,
But vows to every purpose must not hold.
Unarm, sweet Hector.

HECTOR Hold you still, I say.
Mine honor keeps the weather of my fate.
Life every man holds dear, but the dear man
Holds honor far more precious-dear than life.

Enter Troilus.

How now, young man, meanest thou to fight today?

ANDROMACHE
Cassandra, call my father to persuade.

Exit Cassandra.

V.iii. Location: Troy. Priam's palace.
4 train tempt, induce **14 sally** sallying, going forth to battle **21 For** because. **would give** want to give **24 vows . . . hold** not every vow must be held sacred **26 keeps the weather of** keeps to the windward side of, takes precedence over **27 dear man** worthy man, man of nobility

HECTOR
No, faith, young Troilus, doff thy harness, youth;
I am today i' th' vein of chivalry.
Let grow thy sinews till their knots be strong,
And tempt not yet the brushes of the war.
Unarm thee, go, and doubt thou not, brave boy,
I'll stand today for thee and me and Troy.

TROILUS
Brother, you have a vice of mercy in you,
Which better fits a lion than a man.

HECTOR
What vice is that? Good Troilus, chide me for it.

TROILUS
When many times the captive Grecian falls,
Even in the fan and wind of your fair sword,
You bid them rise and live.

HECTOR
O, 'tis fair play.

TROILUS
Fool's play, by heaven, Hector.

HECTOR
How now, how now?

TROILUS
For th' love of all the gods,
Let's leave the hermit Pity with our mother,
And when we have our armors buckled on,
The venom'd vengeance ride upon our swords,
Spur them to ruthful work, rein them from ruth.

HECTOR
Fie, savage, fie!

TROILUS
Hector, then 'tis wars.

HECTOR
Troilus, I would not have you fight today.

TROILUS
Who should withhold me?
Not fate, obedience, nor the hand of Mars
Beck'ning with fiery truncheon my retire,
Not Priamus and Hecuba on knees,
Their eyes o'ergalled with recourse of tears,
Nor you, my brother, with your true sword drawn,
Oppos'd to hinder me, should stop my way,
[But by my ruin.]

Enter Priam and Cassandra.

CASSANDRA
Lay hold upon him, Priam, hold him fast;
He is thy crutch. Now if thou lose thy stay,
Thou on him leaning, and all Troy on thee,
Fall all together.

PRIAM
Come, Hector, come, go back.
Thy wife hath dreamt, thy mother hath had visions,
Cassandra doth foresee, and I myself
Am like a prophet suddenly enrapt
To tell thee that this day is ominous.
Therefore, come back.

HECTOR
Aeneas is a-field,
And I do stand engag'd to many Greeks,
Even in the faith of valor, to appear
This morning to them.

PRIAM
Ay, but thou shalt not go.

HECTOR
I must not break my faith.
You know me dutiful; therefore, dear sir,
Let me not shame respect, but give me leave
To take that course by your consent and voice,
Which you do here forbid me, royal Priam.

CASSANDRA
O Priam, yield not to him!

ANDROMACHE
Do not, dear father.

HECTOR
Andromache, I am offended with you.
Upon the love you bear me, get you in.
Exit Andromache.

TROILUS
This foolish, dreaming, superstitious girl
Makes all these bodements.

CASSANDRA
O, farewell, dear Hector!
Look how thou diest, look how thy eye turns pale!
Look how thy wounds do bleed at many vents!
Hark, how Troy roars, how Hecuba cries out,
How poor Andromache shrills her dolors forth!
Behold, distraction, frenzy, and amazement,
Like witless antics, one another meet,
And all cry, Hector! Hector's dead! O Hector!

TROILUS
Away! away!

CASSANDRA
Farewell. Yet soft! Hector, I take my leave,
Thou dost thyself and all our Troy deceive. [*Exit.*]

HECTOR
You are amaz'd, my liege, at her exclaim.
Go in and cheer the town. We'll forth and fight,
Do deeds worth praise, and tell you them at night.

PRIAM
Farewell. The gods with safety stand about thee!
[*Exeunt severally Priam and Hector.*] *Alarum.*

TROILUS
They are at it, hark! Proud Diomed, believe,
I come to lose my arm, or win my sleeve.

Enter Pandarus.

PANDARUS Do you hear, my lord? Do you hear?

TROILUS
What now?

PANDARUS Here's a letter come from yond poor girl.
[*Gives letter.*]

TROILUS
Let me read.

PANDARUS A whoreson tisick, a whoreson rascally tisick so troubles me, and the foolish fortune of this girl, and what one thing, what another, that I shall leave you one o' th's days; and I have a rheum in mine eyes too, and such an ache in my bones that, unless a man

34 brushes hostile encounters **38 better fits a lion** (Lions were thought to be merciful to submissive prey.) **40 captive** overpowered in battle **48 ruthful** lamentable, i.e., causing lamentation. **ruth** pity, mercy **49 then 'tis wars** i.e., war is like that **53 truncheon** staff of office. **retire** withdrawal **55 o'ergalled** inflamed. **recourse** flowing down repeatedly **60 stay** prop

69 faith of valor word of honor **73 shame respect** i.e., violate my filial duty **80 Makes** causes. **bodements** omens of ill fortune **86 antics** fools **91 amaz'd** dumbstruck **101 tisick** consumptive cough

were curs'd, I cannot tell what to think on 't. What says she there?

TROILUS
Words, words, mere words, no matter from the
heart;
Th' effect doth operate another way.
[*Tears the letter.*]
Go, wind, to wind, there turn and change together.
My love with words and errors still she feeds,
But edifies another with her deeds. *Exeunt.*

[SCENE IV]

[*Alarum.*] *Enter Thersites. Excursions.*

THERSITES Now they are clapper-clawing one another; I'll go look on. That dissembling abominable varlet, Diomed, has got that same scurvy doting foolish young knave's sleeve of Troy there in his helm. I would fain see them meet, that that same young Troyan ass, that loves the whore there, might send that Greekish whoremasterly villain, with the sleeve, back to the dissembling luxurious drab, of a sleeveless errand. O' th' t'other side, the policy of those crafty swearing rascals, that stale old mouse-eaten dry cheese, Nestor, and that same dog-fox, Ulysses, is not prov'd worth a blackberry. They set me up, in policy, that mongrel cur, Ajax, against that dog of as bad a kind, Achilles. And now is the cur Ajax prouder than the cur Achilles, and will not arm today, whereupon the Grecians begin to proclaim barbarism, and policy grows into an ill opinion.

[*Enter Diomedes, Troilus following.*]

Soft! Here comes sleeve, and t' other.

TROILUS
Fly not; for shouldst thou take the river Styx,
I would swim after.

DIOMEDES Thou dost miscall retire.
I do not fly, but advantageous care
Withdrew me from the odds of multitude.
Have at thee!

THERSITES Hold thy whore, Grecian!—Now for thy whore, Troyan!—Now the sleeve, now the sleeve!

[*Exeunt Troilus and Diomedes, fighting.*]

Enter Hector.

HECTOR
What art thou, Greek? Art thou for Hector's match?
Art thou of blood and honor?

THERSITES No, no, I am a rascal, a scurvy railing knave, a very filthy rogue.

HECTOR
I do believe thee. Live. [*Exit.*]

THERSITES God-a-mercy, that thou wilt believe me; but a plague break thy neck for frighting me! What's become of the wenching rogues? I think they have swallow'd one another. I would laugh at that miracle—yet, in a sort, lechery eats itself. I'll seek them. *Exit.*

[SCENE V]

Enter Diomedes and Servant.

DIOMEDES
Go, go, my servant, take thou Troilus' horse;
Present the fair steed to my lady Cressid.
Fellow, commend my service to her beauty;
Tell her I have chastis'd the amorous Troyan,
And am her knight by proof.

SERVANT I go, my lord. [*Exit.*]

Enter Agamemnon.

AGAMEMNON
Renew, renew! The fierce Polydamas
Hath beat down Menon; bastard Margarelon
Hath Doreus prisoner,
And stands colossus-wise, waving his beam,
Upon the pashed corses of the kings
Epistrophus and Cedius; Polyxenes is slain,
Amphimachus and Thoas deadly hurt,
Patroclus ta'en or slain, and Palamedes
Sore hurt and bruis'd. The dreadful Sagittary
Appals our numbers. Haste we, Diomed,
To reinforcement, or we perish all.

Enter Nestor.

NESTOR
Go, bear Patroclus' body to Achilles,
And bid the snail-pac'd Ajax arm for shame.
There is a thousand Hectors in the field.
Now here he fights on Galathe his horse,
And there lacks work; anon he's there afoot,
And there they fly or die, like scaled sculls
Before the belching whale; then is he yonder,
And there the strawy Greeks, ripe for his edge,
Fall down before him, like the mower's swath.
Here, there, and every where, he leaves and takes,
Dexterity so obeying appetite
That what he will he does, and does so much
That proof is call'd impossibility.

Enter Ulysses.

112 s.d. Exeunt (In the Folio version, Pandarus is angrily dismissed at this point, in the lines printed by the Quarto at V.x.32–34.)

V.iv. Location: Plains between Troy and the Greek camp.
1 clapper-clawing mauling, thrashing **8 luxurious** lecherous. **sleeveless** futile **12 set me** set. (*Me* is the ethical dative.) **16 proclaim barbarism** i.e., declare they will be governed by "policy" or established government no longer **20 miscall retire** call my retirement by the wrong name of retreat **21–22 advantageous . . . multitude** care for my own advantage prompted me to withdraw from facing heavy odds **27 blood** noble blood

35 in a sort in a way

V.v. Location: Plains between Troy and the Greek camp still. The battle scene is virtually uninterrupted to the play's end.
9 beam lance **10 pashed corses** battered corpses **14 Sagittary** (Literally, the archer; a centaur, i.e., a monster half man, half horse, who according to medieval legends fought in the Trojan War against the Greeks.) **15 Appals our numbers** dismays our troops **22 scaled sculls** scattering schools of fish **24 strawy** like straw ready for mowing **26 leaves and takes** i.e., leaves one dead and takes on another (?) **29 proof** fact, accomplished deed

ULYSSES
O, courage, courage, princes! Great Achilles
Is arming, weeping, cursing, vowing vengeance.
Patroclus' wounds have rous'd his drowsy blood,
Together with his mangled Myrmidons,
That noseless, handless, hack'd and chipp'd, come to him,
Crying on Hector. Ajax hath lost a friend
And foams at mouth, and he is arm'd and at it,
Roaring for Troilus, who hath done today
Mad and fantastic execution,
Engaging and redeeming of himself
With such a careless force and forceless care
As if that luck, in very spite of cunning,
Bade him win all.

Enter Ajax.

AJAX
Troilus! Thou coward Troilus! *Exit.*
DIOMEDES
Ay, there, there.
NESTOR
So, so, we draw together. *Exit.*

Enter Achilles.

ACHILLES
Where is this Hector?
Come, come, thou boy-queller, show thy face!
Know what it is to meet Achilles angry.
Hector! Where's Hector? I will none but Hector.
Exit [with others].

[SCENE VI]

Enter Ajax.

AJAX
Troilus, thou coward Troilus, show thy head!

Enter Diomedes.

DIOMEDES
Troilus, I say! Where's Troilus?
AJAX
What wouldst thou?
DIOMEDES
I would correct him.
AJAX
Were I the general, thou shouldst have my office
Ere that correction. Troilus, I say! What, Troilus!

Enter Troilus.

TROILUS
O traitor Diomed! Turn thy false face, thou traitor,
And pay thy life thou owest me for my horse!
DIOMEDES
Ha, art thou there?
AJAX
I'll fight with him alone. Stand, Diomed.
DIOMEDES
He is my prize. I will not look upon.
TROILUS
Come, both you cogging Greeks, have at you both!
[Exeunt, fighting.]

[Enter Hector.]

HECTOR
Yea, Troilus? O, well fought, my youngest brother!

Enter Achilles.

ACHILLES
Now do I see thee, ha! Have at thee, Hector!
[They fight; Achilles tires.]
HECTOR
Pause, if thou wilt.
ACHILLES
I do disdain thy courtesy, proud Troyan.
Be happy that my arms are out of use.
My rest and negligence befriends thee now,
But thou anon shalt hear of me again;
Till when, go seek thy fortune. *Exit.*
HECTOR
Fare thee well.
I would have been much more a fresher man,
Had I expected thee. How now, my brother!

Enter Troilus.

TROILUS
Ajax hath ta'en Aeneas! Shall it be?
No, by the flame of yonder glorious heaven,
He shall not carry him. I'll be ta'en too,
Or bring him off. Fate, hear me what I say!
I reck not though I end my life today. *Exit.*

Enter one in armor.

HECTOR
Stand, stand, thou Greek; thou art a goodly mark.
No? Wilt thou not? I like thy armor well;
I'll frush it and unlock the rivets all,
But I'll be master of it. *[Exit one in armor.]* Wilt thou not, beast, abide?
Why, then fly on, I'll hunt thee for thy hide.
Exit [in pursuit].

[SCENE VII]

Enter Achilles, with Myrmidons.

ACHILLES
Come here about me, you my Myrmidons;
Mark what I say. Attend me where I wheel.
Strike not a stroke, but keep yourselves in breath,
And when I have the bloody Hector found,
Empale him with your weapons round about;
In fellest manner execute your aims.

39 Engaging committing to battle **40 forceless care** easy dexterity **45 boy-queller** boy killer; i.e., slayer of Patroclus

V.vi. Location: As before; the battle continues.
5 Ere that correction i.e., sooner than take from me the privilege of chastising Troilus **9 Stand** i.e., stand aside **10 look upon** remain an onlooker **11 cogging** deceitful **24 carry him** i.e., into captivity **25 bring him off** rescue him **29 frush** bruise

V.vii. Location: As before; the battle continues.
5 Empale fence

Follow me, sirs, and my proceedings eye.
It is decreed Hector the great must die. *Exeunt.*

Enter Thersites; Menelaus [*and*] *Paris* [*fighting*].

THERSITES The cuckold and the cuckold-maker are at it.
Now, bull! Now, dog! 'Loo, Paris, 'loo! Now my dou- 10
ble-horn'd Spartan! 'Loo, Paris, 'loo! The bull has the 11
game. Ware horns, ho! 12

Exeunt Paris and Menelaus.

Enter Bastard [*Margarelon*].

MARGARELON
Turn, slave, and fight.

THERSITES What art thou?

MARGARELON
A bastard son of Priam's.

THERSITES I am a bastard too; I love bastards. I am bastard begot, bastard instructed, bastard in mind, bastard in valor, in every thing illegitimate. One bear will not bite another, and wherefore should one bastard? Take heed, the quarrel's most ominous to us. If the son of a whore fight for a whore, he tempts judgment. Farewell, bastard. [*Exit.*]

MARGARELON
The devil take thee, coward! *Exit.*

[SCENE VIII]

Enter Hector, [*bearing the armor he has taken*].

HECTOR
Most putrefied core, so fair without, 1
Thy goodly armor thus hath cost thy life.
Now is my day's work done; I'll take good breath.
Rest, sword; thou hast thy fill of blood and death.
[*Puts off his helmet and shield.*]

Enter Achilles and Myrmidons.

ACHILLES
Look, Hector, how the sun begins to set,
How ugly night comes breathing at his heels.
Even with the vail and dark'ning of the sun, 7
To close the day up, Hector's life is done.

HECTOR
I am unarm'd. Forego this vantage, Greek.

ACHILLES
Strike, fellows, strike! This is the man I seek.
[*Hector falls.*]
So, Ilion, fall thou next! Come, Troy, sink down!
Here lies thy heart, thy sinews, and thy bone.
On, Myrmidons, and cry you all amain,
"Achilles hath the mighty Hector slain."
Retreat [*sounded*].
Hark! A retire upon our Grecian part.

MYRMIDON
The Troyans' trumpet sound the like, my lord.

ACHILLES
The dragon wing of night o'erspreads the earth,
And, stickler-like, the armies separates. 18
My half-supp'd sword, that frankly would have fed, 19
Pleas'd with this dainty bait, thus goes to bed.
[*Sheathes his sword.*]
Come, tie his body to my horse's tail;
Along the field I will the Troyan trail.
Exeunt [*with Hector's body*].

[SCENE IX]

Enter Agamemnon, Ajax, Menelaus, Nestor, Diomedes, and the rest, marching. [*Shouts within.*]

AGAMEMNON
Hark! Hark! What shout is that?

NESTOR
Peace, drums!

SOLDIERS *(Within)*
Achilles! Achilles! Hector's slain! Achilles!

DIOMEDES
The bruit is, Hector's slain, and by Achilles. 4

AJAX
If it be so, yet bragless let it be;
Great Hector was as good a man as he.

AGAMEMNON
March patiently along. Let one be sent
To pray Achilles see us at our tent.
If in his death the gods have us befriended,
Great Troy is ours, and our sharp wars are ended.
Exeunt.

[SCENE X]

Enter Aeneas, Paris, Antenor, [*and*] *Deiphobus.*

AENEAS
Stand, ho! Yet are we masters of the field.
Never go home; here starve we out the night.

Enter Troilus.

TROILUS
Hector is slain.

ALL Hector! The gods forbid!

TROILUS
He's dead, and at the murderer's horse's tail,
In beastly sort, dragg'd through the shameful field.

10 bull i.e., Menelaus, a cuckold, a horned creature. **'Loo** (A cry to incite a dog against the bull in the sport of bull-baiting in Shakespeare's England.) **11–12 has the game** wins

V.viii. Location: As before; the battle continues.
1 core i.e., the body of the Greek from whom Hector has taken the armor **7 vail** going down

18 stickler-like like an umpire **19 frankly** freely

V.ix. Location: As before; the battle has concluded.
4 bruit rumor, noise

V.x. Location: Plains between Troy and the Greek camp still, after the battle.

Frown on, you heavens, effect your rage with speed!
Sit, gods, upon your thrones, and smile at Troy! 7
I say, at once let your brief plagues be mercy, 8
And linger not our sure destructions on!

AENEAS
My lord, you do discomfort all the host.

TROILUS
You understand me not that tell me so.
I do not speak of flight, of fear, of death, 12
But dare all imminence that gods and men 13
Address their dangers in. Hector is gone. 14
Who shall tell Priam so, or Hecuba?
Let him that will a screech-owl aye be call'd
Go in to Troy, and say there, Hector's dead.
There is a word will Priam turn to stone,
Make wells and Niobes of the maids and wives, 19
Cold statues of the youth, and, in a word,
Scare Troy out of itself. [But march away.
Hector is dead.] There is no more to say.
Stay yet. You vile abominable tents,
Thus proudly pight upon our Phrygian plains, 24
Let Titan rise as early as he dare, 25
I'll through and through you! And, thou great-siz'd coward, 26
No space of earth shall sunder our two hates.
I'll haunt thee like a wicked conscience still,
That moldeth goblins swift as frenzy's thoughts.
Strike a free march to Troy! With comfort go.
Hope of revenge shall hide our inward woe.
[*Exeunt Aeneas and Trojans.*]

Enter Pandarus.

PANDARUS But hear you, hear you!

TROILUS
Hence, broker-lackey! Ignomy and shame
Pursue thy life, and live aye with thy name!
Exeunt all but Pandarus.

PANDARUS A goodly medicine for my aching bones! O
world, world, world! Thus is the poor agent despis'd!
O traders and bawds, how earnestly are you set 37
a-work, and how ill requited! Why should our en-
deavor be so lov'd and the performance so loath'd?
What verse for it? What instance for it? Let me see:

Full merrily the humble-bee doth sing,
Till he hath lost his honey and his sting;
And being once subdu'd in armed tail,
Sweet honey and sweet notes together fail.

Good traders in the flesh, set this in your painted 45
cloths: 46
As many as be here of Pandar's hall, 47
Your eyes, half out, weep out at Pandar's fall; 48
Or if you cannot weep, yet give some groans,
Though not for me, yet for your aching bones. 50
Brethren and sisters of the hold-door trade, 51
Some two months hence my will shall here be made.
It should be now, but that my fear is this,
Some galled goose of Winchester would hiss. 54
Till then I'll sweat and seek about for eases, 55
And at that time bequeath you my diseases. [*Exit.*]

7 smile i.e., mockingly **8 let . . . mercy** i.e., let your afflictions end us quickly, be mercifully brief **12 of flight** i.e., merely of disordered retreat **13–14 dare . . . in** i.e., I speak direly, calling up all the impending evils that gods and men invoke when they warn of disaster **19 Niobes** (Niobe boasted that her six sons and six daughters made her superior to Latona, mother of Apollo and Diana, for which she was punished by seeing them put to death by the arrows of these two deities. While weeping she was changed into a stone, but her tears continued to flow from the rock.) **24 pight** pitched **25 Titan** i.e., Helios, the sun god, one of the Titans **26 coward** i.e., Achilles, craven slayer of Hector **37 traders** i.e., traders in sex **45–46 painted cloths** cheap wall hangings worked or painted with scenes and mottoes **47 hall** fraternity **48 half out** i.e., already half eaten away by venereal disease

50 aching bones (A symptom of venereal disease.) **51 hold-door trade** i.e., brothel-keeping **54 galled . . . Winchester** i.e., a prostitute having venereal disease; so called because the brothels of Southwark were under the jurisdiction of the Bishop of Winchester **55 sweat** (A common treatment for venereal disease.)

The Histories

The First Part of King Henry the Sixth

The Second Part of King Henry the Sixth

The Third Part of King Henry the Sixth

The Tragedy of King Richard the Third

The Life and Death of King John

The Tragedy of King Richard the Second

The First Part of King Henry the Fourth

The Second Part of King Henry the Fourth

The Life of King Henry the Fifth

The Famous History of
the Life of King Henry the Eighth

The First Part of King Henry the Sixth

Throughout much of the fifteenth century, England had suffered the ravages of civil war. From the long struggles between the Lancastrians and the Yorkists, the so-called Wars of the Roses, the country had emerged in 1485 shaken but united at last under the strong rule of the Tudors. To Elizabethan Englishmen, this period of civil war was a still-recent event that had tested and almost destroyed England's nationhood. Elizabethans were, moreover, still troubled by political and dynastic uncertainties of their own. Queen Elizabeth, granddaughter of the first Tudor king, Henry VII, was unmarried and aging, her successor unchosen. Her Catholic enemies at home and abroad plotted a return to the ancient faith renounced by Henry VIII in his reformation of the church. Spain had attempted an invasion of England with the great Armada in 1588, perhaps two years before Shakespeare began writing his *Henry VI* plays. It was in such an era of crisis and patriotic excitement that the *Henry VI* plays first appeared. Indeed, they helped to establish the vogue of the English history play, which was to flourish throughout the decade of the 1590's. England's civil wars could be studied and analyzed now, from a perspective of over one hundred years later, as a key to the present time. At hand was a new edition of Holinshed's chronicles, 1587, along with the earlier chronicle writings of Fabyan, Stow, Grafton, Edward Hall's *Union of the Two Noble and Illustre Famelies of Lancastre and Yorke,* John Foxe's *Actes and Monuments of Martyrs,* and *A Myrroure for Magistrates.*

How had these wars begun? Elizabethan Englishmen searched for an answer not in economic or social terms, but in religious and moral ones. According to a traditional and government-sponsored explanation, formulated most comprehensively by Edward Hall and familiar to Shakespeare whether he accepted it fully or not, the Wars of the Roses were a manifestation of God's wrath, a divine punishment inflicted on the English people for their wayward behavior. The people and their rulers had brought civil war on themselves by self-serving ambition, arrogance, and disloyalty. King Henry VI's grandfather, Henry IV, had come to the throne in 1399 by deposing and then executing his own cousin Richard II (a momentous event to be portrayed by Shakespeare in a later history play). Henry VI was himself an infant when he succeeded to the throne in 1422, owing to the untimely death of his father Henry V. Too young at first to rule, and never blessed with his father's ability to act decisively, Henry VI was utterly unable to halt the struggle for power that developed among members of his large but discordant family. Ultimately, his very title to the throne was challenged by his kinsman Richard Plantagenet, Duke of York, who claimed to be rightful king by virtue of his descent from Henry IV's uncle, Lionel, Duke of Clarence. The Yorkist faction marched to battle against Henry VI's Lancastrian faction (so named because for generations the family had been possessors of the dukedom of Lancaster), and the war was on.

All these harrowing misfortunes were the result, according to Tudor historians, of God's anger toward a rebellious people. The outcome of the war confirmed this pattern: universal devastation and the deaths of those most responsible for the conflict led eventually to appeasement of God's anger and a restoration of order. Richard Plantagenet died in the struggle, as did Henry VI, Henry's son Edward, and much of the English nobility. Richard's son Edward survived to become Edward IV; but his manner of obtaining the throne was so manifestly offensive to Providence that (according to the theory) he suffered a retributive death at the hands of an angry God and was succeeded by his younger brother, Richard III. This last Yorkist ruler governed only two years, 1483–1485, and it was through Richard's insane vengeance that God finally settled all his scores against the wayward English people. Having completed this purgation, God chose as his instrument of a new order Henry Tudor, Earl of Richmond, Henry VII. Although Henry's return to England and defeat of Richard at the battle of Bosworth Field might outwardly resemble Henry IV's seizure of power from Richard II, the difference was crucial to Tudor historians. Richard III had to be seen not as a flawed legitimate monarch but as a mad usurper and tyrant; his defeat was not the disobedient act of one man but a rising up of the entire English nation at the prompting of divine command. Henry VII's accession to power was to be viewed not as a precedent for further rebellion but as a manifestation of divine will without parallel in human history.

The essence of this providential view of events was that divine retribution and eventual reconciliation revealed themselves in the history of the war. The theory of course served the interests of the Tudor state, and was in part a propaganda weapon calculatedly employed by the ruling class. Shakespeare's commitment to it should not be taken for granted, and indeed a number of recent studies have expressed a profound skepticism toward the theory as the basis of Shakespeare's dramaturgy. Especially in his later tetralogy or four-play series from *Richard II* to *Henry V,* Shakespeare reveals considerably more interest in the clash of personalities than in patterns of divine retribution. Shakespeare does not endorse the orthodox view that Bolingbroke's seizure of the throne is a violation of divine purpose for which he and England must be humbled; instead, Shakespeare portrays the issues as many-sided and subject to varying interpretations.

Throughout his history plays, indeed, Shakespeare avoids expressing the Tudor providential view of recent history through didactic narrators or chorus figures who might seem to represent the point of view of the entire plays; instead, he puts this providential interpretation into the mouths of avowedly biased and self-interested characters whose motives and testimony the audience can then evaluate as it sees fit. In Shakespeare's depiction of the Lancastrian-Yorkist conflict, neither side maintains a consistent ideological position, but instead shifts argument as required by the expediency of the moment. Although in his earlier tetralogy from *1 Henry VI* to *Richard III* Shakespeare does sometimes allow his contending characters to hearken back to the deposition of Richard II in order to explain the misfortunes of England's civil wars, those characters speak from self-interest and interpret history to their own advantage.

The individual plays of this earlier tetralogy, if seen or read separately, do not consistently comfort the spectator or reader with an assurance that all is working out according to God's plan. At the end of *1 Henry VI,* King Henry has surrendered to a disastrous marriage and has lost most of France; at the end of *2 Henry VI* the good Duke Humphrey of Gloucester is dead and his opportunistic political enemies are about to turn King Henry out of his throne. The hostilities of Lancaster and York end at the conclusion of *3 Henry VI,* to be sure, but prospects for a stable peace are ominous in view of Richard of Gloucester's baleful presence. The reciprocity of slaughter visited on both sides appears to stem as much from man's insane desire for vengeance as from God's evening of the score. Only in *Richard III* do we retroactively see a pattern of divine anger, retribution, and eventual appeasement that can then be applied to the tetralogy as a continuous narrative. E. M. W. Tillyard's argument for a providential reading of these plays is based not coincidentally on a view of the tetralogy as a cohesive whole. What about the playgoers who saw the plays one at a time? The plays, so far as we know, were written and produced singly and were never staged in a continuous series. Even though the tetralogy as a whole may harmonize in part with the chronicles of Edward Hall and others, written to glorify the Tudor state and to give thanks for its having ended the prolonged anarchy of the fifteenth century, we can see that Shakespeare is no apologist for the Tudor state. He gives expression to a widely felt distrust of political chaos. A pattern of divine wrath and appeasement, seen retrospectively in *Richard III,* provides at last a causal explanation of England's darkest hour. More immediately, in each individual play, the overriding cosmic irony stressing the gulf between foolish humanity and the inscrutable intentions of Providence offers a potentially stirring conflict of which Shakespeare makes rich use.

Shakespeare wrote his first tetralogy some time between 1589 and 1594. Just how much of this first tetralogy may have been planned out when Shakespeare began work is hard to say. In fact the very order of composition has long been in dispute. Despite the commonsense pleading of Dr. Johnson that Part II follows from Part I as a logical consequence, some scholars argue that Part I was composed last. One piece of evidence is that a corrupt version of Part II was published in quarto version in 1594 as *The First part of the Contention betwixt the two famous Houses of Yorke and Lancaster,* and a corrupt version of Part III in octavo in 1595 as *The true Tragedie of Richard Duke of Yorke.* Part I had to await publication in the Folio of 1623, and was registered for publication at that time as "The thirde parte of Henry the sixt." It seems odd, moreover, that Parts II and III make no mention of Lord Talbot, so prominent in Part I. If, however, as seems likely, the early printed versions of Parts II and III were memorial reconstructions without the authority of the official prompt book, the claim of Part II to have been written first may be unsubstantial. The very fact of prior publication of Parts II and III could explain why Part I was called "The thirde parte" in 1623. Although Talbot is not mentioned in Parts II and III, these texts do recall important aspects of Part I. It is certainly possible that Shakespeare wrote all three parts in normal order.

Equally vexing is the question of authorship. Many Elizabethan plays were written by teams of authors, and Shakespeare might have collaborated, especially at the beginning of his career. Perhaps he rewrote older works by such writers as Nashe, Greene, and Marlowe. Yet the theories of multiple authorship, once a commonplace of scholarship, are now generally in disfavor. Greene's famous resentment toward Shakespeare as the "vpstart crow beautified with our feathers" seems more the envy of a lesser talent than the righteous indignation of one who has been plagiarized. The chief criteria used to "disintegrate" the plays into the hands of various supposed contributors are those of taste and style: for example, the low comic scenes of Joan of Arc were long held to be too coarse for Shakespeare's genius. Today most critics see a consistency of view throughout the *Henry VI* plays despite minor inconsistencies of fact that might be the result of simple error or of using multiple sources, and find nothing in these plays inimical to Shakespeare's budding genius. This belief confirms the judgment of Heminges and Condell, Shakespeare's fellow actors and editors of the 1623 Folio, who placed all the *Henry VI* plays among Shakespeare's collected works in their historical order.

If Shakespeare was at least chiefly responsible for the

Henry VI series, he may also have been an important innovator in the new genre of the history play. Only the anonymous *Famous Victories of Henry V* is certainly earlier in dealing with recent English history. There were, to be sure, plays about legendary British history such as *Gorboduc* or *The Misfortunes of Arthur,* or about far-off lands such as *Cambises* or Marlowe's *Tamburlaine.* All these plays had explored by analogue political questions fascinating to Elizabethan England, and *Tamburlaine*'s immense success had certainly established a vogue for grand scenes of military conquest. Still, the English history play as a recognizable form came into being with *Henry VI.* The success was evidently tremendous and established Shakespeare as a major playwright.

1 Henry VI, like all the plays in this first tetralogy, comprises a large number of episodes, a sizable cast of characters, and a wide geographical range. The subject is England's loss of French territories because of political division at home. The structure of the play is one of sequential action displayed in great variety and in alternating scenes that are thematically juxtaposed and contrasted with one another. In the rapid shifting back and forth between the English and French court, for example, Shakespeare establishes a paradoxical theme: France triumphs in England's weakness, not in her own strength. The French court is merely one of debased sexual frivolity. The English are naturally superior but are torn apart by internal dissension, by a "jarring discord of nobility" and a "shouldering of each other in the court" among those attempting to take advantage of Henry VI's weak minority rule and his vulnerable genealogical claim. Two of young Henry's kinsmen jockeying for position are Humphrey, Duke of Gloucester, and the Bishop of Winchester. Humphrey's intentions are virtuous, but he is unable to prevent the opportunistic scheming of his rival. Winchester, despite his ecclesiastical calling, is a man of evil ambition and corrupt life, wholly intent on destroying the rightminded Gloucester. Shakespeare employs derisive anticlerical humor against Winchester, and enlists the Protestant sympathies of his Elizabethan audience against the meddling Catholic church attempting to exploit England's weak kingship for its own ulterior purposes.

Even so, the menace threatening England is not seen as a Catholic conspiracy throughout; Winchester is only one opportunist fishing in troubled waters. Of greater danger in the long run is Richard Plantagenet, scion of the Yorkist claim. From the start, Shakespeare portrays him as cunning, able to ingratiate himself and bide his time, ultimately ruthless. In these qualities he ominously foreshadows his youngest son and namesake, Richard III. In this play, Plantagenet's strategy is to allow England to wear herself down by the various conflicts at court and military losses abroad; once the situation is reduced to anarchy, Plantagenet will be able to move in. The strategy works only too well.

Chief defender of England's military might in France, and eventual victim of the bickering among the English nobility, is Lord Talbot. He is the heroic figure of this play with whom Elizabethan audiences identified. He pleads for political and military unity against the French, and demonstrates that with such unity England would be invincible. Talbot is "the terror of the French," able to hold off a troop of French soldiers with his bare fists, reputed to twist bars of steel. As the embodiment of chivalry, he delivers a richly deserved rebuke to Sir John Falstaff (historically "Fastolfe," but called "Falstaff" in the Folio text of this play), the cowardly soldier who foreshadows the fat knight of *1 Henry IV.* In *1 Henry VI,* cowardice and honor are rendered in black and white extremes. Talbot is a model general, illustrating all the qualities of great leadership advocated by the textbooks of the age: he is a stirring orator, fearless, witty, and concerned with a proper lasting fame. In the touching scenes with his son, Talbot rises triumphantly above death to become the immortal embodiment of brave soldiership. His unnecessary death offers a devastating comment on the weak leadership that has allowed authority in France to be divided among political rivals.

The relations between men and women in this play are also used to create thematic contrasts. Talbot's chief military rival in France is Joan of Arc; and, although many earlier scholars have wanted to deny Shakespeare's authorship of the Joan of Arc scenes, their thematic function is central. As a woman in armor, Joan is the embodiment of the domineering Amazonian woman to whom the effete and self-indulgent dauphin, Charles, weakly capitulates. The sexual roles have been reversed; Venus triumphs over Mars. Joan also attempts to practice her witchcraft on Talbot and his son, but in vain. Talbot's sense of duty never succumbs to Circean voluptuousness. In his encounter with the Countess of Auvergne, Talbot resourcefully outwits another woman who, like Joan, seeks to entrap him. The Countess finally submits to Talbot's courteous but firm authority, thereby reestablishing the traditional relationship of male and female. Talbot stands for every kind of decency and order that ought to prevail, but is senselessly destroyed through England's political division.

The last woman introduced in the play, Margaret of Anjou, is another domineering female. Her adulterous relationship with the fleshly Suffolk, and her ascendancy over the weak Henry VI, are to be of fateful consequence in the ensuing plays. Her scenes, although once dismissed as an afterthought linking *1 Henry VI* with the following plays, in fact recapitulate the motifs of female dominance with great dramatic effect. Young Henry VI is no Talbot; inexperienced in love and highly impressionable, he surrenders to the mere description of a woman he has not even seen, and refuses a politically advantageous match arranged by Duke Humphrey in order that he may marry a conniving Frenchwoman without dowry. The marriage also anticipates that of Edward IV (in *3 Henry VI*) to a penniless widow who has caught his roving eye, when Edward could have obtained a handsome dowry and a favorable alliance by marrying the French King's sister-in-law. Such dismal triumphs of passion over reason are emblematic of the general decay among the English aristocracy. Despite Henry's weakness, he is the central character of this play after all, and his enervating surrender in love is a fitting anticlimax with which to end the first installment of England's decline.

The First Part of King Henry the Sixth

[*Dramatis Personae*

KING HENRY THE SIXTH.

DUKE OF GLOUCESTER, *uncle to the King, and Protector.*

DUKE OF BEDFORD, *uncle to the King, and Regent of France.*

THOMAS BEAUFORT, DUKE OF EXETER, *great-uncle to the King.*

HENRY BEAUFORT, *great-uncle to the King,* BISHOP OF WINCHESTER, *and afterwards* CARDINAL.

JOHN BEAUFORT, EARL, *afterwards* DUKE, OF SOMERSET.

RICHARD PLANTAGENET, *son of Richard late Earl of Cambridge, afterwards* DUKE OF YORK.

EARL OF WARWICK.

EARL OF SALISBURY.

WILLIAM DE LA POLE, EARL OF SUFFOLK.

LORD TALBOT, *afterwards Earl of Shrewsbury.*

JOHN TALBOT, *his son.*

EDMUND MORTIMER, *Earl of March.*

SIR JOHN FALSTAFF.

SIR WILLIAM LUCY.

SIR WILLIAM GLANSDALE.

SIR THOMAS GARGRAVE.

MAYOR OF LONDON.

WOODVILLE, *Lieutenant of the Tower.*

VERNON, *of the White Rose or York faction.*

BASSET, *of the Red Rose or Lancaster faction.*

LAWYER. *Mortimer's* KEEPERS.

CHARLES, *Dauphin, and afterwards King, of France.*

REIGNIER, *Duke of Anjou, and titular King of Naples.*

DUKE OF BURGUNDY.

DUKE OF ALENCON.

BASTARD OF ORLEANS.

GOVERNOR OF PARIS.

MASTER-GUNNER OF ORLEANS, *and his* SON.

GENERAL, *of the French forces in Bordeaux.*

A French SERGEANT. PORTER.

An old SHEPHERD, *father to Joan la Pucelle.*

MARGARET, *daughter to Reignier, afterwards married to King Henry.*

COUNTESS OF AUVERGNE.

JOAN LA PUCELLE, *commonly called Joan of Arc.*

LORDS, WARDERS *of the Tower,* HERALD,
OFFICERS, PAPAL LEGATE, AMBASSADORS,
SOLDIERS, MESSENGERS, *and* ATTENDANTS.

FIENDS *appearing to La Pucelle.*

SCENE: *Partly in England, and partly in France.*]

ACT I • SCENE I

Dead March. Enter the Funeral of King Henry the Fifth, attended on by the Duke of Bedford, Regent of France; the Duke of Gloucester, Protector; the Duke of Exeter, [*the Earl of*] *Warwick, the Bishop of Winchester, and the Duke of Somerset,* [*Heralds, etc.*].

BEDFORD
Hung be the heavens with black, yield day to night! 1
Comets, importing change of times and states,
Brandish your crystal tresses in the sky 3
And with them scourge the bad revolting stars
That have consented unto Henry's death—
King Henry the Fifth, too famous to live long!
England ne'er lost a king of so much worth.

GLOUCESTER
England ne'er had a king until his time.
Virtue he had, deserving to command. 9
His brandish'd sword did blind men with his beams; 10
His arms spread wider than a dragon's wings;
His sparkling eyes, replete with wrathful fire,
More dazzled and drove back his enemies
Than midday sun fierce bent against their faces.
What should I say? His deeds exceed all speech.
He ne'er lift up his hand but conquered. 16

EXETER
We mourn in black. Why mourn we not in blood?
Henry is dead and never shall revive.
Upon a wooden coffin we attend,
And death's dishonorable victory
We with our stately presence glorify,
Like captives bound to a triumphant car. 22
What? Shall we curse the planets of mishap
That plotted thus our glory's overthrow?
Or shall we think the subtle-witted French
Conjurers and sorcerers, that, afraid of him,
By magic verses have contriv'd his end?

WINCHESTER
He was a king bless'd of the King of kings.
Unto the French the dreadful Judgment Day
So dreadful will not be as was his sight.
The battles of the Lord of hosts he fought;
The church's prayers made him so prosperous.

GLOUCESTER
The church? Where is it? Had not churchmen pray'd, 33
His thread of life had not so soon decay'd. 34
None do you like but an effeminate prince,
Whom, like a schoolboy, you may overawe.

WINCHESTER
Gloucester, whate'er we like, thou art Protector 37
And lookest to command the Prince and realm.
Thy wife is proud. She holdeth thee in awe 39
More than God or religious churchmen may.

GLOUCESTER
Name not religion, for thou lov'st the flesh,
And ne'er throughout the year to church thou go'st
Except it be to pray against thy foes.

BEDFORD
Cease, cease these jars and rest your minds in peace! 44
Let's to the altar. Heralds, wait on us.
Instead of gold, we'll offer up our arms,
Since arms avail not now that Henry's dead.
Posterity, await for wretched years, 48
When at their mothers' moist'ned eyes babes shall suck, 49
Our isle be made a nourish of salt tears, 50
And none but women left to wail the dead.
Henry the Fifth, thy ghost I invocate:
Prosper this realm, keep it from civil broils,
Combat with adverse planets in the heavens!
A far more glorious star thy soul will make
Than Julius Caesar or bright——

Enter a Messenger.

FIRST MESSENGER
My honorable lords, health to you all!
Sad tidings bring I to you out of France,
Of loss, of slaughter, and discomfiture.
Guienne, Champagne, Rheims, Orleans, 60
Paris, Guysors, Poitiers, are all quite lost.

BEDFORD
What say'st thou, man, before dead Henry's corse?
Speak softly, or the loss of those great towns
Will make him burst his lead and rise from death. 64

GLOUCESTER
Is Paris lost? Is Rouen yielded up?
If Henry were recall'd to life again,
These news would cause him once more yield the ghost.

EXETER
How were they lost? What treachery was us'd?

FIRST MESSENGER
No treachery, but want of men and money.
Amongst the soldiers this is muttered,
That here you maintain several factions,

I.i. Location: Westminster Abbey.
1 Hung . . . black (A metaphor from the theatrical practice of draping the "heavens" or roof projecting over the stage in black when a tragedy was to be performed.) **3 crystal** bright, shining. **tresses** hair, i.e., the trail of the comet **9 Virtue** excellence, authority **10 his beams** its beams **16 lift** lifted. **but conquered** without conquering **22 car** chariot

33 pray'd (with pun on *prey'd;* also in l. 43) **34 decay'd** been destroyed **37 Protector** head of state during the king's minority **39 Thy wife is proud** (A reference to Gloucester's ambitious wife, Eleanor, whose inordinate desire for greatness is depicted in *2 Henry VI.*) **44 jars** discords **48 await for** expect **49 When . . . suck** i.e., when mothers will feed their children with tears only **50 nourish . . . tears** i.e., a nurse feeding with tears only **60 Champagne** the city of Compiegne **64 lead** leaden inner coffin or wrapping, inside the wooden coffin (l. 19)

And whilst a field should be dispatch'd and fought,
You are disputing of your generals.
One would have ling'ring wars with little cost;
Another would fly swift, but wanteth wings;
A third thinks, without expense at all,
By guileful fair words peace may be obtain'd.
Awake, awake, English nobility!
Let not sloth dim your honors new begot.
Cropp'd are the flower-de-luces in your arms;
Of England's coat one half is cut away. [*Exit.*]

EXETER
Were our tears wanting to this funeral,
These tidings would call forth her flowing tides.

BEDFORD
Me they concern; Regent I am of France.
Give me my steeled coat. I'll fight for France.
Away with these disgraceful wailing robes!
Wounds will I lend the French instead of eyes,
To weep their intermissive miseries.

Enter to them another Messenger, [*with letters*].

SECOND MESSENGER
Lords, view these letters full of bad mischance.
France is revolted from the English quite,
Except some petty towns of no import.
The Dauphin Charles is crowned king in Rheims;
The Bastard of Orleans with him is join'd;
Reignier, Duke of Anjou, doth take his part;
The Duke of Alençon flieth to his side. *Exit.*

EXETER
The Dauphin crowned king? All fly to him?
O, whither shall we fly from this reproach?

GLOUCESTER
We will not fly, but to our enemies' throats!
Bedford, if thou be slack, I'll fight it out.

BEDFORD
Gloucester, why doubt'st thou of my forwardness?
An army have I muster'd in my thoughts,
Wherewith already France is overrun.

Enter another Messenger.

THIRD MESSENGER
My gracious lords, to add to your laments,
Wherewith you now bedew King Henry's hearse,
I must inform you of a dismal fight
Betwixt the stout Lord Talbot and the French.

WINCHESTER
What? Wherein Talbot overcame, is 't so?

THIRD MESSENGER
O, no! Wherein Lord Talbot was o'erthrown.
The circumstance I'll tell you more at large.
The tenth of August last this dreadful lord,
Retiring from the siege of Orleans,
Having full scarce six thousand in his troop,
By three and twenty thousand of the French
Was round encompassed and set upon.
No leisure had he to enrank his men.
He wanted pikes to set before his archers,
Instead whereof sharp stakes pluck'd out of hedges
They pitched in the ground confusedly,
To keep the horsemen off from breaking in.
More than three hours the fight continued,
Where valiant Talbot above human thought
Enacted wonders with his sword and lance.
Hundreds he sent to hell, and none durst stand him;
Here, there, and every where, enrag'd he slew.
The French exclaim'd the devil was in arms;
All the whole army stood agaz'd on him.
His soldiers, spying his undaunted spirit,
"A Talbot, a Talbot!" cried out amain
And rush'd into the bowels of the battle.
Here had the conquest fully been seal'd up
If Sir John Falstaff had not play'd the coward.
He, being in the vaward, plac'd behind
With purpose to relieve and follow them,
Cowardly fled, not having struck one stroke.
Hence grew the general wrack and massacre.
Enclosed were they with their enemies.
A base Walloon, to win the Dauphin's grace,
Thrust Talbot with a spear into the back,
Whom all France with their chief assembled strength
Durst not presume to look once in the face.

BEDFORD
Is Talbot slain? Then I will slay myself
For living idly here in pomp and ease
Whilst such a worthy leader, wanting aid,
Unto his dastard foemen is betray'd.

THIRD MESSENGER
O no, he lives, but is took prisoner,
And Lord Scales with him, and Lord Hungerford;
Most of the rest slaughter'd or took likewise.

BEDFORD
His ransom there is none but I shall pay.
I'll hale the Dauphin headlong from his throne;
His crown shall be the ransom of my friend.
Four of their lords I'll change for one of ours.
Farewell, my masters; to my task will I.
Bonfires in France forthwith I am to make,
To keep our great Saint George's feast withal.
Ten thousand soldiers with me I will take,
Whose bloody deeds shall make all Europe quake.

THIRD MESSENGER
So you had need, for Orleans is besieg'd;
The English army is grown weak and faint;

72 field battle **73 of** about **75 wanteth** lacks **80 flower-de-luces** the *fleurs-de-lis,* or iris, national emblem of France. (According to the Treaty of Troyes, 1420, the crown of France was ceded to England but was nominally to belong to the French king, Charles VI, as long as he lived. Henry V's title was designated "King of England and Heir of France." At his death this title passed to Henry VI; but within two months after this took place, Charles VI died and his son Charles VII was proclaimed king. The loss of the French crown would deprive the English king of the right to display the *fleur-de-lis* in his coat of arms.) **82 wanting** lacking **84 Regent** ruler in the king's absence **87–88 Wounds . . . weep** i.e., I'll make the French shed blood instead of weep tears **88 intermissive** intermittent but now to be resumed **105 dismal** savage, terrible **109 circumstance** particulars. **at large** in full detail

110 dreadful to be dreaded **112 full scarce** scarce full, barely **116 wanted pikes** lacked ironbound stakes, sharpened at the ends and set in the ground in front of archers as protection against cavalry **126 agaz'd on** astounded at **128 amain** with full force **130 seal'd up** completed **131 Falstaff** ("Fastolfe" in the chronicles; but the Shakespearean spelling used here shows us the origin of the name used in the *Henry IV* plays.) **132 vaward** vanguard **136 with** by **137 Walloon** an inhabitant of that province, now a part of southern Belgium **151 change** i.e., kill in exchange **154 Saint George's feast** the twenty-third of April. (St. George was the patron saint of England. To celebrate his day in France would be to assert England's claim to that territory.)

The Earl of Salisbury craveth supply,
And hardly keeps his men from mutiny,
Since they, so few, watch such a multitude. *[Exit.]*

EXETER
Remember, lords, your oaths to Henry sworn,
Either to quell the Dauphin utterly,
Or bring him in obedience to your yoke.

BEDFORD
I do remember it, and here take my leave
To go about my preparation. *Exit Bedford.*

GLOUCESTER
I'll to the Tower with all the haste I can
To view th' artillery and munition,
And then I will proclaim young Henry king.
Exit Gloucester.

EXETER
To Eltham will I, where the young King is,
Being ordain'd his special governor,
And for his safety there I'll best devise. *Exit.*

WINCHESTER
Each hath his place and function to attend.
I am left out; for me nothing remains.
But long I will not be Jack out of office.
The King from Eltham I intend to steal
And sit at chiefest stern of public weal. *Exit.*

[SCENE II]

Sound a flourish. Enter Charles, Alençon, and Reignier, marching with drum and Soldiers.

CHARLES
Mars his true moving, even as in the heavens
So in the earth, to this day is not known.
Late did he shine upon the English side;
Now we are victors, upon us he smiles.
What towns of any moment but we have?
At pleasure here we lie near Orleans;
Otherwhiles the famish'd English, like pale ghosts,
Faintly besiege us one hour in a month.

ALENÇON
They want their porridge and their fat bull-beeves.
Either they must be dieted like mules
And have their provender tied to their mouths,
Or piteous they will look, like drowned mice.

REIGNIER
Let's raise the siege. Why live we idly here?
Talbot is taken, whom we wont to fear.
Remaineth none but mad-brain'd Salisbury,
And he may well in fretting spend his gall—
Nor men nor money hath he to make war.

CHARLES
Sound, sound alarum! We will rush on them.
Now for the honor of the forlorn French!
Him I forgive my death that killeth me
When he sees me go back one foot or fly. *Exeunt.*

Here alarum. They are beaten back by the English with great loss. Enter Charles, Alençon, and Reignier.

CHARLES
Who ever saw the like? What men have I!
Dogs, cowards, dastards! I would ne'er have fled,
But that they left me 'midst my enemies.

REIGNIER
Salisbury is a desperate homicide;
He fighteth as one weary of his life.
The other lords, like lions wanting food,
Do rush upon us as their hungry prey.

ALENÇON
Froissart, a countryman of ours, records
England all Olivers and Rowlands bred
During the time Edward the Third did reign.
More truly now may this be verified,
For none but Samsons and Goliases
It sendeth forth to skirmish. One to ten!
Lean raw-bon'd rascals! Who would e'er suppose
They had such courage and audacity?

CHARLES
Let's leave this town; for they are hare-brain'd slaves,
And hunger will enforce them to be more eager.
Of old I know them. Rather with their teeth
The walls they'll tear down than forsake the siege.

REIGNIER
I think by some odd gimmors or device
Their arms are set, like clocks, still to strike on;
Else ne'er could they hold out so as they do.
By my consent, we'll even let them alone.

ALENÇON
Be it so.

Enter the Bastard of Orleans.

BASTARD
Where's the Prince Dauphin? I have news for him.

CHARLES
Bastard of Orleans, thrice welcome to us.

BASTARD
Methinks your looks are sad, your cheer appall'd.
Hath the late overthrow wrought this offense?
Be not dismay'd, for succor is at hand.

159 supply reinforcements **167 Tower** Tower of London, ancient palace-fortress, later a prison for persons of eminence **170 Eltham** a royal residence southeast of London **175 Jack out of office** i.e., an unimportant fellow with nothing to do **177 at chiefest stern** in the steersman's seat; i.e., in a position of supreme control

I.ii. Location: France. Before Orleans.
1 Mars . . . moving Mars' precise orbit. (The planet's seemingly eccentric orbit was a source of perplexity in Shakespeare's day; here, its influence on earth in human affairs is likewise mysterious. Mars is also the god of war.) **3 Late** lately, recently **5 What . . . have** what towns of any consequence do we not possess **7 Otherwhiles** at times **10 dieted** fed. (The eating of beef, l. 9, was believed to confer courage.) **13 raise the siege** i.e., cause the English to abandon their siege **14 wont** were accustomed

16 spend expend, waste. **gall** i.e., bitterness of spirit **17 Nor** neither **18 alarum** call to arms **28 hungry prey** prey of their hunger **29 Froissart** a fourteenth-century French chronicler who wrote of contemporary events in Flanders, France, Spain, and England **30 Olivers and Rowlands** paladins in the Charlemagne legends, the most famous of the twelve for their daring exploits **33 Samsons, Goliases** (i.e., Goliaths), Biblical characters typifying great physical strength **35 rascals** young, lean, or inferior deer of a herd **41 gimmors** gimmals, joints or connecting parts for transmitting motion **42 still** continually **48 cheer appall'd** countenance made pale

A holy maid hither with me I bring,
Which by a vision sent to her from heaven
Ordained is to raise this tedious siege
And drive the English forth the bounds of France.
The spirit of deep prophecy she hath,
Exceeding the nine sibyls of old Rome. 56
What's past and what's to come she can descry.
Speak, shall I call her in? Believe my words,
For they are certain and unfallible.

CHARLES
Go, call her in. [*Bastard goes to the door.*] But first, to try her skill,
Reignier, stand thou as Dauphin in my place.
Question her proudly, let thy looks be stern.
By this means shall we sound what skill she hath. 63
[*They exchange places.*]

Enter Joan Pucelle, [*the Bastard escorting her*].

REIGNIER
Fair maid, is 't thou wilt do these wondrous feats?

PUCELLE
Reignier, is 't thou that thinkest to beguile me?
Where is the Dauphin? Come, come from behind;
I know thee well, though never seen before.
Be not amaz'd, there's nothing hid from me.
In private will I talk with thee apart.
Stand back, you lords, and give us leave awhile.
[*The lords stand aside.*]

REIGNIER
She takes upon her bravely at first dash. 71

PUCELLE
Dauphin, I am by birth a shepherd's daughter,
My wit untrain'd in any kind of art.
Heaven and our Lady gracious hath it pleas'd
To shine on my contemptible estate.
Lo, whilst I waited on my tender lambs,
And to sun's parching heat display'd my cheeks,
God's mother deigned to appear to me
And in a vision full of majesty
Will'd me to leave my base vocation
And free my country from calamity.
Her aid she promis'd and assur'd success.
In complete glory she reveal'd herself;
And, whereas I was black and swart before, 84
With those clear rays which she infus'd on me
That beauty am I bless'd with which you may see.
Ask me what question thou canst possible,
And I will answer unpremeditated.
My courage try by combat, if thou dar'st,
And thou shalt find that I exceed my sex.
Resolve on this: thou shalt be fortunate 91
If thou receive me for thy warlike mate. 92

CHARLES
Thou hast astonish'd me with thy high terms. 93
Only this proof I'll of thy valor make: 94
In single combat thou shalt buckle with me, 95
And if thou vanquishest, thy words are true.
Otherwise I renounce all confidence. 97

PUCELLE
I am prepar'd. Here is my keen-edg'd sword,
Deck'd with five flower-de-luces on each side,
The which at Touraine, in Saint Katharine's churchyard,
Out of a great deal of old iron I chose forth.

CHARLES
Then come, a' God's name! I fear no woman. 102

PUCELLE
And while I live, I'll ne'er fly from a man.
Here they fight, and Joan la Pucelle overcomes.

CHARLES
Stay, stay thy hands! Thou art an Amazon
And fightest with the sword of Deborah. 105

PUCELLE
Christ's mother helps me, else I were too weak.

CHARLES
Whoe'er helps thee, 'tis thou that must help me!
Impatiently I burn with thy desire; 108
My heart and hands thou hast at once subdu'd.
Excellent Pucelle, if thy name be so,
Let me thy servant and not sovereign be.
'Tis the French Dauphin sueth to thee thus.

PUCELLE
I must not yield to any rites of love,
For my profession 's sacred from above.
When I have chased all thy foes from hence,
Then will I think upon a recompense.

CHARLES
Meantime, look gracious on thy prostrate thrall.

REIGNIER [*To Alençon*]
My lord, methinks, is very long in talk.

ALENÇON
Doubtless he shrives this woman to her smock; 119
Else ne'er could he so long protract his speech.

REIGNIER
Shall we disturb him, since he keeps no mean? 121

ALENÇON
He may mean more than we poor men do know.
These women are shrewd tempters with their tongues.

REIGNIER [*To Charles*]
My lord, where are you? What devise you on? 124
Shall we give o'er Orleans, or no?

PUCELLE
Why, no, I say, distrustful recreants! 126
Fight till the last gasp. I'll be your guard.

CHARLES
What she says I'll confirm. We'll fight it out.

PUCELLE
Assign'd am I to be the English scourge.

56 nine . . . Rome inspired women of the ancient world. (Not only of Rome, however; the phrase here is probably owing to a confusion with the Cumaean sibyl who came to Tarquin with nine prophetic books.) **63 sound** test, determine **63 s.d. Pucelle** virgin **71 takes . . . bravely** plays her part well **84 black and swart** i.e., heavily tanned **91 Resolve on** be sure of **92 warlike mate** (with sexual suggestion, as in the military terms throughout this interview) **93 high** lofty **94 proof** trial, test

95 buckle join in close combat (with bawdy suggestion) **97 confidence** (1) trust in your speech (2) intimacy **102 a'** in **105 Deborah** Hebrew prophetess who "judged" Israel in the fourteenth century B.C. (She led an army against the Canaanite oppressors, whom she overcame; Judges 4, 5.) **108 thy desire** desire for you **119 shrives** hears confession, i.e., examines. **to her smock** to her undergarment, i.e., completely (with bawdy suggestion) **121 keeps no mean** observes no middle position, is immoderate **124 devise** decide **126 recreants** cowards

This night the siege assuredly I'll raise.
Expect Saint Martin's summer, halcyon days,
Since I have entered into these wars.
Glory is like a circle in the water,
Which never ceaseth to enlarge itself
Till by broad spreading it disperse to nought.
With Henry's death the English circle ends;
Dispersed are the glories it included.
Now am I like that proud insulting ship
Which Caesar and his fortune bare at once.

CHARLES
Was Mahomet inspired with a dove?
Thou with an eagle art inspired then.
Helen, the mother of great Constantine,
Nor yet Saint Philip's daughters, were like thee.
Bright star of Venus, fall'n down on the earth,
How may I reverently worship thee enough?

ALENÇON
Leave off delays, and let us raise the siege.

REIGNIER
Woman, do what thou canst to save our honors.
Drive them from Orleans and be immortaliz'd.

CHARLES
Presently we'll try. Come, let's away about it.
No prophet will I trust, if she prove false. *Exeunt.*

[SCENE III]

Enter [*the Duke of*] *Gloucester, with his Servingmen* [*in blue coats*].

GLOUCESTER
I am come to survey the Tower this day.
Since Henry's death, I fear, there is conveyance.
Where be these warders, that they wait not here?
Open the gates! 'Tis Gloucester that calls.

FIRST WARDER [*Within*]
Who's there that knocks so imperiously?

FIRST SERVINGMAN
It is the noble Duke of Gloucester.

SECOND WARDER [*Within*]
Whoe'er he be, you may not be let in.

FIRST SERVINGMAN
Villains, answer you so the Lord Protector?

FIRST WARDER [*Within*]
The Lord protect him! So we answer him.
We do no otherwise than we are will'd.

GLOUCESTER
Who willed you? Or whose will stands but mine?
There's none Protector of the realm but I.—
Break up the gates, I'll be your warrantize.
Shall I be flouted thus by dunghill grooms?

Gloucester's men rush at the Tower Gates, and Woodville the Lieutenant speaks within.

WOODVILLE
What noise is this? What traitors have we here?

GLOUCESTER
Lieutenant, is it you whose voice I hear?
Open the gates. Here's Gloucester that would enter.

WOODVILLE
Have patience, noble Duke. I may not open;
The Cardinal of Winchester forbids.
From him I have express commandement
That thou nor none of thine shall be let in.

GLOUCESTER
Faint-hearted Woodville, prizest him 'fore me?
Arrogant Winchester, that haughty prelate,
Whom Henry, our late sovereign, ne'er could brook?
Thou art no friend to God or to the King.
Open the gates, or I'll shut thee out shortly.

SERVINGMEN
Open the gates unto the Lord Protector,
Or we'll burst them open, if that you come not quickly.

Enter to the Protector at the Tower Gates Winchester and his men in tawny coats.

WINCHESTER
How now, ambitious Humphrey, what means this?

GLOUCESTER
Peel'd priest, dost thou command me to be shut out?

WINCHESTER
I do, thou most usurping proditor,
And not Protector, of the king or realm.

GLOUCESTER
Stand back, thou manifest conspirator,
Thou that contrivedst to murder our dead lord,
Thou that giv'st whores indulgences to sin.
I'll canvass thee in thy broad cardinal's hat,
If thou proceed in this thy insolence.

WINCHESTER
Nay, stand thou back. I will not budge a foot.
This be Damascus, be thou cursed Cain,
To slay thy brother Abel, if thou wilt.

GLOUCESTER
I will not slay thee, but I'll drive thee back.
Thy scarlet robes as a child's bearing-cloth
I'll use to carry thee out of this place.

WINCHESTER
Do what thou dar'st! I beard thee to thy face.

131 Saint Martin's summer i.e., Indian summer; St. Martin's Day is November 11. **halcyon days** i.e., unseasonable calm. (The halcyon is the kingfisher, which, according to fable, nested at midwinter on the seas, which became calm for that purpose.) **138–139 Now . . . once** (North's translation of Plutarch relates how Caesar, encountering a storm at sea, said to the mariners, "Fear not, for thou hast Caesar and his fortune with thee.") **140 Was . . . dove** (Mohammed supposedly claimed that he received divine inspiration from a dove whispering in his ear.) **142 Helen** mother of the Emperor Constantine and supposed discoverer of the holy cross and sepulcher of the Lord **143 Saint Philip's daughters** the four daughters of Philip the Evangelist, said in Acts 21:9 to have the power of prophecy **149 Presently** immediately

I.iii. Location: London. Before the Tower.
s.d. blue coats (Customarily worn by servingmen.) **1 survey** inspect **2 conveyance** trickery **10 will'd** commanded

13 warrantize guarantee **14 s.d. rush . . . Gates** (Gloucester's men assault the facade of the tiring house wall backstage, which represents the Tower Gates; Woodville and the warders are "within," or behind that wall, invisible to the audience.) **24 brook** endure **26 I'll . . . shortly** i.e., I'll take possession and shut you out **28 s.d. tawny coats** (Customarily worn by attendants of a mighty churchman.) **30 Peel'd** shaven, tonsured **31 proditor** traitor **34–35 Thou . . . sin** (Gloucester, in his bill of particulars against Winchester, charged that the cleric had suborned someone to attempt the murder of Henry V. Here he refers also to the fact that Winchester collected revenues from houses of prostitution on the south bank of the Thames.) **36 canvass** i.e., deal with severely. (The metaphor is that of tossing someone in a canvas or blanket as sport or punishment.) **39 Damascus** a city reputed to have been built on the site of Cain's slaying of Abel **40 thy brother** (Winchester was Gloucester's half-uncle.) **42 bearing-cloth** christening robe **44 beard** openly defy

GLOUCESTER
What, am I dar'd and bearded to my face?
Draw, men, for all this privileged place— 46
Blue coats to tawny coats. Priest, beware your beard.
I mean to tug it and to cuff you soundly.
Under my feet I stamp thy cardinal's hat.
In spite of Pope or dignities of church, 50
Here by the cheeks I'll drag thee up and down.

WINCHESTER
Gloucester, thou wilt answer this before the Pope. 52

GLOUCESTER
Winchester goose, I cry, a rope, a rope! 53
Now beat them hence. Why do you let them stay?
Thee I'll chase hence, thou wolf in sheep's array.
Out, tawny coats! Out, scarlet hypocrite!

Here Gloucester's men beat out the Cardinal's men, and enter in the hurly-burly the Mayor of London and his Officers.

MAYOR
Fie, lords, that you, being supreme magistrates,
Thus contumeliously should break the peace! 58

GLOUCESTER
Peace, Mayor! Thou know'st little of my wrongs.
Here's Beaufort, that regards nor God nor king,
Hath here distrain'd the Tower to his use. 61

WINCHESTER
Here's Gloucester, a foe to citizens,
One that still motions war and never peace, 63
O'ercharging your free purses with large fines, 64
That seeks to overthrow religion
Because he is Protector of the realm,
And would have armor here out of the Tower,
To crown himself king and suppress the Prince. 68

GLOUCESTER
I will not answer thee with words, but blows.
Here they skirmish again.

MAYOR
Nought rests for me in this tumultuous strife
But to make open proclamation.
Come, officer, as loud as e'er thou canst,
Cry.

[OFFICER] All manner of men assembled here in arms this day against God's peace and the King's, we charge and command you, in his Highness' name, to repair to your several dwelling-places, and not to wear, handle, or use any sword, weapon, or dagger, henceforward, upon pain of death. 79

GLOUCESTER
Cardinal, I'll be no breaker of the law;
But we shall meet, and break our minds at large. 81

WINCHESTER
Gloucester, we'll meet to thy cost, be sure.
Thy heart-blood I will have for this day's work.

MAYOR
I'll call for clubs, if you will not away. 84
This cardinal's more haughty than the devil.

GLOUCESTER
Mayor, farewell. Thou dost but what thou mayst.

WINCHESTER
Abominable Gloucester, guard thy head;
For I intend to have it ere long.
Exeunt, [severally, Gloucester and Winchester with their Servingmen].

MAYOR
See the coast clear'd, and then we will depart.
Good God, these nobles should such stomachs bear! 90
I myself fight not once in forty year. *Exeunt.*

[SCENE IV]

Enter the Master Gunner of Orleans and his Boy.

MASTER GUNNER
Sirrah, thou know'st how Orleans is besieg'd, 1
And how the English have the suburbs won.

BOY
Father, I know, and oft have shot at them,
Howe'er unfortunate I miss'd my aim.

MASTER GUNNER
But now thou shalt not. Be thou rul'd by me.
Chief master-gunner am I of this town;
Something I must do to procure me grace. 7
The Prince's espials have informed me 8
How the English, in the suburbs close intrench'd,
Wont through a secret grate of iron bars 10
In yonder tower to overpeer the city,
And thence discover how with most advantage
They may vex us with shot or with assault.
To intercept this inconvenience, 14
A piece of ordnance 'gainst it I have plac'd, 15
And even these three days have I watch'd,
If I could see them.
Now do thou watch, for I can stay no longer.
If thou spy'st any, run and bring me word,
And thou shalt find me at the governor's. *Exit.*

BOY
Father, I warrant you; take you no care.
I'll never trouble you, if I may spy them. *Exit.* 22

Enter Salisbury and Talbot on the turrets, with [Sir William Glansdale, Sir Thomas Gargrave, and] others.

SALISBURY
Talbot, my life, my joy, again return'd?
How wert thou handled being prisoner?
Or by what means gots thou to be releas'd? 25

46 privileged place (The Tower, as a royal residence, was one of the precincts where drawing of weapons was forbidden by the law of arms; cf. II.iv.86, note.) **50 dignities** dignitaries **52 answer** render an account of, pay for **53 Winchester goose** (Slang for a symptom of venereal disease.) **58 contumeliously** arrogantly, contemptuously **61 distrain'd** confiscated **63 still motions** incessantly advocates **64 O'ercharging . . . purses** overburdening you with excessive taxation **68 Prince** i.e., Henry VI **79 pain** punishment **81 break our minds** (1) reveal our purposes (2) crack our heads. **at large** at length

84 call for clubs i.e., sound the rallying cry for London apprentices armed with clubs **90 stomachs** i.e., angry tempers

I.iv. Location: France. Orleans.
1 Sirrah (Customary form of address to an inferior.) **7 grace** honor, credit **8 espials** spies **10 Wont** are accustomed **14 inconvenience** mischief **15 'gainst** directed toward **22 s.d. turrets** i.e., some high point of vantage in the theatre, above the main stage **25 gots** gottest

Discourse, I prithee, on this turret's top.

TALBOT

The Duke of Bedford had a prisoner
Call'd the brave Lord Ponton de Santrailles;
For him was I exchang'd and ransomed.
But with a baser man of arms by far 30
Once in contempt they would have barter'd me;
Which I disdaining scorn'd, and craved death
Rather than I would be so pill'd esteem'd. 33
In fine, redeem'd I was as I desir'd. 34
But O, the treacherous Falstaff wounds my heart,
Whom with my bare fists I would execute
If I now had him brought into my power.

SALISBURY

Yet tell'st thou not how thou wert entertain'd. 38

TALBOT

With scoffs and scorns and contumelious taunts.
In open market-place produc'd they me
To be a public spectacle to all.
Here, said they, is the terror of the French,
The scarecrow that affrights our children so.
Then broke I from the officers that led me,
And with my nails digg'd stones out of the ground
To hurl at the beholders of my shame.
My grisly countenance made others fly;
None durst come near for fear of sudden death.
In iron walls they deem'd me not secure;
So great fear of my name 'mongst them were spread
That they suppos'd I could rend bars of steel
And spurn in pieces posts of adamant. 52
Wherefore a guard of chosen shot I had 53
That walk'd about me every minute while; 54
And if I did but stir out of my bed,
Ready they were to shoot me to the heart. 56

Enter the Boy with a linstock.

SALISBURY

I grieve to hear what torments you endur'd.
But we will be reveng'd sufficiently.
Now it is supper time in Orleans.
Here, through this grate, I count each one
And view the Frenchmen how they fortify.
Let us look in; the sight will much delight thee.
Sir Thomas Gargrave, and Sir William Glansdale,
Let me have your express opinions 64
Where is best place to make our batt'ry next.

GARGRAVE

I think, at the north gate; for there stands lords.

GLANSDALE

And I, here, at the bulwark of the bridge.

TALBOT

For aught I see, this city must be famish'd, 68
Or with light skirmishes enfeebled. 69

Here they shoot, and Salisbury falls down [together with Gargrave].

SALISBURY

O Lord, have mercy on us, wretched sinners!

GARGRAVE

O Lord, have mercy on me, woeful man!

TALBOT

What chance is this that suddenly hath cross'd us?
Speak, Salisbury; at least, if thou canst, speak.
How far'st thou, mirror of all martial men? 74
One of thy eyes and thy cheek's side struck off!
Accursed tower! Accursed fatal hand
That hath contriv'd this woeful tragedy!
In thirteen battles Salisbury o'ercame;
Henry the Fifth he first train'd to the wars;
Whilst any trump did sound, or drum struck up,
His sword did ne'er leave striking in the field.
Yet liv'st thou, Salisbury? Though thy speech doth fail,
One eye thou hast to look to heaven for grace.
The sun with one eye vieweth all the world.
Heaven, be thou gracious to none alive,
If Salisbury wants mercy at thy hands! 86
Bear hence his body; I will help to bury it.
Sir Thomas Gargrave, hast thou any life?
Speak unto Talbot; nay, look up to him.
Salisbury, cheer thy spirit with this comfort;
Thou shalt not die whiles—
He beckons with his hand and smiles on me,
As who should say "When I am dead and gone,
Remember to avenge me on the French."
Plantagenet, I will; and like thee, 95
Play on the lute, beholding the towns burn.
Wretched shall France be only in my name. 97

Here an alarum, and it thunders and lightens.

What stir is this? What tumult 's in the heavens?
Whence cometh this alarum and the noise?

Enter a Messenger.

MESSENGER

My lord, my lord, the French have gather'd head! 100
The Dauphin, with one Joan la Pucelle join'd,
A holy prophetess new risen up,
Is come with a great power to raise the siege. 103

Here Salisbury lifteth himself up and groans.

TALBOT

Hear, hear how dying Salisbury doth groan!
It irks his heart he cannot be reveng'd.
Frenchmen, I'll be a Salisbury to you.
Pucelle or puzzel, dolphin or dogfish, 107
Your hearts I'll stamp out with my horse's heels,
And make a quagmire of your mingled brains.
Convey me Salisbury into his tent, 110
And then we'll try what these dastard Frenchmen dare. *Alarum. Exeunt, [bearing out the bodies].*

30 baser of lower rank **33 pill'd** peeled, i.e., despoiled of honor **34 In fine** finally. **redeem'd** ransomed **38 entertain'd** treated **52 spurn** kick **53 chosen shot** carefully selected marksmen **54 every minute while** i.e., constantly **56 s.d. linstock** forked stick used to hold a lighted match for firing cannon **64 express** precise **68 famish'd** reduced to famine **69 s.d. Here they shoot** i.e., the French. (Probably offstage.)

74 mirror example **86 wants** lacks **95 Plantagenet** (The Earl of Salisbury was Thomas Montacute; he was descended from the Plantagenet Edward I.) **like thee** (Salisbury is being compared to Nero, who played music while Rome burned.) **97 only in** at the mere sound of **100 gather'd head** drawn their forces together **103 power** army **107 puzzel** drab, slut (with pun on *pucelle,* maid). **dolphin** (The normal Folio Elizabethan spelling of *Dauphin;* with a pun on *dogfish.*) **110 me** for my benefit. (The ethical dative.)

[SCENE V]

Here an alarum again, and Talbot pursueth the Dauphin, and driveth him. Then enter Joan la Pucelle, driving Englishmen before her [and exit after them]. Then [re-]enter Talbot.

TALBOT
Where is my strength, my valor, and my force?
Our English troops retire, I cannot stay them;
A woman clad in armor chaseth them.

Enter Pucelle.

Here, here she comes. I'll have a bout with thee;
Devil or devil's dam, I'll conjure thee.
Blood will I draw on thee—thou art a witch—
And straightway give thy soul to him thou serv'st.

PUCELLE
Come, come, 'tis only I that must disgrace thee.
Here they fight.

TALBOT
Heavens, can you suffer hell so to prevail?
My breast I'll burst with straining of my courage
And from my shoulders crack my arms asunder,
But I will chastise this high-minded strumpet.
They fight again.

PUCELLE
Talbot, farewell; thy hour is not yet come.
I must go victual Orleans forthwith.

A short alarum. Then enter the town with Soldiers.

O'ertake me, if thou canst! I scorn thy strength.
Go, go, cheer up thy hungry-starved men;
Help Salisbury to make his testament.
This day is ours, as many more shall be. *Exit.*

TALBOT
My thoughts are whirled like a potter's wheel;
I know not where I am, nor what I do.
A witch, by fear, not force, like Hannibal,
Drives back our troops and conquers as she lists.
So bees with smoke and doves with noisome stench
Are from their hives and houses driven away.
They call'd us, for our fierceness, English dogs;
Now, like to whelps, we crying run away.
A short alarum.
Hark, countrymen! Either renew the fight,
Or tear the lions out of England's coat,
Renounce your soil, give sheep in lions' stead.
Sheep run not half so treacherous from the wolf,
Or horse or oxen from the leopard,
As you fly from your oft-subdued slaves.
Alarum. Here another skirmish.
It will not be. Retire into your trenches.
You all consented unto Salisbury's death,
For none would strike a stroke in his revenge.
Pucelle is ent'red into Orleans
In spite of us or aught that we could do.
O, would I were to die with Salisbury!
The shame hereof will make me hide my head.
Exit Talbot. Alarum; retreat.

[SCENE VI]

Flourish. Enter, on the walls, Pucelle, Dauphin [Charles], Reignier, Alençon, and Soldiers.

PUCELLE
Advance our waving colors on the walls;
Rescu'd is Orleans from the English!
Thus Joan la Pucelle hath perform'd her word.

CHARLES
Divinest creature, Astraea's daughter,
How shall I honor thee for this success?
Thy promises are like Adonis' garden,
That one day bloom'd and fruitful were the next.
France, triumph in thy glorious prophetess!
Recover'd is the town of Orleans.
More blessed hap did ne'er befall our state.

REIGNIER
Why ring not out the bells aloud throughout the town?
Dauphin, command the citizens make bonfires
And feast and banquet in the open streets
To celebrate the joy that God hath given us.

ALENÇON
All France will be replete with mirth and joy
When they shall hear how we have play'd the men.

CHARLES
'Tis Joan, not we, by whom the day is won;
For which I will divide my crown with her,
And all the priests and friars in my realm
Shall in procession sing her endless praise.
A statelier pyramis to her I'll rear
Than Rhodope's of Memphis ever was.
In memory of her when she is dead,
Her ashes, in an urn more precious
Than the rich-jewel'd coffer of Darius,
Transported shall be at high festivals
Before the kings and queens of France.
No longer on Saint Denis will we cry,

I.v. Location: Scene continues at Orleans.
5 dam dame, mother **6 Blood . . . witch** (Anyone who succeeded in drawing blood from a witch was thought to be invulnerable to her magic.) **7 him** i.e., the devil **12 But I will** if I do not. **high-minded** arrogant **14 victual** supply with provisions **14 s.d. enter** i.e., they, the French, enter Orleans; Joan follows four lines later **21 Hannibal** Carthaginian general who once repulsed a Roman army by tying firebrands to the horns of a herd of oxen and driving the animals toward the Romans **22 lists** pleases **28 lions . . . coat** i.e., the three lions passant displayed in the English coat of arms **29 soil** country. **give** display (on coat of arms) **30 treacherous** i.e., cowardly

35 his revenge revenge of him **39 s.d. retreat** trumpet call to signal a retreat

I.vi. Location: Scene continues at Orleans.
s.d. on the walls i.e., in the gallery backstage, above the main doors of the tiring house façade. (When Joan enters Orleans in I.v., she enters the tiring house through one of its doors, and that tiring house façade remains the visual equivalent of the walls of Orleans through II.i.) **1 Advance** lift up **4 Astraea** goddess of Justice **6 Adonis' garden** mythical garden of eternal fecundity **21 pyramis** pyramid **22 Rhodope** a Greek courtesan who became the wife of the King of Egypt. (A legend was current that she built the third pyramid.) **Memphis** an ancient city of Egypt near which stand the pyramids of Ramses II **25 Darius** King of Persia conquered by Alexander the Great, who, according to legend, used Darius' *rich-jewel'd coffer* to carry about the poems of Homer **28 Saint Denis** patron saint of France

But Joan la Pucelle shall be France's saint.
Come in, and let us banquet royally,
After this golden day of victory. *Flourish. Exeunt.*

ACT II • SCENE I

Enter a [French] Sergeant of a band, with two Sentinels.

SERGEANT
Sirs, take your places and be vigilant.
If any noise or soldier you perceive
Near to the walls, by some apparent sign 3
Let us have knowledge at the court of guard. 4

FIRST SENTINEL
Sergeant, you shall. [*Exit Sergeant.*] Thus are poor servitors,
When others sleep upon their quiet beds,
Constrain'd to watch in darkness, rain, and cold. 7

Enter Talbot, Bedford, and Burgundy, [and forces,] with scaling-ladders.

TALBOT
Lord Regent, and redoubted Burgundy,
By whose approach the regions of Artois,
Wallon, and Picardy are friends to us,
This happy night the Frenchmen are secure, 11
Having all day carous'd and banqueted.
Embrace we then this opportunity
As fitting best to quittance their deceit 14
Contriv'd by art and baleful sorcery. 15

BEDFORD
Coward of France, how much he wrongs his fame, 16
Despairing of his own arm's fortitude,
To join with witches and the help of hell!

BURGUNDY
Traitors have never other company.
But what's that Pucelle whom they term so pure?

TALBOT
A maid, they say.

BEDFORD
A maid, and be so martial?

BURGUNDY
Pray God she prove not masculine ere long, 22
If underneath the standard of the French
She carry armor as she hath begun.

TALBOT
Well, let them practice and converse with spirits.
God is our fortress, in whose conquering name
Let us resolve to scale their flinty bulwarks.

BEDFORD
Ascend, brave Talbot. We will follow thee.

TALBOT
Not all together. Better far, I guess,
That we do make our entrance several ways; 30
That, if it chance the one of us do fail,
The other yet may rise against their force.

BEDFORD
Agreed. I'll to yond corner.

BURGUNDY
And I to this.

TALBOT
And here will Talbot mount, or make his grave.
Now, Salisbury, for thee, and for the right
Of English Henry, shall this night appear
How much in duty I am bound to both.

FIRST SENTINEL
Arm, arm! The enemy doth make assault! 38
[*The English scale the walls, Talbot in the center.*]
Cry: "Saint George! A Talbot!"

The French leap o'er the walls in their shirts. Enter, several ways, [the] Bastard [of Orleans], Alençon, [and] Reignier, half ready, and half unready.

ALENÇON
How now, my lords? What, all unready so?

BASTARD
Unready? Ay, and glad we scap'd so well.

REIGNIER
'Twas time, I trow, to wake and leave our beds, 41
Hearing alarums at our chamber-doors.

ALENÇON
Of all exploits since first I follow'd arms,
Ne'er heard I of a warlike enterprise
More venturous or desperate than this.

BASTARD
I think this Talbot be a fiend of hell.

REIGNIER
If not of hell, the heavens sure favor him.

ALENÇON
Here cometh Charles. I marvel how he sped. 48

Enter Charles and Joan [la Pucelle].

BASTARD
Tut, holy Joan was his defensive guard.

CHARLES
Is this thy cunning, thou deceitful dame? 50
Didst thou at first, to flatter us withal, 51
Make us partakers of a little gain
That now our loss might be ten times so much?

PUCELLE
Wherefore is Charles impatient with his friend?
At all times will you have my power alike?
Sleeping or waking must I still prevail,
Or will you blame and lay the fault on me?
Improvident soldiers! Had your watch been good,
This sudden mischief never could have fall'n.

II.i. Location: Before Orleans, as in the previous scenes; the time is later that night. **3 apparent** plain **4 court of guard** guard house **7 s.d. Burgundy** the Duke of Burgundy, allied to the English by the Treaty of Troyes, 1420. (His support brought with it the cooperation of territories near to Burgundy, in the Low Countries, such as Wallon and Picardy.) **11 secure** overconfident **14 quittance** requite **15 art** i.e., black magic **16 Coward of France** i.e., the Dauphin. **fame** reputation **22 prove not masculine** i.e., turn out to be carrying a male child. (The bawdy punning continues in *standard,* "that which stands up," *carry armor,* "bear the weight of a man," *practice and converse,* "engage in sexual contact," etc.)

30 several ways i.e., on ladders at different points. (The three leaders place their ladders against the tiring house façade, one in the middle for Talbot and one on each wing, and actually ascend to the gallery or top of the "walls" where they surprise the French. Some of the French, thus surprised, leap from the gallery down onto the main stage, where the Bastard, Alençon, and others consult in a state of disorder about their situation.) **38 s.d. unready** not fully clothed. (This scene is based on an incident occurring at Le Mans, a year prior to the siege of Orleans.) **41 trow** believe **48 sped** fared **50 cunning** skill **51 flatter** i.e., with false hopes

CHARLES
Duke of Alençon, this was your default,
That, being captain of the watch tonight,
Did look no better to that weighty charge.

ALENÇON
Had all your quarters been as safely kept
As that whereof I had the government,
We had not been thus shamefully surpris'd.

BASTARD
Mine was secure.

REIGNIER
And so was mine, my lord.

CHARLES
And, for myself, most part of all this night
Within her quarter and mine own precinct
I was employ'd in passing to and fro,
About relieving of the sentinels.
Then how or which way should they first break in?

PUCELLE
Question, my lords, no further of the case,
How or which way. 'Tis sure they found some place
But weakly guarded, where the breach was made.
And now there rests no other shift but this:
To gather our soldiers, scatter'd and dispers'd,
And lay new platforms to endamage them.

Alarum. Enter a[*n English*] *Soldier, crying "A Talbot! A Talbot!" They fly, leaving their clothes behind.*

SOLDIER
I'll be so bold to take what they have left.
The cry of Talbot serves me for a sword,
For I have loaden me with many spoils,
Using no other weapon but his name.
Exit, [*bearing spoils*].

[SCENE II]

Enter Talbot, Bedford, Burgundy, [*a Captain, and others*]*, their drums beating a dead march.*

BEDFORD
The day begins to break, and night is fled,
Whose pitchy mantle overveil'd the earth.
Here sound retreat, and cease our hot pursuit.
Retreat [*sounded*].

TALBOT
Bring forth the body of old Salisbury,
And here advance it in the market-place,
The middle center of this cursed town.
[*Salisbury's body is borne in.*]
Now have I paid my vow unto his soul;
For every drop of blood was drawn from him
There hath at least five Frenchmen died tonight.
And that hereafter ages may behold
What ruin happened in revenge of him,
Within their chiefest temple I'll erect
A tomb, wherein his corpse shall be interr'd;
Upon the which, that everyone may read,
Shall be engrav'd the sack of Orleans,
The treacherous manner of his mournful death,
And what a terror he had been to France.
But, lords, in all our bloody massacre,
I muse we met not with the Dauphin's grace,
His new-come champion, virtuous Joan of Arc,
Nor any of his false confederates.

BEDFORD
'Tis thought, Lord Talbot, when the fight began,
Rous'd on the sudden from their drowsy beds,
They did amongst the troops of armed men
Leap o'er the walls for refuge in the field.

BURGUNDY
Myself, as far as I could well discern
For smoke and dusky vapors of the night,
Am sure I scar'd the Dauphin and his trull,
When arm in arm they both came swiftly running,
Like to a pair of loving turtle-doves
That could not live asunder day or night.
After that things are set in order here,
We'll follow them with all the power we have.

Enter a Messenger.

MESSENGER
All hail, my lords! Which of this princely train
Call ye the warlike Talbot, for his acts
So much applauded through the realm of France?

TALBOT
Here is the Talbot. Who would speak with him?

MESSENGER
The virtuous lady, Countess of Auvergne,
With modesty admiring thy renown,
By me entreats, great lord, thou wouldst vouchsafe
To visit her poor castle where she lies,
That she may boast she hath beheld the man
Whose glory fills the world with loud report.

BURGUNDY
Is it even so? Nay, then, I see our wars
Will turn unto a peaceful comic sport,
When ladies crave to be encount'red with.
You may not, my lord, despise her gentle suit.

TALBOT
Ne'er trust me then; for when a world of men
Could not prevail with all their oratory,
Yet hath a woman's kindness overrul'd;
And therefore tell her I return great thanks,
And in submission will attend on her.
Will not your honors bear me company?

BEDFORD
No, truly, 'tis more than manners will;
And I have heard it said, unbidden guests
Are often welcomest when they are gone.

61 tonight i.e., this previous night **68 her** i.e., Joan's (with a bawdy suggestion, continued in *passing to and fro,* l. 69) **75 rests** remains. **shift** strategy **77 platforms** plans

II.ii. Location: Orleans. Within the town.
5 advance raise aloft (on a bier) **8 was** that was

19 muse wonder **20 virtuous** (Said ironically.) **28 trull** strumpet (i.e., Joan) **41 lies** dwells **43 report** (1) acclaim (2) noise of battle **54 will** require, allow

TALBOT
Well then, alone, since there's no remedy,
I mean to prove this lady's courtesy.
Come hither, captain. *(Whispers.)* You perceive my mind?

CAPTAIN
I do, my lord, and mean accordingly. *Exeunt.*

[SCENE III]

Enter [the] Countess [and her Porter].

COUNTESS
Porter, remember what I gave in charge,
And when you have done so, bring the keys to me.

PORTER
Madam, I will. *Exit.*

COUNTESS
The plot is laid. If all things fall out right,
I shall as famous be by this exploit
As Scythian Tomyris by Cyrus' death.
Great is the rumor of this dreadful knight,
And his achievements of no less account.
Fain would mine eyes be witness with mine ears,
To give their censure of these rare reports.

Enter Messenger and Talbot.

MESSENGER
Madam,
According as your ladyship desir'd,
By message crav'd, so is Lord Talbot come.

COUNTESS
And he is welcome. What? Is this the man?

MESSENGER
Madam, it is.

COUNTESS Is this the scourge of France?
Is this the Talbot, so much fear'd abroad
That with his name the mothers still their babes?
I see report is fabulous and false.
I thought I should have seen some Hercules,
A second Hector, for his grim aspect
And large proportion of his strong-knit limbs.
Alas, this is a child, a silly dwarf!
It cannot be this weak and writhled shrimp
Should strike such terror to his enemies.

TALBOT
Madam, I have been bold to trouble you;
But since your ladyship is not at leisure,
I'll sort some other time to visit you. *[Going.]*

COUNTESS
What means he now? Go ask him whither he goes.

MESSENGER
Stay, my Lord Talbot, for my lady craves
To know the cause of your abrupt departure.

TALBOT
Marry, for that she's in a wrong belief,
I go to certify her Talbot's here.

Enter Porter with keys.

COUNTESS
If thou be he, then art thou prisoner.

TALBOT
Prisoner? To whom?

COUNTESS To me, blood-thirsty lord;
And for that cause I train'd thee to my house.
Long time thy shadow hath been thrall to me,
For in my gallery thy picture hangs;
But now the substance shall endure the like,
And I will chain these legs and arms of thine,
That hast by tyranny these many years
Wasted our country, slain our citizens,
And sent our sons and husbands captivate.

TALBOT
Ha, ha, ha!

COUNTESS
Laughest thou, wretch? Thy mirth shall turn to moan.

TALBOT
I laugh to see your ladyship so fond
To think that you have aught but Talbot's shadow
Whereon to practice your severity.

COUNTESS
Why, art not thou the man?

TALBOT I am indeed.

COUNTESS
Then have I substance too.

TALBOT
No, no, I am but shadow of myself.
You are deceiv'd, my substance is not here;
For what you see is but the smallest part
And least proportion of humanity.
I tell you, madam, were the whole frame here,
It is of such a spacious lofty pitch
Your roof were not sufficient to contain 't.

COUNTESS
This is a riddling merchant for the nonce!
He will be here, and yet he is not here.
How can these contrarieties agree?

TALBOT
That will I show you presently.

Winds his horn. Drums strike up. A peal of ordnance. Enter Soldiers.

How say you, madam? Are you now persuaded
That Talbot is but shadow of himself?
These are his substance, sinews, arms, and strength,
With which he yoketh your rebellious necks,
Razeth your cities, and subverts your towns,
And in a moment makes them desolate.

58 prove test **60 mean** i.e., intend to act

II.iii. Location: Auvergne. The Countess' castle.
1 gave in charge commanded **6 Scythian Tomyris** tribal queen of the Massagetae, who slew Cyrus the Great when he invaded her territory and, in revenge for her son's death, had the head of Cyrus placed in a wineskin filled with blood **7 dreadful** inspiring dread **10 censure** judgment. **rare** remarkable **16 abroad** everywhere **17 still** quiet **19–20 Hercules, Hector** (Types of great physical strength.) **21 proportion** size **22 silly** i.e., frail, mere **23 writhled** wrinkled **27 sort** choose

31 Marry (A mild interjection.) **for that** because **35 train'd** lured, enticed **36 shadow** image, likeness. **thrall** enslaved **42 captivate** taken captive **45 fond** foolish **53 proportion of humanity** (1) part of the whole man (2) portion of my army **54 frame** structure, construct, i.e., of man and of the army **55 pitch** height **57 riddling merchant** dealer in riddles. **nonce** occasion **60 presently** immediately **60 s.d. Winds** sounds **65 subverts** overthrows

COUNTESS
Victorious Talbot, pardon my abuse.
I find thou art no less than fame hath bruited
And more than may be gathered by thy shape.
Let my presumption not provoke thy wrath,
For I am sorry that with reverence
I did not entertain thee as thou art.

TALBOT
Be not dismay'd, fair lady, nor misconster
The mind of Talbot, as you did mistake
The outward composition of his body.
What you have done hath not offended me;
Nor other satisfaction do I crave
But only, with your patience, that we may
Taste of your wine and see what cates you have;
For soldiers' stomachs always serve them well.

COUNTESS
With all my heart, and think me honored
To feast so great a warrior in my house. *Exeunt.*

[SCENE IV]

Enter Richard Plantagenet, Warwick, Somerset, [William de la] Pole [Earl of Suffolk, Vernon], and others [including a Lawyer].

PLANTAGENET
Great lords and gentlemen, what means this silence?
Dare no man answer in a case of truth?

SUFFOLK
Within the Temple hall we were too loud.
The garden here is more convenient.

PLANTAGENET
Then say at once if I maintain'd the truth;
Or else was wrangling Somerset in th' error?

SUFFOLK
Faith, I have been a truant in the law,
And never yet could frame my will to it,
And therefore frame the law unto my will.

SOMERSET
Judge you, my Lord of Warwick, then, between us.

WARWICK
Between two hawks, which flies the higher pitch,
Between two dogs, which hath the deeper mouth,
Between two blades, which bears the better temper,
Between two horses, which doth bear him best,
Between two girls, which hath the merriest eye,
I have perhaps some shallow spirit of judgment;
But in these nice sharp quillets of the law,
Good faith, I am no wiser than a daw.

PLANTAGENET
Tut, tut, here is a mannerly forbearance.
The truth appears so naked on my side
That any purblind eye may find it out.

SOMERSET
And on my side it is so well apparel'd,
So clear, so shining, and so evident,
That it will glimmer through a blind man's eye.

PLANTAGENET
Since you are tongue-tied and so loath to speak,
In dumb significants proclaim your thoughts.
Let him that is a true-born gentleman
And stands upon the honor of his birth,
If he suppose that I have pleaded truth,
From off this brier pluck a white rose with me.
[*Plucks a white rose.*]

SOMERSET
Let him that is no coward nor no flatterer,
But dare maintain the party of the truth,
Pluck a red rose from off this thorn with me.
[*Plucks a red rose. The others similarly pluck roses as they choose sides.*]

WARWICK
I love no colors, and without all color
Of base insinuating flattery
I pluck this white rose with Plantagenet.

SUFFOLK
I pluck this red rose with young Somerset
And say withal I think he held the right.

VERNON
Stay, lords and gentlemen, and pluck no more,
Till you conclude that he upon whose side
The fewest roses are cropp'd from the tree
Shall yield the other in the right opinion.

SOMERSET
Good Master Vernon, it is well objected.
If I have fewest, I subscribe in silence.

PLANTAGENET
And I.

VERNON
Then for the truth and plainness of the case,
I pluck this pale and maiden blossom here,
Giving my verdict on the white rose side.

SOMERSET
Prick not your finger as you pluck it off,
Lest bleeding you do paint the white rose red
And fall on my side so, against your will.

VERNON
If I, my lord, for my opinion bleed,
Opinion shall be surgeon to my hurt
And keep me on the side where still I am.

SOMERSET
Well, well, come on, who else?

67 abuse (1) error (2) deception **68 fame** report. **bruited** reported, rumored **72 entertain** receive **73 misconster** misconstrue **78 patience** permission **79 cates** delicacies, dainty confections **80 stomachs** (1) appetites (2) bravery

II.iv. Location: London. The Temple Garden. (The Temple was a district of London taking its name from the Knights Templars, who owned it during the twelfth and thirteenth centuries. Its buildings were converted into Inns of Court, housing the legal societies of London, including the Inner Temple and the Middle Temple, in the fourteenth century.)
3 were would have been **6 Or else** i.e., in other words (?). (Or Plantagenet may be saying, ll. 5–6, with intended humor, am I right or is Somerset wrong?) **8 frame** adapt **11 pitch** elevation in flight **12 mouth** voice **14 bear him** carry himself **17 nice** subtle, precise. **quillets** subtle distinctions **18 daw** jackdaw. (A type of foolishness.)

21 purblind dimsighted **26 dumb significants** silent tokens, signs **29 pleaded** argued. (One of many legal terms occurring throughout this scene.) **30 white rose** badge of the house of York **32 party** side (in law) **33 red rose** badge of the house of Lancaster **34 colors** pretexts **36 Plantagenet** (The nickname of Geoffrey of Anjou, founder of the Angevin dynasty, that ruled England from the reign of Geoffrey's son, Henry II, to that of Richard III. None of Geoffrey's descendants assumed the name until Richard Duke of York adopted it in order to proclaim his superior right to the crown.) **38 withal** besides **43 objected** urged **44 subscribe** submit **53 Opinion** public opinion, i.e., my reputation (punning on *opinion* in the sense of "conviction" in the previous line)

LAWYER [*To Somerset*]
Unless my study and my books be false,
The argument you held was wrong in you;
In sign whereof I pluck a white rose too.

PLANTAGENET
Now, Somerset, where is your argument?

SOMERSET
Here in my scabbard, meditating that
Shall dye your white rose in a bloody red.

PLANTAGENET
Meantime your cheeks do counterfeit our roses;
For pale they look with fear, as witnessing
The truth on our side.

SOMERSET No, Plantagenet,
'Tis not for fear, but anger, that thy cheeks
Blush for pure shame to counterfeit our roses,
And yet thy tongue will not confess thy error.

PLANTAGENET
Hath not thy rose a canker, Somerset?

SOMERSET
Hath not thy rose a thorn, Plantagenet?

PLANTAGENET
Ay, sharp and piercing, to maintain his truth,
Whiles thy consuming canker eats his falsehood.

SOMERSET
Well, I'll find friends to wear my bleeding roses
That shall maintain what I have said is true,
Where false Plantagenet dare not be seen.

PLANTAGENET
Now, by this maiden blossom in my hand,
I scorn thee and thy fashion, peevish boy.

SUFFOLK
Turn not thy scorns this way, Plantagenet.

PLANTAGENET
Proud Pole, I will, and scorn both him and thee.

SUFFOLK
I'll turn my part thereof into thy throat.

SOMERSET
Away, away, good William de la Pole!
We grace the yeoman by conversing with him.

WARWICK
Now, by God's will, thou wrong'st him, Somerset.
His grandfather was Lionel Duke of Clarence,
Third son to the third Edward, King of England.
Spring crestless yeomen from so deep a root?

PLANTAGENET
He bears him on the place's privilege,
Or durst not, for his craven heart, say thus.

SOMERSET
By him that made me, I'll maintain my words
On any plot of ground in Christendom.
Was not thy father, Richard Earl of Cambridge,
For treason executed in our late king's days?
And, by his treason, stand'st not thou attainted,
Corrupted, and exempt from ancient gentry?
His trespass yet lives guilty in thy blood,
And, till thou be restor'd, thou art a yeoman.

PLANTAGENET
My father was attached, not attainted,
Condemn'd to die for treason, but no traitor;
And that I'll prove on better men than Somerset,
Were growing time once ripened to my will.
For your partaker Pole and you yourself,
I'll note you in my book of memory
To scourge you for this apprehension.
Look to it well and say you are well warn'd.

SOMERSET
Ah, thou shalt find us ready for thee still;
And know us by these colors for thy foes,
For these my friends in spite of thee shall wear.

PLANTAGENET
And, by my soul, this pale and angry rose,
As cognizance of my blood-drinking hate,
Will I for ever and my faction wear,
Until it wither with me to my grave
Or flourish to the height of my degree.

SUFFOLK
Go forward, and be chok'd with thy ambition!
And so farewell until I meet thee next. *Exit.*

SOMERSET
Have with thee, Pole. Farewell, ambitious Richard. *Exit.*

PLANTAGENET
How I am brav'd and must perforce endure it!

WARWICK
This blot that they object against your house
Shall be wip'd out in the next parliament
Call'd for the truce of Winchester and Gloucester;
And if thou be not then created York,
I will not live to be accounted Warwick.
Meantime, in signal of my love to thee,
Against proud Somerset and William Pole,
Will I upon thy party wear this rose.
And here I prophesy: this brawl today,
Grown to this faction in the Temple garden,
Shall send, between the red rose and the white,
A thousand souls to death and deadly night.

PLANTAGENET
Good Master Vernon, I am bound to you
That you on my behalf would pluck a flower.

VERNON
In your behalf still will I wear the same.

60 that that which **62 counterfeit** imitate **68 canker** cankerworm (that feeds on buds) **70 his** its **76 fashion** sort **78 Pole** family name of the Duke of Suffolk. (See also l. 80.) **79 I'll . . . throat** I'll throw the lies or slanders back into the throat from which they proceeded **81 grace** do honor to. **yeoman** a small freeholder, below the rank of landed gentleman. (A jibe at Plantagenet for having lost his lands and titles when his father, Richard Earl of Cambridge, was executed in 1415 by Henry V for treason.) **83 His . . . Clarence** (Lionel was actually Richard's maternal great-great-grandfather; but Edmund Duke of York, fifth son of Edward III, was his paternal grandfather. Richard thus could trace his descent from Edward III through both Lionel and Edmund.) **85 crestless** lacking heraldic titles (with a suggestion also of cowardice) **86 He . . . privilege** i.e., Somerset presumes upon the safety of a privileged place (since engaging in quarrels with drawn weapons was prohibited in certain precincts including the official residences of the sovereign; in fact, however, the Inns of Court were not thus privileged)

91 late king i.e., Henry V **92 attainted** convicted and condemned. (According to law, the heirs of a person so attainted were deprived of all the rights and titles of their forebears; their blood was pronounced *corrupted.*) **93 exempt** excluded **96 attached, not attainted** (Historically, as Plantagenet insists, his father was *attached,* i.e., arrested, and summarily executed for treason without a bill of attainder.) **99 Were . . . will** i.e., if the unfolding of time provides me opportunity **100 For your partaker** as for your supporter **102 apprehension** conception **105 know . . . foes** i.e., recognize us by these red badges as your enemies **108 cognizance** badge **111 degree** noble rank **114 Have with thee** let us go **115 brav'd** defied. **perforce** necessarily **116 object** urge, allege **118 Call'd . . . of** assembled to make peace between **121 signal** token

LAWYER
And so will I.
PLANTAGENET
Thanks, gentle sir.
Come, let us four to dinner. I dare say
This quarrel will drink blood another day. *Exeunt.*

[SCENE V]

Enter Mortimer, brought in a chair, and Jailers.

MORTIMER
Kind keepers of my weak decaying age,
Let dying Mortimer here rest himself.
Even like a man new haled from the rack,
So fare my limbs with long imprisonment;
And these grey locks, the pursuivants of death, 5
Nestor-like aged in an age of care, 6
Argue the end of Edmund Mortimer. 7
These eyes, like lamps whose wasting oil is spent,
Wax dim, as drawing to their exigent; 9
Weak shoulders, overborne with burdening grief,
And pithless arms, like to a withered vine
That droops his sapless branches to the ground.
Yet are these feet, whose strengthless stay is numb, 13
Unable to support this lump of clay,
Swift-winged with desire to get a grave,
As witting I no other comfort have. 16
But tell me, keeper, will my nephew come?
FIRST KEEPER
Richard Plantagenet, my lord, will come.
We sent unto the Temple, unto his chamber,
And answer was return'd that he will come.
MORTIMER
Enough. My soul shall then be satisfied.
Poor gentleman, his wrong doth equal mine. 22
Since Henry Monmouth first began to reign, 23
Before whose glory I was great in arms,
This loathsome sequestration have I had; 25
And even since then hath Richard been obscur'd,
Depriv'd of honor and inheritance.
But now the arbitrator of despairs,
Just death, kind umpire of men's miseries,
With sweet enlargement doth dismiss me hence. 30
I would his troubles likewise were expir'd,
That so he might recover what was lost.

Enter Richard [Plantagenet].

FIRST KEEPER
My lord, your loving nephew now is come.
MORTIMER
Richard Plantagenet, my friend, is he come?
PLANTAGENET
Ay, noble uncle, thus ignobly us'd,
Your nephew, late despised Richard, comes. 36
MORTIMER
Direct mine arms I may embrace his neck,
And in his bosom spend my latter gasp. 38
O, tell me when my lips do touch his cheeks,
That I may kindly give one fainting kiss.
[*Embraces Richard.*]
And now declare, sweet stem from York's great stock,
Why didst thou say of late thou wert despis'd?
PLANTAGENET
First, lean thine aged back against mine arm,
And, in that ease, I'll tell thee my disease. 44
This day, in argument upon a case,
Some words there grew 'twixt Somerset and me;
Among which terms he us'd his lavish tongue
And did upbraid me with my father's death;
Which obloquy set bars before my tongue,
Else with the like I had requited him.
Therefore, good uncle, for my father's sake,
In honor of a true Plantagenet,
And for alliance sake, declare the cause 53
My father, Earl of Cambridge, lost his head.
MORTIMER
That cause, fair nephew, that imprison'd me
And hath detain'd me all my flow'ring youth
Within a loathsome dungeon, there to pine,
Was cursed instrument of his decease.
PLANTAGENET
Discover more at large what cause that was, 59
For I am ignorant and cannot guess.
MORTIMER
I will, if that my fading breath permit
And death approach not ere my tale be done.
Henry the Fourth, grandfather to this king,
Depos'd his nephew Richard, Edward's son, 64
The first-begotten and the lawful heir
Of Edward king, the third of that descent;
During whose reign the Percies of the north, 67
Finding his usurpation most unjust,
Endeavor'd my advancement to the throne.
The reason mov'd these warlike lords to this 70
Was for that—young King Richard thus remov'd,
Leaving no heir begotten of his body—
I was the next by birth and parentage;
For by my mother I derived am 74
From Lionel Duke of Clarence, third son
To King Edward the Third; whereas he 76
From John of Gaunt doth bring his pedigree,
Being but fourth of that heroic line.
But mark. As in this haughty great attempt 79

II.v. Location: The Tower of London.
5 pursuivants heralds **6 Nestor-like** i.e., extremely old. (Nestor, the oldest of the Greek chieftains at the siege of Troy, came to represent a type of old age.) **7 Argue** portend **9 exigent** end **13 stay** support **16 witting** knowing **22 his wrong** i.e., the wrong done him **23 Henry Monmouth** i.e., Henry V **25 sequestration** imprisonment. (Shakespeare, following the chroniclers, confuses Edmund Mortimer, great-grandson of Lionel Duke of Clarence and hence potential heir to the throne, with his cousin Sir John Mortimer, who was imprisoned and finally executed for agitating in behalf of Edmund's royal claim. Edmund remained loyal to Henry V.) **30 enlargement** release from confinement

36 late lately **38 latter** last **44 disease** un-ease, trouble, grievance **53 alliance** kinship's **59 Discover** make known. **at large** at length **64 nephew** kinsman. (Here, cousin.) **67 whose** i.e., Henry IV's **70 mov'd** i.e., which moved **74 mother** (Shakespeare appears to confuse this Edmund with his uncle, Edmund Mortimer, second son of Lionel's daughter Philippa.) **76 he** i.e., Henry VI, or perhaps Henry IV. (See l. 63.) **79 haughty** proud

They labored to plant the rightful heir,
I lost my liberty and they their lives.
Long after this, when Henry the Fifth,
Succeeding his father Bolingbroke, did reign,
Thy father, Earl of Cambridge, then deriv'd
From famous Edmund Langley, Duke of York,
Marrying my sister that thy mother was,
Again, in pity of my hard distress,
Levied an army, weening to redeem
And have install'd me in the diadem.
But, as the rest, so fell that noble earl
And was beheaded. Thus the Mortimers,
In whom the title rested, were suppress'd.

PLANTAGENET
Of which, my lord, your honor is the last.

MORTIMER
True, and thou seest that I no issue have,
And that my fainting words do warrant death.
Thou art my heir. The rest I wish thee gather;
But yet be wary in thy studious care.

PLANTAGENET
Thy grave admonishments prevail with me.
But yet, methinks, my father's execution
Was nothing less than bloody tyranny.

MORTIMER
With silence, nephew, be thou politic.
Strong-fixed is the house of Lancaster
And like a mountain, not to be remov'd.
But now thy uncle is removing hence,
As princes do their courts, when they are cloy'd
With long continuance in a settled place.

PLANTAGENET
O uncle, would some part of my young years
Might but redeem the passage of your age!

MORTIMER
Thou dost then wrong me, as that slaughterer doth
Which giveth many wounds when one will kill.
Mourn not, except thou sorrow for my good;
Only give order for my funeral.
And so farewell, and fair be all thy hopes,
And prosperous be thy life in peace and war! *Dies.*

PLANTAGENET
And peace, no war, befall thy parting soul!
In prison hast thou spent a pilgrimage
And like a hermit overpass'd thy days.
Well, I will lock his counsel in my breast,
And what I do imagine let that rest.
Keepers, convey him hence, and I myself
Will see his burial better than his life.
Exeunt [Keepers, bearing out the body of Mortimer].
Here dies the dusky torch of Mortimer,
Chok'd with ambition of the meaner sort.
And for those wrongs, those bitter injuries,
Which Somerset hath offer'd to my house,
I doubt not but with honor to redress;
And therefore haste I to the parliament,
Either to be restored to my blood
Or make my will th' advantage of my good. *Exit.*

ACT III • SCENE I

Flourish. Enter King, Exeter, Gloucester, Winchester, Warwick, Somerset, Suffolk, Richard Plantagenet, [and others]. Gloucester offers to put up a bill; Winchester snatches it, [and] tears it.

WINCHESTER
Com'st thou with deep premeditated lines,
With written pamphlets studiously devis'd,
Humphrey of Gloucester? If thou canst accuse,
Or aught intend'st to lay unto my charge,
Do it without invention, suddenly,
As I with sudden and extemporal speech
Purpose to answer what thou canst object.

GLOUCESTER
Presumptuous priest, this place commands my patience,
Or thou shouldst find thou hast dishonor'd me.
Think not, although in writing I preferr'd
The manner of thy vile outrageous crimes,
That therefore I have forg'd, or am not able
Verbatim to rehearse the method of my pen.
No, prelate, such is thy audacious wickedness,
Thy lewd, pestiferous, and dissentious pranks,
As very infants prattle of thy pride.
Thou art a most pernicious usurer,
Froward by nature, enemy to peace,
Lascivious, wanton, more than well beseems
A man of thy profession and degree.
And for thy treachery, what's more manifest?
In that thou laid'st a trap to take my life,
As well at London bridge as at the Tower.
Beside, I fear me, if thy thoughts were sifted,
The King, thy sovereign, is not quite exempt
From envious malice of thy swelling heart.

WINCHESTER
Gloucester, I do defy thee. Lords, vouchsafe
To give me hearing what I shall reply.
If I were covetous, ambitious, or perverse,
As he will have me, how am I so poor?
Or how haps it I seek not to advance
Or raise myself, but keep my wonted calling?
And for dissension, who preferreth peace
More than I do, except I be provok'd?
No, my good lords, it is not that offends;
It is not that that hath incens'd the Duke.

88 weening thinking **89 install'd . . . diadem** crowned me king **95 warrant** promise, assure **96 gather** infer **97 studious** diligent **104 removing hence** departing from here, i.e., dying **111 except** unless **112 give order** make arrangements **117 overpass'd** passed **119 let that rest** leave it alone, i.e., let that be my business **123 meaner sort** those whose claim to the throne was inferior to his, i.e., the Lancastrians

128 blood hereditary rights **129 Or . . . good** or make my will-power the means of achieving my ambition

III.i. Location: London. The Parliament house.
s.d. bill (Here, a written accusation.) **5 invention** premeditated design. **suddenly** extempore **7 object** urge, present **10 preferr'd** put forward. (See I.iii.35–36 and note.) **13 Verbatim . . . pen** orally to recount what I have written **15 lewd** wicked **16 As that** **18 Froward** perverse **23 at London bridge** (Gloucester's articles of accusation against Winchester presented to the Parliament stated that the latter had "set men of armes and archers, at the ende of London bridge next Southwerke," to prevent Gloucester's going to Eltham to interfere with the Bishop's plans regarding the young King.) **34 except** unless **35 that** that which

It is because no one should sway but he,
No one but he should be about the King;
And that engenders thunder in his breast
And makes him roar these accusations forth.
But he shall know I am as good—

GLOUCESTER As good?
Thou bastard of my grandfather! 42

WINCHESTER
Ay, lordly sir! For what are you, I pray,
But one imperious in another's throne?

GLOUCESTER
Am I not Protector, saucy priest?

WINCHESTER
And am not I a prelate of the church?

GLOUCESTER
Yes, as an outlaw in a castle keeps 47
And useth it to patronage his theft. 48

WINCHESTER
Unreverent Gloucester!

GLOUCESTER Thou art reverent
Touching thy spiritual function, not thy life. 50

WINCHESTER
Rome shall remedy this.

WARWICK Roam thither, then.

SOMERSET [*To Warwick*]
My lord, it were your duty to forbear. 52

WARWICK
Ay, see the Bishop be not overborne. 53

SOMERSET
Methinks my lord should be religious 54
And know the office that belongs to such.

WARWICK
Methinks his lordship should be humbler.
It fitteth not a prelate so to plead.

SOMERSET
Yes, when his holy state is touch'd so near. 58

WARWICK
State holy or unhallow'd, what of that?
Is not his Grace Protector to the King? 60

PLANTAGENET [*Aside*]
Plantagenet, I see, must hold his tongue,
Lest it be said "Speak, sirrah, when you should;
Must your bold verdict enter talk with lords?" 63
Else would I have a fling at Winchester.

KING
Uncles of Gloucester and of Winchester,
The special watchmen of our English weal, 66
I would prevail, if prayers might prevail,
To join your hearts in love and amity.
O, what a scandal is it to our crown
That two such noble peers as ye should jar! 70
Believe me, lords, my tender years can tell 71
Civil dissension is a viperous worm
That gnaws the bowels of the commonwealth.

A noise within, "Down with the tawny-coats!"

What tumult's this?

WARWICK An uproar, I dare warrant,
Begun through malice of the Bishop's men.

A noise again, "Stones! Stones!"

Enter Mayor.

MAYOR
O, my good lords, and virtuous Henry,
Pity the city of London, pity us!
The Bishop and the Duke of Gloucester's men, 80
Forbidden late to carry any weapon, 81
Have fill'd their pockets full of pebble stones
And, banding themselves in contrary parts, 83
Do pelt so fast at one another's pate
That many have their giddy brains knock'd out.
Our windows are broke down in every street
And we for fear compell'd to shut our shops.

Enter [Servingmen of both parties], in skirmish with bloody pates.

KING
We charge you, on allegiance to ourself,
To hold your slaught'ring hands and keep the peace.
Pray, uncle Gloucester, mitigate this strife.

FIRST SERVINGMAN Nay, if we be forbidden stones, we'll fall to it with our teeth.

SECOND SERVINGMAN
Do what ye dare, we are as resolute. *Skirmish again.*

GLOUCESTER
You of my household, leave this peevish broil 94
And set this unaccustom'd fight aside. 95

THIRD SERVINGMAN
My lord, we know your Grace to be a man
Just and upright, and for your royal birth,
Inferior to none but to his Majesty;
And ere that we will suffer such a prince, 99
So kind a father of the commonweal,
To be disgraced by an inkhorn mate, 101
We and our wives and children all will fight
And have our bodies slaught'red by thy foes.

FIRST SERVINGMAN
Ay, and the very parings of our nails
Shall pitch a field when we are dead. *Begin again.*

GLOUCESTER Stay, stay, I say! 105
And if you love me, as you say you do,
Let me persuade you to forbear awhile.

KING
O, how this discord doth afflict my soul!
Can you, my Lord of Winchester, behold
My sighs and tears and will not once relent?
Who should be pitiful, if you be not?
Or who should study to prefer a peace, 112
If holy churchmen take delight in broils?

42 Thou bastard (Winchester—son of John of Gaunt and Catherine Swynford before their marriage—was, with his two brothers and one sister, legitimatized by act of Parliament in Richard II's reign.) **47 keeps** dwells **48 patronage** maintain **50 Touching . . . function** i.e., in ecclesiastical title only **52 were** should be **53 overborne** prevailed over **54 my lord** i.e., Winchester. **should be** i.e., should be regarded as. (But Warwick, two lines below, uses the phrase in the sense *ought to be*.) **58 state** degree, rank. **touch'd so near** so closely concerned **60 his Grace** i.e., Gloucester **63 bold verdict** audacious opinion. **enter talk** hold conversation **66 weal** common good **70 jar** quarrel **71 my tender years** (The King was actually five years old at the time of this episode.)

80 Bishop i.e., Bishop's **81 late** lately **83 contrary parts** contending factions **94 peevish** petty, senseless **95 unaccustom'd** contrary to custom and normality **99 ere that** before **101 inkhorn mate** scribbler. (Alludes scornfully to Winchester as a cleric or clerk.) **105 pitch a field** fight a battle **112 prefer** propose, assist in arranging

WARWICK
Yield, my Lord Protector, yield, Winchester,
Except you mean with obstinate repulse
To slay your sovereign and destroy the realm.
You see what mischief and what murder too
Hath been enacted through your enmity.
Then be at peace, except ye thirst for blood.

WINCHESTER
He shall submit, or I will never yield.

GLOUCESTER
Compassion on the King commands me stoop,
Or I would see his heart out ere the priest
Should ever get that privilege of me.

WARWICK
Behold, my Lord of Winchester, the Duke
Hath banish'd moody discontented fury,
As by his smoothed brows it doth appear.
Why look you still so stern and tragical?

GLOUCESTER
Here, Winchester, I offer thee my hand.
[*Offers his hand, which Winchester refuses.*]

KING
Fie, uncle Beaufort! I have heard you preach
That malice was a great and grievous sin;
And will not you maintain the thing you teach,
But prove a chief offender in the same?

WARWICK
Sweet King! The Bishop hath a kindly gird.
For shame, my Lord of Winchester, relent!
What, shall a child instruct you what to do?

WINCHESTER
Well, Duke of Gloucester, I will yield to thee;
Love for thy love and hand for hand I give.
[*They clasp hands.*]

GLOUCESTER [*Aside*]
Ay, but, I fear me, with a hollow heart.—
See here, my friends and loving countrymen,
This token serveth for a flag of truce
Betwixt ourselves and all our followers.
So help me God, as I dissemble not!

WINCHESTER [*Aside*]
So help me God, as I intend it not!

KING
O loving uncle, kind Duke of Gloucester,
How joyful am I made by this contract!
Away, my masters. Trouble us no more,
But join in friendship, as your lords have done.

FIRST SERVINGMAN
Content. I'll to the surgeon's.

SECOND SERVINGMAN And so will I.

THIRD SERVINGMAN
And I will see what physic the tavern affords.
Exeunt [*Servingmen, Mayor, etc.*].

WARWICK [*Proferring scroll*]
Accept this scroll, most gracious sovereign,
Which in the right of Richard Plantagenet
We do exhibit to your Majesty.

GLOUCESTER
Well urg'd, my Lord of Warwick. For, sweet prince,
An if your Grace mark every circumstance,
You have great reason to do Richard right,
Especially for those occasions
At Eltham Place I told your Majesty.

KING
And those occasions, uncle, were of force.
Therefore, my loving lords, our pleasure is
That Richard be restored to his blood.

WARWICK
Let Richard be restored to his blood;
So shall his father's wrongs be recompens'd.

WINCHESTER
As will the rest, so willeth Winchester.

KING
If Richard will be true, not that alone
But all the whole inheritance I give
That doth belong unto the house of York,
From whence you spring by lineal descent.

PLANTAGENET
Thy humble servant vows obedience
And humble service till the point of death.

KING
Stoop then and set your knee against my foot,
[*Richard kneels.*]
And in reguerdon of that duty done,
I girt thee with the valiant sword of York.
Rise, Richard, like a true Plantagenet,
And rise created princely Duke of York.
[*Richard rises.*]

PLANTAGENET
And so thrive Richard as thy foes may fall!
And as my duty springs, so perish they
That grudge one thought against your Majesty!

ALL
Welcome, high prince, the mighty Duke of York!

SOMERSET [*Aside*]
Perish, base prince, ignoble Duke of York!

GLOUCESTER
Now will it best avail your Majesty
To cross the seas and to be crown'd in France.
The presence of a king engenders love
Amongst his subjects and his loyal friends,
As it disanimates his enemies.

KING
When Gloucester says the word, King Henry goes,
For friendly counsel cuts off many foes.

GLOUCESTER
Your ships already are in readiness.
Sennet. Flourish. Exeunt. Manet Exeter.

EXETER
Ay, we may march in England or in France,
Not seeing what is likely to ensue.
This late dissension grown betwixt the peers
Burns under feigned ashes of forg'd love
And will at last break out into a flame.

115 Except unless. **repulse** refusal **123 privilege** advantage **125 moody** haughty **133 kindly gird** appropriate rebuke **146 masters** (Condescending term of address to servants.) **149 physic** remedy

154 An if if **156 occasions** reasons **158 of force** compelling **160 blood** hereditary right, inherited from his father **171 reguerdon** reward **172 girt** gird **184 disanimates** discourages **187 s.d. Sennet** set of notes played on a trumpet as a signal for the approach or departure of processions

As fest'red members rot but by degree,
Till bones and flesh and sinews fall away,
So will this base and envious discord breed.
And now I fear that fatal prophecy
Which in the time of Henry nam'd the Fifth
Was in the mouth of every sucking babe:
That Henry born at Monmouth should win all
And Henry born at Windsor lose all;
Which is so plain that Exeter doth wish
His days may finish ere that hapless time. *Exit.*

SCENE II

Enter Pucelle disguis'd, with four Soldiers with sacks upon their backs.

PUCELLE
These are the city gates, the gates of Rouen,
Through which our policy must make a breach.
Take heed, be wary how you place your words;
Talk like the vulgar sort of market men
That come to gather money for their corn.
If we have entrance, as I hope we shall,
And that we find the slothful watch but weak,
I'll by a sign give notice to our friends,
That Charles the Dauphin may encounter them.

FIRST SOLDIER
Our sacks shall be a mean to sack the city,
And we be lords and rulers over Rouen.
Therefore we'll knock. *Knock.*

WATCH [*Within*] Che la?

PUCELLE
Paysans, la pauvre gens de France,
Poor market folks that come to sell their corn.

WATCH [*Opening the gates*]
Enter, go in; the market bell is rung.

PUCELLE
Now, Rouen, I'll shake thy bulwarks to the ground.
Exeunt [*to the town*].

Enter Charles, [*the*] *Bastard* [*of Orleans*], *Alençon,* [*Reignier, and forces*].

CHARLES
Saint Denis bless this happy stratagem!
And once again we'll sleep secure in Rouen.

BASTARD
Here ent'red Pucelle and her practisants.
Now she is there, how will she specify
Where is the best and safest passage in?

REIGNIER
By thrusting out a torch from yonder tower,
Which, once discern'd, shows that her meaning is,
No way to that, for weakness, which she ent'red.

Enter Pucelle on the top, thrusting out a torch burning.

PUCELLE
Behold, this is the happy wedding torch
That joineth Rouen unto her countrymen,
But burning fatal to the Talbonites! [*Exit.*]

BASTARD
See, noble Charles, the beacon of our friend!
The burning torch in yonder turret stands.

CHARLES
Now shine it like a comet of revenge,
A prophet to the fall of all our foes!

REIGNIER
Defer no time! Delays have dangerous ends.
Enter, and cry "The Dauphin!" presently,
And then do execution on the watch.
Alarum. [*They storm the gates.*]

An alarum. [*Enter*] *Talbot in an excursion* [*from within*].

TALBOT
France, thou shalt rue this treason with thy tears,
If Talbot but survive thy treachery.
Pucelle, that witch, that damned sorceress,
Hath wrought this hellish mischief unawares,
That hardly we escap'd the pride of France. *Exit.*

An alarum. Excursions. Bedford, brought in sick in a chair. Enter Talbot and Burgundy without; within, Pucelle, Charles, Bastard, [*Alençon,*] *and Reignier, on the walls.*

PUCELLE
Good morrow, gallants, want ye corn for bread?
I think the Duke of Burgundy will fast
Before he'll buy again at such a rate.
'Twas full of darnel. Do you like the taste?

BURGUNDY
Scoff on, vile fiend and shameless courtesan!
I trust ere long to choke thee with thine own
And make thee curse the harvest of that corn.

CHARLES
Your Grace may starve, perhaps, before that time.

BEDFORD
O, let no words, but deeds, revenge this treason!

PUCELLE
What will you do, good greybeard, break a lance,
And run a-tilt at Death within a chair?

TALBOT
Foul fiend of France, and hag of all despite,
Encompass'd with thy lustful paramours!
Becomes it thee to taunt his valiant age
And twit with cowardice a man half dead?
Damsel, I'll have a bout with you again,
Or else let Talbot perish with this shame.

III.ii. Location: France. Before Rouen.
1 Rouen (As at Orleans in I.v through II.i, the city gates here are represented by doors in the tiring house façade, the "walls" of Rouen. Appearances "on the walls," as at l. 41, take place on the gallery backstage.) **2 policy** stratagem **4 vulgar** common **5 corn** grain **7 that** if **13 Che la** qui est la, who is there. (Rustic French.) **20 practisants** conspirators **25 to** is comparable to

25 s.d. on the top i.e., at some upper vantage point in the theatre **28 Talbonites** followers of Talbot **31 shine it** may it shine **34 presently** immediately **35 s.d. excursion** skirmish, sortie **39 unawares** unexpectedly **40 pride** princely power **40 s.d. Bedford . . . sick** (Actually, Bedford outlived Joan of Arc by four years. The entire episode of the capture of Orleans, as presented here, is unhistorical; the English did not relinquish the city until some eighteen years after Joan's death.) **without** i.e., on the main stage. **within** i.e., in the gallery backstage **44 darnel** injurious weed **46 thine own** i.e., your own bread **51 run a-tilt at** joust with. **within** i.e., sitting in **52 of all despite** thoroughly despicable

PUCELLE
Are ye so hot, sir? Yet, Pucelle, hold thy peace.
If Talbot do but thunder, rain will follow.
They [the English] whisper together in council.
God speed the parliament! Who shall be the speaker?

TALBOT
Dare ye come forth and meet us in the field?

PUCELLE
Belike your lordship takes us then for fools,
To try if that our own be ours or no.

TALBOT
I speak not to that railing Hecate, 64
But unto thee, Alençon, and the rest.
Will ye, like soldiers, come and fight it out?

ALENÇON
Signior, no.

TALBOT
Signior, hang! Base muleters of France! 68
Like peasant footboys do they keep the walls
And dare not take up arms like gentlemen.

PUCELLE
Away, captains. Let's get us from the walls,
For Talbot means no goodness by his looks.
God buy, my lord. We came but to tell you 73
That we are here. *Exeunt from the walls.*

TALBOT
And there will we be too, ere it be long,
Or else reproach be Talbot's greatest fame!
Vow, Burgundy, by honor of thy house,
Prick'd on by public wrongs sustain'd in France, 78
Either to get the town again or die.
And I, as sure as English Henry lives
And as his father here was conqueror, 81
As sure as in this late-betrayed town
Great Cordelion's heart was buried, 83
So sure I swear to get the town or die.

BURGUNDY
My vows are equal partners with thy vows.

TALBOT
But, ere we go, regard this dying prince, 86
The valiant Duke of Bedford. Come, my lord,
We will bestow you in some better place,
Fitter for sickness and for crazy age. 89

BEDFORD
Lord Talbot, do not so dishonor me.
Here will I sit before the walls of Rouen
And will be partner of your weal or woe.

BURGUNDY
Courageous Bedford, let us now persuade you.

BEDFORD
Not to be gone from hence; for once I read
That stout Pendragon in his litter sick 95
Came to the field and vanquished his foes.
Methinks I should revive the soldiers' hearts,
Because I ever found them as myself.

TALBOT
Undaunted spirit in a dying breast!
Then be it so. Heavens keep old Bedford safe!
And now no more ado, brave Burgundy,
But gather we our forces out of hand 102
And set upon our boasting enemy.
Exeunt [all but Bedford and Attendants].

An alarum. Excursions. Enter Sir John Falstaff and a Captain.

CAPTAIN
Whither away, Sir John Falstaff, in such haste?

FALSTAFF
Whither away? To save myself by flight.
We are like to have the overthrow again.

CAPTAIN
What? Will you fly, and leave Lord Talbot?

FALSTAFF
Ay,
All the Talbots in the world, to save my life. *Exit.*

CAPTAIN
Cowardly knight, ill fortune follow thee! *Exit.*

Retreat. Excursions. Pucelle, Alençon, and Charles fly.

BEDFORD
Now, quiet soul, depart when heaven please,
For I have seen our enemies' overthrow.
What is the trust or strength of foolish man?
They that of late were daring with their scoffs
Are glad and fain by flight to save themselves. 114
Bedford dies, and is carried in by two in his chair.

An alarum. Enter Talbot, Burgundy, and the rest.

TALBOT
Lost and recovered in a day again!
This is a double honor, Burgundy.
Yet heavens have glory for this victory!

BURGUNDY
Warlike and martial Talbot, Burgundy
Enshrines thee in his heart and there erects
Thy noble deeds as valor's monuments.

TALBOT
Thanks, gentle Duke. But where is Pucelle now? 121
I think her old familiar is asleep. 122
Now where's the Bastard's braves, and Charles his glikes? 123
What, all amort? Rouen hangs her head for grief 124
That such a valiant company are fled.
Now will we take some order in the town, 126
Placing therein some expert officers,
And then depart to Paris to the King,
For there young Henry with his nobles lie.

BURGUNDY
What wills Lord Talbot pleaseth Burgundy.

64 Hecate goddess of night and of black magic **68 muleters** mule drivers **73 God buy** God be with you, i.e., good-by **78 Prick'd on** goaded **81 father . . . conqueror** (Henry V captured Rouen in 1419.) **83 Great . . . heart** (According to Holinshed, Richard Coeur-de-Lion, "the lion-hearted," King of England, 1189–1199, had willed that "his heart be conueied vnto Rouen, and there buried; in testimonie of the loue which he had euer borne vnto that citie.") **86 regard** attend to **89 crazy** decrepit **95 Pendragon** (According to Holinshed, it was the brother of Uther Pendragon who, "euen sicke as he was, caused himselfe to be carried forth *in a litter;* with whose presence his people were so incouraged, that incountring with the Saxons, they wan the victorie." Geoffrey of Monmouth, on the other hand, credits this feat to Uther himself. Uther was father of King Arthur.)

102 out of hand at once **114 fain** eager **121 gentle** noble **122 familiar** demon **123 braves** boasts. **Charles his glikes** Charles' gibes, jests **124 amort** sick to death, dispirited **126 take some order** establish order

TALBOT

But yet, before we go, let's not forget
The noble Duke of Bedford late deceas'd,
But see his exequies fulfill'd in Rouen. 133
A braver soldier never couched lance,
A gentler heart did never sway in court. 135
But kings and mightiest potentates must die,
For that's the end of human misery. *Exeunt.*

SCENE III

Enter Charles, [the] Bastard [of Orleans], Alençon, Pucelle, [and forces].

PUCELLE

Dismay not, princes, at this accident,
Nor grieve that Rouen is so recovered.
Care is no cure, but rather corrosive,
For things that are not to be remedied.
Let frantic Talbot triumph for a while
And like a peacock sweep along his tail;
We'll pull his plumes and take away his train, 7
If Dauphin and the rest will be but rul'd.

CHARLES

We have been guided by thee hitherto
And of thy cunning had no diffidence. 10
One sudden foil shall never breed distrust. 11

BASTARD

Search out thy wit for secret policies, 12
And we will make thee famous through the world.

ALENÇON

We'll set thy statue in some holy place,
And have thee reverenc'd like a blessed saint.
Employ thee then, sweet virgin, for our good.

PUCELLE

Then thus it must be, this doth Joan devise:
By fair persuasions, mix'd with sug'red words,
We will entice the Duke of Burgundy
To leave the Talbot and to follow us.

CHARLES

Ay, marry, sweeting, if we could do that,
France were no place for Henry's warriors,
Nor should that nation boast it so with us,
But be extirped from our provinces. 24

ALENÇON

Forever should they be expuls'd from France
And not have title of an earldom here.

PUCELLE

Your honors shall perceive how I will work
To bring this matter to the wished end.
Drum sounds afar off.
Hark, by the sound of drum you may perceive
Their powers are marching unto Paris-ward.

Here sound an English march. [Enter, and pass over at a distance, Talbot and his forces.]

There goes the Talbot, with his colors spread,
And all the troops of English after him.

French march. [Enter the Duke of Burgundy and forces.]

Now in the rearward comes the Duke and his.
Fortune in favor makes him lag behind. 34
Summon a parley; we will talk with him.
Trumpets sound a parley.

CHARLES

A parley with the Duke of Burgundy!

BURGUNDY

Who craves a parley with the Burgundy?

PUCELLE

The princely Charles of France, thy countryman.

BURGUNDY

What say'st thou, Charles? For I am marching hence.

CHARLES

Speak, Pucelle, and enchant him with thy words.

PUCELLE

Brave Burgundy, undoubted hope of France! 41
Stay, let thy humble handmaid speak to thee.

BURGUNDY

Speak on; but be not over-tedious.

PUCELLE

Look on thy country, look on fertile France,
And see the cities and the towns defac'd
By wasting ruin of the cruel foe.
As looks the mother on her lowly babe
When death doth close his tender-dying eyes,
See, see the pining malady of France!
Behold the wounds, the most unnatural wounds,
Which thou thyself hast given her woeful breast.
O, turn thy edged sword another way;
Strike those that hurt, and hurt not those that help!
One drop of blood drawn from thy country's bosom
Should grieve thee more than streams of foreign gore.
Return thee therefore with a flood of tears,
And wash away thy country's stained spots.

BURGUNDY

Either she hath bewitch'd me with her words,
Or nature makes me suddenly relent.

PUCELLE

Besides, all French and France exclaims on thee, 60
Doubting thy birth and lawful progeny. 61
Who join'st thou with but with a lordly nation
That will not trust thee but for profit's sake?
When Talbot hath set footing once in France
And fashion'd thee that instrument of ill,
Who then but English Henry will be lord,
And thou be thrust out like a fugitive?
Call we to mind, and mark but this for proof:
Was not the Duke of Orleans thy foe?
And was he not in England prisoner?
But when they heard he was thine enemy,
They set him free without his ransom paid,
In spite of Burgundy and all his friends.

133 exequies funeral rites **135 sway** exercise influence

III.iii. Location: Plains near Rouen.
7 train (1) peacock's tail (2) army **10 diffidence** distrust **11 foil** repulse, defeat **12 policies** stratagems **24 extirped** rooted out

34 in favor benevolently, i.e., in our favor **41 undoubted** i.e., whose bravery and strength are sure bulwarks **60 exclaims on** denounces, accuses **61 progeny** ancestry

See, then, thou fight'st against thy countrymen
And join'st with them will be thy slaughter-men. 75
Come, come, return. Return, thou wandering lord!
Charles and the rest will take thee in their arms.

BURGUNDY
I am vanquished. These haughty words of hers 78
Have batt'red me like roaring cannon-shot,
And made me almost yield upon my knees.—
Forgive me, country, and sweet countrymen!
And, lords, accept this hearty kind embrace.
My forces and my power of men are yours.
So farewell, Talbot. I'll no longer trust thee.

PUCELLE [*Aside*]
Done like a Frenchman—turn, and turn again!

CHARLES
Welcome, brave Duke! Thy friendship makes us fresh.

BASTARD
And doth beget new courage in our breasts.

ALENÇON
Pucelle hath bravely play'd her part in this,
And doth deserve a coronet of gold.

CHARLES
Now let us on, my lords, and join our powers,
And seek how we may prejudice the foe. *Exeunt.* 91

SCENE IV

Enter the King, Gloucester, Winchester, [*Richard Duke of*] *York, Suffolk, Somerset, Warwick, Exeter,* [*Vernon, wearing a white rose, Basset, wearing a red rose, and others*]. *To them, with his Soldiers, Talbot.*

TALBOT
My gracious prince, and honorable peers,
Hearing of your arrival in this realm,
I have awhile given truce unto my wars
To do my duty to my sovereign; 4
In sign whereof, this arm, that hath reclaim'd
To your obedience fifty fortresses,
Twelve cities, and seven walled towns of strength,
Beside five hundred prisoners of esteem,
Lets fall his sword before your Highness' feet,
And with submissive loyalty of heart
Ascribes the glory of his conquest got
First to my God and next unto your Grace. [*Kneels.*]

KING
Is this the Lord Talbot, uncle Gloucester,
That hath so long been resident in France?

GLOUCESTER
Yes, if it please your Majesty, my liege.

75 them those who **78 I am vanquished** (Historically, Burgundy did not desert the English alliance until four years after Joan's death. This desertion occurred five years before the Duke of Orleans was released by the English; see ll. 69–73.) **91 prejudice** harm

III.iv. Location: Paris. The palace.
4 duty homage

KING
Welcome, brave captain and victorious lord!
When I was young, as yet I am not old,
I do remember how my father said 18
A stouter champion never handled sword.
Long since we were resolved of your truth, 20
Your faithful service, and your toil in war;
Yet never have you tasted our reward,
Or been reguerdon'd with so much as thanks, 23
Because till now we never saw your face.
Therefore, stand up, and for these good deserts
We here create you Earl of Shrewsbury;
And in our coronation take your place.
Sennet. Flourish. Exeunt. Mane[*n*]*t Vernon and Basset.*

VERNON
Now, sir, to you, that were so hot at sea, 28
Disgracing of these colors that I wear 29
In honor of my noble Lord of York:
Dar'st thou maintain the former words thou spak'st?

BASSET
Yes, sir; as well as you dare patronage 32
The envious barking of your saucy tongue
Against my lord the Duke of Somerset.

VERNON
Sirrah, thy lord I honor as he is.

BASSET
Why, what is he? As good a man as York.

VERNON
Hark ye; not so. In witness, take ye that.
Strikes him.

BASSET
Villain, thou knowest the law of arms is such 38
That whoso draws a sword, 'tis present death, 39
Or else this blow should broach thy dearest blood. 40
But I'll unto his Majesty, and crave
I may have liberty to venge this wrong,
When thou shalt see I'll meet thee to thy cost.

VERNON
Well, miscreant, I'll be there as soon as you,
And after meet you, sooner than you would. *Exeunt.*

ACT IV • SCENE I

Enter King, Gloucester, Winchester, [*Richard Duke of*] *York, Suffolk, Somerset, Warwick, Talbot, Exeter, Governor* [*of Paris, and others*].

GLOUCESTER
Lord Bishop, set the crown upon his head.

18 I . . . said (Historically, Henry VI was an infant of nine months at his father's death.) **20 we** i.e., I. (The royal "we.") **resolved** convinced **23 reguerdon'd** rewarded **28 so hot at sea** (The details of this quarrel are given below, IV.i.87–97.) **29 these colors** i.e., the white rose of York **32 patronage** defend **38 law of arms** (This law forbade the drawing of weapons near a royal residence; see I.iii.46 and note, and II.iv.86 and note.) **39 present** instant **40 broach** tap, draw. **dearest blood** i.e., life blood

IV.i. Location: Paris. Scene continues. (The action appears to go on immediately after the events of III.iv.)
s.d. York i.e., Richard Plantagenet, created Duke of York in III.i and hereafter identified by the speech-prefix YORK

WINCHESTER
God save King Henry, of that name the sixth!
[*The King is crowned.*]

GLOUCESTER
Now, Governor of Paris, take your oath,
[*Governor kneels.*]
That you elect no other king but him, 4
Esteem none friends but such as are his friends,
And none your foes but such as shall pretend 6
Malicious practices against his state. 7
This shall ye do, so help you righteous God!
[*Governor retires.*]

Enter [*Sir John*] *Falstaff.*

FALSTAFF
My gracious sovereign, as I rode from Calais,
To haste unto your coronation,
A letter was deliver'd to my hands,
Writ to your Grace from th' Duke of Burgundy.
[*Presents letter.*]

TALBOT
Shame to the Duke of Burgundy and thee!
I vow'd, base knight, when I did meet thee next,
To tear the garter from thy craven's leg, 15
[*Plucking it off.*]
Which I have done, because unworthily
Thou wast installed in that high degree.
Pardon me, princely Henry, and the rest.
This dastard, at the battle of Poitiers, 19
When but in all I was six thousand strong
And that the French were almost ten to one,
Before we met or that a stroke was given,
Like to a trusty squire did run away; 23
In which assault we lost twelve hundred men.
Myself and divers gentlemen beside
Were there surpris'd and taken prisoners.
Then judge, great lords, if I have done amiss,
Or whether that such cowards ought to wear
This ornament of knighthood, yea or no?

GLOUCESTER
To say the truth, this fact was infamous 30
And ill beseeming any common man,
Much more a knight, a captain, and a leader.

TALBOT
When first this order was ordain'd, my lords,
Knights of the garter were of noble birth,
Valiant and virtuous, full of haughty courage, 35
Such as were grown to credit by the wars— 36
Not fearing death, nor shrinking for distress,
But always resolute in most extremes. 38
He then that is not furnish'd in this sort 39
Doth but usurp the sacred name of knight,
Profaning this most honorable order,
And should, if I were worthy to be judge,
Be quite degraded, like a hedge-born swain 43
That doth presume to boast of gentle blood.

KING
Stain to thy countrymen, thou hear'st thy doom.
Be packing, therefore, thou that wast a knight. 46
Henceforth we banish thee, on pain of death.
[*Exit Falstaff.*]
And now, my Lord Protector, view the letter
Sent from our uncle Duke of Burgundy. 49

GLOUCESTER [*Taking the letter*]
What means his Grace, that he hath chang'd his
style? 50
No more but, plain and bluntly, "To the King"?
Hath he forgot he is his sovereign?
Or doth this churlish superscription
Pretend some alteration in good will? 54
What's here? [*Reads.*] "I have, upon especial cause,
Mov'd with compassion of my country's wrack,
Together with the pitiful complaints
Of such as your oppression feeds upon,
Forsaken your pernicious faction
And join'd with Charles, the rightful King of
France." 60
O monstrous treachery! Can this be so,
That in alliance, amity, and oaths,
There should be found such false dissembling guile?

KING
What? Doth my uncle Burgundy revolt?

GLOUCESTER
He doth, my lord, and is become your foe.

KING
Is that the worst this letter doth contain?

GLOUCESTER
It is the worst, and all, my lord, he writes.

KING
Why, then, Lord Talbot there shall talk with him
And give him chastisement for this abuse.
How say you, my lord? Are you not content?

TALBOT
Content, my liege? Yes. But that I am prevented, 71
I should have begg'd I might have been employ'd.

KING
Then gather strength and march unto him straight. 73
Let him perceive how ill we brook his treason 74
And what offense it is to flout his friends.

TALBOT
I go, my lord, in heart desiring still 76
You may behold confusion of your foes. [*Exit.*] 77

Enter Vernon and Basset, [*wearing a white and a red rose respectively, as before*].

VERNON
Grant me the combat, gracious sovereign. 78

BASSET
And me, my lord, grant me the combat too.

4 elect acknowledge **6 pretend** purpose, intend **7 practices** stratagems **15 garter** badge of the Knights of the Garter, a ribbon of blue velvet edged and buckled with gold, worn below the left knee. (Historically, the garter was apparently taken from Fastolfe by the Duke of Bedford; Talbot, who was a captive of the French at the time of Henry VI's coronation in Paris, was opposed to the restoration of the garter to Fastolfe.) **19 Poitiers** (Seemingly confused with *Patay.*) **23 trusty squire** (Said contemptuously.) **30 fact** deed **35 haughty** exalted **36 credit** renown **38 most** greatest **39 furnish'd . . . sort** endowed thus

43 degraded lowered in rank. **hedge-born swain** lowly-born rustic **46 Be packing** be off **49 uncle** (The Lancastrian and Burgundian houses were allied by the marriage of the Duke of Bedford, the King's uncle, to Anne, sister of the Duke of Burgundy.) **50 style** form of address **54 Pretend** portend, import **71 prevented** anticipated **73 straight** immediately **74 brook** endure **76 still** always **77 confusion** destruction **78 the combat** permission to fight

YORK
This is my servant. Hear him, noble prince.

SOMERSET
And this is mine. Sweet Henry, favor him.

KING
Be patient, lords, and give them leave to speak.
Say, gentlemen, what makes you thus exclaim?
And wherefore crave you combat, or with whom?

VERNON
With him, my lord, for he hath done me wrong.

BASSET
And I with him, for he hath done me wrong.

KING
What is that wrong whereof you both complain?
First let me know, and then I'll answer you.

BASSET
Crossing the sea from England into France,
This fellow here, with envious carping tongue,
Upbraided me about the rose I wear,
Saying the sanguine color of the leaves
Did represent my master's blushing cheeks,
When stubbornly he did repugn the truth
About a certain question in the law
Argu'd betwixt the Duke of York and him;
With other vile and ignominious terms.
In confutation of which rude reproach,
And in defense of my lord's worthiness,
I crave the benefit of law of arms.

VERNON
And that is my petition, noble lord.
For though he seem with forged quaint conceit
To set a gloss upon his bold intent,
Yet know, my lord, I was provok'd by him,
And he first took exceptions at this badge,
Pronouncing that the paleness of this flower
Bewray'd the faintness of my master's heart.

YORK
Will not this malice, Somerset, be left?

SOMERSET
Your private grudge, my Lord of York, will out,
Though ne'er so cunningly you smother it.

KING
Good Lord, what madness rules in brainsick men,
When for so slight and frivolous a cause
Such factious emulations shall arise!
Good cousins both, of York and Somerset,
Quiet yourselves, I pray, and be at peace.

YORK
Let this dissension first be tried by fight,
And then your Highness shall command a peace.

SOMERSET
The quarrel toucheth none but us alone;
Betwixt ourselves let us decide it then.

YORK
There is my pledge. Accept it, Somerset.
[*Throws down a gage.*]

VERNON
Nay, let it rest where it began at first.

BASSET [*To Somerset*]
Confirm it so, mine honorable lord.

GLOUCESTER
Confirm it so? Confounded be your strife!
And perish ye, with your audacious prate!
Presumptuous vassals, are you not asham'd
With this immodest clamorous outrage
To trouble and disturb the King and us?
And you, my lords, methinks you do not well
To bear with their perverse objections,
Much less to take occasion from their mouths
To raise a mutiny betwixt yourselves.
Let me persuade you take a better course.

EXETER
It grieves his Highness. Good my lords, be friends.

KING
Come hither, you that would be combatants:
Henceforth I charge you, as you love our favor,
Quite to forget this quarrel and the cause.
And you, my lords: remember where we are,
In France, amongst a fickle wavering nation.
If they perceive dissension in our looks
And that within ourselves we disagree,
How will their grudging stomachs be provok'd
To willful disobedience, and rebel?
Beside, what infamy will there arise
When foreign princes shall be certified
That for a toy, a thing of no regard,
King Henry's peers and chief nobility
Destroy'd themselves, and lost the realm of France?
O, think upon the conquest of my father,
My tender years, and let us not forego
That for a trifle that was bought with blood!
Let me be umpire in this doubtful strife.
I see no reason, if I wear this rose,
[*Putting on a red rose.*]
That anyone should therefore be suspicious
I more incline to Somerset than York.
Both are my kinsmen, and I love them both.
As well they may upbraid me with my crown,
Because, forsooth, the King of Scots is crown'd.
But your discretions better can persuade
Than I am able to instruct or teach;
And therefore, as we hither came in peace,
So let us still continue peace and love.
Cousin of York, we institute your Grace
To be our regent in these parts of France.
And, good my Lord of Somerset, unite
Your troops of horsemen with his bands of foot;
And, like true subjects, sons of your progenitors,
Go cheerfully together and digest
Your angry choler on your enemies.
Ourself, my Lord Protector, and the rest
After some respite will return to Calais;
From thence to England, where I hope ere long

80 servant i.e., follower **92 sanguine** blood-red. **leaves** petals **94 repugn** oppose, resist **100 benefit . . . arms** right to protect one's honor in a duel **102 quaint conceit** ingenious device **103 gloss** speciously fair appearance **107 Bewray'd** revealed **108 left** i.e., forgotten **109 out** appear, be revealed **113 emulations** contentions between rivals **114 cousins** kinsmen **118 toucheth** concerns **120 pledge** i.e., a glove or gauntlet flung down as a gage in a duel

121 let . . . first i.e., let the quarrel remain with me and Basset, who began it. (Basset similarly asks his lord, Somerset, to confirm this arrangement.) **129 objections** charges, accusations **141 grudging stomachs** resentful tempers **144 certified** informed **145 toy** trifle **150 That . . . that** for a trifle that which **167 digest** disperse, dissipate

To be presented, by your victories,
With Charles, Alençon, and that traitorous rout.

Flourish. Exeunt. Man[n]t York, Warwick, Exeter, [and] Vernon.

WARWICK
My Lord of York, I promise you, the King
Prettily, methought, did play the orator.

YORK
And so he did; but yet I like it not,
In that he wears the badge of Somerset.

WARWICK
Tush, that was but his fancy. Blame him not.
I dare presume, sweet prince, he thought no harm.

YORK
An if I wist he did—But let it rest.
Other affairs must now be managed.

Exeunt. Manet Exeter.

EXETER
Well didst thou, Richard, to suppress thy voice;
For, had the passions of thy heart burst out,
I fear we should have seen decipher'd there
More rancorous spite, more furious raging broils,
Than yet can be imagin'd or suppos'd.
But howsoe'er, no simple man that sees
This jarring discord of nobility,
This shouldering of each other in the court,
This factious bandying of their favorites,
But that it doth presage some ill event.
'Tis much when scepters are in children's hands,
But more when envy breeds unkind division.
There comes the ruin, there begins confusion. *Exit.*

[SCENE II]

Enter Talbot, with trump and drum [and forces], before Bordeaux.

TALBOT
Go to the gates of Bordeaux, trumpeter.
Summon their general unto the wall.

[Trumpet] sounds. Enter General [and others], aloft.

English John Talbot, captains, calls you forth,
Servant in arms to Harry King of England,
And thus he would: Open your city gates,
Be humble to us, call my sovereign yours,
And do him homage as obedient subjects,
And I'll withdraw me and my bloody power.
But if you frown upon this proffer'd peace,
You tempt the fury of my three attendants,
Lean famine, quartering steel, and climbing fire,
Who in a moment even with the earth
Shall lay your stately and air-braving towers,
If you forsake the offer of their love.

GENERAL
Thou ominous and fearful owl of death,
Our nation's terror and their bloody scourge,
The period of thy tyranny approacheth.
On us thou canst not enter but by death;
For, I protest, we are well fortified
And strong enough to issue out and fight.
If thou retire, the Dauphin, well appointed,
Stands with the snares of war to tangle thee.
On either hand thee there are squadrons pitch'd,
To wall thee from the liberty of flight;
And no way canst thou turn thee for redress,
But death doth front thee with apparent spoil
And pale destruction meets thee in the face.
Ten thousand French have ta'en the sacrament
To rive their dangerous artillery
Upon no Christian soul but English Talbot.
Lo, there thou stand'st, a breathing valiant man,
Of an invincible unconquer'd spirit.
This is the latest glory of thy praise
That I, thy enemy, due thee withal;
For ere the glass, that now begins to run,
Finish the process of his sandy hour,
These eyes, that see thee now well colored,
Shall see thee withered, bloody, pale, and dead.

Drum afar off.

Hark, Hark! The Dauphin's drum, a warning bell,
Sings heavy music to thy timorous soul;
And mine shall ring thy dire departure out.

Exit [with his men].

TALBOT
He fables not; I hear the enemy.
Out, some light horsemen, and peruse their wings.

[Exeunt some.]

O, negligent and heedless discipline!
How are we park'd and bounded in a pale,
A little herd of England's timorous deer,
Maz'd with a yelping kennel of French curs!
If we be English deer, be then in blood:
Not rascal-like, to fall down with a pinch,
But rather, moody-mad and desperate stags,
Turn on the bloody hounds with heads of steel
And make the cowards stand aloof at bay.
Sell every man his life as dear as mine,
And they shall find dear deer of us, my friends.
God and Saint George, Talbot and England's right,
Prosper our colors in this dangerous fight! *[Exeunt.]*

173 rout rabble **180 An . . . wist** if I knew for certain **190 bandying** contending. **favorites** followers **191 event** outcome **193 unkind** unnatural

IV.ii. Location: France. Before Bordeaux.
1 gates (As before at Orleans and Rouen, these city gates are represented by a door in the tiring house façade, which is imagined to be the walls of Bordeaux. Occupants of Bordeaux appearing *aloft* or on the walls are seen in the gallery backstage.) **5 would** wishes

11 quartering dismembering **13 air-braving** defying the heavens (by their height) **17 period** termination **21 appointed** equipped **23 thee** i.e., of you. **pitch'd** set in battle array **26 front** face. **apparent spoil** obvious destruction **28 ta'en the sacrament** i.e., confirmed their solemn oaths by taking the sacrament **29 rive** burst, fire **34 due** endue, invest **35 glass** hourglass **37 well colored** in health **41 departure** i.e., death **43 peruse** survey, reconnoitre **45 park'd** enclosed. **pale** fenced-in space **47 Maz'd with** (1) bewildered, amazed by (2) enclosed by, as in a labyrinth (?) **48 in blood** in prime condition **49 rascal-like** like young or inferior deer. **pinch** nip

[SCENE III]

Enter a Messenger that meets York. Enter York with trumpet and many Soldiers.

YORK
Are not the speedy scouts return'd again,
That dogg'd the mighty army of the Dauphin?

MESSENGER
They are return'd, my lord, and give it out
That he is march'd to Bordeaux with his power,
To fight with Talbot. As he march'd along,
By your espials were discovered
Two mightier troops than that the Dauphin led,
Which join'd with him and made their march for
Bordeaux. [*Exit.*]

YORK
A plague upon that villain Somerset,
That thus delays my promised supply
Of horsemen, that were levied for this siege!
Renowned Talbot doth expect my aid,
And I am louted by a traitor villain 13
And cannot help the noble chevalier.
God comfort him in this necessity!
If he miscarry, farewell wars in France. 16

Enter another Messenger, [Sir William Lucy].

LUCY
Thou princely leader of our English strength,
Never so needful on the earth of France,
Spur to the rescue of the noble Talbot,
Who now is girdled with a waist of iron
And hemm'd about with grim destruction.
To Bordeaux, warlike Duke! To Bordeaux, York!
Else, farewell Talbot, France, and England's honor.

YORK
O God, that Somerset, who in proud heart
Doth stop my cornets, were in Talbot's place! 25
So should we save a valiant gentleman
By forfeiting a traitor and a coward.
Mad ire and wrathful fury makes me weep,
That thus we die, while remiss traitors sleep.

LUCY
O, send some succor to the distress'd lord! 30

YORK
He dies, we lose; I break my warlike word;
We mourn, France smiles; we lose, they daily get;
All 'long of this vile traitor Somerset. 33

LUCY
Then God take mercy on brave Talbot's soul,
And on his son young John, who two hours since
I met in travel toward his warlike father!
This seven years did not Talbot see his son,
And now they meet where both their lives are done.

YORK
Alas, what joy shall noble Talbot have
To bid his young son welcome to his grave?
Away! Vexation almost stops my breath,
That sund'red friends greet in the hour of death.
Lucy, farewell. No more my fortune can 43
But curse the cause I cannot aid the man.
Maine, Blois, Poitiers, and Tours, are won away,
'Long all of Somerset and his delay.
Exit [*with his soldiers*].

LUCY
Thus, while the vulture of sedition
Feeds in the bosom of such great commanders,
Sleeping neglection doth betray to loss
The conquest of our scarce-cold conqueror,
That ever-living man of memory, 51
Henry the Fifth. Whiles they each other cross,
Lives, honors, lands, and all hurry to loss.

IV.iii. Location: France. Plains in Gascony.
13 louted made a fool of, mocked **16 miscarry** come to grief **25 cornets** cavalry units **30 distress'd** in difficulties **33 'long of** on account of

43 can is able to do **51 ever-living . . . memory** man of ever-living memory

[SCENE IV]

Enter Somerset, with his army; [a Captain of Talbot's with him].

SOMERSET
It is too late; I cannot send them now.
This expedition was by York and Talbot
Too rashly plotted. All our general force 3
Might with a sally of the very town 4
Be buckled with. The over-daring Talbot 5
Hath sullied all his gloss of former honor
By this unheedful, desperate, wild adventure.
York set him on to fight and die in shame,
That, Talbot dead, great York might bear the name. 9

CAPTAIN
Here is Sir William Lucy, who with me
Set from our o'ermatch'd forces forth for aid.

[*Sir William Lucy comes forward.*]

SOMERSET
How now, Sir William, whither were you sent?

LUCY
Whither, my lord? From bought and sold Lord
Talbot,
Who, ring'd about with bold adversity,
Cries out for noble York and Somerset
To beat assailing death from his weak legions;
And whiles the honorable captain there
Drops bloody sweat from his war-wearied limbs,
And, in advantage ling'ring, looks for rescue, 19
You, his false hopes, the trust of England's honor,
Keep off aloof with worthless emulation. 21
Let not your private discord keep away
The levied succors that should lend him aid,

IV.iv. Location: France. Scene continues. Lucy does not leave the stage.
3–5 All . . . with i.e., our entire army might be successfully encountered by a sortie of the mere French garrison in Bordeaux, unsupported by the other French armies coming to the relief of Bordeaux **9 That** so that. **bear the name** i.e., receive all honor as supreme commander in France **19 in advantage ling'ring** making the best he can out of delaying tactics (?) **21 worthless emulation** ignoble rivalry

While he, renowned noble gentleman,
Yield up his life unto a world of odds.
Orleans the Bastard, Charles, Burgundy,
Alençon, Reignier, compass him about,
And Talbot perisheth by your default.

SOMERSET
York set him on. York should have sent him aid.

LUCY
And York as fast upon your Grace exclaims, 30
Swearing that you withhold his levied host,
Collected for this expedition.

SOMERSET
York lies. He might have sent and had the horse. 33
I owe him little duty, and less love,
And take foul scorn to fawn on him by sending. 35

LUCY
The fraud of England, not the force of France,
Hath now entrapp'd the noble-minded Talbot.
Never to England shall he bear his life,
But dies betray'd to fortune by your strife.

SOMERSET
Come, go. I will dispatch the horsemen straight.
Within six hours they will be at his aid.

LUCY
Too late comes rescue. He is ta'en or slain;
For fly he could not, if he would have fled;
And fly would Talbot never, though he might.

SOMERSET
If he be dead, brave Talbot, then adieu!

LUCY
His fame lives in the world, his shame in you.
Exeunt.

[SCENE V]

Enter Talbot and his son [John].

TALBOT
O young John Talbot, I did send for thee
To tutor thee in stratagems of war,
That Talbot's name might be in thee reviv'd
When sapless age and weak unable limbs
Should bring thy father to his drooping chair.
But, O malignant and ill-boding stars!
Now thou art come unto a feast of death,
A terrible and unavoided danger. 8
Therefore, dear boy, mount on my swiftest horse,
And I'll direct thee how thou shalt escape
By sudden flight. Come, dally not, be gone.

JOHN
Is my name Talbot? And am I your son?
And shall I fly? O, if you love my mother,
Dishonor not her honorable name
To make a bastard and a slave of me!

30 upon . . . exclaims accuses your Grace **33 might . . . had** i.e., had and could have sent **35 take foul scorn** consider it humiliating

IV.v. Location: France. A field of battle near Bordeaux.
8 unavoided unavoidable

The world will say he is not Talbot's blood,
That basely fled when noble Talbot stood.

TALBOT
Fly, to revenge my death, if I be slain.

JOHN
He that flies so will ne'er return again.

TALBOT
If we both stay, we both are sure to die.

JOHN
Then let me stay, and, father, do you fly.
Your loss is great, so your regard should be; 22
My worth unknown, no loss is known in me.
Upon my death the French can little boast;
In yours they will, in you all hopes are lost.
Flight cannot stain the honor you have won;
But mine it will, that no exploit have done.
You fled for vantage, every one will swear; 28
But, if I bow, they'll say it was for fear.
There is no hope that ever I will stay,
If the first hour I shrink and run away.
Here on my knee I beg mortality, 32
Rather than life preserv'd with infamy.

TALBOT
Shall all thy mother's hopes lie in one tomb?

JOHN
Ay, rather than I'll shame my mother's womb.

TALBOT
Upon my blessing, I command thee go.

JOHN
To fight I will, but not to fly the foe.

TALBOT
Part of thy father may be sav'd in thee.

JOHN
No part of him but will be shame in me.

TALBOT
Thou never hadst renown, nor canst not lose it.

JOHN
Yes, your renowned name. Shall flight abuse it?

TALBOT
Thy father's charge shall clear thee from that stain.

JOHN
You cannot witness for me, being slain. 43
If death be so apparent, then both fly.

TALBOT
And leave my followers here to fight and die?
My age was never tainted with such shame. 46

JOHN
And shall my youth be guilty of such blame?
No more can I be severed from your side
Than can yourself yourself in twain divide.
Stay, go, do what you will—the like do I;
For live I will not, if my father die.

TALBOT
Then here I take my leave of thee, fair son,
Born to eclipse thy life this afternoon.
Come, side by side together live and die,
And soul with soul from France to heaven fly.
Exeunt.

22 regard heed for yourself **28 vantage** military advantage **32 mortality** death **43 being slain** i.e., you having been slain **46 age** lifetime

[SCENE VI]

Alarum. Excursions, wherein Talbot's Son is hemmed about, and Talbot rescues him.

TALBOT
Saint George and victory! Fight, soldiers, fight!
The Regent hath with Talbot broke his word
And left us to the rage of France his sword.
Where is John Talbot? Pause, and take thy breath.
I gave thee life and rescu'd thee from death.

JOHN
O, twice my father, twice am I thy son!
The life thou gav'st me first was lost and done,
Till with thy warlike sword, despite of fate,
To my determin'd time thou gav'st new date.

TALBOT
When from the Dauphin's crest thy sword struck fire,
It warm'd thy father's heart with proud desire
Of bold-fac'd victory. Then leaden age,
Quicken'd with youthful spleen and warlike rage,
Beat down Alençon, Orleans, Burgundy,
And from the pride of Gallia rescued thee.
The ireful bastard Orleans, that drew blood
From thee, my boy, and had the maidenhood
Of thy first fight, I soon encountered,
And interchanging blows I quickly shed
Some of his bastard blood; and in disgrace
Bespoke him thus: "Contaminated, base,
And misbegotten blood I spill of thine,
Mean and right poor, for that pure blood of mine
Which thou didst force from Talbot, my brave boy."
Here, purposing the Bastard to destroy,
Came in strong rescue. Speak, thy father's care.
Art thou not weary, John? How dost thou fare?
Wilt thou yet leave the battle, boy, and fly,
Now thou art seal'd the son of chivalry?
Fly, to revenge my death when I am dead.
The help of one stands me in little stead.
O, too much folly is it, well I wot,
To hazard all our lives in one small boat!
If I today die not with Frenchmen's rage,
Tomorrow I shall die with mickle age.
By me they nothing gain an if I stay;
'Tis but the short'ning of my life one day.
In thee thy mother dies, our household's name,
My death's revenge, thy youth, and England's fame.
All these and more we hazard by thy stay;
All these are sav'd if thou wilt fly away.

JOHN
The sword of Orleans hath not made me smart;
These words of yours draw life-blood from my heart.
On that advantage, bought with such a shame,
To save a paltry life and slay bright fame,
Before young Talbot from old Talbot fly,
The coward horse that bears me fall and die!
And like me to the peasant boys of France,
To be shame's scorn and subject of mischance!
Surely, by all the glory you have won,
An if I fly, I am not Talbot's son.
Then talk no more of flight. It is no boot.
If son to Talbot, die at Talbot's foot.

TALBOT
Then follow thou thy desp'rate sire of Crete,
Thou Icarus. Thy life to me is sweet.
If thou wilt fight, fight by thy father's side;
And, commendable prov'd, let's die in pride.
Exeunt.

IV.vi. Location: The battlefield still, moments later; the scene is continuous.
2 The Regent i.e., the Duke of York. (Cf. IV.i.162–163.) **3 France his** France's **9 determin'd** having been determined to end. **date** limit, termination **13 spleen** i.e., courage, ardor **15 Gallia** France **20 in disgrace** by way of insult **23 Mean** base, inferior **25 purposing** as I purposed **29 seal'd** certified **32 wot** know **35 mickle** great **42 smart** feel pain

44 On that advantage i.e., to gain that advantage of safety **47 fall** i.e., may it fall **48 like** liken **52 boot** profit, advantage **55 Thou Icarus** (Daedalus of Crete and his son Icarus escaped from the labyrinth by means of wings that the father's ingenuity had devised. As they flew across the sea, Icarus mounted too high, the sun's heat melted the wax by which his wings were attached, and he fell into the sea, hence called the Icarian Sea, and was lost.)

[SCENE VII]

Alarum. Excursions. Enter old Talbot led [by a Servant].

TALBOT
Where is my other life? Mine own is gone.
O, where's young Talbot? Where is valiant John?
Triumphant Death, smear'd with captivity,
Young Talbot's valor makes me smile at thee.
When he perceiv'd me shrink and on my knee,
His bloody sword he brandish'd over me,
And like a hungry lion, did commence
Rough deeds of rage and stern impatience.
But when my angry guardant stood alone,
Tend'ring my ruin and assail'd of none,
Dizzy-ey'd fury and great rage of heart
Suddenly made him from my side to start
Into the clust'ring battle of the French;
And in that sea of blood my boy did drench
His over-mounting spirit; and there died
My Icarus, my blossom, in his pride.

Enter [Soldiers], with John Talbot, borne.

SERVANT
O my dear lord, lo, where your son is borne!

TALBOT
Thou antic Death, which laugh'st us here to scorn,

IV.vii. Location: The battlefield still; the scene is continuous.
3 smear'd with captivity i.e., stained with the blood of your victims (?) **5 shrink** retire in battle **9 guardant** guardian **10 Tend'ring** being concerned for **13 battle** army **14 drench** drown **18 antic** i.e., grinning. (A personification probably suggested by grotesque pictorial representations of the Middle Ages and early Renaissance, such as the Dance of Death.)

Anon, from thy insulting tyranny,
Coupled in bonds of perpetuity,
Two Talbots, winged through the lither sky, 21
In thy despite shall scape mortality.
O thou, whose wounds become hard-favored Death, 23
Speak to thy father ere thou yield thy breath!
Brave Death by speaking, whether he will or no; 25
Imagine him a Frenchman and thy foe.
Poor boy! He smiles, methinks, as who should say, 27
Had Death been French, then Death had died today.
Come, come, and lay him in his father's arms.
[John is laid in his father's arms.]
My spirit can no longer bear these harms.
Soldiers, adieu! I have what I would have,
Now my old arms are young John Talbot's grave. 32
Dies.

Enter Charles, Alençon, Burgundy, Bastard, and Pucelle, [and forces].

CHARLES
Had York and Somerset brought rescue in,
We should have found a bloody day of this.

BASTARD
How the young whelp of Talbot's, raging wood, 35
Did flesh his puny sword in Frenchmen's blood! 36

PUCELLE
Once I encount'red him, and thus I said:
"Thou maiden youth, be vanquish'd by a maid." 38
But, with a proud majestical high scorn,
He answer'd thus: "Young Talbot was not born
To be the pillage of a giglot wench." 41
So, rushing in the bowels of the French,
He left me proudly, as unworthy fight.

BURGUNDY
Doubtless he would have made a noble knight.
See where he lies inhearsed in the arms 45
Of the most bloody nurser of his harms! 46

BASTARD
Hew them to pieces, hack their bones asunder,
Whose life was England's glory, Gallia's wonder.

CHARLES
O, no, forbear! For that which we have fled
During the life, let us not wrong it dead.

Enter [Sir William] Lucy [attended; Herald of the French preceding].

LUCY
Herald, conduct me to the Dauphin's tent,
To know who hath obtain'd the glory of the day.

CHARLES
On what submissive message art thou sent?

LUCY
Submission, Dauphin? 'Tis a mere French word.
We English warriors wot not what it means.
I come to know what prisoners thou hast ta'en
And to survey the bodies of the dead.

CHARLES
For prisoners ask'st thou? Hell our prison is. 58
But tell me whom thou seek'st.

LUCY
But where's the great Alcides of the field, 60
Valiant Lord Talbot, Earl of Shrewsbury,
Created, for his rare success in arms,
Great Earl of Washford, Waterford, and Valence,
Lord Talbot of Goodrig and Urchinfield,
Lord Strange of Blackmere, Lord Verdun of Alton,
Lord Cromwell of Wingfield, Lord Furnival of Sheffield,
The thrice-victorious Lord of Falconbridge,
Knight of the noble order of Saint George,
Worthy Saint Michael, and the Golden Fleece,
Great marshal to Henry the Sixth 70
Of all his wars within the realm of France?

PUCELLE
Here is a silly stately style indeed!
The Turk, that two and fifty kingdoms hath,
Writes not so tedious a style as this.
Him that thou magnifi'st with all these titles
Stinking and fly-blown lies here at our feet.

LUCY
Is Talbot slain, the Frenchmen's only scourge,
Your kingdom's terror and black Nemesis? 78
O, were mine eyeballs into bullets turn'd,
That I in rage might shoot them at your faces!
O, that I could but call these dead to life!
It were enough to fright the realm of France.
Were but his picture left amongst you here,
It would amaze the proudest of you all.
Give me their bodies, that I may bear them hence
And give them burial as beseems their worth.

PUCELLE
I think this upstart is old Talbot's ghost,
He speaks with such a proud commanding spirit.
For God's sake, let him have 'em! To keep them here,
They would but stink and putrefy the air.

CHARLES
Go, take their bodies hence.

LUCY
I'll bear them hence; but from their ashes shall be rear'd
A phoenix that shall make all France afeard. 93

CHARLES
So we be rid of them, do with 'em what thou wilt.
And now to Paris in this conquering vein.
All will be ours, now bloody Talbot's slain. *Exeunt.*
[The bodies are borne out.]

21 lither yielding **23 become . . . Death** make Death, otherwise hideous, beautiful **25 Brave** defy **27 as who** as if one **32 s.d. Dies** (Historically, Talbot did not die until some twenty-two years after Henry VI's coronation in Paris. Talbot's campaign in the Bordeaux region was successful, and included the taking of the city.) **35 wood** mad **36 flesh** use for the first time in battle **38 maiden** i.e., not yet initiated in warfare **41 giglot** wanton **45 inhearsed** as in a coffin **46 nurser . . . harms** i.e., sire of his capacity for doing harm to his enemy

58 Hell . . . is i.e., we have slain rather than taking prisoner **60 Alcides** Hercules. (Literally, descendant of Alcaeus, who was the father of Hercules' stepfather.) **78 Nemesis** the personification of retribution for arrogance **93 phoenix** fabulous bird, the only one of its kind, which every five hundred years built itself a funeral pile and died upon it; from the ashes a new phoenix arose

[ACT V] • SCENE [I]

Sennet. Enter King, Gloucester, and Exeter.

KING
Have you perus'd the letters from the Pope,
The Emperor, and the Earl of Armagnac?

GLOUCESTER
I have, my lord, and their intent is this:
They humbly sue unto your excellence
To have a godly peace concluded of
Between the realms of England and of France.

KING
How doth your Grace affect their motion?

GLOUCESTER
Well, my good lord, and as the only means
To stop effusion of our Christian blood
And stablish quietness on every side.

KING
Ay, marry, uncle; for I always thought
It was both impious and unnatural
That such immanity and bloody strife
Should reign among professors of one faith.

GLOUCESTER
Beside, my lord, the sooner to effect
And surer bind this knot of amity,
The Earl of Armagnac, near knit to Charles,
A man of great authority in France,
Proffers his only daughter to your Grace
In marriage, with a large and sumptuous dowry.

KING
Marriage, uncle! Alas, my years are young,
And fitter is my study and my books
Than wanton dalliance with a paramour.
Yet call th' ambassadors; and, as you please,
So let them have their answers everyone.
I shall be well content with any choice
Tends to God's glory and my country's weal.

Enter Winchester [in Cardinal's habit], and three Ambassadors, [one a Papal Legate].

EXETER [*Aside*]
What? Is my Lord of Winchester install'd,
And call'd unto a cardinal's degree?
Then I perceive that will be verified
Henry the Fifth did sometime prophesy:
"If once he come to be a cardinal,
He'll make his cap co-equal with the crown."

KING
My Lords Ambassadors, your several suits
Have been consider'd and debated on.
Your purpose is both good and reasonable;
And therefore are we certainly resolv'd
To draw conditions of a friendly peace,
Which by my Lord of Winchester we mean
Shall be transported presently to France.

GLOUCESTER [*To the Ambassador from Armagnac*]
And for the proffer of my lord your master,
I have inform'd his Highness so at large
As, liking of the lady's virtuous gifts,
Her beauty, and the value of her dower,
He doth intend she shall be England's queen.

KING
In argument and proof of which contract,
Bear her this jewel, pledge of my affection.
[*Presents jewel.*]
And so, my Lord Protector, see them guarded
And safely brought to Dover, wherein shipp'd,
Commit them to the fortune of the sea.
Exeunt [*all but Winchester and Legate*].

WINCHESTER
Stay, my lord legate. You shall first receive
The sum of money which I promised
Should be delivered to his Holiness
For clothing me in these grave ornaments.

LEGATE
I will attend upon your lordship's leisure.
[*Steps aside.*]

WINCHESTER [*Aside*]
Now Winchester will not submit, I trow,
Or be inferior to the proudest peer.
Humphrey of Gloucester, thou shalt well perceive
That neither in birth or for authority
The Bishop will be overborne by thee.
I'll either make thee stoop and bend thy knee,
Or sack this country with a mutiny. *Exeunt.*

SCENE [II]

Enter Charles, Burgundy, Alençon, Bastard, Reignier, and Joan [la Pucelle, with forces].

CHARLES
These news, my lords, may cheer our drooping spirits:
'Tis said the stout Parisians do revolt
And turn again unto the warlike French.

ALENÇON
Then march to Paris, royal Charles of France,
And keep not back your powers in dalliance.

PUCELLE
Peace be amongst them, if they turn to us;
Else, ruin combat with their palaces!

V.i. Location: London. The palace.
1–2 Pope . . . Armagnac (During the year 1434–35 efforts were made by the Emperor Sigismund and other potentates to effect a peace. The marriage proposal of the King to the Earl of Armagnac's daughter, however, was made eight or nine years later.) **7 affect their motion** incline toward their proposal **13 immanity** atrocious savagery **17 knit** i.e., by ties of kinship **27 Tends** which tends **29 call'd . . . degree** (Winchester's newly being made a cardinal is inconsistent with I.iii.19 and 36.) **31 sometime** at one time **33 cap** i.e., Cardinal's scullcap

42 at large in full **49 shipp'd** embarked **54 grave ornaments** i.e., solemn robes of ecclesiastical office

V.ii. Location: France. Fields before Angiers.
2 stout courageous **5 powers** forces **7 Else . . . palaces** otherwise, let ruin destroy their palaces

Enter Scout.

SCOUT
Success unto our valiant general,
And happiness to his accomplices!

CHARLES
What tidings send our scouts? I prithee, speak.

SCOUT
The English army, that divided was
Into two parties, is now conjoin'd in one
And means to give you battle presently.

CHARLES
Somewhat too sudden, sirs, the warning is,
But we will presently provide for them.

BURGUNDY
I trust the ghost of Talbot is not there.
Now he is gone, my lord, you need not fear.

PUCELLE
Of all base passions, fear is most accurs'd.
Command the conquest, Charles, it shall be thine,
Let Henry fret and all the world repine.

CHARLES
Then on, my lords; and France be fortunate!
Exeunt.

[SCENE III]

Alarum. Excursions. Enter Joan la Pucelle.

PUCELLE
The Regent conquers, and the Frenchmen fly.
Now help, ye charming spells and periapts,
And ye choice spirits that admonish me
And give me signs of future accidents. *Thunder.*
You speedy helpers, that are substitutes
Under the lordly monarch of the north,
Appear and aid me in this enterprise.

Enter Fiends.

This speedy and quick appearance argues proof
Of your accustom'd diligence to me.
Now, ye familiar spirits, that are cull'd
Out of the powerful regions under earth,
Help me this once, that France may get the field.
They walk, and speak not.
O, hold me not with silence over-long!
Where I was wont to feed you with my blood,
I'll lop a member off and give it you
In earnest of a further benefit,
So you do condescend to help me now.
They hang their heads.
No hope to have redress? My body shall
Pay recompense, if you will grant my suit.
They shake their heads.
Cannot my body nor blood-sacrifice
Entreat you to your wonted furtherance?
Then take my soul, my body, soul, and all,
Before that England give the French the foil.
They depart.
See, they forsake me! Now the time is come
That France must vail her lofty-plumed crest
And let her head fall into England's lap.
My ancient incantations are too weak,
And hell too strong for me to buckle with.
Now, France, thy glory droopeth to the dust. *Exit.*

Excursions. Burgundy and York fight hand to hand. French fly. [Pucelle is brought in captive.]

YORK
Damsel of France, I think I have you fast.
Unchain your spirits now with spelling charms
And try if they can gain your liberty.
A goodly prize, fit for the devil's grace!
See, how the ugly witch doth bend her brows,
As if, with Circe, she would change my shape!

PUCELLE
Chang'd to a worser shape thou canst not be.

YORK
O, Charles the Dauphin is a proper man!
No shape but his can please your dainty eye.

PUCELLE
A plaguing mischief light on Charles and thee!
And may ye both be suddenly surpris'd
By bloody hands, in sleeping on your beds!

YORK
Fell banning hag, enchantress, hold thy tongue!

PUCELLE
I prithee, give me leave to curse awhile.

YORK
Curse, miscreant, when thou com'st to the stake.
Exeunt.

Alarum. Enter Suffolk, with Margaret in his hand.

SUFFOLK
Be what thou wilt, thou art my prisoner.
Gazes on her.
O fairest beauty, do not fear nor fly!
For I will touch thee but with reverent hands.
I kiss these fingers for eternal peace,
And lay them gently on thy tender side.
Who art thou? Say, that I may honor thee.

MARGARET
Margaret my name, and daughter to a king,
The King of Naples, whosoe'er thou art.

SUFFOLK
An earl I am, and Suffolk am I call'd.
Be not offended, nature's miracle,
Thou art allotted to be ta'en by me.
So doth the swan her downy cygnets save,
Keeping them prisoner underneath her wings.

9 accomplices allies

V.iii. Location: Before Angiers still. The scene is continuous.
1 The Regent i.e., the Duke of York **2 charming** working by charms. **periapts** amulets **3 admonish** forewarn **4 accidents** occurrences **5 substitutes** deputies, agents **6 north** (Evil spirits were frequently associated with the north.) **12 get the field** win the battle **16 earnest** partial payment

21 wonted furtherance customary aid **23 foil** defeat **25 vail** lower **27 ancient** former **31 spirits** i.e., the demons—"familiars"—attending on Joan. (Cf. I. 10.) **spelling charms** charms that cast a spell **35 Circe** sorceress celebrated for her power to change men into swine **37 proper** handsome. (Said sardonically.) **38 dainty** fastidious **42 Fell** fierce, cruel. **banning** cursing **48 for** in token of

Yet, if this servile usage once offend,
Go and be free again as Suffolk's friend.

She is going.

O, stay! [*Aside.*] I have no power to let her pass;
My hand would free her, but my heart says no.
As plays the sun upon the glassy streams,
Twinkling another counterfeited beam,
So seems this gorgeous beauty to mine eyes.
Fain would I woo her, yet I dare not speak.
I'll call for pen and ink, and write my mind.
Fie, de la Pole, disable not thyself.
Hast not a tongue? Is she not here?
Wilt thou be daunted at a woman's sight?
Ay, beauty's princely majesty is such,
Confounds the tongue and makes the senses rough.

MARGARET
Say, Earl of Suffolk—if thy name be so—
What ransom must I pay before I pass?
For I perceive I am thy prisoner.

SUFFOLK [*Aside*]
How canst thou tell she will deny thy suit,
Before thou make a trial of her love?

MARGARET
Why speak'st thou not? What ransom must I pay?

SUFFOLK [*Aside*]
She's beautiful, and therefore to be woo'd;
She is a woman, therefore to be won.

MARGARET
Wilt thou accept of ransom, yea, or no?

SUFFOLK [*Aside*]
Fond man, remember that thou hast a wife.
Then how can Margaret be thy paramour?

MARGARET
I were best to leave him, for he will not hear.

SUFFOLK [*Aside*]
There all is marr'd; there lies a cooling card.

MARGARET
He talks at random. Sure the man is mad.

SUFFOLK [*Aside*]
And yet a dispensation may be had.

MARGARET
And yet I would that you would answer me.

SUFFOLK [*Aside*]
I'll win this Lady Margaret. For whom?
Why, for my king. Tush, that's a wooden thing!

MARGARET
He talks of wood. It is some carpenter.

SUFFOLK [*Aside*]
Yet so my fancy may be satisfied,
And peace established between these realms.
But there remains a scruple in that too;
For though her father be the King of Naples,
Duke of Anjou and Maine, yet is he poor,
And our nobility will scorn the match.

MARGARET
Hear ye, captain, are you not at leisure?

SUFFOLK [*Aside*]
It shall be so, disdain they ne'er so much.
Henry is youthful and will quickly yield.—
Madam, I have a secret to reveal.

MARGARET [*Aside*]
What though I be enthrall'd? He seems a knight,
And will not any way dishonor me.

SUFFOLK
Lady, vouchsafe to listen what I say.

MARGARET [*Aside*]
Perhaps I shall be rescu'd by the French,
And then I need not crave his courtesy.

SUFFOLK
Sweet madam, give me hearing in a cause—

MARGARET [*Aside*]
Tush, women have been captivate ere now.

SUFFOLK
Lady, wherefore talk you so?

MARGARET
I cry you mercy, 'tis but quid for quo.

SUFFOLK
Say, gentle Princess, would you not suppose
Your bondage happy, to be made a queen?

MARGARET
To be a queen in bondage is more vile
Than is a slave in base servility;
For princes should be free.

SUFFOLK And so shall you,
If happy England's royal king be free.

MARGARET
Why, what concerns his freedom unto me?

SUFFOLK
I'll undertake to make thee Henry's queen,
To put a golden scepter in thy hand,
And set a precious crown upon thy head,
If thou wilt condescend to be my—

MARGARET What?

SUFFOLK
His love.

MARGARET
I am unworthy to be Henry's wife.

SUFFOLK
No, gentle madam. I unworthy am
To woo so fair a dame to be his wife
And have no portion in the choice myself.
How say you, madam, are ye so content?

MARGARET
An if my father please, I am content.

SUFFOLK
Then call our captains and our colors forth.
And, madam, at your father's castle walls
We'll crave a parley, to confer with him.

Sound [a parley]. Enter Reignier on the walls.

See, Reignier, see, thy daughter prisoner!

REIGNIER
To whom?

62 As . . . streams just as the sun plays upon the glassy surface of a stream **63 Twinkling** causing to twinkle. **counterfeited** i.e., reflected **67 disable** disparage **71 Confounds** that it confounds **81 Fond** foolish **84 cooling card** something that cools one's ardor or dashes one's hopes **86 dispensation** papal permission (to divorce a wife) **89 wooden** stupid. (I.e., either King Henry, or Suffolk's plan.)

101 enthrall'd captured **107 captivate** taken captive **109 cry you mercy** beg your pardon. **quid for quo** tit for tat **130 s.d. on the walls** (As in previous sieges, the "walls" of Angiers are here represented by the tiring house façade, with Reignier appearing above, in the gallery backstage.)

SUFFOLK To me.
REIGNIER Suffolk, what remedy?
I am a soldier, and unapt to weep
Or to exclaim on fortune's fickleness.

SUFFOLK
Yes, there is remedy enough, my lord.
Consent, and for thy honor give consent,
Thy daughter shall be wedded to my king,
Whom I with pain have woo'd and won thereto;
And this her easy-held imprisonment
Hath gain'd thy daughter princely liberty.

REIGNIER
Speaks Suffolk as he thinks?
SUFFOLK Fair Margaret knows
That Suffolk doth not flatter, face, or feign.

REIGNIER
Upon thy princely warrant, I descend
To give thee answer of thy just demand.
[Exit from the walls.]

SUFFOLK
And here I will expect thy coming.

Trumpets sound. Enter Reignier [below].

REIGNIER
Welcome, brave earl, into our territories.
Command in Anjou what your honor pleases.

SUFFOLK
Thanks, Reignier, happy for so sweet a child,
Fit to be made companion with a king.
What answer makes your Grace unto my suit?

REIGNIER
Since thou dost deign to woo her little worth
To be the princely bride of such a lord,
Upon condition I may quietly
Enjoy mine own, the country Maine and Anjou,
Free from oppression or the stroke of war,
My daughter shall be Henry's, if he please.

SUFFOLK
That is her ransom. I deliver her,
And those two counties I will undertake
Your Grace shall well and quietly enjoy.

REIGNIER
And I again, in Henry's royal name,
As deputy unto that gracious king,
Give thee her hand, for sign of plighted faith.

SUFFOLK
Reignier of France, I give thee kingly thanks,
Because this is in traffic of a king.
[*Aside.*] And yet, methinks, I could be well content
To be mine own attorney in this case.—
I'll over then to England with this news,
And make this marriage to be solemniz'd.
So farewell, Reignier. Set this diamond safe
In golden palaces, as it becomes.

REIGNIER
I do embrace thee, as I would embrace
The Christian prince, King Henry, were he here.
[He embraces Suffolk.]

MARGARET
Farewell, my lord. Good wishes, praise, and prayers
Shall Suffolk ever have of Margaret. *She is going.*

SUFFOLK
Farewell, sweet madam—but hark you, Margaret—
No princely commendations to my king?

MARGARET
Such commendations as becomes a maid,
A virgin, and his servant, say to him.

SUFFOLK
Words sweetly plac'd and modestly directed.
But, madam, I must trouble you again—
No loving token to his Majesty?

MARGARET
Yes, my good lord, a pure unspotted heart,
Never yet taint with love, I send the King.

SUFFOLK
And this withal. *Kiss her.*

MARGARET
That for thyself. I will not so presume
To send such peevish tokens to a king.
[Exeunt Reignier and Margaret.]

SUFFOLK
O, wert thou for myself! But, Suffolk, stay.
Thou mayest not wander in that labyrinth;
There Minotaurs and ugly treasons lurk.
Solicit Henry with her wondrous praise;
Bethink thee on her virtues that surmount,
And natural graces that extinguish art;
Repeat their semblance often on the seas,
That, when thou com'st to kneel at Henry's feet,
Thou mayest bereave him of his wits with wonder.
Exit.

[SCENE IV]

Enter York, Warwick, Shepherd, [and] Pucelle [guarded].

YORK
Bring forth that sorceress condemn'd to burn.

SHEPHERD
Ah, Joan, this kills thy father's heart outright!
Have I sought every country far and near,
And, now it is my chance to find thee out,
Must I behold thy timeless cruel death?
Ah, Joan, sweet daughter Joan, I'll die with thee!

PUCELLE
Decrepit miser, base ignoble wretch!
I am descended of a gentler blood.
Thou art no father nor no friend of mine.

142 face show a false face, deceive **145 expect** await **160 again** in return. (Reignier gives back his daughter into the hands of Suffolk, who has released her to her father three lines earlier.) **161 As deputy** i.e., to you, Suffolk, as deputy **164 traffic** business **170 as it becomes** as befits such a jewel

183 taint tainted **184 withal** in addition **186 peevish** trivial **188 labyrinth** a structure built by Daedalus consisting of intricate passageways where the Minotaur—a monster born from the union of the Cretan king's wife with a bull—was confined **190 her wondrous praise** praise of her wondrous beauty **192 extinguish** eclipse **193 Repeat their semblance** rehearse mentally the image of her virtues

V.iv. Location: France. Camp of the Duke of York in Anjou.
4 find thee out discover you **5 timeless** premature **7 miser** wretch **8 gentler** more noble **9 friend** kinsman

SHEPHERD

Out, out! My lords, an please you, 'tis not so.
I did beget her, all the parish knows.
Her mother liveth yet, can testify
She was the first fruit of my bach'lorship.

WARWICK

Graceless, wilt thou deny thy parentage?

YORK

This argues what her kind of life hath been,
Wicked and vile; and so her death concludes.

SHEPHERD

Fie, Joan, that thou wilt be so obstacle!
God knows thou art a collop of my flesh,
And for thy sake have I shed many a tear.
Deny me not, I prithee, gentle Joan.

PUCELLE

Peasant, avaunt! You have suborn'd this man
Of purpose to obscure my noble birth.

SHEPHERD

'Tis true, I gave a noble to the priest
The morn that I was wedded to her mother.
Kneel down and take my blessing, good my girl.
Wilt thou not stoop? Now cursed be the time
Of thy nativity! I would the milk
Thy mother gave thee when thou suck'dst her breast
Had been a little ratsbane for thy sake!
Or else, when thou didst keep my lambs a-field,
I wish some ravenous wolf had eaten thee!
Dost thou deny thy father, cursed drab?
O, burn her, burn her! Hanging is too good. *Exit.*

YORK

Take her away, for she hath liv'd too long,
To fill the world with vicious qualities.

PUCELLE

First, let me tell you whom you have condemn'd:
Not me begotten of a shepherd swain,
But issued from the progeny of kings,
Virtuous and holy, chosen from above
By inspiration of celestial grace
To work exceeding miracles on earth.
I never had to do with wicked spirits.
But you, that are polluted with your lusts,
Stain'd with the guiltless blood of innocents,
Corrupt and tainted with a thousand vices—
Because you want the grace that others have,
You judge it straight a thing impossible
To compass wonders but by help of devils.
No, misconceived! Joan of Arc hath been
A virgin from her tender infancy,
Chaste and immaculate in very thought,
Whose maiden blood, thus rigorously effus'd,
Will cry for vengeance at the gates of heaven.

YORK

Ay, ay. Away with her to execution.

WARWICK

And hark ye, sirs: because she is a maid,
Spare for no faggots, let there be enow.
Place barrels of pitch upon the fatal stake,
That so her torture may be shortened.

PUCELLE

Will nothing turn your unrelenting hearts?
Then, Joan, discover thine infirmity,
That warranteth by law to be thy privilege.
I am with child, ye bloody homicides!
Murder not then the fruit within my womb,
Although ye hale me to a violent death.

YORK

Now heaven forfend! The holy maid with child?

WARWICK

The greatest miracle that e'er ye wrought.
Is all your strict preciseness come to this?

YORK

She and the Dauphin have been juggling.
I did imagine what would be her refuge.

WARWICK

Well, go to. We'll have no bastards live,
Especially since Charles must father it.

PUCELLE

You are deceiv'd. My child is none of his.
It was Alençon that enjoy'd my love.

YORK

Alençon, that notorious Machiavel?
It dies, an if it had a thousand lives.

PUCELLE

O, give me leave, I have deluded you.
'Twas neither Charles nor yet the Duke I nam'd,
But Reignier, King of Naples, that prevail'd.

WARWICK

A married man! That's most intolerable.

YORK

Why, here's a girl! I think she knows not well,
There were so many, whom she may accuse.

WARWICK

It's sign she hath been liberal and free.

YORK

And yet, forsooth, she is a virgin pure!
Strumpet, thy words condemn thy brat and thee.
Use no entreaty, for it is in vain.

PUCELLE

Then lead me hence; with whom I leave my curse.
May never glorious sun reflex his beams
Upon the country where you make abode,
But darkness and the gloomy shade of death
Environ you, till mischief and despair
Drive you to break your necks or hang yourselves!
Exit [guarded].

YORK

Break thou in pieces and consume to ashes,
Thou foul accursed minister of hell!

Enter [Winchester, now] Cardinal [Beaufort, with letters, attended].

CARDINAL

Lord Regent, I do greet your excellence

16 concludes (1) confirms (2) ends **17 obstacle** obstinate **18 collop** slice **23 noble** coin worth 6 shillings 8 pence **32 drab** whore **46 want** lack **47 straight** straightway, at once **49 misconceived** you who have a wrong idea **52 rigorously effus'd** mercilessly shed **56 enow** enough

60 discover reveal **61 privilege** i.e., to be spared until the birth of her supposed child **65 forfend** forbid. (Said sardonically.) **67 preciseness** propriety, modesty **71 must father it** is evidently the father **74 Machiavel** (In the popular Elizabethan conception, Niccolo Machiavelli, Italian political philosopher, symbolized political immorality and ruthless ambition.) **82 liberal** unrestrained, licentious

With letters of commission from the King.
For know, my lords, the states of Christendom,
Mov'd with remorse of these outrageous broils,
Have earnestly implor'd a general peace
Betwixt our nation and the aspiring French;
And here at hand the Dauphin and his train
Approacheth, to confer about some matter.

YORK
Is all our travail turn'd to this effect?
After the slaughter of so many peers,
So many captains, gentlemen, and soldiers,
That in this quarrel have been overthrown
And sold their bodies for their country's benefit,
Shall we at last conclude effeminate peace?
Have we not lost most part of all the towns,
By treason, falsehood, and by treachery,
Our great progenitors had conquered?
O, Warwick, Warwick! I foresee with grief
The utter loss of all the realm of France.

WARWICK
Be patient, York. If we concluded a peace,
It shall be with such strict and severe covenants
As little shall the Frenchmen gain thereby.

Enter Charles, Alençon, Bastard, Reignier, [*and others*].

CHARLES
Since, lords of England, it is thus agreed
That peaceful truce shall be proclaim'd in France,
We come to be informed by yourselves
What the conditions of that league must be.

YORK
Speak, Winchester, for boiling choler chokes
The hollow passage of my poison'd voice,
By sight of these our baleful enemies.

CARDINAL
Charles, and the rest, it is enacted thus:
That, in regard King Henry gives consent,
Of mere compassion and of lenity,
To ease your country of distressful war
And suffer you to breathe in fruitful peace,
You shall become true liegemen to his crown.
And, Charles, upon condition thou wilt swear
To pay him tribute and submit thyself,
Thou shalt be plac'd as viceroy under him,
And still enjoy thy regal dignity.

ALENÇON
Must he be then as shadow of himself?
Adorn his temples with a coronet,
And yet, in substance and authority,
Retain but privilege of a private man?
This proffer is absurd and reasonless.

CHARLES
'Tis known already that I am possess'd
With more than half the Gallian territories,
And therein reverenc'd for their lawful king.
Shall I, for lucre of the rest unvanquish'd,
Detract so much from that prerogative
As to be call'd but viceroy of the whole?
No, Lord Ambassador, I'll rather keep
That which I have than, coveting for more,
Be cast from possibility of all.

YORK
Insulting Charles, hast thou by secret means
Us'd intercession to obtain a league,
And, now the matter grows to compromise,
Stand'st thou aloof upon comparison?
Either accept the title thou usurp'st,
Of benefit proceeding from our king
And not of any challenge of desert,
Or we will plague thee with incessant wars.

REIGNIER [*Aside to Charles*]
My lord, you do not well in obstinacy
To cavil in the course of this contract.
If once it be neglected, ten to one
We shall not find like opportunity.

ALENÇON [*Aside to Charles*]
To say the truth, it is your policy
To save your subjects from such massacre
And ruthless slaughters as are daily seen
By our proceeding in hostility;
And therefore take this compact of a truce,
Although you break it when your pleasure serves.

WARWICK
How say'st thou, Charles? Shall our condition stand?

CHARLES
It shall;
Only reserv'd, you claim no interest
In any of our towns of garrison.

YORK
Then swear allegiance to his Majesty,
As thou art knight, never to disobey
Nor be rebellious to the crown of England,
Thou, nor thy nobles, to the crown of England.
[*Charles and his nobles give tokens of fealty.*]
So, now dismiss your army when ye please;
Hang up your ensigns, let your drums be still,
For here we entertain a solemn peace. *Exeunt.*

[SCENE V]

Enter Suffolk in conference with the King, Gloucester, and Exeter.

KING
Your wondrous rare description, noble earl,
Of beauteous Margaret hath astonish'd me.
Her virtues graced with external gifts
Do breed love's settled passions in my heart;
And like as rigor of tempestuous gusts
Provokes the mightiest hulk against the tide,

102 travail labor **114 covenants** articles of agreement **120 choler** i.e., anger **124 in regard** inasmuch as **125 Of mere** out of pure

142 Detract . . . prerogative i.e., yield up my right to be called king in the territories I already possess **146 cast** excluded **149 grows to compromise** moves toward a peaceful settlement **150 upon comparison** i.e., quibbling about the proposed articles **152 Of benefit** as a feudal bestowal **153 challenge of desert** claim of inherent right **156 cavil** raise frivolous or fault-finding objections **159 policy** politic course **165 condition** treaty, contract **168 towns of garrison** fortified towns

V.v. Location: London. The palace.
4 settled fixed, rooted **6 Provokes** drives. **hulk** vessel

So am I driven by breath of her renown
Either to suffer shipwrack or arrive
Where I may have fruition of her love.

SUFFOLK

Tush, my good lord, this superficial tale
Is but a preface of her worthy praise.
The chief perfections of that lovely dame,
Had I sufficient skill to utter them,
Would make a volume of enticing lines
Able to ravish any dull conceit;
And, which is more, she is not so divine,
So full replete with choice of all delights,
But with as humble lowliness of mind
She is content to be at your command—
Command, I mean, of virtuous chaste intents,
To love and honor Henry as her lord.

KING

And otherwise will Henry ne'er presume.
Therefore, my Lord Protector, give consent
That Marg'ret may be England's royal queen.

GLOUCESTER

So should I give consent to flatter sin.
You know, my lord, your Highness is betroth'd
Unto another lady of esteem.
How shall we then dispense with that contract,
And not deface your honor with reproach?

SUFFOLK

As doth a ruler with unlawful oaths;
Or one that, at a triumph having vow'd
To try his strength, forsaketh yet the lists
By reason of his adversary's odds.
A poor earl's daughter is unequal odds,
And therefore may be broke without offense.

GLOUCESTER

Why, what, I pray, is Margaret more than that?
Her father is no better than an earl,
Although in glorious titles he excel.

SUFFOLK

Yes, my lord, her father is a king,
The King of Naples and Jerusalem,
And of such great authority in France
As his alliance will confirm our peace
And keep the Frenchmen in allegiance.

GLOUCESTER

And so the Earl of Armagnac may do,
Because he is near kinsman unto Charles.

EXETER

Beside, his wealth doth warrant a liberal dower,
Where Reignier sooner will receive than give.

SUFFOLK

A dow'r, my lords? Disgrace not so your king
That he should be so abject, base, and poor,
To choose for wealth and not for perfect love.
Henry is able to enrich his queen,
And not to seek a queen to make him rich.
So worthless peasants bargain for their wives,
As marketmen for oxen, sheep, or horse.
Marriage is a matter of more worth
Than to be dealt in by attorneyship.
Not whom we will, but whom his Grace affects,
Must be companion of his nuptial bed.
And therefore, lords, since he affects her most,
Most of all these reasons bindeth us
In our opinions she should be preferr'd.
For what is wedlock forced but a hell,
An age of discord and continual strife?
Whereas the contrary bringeth bliss,
And is a pattern of celestial peace.
Whom should we match with Henry, being a king,
But Margaret, that is daughter to a king?
Her peerless feature, joined with her birth,
Approves her fit for none but for a king.
Her valiant courage and undaunted spirit,
More than in women commonly is seen,
Will answer our hope in issue of a king;
For Henry, son unto a conqueror,
Is likely to beget more conquerors,
If with a lady of so high resolve
As is fair Margaret he be link'd in love.
Then yield, my lords, and here conclude with me
That Margaret shall be queen, and none but she.

KING

Whether it be through force of your report,
My noble Lord of Suffolk, or for that
My tender youth was never yet attaint
With any passion of inflaming love,
I cannot tell; but this I am assur'd,
I feel such sharp dissension in my breast,
Such fierce alarums both of hope and fear,
As I am sick with working of my thoughts.
Take, therefore, shipping; post, my lord, to France;
Agree to any covenants, and procure
That Lady Margaret do vouchsafe to come
To cross the seas to England and be crown'd
King Henry's faithful and anointed queen.
For your expenses and sufficient charge,
Among the people gather up a tenth.
Be gone, I say; for till you do return,
I rest perplexed with a thousand cares.
And you, good uncle, banish all offense.
If you do censure me by what you were,
Not what you are, I know it will excuse
This sudden execution of my will.
And so, conduct me where, from company,
I may revolve and ruminate my grief. *Exit.*

GLOUCESTER

Ay, grief, I fear me, both at first and last.
Exit Gloucester [*with Exeter*].

SUFFOLK

Thus Suffolk hath prevail'd; and thus he goes,
As did the youthful Paris once to Greece,
With hope to find the like event in love,
But prosper better than the Trojan did.
Margaret shall now be Queen, and rule the King;
But I will rule both her, the King, and realm. *Exit.*

11 her worthy praise praise she is truly worth **15 conceit** imagination **25 flatter** countenance, excuse **27 another lady** i.e., the Earl of Armagnac's daughter. (See V.i.17 f.) **31 triumph** tournament **32 lists** place of combat in a tournament **42 As** that **46 warrant** guarantee

56 attorneyship proxy **57 affects** desires **68 feature** figure **80 for that** because **81 attaint** infected **87 post** hasten **92 charge** money **93 gather up a tenth** levy a tax of ten percent of the produce of lands and industry **95 rest** remain **97–98 censure . . . are** i.e., judge me (in my lovesickness) in comparison to your own youthful ways, not to your present wisdom **100 from company** i.e., alone **104 Paris** Trojan prince whose abduction of Helen of Sparta instigated the Trojan war

The Second Part of King Henry the Sixth

We have already, in the introduction to *1 Henry VI,* surveyed Shakespeare's use of his chronicle sources, including the providential myth of fifteenth-century history, and have established the importance of regarding each play as a separate entity as well as part of a series. *2 Henry VI* picks up where the first play ends (in the year 1445) and continues down to the very eve of actual civil war at the Battle of St. Albans (1455). The major events portrayed are the downfall of Humphrey, Duke of Gloucester, and the angry stirrings of the commons leading finally to Jack Cade's rebellion. Popular agitation brings about the death of the Duke of Suffolk, thereby claiming the life of one of those most cynically responsible for England's troubles. The villainous Cardinal of Winchester also dies a horrible and edifying death, suggesting that divine retribution is beginning to reveal its inexorable force. Yet throughout this declining action we witness as countermovement the ominous rise of Richard Plantagenet, Duke of York.

Richard's strategy, like that of his namesake in *Richard III,* is to exploit antagonisms at the English court, turning feuding nobles against one another until his potential rivals for power have destroyed themselves. In particular, he takes advantage of the animosity between the new Queen Margaret and Duke Humphrey. Margaret, daughter of a foreign prince, is a consort in the autocratic European style. She haughtily insists on the privileges of her exalted rank and spurns those who govern in the name of justice. "Is this the guise, Is this the fashion in the court of England?" she incredulously inquires of Suffolk, her lover and political ally (I,iii). Suffolk is an apt mate for Margaret, since he too oppresses the commons. A petition "against the Duke of Suffolk, for enclosing the commons of Melford" is one of many heartfelt grievances brought to the attention of the throne by the common people. Margaret naturally resents the moderate and fairminded counsel of Duke Humphrey, who urges King Henry to remedy the distress of the commons.

Richard of York has no inherent admiration for Suffolk and Margaret, but cynically backs them as a way of destroying the good Duke of Gloucester. He advises his partners Salisbury and Warwick, "Wink at the Duke of Suffolk's insolence, At Beaufort's pride, at Somerset's ambition, At Buckingham and all the crew of them, Till they have snar'd the shepherd of the flock, That virtuous prince, the good Duke Humphrey" (II,ii). Regrettably, Humphrey has a fatal weakness through which he can be pulled down: the ambition of his wife, Eleanor. Intent on being first lady of the land, Eleanor comes into inevitable conflict with the remorseless Queen Margaret. Winchester and Suffolk, knowing Eleanor's self-blinding pride, find it pathetically easy to plant spies in her household who will encourage her penchant for witchcraft. Humphrey is never contaminated personally by his wife's pride, but is doomed nonetheless. King Henry knows of Humphrey's goodness but cannot save him. This dismaying fall of a courageous moderate, highlighted in the title of the 1594 quarto text ("with the death of the good Duke Humphrey"), singles Humphrey out as the most prominent victim of the second play, like Talbot in Part I. He is cut down by an insincere and temporary alliance of extremists from both sides: those like Margaret and Suffolk who cling to despotic privilege, and those like York who wish to stir up the commons for their own ulterior purposes. In times of confrontation the middle position is inherently vulnerable, and its destruction leads to escalating polarization.

As York both foresees and desires, the commons are indeed unruly when deprived of Humphrey's moderating leadership. Shakespeare has already shown that they tend to ape the quarrels of their elders (as in the ludicrous duels between Horner the Armorer and his man Peter Thump), and are superstitiously gullible (as in the episode of Simpcox the fraudulent blind man). Now, no longer able to petition through channels, their voice becomes importunate. "The commons, like an angry hive of bees That want their leader, scatter up and down And care not who they sting in his revenge" (III,ii). At first their grievances are plausible and their wrath directed at guilty objects. They suspect rightly that their hero, Humphrey, has been destroyed by Suffolk and the Cardinal, and they demand Suffolk's banishment. The request is laudable, but the peremptory tone suggests that the people are beginning to feel their own political power. Unless Suffolk is banished, they warn, they will take him by force from the palace. Poor King Henry, lamenting the lost conciliatory authority of Humphrey, aptly points up the central issue of royal prerogative: "And had I not been cited so by them, Yet did I purpose as they do entreat" (III,ii). In the perspective of this play, Henry's yielding to popular force is regrettable, but he has no alternative. Equally lamentable is the execution of Suffolk by private citizens taking justice into their own hands. However much this despot deserved to be condemned, his murder is an affront to justice. Servant has turned against master; the commons have tasted blood.

The popular rebellion itself, Cade's uprising, is a grotesque travesty of popular longings for social justice, and suggests that any movement of this sort is bound to end in absurdity. Shakespeare, for all his appreciative depiction of individual commoners, never credits them with collective political sagacity once they are demonstrating for their rights. In fact Shakespeare unhistorically brings together the worst excesses of the Cade rebellion itself (1450) and the famous Peasants' Revolt of 1381 in order to exaggerate the dangers of popular agitation. The Cade scenes abound in the degrading comedy of grandiose pretentiousness. We laugh at the contrast between Cade's professed Utopian notions of abundant food and drink for all, and his petty ambition to be king. He kills those who refer to him as Jack Cade rather than by his pretended title of Lord Mortimer. His movement is fiercely anti-intellectual. Yet the sour joke does not indict the commons alone. Cade's insolent pretentions and his claptrap genealogical claims are a recognizable parody of aristocratic behavior. More importantly, we remember that Cade was whetted on to his rebellion by the demagogic York. That schemer has "seduced" Cade to make commotion while York himself raises a huge personal army and advances his fortunes in Ireland. "This devil here shall be my substitute" (III,i). The commons can indeed prove irresponsible when goaded, but throughout *2 Henry VI* feuding aristocrats must bear the chief blame for causing popular discontent.

Prophecy assumes a structural importance in *2 Henry VI* that is to be accentuated in later plays of the tetralogy. As in ancient Greek drama, prophecies are always eventually fulfilled. They reveal divine necessity, but in such ambiguous and riddling language that the persons affected by the prophecy do not comprehend the true nature of the utterance until the event itself is upon them. In this play, for example, the spirit conjured to appear before the Duchess of Gloucester (I,iv) predicts that Suffolk will die "by water" and that Somerset should "shun castles." What sorts of warnings are these? When his time comes, Suffolk dies at the hands of a man named Walter (pronounced "water," though Suffolk tries desperately to insist on the French "Gualtier"), whereas Somerset dies at the Castle Inn near St. Albans, at the play's end. Through such paltry quibbles, as in *Macbeth,* great men are misled into a false security. No less riddling is the prophecy about King Henry and his political antagonist: "The duke yet lives that Henry shall depose; But him outlive, and die a violent death." The first phrase of this oracle is perfectly ambiguous: it can mean that a still-living duke will depose Henry, or that Henry will depose this duke. Both interpretations turn out to be valid; during the wars of Lancaster and York shown in *3 Henry VI,* King Henry and his Yorkist opponent will by turns take the throne from one another. Eventually, too, in *3 Henry VI* and *Richard III,* Edward of York will outlive Henry only to die a retributive death. In such prophecy there is already the concept of an eye for an eye, a Lancastrian for a Yorkist, through which Providence will finally impose its penalty on a rebellious people. Prophecy then serves not to allow man to escape his destiny, which is unavoidable, but to give man the opportunity to perceive at last the pattern of divine justice. The audience realizes that prophecy is a divine warning too often unheeded by foolish man, and acknowledges the necessity of a fulfillment that is tragic and dispiriting but is also comforting to the extent that it shows the heavens to be just.

This comfort is slow to arrive; much of it is reserved for *Richard III.* In *2 Henry VI,* England's political and moral decline remains unchecked. The commons' rebellion, cynically fomented by Richard, Duke of York, has established the precedent for further rebellion. Knowing his enemies to be weak and divided, Richard no longer conceals the ambition that has led him to accept an assignment in Ireland and thereby raise an army. His excuse for returning to England in arms, to rid King Henry of the hated adviser Somerset, is similarly shown to be no more than a pretext for declaring open civil war. His final justification for challenging King Henry, despite all the fine talk about genealogies, is that Richard has the ambition and the raw power to carry out his plan. Henry's assertions of right are no less governed by expediency, for he privately confesses the weakness of his claim. The admirable example, shown late in this play, of a Kentish gentleman named Iden who is content to live peaceably on his estate, serves as a contrast to the dismaying ambitions that have seized not only Richard of York and his allies but also the remorseless Queen Margaret and those loyal to her. If, as A. P. Rossiter has cogently argued, *2 Henry VI* is a "morality of state" in which forces of good and evil struggle for the soul of that beleagured heroine, Respublica or the commonwealth, then the play must ultimately be viewed as one in which the forces of good do not fare well. To be sure, the haughty Suffolk meets his dire fate, though by a means that encourages further private revenge; Somerset falls as predicted at St. Albans; and Winchester suffers a death of edifying horror. Still, Richard of York and Queen Margaret, having profited from the victimization of the virtuous Duke Humphrey, are more powerful than ever, and Richard's son and namesake is only beginning to make his presence felt. Many scores remain to be settled at the close of *2 Henry VI.*

The Second Part of King Henry the Sixth

[*Dramatis Personae*

KING HENRY THE SIXTH.
HUMPHREY, DUKE OF GLOUCESTER, *his uncle.*
CARDINAL BEAUFORT, *Bishop of Winchester, great-uncle to the King.*
RICHARD PLANTAGENET, DUKE OF YORK.
EDWARD *and* RICHARD, *his sons.*
DUKE OF SOMERSET.
WILLIAM DE LA POLE, EARL *then* DUKE OF SUFFOLK.
DUKE OF BUCKINGHAM.
LORD CLIFFORD.
YOUNG CLIFFORD, *his son.*
EARL OF SALISBURY.
EARL OF WARWICK.
LORD SCALES.
LORD SAY.
SIR HUMPHREY STAFFORD, *and* WILLIAM STAFFORD, *his brother.*
SIR JOHN STANLEY.
VAUX.
MATTHEW GOFFE.
ALEXANDER IDEN, *a Kentish gentleman.*
A LIEUTENANT, MASTER, *and* MASTER'S MATE, *and* WALTER WHITMORE.
Two GENTLEMEN, *prisoners with Suffolk.*
JOHN HUME *and* JOHN SOUTHWELL, *priests.*
ROGER BOLINGBROKE, *a conjurer.*
THOMAS HORNER, *an armorer.* PETER THUMP, *his man.*
CLERK OF CHARTHAM. MAYOR OF SAINT ALBANS.
SIMPCOX, *an impostor.*
JACK CADE, *a rebel.*
GEORGE BEVIS, JOHN HOLLAND, DICK *the Butcher,* SMITH *the weaver,* MICHAEL, *etc., followers of Cade.*
Two MURDERERS.

MARGARET, *Queen to King Henry.*
ELEANOR, *Duchess of Gloucester.*
MARGERY JOURDAIN, *a witch.*
WIFE *to Simpcox.*

LORDS, LADIES, *and* ATTENDANTS, PETITIONERS, ALDERMEN, *a* HERALD, *a* BEADLE, SHERIFF, *and* OFFICERS, CITIZENS, PRENTICES, FALCONERS, GUARDS, SOLDIERS, MESSENGERS, *etc.*

A SPIRIT.

SCENE: *England.*]

ACT I • SCENE I

Flourish of trumpets, then hautboys. Enter [the] King, Duke Humphrey [of Gloucester], Salisbury, Warwick, and [Cardinal] Beaufort, on the one side; the Queen, Suffolk, York, Somerset, and Buckingham, on the other.

SUFFOLK
As by your high imperial Majesty
I had in charge at my depart for France, 2
As procurator to your Excellence, 3
To marry Princess Margaret for your Grace,
So, in the famous ancient city Tours,
In presence of the Kings of France and Sicil, 6
The Dukes of Orleans, Calaber, Bretagne, and Alençon, 7
Seven earls, twelve barons, and twenty reverend bishops,
I have perform'd my task and was espous'd;
And humbly now upon my bended knee, [*Kneels.*]
In sight of England and her lordly peers,
Deliver up my title in the Queen
To your most gracious hands, that are the substance
Of that great shadow I did represent: 14
The happiest gift that ever marquess gave,
The fairest queen that ever king receiv'd.

KING
Suffolk, arise. Welcome, Queen Margaret. [*Suffolk rises.*]
I can express no kinder sign of love 18
Than this kind kiss. [*Kisses her.*] O Lord, that lends me life, 19
Lend me a heart replete with thankfulness!
For thou hast given me in this beauteous face
A world of earthly blessings to my soul,
If sympathy of love unite our thoughts.

QUEEN
Great King of England and my gracious lord,
The mutual conference that my mind hath had,
By day, by night, waking and in my dreams,
In courtly company or at my beads,
With you, mine alder-liefest sovereign, 28
Makes me the bolder to salute my king
With ruder terms, such as my wit affords
And over-joy of heart doth minister. 31

KING
Her sight did ravish, but her grace in speech,
Her words yclad with wisdom's majesty, 33
Makes me from wond'ring fall to weeping joys,
Such is the fullness of my heart's content.
Lords, with one cheerful voice welcome my love.

ALL (*Kneeling*)
Long live Queen Margaret, England's happiness!

I.i. Location: London. The palace.
s.d. Flourish fanfare. **hautboys** oboes **2 had in charge** was commissioned. **depart** departure **3 procurator** agent, proxy **6 Sicil** Sicily. (Titularly ruled by Margaret's father, the Duke of Anjou.) **7 Calaber** Calabria, in southern Italy **14 shadow** image, i.e., of royalty **18 kinder** more natural **19 kind** loving **28 alder-liefest** most loved **31 minister** supply **33 yclad** clad, clothed

QUEEN
We thank you all. *Flourish.*

SUFFOLK
My Lord Protector, so it please your Grace,
Here are the articles of contracted peace
Between our sovereign and the French King Charles,
For eighteen months concluded by consent.

GLOUCESTER *(Reads)* "Imprimis, It is agreed between 43
the French King Charles, and William de la Pole, Mar- 44
quess of Suffolk, ambassador for Henry King of En- 45
gland, that the said Henry shall espouse the Lady Mar-
garet, daughter unto Reignier King of Naples, Sicilia,
and Jerusalem, and crown her Queen of England ere
the thirtieth of May next ensuing. Item, that the duchy 49
of Anjou and the county of Maine shall be releas'd and
deliver'd to the King her father"—
[*Lets the paper fall.*]

KING
Uncle, how now?

GLOUCESTER Pardon me, gracious lord;
Some sudden qualm hath struck me at the heart
And dimm'd mine eyes, that I can read no further.

KING
Uncle of Winchester, I pray, read on.

CARDINAL [*Reads*] "Item, It is further agreed between
them, that the duchies of Anjou and Maine shall be
releas'd and deliver'd over to the King her father, and
she sent over of the King of England's own proper cost 59
and charges, without having any dowry."

KING
They please us well. Lord Marquess, kneel down.
[*Suffolk kneels.*]
We here create thee the first Duke of Suffolk,
And girt thee with the sword. Cousin of York, 63
We here discharge your Grace from being Regent
I' th' parts of France, till term of eighteen months 65
Be full expir'd. Thanks, uncle Winchester,
Gloucester, York, Buckingham, Somerset,
Salisbury, and Warwick;
We thank you all for this great favor done,
In entertainment to my princely queen.
Come, let us in, and with all speed provide
To see her coronation be perform'd.
Exeunt King, Queen, and Suffolk.
Mane[*n*]*t the rest.*

GLOUCESTER
Brave peers of England, pillars of the state,
To you Duke Humphrey must unload his grief,
Your grief, the common grief of all the land.
What? Did my brother Henry spend his youth, 76
His valor, coin, and people, in the wars?
Did he so often lodge in open field,
In winter's cold and summer's parching heat,
To conquer France, his true inheritance?
And did my brother Bedford toil his wits
To keep by policy what Henry got? 82
Have you yourselves, Somerset, Buckingham,
Brave York, Salisbury, and victorious Warwick,
Receiv'd deep scars in France and Normandy?
Or hath mine uncle Beaufort and myself,
With all the learned council of the realm,
Studied so long, sat in the council-house
Early and late, debating to and fro
How France and Frenchmen might be kept in awe, 90
And had his Highness in his infancy
Crowned in Paris in despite of foes?
And shall these labors and these honors die?
Shall Henry's conquest, Bedford's vigilance,
Your deeds of war, and all our counsel die?
O peers of England, shameful is this league!
Fatal this marriage, canceling your fame,
Blotting your names from books of memory,
Rasing the characters of your renown, 99
Defacing monuments of conquer'd France,
Undoing all, as all had never been!

CARDINAL
Nephew, what means this passionate discourse,
This peroration with such circumstance? 103
For France, 'tis ours; and we will keep it still. 104

GLOUCESTER
Ay, uncle, we will keep it if we can,
But now it is impossible we should.
Suffolk, the new-made duke that rules the roast, 107
Hath given the duchy of Anjou, and Maine,
Unto the poor King Reignier, whose large style 109
Agrees not with the leanness of his purse.

SALISBURY
Now, by the death of Him that died for all,
These counties were the keys of Normandy.
But wherefore weeps Warwick, my valiant son?

WARWICK
For grief that they are past recovery;
For, were there hope to conquer them again,
My sword should shed hot blood, mine eyes no
tears.
Anjou and Maine? Myself did win them both;
Those provinces these arms of mine did conquer.
And are the cities, that I got with wounds,
Deliver'd up again with peaceful words?
Mort Dieu! 121

YORK
For Suffolk's duke, may he be suffocate, 122
That dims the honor of this warlike isle!
France should have torn and rent my very heart
Before I would have yielded to this league.
I never read but England's kings have had
Large sums of gold and dowries with their wives;
And our King Henry gives away his own,
To match with her that brings no vantages. 129

GLOUCESTER
A proper jest, and never heard before,
That Suffolk should demand a whole fifteenth 131

43 Imprimis in the first place **44–45 Marquess** (William de la Pole was fourth Earl and then first Duke of Suffolk; he did not hold the title of Marquess.) **49 Item** also **59 of** at. **proper** personal **63 girt** gird **65 term . . . months** i.e., the period of the truce between England and France **76 Henry** i.e., Henry V **82 policy** prudent management

99 Rasing the characters erasing the records **103 circumstance** detail **104 still** always **107 rules the roast** i.e., domineers **109 large style** lavish title **121 Mort Dieu** by God's (Christ's) death **122 For** as for **129 vantages** benefits, profits **131 whole fifteenth** i.e., tax levy consisting of one-fifteenth of the produce of lands and industry. (Cf. *1 Henry VI*, V.v.92–93, where the figure is put at one tenth.)

For costs and charges in transporting her!
She should have stay'd in France and starv'd in France,
Before—

CARDINAL
My Lord of Gloucester, now ye grow too hot.
It was the pleasure of my lord the King.

GLOUCESTER
My Lord of Winchester, I know your mind.
'Tis not my speeches that you do mislike,
But 'tis my presence that doth trouble ye.
Rancor will out. Proud prelate, in thy face
I see thy fury. If I longer stay,
We shall begin our ancient bickerings.
Lordings, farewell; and say, when I am gone,
I prophesied France will be lost ere long.

Exit Humphrey.

CARDINAL
So, there goes our Protector in a rage.
'Tis known to you he is mine enemy,
Nay, more, an enemy unto you all,
And no great friend, I fear me, to the King.
Consider, lords, he is the next of blood,
And heir apparent to the English crown.
Had Henry got an empire by his marriage,
And all the wealthy kingdoms of the west,
There's reason he should be displeas'd at it.
Look to it, lords, let not his smoothing words
Bewitch your hearts; be wise and circumspect.
What though the common people favor him,
Calling him "Humphrey, the good Duke of Gloucester,"
Clapping their hands, and crying with loud voice,
"Jesu maintain your royal Excellence!"
With "God preserve the good Duke Humphrey!"
I fear me, lords, for all this flattering gloss,
He will be found a dangerous Protector.

BUCKINGHAM
Why should he, then, protect our sovereign,
He being of age to govern of himself?
Cousin of Somerset, join you with me,
And all together, with the Duke of Suffolk,
We'll quickly hoise Duke Humphrey from his seat.

CARDINAL
This weighty business will not brook delay;
I'll to the Duke of Suffolk presently.

Exit Cardinal.

SOMERSET
Cousin of Buckingham, though Humphrey's pride
And greatness of his place be grief to us,
Yet let us watch the haughty Cardinal;
His insolence is more intolerable
Than all the princes in the land beside.
If Gloucester be displac'd, he'll be Protector.

BUCKINGHAM
Or thou or I, Somerset, will be Protector,
Despite Duke Humphrey or the Cardinal.

Exeunt Buckingham and Somerset.

SALISBURY
Pride went before, ambition follows him.
While these do labor for their own preferment,
Behooves it us to labor for the realm.
I never saw but Humphrey Duke of Gloucester
Did bear him like a noble gentleman.
Oft have I seen the haughty Cardinal,
More like a soldier than a man o' th' church,
As stout and proud as he were lord of all,
Swear like a ruffian and demean himself
Unlike the ruler of a commonweal.
Warwick, my son, the comfort of my age,
Thy deeds, thy plainness, and thy housekeeping
Hath won the greatest favor of the commons,
Excepting none but good Duke Humphrey.
And, brother York, thy acts in Ireland,
In bringing them to civil discipline,
Thy late exploits done in the heart of France,
When thou wert Regent for our sovereign,
Have made thee fear'd and honor'd of the people.
Join we together, for the public good,
In what we can, to bridle and suppress
The pride of Suffolk and the Cardinal,
With Somerset's and Buckingham's ambition;
And, as we may, cherish Duke Humphrey's deeds,
While they do tend the profit of the land.

WARWICK
So God help Warwick, as he loves the land,
And common profit of his country!

YORK
And so says York—[*Aside.*] for he hath greatest cause.

SALISBURY
Then let's make haste away, and look unto the main.

WARWICK
Unto the main? O father, Maine is lost;
That Maine which by main force Warwick did win,
And would have kept so long as breath did last!
Main chance, father, you meant; but I meant Maine,
Which I will win from France, or else be slain.

Exeunt Warwick and Salisbury. Manet York.

YORK
Anjou and Maine are given to the French;
Paris is lost; the state of Normandy
Stands on a tickle point, now they are gone.
Suffolk concluded on the articles,
The peers agreed, and Henry was well pleas'd
To change two dukedoms for a duke's fair daughter.
I cannot blame them all. What is 't to them?
'Tis thine they give away, and not their own.

149 next of blood i.e., in line to succeed to the throne, as Henry's eldest uncle. (Henry was as yet childless.) **152 the wealthy . . . west** (Possibly an anachronistic reference to New World possessions.) **161 gloss** i.e., specious talk **167 hoise** hoist **168 brook** endure, permit **169 presently** immediately **170 Cousin** kinsman **176 Or** either

178 Pride i.e., Winchester. **ambition** i.e., Buckingham and Somerset **185 stout** haughty. **as** as if **186 demean** conduct **189 housekeeping** hospitality **192 brother** i.e., brother-in-law; see note to l. 238 below **205 greatest cause** i.e., as hopeful claimant to the throne **206 unto the main** to the most important business (with several puns in the following lines: [1] *Maine,* a French province lost in the treaty [2] *main force,* brute force [3] *Main chance,* a gambling term from the dice game called hazard) **214 tickle** unstable, insecure **219 thine** (York speaks to himself.)

Pirates may make cheap pennyworths of their pillage 220
And purchase friends and give to courtezans,
Still reveling like lords till all be gone, 222
While as the silly owner of the goods 223
Weeps over them and wrings his hapless hands
And shakes his head and trembling stands aloof,
While all is shar'd and all is borne away,
Ready to starve and dare not touch his own.
So York must sit and fret and bite his tongue,
While his own lands are bargain'd for and sold.
Methinks the realms of England, France, and Ireland
Bear that proportion to my flesh and blood 231
As did the fatal brand Althaea burnt 232
Unto the Prince's heart of Calydon.
Anjou and Maine both given unto the French!
Cold news for me, for I had hope of France,
Even as I have of fertile England's soil.
A day will come when York shall claim his own;
And therefore I will take the Nevils' parts 238
And make a show of love to proud Duke Humphrey,
And, when I spy advantage, claim the crown,
For that's the golden mark I seek to hit.
Nor shall proud Lancaster usurp my right, 242
Nor hold the scepter in his childish fist,
Nor wear the diadem upon his head,
Whose church-like humors fits not for a crown. 245
Then, York, be still awhile, till time do serve.
Watch thou and wake when others be asleep,
To pry into the secrets of the state,
Till Henry, surfeiting in joys of love,
With his new bride and England's dear-bought queen,
And Humphrey with the peers be fall'n at jars. 251
Then will I raise aloft the milk-white rose, 252
With whose sweet smell the air shall be perfum'd,
And in my standard bear the arms of York,
To grapple with the house of Lancaster;
And force perforce I'll make him yield the crown, 256
Whose bookish rule hath pull'd fair England down. 257

Exit York.

[SCENE II]

Enter Duke Humphrey and his wife Eleanor.

DUCHESS

Why droops my lord, like overripen'd corn, 1
Hanging the head at Ceres' plenteous load? 2
Why doth the great Duke Humphrey knit his brows,
As frowning at the favors of the world? 4
Why are thine eyes fix'd to the sullen earth,
Gazing on that which seems to dim thy sight?
What seest thou there? King Henry's diadem,
Enchas'd with all the honors of the world? 8
If so, gaze on, and grovel on thy face,
Until thy head be circled with the same.
Put forth thy hand, reach at the glorious gold.
What, is 't too short? I'll lengthen it with mine;
And, having both together heav'd it up,
We'll both together lift our heads to heaven,
And never more abase our sight so low
As to vouchsafe one glance unto the ground.

GLOUCESTER

O Nell, sweet Nell, if thou dost love thy lord,
Banish the canker of ambitious thoughts!
And may that thought, when I imagine ill
Against my king and nephew, virtuous Henry,
Be my last breathing in this mortal world!
My troublous dream this night doth make me sad. 22

DUCHESS

What dream'd my lord? Tell me, and I'll requite it
With sweet rehearsal of my morning's dream. 24

GLOUCESTER

Methought this staff, mine office-badge in court,
Was broke in twain—by whom, I have forgot,
But, as I think, it was by th' Cardinal—
And on the pieces of the broken wand
Were plac'd the heads of Edmund Duke of Somerset,
And William de la Pole, first Duke of Suffolk.
This was my dream. What it doth bode, God knows.

DUCHESS

Tut, this was nothing but an argument 32
That he that breaks a stick of Gloucester's grove
Shall lose his head for his presumption.
But list to me, my Humphrey, my sweet duke:
Methought I sat in seat of majesty
In the cathedral church of Westminster,
And in that chair where kings and queens are crown'd,
Where Henry and Dame Margaret kneel'd to me
And on my head did set the diadem.

GLOUCESTER

Nay, Eleanor, then must I chide outright.
Presumptuous dame, ill-nurtur'd Eleanor, 42
Art thou not second woman in the realm,
And the Protector's wife, belov'd of him?
Hast thou not worldly pleasure at command
Above the reach or compass of thy thought?
And wilt thou still be hammering treachery, 47
To tumble down thy husband and thyself
From top of honor to disgrace's feet?
Away from me, and let me hear no more!

220 cheap pennyworths bargains **222 Still** continually **223 While as** while. **silly** wretched, helpless **231 proportion** relationship **232 Althaea** mother of Meleager, prince of Calydon. (At his birth she was told that her son would live only as long as a brand of wood remained unconsumed. She snatched the brand from the fire; but years later, when Meleager quarreled with Althaea's brothers and slew them, she resentfully threw the fatal brand into the fire, thus causing his death.) **238 the Nevils'** i.e., Salisbury's and his son Warwick's (to whom Richard of York was allied by marriage, having married Cecille or Cicely Neville, Salisbury's sister) **242 Lancaster** i.e., Henry VI **245 humors** temperament **251 at jars** in discords, quarreling **252 milk-white rose** (Emblem of the Yorkist dynasty.) **256 force perforce** by violent compulsion **257 bookish** scholarly and ineffectual

I.ii. Location: The Duke of Gloucester's house.
1 corn grain **2 Ceres** goddess of the harvest and agriculture

4 As as if **8 Enchas'd** adorned as with gems **22 this night** this past night **24 rehearsal** recounting **32 argument** proof, evidence **42 ill-nurtur'd** ill-bred **47 hammering** i.e., devising

DUCHESS
What, what, my lord? Are you so choleric
With Eleanor, for telling but her dream?
Next time I'll keep my dreams unto myself,
And not be check'd. 54
GLOUCESTER
Nay, be not angry; I am pleas'd again.

Enter Messenger.

MESSENGER
My Lord Protector, 'tis his Highness' pleasure
You do prepare to ride unto Saint Albans,
Where as the King and Queen do mean to hawk. 58
GLOUCESTER
I go. Come, Nell, thou wilt ride with us?
DUCHESS
Yes, my good lord, I'll follow presently.
Exit Humphrey [*with Messenger*].
Follow I must; I cannot go before,
While Gloucester bears this base and humble mind.
Were I a man, a duke, and next of blood,
I would remove these tedious stumbling-blocks
And smooth my way upon their headless necks;
And, being a woman, I will not be slack
To play my part in Fortune's pageant. 67
Where are you there? Sir John! Nay, fear not, man, 68
We are alone; here's none but thee and I.

Enter Hume.

HUME
Jesus preserve your royal Majesty!
DUCHESS
What say'st thou? Majesty? I am but Grace. 71
HUME
But, by the grace of God, and Hume's advice,
Your Grace's title shall be multiplied.
DUCHESS
What say'st thou, man? Hast thou as yet conferr'd
With Margery Jourdain, the cunning witch,
With Roger Bolingbroke, the conjurer?
And will they undertake to do me good?
HUME
This they have promised, to show your Highness
A spirit rais'd from depth of underground
That shall make answer to such questions
As by your Grace shall be propounded him.
DUCHESS
It is enough. I'll think upon the questions.
When from Saint Albans we do make return,
We'll see these things effected to the full.
Here, Hume, take this reward. [*Gives money.*] Make merry, man,
With thy confederates in this weighty cause.
Exit Eleanor.
HUME
Hume must make merry with the Duchess' gold.
Marry, and shall! But, how now, Sir John Hume? 88
Seal up your lips, and give no words but mum;
The business asketh silent secrecy.
Dame Eleanor gives gold to bring the witch;
Gold cannot come amiss, were she a devil.
Yet have I gold flies from another coast; 93
I dare not say, from the rich Cardinal
And from the great and new-made Duke of Suffolk,
Yet I do find it so; for, to be plain,
They, knowing Dame Eleanor's aspiring humor, 97
Have hired me to undermine the Duchess
And buzz these conjurations in her brain.
They say, "A crafty knave does need no broker,"
Yet am I Suffolk and the Cardinal's broker.
Hume, if you take not heed, you shall go near
To call them both a pair of crafty knaves.
Well, so it stands; and thus, I fear, at last
Hume's knavery will be the Duchess' wrack,
And her attainture will be Humphrey's fall. 106
Sort how it will, I shall have gold for all. *Exit.* 107

[SCENE III]

Enter three or four Petitioners, [*Peter,*] *the Armorer's man, being one.*

FIRST PETITIONER My masters, let's stand close. My Lord Protector will come this way by and by, and then
we may deliver our supplications in the quill. 3
SECOND PETITIONER Marry, the Lord protect him, for he's a good man! Jesu bless him!

Enter Suffolk and Queen.

PETER Here 'a comes, methinks, and the Queen with him. I'll be the first, sure. [*Starts forward.*]
SECOND PETITIONER Come back, fool. This is the Duke of Suffolk, and not my Lord Protector.
SUFFOLK How now, fellow? Wouldst anything with me?
FIRST PETITIONER I pray, my lord, pardon me; I took ye for my Lord Protector.
QUEEN [*Reads*] "To my Lord Protector"? Are your supplications to his lordship? Let me see them. What is thine?
FIRST PETITIONER Mine is, an 't please your Grace, 17
against John Goodman, my Lord Cardinal's man, for keeping my house, and lands, and wife and all, from me.
SUFFOLK Thy wife too? That's some wrong, indeed. What's yours? What's here? [*Reads.*] "Against the
Duke of Suffolk, for enclosing the commons of Mel- 23
ford." How now, sir knave?
SECOND PETITIONER Alas, sir, I am but a poor petitioner of our whole township.

54 check'd rebuked **58 Where as** where **67 pageant** spectacular entertainment **68 Sir John** (Conventional form of addressing a priest.) **71 Grace** (Appropriate address to a duchess.) **88 Marry, and shall** i.e., indeed he will

93 flies i.e., that flies, approaches. **coast** quarter, source **97 humor** temperament, fancy **100 They say** people say. **broker** agent **105 wrack** destruction, ruin **106 attainture** conviction and disgrace **107 Sort . . . will** turn out which way it will. **for all** i.e., in any case

I.iii. Location: London. The palace.
3 in the quill i.e., simultaneously, in a body **17 an 't** if it **23 enclosing the commons** the action of a lord of a manor in enclosing or converting into private property lands formerly undivided and used by the community as a whole

PETER [*Giving his petition*] Against my master, Thomas Horner, for saying that the Duke of York was rightful heir to the crown.

QUEEN What say'st thou? Did the Duke of York say he was rightful heir to the crown?

PETER That my master was? No, forsooth; my master said that he was, and that the King was an usurper.

SUFFOLK Who is there? (*Enter Servant.*) Take this fellow in, and send for his master with a pursuivant presently. We'll hear more of your matter before the King.

Exit [*Servant with Peter*].

QUEEN
And as for you, that love to be protected
Under the wings of our Protector's grace,
Begin your suits anew, and sue to him.

Tear the supplication.

Away, base cullions! Suffolk, let them go.

ALL Come, let's be gone. *Exeunt.*

QUEEN
My Lord of Suffolk, say, is this the guise,
Is this the fashion in the court of England?
Is this the government of Britain's isle,
And this the royalty of Albion's king?
What, shall King Henry be a pupil still
Under the surly Gloucester's governance?
Am I a queen in title and in style,
And must be made a subject to a duke?
I tell thee, Pole, when in the city Tours
Thou ran'st a-tilt in honor of my love
And stol'st away the ladies' hearts of France,
I thought King Henry had resembled thee
In courage, courtship, and proportion;
But all his mind is bent to holiness,
To number Ave-Maries on his beads;
His champions are the prophets and apostles,
His weapons holy saws of sacred writ,
His study is his tilt-yard, and his loves
Are brazen images of canonized saints.
I would the college of the Cardinals
Would choose him Pope and carry him to Rome,
And set the triple crown upon his head;
That were a state fit for his holiness.

SUFFOLK
Madam, be patient. As I was cause
Your Highness came to England, so will I
In England work your Grace's full content.

QUEEN
Beside the haughty Protector, have we Beaufort
The imperious churchman, Somerset, Buckingham,
And grumbling York; and not the least of these
But can do more in England than the King.

SUFFOLK
And he of these that can do most of all
Cannot do more in England than the Nevils;
Salisbury and Warwick are no simple peers.

QUEEN
Not all these lords do vex me half so much
As that proud dame, the Lord Protector's wife.
She sweeps it through the court with troops of ladies,
More like an empress than Duke Humphrey's wife.
Strangers in court do take her for the Queen.
She bears a duke's revenues on her back,
And in her heart she scorns our poverty.
Shall I not live to be aveng'd on her?
Contemptuous base-born callet as she is,
She vaunted 'mongst her minions t' other day,
The very train of her worst wearing gown
Was better worth than all my father's lands,
Till Suffolk gave two dukedoms for his daughter.

SUFFOLK
Madam, myself have lim'd a bush for her,
And plac'd a quire of such enticing birds
That she will light to listen to the lays,
And never mount to trouble you again.
So let her rest. And, madam, list to me,
For I am bold to counsel you in this.
Although we fancy not the Cardinal,
Yet must we join with him and with the lords
Till we have brought Duke Humphrey in disgrace.
As for the Duke of York, this late complaint
Will make but little for his benefit.
So, one by one, we'll weed them all at last,
And you yourself shall steer the happy helm.

Sound a sennet. Enter the King, Duke Humphrey [*of Gloucester*], *Cardinal* [*Beaufort*], *Buckingham, York,* [*Somerset,*] *Salisbury, Warwick, and the Duchess* [*of Gloucester*].

KING
For my part, noble lords, I care not which;
Or Somerset or York, all's one to me.

YORK
If York have ill demean'd himself in France,
Then let him be denay'd the regentship.

SOMERSET
If Somerset be unworthy of the place,
Let York be Regent; I will yield to him.

WARWICK
Whether your Grace be worthy, yea or no,
Dispute not that. York is the worthier.

CARDINAL
Ambitious Warwick, let thy betters speak.

WARWICK
The Cardinal's not my better in the field.

BUCKINGHAM
All in this presence are thy betters, Warwick.

WARWICK
Warwick may live to be the best of all.

35 pursuivant officer-at-arms **40 cullions** base fellows. (Originally, *cullion* meant *testicle*.) **42 guise** custom, manner **45 Albion's** England's **50 Pole** i.e., Suffolk **51 ran'st a-tilt** jousted in a tournament **54 courtship** courtly manners. **proportion** carriage, build **58 saws** sayings

83 callet lewd woman **84 vaunted** boasted. **minions** followers, attendants (with overtones of *saucy women*) **85–87 The very . . . daughter** i.e., (Eleanor boasted that) the mere trailing part of her least expensive gown was worth more than all the lands possessed by the Duke of Anjou until Suffolk arranged a dowry whereby the Duke received two rich dukedoms (Anjou and Maine) in return for the marriage of me, his daughter, to King Henry **88 lim'd a bush** set a trap. (A metaphor from the practice of catching birds by putting sticky birdlime on twigs of trees.) **89 enticing birds** i.e., decoys **90 light** alight. **lays** songs **97 late complaint** i.e., recent allegation made by Peter that his master, the armorer, had spoken of York as the proper King of England **100 s.d. sennet** trumpet signal for the approach or departure of processions **102 Or** either **103 have . . . himself** has conducted himself badly **104 denay'd** denied

SALISBURY
Peace, son! And show some reason, Buckingham,
Why Somerset should be preferr'd in this.
QUEEN
Because the King, forsooth, will have it so.
GLOUCESTER
Madam, the King is old enough himself
To give his censure. These are no women's matters. 117
QUEEN
If he be old enough, what needs your Grace
To be Protector of his Excellence?
GLOUCESTER
Madam, I am Protector of the realm,
And at his pleasure will resign my place.
SUFFOLK
Resign it then and leave thine insolence.
Since thou wert king—as who is king but thou?—
The commonwealth hath daily run to wrack,
The Dauphin hath prevail'd beyond the seas, 125
And all the peers and nobles of the realm
Have been as bondmen to thy sovereignty.
CARDINAL
The commons hast thou rack'd; the clergy's bags 128
Are lank and lean with thy extortions.
SOMERSET
Thy sumptuous buildings and thy wife's attire
Have cost a mass of public treasury.
BUCKINGHAM
Thy cruelty in execution
Upon offenders hath exceeded law
And left thee to the mercy of the law.
QUEEN
Thy sale of offices and towns in France,
If they were known, as the suspect is great, 136
Would make thee quickly hop without thy head.
Exit Humphrey. [*The Queen drops her fan.*]
Give me my fan. What, minion, can ye not?
She gives the Duchess a box on the ear.
I cry you mercy, madam. Was it you? 139
DUCHESS
Was 't I? Yea, I it was, proud Frenchwoman.
Could I come near your beauty with my nails,
I'd set my ten commandments in your face. 142
KING
Sweet aunt, be quiet; 'twas against her will. 143
DUCHESS
Against her will, good King? Look to 't in time;
She'll hamper thee, and dandle thee like a baby. 145
Though in this place most master wear no breeches, 146
She shall not strike Dame Eleanor unreveng'd.
Exit Eleanor.
BUCKINGHAM [*To Cardinal*]
Lord Cardinal, I will follow Eleanor,
And listen after Humphrey, how he proceeds. 149
She's tickled now; her fume needs no spurs, 150
She'll gallop far enough to her destruction.
Exit Buckingham.

Enter Humphrey.

GLOUCESTER
Now, lords, my choler being overblown 152
With walking once about the quadrangle,
I come to talk of commonwealth affairs.
As for your spiteful false objections,
Prove them, and I lie open to the law;
But God in mercy so deal with my soul
As I in duty love my king and country!
But, to the matter that we have in hand:
I say, my sovereign, York is meetest man 160
To be your Regent in the realm of France.
SUFFOLK
Before we make election, give me leave 162
To show some reason, of no little force,
That York is most unmeet of any man.
YORK
I'll tell thee, Suffolk, why I am unmeet:
First, for I cannot flatter thee in pride; 166
Next, if I be appointed for the place,
My Lord of Somerset will keep me here
Without discharge, money, or furniture, 169
Till France be won into the Dauphin's hands.
Last time I danc'd attendance on his will 171
Till Paris was besieg'd, famish'd, and lost.
WARWICK
That can I witness; and a fouler fact 173
Did never traitor in the land commit.
SUFFOLK
Peace, headstrong Warwick!
WARWICK
Image of pride, why should I hold my peace?

Enter [*Horner, the*] *Armorer, and his man* [*Peter, guarded*].

SUFFOLK
Because here is a man accus'd of treason.
Pray God the Duke of York excuse himself!
YORK
Doth anyone accuse York for a traitor?
KING
What mean'st thou, Suffolk? Tell me, what are these? 180
SUFFOLK
Please it your Majesty, this is the man
That doth accuse his master of high treason.
His words were these: that Richard Duke of York
Was rightful heir unto the English crown
And that your Majesty was an usurper.
KING
Say, man, were these thy words?
HORNER An 't shall please your Majesty, I never said nor thought any such matter. God is my witness, I am falsely accus'd by the villain.

117 censure opinion **125 Dauphin** (Suffolk here uses the title of the heir-apparent of France to refer to King Charles VII because Suffolk, like all Englishmen, considers Henry the rightful King of France.) **128 rack'd** (Literally, tortured; here, strained beyond endurance in matters of taxation.) **136 suspect** suspicion **139 cry you mercy** beg your pardon **142 ten commandments** i.e., ten fingers **143 against her will** unintentional **145 hamper** (1) fetter (2) cradle **146 most master** the one most in command (i.e., the Queen) **149 listen** inquire **150 tickled** vexed, irritated. **fume** smoke, i.e., rage

152 choler . . . overblown anger being dissipated **160 meetest** fittest **162 election** choice **166 for** because **169 discharge** payment of what is owed. **furniture** military equipment **171 Last time** (See *1 Henry VI*, V.iii.) **173 fact** deed

PETER By these ten bones, my lords, he did speak them to me in the garret one night, as we were scouring my Lord of York's armor.

YORK
Base dunghill villain and mechanical,
I'll have thy head for this thy traitor's speech.
I do beseech your royal Majesty,
Let him have all the rigor of the law.

HORNER Alas, my lord, hang me if ever I spake the words. My accuser is my prentice; and when I did correct him for his fault the other day, he did vow upon his knees he would be even with me. I have good witness of this; therefore I beseech your Majesty, do not cast away an honest man for a villain's accusation.

KING
Uncle, what shall we say to this in law?

GLOUCESTER
This doom, my lord, if I may judge:
Let Somerset be Regent o'er the French,
Because in York this breeds suspicion;
And let these have a day appointed them
For single combat in convenient place,
For he hath witness of his servant's malice.
This is the law, and this Duke Humphrey's doom.

[KING
Then be it so. My lord of Somerset,
We make your Grace Regent over the French.]

SOMERSET
I humbly thank your royal Majesty.

HORNER And I accept the combat willingly.

PETER Alas, my lord, I cannot fight; for God's sake, pity my case. The spite of man prevaileth against me. O Lord, have mercy upon me! I shall never be able to fight a blow. O Lord, my heart!

GLOUCESTER
Sirrah, or you must fight, or else be hang'd.

KING Away with them to prison; and the day of combat shall be the last of the next month. Come, Somerset, we'll see thee sent away. *Flourish. Exeunt.*

[SCENE IV]

Enter [Margery Jourdain] the Witch, the two Priests [Hume and Southwell], and Bolingbroke.

HUME Come, my masters. The Duchess, I tell you, expects performance of your promises.

BOLINGBROKE Master Hume, we are therefore provided. Will her ladyship behold and hear our exorcisms?

HUME Ay, what else? Fear you not her courage.

BOLINGBROKE I have heard her reported to be a woman of an invincible spirit. But it shall be convenient, Master Hume, that you be by her aloft, while we be busy below; and so, I pray you, go, in God's name, and leave us. *(Exit Hume.)* Mother Jourdain, be you prostrate and grovel on the earth. John Southwell, read you; and let us to our work.
[Margery Jourdain prostrates herself.]

Enter [Duchess] Eleanor aloft, [Hume following].

DUCHESS Well said, my masters, and welcome all. To this gear, the sooner the better.

BOLINGBROKE
Patience, good lady; wizards know their times.
Deep night, dark night, the silent of the night,
The time of night when Troy was set on fire;
The time when screech-owls cry and ban-dogs howl
And spirits walk and ghosts break up their graves,
That time best fits the work we have in hand.
Madam, sit you and fear not. Whom we raise,
We will make fast within a hallow'd verge.

Here [they] do the ceremonies belonging, and make the circle; Bolingbroke or Southwell reads, Conjuro te, *etc. It thunders and lightens terribly; then the Spirit riseth.*

SPIRIT Adsum.

MARGERY JOURDAIN Asmath,
By the eternal God, whose name and power
Thou tremblest at, answer that I shall ask;
For, till thou speak, thou shalt not pass from hence.

SPIRIT
Ask what thou wilt. That I had said and done!

BOLINGBROKE *[Reading out of a paper]*
"First of the King: what shall of him become?"

SPIRIT
The duke yet lives that Henry shall depose;
But him outlive, and die a violent death.
[As the Spirit speaks, Southwell writes the answer.]

BOLINGBROKE
"What fates await the Duke of Suffolk?"

SPIRIT
By water shall he die, and take his end.

BOLINGBROKE
"What shall befall the Duke of Somerset?"

SPIRIT
Let him shun castles;
Safer shall he be upon the sandy plains
Than where castles mounted stand.
Have done, for more I hardly can endure.

BOLINGBROKE
Descend to darkness and the burning lake!
False fiend, avoid!
Thunder and lightning. Exit Spirit, [sinking down again].

Enter the Duke of York and the Duke of Buckingham with their Guard and break in.

190 bones i.e., fingers **193 mechanical** common workman **205 doom** judgment **208 these** i.e., Peter and Horner **220 Sirrah** (Customary form of address to servants.)

I.iv. Location: Gloucester's garden.
4–5 exorcisms conjurations **6 Fear** doubt

15 gear business **19 ban-dogs** leashed watchdogs **23 hallow'd verge** magic circle. **23 s.d. the ceremonies belonging** i.e., the "hocus-pocus" necessary to conjure spirits, such as drawing a magic circle and reciting a formula. **Conjuro te** I conjure you. **riseth** (Presumably a trap door is used on the main stage.) **24 Adsum** I am here **25 Asmath** (Perhaps *Asnath*, an anagram for *Sathan*.) **27 that** that which **29 That** would that **31–32 The duke . . . death** (The first line of the prophecy, as is characteristic of such utterances, is capable of a double construction: *whom Henry will depose*, or *who will depose Henry*. The second line is fulfilled in *3 Henry VI* in the deaths of Henry VI and Edward IV.) **39 Have done** finish up **41 False** treacherous. **avoid** begone

YORK
Lay hands upon these traitors and their trash.
Beldam, I think we watch'd you at an inch. 43
What, madam, are you there? The King and commonweal
Are deeply indebted for this piece of pains. 45
My Lord Protector will, I doubt it not,
See you well guerdon'd for these good deserts. 47

DUCHESS
Not half so bad as thine to England's king,
Injurious Duke, that threatest where's no cause. 49

BUCKINGHAM
True, madam, none at all. What call you this?
[*Shows her the papers he has seized.*]
Away with them! Let them be clapp'd up close, 51
And kept asunder. You, madam, shall with us.
Stafford, take her to thee. 53
[*Exeunt above Duchess and Hume, guarded.*]
We'll see your trinkets here all forthcoming. 54
All, away! *Exit* [*guard with Jourdain, Southwell, etc.*].

YORK
Lord Buckingham, methinks you watch'd her well.
A pretty plot, well chosen to build upon! 57
Now, pray, my lord, let's see the devil's writ.
What have we here? *Reads.*
"The duke yet lives that Henry shall depose;
But him outlive, and die a violent death."
Why, this is just "Aio te, Aeacida, 62
Romanos vincere posse." Well, to the rest: 63
"Tell me what fate awaits the Duke of Suffolk?"
"By water shall he die, and take his end."
"What shall betide the Duke of Somerset?"
"Let him shun castles;
Safer shall he be upon the sandy plains
Than where castles mounted stand."
Come, come, my lords, these oracles
Are hardly attain'd, and hardly understood. 71
The King is now in progress towards Saint Albans,
With him the husband of this lovely lady.
Thither goes these news, as fast as horse can carry them—
A sorry breakfast for my Lord Protector.

BUCKINGHAM
Your Grace shall give me leave, my Lord of York,
To be the post, in hope of his reward. 77

YORK
At your pleasure, my good lord. [*Exit Buckingham.*]
Who's within there, ho!

Enter a Servingman.

Invite my Lords of Salisbury and Warwick
To sup with me tomorrow night. Away! *Exeunt.*

43 Beldam witch, hag. **at an inch** i.e., closely **45 piece of pains** trouble undergone. (Said ironically.) **47 guerdon'd** rewarded. **deserts** deserving acts. (Said ironically.) **49 Injurious** insulting **51 clapp'd up close** imprisoned closely **53 Stafford** (Presumably one of Buckingham's kinsmen, perhaps Sir Humphrey Stafford, acting as an officer of the arresting guard.) **54 trinkets** trifles, rubbish (used in performing magical acts, and now confiscated to be *forthcoming*, used as legal evidence) **57 plot** clever plan (with pun on the sense of *plot of ground*) **62 just** precisely **62–63 Aio . . . posse** I say that you, Aeacides, the Romans can conquer. (This prophecy, given by the Delphic oracle to Pyrrhus, descendant of Aeacus, is grammatically ambiguous in just the same fashion as the English oracle about Henry and the Yorkists, ll. 31–32.) **71 hardly attain'd** with difficulty obtained, or comprehended **77 post** messenger

[ACT II • SCENE I]

Enter the King, Queen [*with her hawk on her fist*], *Protector* [*Gloucester*], *Cardinal, and Suffolk, with Falconers halloing.*

QUEEN
Believe me, lords, for flying at the brook, 1
I saw not better sport these seven years' day. 2
Yet, by your leave, the wind was very high,
And ten to one old Joan had not gone out. 4

KING [*To Gloucester*]
But what a point, my lord, your falcon made, 5
And what a pitch she flew above the rest! 6
To see how God in all his creatures works!
Yea, man and birds are fain of climbing high. 8

SUFFOLK
No marvel, an it like your Majesty, 9
My Lord Protector's hawks do tow'r so well; 10
They know their master loves to be aloft
And bears his thoughts above his falcon's pitch.

GLOUCESTER
My lord, 'tis but a base ignoble mind
That mounts no higher than a bird can soar.

CARDINAL
I thought as much. He would be above the clouds.

GLOUCESTER
Ay, my Lord Cardinal, how think you by that?
Were it not good your Grace could fly to heaven?

KING
The treasury of everlasting joy.

CARDINAL
Thy heaven is on earth; thine eyes and thoughts
Beat on a crown, the treasure of thy heart.
Pernicious Protector, dangerous peer,
That smooth'st it so with King and commonweal! 22

GLOUCESTER
What, Cardinal, is your priesthood grown peremptory?
Tantaene animis coelestibus irae? 24
Churchmen so hot? Good uncle, hide such malice;
With such holiness can you do it?

SUFFOLK
No malice, sir, no more than well becomes
So good a quarrel and so bad a peer.

GLOUCESTER
As who, my lord?

SUFFOLK Why, as you, my lord,
An 't like your lordly Lord-Protectorship.

GLOUCESTER
Why, Suffolk, England knows thine insolence.

QUEEN
And thy ambition, Gloucester.

II.i. Location: St. Albans.
1 flying . . . brook i.e., hawking for waterfowl **2 these . . . day** in seven years' time **4 old . . . out** i.e., the hawk named old Joan would not have flown out against such a high wind **5 point** advantageous position from which the hawk attacks the bird **6 pitch** height to which a hawk soars before descending on its prey **8 fain** fond **9 an it like** if it please **10 hawks** (Refers not only to the hawks flown by Gloucester in this hunt, but also to the falcon with a maiden's head portrayed on his heraldic badge.) **tow'r** rise wheeling up to the *point* from which the hawk swoops down **22 smooth'st it** flatters **24 Tantaene . . . irae** is there such resentment in heavenly minds. (Virgil, Aeneid, I.11.)

KING I prithee, peace,
Good queen, and whet not on these furious peers;
For blessed are the peacemakers on earth.

CARDINAL
Let me be blessed for the peace I make,
Against this proud Protector, with my sword!

GLOUCESTER [*Aside to Cardinal*]
Faith, holy uncle, would 'twere come to that!

CARDINAL [*Aside to Gloucester*]
Marry, when thou dar'st.

GLOUCESTER [*Aside to Cardinal*]
Make up no factious numbers for the matter;
In thine own person answer thy abuse.

CARDINAL [*Aside to Gloucester*]
Ay, where thou dar'st not peep. And if thou dar'st,
This evening, on the east side of the grove.

KING
How now, my lords?

CARDINAL Believe me, cousin Gloucester,
Had not your man put up the fowl so suddenly,
We had had more sport. [*Aside to Gloucester.*] Come with thy two-hand sword.

GLOUCESTER
True, uncle.

CARDINAL [*Aside to Gloucester*]
Are ye advis'd? The east side of the grove?

GLOUCESTER [*Aside to Cardinal*]
Cardinal, I am with you.

KING Why, how now, uncle Gloucester?

GLOUCESTER
Talking of hawking; nothing else, my lord.
[*Aside to Cardinal.*] Now by God's mother, priest, I'll shave your crown for this,
Or all my fence shall fail.

CARDINAL [*Aside to Gloucester*] Medice, teipsum—
Protector, see to 't well, protect yourself.

KING
The winds grow high; so do your stomachs, lords.
How irksome is this music to my heart!
When such strings jar, what hope of harmony?
I pray, my lords, let me compound this strife.

Enter one [*a Townsman of Saint Albans*] *crying "A miracle!"*

GLOUCESTER
What means this noise?
Fellow, what miracle dost thou proclaim?

TOWNSMAN
A miracle! A miracle!

SUFFOLK
Come to the King and tell him what miracle.

TOWNSMAN
Forsooth, a blind man at Saint Albans shrine,
Within this half-hour, hath receiv'd his sight—
A man that ne'er saw in his life before.

KING
Now, God be prais'd, that to believing souls
Gives light in darkness, comfort in despair!

Enter the Mayor of Saint Albans and his brethren, bearing the man [*Simpcox*], *between two in a chair,* [*Simpcox's Wife and others following*].

CARDINAL
Here comes the townsmen on procession,
To present your Highness with the man.

KING
Great is his comfort in this earthly vale,
Although by his sight his sin be multiplied.

GLOUCESTER
Stand by, my masters. Bring him near the King;
His Highness' pleasure is to talk with him.

KING
Good fellow, tell us here the circumstance,
That we for thee may glorify the Lord.
What, hast thou been long blind and now restor'd?

SIMPCOX
Born blind, an 't please your Grace.

WIFE Ay, indeed, was he.

SUFFOLK What woman is this?

WIFE His wife, an 't like your worship.

GLOUCESTER Hadst thou been his mother, thou couldst have better told.

KING
Where wert thou born?

SIMPCOX
At Berwick in the north, an 't like your Grace.

KING
Poor soul, God's goodness hath been great to thee.
Let never day nor night unhallowed pass,
But still remember what the Lord hath done.

QUEEN
Tell me, good fellow, cam'st thou here by chance,
Or of devotion, to this holy shrine?

SIMPCOX
God knows, of pure devotion, being call'd
A hundred times and oftener, in my sleep,
By good Saint Alban, who said, "Simon, come,
Come, offer at my shrine, and I will help thee."

WIFE
Most true, forsooth; and many time and oft
Myself have heard a voice to call him so.

CARDINAL
What, art thou lame?

SIMPCOX Ay, God Almighty help me!

SUFFOLK
How cam'st thou so?

SIMPCOX A fall off of a tree.

WIFE
A plum-tree, master.

GLOUCESTER How long hast thou been blind?

SIMPCOX
O, born so, master.

GLOUCESTER What, and wouldst climb a tree?

39 Make . . . numbers i.e., do not raise a party of your quarrelsome supporters **40 abuse** offense, insult **44 put . . . fowl** startled the game into flight **47 advis'd** agreed **51 fence** skill in fighting with a sword. **Medice, teipsum** physician, [heal] thyself. (Luke 4:23.) **53 stomachs** tempers **56 compound** settle **56 s.d. Saint Albans** a shrine and a town named for St. Alban, supposedly the first Christian martyr in Britain, executed under the edicts of Diocletian in the third century for sheltering a Christian priest

69 his sight . . . multiplied i.e., he may now be guilty of more sins, being able to see **84 unhallowed** unblessed **85 still** continually **90 Simon** (His proper name; *Simpcox* is a variant.)

SIMPCOX
But that in all my life, when I was a youth.

WIFE
Too true, and bought his climbing very dear.

GLOUCESTER
Mass, thou lov'dst plums well, that wouldst venture so.

SIMPCOX
Alas, good master, my wife desired some damsons,
And made me climb, with danger of my life.

GLOUCESTER
A subtle knave! But yet it shall not serve.
Let me see thine eyes. Wink now; now open them.
In my opinion yet thou see'st not well.

SIMPCOX
Yes, master, clear as day, I thank God and Saint Alban.

GLOUCESTER
Say'st thou me so? What color is this cloak of?

SIMPCOX
Red, master, red as blood.

GLOUCESTER
Why, that's well said. What color is my gown of?

SIMPCOX
Black, forsooth, coal-black as jet.

KING
Why, then, thou know'st what color jet is of?

SUFFOLK
And yet, I think, jet did he never see.

GLOUCESTER
But cloaks and gowns, before this day, a many.

WIFE
Never, before this day, in all his life.

GLOUCESTER Tell me, sirrah, what's my name?

SIMPCOX Alas, master, I know not.

GLOUCESTER What's his name?

SIMPCOX I know not.

GLOUCESTER Nor his?

SIMPCOX No, indeed, master.

GLOUCESTER What's thine own name?

SIMPCOX Saunder Simpcox, an if it please you, master.

GLOUCESTER Then, Saunder, sit there, the lying'st knave in Christendom. If thou hadst been born blind, thou mightst as well have known all our names as thus to name the several colors we do wear. Sight may distinguish of colors, but suddenly to nominate them all, it is impossible. My lords, Saint Alban here hath done a miracle; and would ye not think his cunning to be great, that could restore this cripple to his legs again?

SIMPCOX O master, that you could!

GLOUCESTER My masters of Saint Albans, have you not beadles in your town, and things call'd whips?

MAYOR Yes, my lord, if it please your Grace.

GLOUCESTER Then send for one presently.

MAYOR Sirrah, go fetch the beadle hither straight.

Exit [an Attendant].

GLOUCESTER Now fetch me a stool hither by and by. [*A stool is brought.*] Now, sirrah, if you mean to save yourself from whipping, leap me over this stool and run away.

SIMPCOX
Alas, master, I am not able to stand alone;
You go about to torture me in vain.

Enter a Beadle with whips.

GLOUCESTER Well, sir, we must have you find your legs. Sirrah beadle, whip him till he leap over that same stool.

BEADLE I will, my lord. Come on, sirrah, off with your doublet quickly.

SIMPCOX Alas, master, what shall I do? I am not able to stand.

After the Beadle hath hit him once, he leaps over the stool and runs away; and they follow and cry, "A miracle!"

KING
O God, seest Thou this, and bearest so long?

QUEEN
It made me laugh to see the villain run.

GLOUCESTER
Follow the knave, and take this drab away.

WIFE
Alas, sir, we did it for pure need.

GLOUCESTER Let them be whipp'd through every market town, till they come to Berwick, from whence they came.

Exit [Wife, with Beadle, Mayor, etc.].

CARDINAL
Duke Humphrey has done a miracle today.

SUFFOLK
True; made the lame to leap and fly away.

GLOUCESTER
But you have done more miracles than I;
You made in a day, my lord, whole towns to fly.

Enter Buckingham.

KING
What tidings with our cousin Buckingham?

BUCKINGHAM
Such as my heart doth tremble to unfold.
A sort of naughty persons, lewdly bent,
Under the countenance and confederacy
Of Lady Eleanor, the Protector's wife,
The ringleader and head of all this rout,
Have practic'd dangerously against your state,
Dealing with witches and with conjurers,
Whom we have apprehended in the fact,
Raising up wicked spirits from under ground,
Demanding of King Henry's life and death
And other of your Highness' Privy Council,
As more at large your Grace shall understand.

CARDINAL [*Aside to Gloucester*]
And so, my Lord Protector, by this means
Your lady is forthcoming yet at London.

98 But that only that one **100 Mass** by the Mass. (An oath.) **101 damsons** a variety of plum **104 Wink** close the eyes **127 nominate** call by name **134 beadles** inferior parish officers who might punish petty offenses **137 straight** immediately **138 by and by** at once

140 me for me. (Ethical dative.) **153 drab** low woman **161 You . . . fly** i.e., you gave away French towns in a day, as part of Queen Margaret's dowry **164 sort** lot, gang. **naughty** wicked. **lewdly** evilly **165 Under . . . confederacy** with the authorization and even cooperation **167 rout** crew **168 practic'd** conspired **170 fact** deed **172 Demanding** inquiring **174 at large** in detail **176 forthcoming** ready to appear (in court)

This news, I think, hath turn'd your weapon's edge;
'Tis like, my lord, you will not keep your hour.

GLOUCESTER [*Aside to Cardinal*]
Ambitious churchman, leave to afflict my heart.
Sorrow and grief have vanquish'd all my powers;
And, vanquish'd as I am, I yield to thee,
Or to the meanest groom.

KING
O God, what mischiefs work the wicked ones,
Heaping confusion on their own heads thereby!

QUEEN
Gloucester, see here the tainture of thy nest,
And look thyself be faultless, thou wert best.

GLOUCESTER
Madam, for myself, to heaven I do appeal
How I have lov'd my king and commonweal;
And, for my wife, I know not how it stands.
Sorry I am to hear what I have heard.
Noble she is; but if she have forgot
Honor and virtue, and convers'd with such
As, like to pitch, defile nobility,
I banish her my bed and company
And give her as a prey to law and shame,
That hath dishonored Gloucester's honest name.

KING
Well, for this night we will repose us here;
Tomorrow toward London back again,
To look into this business thoroughly
And call these foul offenders to their answers
And poise the cause in justice' equal scales,
Whose beam stands sure, whose rightful cause
prevails. *Flourish. Exeunt.*

[SCENE II]

Enter York, Salisbury, and Warwick.

YORK
Now, my good Lords of Salisbury and Warwick,
Our simple supper ended, give me leave
In this close walk to satisfy myself,
In craving your opinion of my title,
Which is infallible, to England's crown.

SALISBURY
My lord, I long to hear it at full.

WARWICK
Sweet York, begin; and if thy claim be good,
The Nevils are thy subjects to command.

YORK
Then thus:
Edward the Third, my lords, had seven sons:
The first, Edward the Black Prince, Prince of Wales;
The second, William of Hatfield, and the third,
Lionel Duke of Clarence; next to whom
Was John of Gaunt, the Duke of Lancaster;
The fifth was Edmund Langley, Duke of York;
The sixth was Thomas of Woodstock, Duke of
Gloucester;
William of Windsor was the seventh and last.
Edward the Black Prince died before his father
And left behind him Richard, his only son,
Who after Edward the Third's death reign'd as king
Till Henry Bolingbroke, Duke of Lancaster,
The eldest son and heir of John of Gaunt,
Crown'd by the name of Henry the Fourth,
Seiz'd on the realm, depos'd the rightful king,
Sent his poor queen to France, from whence she
came,
And him to Pomfret; where, as all you know,
Harmless Richard was murdered traitorously.

WARWICK
Father, the Duke hath told the truth;
Thus got the house of Lancaster the crown.

YORK
Which now they hold by force and not by right;
For Richard, the first son's heir, being dead,
The issue of the next son should have reign'd.

SALISBURY
But William of Hatfield died without an heir.

YORK
The third son, Duke of Clarence, from whose line
I claim the crown, had issue, Philippe, a daughter,
Who married Edmund Mortimer, Earl of March.
Edmund had issue, Roger Earl of March;
Roger had issue, Edmund, Anne, and Eleanor.

SALISBURY
This Edmund, in the reign of Bolingbroke,
As I have read, laid claim unto the crown,
And, but for Owen Glendower, had been king,
Who kept him in captivity till he died.
But to the rest.

YORK His eldest sister, Anne,
My mother, being heir unto the crown,
Married Richard Earl of Cambridge, who was son
To Edmund Langley, Edward the Third's fifth son.
By her I claim the kingdom. She was heir
To Roger Earl of March, who was the son
Of Edmund Mortimer, who married Philippe,
Sole daughter unto Lionel Duke of Clarence.
So, if the issue of the elder son
Succeed before the younger, I am king.

WARWICK
What plain proceeding is more plain than this?
Henry doth claim the crown from John of Gaunt,
The fourth son; York claims it from the third.
Till Lionel's issue fails, his should not reign.
It fails not yet, but flourishes in thee

178 hour appointment (for the duel between Gloucester and the Cardinal) **180 leave to afflict** cease afflicting **183 meanest** of lowest degree **185 confusion** destruction **186 tainture** defilement **187 look** take care, see to it. **thou wert best** you'd be well advised **188, 190 for** as for **193 convers'd** had to do with **202 poise** weigh **203 beam** bar on which the scales are suspended. **stands sure** is perfectly level

II.ii. Location: London. The Duke of York's garden.
3 close private

19 Richard i.e., Richard II **39 This Edmund** (A historical error, found also in the chronicles, of confusing Edmund Mortimer, fifth Earl of March, who was named heir to the throne by Richard II, with his uncle Edmund, brother of Roger, who married Glendower's daughter. See *1 Henry VI,* II.v and *1 Henry IV,* I.iii.) **56 his** i.e., John of Gaunt's **57 It fails not** i.e., Lionel's line of descent does not die out

And in thy sons, fair slips of such a stock.
Then, father Salisbury, kneel we together,
And in this private plot be we the first
That shall salute our rightful sovereign
With honor of his birthright to the crown.

BOTH [*Kneeling*]
Long live our sovereign Richard, England's king!

YORK
We thank you, lords. But I am not your king
Till I be crown'd and that my sword be stain'd
With heart-blood of the house of Lancaster;
And that's not suddenly to be perform'd,
But with advice and silent secrecy.
Do you as I do in these dangerous days:
Wink at the Duke of Suffolk's insolence,
At Beaufort's pride, at Somerset's ambition,
At Buckingham and all the crew of them,
Till they have snar'd the shepherd of the flock,
That virtuous prince, the good Duke Humphrey.
'Tis that they seek, and they in seeking that
Shall find their deaths, if York can prophesy.

SALISBURY
My lord, break we off; we know your mind at full.

WARWICK
My heart assures me that the Earl of Warwick
Shall one day make the Duke of York a king.

YORK
And, Nevil, this I do assure myself:
Richard shall live to make the Earl of Warwick
The greatest man in England but the King. *Exeunt.*

[SCENE III]

Sound trumpets. Enter the King and State, [*the Queen, Gloucester, York, Suffolk, Salisbury, and others,*] *with Guard, to banish the Duchess* [*of Gloucester, who is brought on under guard with Margery Jourdain, Southwell, Hume, and Bolingbroke*].

KING
Stand forth, Dame Eleanor Cobham, Gloucester's wife.
In sight of God and us, your guilt is great.
Receive the sentence of the law for sins
Such as by God's book are adjudg'd to death.
[*To Margery and the others.*]
You four, from hence to prison back again;
From thence unto the place of execution.
The witch in Smithfield shall be burnt to ashes,
And you three shall be strangled on the gallows.
[*To the Duchess.*]
You, madam, for you are more nobly born,
Despoiled of your honor in your life,
Shall, after three days' open penance done,
Live in your country here in banishment,
With Sir John Stanley, in the Isle of Man.

DUCHESS
Welcome is banishment. Welcome were my death.

GLOUCESTER
Eleanor, the law, thou see'st, hath judged thee.
I cannot justify whom the law condemns.
[*Exeunt Duchess and other prisoners, guarded.*]
Mine eyes are full of tears, my heart of grief.
Ah, Humphrey, this dishonor in thine age
Will bring thy head with sorrow to the ground!
I beseech your Majesty, give me leave to go;
Sorrow would solace and mine age would ease.

KING
Stay, Humphrey Duke of Gloucester, ere thou go,
Give up thy staff. Henry will to himself
Protector be; and God shall be my hope,
My stay, my guide, and lantern to my feet.
And go in peace, Humphrey, no less belov'd
Than when thou wert Protector to thy king.

QUEEN
I see no reason why a king of years
Should be to be protected like a child.
God and King Henry govern England's realm.
Give up your staff, sir, and the King his realm.

GLOUCESTER
My staff? Here, noble Henry, is my staff.
[*He hands over his staff.*]
As willingly do I the same resign
As ere thy father Henry made it mine;
And even as willingly at thy feet I leave it
As others would ambitiously receive it.
Farewell, good King. When I am dead and gone,
May honorable peace attend thy throne!
Exit Gloucester.

QUEEN
Why, now is Henry king, and Margaret queen,
And Humphrey Duke of Gloucester scarce himself,
That bears so shrewd a maim. Two pulls at once:
His lady banish'd, and a limb lopp'd off.
This staff of honor raught, there let it stand
Where it best fits to be, in Henry's hand.

SUFFOLK
Thus droops this lofty pine and hangs his sprays;
Thus Eleanor's pride dies in her youngest days.

YORK
Lords, let him go. Please it your Majesty,
This is the day appointed for the combat,
And ready are the appellant and defendant,
The armorer and his man, to enter the lists,
So please your Highness to behold the fight.

QUEEN
Ay, good my lord; for purposely therefore
Left I the court, to see this quarrel tried.

58 slips cuttings **60 plot** plot of ground **68 advice** careful reflection **70 Wink at** shut your eyes to

II.iii. Location: London. A hall of justice.
4 by God's book i.e., according to the commandments in the Bible against witches, Exodus 22:18, and enchantments, Leviticus 19:26 **9 for** because **10 Despoiled** deprived

13 With . . . Stanley (An error for Sir Thomas Stanley, the Duchess' custodian and the Lord Stanley of *Richard III.*) **21 would** would have **23 staff** staff of office **28 of years** who is of age **31 King his** King's **41 bears . . . maim** endures so grievous a multilation. **pulls** pluckings **43 raught** attained, seized **45 lofty pine** (An emblem adopted by Henry IV, Gloucester's father.) **46 her youngest days** i.e., when her ambition and pride are at their height (?) **49 appellant** challenger

KING
A' God's name, see the lists and all things fit.
Here let them end it, and God defend the right!

YORK
I never saw a fellow worse bestead,
Or more afraid to fight, than is the appellant,
The servant of this armorer, my lords.

Enter at one door, the Armorer [*Horner*] *and his Neighbors, drinking to him so much that he is drunk; and he enters with a drum before him and his staff with a sand-bag fastened to it; and at the other door his man* [*Peter*], *with a drum and sand-bag, and Prentices drinking to him.*

FIRST NEIGHBOR Here, neighbor Horner, I drink to you in a cup of sack; and fear not, neighbor, you shall do well enough.

SECOND NEIGHBOR And here, neighbor, here's a cup of charneco.

THIRD NEIGHBOR And here's a pot of good double beer, neighbor. Drink, and fear not your man.

HORNER Let it come, i' faith, and I'll pledge you all; and a fig for Peter!

FIRST PRENTICE Here, Peter, I drink to thee, and be not afraid.

SECOND PRENTICE Be merry, Peter, and fear not thy master. Fight for credit of the prentices.

PETER I thank you all. Drink, and pray for me, I pray you, for I think I have taken my last draught in this world. Here, Robin, an if I die, I give thee my apron; and, Will, thou shalt have my hammer; and here, Tom, take all the money that I have. [*Gives away his things.*] O Lord bless me, I pray God, for I am never able to deal with my master, he hath learn'd so much fence already.

SALISBURY Come, leave your drinking, and fall to blows. Sirrah, what's thy name?

PETER Peter, forsooth.

SALISBURY Peter? What more?

PETER Thump.

SALISBURY Thump? Then see thou thump thy master well.

HORNER Masters, I am come hither, as it were, upon my man's instigation, to prove him a knave and myself an honest man; and touching the Duke of York, I will take my death, I never meant him any ill, nor the King, nor the Queen. And therefore, Peter, have at thee with a downright blow!

YORK
Dispatch. This knave's tongue begins to double.
Sound, trumpets, alarum to the combatants!

[*Alarum.*] *They fight, and Peter strikes him down.*

HORNER Hold, Peter, hold! I confess, I confess treason. [*Dies.*]

YORK Take away his weapon. Fellow, thank God, and the good wine in thy master's way.

PETER O God, have I overcome mine enemies in this presence? O Peter, thou hast prevail'd in right!

KING
Go, take hence that traitor from our sight;
For by his death we do perceive his guilt,
And God in justice hath reveal'd to us
The truth and innocence of this poor fellow,
Which he had thought to have murder'd wrongfully.
Come, fellow, follow us for thy reward.

Sound a flourish. Exeunt.

[SCENE IV]

Enter Duke Humphrey [*of Gloucester*] *and his Men in mourning cloaks.*

GLOUCESTER
Thus sometimes hath the brightest day a cloud,
And after summer evermore succeeds
Barren winter, with his wrathful nipping cold;
So cares and joys abound, as seasons fleet.
Sirs, what's o'clock?

SERVANT Ten, my lord.

GLOUCESTER
Ten is the hour that was appointed me
To watch the coming of my punish'd duchess.
Uneath may she endure the flinty streets,
To tread them with her tender-feeling feet.
Sweet Nell, ill can thy noble mind abrook
The abject people gazing on thy face,
With envious looks laughing at thy shame,
That erst did follow thy proud chariot-wheels
When thou didst ride in triumph through the streets.
But, soft! I think she comes, and I'll prepare
My tear-stain'd eyes to see her miseries.

Enter the Duchess [*of Gloucester, barefoot*], *in a white sheet,* [*with verses pinned upon her back,*] *and a taper burning in her hand; with* [*Sir John Stanley,*] *the Sheriff, and Officers,* [*followed by a crowd*].

SERVANT
So please your Grace, we'll take her from the sheriff.

GLOUCESTER
No, stir not, for your lives. Let her pass by.

DUCHESS
Come you, my lord, to see my open shame?
Now thou dost penance too. Look how they gaze!
See how the giddy multitude do point
And nod their heads and throw their eyes on thee!
Ah, Gloucester, hide thee from their hateful looks,
And, in thy closet pent up, rue my shame,
And ban thine enemies, both mine and thine!

54 A' in **56 bestead** prepared **60 sack** a dry Spanish or Canary wine **63 charneco** a sweet Portuguese wine **64 double** strong **67 fig** (Sign of contempt made by putting the thumb between the first and second fingers.) **79 fence** skill in fencing **90 take my death** i.e., take an oath on pain of death **91–92 have at thee** here I come at you **93 double** thicken (as an intoxicated person's)

104 Which he i.e., whom Horner

II.iv. Location: London. A street.
4 fleet flow by **8 Uneath** with difficulty, scarcely **10 abrook** endure **11 abject** lowly born **12 envious** full of malice **13 erst** formerly **24 closet** private room **25 ban** curse

GLOUCESTER
Be patient, gentle Nell, forget this grief.

DUCHESS
Ah, Gloucester, teach me to forget myself!
For whilst I think I am thy married wife
And thou a prince, Protector of this land,
Methinks I should not thus be led along,
Mail'd up in shame, with papers on my back,
And follow'd with a rabble that rejoice
To see my tears and hear my deep-fet groans.
The ruthless flint doth cut my tender feet,
And when I start, the envious people laugh
And bid me be advised how I tread.
Ah, Humphrey, can I bear this shameful yoke?
Trowest thou that e'er I'll look upon the world,
Or count them happy that enjoy the sun?
No, dark shall be my light and night my day;
To think upon my pomp shall be my hell.
Sometime I'll say, I am Duke Humphrey's wife,
And he a prince and ruler of the land;
Yet so he rul'd and such a prince he was
As he stood by whilst I, his forlorn duchess,
Was made a wonder and a pointing-stock
To every idle rascal follower.
But be thou mild and blush not at my shame,
Nor stir at nothing till the axe of death
Hang over thee, as, sure, it shortly will.
For Suffolk, he that can do all in all
With her that hateth thee and hates us all,
And York and impious Beaufort, that false priest,
Have all lim'd bushes to betray thy wings,
And, fly thou how thou canst, they'll tangle thee.
But fear not thou, until thy foot be snar'd,
Nor never seek prevention of thy foes.

GLOUCESTER
Ah, Nell, forbear! Thou aimest all awry.
I must offend before I be attainted;
And had I twenty times so many foes,
And each of them had twenty times their power,
All these could not procure me any scathe
So long as I am loyal, true, and crimeless.
Wouldst have me rescue thee from this reproach?
Why, yet thy scandal were not wip'd away,
But I in danger for the breach of law.
Thy greatest help is quiet, gentle Nell.
I pray thee, sort thy heart to patience;
These few days' wonder will be quickly worn.

Enter a Herald.

HERALD
I summon your Grace to his Majesty's parliament,
Holden at Bury the first of this next month.

GLOUCESTER
And my consent ne'er ask'd herein before?
This is close dealing. Well, I will be there.
[*Exit Herald.*]
My Nell, I take my leave. And, master sheriff,
Let not her penance exceed the King's commission.

SHERIFF
An 't please your Grace, here my commission stays,
And Sir John Stanley is appointed now
To take her with him to the Isle of Man.

GLOUCESTER
Must you, Sir John, protect my lady here?

STANLEY
So am I given in charge, may 't please your Grace.

GLOUCESTER
Entreat her not the worse in that I pray
You use her well. The world may laugh again,
And I may live to do you kindness if
You do it her. And so, Sir John, farewell.

DUCHESS
What, gone, my lord, and bid me not farewell?

GLOUCESTER
Witness my tears, I cannot stay to speak.
Exit Gloucester [*with his Men*].

DUCHESS
Art thou gone too? All comfort go with thee!
For none abides with me. My joy is death—
Death, at whose name I oft have been afear'd,
Because I wish'd this world's eternity.
Stanley, I prithee, go, and take me hence;
I care not whither, for I beg no favor,
Only convey me where thou art commanded.

STANLEY
Why, madam, that is to the Isle of Man,
There to be us'd according to your state.

DUCHESS
That's bad enough, for I am but reproach;
And shall I then be us'd reproachfully?

STANLEY
Like to a duchess, and Duke Humphrey's lady;
According to that state you shall be us'd.

DUCHESS
Sheriff, farewell, and better than I fare,
Although thou hast been conduct of my shame.

SHERIFF
It is my office; and madam, pardon me.

DUCHESS
Ay, ay, farewell, thy office is discharg'd.
Come, Stanley, shall we go?

STANLEY
Madam, your penance done, throw off this sheet,
And go we to attire you for our journey.

DUCHESS
My shame will not be shifted with my sheet.
No, it will hang upon my richest robes
And show itself, attire me how I can.
Go, lead the way; I long to see my prison. *Exeunt.*

31 Mail'd up enveloped. (Used in hawking to prevent the hawk from struggling, just as Eleanor is wrapped in a white sheet.) **papers on my back** (The verses pinned upon her back describe the sin for which she is doing penance.) **33 deep-fet** fetched from the depths **35 start** flinch, wince **36 advised** careful **38 Trowest thou** do you believe **46 pointing-stock** one pointed at in scorn **52 her** i.e., Queen Margaret **54 lim'd** put out sticky birdlime as a trap **56 fear not thou** i.e., you are not properly wary. (Or the Duchess may be ironically urging him to wait until it is too late.) **57 prevention** forestalling **59 attainted** condemned for treason or other serious wrongdoing **62 scathe** injury **65 were not** would not be **68 sort** adapt **69 worn** i.e., forgotten **71 Holden at Bury** to be held at Bury St. Edmunds (in Suffolk)

73 close secret, underhand **76 stays** stops, ends **81 Entreat** treat **90 this world's eternity** endless worldly success **95 state** noble rank. (But Eleanor plays on *state* in the sense of "condition.") **96 I . . . reproach** I am the embodiment of reproach or disgrace **100 better . . . fare** may you fare better than I **101 conduct** conductor **107 shifted** changed (with a pun on *shift,* a chemise)

[ACT III • SCENE I]

Sound a sennet. Enter King, Queen, Cardinal [Beaufort], Suffolk, York, Buckingham, Salisbury, and Warwick to the Parliament.

KING
I muse my Lord of Gloucester is not come.
'Tis not his wont to be the hindmost man,
Whate'er occasion keeps him from us now.

QUEEN
Can you not see? Or will ye not observe
The strangeness of his alter'd countenance?
With what a majesty he bears himself,
How insolent of late he is become,
How proud, how peremptory, and unlike himself?
We know the time since he was mild and affable,
And if we did but glance a far-off look,
Immediately he was upon his knee,
That all the court admir'd him for submission;
But meet him now, and, be it in the morn,
When every one will give the time of day,
He knits his brow and shows an angry eye
And passeth by with stiff unbowed knee,
Disdaining duty that to us belongs.
Small curs are not regarded when they grin,
But great men tremble when the lion roars—
And Humphrey is no little man in England.
First note that he is near you in descent,
And, should you fall, he is the next will mount.
Me seemeth then it is no policy,
Respecting what a rancorous mind he bears
And his advantage following your decease,
That he should come about your royal person
Or be admitted to your Highness' Council.
By flattery hath he won the commons' hearts;
And when he please to make commotion,
'Tis to be fear'd they all will follow him.
Now 'tis the spring, and weeds are shallow-rooted;
Suffer them now, and they'll o'ergrow the garden
And choke the herbs for want of husbandry.
The reverent care I bear unto my lord
Made me collect these dangers in the Duke.
If it be fond, call it a woman's fear—
Which fear, if better reasons can supplant,
I will subscribe and say I wrong'd the Duke.
My Lord of Suffolk, Buckingham, and York,
Reprove my allegation, if you can,
Or else conclude my words effectual.

SUFFOLK
Well hath your Highness seen into this Duke,
And, had I first been put to speak my mind,
I think I should have told your Grace's tale.
The Duchess by his subornation,
Upon my life, began her devilish practices;
Or, if he were not privy to those faults,
Yet, by reputing of his high descent—
As next the King he was successive heir,
And such high vaunts of his nobility—
Did instigate the bedlam brain-sick Duchess
By wicked means to frame our sovereign's fall.
Smooth runs the water where the brook is deep,
And in his simple show he harbors treason.
The fox barks not when he would steal the lamb.
No, no, my sovereign; Gloucester is a man
Unsounded yet and full of deep deceit.

CARDINAL
Did he not, contrary to form of law,
Devise strange deaths for small offenses done?

YORK
And did he not, in his protectorship,
Levy great sums of money through the realm
For soldiers' pay in France, and never sent it,
By means whereof the towns each day revolted?

BUCKINGHAM
Tut, these are petty faults to faults unknown,
Which time will bring to light in smooth Duke
Humphrey.

KING
My lords, at once: the care you have of us,
To mow down thorns that would annoy our foot,
Is worthy praise; but, shall I speak my conscience,
Our kinsman Gloucester is as innocent
From meaning treason to our royal person
As is the sucking lamb or harmless dove.
The Duke is virtuous, mild, and too well given
To dream on evil or to work my downfall.

QUEEN
Ah, what's more dangerous than this fond affiance!
Seems he a dove? His feathers are but borrow'd,
For he's disposed as the hateful raven.
Is he a lamb? His skin is surely lent him,
For he's inclin'd as is the ravenous wolves.
Who cannot steal a shape that means deceit?
Take heed, my lord. The welfare of us all
Hangs on the cutting short that fraudful man.

Enter Somerset.

SOMERSET
All health unto my gracious sovereign!

KING
Welcome, Lord Somerset. What news from France?

SOMERSET
That all your interest in those territories
Is utterly bereft you. All is lost.

KING
Cold news, Lord Somerset; but God's will be done!

YORK [*Aside*]
Cold news for me, for I had hope of France
As firmly as I hope for fertile England.
Thus are my blossoms blasted in the bud,
And caterpillars eat my leaves away;

III.i. Location: The Abbey at Bury St. Edmunds.
1 muse wonder **2 wont** custom **9 know** remember. **since** when **14 give . . . day** say good morning **18 grin** bare their teeth **22 will mount** who will mount the throne **23 Me seemeth** it seems to me. **policy** prudent course **24 Respecting** considering **33 husbandry** proper cultivation **35 collect** gather, infer **36 fond** foolish **38 subscribe** agree. (Literally, *undersign*.) **40 Reprove** disprove **45 subornation** instigation **46 Upon my life** i.e., I swear this on pain of death. **practices** intrigues

48 reputing boasting **51 bedlam** crazy **52 frame** devise **54 show** outward appearance **57 Unsounded** with depths still undiscovered **64 to** compared to **66 at once** all of you; or, without more ado **72 well given** kindly disposed **74 fond affiance** foolish confidence **79 Who . . . deceit** who is there, intending to deceive, that cannot assume an appropriate disguise

But I will remedy this gear ere long,
Or sell my title for a glorious grave.

Enter Gloucester.

GLOUCESTER
All happiness unto my lord the King!
Pardon, my liege, that I have stay'd so long.

SUFFOLK
Nay, Gloucester, know that thou art come too soon,
Unless thou wert more loyal than thou art.
I do arrest thee of high treason here.

GLOUCESTER
Well, Suffolk, thou shalt not see me blush
Nor change my countenance for this arrest.
A heart unspotted is not easily daunted.
The purest spring is not so free from mud
As I am clear from treason to my sovereign.
Who can accuse me? Wherein am I guilty?

YORK
'Tis thought, my lord, that you took bribes of France,
And, being Protector, stay'd the soldiers' pay,
By means whereof his Highness hath lost France.

GLOUCESTER
Is it but thought so? What are they that think it?
I never robb'd the soldiers of their pay,
Nor ever had one penny bribe from France.
So help me God as I have watch'd the night,
Ay, night by night, in studying good for England!
That doit that e'er I wrested from the King,
Or any groat I hoarded to my use,
Be brought against me at my trial day!
No! Many a pound of mine own proper store,
Because I would not tax the needy commons,
Have I dispursed to the garrisons,
And never ask'd for restitution.

CARDINAL
It serves you well, my lord, to say so much.

GLOUCESTER
I say no more than truth, so help me God!

YORK
In your protectorship you did devise
Strange tortures for offenders never heard of,
That England was defam'd by tyranny.

GLOUCESTER
Why, 'tis well known that, whiles I was Protector,
Pity was all the fault that was in me;
For I should melt at an offender's tears,
And lowly words were ransom for their fault.
Unless it were a bloody murderer,
Or foul felonious thief that fleec'd poor passengers,
I never gave them condign punishment.
Murder indeed, that bloody sin, I tortur'd
Above the felon or what trespass else.

SUFFOLK
My lord, these faults are easy, quickly answer'd;
But mightier crimes are laid unto your charge,
Whereof you cannot easily purge yourself.
I do arrest you in his Highness' name,
And here commit you to my Lord Cardinal
To keep, until your further time of trial.

KING
My Lord of Gloucester, 'tis my special hope
That you will clear yourself from all suspense.
My conscience tells me you are innocent.

GLOUCESTER
Ah, gracious lord, these days are dangerous!
Virtue is chok'd with foul ambition
And charity chas'd hence by rancor's hand;
Foul subornation is predominant
And equity exil'd your Highness' land.
I know their complot is to have my life,
And, if my death might make this island happy
And prove the period of their tyranny,
I would expend it with all willingness.
But mine is made the prologue to their play;
For thousands more, that yet suspect no peril,
Will not conclude their plotted tragedy.
Beaufort's red sparkling eyes blab his heart's malice,
And Suffolk's cloudy brow his stormy hate;
Sharp Buckingham unburdens with his tongue
The envious load that lies upon his heart;
And dogged York, that reaches at the moon,
Whose overweening arm I have pluck'd back,
By false accuse doth level at my life.
[*To the Queen.*] And you, my sovereign lady, with the rest,
Causeless have laid disgraces on my head
And with your best endeavor have stirr'd up
My liefest liege to be mine enemy.
Ay, all of you have laid your heads together—
Myself had notice of your conventicles—
And all to make away my guiltless life.
I shall not want false witness to condemn me,
Nor store of treasons to augment my guilt.
The ancient proverb will be well effected:
"A staff is quickly found to beat a dog."

CARDINAL
My liege, his railing is intolerable.
If those that care to keep your royal person
From treason's secret knife and traitors' rage
Be thus upbraided, chid, and rated at,
And the offender granted scope of speech,
'Twill make them cool in zeal unto your Grace.

SUFFOLK
Hath he not twit our sovereign lady here
With ignominious words, though clerkly couch'd,
As if she had suborned some to swear
False allegations to o'erthrow his state?

QUEEN
But I can give the loser leave to chide.

GLOUCESTER
Far truer spoke than meant. I lose, indeed;
Beshrew the winners, for they play'd me false!

91 gear business **94 stay'd** delayed **105 stay'd** held back **110 watch'd the night** remained awake all night **112, 113 doit, groat** coins of small value **115 proper** personal **117 dispursed** disbursed **123 That** so that **126 should** would **127 lowly** humble **130 condign** worthily deserved **132 Above . . . else** beyond any other kind of felony or misdemeanor **133 easy** slight

140 suspense i.e., doubt as to your innocence **145 subornation** instigating others to commit crimes, including perjury **146 exil'd** exiled from **147 complot** plot, conspiracy **149 prove the period** turn out to be the end **160 accuse** accusation. **level** aim **164 liefest liege** dearest sovereign **166 conventicles** private or secret meetings **168 want** lack **175 rated** scolded **176 scope** freedom **178 twit** twitted **179 clerkly couch'd** learnedly and cleverly phrased **182 leave** permission **184 Beshrew** curse

And well such losers may have leave to speak.

BUCKINGHAM
He'll wrest the sense and hold us here all day.
Lord Cardinal, he is your prisoner.

CARDINAL
Sirs, take away the Duke, and guard him sure.

GLOUCESTER
Ah, thus King Henry throws away his crutch
Before his legs be firm to bear his body.
Thus is the shepherd beaten from thy side
And wolves are gnarling who shall gnaw thee first.
Ah, that my fear were false, ah, that it were!
For, good King Henry, thy decay I fear.
Exit Gloucester [*guarded*].

KING [*Rising*]
My lord, what to your wisdoms seemeth best,
Do or undo, as if ourself were here.

QUEEN
What, will your Highness leave the parliament?

KING
Ay, Margaret. My heart is drown'd with grief,
Whose flood begins to flow within mine eyes,
My body round engirt with misery;
For what's more miserable than discontent?
Ah, uncle Humphrey, in thy face I see
The map of honor, truth, and loyalty;
And yet, good Humphrey, is the hour to come
That e'er I prov'd thee false or fear'd thy faith.
What louring star now envies thy estate,
That these great lords and Margaret our queen
Do seek subversion of thy harmless life?
Thou never didst them wrong nor no man wrong.
And as the butcher takes away the calf
And binds the wretch and beats it when it strays,
Bearing it to the bloody slaughter-house,
Even so remorseless have they borne him hence;
And as the dam runs lowing up and down,
Looking the way her harmless young one went,
And can do nought but wail her darling's loss,
Even so myself bewails good Gloucester's case
With sad unhelpful tears, and with dimm'd eyes
Look after him and cannot do him good,
So mighty are his vowed enemies.
His fortunes I will weep, and 'twixt each groan
Say "Who's a traitor? Gloucester he is none."
Exeunt [*King, Buckingham, Salisbury, and Warwick with attendants; Somerset remains apart*].

QUEEN
Free lords, cold snow melts with the sun's hot
beams.
Henry my lord is cold in great affairs,
Too full of foolish pity; and Gloucester's show
Beguiles him, as the mournful crocodile
With sorrow snares relenting passengers,
Or as the snake, roll'd in a flow'ring bank,
With shining checker'd slough, doth sting a child
That for the beauty thinks it excellent.
Believe me, lords, were none more wise than I—
And yet herein I judge mine own wit good—
This Gloucester should be quickly rid the world,
To rid us from the fear we have of him.

CARDINAL
That he should die is worthy policy,
But yet we want a color for his death.
'Tis meet he be condemn'd by course of law.

SUFFOLK
But, in my mind, that were no policy.
The King will labor still to save his life,
The commons haply rise to save his life;
And yet we have but trivial argument,
More than mistrust, that shows him worthy death.

YORK
So that, by this, you would not have him die.

SUFFOLK
Ah, York, no man alive so fain as I!

YORK
'Tis York that hath more reason for his death.
But, my Lord Cardinal, and you, my Lord of
Suffolk,
Say as you think, and speak it from your souls:
Were 't not all one, an empty eagle were set
To guard the chicken from a hungry kite,
As place Duke Humphrey for the King's Protector?

QUEEN
So the poor chicken should be sure of death.

SUFFOLK
Madam, 'tis true; and were 't not madness, then,
To make the fox surveyor of the fold?
Who, being accus'd a crafty murderer,
His guilt should be but idly posted over,
Because his purpose is not executed.
No, let him die in that he is a fox,
By nature prov'd an enemy to the flock,
Before his chaps be stain'd with crimson blood,
As Humphrey, prov'd by reasons, to my liege.
And do not stand on quillets how to slay him—
Be it by gins, by snares, by subtlety,
Sleeping or waking, 'tis no matter how,
So he be dead. For that is good deceit
Which mates him first that first intends deceit.

QUEEN
Thrice-noble Suffolk, 'tis resolutely spoke.

SUFFOLK
Not resolute, except so much were done,
For things are often spoke and seldom meant;
But that my heart accordeth with my tongue,
Seeing the deed is meritorious,
And to preserve my sovereign from his foe,
Say but the word, and I will be his priest.

186 wrest the sense twist the meaning **192 gnarling** snarling **194 decay** downfall **205 fear'd thy faith** doubted your loyalty **214 dam** mother **223 Free** noble **229 slough** skin

236 color pretext **238 were no policy** would be a poor stratagem **239 still** continually **240 haply** perhaps **241 argument** evidence **242 More than mistrust** other than suspicion **243 by this** i.e., by this reasoning **244 fain** glad, eager **248 all one** all the same, the same thing. **empty** hungry **249 kite** scavenger bird, a kind of hawk **255 idly posted over** foolishly ignored or hastened over. (I.e., it would be foolish to place a fox in charge of a chicken coop and then exonerate him of being a killer simply because he hasn't yet killed the chickens.) **259 chaps** chops, jaws **260 prov'd** i.e., proved to be an enemy **261 quillets** subtle distinctions or disputes **262 gins** engines, traps **265 mates** checkmates, foils (i.e., strikes quickly before the enemy can move first) **267 except . . . done** unless what I've spoken is converted into action **269 that** i.e., to prove that **272 be his priest** i.e., perform the last rites for him, preside over his death

CARDINAL
But I would have him dead, my Lord of Suffolk,
Ere you can take due orders for a priest.
Say you consent and censure well the deed,
And I'll provide his executioner,
I tender so the safety of my liege.

SUFFOLK
Here is my hand, the deed is worthy doing.

QUEEN
And so say I.

YORK
And I. And now we three have spoke it,
It skills not greatly who impugns our doom.

Enter a Post.

POST
Great lords, from Ireland am I come amain,
To signify that rebels there are up
And put the Englishmen unto the sword.
Send succors, lords, and stop the rage betime,
Before the wound do grow uncurable;
For, being green, there is great hope of help. [*Exit.*]

CARDINAL
A breach that craves a quick expedient stop!
What counsel give you in this weighty cause?

YORK
That Somerset be sent as Regent thither.
'Tis meet that lucky ruler be employ'd—
Witness the fortune he hath had in France.

SOMERSET [*Coming forward*]
If York, with all his far-fet policy,
Had been the Regent there instead of me,
He never would have stay'd in France so long.

YORK
No, not to lose it all, as thou hast done.
I rather would have lost my life betimes
Than bring a burden of dishonor home
By staying there so long till all were lost.
Show me one scar character'd on thy skin.
Men's flesh preserv'd so whole do seldom win.

QUEEN
Nay, then, this spark will prove a raging fire,
If wind and fuel be brought to feed it with.
No more, good York; sweet Somerset, be still.
Thy fortune, York, hadst thou been Regent there,
Might happily have prov'd far worse than his.

YORK
What, worse than nought? Nay, then, a shame take all!

SOMERSET
And, in the number, thee that wishest shame!

CARDINAL
My Lord of York, try what your fortune is.
Th' uncivil kerns of Ireland are in arms
And temper clay with blood of Englishmen.
To Ireland will you lead a band of men,
Collected choicely, from each county some,
And try your hap against the Irishmen?

YORK
I will, my lord, so please his Majesty.

SUFFOLK
Why, our authority is his consent,
And what we do establish he confirms.
Then, noble York, take thou this task in hand.

YORK
I am content. Provide me soldiers, lords,
Whiles I take order for mine own affairs.

SUFFOLK
A charge, Lord York, that I will see perform'd.
But now return we to the false Duke Humphrey.

CARDINAL
No more of him; for I will deal with him
That henceforth he shall trouble us no more.
And so break off; the day is almost spent.
Lord Suffolk, you and I must talk of that event.

YORK
My Lord of Suffolk, within fourteen days
At Bristol I expect my soldiers,
For there I'll ship them all for Ireland.

SUFFOLK
I'll see it truly done, my Lord of York.
Exeunt. Manet York.

YORK
Now, York, or never, steel thy fearful thoughts,
And change misdoubt to resolution.
Be that thou hop'st to be, or what thou art
Resign to death; it is not worth th' enjoying.
Let pale-fac'd fear keep with the mean-born man,
And find no harbor in a royal heart.
Faster than springtime show'rs comes thought on thought,
And not a thought but thinks on dignity.
My brain more busy than the laboring spider
Weaves tedious snares to trap mine enemies.
Well, nobles, well, 'tis politicly done,
To send me packing with an host of men.
I fear me you but warm the starved snake,
Who, cherish'd in your breasts, will sting your hearts.
'Twas men I lack'd, and you will give them me;
I take it kindly. Yet be well assur'd
You put sharp weapons in a madman's hands.
Whiles I in Ireland nourish a mighty band,
I will stir up in England some black storm
Shall blow ten thousand souls to heaven or hell;
And this fell tempest shall not cease to rage
Until the golden circuit on my head,
Like to the glorious sun's transparent beams,
Do calm the fury of this mad-bred flaw.

274 take . . . priest (1) make arrangements to have a priest there (2) prepare yourself for the priesthood **275 censure well** approve **277 tender** am concerned for, care for **281 skills not** makes no great difference. **impugns our doom** questions our decision **282 amain** with full speed **285 betime** early, swiftly **287 green** fresh **291 meet** fitting. (Said ironically; York is hostile toward Somerset.) **293 far-fet** far-fetched, artful, deep. (Said ironically.) **297 betimes** forthwith **300 character'd** inscribed **306 happily** haply, perhaps **308 in the number** i.e., among the "all" to whom York wishes shame **310 uncivil kerns** disorderly and irregular light-armed Irish soldiers

311 temper clay moisten the soil **320 take order for** arrange **325 break off** cease conversation **326 event** affair, business **332 misdoubt** suspicion, fear **335 keep** dwell **338 dignity** i.e., the dignity of high office—kingship **340 tedious** intricate **341 politicly** shrewdly. (Said ironically.) **343 starved** i.e., deathlike with cold **350 Shall** that shall **351 fell** fierce **354 mad-bred** produced by madness (i.e., by mismanagement, faction, and ambition at court). **flaw** squall, tempest

And, for a minister of my intent,
I have seduc'd a headstrong Kentishman,
John Cade of Ashford,
To make commotion, as full well he can,
Under the title of John Mortimer.
In Ireland have I seen this stubborn Cade
Oppose himself against a troop of kerns,
And fought so long, till that his thighs with darts
Were almost like a sharp-quill'd porpentine;
And, in the end being rescued, I have seen
Him caper upright like a wild Morisco,
Shaking the bloody darts as he his bells.
Full often, like a shag-hair'd crafty kern,
Hath he conversed with the enemy,
And undiscover'd come to me again
And given me notice of their villainies.
This devil here shall be my substitute;
For that John Mortimer, which now is dead,
In face, in gait, in speech, he doth resemble.
By this I shall perceive the commons' mind,
How they affect the house and claim of York.
Say he be taken, rack'd, and tortured,
I know no pain they can inflict upon him
Will make him say I mov'd him to those arms.
Say that he thrive, as 'tis great like he will,
Why then from Ireland come I with my strength
And reap the harvest which that rascal sow'd.
For, Humphrey being dead, as he shall be,
And Henry put apart, the next for me. *Exit.*

[SCENE II]

Enter two or three running over the stage, from the murder of Duke Humphrey.

FIRST MURDERER
Run to my Lord of Suffolk. Let him know
We have dispatch'd the Duke, as he commanded.

SECOND MURDERER
O that it were to do! What have we done?
Didst ever hear a man so penitent?

Enter Suffolk.

FIRST MURDERER
Here comes my lord.

SUFFOLK
Now, sirs, have you dispatch'd this thing?

FIRST MURDERER
Ay, my good lord, he's dead.

SUFFOLK
Why, that's well said. Go get you to my house.
I will reward you for this venturous deed.
The King and all the peers are here at hand.
Have you laid fair the bed? Is all things well,
According as I gave directions?

FIRST MURDERER
'Tis, my good lord.

SUFFOLK
Away! Be gone. *Exeunt [Murderers].*

Sound trumpets. Enter the King, the Queen, Cardinal [Beaufort], Somerset, with Attendants.

KING
Go call our uncle to our presence straight.
Say we intend to try his Grace today,
If he be guilty, as 'tis published.

SUFFOLK
I'll call him presently, my noble lord. *Exit.*

KING
Lords, take your places; and, I pray you all,
Proceed no straiter 'gainst our uncle Gloucester
Than from true evidence of good esteem
He be approv'd in practice culpable.
[They take their places.]

QUEEN
God forbid any malice should prevail,
That faultless may condemn a nobleman!
Pray God he may acquit him of suspicion!

KING
I thank thee, Meg. These words content me much.

Enter Suffolk.

How now? Why look'st thou pale? Why tremblest thou?
Where is our uncle? What's the matter, Suffolk?

SUFFOLK
Dead in his bed, my lord. Gloucester is dead.

QUEEN
Marry, God forfend!

CARDINAL
God's secret judgment. I did dream tonight
The Duke was dumb and could not speak a word.
King swoons.

QUEEN
How fares my lord? Help, lords, the King is dead!

SOMERSET
Rear up his body; wring him by the nose.

QUEEN
Run, go, help, help! O Henry, ope thine eyes!
[They revive the King.]

SUFFOLK
He doth revive again. Madam, be patient.

KING
O heavenly God!

QUEEN
How fares my gracious lord?

SUFFOLK
Comfort, my sovereign! Gracious Henry, comfort!

355 minister agent **359 Mortimer** (The name of a powerful family claiming descent from Lionel Duke of Clarence and hence entitled to the crown. See *1 Henry VI*, II.v.) **362 darts** light spears **363 porpentine** porcupine **365 Morisco** morris dancer, always fancily or grotesquely dressed; or the dance itself **366 he** i.e., the morris dancer **375 affect** incline toward **378 Will** that will. **mov'd** incited, prompted **379 great like** very likely

III.ii. Location: Bury St. Edmunds. A room of state, with seats prepared as for a trial.
3 that . . . do i.e., that it were not done

15 straight straightway **17 If** whether. **published** publicly proclaimed **20 straiter** more severely **21 of good esteem** worthy of belief **22 approv'd** proved **24 faultless** (Modifies *nobleman*.) **30 forfend** forbid **31 tonight** this past night **34 wring . . . nose** (Evidently a common first-aid remedy for restoring consciousness; cf. *Venus and Adonis*, 475.)

KING

What, doth my Lord of Suffolk comfort me?
Came he right now to sing a raven's note,
Whose dismal tune bereft my vital pow'rs,
And thinks he that the chirping of a wren,
By crying comfort from a hollow breast,
Can chase away the first-conceived sound?
Hide not thy poison with such sug'red words.
Lay not thy hands on me; forbear, I say!
Their touch affrights me as a serpent's sting.
Thou baleful messenger, out of my sight!
Upon thy eyeballs murderous tyranny
Sits in grim majesty, to fright the world.
Look not upon me, for thine eyes are wounding.
Yet do not go away. Come, basilisk,
And kill the innocent gazer with thy sight;
For in the shade of death I shall find joy,
In life but double death, now Gloucester's dead.

QUEEN

Why do you rate my Lord of Suffolk thus?
Although the Duke was enemy to him,
Yet he most Christian-like laments his death.
And for myself, foe as he was to me,
Might liquid tears or heart-offending groans
Or blood-consuming sighs recall his life,
I would be blind with weeping, sick with groans,
Look pale as primrose with blood-drinking sighs,
And all to have the noble Duke alive.
What know I how the world may deem of me?
For it is known we were but hollow friends.
It may be judg'd I made the Duke away;
So shall my name with slander's tongue be
wounded,
And princes' courts be fill'd with my reproach.
This get I by his death. Ay me, unhappy,
To be a queen, and crown'd with infamy!

KING

Ah, woe is me for Gloucester, wretched man!

QUEEN

Be woe for me, more wretched than he is.
What, dost thou turn away and hide thy face?
I am no loathsome leper. Look on me.
What? Art thou, like the adder, waxen deaf?
Be poisonous too, and kill thy forlorn queen.
Is all thy comfort shut in Gloucester's tomb?
Why, then, Dame Margaret was ne'er thy joy.
Erect his statue and worship it,
And make my image but an alehouse sign.
Was I for this nigh wrack'd upon the sea
And twice by awkward wind from England's bank
Drove back again unto my native clime?
What boded this, but well forewarning wind
Did seem to say, "Seek not a scorpion's nest,
Nor set no footing on this unkind shore"?
What did I then but curs'd the gentle gusts
And he that loos'd them forth their brazen caves,
And bid them blow towards England's blessed
shore,
Or turn our stern upon a dreadful rock?
Yet Aeolus would not be a murderer,
But left that hateful office unto thee.
The pretty-vaulting sea refus'd to drown me,
Knowing that thou wouldst have me drown'd on
shore
With tears as salt as sea, through thy unkindness.
The splitting rocks cow'r'd in the sinking sands
And would not dash me with their ragged sides,
Because thy flinty heart, more hard than they,
Might in thy palace perish Margaret.
As far as I could ken thy chalky cliffs,
When from thy shore the tempest beat us back,
I stood upon the hatches in the storm,
And when the dusky sky began to rob
My earnest-gaping sight of thy land's view,
I took a costly jewel from my neck—
A heart it was, bound in with diamonds—
And threw it towards thy land. The sea receiv'd it,
And so I wish'd thy body might my heart.
And even with this I lost fair England's view,
And bid mine eyes be packing with my heart,
And call'd them blind and dusky spectacles,
For losing ken of Albion's wished coast.
How often have I tempted Suffolk's tongue,
The agent of thy foul inconstancy,
To sit and witch me, as Ascanius did
When he to madding Dido would unfold
His father's acts commenc'd in burning Troy!
Am I not witch'd like her, or thou not false like
him?
Ay me, I can no more! Die, Margaret!
For Henry weeps that thou dost live so long.

Noise within. Enter Warwick, [Salisbury,] and many Commons.

WARWICK

It is reported, mighty sovereign,
That good Duke Humphrey traitorously is murd'red
By Suffolk and the Cardinal Beaufort's means.
The commons, like an angry hive of bees
That want their leader, scatter up and down
And care not who they sting in his revenge.
Myself have calm'd their spleenful mutiny,
Until they hear the order of his death.

KING

That he is dead, good Warwick, 'tis too true;
But how he died God knows, not Henry.
Enter his chamber, view his breathless corpse,
And comment then upon his sudden death.

40 right now just now. **raven's note** a supposed omen of death **52 basilisk** fabulous reptile, said to kill by its look **56 rate** berate **60, 61, 63 heart-offending, blood-consuming, blood-drinking** (It was commonly believed that groans and sighs cost the heart a drop of blood.) **76 waxen** grown **83 awkward** adverse **85 but** but that **89 he** i.e., Aeolus, god of the winds. **forth** forth from

99 Because so that **100 perish** cause to perish **101 ken** discern **111 be packing** be gone **112 spectacles** instruments of sight **113 Albion's** England's **115 agent** i.e., arranger of the marriage agreement between Henry and Margaret **116 witch** bewitch. **Ascanius** young son of Aeneas. (In Virgil's *Aeneid*, Book I, during Aeneas' narration of his adventures and misfortunes in the court of Queen Dido, Aeneas' mother Venus sends Cupid disguised as Ascanius to inflict the Queen with love for Aeneas.) **117 madding** becoming frantic (with love) **126 want** lack **127 his revenge** revenge of him **128 spleenful** wrathful **129 order** manner **133 comment . . . upon** explain

WARWICK
That shall I do, my liege. Stay, Salisbury,
With the rude multitude till I return. [*Exit.*]
[*Exit Salisbury with the Commons.*]

KING
O Thou that judgest all things, stay my thoughts, 136
My thoughts, that labor to persuade my soul
Some violent hands were laid on Humphrey's life!
If my suspect be false, forgive me, God, 139
For judgment only doth belong to Thee.
Fain would I go to chafe his paly lips 141
With twenty thousand kisses, and to drain
Upon his face an ocean of salt tears,
To tell my love unto his dumb deaf trunk
And with my fingers feel his hand unfeeling.
But all in vain are these mean obsequies; 146

Bed put forth [*bearing Gloucester's body. Enter Warwick*].

And to survey his dead and earthy image,
What were it but to make my sorrow greater?

WARWICK
Come hither, gracious sovereign, view this body.

KING
That is to see how deep my grave is made,
For with his soul fled all my worldly solace;
For seeing him I see my life in death.

WARWICK
As surely as my soul intends to live
With that dread King that took our state upon him 154
To free us from his Father's wrathful curse,
I do believe that violent hands were laid
Upon the life of this thrice-famed Duke. 157

SUFFOLK
A dreadful oath, sworn with a solemn tongue!
What instance gives Lord Warwick for his vow? 159

WARWICK
See how the blood is settled in his face.
Oft have I seen a timely-parted ghost, 161
Of ashy semblance, meager, pale, and bloodless,
Being all descended to the laboring heart, 163
Who, in the conflict that it holds with death, 164
Attracts the same for aidance 'gainst the enemy, 165
Which with the heart there cools and ne'er returneth
To blush and beautify the cheek again. 167
But see, his face is black and full of blood,
His eyeballs further out than when he lived,
Staring full ghastly, like a strangled man;
His hair uprear'd, his nostrils stretch'd with struggling;
His hands abroad display'd, as one that grasp'd 172
And tugg'd for life and was by strength subdu'd.
Look, on the sheets his hair, you see, is sticking;
His well-proportion'd beard made rough and rugged,
Like to the summer's corn by tempest lodg'd. 176
It cannot be but he was murd'red here.
The least of all these signs were probable. 178

SUFFOLK
Why, Warwick, who should do the Duke to death?
Myself and Beaufort had him in protection,
And we, I hope, sir, are no murderers.

WARWICK
But both of you were vow'd Duke Humphrey's foes,
And you [*To Cardinal*], forsooth, had the good Duke to keep.
'Tis like you would not feast him like a friend, 184
And 'tis well seen he found an enemy.

QUEEN
Then you, belike, suspect these noblemen 186
As guilty of Duke Humphrey's timeless death. 187

WARWICK
Who finds the heifer dead and bleeding fresh
And sees fast by a butcher with an axe, 189
But will suspect 'twas he that made the slaughter?
Who finds the partridge in the puttock's nest 191
But may imagine how the bird was dead,
Although the kite soar with unbloodied beak?
Even so suspicious is this tragedy.

QUEEN
Are you the butcher, Suffolk? Where's your knife?
Is Beaufort term'd a kite? Where are his talons?

SUFFOLK
I wear no knife to slaughter sleeping men;
But here's a vengeful sword, rusted with ease, 198
That shall be scoured in his rancorous heart
That slanders me with murder's crimson badge.
Say, if thou dar'st, proud Lord of Warwickshire,
That I am faulty in Duke Humphrey's death.
[*Exeunt Cardinal, Somerset, and others.*]

WARWICK
What dares not Warwick, if false Suffolk dare him?

QUEEN
He dares not calm his contumelious spirit, 204
Nor cease to be an arrogant controller, 205
Though Suffolk dare him twenty thousand times.

WARWICK
Madam, be still—with reverence may I say—
For every word you speak in his behalf
Is slander to your royal dignity.

SUFFOLK
Blunt-witted lord, ignoble in demeanor!
If ever lady wrong'd her lord so much,
Thy mother took into her blameful bed
Some stern untutor'd churl, and noble stock 213
Was graft with crab-tree slip—whose fruit thou art 214
And never of the Nevils' noble race.

WARWICK
But that the guilt of murder bucklers thee, 216
And I should rob the deathsman of his fee,
Quitting thee thereby of ten thousand shames, 218

136 stay hold back **139 suspect** suspicion **141 chafe** rub, warm. **paly** pale **146 mean obsequies** deficient funeral rites **154 King** i.e., Christ. **state** i.e., human nature **157 thrice-famed** very famous **159 instance** proof **161 timely-parted ghost** the remains of one having died in the natural course of time **163 Being all descended** i.e., the blood having all descended **164 Who,** i.e., the heart **165 the same** i.e., the blood. **aidance** aid. **the enemy,** i.e., death **167 blush** cause to blush, take on sanguine color **172 abroad display'd** i.e., spread out

176 corn grain. **lodg'd** beaten down **178 probable** sufficient confirmation **184 like** likely **186 belike** perchance **187 timeless** untimely **189 fast by** close by **191 puttock's** kite's **198 ease** i.e., disuse **204 contumelious** contemptuous, contentious **205 controller** critic, detractor **213 stern** rough **214 graft** grafted. **slip** cutting (with a possible play on the sense of *moral lapse*) **216 bucklers** shields **218 Quitting** ridding

And that my sovereign's presence makes me mild,
I would, false murd'rous coward, on thy knee
Make thee beg pardon for thy passed speech
And say it was thy mother that thou meant'st,
That thou thyself wast born in bastardy;
And after all this fearful homage done,
Give thee thy hire and send thy soul to hell,
Pernicious blood-sucker of sleeping men!

SUFFOLK
Thou shalt be waking while I shed thy blood,
If from this presence thou dar'st go with me.

WARWICK
Away even now, or I will drag thee hence!
Unworthy though thou art, I'll cope with thee
And do some service to Duke Humphrey's ghost.
Exeunt [Suffolk and Warwick].

KING
What stronger breastplate than a heart untainted!
Thrice is he arm'd that hath his quarrel just,
And he but naked, though lock'd up in steel,
Whose conscience with injustice is corrupted.
A noise within.

QUEEN
What noise is this?

Enter Suffolk and Warwick, with their weapons drawn.

KING
Why, how now, lords? Your wrathful weapons drawn
Here in our presence? Dare you be so bold?
Why, what tumultuous clamor have we here?

SUFFOLK
The trait'rous Warwick, with the men of Bury,
Set all upon me, mighty sovereign.

Enter Salisbury.

SALISBURY [*To the Commons, within*]
Sirs, stand apart. The King shall know your mind.—
Dread lord, the commons send you word by me,
Unless Lord Suffolk straight be done to death,
Or banished fair England's territories,
They will by violence tear him from your palace
And torture him with grievous ling'ring death.
They say, by him the good Duke Humphrey died;
They say, in him they fear your Highness' death;
And mere instinct of love and loyalty,
Free from a stubborn opposite intent,
As being thought to contradict your liking,
Makes them thus forward in his banishment.
They say, in care of your most royal person,
That if your Highness should intend to sleep
And charge that no man should disturb your rest
In pain of your dislike or pain of death,
Yet, notwithstanding such a strait edict,
Were there a serpent seen, with forked tongue,
That slily glided towards your Majesty,
It were but necessary you were wak'd,
Lest, being suffer'd in that harmful slumber,
The mortal worm might make the sleep eternal.
And therefore do they cry, though you forbid,
That they will guard you, whe'er you will or no,
From such fell serpents as false Suffolk is—
With whose envenomed and fatal sting,
Your loving uncle, twenty times his worth,
They say is shamefully bereft of life.

COMMONS (*Within*)
An answer from the King, my Lord of Salisbury!

SUFFOLK
'Tis like the commons, rude unpolish'd hinds,
Could send such message to their sovereign!
[*To Salisbury.*] But you, my lord, were glad to be employ'd,
To show how quaint an orator you are.
But all the honor Salisbury hath won
Is that he was the lord ambassador
Sent from a sort of tinkers to the King.

COMMONS (*Within*)
An answer from the King, or we will all break in!

KING
Go, Salisbury, and tell them all from me,
I thank them for their tender loving care;
And had I not been cited so by them,
Yet did I purpose as they do entreat.
For, sure, my thoughts do hourly prophesy
Mischance unto my state by Suffolk's means.
And therefore, by His majesty I swear,
Whose far unworthy deputy I am,
He shall not breathe infection in this air
But three days longer, on the pain of death.
[*Exit Salisbury.*]

QUEEN
O Henry, let me plead for gentle Suffolk!

KING
Ungentle queen, to call him gentle Suffolk!
No more, I say! If thou dost plead for him,
Thou wilt but add increase unto my wrath.
Had I but said, I would have kept my word,
But when I swear, it is irrevocable. [*To Suffolk.*]
If, after three days' space, thou here be'st found
On any ground that I am ruler of,
The world shall not be ransom for thy life.
Come, Warwick, come, good Warwick, go with me.
I have great matters to impart to thee.
Exit [with all but Queen and Suffolk].

QUEEN
Mischance and sorrow go along with you!
Heart's discontent and sour affliction
Be playfellows to keep you company!
There's two of you; the devil make a third,
And threefold vengeance tend upon your steps!

SUFFOLK
Cease, gentle queen, these execrations,

221 passed just spoken **224 fearful homage** craven submission **225 hire** reward **227 waking** (Warwick has accused Suffolk of killing Gloucester in his sleep.) **230 cope with** encounter **250 mere instinct** pure impulse **251–252 Free . . . liking** innocent of any stubborn willfulness that might be interpreted as crossing your wishes **253 forward** bold, insistent **258 strait** strict

262 being suffer'd you being permitted to remain **263 mortal worm** deadly serpent **265 whe'er** whether **266 fell** cruel **271 like** likely. (Said ironically.) **hinds** boors, rustics **274 quaint** skilled, clever **277 sort** gang **281 cited** incited, urged **285 His** i.e., God's **287 breathe** breathe out, spread **289 gentle** noble **293 but said** merely spoken, without an oath **303 two** i.e., the King and Warwick

And let thy Suffolk take his heavy leave.

QUEEN
Fie, coward woman and soft-hearted wretch!
Hast thou not spirit to curse thine enemy?

SUFFOLK
A plague upon them, wherefore should I curse them?
Would curses kill, as doth the mandrake's groan,
I would invent as bitter-searching terms,
As curst, as harsh, and horrible to hear,
Deliver'd strongly through my fixed teeth,
With full as many signs of deadly hate,
As lean-fac'd Envy in her loathsome cave.
My tongue should stumble in mine earnest words,
Mine eyes should sparkle like the beaten flint,
Mine hair be fix'd an end, as one distract;
Ay, every joint should seem to curse and ban;
And even now my burden'd heart would break,
Should I not curse them. Poison be their drink!
Gall, worse than gall, the daintiest that they taste!
Their sweetest shade a grove of cypress trees!
Their chiefest prospect murd'ring basilisks!
Their softest touch as smart as lizards' stings!
Their music frightful as the serpent's hiss,
And boding screech-owls make the consort full!
All the foul terrors in dark-seated hell—

QUEEN
Enough, sweet Suffolk. Thou torment'st thyself,
And these dread curses, like the sun 'gainst glass,
Or like an overcharged gun, recoil,
And turns the force of them upon thyself.

SUFFOLK
You bade me ban, and will you bid me leave?
Now, by the ground that I am banish'd from,
Well could I curse away a winter's night,
Though standing naked on a mountain top,
Where biting cold would never let grass grow,
And think it but a minute spent in sport.

QUEEN
O, let me entreat thee cease! Give me thy hand,
That I may dew it with my mournful tears;
Nor let the rain of heaven wet this place
To wash away my woeful monuments.
[*Kisses his hand.*]
O, could this kiss be printed in thy hand,
That thou mightst think upon these by the seal,
Through whom a thousand sighs are breath'd for thee!
So, get thee gone, that I may know my grief;
'Tis but surmis'd whiles thou art standing by,
As one that surfeits thinking on a want.
I will repeal thee, or, be well assur'd,
Adventure to be banished myself;
And banished I am, if but from thee.
Go, speak not to me. Even now be gone.
O, go not yet! Even thus two friends condemn'd
Embrace and kiss and take ten thousand leaves,
Loather a hundred times to part than die.
[*They embrace.*]
Yet now farewell, and farewell life with thee!

SUFFOLK
Thus is poor Suffolk ten times banished,
Once by the King, and three times thrice by thee.
'Tis not the land I care for, wert thou thence.
A wilderness is populous enough,
So Suffolk had thy heavenly company;
For where thou art, there is the world itself,
With every several pleasure in the world,
And where thou art not, desolation.
I can no more. Live thou to joy thy life;
Myself no joy in nought but that thou liv'st.

Enter Vaux.

QUEEN
Whither goes Vaux so fast? What news, I prithee?

VAUX
To signify unto his Majesty
That Cardinal Beaufort is at point of death;
For suddenly a grievous sickness took him,
That makes him gasp and stare and catch the air,
Blaspheming God and cursing men on earth.
Sometime he talks as if Duke Humphrey's ghost
Were by his side; sometime he calls the King,
And whispers to his pillow as to him
The secrets of his overcharged soul;
And I am sent to tell his Majesty
That even now he cries aloud for him.

QUEEN
Go tell this heavy message to the King. *Exit* [*Vaux*].
Ay me, what is this world? What news are these!
But wherefore grieve I at an hour's poor loss,
Omitting Suffolk's exile, my soul's treasure?
Why only, Suffolk, mourn I not for thee,
And with the southern clouds contend in tears,
Theirs for the earth's increase, mine for my sorrows?
Now get thee hence. The King, thou know'st, is coming.
If thou be found by me, thou art but dead.

SUFFOLK
If I depart from thee, I cannot live,
And, in thy sight to die, what were it else
But like a pleasant slumber in thy lap?
Here could I breathe my soul into the air,
As mild and gentle as the cradle-babe
Dying with mother's dug between its lips—
Where, from thy sight, I should be raging mad
And cry out for thee to close up mine eyes,
To have thee with thy lips to stop my mouth.
So shouldst thou either turn my flying soul,
Or I should breathe it so into thy body,

306 heavy sorrowful **310 mandrake's groan** (Folk belief held that when the forked and man-shaped mandrake root was pulled from the ground, it uttered a shriek that was fatal to the hearer or would drive him mad; cf. *Romeo and Juliet,* IV.iii.47–49.) **312 curst** malignant **318 an** on. **distract** mad **319 ban** curse **323 cypress trees** (Associated with death because they were often planted near graveyards.) **324 prospect** view. **basilisks.** (See l. 52 above.) **325 smart** stinging **327 consort** ensemble of musicians **331 overcharged** overloaded **333 leave** leave off **342 monuments** i.e., traces of her tears **344 these** i.e., my lips. **seal** imprint **345 Through whom** i.e., through which lips **346 know** fully comprehend **348 As . . . want** like a person (such as myself) who, enjoying plenty, anticipates a time of deprivation **349 repeal thee** bring about your recall **350 Adventure** risk

361 So so long as **363 several** distinct **381 an hour's** (i.e., the Cardinal has figuratively but an hour left to live in any case.) **382 Omitting** neglecting **384 southern** i.e., especially moist **387 by me** near me **393 dug** breast **397 turn** turn back, i.e., prevent the soul's escape, preserve my life. (The soul was thought to leave the body through the mouth.)

And then it liv'd in sweet Elysium. 399
To die by thee were but to die in jest; 400
From thee to die were torture more than death. 401
O, let me stay, befall what may befall!

QUEEN
Away! Though parting be a fretful corrosive, 403
It is applied to a deathful wound. 404
To France, sweet Suffolk. Let me hear from thee,
For wheresoe'er thou art in this world's globe,
I'll have an Iris that shall find thee out. 407

SUFFOLK
I go.

QUEEN
And take my heart with thee.

SUFFOLK
A jewel, lock'd into the woefull'st cask
That ever did contain a thing of worth.
Even as a splitted bark, so sunder we.
This way fall I to death.

QUEEN
This way for me.
Exeunt [severally].

[SCENE III]

Enter the King, Salisbury, and Warwick, to the Cardinal in bed, [raving and staring as if mad].

KING
How fares my lord? Speak, Beaufort, to thy sovereign.

CARDINAL
If thou be'st Death, I'll give thee England's treasure,
Enough to purchase such another island,
So thou wilt let me live, and feel no pain. 4

KING
Ah, what a sign it is of evil life,
Where death's approach is seen so terrible!

WARWICK
Beaufort, it is thy sovereign speaks to thee.

CARDINAL
Bring me unto my trial when you will.
Died he not in his bed? Where should he die? 9
Can I make men live, whe'er they will or no?
O, torture me no more! I will confess.
Alive again? Then show me where he is.
I'll give a thousand pound to look upon him.
He hath no eyes, the dust hath blinded them.
Comb down his hair. Look, look! It stands upright,
Like lime-twigs set to catch my winged soul. 16
Give me some drink, and bid the apothecary
Bring the strong poison that I bought of him.

KING
O thou eternal Mover of the heavens,
Look with a gentle eye upon this wretch!
O, beat away the busy meddling fiend
That lays strong siege unto this wretch's soul
And from his bosom purge this black despair!

WARWICK
See, how the pangs of death do make him grin!

SALISBURY
Disturb him not. Let him pass peaceably.

KING
Peace to his soul, if God's good pleasure be!
Lord Card'nal, if thou think'st on heaven's bliss,
Hold up thy hand, make signal of thy hope.
[Cardinal dies.]
He dies, and makes no sign. O God, forgive him!

WARWICK
So bad a death argues a monstrous life.

KING
Forbear to judge, for we are sinners all.
Close up his eyes and draw the curtain close, 32
And let us all to meditation. *[Bed curtains are closed.]*
Exeunt.

[ACT IV • SCENE I]

Alarum [within]. Fight at sea. Ordnance goes off. Enter Lieutenant, [a Master, a Master's Mate, Walter Whitmore, and others; with them] Suffolk [disguised], and others, [prisoners].

LIEUTENANT
The gaudy, blabbing, and remorseful day 1
Is crept into the bosom of the sea,
And now loud-howling wolves arouse the jades 3
That drag the tragic melancholy night,
Who, with their drowsy, slow, and flagging wings
Clip dead men's graves, and from their misty jaws 6
Breathe foul contagious darkness in the air.
Therefore bring forth the soldiers of our prize; 8
For, whilst our pinnace anchors in the Downs, 9
Here shall they make their ransom on the sand,
Or with their blood stain this discolored shore. 11
Master, this prisoner freely give I thee; 12
And thou that art his mate, make boot of this; 13
The other, Walter Whitmore, is thy share. 14
[Three gentlemen-prisoners, one of them Suffolk, are apportioned and handed over.]

FIRST GENTLEMAN
What is my ransom, master? Let me know.

MASTER
A thousand crowns, or else lay down your head.

MATE *[To his gentleman-prisoner]*
And so much shall you give, or off goes yours.

LIEUTENANT
What, think you much to pay two thousand crowns,
And bear the name and port of gentlemen? 19

399 liv'd would live. **Elysium** classical abode after death of those favored by the gods **400 in jest** i.e., not truly to die at all. (*To die* carries the suggestion of experiencing orgasm.) **401 From** away from **403 fretful corrosive** painful and caustic course of treatment **404 deathful** fatal (since Suffolk's remaining would prove fatal) **407 Iris** Juno's messenger

III.iii. Location: London. The Cardinal's bedchamber.
4 So provided **9 he** i.e., Gloucester **16 lime-twigs** twigs smeared with sticky lime to trap birds

32 curtain bedcurtain. (The bed itself, presumably "thrust out" on stage for this brief scene, would have to be removed at this point.)

IV.i. Location: The coast of Kent.
1 blabbing telltale, revealing. **remorseful** causing remorse **3 jades** i.e., the dragons of Hecate that draw the chariot of the night **6 Clip** embrace **8 soldiers . . . prize** i.e., those we have captured **9 pinnace** one-masted vessel. **Downs** anchorage off the Kentish coast **11 discolored** i.e., to be discolored by blood **12 this prisoner** i.e., the First Gentleman **13 his** i.e., the ship master's. **make . . . this** i.e., make a profit by ransoming this Second Gentleman **14 The other** i.e., Suffolk **19 port** demeanor

Cut both the villains' throats, for die you shall.
The lives of those which we have lost in fight
Be counterpois'd with such a petty sum!

FIRST GENTLEMAN
I'll give it, sir, and therefore spare my life.

SECOND GENTLEMAN
And so will I, and write home for it straight.

WHITMORE [*To Suffolk*]
I lost mine eye in laying the prize aboard,
And therefore to revenge it, shalt thou die;
And so should these, if I might have my will.

LIEUTENANT
Be not so rash. Take ransom, let him live.

SUFFOLK
Look on my George; I am a gentleman.
Rate me at what thou wilt, thou shalt be paid.

WHITMORE
And so am I. My name is Walter Whitmore.
[*Suffolk starts.*]
How now, why starts thou? What, doth death affright?

SUFFOLK
Thy name affrights me, in whose sound is death.
A cunning man did calculate my birth
And told me that by water I should die.
Yet let not this make thee be bloody-minded;
Thy name is Gualtier, being rightly sounded.

WHITMORE
Gualtier or Walter, which it is, I care not.
Never yet did base dishonor blur our name
But with our sword we wip'd away the blot;
Therefore, when merchant-like I sell revenge,
Broke be my sword, my arms torn and defac'd,
And I proclaim'd a coward through the world!

SUFFOLK [*Revealing his face*]
Stay, Whitmore; for thy prisoner is a prince,
The Duke of Suffolk, William de la Pole.

WHITMORE
The Duke of Suffolk muffled up in rags?

SUFFOLK
Ay, but these rags are no part of the Duke.
[Jove sometime went disguis'd, and why not I?]

LIEUTENANT
But Jove was never slain, as thou shalt be.

SUFFOLK
Obscure and lousy swain, King Henry's blood,
The honorable blood of Lancaster,
Must not be shed by such a jaded groom.
Hast thou not kiss'd thy hand and held my stirrup?
Bare-headed plodded by my foot-cloth mule
And thought thee happy when I shook my head?
How often hast thou waited at my cup,
Fed from my trencher, kneel'd down at the board,
When I have feasted with Queen Margaret?
Remember it and let it make thee crestfall'n,
Ay, and allay this thy abortive pride.
How in our voiding lobby hast thou stood
And duly waited for my coming forth?
This hand of mine hath writ in thy behalf,
And therefore shall it charm thy riotous tongue.

WHITMORE
Speak, captain, shall I stab the forlorn swain?

LIEUTENANT
First let my words stab him, as he hath me.

SUFFOLK
Base slave, thy words are blunt and so art thou.

LIEUTENANT
Convey him hence, and on our longboat's side
Strike off his head.

SUFFOLK Thou dar'st not, for thy own.

LIEUTENANT
Yes, Pole.

SUFFOLK Pole?

LIEUTENANT Pool! Sir Pool! Lord!
Ay, kennel, puddle, sink, whose filth and dirt
Troubles the silver spring where England drinks.
Now will I dam up this thy yawning mouth
For swallowing the treasure of the realm.
Thy lips that kiss'd the Queen shall sweep the ground,
And thou that smil'dst at good Duke Humphrey's death
Against the senseless winds shalt grin in vain,
Who in contempt shall hiss at thee again.
And wedded be thou to the hags of hell
For daring to affy a mighty lord
Unto the daughter of a worthless king,
Having neither subject, wealth, nor diadem.
By devilish policy art thou grown great,
And, like ambitious Sylla, overgorg'd
With gobbets of thy mother's bleeding heart.
By thee Anjou and Maine were sold to France.
The false revolting Normans thorough thee
Disdain to call us lord, and Picardy
Hath slain their governors, surpris'd our forts,
And sent the ragged soldiers wounded home.
The princely Warwick, and the Nevils all,
Whose dreadful swords were never drawn in vain,
As hating thee, are rising up in arms;
And now the house of York, thrust from the crown
By shameful murder of a guiltless king
And lofty, proud, encroaching tyranny,
Burns with revenging fire, whose hopeful colors
Advance our half-fac'd sun, striving to shine,

25 laying . . . aboard boarding the captured ship **29 George** the gold or jeweled figure of St. George, worn as the insignium of the Order of the Knights of the Garter **30 Rate** value, assess **33 Thy name** (I.e., *Walter,* pronounced like "water." In l. 37 below, Suffolk tries to avert the prophecy referred to in ll. 34–35 [cf. I.iv.33–34] by urging the French form of the name, *Gualtier* or *Gaultier.*) **34 A . . . birth** a fortune-teller cast my horoscope **41 sell revenge** i.e., give up revenge (for my lost eye) in return for ransom money **42 arms** coat of arms **50 lousy** louse-infested. **King Henry's blood** (Suffolk's claim to be connected to the house of Lancaster was a dubious one.) **52 jaded** ignoble (with a play in the next line on one who deals with *jades,* or horses) **54 foot-cloth** with a large, richly ornamented cloth laid over the back of a horse or mule, hanging down to the ground on each side **55 shook** i.e., nodded **57 trencher** wooden dish or plate

59 crestfall'n (1) downcast, abashed (2) deprived of the coat of arms boasted of in l. 42 **60 abortive** monstrous **61 our voiding lobby** my ante-room **63 writ . . . behalf** i.e., written to recommend you, or because you cannot write **64 charm** put a spell on, silence **65 captain** (Appropriate courtesy title for the Lieutenant, since he is commander of a vessel.) **69 for thy own** i.e., for fear of losing your own head **70 Pole, Pool** (with verbal pay on *poll,* head, *Pole,* Suffolk's family name, and *pool,* a pool of water, all similar in pronunciation) **71 kennel** gutter. **sink** cesspool **77 senseless** insensible. (Suffolk's head is to be put up on display.) **78 Who** which, i.e., the winds **80 affy** betroth. **lord** i.e., King Henry **84 ambitious Sylla** i.e., Sulla, Roman dictator of the second and first centuries B.C., notorious for his cruel proceedings against his adversaries **85 gobbets** pieces of raw flesh. **mother's** i.e., England's **87 thorough** through **95 shameful . . . king** i.e., the murder of Richard II by Bolingbroke, who thereupon sidestepped the Yorkist claim and became King Henry IV **98 Advance** raise, display. **half-fac'd sun** (Edward III's and Richard II's banner displayed the rays of the sun dispersing themselves out of a cloud.)

Under the which is writ "Invitis nubibus." 99
The commons here in Kent are up in arms,
And, to conclude, reproach and beggary
Is crept into the palace of our King,
And all by thee. Away! Convey him hence.

SUFFOLK
O that I were a god, to shoot forth thunder
Upon these paltry, servile, abject drudges!
Small things make base men proud. This villain here,
Being captain of a pinnace, threatens more
Than Bargulus the strong Illyrian pirate. 108
Drones suck not eagles' blood, but rob beehives. 109
It is impossible that I should die
By such a lowly vassal as thyself.
Thy words move rage and not remorse in me.

[LIEUTENANT
Ay, but my deeds shall stay thy fury soon.]

[SUFFOLK]
I go of message from the Queen to France; 114
I charge thee waft me safely cross the Channel. 115

WHITMORE
Come, Suffolk, I must waft thee to thy death.

SUFFOLK
Paene gelidus timor occupat artus. It is thee I fear. 117

WHITMORE
Thou shalt have cause to fear before I leave thee.
What, are ye daunted now? Now will ye stoop?

FIRST GENTLEMAN [*To Suffolk*]
My gracious lord, entreat him, speak him fair. 120

SUFFOLK
Suffolk's imperial tongue is stern and rough,
Us'd to command., untaught to plead for favor.
Far be it we should honor such as these
With humble suit. No, rather let my head
Stoop to the block than these knees bow to any
Save to the God of heaven and to my king;
And sooner dance upon a bloody pole
Than stand uncover'd to the vulgar groom. 128
True nobility is exempt from fear.
More can I bear than you dare execute.

LIEUTENANT
Hale him away, and let him talk no more. 131

SUFFOLK
Come, soldiers, show what cruelty ye can,
That this my death may never be forgot!
Great men oft die by vile bezonians: 134
A Roman sworder and banditto slave 135
Murder'd sweet Tully; Brutus' bastard hand 136
Stabb'd Julius Caesar; savage islanders 137
Pompey the Great; and Suffolk dies by pirates.
Exit Walter [*Whitmore and others*] *with Suffolk.*

LIEUTENANT
And as for these whose ransom we have set,
It is our pleasure one of them depart;
Therefore come you with us and let him go.
Exeunt Lieutenant and the rest.
Manet the First Gentleman.

Enter Walter [*Whitmore*] *with the body* [*of Suffolk*].

WHITMORE
There let his head and lifeless body lie,
Until the Queen his mistress bury it. *Exit Walter.*

FIRST GENTLEMAN
O barbarous and bloody spectacle!
His body will I bear unto the King.
If he revenge it not, yet will his friends;
So will the Queen, that living held him dear.
[*Exit with the body.*]

[SCENE II]

Enter [*George*] *Bevis and John Holland,* [*with long staves*].

BEVIS Come, and get thee a sword, though made of a lath. They have been up these two days. 2

HOLLAND They have the more need to sleep now, then.

BEVIS I tell thee, Jack Cade the clothier means to dress the commonwealth, and turn it, and set a new nap 5
upon it.

HOLLAND So he had need, for 'tis threadbare. Well, I say it was never merry world in England since gentlemen came up. 9

BEVIS O miserable age! Virtue is not regarded in handicrafts-men.

HOLLAND The nobility think scorn to go in leather aprons.

BEVIS Nay, more, the King's Council are no good workmen.

HOLLAND True; and yet it is said, labor in thy vocation; which is as much to say as, let the magistrates be laboring men; and therefore should we be magistrates.

BEVIS Thou hast hit it; for there's no better sign of a brave mind than a hard hand. 20

HOLLAND I see them! I see them! There's Best's son, the tanner of Wingham— 22

BEVIS He shall have the skins of our enemies, to make dog's-leather of. 24

HOLLAND And Dick the Butcher—

BEVIS Then is sin struck down like an ox, and iniquity's throat cut like a calf.

HOLLAND And Smith the weaver—

BEVIS Argo, their thread of life is spun. 29

HOLLAND Come, come, let's fall in with them.

99 Invitis nubibus in spite of the clouds **108 Bargulus** (A name mentioned in Cicero's *De Officiis,* II.xi; perhaps confused with Bardylis, a Balkan chieftain of the 4th century B.C.) **109 Drones** beetles, worthless parasites **114 of message** as messenger **115 waft** transport, convey **117 Paene . . . artus** cold fear takes hold of my limbs almost entirely **120 fair** courteously **128 uncover'd** bareheaded **131 Hale** haul **134 bezonians** needy beggars, rascals **135 sworder** gladiator. **banditto** bandit **136 Tully** Cicero. **bastard** (According to an unreliable tradition, Brutus was thought to be Caesar's bastard son.) **137 savage islanders** i.e., inhabitants of Lesbos. (But Plutarch reports, quite to the contrary, that Pompey the Great was stabbed by his former officers at the instigation of Ptolemy, in Egypt after his defeat by Caesar at Pharsalus.)

IV.ii. Location: Blackheath, a heath in Kent near London.
s.d. John Holland (The name of the actor assigned to a bit part in this scene; probably *George Bevis* is similarly a hired man in the company.) **2 lath** wood strip (often used by the comic Vice character in morality plays). **up** i.e., up in arms **5 turn** turn inside out (as a way of refurbishing old cloth). **nap** fuzz or down on the surface of cloth **9 came up** came into fashion, rose to prominence **20 hard** callused **22 Wingham** a village near Canterbury **24 dog's-leather** (Used in the manufacture of gloves.) **29 Argo** i.e., ergo, therefore

Drum. Enter Cade, Dick Butcher, Smith the Weaver, and a Sawyer, with infinite numbers, [bearing long staves].

CADE We John Cade, so term'd of our suppos'd father—

DICK [*Aside*] Or rather, of stealing a cade of herrings.

CADE For our enemies shall fall before us, inspir'd with the spirit of putting down kings and princes—command silence.

DICK Silence!

CADE My father was a Mortimer—

DICK [*Aside*] He was an honest man, and a good bricklayer.

CADE My mother a Plantagenet—

DICK [*Aside*] I knew her well; she was a midwife.

CADE My wife descended of the Lacies—

DICK [*Aside*] She was, indeed, a pedler's daughter, and sold many laces.

SMITH [*Aside*] But now of late, not able to travel with her furr'd pack, she washes bucks here at home.

CADE Therefore am I of an honorable house.

DICK [*Aside*] Ay, by my faith, the field is honorable; and there was he born, under a hedge, for his father had never a house but the cage.

CADE Valiant I am.

SMITH [*Aside*] 'A must needs; for beggary is valiant.

CADE I am able to endure much.

DICK [*Aside*] No question of that; for I have seen him whipp'd three market-days together.

CADE I fear neither sword nor fire.

SMITH [*Aside*] He need not fear the sword, for his coat is of proof.

DICK [*Aside*] But methinks he should stand in fear of fire, being burnt i' th' hand for stealing of sheep.

CADE Be brave, then, for your captain is brave, and vows reformation. There shall be in England seven halfpenny loaves sold for a penny, the three-hoop'd pot shall have ten hoops, and I will make it felony to drink small beer. All the realm shall be in common, and in Cheapside shall my palfry go to grass. And when I am king, as king I will be—

ALL God save your Majesty!

CADE I thank you, good people—there shall be no money; all shall eat and drink on my score; and I will apparel them all in one livery, that they may agree like brothers and worship me their lord.

DICK The first thing we do, let's kill all the lawyers.

CADE Nay, that I mean to do. Is not this a lamentable thing, that of the skin of an innocent lamb should be made parchment? That parchment, being scribbled o'er, should undo a man? Some say the bee stings, but I say, 'tis the bee's wax; for I did but seal once to a thing, and I was never mine own man since. How now? Who's there?

Enter [some, bringing forward] a Clerk [of Chartham].

SMITH The clerk of Chartham. He can write and read and cast account.

CADE O monstrous!

SMITH We took him setting of boys' copies.

CADE Here's a villain!

SMITH H'as a book in his pocket with red letters in 't.

CADE Nay, then, he is a conjurer.

DICK Nay, he can make obligations, and write court-hand.

CADE I am sorry for 't. The man is a proper man, of mine honor; unless I find him guilty, he shall not die. Come hither, sirrah, I must examine thee. What is thy name?

CLERK Emmanuel.

DICK They use to write it on the top of letters. 'Twill go hard with you.

CADE Let me alone.—Dost thou use to write thy name? Or hast thou a mark to thyself, like an honest plain-dealing man?

CLERK Sir, I thank God, I have been so well brought up that I can write my name.

ALL He hath confess'd. Away with him! He's a villain and a traitor.

CADE Away with him, I say! Hang him with his pen and inkhorn about his neck. *Exit one with the Clerk.*

Enter Michael.

MICHAEL Where's our general?

CADE Here I am, thou particular fellow.

MICHAEL Fly, fly, fly! Sir Humphrey Stafford and his brother are hard by, with the King's forces.

CADE Stand, villain, stand, or I'll fell thee down. He shall be encount'red with a man as good as himself. He is but a knight, is 'a?

MICHAEL No.

CADE To equal him, I will make myself a knight presently. [*Kneels.*] Rise up Sir John Mortimer. [*Rises.*] Now have at him!

Enter Sir Humphrey Stafford and his Brother, with drum and Soldiers.

STAFFORD
Rebellious hinds, the filth and scum of Kent,
Mark'd for the gallows, lay your weapons down!
Home to your cottages, forsake this groom.
The King is merciful, if you revolt.

33 cade barrel, cask **34 For** because. **fall** (with a pun on the Latin *cado,* I fall) **38 Mortimer** (See III.i.359 and note.) **39–40 bricklayer** (with a play on *mortarer,* Mortimer) **43 Lacies** the family name of the Earls of Lincoln. (But Dick makes an obvious pun on *laces.*) **47 furr'd pack** pedlar's pack made of hides turned hair outward (with a pun on *herd of deer*). **bucks** soiled clothes treated with *buck* or lye **51 cage** prison for petty malefactors **53 'A must needs** he has to be. **valiant** sturdy, able to work. (Ordnances forbade those who were sturdy to beg.) **56 whipp'd** i.e., for vagabondage **59 of proof** (1) tried by experience and hence reliable (2) well-worn **61 burnt i' th' hand** branded **64–65 three-hoop'd pot** wooden quart-pot made with three metal bands or staves. (A ten-hooped pot would presumably hold a lot more.) **66 small** weak. (Cade intends that everyone shall drink strong beer.) **be in common** belong to everyone **67 Cheapside** chief location for markets in London **71 on my score** at my expense

79 seal i.e., sign and seal (with sealing wax) a legal agreement **82 Chartham** a town near Canterbury **83 cast account** i.e., do arithmetic **85 setting . . . copies** writing out words, etc., as models to be reproduced by schoolboys **87 book . . . in 't** a schoolbook, probably a primer, with "rubricated" or red-lettered capitals **89 make obligations** draw up bonds **89–90 court-hand** professional hand, used in preparing legal documents **91 proper** handsome-looking. **of** upon **95 Emmanuel** i.e., God with us. (Used frequently as heading for letters and documents.) **108 particular** private (as opposed to *general* in the previous line) **114 No** i.e., he is only a knight **118 hinds** peasants **121 revolt** turn back

BROTHER
But angry, wrathful, and inclin'd to blood,
If you go forward. Therefore yield, or die.

CADE
As for these silken-coated slaves, I pass not.
It is to you, good people, that I speak,
Over whom, in time to come, I hope to reign;
For I am rightful heir unto the crown.

STAFFORD
Villain, thy father was a plasterer,
And thou thyself a shearman, art thou not?

CADE
And Adam was a gardener.

BROTHER
And what of that?

CADE
Marry, this: Edmund Mortimer, Earl of March,
Married the Duke of Clarence' daughter, did he not?

STAFFORD
Ay, sir.

CADE
By her he had two children at one birth.

BROTHER
That's false.

CADE
Ay, there's the question. But I say 'tis true.
The elder of them, being put to nurse,
Was by a beggar-woman stol'n away,
And, ignorant of his birth and parentage,
Became a bricklayer when he came to age.
His son am I. Deny it, if you can.

DICK
Nay, 'tis too true. Therefore he shall be king.

SMITH Sir, he made a chimney in my father's house, and the bricks are alive at this day to testify it. Therefore deny it not.

STAFFORD
And will you credit this base drudge's words,
That speaks he knows not what?

ALL
Ay, marry, will we. Therefore get ye gone.

BROTHER
Jack Cade, the Duke of York hath taught you this.

CADE [*Aside*] He lies, for I invented it myself.—Go to, sirrah, tell the King from me, that, for his father's sake, Henry the Fifth, in whose time boys went to span-counter for French crowns, I am content he shall reign; but I'll be Protector over him.

DICK And furthermore, we'll have the Lord Say's head for selling the dukedom of Maine.

CADE And good reason; for thereby is England main'd, and fain to go with a staff, but that my puissance holds it up. Fellow kings, I tell you that that Lord Say hath gelded the commonwealth and made it an eunuch; and more than that, he can speak French, and therefore he is a traitor.

STAFFORD
O gross and miserable ignorance!

CADE Nay, answer, if you can. The Frenchmen are our enemies. Go to, then, I ask but this: can he that speaks with the tongue of an enemy be a good counselor, or no?

ALL No, no! And therefore we'll have his head.

BROTHER
Well, seeing gentle words will not prevail,
Assail them with the army of the King.

STAFFORD
Herald, away, and throughout every town
Proclaim them traitors that are up with Cade,
That those which fly before the battle ends
May, even in their wives' and children's sight,
Be hang'd up for example at their doors.
And you that be the King's friends, follow me.
Exeunt [the two Staffords, and soldiers].

CADE
And you that love the commons, follow me.
Now show yourselves men; 'tis for liberty!
We will not leave one lord, one gentleman.
Spare none but such as go in clouted shoon,
For they are thrifty honest men and such
As would, but that they dare not, take our parts.

DICK They are all in order and march toward us.

CADE But then are we in order when we are most out of order. Come, march forward. *[Exeunt.]*

[SCENE III]

Alarums to the fight, wherein both the Staffords are slain. Enter Cade and the rest.

CADE Where's Dick, the butcher of Ashford?

DICK Here, sir.

CADE They fell before thee like sheep and oxen, and thou behavedst thyself as if thou hadst been in thine own slaughter-house. Therefore thus will I reward thee: the Lent shall be as long again as it is, and thou shalt have a license to kill for a hundred lacking one.

DICK I desire no more.

CADE And, to speak truth, thou deserv'st no less. This monument of the victory will I bear [*Putting on Sir Humphrey's armor*]; and the bodies shall be dragg'd at my horse heels till I do come to London, where we will have the Mayor's sword borne before us.

DICK If we mean to thrive and do good, break open the jails and let out the prisoners.

CADE Fear not that, I warrant thee. Come, let's march towards London. *Exeunt.*

124 pass care **129 shearman** one who shears the nap (see l. 5) from woolen cloth during its manufacture **143 too** very **144 he** i.e., Cade's father **153–154 span-counter** a boys' game in which one throws a counter or piece of money that the other wins if he can throw another that hits it or falls within a span (nine inches) of it **154 crowns** (1) coins (2) kingdoms **156 Lord Say** (A peer implicated with Suffolk in the loss of Anjou and Maine.) **158 main'd** maimed (with a pun on *Maine*) **159 fain** obliged

174 That . . . fly i.e., so that those cowardly traitors who will surely flee **181 clouted shoon** hobnailed shoes

IV.iii. Location: Scene continues at Blackheath.
s.d. (The bodies of the slain Staffords must be removed at some point.) **6–7 Lent . . . one** (For Dick the butcher's benefit, Cade proposes to double the length of Lent, during which animals could be butchered only by special license in order to supply the sick and others with particular needs; and during this period, Dick is to have license either to kill 99 animals a week or to supply 99 persons.) **16 Fear** doubt

[SCENE IV]

Enter the King with a supplication, and the Queen with Suffolk's head, the Duke of Buckingham, and the Lord Say.

QUEEN
Oft have I heard that grief softens the mind
And makes it fearful and degenerate.
Think therefore on revenge and cease to weep.
But who can cease to weep and look on this?
Here may his head lie on my throbbing breast,
But where's the body that I should embrace?

BUCKINGHAM What answer makes your Grace to the rebels' supplication?

KING
I'll send some holy bishop to entreat,
For God forbid so many simple souls
Should perish by the sword! And I myself,
Rather than bloody war shall cut them short,
Will parley with Jack Cade their general.
But stay, I'll read it over once again.

QUEEN
Ah, barbarous villains! Hath this lovely face
Rul'd, like a wandering planet, over me,
And could it not enforce them to relent
That were unworthy to behold the same?

KING
Lord Say, Jack Cade hath sworn to have thy head.

SAY
Ay, but I hope your Highness shall have his.

KING
How now, madam?
Still lamenting and mourning for Suffolk's death?
I fear me, love, if that I had been dead,
Thou wouldst not have mourn'd so much for me.

QUEEN
No, my love, I should not mourn, but die for thee.

Enter a Messenger.

KING
How now, what news? Why com'st thou in such haste?

FIRST MESSENGER
The rebels are in Southwark. Fly, my lord!
Jack Cade proclaims himself Lord Mortimer,
Descended from the Duke of Clarence' house,
And calls your Grace usurper openly
And vows to crown himself in Westminster.
His army is a ragged multitude
Of hinds and peasants, rude and merciless.
Sir Humphrey Stafford and his brother's death
Hath given them heart and courage to proceed.
All scholars, lawyers, courtiers, gentlemen,
They call false caterpillars and intend their death.

KING
O graceless men! They know not what they do.

BUCKINGHAM
My gracious lord, retire to Killingworth,
Until a power be rais'd to put them down.

QUEEN
Ah, were the Duke of Suffolk now alive,
These Kentish rebels would be soon appeas'd!

KING
Lord Say, the traitors hateth thee;
Therefore away with us to Killingworth.

SAY
So might your Grace's person be in danger.
The sight of me is odious in their eyes;
And therefore in this city will I stay
And live alone as secret as I may.

Enter another Messenger.

SECOND MESSENGER
Jack Cade hath gotten London bridge!
The citizens fly and forsake their houses.
The rascal people, thirsting after prey,
Join with the traitor, and they jointly swear
To spoil the city and your royal court.

BUCKINGHAM
Then linger not, my lord. Away, take horse!

KING
Come, Margaret. God, our hope, will succor us.

QUEEN
My hope is gone, now Suffolk is deceas'd.

KING [*To Say*]
Farewell, my lord. Trust not the Kentish rebels.

BUCKINGHAM
Trust nobody, for fear you be betray'd.

SAY
The trust I have is in mine innocence,
And therefore am I bold and resolute. *Exeunt.*

IV.iv. Location: London. The palace.
16 wandering i.e., not fixed, like the stars **27 Southwark** suburb on the south bank of the Thames, just across the river from London

39 Killingworth Kenilworth (in Warwickshire) **40 power** army **42 appeas'd** pacified **53 spoil** despoil, sack

[SCENE V]

Enter Lord Scales upon the Tower, walking. Then enter two or three Citizens below.

SCALES
How now, is Jack Cade slain?

FIRST CITIZEN No, my lord, nor likely to be slain; for they have won the bridge, killing all those that withstand them. The Lord Mayor craves aid of your honor from the Tower to defend the city from the rebels.

SCALES
Such aid as I can spare you shall command.
But I am troubled here with them myself;
The rebels have assay'd to win the Tower.

IV.v. Location: London. The Tower.
s.d. upon the Tower i.e., probably in the rear gallery above the main stage

But get you to Smithfield and gather head,
And thither I will send you Matthew Goffe.
Fight for your king, your country, and your lives.
And so, farewell, for I must hence again. *Exeunt.*

[SCENE VI]

Enter Jack Cade and the rest, and strikes his staff on London Stone.

CADE Now is Mortimer lord of this city. And here, sitting upon London Stone, I charge and command that, of the city's cost, the pissing-conduit run nothing but claret wine this first year of our reign. And now henceforward it shall be treason for any that calls me other than Lord Mortimer.

Enter a Soldier, running.

SOLDIER Jack Cade! Jack Cade!
CADE Knock him down there. *They kill him.*
SMITH If this fellow be wise, he'll never call ye Jack Cade more. I think he hath a very fair warning.
DICK My lord, there's an army gather'd together in Smithfield.
CADE Come, then, let's go fight with them. But first go and set London bridge on fire, and, if you can, burn down the Tower too. Come, let's away. *Exeunt omnes.*

[SCENE VII]

Alarums. Matthew Goffe is slain, and all the rest. Then enter Jack Cade, with his company.

CADE So, sirs. Now go some and pull down the Savoy; others to th' Inns of Court; down with them all.
DICK I have a suit unto your lordship.
CADE Be it a lordship, thou shalt have it for that word.
DICK Only that the laws of England may come out of your mouth.
HOLLAND [*Aside*] Mass, 'twill be sore law then, for he was thrust in the mouth with a spear, and 'tis not whole yet.
SMITH [*Aside*] Nay, John, it will be stinking law, for his breath stinks with eating toasted cheese.
CADE I have thought upon it, it shall be so. Away, burn all the records of the realm. My mouth shall be the parliament of England.
HOLLAND [*Aside*] Then we are like to have biting statutes, unless his teeth be pull'd out.
CADE And henceforward all things shall be in common.

Enter a Messenger.

MESSENGER My lord, a prize, a prize! Here's the Lord Say, which sold the towns in France; he that made us pay one and twenty fifteens, and one shilling to the pound, the last subsidy.

Enter George [Bevis], with the Lord Say.

CADE Well, he shall be beheaded for it ten times. Ah, thou say, thou serge, nay, thou buckram lord! Now art thou within point-blank of our jurisdiction regal. What canst thou answer to my Majesty for giving up of Normandy unto Mounsieur Basimecu, the Dauphin of France? Be it known unto thee by these presence, even the presence of Lord Mortimer, that I am the besom that must sweep the court clean of such filth as thou art. Thou hast most traitorously corrupted the youth of the realm in erecting a grammar school; and whereas, before, our forefathers had no other books but the score and the tally, thou hast caus'd printing to be us'd, and contrary to the King his crown and dignity, thou hast built a paper-mill. It will be prov'd to thy face that thou hast men about thee that usually talk of a noun and a verb, and such abominable words as no Christian ear can endure to hear. Thou hast appointed justices of peace, to call poor men before them about matters they were not able to answer. Moreover, thou hast put them in prison, and because they could not read, thou hast hang'd them, when, indeed, only for that cause they have been most worthy to live. Thou dost ride in a foot-cloth, dost thou not?
SAY What of that?
CADE Marry, thou oughtst not to let thy horse wear a cloak, when honester men than thou go in their hose and doublets.
DICK And work in their shirt too; as myself, for example, that am a butcher.
SAY You men of Kent—
DICK What say you of Kent?
SAY Nothing but this; 'tis "bona terra, mala gens."
CADE Away with him, away with him! He speaks Latin.
SAY
Hear me but speak, and bear me where you will.
Kent, in the Commentaries Caesar writ,

9 Smithfield area of open fields to the northwest, just outside London's walls. **head** an armed force

IV.vi. Location: London.
s.d. London Stone ancient landmark, located in Canon Street **3 pissing-conduit** popular name of a conduit, or common fountain, near the Royal Exchange

IV.vii. Location: London. The rebellion continues.
s.d. (The bodies of Goffe and other slain must be removed at some point.) **1 the Savoy** (This palace, residence of the Duke of Lancaster, was actually destroyed during Wat Tyler's rebellion in 1381 and not rebuilt until the sixteenth century.) **2 Inns of Court** sets of buildings in London belonging to legal societies training persons in the law

20–21 one . . . subsidy (An exaggeratedly inflated estimate of personal property taxes that were levied on special occasions; see I.i.131–34.) **23 say, serge, buckram** kinds of cloth, respectively of silk, wool, and coarse linen **26 Basimecu** "baise-mon-cul," kiss my arse **27–28 these presence** i.e., these presents, this present document. (A legal phrase.) **29 besom** broom **33 score . . . tally** means of reckoning accounts or keeping score, in which a stick was notched and then split transversely, thereby giving both debtor and creditor a record of what was owed **34 printing** (An anachronism; the first printing press was set up in England twenty-seven years after Cade's rebellion, and the first paper-mill over a century later.) **King his** King's **37 usually** habitually **42 could not read** i.e., could not demonstrate their literacy in Latin and thereby claim exemption from civil prosecution through "benefit of clergy" **44 foot-cloth** richly ornamented horse covering; see IV.i.54 note **47–48 hose and doublets** breeches and jacket (without a cloak) **53 bona . . . gens** good land, bad people

Is term'd the civil'st place of all this isle.
Sweet is the country, because full of riches,
The people liberal, valiant, active, wealthy,
Which makes me hope you are not void of pity.
I sold not Maine, I lost not Normandy,
Yet, to recover them, would lose my life.
Justice with favor have I always done;
Pray'rs and tears have mov'd me, gifts could never.
When have I aught exacted at your hands
But to maintain the King, the realm, and you?
Large gifts have I bestow'd on learned clerks,
Because my book preferr'd me to the King;
And, seeing ignorance is the curse of God,
Knowledge the wing wherewith we fly to heaven,
Unless you be possess'd with devilish spirits
You cannot but forbear to murder me.
This tongue hath parley'd unto foreign kings
For your behoof—

CADE Tut, when struck'st thou one blow in the field?

SAY
Great men have reaching hands. Oft have I struck
Those that I never saw, and struck them dead.

BEVIS O monstrous coward! What, to come behind folks?

SAY
These cheeks are pale for watching for your good.

CADE Give him a box o' th' ear and that will make 'em red again.

SAY
Long sitting to determine poor men's causes
Hath made me full of sickness and diseases.

CADE Ye shall have a hempen caudle then and the help of hatchet.

DICK Why dost thou quiver, man?

SAY
The palsy, and not fear, provokes me.

CADE Nay, he nods at us, as who should say, I'll be even with you. I'll see if his head will stand steadier on a pole, or no. Take him away, and behead him.

SAY
Tell me wherein have I offended most?
Have I affected wealth or honor? Speak.
Are my chests fill'd up with extorted gold?
Is my apparel sumptuous to behold?
Whom have I injur'd, that ye seek my death?
These hands are free from guiltless blood-shedding,
This breast from harboring foul deceitful thoughts.
O, let me live!

CADE [*Aside*] I feel remorse in myself with his words, but I'll bridle it. He shall die, an it be for pleading so well for his life.—Away with him! He has a familiar under his tongue; he speaks not a' God's name. Go, take him away, I say, and strike off his head presently; and then break into his son-in-law's house, Sir James Cromer, and strike off his head, and bring them both upon two poles hither.

ALL It shall be done.

SAY
Ah, countrymen! If when you make your pray'rs,
God should be so obdurate as yourselves,
How would it fare with your departed souls?
And therefore yet relent, and save my life.

CADE
Away with him! And do as I command ye.
[Exeunt some with Lord Say.]
The proudest peer in the realm shall not wear a head on his shoulders, unless he pay me tribute. There shall not a maid be married, but she shall pay to me her maidenhead ere they have it. Men shall hold of me in capite; and we charge and command that their wives be as free as heart can wish or tongue can tell.

DICK My lord, when shall we go to Cheapside and take up commodities upon our bills?

CADE Marry, presently.

ALL O, brave!

Enter one with the heads [of Lord Say and Sir John Cromer upon two poles].

CADE But is not this braver? Let them kiss one another, for they lov'd well when they were alive. [*The heads are made to touch one another.*] Now part them again, lest they consult about the giving up of some more towns in France. Soldiers, defer the spoil of the city until night, for with these borne before us, instead of maces, will we ride through the streets, and at every corner have them kiss. Away! *Exeunt.*

[SCENE VIII]

Alarum and retreat. Enter again Cade and all his rabblement.

CADE Up Fish Street! Down Saint Magnus' Corner! Kill and knock down! Throw them into Thames! *(Sound a parley.)* What noise is this I hear? Dare any be so bold to sound retreat or parley, when I command them kill?

Enter Buckingham and old Clifford [attended].

BUCKINGHAM
Ay, here they be that dare and will disturb thee.
Know, Cade, we come ambassadors from the King
Unto the commons whom thou hast misled,
And here pronounce free pardon to them all
That will forsake thee and go home in peace.

CLIFFORD
What say ye, countrymen? Will ye relent,
And yield to mercy whilst 'tis offered you,

64 favor compassion **68 clerks** scholars **69 book** learning **84 sitting** i.e., on the judge's bench **86 caudle** warm gruel, given to sick people. (*Hempen caudle* means that his restorative is to be a hanging.) **94 affected** preferred, striven for **103 familiar** familiar spirit, attendant demon **104 a'** in

118–119 in capite as tenent in chief, i.e., directly from the crown. The Latin *caput,* head, also puns on *maidenhead.*) **120 free** (1) legally unincumbered (2) licentious **121–122 take . . . bills** obtain goods on credit (with a pun on *bills,* military weapons having wooden handles and a blade or ax-shaped head) **124 brave** fine, splendid **129 spoil** plundering **131 maces** staves of office carried by sergeants

IV.viii. Location: London or Southwark. The rebellion continues.
1 Fish Street, Saint Magnus' Corner locations in London near London Bridge, directly across from Southwark **4 parley** trumpet signal requesting a conference between the contending forces

Or let a rebel lead you to your deaths?
Who loves the King and will embrace his pardon,
Fling up his cap, and say "God save his Majesty!"
Who hateth him and honors not his father,
Henry the Fifth, that made all France to quake,
Shake he his weapon at us and pass by.

ALL God save the King! God save the King!

CADE What, Buckingham and Clifford, are ye so brave? And you, base peasants, do ye believe him? Will you needs be hang'd with your pardons about your necks? Hath my sword therefore broke through London gates, that you should leave me at the White Hart in Southwark? I thought ye would never have given out these arms till you had recover'd your ancient freedom. But you are all recreants and dastards, and delight to live in slavery to the nobility. Let them break your backs with burdens, take your houses over your heads, ravish your wives and daughters before your faces. For me, I will make shift for one; and so, God's curse light upon you all!

ALL We'll follow Cade, we'll follow Cade!

CLIFFORD
Is Cade the son of Henry the Fifth,
That thus you do exclaim you'll go with him?
Will he conduct you through the heart of France,
And make the meanest of you earls and dukes?
Alas, he hath no home, no place to fly to,
Nor knows he how to live but by the spoil,
Unless by robbing of your friends and us.
Were 't not a shame that, whilst you live at jar,
The fearful French, whom you late vanquished,
Should make a start o'er seas and vanquish you?
Methinks already in this civil broil
I see them lording it in London streets,
Crying "Villiago!" unto all they meet.
Better ten thousand base-born Cades miscarry
Than you should stoop unto a Frenchman's mercy.
To France, to France, and get what you have lost!
Spare England, for it is your native coast.
Henry hath money, you are strong and manly;
God on our side, doubt not of victory.

ALL A Clifford! A Clifford! We'll follow the King and Clifford!

CADE [*Aside*] Was ever feather so lightly blown to and fro as this multitude? The name of Henry the Fifth hales them to an hundred mischiefs and makes them leave me desolate. I see them lay their heads together to surprise me. My sword make way for me, for here is no staying.—In despite of the devils and hell, have through the very middest of you! And heavens and honor be witness that no want of resolution in me, but only my followers' base and ignominious treasons, makes me betake me to my heels.

Exit [Cade, running through the crowd with drawn sword].

BUCKINGHAM
What, is he fled? Go some, and follow him;
And he that brings his head unto the King
Shall have a thousand crowns for his reward.
Exeunt some of them.
Follow me, soldiers. We'll devise a mean
To reconcile you all unto the King. *Exeunt omnes.*

[SCENE IX]

Sound trumpets. Enter King, Queen, and Somerset, on the terrace [aloft].

KING
Was ever king that joy'd an earthly throne,
And could command no more content than I?
No sooner was I crept out of my cradle
But I was made a king, at nine months old.
Was never subject long'd to be a king
As I do long and wish to be a subject.

Enter Buckingham and [old] Clifford.

BUCKINGHAM
Health and glad tidings to your Majesty!

KING
Why, Buckingham, is the traitor Cade surpris'd?
Or is he but retir'd to make him strong?

Enter [below] multitudes, with halters about their necks.

CLIFFORD
He is fled, my lord, and all his powers do yield,
And humbly thus, with halters on their necks,
Expect your Highness' doom, of life or death.

KING
Then, heaven, set ope thy everlasting gates
To entertain my vows of thanks and praise!
Soldiers, this day have you redeem'd your lives
And show'd how well you love your prince and country.
Continue still in this so good a mind,
And Henry, though he be infortunate,
Assure yourselves, will never be unkind.
And so, with thanks and pardon to you all,
I do dismiss you to your several countries.

ALL
God save the King! God save the King!

Enter a Messenger.

MESSENGER
Please it your Grace to be advertised
The Duke of York is newly come from Ireland,
And with a puissant and a mighty power

19 brave haughty **21 pardons . . . necks** (I.e., the pardons would be not only worthless but also the very means of their hanging.) **23 White Hart** a famous inn in Southwark **24 out** up **26 recreants** those who break faith, cowards **30 make shift** manage **40 at jar** in discord **42 make a start** suddenly arouse themselves **45 Villiago** rascal, villian. (Italian.) **46 miscarry** encounter misfortune **56 hales** draws **58 surprise** capture **59–60 have through** i.e., here I come through

67 mean means

IV.ix. Location: Kenilworth Castle in Warwickshire.
s.d. terrace i.e., probably in the gallery to the rear above the main stage **1 joy'd** enjoyed **12 Expect** await. **doom** judgment **14 entertain** receive **21 countries** localities **23 advertised** informed

Of gallowglasses and stout kerns
Is marching hitherward in proud array,
And still proclaimeth, as he comes along,
His arms are only to remove from thee
The Duke of Somerset, whom he terms a traitor.

KING
Thus stands my state, 'twixt Cade and York distress'd,
Like to a ship that, having scap'd a tempest,
Is straightway calm'd and boarded with a pirate.
But now is Cade driven back, his men dispers'd,
And now is York in arms to second him.
I pray thee, Buckingham, go and meet him,
And ask him what's the reason of these arms.
Tell him I'll send Duke Edmund to the Tower;
And, Somerset, we will commit thee thither,
Until his army be dismiss'd from him.

SOMERSET
My lord,
I'll yield myself to prison willingly,
Or unto death, to do my country good.

KING
In any case, be not too rough in terms,
For he is fierce and cannot brook hard language.

BUCKINGHAM
I will, my lord, and doubt not so to deal
As all things shall redound unto your good.

KING
Come, wife, let's in, and learn to govern better;
For yet may England curse my wretched reign.
Flourish. Exeunt.

[SCENE X]

Enter Cade.

CADE Fie on ambition! Fie on myself, that have a sword, and yet am ready to famish! These five days have I hid me in these woods and durst not peep out, for all the country is laid for me; but now am I so hungry that, if I might have a lease of my life for a thousand years, I could stay no longer. Wherefore, on a brick wall have I climb'd into this garden, to see if I can eat grass, or pick a sallet another while, which is not amiss to cool a man's stomach this hot weather. And I think this word "sallet" was born to do me good; for many a time, but for a sallet, my brain-pan had been cleft with a brown bill; and many a time, when I have been dry and bravely marching, it hath serv'd me instead of a quart pot to drink in; and now the word "sallet" must serve me to feed on.

Enter Iden, [followed at a distance by his attendants].

IDEN
Lord, who would live turmoiled in the court,
And may enjoy such quiet walks as these?
This small inheritance my father left me
Contenteth me, and worth a monarchy.
I seek not to wax great by others' waning,
Or gather wealth, I care not with what envy.
Sufficeth that I have maintains my state
And sends the poor well pleased from my gate.

CADE [*Aside*] Here's the lord of the soil come to seize me for a stray, for entering his fee-simple without leave.—Ah, villain, thou wilt betray me, and get a thousand crowns of the King by carrying my head to him; but I'll make thee eat iron like an ostrich, and swallow my sword like a great pin, ere thou and I part.

IDEN
Why, rude companion, whatsoe'er thou be,
I know thee not. Why, then, should I betray thee?
Is 't not enough to break into my garden,
And, like a thief, to come to rob my grounds,
Climbing my walls in spite of me the owner,
But thou wilt brave me with these saucy terms?

CADE Brave thee? Ay, by the best blood that ever was broach'd, and beard thee too. Look on me well. I have eat no meat these five days; yet, come thou and thy five men, and if I do not leave you all as dead as a doornail, I pray God I may never eat grass more.

IDEN
Nay, it shall ne'er be said, while England stands,
That Alexander Iden, an esquire of Kent,
Took odds to combat a poor famish'd man.
Oppose thy steadfast-gazing eyes to mine,
See if thou canst outface me with thy looks.
Set limb to limb, and thou art far the lesser;
Thy hand is but a finger to my fist,
Thy leg a stick compared with this truncheon;
My foot shall fight with all the strength thou hast;
And if mine arm be heaved in the air,
Thy grave is digg'd already in the earth.
As for words, whose greatness answers words,
Let this my sword report what speech forbears.

CADE By my valor, the most complete champion that ever I heard! Steel, if thou turn the edge, or cut not out the burly-bon'd clown in chines of beef ere thou sleep in thy sheath, I beseech God on my knees thou mayst be turn'd to hobnails. *Here they fight.* [*Cade falls.*] O, I am slain! Famine and no other hath slain me. Let ten thousand devils come against me, and give me but

26 gallowglasses, kerns Irish footsoldiers, armed with heavy and light weapons respectively **33 calm'd** becalmed **34 But now** even now, just now **38 Duke Edmund** i.e., Edmund Beaufort, the Duke of Somerset **45 brook** endure **49 yet** until now

IV.x. Location: Kent. Iden's garden.
4 is laid is laying in wait **6 stay** wait **8 sallet** salad greens (with a pun in the following lines on *sallet,* light helmet) **12 brown bill** brownhandled weapon with a blade or ax-shaped head

22 Sufficeth . . . state it suffices that what I have supports my manner of life **23 And . . . gate** i.e., and also provides enough to feed the poor who come to my gate **25 stray** trespasser. **fee-simple** estate belonging to an owner and his heirs forever **30 rude companion** base fellow **35 brave** defy, taunt. **saucy** insolent **36 best blood** i.e., Christ's blood **37 broach'd** tapped, shed. **beard** defy **38 eat** eaten. (Pronounced "et.") **43 odds** advantage **48 truncheon** heavy staff (i.e., Iden's leg) **50–51 And . . . earth** i.e., if I but lift my arm, you're as good as dead already **52 whose . . . words** i.e., I whose might is more than a match for your words **54 complete** accomplished **55 turn the edge** fail to cut **56 chines** roasts **58 turn'd to hobnails** i.e., melted down and recast as nails

the ten meals I have lost, and I'd defy them all. Wither, garden, and be henceforth a burying-place to all that do dwell in this house, because the unconquer'd soul of Cade is fled.

IDEN
Is 't Cade that I have slain, that monstrous traitor?
Sword, I will hallow thee for this thy deed,
And hang thee o'er my tomb when I am dead.
Ne'er shall this blood be wiped from thy point,
But thou shalt wear it as a herald's coat
To emblaze the honor that thy master got.

CADE Iden, farewell, and be proud of thy victory. Tell Kent from me, she hath lost her best man, and exhort all the world to be cowards; for I, that never fear'd any, am vanquish'd by famine, not by valor. *Dies.*

IDEN
How much thou wrong'st me, heaven be my judge.
Die, damned wretch, the curse of her that bare thee!
And as I thrust thy body in with my sword,
[*Stabs Cade's body.*]
So wish I, I might thrust thy soul to hell.
Hence will I drag thee headlong by the heels
Unto a dunghill, which shall be thy grave,
And there cut off thy most ungracious head,
Which I will bear in triumph to the King,
Leaving thy trunk for crows to feed upon.
Exit [*dragging out the body, with his servants*].

[ACT V • SCENE I]

Enter York, and his army of Irish, with drum and colors.

YORK
From Ireland thus comes York to claim his right,
And pluck the crown from feeble Henry's head.
Ring, bells, aloud, burn, bonfires, clear and bright,
To entertain great England's lawful king.
Ah, sancta majestas! Who would not buy thee dear?
Let them obey that knows not how to rule;
This hand was made to handle nought but gold.
I cannot give due action to my words,
Except a sword or scepter balance it.
A scepter shall it have, have I a soul,
On which I'll toss the flow'r-de-luce of France.

Enter Buckingham.

Whom have we here? Buckingham, to disturb me?
The King hath sent him, sure. I must dissemble.

BUCKINGHAM
York, if thou meanest well, I greet thee well.

YORK
Humphrey of Buckingham, I accept thy greeting.
Art thou a messenger, or come of pleasure?

BUCKINGHAM
A messenger from Henry, our dread liege,
To know the reason of these arms in peace;
Or why thou, being a subject as I am,
Against thy oath and true allegiance sworn,
Should raise so great a power without his leave,
Or dare to bring thy force so near the court.

YORK [*Aside*]
Scarce can I speak, my choler is so great.
O, I could hew up rocks and fight with flint,
I am so angry at these abject terms!
And now, like Ajax Telamonius,
On sheep or oxen could I spend my fury.
I am far better born than is the King,
More like a king, more kingly in my thoughts.
But I must make fair weather yet a while,
Till Henry be more weak and I more strong.—
Buckingham, I prithee, pardon me,
That I have given no answer all this while;
My mind was troubled with deep melancholy.
The cause why I have brought this army hither
Is to remove proud Somerset from the King,
Seditious to his Grace and to the state.

BUCKINGHAM
That is too much presumption on thy part.
But if thy arms be to no other end,
The King hath yielded unto thy demand.
The Duke of Somerset is in the Tower.

YORK
Upon thine honor, is he prisoner?

BUCKINGHAM
Upon mine honor, he is prisoner.

YORK
Then, Buckingham, I do dismiss my pow'rs.
Soldiers, I thank you all. Disperse yourselves;
Meet me tomorrow in Saint George's field,
You shall have pay and everything you wish.
[*Exeunt Soldiers.*]
And let my sovereign, virtuous Henry,
Command my eldest son, nay, all my sons,
As pledges of my fealty and love;
I'll send them all as willing as I live.
Lands, goods, horse, armor, anything I have,
Is his to use, so Somerset may die.

BUCKINGHAM
York, I commend this kind submission.
We twain will go into his Highness' tent.
[*They walk arm in arm.*]

Enter King and Attendants.

KING
Buckingham, doth York intend no harm to us,

70 emblaze proclaim as by a heraldic device **79 headlong** at full length

V.i. Location: Fields between London and St. Albans, near the Castle Inn.
s.d. drum and colors drummer and flagbearer **5 sancta majestas** sacred majesty **9 Except** unless **10 have I** i.e., just as sure as I have **11 toss** carry aloft on the point of a pike. **flow'r-de-luce** France's national emblem

25 abject terms degrading, insulting words **26 Ajax Telamonius** Ajax the son of Telamon, one of the Greek heroes of the Trojan War who, when the weapons of Achilles were allotted to Odysseus, slaughtered in his fury a flock of sheep, mistaking them for the enemy **30 make fair weather** i.e., dissemble **46 Saint George's field** an open area south of the Thames River near Southwark **49 Command** hold under his authority **50 pledges** hostages **53 so** so long as

That thus he marcheth with thee arm in arm?

YORK
In all submission and humility
York doth present himself unto your Highness.

KING
Then what intends these forces thou dost bring?

YORK
To heave the traitor Somerset from hence,
And fight against that monstrous rebel Cade,
Who since I heard to be discomfited. 63

Enter Iden, with Cade's head.

IDEN
If one so rude and of so mean condition 64
May pass into the presence of a king,
Lo, I present your Grace a traitor's head,
The head of Cade, whom I in combat slew.

KING
The head of Cade? Great God, how just art Thou!
O, let me view his visage, being dead,
That living wrought me such exceeding trouble.
Tell me, my friend, art thou the man that slew him?

IDEN
I was, an 't like your Majesty.

KING
How art thou call'd, and what is thy degree?

IDEN
Alexander Iden, that's my name,
A poor esquire of Kent that loves his king.

BUCKINGHAM
So please it you, my lord, 'twere not amiss
He were created knight for his good service.

KING
Iden, kneel down. [*He kneels.*] Rise up a knight.
We give thee for reward a thousand marks,
And will that thou henceforth attend on us.

IDEN
May Iden live to merit such a bounty,
And never live but true unto his liege! [*Rises.*]

Enter Queen and Somerset.

KING
See, Buckingham, Somerset comes with th' Queen.
Go bid her hide him quickly from the Duke. 84

QUEEN
For thousand Yorks he shall not hide his head,
But boldly stand and front him to his face. 86

YORK
How now? Is Somerset at liberty?
Then, York, unloose thy long-imprisoned thoughts,
And let thy tongue be equal with thy heart.
Shall I endure the sight of Somerset?
False king, why hast thou broken faith with me,
Knowing how hardly I can brook abuse? 92
King did I call thee? No, thou art not king,
Not fit to govern and rule multitudes,
Which dar'st not, no, nor canst not rule a traitor.
That head of thine doth not become a crown;
Thy hand is made to grasp a palmer's staff, 97
And not to grace an aweful princely scepter. 98
That gold must round engirt these brows of mine,
Whose smile and frown, like to Achilles' spear,
Is able with the change to kill and cure.
Here is a hand to hold a scepter up
And with the same to act controlling laws. 103
Give place. By heaven, thou shalt rule no more
O'er him whom heaven created for thy ruler.

SOMERSET
O monstrous traitor! I arrest thee, York,
Of capital treason 'gainst the King and crown.
Obey, audacious traitor, kneel for grace.

YORK
Wouldst have me kneel? First let me ask of these, 109
If they can brook I bow a knee to man.
Sirrah, call in my sons to be my bail.
[*Exit Attendant.*]
I know, ere they will have me go to ward, 112
They'll pawn their swords for my enfranchisement. 113

QUEEN
Call hither Clifford. Bid him come amain, 114
To say if that the bastard boys of York
Shall be the surety for their traitor father.
[*Exit Attendant.*]

YORK
O blood-bespotted Neapolitan, 117
Outcast of Naples, England's bloody scourge!
The sons of York, thy betters in their birth,
Shall be their father's bail, and bane to those
That for my surety will refuse the boys!

Enter Edward and Richard [Plantagenet, with drum and Soldiers, at one door].

See where they come. I'll warrant they'll make it good.

Enter [old] Clifford [and his Son, with drum and Soldiers, at the other door].

QUEEN
And here comes Clifford to deny their bail.

CLIFFORD
Health and all happiness to my lord the King!
[*Kneels.*]

YORK
I thank thee, Clifford. Say, what news with thee?
Nay, do not fright us with an angry look.
We are thy sovereign, Clifford, kneel again.
For thy mistaking so, we pardon thee.

CLIFFORD
This is my king, York, I do not mistake,
But thou mistakes me much to think I do.

63 discomfited routed **64 rude** uncultivated. **mean condition** low rank **80 will** command **84 the Duke** i.e., of York **86 front** confront **92 brook abuse** tolerate deception **95 Which** who

97 palmer's pilgrim's **98 aweful** awe-inspiring **100 Achilles' spear** (Telephus, wounded by Achilles' spear, learned from an oracle that he could be cured only by the wounder. He was eventually cured by an application of rust from the point of the spear.) **103 act** enact **109 these** i.e., his sons, who are waiting outside; or possibly his hands or weapons **112 to ward** into custody **113 pawn** pledge. **enfranchisement** freedom **114 amain** swiftly **117 Neapolitan** (Margaret's father Reignier or René was titular King of Naples.) **120 bane** destruction

To Bedlam with him! Is the man grown mad? 131

KING

Ay, Clifford, a bedlam and ambitious humor 132
Makes him oppose himself against his king.

CLIFFORD

He is a traitor. Let him to the Tower,
And chop away that factious pate of his.

QUEEN

He is arrested, but will not obey.
His sons, he says, shall give their words for him.

YORK

Will you not, sons?

EDWARD

Ay, noble father, if our words will serve.

RICHARD

And if words will not, then our weapons shall.

CLIFFORD

Why, what a brood of traitors have we here!

YORK

Look in a glass, and call thy image so. 142
I am thy king, and thou a false-heart traitor.
Call hither to the stake my two brave bears, 144
That with the very shaking of their chains
They may astonish these fell-lurking curs.
Bid Salisbury and Warwick come to me.
[*An attendant goes to summon them.*]

Enter the Earls of Warwick and Salisbury, [*with drum and Soldiers*].

CLIFFORD

Are these thy bears? We'll bait thy bears to death,
And manacle the bear 'ard in their chains, 149
If thou dar'st bring them to the baiting place. 150

RICHARD

Oft have I seen a hot o'erweening cur 151
Run back and bite, because he was withheld, 152
Who, being suffer'd, with the bear's fell paw 153
Hath clapp'd his tail between his legs and cried;
And such a piece of service will you do,
If you oppose yourselves to match Lord Warwick. 156

CLIFFORD

Hence, heap of wrath, foul indigested lump, 157
As crooked in thy manners as thy shape!

YORK

Nay, we shall heat you thoroughly anon.

CLIFFORD

Take heed, lest by your heat you burn yourselves.

KING

Why, Warwick, hath thy knee forgot to bow?
Old Salisbury, shame to thy silver hair,
Thou mad misleader of thy brain-sick son!
What, wilt thou on thy death-bed play the ruffian,
And seek for sorrow with thy spectacles? 165
O, where is faith? O, where is loyalty?
If it be banish'd from the frosty head,
Where shall it find a harbor in the earth?
Wilt thou go dig a grave to find out war,
And shame thine honorable age with blood?
Why art thou old, and want'st experience? 171
Or wherefore dost abuse it if thou hast it?
For shame! In duty bend thy knee to me
That bows unto the grave with mickle age. 174

SALISBURY

My lord, I have considered with myself
The title of this most renowned duke,
And in my conscience do repute his Grace
The rightful heir to England's royal seat.

KING

Hast thou not sworn allegiance unto me?

SALISBURY

I have.

KING

Canst thou dispense with heaven for such an oath? 181

SALISBURY

It is great sin to swear unto a sin,
But greater sin to keep a sinful oath.
Who can be bound by any solemn vow
To do a murd'rous deed, to rob a man,
To force a spotless virgin's chastity,
To reave the orphan of his patrimony, 187
To wring the widow from her custom'd right, 188
And have no other reason for this wrong
But that he was bound by a solemn oath?

QUEEN

A subtle traitor needs no sophister. 191

KING

Call Buckingham, and bid him arm himself.

YORK

Call Buckingham, and all the friends thou hast,
I am resolv'd for death or dignity.

CLIFFORD

The first I warrant thee, if dreams prove true.

WARWICK

You were best to go to bed and dream again,
To keep thee from the tempest of the field.

CLIFFORD

I am resolv'd to bear a greater storm
Than any thou canst conjure up today;
And that I'll write upon thy burgonet, 200
Might I but know thee by thy household badge.

WARWICK

Now, by my father's badge, old Nevil's crest, 202
The rampant bear chain'd to the ragged staff,
This day I'll wear aloft my burgonet,

131 Bedlam hospital of St. Mary of Bethlehem in London, used as an asylum for the mentally deranged **132 bedlam** mad. **humor** disposition **142 glass** looking-glass **144 brave bears** i.e., Salisbury and his son Warwick. (Cf. ll. 202–03 below, where Warwick describes the badge of his house as a "rampant bear chain'd to the ragged staff." The image is from bearbaiting, in which bears were chained to a stake and attacked by *fell-lurking curs,* cruelly waiting dogs, l. 146.) **149 bear 'ard** bear-ward or bear-herd (i.e., York) **150 baiting place** bear pit **151 hot o'erweening** hot-tempered and overconfident **152 bite** i.e., at his trainer who is restraining him **153 suffer'd** permitted (to attack the bear). **with** i.e., struck by. **fell** fierce, terrible **156 oppose yourselves** set yourselves up as opponents **157 indigested** ill-formed. **lump** (Bear cubs were supposedly born unformed and had to be licked into shape by their mother. See *3 Henry VI,* III.ii.161, where Richard's hunched back and other deformities are compared with those of "an unlick'd bear-whelp.")

165 spectacles i.e., eyes **171 want'st** lack **174 That bows** you that bow. **mickle** great **181 dispense with** make dispensation with **187 reave** bereave **188 custom'd right** i.e., to inherit a portion of her husband's estate **191 sophister** equivocator, expert in casuistry **200 burgonet** light helmet or steel cap (upon which the wearer's heraldic device was often mounted) **202 old Nevil's crest** (The Nevils' crest was in fact a bull; Warwick inherited his badge of a chained bear from his wife's family, the Beauchamps.)

As on a mountain top the cedar shows
That keeps his leaves in spite of any storm,
Even to affright thee with the view thereof.

CLIFFORD
And from thy burgonet I'll rend thy bear
And tread it under foot with all contempt,
Despite the bear 'ard that protects the bear.

YOUNG CLIFFORD
And so to arms, victorious father,
To quell the rebels and their complices.

RICHARD
Fie! Charity, for shame! Speak not in spite,
For you shall sup with Jesu Christ tonight.

YOUNG CLIFFORD
Foul stigmatic, that's more than thou canst tell.

RICHARD
If not in heaven, you'll surely sup in hell.
Exeunt [*severally*].

[SCENE II]

[*Alarums to the battle.*] *Enter Warwick.*

WARWICK
Clifford of Cumberland, 'tis Warwick calls!
And if thou dost not hide thee from the bear,
Now, when the angry trumpet sounds alarum
And dead men's cries do fill the empty air,
Clifford, I say, come forth and fight with me.
Proud northern lord, Clifford of Cumberland,
Warwick is hoarse with calling thee to arms.

Enter York.

How now, my noble lord? What, all afoot?

YORK
The deadly-handed Clifford slew my steed,
But match to match I have encount'red him
And made a prey for carrion kites and crows
Even of the bonny beast he lov'd so well.

Enter [*old*] *Clifford.*

WARWICK
Of one or both of us the time is come.

YORK
Hold, Warwick, seek thee out some other chase,
For I myself must hunt this deer to death.

WARWICK
Then, nobly, York! 'Tis for a crown thou fight'st.
As I intend, Clifford, to thrive today,
It grieves my soul to leave thee unassail'd.
Exit Warwick.

CLIFFORD
What seest thou in me, York? Why dost thou pause?

YORK
With thy brave bearing should I be in love,
But that thou art so fast mine enemy.

CLIFFORD
Nor should thy prowess want praise and esteem,
But that 'tis shown ignobly and in treason.

YORK
So let it help me now against thy sword
As I in justice and true right express it.

CLIFFORD
My soul and body on the action both!

YORK
A dreadful lay! Address thee instantly.
[*They fight, and Clifford falls.*]

CLIFFORD
La fin couronne les oeuvres. [*Dies.*]

YORK
Thus war hath given thee peace, for thou art still.
Peace with his soul, heaven, if it be thy will! [*Exit.*]

Enter young Clifford.

YOUNG CLIFFORD
Shame and confusion! All is on the rout.
Fear frames disorder, and disorder wounds
Where it should guard. O war, thou son of hell,
Whom angry heavens do make their minister,
Throw in the frozen bosoms of our part
Hot coals of vengeance! Let no soldier fly.
He that is truly dedicate to war
Hath no self-love, nor he that loves himself
Hath not essentially but by circumstance
The name of valor. [*Seeing his dead father.*] O, let the vile world end,
And the premised flames of the last day
Knit earth and heaven together!
Now let the general trumpet blow his blast,
Particularities and petty sounds
To cease! Wast thou ordain'd, dear father,
To lose thy youth in peace, and to achieve
The silver livery of advised age,
And in thy reverence and thy chair-days, thus
To die in ruffian battle? Even at this sight
My heart is turn'd to stone; and while 'tis mine,
It shall be stony. York not our old men spares;
No more will I their babes. Tears virginal
Shall be to me even as the dew to fire,
And beauty, that the tyrant oft reclaims,
Shall to my flaming wrath be oil and flax.
Henceforth I will not have to do with pity.
Meet I an infant of the house of York,
Into as many gobbets will I cut it
As wild Medea young Absyrtus did.
In cruelty will I seek out my fame.
Come, thou new ruin of old Clifford's house.
As did Aeneas old Anchises bear,

215 stigmatic one branded with the mark of his crime (just as Richard is marked by his deformities)

V.ii. Location: Scene continues at the battlefield near the Castle Inn.
14 chase game **20 bearing** demeanor **21 fast** completely

26 action outcome of action **27 lay** wager, oath. **Address thee** prepare yourself **28 La . . . oeuvres** the end crowns the work **32 frames** causes **35 frozen** i.e., unwarmed by wrathful courage. **part** party, faction **37 dedicate** dedicated **38 nor** conversely **39 not . . . circumstance** not by any virtue of his own, but only outwardly **41 premised** foreordained. **last day** Day of Judgment **44 Particularities** individual affairs **46 lose** expend **47 advised** wise, prudent **48 chair-days** i.e., inactive years of old age **53 dew to fire** (Water finely sprayed on a fire was thought to cause it to burn hotter.) **54 that . . . reclaims** which often softens the temper of the tyrant **58 gobbets** pieces, lumps of flesh **59 Medea** daughter of Aeetes, King of Colchis, who helped Jason recover the Golden Fleece and fled with him. (To delay her father's pursuit, she killed her brother Absyrtus and left his dismembered body in the father's path.) **62 Aeneas, Anchises** (In Virgil's *Aeneid*, Aeneas, fleeing from Troy, carried his aged father on his shoulders.)

So bear I thee upon my manly shoulders;
But then Aeneas bare a living load, 64
Nothing so heavy as these woes of mine. 65
[Exit, bearing off his father.]

Enter Richard and Somerset to fight. [Somerset is killed under the sign of the Castle Inn.]

RICHARD
So, lie thou there;
For underneath an alehouse' paltry sign,
The Castle in Saint Albans, Somerset
Hath made the wizard famous in his death. 69
Sword, hold thy temper; heart, be wrathful still.
Priests pray for enemies, but princes kill. *[Exit.]* 71

Fight. Excursions. Enter King, Queen, and others.

QUEEN
Away, my lord! You are slow. For shame, away!

KING
Can we outrun the heavens? Good Margaret, stay.

QUEEN
What are you made of? You'll nor fight nor fly. 74
Now is it manhood, wisdom, and defense
To give the enemy way, and to secure us 76
By what we can, which can no more but fly. 77
Alarum afar off.
If you be ta'en, we then should see the bottom
Of all our fortunes; but if we haply scape,
As well we may, if not through your neglect, 80
We shall to London get, where you are lov'd
And where this breach now in our fortunes made
May readily be stopp'd.

Enter [young] Clifford.

YOUNG CLIFFORD
But that my heart's on future mischief set,
I would speak blasphemy ere bid you fly;
But fly you must. Uncurable discomfit 86
Reigns in the hearts of all our present parts. 87
Away, for your relief! And we will live
To see their day and them our fortune give. 89
Away, my lord, away! *Exeunt.*

[SCENE III]

Alarum. Retreat. Enter York, Richard, Warwick, and Soldiers, with drum and colors.

YORK
Of Salisbury, who can report of him,
That winter lion, who in rage forgets 2
Aged contusions and all brush of time, 3
And, like a gallant in the brow of youth, 4
Repairs him with occasion? This happy day 5
Is not itself, nor have we won one foot,
If Salisbury be lost.

RICHARD
My noble father,
Three times today I holp him to his horse, 8
Three times bestrid him; thrice I led him off, 9
Persuaded him from any further act.
But still, where danger was, still there I met him; 11
And like rich hangings in a homely house, 12
So was his will in his old feeble body.
But, noble as he is, look where he comes.

Enter Salisbury.

SALISBURY
Now, by my sword, well hast thou fought today!
By th' mass, so did we all. I thank you, Richard.
God knows how long it is I have to live,
And it hath pleas'd him that three times today
You have defended me from imminent death.
Well, lords, we have not got that which we have; 20
'Tis not enough our foes are this time fled,
Being opposites of such repairing nature. 22

YORK
I know our safety is to follow them;
For, as I hear, the King is fled to London,
To call a present court of parliament.
Let us pursue him ere the writs go forth. 26
What says Lord Warwick? Shall we after them?

WARWICK
After them? Nay, before them, if we can.
Now, by my faith, lords, 'twas a glorious day.
Saint Albans battle won by famous York
Shall be eterniz'd in all age to come. 31
Sound drum and trumpets, and to London all,
And more such days as these to us befall! *Exeunt.*

64 bare bore **65 Nothing** not at all **69 Hath . . . death** i.e., has confirmed by his death the prophecy that he would die "where castles mounted stand." (See I.iv.36–38.) **71 s.d. Exit** (The body of the slain Somerset must be removed at some point.) **Excursions** sorties **74 nor . . . nor** neither . . . nor **76 secure us** save ourselves **77 what** whatever means. **which** (we) who **80 if not** unless **86 Uncurable discomfit** hopeless defeat **87 our present parts** those forces still remaining on our side **89 To . . . give** to see a day of success like theirs and let them experience our misfortune

V.iii. Location: Scene continues at the battlefield.
2 winter i.e., aged

3 brush collision **4 gallant** young man of fashion. **brow** i.e., crown, height **5 Repairs . . . occasion** i.e., renews his strength with the opportunity of further military action **8 holp** helped **9 bestrid him** i.e., stood over him to defend him when he was down **11 still** continually **12 hangings** tapestries. **homely** modest **20 not . . . have** i.e., not decisively overwhelmed the forces we today defeated in order to secure the whole country **22 Being . . . nature** they being adversaries with such ability to recover quickly **26 writs** official summons issued by the King to members of parliament **31 eterniz'd** immortalized

The Third Part of King Henry the Sixth

Like the earlier plays in this series already examined, *3 Henry VI* must be seen not only as a part of that series but as a play in its own right, presumably seen on its first showing by an Elizabethan audience who, though aware of a larger context, witnessed this dramatic action as a self-contained event. Because *3 Henry VI* represents nearly the entire military phase of the civil war, it is the most crowded and bustling play of the series. Historically it covers the period from the battles of Wakefield and second St. Albans (1460–1461) to the decisive Yorkist victories at Barnet and Tewkesbury (1471). These and other battles are actually represented on stage. The conventional method of representing armed conflict is by means of alarums and excursions, employing as many soldiers as the acting company could muster, with martial music and numerous entrances and exits in rapid succession. Battles are usually preceded by florid boastful rhetorical exchanges, or *flytings,* between the combatants. The military contests focus on heroic confrontations between individual leaders. Staging of battles often uses the Elizabethan playhouse to its physical capacity, with appearances "on the walls" of some town (i.e., from the upper gallery), scaling operations, sieges, and the like. *3 Henry VI* abounds in spectacular deaths, often performed as gruesome rituals. Young Rutland is dragged from his tutor by the implacable Clifford, and Richard of York is mocked with a paper crown by Queen Margaret; Clifford dies with an arrow in his neck and Warwick the kingmaker dies lamenting the vanity of all earthly achievement; King Henry dies in the Tower, a defenseless prisoner in the hands of Richard of Gloucester. The play is perhaps confusing to the reader, but breathes with violent energy on stage.

The action lacks a single central character. The title of the 1595 octavo edition pairs the deaths of Richard of York and of King Henry as the play's most memorable episodes; and in this dual focus we see the dominant motif of reciprocity, a Yorkist death for a Lancastrian death. This pattern will continue into *Richard III,* for *3 Henry VI* ends with an ominous amount of unfinished business; Clarence, for example, later sees that he must die in atonement for his part in the slaughter of Edward, the Lancastrian Prince of Wales. Just as the deaths are balanced and contrasted with one another, the military action also seesaws back and forth. Both Henry VI and Edward IV are at times imprisoned. The wheel of fortune elevates one side and then the other. Political alliances shift the balance of power one way and then the other. The action is painfully indecisive, the carnage pointlessly leading only to further violence. The spectacle is made infinitely more agonizing by the realization that all this is a family quarrel. The commons suffer accordingly: we witness the grief of a father who has mistakenly killed his son in battle, and a son who has killed his father (II,v). The people, seldom seen, are no longer political troublemakers but mere victims, waiting patiently for an end. A recurrent emblem used to convey the utter futility of this war is the molehill. York is mockingly crowned before his execution on a molehill, and King Henry retires from a battle to a molehill in order to meditate on the happy contemplative life he has been denied. The molehill suggests the ironic perversity of man's quest for worldly power, whereby those who possess power are incapable of exercising it wisely, and those who burn with ambition are denied legitimate opportunity.

One sure sign of moral chaos throughout this play is the phenomenon of oath-breaking. In the opening scene, Richard of York accepts under oath an obligation to honor Henry VI as his king in return for being named king after Henry's death, but is soon talked out of his promise by his son Richard on the specious grounds that the oath was not made before "a true and lawful magistrate" (I,ii). This masterful equivocation prepares us for Richard's later perfidies. (In Shakespeare's sources, especially Hall, Parliament plays a major role in working out the compromise between York and Henry; Shakespeare shows us instead a personal agreement made between two contending leaders on the basis of private will and assertion of military power, and easily broken on the same pragmatic grounds.) King Henry is no less forsworn in denying to his own son the crown bestowed on him as birthright by sacred law and custom. Lewis the French King excuses his shifting of alliance from King Henry to the Yorkists on grounds of simple expediency. Clarence forswears his oaths made to his brother Edward and changes sides in the wars, offended at Edward's perfidy in having renounced his intent to marry the French King's sister-in-law. Soon Clarence is back again in the Yorkist camp, having now betrayed the promises he made to the Lancastrians. Warwick the kingmaker forswears his oaths to Edward because Edward has undermined Warwick's embassy to France. Where in fact do truth and justice reside, now that England is governed by two kings who are both forsworn? The common people sense this dilemma, as revealed in the attitudes of two gamekeepers: they capture Henry to whom they were once loyal because they are now "sworn in all allegiance" to

Edward, but would be true subjects again to Henry "If he were seated as King Edward is" (III,i). Political and military reality governs political ethics; the ruler to be acknowledged is he who can establish control.

Another sign of moral decay in this play is the dominance of vengeful purpose. *3 Henry VI* indeed can be viewed as a kind of revenge play in which Richard of Gloucester finally emerges as the consummate avenger in a society of avengers. In the opening confrontation between the Yorkists and Lancastrians, Warwick taunts the Lancastrians with having lost many of their fathers in the recent military action at St. Albans; the fathers of Northumberland, Westmorland, and Clifford have all fallen in that one battle. (Historically, Westmorland and Clifford appear to be the same man with the same father, Old Clifford of *2 Henry VI;* Shakespeare gives us more fatherless sons by this division of one man into two.) The sons of course vow vengeance. Clifford, renowned as "the butcher" for his cruelty, exacts a terrible price for his father's death through the slaughter of the defenseless young Rutland and the mocking execution of Rutland's father the Duke of York. York's surviving sons take vengeance not only on Clifford but on King Henry, his son Edward, and many others. Warwick turns against Edward of York more to avenge an insult than to aid Henry, and is himself cut down by the Yorkists at Barnet (IV,ii). The implacable pattern of an eye for an eye eventually takes on a providential meaning, especially as seen from the hindsight of *Richard III,* but our experiencing of its working out in this play involves much brutality and horror.

As in earlier plays of the series, the relationships between men and women echo the discord of the English nation, and contribute in turn to further discord. Margaret of Anjou, the remorseless defender of her son Edward's claim, acts with increasingly masculine authority while her ineffectual husband abdicates responsibility. She is the Lancastrian general, resourceful in battle and often victorious, implacable in vengeance. This inversion of male and female roles is reflected on the Yorkist side by Edward IV's disastrous marriage with Lady Elizabeth Grey. She is the widow of a Lancastrian soldier with no family position or political power to bring to the marriage—nothing, in fact, but her ambition on behalf of her kinsmen. Edward's attraction to her is fleshly indulgence in defiance of more prudent considerations. To make matters worse, Warwick is at that very moment negotiating a highly favorable alliance with the King of France. Edward IV thus unconsciously apes the earlier willfulness of his counterpart, Henry VI. Edward IV's snubbing of Warwick leads to the defection of that powerful leader, and through him the defection of Edward's brother Clarence who has succumbed to the charms of Warwick's daughter Isabel. And whereas *1 Henry VI* at least counterbalances the uxoriousness of Henry with the positive example of Lord Talbot, *3 Henry VI* fails to discover any such central noble character. (To be sure, we are briefly introduced to the young Earl of Richmond, who is to be Henry VII, but only as a glimpse of a hopeful future.) The almost total lack of any distinctly virtuous character gives to *3 Henry VI* its predominantly dismaying and helpless mood. The heroes have been destroyed.

Richard of Gloucester alone seems to profit from England's decline. Like his father York, his strategy has been to let England flay herself into anarchic vulnerability. Once the father York has disappeared from the scene, young Richard's malevolent character becomes increasingly apparent. No longer merely one of York's brave sons, Richard is the new genius of discord. His bravura soliloquy in III,ii is often included in performances of *Richard III,* for it yields rich clues to his emerging character: he is ambitious, ruthless, deformed from birth, and above all a consummate deceiver. To the audience he boasts of his ability, claiming that as a hypocrite he will excel the combined talents of Nestor, Ulysses, Sinon, Proteus, and Machiavelli. The superb self-assurance is arresting, the heartless consistency admirable even though despicable. In a second soliloquy, virtually at the end of the play, having already dispatched Henry VI and his son Edward, Richard confides to the audience that Clarence is to be his next victim. And although Richard pledges fealty to his young nephew Edward, the Yorkist crown prince, at the Yorkist victory celebration with which the play ends, we know that Richard's kiss of peace is no more trustworthy than Judas' kissing of Christ. All those standing between Richard and the throne are to be eliminated. Clearly, the pious longings for peace expressed by King Edward IV are to be cruelly violated.

The Third Part of King Henry The Sixth

[*Dramatis Personae*

KING HENRY THE SIXTH.
EDWARD, PRINCE OF WALES, *his son.*
LEWIS XI. KING OF FRANCE.
DUKE OF SOMERSET.
DUKE OF EXETER.
EARL OF OXFORD.
EARL OF NORTHUMBERLAND.
EARL OF WESTMORLAND.
LORD CLIFFORD.
RICHARD PLANTAGENET, DUKE OF YORK.
EDWARD, *Earl of March, afterwards* KING EDWARD IV., } *his sons.*
EDMUND, EARL OF RUTLAND, }
GEORGE, *afterwards* DUKE OF CLARENCE, }
RICHARD, *afterwards* DUKE OF GLOUCESTER, }
DUKE OF NORFOLK.
MARQUESS OF MONTAGUE.
EARL OF WARWICK.
EARL OF PEMBROKE.
LORD HASTINGS.
LORD STAFFORD.
SIR JOHN MORTIMER, } *uncles to the Duke of York.*
SIR HUGH MORTIMER, }
HENRY, EARL OF RICHMOND, *a youth.*
LORD RIVERS, *brother to Lady Grey.*
SIR WILLIAM STANLEY.
SIR JOHN MONTGOMERY.
SIR JOHN SOMERVILLE.
TUTOR *to Rutland.* MAYOR OF YORK.
LIEUTENANT *of the Tower. A* NOBLEMAN.
Two KEEPERS. *A* HUNTSMAN.
A SON *that has killed his father.*
A FATHER *that has killed his son.*

QUEEN MARGARET.
LADY GREY, *afterwards queen to Edward IV.*
BONA, *sister to the French queen.*

SOLDIERS, ATTENDANTS, MESSENGERS, WATCHMEN, *etc.*

SCENE: *England and France.*]

ACT I • SCENE I

Alarum. Enter [Richard] Plantagenet [Duke of York], Edward, Richard, Norfolk, Montague, Warwick, [with drum] and Soldiers, [wearing white roses in their hats].

WARWICK
I wonder how the King escap'd our hands.

YORK
While we pursu'd the horsemen of the north,
He slily stole away and left his men;
Whereat the great Lord of Northumberland,
Whose warlike ears could never brook retreat,
Cheer'd up the drooping army, and himself,
Lord Clifford, and Lord Stafford, all abreast,
Charg'd our main battle's front, and breaking in
Were by the swords of common soldiers slain.

EDWARD
Lord Stafford's father, Duke of Buckingham,
Is either slain or wounded dangerous;
I cleft his beaver with a downright blow.
That this is true, father, behold his blood.
[*Shows his bloody sword.*]

MONTAGUE
And, brother, here's the Earl of Wiltshire's blood,
Whom I encount'red as the battles join'd.
[*Shows sword.*]

RICHARD
Speak thou for me and tell them what I did.
[*Showing the Duke of Somerset's head.*]

YORK
Richard hath best deserv'd of all my sons.
But is your Grace dead, my Lord of Somerset?

NORFOLK
Such hope have all the line of John of Gaunt!

RICHARD
Thus do I hope to shake King Henry's head.

WARWICK
And so do I. Victorious Prince of York,
Before I see thee seated in that throne
Which now the house of Lancaster usurps,
I vow by heaven these eyes shall never close.
This is the palace of the fearful king,
And this the regal seat. Possess it, York,
For this is thine and not King Henry's heirs'.

YORK
Assist me, then, sweet Warwick, and I will,
For hither we have broken in by force.

I.i. Location: London. The Parliament House (see ll. 35–39, 71, etc.,) but also referred to as King Henry VI's palace; see l. 25. The chair of state is onstage, probably on a raised platform.
s.d. Alarum trumpet call to arms. (York and his followers, in hot pursuit of King Henry, have just arrived from St. Albans.) **5 brook** endure. **retreat** the call sounding retreat **8 battle's** army's **9 Were . . . slain** (In *2 Henry VI*, V.ii, it is York who kills Clifford.) **12 beaver** face guard of a helmet, i.e., here the helmet itself **14 brother** (Montague was brother to Warwick. His father, Salisbury of *2 Henry VI*, was brother-in-law of York.) **18 But . . . Somerset** i.e., are you really dead, my lord? (Like his son, York contemptuously addresses his slain enemy.) **19 Such . . . Gaunt** (The descendants of John of Gaunt, to whom Norfolk wishes ill luck, include Edmund Beaufort, second Duke of Somerset, and King Henry VI.) **22 Before** i.e., until

NORFOLK
We'll all assist you. He that flies shall die.

YORK
Thanks, gentle Norfolk. Stay by me, my lords,
And, soldiers, stay and lodge by me this night.
They go up [to the chair of state].

WARWICK
And when the King comes, offer him no violence,
Unless he seek to thrust you out perforce. 34

YORK
The Queen this day here holds her parliament,
But little thinks we shall be of her council.
By words or blows here let us win our right.

RICHARD
Arm'd as we are, let's stay within this house.

WARWICK
The bloody parliament shall this be call'd,
Unless Plantagenet, Duke of York, be king,
And bashful Henry depos'd, whose cowardice
Hath made us by-words to our enemies. 42

YORK
Then leave me not, my lords. Be resolute.
I mean to take possession of my right.

WARWICK
Neither the King, nor he that loves him best,
The proudest he that holds up Lancaster, 46
Dares stir a wing if Warwick shake his bells. 47
I'll plant Plantagenet, root him up who dares.
Resolve thee, Richard; claim the English crown. 49

Flourish. Enter King Henry, Clifford, Northumberland, Westmorland, Exeter, and the rest.

KING HENRY
My lords, look where the sturdy rebel sits,
Even in the chair of state. Belike he means,
Back'd by the power of Warwick, that false peer,
To aspire unto the crown and reign as king.
Earl of Northumberland, he slew thy father,
And thine, Lord Clifford, and you both have vow'd revenge
On him, his sons, his favorites, and his friends.

NORTHUMBERLAND
If I be not, heavens be reveng'd on me! 57

CLIFFORD
The hope thereof makes Clifford mourn in steel. 58

WESTMORLAND
What, shall we suffer this? Let's pluck him down.
My heart for anger burns. I cannot brook it.

KING HENRY
Be patient, gentle Earl of Westmorland.

CLIFFORD
Patience is for poltroons, such as he. 62
He durst not sit there, had your father liv'd.
My gracious lord, here in the parliament
Let us assail the family of York.

NORTHUMBERLAND
Well hast thou spoken, cousin. Be it so. 66

KING HENRY
Ah, know you not the city favors them, 67
And they have troops of soldiers at their beck?

EXETER
But when the Duke is slain, they'll quickly fly.

KING HENRY
Far be the thought of this from Henry's heart,
To make a shambles of the parliament house! 71
Cousin of Exeter, frowns, words, and threats
Shall be the war that Henry means to use.
Thou factious Duke of York, descend my throne,
And kneel for grace and mercy at my feet!
I am thy sovereign.

YORK
I am thine.

EXETER
For shame, come down. He made thee Duke of York. 77

YORK
It was my inheritance, as the earldom was. 78

EXETER
Thy father was a traitor to the crown. 79

WARWICK
Exeter, thou art a traitor to the crown
In following this usurping Henry.

CLIFFORD
Whom should he follow but his natural king?

WARWICK
True, Clifford. That's Richard Duke of York.

KING HENRY
And shall I stand, and thou sit in my throne?

YORK
It must and shall be so. Content thyself.

WARWICK
Be Duke of Lancaster; let him be King.

WESTMORLAND
He is both King and Duke of Lancaster,
And that the Lord of Westmorland shall maintain.

WARWICK
And Warwick shall disprove it. You forget
That we are those which chas'd you from the field
And slew your fathers, and with colors spread
March'd through the city to the palace gates.

NORTHUMBERLAND
Yes, Warwick, I remember it to my grief;
And, by his soul, thou and thy house shall rue it. 94

WESTMORLAND
Plantagenet, of thee and these thy sons,
Thy kinsmen and thy friends, I'll have more lives
Than drops of blood were in my father's veins. 97

34 perforce by force **42 by-words** i.e., objects of scorn. **our enemies** i.e., the French **46 he . . . up** person that supports **47 shake his bells** (Bells were sometimes fastened to the legs of a falcon to incite it to greater ferocity.) **49 Resolve thee** be resolute **49 s.d. Flourish** trumpet fanfare **57 be not** i.e., be not revenged **58 in steel** i.e., in armor, not in mourning attire **62 poltroons** arrant cowards

66 cousin kinsman **67 the city** i.e., London **71 shambles** slaughterhouse **77–78 He . . . was** (Cf. *1 Henry VI*, III.i.161–174, where the King restored to Richard the whole inheritance of the house of York, which included the earldom of March.) **79 Thy . . . crown** (On the execution of Richard, Earl of Cambridge, for treason by Henry V, see *Henry V*, II.ii and *1 Henry VI*, II.iv.90–94, II.v.84–91.) **94 his** i.e., the second Earl of Northumberland's, who fell at St. Albans on the Lancastrian side. (This event is not shown in *2 Henry VI*.) The speaker is the third earl. **97 my father's** (Thomas de Clifford fell at St. Albans; see *2 Henry VI*, V.ii. His title of Earl of Westmorland descended to his son, John de Clifford, who is seemingly to be identified both with the *Westmorland* who speaks here and the *Clifford* who speaks next. Shakespeare portrays these two men as "cousins" or kinsmen; see l. 182.

CLIFFORD
Urge it no more, lest that, instead of words,
I send thee, Warwick, such a messenger
As shall revenge his death before I stir.

WARWICK
Poor Clifford, how I scorn his worthless threats!

YORK
Will you we show our title to the crown?
If not, our swords shall plead it in the field.

KING HENRY
What title hast thou, traitor, to the crown?
Thy father was, as thou art, Duke of York,
Thy grandfather, Roger Mortimer, Earl of March.
I am the son of Henry the Fifth,
Who made the Dauphin and the French to stoop
And seiz'd upon their towns and provinces.

WARWICK
Talk not of France, sith thou hast lost it all.

KING HENRY
The Lord Protector lost it, and not I.
When I was crown'd I was but nine months old.

RICHARD
You are old enough now, and yet, methinks, you lose.
Father, tear the crown from the usurper's head.

EDWARD
Sweet father, do so; set it on your head.

MONTAGUE [*To York*]
Good brother, as thou lov'st and honorest arms,
Let's fight it out and not stand cavilling thus.

RICHARD
Sound drums and trumpets, and the King will fly.

YORK
Sons, peace!

KING HENRY
Peace, thou! And give King Henry leave to speak.

WARWICK
Plantagenet shall speak first. Hear him, lords,
And be you silent and attentive too,
For he that interrupts him shall not live.

KING HENRY
Think'st thou that I will leave my kingly throne,
Wherein my grandsire and my father sat?
No! First shall war unpeople this my realm;
Ay, and their colors, often borne in France,
And now in England to our heart's great sorrow,
Shall be my winding-sheet. Why faint you, lords?
My title's good, and better far than his.

WARWICK
Prove it, Henry, and thou shalt be king.

KING HENRY
Henry the Fourth by conquest got the crown.

YORK
'Twas by rebellion against his king.

KING HENRY [*Aside*]
I know not what to say; my title 's weak.—
Tell me, may not a king adopt an heir?

YORK
What then?

KING HENRY
An if he may, then am I lawful king;
For Richard, in the view of many lords,
Resign'd the crown to Henry the Fourth,
Whose heir my father was, and I am his.

YORK
He rose against him, being his sovereign,
And made him to resign his crown perforce.

WARWICK
Suppose, my lords, he did it unconstrain'd,
Think you 'twere prejudicial to his crown?

EXETER
No, for he could not so resign his crown
But that the next heir should succeed and reign.

KING HENRY
Art thou against us, Duke of Exeter?

EXETER
His is the right, and therefore pardon me.

YORK
Why whisper you, my lords, and answer not?

EXETER
My conscience tells me he is lawful king.

KING HENRY [*Aside*]
All will revolt from me, and turn to him.

NORTHUMBERLAND
Plantagenet, for all the claim thou lay'st,
Think not that Henry shall be so depos'd.

WARWICK
Depos'd he shall be, in despite of all.

NORTHUMBERLAND
Thou art deceiv'd. 'Tis not thy southern power
Of Essex, Norfolk, Suffolk, nor of Kent,
Which makes thee thus presumptuous and proud,
Can set the Duke up in despite of me.

CLIFFORD
King Henry, be thy title right or wrong,
Lord Clifford vows to fight in thy defense.
May that ground gape and swallow me alive,
Where I shall kneel to him that slew my father!

KING HENRY
O Clifford, how thy words revive my heart!

YORK
Henry of Lancaster, resign thy crown.
What mutter you, or what conspire you, lords?

WARWICK
Do right unto this princely Duke of York,
Or I will fill the house with armed men,
And over the chair of state, where now he sits,
Write up his title with usurping blood.

He stamps with his foot, and the Soldiers show themselves.

KING HENRY
My Lord of Warwick, hear but one word:
Let me for this my lifetime reign as king.

YORK
Confirm the crown to me and to mine heirs,

100 his i.e., old Clifford's; see previous note **102 Will you** do you desire **105 Thy . . . York** (Shakespeare's historical inaccuracy; Richard's father was never Duke of York. That title belonged to his oldest brother, Edward, who died at Agincourt; it was given by Henry VI to Richard.) **110 sith** since **111 Lord Protector** i.e., Humphrey, Duke of Gloucester **129 winding-sheet** sheet in which a corpse was wrapped. **faint** lose heart

137 An if if **141 being** i.e., Richard, who was **148 His** i.e., York's

And thou shalt reign in quiet while thou liv'st.

KING HENRY
I am content. Richard Plantagenet,
Enjoy the kingdom after my decease.

CLIFFORD
What wrong is this unto the prince your son!

WARWICK
What good is this to England and himself!

WESTMORLAND
Base, fearful, and despairing Henry!

CLIFFORD
How hast thou injur'd both thyself and us!

WESTMORLAND
I cannot stay to hear these articles.

NORTHUMBERLAND
Nor I.

CLIFFORD
Come, cousin, let us tell the Queen these news.

WESTMORLAND
Farewell, faint-hearted and degenerate king,
In whose cold blood no spark of honor bides.
[Exit with his men.]

NORTHUMBERLAND
Be thou a prey unto the house of York,
And die in bands for this unmanly deed!
[Exit with his men.]

CLIFFORD
In dreadful war mayst thou be overcome,
Or live in peace abandon'd and despis'd!
[Exit with his men.]

WARWICK
Turn this way, Henry, and regard them not.

EXETER
They seek revenge and therefore will not yield.

KING HENRY
Ah, Exeter!

WARWICK Why should you sigh, my lord?

KING HENRY
Not for myself, Lord Warwick, but my son,
Whom I unnaturally shall disinherit.
But be it as it may: *[To York.]* I here entail
The crown to thee and to thine heirs forever,
Conditionally, that here thou take an oath
To cease this civil war, and, whilst I live,
To honor me as thy king and sovereign,
And neither by treason nor hostility
To seek to put me down and reign thyself.

YORK
This oath I willingly take and will perform.

WARWICK
Long live King Henry! Plantagenet, embrace him.
[York embraces Henry.]

KING HENRY
And long live thou and these thy forward sons!

YORK
Now York and Lancaster are reconcil'd.

EXETER
Accurs'd be he that seeks to make them foes!

Sennet. Here they come down.

YORK
Farewell, my gracious lord. I'll to my castle.
[Exeunt York and his sons with their men.]

WARWICK
And I'll keep London with my soldiers.
[Exit Warwick with his men.]

NORFOLK
And I to Norfolk with my followers.
[Exit Norfolk with his men.]

MONTAGUE
And I unto the sea from whence I came.
[Exit Montague with his men.]

KING HENRY
And I, with grief and sorrow, to the court.

Enter the Queen [Margaret and Edward, Prince of Wales].

EXETER
Here comes the Queen, whose looks bewray her anger.
I'll steal away.

KING HENRY Exeter, so will I. *[Starts to leave.]*

QUEEN MARGARET
Nay, go not from me; I will follow thee.

KING HENRY
Be patient, gentle Queen, and I will stay.

QUEEN MARGARET
Who can be patient in such extremes?
Ah, wretched man! Would I had died a maid,
And never seen thee, never borne thee son,
Seeing thou hast prov'd so unnatural a father!
Hath he deserv'd to lose his birthright thus?
Hadst thou but lov'd him half so well as I,
Or felt that pain which I did for him once,
Or nourish'd him as I did with my blood,
Thou wouldst have left thy dearest heart-blood there,
Rather than have made that savage Duke thine heir
And disinherited thine only son.

PRINCE
Father, you cannot disinherit me.
If you be king, why should not I succeed?

KING HENRY
Pardon me, Margaret. Pardon me, sweet son.
The Earl of Warwick and the Duke enforc'd me.

QUEEN MARGARET
Enforc'd thee? Art thou king, and wilt be forc'd?
I shame to hear thee speak. Ah, timorous wretch!
Thou hast undone thyself, thy son, and me,
And giv'n unto the house of York such head
As thou shalt reign but by their sufferance.
To entail him and his heirs unto the crown,
What is it but to make thy sepulcher
And creep into it far before thy time?
Warwick is chancellor and the lord of Calais;

180 articles terms of agreement **186 bands** bonds, fetters **194 entail** bequeath irrevocably **203 forward** ardent, zealous

205 s.d. Sennet trumpet notes announcing the approach of a procession **206 castle** i.e., Sandal castle in Yorkshire. (See next scene.) **209 unto the sea** (Actually, Montague appears in scene ii at Sandal castle, not at the sea; possibly he is confused here with his uncle, William Neville, Baron Falconbridge. See l. 239 below.) **211 bewray** betray, reveal **233 head** i.e., free rein

Stern Falconbridge commands the narrow seas,
The Duke is made Protector of the realm,
And yet shalt thou be safe? Such safety finds
The trembling lamb environed with wolves.
Had I been there, which am a silly woman,
The soldiers should have toss'd me on their pikes
Before I would have granted to that act.
But thou preferr'st thy life before thine honor;
And seeing thou dost, I here divorce myself
Both from thy table, Henry, and thy bed,
Until that act of parliament be repeal'd
Whereby my son is disinherited.
The northern lords that have forsworn thy colors
Will follow mine, if once they see them spread;
And spread they shall be, to thy foul disgrace
And utter ruin of the house of York.
Thus do I leave thee. Come, son, let's away.
Our army is ready. Come, we'll after them.

KING HENRY
Stay, gentle Margaret, and hear me speak.

QUEEN MARGARET
Thou hast spoke too much already. Get thee gone.

KING HENRY
Gentle son Edward, thou wilt stay with me?

QUEEN MARGARET
Ay, to be murder'd by his enemies!

PRINCE
When I return with victory from the field
I'll see your Grace. Till then I'll follow her.

QUEEN MARGARET
Come, son, away. We may not linger thus.
[Exeunt Queen Margaret and the Prince.]

KING HENRY
Poor queen! How love to me and to her son
Hath made her break out into terms of rage!
Reveng'd may she be on that hateful Duke,
Whose haughty spirit, winged with desire,
Will cost my crown, and like an empty eagle
Tire on the flesh of me and of my son!
The loss of those three lords torments my heart.
I'll write unto them and entreat them fair.
Come, cousin, you shall be the messenger.

EXETER
And I, I hope, shall reconcile them all.
Flourish. Exeunt.

[SCENE II]

Enter Richard, Edward, and Montague.

RICHARD
Brother, though I be youngest, give me leave.

EDWARD
No, I can better play the orator.

MONTAGUE
But I have reasons strong and forcible.

Enter the Duke of York.

YORK
Why, how now, sons and brother, at a strife?
What is your quarrel? How began it first?

EDWARD
No quarrel, but a slight contention.

YORK
About what?

RICHARD
About that which concerns your Grace and us:
The crown of England, father, which is yours.

YORK
Mine, boy? Not till King Henry be dead.

RICHARD
Your right depends not on his life or death.

EDWARD
Now you are heir, therefore enjoy it now.
By giving the house of Lancaster leave to breathe,
It will outrun you, father, in the end.

YORK
I took an oath that he should quietly reign.

EDWARD
But for a kingdom any oath may be broken.
I would break a thousand oaths to reign one year.

RICHARD
No. God forbid your Grace should be forsworn.

YORK
I shall be, if I claim by open war.

RICHARD
I'll prove the contrary, if you'll hear me speak.

YORK
Thou canst not, son. It is impossible.

RICHARD
An oath is of no moment, being not took
Before a true and lawful magistrate
That hath authority over him that swears.
Henry had none, but did usurp the place.
Then, seeing 'twas he that made you to depose,
Your oath, my lord, is vain and frivolous.
Therefore, to arms! And, father, do but think
How sweet a thing it is to wear a crown,
Within whose circuit is Elysium
And all that poets feign of bliss and joy.
Why do we linger thus? I cannot rest
Until the white rose that I wear be dy'd
Even in the lukewarm blood of Henry's heart.

YORK
Richard, enough. I will be king, or die.
Brother, thou shalt to London presently,
And whet on Warwick to this enterprise.
Thou, Richard, shalt to the Duke of Norfolk,
And tell him privily of our intent.
You, Edward, shall unto my Lord Cobham,

239 Falconbridge i.e., William Neville or his son Thomas. (See l. 209 above, and note.) **narrow seas** i.e., English Channel **240 Duke** i.e., Duke of York **242 environed** surrounded **243 silly** helpless **244 pikes** long steel-pointed or ax-like weapons **245 granted** yielded **268 cost** i.e., deprive me of. **empty** hungry **269 Tire** feed ravenously **271 fair** civilly, kindly

I.ii. Location: Sandal Castle (the Duke of York's castle) in Yorkshire.
1 give me leave permit me (to speak first)

4 brother (See I.i.14, note.) **13 to breathe** i.e., to enjoy a respite **22 moment** significance **26 depose** take an oath **30 Elysium** the classical abode after life of those loved of the gods **36 presently** immediately **39 privily** secretly

With whom the Kentishmen will willingly rise.
In them I trust, for they are soldiers,
Witty, courteous, liberal, full of spirit.
While you are thus employ'd, what resteth more 44
But that I seek occasion how to rise,
And yet the King not privy to my drift, 46
Nor any of the house of Lancaster?

Enter a Messenger.

But, stay, what news? Why com'st thou in such
post? 48

MESSENGER
The Queen with all the northern earls and lords
Intend here to besiege you in your castle.
She is hard by with twenty thousand men,
And therefore fortify your hold, my lord. 52

YORK
Ay, with my sword. What, think'st thou that we
fear them?
Edward and Richard, you shall stay with me;
My brother Montague shall post to London.
Let noble Warwick, Cobham, and the rest,
Whom we have left protectors of the King,
With pow'rful policy strengthen themselves, 58
And trust not simple Henry nor his oaths.

MONTAGUE
Brother, I go. I'll win them, fear it not.
And thus most humbly I do take my leave.
Exit Montague.

Enter [Sir John] Mortimer and [Sir Hugh,] his Brother.

YORK
Sir John and Sir Hugh Mortimer, mine uncles,
You are come to Sandal in a happy hour.
The army of the Queen mean to besiege us.

SIR JOHN
She shall not need. We'll meet her in the field.

YORK
What, with five thousand men?

RICHARD
Ay, with five hundred, father, for a need. 67
A woman's general. What should we fear?
A march afar off.

EDWARD
I hear their drums. Let's set our men in order,
And issue forth and bid them battle straight. 70

YORK
Five men to twenty! Though the odds be great,
I doubt not, uncle, of our victory.
Many a battle have I won in France
When as the enemy hath been ten to one. 74
Why should I not now have the like success?
Alarum. Exeunt.

44 what resteth more what else remains **46 privy to** aware of **48 post** haste **52 hold** stronghold, castle **58 policy** stratagem, cunning **67 for a need** if necessary **70 straight** immediately **74 When as** when

[SCENE III]

[Alarums.] Enter Rutland and his Tutor.

RUTLAND
Ah, whither shall I fly to scape their hands?
Ah, tutor, look where bloody Clifford comes!

Enter Clifford [and Soldiers].

CLIFFORD
Chaplain, away! Thy priesthood saves thy life.
As for the brat of this accursed Duke, 4
Whose father slew my father, he shall die.

TUTOR
And I, my lord, will bear him company.

CLIFFORD
Soldiers, away with him!

TUTOR
Ah, Clifford, murder not this innocent child,
Lest thou be hated both of God and man!
Exit [dragged off by Soldiers].

CLIFFORD
How now, is he dead already? Or is it fear
That makes him close his eyes? I'll open them.

RUTLAND
So looks the pent-up lion o'er the wretch 12
That trembles under his devouring paws;
And so he walks, insulting o'er his prey, 14
And so he comes, to rend his limbs asunder.
Ah, gentle Clifford, kill me with thy sword
And not with such a cruel threat'ning look!
Sweet Clifford, hear me speak before I die!
I am too mean a subject for thy wrath. 19
Be thou reveng'd on men, and let me live. 20

CLIFFORD
In vain thou speak'st, poor boy. My father's blood
Hath stopp'd the passage where thy words should
enter.

RUTLAND
Then let my father's blood open it again.
He is a man, and, Clifford, cope with him.

CLIFFORD
Had I thy brethren here, their lives and thine
Were not revenge sufficient for me;
No, if I digg'd up thy forefathers' graves
And hung their rotten coffins up in chains,
It could not slake mine ire, nor ease my heart.
The sight of any of the house of York 30
Is as a fury to torment my soul;
And till I root out their accursed line
And leave not one alive, I live in hell.
Therefore— *[Lifting his hand.]*

RUTLAND
O, let me pray before I take my death!

I.iii. Location: Field of battle between Sandal Castle and Wakefield. The action follows continuously from the previous scene.
4 Duke i.e., Duke of York, who killed old Clifford in *2 Henry VI*, V.ii. **12 pent-up** caged, hence fierce and hungry **14 insulting** gloating, exulting **19 mean** lowly. (Rutland appeals to the popular notion that because the lion was a royal beast it would show compassion to women and children. See II.ii.11–12.)

To thee I pray. Sweet Clifford, pity me!

CLIFFORD
Such pity as my rapier's point affords.

RUTLAND
I never did thee harm. Why wilt thou slay me?

CLIFFORD
Thy father hath.

RUTLAND
But 'twas ere I was born.
Thou hast one son. For his sake pity me,
Lest in revenge thereof, sith God is just, 41
He be as miserably slain as I.
Ah, let me live in prison all my days,
And when I give occasion of offense,
Then let me die, for now thou hast no cause.

CLIFFORD
No cause?
Thy father slew my father; therefore, die.
[Stabs him.]

RUTLAND
Di faciant laudis summa sit ista tuae! *[Dies.]* 48

CLIFFORD
Plantagenet, I come, Plantagenet!
And this thy son's blood cleaving to my blade
Shall rust upon my weapon, till thy blood,
Congeal'd with this, do make me wipe off both.
Exit.
[Rutland's body is carried off.]

[SCENE IV]

Alarum. Enter Richard, Duke of York.

YORK
The army of the Queen hath got the field.
My uncles both are slain in rescuing me, 2
And all my followers to the eager foe
Turn back and fly, like ships before the wind 4
Or lambs pursu'd by hunger-starved wolves.
My sons—God knows what hath bechanced them;
But this I know, they have demean'd themselves 7
Like men born to renown by life or death.
Three times did Richard make a lane to me,
And thrice cried "Courage, father, fight it out!"
And full as oft came Edward to my side
With purple falchion, painted to the hilt 12
In blood of those that had encount'red him.
And when the hardiest warriors did retire,
Richard cried, "Charge, and give no foot of ground!"
And cried "A crown, or else a glorious tomb!
A scepter, or an earthly sepulcher!"
With this, we charg'd again, but, out, alas! 18
We bodg'd again, as I have seen a swan 19
With bootless labor swim against the tide 20
And spend her strength with overmatching waves. 21
A short alarum within.
Ah, hark! The fatal followers do pursue,
And I am faint and cannot fly their fury;
And, were I strong, I would not shun their fury.
The sands are numb'red that make up my life. 25
Here must I stay, and here my life must end.

Enter the Queen [Margaret], Clifford, Northumberland, the young Prince, and Soldiers.

Come, bloody Clifford, rough Northumberland,
I dare your quenchless fury to more rage.
I am your butt, and I abide your shot. 29

NORTHUMBERLAND
Yield to our mercy, proud Plantagenet.

CLIFFORD
Ay, to such mercy as his ruthless arm,
With downright payment, show'd unto my father.
Now Phaethon hath tumbled from his car, 33
And made an evening at the noontide prick. 34

YORK
My ashes, as the phoenix, may bring forth 35
A bird that will revenge upon you all;
And in that hope I throw mine eyes to heaven,
Scorning whate'er you can afflict me with.
Why come you not? What? Multitudes, and fear?

CLIFFORD
So cowards fight when they can fly no further;
So doves do peck the falcon's piercing talons;
So desperate thieves, all hopeless of their lives,
Breathe out invectives 'gainst the officers.

YORK
O Clifford, but bethink thee once again,
And in thy thought o'errun my former time; 45
And, if thou canst for blushing, view this face,
And bite thy tongue, that slanders him with cowardice
Whose frown hath made thee faint and fly ere this!

CLIFFORD
I will not bandy with thee word for word, 49
But buckler with thee blows, twice two for one. 50

QUEEN MARGARET
Hold, valiant Clifford! For a thousand causes
I would prolong awhile the traitor's life.
Wrath makes him deaf. Speak thou, Northumberland.

NORTHUMBERLAND
Hold, Clifford, do not honor him so much
To prick thy finger, though to wound his heart.
What valor were it, when a cur doth grin, 56
For one to thrust his hand between his teeth,
When he might spurn him with his foot away?

41 sith since **48 Di . . . tuae** The gods grant that this may be the height of thy glory. (Ovid, *Heroides,* II.66.)

I.iv. Location: The battle of Wakefield continues.
2 uncles i.e., Sir John and Sir Hugh Mortimer **4 Turn back** turn their backs **7 demean'd** conducted **12 falchion** curved sword **18 out** (An expression of reproach.)

19 bodg'd gave way, budged **20 bootless** fruitless **21 with** against **25 sands** (of the hourglass) **29 butt** target **33 Phaethon** son of the sun god, who begged his father to allow him to drive the chariot of the sun; he drove it so near the earth that Zeus destroyed him with a thunderbolt **34 noontide prick** exact point of noon on a sundial **35 phoenix** fabulous bird that was consumed through spontaneous combustion and was reborn from its own ashes **45 o'errun** review **49 bandy** exchange **50 buckler** join in close combat, grapple **56 grin** show its teeth

It is war's prize to take all vantages, 59
And ten to one is no impeach of valor. 60
[*They lay hands on York, who struggles.*]

CLIFFORD
Ay, ay, so strives the woodcock with the gin. 61

NORTHUMBERLAND
So doth the cony struggle in the net. 62

YORK
So triumph thieves upon their conquer'd booty;
So true men yield, with robbers so o'ermatch'd. 64

NORTHUMBERLAND
What would your Grace have done unto him now?

QUEEN MARGARET
Brave warriors, Clifford and Northumberland,
Come, make him stand upon this molehill here
That raught at mountains with outstretched arms, 68
Yet parted but the shadow with his hand. 69
What, was it you that would be England's king?
Was 't you that revel'd in our parliament, 71
And made a preachment of your high descent?
Where are your mess of sons to back you now, 73
The wanton Edward, and the lusty George?
And where's that valiant crook-back prodigy, 75
Dicky your boy, that with his grumbling voice
Was wont to cheer his dad in mutinies?
Or, with the rest, where is your darling Rutland?
Look, York! I stain'd this napkin with the blood 79
That valiant Clifford, with his rapier's point,
Made issue from the bosom of the boy;
And if thine eyes can water for his death,
I give thee this to dry thy cheeks withal.
[*Gives him the bloodstained cloth.*]
Alas, poor York, but that I hate thee deadly,
I should lament thy miserable state.
I prithee, grieve, to make me merry, York.
What, hath thy fiery heart so parch'd thine entrails
That not a tear can fall for Rutland's death?
Why art thou patient, man? Thou shouldst be mad;
And I, to make thee mad, do mock thee thus.
Stamp, rave, and fret, that I may sing and dance.
Thou wouldst be fee'd, I see, to make me sport. 92
York cannot speak, unless he wear a crown.
A crown for York! And, lords, bow low to him.
Hold you his hands, whilst I do set it on.
[*Putting a paper crown on his head.*]
Ay, marry, sir, now looks he like a king! 96
Ay, this is he that took King Henry's chair,
And this is he was his adopted heir.
But how is it that great Plantagenet
Is crown'd so soon, and broke his solemn oath?
As I bethink me, you should not be king
Till our King Henry had shook hands with death.
And will you pale your head in Henry's glory, 103
And rob his temples of the diadem,
Now in his life, against your holy oath?
O, 'tis a fault too too unpardonable!
Off with the crown, and, with the crown, his head;
And, whilst we breathe, take time to do him dead. 108

CLIFFORD
That is my office, for my father's sake.

QUEEN MARGARET
Nay, stay; let's hear the orisons he makes. 110

YORK
She-wolf of France, but worse than wolves of France,
Whose tongue more poisons than the adder's tooth!
How ill-beseeming is it in thy sex
To triumph, like an Amazonian trull, 114
Upon their woes whom fortune captivates!
But that thy face is, vizard-like, unchanging, 116
Made impudent with use of evil deeds,
I would assay, proud queen, to make thee blush. 118
To tell thee whence thou cam'st, of whom deriv'd,
Were shame enough to shame thee, wert thou not shameless.
Thy father bears the type of King of Naples, 121
Of both the Sicils and Jerusalem, 122
Yet not so wealthy as an English yeoman. 123
Hath that poor monarch taught thee to insult?
It needs not, nor it boots thee not, proud Queen, 125
Unless the adage must be verified,
That beggars mounted run their horse to death.
'Tis beauty that doth oft make women proud;
But, God he knows, thy share thereof is small.
'Tis virtue that doth make them most admir'd;
The contrary doth make thee wond'red at.
'Tis government that makes them seem divine; 132
The want thereof makes thee abominable.
Thou art as opposite to every good
As the Antipodes are unto us, 135
Or as the south to the septentrion. 136
O tiger's heart wrapt in a woman's hide!
How couldst thou drain the life-blood of the child,
To bid the father wipe his eyes withal,
And yet be seen to bear a woman's face?
Women are soft, mild, pitiful, and flexible; 141
Thou stern, obdurate, flinty, rough, remorseless.
Bid'st thou me rage? Why, now thou hast thy wish.
Wouldst have me weep? Why, now thou hast thy will.
For raging wind blows up incessant showers,
And, when the rage allays, the rain begins. [*Weeps.*] 146
These tears are my sweet Rutland's obsequies, 147
And every drop cries vengeance for his death
'Gainst thee, fell Clifford, and thee, false Frenchwoman. 149

NORTHUMBERLAND
Beshrew me, but his passion moves me so 150

59 prize reward, benefit **60 impeach** calling in question **61 woodcock** (A proverbially stupid bird.) **gin** engine, trap **62 cony** rabbit **64 true** honest **68 That raught** he that reached **69 but** only **71 revel'd** rioted **73 mess** group of four **75 prodigy** monster **79 napkin** handkerchief **92 fee'd** paid **96 marry** i.e., indeed. (Originally an oath by the Virgin Mary.) **103 pale** encircle

108 breathe rest **110 orisons** prayers **114 Amazonian** from the race of legendary female warriors. **trull** wench **116 But that** were it not that. **vizard-like** mask-like **118 assay** essay, attempt **121 type** title **122 both the Sicils** i.e., Sicily and Naples (known as the Kingdom of the Two Sicilies) **123 yeoman** landowner below rank of gentleman **125 needs not** is unnecessary. **boots** profits **132 government** self-government **135 Antipodes** people dwelling on the opposite side of the world **136 septentrion** the seven stars, i.e., the Big Dipper, representing the north **141 pitiful** capable of pity **146 allays** abates **147 obsequies** funeral observances **149 fell** cruel **150 Beshrew** curse

That hardly can I check my eyes from tears.

YORK

That face of his the hungry cannibals
Would not have touch'd, would not have stain'd with blood.
But you are more inhuman, more inexorable,
O, ten times more, than tigers of Hyrcania.
See, ruthless queen, a hapless father's tears!
This cloth thou dip'dst in blood of my sweet boy,
And I with tears do wash the blood away.
Keep thou the napkin, and go boast of this;
[Gives back the bloodstained cloth.]
And if thou tell'st the heavy story right,
Upon my soul, the hearers will shed tears.
Yea even my foes will shed fast-falling tears
And say, "Alas, it was a piteous deed!"
There, take the crown, and, with the crown, my curse; *[Removes his paper crown.]*
And in thy need such comfort come to thee
As now I reap at thy too cruel hand!
Hard-hearted Clifford, take me from the world.
My soul to heaven, my blood upon your heads!

NORTHUMBERLAND

Had he been slaughterman to all my kin,
I should not for my life but weep with him,
To see how inly sorrow gripes his soul.

QUEEN MARGARET

What, weeping-ripe, my Lord Northumberland?
Think but upon the wrong he did us all,
And that will quickly dry thy melting tears.

CLIFFORD

Here's for my oath, here's for my father's death.
[Stabbing him.]

QUEEN MARGARET

And here's to right our gentlehearted king.
[Stabbing him.]

YORK

Open Thy gate of mercy, gracious God!
My soul flies through these wounds to seek out Thee. *[Dies.]*

QUEEN MARGARET

Off with his head, and set it on York gates,
So York may overlook the town of York.
Flourish. Exeunt [with the body].

[ACT II • SCENE I]

A march. Enter Edward, Richard, and their power.

EDWARD

I wonder how our princely father scap'd,
Or whether he be scap'd away or no
From Clifford's and Northumberland's pursuit.
Had he been ta'en, we should have heard the news;
Had he been slain, we should have heard the news;
Or had he scap'd, methinks we should have heard
The happy tidings of his good escape.
How fares my brother? Why is he so sad?

RICHARD

I cannot joy, until I be resolv'd
Where our right valiant father is become.
I saw him in the battle range about,
And watch'd him how he singled Clifford forth.
Methought he bore him in the thickest troop
As doth a lion in a herd of neat,
Or as a bear, encompass'd round with dogs,
Who having pinch'd a few and made them cry,
The rest stand all aloof, and bark at him.
So far'd our father with his enemies,
So fled his enemies my warlike father.
Methinks 'tis prize enough to be his son.
See how the morning opes her golden gates,
And takes her farewell of the glorious sun!
How well resembles it the prime of youth,
Trimm'd like a younker prancing to his love!

EDWARD

Dazzle mine eyes, or do I see three suns?

RICHARD

Three glorious suns, each one a perfect sun,
Not separated with the racking clouds,
But sever'd in a pale clear-shining sky.
See, see! They join, embrace, and seem to kiss,
As if they vow'd some league inviolable.
Now are they but one lamp, one light, one sun.
In this the heaven figures some event.

EDWARD

'Tis wondrous strange, the like yet never heard of.
I think it cites us, brother, to the field,
That we, the sons of brave Plantagenet,
Each one already blazing by our meeds,
Should notwithstanding join our lights together
And overshine the earth as this the world.
Whate'er it bodes, henceforward will I bear
Upon my target three fair-shining suns.

RICHARD

Nay, bear three daughters. By your leave I speak it,
You love the breeder better than the male.

Enter one [a Messenger] blowing [a horn].

But what art thou, whose heavy looks foretell
Some dreadful story hanging on thy tongue?

MESSENGER

Ah, one that was a woeful looker-on
When as the noble Duke of York was slain,
Your princely father and my loving lord!

EDWARD

O, speak no more, for I have heard too much.

151 check restrain **155 Hyrcania** region of the ancient Persian empire, reputed to abound in wild beasts. (See *Aeneid*, IV.366–367.) **171 inly** inward

II.i. Location: A plain near Mortimer's Cross in Herefordshire, near the Welsh border, several days after the battle of Wakefield.

9 resolv'd informed **10 Where . . . become** i.e., what is become of him **14 neat** cattle **16 pinch'd** bit **19 fled his enemies** his enemies fled from **22 farewell** (The dawn is pictured as remaining behind while the sun ascends the sky.) **24 Trimm'd** dressed up. **younker** young man **25 three suns** (According to the chronicles, it was because Edward saw three suns as a favorable omen before the battle of Mortimer's Cross, in which he triumphed, that he chose the bright sun as his badge.) **27 racking** driving, scudding **32 figures** prefigures **34 cites** incites, impels **36 meeds** worth, deserts **38 this** i.e., this phenomenon **40 target** shield **41 daughters** i.e., instead of sons or "suns" **42 breeder** female. (Richard jokes about Edward's weakness for women, to be demonstrated in III.ii and following.) **42 s.d. blowing a horn** (Post-riders thus announced themselves.) **46 When as** when

RICHARD
Say how he died, for I will hear it all.

MESSENGER
Environed he was with many foes,
And stood against them, as the hope of Troy
Against the Greeks that would have ent'red Troy.
But Hercules himself must yield to odds;
And many strokes, though with a little axe,
Hews down and fells the hardest-timber'd oak.
By many hands your father was subdu'd,
But only slaught'red by the ireful arm
Of unrelenting Clifford and the Queen,
Who crown'd the gracious Duke in high despite,
Laugh'd in his face; and when with grief he wept,
The ruthless Queen gave him to dry his cheeks
A napkin steeped in the harmless blood
Of sweet young Rutland, by rough Clifford slain.
And after many scorns, many foul taunts,
They took his head, and on the gates of York
They set the same; and there it doth remain,
The saddest spectacle that e'er I view'd.

EDWARD
Sweet Duke of York, our prop to lean upon,
Now thou art gone, we have no staff, no stay.
O Clifford, boist'rous Clifford! Thou hast slain
The flow'r of Europe for his chivalry;
And treacherously hast thou vanquish'd him,
For hand to hand he would have vanquish'd thee.
Now my soul's palace is become a prison.
Ah, would she break from hence, that this my body
Might in the ground be closed up in rest!
For never henceforth shall I joy again,
Never, O never, shall I see more joy!

RICHARD
I cannot weep, for all my body's moisture
Scarce serves to quench my furnace-burning heart;
Nor can my tongue unload my heart's great burden,
For selfsame wind that I should speak withal
Is kindling coals that fires all my breast
And burns me up with flames that tears would quench.
To weep is to make less the depth of grief.
Tears then for babes; blows and revenge for me!
Richard, I bear thy name. I'll venge thy death,
Or die renowned by attempting it.

EDWARD
His name that valiant Duke hath left with thee;
His dukedom and his chair with me is left.

RICHARD
Nay, if thou be that princely eagle's bird,
Show thy descent by gazing 'gainst the sun;
For chair and dukedom, throne and kingdom say
Either that is thine, or else thou wert not his.

March. Enter Warwick, Marquess Montague, and their army.

WARWICK
How now, fair lords? What fare? What news abroad?

RICHARD
Great Lord of Warwick, if we should recount
Our baleful news, and at each word's deliverance
Stab poniards in our flesh till all were told,
The words would add more anguish than the wounds.
O valiant lord, the Duke of York is slain!

EDWARD
O Warwick, Warwick! That Plantagenet,
Which held thee dearly as his soul's redemption,
Is by the stern Lord Clifford done to death.

WARWICK
Ten days ago I drown'd these news in tears;
And now, to add more measure to your woes,
I come to tell you things sith then befall'n.
After the bloody fray at Wakefield fought,
Where your brave father breath'd his latest gasp,
Tidings, as swiftly as the posts could run,
Were brought me of your loss and his depart.
I, then in London, keeper of the King,
Muster'd my soldiers, gathered flocks of friends,
[And very well appointed, as I thought,]
March'd toward Saint Albans to intercept the Queen,
Bearing the King in my behalf along;
For by my scouts I was advertised
That she was coming with a full intent
To dash our late decree in parliament
Touching King Henry's oath and your succession.
Short tale to make, we at Saint Albans met,
Our battles join'd, and both sides fiercely fought.
But whether 'twas the coldness of the King,
Who look'd full gently on his warlike queen,
That robb'd my soldiers of their heated spleen,
Or whether 'twas report of her success,
Or more than common fear of Clifford's rigor,
Who thunders to his captives blood and death,
I cannot judge; but, to conclude with truth,
Their weapons like to lightning came and went;
Our soldiers', like the night-owl's lazy flight,
Or like an idle thresher with a flail,
Fell gently down, as if they struck their friends.
I cheer'd them up with justice of our cause,
With promise of high pay and great rewards,
But all in vain. They had no heart to fight,
And we in them no hope to win the day,
So that we fled: the King unto the Queen;
Lord George your brother, Norfolk and myself,
In haste, post-haste, are come to join with you;
For in the marches here we heard you were,
Making another head to fight again.

EDWARD
Where is the Duke of Norfolk, gentle Warwick?

50 Environed surrounded **51 hope of Troy** i.e., Hector **70 boist'rous** savage **74 soul's palace** i.e., body **78 see more joy** see joy any more **90 his chair** i.e., the throne **91 bird** i.e., offspring **92 gazing . . . sun** (According to Pliny and other writers, eagles could gaze unblinkingly at the sun and would test their young by forcing them to do so.) **94 that** i.e., the throne, symbolized by the sun. **his** i.e., Plantagenet's son

98 poniards daggers **106 sith** since **108 latest** last **110 depart** departure, i.e., death **113 appointed** equipped **115 in my behalf** for my advantage **116 advertised** informed **118 dash** overthrow **121 battles** armies **124 heated spleen** i.e., courage roused to a high pitch **131 flail** threshing tool **138 Lord George** i.e., George, later Duke of Clarence, brother to Edward and Richard **140 marches** borders (of Wales) **141 Making another head** raising another armed force

And when came George from Burgundy to England?

WARWICK

Some six miles off the Duke is with the soldiers;
And for your brother, he was lately sent
From your kind aunt, Duchess of Burgundy,
With aid of soldiers to this needful war.

RICHARD

'Twas odds, belike, when valiant Warwick fled.
Oft have I heard his praises in pursuit,
But ne'er till now his scandal of retire.

WARWICK

Nor now my scandal, Richard, dost thou hear;
For thou shalt know this strong right hand of mine
Can pluck the diadem from faint Henry's head,
And wring the aweful scepter from his fist,
Were he as famous and as bold in war
As he is fam'd for mildness, peace, and prayer.

RICHARD

I know it well, Lord Warwick. Blame me not.
'Tis love I bear thy glories make me speak.
But in this troublous time what's to be done?
Shall we go throw away our coats of steel,
And wrap our bodies in black mourning gowns,
Numb'ring our Ave-Maries with our beads?
Or shall we on the helmets of our foes
Tell our devotion with revengeful arms?
If for the last, say ay, and to it, lords.

WARWICK

Why, therefore Warwick came to seek you out,
And therefore comes my brother Montague.
Attend me, lords. The proud insulting Queen,
With Clifford and the haught Northumberland,
And of their feather many moe proud birds,
Have wrought the easy-melting King like wax.
He swore consent to your succession,
His oath enrolled in the parliament,
And now to London all the crew are gone
To frustrate both his oath and what beside
May make against the house of Lancaster.
Their power, I think, is thirty thousand strong.
Now, if the help of Norfolk and myself,
With all the friends that thou, brave Earl of March,
Amongst the loving Welshmen canst procure,
Will but amount to five and twenty thousand,
Why, via! To London will we march,
And once again bestride our foaming steeds,
And once again cry "Charge!" upon our foes,
But never once again turn back and fly.

RICHARD

Ay, now methinks I hear great Warwick speak.
Ne'er may he live to see a sunshine day
That cries "Retire!" if Warwick bid him stay.

EDWARD

Lord Warwick, on thy shoulder will I lean;
And when thou fail'st—as God forbid the hour!—
Must Edward fall, which peril heaven forfend!

WARWICK

No longer Earl of March, but Duke of York;
The next degree is England's royal throne.
For King of England shalt thou be proclaim'd
In every borough as we pass along;
And he that throws not up his cap for joy
Shall for the fault make forfeit of his head.
King Edward, valiant Richard, Montague,
Stay we no longer, dreaming of renown,
But sound the trumpets, and about our task.

RICHARD

Then, Clifford, were thy heart as hard as steel,
As thou hast shown it flinty by thy deeds,
I come to pierce it, or to give thee mine.

EDWARD

Then strike up drums. God and Saint George for us!

Enter a Messenger.

WARWICK

How now? What news?

MESSENGER

The Duke of Norfolk sends you word by me
The Queen is coming with a puissant host;
And craves your company for speedy counsel.

WARWICK

Why then it sorts, brave warriors. Let's away.

Exeunt omnes.

[SCENE II]

Flourish. Enter the King [Henry], the Queen [Margaret], Clifford, Northumberland, and young Prince, with drum and trumpets. [York's head is set above the gates.]

QUEEN MARGARET

Welcome, my lord, to this brave town of York.
Yonder's the head of that arch-enemy
That sought to be encompass'd with your crown.
Doth not the object cheer your heart, my lord?

KING HENRY

Ay, as the rocks cheer them that fear their wrack.
To see this sight, it irks my very soul.
Withhold revenge, dear God! 'Tis not my fault,
Nor wittingly have I infring'd my vow.

CLIFFORD

My gracious liege, this too much lenity
And harmful pity must be laid aside.
To whom do lions cast their gentle looks?
Not to the beast that would usurp their den.
Whose hand is that the forest bear doth lick?
Not his that spoils her young before her face.

146 Duchess of Burgundy (A granddaughter of John of Gaunt and distant relative of Richard of York, to whom, according to the chroniclers, both George and Richard were sent for protection after York's execution.) **148 'Twas odds, belike** i.e., no doubt the odds were very heavy **149 in pursuit** i.e., for pursuing the enemy **150 his . . . retire** i.e., condemnation of him for retreating **154 aweful** awe-inspiring **158 make** which makes **162 beads** rosary beads (used in reciting *Ave-Maries,* or Hail Marys) **164 Tell our devotion** (1) count off our prayers (2) proclaim our love. (Said ironically.) **169 haught** haughty **170 moe** more **171 wrought** worked on, manipulated **176 make** be effective **179 Earl of March** i.e., Edward, who at his father's death inherited this with other titles **182 via** forward **187 he** i.e., anyone

191 forfend forbid **193 degree** step, rank **207 puissant** powerful **209 sorts** is fitting

II.ii. Location: Before York.
1 brave fine **5 wrack** shipwreck, destruction **14 spoils** destroys

Who scapes the lurking serpent's mortal sting?
Not he that sets his foot upon her back.
The smallest worm will turn, being trodden on,
And doves will peck in safeguard of their brood.
Ambitious York did level at thy crown, 19
Thou smiling while he knit his angry brows.
He, but a duke, would have his son a king,
And raise his issue, like a loving sire; 22
Thou, being a king, bless'd with a goodly son,
Didst yield consent to disinherit him,
Which argued thee a most unloving father.
Unreasonable creatures feed their young; 26
And though man's face be fearful to their eyes,
Yet, in protection of their tender ones,
Who hath not seen them, even with those wings
Which sometime they have us'd with fearful flight,
Make war with him that climb'd unto their nest,
Offering their own lives in their young's defense?
For shame, my liege, make them your precedent!
Were it not pity that this goodly boy
Should lose his birthright by his father's fault,
And long hereafter say unto his child,
"What my great-grandfather and grandsire got,
My careless father fondly gave away"? 38
Ah, what a shame were this! Look on the boy,
And let his manly face, which promiseth
Successful fortune, steel thy melting heart
To hold thine own and leave thine own with him.

KING HENRY
Full well hath Clifford play'd the orator,
Inferring arguments of mighty force. 44
But, Clifford, tell me, didst thou never hear
That things ill got had ever bad success? 46
And happy always was it for that son 47
Whose father for his hoarding went to hell? 48
I'll leave my son my virtuous deeds behind;
And would my father had left me no more!
For all the rest is held at such a rate 51
As brings a thousandfold more care to keep
Than in possession any jot of pleasure.
Ah, cousin York, would thy best friends did know
How it doth grieve me that thy head is here!

QUEEN MARGARET
My lord, cheer up your spirits. Our foes are nigh,
And this soft courage makes your followers faint. 57
You promis'd knighthood to our forward son.
Unsheathe your sword, and dub him presently.
Edward, kneel down. [*The Prince kneels.*]

KING HENRY
Edward Plantagenet, arise a knight,
And learn this lesson: Draw thy sword in right.

PRINCE [*Rising*]
My gracious father, by your kingly leave,
I'll draw it as apparent to the crown, 64
And in that quarrel use it to the death.

CLIFFORD
Why, that is spoken like a toward prince. 66

Enter a Messenger.

MESSENGER
Royal commanders, be in readiness,
For with a band of thirty thousand men
Comes Warwick, backing of the Duke of York, 69
And in the towns, as they do march along,
Proclaims him king, and many fly to him.
Darraign your battle, for they are at hand. 72

CLIFFORD
I would your Highness would depart the field.
The Queen hath best success when you are absent.

QUEEN MARGARET
Ay, good my lord, and leave us to our fortune.

KING HENRY
Why, that's my fortune too. Therefore I'll stay.

NORTHUMBERLAND
Be it with resolution then to fight.

PRINCE
My royal father, cheer these noble lords
And hearten those that fight in your defense.
Unsheathe your sword, good father; cry "Saint George!" 80

March. Enter Edward, Warwick, Richard, [George of] Clarence, Norfolk, Montague, and Soldiers.

EDWARD
Now, perjur'd Henry, wilt thou kneel for grace, 81
And set thy diadem upon my head,
Or bide the mortal fortune of the field? 83

QUEEN MARGARET
Go, rate thy minions, proud insulting boy! 84
Becomes it thee to be thus bold in terms 85
Before thy sovereign and thy lawful king?

EDWARD
I am his king, and he should bow his knee.
I was adopted heir by his consent.
Since when, his oath is broke; for, as I hear,
You, that are king, though he do wear the crown,
Have caus'd him, by new act of parliament,
To blot out me, and put his own son in.

CLIFFORD
And reason too.
Who should succeed the father but the son?

RICHARD
Are you there, butcher? O, I cannot speak! 95

CLIFFORD
Ay, crook-back, here I stand to answer thee,
Or any he the proudest of thy sort. 97

RICHARD
'Twas you that kill'd young Rutland, was it not?

CLIFFORD
Ay, and old York, and yet not satisfied.

RICHARD
For God's sake, lords, give signal to the fight.

19 level aim **22 raise** raise in dignity **26 Unreasonable** not endowed with reason **38 fondly** foolishly **44 Inferring** alleging, adducing **46 success** outcome **47–48 And . . . hell** i.e., the son may be happy to inherit wealth, but the father who obtained that wealth by hoarding and miserly grasping will go to hell **51 rate** cost **57 faint** faint-hearted **64 apparent** heir **66 toward** ready, bold

69 Duke of York i.e., Edward **72 Darraign your battle** set your army in battle array **80 s.d. George of Clarence** (Actually, George is not made Duke of Clarence until II.vi.104.) **81 grace** mercy, pardon **83 bide** wait for. **mortal** fatal **84 rate thy minions** chide your followers or favorites **85 terms** language **95 butcher** (Clifford was nicknamed "the butcher" for his cruelty.) **97 any he** any man. **sort** gang

WARWICK
What say'st thou, Henry, wilt thou yield the crown?

QUEEN MARGARET
Why, how now, long-tongu'd Warwick, dare you
speak?
When you and I met at Saint Albans last,
Your legs did better service than your hands.

WARWICK
Then 'twas my turn to fly, and now 'tis thine.

CLIFFORD
You said so much before, and yet you fled.

WARWICK
'Twas not your valor, Clifford, drove me thence.

NORTHUMBERLAND
No, nor your manhood that durst make you stay.

RICHARD
Northumberland, I hold thee reverently.
Break off the parley, for scarce I can refrain 110
The execution of my big-swoll'n heart 111
Upon that Clifford, that cruel child-killer.

CLIFFORD
I slew thy father, call'st thou him a child?

RICHARD
Ay, like a dastard and a treacherous coward,
As thou didst kill our tender brother Rutland;
But ere sunset I'll make thee curse the deed.

KING HENRY
Have done with words, my lords, and hear me
speak.

QUEEN MARGARET
Defy them then, or else hold close thy lips.

KING HENRY
I prithee, give no limits to my tongue.
I am a king, and privileg'd to speak.

CLIFFORD
My liege, the wound that bred this meeting here
Cannot be cur'd by words. Therefore be still.

RICHARD
Then, executioner, unsheathe thy sword.
By Him that made us all, I am resolv'd 124
That Clifford's manhood lies upon his tongue. 125

EDWARD
Say, Henry, shall I have my right, or no?
A thousand men have broke their fasts today 127
That ne'er shall dine unless thou yield the crown.

WARWICK
If thou deny, their blood upon thy head, 129
For York in justice puts his armor on.

PRINCE
If that be right which Warwick says is right,
There is no wrong, but every thing is right.

RICHARD
Whoever got thee, there thy mother stands; 133
For, well I wot, thou hast thy mother's tongue. 134

QUEEN MARGARET
But thou art neither like thy sire nor dam,
But like a foul misshapen stigmatic, 136
Mark'd by the destinies to be avoided,
As venom toads, or lizards' dreadful stings. 138

RICHARD
Iron of Naples hid with English gilt, 139
Whose father bears the title of a king—
As if a channel should be call'd the sea— 141
Sham'st thou not, knowing whence thou art
extraught, 142
To let thy tongue detect thy base-born heart? 143

EDWARD
A wisp of straw were worth a thousand crowns, 144
To make this shameless callet know herself. 145
Helen of Greece was fairer far than thou,
Although thy husband may be Menelaus; 147
And ne'er was Agamemnon's brother wrong'd 148
By that false woman, as this king by thee.
His father revel'd in the heart of France, 150
And tam'd the King, and made the Dauphin stoop;
And had he match'd according to his state, 152
He might have kept that glory to this day.
But when he took a beggar to his bed,
And grac'd thy poor sire with his bridal day, 155
Even then that sunshine brew'd a show'r for him
That wash'd his father's fortunes forth of France 157
And heap'd sedition on his crown at home.
For what hath broach'd this tumult but thy pride? 159
Hadst thou been meek, our title still had slept, 160
And we, in pity of the gentle King,
Had slipp'd our claim until another age. 162

GEORGE
But when we saw our sunshine made thy spring, 163
And that thy summer bred us no increase, 164
We set the axe to thy usurping root;
And though the edge hath something hit ourselves, 166
Yet know thou, since we have begun to strike,
We'll never leave till we have hewn thee down
Or bath'd thy growing with our heated bloods.

EDWARD
And, in this resolution, I defy thee,
Not willing any longer conference,
Since thou deniedst the gentle King to speak.
Sound trumpets! Let our bloody colors wave!
And either victory, or else a grave.

QUEEN MARGARET
Stay, Edward.

EDWARD
No, wrangling woman, we'll no longer stay.
These words will cost ten thousand lives this day.
Exeunt omnes.

110 refrain give up **111 execution** i.e., giving practical effect to my passion **124 resolv'd** convinced **125 lies . . . tongue** i.e., consists only in words **127 broke their fasts** i.e., had breakfast **129 deny** refuse **133 got** begot, sired **134 wot** know

136 stigmatic one branded with the mark of his crime or deformity. (See *2 Henry VI*, V.i.215.) **138 venom** venomous **139 Iron . . . gilt** i.e., you cheap product of Naples (being daughter of the titular King of Naples), being gilded over by an English marriage **141 As . . . sea** i.e., comparing your father to a king is like comparing a gutter *(channel)* to the sea **142 extraught** descended, extracted **143 detect** expose **144 wisp of straw** (A traditional way of marking or branding a scolding woman.) **145 callet** lewd woman **147 Menelaus** husband of Helen of Greece, whose abduction led to the Trojan War. (By implication, King Henry is the cuckolded husband just as Menelaus was.) **148 Agamemnon** brother of Menelaus and leader of the Greeks in the Trojan War **150 His father** i.e., Henry V **152 had . . . state** i.e., if Henry VI had married someone equal to him in social position **155 grac'd** honored. **thy poor sire** i.e., Reignier, King of Naples **157 of** out of **159 broach'd** set flowing, started **160 title** claim to the throne **162 slipp'd** postponed **163 But . . . spring** i.e., but when we saw you reaping all the benefit of what should be ours **164 increase** harvest **166 something** somewhat

[SCENE III]

Alarum. Excursions. Enter Warwick.

WARWICK
Forspent with toil, as runners with a race,
I lay me down a little while to breathe;
For strokes receiv'd, and many blows repaid,
Have robb'd my strong-knit sinews of their strength,
And spite of spite needs must I rest awhile.

Enter Edward, running.

EDWARD
Smile, gentle heaven, or strike, ungentle death!
For this world frowns, and Edward's sun is clouded.
WARWICK
How now, my lord, what hap? What hope of good?

Enter [George of] Clarence.

GEORGE
Our hap is loss, our hope but sad despair,
Our ranks are broke, and ruin follows us.
What counsel give you? Whither shall we fly?
EDWARD
Bootless is flight. They follow us with wings,
And weak we are and cannot shun pursuit.

Enter Richard.

RICHARD
Ah, Warwick, why hast thou withdrawn thyself?
Thy brother's blood the thirsty earth hath drunk,
Broach'd with the steely point of Clifford's lance;
And in the very pangs of death he cried,
Like to a dismal clangor heard from far,
"Warwick, revenge! Brother, revenge my death!"
So, underneath the belly of their steeds,
That stain'd their fetlocks in his smoking blood,
The noble gentleman gave up the ghost.
WARWICK
Then let the earth be drunken with our blood!
I'll kill my horse, because I will not fly.
Why stand we like soft-hearted women here,
Wailing our losses, whiles the foe doth rage,
And look upon, as if the tragedy
Were play'd in jest by counterfeiting actors?
Here on my knee I vow to God above [*Kneels.*]
I'll never pause again, never stand still,
Till either death hath clos'd these eyes of mine
Or fortune given me measure of revenge.
EDWARD
O Warwick, I do bend my knee with thine,
And in this vow do chain my soul to thine!
[*Kneels.*]
And, ere my knee rise from the earth's cold face,
I throw my hands, mine eyes, my heart to thee,
Thou setter up and plucker down of kings,
Beseeching thee, if with thy will it stands
That to my foes this body must be prey,
Yet that thy brazen gates of heaven may ope
And give sweet passage to my sinful soul!
[*They rise.*]
Now, lords, take leave until we meet again,
Where'er it be, in heaven or in earth.
RICHARD
Brother, give me thy hand; and, gentle Warwick,
[*They embrace.*]
Let me embrace thee in my weary arms.
I, that did never weep, now melt with woe
That winter should cut off our springtime so.
WARWICK
Away, away! Once more, sweet lords, farewell.
GEORGE
Yet let us all together to our troops,
And give them leave to fly that will not stay,
And call them pillars that will stand to us;
And, if we thrive, promise them such rewards
As victors wear at the Olympian games.
This may plant courage in their quailing breasts;
For yet is hope of life and victory.
Forslow no longer, make we hence amain. *Exeunt.*

[SCENE IV]

Excursions. Enter Richard and Clifford [meeting].

RICHARD
Now, Clifford, I have singled thee alone.
Suppose this arm is for the Duke of York,
And this for Rutland—both bound to revenge,
Wert thou environ'd with a brazen wall.
CLIFFORD
Now, Richard, I am with thee here alone.
This is the hand that stabb'd thy father York,
And this the hand that slew thy brother Rutland,
And here's the heart that triumphs in their death
And cheers these hands that slew thy sire and brother
To execute the like upon thyself.
And so, have at thee!
They fight. Warwick comes; Clifford flies.
RICHARD
Nay, Warwick, single out some other chase,
For I myself will hunt this wolf to death.
Exeunt.

II.iii. Location: The field of battle before the gates of York, immediately following the preceding scene. (Historically, the field of battle is between Towton and Saxton in Yorkshire.)
1 Forspent exhausted **2 breathe** rest **5 spite of spite** i.e., come what may **12 Bootless** useless **15 Thy brother's blood** (Warwick's half-brother, the Bastard of Salisbury, not among the *Dramatis Personae* of this play, was killed at Ferrybridge shortly before the battle of Towton.) **16 Broach'd** set flowing **27 upon** on

36 thee i.e., God **56 Forslow** delay

II.iv. Location: Scene continues at the battlefield.
4 environ'd surrounded **12 chase** prey

[SCENE V]

Alarum. Enter King Henry alone.

KING HENRY
This battle fares like to the morning's war,
When dying clouds contend with growing light,
What time the shepherd, blowing of his nails, 3
Can neither call it perfect day nor night.
Now sways it this way, like a mighty sea
Forc'd by the tide to combat with the wind;
Now sways it that way, like the selfsame sea
Forc'd to retire by fury of the wind.
Sometime the flood prevails, and then the wind;
Now one the better, then another best;
Both tugging to be victors, breast to breast,
Yet neither conqueror nor conquered;
So is the equal poise of this fell war. 13
Here on this molehill will I sit me down. [*Sits.*]
To whom God will, there be the victory!
For Margaret my queen, and Clifford too,
Have chid me from the battle, swearing both
They prosper best of all when I am thence.
Would I were dead, if God's good will were so!
For what is in this world but grief and woe?
O God! Methinks it were a happy life
To be no better than a homely swain,
To sit upon a hill, as I do now,
To carve out dials quaintly, point by point, 24
Thereby to see the minutes how they run:
How many makes the hour full complete,
How many hours brings about the day,
How many days will finish up the year,
How many years a mortal man may live.
When this is known, then to divide the times:
So many hours must I tend my flock,
So many hours must I take my rest,
So many hours must I contemplate,
So many hours must I sport myself,
So many days my ewes have been with young,
So many weeks ere the poor fools will ean, 36
So many years ere I shall shear the fleece.
So minutes, hours, days, months, and years,
Pass'd over to the end they were created, 39
Would bring white hairs unto a quiet grave.
Ah, what a life were this, how sweet, how lovely!
Gives not the hawthorn bush a sweeter shade
To shepherds looking on their silly sheep 43
Than doth a rich embroider'd canopy
To kings that fear their subjects' treachery?
O, yes, it doth, a thousandfold it doth.
And to conclude, the shepherd's homely curds,
His cold thin drink out of his leather bottle,
His wonted sleep under a fresh tree's shade, 49
All which secure and sweetly he enjoys,
Is far beyond a prince's delicates— 51
His viands sparkling in a golden cup,
His body couched in a curious bed— 53
When care, mistrust, and treason waits on him.

Alarum. Enter a Son that hath killed his father, at one door [bearing in the dead body].

SON
Ill blows the wind that profits nobody.
This man, whom hand to hand I slew in fight,
May be possessed with some store of crowns; 57
And I, that haply take them from him now, 58
May yet ere night yield both my life and them
To some man else, as this dead man doth me.
Who's this? O God! It is my father's face,
Whom in this conflict I unwares have kill'd.
O heavy times, begetting such events!
From London by the King was I press'd forth; 64
My father, being the Earl of Warwick's man,
Came on the part of York, press'd by his master; 66
And I, who at his hands receiv'd my life,
Have by my hands of life bereaved him.
Pardon me, God, I knew not what I did!
And pardon, father, for I knew not thee!
My tears shall wipe away these bloody marks;
And no more words till they have flow'd their fill.
[*Weeps.*]

KING HENRY
O piteous spectacle! O bloody times!
Whiles lions war and battle for their dens,
Poor harmless lambs abide their enmity. 75
Weep, wretched man, I'll aid thee tear for tear;
And let our hearts and eyes, like civil war,
Be blind with tears, and break o'ercharg'd with
grief. 78

Enter at another door, a Father that hath killed his son, bearing of his son.

FATHER
Thou that so stoutly hast resisted me,
Give me thy gold, if thou hast any gold;
For I have bought it with an hundred blows.
But let me see: is this our foeman's face?
Ah, no, no, no, it is mine only son!
Ah, boy, if any life be left in thee,
Throw up thine eye! See, see what show'rs arise,
Blown with the windy tempest of my heart,
Upon thy wounds, that kills mine eye and heart!
O, pity, God, this miserable age! [*Weeps.*]
What stratagems, how fell, how butcherly, 89
Erroneous, mutinous, and unnatural, 90
This deadly quarrel daily doth beget!
O boy, thy father gave thee life too soon,
And hath bereft thee of thy life too late! 93

II.v. Location: The battlefield, as before.
3 What time when. **of** on (to warm them) **13 poise** balance. **fell** cruel **24 dials** sundials. **quaintly** artfully, intricately **36 ean** bring forth (lambs) **39 end they** end for which they **43 silly** innocent, helpless **49 wonted** accustomed

51 delicates luxuries **53 curious** skillfully and daintily made **57 crowns** i.e., coins, money **58 haply** by chance **64 press'd forth** impressed into military service **66 part** party, side **75 abide** endure, pay for **78 o'ercharg'd** overfilled **89 stratagems** deeds of violence. **fell** cruel **90 Erroneous** criminal **93 late** lately

KING HENRY
Woe above woe, grief more than common grief!
O that my death would stay these ruthful deeds!
O, pity, pity, gentle heaven, pity!
The red rose and the white are on his face,
The fatal colors of our striving houses.
The one his purple blood right well resembles;
The other his pale cheeks, methinks, presenteth.
Wither one rose, and let the other flourish;
If you contend, a thousand lives must wither.

SON
How will my mother for a father's death
Take on with me and ne'er be satisfied!

FATHER
How will my wife for slaughter of my son
Shed seas of tears and ne'er be satisfied!

KING HENRY
How will the country for these woeful chances
Misthink the King and not be satisfied!

SON
Was ever son so ru'd a father's death?

FATHER
Was ever father so bemoan'd his son?

KING HENRY
Was ever king so griev'd for subjects' woe?
Much is your sorrow; mine ten times so much.

SON
I'll bear thee hence, where I may weep my fill.
[Exit with the body.]

FATHER
These arms of mine shall be thy winding sheet;
My heart, sweet boy, shall be thy sepulcher,
For from my heart thine image ne'er shall go.
My sighing breast shall be thy funeral bell;
And so obsequious will thy father be,
E'en for the loss of thee, having no more,
As Priam was for all his valiant sons.
I'll bear thee hence, and let them fight that will,
For I have murdered where I should not kill.
Exit [with the body].

KING HENRY
Sad-hearted men, much overgone with care,
Here sits a king more woeful than you are.

Alarums. Excursions. Enter the Queen [Margaret], the Prince, and Exeter.

PRINCE
Fly, father, fly! For all your friends are fled,
And Warwick rages like a chafed bull.
Away! For death doth hold us in pursuit.

QUEEN MARGARET
Mount you, my lord; towards Berwick post amain.
Edward and Richard, like a brace of greyhounds
Having the fearful flying hare in sight,
With fiery eyes sparkling for very wrath,
And bloody steel grasp'd in their ireful hands,
Are at our backs; and therefore hence amain.

EXETER
Away! For vengeance comes along with them.
Nay, stay not to expostulate, make speed!
Or else come after. I'll away before.

KING HENRY
Nay, take me with thee, good sweet Exeter.
Not that I fear to stay, but love to go
Whither the Queen intends. Forward; away! *Exeunt.*

[SCENE VI]

A loud alarum. Enter Clifford, wounded, [with an arrow in his neck].

CLIFFORD
Here burns my candle out; ay, here it dies,
Which, whiles it lasted, gave King Henry light.
O Lancaster, I fear thy overthrow
More than my body's parting with my soul!
My love and fear glu'd many friends to thee;
And, now I fall, thy tough commixture melts,
Impairing Henry, strength'ning misproud York.
[The common people swarm like summer flies;]
And whither fly the gnats but to the sun?
And who shines now but Henry's enemies?
O Phoebus, hadst thou never given consent
That Phaethon should check thy fiery steeds,
Thy burning car never had scorch'd the earth!
And, Henry, hadst thou sway'd as kings should do,
Or as thy father and his father did,
Giving no ground unto the house of York,
They never then had sprung like summer flies;
I and ten thousand in this luckless realm
Had left no mourning widows for our death,
And thou this day hadst kept thy chair in peace.
For what doth cherish weeds but gentle air?
And what makes robbers bold but too much lenity?
Bootless are plaints, and cureless are my wounds;
No way to fly, nor strength to hold out flight.
The foe is merciless, and will not pity,
For at their hands I have deserv'd no pity.
The air hath got into my deadly wounds,
And much effuse of blood doth make me faint.
Come, York and Richard, Warwick and the rest;
I stabb'd your fathers' bosoms, split my breast.
[He faints.]

Alarum and retreat. Enter Edward, Warwick, Richard, and Soldiers, Montague, and [George of] Clarence.

95 ruthful pitiful **100 presenteth** represents **104 Take on with** cry out against. **satisfied** comforted **108 Misthink** think ill of **118 obsequious** dutiful in manifesting regard for the dead **120 Priam** King of Troy, whose fifty sons fell in the war against the Greeks **123 overgone** overcome **126 chafed** enraged **128 Berwick** Berwick-on-Tweed, on the Scottish border at the North Sea shore. **post amain** hasten with full speed

II.vi. Location: The battlefield, as before.
5 My love and fear love and fear of me **6 commixture** compound (i.e., the "glue" that held many friends) **7 Impairing** weakening. **misproud** falsely proud **9 the sun** (Refers to Edward's emblem.) **12 Phaethon** (See I.iv.33, note). **check** control, manage **13 car** chariot **14 sway'd** reigned **20 chair** throne **21 cherish** foster, encourage **23 Bootless** fruitless **24 hold out** sustain **28 effuse** effusion

EDWARD
Now breathe we, lords. Good fortune bids us pause,
And smooth the frowns of war with peaceful looks.
Some troops pursue the bloody-minded Queen,
That led calm Henry, though he were a king,
As doth a sail, fill'd with a fretting gust,
Command an argosy to stem the waves.
But think you, lords, that Clifford fled with them?

WARWICK
No, 'tis impossible he should escape;
For, though before his face I speak the words,
Your brother Richard mark'd him for the grave;
And wheresoe'er he is, he's surely dead.
Clifford groans [*and dies*].

EDWARD
Whose soul is that which takes her heavy leave?

RICHARD
A deadly groan, like life and death's departing.

EDWARD
See who it is, and, now the battle's ended,
If friend or foe, let him be gently used.

RICHARD
Revoke that doom of mercy, for 'tis Clifford,
Who, not contented that he lopp'd the branch
In hewing Rutland when his leaves put forth,
But set his murd'ring knife unto the root
From whence that tender spray did sweetly spring,
I mean our princely father, Duke of York.

WARWICK
From off the gates of York fetch down the head,
Your father's head, which Clifford placed there;
Instead whereof let this supply the room.
Measure for measure must be answered.

EDWARD
Bring forth that fatal screech-owl to our house,
That nothing sung but death to us and ours.
[*Clifford's body is dragged in front of York gates.*]
Now death shall stop his dismal threat'ning sound,
And his ill-boding tongue no more shall speak.

WARWICK
I think his understanding is bereft.
Speak, Clifford, dost thou know who speaks to thee?—
Dark cloudy death o'ershades his beams of life,
And he nor sees nor hears us what we say.

RICHARD
O, would he did! And so perhaps he doth.
'Tis but his policy to counterfeit,
Because he would avoid such bitter taunts
Which in the time of death he gave our father.

GEORGE
If so thou think'st, vex him with eager words.

RICHARD
Clifford, ask mercy and obtain no grace.

EDWARD
Clifford, repent in bootless penitence.

WARWICK
Clifford, devise excuses for thy faults.

GEORGE
While we devise fell tortures for thy faults.

RICHARD
Thou didst love York, and I am son to York.

EDWARD
Thou pitied'st Rutland; I will pity thee.

GEORGE
Where's Captain Margaret, to fence you now?

WARWICK
They mock thee, Clifford. Swear as thou wast wont.

RICHARD
What, not an oath? Nay, then the world goes hard
When Clifford cannot spare his friends an oath.
I know by that he's dead; and, by my soul,
If this right hand would buy two hours' life,
That I in all despite might rail at him,
This hand should chop it off, and with the issuing blood
Stifle the villain whose unstanched thirst
York and young Rutland could not satisfy.

WARWICK
Ay, but he's dead. Off with the traitor's head,
And rear it in the place your father's stands.
And now to London with triumphant march,
There to be crowned England's royal king;
From whence shall Warwick cut the sea to France,
And ask the Lady Bona for thy queen.
So shalt thou sinew both these lands together,
And, having France thy friend, thou shalt not dread
The scatt'red foe that hopes to rise again;
For though they cannot greatly sting to hurt,
Yet look to have them buzz to offend thine ears.
First will I see the coronation,
And then to Brittany I'll cross the sea
To effect this marriage, so it please my lord.

EDWARD
Even as thou wilt, sweet Warwick, let it be;
For in thy shoulder do I build my seat,
And never will I undertake the thing
Wherein thy counsel and consent is wanting.
Richard, I will create thee Duke of Gloucester,
And George, of Clarence. Warwick, as ourself,
Shall do and undo as him pleaseth best.

RICHARD
Let me be Duke of Clarence, George of Gloucester;
For Gloucester's dukedom is too ominous.

WARWICK
Tut, that's a foolish observation.
Richard, be Duke of Gloucester. Now to London,
To see these honors in possession. *Exeunt.*

35 fretting blowing in gusts (with a suggestion also of *nagging*) **36 argosy** large merchant vessel **39 his** i.e., Richard's **46 doom** judgment **54 this** i.e., Clifford's head **55 answered** given in return **56 screech-owl** (A conventional omen of death, here likened to Clifford.) **63 nor . . . nor** neither . . . nor **65 policy** stratagem **68 eager** biting, bitter

72 fell cruel **75 fence** defend **76 wont** accustomed **83 unstanched** unquenchable **90 Lady Bona** daughter of the Duke of Savoy and sister to the Queen of France **91 sinew** join (as with sinew) **100 in thy shoulder** i.e., with your support. **seat** throne **107 Gloucester's . . . ominous** (Three dukes of Gloucester had met with violent deaths: Hugh Spenser, a favorite of Edward II, Thomas of Woodstock, youngest son of Edward III [see *Richard II*, I.i], and Humphrey, uncle of Henry VI [see *2 Henry VI*, III.ii].) **110 in possession** i.e., in our possession

[ACT III • SCENE I]

Enter [*two Keepers*] *with cross-bows in their hands.*

FIRST KEEPER
Under this thick-grown brake we'll shroud ourselves,
For through this laund anon the deer will come;
And in this covert will we make our stand,
Culling the principal of all the deer.

SECOND KEEPER
I'll stay above the hill, so both may shoot.

FIRST KEEPER
That cannot be. The noise of thy cross-bow
Will scare the herd, and so my shoot is lost.
Here stand we both, and aim we at the best;
And, for the time shall not seem tedious,
I'll tell thee what befell me on a day
In this self place where now we mean to stand.

SECOND KEEPER
Here comes a man. Let's stay till he be past.
[*They remain concealed.*]

Enter the King [*Henry, disguised,*] *with a prayer book.*

KING HENRY
From Scotland am I stol'n, even of pure love,
To greet mine own land with my wishful sight.
No, Harry, Harry, 'tis no land of thine!
Thy place is fill'd, thy scepter wrung from thee,
Thy balm wash'd off wherewith thou wast anointed.
No bending knee will call thee Caesar now,
No humble suitors press to speak for right,
No, not a man comes for redress of thee;
For how can I help them, and not myself?

FIRST KEEPER [*Aside*]
Ay, here's a deer whose skin's a keeper's fee:
This is the quondam king. Let's seize upon him.

KING HENRY
Let me embrace thee, sour adversity,
For wise men say it is the wisest course.

SECOND KEEPER [*Aside*]
Why linger we? Let us lay hands upon him.

FIRST KEEPER [*Aside*]
Forbear awhile. We'll hear a little more.

KING HENRY
My queen and son are gone to France for aid;
And, as I hear, the great commanding Warwick
Is thither gone, to crave the French king's sister
To wife for Edward. If this news be true,
Poor queen and son, your labor is but lost,
For Warwick is a subtle orator,
And Lewis a prince soon won with moving words.
By this account then Margaret may win him,
For she's a woman to be pitied much.
Her sighs will make a batt'ry in his breast,
Her tears will pierce into a marble heart;
The tiger will be mild whiles she doth mourn;
And Nero will be tainted with remorse
To hear and see her plaints, her brinish tears.
Ay, but she's come to beg, Warwick, to give;
She, on his left side, craving aid for Henry,
He, on his right, asking a wife for Edward.
She weeps, and says her Henry is depos'd;
He smiles, and says his Edward is install'd;
That she, poor wretch, for grief can speak no more,
Whiles Warwick tells his title, smooths the wrong,
Inferreth arguments of mighty strength,
And in conclusion wins the King from her
With promise of his sister, and what else,
To strengthen and support King Edward's place.
O Margaret, thus 'twill be, and thou, poor soul,
Art then forsaken, as thou went'st forlorn!
[*The Keepers come forward.*]

SECOND KEEPER
Say, what art thou that talk'st of kings and queens?

KING HENRY
More than I seem, and less than I was born to.
A man at least, for less I should not be;
And men may talk of kings, and why not I?

SECOND KEEPER
Ay, but thou talk'st as if thou wert a king.

KING HENRY
Why, so I am, in mind, and that's enough.

SECOND KEEPER
But, if thou be a king, where is thy crown?

KING HENRY
My crown is in my heart, not on my head;
Not deck'd with diamonds and Indian stones,
Nor to be seen. My crown is call'd content;
A crown it is that seldom kings enjoy.

SECOND KEEPER
Well, if you be a king crown'd with content,
Your crown content and you must be contented
To go along with us. For, as we think,
You are the king King Edward hath depos'd;
And we his subjects sworn in all allegiance
Will apprehend you as his enemy.

KING HENRY
But did you never swear, and break an oath?

SECOND KEEPER
No, never such an oath; nor will not now.

KING HENRY
Where did you dwell when I was King of England?

SECOND KEEPER
Here in this country where we now remain.

KING HENRY
I was anointed king at nine months old;
My father and my grandfather were kings,
And you were sworn true subjects unto me.

III.i. Location: A forest in the north of England, near the Scottish border.
s.d. Keepers gamekeepers **1 brake** thicket **2 laund** glade **8 at the best** as best we can **9 for** so that **11 self** same, very **13 of** out of **14 wishful** longing **19 speak for right** plead for justice **20 of** from **22 fee** perquisite. (I.e., the gamekeeper will get a reward for capturing the King.) **23 quondam** one-time, former

37 batt'ry breach **40 Nero** Roman emperor famed for his cruelty. **tainted** touched, affected **41 brinish** salty **47 That** so that **48 his title** i.e., Edward's royal claim. **smooths** explains away **49 Inferreth** adduces **51 and what else** i.e., and whatever else he may think to offer

And tell me, then, have you not broke your oaths?

FIRST KEEPER
No, for we were subjects but while you were king.

KING HENRY
Why, am I dead? Do I not breathe a man?
Ah, simple men, you know not what you swear!
Look, as I blow this feather from my face,
And as the air blows it to me again,
Obeying with my wind when I do blow,
And yielding to another when it blows,
Commanded always by the greater gust—
Such is the lightness of you common men.
But do not break your oaths, for of that sin
My mild entreaty shall not make you guilty.
Go where you will, the king shall be commanded;
And be you kings, command, and I'll obey.

FIRST KEEPER
We are true subjects to the king, King Edward.

KING HENRY
So would you be again to Henry,
If he were seated as King Edward is.

FIRST KEEPER
We charge you, in God's name, and the King's,
To go with us unto the officers.

KING HENRY
In God's name, lead. Your King's name be obey'd,
And what God will, that let your King perform;
And what he will, I humbly yield unto. *Exeunt.*

[SCENE II]

Enter King Edward, Gloucester, Clarence, [and] Lady Grey.

KING EDWARD
Brother of Gloucester, at Saint Albans field
This lady's husband, Sir Richard Grey, was slain,
His land then seiz'd on by the conqueror.
Her suit is now to repossess those lands,
Which we in justice cannot well deny,
Because in quarrel of the house of York
The worthy gentleman did lose his life.

GLOUCESTER
Your Highness shall do well to grant her suit.
It were dishonor to deny it her.

KING EDWARD
It were no less; but yet I'll make a pause.

GLOUCESTER [*Aside to Clarence*]
Yea, is it so?
I see the lady hath a thing to grant,
Before the King will grant her humble suit.

CLARENCE [*Aside to Gloucester*]
He knows the game. How true he keeps the wind!

GLOUCESTER [*Aside to Clarence*]
Silence!

KING EDWARD
Widow, we will consider of your suit;
And come some other time to know our mind.

LADY GREY
Right gracious lord, I cannot brook delay.
May it please your Highness to resolve me now,
And what your pleasure is shall satisfy me.

GLOUCESTER [*Aside to Clarence*]
Ay, widow? Then I'll warrant you all your lands,
An if what pleases him shall pleasure you.
Fight closer, or, good faith, you'll catch a blow.

CLARENCE [*Aside to Gloucester*]
I fear her not, unless she chance to fall.

GLOUCESTER [*Aside to Clarence*]
God forbid that, for he'll take vantages.

KING EDWARD
How many children hast thou, widow? Tell me.

CLARENCE [*Aside to Gloucester*]
I think he means to beg a child of her.

GLOUCESTER [*Aside to Clarence*]
Nay, then, whip me; he'll rather give her two.

LADY GREY
Three, my most gracious lord.

GLOUCESTER [*Aside to Clarence*]
You shall have four, if you'll be rul'd by him.

KING EDWARD
'Twere pity they should lose their father's lands.

LADY GREY
Be pitiful, dread lord, and grant it then.

KING EDWARD
Lords, give us leave. I'll try this widow's wit.

GLOUCESTER [*Aside to Clarence*]
Ay, good leave have you; for you will have leave
Till youth take leave and leave you to the crutch.
[*Gloucester and Clarence retire.*]

KING EDWARD
Now tell me, madam, do you love your children?

LADY GREY
Ay, full as dearly as I love myself.

KING EDWARD
And would you not do much to do them good?

LADY GREY
To do them good I would sustain some harm.

KING EDWARD
Then get your husband's lands, to do them good.

LADY GREY
Therefore I came unto your Majesty.

KING EDWARD
I'll tell you how these lands are to be got.

LADY GREY
So shall you bind me to your Highness' service.

KING EDWARD
What service wilt thou do me if I give them?

80 but only **83 this feather** (Henry may take a feather from his hat.)

III.ii. Location: London. The palace.
s.d. Gloucester, Clarence i.e., Richard and George, King Edward's brothers, made dukes in II.vi.103–104 **2 Sir Richard Grey** (An error for *Sir John Grey*, who fell at the second battle of St. Albans fighting on the Lancastrian side; cf. *Richard III*, I.iii.126-129.) **14 keeps the wind** hunts downwind (to prevent the game from catching the scent)

18 brook tolerate **19 resolve me** answer me, end my uncertainty **21 warrant** guarantee **22 An if** if. **pleasure** please **23 Fight closer . . . catch a blow** (The dueling terms here are used with sexual double meaning, as also in *fall* and *vantages*, ll. 24, 25. See also *a thing*, l. 12, *beg a child*, l. 27, *crutch*, i.e., crotch, l. 35, *service*, l. 43, and *shift*, i.e., a woman's smock, l. 108, for other sexual double entendres.) **24 fear** i.e., fear for **27 beg a child** i.e., seek for self-interested motives to be appointed guardian of some rich young ward (with sexual double meaning) **28 whip me** i.e., I'll bet a whipping the King has other designs **33 give us leave** pardon us, i.e., leave us to confer alone **34–35 Ay . . . crutch** yes, may you be pardoned, for you will take liberties, until your youth bids you farewell and leaves you hobbling on a crutch (too old for lovemaking)

LADY GREY
What you command that rests in me to do.
KING EDWARD
But you will take exceptions to my boon. 46
LADY GREY
No, gracious lord, except I cannot do it. 47
KING EDWARD
Ay, but thou canst do what I mean to ask.
LADY GREY
Why, then I will do what your Grace commands.
GLOUCESTER [*Aside to Clarence*]
He plies her hard; and much rain wears the marble.
CLARENCE [*Aside to Gloucester*]
As red as fire? Nay then, her wax must melt. 51
LADY GREY
Why stops my lord? Shall I not hear my task?
KING EDWARD
An easy task. 'Tis but to love a king.
LADY GREY
That's soon perform'd, because I am a subject.
KING EDWARD
Why, then, thy husband's lands I freely give thee.
LADY GREY
I take my leave with many thousand thanks.
[*She curtsies, preparing to go.*]
GLOUCESTER [*Aside to Clarence*]
The match is made; she seals it with a cur'sy.
KING EDWARD
But stay thee. 'Tis the fruits of love I mean.
LADY GREY
The fruits of love I mean, my loving liege.
KING EDWARD
Ay, but, I fear me, in another sense. 60
What love, think'st thou, I sue so much to get?
LADY GREY
My love till death, my humble thanks, my prayers—
That love which virtue begs and virtue grants.
KING EDWARD
No, by my troth, I did not mean such love.
LADY GREY
Why then you mean not as I thought you did.
KING EDWARD
But now you partly may perceive my mind.
LADY GREY
My mind will never grant what I perceive
Your Highness aims at, if I aim aright. 68
KING EDWARD
To tell thee plain, I aim to lie with thee.
LADY GREY
To tell you plain, I had rather lie in prison. 70
KING EDWARD
Why then thou shalt not have thy husband's lands.
LADY GREY
Why then mine honesty shall be my dower; 72
For by that loss I will not purchase them.
KING EDWARD
Therein thou wrong'st thy children mightily.
LADY GREY
Herein your Highness wrongs both them and me.
But, mighty lord, this merry inclination
Accords not with the sadness of my suit. 77
Please you dismiss me, either with "ay" or "no."
KING EDWARD
Ay, if thou wilt say "ay" to my request;
No, if thou dost say "no" to my demand.
LADY GREY
Then, no, my lord. My suit is at an end.
GLOUCESTER [*Aside to Clarence*]
The widow likes him not, she knits her brows.
CLARENCE [*Aside to Gloucester*]
He is the bluntest wooer in Christendom.
KING EDWARD [*Aside*]
Her looks doth argue her replete with modesty; 84
Her words doth show her wit incomparable;
All her perfections challenge sovereignty. 86
One way or other, she is for a king,
And she shall be my love, or else my queen.—
Say that King Edward take thee for his queen?
LADY GREY
'Tis better said than done, my gracious lord.
I am a subject fit to jest withal,
But far unfit to be a sovereign.
KING EDWARD
Sweet widow, by my state I swear to thee 93
I speak no more than what my soul intends,
And that is, to enjoy thee for my love.
LADY GREY
And that is more than I will yield unto.
I know I am too mean to be your queen,
And yet too good to be your concubine.
KING EDWARD
You cavil, widow. I did mean my queen.
LADY GREY
'Twill grieve your Grace my sons should call you father.
KING EDWARD
No more than when my daughters call thee mother.
Thou art a widow, and thou hast some children;
And, by God's mother, I, being but a bachelor,
Have other some. Why, 'tis a happy thing 104
To be the father unto many sons.
Answer no more, for thou shalt be my queen.
GLOUCESTER [*Aside to Clarence*]
The ghostly father now hath done his shrift. 107
CLARENCE [*Aside to Gloucester*]
When he was made a shriver, 'twas for shift. 108
KING EDWARD
Brothers, you muse what chat we two have had. 109
GLOUCESTER
The widow likes it not, for she looks very sad. 110
KING EDWARD
You'd think it strange if I should marry her.
CLARENCE
To who, my lord?

46 my boon the request I ask **47 except** unless **51 As red as fire** i.e., Edward is hotly importunate **68 aim** guess **70 lie** be confined **72 honesty** chastity, virtue

77 sadness seriousness **84 argue her** show her to be **86 challenge** lay claim to **93 state** i.e., kingship **104 other some** some others **107 ghostly father** spiritual father, confessor. **done his shrift** finished hearing confession **108 for shift** to serve a devious purpose (with bawdy suggestion; see note to l. 23) **109 muse** wonder **110 sad** serious

KING EDWARD Why, Clarence, to myself.

GLOUCESTER
That would be ten days' wonder at the least.

CLARENCE
That's a day longer than a wonder lasts. 114

GLOUCESTER
By so much is the wonder in extremes.

KING EDWARD
Well, jest on, brothers. I can tell you both
Her suit is granted for her husband's lands.

Enter a Nobleman.

NOBLEMAN
My gracious lord, Henry your foe is taken,
And brought your prisoner to your palace gate.

KING EDWARD
See that he be convey'd unto the Tower.
And go we, brothers, to the man that took him,
To question of his apprehension. 122
Widow, go you along. Lords, use her honorably.
Exeunt. Manet Richard [*of Gloucester*]

GLOUCESTER
Ay, Edward will use women honorably.
Would he were wasted, marrow, bones, and all,
That from his loins no hopeful branch may spring,
To cross me from the golden time I look for! 127
And yet, between my soul's desire and me—
The lustful Edward's title buried— 129
Is Clarence, Henry, and his son young Edward,
And all the unlook'd-for issue of their bodies, 131
To take their rooms, ere I can place myself. 132
A cold premeditation for my purpose! 133
Why, then, I do but dream on sovereignty,
Like one that stands upon a promontory
And spies a far-off shore where he would tread,
Wishing his foot were equal with his eye, 137
And chides the sea that sunders him from thence,
Saying, he'll lade it dry to have this way. 139
So do I wish the crown, being so far off;
And so I chide the means that keeps me from it; 141
And so, I say, I'll cut the causes off, 142
Flattering me with impossibilities. 143
My eye's too quick, my heart o'erweens too much, 144
Unless my hand and strength could equal them.
Well, say there is no kingdom then for Richard;
What other pleasure can the world afford?
I'll make my heaven in a lady's lap,
And deck my body in gay ornaments,
And witch sweet ladies with my words and looks. 150
O miserable thought, and more unlikely
Than to accomplish twenty golden crowns!
Why, love forswore me in my mother's womb;
And, for I should not deal in her soft laws, 154
She did corrupt frail nature with some bribe,
To shrink mine arm up like a wither'd shrub;
To make an envious mountain on my back, 157
Where sits deformity to mock my body;
To shape my legs of an unequal size;
To disproportion me in every part,
Like to a chaos, or an unlick'd bear-whelp 161
That carries no impression like the dam. 162
And am I then a man to be belov'd?
O monstrous fault, to harbor such a thought!
Then, since this earth affords no joy to me
But to command, to check, to o'erbear such 166
As are of better person than myself,
I'll make my heaven to dream upon the crown,
And, whiles I live, t' account this world but hell,
Until my mis-shap'd trunk that bears this head
Be round impaled with a glorious crown. 171
And yet I know not how to get the crown,
For many lives stand between me and home; 173
And I—like one lost in a thorny wood,
That rends the thorns and is rent with the thorns,
Seeking a way and straying from the way,
Not knowing how to find the open air,
But toiling desperately to find it out—
Torment myself to catch the English crown;
And from that torment I will free myself,
Or hew my way out with a bloody axe.
Why, I can smile, and murder whiles I smile,
And cry "Content" to that which grieves my heart,
And wet my cheeks with artificial tears,
And frame my face to all occasions.
I'll drown more sailors than the mermaid shall; 186
I'll slay more gazers than the basilisk; 187
I'll play the orator as well as Nestor, 188
Deceive more slily than Ulysses could, 189
And, like a Sinon, take another Troy. 190
I can add colors to the chameleon,
Change shapes with Proteus for advantages, 192
And set the murderous Machiavel to school. 193
Can I do this, and cannot get a crown?
Tut, were it farther off, I'll pluck it down. *Exit.*

[SCENE III]

Flourish. Enter Lewis the French King, his sister Bona, his Admiral, call'd Bourbon, Prince Edward, Queen Margaret, and the Earl of Oxford. Lewis sits, and riseth up again.

KING LEWIS
Fair Queen of England, worthy Margaret,
Sit down with us. It ill befits thy state 2

114 a day longer (Refers to the proverbial expression "a nine days' wonder.") **122 of his apprehension** about his being taken **127 cross** thwart, frustrate **129 buried** i.e., eliminated by his death **131 unlook'd for** unforeseeable **132 rooms** places **133 cold premeditation** discouraging prospect **137 equal with his eye** i.e., able to achieve what he views **139 lade** empty (by ladling, scooping) **141 means** obstacles **142 causes** i.e., of my impatience **143 Flattering . . . impossibilities** i.e., deceiving myself with vain hopes **144 o'erweens** presumes **150 witch** bewitch **154 for** so that

157 envious spiteful, detested **161 unlick'd bear-whelp** (It was a popular notion that bears licked their shapeless newly born cubs into a proper shape.) **162 impression** shape **166 check** control. **o'erbear** dominate **171 impaled** enclosed **173 home** i.e., the goal **186 mermaid** (Mermaids allegedly had the power to lure sailors to destruction by their singing or weeping.) **187 basilisk** fabulous reptile said to kill by its gaze **188–189 Nestor, Ulysses** Greek leaders in the Trojan war, noted respectively for aged wisdom and cunning **190 Sinon** Greek warrior who allowed himself to be taken captive by the Trojans, and then, feigning resentment toward his Greek companions, persuaded Priam to bring the wooden horse within the city walls by which Troy was taken **192 Proteus** old man of the sea, able to assume different shapes. **for advantages** to suit my purpose **193 set . . . school** teach Machiavelli how to be ruthless. (On Machiavelli, see *1 Henry VI*, V.iv.74 note.)

III.iii. Location: France. The King's palace. A throne and a seat are provided.
2 state rank

And birth, that thou shouldst stand while Lewis doth sit.

QUEEN MARGARET
No, mighty King of France. Now Margaret
Must strike her sail and learn awhile to serve
Where kings command. I was, I must confess,
Great Albion's queen in former golden days.
But now mischance hath trod my title down,
And with dishonor laid me on the ground,
Where I must take like seat unto my fortune,
And to my humble seat conform myself.

KING LEWIS
Why, say, fair Queen, whence springs this deep despair?

QUEEN MARGARET
From such a cause as fills mine eyes with tears
And stops my tongue, while heart is drown'd in cares.

KING LEWIS
Whate'er it be, be thou still like thyself,
And sit thee by our side. *(Seats her by him.)* Yield not thy neck
To fortune's yoke, but let thy dauntless mind
Still ride in triumph over all mischance.
Be plain, Queen Margaret, and tell thy grief.
It shall be eas'd, if France can yield relief.

QUEEN MARGARET
Those gracious words revive my drooping thoughts
And give my tongue-tied sorrows leave to speak.
Now, therefore, be it known to noble Lewis,
That Henry, sole possessor of my love,
Is, of a king, become a banish'd man,
And forc'd to live in Scotland a forlorn,
While proud ambitious Edward Duke of York
Usurps the regal title and the seat
Of England's true-anointed lawful king.
This is the cause that I, poor Margaret,
With this my son, Prince Edward, Henry's heir,
Am come to crave thy just and lawful aid;
And if thou fail us, all our hope is done.
Scotland hath will to help, but cannot help;
Our people and our peers are both misled,
Our treasure seiz'd, our soldiers put to flight,
And, as thou seest, ourselves in heavy plight.

KING LEWIS
Renowned Queen, with patience calm the storm,
While we bethink a means to break it off.

QUEEN MARGARET
The more we stay, the stronger grows our foe.

KING LEWIS
The more I stay, the more I'll succor thee.

QUEEN MARGARET
O, but impatience waiteth on true sorrow.
And see where comes the breeder of my sorrow!

Enter Warwick.

5 strike her sail lower her sail, i.e., act deferentially, as the captain of a sea vessel does to one of higher rank **7 Albion's** England's **15 like thyself** i.e., as befits your title **20 France** i.e., the King of France **25 of** instead of **26 forlorn** outcast **39 break it off** i.e., cease the storm of grief **40 stay** delay **41 The . . . thee** i.e., the longer preparation I make, the greater help I can give you **42 waiteth on** attends, accompanies

KING LEWIS
What's he approacheth boldly to our presence?

QUEEN MARGARET
Our Earl of Warwick, Edward's greatest friend.

KING LEWIS
Welcome, brave Warwick! What brings thee to France? *He descends. She ariseth.*

QUEEN MARGARET
Ay, now begins a second storm to rise,
For this is he that moves both wind and tide.

WARWICK
From worthy Edward, King of Albion,
My lord and sovereign, and thy vowed friend,
I come, in kindness and unfeigned love,
First, to do greetings to thy royal person,
And then to crave a league of amity;
And lastly, to confirm that amity
With nuptial knot, if thou vouchsafe to grant
That virtuous Lady Bona, thy fair sister,
To England's king in lawful marriage.

QUEEN MARGARET [*Aside*]
If that go forward, Henry's hope is done.

WARWICK *(Speaking to Bona)*
And, gracious madam, in our king's behalf,
I am commanded, with your leave and favor,
Humbly to kiss your hand, and with my tongue
To tell the passion of my sovereign's heart—
Where fame, late ent'ring at his heedful ears,
Hath plac'd thy beauty's image and thy virtue.

QUEEN MARGARET
King Lewis and Lady Bona, hear me speak
Before you answer Warwick. His demand
Springs not from Edward's well-meant honest love,
But from deceit bred by necessity.
For how can tyrants safely govern home
Unless abroad they purchase great alliance?
To prove him tyrant this reason may suffice,
That Henry liveth still; but were he dead,
Yet here Prince Edward stands, King Henry's son.
Look, therefore, Lewis, that by this league and marriage
Thou draw not on thy danger and dishonor.
For though usurpers sway the rule awhile,
Yet heav'ns are just, and time suppresseth wrongs.

WARWICK
Injurious Margaret!

PRINCE
And why not queen?

WARWICK
Because thy father Henry did usurp,
And thou no more art prince than she is queen.

OXFORD
Then Warwick disannuls great John of Gaunt,
Which did subdue the greatest part of Spain;
And, after John of Gaunt, Henry the Fourth,
Whose wisdom was a mirror to the wisest;
And after that wise prince, Henry the Fifth,
Who by his prowess conquered all France.
From these our Henry lineally descends.

44 he he who **56 sister** i.e., sister-in-law **63 fame** report. **late** lately **75 draw not on** do not bring about **76 sway** exercise **78 Injurious** insulting **81 disannuls** cancels, takes no account of

WARWICK
Oxford, how haps it, in this smooth discourse,
You told not how Henry the Sixth hath lost
All that which Henry the Fifth had gotten?
Methinks these peers of France should smile at that.
But for the rest: you tell a pedigree
Of threescore and two years—a silly time
To make prescription for a kingdom's worth.

OXFORD
Why, Warwick, canst thou speak against thy liege,
Whom thou obeyed'st thirty and six years,
And not bewray thy treason with a blush?

WARWICK
Can Oxford, that did ever fence the right,
Now buckler falsehood with a pedigree?
For shame! Leave Henry, and call Edward king.

OXFORD
Call him my king by whose injurious doom
My elder brother, the Lord Aubrey Vere,
Was done to death? And more than so, my father,
Even in the downfall of his mellow'd years,
When nature brought him to the door of death?
No, Warwick, no! While life upholds this arm,
This arm upholds the house of Lancaster.

WARWICK
And I the house of York.

KING LEWIS
Queen Margaret, Prince Edward, and Oxford,
Vouchsafe, at our request, to stand aside,
While I use further conference with Warwick.
They stand aloof.

QUEEN MARGARET
Heavens grant that Warwick's words bewitch him not!

KING LEWIS
Now, Warwick, tell me, even upon thy conscience,
Is Edward your true king? For I were loath
To link with him that were not lawful chosen.

WARWICK
Thereon I pawn my credit and mine honor.

KING LEWIS
But is he gracious in the people's eye?

WARWICK
The more that Henry was unfortunate.

KING LEWIS
Then further, all dissembling set aside,
Tell me for truth the measure of his love
Unto our sister Bona.

WARWICK Such it seems
As may beseem a monarch like himself.
Myself have often heard him say and swear
That this his love was an eternal plant,
Whereof the root was fix'd in virtue's ground,
The leaves and fruit maintain'd with beauty's sun,
Exempt from envy, but not from disdain,
Unless the Lady Bona quit his pain.

KING LEWIS
Now, sister, let us hear your firm resolve.

BONA
Your grant, or your denial, shall be mine.
(Speaks to Warwick.)
Yet I confess that often ere this day,
When I have heard your king's desert recounted,
Mine ear hath tempted judgment to desire.

KING LEWIS
Then, Warwick, thus: our sister shall be Edward's.
And now forthwith shall articles be drawn
Touching the jointure that your king must make,
Which with her dowry shall be counterpois'd.
Draw near, Queen Margaret, and be a witness
That Bona shall be wife to the English king.
[Margaret, Edward, and Oxford come forward.]

PRINCE
To Edward, but not to the English king.

QUEEN MARGARET
Deceitful Warwick! It was thy device
By this alliance to make void my suit.
Before thy coming, Lewis was Henry's friend.

KING LEWIS
And still is friend to him and Margaret.
But if your title to the crown be weak,
As may appear by Edward's good success,
Then 'tis but reason that I be releas'd
From giving aid which late I promised.
Yet shall you have all kindness at my hand
That your estate requires and mine can yield.

WARWICK
Henry now lives in Scotland at his ease,
Where, having nothing, nothing can he lose.
And as for you yourself, our quondam queen,
You have a father able to maintain you;
And better 'twere you troubled him than France.

QUEEN MARGARET
Peace, impudent and shameless Warwick,
Proud setter-up and puller-down of kings!
I will not hence, till, with my talk and tears,
Both full of truth, I make King Lewis behold
Thy sly conveyance and thy lord's false love;
For both of you are birds of selfsame feather.
Post blowing a horn within.

KING LEWIS
Warwick, this is some post to us or thee.

Enter the Post.

POST *(Speaks to Warwick)*
My Lord Ambassador, these letters are for you,
Sent from your brother, Marquess Montague.
(To Lewis.) These from our king unto your Majesty.
(To Margaret.) And, madam, these for you; from whom I know not. *They all read their letters.*

OXFORD *[To Edward]*
I like it well that our fair queen and mistress

93 threescore and two i.e., from 1399, the date of Henry IV's accession, to 1461, that of Edward's. **silly** i.e., ridiculously short **94 prescription** claim founded upon long use and *de facto* possession **97 bewray** betray, reveal **98 fence** defend **99 buckler** shield, protect **101 doom** judgment **102 Lord Aubrey Vere** the eldest son of the twelfth Earl of Oxford, John de Vere. (Both he and his father were attainted and executed for treason by the Yorkists in 1462.) **103 more than so** even more than that **122 beseem** befit **127 envy** ill will, malice. **but . . . disdain** i.e., his love will wither if the lady disdains him. (Warwick uses the stock hyperbole of Petrarchan devotion.)

128 quit requite, alleviate **130 grant** granting, agreeing **132 desert** deserving **136 jointure** marriage settlement **137 counterpois'd** matched, balanced in amount **153 quondam** former **160 conveyance** underhand dealing **161 s.d. Post** messenger

Smiles at her news, while Warwick frowns at his.

PRINCE [*To Oxford*]
Nay, mark how Lewis stamps, as he were nettled.
I hope all's for the best.

KING LEWIS
Warwick, what are thy news? And yours, fair Queen?

QUEEN MARGARET
Mine, such as fill my heart with unhop'd joys.

WARWICK
Mine, full of sorrow and heart's discontent.

KING LEWIS
What, has your king married the Lady Grey?
And now, to soothe your forgery and his,
Sends me a paper to persuade me patience?
Is this th' alliance that he seeks with France?
Dare he presume to scorn us in this manner?

QUEEN MARGARET
I told your Majesty as much before.
This proveth Edward's love and Warwick's honesty.

WARWICK
King Lewis, I here protest, in sight of heaven,
And by the hope I have of heavenly bliss,
That I am clear from this misdeed of Edward's—
No more my king, for he dishonors me,
But most himself, if he could see his shame.
Did I forget that by the house of York
My father came untimely to his death?
Did I let pass th' abuse done to my niece?
Did I impale him with the regal crown?
Did I put Henry from his native right?
And am I guerdon'd at the last with shame?
Shame on himself! For my desert is honor;
And, to repair my honor lost for him,
I here renounce him and return to Henry.
My noble Queen, let former grudges pass,
And henceforth I am thy true servitor.
I will revenge his wrong to Lady Bona
And replant Henry in his former state.

QUEEN MARGARET
Warwick, these words have turn'd my hate to love;
And I forgive and quite forget old faults,
And joy that thou becom'st King Henry's friend.

WARWICK
So much his friend, ay, his unfeigned friend,
That, if King Lewis vouchsafe to furnish us
With some few bands of chosen soldiers,
I'll undertake to land them on our coast
And force the tyrant from his seat by war.
'Tis not his new-made bride shall succor him.
And as for Clarence, as my letters tell me,
He's very likely now to fall from him,
For matching more for wanton lust than honor,
Or than for strength and safety of our country.

BONA
Dear brother, how shall Bona be reveng'd
But by thy help to this distressed queen?

QUEEN MARGARET
Renowned prince, how shall poor Henry live,
Unless thou rescue him from foul despair?

BONA
My quarrel and this English queen's are one.

WARWICK
And mine, fair lady Bona, joins with yours.

KING LEWIS
And mine with hers, and thine, and Margaret's.
Therefore at last I firmly am resolv'd
You shall have aid.

QUEEN MARGARET
Let me give humble thanks for all at once.

KING LEWIS
Then, England's messenger, return in post,
And tell false Edward, thy supposed king,
That Lewis of France is sending over masquers
To revel it with him and his new bride.
Thou seest what's pass'd. Go fear thy king withal.

BONA
Tell him, in hope he'll prove a widower shortly,
I'll wear the willow garland for his sake.

QUEEN MARGARET
Tell him, my mourning weeds are laid aside,
And I am ready to put armor on.

WARWICK
Tell him from me that he hath done me wrong,
And therefore I'll uncrown him ere 't be long.
There's thy reward. [*Gives money.*] Be gone.

Exit Post.

KING LEWIS
But, Warwick,
Thou and Oxford, with five thousand men,
Shall cross the seas, and bid false Edward battle;
And, as occasion serves, this noble queen
And prince shall follow with a fresh supply.
Yet, ere thou go, but answer me one doubt:
What pledge have we of thy firm loyalty?

WARWICK
This shall assure my constant loyalty,
That, if our queen and this young prince agree,
I'll join mine eldest daughter and my joy
To him forthwith in holy wedlock bands.

QUEEN MARGARET
Yes, I agree, and thank you for your motion.
Son Edward, she is fair and virtuous,
Therefore delay not, give thy hand to Warwick,
And, with thy hand, thy faith irrevocable
That only Warwick's daughter shall be thine.

PRINCE
Yes, I accept her, for she well deserves it;
And here, to pledge my vow, I give my hand.

He gives his hand to Warwick.

KING LEWIS
Why stay we now? These soldiers shall be levied,
And thou, Lord Bourbon, our high admiral,

175 forgery deceit **187 My father** i.e., Salisbury (who, according to the chronicles, was captured at Wakefield and beheaded by the Lancastrians) **188 abuse . . . niece** (The chronicles report that Edward attempted to "deflower" Warwick's niece while a guest in his house.) **189 impale him** i.e., encircle his head **191 guerdon'd** rewarded **210 matching** marrying

222 in post in haste **224 masquers** dancers in a mask or court revels. (Said ironically.) **226 fear** frighten **228 willow garland** (Symbol of a forsaken lover; said here contemptuously.) **229 weeds** garments **238 but** only **242 eldest daughter** (A historical inaccuracy; Prince Edward was betrothed to a younger daughter of Warwick, Anne, who later married Richard of Gloucester; the eldest daughter, Isabella, was already the wife of the Duke of Clarence.) **244 motion** proposal

Shall waft them over with our royal fleet.
I long till Edward fall by war's mischance,
For mocking marriage with a dame of France.
Exeunt. Manet Warwick.

WARWICK
I came from Edward as ambassador,
But I return his sworn and mortal foe.
Matter of marriage was the charge he gave me,
But dreadful war shall answer his demand.
Had he none else to make a stale but me?
Then none but I shall turn his jest to sorrow.
I was the chief that rais'd him to the crown,
And I'll be chief to bring him down again—
Not that I pity Henry's misery,
But seek revenge on Edward's mockery. *Exit.*

[ACT IV • SCENE I]

Enter Richard [Duke of Gloucester], Clarence, Somerset, and Montague.

GLOUCESTER
Now tell me, brother Clarence, what think you
Of this new marriage with the Lady Grey?
Hath not our brother made a worthy choice?

CLARENCE
Alas, you know, 'tis far from hence to France;
How could he stay till Warwick made return?

SOMERSET
My lords, forbear this talk. Here comes the King.

Flourish. Enter King Edward, Lady Grey [as Queen Elizabeth], Pembroke, Stafford, Hastings. Four stand on one side and four on the other.

GLOUCESTER
And his well-chosen bride.

CLARENCE
I mind to tell him plainly what I think.

KING EDWARD
Now, brother of Clarence, how like you our choice,
That you stand pensive, as half malcontent?

CLARENCE
As well as Lewis of France, or the Earl of Warwick,
Which are so weak of courage and in judgment
That they'll take no offense at our abuse.

KING EDWARD
Suppose they take offense without a cause;
They are but Lewis and Warwick, I am Edward,
Your king and Warwick's, and must have my will.

GLOUCESTER
And shall have your will, because our king.
Yet hasty marriage seldom proveth well.

KING EDWARD
Yea, brother Richard, are you offended too?

GLOUCESTER
Not I.
No, God forbid that I should wish them sever'd
Whom God hath join'd together! Ay, and 'twere pity
To sunder them that yoke so well together.

KING EDWARD
Setting your scorns and your mislike aside,
Tell me some reason why the Lady Grey
Should not become my wife and England's queen.
And you too, Somerset and Montague,
Speak freely what you think.

CLARENCE
Then this is mine opinion: that King Lewis
Becomes your enemy for mocking him
About the marriage of the Lady Bona.

GLOUCESTER
And Warwick, doing what you gave in charge,
Is now dishonored by this new marriage.

KING EDWARD
What if both Lewis and Warwick be appeas'd
By such invention as I can devise?

MONTAGUE
Yet, to have join'd with France in such alliance
Would more have strength'ned this our commonwealth
'Gainst foreign storms than any home-bred marriage.

HASTINGS
Why, knows not Montague that of itself
England is safe, if true within itself?

MONTAGUE
But the safer when 'tis back'd with France.

HASTINGS
'Tis better using France than trusting France.
Let us be back'd with God and with the seas
Which He hath giv'n for fence impregnable,
And with their helps only defend ourselves;
In them and in ourselves our safety lies.

CLARENCE
For this one speech Lord Hastings well deserves
To have the heir of the Lord Hungerford.

KING EDWARD
Ay, what of that? It was my will and grant,
And for this once my will shall stand for law.

GLOUCESTER
And yet methinks your Grace hath not done well
To give the heir and daughter of Lord Scales
Unto the brother of your loving bride.
She better would have fitted me or Clarence.
But in your bride you bury brotherhood.

CLARENCE
Or else you would not have bestow'd the heir
Of the Lord Bonville on your new wife's son,
And leave your brothers to go speed elsewhere.

253 waft convey by water **260 stale** dupe, laughingstock

IV.i. Location: London. The palace.
5 stay wait. (Said ironically.) **6 s.d. Four stand** i.e., the four already on stage. Edward is seemingly in the middle. **8 mind** intend **10 malcontent** discontented **13 abuse** insult. (Clarence speaks scornfully, as does Gloucester in ll. 21–23.)

24 mislike displeasure **32 gave in charge** commissioned **35 invention** scheme, plan **48 To . . . Hungerford** (Clarence objects to the marriage of Lord Hastings to the daughter of Lord Hungerford.) **53 brother** i.e., Lord Anthony Rivers (whose marriage to the daughter of Lord Scales was one of the advancements of Queen Elizabeth's kindred so much resented by Edward's brothers and other noble supporters) **57 son** i.e., Sir Thomas Grey, Marquess Dorset, another of the Queen's upstart relatives advanced by Edward **58 speed** prosper

KING EDWARD
Alas, poor Clarence! Is it for a wife
That thou art malcontent? I will provide thee.

CLARENCE
In choosing for yourself, you show'd your judgment,
Which being shallow, you shall give me leave
To play the broker in mine own behalf;
And to that end I shortly mind to leave you.

KING EDWARD
Leave me, or tarry, Edward will be king,
And not be tied unto his brother's will.

QUEEN ELIZABETH
My lords, before it pleas'd his Majesty
To raise my state to title of a queen,
Do me but right, and you must all confess
That I was not ignoble of descent;
And meaner than myself have had like fortune. 71
But as this title honors me and mine,
So your dislikes, to whom I would be pleasing,
Doth cloud my joys with danger and with sorrow. 74

KING EDWARD
My love, forbear to fawn upon their frowns.
What danger or what sorrow can befall thee
So long as Edward is thy constant friend
And their true sovereign, whom they must obey?
Nay, whom they shall obey, and love thee too,
Unless they seek for hatred at my hands;
Which if they do, yet will I keep thee safe,
And they shall feel the vengeance of my wrath.

GLOUCESTER [*Aside*]
I hear, yet say not much, but think the more.

Enter a Post.

KING EDWARD
Now, messenger, what letters or what news
From France?

POST
My sovereign liege, no letters; and few words,
But such as I, without your special pardon,
Dare not relate.

KING EDWARD
Go to, we pardon thee. Therefore, in brief,
Tell me their words as near as thou canst guess
them. 90
What answer makes King Lewis unto our letters?

POST
At my depart, these were his very words:
"Go tell false Edward, the supposed king,
That Lewis of France is sending over masquers
To revel it with him and his new bride."

KING EDWARD
Is Lewis so brave? Belike he thinks me Henry. 96
But what said Lady Bona to my marriage?

POST
These were her words, utt'red with mild disdain:
"Tell him, in hope he'll prove a widower shortly,
I'll wear the willow garland for his sake."

KING EDWARD
I blame not her, she could say little less;
She had the wrong. But what said Henry's queen?
For I have heard that she was there in place.

POST
"Tell him," quoth she, "my mourning weeds are
done,
And I am ready to put armor on."

KING EDWARD
Belike she minds to play the Amazon.
But what said Warwick to these injuries?

POST
He, more incens'd against your Majesty
Than all the rest, discharg'd me with these words:
"Tell him from me that he hath done me wrong,
And therefore I'll uncrown him ere 't be long."

KING EDWARD
Ha? Durst the traitor breathe out so proud words?
Well, I will arm me, being thus forewarn'd.
They shall have wars and pay for their presumption.
But say, is Warwick friends with Margaret?

POST
Ay, gracious sovereign, they are so link'd in
friendship
That young Prince Edward marries Warwick's
daughter.

CLARENCE
Belike the elder; Clarence will have the younger. 118
Now, brother king, farewell, and sit you fast,
For I will hence to Warwick's other daughter,
That, though I want a kingdom, yet in marriage 121
I may not prove inferior to yourself.
You that love me and Warwick, follow me.
Exit Clarence, and Somerset follows.

GLOUCESTER [*Aside*]
Not I.
My thoughts aim at a further matter. I
Stay not for the love of Edward, but the crown.

KING EDWARD
Clarence and Somerset both gone to Warwick?
Yet am I arm'd against the worst can happen; 128
And haste is needful in this desp'rate case.
Pembroke and Stafford, you in our behalf
Go levy men, and make prepare for war. 131
They are already, or quickly will be, landed.
Myself in person will straight follow you.
Exeunt Pembroke and Stafford.
But, ere I go, Hastings and Montague,
Resolve my doubt. You twain, of all the rest,
Are near to Warwick by blood and by alliance.
Tell me if you love Warwick more than me?
If it be so, then both depart to him;
I rather wish you foes than hollow friends.
But if you mind to hold your true obedience, 140
Give me assurance with some friendly vow,
That I may never have you in suspect. 142

MONTAGUE
So God help Montague as he proves true!

71 meaner more lowly **74 danger** apprehension **90 guess** i.e, reproduce from memory **96 Belike** perhaps

118 the elder (Cf. III.iii.242, note.) **121 want** lack **128 can** that can **131 prepare** preparation **140 mind** intend **142 suspect** suspicion

HASTINGS
And Hastings as he favors Edward's cause!

KING EDWARD
Now, brother Richard, will you stand by us?

GLOUCESTER
Ay, in despite of all that shall withstand you.

KING EDWARD
Why, so, then am I sure of victory.
Now therefore let us hence, and lose no hour
Till we meet Warwick with his foreign pow'r.

Exeunt.

[SCENE II]

Enter Warwick and Oxford in England, with French soldiers.

WARWICK
Trust me, my lord, all hitherto goes well.
The common people by numbers swarm to us.

Enter Clarence and Somerset.

But see where Somerset and Clarence comes!
Speak suddenly, my lords, are we all friends?

CLARENCE
Fear not that, my lord.

WARWICK
Then, gentle Clarence, welcome unto Warwick;
And welcome, Somerset! I hold it cowardice
To rest mistrustful where a noble heart
Hath pawn'd an open hand in sign of love; 9
Else might I think that Clarence, Edward's brother,
Were but a feigned friend to our proceedings.
But welcome, sweet Clarence, my daughter shall be thine.
And now what rests but, in night's coverture, 13
Thy brother being carelessly encamp'd,
His soldiers lurking in the towns about, 15
And but attended by a simple guard, 16
We may surprise and take him at our pleasure?
Our scouts have found the adventure very easy;
That as Ulysses and stout Diomede 19
With sleight and manhood stole to Rhesus' tents, 20
And brought from thence the Thracian fatal steeds, 21
So we, well cover'd with the night's black mantle,
At unawares may beat down Edward's guard 23
And seize himself. I say not, slaughter him,
For I intend but only to surprise him. 25
You that will follow me to this attempt,
Applaud the name of Henry with your leader.

They all cry, "Henry!"

Why, then, let's on our way in silent sort.
For Warwick and his friends, God and Saint George!

Exeunt.

IV.ii. Location: A plain in Warwickshire.
9 pawn'd pledged **13 rests** remains **in night's coverture** under cover of night **15 lurking** idling, lodging **16 simple** mere **19–21 Ulysses . . . steeds** (In Book X of the *Iliad,* Ulysses and Diomedes under cover of night stealthily enter the camp of the Thracian leader Rhesus, slay him and twelve of his men, and lead away his horses. The horses are called *fatal steeds* because of a prophecy foretelling that Troy would not fall if once these horses drank from the River Xanthus and grazed on the Trojan plain.) **23 At unawares** unexpectedly, suddenly **25 surprise** capture

[SCENE III]

Enter three Watchmen, to guard the King's tent.

FIRST WATCH
Come on, my masters, each man take his stand.
The King by this is set him down to sleep. 2

SECOND WATCH
What, will he not to bed?

FIRST WATCH
Why, no, for he hath made a solemn vow
Never to lie and take his natural rest
Till Warwick or himself be quite suppress'd.

SECOND WATCH
Tomorrow then belike shall be the day,
If Warwick be so near as men report.

THIRD WATCH
But say, I pray, what nobleman is that
That with the King here resteth in his tent?

FIRST WATCH
'Tis the Lord Hastings, the King's chiefest friend.

THIRD WATCH
O, is it so? But why commands the King
That his chief followers lodge in towns about him,
While he himself keeps in the cold field? 14

SECOND WATCH
'Tis the more honor, because more dangerous.

THIRD WATCH
Ay, but give me worship and quietness; 16
I like it better than a dangerous honor.
If Warwick knew in what estate he stands, 18
'Tis to be doubted he would waken him. 19

FIRST WATCH
Unless our halberds did shut up his passage. 20

SECOND WATCH
Ay, wherefore else guard we his royal tent,
But to defend his person from night-foes?

Enter Warwick, Clarence, Oxford, Somerset, and French soldiers, silent all.

WARWICK
This is his tent; and see where stand his guard.
Courage, my masters! Honor now or never!
But follow me, and Edward shall be ours. 25

FIRST WATCH
Who goes there?

SECOND WATCH
Stay, or thou diest!

IV.iii. Location: Edward's camp, near Warwick.
2 by this by this time **14 keeps** lodges **16 worship** ease and dignity **18 estate** situation. **he** i.e., King Edward **19 doubted** feared **20 halberds** long-handled weapons bearing axe-like heads **25 But** only

Warwick and the rest cry all, "Warwick! Warwick!" and set upon the Guard, who fly, crying, "Arm! Arm!" Warwick and the rest following them.

The drum playing and trumpet sounding, enter Warwick, Somerset, and the rest, bringing the King [Edward] out in his gown, sitting in a chair. Richard [of Gloucester] and Hastings fly over the stage.

SOMERSET
What are they that fly there?

WARWICK
Richard and Hastings. Let them go. Here is
The Duke.

KING EDWARD The Duke? Why, Warwick, when we parted,
Thou call'dst me King.

WARWICK Ay, but the case is alter'd.
When you disgrac'd me in my embassade, 32
Then I degraded you from being king,
And come now to create you Duke of York.
Alas, how should you govern any kingdom,
That know not how to use ambassadors,
Nor how to be contented with one wife,
Nor how to use your brothers brotherly,
Nor how to study for the people's welfare,
Nor how to shroud yourself from enemies? 40

KING EDWARD
Yea, brother of Clarence, art thou here too?
Nay, then I see that Edward needs must down. 42
Yet, Warwick, in despite of all mischance,
Of thee thyself and all thy complices, 44
Edward will always bear himself as king.
Though fortune's malice overthrow my state,
My mind exceeds the compass of her wheel. 47

WARWICK
Then, for his mind, be Edward England's king, 48
Takes off his crown.
But Henry now shall wear the English crown,
And be true king indeed, thou but the shadow.
My lord of Somerset, at my request
See that forthwith Duke Edward be convey'd
Unto my brother, Archbishop of York. 53
When I have fought with Pembroke and his fellows,
I'll follow you, and tell what answer
Lewis and the Lady Bona send to him.
Now, for a while farewell, good Duke of York.
They lead him out forcibly.

KING EDWARD
What fates impose, that men must needs abide.
It boots not to resist both wind and tide. 59
Exit [guarded, with Somerset].

OXFORD
What now remains, my lords, for us to do
But march to London with our soldiers?

WARWICK
Ay, that's the first thing that we have to do,
To free King Henry from imprisonment
And see him seated in the regal throne. *Exeunt.*

[SCENE IV]

Enter Rivers and Lady Grey [Queen Elizabeth].

RIVERS
Madam, what makes you in this sudden change? 1

QUEEN ELIZABETH
Why, brother Rivers, are you yet to learn
What late misfortune is befall'n King Edward?

RIVERS
What? Loss of some pitch'd battle against Warwick?

QUEEN ELIZABETH
No, but the loss of his own royal person.

RIVERS
Then is my sovereign slain?

QUEEN ELIZABETH
Ay, almost slain, for he is taken prisoner,
Either betray'd by falsehood of his guard
Or by his foe surpris'd at unawares;
And, as I further have to understand,
Is new committed to the Bishop of York, 11
Fell Warwick's brother, and by that our foe. 12

RIVERS
These news I must confess are full of grief,
Yet, gracious madam, bear it as you may.
Warwick may lose, that now hath won the day.

QUEEN ELIZABETH
Till then fair hope must hinder life's decay. 16
And I the rather wean me from despair
For love of Edward's offspring in my womb.
This is it that makes me bridle passion
And bear with mildness my misfortune's cross.
Ay, ay, for this I draw in many a tear
And stop the rising of blood-sucking sighs, 22
Lest with my sighs or tears I blast or drown 23
King Edward's fruit, true heir to th' English crown.

RIVERS
But, madam, where is Warwick then become?

QUEEN ELIZABETH
I am inform'd that he comes towards London,
To set the crown once more on Henry's head.
Guess thou the rest. King Edward's friends must down.
But, to prevent the tyrant's violence— 29
For trust not him that hath once broken faith—
I'll hence forthwith unto the sanctuary,
To save, at least, the heir of Edward's right. 32

32 embassade ambassadorial mission **40 shroud** conceal, shield **42 needs must down** must fall of necessity **44 complices** accomplices **47 My . . . wheel** i.e., my spirit rises above the misery of Fortune and her wheel **48 for his mind** i.e., in his own thoughts **53 Archbishop of York** i.e., George Neville **59 boots** avails

IV.iv. Location: London. The palace.
1 makes . . . change causes this sudden change (of mood) in you **11 new** newly. **Bishop** i.e., Archbishop **12 Fell** cruel. **by that** i.e., by that token **16 hope . . decay** i.e., only hope can hold off my downfall and death **22 blood-sucking sighs** (Sighs were thought to cost the heart a drop of blood; cf. *2 Henry VI*, III.ii.61, 63 and note.) **23 blast** wither, blight **29 prevent** forestall **32 right** royal claim

There shall I rest secure from force and fraud.
Come, therefore, let us fly while we may fly.
If Warwick take us we are sure to die. *Exeunt.*

[SCENE V]

Enter Richard [Duke of Gloucester], Lord Hastings, and Sir William Stanley.

GLOUCESTER
Now, my Lord Hastings and Sir William Stanley,
Leave off to wonder why I drew you hither 2
Into this chiefest thicket of the park. 3
Thus stands the case: you know our king, my brother,
Is prisoner to the Bishop here, at whose hands
He hath good usage and great liberty,
And, often but attended with weak guard,
Comes hunting this way to disport himself. 8
I have advertis'd him by secret means 9
That if about this hour he make this way
Under the color of his usual game, 11
He shall here find his friends with horse and men
To set him free from his captivity.

Enter King Edward and a Huntsman with him.

HUNTSMAN
This way, my lord, for this way lies the game.
KING EDWARD
Nay, this way, man, see where the huntsmen stand.
Now, brother of Gloucester, Lord Hastings, and the rest,
Stand you thus close to steal the Bishop's deer? 17
GLOUCESTER
Brother, the time and case requireth haste.
Your horse stands ready at the park-corner.
KING EDWARD
But whither shall we then?
HASTINGS To Lynn, my lord— 20
And shipp'd from thence to Flanders?
GLOUCESTER
Well guess'd, believe me, for that was my meaning.
KING EDWARD
Stanley, I will requite thy forwardness. 23
GLOUCESTER
But wherefore stay we? 'Tis no time to talk.
KING EDWARD
Huntsman, what say'st thou? Wilt thou go along?
HUNTSMAN
Better do so than tarry and be hang'd.
GLOUCESTER
Come then, away. Let's ha' no more ado.
KING EDWARD
Bishop, farewell! Shield thee from Warwick's frown,
And pray that I may repossess the crown. *Exeunt.*

[SCENE VI]

Flourish. Enter King Henry the Sixth, Clarence, Warwick, Somerset, young Henry [Earl of Richmond], Oxford, Montague, and Lieutenant [of the Tower].

KING HENRY
Master Lieutenant, now that God and friends
Have shaken Edward from the regal seat,
And turn'd my captive state to liberty,
My fear to hope, my sorrows unto joys,
At our enlargement what are thy due fees? 5
LIEUTENANT
Subjects may challenge nothing of their sov'reigns; 6
But if an humble prayer may prevail,
I then crave pardon of your Majesty.
KING HENRY
For what, Lieutenant? For well using me?
Nay, be thou sure I'll well requite thy kindness
For that it made my imprisonment a pleasure—
Ay, such a pleasure as incaged birds
Conceive when after many moody thoughts
At last by notes of household harmony
They quite forget their loss of liberty.
But, Warwick, after God, thou set'st me free,
And chiefly therefore I thank God and thee.
He was the author, thou the instrument.
Therefore, that I may conquer fortune's spite
By living low, where fortune cannot hurt me,
And that the people of this blessed land
May not be punish'd with my thwarting stars, 22
Warwick, although my head still wear the crown,
I here resign my government to thee,
For thou art fortunate in all thy deeds.
WARWICK
Your Grace hath still been fam'd for virtuous, 26
And now may seem as wise as virtuous
By spying and avoiding fortune's malice,
For few men rightly temper with the stars. 29
Yet in this one thing let me blame your Grace,
For choosing me when Clarence is in place. 31
CLARENCE
No, Warwick, thou art worthy of the sway, 32
To whom the heav'ns in thy nativity
Adjudg'd an olive branch and laurel crown, 34
As likely to be blest in peace and war;
And therefore I yield thee my free consent.
WARWICK
And I choose Clarence only for Protector.

IV.v. Location: A park near Middleham Castle in Yorkshire, belonging to the Archbishop of York.
2 Leave off cease **3 chiefest thicket** thickest copse **8 disport** amuse **9 advertis'd** notified **11 color** pretext **17 close** concealed **20 Lynn** King's Lynn, a seaport in Norfolk **23 forwardness** zeal

IV.vi. Location: London. The Tower.
5 enlargement release from confinement **6 challenge** claim as a right **22 thwarting** crossing (in their astrological influence) **26 still** always **29 temper . . . stars** blend or accord with their destiny **31 in place** present **32 sway** rule **34 olive branch** (Symbol of peace.) **laurel crown** (Symbol of honor in war.)

KING HENRY
Warwick and Clarence, give me both your hands.
[The King joins their hands.]
Now join your hands, and with your hands your hearts,
That no dissension hinder government.
I make you both Protectors of this land,
While I myself will lead a private life
And in devotion spend my latter days,
To sin's rebuke and my Creator's praise.

WARWICK
What answers Clarence to his sovereign's will?

CLARENCE
That he consents, if Warwick yield consent;
For on thy fortune I repose myself.

WARWICK
Why, then, though loath, yet must I be content.
We'll yoke together, like a double shadow
To Henry's body, and supply his place—
I mean, in bearing weight of government
While he enjoys the honor and his ease.
And, Clarence, now then it is more than needful
Forthwith that Edward be pronounc'd a traitor,
And all his lands and goods be confiscate.

CLARENCE
What else? And that succession be determined.

WARWICK
Ay, therein Clarence shall not want his part.

KING HENRY
But, with the first of all your chief affairs,
Let me entreat, for I command no more,
That Margaret your queen and my son Edward
Be sent for, to return from France with speed;
For, till I see them here, by doubtful fear
My joy of liberty is half eclips'd.

CLARENCE
It shall be done, my sovereign, with all speed.

KING HENRY
My Lord of Somerset, what youth is that
Of whom you seem to have so tender care?

SOMERSET
My liege, it is young Henry, Earl of Richmond.

KING HENRY
Come hither, England's hope. *(Lays his hand on his head.)* If secret powers
Suggest but truth to my divining thoughts,
This pretty lad will prove our country's bliss.
His looks are full of peaceful majesty,
His head by nature fram'd to wear a crown,
His hand to wield a scepter, and himself
Likely in time to bless a regal throne.
Make much of him, my lords, for this is he
Must help you more than you are hurt by me.

Enter a Post.

WARWICK
What news, my friend?

POST
That Edward is escaped from your brother,
And fled, as he hears since, to Burgundy.

WARWICK
Unsavory news! But how made he escape?

POST
He was convey'd by Richard Duke of Gloucester
And the Lord Hastings, who attended him
In secret ambush on the forest side
And from the Bishop's huntsmen rescu'd him;
For hunting was his daily exercise.

WARWICK
My brother was too careless of his charge.
But let us hence, my sovereign, to provide
A salve for any sore that may betide.
Exeunt. Mane[n]t Somerset, Richmond, and Oxford.

SOMERSET
My lord, I like not of this flight of Edward's;
For doubtless Burgundy will yield him help,
And we shall have more wars before 't be long.
As Henry's late presaging prophecy
Did glad my heart with hope of this young Richmond,
So doth my heart misgive me, in these conflicts
What may befall him, to his harm and ours.
Therefore, Lord Oxford, to prevent the worst,
Forthwith we'll send him hence to Brittany,
Till storms be past of civil enmity.

OXFORD
Ay, for if Edward repossess the crown,
'Tis like that Richmond with the rest shall down.

SOMERSET
It shall be so; he shall to Brittany.
Come, therefore, let's about it speedily. *Exeunt.*

[SCENE VII]

Flourish. Enter [King] Edward, Richard [Duke of Gloucester], Hastings, and Soldiers, [a troop of Hollanders].

KING EDWARD
Now, brother Richard, Lord Hastings, and the rest,
Yet thus far fortune maketh us amends,
And says that once more I shall interchange
My waned state for Henry's regal crown.
Well have we pass'd and now repass'd the seas,
And brought desired help from Burgundy.
What then remains, we being thus arriv'd
From Ravenspurgh haven before the gates of York,
But that we enter, as into our dukedom?

56 succession be determined the order of succession to the throne (in view of Edward's removal) be definitely established **57 want** lack. (Clarence would have an interest in the crown previously claimed by his brother and willed to him after Henry's death.) **67 Henry . . . Richmond** Henry Tudor, later Henry VII and founder of the Tudor dynasty **69 divining** foreseeing the future

79 he i.e., Warwick's brother, the Archbishop of York **81 convey'd** spirited away **82 attended** awaited **88 betide** occur, develop **100 down** fall

IV. vii. Location: Before York.
8 Ravenspurgh former seaport on the Yorkshire coast, at the mouth of the River Humber

GLOUCESTER
The gates made fast? Brother, I like not this;
For many men that stumble at the threshold
Are well foretold that danger lurks within.

KING EDWARD
Tush, man, abodements must not now affright us.
By fair or foul means we must enter in,
For hither will our friends repair to us.

HASTINGS
My liege, I'll knock once more to summon them.

Enter, on the walls, the Mayor of York, and his Brethren [the Aldermen].

MAYOR
My lords, we were forewarned of your coming,
And shut the gates for safety of ourselves;
For now we owe allegiance unto Henry.

KING EDWARD
But, Master Mayor, if Henry be your king,
Yet Edward at the least is Duke of York.

MAYOR
True, my good lord; I know you for no less.

KING EDWARD
Why, and I challenge nothing but my dukedom,
As being well content with that alone.

GLOUCESTER [*Aside*]
But when the fox hath once got in his nose,
He'll soon find means to make the body follow.

HASTINGS
Why, Master Mayor, why stand you in a doubt?
Open the gates; we are King Henry's friends.

MAYOR
Ay, say you so? The gates shall then be opened.
He descends [with the Aldermen].

GLOUCESTER
A wise stout captain, and soon persuaded!

HASTINGS
The good old man would fain that all were well,
So 'twere not 'long of him; but being ent'red,
I doubt not, I, but we shall soon persuade
Both him and all his brothers unto reason.

Enter [below] the Mayor and two Aldermen.

KING EDWARD
So, Master Mayor, these gates must not be shut
But in the night or in the time of war.
What, fear not, man, but yield me up the keys,
Takes his keys.
For Edward will defend the town and thee,
And all those friends that deign to follow me.

March. Enter Montgomery, with drum and Soldiers.

GLOUCESTER
Brother, this is Sir John Montgomery,
Our trusty friend, unless I be deceiv'd.

KING EDWARD
Welcome, Sir John! But why come you in arms?

MONTGOMERY
To help King Edward in his time of storm,
As every loyal subject ought to do.

KING EDWARD
Thanks, good Montgomery; but we now forget
Our title to the crown and only claim
Our dukedom till God please to send the rest.

MONTGOMERY
Then fare you well, for I will hence again.
I came to serve a king and not a duke.
Drummer, strike up, and let us march away.
The drum begins to march.

KING EDWARD
Nay, stay, Sir John, awhile, and we'll debate
By what safe means the crown may be recover'd.

MONTGOMERY
What talk you of debating? In few words,
If you'll not here proclaim yourself our king,
I'll leave you to your fortune and be gone
To keep them back that come to succor you.
Why shall we fight, if you pretend no title?

GLOUCESTER
Why, brother, wherefore stand you on nice points?

KING EDWARD
When we grow stronger, then we'll make our claim;
Till then, 'tis wisdom to conceal our meaning.

HASTINGS
Away with scrupulous wit! Now arms must rule.

GLOUCESTER
And fearless minds climb soonest unto crowns.
Brother, we will proclaim you out of hand;
The bruit thereof will bring you many friends.

KING EDWARD
Then be it as you will. For 'tis my right,
And Henry but usurps the diadem.

MONTGOMERY
Ay, now my sovereign speaketh like himself,
And now will I be Edward's champion.

HASTINGS
Sound trumpet! Edward shall be here proclaim'd.
Come, fellow soldier, make thou proclamation.
[Gives him a paper.] Flourish. Sound.

SOLDIER [*Reads*] "Edward the Fourth, by the grace of God, King of England and France, and lord of Ireland, etc."

MONTGOMERY
And whosoe'er gainsays King Edward's right,
By this I challenge him to single fight.
Throws down his gauntlet.

ALL Long live Edward the Fourth!

KING EDWARD
Thanks, brave Montgomery, and thanks unto you all.
If fortune serve me, I'll requite this kindness.
Now, for this night, let's harbor here in York;

13 abodements omens (such as stumbling at the threshold, a conventional sign of bad luck) **16 s.d. on the walls** (In this scene, the back wall of the stage, or tiring house façade, is imagined to be the walls of York; a door in the façade represents the gates; and persons in the rear gallery above the stage are *on the walls.*) **23 challenge** claim **29 s.d. descends** (The Mayor and aldermen descend from the rear gallery behind the scenes, and then enter below through the door representing the gates of York.) **31 fain** be glad **32 So . . . him** as long as he does not bear the responsibility **39 deign** are willing **40 Sir John Montgomery** (Called *Sir Thomas* in the chronicles.)

57 pretend claim **58 nice points** overscrupulous details **61 scrupulous wit** cautious or prudent reasoning **63 out of hand** at once **64 bruit** rumor, report

And when the morning sun shall raise his car 80
Above the border of this horizon,
We'll forward towards Warwick and his mates;
For well I wot that Henry is no soldier.
Ah, froward Clarence, how evil it beseems thee 84
To flatter Henry and forsake thy brother!
Yet, as we may, we'll meet both thee and Warwick.
Come on, brave soldiers. Doubt not of the day, 87
And, that once gotten, doubt not of large pay.
Exeunt.

[SCENE VIII]

Flourish. Enter the King [Henry], Warwick, Montague, Clarence, Oxford, and Exeter.

WARWICK
What counsel, lords? Edward from Belgia, 1
With hasty Germans and blunt Hollanders, 2
Hath pass'd in safety through the narrow seas,
And with his troops doth march amain to London, 4
And many giddy people flock to him.

KING HENRY
Let's levy men, and beat him back again.

CLARENCE
A little fire is quickly trodden out
Which, being suffer'd, rivers cannot quench. 8

WARWICK
In Warwickshire I have true-hearted friends,
Not mutinous in peace, yet bold in war.
Those will I muster up. And thou, son Clarence, 11
Shalt stir up in Suffolk, Norfolk, and in Kent,
The knights and gentlemen to come with thee.
Thou, brother Montague, in Buckingham,
Northampton, and in Leicestershire, shalt find
Men well inclin'd to hear what thou command'st.
And thou, brave Oxford, wondrous well belov'd,
In Oxfordshire shalt muster up thy friends.
My sovereign, with the loving citizens,
Like to his island girt in with the ocean,
Or modest Dian circled with her nymphs, 21
Shall rest in London till we come to him.
Fair lords, take leave and stand not to reply. 23
Farewell, my sovereign.

KING HENRY
Farewell, my Hector, and my Troy's true hope. 25

CLARENCE
In sign of truth, I kiss your Highness' hand.

KING HENRY
Well-minded Clarence, be thou fortunate!

MONTAGUE
Comfort, my lord; and so I take my leave.

OXFORD
And thus I seal my truth, and bid adieu.
[They kiss Henry's hand.]

KING HENRY
Sweet Oxford, and my loving Montague,
And all at once, once more a happy farewell. 31

WARWICK
Farewell, sweet lords. Let's meet at Coventry.
Exeunt [all but King Henry and Exeter].

KING HENRY
Here at the palace will I rest awhile.
Cousin of Exeter, what thinks your lordship?
Methinks the power that Edward hath in field
Should not be able to encounter mine.

EXETER
The doubt is that he will seduce the rest. 37

KING HENRY
That's not my fear. My meed hath got me fame. 38
I have not stopp'd mine ears to their demands,
Nor posted off their suits with slow delays. 40
My pity hath been balm to heal their wounds,
My mildness hath allay'd their swelling griefs,
My mercy dried their water-flowing tears.
I have not been desirous of their wealth,
Nor much oppress'd them with great subsidies, 45
Nor forward of revenge, though they much err'd. 46
Then why should they love Edward more than me?
No, Exeter, these graces challenge grace; 48
And when the lion fawns upon the lamb,
The lamb will never cease to follow him.
Shout within, "A Lancaster! A Lancaster!"

EXETER
Hark, hark, my lord! What shouts are these?

Enter [King] Edward and his Soldiers [with Gloucester].

KING EDWARD
Seize on the shame-fac'd Henry, bear him hence, 52
And once again proclaim us king of England!
You are the fount that makes small brooks to flow.
Now stops thy spring; my sea shall suck them dry,
And swell so much the higher by their ebb.
Hence with him to the Tower; let him not speak.
Exit [Guard] with King Henry.
And, lords, towards Coventry bend we our course,
Where peremptory Warwick now remains. 59
The sun shines hot, and, if we use delay, 60
Cold biting winter mars our hop'd-for hay. 61

GLOUCESTER
Away betimes, before his forces join, 62
And take the great-grown traitor unawares.
Brave warriors, march amain towards Coventry.
Exeunt.

80 his car i.e. Phoebus' chariot **84 froward** perverse **87 the day** the day's outcome

IV.viii. Location: The Bishop of London's palace.
1 Belgia i.e., the Low Countries **2 hasty** quick-tempered. **blunt** merciless **4 amain** with full speed **8 suffer'd** allowed **11 son** i.e., son-in-law **21 modest Dian** chaste Diana, goddess of the moon and of chastity **23 stand** wait **25 Hector** i.e., chief protector of Troy. (England derived its legendary descent from Troy, through Brutus, great-grandson of Aeneas, supposed founder of the English nation.)

31 at once together **37 doubt** fear, danger **38 My . . . fame** my merits (for dealing generously and justly) have established my reputation **40 posted off** put off **45 subsidies** taxes **46 forward of** eager for **48 challenge grace** claim favor **52 shame-fac'd** shamefast, shy **59 peremptory** overbearing **60–61 The sun . . . hay** i.e., make hay while the sun shines **62 betimes** quickly

[ACT V • SCENE I]

Enter Warwick, the Mayor of Coventry, two Messengers, and others upon the walls.

WARWICK
Where is the post that came from valiant Oxford?
How far hence is thy lord, mine honest fellow?
FIRST MESSENGER
By this at Dunsmore, marching hitherward. 3
WARWICK
How far off is our brother Montague?
Where is the post that came from Montague?
SECOND MESSENGER
By this at Daintry, with a puissant troop. 6

Enter [*Sir John*] *Somerville* [*aloft*].

WARWICK
Say, Somerville, what says my loving son?
And, by thy guess, how nigh is Clarence now?
SOMERVILLE
At Southam I did leave him with his forces, 9
And do expect him here some two hours hence.
[*Drum heard.*]
WARWICK
Then Clarence is at hand. I hear his drum.
SOMERVILLE
It is not his, my lord. Here Southam lies. [*Points.*]
The drum your honor hears marcheth from Warwick. 13
WARWICK
Who should that be? Belike unlook'd-for friends.
SOMERVILLE
They are at hand, and you shall quickly know.

March. Flourish. Enter [*King*] *Edward, Richard* [*Duke of Gloucester*], *and Soldiers* [*below*].

KING EDWARD
Go, trumpet, to the walls, and sound a parle. 16
GLOUCESTER
See how the surly Warwick mans the wall!
WARWICK
O unbid spite! Is sportful Edward come? 18
Where slept our scouts, or how are they seduc'd,
That we could hear no news of his repair? 20
KING EDWARD
Now, Warwick, wilt thou ope the city gates,
Speak gentle words and humbly bend thy knee,
Call Edward king, and at his hands beg mercy?
And he shall pardon thee these outrages.
WARWICK
Nay, rather, wilt thou draw thy forces hence, 25
Confess who set thee up and pluck'd thee down,
Call Warwick patron and be penitent?
And thou shalt still remain the Duke of York.
GLOUCESTER
I thought, at least, he would have said "the King";
Or did he make the jest against his will?
WARWICK
Is not a dukedom, sir, a goodly gift?
GLOUCESTER
Ay, by my faith, for a poor earl to give.
I'll do thee service for so good a gift. 33
WARWICK
'Twas I that gave the kingdom to thy brother.
KING EDWARD
Why then 'tis mine, if but by Warwick's gift.
WARWICK
Thou art no Atlas for so great a weight; 36
And, weakling, Warwick takes his gift again,
And Henry is my king, Warwick his subject.
KING EDWARD
But Warwick's king is Edward's prisoner.
And, gallant Warwick, do but answer this:
What is the body when the head is off?
GLOUCESTER
Alas, that Warwick had no more forecast, 42
But, whiles he thought to steal the single ten, 43
The King was slily finger'd from the deck!
You left poor Henry at the Bishop's palace,
And, ten to one, you'll meet him in the Tower.
KING EDWARD
'Tis even so. Yet you are Warwick still.
GLOUCESTER
Come, Warwick, take the time. Kneel down, kneel down. 48
Nay, when? Strike now, or else the iron cools. 49
WARWICK
I had rather chop this hand off at a blow,
And with the other fling it at thy face,
Than bear so low a sail, to strike to thee.
KING EDWARD
Sail how thou canst, have wind and tide thy friend,
This hand, fast wound about thy coal-black hair,
Shall, whiles thy head is warm and new cut off,
Write in the dust this sentence with thy blood,
"Wind-changing Warwick now can change no more."

Enter Oxford, with drum and colors.

WARWICK
O cheerful colors! See where Oxford comes!
OXFORD
Oxford, Oxford, for Lancaster!
[*He and his forces enter the city.*]
GLOUCESTER
The gates are open, let us enter too.
KING EDWARD
So other foes may set upon our backs.

V.i. Location: Coventry. Before the walls.
s.d. upon the walls (As in IV.vii, the *walls* of this town are the tiring house façade backstage, and those appearing *on the walls* are in the rear gallery above the stage.) **3, 6, 9, 13 Dunsmore, Daintry** (i.e., Daventry), **Southam, Warwick** (Towns within a day's march of Coventry.) **16 parle** trumpet call for a parley **18 unbid** unwelcome. **spite** vexatious circumstance. **sportful** lascivious **20 repair** approach **25 draw** withdraw

33 do thee service i.e., pay feudal homage. (Said ironically.) **36 Atlas** the Titan in classical myth who carried the world on his shoulders **42 forecast** forethought **43 single ten** mere ten-card. (Less valuable than the king-card.) **48 time** opportunity **49 when** i.e., when are you going to act. **Strike . . . cools** i.e., strike while the iron is hot. (But *strike* also means to lower sail, yield; hence Warwick's refusal to *bear so low a sail*, i.e., offer tokens of submission, in l. 52. Cf. III.iii.5, note.) **57 Wind-changing** i.e., shifting like a weathervane

Stand we in good array, for they no doubt
Will issue out again and bid us battle.
If not, the city being but of small defense,
We'll quickly rouse the traitors in the same. 65
[Oxford appears above, on the walls.]

WARWICK
O, welcome, Oxford, for we want thy help.

Enter Montague, with drum and colors.

MONTAGUE
Montague, Montague, for Lancaster!
[He and his forces enter the city.]

GLOUCESTER
Thou and thy brother both shall buy this treason
Even with the dearest blood your bodies bear.

KING EDWARD
The harder match'd, the greater victory.
My mind presageth happy gain and conquest.

Enter Somerset, with drum and colors.

SOMERSET
Somerset, Somerset, for Lancaster!
[He and his forces enter the city.]

GLOUCESTER
Two of thy name, both Dukes of Somerset, 73
Have sold their lives unto the house of York,
And thou shalt be the third, if this sword hold.

Enter Clarence, with drum and colors.

WARWICK
And lo, where George of Clarence sweeps along,
Of force enough to bid his brother battle;
With whom an upright zeal to right prevails
More than the nature of a brother's love!
[Gloucester and Clarence whisper together.]
Come, Clarence, come; thou wilt, if Warwick call.

CLARENCE
Father of Warwick, know you what this means?
[Takes his red rose out of his hat and throws it at Warwick.]
Look here, I throw my infamy at thee.
I will not ruinate my father's house,
Who gave his blood to lime the stones together, 84
And set up Lancaster. Why, trowest thou, Warwick, 85
That Clarence is so harsh, so blunt, unnatural,
To bend the fatal instruments of war
Against his brother and his lawful king?
Perhaps thou wilt object my holy oath. 89
To keep that oath were more impiety
Than Jephthah when he sacrific'd his daughter. 91
I am so sorry for my trespass made
That, to deserve well at my brother's hands,
I here proclaim myself thy mortal foe,
With resolution, wheresoe'er I meet thee—
As I will meet thee, if thou stir abroad— 96
To plague thee for thy foul misleading me.
And so, proud-hearted Warwick, I defy thee,
And to my brother turn my blushing cheeks.
Pardon me, Edward, I will make amends;
And, Richard, do not frown upon my faults,
For I will henceforth be no more unconstant.

KING EDWARD
Now welcome more, and ten times more belov'd,
Than if thou never hadst deserv'd our hate!

GLOUCESTER
Welcome, good Clarence. This is brother-like.

WARWICK
O passing traitor, perjur'd and unjust! 106

KING EDWARD
What, Warwick, wilt thou leave the town and fight?
Or shall we beat the stones about thine ears?

WARWICK
Alas, I am not coop'd here for defense!
I will away towards Barnet presently, 110
And bid thee battle, Edward, if thou dar'st.

KING EDWARD
Yes, Warwick, Edward dares, and leads the way.
Lords, to the field! Saint George and victory!

Exeunt [King Edward and his company]. March. Warwick and his company follows [out of the city].

[SCENE II]

Alarum and excursions. Enter [King] Edward, bringing forth Warwick wounded.

KING EDWARD
So, lie thou there. Die thou, and die our fear,
For Warwick was a bug that fear'd us all. 2
Now, Montague, sit fast. I seek for thee,
That Warwick's bones may keep thine company.
Exit.

WARWICK
Ah, who is nigh? Come to me, friend or foe,
And tell me who is victor, York or Warwick?
Why ask I that? My mangled body shows,
My blood, my want of strength, my sick heart shows,
That I must yield my body to the earth
And, by my fall, the conquest to my foe.
Thus yields the cedar to the axe's edge,
Whose arms gave shelter to the princely eagle, 12
Under whose shade the ramping lion slept, 13
Whose top-branch overpeer'd Jove's spreading tree 14

65 rouse cause (an animal) to rise from its lair **73 Two of thy name** i.e., Edmund Beaufort, second Duke of Somerset, killed at St. Albans in 1455, and his son Henry (not a character in this play), beheaded in 1464 for his Lancastrian sympathies. (The duke addressed here is Henry's brother Edmund, fourth duke.) **84 lime** cement **85 trowest thou** do you think **89 object** urge **91 Jephthah** (See Judges 11:30 ff. for the account of Jephthah's vow to sacrifice, if victorious, the first living creature that came to meet him on his return. His daughter was the victim.) **96 abroad** from home

106 passing surpassing **110 Barnet** a town in Hertfordshire, about ten miles north of London. (Warwick's illogical proposal that the armies meet at Barnet, some seventy-five miles from Coventry, is a result of Shakespeare's telescoping and rearranging of historical events.)

V.ii. Location: A field of battle near Barnet. (Despite the distance from Coventry to Barnet, the sense here is of virtually continuous action.)
2 bug bugbear, goblin. **fear'd** frightened **12, 13 eagle, lion** (Royal emblems; Warwick, the lofty *cedar* in this metaphor, has at times given his protection to both Edward and Henry.) **13 ramping** rampant, upreared **14 Jove's spreading tree** i.e., the oak

And kept low shrubs from winter's pow'rful wind.
These eyes, that now are dimm'd with death's black veil,
Have been as piercing as the midday sun,
To search the secret treasons of the world.
The wrinkles in my brows, now fill'd with blood,
Were lik'ned oft to kingly sepulchers;
For who liv'd king, but I could dig his grave?
And who durst smile when Warwick bent his brow?
Lo, now my glory smear'd in dust and blood!
My parks, my walks, my manors that I had,
Even now forsake me, and of all my lands
Is nothing left me but my body's length.
Why, what is pomp, rule, reign, but earth and dust?
And, live we how we can, yet die we must.

Enter Oxford and Somerset.

SOMERSET
Ah, Warwick, Warwick! Wert thou as we are,
We might recover all our loss again.
The Queen from France hath brought a puissant power;
Even now we heard the news. Ah, couldst thou fly!

WARWICK
Why, then I would not fly. Ah, Montague,
If thou be there, sweet brother, take my hand,
And with thy lips keep in my soul awhile!
Thou lov'st me not, for, brother, if thou didst,
Thy tears would wash this cold congealed blood
That glues my lips and will not let me speak.
Come quickly, Montague, or I am dead.

SOMERSET
Ah, Warwick, Montague hath breath'd his last,
And to the latest gasp cried out for Warwick
And said "Commend me to my valiant brother."
And more he would have said, and more he spoke,
Which sounded like a cannon in a vault,
That mought not be distinguish'd; but at last
I well might hear, delivered with a groan,
"O, farewell, Warwick!"

WARWICK
Sweet rest his soul! Fly, lords, and save yourselves,
For Warwick bids you all farewell, to meet in heaven. *[Dies.]*

OXFORD
Away, away, to meet the Queen's great power!
Here they bear away his body. Exeunt.

[SCENE III]

Flourish. Enter King Edward in triumph, with Richard [Duke of Gloucester], Clarence, and the rest.

KING EDWARD
Thus far our fortune keeps an upward course,
And we are grac'd with wreaths of victory.

31 puissant powerful **35 with thy lips** i.e., with a kiss. (The soul was thought to leave the body through the mouth.) **41 latest** last **45 mought** might

V.iii. Location: The field of battle near Barnet, as before.

But, in the midst of this bright-shining day,
I spy a black, suspicious, threat'ning cloud
That will encounter with our glorious sun,
Ere he attain his easeful western bed:
I mean, my lords, those powers that the Queen
Hath rais'd in Gallia have arriv'd our coast
And, as we hear, march on to fight with us.

CLARENCE
A little gale will soon disperse that cloud
And blow it to the source from whence it came.
The very beams will dry those vapors up,
For every cloud engenders not a storm.

GLOUCESTER
The Queen is valued thirty thousand strong,
And Somerset, with Oxford, fled to her.
If she have time to breathe, be well assur'd
Her faction will be full as strong as ours.

KING EDWARD
We are advertis'd by our loving friends
That they do hold their course toward Tewkesbury.
We, having now the best at Barnet field,
Will thither straight, for willingness rids way;
And, as we march, our strength will be augmented
In every county as we go along.
Strike up the drum, cry "Courage!" and away.
Exeunt.

[SCENE IV]

Flourish. March. Enter the Queen [Margaret], young [Prince] Edward, Somerset, Oxford, and Soldiers.

QUEEN MARGARET
Great lords, wise men ne'er sit and wail their loss,
But cheerly seek how to redress their harms.
What though the mast be now blown overboard,
The cable broke, the holding-anchor lost,
And half our sailors swallow'd in the flood?
Yet lives our pilot still. Is 't meet that he
Should leave the helm and, like a fearful lad,
With tearful eyes add water to the sea,
And give more strength to that which hath too much,
Whiles, in his moan, the ship splits on the rock,
Which industry and courage might have sav'd?
Ah, what a shame, ah, what a fault were this!
Say Warwick was our anchor. What of that?
And Montague our topmast. What of him?
Our slaught'red friends the tackles. What of these?
Why, is not Oxford here another anchor?
And Somerset another goodly mast?
The friends of France our shrouds and tacklings?

8 Gallia France. **arriv'd** reached **16 breathe** i.e., muster her strength **18 advertis'd** notified **19 Tewkesbury** a town in Gloucestershire **21 rids way** annihilates distance, makes the way seem short

V.iv. Location: Plains near Tewkesbury.
2 cheerly cheerfully **15 tackles** ropes and blocks for raising and lowering sails **18 shrouds** ropes or cables supporting the mast

And, though unskillful, why not Ned and I
For once allow'd the skillful pilot's charge?
We will not from the helm to sit and weep,
But keep our course, though the rough wind say no,
From shelves and rocks that threaten us with wrack.
As good to chide the waves as speak them fair.
And what is Edward but a ruthless sea?
What Clarence but a quicksand of deceit?
And Richard but a ragged fatal rock?
All these the enemies to our poor bark.
Say you can swim, alas, 'tis but a while;
Tread on the sand, why, there you quickly sink;
Bestride the rock, the tide will wash you off,
Or else you famish—that's a threefold death.
This speak I, lords, to let you understand,
If case some one of you would fly from us,
That there's no hop'd-for mercy with the brothers
More than with ruthless waves, with sands and rocks.
Why, courage then! What cannot be avoided
'Twere childish weakness to lament or fear.

PRINCE
Methinks a woman of this valiant spirit
Should, if a coward heard her speak these words,
Infuse his breast with magnanimity
And make him, naked, foil a man at arms.
I speak not this as doubting any here;
For did I but suspect a fearful man,
He should have leave to go away betimes,
Lest in our need he might infect another
And make him of like spirit to himself.
If any such be here—as God forbid!—
Let him depart before we need his help.

OXFORD
Women and children of so high a courage,
And warriors faint! Why, 'twere perpetual shame.
O brave young prince! Thy famous grandfather
Doth live again in thee. Long mayst thou live
To bear his image and renew his glories!

SOMERSET
And he that will not fight for such a hope,
Go home to bed, and, like the owl by day,
If he arise, be mock'd and wond'red at.

QUEEN MARGARET
Thanks, gentle Somerset; sweet Oxford, thanks.

PRINCE
And take his thanks that yet hath nothing else.

Enter a Messenger.

MESSENGER
Prepare you, lords, for Edward is at hand,
Ready to fight. Therefore be resolute.

OXFORD
I thought no less. It is his policy
To haste thus fast, to find us unprovided.

SOMERSET
But he's deceiv'd; we are in readiness.

QUEEN MARGARET
This cheers my heart, to see your forwardness.

OXFORD
Here pitch our battle. Hence we will not budge.

Flourish and march. Enter [King] Edward, Richard [Duke of Gloucester], Clarence, and Soldiers.

KING EDWARD
Brave followers, yonder stands the thorny wood,
Which, by the heavens' assistance and your strength,
Must by the roots be hewn up yet ere night.
I need not add more fuel to your fire,
For well I wot ye blaze to burn them out.
Give signal to the fight, and to it, lords!

QUEEN MARGARET
Lords, knights, and gentlemen, what I should say
My tears gainsay; for every word I speak,
Ye see, I drink the water of mine eye.
Therefore, no more but this: Henry, your sovereign,
Is prisoner to the foe, his state usurp'd,
His realm a slaughter-house, his subjects slain,
His statutes cancel'd, and his treasure spent;
And yonder is the wolf that makes this spoil.
You fight in justice. Then, in God's name, lords,
Be valiant and give signal to the fight.

Alarum. Retreat. Excursions [in which Queen Margaret, Prince Edward, Oxford, and Somerset are taken]. Exeunt.

[SCENE V]

Flourish. Enter [King] Edward, Richard [Duke of Gloucester], Queen [Margaret, as prisoner], Clarence; Oxford, Somerset [as prisoners].

KING EDWARD
Now here a period of tumultuous broils.
Away with Oxford to Hames Castle straight.
For Somerset, off with his guilty head.
Go, bear them hence. I will not hear them speak.

OXFORD
For my part, I'll not trouble thee with words.

SOMERSET
Nor I, but stoop with patience to my fortune.

Exeunt [Oxford and Somerset, guarded].

QUEEN MARGARET
So part we sadly in this troublous world,
To meet with joy in sweet Jerusalem.

KING EDWARD
Is proclamation made, that who finds Edward

20 charge responsibility **23 shelves** sandbanks, shoals. **wrack** ruin **24 As good to** i.e., one might as well. **speak them fair** address them courteously **34 If in** **42 naked** unarmed. **foil** defeat. **man at arms** armed soldier **45 betimes** at once **52 grandfather** i.e., Henry V **59 his . . . else** i.e., my thanks, I who as yet have nothing else to give **63 unprovided** unprepared

66 pitch our battle draw up our armies **71 wot** know **74 gainsay** forbid

V.v. Location: Scene continues at the battlefield near Tewkesbury.
1 period termination **2 Hames Castle** i.e., Hammes Castle near Calais (where Oxford was indeed confined, but not until his capture some three years after Tewkesbury)

Shall have a high reward, and he his life?

GLOUCESTER
It is. And lo, where youthful Edward comes!

Enter [Soldiers, with] the Prince [Edward].

KING EDWARD
Bring forth the gallant, let us hear him speak.
What, can so young a thorn begin to prick?
Edward, what satisfaction canst thou make
For bearing arms, for stirring up my subjects,
And all the trouble thou hast turn'd me to?

PRINCE
Speak like a subject, proud ambitious York!
Suppose that I am now my father's mouth;
Resign thy chair, and where I stand kneel thou,
Whilst I propose the selfsame words to thee,
Which, traitor, thou wouldst have me answer to.

QUEEN MARGARET
Ah, that thy father had been so resolv'd!

GLOUCESTER
That you might still have worn the petticoat,
And ne'er have stol'n the breech from Lancaster.

PRINCE
Let Aesop fable in a winter's night;
His currish riddles sorts not with this place.

GLOUCESTER
By heaven, brat, I'll plague ye for that word.

QUEEN MARGARET
Ay, thou wast born to be a plague to men.

GLOUCESTER
For God's sake, take away this captive scold.

PRINCE
Nay, take away this scolding crook-back rather.

KING EDWARD
Peace, willful boy, or I will charm your tongue.

CLARENCE
Untutor'd lad, thou art too malapert.

PRINCE
I know my duty; you are all undutiful.
Lascivious Edward, and thou perjur'd George,
And thou misshapen Dick, I tell ye all
I am your better, traitors as ye are,
And thou usurp'st my father's right and mine.

KING EDWARD
Take that, thou likeness of this railer here!
Stabs him.

GLOUCESTER
Sprawl'st thou? Take that, to end thy agony.
Richard stabs him.

CLARENCE
And there's for twitting me with perjury.
Clarence stabs him.

QUEEN MARGARET
O, kill me too!

GLOUCESTER
Marry, and shall. *Offers to kill her.*

KING EDWARD
Hold, Richard, hold, for we have done too much.

GLOUCESTER
Why should she live, to fill the world with words?
[Margaret swoons.]

KING EDWARD
What, doth she swoon? Use means for her recovery.

GLOUCESTER *[To Clarence]*
Clarence, excuse me to the King my brother;
I'll hence to London on a serious matter.
Ere ye come there, be sure to hear some news.

CLARENCE
What? What?

GLOUCESTER
The Tower, the Tower. *Exit.*

QUEEN MARGARET *[Reviving]*
O Ned, sweet Ned, speak to thy mother, boy!
Canst thou not speak? O traitors, murderers!
They that stabb'd Caesar shed no blood at all,
Did not offend, nor were not worthy blame,
If this foul deed were by to equal it.
He was a man; this, in respect, a child,
And men ne'er spend their fury on a child.
What's worse than murderer, that I may name it?
No, no, my heart will burst, an if I speak;
And I will speak, that so my heart may burst.
Butchers and villains, bloody cannibals!
How sweet a plant have you untimely cropp'd!
You have no children, butchers; if you had,
The thought of them would have stirr'd up remorse.
But if you ever chance to have a child,
Look in his youth to have him so cut off
As, deathsmen, you have rid this sweet young
prince!

KING EDWARD
Away with her. Go, bear her hence perforce.

QUEEN MARGARET
Nay, never bear me hence, dispatch me here;
Here sheathe thy sword, I'll pardon thee my death.
What, wilt thou not? Then, Clarence, do it thou.

CLARENCE
By heaven, I will not do thee so much ease.

QUEEN MARGARET
Good Clarence, do; sweet Clarence, do thou do it.

CLARENCE
Didst thou not hear me swear I would not do it?

QUEEN MARGARET
Ay, but thou usest to forswear thyself.
'Twas sin before, but now 'tis charity.
What, wilt thou not? Where is that devil's butcher,
Hard-favor'd Richard? Richard, where art thou?
Thou art not here. Murder is thy alms-deed;
Petitioners for blood thou ne'er put'st back.

KING EDWARD
Away, I say! I charge ye, bear her hence.

14 satisfaction recompense **19 chair** throne **24 breech** breeches, symbol of male authority **25 Aesop** Greek teller of fables (who, like Gloucester, was reputed to have been deformed). **in . . . night** i.e., in a setting fitted for such childish tales **26 His . . . place** his mean riddles are inappropriate to this place. (Prince Edward is retorting to Gloucester's jibe, denying the allegation that his father was henpecked.) **31 charm** cast a spell upon, i.e., silence **32 malapert** saucy **38 this railer here** i.e., Queen Margaret **39 Sprawl'st thou** i.e., are you twitching in the throes of death

42 Marry, and shall i.e., indeed, I will **48 be sure** expect **55 equal** compare with **56 respect** comparison **67 rid** removed, killed **75 thou usest** you are accustomed **78 Hard-favor'd** ugly **79 alms-deed** act of charity **80 Petitioners . . . back** you never turn away men asking for blood

QUEEN MARGARET
So come to you and yours, as to this prince!
Exit Queen [led out forcibly].

KING EDWARD
Where's Richard gone?

CLARENCE
To London, all in post; and, as I guess,
To make a bloody supper in the Tower.

KING EDWARD
He's sudden, if a thing comes in his head.
Now march we hence. Discharge the common sort
With pay and thanks, and let's away to London
And see our gentle queen how well she fares.
By this, I hope, she hath a son for me. *Exeunt.*

[SCENE VI]

Enter Henry the Sixth and Richard [Duke of Gloucester], with the Lieutenant, on the walls.

GLOUCESTER
Good day, my lord. What, at your book so hard?

KING HENRY
Ay, my good lord—my lord, I should say rather.
'Tis sin to flatter. "Good" was little better.
"Good Gloucester" and "good devil" were alike,
And both preposterous; therefore, not "good lord."

GLOUCESTER
Sirrah, leave us to ourselves. We must confer.
[Exit Lieutenant.]

KING HENRY
So flies the reakless shepherd from the wolf;
So first the harmless sheep doth yield his fleece
And next his throat unto the butcher's knife.
What scene of death hath Roscius now to act?

GLOUCESTER
Suspicion always haunts the guilty mind;
The thief doth fear each bush an officer.

KING HENRY
The bird that hath been limed in a bush,
With trembling wings misdoubteth every bush;
And I, the hapless male to one sweet bird,
Have now the fatal object in my eye
Where my poor young was lim'd, was caught, and kill'd.

GLOUCESTER
Why, what a peevish fool was that of Crete,
That taught his son the office of a fowl!
And yet, for all his wings, the fool was drown'd.

KING HENRY
I, Daedalus; my poor boy, Icarus;
Thy father, Minos, that denied our course;
The sun that sear'd the wings of my sweet boy,
Thy brother Edward; and thyself the sea
Whose envious gulf did swallow up his life.
Ah, kill me with thy weapon, not with words!
My breast can better brook thy dagger's point
Than can my ears that tragic history.
But wherefore dost thou come? Is 't for my life?

GLOUCESTER
Think'st thou I am an executioner?

KING HENRY
A persecutor, I am sure, thou art.
If murdering innocents be executing,
Why, then thou art an executioner.

GLOUCESTER
Thy son I kill'd for his presumption.

KING HENRY
Hadst thou been kill'd when first thou didst presume,
Thou hadst not liv'd to kill a son of mine.
And thus I prophesy, that many a thousand,
Which now mistrust no parcel of my fear,
And many an old man's sigh and many a widow's,
And many an orphan's water-standing eye—
Men for their sons, wives for their husbands,
Orphans for their parents' timeless death—
Shall rue the hour that ever thou wast born.
The owl shriek'd at thy birth—an evil sign;
The night-crow cried, aboding luckless time;
Dogs howl'd, and hideous tempest shook down trees;
The raven rook'd her on the chimney's top,
And chatt'ring pies in dismal discords sung.
Thy mother felt more than a mother's pain,
And yet brought forth less than a mother's hope,
To wit, an indigested and deformed lump,
Not like the fruit of such a goodly tree.
Teeth hadst thou in thy head when thou wast born,
To signify thou cam'st to bite the world;
And, if the rest be true which I have heard,
Thou cam'st—

GLOUCESTER
I'll hear no more. Die, prophet, in thy speech.
Stabs him.
For this, amongst the rest, was I ordain'd.

KING HENRY
Ay, and for much more slaughter after this.
O, God forgive my sins, and pardon thee! *Dies.*

GLOUCESTER
What, will the aspiring blood of Lancaster
Sink in the ground? I thought it would have mounted.
See how my sword weeps for the poor king's death!
O, may such purple tears be alway shed
From those that wish the downfall of our house!

84 post haste **87 common sort** ordinary soldiers **90 this** this time

V.vi. Location: London. The Tower.
1 book i.e., book of devotion **3 little better** i.e., little more than flattery **5 preposterous** unnatural **6 Sirrah** (Customary form of address to inferiors.) **7 reakless** heedless **10 Roscius** celebrated Roman actor much admired by Cicero, thought by the Elizabethans to have been a tragedian **12 an officer** to be an arresting officer **13 limed** snared with birdlime, a sticky substance smeared on branches **14 misdoubteth** is mistrustful of **15 male** father, begetter. **bird** chick, offspring **18 peevish** silly. (For the story of Daedalus and Icarus of Crete, see *1 Henry VI*, IV.vi.55, note.)

27 brook endure **38 mistrust . . . fear** i.e., feel none of the suspicion that I feel **40 water-standing** i.e., filled with tears **42 timeless** untimely **45 night-crow** nightjar or owl. **aboding** foreboding **47 rook'd her** alighted, roosted **48 pies** magpies **64 purple** blood-red

If any spark of life be yet remaining,
Down, down to hell, and say I sent thee thither!
Stabs him again.
I, that have neither pity, love, nor fear.
Indeed, 'tis true that Henry told me of;
For I have often heard my mother say
I came into the world with my legs forward.
Had I not reason, think ye, to make haste,
And seek their ruin that usurp'd our right?
The midwife wonder'd and the women cried,
"O, Jesus bless us, he is born with teeth!"
And so I was, which plainly signified
That I should snarl and bite and play the dog.
Then, since the heavens have shap'd my body so,
Let hell make crook'd my mind to answer it. 79
I have no brother, I am like no brother;
And this word "love," which greybeards call divine,
Be resident in men like one another
And not in me. I am myself alone.
Clarence, beware. Thou keep'st me from the light;
But I will sort a pitchy day for thee; 85
For I will buzz abroad such prophecies
That Edward shall be fearful of his life,
And then, to purge his fear, I'll be thy death.
King Henry and the Prince his son are gone;
Clarence, thy turn is next, and then the rest,
Counting myself but bad till I be best. 91
I'll throw thy body in another room
And triumph, Henry, in thy day of doom.
Exit [with the body].

[SCENE VII]

Flourish, Enter King [Edward], Queen [Elizabeth], Clarence, Richard [Duke of Gloucester], Hastings, Nurse [with the young Prince], and Attendants.

KING EDWARD
Once more we sit in England's royal throne,
Repurchas'd with the blood of enemies.
What valiant foemen, like to autumn's corn, 3
Have we mow'd down in tops of all their pride! 4
Three Dukes of Somerset, threefold renown'd
For hardy and undoubted champions; 6
Two Cliffords, as the father and the son, 7
And two Northumberlands—two braver men
Ne'er spurr'd their coursers at the trumpet's sound; 9
With them, the two brave bears, Warwick and Montague, 10
That in their chains fetter'd the kingly lion
And made the forest tremble when they roar'd.
Thus have we swept suspicion from our seat 13
And made our footstool of security.
Come hither, Bess, and let me kiss my boy.
[Kisses his son.]
Young Ned, for thee, thine uncles and myself
Have in our armors watch'd the winter's night, 17
Went all afoot in summer's scalding heat,
That thou mightst repossess the crown in peace;
And of our labors thou shalt reap the gain.

GLOUCESTER *[Aside]*
I'll blast his harvest, if your head were laid; 21
For yet I am not look'd on in the world. 22
This shoulder was ordain'd so thick to heave,
And heave it shall some weight, or break my back.
Work thou the way, and thou shalt execute. 25

KING EDWARD
Clarence and Gloucester, love my lovely queen,
And kiss your princely nephew, brothers both.

CLARENCE
The duty that I owe unto your Majesty
I seal upon the lips of this sweet babe.
[Kisses the Prince.]

QUEEN ELIZABETH
Thanks, noble Clarence; worthy brother, thanks.

GLOUCESTER
And, that I love the tree from whence thou sprang'st,
Witness the loving kiss I give the fruit. *[Kiss.]*
[Aside.] To say the truth, so Judas kiss'd his master,
And cried "All hail!" when as he meant all harm.

KING EDWARD
Now am I seated as my soul delights,
Having my country's peace and brothers' loves.

CLARENCE
What will your Grace have done with Margaret?
Reignier, her father, to the King of France
Hath pawn'd the Sicils and Jerusalem, 39
And hither have they sent it for her ransom. 40

KING EDWARD
Away with her, and waft her hence to France. 41
And now what rests but that we spend the time
With stately triumphs, mirthful comic shows, 43
Such as befits the pleasure of the court?
Sound drums and trumpets! Farewell sour annoy!
For here, I hope, begins our lasting joy.
Exeunt omnes.

79 answer match **85 sort** select. **pitchy** black **91 bad** unfortunate

V.vii. Location: London. The palace.
3 corn grain **4 in tops** at the height **6 undoubted** fearless **7 as** to wit **9 coursers** horses **10 bears** (Refers to the Neville family emblem.) **13 seat** throne

17 watch'd stayed awake throughout **21 if . . . laid** i.e., once you are laid out on the bier in death **22 look'd on** heeded, respected **25 Work thou** (Addressed to himself, indicating his head.) **thou shalt** (Addressed to his shoulder and arm.) **39 the Sicils** (See note to I.iv.122.) **40 it** i.e., the money raised by "pawn" **41 waft** convey by water **43 triumphs** festivities

The Tragedy of King Richard the Third

Richard III begins where *3 Henry VI* left off, and completes the action of the four-play series. On the basis of its Senecan style, the play appears to have been written soon after its predecessors, some time between 1591 and 1594. Richard's evil character, which had already begun to emerge in the last of the *Henry VI* plays, now stands fully revealed. His opening soliloquy depends for its ironically mocking effect on our familiarity with recent events. An end to the Yorkist-Lancastrian hostilities has come at last; but with his genius for evil, Richard looks upon a time of peace only with envy and contempt. His intense self-assertion and his aggressive energy must find new employment. No peace can withstand the machinations of this consummate deceiver who has given his nephew Edward the kiss of Judas during the Yorkist triumph concluding *3 Henry VI.*

Richard dominates the play of *Richard III* to an extraordinary extent. He is the central character that the earlier plays, especially *3 Henry VI,* lacked. He is on stage almost continuously and, until the end, completely manipulates the actions of others. As chief actor and stage manager in his own drama, Richard chortlingly takes the audience into his confidence. His revelation of his plotting serves as a structural device for the play even as it manipulates and directs the audience's attention; we know in advance that Clarence's turn is next, that Richard will then attempt to woo the Lady Anne, and so forth. The dramatic excitement we experience in watching the action is not that of wondering what will happen next, but in seeing how cleverly the preannounced plans will be executed. Not until the rise of Richmond near the end of the play does Richard meet effective opposition, though quite early the voice of the deposed Queen Margaret is raised against him (I,iii). Margaret's curses upon the enemies of the Lancastrian House and her warning to Buckingham also serve as a structural device preparing us for what will happen, and they complement Richard's gloating and sardonic tone by striking a bitter and ominous note. Again the dramatic interest lies in the way the fates of the characters come upon them; these persons fall victim to Richard's machinations, and yet their downfalls also fulfill a larger providential scheme of retribution for injustice and wickedness.

Richard's ability as an actor is seemingly limitless. He has already boasted, in *3 Henry VI,* that he can deceive more slyly than Ulysses, Sinon, or Machiavelli, and put on more false shapes than Proteus. To us as audience he is cynically candid and boastful, setting us up in advance to watch his unbelievable performances. In an instant, before our eyes, he is the concerned younger brother of Clarence, sharing a hatred of Queen Elizabeth and her kindred; or he is the jocular uncle of the little princes; or he is the pious recluse studying divinity with his clerical teachers, reluctant to accept the responsibilities of state that are thrust upon him by his importunate subjects (that is to say, by Catesby and Buckingham, who are also actors in this staged scene). Yet none of these bravura performances can match the wooing of the Lady Anne.

Is the wooing of the Lady Anne credible? One key to credibility must lie in superb acting. The actor of Richard must transform himself from the gloating villain we know in soliloquy to the grief-stricken lover. Richard's argument is, after all, speciously plausible: that he has killed Anne's husband and his father out of desperate love for her. The argument appeals to vanity, that most fatal of human weaknesses. What power Anne suddenly appears to have over Richard! She can spare his life, or kill him. Richard shrewdly judges her as one not able to kill, and so risks offering her his sword. As stage manager, he has altered her role from that of sincere mourner to the stereotype of the proud woman worshiped by her groveling servant in love. With superb irony, Richard has inverted the appearance and the reality of control in this struggle between man and woman. He wins mastery by flattering her that only she can spare his miserable life. The very impossibility of what Richard has achieved merely illustrates his thesis that ordinary men and women can be made to believe anything, and betray their own best instincts, by "the plain devil and dissembling looks." Richard is of course devillike; his role as actor stems from that of the Vice in the morality play, brilliantly comic and sinister. Yet even the devil can prevail over his victims only when they acquiesce in evil. The devil can deceive the senses, but acceptance of evil is still an act of the perverted will. Anne is guilty, however much we can appreciate the mesmerizing power of Richard's personality. By the end of the scene she violates everything she had held sacred.

The image of Richard as devil or Vice raises the question of motivation and of symbolic meaning. Is Richard a human character propelled toward the throne by his insatiable ambition, like Macbeth? Is there a clue to his behavior in his ugliness and misanthropy? Modern psychological criticism might well be tempted to examine Richard's childhood: by his own admission, he was born feet forward, hunchbacked, withered in one arm, and already toothed ("which plainly signified That I should snarl and bite and play the dog," *3 Henry VI,* V,vi). One might argue that he compensates for his ugliness and unlovability by resolving to domineer. Feeling unwanted, he despises all men and undertakes to prove them weak and corrupt. This reading is not without merit; indeed, no matter how extraordinary Richard's behavior, he does seem plausible. He expresses a universal human penchant for cruelty and senseless domination. Yet the proposition that Richard is evil *because* he was born ugly can be logically reversed as well: he was born ugly *because* he is evil.

This concept, owing much to Renaissance notions of Platonic correspondence between outer appearances and inner qualities, is grounded on the idea of a vast struggle between the forces of absolute good and absolute evil in the cosmos, one in which every event in human life has divine meaning and cause. Richard's birth is a physical manifestation of that divine meaning. Providential destiny, having determined the need for a genius of evil at this point in English history, decrees that Richard shall be born. The teeth and hunched back merely give evidence of what is already predetermined. In the apt words of the choric Queen Margaret, Richard was "seal'd in thy nativity The slave of nature and the son of hell" (I,iii). Although Richard is also plausible as a man, he is in part an emissary of the devil, and ultimately serves the righteous purpose of divine Providence in human affairs. Such a symbolic reading clarifies our impression that Richard is fundamentally unlike many of Shakespeare's human villains such as Macbeth or King Claudius. Richard belongs instead to a special group of villains including Iago in *Othello* and Edmund in *King Lear.* Like them, Richard is driven both by human motivation and by his preexistent evil genius; he displays the "motiveless malignity" ascribed by Coleridge to Iago.

Such a reading helps explain not only Richard's delight in evil, but explains also the necessity for so much evil and suffering in England's civil wars. This theory of history owes much to Edward Hall's *Union of the Two Noble and Illustre Famelies of Lancastre and Yorke,* Shakespeare's chief source for his *Henry VI* plays. In addition, *Richard III* is particularly indebted to Polydore Vergil's *Anglica Historia* (1534) and to *The History of King Richard the Third* attributed to Sir Thomas More (published1557). This latter work, adopted in turn by Hall, Grafton, and Holinshed, purposefully blackens Richard's character. He becomes a study in the nature of tyranny, an object lesson to future rulers and their subjects. He is, moreover, a result of the curse placed by God on the English people for their sinful disobedience. Richard III functions as the scourge of God, destroying God's enemies until he too is destroyed for his own colossal evil.

Henry VII, in this Tudor explanation, becomes God's minister chosen to destroy the scourge and thereafter to fulfill a new and happy covenant between God and man. Although modern historians more impartially regard the defeat of Richard III at Bosworth Field in 1485 as a political overthrow not unlike Henry IV's overthrow of Richard II, and stress that Richard III was a talented administrator guilty of no worse political crimes than his more fortunate successor, Tudor Englishmen could not find meaning in such a neutral interpretation. History had to reveal God's intention. Henry VII's accession could not be viewed as parallel to the rebellion of Henry IV against Richard II, but was seen as a divinely sanctioned deliverance of the English nation, a blessing continued in the reign of Elizabeth I. Accordingly, the Tudor myth stressed the tyrannical nature of Richard III's seizure of power and conversely minimized the political element in Henry VII's takeover. Bosworth Field was an act of God, a rising up of some irresistible force, and under no circumstances a precedent for future rebellion.

In the *Henry VI* plays, Shakespeare puts considerable distance between himself and the Tudor orthodox reading of history, allowing the grim realities of civil war to speak for themselves. In *Richard III,* however, the pattern shown in the chronicles provides Shakespeare an essential structural device. Viewing the civil wars in retrospect, *Richard III* discovers at last a cohesive sense in which England's suffering has fulfilled a necessary plan of fall from innocence leading through sin and penitence to regeneration. Evil is seen at last as something through which good triumphs, in English history as in the story of man's fall from grace.

This providential scheme imposes a double irony on *Richard III.* In the short run, Richard appears to be complete master over his victims. "Your imprisonment shall not be long," Richard assures his brother Clarence. "I will deliver you, or else lie for you." The audience, already let in on the secret, can shiver at the grisly humor of these double entendres. Clarence will indeed soon be delivered—to his death. Richard's henchmen are fond of such jokes too. When Lord Hastings is on his way to the Tower, from which he will never return, and announces his intention of staying for dinner in the Tower, Buckingham observes aside, "And supper too, although thou know'st it not." Shortly before, Catesby has assured Hastings of Richard's and Buckingham's favor toward him: "The princes both make high account of you— [*Aside*] For they account his head upon the Bridge" (III,ii). Richard has a phrase for such wit: "Thus, like the formal Vice, Iniquity, I moralize two meanings in one word" (III,i). The point of such ironies is always the same: the devil is cleverer than his victims, deceiving them through equivocation, triumphing in their spiritual blindness.

The delayed irony of the play, however, ultimately repudiates the seemingly nihilistic conclusions of the early scenes. Richard, too, is blind to the significance of God's actions: he is God's scourge, fulfilling a divine plan even in the process of what he gloatingly regards as his own self-aggrandizement. Divine plans are always complex, inscrutable to the minds of mortals, understood least by those who unwittingly execute them. In attempting to prove his own contention that human nature is bestial and that a Machiavellian man of utter self-confidence can force his way to the top, flouting all conventions of morality, Richard has succeeded in demonstrating exactly the opposite. He is the proverbial beguiler beguiled.

This pattern, finding divine causality in all the suffering of the civil wars, argues that virtually all of Richard's victims deserve their fate because they have offended God. Prophecies and dreams give structure to the sequence of retributive actions, and keep grim score. As the choric Margaret observes, a York must pay for a Lancaster, eye for an eye: Edward IV for Henry VI, young Edward V for Henry VI's son Edward. Thus the Yorkist princes, though guiltless, die for their family's sins. The Yorkist Queen Elizabeth, like the Lancastrian Margaret, must outlive her husband into impotent old age, bewailing her children's cruel deaths. Clarence sees his death as punishment for breaking his oath at the battle of Tewkesbury and for his part in murdering Henry VI's son, Prince Edward. The Queen's kindred have been guilty of ambition, and Lord Hastings in turn is vulnerable because he has been willing to plot with Richard against the Queen's kindred. Margaret's curses serve both to warn the characters of their fates (a warning they blindly ignore) and to invite each person to curse himself unwittingly but with ironic appropriateness. The Lady Anne wishes unquietness on any woman so insane as to marry Richard. Buckingham protests in a most sacred oath that whenever he turns again on the Queen's kindred, he will deserve to be punished by the treachery of his dearest friend (i.e., of Richard). Dreams serve the same purpose of divine warning, giving Clarence a grotesque intimation of his death by drowning (in a butt of malmsey wine), and warning Hastings (through Stanley's dream) that the boar, Richard, will raze off his helm. Thus the English court punishes itself through Richard. He is the essence of the courtiers' factionalism, able to succeed as he does only because they forswear their most holy vows and conspire to destroy one another. They deserve to be outwitted at their own dismal game. Yet their falls are curative as well; again and again, Richard's victims acknowledge the justice of their undoings and penitently implore Divine forgiveness. Richard alone finds conscience a torment rather than a voice of comfort and wisdom.

As in *3 Henry VI,* the people have little to do with the action of the play. They are choric spokesmen and bystanders, virtuous in their attitude (except for the two suborned murderers of Clarence). In their plain folk wisdom they see the folly and evil their betters ignore: "O, full of danger is the Duke of Gloucester, And the Queen's sons and brothers haught and proud" (II,iii). And although they accept Richard as ruler, they do so most reluctantly; Buckingham's first attempt to persuade the people to this course meets with apathy and silence. Their wisdom is to be patient and "leave it all to God." In the fullness of time, this passive obedience brings its just reward.

The Tragedy of King Richard the Third

[*Dramatis Personae*

KING EDWARD THE FOURTH.
EDWARD, PRINCE OF WALES, afterwards KING EDWARD V, } *sons to the King.*
RICHARD, DUKE OF YORK, } *sons to the King.*
GEORGE, DUKE OF CLARENCE, } *brothers to the King.*
RICHARD, DUKE OF GLOUCESTER, *afterwards* KING RICHARD III, } *brothers to the King.*
A young son of Clarence, (EDWARD PLANTAGENET, *Earl of Warwick*).
HENRY, EARL OF RICHMOND, *afterwards* KING HENRY VII.
CARDINAL BOURCHIER, ARCHBISHOP OF CANTERBURY.
THOMAS ROTHERHAM, ARCHBISHOP OF YORK.
JOHN MORTON, BISHOP OF ELY.
DUKE OF BUCKINGHAM.
DUKE OF NORFOLK.
EARL OF SURREY, *his son.*
ANTHONY WOODVILLE, EARL RIVERS, *brother to Elizabeth.*
MARQUESS OF DORSET *and* LORD GREY, *sons to Elizabeth.*
EARL OF OXFORD.
LORD HASTINGS.
LORD STANLEY, *called also* EARL OF DERBY.
LORD LOVEL.
SIR THOMAS VAUGHAN.
SIR RICHARD RATCLIFFE.
SIR WILLIAM CATESBY.
SIR JAMES TYRREL.
SIR JAMES BLUNT.
SIR WALTER HERBERT.
SIR ROBERT BRAKENBURY, *Lieutenant of the Tower.*
SIR WILLIAM BRANDON.
CHRISTOPHER URSWICK, *a priest. Another* PRIEST.
TRESSEL *and* BERKELEY, *gentlemen attending on the Lady Anne.*
KEEPER *in the Tower.*
LORD MAYOR OF LONDON. SHERIFF OF WILTSHIRE.

ELIZABETH, *Queen to King Edward IV.*
MARGARET, *widow of King Henry VI.*
DUCHESS OF YORK, *mother to King Edward IV, Clarence, and Gloucester.*
LADY ANNE, *widow of Edward Prince of Wales, son to King Henry VI; afterwards married to Richard.*

A young daughter of Clarence, (MARGARET PLANTAGENET, *Countess of Salisbury.*)

GHOSTS *of those murdered by Richard III,* LORDS *and other* ATTENDANTS; *A* PURSUIVANT, PAGE, SCRIVENER, BISHOPS, ALDERMEN, COUNCILORS, CITIZENS, MURDERERS, MESSENGERS, SOLDIERS, *etc.*

SCENE: *England.*]

ACT I • SCENE I

Enter Richard, Duke of Gloucester, solus.

GLOUCESTER
Now is the winter of our discontent
Made glorious summer by this sun of York;
And all the clouds that low'r'd upon our house
In the deep bosom of the ocean buried.
Now are our brows bound with victorious wreaths,
Our bruised arms hung up for monuments,
Our stern alarums chang'd to merry meetings,
Our dreadful marches to delightful measures.
Grim-visag'd war hath smooth'd his wrinkled front;
And now, instead of mounting barbed steeds
To fright the souls of fearful adversaries,
He capers nimbly in a lady's chamber
To the lascivious pleasing of a lute.
But I, that am not shap'd for sportive tricks,
Nor made to court an amorous looking-glass;
I, that am rudely stamp'd, and want love's majesty
To strut before a wanton ambling nymph;
I, that am curtail'd of this fair proportion,
Cheated of feature by dissembling nature,
Deform'd, unfinish'd, sent before my time
Into this breathing world, scarce half made up,
And that so lamely and unfashionable
That dogs bark at me as I halt by them—
Why, I, in this weak piping time of peace,
Have no delight to pass away the time,
Unless to see my shadow in the sun
And descant on mine own deformity.
And therefore, since I cannot prove a lover
To entertain these fair well-spoken days,
I am determined to prove a villain
And hate the idle pleasures of these days.
Plots have I laid, inductions dangerous,
By drunken prophecies, libels, and dreams,
To set my brother Clarence and the King
In deadly hate the one against the other;
And if King Edward be as true and just
As I am subtle, false, and treacherous,
This day should Clarence closely be mew'd up
About a prophecy, which says that G
Of Edward's heirs the murderer shall be.
Dive, thoughts, down to my soul; here Clarence comes.

Enter Clarence, guarded, and Brakenbury, [Lieutenant of the Tower].

Brother, good day. What means this armed guard
That waits upon your Grace?

CLARENCE
His Majesty,
Tend'ring my person's safety, hath appointed
This conduct to convey me to the Tower.

GLOUCESTER
Upon what cause?

CLARENCE
Because my name is George.

GLOUCESTER
Alack, my lord, that fault is none of yours.
He should, for that, commit your godfathers.
O, belike his Majesty hath some intent
That you should be new christ'ned in the Tower.
But what's the matter, Clarence, may I know?

CLARENCE
Yea, Richard, when I know; but I protest
As yet I do not. But, as I can learn,
He hearkens after prophecies and dreams,
And from the cross-row plucks the letter G,
And says a wizard told him that by G
His issue disinherited should be;
And, for my name of George begins with G,
It follows in his thought that I am he.
These, as I learn, and such like toys as these
Hath mov'd his Highness to commit me now.

GLOUCESTER
Why, this it is, when men are rul'd by women.
'Tis not the King that sends you to the Tower;
My Lady Grey his wife, Clarence, 'tis she
That tempers him to this extremity.
Was it not she, and that good man of worship,
Anthony Woodville, her brother there,
That made him send Lord Hastings to the Tower,
From whence this present day he is delivered?
We are not safe, Clarence, we are not safe.

CLARENCE
By heaven, I think there is no man secure
But the Queen's kindred and night-walking heralds
That trudge betwixt the King and Mistress Shore.

I.i. Location: London. A street.
2 sun (Edward IV's badge displayed three suns; with a pun on *son.*) **6 arms** armor. **monuments** trophies **7 alarums** call to arms **8 measures** stately dances **9 front** forehead **10 barbed** armored **11 fearful** frightened **14 sportive** amorous **16 want** lack **17 ambling** walking affectedly, i.e., wantonly **18 proportion** shape **19 feature** shapeliness of body **23 halt** limp **24 piping time** i.e., a time when the music heard is that of pipes and not fifes and drums **27 descant** compose variations, warble, comment on **29 entertain** pass away pleasurably **32 inductions** preparations

38 mew'd up confined (like a hawk) **39 prophecy . . . G** (The prophecy is mentioned in the chronicles; the quibble is that G stands for Gloucester and not for George, the given name of the Duke of Clarence.) **44 Tend'ring** having care for **45 conduct** escort **49 belike** probably **50 new christ'ned** (Anticipates, ironically, Clarence's death by drowning in I.iv.) **55 cross-row** Christ-cross-row, or alphabet (so called from the cross printed before the alphabet in the hornbook) **58 for** because **60 toys** trifles **61 commit** arrest **64 My Lady Grey** (A disrespectful reference to the Queen, whose maiden name was Elizabeth Woodville and who, when the King married her, was the widow of Sir John Grey.) **65 tempers** molds, persuades **67 Woodville** i.e., Earl Rivers (whom Richard also disrespectfully refers to by his family name rather than by his recently acquired title) **72 night-walking heralds** i.e., secret messengers for an assignation **73 Mistress Shore** Jane Shore, the King's mistress, and wife of a goldsmith in Lombard Street. (The title *Mistress* is a respectful form of address for any woman, married or unmarried.)

Heard you not what an humble suppliant
Lord Hastings was to her for his delivery?

GLOUCESTER

Humbly complaining to her deity 76
Got my Lord Chamberlain his liberty. 77
I'll tell you what; I think it is our way, 78
If we will keep in favor with the King,
To be her men and wear her livery.
The jealous o'erworn widow and herself, 81
Since that our brother dubb'd them gentlewomen, 82
Are mighty gossips in our monarchy. 83

BRAKENBURY

I beseech your Graces both to pardon me:
His Majesty hath straitly given in charge 85
That no man shall have private conference,
Of what degree soever, with your brother.

GLOUCESTER

Even so? An please your worship, Brakenbury, 88
You may partake of anything we say.
We speak no treason, man. We say the King
Is wise and virtuous, and his noble queen
Well struck in years, fair, and not jealous. 92
We say that Shore's wife hath a pretty foot,
A cherry lip, a bonny eye, a passing pleasing
tongue; 94
And that the Queen's kindred are made gentlefolks.
How say you, sir? Can you deny all this?

BRAKENBURY

With this, my lord, myself have nought to do.

GLOUCESTER

Naught to do with Mistress Shore? I tell thee, fellow, 98
He that doth naught with her, excepting one,
Were best to do it secretly, alone.

BRAKENBURY

What one, my lord?

GLOUCESTER

Her husband, knave. Wouldst thou betray me? 102

BRAKENBURY

I beseech your Grace to pardon me, and withal 103
Forbear your conference with the noble Duke.

CLARENCE

We know thy charge, Brakenbury, and will obey.

GLOUCESTER

We are the Queen's abjects, and must obey. 106
Brother, farewell. I will unto the King;
And whatsoe'er you will employ me in,
Were it to call King Edward's widow sister, 109
I will perform it to enfranchise you. 110
Meantime, this deep disgrace in brotherhood
Touches me deeper than you can imagine. 112

76 her deity (A mock title for Jane Shore, suggesting she is even more elevated than *her Grace* or *her Majesty*.) **77 Lord Chamberlain** i.e., Lord Hastings **78 our way** i.e., our only way (to succeed) **81 widow** i.e., Queen Elizabeth. (See l. 64, note.) **herself** i.e., Jane Shore **82 gentlewomen** (A sneer at the Queen's family, which was gentle but not noble until after her marriage with the King; Jane Shore was, of course, neither gentle nor noble.) **83 mighty gossips** i.e., influential busybodies **85 straitly . . . charge** strictly ordered **88 An** if (it) **92 Well struck** i.e., well along. **not jealous** (Implies there are things she might be jealous about.) **94 passing** surpassingly **98 Naught** (Richard quibbles on the meanings *nothing* and *the sexual act*.) **102 betray me** i.e., into naming the King as a person who does "naught" with Mistress Shore **103 withal** at the same time **106 abjects** abjectly servile subjects **109 King Edward's widow** i.e., the widow whom Edward has made queen **110 enfranchise** release from imprisonment **112 Touches . . . imagine** (1) distresses me more than can be imagined (2) concerns me (in my personal ambition) more than you could possibly guess

CLARENCE

I know it pleaseth neither of us well.

GLOUCESTER

Well, your imprisonment shall not be long;
I will deliver you, or else lie for you. 115
Meantime, have patience.

CLARENCE I must perforce. Farewell. 116

Exit Clarence [with Brakenbury and Guard].

GLOUCESTER

Go tread the path that thou shalt ne'er return.
Simple, plain Clarence, I do love thee so,
That I will shortly send thy soul to heaven,
If heaven will take the present at our hands.
But who comes here? The new-delivered Hastings?

Enter Lord Hastings.

HASTINGS

Good time of day unto my gracious lord.

GLOUCESTER

As much unto my good Lord Chamberlain.
Well are you welcome to this open air.
How hath your lordship brook'd imprisonment? 125

HASTINGS

With patience, noble lord, as prisoners must.
But I shall live, my lord, to give them thanks 127
That were the cause of my imprisonment.

GLOUCESTER

No doubt, no doubt; and so shall Clarence too,
For they that were your enemies are his,
And have prevail'd as much on him as you.

HASTINGS

More pity that the eagles should be mew'd,
Whiles kites and buzzards prey at liberty. 133

GLOUCESTER

What news abroad? 134

HASTINGS

No news so bad abroad as this at home:
The King is sickly, weak, and melancholy,
And his physicians fear him mightily. 137

GLOUCESTER

Now, by Saint John, that news is bad indeed!
O, he hath kept an evil diet long,
And overmuch consum'd his royal person.
'Tis very grievous to be thought upon.
Where is he, in his bed?

HASTINGS

He is.

GLOUCESTER

Go you before, and I will follow you. *Exit Hastings.*
He cannot live, I hope, and must not die
Till George be pack'd with post-horse up to heaven. 146
I'll in, to urge his hatred more to Clarence
With lies well steel'd with weighty arguments; 148
And, if I fail not in my deep intent,
Clarence hath not another day to live.

115 lie for you (1) take your place in prison (2) tell lies about you **116 perforce** necessarily **125 brook'd** endured **127 give them thanks** i.e., pay them off. (Said ironically.) **133 kites** scavengers of the hawk family **134 abroad** at large, circulating **137 fear** fear for **146 with post-horse** by post horses, i.e., by swiftest possible means **148 steel'd** reinforced

Which done, God take King Edward to his mercy,
And leave the world for me to bustle in!
For then I'll marry Warwick's youngest daughter. 153
What though I kill'd her husband and her father?
The readiest way to make the wench amends
Is to become her husband and her father,
The which will I; not all so much for love
As for another secret close intent, 158
By marrying her which I must reach unto.
But yet I run before my horse to market.
Clarence still breathes, Edward still lives and reigns;
When they are gone, then must I count my gains.
Exit.

SCENE II

Enter the corse of [*King*] *Henry the Sixth, with Halberds to guard it; Lady Anne being the mourner* [*attended by Tressel and Berkeley*].

ANNE
Set down, set down your honorable load—
If honor may be shrouded in a hearse—
Whilst I awhile obsequiously lament 3
Th' untimely fall of virtuous Lancaster.
Poor key-cold figure of a holy king, 5
Pale ashes of the house of Lancaster,
Thou bloodless remnant of that royal blood,
Be it lawful that I invocate thy ghost 8
To hear the lamentations of poor Anne,
Wife to thy Edward, to thy slaught'red son,
Stabb'd by the selfsame hand that made these wounds!
Lo, in these windows that let forth thy life,
I pour the helpless balm of my poor eyes. 13
O, cursed be the hand that made these holes!
Cursed the heart that had the heart to do it!
Cursed the blood that let this blood from hence!
More direful hap betide that hated wretch, 17
That makes us wretched by the death of thee,
Than I can wish to wolves, to spiders, toads,
Or any creeping venom'd thing that lives!
If ever he have child, abortive be it,
Prodigious, and untimely brought to light, 22
Whose ugly and unnatural aspect
May fright the hopeful mother at the view,
And that be heir to his unhappiness! 25
If ever he have wife, let her be made
More miserable by the life of him
Than I am made by my young lord and thee! 28
Come, now towards Chertsey with your holy load, 29
Taken from Paul's to be interred there; 30
And still as you are weary of this weight, 31
Rest you, whiles I lament King Henry's corse.

Enter Richard, Duke of Gloucester.

GLOUCESTER
Stay, you that bear the corse, and set it down.

ANNE
What black magician conjures up this fiend
To stop devoted charitable deeds? 35

GLOUCESTER
Villains, set down the corse, or, by Saint Paul,
I'll make a corse of him that disobeys.

GENTLEMAN [*Advancing with his halberd lowered*]
My lord, stand back, and let the coffin pass.

GLOUCESTER
Unmanner'd dog, stand thou, when I command! 39
Advance thy halberd higher than my breast, 40
Or, by Saint Paul, I'll strike thee to my foot,
And spurn upon thee, beggar, for thy boldness. 42

ANNE
What do you tremble? Are you all afraid? 43
Alas, I blame you not, for you are mortal,
And mortal eyes cannot endure the devil.
Avaunt, thou dreadful minister of hell! 46
Thou hadst but power over his mortal body,
His soul thou canst not have. Therefore be gone.

GLOUCESTER
Sweet saint, for charity, be not so curst. 49

ANNE
Foul devil, for God's sake hence, and trouble us not,
For thou hast made the happy earth thy hell,
Fill'd it with cursing cries and deep exclaims. 52
If thou delight to view thy heinous deeds,
Behold this pattern of thy butcheries. 54
[*She uncovers the corpse.*]
O, gentlemen, see, see dead Henry's wounds
Open their congeal'd mouths and bleed afresh! 56
Blush, blush, thou lump of foul deformity;
For 'tis thy presence that exhales this blood 58
From cold and empty veins where no blood dwells.
Thy deeds inhuman and unnatural
Provokes this deluge most unnatural.
O God, which this blood mad'st, revenge his death!
O earth, which this blood drink'st, revenge his death!
Either heav'n with lightning strike the murd'rer dead,
Or earth gape open wide and eat him quick, 65
As thou dost swallow up this good king's blood,
Which his hell-govern'd arm hath butchered!

153 Warwick's youngest daughter the Lady Anne Neville (regarded by Shakespeare, following the chronicles, as widow of Edward Prince of Wales, son of King Henry VI, though in fact they were only betrothed) **158 intent** design. (I.e., Richard hopes to ally himself with the house of Lancaster to bolster his claim to the throne.)

I.ii. Location: London. A street.
s.d. corse corpse. **Halberds** guards with long poleaxes **3 obsequiously** as befits a funeral, mournfully **5 key-cold** extremely cold, cold as a metal key. (Proverbial.) **8 invocate** invoke **13 helpless** useless, unavailing **17 hap betide** fortune befall **22 Prodigious** monstrous, unnatural **25 unhappiness** evil nature

28 by i.e., by the deaths of **29 Chertsey** monastery in Surrey, near London, where King Henry's body is to be buried **30 Paul's** St. Paul's Cathedral in London **31 still as** as often as **35 devoted** holy **39 stand** halt **40 Advance . . . breast** raise your halberd upright **42 spurn** trample **43 What** why **46 Avaunt** be gone **49 curst** spiteful, shrewish **52 exclaims** exclamations **54 pattern** example **56 bleed afresh** (A phenomenon popularly supposed to occur in the presence of the murderer.) **58 exhales** draws out **65 quick** alive

GLOUCESTER
Lady, you know no rules of charity,
Which renders good for bad, blessings for curses.
ANNE
Villain, thou know'st nor law of God nor man. 70
No beast so fierce but knows some touch of pity.
GLOUCESTER
But I know none, and therefore am no beast.
ANNE
O wonderful, when devils tell the truth!
GLOUCESTER
More wonderful, when angels are so angry.
Vouchsafe, divine perfection of a woman,
Of these supposed crimes to give me leave
By circumstance but to acquit myself. 77
ANNE
Vouchsafe, defus'd infection of a man, 78
Of these known evils, but to give me leave,
By circumstance, to curse thy cursed self.
GLOUCESTER
Fairer than tongue can name thee, let me have
Some patient leisure to excuse myself.
ANNE
Fouler than heart can think thee, thou canst make
No excuse current but to hang thyself. 84
GLOUCESTER
By such despair I should accuse myself.
ANNE
And by despairing shalt thou stand excused
For doing worthy vengeance on thyself
That didst unworthy slaughter upon others.
GLOUCESTER
Say that I slew them not?
ANNE Then say they were not slain.
But dead they are, and, devilish slave, by thee.
GLOUCESTER
I did not kill your husband.
ANNE Why, then he is alive.
GLOUCESTER
Nay, he is dead, and slain by Edward's hands.
ANNE
In thy foul throat thou li'st! Queen Margaret saw
Thy murd'rous falchion smoking in his blood, 94
The which thou once didst bend against her breast, 95
But that thy brothers beat aside the point.
GLOUCESTER
I was provoked by her sland'rous tongue,
That laid their guilt upon my guiltless shoulders.
ANNE
Thou wast provoked by thy bloody mind,
That never dream'st on aught but butcheries.
Didst thou not kill this king?
GLOUCESTER I grant ye.
ANNE
Dost grant me, hedgehog? Then God grant me too 102
Thou mayst be damned for that wicked deed!
O, he was gentle, mild, and virtuous!
GLOUCESTER
The better for the King of Heaven that hath him.
ANNE
He is in heaven, where thou shalt never come.
GLOUCESTER
Let him thank me that holp to send him thither; 107
For he was fitter for that place than earth.
ANNE
And thou unfit for any place but hell.
GLOUCESTER
Yes, one place else, if you will hear me name it.
ANNE
Some dungeon.
GLOUCESTER Your bed-chamber.
ANNE
Ill rest betide the chamber where thou liest!
GLOUCESTER
So will it, madam, till I lie with you.
ANNE
I hope so.
GLOUCESTER I know so. But, gentle Lady Anne,
To leave this keen encounter of our wits
And fall something into a slower method,
Is not the causer of the timeless deaths 117
Of these Plantagenets, Henry and Edward,
As blameful as the executioner?
ANNE
Thou wast the cause, and most accurs'd effect. 120
GLOUCESTER
Your beauty was the cause of that effect— 121
Your beauty, that did haunt me in my sleep
To undertake the death of all the world,
So I might live one hour in your sweet bosom.
ANNE
If I thought that, I tell thee, homicide,
These nails should rend that beauty from my cheeks.
GLOUCESTER
These eyes could not endure that beauty's wrack; 127
You should not blemish it, if I stood by.
As all the world is cheered by the sun,
So I by that. It is my day, my life.
ANNE
Black night o'ershade thy day, and death thy life!
GLOUCESTER
Curse not thyself, fair creature—thou art both.
ANNE
I would I were, to be reveng'd on thee.
GLOUCESTER
It is a quarrel most unnatural
To be reveng'd on him that loveth thee.
ANNE
It is a quarrel just and reasonable
To be reveng'd on him that kill'd my husband.
GLOUCESTER
He that bereft thee, lady, of thy husband,

70 nor . . . nor neither . . . nor **77 circumstance** detailed argument **78 defus'd** diffused, disordered, shapeless **84 current** genuine, acceptable (as in coinage) **94 falchion** curved sword **95 bend** direct, aim **102 hedgehog** (Richard's heraldic emblem featured a boar or wild hog.)

107 holp helped **117 timeless** untimely **120 effect** agent **121 effect** result **127 wrack** destruction

Did it to help thee to a better husband.
ANNE
His better doth not breathe upon the earth.
GLOUCESTER
He lives that loves thee better than he could. 141
ANNE
Name him.
GLOUCESTER Plantagenet.
ANNE Why, that was he.
GLOUCESTER
The selfsame name, but one of better nature.
ANNE
Where is he?
GLOUCESTER Here. *[She] spits at him.*
Why dost thou spit at me?
ANNE
Would it were mortal poison, for thy sake!
GLOUCESTER
Never came poison from so sweet a place.
ANNE
Never hung poison on a fouler toad. 147
Out of my sight! Thou dost infect mine eyes.
GLOUCESTER
Thine eyes, sweet lady, have infected mine. 149
ANNE
Would they were basilisks, to strike thee dead! 150
GLOUCESTER
I would they were, that I might die at once;
For now they kill me with a living death.
Those eyes of thine from mine have drawn salt tears,
Sham'd their aspects with store of childish drops; 154
These eyes, which never shed remorseful tear—
No, when my father York and Edward wept
To hear the piteous moan that Rutland made 157
When black-fac'd Clifford shook his sword at him; 158
Nor when thy warlike father, like a child, 159
Told the sad story of my father's death,
And twenty times made pause to sob and weep,
That all the standers-by had wet their cheeks, 162
Like trees bedash'd with rain—in that sad time
My manly eyes did scorn an humble tear;
And what these sorrows could not thence exhale,
Thy beauty hath, and made them blind with weeping.
I never sued to friend nor enemy; 167
My tongue could never learn sweet smoothing words; 168
But, now thy beauty is propos'd my fee, 169
My proud heart sues and prompts my tongue to speak. *She looks scornfully at him.*
Teach not thy lip such scorn, for it was made
For kissing, lady, not for such contempt.
If thy revengeful heart cannot forgive,
Lo, here I lend thee this sharp-pointed sword,
Which if thou please to hide in this true breast,
And let the soul forth that adoreth thee,
I lay it naked to the deadly stroke
And humbly beg the death upon my knee.
He lays his breast open; she offers at [it] with his sword.
Nay, do not pause; for I did kill King Henry—
But 'twas thy beauty that provoked me.
Nay, now dispatch; 'twas I that stabb'd young Edward—
But 'twas thy heavenly face that set me on. 182
She falls the sword.
Take up the sword again, or take up me.
ANNE
Arise, dissembler. Though I wish thy death,
I will not be thy executioner.
GLOUCESTER
Then bid me kill myself, and I will do it.
ANNE
I have already.
GLOUCESTER That was in thy rage.
Speak it again, and, even with the word,
This hand, which, for thy love, did kill thy love,
Shall, for thy love, kill a far truer love.
To both their deaths shalt thou be accessary.
ANNE
I would I knew thy heart.
GLOUCESTER
'Tis figur'd in my tongue. 193
ANNE
I fear me both are false.
GLOUCESTER
Then never man was true.
ANNE
Well, well, put up your sword.
GLOUCESTER
Say, then, my peace is made.
ANNE
That shalt thou know hereafter.
GLOUCESTER
But shall I live in hope?
ANNE
All men, I hope, live so.
GLOUCESTER
Vouchsafe to wear this ring.
[ANNE
To take is not to give.]
[He slips the ring on her finger.]
GLOUCESTER
Look how my ring encompasseth thy finger,
Even so thy breast encloseth my poor heart;
Wear both of them, for both of them are thine.
And if thy poor devoted servant may 206
But beg one favor at thy gracious hand,
Thou dost confirm his happiness forever.
ANNE
What is it?
GLOUCESTER
That it may please you leave these sad designs

141 He lives i.e., there is a man. **he** i.e., Prince Edward **147 poison . . . toad** (Toads were popularly regarded as poisonous.) **149 infected** i.e., with love (since love was thought to enter through the eyes) **150 basilisks** fabulous reptiles reputed to kill by their looks **154 aspects** appearance **157 Rutland** second son of Richard Duke of York. (See *3 Henry VI*, I.iii for his death scene.) **158 black-fac'd** i.e., foreboding in appearance **159 thy warlike father** i.e., the Earl of Warwick **162 That** so that **167 sued** supplicated, appealed **168 smoothing** flattering **169 propos'd my fee** offered as my reward

182 s.d. falls lets fall **193 figur'd** portrayed **206 servant** i.e., lover, one whom she may command

To him that hath most cause to be a mourner,
And presently repair to Crosby House,
Where, after I have solemnly interr'd
At Chertsey monast'ry this noble king,
And wet his grave with my repentant tears,
I will with all expedient duty see you.
For divers unknown reasons, I beseech you,
Grant me this boon.

ANNE
With all my heart; and much it joys me too,
To see you are become so penitent.
Tressel and Berkeley, go along with me.

GLOUCESTER
Bid me farewell.

ANNE
'Tis more than you deserve;
But since you teach me how to flatter you,
Imagine I have said farewell already.
Exeunt two [Tressel and Berkeley] with Anne.

[GLOUCESTER
Sirs, take up the corse.]

GENTLEMAN
Towards Chertsey, noble lord?

GLOUCESTER
No, to White-Friars. There attend my coming.
Exeunt [bearers with] corse.
Was ever woman in this humor woo'd?
Was ever woman in this humor won?
I'll have her, but I will not keep her long.
What? I, that kill'd her husband and his father,
To take her in her heart's extremest hate,
With curses in her mouth, tears in her eyes,
The bleeding witness of my hatred by,
Having God, her conscience, and these bars
against me,
And I no friends to back my suit withal,
But the plain devil and dissembling looks?
And yet to win her! All the world to nothing!
Ha!
Hath she forgot already that brave prince,
Edward, her lord, whom I, some three months
since,
Stabb'd in my angry mood at Tewkesbury?
A sweeter and a lovelier gentleman,
Fram'd in the prodigality of nature,
Young, valiant, wise, and, no doubt, right royal,
The spacious world cannot again afford.
And will she yet abase her eyes on me,
That cropp'd the golden prime of this sweet prince,
And made her widow to a woeful bed?
On me, whose all not equals Edward's moi'ty?
On me, that halts and am misshapen thus?
My dukedom to a beggarly denier,
I do mistake my person all this while!
Upon my life, she finds, although I cannot,
Myself to be a marv'lous proper man.
I'll be at charges for a looking-glass,
And entertain a score or two of tailors
To study fashions to adorn my body.
Since I am crept in favor with myself,
I will maintain it with some little cost.
But first I'll turn yon fellow in his grave,
And then return lamenting to my love.
Shine out, fair sun, till I have bought a glass,
That I may see my shadow as I pass. *Exit.*

212 presently at once. **Crosby House** (One of Richard's London dwellings; built originally by Sir John Crosby.) **216 expedient** expeditious **217 unknown** secret **226 White-Friars** the Carmelite priory in London. **attend** await **237 All . . . nothing** i.e., against infinite odds **243 in . . . nature** i.e., in nature's most lavish mood **246 abase** lower, devalue **247 cropp'd** cut short **249 moi'ty** half of (Edward's virtues) **251 denier** small copper coin, the twelfth part of a sou **254 proper** handsome **255 be . . . for** undertake the expense of

256 entertain retain, employ **260 in** into

SCENE III

Enter the Queen Mother [Elizabeth], Lord Rivers, [Marquess of Dorset,] and Lord Grey.

RIVERS
Have patience, madam. There's no doubt his
Majesty
Will soon recover his accustom'd health.

GREY
In that you brook it ill, it makes him worse.
Therefore, for God's sake, entertain good comfort,
And cheer his Grace with quick and merry eyes.

QUEEN ELIZABETH
If he were dead, what would betide on me?

GREY
No other harm but loss of such a lord.

QUEEN ELIZABETH
The loss of such a lord includes all harms.

GREY
The heavens have bless'd you with a goodly son,
To be your comforter when he is gone.

QUEEN ELIZABETH
Ah, he is young, and his minority
Is put unto the trust of Richard Gloucester,
A man that loves not me, nor none of you.

RIVERS
Is it concluded he shall be Protector?

QUEEN ELIZABETH
It is determin'd, not concluded yet;
But so it must be, if the King miscarry.

Enter Buckingham and [Lord Stanley Earl of] Derby.

GREY
Here come the lords of Buckingham and Derby.

BUCKINGHAM
Good time of day unto your royal Grace!

STANLEY
God make your Majesty joyful, as you have been!

QUEEN ELIZABETH
The Countess Richmond, good my Lord of Derby,
To your good prayer will scarcely say amen.

I.iii. Location: London. The palace.
3 brook endure **6 betide on** become of **15 determin'd, not concluded** i.e., decided though not officially announced **16 miscarry** perish **20 Countess Richmond** i.e., Margaret Beaufort (1443–1509), who married successively Edmund Tudor Earl of Richmond, Lord Henry Stafford, and Thomas Lord Stanley (here called the Earl of Derby), to whom she is currently married. By the Earl of Richmond she was mother of the future Henry VII.

Yet, Derby, notwithstanding she's your wife,
And loves not me, be you, good lord, assur'd
I hate not you for her proud arrogance.

STANLEY

I do beseech you, either not believe
The envious slanders of her false accusers,
Or, if she be accus'd on true report,
Bear with her weakness, which, I think, proceeds
From wayward sickness, and no grounded malice.

QUEEN ELIZABETH

Saw you the King today, my Lord of Derby?

STANLEY

But now the Duke of Buckingham and I 31
Are come from visiting his Majesty.

QUEEN ELIZABETH

What likelihood of his amendment, lords?

BUCKINGHAM

Madam, good hope; his Grace speaks cheerfully.

QUEEN ELIZABETH

God grant him health! Did you confer with him?

BUCKINGHAM

Ay, madam. He desires to make atonement
Between the Duke of Gloucester and your brothers, 37
And between them and my Lord Chamberlain,
And sent to warn them to his royal presence. 39

QUEEN ELIZABETH

Would all were well! But that will never be.
I fear our happiness is at the height.

Enter Richard [*Duke of Gloucester, and Lord Hastings*].

GLOUCESTER

They do me wrong, and I will not endure it!
Who is it that complains unto the King
That I, forsooth, am stern and love them not?
By holy Paul, they love his Grace but lightly
That fill his ears with such dissentious rumors.
Because I cannot flatter and look fair, 47
Smile in men's faces, smooth, deceive, and cog, 48
Duck with French nods and apish courtesy, 49
I must be held a rancorous enemy.
Cannot a plain man live and think no harm,
But thus his simple truth must be abus'd
With silken, sly, insinuating Jacks? 53

GREY

To who in all this presence speaks your Grace?

GLOUCESTER

To thee, that hast nor honesty nor grace. 55
When have I injur'd thee? When done thee wrong?
Or thee? Or thee? Or any of your faction?
A plague upon you all! His royal Grace—
Whom God preserve better than you would wish!—
Cannot be quiet scarce a breathing while 60
But you must trouble him with lewd complaints. 61

QUEEN ELIZABETH

Brother of Gloucester, you mistake the matter.
The King, on his own royal disposition, 63
And not provok'd by any suitor else,
Aiming, belike, at your interior hatred,
That in your outward action shows itself
Against my children, brothers, and myself,
Makes him to send, that he may learn the ground. 68

GLOUCESTER

I cannot tell. The world is grown so bad
That wrens make prey where eagles dare not perch.
Since every Jack became a gentleman,
There's many a gentle person made a Jack.

QUEEN ELIZABETH

Come, come, we know your meaning, brother Gloucester;
You envy my advancement and my friends'. 74
God grant we never may have need of you!

GLOUCESTER

Meantime, God grants that I have need of you:
Our brother is imprison'd by your means,
Myself disgrac'd, and the nobility
Held in contempt, while great promotions
Are daily given to ennoble those
That scarce some two days since were worth a noble. 81

QUEEN ELIZABETH

By Him that rais'd me to this careful height 82
From that contented hap which I enjoy'd, 83
I never did incense his Majesty
Against the Duke of Clarence, but have been
An earnest advocate to plead for him.
My lord, you do me shameful injury
Falsely to draw me in these vile suspects. 88

GLOUCESTER

You may deny that you were not the mean
Of my Lord Hastings' late imprisonment.

RIVERS

She may, my lord, for—

GLOUCESTER

She may, Lord Rivers! Why, who knows not so?
She may do more, sir, than denying that:
She may help you to many fair preferments,
And then deny her aiding hand therein,
And lay those honors on your high desert. 96
What may she not? She may, ay, marry, may she— 97

RIVERS

What, marry, may she?

GLOUCESTER

What, marry, may she? Marry with a king,
A bachelor, and a handsome stripling too;
I wis your grandam had a worser match. 101

QUEEN ELIZABETH

My Lord of Gloucester, I have too long borne
Your blunt upbraidings and your bitter scoffs.

31 But now just now **37 brothers** (Only one brother, Earl Rivers, is mentioned in the play, though historically Elizabeth had others; Shakespeare may be thinking of other kinsmen, including her sons, whom she helped to advance.) **39 warn** summon **47 fair** courteously **48 smooth** flatter. **cog** cheat **49 Duck . . . nods** i.e., bow affectedly **53 Jacks** lowbred persons **55 grace** sense of duty or propriety (playing upon *your Grace* in the preceding line) **60 breathing while** i.e., moment of rest **61 lewd** vile, base

63 disposition inclination **68 Makes him** causes him. (The implied subject is "The king's own disposition.") **ground** cause (of your ill will) **74 friends'** i.e., kinsmen's **81 noble** (1) gold coin worth 6 shillings, 8 pence (2) nobleman **82 careful** full of cares **83 hap** fortune **88 in** into. **suspects** suspicions **96 lay . . . on** attribute these high honors to **97 marry** i.e., indeed (followed by a pun on *wed*) **101 I wis** certainly

By heaven, I will acquaint his Majesty
Of those gross taunts that oft I have endur'd.
I had rather be a country servant maid
Than a great queen with this condition,
To be so baited, scorn'd, and stormed at.

Enter old Queen Margaret [*behind*].

Small joy have I in being England's queen.

QUEEN MARGARET [*Aside*]
And less'ned be that small, God I beseech him!
Thy honor, state, and seat is due to me.

GLOUCESTER
What? Threat you me with telling of the King?
[Tell him, and spare not. Look what I have said]
I will avouch 't in presence of the King.
I dare adventure to be sent to th' Tower.
'Tis time to speak; my pains are quite forgot.

QUEEN MARGARET [*Aside*]
Out, devil! I do remember them too well:
Thou kill'dst my husband Henry in the Tower,
And Edward, my poor son, at Tewkesbury.

GLOUCESTER
Ere you were queen, ay, or your husband king,
I was a pack-horse in his great affairs,
A weeder-out of his proud adversaries,
A liberal rewarder of his friends.
To royalize his blood I spent mine own.

QUEEN MARGARET [*Aside*]
Ay, and much better blood than his or thine.

GLOUCESTER
In all which time you and your husband Grey
Were factious for the house of Lancaster;
And, Rivers, so were you. Was not your husband
In Margaret's battle at Saint Albans slain?
Let me put in your minds, if you forget,
What you have been ere this, and what you are;
Withal, what I have been, and what I am.

QUEEN MARGARET [*Aside*]
A murd'rous villain, and so still thou art.

GLOUCESTER
Poor Clarence did forsake his father, Warwick,
Ay, and forswore himself—which Jesu pardon!—

QUEEN MARGARET [*Aside*]
Which God revenge!

GLOUCESTER
To fight on Edward's party for the crown;
And for his meed, poor lord, he is mewed up.
I would to God my heart were flint, like Edward's,
Or Edward's soft and pitiful, like mine.
I am too childish-foolish for this world.

QUEEN MARGARET [*Aside*]
Hie thee to hell for shame, and leave this world,
Thou cacodemon! There thy kingdom is.

RIVERS
My Lord of Gloucester, in those busy days
Which here you urge to prove us enemies,
We follow'd then our lord, our sovereign king.
So should we you, if you should be our king.

GLOUCESTER
If I should be? I had rather be a pedlar.
Far be it from my heart, the thought thereof!

QUEEN ELIZABETH
As little joy, my lord, as you suppose
You should enjoy, were you this country's king,
As little joy you may suppose in me
That I enjoy, being the queen thereof.

QUEEN MARGARET [*Aside*]
A little joy enjoys the queen thereof,
For I am she, and altogether joyless.
I can no longer hold me patient. [*Advancing.*]
Hear me, you wrangling pirates, that fall out
In sharing that which you have pill'd from me!
Which of you trembles not that looks on me?
If not, that I am queen, you bow like subjects,
Yet that, by you depos'd, you quake like rebels?
Ah, gentle villain, do not turn away!

GLOUCESTER
Foul wrinkled witch, what mak'st thou in my sight?

QUEEN MARGARET
But repetition of what thou hast marr'd;
That will I make before I let thee go.

GLOUCESTER
Wert thou not banished on pain of death?

QUEEN MARGARET
I was; but I do find more pain in banishment
Than death can yield me here by my abode.
A husband and a son thou ow'st to me;
And thou a kingdom; all of you allegiance.
This sorrow that I have, by right is yours,
And all the pleasures you usurp are mine.

GLOUCESTER
The curse my noble father laid on thee
When thou didst crown his warlike brows with paper
And with thy scorns drew'st rivers from his eyes,
And then, to dry them, gav'st the Duke a clout
Steep'd in the faultless blood of pretty Rutland—
His curses then, from bitterness of soul
Denounc'd against thee, are all fall'n upon thee;
And God, not we, hath plagu'd thy bloody deed.

QUEEN ELIZABETH
So just is God, to right the innocent.

HASTINGS
O, 'twas the foulest deed to slay that babe,
And the most merciless, that e'er was heard of!

108 baited harassed **108 s.d. Queen Margaret** (Historically, Queen Margaret was held prisoner in England for five years following Tewkesbury and then was sent to France; see note to l. 166 below.) **111 state** degree, high rank. **seat** throne **113 Look what** whatever **115 adventure to be** risk being **116 pains** efforts (in King Edward's behalf) **117 Out** (An exclamation of anger.) **121 pack-horse** work-horse, beast of burden **128 husband** (Queen Elizabeth's first husband, Sir John Grey, fell fighting on the Lancastrian side at St. Albans.) **134 father** i.e., father-in-law. (See *3 Henry VI*, IV.i, when Clarence deserted his brothers to marry Warwick's daughter Isabella and supported the Lancastrian cause for a time; thereafter he forswore his oath to Warwick by returning to fight on Edward's "party" or side.) **138 meed** reward. **mewed** caged (like a hawk)

143 cacodemon evil spirit **145 urge** cite **158 pill'd** pillaged, robbed **160–161 If . . . rebels** i.e., even if you do not bow low to me as your queen, you quake as rebels who have deposed me **162 gentle** nobly born **163 mak'st thou** are you doing **164 But . . . marr'd** only reciting your crimes **166 banished** (Margaret was banished in 1464, returned to England in 1471, and after the Battle of Tewkesbury was confined in the Tower until 1476 when she returned to France, dying there in 1482, one year before the historical time of this scene.) **169 thou** i.e., Richard **170 thou** i.e., Elizabeth **173 The curse** (See *3 Henry VI*, I.iv. 164–166.) **176 clout** cloth, handkerchief **182 that babe** i.e., Rutland

RIVERS
Tyrants themselves wept when it was reported.

DORSET
No man but prophesied revenge for it.

BUCKINGHAM
Northumberland, then present, wept to see it.

QUEEN MARGARET
What? Were you snarling all before I came,
Ready to catch each other by the throat,
And turn you all your hatred now on me?
Did York's dread curse prevail so much with heaven
That Henry's death, my lovely Edward's death,
Their kingdom's loss, my woeful banishment,
Should all but answer for that peevish brat?
Can curses pierce the clouds and enter heaven?
Why then give way, dull clouds, to my quick curses!
Though not by war, by surfeit die your king,
As ours by murder, to make him a king!
Edward thy son, that now is Prince of Wales,
For Edward our son, that was Prince of Wales,
Die in his youth by like untimely violence!
Thyself a queen, for me that was a queen,
Outlive thy glory, like my wretched self!
Long mayst thou live to wail thy children's death,
And see another, as I see thee now,
Deck'd in thy rights, as thou art stall'd in mine!
Long die thy happy days before thy death,
And, after many length'ned hours of grief,
Die neither mother, wife, nor England's queen!
Rivers and Dorset, you were standers by,
And so wast thou, Lord Hastings, when my son
Was stabb'd with bloody daggers: God, I pray him,
That none of you may live his natural age,
But by some unlook'd accident cut off!

GLOUCESTER
Have done thy charm, thou hateful wither'd hag!

QUEEN MARGARET
And leave out thee? Stay, dog, for thou shalt hear me.
If heaven have any grievous plague in store
Exceeding those that I can wish upon thee,
O, let them keep it till thy sins be ripe,
And then hurl down their indignation
On thee, the troubler of the poor world's peace!
The worm of conscience still begnaw thy soul!
Thy friends suspect for traitors while thou liv'st,
And take deep traitors for thy dearest friends!
No sleep close up that deadly eye of thine,
Unless it be while some tormenting dream
Affrights thee with a hell of ugly devils!
Thou elvish-mark'd, abortive, rooting hog,
Thou that wast seal'd in thy nativity
The slave of nature and the son of hell!
Thou slander of thy heavy mother's womb,
Thou loathed issue of thy father's loins,
Thou rag of honor, thou detested—

GLOUCESTER
Margaret.

QUEEN MARGARET Richard!

GLOUCESTER Ha!

QUEEN MARGARET I call thee not.

GLOUCESTER
I cry thee mercy then, for I did think
That thou hadst call'd me all these bitter names.

QUEEN MARGARET
Why, so I did, but look'd for no reply.
O, let me make the period to my curse!

GLOUCESTER
'Tis done by me, and ends in "Margaret."

QUEEN ELIZABETH
Thus have you breath'd your curse against yourself.

QUEEN MARGARET
Poor painted queen, vain flourish of my fortune!
Why strew'st thou sugar on that bottled spider,
Whose deadly web ensnareth thee about?
Fool, fool, thou whet'st a knife to kill thyself.
The day will come that thou shalt wish for me
To help thee curse this poisonous bunch-back'd toad.

HASTINGS
False-boding woman, end thy frantic curse,
Lest to thy harm thou move our patience.

QUEEN MARGARET
Foul shame upon you! You have all mov'd mine.

RIVERS
Were you well serv'd, you would be taught your duty.

QUEEN MARGARET
To serve me well, you all should do me duty,
Teach me to be your queen, and you my subjects.
O, serve me well, and teach yourselves that duty!

DORSET
Dispute not with her; she is lunatic.

QUEEN MARGARET
Peace, Master Marquess, you are malapert.
Your fire-new stamp of honor is scarce current.
O, that your young nobility could judge
What 'twere to lose it and be miserable!
They that stand high have many blasts to shake them,
And if they fall, they dash themselves to pieces.

GLOUCESTER
Good counsel, marry! Learn it, learn it, Marquess.

DORSET
It touches you, my lord, as much as me.

GLOUCESTER
Ay, and much more; but I was born so high.
Our aery buildeth in the cedar's top,
And dallies with the wind and scorns the sun.

185 No . . . prophesied there was no one who did not prophesy **193 but answer for** merely atone for, equal **195 quick** lively, piercing **196 surfeit** dissipated living **205 stall'd** installed **209–210 Rivers, Dorset, Hastings** (Not present in Shakespeare's dramatization of the event in *3 Henry VI,* V.v, but named in the chronicles as having been present.) **213 unlook'd** unanticipated **214 charm** magic curse, pronounced by a witch **218 them** i.e., the heavens, heaven **221 still begnaw** continually gnaw **227 elvish-mark'd** marked by elves at birth. **hog** (Alludes to Richard's badge, the wild boar.) **228 seal'd** stamped **229 slave of nature** i.e., by the malignancy of nature (as seen in his deformity) **230 heavy** sorrowful

234 cry thee mercy beg your pardon. (Said sarcastically.) **237 period** conclusion **240 painted** counterfeit. **vain . . . fortune** i.e., mere ornament of a position which is mine by right **241 bottled** bottle-shaped, swollen **246 False-boding** falsely prophesying **249 well serv'd** treated as you deserve. (But Margaret turns the phrase around to mean *served as befitting one of royal rank.*) **your duty** your place (i.e., to be obedient) **254 malapert** impudent **255 fire-new** newly coined. **current** genuine as legal tender **263 aery** eagle's brood

QUEEN MARGARET
And turns the sun to shade; alas, alas!
Witness my son, now in the shade of death,
Whose bright out-shining beams thy cloudy wrath
Hath in eternal darkness folded up.
Your aery buildeth in our aery's nest.
O God, that seest it, do not suffer it!
As it is won with blood, lost be it so!

BUCKINGHAM
Peace, peace, for shame, if not for charity!

QUEEN MARGARET
Urge neither charity nor shame to me.
[*Turning to the others.*]
Uncharitably with me have you dealt,
And shamefully my hopes by you are butcher'd.
My charity is outrage, life my shame,
And in that shame still live my sorrow's rage!

BUCKINGHAM
Have done, have done.

QUEEN MARGARET
O princely Buckingham, I'll kiss thy hand
In sign of league and amity with thee.
Now fair befall thee and thy noble house!
Thy garments are not spotted with our blood,
Nor thou within the compass of my curse.

BUCKINGHAM
Nor no one here; for curses never pass
The lips of those that breathe them in the air.

QUEEN MARGARET
I will not think but they ascend the sky,
And there awake God's gentle-sleeping peace.
O Buckingham, take heed of yonder dog.
Look when he fawns, he bites; and when he bites,
His venom tooth will rankle to the death.
Have not to do with him, beware of him;
Sin, death, and hell have set their marks on him,
And all their ministers attend on him.

GLOUCESTER
What doth she say, my Lord of Buckingham?

BUCKINGHAM
Nothing that I respect, my gracious lord.

QUEEN MARGARET
What, dost thou scorn me for my gentle counsel?
And soothe the devil that I warn thee from?
O, but remember this another day,
When he shall split thy very heart with sorrow,
And say poor Margaret was a prophetess!
Live each of you the subjects to his hate,
And he to yours, and all of you to God's! *Exit.*

BUCKINGHAM
My hair doth stand an end to hear her curses.

RIVERS
And so doth mine. I muse why she's at liberty.

GLOUCESTER
I cannot blame her. By God's holy mother,
She hath had too much wrong, and I repent
My part thereof that I have done to her.

QUEEN ELIZABETH
I never did her any, to my knowledge.

GLOUCESTER
Yet you have all the vantage of her wrong.
I was too hot to do somebody good
That is too cold in thinking of it now.
Marry, as for Clarence, he is well repaid;
He is frank'd up to fatting for his pains—
God pardon them that are the cause thereof!

RIVERS
A virtuous and a Christian-like conclusion,
To pray for them that have done scathe to us.

GLOUCESTER
So do I ever—*(Speaks to himself.)* being well advis'd.
For had I curs'd now, I had curs'd myself.

Enter Catesby.

CATESBY
Madam, his Majesty doth call for you,
And for your Grace, and yours, my gracious lord.

QUEEN ELIZABETH
Catesby, I come. Lords, will you go with me?

RIVERS
We wait upon your Grace. *Exeunt all but Gloucester.*

GLOUCESTER
I do the wrong, and first begin to brawl.
The secret mischiefs that I set abroach
I lay unto the grievous charge of others.
Clarence, who I indeed have cast in darkness,
I do beweep to many simple gulls—
Namely, to Derby, Hastings, Buckingham—
And tell them 'tis the Queen and her allies
That stir the King against the Duke my brother.
Now they believe it, and withal whet me
To be reveng'd on Rivers, Dorset, Grey.
But then I sigh, and, with a piece of scripture,
Tell them that God bids us do good for evil.
And thus I clothe my naked villainy
With odd old ends stol'n forth of holy writ,
And seem a saint, when most I play the devil.

Enter two Murderers.

But, soft! Here come my executioners.
How now, my hardy, stout, resolved mates,
Are you now going to dispatch this thing?

FIRST MURDERER
We are, my lord, and come to have the warrant
That we may be admitted where he is.

GLOUCESTER
Well thought upon. I have it here about me.
[*Gives the warrant.*]
When you have done, repair to Crosby Place.
But sirs, be sudden in the execution,
Withal obdurate, do not hear him plead;

265 sun (with a play on *son* in the next line) **276 My . . . outrage** i.e., instead of charity I receive outrage **281 fair befall** good luck to **284–285 curses . . . air** i.e., curses have no effect, are mere speech **286 I . . . but** I must believe that **289 Look when** whenever **290 venom** envenomed. **rankle** cause a festering wound **295 respect** heed **297 soothe** flatter **303 an** on **304 muse** wonder

309 vantage of advantage derived from **310 hot** eager (in helping Edward to the throne) **311 That . . . cold** who is too ungrateful **313 frank'd up** shut up in a frank or sty. **to fatting** to be fattened (for slaughter) **316 scathe** harm **322 wait upon** attend **324 set abroach** set flowing, begin **325 lay . . . of** impute as a serious accusation against **327 gulls** credulous persons **334 for** in return for **339 resolved** resolute **344 repair** betake yourselves

For Clarence is well-spoken, and perhaps
May move your hearts to pity if you mark him.

FIRST MURDERER
Tut, tut, my lord, we will not stand to prate;
Talkers are no good doers. Be assur'd
We go to use our hands and not our tongues.

GLOUCESTER
Your eyes drop millstones, when fools' eyes fall
tears.
I like you, lads; about your business straight.
Go, go, dispatch.

FIRST MURDERER We will, my noble lord. [*Exeunt.*]

SCENE IV

Enter Clarence and Keeper.

KEEPER
Why looks your Grace so heavily today?

CLARENCE
O, I have pass'd a miserable night,
So full of fearful dreams, of ugly sights,
That, as I am a Christian faithful man,
I would not spend another such a night
Though 'twere to buy a world of happy days,
So full of dismal terror was the time!

KEEPER
What was your dream, my lord? I pray you tell me.

CLARENCE
Methoughts that I had broken from the Tower,
And was embark'd to cross to Burgundy,
And in my company my brother Gloucester,
Who from my cabin tempted me to walk
Upon the hatches. Thence we look'd toward
England,
And cited up a thousand heavy times,
During the wars of York and Lancaster,
That had befall'n us. As we pac'd along
Upon the giddy footing of the hatches,
Methought that Gloucester stumbled, and, in falling,
Struck me, that thought to stay him, overboard,
Into the tumbling billows of the main.
O Lord, methought what pain it was to drown!
What dreadful noise of water in mine ears!
What sights of ugly death within mine eyes!
Methoughts I saw a thousand fearful wracks;
A thousand men that fishes gnaw'd upon;
Wedges of gold, great anchors, heaps of pearl,
Inestimable stones, unvalued jewels,
All scatt'red in the bottom of the sea.
Some lay in dead men's skulls; and, in the holes
Where eyes did once inhabit, there were crept,
As 'twere in scorn of eyes, reflecting gems,
That woo'd the slimy bottom of the deep,
And mock'd the dead bones that lay scatt'red by.

KEEPER
Had you such leisure in the time of death
To gaze upon these secrets of the deep?

CLARENCE
Methought I had, and often did I strive
To yield the ghost; but still the envious flood
Stopp'd in my soul, and would not let it forth
To find the empty, vast, and wand'ring air,
But smother'd it within my panting bulk,
Who almost burst to belch it in the sea.

KEEPER
Awak'd you not in this sore agony?

CLARENCE
No, no, my dream was lengthen'd after life.
O, then began the tempest to my soul!
I pass'd, methought, the melancholy flood,
With that sour ferryman which poets write of,
Unto the kingdom of perpetual night.
The first that there did greet my stranger soul
Was my great father-in-law, renowned Warwick,
Who spake aloud, "What scourge for perjury
Can this dark monarchy afford false Clarence?"
And so he vanish'd. Then came wand'ring by
A shadow like an angel, with bright hair
Dabbled in blood, and he shriek'd out aloud,
"Clarence is come—false, fleeting, perjur'd Clarence,
That stabb'd me in the field by Tewkesbury.
Seize on him, Furies, take him unto torment!"
With that, methought, a legion of foul fiends
Environ'd me, and howled in mine ears
Such hideous cries that with the very noise
I trembling wak'd, and for a season after
Could not believe but that I was in hell,
Such terrible impression made my dream.

KEEPER
No marvel, lord, though it affrighted you.
I am afraid, methinks, to hear you tell it.

CLARENCE
Ah, keeper, keeper, I have done these things,
That now give evidence against my soul,
For Edward's sake; and see how he requites me!
O God! If my deep pray'rs cannot appease thee,
But thou wilt be aveng'd on my misdeeds,
Yet execute thy wrath in me alone!
O, spare my guiltless wife and my poor children!
Keeper, I prithee sit by me awhile.
My soul is heavy, and I fain would sleep.

KEEPER
I will, my lord. God give your Grace good rest!
[*Clarence sleeps.*]

Enter Brakenbury, the Lieutenant.

BRAKENBURY
Sorrow breaks seasons and reposing hours,

352 fall let fall

I.iv. Location: London. The Tower.
10 Burgundy (Clarence and Richard, according to the chronicles, had been sent to Burgundy for protection following their father's death.) **13 hatches** moveable planks forming a deck **14 cited up** recalled **19 stay** hold, steady **27 Inestimable** precious and innumerable. **unvalued** priceless

40 bulk body **45 melancholy flood** i.e., River Styx **46 ferryman** i.e., Charon, who ferried souls to Hades, *the kingdom of perpetual night* (l. 47) **48 stranger** i.e., newly arrived **53 shadow** i.e., ghost of Edward Prince of Wales, son of Henry VI **55 fleeting** fickle, deceitful **74 fain** willingly **76 breaks seasons** i.e., disrupts the normal rhythms of life. **reposing hours** i.e., hours properly devoted to sleep

Makes the night morning, and the noontide night.
Princes have but their titles for their glories,
An outward honor for an inward toil,
And, for unfelt imaginations,
They often feel a world of restless cares;
So that, between their titles and low name,
There's nothing differs but the outward fame.

Enter two Murderers.

FIRST MURDERER Ho! Who's here?

BRAKENBURY
What would'st thou, fellow, and how cam'st thou hither?

FIRST MURDERER I would speak with Clarence, and I came hither on my legs.

BRAKENBURY
What, so brief?

SECOND MURDERER 'Tis better, sir, than to be tedious. Let him see our commission, and talk no more.

[Brakenbury] reads [it].

BRAKENBURY
I am, in this, commanded to deliver
The noble Duke of Clarence to your hands.
I will not reason what is meant hereby,
Because I will be guiltless from the meaning.
There lies the Duke asleep, and there the keys.
[Gives keys.]
I'll to the King and signify to him
That thus I have resign'd to you my charge.

FIRST MURDERER You may, sir, 'tis a point of wisdom. Fare you well. *Exit [Brakenbury with Keeper].*

SECOND MURDERER What, shall we stab him as he sleeps?

FIRST MURDERER No. He'll say 'twas done cowardly, when he wakes.

SECOND MURDERER Why, he shall never wake until the great Judgment Day.

FIRST MURDERER Why, then he'll say we stabb'd him sleeping.

SECOND MURDERER The urging of that word "judgment" hath bred a kind of remorse in me.

FIRST MURDERER What, art thou afraid?

SECOND MURDERER Not to kill him, having a warrant, but to be damn'd for killing him, from the which no warrant can defend me.

FIRST MURDERER I thought thou hadst been resolute.

SECOND MURDERER So I am—to let him live.

FIRST MURDERER I'll back to the Duke of Gloucester, and tell him so.

SECOND MURDERER Nay, I prithee, stay a little. I hope this passionate humor of mine will change. It was wont to hold me but while one tells twenty.

FIRST MURDERER How dost thou feel thyself now?

SECOND MURDERER Faith, some certain dregs of conscience are yet within me.

FIRST MURDERER Remember our reward when the deed 's done.

SECOND MURDERER 'Zounds, he dies! I had forgot the reward.

FIRST MURDERER Where's thy conscience now?

SECOND MURDERER O, in the Duke of Gloucester's purse.

FIRST MURDERER When he opens his purse to give us our reward, thy conscience flies out.

SECOND MURDERER 'Tis no matter, let it go. There's few or none will entertain it.

FIRST MURDERER What if it come to thee again?

SECOND MURDERER I'll not meddle with it; it makes a man a coward. A man cannot steal, but it accuseth him; a man cannot swear, but it checks him; a man cannot lie with his neighbor's wife, but it detects him. 'Tis a blushing shamefac'd spirit that mutinies in a man's bosom. It fills a man full of obstacles. It made me once restore a purse of gold that by chance I found. It beggars any man that keeps it. It is turn'd out of towns and cities for a dangerous thing, and every man that means to live well endeavors to trust to himself and live without it.

FIRST MURDERER 'Zounds, 'tis even now at my elbow, persuading me not to kill the Duke.

SECOND MURDERER Take the devil in thy mind, and believe him not. He would insinuate with thee but to make thee sigh.

FIRST MURDERER I am strong-fram'd, he cannot prevail with me.

SECOND MURDERER Spoke like a tall man that respects thy reputation. Come, shall we fall to work?

FIRST MURDERER Take him on the costard with the hilts of thy sword, and then throw him into the malmsey-butt in the next room.

SECOND MURDERER O excellent device! And make a sop of him.

FIRST MURDERER Soft, he wakes.

SECOND MURDERER Strike!

FIRST MURDERER No, we'll reason with him.

CLARENCE
Where art thou, keeper? Give me a cup of wine.

SECOND MURDERER
You shall have wine enough, my lord, anon.

CLARENCE
In God's name, what art thou?

FIRST MURDERER
A man, as you are.

CLARENCE
But not, as I am, royal.

FIRST MURDERER
Nor you, as we are, loyal.

CLARENCE
Thy voice is thunder, but thy looks are humble.

FIRST MURDERER
My voice is now the King's, my looks mine own.

CLARENCE
How darkly and how deadly dost thou speak!

80 for unfelt imaginations in return for glories that are only imagined **82 low name** i.e., the lowly position of ordinary men **83 fame** reputation **94 will be** wish to be **119 passionate humor** compassionate mood **120 tells** counts

126 'Zounds i.e., by God's (Christ's) wounds **134 entertain it** receive it, give it welcome **138 checks** reproves **149–150 Take . . . not** i.e., listen to the devil and don't heed the devil conscience **150 insinuate** ingratiate himself **154 tall** brave **156 costard** head. (Literally, a kind of apple.) **157–158 malmsey-butt** wine barrel. (Malmsey is a sweet wine.) **159 sop** bread or cake soaked in wine

Your eyes do menace me. Why look you pale?
Who sent you hither? Wherefore do you come?

SECOND MURDERER
To, to, to—

CLARENCE
To murder me?

BOTH
Ay, ay.

CLARENCE
You scarcely have the hearts to tell me so,
And therefore cannot have the hearts to do it.
Wherein, my friends, have I offended you?

FIRST MURDERER
Offended us you have not, but the King.

CLARENCE
I shall be reconcil'd to him again.

SECOND MURDERER
Never, my lord; therefore prepare to die.

CLARENCE
Are you drawn forth among a world of men 184
To slay the innocent? What is my offense?
Where is the evidence that doth accuse me?
What lawful quest have given their verdict up 187
Unto the frowning judge? Or who pronounc'd
The bitter sentence of poor Clarence' death?
Before I be convict by course of law, 190
To threaten me with death is most unlawful.
I charge you, as you hope to have redemption
[By Christ's dear blood shed for our grievous sins,]
That you depart and lay no hands on me.
The deed you undertake is damnable.

FIRST MURDERER
What we will do, we do upon command.

SECOND MURDERER
And he that hath commanded is our king.

CLARENCE
Erroneous vassals! The great King of kings 198
Hath in the table of his law commanded 199
That thou shalt do no murder. Will you, then,
Spurn at his edict and fulfill a man's?
Take heed; for he holds vengeance in his hand,
To hurl upon their heads that break his law.

SECOND MURDERER
And that same vengeance doth he hurl on thee,
For false forswearing and for murder too.
Thou didst receive the sacrament to fight 206
In quarrel of the house of Lancaster.

FIRST MURDERER
And, like a traitor to the name of God,
Didst break that vow, and with thy treacherous
blade
Unrip'dst the bowels of thy sov'reign's son. 210

SECOND MURDERER
Whom thou wast sworn to cherish and defend.

FIRST MURDERER
How canst thou urge God's dreadful law to us,
When thou hast broke it in such dear degree? 213

CLARENCE
Alas! For whose sake did I that ill deed?
For Edward, for my brother, for his sake.
He sends you not to murder me for this,
For in that sin he is as deep as I.
If God will be avenged for the deed,
O, know you yet, he doth it publicly!
Take not the quarrel from his pow'rful arm.
He needs no indirect or lawless course
To cut off those that have offended him.

FIRST MURDERER
Who made thee, then, a bloody minister,
When gallant-springing brave Plantagenet, 224
That princely novice, was struck dead by thee? 225

CLARENCE
My brother's love, the devil, and my rage. 226

FIRST MURDERER
Thy brother's love, our duty, and thy faults
Provoke us hither now to slaughter thee.

CLARENCE
O, if you do love my brother, hate not me!
I am his brother, and I love him well.
If you are hir'd for meed, go back again, 231
And I will send you to my brother Gloucester,
Who shall reward you better for my life
Than Edward will for tidings of my death.

SECOND MURDERER
You are deceiv'd, your brother Gloucester hates you.

CLARENCE
O, no, he loves me, and he holds me dear.
Go you to him from me.

FIRST MURDERER
Ay, so we will.

CLARENCE
Tell him, when that our princely father York
Bless'd his three sons with his victorious arm,
[And charg'd us from his soul to love each other,]
He little thought of this divided friendship.
Bid Gloucester think on this, and he will weep.

FIRST MURDERER
Ay, millstones, as he lessoned us to weep. 243

CLARENCE
O, do not slander him, for he is kind.

FIRST MURDERER
Right, as snow in harvest. Come, you deceive
yourself. 245
'Tis he that sends us to destroy you here.

CLARENCE
It cannot be; for he bewept my fortune,
And hugg'd me in his arms, and swore with sobs
That he would labor my delivery. 249

FIRST MURDERER
Why, so he doth, when he delivers you

184 drawn . . . men especially selected from the whole human race **187 quest** inquest, i.e., jury **190 convict** convicted **198 Erroneous vassals** sinful and mistaken wretches **199 table** tablet **206 receive the sacrament** i.e., swear upon the sacrament **210 sov'reign's son** i.e., Prince Edward, son of Henry VI

213 dear grievous **224 gallant-springing** i.e., gallant and sprightly, aspiring. **Plantagenet** (Originally, a nickname for Geoffrey of Anjou, father of Henry II and founder of the dynasty that ruled England until 1485; the name is thus appropriate to the Lancastrian Prince Edward, though the Yorkist Richard Plantagenet had attempted to take the name for his own.) **225 novice** youth **226 My brother's love** i.e., my love for my brother **231 meed** financial reward **243 lessoned** taught **245 Right . . . harvest** i.e., he's just as kind and natural—that is, both affectionate and with the natural feelings of a brother—as is snow at harvest time **249 labor my delivery** work for my release

From this earth's thralldom to the joys of heaven.

SECOND MURDERER
Make peace with God, for you must die, my lord.

CLARENCE
Have you that holy feeling in your souls
To counsel me to make my peace with God,
And are you yet to your own souls so blind
That you will war with God by murd'ring me?
O, sirs, consider, they that set you on
To do this deed will hate you for the deed.

SECOND MURDERER
What shall we do?

CLARENCE Relent, and save your souls.
Which of you, if you were a prince's son,
Being pent from liberty, as I am now,
If two such murderers as yourselves came to you,
Would not entreat for life?

FIRST MURDERER
Relent? No. 'Tis cowardly and womanish.

CLARENCE
Not to relent is beastly, savage, devilish.
My friend [*To Second Murderer.*], I spy some pity in thy looks.
O, if thine eye be not a flatterer,
Come thou on my side, and entreat for me,
As you would beg, were you in my distress.
A begging prince what beggar pities not?

SECOND MURDERER
Look behind you, my lord.

FIRST MURDERER
Take that, and that! *(Stabs him.)* If all this will not do,
I'll drown you in the malmsey-butt within.
Exit [*with the body*].

SECOND MURDERER
A bloody deed, and desperately dispatch'd!
How fain, like Pilate, would I wash my hands
Of this most grievous murder!

Enter First Murderer.

FIRST MURDERER
How now? What mean'st thou, that thou help'st me not?
By heaven, the Duke shall know how slack you have been!

SECOND MURDERER
I would he knew that I had sav'd his brother!
Take thou the fee, and tell him what I say,
For I repent me that the Duke is slain. *Exit.*

FIRST MURDERER
So do not I. Go, coward as thou art.
Well, I'll go hide his body in some hole,
Till that the Duke give order for his burial;
And when I have my meed, I will away;
For this will out, and then I must not stay. *Exit.*

261 pent shut up **286 this** i.e., this murder

ACT II • SCENE I

Flourish. Enter the King [*Edward*], *sick, the Queen* [*Elizabeth*], *Lord Marquess Dorset,* [*Grey,*] *Rivers, Hastings, Catesby, Buckingham,* [*and others*].

KING EDWARD
Why, so. Now have I done a good day's work.
You peers, continue this united league.
I every day expect an embassage
From my Redeemer to redeem me hence;
And more in peace my soul shall part to heaven,
Since I have made my friends at peace on earth.
Rivers and Hastings, take each other's hand;
Dissemble not your hatred, swear your love.

RIVERS
By heaven, my soul is purg'd from grudging hate,
[*Takes Hastings' hand.*]
And with my hand I seal my true heart's love.

HASTINGS
So thrive I, as I truly swear the like!

KING EDWARD
Take heed you dally not before your king,
Lest he that is the supreme King of kings
Confound your hidden falsehood, and award
Either of you to be the other's end.

HASTINGS
So prosper I, as I swear perfect love!

RIVERS
And I, as I love Hastings with my heart!

KING EDWARD
Madam, yourself is not exempt from this,
Nor you, son Dorset, Buckingham, nor you;
You have been factious one against the other.
Wife, love Lord Hastings, let him kiss your hand;
And what you do, do it unfeignedly.

QUEEN ELIZABETH
There, Hastings; I will never more remember
Our former hatred, so thrive I and mine!
[*Hastings kisses her hand.*]

KING EDWARD
Dorset, embrace him; Hastings, love Lord Marquess.

DORSET
This interchange of love, I here protest,
Upon my part shall be inviolable.

HASTINGS
And so swear I. [*They embrace.*]

KING EDWARD
Now, princely Buckingham, seal thou this league
With thy embracements to my wife's allies,
And make me happy in your unity.

BUCKINGHAM
Whenever Buckingham doth turn his hate

II.i. Location: London. The palace.
s.d. Flourish trumpet call to announce the arrival of a distinguished person **8 Dissemble** conceal, disguise (under a false appearance of love) **12 dally** trifle **15 Either . . . end** i.e., each of you to die at the hands of the other

Upon your Grace [*To the Queen*], but with all
duteous love
Doth cherish you and yours, God punish me
With hate in those where I expect most love!
When I have most need to employ a friend,
And most assured that he is a friend,
Deep, hollow, treacherous, and full of guile
Be he unto me! This do I beg of God,
When I am cold in love to you or yours.
[*They*] *embrace.*

KING EDWARD
A pleasing cordial, princely Buckingham,
Is this thy vow unto my sickly heart.
There wanteth now our brother Gloucester here
To make the blessed period of this peace.

BUCKINGHAM
And, in good time,
Here comes Sir Richard Ratcliffe and the Duke.

Enter Ratcliffe and Gloucester.

GLOUCESTER
Good morrow to my sovereign king and queen;
And, princely peers, a happy time of day!

KING EDWARD
Happy, indeed, as we have spent the day.
Gloucester, we have done deeds of charity,
Made peace of enmity, fair love of hate,
Between these swelling wrong-incensed peers.

GLOUCESTER
A blessed labor, my most sovereign lord.
Among this princely heap, if any here,
By false intelligence, or wrong surmise,
Hold me a foe;
If I unwittingly, or in my rage,
Have aught committed that is hardly borne
By any in this presence, I desire
To reconcile me to his friendly peace.
'Tis death to me to be at enmity;
I hate it, and desire all good men's love.
First, madam, I entreat true peace of you,
Which I will purchase with my duteous service;
Of you, my noble cousin Buckingham,
If ever any grudge were lodg'd between us;
Of you and you, Lord Rivers and of Dorset,
That all without desert have frown'd on me;
Dukes, earls, lords, gentlemen—indeed, of all.
I do not know that Englishman alive
With whom my soul is any jot at odds
More than the infant that is born tonight.
I thank my God for my humility.

QUEEN ELIZABETH
A holy day shall this be kept hereafter.
I would to God all strifes were well compounded.
My sovereign lord, I do beseech your Highness
To take our brother Clarence to your grace.

GLOUCESTER
Why, madam, have I off'red love for this,
To be so flouted in this royal presence?
Who knows not that the gentle Duke is dead?
They all start.
You do him injury to scorn his corse.

KING EDWARD
Who knows not he is dead? Who knows he is?

QUEEN ELIZABETH
All-seeing heaven, what a world is this!

BUCKINGHAM
Look I so pale, Lord Dorset, as the rest?

DORSET
Ay, my good lord; and no man in this presence
But his red color hath forsook his cheeks.

KING EDWARD
Is Clarence dead? The order was revers'd.

GLOUCESTER
But he, poor man, by your first order died,
And that a winged Mercury did bear;
Some tardy cripple bare the countermand,
That came too lag to see him buried.
God grant that some, less noble and less loyal,
Nearer in bloody thoughts, but not in blood,
Deserve not worse than wretched Clarence did,
And yet go current from suspicion!

Enter [*Lord Stanley*] *Earl of Derby.*

STANLEY
A boon, my sovereign, for my service done!
[*Kneels.*]

KING EDWARD
I pray thee, peace. My soul is full of sorrow.

STANLEY
I will not rise unless your Highness hear me.

KING EDWARD
Then say at once what is it thou requests.

STANLEY
The forfeit, sovereign, of my servant's life,
Who slew today a riotous gentleman
Lately attendant on the Duke of Norfolk.

KING EDWARD
Have I a tongue to doom my brother's death,
And shall that tongue give pardon to a slave?
My brother kill'd no man; his fault was thought,
And yet his punishment was bitter death.
Who sued to me for him? Who, in my wrath,
Kneel'd at my feet, and bid me be advis'd?
Who spoke of brotherhood? Who spoke of love?
Who told me how the poor soul did forsake
The mighty Warwick, and did fight for me?
Who told me, in the field at Tewkesbury,
When Oxford had me down, he rescued me,
And said, "Dear brother, live, and be a king"?
Who told me, when we both lay in the field
Frozen almost to death, how he did lap me

33 but i.e., nor **41 cordial** restorative **43 wanteth** is lacking **44 period** conclusion **52 swelling** i.e., with anger or rivalry **54 heap** assembly **55 false intelligence** being misinformed **58 hardly borne** taken amiss, deeply resented **68 all without desert** wholly without my having deserved it **72 More than the infant** i.e., more than is that infant's soul **75 compounded** settled

85 presence i.e., royal presence **90 bare** bore **91 lag** late **92–95 God . . . suspicion** i.e., (ironically), pray God there be not persons who deserve worse than Clarence got, persons less noble or related by blood to the King than he although closely involved in bloody plots, who yet go undetected. (Richard means the Queen and her kindred.) **95 go current** are accepted at face value (like legal currency) **96 A boon** (I crave) a favor **100 forfeit** i.e., the remission of the forfeit **108 advis'd** cautious **113 Oxford** (See *3 Henry VI*, V.v.2 and note; this episode has no historical basis.)

Even in his garments, and did give himself,
All thin and naked, to the numb cold night?
All this from my remembrance brutish wrath
Sinfully pluck'd, and not a man of you
Had so much grace to put it in my mind.
But when your carters or your waiting vassals
Have done a drunken slaughter, and defac'd
The precious image of our dear Redeemer,
You straight are on your knees for pardon, pardon;
And I, unjustly too, must grant it you.
[Stanley rises.]
But for my brother not a man would speak,
Nor I, ungracious, speak unto myself
For him, poor soul. The proudest of you all
Have been beholding to him in his life;
Yet none of you would once beg for his life.
O God, I fear thy justice will take hold
On me, and you, and mine, and yours for this!
Come, Hastings, help me to my closet. Ah, poor
Clarence! *Exeunt some with King and Queen.*

GLOUCESTER
This is the fruits of rashness! Mark'd you not
How that the guilty kindred of the Queen
Look'd pale when they did hear of Clarence' death?
O, they did urge it still unto the King!
God will revenge it. Come, lords, will you go
To comfort Edward with our company?

BUCKINGHAM
We wait upon your Grace. *Exeunt.*

SCENE II

Enter the old Duchess of York, with the two children of Clarence, [Edward and Margaret Plantagenet].

BOY
Good grandam, tell us, is our father dead?

DUCHESS
No, boy.

GIRL
Why do you weep so oft, and beat your breast,
And cry "O Clarence, my unhappy son"?

BOY
Why do you look on us, and shake your head,
And call us orphans, wretches, castaways,
If that our noble father were alive?

DUCHESS
My pretty cousins, you mistake me both.
I do lament the sickness of the King,
As loath to lose him, not your father's death;
It were lost sorrow to wail one that's lost.

BOY
Then, you conclude, my grandam, he is dead.
The King mine uncle is to blame for it.
God will revenge it, whom I will importune
With earnest prayers all to that effect.

GIRL
And so will I.

DUCHESS
Peace, children, peace, the King doth love you well.
Incapable and shallow innocents,
You cannot guess who caus'd your father's death.

BOY
Grandam, we can; for my good uncle Gloucester
Told me the King, provok'd to it by the Queen,
Devis'd impeachments to imprison him;
And when my uncle told me so, he wept,
And pitied me, and kindly kiss'd my cheek;
Bade me rely on him as on my father,
And he would love me dearly as a child.

DUCHESS
Ah, that deceit should steal such gentle shape,
And with a virtuous visor hide deep vice!
He is my son—ay, and therein my shame;
Yet from my dugs he drew not this deceit.

BOY
Think you my uncle did dissemble, grandam?

DUCHESS
Ay, boy.

BOY
I cannot think it. Hark, what noise is this?

Enter the Queen [Elizabeth], with her hair about her ears; Rivers and Dorset after her.

QUEEN ELIZABETH
Ah, who shall hinder me to wail and weep,
To chide my fortune, and torment myself?
I'll join with black despair against my soul,
And to myself become an enemy.

DUCHESS
What means this scene of rude impatience?

QUEEN ELIZABETH
To make an act of tragic violence.
Edward, my lord, thy son, our king, is dead!
Why grow the branches when the root is gone?
Why wither not the leaves that want their sap?
If you will live, lament; if die, be brief,
That our swift-winged souls may catch the King's,
Or, like obedient subjects, follow him
To his new kingdom of ne'er-changing night.

DUCHESS
Ah, so much interest have I in thy sorrow
As I had title in thy noble husband!
I have bewept a worthy husband's death,
And liv'd with looking on his images;
But now two mirrors of his princely semblance
Are crack'd in pieces by malignant death,
And I for comfort have but one false glass,
That grieves me when I see my shame in him.
Thou art a widow; yet thou art a mother,

134 closet private chambers

II.ii. Location: London. The palace.
8 cousins kinsmen

18 Incapable unable to understand **22 impeachments** accusations **28 visor** mask **38 rude** violent **39 make** perform. (Continues the theatrical metaphor in the previous line.) **40 Edward . . . dead** (Clarence's death, February 1478, and Edward IV's death, April 1483, are treated as if they had occurred near together.) **48 title** i.e., as mother of the King **50 images** likenesses; here, children **51 two mirrors** i.e., Edward and Clarence. (She does not count Rutland.) **53 false glass** i.e., Richard

And hast the comfort of thy children left;
But death hath snatch'd my husband from mine arms,
And pluck'd two crutches from my feeble hands,
Clarence and Edward. O, what cause have I, 59
Thine being but a moi'ty of my moan, 60
To overgo thy woes and drown thy cries! 61

BOY
Ah, aunt! You wept not for our father's death.
How can we aid you with our kindred tears? 63

GIRL
Our fatherless distress was left unmoan'd;
Your widow-dolor likewise be unwept! 65

QUEEN ELIZABETH
Give me no help in lamentation;
I am not barren to bring forth complaints. 67
All springs reduce their currents to mine eyes, 68
That I, being govern'd by the watery moon,
May send forth plenteous tears to drown the world!
Ah for my husband, for my dear lord Edward!

CHILDREN
Ah for our father, for our dear lord Clarence!

DUCHESS
Alas for both, both mine, Edward and Clarence!

QUEEN ELIZABETH
What stay had I but Edward? And he's gone. 74

CHILDREN
What stay had we but Clarence? And he's gone.

DUCHESS
What stays had I but they? And they are gone.

QUEEN ELIZABETH
Was never widow had so dear a loss! 77

CHILDREN
Were never orphans had so dear a loss!

DUCHESS
Was never mother had so dear a loss!
Alas, I am the mother of these griefs!
Their woes are parcel'd, mine is general. 81
She for an Edward weeps, and so do I;
I for a Clarence weep, so doth not she.
These babes for Clarence weep, and so do I;
I for an Edward weep, so do not they.
Alas, you three, on me, threefold distress'd,
Pour all your tears! I am your sorrow's nurse,
And I will pamper it with lamentation. 88

DORSET [*To Queen Elizabeth*]
Comfort, dear mother. God is much displeas'd
That you take with unthankfulness his doing.
In common worldly things 'tis call'd ungrateful
With dull unwillingness to repay a debt
Which with a bounteous hand was kindly lent;
Much more to be thus opposite with heaven, 94
For it requires the royal debt it lent you. 95

RIVERS
Madam, bethink you like a careful mother
Of the young Prince your son. Send straight for him;
Let him be crown'd. In him your comfort lives.
Drown desperate sorrow in dead Edward's grave,
And plant your joys in living Edward's throne.

Enter Richard [Duke of Gloucester], Buckingham, [Lord Stanley Earl of] Derby, Hastings, and Ratcliffe.

GLOUCESTER
Sister, have comfort. All of us have cause
To wail the dimming of our shining star,
But none can help our harms by wailing them.
Madam, my mother, I do cry you mercy; 104
I did not see your Grace. Humbly on my knee
I crave your blessing. [*Kneels.*]

DUCHESS
God bless thee; and put meekness in thy breast,
Love, charity, obedience, and true duty!

GLOUCESTER
Amen! [*Aside.*] And make me die a good old man!
That is the butt-end of a mother's blessing;
I marvel that her Grace did leave it out.

BUCKINGHAM
You cloudy princes and heart-sorrowing peers, 112
That bear this heavy mutual load of moan, 113
Now cheer each other in each other's love.
Though we have spent our harvest of this king,
We are to reap the harvest of his son.
The broken rancor of your high-swoll'n hates,
But lately splinter'd, knit, and join'd together, 118
Must gently be preserv'd, cherish'd, and kept. 119
Me seemeth good that, with some little train, 120
Forthwith from Ludlow the young Prince be fet 121
Hither to London, to be crown'd our king.

RIVERS
Why with some little train, my Lord of Buckingham?

BUCKINGHAM
Marry, my lord, lest, by a multitude, 124
The new-heal'd wound of malice should break out,
Which would be so much the more dangerous
By how much the estate is green and yet ungovern'd. 127
Where every horse bears his commanding rein 128
And may direct his course as please himself,
As well the fear of harm, as harm apparent, 130
In my opinion, ought to be prevented.

GLOUCESTER
I hope the King made peace with all of us;
And the compact is firm and true in me.

RIVERS
And so in me; and so, I think, in all.

59 what . . . I what a cause I have **60 moi'ty of my moan** half (the cause) of my grief **61 overgo** exceed **63 kindred tears** i.e., tears of kinsmen **65 widow-dolor** widow'd grief **67 barren to** unable to **68 All springs reduce** let all springs bring **74 stay** support **77 dear** grievous **81 Their . . . parcel'd** i.e., the woes of Queen Elizabeth and these children are single **88 pamper** i.e., sustain **94 opposite with** in opposition to **95 For it requires** because it calls back

104 cry you mercy beg your pardon **112 cloudy** clouded with grief **113 moan** lamentation **118 But lately splinter'd** only recently bound together (as with a splint) **119 Must . . . preserv'd** i.e., the recent mending of differences must be preserved **120 Me seemeth** it seems to me. **train** entourage **121 Ludlow** royal castle in Shropshire, near the Welsh border. **fet** fetched **124 multitude** i.e., large train or entourage **127 estate** state, government. **green** i.e., newly established **128 bears . . . rein** controls the reins that ought to control him **130 As well . . . as** both . . . and. **apparent** evident, real

Yet since it is but green, it should be put
To no apparent likelihood of breach,
Which haply by much company might be urg'd. 137
Therefore I say with noble Buckingham
That it is meet so few should fetch the Prince.

HASTINGS
And so say I.

GLOUCESTER
Then be it so; and go we to determine
Who they shall be that straight shall post to Ludlow. 142
Madam, and you, my sister, will you go
To give your censures in this business? 144

[QUEEN ELIZABETH, DUCHESS
With all our hearts.]

Exeunt. Mane[n]t Buckingham and Richard.

BUCKINGHAM
My lord, whoever journeys to the Prince,
For God sake, let not us two stay at home;
For by the way I'll sort occasion, 148
As index to the story we late talk'd of, 149
To part the Queen's proud kindred from the Prince.

GLOUCESTER
My other self, my counsel's consistory, 151
My oracle, my prophet! My dear cousin,
I, as a child, will go by thy direction.
Toward Ludlow then, for we'll not stay behind.

Exeunt.

SCENE III

Enter one Citizen at one door, and another at the other.

FIRST CITIZEN
Good morrow, neighbor. Whither away so fast?

SECOND CITIZEN
I promise you, I scarcely know myself. 2
Hear you the news abroad?

FIRST CITIZEN
Yes, that the King is dead.

SECOND CITIZEN
Ill news, by 'r lady; seldom comes the better. 5
I fear, I fear 'twill prove a giddy world.

Enter another Citizen.

THIRD CITIZEN
Neighbors, God speed!

FIRST CITIZEN
Give you good morrow, sir.

THIRD CITIZEN
Doth the news hold of good King Edward's death?

SECOND CITIZEN
Ay, sir, it is too true, God help the while!

THIRD CITIZEN
Then, masters, look to see a troublous world.

FIRST CITIZEN
No, no; by God's good grace his son shall reign.

THIRD CITIZEN
Woe to that land that's govern'd by a child!

SECOND CITIZEN
In him there is a hope of government,
Which in his nonage, council under him, 14
And in his full and ripened years, himself,
No doubt, shall then and till then govern well.

FIRST CITIZEN
So stood the state when Henry the Sixth
Was crown'd in Paris but at nine months old.

THIRD CITIZEN
Stood the state so? No, no, good friends, God wot, 19
For then this land was famously enrich'd
With politic grave counsel; then the King 21
Had virtuous uncles to protect his Grace.

FIRST CITIZEN
Why, so hath this, both by his father and mother.

THIRD CITIZEN
Better it were they all came by his father,
Or by his father there were none at all;
For emulation who shall now be nearest
Will touch us all too near, if God prevent not.
O, full of danger is the Duke of Gloucester,
And the Queen's sons and brothers haught and proud! 29
And were they to be rul'd, and not to rule,
This sickly land might solace as before. 31

FIRST CITIZEN
Come, come, we fear the worst. All will be well.

THIRD CITIZEN
When clouds are seen, wise men put on their cloaks;
When great leaves fall, then winter is at hand;
When the sun sets, who doth not look for night?
Untimely storms makes men expect a dearth.
All may be well; but, if God sort it so, 37
'Tis more than we deserve, or I expect.

SECOND CITIZEN
Truly, the hearts of men are full of fear.
You cannot reason almost with a man 40
That looks not heavily and full of dread. 41

THIRD CITIZEN
Before the days of change, still is it so. 42
By a divine instinct men's minds mistrust 43
Ensuing danger; as, by proof, we see
The water swell before a boist'rous storm.
But leave it all to God. Whither away?

SECOND CITIZEN
Marry, we were sent for to the justices.

THIRD CITIZEN
And so was I. I'll bear you company. *Exeunt.*

137 haply perhaps. **urg'd** encouraged, provoked **142 post** hasten **144 censures** judgments **148 sort** find, contrive **149 index** prologue. **late** lately **151 consistory** council chamber

II.iii. Location: London. A street.
2 promise assure **5 by 'r lady** by Our Lady

14 nonage minority. **council under him** i.e., aided by wise counsel **19 wot** knows **21 politic** sagacious **29 haught** haughty **31 solace** be happy, have comfort **37 sort** dispose **40 You . . . man** there is scarcely anyone with whom you can talk **41 heavily** sad **42 still** ever **43 mistrust** suspect, fear

SCENE IV

Enter [the] Archbishop [of York], [the] young [Duke of] York, the Queen [Elizabeth], and the Duchess [of York].

ARCHBISHOP
Last night, I hear, they lay at Stony-Stratford,
And at Northampton they do rest tonight.
Tomorrow, or next day, they will be here.
DUCHESS
I long with all my heart to see the Prince.
I hope he is much grown since last I saw him.
QUEEN ELIZABETH
But I hear, no; they say my son of York
Has almost overta'en him in his growth.
YORK
Ay, mother; but I would not have it so.
DUCHESS
Why, my young cousin, it is good to grow.
YORK
Grandam, one night, as we did sit at supper,
My uncle Rivers talk'd how I did grow
More than my brother. "Ay," quoth my uncle Gloucester,
"Small herbs have grace, great weeds do grow apace."
And since, methinks, I would not grow so fast,
Because sweet flow'rs are slow and weeds make haste.
DUCHESS
Good faith, good faith, the saying did not hold
In him that did object the same to thee.
He was the wretched'st thing when he was young,
So long a-growing and so leisurely,
That, if this rule were true, he should be gracious.
ARCHBISHOP
And so no doubt he is, my gracious madam.
DUCHESS
I hope he is; but yet let mothers doubt.
YORK
Now, by my troth, if I had been remember'd,
I could have given my uncle's Grace a flout,
To touch his growth nearer than he touch'd mine.
DUCHESS
How, my young York? I prithee, let me hear it.
YORK
Marry, they say my uncle grew so fast
That he could gnaw a crust at two hours old;
'Twas full two years ere I could get a tooth.
Grandam, this would have been a biting jest.
DUCHESS
I prithee, pretty York, who told thee this?
YORK
Grandam, his nurse.
DUCHESS
His nurse? Why, she was dead ere thou wast born.
YORK
If 'twere not she, I cannot tell who told me.
QUEEN ELIZABETH
A parlous boy! Go to, you are too shrewd.
DUCHESS
Good madam, be not angry with the child.
QUEEN ELIZABETH
Pitchers have ears.

Enter a Messenger.

ARCHBISHOP
Here comes a messenger. What news?
MESSENGER
Such news, my lord, as grieves me to report.
QUEEN ELIZABETH
How doth the Prince?
MESSENGER Well, madam, and in health.
DUCHESS
What is thy news?
MESSENGER
Lord Rivers and Lord Grey are sent to Pomfret,
And with them Sir Thomas Vaughan, prisoners.
DUCHESS
Who hath committed them?
MESSENGER The mighty dukes
Gloucester and Buckingham.
ARCHBISHOP For what offense?
MESSENGER
The sum of all I can, I have disclos'd.
Why or for what the nobles were committed
Is all unknown to me, my gracious lord.
QUEEN ELIZABETH
Ay me, I see the ruin of my house!
The tiger now hath seiz'd the gentle hind;
Insulting tyranny begins to jut
Upon the innocent and aweless throne.
Welcome, destruction, blood, and massacre!
I see, as in a map, the end of all.
DUCHESS
Accursed and unquiet wrangling days,
How many of you have mine eyes beheld!
My husband lost his life to get the crown;
And often up and down my sons were toss'd,
For me to joy and weep their gain and loss;
And being seated, and domestic broils
Clean overblown, themselves, the conquerors,
Make war upon themselves, brother to brother,
Blood to blood, self against self. O, preposterous
And frantic outrage, end thy damned spleen,

II.iv. Location: London. The palace.
1 Stony-Stratford town in Buckinghamshire **2 Northampton** town in Northamptonshire, and hence farther from London than Stony-Stratford. The Prince was taken back to Northampton after the arrest of Rivers, Grey, and Vaughan; but since the Archbishop does not yet know of that arrest, his speech doesn't make sense dramatically. The quartos reverse the order in which the two towns are named. **13 grace** virtuous qualities **16 hold** pertain **17 In him** i.e., in Richard. **object . . . to** i.e., apply this saying to **23 troth** truth, faith. **been remember'd** considered, recollected **24 my . . . flout** his Grace, my uncle, a mocking gibe **25 touch . . . nearer** i.e., taunt him about his growth more tellingly **30 biting** (with a play on the idea of *teething*)

35 parlous cunning, precocious. **Go to** (An expression of remonstrance.) **shrewd** sharp-tongued **37 Pitchers have ears** i.e., little pitchers have large ears. (Proverbial.) **42 Pomfret** castle in Yorkshire **50 hind** doe **51 jut** encroach **52 aweless** inspiring no awe (because of the youth of the King) **54 map** i.e., of future events **60 seated** i.e., on the throne **64 spleen** i.e., malice, hatred

Or let me die, to look on death no more!

QUEEN ELIZABETH
Come, come, my boy, we will to sanctuary.
Madam, farewell.

DUCHESS Stay, I will go with you.

QUEEN ELIZABETH
You have no cause.

ARCHBISHOP [*To the Queen*] My gracious lady, go,
And thither bear your treasure and your goods.
For my part, I'll resign unto your Grace
The seal I keep; and so betide to me
As well I tender you and all of yours!
Go, I'll conduct you to the sanctuary. *Exeunt.*

ACT III • SCENE I

The trumpets sound. Enter [*the*] *young Prince* [*Edward*], *the Dukes of Gloucester and Buckingham,* [*Lord*] *Cardinal* [*Bourchier, Catesby*], *etc.*

BUCKINGHAM
Welcome, sweet Prince, to London, to your chamber.

GLOUCESTER
Welcome, dear cousin, my thoughts' sovereign.
The weary way hath made you melancholy.

PRINCE
No, uncle, but our crosses on the way
Have made it tedious, wearisome, and heavy.
I want more uncles here to welcome me.

GLOUCESTER
Sweet Prince, the untainted virtue of your years
Hath not yet div'd into the world's deceit.
Nor more can you distinguish of a man
Than of his outward show—which, God he knows,
Seldom or never jumpeth with the heart.
Those uncles which you want were dangerous.
Your Grace attended to their sug'red words
But look'd not on the poison of their hearts.
God keep you from them, and from such false friends!

PRINCE
God keep me from false friends! But they were none.

GLOUCESTER
My lord, the Mayor of London comes to greet you.

Enter [*the*] *Lord Mayor* [*and his train*].

MAYOR
God bless your Grace with health and happy days!

PRINCE
I thank you, good my lord; and thank you all.
[*Mayor and his train stand aside.*]
I thought my mother, and my brother York,
Would long ere this have met us on the way.
Fie, what a slug is Hastings, that he comes not
To tell us whether they will come or no!

Enter Lord Hastings.

BUCKINGHAM
And, in good time, here comes the sweating lord.

PRINCE
Welcome, my lord. What, will our mother come?

HASTINGS
On what occasion, God he knows, not I,
The Queen your mother, and your brother York,
Have taken sanctuary. The tender Prince
Would fain have come with me to meet your Grace,
But by his mother was perforce withheld.

BUCKINGHAM
Fie, what an indirect and peevish course
Is this of hers! Lord Cardinal, will your Grace
Persuade the Queen to send the Duke of York
Unto his princely brother presently?
If she deny, Lord Hastings, go with him,
And from her jealous arms pluck him perforce.

CARDINAL
My Lord of Buckingham, if my weak oratory
Can from his mother win the Duke of York,
Anon expect him here; but if she be obdurate
To mild entreaties, God in heaven forbid
We should infringe the holy privilege
Of blessed sanctuary! Not for all this land
Would I be guilty of so deep a sin.

BUCKINGHAM
You are too senseless-obstinate, my lord,
Too ceremonious and traditional.
Weigh it but with the grossness of this age,
You break not sanctuary in seizing him.
The benefit thereof is always granted
To those whose dealings have deserv'd the place
And those who have the wit to claim the place.
This Prince hath neither claim'd it nor deserv'd it,
And therefore, in mine opinion, cannot have it.
Then, taking him from thence that is not there,
You break no privilege nor charter there.
Oft have I heard of sanctuary men,
But sanctuary children never till now.

CARDINAL
My lord, you shall o'errule my mind for once.
Come on, Lord Hastings, will you go with me?

HASTINGS
I go, my lord.

PRINCE
Good lords, make all the speedy haste you may.
[*Exeunt Cardinal and Hastings.*]
Say, uncle Gloucester, if our brother come,

66 sanctuary (Queen Elizabeth, with her son, daughters, and kinsmen, lodged in the precincts of Westminster Abbey which served as a legal refuge for criminals and persons in danger of their lives.) **71 seal** seal of office **71–72 so . . . you** may my fortunes be measured by the care I take of you

III.i. Location: London. A street.
1 chamber (London was called the *camera regis,* or King's chamber.) **4 crosses** vexations (i.e., the arrests of the Queen's kindred) **6 want** (1) lack (2) wish **11 jumpeth** agrees

22 slug sluggard **26 On what occasion** for what reason **30 perforce** by force **31 peevish** perverse **34 presently** at once **45 ceremonious** bound by formalities **46 grossness** lack of moral refinement

Where shall we sojourn till our coronation?

GLOUCESTER
Where it seems best unto your royal self.
If I may counsel you, some day or two
Your Highness shall repose you at the Tower;
Then where you please, and shall be thought most fit
For your best health and recreation.

PRINCE
I do not like the Tower, of any place.
Did Julius Caesar build that place, my lord?

BUCKINGHAM
He did, my gracious lord, begin that place,
Which, since, succeeding ages have re-edified.

PRINCE
Is it upon record, or else reported
Successively from age to age, he built it?

BUCKINGHAM
Upon record, my gracious lord.

PRINCE
But say, my lord, it were not regist'red,
Methinks the truth should live from age to age,
As 'twere retail'd to all posterity,
Even to the general all-ending day.

GLOUCESTER [*Aside*]
So wise so young, they say, do never live long.

PRINCE
What say you, uncle?

GLOUCESTER
I say, without characters fame lives long.
[*Aside.*] Thus, like the formal Vice, Iniquity,
I moralize two meanings in one word.

PRINCE
That Julius Caesar was a famous man;
With what his valor did enrich his wit,
His wit set down to make his valor live.
Death makes no conquest of this conqueror,
For now he lives in fame, though not in life.
I'll tell you what, my cousin Buckingham—

BUCKINGHAM
What, my gracious lord?

PRINCE
An if I live until I be a man,
I'll win our ancient right in France again,
Or die a soldier, as I liv'd a king.

GLOUCESTER [*Aside*]
Short summers lightly have a forward spring.

Enter young York, Hastings, [*and the*] *Cardinal.*

BUCKINGHAM
Now, in good time, here comes the Duke of York.

PRINCE
Richard of York, how fares our loving brother?

YORK
Well, my dread lord—so must I call you now.

PRINCE
Ay, brother, to our grief, as it is yours.
Too late he died that might have kept that title,
Which by his death hath lost much majesty.

GLOUCESTER
How fares our cousin, noble Lord of York?

YORK
I thank you, gentle uncle. O, my lord,
You said that idle weeds are fast in growth;
The Prince my brother hath outgrown me far.

GLOUCESTER
He hath, my lord.

YORK
And therefore is he idle?

GLOUCESTER
O, my fair cousin, I must not say so.

YORK
Then he is more beholding to you than I.

GLOUCESTER
He may command me as my sovereign,
But you have power in me as in a kinsman.

YORK
I pray you, uncle, give me this dagger.

GLOUCESTER
My dagger, little cousin? With all my heart.

PRINCE
A beggar, brother?

YORK
Of my kind uncle, that I know will give;
And being but a toy, which is no grief to give.

GLOUCESTER
A greater gift than that I'll give my cousin.

YORK
A greater gift? O, that's the sword to it.

GLOUCESTER
Ay, gentle cousin, were it light enough.

YORK
O, then, I see, you will part but with light gifts;
In weightier things you'll say a beggar nay.

GLOUCESTER
It is too heavy for your Grace to wear.

YORK
I weigh it lightly, were it heavier.

GLOUCESTER
What, would you have my weapon, little lord?

YORK
I would, that I might thank you as you call me.

GLOUCESTER
How?

YORK
Little.

65 Tower (Although in the fifteenth century, the historical time this play represents, the Tower of London was a royal palace, by Shakespeare's day it had acquired a sinister reputation.) **68 of any place** of all places **71 re-edified** rebuilt **72 upon record** in the written record. **reported** i.e., by oral tradition **75 say** suppose. **regist'red** written down **77 retail'd** handed down from one to another **78 general . . . day** Day of Judgment **81 without characters** (1) even lacking written records (2) even in the absence of moral character **82 formal Vice** i.e., the conventional Vice figure of the morality play, a comic tempter to evil who would habitually *moralize two meanings in one word,* that is, play on double meanings in a single phrase as Richard does in the phrase *live long* **85 With what** with that with which **85–86 With . . . live** i.e., taking his military achievements, whereby his bravery as a soldier added stature to his understanding, he used his understanding to set down in writing an account (the *Gallic Wars*) that would make his valor immortal **94 lightly** commonly, often. **forward** early. (Alludes to Edward's precociousness.)

96 our i.e., my. (The royal "we.") **97 dread** inspiring reverential fear (as King) **99 late** lately **103 idle** useless **118 light** trivial **121 weigh it lightly** consider it a trifle (playing on the literal meanings of *light* and *heavy*)

PRINCE
My Lord of York will still be cross in talk.
Uncle, your Grace knows how to bear with him.

YORK
You mean, to bear me, not to bear with me.
Uncle, my brother mocks both you and me:
Because that I am little, like an ape,
He thinks that you should bear me on your
shoulders.

BUCKINGHAM [*Aside to Hastings*]
With what a sharp-provided wit he reasons!
To mitigate the scorn he gives his uncle,
He prettily and aptly taunts himself.
So cunning and so young is wonderful.

GLOUCESTER
My lord, will 't please you pass along?
Myself and my good cousin Buckingham
Will to your mother, to entreat of her
To meet you at the Tower and welcome you.

YORK
What, will you go unto the Tower, my lord?

PRINCE
My Lord Protector needs will have it so.

YORK
I shall not sleep in quiet at the Tower.

GLOUCESTER
Why, what should you fear?

YORK
Marry, my uncle Clarence' angry ghost.
My grandam told me he was murd'red there.

PRINCE
I fear no uncles dead.

GLOUCESTER
Nor none that live, I hope.

PRINCE
An if they live, I hope I need not fear.
But come, my lord; with a heavy heart,
Thinking on them, go I unto the Tower.
[*A sennet.*] *Exeunt Prince, York, Hastings,*
[*Cardinal, and others*]. *Mane*[*n*]*t*
Richard, Buckingham, [*and Catesby*].

BUCKINGHAM
Think you, my lord, this little prating York
Was not incensed by his subtle mother
To taunt and scorn you thus opprobriously?

GLOUCESTER
No doubt, no doubt. O, 'tis a perilous boy,
Bold, quick, ingenious, forward, capable.
He is all the mother's, from the top to toe.

BUCKINGHAM
Well, let them rest. Come hither, Catesby.
Thou art sworn as deeply to effect what we intend
As closely to conceal what we impart.
Thou know'st our reasons urg'd upon the way.
What think'st thou? Is it not an easy matter
To make William Lord Hastings of our mind
For the installment of this noble Duke
In the seat royal of this famous isle?

CATESBY
He for his father's sake so loves the Prince
That he will not be won to aught against him.

BUCKINGHAM
What think'st thou, then, of Stanley? Will not he?

CATESBY
He will do all in all as Hastings doth.

BUCKINGHAM
Well, then, no more but this: go, gentle Catesby,
And, as it were far off, sound thou Lord Hastings,
How he doth stand affected to our purpose,
And summon him tomorrow to the Tower
To sit about the coronation.
If thou dost find him tractable to us,
Encourage him, and tell him all our reasons.
If he be leaden, icy, cold, unwilling,
Be thou so too; and so break off the talk,
And give us notice of his inclination.
For we tomorrow hold divided councils,
Wherein thyself shalt highly be employ'd.

GLOUCESTER
Commend me to Lord William. Tell him, Catesby,
His ancient knot of dangerous adversaries
Tomorrow are let blood at Pomfret Castle;
And bid my lord, for joy of this good news,
Give Mistress Shore one gentle kiss the more.

BUCKINGHAM
Good Catesby, go, effect this business soundly.

CATESBY
My good lords both, with all the heed I can.

GLOUCESTER
Shall we hear from you, Catesby, ere we sleep?

CATESBY
You shall, my lord.

GLOUCESTER
At Crosby House, there shall you find us both.
Exit Catesby.

BUCKINGHAM
Now, my lord, what shall we do, if we perceive
Lord Hastings will not yield to our complots?

GLOUCESTER
Chop off his head. Something we will determine.
And look when I am king, claim thou of me
The earldom of Hereford, and all the moveables
Whereof the King my brother was possess'd.

BUCKINGHAM
I'll claim that promise at your Grace's hand.

GLOUCESTER
And look to have it yielded with all kindness.

126 still always. **cross** perverse in twisting words **131 bear me . . . shoulders** (At fairs, the bear commonly carried an ape on his back. The speech is doubtless an allusion to Richard's hump, and puns triply on *bear with,* put up with, *bear,* carry, and *bear,* an animal.) **132 sharp-provided** keenly thought out **148 they** i.e., Rivers and Grey. (Grey was in fact Edward's step-brother, not his uncle.) **150 s.d. sennet** trumpet call to announce the approach or departure of processions **152 incensed** incited **154 perilous** i.e., parlous, clever, but also dangerous **157 let them rest** leave them for the moment

160 the way i.e., the journey to London from Ludlow **165 He . . . sake** i.e., Hastings for King Edward IV's sake **171 doth stand affected** is disposed **173 sit** sit in council **179 divided councils** (While the regular council meets about the coronation, Richard plans also to have his own private consultation at Crosby House.) **181 Lord William** i.e., Hastings **183 are let blood** i.e., will be executed **185 Mistress Shore** (According to Thomas More, Jane Shore had become the mistress of Hastings after the death of Edward IV.) **192 complots** conspiracies **194 look when** as soon as **195 moveables** personal property, other than real estate

Come, let us sup betimes, that afterwards
We may digest our complots in some form. *Exeunt.*

SCENE II

Enter a Messenger to the door of Hastings.

MESSENGER
My lord! My lord!

HASTINGS [*Within*]
Who knocks?

MESSENGER
One from the Lord Stanley.

HASTINGS [*Within*]
What is 't o'clock?

MESSENGER
Upon the stroke of four.

Enter Lord Hastings.

HASTINGS
Cannot my Lord Stanley sleep these tedious nights?

MESSENGER
So it appears by that I have to say.
First, he commends him to your noble self.

HASTINGS
What then?

MESSENGER
Then certifies your lordship that this night
He dreamt the boar had razed off his helm.
Besides, he says there are two councils kept,
And that may be determin'd at the one
Which may make you and him to rue at th' other.
Therefore he sends to know your lordship's pleasure,
If you will presently take horse with him
And with all speed post with him toward the north,
To shun the danger that his soul divines.

HASTINGS
Go, fellow, go, return unto thy lord.
Bid him not fear the separated Council.
His honor and myself are at the one,
And at the other is my good friend Catesby,
Where nothing can proceed that toucheth us
Whereof I shall not have intelligence.
Tell him his fears are shallow, without instance.
And for his dreams, I wonder he's so simple
To trust the mock'ry of unquiet slumbers.
To fly the boar before the boar pursues
Were to incense the boar to follow us
And make pursuit where he did mean no chase.
Go, bid thy master rise and come to me,
And we will both together to the Tower
Where, he shall see, the boar will use us kindly.

MESSENGER
I'll go, my lord, and tell him what you say.
Exit.

Enter Catesby.

CATESBY
Many good morrows to my noble lord!

HASTINGS
Good morrow, Catesby. You are early stirring.
What news, what news, in this our tott'ring state?

CATESBY
It is a reeling world, indeed, my lord,
And I believe will never stand upright
Till Richard wear the garland of the realm.

HASTINGS
How? Wear the garland? Dost thou mean the crown?

CATESBY
Ay, my good lord.

HASTINGS
I'll have this crown of mine cut from my shoulders
Before I'll see the crown so foul misplac'd.
But canst thou guess that he doth aim at it?

CATESBY
Ay, on my life, and hopes to find you forward
Upon his party for the gain thereof;
And thereupon he sends you this good news,
That this same very day your enemies,
The kindred of the Queen, must die at Pomfret.

HASTINGS
Indeed, I am no mourner for that news,
Because they have been still my adversaries.
But that I'll give my voice on Richard's side
To bar my master's heirs in true descent,
God knows I will not do it, to the death.

CATESBY
God keep your lordship in that gracious mind!

HASTINGS
But I shall laugh at this a twelvemonth hence,
That they which brought me in my master's hate,
I live to look upon their tragedy.
Well, Catesby, ere a fortnight make me older,
I'll send some packing that yet think not on 't.

CATESBY
'Tis a vile thing to die, my gracious lord,
When men are unprepar'd and look not for it.

HASTINGS
O monstrous, monstrous! And so falls it out
With Rivers, Vaughan, Grey; and so 'twill do
With some men else, that think themselves as safe
As thou and I—who, as thou know'st, are dear
To princely Richard and to Buckingham.

CATESBY
The princes both make high account of you—
[*Aside.*] For they account his head upon the bridge.

199 betimes soon **200 digest** arrange, perfect

III.ii. Location: Before Lord Hastings' house.
10 certifies informs **11 boar** i.e., Richard. **razed** torn, slashed **14 at th' other** i.e., the regular council meeting in the Tower, in which Hastings and Stanley will participate **25 without instance** lacking evidence

43 crown i.e., head. (Recalls Stanley's dream in l. 11 and anticipates Hastings' execution by beheading.) **47 Upon his party** on his side **52 still** always **55 to the death** i.e., though I lose my life **58 they which** i.e., regarding those who **59 I live** i.e., I shall live **69 high account** great estimation. (The quibble on *high* appears in the next line.) **70 the bridge** London Bridge, on a tower of which the heads of traitors were exposed

HASTINGS
I know they do, and I have well deserv'd it.

Enter Lord Stanley [Earl of Derby].

Come on, come on, where is your boar-spear, man?
Fear you the boar, and go so unprovided?

STANLEY
My lord, good morrow. Good morrow, Catesby.
You may jest on, but, by the holy rood, 75
I do not like these several councils, I. 76

HASTINGS
My lord,
I hold my life as dear as you do yours,
And never in my days, I do protest,
Was it so precious to me as 'tis now.
Think you, but that I know our state secure,
I would be so triumphant as I am?

STANLEY
The lords at Pomfret, when they rode from London, 83
Were jocund, and suppos'd their states were sure, 84
And they indeed had no cause to mistrust;
But yet you see how soon the day o'ercast. 86
This sudden stab of rancor I misdoubt. 87
Pray God, I say, I prove a needless coward!
What, shall we toward the Tower? The day is spent. 89

HASTINGS
Come, come, have with you. Wot you what, my lord? 90
Today the lords you talk of are beheaded.

STANLEY
They, for their truth, might better wear their heads 92
Than some that have accus'd them wear their hats. 93
But come, my lord, let's away. 94

Enter a Pursuivant.

HASTINGS
Go on before. I'll talk with this good fellow.
Exit Lord Stanley [Earl of Derby], and Catesby.
How now, sirrah? How goes the world with thee? 96

PURSUIVANT
The better that your lordship please to ask.

HASTINGS
I tell thee, man, 'tis better with me now
Than when thou met'st me last where now we meet.
Then was I going prisoner to the Tower,
By the suggestion of the Queen's allies; 101
But now, I tell thee—keep it to thyself—
This day those enemies are put to death,
And I in better state than e'er I was.

PURSUIVANT
God hold it, to your honor's good content! 105

HASTINGS
Gramercy, fellow. There, drink that for me. 106
Throws him his purse.

PURSUIVANT
I thank your honor. *Exit Pursuivant.*

Enter a Priest.

PRIEST
Well met, my lord. I am glad to see your honor.

HASTINGS
I thank thee, good Sir John, with all my heart. 109
I am in your debt for your last exercise; 110
Come the next Sabbath, and I will content you.
[He whispers in his ear.]

PRIEST
I'll wait upon your lordship.

Enter Buckingham.

BUCKINGHAM
What, talking with a priest, Lord Chamberlain?
Your friends at Pomfret, they do need the priest;
Your honor hath no shriving work in hand. 115

HASTINGS
Good faith, and when I met this holy man,
The men you talk of came into my mind.
What, go you toward the Tower?

BUCKINGHAM
I do, my lord, but long I cannot stay there.
I shall return before your lordship thence.

HASTINGS
Nay, like enough, for I stay dinner there. 121

BUCKINGHAM *[Aside]*
And supper too, although thou know'st it not.—
Come, will you go?

HASTINGS I'll wait upon your lordship.
Exeunt.

SCENE III

Enter Sir Richard Ratcliffe, with Halberds, carrying the nobles [Rivers, Grey, and Vaughan] to death at Pomfret.

[RATCLIFFE
Come, bring forth the prisoners.]

RIVERS
Sir Richard Ratcliffe, let me tell thee this:
Today shalt thou behold a subject die
For truth, for duty, and for loyalty.

GREY
God bless the Prince from all the pack of you!
A knot you are of damned blood-suckers.

VAUGHAN
You live that shall cry woe for this hereafter.

RATCLIFFE
Dispatch. The limit of your lives is out.

RIVERS
O Pomfret, Pomfret! O thou bloody prison,

75 holy rood i.e., the cross of Christ **76 several** separate **83 London** (An error for Ludlow?) **84 jocund** merry **86 o'ercast** became overcast **87 misdoubt** fear. (I.e., I fear more such sudden attacks.) **89 spent** i.e., well advanced (although the scene began at 4:00 a.m.) **90 have with you** I'll go with you. **Wot** know **92 for their truth** as far as their honesty is concerned **93 wear their hats** i.e., hold their offices **94 s.d. Pursuivant** attendant on a herald with authority to serve warrants **96 sirrah** (Form of address to inferiors.) **101 suggestion** instigation **105 hold it** continue it (i.e., the better state) **106 Gramercy** much thanks

109 Sir John (Common title for addressing any priest.) **110 exercise** sermon or religious service **115 shriving work** confession and absolution **121 stay** stay for

III.iii. Location: Pomfret Castle.

Fatal and ominous to noble peers!
Within the guilty closure of thy walls
Richard the Second here was hack'd to death;
And, for more slander to thy dismal seat,
We give to thee our guiltless blood to drink.

GREY
Now Margaret's curse is fall'n upon our heads,
When she exclaim'd on Hastings, you, and I,
For standing by when Richard stabb'd her son.

RIVERS
Then curs'd she Richard, then curs'd she
Buckingham,
Then curs'd she Hastings. O, remember, God,
To hear her pray'r for them, as now for us!
And for my sister and her princely sons,
Be satisfied, dear God, with our true blood,
Which, as thou know'st, unjustly must be spilt.

RATCLIFFE
Make haste; the hour of death is expiate.

RIVERS
Come, Grey, come, Vaughan, let us here embrace.
[*They embrace.*]
Farewell, until we meet again in heaven. *Exeunt.*

SCENE IV

Enter Buckingham, [*Lord Stanley Earl of*] *Derby, Hastings, Bishop of Ely, Norfolk, Ratcliffe, Lovel, with others, at a table.*

HASTINGS
Now, noble peers, the cause why we are met
Is to determine of the coronation.
In God's name, speak. When is the royal day?

BUCKINGHAM
Is all things ready for the royal time?

STANLEY
It is, and wants but nomination.

ELY
Tomorrow, then, I judge a happy day.

BUCKINGHAM
Who knows the Lord Protector's mind herein?
Who is most inward with the noble Duke?

ELY
Your Grace, we think, should soonest know his
mind.

BUCKINGHAM
We know each other's faces; for our hearts,
He knows no more of mine than I of yours,
Or I of his, my lord, than you of mine.
Lord Hastings, you and he are near in love.

HASTINGS
I thank his Grace, I know he loves me well;
But, for his purpose in the coronation,
I have not sounded him, nor he deliver'd
His gracious pleasure any way therein.
But you, my honorable lords, may name the time,
And in the Duke's behalf I'll give my voice,
Which I presume he'll take in gentle part.

Enter Gloucester.

ELY
In happy time, here comes the Duke himself.

GLOUCESTER
My noble lords and cousins all, good morrow.
I have been long a sleeper; but I trust
My absence doth neglect no great design,
Which by my presence might have been concluded.

BUCKINGHAM
Had you not come upon your cue, my lord,
William Lord Hastings had pronounc'd your part,
I mean your voice for crowning of the King.

GLOUCESTER
Than my Lord Hastings no man might be bolder.
His lordship knows me well, and loves me well.—
My lord of Ely, when I was last in Holborn,
I saw good strawberries in your garden there.
I do beseech you send for some of them.

ELY
Marry, and will, my lord, with all my heart.
Exit Bishop.

GLOUCESTER
Cousin of Buckingham, a word with you.
[*Drawing him aside.*]
Catesby hath sounded Hastings in our business,
And finds the testy gentleman so hot
That he will lose his head ere give consent
His master's child, as worshipfully he terms it,
Shall lose the royalty of England's throne.

BUCKINGHAM
Withdraw yourself a while, I'll go with you.
Exeunt [*Gloucester and Buckingham*].

STANLEY
We have not yet set down this day of triumph.
Tomorrow, in my judgment, is too sudden,
For I myself am not so well provided
As else I would be, were the day prolong'd.

Enter the Bishop of Ely.

ELY
Where is my lord the Duke of Gloucester?
I have sent for these strawberries.

HASTINGS
His Grace looks cheerfully and smooth this morning;
There's some conceit or other likes him well,
When that he bids good morrow with such spirit.
I think there's never a man in Christendom
Can lesser hide his love or hate than he;
For by his face straight shall you know his heart.

STANLEY
What of his heart perceive you in his face
By any livelihood he show'd today?

13 for . . . seat i.e., to add further to the evil reputation of this place **24 expiate** fully come

III.iv. Location: London. The Tower.
2 determine of decide upon **5 nomination** naming of a date **8 inward** intimate

45 prolong'd postponed **49 conceit** fancy, idea. **likes** pleases **55 livelihood** vivacity

HASTINGS
Marry, that with no man here he is offended;
For, were he, he had shown it in his looks.

[STANLEY
I pray God he be not, I say.]

Enter Richard and Buckingham.

GLOUCESTER
I pray you all, tell me what they deserve
That do conspire my death with devilish plots
Of damned witchcraft, and that have prevail'd
Upon my body with their hellish charms?

HASTINGS
The tender love I bear your Grace, my lord,
Makes me most forward in this princely presence
To doom th' offenders, whosoe'er they be:
I say, my lord, they have deserved death.

GLOUCESTER
Then be your eyes the witness of their evil.
[Bares his arm.]
Look how I am bewitch'd! Behold mine arm
Is, like a blasted sapling, wither'd up.
And this is Edward's wife, that monstrous witch,
Consorted with that harlot strumpet Shore,
That by their witchcraft thus have marked me.

HASTINGS
If they have done this deed, my noble lord—

GLOUCESTER
If? Thou protector of this damned strumpet,
Talk'st thou to me of "ifs"? Thou art a traitor.
Off with his head! Now, by Saint Paul I swear,
I will not dine until I see the same.
Lovel and Ratcliffe, look that it be done.
The rest that love me, rise and follow me.
Exeunt. Mane[n]t Lovel and Ratcliffe, with the Lord Hastings.

HASTINGS
Woe, woe for England! Not a whit for me,
For I, too fond, might have prevented this.
Stanley did dream the boar did raze our helms,
But I did scorn it and disdain to fly.
Three times today my foot-cloth horse did stumble,
And started, when he look'd upon the Tower,
As loath to bear me to the slaughter-house.
O, now I need the priest that spake to me!
I now repent I told the pursuivant,
As too triumphing, how mine enemies
Today at Pomfret bloodily were butcher'd,
And I myself secure in grace and favor.
O Margaret, Margaret, now thy heavy curse
Is lighted on poor Hastings' wretched head!

RATCLIFFE
Come, come, dispatch. The Duke would be at dinner.
Make a short shrift. He longs to see your head.

HASTINGS
O momentary grace of mortal men,
Which we more hunt for than the grace of God!
Who builds his hope in air of your good looks
Lives like a drunken sailor on a mast,
Ready, with every nod, to tumble down
Into the fatal bowels of the deep.

LOVEL
Come, come, dispatch. 'Tis bootless to exclaim.

HASTINGS
O bloody Richard! Miserable England!
I prophesy the fearfull'st time to thee
That ever wretched age hath look'd upon.
Come, lead me to the block; bear him my head.
They smile at me who shortly shall be dead.
Exeunt.

[SCENE V]

Enter Richard [of Gloucester] and Buckingham in rotten armor, marvelous ill-favored.

GLOUCESTER
Come, cousin, canst thou quake, and change thy color,
Murder thy breath in middle of a word,
And then again begin, and stop again,
As if thou wert distraught and mad with terror?

BUCKINGHAM
Tut, I can counterfeit the deep tragedian,
Speak and look back, and pry on every side,
Tremble and start at wagging of a straw;
Intending deep suspicion, ghastly looks
Are at my service, like enforced smiles;
And both are ready in their offices,
At any time, to grace my stratagems.
But what, is Catesby gone?

GLOUCESTER
He is; and, see, he brings the Mayor along.

Enter the Mayor and Catesby.

BUCKINGHAM
Lord Mayor—

GLOUCESTER
Look to the drawbridge there!

BUCKINGHAM
Hark, a drum!

GLOUCESTER
Catesby, o'erlook the walls.

BUCKINGHAM
Lord Mayor, the reason we have sent—

GLOUCESTER
Look back, defend thee, here are enemies!

BUCKINGHAM
God and our innocency defend and guard us!

Enter Lovel and Ratcliffe, with Hastings' head.

71 Consorted associated **78 look** see to it **81 fond** foolish **84 foot-cloth** large, richly ornamented cloth laid over the back of a horse and hanging to the ground on each side. **stumble** (An omen of misfortune.) **95 shrift** confession **96 grace** favor, fortune

98 Who he who. **in . . . looks** on the outward appearance of your kind glances **102 bootless** unavailing

III.v. Location: London. The Tower walls.
s.d. rotten rusty. **ill-favored** ugly **6 pry** peer **8 Intending** pretending **10 offices** uses, functions **17 o'erlook** inspect

GLOUCESTER
Be patient, they are friends, Ratcliffe and Lovel.
LOVEL
Here is the head of that ignoble traitor,
The dangerous and unsuspected Hastings.
GLOUCESTER
So dear I lov'd the man that I must weep.
I took him for the plainest harmless creature
That breath'd upon the earth a Christian;
Made him my book, wherein my soul recorded
The history of all her secret thoughts.
So smooth he daub'd his vice with show of virtue
That, his apparent open guilt omitted—
I mean, his conversation with Shore's wife—
He liv'd from all attainder of suspects.
BUCKINGHAM
Well, well, he was the covert'st shelt'red traitor
That ever liv'd. [Look ye, my Lord Mayor,]
Would you imagine, or almost believe,
Were 't not that, by great preservation
We live to tell it, that the subtle traitor
This day had plotted, in the Council House,
To murder me and my good Lord of Gloucester?
MAYOR
Had he done so?
GLOUCESTER
What, think you we are Turks or infidels?
Or that we would, against the form of law,
Proceed thus rashly in the villain's death,
But that the extreme peril of the case,
The peace of England, and our persons' safety,
Enforc'd us to this execution?
MAYOR
Now fair befall you! He deserv'd his death,
And your good graces both have well proceeded
To warn false traitors from the like attempts.
BUCKINGHAM
I never look'd for better at his hands
After he once fell in with Mistress Shore.
Yet had we not determin'd he should die
Until your lordship came to see his end,
Which now the loving haste of these our friends,
Something against our meanings, have prevented;
Because, my lord, I would have had you heard
The traitor speak and timorously confess
The manner and the purpose of his treasons,
That you might well have signified the same
Unto the citizens, who haply may
Misconster us in him and wail his death.
MAYOR
But, my good lord, your Grace's words shall serve
As well as I had seen and heard him speak.
And do not doubt, right noble princes both,
But I'll acquaint our duteous citizens
With all your just proceedings in this case.

GLOUCESTER
And to that end we wish'd your lordship here,
T' avoid the censures of the carping world.
BUCKINGHAM
Which since you come too late of our intent,
Yet witness what you hear we did intend.
And so, my good Lord Mayor, we bid farewell.
Exit Mayor.
GLOUCESTER
Go, after, after, cousin Buckingham.
The Mayor towards Guildhall hies him in all post.
There, at your meetest vantage of the time,
Infer the bastardy of Edward's children.
Tell them how Edward put to death a citizen
Only for saying he would make his son
Heir to the crown—meaning indeed his house,
Which, by the sign thereof, was termed so.
Moreover, urge his hateful luxury
And bestial appetite in change of lust;
Which stretch'd unto their servants, daughters, wives,
Even where his raging eye or savage heart,
Without control, lusted to make a prey.
Nay, for a need, thus far come near my person:
Tell them, when that my mother went with child
Of that insatiate Edward, noble York
My princely father then had wars in France,
And, by true computation of the time,
Found that the issue was not his begot—
Which well appeared in his lineaments,
Being nothing like the noble Duke my father.
Yet touch this sparingly, as 'twere far off,
Because, my lord, you know my mother lives.
BUCKINGHAM
Doubt not, my lord, I'll play the orator
As if the golden fee for which I plead
Were for myself. And so, my lord, adieu.
GLOUCESTER
If you thrive well, bring them to Baynard's Castle,
Where you shall find me well accompanied
With reverend fathers and well-learned bishops.
BUCKINGHAM
I go; and towards three or four o'clock
Look for the news that the Guildhall affords.
Exit Buckingham.
GLOUCESTER
Go, Lovel, with all speed to Doctor Shaw.
[*To Catesby.*] Go thou to Friar Penker. Bid them both
Meet me within this hour at Baynard's Castle.
Exeunt [*Lovel and Catesby*].
[*To Ratcliffe.*] Now will I go to take some privy order

27 book i.e., table book or diary **30 his . . . omitted** apart from his manifest open guilt **31 conversation** sexual intimacy **32 attainder of suspects** stain of suspicion **33 shelt'red** most hidden **35 almost** even **36 great preservation** i.e., fortunate escape through forestalling evil **48 proceeded** done **55 Something . . . meanings** somewhat contrary to our intent. **have prevented** has anticipated **60 haply** perchance **61 Misconster . . . him** i.e., misconstrue our intentions regarding him

69 of regarding **70 witness** bear witness to **73 Guildhall** central hall for municipal affairs. **post** haste **74 meetest vantage** most suitable opportunity **75 Infer** allege, adduce **78 the crown** i.e., a tavern in Cheapside identified by the sign of the Crown **80 luxury** lechery **81 in . . . lust** i.e., constantly desiring new mistresses **85 for a need** in case of necessity **86–87 went . . . Of** was pregnant with **96 golden fee** i.e., the crown **98 Baynard's Castle** residence on the north bank of the Thames. It was founded by Baynard, a nobleman in the time of the Conquest, and belonged to Richard's father. **103, 104 Doctor Shaw, Friar Penker** (Well-known divines who delivered sermons in Richard's favor.) **106 take . . . order** make some secret disposition

To draw the brats of Clarence out of sight,
And to give order that no manner person
Have any time recourse unto the princes. *Exeunt.*

[SCENE VI]

Enter a Scrivener [*with a paper in his hand*].

SCRIVENER
Here is the indictment of the good Lord Hastings,
Which in a set hand fairly is engross'd,
That it may be today read o'er in Paul's.
And mark how well the sequel hangs together:
Eleven hours I have spent to write it over,
For yesternight by Catesby was it sent me;
The precedent was full as long a-doing.
And yet within these five hours Hastings liv'd,
Untainted, unexamin'd, free, at liberty.
Here's a good world the while! Who is so gross
That cannot see this palpable device?
Yet who so bold but says he sees it not?
Bad is the world, and all will come to nought
When such ill dealing must be seen in thought.
Exit.

[SCENE VII]

Enter Richard [*of Gloucester*] *and Buckingham, at several doors.*

GLOUCESTER
How now, how now, what say the citizens?
BUCKINGHAM
Now, by the holy mother of our Lord,
The citizens are mum, say not a word.
GLOUCESTER
Touch'd you the bastardy of Edward's children?
BUCKINGHAM
I did; with his contract with Lady Lucy,
And his contract by deputy in France;
Th' unsatiate greediness of his desire,
And his enforcement of the city wives;
His tyranny for trifles; his own bastardy,
As being got, your father then in France,
And his resemblance, being not like the Duke.
Withal I did infer your lineaments,
Being the right idea of your father,
Both in your form and nobleness of mind;
Laid open all your victories in Scotland,
Your discipline in war, wisdom in peace,
Your bounty, virtue, fair humility;
Indeed, left nothing fitting for your purpose
Untouch'd, or slightly handled, in discourse.
And when my oratory drew toward end,
I bid them that did love their country's good
Cry, "God save Richard, England's royal king!"
GLOUCESTER
And did they so?
BUCKINGHAM
No, so God help me, they spake not a word,
But, like dumb statues or breathing stones,
Star'd each on other, and look'd deadly pale.
Which when I saw, I reprehended them,
And ask'd the Mayor what meant this willful silence.
His answer was, the people were not us'd
To be spoke to but by the recorder.
Then he was urg'd to tell my tale again:
"Thus saith the Duke, thus hath the Duke inferr'd,"—
But nothing spoke in warrant from himself.
When he had done, some followers of mine own,
At lower end of the hall, hurl'd up their caps,
And some ten voices cried, "God save King Richard!"
And thus I took the vantage of those few:
"Thanks, gentle citizens and friends," quoth I,
"This general applause and cheerful shout
Argues your wisdom and your love to Richard"—
And even here brake off, and came away.
GLOUCESTER
What tongueless blocks were they! Would they not speak?
[BUCKINGHAM
No, by my troth, my lord.]
GLOUCESTER
Will not the Mayor then and his brethren come?
BUCKINGHAM
The Mayor is here at hand. Intend some fear;
Be not you spoke with but by mighty suit.
And look you get a prayer-book in your hand,
And stand between two churchmen, good my lord,
For on that ground I'll make a holy descant;
And be not easily won to our requests.
Play the maid's part, still answer nay, and take it.
GLOUCESTER
I go; and if you plead as well for them
As I can say nay to thee for myself,
No doubt we'll bring it to a happy issue.
BUCKINGHAM
Go, go, up to the leads. The Lord Mayor knocks.
[*Exit Gloucester.*]

Enter the Mayor, [*Aldermen,*] *and Citizens.*

109 any time at any time. **recourse** access, admittance

III.vi. Location: London. A street.
2 in . . . engross'd is written out in a style of script used for legal documents **3 Paul's** i.e., St. Paul's Cathedral **4 the sequel** what follows **7 precedent** prepared indictment serving as a first draft **9 Untainted** unaccused **10 gross** dull, stupid **14 seen in thought** i.e., perceived in silence

III.vii. Location: Baynard's castle.
s.d. several separate **5 Lady Lucy** Elizabeth Lucy (by whom Edward had a child, though there was no formal contract of betrothal) **6 deputy** (See *3 Henry VI*, III.iii.49 ff., where Warwick, as deputy, contracts with Louis XI of France for the marriage of King Edward to Lady Bona, sister of the French queen.) **8 enforcement** forcible seduction **9 tyranny for trifles** harsh punishment of minor offenses **10 got** begot **13 right idea** exact image

15 victories in Scotland (Richard had commanded the English forces in the Scottish expedition of 1482.) **30 recorder** a city official **33 in . . . himself** on his own authority **41 brake** broke **45 Intend** pretend **46 mighty suit** importunate entreaty **49 descant** variation composed on a theme (called a *ground*) **55 leads** flat lead coverings for roof; hence, the roof itself

Welcome, my lord. I dance attendance here;
I think the Duke will not be spoke withal. 57

Enter Catesby.

Now, Catesby, what says your Lord to my request?

CATESBY
He doth entreat your Grace, my noble lord,
To visit him tomorrow or next day.
He is within, with two right reverend fathers,
Divinely bent to meditation,
And in no worldly suits would he be mov'd,
To draw him from his holy exercise.

BUCKINGHAM
Return, good Catesby, to the gracious Duke.
Tell him, myself, the Mayor and Aldermen,
In deep designs, in matter of great moment,
No less importing than our general good, 68
Are come to have some conference with his Grace.

CATESBY
I'll signify so much unto him straight. *Exit.*

BUCKINGHAM
Ah, ha, my lord, this prince is not an Edward!
He is not lulling on a lewd love-bed, 72
But on his knees at meditation;
Not dallying with a brace of courtezans,
But meditating with two deep divines; 75
Not sleeping, to engross his idle body, 76
But praying, to enrich his watchful soul.
Happy were England, would this virtuous prince
Take on his Grace the sovereignty thereof;
But, sure, I fear, we shall not win him to it.

MAYOR
Marry, God defend his Grace should say us nay! 81

BUCKINGHAM
I fear he will. Here Catesby comes again.

Enter Catesby.

Now, Catesby, what says his Grace?

CATESBY My lord,
He wonders to what end you have assembled
Such troops of citizens to come to him,
His Grace not being warn'd thereof before.
He fears, my lord, you mean no good to him.

BUCKINGHAM
Sorry I am my noble cousin should
Suspect me that I mean no good to him.
By heaven, we come to him in perfect love,
And so once more return and tell his Grace.
Exit [Catesby].
When holy and devout religious men
Are at their beads, 'tis much to draw them thence,
So sweet is zealous contemplation. 94

Enter Richard aloft, between two Bishops. [Catesby returns, below.]

MAYOR
See where his Grace stands, 'tween two clergymen!

BUCKINGHAM
Two props of virtue for a Christian prince,
To stay him from the fall of vanity. 97
And, see, a book of prayer in his hand,
True ornaments to know a holy man. 99
Famous Plantagenet, most gracious prince,
Lend favorable ear to our requests,
And pardon us the interruption
Of thy devotion and right Christian zeal.

GLOUCESTER
My lord, there needs no such apology.
I do beseech your Grace to pardon me,
Who, earnest in the service of my God,
Deferr'd the visitation of my friends.
But, leaving this, what is your Grace's pleasure?

BUCKINGHAM
Even that, I hope, which pleaseth God above,
And all good men of this ungovern'd isle.

GLOUCESTER
I do suspect I have done some offense
That seems disgracious in the city's eye, 112
And that you come to reprehend my ignorance.

BUCKINGHAM
You have, my lord. Would it might please your Grace,
On our entreaties, to amend your fault!

GLOUCESTER
Else wherefore breathe I in a Christian land? 116

BUCKINGHAM
Know then, it is your fault that you resign
The supreme seat, the throne majestical,
The sceptred office of your ancestors,
Your state of fortune and your due of birth, 120
The lineal glory of your royal house,
To the corruption of a blemish'd stock;
Whiles, in the mildness of your sleepy thoughts, 123
Which here we waken to our country's good,
The noble isle doth want her proper limbs; 125
Her face defac'd with scars of infamy,
Her royal stock graft with ignoble plants, 127
And almost should'red in the swallowing gulf 128
Of dark forgetfulness and deep oblivion.
Which to recure, we heartily solicit 130
Your gracious self to take on you the charge
And kingly government of this your land—
Not as protector, steward, substitute,
Or lowly factor for another's gain, 134
But as successively from blood to blood, 135
Your right of birth, your empery, your own. 136
For this, consorted with the citizens, 137
Your very worshipful and loving friends,
And by their vehement instigation,

57 withal with **68 No less importing** concerned with nothing less **72 lulling** lolling **75 deep** learned **76 engross** fatten **81 defend** forbid **94 s.d. aloft** i.e., on the gallery above the stage, rear. (The tiring house façade in this scene is imagined to be the façade of Baynard's Castle.)

97 stay sustain. **of** caused by **99 ornaments** i.e., the bishops as well as the prayer book **112 disgracious** unbecoming **116 Else** otherwise **120 state of fortune** position to which fortune entitles you **123 sleepy** reposeful **125 want her proper** lack its own **127 graft** engrafted **128 should'red in** jostled into, or immersed up to the shoulders in **130 recure** restore, make whole **134 factor** agent **135 successively** in order of succession **136 empery** realm of your sole rule **137 consorted** associated, leagued

In this just cause come I to move your Grace.

GLOUCESTER

I cannot tell if to depart in silence,
Or bitterly to speak in your reproof,
Best fitteth my degree or your condition. 143
If not to answer, you might haply think
Tongue-tied ambition, not replying, yielded 145
To bear the golden yoke of sovereignty,
Which fondly you would here impose on me. 147
If to reprove you for this suit of yours,
So season'd with your faithful love to me, 149
Then, on the other side, I check'd my friends. 150
Therefore, to speak, and to avoid the first,
And then, in speaking, not to incur the last,
Definitively thus I answer you. 153
Your love deserves my thanks, but my desert
Unmeritable shuns your high request. 155
First, if all obstacles were cut away,
And that my path were even to the crown, 157
As the ripe revenue and due of birth, 158
Yet so much is my poverty of spirit,
So mighty and so many my defects,
That I would rather hide me from my greatness— 161
Being a bark to brook no mighty sea— 162
Than in my greatness covet to be hid 163
And in the vapor of my glory smother'd.
But, God be thank'd, there is no need of me,
And much I need to help you, were there need. 166
The royal tree hath left us royal fruit,
Which, mellow'd by the stealing hours of time,
Will well become the seat of majesty,
And make, no doubt, us happy by his reign.
On him I lay that you would lay on me,
The right and fortune of his happy stars,
Which God defend that I should wring from him!

BUCKINGHAM

My lord, this argues conscience in your Grace;
But the respects thereof are nice and trivial, 175
All circumstances well considered.
You say that Edward is your brother's son.
So say we too, but not by Edward's wife;
For first was he contract to Lady Lucy—
Your mother lives a witness to his vow— 180
And afterward by substitute betroth'd 181
To Bona, sister to the King of France. 182
These both put off, a poor petitioner,
A care-craz'd mother to a many sons,
A beauty-waning and distressed widow,
Even in the afternoon of her best days,
Made prize and purchase of his wanton eye, 187
Seduc'd the pitch and height of his degree 188
To base declension and loath'd bigamy. 189
By her, in his unlawful bed, he got
This Edward, whom our manners call the Prince. 191
More bitterly could I expostulate,
Save that, for reverence to some alive, 193
I give a sparing limit to my tongue.
Then, good my lord, take to your royal self
This proffer'd benefit of dignity;
If not to bless us and the land withal,
Yet to draw forth your noble ancestry
From the corruption of abusing times
Unto a lineal true-derived course.

MAYOR

Do, good my lord, your citizens entreat you.

BUCKINGHAM

Refuse not, mighty lord, this proffer'd love.

CATESBY

O, make them joyful, grant their lawful suit!

GLOUCESTER

Alas, why would you heap this care on me?
I am unfit for state and majesty.
I do beseech you, take it not amiss;
I cannot nor I will not yield to you.

BUCKINGHAM

If you refuse it—as, in love and zeal, 208
Loath to depose the child, your brother's son;
As well we know your tenderness of heart 210
And gentle, kind, effeminate remorse, 211
Which we have noted in you to your kindred,
And egally indeed to all estates— 213
Yet know, whe'er you accept our suit or no, 214
Your brother's son shall never reign our king;
But we will plant some other in the throne,
To the disgrace and downfall of your house.
And in this resolution here we leave you.—
Come, citizens. 'Zounds! I'll entreat no more.

[GLOUCESTER

O, do not swear, my lord of Buckingham.]

Exeunt [Buckingham, Mayor, Aldermen, and the citizens].

CATESBY

Call them again, sweet prince, accept their suit.
If you deny them, all the land will rue it.

GLOUCESTER

Will you enforce me to a world of cares?
Call them again. I am not made of stones,
But penetrable to your kind entreaties,
Albeit against my conscience and my soul.

Enter Buckingham and the rest.

Cousin of Buckingham, and sage, grave men,
Since you will buckle fortune on my back,
To bear her burden, whe'er I will or no,
I must have patience to endure the load.

143 degree rank. **condition** social status **145 Tongue-tied** silent. (I.e., silence gives consent.) **yielded** consented **147 fondly** foolishly **149 season'd** i.e., made agreeable or palatable **150 check'd** rebuked, i.e., would rebuke **153 Definitively** once and for all **155 Unmeritable** undeserving **157 even** smooth **158 ripe revenue** possession ready to be inherited **161 my greatness** i.e., my claim to the throne **162 bark** small sailing vessel. **brook** endure **163 Than . . . hid** than wish to be enveloped in my greatness, i.e., the throne **166 I need** I lack the ability requisite **175 respects thereof** considerations by which you support your argument. **nice** overscrupulous **180 Your . . . vow** (According to the chronicles, Richard's mother, in opposing Edward's intention of marrying Lady Grey because it was interfering with the negotiations for his marriage to Lady Bona of Savoy, asserted that Lady Elizabeth Lucy was already Edward's trothplight wife. Cf. III.v.75 and vii.6.) **181 substitute** proxy **182 sister** i.e., sister-in-law, the Queen's sister **187 purchase** booty

188 Seduc'd debased. **pitch** height, highest point (as in falconry) **189 declension** falling away from a high standard **191 manners** sense of politeness **193 some alive** i.e., the Duchess of York. (See III.v.93–94.) **208 as** from being **210 As . . . know** since we know well **211 kind, effeminate remorse** natural, tender pity **213 egally** equally. **estates** ranks. (I.e., this virtue is found in Richard's treatment of everyone.) **214 whe'er** whether

But if black scandal or foul-fac'd reproach
Attend the sequel of your imposition,
Your mere enforcement shall acquittance me
From all the impure blots and stains thereof;
For God doth know, and you may partly see,
How far I am from the desire of this.

MAYOR
God bless your Grace! We see it, and will say it.

GLOUCESTER
In saying so, you shall but say the truth.

BUCKINGHAM
Then I salute you with this royal title:
Long live King Richard, England's worthy king!

MAYOR AND CITIZENS
Amen.

BUCKINGHAM
Tomorrow may it please you to be crown'd?

GLOUCESTER
Even when you please, for you will have it so.

BUCKINGHAM
Tomorrow, then, we will attend your Grace.
And so most joyfully we take our leave.

GLOUCESTER [*To the Bishops*]
Come, let us to our holy work again.—
Farewell, my cousin; farewell, gentle friends. *Exeunt.*

ACT IV • SCENE I

Enter [*at one door*] *the Queen* [*Elizabeth,*] *the Duchess of York, and Marquess* [*of*] *Dorset;* [*at another door*] *Anne Duchess of Gloucester* [*leading Lady Margaret Plantagenet, Clarence's young daughter*].

DUCHESS
Who meets us here? My niece Plantagenet
Led in the hand of her kind aunt of Gloucester?
Now, for my life, she's wand'ring to the Tower,
On pure heart's love to greet the tender Prince.
Daughter, well met.

ANNE
God give your Graces both
A happy and a joyful time of day!

QUEEN ELIZABETH
As much to you, good sister! Whither away?

ANNE
No farther than the Tower; and, as I guess,
Upon the like devotion as yourselves,
To gratulate the gentle princes there.

QUEEN ELIZABETH
Kind sister, thanks. We'll enter all together.

Enter [*Brakenbury*] *the Lieutenant.*

And, in good time, here the Lieutenant comes.
Master Lieutenant, pray you, by your leave,
How doth the Prince, and my young son of York?

BRAKENBURY
Right well, dear madam. By your patience,
I may not suffer you to visit them;
The King hath strictly charg'd the contrary.

QUEEN ELIZABETH
The King? Who's that?

BRAKENBURY
I mean the Lord Protector.

QUEEN ELIZABETH
The Lord protect him from that kingly title!
Hath he set bounds between their love and me?
I am their mother; who shall bar me from them?

DUCHESS
I am their father's mother; I will see them.

ANNE
Their aunt I am in law, in love their mother;
Then bring me to their sights. I'll bear thy blame
And take thy office from thee, on my peril.

BRAKENBURY
No, madam, no; I may not leave it so.
I am bound by oath, and therefore pardon me.
Exit Lieutenant.

Enter [*Lord*] *Stanley* [*Earl of Derby*].

STANLEY
Let me but meet you, ladies, one hour hence,
And I'll salute your Grace of York as mother,
And reverend looker on, of two fair queens.
[*To Anne.*] Come, madam, you must straight to
Westminster,
There to be crowned Richard's royal queen.

QUEEN ELIZABETH
Ah, cut my lace asunder,
That my pent heart may have some scope to beat,
Or else I swoon with this dead-killing news!

ANNE
Despiteful tidings! O unpleasing news!

DORSET
Be of good cheer. Mother, how fares your Grace?

QUEEN ELIZABETH
O Dorset, speak not to me, get thee gone!
Death and destruction dogs thee at thy heels;
Thy mother's name is ominous to children.
If thou wilt outstrip death, go cross the seas
And live with Richmond, from the reach of hell.
Go, hie thee, hie thee from this slaughter-house,
Lest thou increase the number of the dead
And make me die the thrall of Margaret's curse,
Nor mother, wife, nor England's counted queen.

STANLEY
Full of wise care is this your counsel, madam.

232 your imposition the duty which you lay upon me **233 mere** absolute, downright. **acquittance** acquit

IV.i. Location: London. Before the Tower.
1 niece i.e., granddaughter **3 for my life** i.e., I'd bet my life **4 On** out of **5 Daughter** i.e., daughter-in-law **7 sister** i.e., sister-in-law **9 like devotion** same devout errand **10 gratulate** greet, salute

20 bounds barriers **25 take . . . thee** i.e., relieve you of the responsibility **26 leave it** i.e., fail to perform my office **29 mother** i.e., mother-in-law (of Elizabeth as widow of Edward, and of Anne as wife of King Richard) **30 looker on** beholder. **two fair queens** i.e., Elizabeth and Anne (since Anne's husband, Richard, is about to be crowned) **33 cut my lace** i.e., of my bodice **42 with Richmond** i.e., with Henry Tudor, Earl of Richmond, at this time in Brittany **46 Nor** neither. **counted** accepted, esteemed

Take all the swift advantage of the hours.
You shall have letters from me to my son 49
In your behalf, to meet you on the way.
Be not ta'en tardy by unwise delay. 51

DUCHESS
O ill-dispersing wind of misery! 52
O my accursed womb, the bed of death!
A cockatrice hast thou hatch'd to the world, 54
Whose unavoided eye is murderous.

STANLEY
Come, madam, come. I in all haste was sent.

ANNE
And I with all unwillingness will go.
O, would to God that the inclusive verge 58
Of golden metal that must round my brow
Were red-hot steel, to sear me to the brains!
Anointed let me be with deadly venom, 61
And die, ere men can say, "God save the Queen!"

QUEEN ELIZABETH
Go, go, poor soul, I envy not thy glory,
To feed my humor wish thyself no harm. 64

ANNE
No? Why? When he that is my husband now
Came to me, as I follow'd Henry's corse,
When scarce the blood was well wash'd from his hands
Which issued from my other angel husband
And that dear saint which then I weeping follow'd—
O, when, I say, I look'd on Richard's face,
This was my wish: "Be thou," quoth I, "accurs'd
For making me, so young, so old a widow! 72
And, when thou wed'st, let sorrow haunt thy bed;
And be thy wife—if any be so mad—
More miserable by the life of thee
Than thou hast made me by my dear lord's death!"
Lo, ere I can repeat this curse again,
Within so small a time, my woman's heart
Grossly grew captive to his honey words 79
And prov'd the subject of mine own soul's curse,
Which hitherto hath held mine eyes from rest;
For never yet one hour in his bed
Did I enjoy the golden dew of sleep,
But with his timorous dreams was still awak'd. 84
Besides, he hates me for my father Warwick,
And will, no doubt, shortly be rid of me.

QUEEN ELIZABETH
Poor heart, adieu! I pity thy complaining.

ANNE
No more than with my soul I mourn for yours.

DORSET
Farewell, thou woeful welcomer of glory!

ANNE
Adieu, poor soul, that tak'st thy leave of it!

DUCHESS [*To Dorset*]
Go thou to Richmond, and good fortune guide thee!
[*To Anne.*] Go thou to Richard, and good angels tend thee!
[*To Queen Elizabeth.*] Go thou to sanctuary, and good thoughts possess thee!
I to my grave, where peace and rest lie with me!
Eighty odd years of sorrow have I seen,
And each hour's joy wrack'd with a week of teen. 96
[*They start to go.*]

QUEEN ELIZABETH
Stay, yet look back with me unto the Tower.
Pity, you ancient stones, those tender babes
Whom envy hath immur'd within your walls— 99
Rough cradle for such little pretty ones!
Rude ragged nurse, old sullen playfellow
For tender princes, use my babies well!
So foolish sorrows bids your stones farewell. *Exeunt.*

SCENE II

Sound a sennet. Enter Richard, in pomp; Buckingham, Catesby, Ratcliffe, Lovel, [*a Page, and others*].

KING RICHARD
Stand all apart. Cousin of Buckingham!
[*The others stand aside, out of earshot.*]

BUCKINGHAM
My gracious sovereign?

KING RICHARD
Give me thy hand.
Sound. [*Here he ascends the throne.*]
Thus high, by thy advice,
And thy assistance, is King Richard seated.
But shall we wear these glories for a day?
Or shall they last, and we rejoice in them?

BUCKINGHAM
Still live they and for ever let them last!

KING RICHARD
Ah, Buckingham, now do I play the touch, 8
To try if thou be current gold indeed: 9
Young Edward lives. Think now what I would speak.

BUCKINGHAM
Say on, my loving lord.

KING RICHARD
Why, Buckingham, I say, I would be king.

BUCKINGHAM
Why, so you are, my thrice renowned lord.

KING RICHARD
Ha! Am I king? 'Tis so. But Edward lives.

BUCKINGHAM
True, noble prince.

49 You . . . from me i.e., I'll dispatch letters in your behalf. **son** i.e., stepson **51 ta'en** taken, caught **52 ill-dispersing** scattering ill fortune **54 cockatrice** basilisk. (See I.ii.150, note.) **58 inclusive verge** enclosing circle, i.e., the crown, here likened to an instrument of torture used to punish regicides or other criminals **61 Anointed** (Anne desires to be anointed with poison rather than with holy oil, as in the ceremony of coronation.) **64 humor** (Here, a passion for revenge.) **72 so old a widow** i.e., destined to live so long as a widow **79 Grossly** stupidly **84 timorous** full of fears. **still** continually

96 wrack'd destroyed. **teen** woe **99 envy** malice

IV.ii. Location: London. The palace.
8 play the touch play the part of a touchstone (to test the quality of gold) **9 current** sterling, genuine

KING RICHARD O bitter consequence,
That Edward still should live! "True, noble prince!"
Cousin, thou wast not wont to be so dull.
Shall I be plain? I wish the bastards dead,
And I would have it suddenly perform'd.
What say'st thou now? Speak suddenly; be brief.

BUCKINGHAM
Your Grace may do your pleasure.

KING RICHARD
Tut, tut, thou art all ice, thy kindness freezes.
Say, have I thy consent that they shall die?

BUCKINGHAM
Give me some little breath, some pause, dear lord,
Before I positively speak in this.
I will resolve you herein presently. *Exit Buckingham.*

CATESBY [*Aside to a stander by*]
The King is angry. See, he gnaws his lip.

KING RICHARD
I will converse with iron-witted fools
And unrespective boys. None are for me
That look into me with considerate eyes.
High-reaching Buckingham grows circumspect.
Boy!

PAGE [*Approaching*]
My lord?

KING RICHARD
Know'st thou not any whom corrupting gold
Will tempt unto a close exploit of death?

PAGE
My lord, I know a discontented gentleman
Whose humble means match not his haughty spirit.
Gold were as good as twenty orators,
And will, no doubt, tempt him to any thing.

KING RICHARD
What is his name?

PAGE His name, my lord, is Tyrrel.

KING RICHARD
I partly know the man. Go call him hither, boy.
Exit [*Page*].
The deep-revolving witty Buckingham
No more shall be the neighbor to my counsels.
Hath he so long held out with me untir'd,
And stops he now for breath? Well, be it so.

Enter [*Lord*] *Stanley* [*Earl of Derby*].

How now, Lord Stanley? What's the news?

STANLEY
Know, my loving lord,
The Marquess Dorset, as I hear, is fled
To Richmond, in the parts where he abides.
[*Stands apart.*]

KING RICHARD
Come hither, Catesby. Rumor it abroad
That Anne, my wife, is very grievous sick;
I will take order for her keeping close.
Inquire me out some mean poor gentleman,
Whom I will marry straight to Clarence' daughter.
The boy is foolish, and I fear not him.
Look how thou dream'st! I say again, give out
That Anne my queen is sick and like to die.
About it, for it stands me much upon
To stop all hopes whose growth may damage me.
[*Exit Catesby.*]
I must be married to my brother's daughter,
Or else my kingdom stands on brittle glass.
Murder her brothers, and then marry her—
Uncertain way of gain! But I am in
So far in blood that sin will pluck on sin.
Tear-falling pity dwells not in this eye.

Enter [*Page, with*] *Tyrrel.*

Is thy name Tyrrel?

TYRREL
James Tyrrel, and your most obedient subject.

KING RICHARD
Art thou, indeed?

TYRREL Prove me, my gracious lord.

KING RICHARD
Dar'st thou resolve to kill a friend of mine?

TYRREL
Please you;
But I had rather kill two enemies.

KING RICHARD
Why, there thou hast it: two deep enemies,
Foes to my rest and my sweet sleep's disturbers
Are they that I would have thee deal upon—
Tyrrel, I mean those bastards in the Tower.

TYRREL
Let me have open means to come to them,
And soon I'll rid you from the fear of them.

KING RICHARD
Thou sing'st sweet music. Hark, come hither, Tyrrel.
Go, by this token. [*Gives him a token.*] Rise, and lend
thine ear. *Whispers.*
There is no more but so. Say it is done,
And I will love thee and prefer thee for it.

TYRREL
I will dispatch it straight. *Exit.*

Enter Buckingham.

BUCKINGHAM
My lord, I have consider'd in my mind
The late request that you did sound me in.

KING RICHARD
Well, let that rest. Dorset is fled to Richmond.

BUCKINGHAM
I hear the news, my lord.

KING RICHARD
Stanley, he is your wife's son. Well, look unto it.

15 bitter consequence i.e., intolerable answer to my words, and an intolerable fact **26 resolve** answer **28 converse** associate. **iron-witted** unfeeling **29 unrespective** thoughtless, heedless **30 considerate** thoughtful **35 close** secret **42 deep-revolving** deeply scheming. **witty** cunning **52 take** give. **close** imprisoned, confined **53 mean poor** of low degree

55 boy i.e., Clarence's eldest son, Edward Plantagenet, Earl of Warwick **58 stands . . . upon** is a matter of the utmost importance to me **60 brother's daughter** i.e., Elizabeth of York, daughter to Edward IV. She later became the queen of Henry VII; see IV.v.7–9 and V.v.29–31. **64 pluck on** draw on **68 Prove** test **70 Please** if it please **76 open** unhampered **81 prefer** promote, advance **84 sound me in** ask me about **87 he** i.e., Richmond

BUCKINGHAM
My lord, I claim the gift, my due by promise,
For which your honor and your faith is pawn'd:
Th' earldom of Hereford and the moveables
Which you have promised I shall possess.

KING RICHARD
Stanley, look to your wife. If she convey
Letters to Richmond, you shall answer it. 93

BUCKINGHAM
What says your Highness to my just request?

KING RICHARD
I do remember me, Henry the Sixth
Did prophesy that Richmond should be king,
When Richmond was a little peevish boy.
A king! Perhaps, [perhaps—

BUCKINGHAM
My lord!

KING RICHARD
How chance the prophet could not at that time
Have told me, I being by, that I should kill him?

BUCKINGHAM
My lord, your promise for the earldom—

KING RICHARD
Richmond! When last I was at Exeter,
The Mayor in courtesy show'd me the castle,
And call'd it Rougemont, at which name I started, 105
Because a bard of Ireland told me once
I should not live long after I saw Richmond.

BUCKINGHAM
My lord!

KING RICHARD
Ay, what's o'clock?

BUCKINGHAM
I am thus bold to put your Grace in mind
Of what you promis'd me.

KING RICHARD
Well, but what's o'clock?

BUCKINGHAM
Upon the stroke of ten.

KING RICHARD
Well, let it strike.

BUCKINGHAM
Why let it strike?

KING RICHARD
Because that, like a Jack, thou keep'st the stroke 114
Betwixt thy begging and my meditation.
I am not in the giving vein today.]

BUCKINGHAM
May it please you to resolve me in my suit. 117

KING RICHARD
Thou troublest me. I am not in the vein.
Exit [with all but Buckingham].

BUCKINGHAM
And is it thus? Repays he my deep service
With such contempt? Made I him king for this?
O, let me think on Hastings, and be gone
To Brecknock, while my fearful head is on! *Exit.* 122

[SCENE III]

Enter Tyrrel.

TYRREL
The tyrannous and bloody act is done,
The most arch deed of piteous massacre 2
That ever yet this land was guilty of.
Dighton and Forrest, who I did suborn
To do this piece of ruthless butchery,
Albeit they were flesh'd villains, bloody dogs, 6
Melted with tenderness and mild compassion,
Wept like to children in their deaths' sad story.
"O, thus," quoth Dighton, "lay the gentle babes."
"Thus, thus," quoth Forrest, "girdling one another
Within their alabaster innocent arms.
Their lips were four red roses on a stalk,
Which in their summer beauty kiss'd each other.
A book of prayers on their pillow lay,
Which once," quoth Forrest, "almost chang'd my mind;
But O! the devil"—there the villain stopp'd;
When Dighton thus told on: "We smothered
The most replenished sweet work of nature 18
That from the prime creation e'er she framed." 19
Hence both are gone with conscience and remorse 20
They could not speak; and so I left them both,
To bear this tidings to the bloody king.

Enter [King] Richard.

And here he comes. All health, my sovereign lord!

KING RICHARD
Kind Tyrrel, am I happy in thy news?

TYRREL
If to have done the thing you gave in charge 25
Beget your happiness, be happy then,
For it is done.

KING RICHARD
But didst thou see them dead?

TYRREL
I did, my lord.

KING RICHARD
And buried, gentle Tyrrel?

TYRREL
The chaplain of the Tower hath buried them;
But where, to say the truth, I do not know.

KING RICHARD
Come to me, Tyrrel, soon at after supper, 31
When thou shalt tell the process of their death. 32
Meantime, but think how I may do thee good,
And be inheritor of thy desire.
Farewell till then.

TYRREL
I humbly take my leave. *[Exit.]*

KING RICHARD
The son of Clarence have I pent up close,

93 it i.e., for it **105 Rougemont** i.e., Red Hill (with a play on *Richmond*) **114 Jack** the figure of a man which strikes the bell on the outside of a clock (with a play on the meaning *lowbred fellow.* Richard's complaint is that Buckingham, like the jack of a clock, being on the point of striking the hour—i.e., speaking his request—breaks the continuity of Richard's reflections.) **117 resolve me** give me a final answer **122 Brecknock** a manor house in Wales. **fearful** full of fears

IV.iii. Location: London. The palace.
2 arch deed i.e., chief or notorious act **6 flesh'd** experienced in bloodshed **18 replenished** complete, perfect **19 prime** first **20 gone with** completely overcome by **25 gave in charge** ordered, commanded **31 after supper** dessert after supper **32 process** story

His daughter meanly have I match'd in marriage,
The sons of Edward sleep in Abraham's bosom,
And Anne my wife hath bid this world good night.
Now, for I know the Britaine Richmond aims
At young Elizabeth, my brother's daughter,
And, by that knot, looks proudly on the crown,
To her go I, a jolly thriving wooer.

Enter Ratcliffe.

RATCLIFFE
My lord!

KING RICHARD
Good or bad news, that thou com'st in so bluntly?

RATCLIFFE
Bad news, my lord. Morton is fled to Richmond,
And Buckingham, back'd with the hardy Welshmen,
Is in the field, and still his power increaseth.

KING RICHARD
Ely with Richmond troubles me more near
Than Buckingham and his rash-levied strength.
Come, I have learn'd that fearful commenting
Is leaden servitor to dull delay;
Delay leads impotent and snail-pac'd beggary.
Then fiery expedition be my wing,
Jove's Mercury, and herald for a king!
Go, muster men. My counsel is my shield;
We must be brief when traitors brave the field.
Exeunt.

SCENE [IV]

Enter old Queen Margaret.

QUEEN MARGARET
So, now prosperity begins to mellow
And drop into the rotten mouth of death.
Here in these confines slily have I lurk'd
To watch the waning of mine enemies.
A dire induction am I witness to,
And will to France, hoping the consequence
Will prove as bitter, black, and tragical.
Withdraw thee, wretched Margaret. Who comes here? [*She steps aside.*]

Enter Duchess [*of York*] *and Queen* [*Elizabeth*].

QUEEN ELIZABETH
Ah, my poor princes! Ah, my tender babes!
My unblown flow'rs, new-appearing sweets!
If yet your gentle souls fly in the air
And be not fix'd in doom perpetual,
Hover about me with your airy wings
And hear your mother's lamentation!

QUEEN MARGARET [*Aside*]
Hover about her; say that right for right
Hath dimm'd your infant morn to aged night.

DUCHESS
So many miseries have craz'd my voice
That my woe-wearied tongue is still and mute.
Edward Plantagenet, why art thou dead?

QUEEN MARGARET [*Aside*]
Plantagenet doth quit Plantagenet.
Edward for Edward pays a dying debt.

QUEEN ELIZABETH
Wilt thou, O God, fly from such gentle lambs,
And throw them in the entrails of the wolf?
When didst thou sleep when such a deed was done?

QUEEN MARGARET [*Aside*]
When holy Harry died, and my sweet son.

DUCHESS
Dead life, blind sight, poor mortal-living ghost,
Woe's scene, world's shame, grave's due by life usurp'd,
Brief abstract and record of tedious days,
Rest thy unrest on England's lawful earth, [*Sits down.*]
Unlawfully made drunk with innocent blood!

QUEEN ELIZABETH
Ah, that thou wouldst as soon afford a grave
As thou canst yield a melancholy seat!
Then would I hide my bones, not rest them here.
Ah, who hath any cause to mourn but we? [*Sits down by her.*]

QUEEN MARGARET [*Coming forward*]
If ancient sorrow be most reverend,
Give mine the benefit of seniory,
And let my griefs frown on the upper hand.
If sorrow can admit society, [*Sits down with them.*]
[Tell o'er your woes again by viewing mine:]
I had an Edward, till a Richard kill'd him;
I had a Harry, till a Richard kill'd him:
Thou hadst an Edward, till a Richard kill'd him;
Thou hadst a Richard, till a Richard kill'd him.

DUCHESS
I had a Richard too, and thou didst kill him;
I had a Rutland too, thou holp'st to kill him.

QUEEN MARGARET
Thou hadst a Clarence too, and Richard kill'd him.
From forth the kennel of thy womb hath crept
A hell-hound that doth hunt us all to death.

37 His . . . marriage (Margaret Plantagenet was about twelve years old when Richard died. Shakespeare may have confused her with Lady Cicely, a daughter of Edward IV, whom Richard, according to Holinshed, intended to marry to "a man found in a cloud, and of an unknown linage and familie.") **38 Abraham's bosom** (See Luke 16:22.) **40 for** because. **Britaine** Breton **41 my brother's** Edward's **42 by that knot** by virtue of that alliance **46 Morton** i.e., John Morton, Bishop of Ely, who had been kept prisoner at Brecknock Castle; he is the Ely of III.iv **51 fearful commenting** timorous talk **52 leaden servitor** sluggish attendant **53 leads** leads to. **beggary** ruin **54 expedition** speed **55 Mercury** messenger of the gods **57 brave** challenge

IV.iv. Location: London. Before the palace.
5 induction beginning (as of a play) **6 consequence** what follows, the sequel and conclusion (as in a play) **10 unblown** unopened. **sweets** flowers

12 doom perpetual i.e., eternal punishment or reward **15 right for right** i.e., a just punishment for an offense against justice **16 dimm'd . . . night** i.e., brought the youthful promise of your children to ruin and death **17 craz'd** cracked **20 quit** requite **21 Edward for Edward** i.e., Edward V, the Yorkist Prince, for Edward the son of Margaret and Henry VI. **dying debt** debt paid through death **24 When** i.e., whenever till now **25 Harry** i.e., Henry VI **26 mortal-living ghost** i.e., a dead person still among the living **27 grave's . . . usurp'd** i.e., one who, by living too long, deprives the grave of its due **28 abstract** epitome **31 thou** i.e., the earth **36 seniory** seniority of claim **37 on . . . hand** i.e., from a place of precedence **40 Edward** i.e., my son, the former Prince of Wales **41 Harry** i.e., my husband, King Henry VI **42 Thou** i.e., Queen Elizabeth. **Edward** i.e., Edward V **43 Richard** i.e., the young Duke of York **44 Richard** i.e., Duke of York, the Duchess' husband and father of Richard III, killed by Margaret's army at the Battle of Wakefield in 1460 **45 Rutland** i.e., Edmund, son of the Duke of York, also killed at Wakefield

That dog, that had his teeth before his eyes
To worry lambs and lap their gentle blood,
That foul defacer of God's handiwork,
That excellent grand tyrant of the earth
That reigns in galled eyes of weeping souls,
Thy womb let loose, to chase us to our graves.
O upright, just, and true-disposing God,
How do I thank thee, that this carnal cur
Preys on the issue of his mother's body,
And makes her pew-fellow with others' moan!

DUCHESS
O Harry's wife, triumph not in my woes!
God witness with me, I have wept for thine.

QUEEN MARGARET
Bear with me. I am hungry for revenge,
And now I cloy me with beholding it.
Thy Edward he is dead, that kill'd my Edward;
Thy other Edward dead, to quit my Edward;
Young York he is but boot, because both they
Match'd not the high perfection of my loss.
Thy Clarence he is dead that stabb'd my Edward;
And the beholders of this frantic play,
Th' adulterate Hastings, Rivers, Vaughan, Grey,
Untimely smother'd in their dusky graves.
Richard yet lives, hell's black intelligencer,
Only reserv'd their factor to buy souls
And send them thither; but at hand, at hand,
Ensues his piteous and unpitied end.
Earth gapes, hell burns, fiends roar, saints pray,
To have him suddenly convey'd from hence.
Cancel his bond of life, dear God, I pray,
That I may live and say, The dog is dead!

QUEEN ELIZABETH
O, thou didst prophesy the time would come
That I should wish for thee to help me curse
That bottled spider, that foul bunch-back'd toad!

QUEEN MARGARET
I call'd thee then vain flourish of my fortune;
I call'd thee then poor shadow, painted queen,
The presentation of but what I was;
The flattering index of a direful pageant;
One heav'd a-high, to be hurl'd down below;
A mother only mock'd with two fair babes;
A dream of what thou wast, a garish flag
To be the aim of every dangerous shot;
A sign of dignity, a breath, a bubble,
A queen in jest, only to fill the scene.
Where is thy husband now? Where be thy brothers?
Where be thy two sons? Wherein dost thou joy?
Who sues and kneels and says "God save the
Queen"?
Where be the bending peers that flattered thee?
Where be the thronging troops that followed thee?
Decline all this, and see what now thou art:
For happy wife, a most distressed widow;
For joyful mother, one that wails the name;
For one being sued to, one that humbly sues;
For queen, a very caitiff crown'd with care;
For she that scorn'd at me, now scorn'd of me;
For she being fear'd of all, now fearing one;
For she commanding all, obey'd of none.
Thus hath the course of justice whirl'd about,
And left thee but a very prey to time,
Having no more but thought of what thou wast
To torture thee the more, being what thou art.
Thou didst usurp my place, and dost thou not
Usurp the just proportion of my sorrow?
Now thy proud neck bears half my burden'd yoke,
From which even here I slip my wearied head,
And leave the burden of it all on thee.
Farewell, York's wife, and queen of sad mischance!
These English woes shall make me smile in France.
[*She starts to leave.*]

QUEEN ELIZABETH
O thou well skill'd in curses, stay awhile,
And teach me how to curse mine enemies!

QUEEN MARGARET
Forbear to sleep the night, and fast the day;
Compare dead happiness with living woe;
Think that thy babes were sweeter than they were,
And he that slew them fouler than he is.
Bett'ring thy loss makes the bad causer worse;
Revolving this will teach thee how to curse.

QUEEN ELIZABETH
My words are dull. O, quicken them with thine!

QUEEN MARGARET
Thy woes will make them sharp, and pierce like
mine. *Exit Margaret.*

DUCHESS
Why should calamity be full of words?

QUEEN ELIZABETH
Windy attorneys to their client's woes,
Airy succeeders of intestate joys,
Poor breathing orators of miseries,
Let them have scope! Though what they will impart
Help nothing else, yet do they ease the heart.

DUCHESS
If so, then be not tongue-tied. Go with me,
And in the breath of bitter words let's smother
My damned son, that thy two sweet sons smother'd.
The trumpet sounds. Be copious in exclaims.

Enter King Richard and his train [*marching, with drums and trumpets*].

KING RICHARD
Who intercepts me in my expedition?

DUCHESS
O, she that might have intercepted thee,

49 teeth (Richard was supposedly born with teeth.) **50 worry** tear to pieces **52 excellent** unparalleled **53 galled** sore with weeping **56 carnal** flesh-eating **58 pew-fellow** i.e., intimate associate **63 Thy Edward** Edward IV. **my Edward** the son of Henry VI **64 other Edward** Edward V. **quit** requite **65 Young York** Richard, Duke of York, the younger of the princes murdered in the Tower. **but boot** merely into the bargain **69 adulterate** adulterous **71 intelligencer** agent, go-between, spy **72 Only . . . factor** chosen above all others as their (hell's) agent **85 index** argument, preface, prologue. **pageant** spectacular entertainment **88–89 garish . . . shot** i.e., standard-bearer, conspicuous in appearance, and thus the target of enemy fire **90 sign** mere token **95 bending** bowing

97 Decline go through in order. (A grammatical metaphor.) **101 caitiff** wretch, slave **102, 103, 104 of** by **111 burden'd** burdensome **122 Bett'ring** magnifying **123 Resolving** meditating on **124 quicken** put life into **127 Windy . . . woes** i.e., words, which are airy pleaders on behalf of one who is suffering **128 succeeders** heirs. **intestate** having died without anything to bequeath **129 breathing** speaking **135 exclaims** exclamations **136 expedition** (1) haste (2) military undertaking

By strangling thee in her accursed womb,
From all the slaughters, wretch, that thou hast done!

QUEEN ELIZABETH
Hid'st thou that forehead with a golden crown,
Where should be branded, if that right were right,
The slaughter of the prince that ow'd that crown,
And the dire death of my poor sons and brothers?
Tell me, thou villain slave, where are my children?

DUCHESS
Thou toad, thou toad, where is thy brother
Clarence?
And little Ned Plantagenet, his son?

QUEEN ELIZABETH
Where is the gentle Rivers, Vaughan, Grey?

DUCHESS
Where is kind Hastings?

KING RICHARD
A flourish, trumpets! Strike alarum, drums!
Let not the heavens hear these tell-tale women
Rail on the Lord's anointed. Strike, I say!
Flourish. Alarums.
Either be patient and entreat me fair,
Or with the clamorous report of war
Thus will I drown your exclamations.

DUCHESS
Art thou my son?

KING RICHARD
Ay, I thank God, my father, and yourself.

DUCHESS
Then patiently hear my impatience.

KING RICHARD
Madam, I have a touch of your condition,
That cannot brook the accent of reproof.

DUCHESS
O, let me speak!

KING RICHARD Do then, but I'll not hear.

DUCHESS
I will be mild and gentle in my words.

KING RICHARD
And brief, good mother, for I am in haste.

DUCHESS
Art thou so hasty? I have stay'd for thee,
God knows, in torment and in agony.

KING RICHARD
And came I not at last to comfort you?

DUCHESS
No, by the holy rood, thou know'st it well,
Thou cam'st on earth to make the earth my hell.
A grievous burden was thy birth to me,
Tetchy and wayward was thy infancy;
Thy school-days frightful, desp'rate, wild, and
furious;
Thy prime of manhood daring, bold, and venturous;
Thy age confirm'd, proud, subtle, sly, and bloody,
More mild, but yet more harmful, kind in hatred.

142 ow'd owned **146 Ned Plantagenet** (See IV.iii.36.) **149 alarum** the cry or signal "allarme" (to arms) **150 tell-tale** tattling, gabbling **152 entreat me fair** treat me with courtesy **158 condition** disposition **163 stay'd** waited **166 holy rood** Christ's cross **169 Tetchy** fretful, peevish **170 frightful** full of fears **172 age confirm'd** riper manhood **173 kind in hatred** concealing hatred under pretense of kindness

What comfortable hour canst thou name
That ever grac'd me with thy company?

KING RICHARD
Faith, none, but Humphrey Hour, that call'd your
Grace
To breakfast once forth of my company.
If I be so disgracious in your eye,
Let me march on, and not offend you, madam.
Strike up the drum.

DUCHESS I prithee, hear me speak.

KING RICHARD
You speak too bitterly.

DUCHESS Hear me a word;
For I shall never speak to thee again.

KING RICHARD
So.

DUCHESS
Either thou wilt die, by God's just ordinance,
Ere from this war thou turn a conqueror,
Or I with grief and extreme age shall perish
And never more behold thy face again.
Therefore take with thee my most grievous curse,
Which, in the day of battle, tire thee more
Than all the complete armor that thou wear'st!
My prayers on the adverse party fight;
And there the little souls of Edward's children
Whisper the spirits of thine enemies
And promise them success and victory.
Bloody thou art, bloody will be thy end;
Shame serves thy life and doth thy death attend.
Exit.

QUEEN ELIZABETH
Though far more cause, yet much less spirit to curse
Abides in me; I say amen to her.

KING RICHARD
Stay, madam; I must talk a word with you.

QUEEN ELIZABETH
I have no more sons of the royal blood
For thee to slaughter. For my daughters, Richard,
They shall be praying nuns, not weeping queens,
And therefore level not to hit their lives.

KING RICHARD
You have a daughter call'd Elizabeth,
Virtuous and fair, royal and gracious.

QUEEN ELIZABETH
And must she die for this? O, let her live,
And I'll corrupt her manners, stain her beauty,
Slander myself as false to Edward's bed,
Throw over her the veil of infamy;
So she may live unscarr'd of bleeding slaughter,
I will confess she was not Edward's daughter.

KING RICHARD
Wrong not her birth, she is a royal princess.

QUEEN ELIZABETH
To save her life, I'll say she is not so.

KING RICHARD
Her life is safest only in her birth.

176 Humphrey Hour (To "dine with Duke Humphrey" was to go hungry. The passage is obscure.) **185 turn** return **196 serves** accompanies **203 level** aim **207 manners** morals

QUEEN ELIZABETH
And only in that safety died her brothers.
KING RICHARD
Lo, at their birth good stars were opposite.
QUEEN ELIZABETH
No, to their lives ill friends were contrary.
KING RICHARD
All unavoided is the doom of destiny.
QUEEN ELIZABETH
True, when avoided grace makes destiny.
My babes were destin'd to a fairer death,
If grace had bless'd thee with a fairer life.
KING RICHARD
You speak as if that I had slain my cousins.
QUEEN ELIZABETH
Cousins, indeed, and by their uncle cozen'd
Of comfort, kingdom, kindred, freedom, life.
Whose hand soever lanch'd their tender hearts,
Thy head, all indirectly, gave direction.
No doubt the murd'rous knife was dull and blunt
Till it was whetted on thy stone-hard heart,
To revel in the entrails of my lambs.
But that still use of grief makes wild grief tame,
My tongue should to thy ears not name my boys
Till that my nails were anchor'd in thine eyes;
And I, in such a desp'rate bay of death,
Like a poor bark, of sails and tackling reft,
Rush all to pieces on thy rocky bosom.
KING RICHARD
Madam, so thrive I in my enterprise
And dangerous success of bloody wars,
As I intend more good to you and yours
Than ever you or yours by me were harm'd!
QUEEN ELIZABETH
What good is cover'd with the face of heaven,
To be discovered, that can do me good?
KING RICHARD
Th' advancement of your children, gentle lady.
QUEEN ELIZABETH
Up to some scaffold, there to lose their heads?
KING RICHARD
Unto the dignity and height of fortune,
The high imperial type of this earth's glory.
QUEEN ELIZABETH
Flatter my sorrow with report of it;
Tell me what state, what dignity, what honor,
Canst thou demise to any child of mine?
KING RICHARD
Even all I have—ay, and myself and all—
Will I withal endow a child of thine,
So in the Lethe of thy angry soul
Thou drown the sad remembrance of those wrongs
Which thou supposest I have done to thee.

216 opposite hostile, antagonistic **217 contrary** opposed **218 unavoided** unavoidable **219 avoided grace** i.e., Richard, in whom grace is void or lacking **223 cozen'd** cheated **225 lanch'd** lanced, pierced **226 all indirectly** even if by indirect means **230 But** except. **still** continual **233 bay** (1) inlet (2) position of a hunted animal turning to face the hounds **234 reft** bereft **237 success** sequel, result **240 cover'd with** hidden by (and therefore not yet revealed to man) **245 imperial type** symbol of rule **248 demise** convey, transmit, lease **251 Lethe** river in the underworld, the waters of which produce forgetfulness

QUEEN ELIZABETH
Be brief, lest that the process of thy kindness
Last longer telling than thy kindness' date.
KING RICHARD
Then know that from my soul I love thy daughter.
QUEEN ELIZABETH
My daughter's mother thinks it with her soul.
KING RICHARD
What do you think?
QUEEN ELIZABETH
That thou dost love my daughter from thy soul.
So from thy soul's love didst thou love her brothers,
And from my heart's love I do thank thee for it.
KING RICHARD
Be not so hasty to confound my meaning.
I mean that with my soul I love thy daughter,
And do intend to make her Queen of England.
QUEEN ELIZABETH
Well then, who dost thou mean shall be her king?
KING RICHARD
Even he that makes her queen. Who else should be?
QUEEN ELIZABETH
What, thou?
KING RICHARD Even so. How think you of it?
QUEEN ELIZABETH
How canst thou woo her?
KING RICHARD That would I learn of you,
As one being best acquainted with her humor.
QUEEN ELIZABETH
And wilt thou learn of me?
KING RICHARD Madam, with all my heart.
QUEEN ELIZABETH
Send to her, by the man that slew her brothers,
A pair of bleeding hearts; thereon engrave
"Edward" and "York"; then haply will she weep.
Therefore present to her—as sometime Margaret
Did to thy father, steep'd in Rutland's blood—
A handkerchief, which, say to her, did drain
The purple sap from her sweet brothers' body;
And bid her wipe her weeping eyes withal.
If this inducement move her not to love,
Send her a letter of thy noble deeds.
Tell her thou mad'st away her uncle Clarence,
Her uncle Rivers, ay, and, for her sake,
Mad'st quick conveyance with her good aunt Anne.
KING RICHARD
You mock me, madam. This is not the way
To win your daughter.
QUEEN ELIZABETH There is no other way,
Unless thou couldst put on some other shape
And not be Richard that hath done all this.
KING RICHARD
Say that I did all this for love of her.
QUEEN ELIZABETH
Nay, then indeed she cannot choose but hate thee,
Having bought love with such a bloody spoil.

254 process story **255 date** term of existence **256 from** with. (But Queen Elizabeth, in the next lines, sarcastically uses the word in the sense *apart from.*) **269 humor** mood **274 sometime** once **275 Rutland's** (See *3 Henry VI,* I.iv.) **283 conveyance with** riddance of **290 spoil** slaughter. (A hunting term.)

KING RICHARD
Look what is done cannot be now amended. 291
Men shall deal unadvisedly sometimes,
Which after-hours gives leisure to repent.
If I did take the kingdom from your sons,
To make amends I'll give it to your daughter.
If I have kill'd the issue of your womb,
To quicken your increase, I will beget 297
Mine issue of your blood upon your daughter.
A grandam's name is little less in love
Than is the doting title of a mother;
They are as children but one step below,
Even of your metal, of your very blood, 302
Of all one pain, save for a night of groans
Endur'd of her for whom you bid like sorrow. 304
Your children were vexation to your youth,
But mine shall be a comfort to your age.
The loss you have is but a son being king,
And by that loss your daughter is made queen.
I cannot make you what amends I would,
Therefore accept such kindness as I can. 310
Dorset, your son, that with a fearful soul
Leads discontented steps in foreign soil,
This fair alliance quickly shall call home
To high promotions and great dignity.
The king that calls your beauteous daughter wife
Familiarly shall call thy Dorset brother;
Again shall you be mother to a king,
And all the ruins of distressful times
Repair'd with double riches of content.
What? We have many goodly days to see.
The liquid drops of tears that you have shed
Shall come again, transform'd to orient pearl, 322
Advantaging their love with interest 323
Of ten times double gain of happiness.
Go, then, my mother, to thy daughter go.
Make bold her bashful years with your experience;
Prepare her ears to hear a wooer's tale;
Put in her tender heart th' aspiring flame
Of golden sovereignty; acquaint the Princess
With the sweet silent hours of marriage joys.
And when this arm of mine hath chastised
The petty rebel, dull-brain'd Buckingham,
Bound with triumphant garlands will I come
And lead thy daughter to a conqueror's bed;
To whom I will retail my conquest won, 335
And she shall be sole victoress, Caesar's Caesar.

QUEEN ELIZABETH
What were I best to say? Her father's brother
Would be her lord? Or shall I say her uncle?
Or, he that slew her brothers and her uncles?
Under what title shall I woo for thee,
That God, the law, my honor, and her love
Can make seem pleasing to her tender years?

KING RICHARD
Infer fair England's peace by this alliance. 343

QUEEN ELIZABETH
Which she shall purchase with still lasting war.

KING RICHARD
Tell her the King, that may command, entreats.

QUEEN ELIZABETH
That at her hands which the King's King forbids.

KING RICHARD
Say she shall be a high and mighty queen.

QUEEN ELIZABETH
To vail the title, as her mother doth. 348

KING RICHARD
Say I will love her everlastingly.

QUEEN ELIZABETH
But how long shall that title "ever" last?

KING RICHARD
Sweetly in force unto her fair life's end.

QUEEN ELIZABETH
But how long fairly shall her sweet life last?

KING RICHARD
As long as heaven and nature lengthens it.

QUEEN ELIZABETH
As long as hell and Richard likes of it.

KING RICHARD
Say I, her sovereign, am her subject low.

QUEEN ELIZABETH
But she, your subject, loathes such sovereignty.

KING RICHARD
Be eloquent in my behalf to her.

QUEEN ELIZABETH
An honest tale speeds best being plainly told. 358

KING RICHARD
Then plainly to her tell my loving tale.

QUEEN ELIZABETH
Plain and not honest is too harsh a style. 360

KING RICHARD
Your reasons are too shallow and too quick. 361

QUEEN ELIZABETH
O no, my reasons are too deep and dead—
Too deep and dead, poor infants, in their graves.

KING RICHARD
Harp not on that string, madam; that is past.

QUEEN ELIZABETH
Harp on it still shall I till heartstrings break.

KING RICHARD
Now, by my George, my garter, and my crown— 366

QUEEN ELIZABETH
Profan'd, dishonor'd, and the third usurp'd.

KING RICHARD
I swear—

QUEEN ELIZABETH By nothing; for this is no oath.
Thy George, profan'd, hath lost his lordly honor;
Thy garter, blemish'd, pawn'd his knightly virtue;
Thy crown, usurp'd, disgrac'd his kingly glory.
If something thou wouldst swear to be believ'd,
Swear then by something that thou hast not
wrong'd.

291 Look what whatever **297 quicken your increase** give new life to your (dead) progeny **302 metal** substance **304 of** by. **bid** endured, bided **310 can** am able (to give) **322 orient** bright, shining **323 Advantaging** augmenting. **love** i.e., the love which prompted tears **335 retail** relate **343 Infer** allege, adduce (as a reason)

348 vail lower, abase as a sign of submission **358 speeds** succeeds **360 too . . . style** i.e., a discordant combination **361 quick** hasty (with a pun on the meaning *alive,* contrasted with *dead* in the next line, just as *shallow* is punningly contrasted with *deep*) **366 George . . . garter** (The George, a badge showing St. George slaying the dragon, was not added to the insignia of the Order of the Garter until the reign of Henry VII or Henry VIII.)

KING RICHARD
Then, by myself—
QUEEN ELIZABETH Thyself is self-misus'd.
KING RICHARD
Now, by the world—
QUEEN ELIZABETH 'Tis full of thy foul wrongs.
KING RICHARD
My father's death—
QUEEN ELIZABETH Thy life hath it dishonor'd.
KING RICHARD
Why then, by God—
QUEEN ELIZABETH God's wrong is most of all.
If thou didst fear to break an oath with Him,
The unity the King my husband made
Thou hadst not broken, nor my brothers died.
If thou hadst fear'd to break an oath by Him,
Th' imperial metal, circling now thy head,
Had grac'd the tender temples of my child,
And both the princes had been breathing here,
Which now, two tender bedfellows for dust,
Thy broken faith hath made the prey for worms.
What canst thou swear by now?
KING RICHARD The time to come.
QUEEN ELIZABETH
That thou hast wronged in the time o'erpast;
For I myself have many tears to wash
Hereafter time, for time past wrong'd by thee.
The children live whose fathers thou hast slaughter'd,
Ungovern'd youth, to wail it in their age;
The parents live whose children thou hast butcher'd,
Old barren plants, to wail it with their age.
Swear not by time to come, for that thou hast
Misus'd ere us'd, by times ill-us'd o'erpast.
KING RICHARD
As I intend to prosper and repent,
So thrive I in my dangerous affairs
Of hostile arms! Myself myself confound!
Heaven and fortune bar me happy hours!
Day, yield me not thy light, nor, night, thy rest!
Be opposite all planets of good luck
To my proceeding, if, with dear heart's love,
Immaculate devotion, holy thoughts,
I tender not thy beauteous princely daughter!
In her consists my happiness and thine;
Without her, follows to myself and thee,
Herself, the land, and many a Christian soul,
Death, desolation, ruin, and decay.
It cannot be avoided but by this;
It will not be avoided but by this.
Therefore, dear mother—I must call you so—
Be the attorney of my love to her.
Plead what I will be, not what I have been,
Not my deserts, but what I will deserve.
Urge the necessity and state of times,
And be not peevish-fond in great designs.
QUEEN ELIZABETH
Shall I be tempted of the devil thus?
KING RICHARD
Ay, if the devil tempt you to do good.
QUEEN ELIZABETH
Shall I forget myself to be myself?
KING RICHARD
Ay, if yourself's remembrance wrong yourself.
QUEEN ELIZABETH
Yet thou didst kill my children.
KING RICHARD
But in your daughter's womb I bury them,
Where in that nest of spicery they will breed
Selves of themselves, to your recomforture.
QUEEN ELIZABETH
Shall I go win my daughter to thy will?
KING RICHARD
And be a happy mother by the deed.
QUEEN ELIZABETH
I go. Write to me very shortly,
And you shall understand from me her mind.
KING RICHARD
Bear her my true love's kiss; and so, farewell.
Exit Queen [*Elizabeth*].
Relenting fool, and shallow, changing woman!

Enter Ratcliffe; [*Catesby following*].

How now, what news?
RATCLIFFE
Most mighty sovereign, on the western coast
Rideth a puissant navy; to our shores
Throng many doubtful hollow-hearted friends,
Unarm'd, and unresolv'd to beat them back.
'Tis thought that Richmond is their admiral;
And there they hull, expecting but the aid
Of Buckingham to welcome them ashore.
KING RICHARD
Some light-foot friend post to the Duke of Norfolk:
Ratcliffe, thyself, or Catesby; where is he?
CATESBY
Here, my good lord.
KING RICHARD Catesby, fly to the Duke.
CATESBY
I will, my lord, with all convenient haste.
KING RICHARD
Ratcliffe, come hither. Post to Salisbury.
When thou com'st thither—[*To Catesby.*] Dull, unmindful villain,
Why stay'st thou here, and go'st not to the Duke?
CATESBY
First, mighty liege, tell me your Highness' pleasure,
What from your Grace I shall deliver to him.
KING RICHARD
O, true, good Catesby. Bid him levy straight
The greatest strength and power that he can make,
And meet me suddenly at Salisbury.

379 unity i.e., the reconciliation between Queen Elizabeth and her enemies **390 Hereafter** after this **392 Ungovern'd** i.e., without a father's guidance or rule **397 As . . . repent** i.e., I swear that as I hope to thrive and intend to repent **399 Myself . . . confound** may I destroy myself **405 tender** have a tender regard for **417 peevish-fond** childishly foolish

420 Shall . . . myself i.e., shall I forget who I am, the person wronged by Richard **421 wrong yourself** i.e., interfere with what is to your advantage **424 nest of spicery** (The fabled phoenix arose anew from the nest of spices, its funeral pyre.) **425 recomforture** comfort, consolation **437 their admiral** i.e., of the *puissant navy* named three lines earlier **438 hull** drift with the sails furled **440 light-foot** swift-footed

CATESBY
I go. *Exit.*

RATCLIFFE
What, may it please you, shall I do at Salisbury?

KING RICHARD
Why, what wouldst thou do there before I go?

RATCLIFFE
Your highness told me I should post before.

KING RICHARD
My mind is chang'd.

Enter Lord Stanley [*Earl of Derby*].

Stanley, what news with you?

STANLEY
None good, my liege, to please you with the hearing,
Nor none so bad, but well may be reported.

KING RICHARD
Hoyday, a riddle! Neither good nor bad!
What need'st thou run so many miles about,
When thou mayest tell thy tale the nearest way?
Once more, what news?

STANLEY
Richmond is on the seas.

KING RICHARD
There let him sink, and be the seas on him!
White-liver'd runagate, what doth he there?

STANLEY
I know not, mighty sovereign, but by guess.

KING RICHARD
Well, as you guess?

STANLEY
Stirr'd up by Dorset, Buckingham, and Morton,
He makes for England, here to claim the crown.

KING RICHARD
Is the chair empty? Is the sword unsway'd?
Is the King dead? The empire unpossess'd?
What heir of York is there alive but we?
And who is England's king but great York's heir?
Then, tell me, what makes he upon the seas?

STANLEY
Unless for that, my liege, I cannot guess.

KING RICHARD
Unless for that he comes to be your liege,
You cannot guess wherefore the Welshman comes.
Thou wilt revolt and fly to him, I fear.

STANLEY
No, my good lord; therefore mistrust me not.

KING RICHARD
Where is thy power, then, to beat him back?
Where be thy tenants and thy followers?
Are they not now upon the western shore,
Safe-conducting the rebels from their ships?

STANLEY
No, my good lord, my friends are in the north.

KING RICHARD
Cold friends to me! What do they in the north,
When they should serve their sovereign in the west?

STANLEY
They have not been commanded, mighty King.
Pleaseth your Majesty to give me leave,
I'll muster up my friends and meet your Grace
Where and what time your Majesty shall please.

KING RICHARD
Ay, thou wouldst be gone to join with Richmond.
But I'll not trust thee.

STANLEY
Most mighty sovereign,
You have no cause to hold my friendship doubtful.
I never was nor never will be false.

KING RICHARD
Go then and muster men, but leave behind
Your son, George Stanley. Look your heart be firm,
Or else his head's assurance is but frail.

STANLEY
So deal with him as I prove true to you.
Exit Stanley [*Earl of Derby*].

Enter a Messenger.

FIRST MESSENGER
My gracious sovereign, now in Devonshire,
As I by friends am well advertised,
Sir Edward Courtney, and the haughty prelate
Bishop of Exeter, his elder brother,
With many moe confederates, are in arms.

Enter another Messenger.

SECOND MESSENGER
In Kent, my liege, the Guildfords are in arms,
And every hour more competitors
Flock to the rebels, and their power grows strong.

Enter another Messenger.

THIRD MESSENGER
My lord, the army of great Buckingham—

KING RICHARD
Out on ye, owls! Nothing but songs of death?
He striketh him.
There, take thou that, till thou bring better news.

THIRD MESSENGER
The news I have to tell your Majesty
Is that by sudden floods and fall of waters
Buckingham's army is dispers'd and scatter'd,
And he himself wand'red away alone,
No man knows whither.

KING RICHARD
I cry thee mercy.
There is my purse to cure that blow of thine.
[*Gives money.*]
Hath any well-advised friend proclaim'd
Reward to him that brings the traitor in?

THIRD MESSENGER
Such proclamation hath been made, my lord.

Enter another Messenger.

455 post hasten **464 White-liver'd runagate** cowardly renegade, fugitive **470 empire** kingdom **476 Welshman** (Richmond was the grandson of Owen Tudor, a Welshman of Anglesea, who fathered three sons and a daughter by Katharine of Valois, widow of Henry V.)

487 Pleaseth may it please **496 assurance** safety **499 advertised** informed **504 competitors** confederates **507 owls** (The cry of the owl was thought to portend death.)

FOURTH MESSENGER

Sir Thomas Lovel and Lord Marquess Dorset,
'Tis said, my liege, in Yorkshire are in arms.
But this good comfort bring I to your Highness:
The Britaine navy is dispers'd by tempest.
Richmond, in Dorsetshire, sent out a boat
Unto the shore, to ask those on the banks
If they were his assistants, yea or no,
Who answer'd him they came from Buckingham
Upon his party. He, mistrusting them,
Hois'd sail and made his course again for Britaine.

KING RICHARD

March on, march on, since we are up in arms,
If not to fight with foreign enemies,
Yet to beat down these rebels here at home.

Enter Catesby.

CATESBY

My liege, the Duke of Buckingham is taken!
That is the best news. That the Earl of Richmond
Is with a mighty power landed at Milford
Is colder news, but yet they must be told.

KING RICHARD

Away towards Salisbury! While we reason here,
A royal battle might be won and lost.
Some one take order Buckingham be brought
To Salisbury. The rest march on with me.
Flourish. Exeunt.

SCENE [V]

Enter [Lord Stanley Earl of] Derby and Sir Christopher [Urswick, a priest].

STANLEY

Sir Christopher, tell Richmond this from me:
That in the sty of the most deadly boar
My son George Stanley is frank'd up in hold.
If I revolt, off goes young George's head;
The fear of that holds off my present aid.
So get thee gone; commend me to thy lord.
Withal say that the Queen hath heartily consented
He should espouse Elizabeth her daughter.
But, tell me, where is princely Richmond now?

CHRISTOPHER

At Pembroke, or at Ha'rford-west, in Wales.

STANLEY

What men of name resort to him?

CHRISTOPHER

Sir Walter Herbert, a renowned soldier,
Sir Gilbert Talbot, Sir William Stanley,
Oxford, redoubted Pembroke, Sir James Blunt,
And Rice ap Thomas, with a valiant crew,
And many other of great name and worth;
And towards London do they bend their power,
If by the way they be not fought withal.

STANLEY

Well, hie thee to thy lord; I kiss his hand.
My letter will resolve him of my mind. [*Gives letter.*]
Farewell. *Exeunt.*

ACT V • SCENE I

Enter Buckingham, with [Sheriff and] Halberds, led to execution.

BUCKINGHAM

Will not King Richard let me speak with him?

SHERIFF

No, my good lord; therefore be patient.

BUCKINGHAM

Hastings, and Edward's children, Grey, and Rivers,
Holy King Henry, and thy fair son Edward,
Vaughan, and all that have miscarried
By underhand corrupted foul injustice,
If that your moody discontented souls
Do through the clouds behold this present hour,
Even for revenge mock my destruction!
This is All-Souls' day, fellow, is it not?

SHERIFF

It is, my lord.

BUCKINGHAM

Why, then All-Souls' day is my body's doomsday.
This is the day which, in King Edward's time,
I wish'd might fall on me, when I was found
False to his children and his wife's allies;
This is the day wherein I wish'd to fall
By the false faith of him whom most I trusted;
This, this All-Souls' day to my fearful soul
Is the determin'd respite of my wrongs.
That high All-Seer which I dallied with
Hath turn'd my feigned prayer on my head
And given in earnest what I begg'd in jest.
Thus doth he force the swords of wicked men
To turn their own points in their masters' bosoms.
Thus Margaret's curse falls heavy on my neck:
"When he," quoth she, "shall split thy heart with sorrow,
Remember Margaret was a prophetess."
Come, lead me, officers, to the block of shame;
Wrong hath but wrong, and blame the due of blame. *Exeunt Buckingham with officers.*

521 Britaine Breton **527 Hois'd** hoisted. **Britaine** Brittany **533 Milford** i.e., Milford Haven on the coast of Wales in the county of Pembroke. (A gap of two years is bridged here. Richmond's first fruitless expedition was in October 1483; his landing at Milford was in August 1485.)

IV.v. Location: London. The house of Lord Stanley, Earl of Derby.
s.d. Sir (Honorific title for a clergyman.) **3 frank'd up in hold** shut up in custody, as in a pig-pen **11 name** rank

14 redoubted dreaded. **Pembroke** i.e., Jasper Tudor, Earl of Pembroke, uncle to Richmond **20 resolve him of** inform him concerning

V.i. Location: Salisbury. An open place.
4 thy i.e., Henry's **5 miscarried** perished **7 discontented** i.e., still seeking vengeance **10 All-Soul's day** November 2, the day on which the Roman Catholic church intercedes for all Christian souls **19 determin'd . . . wrongs** i.e., the preordained date to which the punishment of my evil practices was respited or postponed

SCENE II

Enter Richmond, Oxford, [*Sir James*] *Blunt,* [*Sir Walter*] *Herbert, and others, with drum and colors.*

RICHMOND
Fellows in arms, and my most loving friends,
Bruis'd underneath the yoke of tyranny,
Thus far into the bowels of the land
Have we march'd on without impediment;
And here receive we from our father Stanley
Lines of fair comfort and encouragement.
The wretched, bloody, and usurping boar,
That spoil'd your summer fields and fruitful vines,
Swills your warm blood like wash, and makes his trough
In your embowel'd bosoms, this foul swine
Is now even in the center of this isle,
Near to the town of Leicester, as we learn.
From Tamworth thither is but one day's march.
In God's name, cheerly on, courageous friends,
To reap the harvest of perpetual peace
By this one bloody trial of sharp war.

OXFORD
Every man's conscience is a thousand men,
To fight against this guilty homicide.

HERBERT
I doubt not but his friends will turn to us.

BLUNT
He hath no friends but what are friends for fear,
Which in his dearest need will fly from him.

RICHMOND
All for our vantage. Then, in God's name, march!
True hope is swift, and flies with swallow's wings;
Kings it makes gods and meaner creatures kings.
Exeunt omnes.

[SCENE III]

Enter King Richard in arms, with Norfolk, Ratcliffe, and the Earl of Surrey [*and others*].

KING RICHARD
Here pitch our tent, even here in Bosworth field.
My Lord of Surrey, why look you so sad?

SURREY
My heart is ten times lighter than my looks.

KING RICHARD
My Lord of Norfolk—

NORFOLK
Here, most gracious liege.

KING RICHARD
Norfolk, we must have knocks; ha! Must we not?

NORFOLK
We must both give and take, my loving lord.

KING RICHARD
Up with my tent! Here will I lie tonight;
[*Soldiers begin to set up King Richard's tent.*]
But where tomorrow? Well, all's one for that.
Who hath descried the number of the traitors?

NORFOLK
Six or seven thousand is their utmost power.

KING RICHARD
Why, our battalia trebles that account.
Besides, the King's name is a tower of strength,
Which they upon the adverse faction want.
Up with the tent! Come, noble gentlemen,
Let us survey the vantage of the ground.
Call for some men of sound direction.
Let's lack no discipline, make no delay,
For, lords, tomorrow is a busy day. *Exeunt.*

Enter [*on the other side of the stage*] *Richmond, Sir William Brandon, Oxford, and Dorset,* [*Blunt, Herbert, and others. Some of the Soldiers pitch Richmond's tent.*]

RICHMOND
The weary sun hath made a golden set,
And, by the bright tract of his fiery car,
Gives token of a goodly day tomorrow.
Sir William Brandon, you shall bear my standard.
Give me some ink and paper in my tent.
I'll draw the form and model of our battle,
Limit each leader to his several charge,
And part in just proportion our small power.
My Lord of Oxford, you, Sir William Brandon,
And you, Sir Walter Herbert, stay with me.
The Earl of Pembroke keeps his regiment;
Good Captain Blunt, bear my good-night to him,
And by the second hour in the morning
Desire the Earl to see me in my tent.
Yet one thing more, good captain, do for me:
Where is Lord Stanley quarter'd, do you know?

BLUNT
Unless I have mista'en his colors much,
Which well I am assur'd I have not done,
His regiment lies half a mile at least
South from the mighty power of the King.

RICHMOND
If without peril it be possible,
Sweet Blunt, make some good means to speak with him,
And give him from me this most needful note.
[*Gives a letter.*]

BLUNT
Upon my life, my lord, I'll undertake it.
And so, God give you quiet rest tonight!

V.ii. Location: A camp near Tamworth.
5 father i.e., stepfather, Lord Stanley, Earl of Derby **8 spoil'd** despoiled **9 wash** hog's wash, swill **10 embowel'd** disemboweled **20 for fear** i.e., out of fearing Richard **24 meaner** of lower degree

V.iii. Location: Bosworth Field.

8 all's . . . that be that as it may **11 battalia** army **13 want** lack **15 vantage of the ground** i.e., way in which the field can best be used for tactical advantage **16 direction** judgment, military skill **20 tract** track. **car** chariot (of Phoebus) **25 Limit** appoint. **several charge** individual command **29 keeps** i.e., is with

RICHMOND
Good night, good Captain Blunt. [*Exit Blunt.*] Come,
gentlemen,
Let us consult upon tomorrow's business.
Into my tent; the dew is raw and cold.
They withdraw into the tent.

Enter [to his tent, King] Richard, Ratcliffe, Norfolk, and Catesby [with others].

KING RICHARD
What is 't o'clock?
CATESBY It's supper-time, my lord;
It's nine o'clock.
KING RICHARD I will not sup tonight.
Give me some ink and paper.
What, is my beaver easier than it was?
And all my armor laid into my tent?
CATESBY
It is, my liege, and all things are in readiness.
KING RICHARD
Good Norfolk, hie thee to thy charge;
Use careful watch, choose trusty sentinels.
NORFOLK
I go, my lord.
KING RICHARD
Stir with the lark tomorrow, gentle Norfolk.
NORFOLK
I warrant you, my lord. [*Exit.*]
KING RICHARD
Catesby!
CATESBY
My lord?
KING RICHARD Send out a pursuivant at arms
To Stanley's regiment. Bid him bring his power
Before sunrising, lest his son George fall
Into the blind cave of eternal night. [*Exit Catesby.*]
Fill me a bowl of wine. Give me a watch.
Saddle white Surrey for the field tomorrow.
Look that my staves be sound, and not too heavy.
Ratcliffe!
RATCLIFFE
My lord?
KING RICHARD
Saw'st thou the melancholy Lord Northumberland?
RATCLIFFE
Thomas the Earl of Surrey and himself,
Much about cockshut time, from troop to troop
Went through the army, cheering up the soldiers,
KING RICHARD
So, I am satisfied. Give me a bowl of wine.
I have not that alacrity of spirit,
Nor cheer of mind, that I was wont to have.
[*Wine is brought.*]
Set it down. Is ink and paper ready?
RATCLIFFE
It is, my lord.
KING RICHARD Bid my guard watch; leave me.
Ratcliffe, about the mid of night come to my tent
And help to arm me. Leave me, I say.
Exit Ratcliffe. [*Richard sleeps.*]

Enter [Lord Stanley Earl of] Derby, to Richmond in his tent, [Lords and others attending].

STANLEY
Fortune and victory sit on thy helm!
RICHMOND
All comfort that the dark night can afford
Be to thy person, noble father-in-law!
Tell me, how fares our loving mother?
STANLEY
I, by attorney, bless thee from thy mother,
Who prays continually for Richmond's good.
So much for that. The silent hours steal on,
And flaky darkness breaks within the east.
In brief—for so the season bids us be—
Prepare thy battle early in the morning,
And put thy fortune to the arbitrement
Of bloody strokes and mortal-staring war.
I, as I may—that which I would I cannot—
With best advantage will deceive the time,
And aid thee in this doubtful shock of arms.
But on thy side I may not be too forward,
Lest, being seen, thy brother, tender George,
Be executed in his father's sight.
Farewell. The leisure and the fearful time
Cuts off the ceremonious vows of love
And ample interchange of sweet discourse,
Which so long sund'red friends should dwell upon.
God give us leisure for these rites of love!
Once more, adieu. Be valiant, and speed well!
RICHMOND
Good lords, conduct him to his regiment.
I'll strive, with troubled thoughts, to take a nap,
Lest leaden slumber peise me down tomorrow,
When I should mount with wings of victory.
Once more, good night, kind lords and gentlemen.
Exeunt. [*Manet Richmond.*]
O Thou, whose captain I account myself,
Look on my forces with a gracious eye;
Put in their hands thy bruising irons of wrath,
That they may crush down with a heavy fall
The usurping helmets of our adversaries!
Make us thy ministers of chastisement,
That we may praise thee in the victory!
To thee I do commend my watchful soul,
Ere I let fall the windows of mine eyes.
Sleeping and waking, O, defend me still! [*Sleeps.*]

50 beaver face-guard or visor of helmet. **easier** more loosely fitting **59 pursuivant at arms** junior officer attendant on a herald **63 watch** watch light, candle marked into equal divisions to show time; or, perhaps, sentinel **64 white Surrey** (The name seems to be Shakespeare's invention. The chroniclers say that Richard was mounted on a "great white courser.") **65 staves** lance shafts **70 cockshut time** evening twilight; possibly, the time at which the poultry are shut up

81 father-in-law i.e., stepfather **86 flaky** streaked with light **87 season** time of day **90 mortal-staring** fatal-visaged **91 that . . . cannot** i.e., I cannot fight openly on your side, though I want to **92 With . . . time** i.e., as best I can will work for our side without seeming to do so **95 brother** i.e., stepbrother. **tender** young, of tender years **97 leisure** i.e., brief time allowed **104 with** i.e., in spite of **105 peise** weigh **116 windows** i.e., eyelids

Enter the Ghost of young Prince Edward, son [to] Harry the Sixth, to Richard.

GHOST *(To Richard)*
Let me sit heavy on thy soul tomorrow!
Think, how thou stab'dst me in my prime of youth
At Tewkesbury. Despair therefore and die!
(To Richmond.) Be cheerful, Richmond, for the wronged souls
Of butcher'd princes fight in thy behalf.
King Henry's issue, Richmond, comforts thee.

Enter the Ghost of Henry the Sixth.

GHOST *(To Richard)*
When I was mortal, my anointed body
By thee was punched full of deadly holes.
Think on the Tower and me. Despair and die!
Harry the Sixth bids thee despair and die!
(To Richmond.) Virtuous and holy, be thou conqueror!
Harry, that prophesied thou shouldst be king,
Doth comfort thee in thy sleep. Live and flourish!

Enter the Ghost of Clarence.

GHOST [*To Richard*]
Let me sit heavy in thy soul tomorrow,
I, that was wash'd to death with fulsome wine,
Poor Clarence, by thy guile betray'd to death!
Tomorrow in the battle think on me,
And fall thy edgeless sword. Despair and die!—
(To Richmond.) Thou offspring of the house of Lancaster,
The wronged heirs of York do pray for thee.
Good angels guard thy battle! Live, and flourish!

Enter the Ghosts of Rivers, Grey, [and] Vaughan.

GHOST OF RIVERS [*To Richard*]
Let me sit heavy in thy soul tomorrow,
Rivers that died at Pomfret! Despair and die!
GHOST OF GREY [*To Richard*]
Think upon Grey, and let thy soul despair!
GHOST OF VAUGHAN [*To Richard*]
Think upon Vaughan, and, with guilty fear,
Let fall thy lance. Despair and die!
ALL *(To Richmond)*
Awake, and think our wrongs in Richard's bosom
Will conquer him! Awake, and win the day!

Enter the Ghosts of the two young Princes.

GHOSTS *(To Richard)*
Dream on thy cousins smothered in the Tower.
Let us be lead within thy bosom, Richard,
And weigh thee down to ruin, shame, and death!
Thy nephews' souls bid thee despair and die!
(To Richmond.) Sleep, Richmond, sleep in peace, and wake in joy.
Good angels guard thee from the boar's annoy!
Live, and beget a happy race of kings!
Edward's unhappy sons do bid thee flourish.

Enter the Ghost of Hastings.

GHOST [*To Richard*]
Bloody and guilty, guiltily awake,
And in a bloody battle end thy days!
Think on Lord Hastings. Despair and die!
(To Richmond.) Quiet untroubled soul, awake, awake!
Arm, fight, and conquer for fair England's sake!

Enter the Ghost of Lady Anne, his Wife.

GHOST [*To Richard*]
Richard, thy wife, that wretched Anne thy wife,
That never slept a quiet hour with thee,
Now fills thy sleep with perturbations.
Tomorrow in the battle think on me,
And fall thy edgeless sword. Despair and die!
(To Richmond.) Thou quiet soul, sleep thou a quiet sleep;
Dream of success and happy victory!
Thy adversary's wife doth pray for thee.

Enter the Ghost of Buckingham.

GHOST [*To Richard*]
The first was I that help'd thee to the crown;
The last was I that felt thy tyranny.
O, in the battle think on Buckingham,
And die in terror of thy guiltiness!
Dream on, dream on, of bloody deeds and death;
Fainting, despair; despairing, yield thy breath!
(To Richmond.) I died for hope ere I could lend thee aid,
But cheer thy heart, and be thou not dismay'd.
God and good angels fight on Richmond's side,
And Richard falls in height of all his pride.

[*The Ghosts vanish.*] *Richard starteth up out of a dream.*

KING RICHARD
Give me another horse! Bind up my wounds!
Have mercy, Jesu!—Soft! I did but dream.
O coward conscience, how dost thou afflict me!
The lights burn blue. It is now dead midnight.
Cold fearful drops stand on my trembling flesh.
What do I fear? Myself? There's none else by.
Richard loves Richard; that is, I am I.
Is there a murderer here? No. Yes, I am.
Then fly. What, from myself? Great reason why:
Lest I revenge. What, myself upon myself?
Alack, I love myself. Wherefore? For any good
That I myself have done unto myself?
O, no! Alas, I rather hate myself
For hateful deeds committed by myself!
I am a villain. Yet I lie, I am not.
Fool, of thyself speak well. Fool, do not flatter.
My conscience hath a thousand several tongues,
And every tongue brings in a several tale,

126 Tower (Where Henry VI was supposed to have been murdered.) **129 prophesied** (See *3 Henry VI* IV.vi.68 ff.) **132 wash'd to death** i.e., drowned in a butt of malmsey. **fulsome** cloying **135 fall** may it fall **151 the boar's annoy** i.e., Richard's attack

173 for hope i.e., for want of hope, hoping in vain to help **180 lights burn blue** (Superstitiously regarded as evidence of the presence of ghosts.) **193 several** different, separate

And every tale condemns me for a villain.
Perjury, perjury, in the highest degree,
Murder, stern murder, in the direst degree,
All several sins, all us'd in each degree, 198
Throng to the bar, crying all, "Guilty! Guilty!" 199
I shall despair. There is no creature loves me,
And if I die, no soul will pity me.
And, wherefore should they, since that I myself
Find in myself no pity to myself?
Methought the souls of all that I had murder'd
Came to my tent, and every one did threat
Tomorrow's vengeance on the head of Richard.

Enter Ratcliffe.

RATCLIFFE
My lord!

KING RICHARD
'Zounds! Who is there?

RATCLIFFE
Ratcliffe, my lord, 'tis I. The early village cock
Hath twice done salutation to the morn.
Your friends are up, and buckle on their armor.

KING RICHARD
O Ratcliffe, I have dream'd a fearful dream!
What think'st thou, will our friends prove all true?

RATCLIFFE
No doubt, my lord.

KING RICHARD O Ratcliffe, I fear, I fear!

RATCLIFFE
Nay, good my lord, be not afraid of shadows.

KING RICHARD
By the apostle Paul, shadows tonight
Have struck more terror to the soul of Richard
Than can the substance of ten thousand soldiers
Armed in proof and led by shallow Richmond. 219
'Tis not yet near day. Come, go with me;
Under our tents I'll play the ease-dropper, 221
To see if any mean to shrink from me.
Exeunt [Richard and Ratcliffe].

Enter the Lords to Richmond, [sitting in his tent].

LORDS
Good morrow, Richmond!

RICHMOND
Cry mercy, lords and watchful gentlemen, 224
That you have ta'en a tardy sluggard here.

LORDS
How have you slept, my lord?

RICHMOND
The sweetest sleep, and fairest-boding dreams
That ever ent'red in a drowsy head,
Have I since your departure had, my lords.
Methought their souls whose bodies Richard murder'd
Came to my tent and cried on victory. 231
I promise you, my soul is very jocund
In the remembrance of so fair a dream.
How far into the morning is it, lords?

LORDS
Upon the stroke of four.

RICHMOND
Why, then 'tis time to arm and give direction.

His oration to his Soldiers.

More than I have said, loving countrymen,
The leisure and enforcement of the time 238
Forbids to dwell upon. Yet remember this:
God and our good cause fight upon our side.
The prayers of holy saints and wronged souls,
Like high-rear'd bulwarks, stand before our faces.
Richard except, those whom we fight against 243
Had rather have us win than him they follow.
For what is he they follow? Truly, gentlemen,
A bloody tyrant and a homicide;
One rais'd in blood, and one in blood establish'd; 247
One that made means to come by what he hath, 248
And slaughtered those that were the means to help him;
A base foul stone, made precious by the foil 250
Of England's chair, where he is falsely set;
One that hath ever been God's enemy.
Then, if you fight against God's enemy,
God will in justice ward you as his soldiers; 254
If you do sweat to put a tyrant down,
You sleep in peace, the tyrant being slain;
If you do fight against your country's foes,
Your country's fat shall pay your pains the hire; 258
If you do fight in safeguard of your wives,
Your wives shall welcome home the conquerors;
If you do free your children from the sword,
Your children's children quits it in your age. 262
Then, in the name of God and all these rights,
Advance your standards, draw your willing swords.
For me, the ransom of my bold attempt 265
Shall be this cold corpse on the earth's cold face; 266
But if I thrive, the gain of my attempt
The least of you shall share his part thereof.
Sound drums and trumpets boldly and cheerfully;
God and Saint George! Richmond and victory!
[Exeunt.]

Enter King Richard, Ratcliffe, [Attendants and Forces].

KING RICHARD
What said Northumberland as touching Richmond?

RATCLIFFE
That he was never trained up in arms.

KING RICHARD
He said the truth. And what said Surrey then?

RATCLIFFE
He smil'd and said "The better for our purpose."

KING RICHARD
He was in the right, and so indeed it is.
The clock striketh.

198 us'd committed. **degree** i.e., of infamy, from bad to worst **199 bar** i.e., bar of justice **219 proof** armor which is proof against weapons **221 ease-dropper** eaves-dropper **224 Cry mercy** I beg your pardon **231 cried on** uttered the cry of. (A hunting term; i.e., *urged on to.*)

238 leisure i.e., brief time allowed **243 except** excepted **247 in blood** by bloodshed **248 made means** i.e., has taken advantage, created opportunity **250 foil** a thin leaf of metal placed under a gem to set it off to advantage **254 ward** protect **258 fat** prosperity, wealth **262 quits** requites **265–266 the ransom . . . face** i.e., if I fail, there will be no question of ransom, but only death

Tell the clock there. Give me a calendar.
Who saw the sun today? [*Takes an almanac.*]

RATCLIFFE Not I, my lord.

KING RICHARD
Then he disdains to shine, for by the book
He should have brav'd the east an hour ago.
A black day will it be to somebody.
Ratcliffe!

RATCLIFFE
My lord?

KING RICHARD The sun will not be seen today;
The sky doth frown and lour upon our army.
I would these dewy tears were from the ground.
Not shine today? Why, what is that to me
More than to Richmond? For the selfsame heaven
That frowns on me looks sadly upon him.

Enter Norfolk.

NORFOLK
Arm, arm, my lord, the foe vaunts in the field!

KING RICHARD
Come, bustle, bustle! Caparison my horse.
Call up Lord Stanley, bid him bring his power.
I will lead forth my soldiers to the plain,
And thus my battle shall be ordered:
My foreward shall be drawn out all in length,
Consisting equally of horse and foot;
Our archers shall be placed in the midst.
John Duke of Norfolk, Thomas Earl of Surrey,
Shall have the leading of this foot and horse.
They thus directed, we will follow
In the main battle, whose puissance on either side
Shall be well winged with our chiefest horse.
This, and Saint George to boot! What think'st thou, Norfolk?

NORFOLK
A good direction, warlike sovereign.
This found I on my tent this morning.
He showeth him a paper.
[*Reads.*] "Jockey of Norfolk, be not so bold,
For Dickon thy master is bought and sold."

KING RICHARD
A thing devised by the enemy.
Go, gentlemen, every man unto his charge.
Let not our babbling dreams affright our souls;
Conscience is but a word that cowards use,
Devis'd at first to keep the strong in awe.
Our strong arms be our conscience, swords our law!
March on, join bravely, let us to it pell-mell;
If not to heaven, then hand in hand to hell.

His oration to his Army.

What shall I say more than I have inferr'd?
Remember whom you are to cope withal:
A sort of vagabonds, rascals, and runaways,
A scum of Britaines, and base lackey peasants,
Whom their o'ercloyed country vomits forth
To desperate adventures and assur'd destruction.
You sleeping safe, they bring to you unrest;
You having lands, and blest with beauteous wives,
They would restrain the one, distain the other.
And who doth lead them but a paltry fellow,
Long kept in Britaine at our mother's cost?
A milksop, one that never in his life
Felt so much cold as over shoes in snow?
Let's whip these stragglers o'er the seas again.
Lash hence these overweening rags of France,
These famish'd beggars, weary of their lives,
Who, but for dreaming on this fond exploit,
For want of means, poor rats, had hang'd themselves.
If we be conquered, let men conquer us,
And not these bastard Britaines, whom our fathers
Have in their own land beaten, bobb'd, and thump'd,
And in record left them the heirs of shame.
Shall these enjoy our lands? Lie with our wives?
Ravish our daughters? [*Drum afar off.*] Hark! I hear their drum.
Fight, gentlemen of England! Fight, bold yeomen!
Draw, archers, draw your arrows to the head!
Spur your proud horses hard, and ride in blood;
Amaze the welkin with your broken staves!

[*Enter a Messenger.*]

What says Lord Stanley? Will he bring his power?

MESSENGER
My lord, he doth deny to come.

KING RICHARD
Off with his son George's head!

NORFOLK
My lord, the enemy is past the marsh.
After the battle let George Stanley die.

KING RICHARD
A thousand hearts are great within my bosom.
Advance our standards, set upon our foes;
Our ancient word of courage, fair Saint George,
Inspire us with the spleen of fiery dragons!
Upon them! Victory sits on our helms. *Exeunt.*

[SCENE IV]

Alarum. Excursions. Enter [Norfolk and forces fighting; to him] Catesby.

CATESBY
Rescue, my Lord of Norfolk, rescue, rescue!
The King enacts more wonders than a man,
Daring an opposite to every danger.

276 Tell count the strokes of. **calendar** almanac **278 book** i.e., the almanac **279 brav'd** made splendid **288 vaunts** boasts his strength **289 Caparison** put on the battle trappings **293 foreward** vanguard **298 directed** deployed **299 main battle** main body of troops **300 winged** flanked. **horse** cavalry **301 to boot** i.e., to give us aid in addition **304 Jockey** i.e., Jack, John **305 Dickon** i.e., Dick, Richard **314 inferr'd** stated **316 sort** gang **317 Britaines** Bretons

322 restrain deprive you of. **distain** defile, sully **324 Britaine** Brittany. **our mother's** (Richmond's mother was not Richard's. This error occurs in the second edition of Holinshed's *Chronicles.* The first edition reads "brothers," the reference being to the fact that Richmond had been supported at the court of the Duke of Brittany at the cost of Charles, Duke of Burgundy, Richard's brother-in-law.) **326 over shoes** i.e., over his shoe-tops **330 fond** foolish **331 want of means** poverty **334 bobb'd** thrashed **335 record** history **341 Amaze the welkin** fright the skies

V.iv. Location: Bosworth Field, as before; action is continuous.
2 than a man than seems possible for a human being **3 Daring . . . danger** boldly facing every danger in battle

His horse is slain, and all on foot he fights,
Seeking for Richmond in the throat of death.
Rescue, fair lord, or else the day is lost!

[Alarums.] Enter [King] Richard.

KING RICHARD
A horse, a horse! My kingdom for a horse!

CATESBY
Withdraw, my lord. I'll help you to a horse.

KING RICHARD
Slave, I have set my life upon a cast,
And I will stand the hazard of the die.
I think there be six Richmonds in the field;
Five have I slain today instead of him.
A horse, a horse! My kingdom for a horse! *[Exeunt.]*

[SCENE V]

Alarum. Enter Richard and Richmond; they fight. Richard is slain. Then, retreat being sounded, [flourish, and] enter Richmond, [Lord Stanley Earl of] Derby bearing the crown, with other Lords, etc.

RICHMOND
God and your arms be prais'd, victorious friends!
The day is ours, the bloody dog is dead.

STANLEY *[Offering him the crown]*
Courageous Richmond, well hast thou acquit thee.
Lo here this long-usurped royalty
From the dead temples of this bloody wretch
Have I pluck'd off, to grace thy brows withal.
Wear it, enjoy it, and make much of it.

RICHMOND
Great God of heaven, say amen to all!
But, tell me, is young George Stanley living?

STANLEY
He is, my lord, and safe in Leicester town,
Whither, if it please you, we may now withdraw us.

RICHMOND
What men of name are slain on either side?

STANLEY
John Duke of Norfolk, Walter Lord Ferrers,
Sir Robert Brakenbury, and Sir William Brandon.

RICHMOND
Inter their bodies as becomes their births.
Proclaim a pardon to the soldiers fled
That in submission will return to us,
And then, as we have ta'en the sacrament,
We will unite the white rose and the red.
Smile heaven upon this fair conjunction,
That long have frown'd upon their enmity!
What traitor hears me, and says not amen?
England hath long been mad, and scarr'd herself;
The brother blindly shed the brother's blood,
The father rashly slaughter'd his own son,
The son, compell'd, been butcher to the sire.
All this divided York and Lancaster,
Divided in their dire division,
O, now, let Richmond and Elizabeth,
The true succeeders of each royal house,
By God's fair ordinance conjoin together!
And let their heirs, God, if thy will be so,
Enrich the time to come with smooth-fac'd peace,
With smiling plenty, and fair prosperous days!
Abate the edge of traitors, gracious Lord,
That would reduce these bloody days again
And make poor England weep in streams of blood!
Let them not live to taste this land's increase
That would with treason wound this fair land's
  peace!
Now civil wounds are stopp'd, peace lives again.
That she may long live here, God say amen! *Exeunt.*

9 cast throw of the dice **10 die** (Singular of *dice*.) **11 six Richmonds** i.e., Richmond himself and five men dressed like him as a safety precaution

V.v. Location: Action continues at Bosworth Field.
18 ta'en the sacrament sworn a sacred oath on the sacrament (to marry Princess Elizabeth, daughter of Edward IV, thereby uniting the houses of York and of Lancaster, white rose and red) **20 conjunction** union. (An astrological metaphor)

35 Abate blunt, render ineffective **36 reduce** bring back

The Life and Death of King John

King John is usually dated on grounds of style between Shakespeare's two historical tetralogies, perhaps shortly before *Richard II* in 1594 or 1595. In structure and characterization it is also transitional from the episodic and morally straightforward first series *(Henry VI* through *Richard III)* to the more tightly organized and sophisticated second *(Richard II* through *Henry V).* It stands alone among Shakespeare's history plays of the 1590's in choosing the early thirteenth century for its subject rather than the fifteenth. Yet the political problems are familiar.

Foremost is the uncertainty of John's claim to the English throne. He occupies that throne by "strong possession" and also seemingly by the last will and testament of his deceased eldest brother, King Richard I. But could such a will disinherit Arthur, the son of John's older brother Geoffrey? English primogeniture specified that property must descend to the eldest son; after Richard's death without direct heirs, his next brother Geoffrey would inherit, and then Geoffrey's son Arthur. Significantly, even John's mother, Queen Elinor, who publicly supports John's claim, privately admits that "strong possession" is much more on their side than "right" (I,i). All parties concede, then, that young Arthur's claim is legally superior.

Yet such a claim raises serious practical questions, because it challenges the status quo. John is *de facto* king, and Arthur a child. To make the dilemma complete, Arthur has no ambitions to rule and seemingly no talent for leadership. Without the unremitting zeal of his widowed mother, Constance, Arthur would retire into the private world of kindness and love where his virtues shine. Moreover, Constance's uncompromising defense of her son's true claim requires her to seek alliance with the French for an invasion of England. Such an appalling prospect of invasion and civil war inevitably poses the question: is the replacement of John by Arthur worth the price? Which is better, an ongoing regime flawed by uncertain claim and political compromises, or restitution of the "right" by violent and potentially self-destructive means?

Shakespeare refuses to simplify the issues. John is neither a monstrous tyrant nor a martyred hero, although both interpretations were available to Shakespeare in sixteenth-century historical writings. Catholic historians of the late Middle Ages such as Polydore Vergil had uniformly condemned John, partly at least because of his interference with the church. The English Reformation brought about a conscious rewriting of history, and in John Bale's play of *King Johan* (1538, with later revisions) the protagonist is unassailably virtuous. Centuries ahead of his time, John comprehends the true interests of the state in fending off the encroachments of the international church. He fails only because his people are superstitious and his aristocrats are the dupes of Catholic meddling. Bale's play is transparently a warning to Tudor England. This portrait of John as a martyr continues unabated in John Foxe's *Actes and Monuments,* and in the chronicles of Grafton and Holinshed that were based on Foxe. Most virulent of all is the play called *The Troublesome Raigne of King John* (c. 1587–1591), once thought to be by Shakespeare and analyzed by one recent editor as a bad quarto of Shakespeare's text, but now almost universally regarded as the work of some more chauvinistic playwright such as Peele. Although generally close to Shakespeare's play in its narrative of events, it also contains scenes of the most degraded anti-Catholic humor, featuring gross abbots who conceal nuns in their private rooms, and the like. Against such a corrupt institution, the Bastard's plundering is wholly justifiable. John and the Bastard would be invincible, were it not for the base Catholic loyalties of the nobility.

Shakespeare consciously declines to endorse either the Catholic or the Protestant interpretation of King John. (Interestingly, neither side showed any interest in Magna Carta; not until the seventeenth century was that event interpreted as a famous precedent for constitutional restraints imposed on the monarchy.) To be sure, some anticlericalism remains still in the play. John grandly proclaims that "no Italian priest Shall tithe or toll in our dominions." John is "supreme head" of the church and state (the actual title claimed by Henry VIII), defending his people against "this meddling priest" with his "juggling witchcraft" (III,i). Yet Shakespeare's King John is not vindictive against the church. He seizes some of its wealth not as a reprisal but to support his costly military campaigns; and, when he is poisoned by a monk, neither John nor anyone else assumes that a Catholic conspiracy is responsible—as it is in *Troublesome Raigne.* Similarly, the baronial opposition to John is motivated not by secret leanings toward Rome but by understandable revulsion at the apparent murder of Arthur.

Shakespeare's balanced treatment need not merely reflect his own political allegiances, whatever they were. Artistically, *King John* is a study of impasse, of tortured political dilemmas to which there can be no clear answer. How do men behave under such trying circumstances? Shakespeare's play is remarkable for its sensitivity and compassion toward all sides. His most completely sympathetic characters are those innocently caught in the political crossfire, like Arthur and the Lady Blanch. Among the major contenders for power, all except the ruthless Dauphin Lewis are guided by worthy intentions, and yet are forced to make unfortunate and self-contradictory compromises. Constance, for all her virtuous singleness of mind, must seek a French invasion of England. King Philip of France, bound to Constance's cause by all the holy vows of heaven, changes his purpose when England offers a profitable marriage-alliance, and then shifts quickly back again when the papacy demands in the name of the church that Philip punish King John for heresy. Philip's conscience is troubled about both decisions, but what is a king to do when faced with practical choices affecting his people's welfare and his own political safety?

Even Pandulph, the papal legate, can be viewed as a well-intentioned statesman caught in the web of political compromise. Presumably he is sincere in his belief that King John's heresy—in particular, his refusal to accept the Pope's choice, Stephen Langton, as Archbishop of Canterbury—represents a grave threat to Catholic Christendom. Yet Pandulph reveals an unprincipled cunning when he teaches King Philip how to "equivocate" a sacred vow, or instructs the apt young Lewis in Machiavellian intrigue. As Pandulph explains, the French can exploit King John's capture of Arthur by invading England in Arthur's name, thereby forcing John to murder his nephew in order to terminate the rival claim to the throne. Arthur's death will in turn drive the English nobility over to the French side. By this stratagem, the seemingly bad luck of Arthur's capture can neatly be turned to the advantage of France and the international church (III,iv). Lewis learns his lesson only too well. What Pandulph has failed to take into account is the insincerity of Lewis' alliance with papal power. When the legate has achieved through the invasion what he wants—the submission of John—and then tries to call off Lewis' army, Pandulph discovers too late that the young Frenchman cares only for war on his own terms. Pandulph's cunning becomes a weapon turned against himself.

John is, like his enemies, a talented man justly punished by his own perjuries. His failings are serious, but they are also understandable. Given the fact that he is king, his desire to maintain rule serves both his own interests and those of political order generally. The deal by which John bargains away his French territories of Angiers, Touraine, Maine, Poitiers, and the rest, in order to win peace with France, is prudent under the circumstances but a blow to those English dreams of greatness which John professes to uphold. When France immediately repudiates this treaty, John merely gets what he deserves for entering such a deal. His surrender of the crown to the papacy is again the canny result of yielding to the least dangerous of the alternatives available but diminishes John's already shaky authority nonetheless. Most heinous is John's determination to be rid of Arthur. He has compelling reasons, to be sure. As Pandulph predicts, the French invasion of England using Arthur's claim as its pretext forces John to consider Arthur as an immediate threat to himself. (Queen Elizabeth had long agonized over a similar problem with her captive, Mary, Queen of Scots; so long as Mary lived, a Catholic and claimant to the throne, English Catholics had a perennial rallying point.) What is a ruling king to do with a rival claimant in his captivity? As Henry IV also discovers once he has captured Richard II, the logic demanding death is inexorable. Yet such a deed is not only murder, but murder of one's close kinsman and murder of the Lord's anointed in the eyes of those believing Arthur to be rightful king. Furthermore, it is a deed calculated to backfire and punish itself by arousing national resentment and rebellion. John quickly regrets his deed, but we suspect that the regret is in part motivated by fear of the consequences. The same unseen power that protects John against his own worst instincts, momentarily saving the boy from Hubert's instruments of torture, also justly prevents John from obtaining any political benefit from this brief reprieve; Hubert is too late, Arthur dies in a fall, the lords are convinced of John's guilt. With fitting irony, John is punished for his deed after he has decided not to do it and after the murder itself has failed to take place.

The word used to sum up the universal political scheming and oath-breaking in this play is "commodity," or self-interest. The word is introduced by the Bastard, the fascinating choric figure of *King John* whose reactions to the events of the play are so important in shaping our own. The Bastard is an outsider from birth and so not beholden to society for its usual tawdry benefits. As the natural son of the great King Richard Coeur de Lion, the Bastard is a kind of folk hero: he is instinctively royal and yet a commoner, a projection of the audience's sentimental fondness for monarchy and at the same time a hero representing all of society. His quarrel with his effete brother Robert over the inheritance of their father's property comically underscores the futility of the dynastic quarrel between King John and Arthur. In both contentions a will left by the deceased confuses the issue of genealogical priority. Thus John, who defends the Bastard's unconventional claim to his inheritance, discovers a natural ally.

The Bastard is strangely drawn to "commodity" at first. He finds it exhilarating to trust his fortune to war and the King's favor, rather than to the easy comfort of a landed estate. The wars enable him to pursue a quest for self-identity. After learning from his reluctant mother who his real father was, the Bastard must venge himself upon the Duke of Austria, who killed his father. When first confronted with the moral ambiguity of the war, the Bastard's response is mischievous, almost Vicelike. He makes the cunning suggestion, for example, that France and England join against the city of Angiers until it surrenders, after which they may resume fighting one another. Clearly this

Machiavellian proposal embodies, even satirizes, the spirit of "commodity." Yet the Bastard is not motivated by self-interest or a cynical delight in duping men, like the bastard Edmund in *King Lear*. This Bastard's illegitimacy has no such ominous cosmic import. Instead he is at first the detached witty observer, wryly amused at the seemingly inherent absurdity of politics. Although he does protest also that he will worship commodity for his own gain, we never see him doing so. Despite his philosophic detachment, he remains loyal to England and to John. In fact he is the play's greatest patriot.

The supreme test for the Bastard, as for all well-meaning characters and for the audience as well, is the death of Arthur. The Bastard must experience disaffection and even revulsion if he is to retain our sympathy as choric interpreter. Yet his chief function is to triumph over that revulsion, and in so doing to act as counterpart to the more rash English lords. They have come hastily to the conclusion that John is guilty of Arthur's death. This is of course true in the main, but they do not know all the circumstances, and truth as always is more complicated than they suppose. Only the Bastard consistently phrases his condemnation in qualified terms: "It is a damned and a bloody work . . . *If* that it be the work of any hand" (IV,iii). Moreover, the lords have concluded that John's guilt justifies their rebellion. Yet they stoop to "commodity" of the very sort they condemn. They fight for the supposed good of England by allying themselves with Lewis of France. Once again, the ironies of cosmic justice demand that such "commodity" be repaid by treachery. The lords are luckily saved just in time by Lord Melun's revelation of Lewis' plan, just as John had been saved from his own headstrong folly by the kindness of Hubert. The Bastard's decision to remain loyal to John thus proves not only prudent but virtuous. He has led our sympathies through disaffection to acceptance. Rebellion only worsens matters by playing into the hands of opportunists. Loyalty to John is still, in a sense, a kind of "commodity," for it involves compromise and acceptance of politics as morally a world unto itself. Nevertheless, loyalty is a conscientious choice, and is rewarded finally by the accession of young Henry III who at last combines political legitimacy and the will to act.

King John was one of Shakespeare's more popular plays on stage in the eighteenth and nineteenth centuries, the roles of Constance and the Bastard being favorites of the leading actors of the time. It has been rarely seen in the twentieth century, though revivals by the Royal Shakespeare Company have taken place in 1970 and 1974. The play has been adapted for performance by Colley Cibber (1745), Richard Valpy (1800), and Friedrich Dürrenmatt (1968).

The Life and Death of King John

[*Dramatis Personae*

KING JOHN.
PRINCE HENRY, *son to the King.*
ARTHUR, *Duke of Britaine, nephew to the King.*
EARL OF PEMBROKE.
EARL OF ESSEX.
EARL OF SALISBURY.
LORD BIGOT.
HUBERT DE BURGH.
ROBERT FAULCONBRIDGE, *son to Sir Robert Faulconbridge.*
PHILIP THE BASTARD, *his half-brother, also called Richard.*
JAMES GURNEY, *servant to Lady Faulconbridge.*
PETER OF POMFRET, *a prophet.*

KING PHILIP *of France.*
LEWIS, *the Dauphin.*
LYMOGES, DUKE OF AUSTRIA.
CARDINAL PANDULPH, *the Pope's legate.*
MELUN, *a French Lord.*
CHATILLION, *ambassador from France to King John.*

QUEEN ELINOR, *mother to King John.*
CONSTANCE, *mother to Arthur, widow of John's elder brother, Geffrey.*
BLANCH OF SPAIN, *niece to King John.*
LADY FAULCONBRIDGE.

LORDS, CITIZENS *of Angiers,* SHERIFF, HERALDS, OFFICERS, SOLDIERS, MESSENGERS, *and other* ATTENDANTS.

SCENE: *Partly in England, and partly in France.*]

ACT I • SCENE I

Enter King John, Queen Elinor, Pembroke, Essex, and Salisbury, with the Chatillion of France.

KING JOHN
Now, say, Chatillion, what would France with us?

CHATILLION
Thus, after greeting, speaks the King of France
In my behavior to the majesty,

I.i. Location: England. King John's palace.
3 In my behavior in my person and conduct

The borrowed majesty, of England here.

ELINOR
A strange beginning: "borrowed majesty"!

KING JOHN
Silence, good mother; hear the embassy. 6

CHATILLION
Philip of France, in right and true behalf
Of thy deceased brother Geffrey's son,
Arthur Plantagenet, lays most lawful claim
To this fair island and the territories,
To Ireland, Poitiers, Anjou, Touraine, Maine,
Desiring thee to lay aside the sword
Which sways usurpingly these several titles, 13
And put the same into young Arthur's hand,
Thy nephew and right royal sovereign.

KING JOHN
What follows if we disallow of this? 16

CHATILLION
The proud control of fierce and bloody war, 17
To enforce these rights so forcibly withheld.

KING JOHN
Here have we war for war and blood for blood,
Controlment for controlment: so answer France.

CHATILLION
Then take my king's defiance from my mouth,
The farthest limit of my embassy.

KING JOHN
Bear mine to him, and so depart in peace.
Be thou as lightning in the eyes of France,
For ere thou canst report I will be there. 25
The thunder of my cannon shall be heard. 26
So hence! Be thou the trumpet of our wrath
And sullen presage of your own decay. 28
An honorable conduct let him have. 29
Pembroke, look to 't. Farewell, Chatillion.
Exeunt Chatillion and Pembroke.

ELINOR
What now, my son! Have I not ever said
How that ambitious Constance would not cease
Till she had kindled France and all the world
Upon the right and party of her son? 34
This might have been prevented and made whole 35
With very easy arguments of love, 36
Which now the manage of two kingdoms must 37
With fearful bloody issue arbitrate.

KING JOHN
Our strong possession and our right for us.

ELINOR
Your strong possession much more than your right,
Or else it must go wrong with you and me—
So much my conscience whispers in your ear,
Which none but heaven and you and I shall hear.

Enter a Sheriff, [who whispers aside to Essex].

ESSEX
My liege, here is the strangest controversy
Come from the country to be judg'd by you
That e'er I heard. Shall I produce the men?

KING JOHN
Let them approach. [*Sheriff goes to summon the men.*]
Our abbeys and our priories shall pay
This expedition's charge.

Enter Robert Faulconbridge, and Philip [his bastard brother].

What men are you? 49

BASTARD
Your faithful subject I, a gentleman
Born in Northamptonshire, and eldest son,
As I suppose, to Robert Faulconbridge,
A soldier, by the honor-giving hand
Of Cordelion knighted in the field. 54

KING JOHN
What art thou?

ROBERT
The son and heir to that same Faulconbridge.

KING JOHN
Is that the elder, and art thou the heir?
You came not of one mother then, it seems.

BASTARD
Most certain of one mother, mighty King—
That is well known—and, as I think, one father.
But for the certain knowledge of that truth
I put you o'er to heaven and to my mother. 62
Of that I doubt, as all men's children may.

ELINOR
Out on thee, rude man! Thou dost shame thy mother
And wound her honor with this diffidence. 65

BASTARD
I, madam? No, I have no reason for it.
That is my brother's plea and none of mine—
The which if he can prove, 'a pops me out 68
At least from fair five hundred pound a year.
Heaven guard my mother's honor and my land!

KING JOHN
A good blunt fellow. Why, being younger born,
Doth he lay claim to thine inheritance?

BASTARD
I know not why, except to get the land.
But once he slander'd me with bastardy. 74
But whe'er I be as true begot or no, 75
That still I lay upon my mother's head; 76
But that I am as well begot, my liege—
Fair fall the bones that took the pains for me!— 78
Compare our faces and be judge yourself.
If old Sir Robert did beget us both

6 embassy message **13 sways** manages, directs **16 disallow of** reject **17 control** compulsion **25 report** (1) deliver message (2) sound like thunder **26 cannon** (An anachronism, since gunpowder was not employed in Europe until the fourteenth century.) **28 sullen presage** dismal portent, omen. **decay** ruin **29 conduct** escort, guard **34 Upon** in behalf of. **party** cause **35 prevented** foreseen **36 arguments of love** amicable negotiation **37 manage** government

49 This expedition's i.e., the war in France **54 Cordelion** Coeur-de-Lion, Lion-heart, i.e., Richard I **62 put you o'er** refer you **65 diffidence** distrust, suspicion **68 'a** he **74 once** in short **75 whe'er** whether **76 lay . . . head** leave to my mother to give account **78 fall** befall

And were our father, and this son like him,
O old Sir Robert, father, on my knee
I give heaven thanks I was not like to thee!

KING JOHN
Why, what a madcap hath heaven lent us here!

ELINOR
He hath a trick of Cordelion's face;
The accent of his tongue affecteth him.
Do you not read some tokens of my son
In the large composition of this man?

KING JOHN
Mine eye hath well examined his parts
And finds them perfect Richard. Sirrah, speak,
What doth move you to claim your brother's land?

BASTARD
Because he hath a half-face, like my father.
With half that face would he have all my land—
A half-fac'd groat five hundred pound a year!

ROBERT
My gracious liege, when that my father liv'd,
Your brother did employ my father much—

BASTARD
Well, sir, by this you cannot get my land.
Your tale must be how he employ'd my mother.

ROBERT
And once dispatch'd him in an embassy
To Germany, there with the Emperor
To treat of high affairs touching that time.
Th' advantage of his absence took the King
And in the mean time sojourn'd at my father's;
Where how he did prevail I shame to speak,
But truth is truth. Large lengths of seas and shores
Between my father and my mother lay,
As I have heard my father speak himself,
When this same lusty gentleman was got.
Upon his death-bed he by will bequeath'd
His lands to me, and took it on his death
That this my mother's son was none of his;
And if he were, he came into the world
Full fourteen weeks before the course of time.
Then, good my liege, let me have what is mine,
My father's land, as was my father's will.

KING JOHN
Sirrah, your brother is legitimate.
Your father's wife did after wedlock bear him,
And if she did play false, the fault was hers—
Which fault lies on the hazards of all husbands
That marry wives. Tell me, how if my brother,
Who, as you say, took pains to get this son,
Had of your father claim'd this son for his?
In sooth, good friend, your father might have kept
This calf, bred from his cow, from all the world;
In sooth he might. Then, if he were my brother's,
My brother might not claim him, nor your father,
Being none of his, refuse him. This concludes:
My mother's son did get your father's heir;
Your father's heir must have your father's land.

ROBERT
Shall then my father's will be of no force
To dispossess that child which is not his?

BASTARD
Of no more force to dispossess me, sir,
Than was his will to get me, as I think.

ELINOR
Whether hadst thou rather be a Faulconbridge
And, like thy brother, to enjoy thy land,
Or the reputed son of Cordelion
Lord of thy presence and no land beside?

BASTARD
Madam, an if my brother had my shape
And I had his, Sir Robert's his, like him,
And if my legs were two such riding-rods,
My arms such eel-skins stuff'd, my face so thin
That in mine ear I durst not stick a rose
Lest men should say "Look, where three-farthings goes!"
And, to his shape, were heir to all this land,
Would I might never stir from off this place,
I would give it every foot to have this face;
I would not be Sir Nob in any case.

ELINOR
I like thee well. Wilt thou forsake thy fortune,
Bequeath thy land to him, and follow me?
I am a soldier and now bound to France.

BASTARD
Brother, take you my land, I'll take my chance.
Your face hath got five hundred pound a year,
Yet sell your face for five pence and 'tis dear.
Madam, I'll follow you unto the death.

ELINOR
Nay, I would have you go before me thither.

BASTARD
Our country manners give our betters way.

KING JOHN
What is thy name?

BASTARD
Philip, my liege, so is my name begun;
Philip, good old Sir Robert's wife's eldest son.

KING JOHN
From henceforth bear his name whose form thou bearest.
Kneel thou down Philip, but rise more great,
Arise Sir Richard, and Plantagenet.
[*Bastard kneels, then rises.*]

BASTARD
Brother by th' mother's side, give me your hand.
My father gave me honor, yours gave land.

85 trick characteristic look **86 affecteth** resembles **88 large composition** general constitution **90 Sirrah** (Customary form of address to inferiors.) **92 half-face** (1) profile (2) defective, scant face **94 half-fac'd groat** i.e., coin bearing the sovereign's profile. (The groat, worth four pence, is a figure for Robert's insignificance, in antithesis to his fortune, five hundred pounds a year.) **95 when that** when **96 Your brother** i.e., Richard Coeur-de-Lion **108 lusty** merry. **got** begot **110 took . . . death** i.e., swore solemnly (the most solemn oath being a deathbed oath) **119 lies on the hazards** is one of the risks **125 if** even if

127 Being . . . his i.e., even if the Bastard were not sired by him. **refuse** disclaim. **concludes** settles the problem **134 Whether** which of two choices **137 Lord of thy presence** i.e., master of your own person **138 an if** if **139 I had. . . him** i.e., I had Sir Robert's shape as my brother now has **140 riding-rods** switches **142 stick a rose** (The Queen's likeness on the three-farthing coin was distinguished from that on the three half-pence by a rose behind her head. The Bastard's taunt is based on the thinness of the coin.) **144 to his shape** in addition to (inheriting) his physical characteristics **147 Nob** (Diminutive of *Robert;* with a possible play on *head.*) **156 give . . . way** yield precedence to our superiors

Now blessed be the hour, by night or day,
When I was got, Sir Robert was away!

ELINOR
The very spirit of Plantagenet!
I am thy grandam, Richard; call me so.

BASTARD
Madam, by chance but not by truth; what though?
Something about, a little from the right,
In at the window, or else o'er the hatch.
Who dares not stir by day must walk by night,
And have is have, however men do catch.
Near or far off, well won is still well shot,
And I am I, howe'er I was begot.

KING JOHN
Go, Faulconbridge, now hast thou thy desire;
A landless knight makes thee a landed squire.
Come, madam, and come, Richard, we must speed
For France, for France, for it is more than need.

BASTARD
Brother, adieu: good fortune come to thee!
For thou wast got i' th' way of honesty.
Exeunt all but Bastard.
A foot of honor better than I was,
But many a many foot of land the worse.
Well, now can I make any Joan a lady.
"Good den, Sir Richard!"—"God-a-mercy, fellow!"—
And if his name be George, I'll call him Peter,
For new-made honor doth forget men's names;
'Tis too respective and too sociable
For your conversion. Now your traveler,
He and his toothpick at my worship's mess,
And when my knightly stomach is suffic'd,
Why then I suck my teeth and catechize
My picked man of countries: "My dear sir,"
Thus, leaning on mine elbow, I begin,
"I shall beseech you"—that is question now;
And then comes answer like an Absey book:
"O sir," says answer, "at your best command;
At your employment; at your service, sir."
"No sir," says question, "I, sweet sir, at yours";
And so, ere answer knows what question would,
Saving in dialogue of compliment,
And talking of the Alps and Apennines,
The Pyrenean and the river Po,
It draws toward supper in conclusion so.
But this is worshipful society
And fits the mounting spirit like myself,
For he is but a bastard to the time
That doth not smack of observation.
And so am I, whether I smack or no;
And not alone in habit and device,
Exterior form, outward accoutrement,
But from the inward motion to deliver
Sweet, sweet, sweet poison for the age's tooth,
Which, though I will not practice to deceive,
Yet, to avoid deceit, I mean to learn;
For it shall strew the footsteps of my rising.
But who comes in such haste in riding-robes?
What woman-post is this? Hath she no husband
That will take pains to blow a horn before her?

Enter Lady Faulconbridge and James Gurney.

O me! 'Tis my mother. How now, good lady?
What brings you here to court so hastily?

LADY FAULCONBRIDGE
Where is that slave, thy brother? Where is he,
That holds in chase mine honor up and down?

BASTARD
My brother Robert, old Sir Robert's son?
Colbrand the giant, that same mighty man?
Is it Sir Robert's son that you seek so?

LADY FAULCONBRIDGE
Sir Robert's son! Ay, thou unreverend boy,
Sir Robert's son. Why scorn'st thou at Sir Robert?
He is Sir Robert's son, and so art thou.

BASTARD
James Gurney, wilt thou give us leave awhile?

GURNEY
Good leave, good Philip.

BASTARD Philip? Sparrow! James,
There's toys abroad; anon I'll tell thee more.
Exit James.
Madam, I was not old Sir Robert's son;
Sir Robert might have eat his part in me
Upon Good Friday and ne'er broke his fast.
Sir Robert could do well—marry, to confess—
Could he get me! Sir Robert could not do it;
We know his handiwork. Therefore, good mother,
To whom am I beholding for these limbs?
Sir Robert never holp to make this leg.

LADY FAULCONBRIDGE
Hast thou conspired with thy brother too,
That for thine own gain shouldst defend mine honor?
What means this scorn, thou most untoward knave?

BASTARD
Knight, knight, good mother, Basilisco-like.
What! I am dubb'd; I have it on my shoulder.

169 not by truth not honorably, not chastely **170 Something about** somewhat roundabout, clandestinely **171 hatch** lower half door. (*O'er the hatch* means clandestinely, out of wedlock.) **177 a landless knight** i.e., the Bastard, who is willing to trade his inheritance for a knighthood **184 Joan** (Frequently used to designate any girl, usually of the lower class.) **185 Good den** good even. (The Bastard imagines himself, in his new title, encountering a lower-class person.) **God-a-mercy** God reward you **188 respective** considerate **189 conversion** change of status, acquistion of *new-made honor* **190 toothpick** (An affectation associated with foreign travel.) **my worship's mess** i.e., my dinner table **192 suck my teeth** (i.e., in contrast to the use of toothpick by the *traveler*) **193 picked** (1) refined (2) having picked his teeth **196 Absey** ABC, primer **200 would** intends, asks **201 dialogue of compliment** polite but inane conversation **207–208 a bastard . . . observation** i.e., not a true son of the times unless he observes and practices obsequiousness

209 so am I i.e., I am a bastard in that sense of scorning polite mannerisms **210 habit** attire. **device** coat of arms **212 from . . . motion** lacking the impulse or inclination **213 Sweet . . . poison** flattery. **tooth** i.e., sweet tooth, appetite **215 deceit** being deceived **216 it . . . rising** i.e., deceitful flattery will inevitably accompany my rise in importance, just as rushes are strewn on the floors of great men **218 woman-post** female messenger **219 blow a horn** (The ordinary signal of approach; with a punning reference to the horn of cuckoldry.) **223 holds in chase** pursues **225 Colbrand the giant** legendary Danish giant slain by Guy of Warwick in a popular romance named after its hero **231 Philip? Sparrow** i.e., call me Philip no more, a name commonly used for sparrows (because of their "Phip"-like chirp), since I'm now Sir Richard **232 toys** rumors, follies, interesting events **234 eat** eaten. (Pronounced *et*.) **237 get** beget **239 beholding** beholden **240 holp** helped **243 untoward** unmannerly **244 Basilisco-like** (The character Basilisco in the play *Solyman and Perseda,* presumably by Kyd, braggart-like insists on his knighthood but nevertheless is called *Knave* by his servant.) **245 dubb'd** made a knight by a touch of the sword on the shoulder

But, mother, I am not Sir Robert's son;
I have disclaim'd Sir Robert and my land;
Legitimation, name, and all is gone.
Then, good my mother, let me know my father;
Some proper man, I hope. Who was it, mother?

LADY FAULCONBRIDGE
Hast thou denied thyself a Faulconbridge?

BASTARD
As faithfully as I deny the devil.

LADY FAULCONBRIDGE
King Richard Cordelion was thy father.
By long and vehement suit I was seduc'd
To make room for him in my husband's bed.
Heaven lay not my transgression to my charge!
Thou art the issue of my dear offense
Which was so strongly urg'd past my defense.

BASTARD
Now, by this light, were I to get again,
Madam, I would not wish a better father.
Some sins do bear their privilege on earth,
And so doth yours; your fault was not your folly.
Needs must you lay your heart at his dispose,
Subjected tribute to commanding love,
Against whose fury and unmatched force
The aweless lion could not wage the fight,
Nor keep his princely heart from Richard's hand.
He that perforce robs lions of their hearts
May easily win a woman's. Ay, my mother,
With all my heart I thank thee for my father!
Who lives and dares but say thou didst not well
When I was got, I'll send his soul to hell.
Come, lady, I will show thee to my kin;
And they shall say, when Richard me begot,
If thou hadst said him nay, it had been sin.
Who says it was, he lies; I say 'twas not. *Exeunt.*

[ACT II] • SCENE [I]

Enter, before Angiers, Philip King of France, Lewis [the] Dauphin, Austria, Constance, Arthur [and Attendants].

KING PHILIP
Before Angiers well met, brave Austria.
Arthur, that great forerunner of thy blood,
Richard, that robb'd the lion of his heart
And fought the holy wars in Palestine,
By this brave duke came early to his grave;
And for amends to his posterity,
At our importance hither is he come,
To spread his colors, boy, in thy behalf,
And to rebuke the usurpation
Of thy unnatural uncle, English John.
Embrace him, love him, give him welcome hither.

ARTHUR
God shall forgive you Cordelion's death
The rather that you give his offspring life,
Shadowing their right under your wings of war.
I give you welcome with a powerless hand,
But with a heart full of unstained love.
Welcome before the gates of Angiers, Duke.

KING PHILIP
A noble boy! Who would not do thee right?

AUSTRIA
Upon thy cheek lay I this zealous kiss,
As seal to this indenture of my love, [*Kisses Arthur.*]
That to my home I will no more return
Till Angiers and the right thou hast in France,
Together with that pale, that white-fac'd shore,
Whose foot spurns back the ocean's roaring tides
And coops from other lands her islanders,
Even till that England, hedg'd in with the main,
That water-walled bulwark, still secure
And confident from foreign purposes,
Even till that utmost corner of the west
Salute thee for her king. Till then, fair boy,
Will I not think of home, but follow arms.

CONSTANCE
O, take his mother's thanks, a widow's thanks,
Till your strong hand shall help to give him strength
To make a more requital to your love!

AUSTRIA
The peace of heaven is theirs that lift their swords
In such a just and charitable war.

KING PHILIP
Well then, to work. Our cannon shall be bent
Against the brows of this resisting town.
Call for our chiefest men of discipline,
To cull the plots of best advantages.
We'll lay before this town our royal bones,
Wade to the market-place in Frenchmen's blood,
But we will make it subject to this boy.

CONSTANCE
Stay for an answer to your embassy,
Lest unadvis'd you stain your swords with blood.
My Lord Chatillion may from England bring
That right in peace which here we urge in war,
And then we shall repent each drop of blood
That hot rash haste so indirectly shed.

Enter Chatillion.

KING PHILIP
A wonder, lady! Lo, upon thy wish,
Our messenger Chatillion is arriv'd.
What England says, say briefly, gentle lord;

250 proper handsome, fine **257 dear** (1) precious, costly (2) loving **259 get** be conceived **261 do . . . earth** i.e., are excusable, venial **263 dispose** disposal **266 aweless lion** (During his imprisonment by the Duke of Austria, according to legend, Coeur-de-Lion slew the Duke's son and as punishment was given to a hungry lion. When the lion attacked him, he slew it by thrusting his hand down its throat and tearing out its heart, which he is supposed to have eaten.) **268 perforce** forcibly

II.i. Location: France. Before Angiers. (The French and Austrian forces enter from opposite sides before the "gates" of Angiers seen backstage.)
s.d. Austria (The Duke of Austria wears a lion-skin which he took from Coeur-de-Lion; see l. 292.) **2 forerunner** ancestor. (Richard was actually not a direct ancestor of Arthur, but his uncle.) **5 By . . . duke** (A confusion of the Duke of Austria with Viscount Limoges, before whose castle Richard was mortally wounded. The roles of the two were combined in *The Troublesome Raigne of King John* as they are in this play.)

7 importance importunity **14 Shadowing** sheltering **23 pale . . . shore** i.e., the chalk cliffs at Dover **25 coops** encloses for defense **27 still** perpetually **34 more** greater **37 bent** directed **39 men of discipline** men trained in military strategy **40 To . . . advantages** to select positions which are most favorable for attack **45 unadvis'd** rashly **49 indirectly** wrongfully, misdirectedly

We coldly pause for thee. Chatillion, speak.

CHATILLION

Then turn your forces from this paltry siege
And stir them up against a mightier task.
England, impatient of your just demands,
Hath put himself in arms. The adverse winds,
Whose leisure I have stay'd, have given him time
To land his legions all as soon as I.
His marches are expedient to this town,
His forces strong, his soldiers confident.
With him along is come the mother-queen,
An Ate, stirring him to blood and strife;
With her her niece, the Lady Blanch of Spain;
With them a bastard of the king's deceas'd;
And all th' unsettled humors of the land,
Rash, inconsiderate, fiery voluntaries,
With ladies' faces and fierce dragons' spleens,
Have sold their fortunes at their native homes,
Bearing their birthrights proudly on their backs,
To make a hazard of new fortunes here.
In brief, a braver choice of dauntless spirits
Than now the English bottoms have waft o'er
Did never float upon the swelling tide
To do offense and scath in Christendom.
The interruption of their churlish drums
Cuts off more circumstance. They are at hand,
Drum beats.
To parley or to fight; therefore prepare.

KING PHILIP

How much unlook'd for is this expedition!

AUSTRIA

By how much unexpected, by so much
We must awake endeavor for defense,
For courage mounteth with occasion.
Let them be welcome then; we are prepar'd.

Enter King [John] of England, Bastard, Queen [Elinor], Blanch, Pembroke, and others.

KING JOHN

Peace be to France, if France in peace permit
Our just and lineal entrance to our own.
If not, bleed France, and peace ascend to heaven,
Whiles we, God's wrathful agent, do correct
Their proud contempt that beats His peace to heaven.

KING PHILIP

Peace be to England, if that war return
From France to England, there to live in peace.
England we love, and for that England's sake
With burden of our armor here we sweat.
This toil of ours should be a work of thine;
But thou from loving England art so far
That thou hast under-wrought his lawful king,
Cut off the sequence of posterity,
Outfaced infant state, and done a rape
Upon the maiden virtue of the crown.
Look here upon thy brother Geffrey's face:
These eyes, these brows, were molded out of his;
This little abstract doth contain that large
Which died in Geffrey, and the hand of time
Shall draw this brief into as huge a volume.
That Geffrey was thy elder brother born,
And this his son. England was Geffrey's right
And this is Geffrey's. In the name of God
How comes it then that thou art call'd a king,
When living blood doth in these temples beat,
Which owe the crown that thou o'ermasterest?

KING JOHN

From whom hast thou this great commission, France,
To draw my answer from thy articles?

KING PHILIP

From that supernal judge, that stirs good thoughts
In any breast of strong authority,
To look into the blots and stains of right.
That judge hath made me guardian to this boy,
Under whose warrant I impeach thy wrong
And by whose help I mean to chastise it.

KING JOHN

Alack, thou dost usurp authority.

KING PHILIP

Excuse it is to beat usurping down.

ELINOR

Who is it thou dost call usurper, France?

CONSTANCE

Let me make answer: thy usurping son.

ELINOR

Out, insolent! Thy bastard shall be king,
That thou mayst be a queen, and check the world!

CONSTANCE

My bed was ever to thy son as true
As thine was to thy husband, and this boy
Liker in feature to his father Geffrey
Than thou and John in manners—being as like
As rain to water, or devil to his dam.
My boy a bastard? By my soul, I think
His father never was so true begot.
It cannot be, an if thou wert his mother.

ELINOR

There's a good mother, boy, that blots thy father.

CONSTANCE

There's a good grandam, boy, that would blot thee.

AUSTRIA

Peace!

53 coldly calmly **58 stay'd** waited for **60 expedient** speedy **63 Ate** Greek goddess of discord **64 niece** i.e., granddaughter **65 of . . . deceas'd** of the deceased king's, i.e., Richard's **66 unsettled humors** i.e., disgruntled individuals **67 voluntaries** volunteers **68 With ladies' faces** i.e., beardless. **fierce dragons' spleens** i.e., utmost fierceness. (The spleen was thought to be the seat of the passions.) **70 Bearing . . . backs** i.e., having sold everything to obtain armor **72 choice** picked company **73 bottoms** i.e., ships. **waft** wafted **75 scath** harm **77 circumstance** detailed reporting **79 expedition** speed **82 occasion** emergency **85 lineal** by right of birth **91 England's** i.e., Arthur's, whose claim to England the French King is supporting **93 This . . . thine** i.e., you should be supporting our cause also, since it is in England's interest

95 under-wrought his undermined its **96 sequence of posterity** lawful succession **97 Outfaced infant state** intimidated the majesty of a boy-king **101 little abstract** abridgement or epitome **101–102 doth . . . Geffrey** contains that which, in its complete form, died in Geffrey **103 draw this brief** enlarge this epitome **106 this** i.e., Angiers, or Arthur himself, or the English crown **109 owe** own **111 draw . . . articles** i.e., make me answer your charges **116 whose** i.e., the supreme judge's, God's. **impeach** accuse **119 Excuse . . . down** i.e., what you call my usurping authority is in fact a resisting and defeating of usurpation **123 check** control **128 dam** mother. (Constance says that Arthur is more like his father, and therefore no bastard, than John is like his mother—a resemblance that would not rule out bastardy, especially when the two are as alike as the devil and his mother. Constance goes on to wonder if John's brother Geffrey might also be a bastard.) **132 blots** slanders

BASTARD Hear the crier.
AUSTRIA What the devil art thou?
BASTARD
One that will play the devil, sir, with you,
An 'a may catch your hide and you alone.
You are the hare of whom the proverb goes,
Whose valor plucks dead lions by the beard.
I'll smoke your skin-coat, an I catch you right.
Sirrah, look to 't; i' faith, I will, i' faith.
BLANCH
O, well did he become that lion's robe
That did disrobe the lion of that robe!
BASTARD
It lies as sightly on the back of him
As great Alcides' shows upon an ass.
But, ass, I'll take that burden from your back,
Or lay on that shall make your shoulders crack.
AUSTRIA
What cracker is this same that deafs our ears
With this abundance of superfluous breath?
King Philip, determine what we shall do straight.
KING PHILIP
Women and fools, break off your conference.
King John, this is the very sum of all:
England and Ireland, Anjou, Touraine, Maine,
In right of Arthur do I claim of thee.
Wilt thou resign them and lay down thy arms?
KING JOHN
My life as soon. I do defy thee, France.
Arthur of Britaine, yield thee to my hand,
And out of my dear love I'll give thee more
Than e'er the coward hand of France can win.
Submit thee, boy.
ELINOR Come to thy grandam, child.
CONSTANCE
Do, child, go to it grandam, child;
Give grandam kingdom, and it grandam will
Give it a plum, a cherry, and a fig.
There's a good grandam.
ARTHUR Good my mother, peace!
I would that I were low laid in my grave.
I am not worth this coil that's made for me.
[*Weeps.*]
ELINOR
His mother shames him so, poor boy, he weeps.
CONSTANCE
Now shame upon you, whe'er she does or no!
His grandam's wrongs, and not his mother's shames,
Draws those heaven-moving pearls from his poor eyes,
Which heaven shall take in nature of a fee.
Ay, with these crystal beads heaven shall be brib'd
To do him justice and revenge on you.
ELINOR
Thou monstrous slanderer of heaven and earth!
CONSTANCE
Thou monstrous injurer of heaven and earth!
Call not me slanderer; thou and thine usurp
The dominations, royalties, and rights
Of this oppressed boy. This is thy eldest son's son,
Infortunate in nothing but in thee.
Thy sins are visited in this poor child;
The canon of the law is laid on him,
Being but the second generation
Removed from thy sin-conceiving womb.
KING JOHN
Bedlam, have done.
CONSTANCE I have but this to say,
That he is not only plagued for her sin,
But God hath made her sin and her the plague
On this removed issue, plagu'd for her
And with her plague; her sin his injury,
Her injury the beadle to her sin,
All punish'd in the person of this child,
And all for her. A plague upon her!
ELINOR
Thou unadvised scold, I can produce
A will that bars the title of thy son.
CONSTANCE
Ay, who doubts that? A will, a wicked will,
A woman's will, a cank'red grandam's will!
KING PHILIP
Peace, lady! Pause, or be more temperate.
It ill beseems this presence to cry aim
To these ill-tuned repetitions.
Some trumpet summon hither to the walls
These men of Angiers. Let us hear them speak
Whose title they admit, Arthur's or John's.

Trumpet sounds. Enter a Citizen upon the walls.

FIRST CITIZEN
Who is it that hath warn'd us to the walls?
KING PHILIP
'Tis France, for England.
KING JOHN England, for itself.
You men of Angiers, and my loving subjects—
KING PHILIP
You loving men of Angiers, Arthur's subjects,
Our trumpet call'd you to this gentle parle—
KING JOHN
For our advantage; therefore hear us first.
These flags of France, that are advanced here

134 Hear the crier (A mocking suggestion by the Bastard that Austria's call for silence likens him to the town crier.) **136 An 'a** if he. **hide** i.e., the lion's skin Austria wears in celebration of his triumph over Richard Coeur-de-Lion **137 the proverb** i.e., "even hares may insult the dead lion." (This proverb occurs in Erasmus' *Adages.*) **139 smoke** thrash, beat **141 he** i.e., Richard Coeur-de-Lion **143 him** i.e., the Duke of Austria **144 Alcides** Hercules, who slew the Nemean lion as one of his twelve labors and thereafter wore its pelt **146 that** that which **147 cracker** i.e., boaster (with a play on *crack,* l. 146) **149 straight** at once **150 fools** children **156 Britaine** Brittany **160 Do . . . grandam** (Contemptuous baby talk.) **165 coil** disturbance, fuss

176 dominations dominions, sovereignties **177 eldest son's son** i.e., eldest grandchild, not son of the eldest son **179 visited** punished **180 canon . . . law** i.e., that the sins of parents shall be visited upon their children to the third and fourth generation **183 Bedlam** lunatic **184 he** i.e., Arthur. **her sin** i.e., Elinor's alleged adultery when she conceived John. (See ll. 124 ff.) **185 her sin** i.e., John, the issue of her sin **186 removed issue** distant descendant, i.e., Arthur. **for her** on her account **187 with her plague** i.e., by the offspring, John, with whom she was cursed. **his injury** i.e., the wrong done to Arthur **188 Her injury** Elinor's wrong deeds, which act as the officer *(beadle)* to incite her son John *(her sin)* on to further wrongs **191 unadvised** rash **192 A will** i.e., according to Holinshed and other chroniclers, the final testament of Richard Coeur-de-Lion naming John as his heir and disinheriting Arthur who had been named heir in a previous will. (But Constance deliberately takes *will* to mean *willfulness.*) **196 ill . . . presence** is not proper in the presence of royalty **196–197 cry aim To** encourage. (An archery term.) **198 trumpet** trumpeter **200 s.d. upon the walls** i.e., in the upper gallery rearstage. (Throughout this scene, the tiring house façade is visualized as the walls of Angiers.) **201 warn'd** summoned **205 parle** parley **207 advanced** raised

Before the eye and prospect of your town,
Have hither march'd to your endamagement.
The cannons have their bowels full of wrath,
And ready mounted are they to spit forth
Their iron indignation 'gainst your walls.
All preparation for a bloody siege
And merciless proceeding by these French
Confronts your city's eyes, your winking gates;
And but for our approach those sleeping stones,
That as a waist doth girdle you about,
By the compulsion of their ordinance
By this time from their fixed beds of lime
Had been dishabited, and wide havoc made
For bloody power to rush upon your peace.
But on the sight of us, your lawful king,
Who painfully with much expedient march
Have brought a countercheck before your gates,
To save unscratch'd your city's threat'ned cheeks,
Behold, the French amaz'd vouchsafe a parle;
And now, instead of bullets wrapp'd in fire,
To make a shaking fever in your walls,
They shoot but calm words folded up in smoke,
To make a faithless error in your ears.
Which trust accordingly, kind citizens,
And let us in, your king, whose labor'd spirits,
Forwearied in this action of swift speed,
Craves harborage within your city walls.

KING PHILIP
When I have said, make answer to us both.
Lo, in this right hand, whose protection
Is most divinely vow'd upon the right
Of him it holds, stands young Plantagenet,
Son to the elder brother of this man,
And king o'er him and all that he enjoys.
For this down-trodden equity, we tread
In warlike march these greens before your town,
Being no further enemy to you
Than the constraint of hospitable zeal
In the relief of this oppressed child
Religiously provokes. Be pleased then
To pay that duty which you truly owe
To him that owes it, namely this young prince;
And then our arms, like to a muzzled bear,
Save in aspect, hath all offense seal'd up.
Our cannons' malice vainly shall be spent
Against th' invulnerable clouds of heaven,
And with a blessed and unvex'd retire,
With unhack'd swords and helmets all unbruis'd,
We will bear home that lusty blood again
Which here we came to spout against your town,
And leave your children, wives, and you in peace.
But if you fondly pass our proffer'd offer,
'Tis not the roundure of your old-fac'd walls
Can hide you from our messengers of war,
Though all these English and their discipline
Were harbor'd in their rude circumference.
Then tell us, shall your city call us lord,
In that behalf which we have challeng'd it?
Or shall we give the signal to our rage
And stalk in blood to our possession?

FIRST CITIZEN
In brief, we are the King of England's subjects.
For him, and in his right, we hold this town.

KING JOHN
Acknowledge then the king, and let me in.

FIRST CITIZEN
That can we not; but he that proves the king,
To him will we prove loyal. Till that time
Have we ramm'd up our gates against the world.

KING JOHN
Doth not the crown of England prove the king?
And if not that, I bring you witnesses,
Twice fifteen thousand hearts of England's breed—

BASTARD
Bastards, and else.

KING JOHN
To verify our title with their lives.

KING PHILIP
As many and as well-born bloods as those—

BASTARD
Some bastards too.

KING PHILIP
Stand in his face to contradict his claim.

FIRST CITIZEN
Till you compound whose right is worthiest,
We for the worthiest hold the right from both.

KING JOHN
Then God forgive the sin of all those souls
That to their everlasting residence,
Before the dew of evening fall, shall fleet,
In dreadful trial of our kingdom's king!

KING PHILIP
Amen, amen! Mount, chevaliers! To arms!

BASTARD
Saint George, that swing'd the dragon, and e'er
since
Sits on 's horse back at mine hostess' door,
Teach us some fence! [*To Austria.*] Sirrah, were I at
home,
At your den, sirrah, with your lioness,
I would set an ox-head to your lion's hide,
And make a monster of you.

AUSTRIA Peace! No more.

BASTARD
O, tremble, for you hear the lion roar.

KING JOHN
Up higher to the plain, where we'll set forth
In best appointment all our regiments.

BASTARD
Speed then, to take advantage of the field.

215 winking closed **218 their** i.e., *these French* (l. 214) **220 dishabited** dislodged **226 amaz'd** stunned **230 faithless error** perfidious lie **232 labor'd** oppressed with labor **233 Forwearied in** exhausted by **236–238 in . . . holds** i.e., led by my right hand, which hand is most sacredly committed to defend the right of the person whose hand it now holds **241 equity** justice, right **248 owes** owns **250 Save in aspect** except in appearance **253 retire** withdrawal **258 fondly pass** foolishly pass up **259 roundure** enclosure, circumference **260 messengers** i.e., cannonballs

264 In . . . which on behalf of him for whom **270 proves** i.e., proves himself, proves to be **276 else** others **278 bloods** men of mettle and of good breeding **280 in his face** opposite to him **281 compound** settle, agree **285 fleet** leave (their bodies) **288 swing'd** whipped, thrashed **289 Sits . . . door** (One of the most common signs at tavern doors was that of St. George and the Dragon.) **290 fence** skill in fencing, defense **292 set an ox-head** i.e., give you the horns of a cuckold

KING PHILIP
It shall be so; and at the other hill
Command the rest to stand. God and our right!
Exeunt. [*The citizens remain above.*]

Here after excursions, enter the Herald of France, with trumpets, to the gates.

FRENCH HERALD
You men of Angiers, open wide your gates,
And let young Arthur, Duke of Britaine, in,
Who by the hand of France this day hath made
Much work for tears in many an English mother,
Whose sons lie scattered on the bleeding ground.
Many a widow's husband groveling lies,
Coldly embracing the discolored earth,
And victory, with little loss, doth play
Upon the dancing banners of the French,
Who are at hand, triumphantly display'd,
To enter conquerors and to proclaim
Arthur of Britaine England's king and yours.

Enter English Herald, with trumpet.

ENGLISH HERALD
Rejoice, you men of Angiers, ring your bells!
King John, your king and England's, doth approach,
Commander of this hot malicious day.
Their armors, that march'd hence so silver-bright,
Hither return all gilt with Frenchmen's blood.
There stuck no plume in any English crest
That is removed by a staff of France.
Our colors do return in those same hands
That did display them when we first march'd forth;
And, like a jolly troop of huntsmen, come
Our lusty English, all with purpled hands,
Dy'd in the dying slaughter of their foes.
Open your gates and give the victors way.

FIRST CITIZEN
Heralds, from off our tow'rs we might behold,
From first to last, the onset and retire
Of both your armies, whose equality
By our best eyes cannot be censured.
Blood hath bought blood, and blows have answer'd blows;
Strength match'd with strength, and power confronted power.
Both are alike, and both alike we like.
One must prove greatest. While they weigh so even,
We hold our town for neither, yet for both.

Enter the two Kings, with their powers, at several doors.

KING JOHN
France, hast thou yet more blood to cast away?
Say, shall the current of our right run on,
Whose passage, vex'd with thy impediment,
Shall leave his native channel and o'erswell
With course disturb'd even thy confining shores,
Unless thou let his silver water keep
A peaceful progress to the ocean?

KING PHILIP
England, thou hast not sav'd one drop of blood
In this hot trial more than we of France,
Rather lost more. And by this hand I swear,
That sways the earth this climate overlooks,
Before we will lay down our just-borne arms
We'll put thee down, 'gainst whom these arms we bear,
Or add a royal number to the dead,
Gracing the scroll that tells of this war's loss
With slaughter coupled to the name of kings.

BASTARD
Ha, majesty! How high thy glory tow'rs
When the rich blood of kings is set on fire!
O, now doth Death line his dead chaps with steel;
The swords of soldiers are his teeth, his fangs;
And now he feasts, mousing the flesh of men,
In undetermin'd differences of kings.
Why stand these royal fronts amazed thus?
Cry "havoc," kings! Back to the stained field,
You equal potents, fiery kindled spirits!
Then let confusion of one part confirm
The other's peace. Till then, blows, blood, and death!

KING JOHN
Whose party do the townsmen yet admit?

KING PHILIP
Speak, citizens, for England. Who's your king?

FIRST CITIZEN
The king of England, when we know the king.

KING PHILIP
Know him in us, that here hold up his right.

KING JOHN
In us, that are our own great deputy,
And bear possession of our person here,
Lord of our presence, Angiers, and of you.

FIRST CITIZEN
A greater pow'r than we denies all this,
And, till it be undoubted, we do lock
Our former scruple in our strong-barr'd gates,
King'd of our fears, until our fears, resolv'd,
Be by some certain king purg'd and depos'd.

BASTARD
By heaven, these scroyles of Angiers flout you, kings,
And stand securely on their battlements
As in a theatre, whence they gape and point
At your industrious scenes and acts of death.
Your royal presences be rul'd by me:
Do like the mutines of Jerusalem,

299 s.d. excursions skirmishes, sorties **314 Commander** victor. **hot malicious day** a day hotly and violently contested **316 gilt** gilded in red **318 staff** spear **323 Dy'd . . . foes** (Huntsmen dipped their hands in the blood of a slain deer to celebrate the slaughter.) **325 First Citizen** (The Folio text reads *Hubert* here and throughout the remainder of this scene.) **328 censured** estimated (?) impugned (?) **333 s.d. powers** armies. **several** separate

344 climate portion of the sky **347 a royal number** i.e., a king's name **350 glory** vainglory **352 chaps** jaws **354 mousing** tearing, gnawing **355 undetermin'd differences** unsettled quarrels **356 royal fronts** i.e., faces of kings **357 Cry "havoc"** proclaim a general slaughter with no taking of prisoners **358 potents** potentates **359 confusion** destruction, overthrow. **part** faction, party **361 yet** now **371 King'd of** ruled by **373 scroyles** scoundrels **378 mutines** mutineers. **Jerusalem** (During the siege of Jerusalem by Titus, A.D. 70, two rival Jewish factions united to resist the Romans.)

Be friends awhile and both conjointly bend
Your sharpest deeds of malice on this town.
By east and west let France and England mount
Their battering cannon charged to the mouths,
Till their soul-fearing clamors have brawl'd down 383
The flinty ribs of this contemptuous city.
I'd play incessantly upon these jades, 385
Even till unfenced desolation 386
Leave them as naked as the vulgar air. 387
That done, dissever your united strengths,
And part your mingled colors once again;
Turn face to face and bloody point to point.
Then, in a moment, Fortune shall cull forth
Out of one side her happy minion, 392
To whom in favor she shall give the day,
And kiss him with a glorious victory.
How like you this wild counsel, mighty states? 395
Smacks it not something of the policy? 396

KING JOHN
Now, by the sky that hangs above our heads,
I like it well. France, shall we knit our pow'rs
And lay this Angiers even with the ground,
Then after fight who shall be king of it?

BASTARD
An if thou hast the mettle of a king,
Being wrong'd as we are by this peevish town, 402
Turn thou the mouth of thy artillery,
As we will ours, against these saucy walls;
And when that we have dash'd them to the ground,
Why then defy each other, and pell-mell
Make work upon ourselves, for heaven or hell.

KING PHILIP
Let it be so. Say, where will you assault?

KING JOHN
We from the west will send destruction
Into this city's bosom.

AUSTRIA
I from the north.

KING PHILIP Our thunder from the south
Shall rain their drift of bullets on this town. 412

BASTARD
O prudent discipline! From north to south 413
Austria and France shoot in each other's mouth.
I'll stir them to it.—Come, away, away!
[*The armies start to move.*]

FIRST CITIZEN
Hear us, great kings! Vouchsafe awhile to stay,
And I shall show you peace and fair-fac'd league,
Win you this city without stroke or wound,
Rescue those breathing lives to die in beds
That here come sacrifices for the field.
Persever not, but hear me, mighty kings.

KING JOHN
Speak on with favor; we are bent to hear. 422

FIRST CITIZEN
That daughter there of Spain, the Lady Blanch,
Is near to England. Look upon the years 424
Of Lewis the Dauphin and that lovely maid.
If lusty love should go in quest of beauty,
Where should he find it fairer than in Blanch?
If zealous love should go in search of virtue, 428
Where should he find it purer than in Blanch?
If love ambitious sought a match of birth, 430
Whose veins bound richer blood than Lady Blanch? 431
Such as she is, in beauty, virtue, birth,
Is the young Dauphin every way complete. 433
If not complete of, say he is not she, 434
And she again wants nothing, to name want, 435
If want it be not that she is not he. 436
He is the half part of a blessed man,
Left to be finished by such as she;
And she a fair divided excellence,
Whose fullness of perfection lies in him.
O, two such silver currents, when they join,
Do glorify the banks that bound them in;
And two such shores to two such streams made one,
Two such controlling bounds shall you be, kings,
To these two princes, if you marry them.
This union shall do more than battery can 446
To our fast-closed gates; for at this match, 447
With swifter spleen than powder can enforce, 448
The mouth of passage shall we fling wide ope,
And give you entrance; but without this match,
The sea enraged is not half so deaf,
Lions more confident, mountains and rocks
More free from motion, no, not Death himself
In mortal fury half so peremptory,
As we to keep this city.

BASTARD Here's a stay 455
That shakes the rotten carcass of old Death
Out of his rags! Here's a large mouth, indeed,
That spits forth death and mountains, rocks and seas,
Talks as familiarly of roaring lions
As maids of thirteen do of puppy-dogs.
What cannoneer begot this lusty blood?
He speaks plain cannon fire and smoke and bounce. 462
He gives the bastinado with his tongue. 463
Our ears are cudgel'd; not a word of his
But buffets better than a fist of France.
'Zounds! I was never so bethump'd with words 466
Since I first call'd my brother's father dad.
[*The French confer apart.*]

ELINOR
Son, list to this conjunction, make this match. 468
Give with our niece a dowry large enough,
For by this knot thou shalt so surely tie
Thy now unsur'd assurance to the crown,
That yon green boy shall have no sun to ripe 472

383 soul-fearing inspiring fear in the soul **385 play . . . jades** i.e., fire cannon repeatedly upon these wretches. (*Jades* are ill-conditioned horses.) **386 unfenced** defenseless **387 vulgar** common **392 minion** favorite **395 states** kings **396 the policy** the art of politics, a canny maneuver **402 peevish** stubborn **412 drift** shower **413 discipline** military skill **422 favor** permission. **bent** inclined

424 near to England a near relative of King John, i.e., his niece **428 zealous** pious **430 of birth** i.e., of equal royal rank **431 bound** contain **433 complete** accomplished, perfect **434–436 If . . . he** (The idea here appears to be that the two young people lack only each other to be perfect in themselves.) **435 wants** lacks **446 battery** artillery **447 match** (1) marriage (2) fire used to ignite gunpowder **448 spleen** i.e., eager violent energy **455 stay** hindrance, obstacle **462 bounce** i.e., the noise of the cannon **463 bastinado** beating with a cudgel **466 'Zounds** by God's (Christ's) wounds **468 list** listen **472 green** youthful, hence unripe

The bloom that promiseth a mighty fruit.
I see a yielding in the looks of France;
Mark, how they whisper. Urge them while their souls
Are capable of this ambition,
Lest zeal, now melted by the windy breath
Of soft petitions, pity, and remorse,
Cool and congeal again to what it was.

FIRST CITIZEN
Why answer not the double majesties
This friendly treaty of our threat'ned town?

KING PHILIP
Speak England first, that hath been forward first
To speak unto this city. What say you?

KING JOHN
If that the Dauphin there, thy princely son,
Can in this book of beauty read "I love,"
Her dowry shall weigh equal with a queen:
For Anjou and fair Touraine, Maine, Poitiers,
And all that we upon this side the sea,
Except this city now by us besieg'd,
Find liable to our crown and dignity,
Shall gild her bridal bed and make her rich
In titles, honors, and promotions,
As she in beauty, education, blood,
Holds hand with any princess of the world.

KING PHILIP
What say'st thou, boy? Look in the lady's face.

LEWIS
I do, my lord, and in her eye I find
A wonder, or a wondrous miracle,
The shadow of myself form'd in her eye,
Which, being but the shadow of your son,
Becomes a sun and makes your son a shadow.
I do protest I never lov'd myself
Till now infixed I beheld myself
Drawn in the flattering table of her eye.
Whispers with Blanch.

BASTARD [*Aside*]
Drawn in the flattering table of her eye!
Hang'd in the frowning wrinkle of her brow!
And quarter'd in her heart! He doth espy
Himself love's traitor. This is pity now,
That, hang'd and drawn and quarter'd, there should be
In such a love so vile a lout as he.

BLANCH
My uncle's will in this respect is mine.
If he see aught in you that makes him like,
That any thing he sees, which moves his liking,
I can with ease translate it to my will;
Or if you will, to speak more properly,
I will enforce it eas'ly to my love.
Further I will not flatter you, my lord,
That all I see in you is worthy love,
Than this: that nothing do I see in you,
Though churlish thoughts themselves should be your judge,
That I can find should merit any hate.

KING JOHN
What say these young ones? What say you, my niece?

BLANCH
That she is bound in honor still to do
What you in wisdom still vouchsafe to say.

KING JOHN
Speak then, Prince Dauphin. Can you love this lady?

LEWIS
Nay, ask me if I can refrain from love,
For I do love her most unfeignedly.

KING JOHN
Then do I give Volquessen, Touraine, Maine,
Poitiers, and Anjou, these five provinces,
With her to thee, and this addition more,
Full thirty thousand marks of English coin.
Philip of France, if thou be pleas'd withal,
Command thy son and daughter to join hands.

KING PHILIP
It likes us well. Young princes, close your hands.
[*Lewis and Blanch exchange pledges of love.*]

AUSTRIA
And your lips too, for I am well assur'd
That I did so when I was first assur'd.

KING PHILIP
Now, citizens of Angiers, ope your gates,
Let in that amity which you have made,
For at Saint Mary's chapel presently
The rites of marriage shall be solemniz'd.
Is not the Lady Constance in this troop?
I know she is not, for this match made up
Her presence would have interrupted much.
Where is she and her son? Tell me, who knows.

LEWIS
She is sad and passionate at your Highness' tent.

KING PHILIP
And, by my faith, this league that we have made
Will give her sadness very little cure.
Brother of England, how may we content
This widow lady? In her right we came,
Which we, God knows, have turn'd another way,
To our own vantage.

KING JOHN We will heal up all,
For we'll create young Arthur Duke of Britaine
And Earl of Richmond, and this rich fair town
We make him lord of. Call the Lady Constance.
Some speedy messenger bid her repair
To our solemnity. I trust we shall,
If not fill up the measure of her will,
Yet in some measure satisfy her so

476 capable of susceptible to. **ambition** i.e., desire to negotiate **477 zeal** i.e., the French king's zeal in Arthur's behalf. (The metaphor is one of melting and hardening wax.) **478 remorse** compassion **481 treaty** proposal **485 book . . . "I love"** (An allusion to Lilly's famous Latin grammar, in which the verb *amo,* "I love," was used as a paradigm.) **490 liable** subject **494 Holds hand with** equals **498 shadow** image, reflection **503 Drawn** pictured. **table** tablet or flat surface on which the picture is painted **504 Drawn** (with a pun on the meaning *disemboweled.* The pun is continued in the next two lines in *Hang'd* and *quarter'd;* Elizabethan punishment for traitors specified that they be hanged, taken down while still alive, drawn, and quartered.) **506 quarter'd** (with a pun on the meaning *lodged*) **509 love** lover **514 properly** exactly

519 churlish sparing of praise **522, 523 still** always **530 marks** (A mark was the equivalent of 13 shillings, 4 pence.) **533 likes** pleases **535 assur'd** betrothed **538 presently** at once **541 made up** arranged, concluded **555 our solemnity** i.e., the wedding

That we shall stop her exclamation. 558
Go we, as well as haste will suffer us, 559
To this unlook'd for, unprepared pomp.
Exeunt [all but the Bastard].

BASTARD
Mad world, mad kings, mad composition! 561
John, to stop Arthur's title in the whole,
Hath willingly departed with a part, 563
And France, whose armor conscience buckled on,
Whom zeal and charity brought to the field
As God's own soldier, rounded in the ear 566
With that same purpose-changer, that sly devil, 567
That broker, that still breaks the pate of faith, 568
That daily break-vow, he that wins of all,
Of kings, of beggars, old men, young men, maids,
Who, having no external thing to lose 571
But the word "maid," cheats the poor maid of that,
That smooth-fac'd gentleman, tickling commodity, 573
Commodity, the bias of the world— 574
The world, who of itself is peised well, 575
Made to run even upon even ground,
Till this advantage, this vile-drawing bias, 577
This sway of motion, this commodity,
Makes it take head from all indifferency, 579
From all direction, purpose, course, intent.
And this same bias, this commodity,
This bawd, this broker, this all-changing word,
Clapp'd on the outward eye of fickle France, 583
Hath drawn him from his own determin'd aid,
From a resolv'd and honorable war,
To a most base and vile-concluded peace.
And why rail I on this commodity?
But for because he hath not woo'd me yet. 588
Not that I have the power to clutch my hand 589
When his fair angels would salute my palm, 590
But for my hand, as unattempted yet, 591
Like a poor beggar, raileth on the rich.
Well, whiles I am a beggar, I will rail
And say there is no sin but to be rich;
And being rich, my virtue then shall be
To say there is no vice but beggary.
Since kings break faith upon commodity, 597
Gain, be my lord, for I will worship thee. *Exit.*

ACT [III] • [SCENE I]

Enter Constance, Arthur, and Salisbury.

CONSTANCE
Gone to be married? Gone to swear a peace?
False blood to false blood join'd! Gone to be friends?

558 exclamation complaint **559 suffer** allow **561 composition** agreement, compromise **563 departed with** given up **566 rounded** whispered **567 With** by **568 broker** go-between **571 Who** i.e., the maids **573 tickling commodity** flattering self-interest **574 bias** swaying influence. (From the game of bowls, in which a weight in the side of a bowl caused it to curve.) **575 peised** balanced, in equilibrium **577 vile-drawing** attracting to evil **579 take . . . indifferency** rush away from all balanced, equal motion **583 Clapp'd on** stuck on. **outward eye** (1) eyeball (2) hole in the bowling ball in which the lead creating the "bias" was inserted. **France** i.e., the King of France **588 But for** merely **589 clutch** (in a gesture of refusal) **590 angels** coins bearing the figure of an angel, worth 10 shillings **591 unattempted** untempted **597 upon** because of

III.i. Location: France. The French King's pavilion.

Shall Lewis have Blanch, and Blanch those
provinces?
It is not so; thou hast misspoke, misheard.
Be well advis'd, tell o'er thy tale again.
It cannot be; thou dost but say 'tis so.
I trust I may not trust thee, for thy word
Is but the vain breath of a common man.
Believe me, I do not believe thee, man;
I have a king's oath to the contrary.
Thou shalt be punish'd for thus frighting me,
For I am sick and capable of fears,
Oppress'd with wrongs, and therefore full of fears,
A widow, husbandless, subject to fears,
A woman, naturally born to fears;
And though thou now confess thou didst but jest,
With my vex'd spirits I cannot take a truce, 17
But they will quake and tremble all this day.
What dost thou mean by shaking of thy head?
Why dost thou look so sadly on my son?
What means that hand upon that breast of thine?
Why holds thine eye that lamentable rheum, 22
Like a proud river peering o'er his bounds? 23
Be these sad signs confirmers of thy words?
Then speak again—not all thy former tale,
But this one word, whether thy tale be true.

SALISBURY
As true as I believe you think them false 27
That give you cause to prove my saying true.

CONSTANCE
O, if thou teach me to believe this sorrow,
Teach thou this sorrow how to make me die,
And let belief and life encounter so
As doth the fury of two desperate men
Which in the very meeting fall and die.
Lewis marry Blanch? O boy, then where art thou?
France friend with England, what becomes of me?
Fellow, be gone! I cannot brook thy sight. 36
This news hath made thee a most ugly man.

SALISBURY
What other harm have I, good lady, done,
But spoke the harm that is by others done?

CONSTANCE
Which harm within itself so heinous is
As it makes harmful all that speak of it.

ARTHUR
I do beseech you, madam, be content. 42

CONSTANCE
If thou, that bid'st me be content, wert grim,
Ugly, and sland'rous to thy mother's womb,
Full of unpleasing blots and sightless stains, 45
Lame, foolish, crooked, swart, prodigious, 46
Patch'd with foul moles and eye-offending marks,
I would not care, I then would be content,
For then I should not love thee, no, nor thou
Become thy great birth nor deserve a crown.
But thou art fair, and at thy birth, dear boy,
Nature and Fortune join'd to make thee great.
Of Nature's gifts thou mayst with lilies boast

17 take a truce make peace **22 lamentable rheum** sad moisture, i.e., tears **23 peering o'er** i.e., overflowing **27 them** i.e., the French **36 brook** endure **42 content** calm **45 sightless** unsightly **46 swart** swarthy

And with the half-blown rose. But Fortune, O,
She is corrupted, chang'd, and won from thee.
Sh' adulterates hourly with thine uncle John,
And with her golden hand hath pluck'd on France
To tread down fair respect of sovereignty,
And made his majesty the bawd to theirs.
France is a bawd to Fortune and King John,
That strumpet Fortune, that usurping John!
Tell me, thou fellow, is not France forsworn?
Envenom him with words, or get thee gone
And leave those woes alone which I alone
Am bound to underbear.

SALISBURY
Pardon me, madam,
I may not go without you to the kings.

CONSTANCE
Thou mayst, thou shalt. I will not go with thee.
I will instruct my sorrows to be proud,
For grief is proud and makes his owner stoop.
To me and to the state of my great grief
Let kings assemble, for my grief's so great
That no supporter but the huge firm earth
Can hold it up. Here I and sorrows sit;
Here is my throne, bid kings come bow to it.
[*Seats herself on the ground.*]

Enter King John, [King Philip of] France, [Lewis the] Dauphin, Blanch, Elinor, Philip [the Bastard], Austria. [and Attendants]. [The two kings are arm in arm.]

KING PHILIP
'Tis true, fair daughter, and this blessed day
Ever in France shall be kept festival.
To solemnize this day the glorious sun
Stays in his course and plays the alchemist,
Turning with splendor of his precious eye
The meager cloddy earth to glittering gold.
The yearly course that brings this day about
Shall never see it but a holy day.

CONSTANCE [*Rising*]
A wicked day, and not a holy day!
What hath this day deserv'd? What hath it done,
That it in golden letters should be set
Among the high tides in the calendar?
Nay, rather turn this day out of the week,
This day of shame, oppression, perjury.
Or, if it must stand still, let wives with child
Pray that their burdens may not fall this day,
Lest that their hopes prodigiously be cross'd.
But on this day let seamen fear no wrack;
No bargains break that are not this day made.
This day, all things begun come to ill end,
Yea, faith itself to hollow falsehood change!

KING PHILIP
By heaven, lady, you shall have no cause
To curse the fair proceedings of this day.
Have I not pawn'd to you my majesty?

CONSTANCE
You have beguil'd me with a counterfeit
Resembling majesty, which, being touch'd and tried,
Proves valueless. You are forsworn, forsworn!
You came in arms to spill mine enemies' blood,
But now in arms you strengthen it with yours.
The grappling vigor and rough frown of war
Is cold in amity and painted peace,
And our oppression hath made up this league.
Arm, arm, you heavens, against these perjur'd kings!
A widow cries; be husband to me, heavens!
Let not the hours of this ungodly day
Wear out the day in peace; but, ere sunset,
Set armed discord 'twixt these perjur'd kings!
Hear me, O, hear me!

AUSTRIA
Lady Constance, peace!

CONSTANCE
War, war, no peace! Peace is to me a war.
O Lymoges, O Austria, thou dost shame
That bloody spoil. Thou slave, thou wretch, thou coward,
Thou little valiant, great in villainy,
Thou ever strong upon the stronger side,
Thou Fortune's champion that dost never fight
But when her humorous ladyship is by
To teach thee safety! Thou art perjur'd too,
And sooth'st up greatness. What a fool art thou,
A ramping fool, to brag and stamp and swear
Upon my party! Thou cold-blooded slave,
Hast thou not spoke like thunder on my side,
Been sworn my soldier, bidding me depend
Upon thy stars, thy fortune, and thy strength,
And dost thou now fall over to my foes?
Thou wear a lion's hide! Doff it for shame,
And hang a calf's-skin on those recreant limbs.

AUSTRIA
O, that a man should speak those words to me!

BASTARD
And hang a calf's-skin on those recreant limbs.

AUSTRIA
Thou dar'st not say so, villain, for thy life.

BASTARD
And hang a calf's-skin on those recreant limbs.

KING JOHN [*To Bastard*]
We like not this. Thou dost forget thyself.

Enter Pandulph.

KING PHILIP
Here comes the holy legate of the Pope.

PANDULPH
Hail, you anointed deputies of heaven!
To thee, King John, my holy errand is.
I Pandulph, of fair Milan cardinal,

54 half-blown only partly opened, still young **56 adulterates** commits adultery **57 golden** i.e., offering gold. **pluck'd on** induced **65 underbear** endure **70 state** majesty **85 golden** i.e., red **86 high tides** i.e., great festivals **89 stand still** remain **91 prodigiously be cross'd** be thwarted by some monstrous birth defect **92 But** except (since this is the most evil of days). **wrack** shipwreck **98 pawn'd** pledged

100 touch'd tested (as one tests gold by rubbing it on a touchstone) **102 in arms** in armor **103 in arms** embracing. **with yours** i.e., by uniting your enemies to your royal house in marriage **105 painted** specious, unreal **106 our oppression** our being oppressed **114 Lymoges** (Cf. II. i.5 note.) **115 spoil** booty, i.e., the lion's pelt that Austria wears **119 humorous** capricious **121 sooth'st up greatness** flatter the influential **122 ramping** making a fierce show **123 Upon my party** in my behalf **127 fall over** go over, desert **129 calf's-skin** (Customarily used to make coats for the fools kept to amuse great families.) **recreant** cowardly, having deserted his cause

And from Pope Innocent the legate here,
Do in his name religiously demand
Why thou against the church, our holy mother,
So willfully dost spurn, and force perforce 142
Keep Stephen Langton, chosen Archbishop
Of Canterbury, from that holy see?
This, in our foresaid holy father's name,
Pope Innocent, I do demand of thee.

KING JOHN
What earthy name to interrogatories 147
Can taste the free breath of a sacred king? 148
Thou canst not, Cardinal, devise a name
So slight, unworthy, and ridiculous,
To charge me to an answer, as the Pope.
Tell him this tale, and from the mouth of England
Add thus much more, that no Italian priest
Shall tithe or toll in our dominions; 154
But as we, under heaven, are supreme head,
So under Him that great supremacy,
Where we do reign, we will alone uphold
Without th' assistance of a mortal hand.
So tell the Pope, all reverence set apart
To him and his usurp'd authority.

KING PHILIP
Brother of England, you blaspheme in this.

KING JOHN
Though you and all the kings of Christendom
Are led so grossly by this meddling priest,
Dreading the curse that money may buy out,
And by the merit of vile gold, dross, dust,
Purchase corrupted pardon of a man
Who in that sale sells pardon from himself, 167
Though you and all the rest, so grossly led,
This juggling witchcraft with revenue cherish,
Yet I alone, alone do me oppose
Against the Pope and, count his friends my foes.

PANDULPH
Then, by the lawful power that I have,
Thou shalt stand curs'd and excommunicate;
And blessed shall he be that doth revolt
From his allegiance to an heretic;
And meritorious shall that hand be call'd,
Canonized and worship'd as a saint,
That takes away by any secret course
Thy hateful life.

CONSTANCE O, lawful let it be
That I have room with Rome to curse awhile! 180
Good father Cardinal, cry thou amen
To my keen curses, for without my wrong 182
There is no tongue hath power to curse him right.

PANDULPH
There's law and warrant, lady, for my curse.

CONSTANCE
And for mine too. When law can do no right,
Let it be lawful that law bar no wrong.
Law cannot give my child his kingdom here,
For he that holds his kingdom holds the law;
Therefore, since law itself is perfect wrong,
How can the law forbid my tongue to curse?

PANDULPH
Philip of France, on peril of a curse,
Let go the hand of that arch-heretic,
And raise the power of France upon his head
Unless he do submit himself to Rome.

ELINOR
Look'st thou pale, France? Do not let go thy hand.

CONSTANCE [*To Elinor*]
Look to that, devil, lest that France repent,
And by disjoining hands, hell lose a soul.

AUSTRIA
King Philip, listen to the Cardinal.

BASTARD
And hang a calf's-skin on his recreant limbs.

AUSTRIA
Well, ruffian, I must pocket up these wrongs, 200
Because—

BASTARD Your breeches best may carry them.

KING JOHN
Philip, what say'st thou to the Cardinal?

CONSTANCE
What should he say, but as the Cardinal?

LEWIS
Bethink you, father; for the difference
Is purchase of a heavy curse from Rome,
Or the light loss of England for a friend.
Forego the easier.

BLANCH That's the curse of Rome.

CONSTANCE
O Lewis, stand fast! The devil tempts thee here
In likeness of a new untrimmed bride. 209

BLANCH
The Lady Constance speaks not from her faith,
But from her need.

CONSTANCE O, if thou grant my need,
Which only lives but by the death of faith, 212
That need must needs infer this principle, 213
That faith would live again by death of need. 214
O then, tread down my need, and faith mounts up; 215
Keep my need up, and faith is trodden down!

KING JOHN
The King is mov'd, and answers not to this.

CONSTANCE
O, be remov'd from him, and answer well!

AUSTRIA
Do so, King Philip; hang no more in doubt.

BASTARD
Hang nothing but a calf's-skin, most sweet lout.

KING PHILIP
I am perplex'd, and know not what to say.

142 spurn oppose scornfully. (Literally, *kick.*) **force perforce** violently **147 What . . . interrogatories** what merely secular authority to present formal interrogations under oath **148 taste** test. (Many editors emend to *task.*) **154 tithe** impose tithes, a tenth of one's income given to the church. **toll** collect taxes **167 Who . . . himself** i.e., who, in selling indulgences, incurs his own damnation. (*From himself* may also suggest that the pardon stems only from him, not from God, and is therefore invalid.) **180 room, Rome** (An obvious pun, pronounced alike in Elizabethan England.) **182 without my wrong** i.e., without recognition of the wrong done to me

200 pocket up submit to **209 untrimmed** i.e., freshly married, unshorn (suggesting she is still a virgin). (Alludes to the temptation of St. Anthony by the devil in the form of a naked woman.) **212 Which . . . faith** i.e., my need is so strong that I must put it ahead of matters of faith **213 needs infer** necessarily imply **214 That . . . need** i.e., my faith will be rekindled once my prior and compelling necessity, Arthur's claim, has been satisfied **215 tread down** i.e., put down by satisfying, subdue

PANDULPH
What canst thou say but will perplex thee more,
If thou stand excommunicate and curs'd?

KING PHILIP
Good reverend father, make my person yours,
And tell me how you would bestow yourself.
This royal hand and mine are newly knit,
And the conjunction of our inward souls
Married in league, coupl'd, and link'd together
With all religious strength of sacred vows.
The latest breath that gave the sound of words
Was deep-sworn faith, peace, amity, true love
Between our kingdoms and our royal selves,
And even before this truce, but new before,
No longer than we well could wash our hands
To clap this royal bargain up of peace,
Heaven knows, they were besmear'd and overstain'd
With slaughter's pencil, where revenge did paint
The fearful difference of incensed kings.
And shall these hands, so lately purg'd of blood,
So newly join'd in love, so strong in both,
Unyoke this seizure and this kind regreet?
Play fast and loose with faith? So jest with heaven,
Make such unconstant children of ourselves,
As now again to snatch our palm from palm,
Unswear faith sworn, and on the marriage-bed
Of smiling peace to march a bloody host,
And make a riot on the gentle brow
Of true sincerity? O, holy sir,
My reverend father, let it not be so!
Out of your grace, devise, ordain, impose
Some gentle order; and then we shall be blest
To do your pleasure and continue friends.

PANDULPH
All form is formless, order orderless,
Save what is opposite to England's love.
Therefore to arms! Be champion of our church,
Or let the church, our mother, breathe her curse,
A mother's curse, on her revolting son.
France, thou mayst hold a serpent by the tongue,
A cased lion by the mortal paw,
A fasting tiger safer by the tooth,
Than keep in peace that hand which thou dost hold.

KING PHILIP
I may disjoin my hand, but not my faith.
[*Lets go of King John's arm.*]

PANDULPH
So mak'st thou faith an enemy to faith,
And like a civil war set'st oath to oath,
Thy tongue against thy tongue. O, let thy vow
First made to heaven, first be to heaven perform'd,
That is, to be the champion of our church!
What since thou swor'st is sworn against thyself
And may not be performed by thyself,
For that which thou hast sworn to do amiss
Is not amiss when it is truly done,
And being not done, where doing tends to ill,
The truth is then most done not doing it.
The better act of purposes mistook
Is to mistake again; though indirect,
Yet indirection thereby grows direct,
And falsehood falsehood cures, as fire cools fire
Within the scorched veins of one new-burn'd.
It is religion that doth make vows kept,
But thou hast sworn against religion,
By what thou swear'st against the thing thou swear'st,
And mak'st an oath the surety for thy truth
Against an oath; the truth thou art unsure
To swear, swears only not to be forsworn,
Else what a mockery should it be to swear!
But thou dost swear only to be forsworn;
And most forsworn, to keep what thou dost swear.
Therefore thy later vows against thy first
Is in thyself rebellion to thyself;
And better conquest never canst thou make
Than arm thy constant and thy nobler parts
Against these giddy loose suggestions,
Upon which better part our pray'rs come in,
If thou vouchsafe them. But if not, then know
The peril of our curses light on thee
So heavy as thou shalt not shake them off,
But in despair die under their black weight.

AUSTRIA
Rebellion, flat rebellion!

BASTARD
Will 't not be?
Will not a calf's-skin stop that mouth of thine?

LEWIS
Father, to arms!

BLANCH
Upon thy wedding-day?
Against the blood that thou hast married?
What, shall our feast be kept with slaughtered men?
Shall braying trumpets and loud churlish drums,
Clamors of hell, be measures to our pomp?
O husband, hear me! Ay, alack, how new
Is "husband" in my mouth! Even for that name,
Which till this time my tongue did ne'er pronounce,
Upon my knee I beg, go not to arms
Against mine uncle. [*Kneels.*]

CONSTANCE
O, upon my knee,
Made hard with kneeling, I do pray to thee,
Thou virtuous Dauphin, alter not the doom
Forethought by heaven!
[*Kneels.*]

BLANCH
Now shall I see thy love. What motive may
Be stronger with thee than the name of wife?

CONSTANCE
That which upholdeth him that thee upholds,
His honor. O, thine honor, Lewis, thine honor!

224 make . . . yours put yourself in my place **225 bestow** conduct **230 latest** most recent **233 even before** just before. **new** immediately **235 clap . . . up** i.e., conclude with a grasping of hands **237 pencil** brush **238 difference** dissension **240 both** i.e., blood and love **241 Unyoke this seizure** disjoin this handclasp. **regreet** returned salutation, counterclasp **259 cased** caged. **mortal** deadly **263 So . . . to faith** i.e., you are trying to set your promise to John against your religious vow to the church **268 since** since then

271 truly done i.e., not done at all, (since, as Pandulph explains two lines later, an ill-considered vow is best performed by not performing it. This is an example of *equivocation,* much deplored by many Elizabethans and regarded as typical of Catholic duplicity.) **281 By . . . swear'st** i.e., by your oath of allegiance to John in direct violation of your prior vows given to the Church **292 suggestions** temptations **296 as** that **298 Will 't not be** i.e., will nothing serve (to keep you quiet) **304 measures** musical accompaniment. **pomp** i.e., wedding ceremony **312 Forethought** destined

LEWIS
I muse your Majesty doth seem so cold, 317
When such profound respects do pull you on. 318

PANDULPH
I will denounce a curse upon his head. 319

KING PHILIP
Thou shalt not need. England, I will fall from thee.

CONSTANCE
O fair return of banish'd majesty! *[Rises.]*

ELINOR
O foul revolt of French inconstancy!

KING JOHN
France, thou shalt rue this hour within this hour.

BASTARD
Old Time the clock-setter, that bald sexton Time,
Is it as he will? Well then, France shall rue.

BLANCH *[Rising]*
The sun's o'ercast with blood. Fair day, adieu!
Which is the side that I must go withal?
I am with both: each army hath a hand,
And in their rage, I having hold of both,
They whirl asunder and dismember me.
Husband, I cannot pray that thou mayst win;
Uncle, I needs must pray that thou mayst lose;
Father, I may not wish the fortune thine; 333
Grandam, I will not wish thy wishes thrive.
Whoever wins, on that side shall I lose;
Assured loss before the match be play'd.

LEWIS
Lady, with me, with me thy fortune lies.

BLANCH
There where my fortune lives, there my life dies.

KING JOHN
Cousin, go draw our puissance together. 339
[Exit Bastard.]
France, I am burn'd up with inflaming wrath,
A rage whose heat hath this condition,
That nothing can allay, nothing but blood—
The blood, and dearest-valued blood, of France.

KING PHILIP
Thy rage shall burn thee up, and thou shalt turn
To ashes, ere our blood shall quench that fire.
Look to thyself, thou art in jeopardy.

KING JOHN
No more than he that threats. To arms let's hie!
Exeunt.

SCENE II

Alarums, excursions. Enter [the] Bastard, with Austria's head.

BASTARD
Now, by my life, this day grows wondrous hot.
Some airy devil hovers in the sky 2
And pours down mischief. Austria's head lie there,
While Philip breathes. *[Puts down the head.]* 4

317 muse wonder **318 respects** considerations **319 denounce** proclaim, call down **333 Father** i.e., father-in-law, King Philip **339 Cousin** kinsman. **puissance** armed force

III.ii. Location: France. Plains near Angiers. The battle is seen as following immediately upon the previous scene.
2 airy devil (Aerial spirits or devils were thought to be the cause of tempests, thunder, lightning, etc.) **4 breathes** i.e., gets his breath

Enter [King] John, Arthur, [and] Hubert.

KING JOHN
Hubert, keep this boy. Philip, make up. 5
My mother is assailed in our tent,
And ta'en, I fear.

BASTARD
My lord, I rescued her;
Her Highness is in safety, fear you not.
But on, my liege, for very little pains
Will bring this labor to an happy end.
Exeunt [with Austria's head].

[SCENE III]

Alarums, excursions, retreat. Enter [King] John, Elinor, Arthur, [the] Bastard, Hubert, [and] Lords.

KING JOHN *[To Elinor]*
So shall it be; your Grace shall stay behind
So strongly guarded. *[To Arthur.]* Cousin, look not sad.
Thy grandam loves thee, and thy uncle will
As dear be to thee as thy father was.

ARTHUR
O, this will make my mother die with grief!

KING JOHN *[To the Bastard]*
Cousin, away for England! Haste before,
And, ere our coming, see thou shake the bags
Of hoarding abbots; imprisoned angels 8
Set at liberty. The fat ribs of peace 9
Must by the hungry now be fed upon.
Use our commission in his utmost force. 11

BASTARD
Bell, book, and candle shall not drive me back, 12
When gold and silver becks me to come on. 13
I leave your Highness. Grandam, I will pray,
If ever I remember to be holy,
For your fair safety; so, I kiss your hand.

ELINOR
Farewell, gentle cousin.

KING JOHN
Coz, farewell. *[Exit Bastard.]* 17

ELINOR
Come hither, little kinsman; hark, a word.
[Takes Arthur aside.]

KING JOHN
Come hither, Hubert. O my gentle Hubert,
We owe thee much! Within this wall of flesh
There is a soul counts thee her creditor
And with advantage means to pay thy love; 22
And, my good friend, thy voluntary oath
Lives in this bosom, dearly cherished.
Give me thy hand. I had a thing to say,
But I will fit it with some better tune.
By heaven, Hubert, I am almost asham'd
To say what good respect I have of thee. 28

5 make up advance, press on

III.iii. Location: Scene continues on the plains near Angiers.
8 angels gold coins (with a common pun) **9 fat ribs of peace** (I.e., in contrast to the skeleton of war, the *bare-ribb'd death* of V.ii.177.) **11 his** its **12 Bell, book, candle** (Articles used in the office of excommunication.) **13 becks** beckons **17 Coz** cousin, i.e., kinsman **22 advantage** interest **28 respect** opinion

HUBERT
I am much bounden to your Majesty.
KING JOHN
Good friend, thou hast no cause to say so yet,
But thou shalt have; and, creep time ne'er so slow,
Yet it shall come for me to do thee good.
I had a thing to say, but let it go.
The sun is in the heaven, and the proud day,
Attended with the pleasures of the world,
Is all too wanton and too full of gauds 36
To give me audience. If the midnight bell 37
Did with his iron tongue and brazen mouth
Sound on into the drowsy race of night; 39
If this same were a churchyard where we stand,
And thou possessed with a thousand wrongs;
Or if that surly spirit, melancholy,
Had bak'd thy blood and made it heavy, thick,
Which else runs tickling up and down the veins,
Making that idiot, laughter, keep men's eyes
And strain their cheeks to idle merriment,
A passion hateful to my purposes;
Or if that thou couldst see me without eyes,
Hear me without thine ears, and make reply
Without a tongue, using conceit alone,
Without eyes, ears, and harmful sound of words—
Then, in despite of brooded watchful day, 52
I would into thy bosom pour my thoughts.
But, ah, I will not! Yet I love thee well,
And, by my troth, I think thou lov'st me well.
HUBERT
So well, that what you bid me undertake,
Though that my death were adjunct to my act,
By heaven, I would do it.
KING JOHN Do not I know thou wouldst?
Good Hubert, Hubert, Hubert, throw thine eye
On yon young boy. I'll tell thee what, my friend,
He is a very serpent in my way,
And wheresoe'er this foot of mine doth tread
He lies before me. Dost thou understand me?
Thou art his keeper.
HUBERT And I'll keep him so
That he shall not offend your Majesty.
KING JOHN Death.
HUBERT
My lord?
KING JOHN A grave.
HUBERT He shall not live.
KING JOHN Enough.
I could be merry now. Hubert, I love thee.
Well, I'll not say what I intend for thee.
Remember.—Madam, fare you well.
I'll send those powers o'er to your Majesty.
ELINOR
My blessing go with thee!
KING JOHN For England, cousin, go. 71
Hubert shall be your man, attend on you
With all true duty. On toward Calais, ho! *Exeunt.*

36 gauds showy ornaments, trifles **37 To give me audience** i.e., for you to hearken to my words **39 race** running, course. (*Face* and *ear* have been suggested as emendations.) **50 conceit** the mental faculty **52 brooded** brooding **70 powers** troops **71 cousin** i.e., Arthur

SCENE [IV]

Enter [King Philip of] France, [Lewis the] Dauphin, Pandulph, [and] Attendants.

KING PHILIP
So, by a roaring tempest on the flood, 1
A whole armado of convicted sail 2
Is scattered and disjoin'd from fellowship.
PANDULPH
Courage and comfort! All shall yet go well.
KING PHILIP
What can go well, when we have run so ill?
Are we not beaten? Is not Angiers lost?
Arthur ta'en prisoner? Divers dear friends slain?
And bloody England into England gone,
O'erbearing interruption, spite of France? 9
LEWIS
What he hath won, that hath he fortified.
So hot a speed with such advice dispos'd, 11
Such temperate order in so fierce a cause,
Doth want example. Who hath read or heard 13
Of any kindred action like to this? 14
KING PHILIP
Well could I bear that England had this praise,
So we could find some pattern of our shame. 16

Enter Constance.

Look who comes here! A grave unto a soul,
Holding th' eternal spirit, against her will,
In the vile prison of afflicted breath. 19
I prithee, lady, go away with me.
CONSTANCE
Lo, now! Now see the issue of your peace. 21
KING PHILIP
Patience, good lady, comfort, gentle Constance!
CONSTANCE
No, I defy all counsel, all redress, 23
But that which ends all counsel, true redress,
Death, death. O amiable, lovely death,
Thou odoriferous stench! Sound rottenness,
Arise forth from the couch of lasting night,
Thou hate and terror to prosperity,
And I will kiss thy detestable bones,
And put my eyeballs in thy vaulty brows,
And ring these fingers with thy household worms,
And stop this gap of breath with fulsome dust, 32
And be a carrion monster like thyself.
Come, grin on me, and I will think thou smil'st,
And buss thee as thy wife. Misery's love, 35
O, come to me!
KING PHILIP O fair affliction, peace!

III.iv. Location: France. The French King's pavilion.
1 flood seas **2 armado** armada, fleet. **convicted** doomed **9 O'erbearing interruption** overthrowing resistance. **spite** in spite **11 with . . . dispos'd** directed with such judgment **13 Doth want example** lacks parallel instance **14 kindred** comparable **16 So** provided. **pattern** precedent **19 prison . . . breath** (The soul was thought to leave the body from the mouth with the last expiring breath.) **21 issue** outcome **23 defy** reject **30 vaulty** arched **32 fulsome** loathsome **35 buss** kiss

CONSTANCE
No, no, I will not, having breath to cry.
O, that my tongue were in the thunder's mouth!
Then with a passion would I shake the world,
And rouse from sleep that fell anatomy
Which cannot hear a lady's feeble voice,
Which scorns a modern invocation.

PANDULPH
Lady, you utter madness, and not sorrow.

CONSTANCE
Thou art not holy to belie me so.
I am not mad. This hair I tear is mine;
[*Tears her hair.*]
My name is Constance; I was Geffrey's wife;
Young Arthur is my son, and he is lost.
I am not mad; I would to heaven I were!
For then, 'tis like I should forget myself.
O, if I could, what grief should I forget?
Preach some philosophy to make me mad,
And thou shalt be canoniz'd, Cardinal;
For being not mad, but sensible of grief,
My reasonable part produces reason
How I may be deliver'd of these woes,
And teaches me to kill or hang myself.
If I were mad, I should forget my son,
Or madly think a babe of clouts were he.
I am not mad. Too well, too well I feel
The different plague of each calamity.

KING PHILIP
Bind up those tresses. O, what love I note
In the fair multitude of those her hairs!
Where but by chance a silver drop hath fall'n,
Even to that drop ten thousand wiry friends
Do glue themselves in sociable grief,
Like true, inseparable, faithful loves,
Sticking together in calamity.

CONSTANCE
To England, if you will.

KING PHILIP
Bind up your hairs.

CONSTANCE
Yes, that I will; and wherefore will I do it?
I tore them from their bonds, and cried aloud,
"O that these hands could so redeem my son,
As they have given these hairs their liberty!"
But now I envy at their liberty,
And will again commit them to their bonds,
[*Binds up her hair.*]
Because my poor child is a prisoner.
And, father Cardinal, I have heard you say
That we shall see and know our friends in heaven.
If that be true, I shall see my boy again;
For since the birth of Cain, the first male child,
To him that did but yesterday suspire,
There was not such a gracious creature born.
But now will canker sorrow eat my bud
And chase the native beauty from his cheek,
And he will look as hollow as a ghost,
As dim and meager as an ague's fit,
And so he'll die; and, rising so again,
When I shall meet him in the court of heaven
I shall not know him. Therefore never, never
Must I behold my pretty Arthur more.

PANDULPH
You hold too heinous a respect of grief.

CONSTANCE
He talks to me that never had a son.

KING PHILIP
You are as fond of grief as of your child.

CONSTANCE
Grief fills the room up of my absent child,
Lies in his bed, walks up and down with me,
Puts on his pretty looks, repeats his words,
Remembers me of all his gracious parts,
Stuffs out his vacant garments with his form;
Then, have I reason to be fond of grief?
Fare you well! Had you such a loss as I,
I could give better comfort than you do.
I will not keep this form upon my head
[*Tears her hair again.*]
When there is such disorder in my wit.
O Lord! My boy, my Arthur, my fair son!
My life, my joy, my food, my all the world!
My widow-comfort, and my sorrows' cure! *Exit.*

KING PHILIP
I fear some outrage, and I'll follow her. *Exit.*

LEWIS
There's nothing in this world can make me joy.
Life is as tedious as a twice-told tale
Vexing the dull ear of a drowsy man;
And bitter shame hath spoil'd the sweet world's taste,
That it yields nought but shame and bitterness.

PANDULPH
Before the curing of a strong disease,
Even in the instant of repair and health,
The fit is strongest; evils that take leave,
On their departure most of all show evil.
What have you lost by losing of this day?

LEWIS
All days of glory, joy, and happiness.

PANDULPH
If you had won it, certainly you had.
No, no; when Fortune means to men most good,
She looks upon them with a threat'ning eye.
'Tis strange to think how much King John hath lost
In this which he accounts so clearly won.
Are not you griev'd that Arthur is his prisoner?

LEWIS
As heartily as he is glad he hath him.

PANDULPH
Your mind is all as youthful as your blood.
Now hear me speak with a prophetic spirit;
For even the breath of what I mean to speak
Shall blow each dust, each straw, each little rub,
Out of the path which shall directly lead

40 fell anatomy cruel skeleton (which was the usual figure of death in pictorial representations) **42 modern** everyday, commonplace **49 like** likely **53 sensible of** capable of feeling **58 babe of clouts** rag doll **63 silver drop** i.e., tear **64 wiry friends** i.e., hairs **68 To England** (Perhaps an answer to Philip's invitation at l. 20; perhaps evidence of textual revision.) **80 suspire** breathe **82 canker** like a cankerworm, feeding on buds

90 heinous a respect terrible an opinion **96 Remembers** reminds **101 form** coiffure **128 rub** obstacle

Thy foot to England's throne. And therefore mark.
John hath seiz'd Arthur, and it cannot be
That, whiles warm life plays in that infant's veins,
The misplac'd John should entertain an hour,
One minute, nay, one quiet breath of rest.
A scepter snatch'd with an unruly hand
Must be as boisterously maintain'd as gain'd;
And he that stands upon a slipp'ry place
Makes nice of no vile hold to stay him up.
That John may stand, then Arthur needs must fall;
So be it, for it cannot be but so.

LEWIS
But what shall I gain by young Arthur's fall?

PANDULPH
You, in the right of Lady Blanch your wife,
May then make all the claim that Arthur did.

LEWIS
And lose it, life and all, as Arthur did.

PANDULPH
How green you are and fresh in this old world!
John lays you plots; the times conspire with you,
For he that steeps his safety in true blood
Shall find but bloody safety, and untrue.
This act so evilly borne shall cool the hearts
Of all his people and freeze up their zeal,
That none so small advantage shall step forth
To check his reign but they will cherish it;
No natural exhalation in the sky,
No scope of nature, no distemper'd day,
No common wind, no customed event
But they will pluck away his natural cause
And call them meteors, prodigies, and signs,
Abortives, presages, and tongues of heaven,
Plainly denouncing vengeance upon John.

LEWIS
May be he will not touch young Arthur's life,
But hold himself safe in his prisonment.

PANDULPH
O, sir, when he shall hear of your approach,
If that young Arthur be not gone already,
Even at that news he dies; and then the hearts
Of all his people shall revolt from him
And kiss the lips of unacquainted change,
And pick strong matter of revolt and wrath
Out of the bloody fingers' ends of John.
Methinks I see this hurly all on foot;
And, O, what better matter breeds for you
Than I have nam'd! The bastard Faulconbridge
Is now in England, ransacking the church,
Offending charity. If but a dozen French
Were there in arms, they would be as a call
To train ten thousand English to their side,
Or as a little snow, tumbled about,
Anon becomes a mountain. O noble Dauphin,
Go with me to the King. 'Tis wonderful
What may be wrought out of their discontent,
Now that their souls are topfull of offense.
For England go. I will whet on the King.

LEWIS
Strong reasons make strange actions. Let us go.
If you say ay, the King will not say no. *Exeunt.*

133 misplac'd i.e., usurping **138 Makes nice of no** is not scrupulous about any **146 lays you plots** i.e., makes plots by which you will profit **147 true blood** blood of a true prince **149 borne** carried out **151 none . . . advantage** no opportunity, however small **153 exhalation** meteor **154 scope of nature** i.e., one of those prodigious phenomena within nature's power **156 his** its **158 Abortives** untimely or monstrous births **166 kiss . . . change** i.e., welcome any change. **unacquainted** unfamiliar **167 pick strong matter of** find compelling reason for **168 Out . . . John** i.e., out of John's bloody-handed deeds **169 hurly** commotion. **on foot** in motion **170 breeds** is ripening **174 call** decoy **175 train** attract

180 topfull of offense brimful of grievance

ACT IV • SCENE I

Enter Hubert and Executioners [with irons].

HUBERT
Heat me these irons hot, and look thou stand
Within the arras. When I strike my foot
Upon the bosom of the ground, rush forth
And bind the boy which you shall find with me
Fast to the chair. Be heedful. Hence, and watch.

FIRST EXECUTIONER
I hope your warrant will bear out the deed.

HUBERT
Uncleanly scruples! Fear not you. Look to 't.
[*The Executioners go to do as they are bid.*]
Young lad, come forth. I have to say with you.

Enter Arthur.

ARTHUR
Good morrow, Hubert.

HUBERT
Good morrow, little prince.

ARTHUR
As little prince, having so great a title
To be more prince, as may be. You are sad.

HUBERT
Indeed, I have been merrier.

ARTHUR
Mercy on me!
Methinks nobody should be sad but I.
Yet I remember, when I was in France,
Young gentlemen would be as sad as night,
Only for wantonness. By my christendom,
So I were out of prison and kept sheep,
I should be as merry as the day is long;
And so I would be here, but that I doubt
My uncle practices more harm to me.
He is afraid of me and I of him.
Is it my fault that I was Geffrey's son?
No, indeed, is 't not; and I would to heaven
I were your son, so you would love me, Hubert.

HUBERT [*Aside*]
If I talk to him, with his innocent prate

IV.i. Location: England. A room in a castle. A chair is provided.
1 look take care **2 Within the arras** behind the wall-hangings. (Evidently the Executioners go out as though to heat their irons and then conceal themselves behind the arras, ready at l. 71 to come forth.) **7 Uncleanly** improper, unbecoming **8 to say** something to speak about **10–11 As . . . be** i.e., I am as little a prince, despite my being entitled to be greater, as is possible **16 for wantonness** out of affected behavior. **By my christendom** as I am a Christian **17 So** provided **19 doubt** fear **20 practices** plots **25 prate** prattle

He will awake my mercy, which lies dead.
Therefore I will be sudden and dispatch.

ARTHUR
Are you sick, Hubert? You look pale today.
In sooth, I would you were a little sick,
That I might sit all night and watch with you.
I warrant I love you more than you do me.

HUBERT [*Aside*]
His words do take possession of my bosom.—
Read here, young Arthur. [*Shows a paper.*]
[*Aside.*] How now, foolish rheum?
Turning dispiteous torture out of door?
I must be brief, lest resolution drop
Out at mine eyes in tender womanish tears.—
Can you not read it? Is it not fair writ?

ARTHUR
Too fairly, Hubert, for so foul effect.
Must you with hot irons burn out both mine eyes?

HUBERT
Young boy, I must.

ARTHUR
And will you?

HUBERT
And I will.

ARTHUR
Have you the heart? When your head did but ache,
I knit my handkercher about your brows—
The best I had, a princess wrought it me—
And I did never ask it you again;
And with my hand at midnight held your head,
And like the watchful minutes to the hour
Still and anon cheer'd up the heavy time,
Saying, "What lack you?" and "Where lies your grief?"
Or "What good love may I perform for you?"
Many a poor man's son would have lien still
And ne'er have spoke a loving word to you,
But you at your sick service had a prince.
Nay, you may think my love was crafty love
And call it cunning. Do, an if you will.
If heaven be pleas'd that you must use me ill,
Why then you must. Will you put out mine eyes?
These eyes that never did nor never shall
So much as frown on you?

HUBERT
I have sworn to do it,
And with hot irons must I burn them out.

ARTHUR
Ah, none but in this iron age would do it!
The iron of itself, though heat red-hot,
Approaching near these eyes, would drink my tears
And quench his fiery indignation
Even in the matter of mine innocence—
Nay, after that, consume away in rust,
But for containing fire to harm mine eye.
Are you more stubborn-hard than hammer'd iron?
An if an angel should have come to me
And told me Hubert should put out mine eyes,
I would not have believ'd him—no tongue but Hubert's.

HUBERT
Come forth. [*Stamps.*]

[*Executioners come forth, with a cord, irons, etc.*]

Do as I bid you do.

ARTHUR
O, save me Hubert, save me! My eyes are out
Even with the fierce looks of these bloody men.

HUBERT
Give me the iron, I say, and bind him here.
[*They start to bind Arthur to a chair.*]

ARTHUR
Alas, what need you be so boist'rous-rough?
I will not struggle, I will stand stone-still.
For heaven sake, Hubert, let me not be bound!
Nay, hear me, Hubert, drive these men away,
And I will sit as quiet as a lamb;
I will not stir, nor winch, nor speak a word,
Nor look upon the iron angerly.
Thrust but these men away, and I'll forgive you,
Whatever torment you do put me to.

HUBERT
Go, stand within; let me alone with him.

FIRST EXECUTIONER
I am best pleas'd to be from such a deed.
[*Executioners retire.*]

ARTHUR
Alas, I then have chid away my friend!
He hath a stern look, but a gentle heart.
Let him come back, that his compassion may
Give life to yours.

HUBERT
Come, boy, prepare yourself.

ARTHUR
Is there no remedy?

HUBERT
None, but to lose your eyes.

ARTHUR
O heaven, that there were but a mote in yours,
A grain, a dust, a gnat, a wandering hair,
Any annoyance in that precious sense!
Then feeling what small things are boisterous there,
Your vile intent must needs seem horrible.

HUBERT
Is this your promise? Go to, hold your tongue.

ARTHUR
Hubert, the utterance of a brace of tongues
Must needs want pleading for a pair of eyes.
Let me not hold my tongue, let me not, Hubert;
Or, Hubert, if you will, cut out my tongue,
So I may keep mine eyes. O, spare mine eyes,
Though to no use but still to look on you!
Lo, by my troth, the instrument is cold
And would not harm me.

HUBERT
I can heat it, boy.

29 sooth truth **34 dispiteous** pitiless **37 fair** handsomely, legibly **43 wrought** i.e., embroidered. **me** for me **46 watchful . . . hour** minutes that mark the progress of the hour **47 Still and anon** continually **49 love** loving assistance **50 lien** lain **52 at your sick service** to serve you in your sickness **60 iron age** degenerate time (with pun on *hot irons*) **61 heat** heated **63 his** its **64 matter . . . innocence** substance betokening my innocence, i.e., my tears **66 But** merely

75 what why **80 winch** recoil, wince **85 from** away from **91 mote** minute particle of anything **93 precious sense** i.e., sight **94 boisterous** painful, irritating **98 want pleading** be inadequate to plead sufficiently

ARTHUR
No, in good sooth. The fire is dead with grief,
Being create for comfort, to be us'd 106
In undeserv'd extremes. See else yourself. 107
There is no malice in this burning coal;
The breath of heaven hath blown his spirit out
And strew'd repentant ashes on his head.

HUBERT
But with my breath I can revive it, boy.

ARTHUR
An if you do, you will but make it blush
And glow with shame of your proceedings, Hubert.
Nay, it perchance will sparkle in your eyes, 114
And, like a dog that is compell'd to fight,
Snatch at his master that doth tarre him on. 116
All things that you should use to do me wrong
Deny their office. Only you do lack 118
That mercy which fierce fire and iron extends, 119
Creatures of note for mercy-lacking uses. 120

HUBERT
Well, see to live; I will not touch thine eye
For all the treasure that thine uncle owes. 122
Yet am I sworn and I did purpose, boy,
With this same very iron to burn them out.

ARTHUR
O, now you look like Hubert! All this while
You were disguis'd.

HUBERT
Peace; no more. Adieu.
Your uncle must not know but you are dead. 127
I'll fill these dogged spies with false reports. 128
And, pretty child, sleep doubtless and secure 129
That Hubert, for the wealth of all the world,
Will not offend thee.

ARTHUR
O heaven! I thank you, Hubert.

HUBERT
Silence! No more. Go closely in with me. 132
Much danger do I undergo for thee. *Exeunt.*

SCENE II

Enter [King] John, Pembroke, Salisbury, and other Lords.

KING JOHN
Here once again we sit, once again crown'd.
And look'd upon, I hope, with cheerful eyes.

PEMBROKE
This "once again," but that your Highness pleas'd,
Was once superfluous. You were crown'd before,
And that high royalty was ne'er pluck'd off,
The faiths of men ne'er stained with revolt.
Fresh expectation troubled not the land
With any long'd-for change or better state.

SALISBURY
Therefore, to be possess'd with double pomp, 9
To guard a title that was rich before, 10
To gild refined gold, to paint the lily,
To throw a perfume on the violet,
To smooth the ice, or add another hue
Unto the rainbow, or with taper-light
To seek the beauteous eye of heaven to garnish, 15
Is wasteful and ridiculous excess.

PEMBROKE
But that your royal pleasure must be done,
This act is as an ancient tale new told,
And in the last repeating troublesome,
Being urged at a time unseasonable.

SALISBURY
In this the antique and well noted face 21
Of plain old form is much disfigured; 22
And, like a shifted wind unto a sail,
It makes the course of thoughts to fetch about, 24
Startles and frights consideration, 25
Makes sound opinion sick and truth suspected,
For putting on so new a fashion'd robe.

PEMBROKE
When workmen strive to do better than well,
They do confound their skill in covetousness; 29
And oftentimes excusing of a fault
Doth make the fault the worse by th' excuse,
As patches set upon a little breach 32
Discredit more in hiding of the fault
Than did the fault before it was so patch'd.

SALISBURY
To this effect, before you were new crown'd,
We breath'd our counsel; but it pleas'd your Highness 36
To overbear it, and we are all well pleas'd, 37
Since all and every part of what we would
Doth make a stand at what your Highness will. 39

KING JOHN
Some reasons of this double coronation
I have possess'd you with, and think them strong; 41
And more, more strong than lesser is my fear, 42
I shall indue you with. Meantime but ask 43
What you would have reform'd that is not well,
And well shall you perceive how willingly
I will both hear and grant you your requests.

PEMBROKE
Then I, as one that am the tongue of these
To sound the purposes of all their hearts, 48
Both for myself and them—but, chief of all,
Your safety, for the which myself and them 50
Bend their best studies—heartily request 51
Th' enfranchisement of Arthur, whose restraint

106 create created **107 extremes** i.e., extreme cruelties **114 sparkle in** scatter sparks into **116 tarre** provoke, incite **118 Deny** refuse to do **119 extends** proffer **120 Creatures . . . uses** things (i.e., fire and iron) noted as instruments of torture **122 owes** owns **127 but** other than that **128 dogged** fierce, malicious **129 doubtless** fearless **132 closely** secretly

IV.ii. Location: England. King John's palace.

9 be possess'd with have possession of **10 guard** trim, ornament; also, protect **15 eye of heaven** i.e., the sun (much too fair and bright to be enhanced by a *taper-light* or candle) **21 well noted** familiar **22 form** custom **24 fetch about** change direction, tack **25 consideration** reflection, i.e., on matters of state **29 confound** destroy, disrupt. **in covetousness** i.e., by their greedy desire to do better **32 breach** hole **36 breath'd** spoke **37 overbear** overrule **39 Doth . . . will** may go no further than what your Highness desires **41 possess'd you with** informed you of **42–43 And . . . with** i.e., and I shall provide you with even more and stronger reasons, strong in proportion as my fear (in Arthur) grows less **48 sound** express **50 them** i.e., they **51 Bend** direct. **studies** efforts

Doth move the murmuring lips of discontent
To break into this dangerous argument:
If what in rest you have in right you hold,
Why then your fears, which, as they say, attend
The steps of wrong, should move you to mew up
Your tender kinsman and to choke his days
With barbarous ignorance and deny his youth
The rich advantage of good exercise.
That the time's enemies may not have this
To grace occasions, let it be our suit
That you have bid us ask his liberty,
Which for our goods we do no further ask
Than whereupon our weal, on you depending,
Counts it your weal he have his liberty.

Enter Hubert.

KING JOHN
Let it be so. I do commit his youth
To your direction. Hubert, what news with you?
[*Taking him apart.*]

PEMBROKE
This is the man should do the bloody deed;
He show'd his warrant to a friend of mine.
The image of a wicked heinous fault
Lives in his eye; that close aspect of his
Doth show the mood of a much troubled breast,
And I do fearfully believe 'tis done,
What we so fear'd he had a charge to do.

SALISBURY
The color of the King doth come and go
Between his purpose and his conscience,
Like heralds 'twixt two dreadful battles set.
His passion is so ripe it needs must break.

PEMBROKE
And when it breaks, I fear will issue thence
The foul corruption of a sweet child's death.

KING JOHN
We cannot hold mortality's strong hand.
Good lords, although my will to give is living,
The suit which you demand is gone and dead.
He tells us Arthur is deceas'd tonight.

SALISBURY
Indeed we fear'd his sickness was past cure.

PEMBROKE
Indeed we heard how near his death he was
Before the child himself felt he was sick.
This must be answer'd either here or hence.

KING JOHN
Why do you bend such solemn brows on me?
Think you I bear the shears of destiny?
Have I commandment on the pulse of life?

SALISBURY
It is apparent foul play, and 'tis shame
That greatness should so grossly offer it.
So thrive it in your game! And so, farewell.

PEMBROKE
Stay yet, Lord Salisbury. I'll go with thee,
And find th' inheritance of this poor child,
His little kingdom of a forced grave.
That blood which ow'd the breadth of all this isle,
Three foot of it doth hold; bad world the while!
This must not be thus borne. This will break out
To all our sorrows, and ere long I doubt.
Exeunt [*Lords*].

KING JOHN
They burn in indignation. I repent.
There is no sure foundation set on blood,
No certain life achiev'd by others' death.—

Enter Messenger.

A fearful eye thou hast. Where is that blood
That I have seen inhabit in those cheeks?
So foul a sky clears not without a storm.
Pour down thy weather: how goes all in France?

MESSENGER
From France to England. Never such a pow'r
For any foreign preparation
Was levied in the body of a land.
The copy of your speed is learn'd by them;
For when you should be told they do prepare,
The tidings comes that they are all arriv'd.

KING JOHN
O, where hath our intelligence been drunk?
Where hath it slept? Where is my mother's care,
That such an army could be drawn in France,
And she not hear of it?

MESSENGER
My liege, her ear
Is stopp'd with dust. The first of April died
Your noble mother; and, as I hear, my lord,
The Lady Constance in a frenzy died
Three days before. But this from rumor's tongue
I idly heard; if true or false I know not.

KING JOHN
Withhold thy speed, dreadful Occasion!
O, make a league with me, till I have pleas'd
My discontented peers! What, mother dead?
How wildly then walks my estate in France!
Under whose conduct came those pow'rs of France
That thou for truth giv'st out are landed here?

MESSENGER
Under the Dauphin.

KING JOHN
Thou hast made me giddy
With these ill tidings.

Enter [*the*] *Bastard and Peter of Pomfret.*

Now, what says the world
To your proceedings? Do not seek to stuff
My head with more ill news, for it is full.

55 in rest in security, peaceably **57 mew up** shut up. (A falconing term.) **61 the time's enemies** enemies of the present state of affairs **62 grace occasions** i.e., suit their purposes **63 That . . . liberty** i.e., let his liberty be the suit which you have bid us ask (at II. 43–46) **64 our goods** our personal benefit **65 whereupon** to the extent that. **weal** welfare **72 close** secret **75 charge** commission **78 battles** armies in battle order **89 answer'd** atoned for. **hence** i.e., in heaven **93 apparent** evident **94 That . . . it** i.e., that a king should flaunt foul play so flagrantly

95 So . . . game may your schemes lead to the same (bad) end **98 forced** imposed by violence **99 ow'd** owned **100 the while** while such things occur **102 doubt** fear **106 fearful** full of fear **109 weather** storm, tempest **111 preparation** expedition **113 copy** example. **your speed** (as when John proceeded to Angiers; see II.i.56 ff.) **116 our intelligence** our spies, spy network **118 drawn** mustered, assembled **125 Occasion** course of events **128 estate** power **129 conduct** command

BASTARD
But if you be afeard to hear the worst,
Then let the worst unheard fall on your head.
KING JOHN
Bear with me, cousin, for I was amaz'd 137
Under the tide; but now I breathe again
Aloft the flood, and can give audience 139
To any tongue, speak it of what it will.
BASTARD
How I have sped among the clergymen, 141
The sums I have collected shall express.
But as I travel'd hither through the land,
I find the people strangely fantasied, 144
Possess'd with rumors, full of idle dreams,
Not knowing what they fear, but full of fear.
And here's a prophet that I brought with me
From forth the streets of Pomfret, whom I found 148
With many hundreds treading on his heels,
To whom he sung, in rude harsh-sounding rhymes,
That, ere the next Ascension-day at noon,
Your Highness should deliver up your crown.
KING JOHN
Thou idle dreamer, wherefore didst thou so?
PETER
Foreknowing that the truth will fall out so.
KING JOHN
Hubert, away with him! Imprison him,
And on that day at noon, whereon he says
I shall yield up my crown, let him be hang'd.
Deliver him to safety, and return, 158
For I must use thee. [*Exit Hubert with Peter.*]
O my gentle cousin, 159
Hear'st thou the news abroad, who are arriv'd?
BASTARD
The French, my lord. Men's mouths are full of it.
Besides, I met Lord Bigot and Lord Salisbury,
With eyes as red as new-enkindled fire,
And others more, going to seek the grave
Of Arthur, whom they say is kill'd tonight
On your suggestion.
KING JOHN Gentle kinsman, go,
And thrust thyself into their companies.
I have a way to win their loves again.
Bring them before me.
BASTARD I will seek them out.
KING JOHN
Nay, but make haste, the better foot before.
O, let me have no subject enemies,
When adverse foreigners affright my towns 172
With dreadful pomp of stout invasion! 173
Be Mercury, set feathers to thy heels, 174
And fly like thought from them to me again.
BASTARD
The spirit of the time shall teach me speed. *Exit.*
KING JOHN
Spoke like a sprightful noble gentleman. 177
Go after him, for he perhaps shall need
Some messenger betwixt me and the peers;
And be thou he.
MESSENGER With all my heart, my liege. [*Exit.*]
KING JOHN
My mother dead!

Enter Hubert.

HUBERT
My lord, they say five moons were seen tonight:
Four fixed, and the fifth did whirl about
The other four in wondrous motion.
KING JOHN
Five moons!
HUBERT Old men and beldams in the streets 185
Do prophesy upon it dangerously.
Young Arthur's death is common in their mouths,
And, when they talk of him, they shake their heads
And whisper one another in the ear;
And he that speaks doth gripe the hearer's wrist,
Whilst he that hears makes fearful action, 191
With wrinkled brows, with nods, with rolling eyes.
I saw a smith stand with his hammer, thus,
The whilst his iron did on the anvil cool,
With open mouth swallowing a tailor's news;
Who, with his shears and measure in his hand,
Standing on slippers, which his nimble haste
Had falsely thrust upon contrary feet,
Told of a many thousand warlike French
That were embattailed and rank'd in Kent. 200
Another lean unwash'd artificer
Cuts off his tale and talks of Arthur's death.
KING JOHN
Why seek'st thou to possess me with these fears?
Why urgest thou so oft young Arthur's death?
Thy hand hath murd'red him. I had a mighty cause
To wish him dead, but thou hadst none to kill him.
HUBERT
No had, my lord? Why, did you not provoke me? 207
KING JOHN
It is the curse of kings to be attended
By slaves that take their humors for a warrant 209
To break within the bloody house of life, 210
And on the winking of authority 211
To understand a law, to know the meaning 212
Of dangerous majesty, when perchance it frowns
More upon humor than advis'd respect. 214
HUBERT
Here is your hand and seal for what I did.
[*Shows his warrant.*]
KING JOHN
O, when the last account 'twixt heaven and earth
Is to be made, then shall this hand and seal
Witness against us to damnation!
How oft the sight of means to do ill deeds
Make deeds ill done! Hadst not thou been by,
A fellow by the hand of nature mark'd,

137 amaz'd bewildered **139 Aloft the flood** riding on the sea's surface **141 sped** succeeded **144 fantasied** full of strange fancies **148 Pomfret** Pontefract, in Yorkshire **158 safety** safe keeping **159 gentle** noble **172 adverse** hostile **173 stout** bold **174 feathers** (Mercury, messenger of the gods, had winged sandals.) **177 sprightful** spirited

185 beldams old women **191 action** gestures **200 embattailed** drawn up in battle array **207 No had** had I not **209 humors** whims **210 bloody . . . life** the body, animated by life blood **211 winking** closing the eyes (i.e., when the person in authority closes his eyes to the law, or gives the merest hint of approving illegality) **212 understand a law** i.e., infer what is being commanded **214 upon humor** through whim. **advis'd respect** careful consideration

Quoted, and sign'd to do a deed of shame, 222
This murder had not come into my mind.
But, taking note of thy abhorr'd aspect,
Finding thee fit for bloody villainy,
Apt, liable to be employ'd in danger, 226
I faintly broke with thee of Arthur's death, 227
And thou, to be endeared to a king,
Made it no conscience to destroy a prince. 229

HUBERT
My lord—

KING JOHN
Hadst thou but shook thy head or made a pause
When I spake darkly what I purposed, 232
Or turn'd an eye of doubt upon my face,
As bid me tell my tale in express words, 234
Deep shame had struck me dumb, made me break off,
And those thy fears might have wrought fears in me.
But thou didst understand me by my signs
And didst in signs again parley with sin,
Yea, without stop didst let thy heart consent,
And consequently thy rude hand to act
The deed which both our tongues held vile to name.
Out of my sight, and never see me more!
My nobles leave me, and my state is brav'd, 243
Even at my gates, with ranks of foreign pow'rs.
Nay, in the body of this fleshly land, 245
This kingdom, this confine of blood and breath, 246
Hostility and civil tumult reigns
Between my conscience and my cousin's death.

HUBERT
Arm you against your other enemies,
I'll make a peace between your soul and you.
Young Arthur is alive. This hand of mine
Is yet a maiden and an innocent hand,
Not painted with the crimson spots of blood.
Within this bosom never ent'red yet
The dreadful motion of a murderous thought, 255
And you have slander'd nature in my form, 256
Which, howsoever rude exteriorly,
Is yet the cover of a fairer mind
Than to be butcher of an innocent child.

KING JOHN
Doth Arthur live? O, haste thee to the peers,
Throw this report on their incensed rage,
And make them tame to their obedience!
Forgive the comment that my passion made
Upon thy feature, for my rage was blind, 264
And foul imaginary eyes of blood 265
Presented thee more hideous than thou art.
O, answer not, but to my closet bring 267
The angry lords with all expedient haste.
I conjure thee but slowly; run more fast. *Exeunt.* 269

222 Quoted, and sign'd particularly designated and marked out **226 liable** suitable **227 faintly broke with** hesitatingly broached the subject with **229 conscience** matter of conscience **232 darkly** indirectly **234 As** as though to. **express** explicit **243 my state is brav'd** my authority is challenged **245 body . . . land** i.e., John's own body. (Uses the figure of the microcosm, in which man is conceived as the epitome of the universe.) **246 confine** (1) territorial limit (2) prison **255 motion** impulse **256 form** outward appearance **264 feature** outward appearance **265 imaginary . . . blood** (Hubert's) eyes, imagined to be bloody in thought **267 closet** private chamber **269 conjure** adjure, urge

SCENE III

Enter Arthur, on the walls, [disguised as a ship-boy].

ARTHUR
The wall is high, and yet will I leap down.
Good ground, be pitiful and hurt me not!
There's few or none do know me; if they did,
This ship-boy's semblance hath disguis'd me quite. 4
I am afraid, and yet I'll venture it.
If I get down, and do not break my limbs,
I'll find a thousand shifts to get away. 7
As good to die and go, as die and stay. [*Leaps down.*]
O me! My uncle's spirit is in these stones.
Heaven take my soul, and England keep my bones!
Dies.

Enter Pembroke, Salisbury [with a letter], and Bigot.

SALISBURY
Lords, I will meet him at Saint Edmundsbury. 11
It is our safety, and we must embrace
This gentle offer of the perilous time.

PEMBROKE
Who brought that letter from the Cardinal?

SALISBURY
The Count Melun, a noble lord of France,
Whose private with me of the Dauphin's love 16
Is much more general than these lines import. 17

BIGOT
Tomorrow morning let us meet him then.

SALISBURY
Or rather than set forward; for 'twill be
Two long days' journey, lords, or ere we meet. 20

Enter [the] Bastard.

BASTARD
Once more today well met, distemper'd lords! 21
The King by me requests your presence straight. 22

SALISBURY
The King hath dispossess'd himself of us.
We will not line his thin bestained cloak
With our pure honors, nor attend the foot
That leaves the print of blood where'er it walks.
Return and tell him so. We know the worst.

BASTARD
Whate'er you think, good words, I think, were best.

SALISBURY
Our griefs, and not our manners, reason now. 29

BASTARD
But there is little reason in your grief;
Therefore 'twere reason you had manners now.

PEMBROKE
Sir, sir, impatience hath his privilege. 32

IV.iii. Location: England. Before the castle.
4 semblance disguise **7 shifts** (1) stratagems (2) changes of costume **11 him** i.e., the Dauphin. **Saint Edmundsbury** Bury St. Edmunds, in Suffolk **16 private** private communication **17 general** all-embracing **20 or ere** before **21 distemper'd** disaffected **22 straight** at once **29 griefs** grievances. **reason** speak **32, 33 his** its

BASTARD
'Tis true, to hurt his master, no man else.
SALISBURY
This is the prison. What is he lies here?
[*Seeing Arthur.*]
PEMBROKE
O death, made proud with pure and princely
beauty!
The earth had not a hole to hide this deed.
SALISBURY
Murder, as hating what himself hath done,
Doth lay it open to urge on revenge.
BIGOT
Or, when he doom'd this beauty to a grave,
Found it too precious-princely for a grave.
SALISBURY
Sir Richard, what think you? Have you beheld,
Or have you read or heard, or could you think?
Or do you almost think, although you see,
That you do see? Could thought, without this object,
Form such another? This is the very top,
The height, the crest, or crest unto the crest,
Of murder's arms. This is the bloodiest shame,
The wildest savagery, the vilest stroke,
That ever wall-ey'd wrath or staring rage
Presented to the tears of soft remorse.
PEMBROKE
All murders past do stand excus'd in this;
And this, so sole and so unmatchable,
Shall give a holiness, a purity,
To the yet unbegotten sin of times,
And prove a deadly bloodshed but a jest,
Exampled by this heinous spectacle.
BASTARD
It is a damned and a bloody work,
The graceless action of a heavy hand—
If that it be the work of any hand.
SALISBURY
If that it be the work of any hand?
We had a kind of light what would ensue.
It is the shameful work of Hubert's hand,
The practice and the purpose of the King,
From whose obedience I forbid my soul,
Kneeling before this ruin of sweet life, [*Kneels.*]
And breathing to his breathless excellence
The incense of a vow, a holy vow,
Never to taste the pleasures of the world,
Never to be infected with delight,
Nor conversant with ease and idleness,
Till I have set a glory to this hand,
By giving it the worship of revenge.
PEMBROKE, BIGOT
Our souls religiously confirm thy words.
[*They kneel, and then all rise.*]

Enter Hubert.

HUBERT
Lords, I am hot with haste in seeking you.
Arthur doth live; the King hath sent for you.
SALISBURY
O, he is bold and blushes not at death.
Avaunt, thou hateful villain, get thee gone!
HUBERT
I am no villain.
SALISBURY Must I rob the law?
[*Drawing his sword.*]
BASTARD
Your sword is bright, sir; put it up again.
SALISBURY
Not till I sheathe it in a murderer's skin.
HUBERT
Stand back, Lord Salisbury, stand back, I say!
[*Draws.*]
By heaven, I think my sword's as sharp as yours.
I would not have you, lord, forget yourself,
Nor tempt the danger of my true defense,
Lest I, by marking of your rage, forget
Your worth, your greatness, and nobility.
BIGOT
Out, dunghill, dar'st thou brave a nobleman?
HUBERT
Not for my life. But yet I dare defend
My innocent life against an emperor.
SALISBURY
Thou art a murderer.
HUBERT Do not prove me so;
Yet I am none. Whose tongue soe'er speaks false,
Not truly speaks; who speaks not truly, lies.
PEMBROKE
Cut him to pieces.
BASTARD Keep the peace, I say. [*Draws.*]
SALISBURY
Stand by, or I shall gall you, Faulconbridge.
BASTARD
Thou wert better gall the devil, Salisbury.
If thou but frown on me, or stir thy foot,
Or teach thy hasty spleen to do me shame,
I'll strike thee dead. Put up thy sword betime,
Or I'll so maul you and your toasting-iron
That you shall think the devil is come from hell.
BIGOT
What wilt thou do, renowned Faulconbridge?
Second a villain and a murderer?
HUBERT
Lord Bigot, I am none.
BIGOT Who kill'd this prince?
HUBERT
'Tis not an hour since I left him well.
I honor'd him, I lov'd him, and will weep
My date of life out for his sweet life's loss. [*Weeps.*]
SALISBURY
Trust not those cunning waters of his eyes,

41 Sir Richard i.e., the Bastard **43 almost** even **44 That** that which **49 wall-ey'd** glaring fiercely **50 remorse** pity **54 times** i.e., future times **55 but** to be only **56 Exampled by** compared with **58 graceless** unholy. **heavy** wicked **61 light** premonition **63 practice** plot, treachery **71 this hand** i.e., either Arthur's hand, or Salisbury's own hand, which he raises in taking an oath **72 worship** honor

77 Avaunt be gone **79 bright** i.e., unused **84 tempt** risk, test **87 brave** insult **90 prove me so** i.e., make me a murderer by tempting me to kill you **94 Stand by** stand aside. **gall** wound **97 spleen** i.e., wrath **98 betime** promptly **99 toasting-iron** sword. (Used contemptuously.) **106 date** duration

For villainy is not without such rheum;
And he, long traded in it, makes it seem 109
Like rivers of remorse and innocency.
Away with me, all you whose souls abhor
Th' uncleanly savors of a slaughter-house, 112
For I am stifled with this smell of sin.

BIGOT
Away toward Bury, to the Dauphin there!

PEMBROKE
There, tell the King, he may inquire us out.
Exeunt Lords.

BASTARD
Here's a good world! Knew you of this fair work?
Beyond the infinite and boundless reach
Of mercy, if thou didst this deed of death,
Art thou damn'd, Hubert.

HUBERT
Do but hear me, sir.

BASTARD
Ha! I'll tell thee what; 120
Thou 'rt damn'd as black—nay, nothing is so black;
Thou art more deep damn'd than Prince Lucifer.
There is not yet so ugly a fiend of hell
As thou shalt be, if thou didst kill this child.

HUBERT
Upon my soul—

BASTARD
If thou didst but consent
To this most cruel act, do but despair;
And if thou want'st a cord, the smallest thread
That ever spider twisted from her womb
Will serve to strangle thee; a rush will be a beam 129
To hang thee on; or wouldst thou drown thyself,
Put but a little water in a spoon,
And it shall be as all the ocean,
Enough to stifle such a villain up.
I do suspect thee very grievously.

HUBERT
If I in act, consent, or sin of thought
Be guilty of the stealing that sweet breath
Which was embounded in this beauteous clay, 137
Let hell want pains enough to torture me.
I left him well.

BASTARD
Go, bear him in thine arms.
I am amaz'd, methinks, and lose my way
Among the thorns and dangers of this world.
[*Hubert picks up Arthur.*]
How easy dost thou take all England up!
From forth this morsel of dead royalty,
The life, the right, and truth of all this realm
Is fled to heaven; and England now is left
To tug and scamble and to part by th' teeth 146
The unowed interest of proud-swelling state. 147
Now for the bare-pick'd bone of majesty
Doth dogged war bristle his angry crest
And snarleth in the gentle eyes of peace.
Now powers from home and discontents at home 151
Meet in one line; and vast confusion waits, 152
As doth a raven on a sick-fall'n beast,
The imminent decay of wrested pomp. 154
Now happy he whose cloak and cincture can 155
Hold out this tempest. Bear away that child
And follow me with speed. I'll to the King.
A thousand businesses are brief in hand, 158
And heaven itself doth frown upon the land.
Exeunt.

109 traded experienced **112 savors** odors **129 rush** reed **137 clay** i.e., Arthur's body **146 scamble** scramble **147 unowed interest** disputed ownership or control **151 powers from home** foreign armies **152 in one line** in united purpose. **waits** waits for

154 wrested pomp usurped majesty **155 cincture** belt **158 are brief in hand** demand immediate action

ACT [V] • SCENE I

Enter King John and Pandulph, [*with*] *Attendants.*

KING JOHN
Thus have I yielded up into your hand
The circle of my glory. [*Giving the crown.*]

PANDULPH
Take again
From this my hand, as holding of the Pope
Your sovereign greatness and authority.
[*Gives back the crown.*]

KING JOHN
Now keep your holy word. Go meet the French,
And from his Holiness use all your power
To stop their marches 'fore we are inflam'd.
Our discontented counties do revolt; 8
Our people quarrel with obedience,
Swearing allegiance and the love of soul 10
To stranger blood, to foreign royalty. 11
This inundation of mistemp'red humor 12
Rests by you only to be qualified. 13
Then pause not, for the present time's so sick
That present med'cine must be minist'red, 15
Or overthrow incurable ensues.

PANDULPH
It was my breath that blew this tempest up,
Upon your stubborn usage of the Pope; 18
But since you are a gentle convertite, 19
My tongue shall hush again this storm of war
And make fair weather in your blust'ring land.
On this Ascension-day, remember well,
Upon your oath of service to the Pope,
Go I to make the French lay down their arms. *Exit.*

KING JOHN
Is this Ascension-day? Did not the prophet
Say that before Ascension-day at noon
My crown I should give off? Even so I have.
I did suppose it should be on constraint;
But, heav'n be thank'd, it is but voluntary.

Enter [*the*] *Bastard.*

BASTARD
All Kent hath yielded; nothing there holds out 30

V.i. Location: England. King John's palace.
8 counties shires; possibly, nobles **10 love of soul** most sincere love **11 stranger** foreign **12–13 This . . . qualified** this imbalance created by the excess of one humor can be reduced to its right proportion only by you **15 present** prompt **18 Upon** resulting from **19 convertite** convert

But Dover castle. London hath receiv'd,
Like a kind host, the Dauphin and his powers.
Your nobles will not hear you, but are gone
To offer service to your enemy,
And wild amazement hurries up and down
The little number of your doubtful friends.

KING JOHN
Would not my lords return to me again,
After they heard young Arthur was alive?

BASTARD
They found him dead and cast into the streets,
An empty casket, where the jewel of life
By some damn'd hand was robb'd and ta'en away.

KING JOHN
That villain Hubert told me he did live.

BASTARD
So, on my soul, he did, for aught he knew.
But wherefore do you droop? Why look you sad?
Be great in act, as you have been in thought.
Let not the world see fear and sad distrust
Govern the motion of a kingly eye.
Be stirring as the time; be fire with fire;
Threaten the threat'ner, and outface the brow
Of bragging horror. So shall inferior eyes,
That borrow their behaviors from the great,
Grow great by your example, and put on
The dauntless spirit of resolution.
Away, and glister like the god of war
When he intendeth to become the field!
Show boldness and aspiring confidence.
What, shall they seek the lion in his den,
And fright him there? And make him tremble there?
O, let it not be said! Forage, and run
To meet displeasure farther from the doors,
And grapple with him ere he come so nigh.

KING JOHN
The legate of the Pope hath been with me,
And I have made a happy peace with him;
And he hath promis'd to dismiss the powers
Led by the Dauphin.

BASTARD
O inglorious league!
Shall we, upon the footing of our land,
Send fair-play orders and make compromise,
Insinuation, parley, and base truce
To arms invasive? Shall a beardless boy,
A cock'red silken wanton, brave our fields,
And flesh his spirit in a warlike soil,
Mocking the air with colors idly spread,
And find no check? Let us, my liege, to arms!
Perchance the Cardinal cannot make your peace;
Or if he do, let it at least be said
They saw we had a purpose of defense.

KING JOHN
Have thou the ordering of this present time.

BASTARD
Away, then, with good courage! Yet, I know,
Our party may well meet a prouder foe. *Exeunt.*

36 doubtful not to be relied on; fearful **55 become** grace, adorn **59 Forage** seek out the enemy as prey **66 upon . . . land** standing on our native soil **67 fair-play orders** chivalric conditions **69 invasive** invading **70 cock'red . . . wanton** spoiled child. **brave** arrogantly display his splendor in **71 flesh** initiate in bloodshed or inure to bloodshed **73 check** restraint **76 of defense** to defend ourselves

SCENE II

Enter, in arms [Lewis the] Dauphin, Salisbury, Melun, Pembroke, Bigot, Soldiers.

LEWIS
My Lord Melun, let this be copied out,
And keep it safe for our remembrance.
[*Gives a document.*]
Return the precedent to these lords again,
That, having our fair order written down,
Both they and we, perusing o'er these notes,
May know wherefore we took the sacrament
And keep our faiths firm and inviolable.

SALISBURY
Upon our sides it never shall be broken.
And, noble Dauphin, albeit we swear
A voluntary zeal and an unurg'd faith
To your proceedings, yet believe me, Prince,
I am not glad that such a sore of time
Should seek a plaster by contemn'd revolt,
And heal the inveterate canker of one wound
By making many. O, it grieves my soul
That I must draw this metal from my side
To be a widow-maker! O, and there
Where honorable rescue and defense
Cries out upon the name of Salisbury!
But such is the infection of the time,
That, for the health and physic of our right,
We cannot deal but with the very hand
Of stern injustice and confused wrong.
And is 't not pity, O my grieved friends,
That we, the sons and children of this isle,
Were born to see so sad an hour as this,
Wherein we step after a stranger, march
Upon her gentle bosom, and fill up
Her enemies' ranks—I must withdraw and weep
Upon the spot of this enforced cause—
To grace the gentry of a land remote,
And follow unacquainted colors here? [*Weeps.*]
What, here? O nation, that thou couldst remove!
That Neptune's arms, who clippeth thee about,
Would bear thee from the knowledge of thyself,
And cripple thee unto a pagan shore,
Where these two Christian armies might combine
The blood of malice in a vein of league,
And not to spend it so unneighborly!

LEWIS
A noble temper dost thou show in this,
And great affections wrestling in thy bosom
Doth make an earthquake of nobility.
O, what a noble combat hast thou fought

V.ii. Location: England. The Dauphin's camp at St. Edmundsbury.
1 this i.e., the agreement with the English lords. (See ll. 30–34 of the preceding scene.) **3 precedent** original document, first draft **4 order** proposal **10 unurg'd** uncompelled **13 plaster** dressing for a wound. **contemn'd** reviled **16 metal** i.e., sword **19 Cries out upon** appeals to **21 physic** medical cure **27 step after** follow (as in a march). **stranger** foreign (leader) **30 spot** stain. **enforced cause** i.e., cause into which I am forced **31 grace** honor **32 unacquainted colors** i.e., the banners of a foreign power **33 remove** depart **34 clippeth** embraces **36 cripple** disable. (Often emended to *grapple.*) **37–38 combine . . . league** i.e., unite the malice they now expend on one another in a league of hostility toward a pagan foe **41 affections** passions

Between compulsion and a brave respect!
Let me wipe off this honorable dew,
That silverly doth progress on thy cheeks.
[*Wipes Salisbury's eyes.*]
My heart hath melted at a lady's tears,
Being an ordinary inundation;
But this effusion of such manly drops,
This show'r, blown up by tempest of the soul,
Startles mine eyes, and makes me more amaz'd
Than had I seen the vaulty top of heaven
Figur'd quite o'er with burning meteors.
Lift up thy brow, renowned Salisbury,
And with a great heart heave away this storm.
Commend these waters to those baby eyes
That never saw the giant world enrag'd,
Nor met with fortune other than at feasts,
Full warm of blood, of mirth, of gossiping.
Come, come; for thou shalt thrust thy hand as deep
Into the purse of rich prosperity
As Lewis himself. So, nobles, shall you all,
That knit your sinews to the strength of mine.

Enter Pandulph.

And even there, methinks, an angel spake.
Look where the holy legate comes apace,
To give us warrant from the hand of heaven,
And on our actions set the name of right
With holy breath.

PANDULPH
Hail, noble prince of France!
The next is this: King John hath reconcil'd
Himself to Rome. His spirit is come in,
That so stood out against the holy church,
The great metropolis and see of Rome.
Therefore thy threat'ning colors now wind up,
And tame the savage spirit of wild war,
That, like a lion fostered up at hand,
It may lie gently at the foot of peace
And be no further harmful than in show.

LEWIS
Your Grace shall pardon me, I will not back.
I am too high-born to be propertied,
To be a secondary at control,
Or useful servingman and instrument,
To any sovereign state throughout the world.
Your breath first kindled the dead coal of wars
Between this chastis'd kingdom and myself,
And brought in matter that should feed this fire;
And now 'tis far too huge to be blown out
With that same weak wind which enkindled it.
You taught me how to know the face of right,
Acquainted me with interest to this land,
Yea, thrust this enterprise into my heart.
And come ye now to tell me John hath made
His peace with Rome? What is that peace to me?
I, by the honor of my marriage-bed,
After young Arthur, claim this land for mine;
And, now it is half-conquer'd, must I back
Because that John hath made his peace with Rome?
Am I Rome's slave? What penny hath Rome borne,
What men provided, what munition sent,
To underprop this action? Is 't not I
That undergo this charge? Who else but I,
And such as to my claim are liable,
Sweat in this business and maintain this war?
Have I not heard these islanders shout out
"Vive le roi!" as I have bank'd their towns?
Have I not here the best cards for the game,
To win this easy match play'd for a crown?
And shall I now give o'er the yielded set?
No, no, on my soul, it never shall be said.

PANDULPH
You look but on the outside of this work.

LEWIS
Outside or inside, I will not return
Till my attempt so much be glorified
As to my ample hope was promised
Before I drew this gallant head of war,
And cull'd these fiery spirits from the world,
To outlook conquest and to win renown
Even in the jaws of danger and of death.
[*Trumpet sounds.*]
What lusty trumpet thus doth summon us?

Enter [the] Bastard.

BASTARD
According to the fair play of the world,
Let me have audience. I am sent to speak.
My holy Lord of Milan, from the King
I come, to learn how you have dealt for him;
And, as you answer, I do know the scope
And warrant limited unto my tongue.

PANDULPH
The Dauphin is too willful-opposite,
And will not temporize with my entreaties.
He flatly says he'll not lay down his arms.

BASTARD
By all the blood that ever fury breath'd,
The youth says well. Now hear our English king,
For thus his royalty doth speak in me.
He is prepar'd, and reason too he should.
This apish and unmannerly approach,
This harness'd masque and unadvised revel,
This unhair'd sauciness and boyish troops,
The King doth smile at, and is well prepar'd
To whip this dwarfish war, these pigmy arms,
From out the circle of his territories.
That hand which had the strength, even at your door,
To cudgel you and make you take the hatch,
To dive like buckets in concealed wells,
To crouch in litter of your stable planks,

44 compulsion what you are compelled to do. **brave respect** gallant consideration (of your country's need) **52 had I seen** if I had seen **53 Figur'd** adorned **64 an angel spake** (1) i.e., Pandulph comes with warrant from "the hand of heaven" (2) a pun on *angel* meaning a coin, in "the purse of rich prosperity" **70 is come in** has submitted **78 shall** must. **back** go back **79 propertied** made a tool of **80 secondary at control** second in command **85 matter** i.e., fuel **89 interest** title, right

100 charge expense **101 liable** subject **104 Vive le roi** long live the king. **bank'd** coasted, skirted **107 give o'er** abandon. **the yielded set** the game already won **113 head** army **115 outlook** stare down **118 fair play** i.e., rules of chivalry **125 temporize** come to an agreement **132 harness'd** in armor. **unadvised revel** ill-considered entertainment **133 unhair'd** beardless, youthful **138 take the hatch** leap over the lower half door; i.e., make a hasty and undignified retreat **140 litter** straw bedding for animals. **planks** floors

To lie like pawns lock'd up in chests and trunks, 141
To hug with swine, to seek sweet safety out
In vaults and prisons, and to thrill and shake
Even at the crying of your nation's crow, 144
Thinking his voice an armed Englishman—
Shall that victorious hand be feebled here,
That in your chambers gave you chastisement?
No! Know the gallant monarch is in arms,
And like an eagle o'er his aery tow'rs, 149
To souse annoyance that comes near his nest. 150
And you degenerate, you ingrate revolts, 151
You bloody Neroes, ripping up the womb 152
Of your dear mother England, blush for shame!
For your own ladies and pale-visag'd maids
Like Amazons come tripping after drums, 155
Their thimbles into armed gauntlets change,
Their needles to lances, and their gentle hearts
To fierce and bloody inclination.

LEWIS
There end thy brave, and turn thy face in peace. 159
We grant thou canst outscold us. Fare thee well.
We hold our time too precious to be spent
With such a brabbler.

PANDULPH Give me leave to speak.

BASTARD
No, I will speak.

LEWIS We will attend to neither.
Strike up the drums, and let the tongue of war
Plead for our interest and our being here.

BASTARD
Indeed, your drums, being beaten, will cry out;
And so shall you, being beaten. Do but start
An echo with the clamor of thy drum,
And even at hand a drum is ready brac'd 169
That shall reverberate all as loud as thine.
Sound but another, and another shall
As loud as thine rattle the welkin's ear 172
And mock the deep-mouth'd thunder. For at hand,
Not trusting to this halting legate here,
Whom he hath us'd rather for sport than need,
Is warlike John; and in his forehead sits
A bare-ribb'd death, whose office is this day 177
To feast upon whole thousands of the French.

LEWIS
Strike up our drums, to find this danger out.

BASTARD
And thou shalt find it, Dauphin, do not doubt.
Exeunt.

SCENE III

Alarums. Enter [King] John and Hubert.

KING JOHN
How goes the day with us? O, tell me, Hubert.

HUBERT
Badly, I fear. How fares your Majesty?

KING JOHN
This fever, that hath troubled me so long,
Lies heavy on me. O, my heart is sick!

Enter a Messenger.

MESSENGER
My lord, your valiant kinsman, Faulconbridge,
Desires your Majesty to leave the field
And send him word by me which way you go.

KING JOHN
Tell him, toward Swinstead, to the abbey there. 8

MESSENGER
Be of good comfort; for the great supply, 9
That was expected by the Dauphin here,
Are wrack'd three nights ago on Goodwin Sands.
This news was brought to Richard but even now.
The French fight coldly, and retire themselves.

KING JOHN
Ay me, this tyrant fever burns me up,
And will not let me welcome this good news.
Set on toward Swinstead. To my litter straight;
Weakness possesseth me, and I am faint. *Exeunt.*

SCENE IV

Enter Salisbury, Pembroke, and Bigot.

SALISBURY
I did not think the King so stor'd with friends.

PEMBROKE
Up once again! Put spirit in the French.
If they miscarry, we miscarry too.

SALISBURY
That misbegotten devil, Faulconbridge,
In spite of spite, alone upholds the day. 5

PEMBROKE
They say King John, sore sick, hath left the field.

Enter Melun, wounded.

MELUN
Lead me to the revolts of England here. 7

SALISBURY
When we were happy we had other names.

PEMBROKE
It is the Count Melun.

SALISBURY Wounded to death.

MELUN
Fly, noble English, you are bought and sold! 10
Unthread the rude eye of rebellion 11

141 pawns articles in pawn **144 crying . . . crow** i.e., crowing of the rooster **149 aery** nest. **tow'rs** soars **150 souse** swoop down upon (as a bird of prey) **151 revolts** rebels **152 Neroes** (The Roman emperor Nero allegedly ripped open the womb of his mother after having murdered her.) **155 Amazons** female warriors of ancient mythology **159 brave** defiant boast **169 ready brac'd** i.e., tightened, ready to be struck **172 welkin's** heaven's, sky's **177 bare-ribb'd death** i.e., death envisaged as a skeleton

V.iii. Location: England. The field of battle.

8 Swinstead i.e., Swineshead, in Lincolnshire **9 supply** reinforcement

V.iv. Location: The field of battle, as before.
5 In spite of spite i.e., despite anything we do **7 revolts** rebels **10 bought and sold** i.e., betrayed **11 Unthread . . . eye** i.e., withdraw from the hazardous undertaking in which you are engaged, just as you would withdraw thread from a needle's eye

And welcome home again discarded faith.
Seek out King John and fall before his feet;
For if the French be lords of this loud day,
He means to recompense the pains you take
By cutting off your heads. Thus hath he sworn,
And I with him, and many moe with me,
Upon the altar at Saint Edmundsbury,
Even on that altar where we swore to you
Dear amity and everlasting love.

SALISBURY
May this be possible? May this be true?

MELUN
Have I not hideous death within my view,
Retaining but a quantity of life,
Which bleeds away, even as a form of wax
Resolveth from his figure 'gainst the fire?
What in the world should make me now deceive,
Since I must lose the use of all deceit?
Why should I then be false, since it is true
That I must die here and live hence by truth?
I say again, if Lewis do win the day,
He is forsworn if e'er those eyes of yours
Behold another day break in the east.
But even this night, whose black contagious breath
Already smokes about the burning crest
Of the old, feeble, and day-wearied sun,
Even this ill night, your breathing shall expire,
Paying the fine of rated treachery
Even with a treacherous fine of all your lives,
If Lewis by your assistance win the day.
Commend me to one Hubert with your king;
The love of him, and this respect besides,
For that my grandsire was an Englishman,
Awakes my conscience to confess all this.
In lieu whereof, I pray you, bear me hence
From forth the noise and rumor of the field,
Where I may think the remnant of my thoughts
In peace, and part this body and my soul
With contemplation and devout desires.

SALISBURY
We do believe thee, and beshrew my soul
But I do love the favor and the form
Of this most fair occasion, by the which
We will untread the steps of damned flight,
And like a bated and retired flood,
Leaving our rankness and irregular course,
Stoop low within those bounds we have o'erlook'd
And calmly run on in obedience
Even to our ocean, to our great King John.
My arm shall give thee help to bear thee hence,
For I do see the cruel pangs of death
Right in thine eye. Away, my friends! New flight,
And happy newness, that intends old right.
Exeunt [leading off Melun].

15 He i.e., the French Dauphin **17 moe** more **25 Resolveth** melts. **his** its **27 use** profit **29 hence** i.e., in heaven **34 smokes** becomes misty **37 fine** penalty. **rated** (1) assessed, evaluated (2) rebuked, chided **38 fine** end (with a pun on *fine* of the previous line) **41 respect** consideration **44 In lieu whereof** in payment for which (information) **45 rumor** noise **49 beshrew** curse **50 favor . . . form** i.e., outward appearance **53 bated** checked, abated **54 rankness** overgrowth, i.e., flooding **55 o'erlook'd** overflowed **61 happy newness** a change for the better. **intends old right** intends to reestablish an ancient right or just cause

SCENE V

Enter [Lewis the] Dauphin and his train.

LEWIS
The sun of heaven methought was loath to set,
But stay'd and made the western welkin blush,
When English measure backward their own ground
In faint retire. O, bravely came we off,
When with a volley of our needless shot,
After such bloody toil, we bid good night,
And wound our tott'ring colors clearly up,
Last in the field, and almost lords of it!

Enter a Messenger.

MESSENGER
Where is my prince, the Dauphin?

LEWIS
Here. What news?

MESSENGER
The Count Melun is slain. The English lords
By his persuasion are again fall'n off,
And your supply, which you have wish'd so long,
Are cast away and sunk on Goodwin Sands.

LEWIS
Ah, foul shrewd news! Beshrew thy very heart!
I did not think to be so sad tonight
As this hath made me. Who was he that said
King John did fly an hour or two before
The stumbling night did part our weary pow'rs?

MESSENGER
Whoever spoke it, it is true, my lord.

LEWIS
Well, keep good quarter and good care tonight.
The day shall not be up so soon as I,
To try the fair adventure of tomorrow. *Exeunt.*

SCENE VI

Enter [the] Bastard and Hubert, severally.

HUBERT
Who's there? Speak, ho! Speak quickly, or I shoot.

BASTARD
A friend. What art thou?

HUBERT
Of the part of England.

BASTARD
Whither dost thou go?

HUBERT
What's that to thee? Why may not I demand
Of thine affairs, as well as thou of mine?

BASTARD
Hubert, I think?

V.v. Location: England. The French camp.
3 measure traverse **4 faint retire** fainthearted retreat **7 tott'ring** flying in tatters. **clearly** completely **14 shrewd** of evil import **18 stumbling** causing to stumble **20 quarter** watch

V.vi. Location: England. An open place in the neighborhood of Swinstead Abbey.
2 Of the part on the side

HUBERT Thou hast a perfect thought.
I will upon all hazards well believe
Thou art my friend, that know'st my tongue so well.
Who art thou?

BASTARD Who thou wilt. And if thou please,
Thou mayst befriend me so much as to think
I come one way of the Plantagenets.

HUBERT
Unkind remembrance! Thou and eyeless night
Have done me shame. Brave soldier, pardon me,
That any accent breaking from thy tongue
Should scape the true acquaintance of mine ear.

BASTARD
Come, come; sans compliment, what news abroad?

HUBERT
Why, here walk I in the black brow of night,
To find you out.

BASTARD Brief, then; and what's the news?

HUBERT
O, my sweet sir, news fitting to the night,
Black, fearful, comfortless, and horrible.

BASTARD
Show me the very wound of this ill news.
I am no woman, I'll not swoon at it.

HUBERT
The King, I fear, is poison'd by a monk.
I left him almost speechless, and broke out
To acquaint you with this evil, that you might
The better arm you to the sudden time,
Than if you had at leisure known of this.

BASTARD
How did he take it? Who did taste to him?

HUBERT
A monk, I tell you, a resolved villain,
Whose bowels suddenly burst out. The King
Yet speaks and peradventure may recover.

BASTARD
Who didst thou leave to tend his Majesty?

HUBERT
Why, know you not? The lords are all come back,
And brought Prince Henry in their company,
At whose request the King hath pardon'd them,
And they are all about his Majesty.

BASTARD
Withhold thine indignation, mighty heaven,
And tempt us not to bear above our power!
I'll tell thee, Hubert, half my power this night,
Passing these flats, are taken by the tide;
These Lincoln Washes have devoured them.
Myself, well mounted, hardly have escap'd.
Away before! Conduct me to the King.
I doubt he will be dead or ere I come. *Exeunt.*

6 perfect correct **12 Unkind remembrance** (Hubert chides his own faulty memory.) **14 accent** speech **16 sans compliment** without the usual civilities **24 out** away **26 to the sudden time** for this emergency **27 at leisure** i.e., later, because of a leisurely report **28 it** i.e., the poison. **Who did taste to him** (A "taster" was supposed to eat a portion of everything the King was to eat in order to protect him from poisoning. The monk who did so here took the poison knowingly—as a *resolved villain*—to insure the King's death.) **34 Prince Henry** i.e., John's son, the future Henry III **38 tempt . . . power** don't try us beyond our power of endurance **39 power** army **40 Passing** traversing. **flats** tidal flatlands in the large inlet called the Wash, between Lincolnshire and Norfolk **44 doubt** fear

SCENE VII

Enter Prince Henry, Salisbury, and Bigot.

PRINCE HENRY
It is too late. The life of all his blood
Is touch'd corruptibly, and his pure brain,
Which some suppose the soul's frail dwelling-house,
Doth by the idle comments that it makes
Foretell the ending of mortality.

Enter Pembroke.

PEMBROKE
His Highness yet doth speak, and holds belief
That, being brought into the open air,
It would allay the burning quality
Of that fell poison which assaileth him.

PRINCE HENRY
Let him be brought into the orchard here.
Doth he still rage? [*Exit Bigot.*]

PEMBROKE He is more patient
Than when you left him; even now he sung.

PRINCE HENRY
O vanity of sickness! Fierce extremes
In their continuance will not feel themselves.
Death, having prey'd upon the outward parts,
Leaves them invisible, and his siege is now
Against the mind, the which he pricks and wounds
With many legions of strange fantasies,
Which, in their throng and press to that last hold,
Confound themselves. 'Tis strange that death should sing.
I am the cygnet to this pale faint swan,
Who chants a doleful hymn to his own death,
And from the organ-pipe of frailty sings
His soul and body to their lasting rest.

SALISBURY
Be of good comfort, Prince, for you are born
To set a form upon that indigest
Which he hath left so shapeless and so rude.

[*King*] *John brought in* [*in a chair*].

KING JOHN
Ay, marry, now my soul hath elbow-room;
It would not out at windows nor at doors.
There is so hot a summer in my bosom
That all my bowels crumble up to dust.
I am a scribbled form, drawn with a pen
Upon a parchment, and against this fire
Do I shrink up.

PRINCE HENRY How fares your Majesty?

KING JOHN
Poison'd—ill fare! Dead, forsook, cast off,

V.vii. Location: England. The orchard in Swinstead Abbey.
5 mortality life **9 fell** cruel **14 In . . . themselves** i.e., by the very intensity of their continuation produce a loss of sensation **16 invisible** imperceptibly (?) insensate (?). **his** its, Death's **19 hold** stronghold (the mind) **20 Confound** destroy, i.e., make incoherent and senseless **21 cygnet** young swan. (It was a popular belief that the swan sang only once in its life, just before it died, as its spirit attempted to pass through its long neck, the *organ-pipe of frailty* of l. 23.) **26 indigest** shapeless mass, i.e., the confused state

And none of you will bid the winter come
To thrust his icy fingers in my maw,
Nor let my kingdom's rivers take their course
Through my burn'd bosom, nor entreat the north
To make his bleak winds kiss my parched lips
And comfort me with cold. I do not ask you much,
I beg cold comfort; and you are so strait 42
And so ingrateful, you deny me that.

PRINCE HENRY
O that there were some virtue in my tears, 44
That might relieve you!

KING JOHN The salt in them is hot.
Within me is a hell, and there the poison
Is as a fiend confin'd to tyrannize
On unreprievable condemned blood.

Enter [the] Bastard.

BASTARD
O, I am scalded with my violent motion
And spleen of speed to see your Majesty! 50

KING JOHN
O cousin, thou art come to set mine eye. 51
The tackle of my heart is crack'd and burn'd, 52
And all the shrouds wherewith my life should sail
Are turned to one thread, one little hair.
My heart hath one poor string to stay it by, 55
Which holds but till thy news be uttered,
And then all this thou seest is but a clod
And module of confounded royalty. 58

BASTARD
The Dauphin is preparing hitherward, 59
Where heaven He knows how we shall answer him; 60
For in a night the best part of my pow'r,
As I upon advantage did remove, 62
Were in the Washes all unwarily
Devoured by the unexpected flood. *[The King dies.]*

SALISBURY
You breathe these dead news in as dead an ear.
My liege! My lord! But now a king, now thus.

PRINCE HENRY
Even so must I run on, and even so stop.
What surety of the world, what hope, what stay, 68
When this was now a king, and now is clay?

BASTARD
Art thou gone so? I do but stay behind
To do the office for thee of revenge,
And then my soul shall wait on thee to heaven, 72
As it on earth hath been thy servant still.
Now, now, you stars that move in your right
spheres, 74
Where be your pow'rs? Show now your mended
faiths, 75
And instantly return with me again
To push destruction and perpetual shame
Out of the weak door of our fainting land.
Straight let us seek, or straight we shall be sought; 79
The Dauphin rages at our very heels.

SALISBURY
It seems you know not, then, so much as we.
The Cardinal Pandulph is within at rest,
Who half an hour since came from the Dauphin,
And brings from him such offers of our peace
As we with honor and respect may take,
With purpose presently to leave this war.

BASTARD
He will the rather do it when he sees
Ourselves well sinewed to our defense.

SALISBURY
Nay, 'tis in a manner done already,
For many carriages he hath dispatch'd 90
To the sea-side, and put his cause and quarrel
To the disposing of the Cardinal,
With whom yourself, myself, and other lords,
If you think meet, this afternoon will post 94
To consummate this business happily.

BASTARD
Let it be so. And you, my noble Prince,
With other princes that may best be spar'd,
Shall wait upon your father's funeral.

PRINCE HENRY
At Worcester must his body be interr'd,
For so he will'd it.

BASTARD Thither shall it then.
And happily may your sweet self put on
The lineal state and glory of the land, 102
To whom, with all submission, on my knee
I do bequeath my faithful services
And true subjection everlastingly. *[Kneels.]*

SALISBURY
And the like tender of our love we make, 106
To rest without a spot for evermore. 107
[All kneel to Prince Henry, and then rise.]

PRINCE HENRY
I have a kind soul that would give you thanks
And knows not how to do it but with tears.

BASTARD
O, let us pay the time but needful woe, 110
Since it hath been beforehand with our griefs.
This England never did, nor never shall,
Lie at the proud foot of a conqueror
But when it first did help to wound itself.
Now these her princes are come home again,
Come the three corners of the world in arms, 116
And we shall shock them. Nought shall make us
rue, 117
If England to itself do rest but true. *Exeunt.*

42 strait niggardly **44 virtue** power **50 spleen** i.e., eagerness **51 set mine eye** close my eyes (in death) **52 tackle** rigging of a ship **55 stay it** support itself **58 module** counterfeit, mere image. **confounded** destroyed **59 preparing** repairing, coming **60 heaven He knows** only God knows. **answer** encounter **62 upon advantage** taking favorable opportunity. **remove** shift position **68 stay** support **72 wait on** attend **74 stars** i.e., nobles. **right spheres** proper orbits (around the throne, like heavenly bodies around the earth) **75 faiths** loyalties (to the crown)

79 Straight at once **90 carriages** baggage vehicles **94 post** hasten **102 lineal state** crown by right of succession **106 tender** offer **107 spot** stain **110 but needful woe** no more weeping than necessary **116 three . . . world** i.e., all the world except England, the fourth corner **117 shock** meet with force

The Tragedy of King Richard the Second

Richard II (c. 1595–1596) is the first in Shakespeare's great four-play historical saga, or tetralogy, that continues with the two parts of *Henry IV* (c. 1596–1598) and concludes with *Henry V* (1599). This second tetralogy completes the action of Shakespeare's great cycle on the Wars of the Roses, begun in the earlier tetralogy on Henry VI and Richard III (c. 1589–1594). Both sequences move from an outbreak of civil faction to the eventual triumph of political stability. Together, they comprise the story of England's long century of political turmoil from the 1390's until Henry Tudor's victory over Richard III in 1485. Yet Shakespeare chose to relate the two halves of this chronicle in reverse order. His crowning statement about kingship in *Henry V* focuses on the earlier historical period, on the education and kingly success of Prince Hal.

With *Richard II,* then, Shakespeare turns to the events which had launched England's century of crisis. These events were still fresh and relevant to Elizabethan minds. Richard and Bolingbroke's contest for the English crown provided a "mirror for magistrates": a sobering example of political wrongdoing and, at least by implication, a rule for political right conduct. One prominent reason for studying history, to an Elizabethan, was to avoid errors of the past. What are the rights and wrongs of Richard's deposition, and to what extent can political lessons be drawn from Shakespeare's presentation?

To begin with, we should not underestimate Richard's attractive qualities, as a man and even as a king. Throughout the play, Richard is consistently more impressive and majestic in appearance than his rival Bolingbroke. Richard fascinates us with his verbal sensitivity, his poetic insight, and his dramatic self-consciousness. He eloquently expounds a sacramental view of kingship, according to which "Not all the water in the rough rude sea Can wash the balm off from an anointed king" (III,ii). Bolingbroke can depose Richard but can never capture the aura of majesty Richard possesses; Bolingbroke may succeed politically, but only at the expense of desecrating an idea. Richard is much more interesting to us as a man than Bolingbroke, more capable of grief, more tender in his personal relationships, more in need of being understood. Indeed, a major factor in Richard's tragedy is the conflict between his public role (wherein he sees himself as divinely appointed, almost superhuman) and his private role (wherein he is emotionally dependent and easily hurt). He confuses what the medieval and Renaissance world knew as the king's "two bodies," the sacramental body of kingship which is eternal, and the human body of a single occupant of the throne whose frail mortal condition is subject to time and fortune. Richard's failure to perceive and act wisely on this difference is part of his tragic predicament, but his increasing insight through suffering into the truth of the distinction is also part of his spiritual growth. His dilemma, however poignantly individual, lies at the heart of kingship. Richard is thus very much a king. Although he sometimes indulges in childish sentimentality, at his best he is superbly refined, perceptive, and poetic.

These qualities notwithstanding, Richard is an incompetent ruler compared with the man who supplants him. Richard himself confesses to the prodigal expense of "too great a court." In order to raise funds, he has been obliged to "farm our royal realm": that is, sell for ready cash the right of collecting taxes to individual courtiers, who are then free to extort what the market will bear (I,iv). Similarly, Richard proposes to issue "blank charters" to his minions, who will then be authorized to fill in the amount of tax to be paid by any hapless subject. These abuses were infamous to Elizabethan audiences as symbols of autocratic misgovernment. No less heinous is Richard's seizure of the dukedom of Lancaster from his cousin Bolingbroke. Although Richard does receive the consent of his council to banish Bolingbroke, he violates the very idea of inheritance of property when he takes away Bolingbroke's title and lands. And, as his uncle the Duke of York remonstrates, Richard's own right to the throne depends on that idea of due inheritance. By offending against the most sacred concepts of order and degree, he teaches others to rebel.

Richard's behavior even prior to the commencement of the play arouses suspicion. The nature of his complicity in the death of his uncle Thomas of Woodstock, Duke of Gloucester, is perhaps never entirely clear, and Gloucester may have given provocation. Indeed, one can sympathize with the predicament of a young ruler prematurely thrust into the center of power by the untimely death of his father, the crown prince, now having to cope with an array of worldly-wise, advice-giving uncles. Nevertheless, Richard is unambiguously guilty of murder in the eyes of Gloucester's widow and of her brother-in-law John of Gaunt, Duke of Lancaster. Apparently, too, Gaunt's son Bolingbroke believes Richard to be a murderer, and brings accusation against Thomas Mowbray, Duke of Norfolk, partly as a means of embarrassing the King whom he cannot accuse directly. Mowbray's lot is an unenviable one: he was in command at Calais when Gloucester was executed there, and he hints that Richard ordered the execution (even though Mowbray alleges that he himself did not carry out the order). For his part, Richard is only too glad to banish the man suspected of having been his agent in murder. Mowbray is a convenient scapegoat.

The polished, ceremonial tone of the play's opening is vitiated, then, by our growing awareness of dirty politics going on behind the display. Our first impression of Richard is of a king devoted to the public display of conciliatory evenhandedness. He listens to the rival claims of Bolingbroke and Mowbray, and, when he cannot reconcile them peacefully, he allows a trial by combat. This trial (I,iii) is replete with ceremonial repetition and ritual. The combatants are duly sworn in the justice of their cause, and God is to decide the quarrel by awarding victory to the champion who speaks the truth. Richard, the presiding officer, is God's anointed deputy on earth. Yet it becomes evident in due course that Richard is a major perpetrator of injustice rather than an impartial judge, that Bolingbroke is after greater objectives than he acknowledges even to himself, and that the banishment of the two contenders is Richard's desperate way of burying a problem he cannot deal with forthrightly. His uncles reluctantly consent to the banishment only because they too see that disaffection has reached alarming proportions.

Bolingbroke's motivation in these opening scenes is perhaps even more obscure than that of Richard. Our first impression of Bolingbroke is of forthrightness, moral indignation, and patriotic zeal. In fact we never really question the earnestness of his outrage at Richard's misgovernance, his longing to avenge a family murder (for Gloucester was his uncle, too), or his bitter disappointment at being banished. Yet we are prompted to ask further: what is the essential cause of the enmity between Bolingbroke and Richard? If Mowbray is only a stalking-horse, is not Gloucester's death also the excuse for pursuing a preexistent animosity? Richard, for one, appears to think so. His portrayal of Bolingbroke as a scheming politician, one who curries favor with the populace in order to build a widely based alliance against the King himself, is telling and prophetic. Bolingbroke, says Richard, acts "As were our England in reversion his, And he our subjects' next degree in hope" (I,iv). This unflattering appraisal might be ascribed to malicious envy on Richard's part, were it not proved by subsequent events to be wholly accurate.

Paradoxically, Richard is far the more prescient of the two contenders for the English throne. It is he, in fact, who perceives from the start that the conflict between them is irreconcilable. He banishes Bolingbroke as his chief rival, and does not doubt what motives will call Bolingbroke home again. Meanwhile, Bolingbroke disclaims any motive for his deed other than love of country and hatred of injustice. Although born with a political canniness that Richard lacks, Bolingbroke does not theorize about the consequences of his acts. As a man of action, he lives in the present. Richard, conversely, a person of exquisite contemplative powers and poetic imagination, does not deign to cope with the practical. He both envies and despises Bolingbroke's easy way with the commoners. Richard cherishes kingship for the majesty and the royal prerogative it confers, not for the power to govern wisely. Thus it is that, despite his perception of what will follow, Richard habitually indulges his worst instincts, buying a moment of giddy pleasure at the expense of long-term disaster.

We cannot doubt Richard's incompetence as a ruler. Does this incompetence condone Bolingbroke's armed rebellion? According to John of Gaunt, to York (despite his later shift of allegiance), and to the Bishop of Carlisle, it does not. The attitude of these men can be summed up by the phrase "passive obedience." As Gaunt expresses the concept, "God's is the quarrel." Because Richard is God's anointed deputy on earth, only God may punish the King's wrongdoing. Gaunt does not question Richard's guilt, but neither does he question God's ability to avenge. Gaunt sees human intervention in God's affair as blasphemous: "for I may never lift An angry arm against His minister" (I,ii). To be sure, Gaunt does acknowledge a solemn duty to offer frank advice to extremists of both sides, and he does so unsparingly. He consents to the banishment of his son, and he rebukes Richard with his dying breath.

This doctrine of passive obedience was familiar to Elizabethans, for they heard it in church periodically in official homilies against rebellion. It was the Tudor state's answer to those who asserted a right to overthrow reputedly evil kings. The argument was logically ingenious. Why are evil rulers permitted to govern from time to time? Presumably because God wishes to test a people or punish them for waywardness. Any king performing such chastisement is a divine "scourge." Accordingly, the worst thing a people can do is to rebel against God's scourge, thereby manifesting more waywardness. Instead, they must attempt to remedy the insolence in their hearts, advise the King to mend his ways, and patiently await God's pardon. If they do so they will not long be disappointed. The doctrine is essentially conservative, defending the status quo. Nevertheless, in *Richard II* it is a moderate position between the extremes of tyranny and rebellion, and is expressed by thoughtful, selfless men. We might be tempted to label it Shakespeare's view, if we did not also perceive that the doctrine is continually placed in ironic conflict with harsh political realities. The character who most reflects the ironies and even ludicrous incongruities of the position is the Duke of York.

York is to an extent a choric character—that is, one who helps direct our viewpoint—because his transfer of loyalties from Richard to Bolingbroke structurally delineates the decline of Richard's fortunes and the concurrent rise of Bolingbroke's. At first York shares with his brother Gaunt a dismay at Richard's willfulness, together with a reluctance to act. It is only when Richard seizes the dukedom of Lancaster that York can no longer hold his tongue. His condemnation is as bitter as that of Gaunt, hinting even at loss of allegiance (II,i). Still, he accepts the responsibility, so cavalierly bestowed by Richard, of governing England in the King's absence. He musters what force he can to oppose Bolingbroke's advance, and lectures against this rebellion with the same vehemence he had used against Richard's despotism. Yet when faced with Bolingbroke's overwhelming military superiority, he accedes rather than fight in behalf of a lost cause. However much this may resemble cowardice or mere expediency, it also displays a pragmatic logic. Once Bolingbroke has become *de facto* king, in York's view he must be acknowledged and obeyed. By a kind of analogy to the doctrine of passive obedience (which more rigorous theorists would never allow), York accepts the status quo as inevitable. He is vigorously ready to defend the new regime, just as he earlier defended Richard's rule.

When, however, this conclusion brings York to the point of turning in his own son Aumerle for a traitor, and quarreling with his wife as to whether their son shall live, the ironic absurdity is apparent. King Henry himself is amused, in one of the play's rare lighthearted moments (V,iii). When a family and a kingdom are divided against one another, there can be no really satisfactory resolution.

We are never entirely convinced that all the fine old medieval theories surrounding kingship—divine right, passive obedience, trial by combat, and the like—can ever wholly explain or remedy the complex and nasty political situation afflicting England. The one man capable of decisive action, in fact, is he who never theorizes at all: Bolingbroke. As we have seen, his avowed motive for opposing Mowbray—simple patriotic indignation—is uttered with such earnestness that we wonder if indeed Bolingbroke has examined in himself those political ambitions so plainly visible to Richard and others. This same discrepancy between surface and depth applies to Bolingbroke's motives in returning to England. We cannot be sure at what time he begins to plot that return; the conspiracy announced by Northumberland (II,i) follows so closely after Richard's violation of Bolingbroke's hereditary rights, and is already so well advanced, that we gain the impression of an already-existing plot, though some of this impression may be simply owing to Shakespeare's characteristic compression of historic time. When Bolingbroke arrives in England, in any case, he protests to York with seemingly passionate sincerity that he comes only for his dukedom of Lancaster (II,iii). If so, why does he set about executing Richard's followers without legal authority, and otherwise setting the kingdom to rights? Does Bolingbroke seriously think he can reclaim his dukedom by force, and then yield to Richard without either maintaining Richard as a puppet king or placing himself in intolerable jeopardy? And can he suppose that his allies, Northumberland and the rest, who have now openly defied the King, will countenance the return to power of one who would never trust them again? It is in this context that York protests, "Well, well, I see the issue of these arms." Not only the deposition of Richard, but Richard's death, are foregone conclusions once Bolingbroke has succeeded in an armed rebellion. There can be no turning back. Yet Bolingbroke simply will not theorize in these terms. He repeatedly admonishes Northumberland for treating Richard harshly, even though Northumberland is only taking upon himself the unpleasant but unavoidable duty of arresting and impeaching a king. When the new King Henry discovers—to his surprise, evidently—that Richard's life is now a burden to the state, he ponders aloud, "Have I no friend will rid me of this living fear?" and then rebukes Exton for proceeding on cue.

The phrase for Bolingbroke's pragmatic spirit, and for his new government, is *"de facto."* Ultimately, the justification for his rule is the very fact of its existence, its functioning. Bolingbroke is the man of the hour. In Yeats' fine maxim, Bolingbroke is the vessel of clay, Richard the vessel of porcelain. One is durable and utilitarian, yet unattractive; the other is exquisite, fragile, impractical. The comparison does not force us to prefer one to the other, even though Yeats himself characteristically sided with beauty against politics. Rather, Shakespeare gives us our choice, allowing us to see in ourselves an inclination toward political and social stability or toward artistic temperament.

The paradox may suggest that the qualities of a good administrator are not those of a sensitive, thoughtful man. However hopeless as a king, Richard stands before us increasingly as an introspective and fascinating person. When his power crumbles, his spirit is enhanced, as though loss of power and royal identity were necessary for the discovery of true values.

In this there is a faint anticipation of King Lear's self-learning, fearfully and preciously bought. The trace is only slight here, because in good part *Richard II* is a political history play rather than a tragedy, and because Richard's self-realization is imperfect. Nevertheless, when Richard faces deposition and separation from his queen, and especially when he is alone in prison expecting to die, he strives to understand his life and through it the general condition of humanity. He perceives a contradiction in heaven's assurances about salvation: Christ promises to receive all God's children, and yet He also warns that it is as hard for a rich man to enter heaven as for a camel to thread a needle's eye (V,v). The paradox echoes the Beatitudes: the last shall be first, the meek shall inherit the earth. Richard, now one of the downtrodden, gropes for an understanding of the vanity of human achievement whereby he can aspire to the victory Christ promised. At his death, that victory seems to him assured: his soul will mount to its seat on high "Whilst my gross flesh sinks downward, here to die."

In this triumph of spirit over flesh, the long downward motion of Richard's worldly fortune is crucially reversed. By the same token, the worldly success of Bolingbroke is shown to be no more than that: worldly success. His archetype is Cain, the primal murderer of a brother. To the extent that the play is a history, Bolingbroke's *de facto* success is still a matter of political relevance; but in the belated movement toward Richard's personal tragedy, we experience a profound countermovement that partly achieves a purgative sense of atonement and reassurance. Whatever Richard may have lost, his gain is also great.

Balance and symmetry are unusually important in *Richard II*. The play begins and ends with elaborate ritual obeisance to the concept of social and monarchic order, and yet in both cases a note of personal disorder refuses to be subdued by the public ceremonial. Shakespeare keeps our response to both Richard and Bolingbroke ambivalent by clouding their respective responsibilities for murder. Just as Richard's role in Gloucester's death remains unclear, so Bolingbroke's role in the assassination of Richard remains equally unclear. Mowbray and Exton, as scapegoats, are in some respects parallel. Because Richard and Bolingbroke are both implicated in the deaths of near kinsmen, both are associated with Cain's murder of Abel. As Bolingbroke rises in worldly fortune, Richard falls; as Richard finds insight and release through suffering, Bolingbroke finds guilt and remorse through distasteful political necessity. Again and again, the ritual effects of staging and style draw our attention to the balanced conflict between the two men and within Richard. Symmetry helps to focus these conflicts in visual and aural ways. In particular, the deposition scene with its spectacle of a coronation in reverse brings the sacramental and human sides of the central figure into poignant dramatic relationship.

The imagery of *Richard II* reinforces structure and meaning. The play is unusual for its extensive use of blank verse and rhyme, and for its interwoven sets of recurring images. England is a garden mismanaged by her royal gardener, so that weeds and caterpillars (e.g., Bushy, Bagot, and Green) flourish. The "garden" scene (III,iv), located at the center of the play, offering a momentary haven of allegorical reflection on the play's hectic events, is central in the development of the garden metaphor. England is also a sick body ill-tended by her royal physician, and a family divided against itself yielding abortive and sterile progeny. Her political ills are attested to by disorders in the cosmos: comets, shooting stars, withered bay trees, weeping rains. Night owls, associated with death, prevail over the larks of morning. The sun, royally associated at first with Richard, deserts him for Bolingbroke and leaves Richard as the Phaethon who has mishandled the sun-god's chariot and so scorched the earth. Linked to the sun image is the prevalent *leit-motif* of ascent and descent. And, touching upon all these, a cluster of Biblical images sees England as a despoiled garden of Eden witnessing a second fall of man. Richard repeatedly brands his enemies and deserters as Judases and Pilates, not always fairly; nonetheless, in his last agony he finds genuine consolation in Christ's example. This poetic method is intensely suitable for a man so self-absorbed in the drama of his existence.

The poetry also confirms the date of *Richard II* as of the so-called lyric period, c. 1594–1596, that also produced *Romeo and Juliet* and *A Midsummer Night's Dream*. The play, registered and carefully published in quarto form in 1597, appears to have drawn on Samuel Daniel's *Civill Wars* (1595) as well as Holinshed's *Chronicles*. For its structure it surely owed something to Marlowe's *Edward II* (c. 1592), and it may have relied on the anonymous *Thomas of Woodstock* (c. 1591–1595) for an understanding of the occasionally obscure events surrounding the death of Richard's uncle. Shakespeare must have known he was dealing with a politically explosive topic often used as a libelous analogy against Queen Elizabeth. The deposition scene is missing from the earlier quartos, as though it had been excised by the censor. And in 1601 the Earl of Essex commissioned Shakespeare's company to perform a revived play about Richard II on the eve of an abortive rebellion, presumably as a means of inciting to riot. Whether the play was Shakespeare's is not certain, but seems likely. The acting company was ultimately exonerated, but not before Elizabeth believed that she was being compared to Richard. However little Shakespeare may have intended the analogy when he wrote, he chose a subject of intense political relevance to Elizabethans, for which the greatest tact was needed.

The Tragedy of King Richard the Second

[*Dramatis Personae*

KING RICHARD THE SECOND.
JOHN OF GAUNT, *Duke of Lancaster,* } *uncles to the King.*
EDMUND OF LANGLEY, DUKE OF YORK, } *uncles to the King.*
HENRY, *surnamed* BOLINGBROKE, *Duke of Hereford, son to John of Gaunt; afterwards* KING HENRY IV.
DUKE OF AUMERLE, *son to the Duke of York.*
THOMAS MOWBRAY, *Duke of Norfolk.*
DUKE OF SURREY.
EARL OF SALISBURY.
LORD BERKELEY.
BUSHY, BAGOT, GREEN, } *favorites to King Richard.*
EARL OF NORTHUMBERLAND.
HENRY PERCY, *surnamed* HOTSPUR, *his son.*
LORD ROSS.
LORD WILLOUGHBY.
LORD FITZWATER.
BISHOP OF CARLISLE.
ABBOT OF WESTMINSTER.
LORD MARSHAL.
SIR STEPHEN SCROOP.
SIR PIERCE OF EXTON.
CAPTAIN *of a band of Welshmen.*

QUEEN *to King Richard.*
DUCHESS OF YORK.
DUCHESS OF GLOUCESTER, *widow of Thomas of Woodstock, Duke of Gloucester.*
LADIES *attending on the Queen.*

LORDS, HERALDS, OFFICERS, SOLDIERS, GARDENERS, KEEPER, MESSENGER, GROOM, *and other* ATTENDANTS.

SCENE: *England and Wales.*]

[ACT I • SCENE I]

Enter King Richard, John of Gaunt, with other Nobles and Attendants.

KING RICHARD
Old John of Gaunt, time-honored Lancaster, 1
Hast thou, according to thy oath and band, 2
Brought hither Henry Hereford thy bold son,
Here to make good the boist'rous late appeal, 4
Which then our leisure would not let us hear, 5
Against the Duke of Norfolk, Thomas Mowbray?

GAUNT
I have, my liege.

KING RICHARD
Tell me, moreover, hast thou sounded him 8
If he appeal the Duke on ancient malice, 9
Or worthily, as a good subject should,
On some known ground of treachery in him?

GAUNT
As near as I could sift him on that argument, 12
On some apparent danger seen in him 13
Aim'd at your Highness, no inveterate malice.

KING RICHARD
Then call them to our presence. [*Exit Attendant.*]
Face to face,
And frowning brow to brow, ourselves will hear
The accuser and the accused freely speak.
High-stomach'd are they both, and full of ire, 18
In rage deaf as the sea, hasty as fire.

Enter Bolingbroke and Mowbray [*with Attendants*].

BOLINGBROKE
Many years of happy days befall
My gracious sovereign, my most loving liege!

MOWBRAY
Each day still better other's happiness,
Until the heavens, envying earth's good hap, 23
Add an immortal title to your crown!

KING RICHARD
We thank you both. Yet one but flatters us,
As well appeareth by the cause you come:
Namely, to appeal each other of high treason.
Cousin of Hereford, what dost thou object 28
Against the Duke of Norfolk, Thomas Mowbray?

BOLINGBROKE
First—heaven be the record to my speech!—
In the devotion of a subject's love,

I.i. Location: A room of state. (Holinshed's *Chronicles* places this scene at Windsor, in 1398.)
1 Old John of Gaunt (Born in 1340 at Ghent; hence the surname *Gaunt.* In 1398 he was fifty-eight years old.) **2 band** bond **4 late** recent. **appeal** accusation, formal challenge or impeachment which the accuser was obliged to maintain in combat **5 our, us** (The royal plural.) **leisure** i.e., lack of leisure **8 sounded** inquired of **9 appeal** accuse. **on . . . malice** on the grounds of a long-standing enmity **12 sift** discover true motives by indirect questioning. **argument** subject **13 apparent** obvious, manifest **18 High-stomach'd** haughty **23 hap** fortune **28 What . . . object** what accusation do you bring

Tend'ring the precious safety of my prince, 32
And free from other misbegotten hate,
Come I appellant to this princely presence. 34
Now, Thomas Mowbray, do I turn to thee,
And mark my greeting well; for what I speak
My body shall make good upon this earth,
Or my divine soul answer it in heaven.
Thou art a traitor and a miscreant, 39
Too good to be so, and too bad to live,
Since the more fair and crystal is the sky,
The uglier seem the clouds that in it fly.
Once more, the more to aggravate the note, 43
With a foul traitor's name stuff I thy throat,
And wish, so please my sovereign, ere I move,
What my tongue speaks my right drawn sword may
prove. 46

MOWBRAY
Let not my cold words here accuse my zeal. 47
'Tis not the trial of a woman's war, 48
The bitter clamor of two eager tongues, 49
Can arbitrate this cause betwixt us twain; 50
The blood is hot that must be cool'd for this.
Yet can I not of such tame patience boast
As to be hush'd and nought at all to say.
First, the fair reverence of your Highness curbs me
From giving reins and spurs to my free speech,
Which else would post until it had return'd 56
These terms of treason doubled down his throat.
Setting aside his high blood's royalty, 58
And let him be no kinsman to my liege, 59
I do defy him, and I spit at him,
Call him a slanderous coward and a villain;
Which to maintain I would allow him odds
And meet him, were I tied to run afoot 63
Even to the frozen ridges of the Alps,
Or any other ground inhabitable 65
Wherever Englishman durst set his foot.
Meantime let this defend my loyalty:
By all my hopes, most falsely doth he lie.

BOLINGBROKE
Pale trembling coward, there I throw my gage, 69
[*Throws down gage.*]
Disclaiming here the kindred of the King, 70
And lay aside my high blood's royalty,
Which fear, not reverence, makes thee to except. 72
If guilty dread have left thee so much strength
As to take up mine honor's pawn, then stoop. 74
By that, and all the rites of knighthood else,
Will I make good against thee, arm to arm,
What I have spoke, or thou canst worse devise. 77

MOWBRAY
I take it up; and by that sword I swear,
[*Takes up the gage.*]
Which gently laid my knighthood on my shoulder,
I'll answer thee in any fair degree
Or chivalrous design of knightly trial;
And when I mount, alive may I not light, 82
If I be traitor or unjustly fight!

KING RICHARD
What doth our cousin lay to Mowbray's charge?
It must be great that can inherit us 85
So much as of a thought of ill in him.

BOLINGBROKE
Look what I speak, my life shall prove it true: 87
That Mowbray hath receiv'd eight thousand nobles 88
In name of lendings for your Highness' soldiers, 89
The which he hath detain'd for lewd employments, 90
Like a false traitor and injurious villain.
Besides I say, and will in battle prove,
Or here or elsewhere to the furthest verge 93
That ever was survey'd by English eye,
That all the treasons for these eighteen years, 95
Complotted and contrived in this land,
Fetch from false Mowbray their first head and
spring. 97
Further I say, and further will maintain
Upon his bad life to make all this good,
That he did plot the Duke of Gloucester's death, 100
Suggest his soon-believing adversaries, 101
And consequently, like a traitor coward, 102
Sluic'd out his innocent soul through streams of
blood—
Which blood, like sacrificing Abel's, cries, 104
Even from the tongueless caverns of the earth, 105
To me for justice and rough chastisement.
And, by the glorious worth of my descent,
This arm shall do it, or this life be spent.

KING RICHARD
How high a pitch his resolution soars! 109
Thomas of Norfolk, what say'st thou to this?

MOWBRAY
O, let my sovereign turn away his face
And bid his ears a little while be deaf,
Till I have told this slander of his blood, 113
How God and good men hate so foul a liar.

KING RICHARD
Mowbray, impartial are our eyes and ears.
Were he my brother, nay, my kingdom's heir,
As he is but my father's brother's son,
Now, by my scepter's awe, I make a vow, 118
Such neighbor nearness to our sacred blood
Should nothing privilege him, nor partialize 120
The unstooping firmness of my upright soul.

32 Tend'ring holding dear **34 appellant** as the accuser **39 miscreant** irreligious villain **43 note** reproach, stigma, i.e., charge of treason **46 right drawn** justly or rightly drawn **47 accuse my zeal** cast doubt on my zeal or loyalty **48 woman's war** i.e., war of words **49 eager** sharp, biting **50 Can** that can **56 post** ride at high speed **58 Setting . . . royalty** disregarding Bolingbroke's royal blood (as grandson of Edward III) **59 let him be** suppose him to be **63 tied** obliged **65 inhabitable** uninhabitable **69 gage** a pledge to combat (usually a glove or gauntlet) **70 kindred** kinship **72 except** use as an excuse **74 pawn** i.e., the gage **77 or . . . devise** or anything worse you can imagine me to have said about you

82 light alight, dismount **85 inherit us** put us in possession of, make us have **87 Look what** whatever **88 nobles** gold coins worth 6 shillings 8 pence **89 lendings** money advanced to soldiers when the regular pay cannot be given **90 lewd** vile, base **93 Or** either **95 these eighteen years** i.e., ever since the Peasants' Revolt of 1381 **97 head and spring** (Synonymous words meaning *origin*.) **100 Duke of Gloucester's death** (Thomas of Woodstock, Duke of Gloucester, a younger son of Edward III and brother of John of Gaunt, was murdered at Calais in September, 1397, while under Mowbray's custody.) **101 Suggest** prompt, incite. **soon-believing** easily persuaded, overcredulous **102 consequently** afterwards **104 Abel's** (For the story of Cain's murder of his brother Abel, the first such murder on earth and the archetype of the killing of a kinsman, see Genesis 4:3–12.) **105 tongueless** resonant but without articulate speech, echoing **109 pitch** highest reach of a falcon's flight **113 slander of** disgrace or reproach to **118 my scepter's awe** the reverence due my scepter **120 nothing** not at all. **partialize** make partial

He is our subject, Mowbray; so art thou.
Free speech and fearless I to thee allow.

MOWBRAY
Then, Bolingbroke, as low as to thy heart
Through the false passage of thy throat, thou liest!
Three parts of that receipt I had for Calais
Disburs'd I duly to his Highness' soldiers;
The other part reserv'd I by consent,
For that my sovereign liege was in my debt
Upon remainder of a dear account,
Since last I went to France to fetch his queen.
Now swallow down that lie. For Gloucester's death,
I slew him not, but to my own disgrace
Neglected my sworn duty in that case.
For you, my noble Lord of Lancaster,
The honorable father to my foe,
Once did I lay an ambush for your life,
A trespass that doth vex my grieved soul;
But ere I last receiv'd the sacrament
I did confess it, and exactly begg'd
Your Grace's pardon, and I hope I had it.
This is my fault. As for the rest appeal'd,
It issues from the rancor of a villain,
A recreant and most degenerate traitor,
Which in myself I boldly will defend,
And interchangeably hurl down my gage
Upon this overweening traitor's foot,
To prove myself a loyal gentleman
Even in the best blood chamber'd in his bosom.
[*Throws down gage. Bolingbroke picks it up.*]
In haste whereof, most heartily I pray
Your Highness to assign our trial day.

KING RICHARD
Wrath-kindled gentlemen, be rul'd by me;
Let's purge this choler without letting blood.
This we prescribe, though no physician;
Deep malice makes too deep incision.
Forget, forgive; conclude and be agreed;
Our doctors say this is no month to bleed.
Good uncle, let this end where it begun;
We'll calm the Duke of Norfolk, you your son.

GAUNT
To be a make-peace shall become my age.
Throw down, my son, the Duke of Norfolk's gage.

KING RICHARD
And, Norfolk, throw down his.

GAUNT
When, Harry, when?
Obedience bids I should not bid again.

KING RICHARD
Norfolk, throw down, we bid; there is no boot.

MOWBRAY [*Kneeling*]
Myself I throw, dread sovereign, at thy foot.
My life thou shalt command, but not my shame.
The one my duty owes; but my fair name,
Despite of death that lives upon my grave,
To dark dishonor's use thou shalt not have.
I am disgrac'd, impeach'd, and baffled here,
Pierc'd to the soul with slander's venom'd spear,
The which no balm can cure but his heart-blood
Which breath'd this poison.

KING RICHARD
Rage must be withstood.
Give me his gage. Lions make leopards tame.

MOWBRAY
Yea, but not change his spots. Take but my shame,
And I resign my gage. My dear dear lord,
The purest treasure mortal times afford
Is spotless reputation; that away,
Men are but gilded loam or painted clay.
A jewel in a ten-times-barr'd-up chest
Is a bold spirit in a loyal breast.
Mine honor is my life; both grow in one;
Take honor from me, and my life is done.
Then, dear my liege, mine honor let me try;
In that I live and for that will I die.

KING RICHARD
Cousin, throw up your gage; do you begin.

BOLINGBROKE
O, God defend my soul from such deep sin!
Shall I seem crestfallen in my father's sight?
Or with pale beggar-fear impeach my height
Before this out-dar'd dastard? Ere my tongue
Shall wound my honor with such feeble wrong,
Or sound so base a parle, my teeth shall tear
The slavish motive of recanting fear
And spit it bleeding in his high disgrace,
Where shame doth harbor, even in Mowbray's face.
[*Exit Gaunt.*]

KING RICHARD
We were not born to sue, but to command;
Which since we cannot do to make you friends,
Be ready, as your lives shall answer it,
At Coventry, upon Saint Lambert's day.
There shall your swords and lances arbitrate
The swelling difference of your settled hate.
Since we cannot atone you, we shall see
Justice design the victor's chivalry.
Lord Marshal, command our officers at arms
Be ready to direct these home alarms.
Exit [*with others*].

126 receipt money received **129 For that** because **130 Upon . . . account** for the balance of a heavy debt **131 Since . . . queen** i.e., since my most recent voyage to France to negotiate the King's marriage (1396) with Isabella, daughter of the French King Charles VI **132 For** as for **132–134 For . . . case** (Mowbray speaks guardedly, but seems to imply that he postponed the execution of Gloucester that he was ordered by Richard to carry out.) **140 exactly** explicitly, formally **142 appeal'd** of which I am charged **144 recreant** faithless, debased **145 Which** which charge **146 interchangeably** in exchange, in turn **150 In haste whereof** to hasten which proof of my innocence **153 Let's. . . blood** let's treat this wrath (caused by an excess of bile or choler) by purgation rather than by medical bloodletting (with a play on *bloodshed in combat*) **156 conclude** come to a final agreement **157 no month to bleed** (Spring and autumn were regarded as the proper times to bleed patients.) **164 boot** remedy

168 Despite . . . lives that will live in spite of death **170 impeach'd** accused. **baffled** disgraced as a recreant knight **173 Which breath'd** of him who uttered **174 Lions . . . tame** (The royal arms showed a lion rampant; Mowbray's emblem was a leopard.) **177 mortal times** our earthly lives **184 try** put to the test **186 throw . . . gage** i.e., throw your gage up to me, thereby ending the quarrel. (Richard is probably seated in an elevated position, as in scene iii.) **189 impeach my height** discredit my high rank **190 out-dar'd** dared down, cowed **191 feeble wrong** dishonorable submission **192 sound . . . parle** trumpet so shameful a negotiation, i.e., consent to such a truce **193 motive** instrument, i.e., the tongue **194 in his** to its, the tongue's **195 s. d. Exit Gaunt** (A stage direction from the Folio, adopted by most editors so that Gaunt will not be required to exit at the end of scene i and then immediately reenter.) **199 Saint Lambert's day** September 17 **202 atone** reconcile **203 design** point out. **chivalry** true knightly qualities (as demonstrated by victory in trial by combat) **205 home alarms** domestic conflicts

[SCENE II]

Enter John of Gaunt with the Duchess of Gloucester.

GAUNT
Alas, the part I had in Woodstock's blood 1
Doth more solicit me than your exclaims 2
To stir against the butchers of his life!
But since correction lieth in those hands 4
Which made the fault that we cannot correct,
Put we our quarrel to the will of heaven,
Who, when they see the hours ripe on earth,
Will rain hot vengeance on offenders' heads.

DUCHESS
Finds brotherhood in thee no sharper spur?
Hath love in thy old blood no living fire?
Edward's seven sons, whereof thyself art one, 11
Were as seven vials of his sacred blood,
Or seven fair branches springing from one root.
Some of those seven are dried by nature's course,
Some of those branches by the Destinies cut;
But Thomas, my dear lord, my life, my Gloucester,
One vial full of Edward's sacred blood,
One flourishing branch of his most royal root,
Is crack'd, and all the precious liquor spilt,
Is hack'd down, and his summer leaves all faded,
By envy's hand and murder's bloody axe. 21
Ah, Gaunt, his blood was thine! That bed, that womb,
That metal, that self mold, that fashioned thee 23
Made him a man; and though thou livest and breathest,
Yet art thou slain in him. Thou dost consent
In some large measure to thy father's death,
In that thou seest thy wretched brother die,
Who was the model of thy father's life. 28
Call it not patience, Gaunt; it is despair.
In suff'ring thus thy brother to be slaught'red,
Thou showest the naked pathway to thy life,
Teaching stern murder how to butcher thee.
That which in mean men we entitle patience 33
Is pale cold cowardice in noble breasts.
What shall I say? To safeguard thine own life,
The best way is to venge my Gloucester's death.

GAUNT
God's is the quarrel, for God's substitute, 37
His deputy anointed in His sight,
Hath caus'd his death, the which if wrongfully, 39
Let heaven revenge; for I may never lift
An angry arm against His minister.

DUCHESS
Where then, alas, may I complain myself?

GAUNT
To God, the widow's champion and defense.

DUCHESS
Why, then, I will. Farewell, old Gaunt.
Thou goest to Coventry, there to behold
Our cousin Hereford and fell Mowbray fight. 46
O, sit my husband's wrongs on Hereford's spear,
That it may enter butcher Mowbray's breast!
Or, if misfortune miss the first career, 49
Be Mowbray's sins so heavy in his bosom
That they may break his foaming courser's back,
And throw the rider headlong in the lists,
A caitiff recreant to my cousin Hereford! 53
Farewell, old Gaunt. Thy sometimes brother's wife 54
With her companion, Grief, must end her life.

GAUNT
Sister, farewell; I must to Coventry.
As much good stay with thee as go with me!

DUCHESS
Yet one word more. Grief boundeth where it falls, 58
Not with the empty hollowness, but weight.
I take my leave before I have begun,
For sorrow ends not when it seemeth done.
Commend me to thy brother, Edmund York. 62
Lo, this is all. Nay, yet depart not so!
Though this be all, do not so quickly go;
I shall remember more. Bid him—ah, what?—
With all good speed at Plashy visit me. 66
Alack, and what shall good old York there see
But empty lodgings and unfurnish'd walls, 68
Unpeopled offices, untrodden stones? 69
And what hear there for welcome but my groans?
Therefore commend me; let him not come there,
To seek out sorrow that dwells everywhere.
Desolate, desolate, will I hence and die!
The last leave of thee takes my weeping eye. *Exeunt.*

[SCENE III]

Enter Lord Marshal and the Duke [of] Aumerle.

MARSHAL
My Lord Aumerle, is Harry Hereford arm'd?

AUMERLE
Yea, at all points, and longs to enter in.

MARSHAL
The Duke of Norfolk, sprightfully and bold, 3
Stays but the summons of the appellant's trumpet.

I.ii. Location: The Duke of Lancaster's palace (? No place is specified, and the scene is not in Holinshed.)
1 part . . . blood my kinship with Thomas of Woodstock, the Duke of Gloucester (i.e., as his older brother) **2 exclaims** exclamations **4 those hands** i.e., Richard's (whom Gaunt charges with responsibility for Gloucester's death) **11 Edward's** Edward III's **21 envy's** malice's **23 metal** substance. **self** selfsame **28 model** likeness, copy **33 mean** lowly **37 God's substitute** i.e., the King, God's deputy on earth **39 his** i.e., Gloucester's

46 cousin kinsman. **fell** fierce **49 misfortune** i.e., Mowbray's downfall. **career** the charge of the horse in a tourney or combat **53 caitiff** base, cowardly **54 sometimes** late **58 boundeth** bounces, rebounds, returns **62 Edmund York** Edmund of Langley, fifth son of Edward III **66 Plashy** Pleshey, Gloucester's country seat, in Essex **68 unfurnish'd** bare **69 offices** service quarters, workrooms

I.iii. Location: The lists at Coventry. Scaffolds or raised seats are provided for the King and his nobles, and chairs for the combatants.
3 sprightfully with high spirit

AUMERLE
Why then, the champions are prepar'd, and stay
For nothing but his Majesty's approach.

The trumpets sound, and the King enters with his nobles [*Gaunt, Bushy, Bagot, Green, and others*]. *When they are set, enter* [*Mowbray*] *the Duke of Norfolk in arms, defendant* [*with a Herald*].

KING RICHARD
Marshal, demand of yonder champion
The cause of his arrival here in arms.
Ask him his name, and orderly proceed
To swear him in the justice of his cause.

MARSHAL
In God's name and the King's, say who thou art
And why thou comest thus knightly clad in arms,
Against what man thou com'st, and what thy quarrel.
Speak truly on thy knighthood and thy oath,
As so defend thee heaven and thy valor!

MOWBRAY
My name is Thomas Mowbray, Duke of Norfolk,
Who hither come engaged by my oath—
Which God defend a knight should violate!—
Both to defend my loyalty and truth
To God, my king, and my succeeding issue,
Against the Duke of Hereford that appeals me,
And, by the grace of God and this mine arm,
To prove him, in defending of myself,
A traitor to my God, my king, and me;
And as I truly fight, defend me heaven!

The trumpets sound. Enter [*Bolingbroke,*] *Duke of Hereford, appellant, in armor* [*with a Herald*].

KING RICHARD
Marshal, ask yonder knight in arms
Both who he is and why he cometh hither
Thus plated in habiliments of war,
And formally, according to our law,
Depose him in the justice of his cause.

MARSHAL
What is thy name? And wherefore com'st thou hither,
Before King Richard in his royal lists?
Against whom comest thou? And what's thy quarrel?
Speak like a true knight, so defend thee heaven!

BOLINGBROKE
Harry of Hereford, Lancaster, and Derby
Am I, who ready here do stand in arms
To prove, by God's grace and my body's valor,
In lists, on Thomas Mowbray, Duke of Norfolk,
That he is a traitor, foul and dangerous,
To God of heaven, King Richard, and to me;
And as I truly fight, defend me heaven!

MARSHAL
On pain of death, no person be so bold
Or daring-hardy as to touch the lists,
Except the Marshal and such officers
Appointed to direct these fair designs.

BOLINGBROKE
Lord Marshal, let me kiss my sovereign's hand
And bow my knee before his Majesty;
For Mowbray and myself are like two men
That vow a long and weary pilgrimage.
Then let us take a ceremonious leave
And loving farewell of our several friends.

MARSHAL
The appellant in all duty greets your Highness,
And craves to kiss your hand and take his leave.

KING RICHARD [*Coming down*]
We will descend and fold him in our arms.
[*He embraces Bolingbroke.*]
Cousin of Hereford, as thy cause is right,
So be thy fortune in this royal fight!
Farewell, my blood; which if today thou shed,
Lament we may, but not revenge thee dead.

BOLINGBROKE
O, let no noble eye profane a tear
For me, if I be gor'd with Mowbray's spear.
As confident as is the falcon's flight
Against a bird, do I with Mowbray fight.
My loving lord, I take my leave of you;
Of you, my noble cousin, Lord Aumerle;
Not sick, although I have to do with death,
But lusty, young, and cheerly drawing breath.
Lo, as at English feasts, so I regreet
The daintiest last, to make the end most sweet.
O thou, the earthly author of my blood,
Whose youthful spirit, in me regenerate,
Doth with a twofold vigor lift me up
To reach at victory above my head,
Add proof unto mine armor with thy prayers,
And with thy blessings steel my lance's point,
That it may enter Mowbray's waxen coat,
And furbish new the name of John a Gaunt,
Even in the lusty havior of his son.

GAUNT
God in thy good cause make thee prosperous!
Be swift like lightning in the execution,
And let thy blows, doubly redoubled,
Fall like amazing thunder on the casque
Of thy adverse pernicious enemy.
Rouse up thy youthful blood, be valiant and live.

BOLINGBROKE
Mine innocency and Saint George to thrive!

MOWBRAY
However God or fortune cast my lot,
There lives or dies, true to King Richard's throne,
A loyal, just, and upright gentleman.
Never did captive with a freer heart

18 defend forbid **28 plated** armored **30 Depose him** take his sworn deposition

43 daring-hardy daringly bold, reckless **47 bow my knee** (Presumably Bolingbroke kneels to Richard, and, at about l. 69, to Gaunt.) **59–60 profane . . . For me** misuse tears by weeping for me **66 lusty** full of vigor. **cheerly** cheerfully **67 regreet** greet, salute **68 The daintiest** i.e., the most tasty, the finest **70 regenerate** born anew **73 proof** invulnerability **75 enter . . . coat** pierce Mowbray's armor as though it were made of wax **76 a** of **77 havior** behavior, deportment **81 amazing** bewildering. **casque** helmet

Cast off his chains of bondage, and embrace
His golden uncontroll'd enfranchisement,
More than my dancing soul doth celebrate
This feast of battle with mine adversary.
Most mighty liege, and my companion peers,
Take from my mouth the wish of happy years. 94
As gentle and as jocund as to jest 95
Go I to fight. Truth hath a quiet breast.

KING RICHARD
Farewell, my lord. Securely I espy 97
Virtue with valor couched in thine eye. 98
Order the trial, Marshal, and begin.

MARSHAL
Harry of Hereford, Lancaster, and Derby,
Receive thy lance; and God defend the right!
[*A lance is given to Bolingbroke.*]

BOLINGBROKE
Strong as a tower in hope, I cry amen.

MARSHAL
Go bear this lance to Thomas, Duke of Norfolk.
[*A lance is given to Norfolk.*]

FIRST HERALD
Harry of Hereford, Lancaster, and Derby
Stands here for God, his sovereign, and himself,
On pain to be found false and recreant,
To prove the Duke of Norfolk, Thomas Mowbray,
A traitor to his God, his king, and him,
And dares him to set forward to the fight.

SECOND HERALD
Here standeth Thomas Mowbray, Duke of Norfolk,
On pain to be found false and recreant,
Both to defend himself and to approve 112
Henry of Hereford, Lancaster, and Derby,
To God, his sovereign, and to him disloyal,
Courageously and with a free desire
Attending but the signal to begin. 116

MARSHAL
Sound, trumpets; and set forward, combatants.
[*A charge sounded. Richard throws down his baton.*]
Stay, the King hath thrown his warder down. 118

KING RICHARD
Let them lay by their helmets and their spears,
And both return back to their chairs again.
Withdraw with us, and let the trumpets sound 121
While we return these dukes what we decree. 122
[*A long flourish. Richard consults apart with Gaunt and others.*]
Draw near,
And list what with our council we have done. 124
For that our kingdom's earth should not be soil'd 125
With that dear blood which it hath fostered;
And for our eyes do hate the dire aspect 127
Of civil wounds plough'd up with neighbors' sword;
And for we think the eagle-winged pride
Of sky-aspiring and ambitious thoughts,
With rival-hating envy, set on you 131
To wake our peace, which in our country's cradle
Draws the sweet infant breath of gentle sleep;
Which, so rous'd up with boist'rous untun'd drums, 134
With harsh-resounding trumpets' dreadful bray,
And grating shock of wrathful iron arms,
Might from our quiet confines fright fair peace
And make us wade even in our kindred's blood:
Therefore, we banish you our territories.
You, cousin Hereford, upon pain of life,
Till twice five summers have enrich'd our fields
Shall not regreet our fair dominions,
But tread the stranger paths of banishment. 143

BOLINGBROKE
Your will be done. This must my comfort be,
That sun that warms you here shall shine on me,
And those his golden beams to you here lent
Shall point on me and gild my banishment.

KING RICHARD
Norfolk, for thee remains a heavier doom,
Which I with some unwillingness pronounce:
The sly slow hours shall not determinate 150
The dateless limit of thy dear exile. 151
The hopeless word of "never to return"
Breathe I against thee, upon pain of life.

MOWBRAY
A heavy sentence, my most sovereign liege,
And all unlook'd for from your Highness' mouth.
A dearer merit, not so deep a maim 156
As to be cast forth in the common air,
Have I deserved at your Highness' hands.
The language I have learn'd these forty years,
My native English, now I must forego;
And now my tongue's use is to me no more
Than an unstringed viol or a harp,
Or like a cunning instrument cas'd up, 163
Or, being open, put into his hands 164
That knows no touch to tune the harmony.
Within my mouth you have enjail'd my tongue,
Doubly portcullis'd with my teeth and lips, 167
And dull unfeeling barren ignorance
Is made my jailer to attend on me.
I am too old to fawn upon a nurse,
Too far in years to be a pupil now.
What is thy sentence then but speechless death,
Which robs my tongue from breathing native breath?

KING RICHARD
It boots thee not to be compassionate. 174
After our sentence plaining comes too late. 175

MOWBRAY
Then thus I turn me from my country's light,

94 Take . . . years i.e., take from me the wish that you may enjoy many happy years **95 gentle** unperturbed in spirit. **to jest** i.e., to a play or entertainment **97 Securely** confidently **98 couched** expressed **112 approve** prove **116 Attending** awaiting **118 warder** staff or truncheon borne by the King when presiding over a trial by combat **121 Withdraw with us** (Addressed to members of the council.) **122 While we return** until I inform **122 s.d. flourish** fanfare **124 list** hear **125 For that** in order that **127 for** because (also in l. 129)

131 envy enmity. **set on you** set you on **134 Which** i.e., which enmity, disturbance of the peace. (Although in literal terms the antecedent of *Which* is *peace* in l. 132.) **143 stranger** alien **150 determinate** put to an end **151 dateless limit** unlimited term. **dear** grievous **156 dearer merit** more valued reward. **maim** injury **163 cunning** skillfully made **164 open** taken from its case **167 portcullis'd** shut in by a portcullis, an iron grating over a gateway that can be raised and lowered **174 boots** avails. **compassionate** full of laments **175 plaining** complaining

To dwell in solemn shades of endless night.
[Starts to leave.]

KING RICHARD
Return again, and take an oath with thee.
Lay on our royal sword your banish'd hands.
[They place their hands on Richard's sword.]
Swear by the duty that you owe to God—
Our part therein we banish with yourselves— 181
To keep the oath that we administer:
You never shall, so help you truth and God,
Embrace each other's love in banishment,
Nor never look upon each other's face,
Nor never write, regreet, nor reconcile
This louring tempest of your home-bred hate;
Nor never by advised purpose meet 188
To plot, contrive, or complot any ill
'Gainst us, our state, our subjects, or our land.

BOLINGBROKE
I swear.

MOWBRAY
And I, to keep all this.

BOLINGBROKE
Norfolk, so far as to mine enemy: 193
By this time, had the King permitted us,
One of our souls had wand'red in the air,
Banish'd this frail sepulcher of our flesh,
As now our flesh is banish'd from this land.
Confess thy treasons ere thou fly the realm.
Since thou hast far to go, bear not along
The clogging burden of a guilty soul.

MOWBRAY
No, Bolingbroke. If ever I were traitor,
My name be blotted from the book of life,
And I from heaven banish'd as from hence!
But what thou art, God, thou, and I do know;
And all too soon, I fear, the King shall rue.
Farewell, my liege. Now no way can I stray; 206
Save back to England, all the world's my way. *Exit.*

KING RICHARD
Uncle, even in the glasses of thine eyes 208
I see thy grieved heart. Thy sad aspect
Hath from the number of his banish'd years
Pluck'd four away. *[To Bolingbroke.]* Six frozen winters spent,
Return with welcome home from banishment.

BOLINGBROKE
How long a time lies in one little word!
Four lagging winters and four wanton springs 214
End in a word; such is the breath of kings.

GAUNT
I thank my liege, that in regard of me
He shortens four years of my son's exile.
But little vantage shall I reap thereby;
For, ere the six years that he hath to spend
Can change their moons and bring their times about,
My oil-dried lamp and time-bewasted light
Shall be extinct with age and endless night;
My inch of taper will be burnt and done,
And blindfold death not let me see my son. 224

KING RICHARD
Why, uncle, thou hast many years to live.

GAUNT
But not a minute, King, that thou canst give.
Shorten my days thou canst with sullen sorrow,
And pluck nights from me, but not lend a morrow;
Thou canst help time to furrow me with age,
But stop no wrinkle in his pilgrimage; 230
Thy word is current with him for my death, 231
But dead, thy kingdom cannot buy my breath. 232

KING RICHARD
Thy son is banish'd upon good advice,
Whereto thy tongue a party-verdict gave. 234
Why at our justice seem'st thou then to lour?

GAUNT
Things sweet to taste prove in digestion sour.
You urg'd me as a judge, but I had rather
You would have bid me argue like a father.
O, had it been a stranger, not my child,
To smooth his fault I should have been more mild. 240
A partial slander sought I to avoid, 241
And in the sentence my own life destroy'd.
Alas, I look'd when some of you should say
I was too strict to make mine own away; 244
But you gave leave to my unwilling tongue
Against my will to do myself this wrong.

KING RICHARD
Cousin, farewell; and, uncle, bid him so.
Six years we banish him, and he shall go.
[Flourish. Exit King Richard with his train.]

AUMERLE *[To Bolingbroke]*
Cousin, farewell. What presence must not know, 249
From where you do remain let paper show.

MARSHAL *[To Bolingbroke]*
My lord, no leave take I, for I will ride,
As far as land will let me, by your side.
[Bolingbroke makes no answer. They retire.]

GAUNT
O, to what purpose dost thou hoard thy words,
That thou returnest no greeting to thy friends?

BOLINGBROKE
I have too few to take my leave of you,
When the tongue's office should be prodigal
To breathe the abundant dolor of the heart.

GAUNT
Thy grief is but thy absence for a time.

BOLINGBROKE
Joy absent, grief is present for that time.

GAUNT
What is six winters? They are quickly gone. 260

181 Our part therein i.e., the duty you owe me as king **188 advised** deliberate, premeditated **193 so . . . enemy** so far as I would speak to or wish success to my sworn enemy **206 stray** take the wrong road **208 glasses** mirrors (here glistening with tears) **214 wanton** luxuriant

224 blindfold death i.e., death which blinds **230 stop . . . pilgrimage** prevent no wrinkle that comes with time **231 current** i.e., as good as current coin, valid **232 dead** i.e., once I am dead. **buy** i.e., restore with a payment **234 a party-verdict** one person's share in a joint verdict **240 smooth** extenuate **241 partial slander** accusation of partiality (on behalf of my son) **244 to . . . away** in making away with my own (son) **249 What . . . know** what I cannot learn from you in person

BOLINGBROKE
To men in joy; but grief makes one hour ten.
GAUNT
Call it a travel that thou tak'st for pleasure.
BOLINGBROKE
My heart will sigh when I miscall it so,
Which finds it an enforced pilgrimage.
GAUNT
The sullen passage of thy weary steps
Esteem as foil wherein thou art to set 266
The precious jewel of thy home return.
BOLINGBROKE
Nay, rather, every tedious stride I make
Will but remember me what a deal of world 269
I wander from the jewels that I love.
Must I not serve a long apprenticehood
To foreign passages, and in the end, 272
Having my freedom, boast of nothing else
But that I was a journeyman to grief? 274
GAUNT
All places that the eye of heaven visits
Are to a wise man ports and happy havens.
Teach thy necessity to reason thus:
There is no virtue like necessity.
Think not the King did banish thee,
But thou the King. Woe doth the heavier sit
Where it perceives it is but faintly borne. 281
Go, say I sent thee forth to purchase honor, 282
And not the King exil'd thee; or suppose
Devouring pestilence hangs in our air
And thou art flying to a fresher clime.
Look what thy soul holds dear, imagine it 286
To lie that way thou goest, not whence thou com'st.
Suppose the singing birds musicians,
The grass whereon thou tread'st the presence strew'd, 289
The flowers fair ladies, and thy steps no more
Than a delightful measure or a dance; 291
For gnarling sorrow hath less power to bite 292
The man that mocks at it and sets it light.
BOLINGBROKE
O, who can hold a fire in his hand
By thinking on the frosty Caucasus?
Or cloy the hungry edge of appetite
By bare imagination of a feast?
Or wallow naked in December snow
By thinking on fantastic summer's heat? 299
O, no, the apprehension of the good
Gives but the greater feeling to the worse.
Fell sorrow's tooth doth never rankle more 302
Than when he bites, but lanceth not the sore. 303
GAUNT
Come, come, my son, I'll bring thee on thy way. 304
Had I thy youth and cause, I would not stay.
BOLINGBROKE
Then, England's ground, farewell; sweet soil, adieu;
My mother, and my nurse, that bears me yet!
Where'er I wander, boast of this I can,
Though banish'd, yet a true born Englishman.
Exeunt.

[SCENE IV]

Enter the King, with Bagot, [Green,] etc. at one door, and the Lord Aumerle at another.

KING RICHARD
We did observe. Cousin Aumerle, 1
How far brought you high Hereford on his way?
AUMERLE
I brought high Hereford, if you call him so,
But to the next highway, and there I left him.
KING RICHARD
And say, what store of parting tears were shed?
AUMERLE
Faith, none for me; except the northeast wind, 6
Which then blew bitterly against our faces,
Awak'd the sleeping rheum, and so by chance 8
Did grace our hollow parting with a tear.
KING RICHARD
What said our cousin when you parted with him?
AUMERLE
"Farewell!"
And, for my heart disdained that my tongue 12
Should so profane the word, that taught me craft 13
To counterfeit oppression of such grief
That words seem'd buried in my sorrow's grave.
Marry, would the word "farewell" have length'ned hours 16
And added years to his short banishment,
He should have had a volume of farewells;
But since it would not, he had none of me. 19
KING RICHARD
He is our cousin, cousin; but 'tis doubt,
When time shall call him home from banishment,
Whether our kinsman come to see his friends. 22
Ourself and Bushy, Bagot here, and Green
Observ'd his courtship to the common people;
How he did seem to dive into their hearts
With humble and familiar courtesy,
What reverence he did throw away on slaves,
Wooing poor craftsmen with the craft of smiles
And patient underbearing of his fortune, 29
As 'twere to banish their affects with him. 30
Off goes his bonnet to an oyster-wench;
A brace of draymen bid God speed him well 32

266 foil thin metal leaf set behind gems to show off their luster; hence, that which sets something off to advantage **269 remember** remind **272 passages** wanderings, experiences **274 journeyman** one who labors for daily wages **281 faintly** faintheartedly **282 purchase** acquire **286 Look what** whatever **289 the presence strew'd** the royal presence chamber strewn with rushes **291 measure** stately, formal dance **292 gnarling** snarling, growling **299 fantastic** imaginary **302 Fell** fierce. **rankle** cause irritation and festering **303 lanceth not** does not open by probing (in order to cleanse the infection) **304 bring** escort

I.iv. Location: The court.
1 We did observe (The scene begins in the midst of a conversation.) **6 for me** for my part **8 rheum** moisture, tears **12 for** because **13 that** i.e., my disdain. (Aumerle says he pretended to be overcome by grief in order to avoid saying an insincere "Farewell" to Bolingbroke.) **16 Marry** indeed. (From the oath, *by the Virgin Mary.*) **19 of** from **22 friends** kinsmen, i.e., us, his cousins **29 underbearing** bearing, endurance **30 affects** affections. (I.e., as if the affections of the common people would go abroad with Bolingbroke and thus desert Richard.) **32 draymen** carters

And had the tribute of his supple knee,
With "Thanks, my countrymen, my loving friends,"
As were our England in reversion his,
And he our subjects' next degree in hope.

GREEN
Well, he is gone, and with him go these thoughts.
Now for the rebels which stand out in Ireland,
Expedient manage must be made, my liege,
Ere further leisure yield them further means
For their advantage and your Highness' loss.

KING RICHARD
We will ourself in person to this war.
And, for our coffers, with too great a court
And liberal largess, are grown somewhat light,
We are enforc'd to farm our royal realm,
The revenue whereof shall furnish us
For our affairs in hand. If that come short,
Our substitutes at home shall have blank charters,
Whereto, when they shall know what men are rich,
They shall subscribe them for large sums of gold
And send them after to supply our wants;
For we will make for Ireland presently.

Enter Bushy.

Bushy, what news?

BUSHY
Old John of Gaunt is grievous sick, my lord,
Suddenly taken; and hath sent post haste
To entreat your Majesty to visit him.

KING RICHARD
Where lies he?

BUSHY
At Ely House.

KING RICHARD
Now put it, God, in the physician's mind
To help him to his grave immediately!
The lining of his coffers shall make coats
To deck our soldiers for these Irish wars.
Come, gentlemen, let's all go visit him.
Pray God we may make haste, and come too late!

[ALL]
Amen. *Exeunt.*

[ACT II • SCENE I]

Enter John of Gaunt sick, with the Duke of York, etc.

GAUNT
Will the King come, that I may breathe my last
In wholesome counsel to his unstaid youth?

YORK
Vex not yourself, nor strive not with your breath;
For all in vain comes counsel to his ear.

GAUNT
O, but they say the tongues of dying men
Enforce attention like deep harmony.
Where words are scarce, they are seldom spent in vain,
For they breathe truth that breathe their words in pain.
He that no more must say is listened more
Than they whom youth and ease have taught to glose.
More are men's ends mark'd than their lives before.
The setting sun, and music at the close,
As the last taste of sweets, is sweetest last,
Writ in remembrance more than things long past.
Though Richard my life's counsel would not hear,
My death's sad tale may yet undeaf his ear.

YORK
No, it is stopp'd with other flattering sounds,
As praises, of whose taste the wise are fond,
Lascivious meters, to whose venom sound
The open ear of youth doth always listen;
Report of fashions in proud Italy,
Whose manners still our tardy apish nation
Limps after in base imitation.
Where doth the world thrust forth a vanity—
So it be new, there's no respect how vile—
That is not quickly buzz'd into his ears?
Then all too late comes counsel to be heard,
Where will doth mutiny with wit's regard.
Direct not him whose way himself will choose.
'Tis breath thou lack'st, and that breath wilt thou lose.

GAUNT
Methinks I am a prophet new inspir'd,
And thus expiring do foretell of him:
His rash fierce blaze of riot cannot last,
For violent fires soon burn out themselves;
Small show'rs last long, but sudden storms are short;
He tires betimes that spurs too fast betimes;
With eager feeding food doth choke the feeder;
Light vanity, insatiate cormorant,
Consuming means, soon preys upon itself.
This royal throne of kings, this sceptred isle,
This earth of majesty, this seat of Mars,
This other Eden, demi-paradise,
This fortress built by Nature for herself
Against infection and the hand of war,
This happy breed of men, this little world,

35 in reversion by right of future succession **37 go** let go **38 stand out** rise in rebellion **39 Expedient manage** expeditious management **43 for** because. **too great a court** i.e., too great an extravagance at court **45 farm** lease the right of collecting taxes, for a present cash payment, to the highest bidder **48 substitutes** deputies. **blank charters** writs authorizing the collection of revenues or forced loans to the crown, blank spaces being left for the names of the parties and the sums they were to provide **50 subscribe them** put down their names **52 presently** at once **58 Ely House** (Palace of the Bishop of Ely in Holborn, a London district.) **61 lining** contents (with pun on lining for coats). **coats** coats of mail, armor

II.i. Location: Ely House.
s.d. Enter John of Gaunt sick (Presumably he is carried in by servants in a chair.)

9 listened listened to **10 glose** flatter, deceive in speech **11 mark'd** noticed **15 my life's counsel** my advice while I lived **16 My . . . tale** my grave dying speech **18 As . . . fond** such as praises, which even wise men are foolishly inclined to hear **19 venom** poisonous **21 proud Italy** (Ascham, Lyly, and other sixteenth-century writers complained of the growing influence of Italian luxury.) **22 still** always. **tardy apish** imitative but behind the times **25 there's no respect** it makes no difference **28 will . . . regard** natural inclination rebels against what reason esteems **33 riot** profligacy **36 betimes** soon, early **38 Light vanity** frivolous dissipation. **cormorant** glutton. (Literally, a voracious seabird.) **39 means** i.e., means of sustenance **44 infection** (1) plague (2) moral pollution

This precious stone set in the silver sea,
Which serves it in the office of a wall
Or as a moat defensive to a house,
Against the envy of less happier lands,
This blessed plot, this earth, this realm, this England,
This nurse, this teeming womb of royal kings,
Fear'd by their breed and famous by their birth,
Renowned for their deeds as far from home,
For Christian service and true chivalry,
As is the sepulcher in stubborn Jewry
Of the world's ransom, blessed Mary's Son,
This land of such dear souls, this dear dear land,
Dear for her reputation through the world,
Is now leas'd out—I die pronouncing it—
Like to a tenement or pelting farm.
England, bound in with the triumphant sea,
Whose rocky shore beats back the envious siege
Of wat'ry Neptune, is now bound in with shame,
With inky blots and rotten parchment bonds.
That England, that was wont to conquer others,
Hath made a shameful conquest of itself.
Ah, would the scandal vanish with my life,
How happy then were my ensuing death!

Enter King [*Richard*] *and Queen,* [*Aumerle, Bushy, Green, Bagot, Ross, and Willoughby,*] *etc.*

YORK
The King is come. Deal mildly with his youth,
For young hot colts being rag'd do rage the more.

QUEEN
How fares our noble uncle, Lancaster?

KING RICHARD
What comfort, man? How is 't with aged Gaunt?

GAUNT
O, how that name befits my composition!
Old Gaunt indeed, and gaunt in being old.
Within me grief hath kept a tedious fast,
And who abstains from meat that is not gaunt?
For sleeping England long time have I watch'd;
Watching breeds leanness, leanness is all gaunt.
The pleasure that some fathers feed upon
Is my strict fast—I mean, my children's looks—
And, therein fasting, hast thou made me gaunt.
Gaunt am I for the grave, gaunt as a grave,
Whose hollow womb inherits nought but bones.

KING RICHARD
Can sick men play so nicely with their names?

GAUNT
No, misery makes sport to mock itself.
Since thou dost seek to kill my name in me,
I mock my name, great King, to flatter thee.

KING RICHARD
Should dying men flatter with those that live?

GAUNT
No, no, men living flatter those that die.

KING RICHARD
Thou, now a-dying, sayest thou flatterest me.

GAUNT
O, no, thou diest, though I the sicker be.

KING RICHARD
I am in health, I breathe, and see thee ill.

GAUNT
Now He that made me knows I see thee ill;
Ill in myself to see, and in thee seeing ill.
Thy death-bed is no lesser than thy land,
Wherein thou liest in reputation sick;
And thou, too careless patient as thou art,
Commit'st thy anointed body to the cure
Of those physicians that first wounded thee.
A thousand flatterers sit within thy crown,
Whose compass is no bigger than thy head;
And yet, incaged in so small a verge,
The waste is no whit lesser than thy land.
O, had thy grandsire with a prophet's eye
Seen how his son's son should destroy his sons,
From forth thy reach he would have laid thy shame,
Deposing thee before thou wert possess'd,
Which art possess'd now to depose thyself.
Why, cousin, wert thou regent of the world
It were a shame to let this land by lease;
But, for thy world enjoying but this land,
Is it not more than shame to shame it so?
Landlord of England art thou now, not king.
Thy state of law is bondslave to the law,
And thou—

KING RICHARD A lunatic lean-witted fool,
Presuming on an ague's privilege,
Darest with thy frozen admonition
Make pale our cheek, chasing the royal blood
With fury from his native residence.
Now, by my seat's right royal majesty,
Wert thou not brother to great Edward's son,
This tongue that runs so roundly in thy head
Should run thy head from thy unreverent shoulders.

GAUNT
O, spare me not, my brother Edward's son,
For that I was his father Edward's son!
That blood already, like the pelican,
Hast thou tapp'd out and drunkenly carous'd.
My brother Gloucester, plain well-meaning soul—
Whom fair befall in heaven 'mongst happy souls!—
May be a precedent and witness good
That thou respect'st not spilling Edward's blood.
Join with the present sickness that I have,

52 by their breed for their ancestral reputation for prowess **55 stubborn Jewry** i.e., Judea, called stubborn because it resisted Christianity **60 tenement** land or property held by a tenant. **pelting** paltry **62 envious** hostile **64 blots . . . bonds** i.e., the blank charters **70 rag'd** enraged **73 composition** constitution **77 watch'd** kept watch at night, been vigilant **81 therein fasting** i.e., since I am starved of the pleasure some fathers have, in seeing happy looks in the next generation **83 inherits** possesses, will receive **84 nicely** playfully, fantastically **85 to mock** of mocking **86 kill . . . me** i.e., by banishing my son

99 physicians i.e., the King's favorites **102 verge** (1) circle, ring (2) the compass about the King's court which extended for twelve miles **104 grandsire** i.e., Edward III **107 possess'd** put in possession of the crown **108 possess'd** seized by a diabolical spirit, an obsession **109 cousin** kinsman **111 But. . . land** i.e., but since you enjoy as your domain only this land of England (rather than the whole world) **113 Landlord** i.e., one who leases out a property **114 Thy . . . the law** i.e., your legal status as King is now subservient to and at the mercy of the law governing contracts, such as blank charters **116 an ague's privilege** i.e., a sick person's right to be testy **117 frozen** (1) chilly (2) caused by a chill **119 his** its **122 roundly** unceremoniously, bluntly **125 For that** because **126 pelican** (The pelican was thought to feed its young with its own blood.) **129 Whom fair befall** to whom may good come **131 thou respect'st not** you care nothing about

And thy unkindness be like crooked age
To crop at once a too long withered flower.
Live in thy shame, but die not shame with thee!
These words hereafter thy tormentors be!
Convey me to my bed, then to my grave.
Love they to live that love and honor have.
Exit [borne off by his Attendants].

KING RICHARD
And let them die that age and sullens have;
For both hast thou, and both become the grave.

YORK
I do beseech your Majesty, impute his words
To wayward sickliness and age in him.
He loves you, on my life, and holds you dear
As Harry Duke of Hereford, were he here.

KING RICHARD
Right, you say true. As Hereford's love, so his;
As theirs, so mine; and all be as it is.

[Enter Northumberland.]

NORTHUMBERLAND
My liege, old Gaunt commends him to your
Majesty.

KING RICHARD
What says he?

NORTHUMBERLAND Nay, nothing, all is said.
His tongue is now a stringless instrument;
Words, life, and all, old Lancaster hath spent.

YORK
Be York the next that must be bankrupt so!
Though death be poor, it ends a mortal woe.

KING RICHARD
The ripest fruit first falls, and so doth he;
His time is spent, our pilgrimage must be.
So much for that. Now for our Irish wars:
We must supplant those rough rug-headed kerns,
Which live like venom where no venom else
But only they have privilege to live.
And, for these great affairs do ask some charge,
Towards our assistance we do seize to us
The plate, coin, revenues, and moveables
Whereof our uncle Gaunt did stand possess'd.

YORK
How long shall I be patient? Ah, how long
Shall tender duty make me suffer wrong?
Not Gloucester's death, nor Hereford's banishment,
Not Gaunt's rebukes, nor England's private wrongs,
Nor the prevention of poor Bolingbroke
About his marriage, nor my own disgrace,
Have ever made me sour my patient cheek,
Or bend one wrinkle on my sovereign's face.
I am the last of noble Edward's sons,
Of whom thy father, Prince of Wales, was first.
In war was never lion rag'd more fierce,
In peace was never gentle lamb more mild,
Than was that young and princely gentleman.
His face thou hast, for even so look'd he,
Accomplish'd with the number of thy hours;
But when he frown'd, it was against the French
And not against his friends. His noble hand
Did win what he did spend, and spent not that
Which his triumphant father's hand had won.
His hands were guilty of no kindred blood,
But bloody with the enemies of his kin.
O Richard! York is too far gone with grief,
Or else he never would compare between.

KING RICHARD
Why, uncle, what's the matter?

YORK O my liege,
Pardon me, if you please; if not, I, pleas'd
Not to be pardoned, am content withal.
Seek you to seize and gripe into your hands
The royalties and rights of banish'd Hereford?
Is not Gaunt dead, and doth not Hereford live?
Was not Gaunt just, and is not Harry true?
Did not the one deserve to have an heir?
Is not his heir a well-deserving son?
Take Hereford's rights away, and take from Time
His charters and his customary rights;
Let not tomorrow then ensue today;
Be not thyself; for how art thou a king
But by fair sequence and succession?
Now, afore God—God forbid I say true!—
If you do wrongfully seize Hereford's rights,
Call in the letters patents that he hath
By his attorneys-general to sue
His livery, and deny his off'red homage,
You pluck a thousand dangers on your head,
You lose a thousand well-disposed hearts,
And prick my tender patience to those thoughts
Which honor and allegiance cannot think.

KING RICHARD
Think what you will, we seize into our hands
His plate, his goods, his money, and his lands.

YORK
I'll not be by the while. My liege, farewell.
What will ensue hereof, there's none can tell;
But by bad courses may be understood
That their events can never fall out good. *Exit.*

KING RICHARD
Go, Bushy, to the Earl of Wiltshire straight.
Bid him repair to us to Ely House
To see this business. Tomorrow next

138 Love they let them desire **139 sullens** sulks, sullenness **140 become** suit **145 Right . . . his** (Richard deliberately takes the opposite of what York had intended to say; Richard jibes that Gaunt is as little fond of the King as is Hereford.) **154 our . . . be** i.e., our journey through life is yet to be completed **156 supplant** expel (from the English territories of Ireland). **rug-headed** shaggy-haired. **kerns** light-armed Irish foot soldiers **157–158 where . . . live** (Allusion to the freedom of Ireland from snakes, traditionally ascribed to St. Patrick). **no venom** no poisonous snakes **159 for** because. **charge** expense **161 moveables** personal property **166 Gaunt's rebukes** i.e., the rebukes given to Gaunt **167–168 prevention . . . marriage** (The chronicles report that Richard had forestalled Bolingbroke's intended marriage with the Duke de Berri's daughter.) **170 wrinkle** i.e., frown

173 was . . . fierce never was there a lion more fiercely enraged **177 Accomplish'd . . . hours** i.e., when he was your age **185 compare between** draw comparisons **188 withal** with that, nonetheless **190 royalties** privileges granted through the King, and belonging in this case to a member of the royal family **195 Take . . . and take** i.e., if you take . . . you take **196 his customary rights** i.e., the right of due inheritance by an heir, a long-established custom **197 ensue** follow **202–204 Call . . . livery** i.e., revoke the royal grant giving him the privilege to sue through his attorneys for possession of his inheritance **204 homage** avowal of allegiance (by which ceremony he would be able legally to secure his inheritance) **214 events** outcomes **215 Earl of Wiltshire** (The King's Lord Treasurer and one of his notorious favorites.) **217 see** see to. **Tomorrow next** tomorrow

We will for Ireland; and 'tis time, I trow.
And we create, in absence of ourself,
Our uncle York Lord Governor of England;
For he is just and always loved us well.
Come on, our queen. Tomorrow must we part.
Be merry, for our time of stay is short.

[Flourish.] Exeunt King and Queen [with attendants]. Manet Northumberland [with Willoughby and Ross].

NORTHUMBERLAND
Well, lords, the Duke of Lancaster is dead.

ROSS
And living too, for now his son is Duke.

WILLOUGHBY
Barely in title, not in revenues.

NORTHUMBERLAND
Richly in both, if justice had her right.

ROSS
My heart is great; but it must break with silence,
Ere 't be disburdened with a liberal tongue.

NORTHUMBERLAND
Nay, speak thy mind; and let him ne'er speak more
That speaks thy words again to do thee harm!

WILLOUGHBY
Tends that thou wouldst speak to the Duke of Hereford?
If it be so, out with it boldly, man.
Quick is mine ear to hear of good towards him.

ROSS
No good at all that I can do for him,
Unless you call it good to pity him,
Bereft and gelded of his patrimony.

NORTHUMBERLAND
Now, afore God, 'tis shame such wrongs are borne
In him, a royal prince, and many moe
Of noble blood in this declining land.
The King is not himself, but basely led
By flatterers; and what they will inform,
Merely in hate, 'gainst any of us all,
That will the King severely prosecute
'Gainst us, our lives, our children, and our heirs.

ROSS
The commons hath he pill'd with grievous taxes,
And quite lost their hearts; the nobles hath he fin'd
For ancient quarrels, and quite lost their hearts.

WILLOUGHBY
And daily new exactions are devis'd,
As blanks, benevolences, and I wot not what.
But what, o' God's name, doth become of this?

NORTHUMBERLAND
Wars hath not wasted it, for warr'd he hath not,
But basely yielded upon compromise
That which his noble ancestors achiev'd with blows.
More hath he spent in peace than they in wars.

ROSS
The Earl of Wiltshire hath the realm in farm.

WILLOUGHBY
The King's grown bankrupt, like a broken man.

NORTHUMBERLAND
Reproach and dissolution hangeth over him.

ROSS
He hath not money for these Irish wars,
His burdenous taxations notwithstanding,
But by the robbing of the banish'd Duke.

NORTHUMBERLAND
His noble kinsman. Most degenerate king!
But, lords, we hear this fearful tempest sing,
Yet seek no shelter to avoid the storm;
We see the wind sit sore upon our sails,
And yet we strike not, but securely perish.

ROSS
We see the very wrack that we must suffer,
And unavoided is the danger now
For suffering so the causes of our wrack.

NORTHUMBERLAND
Not so. Even through the hollow eyes of death
I spy life peering; but I dare not say
How near the tidings of our comfort is.

WILLOUGHBY
Nay, let us share thy thoughts, as thou dost ours.

ROSS
Be confident to speak, Northumberland.
We three are but thyself, and, speaking so,
Thy words are but as thoughts. Therefore, be bold.

NORTHUMBERLAND
Then thus: I have from Le Port Blanc, a bay
In Britaine, receiv'd intelligence
That Harry Duke of Hereford, Rainold Lord Cobham,
[Thomas, son and heir to the Earl of Arundel,]
That late broke from the Duke of Exeter,
His brother, Archbishop late of Canterbury,
Sir Thomas Erpingham, Sir John Ramston,
Sir John Norbery, Sir Robert Waterton, and Francis Quoint,
All these well furnished by the Duke of Britaine
With eight tall ships, three thousand men of war,
Are making hither with all due expedience
And shortly mean to touch our northern shore.
Perhaps they had ere this, but that they stay
The first departing of the King for Ireland.
If then we shall shake off our slavish yoke,
Imp out our drooping country's broken wing,
Redeem from broking pawn the blemish'd crown,
Wipe off the dust that hides our scepter's gilt,

218 trow believe **228 great** i.e., great with sorrow **232 Tends . . . to** does what you wish to say concern **239 moe** more **242 inform** charge, report as spies **243 Merely in hate** out of pure hatred **246 pill'd** peeled, skinned, plundered **250 blanks** blank charters. **benevolences** forced loans to the crown (not actually employed until considerably later, in 1473). **wot** know

265 sore sorely, grievously **266 strike** (1) furl the sails (2) strike blows. **securely** heedlessly, overconfidently **268 unavoided** unavoidable **269 suffering** permitting **278 Britaine** Brittany **280** (This line, or a similarly worded version, was probably censored.) **281 late broke from** lately escaped from the custody of. (Holinshed records that "the earle of Arundels sonne, named Thomas, which was kept in the duke of Exeters house, escaped out of the realme . . . and went to his vncle Thomas Arundell late archbiship of Canturburie.") **282 His** i.e., the Earl of Arundel's. **late** until recently **286 tall** stately. **men of war** troops **287 expedience** expedition, speed **289–290 stay . . . King** wait until the King departs **292 Imp out** piece out. (A term from falconry meaning to attach new feathers to a disabled wing of a bird.) **293 broking pawn** the security held by a pawnbroker **294 gilt** gold (with pun on *guilt*)

And make high majesty look like itself,
Away with me in post to Ravenspurgh;
But if you faint, as fearing to do so,
Stay and be secret, and myself will go.

ROSS
To horse, to horse! Urge doubts to them that fear.

WILLOUGHBY
Hold out my horse, and I will first be there. *Exeunt.*

[SCENE II]

Enter the Queen, Bushy, [and] Bagot.

BUSHY
Madam, your Majesty is too much sad.
You promis'd, when you parted with the King,
To lay aside life-harming heaviness
And entertain a cheerful disposition.

QUEEN
To please the King I did; to please myself
I cannot do it. Yet I know no cause
Why I should welcome such a guest as grief,
Save bidding farewell to so sweet a guest
As my sweet Richard. Yet again, methinks,
Some unborn sorrow, ripe in fortune's womb,
Is coming towards me, and my inward soul
With nothing trembles. At some thing it grieves,
More than with parting from my lord the King.

BUSHY
Each substance of a grief hath twenty shadows,
Which shows like grief itself, but is not so;
For sorrow's eyes, glazed with blinding tears,
Divides one thing entire to many objects,
Like perspectives, which rightly gaz'd upon
Show nothing but confusion, ey'd awry
Distinguish form. So your sweet Majesty,
Looking awry upon your lord's departure,
Find shapes of grief, more than himself, to wail,
Which, look'd on as it is, is nought but shadows
Of what it is not. Then, thrice-gracious Queen,
More than your lord's departure weep not. More is not seen,
Or if it be, 'tis with false sorrow's eye,
Which for things true weeps things imaginary.

QUEEN
It may be so, but yet my inward soul
Persuades me it is otherwise. Howe'er it be,
I cannot but be sad—so heavy sad
As, though on thinking on no thought I think,
Makes me with heavy nothing faint and shrink.

BUSHY
'Tis nothing but conceit, my gracious lady.

QUEEN
'Tis nothing less. Conceit is still deriv'd
From some forefather grief. Mine is not so,
For nothing hath begot my something grief,
Or something hath the nothing that I grieve.
'Tis in reversion that I do possess;
But what it is, that is not yet known—what,
I cannot name. 'Tis nameless woe, I wot.

[Enter Green.]

GREEN
God save your Majesty! And well met, gentlemen.
I hope the King is not yet shipp'd for Ireland.

QUEEN
Why hopest thou so? 'Tis better hope he is,
For his designs crave haste, his haste good hope.
Then wherefore dost thou hope he is not shipp'd?

GREEN
That he, our hope, might have retir'd his power,
And driven into despair an enemy's hope,
Who strongly hath set footing in this land.
The banish'd Bolingbroke repeals himself,
And with uplifted arms is safe arriv'd
At Ravenspurgh.

QUEEN
Now God in heaven forbid!

GREEN
Ah, madam, 'tis too true; and that is worse,
The Lord Northumberland, his son young Harry Percy,
The Lords of Ross, Beaumond, and Willoughby,
With all their powerful friends, are fled to him.

BUSHY
Why have you not proclaim'd Northumberland
And all the rest revolted faction traitors?

GREEN
We have, whereupon the Earl of Worcester
Hath broken his staff, resign'd his stewardship,
And all the household servants fled with him
To Bolingbroke.

QUEEN
So, Green, thou art the midwife to my woe,
And Bolingbroke my sorrow's dismal heir.
Now hath my soul brought forth her prodigy,
And I, a gasping new-deliver'd mother,
Have woe to woe, sorrow to sorrow join'd.

BUSHY
Despair not, madam.

QUEEN
Who shall hinder me?
I will despair, and be at enmity
With cozening hope. He is a flatterer,

296 post haste. **Ravenspurgh** a busy seaport in Yorkshire on the Humber River, destroyed since by the sea **297 faint** are fainthearted **300 Hold . . . and** if my horse holds out

II.ii. Location: Windsor Castle.
4 entertain put on **14 Each . . . shadows** i.e., for every real grief there exist twenty imagined ones **18 perspectives** (In ll. 16–17, Bushy seems to have in mind a glass with many lenses, able to multiply images of the object being viewed; in ll. 18–20, *perspectives* are pictures of figures made to appear distorted or confused except when viewed obliquely, *ey'd awry*.). **rightly** directly, straight **20 Distinguish form** make the form distinct and normal

33 conceit fancy **34 'Tis nothing less** i.e., it is anything but that. **still** always **36 something** i.e., substantial **37 something . . . grieve** the unsubstantial grief, the nothing, that I grieve about has something to it, some substance **38–40 'Tis . . . name** i.e., my grief is like a legacy that will come to me at some future time, but I cannot tell its nature yet **46 retir'd** drawn back. **power** army **49 repeals** recalls (from exile) **50 uplifted arms** brandished weapons **52 that** what **57 rest** rest of the **59 broken his staff** broken his badge of office (in token of resignation as Lord High Steward. Worcester is brother of the Earl of Northumberland.) **63 dismal heir** ill-omened offspring **64 prodigy** monstrous birth **69 cozening** cheating

A parasite, a keeper back of death,
Who gently would dissolve the bands of life, 71
Which false hope lingers in extremity. 72

[Enter York.]

GREEN
Here comes the Duke of York.

QUEEN
With signs of war about his aged neck. 74
O, full of careful business are his looks! 75
Uncle, for God's sake, speak comfortable words. 76

YORK
Should I do so, I should belie my thoughts.
Comfort's in heaven, and we are on the earth,
Where nothing lives but crosses, cares, and grief.
Your husband, he is gone to save far off,
Whilst others come to make him lose at home.
Here am I left to underprop his land,
Who, weak with age, cannot support myself.
Now comes the sick hour that his surfeit made;
Now shall he try his friends that flatter'd him.

[Enter a Servingman.]

SERVINGMAN
My lord, your son was gone before I came. 86

YORK
He was? Why, so, go all which way it will!
The nobles they are fled, the commons they are cold,
And will, I fear, revolt on Hereford's side.
Sirrah, get thee to Plashy, to my sister Gloucester; 90
Bid her send me presently a thousand pound.
Hold, take my ring.

SERVINGMAN
My lord, I had forgot to tell your lordship:
Today, as I came by, I called there—
But I shall grieve you to report the rest.

YORK
What is 't, knave? 96

SERVINGMAN
An hour before I came, the Duchess died.

YORK
God for his mercy, what a tide of woes
Comes rushing on this woeful land at once!
I know not what to do. I would to God,
So my untruth had not provok'd him to it, 101
The King had cut off my head with my brother's. 102
What, are there no posts dispatch'd for Ireland?
How shall we do for money for these wars?
Come, sister—cousin, I would say—pray, pardon me.
Go, fellow, get thee home, provide some carts
And bring away the armor that is there.
[Exit Servingman.]
Gentlemen, will you go muster men?
If I know how or which way to order these affairs
Thus disorderly thrust into my hands,
Never believe me. Both are my kinsmen:
Th' one is my sovereign, whom both my oath
And duty bids defend; t' other again
Is my kinsman, whom the King hath wrong'd,
Whom conscience and my kindred bids to right.
Well, somewhat we must do. Come, cousin,
I'll dispose of you. Gentlemen, 117
Go muster up your men, and meet me presently
At Berkeley. I should to Plashy too, 119
But time will not permit. All is uneven,
And everything is left at six and seven. 121
Exeunt Duke [of York], Queen.
Manent Bushy, [Bagot,] Green.

BUSHY
The wind sits fair for news to go to Ireland,
But none returns. For us to levy power
Proportionable to the enemy
Is all unpossible.

GREEN
Besides, our nearness to the King in love
Is near the hate of those love not the King. 127

BAGOT
And that's the wavering commons, for their love
Lies in their purses, and whoso empties them
By so much fills their hearts with deadly hate.

BUSHY
Wherein the King stands generally condemn'd.

BAGOT
If judgment lie in them, then so do we, 132
Because we ever have been near the King.

GREEN
Well, I will for refuge straight to Bristol castle.
The Earl of Wiltshire is already there.

BUSHY
Thither will I with you, for little office 136
Will the hateful commons perform for us, 137
Except like curs to tear us all to pieces.
Will you go along with us?

BAGOT
No, I will to Ireland to his Majesty.
Farewell. If heart's presages be not vain,
We three here part that ne'er shall meet again.

BUSHY
That's as York thrives to beat back Bolingbroke.

GREEN
Alas, poor duke! The task he undertakes
Is numb'ring sands and drinking oceans dry.
Where one on his side fights, thousands will fly.
Farewell at once, for once, for all, and ever.

BUSHY
Well, we may meet again.

BAGOT
I fear me, never.
[Exeunt.]

71 bands bonds **72 lingers** causes to linger **74 signs of war** (York is in armor.) **75 careful business** worried preoccupation **76 comfortable** affording comfort **86 your son** i.e., the Duke of Aumerle **90 sister** i.e., sister-in-law **96 knave** i.e., fellow **101 untruth** disloyalty **102 brother's** i.e., the Duke of Gloucester's

117 dispose of make arrangements for **119 Berkeley** a castle near Bristol **121 at six and seven** i.e., in confusion **127 those love** those who love **132 If . . . we** i.e., if the power to pass judgment is given to the wavering commons, then we too stand condemned **136 office** service **137 hateful** full of hate, angry

[SCENE III]

Enter [Bolingbroke, Duke of] Hereford, [and] Northumberland [with Forces].

BOLINGBROKE
How far is it, my lord, to Berkeley now?

NORTHUMBERLAND
Believe me, noble lord,
I am a stranger here in Gloucestershire.
These high wild hills and rough uneven ways
Draws out our miles and makes them wearisome;
And yet your fair discourse hath been as sugar,
Making the hard way sweet and delectable.
But I bethink me what a weary way
From Ravenspurgh to Cotshall will be found 9
In Ross and Willoughby, wanting your company,
Which, I protest, hath very much beguil'd
The tediousness and process of my travel. 12
But theirs is sweet'ned with the hope to have
The present benefit which I possess;
And hope to joy is little less in joy
Than hope enjoy'd. By this the weary lords 16
Shall make their way seem short, as mine hath done
By sight of what I have, your noble company.

BOLINGBROKE
Of much less value is my company
Than your good words. But who comes here?

Enter Harry Percy.

NORTHUMBERLAND
It is my son, young Harry Percy,
Sent from my brother Worcester, whencesoever. 22
Harry, how fares your uncle? 23

PERCY
I had thought, my lord, to have learn'd his health of you.

NORTHUMBERLAND
Why, is he not with the Queen?

PERCY
No, my good lord. He hath forsook the court,
Broken his staff of office, and dispers'd
The household of the King.

NORTHUMBERLAND
What was his reason?
He was not so resolv'd when last we spake together.

PERCY
Because your lordship was proclaimed traitor.
But he, my lord, is gone to Ravenspurgh
To offer service to the Duke of Hereford,
And sent me over by Berkeley to discover
What power the Duke of York had levied there,
Then with directions to repair to Ravenspurgh.

NORTHUMBERLAND
Have you forgot the Duke of Hereford, boy?

PERCY
No, my good lord, for that is not forgot
Which ne'er I did remember. To my knowledge,
I never in my life did look on him.

NORTHUMBERLAND
Then learn to know him now. This is the Duke.

PERCY
My gracious lord, I tender you my service, 41
Such as it is, being tender, raw, and young,
Which elder days shall ripen and confirm
To more approved service and desert. 44

BOLINGBROKE
I thank thee, gentle Percy; and be sure
I count myself in nothing else so happy
As in a soul rememb'ring my good friends;
And, as my fortune ripens with thy love,
It shall be still thy true love's recompense.
My heart this covenant makes, my hand thus seals it.

NORTHUMBERLAND
How far is it to Berkeley? And what stir
Keeps good old York there with his men of war?

PERCY
There stands the castle, by yon tuft of trees,
Mann'd with three hundred men, as I have heard,
And in it are the Lords of York, Berkeley, and Seymour,
None else of name and noble estimate.

[Enter Ross and Willoughby.]

NORTHUMBERLAND
Here come the Lords of Ross and Willoughby,
Bloody with spurring, fiery-red with haste.

BOLINGBROKE
Welcome, my lords. I wot your love pursues
A banish'd traitor. All my treasury
Is yet but unfelt thanks, which more enrich'd 61
Shall be your love and labor's recompense.

ROSS
Your presence makes us rich, most noble lord.

WILLOUGHBY
And far surmounts our labor to attain it.

BOLINGBROKE
Evermore thanks, the exchequer of the poor, 65
Which, till my infant fortune comes to years, 66
Stands for my bounty. But who comes here?

[Enter Berkeley.]

NORTHUMBERLAND
It is my Lord of Berkeley, as I guess.

BERKELEY
My Lord of Hereford, my message is to you.

BOLINGBROKE
My lord, my answer is—to Lancaster;
And I am come to seek that name in England;
And I must find that title in your tongue,
Before I make reply to aught you say.

II.iii. Location: Wilds in Gloucestershire, near Berkeley castle.
9 Cotshall Cotswold, hilly district in Gloucestershire **12 tediousness and process** tedious process **16 this** this expectation **22 whencesoever** from wherever he is **23 your uncle** i.e., the Earl of Worcester

41 my service (Presumably Percy kneels to Bolingbroke, and so do Ross and Willoughby when they enter.) **44 approved** proven, demonstrated **61 unfelt** impalpable, expressed in words, not gifts. **more enrich'd** i.e., with still more thanks added; or, with substantial gifts at a later date **65 Evermore . . . poor** i.e., receive still more thanks, the treasury of those poor people like myself who can repay favors in no other way **66 comes to years** reaches maturity **70 Lancaster** (Bolingbroke will enter into no negotiations unless his proper title is given him, the title taken away by Richard.)

BERKELEY
Mistake me not, my lord, 'tis not my meaning
To rase one title of your honor out.
To you, my lord, I come, what lord you will,
From the most gracious regent of this land,
The Duke of York, to know what pricks you on
To take advantage of the absent time
And fright our native peace with self-borne arms.

[*Enter York attended.*]

BOLINGBROKE
I shall not need transport my words by you;
Here comes his Grace in person. My noble uncle!
[*Kneels.*]

YORK
Show me thy humble heart, and not thy knee,
Whose duty is deceivable and false.

BOLINGBROKE
My gracious uncle—

YORK
Tut, tut!
Grace me no grace, nor uncle me no uncle.
I am no traitor's uncle; and that word "grace"
In an ungracious mouth is but profane.
Why have those banish'd and forbidden legs
Dar'd once to touch a dust of England's ground?
But then more "why?" Why have they dar'd to march
So many miles upon her peaceful bosom,
Frighting her pale-fac'd villages with war
And ostentation of despised arms?
Com'st thou because the anointed King is hence?
Why, foolish boy, the King is left behind,
And in my loyal bosom lies his power.
Were I but now the lord of such hot youth
As when brave Gaunt, thy father, and myself
Rescued the Black Prince, that young Mars of men,
From forth the ranks of many thousand French,
O, then how quickly should this arm of mine,
Now prisoner to the palsy, chastise thee
And minister correction to thy fault!

BOLINGBROKE
My gracious uncle, let me know my fault.
On what condition stands it and wherein?

YORK
Even in condition of the worst degree,
In gross rebellion and detested treason.
Thou art a banish'd man, and here art come,
Before the expiration of thy time,
In braving arms against thy sovereign.

BOLINGBROKE
As I was banish'd, I was banish'd Hereford;
But as I come, I come for Lancaster.
And, noble uncle, I beseech your Grace
Look on my wrongs with an indifferent eye.
You are my father, for methinks in you
I see old Gaunt alive. O, then, my father,
Will you permit that I shall stand condemn'd
A wandering vagabond, my rights and royalties
Pluck'd from my arms perforce, and given away
To upstart unthrifts? Wherefore was I born?
If that my cousin king be King of England,
It must be granted I am Duke of Lancaster.
You have a son, Aumerle, my noble cousin;
Had you first died, and he been thus trod down,
He should have found his uncle Gaunt a father
To rouse his wrongs and chase them to the bay.
I am denied to sue my livery here,
And yet my letters-patents give me leave.
My father's goods are all distrain'd and sold,
And these, and all, are all amiss employ'd.
What would you have me do? I am a subject,
And I challenge law. Attorneys are denied me,
And therefore personally I lay my claim
To my inheritance of free descent.

NORTHUMBERLAND
The noble Duke hath been too much abused.

ROSS
It stands your Grace upon to do him right.

WILLOUGHBY
Base men by his endowments are made great.

YORK
My lords of England, let me tell you this:
I have had feeling of my cousin's wrongs,
And labor'd all I could to do him right;
But in this kind to come, in braving arms,
Be his own carver and cut out his way,
To find out right with wrong—it may not be;
And you that do abet him in this kind
Cherish rebellion and are rebels all.

NORTHUMBERLAND
The noble Duke hath sworn his coming is
But for his own, and for the right of that
We all have strongly sworn to give him aid;
And let him never see joy that breaks that oath!

YORK
Well, well, I see the issue of these arms.
I cannot mend it, I must needs confess,
Because my power is weak and all ill left;
But if I could, by Him that gave me life,
I would attach you all and make you stoop
Unto the sovereign mercy of the King.
But since I cannot, be it known unto you
I do remain as neuter. So fare you well—
Unless you please to enter in the castle
And there repose you for this night.

BOLINGBROKE
An offer, uncle, that we will accept;
But we must win your Grace to go with us
To Bristol castle, which they say is held
By Bushy, Bagot, and their complices,

75 rase erase **79 the absent time** i.e., the time of the King's absence **80 self-borne** i.e., borne for oneself, not for the King **84 deceivable** deceitful, deceptive **91 dust** a particle of dust **95 ostentation** display. **despised** despicable **107 condition** i.e., defect in me. **wherein** in what does it consist **112 braving** defiant **114 for Lancaster** i.e., under the title of Lancaster **116 indifferent** impartial

122 unthrifts spendthrifts **126 first** i.e., before Gaunt **128 rouse** chase from cover, expose. **the bay** the extremity where the hunted animal turns on its pursuers **129 sue my livery** sue for possession of hereditary rights. (See II.i. 202–204 and note.) **131 distrain'd** seized by legal process **134 challenge law** claim my legal rights **136 of free descent** by legal succession **138 stands . . . upon** is incumbent upon your Grace **139 his endowments** i.e., his properties which they have seized **143 kind** fashion **152 issue** outcome **154 ill left** left with inadequate means **156 attach** arrest **159 neuter** neutral **165 Bagot** (According to II.ii.140, Bagot had gone to Ireland.)

The caterpillars of the commonwealth,
Which I have sworn to weed and pluck away.

YORK

It may be I will go with you; but yet I'll pause,
For I am loath to break our country's laws.
Nor friends nor foes, to me welcome you are. 170
Things past redress are now with me past care.
Exeunt.

[SCENE IV]

Enter Earl of Salisbury and a Welsh Captain.

WELSH CAPTAIN

My Lord of Salisbury, we have stay'd ten days,
And hardly kept our countrymen together, 2
And yet we hear no tidings from the King.
Therefore we will disperse ourselves. Farewell.

SALISBURY

Stay yet another day, thou trusty Welshman.
The King reposeth all his confidence in thee.

WELSH CAPTAIN

'Tis thought the King is dead. We will not stay.
The bay-trees in our country are all wither'd
And meteors fright the fixed stars of heaven;
The pale-fac'd moon looks bloody on the earth,
And lean-look'd prophets whisper fearful change; 11
Rich men look sad, and ruffians dance and leap,
The one in fear to lose what they enjoy,
The other to enjoy by rage and war. 14
These signs forerun the death or fall of kings.
Farewell. Our countrymen are gone and fled,
As well assured Richard their king is dead. [*Exit.*] 17

SALISBURY

Ah, Richard, with the eyes of heavy mind
I see thy glory like a shooting star
Fall to the base earth from the firmament.
Thy sun sets weeping in the lowly west,
Witnessing storms to come, woe, and unrest. 22
Thy friends are fled to wait upon thy foes, 23
And crossly to thy good all fortune goes. [*Exit.*] 24

[ACT III • SCENE I]

Enter [Bolingbroke,] Duke of Hereford, York, Northumberland, [Ross, Percy, Willoughby, with] Bushy and Green, prisoners.

BOLINGBROKE

Bring forth these men.
Bushy and Green, I will not vex your souls—
Since presently your souls must part your bodies— 3
With too much urging your pernicious lives, 4
For 'twere no charity; yet, to wash your blood
From off my hands, here in the view of men
I will unfold some causes of your deaths.
You have misled a prince, a royal king,
A happy gentleman in blood and lineaments, 9
By you unhappied and disfigured clean. 10
You have in manner with your sinful hours 11
Made a divorce betwixt his queen and him,
Broke the possession of a royal bed,
And stain'd the beauty of a fair queen's cheeks
With tears drawn from her eyes by your foul wrongs.
Myself, a prince by fortune of my birth,
Near to the King in blood, and near in love
Till you did make him misinterpret me,
Have stoop'd my neck under your injuries,
And sigh'd my English breath in foreign clouds, 20
Eating the bitter bread of banishment;
Whilst you have fed upon my signories, 22
Dispark'd my parks and fell'd my forest woods, 23
From my own windows torn my household coat, 24
Ras'd out my imprese, leaving me no sign, 25
Save men's opinions and my living blood,
To show the world I am a gentleman.
This and much more, much more than twice all this,
Condemns you to the death. See them delivered over
To execution and the hand of death.

BUSHY

More welcome is the stroke of death to me
Than Bolingbroke to England. Lords, farewell.

GREEN

My comfort is that heaven will take our souls
And plague injustice with the pains of hell.

BOLINGBROKE

My Lord Northumberland, see them dispatch'd.
[*Exeunt Northumberland and others, with the prisoners.*]
Uncle, you say the Queen is at your house.
For God's sake, fairly let her be entreated. 37
Tell her I send to her my kind commends; 38
Take special care my greetings be delivered.

YORK

A gentleman of mine I have dispatch'd
With letters of your love to her at large. 41

BOLINGBROKE

Thanks, gentle uncle. Come, lords, away,
To fight with Glendower and his complices. 43
Awhile to work, and after holiday. *Exeunt.* 44

170 Nor neither as

II.iv. Location: A camp in Wales.
2 hardly with difficulty **11 lean-look'd** lean-looking **14 to . . . rage** in hopes of enjoying by violence **17 As** as being **22 Witnessing** betokening **23 wait upon** attend, offer allegiance to **24 crossly** adversely

III.i. Location: Bristol. Before the castle.

3 presently immediately **4 urging** emphasizing as reasons (for your executions) **9 happy** fortunate **10 unhappied** made wretched, ruined. **clean** completely **11 in manner** as it were **20 foreign clouds** i.e., the air of foreign lands **22 signories** estates **23 Dispark'd** thrown open to uses other than hunting and forestry **24 my household coat** coat of arms (frequently emblazoned on stained or painted windows) **25 Ras'd out** erased. **imprese** heraldic device, emblematic design **37 entreated** treated **38 commends** regards, commendations **41 at large** conveyed in full **43 Glendower** (Owen Glendower was not, according to the chronicles, at this time in arms against Bolingbroke. Possibly he is to be identified here with the Welsh captain of the preceding scene.) **44 after** afterwards

[SCENE II]

[Drums. Flourish and colors.] Enter the King, Aumerle, [the Bishop of] Carlisle, etc. [with Soldiers].

KING RICHARD
Barkloughly castle call they this at hand?
AUMERLE
Yea, my lord. How brooks your Grace the air,
After your late tossing on the breaking seas?
KING RICHARD
Needs must I like it well. I weep for joy
To stand upon my kingdom once again.
Dear earth, I do salute thee with my hand,
Though rebels wound thee with their horses' hoofs.
As a long-parted mother with her child
Plays fondly with her tears and smiles in meeting,
So, weeping, smiling, greet I thee, my earth,
And do thee favors with my royal hands.
Feed not thy sovereign's foe, my gentle earth,
Nor with thy sweets comfort his ravenous sense,
But let thy spiders, that suck up thy venom,
And heavy-gaited toads lie in their way,
Doing annoyance to the treacherous feet
Which with usurping steps do trample thee.
Yield stinging nettles to mine enemies;
And when they from thy bosom pluck a flower,
Guard it, I pray thee, with a lurking adder
Whose double tongue may with a mortal touch
Throw death upon thy sovereign's enemies.
Mock not my senseless conjuration, lords.
This earth shall have a feeling, and these stones
Prove armed soldiers, ere her native king
Shall falter under foul rebellion's arms.
CARLISLE
Fear not, my lord. That Power that made you king
Hath power to keep you king in spite of all.
The means that heavens yield must be embrac'd,
And not neglected; else, heaven would,
And we will not. Heaven's offer we refuse,
The proffered means of succor and redress.
AUMERLE
He means, my lord, that we are too remiss,
Whilst Bolingbroke, through our security,
Grows strong and great in substance and in power.
KING RICHARD
Discomfortable cousin, know'st thou not
That when the searching eye of heaven is hid
Behind the globe, that lights the lower world,
Then thieves and robbers range abroad unseen
In murders and in outrage boldly here;
But when from under this terrestrial ball
He fires the proud tops of the eastern pines
And darts his light through every guilty hole,
Then murders, treasons, and detested sins,
The cloak of night being pluck'd from off their backs,
Stand bare and naked, trembling at themselves?
So when this thief, this traitor, Bolingbroke,
Who all this while hath revel'd in the night
Whilst we were wand'ring with the antipodes,
Shall see us rising in our throne, the east,
His treasons will sit blushing in his face,
Not able to endure the sight of day,
But self-affrighted tremble at his sin.
Not all the water in the rough rude sea
Can wash the balm off from an anointed king;
The breath of worldly men cannot depose
The deputy elected by the Lord.
For every man that Bolingbroke hath press'd
To lift shrewd steel against our golden crown,
God for his Richard hath in heavenly pay
A glorious angel. Then, if angels fight,
Weak men must fall, for heaven still guards the right.

Enter Salisbury.

Welcome, my lord. How far off lies your power?
SALISBURY
Nor near nor farther off, my gracious lord,
Than this weak arm. Discomfort guides my tongue
And bids me speak of nothing but despair.
One day too late, I fear me, noble lord,
Hath clouded all thy happy days on earth.
O, call back yesterday, bid time return,
And thou shalt have twelve thousand fighting men!
Today, today, unhappy day, too late,
O'erthrows thy joys, friends, fortune, and thy state;
For all the Welshmen, hearing thou wert dead,
Are gone to Bolingbroke, dispers'd, and fled.
AUMERLE
Comfort, my liege. Why looks your Grace so pale?
KING RICHARD
But now the blood of twenty thousand men
Did triumph in my face, and they are fled;
And, till so much blood thither come again,
Have I not reason to look pale and dead?
All souls that will be safe, fly from my side,
For time hath set a blot upon my pride.
AUMERLE
Comfort, my liege. Remember who you are.
KING RICHARD
I had forgot myself. Am I not king?
Awake, thou coward majesty, thou sleepest!
Is not the king's name twenty thousand names?
Arm, arm, my name! A puny subject strikes
At thy great glory. Look not to the ground,

III.ii. Location: The coast of Wales, near Barkloughly castle.
1 Barkloughly i.e., Harlech **2 brooks** enjoys **3 late** recent **8 long-parted mother with** a mother long parted from **13 sweets** i.e., bounty. **sense** appetite **21 double** forked. **mortal** deadly **23 senseless conjuration** solemn entreaty of senseless things **25 native** entitled (to the crown) by birth, rightful. (Richard was born at Bordeaux.) **30–31 else . . . not** i.e., otherwise we spurn heaven's will **34 security** overconfidence **36 Discomfortable** uncomforting, discouraging **38 globe** earth. **that** i.e., the *eye of heaven,* the sun

49 antipodes people on the other side of the world; here, the Irish **55 balm** consecrated oil used in anointing a king **56 worldly** earthly **58 press'd** impressed, forced into the ranks **59 shrewd** keen, biting **62 still** always **64 near** nearer **65 Discomfort** discouragement

Ye favorites of a king. Are we not high?
High be our thoughts. I know my uncle York
Hath power enough to serve our turn. But who
comes here?

Enter Scroop.

SCROOP
More health and happiness betide my liege
Than can my care-tun'd tongue deliver him!

KING RICHARD
Mine ear is open and my heart prepar'd.
The worst is worldly loss thou canst unfold.
Say, is my kingdom lost? Why, 'twas my care;
And what loss is it to be rid of care?
Strives Bolingbroke to be as great as we?
Greater he shall not be; if he serve God,
We'll serve Him too, and be his fellow so.
Revolt our subjects? That we cannot mend;
They break their faith to God as well as us.
Cry woe, destruction, ruin, and decay;
The worst is death, and death will have his day.

SCROOP
Glad am I that your Highness is so arm'd
To bear the tidings of calamity.
Like an unseasonable stormy day,
Which makes the silver rivers drown their shores
As if the world were all dissolv'd to tears,
So high above his limits swells the rage 109
Of Bolingbroke, covering your fearful land
With hard bright steel, and hearts harder than steel.
White-beards have arm'd their thin and hairless
scalps 112
Against thy Majesty; boys, with women's voices,
Strive to speak big, and clap their female joints 114
In stiff unwieldy arms against thy crown.
Thy very beadsmen learn to bend their bows 116
Of double-fatal yew against thy state; 117
Yea, distaff-women manage rusty bills 118
Against thy seat. Both young and old rebel, 119
And all goes worse than I have power to tell.

KING RICHARD
Too well, too well thou tell'st a tale so ill.
Where is the Earl of Wiltshire? Where is Bagot? 122
What is become of Bushy? Where is Green,
That they have let the dangerous enemy
Measure our confines with such peaceful steps? 125
If we prevail, their heads shall pay for it.
I warrant they have made peace with Bolingbroke.

SCROOP
Peace have they made with him indeed, my lord

KING RICHARD
O villains, vipers, damn'd without redemption!
Dogs easily won to fawn on any man!
Snakes, in my heart-blood warm'd, that sting my
heart!
Three Judases, each one thrice worse than Judas!
Would they make peace? Terrible hell
Make war upon their spotted souls for this! 134

SCROOP
Sweet love, I see, changing his property, 135
Turns to the sourest and most deadly hate.
Again uncurse their souls. Their peace is made
With heads, and not with hands. Those whom you
curse
Have felt the worst of death's destroying wound
And lie full low, grav'd in the hollow ground.

AUMERLE
Is Bushy, Green, and the Earl of Wiltshire dead?

SCROOP
Ay, all of them at Bristol lost their heads.

AUMERLE
Where is the Duke my father with his power?

KING RICHARD
No matter where. Of comfort no man speak!
Let's talk of graves, of worms, and epitaphs,
Make dust our paper, and with rainy eyes
Write sorrow on the bosom of the earth.
Let's choose executors and talk of wills.
And yet not so, for what can we bequeath
Save our deposed bodies to the ground?
Our lands, our lives, and all are Bolingbroke's,
And nothing can we call our own but death
And that small model of the barren earth 153
Which serves as paste and cover to our bones. 154
For God's sake, let us sit upon the ground
And tell sad stories of the death of kings!
How some have been depos'd, some slain in war,
Some haunted by the ghosts they have depos'd, 158
Some poisoned by their wives, some sleeping
kill'd—
All murdered; for within the hollow crown
That rounds the mortal temples of a king
Keeps Death his court, and there the antic sits, 162
Scoffing his state and grinning at his pomp, 163
Allowing him a breath, a little scene, 164
To monarchize, be fear'd, and kill with looks, 165
Infusing him with self and vain conceit, 166
As if this flesh which walls about our life
Were brass impregnable; and humor'd thus 168
Comes at the last and with a little pin
Bores through his castle wall, and farewell king!
Cover your heads, and mock not flesh and blood
With solemn reverence. Throw away respect,
Tradition, form, and ceremonious duty,
For you have but mistook me all this while.
I live with bread like you, feel want,

109 his limits its banks **112 thin** sparsely haired **114 clap** thrust. **female** i.e., weak and delicate **116 beadsmen** old almsmen or pensioners whose duty it was to pray for a benefactor; here, for the king **117 double-fatal** doubly fatal (since the wood of the yew was used for bows and since its foliage and berries are poisonous) **118–119 distaff-women . . . seat** spinning-women wield rusty pikes (long-handled axes) against your throne **122 Bagot** (Although the King names Bagot here, he mentions only *three Judases* in l. 132 and Aumerle does not ask about Bagot in l. 141; in III.iv. we learn that Bagot is not executed along with the other three, but reappears instead in IV.i.) **125 Measure our confines** travel over our kingdom. **peaceful** unopposed

134 spotted stained with treason **135 his property** its distinctive quality **153 model** mold, i.e., the body **154 paste** pastry, pie crust **158 ghosts** i.e., ghosts of kings **162 antic** grotesque figure, jester **163 Scoffing his state** scoffing at the king's regality. **pomp** ceremony, splendor **164 breath** breathing space, moment **165 monarchize** play the monarch **166 self and vain conceit** vain conceit of himself **168 humor'd thus** having satisfied his humor or whim (referring to Death); or possibly *humored* or *indulged* (referring to the King)

Taste grief, need friends. Subjected thus,
How can you say to me I am a king?

CARLISLE
My lord, wise men ne'er sit and wail their woes,
But presently prevent the ways to wail.
To fear the foe, since fear oppresseth strength,
Gives in your weakness strength unto your foe,
And so your follies fight against yourself.
Fear, and be slain—no worse can come to fight,
And fight and die is death destroying death,
Where fearing dying pays death servile breath.

AUMERLE
My father hath a power. Inquire of him,
And learn to make a body of a limb.

KING RICHARD
Thou chid'st me well. Proud Bolingbroke, I come
To change blows with thee for our day of doom.
This ague fit of fear is overblown;
An easy task it is to win our own.
Say, Scroop, where lies our uncle with his power?
Speak sweetly, man, although thy looks be sour.

SCROOP
Men judge by the complexion of the sky
The state and inclination of the day.
So may you by my dull and heavy eye;
My tongue hath but a heavier tale to say.
I play the torturer, by small and small
To lengthen out the worst that must be spoken:
Your uncle York is join'd with Bolingbroke,
And all your northern castles yielded up,
And all your southern gentlemen in arms
Upon his party.

KING RICHARD Thou hast said enough.
[*To Aumerle.*] Beshrew thee, cousin, which didst lead me forth
Of that sweet way I was in to despair!
What say you now? What comfort have we now?
By heaven, I'll hate him everlastingly
That bids me be of comfort any more.
Go to Flint castle. There I'll pine away;
A king, woe's slave, shall kingly woe obey.
That power I have, discharge; and let them go
To ear the land that hath some hope to grow,
For I have none. Let no man speak again
To alter this, for counsel is but vain.

AUMERLE
My liege, one word.

KING RICHARD He does me double wrong
That wounds me with the flatteries of his tongue.
Discharge my followers. Let them hence away,
From Richard's night to Bolingbroke's fair day.
[*Exeunt.*]

176 Subjected made subject to grief, want, etc. (with pun on *being treated like a subject*) **179 prevent . . . wail** block off the paths leading to grief **183 Fear . . . fight** i.e., if you fear you are sure to be slain, and no worse fate can come to you if you fight **184–185 fight . . . breath** to die fighting is to conquer death in the very act of dying, whereas to die fearfully pays to death the tribute of servility **186 power** army. **of** about **187 learn . . . limb** i.e., discover how to make a partial force substitute for a complete one **189 change** exchange. **for . . . doom** i.e., in order to settle our fates, which of us is to die now **190 is overblown** has blown over **191 our own** i.e., my own kingdom **198 by small and small** little by little **204 Beshrew** confound. (Literally, *curse.*) **209 Flint castle** (Near Chester.) **212 ear** plough

[SCENE III]

Enter [with drum and colors] Bolingbroke, York, Northumberland, [Attendants, and forces].

BOLINGBROKE
So that by this intelligence we learn
The Welshmen are dispers'd, and Salisbury
Is gone to meet the King, who lately landed
With some few private friends upon this coast.

NORTHUMBERLAND
The news is very fair and good, my lord:
Richard not far from hence hath hid his head.

YORK
It would beseem the Lord Northumberland
To say "King Richard." Alack the heavy day
When such a sacred king should hide his head.

NORTHUMBERLAND
Your Grace mistakes. Only to be brief
Left I his title out.

YORK The time hath been,
Would you have been so brief with him, he would
Have been so brief with you to shorten you,
For taking so the head, your whole head's length.

BOLINGBROKE
Mistake not, uncle, further than you should.

YORK
Take not, good cousin, further than you should,
Lest you mistake the heavens are over our heads.

BOLINGBROKE
I know it, uncle, and oppose not myself
Against their will. But who comes here?

Enter Percy.

Welcome, Harry. What, will not this castle yield?

PERCY
The castle royally is mann'd, my lord,
Against thy entrance.

BOLINGBROKE
Royally? Why, it contains no king?

PERCY
Yes, my good lord,
It doth contain a king. King Richard lies
Within the limits of yon lime and stone,
And with him are the Lord Aumerle, Lord Salisbury,
Sir Stephen Scroop, besides a clergyman
Of holy reverence—who, I cannot learn.

NORTHUMBERLAND
O, belike it is the Bishop of Carlisle.

BOLINGBROKE
Noble lords,
Go to the rude ribs of that ancient castle;
Through brazen trumpet send the breath of parley

III.iii. Location: Wales. Before Flint Castle.
1 intelligence information **13 to** as to **14 taking so the head** i.e., presumptuously omitting thus his title **17 mistake** fail to perceive that. (Plays on Bolingbroke's use of *mistake,* just as York has punned on *brief* and *head.*)

Into his ruin'd ears, and thus deliver:
Henry Bolingbroke
On both his knees doth kiss King Richard's hand
And sends allegiance and true faith of heart
To his most royal person, hither come
Even at his feet to lay my arms and power,
Provided that my banishment repeal'd
And lands restor'd again be freely granted.
If not, I'll use the advantage of my power,
And lay the summer's dust with show'rs of blood
Rain'd from the wounds of slaughtered
  Englishmen—
The which, how far off from the mind of
  Bolingbroke
It is, such crimson tempest should bedrench
The fresh green lap of fair King Richard's land,
My stooping duty tenderly shall show.
Go signify as much, while here we march
Upon the grassy carpet of this plain.

[*Northumberland and attendants advance to the castle.*]

Let's march without the noise of threat'ning drum,
That from this castle's tottered battlements
Our fair appointments may be well perus'd.
Methinks King Richard and myself should meet
With no less terror than the elements
Of fire and water, when their thund'ring shock
At meeting tears the cloudy cheeks of heaven.
Be he the fire, I'll be the yielding water;
The rage be his, whilst on the earth I rain
My waters—on the earth, and not on him.
March on, and mark King Richard how he looks.

The trumpets sound [*a parle without and answer within, then a flourish. King*] *Richard appeareth on the walls* [*with the Bishop of Carlisle, Aumerle, Scroop, and Salisbury*].

See, see, King Richard doth himself appear,
As doth the blushing discontented sun
From out the fiery portal of the east,
When he perceives the envious clouds are bent
To dim his glory and to stain the track
Of his bright passage to the occident.

YORK
Yet looks he like a king. Behold, his eye,
As bright as is the eagle's, lightens forth
Controlling majesty. Alack, alack, for woe,
That any harm should stain so fair a show!

KING RICHARD [*To Northumberland*]
We are amaz'd; and thus long have we stood
To watch the fearful bending of thy knee,
Because we thought ourself thy lawful king.
And if we be, how dare thy joints forget
To pay their aweful duty to our presence?
If we be not, show us the hand of God
That hath dismiss'd us from our stewardship;
For well we know, no hand of blood and bone
Can gripe the sacred handle of our scepter,
Unless he do profane, steal, or usurp.
And though you think that all, as you have done,
Have torn their souls by turning them from us,
And we are barren and bereft of friends,
Yet know, my master, God omnipotent,
Is mustering in his clouds on our behalf
Armies of pestilence; and they shall strike
Your children yet unborn and unbegot,
That lift your vassal hands against my head
And threat the glory of my precious crown.
Tell Bolingbroke—for yon methinks he stands—
That every stride he makes upon my land
Is dangerous treason. He is come to open
The purple testament of bleeding war;
But, ere the crown he looks for live in peace,
Ten thousand bloody crowns of mothers' sons
Shall ill become the flower of England's face,
Change the complexion of her maid-pale peace
To scarlet indignation, and bedew
Her pastures' grass with faithful English blood.

NORTHUMBERLAND
The King of heaven forbid our lord the King
Should so with civil and uncivil arms
Be rush'd upon! Thy thrice noble cousin,
Harry Bolingbroke, doth humbly kiss thy hand;
And by the honorable tomb he swears
That stands upon your royal grandsire's bones,
And by the royalties of both your bloods,
Currents that spring from one most gracious head,
And by the buried hand of warlike Gaunt,
And by the worth and honor of himself,
Comprising all that may be sworn or said,
His coming hither hath no further scope
Than for his lineal royalties, and to beg
Enfranchisement immediate on his knees;
Which on thy royal party granted once,
His glittering arms he will commend to rust,
His barbed steeds to stables, and his heart
To faithful service of your Majesty.
This swears he, as he is a prince, is just;
And, as I am a gentleman, I credit him.

KING RICHARD
Northumberland, say thus the King returns:
His noble cousin is right welcome hither,
And all the number of his fair demands
Shall be accomplish'd without contradiction.
With all the gracious utterance thou hast
Speak to his gentle hearing kind commends.

[*Northumberland retires to Bolingbroke and York.*]

34 his ruin'd ears i.e., its (the castle's) ancient and battered loopholes **40 my banishment repeal'd** i.e., the revocation of my banishment **48 stooping duty** submissive kneeling **52 tottered** tattered, saw-toothed **53 appointments** equipment **56 fire and water** i.e., lightning and rain **59–60 rain . . . earth** i.e., weep contritely as I kneel **61 s.d. parle** trumpet summons to a negotiation. **on the walls** i.e., in the gallery of the tiring house, above, to the rear of the stage **63 blushing** i.e., turning red with anger **65 he** i.e., the sun. **envious** hostile **68 he** i.e., King Richard **69 lightens forth** flashes out, like lightning **76 aweful** reverential, full of awe

83 torn . . . us i.e., turned traitor to Richard at peril to their souls **85 know** know that **89 That** of you that **93–94 open . . . testament** begin to carry out a bequest of blood to England. (Blood was often said to be purple.) **96 crowns** heads (playing on *crown* in l. 95) **97 flower . . . face** the blooming face of England **102 civil** used in civil strife. **uncivil** barbarous, violent **113 lineal royalties** hereditary rights as one of royal blood **114 Enfranchisement** freedom (from banishment) **115 party** part **116 commend** give over **117 barbed** armored **121 returns** answers **126 commends** regards

[*To Aumerle.*] We do debase ourselves, cousin, do
we not,
To look so poorly and to speak so fair?
Shall we call back Northumberland, and send
Defiance to the traitor, and so die?

AUMERLE
No, good my lord. Let's fight with gentle words
Till time lend friends, and friends their helpful
swords.

KING RICHARD
O God, O God, that e'er this tongue of mine,
That laid the sentence of dread banishment
On yon proud man, should take it off again
With words of sooth! O that I were as great 136
As is my grief, or lesser than my name!
Or that I could forget what I have been,
Or not remember what I must be now!
Swell'st thou, proud heart? I'll give thee scope to
beat,
Since foes have scope to beat both thee and me.
[*Northumberland returns to the castle.*]

AUMERLE
Northumberland comes back from Bolingbroke.

KING RICHARD
What must the King do now? Must he submit?
The King shall do it. Must he be depos'd?
The King shall be contented. Must he lose
The name of king? A' God's name, let it go. 146
I'll give my jewels for a set of beads, 147
My gorgeous palace for a hermitage,
My gay apparel for an almsman's gown, 149
My figur'd goblets for a dish of wood, 150
My scepter for a palmer's walking-staff, 151
My subjects for a pair of carved saints,
And my large kingdom for a little grave,
A little little grave, an obscure grave;
Or I'll be buried in the king's highway,
Some way of common trade, where subjects' feet 156
May hourly trample on their sovereign's head;
For on my heart they tread now whilst I live,
And, buried once, why not upon my head?
Aumerle, thou weep'st, my tender-hearted cousin!
We'll make foul weather with despised tears;
Our sighs and they shall lodge the summer corn, 162
And make a dearth in this revolting land.
Or shall we play the wantons with our woes, 164
And make some pretty match with shedding tears? 165
As thus, to drop them still upon one place, 166
Till they have fretted us a pair of graves 167
Within the earth; and, therein laid—there lies
Two kinsmen digg'd their graves with weeping
eyes. 169
Would not this ill do well? Well, well, I see
I talk but idly, and you laugh at me.—
Most mighty prince, my Lord Northumberland,
What says King Bolingbroke? Will his Majesty
Give Richard leave to live till Richard die?
You make a leg, and Bolingbroke says ay. 175

NORTHUMBERLAND
My lord, in the base court he doth attend 176
To speak with you; may it please you to come
down.

KING RICHARD
Down, down I come, like glist'ring Phaethon, 178
Wanting the manage of unruly jades. 179
In the base court? Base court, where kings grow
base,
To come at traitors' calls and do them grace.
In the base court? Come down? Down, court!
Down, king!
For night-owls shriek where mounting larks should
sing. [*Exeunt from above.*]

BOLINGBROKE
What says his Majesty?

NORTHUMBERLAND Sorrow and grief of heart
Makes him speak fondly, like a frantic man. 185
Yet he is come.

[*Enter King Richard and his attendants below.*]

BOLINGBROKE
Stand all apart,
And show fair duty to his Majesty. *He kneels down.*
My gracious lord—

KING RICHARD
Fair cousin, you debase your princely knee 190
To make the base earth proud with kissing it. 191
Me rather had my heart might feel your love 192
Than my unpleased eye see your courtesy.
Up, cousin, up; your heart is up, I know,
Thus high at least [*Touching his crown*], although
your knee be low.

BOLINGBROKE [*Rising*]
My gracious lord, I come but for mine own.

KING RICHARD
Your own is yours, and I am yours, and all.

BOLINGBROKE
So far be mine, my most redoubted lord, 198
As my true service shall deserve your love.

KING RICHARD
Well you deserve. They well deserve to have
That know the strong'st and surest way to get.—
[*To York, who weeps.*] Uncle, give me your hands.
Nay, dry your eyes;
Tears show their love, but want their remedies.— 203
[*To Bolingbroke.*] Cousin, I am too young to be your
father,
Though you are old enough to be my heir.
What you will have, I'll give, and willing too;
For do we must what force will have us do.
Set on towards London, cousin, is it so?

136 sooth cajolery, flattery **146 A'** in **147 set of beads** rosary **149 almsman's** one who lives on alms or charity **150 figur'd** ornamented, embossed **151 palmer's** pilgrim's **156 trade** passage **162 lodge** beat down. **corn** grain **164 play the wantons** sport, frolic **165 match** game, contest **166 still** continually **167 fretted us** eaten away for us, worn (with a pun on *complained*) **169 digg'd** who dug

175 a leg an obeisance **176 base court** outer or lower court of a castle **178 glist'ring** glistening, glittering. **Phaethon** son of the sun-god, whose chariot he attempted to steer across the sky; unable to control the horses of the sun, he was hurled from the chariot by Jupiter **179 Wanting . . . jades** lacking the skill in horsemanship to control unruly nags **185 fondly** foolishly. **frantic** mad **190–191 debase . . . base** (Continues the word-play on *base* in l. 180.) **192 Me rather had** I had rather **198 redoubted** dread **203 want their remedies** lack remedies for what caused them

BOLINGBROKE
Yea, my good lord.
KING RICHARD Then I must not say no.
[*Flourish. Exeunt.*]

[SCENE IV]

Enter the Queen with [*two Ladies,*] *her Attendants.*

QUEEN
What sport shall we devise here in this garden,
To drive away the heavy thought of care?
LADY
Madam, we'll play at bowls.
QUEEN
'Twill make me think the world is full of rubs, 4
And that my fortune runs against the bias. 5
LADY
Madam, we'll dance.
QUEEN
My legs can keep no measure in delight, 7
When my poor heart no measure keeps in grief. 8
Therefore, no dancing, girl; some other sport.
LADY
Madam, we'll tell tales.
QUEEN
Of sorrow or of joy?
LADY Of either, madam.
QUEEN
Of neither, girl;
For if of joy, being altogether wanting, 13
It doth remember me the more of sorrow; 14
Or if of grief, being altogether had,
It adds more sorrow to my want of joy.
For what I have I need not to repeat,
And what I want it boots not to complain. 18
LADY
Madam, I'll sing.
QUEEN 'Tis well that thou hast cause;
But thou shouldst please me better, wouldst thou weep.
LADY
I could weep, madam, would it do you good.
QUEEN
And I could sing, would weeping do me good,
And never borrow any tear of thee.

Enter Gardeners [*a Master and two Men*].

But stay, here come the gardeners.
Let's step into the shadow of these trees.
My wretchedness unto a row of pins, 26
They will talk of state, for everyone doth so 27
Against a change; woe is forerun with woe. 28
[*Queen and Ladies retire.*]
GARDENER
Go bind thou up yon dangling apricocks, 29
Which, like unruly children, make their sire
Stoop with oppression of their prodigal weight.
Give some supportance to the bending twigs.
Go thou, and like an executioner
Cut off the heads of too fast growing sprays
That look too lofty in our commonwealth.
All must be even in our government. 36
You thus employ'd, I will go root away
The noisome weeds which without profit suck
The soil's fertility from wholesome flowers.
MAN
Why should we in the compass of a pale 40
Keep law and form and due proportion,
Showing, as in a model, our firm estate,
When our sea-walled garden, the whole land,
Is full of weeds, her fairest flowers chok'd up,
Her fruit-trees all unprun'd, her hedges ruin'd,
Her knots disordered, and her wholesome herbs 46
Swarming with caterpillars?
GARDENER Hold thy peace.
He that hath suffered this disordered spring 48
Hath now himself met with the fall of leaf.
The weeds which his broad-spreading leaves did shelter,
That seem'd in eating him to hold him up,
Are pluck'd up root and all by Bolingbroke,
I mean the Earl of Wiltshire, Bushy, Green.
MAN
What, are they dead?
GARDENER They are; and Bolingbroke
Hath seiz'd the wasteful King. O, what pity is it
That he had not so trimm'd and dress'd his land
As we this garden! We at time of year 57
Do wound the bark, the skin of our fruit-trees,
Lest, being over-proud in sap and blood,
With too much riches it confound itself;
Had he done so to great and growing men,
They might have liv'd to bear and he to taste
Their fruits of duty. Superfluous branches
We lop away, that bearing boughs may live;
Had he done so, himself had borne the crown
Which waste of idle hours hath quite thrown down.
MAN
What, think you the King shall be depos'd?
GARDENER
Depress'd he is already, and depos'd 68
'Tis doubt he will be. Letters came last night 69
To a dear friend of the good Duke of York's,
That tell black tidings.
QUEEN [*Coming forward*] O, I am press'd to death 71
Through want of speaking! Thou, old Adam's likeness, 72
Set to dress this garden, how dares 73
Thy harsh rude tongue sound this unpleasing news?

III.iv. Location: Langley. The Duke of York's garden.
4 rubs impediments (in the game of bowls) **5 against the bias** i.e., contrary, athwart. (Literally, not following the naturally curved path of a bowl.) **7 measure** a stately slow dance **8 measure** moderation **13 wanting** lacking **14 remember** remind **18 boots** avails **26 My . . . unto** i.e., I'll wager my wretchedness against **27 state** statecraft, politics **28 Against** anticipating

29 apricocks apricots **36 even** equal **40 pale** enclosure, enclosed garden **46 knots** flower beds laid out in patterns **48 suffered** allowed **57 at . . . year** in the appropriate season **68 Depress'd** brought low **69 'Tis doubt** there is fear **71 press'd to death** (Allusion to the *peine forte et dure,* inflicted by pressure of heavy weights upon the chests of indicted persons who refused to plead and remained silent.) **72 old Adam** (In his role as the first gardener.) **73 dress** cultivate

What Eve, what serpent, hath suggested thee
To make a second fall of cursed man?
Why dost thou say King Richard is depos'd?
Dar'st thou, thou little better thing than earth,
Divine his downfall? Say, where, when, and how
Cam'st thou by this ill tidings? Speak, thou wretch.

GARDENER
Pardon me, madam. Little joy have I
To breathe this news, yet what I say is true.
King Richard, he is in the mighty hold
Of Bolingbroke. Their fortunes both are weigh'd.
In your lord's scale is nothing but himself,
And some few vanities that make him light;
But in the balance of great Bolingbroke,
Besides himself, are all the English peers,
And with that odds he weighs King Richard down.
Post you to London, and you will find it so;
I speak no more than everyone doth know.

QUEEN
Nimble mischance, that art so light of foot,
Doth not thy embassage belong to me,
And am I last that knows it? O, thou thinkest
To serve me last, that I may longest keep
Thy sorrow in my breast. Come, ladies, go
To meet at London London's king in woe.
What, was I born to this, that my sad look
Should grace the triumph of great Bolingbroke?
Gard'ner, for telling me these news of woe,
Pray God the plants thou graft'st may never grow.
Exit [with Ladies].

GARDENER
Poor queen! So that thy state might be no worse,
I would my skill were subject to thy curse.
Here did she fall a tear; here in this place
I'll set a bank of rue, sour herb of grace.
Rue, even for ruth, here shortly shall be seen,
In the remembrance of a weeping queen. *Exeunt.*

[ACT IV • SCENE I]

Enter Bolingbroke with the Lords [Aumerle, Northumberland, Percy, Fitzwater, Surrey, the Bishop of Carlisle, the Abbot of Westminster, and another Lord, Herald, Officers] to Parliament. [The throne is provided on stage.]

BOLINGBROKE
Call forth Bagot.

Enter [Officers with] Bagot.

Now, Bagot, freely speak thy mind,
What thou dost know of noble Gloucester's death,
Who wrought it with the King, and who perform'd
The bloody office of his timeless end.

BAGOT
Then set before my face the Lord Aumerle.

BOLINGBROKE
Cousin, stand forth, and look upon that man.
[Aumerle comes forward.]

BAGOT
My Lord Aumerle, I know your daring tongue
Scorns to unsay what once it hath deliver'd.
In that dead time when Gloucester's death was plotted,
I heard you say, "Is not my arm of length,
That reacheth from the restful English court
As far as Calais, to mine uncle's head?"
Amongst much other talk, that very time,
I heard you say that you had rather refuse
The offer of an hundred thousand crowns
Than Bolingbroke's return to England—
Adding withal, how blest this land would be
In this your cousin's death.

AUMERLE
Princes and noble lords,
What answer shall I make to this base man?
Shall I so much dishonor my fair stars
On equal terms to give him chastisement?
Either I must, or have mine honor soil'd
With the attainder of his slanderous lips.
[Throws down his gage.]
There is my gage, the manual seal of death,
That marks thee out for hell. I say thou liest,
And will maintain what thou hast said is false
In thy heart-blood, though being all too base
To stain the temper of my knightly sword.

BOLINGBROKE
Bagot, forbear; thou shalt not take it up.

AUMERLE
Excepting one, I would he were the best
In all this presence that hath mov'd me so.

FITZWATER *[Throwing down a gage]*
If that thy valor stand on sympathy,
There is my gage, Aumerle, in gage to thine.
By that fair sun which shows me where thou stand'st,
I heard thee say, and vauntingly thou spak'st it,
That thou wert cause of noble Gloucester's death.
If thou deniest it twenty times, thou liest;
And I will turn thy falsehood to thy heart,
Where it was forged, with my rapier's point.

AUMERLE *[Taking up the gage]*
Thou dar'st not, coward, live to see that day.

FITZWATER
Now, by my soul, I would it were this hour.

AUMERLE
Fitzwater, thou art damn'd to hell for this.

75 suggested tempted **79 Divine** prophesy **93 embassage** message **96 Thy sorrow** the sorrow that you (mischance) report **99 Bolingbroke** (The original spelling, *Bullingbrooke,* indicates the rhyme with *look* in the previous line, pronounced something like *bruke* and *luke.*) **102 So that** provided **104 fall** let fall **105 rue** "herb of grace," a plant symbolical of repentance, ruth, or sorrow for another's misery

IV.i. Location: Westminster Hall.
4 Who . . . King who prevailed upon the King to have the murder performed

5 timeless untimely **10 dead** dark, silent **11 of length** long **12 restful** i.e., untroubled by Gloucester **14 that very time** (An inconsistency; Gloucester's death occurred before Bolingbroke left England.) **17 Than . . . return** than have Bolingbroke return **22 stars** i.e., sphere, fortune, rank **23 On . . . chastisement** as to challenge him as my equal **25 attainder** dishonoring accusation **26 manual . . . death** death warrant sealed by my hand **32 one** i.e., Bolingbroke. **best** highest in rank **34 stand on sympathy** i.e., requires correspondence of rank in your opponent

PERCY
Aumerle, thou liest. His honor is as true
In this appeal as thou art all unjust; 46
[*Throws down a gage.*]
And that thou art so, there I throw my gage,
To prove it on thee to the extremest point
Of mortal breathing. Seize it, if thou dar'st.

AUMERLE [*Taking up the gage*]
An if I do not, may my hands rot off
And never brandish more revengeful steel
Over the glittering helmet of my foe!

ANOTHER LORD [*Throwing down a gage*]
I task the earth to the like, forsworn Aumerle; 53
And spur thee on with full as many lies 54
As may be holloa'd in thy treacherous ear
From sun to sun. There is my honor's pawn;
Engage it to the trial, if thou darest. 57

AUMERLE [*Taking up the gage*]
Who sets me else? By heaven, I'll throw at all! 58
I have a thousand spirits in one breast,
To answer twenty thousand such as you.

SURREY
My Lord Fitzwater, I do remember well
The very time Aumerle and you did talk.

FITZWATER
'Tis very true. You were in presence then, 63
And you can witness with me this is true.

SURREY
As false, by heaven, as heaven itself is true.

FITZWATER
Surrey, thou liest.

SURREY Dishonorable boy!
That lie shall lie so heavy on my sword
That it shall render vengeance and revenge,
Till thou the lie-giver and that lie do lie
In earth as quiet as thy father's skull.
In proof whereof, there is my honor's pawn.
[*Throws down a gage.*]
Engage it to the trial, if thou dar'st.

FITZWATER [*Taking up the gage*]
How fondly dost thou spur a forward horse! 73
If I dare eat, or drink, or breathe, or live,
I dare meet Surrey in a wilderness, 75
And spit upon him, whilst I say he lies,
And lies, and lies. There is my bond of faith,
To tie thee to my strong correction.
[*Throws down a gage.*]
As I intend to thrive in this new world, 79
Aumerle is guilty of my true appeal.
Besides, I heard the banish'd Norfolk say
That thou, Aumerle, didst send two of thy men
To execute the noble Duke at Calais.

AUMERLE
Some honest Christian trust me with a gage,
That Norfolk lies. [*Borrows a gage, and throws it down.*] Here do I throw down this,
If he may be repeal'd, to try his honor. 86

BOLINGBROKE
These differences shall all rest under gage 87
Till Norfolk be repeal'd. Repeal'd he shall be,
And, though mine enemy, restor'd again
To all his lands and signories. When he is return'd,
Against Aumerle we will enforce his trial.

CARLISLE
That honorable day shall never be seen.
Many a time hath banish'd Norfolk fought
For Jesu Christ in glorious Christian field,
Streaming the ensign of the Christian cross 95
Against black pagans, Turks, and Saracens;
And, toil'd with works of war, retir'd himself 97
To Italy, and there at Venice gave
His body to that pleasant country's earth,
And his pure soul unto his captain Christ,
Under whose colors he had fought so long.

BOLINGBROKE
Why, Bishop, is Norfolk dead?

CARLISLE
As surely as I live, my lord.

BOLINGBROKE
Sweet peace conduct his sweet soul to the bosom 104
Of good old Abraham! Lords appellants, 105
Your differences shall all rest under gage
Till we assign you to your days of trial. 107

Enter York.

YORK
Great Duke of Lancaster, I come to thee
From plume-pluck'd Richard, who with willing soul
Adopts thee heir, and his high scepter yields
To the possession of thy royal hand.
Ascend his throne, descending now from him,
And long live Henry, fourth of that name!

BOLINGBROKE
In God's name, I'll ascend the regal throne.

CARLISLE
Marry, God forbid!
Worst in this royal presence may I speak, 116
Yet best beseeming me to speak the truth. 117
Would God that any in this noble presence
Were enough noble to be upright judge
Of noble Richard! Then true noblesse would 120
Learn him forbearance from so foul a wrong. 121
What subject can give sentence on his king?
And who sits here that is not Richard's subject?
Thieves are not judg'd but they are by to hear, 124
Although apparent guilt be seen in them; 125
And shall the figure of God's majesty,
His captain, steward, deputy elect,
Anointed, crowned, planted many years,
Be judg'd by subject and inferior breath,

46 appeal accusation. **all unjust** totally false **53 I . . . like** i.e., I burden the ground with another gage **54 lies** accusations of lying; challenges to combat **57 Engage . . . trial** take it up as a pledge to combat **58 sets me** puts up stakes against me, i.e., challenges me to a game. **throw** (1) throw dice (2) throw down gages **63 in presence** i.e., present at court **73 fondly** foolishly. **forward** willing **75 in a wilderness** i.e., where fighting might go on uninterrupted to the death **79 in . . . world** i.e., under the new king

86 repeal'd recalled from exile. **try** test **87 under gage** as challenges **95 Streaming** flying **97 toil'd** wearied **104–105 bosom . . . Abraham** i.e., heaven. (See Luke 16:22.) **105 Lords appellants** lords who appear as formal accusers **107 s. d. Enter York** (Some editors suggest that Richard's scepter etc. are brought in at l. 162, but York here invites Bolingbroke to ascend the throne with the surrendered scepter, and so perhaps the regalia are brought on here.) **116 Worst** least in rank **117 best beseeming me** i.e., most befitting to me as a clergyman **120 noblesse** nobleness **121 Learn him forbearance** teach him to forbear **124 judg'd . . . by** condemned unless they are present **125 apparent** manifest

And he himself not present? O, forfend it, God,
That in a Christian climate souls refin'd
Should show so heinous, black, obscene a deed!
I speak to subjects, and a subject speaks,
Stirr'd up by God, thus boldly for his king.
My Lord of Hereford here, whom you call king,
Is a foul traitor to proud Hereford's king.
And if you crown him, let me prophesy:
The blood of English shall manure the ground,
And future ages groan for this foul act;
Peace shall go sleep with Turks and infidels,
And in this seat of peace tumultuous wars
Shall kin with kin and kind with kind confound;
Disorder, horror, fear, and mutiny
Shall here inhabit, and this land be call'd
The field of Golgotha and dead men's skulls.
O, if you raise this house against this house,
It will the woefullest division prove
That ever fell upon this cursed earth.
Prevent it, resist it, let it not be so,
Lest child, child's children, cry against you "woe!"

NORTHUMBERLAND
Well have you argued, sir; and, for your pains,
Of capital treason we arrest you here.
My Lord of Westminster, be it your charge
To keep him safely till his day of trial.
[*Carlisle is taken into custody.*]
[May it please you, lords, to grant the commons'
suit.

BOLINGBROKE
Fetch hither Richard, that in common view
He may surrender; so we shall proceed
Without suspicion.

YORK I will be his conduct. *Exit.*

BOLINGBROKE
Lords, you that here are under our arrest,
Procure your sureties for your days of answer.
Little are we beholding to your love,
And little look'd for at your helping hands.

Enter Richard and York.

KING RICHARD
Alack, why am I sent for to a king,
Before I have shook off the regal thoughts
Wherewith I reign'd? I hardly yet have learn'd
To insinuate, flatter, bow, and bend my knee.
Give sorrow leave awhile to tutor me
To this submission. Yet I well remember
The favors of these men. Were they not mine?
Did they not sometime cry, "All hail!" to me?
So Judas did to Christ. But he, in twelve,
Found truth in all but one; I, in twelve thousand,
none.
God save the King! Will no man say amen?
Am I both priest and clerk? Well then, amen.
God save the King, although I be not he;
And yet, amen, if heaven do think him me.
To do what service am I sent for hither?

YORK
To do that office of thine own good will
Which tired majesty did make thee offer,
The resignation of thy state and crown
To Henry Bolingbroke.

KING RICHARD
Give me the crown. [*He takes the crown.*] Here,
cousin, seize the crown.
Here, cousin,
On this side my hand, and on that side thine.
Now is this golden crown like a deep well
That owes two buckets, filling one another,
The emptier ever dancing in the air,
The other down, unseen, and full of water.
That bucket down and full of tears am I,
Drinking my griefs, whilst you mount up on high.

BOLINGBROKE
I thought you had been willing to resign.

KING RICHARD
My crown I am, but still my griefs are mine.
You may my glories and my state depose,
But not my griefs. Still am I king of those.

BOLINGBROKE
Part of your cares you give me with your crown.

KING RICHARD
Your cares set up do not pluck my cares down.
My care is loss of care, by old care done;
Your care is gain of care, by new care won.
The cares I give I have, though given away;
They tend the crown, yet still with me they stay.

BOLINGBROKE
Are you contented to resign the crown?

KING RICHARD
Ay, no; no, ay; for I must nothing be;
Therefore no no, for I resign to thee.
Now mark me how I will undo myself:
[*He yields his crown and scepter.*]
I give this heavy weight from off my head
And this unwieldy scepter from my hand,
The pride of kingly sway from out my heart;
With mine own tears I wash away my balm,
With mine own hands I give away my crown,
With mine own tongue deny my sacred state,
With mine own breath release all duteous oaths.
All pomp and majesty I do forswear;
My manors, rents, revenues I forgo;
My acts, decrees, and statutes I deny.
God pardon all oaths that are broke to me!
God keep all vows unbroke are made to thee!
Make me, that nothing have, with nothing griev'd,

130 forfend forbid **131 souls refin'd** civilized people **132 obscene** odious, repulsive **142 Shall . . . confound** shall destroy kinsmen by means of kinsmen and fellow-countrymen by means of fellow-countrymen **145 Golgotha** "the place of a skull," Calvary. (See Mark 15:22.) **146 this house . . . this house** i.e., Lancaster against York. (See Mark 3:25.) **155 the commons' suit** request of the commons (i.e., that Richard be formally tried and the causes of his deposition made public. This line begins the abdication passage omitted in early quartos of the play.) **157 surrender** i.e., surrender the crown, abdicate **158 conduct** escort **160 sureties** persons who will guarantee your appearance **161 beholding** beholden, indebted **169 favors** (1) faces (2) benefits

174 priest and clerk (In religious services, the clerk or assistant would say "Amen" to the priest's prayers.) **186 owes** owns, has **196–200 Your . . . stay** i.e., Your assuming the cares of office does not assuage my griefs. My grief is loss of kingly responsibility, destroyed by a failure in diligence; your concern is gaining of kingly responsibility, won by zealous effort. The anxieties I transfer to you I also keep for myself, despite my giving them to you; they accompany the crown, and yet still remain with me. **202 Ay** i.e., I. (But, says Richard, I am nothing, and therefore "Ay" is "I" or "nothing," that is, "no.") **203 no no . . . thee** (Richard plays on the logic that a double negative equals a positive.) **216 are** that are

And thou with all pleas'd, that hast all achiev'd!
Long mayst thou live in Richard's seat to sit,
And soon lie Richard in an earthy pit!
God save King Henry, unking'd Richard says,
And send him many years of sunshine days!—
What more remains?

NORTHUMBERLAND [*Presenting a paper*]
No more, but that you read
These accusations and these grievous crimes
Committed by your person and your followers
Against the state and profit of this land;
That, by confessing them, the souls of men
May deem that you are worthily depos'd.

KING RICHARD
Must I do so? And must I ravel out
My weav'd-up follies? Gentle Northumberland,
If thy offenses were upon record,
Would it not shame thee in so fair a troop
To read a lecture of them? If thou wouldst,
There shouldst thou find one heinous article,
Containing the deposing of a king
And cracking the strong warrant of an oath,
Mark'd with a blot, damn'd in the book of heaven.
Nay, all of you that stand and look upon me,
Whilst that my wretchedness doth bait myself,
Though some of you, with Pilate, wash your hands,
Showing an outward pity, yet you Pilates
Have here deliver'd me to my sour cross,
And water cannot wash away your sin.

NORTHUMBERLAND
My lord, dispatch. Read o'er these articles.

KING RICHARD
Mine eyes are full of tears, I cannot see.
And yet salt water blinds them not so much
But they can see a sort of traitors here.
Nay, if I turn mine eyes upon myself,
I find myself a traitor with the rest;
For I have given here my soul's consent
T' undeck the pompous body of a king,
Made glory base and sovereignty a slave,
Proud majesty a subject, state a peasant.

NORTHUMBERLAND
My lord—

KING RICHARD
No lord of thine, thou haught insulting man,
Nor no man's lord. I have no name, no title,
No, not that name was given me at the font,
But 'tis usurp'd. Alack the heavy day,
That I have worn so many winters out
And know not now what name to call myself!
O that I were a mockery king of snow,
Standing before the sun of Bolingbroke,
To melt myself away in water-drops!
Good king, great king, and yet not greatly good,
An if my word be sterling yet in England,
Let it command a mirror hither straight,
That it may show me what a face I have,
Since it is bankrupt of his majesty.

BOLINGBROKE
Go some of you and fetch a looking-glass.
[*Exit an attendant.*]

NORTHUMBERLAND
Read o'er this paper while the glass doth come.

KING RICHARD
Fiend, thou torments me ere I come to hell!

BOLINGBROKE
Urge it no more, my Lord Northumberland.

NORTHUMBERLAND
The commons will not then be satisfied.

KING RICHARD
They shall be satisfied. I'll read enough,
When I do see the very book indeed
Where all my sins are writ, and that's myself.

Enter one with a glass.

Give me that glass, and therein will I read.
[*He takes the looking-glass.*]
No deeper wrinkles yet? Hath sorrow struck
So many blows upon this face of mine,
And made no deeper wounds? O flatt'ring glass,
Like to my followers in prosperity,
Thou dost beguile me! Was this face the face
That every day under his household roof
Did keep ten thousand men? Was this the face
That, like the sun, did make beholders wink?
Is this the face which fac'd so many follies,
And was at last out-fac'd by Bolingbroke?
A brittle glory shineth in this face—
As brittle as the glory is the face,
[*Dashes the looking-glass against the ground.*]
For there it is, crack'd in an hundred shivers.
Mark, silent king, the moral of this sport,
How soon my sorrow hath destroy'd my face.

BOLINGBROKE
The shadow of your sorrow hath destroy'd
The shadow of your face.

KING RICHARD
Say that again.
The shadow of my sorrow? Ha! Let's see.
'Tis very true, my grief lies all within;
And these external manners of laments
Are merely shadows to the unseen grief
That swells with silence in the tortur'd soul.
There lies the substance; and I thank thee, King,
For thy great bounty, that not only giv'st
Me cause to wail, but teachest me the way
How to lament the cause. I'll beg one boon,
And then be gone and trouble you no more.
Shall I obtain it?

BOLINGBROKE
Name it, fair cousin.

KING RICHARD
"Fair cousin"? I am greater than a king.
For when I was a king, my flatterers
Were then but subjects; being now a subject,
I have a king here to my flatterer.

226 state and profit ordered prosperity **239 bait** torment, harass (as in bearbaiting) **240 wash your hands** (See Matthew 27:24. Richard persistently compares himself with Christ; see also III.ii. 132; IV.i.171.) **242 sour** bitter **247 sort** gang **251 pompous** stately, splendid **253 state** royalty **255 haught** haughty **265 sterling** current

282 Was this face (An echo of Marlowe's *Doctor Faustus,* in which the protagonist addresses Helen of Troy.) **285 wink** close the eyes, blink **286 fac'd** countenanced **293 shadow** outward show; or, overshadowing nature **294 shadow** reflection (in the mirror) **298 shadows to** physical (and therefore imperfect) manifestations of **301 that** who **309 to** as

Being so great, I have no need to beg.

BOLINGBROKE
Yet ask.

KING RICHARD
And shall I have?

BOLINGBROKE
You shall.

KING RICHARD
Then give me leave to go.

BOLINGBROKE
Whither?

KING RICHARD
Whither you will, so I were from your sights.

BOLINGBROKE
Go some of you, convey him to the Tower.

KING RICHARD
O, good! Convey? Conveyers are you all,
That rise thus nimbly by a true king's fall.]

[Exeunt King Richard, some Lords, and a Guard.]

BOLINGBROKE
On Wednesday next we solemnly proclaim
Our coronation. Lords, be ready all.

Exeunt. Manent [the Abbot of] Westminster, [the Bishop of] Carlisle, Aumerle.

ABBOT
A woeful pageant have we here beheld.

CARLISLE
The woe's to come, the children yet unborn,
Shall feel this day as sharp to them as thorn.

AUMERLE
You holy clergymen, is there no plot
To rid the realm of this pernicious blot?

ABBOT
My lord,
Before I freely speak my mind herein,
You shall not only take the sacrament
To bury mine intents, but also to effect
Whatever I shall happen to devise.
I see your brows are full of discontent,
Your hearts of sorrow, and your eyes of tears.
Come home with me to supper; I'll lay
A plot shall show us all a merry day. *Exeunt.*

[ACT V • SCENE I]

Enter the Queen with [Ladies,] her Attendants.

QUEEN
This way the King will come. This is the way
To Julius Caesar's ill-erected tower,
To whose flint bosom my condemned lord
Is doom'd a prisoner by proud Bolingbroke.
Here let us rest, if this rebellious earth
Have any resting for her true king's queen.

Enter Richard [and Guard].

But soft, but see, or rather do not see
My fair rose wither. Yet look up, behold,
That you in pity may dissolve to dew,
And wash him fresh again with true-love tears.
Ah, thou, the model where old Troy did stand,
Thou map of honor, thou King Richard's tomb,
And not King Richard! Thou most beauteous inn,
Why should hard-favor'd grief be lodg'd in thee,
When triumph is become an alehouse guest?

KING RICHARD
Join not with grief, fair woman, do not so,
To make my end too sudden. Learn, good soul,
To think our former state a happy dream,
From which awak'd, the truth of what we are
Shows us but this. I am sworn brother, sweet,
To grim Necessity, and he and I
Will keep a league till death. Hie thee to France
And cloister thee in some religious house.
Our holy lives must win a new world's crown,
Which our profane hours here have thrown down.

QUEEN
What, is my Richard both in shape and mind
Transform'd and weak'ned? Hath Bolingbroke depos'd
Thine intellect? Hath he been in thy heart?
The lion dying thrusteth forth his paw,
And wounds the earth, if nothing else, with rage
To be o'erpow'r'd; and wilt thou, pupil-like,
Take the correction, mildly kiss the rod,
And fawn on rage with base humility,
Which art a lion and the king of beasts?

KING RICHARD
A king of beasts, indeed! If aught but beasts,
I had been still a happy king of men.
Good sometimes queen, prepare thee hence for France.
Think I am dead and that even here thou takest,
As from my death-bed, thy last living leave.
In winter's tedious nights sit by the fire
With good old folks and let them tell thee tales
Of woeful ages long ago betid;
And ere thou bid good night, to quite their griefs,
Tell thou the lamentable tale of me
And send the hearers weeping to their beds.
For why, the senseless brands will sympathize
The heavy accent of thy moving tongue,
And in compassion weep the fire out;
And some will mourn in ashes, some coal-black,
For the deposing of a rightful king.

Enter Northumberland [and others].

NORTHUMBERLAND
My lord, the mind of Bolingbroke is chang'd;

317 convey escort **318 Convey** steal **324 Shall** who shall **330 To . . . intents** to conceal my plans **335 shall** that shall

V.i. Location: London. A street leading to the Tower.
2 Caesar's (The Tower, ascribed by tradition to Julius Caesar, was built by William the Conqueror to hold the city in subordination.) **ill-erected** erected for evil ends, or with evil results

11 thou . . . stand i.e., you ruined majesty, pattern of fallen greatness like the desolate waste where Troy once stood **12 map of honor** i.e., the mere outline of a once-glorious honor **13 inn** mansion **15 is . . . guest** i.e., lodges in such a lowly house as Bolingbroke **24 new world's** heaven's **31 To be** at being **35 king of beasts** (1) lion (2) ruler over beastly men **37 sometimes** sometime, former **42 Of . . . betid** of woe that happened ages ago **43 quite their griefs** requite their tales of woe **46 For why** because. **brands** firebrands. **sympathize** respond to

You must to Pomfret, not unto the Tower. 52
And, madam, there is order ta'en for you; 53
With all swift speed you must away to France.

KING RICHARD
Northumberland, thou ladder wherewithal
The mounting Bolingbroke ascends my throne,
The time shall not be many hours of age
More than it is, ere foul sin gathering head 58
Shall break into corruption. Thou shalt think, 59
Though he divide the realm and give thee half,
It is too little, helping him to all;
He shall think that thou, which knowest the way
To plant unrightful kings, wilt know again,
Being ne'er so little urg'd, another way
To pluck him headlong from the usurped throne. 65
The love of wicked men converts to fear, 66
That fear to hate, and hate turns one or both 67
To worthy danger and deserved death. 68

NORTHUMBERLAND
My guilt be on my head, and there an end.
Take leave and part, for you must part forthwith. 70

KING RICHARD
Doubly divorc'd! Bad men, you violate
A twofold marriage, 'twixt my crown and me,
And then betwixt me and my married wife.—
Let me unkiss the oath 'twixt thee and me; 74
And yet not so, for with a kiss 'twas made.
Part us, Northumberland: I towards the north,
Where shivering cold and sickness pines the clime; 77
My wife to France, from whence, set forth in pomp,
She came adorned hither like sweet May,
Sent back like Hallowmas or short'st of day. 80

QUEEN
And must we be divided? Must we part?

KING RICHARD
Ay, hand from hand, my love, and heart from heart.

QUEEN
Banish us both and send the King with me.

NORTHUMBERLAND
That were some love but little policy. 84

QUEEN
Then whither he goes, thither let me go.

KING RICHARD
So two, together weeping, make one woe.
Weep thou for me in France, I for thee here;
Better far off than, near, be ne'er the near. 88
Go count thy way with sighs, I mine with groans.

QUEEN
So longest way shall have the longest moans.

KING RICHARD
Twice for one step I'll groan, the way being short,
And piece the way out with a heavy heart.
Come, come, in wooing sorrow let's be brief,
Since, wedding it, there is such length in grief.
One kiss shall stop our mouths, and dumbly part;
Thus give I mine, and thus take I thy heart.
[*They kiss.*]

QUEEN
Give me mine own again. 'Twere no good part 97
To take on me to keep and kill thy heart. [*Kiss.*] 98
So, now I have mine own again, be gone,
That I may strive to kill it with a groan.

KING RICHARD
We make woe wanton with this fond delay. 101
Once more, adieu! The rest let sorrow say. *Exeunt.*

[SCENE II]

Enter Duke of York and the Duchess.

DUCHESS
My lord, you told me you would tell the rest,
When weeping made you break the story off,
Of our two cousins coming into London. 3

YORK
Where did I leave?

DUCHESS
At that sad stop, my lord, 4
Where rude misgovern'd hands from windows' tops 5
Threw dust and rubbish on King Richard's head.

YORK
Then, as I said, the Duke, great Bolingbroke,
Mounted upon a hot and fiery steed
Which his aspiring rider seem'd to know, 9
With slow but stately pace kept on his course,
Whilst all tongues cried, "God save thee, Bolingbroke!"
You would have thought the very windows spake,
So many greedy looks of young and old
Through casements darted their desiring eyes
Upon his visage, and that all the walls
With painted imagery had said at once, 16
"Jesu preserve thee! Welcome, Bolingbroke!"
Whilst he, from the one side to the other turning,
Bareheaded, lower than his proud steed's neck,
Bespake them thus: "I thank you, countrymen."
And thus still doing, thus he pass'd along.

DUCHESS
Alack, poor Richard! Where rode he the whilst?

YORK
As in a theatre the eyes of men,
After a well-grac'd actor leaves the stage,
Are idly bent on him that enters next, 25
Thinking his prattle to be tedious,
Even so, or with much more contempt, men's eyes
Did scowl on gentle Richard. No man cried, "God save him!"

52 Pomfret Pontefract in Yorkshire **53 order ta'en** arrangement made **58 gathering head** gathering to a head **59 corruption** putrid matter, pus **65 To** how to **66 converts** changes **67 That fear** i.e., that fear changes. **one or both** i.e., the new king or his partner, or both **68 worthy** well-merited **70 part . . . part** separate . . . depart **74 unkiss** annul with a kiss (regarded as the seal of a ceremonial bond) **77 pines** afflicts, distresses **80 Hallowmas** All Saints' Day (November 1), regarded as the beginning of winter. **short'st of day** the winter solstice **84 policy** political practicality **88 Better . . . the near** i.e., better to be far apart than near and yet unable to meet. (The second *near* means *nearer.*)

97–98 'Twere . . . me it would not be wise of me to take it upon myself **101 We . . . wanton** we sport with our grief. **fond** both foolish and affectionate

V.ii. Location: The Duke of York's palace.
3 cousins kinsmen, i.e., nephews **4 leave** leave off **5 misgovern'd** unruly. **windows' tops** upper windows **9 Which . . . know** which seemed to know its ambitious rider **16 With painted imagery** i.e., painted with crowds of people, as on a tapestry depicting a procession **25 idly** indifferently

No joyful tongue gave him his welcome home,
But dust was thrown upon his sacred head—
Which with such gentle sorrow he shook off,
His face still combating with tears and smiles,
The badges of his grief and patience,
That had not God, for some strong purpose, steel'd
The hearts of men, they must perforce have melted
And barbarism itself have pitied him.
But heaven hath a hand in these events,
To whose high will we bound our calm contents.
To Bolingbroke are we sworn subjects now,
Whose state and honor I for aye allow.

DUCHESS
Here comes my son Aumerle.

[Enter Aumerle.]

YORK Aumerle that was;
But that is lost for being Richard's friend,
And, madam, you must call him Rutland now.
I am in parliament pledge for his truth
And lasting fealty to the new-made king.

DUCHESS
Welcome, my son. Who are the violets now
That strew the green lap of the new-come spring?

AUMERLE
Madam, I know not, nor I greatly care not.
God knows I had as lief be none as one.

YORK
Well, bear you well in this new spring of time,
Lest you be cropp'd before you come to prime.
What news from Oxford? Do those justs and triumphs hold?

AUMERLE
For aught I know, my lord, they do.

YORK
You will be there, I know.

AUMERLE
If God prevent not, I purpose so.

YORK
What seal is that, that hangs without thy bosom?
Yea, look'st thou pale? Let me see the writing.

AUMERLE
My lord, 'tis nothing.

YORK No matter, then, who see it.
I will be satisfied. Let me see the writing.

AUMERLE
I do beseech your Grace to pardon me.
It is a matter of small consequence,
Which for some reasons I would not have seen.

YORK
Which for some reasons, sir, I mean to see.
I fear, I fear—

DUCHESS What should you fear?
'Tis nothing but some bond that he is ent'red into
For gay apparel 'gainst the triumph day.

YORK
Bound to himself? What doth he with a bond
That he is bound to? Wife, thou art a fool.
Boy, let me see the writing.

AUMERLE
I do beseech you, pardon me. I may not show it.

YORK
I will be satisfied. Let me see it, I say.
He plucks it out of his bosom and reads it.
Treason! Foul treason! Villain! Traitor! Slave!

DUCHESS
What is the matter, my lord?

YORK
Ho! Who is within there?

[Enter a servant.]

Saddle my horse.
God for his mercy, what treachery is here?

DUCHESS
Why, what is it, my lord?

YORK
Give me my boots, I say. Saddle my horse.
[Exit Servant.]
Now, by mine honor, by my life, by my troth,
I will appeach the villain.

DUCHESS What is the matter?

YORK
Peace, foolish woman.

DUCHESS
I will not peace. What is the matter, Aumerle?

AUMERLE
Good mother, be content. It is no more
Than my poor life must answer.

DUCHESS Thy life answer?

YORK
Bring me my boots! I will unto the King.

His Man enters with his boots.

DUCHESS
Strike him, Aumerle. Poor boy, thou art amaz'd.—
[*To York's Man.*] Hence, villain! Never more come in my sight.

YORK
Give me my boots, I say.
[His man helps him on with his boots, and exit.]

DUCHESS
Why, York, what wilt thou do?
Wilt thou not hide the trespass of thine own?
Have we more sons? Or are we like to have?
Is not my teeming date drunk up with time?
And wilt thou pluck my fair son from mine age,
And rob me of a happy mother's name?

38 we . . . contents i.e., we bind ourselves to be calmly content **40 state** i.e., royal title. **allow** acknowledge **41 Aumerle that was** (Aumerle, as a member of Richard's party, lost his dukedom, though he remained Earl of Rutland.) **44 truth** loyalty **46–47 Who . . . spring** i.e., who are the favorites of the new king **50 bear you** bear yourself **52 Do . . . hold** are those tourneys and pageants going forward. (According to Holinshed, these tourneys at Oxford were part of a conspiracy against Bolingbroke by the Abbott of Westminster and others; the new king was to be invited to attend, and there be assassinated.) **56 seal** i.e., seal attached to the border of a document

66 'gainst in anticipation of **75 God** i.e., I pray God **78 troth** faith, allegiance **79 appeach** inform against, publicly accuse **85 Strike him** i.e., strike the servant. **amaz'd** confused, bewildered **90 Have we more sons** (Historically, this Duchess of York was the Duke's second wife and was not Aumerle's mother.) **91 teeming date** period of childbearing

Is he not like thee? Is he not thine own?

YORK
Thou fond mad woman,
Wilt thou conceal this dark conspiracy?
A dozen of them here have ta'en the sacrament,
And interchangeably set down their hands,
To kill the King at Oxford.

DUCHESS
He shall be none;
We'll keep him here. Then what is that to him?

YORK
Away, fond woman! Were he twenty times my son,
I would appeach him.

DUCHESS
Hadst thou groan'd for him
As I have done, thou wouldst be more pitiful.
But now I know thy mind. Thou dost suspect
That I have been disloyal to thy bed,
And that he is a bastard, not thy son.
Sweet York, sweet husband, be not of that mind!
He is as like thee as a man may be,
Not like to me, or any of my kin,
And yet I love him.

YORK
Make way, unruly woman! *Exit.*

DUCHESS
After, Aumerle! Mount thee upon his horse,
Spur post, and get before him to the King,
And beg thy pardon ere he do accuse thee.
I'll not be long behind. Though I be old,
I doubt not but to ride as fast as York.
And never will I rise up from the ground
Till Bolingbroke have pardon'd thee. Away, be gone! *[Exeunt.]*

[SCENE III]

Enter [Bolingbroke, now] King [Henry], with his Nobles [Percy and others].

KING HENRY
Can no man tell me of my unthrifty son?
'Tis full three months since I did see him last.
If any plague hang over us, 'tis he.
I would to God, my lords, he might be found.
Inquire at London, 'mongst the taverns there,
For there, they say, he daily doth frequent,
With unrestrained loose companions,
Even such, they say, as stand in narrow lanes
And beat our watch, and rob our passengers—
Which he, young wanton and effeminate boy,
Takes on the point of honor to support
So dissolute a crew.

PERCY
My lord, some two days since I saw the Prince,
And told him of those triumphs held at Oxford.

KING HENRY
And what said the gallant?

PERCY
His answer was, he would unto the stews,
And from the common'st creature pluck a glove,
And wear it as a favor, and with that
He would unhorse the lustiest challenger.

KING HENRY
As dissolute as desperate! Yet through both
I see some sparks of better hope, which elder years
May happily bring forth. But who comes here?

Enter Aumerle, amazed.

AUMERLE
Where is the King?

KING HENRY
What means our cousin, that he stares and looks
So wildly?

AUMERLE
God save your Grace! I do beseech your Majesty
To have some conference with your Grace alone.

KING HENRY
Withdraw yourselves, and leave us here alone.
[Exeunt Percy and Lords.]
What is the matter with our cousin now?

AUMERLE *[Kneeling]*
For ever may my knees grow to the earth,
My tongue cleave to my roof within my mouth,
Unless a pardon ere I rise or speak.

KING HENRY
Intended or committed was this fault?
If on the first, how heinous e'er it be,
To win thy after-love I pardon thee.

AUMERLE
Then give me leave that I may turn the key,
That no man enter till my tale be done.

KING HENRY
Have thy desire.
[Aumerle locks the door.] The Duke of York knocks at the door and crieth.

YORK *[Within]*
My liege, beware! Look to thyself.
Thou hast a traitor in thy presence there.

KING HENRY
Villain, I'll make thee safe. *[Drawing.]*

AUMERLE
Stay thy revengeful hand. Thou hast no cause to fear.

YORK *[Within]*
Open the door, secure, foolhardy King!
Shall I for love speak treason to thy face?
Open the door, or I will break it open.
[King Henry unlocks the door.]

[Enter York.]

KING HENRY
What is the matter, uncle? Speak.

95 fond foolish **97–99 A dozen . . . Oxford** ("Hervpon was an indenture sextipartite made, sealed with their seales, and signed with their hands, in the which each stood bound to other, to do their whole indeuor for the accomplishing of their purposed exploit." [Holinshed]) **100 that** i.e., the plot **103 pitiful** pitying **111 his horse** i.e., one of York's horses **112 Spur post** ride as fast as possible

V.iii. Location: A royal palace (i.e., Windsor Castle).
1 unthrifty profligate **9 passengers** passers-by, wayfarers **10 Which** i.e., as to which. **wanton** spoiled, pampered. **effeminate** self-indulgent

14 held i.e., to be held **16 stews** brothels **22 happily** with good fortune **43 secure** unsuspecting, heedless **44 speak . . . face** i.e., speak so disrespectfully as to call you *secure* and *foolhardy*

Recover breath; tell us how near is danger,
That we may arm us to encounter it.

YORK [*Giving letter*]
Peruse this writing here, and thou shalt know
The treason that my haste forbids me show. 50

AUMERLE
Remember, as thou read'st, thy promise pass'd.
I do repent me. Read not my name there;
My heart is not confederate with my hand.

YORK
It was, villain, ere thy hand did set it down.
I tore it from the traitor's bosom, King;
Fear, and not love, begets his penitence.
Forget to pity him, lest thy pity prove
A serpent that will sting thee to the heart.

KING HENRY
O heinous, strong, and bold conspiracy!
O loyal father of a treacherous son,
Thou sheer, immaculate, and silver fountain, 61
From whence this stream through muddy passages
Hath held his current and defil'd himself,
Thy overflow of good converts to bad, 64
And thy abundant goodness shall excuse
This deadly blot in thy digressing son. 66

YORK
So shall my virtue be his vice's bawd,
And he shall spend mine honor with his shame,
As thriftless sons their scraping fathers' gold. 69
Mine honor lives when his dishonor dies,
Or my sham'd life in his dishonor lies.
Thou kill'st me in his life; giving him breath,
The traitor lives, the true man's put to death.

DUCHESS [*Within*]
What ho, my liege! For God's sake, let me in.

KING HENRY
What shrill-voic'd suppliant makes this eager cry?

DUCHESS [*Within*]
A woman, and thy aunt, great King. 'Tis I.
Speak with me, pity me, open the door!
A beggar begs that never begg'd before.

KING HENRY
Our scene is alt'red from a serious thing,
And now chang'd to "The Beggar and the King." 80
My dangerous cousin, let your mother in.
I know she is come to pray for your foul sin.

YORK
If thou do pardon whosoever pray,
More sins for this forgiveness prosper may.
This fest'red joint cut off, the rest rest sound;
This let alone will all the rest confound.

[*Aumerle opens the door. Enter Duchess.*]

DUCHESS
O King, believe not this hard-hearted man!
Love loving not itself, none other can. 88

YORK
Thou frantic woman, what dost thou make here? 89
Shall thy old dugs once more a traitor rear?

DUCHESS
Sweet York, be patient. Hear me, gentle liege.
[*Kneels.*]

KING HENRY
Rise up, good aunt.

DUCHESS
Not yet, I thee beseech.
For ever will I walk upon my knees,
And never see day that the happy sees,
Till thou give joy, until thou bid me joy,
By pardoning Rutland, my transgressing boy.

AUMERLE
Unto my mother's prayers I bend my knee. [*Kneels.*]

YORK
Against them both my true joints bended be.
[*Kneels.*]
Ill mayst thou thrive, if thou grant any grace!

DUCHESS
Pleads he in earnest? Look upon his face. 100
His eyes do drop no tears, his prayers are in jest;
His words come from his mouth, ours from our
breast.
He prays but faintly and would be denied;
We pray with heart and soul and all beside.
His weary joints would gladly rise, I know;
Our knees still kneel till to the ground they grow. 106
His prayers are full of false hypocrisy;
Ours of true zeal and deep integrity.
Our prayers do out-pray his; then let them have
That mercy which true prayer ought to have.

KING HENRY
Good aunt, stand up.

DUCHESS
Nay, do not say, "stand up."
Say "pardon" first, and afterwards "stand up."
An if I were thy nurse, thy tongue to teach,
"Pardon" should be the first word of thy speech.
I never long'd to hear a word till now;
Say "pardon," King; let pity teach thee how.
The word is short, but not so short as sweet;
No word like "pardon" for kings' mouths so meet.

YORK
Speak it in French, King; say "pardonne moy." 119

DUCHESS
Dost thou teach pardon pardon to destroy?
Ah, my sour husband, my hard-hearted lord,
That sets the word itself against the word!
Speak "pardon" as 'tis current in our land;
The chopping French we do not understand. 124
Thine eye begins to speak; set thy tongue there,
Or in thy piteous heart plant thou thine ear,
That hearing how our plaints and prayers do pierce,
Pity may move thee "pardon" to rehearse. 128

KING HENRY
Good aunt, stand up.

DUCHESS
I do not sue to stand.

50 haste . . . show i.e., breathlessness prevents me from revealing **61 sheer** clear, pure **64 converts** changes **66 digressing** transgressing **69 scraping** parsimonious **80 The Beggar . . . King** (Probably one of Shakespeare's many allusions to the ballad of King Cophetua and the Beggar Maid.) **88 Love . . . can** i.e., he who does not love his own kin can love no one else, not even the King

89 make do **106 still** continually **119 pardonne moy** pardonnez moi, excuse me. (An affectedly polite refusal.) **124 chopping** shifting suddenly, changing the sense **128 rehearse** repeat

Pardon is all the suit I have in hand.

KING HENRY

I pardon him, as God shall pardon me.

DUCHESS

O happy vantage of a kneeling knee!
Yet am I sick for fear. Speak it again;
Twice saying "pardon" doth not pardon twain,
But makes one pardon strong.

KING HENRY With all my heart
I pardon him.

DUCHESS A god on earth thou art. [*All rise.*]

KING HENRY

But for our trusty brother-in-law and the
Abbot, 137
With all the rest of that consorted crew, 138
Destruction straight shall dog them at the heels.
Good uncle, help to order several powers 140
To Oxford, or where'er these traitors are.
They shall not live within this world, I swear,
But I will have them, if I once know where.
Uncle, farewell, and, cousin, adieu.
Your mother well hath pray'd, and prove you true. 145

DUCHESS

Come, my old son. I pray God make thee new.
Exeunt.

[SCENE IV]

Enter Sir Pierce [of] Exton [and Servants].

EXTON

Didst thou not mark the King, what words he
spake,
"Have I no friend will rid me of this living fear?"
Was it not so?

FIRST MAN These were his very words.

EXTON

"Have I no friend?" quoth he. He spake it
twice,
And urg'd it twice together, did he not?

FIRST MAN

He did.

EXTON

And speaking it, he wishtly look'd on me, 7
As who should say, "I would thou wert the man
That would divorce this terror from my heart"—
Meaning the king at Pomfret. Come, let's go.
I am the King's friend, and will rid his foe. 11
[*Exeunt.*]

[SCENE V]

Enter Richard alone.

KING RICHARD

I have been studying how I may compare
This prison where I live unto the world;
And, for because the world is populous, 3
And here is not a creature but myself,
I cannot do it. Yet I'll hammer it out.
My brain I'll prove the female to my soul,
My soul the father, and these two beget
A generation of still-breeding thoughts; 8
And these same thoughts people this little world,
In humors like the people of this world, 10
For no thought is contented. The better sort,
As thoughts of things divine, are intermix'd
With scruples and do set the word itself 13
Against the word, 14
As thus, "Come, little ones," and then again, 15
"It is as hard to come as for a camel 16
To thread the postern of a small needle's eye." 17
Thoughts tending to ambition, they do plot
Unlikely wonders—how these vain weak nails
May tear a passage through the flinty ribs
Of this hard world, my ragged prison walls, 21
And, for they cannot, die in their own pride. 22
Thoughts tending to content flatter themselves
That they are not the first of fortune's slaves,
Nor shall not be the last—like seely beggars 25
Who, sitting in the stocks, refuge their shame 26
That many have and others must sit there;
And in this thought they find a kind of ease,
Bearing their own misfortunes on the back
Of such as have before endur'd the like.
Thus play I in one person many people,
And none contented. Sometimes am I king;
Then treasons make me wish myself a beggar,
And so I am. Then crushing penury
Persuades me I was better when a king;
Then am I king'd again, and by and by
Think that I am unking'd by Bolingbroke,
And straight am nothing. But whate'er I be,
Nor I nor any man that but man is 39
With nothing shall be pleas'd, till he be eas'd
With being nothing. Music do I hear? 41
The music plays.
Ha, ha, keep time! How sour sweet music is,
When time is broke and no proportion kept!
So is it in the music of men's lives.
And here have I the daintiness of ear
To check time broke in a disordered string; 46
But for the concord of my state and time

137 brother-in-law i.e., the Duke of Exeter, who had married Bolingbroke's sister **138 consorted** confederate **140 powers** forces **145 prove you true** may you prove loyal

V.iv. Location: Windsor Castle. The opening stage direction in the Quarto reads *Manet Sir Pierce Exton, etc.*, suggesting continuity of action with a preceding scene.
7 wishtly intently **11 rid** rid him of

V.v. Location: Pomfret Castle. A dungeon.
3 for because because **8 still-breeding** constantly breeding **10 humors** temperaments, peculiar fancies **13 scruples** doubts **13–14 do set . . . word** i.e., oppose one Scriptural passage against its apparent opposite **15–17 Come . . . eye** (See Matthew 19:14, 24.) **17 postern** narrow gate **21 ragged** rugged **22 for** because. **pride** prime **25 seely** simpleminded **26 refuge their shame** i.e., rationalize their disgrace by reflecting **39 Nor** neither **41 being nothing** i.e., being dead **46 check** rebuke

Had not an ear to hear my true time broke.
I wasted time, and now doth time waste me;
For now hath time made me his numb'ring clock. 50
My thoughts are minutes, and with sighs they jar 51
Their watches on unto mine eyes, the outward
watch, 52
Whereto my finger, like a dial's point, 53
Is pointing still, in cleansing them from tears.
Now sir, the sound that tells what hour it is
Are clamorous groans, which strike upon my heart,
Which is the bell. So sighs and tears and groans
Show minutes, times, and hours. But my time 58
Runs posting on in Bolingbroke's proud joy, 59
While I stand fooling here, his Jack of the clock. 60
This music mads me. Let it sound no more, 61
For though it have holp madmen to their wits, 62
In me it seems it will make wise men mad.
Yet blessing on his heart that gives it me!
For 'tis a sign of love; and love to Richard
Is a strange brooch in this all-hating world. 66

Enter a Groom of the Stable.

GROOM
Hail, royal prince!

KING RICHARD Thanks, noble peer!
The cheapest of us is ten groats too dear. 68
What art thou, and how comest thou hither,
Where no man never comes but that sad dog
That brings me food to make misfortune live?

GROOM
I was a poor groom of thy stable, King,
When thou wert king; who, traveling towards York,
With much ado at length have gotten leave
To look upon my sometimes royal master's face. 75
O, how it ern'd my heart when I beheld 76
In London streets, that coronation-day,
When Bolingbroke rode on roan Barbary,
That horse that thou so often hast bestrid,
That horse that I so carefully have dress'd!

KING RICHARD
Rode he on Barbary? Tell me, gentle friend,
How went he under him?

GROOM
So proudly as if he disdain'd the ground.

KING RICHARD
So proud that Bolingbroke was on his back!
That jade hath eat bread from my royal hand; 85
This hand hath made him proud with clapping him. 86
Would he not stumble? Would he not fall down,
Since pride must have a fall, and break the neck
Of that proud man that did usurp his back?
Forgiveness, horse! Why do I rail on thee,
Since thou, created to be aw'd by man,
Wast born to bear? I was not made a horse;
And yet I bear a burden like an ass,
Spurr'd, gall'd, and tir'd by jauncing Bolingbroke. 94

Enter one [a Keeper] to Richard with meat.

KEEPER
Fellow, give place. Here is no longer stay.

KING RICHARD
If thou love me, 'tis time thou wert away.

GROOM
What my tongue dares not, that my heart shall say.
Exit Groom.

KEEPER
My lord, will 't please you to fall to?

KING RICHARD
Taste of it first, as thou art wont to do. 99

KEEPER
My lord, I dare not. Sir Pierce of Exton, who
Lately came from the King, commands the contrary.

KING RICHARD
The devil take Henry of Lancaster and thee!
Patience is stale, and I am weary of it.
[Beats the keeper.]

KEEPER
Help, help, help!
The Murderers [Exton and Servants] rush in.

KING RICHARD
How now, what means death in this rude assault?
Villain, thy own hand yields thy death's instrument.
[Snatching an axe from a Servant and killing him.]
Go thou, and fill another room in hell. 107
[He kills another.] Here Exton strikes him down.
That hand shall burn in never-quenching fire
That staggers thus my person. Exton, thy fierce hand
Hath with the King's blood stain'd the King's own
land.
Mount, mount, my soul! Thy seat is up on high,
Whilst my gross flesh sinks downward, here to die.
[Dies.]

EXTON
As full of valor as of royal blood!
Both have I spill'd. O would the deed were good!
For now the devil, that told me I did well,
Says that this deed is chronicled in hell.
This dead king to the living king I'll bear.
Take hence the rest, and give them burial here.
[Exeunt, with the bodies.]

[SCENE VI]

[Flourish.] Enter Bolingbroke [as King], with the Duke of York, [other Lords, and Attendants].

KING HENRY
Kind uncle York, the latest news we hear

50 numb'ring clock i.e., a clock that numbers hours and minutes (not an hourglass) **51–52 with . . . watch** i.e., by means of sighs, occurring as regularly as the swinging of a clock's pendulum, my thoughts tick away, marking periods of time and transferring these manifestations to my eyes, which are like the face of the clock **53 dial's point** clock hand **58 times** quarters and halves **59 posting** hastening **60 Jack of the clock** manikin which struck the bell on a clock **61 mads** maddens **62 holp** helped **66 strange brooch** rare ornament **68 ten groats too dear** (There is a pun on *royal* and *noble* in the preceding lines. A royal [10s.] is worth 10 groats [ten times 4d.] more than a noble [6s. 8d.] is; hence, Richard is saying that he, "the cheapest of us" because he is a prisoner, is worth no more than the groom, whom he greets as "noble.") **75 sometimes** former **76 ern'd** grieved **85 eat** eaten. (Pronounced *et*.) **86 clapping** patting, stroking

94 jauncing making the horse prance up and down **99 Taste . . . first** i.e., to ensure that it isn't poisoned **107 room** place

V.vi. Location: Windsor Castle.

Is that the rebels have consum'd with fire
Our town of Ciceter in Gloucestershire; 3
But whether they be ta'en or slain we hear not.

Enter Northumberland.

Wecome, my lord. What is the news?

NORTHUMBERLAND
First, to thy sacred state wish I all happiness.
The next news is, I have to London sent
The heads of Salisbury, Spencer, Blunt, and Kent.
The manner of their taking may appear 9
At large discoursed in this paper here. [*Gives paper.*]

KING HENRY
We thank thee, gentle Percy, for thy pains,
And to thy worth will add right worthy gains. 12

Enter Lord Fitzwater.

FITZWATER
My lord, I have from Oxford sent to London
The heads of Brocas and Sir Bennet Seely,
Two of the dangerous consorted traitors
That sought at Oxford thy dire overthrow.

KING HENRY
Thy pains, Fitzwater, shall not be forgot;
Right noble is thy merit, well I wot.

Enter Henry Percy [*and the Bishop of Carlisle*].

PERCY
The grand conspirator, Abbot of Westminster,
With clog of conscience and sour melancholy 20
Hath yielded up his body to the grave;
But here is Carlisle living, to abide 22
Thy kingly doom and sentence of his pride. 23

KING HENRY
Carlisle, this is your doom:
Choose out some secret place, some reverend room, 25
More than thou hast, and with it joy thy life. 26
So as thou liv'st in peace, die free from strife;
For though mine enemy thou hast ever been,
High sparks of honor in thee have I seen.

Enter Exton, with [*Attendants bearing*] *the coffin.*

EXTON
Great King, within this coffin I present
Thy buried fear. Herein all breathless lies
The mightiest of thy greatest enemies,
Richard of Bordeaux, by me hither brought.

KING HENRY
Exton, I thank thee not, for thou hast wrought
A deed of slander with thy fatal hand 35
Upon my head and all this famous land.

EXTON
From your own mouth, my lord, did I this deed.

KING HENRY
They love not poison that do poison need,
Nor do I thee. Though I did wish him dead,
I hate the murderer, love him murdered.

3 Ciceter i.e., Cirencester **9 taking** capture **12 worth** (1) deserving (2) present worth **20 clog** burden **22 abide** await **23 doom** judgment **25 reverend room** place suitable to religious retirement **26 joy** gladden, enjoy **35 deed of slander** i.e., a deed sure to arouse slanderous talk about the new king

The guilt of conscience take thou for thy labor,
But neither my good word nor princely favor.
With Cain go wander thorough shades of night, 43
And never show thy head by day nor light.
Lords, I protest, my soul is full of woe,
That blood should sprinkle me to make me grow.
Come, mourn with me for what I do lament,
And put on sullen black incontinent. 48
I'll make a voyage to the Holy Land,
To wash this blood off from my guilty hand.
March sadly after. Grace my mournings here, 51
In weeping after this untimely bier.
[*Exeunt in procession, following the coffin.*]

43 Cain murderer of his brother Abel; see I.i.104. **thorough** through **48 incontinent** immediately **51 Grace** dignify

The First Part of King Henry the Fourth

The opening of *1 Henry IV* is taut and grave in tone. England is "shaken" and "wan with care." The troubles of *Richard II,* to which this play (1596–1597) is a close sequel, have not been left behind. However much King Henry would prefer to unite his countrymen against a common foreign enemy in a crusade to the holy lands, he is prevented from doing so by continuing civil war. The impassioned rhetoric of his opening speech proclaiming a new era of peace can only end in anticlimax, for the actual purpose of this meeting in council is to receive and assess reports of military action against the throne.

Henry's current troubles are in the far reaches of his kingdom: Scots in the north, Welsh in the west. Fighting for Henry on these two fronts are the nobles of the Percy family who helped him to power: Henry Percy ("Hotspur"), his father the Earl of Northumberland, his uncle the Earl of Worcester, and his brother-in-law Edmund Mortimer the Earl of March. Apparently they have fought bravely. Yet we soon sense that all is not well between the new king and those who rebelled with him against Richard. A quarrel breaks out because Hotspur refuses to deliver to Henry some prisoners as required by feudal obedience. The matter of the ransom money is only a technicality; what is really at issue? In part, it is Henry's insistence on being obeyed on principle. Admiring Hotspur inordinately, the King feels he must discipline affectionately this fine young warrior as a father would discipline his son. Even more deeply, however, the issue of the prisoners galls Henry because of the proviso that he ransom Mortimer, captured by the Welsh. Henry does not forget that Mortimer is his chief rival for the English crown, being descended from the Duke of Clarence (elder brother to Henry's father, Gaunt), and proclaimed by Richard heir to the throne. Mortimer is the last person Henry would wish ransomed. Moreover, the King suspects Mortimer of having fought with something less than total zeal against the Welsh Glendower. Mortimer's marriage to Glendower's daughter confirms the King's worst fears. Henry knows Northumberland and Worcester to be expert in treasonous plotting, since they conspired with him to overthrow Richard. Now, Henry believes, these Percies are extending their alliance by a series of calculated marriages in order to seize power once again. This time their claimant is Mortimer.

Shakespeare's sympathies are many-sided. The Percy clan is in fact organizing against Henry, but not without cause. As they see it, the man they helped to the throne has done little for them since. His manner of disciplining them sounds too much like hostility and ingratitude. Other counselors attend the King constantly while Worcester is banished from court. In such an atmosphere of distrust, suspicion breeds still more suspicion. The situation has polarized, surely more than either party originally intended.

Hotspur is the most attractive of the rebels, to us as to King Henry. He is outspoken, courageous, witty, domineering in conversation. Above all, he is a disciple of manliness, loyalty, chivalry, bravery in battle—the attributes of an upstanding and somewhat old-fashioned sense of honor. Yet a fatal defect dwells even in these attractive qualities. Hotspur is impatient, proud, unwilling to tolerate a rival—be it Glendower or Prince Hal. In his very first speech, purporting to explain his refusal to deliver the prisoners, he brilliantly satirizes an effete courtier who had come to him from King Henry in the midst of a battle. The satire betrays many harsh qualities in Hotspur: the self-indulgent wrath which returns fully to him even in recollection of the encounter, the pride in his own stoical indifference to suffering, and especially the obsessive character (revealed in the repetitive pattern of the rhetoric) of his contempt for courtiers generally. Surely his scorn for stay-at-home politicians is directed in part at King Henry himself. All courtiers are to Hotspur effeminate, perfume-wearing, affected in mannerism and speech, scarcely masculine. This preoccupation of Hotspur makes him extraordinarily prone to one-sided judgments. Like most excessive devotees of chivalry, he divides mankind into sheep and goats: those who are gentlemen, like himself, and those who are beneath contempt. The "vile politician" Bolingbroke and his son the "sword-and-buckler Prince of Wales" fall into the latter category.

Prone as he is to such an overly simple view of political behavior, Hotspur can see no good in the King's cause and no evil in his own. He is a poor listener because of his obsession, and yet an easy prey to his uncle and father who require his leadership for their cause. They need only implant the suggestion that King Henry is acting from a political motive in his refusal to ransom Mortimer, and Hotspur is ready to leap incautiously to the defense of their cause. The great irony is that Hotspur fails to see political motives in the machinations of his own relatives. While he fights for bright honor, they maneuver cautiously for position and prove uncertain allies when the hour of battle approaches. Most crucially, they betray Hotspur in the pre-battle negotiations, at which he is not present. As Worcester explains to Vernon during their return to rebel headquarters (V,ii), they cannot let Hospur know of the King's offer to settle matters by a general pardon. Although, as they realize, the King could pardon Hotspur's youth, there can be no turning back for themselves. Thus the honor for which Hotspur fights is at bottom a lie, and the mutual esteem that might have grown between him and a much-reformed Prince of Wales is thwarted by the polarization of attitudes in the two camps. Hotspur's brand of honor is the victim of its own excess, and lends some credence to Falstaff's wry conclusion that honor "is a mere scutcheon."

The contrasting of Falstaff and Hotspur on the theme of honor suggests that they are dramatic "foils" to one another, representing extremes between which Hal must choose. Shakespeare uses this "foil" device structurally and consciously; for example, he has considerably reduced the age of the Hotspur he found in Holinshed's *Chronicles* in order to accentuate the similarity between Hotspur and Hal. Conversely, to emphasize the contrast between Falstaff and Hotspur, Shakespeare envisages Falstaff as old (nearly sixty, by his own admission), fat, humorous, and without honor. Falstaff's vices are Hotspur's virtues, and the reverse. Whereas Hotspur offers to Hal a model of chivalric striving and attention to duty, Falstaff is a highwayman and liar. On the other hand, Hotspur is a fanatic, unbending and self-absorbed even in the company of his sprightly wife Kate, irritated by music and poetry; Falstaff is the epitome of merriment and *joie de vivre*. We excuse much in him because he lusts after life with such an appetite, and ingratiates himself to others by inviting them to laugh at his expense.

The two most pronounced motifs of the first scene between Hal and Falstaff (I,ii) are the hanging of thieves and temptation to sinfulness. Beneath the gay surface of their raillery, the two are already debating the need for the ultimate rejection of Falstaff. Can their relationship continue unchanged into the reign of Henry V? Will there be gallows standing, and justice for highwaymen? Will "Monsieur Remorse," as Poins calls Falstaff, ever sincerely repent? Will the Prince, for that matter? To allay our fears, Hal soliloquizes at scene's end, vowing his determination to use these scapegrace companions as mere "foils" to his triumphal reformation at the appropriate time. But this explanation raises an opposite danger in our sympathies: is he callously using his companions merely to create a self-serving myth of Prince Hal, the Politician with the Common Touch? Is Francis the "drawer" or tapster no more to Hal than a butt for his raillery? Since the rejection of Falstaff is, by Hal's own words, already determined, can we credit him with a serious friendship? Where do Shakespeare's sympathies lie, with the need for political order or with the hedonistic spirit of youth? Perhaps he recognizes the validity of both, and accordingly shows us a prince who is genuinely fond of Falstaff's exuberant company, but who also knows that he is a king's son and must sooner or later accept the consequences of that unsought role. Falstaff's gift to him is youthful irresponsibility, which must be cherished (by all of us) even though it cannot last.

In the Gadshill robbery, Falstaff reveals that his "cowardice" differs from the natural craven fear of Bardolph and Peto. He fights no longer than he sees "reason," that is, not against unfair odds such as two athletic young men in the dark (or later, at Shrewsbury, against the burly Scots giant, the Douglas). A man could get killed that way. Falstaff's cowardice, then, is philosophic, seen by himself in a humorous perspective. The same is true of his lying about the robbery. However much Hal exults in exposing Falstaff as a fraud, we cannot dismiss the possibility that Falstaff may see through the Prince's scheme, and may then feed Hal the expectedly outlandish lie (two men in buckram become eleven men) as a means of begging for affection. Falstaff's only way of pleading his cause is to tickle the Prince's fancy, in his role as a kind of court fool. What Falstaff most wants is to be loved and retained for what he is; and that, poignantly enough, is the one thing the mature Henry V cannot grant.

Throughout *1 Henry IV,* Shakespeare seems interested in the relationships between fathers and sons. These relationships help structure the comparisons and contrasts among "foil" characters. Falstaff is a foil not only to Hotspur, but also to Henry IV; that is, despite all his insistence on youthful irresponsibility, Falstaff acts as a kind of parental figure to Hal. In the tavern scene (II,iv), Falstaff and Hal take turns playing king and crown prince, and in both roles Falstaff wittily argues his case as companion and guide to the heir to the throne. Is it better to be old and merry, fat and loved, or to be hated like Pharaoh's lean kine? Falstaff argues against the gravity of council meetings with the same amused fervor he later directs at the grinning honor of a dead hero. Hal, in his turn as king, questions the propriety of a "devil" haunting the crown prince "in the likeness of an old man," a "reverend vice," a "grey iniquity," a "father ruffian." For all the good humor in this exchange, both men are asking whether Falstaff or King Henry serves Hal as the better model. Hal anticipates some of the very arguments his father will use against him next day at court, and indeed the insistent presence of that sober adult world makes itself felt even in the tavern. To Falstaff's moving litany, urging that Hal "banish not him thy Harry's company; banish plump Jack, and banish all the world," the Prince can only reply, "I do, I will."

Hotspur too is regarded as a son by more than one father. King Henry only half-jokingly wishes it could be proved that some night-tripping fairy had exchanged his Harry in the cradle for Harry Percy (I,i). Paradoxically, the King admires Hotspur all the more for standing up to him, just as another imperious father-figure, Owen Glendower, bestows grudging but real admiration on Hotspur for his outspokenness (III,i). Hotspur's rebellious ways are cherished because they seem to promise manliness and fame; Hal's rebellious ways are feared and despised because they seem to reject the values of duty and leadership on which King Henry bases his self-respect. In these terms, the play must resolve Hal's coming of age, his acceptance of his role as true son of the King and his proving to the King of the son's worth. Hal must find his adult self, a self that differs greatly from that of King Henry, but must do so in a way that preserves the integrity of their relationship and the real debt he owes the father.

These conflicts reach their climax and resolution at the field of Shrewsbury in Act V. Hal's worth must be proven at Hotspur's expense. The rivalry between the two has been intense throughout the play, as seen for example in Hal's brilliant mimicking of Hotspur's devotion to bloodshed (II,iv). Aware that his tarnished reputation puts him at a disadvantage, Hal speaks nobly of his rival and impresses even the adversary camp with his regal bearing (V,i). He rescues his father in the battle, thereby proving to King Henry that the son does not wish to supplant the father as the father had feared. After the battle, Hal frees his Scottish adversary Douglas in a display of princely magnificence. Meantime, Hal has put considerable distance between himself and Falstaff, though sensitive still to the warmth of old memories. When he sees Hotspur and Falstaff on the ground together, seemingly both dead, Hal views as in a tableau the contrasting models between which he has shaped his own identity. Yet Falstaff is not dead. He rises to mutilate Hotspur's body and to claim the honor due Hal for Hotspur's death. For all Falstaff's witty commentary at the expense of honor, his own opposite course is unsuited to a time of war or to Hal's new public role. Falstaff's abuse of military conscription, his carrying a bottle of sack in place of a pistol, show him at his wittiest still, but in a world that may not tolerate such pranks. The merry games are out of place, childish. With characteristic generosity and imprudence, Hal gives the credit for Hotspur's death to Falstaff who claims it so cravenly. Even so, the magic of their association has vanished. The time of manhood is upon Hal.

Shakespeare's chief sources for this play and for *2 Henry IV* are the chronicles, especially Holinshed's 1587 edition, Samuel Daniel's *The First Fowre Bookes of the Civile Wars* (1595), and a play called *The Famous Victories of Henry V*. See Appendix II for an analysis of his use of these and other materials.

The First Part of King Henry the Fourth

[*Dramatis Personae*

KING HENRY THE FOURTH.
HENRY, PRINCE OF WALES, } *sons to the King.*
PRINCE JOHN OF LANCASTER, }
EARL OF WESTMORLAND.
SIR WALTER BLUNT.
THOMAS PERCY, EARL OF WORCESTER.
HENRY PERCY, EARL OF NORTHUMBERLAND.
HENRY PERCY, *surnamed* HOTSPUR, *his son.*
EDMUND MORTIMER, *Earl of March.*
RICHARD SCROOP, ARCHBISHOP OF YORK.
ARCHIBALD, EARL OF DOUGLAS.
OWEN GLENDOWER.
SIR RICHARD VERNON.
SIR JOHN FALSTAFF.
SIR MICHAEL, *of the household of the Archbishop of York.*
EDWARD POINS.
GADSHILL.
PETO.
BARDOLPH.

LADY PERCY, *wife to Hotspur, and sister to Mortimer.*
LADY MORTIMER, *daughter to Glendower, and wife to Mortimer.*
MISTRESS QUICKLY, *hostess of a tavern in Eastcheap.*

LORDS, OFFICERS, SHERIFF, VINTNER, CHAMBERLAIN, OSTLER, DRAWERS, *two* CARRIERS, TRAVELERS, *and* ATTENDANTS.

SCENE: *England and Wales.*]

[ACT I • SCENE I]

Enter the King, Lord John of Lancaster, [*the*] *Earl of Westmorland,* [*Sir Walter Blunt,*] *with others.*

KING
So shaken as we are, so wan with care,
Find we a time for frighted peace to pant,
And breathe short-winded accents of new broils
To be commenc'd in stronds afar remote.

I.i. Location: London. The palace.
2 Find we let us find **3 accents** words **4 stronds afar remote** far-off strands, shores, i.e., of the Holy Land (to which, at the end of *Richard II*, Henry has pledged himself to a crusade)

No more the thirsty entrance of this soil 5
Shall daub her lips with her own children's blood;
No more shall trenching war channel her fields, 7
Nor bruise her flow'rets with the armed hoofs
Of hostile paces. Those opposed eyes, 9
Which, like the meteors of a troubled heaven,
All of one nature, of one substance bred,
Did lately meet in the intestine shock 12
And furious close of civil butchery, 13
Shall now, in mutual well-beseeming ranks,
March all one way and be no more oppos'd
Against acquaintance, kindred, and allies.
The edge of war, like an ill-sheathed knife,
No more shall cut his master. Therefore, friends, 18
As far as to the sepulcher of Christ—
Whose soldier now, under whose blessed cross
We are impressed and engag'd to fight— 21
Forthwith a power of English shall we levy, 22
Whose arms were molded in their mothers' womb
To chase these pagans in those holy fields
Over whose acres walk'd those blessed feet
Which fourteen hundred years ago were nail'd
For our advantage on the bitter cross.
But this our purpose now is twelve month old,
And bootless 'tis to tell you we will go. 29
Therefore we meet not now. Then let me hear
Of you, my gentle cousin Westmorland, 31
What yesternight our council did decree
In forwarding this dear expedience. 33

WESTMORLAND
My liege, this haste was hot in question, 34
And many limits of the charge set down 35
But yesternight, when all athwart there came 36
A post from Wales loaden with heavy news, 37
Whose worst was that the noble Mortimer,
Leading the men of Herefordshire to fight
Against the irregular and wild Glendower,
Was by the rude hands of that Welshman taken,
A thousand of his people butchered—
Upon whose dead corpse there was such misuse, 43
Such beastly shameless transformation, 44
By those Welshwomen done as may not be
Without much shame retold or spoken of.

KING
It seems then that the tidings of this broil
Brake off our business for the Holy Land.

WESTMORLAND
This match'd with other did, my gracious lord; 49
For more uneven and unwelcome news 50
Came from the north, and thus it did import:
On Holy-rood day, the gallant Hotspur there, 52
Young Harry Percy, and brave Archibald,
That ever-valiant and approved Scot,
At Holmedon met, 55
Where they did spend a sad and bloody hour,
As by discharge of their artillery, 57
And shape of likelihood, the news was told; 58
For he that brought them, in the very heat 59
And pride of their contention did take horse, 60
Uncertain of the issue any way.

KING
Here is a dear, a true industrious friend,
Sir Walter Blunt, new lighted from his horse,
Stain'd with the variation of each soil
Betwixt that Holmedon and this seat of ours;
And he hath brought us smooth and welcome news.
The Earl of Douglas is discomfited;
Ten thousand bold Scots, two and twenty knights,
Balk'd in their own blood, did Sir Walter see 69
On Holmedon's plains. Of prisoners, Hotspur took
Mordake Earl of Fife and eldest son 71
To beaten Douglas, and the Earl of Athol,
Of Murray, Angus, and Menteith.
And is not this an honorable spoil?
A gallant prize? Ha, cousin, is it not?

WESTMORLAND
In faith, it is a conquest for a prince to boast of.

KING
Yea, there thou mak'st me sad, and mak'st me sin
In envy that my Lord Northumberland
Should be the father to so blest a son—
A son who is the theme of honor's tongue,
Amongst a grove the very straightest plant, 81
Who is sweet Fortune's minion and her pride, 82
Whilst I, by looking on the praise of him,
See riot and dishonor stain the brow
Of my young Harry. O that it could be prov'd
That some night-tripping fairy had exchang'd
In cradle-clothes our children where they lay,
And call'd mine Percy, his Plantagenet! 88
Then would I have his Harry, and he mine.
But let him from my thoughts. What think you, coz, 90
Of this young Percy's pride? The prisoners
Which he in this adventure hath surpris'd 92
To his own use he keeps, and sends me word 93
I shall have none but Mordake Earl of Fife. 94

WESTMORLAND
This is his uncle's teaching, this is Worcester,
Malevolent to you in all aspects, 96
Which makes him prune himself, and bristle up 97
The crest of youth against your dignity.

KING
But I have sent for him to answer this;
And for this cause awhile we must neglect
Our holy purpose to Jerusalem.
Cousin, on Wednesday next our council we
Will hold at Windsor. So inform the lords.

5 thirsty entrancei.e., parched mouth **7 trenching** cutting **9 paces** horses' tread **12 intestine** internal **13 close** hand-to-hand encounter **18 his** its **21 impressed** conscripted **22 power** army **29 bootless** useless **31 gentle cousin** noble kinsman **33 dear expedience** urgent expedition **34 hot in question** being hotly debated **35 limits . . . charge** particulars of military responsibility **36 athwart** at cross purposes, contrarily **37 post** messenger **43 corpse** corpses **44 transformation** mutilation **49 other** i.e., other news **50 uneven** disconcerting, distressing **52 Holy-rood day** September 14 **55 Holmedon** Humbleton in Northumberland

57 by i.e., judging from **58 shape of likelihood** apparent likelihood **59 them** i.e., the news **60 pride** height **69 Balk'd** heaped up in balks or ridges **71 Mordake** i.e., Murdoch, son of the Earl of Albany **81 plant** i.e., tree **82 minion** favorite **88 Plantagenet** (Family name of English royalty since Henry II.) **90 let him** let him go. **coz** cousin, i.e., kinsman **92 surpris'd** ambushed, captured **93 To . . . use** i.e., to collect ransom for them **94 none but Mordake** (Since Mordake was of royal blood, being grandson to Robert II of Scotland, Hotspur could not claim him as his prisoner according to the law of arms.) **96 Malevolent, aspects** (Astrological terms.) **97 Which . . . himself** i.e., which teaching makes Hotspur preen himself (as a falcon preens its feathers)

But come yourself with speed to us again,
For more is to be said and to be done
Than out of anger can be uttered.

WESTMORLAND
I will, my liege. *Exeunt.*

[SCENE II]

Enter Prince of Wales and Sir John Falstaff.

FALSTAFF Now, Hal, what time of day is it, lad?

PRINCE Thou art so fat-witted with drinking of old sack and unbuttoning thee after supper, and sleeping upon benches after noon, that thou hast forgotten to demand that truly which thou wouldst truly know. What a devil hast thou to do with the time of the day? Unless hours were cups of sack, and minutes capons, and clocks the tongues of bawds, and dials the signs of leaping-houses, and the blessed sun himself a fair hot wench in flame-color'd taffeta, I see no reason why thou shouldst be so superfluous to demand the time of the day.

FALSTAFF Indeed, you come near me now, Hal; for we that take purses go by the moon and the seven stars, and not by Phoebus, he, "that wand'ring knight so fair." And, I prithee, sweet wag, when thou art king, as, God save thy Grace—Majesty I should say, for grace thou wilt have none—

PRINCE What, none?

FALSTAFF No, by my troth, not so much as will serve to be prologue to an egg and butter.

PRINCE Well, how then? Come, roundly, roundly.

FALSTAFF Marry, then, sweet wag, when thou art king, let not us that are squires of the night's body be call'd thieves of the day's beauty. Let us be Diana's foresters, gentlemen of the shade, minions of the moon; and let men say we be men of good government, being govern'd, as the sea is, by our noble and chaste mistress the moon, under whose countenance we steal.

PRINCE Thou sayest well, and it holds well too; for the fortune of us that are the moon's men doth ebb and flow like the sea, being govern'd, as the sea is, by the moon. As, for proof, now: a purse of gold most resolutely snatch'd on Monday night and most dissolutely spent on Tuesday morning; got with swearing "Lay by," and spent with crying "Bring in"; now in as low an ebb as the foot of the ladder, and by and by in as high a flow as the ridge of the gallows.

FALSTAFF By the Lord, thou say'st true, lad. And is not my hostess of the tavern a most sweet wench?

PRINCE As the honey of Hybla, my old lad of the castle. And is not a buff jerkin a most sweet robe of durance?

FALSTAFF How now, how now, mad wag, what, in thy quips and thy quiddities? What a plague have I to do with a buff jerkin?

PRINCE Why, what a pox have I to do with my hostess of the tavern?

FALSTAFF Well, thou hast call'd her to a reckoning many a time and oft.

PRINCE Did I ever call for thee to pay thy part?

FALSTAFF No; I'll give thee thy due, thou hast paid all there.

PRINCE Yea, and elsewhere, so far as my coin would stretch; and where it would not, I have us'd my credit.

FALSTAFF Yea, and so us'd it that, were it not here apparent that thou art heir apparent—But, I prithee, sweet wag, shall there be gallows standing in England when thou art king? And resolution thus fubb'd as it is with the rusty curb of old father antic the law? Do not thou, when thou art king, hang a thief.

PRINCE No; thou shalt.

FALSTAFF Shall I? O rare! By the Lord, I'll be a brave judge.

PRINCE Thou judgest false already. I mean, thou shalt have the hanging of the thieves and so become a rare hangman.

FALSTAFF Well, Hal, well; and in some sort it jumps with my humor as well as waiting in the court, I can tell you.

PRINCE For obtaining of suits?

FALSTAFF Yea, for obtaining of suits, whereof the hangman hath no lean wardrobe. 'Sblood, I am as melancholy as a gib cat or a lugg'd bear.

PRINCE Or an old lion, or a lover's lute.

FALSTAFF Yea, or the drone of a Lincolnshire bagpipe.

PRINCE What sayest thou to a hare, or the melancholy of Moor-ditch?

FALSTAFF Thou hast the most unsavory similes, and art indeed the most comparative, rascalliest, sweet young prince. But, Hal, I prithee trouble me no more with vanity. I would to God thou and I knew where a commodity of good names were to be bought. An old lord of the council rated me the other day in the street about you, sir, but I mark'd him not; and yet he talk'd very wisely, but I regarded him not; and yet he talk'd wisely, and in the street too.

PRINCE Thou didst well, for wisdom cries out in the streets, and no man regards it.

I.ii. Location: London. An apartment of the Prince's.
2 sack a Spanish white wine **8 dials** clocks **9 leaping-houses** houses of prostitution **10 taffeta** (Commonly worn by prostitutes.) **13 you . . . now** i.e., you've scored a point on me **14 the seven stars** the Pleiades **15–16 Phoebus . . . fair** (Phoebus, god of the sun, is here equated with the wandering knight of a ballad or popular romance.) **17 Grace** royal highness (with pun on *spiritual grace* and also on *"grace"* or blessing before a meal) **20 troth** faith **21 prologue . . . butter** i.e., grace before a brief meal **22 roundly** i.e., out with it **23 Marry** indeed. (Literally, *by the Virgin Mary*.) **25 Diana's foresters** (An elegant name for thieves by night; Diana is goddess of the moon and the hunt.) **26 minions** favorites **27 government** conduct **29 countenance** (1) face (2) patronage, approval. **steal** (1) move stealthily (2) rob **30 it holds well** the comparison is apt **35–36 Lay by** (A cry of highwaymen, like "Hands up!") **36 Bring in** (An order given to a waiter in a tavern.) **37 ladder** i.e., gallows ladder

41 Hybla (A mountain range in Sicily near Syracuse, famed for honey.) **old . . . castle** (1) a roisterer (2) the name, Sir John Oldcastle, borne by Falstaff in the earlier version of the Henry IV plays **42 buff jerkin** a leather jacket worn by officers of the law. **durance** (1) imprisonment (2) durability **44 quiddities** subtleties of speech **46 pox** syphilis. (Here, *what a pox* is used as an expletive, like "what the devil.") **48 reckoning** settlement of the bill (with bawdy suggestion) **58 resolution** courage (of a highwayman). **fubb'd** cheated **59 antic** buffoon **62 brave** excellent **67–68 jumps . . . humor** suits my temperament **68 waiting in the court** being in attendance at the royal court **70 suits** petitions. (But Falstaff uses the word to mean *suits of clothes;* clothes belonging to an executed man were given to the executioner.) **72 'Sblood** by his (Christ's) blood **73 gib cat** tomcat. **lugg'd bear** bear led by a chain and baited by dogs **76 hare** (A proverbially melancholy animal.) **77 Moor-ditch** (A foul ditch draining Moorfields, outside London walls.) **79 comparative** given to abusive comparisons **81 vanity** worldliness **81–82 commodity** supply **83 rated** chastised **87–88 wisdom . . . it** (An allusion to Proverbs 1:20–24.)

FALSTAFF O, thou hast damnable iteration, and art in- 89
deed able to corrupt a saint. Thou hast done much
harm upon me, Hal, God forgive thee for it! Before I
knew thee, Hal, I knew nothing; and now am I, if a 92
man should speak truly, little better than one of the
wicked. I must give over this life, and I will give it
over. By the Lord, an I do not, I am a villain. I'll be 95
damn'd for never a king's son in Christendom.

PRINCE Where shall we take a purse tomorrow, Jack?

FALSTAFF 'Zounds, where thou wilt, lad, I'll make one. 98
An I do not, call me villain and baffle me. 99

PRINCE I see a good amendment of life in thee—from
praying to purse-taking.

FALSTAFF Why, Hal, 'tis my vocation, Hal. 'Tis no sin
for a man to labor in his vocation.

Enter Poins.

Poins! Now shall we know if Gadshill have set a 104
match. O, if men were to be sav'd by merit, what 105
hole in hell were hot enough for him? This is the
most omnipotent villain that ever cried "Stand" to a 107
true man. 108

PRINCE Good morrow, Ned.

POINS Good morrow, sweet Hal. What says Monsieur
Remorse? What says Sir John Sack and Sugar? Jack,
how agrees the devil and thee about thy soul, that
thou soldest him on Good Friday last for a cup of Ma-
deira and a cold capon's leg?

PRINCE Sir John stands to his word, the devil shall have
his bargain; for he was never yet a breaker of pro-
verbs. He will give the devil his due.

POINS Then art thou damn'd for keeping thy word with
the devil.

PRINCE Else he had been damn'd for cozening the 120
devil.

POINS But, my lads, my lads, tomorrow morning, by
four o'clock early, at Gads Hill, there are pilgrims 123
going to Canterbury with rich offerings, and traders
riding to London with fat purses. I have vizards for 125
you all; you have horses for yourselves. Gadshill lies 126
tonight in Rochester. I have bespoke supper tomorrow
night in Eastcheap. We may do it as secure as sleep. If
you will go, I will stuff your purses full of crowns; if
you will not, tarry at home and be hang'd.

FALSTAFF Hear ye, Yedward, if I tarry at home and go 131
not, I'll hang you for going.

POINS You will, chops? 133

FALSTAFF Hal, wilt thou make one?

PRINCE Who, I rob? I a thief? Not I, by my faith.

FALSTAFF There's neither honesty, manhood, nor good
fellowship in thee, nor thou cam'st not of the blood
royal, if thou darest not stand for ten shillings. 138

PRINCE Well then, once in my days I'll be a madcap.

FALSTAFF Why, that's well said.

PRINCE Well, come what will, I'll tarry at home.

FALSTAFF By the Lord, I'll be a traitor then, when thou
art king.

PRINCE I care not.

POINS Sir John, I prithee leave the Prince and me alone.
I will lay him down such reasons for this adventure
that he shall go.

FALSTAFF Well, God give thee the spirit of persuasion
and him the ears of profiting, that what thou speakest
may move and what he hears may be believ'd, that
the true prince may, for recreation sake, prove a false
thief; for the poor abuses of the time want counte- 152
nance. Farewell. You shall find me in Eastcheap. 153

PRINCE Farewell, thou latter spring! Farewell, All-hal- 154
lown summer! *[Exit Falstaff.]* 155

POINS Now, my good sweet honey lord, ride with us
tomorrow. I have a jest to execute that I cannot manage
alone. Falstaff, Bardolph, Peto, and Gadshill shall rob
those men that we have already waylaid; yourself and 159
I will not be there; and when they have the booty, if
you and I do not rob them, cut this head off from my
shoulders.

PRINCE How shall we part with them in setting forth?

POINS Why, we will set forth before or after them, and
appoint them a place of meeting, wherein it is at our
pleasure to fail; and then will they adventure upon the
exploit themselves, which they shall have no sooner
achiev'd but we'll set upon them.

PRINCE Yea, but 'tis like that they will know us by our
horses, by our habits, and by every other appoint- 170
ment, to be ourselves. 171

POINS Tut, our horses they shall not see—I'll tie them
in the wood; our vizards we will change after we leave
them; and, sirrah, I have cases of buckram for the 174
nonce, to immask our noted outward garments. 175

PRINCE Yea, but I doubt they will be too hard for us. 176

POINS Well, for two of them, I know them to be as true-
bred cowards as ever turn'd back; and for the third, if
he fight longer than he sees reason, I'll forswear arms.
The virtue of this jest will be the incomprehensible lies 180
that this same fat rogue will tell us when we meet at
supper—how thirty, at least, he fought with, what
wards, what blows, what extremities he endur'd; and 183
in the reproof of this lives the jest. 184

PRINCE Well, I'll go with thee. Provide us all things nec-
essary and meet me tomorrow night in Eastcheap.
There I'll sup. Farewell.

POINS Farewell, my lord. *Exit Poins.*

PRINCE
I know you all, and will awhile uphold
The unyok'd humor of your idleness. 190

89 iteration repetition (of Biblical texts, with a neat twist) **92 nothing** i.e., no evil **95 an** if **98 'Zounds** by his (Christ's) wounds. **make one** be one of the party **99 baffle** disgrace as a recreant knight **104 Gadshill** (The name of one of the highwaymen.) **104–105 set a match** arranged a robbery **105 by merit** i.e., according to their deservings rather than by God's grace **107 omnipotent** utter **108 true** honest **120 cozening** cheating **123 Gads Hill** (Location near Rochester on the road from London to Canterbury; one of the highwaymen is called *Gadshill.*) **125 vizards** masks **126 lies** lodges **131 Yedward** (Nickname for *Edward,* Poins' first name.) **133 chops** i.e., fat jaws or cheeks **138 stand . . . shillings** (1) stand up and fight for money (2) be worth 10s., the value of the *royal* or gold coin alluded to in *blood royal* (ll. 137–138)

152–153 want countenance lack encouragement and protection (from men of rank) **154–155 All-hallown summer** (Cf. "Indian summer"; Falstaff's summer or "latter spring," i.e., his youth, has lasted to All Saints' Day, November 1.) **159 waylaid** set an ambush for **170 habits** garments **170–171 appointment** accoutrement **174 sirrah** (Usually addressed to an inferior; here, a sign of intimacy.) **174–175 cases . . . nonce** suits of buckram, a stiff-finished heavily sized fabric, for the purpose **175 noted** known **176 doubt** fear. **too hard** too formidable **180 incomprehensible** boundless **183 wards** parries **184 reproof** disproof **190 idleness** frivolity

Yet herein will I imitate the sun,
Who doth permit the base contagious clouds
To smother up his beauty from the world,
That, when he please again to be himself,
Being wanted, he may be more wond'red at
By breaking through the foul and ugly mists
Of vapors that did seem to strangle him.
If all the year were playing holidays,
To sport would be as tedious as to work;
But when they seldom come, they wish'd for come,
And nothing pleaseth but rare accidents.
So, when this loose behavior I throw off
And pay the debt I never promised,
By how much better than my word I am,
By so much shall I falsify men's hopes;
And like bright metal on a sullen ground,
My reformation, glitt'ring o'er my fault,
Shall show more goodly and attract more eyes
Than that which hath no foil to set it off.
I'll so offend to make offense a skill,
Redeeming time when men think least I will. *Exit.*

[SCENE III]

Enter the King, Northumberland, Worcester, Hotspur, Sir Walter Blunt, with others.

KING
My blood hath been too cold and temperate,
Unapt to stir at these indignities,
And you have found me, for accordingly
You tread upon my patience. But be sure
I will from henceforth rather be myself,
Mighty and to be fear'd, than my condition,
Which hath been smooth as oil, soft as young down,
And therefore lost that title of respect
Which the proud soul ne'er pays but to the proud.

WORCESTER
Our house, my sovereign liege, little deserves
The scourge of greatness to be us'd on it—
And that same greatness too which our own hands
Have holp to make so portly.

NORTHUMBERLAND
My lord—

KING
Worcester, get thee gone, for I do see
Danger and disobedience in thine eye.
O, sir, your presence is too bold and peremptory,
And majesty might never yet endure
The moody frontier of a servant brow.
You have good leave to leave us. When we need
Your use and counsel, we shall send for you.
Exit Worcester.
[*To Northumberland.*] You were about to speak.

NORTHUMBERLAND
Yea, my good lord.
Those prisoners in your Highness' name demanded,
Which Harry Percy here at Holmedon took,
Were, as he says, not with such strength denied
As is delivered to your Majesty.
Either envy, therefore, or misprision
Is guilty of this fault, and not my son.

HOTSPUR
My liege, I did deny no prisoners.
But I remember, when the fight was done,
When I was dry with rage and extreme toil,
Breathless and faint, leaning upon my sword,
Came there a certain lord, neat and trimly dress'd,
Fresh as a bridegroom, and his chin new reap'd
Show'd like a stubble-land at harvest-home.
He was perfumed like a milliner,
And 'twixt his finger and his thumb he held
A pouncet-box, which ever and anon
He gave his nose and took 't away again,
Who therewith angry, when it next came there,
Took it in snuff; and still he smil'd and talk'd,
And as the soldiers bore dead bodies by
He call'd them untaught knaves, unmannerly,
To bring a slovenly unhandsome corse
Betwixt the wind and his nobility.
With many holiday and lady terms
He questioned me, amongst the rest demanded
My prisoners in your Majesty's behalf.
I then, all smarting with my wounds being cold,
To be so pest'red with a popinjay,
Out of my grief and my impatience
Answer'd neglectingly I know not what,
He should, or he should not; for he made me mad
To see him shine so brisk and smell so sweet
And talk so like a waiting-gentlewoman
Of guns and drums and wounds—God save the mark!—
And telling me the sovereignest thing on earth
Was parmaceti for an inward bruise;
And that it was great pity, so it was,
This villainous saltpeter should be digg'd
Out of the bowels of the harmless earth,
Which many a good tall fellow had destroy'd
So cowardly, and but for these vile guns

192 contagious noxious **194 That** so that **195 wanted** lacked **201 accidents** events **205 hopes** expectations **206 sullen ground** dark background, like a *foil.* (See l. 209.) **209 foil** metal sheet laid contrastingly behind a jewel to set off its luster **210 to** as to. **skill** i.e., clever tactic, a positive good **211 Redeeming time** i.e., making amends for lost time

I.iii. Location: London. The palace.
3 found me i.e., found me so **5 myself** i.e., my royal self **6 my condition** my natural (mild) disposition **13 holp** helped. **portly** majestic, prosperous

19 moody frontier i.e., angry brow, frown. (*Frontier* literally means *outwork* or *fortification.*) **26 delivered** reported **27 envy** malice. **misprision** misunderstanding **34 chin new reap'd** i.e., with beard newly trimmed according to the latest fashion, not like a soldier's beard **35 Show'd** looked. **harvest-home** end of harvest, fields being neat and bare **36 milliner** man dealing in fancy articles such as gloves and hats **38 pouncet-box** perfume box with perforated lid **40 Who** i.e., his nose **41 Took it in snuff** (1) inhaled it (2) took offense. **still** continually **46 holiday and lady** dainty and effeminate **47 questioned** conversed with **50 popinjay** parrot **51 grief** pain **56 God . . . mark** (Probably originally a formula to avert evil omen; here, an expression of impatience.) **57 sovereignest** most efficacious **58 parmaceti** spermaceti, sperm from the whale **62 tall** brave

He would himself have been a soldier.
This bald unjointed chat of his, my lord, 65
I answer'd indirectly, as I said;
And I beseech you, let not his report
Come current for an accusation 68
Betwixt my love and your high Majesty.

BLUNT
The circumstance considered, good my lord,
Whate'er Lord Harry Percy then had said
To such a person and in such a place,
At such a time, with all the rest retold,
May reasonably die, and never rise
To do him wrong, or any way impeach 75
What then he said, so he unsay it now. 76

KING
Why, yet he doth deny his prisoners,
But with proviso and exception,
That we at our own charge shall ransom straight 79
His brother-in-law, the foolish Mortimer, 80
Who, on my soul, hath willfully betray'd
The lives of those that he did lead to fight
Against that great magician, damn'd Glendower,
Whose daughter, as we hear, that Earl of March 84
Hath lately married. Shall our coffers, then,
Be emptied to redeem a traitor home?
Shall we buy treason, and indent with fears, 87
When they have lost and forfeited themselves?
No, on the barren mountains let him starve!
For I shall never hold that man my friend
Whose tongue shall ask me for one penny cost
To ransom home revolted Mortimer.

HOTSPUR
Revolted Mortimer!
He never did fall off, my sovereign liege,
But by the chance of war. To prove that true
Needs no more but one tongue for all those wounds,
Those mouthed wounds, which valiantly he took, 97
When on the gentle Severn's sedgy bank,
In single opposition, hand to hand,
He did confound the best part of an hour 100
In changing hardiment with great Glendower. 101
Three times they breath'd and three times did they drink, 102
Upon agreement, of swift Severn's flood,
Who then, affrighted with their bloody looks,
Ran fearfully among the trembling reeds,
And hid his crisp head in the hollow bank 106
Bloodstained with these valiant combatants.
Never did base and rotten policy 108
Color her working with such deadly wounds, 109
Nor never could the noble Mortimer
Receive so many, and all willingly.
Then let not him be slandered with revolt.

KING
Thou dost belie him, Percy, thou dost belie him!
He never did encounter with Glendower.
I tell thee,
He durst as well have met the devil alone
As Owen Glendower for an enemy.
Art thou not asham'd? But, sirrah, henceforth
Let me not hear you speak of Mortimer.
Send me your prisoners with the speediest means,
Or you shall hear in such a kind from me
As will displease you. My Lord Northumberland,
We license your departure with your son.
Send us your prisoners, or you will hear of it.
Exit King [with Blunt, and train].

HOTSPUR
An if the devil come and roar for them,
I will not send them. I will after straight 126
And tell him so, for I will ease my heart,
Albeit I make a hazard of my head.

NORTHUMBERLAND
What, drunk with choler? Stay and pause awhile. 129
Here comes your uncle.

Enter Worcester.

HOTSPUR
Speak of Mortimer?
'Zounds, I will speak of him, and let my soul
Want mercy if I do not join with him!
Yea, on his part I'll empty all these veins,
And shed my dear blood drop by drop in the dust,
But I will lift the down-trod Mortimer
As high in the air as this unthankful king,
As this ingrate and cank'red Bolingbroke. 137

NORTHUMBERLAND
Brother, the King hath made your nephew mad.

WORCESTER
Who struck this heat up after I was gone?

HOTSPUR
He will, forsooth, have all my prisoners; 140
And when I urg'd the ransom once again
Of my wife's brother, then his cheek look'd pale,
And on my face he turn'd an eye of death,
Trembling even at the name of Mortimer.

WORCESTER
I cannot blame him. Was not he proclaim'd
By Richard, that dead is, the next of blood?

NORTHUMBERLAND
He was; I heard the proclamation.
And then it was when the unhappy king—
Whose wrongs in us God pardon!—did set forth 149
Upon his Irish expedition;
From whence he intercepted did return 151
To be depos'd and shortly murdered.

WORCESTER
And for whose death we in the world's wide mouth
Live scandaliz'd and foully spoken of.

65 bald trivial **68 Come current** be taken as valid **75 impeach** discredit **76 so** provided that **79 straight** straightway, at once **80, 84 Mortimer, Earl of March** (There were two Edmund Mortimers; Shakespeare confuses them and combines their stories. It was the uncle [1376–1409?] who was captured by Glendower and married Glendower's daughter; it was the nephew [1391–1425], fifth Earl of March, who was proclaimed heir presumptive to King Richard II after the death of his father, the fourth earl, whom Richard had named as his heir. The uncle was brother to the fourth earl and to Hotspur's wife Elizabeth, called Kate in this play.) **87 indent with fears** i.e., make a bargain or come to terms with those we fear **97 mouthed** gaping and eloquent **100 confound** consume **101 changing hardiment** exchanging blows, matching valor **102 breath'd** paused for breath **106 crisp** curly, i.e., rippled **108 policy** cunning **109 Color** disguise

126 will after will go after **129 choler** anger **137 cank'red** spoiled, malignant **140 forsooth** indeed **149 in us** caused by our doings **151 intercepted** interrupted

HOTSPUR
But, soft, I pray you; did King Richard then
Proclaim my brother Edmund Mortimer 156
Heir to the crown?
NORTHUMBERLAND He did; myself did hear it.
HOTSPUR
Nay, then I cannot blame his cousin king,
That wish'd him on the barren mountains starve.
But shall it be that you, that set the crown
Upon the head of this forgetful man
And for his sake wear the detested blot
Of murderous subornation—shall it be 163
That you a world of curses undergo,
Being the agents, or base second means,
The cords, the ladder, or the hangman rather?
O, pardon me that I descend so low
To show the line and the predicament 168
Wherein you range under this subtle king! 169
Shall it for shame be spoken in these days,
Or fill up chronicles in time to come,
That men of your nobility and power
Did gage them both in an unjust behalf, 173
As both of you—God pardon it!—have done,
To put down Richard, that sweet lovely rose,
And plant this thorn, this canker, Bolingbroke? 176
And shall it in more shame be further spoken,
That you are fool'd, discarded, and shook off
By him for whom these shames ye underwent?
No! Yet time serves wherein you may redeem
Your banish'd honors and restore yourselves
Into the good thoughts of the world again;
Revenge the jeering and disdain'd contempt 183
Of this proud king, who studies day and night
To answer all the debt he owes to you 185
Even with the bloody payment of your deaths.
Therefore, I say—
WORCESTER Peace, cousin, say no more.
And now I will unclasp a secret book,
And to your quick-conceiving discontents 189
I'll read you matter deep and dangerous,
As full of peril and adventurous spirit
As to o'er-walk a current roaring loud
On the unsteadfast footing of a spear.
HOTSPUR
If he fall in, good night, or sink or swim! 194
Send danger from the east unto the west,
So honor cross it from the north to south, 196
And let them grapple. O, the blood more stirs
To rouse a lion than to start a hare!
NORTHUMBERLAND
Imagination of some great exploit
Drives him beyond the bounds of patience.
HOTSPUR
By heaven, methinks it were an easy leap
To pluck bright honor from the pale-fac'd moon,
Or dive into the bottom of the deep,
Where fathom-line could never touch the ground,
And pluck up drowned honor by the locks,
So he that doth redeem her thence might wear
Without corrival all her dignities; 207
But out upon this half-fac'd fellowship! 208
WORCESTER
He apprehends a world of figures here, 209
But not the form of what he should attend. 210
Good cousin, give me audience for a while.
HOTSPUR
I cry you mercy.
WORCESTER Those same noble Scots 212
That are your prisoners—
HOTSPUR I'll keep them all!
By God, he shall not have a Scot of them,
No, if a Scot would save his soul, he shall not!
I'll keep them, by this hand!
WORCESTER You start away
And lend no ear unto my purposes.
Those prisoners you shall keep.
HOTSPUR Nay, I will; that's flat.
He said he would not ransom Mortimer,
Forbade my tongue to speak of Mortimer,
But I will find him when he lies asleep,
And in his ear I'll holla "Mortimer!"
Nay, I'll have a starling shall be taught to speak
Nothing but "Mortimer," and give it him,
To keep his anger still in motion. 226
WORCESTER
Hear you, cousin, a word.
HOTSPUR
All studies here I solemnly defy, 228
Save how to gall and pinch this Bolingbroke,
And that same sword-and-buckler Prince of Wales; 230
But that I think his father loves him not
And would be glad he met with some mischance,
I would have him poisoned with a pot of ale.
WORCESTER
Farewell, kinsman. I'll talk to you
When you are better temper'd to attend.
NORTHUMBERLAND
Why, what a wasp-stung and impatient fool
Art thou to break into this woman's mood,
Tying thine ear to no tongue but thine own!
HOTSPUR
Why, look you, I am whipp'd and scourg'd with rods,
Nettled and stung with pismires, when I hear 240
Of this vile politician, Bolingbroke. 241
In Richard's time—what do you call the place?—
A plague upon it, it is in Gloucestershire;
'Twas where the madcap duke his uncle kept, 244
His uncle York; where I first bow'd my knee
Unto this king of smiles, this Bolingbroke—
'Sblood!—

156 brother i.e., brother-in-law **163 murderous subornation** the suborning of or inciting to murder **168 line** station, rank; also, hangman's rope. **predicament** category; also, dangerous situation **169 range** i.e., are classified **173 gage** engage, pledge **176 canker** (1) canker rose or dog rose, wild and unfragrant (2) ulcer **183 disdain'd** disdainful **185 answer** satisfy, discharge **189 quick-conceiving** comprehending quickly **194 If . . . swim** i.e., such a man, walking over a roaring stream, is doomed if he fall in, whether he sink or swim **196 So** provided that. (Also at l. 206.)

207 corrival rival, competitor **208 out . . . fellowship** down with this paltry business of sharing glory with others **209 figures** figures of the imagination, or figures of speech **210 attend** give attention to **212 cry you mercy** beg your pardon **226 still** continually **228 defy** renounce **230 sword-and-buckler** (Arms improper for a prince, who should carry rapier and dagger.) **240 pismires** ants. (From the urinous smell of an anthill.) **241 politician** deceitful schemer **244 kept** dwelled

When you and he came back from Ravenspurgh—

NORTHUMBERLAND
At Berkeley castle.

HOTSPUR
You say true.
Why, what a candy deal of courtesy
This fawning greyhound then did proffer me!
"Look when his infant fortune came to age,"
And "gentle Harry Percy," and "kind cousin"—
O, the devil take such cozeners!—God forgive me!
Good uncle, tell your tale; I have done.

WORCESTER
Nay, if you have not, to it again;
We will stay your leisure.

HOTSPUR
I have done, i' faith.

WORCESTER
Then once more to your Scottish prisoners.
Deliver them up without their ransom straight,
And make the Douglas' son your only mean
For powers in Scotland, which, for divers reasons
Which I shall send you written, be assur'd
Will easily be granted. [*To Northumberland.*] You, my lord,
Your son in Scotland being thus employ'd,
Shall secretly into the bosom creep
Of that same noble prelate well belov'd,
The Archbishop.

HOTSPUR
Of York, is it not?

WORCESTER
True; who bears hard
His brother's death at Bristol, the Lord Scroop.
I speak not this in estimation,
As what I think might be, but what I know
Is ruminated, plotted, and set down,
And only stays but to behold the face
Of that occasion that shall bring it on.

HOTSPUR
I smell it. Upon my life, it will do well.

NORTHUMBERLAND
Before the game is afoot thou still let'st slip.

HOTSPUR
Why, it cannot choose but be a noble plot.
And then the power of Scotland and of York,
To join with Mortimer, ha?

WORCESTER
And so they shall.

HOTSPUR
In faith, it is exceedingly well aim'd.

WORCESTER
And 'tis no little reason bids us speed,
To save our heads by raising of a head;
For, bear ourselves as even as we can,
The King will always think him in our debt,
And think we think ourselves unsatisfied,
Till he hath found a time to pay us home.
And see already how he doth begin
To make us strangers to his looks of love.

HOTSPUR
He does, he does. We'll be reveng'd on him.

WORCESTER
Cousin, farewell. No further go in this
Than I by letters shall direct your course.
When time is ripe, which will be suddenly,
I'll steal to Glendower and Lord Mortimer,
Where you and Douglas and our pow'rs at once,
As I will fashion it, shall happily meet
To bear our fortunes in our own strong arms,
Which now we hold at much uncertainty.

NORTHUMBERLAND
Farewell, good brother. We shall thrive, I trust.

HOTSPUR
Uncle, adieu. O, let the hours be short
Till fields and blows and groans applaud our sport!
Exeunt.

[ACT II • SCENE I]

Enter a Carrier with a lantern in his hand.

FIRST CARRIER Heigh-ho! An it be not four by the day, I'll be hang'd. Charles' wain is over the new chimney, and yet our horse not pack'd. What, ostler!

OSTLER [*Within*] Anon, anon.

FIRST CARRIER I prithee, Tom, beat Cut's saddle, put a few flocks in the point. Poor jade is wrung in the withers out of all cess.

Enter another Carrier.

SECOND CARRIER Peas and beans are as dank here as a dog, and that is the next way to give poor jades the bots. This house is turn'd upside down since Robin Ostler died.

FIRST CARRIER Poor fellow, never joy'd since the price of oats rose. It was the death of him.

SECOND CARRIER I think this be the most villainous house in all London road for fleas. I am stung like a tench.

FIRST CARRIER Like a tench? By the mass, there is ne'er a king christen could be better bit than I have been since the first cock.

SECOND CARRIER Why, they will allow us ne'er a jordan, and then we leak in your chimney, and your chamber-lie breeds fleas like a loach.

251 candy sugared, flattering **253 Look when** whenever **255 cozeners** cheats (with pun on *cousins*) **258 stay** await **260 Deliver them up** free them **261 the Douglas' son** i.e., Mordake. (See I.i.71 and note). **mean** means, agent **262 For powers** for raising an army **270 bears hard** resents **272 estimation** guesswork **278 still let'st slip** always let loose the dogs **284 head** army **285 even** carefully **286 him** himself **288 home** fully

302 fields battlefields

II.i. Location: Rochester. An innyard.
s.d. Carrier one whose trade was conveying goods, usually by pack horses **1 by the day** in the morning **2 Charles' wain** the constellation of the Great Bear **3 horse** horses. **ostler** hostler, groom **4 Anon** right away, coming **5 beat** soften. **Cut's saddle** packsaddle of the horse named *Cut,* meaning "bob-tailed" **6 flocks** tufts of wool. **point** pommel of the saddle. **jade** nag **6–7 wrung . . . withers** chafed (by his saddle) on the ridge between his shoulder bones **7 cess** measure, estimate **8 Peas and beans** i.e., horse fodder **9 next** nearest, quickest **10 bots** intestinal maggots **16 tench** a spotted fish, whose spots may have been likened to flea bites **18 king christen** Christian king **19 first cock** i.e., midnight **20 jordan** chamberpot **21 chimney** fireplace **21–22 chamber-lie** urine **22 like a loach** i.e., as fast as a loach, a prolific fish, breeds loaches

FIRST CARRIER What, ostler! Come away and be hang'd! Come away.

SECOND CARRIER I have a gammon of bacon and two razes of ginger, to be deliver'd as far as Charing-cross.

FIRST CARRIER God's body, the turkeys in my pannier are quite starv'd. What, ostler! A plague on thee! Hast thou never an eye in thy head? Canst not hear? An 'twere not as good deed as drink to break the pate on thee, I am a very villain. Come, and be hang'd! Hast no faith in thee?

Enter Gadshill.

GADSHILL Good morrow, carriers, what's o'clock?

FIRST CARRIER I think it be two o'clock.

GADSHILL I prithee lend me thy lantern, to see my gelding in the stable.

FIRST CARRIER Nay, by God, soft, I know a trick worth two of that, i' faith.

GADSHILL I pray thee, lend me thine.

SECOND CARRIER Ay, when, canst tell? Lend me thy lantern, quoth he! Marry, I'll see thee hang'd first.

GADSHILL Sirrah carrier, what time do you mean to come to London?

SECOND CARRIER Time enough to go to bed with a candle, I warrant thee. Come, neighbor Mugs, we'll call up the gentlemen. They will along with company, for they have great charge. *Exeunt [Carriers].*

GADSHILL What, ho! Chamberlain!

Enter Chamberlain.

CHAMBERLAIN At hand, quoth pick-purse.

GADSHILL That's even as fair as—at hand, quoth the chamberlain; for thou variest no more from picking of purses than giving direction doth from laboring; thou layest the plot how.

CHAMBERLAIN Good morrow, Master Gadshill. It holds current that I told you yesternight: there's a franklin in the wild of Kent hath brought three hundred marks with him in gold. I heard him tell it to one of his company last night at supper—a kind of auditor, one that hath abundance of charge too, God knows what. They are up already, and call for eggs and butter. They will away presently.

GADSHILL Sirrah, if they meet not with Saint Nicholas' clerks, I'll give thee this neck.

CHAMBERLAIN No, I'll none of it. I pray thee, keep that for the hangman, for I know thou worshipest Saint Nicholas as truly as a man of falsehood may.

GADSHILL What talkest thou to me of the hangman? If I hang, I'll make a fat pair of gallows; for if I hang, old Sir John hangs with me, and thou knowest he is no starveling. Tut, there are other Troyans that thou dream'st not of, the which for sport sake are content to do the profession some grace, that would, if matters should be look'd into, for their own credit sake make all whole. I am join'd with no foot land-rakers, no long-staff sixpenny strikers, none of these mad mustachio purple-hu'd malt-worms, but with nobility and tranquillity, burgomasters and great oney'rs, such as can hold in, such as will strike sooner than speak, and speak sooner than drink, and drink sooner than pray. And yet, 'zounds, I lie, for they pray continually to their saint, the commonwealth, or rather, not pray to her, but prey on her, for they ride up and down on her and make her their boots.

CHAMBERLAIN What, the commonwealth their boots? Will she hold out water in foul way?

GADSHILL She will, she will. Justice hath liquor'd her. We steal as in a castle, cocksure. We have the receipt of fern-seed, we walk invisible.

CHAMBERLAIN Nay, by my faith, I think you are more beholding to the night than to fern-seed for your walking invisible.

GADSHILL Give me thy hand. Thou shalt have a share in our purchase, as I am a true man.

CHAMBERLAIN Nay, rather let me have it as you are a false thief.

GADSHILL Go to; "homo" is a common name to all men. Bid the ostler bring my gelding out of the stable. Farewell, you muddy knave. *[Exeunt severally.]*

[SCENE II]

Enter Prince, Poins, Peto, [and Bardolph].

POINS Come, shelter, shelter! I have remov'd Falstaff's horse, and he frets like a gumm'd velvet.

PRINCE Stand close. *[They step aside.]*

Enter Falstaff.

FALSTAFF Poins! Poins, and be hang'd! Poins!

PRINCE *[Coming forward]* Peace, ye fat-kidney'd rascal! What a brawling dost thou keep!

FALSTAFF Where's Poins, Hal?

PRINCE He is walk'd up to the top of the hill. I'll go seek him. *[Steps aside.]*

FALSTAFF I am accurs'd to rob in that thief's company. The rascal hath remov'd my horse, and tied him I

23 Come away come along **25 gammon of bacon** ham **26 razes** roots **27 pannier** basket **30–31 to break . . . thee** to give you a blow on the head **40 Ay . . . tell** i.e., never **46–47 They . . . charge** i.e., they wish to travel in company, because they have lots of valuable cargo **48 Chamberlain** (Male equivalent of a chambermaid.) **49 At . . . pick-purse** i.e., I am right beside you, as the pick-purse said **50 fair** apt **52–53 thou . . . how** i.e., you don't actually do the stealing, but you give directions, like a master workman to his apprentices **54–55 holds current that** holds true what **55 franklin** a small farmer owning his own land **56 wild** weald, wooded region. **marks** coins of the value of 13 shillings 6 pence **62–63 Saint Nicholas' clerks** highwaymen. (St. Nicholas was popularly supposed the patron of thieves.) **64 I'll none** I want none

70 Troyans i.e., Trojans, slang for *sports* or *roisterers* **72 profession** i.e., robbery. **grace** credit, favor **74 join'd** associated. **foot land-rakers** footpads **75 long-staff sixpenny strikers** robbers with long staves who would knock down their victims for sixpence **75–76 mustachio purple-hu'd malt-worms** common drunkards with mustaches stained with drink **77 tranquillity** those who lead easy lives. **oney'rs** ones (?) **78 hold in** keep a secret **83 boots** booty (with pun on *boots,* shoes) **85 Will . . . way** will she let you go dry in muddy roads, i.e., will she protect you in tight places **86 liquor'd** (1) made waterproof by oiling (2) bribed **87 as in a castle** i.e., in complete security **88 of fern-seed** i.e., of becoming invisible (since fern-seed, almost invisible itself, was popularly supposed to render its possessor invisible) **93 purchase** booty **96 homo . . . men** i.e., the Latin name for man applies to all types **98 muddy** stupid

II.ii. Location: The highway, near Gadshill.
2 frets chafes (with pun on another meaning of the word applying to *gumm'd velvet,* velvet stiffened with gum and therefore liable to *fret* or wear) **3 close** concealed **6 keep** keep up

know not where. If I travel but four foot by the squier further afoot, I shall break my wind. Well, I doubt not but to die a fair death for all this, if I scape hanging for killing that rogue. I have forsworn his company hourly any time this two and twenty years, and yet I am bewitch'd with the rogue's company. If the rascal have not given me medicines to make me love him, I'll be hang'd; it could not be else, I have drunk medicines. Poins! Hal! A plague upon you both! Bardolph! Peto! I'll starve ere I'll rob a foot further. An 'twere not as good a deed as drink to turn true man and to leave these rogues, I am the veriest varlet that ever chew'd with a tooth. Eight yards of uneven ground is threescore and ten miles afoot with me, and the stony-hearted villains know it well enough. A plague upon it when thieves cannot be true one to another! *(They whistle.)* Whew! A plague upon you all! Give me my horse, you rogues, give me my horse, and be hang'd!

PRINCE [*Coming forward*] Peace, ye fat-guts! Lie down. Lay thine ear close to the ground and list if thou canst hear the tread of travelers.

FALSTAFF Have you any levers to lift me up again, being down? 'Sblood, I'll not bear mine own flesh so far afoot again for all the coin in thy father's exchequer. What a plague mean ye to colt me thus?

PRINCE Thou liest. Thou art not colted, thou art uncolted.

FALSTAFF I prithee, good Prince Hal, help me to my horse, good king's son.

PRINCE Out, ye rogue! Shall I be your ostler?

FALSTAFF Go hang thyself in thine own heir-apparent garters! If I be ta'en, I'll peach for this. An I have not ballads made on you all and sung to filthy tunes, let a cup of sack be my poison. When a jest is so forward, and afoot too! I hate it.

Enter Gadshill.

GADSHILL Stand.

FALSTAFF So I do, against my will.

POINS [*Coming forward with Bardolph and Peto*] O, 'tis our setter. I know his voice.

BARDOLPH What news?

GADSHILL Case ye, case ye, on with your vizards. There's money of the King's coming down the hill; 'tis going to the King's exchequer.

FALSTAFF You lie, ye rogue, 'tis going to the King's tavern.

GADSHILL There's enough to make us all.

FALSTAFF To be hang'd.

PRINCE Sirs, you four shall front them in the narrow lane; Ned Poins and I will walk lower. If they scape from your encounter, then they light on us.

PETO How many be there of them?

GADSHILL Some eight or ten.

FALSTAFF 'Zounds, will they not rob us?

PRINCE What, a coward, Sir John Paunch?

FALSTAFF Indeed, I am not John of Gaunt, your grandfather, but yet no coward, Hal.

PRINCE Well, we leave that to the proof.

POINS Sirrah Jack, thy horse stands behind the hedge. When thou need'st him, there thou shalt find him. Farewell, and stand fast.

FALSTAFF Now cannot I strike him, if I should be hang'd.

PRINCE [*To Poins*] Ned, where are our disguises?

POINS [*To Prince*] Here, hard by. Stand close.

[*Exeunt Prince and Poins.*]

FALSTAFF Now, my masters, happy man be his dole, say I. Every man to his business.

Enter the Travelers.

FIRST TRAVELER Come, neighbor. The boy shall lead our horses down the hill; we'll walk afoot awhile, and ease our legs.

THIEVES Stand!

TRAVELERS Jesus bless us!

FALSTAFF Strike! Down with them! Cut the villains' throats! Ah, whoreson caterpillars! Bacon-fed knaves! They hate us youth. Down with them! Fleece them!

TRAVELERS O, we are undone, both we and ours forever!

FALSTAFF Hang ye, gorbellied knaves, are ye undone? No, ye fat chuffs, I would your store were here! On, bacons, on! What, ye knaves! Young men must live. You are grandjurors, are ye? We'll jure ye, 'faith.

Here they rob them and bind them. Exeunt.

Enter the Prince and Poins [*in buckram*].

PRINCE The thieves have bound the true men. Now could thou and I rob the thieves and go merrily to London, it would be argument for a week, laughter for a month, and a good jest for ever.

POINS Stand close. I hear them coming.

Enter the Thieves again.

FALSTAFF Come, my masters, let us share, and then to horse before day. An the Prince and Poins be not two arrant cowards, there's no equity stirring. There's no more valor in that Poins than in a wild duck.

PRINCE Your money!

POINS Villains!

As they are sharing, the Prince and Poins set upon them. They all run away, and Falstaff, after a blow or two, runs away too, leaving the booty behind them.

12 squier square, foot-rule **14 for all** despite all **18 medicines** love potions **22 turn true man** turn honest; turn informer **36 colt** cheat, trick **43 peach** inform on you **50 setter** arranger of the robbery. (See I.ii. 104–105 and note.) **52 Case ye** put on your masks **57 make us all** make our fortunes

66 Gaunt i.e., Ghent (but punning on *gaunt*, thin) **68 proof** test **72–73 Now . . . hang'd** (Falstaff wishes he could hit Poins, who is too quick for him.) **76 happy . . . dole** may happiness be every man's portion or lot **84 caterpillars** i.e., parasites **88 gorbellied** big-bellied **89 chuffs** churls, rich but miserly. **store** total wealth **90 bacons** fat men **91 grandjurors** i.e., men of wealth, able to serve on juries **94 argument** a subject for conversation **99 equity** judgment, discernment

PRINCE
Got with much ease. Now merrily to horse.
The thieves are all scattered and possess'd with fear
So strongly that they dare not meet each other;
Each takes his fellow for an officer.
Away, good Ned. Falstaff sweats to death,
And lards the lean earth as he walks along.
Were 't not for laughing, I should pity him.

POINS
How the fat rogue roar'd! *Exeunt.*

[SCENE III]

Enter Hotspur, solus, reading a letter.

HOTSPUR "But, for mine own part, my lord, I could be well contented to be there, in respect of the love I bear your house." He could be contented; why is he not, then? In respect of the love he bears our house! He shows in this, he loves his own barn better than he loves our house. Let me see some more. "The purpose you undertake is dangerous"—why, that's certain. 'Tis dangerous to take a cold, to sleep, to drink; but I tell you, my lord fool, out of this nettle, danger, we pluck this flower, safety. "The purpose you undertake is dangerous, the friends you have nam'd uncertain, the time itself unsorted, and your whole plot too light for the counterpoise of so great an opposition." Say you so, say you so? I say unto you again, you are a shallow, cowardly hind, and you lie. What a lack-brain is this! By the Lord, our plot is a good plot as ever was laid, our friends true and constant; a good plot, good friends, and full of expectation; an excellent plot, very good friends. What a frosty-spirited rogue is this! Why, my Lord of York commends the plot and the general course of the action. 'Zounds, an I were now by this rascal, I could brain him with his lady's fan. Is there not my father, my uncle, and myself? Lord Edmund Mortimer, my lord of York, and Owen Glendower? Is there not besides the Douglas? Have I not all their letters to meet me in arms by the ninth of the next month? And are they not some of them set forward already? What a pagan rascal is this! An infidel! Ha! You shall see now in very sincerity of fear and cold heart, will he to the King and lay open all our proceedings. O, I could divide myself and go to buffets, for moving such a dish of skim milk with so honorable an action! Hang him! Let him tell the King, we are prepar'd. I will set forward tonight.

Enter his Lady.

How now, Kate? I must leave you within these two hours.

LADY
O, my good lord, why are you thus alone?
For what offense have I this fortnight been
A banish'd woman from my Harry's bed?
Tell me, sweet lord, what is 't that takes from thee
Thy stomach, pleasure, and thy golden sleep?
Why dost thou bend thine eyes upon the earth,
And start so often when thou sit'st alone?
Why hast thou lost the fresh blood in thy cheeks,
And given my treasures and my rights of thee
To thick-ey'd musing and curs'd melancholy?
In thy faint slumbers I by thee have watch'd,
And heard thee murmur tales of iron wars,
Speak terms of manage to thy bounding steed,
Cry, "Courage! To the field!" And thou hast talk'd
Of sallies and retires, of trenches, tents,
Of palisadoes, frontiers, parapets,
Of basilisks, of cannon, culverin,
Of prisoners' ransom, and of soldiers slain,
And all the currents of a heady fight.
Thy spirit within thee hath been so at war,
And thus hath so bestirr'd thee in thy sleep,
That beads of sweat have stood upon thy brow
Like bubbles in a late-disturbed stream,
And in thy face strange motions have appear'd,
Such as we see when men restrain their breath
On some great sudden hest. O, what portents are these?
Some heavy business hath my lord in hand,
And I must know it, else he loves me not.

HOTSPUR
What, ho!

[*Enter Servant.*]

Is Gilliams with the packet gone?

SERVANT
He is, my lord, an hour ago.

HOTSPUR
Hath Butler brought those horses from the sheriff?

SERVANT
One horse, my lord, he brought even now.

HOTSPUR
What horse? Roan, a crop-ear, is it not?

SERVANT
It is, my lord.

HOTSPUR That roan shall be my throne.
Well, I will back him straight. O esperance!
Bid Butler lead him forth into the park.
[*Exit Servant.*]

LADY
But hear you, my lord.

HOTSPUR
What say'st thou, my lady?

II.iii. Location: Warkworth Castle in Northumberland.
3 house family **12 unsorted** unsuitable **13 for . . . of** to counterbalance **15 hind** menial, peasant **18 expectation** promise **20 Lord of York** i.e., Archbishop Scroop **28 pagan** unbelieving **31–32 divide . . . buffets** i.e., fight with myself

41 stomach appetite **45 And . . . thee** i.e., and given what I treasure in you and have a right, as wife, to share **46 thick-ey'd musing** i.e., staring vacantly **47 faint** i.e., restless. **watch'd** lain awake **49 manage** horsemanship **52 palisadoes** stakes set in the ground for defense. **frontiers** outworks, ramparts **53 basilisks** large cannon. **culverin** long cannon **55 heady** headlong **62 hest** command **63 heavy** weighty; sorrowful **71 esperance** hope. (The motto of the Percy family.)

LADY
What is it carries you away?

HOTSPUR
Why, my horse, my love, my horse.

LADY
Out, you mad-headed ape!
A weasel hath not such a deal of spleen
As you are toss'd with. In faith,
I'll know your business, Harry, that I will.
I fear my brother Mortimer doth stir
About his title, and hath sent for you
To line his enterprise; but if you go—

HOTSPUR
So far afoot, I shall be weary, love.

LADY
Come, come, you paraquito, answer me
Directly unto this question that I ask.
In faith, I'll break thy little finger, Harry,
An if thou wilt not tell me all things true.

HOTSPUR
Away,
Away, you trifler! Love? I love thee not,
I care not for thee, Kate. This is no world
To play with mammets and to tilt with lips.
We must have bloody noses and crack'd crowns,
And pass them current too. God's me, my horse!
What say'st thou, Kate? What would'st thou have with me?

LADY
Do you not love me? Do you not, indeed?
Well, do not then, for since you love me not
I will not love myself. Do you not love me?
Nay, tell me if you speak in jest or no.

HOTSPUR
Come, wilt thou see me ride?
And when I am a-horseback, I will swear
I love thee infinitely. But hark you, Kate:
I must not have you henceforth question me
Whither I go, nor reason whereabout.
Whither I must, I must; and, to conclude,
This evening must I leave you, gentle Kate.
I know you wise, but yet no farther wise
Than Harry Percy's wife; constant you are,
But yet a woman; and for secrecy,
No lady closer, for I well believe
Thou wilt not utter what thou dost not know,
And so far will I trust thee, gentle Kate.

LADY
How! So far?

HOTSPUR
Not an inch further. But hark you, Kate:
Whither I go, thither shall you go too.
Today will I set forth, tomorrow you.
Will this content you, Kate?

LADY
It must of force. *Exeunt.*

82 **title** claim to the throne 83 **line** strengthen 85 **paraquito** little parrot. (A term of endearment.) 91 **mammets** dolls; or else, breasts 92 **crowns** (1) heads (2) coins worth 5 shillings. (Cracked coins would not "pass current," as Hotspur jokes in the next line.) 93 **God's me** God save me 103 **reason whereabout** discuss about what 116 **of force** perforce

[SCENE IV]

Enter Prince and Poins.

PRINCE Ned, prithee, come out of that fat room, and lend me thy hand to laugh a little.

POINS Where hast been, Hal?

PRINCE With three or four loggerheads amongst three or four score hogsheads. I have sounded the very base-string of humility. Sirrah, I am sworn brother to a leash of drawers, and can call them all by their christen names, as Tom, Dick, and Francis. They take it already upon their salvation that, though I be but Prince of Wales, yet I am the king of courtesy, and tell me flatly I am no proud Jack like Falstaff, but a Corinthian, a lad of mettle, a good boy—by the Lord, so they call me!—and when I am King of England I shall command all the good lads in Eastcheap. They call drinking deep, dyeing scarlet; and when you breathe in your watering, they cry "hem!" and bid you play it off. To conclude, I am so good a proficient in one quarter of an hour that I can drink with any tinker in his own language during my life. I tell thee, Ned, thou hast lost much honor that thou wert not with me in this action. But, sweet Ned—to sweeten which name of Ned, I give thee this pennyworth of sugar, clapp'd even now into my hand by an under-skinker, one that never spake other English in his life than "Eight shillings and sixpence," and "You are welcome," with this shrill addition, "Anon, anon, sir! Score a pint of bastard in the Half-moon," or so. But, Ned, to drive away the time till Falstaff come, I prithee do thou stand in some by-room, while I question my puny drawer to what end he gave me the sugar; and do thou never leave calling "Francis," that his tale to me may be nothing but "Anon." Step aside, and I'll show thee a precedent.

POINS Francis!

PRINCE Thou art perfect.

POINS Francis! [*Exit Poins.*]

Enter [*Francis, a*] *Drawer.*

FRANCIS Anon, anon, sir. Look down into the Pomgarnet, Ralph.

PRINCE Come hither, Francis.

FRANCIS My lord?

PRINCE How long hast thou to serve, Francis?

FRANCIS Forsooth, five years, and as much as to—

POINS [*Within*] Francis!

FRANCIS Anon, anon, sir.

PRINCE Five year! By 'r lady, a long lease for the clink-

II.iv. Location: A tavern in Eastcheap, London, usually identified as the Boar's Head. Some tavern furniture, including stools, is provided on stage.
1 **fat** stuffy; or, a vat-room 4 **loggerheads** blockheads 7 **leash of drawers** i.e., three waiters. **christen** given at christening 11 **Corinthian** i.e., gay blade, good sport. (Corinth was reputed to be licentious.) 15–16 **breathe . . . watering** pause for breath in your drinking 16 **play** drink 22 **sugar** (Used to sweeten wine.) 23 **under-skinker** assistant to a waiter or bartender 26 **Anon** right away, coming. **Score** charge 26–27 **bastard** (A sweet Spanish wine.) 27 **Half-moon** (The name of a room in the inn.) 33 **precedent** example 37–38 **Pomgarnet** Pomegranate. (Another room in the inn.) 41 **serve** i.e., serve out your apprenticeship 45 **By'r lady** by Our Lady

ing of pewter. But, Francis, darest thou be so valiant as to play the coward with thy indenture and show it a fair pair of heels and run from it?

FRANCIS O Lord, sir, I'll be sworn upon all the books in England, I could find in my heart—

POINS [*Within*] Francis!

FRANCIS Anon, sir.

PRINCE How old art thou, Francis?

FRANCIS Let me see—about Michaelmas next I shall be—

POINS [*Within*] Francis!

FRANCIS Anon, sir. Pray stay a little, my lord.

PRINCE Nay, but hark you, Francis: for the sugar thou gavest me, 'twas a pennyworth, was 't not?

FRANCIS O Lord, I would it had been two!

PRINCE I will give thee for it a thousand pound. Ask me when thou wilt, and thou shalt have it.

POINS [*Within*] Francis!

FRANCIS Anon, anon.

PRINCE Anon, Francis? No, Francis; but tomorrow, Francis; or, Francis, a' Thursday; or indeed, Francis, when thou wilt. But, Francis—

FRANCIS My lord?

PRINCE Wilt thou rob this leathern jerkin, crystal-button, not-pated, agate-ring, puke-stocking, caddis-garter, smooth-tongue, Spanish-pouch—

FRANCIS O Lord, sir, who do you mean?

PRINCE Why, then, your brown bastard is your only drink; for look you, Francis, your white canvas doublet will sully. In Barbary, sir, it cannot come to so much.

FRANCIS What, sir?

POINS [*Within*] Francis!

PRINCE Away, you rogue! Dost thou not hear them call?

Here they both call him; the drawer stands amazed, not knowing which way to go.

Enter Vintner.

VINTNER What, stand'st thou still, and hear'st such a calling? Look to the guests within. [*Exit Francis.*] My lord, old Sir John, with half-a-dozen more, are at the door. Shall I let them in?

PRINCE Let them alone awhile, and then open the door. [*Exit Vintner.*] Poins!

Enter Poins.

POINS Anon, anon, sir.

PRINCE Sirrah, Falstaff and the rest of the thieves are at the door. Shall we be merry?

POINS As merry as crickets, my lad. But hark ye, what cunning match have you made with this jest of the drawer? Come, what's the issue?

PRINCE I am now of all humors that have show'd themselves humors since the old days of goodman Adam to the pupil age of this present twelve o'clock at midnight.

[*Enter Francis, hurrying across the stage with wine.*]

What's o'clock, Francis?

FRANCIS Anon, anon, sir. [*Exit.*]

PRINCE That ever this fellow should have fewer words than a parrot, and yet the son of a woman! His industry is upstairs and downstairs, his eloquence the parcel of a reckoning. I am not yet of Percy's mind, the Hotspur of the north, he that kills me some six or seven dozen of Scots at a breakfast, washes his hands, and says to his wife, "Fie upon this quiet life! I want work." "O my sweet Harry," says she, "how many hast thou kill'd today?" "Give my roan horse a drench," says he, and answers, "Some fourteen," an hour after, "a trifle, a trifle." I prithee, call in Falstaff. I'll play Percy, and that damn'd brawn shall play Dame Mortimer his wife. "Rivo!" says the drunkard. Call in ribs, call in tallow.

Enter Falstaff, [*Gadshill, Bardolph, and Peto; Francis following with wine*].

POINS Welcome, Jack. Where hast thou been?

FALSTAFF A plague of all cowards, I say, and a vengeance too! Marry and amen! Give me a cup of sack, boy. Ere I lead this life long, I'll sew netherstocks, and mend them and foot them too. A plague of all cowards! Give me a cup of sack, rogue. Is there no virtue extant? *He drinketh.*

PRINCE Didst thou never see Titan kiss a dish of butter, pitiful-hearted Titan, that melted at the sweet tale of the sun's? If thou didst, then behold that compound.

FALSTAFF You rogue, here's lime in this sack too. There is nothing but roguery to be found in villainous man, yet a coward is worse than a cup of sack with lime in it. A villainous coward! Go thy ways, old Jack, die when thou wilt; if manhood, good manhood, be not forgot upon the face of the earth, then am I a shotten herring. There lives not three good men unhang'd in England, and one of them is fat and grows old, God help the while! A bad world, I say. I would I were a weaver; I could sing psalms or any thing. A plague of all cowards, I say still.

PRINCE How now, wool-sack, what mutter you?

FALSTAFF A king's son! If I do not beat thee out of thy kingdom with a dagger of lath, and drive all thy sub-

47 indenture contract of apprenticeship **49 books** i.e., Bibles **54 Michaelmas** September 29 **69–71 Wilt . . . Spanish-pouch** i.e., will you rob your master of your services by running away, he who is characterized by a leather jacket, transparent buttons, cropped hair, a ring with small figures in an agate stone for a seal, dark woolen stockings, worsted garters, an ingratiating flattering manner of speech, a pouch of Spanish leather **73–76 Why . . . much** (The Prince talks seeming nonsense in order to bewilder Francis; but he also implies that Francis should endure his life in the tavern rather than run away, choosing *brown bastard,* a sweet Spanish wine, instead of a fancy *white canvas doublet.*) **75 it** i.e., sugar **91 issue** outcome, point

92–95 I . . . midnight i.e., I'm now in a mood for anything that has happened in the whole history of the world **93 goodman** (Title for a farmer.) **94 pupil** youthful **100–101 parcel . . . reckoning** items of a bill **102 kills me** i.e., kills. (*Me* is the ethical dative.) **107 drench** dose of medicine. **says he** i.e., he tells a servant **109 brawn** fat boar **110 Rivo** (An exclamation of uncertain meaning, but related to drinking.) **113 of** on **115 netherstocks** stockings (the sewing or mending of which is a menial occupation) **119 Titan** i.e., the sun **120 that** i.e., the butter **121 compound** melting butter, i.e., Falstaff **122 lime in this sack** i.e., lime added to make the wine sparkle **127–128 shotten herring** a herring that has cast its roe and is consequently thin **130 the while** i.e., in these bad times **131 weaver** (Many psalm-singing Protestant immigrants from the Low Countries were weavers.) **135 dagger of lath** (The Vice, stock comic figure in morality plays, was so armed.)

jects afore thee like a flock of wild geese, I'll never wear hair on my face more. You, Prince of Wales!

PRINCE Why, you whoreson round man, what's the matter?

FALSTAFF Are not you a coward? Answer me to that. And Poins there?

POINS 'Zounds, ye fat paunch, an ye call me coward, by the Lord, I'll stab thee.

FALSTAFF I call thee coward? I'll see thee damn'd ere I call thee coward, but I would give a thousand pound I could run as fast as thou canst. You are straight enough in the shoulders, you care not who sees your back. Call you that backing of your friends? A plague upon such backing! Give me them that will face me. Give me a cup of sack. I am a rogue if I drunk today.

PRINCE O villain, thy lips are scarce wip'd since thou drunk'st last.

FALSTAFF All's one for that. *(He drinketh.)* A plague of all cowards, still say I.

PRINCE What's the matter?

FALSTAFF What's the matter? There be four of us here have ta'en a thousand pound this day morning.

PRINCE Where is it, Jack, where is it?

FALSTAFF Where is it? Taken from us it is. A hundred upon poor four of us.

PRINCE What, a hundred, man?

FALSTAFF I am a rogue if I were not at half-sword with a dozen of them two hours together. I have scap'd by miracle. I am eight times thrust through the doublet, four through the hose, my buckler cut through and through, my sword hack'd like a hand-saw—ecce signum! I never dealt better since I was a man. All would not do. A plague of all cowards! Let them speak. If they speak more or less than truth, they are villains and the sons of darkness.

PRINCE Speak, sirs. How was it?

GADSHILL We four set upon some dozen—

FALSTAFF Sixteen at least, my lord.

GADSHILL And bound them.

PETO No, no, they were not bound.

FALSTAFF You rogue, they were bound, every man of them, or I am a Jew else, an Ebrew Jew.

GADSHILL As we were sharing, some six or seven fresh men set upon us—

FALSTAFF And unbound the rest, and then come in the other.

PRINCE What, fought you with them all?

FALSTAFF All? I know not what you call all, but if I fought not with fifty of them, I am a bunch of radish. If there were not two or three and fifty upon poor old Jack, then am I no two-legg'd creature.

PRINCE Pray God you have not murd'red some of them.

FALSTAFF Nay, that's past praying for. I have pepper'd two of them. Two I am sure I have paid, two rogues in buckram suits. I tell thee what, Hal, if I tell thee a lie, spit in my face, call me horse. Thou knowest my old ward. Here I lay, and thus I bore my point. [*He demonstrates his stance.*] Four rogues in buckram let drive at me—

PRINCE What, four? Thou saidst but two even now.

FALSTAFF Four, Hal, I told thee four.

POINS Ay, ay, he said four.

FALSTAFF These four came all afront, and mainly thrust at me. I made me no more ado but took all their seven points in my target, thus.

PRINCE Seven? Why, there were but four even now.

FALSTAFF In buckram?

POINS Ay, four, in buckram suits.

FALSTAFF Seven, by these hilts, or I am a villain else.

PRINCE [*Aside to Poins*] Prithee let him alone. We shall have more anon.

FALSTAFF Dost thou hear me, Hal?

PRINCE Ay, and mark thee too, Jack.

FALSTAFF Do so, for it is worth the list'ning to. These nine in buckram that I told thee of—

PRINCE So, two more already.

FALSTAFF Their points being broken—

POINS Down fell their hose.

FALSTAFF Began to give me ground; but I follow'd me close, came in foot and hand; and with a thought seven of the eleven I paid.

PRINCE O monstrous! Eleven buckram men grown out of two!

FALSTAFF But, as the devil would have it, three misbegotten knaves in Kendal green came at my back and let drive at me; for it was so dark, Hal, that thou couldst not see thy hand.

PRINCE These lies are like their father that begets them, gross as a mountain, open, palpable. Why, thou clay-brain'd guts, thou knotty-pated fool, thou whoreson, obscene, greasy tallow-catch—

FALSTAFF What, art thou mad? Art thou mad? Is not the truth the truth?

PRINCE Why, how couldst thou know these men in Kendal green, when it was so dark thou couldst not see thy hand? Come, tell us your reason. What sayest thou to this?

POINS Come, your reason, Jack, your reason.

FALSTAFF What, upon compulsion? 'Zounds, an I were at the strappado, or all the racks in the world, I would not tell you on compulsion. Give you a reason on compulsion? If reasons were as plentiful as blackberries, I would give no man a reason upon compulsion, I.

PRINCE I'll be no longer guilty of this sin. This sanguine coward, this bed-presser, this horse-backbreaker, this huge hill of flesh—

FALSTAFF 'Sblood, you starveling, you elf-skin, you dried neat's tongue, you bull's pizzle, you stock-fish! O for breath to utter what is like thee! You tailor's yard, you sheath, you bowcase, you vile standing tuck—

153 All's . . . that i.e., no matter **162 at half-sword** fighting at close quarters **164 doublet** Elizabethan upper garment like a jacket **165 hose** close-fitting breeches. **buckler** shield **166–167 ecce signum** behold the proof. (Familiar words from the Mass.) **181 other** others **192 ward** defensive stance, parry. **lay** stood

198 afront abreast. **mainly** powerfully **199 made me** i.e., made. (*Me* is the ethical dative.) **200 target** shield **204 by these hilts** by my sword-hilt. **villain** i.e., no gentleman **212 points** sword points. (But Poins puns on the sense of *laces by which the hose were attached to the doublet.*) **214 follow'd me** i.e., followed **215 with a thought** quick as a thought **220 Kendal** a town known for its textiles **225 knotty-pated** thickheaded **226 tallow-catch** tallow tub **235 strappado** a kind of torture **237 reasons . . . blackberries** (Falstaff puns on *raisins*, pronounced nearly like *reasons*.) **239 sanguine** ruddy **243 neat's** ox's. **stock-fish** dried cod **246 tuck** rapier

PRINCE Well, breathe awhile, and then to it again, and when thou hast tir'd thyself in base comparisons, hear me speak but this.

POINS Mark, Jack.

PRINCE We two saw you four set on four and bound them, and were masters of their wealth. Mark now how a plain tale shall put you down. Then did we two set on you four, and, with a word, outfac'd you from your prize, and have it, yea, and can show it you here in the house. And, Falstaff, you carried your guts away as nimbly, with as quick dexterity, and roar'd for mercy, and still run and roar'd, as ever I heard bull-calf. What a slave art thou, to hack thy sword as thou hast done, and then say it was in fight! What trick, what device, what starting-hole canst thou now find out to hide thee from this open and apparent shame?

POINS Come, let's hear, Jack. What trick hast thou now?

FALSTAFF By the Lord, I knew ye as well as he that made ye. Why, hear you, my masters, was it for me to kill the heir-apparent? Should I turn upon the true prince? Why, thou knowest I am as valiant as Hercules, but beware instinct. The lion will not touch the true prince. Instinct is a great matter; I was now a coward on instinct. I shall think the better of myself and thee during my life—I for a valiant lion, and thou for a true prince. But by the Lord, lads, I am glad you have the money. Hostess, clap to the doors! Watch tonight, pray tomorrow. Gallants, lads, boys, hearts of gold, all the titles of good fellowship come to you! What, shall we be merry? Shall we have a play extempore?

PRINCE Content; and the argument shall be thy running away.

FALSTAFF Ah, no more of that, Hal, an thou lovest me!

Enter Hostess.

HOSTESS
O Jesu, my lord the Prince!

PRINCE How now, my lady the hostess? What say'st thou to me?

HOSTESS Marry, my lord, there is a nobleman of the court at door would speak with you. He says he comes from your father.

PRINCE Give him as much as will make him a royal man, and send him back again to my mother.

FALSTAFF What manner of man is he?

HOSTESS An old man.

FALSTAFF What doth gravity out of his bed at midnight? Shall I give him his answer?

PRINCE Prithee, do, Jack.

FALSTAFF Faith, and I'll send him packing. *Exit.*

PRINCE Now, sirs. By 'r lady, you fought fair; so did you, Peto; so did you, Bardolph. You are lions too, you ran away upon instinct, you will not touch the true prince; no, fie!

BARDOLPH Faith, I ran when I saw others run.

PRINCE Faith, tell me now in earnest, how came Falstaff's sword so hack'd?

PETO Why, he hack'd it with his dagger, and said he would swear truth out of England but he would make you believe it was done in fight, and persuaded us to do the like.

BARDOLPH Yea, and to tickle our noses with spear-grass to make them bleed, and then to beslubber our garments with it and swear it was the blood of true men. I did that I did not this seven year before, I blush'd to hear his monstrous devices.

PRINCE O villain, thou stolest a cup of sack eighteen years ago, and wert taken with the manner, and ever since thou hast blush'd extempore. Thou hadst fire and sword on thy side, and yet thou ran'st away. What instinct hadst thou for it?

BARDOLPH My lord, do you see these meteors? Do you behold these exhalations?
[*Pointing to his own face.*]

PRINCE I do.

BARDOLPH What think you they portend?

PRINCE Hot livers and cold purses.

BARDOLPH Choler, my lord, if rightly taken.

PRINCE No, if rightly taken, halter.

Enter Falstaff.

Here comes lean Jack, here comes bare-bone. How now, my sweet creature of bombast? How long is 't ago, Jack, since thou sawest thine own knee?

FALSTAFF My own knee? When I was about thy years, Hal, I was not an eagle's talent in the waist; I could have crept into any alderman's thumb-ring. A plague of sighing and grief! It blows a man up like a bladder. There's villainous news abroad. Here was Sir John Bracy from your father. You must to the court in the morning. That same mad fellow of the north, Percy, and he of Wales that gave Amamon the bastinado and made Lucifer cuckold and swore the devil his true liegeman upon the cross of a Welsh hook—what a plague call you him?

POINS Owen Glendower.

FALSTAFF Owen, Owen, the same; and his son-in-law Mortimer, and old Northumberland, and that sprightly Scot of Scots, Douglas, that runs a-horseback up a hill perpendicular—

PRINCE He that rides at high speed and with his pistol kills a sparrow flying.

FALSTAFF You have hit it.

PRINCE So did he never the sparrow.

254 with a word in a word. **outfac'd** frightened **261 starting-hole** point of shelter (like a rabbit's hole) **273 Watch** stay awake. (See Matthew 26:41.) **287–288 Give . . . man** (Hal puns on the value of coins: a *noble* was worth 6 shillings 8 pence, a *royal* 10 shillings.)

303 but he would if he did not **309 that** what **312 taken . . . manner** caught with the goods **313 fire** i.e., a red nose and complexion caused by heavy drinking **316, 317 meteors, exhalations** i.e., the red blotches on Bardolph's face **319 portend** signify. (Continues the metaphor of astrological influence begun in *meteors* and *exhalations.*) **320 Hot . . . purses** i.e., livers inflamed by drink and purses made empty by spending **321 Choler** a choleric or combative temperament. **taken** understood. (But the Prince, in his next speech, uses the word to mean *arrested;* he also puns on *choler, collar,* i.e., halter or hangman's noose.) **324 bombast** cotton padding **327 talent** talon **333 Amamon** (The name of a demon.) **bastinado** beating on the soles of the feet **334 made . . . cuckold** i.e., gave Lucifer his horns, the sign of cuckoldry **335 liegeman** subject. **Welsh hook** curved-bladed pike

FALSTAFF Well, that rascal hath good mettle in him; he will not run.

PRINCE Why, what a rascal art thou then, to praise him so for running!

FALSTAFF A-horseback, ye cuckoo; but afoot he will not budge a foot.

PRINCE Yes, Jack, upon instinct.

FALSTAFF I grant ye, upon instinct. Well, he is there too, and one Mordake, and a thousand blue-caps more. Worcester is stol'n away tonight. Thy father's beard is turn'd white with the news. You may buy land now as cheap as stinking mack'rel.

PRINCE Why, then, it is like, if there come a hot June and this civil buffeting hold, we shall buy maiden-heads as they buy hob-nails, by the hundreds.

FALSTAFF By the mass, lad, thou sayest true; it is like we shall have good trading that way. But tell me, Hal, art not thou horrible afeard? Thou being heir-apparent, could the world pick thee out three such enemies again as that fiend Douglas, that spirit Percy, and that devil Glendower? Art thou not horribly afraid? Doth not thy blood thrill at it?

PRINCE Not a whit, i' faith. I lack some of thy instinct.

FALSTAFF Well, thou wilt be horribly chid tomorrow when thou comest to thy father. If thou love me, practice an answer.

PRINCE Do thou stand for my father, and examine me upon the particulars of my life.

FALSTAFF Shall I? Content. This chair shall be my state, this dagger my scepter, and this cushion my crown.

[*Falstaff establishes himself on his "throne."*]

PRINCE Thy state is taken for a join'd-stool, thy golden scepter for a leaden dagger, and thy precious rich crown for a pitiful bald crown!

FALSTAFF Well, an the fire of grace be not quite out of thee, now shalt thou be mov'd. Give me a cup of sack to make my eyes look red, that it may be thought I have wept; for I must speak in passion, and I will do it in King Cambyses' vein.

PRINCE Well, here is my leg. [*He makes obeisance.*]

FALSTAFF And here is my speech. Stand aside, nobility.

HOSTESS O Jesu, this is excellent sport, i' faith!

FALSTAFF
Weep not, sweet queen, for trickling tears are vain.

HOSTESS O, the father, how he holds his countenance!

FALSTAFF
For God's sake, lords, convey my tristful queen,
For tears do stop the floodgates of her eyes.

HOSTESS O Jesu, he doth it as like one of these harlotry players as ever I see!

FALSTAFF
Peace, good pint-pot; peace, good tickle-brain.—
Harry, I do not only marvel where thou spendest thy time, but also how thou art accompanied; for though the camomile, the more it is trodden on, the faster it grows, yet youth, the more it is wasted, the sooner it wears. That thou art my son I have partly thy mother's word, partly my own opinion, but chiefly a villainous trick of thine eye and a foolish hanging of thy nether lip, that doth warrant me. If then thou be son to me, here lies the point: why, being son to me, art thou so pointed at? Shall the blessed sun of heaven prove a micher and eat blackberries? A question not to be ask'd. Shall the son of England prove a thief and take purses? A question to be ask'd. There is a thing, Harry, which thou hast often heard of, and it is known to many in our land by the name of pitch. This pitch, as ancient writers do report, doth defile; so doth the company thou keepest. For, Harry, now I do not speak to thee in drink, but in tears; not in pleasure, but in passion; not in words only, but in woes also. And yet there is a virtuous man whom I have often noted in thy company, but I know not his name.

PRINCE What manner of man, an it like your Majesty?

FALSTAFF A goodly portly man, i' faith, and a corpulent; of a cheerful look, a pleasing eye, and a most noble carriage; and, as I think, his age some fifty, or, by 'r lady, inclining to threescore; and now I remember me, his name is Falstaff. If that man should be lewdly given, he deceiveth me; for, Harry, I see virtue in his looks. If then the tree may be known by the fruit, as the fruit by the tree, then, peremptorily I speak it, there is virtue in that Falstaff. Him keep with, the rest banish. And tell me now, thou naughty varlet, tell me, where hast thou been this month?

PRINCE Dost thou speak like a king? Do thou stand for me, and I'll play my father.

FALSTAFF Depose me? If thou dost it half so gravely, so majestically, both in word and matter, hang me up by the heels for a rabbit-sucker or a poulter's hare.

[*Hal takes Falstaff's place on the "throne."*]

PRINCE Well, here I am set.

FALSTAFF And here I stand. Judge, my masters.

PRINCE Now, Harry, whence come you?

FALSTAFF My noble lord, from Eastcheap.

PRINCE The complaints I hear of thee are grievous.

FALSTAFF 'Sblood, my lord, they are false.—Nay, I'll tickle ye for a young prince, i' faith.

PRINCE Swearest thou, ungracious boy? Henceforth ne'er look on me. Thou art violently carried away from grace. There is a devil haunts thee in the likeness of an old fat man; a tun of man is thy companion. Why dost thou converse with that trunk of humors, that bolting-hutch of beastliness, that swoll'n parcel of dropsies, that huge bombard of sack, that stuff'd cloak-bag of guts, that roasted Manningtree ox with the pudding in his belly, that reverend Vice, that grey iniquity, that

354 blue-caps Scottish soldiers **359 hold** continue **374 state** chair of state, throne **376 join'd-stool** a stool made by a joiner or furniture-maker **383 in . . . vein** i.e., in the ranting and (by Shakespeare's time) old-fashioned style of Thomas Preston's *Cambyses,* an early Elizabethan tragedy **389 holds his countenance** keeps a straight face **390 convey** escort away. **tristful** sorrowing **392 harlotry** scurvy, vagabond

397 camomile (This parodies the style of Lyly's *Euphues* and exaggerates the balance and alliteration of the style.) **402 warrant** assure **405 micher** truant **409–410 pitch . . . defile** (An allusion to the familiar proverb from Ecclesiasticus 13:1 about the defilement of touching pitch.) **421 lewdly** wickedly **423 If . . . by the fruit** (See Matthew 12:33.) **432 rabbit-sucker** unweaned rabbit. **poulter's** poulterer's **438 'Sblood** i.e., by Christ's blood **439 tickle ye for** amuse you in the role of **444 converse** associate. **humors** body fluids, diseases **444–445 bolting-hutch** large flour bin **446 bombard** leathern drinking vessel **447 Manningtree ox** (Manningtree, a town in Essex, had noted fairs where, no doubt, oxen were roasted whole.) **pudding** stuffing **448 Vice, iniquity** (Names for the chief comic character and tempter in the morality play.)

father ruffian, that vanity in years? Wherein is he good, but to taste sack and drink it? Wherein neat and cleanly, but to carve a capon and eat it? Wherein cunning, but in craft? Wherein crafty, but in villainy? Wherein villainous, but in all things? Wherein worthy, but in nothing?

FALSTAFF I would your Grace would take me with you. Whom means your Grace?

PRINCE That villainous abominable misleader of youth, Falstaff, that old white-bearded Satan.

FALSTAFF My lord, the man I know.

PRINCE I know thou dost.

FALSTAFF But to say I know more harm in him than in myself, were to say more than I know. That he is old, the more the pity, his white hairs do witness it; but that he is, saving your reverence, a whoremaster, that I utterly deny. If sack and sugar be a fault, God help the wicked! If to be old and merry be a sin, then many an old host that I know is damn'd. If to be fat be to be hated, then Pharaoh's lean kine are to be lov'd. No, my good lord, banish Peto, banish Bardolph, banish Poins; but for sweet Jack Falstaff, kind Jack Falstaff, true Jack Falstaff, valiant Jack Falstaff, and therefore more valiant being, as he is, old Jack Falstaff, banish not him thy Harry's company, banish not him thy Harry's company—banish plump Jack, and banish all the world.

PRINCE I do, I will. *[A knocking heard. Exeunt Hostess, Francis, and Bardolph.]*

Enter Bardolph, running.

BARDOLPH O, my lord, my lord! The sheriff with a most monstrous watch is at the door.

FALSTAFF Out, ye rogue! Play out the play. I have much to say in the behalf of that Falstaff.

Enter the Hostess.

HOSTESS O Jesu, my lord, my lord!

PRINCE Heigh, heigh! The devil rides upon a fiddlestick. What's the matter?

HOSTESS The sheriff and all the watch are at the door. They are come to search the house. Shall I let them in?

FALSTAFF Dost thou hear, Hal? Never call a true piece of gold a counterfeit. Thou art essentially mad, without seeming so.

PRINCE And thou a natural coward, without instinct.

FALSTAFF I deny your major. If you will deny the sheriff, so; if not, let him enter. If I become not a cart as well as another man, a plague on my bringing up! I hope I shall as soon be strangled with a halter as another.

PRINCE Go, hide thee behind the arras. The rest walk up above. Now, my masters, for a true face and good conscience.

FALSTAFF Both which I have had, but their date is out, and therefore I'll hide me. *[He hides behind the arras.]*

PRINCE Call in the sheriff. *[Exeunt all except the Prince and Peto.]*

Enter Sheriff and the Carrier.

Now, Master Sheriff, what is your will with me?

SHERIFF
First, pardon me, my lord. A hue and cry
Hath followed certain men unto this house.

PRINCE
What men?

SHERIFF
One of them is well known, my gracious lord,
A gross fat man.

CARRIER As fat as butter.

PRINCE
The man, I do assure you, is not here,
For I myself at this time have employ'd him.
And, sheriff, I will engage my word to thee
That I will, by tomorrow dinner-time,
Send him to answer thee, or any man,
For anything he shall be charg'd withal;
And so let me entreat you leave the house.

SHERIFF
I will, my lord. There are two gentlemen
Have in this robbery lost three hundred marks.

PRINCE
It may be so. If he have robb'd these men,
He shall be answerable; and so farewell.

SHERIFF
Good night, my noble lord.

PRINCE
I think it is good morrow, is it not?

SHERIFF
Indeed, my lord, I think it be two o'clock.
Exit [with Carrier].

PRINCE This oily rascal is known as well as Paul's. Go call him forth.

PETO *[Discovering Falstaff]* Falstaff!—Fast asleep behind the arras, and snorting like a horse.

PRINCE Hark, how hard he fetches breath. Search his pockets. *(He searcheth his pockets, and findeth certain papers.)* What hast thou found?

PETO Nothing but papers, my lord.

PRINCE Let's see what they be. Read them.

PETO *[Reads]*

Item, A capon, ... 2s. 2d.
Item, Sauce, ... 4d.
Item, Sack, two gallons, ... 5s. 8d.
Item, Anchovies and sack after supper, ... 2s. 6d.
Item, Bread, ... ob.

PRINCE O monstrous! But one half-pennyworth of

449 vanity person given to worldly desires **451 cleanly** deft **451–452 cunning** skillful **455 take me with you** i.e., let me catch up with your meaning **464 saving your reverence** i.e., with my apology for using offensive language **468 Pharaoh's lean kine** (See Genesis 41:3–4, 18–21.) **478 watch** posse of constables **482–483 The . . . fiddlestick** i.e., here's much ado about nothing **486–488 Dost . . . seeming so** (In this difficult passage, Falstaff seems to suggest that he is true gold, not counterfeit, and so should not be betrayed to the watch by the Prince who, he hopes, is not merely playacting at the tavern but is truly one of its madcap members.) **490 major** major premise **491 cart** i.e., hangman's cart **495 arras** wall-hanging of tapestry

509 engage pledge **519 morrow** morning **521 Paul's** St. Paul's Cathedral **534 ob.** obolus, i.e., halfpenny

bread to this intolerable deal of sack! What there is else, keep close; we'll read it at more advantage. There let him sleep till day. I'll to the court in the morning. We must all to the wars, and thy place shall be honorable. I'll procure this fat rogue a charge of foot, and I know his death will be a march of twelve score. The money shall be paid back again with advantage. Be with me betimes in the morning; and so, good morrow, Peto.

PETO Good morrow, good my lord.

Exeunt [severally. Falstaff is concealed once more behind the arras].

[ACT III • SCENE I]

Enter Hotspur, Worcester, Lord Mortimer, [and] Owen Glendower.

MORTIMER
These promises are fair, the parties sure,
And our induction full of prosperous hope.

HOTSPUR
Lord Mortimer, and cousin Glendower,
Will you sit down? And uncle Worcester—
[They sit.]
A plague upon it, I have forgot the map.

GLENDOWER [*Producing a map*]
No, here it is. Sit, cousin Percy,
Sit, good cousin Hotspur—for by that name
As oft as Lancaster doth speak of you
His cheek looks pale, and with a rising sigh
He wisheth you in heaven.

HOTSPUR
And you in hell,
As oft as he hears Owen Glendower spoke of.

GLENDOWER
I cannot blame him. At my nativity
The front of heaven was full of fiery shapes,
Of burning cressets, and at my birth
The frame and huge foundation of the earth
Shak'd like a coward.

HOTSPUR
Why, so it would have done
At the same season, if your mother's cat
Had but kitten'd, though yourself had never been
born.

GLENDOWER
I say the earth did shake when I was born.

HOTSPUR
And I say the earth was not of my mind,
If you suppose as fearing you it shook.

GLENDOWER
The heavens were all on fire, the earth did tremble.

HOTSPUR
O, then the earth shook to see the heavens on fire,
And not in fear of your nativity.
Diseased nature oftentimes breaks forth
In strange eruptions; oft the teeming earth
Is with a kind of colic pinch'd and vex'd
By the imprisoning of unruly wind
Within her womb, which, for enlargement striving,
Shakes the old beldam earth and topples down
Steeples and moss-grown towers. At your birth
Our grandam earth, having this distemp'rature,
In passion shook.

GLENDOWER
Cousin, of many men
I do not bear these crossings. Give me leave
To tell you once again that at my birth
The front of heaven was full of fiery shapes,
The goats ran from the mountains, and the herds
Were strangely clamorous to the frighted fields.
These signs have mark'd me extraordinary,
And all the courses of my life do show
I am not in the roll of common men.
Where is he living, clipp'd in with the sea
That chides the banks of England, Scotland, Wales,
Which calls me pupil, or hath read to me?
And bring him out that is but woman's son
Can trace me in the tedious ways of art
And hold me pace in deep experiments.

HOTSPUR
I think there's no man speaks better Welsh.
I'll to dinner.

MORTIMER
Peace, cousin Percy; you will make him mad.

GLENDOWER
I can call spirits from the vasty deep.

HOTSPUR
Why, so can I, or so can any man;
But will they come when you do call for them?

GLENDOWER
Why, I can teach you, cousin, to command the devil.

HOTSPUR
And I can teach thee, coz, to shame the devil
By telling truth. Tell truth and shame the devil.
If thou have power to raise him, bring him hither,
And I'll be sworn I have power to shame him
hence.
O, while you live, tell truth and shame the devil!

MORTIMER
Come, come, no more of this unprofitable chat.

GLENDOWER
Three times hath Henry Bolingbroke made head
Against my power; thrice from the banks of Wye
And sandy-bottom'd Severn have I sent him
Bootless home and weather-beaten back.

HOTSPUR
Home without boots, and in foul weather too!

537 close hidden. **advantage** favorable opportunity **540 charge of foot** command of a company of infantry **541 twelve score** i.e., 240 yards **542 advantage** interest **543 betimes** early **545 s.d. Exeunt . . . arras** (On stage, the arras is evidently arranged so that Falstaff can exit behind it once the scene is over.)

III.i. Location: Wales. Glendower's castle. (Holinshed places a meeting of the rebel deputies at Bangor in the Archdeacon's house, but in this present "unhistorical" scene as invented by Shakespeare Glendower is host throughout.) Seats are provided on stage.
2 induction beginning. **prosperous hope** hope of prospering **7 Lancaster** i.e., King Henry, here demoted to Duke of Lancaster **13 front** forehead **14 cressets** lights burning in baskets atop long poles; hence, meteors

29 enlargement release **30 beldam** grandmother **42 clipp'd in with** enclosed by **44 Which** who. **read to** instructed **46 Can . . . art** who can follow me in the laborious ways of magic **47 hold me pace** keep up with me. **deep** occult **48 Welsh** i.e., incomprehensible boasting **51 vasty deep** lower world **61 made head** raised a force **62 power** army **64 Bootless** without advantage

How scapes he agues, in the devil's name?

GLENDOWER

Come, here is the map. Shall we divide our right
According to our threefold order ta'en? 68

MORTIMER

The Archdeacon hath divided it 69
Into three limits very equally:
England, from Trent and Severn hitherto, 71
By south and east is to my part assign'd;
All westward, Wales beyond the Severn shore,
And all the fertile land within that bound,
To Owen Glendower; and, dear coz, to you
The remnant northward, lying off from Trent.
And our indentures tripartite are drawn, 77
Which being sealed interchangeably—
A business that this night may execute—
Tomorrow, cousin Percy, you and I
And my good Lord of Worcester will set forth
To meet your father and the Scottish power,
As is appointed us, at Shrewsbury.
My father Glendower is not ready yet, 84
Nor shall we need his help these fourteen days.
Within that space you may have drawn together 86
Your tenants, friends, and neighboring gentlemen.

GLENDOWER

A shorter time shall send me to you, lords;
And in my conduct shall your ladies come, 89
From whom you now must steal and take no leave,
For there will be a world of water shed
Upon the parting of your wives and you.

HOTSPUR [*Consulting the map*]

Methinks my moi'ty, north from Burton here, 93
In quantity equals not one of yours.
See how this river comes me cranking in, 95
And cuts me from the best of all my land
A huge half-moon, a monstrous cantle out. 97
I'll have the current in this place damm'd up,
And here the smug and silver Trent shall run 99
In a new channel, fair and evenly.
It shall not wind with such a deep indent
To rob me of so rich a bottom here. 102

GLENDOWER

Not wind? It shall, it must! You see it doth.

MORTIMER

Yea, but mark how he bears his course, and runs
me up
With like advantage on the other side,
Gelding the opposed continent as much 106
As on the other side it takes from you.

WORCESTER

Yea, but a little charge will trench him here 108
And on this north side win this cape of land;
And then he runs straight and even.

HOTSPUR

I'll have it so. A little charge will do it.

GLENDOWER

I'll not have it alt'red.

HOTSPUR Will not you?

GLENDOWER

No, nor you shall not.

HOTSPUR Who shall say me nay?

GLENDOWER

Why, that will I.

HOTSPUR

Let me not understand you, then; speak it in Welsh.

GLENDOWER

I can speak English, lord, as well as you;
For I was train'd up in the English court,
Where, being but young, I framed to the harp
Many an English ditty lovely well,
And gave the tongue a helpful ornament— 120
A virtue that was never seen in you.

HOTSPUR

Marry, and I am glad of it with all my heart!
I had rather be a kitten and cry mew
Than one of these same meter ballad-mongers.
I had rather hear a brazen canstick turn'd, 125
Or a dry wheel grate on the axle-tree,
And that would set my teeth nothing on edge,
Nothing so much as mincing poetry.
'Tis like the forc'd gait of a shuffling nag. 129

GLENDOWER

Come, you shall have Trent turn'd.

HOTSPUR

I do not care. I'll give thrice so much land
To any well-deserving friend;
But in the way of bargain, mark ye me,
I'll cavil on the ninth part of a hair.
Are the indentures drawn? Shall we be gone?

GLENDOWER

The moon shines fair; you may away by night.
I'll haste the writer, and withal 137
Break with your wives of your departure hence. 138
I am afraid my daughter will run mad,
So much she doteth on her Mortimer. *Exit.*

MORTIMER

Fie, cousin Percy, how you cross my father!

HOTSPUR

I cannot choose. Sometime he angers me
With telling me of the moldwarp and the ant, 143
Of the dreamer Merlin and his prophecies, 144
And of a dragon and a finless fish,
A clip-wing'd griffin and a moulten raven, 146
A couching lion and a ramping cat, 147
And such a deal of skimble-skamble stuff 148

68 order ta'en arrangements made **69 Archdeacon** i.e., the Archdeacon of Bangor, in whose house, according to Holinshed, a meeting took place between deputies of the rebel leaders **71 hitherto** to this point **77 tripartite** i.e., drawn up in triplicate, each document sealed *interchangeably* (l. 78) with the seal of all signatories. **drawn** drawn up **84 father** i.e., father-in-law **86 may** will be able to **89 conduct** escort **93 moi'ty** share **95 comes me cranking in** comes bending in on my share **97 cantle** piece **99 smug** smooth **102 bottom** valley **106 Gelding . . . continent** cutting off from the land which it bounds on the opposite side **108 charge** expenditure. **trench** provide a new channel

120 gave . . . ornament i.e., added to the words a pleasing ornament of music; also, gave to the English tongue the ornament of music and poetry **125 canstick turn'd** candlestick turned on a lathe **129 shuffling** hobbled **137 writer** i.e., scrivener who would be drawing the indentures **138 Break with** inform **143 moldwarp** mole. (Holinshed tells us that the division was arranged because of a prophecy which represented King Henry as the mole and the others as the dragon, the lion, and the wolf, who should divide the land among them.) **144 Merlin** the bard, prophet, and magician of Arthurian story, Welsh in origin **146 griffin** a fabulous beast, half lion, half eagle **147 couching** *couchant,* crouching. (Heraldic term.) **ramping** rampant, advancing on its hind legs. (Hotspur is ridiculing the heraldic emblems which Glendower holds so dear.) **148 skimble-skamble** foolish, nonsensical

As puts me from my faith. I tell you what:
He held me last night at least nine hours
In reckoning up the several devils' names
That were his lackeys. I cried "hum," and "well, go to,"
But mark'd him not a word. O, he is as tedious
As a tired horse, a railing wife,
Worse than a smoky house. I had rather live
With cheese and garlic in a windmill, far,
Than feed on cates and have him talk to me
In any summer house in Christendom.

MORTIMER
In faith, he is a worthy gentleman,
Exceedingly well read, and profited
In strange concealments, valiant as a lion
And wondrous affable, and as bountiful
As mines of India. Shall I tell you, cousin?
He holds your temper in a high respect
And curbs himself even of his natural scope
When you come 'cross his humor. Faith, he does.
I warrant you that man is not alive
Might so have tempted him as you have done,
Without the taste of danger and reproof.
But do not use it oft, let me entreat you.

WORCESTER
In faith, my lord, you are too willful-blame,
And since your coming hither have done enough
To put him quite besides his patience.
You must needs learn, lord, to amend this fault.
Though sometimes it show greatness, courage, blood—
And that's the dearest grace it renders you—
Yet oftentimes it doth present harsh rage,
Defect of manners, want of government,
Pride, haughtiness, opinion, and disdain,
The least of which haunting a nobleman
Loseth men's hearts and leaves behind a stain
Upon the beauty of all parts besides,
Beguiling them of commendation.

HOTSPUR
Well, I am school'd. Good manners be your speed!
Here come our wives, and let us take our leave.

Enter Glendower with the ladies.

MORTIMER
This is the deadly spite that angers me:
My wife can speak no English, I no Welsh.

GLENDOWER
My daughter weeps. She'll not part with you;
She'll be a soldier too, she'll to the wars.

MORTIMER
Good father, tell her that she and my aunt Percy
Shall follow in your conduct speedily.

Glendower speaks to her in Welsh, and she answers him in the same.

GLENDOWER
She is desperate here; a peevish self-will'd harlotry,
One that no persuasion can do good upon.

The lady speaks in Welsh.

MORTIMER
I understand thy looks. That pretty Welsh
Which thou pourest down from these swelling heavens
I am too perfect in; and, but for shame,
In such a parley should I answer thee.

The lady again in Welsh.

I understand thy kisses and thou mine,
And that's a feeling disputation.
But I will never be a truant, love,
Till I have learn'd thy language; for thy tongue
Makes Welsh as sweet as ditties highly penn'd,
Sung by a fair queen in a summer's bower,
With ravishing division, to her lute.

GLENDOWER
Nay, if you melt, then will she run mad.

The lady speaks again in Welsh.

MORTIMER
O, I am ignorance itself in this!

GLENDOWER
She bids you on the wanton rushes lay you down
And rest your gentle head upon her lap,
And she will sing the song that pleaseth you
And on your eyelids crown the god of sleep,
Charming your blood with pleasing heaviness,
Making such difference 'twixt wake and sleep
As is the difference betwixt day and night
The hour before the heavenly-harness'd team
Begins his golden progress in the east.

MORTIMER
With all my heart I'll sit and hear her sing.
By that time will our book, I think, be drawn.

GLENDOWER
Do so;
And those musicians that shall play to you
Hang in the air a thousand leagues from hence,
And straight they shall be here. Sit, and attend.

[Mortimer reclines with his head in his wife's lap.]

HOTSPUR Come, Kate, thou art perfect in lying down; come, quick, quick, that I may lay my head in thy lap.

LADY PERCY Go, ye giddy goose.

[Hotspur lies with his head in Kate's lap.] The music plays.

HOTSPUR
Now I perceive the devil understands Welsh;
And 'tis no marvel he is so humorous.
By 'r lady, he is a good musician.

151 several various **157 cates** delicacies **160 profited** proficient **161 concealments** occult practices **165 scope** freedom of speech **171 willful-blame** blameworthy for too much self-will **173 besides** out of **175 blood** spirit **176 dearest grace** best credit **177 present** represent **178 want of government** lack of self-control **179 opinion** vanity, arrogance **182 all parts besides** all other abilities **183 Beguiling** depriving **184 be your speed** give you good fortune **186 spite** vexation **190 aunt** (Percy's wife, here called Kate, was aunt of Edmund Mortimer, the fifth Earl of March, but was sister-in-law to the Sir Edward Mortimer who married Glendower's daughter.)

192 here on this point. **peevish self-will'd harlotry** childish willful silly wench **194 That pretty Welsh** i.e., your eloquent tears **195 heavens** i.e., eyes **196 perfect** proficient **197 such a parley** i.e., the same language (of weeping) **199 disputation** conversation **202 highly** eloquently, nobly **204 division** variation (in music) **207 wanton** soft, luxurious **211 heaviness** drowsiness **217 book** document, indentures **226 humorous** whimsical, capricious

LADY PERCY Then should you be nothing but musical, for you are altogether govern'd by humors. Lie still, ye thief, and hear the lady sing in Welsh.

HOTSPUR I had rather hear Lady, my brach, howl in Irish.

LADY PERCY Wouldst thou have thy head broken?

HOTSPUR No.

LADY PERCY Then be still.

HOTSPUR Neither, 'tis a woman's fault.

LADY PERCY Now God help thee!

HOTSPUR To the Welsh lady's bed.

LADY PERCY What's that?

HOTSPUR Peace, she sings.

Here the lady sings a Welsh song.

HOTSPUR Come, Kate, I'll have your song too.

LADY PERCY Not mine, in good sooth.

HOTSPUR Not yours, in good sooth! Heart, you swear like a comfit-maker's wife. "Not you, in good sooth," and "as true as I live," and "as God shall mend me," and "as sure as day,"
And givest such sarcenet surety for thy oaths
As if thou never walk'st further than Finsbury.
Swear me, Kate, like a lady as thou art,
A good mouth-filling oath, and leave "in sooth,"
And such protest of pepper-gingerbread,
To velvet-guards and Sunday-citizens.
Come, sing.

LADY PERCY I will not sing.

HOTSPUR 'Tis the next way to turn tailor, or be redbreast teacher. An the indentures be drawn, I'll away within these two hours; and so, come in when ye will. *Exit.*

GLENDOWER
Come, come, Lord Mortimer. You are as slow
As hot Lord Percy is on fire to go.
By this our book is drawn; we'll but seal,
And then to horse immediately.

MORTIMER
With all my heart. *Exeunt.*

[SCENE II]

Enter the King, Prince of Wales, and others.

KING
Lords, give us leave. The Prince of Wales and I
Must have some private conference; but be near at hand,
For we shall presently have need of you.
Exeunt Lords.
I know not whether God will have it so
For some displeasing service I have done,
That, in his secret doom, out of my blood
He'll breed revengement and a scourge for me;
But thou dost in thy passages of life
Make me believe that thou art only mark'd
For the hot vengeance and the rod of heaven
To punish my mistreadings. Tell me else,
Could such inordinate and low desires,
Such poor, such bare, such lewd, such mean attempts,
Such barren pleasures, rude society,
As thou art match'd withal and grafted to,
Accompany the greatness of thy blood
And hold their level with thy princely heart?

PRINCE
So please your Majesty, I would I could
Quit all offenses with as clear excuse
As well as I am doubtless I can purge
Myself of many I am charg'd withal.
Yet such extenuation let me beg
As, in reproof of many tales devis'd,
Which oft the ear of greatness needs must hear
By smiling pick-thanks and base newsmongers,
I may, for some things true, wherein my youth
Hath faulty wand'red and irregular,
Find pardon on my true submission.

KING
God pardon thee! Yet let me wonder, Harry,
At thy affections, which do hold a wing
Quite from the flight of all thy ancestors.
Thy place in council thou hast rudely lost,
Which by thy younger brother is supplied,
And art almost an alien to the hearts
Of all the court and princes of my blood.
The hope and expectation of thy time
Is ruin'd, and the soul of every man
Prophetically do forethink thy fall.
Had I so lavish of my presence been,
So common-hackney'd in the eyes of men,
So stale and cheap to vulgar company,
Opinion, that did help me to the crown,
Had still kept loyal to possession
And left me in reputeless banishment,
A fellow of no mark nor likelihood.
By being seldom seen, I could not stir
But like a comet I was wond'red at,
That men would tell their children, "This is he!"
Others would say, "Where, which is Bolingbroke?"
And then I stole all courtesy from heaven,
And dress'd myself in such humility
That I did pluck allegiance from men's hearts,

231 brach bitch hound **236 Neither** i.e., I won't do that either **243 Heart** i.e., by Christ's heart **244 comfit-maker's** confectioner's **247 sarcenet** soft, flimsy (from the soft silken material known as *sarcenet*) **248 Finsbury** a field just outside London frequented by the London citizenry. (Hotspur jokes with Kate as though she were a citizen's wife, using the pious and modest oaths of such people.) **251 protest . . . gingerbread** i.e., mealy-mouthed protestations **252 velvet-guards** i.e., wives who wear velvet trimming **255 next** nearest, quickest. **turn tailor** (Tailors were noted for singing.) **255–256 be redbreast teacher** i.e., teach birds to sing **260 By this** by this time

III.ii. Location: London. The palace.

6 doom judgment **8 passages** course, conduct **10 For** as, to be **13 lewd** low, base. **attempts** undertakings **17 hold . . . with** i.e., continue to find sanction in **19 Quit** acquit myself of **20 doubtless** certain **23 in reproof** upon disproof **25 pick-thanks** flatterers. **newsmongers** talebearers **28 submission** admission of fault **30 affections** inclinations. **hold a wing** fly a course **31 from** at variance with **32 rudely** by violence. (According to an apocryphal story, Hal boxed the ears of the Lord Chief Justice and was sent to prison for it; see *2 Henry IV*, I.ii. 54–55, 192, and V.ii. 70–71.) **36 time** time of life, youth **42 Opinion** i.e., public opinion **43 to possession** i.e., to Richard II's sovereignty **50 I . . . heaven** i.e., I assumed a bearing of the utmost graciousness

Loud shouts and salutations from their mouths,
Even in the presence of the crowned King.
Thus did I keep my person fresh and new,
My presence, like a robe pontifical,
Ne'er seen but wond'red at; and so my state,
Seldom but sumptuous, show'd like a feast
And won by rareness such solemnity.
The skipping King, he ambled up and down
With shallow jesters and rash bavin wits,
Soon kindled and soon burnt; carded his state,
Mingled his royalty with cap'ring fools,
Had his great name profaned with their scorns,
And gave his countenance, against his name,
To laugh at gibing boys and stand the push
Of every beardless vain comparative;
Grew a companion to the common streets,
Enfeoff'd himself to popularity,
That, being daily swallowed by men's eyes,
They surfeited with honey and began
To loathe the taste of sweetness, whereof a little
More than a little is by much too much.
So when he had occasion to be seen,
He was but as the cuckoo is in June,
Heard, not regarded—seen, but with such eyes
As, sick and blunted with community,
Afford no extraordinary gaze,
Such as is bent on sun-like majesty
When it shines seldom in admiring eyes;
But rather drows'd and hung their eyelids down,
Slept in his face and rend'red such aspect
As cloudy men use to their adversaries,
Being with his presence glutted, gorg'd, and full.
And in that very line, Harry, standest thou;
For thou hast lost thy princely privilege
With vile participation. Not an eye
But is a-weary of thy common sight,
Save mine, which hath desir'd to see thee more—
Which now doth that I would not have it do,
Make blind itself with foolish tenderness.

PRINCE
I shall hereafter, my thrice gracious lord,
Be more myself.

KING For all the world
As thou art to this hour was Richard then
When I from France set foot at Ravenspurgh,
And even as I was then is Percy now.
Now, by my scepter, and my soul to boot,
He hath more worthy interest to the state
Than thou the shadow of succession.
For of no right, nor color like to right,
He doth fill fields with harness in the realm,
Turns head against the lion's armed jaws,
And, being no more in debt to years than thou,
Leads ancient lords and reverend bishops on
To bloody battles and to bruising arms.
What never-dying honor hath he got
Against renowned Douglas! Whose high deeds,
Whose hot incursions and great name in arms
Holds from all soldiers chief majority
And military title capital
Through all the kingdoms that acknowledge Christ.
Thrice hath this Hotspur, Mars in swathling clothes,
This infant warrior, in his enterprises
Discomfited great Douglas, ta'en him once,
Enlarged him and made a friend of him,
To fill the mouth of deep defiance up
And shake the peace and safety of our throne.
And what say you to this? Percy, Northumberland,
The Archbishop's Grace of York, Douglas, Mortimer,
Capitulate against us and are up.
But wherefore do I tell these news to thee?
Why, Harry, do I tell thee of my foes,
Which art my nearest and dearest enemy?
Thou that art like enough, through vassal fear,
Base inclination, and the start of spleen,
To fight against me under Percy's pay,
To dog his heels and curtsy at his frowns,
To show how much thou art degenerate.

PRINCE
Do not think so. You shall not find it so.
And God forgive them that so much have sway'd
Your Majesty's good thoughts away from me!
I will redeem all this on Percy's head,
And in the closing of some glorious day
Be bold to tell you that I am your son,
When I will wear a garment all of blood
And stain my favors in a bloody mask,
Which, wash'd away, shall scour my shame with it.
And that shall be the day, whene'er it lights,
That this same child of honor and renown,
This gallant Hotspur, this all-praised knight,
And your unthought-of Harry chance to meet.
For every honor sitting on his helm,
Would they were multitudes, and on my head
My shames redoubled! For the time will come
That I shall make this northern youth exchange
His glorious deeds for my indignities.
Percy is but my factor, good my lord,
To engross up glorious deeds on my behalf;
And I will call him to so strict account
That he shall render every glory up,
Yea, even the slightest worship of his time,
Or I will tear the reckoning from his heart.
This in the name of God I promise here,
The which if He be pleas'd I shall perform,

57 state i.e., public appearances **59 such solemnity** i.e., the solemnity appropriate to a festival **60 skipping** flighty **61 bavin** brushwood, soon burnt out **62 carded** debased. (A term applied to the adulteration of wool.) **state** royal status **64 their scorns** i.e., the scornful opinion people had of these favorites **65 gave . . . name** lent his authority, to the detriment of his royal dignity and reputation **66 stand the push** put up with the impudence **67 comparative** maker of comparisons, wisecracker **69 Enfeoff'd himself** gave himself up **77 community** commonness **82 aspect** look **83 cloudy** sullen. (Also refers back to the image of the sun.) **87 vile participation** base association or companionship **90 that** that which **91 tenderness** i.e., tears **98–99 He . . . succession** i.e., even this rebel Hotspur has a better claim to the throne than you, the mere shadow of an heir **100 of no right** having no rightful claim. **color** pretext **101 harness** armor, i.e., men in armor

102 Turns head leads an armed force. **lion's** i.e., King's **109 majority** preeminence **110 capital** chief, principal **112 swathling** swaddling **115 Enlarged** freed **116 To . . . up** i.e., to swell the roar of deep defiance **119 The Archbishop's Grace** i.e., his Grace the Archbishop **120 Capitulate** form a league. **up** up in arms **124 like** likely. **vassal** slavish **125 Base inclination** inclination for baseness. **start of spleen** perversity **136 favors** features **138 lights** dawns **147 factor** agent **148 engross** amass, buy up **151 worship of his time** honor of his youthful lifetime

I do beseech your Majesty may salve
The long-grown wounds of my intemperance. 156
If not, the end of life cancels all bands, 157
And I will die a hundred thousand deaths
Ere break the smallest parcel of this vow.

KING
A hundred thousand rebels die in this!
Thou shalt have charge and sovereign trust herein. 161

Enter Blunt.

How now, good Blunt? Thy looks are full of speed.

BLUNT
So hath the business that I come to speak of.
Lord Mortimer of Scotland hath sent word 164
That Douglas and the English rebels met
The eleventh of this month at Shrewsbury.
A mighty and a fearful head they are, 167
If promises be kept on every hand,
As ever off'red foul play in a state.

KING
The Earl of Westmorland set forth today,
With him my son, Lord John of Lancaster;
For this advertisement is five days old. 172
On Wednesday next, Harry, you shall set forward;
On Thursday we ourselves will march. Our meeting 174
Is Bridgenorth. And, Harry, you shall march 175
Through Gloucestershire; by which account,
Our business valued, some twelve days hence 177
Our general forces at Bridgenorth shall meet.
Our hands are full of business. Let's away!
Advantage feeds him fat while men delay. *Exeunt.* 180

[SCENE III]

Enter Falstaff and Bardolph.

FALSTAFF Bardolph, am I not fall'n away vilely since this 1
last action? Do I not bate? Do I not dwindle? Why, my 2
skin hangs about me like an old lady's loose gown; I
am wither'd like an old apple-john. Well, I'll repent, 4
and that suddenly, while I am in some liking. I shall 5
be out of heart shortly, and then I shall have no 6
strength to repent. An I have not forgotten what the
inside of a church is made of, I am a peppercorn, a 8
brewer's horse. The inside of a church! Company, vil- 9
lainous company, hath been the spoil of me.

BARDOLPH Sir John, you are so fretful you cannot live long.

FALSTAFF Why, there is it. Come sing me a bawdy
song; make me merry. I was as virtuously given as a 14
gentleman need to be, virtuous enough: swore little,
dic'd not above seven times—a week, went to a
bawdy-house not above once in a quarter—of an
hour, paid money that I borrow'd—three or four
times, liv'd well and in good compass; and now I live 19
out of all order, out of all compass.

BARDOLPH Why, you are so fat, Sir John, that you must needs be out of all compass, out of all reasonable compass, Sir John.

FALSTAFF Do thou amend thy face, and I'll amend my
life. Thou art our admiral, thou bearest the lantern in 25
the poop, but 'tis in the nose of thee. Thou art the
Knight of the Burning Lamp.

BARDOLPH Why, Sir John, my face does you no harm.

FALSTAFF No, I'll be sworn, I make as good use of it as
many a man doth of a death's-head or a memento 30
mori. I never see thy face but I think upon hell-fire and 31
Dives that liv'd in purple; for there he is in his robes, 32
burning, burning. If thou wert any way given to vir-
tue, I would swear by thy face; my oath should be "By 34
this fire, that's God's angel." But thou art altogether 35
given over, and wert indeed, but for the light in thy 36
face, the son of utter darkness. When thou ran'st up
Gads Hill in the night to catch my horse, if I did not
think thou hadst been an ignis fatuus or a ball of wild- 39
fire, there's no purchase in money. O, thou art a per- 40
petual triumph, an everlasting bonfire-light! Thou 41
hast sav'd me a thousand marks in links and torches, 42
walking with thee in the night betwixt tavern and tav-
ern; but the sack that thou hast drunk me would have
bought me lights as good cheap at the dearest chan- 45
dler's in Europe. I have maintain'd that salamander of 46
yours with fire any time this two and thirty years. God
reward me for it!

BARDOLPH 'Sblood, I would my face were in your belly! 49

FALSTAFF God-a-mercy! So should I be sure to be heart-burn'd.

Enter Hostess.

How now, Dame Partlet the hen? Have you inquir'd 52
yet who pick'd my pocket?

HOSTESS Why, Sir John, what do you think, Sir John?
Do you think I keep thieves in my house? I have
search'd, I have inquir'd, so has my husband, man by
man, boy by boy, servant by servant. The tithe of a 57
hair was never lost in my house before.

FALSTAFF Ye lie, hostess. Bardolph was shav'd and lost many a hair; and I'll be sworn my pocket was pick'd. Go to, you are a woman, go.

HOSTESS Who, I? No, I defy thee! God's light, I was never call'd so in mine own house before.

156 intemperance dissolute living **157 bands** bonds **161 charge** command (of troops) **164 Lord Mortimer of Scotland** (A Scottish nobleman, unrelated to Glendower's son-in-law.) **167 head** armed force **172 advertisement** tidings, news **174 meeting** place of rendezvous **175 Bridgenorth** a town near Shrewsbury **177 Our business valued** estimating how long our business will take **180 Advantage . . . fat** opportunity (for rebellion) prospers

III.iii. Location: A tavern in Eastcheap, as in II.iv.
1 fall'n away shrunk **2 action** i.e., the robbery at Gadshill. **bate** lose weight **4 apple-john** a kind of apple still in good eating condition when shriveled **5 liking** (1) good bodily condition (2) inclination **6 out of heart** disinclined, disheartened **8 peppercorn** unground dried pepper berry **9 brewer's horse** i.e., one that is old, withered, and decrepit **14 given** inclined

19 compass reasonable limits; also, in Bardolph's speech, girth, circumference **25 admiral** flagship. **lantern** i.e., a light for the rest of the fleet to follow; here applied to Bardolph's inflamed nose, red from overdrinking **30–31 memento mori** reminder of death, such as a death's head or a skull engraved on a seal ring **32 Dives** the rich man who went to hell, referred to in Luke 16:19–31 **34–35 By . . . angel** (A biblical echo, perhaps to Psalms 104:4, Hebrews 1:7, or Exodus 3:2.) **36 given over** abandoned to wickedness **39 ignis fatuus** will-o'-the-wisp **39–40 wildfire** fireworks; lightning; will-o'-the-wisp **41 triumph** procession led by torches **42 links** torches, flares **45 good cheap** cheap. **dearest** most expensive **46 salamander** lizard reputed to be able to live in fire **49 I . . . belly** (A proverb meaning *I wish I were rid of this irritation;* stock response to an insult based on physical deformity.) **52 Partlet** (Traditional name of a hen.) **57 tithe** tenth part

FALSTAFF Go to, I know you well enough.

HOSTESS No, Sir John, you do not know me, Sir John. I know you, Sir John. You owe me money, Sir John, and now you pick a quarrel to beguile me of it. I bought you a dozen of shirts to your back.

FALSTAFF Dowlas, filthy dowlas. I have given them away to bakers' wives; they have made bolters of them.

HOSTESS Now, as I am a true woman, holland of eight shillings an ell. You owe money here besides, Sir John, for your diet and by-drinkings, and money lent you, four and twenty pound.

FALSTAFF He had his part of it. Let him pay.

HOSTESS He? Alas, he is poor, he hath nothing.

FALSTAFF How, poor? Look upon his face. What call you rich? Let them coin his nose, let them coin his cheeks. I'll not pay a denier. What, will you make a younker of me? Shall I not take mine ease in mine inn but I shall have my pocket pick'd? I have lost a seal-ring of my grandfather's worth forty mark.

HOSTESS O Jesu, I have heard the Prince tell him, I know not how oft, that that ring was copper!

FALSTAFF How? The Prince is a Jack, a sneak-up. 'Sblood, an he were here, I would cudgel him like a dog, if he would say so.

Enter the Prince [with Peto], marching, and Falstaff meets them playing upon his truncheon like a fife.

How now, lad, is the wind in that door, i' faith? Must we all march?

BARDOLPH Yea, two and two, Newgate fashion.

HOSTESS My lord, I pray you hear me.

PRINCE What say'st thou, Mistress Quickly? How doth thy husband? I love him well; he is an honest man.

HOSTESS Good my lord, hear me.

FALSTAFF Prithee let her alone, and list to me.

PRINCE What say'st thou, Jack?

FALSTAFF The other night I fell asleep here behind the arras and had my pocket pick'd. This house is turn'd bawdy-house; they pick pockets.

PRINCE What didst thou lose, Jack?

FALSTAFF Wilt thou believe me, Hal? Three or four bonds of forty pound apiece, and a seal-ring of my grandfather's.

PRINCE A trifle, some eight-penny matter.

HOSTESS So I told him, my lord, and I said I heard your Grace say so; and, my lord, he speaks most vilely of you, like a foul-mouth'd man as he is, and said he would cudgel you.

PRINCE What? He did not?

HOSTESS There's neither faith, truth, nor womanhood in me else.

FALSTAFF There's no more faith in thee than in a stew'd prune, nor no more truth in thee than in a drawn fox; and for womanhood, Maid Marian may be the deputy's wife of the ward to thee. Go, you thing, go.

HOSTESS Say, what thing? What thing?

FALSTAFF What thing? Why, a thing to thank God on.

HOSTESS I am no thing to thank God on, I would thou shouldst know it! I am an honest man's wife, and, setting thy knighthood aside, thou art a knave to call me so.

FALSTAFF Setting thy womanhood aside, thou art a beast to say otherwise.

HOSTESS Say, what beast, thou knave, thou?

FALSTAFF What beast? Why, an otter.

PRINCE An otter, Sir John! Why an otter?

FALSTAFF Why, she's neither fish nor flesh; a man knows not where to have her.

HOSTESS Thou art an unjust man in saying so. Thou or any man knows where to have me, thou knave, thou!

PRINCE Thou say'st true, hostess, and he slanders thee most grossly.

HOSTESS So he doth you, my lord, and said this other day you ought him a thousand pound.

PRINCE Sirrah, do I owe you a thousand pound?

FALSTAFF A thousand pound, Hal? A million! Thy love is worth a million; thou owest me thy love.

HOSTESS Nay, my lord, he call'd you Jack, and said he would cudgel you.

FALSTAFF Did I, Bardolph?

BARDOLPH Indeed, Sir John, you said so.

FALSTAFF Yea, if he said my ring was copper.

PRINCE I say 'tis copper. Darest thou be as good as thy word now?

FALSTAFF Why, Hal, thou knowest, as thou art but man, I dare; but as thou art prince, I fear thee as I fear the roaring of the lion's whelp.

PRINCE And why not as the lion?

FALSTAFF The King himself is to be fear'd as the lion. Dost thou think I'll fear thee as I fear thy father? Nay, an I do, I pray God my girdle break.

PRINCE O, if it should, how would thy guts fall about thy knees! But, sirrah, there's no room for faith, truth, nor honesty in this bosom of thine; it is all fill'd up with guts and midriff. Charge an honest woman with picking thy pocket! Why, thou whoreson, impudent, emboss'd rascal, if there were anything in thy pocket but tavern-reckonings, memorandums of bawdy-houses, and one poor pennyworth of sugar-candy to make thee long-winded, if thy pocket were enrich'd with any other injuries but these, I am a villain. And yet you will stand to it; you will not pocket up wrong. Art thou not asham'd?

FALSTAFF Dost thou hear, Hal? Thou knowest in the state of innocency Adam fell; and what should poor Jack Falstaff do in the days of villainy? Thou seest I

69 Dowlas a coarse kind of linen **70 bolters** cloths for sifting flour **72 holland** fine linen **73 ell** a measure of 45 inches **74 by-drinkings** drinks between meals **80 denier** one twelfth of a French sou; type of very small coin **81 younker** i.e., greenhorn **86 Jack** knave, rascal. **sneak-up** sneak **88 s.d. truncheon** officer's staff **89 door** i.e., quarter **91 Newgate** (A famous city prison in London. Prisoners marched two by two.) **113–114 stew'd prune** (Customarily associated with bawdy houses.)

114 drawn fox fox driven from cover and wily in getting back **115–116 Maid . . . thee** i.e., Maid Marian, disreputable woman in Robin Hood ballads, morris dances, and the like, was a model of respectability compared with you **129 have** understand (with suggestion of enjoying sexually) **135 ought** owed **158 emboss'd** swollen (with fat) **162 injuries** i.e., those things you claim to have lost, thereby suffering harm **163 stand to it** make a stand, insist on your supposed rights. **pocket up** endure silently

have more flesh than another man, and therefore more frailty. You confess then you pick'd my pocket?

PRINCE It appears so by the story.

FALSTAFF Hostess, I forgive thee. Go make ready breakfast. Love thy husband, look to thy servants, cherish thy guests. Thou shalt find me tractable to any honest
reason; thou seest I am pacified still. Nay, prithee, be 174
gone. *(Exit Hostess.)* Now, Hal, to the news at court: for the robbery, lad, how is that answer'd?

PRINCE O, my sweet beef, I must still be good angel to thee. The money is paid back again.

FALSTAFF O, I do not like that paying back. 'Tis a double labor.

PRINCE I am good friends with my father and may do anything.

FALSTAFF Rob me the exchequer the first thing thou
doest, and do it with unwash'd hands too. 184

BARDOLPH Do, my lord.

PRINCE I have procur'd thee, Jack, a charge of foot. 186

FALSTAFF I would it had been of horse. Where shall I find one that can steal well? O for a fine thief, of the age of two and twenty or thereabouts! I am heinously
unprovided. Well, God be thank'd for these rebels, 190
they offend none but the virtuous. I laud them, I praise them.

PRINCE Bardolph!

BARDOLPH My lord?

PRINCE
Go bear this letter to Lord John of Lancaster,
To my brother John; this to my Lord of
 Westmorland. [*Gives letters. Exit Bardolph.*]
Go, Peto, to horse, to horse, for thou and I
Have thirty miles to ride yet ere dinner-time.
 [*Exit Peto.*]
Jack, meet me tomorrow in the Temple Hall 199
At two o'clock in the afternoon.
There shalt thou know thy charge, and there receive
Money and order for their furniture. 202
The land is burning. Percy stands on high,
And either we or they must lower lie. [*Exit.*]

FALSTAFF
Rare words! Brave world! Hostess, my breakfast,
 come! 205
O, I could wish this tavern were my drum! [*Exit.*] 206

[ACT IV • SCENE I]

[*Enter Hotspur, Worcester, and Douglas.*]

HOTSPUR
Well said, my noble Scot. If speaking truth
In this fine age were not thought flattery,
Such attribution should the Douglas have 3
As not a soldier of this season's stamp 4
Should go so general current through the world. 5
By God, I cannot flatter; I do defy 6
The tongues of soothers! But a braver place 7
In my heart's love hath no man than yourself.
Nay, task me to my word; approve me, lord. 9

DOUGLAS
Thou art the king of honor.
No man so potent breathes upon the ground
But I will beard him.

Enter one [*a Messenger*] *with letters.*

HOTSPUR Do so, and 'tis well.— 12
What letters hast thou there?—I can but thank you.

MESSENGER
These letters come from your father.

HOTSPUR
Letters from him! Why comes he not himself?

MESSENGER
He cannot come, my lord. He is grievous sick.

HOTSPUR
'Zounds! How has he the leisure to be sick
In such a justling time? Who leads his power? 18
Under whose government come they along?

MESSENGER
His letters bears his mind, not I, my lord.
 [*Hotspur reads the letter.*]

WORCESTER
I prithee tell me, doth he keep his bed?

MESSENGER
He did, my lord, four days ere I set forth,
And at the time of my departure thence
He was much fear'd by his physicians. 24

WORCESTER
I would the state of time had first been whole 25
Ere he by sickness had been visited.
His health was never better worth than now.

HOTSPUR
Sick now? Droop now? This sickness doth infect
The very life-blood of our enterprise;
'Tis catching hither, even to our camp.
He writes me here that inward sickness—
And that his friends by deputation could not 32
So soon be drawn, nor did he think it meet 33
To lay so dangerous and dear a trust
On any soul remov'd but on his own.
Yet doth he give us bold advertisement 36
That with our small conjunction we should on, 37
To see how fortune is dispos'd to us;
For, as he writes, there is no quailing now,
Because the King is certainly possess'd 40
Of all our purposes. What say you to it?

WORCESTER
Your father's sickness is a maim to us.

174 still always **184 with unwash'd hands** i.e., at once **186 charge of foot** command of a company of infantry **190 unprovided** unprepared **199 Temple Hall** i.e., at the Inner Temple, one of the Inns of Court **202 furniture** equipment, furnishing **205 Brave** splendid **206 drum** (Possibly Falstaff means that he wishes he could continue to enjoy this tavern instead of risking his life in battle.)

IV.i. Location: The rebel camp near Shrewsbury.
3 attribution praise, tribute

4 stamp coinage **5 go . . . current** be so widely accepted and acclaimed. (Continues the metaphor of coinage.) **6 defy** proclaim against **7 soothers** flatterers. **braver** better, dearer **9 task . . . word** challenge me to make good my word. **approve** test **12 But . . . him** but that I will defy him **18 justling** jostling, busy **24 fear'd** feared for **25 time** the times **32 by deputation** through deputies **33 drawn** assembled **36 advertisement** counsel, advice **37 conjunction** joint force **40 possess'd** informed

HOTSPUR
A perilous gash, a very limb lopp'd off.
And yet, in faith, it is not! His present want
Seems more than we shall find it. Were it good
To set the exact wealth of all our states
All at one cast? To set so rich a main
On the nice hazard of one doubtful hour?
It were not good, for therein should we read
The very bottom and the soul of hope,
The very list, the very utmost bound
Of all our fortunes.

DOUGLAS
Faith, and so we should;
Where now remains a sweet reversion,
We may boldly spend upon the hope
Of what is to come in.
A comfort of retirement lives in this.

HOTSPUR
A rendezvous, a home to fly unto,
If that the devil and mischance look big
Upon the maidenhead of our affairs.

WORCESTER
But yet I would your father had been here.
The quality and hair of our attempt
Brooks no division. It will be thought
By some, that know not why he is away,
That wisdom, loyalty, and mere dislike
Of our proceedings kept the Earl from hence.
And think how such an apprehension
May turn the tide of fearful faction
And breed a kind of question in our cause.
For well you know we of the off'ring side
Must keep aloof from strict arbitrement,
And stop all sight-holes, every loop from whence
The eye of reason may pry in upon us.
This absence of your father's draws a curtain
That shows the ignorant a kind of fear
Before not dreamt of.

HOTSPUR
You strain too far.
I rather of his absence make this use:
It lends a luster and more great opinion,
A larger dare to our great enterprise,
Than if the Earl were here; for men must think,
If we without his help can make a head
To push against a kingdom, with his help
We shall o'erturn it topsy-turvy down.
Yet all goes well, yet all our joints are whole.

DOUGLAS
As heart can think. There is not such a word
Spoke of in Scotland as this term of fear.

Enter Sir Richard Vernon.

HOTSPUR
My cousin Vernon, welcome, by my soul.

VERNON
Pray God my news be worth a welcome, lord.
The Earl of Westmorland, seven thousand strong,
Is marching hitherwards; with him Prince John.

HOTSPUR
No harm. What more?

VERNON
And further I have learn'd
The King himself in person is set forth,
Or hitherwards intended speedily,
With strong and mighty preparation.

HOTSPUR
He shall be welcome too. Where is his son,
The nimble-footed madcap Prince of Wales,
And his comrades, that daff'd the world aside
And bid it pass?

VERNON
All furnish'd, all in arms;
All plum'd like estridges, that with the wind
Bated like eagles having lately bath'd,
Glittering in golden coats, like images,
As full of spirit as the month of May
And gorgeous as the sun at midsummer;
Wanton as youthful goats, wild as young bulls.
I saw young Harry, with his beaver on,
His cushes on his thighs, gallantly arm'd,
Rise from the ground like feathered Mercury,
And vaulted with such ease into his seat
As if an angel dropp'd down from the clouds
To turn and wind a fiery Pegasus
And witch the world with noble horsemanship.

HOTSPUR
No more, no more! Worse than the sun in March
This praise doth nourish agues. Let them come.
They come like sacrifices in their trim,
And to the fire-ey'd maid of smoky war
All hot and bleeding will we offer them.
The mailed Mars shall on his altar sit
Up to the ears in blood. I am on fire
To hear this rich reprisal is so nigh,
And yet not ours. Come, let me taste my horse,
Who is to bear me like a thunderbolt
Against the bosom of the Prince of Wales.
Harry to Harry shall, hot horse to horse,
Meet and ne'er part till one drop down a corse.
O that Glendower were come!

VERNON
There is more news:
I learn'd in Worcester, as I rode along,
He cannot draw his power this fourteen days.

DOUGLAS
That's the worst tidings that I hear of yet.

WORCESTER
Ay, by my faith, that bears a frosty sound.

HOTSPUR
What may the King's whole battle reach unto?

44 want absence **46 To . . . states** to stake the absolute total of our resources **47 cast** throw of the dice. **main** stake in gambling; also, an army **48 nice** precarious, delicate **51 list** limit **53 reversion** (Literally, part of an estate yet to be inherited.) **56 retirement** something to fall back on **58 big** threatening **59 maidenhead** i.e., commencement **61 hair** kind, nature **62 Brooks** tolerates **64 mere** absolute **67 fearful faction** timid support **69 off'ring side** side which attacks **70 strict arbitrement** just inquiry or investigation **71 loop** loophole **73 draws** draws aside, opens **77 opinion** renown **80 make a head** raise an armed force **83 Yet** still. **joints** limbs

92 intended i.e., intends to come **96 daff'd** put aside with a gesture **97 furnish'd** equipped **98 estridges** ostriches. (Refers to ostrich plumes on crests.) **99 Bated** flapped their wings. (From falconry.) **100 images** gilded statues **103 Wanton** sportive, frolicsome **104 beaver** visor; hence, helmet **105 cushes** cuisses, armor for the thighs **107 seat** i.e., saddle **109 wind** wheel. **Pegasus** winged horse of Greek mythology **110 witch** bewitch **111–112 Worse . . . agues** (The spring sun was believed to give impetus to chills and fevers, by drawing up vapors.) **113 trim** fine apparel, trappings **114 maid** i.e., Bellona, goddess of war **116 mailed** dressed in mail, armor **118 reprisal** prize **126 draw his power** muster his army **129 battle** army

VERNON
To thirty thousand.

HOTSPUR Forty let it be!
My father and Glendower being both away,
The powers of us may serve so great a day.
Come, let us take a muster speedily.
Doomsday is near; die all, die merrily.

DOUGLAS
Talk not of dying. I am out of fear
Of death or death's hand for this one half year.

Exeunt.

[SCENE II]

Enter Falstaff, [and] Bardolph.

FALSTAFF Bardolph, get thee before to Coventry; fill me a bottle of sack. Our soldiers shall march through; we'll to Sutton Co'fil' tonight.

BARDOLPH Will you give me money, captain?

FALSTAFF Lay out, lay out.

BARDOLPH This bottle makes an angel.

FALSTAFF An if it do, take it for thy labor; an if it make twenty, take them all; I'll answer the coinage. Bid my lieutenant Peto meet me at town's end.

BARDOLPH I will, captain. Farewell. *Exit.*

FALSTAFF If I be not asham'd of my soldiers, I am a sous'd gurnet. I have misus'd the King's press damnably. I have got, in exchange of a hundred and fifty soldiers, three hundred and odd pounds. I press me none but good householders, yeomen's sons, inquire me out contracted bachelors, such as had been ask'd twice on the banns—such a commodity of warm slaves as had as lief hear the devil as a drum, such as fear the report of a caliver worse than a struck fowl or a hurt wild duck. I press'd me none but such toasts-and-butter, with hearts in their bellies no bigger than pins' heads, and they have bought out their services; and now my whole charge consists of ancients, corporals, lieutenants, gentlemen of companies—slaves as ragged as Lazarus in the painted cloth, where the glutton's dogs lick'd his sores, and such as indeed were never soldiers, but discarded unjust servingmen, younger sons to younger brothers, revolted tapsters, and ostlers trade-fall'n, the cankers of a calm world and a long peace, ten times more dishonorable ragged than an old feaz'd ancient. And such have I, to fill up the rooms of them as have bought out their services, that you would think that I had a hundred and fifty totter'd prodigals lately come from swine-keeping, from eating draff and husks. A mad fellow met me on the way and told me I had unloaded all the gibbets and press'd the dead bodies. No eye hath seen such scarecrows. I'll not march through Coventry with them, that's flat. Nay, and the villains march wide betwixt the legs, as if they had gyves on, for indeed I had the most of them out of prison. There's not a shirt and a half in all my company, and the half shirt is two napkins tack'd together and thrown over the shoulders like a herald's coat without sleeves; and the shirt, to say the truth, stol'n from my host at Saint Albans, or the red-nose innkeeper of Daventry. But that's all one, they'll find linen enough on every hedge.

Enter the Prince [and the] Lord of Westmorland.

PRINCE How now, blown Jack? How now, quilt?

FALSTAFF What, Hal? How now, mad wag? What a devil dost thou in Warwickshire? My good Lord of Westmorland, I cry you mercy. I thought your honor had already been at Shrewsbury.

WESTMORLAND Faith, Sir John, 'tis more than time that I were there, and you too; but my powers are there already. The King, I can tell you, looks for us all. We must away all night.

FALSTAFF Tut, never fear me. I am as vigilant as a cat to steal cream.

PRINCE I think, to steal cream indeed, for thy theft hath already made thee butter. But tell me, Jack, whose fellows are these that come after?

FALSTAFF Mine, Hal, mine.

PRINCE I did never see such pitiful rascals.

FALSTAFF Tut, tut; good enough to toss; food for powder, food for powder. They'll fill a pit as well as better. Tush, man, mortal men, mortal men.

WESTMORLAND Ay, but, Sir John, methinks they are exceeding poor and bare, too beggarly.

FALSTAFF Faith, for their poverty, I know not where they had that, and for their bareness, I am sure they never learn'd that of me.

PRINCE No, I'll be sworn, unless you call three fingers in the ribs bare. But, sirrah, make haste. Percy is already in the field. *Exit.*

FALSTAFF What, is the King encamp'd?

WESTMORLAND He is, Sir John. I fear we shall stay too long. *[Exit.]*

FALSTAFF Well,
To the latter end of a fray and the beginning of a feast
Fits a dull fighter and a keen guest. *Exit.*

IV.ii. Location: A public road near Coventry.
3 Sutton Co'fil' Sutton Coldfield, in Warwickshire near Coventry **5 Lay out** i.e., pay for it yourself **6 makes an angel** i.e., makes ten shillings I've spent for you. (But Falstaff answers as though Bardolph had profited from the transaction.) **8 answer** be responsible for **12 sous'd gurnet** a kind of pickled fish. **King's press** royal warrant for the impressment of troops **14 press** draft, conscript **15 yeomen's** small freeholders' **16 contracted** engaged to be married **17 banns** public announcements, declared on three Sundays in succession, of an intent to marry. **warm** i.e., loving their comfort **19 caliver** musket. **struck** wounded **22 bought . . . services** i.e., paid, bribed, to be released from military duty **23 charge** company, troop. **ancients** ensigns, standardbearers. (By appointing a disproportionate number of junior officers, Falstaff has made it possible to collect for himself their more substantial pay.) **24 gentlemen of companies** gentlemen volunteers **25 painted cloth** cheap hangings for a room. (For the story of Lazarus the beggar and Dives the rich man, see Luke 16:19–31.) **27 unjust** dishonest **28 revolted** runaway **29 trade-fall'n** unemployed. **cankers** cankerworms that destroy leaves and buds. (Used figuratively.)

31 feaz'd ancient frayed flag **33 totter'd** tattered **34 prodigals** (See Luke 15:15–16.) **35 draff** hogwash **40 gyves** fetters **45, 46 Saint Albans, Daventry** (Towns north and west of London, on the road to Coventry.) **47 hedge** (Where wet linen was spread out to dry.) **48 blown** swollen, inflated; also, short of wind **51 cry you mercy** beg your pardon **56 must away** must march **57 fear** worry about **64 toss** i.e., on a pike

[SCENE III]

Enter Hotspur, Worcester, Douglas, [and] Vernon.

HOTSPUR
We'll fight with him tonight.
WORCESTER It may not be.
DOUGLAS
You give him then advantage.
VERNON Not a whit.
HOTSPUR
Why say you so? Looks he not for supply?
VERNON
So do we.
HOTSPUR His is certain, ours is doubtful.
WORCESTER
Good cousin, be advis'd, stir not tonight.
VERNON
Do not, my lord.
DOUGLAS You do not counsel well.
You speak it out of fear and cold heart.
VERNON
Do me no slander, Douglas. By my life,
And I dare well maintain it with my life,
If well-respected honor bid me on,
I hold as little counsel with weak fear
As you, my lord, or any Scot that this day lives.
Let it be seen tomorrow in the battle
Which of us fears.
DOUGLAS Yea, or tonight.
VERNON Content.
HOTSPUR
Tonight, say I.
VERNON
Come, come, it may not be. I wonder much,
Being men of such great leading as you are,
That you foresee not what impediments
Drag back our expedition. Certain horse
Of my cousin Vernon's are not yet come up.
Your uncle Worcester's horse came but today,
And now their pride and mettle is asleep,
Their courage with hard labor tame and dull,
That not a horse is half the half of himself.
HOTSPUR
So are the horses of the enemy
In general journey-bated and brought low.
The better part of ours are full of rest.
WORCESTER
The number of the King exceedeth our.
For God's sake, cousin, stay till all come in.
The trumpet sounds a parley.

Enter Sir Walter Blunt.

BLUNT
I come with gracious offers from the King,
If you vouchsafe me hearing and respect.
HOTSPUR
Welcome, Sir Walter Blunt; and would to God
You were of our determination!
Some of us love you well; and even those some
Envy your great deservings and good name
Because you are not of our quality,
But stand against us like an enemy.
BLUNT
And God defend but still I should stand so,
So long as out of limit and true rule
You stand against anointed majesty.
But to my charge. The King hath sent to know
The nature of your griefs, and whereupon
You conjure from the breast of civil peace
Such bold hostility, teaching his duteous land
Audacious cruelty. If that the King
Have any way your good deserts forgot,
Which he confesseth to be manifold,
He bids you name your griefs, and with all speed
You shall have your desires with interest
And pardon absolute for yourself and these
Herein misled by your suggestion.
HOTSPUR
The King is kind; and well we know the King
Knows at what time to promise, when to pay.
My father and my uncle and myself
Did give him that same royalty he wears,
And when he was not six-and-twenty strong,
Sick in the world's regard, wretched and low,
A poor unminded outlaw sneaking home,
My father gave him welcome to the shore;
And when he heard him swear and vow to God
He came but to be Duke of Lancaster,
To sue his livery and beg his peace,
With tears of innocency and terms of zeal,
My father, in kind heart and pity mov'd,
Swore him assistance, and perform'd it too.
Now when the lords and barons of the realm
Perceiv'd Northumberland did lean to him,
The more and less came in with cap and knee,
Met him in boroughs, cities, villages,
Attended him on bridges, stood in lanes,
Laid gifts before him, proffer'd him their oaths,
Gave him their heirs as pages, followed him
Even at the heels in golden multitudes.
He presently, as greatness knows itself,
Steps me a little higher than his vow
Made to my father, while his blood was poor,
Upon the naked shore at Ravenspurgh,
And now, forsooth, takes on him to reform
Some certain edicts and some strait decrees
That lie too heavy on the commonwealth,
Cries out upon abuses, seems to weep
Over his country's wrongs; and by this face,

IV.iii. Location: The rebel camp near Shrewsbury.
3 supply reinforcements **10 well-respected** well weighed or considered **17 leading** leadership **19 expedition** speedy progress. **horse** cavalry **26 journey-bated** tired from the journey **28 our** our number **29 s.d. parley** trumpet summons to a conference

33 determination persuasion (in the fight) **34 those some** i.e., those few others who dislike you **36 quality** party **38 defend** forbid **51 suggestion** instigation **62 sue his livery** sue as an heir come of age for the delivery of his lands. **beg his peace** i.e., request to be reconciled to King Richard **68 more and less** persons of all ranks. **with . . . knee** i.e., with cap in hand and with bended knee **70 stood in lanes** stood row-deep along the roads **72 Gave . . . heirs** i.e., to serve him **73 golden** majestic **74 knows itself** perceives its own strength **75 Steps me** i.e., steps. (*Me* is the ethical dative.) **76 blood** spirit, temper. **poor** i.e., unambitious **79 strait** strict **82 face** show, pretense

This seeming brow of justice, did he win
The hearts of all that he did angle for;
Proceeded further—cut me off the heads
Of all the favorites that the absent King
In deputation left behind him here,
When he was personal in the Irish war.

BLUNT
Tut, I came not to hear this.

HOTSPUR
Then to the point.
In short time after, he depos'd the King,
Soon after that, depriv'd him of his life,
And in the neck of that task'd the whole state;
To make that worse, suff'red his kinsman March—
Who is, if every owner were well plac'd,
Indeed his king—to be engag'd in Wales,
There without ransom to lie forfeited;
Disgrac'd me in my happy victories,
Sought to entrap me by intelligence;
Rated mine uncle from the council-board;
In rage dismiss'd my father from the court;
Broke oath on oath, committed wrong on wrong,
And in conclusion drove us to seek out
This head of safety, and withal to pry
Into his title, the which we find
Too indirect for long continuance.

BLUNT
Shall I return this answer to the King?

HOTSPUR
Not so, Sir Walter. We'll withdraw awhile.
Go to the King; and let there be impawn'd
Some surety for a safe return again,
And in the morning early shall mine uncle
Bring him our purposes. And so farewell.

BLUNT
I would you would accept of grace and love.

HOTSPUR
And may be so we shall.

BLUNT
Pray God you do. [*Exeunt.*]

[SCENE IV]

Enter [*the*] *Archbishop of York,* [*and*] *Sir Michael.*

ARCHBISHOP [*Giving letters*]
Hie, good Sir Michael, bear this sealed brief
With winged haste to the Lord Marshal;
This to my cousin Scroop, and all the rest
To whom they are directed. If you knew
How much they do import, you would make haste.

SIR MICHAEL
My good lord, I guess their tenor.

ARCHBISHOP
Like enough you do.
Tomorrow, good Sir Michael, is a day
Wherein the fortune of ten thousand men
Must bide the touch; for, sir, at Shrewsbury,
As I am truly given to understand,
The King with mighty and quick-raised power
Meets with Lord Harry. And I fear, Sir Michael,
What with the sickness of Northumberland,
Whose power was in the first proportion,
And what with Owen Glendower's absence thence,
Who with them was a rated sinew too
And comes not in, o'er-rul'd by prophecies,
I fear the power of Percy is too weak
To wage an instant trial with the King.

SIR MICHAEL
Why, my good lord, you need not fear;
There is Douglas and Lord Mortimer.

ARCHBISHOP
No, Mortimer is not there.

SIR MICHAEL
But there is Mordake, Vernon, Lord Harry Percy,
And there is my Lord of Worcester, and a head
Of gallant warriors, noble gentlemen.

ARCHBISHOP
And so there is. But yet the King hath drawn
The special head of all the land together:
The Prince of Wales, Lord John of Lancaster,
The noble Westmorland, and warlike Blunt,
And many moe corrivals and dear men
Of estimation and command in arms.

SIR MICHAEL
Doubt not, my lord, they shall be well oppos'd.

ARCHBISHOP
I hope no less, yet needful 'tis to fear;
And, to prevent the worst, Sir Michael, speed.
For if Lord Percy thrive not, ere the King
Dismiss his power he means to visit us,
For he hath heard of our confederacy,
And 'tis but wisdom to make strong against him.
Therefore make haste. I must go write again
To other friends; and so farewell, Sir Michael.
Exeunt.

[ACT V • SCENE I]

Enter the King, Prince of Wales, Lord John of Lancaster, Sir Walter Blunt, [*and*] *Falstaff.*

KING
How bloodily the sun begins to peer
Above yon busky hill! The day looks pale
At his distemp'rature.

PRINCE
The southern wind
Doth play the trumpet to his purposes,

85 cut me i.e., cut **88 personal** in person **92 in . . . that** next, immediately after. **task'd** laid taxes upon **95 engag'd** held as hostage **97 happy** fortunate **98 intelligence** secret information, i.e., from spies **99 Rated** scolded **103 head of safety** armed force for our protection **108 impawn'd** pledged

IV.iv. Location: York. The Archbishop's palace.
1 brief letter, dispatch **2 Lord Marshal** i.e., Thomas Mowbray, son of the Duke of Norfolk who is exiled in *Richard II*, and a longtime enemy of the new King **3 Scroop** i.e., perhaps Sir Stephen Scroop of *Richard II*, III.ii.91–218, or Lord Scroop of Masham of *Henry V*, II.ii

10 bide the touch be put to the test (like gold) **15 in . . . proportion** of the largest size **17 rated sinew** main strength or support reckoned upon **25 head** troop **31 moe corrivals** more partners in the enterprise **32 estimation** reputation, importance **37 he** i.e., the King

V.i. Location: The King's camp near Shrewsbury.
2 busky bosky, bushy **3 his distemp'rature** i.e., the sun's unhealthy appearance **4 trumpet** trumpeter. **his** its, the sun's

And by his hollow whistling in the leaves
Foretells a tempest and a blust'ring day.

KING
Then with the losers let it sympathize,
For nothing can seem foul to those that win.
The trumpet sounds.

Enter Worcester [and Vernon].

How now, my Lord of Worcester? 'Tis not well
That you and I should meet upon such terms
As now we meet. You have deceiv'd our trust,
And made us doff our easy robes of peace
To crush our old limbs in ungentle steel.
This is not well, my lord, this is not well.
What say you to it? Will you again unknit
This churlish knot of all-abhorred war,
And move in that obedient orb again 17
Where you did give a fair and natural light,
And be no more an exhal'd meteor, 19
A prodigy of fear, and a portent 20
Of broached mischief to the unborn times? 21

WORCESTER
Hear me, my liege:
For mine own part, I could be well content
To entertain the lag-end of my life 24
With quiet hours, for I protest
I have not sought the day of this dislike.

KING
You have not sought it? How comes it, then?

FALSTAFF Rebellion lay in his way, and he found it.

PRINCE Peace, chewet, peace! 29

WORCESTER
It pleas'd your Majesty to turn your looks
Of favor from myself and all our house;
And yet I must remember you, my lord, 32
We were the first and dearest of your friends.
For you my staff of office did I break
In Richard's time, and posted day and night
To meet you on the way, and kiss your hand,
When yet you were in place and in account
Nothing so strong and fortunate as I.
It was myself, my brother, and his son
That brought you home, and boldly did outdare
The dangers of the time. You swore to us,
And you did swear that oath at Doncaster,
That you did nothing purpose 'gainst the state,
Nor claim no further than your new-fall'n right, 44
The seat of Gaunt, dukedom of Lancaster.
To this we swore our aid. But in short space
It rain'd down fortune show'ring on your head,
And such a flood of greatness fell on you—
What with our help, what with the absent King,
What with the injuries of a wanton time, 50
The seeming sufferances that you had borne, 51
And the contrarious winds that held the King
So long in his unlucky Irish wars
That all in England did repute him dead—
And from this swarm of fair advantages
You took occasion to be quickly woo'd
To gripe the general sway into your hand;
Forgot your oath to us at Doncaster;
And being fed by us you us'd us so
As that ungentle gull, the cuckoo's bird, 60
Useth the sparrow; did oppress our nest,
Grew by our feeding to so great a bulk
That even our love durst not come near your sight 63
For fear of swallowing; but with nimble wing
We were enforc'd, for safety sake, to fly
Out of your sight and raise this present head, 66
Whereby we stand opposed by such means 67
As you yourself have forg'd against yourself
By unkind usage, dangerous countenance, 69
And violation of all faith and troth
Sworn to us in your younger enterprise.

KING
These things indeed you have articulate, 72
Proclaim'd at market-crosses, read in churches,
To face the garment of rebellion 74
With some fine color that may please the eye 75
Of fickle changelings and poor discontents, 76
Which gape and rub the elbow at the news 77
Of hurlyburly innovation. 78
And never yet did insurrection want 79
Such water-colors to impaint his cause, 80
Nor moody beggars, starving for a time
Of pellmell havoc and confusion.

PRINCE
In both your armies there is many a soul 83
Shall pay full dearly for this encounter,
If once they join in trial. Tell your nephew
The Prince of Wales doth join with all the world
In praise of Henry Percy. By my hopes, 87
This present enterprise set off his head, 88
I do not think a braver gentleman,
More active-valiant or more valiant-young,
More daring or more bold, is now alive
To grace this latter age with noble deeds.
For my part, I may speak it to my shame,
I have a truant been to chivalry;
And so I hear he doth account me too.
Yet this before my father's Majesty:
I am content that he shall take the odds
Of his great name and estimation, 98
And will, to save the blood on either side,
Try fortune with him in a single fight.

KING
And, Prince of Wales, so dare we venture thee,

17 orb orbit, sphere of action **19 exhal'd meteor** (Meteors were believed to be vapors drawn up or *exhal'd* by the sun and visible as streaks of light; they were regarded as ill omens.) **20 prodigy of fear** fearful omen **21 broached** set flowing, already begun **24 entertain** occupy **29 chewet** chough, jackdaw. (Here, a chatterer.) **32 remember** remind **44 new-fall'n** recently inherited (by the death of John of Gaunt) **50 injuries** abuses, evils. **wanton** lawless **51 sufferances** suffering, distress

60 ungentle gull rude young bird, still unfledged. **cuckoo's bird** cuckoo's young offspring. (The cuckoo lays its eggs in other birds' nests.) **63 our love** we in our love **66 head** armed force **67 opposed . . . means** in opposition to you, using such means **69 dangerous** menacing **72 articulate** set forth, specified **74 face** trim, adorn **75 color** (1) hue (2) specious appearance **76 changelings** turncoats **77 rub the elbow** i.e., hug themselves with delight **78 innovation** rebellion **79 want** lack **80 water-colors** i.e., thin excuses. (See *color*, l. 75.) **83 both your** i.e., your and our **87 hopes** i.e., hopes of salvation **88 This . . . head** i.e., if this present rebellion is taken from his account, not held against him **98 estimation** reputation

Albeit considerations infinite
Do make against it. No, good Worcester, no,
We love our people well; even those we love
That are misled upon your cousin's part.
And, will they take the offer of our grace,
Both he and they and you, yea, every man
Shall be my friend again, and I'll be his.
So tell your cousin, and bring me word
What he will do. But if he will not yield,
Rebuke and dread correction wait on us,
And they shall do their office. So, be gone.
We will not now be troubled with reply.
We offer fair; take it advisedly.

Exeunt Worcester [*and Vernon*].

PRINCE
It will not be accepted, on my life.
The Douglas and the Hotspur both together
Are confident against the world in arms.

KING
Hence, therefore, every leader to his charge;
For, on their answer, will we set on them,
And God befriend us as our cause is just!

Exeunt. Manent Prince, Falstaff.

FALSTAFF Hal, if thou see me down in the battle and bestride me, so; 'tis a point of friendship.

PRINCE Nothing but a colossus can do thee that friendship. Say thy prayers, and farewell.

FALSTAFF I would 'twere bed-time, Hal, and all well.

PRINCE Why, thou owest God a death. [*Exit.*]

FALSTAFF 'Tis not due yet; I would be loath to pay him before his day. What need I be so forward with him that calls not on me? Well, 'tis no matter; honor pricks me on. Yea, but how if honor prick me off when I come on? How then? Can honor set to a leg? No. Or an arm? No. Or take away the grief of a wound? No. Honor hath no skill in surgery, then? No. What is honor? A word. What is in that word honor? What is that honor? Air. A trim reckoning! Who hath it? He that died a' Wednesday. Doth he feel it? No. Doth he hear it? No. 'Tis insensible, then? Yea, to the dead. But will it not live with the living? No. Why? Detraction will not suffer it. Therefore I'll none of it. Honor is a mere scutcheon. And so ends my catechism.

Exit.

[SCENE II]

Enter Worcester, [*and*] *Sir Richard Vernon.*

WORCESTER
O, no, my nephew must not know, Sir Richard,
The liberal and kind offer of the King.

VERNON
'Twere best he did.

WORCESTER Then are we all undone.
It is not possible, it cannot be,
The King should keep his word in loving us;
He will suspect us still and find a time
To punish this offense in other faults.
Supposition all our lives shall be stuck full of eyes;
For treason is but trusted like the fox,
Who, never so tame, so cherish'd, and lock'd up,
Will have a wild trick of his ancestors.
Look how we can, or sad or merrily,
Interpretation will misquote our looks,
And we shall feed like oxen at a stall,
The better cherish'd still the nearer death.
My nephew's trespass may be well forgot;
It hath the excuse of youth and heat of blood,
And an adopted name of privilege,
A hare-brain'd Hotspur, govern'd by a spleen.
All his offenses live upon my head
And on his father's. We did train him on,
And, his corruption being ta'en from us,
We as the spring of all shall pay for all.
Therefore, good cousin, let not Harry know
In any case the offer of the King.

Enter Hotspur [*and Douglas, with soldiers*].

VERNON
Deliver what you will; I'll say 'tis so.
Here comes your cousin.

HOTSPUR My uncle is return'd.
Deliver up my Lord of Westmorland.
Uncle, what news?

WORCESTER
The King will bid you battle presently.

DOUGLAS
Defy him by the Lord of Westmorland.

HOTSPUR
Lord Douglas, go you and tell him so.

DOUGLAS
Marry, and shall, and very willingly. *Exit Douglas.*

WORCESTER
There is no seeming mercy in the King.

HOTSPUR
Did you beg any? God forbid!

WORCESTER
I told him gently of our grievances,
Of his oath-breaking, which he mended thus,
By now forswearing that he is forsworn.
He calls us rebels, traitors, and will scourge
With haughty arms this hateful name in us.

Enter Douglas.

DOUGLAS
Arm, gentlemen, to arms! For I have thrown

102 Albeit although. (But sometimes interpreted as meaning *were it not that.*) **111 wait on us** are in attendance upon us **122 so** well and good **126 thou . . . death** (Proverbial, with a pun on *debt.*) **130 prick me off** mark me off (as one dead) **131 set to** graft on **132 grief** pain **138 Detraction** slander **140 scutcheon** heraldic emblem carried in funerals, displayed on coaches, etc.; it was the lowest form of symbol, having no pennon or other insignia

V.ii. Location: Near the rebel camp.

8 Supposition suspicous conjecture **10 never so** however **12 or sad** either sad **18 adopted . . . privilege** i.e., a nickname, "hotspur," to justify his rashness **19 spleen** hot temper **21 train** incite, draw **22 his . . . us** i.e., since his guilt originated in us **23 spring** source **26 Deliver** report **28 Deliver up** release (as hostage; see IV.iii.108–109)

A brave defiance in King Henry's teeth,
And Westmorland, that was engag'd, did bear it;
Which cannot choose but bring him quickly on.

WORCESTER
The Prince of Wales stepp'd forth before the King,
And, nephew, challeng'd you to single fight.

HOTSPUR
O, would the quarrel lay upon our heads,
And that no man might draw short breath today
But I and Harry Monmouth! Tell me, tell me,
How show'd his tasking? Seem'd it in contempt?

VERNON
No, by my soul. I never in my life
Did hear a challenge urg'd more modestly,
Unless a brother should a brother dare
To gentle exercise and proof of arms.
He gave you all the duties of a man,
Trimm'd up your praises with a princely tongue,
Spoke your deservings like a chronicle,
Making you ever better than his praise
By still dispraising praise valued with you;
And, which became him like a prince indeed,
He made a blushing cital of himself,
And chid his truant youth with such a grace
As if he mast'red there a double spirit
Of teaching and of learning instantly.
There did he pause. But let me tell the world,
If he outlive the envy of this day,
England did never owe so sweet a hope,
So much misconstrued in his wantonness.

HOTSPUR
Cousin, I think thou art enamored
On his follies. Never did I hear
Of any prince so wild a liberty.
But be he as he will, yet once ere night
I will embrace him with a soldier's arm,
That he shall shrink under my courtesy.
Arm, arm with speed! And, fellows, soldiers,
friends,
Better consider what you have to do
Than I, that have not well the gift of tongue,
Can lift your blood up with persuasion.

Enter a Messenger.

FIRST MESSENGER
My lord, here are letters for you.

HOTSPUR
I cannot read them now.
O gentlemen, the time of life is short!
To spend that shortness basely were too long
If life did ride upon a dial's point,
Still ending at the arrival of an hour.
An if we live, we live to tread on kings;
If die, brave death, when princes die with us!
Now, for our consciences, the arms are fair
When the intent of bearing them is just.

Enter another [Messenger].

SECOND MESSENGER
My lord, prepare. The King comes on apace.

HOTSPUR
I thank him that he cuts me from my tale,
For I profess not talking. Only this—
Let each man do his best. And here draw I
A sword, whose temper I intend to stain
With the best blood that I can meet withal
In the adventure of this perilous day.
Now, Esperance! Percy! And set on.
Sound all the lofty instruments of war,
And by that music let us all embrace;
For, heaven to earth, some of us never shall
A second time do such a courtesy.

Here they embrace. [*Exeunt.*]

[SCENE III]

The trumpets sound. The King enters with his power [and passes over the stage]. Alarum to the battle. Then enter Douglas and Sir Walter Blunt [dressed like King Henry].

BLUNT
What is thy name, that in the battle thus
Thou crossest me? What honor dost thou seek
Upon my head?

DOUGLAS
Know then, my name is Douglas,
And I do haunt thee in the battle thus
Because some tell me that thou art a king.

BLUNT
They tell thee true.

DOUGLAS
The Lord of Stafford dear today hath bought
Thy likeness, for instead of thee, King Harry,
This sword hath ended him. So shall it thee,
Unless thou yield thee as my prisoner.

BLUNT
I was not born a yielder, thou proud Scot,
And thou shalt find a king that will revenge
Lord Stafford's death. *They fight. Douglas kills Blunt.*

Then enter Hotspur.

HOTSPUR
O Douglas, hadst thou fought at Holmedon thus,
I never had triumph'd upon a Scot.

DOUGLAS
All's done, all's won; here breathless lies the King.

HOTSPUR
Where?

42 brave proud **43 engag'd** held as hostage **50 tasking** challenge **52 urg'd** put forward **54 proof** test **55 duties** due merits **59 dispraising** disparaging. **valued** compared **61 cital** impeachment **64 instantly** simultaneously **66 envy** hostility **67 owe** own **68 wantonness** playful sportiveness **71 liberty** licentiousness **83 If** even if. **dial's point** hand of watch or clock **84 Still . . . hour** ineluctably concluding within an hour's time **86 brave** glorious

87 for as for. **fair** just **99 heaven to earth** i.e., I'll wager heaven against earth

V.iii. Location: Shewsbury field.
s.d. power army. **Alarum** trumpet signal to advance

DOUGLAS
Here.

HOTSPUR
This, Douglas? No. I know this face full well.
A gallant knight he was; his name was Blunt,
Semblably furnish'd like the King himself.

DOUGLAS
A fool go with thy soul, whither it goes!
A borrowed title hast thou bought too dear.
Why didst thou tell me that thou wert a king?

HOTSPUR
The King hath many marching in his coats.

DOUGLAS
Now, by my sword, I will kill all his coats!
I'll murder all his wardrobe, piece by piece,
Until I meet the King.

HOTSPUR
Up, and away!
Our soldiers stand full fairly for the day. *[Exeunt.]*

Alarum. Enter Falstaff, solus.

FALSTAFF Though I could scape shot-free at London, I fear the shot here; here's no scoring but upon the pate. Soft, who are you? Sir Walter Blunt. There's honor for you. Here's no vanity! I am as hot as molten lead, and as heavy too. God keep lead out of me! I need no more weight than mine own bowels. I have led my ragamuffins where they are pepper'd. There's not three of my hundred and fifty left alive, and they are for the town's end, to beg during life. But who comes here?

Enter the Prince.

PRINCE
What, stands thou idle here? Lend me thy sword.
Many a nobleman lies stark and stiff
Under the hoofs of vaunting enemies,
Whose deaths are yet unreveng'd. I prithee,
Lend me thy sword.

FALSTAFF O Hal, I prithee, give me leave to breathe awhile. Turk Gregory never did such deeds in arms as I have done this day. I have paid Percy, I have made him sure.

PRINCE
He is, indeed, and living to kill thee.
I prithee, lend me thy sword.

FALSTAFF Nay, before God, Hal, if Percy be alive, thou gets not my sword; but take my pistol, if thou wilt.

PRINCE
Give it me. What, is it in the case?

FALSTAFF Ay, Hal, 'tis hot, 'tis hot. There's that will sack a city.

The Prince draws it out, and finds it to be a bottle of sack.

PRINCE
What, is it a time to jest and dally now?
He throws the bottle at him. Exit.

FALSTAFF Well, if Percy be alive, I'll pierce him. If he do come in my way, so; if he do not, if I come in his willingly, let him make a carbonado of me. I like not such grinning honor as Sir Walter hath. Give me life, which if I can save, so; if not, honor comes unlook'd for, and there's an end. *[Exit.]*

[SCENE IV]

Alarum. Excursions. Enter the King, the Prince, Lord John of Lancaster, [and] Earl of Westmorland.

KING
I prithee,
Harry, withdraw thyself; thou bleedest too much.
Lord John of Lancaster, go you with him.

LANCASTER
Not I, my lord, unless I did bleed too.

PRINCE
I beseech your Majesty make up,
Lest your retirement do amaze your friends.

KING
I will do so.
My Lord of Westmorland, lead him to his tent.

WESTMORLAND
Come, my lord, I'll lead you to your tent.

PRINCE
Lead me, my lord? I do not need your help.
And God forbid a shallow scratch should drive
The Prince of Wales from such a field as this,
Where stain'd nobility lies trodden on,
And rebels' arms triumph in massacres!

LANCASTER
We breathe too long. Come, cousin Westmorland,
Our duty this way lies. For God's sake, come.
[Exeunt Prince John and Westmorland.]

PRINCE
By God, thou hast deceiv'd me, Lancaster!
I did not think thee lord of such a spirit.
Before, I lov'd thee as a brother, John,
But now, I do respect thee as my soul.

KING
I saw him hold Lord Percy at the point
With lustier maintenance than I did look for
Of such an ungrown warrior.

PRINCE
O, this boy lends mettle to us all! *Exit.*

[Enter Douglas.]

21 Sembably furnish'd similarly accoutered **22 A . . . soul** i.e., may the stigma of "fool" accompany your soul (for having dressed as a decoy of King Henry) **29 stand . . . day** i.e., seem in an auspicious position, likely to win the victory **30 shot-free** without paying the tavern bill **31 scoring** (1) cutting (2) marking up of charges, by notches on a stick or on the inn door **33 vanity** trifling **38 town's end** i.e., city gate, frequented by beggars **45 Turk Gregory** (Possibly a sort of combined allusion to the famous Pope Gregory the Great and to the Grand Turk.) **46–47 made him sure** made sure of him. (But Hal takes *sure* in a different sense, meaning "safe.")

56 Percy . . . pierce (Elizabethan pronunciation rendered the pun more obvious than it is now.) **58 carbonado** meat scored across for broiling

V.iv. Location: Scene continues at Shrewsbury field.
s.d. Excursions sorties. (The fallen body of Blunt may be removed at some point, or may be on stage still in V.iv when Hal kills Hotspur.) **5 make up** go forward **6 amaze** alarm **22 lustier maintenance** more vigorous bearing

DOUGLAS
Another king? They grow like Hydra's heads.
I am the Douglas, fatal to all those
That wear those colors on them. What art thou
That counterfeit'st the person of a king?

KING
The King himself, who, Douglas, grieves at heart
So many of his shadows thou hast met
And not the very King. I have two boys
Seek Percy and thyself about the field;
But, seeing thou fall'st on me so luckily,
I will assay thee and defend thyself.

DOUGLAS
I fear thou art another counterfeit;
And yet, in faith, thou bearest thee like a king.
But mine I am sure thou art, whoe'er thou be,
And thus I win thee.
They fight; the King being in danger, enter Prince of Wales.

PRINCE
Hold up thy head, vile Scot, or thou art like
Never to hold it up again! The spirits
Of valiant Shirley, Stafford, Blunt, are in my arms.
It is the Prince of Wales that threatens thee,
Who never promiseth but he means to pay.
They fight. Douglas flieth.
Cheerly, my lord. How fares your Grace?
Sir Nicholas Gawsey hath for succor sent,
And so hath Clifton. I'll to Clifton straight.

KING
Stay, and breathe awhile.
Thou hast redeem'd thy lost opinion,
And show'd thou mak'st some tender of my life
In this fair rescue thou hast brought to me.

PRINCE
O God, they did me too much injury
That ever said I heark'ned for your death.
If it were so, I might have let alone
The insulting hand of Douglas over you,
Which would have been as speedy in your end
As all the poisonous potions in the world,
And sav'd the treacherous labor of your son.

KING
Make up to Clifton; I'll to Sir Nicholas Gawsey.
Exit King.

Enter Hotspur.

HOTSPUR
If I mistake not, thou art Harry Monmouth.

PRINCE
Thou speak'st as if I would deny my name.

HOTSPUR
My name is Harry Percy.

PRINCE
Why, then I see
A very valiant rebel of the name.
I am the Prince of Wales; and think not, Percy,
To share with me in glory any more.
Two stars keep not their motion in one sphere,
Nor can one England brook a double reign
Of Harry Percy and the Prince of Wales.

HOTSPUR
Nor shall it, Harry, for the hour is come
To end the one of us; and would to God
Thy name in arms were now as great as mine!

PRINCE
I'll make it greater ere I part from thee,
And all the budding honors on thy crest
I'll crop to make a garland for my head.

HOTSPUR
I can no longer brook thy vanities. *They fight.*

Enter Falstaff.

FALSTAFF Well said, Hal! To it, Hal! Nay, you shall find no boy's play here, I can tell you.

Enter Douglas. He fighteth with Falstaff, who falls down as if he were dead. [*Exit Douglas.*] *The Prince killeth Percy.*

HOTSPUR
O, Harry, thou hast robb'd me of my youth!
I better brook the loss of brittle life
Than those proud titles thou hast won of me;
They wound my thoughts worse than thy sword my flesh.
But thoughts, the slaves of life, and life, time's fool,
And time, that takes survey of all the world,
Must have a stop. O, I could prophesy,
But that the earthy and cold hand of death
Lies on my tongue. No, Percy, thou art dust,
And food for— [*Dies.*]

PRINCE
For worms, brave Percy. Fare thee well, great heart!
Ill-weav'd ambition, how much art thou shrunk!
When that this body did contain a spirit,
A kingdom for it was too small a bound;
But now two paces of the vilest earth
Is room enough. This earth that bears thee dead
Bears not alive so stout a gentleman.
If thou wert sensible of courtesy,
I should not make so dear a show of zeal.
But let my favors hide thy mangled face;
And, even in thy behalf, I'll thank myself
For doing these fair rites of tenderness.
[*He covers Hotspur's face with a scarf or other favor.*]
Adieu, and take thy praise with thee to heaven!
Thy ignominy sleep with thee in the grave,
But not remember'd in thy epitaph!
He spieth Falstaff on the ground.
What, old acquaintance? Could not all this flesh
Keep in a little life? Poor Jack, farewell!
I could have better spar'd a better man.

25 Hydra's heads (The heads of the Lernaean Hydra grew again as fast as they were cut off.) **30 shadows** likenesses **32 Seek** who seek **34 assay** challenge **48 opinion** reputation **49 mak'st . . . of** have some care for **52 heark'ned** listened (as for welcome news) **54 insulting** exulting

66 brook endure **81 thoughts . . . fool** i.e., our mental consciousness, which is dependent on physical existence, and our life itself, which is subject to time **93 stout** valiant **94 sensible of courtesy** i.e., able to hear my praise **95 dear** handsome, rich. **zeal** admiration **96 favors** plume, scarf, glove, or similar article

O, I should have a heavy miss of thee
If I were much in love with vanity!
Death hath not struck so fat a deer today,
Though many dearer, in this bloody fray.
Embowel'd will I see thee by and by.
Till then in blood by noble Percy lie. *Exit.*

Falstaff riseth up.

FALSTAFF Embowel'd! If thou embowel me today, I'll give you leave to powder me and eat me too tomorrow. 'Sblood, 'twas time to counterfeit, or that hot termagant Scot had paid me scot and lot too. Counterfeit? I lie, I am no counterfeit. To die is to be a counterfeit, for he is but the counterfeit of a man who hath not the life of a man; but to counterfeit dying, when a man thereby liveth, is to be no counterfeit, but the true and perfect image of life indeed. The better part of valor is discretion, in the which better part I have sav'd my life. 'Zounds, I am afraid of this gunpowder Percy, though he be dead. How if he should counterfeit too and rise? By my faith, I am afraid he would prove the better counterfeit. Therefore I'll make him sure; yea, and I'll swear I kill'd him. Why may not he rise as well as I? Nothing confutes me but eyes, and nobody sees me. Therefore, sirrah [*Stabbing him*], with a new wound in your thigh, come you along with me.

He takes up Hotspur on his back.

Enter Prince [and] John of Lancaster.

PRINCE
Come, brother John; full bravely hast thou flesh'd
Thy maiden sword.

LANCASTER But, soft, whom have we here?
Did you not tell me this fat man was dead?

PRINCE
I did; I saw him dead,
Breathless and bleeding on the ground. Art thou alive?
Or is it fantasy that plays upon our eyesight?
I prithee, speak. We will not trust our eyes
Without our ears. Thou art not what thou seem'st.

FALSTAFF No, that's certain, I am not a double man; but if I be not Jack Falstaff, then am I a Jack. There is Percy [*Throwing the body down*]. If your father will do me any honor, so; if not, let him kill the next Percy himself. I look to be either earl or duke, I can assure you.

PRINCE
Why, Percy I kill'd myself and saw thee dead.

FALSTAFF Didst thou? Lord, Lord, how this world is given to lying! I grant you I was down and out of breath, and so was he; but we rose both at an instant and fought a long hour by Shrewsbury clock. If I may be believ'd, so; if not, let them that should reward valor bear the sin upon their own heads. I'll take it upon my death, I gave him this wound in the thigh. If the man were alive and would deny it, 'zounds, I would make him eat a piece of my sword.

LANCASTER
This is the strangest tale that ever I heard.

PRINCE
This is the strangest fellow, brother John.
Come, bring your luggage nobly on your back.
For my part, if a lie may do thee grace,
I'll gild it with the happiest terms I have.

A retreat is sounded.

The trumpet sounds retreat; the day is our.
Come, brother, let us to the highest of the field,
To see what friends are living, who are dead.

Exeunt [Prince of Wales and Lancaster].

FALSTAFF I'll follow, as they say, for reward. He that rewards me, God reward him! If I do grow great, I'll grow less; for I'll purge, and leave sack, and live cleanly as a nobleman should do.

Exit [with body].

[SCENE V]

The trumpets sound. Enter the King, Prince of Wales, Lord John of Lancaster, Earl of Westmorland, with Worcester and Vernon prisoners.

KING
Thus ever did rebellion find rebuke.
Ill-spirited Worcester! Did not we send grace,
Pardon, and terms of love to all of you?
And wouldst thou turn our offers contrary?
Misuse the tenor of thy kinsman's trust?
Three knights upon our party slain today,
A noble earl, and many a creature else
Had been alive this hour,
If like a Christian thou hadst truly borne
Betwixt our armies true intelligence.

WORCESTER
What I have done my safety urg'd me to;
And I embrace this fortune patiently,
Since not to be avoided it falls on me.

KING
Bear Worcester to the death and Vernon too.
Other offenders we will pause upon.

[Exeunt Worcester and Vernon, guarded.]

How goest the field?

PRINCE
The noble Scot, Lord Douglas, when he saw
The fortune of the day quite turn'd from him,
The noble Percy slain, and all his men
Upon the foot of fear, fled with the rest;
And falling from a hill, he was so bruis'd

105 heavy (1) serious (2) corpulent **106 vanity** frivolity **109 Embowel'd** disemboweled, i.e., for embalming and burial **112 powder** salt **113–114 termagent** violent. (Derived from the name of a heathen god of the Saracens in medieval drama.) **114 scot and lot** i.e., completely. ("Scot" and "lot" were parish taxes.) **119 part** quality **129 flesh'd** initiated (in battle) **137 double man** (1) specter (2) two men **138 Jack** knave

155 grace credit **157 our** ours **158 highest** highest vantage point **162 purge** (1) reduce in weight, using laxatives (2) repent

V.v. Location: The command post of the King.
5 Misuse . . . trust i.e., abuse Hotspur's confidence (by concealing the generosity of my offer, in your role as emissary) **20 Upon . . . fear** fearfully in flight

That the pursuers took him. At my tent
The Douglas is; and I beseech your Grace
I may dispose of him.

KING With all my heart.

PRINCE
Then, brother John of Lancaster, to you
This honorable bounty shall belong. 26
Go to the Douglas, and deliver him
Up to his pleasure, ransomless and free.
His valors shown upon our crests today
Have taught us how to cherish such high deeds
Even in the bosom of our adversaries.

LANCASTER
I thank your Grace for this high courtesy,
Which I shall give away immediately. 33

KING
Then this remains, that we divide our power.
You, son John, and my cousin Westmorland
Towards York shall bend you with your dearest speed,
To meet Northumberland and the prelate Scroop,
Who, as we hear, are busily in arms.
Myself and you, son Harry, will towards Wales,
To fight with Glendower and the Earl of March.
Rebellion in this land shall lose his sway,
Meeting the check of such another day;
And since this business so fair is done,
Let us not leave till all our own be won. *Exeunt.* 44

26 bounty assignment, act of benevolence **33 give away** report (to the Douglas) **44 leave** leave off

The Second Part of King Henry the Fourth

Shakespeare wrote *2 Henry IV* quite soon after *1 Henry IV,* perhaps in 1597, partly no doubt to capitalize on the enormous theatrical success of Falstaff, partly to finish the story of Falstaff's rejection. (He also devoted some time during this period, perhaps at Queen Elizabeth's request, to the pleasant task of showing Falstaff in love; for a discussion of the probable sequence of events, and the creating of new "humors" types like Pistol and Nym, see the introduction to *The Merry Wives of Windsor.*) In writing *2 Henry IV,* Shakespeare drew on materials similar to those used for *1 Henry IV,* notably Holinshed and *The Famous Victories of Henry V.* Moreover, he undertook to write a play that structurally is much like its predecessor, revealing more similarity between plays than one can find elsewhere in Shakespeare. Even the three *Henry VI* plays do not reiterate structural patterns to the same degree. Is Shakespeare repeating himself, rewriting the earlier play, and if so why? Is *2 Henry IV* essentially a way of giving audiences more of what they had found so entertaining in the earlier play?

The structural pattern runs as follows. In both plays, Shakespeare alternates between scenes of political seriousness and scenes of comic irresponsibility, juxtaposing a rebellion in the land with a rebellion in the King's own family. In *1 Henry IV* we move from a council of war (I,i) to a planning of the robbery at Gad's Hill (I,ii). The scenes comment on one another by their nearness and by their mutual concern with lawlessness. Similarly in *2 Henry IV* we are at first introduced to a political rebellion in the north of England, after which we encounter Falstaff and Prince Hal's Page. In both plays, Act II scene ii shows us Hal with Poins, setting up a future meeting to discomfit Falstaff, and in both plays Act II scene iv is a long, centrally-located scene at the tavern involving Hal and Falstaff in a contest of wits devised to expose Falstaff as a resourceful liar. The festivities of both scenes are brought to an end by a knocking at the door. (The act-scene divisions are probably not Shakespeare's, for they do not appear in the early quartos of either play; nevertheless, the structural location of these scenes is similar.) Between these linked scenes of comic action, we turn in both plays to the rebel camp of the Percies for a discussion of military planning against King Henry (II,iii). In both plays Falstaff goes off supposedly to fight against the rebels, but instead manages to abuse his authority as recruiting officer and to garner undeserved honors, either through wounding the dead Hotspur in the leg or through capturing Colevile of the Dale with the aid of an inflated reputation. The battle scenes are punctuated by Falstaff's wry soliloquies; his disputation on wine in *2 Henry IV* (IV,iii) serves a function like that of his better-known catechism on honor in *1 Henry IV* (V,i). Both plays give us a climactic turning in the confrontation between Hal and his father; the son is penitent for his waywardness, the father lectures on statecraft, and the prodigal son is recovered into kingly grace. Hal goes on thereafter to win public honor and to prove himself his father's true son. Even the rejection of Falstaff, with which the second play ends, finds its counterpart in *1 Henry IV* in Hal's impatience with Falstaff during the battle of Shrewsbury, his elegy over the seemingly dead body of his onetime companion, and his resolve to be henceforth a prince.

These resemblances, and still others, are further highlighted when we realize that Shakespeare continues to use in his second play the structural device of foils, or paired characters around Hal who help define alternative models of conduct. The father is, as before, an awesome figure of authority, one whose sternness Hal never fully adopts and yet one whose public role as king Hal must inherit. Falstaff, as before, offers himself as a companion in revelry, dissipation, and *joie de vivre,* and must be rejected even though much of what he says offers insight into the coldness of King Henry and especially of Hal's dutiful brother Prince John. Yet the chief purpose of these recapitulations is to state profound differences. *2 Henry IV* does not simply go over familiar material. Repeatedly, the similarities of situation reveal how much Hal has still to learn, how much Falstaff has changed, and how much more complicated the political process is than it first appeared. The foils in this play set off not honor, as in *1 Henry IV,* but two related matters: rumor or reputation, and justice.

Rumor begins the play—quite literally, since Rumor is presented to us in allegorized form as portrayed by Virgil, painted full of tongues, spreading false information about the battle of Shrewsbury just ended. Rumor takes particular delight in its most cruel trick of all, raising false hopes and then dashing them. In the scene following at the Percies' household, we see rumor as it manifests itself in the real world of men, beguiling Northumberland with the "news" of his son Hotspur's triumph only to disappoint him afterwards with the stark truth of defeat and death. What is the function of the uncharacteristic allegory at the start of this play? It serves first to establish a new dispiriting tone. The rebels are in disarray, their cause in jeopardy. Hotspur is dead, and with him has died the bright honor of his cause. His kinsmen, always more Machiavellian than he, are now warier than ever. Northumberland is persuaded, in a later scene, to prevaricate to his allies and withdraw to Scotland when they most need his support, waiting to come in on their side only when he can be sure of success. The atmosphere of *Realpolitik* and of dealing in false appearances is a consequence of a world governed by rumor. The rebels' case is never as attractive in this play as in *1 Henry IV;* Hotspur's idealism and chivalry are sorely missed.

Rumor has profound consequences for the King's side as well, and for Falstaff and Prince Hal. Falstaff rides on false reputation through the early scenes of *2 Henry IV.* He evades arrest at the hands of the Lord Chief Justice because of his presumed deeds at Shrewsbury, deeds which we know to be illusory. His day's service at Shrewsbury "hath a little gilded over" his "night's exploits on Gad's Hill," as the Lord Chief Justice reluctantly concedes (I,ii). His reputation makes possible his capture of Colevile of the Dale at Gaultree Forest, even though by this time Falstaff's reputation is clearly beginning to wear thin.

Conversely, Hal discovers that his reputation for prodigality will not leave him. Despite the fact that the King has severed Falstaff from Hal (I,ii), so that Hal scarcely knows of Falstaff's whereabouts until he agrees to a kind of reunion for old times' sake at the tavern, Hal begins to realize that everyone assumes the worst of him and expects his future reign to be one of continual riot. He himself characterizes his visit to the tavern, in order to see Falstaff again, as a base "transformation" like those Ovidian portrayals of Jove in lowly human disguise. Talking with Poins in II,ii, Hal professes to be "exceeding weary" of the "disgrace" it is in him to remember all his vile companions, including Poins, and he sardonically congratulates his companion on thinking like everyone else when Poins assumes that any weeping on Hal's part for his father's death would be no more than princely hypocrisy. "Let the end try the man," says Hal, in what should be a plain notice of his reformation, but no one credits him with sincerity. When his father does take to his deathbed, surrounded by hushed courtiers, Hal, until now notably absent from court, enters with exaggerated offhandedness as though eschewing the show of mourning which he knows cannot be believed in him. His taking the crown from the pillow of his seemingly dead father strikes King Henry and his courtiers as one last confirmation of Hal's desire to supplant the father, and indeed we too are forced to wonder at Hal's imprudence. (The parricidal overtones in one of Shakespeare's sources, *The Famous Victories of Henry V,* are much more on the surface than in Shakespeare's play.)

The structural recapitulations of *2 Henry IV,* then, in which Hal first jests with Falstaff at the tavern and afterwards confronts his father at court, are no mere repetitions; they stress the dreary fact that a reputation for riotous conduct persists, that a father's embracing of his son must lapse into renewed distrust, that "reformation" is not the simple process Hal once supposed. Reformation is first a matter of improving one's own conduct, but it is also a matter of improving one's image. This is not a happy revelation to a young man impatient of ceremony and public display, but it is the way of the world, and an integral part of any successful kingship. King Henry's last advice to Hal, in fact, once they have been reconciled anew, concerns the manipulations of appearances in the name of statecraft; the father urges the son to resolve civil strife by going to war against some foreign enemy. He must "busy giddy minds With foreign quarrels" (IV,v). Hal will adopt this stratagem in *Henry V* by warring against the French. Meantime, in *2 Henry IV,* he must overcome his reputation not only with his father but with the Lord Chief Justice, his brother John, and the nobles of the court. Not until the play's end do they believe other than that Hal will turn riot lose in his kingdom. The intransigent nature of false "rumor" or reputation does much to explain why the new king must reject Falstaff so publicly and so sharply. He has in fact already rejected Falstaff in the sense of leaving him, but no one has taken the point—least of all Falstaff, who now presses in upon the new king with hopes of reward and license to act as he pleases. "The laws of England are at my commandment," he exults (V,iii). Only a public repudiation can meet the demands of kingship by making full use of the act's symbolic value. Hal must reject Falstaff not only in his heart but in the view of his nation. It is a distasteful act, perhaps to him as to us, but is made necessary by the political exigencies of the moment.

The play's concern with justice emerges in the first confrontation between the Lord Chief Justice and Falstaff (I,ii). The one represents law, the other license. Who is to represent and administer the law in Henry V's reign? The Lord Chief Justice is a firm and austere figure, a deputy or substitute for the father-king, one who has presumed to imprison Hal for resisting his authority. This Lord Chief Justice does not expect to remain in office once the new king is crowned; like other serious characters in the play, and ourselves as well, he longs for reassurance in the troubled times of civil war and change of administration under a monarchy. In contrast to this somewhat awesome parental figure, Falstaff offers hedonism and irresponsibility. His wit is in a sense no less engaging than in *1 Henry IV.* His scenes with Shallow and Silence, as they choose soldiers for the upcoming campaign or prepare for the golden time they anticipate, are as funny as the best of Falstaff. The pairing of the Lord Chief Justice and Falstaff as foils might suggest at first that one is lacking where the other is strong, and that Hal must steer between extremes.

Yet this play does not give us a genuine debate on justice like that on honor in *1 Henry IV,* where Falstaff's comments on honor strike home because of Hotspur's fanaticism. The Lord Chief Justice of this play is essentially in the right, however austere, and Falstaff is essentially in the wrong, however funny. The Lord Chief Justice sees through Falstaff, and patiently bides his time. Falstaff's excesses are more pronounced than in the earlier play. We see him with Doll Tearsheet, a whore, in maudlin, drunken conversation. He is associated with images of disease—gout, the pox or syphilis, consumption, lameness—and of purging. His lying is not as consistently clever as before. Hal recalls the brilliant lie about the Gad's Hill robbery, and credits Falstaff with having seen through the Prince's trick on that occasion (II,iv), but in the second tavern scene Falstaff can only mutter incoherently that he had no idea that Hal was behind him in disguise listening to his foul-mouthed reproaches. Falstaff's rioting with Pistol disturbs the peace, and in such brawls homicides occur necessitating arrest and punishment (V,iv). When Falstaff appears with the diminutive Page, as in scene ii, we are forcefully reminded of the grossness of his body, though he too laughs at this. His mooching off Mistress Quickly, and his breach of promise of marriage to her, though hinted at in the earlier play, are much more open here; the humor is keen, but we cannot forget that Falstaff is victimizing a woman. Law suits and arrests are more prominent in this play than in its predecessor. Falstaff's abuse of authority to recruit soldiers, about which he discourses wittily in the earlier play, is here fully shown both in its hilarity and in its lawless consequences.

Falstaff's new companions, Pistol, Doll, and then Justice Shallow and Justice Silence, sharpen our perception of Falstaff's increasingly flagrant lawlessness. Shallow and Silence are, by their very profession, counterparts to the Lord Chief Justice. In their complacent interest in their own prosperity ("How a good yoke of bullocks at Stamford fair?" III,ii), in their countenancing of bribery by their subordinates (V,i), and in Shallow's foxy aspirations to deceive Falstaff before Falstaff can deceive him, these pillars of rural respectability reveal how far injustice has permeated the English countryside. They are fit companions for Falstaff when he hears the news of his rejection, and are suitably victimized by Falstaff's inability to repay a loan advanced to him from motives of self-interest. These old men, myopically recollecting the jolly days of their youth, accentuate Falstaff's physical frailty and aging. Falstaff mocks the stories of their escapades, but he too, as he confesses to Doll over his drink, is old. The necessary course of justice is made plain by the structural configurations of the play. Falstaff and his companions seek lawlessness and must be rebuked; the Lord Chief Justice, who fears rejection, must instead be embraced by Hal explicitly as a father-figure ("You shall be as a father to my youth," V,ii) in order to reaffirm public decency. The Lord Chief Justice is to bear "the balance and the sword" as emblems of justice and its stern role in maintaining order; Falstaff is dismissed as "the tutor and feeder of my riots." These necessities are plain, even though they do not answer the emotionally complicated issue of Hal's (and our) fondness for the companion of his youth.

Hal's brother, Prince John of Lancaster, is another opposite to Falstaff. Here the contrast is less prejudicial to Falstaff. Prince John takes charge of his ailing father's wars, and engineers a surrender of the rebels at Gaultree Forest that is a triumph of equivocation and double dealing. It also saves the nation from further civil conflict, at least for the time being, and establishes the peace which Hal inherits and turns to his advantage against France. What are we to make of what has been called John's "dastardly treachery"? It seems all too much in keeping with the *Realpolitik* that has characterized the conduct of both sides heretofore, and may thus be said to be a suitable conclusion. The "revolutions of the times" (III,i) are those in which friendships cool and dire prophecies from the days of Richard II are recalled. The only justification possible for what John does is that it succeeds. It surely lacks the glory and honor attendant on the conflict of Hal and Hotspur in *1 Henry IV*. Not coincidentally, Hal is far away from Gaultree Forest when this dismal surrender is brought about. Prince John is a master at knowing how to "construe the times in their necessities" (IV,i). His acts scarcely represent justice any more than honor. "Is this proceeding just and honorable?" ask the betrayed rebels (IV,ii), and are answered merely "Is your assembly so?" The end justifies the means. Falstaff's observations at Prince John's expense therefore have point. John is, as Falstaff characterizes him, "sober blooded"; he drinks no wine, and relies not on valor but on sagacity. Falstaff hopes that Hal will prove more valiant, tempering "the cold blood he did naturally inherit of his father" (IV,iii) with the imbibing of sherry and other pleasures learned from Falstaff. Whatever the merits of drinking as an inducement to courage, we do perceive that Prince John is too much his father's son, and that Hal will avoid this cold extreme in his quest for a kingly identity that is both symbol and substance.

Hal has thus learned something from Falstaff, if only as a caution against extremes, and partly for this reason his rejection of Falstaff must come as a shock no matter how inevitable and "right." Hal may well appear to dwindle in the process, for he has given up a good deal of his private self to adopt the public role thrust upon him. He accepts that public role not unwillingly, but may also perceive that he does so at some cost to himself—and to Falstaff. His terms of rejection are not wholly ungenerous—he allows the possibility of Falstaff's returning to court if he reforms, and makes financial allowance so that Falstaff will have no need to continue in crime—but the finality of the action remains stunning. We are left with a broken Falstaff, trying to deceive himself into believing that all will be well, and with intimations of a French war that will absorb the energies of the new king and his father's erstwhile political enemies as well. The emergence of Hal into his public role is complete.

The Second Part of King Henry the Fourth

The Actors' Names

RUMOR, *the Presenter.*
KING HENRY THE FOURTH.
PRINCE HENRY, *afterwards crowned* KING HENRY THE FIFTH.

PRINCE JOHN OF LANCASTER,
HUMPHREY [DUKE] OF GLOUCESTER,
THOMAS [DUKE] OF CLARENCE,
} *sons to Henry IV and brethren to Henry V.*

[EARL OF] NORTHUMBERLAND,
[SCROOP,] THE ARCHBISHOP OF YORK,
[LORD] MOWBRAY,
[LORD] HASTING,
LORD BARDOLPH,
TRAVERS,
MORTON,
[SIR JOHN] COLEVILE,
} *opposites against King Henry IV.*

[EARL OF] WARWICK,
[EARL OF] WESTMORLAND,
[EARL OF] SURREY,
GOWER,
HARCOURT,
[BLUNT,]
LORD CHIEF JUSTICE,
[*His* SERVANT,]
} *of the King's party.*

POINS
[SIR JOHN] FALSTAFF,
BARDOLPH,
PISTOL,
PETO,
[FALSTAFF'S] PAGE,
} *irregular humorists.*

SHALLOW,
SILENCE,
} *both country justices.*

DAVY, *servant to Shallow.*
FANG *and* SNARE, *two sergeants.*
MOULDY, SHADOW, WART, FEEBLE, [*and*] BULLCALF, *country soldiers.*
[FRANCIS, *a drawer.*]

NORTHUMBERLAND'S WIFE.
PERCY'S WIDOW [LADY PERCY].
HOSTESS QUICKLY.
DOLL TEARSHEET.

[LORDS *and* ATTENDANTS; PORTER,] DRAWERS, BEADLES, GROOMS, [*etc.*]
[*A Dancer, speaker of the*] EPILOGUE.

[SCENE: *England.*]

[INDUCTION]

Enter Rumor, painted full of tongues.

RUMOR

Open your ears, for which of you will stop
The vent of hearing when loud Rumor speaks?
I, from the orient to the drooping west,
Making the wind my post-horse, still unfold 4
The acts commenced on this ball of earth.
Upon my tongues continual slanders ride,
The which in every language I pronounce,
Stuffing the ears of men with false reports.
I speak of peace, while covert enmity
Under the smile of safety wounds the world.
And who but Rumor, who but only I,
Make fearful musters and prepar'd defense,
Whiles the big year, swoll'n with some other grief, 13
Is thought with child by the stern tyrant War,
And no such matter? Rumor is a pipe
Blown by surmises, jealousies, conjectures, 16
And of so easy and so plain a stop 17
That the blunt monster with uncounted heads, 18
The still-discordant wav'ring multitude,
Can play upon it. But what need I thus 20
My well-known body to anatomize 21
Among my household? Why is Rumor here? 22
I run before King Harry's victory,
Who in a bloody field by Shrewsbury
Hath beaten down young Hotspur and his troops,
Quenching the flame of bold rebellion
Even with the rebels' blood. But what mean I
To speak so true at first? My office is
To noise abroad that Harry Monmouth fell 29
Under the wrath of noble Hotspur's sword,
And that the King before the Douglas' rage
Stoop'd his anointed head as low as death.
This have I rumor'd through the peasant towns 33
Between that royal field of Shrewsbury
And this worm-eaten hold of ragged stone, 35
Where Hotspur's father, old Northumberland,
Lies crafty-sick. The posts come tiring on, 37

Induction. Location: Although the allegory of Rumor, based ultimately on Virgil's depiction of *Fama* as full of eyes, ears, and tongues, in the *Aeneid* (iv. 179–190), is timeless, Rumor is here represented as standing in front of Northumberland's castle, Warkworth. The play is supposed to open immediately after the battle of Shrewsbury, in which Henry Percy, or Hotspur, and the Scottish Earl of Douglas have been overthrown. We are concerned first of all with the news of the battle, with which *1 Henry IV* ended.
4 still continually **13 big** swollen, pregnant with disaster **16 jealousies** suspicions **17 of . . . stop** i.e., whose stops or openings are so easily played on **18 blunt** stupid, dull-witted **20 what** why **21 anatomize** lay open minutely, explain **22 household** retinue, i.e., the audience **29 Harry Monmouth** Prince Hal (who was born at Monmouth in Wales) **33 peasant** rural, provincial **35 hold** stronghold, fortress **37 crafty-sick** feigning sickness. **The . . . on** the messengers gallop hard, exhausted by their effort

And not a man of them brings other news
Than they have learn'd of me. From Rumor's
tongues
They bring smooth comforts false, worse than true
wrongs. *Exit Rumor.*

[ACT I • SCENE I]

Enter the Lord Bardolph at one door.

LORD BARDOLPH
Who keeps the gate here, ho?

[Enter the Porter.]

Where is the Earl?

PORTER
What shall I say you are?

LORD BARDOLPH
Tell thou the Earl
That the Lord Bardolph doth attend him here.

PORTER
His lordship is walk'd forth into the orchard.
Please it your honor knock but at the gate,
And he himself will answer.

Enter the Earl [of] Northumberland [in a nightcap, supporting himself with a crutch].

LORD BARDOLPH
Here comes the Earl.
[Exit Porter.]

NORTHUMBERLAND
What news, Lord Bardolph? Every minute now
Should be the father of some stratagem.
The times are wild. Contention, like a horse
Full of high feeding, madly hath broke loose
And bears down all before him.

LORD BARDOLPH
Noble Earl,
I bring you certain news from Shrewsbury.

NORTHUMBERLAND
Good, an God will!

LORD BARDOLPH
As good as heart can wish.
The King is almost wounded to the death,
And, in the fortune of my lord your son,
Prince Harry slain outright, and both the Blunts
Kill'd by the hand of Douglas. Young Prince John
And Westmorland and Stafford fled the field,
And Harry Monmouth's brawn, the hulk Sir John,
Is prisoner to your son. O, such a day,
So fought, so followed, and so fairly won,
Came not till now to dignify the times
Since Caesar's fortunes!

NORTHUMBERLAND
How is this deriv'd?
Saw you the field? Came you from Shrewsbury?

LORD BARDOLPH
I spake with one, my lord, that came from thence,
A gentleman well bred and of good name,
That freely rend'red me these news for true.

Enter Travers.

NORTHUMBERLAND
Here comes my servant Travers, who I sent
On Tuesday last to listen after news.

LORD BARDOLPH
My lord, I over-rode him on the way,
And he is furnish'd with no certainties
More than he haply may retail from me.

NORTHUMBERLAND
Now, Travers, what good tidings comes with you?

TRAVERS
My lord, Sir John Umfrevile turn'd me back
With joyful tidings, and, being better hors'd,
Outrode me. After him came spurring hard
A gentleman, almost forspent with speed,
That stopp'd by me to breathe his bloodied horse.
He ask'd the way to Chester; and of him
I did demand what news from Shrewsbury.
He told me that rebellion had bad luck
And that young Harry Percy's spur was cold.
With that, he gave his able horse the head,
And bending forward struck his armed heels
Against the panting sides of his poor jade
Up to the rowel-head, and starting so
He seem'd in running to devour the way,
Staying no longer question.

NORTHUMBERLAND
Ha? Again.
Said he young Harry Percy's spur was cold?
Of Hotspur, Coldspur? That rebellion
Had met ill luck?

LORD BARDOLPH
My lord, I'll tell you what:
If my young lord your son have not the day,
Upon mine honor, for a silken point
I'll give my barony. Never talk of it.

NORTHUMBERLAND
Why should that gentleman that rode by Travers
Give then such instances of loss?

LORD BARDOLPH
Who, he?
He was some hilding fellow that had stol'n
The horse he rode on, and, upon my life,
Spoke at a venture. Look, here comes more news.

Enter Morton.

NORTHUMBERLAND
Yea, this man's brow, like to a title-leaf,
Foretells the nature of a tragic volume.
So looks the strand whereon the imperious flood
Hath left a witness'd usurpation.
Say, Morton, didst thou come from Shrewsbury?

MORTON
I ran from Shrewsbury, my noble lord;

I.i. Location: Warkworth. Before Northumberland's castle.
s.d. Lord Bardolph (An ally of the Percies, not to be confused with Bardolph, Falstaff's red-faced companion.) **10 high feeding** too-rich fodder **13 an** if **15 in the fortune** by the good fortune **19 brawn** fat boar **21 followed** carried through **23 fortunes** successes. **deriv'd** learned, obtained

30 over-rode overtook **37 forspent** exhausted **38 bloodied** i.e., with spurring **46 rowel-head** the end of the spur, in which the barbed wheel turns **48 Staying** waiting for **52 day** victory **53 point** tag for fastening clothes (i.e., something of very small value) **57 hilding** good-for-nothing **60 title-leaf** title-page **62 strand** shore **63 witness'd usurpation** evidence of its (the sea's) invasion, encroachment

Where hateful death put on his ugliest mask
To fright our party.

NORTHUMBERLAND How doth my son and brother?
Thou tremblest, and the whiteness in thy cheek
Is apter than thy tongue to tell thy errand.
Even such a man, so faint, so spiritless,
So dull, so dead in look, so woebegone,
Drew Priam's curtain in the dead of night,
And would have told him half his Troy was burnt;
But Priam found the fire ere he his tongue,
And I my Percy's death ere thou report'st it.
This thou wouldst say, "Your son did thus and thus;
Your brother thus; so fought the noble Douglas"—
Stopping my greedy ear with their bold deeds.
But in the end, to stop my ear indeed,
Thou hast a sigh to blow away this praise,
Ending with "Brother, son, and all are dead."

MORTON
Douglas is living, and your brother, yet;
But, for my lord your son—

NORTHUMBERLAND Why, he is dead.
See what a ready tongue suspicion hath!
He that but fears the thing he would not know
Hath by instinct knowledge from others' eyes
That what he fear'd is chanced. Yet speak, Morton.
Tell thou an Earl his divination lies,
And I will take it as a sweet disgrace
And make thee rich for doing me such wrong.

MORTON
You are too great to be by me gainsaid.
Your spirit is too true, your fears too certain.

NORTHUMBERLAND
Yet, for all this, say not that Percy's dead.
I see a strange confession in thine eye.
Thou shak'st thy head and hold'st it fear or sin
To speak a truth. If he be slain, say so.
The tongue offends not that reports his death;
And he doth sin that doth belie the dead,
Not he which says the dead is not alive.
Yet the first bringer of unwelcome news
Hath but a losing office, and his tongue
Sounds ever after as a sullen bell,
Rememb'red tolling a departing friend.

LORD BARDOLPH
I cannot think, my lord, your son is dead.

MORTON
I am sorry I should force you to believe
That which I would to God I had not seen;
But these mine eyes saw him in bloody state,
Rend'ring faint quittance, wearied and outbreath'd,
To Harry Monmouth, whose swift wrath beat down
The never-daunted Percy to the earth,
From whence with life he never more sprung up.
In few, his death, whose spirit lent a fire
Even to the dullest peasant in his camp,
Being bruited once, took fire and heat away
From the best-temper'd courage in his troops;
For from his metal was his party steel'd,
Which once in him abated, all the rest
Turn'd on themselves, like dull and heavy lead.
And as the thing that's heavy in itself
Upon enforcement flies with greatest speed,
So did our men, heavy in Hotspur's loss,
Lend to this weight such lightness with their fear
That arrows fled not swifter toward their aim
Than did our soldiers, aiming at their safety,
Fly from the field. Then was that noble Worcester
So soon ta'en prisoner; and that furious Scot,
The bloody Douglas, whose well-laboring sword
Had three times slain th' appearance of the King,
Gan vail his stomach and did grace the shame
Of those that turn'd their backs, and in his flight,
Stumbling in fear, was took. The sum of all
Is that the King hath won, and hath sent out
A speedy power to encounter you, my lord,
Under the conduct of young Lancaster
And Westmorland. This is the news at full.

NORTHUMBERLAND
For this I shall have time enough to mourn.
In poison there is physic; and these news,
Having been well, that would have made me sick,
Being sick, have in some measure made me well.
And as the wretch whose fever-weak'ned joints
Like strengthless hinges buckle under life,
Impatient of his fit, breaks like a fire
Out of his keeper's arms, even so my limbs,
Weakened with grief, being now enrag'd with grief,
Are thrice themselves. Hence, therefore, thou nice crutch! *[He throws away his crutch.]*
A scaly gauntlet now with joints of steel
Must glove this hand. And hence, thou sickly coif! *[He takes off his nightcap.]*
Thou art a guard too wanton for the head
Which princes, flesh'd with conquest, aim to hit.
Now bind my brows with iron, and approach
The ragged'st hour that time and spite dare bring
To frown upon th' enrag'd Northumberland!
Let heaven kiss earth! Now let not Nature's hand
Keep the wild flood confin'd! Let order die!
And let this world no longer be a stage
To feed contention in a ling'ring act;
But let one spirit of the first-born Cain
Reign in all bosoms, that, each heart being set
On bloody courses, the rude scene may end,
And darkness be the burier of the dead!

TRAVERS
This strained passion doth you wrong, my lord.

72 Priam King of Troy. **curtain** bedcurtain **78 Stopping** filling **87 is chanced** has occurred **91 gainsaid** contradicted **93 for** in spite of **101 losing office** i.e., thankless task **103 tolling** ringing the funeral bell for **108 quittance** requital, i.e., resistance **112 In few** in few words **114 bruited** noised abroad, reported

115 best-temper'd i.e., like the highest quality steel **116 metal** (1) steel, continuing the metaphor of l. 115 (2) mettle, courage **117 abated** (1) blunted (2) slackened **118 Turn'd on themselves** (1) bent backwards (2) turned and ran **120 Upon enforcement** when set forcibly in motion **128 appearance of the King** i.e., warriors dressed like the King. (See *1 Henry IV*, V.iii and V.iv.25–38.) **129 Gan . . . stomach** began to abate or lower his courage. **grace** sanction (by his own running away) **134 conduct** command **137 physic** medicine **138 Having** I having. **that** i.e., the news which **141 buckle under life** bend under the stress of living **143 keeper's** nurse's **144 grief . . . grief** pain and sickness . . . sorrow **145 nice** delicate, effeminate **146 scaly** i.e., mailed **147 sickly coif** close-fitting cap worn by an invalid **148 wanton** effeminate, luxurious **149 flesh'd** inflamed by foretaste of blood and success **151 ragged'st** roughest **156 in . . . act** as in a slow-moving play **157 of . . . Cain** i.e., of murder **161 strained** excessive

LORD BARDOLPH
Sweet Earl, divorce not wisdom from your honor.

MORTON
The lives of all your loving complices
Lean on your health; the which, if you give o'er
To stormy passion, must perforce decay.
[You cast th' event of war, my noble lord,
And summ'd the account of chance, before you said,
"Let us make head." It was your presurmise
That, in the dole of blows, your son might drop.
You knew he walk'd o'er perils, on an edge,
More likely to fall in than to get o'er;
You were advis'd his flesh was capable
Of wounds and scars, and that his forward spirit
Would lift him where most trade of danger rang'd.
Yet did you say "Go forth." And none of this,
Though strongly apprehended, could restrain
The stiff-borne action. What hath then befall'n,
Or what hath this bold enterprise brought forth,
More than that being which was like to be?]

LORD BARDOLPH
We all that are engaged to this loss
Knew that we ventured on such dangerous seas
That if we wrought out life 'twas ten to one.
And yet we ventur'd, for the gain propos'd
Chok'd the respect of likely peril fear'd;
And since we are o'erset, venture again.
Come, we will all put forth, body and goods.

MORTON
'Tis more than time. And, my most noble lord,
I hear for certain, and dare speak the truth,
[The gentle Archbishop of York is up
With well-appointed pow'rs. He is a man
Who with a double surety binds his followers.
My lord your son had only but the corpse,
But shadows and the shows of men, to fight;
For that same word, rebellion, did divide
The action of their bodies from their souls,
And they did fight with queasiness, constrain'd,
As men drink potions, that their weapons only
Seem'd on our side. But for their spirits and souls,
This word, rebellion, it had froze them up,
As fish are in a pond. But now the Bishop
Turns insurrection to religion.
Suppos'd sincere and holy in his thoughts,
He's follow'd both with body and with mind,
And doth enlarge his rising with the blood
Of fair King Richard, scrap'd from Pomfret stones;
Derives from heaven his quarrel and his cause;
Tells them he doth bestride a bleeding land,
Gasping for life under great Bolingbroke;
And more and less do flock to follow him.]

NORTHUMBERLAND
I knew of this before; but, to speak truth,
This present grief had wip'd it from my mind.
Go in with me, and counsel every man
The aptest way for safety and revenge.
Get posts and letters, and make friends with
speed—
Never so few, and never yet more need. *Exeunt.*

[SCENE II]

Enter Sir John [Falstaff] alone, with his Page bearing his sword and buckler.

FALSTAFF Sirrah, you giant, what says the doctor to my water?

PAGE He said, sir, the water itself was a good healthy water; but, for the party that ow'd it, he might have moe diseases than he knew for.

FALSTAFF Men of all sorts take a pride to gird at me. The brain of this foolish-compounded clay, man, is not able to invent any thing that intends to laughter more than I invent or is invented on me. I am not only witty in myself, but the cause that wit is in other men. I do here walk before thee like a sow that hath overwhelm'd all her litter but one. If the Prince put thee into my service for any other reason than to set me off, why then I have no judgment. Thou whoreson mandrake, thou art fitter to be worn in my cap than to wait at my heels. I was never mann'd with an agate till now; but I will inset you neither in gold nor silver, but in vile apparel, and send you back again to your master, for a jewel—the juvenal, the Prince your master, whose chin is not yet fledge. I will sooner have a beard grow in the palm of my hand than he shall get one on his cheek, and yet he will not stick to say his face is a face-royal. God may finish it when he will, 'tis not a hair amiss yet. He may keep it still at a face-royal, for a barber shall never earn sixpence out of it; and yet he'll be crowing as if he had writ man ever since his father was a bachelor. He may keep his own grace, but he's almost out of mine, I can assure him. What said Master Dommelton about the satin for my short cloak and my slops?

PAGE He said, sir, you should procure him better assurance than Bardolph. He would not take his band and yours; he lik'd not the security.

FALSTAFF Let him be damn'd, like the glutton! Pray God his tongue be hotter! A whoreson Achitophel! A

163 complices allies **166 cast th' event** calculated the outcome **168 make head** raise an army **169 dole** dealing out, distribution **172 advis'd** aware **173 Of** of receiving **174 trade** trafficking **177 stiff-borne** obstinately carried out **179 being** event; having occurred **180 engaged to** involved in **182 if . . . one** if we came out alive we survived ten to one odds **184 Chok'd the respect** suppressed the consideration **189 Archbishop of York** i.e., Archbishop Scroop. **up** in arms **190 well-appointed pow'rs** well-equipped armed forces **192 corpse** i.e., corpses, living bodies without their souls **193 to fight** to use for fighting **204 enlarge his rising** enhance the merit of his insurrection **205 Pomfret** i.e., Pontefract Castle in Yorkshire, where Richard II was murdered **208 Bolingbroke** i.e., King Henry IV, here deprived of his title by the Archbishop **209 more and less** all classes

212 counsel every man let every man give advice as to **214 posts** messengers. **make** collect

I.ii. Location: London. A street.
s.d. buckler shield **1–2 to my water** about my urine sample **4 ow'd** owned **5 moe** more. **knew for** was aware of **6 gird** jeer **7 foolish-compounded** composed of folly **8 intends** tends **14–15 mandrake** plant with a forked man-shaped root **16 mann'd . . . agate** i.e., provided with a servant as small as the little figures cut in agate stone for jewelry and seal-rings **19 juvenal** youth **20 fledge** covered with down **23 face-royal** (punning on the *royal,* a coin with the King's face stamped on it) **24 at** at the value of **26 writ man** i.e., attained manhood **27 grace** (1) title suited to his royal rank (2) favor **30 slops** loose breeches **32 Bardolph** (One of Falstaff's followers, not the Lord Bardolph of scene i.) **band** bond **34 the glutton** (A reference to the parable of Dives the rich man, Luke 16:19–31.) **35 hotter** i.e., than Dives' tongue in hell. **Achitophel** abettor of Absalom's treason against David. (II Samuel, chaps. 15–17.)

rascally yea-forsooth knave, to bear a gentleman in hand, and then stand upon security! The whoreson smooth-pates do now wear nothing but high shoes, and bunches of keys at their girdles; and if a man is through with them in honest taking up, then they must stand upon security. I had as lief they would put ratsbane in my mouth as offer to stop it with security. I look'd 'a should have sent me two and twenty yards of satin, as I am a true knight, and he sends me security. Well, he may sleep in security, for he hath the horn of abundance, and the lightness of his wife shines through it. And yet cannot he see, though he have his own lantern to light him. Where's Bardolph?

PAGE He's gone into Smithfield to buy your worship a horse.

FALSTAFF I bought him in Paul's, and he'll buy me a horse in Smithfield. An I could get me but a wife in the stews, I were mann'd, hors'd, and wiv'd.

Enter [*the*] *Lord Chief Justice* [*and Servant*].

PAGE Sir, here comes the nobleman that committed the Prince for striking him about Bardolph.

FALSTAFF Wait close; I will not see him. [*Tries to slip away.*]

CHIEF JUSTICE What's he that goes there?

SERVANT Falstaff, an 't please your lordship.

CHIEF JUSTICE He that was in question for the robb'ry?

SERVANT He, my lord. But he hath since done good service at Shrewsbury, and, as I hear, is now going with some charge to the Lord John of Lancaster.

CHIEF JUSTICE What, to York? Call him back again.

SERVANT Sir John Falstaff!

FALSTAFF Boy, tell him I am deaf.

PAGE You must speak louder; my master is deaf.

CHIEF JUSTICE I am sure he is, to the hearing of anything good. Go, pluck him by the elbow; I must speak with him.

SERVANT Sir John!

FALSTAFF What, a young knave, and begging? Is there not wars? Is there not employment? Doth not the King lack subjects? Do not the rebels need soldiers? Though it be a shame to be on any side but one, it is worse shame to beg than to be on the worst side, were it worse than the name of rebellion can tell how to make it.

SERVANT You mistake me, sir.

FALSTAFF Why, sir, did I say you were an honest man? Setting my knighthood and my soldiership aside, I had lied in my throat if I had said so.

SERVANT I pray you, sir, then set your knighthood and your soldiership aside, and give me leave to tell you you lie in your throat if you say I am any other than an honest man.

FALSTAFF I give thee leave to tell me so? I lay aside that which grows to me? If thou get'st any leave of me, hang me; if thou tak'st leave, thou wert better be hang'd. You hunt counter. Hence! Avaunt!

SERVANT Sir, my lord would speak with you.

CHIEF JUSTICE Sir John Falstaff, a word with you.

FALSTAFF My good lord! God give your lordship good time of day. I am glad to see your lordship abroad. I heard say your lordship was sick. I hope your lordship goes abroad by advice. Your lordship, though not clean past your youth, have yet some smack of an ague in you, some relish of the saltness of time in you, and I most humbly beseech your lordship to have a reverent care of your health.

CHIEF JUSTICE Sir John, I sent for you before your expedition to Shrewsbury.

FALSTAFF An 't please your lordship, I hear his Majesty is return'd with some discomfort from Wales.

CHIEF JUSTICE I talk not of his Majesty. You would not come when I sent for you.

FALSTAFF And I hear, moreover, his Highness is fall'n into this same whoreson apoplexy.

CHIEF JUSTICE Well, God mend him! I pray you, let me speak with you.

FALSTAFF This apoplexy, as I take it, is a kind of lethargy, an 't please your lordship, a kind of sleeping in the blood, a whoreson tingling.

CHIEF JUSTICE What tell you me of it? Be it as it is.

FALSTAFF It hath it original from much grief, from study, and perturbation of the brain. I have read the cause of his effects in Galen. It is a kind of deafness.

CHIEF JUSTICE I think you are fall'n into the disease, for you hear not what I say to you.

FALSTAFF Very well, my lord, very well. Rather, an 't please you, it is the disease of not list'ning, the malady of not marking, that I am troubled withal.

CHIEF JUSTICE To punish you by the heels would amend the attention of your ears, and I care not if I do become your physician.

FALSTAFF I am as poor as Job, my lord, but not so patient. Your lordship may minister the potion of imprisonment to me in respect of poverty; but how I should be your patient to follow your prescriptions, the wise may make some dram of a scruple, or indeed a scruple itself.

CHIEF JUSTICE I sent for you, when there were matters against you for your life, to come speak with me.

FALSTAFF As I was then advis'd by my learned counsel in the laws of this land-service, I did not come.

36 yea-forsooth i.e., yes-man **36–37 bear . . . in hand** delude one with false hopes **38 smooth-pates** (Alludes to the short hair of tradesmen.) **38–39 high shoes . . . keys** (Indications of their financial prosperity and pride.) **39–41 if a man . . . security** if a man straightforwardly orders goods with them on credit, then they demand payment before making delivery **43 look'd 'a** expected that he **46 horn of abundance** (1) cornucopia (2) cockold's horn, a sign of his wife's infidelity. **lightness** (1) wantonness (2) light showing through a lantern (which would have windows of *horn,* thereby giving the cuckold a lantern in his own forehead) **49 Smithfield** district near Saint Paul's cathedral, famous as a livestock market **51 Paul's** i.e., St. Paul's Cathedral churchyard, resort of servingmen seeking employment **53 stews** brothels. **I . . . wiv'd** (Proverbially, to be thus manned, horsed, and wived at St. Paul's, Smithfield, and the stews respectively, was to be taken for a sucker.) **54 committed** i.e., to prison. (According to an apocryphal story, Hal boxed the ears of the Lord Chief Justice; see *1 Henry IV,* III.ii. 32–33 and note, and *2 Henry IV,* V. ii. 70–71 and note.) **59 in question** under judicial examination **62 charge** command of soldiers **77 make** regard

87 grows to is an integral part of **89 hunt counter** i.e., run backward on the trail. (A hunting term.) **95 by advice** by medical advice **113 What** why **114 it original** its origin **116 his** its. **Galen** the famous Greek authority on medicine **122 punish . . . heels** i.e., by setting you in the stocks or fetters **127 in . . . poverty** i.e., by reason of my being too poor to pay a fine **129 make . . . scruple** entertain some small portion of doubt. (*Dram* and *scruple* are small apothecaries' weights.) **132 for your life** i.e., carrying the death penalty **134 land-service** military service (with a pun on avoiding the "service" of a legal summons)

CHIEF JUSTICE Well, the truth is, Sir John, you live in great infamy.

FALSTAFF He that buckles himself in my belt cannot live in less.

CHIEF JUSTICE Your means are very slender, and your waste is great.

FALSTAFF I would it were otherwise; I would my means were greater, and my waist slenderer.

CHIEF JUSTICE You have misled the youthful Prince.

FALSTAFF The young Prince hath misled me. I am the fellow with the great belly, and he my dog.

CHIEF JUSTICE Well, I am loath to gall a new-heal'd wound. Your day's service at Shrewsbury hath a little gilded over your night's exploit on Gads Hill. You may thank th' unquiet time for your quiet o'erposting that action.

FALSTAFF My lord?

CHIEF JUSTICE But since all is well, keep it so. Wake not a sleeping wolf.

FALSTAFF To wake a wolf is as bad as smell a fox.

CHIEF JUSTICE What, you are as a candle, the better part burnt out.

FALSTAFF A wassail candle, my lord, all tallow. If I did say of wax, my growth would approve the truth.

CHIEF JUSTICE There is not a white hair on your face but should have his effect of gravity.

FALSTAFF His effect of gravy, gravy, gravy.

CHIEF JUSTICE You follow the young Prince up and down, like his ill angel.

FALSTAFF Not so, my lord. Your ill angel is light, but I hope he that looks upon me will take me without weighing. And yet in some respects I grant I cannot go. I cannot tell. Virtue is of so little regard in these costermongers' times that true valor is turn'd berrord; pregnancy is made a tapster, and his quick wit wasted in giving reckonings. All the other gifts appertinent to man, as the malice of this age shapes them, are not worth a gooseberry. You that are old consider not the capacities of us that are young; you do measure the heat of our livers with the bitterness of your galls. And we that are in the vaward of our youth, I must confess, are wags too.

CHIEF JUSTICE Do you set down your name in the scroll of youth, that are written down old with all the characters of age? Have you not a moist eye, a dry hand, a yellow cheek, a white beard, a decreasing leg, an increasing belly? Is not your voice broken, your wind short, your chin double, your wit single, and every part about you blasted with antiquity? And will you yet call yourself young? Fie, fie, fie, Sir John!

FALSTAFF My lord, I was born about three of the clock in the afternoon, with a white head and something a round belly. For my voice, I have lost it with halloing and singing of anthems. To approve my youth further, I will not. The truth is, I am only old in judgment and understanding; and he that will caper with me for a thousand marks, let him lend me the money, and have at him! For the box of the ear that the Prince gave you, he gave it like a rude prince, and you took it like a sensible lord. I have check'd him for it, and the young lion repents—[*Aside.*] marry, not in ashes and sackcloth, but in new silk and old sack.

CHIEF JUSTICE Well, God send the Prince a better companion!

FALSTAFF God send the companion a better prince! I cannot rid my hands of him.

CHIEF JUSTICE Well, the King hath sever'd you and Prince Harry. I hear you are going with Lord John of Lancaster against the Archbishop and the Earl of Northumberland.

FALSTAFF Yea, I thank your pretty sweet wit for it. But look you pray, all you that kiss my lady Peace at home, that our armies join not in a hot day; for, by the Lord, I take but two shirts out with me, and I mean not to sweat extraordinarily. If it be a hot day, and I brandish anything but a bottle, I would I might never spit white again. There is not a dangerous action can peep out his head but I am thrust upon it. Well, I cannot last ever. But it was alway yet the trick of our English nation, if they have a good thing, to make it too common. If ye will needs say I am an old man, you should give me rest. I would to God my name were not so terrible to the enemy as it is. I were better to be eaten to death with a rust than to be scour'd to nothing with perpetual motion.

CHIEF JUSTICE Well, be honest, be honest; and God bless your expedition!

FALSTAFF Will your lordship lend me a thousand pound to furnish me forth?

CHIEF JUSTICE Not a penny, not a penny. You are too impatient to bear crosses. Fare you well. Commend me to my cousin Westmorland.

[*Exeunt Chief Justice and Servant.*]

FALSTAFF If I do, fillip me with a three-man beetle. A man can no more separate age and covetousness than 'a can part young limbs and lechery; but the gout galls the one, and the pox pinches the other, and so both the degrees prevent my curses. Boy!

PAGE Sir?

FALSTAFF What money is in my purse?

PAGE Seven groats and two pence.

FALSTAFF I can get no remedy against this consumption of the purse; borrowing only lingers and lingers it out, but the disease is incurable. [*Gives letters.*] Go bear this letter to my Lord of Lancaster, this to the Prince,

148 exploit i.e., the famous robbery in *1 Henry IV,* II.ii **149 o'erposting** escaping the consequences of **154 smell a fox** suspect something. (Cf. *smell a rat.*) **157 wassail candle** large candle lighted up at a feast **158 wax** beeswax (with a pun on *growth*). **approve** prove **160 his effect** its sign **163 ill angel** evil attendant spirit. (But Falstaff quibbles on the meaning "a clipped angel," a coin worth 6 shillings 8 pence.) **164 light** i.e., underweight (because the coin is "clipped") **167 go** (1) walk (2) pass current **168 costermongers'** i.e., commercial. (A costermonger is a hawker of fruits or vegetables.) **berrord** bear-ward or bear-herd, one who handles tame bears **169 pregnancy** quickness (of wit), intellectual capacity **170 reckonings** tavern bills **174 heat . . . galls** (The liver was thought to be the source of passion and to be active in youth; the gall was thought the seat of melancholy and rancor, and to be prevalent in age.) **175 vaward** vanguard, forefront **178–179 characters** (1) characteristics (2) letters

186 something a a somewhat **187 halloing** shouting to hounds **188 approve** prove **190 caper** dance **191 marks** coins worth 13 shillings, 4 pence **192 box of the ear** (See note to l. 54, above.) **194 check'd** rebuked **195 marry** indeed. (Literally, *by the Virgin Mary.*) **196 sack** a white Spanish wine **210 spit white** i.e., from thirst **225 crosses** (1) afflictions (2) silver coins stamped with the figure of the cross **227 fillip** knock. **three-man beetle** a huge pile-driving mallet requiring three men to wield it **231 prevent** anticipate **234 groats** coins worth 4 pence

this to the Earl of Westmorland, and this to old Mistress Ursula, whom I have weekly sworn to marry since I perceiv'd the first white hair of my chin. About it. You know where to find me. [*Exit Page.*] A pox of this gout! Or, a gout of this pox! For the one or the other plays the rogue with my great toe. 'Tis no matter if I do halt; I have the wars for my color, and my pension shall seem the more reasonable. A good wit will make use of anything. I will turn diseases to commodity. [*Exit.*]

[SCENE III]

Enter th' Archbishop [*of York*], *Thomas Mowbray (Earl Marshal), the Lord Hastings, and* [*Lord*] *Bardolph.*

ARCHBISHOP
Thus have you heard our cause and known our means;
And, my most noble friends, I pray you all
Speak plainly your opinions of our hopes.
And first, Lord Marshal, what say you to it?

MOWBRAY
I well allow the occasion of our arms,
But gladly would be better satisfied
How in our means we should advance ourselves
To look with forehead bold and big enough
Upon the power and puissance of the King.

HASTINGS
Our present musters grow upon the file
To five and twenty thousand men of choice;
And our supplies live largely in the hope
Of great Northumberland, whose bosom burns
With an incensed fire of injuries.

LORD BARDOLPH
The question then, Lord Hastings, standeth thus:
Whether our present five and twenty thousand
May hold up head without Northumberland?

HASTINGS
With him, we may.

LORD BARDOLPH Yea, marry, there's the point.
But if without him we be thought too feeble,
My judgment is we should not step too far
[Till we had his assistance by the hand;
For in a theme so bloody-fac'd as this
Conjecture, expectation, and surmise
Of aids incertain should not be admitted.]

ARCHBISHOP
'Tis very true, Lord Bardolph, for indeed
It was young Hotspur's case at Shrewsbury.

LORD BARDOLPH
It was, my lord; who lin'd himself with hope,
Eating the air on promise of supply,
Flatt'ring himself in project of a power
Much smaller than the smallest of his thoughts,
And so, with great imagination
Proper to madmen, led his powers to death
And winking leapt into destruction.

HASTINGS
But, by your leave, it never yet did hurt
To lay down likelihoods and forms of hope.

LORD BARDOLPH
[Yes, if this present quality of war—
Indeed the instant action, a cause on foot—
Lives so in hope, as in an early spring
We see th' appearing buds, which to prove fruit,
Hope gives not so much warrant as despair
That frosts will bite them. When we mean to build,
We first survey the plot, then draw the model;
And when we see the figure of the house,
Then must we rate the cost of the erection,
Which if we find outweighs ability,
What do we then but draw anew the model
In fewer offices, or at least desist
To build at all? Much more, in this great work,
Which is almost to pluck a kingdom down
And set another up, should we survey
The plot of situation and the model,
Consent upon a sure foundation,
Question surveyors, know our own estate,
How able such a work to undergo,
To weigh against his opposite; or else]
We fortify in paper and in figures,
Using the names of men instead of men,
Like one that draws the model of a house
Beyond his power to build it, who, half through,
Gives o'er and leaves his part-created cost
A naked subject to the weeping clouds
And waste for churlish winter's tyranny.

HASTINGS
Grant that our hopes, yet likely of fair birth,
Should be still-born, and that we now possess'd
The utmost man of expectation,
I think we are a body strong enough,
Even as we are, to equal with the King.

LORD BARDOLPH
What, is the King but five and twenty thousand?

HASTINGS
To us no more, nay, not so much, Lord Bardolph.
For his divisions, as the times do brawl,
Are in three heads: one power against the French,
And one against Glendower; perforce a third
Must take up us. So is the unfirm King

245 halt limp. **color** excuse **247–248 commodity** profit

I.iii. Location: York. The Archbishop's palace.
s.d. Thomas Mowbray son of Thomas Mowbray, Duke of Norfolk, who was banished by Richard II **5 allow . . . arms** concede the justice of our arming **7 in** with **10 file** roll **11 men of choice** choice men **12 supplies** reinforcements **22 theme** business **27 lin'd** strengthened

29 project . . . power anticipation of the arrival of an armed force **33 winking** shutting his eyes **36–41 Yes . . . them** i.e., Yes (replying to Lord Hastings) it can do hurt to be too hopeful about war; if, for example, this present business of war—indeed, the very campaign we anticipate, the matter that is now afoot—depends merely on such desperate hopes as we experience about buds appearing too early in the spring, since in reality hope gives us not so much warrant to expect their maturing into fruit than despair that frosts will bite them. (The text is almost certainly corrupt here.) **42 model** plan **43 figure** design **44 rate** estimate **45 ability** i.e., ability to pay **47 offices** rooms. **at least** at the worst **52 Consent** agree **53 surveyors** architects. **estate** wealth **55 his opposite** adverse conditions **56 in paper** merely on paper **60 part-created cost** partly finished splendor **61 naked subject** exposed (i.e., helpless) victim **65 The . . . expectation** i.e., all the men that we might hope to have **70 as . . . brawl** in accordance with the discordant necessity of the time **73 take up** encounter, oppose

In three divided, and his coffers sound
With hollow poverty and emptiness.

ARCHBISHOP
That he should draw his several strengths together,
And come against us in full puissance,
Need not be dreaded.

HASTINGS
If he should do so,
To French and Welsh he leaves his back unarm'd,
They baying him at the heels. Never fear that.

LORD BARDOLPH
Who is it like should lead his forces hither?

HASTINGS
The Duke of Lancaster and Westmorland;
Against the Welsh, himself and Harry Monmouth.
But who is substituted 'gainst the French,
I have no certain notice.

[ARCHBISHOP
Let us on,
And publish the occasion of our arms.
The commonwealth is sick of their own choice;
Their over-greedy love hath surfeited.
An habitation giddy and unsure
Hath he that buildeth on the vulgar heart.
O thou fond many, with what loud applause
Didst thou beat heaven with blessing Bolingbroke,
Before he was what thou wouldst have him be!
And being now trimm'd in thine own desires,
Thou, beastly feeder, art so full of him
That thou provok'st thyself to cast him up.
So, so, thou common dog, didst thou disgorge
Thy glutton bosom of the royal Richard;
And now thou wouldst eat thy dead vomit up,
And howl'st to find it. What trust is in these times?
They that, when Richard liv'd, would have him die,
Are now become enamor'd on his grave.
Thou, that threw'st dust upon his goodly head
When through proud London he came sighing on
After th' admired heels of Bolingbroke,
Criest now "O earth, yield us that king again,
And take thou this!" O thoughts of men accurs'd!
Past and to come seems best; things present worst.]

MOWBRAY
Shall we go draw our numbers and set on?

HASTINGS
We are time's subjects, and time bids be gone.
Exeunt.

[ACT II • SCENE I]

Enter Hostess [Quickly] of the Tavern and an Officer or two [Fang and another, followed by Snare].

HOSTESS Master Fang, have you ent'red the action?

FANG It is ent'red.

HOSTESS Where's your yeoman? Is 't a lusty yeoman? Will 'a stand to 't?

FANG [*To Officer*] Sirrah, where's Snare?

HOSTESS O Lord, ay, good Master Snare.

SNARE Here, here.

FANG Snare, we must arrest Sir John Falstaff.

HOSTESS Yea, good Master Snare, I have ent'red him and all.

SNARE It may chance cost some of us our lives, for he will stab.

HOSTESS Alas the day, take heed of him! He stabb'd me in mine own house, most beastly, in good faith. 'A cares not what mischief he does, if his weapon be out. He will foin like any devil; he will spare neither man, woman, nor child.

FANG If I can close with him, I care not for his thrust.

HOSTESS No, nor I neither. I'll be at your elbow.

FANG An I but fist him once, and 'a come but within my vice—

HOSTESS I am undone by his going. I warrant you, he's an infinitive thing upon my score. Good Master Fang, hold him sure. Good Master Snare, let him not scape. 'A comes continuantly to Pie-corner—saving your manhoods—to buy a saddle; and he is indited to dinner to the Lubber's Head in Lumbert street, to Master Smooth's the silkman. I pray you, since my exion is ent'red and my case so openly known to the world, let him be brought in to his answer. A hundred mark is a long one for a poor lone woman to bear; and I have borne, and borne, and borne, and have been fubb'd off, and fubb'd off, and fubb'd off, from this day to that day, that it is a shame to be thought on. There is no honesty in such dealing, unless a woman should be made an ass and a beast, to bear every knave's wrong. Yonder he comes, and that arrant malmsey-nose knave, Bardolph, with him. Do your offices, do your offices. Master Fang and Master Snare, do me, do me, do me your offices.

Enter Sir John [Falstaff], and Bardolph, and the Boy [Page].

FALSTAFF How now, whose mare's dead? What's the matter?

FANG Sir John, I arrest you at the suit of Mistress Quickly.

FALSTAFF Away, varlets! Draw, Bardolph. Cut me off the villain's head. Throw the quean in the channel.
[*They draw.*]

HOSTESS Throw me in the channel? I'll throw thee in the channel. Wilt thou? Wilt thou? Thou bastardly rogue! Murder, murder! Ah, thou honeysuckle villain! Wilt

74 sound resound, echo **76 several strengths** various armies **81 Who . . . should** who is likely to **84 substituted** delegated **90 vulgar** common, plebeian **91 fond many** foolish multitude **92 beat heaven** assail heaven with prayers **94 trimm'd in** furnished with, dressed in **109 draw our numbers** assemble or muster our forces. **set on** march

II.i. Location: London. A street.
1 ent'red the action begun the lawsuit

3 yeoman sheriff's man **4 Will . . . to 't** will he fight boldly **9 ent'red** brought action against in court **16 foin** thrust in fencing; with sexual double meaning, as also in *stabb'd, weapon, thrust, ent'red, case* (female pudendum), *open to the world, brought in, long one, borne, fubb'd off* (meaning also to be put off with excuses), *stand to me,* etc. **18 close** grapple **20 fist** i.e., seize **21 vice** vise, grip **23 infinitive** (Hostess Quickly's malapropism for *infinite,* endless.) **score** accounts **25 continuantly** (Perhaps a mixup of *continually* and *incontinently,* immediately.) **Pie-corner** a corner in the Smithfield district of London known for its cooks' shops **25–26 saving your manhoods** i.e., with apologies for mentioning anything so indelicate **26 indited** i.e., invited **27 Lubber's Head** i.e., Libbard's Head, Leopard's Head Inn. **Lumbert** i.e., Lombard **28 exion** action, lawsuit **30 mark** (Worth 13 shillings 4 pence.) **37–38 malmsey-nose** red-nosed (from drinking Malmsey, a sweet red wine) **41 whose mare's dead** i.e., what's all the fuss about **46 quean** slut, hussy. **channel** street gutter **49 honeysuckle** (For *homicidal.*)

thou kill God's officers and the King's? Ah, thou honeyseed rogue! Thou art a honeyseed, a man-queller, and a woman-queller.

FALSTAFF Keep them off, Bardolph.

OFFICERS A rescue! A rescue!

HOSTESS Good people, bring a rescue or two. Thou wo 't, wo 't thou? Thou wo 't, wo 't ta? Do, do, thou rogue! Do, thou hempseed!

FALSTAFF Away, you scullion, you rampallian, you fustilarian! I'll tickle your catastrophe.

Enter [the] Lord Chief Justice, and his men.

CHIEF JUSTICE
What is the matter? Keep the peace here, ho!

HOSTESS Good my lord, be good to me. I beseech you, stand to me.

CHIEF JUSTICE
How now, Sir John? What are you brawling here?
Doth this become your place, your time, and business?
You should have been well on your way to York.
Stand from him, fellow. Wherefore hang'st thou upon him?

HOSTESS O my most worshipful lord, an 't please your Grace, I am a poor widow of Eastcheap, and he is arrested at my suit.

CHIEF JUSTICE For what sum?

HOSTESS It is more than for some, my lord; it is for all I have. He hath eaten me out of house and home; he hath put all my substance into that fat belly of his. But I will have some of it out again, or I will ride thee o' nights like the mare.

FALSTAFF I think I am as like to ride the mare, if I have any vantage of ground to get up.

CHIEF JUSTICE How comes this, Sir John? What man of good temper would endure this tempest of exclamation? Are you not asham'd to enforce a poor widow to so rough a course to come by her own?

FALSTAFF What is the gross sum that I owe thee?

HOSTESS Marry, if thou wert an honest man, thyself and the money too. Thou didst swear to me upon a parcel-gilt goblet, sitting in my Dolphin chamber, at the round table, by a sea-coal fire, upon Wednesday in Wheeson week, when the Prince broke thy head for liking his father to a singing-man of Windsor, thou didst swear to me then, as I was washing thy wound, to marry me and make me my lady thy wife. Canst thou deny it? Did not goodwife Keech, the butcher's wife, come in then and call me gossip Quickly? Coming in to borrow a mess of vinegar, telling us she had a good dish of prawns, whereby thou didst desire to eat some, whereby I told thee they were ill for a green wound? And didst thou not, when she was gone down stairs, desire me to be no more so familiarity with such poor people, saying that ere long they should call me madam? And didst thou not kiss me and bid me fetch thee thirty shillings? I put thee now to thy book-oath. Deny it if thou canst.

FALSTAFF My lord, this is a poor mad soul, and she says up and down the town that her eldest son is like you. She hath been in good case, and the truth is, poverty hath distracted her. But for these foolish officers, I beseech you I may have redress against them.

CHIEF JUSTICE Sir John, Sir John, I am well acquainted with your manner of wrenching the true cause the false way. It is not a confident brow, nor the throng of words that come with such more than impudent sauciness from you, can thrust me from a level consideration. You have, as it appears to me, practic'd upon the easy-yielding spirit of this woman, and made her serve your uses both in purse and in person.

HOSTESS Yea, in truth, my lord.

CHIEF JUSTICE Pray thee, peace. Pay her the debt you owe her, and unpay the villainy you have done her. The one you may do with sterling money, and the other with current repentance.

FALSTAFF My lord, I will not undergo this sneap without reply. You call honorable boldness impudent sauciness. If a man will make curtsy and say nothing, he is virtuous. No, my lord, my humble duty remember'd, I will not be your suitor. I say to you, I do desire deliverance from these officers, being upon hasty employment in the King's affairs.

CHIEF JUSTICE You speak as having power to do wrong. But answer in th' effect of your reputation, and satisfy the poor woman.

FALSTAFF Come hither, hostess.

Enter a Messenger [Gower].

CHIEF JUSTICE Now, Master Gower, what news?

GOWER
The King, my lord, and Harry Prince of Wales
Are near at hand. The rest the paper tells.
[*Gives letter. The Chief Justice reads.*]

FALSTAFF [*To Mistress Quickly*] As I am a gentleman.

HOSTESS Faith, you said so before.

FALSTAFF As I am a gentleman. Come, no more words of it.

HOSTESS By this heav'nly ground I tread on, I must be fain to pawn both my plate and the tapestry of my dining-chambers.

FALSTAFF Glasses, glasses, is the only drinking. And for thy walls, a pretty slight drollery, or the story of the Prodigal, or the German hunting in water work, is worth a thousand of these bed-hangers and these fly-

50–51 honeyseed (For *homicide.*) **51 man-queller** murderer **56 wo' t thou** wilt thou **57 hempseed** (Alludes to the hangman's rope.) **58 scullion** kitchen wench. **rampallian** scoundrel **58–59 fustilarian** fat, frowsy woman **59 catastrophe** backside **62 stand to** help (with bawdy suggestion) **74–75 o' nights** by night **75 mare** nightmare **77 get up** mount **84–85 parcel-gilt** partly gilded **85 Dolphin chamber** (The name of a room in her inn.) **86 sea-coal** bituminous coal, brought in by sea **87 Wheeson** Whitsun (Pentecost). **broke** hit, made a cut on **88 liking** likening **91 goodwife** (Title of a married woman.) **Keech** (Literally, "a lump of tallow.") **92 gossip** (Literally, a fellow godparent; hence, a female friend.) **93 mess** quantity **94 prawns** shrimps. **whereby** whereupon **95 green** raw

101 book-oath oath on a Bible **104 in good case** well to do **105 distracted her** driven her mad **111 level** fair-minded, evenhanded **119 current** genuine (with an allusion to current coin) **120 sneap** reproof **123–124 my . . . remember'd** i.e., with all due consideration of the respect I owe to your position **128 in . . . reputation** i.e., in a manner becoming a man of your reputation **139 fain** obliged, content **141 Glasses . . . drinking** i.e., glasses are all the fashion now for drinking, instead of metal tankards **142 drollery** comic picture **143 water work** water color **144 bed-hangers** curtains around a four-poster bed

bitten tapestries. Let it be ten pound, if thou canst.
Come, and 'twere not for thy humors, there's not a 146
better wench in England. Go, wash thy face, and draw 147
the action. Come, thou must not be in this humor
with me. Dost not know me? Come, come, I know
thou wast set on to this.

HOSTESS Pray thee, Sir John, let it be but twenty nobles. 151
'I faith, I am loath to pawn my plate, so God save
me, la!

FALSTAFF Let it alone; I'll make other shift. You'll be a 154
fool still.

HOSTESS Well, you shall have it, though I pawn my
gown. I hope you'll come to supper. You'll pay me all
together?

FALSTAFF Will I live? [*To Bardolph.*] Go, with her, with
her; hook on, hook on. 160

HOSTESS Will you have Doll Tearsheet meet you at
supper?

FALSTAFF No more words. Let's have her.

Exeunt Hostess and Sergeant [*Fang, Bardolph, and others*].

CHIEF JUSTICE I have heard better news.

FALSTAFF What's the news, my lord?

CHIEF JUSTICE Where lay the King tonight? 166

GOWER At Basingstoke, my lord. 167

FALSTAFF I hope, my lord, all's well. What is the news,
my lord?

CHIEF JUSTICE Come all his forces back?

GOWER
No; fifteen hundred foot, five hundred horse,
Are march'd up to my lord of Lancaster, 172
Against Northumberland and the Archbishop.

FALSTAFF Comes the King back from Wales, my noble
lord?

CHIEF JUSTICE You shall have letters of me presently.
Come, go along with me, good Master Gower.

[*Starts to go.*]

FALSTAFF My lord!

CHIEF JUSTICE What's the matter?

FALSTAFF Master Gower, shall I entreat you with me to
dinner?

GOWER I must wait upon my good lord here, I thank
you, good Sir John.

CHIEF JUSTICE Sir John, you loiter here too long, being 184
you are to take soldiers up in counties as you go. 185

FALSTAFF Will you sup with me, Master Gower?

CHIEF JUSTICE What foolish master taught you these
manners, Sir John?

FALSTAFF Master Gower, if they become me not, he was
a fool that taught them me. This is the right fencing
grace, my lord—tap for tap, and so part fair. 191

CHIEF JUSTICE Now the Lord lighten thee! Thou art a 192
great fool. [*Exeunt severally.*]

146 humors whims, vagaries **147 draw** withdraw **151 nobles** coins current at 6 shillings 8 pence **154 shift** expedient **160 hook on** i.e., follow her **166 tonight** this past night **167 Basingstoke** a town in Hampshire **172 to** i.e., led by **184–185 being . . . up** seeing that you are to levy soldiers **191 grace** form, style. (Falstaff is saying that by refusing to answer the Chief Justice's questions in ll. 180 ff., Falstaff is only paying him back tit for tat for ignoring Falstaff's questions, ll. 165–177.) **192 lighten** (1) enlighten (2) reduce in weight

[SCENE II]

Enter the Prince [*Henry*], *Poins, with others.*

PRINCE Before God, I am exceeding weary.

POINS Is 't come to that? I had thought weariness durst
not have attach'd one of so high blood. 3

PRINCE Faith, it does me, though it discolors the com- 4
plexion of my greatness to acknowledge it. Doth it not 5
show vilely in me to desire small beer? 6

POINS Why, a prince should not be so loosely studied 7
as to remember so weak a composition. 8

PRINCE Belike then my appetite was not princely got, 9
for, by my troth, I do now remember the poor crea-
ture, small beer. But indeed these humble considera-
tions make me out of love with my greatness. What a
disgrace is it to me to remember thy name! Or to know
thy face tomorrow! Or to take note how many pair of
silk stockings thou hast, viz., these, and those that
were thy peach-color'd ones! Or to bear the inventory
of thy shirts, as, one for superfluity, and another for 17
use! But that the tennis-court-keeper knows better 18
than I; for it is a low ebb of linen with thee when thou 19
keepest not racket there, as thou hast not done a great 20
while, because the rest of the low countries have made 21
a shift to eat up thy holland. And God knows whether 22
those that bawl out the ruins of thy linen shall inherit 23
his kingdom. But the midwives say the children are
not in the fault, whereupon the world increases, and
kindreds are mightily strengthen'd.

POINS How ill it follows, after you have labor'd so hard,
you should talk so idly! Tell me, how many good
young princes would do so, their fathers being so sick
as yours at this time is?

PRINCE Shall I tell thee one thing, Poins?

POINS Yes, faith, and let it be an excellent good thing.

PRINCE It shall serve among wits of no higher breeding
than thine.

POINS Go to. I stand the push of your one thing that 35
you will tell.

PRINCE Marry, I tell thee it is not meet that I should be
sad, now my father is sick. Albeit I could tell to thee,
as to one it pleases me, for fault of a better, to call my
friend, I could be sad, and sad indeed too.

POINS Very hardly upon such a subject. 41

PRINCE By this hand, thou thinkest me as far in the
devil's book as thou and Falstaff for obduracy and per-
sistency. Let the end try the man. But I tell thee, my
heart bleeds inwardly that my father is so sick. And

II.ii. Location: London. Prince Henry's dwelling.
3 attach'd seized **4–5 discolors . . . greatness** i.e., makes me blush **6 small beer** weak kind of beer **7 studied** versed, inclined **8 so . . . composition** i.e., weak beer, trifles **9 got** begotten **17 for superfluity** as a clean change (of shirt) **18–21 But . . . while** i.e., the keeper of the tennis court knows that Poins' inventory of shirts is at a low ebb, that he does not have a spare clean shirt to shift into, because he has not been seen at the tennis court lately **21 the low countries** i.e., the brothels where Poins spends his money (with a pun on *the Netherlands*) **21–22 made a shift** contrived (with a pun on *shift*, shirt) **22 eat . . . holland** i.e., used up all the money you would spend on a linen shirt (with a pun on *Holland* as one of the Low Countries) **23 those . . . linen** i.e., your bastards, who wear your cast-off shirts made into swaddling clothes **35 push** attack, thrust **41 Very hardly** scarcely, with difficulty

keeping such vile company as thou art hath in reason taken from me all ostentation of sorrow.

POINS The reason?

PRINCE What wouldst thou think of me, if I should weep?

POINS I would think thee a most princely hypocrite.

PRINCE It would be every man's thought, and thou art a blessed fellow to think as every man thinks. Never a man's thought in the world keeps the roadway better than thine. Every man would think me an hypocrite indeed. And what accites your most worshipful thought to think so?

POINS Why, because you have been so lewd and so much engraff'd to Falstaff.

PRINCE And to thee.

POINS By this light, I am well spoke on; I can hear it with mine own ears. The worst that they can say of me is that I am a second brother and that I am a proper fellow of my hands, and those two things I confess I cannot help. By the mass, here comes Bardolph.

Enter Bardolph and Boy [*Page*].

PRINCE And the boy that I gave Falstaff. 'A had him from me Christian, and look if the fat villain have not transform'd him ape.

BARDOLPH God save your Grace!

PRINCE And yours, most noble Bardolph!

POINS Come, you virtuous ass, you bashful fool, must you be blushing? Wherefore blush you now? What a maidenly man-at-arms are you become! Is 't such a matter to get a pottle-pot's maidenhead?

PAGE 'A calls me e'en now, my lord, through a red lattice, and I could discern no part of his face from the window. At last I spied his eyes, and methought he had made two holes in the ale-wife's new petticoat and so peep'd through.

PRINCE Has not the boy profited?

BARDOLPH Away, you whoreson upright rabbit, away!

PAGE Away, you rascally Althaea's dream, away!

PRINCE Instruct us, boy. What dream, boy?

PAGE Marry, my lord, Althaea dreamt she was deliver'd of a fire-brand, and therefore I call him her dream.

PRINCE A crown's worth of good interpretation. There 'tis, boy. [*Gives money.*]

POINS O, that this blossom could be kept from cankers! Well, there is sixpence to preserve thee. [*Gives money.*]

BARDOLPH An you do not make him hang'd among you, the gallows shall have wrong.

PRINCE And how doth thy master, Bardolph?

BARDOLPH Well, my lord. He heard of your Grace's coming to town. There's a letter for you. [*Gives letter.*]

POINS Deliver'd with good respect. And how doth the martlemas, your master?

BARDOLPH In bodily health, sir.

POINS Marry, the immortal part needs a physician, but that moves not him. Though that be sick, it dies not.

PRINCE I do allow this wen to be as familiar with me as my dog, and he holds his place, for look you how he writes. [*Shows letter to Poins.*]

POINS [*Reading the superscription*] "John Falstaff, knight."—Every man must know that, as oft as he has occasion to name himself; even like those that are kin to the King, for they never prick their finger but they say, "There's some of the King's blood spilt." "How comes that?" says he, that takes upon him not to conceive. The answer is as ready as a borrower's cap, "I am the King's poor cousin, sir."

PRINCE Nay, they will be kin to us, or they will fetch it from Japhet. But the letter. [*Reads.*] "Sir John Falstaff, knight, to the son of the King nearest his father, Harry Prince of Wales, greeting."

POINS Why, this is a certificate.

PRINCE Peace! [*Reads.*] "I will imitate the honorable Romans in brevity."

POINS He sure means brevity in breath, short-winded.

[PRINCE *Reads*] "I commend me to thee, I commend thee, and I leave thee. Be not too familiar with Poins, for he misuses thy favors so much that he swears thou art to marry his sister Nell. Repent at idle times as thou may'st; and so, farewell.

"Thine, by yea and no, which is as much as to say, as thou usest him, Jack Falstaff with my familiars, John with my brothers and sisters, and Sir John with all Europe."

POINS My lord, I'll steep this letter in sack and make him eat it.

PRINCE That's to make him eat twenty of his words. But do you use me thus, Ned? Must I marry your sister?

POINS God send the wench no worse fortune! But I never said so.

PRINCE Well, thus we play the fools with the time, and the spirits of the wise sit in the clouds and mock us. Is your master here in London?

BARDOLPH Yea, my lord.

PRINCE Where sups he? Doth the old boar feed in the old frank?

BARDOLPH At the old place, my lord, in Eastcheap.

PRINCE What company?

PAGE Ephesians, my lord, of the old church.

PRINCE Sup any women with him?

PAGE None, my lord, but old Mistress Quickly and Mistress Doll Tearsheet.

PRINCE What pagan may that be?

47 ostentation outward indication **56 accites** induces (with a quibble on *summons*) **58 lewd** base **59 engraff'd** closely attached **63 second brother** i.e., a younger son, without inheritance **63–64 proper . . . hands** i.e., good fighter **72 blushing** i.e., red-faced (from drink) **74 get . . . maidenhead** i.e., drink up a two-quart tankard of ale **75–76 red lattice** (Red lattices identified taverns.) **76 discern** distinguish **82 Althaea's dream** (Althaea dreamed that her newborn son would live only so long as a brand on the fire lasted. The Page mistakenly relates Hecuba's dream: when pregnant with Paris, Hecuba dreamed she would be delivered of a firebrand that would destroy Troy.) **86 crown** i.e., five shillings **88 cankers** cankerworms, worms that destroy buds and leaves **89 to preserve thee** (Allusion to the cross on the sixpence.)

95 good respect proper ceremony. (Said ironically.) **96 martlemas** i.e., Martinmas beef, beef slaughtered on November 11 (and fattened beforehand) **100 wen** swelling, tumor **104 Every . . . that** i.e., Falstaff wants to make sure that everyone is aware of his knightly rank **108–109 takes . . . conceive** pretends not to understand **109 as ready . . . cap** i.e., as quick in coming forth as a cap is doffed by one seeking aid **111–112 fetch . . . Japhet** i.e., trace their ancestry back to Japhet, one of the sons of Noah. (Genesis 10:2–5.) **115 certificate** legal document **124 by yea and no** (A Puritan oath.) **130 twenty** i.e., a considerable number **139 frank** sty, pen. (Often thought to refer to the Boar's Head Tavern.) **142 Ephesians . . . church** i.e., good fellows of the usual, disreputable fellowship **146 pagan** i.e., harlot

PAGE A proper gentlewoman, sir, and a kinswoman of my master's.

PRINCE Even such kin as the parish heifers are to the town bull. Shall we steal upon them, Ned, at supper?

POINS I am your shadow, my lord; I'll follow you.

PRINCE Sirrah, you boy, and Bardolph, no word to your master that I am yet come to town. There's for your silence. [*Gives money.*]

BARDOLPH I have no tongue, sir.

PAGE And for mine, sir, I will govern it.

PRINCE Fare you well; go. [*Exeunt Bardolph and Page.*] This Doll Tearsheet should be some road.

POINS I warrant you, as common as the way between Saint Albans and London.

PRINCE How might we see Falstaff bestow himself tonight in his true colors, and not ourselves be seen?

POINS Put on two leathern jerkins and aprons, and wait upon him at his table as drawers.

PRINCE From a God to a bull? A heavy descension! It was Jove's case. From a prince to a prentice? A low transformation! That shall be mine, for in every thing the purpose must weigh with the folly. Follow me, Ned. *Exeunt.*

[SCENE III]

Enter Northumberland, his Wife [*Lady Northumberland*], *and the Wife to Harry Percy* [*Lady Percy*].

NORTHUMBERLAND
I pray thee, loving wife, and gentle daughter,
Give even way unto my rough affairs.
Put not you on the visage of the times
And be like them to Percy troublesome.

LADY NORTHUMBERLAND
I have given over, I will speak no more.
Do what you will; your wisdom be your guide.

NORTHUMBERLAND
Alas, sweet wife, my honor is at pawn,
And, but my going, nothing can redeem it.

LADY PERCY
O yet, for God's sake, go not to these wars!
The time was, father, that you broke your word,
When you were more endear'd to it than now,
When your own Percy, when my heart's dear Harry,
Threw many a northward look to see his father
Bring up his powers; but he did long in vain.
Who then persuaded you to stay at home?
There were two honors lost, yours and your son's.
For yours, the God of heaven brighten it!
For his, it stuck upon him as the sun
In the grey vault of heaven, and by his light
Did all the chivalry of England move
To do brave acts. He was indeed the glass
Wherein the noble youth did dress themselves.
[He had no legs that practic'd not his gait;
And speaking thick, which nature made his blemish,
Became the accents of the valiant,
For those that could speak low and tardily
Would turn their own perfection to abuse
To seem like him. So that in speech, in gait,
In diet, in affections of delight,
In military rules, humors of blood,
He was the mark and glass, copy and book,
That fashion'd others. And him, O wondrous him!
O miracle of men! Him did you leave,
Second to none, unseconded by you,
To look upon the hideous god of war
In disadvantage, to abide a field
Where nothing but the sound of Hotspur's name
Did seem defensible. So you left him.
Never, O never, do his ghost the wrong
To hold your honor more precise and nice
With others than with him! Let them alone.
The Marshal and the Archbishop are strong.
Had my sweet Harry had but half their numbers,
Today might I, hanging on Hotspur's neck,
Have talk'd of Monmouth's grave.]

NORTHUMBERLAND Beshrew your heart,
Fair daughter, you do draw my spirits from me
With new lamenting ancient oversights.
But I must go and meet with danger there,
Or it will seek me in another place
And find me worse provided.

LADY NORTHUMBERLAND O, fly to Scotland,
Till that the nobles and the armed commons
Have of their puissance made a little taste.

LADY PERCY
If they get ground and vantage of the King,
Then join you with them, like a rib of steel,
To make strength stronger; but, for all our loves,
First let them try themselves. So did your son;
He was so suff'red. So came I a widow,
And never shall have length of life enough
To rain upon remembrance with mine eyes,
That it may grow and sprout as high as heaven,
For recordation to my noble husband.

NORTHUMBERLAND
Come, come, go in with me. 'Tis with my mind
As with the tide swell'd up unto his height,
That makes a still-stand, running neither way.
Fain would I go to meet the Archbishop,
But many thousand reasons hold me back.
I will resolve for Scotland. There am I,
Till time and vantage crave my company. *Exeunt.*

158 road i.e., common whore **161 bestow** behave **163 jerkins** jackets **164 drawers** tapsters, tavern waiters **165 heavy descension** grievous descent **166 Jove's case** (Jupiter, for the love of Europa, transformed himself into a bull.) **168 weigh with** match, balance

II.iii. Location: Warkworth. Before Northumberland's castle.
1 daughter i.e., daughter-in-law **2 even way** free scope **8 but** except for **11 endear'd** pledged **17 For** as for **19 grey** sky-blue

21 glass mirror **23 He** i.e., any man **24 thick** impulsively, impetuously **27 turn . . . abuse** i.e., debase their own manner of speech and adopt his **29 affections of delight** choice of pleasurable occupations **30 humors of blood** temperament **31 mark** pattern **34 unseconded** unsupported **36 In disadvantage** i.e., outnumbered. **abide a field** fight a battle **38 defensible** able to make defense **40 nice** punctilious **45 Monmouth's** i.e., Prince Hal's (since he was born at Monmouth) **47 new lamenting** lamenting anew **57 suff'red** allowed to proceed. **came** became **61 recordation** remembrance, memorial

[SCENE IV]

Enter a Drawer or two [*Francis and another*].

FRANCIS What the devil hast thou brought there? Apple-johns? Thou knowest Sir John cannot endure an apple-john.

SECOND DRAWER Mass, thou say'st true. The Prince once set a dish of apple-johns before him, and told him there were five more Sir Johns, and, putting off his hat, said "I will now take my leave of these six dry, round, old, wither'd knights." It ang'red him to the heart. But he hath forgot that.

FRANCIS Why, then, cover, and set them down. And see if thou canst find out Sneak's noise; Mistress Tearsheet would fain hear some music.

Enter Will [*a third Drawer*].

THIRD DRAWER Dispatch! The room where they supp'd is too hot; they'll come in straight.

FRANCIS Sirrah, here will be the Prince and Master Poins anon, and they will put on two of our jerkins and aprons, and Sir John must not know of it. Bardolph hath brought word.

THIRD DRAWER By the mass, here will be old Utis. It will be an excellent stratagem.

SECOND DRAWER I'll see if I can find out Sneak. *Exit.*

Enter Mistress Quickly [*the Hostess*] *and Doll Tearsheet.*

HOSTESS I' faith, sweetheart, methinks now you are in an excellent good temperality. Your pulsidge beats as extraordinarily as heart would desire, and your color, I warrant you, is as red as any rose, in good truth, la! But, i' faith, you have drunk too much canaries, and that's a marvelous searching wine, and it perfumes the blood ere one can say, "What's this?" How do you now?

DOLL Better than I was. Hem!

HOSTESS Why, that's well said. A good heart's worth gold. Lo, here comes Sir John.

Enter Sir John [*Falstaff*].

FALSTAFF [*Singing*] "When Arthur first in court"— Empty the jordan. [*Exit a Drawer.*]—[*Singing.*] "And was a worthy king." How now, Mistress Doll?

HOSTESS Sick of a calm, yea, good faith.

FALSTAFF So is all her sect. An they be once in a calm, they are sick.

DOLL A pox damn you, you muddy rascal, is that all the comfort you give me?

FALSTAFF You make fat rascals, Mistress Doll.

DOLL I make them? Gluttony and diseases make them; I make them not.

FALSTAFF If the cook help to make the gluttony, you help to make the diseases, Doll. We catch of you, Doll, we catch of you. Grant that, my poor virtue, grant that.

DOLL Yea, joy, our chains and our jewels.

FALSTAFF "Your brooches, pearls, and ouches." For to serve bravely is to come halting off, you know; to come off the breach with his pike bent bravely, and to surgery bravely; to venture upon the charg'd chambers bravely—

DOLL Hang yourself, you muddy conger, hang yourself!

HOSTESS By my troth, this is the old fashion. You two never meet but you fall to some discord. You are both, i' good truth, as rheumatic as two dry toasts; you cannot one bear with another's confirmities. What the good-year! One must bear, and that must be you [*To Doll*]. You are the weaker vessel, as they say, the emptier vessel.

DOLL Can a weak empty vessel bear such a huge full hogshead? There's a whole merchant's venture of Bordeaux stuff in him; you have not seen a hulk better stuff'd in the hold. Come, I'll be friends with thee, Jack. Thou art going to the wars, and whether I shall ever see thee again or no, there is nobody cares.

Enter Drawer.

DRAWER Sir, Ancient Pistol's below, and would speak with you.

DOLL Hang him, swaggering rascal! Let him not come hither. It is the foul-mouth'd'st rogue in England.

HOSTESS If he swagger, let him not come here. No, by my faith, I must live among my neighbors. I'll no swaggerers. I am in good name and fame with the very best. Shut the door, there comes no swaggerers here. I have not liv'd all this while to have swaggering now. Shut the door, I pray you.

FALSTAFF Dost thou hear, Hostess?

HOSTESS Pray ye, pacify yourself, Sir John. There comes no swaggerers here.

FALSTAFF Dost thou hear? It is mine ancient.

HOSTESS Tilly-fally, Sir John, ne'er tell me. Your ancient swagg'rer comes not in my doors. I was before Master Tisick, the debuty, t' other day, and, as he said to me, 'twas no longer ago than Wedn'sday last, i' good faith, "Neighbor Quickly," says he—Master Dumbe, our minister was by then—"Neighbor Quickly," says he, "receive those that are civil, for," said he, "you are in an ill name." Now 'a said so, I can tell whereupon. "For," says he, "you are an honest woman, and well thought on; therefore take heed what guests you re-

II.iv. London. A tavern in Eastcheap, usually identified as the Boar's Head. Some tavern furniture is provided.
2 Apple-johns a kind of apple eaten when shriveled and withered **4 Mass** i.e., by the Mass **10 cover** spread the cloth, set the table **11 noise** band of musicians **13 Dispatch** hurry up **19 old Utis** i.e., rare fun **23 temperality** i.e., temper. **pulsidge** i.e., pulse **24 extraordinarily** i.e., ordinarily **26 canaries** (A light, sweet wine from the Canary Islands.) **27 searching** potent **33 When . . . court** (A fragment from the ballad "Sir Launcelot du Lake.") **34 jordan** chamber-pot **36 calm** i.e., qualm **37 sect** sex

41 rascals (1) lean deer (2) good-for-nothings **47 Yea . . . jewels** i.e., yes, indeed, you *catch* or steal our valuables **48 ouches** jewels. (The line is from a ballad.) **51–52 charg'd chambers** small cannon; with bawdy double meaning, as also in *breach, pike, surgery* (venereal treatment), *conger* (eel, with sexual connotation), *bear* **57 rheumatic** (Blunder for *choleric* or *splenetic?*) **58 confirmities** (For *infirmities.*) **58–59 What the good-year** (An expletive, meaning something like *what the devil.*) **63–64 Bordeaux stuff** i.e., wine **68 Ancient** ensign, standard-bearer **82 Tilly-fally** i.e., fiddlesticks **84 Tisick** (Literally, a cough or consumption.) **debuty** deputy

ceive. Receive," says he, "no swaggering companions." There comes none here. You would bless you to hear what he said. No, I'll no swagg'rers.

FALSTAFF He's no swagg'rer, hostess; a tame cheater, i' faith; you may stroke him as gently as a puppy greyhound. He'll not swagger with a Barbary hen, if her feathers turn back in any show of resistance. Call him up, drawer. *[Exit Drawer.]*

HOSTESS Cheater, call you him? I will bar no honest man my house, nor no cheater, but I do not love swaggering, by my troth. I am the worse when one says swagger. Feel, masters, how I shake; look you, I warrant you.

DOLL So you do, hostess.

HOSTESS Do I? Yea, in very truth, do I, an 'twere an aspen leaf. I cannot abide swagg'rers.

Enter Ancient Pistol, [Bardolph,] and Boy [Page].

PISTOL God save you, Sir John!

FALSTAFF Welcome, Ancient Pistol. Here, Pistol, I charge you with a cup of sack. Do you discharge upon mine hostess.

PISTOL I will discharge upon her, Sir John, with two bullets.

FALSTAFF She is pistol-proof, sir; you shall hardly offend her.

HOSTESS Come, I'll drink no proofs nor no bullets. I'll drink no more than will do me good, for no man's pleasure, I.

PISTOL Then to you, Mistress Dorothy; I will charge you.

DOLL Charge me? I scorn you, scurvy companion. What, you poor, base, rascally, cheating, lack-linen mate? Away, you moldy rogue, away! I am meat for your master.

PISTOL I know you, Mistress Dorothy.

DOLL Away, you cut-purse rascal! You filthy bung, away! By this wine, I'll thrust my knife in your moldy chaps, an you play the saucy cuttle with me. Away, you bottle-ale rascal! You basket-hilt stale juggler, you! Since when, I pray you, sir? God's light, with two points on your shoulder? Much!

PISTOL God let me not live, but I will murder your ruff for this.

FALSTAFF No more, Pistol; I would not have you go off here. Discharge yourself of our company, Pistol.

HOSTESS No, good Captain Pistol, not here, sweet captain.

DOLL Captain? Thou abominable damn'd cheater, art thou not asham'd to be call'd captain? An captains were of my mind, they would truncheon you out for taking their names upon you before you have earn'd them. You a captain? You slave, for what? For tearing a poor whore's ruff in a bawdy-house? He a captain? Hang him, rogue! He lives upon moldy stew'd prunes and dried cakes. A captain? God's light, these villains will make the word as odious as the word "occupy," which was an excellent good word before it was ill sorted. Therefore captains had need look to 't.

BARDOLPH Pray thee go down, good ancient.

FALSTAFF Hark thee hither, Mistress Doll.

PISTOL Not I. I tell thee what, Corporal Bardolph, I could tear her. I'll be reveng'd of her.

PAGE Pray thee go down.

PISTOL I'll see her damn'd first, to Pluto's damned lake,
by this hand, to th' infernal deep,
With Erebus and tortures vile also.
Hold hook and line, say I.
Down, down, dogs! Down, faitors!
Have we not Hiren here?

HOSTESS Good Captain Peesel, be quiet; 'tis very late, i' faith. I beseek you now, aggravate your choler.

PISTOL
These be good humors, indeed! Shall pack-horses
And hollow pamper'd jades of Asia,
Which cannot go but thirty mile a day,
Compare with Caesars, and with Cannibals,
And Troiant Greeks? Nay, rather damn them with
King Cerberus, and let the welkin roar.
Shall we fall foul for toys?

HOSTESS By my troth, captain, these are very bitter words.

BARDOLPH Be gone, good ancient. This will grow to a brawl anon.

PISTOL
Die men like dogs! Give crowns like pins! Have we
not Hiren here?

HOSTESS O' my word, captain, there's none such here. What the good-year, do you think I would deny her? For God's sake, be quiet.

PISTOL
Then feed, and be fat, my fair Calipolis.
Come, give 's some sack.
"Si fortune me tormente, sperato me contento."
Fear we broadsides? No, let the fiend give fire.
Give me some sack, and, sweetheart, lie thou there.
[Laying down his sword.]
Come we to full points here, and are etceteras
nothing?

FALSTAFF Pistol, I would be quiet.

92–93 companions ruffians **95 cheater** decoy in a team of confidence men **97 Barbary hen** guinea hen. (Slang term for a prostitute.) **100 Cheater** (Mistress Quickly may understand the word as *escheator,* an officer of the King's exchequer.) **110 charge** pledge, drink to. **discharge upon** toast; with bawdy double meaning; see also *charge, Pistol, bullets* (testicles), *meat* (slang for *whore*), etc. **114–115 offend** wound **123 mate** low fellow. **meat** (with a pun on *mate;* pronounced alike) **126 bung** pickpocket **128 chaps** chops, cheeks. **cuttle** cut-throat or cutpurse **129 baskethilt** basketlike hilt or handguard for a practice weapon only; see III.ii. 65, note. (Doll scornfully accuses Pistol of avoiding danger by not using a real sword.) **juggler** imposter **131 points** lace tags (for securing armor to the shoulders) **140 truncheon** cudgel

144 stew'd prunes (Associated with brothels.) **146 occupy** fornicate **154 Pluto's damned lake** the river of the underworld **156 Erebus** the underworld **158 faitors** imposters, cheats **159 Hiren** i.e., Pistol's fanciful name for his sword, with a seeming allusion to a lost play by Peele, *The Turkish Mahomet and Hiren the Fair Greek. Hiren* means Irene. (Throughout, Pistol's colorful speech is full of echoes from the contemporary theatre.) **161 beseek** beseech. **aggravate** (For *moderate.*) **162 humors** whimsies of conduct **162–166 Shall . . . Greeks** (Misquotation from Marlowe's *Second Part of Tamburlaine,* IV.iv.1–2.) **165 Cannibals** (For *Hannibals.*) **166 Troiant** Trojan **167 Cerberus** three-headed dog guarding the entrance to Hades. **welkin** heavens **168 fall . . . toys** fall out over trifles **177 Then . . . Calipolis** (Garbled version of a line in Peele's *The Battle of Alcazar,* II.iii. 70.) **179 Si . . . contento** if fortune torments me, hope contents me. (An ignorant medley of Spanish and Italian.) **180 give fire** shoot **182 full points** full stops, periods; also, swords' points

PISTOL
Sweet knight, I kiss thy neaf. 184
What, we have seen the seven stars. 185
DOLL For God's sake, thrust him downstairs. I cannot
endure such a fustian rascal. 187
PISTOL
Thrust him down stairs? Know we not Galloway nags? 188
FALSTAFF Quoit him down, Bardolph, like a shove- 189
groat shilling. Nay, an 'a do nothing but speak noth- 190
ing, 'a shall be nothing here. 191
BARDOLPH Come, get you downstairs.
PISTOL
What, shall we have incision? Shall we imbrue? 193
[Snatching up his sword.]
Then death rock me asleep, abridge my doleful
days! 194
Why, then, let grievous, ghastly, gaping wounds
Untwine the Sisters Three! Come, Atropos, I say! 196
HOSTESS Here's goodly stuff toward!
FALSTAFF Give me my rapier, boy.
DOLL I pray thee, Jack, I pray thee, do not draw.
FALSTAFF Get you down stairs.
[Drawing, and driving Pistol out.]
HOSTESS Here's a goodly tumult! I'll forswear keeping
house afore I'll be in these tirrits and frights. So, mur- 202
der, I warrant now. Alas, alas, put up your naked
weapons, put up your naked weapons.
[Exeunt Pistol and Bardolph.]
DOLL I pray thee, Jack, be quiet; the rascal's gone. Ah,
you whoreson little valiant villain, you!
HOSTESS Are you not hurt i' th' groin? Methought 'a
made a shrewd thrust at your belly.

[Enter Bardolph.]

FALSTAFF Have you turn'd him out o' doors?
BARDOLPH Yea, sir. The rascal's drunk. You have hurt
him, sir, i' th' shoulder.
FALSTAFF A rascal! To brave me?
DOLL Ah, you sweet little rogue, you! Alas, poor ape,
how thou sweat'st! Come, let me wipe thy face. Come
on, you whoreson chops. Ah, rogue, i' faith, I love 215
thee. Thou art as valorous as Hector of Troy, worth 216
five of Agamemnon, and ten times better than the 217
Nine Worthies. Ah, villain! 218
FALSTAFF A rascally slave! I will toss the rogue in a
blanket.
DOLL Do, an thou dar'st for thy heart. An thou dost, I'll
canvass thee between a pair of sheets. 222

Enter Music.

PAGE The music is come, sir.
FALSTAFF Let them play. Play, sirs. Sit on my knee,
Doll. A rascal bragging slave! The rogue fled from me
like quicksilver.
DOLL *[Sitting on his knee]* I' faith, and thou follow'dst
him like a church. Thou whoreson little tidy Bartholo- 228
mew boar-pig, when wilt thou leave fighting o' days 229
and foining o' nights, and begin to patch up thine old 230
body for heaven?

Enter [behind] Prince and Poins [disguised].

FALSTAFF Peace, good Doll, do not speak like a death's-
head; do not bid me remember mine end.
DOLL Sirrah, what humor's the Prince of?
FALSTAFF A good shallow young fellow. 'A would have
made a good pantler, 'a would ha' chipp'd bread well. 236
DOLL They say Poins has a good wit.
FALSTAFF He a good wit? Hang him, baboon! His wit's
as thick as Tewkesbury mustard. There's no more con- 239
ceit in him than is in a mallet. 240
DOLL Why does the Prince love him so, then?
FALSTAFF Because their legs are both of a bigness, and
'a plays at quoits well, and eats conger and fennel, and 243
drinks off candles' ends for flap-dragons, and rides the 244
wild-mare with the boys, and jumps upon join'd- 245
stools, and swears with a good grace, and wears his 246
boots very smooth, like unto the sign of the Leg, and 247
breeds no bate with telling of discreet stories; and such 248
other gambol faculties 'a has, that show a weak mind 249
and an able body, for the which the Prince admits
him. For the Prince himself is such another; the
weight of a hair will turn the scales between their
avoirdupois.
PRINCE *[To Poins]* Would not this nave of a wheel have 254
his ears cut off? 255
POINS Let's beat him before his whore.
PRINCE Look whe'er the wither'd elder hath not his poll 257
claw'd like a parrot. 258
POINS Is it not strange that desire should so many years
outlive performance?
FALSTAFF Kiss me, Doll.
PRINCE *[To Poins]* Saturn and Venus this year in con- 262
junction? What says th' almanac to that? 263
POINS And look whether the fiery Trigon, his man, be 264
not lisping to his master's old tables, his note-book, 265
his counsel-keeper.
FALSTAFF Thou dost give me flattering busses. 267
DOLL By my troth, I kiss thee with a most constant
heart.

184 neaf fist **185 the seven stars** the Pleiades. (Pistol means they have enjoyed themselves at night.) **187 fustian** bombast, worthless **188 Galloway nags** an inferior breed of Irish horses **189 Quoit** throw **189–190 shove-groat shilling** an Edward VI shilling used in shove-groat, a game in which the coins were shoved toward a mark **190–191 speak nothing** speak nonsense **191 nothing here** gone from here **193 incision** bloodshed. **imbrue** shed blood **194 death . . . asleep** (Quotation from a current poem about Anne Boleyn and her brother as they awaited execution.) **196 Sisters Three** i.e., the three Fates, Clotho, Lachesis, and Atropos. Atropos severed the thread of life. **202 tirrits** fits of temper **215 chops** fat jaws **216 Hector of Troy** leader of the Trojans; the type of valor **217 Agamemnon** leader of the Greeks at Troy **218 Nine Worthies** Arthur, Charlemagne, Godfrey of Boulogne; Hector, Alexander, Julius Caesar; Joshua, David, Judas Maccabaeus **222 canvass** toss. (Doll gives a sexual interpretation to Falstaff's phrase, *toss . . . in a blanket,* which means to subject a coward to ignominious treatment.) **222 s.d. Music** musicians

228 a church i.e., a ponderous structure (?) **228–229 Bartholomew boar-pig** (Allusion to the serving of roast pig at Bartholomew Fair, August 24, in Smithfield.) **230 foining** thrusting, fornicating **236 pantler** pantryworker. **chipp'd bread** cut off the hard bread crusts **239 Tewkesbury mustard** (Tewkesbury in Gloucestershire was famous for mustard balls.) **239–240 conceit** wit **243 conger and fennel** conger eel seasoned with a yellow-flowered herb **244 drinks . . . flap-dragons** i.e., drinks liquor with a lighted candle floating in it. (An act of bravado.) **245 wild-mare** seesaw **245–246 join'd-stools** stools made by a *joiner* or craftsman in furniture etc. **247 smooth** i.e., well-fitting. **sign . . . Leg** sign over a bootmaker's shop **248 breeds no bate** causes no strife **249 gambol** sportive **254 nave** hub. (Refers to Falstaff's rotundity; with a pun on *knave*.) **254–255 have . . . off** i.e., as the punishment for slandering royalty **257–258 poll . . . parrot** (Doll is scratching Falstaff's head, his *poll*.) **262–263 Saturn . . . conjunction** i.e., the planets that govern age and love near one another in the heavens **264 fiery Trigon** (One quarter of the zodiac, Aries, Leo, and Sagittarius, was characterized as fiery; the other three quarters were watery, airy, and earthy. The joke here is directed against Bardolph's fiery face.) **265 lisping . . . note-book** making love to Falstaff's old confidante, i.e., Mistress Quickly. **tables** notebook **267 busses** kisses

FALSTAFF I am old, I am old.

DOLL I love thee better than I love e'er a scurvy young boy of them all.

FALSTAFF What stuff wilt have a kirtle of? I shall receive money o' Thursday; shalt have a cap tomorrow. A merry song, come. It grows late; we'll to bed. Thou 'lt forget me when I am gone.

DOLL By my troth, thou 'lt set me a-weeping an thou say'st so. Prove that ever I dress myself handsome till thy return—well, hearken a' th' end.

FALSTAFF Some sack, Francis.

PRINCE, POINS Anon, anon, sir. [*Coming forward.*]

FALSTAFF Ha? A bastard son of the King's? And art not thou Poins his brother?

PRINCE Why, thou globe of sinful continents, what a life dost thou lead!

FALSTAFF A better than thou. I am a gentleman, thou art a drawer.

PRINCE Very true, sir, and I come to draw you out by the ears.

HOSTESS O, the Lord preserve thy Grace! By my troth, welcome to London. Now, the Lord bless that sweet face of thine! O Jesu, are you come from Wales?

FALSTAFF Thou whoreson mad compound of majesty, by this light flesh and corrupt blood, thou art welcome.

DOLL How, you fat fool! I scorn you.

POINS My lord, he will drive you out of your revenge and turn all to a merriment, if you take not the heat.

PRINCE You whoreson candle-mine, you, how vilely did you speak of me even now before this honest, virtuous, civil gentlewoman!

HOSTESS God's blessing of your good heart! And so she is, by my troth.

FALSTAFF Didst thou hear me?

PRINCE Yea, and you knew me, as you did when you ran away by Gads Hill. You knew I was at your back, and spoke it on purpose to try my patience.

FALSTAFF No, no, no; not so. I did not think thou wast within hearing.

PRINCE I shall drive you then to confess the willful abuse, and then I know how to handle you.

FALSTAFF No abuse, Hal, o' mine honor, no abuse.

PRINCE Not to dispraise me, and call me pantler and bread-chipper and I know not what?

FALSTAFF No abuse, Hal.

POINS No abuse?

FALSTAFF No abuse, Ned, i' th' world; honest Ned, none. I disprais'd him before the wicked, that the wicked might not fall in love with thee [*To Hal*]; in which doing, I have done the part of a careful friend and a true subject, and thy father is to give me thanks for it. No abuse, Hal. None, Ned, none. No, faith, boys, none.

PRINCE See now, whether pure fear and entire cowardice doth not make thee wrong this virtuous gentlewoman to close with us. Is she of the wicked? Is thine hostess here of the wicked? Or is thy boy of the wicked? Or honest Bardolph, whose zeal burns in his nose, of the wicked?

POINS Answer, thou dead elm, answer.

FALSTAFF The fiend hath prick'd down Bardolph irrecoverable, and his face is Lucifer's privy-kitchen, where he doth nothing but roast malt-worms. For the boy, there is a good angel about him, but the devil blinds him too.

PRINCE For the women?

FALSTAFF For one of them, she's in hell already, and burns poor souls. For th' other, I owe her money, and whether she be damn'd for that I know not.

HOSTESS No, I warrant you.

FALSTAFF No, I think thou art not; I think thou art quit for that. Marry, there is another indictment upon thee, for suffering flesh to be eaten in thy house, contrary to the law, for the which I think thou wilt howl.

HOSTESS All vict'lers do so. What's a joint of mutton or two in a whole Lent?

PRINCE You, gentlewoman—

DOLL What says your Grace?

FALSTAFF His grace says that which his flesh rebels against. *Peto knocks at door.*

HOSTESS Who knocks so loud at door? Look to th' door there, Francis.

[*Francis goes to the door. Enter Peto.*]

PRINCE
Peto, how now, what news?

PETO
The King your father is at Westminster,
And there are twenty weak and wearied posts
Come from the north. And as I came along
I met and overtook a dozen captains,
Bare-headed, sweating, knocking at the taverns,
And asking everyone for Sir John Falstaff.

PRINCE
By heaven, Poins, I feel me much to blame,
So idly to profane the precious time,
When tempest of commotion, like the south
Borne with black vapor, doth begin to melt
And drop upon our bare unarmed heads.
Give me my sword and cloak. Falstaff, good night.
Exeunt Prince and Poins, [*Peto, and Bardolph*].

FALSTAFF Now comes in the sweetest morsel of the night, and we must hence and leave it unpick'd. [*Knocking within.*] More knocking at the door!

[*Enter Bardolph.*]

How now, what's the matter?

BARDOLPH
You must away to court, sir, presently.

273 stuff material. **kirtle** skirt **279 hearken a' th' end** i.e., wait to see how it turns out **284 globe** (1) terrestrial globe (2) sphere. **continents** (1) the continents of the earth (2) contents **294 light . . . blood** i.e., Doll **298 if . . . heat** if you don't strike while the iron is hot **299 candle-mine** magazine or storehouse of tallow **305–306 Yea . . . Gads Hill** (See *1 Henry IV,* II.iv.) **324 entire** sheer

326 close come to terms, agree **331 prick'd down** marked, or designated **333 malt-worms** topers, drunkards **335 blinds** (A textual crux. F reads *outbids;* sometimes emended to *attends.*) **338 burns** i.e., infects with venereal disease **341–342 quit for that** (1) acquitted of that charge (2) saved on that score **343 flesh to be eaten** (Allusion to enactments to prevent the sale of meat in Lent; with sexual double entendre on *mutton,* whore.) **345 vict'lers** victuallers **349 grace** (1) royal grace (2) inclination toward spiritual grace **355 posts** messengers **362 commotion** insurrection. **south** south wind (regarded as a breeder of tempests) **363 Borne** laden

A dozen captains stay at door for you.

FALSTAFF [*To the Page*] Pay the musicians, sirrah. Farewell, hostess; farewell, Doll. You see, my good wenches, how men of merit are sought after. The undeserver may sleep, when the man of action is call'd on. Farewell, good wenches. If I be not sent away post, I will see you again ere I go.

DOLL I cannot speak. If my heart be not ready to burst—well, sweet Jack, have a care of thyself.

FALSTAFF Farewell, farewell.

Exit [*with Bardolph and Page*].

HOSTESS Well, fare thee well. I have known thee these twenty-nine years, come peascod-time, but an honester and truer-hearted man—well, fare thee well.

BARDOLPH [*Within*] Mistress Tearsheet!

HOSTESS What's the matter?

BARDOLPH [*Within*] Bid Mistress Tearsheet come to my master.

HOSTESS O, run, Doll, run; run, good Doll. Come. [*To Bardolph within.*] She comes blubber'd.—Yea, will you come, Doll? *Exeunt.*

[ACT III • SCENE I]

Enter the King in his nightgown, alone [*with a Page*].

KING

Go call the Earls of Surrey and of Warwick;
But, ere they come, bid them o'er-read these letters,
And well consider of them. Make good speed.

[*Gives letters. Exit Page.*]

How many thousand of my poorest subjects
Are at this hour asleep! O sleep, O gentle sleep,
Nature's soft nurse, how have I frighted thee,
That thou no more wilt weigh my eyelids down
And steep my senses in forgetfulness?
Why rather, sleep, liest thou in smoky cribs,
Upon uneasy pallets stretching thee
And hush'd with buzzing night-flies to thy slumber,
Than in the perfum'd chambers of the great,
Under the canopies of costly state,
And lull'd with sound of sweetest melody?
O thou dull god, why liest thou with the vile
In loathsome beds, and leavest the kingly couch
A watch-case or a common 'larum-bell?
Wilt thou upon the high and giddy mast
Seal up the ship-boy's eyes, and rock his brains
In cradle of the rude imperious surge
And in the visitation of the winds,
Who take the ruffian billows by the top,
Curling their monstrous heads and hanging them
With deafing clamor in the slippery clouds,
That, with the hurly, death itself awakes?
Canst thou, O partial sleep, give thy repose
To the wet sea-boy in an hour so rude,
And, in the calmest and most stillest night,
With all appliances and means to boot,
Deny it to a king? Then happy low, lie down!
Uneasy lies the head that wears a crown.

Enter Warwick, Surrey, and Sir John Blunt.

WARWICK

Many good morrows to your Majesty!

KING

Is it good morrow, lords?

WARWICK

'Tis one o'clock, and past.

KING

Why, then, good morrow to you all, my lords.
Have you read o'er the letters that I sent you?

WARWICK

We have, my liege.

KING

Then you perceive the body of our kingdom
How foul it is, what rank diseases grow,
And with what danger, near the heart of it.

WARWICK

It is but as a body yet distempered,
Which to his former strength may be restor'd
With good advice and little medicine.
My Lord Northumberland will soon be cool'd.

KING

O God, that one might read the book of fate,
And see the revolution of the times
Make mountains level, and the continent,
Weary of solid firmness, melt itself
Into the sea, and other times to see
The beachy girdle of the ocean
Too wide for Neptune's hips, how chance's mocks
And changes fill the cup of alteration
With divers liquors! O, if this were seen,
The happiest youth, viewing his progress through,
What perils past, what crosses to ensue,
Would shut the book, and sit him down and die.
'Tis not ten years gone
Since Richard and Northumberland, great friends,
Did feast together, and in two years after
Were they at wars. It is but eight years since
This Percy was the man nearest my soul,
Who like a brother toil'd in my affairs
And laid his love and life under my foot,
Yea, for my sake, even to the eyes of Richard
Gave him defiance. But which of you was by—
[*To Warwick.*] You, cousin Nevil, as I may
remember—
When Richard, with his eye brimful of tears,
Then check'd and rated by Northumberland,
Did speak these words, now prov'd a prophecy?
"Northumberland, thou ladder by the which

376 post immediately **382 peascod-time** i.e., early summer, when peas are still unripe **389 blubber'd** disfigured with weeping

III.i. Location: Westminster. The palace.
s.d. nightgown dressing gown **9 cribs** hovels **10 thee** thyself **15 dull** drowsy. **vile** low in rank **17 watch-case** sentry box **25 That** so that. **hurly** tumult

30 low humble persons **39 rank** festering **41 distempered** sick **47 continent** dry land **51 Too wide** i.e., vast in expanse, when the ocean recedes. **chance's mocks** (A textual crux. Q and F read *chances mocks;* sometimes emended to *chances mock.*) **54 progress through** life's progress from beginning to end **55 crosses** afflictions **61 This Percy** i.e., Northumberland **63 under my foot** i.e., under my control **64 to the eyes** i.e., face to face **66 Nevil** (An error; this Earl of Warwick's surname is Beauchamp.) **68 check'd and rated** rebuked **70–77 Northumberland . . . corruption** (See *Richard II,* V.i.55 ff.)

My cousin Bolingbroke ascends my throne"—
Though then, God knows, I had no such intent,
But that necessity so bow'd the state
That I and greatness were compell'd to kiss—
"The time shall come," thus did he follow it,
"The time will come, that foul sin, gathering head,
Shall break into corruption"— so went on, 77
Foretelling this same time's condition
And the division of our amity.

WARWICK
There is a history in all men's lives,
Figuring the nature of the times deceas'd, 81
The which observ'd, a man may prophesy,
With a near aim, of the main chance of things 83
As yet not come to life, which in their seeds
And weak beginnings lie intreasured. 85
Such things become the hatch and brood of time,
And by the necessary form of this 87
King Richard might create a perfect guess
That great Northumberland, then false to him,
Would of that seed grow to a greater falseness,
Which should not find a ground to root upon,
Unless on you.

KING Are these things then necessities?
Then let us meet them like necessities.
And that same word even now cries out on us. 94
They say the Bishop and Northumberland
Are fifty thousand strong.

WARWICK It cannot be, my lord.
Rumor doth double, like the voice and echo,
The numbers of the fear'd. Please it your Grace
To go to bed. Upon my soul, my lord,
The powers that you already have sent forth
Shall bring this prize in very easily.
To comfort you the more, I have receiv'd
A certain instance that Glendower is dead. 103
Your Majesty hath been this fortnight ill,
And these unseason'd hours perforce must add 105
Unto your sickness.

KING I will take your counsel.
And were these inward wars once out of hand, 107
We would, dear lords, unto the Holy Land. *Exeunt.*

[SCENE II]

Enter Justice Shallow and Justice Silence, [meeting; with Mouldy, Shadow, Wart, Feeble, Bullcalf, and Servants behind].

SHALLOW Come on, come on, come on, give me your hand, sir, give me your hand, sir. An early stirrer, by the rood! And how doth my good cousin Silence? 3

SILENCE Good morrow, good cousin Shallow.

SHALLOW And how doth my cousin, your bedfellow? And your fairest daughter and mine, my goddaughter Ellen?

SILENCE Alas, a black ousel, cousin Shallow! 8

SHALLOW By yea and no, sir. I dare say my cousin William is become a good scholar. He is at Oxford still, is he not?

SILENCE Indeed, sir, to my cost.

SHALLOW 'A must, then, to the Inns o' Court shortly. I 13
was once of Clement's Inn, where I think they will talk 14
of mad Shallow yet.

SILENCE You were call'd "lusty Shallow" then, cousin. 16

SHALLOW By the mass, I was call'd anything; and I would have done anything indeed too, and roundly too. There was I, and Little John Doit of Staffordshire, and black George Barnes, and Francis Pickbone, and
Will Squele, a Cotsole man. You had not four such 21
swinge-bucklers in all the Inns o' Court again. And I 22
may say to you, we knew where the bona-robas were 23
and had the best of them all at commandment. Then
was Jack Falstaff, now Sir John, a boy, and page to 25
Thomas Mowbray, Duke of Norfolk. 26

SILENCE This Sir John, cousin, that comes hither anon about soldiers?

SHALLOW The same Sir John, the very same. I see him 29
break Skoggin's head at the court-gate, when 'a was a 30
crack not thus high. And the very same day did I fight 31
with one Sampson Stockfish, a fruiterer, behind
Gray's Inn. Jesu, Jesu, the mad days that I have spent! 33
And to see how many of my old acquaintance are dead!

SILENCE We shall all follow, cousin.

SHALLOW Certain, 'tis certain, very sure, very sure. Death, as the Psalmist saith, is certain to all, all shall
die. How a good yoke of bullocks at Stamford fair? 39

SILENCE By my troth, I was not there.

SHALLOW Death is certain. Is old Double of your town living yet?

SILENCE Dead, sir.

SHALLOW Jesu, Jesu, dead! 'A drew a good bow; and
dead? 'A shot a fine shoot. John a Gaunt lov'd him 45
well, and betted much money on his head. Dead? 'A
would have clapp'd i' th' clout at twelve score, and 47
carried you a forehand shaft a fourteen and fourteen 48
and a half, that it would have done a man's heart good 49
to see. How a score of ewes now?

SILENCE Thereafter as they be, a score of good ewes 51
may be worth ten pounds.

SHALLOW And is old Double dead?

SILENCE Here come two of Sir John Falstaff's men, as I think.

81 Figuring depicting. **deceas'd** past **83 main chance** general probability **85 intreasured** stored up **87 necessary . . . this** logical consequence of this principle **94 cries out on** denounces **103 instance** proof **105 unseason'd** unseasonable **107 inward** civil. **out of hand** done with

III.ii. Location: Gloucestershire. Before Justice Shallow's house. A table and chairs must be provided on stage.
3 rood cross

8 ousel blackbird. (I.e., Ellen is *black* or dark-complexioned, not fair.) **13 Inns o' Court** legal societies of London **14 Clement's Inn** one of the Inns of Chancery; in Shallow's time, these institutions prepared one for the Inns of Court **16 lusty** merry **21 Cotsole** from the Cotswold Hills in Gloucestershire **22 swinge-bucklers** swashbucklers, roisterers **23 bona-robas** showily dressed harlots **25–26 page to Thomas Mowbray** (Both Sir John Oldcastle, Falstaff's original, and Sir John Fastolfe, for whom Falstaff was renamed, were pages to the Duke of Norfolk, who figures in the play *Richard II*.) **29 see** saw **30 Skoggin** (Perhaps John Skogan, court jester to Edward IV and protagonist of an Elizabethan jestbook known as "Skogan's Jests.") **31 crack** pert little boy **33 Gray's Inn** one of the Inns of Court **39 How** how much (is the asking price for) **45 John a Gaunt** (Father of Henry IV.) **47 clapp'd . . . score** hit the bull's eye at 240 yards **48–49 carried . . . half** i.e., could shoot a heavy arrow in a straight line rather than in a curved trajectory for a distance of 280 to 290 yards **51 Thereafter . . . be** according to their quality

Enter Bardolph and one with him.

SHALLOW Good morrow, honest gentlemen.

BARDOLPH I beseech you, which is Justice Shallow?

SHALLOW I am Robert Shallow, sir, a poor esquire of this county, and one of the King's justices of the peace. What is your good pleasure with me?

BARDOLPH My captain, sir, commends him to you, my 61
captain, Sir John Falstaff, a tall gentleman, by heaven, 62
and a most gallant leader.

SHALLOW He greets me well, sir. I knew him a good
backsword man. How doth the good knight? May I 65
ask how my lady his wife doth?

BARDOLPH Sir, pardon; a soldier is better accommo- 67
dated than with a wife. 68

SHALLOW It is well said, in faith, sir, and it is well said indeed too. Better accommodated! It is good, yea, indeed, is it. Good phrases are surely, and ever were, very commendable. Accommodated! It comes of "accommodo." Very good, a good phrase.

BARDOLPH Pardon sir, I have heard the word. Phrase
call you it? By this day, I know not the phrase. But I
will maintain the word with my sword to be a soldier-
like word, and a word of exceeding good command,
by heaven. Accommodated; that is, when a man is, as
they say, accommodated; or when a man is, being,
whereby 'a may be thought to be accommodated, 80
which is an excellent thing.

Enter Falstaff.

SHALLOW It is very just.—Look, here comes good Sir
John. Give me your good hand, give me your wor-
ship's good hand. By my troth, you like well and bear 84
your years very well. Welcome, good Sir John.

FALSTAFF I am glad to see you well, good Master Robert Shallow. Master Surecard, as I think?

SHALLOW No, Sir John, it is my cousin Silence, in com- 88
mission with me. 89

FALSTAFF Good Master Silence, it well befits you should
be of the peace. 91

SILENCE Your good worship is welcome.

FALSTAFF Fie, this is hot weather, gentlemen. Have you
provided me here half a dozen sufficient men? 94

SHALLOW Marry, have we, sir. Will you sit?
[*They sit at a table.*]

FALSTAFF Let me see them, I beseech you.

SHALLOW Where's the roll? Where's the roll? Where's the roll? Let me see, let me see, let me see. So, so, so, so, so, so, so; yea, marry, sir. Ralph Mouldy! Let them appear as I call; let them do so, let them do so. Let me see, where is Mouldy?

MOULDY [*Stepping forward*] Here, an 't please you.

SHALLOW What think you, Sir John? A good-limb'd fel-
low, young, strong, and of good friends. 104

FALSTAFF Is thy name Mouldy?

MOULDY Yea, an 't please you.

FALSTAFF 'Tis the more time thou wert us'd.

SHALLOW Ha, ha, ha! Most excellent, i' faith! Things that are moldy lack use. Very singular good, in faith, well said, Sir John, very well said.

[FALSTAFF Prick him.] 111
[*Shallow writes on the muster-roll.*]

MOULDY I was prick'd well enough before, an you 112
could have let me alone. My old dame will be undone 113
now for one to do her husbandry and her drudgery. 114
You need not to have prick'd me. There are other men
fitter to go out than I.

FALSTAFF Go to. Peace, Mouldy, you shall go. Mouldy,
it is time you were spent. 118

MOULDY Spent?

SHALLOW Peace, fellow, peace. Stand aside. Know you
where you are? For th' other, Sir John, let me see: Si- 121
mon Shadow!

FALSTAFF Yea, marry, let me have him to sit under. He's like to be a cold soldier.

SHALLOW Where's Shadow?

SHADOW [*Stepping forward*] Here, sir.

FALSTAFF Shadow, whose son art thou?

SHADOW My mother's son, sir.

FALSTAFF Thy mother's son! Like enough, and thy fa- 129
ther's shadow. So the son of the female is the shadow 130
of the male. It is often so, indeed; but much of the
father's substance!

SHALLOW Do you like him, Sir John?

FALSTAFF Shadow will serve for summer. Prick him
[*Aside*], for we have a number of shadows fill up the 135
muster-book.

SHALLOW Thomas Wart!

FALSTAFF Where's he?

WART [*Stepping forward*] Here, sir.

FALSTAFF Is thy name Wart?

WART Yea, sir.

FALSTAFF Thou art a very ragged wart.

SHALLOW Shall I prick him, Sir John?

FALSTAFF It were superfluous, for his apparel is built
upon his back and the whole frame stands upon pins. 145
Prick him no more.

SHALLOW Ha, ha, ha! You can do it, sir; you can do it. 147
I commend you well. Francis Feeble!

FEEBLE [*Stepping forward*] Here, sir.

FALSTAFF What trade art thou, Feeble?

FEEBLE A woman's tailor, sir.

SHALLOW Shall I prick him, sir?

FALSTAFF You may. But if he had been a man's tailor,
he'd a' prick'd you. Wilt thou make as many holes in 154
an enemy's battle as thou hast done in a woman's pet- 155
ticoat?

FEEBLE I will do my good will, sir. You can have no more.

FALSTAFF Well said, good woman's tailor! Well said, courageous Feeble! Thou wilt be as valiant as the

61 commends him sends his respects **62 tall** valiant **65 backsword** stick with a basket hilt used for fencing practice. (See II.iv.129, note.) **67–68 accommodated** furnished, equipped. (A bit of fine language on Bardolph's part.) **84 like well** are in good condition **88–89 in . . . me** a fellow Justice of the Peace **91 of the peace** i.e., a magistrate (with a play on the name *Silence*, peace) **94 sufficient** fit for service **104 of good friends** well-connected by family

111 Prick choose, designate **112 prick'd** i.e., goaded by nagging **113 dame** mother **114 husbandry** farm work **118 spent** used up **121 other** others **129 son** (with play on *sun*) **130 shadow** i.e., image, copy. (But, Falstaff jests, the father is only dimly copied in a bastard son who lacks the true substance of his purported father.) **135 shadows** i.e., fictitious names for which the officer in charge receives pay **145 the whole . . . pins** i.e., he's pinned together, badly made physically, and therefore needs no more pinpricks **147 can** know how to. **do it** i.e., make a joke **154 prick'd** attired **155 battle** line of battle

wrathful dove or most magnanimous mouse. Prick the woman's tailor. Well, Master Shallow, deep, Master Shallow.

FEEBLE I would Wart might have gone, sir.

FALSTAFF I would thou wert a man's tailor, that thou mightst mend him and make him fit to go. I cannot put him to a private soldier that is the leader of so many thousands. Let that suffice, most forcible Feeble.

FEEBLE It shall suffice, sir.

FALSTAFF I am bound to thee, reverend Feeble. Who is next?

SHALLOW Peter Bullcalf o' th' green!

FALSTAFF Yea, marry, let's see Bullcalf.

BULLCALF [*Stepping forward*] Here, sir.

FALSTAFF 'Fore God, a likely fellow! Come, prick me Bullcalf till he roar again.

BULLCALF O Lord! Good my lord captain—

FALSTAFF What, dost thou roar before thou art prick'd?

BULLCALF O Lord, sir! I am a diseas'd man.

FALSTAFF What disease hast thou?

BULLCALF A whoreson cold, sir, a cough, sir, which I caught with ringing in the King's affairs upon his coronation-day, sir.

FALSTAFF Come, thou shalt go to the wars in a gown. We will have away thy cold, and I will take such order that thy friends shall ring for thee. Is here all?

SHALLOW Here is two more call'd than your number; you must have but four here, sir. And so, I pray you, go in with me to dinner.

FALSTAFF Come, I will go drink with you, but I cannot tarry dinner. I am glad to see you, by my troth, Master Shallow.

SHALLOW O, Sir John, do you remember since we lay all night in the Windmill in Saint George's field?

FALSTAFF No more of that, good Master Shallow, no more of that.

SHALLOW Ha! 'Twas a merry night. And is Jane Nightwork alive?

FALSTAFF She lives, Master Shallow.

SHALLOW She never could away with me.

FALSTAFF Never, never; she would always say she could not abide Master Shallow.

SHALLOW By the mass, I could anger her to th' heart. She was then a bona-roba. Doth she hold her own well?

FALSTAFF Old, old, Master Shallow.

SHALLOW Nay, she must be old. She cannot choose but be old. Certain she's old, and had Robin Nightwork by old Nightwork before I came to Clement's Inn.

SILENCE That's fifty-five years ago.

SHALLOW Ha, cousin Silence, that thou hadst seen that that this knight and I have seen! Ha, Sir John, said I well?

FALSTAFF We have heard the chimes at midnight, Master Shallow.

SHALLOW That we have, that we have, that we have, in faith, Sir John, we have. Our watchword was "Hem boys!" Come, let's to dinner, come, let's to dinner. Jesus, the days that we have seen! Come, come.

Exeunt [*Falstaff and the Justices*].

BULLCALF Good Master Corporate Bardolph, stand my friend, and here's four Harry ten shillings in French crowns for you. [*Gives money.*] In very truth, sir, I had as lief be hang'd, sir, as go. And yet, for mine own part, sir, I do not care, but rather, because I am unwilling, and, for mine own part, have a desire to stay with my friends. Else, sir, I did not care, for mine own part, so much.

BARDOLPH Go to, stand aside.

MOULDY And, good master corporal captain, for my old dame's sake, stand my friend. She has nobody to do anything about her when I am gone, and she is old, and cannot help herself. [*Gives money.*] You shall have forty, sir.

BARDOLPH Go to, stand aside.

FEEBLE By my troth, I care not. A man can die but once. We owe God a death. I'll ne'er bear a base mind. An 't be my destiny, so; an 't be not, so. No man's too good to serve 's prince. And let it go which way it will, he that dies this year is quit for the next.

BARDOLPH Well said. Th' art a good fellow.

FEEBLE Faith, I'll bear no base mind.

Enter Falstaff and the Justices.

FALSTAFF Come, sir, which men shall I have?

SHALLOW Four of which you please.

BARDOLPH [*To Falstaff*] Sir, a word with you. [*Aside.*] I have three pound to free Mouldy and Bullcalf.

FALSTAFF Go to, well.

SHALLOW Come, Sir John, which four will you have?

FALSTAFF Do you choose for me.

SHALLOW Marry, then, Mouldy, Bullcalf, Feeble, and Shadow.

FALSTAFF Mouldy and Bullcalf. For you, Mouldy, stay at home till you are past service; and for your part, Bullcalf, grow till you come unto it. I will none of you.

SHALLOW Sir John, Sir John, do not yourself wrong. They are your likeliest men, and I would have you serv'd with the best.

FALSTAFF Will you tell me, Master Shallow, how to choose a man? Care I for the limb, the thews, the stature, bulk, and big assemblance of a man? Give me the spirit, Master Shallow. Here's Wart; you see what a ragged appearance it is. 'A shall charge you and discharge you with the motion of a pewterer's hammer, come off and on swifter than he that gibbets on the brewer's bucket. And this same half-fac'd fellow, Shadow; give me this man. He presents no mark to

167 to in the character of **168 thousands** i.e., of vermin, lice **182–183 ringing . . . day** i.e., ringing the church bells to celebrate the anniversary of the King's coronation **184 gown** dressing gown **185 have away** do away with. **take such order** provide **186 for thee** (1) in your place (2) at your death **191 tarry** wait for **193 since** when **194 Windmill** a brothel. **Saint George's field** a popular place of resort on the south bank of the Thames **200 away with** tolerate

217–218 Hem boys i.e., down the hatch **220 Corporate** (For *Corporal.*) **221 Harry ten shillings** i.e., money coined in the reign of Henry VII, current in late Elizabethan times at half the face value. The reference is anachronistic. Four such coins would be worth 20 shillings, or one pound. Bullcalf gives his bribe in *French crowns,* worth 4 shillings each; presumably he gives five such coins. **233 forty** i.e., forty shillings **239 quit** free, clear **251 For** as for **258 thews** strength **259 assemblance** appearance **261–262 charge . . . discharge you** load and fire **262 motion . . . hammer** i.e., precise, regular motion **263–264 come . . . bucket** raise and lower his musket quicker than a brewer's man raises and lowers the beam (bucket) of the brewer's yoke across his shoulders

the enemy; the foeman may with as great aim level at the edge of a penknife. And for a retreat, how swiftly will this Feeble the woman's tailor run off! O, give me the spare men, and spare me the great ones. Put me a caliver into Wart's hand, Bardolph.

BARDOLPH [*Giving Wart a musket*] Hold, Wart, traverse. Thus, thus, thus.

FALSTAFF Come, manage me your caliver. So. [*Wart performs maneuvers with the musket.*] Very well. Go to. Very good, exceeding good. O, give me always a little, lean, old, chopp'd, bald shot. Well said, i' faith, Wart, th' art a good scab. Hold, there's a tester for thee. [*Gives sixpence.*]

SHALLOW He is not his craft's master; he doth not do it right. I remember at Mile-end Green, when I lay at Clement's Inn—I was then Sir Dagonet in Arthur's show—there was a little quiver fellow, and 'a would manage you his piece thus [*Shallow demonstrates*], and 'a would about and about, and come you in and come you in. "Rah, tah, tah," would 'a say, "Bounce," would 'a say, and away again would 'a go, and again would 'a come. I shall ne'er see such a fellow.

FALSTAFF These fellows will do well, Master Shallow. God keep you, Master Silence. I will not use many words with you. Fare you well, gentlemen both. I thank you. I must a dozen mile tonight. Bardolph, give the soldiers coats.

SHALLOW Sir John, the Lord bless you! God prosper your affairs! God send us peace! At your return, visit our house; let our old acquaintance be renew'd. Peradventure I will with ye to the court.

FALSTAFF 'Fore God, would you would.

SHALLOW Go to; I have spoke at a word. God keep you.

FALSTAFF Fare you well, gentle gentlemen. *Exeunt* [*Justices.*] On, Bardolph; lead the men away. [*Exeunt Bardolph, Recruits, etc.*] As I return, I will fetch off these justices. I do see the bottom of Justice Shallow. Lord, Lord, how subject we old men are to this vice of lying! This same starv'd justice hath done nothing but prate to me of the wildness of his youth, and the feats he hath done about Turnbull Street, and every third word a lie, duer paid to the hearer than the Turk's tribute. I do remember him at Clement's Inn like a man made after supper of a cheese-paring. When 'a was naked, he was, for all the world, like a fork'd radish, with a head fantastically carv'd upon it with a knife. 'A was so forlorn that his dimensions to any thick sight were invisible. 'A was the very genius of famine, yet lecherous as a monkey, and the whores call'd him mandrake. 'A came ever in the rearward of the fashion, and sung those tunes to the overscutch'd huswives that he heard the carmen whistle, and sware they were his fancies or his good-nights. And now is this Vice's dagger become a squire, and talks as familiarly of John a Gaunt as if he had been sworn brother to him, and I'll be sworn 'a ne'er saw him but once in the Tilt-yard, and then he burst his head for crowding among the marshal's men. I saw it, and told John a Gaunt he beat his own name, for you might have thrust him and all his apparel into an eel-skin; the case of a treble hautboy was a mansion for him, a court. And now has he land and beefs. Well, I'll be acquainted with him if I return, and 't shall go hard but I'll make him a philosopher's two stones to me. If the young dace be a bait for the old pike, I see no reason in the law of nature but I may snap at him. Let time shape, and there an end. [*Exit.*]

[ACT IV • SCENE I]

Enter the Archbishop [*of York*], *Mowbray,* [*Lord*] *Bardolph, Hastings,* [*and others,*] *within the Forest of Gaultree.*

ARCHBISHOP
What is this forest call'd?
HASTINGS
'Tis Gaultree Forest, an 't shall please your Grace.
ARCHBISHOP
Here stand, my lords, and send discoverers forth
To know the numbers of our enemies.
HASTINGS
We have sent forth already.
ARCHBISHOP 'Tis well done.
My friends and brethren in these great affairs,
I must acquaint you that I have receiv'd
New-dated letters from Northumberland,
Their cold intent, tenor, and substance, thus:
Here doth he wish his person, with such powers
As might hold sortance with his quality,
The which he could not levy. Whereupon
He is retir'd, to ripe his growing fortunes,
To Scotland, and concludes in hearty prayers
That your attempts may overlive the hazard
And fearful meeting of their opposite.
MOWBRAY
Thus do the hopes we have in him touch ground
And dash themselves to pieces.

Enter Messenger.

HASTINGS Now, what news?
MESSENGER
West of this forest, scarcely off a mile,

266 level aim **270 caliver** light musket **271 traverse** march, or take aim **276 chopp'd** chapped. **shot** marksman **277 scab** (punning on the name *Wart*). **tester** sixpence **279 Mile-end Green** a drilling ground for citizen soldiers, to the east of London **280–281 Sir . . . show** (An exhibition of archery was held annually at Mile-end Green called "Arthur's show," in which each archer took the name of one of King Arthur's knights; Shallow played the part of Sir Dagonet, Arthur's fool.) **281 quiver** nimble **283 come you in** thrust at one **284 Bounce** bang **297 at a word** in all sincerity **300 fetch off** get the better of **305 Turnbull Street** a street in Clerkenwell, ill-reputed **306 duer** more promptly **306–307 Turk's tribute** tribute money paid annually to the Sultan of Turkey by merchants and others **311 forlorn** meager, thin **312 thick** imperfect. **invisible** (Some editors retain the reading of Q and F, *invincible*, as meaning "invisible.") **genius** spirit, personification **314 mandrake** root of a plant, said to resemble the body of a man **315–316 overscutch'd huswives** outworn and often-whipped prostitutes

316 carmen wagoners **317 fancies . . . good-nights** types of songs (of which he claims authorship) **318 Vice's dagger** (The Vice, or comic character of the morality plays, was armed with a wooden dagger.) **321 Tilt-yard** arena for jousting at Westminster. **he** i.e., John of Gaunt. **his** i.e., Shallow's **323 beat his own name** i.e., was thrashing a gaunt person **324 case** instrument case **325 hautboy** oboe **328 a philosopher's two stones** i.e., yield twice as much as the philosopher's stone, which was supposed to change ordinary metals into gold (with a possible play on *stones* meaning *testicles*) **329 dace** small fish used for live bait

IV.i. Location: Yorkshire. Gaultree Forest.
3 discoverers scouts **8 New** recently **10 powers** forces **11 hold sortance** accord. **quality** rank **13 ripe** make ripe **15 overlive** outlive **16 opposite** adversary

In goodly form comes on the enemy;
And, by the ground they hide, I judge their number
Upon or near the rate of thirty thousand.

MOWBRAY
The just proportion that we gave them out.
Let us sway on and face them in the field.

ARCHBISHOP
What well-appointed leader fronts us here?

Enter Westmorland.

MOWBRAY
I think it is my Lord of Westmorland.

WESTMORLAND
Health and fair greeting from our general,
The Prince, Lord John and Duke of Lancaster.

ARCHBISHOP
Say on, my Lord of Westmorland, in peace,
What doth concern your coming.

WESTMORLAND [Then, my lord,]
Unto your Grace do I in chief address
The substance of my speech. If that rebellion
Came like itself, in base and abject routs,
Led on by bloody youth, guarded with rags,
And countenanc'd by boys and beggary,
I say, if damn'd commotion so appear'd,
In his true, native, and most proper shape,
You, reverend father, and these noble lords
Had not been here, to dress the ugly form
Of base and bloody insurrection
With your fair honors. You, Lord Archbishop,
Whose see is by a civil peace maintain'd,
Whose beard the silver hand of peace hath touch'd,
Whose learning and good letters peace hath tutor'd,
Whose white investments figures innocence,
The dove, and very blessed spirit of peace,
Wherefore do you so ill translate yourself
Out of the speech of peace that bears such grace,
Into the harsh and boist'rous tongue of war,
Turning your books to graves, your ink to blood,
Your pens to lances, and your tongue divine
To a loud trumpet and a point of war?

ARCHBISHOP
Wherefore do I this? So the question stands.
Briefly to this end: we are all diseas'd,
[And with our surfeiting and wanton hours
Have brought ourselves into a burning fever,
And we must bleed for it; of which disease
Our late king, Richard, being infected, died.
But, my most noble Lord of Westmorland,
I take not on me here as a physician,
Nor do I as an enemy to peace
Troop in the throngs of military men,
But rather show awhile like fearful war
To diet rank minds sick of happiness
And purge th' obstructions which begin to stop
Our very veins of life. Hear me more plainly.
I have in equal balance justly weigh'd
What wrongs our arms may do, what wrongs we suffer,
And find our griefs heavier than our offenses.
We see which way the stream of time doth run,
And are enforc'd from our most quiet there
By the rough torrent of occasion,
And have the summary of all our griefs,
When time shall serve, to show in articles;
Which long ere this we offer'd to the King,
And might by no suit gain our audience.
When we are wrong'd and would unfold our griefs,
We are denied access unto his person
Even by those men that most have done us wrong.]
The dangers of the days but newly gone,
Whose memory is written on the earth
With yet appearing blood, and the examples
Of every minute's instance, present now,
Hath put us in these ill-beseeming arms,
Not to break peace or any branch of it,
But to establish here a peace indeed,
Concurring both in name and quality.

WESTMORLAND
Whenever yet was your appeal denied?
Wherein have you been galled by the King?
What peer hath been suborn'd to grate on you,
That you should seal this lawless bloody book
Of forg'd rebellion with a seal divine
And consecrate commotion's bitter edge?

ARCHBISHOP
My brother general, the commonwealth,
To brother born an household cruelty,
I make my quarrel in particular.

WESTMORLAND
There is no need of any such redress;
Or if there were, it not belongs to you.

MOWBRAY
Why not to him in part, and to us all
That feel the bruises of the days before,
And suffer the condition of these times
To lay a heavy and unequal hand
Upon our honors?

WESTMORLAND [O, my good Lord Mowbray,
Construe the times to their necessities,
And you shall say indeed it is the time,
And not the King, that doth you injuries.
Yet for your part, it not appears to me
Either from the King or in the present time
That you should have an inch of any ground
To build a grief on. Were you not restor'd
To all the Duke of Norfolk's signories,

22 rate estimate **23 just . . . out** precise number that we estimated **24 sway on** move on **25 well-appointed** well-armed. **fronts** confronts **33 routs** mobs **34 bloody** passionate. **guarded** adorned, trimmed **35 countenanc'd** supported **36 commotion** tumult, sedition **42 see** diocese. **civil** orderly, law-abiding **44 good letters** scholarship **45 investments** vestments. **figures** symbolize **47 translate** transform **52 point of war** trumpet signal of war **55–79 And . . . wrong** (Omitted from Q1 probably because of censorship, since these lines plead the cause of rebellion; also ll. 103–139.) **55 wanton** self-indulgent **57 bleed** be bled (as a medical treatment) **60 take . . . as** do not now undertake the role of **63 show** appear

64 rank swollen, obese **69 griefs** grievances **72 occasion** circumstances **74 articles** specified items **83 Of . . . instance** occurring every minute **87 Concurring . . . quality** i.e., a peace that will be both in name and in fact **89 galled** injured, made sore with chafing **90 suborn'd . . . on** induced to annoy **94–96 My brother . . . particular** (The text is almost certainly corrupt here, but the general sense seems to be: "I am rebelling against my brother-Englishmen because they have wronged me, which amounts to their being cruel to a member of their own family.") **102 unequal** unjust **104 to** according to. **their necessities** i.e., that which is necessary in a time of disorder and civil strife **111 signories** properties, estates

Your noble and right well rememb'red father's?

MOWBRAY
What thing, in honor, had my father lost,
That need to be reviv'd and breath'd in me?
The King that lov'd him, as the state stood then,
Was force perforce compell'd to banish him;
And then that Henry Bolingbroke and he,
Being mounted and both roused in their seats,
Their neighing coursers daring of the spur,
Their armed staves in charge, their beavers down,
Their eyes of fire sparkling through sights of steel,
And the loud trumpet blowing them together,
Then, then, when there was nothing could have stay'd
My father from the breast of Bolingbroke,
O, when the King did throw his warder down—
His own life hung upon the staff he threw—
Then threw he down himself and all their lives
That by indictment and by dint of sword
Have since miscarried under Bolingbroke.

WESTMORLAND
You speak, Lord Mowbray, now you know not what.
The Earl of Hereford was reputed then
In England the most valiant gentleman.
Who knows on whom fortune would then have smil'd?
But if your father had been victor there,
He ne'er had borne it out of Coventry;
For all the country in a general voice
Cried hate upon him, and all their prayers and love
Were set on Hereford, whom they doted on
And bless'd and grac'd indeed, more than the King.]
But this is mere digression from my purpose.
Here come I from our princely general
To know your griefs, to tell you from his Grace
That he will give you audience; and wherein
It shall appear that your demands are just,
You shall enjoy them, every thing set off
That might so much as think you enemies.

MOWBRAY
But he hath forc'd us to compel this offer,
And it proceeds from policy, not love.

WESTMORLAND
Mowbray, you overween to take it so.
This offer comes from mercy, not from fear.
For, lo, within a ken our army lies,
Upon mine honor, all too confident
To give admittance to a thought of fear.
Our battle is more full of names than yours,
Our men more perfect in the use of arms,
Our armor all as strong, our cause the best.
Then reason will our hearts should be as good.
Say you not then our offer is compell'd.

MOWBRAY
Well, by my will we shall admit no parley.

WESTMORLAND
That argues but the shame of your offense.
A rotten case abides no handling.

HASTINGS
Hath the Prince John a full commission,
In very ample virtue of his father,
To hear and absolutely to determine
Of what conditions we shall stand upon?

WESTMORLAND
That is intended in the general's name.
I muse you make so slight a question.

ARCHBISHOP
Then take, my Lord of Westmorland, this schedule,
[*Gives document.*]
For this contains our general grievances.
Each several article herein redress'd,
All members of our cause, both here and hence,
That are insinewed to this action,
Acquitted by a true substantial form
And present execution of our wills
To us and to our purposes confin'd,
We come within our awful banks again
And knit our powers to the arm of peace.

WESTMORLAND
This will I show the general. Please you, lords,
In sight of both our battles we may meet,
And either end in peace—which God so frame!—
Or to the place of diff'rence call the swords
Which must decide it.

ARCHBISHOP My lord, we will do so.
Exit Westmorland.

MOWBRAY
There is a thing within my bosom tells me
That no conditions of our peace can stand.

HASTINGS
Fear you not that. If we can make our peace
Upon such large terms and so absolute
As our conditions shall consist upon,
Our peace shall stand as firm as rocky mountains.

MOWBRAY
Yea, but our valuation shall be such
That every slight and false-derived cause,
Yea, every idle, nice, and wanton reason,
Shall to the King taste of this action,
That, were our royal faiths martyrs in love,
We shall be winnow'd with so rough a wind
That even our corn shall seem as light as chaff
And good from bad find no partition.

114 breath'd given the breath of life **116 force perforce** willy-nilly. (For the banishment of Mowbray by Richard II, see *Richard II*, I.i and iii.) **118 seats** saddles **120 armed . . . charge** lances ready for the charge. **beavers** movable visors of helmets **121 sights** eye slits **125 warder** staff of command **129 miscarried** died **131 Earl of Hereford** i.e., Bolingbroke, later King Henry IV **135 borne . . . Coventry** i.e., carried away the prize from the site of the intended trial by combat **145 set off** put out of consideration, removed **149 overween** are arrogant or presumptuous **151 ken** seeing distance **154 battle** army. **names** noble names **157 reason will** i.e., it is reasonable that

159 by my will i.e., as far as I'm concerned **161 abides** tolerates **163 virtue** authority **165 what** whatever. **stand** insist **166 intended** understood, implied. **name** i.e., title **167 muse** wonder **170 Each . . . herein** provided that each separate article herein is **172 insinewed** joined as by strong sinews **173 substantial form** formal agreement **174 present . . . wills** immediate fulfillment of our desires **175 To . . . confin'd** i.e., as regards us and our plans **176 awful banks** banks or bounds of respect **179 battles** armies **180 frame** bring about **181 diff'rence** conflict **186 large** liberal **189 our . . . such** i.e., we shall be so considered by the King **191 idle . . . wanton** foolish, petty, and frivolous **193 That . . . love** i.e., so that even if our allegiance to the King were as strong as the devotion of martyrs **195 corn** grain, wheat **196 partition** distinction

ARCHBISHOP
No, no, my lord. Note this: the King is weary
Of dainty and such picking grievances.
For he hath found to end one doubt by death
Revives two greater in the heirs of life,
And therefore will he wipe his tables clean
And keep no tell-tale to his memory
That may repeat and history his loss
To new remembrance. For full well he knows
He cannot so precisely weed this land
As his misdoubts present occasion.
His foes are so enrooted with his friends
That, plucking to unfix an enemy,
He doth unfasten so and shake a friend.
So that this land, like an offensive wife
That hath enrag'd him on to offer strokes,
As he is striking, holds his infant up
And hangs resolv'd correction in the arm
That was uprear'd to execution.

HASTINGS
Besides, the King hath wasted all his rods
On late offenders, that he now doth lack
The very instruments of chastisement,
So that his power, like to a fangless lion,
May offer, but not hold.

ARCHBISHOP 'Tis very true.
And therefore be assur'd, my good Lord Marshal,
If we do now make our atonement well,
Our peace will, like a broken limb united,
Grow stronger for the breaking.

MOWBRAY Be it so.
Here is return'd my Lord of Westmorland.

Enter Westmorland.

WESTMORLAND
The Prince is here at hand. Pleaseth your lordship
To meet his Grace just distance 'tween our armies.

MOWBRAY
Your Grace of York, in God's name then set
forward.

ARCHBISHOP
Before, and greet his Grace.—My lord, we come.

[SCENE II]

Enter Prince John [of Lancaster] and his army.

PRINCE JOHN
You are well encount'red here, my cousin Mowbray.
Good day to you, gentle Lord Archbishop.
And so to you, Lord Hastings, and to all.
My Lord of York, it better show'd with you
When that your flock, assembled by the bell,
Encircled you to hear with reverence
Your exposition on the holy text
Than now to see you here an iron man,
Cheering a rout of rebels with your drum,
Turning the word to sword and life to death.
That man that sits within a monarch's heart
And ripens in the sunshine of his favor,
Would he abuse the countenance of the King,
Alack, what mischiefs might he set abroach
In shadow of such greatness! With you, Lord
Bishop,
It is even so. Who hath not heard it spoken
How deep you were within the books of God,
To us the speaker in his parliament,
To us th' imagin'd voice of God himself,
The very opener and intelligencer
Between the grace, the sanctities of heaven
And our dull workings? O, who shall believe
But you misuse the reverence of your place,
Employ the countenance and grace of heav'n,
As a false favorite doth his prince's name,
In deeds dishonorable? You have ta'en up,
Under the counterfeited zeal of God,
The subjects of his substitute, my father,
And both against the peace of heaven and him
Have here up-swarm'd them.

ARCHBISHOP Good my Lord of Lancaster,
I am not here against your father's peace;
But, as I told my Lord of Westmorland,
The time misord'red doth, in common sense,
Crowd us and crush us to this monstrous form
To hold our safety up. I sent your Grace
The parcels and particulars of our grief,
The which hath been with scorn shov'd from the
court,
Whereon this Hydra son of war is born,
Whose dangerous eyes may well be charm'd asleep
With grant of our most just and right desires,
And true obedience, of this madness cur'd,
Stoop tamely to the foot of majesty.

MOWBRAY
If not, we ready are to try our fortunes
To the last man.

HASTINGS And though we here fall down,
We have supplies to second our attempt;
If they miscarry, theirs shall second them,
And so success of mischief shall be born
And heir from heir shall hold this quarrel up
Whiles England shall have generation.

198 picking fastidious, trivial **199 doubt** danger **201 tables** tablets, notebooks **203 history** record, chronicle **205 precisely** thoroughly **213 hangs resolv'd correction** checks the punishment that was intended **215 wasted** exhausted, spent. **rods** whipping rods **216 late** (other) recent **219 offer . . . hold** offer violence, but not hold fast **221 atonement** reconciliation **225 Pleaseth** may it please **226 just** exact **228 Before** i.e., go before

IV.ii. Location: This scene is apparently continuous with the previous scene. In Q, Prince John and his army enter before the last two lines of IV.i.
1 cousin (Normal address of royal family to a Duke.)

4 it . . . you it showed you to better advantage **8 iron man** warrior clad in armor **9 rout** mob **10 the word** i.e., the word of God, the Scripture **13 Would he** if he should choose to. **countenance** favor **14 set abroach** set aflowing, begin **16 even** just **18 speaker** i.e., spokesman for God, just as the speaker of Parliament spoke in the name of the King **20 opener** revealer. **intelligencer** interpreter, agent **22 dull workings** imperfect human spirit **26 ta'en up** enlisted **28 substitute** deputy **33 time misord'red** disorders of the time **36 parcels** items, details **38 Hydra** (The Lernaean Hydra was a fabulous monster with several heads; when one was cut off, others grew in its place.) **45 supplies** forces in reserve **47 success** succession **49 generation** issue, offspring

PRINCE JOHN
You are too shallow, Hastings, much too shallow,
To sound the bottom of the after-times.

WESTMORLAND
Pleaseth your Grace to answer them directly
How far forth you do like their articles.

PRINCE JOHN
I like them all, and do allow them well,
And swear here, by the honor of my blood,
My father's purposes have been mistook,
And some about him have too lavishly
Wrested his meaning and authority.
My lord, these griefs shall be with speed redress'd,
Upon my soul, they shall. If this may please you,
Discharge your powers unto their several counties,
As we will ours; and here between the armies
Let's drink together friendly and embrace,
That all their eyes may bear those tokens home
Of our restored love and amity.

ARCHBISHOP
I take your princely word for these redresses.

PRINCE JOHN
I give it you, and will maintain my word.
And thereupon I drink unto your Grace.
[*They drink together, and embrace.*]

HASTINGS
Go, captain, and deliver to the army
This news of peace. Let them have pay, and part.
I know it will well please them. Hie thee, captain.
[*Exit Officer.*]

ARCHBISHOP
To you, my noble Lord of Westmorland.

WESTMORLAND
I pledge your Grace; and, if you knew what pains
I have bestow'd to breed this present peace,
You would drink freely. But my love to ye
Shall show itself more openly hereafter.

ARCHBISHOP
I do not doubt you.

WESTMORLAND I am glad of it.
Health to my lord and gentle cousin, Mowbray.

MOWBRAY
You wish me health in very happy season,
For I am, on the sudden, something ill.

ARCHBISHOP
Against ill chances men are ever merry,
But heaviness foreruns the good event.

WESTMORLAND
Therefore be merry, coz, since sudden sorrow
Serves to say thus, "Some good thing comes
tomorrow."

ARCHBISHOP
Believe me, I am passing light in spirit.

MOWBRAY
So much the worse, if your own rule be true.
Shout [*within*].

51 sound . . . after-times predict what the future will bring **52 Pleaseth** may it please **54 allow** approve, sanction **57 lavishly** loosely, negligently **58 Wrested** twisted **70 part** depart **80 something** somewhat **81 Against** when about to face **82 heaviness . . . event** sadness comes over men prior to a happy outcome **85 passing** surpassingly

PRINCE JOHN
The word of peace is rend'red. Hark, how they
shout!

MOWBRAY
This had been cheerful after victory.

ARCHBISHOP
A peace is of the nature of a conquest,
For then both parties nobly are subdu'd,
And neither party loser.

PRINCE JOHN Go, my lord,
And let our army be discharged too.
[*Exit Westmorland.*]
And, good my lord, so please you, let our trains
March by us, that we may peruse the men
We should have cop'd withal.

ARCHBISHOP Go, good Lord Hastings,
And, ere they be dismiss'd, let them march by.
[*Exit Hastings.*]

PRINCE JOHN
I trust, lords, we shall lie tonight together.

Enter Westmorland.

Now cousin, wherefore stands our army still?

WESTMORLAND
The leaders, having charge from you to stand,
Will not go off until they hear you speak.

PRINCE JOHN
They know their duties.

Enter Hastings.

HASTINGS
My lord, our army is dispers'd already.
Like youthful steers unyok'd, they take their courses
East, west, north, south, or, like a school broke up,
Each hurries toward his home and sporting-place.

WESTMORLAND
Good tidings, my Lord Hastings, for the which
I do arrest thee, traitor, of high treason.
And you, Lord Archbishop, and you, Lord
Mowbray,
Of capital treason I attach you both.

MOWBRAY
Is this proceeding just and honorable?

WESTMORLAND
Is your assembly so?

ARCHBISHOP
Will you thus break your faith?

PRINCE JOHN I pawn'd thee none.
I promis'd you redress of these same grievances
Whereof you did complain, which, by mine honor,
I will perform with a most Christian care.
But for you rebels, look to taste the due
Meet for rebellion [and such acts as yours.]
Most shallowly did you these arms commence,
Fondly brought here and foolishly sent hence.

87 rend'red proclaimed **93 trains** armies **95 cop'd withal** encountered, fought with **105 sporting-place** playground **109 capital** punishable by death. **attach** arrest **112 pawn'd** pledged **119 Fondly** foolishly

Strike up our drums, pursue the scatt'red stray.
God, and not we, hath safely fought today.
Some guard these traitors to the block of death,
Treason's true bed and yielder up of breath.

[Exeunt.]

[SCENE III]

Alarum. Excursions. Enter Falstaff [and Colevile, meeting].

FALSTAFF What's your name, sir? Of what condition are you, and of what place?

COLEVILE I am a knight, sir, and my name is Colevile of the Dale.

FALSTAFF Well, then, Colevile is your name, a knight is your degree, and your place the Dale. Colevile shall be still your name, a traitor your degree, and the dungeon your place, a place deep enough; so shall you be still Colevile of the Dale.

COLEVILE Are not you Sir John Falstaff?

FALSTAFF As good a man as he, sir, whoe'er I am. Do ye yield, sir? Or shall I sweat for you? If I do sweat, they are the drops of thy lovers, and they weep for thy death. Therefore rouse up fear and trembling, and do observance to my mercy.

COLEVILE I think you are Sir John Falstaff, and in that thought yield me.

FALSTAFF I have a whole school of tongues in this belly of mine, and not a tongue of them all speaks any other word but my name. An I had but a belly of any indifferency, I were simply the most active fellow in Europe. My womb, my womb, my womb undoes me. Here comes our general.

Enter [Prince] John [of Lancaster], Westmorland, [Blunt,] and the rest.

PRINCE JOHN
The heat is past; follow no further now.
Call in the powers, good cousin Westmorland.
[Exit Westmorland.] Retreat [sounded].
Now, Falstaff, where have you been all this while?
When everything is ended, then you come.
These tardy tricks of yours will, on my life,
One time or other break some gallows' back.

FALSTAFF I would be sorry, my lord, but it should be thus. I never knew yet but rebuke and check was the reward of valor. Do you think me a swallow, an arrow, or a bullet? Have I, in my poor and old motion, the expedition of thought? I have speeded hither with the very extremest inch of possibility. I have found'red nine score and odd posts, and here, travel-tainted as I am, have, in my pure and immaculate valor, taken Sir John Colevile of the Dale, a most furious knight and valorous enemy. But what of that? He saw me, and yielded, that I may justly say, with the hook-nos'd fellow of Rome, "I came, saw, and overcame."

PRINCE JOHN It was more of his courtesy than your deserving.

FALSTAFF I know not. Here is he, and here I yield him. And I beseech your Grace, let it be book'd with the rest of this day's deeds, or, by the Lord, I will have it in a particular ballad else, with mine own picture on the top of 't, Colevile kissing my foot. To the which course if I be enforc'd, if you do not all show like gilt twopences to me, and I in the clear sky of fame o'ershine you as much as the full moon doth the cinders of the element, which show like pins' heads to her, believe not the word of the noble. Therefore let me have right, and let desert mount.

PRINCE JOHN Thine's too heavy to mount.

FALSTAFF Let it shine, then.

PRINCE JOHN Thine's too thick to shine.

FALSTAFF Let it do something, my good lord, that may do me good, and call it what you will.

PRINCE JOHN Is thy name Colevile?

COLEVILE It is, my lord.

PRINCE JOHN A famous rebel art thou, Colevile.

FALSTAFF And a famous true subject took him.

COLEVILE
I am, my lord, but as my betters are
That led me hither. Had they been rul'd by me,
You should have won them dearer than you have.

FALSTAFF I know not how they sold themselves. But thou, like a kind fellow, gavest thyself away gratis, and I thank thee for thee.

Enter Westmorland.

PRINCE JOHN
Now, have you left pursuit?

WESTMORLAND
Retreat is made and execution stay'd.

PRINCE JOHN
Send Colevile with his confederates
To York, to present execution.
Blunt, lead him hence, and see you guard him sure.
[Exeunt Blunt and others with Colevile.]
And now dispatch we toward the court, my lords.
I hear the King my father is sore sick.
Our news shall go before us to his Majesty,
Which, cousin, you shall bear to comfort him,
And we with sober speed will follow you.

FALSTAFF My lord, I beseech you give me leave to go through Gloucestershire, and, when you come to court, stand my good lord in your good report.

120 stray stragglers

IV.iii. Location: Gaultree Forest, as before.
1 condition rank **13 drops** tears. **lovers** friends **15 observance** reverence, homage **18 school** crowd. (I.e., his belly eloquently identifies him.) **20–21 indifferency** moderate size **22 womb** belly **24 heat** pursuit, race **30–31 but . . . thus** if it were not thus **31 check** reprimand **34 expedition** speed **35 found'red** made lame **36 posts** post horses

40–41 hook-nos'd . . . Rome i.e., Julius Caesar **45 book'd** recorded by the chroniclers **47 a particular ballad** a broadside ballad written and published for the particular occasion **49 show** look **49–50 gilt twopences** coins gilded to pass for half-crowns of the same size **50 to** compared to **51–52 cinders . . . element** i.e., stars **54 desert mount** merit be promoted **57 thick** (1) opaque (2) heavy **66 dearer** i.e., at greater military cost **71 Retreat . . . stay'd** the order for withdrawal has been sounded and the slaughter has been stopped **73 present** immediate **75 dispatch we** let us hasten **82 stand my good lord** act as my patron

PRINCE JOHN
Fare you well, Falstaff. I, in my condition, 83
Shall better speak of you than you deserve.
[Exeunt all but Falstaff.]

FALSTAFF I would you had but the wit; 'twere better
than your dukedom. Good faith, this same young
sober-blooded boy doth not love me, nor a man can-
not make him laugh. But that's no marvel, he drinks
no wine. There's never none of these demure boys
come to any proof, for thin drink doth so over-cool 90
their blood, and making many fish-meals, that they
fall into a kind of male green-sickness, and then, when 92
they marry, they get wenches. They are generally fools 93
and cowards, which some of us should be too, but for
inflammation. A good sherris-sack hath a twofold op- 95
eration in it. It ascends me into the brain, dries me 96
there all the foolish and dull and crudy vapors which 97
environ it, makes it apprehensive, quick, forgetive, 98
full of nimble, fiery, and delectable shapes, which, de-
liver'd o'er to the voice, the tongue, which is the birth,
becomes excellent wit. The second property of your 101
excellent sherris is the warming of the blood, which,
before cold and settled, left the liver white and pale, 103
which is the badge of pusillanimity and cowardice.
But the sherris warms it and makes it course from the
inwards to the parts' extremes. It illumineth the face,
which as a beacon gives warning to all the rest of this
little kingdom, man, to arm; and then the vital com- 108
moners and inland petty spirits muster me all to their 109
captain, the heart, who, great and puff'd up with this
retinue, doth any deed of courage; and this valor
comes of sherris. So that skill in the weapon is nothing
without sack, for that sets it a-work; and learning a
mere hoard of gold kept by a devil, till sack com- 114
mences it and sets it in act and use. Hereof comes it 115
that Prince Harry is valiant, for the cold blood he did
naturally inherit of his father, he hath, like lean, ster-
ile, and bare land, manur'd, husbanded, and till'd
with excellent endeavor of drinking good and good
store of fertile sherris, that he is become very hot and
valiant. If I had a thousand sons, the first humane
principle I would teach them should be to forswear
thin potations and to addict themselves to sack.

Enter Bardolph.

How now, Bardolph?

BARDOLPH The army is discharged all and gone.

FALSTAFF Let them go. I'll through Gloucestershire, and
there will I visit Master Robert Shallow, esquire. I have
him already temp'ring between my finger and my 128
thumb, and shortly will I seal with him. Come away. 129
[Exeunt.]

83 **condition** i.e., function as commander 90 **come to any proof** stand up well under testing. **thin drink** i.e., beer 92 **green-sickness** a kind of anemia thought to affect young women 93 **get wenches** beget girls 95 **inflammation** excitement with liquor. **sherris-sack** sherry 96 **ascends me** i.e., ascends. (*Me* is the ethical dative.) 97 **crudy** curded 98 **apprehensive** quick to perceive. **forgetive** inventive 101 **wit** mental capacity 103 **liver** (Thought to be the seat of courage.) 108–109 **vital . . . spirits** vital spirits of man's internal region 114–115 **commences it** transforms its potential into actuality 128 **temp'ring** softening (like a piece of wax) 129 **seal with** i.e., make use of; seal a bargain with (continuing the metaphor of sealing-wax)

[SCENE IV]

Enter the King, Warwick, Thomas Duke of Clarence, Humphrey [Duke] of Gloucester, [and others].

KING
Now, lords, if God doth give successful end
To this debate that bleedeth at our doors, 2
We will our youth lead on to higher fields 3
And draw no swords but what are sanctified.
Our navy is address'd, our power collected, 5
Our substitutes in absence well invested, 6
And everything lies level to our wish. 7
Only we want a little personal strength, 8
And pause us till these rebels, now afoot,
Come underneath the yoke of government.

WARWICK
Both which we doubt not but your Majesty
Shall soon enjoy.

KING Humphrey, my son of Gloucester,
Where is the Prince your brother?

GLOUCESTER
I think he's gone to hunt, my lord, at Windsor.

KING
And how accompanied?

GLOUCESTER I do not know, my lord.

KING
Is not his brother, Thomas of Clarence, with him?

GLOUCESTER
No, my good lord, he is in presence here. 17

CLARENCE
What would my lord and father?

KING
Nothing but well to thee, Thomas of Clarence.
How chance thou art not with the Prince thy
brother?
He loves thee, and thou dost neglect him, Thomas;
Thou hast a better place in his affection
Than all thy brothers. Cherish it, my boy,
And noble offices thou mayst effect
Of mediation, after I am dead,
Between his greatness and thy other brethren.
Therefore omit him not, blunt not his love, 27
Nor lose the good advantage of his grace 28
By seeming cold or careless of his will.
For he is gracious, if he be observ'd. 30
He hath a tear for pity and a hand
Open as day for meting charity. 32
Yet notwithstanding, being incens'd, he is flint, 33

IV.iv. Location: King Henry's Palace at Westminster. The Jerusalem Chamber (so called for its various inscriptions concerning Jerusalem; it adjoined Westminster Abbey).
2 **debate** strife 3 **higher fields** i.e., a crusade to Palestine 5 **address'd** ready, prepared 6 **substitutes** deputies. **invested** empowered 7 **level** conformable 8 **want** lack 17 **in presence** present at court 27 **omit** neglect 28 **grace** favor 30 **observ'd** paid proper respect 32 **meting** dealing out 33 **flint** i.e., in emitting fire

As humorous as winter, and as sudden
As flaws congealed in the spring of day.
His temper, therefore, must be well observ'd.
Chide him for faults, and do it reverently,
When you perceive his blood inclin'd to mirth;
But, being moody, give him line and scope,
Till that his passions, like a whale on ground,
Confound themselves with working. Learn this, Thomas,
And thou shalt prove a shelter to thy friends,
A hoop of gold to bind thy brothers in,
That the united vessel of their blood,
Mingled with venom of suggestion—
As, force perforce, the age will pour it in—
Shall never leak, though it do work as strong
As aconitum or rash gunpowder.

CLARENCE
I shall observe him with all care and love.

KING
Why art thou not at Windsor with him, Thomas?

CLARENCE
He is not there today; he dines in London.

KING
And how accompanied? [Canst thou tell that?]

CLARENCE
With Poins, and other his continual followers.

KING
Most subject is the fattest soil to weeds,
And he, the noble image of my youth,
Is overspread with them. Therefore my grief
Stretches itself beyond the hour of death.
The blood weeps from my heart when I do shape
In forms imaginary th' unguided days
And rotten times that you shall look upon
When I am sleeping with my ancestors.
For when his headstrong riot hath no curb,
When rage and hot blood are his counselors,
When means and lavish manners meet together,
O, with what wings shall his affections fly
Towards fronting peril and oppos'd decay!

WARWICK
My gracious lord, you look beyond him quite.
The Prince but studies his companions
Like a strange tongue, wherein, to gain the language,
'Tis needful that the most immodest word
Be look'd upon and learn'd, which, once attain'd,
Your Highness knows, comes to no further use
But to be known and hated. So, like gross terms,
The Prince will in the perfectness of time
Cast off his followers, and their memory
Shall as a pattern or a measure live,
By which his Grace must mete the lives of other,
Turning past evils to advantages.

KING
'Tis seldom when the bee doth leave her comb
In the dead carrion.

Enter Westmorland.

Who's here? Westmorland?

WESTMORLAND
Health to my sovereign, and new happiness
Added to that that I am to deliver!
Prince John your son doth kiss your Grace's hand.
Mowbray, the Bishop Scroop, Hastings, and all
Are brought to the correction of your law.
There is not now a rebel's sword unsheath'd,
But Peace puts forth her olive everywhere.
The manner how this action hath been borne
Here at more leisure may your Highness read,
With every course in his particular.
[*Gives document.*]

KING
O Westmorland, thou art a summer bird,
Which ever in the haunch of winter sings
The lifting up of day.

Enter Harcourt.

Look, here's more news.

HARCOURT
From enemies heaven keep your Majesty,
And, when they stand against you, may they fall
As those that I am come to tell you of!
The Earl Northumberland and the Lord Bardolph,
With a great power of English and of Scots,
Are by the shrieve of Yorkshire overthrown.
The manner and true order of the fight
This packet, please it you, contains at large.
[*Gives letters.*]

KING
And wherefore should these good news make me sick?
Will Fortune never come with both hands full,
But write her fair words still in foulest letters?
She either gives a stomach and no food—
Such are the poor, in health; or else a feast
And takes away the stomach—such are the rich,
That have abundance and enjoy it not.
I should rejoice now at this happy news,
And now my sight fails, and my brain is giddy.
O me! Come near me. Now I am much ill.
[*King swoons. Several come to his aid.*]

GLOUCESTER
Comfort, your Majesty!

CLARENCE
O my royal father!

WESTMORLAND
My sovereign lord, cheer up yourself, look up.

WARWICK
Be patient, princes. You do know these fits

34 humorous unpredictable in mood **35 flaws congealed** snowflakes. **spring of day** early morning **41 Confound** exhaust, consume. **working** struggling **45 suggestion** insinuation **48 aconitum** a strong poison extracted from monkshood. **rash** quick-acting **54 fattest** richest **64 lavish** unrestrained, licentious **66 fronting . . . decay** danger and ruin which confront him **67 look beyond** misjudge **73 like gross terms** just as with coarse expressions **77 mete** measure, appraise. **other** others

79–80 'Tis . . . carrion rarely does the bee that has placed her comb in dead carrion leave her honeycomb; i.e., the Prince will not forsake his corrupt delights **90 course . . . particular** event or phase set forth in detail **92 haunch** latter end **93 lifting up** dawn **99 shrieve** sheriff

Are with his Highness very ordinary.
Stand from him, give him air; he'll straight be well.

CLARENCE
No, no, he cannot long hold out these pangs.
Th' incessant care and labor of his mind
Hath wrought the mure that should confine it in
So thin that life looks through [and will break out.]

GLOUCESTER
The people fear me, for they do observe
Unfather'd heirs and loathly births of nature.
The seasons change their manners, as the year
Had found some months asleep and leapt them
over.

CLARENCE
The river hath thrice flow'd, no ebb between,
And the old folk, time's doting chronicles,
Say it did so a little time before
That our great-grandsire, Edward, sick'd and died.

WARWICK
Speak lower, princes, for the King recovers.

GLOUCESTER
This apoplexy will certain be his end.

KING
I pray you, take me up, and bear me hence
Into some other chamber. [Softly, pray.]

[SCENE V]

[The King is borne to another part of the stage, to bed.]

[KING]
Let there be no noise made, my gentle friends,
Unless some dull and favorable hand
Will whisper music to my weary spirit.

WARWICK
Call for the music in the other room.

KING
Set me the crown upon my pillow here.

CLARENCE
His eye is hollow, and he changes much.

WARWICK
Less noise, less noise!
[*The crown is placed on the King's pillow.*]

Enter [*Prince*] *Harry.*

PRINCE
Who saw the Duke of Clarence?

CLARENCE
I am here, brother, full of heaviness.

PRINCE
How now, rain within doors, and none abroad?
How doth the King?

GLOUCESTER
Exceeding ill.

PRINCE
Heard he the good news yet? Tell it him.

GLOUCESTER
He alter'd much upon the hearing it.

PRINCE
If he be sick with joy, he'll recover without physic.

WARWICK
Not so much noise, my lords. Sweet Prince,
speak low.
The King your father is dispos'd to sleep.

CLARENCE
Let us withdraw into the other room.

WARWICK
Will 't please your Grace to go along with us?

PRINCE
No, I will sit and watch here by the King.
[*Exeunt all but the Prince.*]
Why doth the crown lie there upon his pillow,
Being so troublesome a bedfellow?
O polish'd perturbation! Golden care!
That keep'st the ports of slumber open wide
To many a watchful night! Sleep with it now!
Yet not so sound and half so deeply sweet
As he whose brow with homely biggen bound
Snores out the watch of night. O majesty!
When thou dost pinch thy bearer, thou dost sit
Like a rich armor worn in heat of day,
That scald'st with safety. By his gates of breath
There lies a downy feather which stirs not.
Did he suspire, that light and weightless down
Perforce must move. My gracious lord! My father!
This sleep is sound indeed. This is a sleep
That from this golden rigol hath divorc'd
So many English kings. Thy due from me
Is tears and heavy sorrows of the blood,
Which nature, love, and filial tenderness
Shall, O dear father, pay thee plenteously.
My due from thee is this imperial crown,
Which, as immediate from thy place and blood,
Derives itself to me. Lo, where it sits,
[*Puts on the crown.*]
Which God shall guard. And put the world's whole
strength
Into one giant arm, it shall not force
This lineal honor from me. This from thee
Will I to mine leave, as 'tis left to me. *Exit.*

KING [*Awaking*]
Warwick! Gloucester! Clarence!

Enter Warwick, Gloucester, Clarence, [*and others*].

CLARENCE
Doth the King call?

WARWICK
What would your Majesty? [How fares your Grace?]

119 wrought the mure made the wall **121 fear** frighten **122 Unfather'd heirs** persons believed to be supernaturally conceived. **loathly births** monstrous offspring **123 as** as if **125 river** i.e., Thames. (Holinshed records this event as having happened on October 12, 1411.) **128 Edward** Edward III

IV.v. Location: The scene is continuous.
2 dull soft, soothing. **favorable** kindly **6 changes** changes color, turns pale **9 rain** i.e., tears

22 perturbation cause of perturbation **23 ports** gates **24 watchful** wakeful. **Sleep with it** i.e., may you (King Henry) sleep with this symbol of care beside you **25 Yet not** i.e., yet your sleep will nonetheless not be **26 biggen** nightcap **28 pinch** torment **30 scald'st with safety** burns while providing safety. **gates of breath** lips **32 suspire** breathe **35 rigol** circle, i.e., crown **37 blood** (1) heart (2) kinship **41 immediate from** nearest to. (Refers to Prince Henry.) **42 Derives itself** descends **45 lineal** inherited

KING
Why did you leave me here alone, my lords?

CLARENCE
We left the Prince my brother here, my liege,
Who undertook to sit and watch by you.

KING
The Prince of Wales? Where is he? Let me see him.
He is not here.

WARWICK
This door is open; he is gone this way.

GLOUCESTER
He came not through the chamber where we stay'd.

KING
Where is the crown? Who took it from my pillow?

WARWICK
When we withdrew, my liege, we left it here.

KING
The Prince hath ta'en it hence. Go, seek him out.
Is he so hasty that he doth suppose
My sleep my death?
Find him, my Lord of Warwick, chide him hither.
[*Exit Warwick.*]
This part of his conjoins with my disease,
And helps to end me. See, sons, what things you are!
How quickly nature falls into revolt
When gold becomes her object!
For this the foolish over-careful fathers
Have broke their sleep with thoughts,
Their brains with care, their bones with industry;
For this they have engrossed and pil'd up
The cank'red heaps of strange-achieved gold;
For this they have been thoughtful to invest
Their sons with arts and martial exercises—
When, like the bee, tolling from every flower
[The virtuous sweets,]
Our thighs pack'd with wax, our mouths with honey,
We bring it to the hive, and, like the bees,
Are murd'red for our pains. This bitter taste
Yields his engrossments to the ending father.

Enter Warwick.

Now, where is he that will not stay so long
Till his friend sickness hath determin'd me?

WARWICK
My lord, I found the Prince in the next room,
Washing with kindly tears his gentle cheeks,
With such a deep demeanor in great sorrow
That tyranny, which never quaff'd but blood,
Would, by beholding him, have wash'd his knife
With gentle eye-drops. He is coming hither.

KING
But wherefore did he take away the crown?

Enter [Prince] Harry [with the crown].

Lo, where he comes. Come hither to me, Harry.
Depart the chamber, leave us here alone.
Exeunt [Warwick and the rest].

PRINCE
I never thought to hear you speak again.

KING
Thy wish was father, Harry, to that thought.
I stay too long by thee, I weary thee.
Dost thou so hunger for mine empty chair
That thou wilt needs invest thee with my honors
Before thy hour be ripe? O foolish youth,
Thou seek'st the greatness that will overwhelm thee.
Stay but a little, for my cloud of dignity
Is held from falling with so weak a wind
That it will quickly drop. My day is dim.
Thou hast stol'n that which after some few hours
Were thine without offense, and at my death
Thou hast seal'd up my expectation.
Thy life did manifest thou lov'dst me not,
And thou wilt have me die assur'd of it.
Thou hid'st a thousand daggers in thy thoughts,
Which thou hast whetted on thy stony heart,
To stab at half an hour of my life.
What, canst thou not forbear me half an hour?
Then get thee gone and dig my grave thyself,
And bid the merry bells ring to thine ear
That thou art crowned, not that I am dead.
Let all the tears that should bedew my hearse
Be drops of balm to sanctify thy head.
Only compound me with forgotten dust;
Give that which gave thee life unto the worms.
Pluck down my officers, break my decrees,
For now a time is come to mock at form.
Harry the Fifth is crown'd. Up, vanity!
Down, royal state! All you sage counselors, hence!
And to the English court assemble now,
From every region, apes of idleness!
Now, neighbor confines, purge you of your scum.
Have you a ruffin that will swear, drink, dance,
Revel the night, rob, murder, and commit
The oldest sins the newest kind of ways?
Be happy, he will trouble you no more.
England shall double gild his treble guilt,
England shall give him office, honor, might;
For the fifth Harry from curb'd license plucks
The muzzle of restraint, and the wild dog
Shall flesh his tooth on every innocent.
O my poor kingdom, sick with civil blows!
When that my care could not withhold thy riots,
What wilt thou do when riot is thy care?
O, thou wilt be a wilderness again,
Peopled with wolves, thy old inhabitants!

PRINCE
O, pardon me, my liege! But for my tears,
The moist impediments unto my speech,
I had forestall'd this dear and deep rebuke

63 part act. **conjoins** unites, joins **68 thoughts** cares **70 engrossed** amassed **71 cank'red** rusting and malignant. **strange-achieved** hard-won (?) **72 thoughtful** careful **74 tolling** taking as toll, collecting **78–79 This . . . father** his storing-up of treasures yields this bitter taste to the dying father **81 determin'd** ended, put an end to **83 kindly** natural **84 deep** intense

103 seal'd up confirmed **114 balm** consecrated oil used in anointing the king at his coronation **115 compound** mix **118 form** ceremony, orderly usages **119 vanity** folly **123 neighbor confines** territories of neighboring countries **124 ruffin** ruffian **132 flesh his tooth on** plunge his teeth into the flesh of **134 care** careful maintenance of discipline **135 care** concern **140 dear** severe (because deeply felt emotionally)

Ere you with grief had spoke and I had heard
The course of it so far. There is your crown;
And He that wears the crown immortally
Long guard it yours! If I affect it more [*Kneels.*] 144
Than as your honor and as your renown,
Let me no more from this obedience rise, 146
Which my most inward true and duteous spirit
Teacheth, this prostrate and exterior bending.
God witness with me, when I here came in,
And found no course of breath within your Majesty,
How cold it struck my heart! If I do feign,
O, let me in my present wildness die
And never live to show th' incredulous world
The noble change that I have purposed!
Coming to look on you, thinking you dead,
And dead almost, my liege, to think you were,
I spake unto this crown as having sense, 157
And thus upbraided it: "The care on thee depending
Hath fed upon the body of my father;
Therefore, thou best of gold art worst of gold.
Other, less fine in carat, is more precious,
Preserving life in med'cine potable; 162
But thou, most fine, most honor'd, most renown'd,
Hast eat thy bearer up." Thus, my most royal liege, 164
Accusing it, I put it on my head,
To try with it, as with an enemy
That had before my face murdered my father,
The quarrel of a true inheritor. 168
But if it did infect my blood with joy,
Or swell my thoughts to any strain of pride, 170
If any rebel or vain spirit of mine
Did with the least affection of a welcome 172
Give entertainment to the might of it,
Let God for ever keep it from my head
And make me as the poorest vassal is
That doth with awe and terror kneel to it!

KING
[O my son,]
God put it in thy mind to take it hence,
That thou mightst win the more thy father's love,
Pleading so wisely in excuse of it!
Come hither, Harry, sit thou by my bed,
[*Prince rises, and sits by the bed.*]
And hear, I think, the very latest counsel 182
That ever I shall breathe. God knows, my son,
By what by-paths and indirect crook'd ways
I met this crown, and I myself know well
How troublesome it sat upon my head.
To thee it shall descend with better quiet,
Better opinion, better confirmation; 188
For all the soil of the achievement goes 189
With me into the earth. It seem'd in me
But as an honor snatch'd with boist'rous hand,
And I had many living to upbraid
My gain of it by their assistances,
Which daily grew to quarrel and to bloodshed,
Wounding supposed peace. All these bold fears
Thou see'st with peril I have answered;
For all my reign hath been but as a scene
Acting that argument. And now my death 198
Changes the mood, for what in me was purchas'd 199
Falls upon thee in a more fairer sort; 200
So thou the garland wear'st successively. 201
Yet, though thou stand'st more sure than I could do,
Thou art not firm enough, since griefs are green. 203
And all my friends, which thou must make thy friends,
Have but their stings and teeth newly ta'en out,
By whose fell working I was first advanc'd 206
And by whose power I well might lodge a fear 207
To be again displac'd. Which to avoid,
I cut them off, and had a purpose now
To lead out many to the Holy Land,
Lest rest and lying still might make them look 211
Too near unto my state. Therefore, my Harry, 212
Be it thy course to busy giddy minds
With foreign quarrels, that action, hence borne out, 214
May waste the memory of the former days. 215
More would I, but my lungs are wasted so
That strength of speech is utterly denied me.
How I came by the crown, O God forgive,
And grant it may with thee in true peace live!

PRINCE
[My gracious liege,]
You won it, wore it, kept it, gave it me.
Then plain and right must my possession be,
Which I with more than with a common pain 223
'Gainst all the world will rightfully maintain.

Enter [*Prince John of*] *Lancaster* [*and Warwick*].

KING
Look, look, here comes my John of Lancaster.

PRINCE JOHN
Health, peace, and happiness to my royal father!

KING
Thou bring'st me happiness and peace, son John;
But health, alack, with youthful wings is flown
From this bare wither'd trunk. Upon thy sight 229
My worldly business makes a period. 230
Where is my Lord of Warwick?

PRINCE
My Lord of Warwick!

[*Warwick comes forward.*]

KING
Doth any name particular belong
Unto the lodging where I first did swoon?

WARWICK
'Tis call'd Jerusalem, my noble lord.

144 affect desire **146 obedience** obeisance **157 as having sense** as if it were capable of sense impressions **162 med'cine potable** potable gold, an elixir, thought from Galen's time to possess magical power to cure **164 eat** eaten. (Pronounced *et*.) **168 The quarrel . . . inheritor** (The prince, as the son and heir of a murdered man, has a quarrel to settle with the murderer.) **170 strain** feeling **172 affection** inclination **182 latest** last **188 opinion** public support **189 soil** stain

198 argument theme **199 mood** state of mind; mode, musical key. **purchas'd** i.e., gained by transaction **200 sort** manner, way **201 garland** crown. **successively** by right of succession **203 griefs are green** grievances are fresh **206 fell working** fierce effort **207 lodge** harbor **211–212 look . . . state** examine too painstakingly my regal status, my claim **214 action . . . out** military action, conducted in other lands **215 waste** efface, obliterate **223 pain** effort **229 Upon thy sight** at the very moment of my seeing you **230 makes a period** comes to an end, rounds out a whole

KING
Laud be to God! Even there my life must end.
It hath been prophesied to me many years
I should not die but in Jerusalem,
Which vainly I suppos'd the Holy Land.
But bear me to that chamber; there I'll lie.
In that Jerusalem shall Harry die. [*Exeunt.*]

[ACT V • SCENE I]

Enter Shallow, Falstaff, and Bardolph [*and Page*].

SHALLOW By cock and pie, sir, you shall not away to- 1
night. What, Davy, I say!
FALSTAFF You must excuse me, Master Robert Shallow.
SHALLOW I will not excuse you, you shall not be
excus'd, excuses shall not be admitted, there is no ex-
cuse shall serve, you shall not be excus'd. Why, Davy!

[*Enter Davy.*]

DAVY Here, sir.
SHALLOW Davy, Davy, Davy, Davy, let me see, Davy,
let me see, Davy, let me see. Yea, marry, William cook,
bid him come hither. Sir John, you shall not be ex-
cus'd.
DAVY Marry, sir, thus, those precepts cannot be serv'd. 12
And, again, sir, shall we sow the hade land with 13
wheat?
SHALLOW With red wheat, Davy. But for William
cook—are there no young pigeons?
DAVY Yes, sir. Here is now the smith's note for shoeing 17
and plough-irons. [*Gives paper.*]
SHALLOW Let it be cast and paid. Sir John, you shall not 19
be excus'd.
DAVY Now, sir, a new link to the bucket must needs be 21
had. And sir, do you mean to stop any of William's
wages, about the sack he lost the other day at Hinckley 23
fair?
SHALLOW 'A shall answer it. Some pigeons, Davy, a 25
couple of short-legg'd hens, a joint of mutton, and any
pretty little tiny kickshaws, tell William cook. 27
[*Davy and Shallow confer privately.*]
DAVY Doth the man of war stay all night, sir?
SHALLOW Yea, Davy. I will use him well. A friend i' th'
court is better than a penny in purse. Use his men
well, Davy, for they are arrant knaves, and will back-
bite.
DAVY No worse than they are backbitten, sir, for they 33
have marvail's foul linen. 34
SHALLOW Well conceited, Davy. About thy business, 35
Davy.
DAVY I beseech you, sir, to countenance William Visor 37
of Woncot against Clement Perkes o' th' hill.
SHALLOW There is many complaints, Davy, against that
Visor. That Visor is an arrant knave, on my knowl-
edge.
DAVY I grant your worship that he is a knave, sir; but
yet, God forbid, sir, but a knave should have some
countenance at his friend's request. An honest man,
sir, is able to speak for himself, when a knave is not.
I have serv'd your worship truly, sir, this eight years;
an I cannot once or twice in a quarter bear out a knave 47
against an honest man, I have little credit with your
worship. The knave is mine honest friend, sir; there-
fore, I beseech you, let him be countenanc'd.
SHALLOW Go to; I say he shall have no wrong. Look 51
about, Davy. [*Exit Davy.*] Where are you, Sir John? 52
Come, come, come, off with your boots. Give me your
hand, Master Bardolph.
BARDOLPH I am glad to see your worship.
SHALLOW I thank thee with all my heart, kind Master
Bardolph. And welcome, my tall fellow [*To the Page*].
Come, Sir John.
FALSTAFF I'll follow you, good Master Robert Shallow.
[*Exit Shallow.*] Bardolph, look to our horses. [*Exeunt
Bardolph and Page.*] If I were saw'd into quantities, I 61
should make four dozen of such bearded hermits'
staves as Master Shallow. It is a wonderful thing to see
the semblable coherence of his men's spirits and his. 64
They, by observing of him, do bear themselves like
foolish justices; he, by conversing with them, is turn'd 66
into a justice-like servingman. Their spirits are so mar-
ried in conjunction with the participation of society 68
that they flock together in consent, like so many wild 69
geese. If I had a suit to Master Shallow, I would humor
his men with the imputation of being near their mas-
ter; if to his men, I would curry with Master Shallow 72
that no man could better command his servants. It is
certain that either wise bearing or ignorant carriage is 74
caught, as men take diseases, one of another. There-
fore let men take heed of their company. I will devise
matter enough out of this Shallow to keep Prince
Harry in continual laughter the wearing out of six
fashions, which is four terms, or two actions, and 'a 79
shall laugh without intervallums. O, it is much that a 80
lie with a slight oath and a jest with a sad brow will 81
do with a fellow that never had the ache in his shoul-
ders! O, you shall see him laugh till his face be like a
wet cloak ill laid up. 84
SHALLOW [*Within*] Sir John!
FALSTAFF I come, Master Shallow, I come, Master
Shallow. [*Exit.*]

V.i. Location: Gloucestershire. Shallow's house.
1 By cock and pie (A mild oath.) **12 precepts** writs, summonses **13 hade land** strip of unploughed land between two ploughed fields **17 note** bill **19 cast** added up **21 link** chain. **bucket** yoke **23 Hinckley** market town not far from Coventry, famous for its fairs **25 answer** pay for **27 kickshaws** fancy dish. (From French *quelque chose.*) **33 backbitten** (with pun on *bitten by vermin*) **34 marvail's** marvelously

35 Well conceited ingeniously punned **37 countenance** favor **47 bear out** support **51–52 Look about** look sharp, be on the alert **61 quantities** pieces **64 semblable coherence** similar or complete agreement **66 conversing** associating **68 with . . . society** by close association **69 consent** agreement **72 curry with** employ flattery with **74 carriage** demeanor, behavior **79 four terms** i.e., of court, Michaelmas, Hilary, Easter, and Trinity, all in all comprising one legal year. **actions** lawsuits **80 intervallums** intervals between terms of court **81 sad** serious **84 ill laid up** carelessly put away so that it wrinkles

[SCENE II]

Enter Warwick [*and the*] *Lord Chief Justice* [*meeting*].

WARWICK
How now, my Lord Chief Justice, whither away?
CHIEF JUSTICE
How doth the King?
WARWICK
Exceeding well. His cares are now all ended.
CHIEF JUSTICE
I hope, not dead.
WARWICK He's walk'd the way of nature;
And to our purposes he lives no more.
CHIEF JUSTICE
I would his Majesty had call'd me with him.
The service that I truly did his life
Hath left me open to all injuries.
WARWICK
Indeed I think the young King loves you not.
CHIEF JUSTICE
I know he doth not, and do arm myself
To welcome the condition of the time,
Which cannot look more hideously upon me
Than I have drawn it in my fantasy.

Enter [*Prince*] *John* [*of Lancaster*], *Thomas* [*of Clarence*], *and Humphrey* [*of Gloucester, with*] *Westmorland,* [*and others*].

WARWICK
Here come the heavy issue of dead Harry.
O that the living Harry had the temper
Of he, the worst of these three gentlemen!
How many nobles then should hold their places,
That must strike sail to spirits of vile sort!
CHIEF JUSTICE
O God, I fear all will be overturn'd.
PRINCE JOHN
Good morrow, cousin Warwick, good morrow.
GLOUCESTER, CLARENCE
Good morrow, cousin.
PRINCE JOHN
We meet like men that had forgot to speak.
WARWICK
We do remember, but our argument
Is all too heavy to admit much talk.
PRINCE JOHN
Well, peace be with him that hath made us heavy!
CHIEF JUSTICE
Peace be with us, lest we be heavier!
GLOUCESTER
O, good my lord, you have lost a friend indeed;
And I dare swear you borrow not that face
Of seeming sorrow, it is sure your own.
PRINCE JOHN
Though no man be assur'd what grace to find,
You stand in coldest expectation.
I am the sorrier; would 'twere otherwise.
CLARENCE
Well, you must now speak Sir John Falstaff fair,
Which swims against your stream of quality.
CHIEF JUSTICE
Sweet princes, what I did, I did in honor,
Led by th' impartial conduct of my soul,
And never shall you see that I will beg
A ragged and forestall'd remission.
If truth and upright innocency fail me,
I'll to the King my master that is dead,
And tell him who hath sent me after him.
WARWICK
Here comes the Prince.

Enter the Prince [*as King Henry the Fifth*] *and Blunt.*

CHIEF JUSTICE
Good morrow; and God save your Majesty!
KING
This new and gorgeous garment, majesty,
Sits not so easy on me as you think.
Brothers, you mix your sadness with some fear.
This is the English, not the Turkish court;
Not Amurath an Amurath succeeds,
But Harry Harry. Yet be sad, good brothers,
For, by my faith, it very well becomes you.
Sorrow so royally in you appears
That I will deeply put the fashion on
And wear it in my heart. Why then, be sad,
But entertain no more of it, good brothers,
Than a joint burden laid upon us all.
For me, by heaven, I bid you be assur'd,
I'll be your father and your brother too.
Let me but bear your love, I'll bear your cares.
Yet weep that Harry's dead, and so will I;
But Harry lives, that shall convert those tears
By number into hours of happiness.
PRINCES
We hope no otherwise from your Majesty.
KING
You all look strangely on me. [*To the Chief Justice.*]
And you most.
You are, I think, assur'd I love you not.
CHIEF JUSTICE
I am assur'd, if I be measur'd rightly,
Your Majesty hath no just cause to hate me.
KING
No?
How might a prince of my great hopes forget
So great indignities you laid upon me?
What? Rate, rebuke, and roughly send to prison

V.ii. Location: Westminster. The palace.
14 heavy issue grieving sons **16 he, the worst** the least worthy **18 strike sail** i.e., salute as a token of submission. (A naval custom.) **22 forgot** forgotten how **23 argument** subject

30 grace to find favor he will find **33 speak . . . fair** speak courteously to Sir John Falstaff **34 swims . . . quality** runs counter to your natural inclination **38 A . . . remission** a half-hearted (beggarly) pardon, which is sure to be refused, or whose effect is gone before it is granted **48 Amurath** a Turkish sultan who, upon succeeding his father, had his brothers strangled **70 Rate** chide

Th' immediate heir of England? Was this easy?
May this be wash'd in Lethe, and forgotten?

CHIEF JUSTICE

I then did use the person of your father.
The image of his power lay then in me.
And, in th' administration of his law,
Whiles I was busy for the commonwealth,
Your Highness pleased to forget my place,
The majesty and power of law and justice,
The image of the King whom I presented,
And struck me in my very seat of judgment;
Whereon, as an offender to your father,
I gave bold way to my authority
And did commit you. If the deed were ill,
Be you contented, wearing now the garland,
To have a son set your decrees at nought,
To pluck down justice from your aweful bench,
To trip the course of law and blunt the sword
That guards the peace and safety of your person,
Nay, more, to spurn at your most royal image
And mock your workings in a second body?
Question your royal thoughts, make the case yours:
Be now the father and propose a son,
Hear your own dignity so much profan'd,
See your most dreadful laws so loosely slighted,
Behold yourself so by a son disdain'd,
And then imagine me taking your part
And in your power soft silencing your son.
After this cold considerance, sentence me,
And, as you are a king, speak in your state
What I have done that misbecame my place,
My person, or my liege's sovereignty.

KING

You are right justice, and you weigh this well.
Therefore still bear the balance and the sword;
And I do wish your honors may increase,
Till you do live to see a son of mine
Offend you and obey you, as I did.
So shall I live to speak my father's words:
"Happy am I, that have a man so bold,
That dares do justice on my proper son;
And not less happy, having such a son
That would deliver up his greatness so
Into the hands of justice." You did commit me;
For which, I do commit into your hand
Th' unstained sword that you have us'd to bear,
With this remembrance, that you use the same
With the like bold, just, and impartial spirit
As you have done 'gainst me. There is my hand.
You shall be as a father to my youth.
My voice shall sound as you do prompt mine ear,
And I will stoop and humble my intents
To your well-practic'd wise directions.
And, princes all, believe me, I beseech you:
My father is gone wild into his grave,
For in his tomb lie my affections,
And with his spirit sadly I survive,
To mock the expectation of the world,
To frustrate prophecies, and to rase out
Rotten opinion, who hath writ me down
After my seeming. The tide of blood in me
Hath proudly flow'd in vanity till now;
Now doth it turn and ebb back to the sea,
Where it shall mingle with the state of floods
And flow henceforth in formal majesty.
Now call we our high court of parliament.
And let us choose such limbs of noble counsel
That the great body of our state may go
In equal rank with the best govern'd nation;
That war, or peace, or both at once, may be
As things acquainted and familiar to us,
[*To Chief Justice*] In which you, father, shall have foremost hand.
Our coronation done, we will accite,
As I before rememb'red, all our state.
And, God consigning to my good intents,
No prince nor peer shall have just cause to say,
God shorten Harry's happy life one day! *Exeunt.*

71 immediate heir next heir in succession. **easy** of small importance, easily forgotten **72 Lethe** the river of forgetfulness in Hades **73 use the person** act as representative **79 presented** represented **83 commit** i.e., to prison **86 aweful** inspiring awe **90 second body** representative, deputy **92 propose** imagine, suppose **97 soft** gently **98 cold considerance** calm reflection **99 state** royal capacity **103 balance, sword** (Emblems of justice.) **109 proper** own **115 remembrance** reminder, admonition **119 sound** speak

123–124 My . . . affections i.e., my wildness, having disappeared with my father's death, is buried along with my father **124 affections** (wild) inclinations **125 sadly** soberly **127 rase out** erase **128 who** which **129 After my seeming** according to what I appeared to be. **blood** passion **130 vanity** folly **132 state of floods** majesty of the ocean **141 accite** summon **142 remem'b'red** mentioned. **state** peers, nobility **143 consigning to** sanctioning

[SCENE III]

Enter Sir John [*Falstaff*], *Shallow, Silence, Davy, Bardolph,* [*and the*] *Page.* [*Davy lays the cloth of table and serves wine.*]

SHALLOW Nay, you shall see my orchard, where, in an arbor, we will eat a last year's pippin of mine own graffing, with a dish of caraways, and so forth. Come, cousin Silence. And then to bed.

FALSTAFF 'Fore God, you have here goodly dwelling and rich.

SHALLOW Barren, barren, barren. Beggars all, beggars all, Sir John. Marry, good air. Spread, Davy, spread, Davy. Well said, Davy.

FALSTAFF This Davy serves you for good uses. He is your servingman and your husband.

SHALLOW A good varlet, a good varlet, a very good varlet, Sir John. By the mass, I have drunk too much sack at supper. A good varlet. Now sit down, now sit down. Come, cousin. [*They sit.*]

SILENCE Ah, sirrah, quoth 'a, we shall
[*Sings.*] "Do nothing but eat, and make good cheer,
And praise God for the merry year,
When flesh is cheap and females dear,

V.iii. Location: Gloucestershire. Shallow's orchard.
2 pippin a kind of apple **3 graffing** grafting. **caraways** caraway seeds (often eaten with apples) **8 Spread** spread the cloth **9 said** done **11 husband** manager of the household **12–13 varlet** servant **16 quoth 'a** said he **19 flesh** meat (with sexual suggestion)

And lusty lads roam here and there
So merrily,
And ever among so merrily."

FALSTAFF There's a merry heart! Good Master Silence, I'll give you a health for that anon.

SHALLOW Give Master Bardolph some wine, Davy.

DAVY Sweet sir, sit, I'll be with you anon. Most sweet sir, sit. Master page, good master page, sit. Proface! What you want in meat, we'll have in drink. But you must bear, the heart's all. [*Exit.*]

SHALLOW Be merry, Master Bardolph, and, my little soldier there, be merry.

SILENCE [*Sings*]
"Be merry, be merry, my wife has all,
For women are shrews, both short and tall.
'Tis merry in hall when beards wags all,
And welcome merry Shrove-tide.
Be merry, be merry."

FALSTAFF I did not think Master Silence had been a man of this mettle.

SILENCE Who, I? I have been merry twice and once ere now.

Enter Davy.

DAVY [*To Bardolph*] There's a dish of leather-coats for you.

SHALLOW Davy!

DAVY Your worship? [*To Bardolph.*] I'll be with you straight.—A cup of wine, sir?

SILENCE [*Sings*]
"A cup of wine that's brisk and fine,
And drink unto thee, leman mine,
And a merry heart lives long-a."

FALSTAFF Well said, Master Silence.

SILENCE An we shall be merry, now comes in the sweet o' th' night.

FALSTAFF Health and long life to you, Master Silence.

SILENCE [*Sings*]
"Fill the cup, and let it come,
I'll pledge you a mile to th' bottom."

SHALLOW Honest Bardolph, welcome. If thou want'st anything, and wilt not call, beshrew thy heart. Welcome, my little tiny thief [*To the Page*], and welcome indeed too. I'll drink to Master Bardolph, and to all the cabileros about London.

DAVY I hope to see London once ere I die.

BARDOLPH An I might see you there, Davy!

SHALLOW By the mass, you'll crack a quart together, ha, will you not, Master Bardolph?

BARDOLPH Yea, sir, in a pottle-pot.

SHALLOW By God's liggens, I thank thee. The knave will stick by thee, I can assure thee that. 'A will not out, 'a; 'tis true bred.

BARDOLPH And I'll stick by him, sir.

SHALLOW Why, there spoke a king. Lack nothing; be merry. (*One knocks at door.*) Look who's at door there, ho! Who knocks? [*Davy goes to the door.*]

FALSTAFF [*To Silence, seeing him drinking*] Why, now you have done me right.

SILENCE [*Sings*]
"Do me right,
And dub me knight,
Samingo."
Is 't not so?

FALSTAFF 'Tis so.

SILENCE Is 't so? Why then, say an old man can do somewhat.

DAVY [*Returning*] An 't please your worship, there's one Pistol come from the court with news.

FALSTAFF From the court? Let him come in.

Enter Pistol.

How now, Pistol?

PISTOL Sir John, God save you!

FALSTAFF What wind blew you hither, Pistol?

PISTOL Not the ill wind which blows no man to good. Sweet knight, thou art now one of the greatest men in this realm.

SILENCE By 'r lady, I think 'a be, but goodman Puff of Barson.

PISTOL Puff?
Puff i' thy teeth, most recreant coward base!
Sir John, I am thy Pistol and thy friend,
And helter-skelter have I rode to thee,
And tidings do I bring, and lucky joys,
And golden times, and happy news of price.

FALSTAFF I pray thee now, deliver them like a man of this world.

PISTOL
A foutre for the world and worldlings base!
I speak of Africa and golden joys.

FALSTAFF
O base Assyrian knight, what is thy news?
Let King Cophetua know the truth thereof.

SILENCE [*Sings*]
"And Robin Hood, Scarlet, and John."

PISTOL
Shall dunghill curs confront the Helicons?
And shall good news be baffled?
Then, Pistol, lay thy head in Furies' lap.

SHALLOW Honest gentleman, I know not your breeding.

PISTOL
Why then, lament therefore.

SHALLOW Give me pardon, sir. If, sir, you come with news from the court, I take it there's but two ways,

22 ever among all the while **27 Proface** (Formula of welcome to a meal, meaning "May it do you good.") **28 want** lack. **meat** food **29 bear** be forbearing **35 Shrove-tide** a season of merrymaking before Lent **39 twice and once** i.e., now and again **41 leather-coats** russet apples **47 leman** sweetheart **53 let it come** i.e., pass it around **54 a mile** i.e., even if it were a mile **59 cabileros** cavaliers, gallants **62 crack** consume **64 pottle-pot** two-quart tankard **65 liggens** (Unexplained.) **66–67 'A will not out** he won't drop out of the drinking, or won't pass out (?)

73 done me right i.e., kept up with me in drinking **76 Samingo** Sir Mingo, or San Domingo, the hero of the song **80 somewhat** something **90 but** except. (Silence interprets *greatest* in the sense of "heaviest.") **goodman** yeoman **97 price** great value **98–99 man of this world** ordinary man **100 foutre** (From the French *foutre,* fornicate.) **101 Africa** (Fabled for wealth.) **102 Assyrian** (Falstaff adopts Pistol's highflown style and metrics.) **103 Cophetua** (King Cophetua married a beggar maid according to the popular ballad, "King Cophetua and the Beggar Maid.") **104 And . . . John** (A scrap from another ballad.) **105 Helicons** i.e., poets. (Mount Helicon was the abode of the Muses.) **106 baffled** disgraced **108–109 breeding** parentage, rank

either to utter them, or conceal them. I am, sir, under the King, in some authority.

PISTOL
Under which king, Besonian? Speak, or die.

SHALLOW
Under King Harry.

PISTOL Harry the Fourth, or Fifth?

SHALLOW
Harry the Fourth.

PISTOL A foutre for thine office!
Sir John, thy tender lambkin now is king;
Harry the Fifth's the man. I speak the truth.
When Pistol lies, do this, and fig me like
The bragging Spaniard.

FALSTAFF
What, is the old King dead?

PISTOL
As nail in door. The things I speak are just.

FALSTAFF Away, Bardolph! Saddle my horse. Master Robert Shallow, choose what office thou wilt in the land, 'tis thine. Pistol, I will double-charge thee with dignities.

BARDOLPH O joyful day! I would not take a knighthood for my fortune.

PISTOL
What? I do bring good news?

FALSTAFF Carry Master Silence to bed. Master Shallow, my Lord Shallow—be what thou wilt, I am fortune's steward—get on thy boots. We'll ride all night. O sweet Pistol! Away, Bardolph! [*Exit Bardolph.*] Come, Pistol, utter more to me, and withal devise something to do thyself good. Boot, boot, Master Shallow! I know the young King is sick for me. Let us take any man's horses; the laws of England are at my commandment. Blessed are they that have been my friends, and woe to my Lord Chief Justice!

PISTOL
Let vultures vile seize on his lungs also!
"Where is the life that late I led?" say they.
Why, here it is. Welcome these pleasant days!
Exeunt.

[SCENE IV]

Enter Beadle and three or four Officers [*with Hostess Quickly and Doll Tearsheet*].

HOSTESS No, thou arrant knave, I would to God that I might die, that I might have thee hang'd. Thou hast drawn my shoulder out of joint.

BEADLE The constables have deliver'd her over to me, and she shall have whipping-cheer, I warrant her. There hath been a man or two lately kill'd about her.

DOLL Nuthook, nuthook, you lie. Come on! I'll tell thee what, thou damn'd tripe-visag'd rascal, an the child I go with do miscarry, thou wert better thou hadst struck thy mother, thou paper-fac'd villain!

HOSTESS O the lord, that Sir John were come! He would make this a bloody day to somebody. But I pray God the fruit of her womb miscarry!

BEADLE If it do, you shall have a dozen of cushions again; you have but eleven now. Come, I charge you both go with me, for the man is dead that you and Pistol beat amongst you.

DOLL I'll tell you what, you thin man in a censer, I will have you as soundly swing'd for this—you blue-bottle rogue, you filthy famish'd correctioner, if you be not swing'd, I'll forswear half-kirtles.

BEADLE Come, come, you she knight-errant, come.

HOSTESS O God, that right should thus overcome might! Well, of sufferance comes ease.

DOLL Come, you rogue, come, bring me to a justice.

HOSTESS Ay, come, you starv'd bloodhound.

DOLL Goodman death, goodman bones!

HOSTESS Thou atomy, thou!

DOLL Come, you thin thing, come, you rascal.

BEADLE Very well. [*Exeunt.*]

[SCENE V]

Enter [*Grooms as*] *strewers of rushes.*

FIRST GROOM More rushes, more rushes.

SECOND GROOM The trumpets have sounded twice.

THIRD GROOM 'Twill be two o'clock ere they come from the coronation. Dispatch, dispatch. [*Exeunt.*]

Trumpets sound, and the King and his train pass over the stage. After them enter Falstaff, Shallow, Pistol, Bardolph, and the Boy [*Page*].

FALSTAFF Stand here by me, Master Shallow, I will make the King do you grace. I will leer upon him as 'a comes by, and do but mark the countenance that he will give me.

PISTOL God bless thy lungs, good knight.

FALSTAFF Come here, Pistol, stand behind me. O, if I had had time to have made new liveries, I would have bestow'd the thousand pound I borrow'd of you. But 'tis no matter; this poor show doth better. This doth infer the zeal I had to see him.

SHALLOW It doth so.

115 Besonian low, beggarly rascal. (From Italian "bisogno," need.) **120 fig** insult with a vulgar gesture consisting in thrusting the thumb between the index and third fingers **126 double-charge** (with a play on Pistol's name) **142 Where . . . led** (Fragment of a ballad.)

V.iv. Location: London. A street.
5 whipping-cheer i.e., a whipping for supper **6 about her** (1) in her company (2) on her account

7 Nuthook hook for pulling down branches in nutting; here, a constable **8, 10 tripe-visag'd, paper-fac'd** (Allusions to the pock-marked and sallow complexion of the Beadle.) **15 eleven now** (The Beadle accuses Doll of using one of the cushions to make her appear pregnant; pregnant women were spared execution.) **18 thin . . . censer** i.e., figure of a man on the lid of a censer or incense burner, embossed in low relief **19 swing'd** thrashed. **blue-bottle** (An allusion to the Beadle's blue coat.) **21 half-kirtles** short skirts **24 sufferance** suffering **28 atomy** (For anatomy, skeleton; an *atomy* is an atom, speck.) **29 rascal** lean deer

V.v. Location: A public place near Westminister Abbey.
1 rushes floor coverings, here used for strewing the streets in the King's path **4 Dispatch** hurry **6 grace** honor. **leer** glance sideways **12 bestow'd** spent. **you** i.e., Justice Shallow **13 poor show** appearing in inferior garments **14 infer** imply

FALSTAFF It shows my earnestness of affection—
SHALLOW It doth so.
FALSTAFF My devotion—
SHALLOW It doth, it doth, it doth.
FALSTAFF As it were, to ride day and night, and not to deliberate, not to remember, not to have patience to shift me— 22
SHALLOW It is best, certain.
FALSTAFF But to stand stain'd with travel, and sweating with desire to see him, thinking of nothing else, putting all affairs else in oblivion, as if there were nothing else to be done but to see him.
PISTOL 'Tis "semper idem," for "obsque hoc nihil est." 28
'Tis all in every part.
SHALLOW 'Tis so, indeed.
PISTOL
My knight, I will inflame thy noble liver, 31
And make thee rage.
Thy Doll, and Helen of thy noble thoughts, 33
Is in base durance and contagious prison, 34
Hal'd thither
By most mechanical and dirty hand. 36
Rouse up revenge from ebon den with fell Alecto's snake, 37
For Doll is in. Pistol speaks nought but truth.
FALSTAFF
I will deliver her.
[Shouts within, and the trumpets sound.]
PISTOL
There roar'd the sea, and trumpet-clangor sounds.

Enter the King and his train, [the Lord Chief Justice among them].

FALSTAFF
God save thy Grace, King Hal, my royal Hal!
PISTOL
The heavens thee guard and keep, most royal imp of fame! 42
FALSTAFF
God save thee, my sweet boy!
KING
My Lord Chief Justice, speak to that vain man.
CHIEF JUSTICE
Have you your wits? Know you what 'tis you speak?
FALSTAFF
My King! My Jove! I speak to thee, my heart!
KING
I know thee not, old man. Fall to thy prayers.
How ill white hairs become a fool and jester!
I have long dreamt of such a kind of man,
So surfeit-swell'd, so old, and so profane,
But, being awak'd, I do despise my dream.
Make less thy body hence, and more thy grace; 52
Leave gormandizing. Know the grave doth gape
For thee thrice wider than for other men.
Reply not to me with a fool-born jest.
Presume not that I am the thing I was,
For God doth know, so shall the world perceive,
That I have turn'd away my former self;
So will I those that kept me company.
When thou dost hear I am as I have been,
Approach me, and thou shalt be as thou wast,
The tutor and the feeder of my riots.
Till then, I banish thee, on pain of death,
As I have done the rest of my misleaders,
Not to come near our person by ten mile.
For competence of life I will allow you, 66
That lack of means enforce you not to evils.
And, as we hear you do reform yourselves,
We will, according to your strengths and qualities,
Give you advancement. Be it your charge, my lord,
To see perform'd the tenor of our word.
Set on. *[Exeunt King and his Train.]*
FALSTAFF Master Shallow, I owe you a thousand pound.
SHALLOW Yea, marry, Sir John, which I beseech you to let me have home with me.
FALSTAFF That can hardly be, Master Shallow. Do not you grieve at this. I shall be sent for in private to him. Look you, he must seem thus to the world. Fear not your advancements; I will be the man yet that shall 80
make you great.
SHALLOW I cannot well perceive how, unless you should give me your doublet and stuff me out with straw. I beseech you, good Sir John, let me have five hundred of my thousand.
FALSTAFF Sir, I will be as good as my word. This that you heard was but a color. 87
SHALLOW A color that I fear you will die in, Sir John.
FALSTAFF Fear no colors. Go with me to dinner. Come, 89
Lieutenant Pistol, come, Bardolph. I shall be sent for soon at night. 91

Enter [the Lord Chief] Justice and Prince John [of Lancaster, with Officers].

CHIEF JUSTICE
Go, carry Sir John Falstaff to the Fleet. 92
Take all his company along with him.
FALSTAFF
My lord, my lord—
CHIEF JUSTICE
I cannot now speak. I will hear you soon.
Take them away.
PISTOL
"Si fortuna me tormenta, spero contenta." 97
Exeunt [all but Prince John and the Chief Justice].

22 shift me change my apparel **28 semper . . . est** "always the same," for "without this there is nothing." (Pistol approvingly rephrases Falstaff's dedication to put his loyalty to the Prince above all else.) **31 liver** (The seat of the passions.) **33 Helen** i.e., Helen of Troy, the type of womanly beauty **34 durance** imprisonment. **contagious** pestilential **36 mechanical** menial, base **37 ebon** black. **Alecto** one of the Furies, who were depicted with snakes twined in their hair **42 imp** scion

52 hence henceforth **66 competence of life** modest allowance **87 color** pretense. (But Shallow uses the word to mean *collar,* hangman's noose.) **89 colors** standards or flags (of the enemy) **91 soon at night** early in the evening **92 Fleet** a famous London prison **97 Si . . . contenta** (See note on II.iv.179, above.)

PRINCE JOHN
I like this fair proceeding of the King's.
He hath intent his wonted followers
Shall all be very well provided for,
But all are banish'd till their conversations 101
Appear more wise and modest to the world.

CHIEF JUSTICE
And so they are.

PRINCE JOHN
The King hath call'd his parliament, my lord.

CHIEF JUSTICE
He hath.

PRINCE JOHN
I will lay odds that, ere this year expire,
We bear our civil swords and native fire 107
As far as France. I heard a bird so sing,
Whose music, to my thinking, pleas'd the King.
Come, will you hence? [*Exeunt.*]

EPILOGUE

[*Spoken by a Dancer.*]

First my fear, then my cur'sy, last my speech. My 1
fear is your displeasure, my cur'sy, my duty, and my
speech, to beg your pardons. If you look for a good
speech now, you undo me, for what I have to say is of
mine own making, and what indeed I should say will,
I doubt, prove mine own marring. But to the purpose, 6
and so to the venture. Be it known to you, as it is very
well, I was lately here in the end of a displeasing play, 8
to pray your patience for it and to promise you a bet-
ter. I meant indeed to pay you with this, which, if like
an ill venture it come unluckily home, I break, and 11
you, my gentle creditors, lose. Here I promis'd you I
would be, and here I commit my body to your mer-
cies. Bate me some and I will pay you some and, as 14
most debtors do, promise you infinitely.

If my tongue cannot entreat you to acquit me, will you command me to use my legs? And yet that were but light payment, to dance out of your debt. But a good conscience will make any possible satisfaction, and so would I. All the gentlewomen here have forgiven me. If the gentlemen will not, then the gentlemen do not agree with the gentlewomen, which was never seen before in such an assembly.

One word more, I beseech you. If you be not too
much cloy'd with fat meat, our humble author will
continue the story, with Sir John in it, and make you 26
merry with fair Katharine of France. Where, for any-
thing I know, Falstaff shall die of a sweat, unless al-
ready a' be kill'd with your hard opinions; for Oldcas- 29
tle died a martyr, and this is not the man. My tongue 30
is weary; when my legs are too, I will bid you good
night; and so I kneel down before you, but, indeed, to
pray for the Queen.

101 conversations conduct **107 civil . . . fire** i.e., our weapons used recently in civil war

Epilogue
1 cur'sy curtsy, obeisance **6 doubt** fear **8 displeasing play** (No satisfactory identification has ever been made.) **11 ill venture** unlucky sending out of merchant vessels. **break** become bankrupt **14 Bate me some** let me off from some portion of the debt **26 Sir John in it** (Shakespeare evidently originally intended to introduce Falstaff into *Henry V;* instead, only his death is reported there in I.i and iii.)

29–30 Oldcastle . . . man i.e., Falstaff was not intended to resemble Sir John Oldcastle, the Lollard venerated by sixteenth-century Puritans as a martyr for their beliefs. (This statement may have been intended to placate Lord Cobham, descendant of Oldcastle, whose resentment of Shakespeare's use of the Oldcastle name in an earlier version of the *Henry IV* plays may have led to the change of the name to Falstaff.)

The Life of King Henry the Fifth

Henry V (1599) is Shakespeare's culminating statement in the genre of the English history play. Unlike the late and atypical *Henry VIII* (1613), separated from the rest of Shakespeare's history plays by some fourteen years and possibly written in collaboration with John Fletcher, *Henry V* sums up the historical themes with which Shakespeare had been fascinated for an entire decade. The play, first published in a "bad" quarto in 1600, must have been written not long after *2 Henry IV*. To be sure, the play does not entirely fulfill the promise made in *2 Henry IV* to "continue the story, with Sir John in it, and make you merry with fair Katharine of France." Falstaff is missing. As before, Shakespeare apparently saw a grand design to his four-play sequence, but improvised when he came to the writing of each part. Despite these minor alterations, however, *Henry V* is clearly intended to bring to fulfillment the education of a Christian prince, and to illustrate the arts of kingship Prince Hal had derived from his experiences in the earlier plays. In a sense, too, *Henry V* sums up the achievement of the English history play not only for Shakespeare but for other popular playwrights as well. The patriotic history play, born in the excitement of the Armada era, had nearly run its course by 1599 and was soon to be supplanted by other dramatic genres such as satire and revenge tragedy.

Henry V has become a controversial play, chiefly because its heroic king can, from the viewpoint of modern history, be looked upon as a warmonger and imperialist. George Bernard Shaw is prominent among those who have recently deplored Henry as a priggish and complacent chauvinist. Historical scholars have argued, on the other hand, that Henry is a perfect model of conduct according to Renaissance notions of statecraft and military leadership. What is Shakespeare's attitude toward his war hero? Does he sympathize with Henry's condescension toward the French, and his ordering every soldier to kill his French prisoners as an act of reprisal? Or is Shakespeare's admiration qualified by ironic reservations? As usual in Shakespeare, the perspective is complex and balanced. The play pulls us in two directions. Although the chorus who "interprets" the play for us approves of Henry's military posture, the grandiose rhetoric of war is consistently undercut by a matter-of-fact revelation of men's self-interested motives. This contrast between rhetorical illusion and political reality extends from the justification of Henry's French campaign to his state marriage with Katharine of France. The irony never amounts to open disillusionment in this play; it is instead the acknowledgment of a special kind of morality pertaining to kingship.

Skill in rhetoric is a key to Henry's success—in defying the French dauphin, in preparing troops for battle, or in wooing the French princess for his queen. As the Archbishop of Canterbury notes approvingly, King Henry's versatility as a rhetorician applies to all the vital disciplines of kingship: Henry can "reason in divinity," "debate of commonwealth affairs," "discourse of war," handle "any cause of policy," and in all such matters speak in "sweet and honey'd sentences" (I,i). Through the arts of language Henry displays piety, learning, administrative sagacity, political cunning, and military intrepidity. Like the contemporary play *Julius Caesar* (1599), *Henry V* is concerned with techniques of persuasion. (The earlier *Richard III* is also a highly rhetorical play, though chiefly through the negative example of tyrannical behavior.) Yet however much we may be swayed emotionally by the rhetoric, we realize that the public figure of Henry V is a mask behind which we can perceive little. Only rarely do we glimpse the affable young companion of the *Henry IV* plays. King Henry has accepted the responsibility of playing a political role. It denies him a private and separate identity, even—or especially—in choosing a wife. And it complicates our task of assessing his sincerity of utterance. Is he genuinely pious, or has he merely learned the usefulness of pious utterance in swaying men's hearts? What especially are his motives for going to war against France?

Shakespeare could have begun this play with the stirring scene (I,ii) in which Hal, urged on by his advisers, issues a defiant challenge to the French ambassadors. Instead, Shakespeare treats us to a prior glimpse beneath the patriotic surface. It seems that the Archbishop of Canterbury, threatened with a bill in parliament designed to take away the better half of the church's possessions, has resolved to parry with a counterproposal, whereby the church will "give" Henry a very substantial sum for his French campaign, provided the offensive tax bill can be conveniently forgotten. The Archbishop has already been negotiating with Henry, and surmises that the plan will work. This revelation is not shocking to us; it merely reveals the political process at work. The faint undercurrent of anticlericalism suggests that Henry is to be admired for putting pressure on his clergy with such success; they are rich and can afford to support the war. In any case, the dramatic effect is to show how men's practical motives affect their rhetoric. When, in the subsequent scene, the Archbishop delivers a public lecture on the English claim to France, we know that this learned prelate has a prior and self-interested commitment to the war. His intricate dynastic argument, which he proclaims to be "as clear as is the summer's sun," gives to the war a much-needed public justification. Henry's questions indicate not only his genuine concern about the legitimacy of his claim, but also his political need for the church's endorsement of his cause; he has already sent into France claiming dukedoms, and must have the church's official approval of those claims before he can proceed. He similarly needs the backing of his nobles, who also have their own reasons for approving the campaign. Henry skillfully orchestrates the scene to produce the desired effect of unanimous and patriotic consent.

Although never directly stated, Henry's own motives for going to war must also combine sincere zeal with calculated self-interest. As King, he longs to recover the French territory which England governed in the great days of Poitiers and Crécy. As a man, he bristles at the contemptuous challenge of the Dauphin; Henry must still strive to overcome his reputation as a wastrel, and must prove himself worthy of honorable comparison with his great ancestors. Politically (and this motive remains most hidden), Henry has absorbed his father's sage advice to "busy giddy minds With foreign quarrels" (*2 Henry IV,* IV,v), to blunt political opposition at home by uniting English resentment against a foreign scapegoat.

The exigencies of war do indeed provide Henry with an opportunity for proceeding against his political enemies. He arrests the Earl of Cambridge, Scroop, and Grey at Southampton on charges of conspiring with France. The scene (II,iv) is, for Shakespeare, uncharacteristically one-sided. We are never even told that Cambridge is the chief pretender to the English throne, son of the Duke of York, married to Anne Mortimer, and founder of the Yorkist claim in the York-Lancastrian wars—the sort of rival whom Shakespeare elsewhere portrays with understanding. Instead, the rhetoric of the Chorus to Act II blatantly warns us to expect "hell and treason." These three conspirators, like Judases, have bargained away their king for gold. The playwright does not give them complex motives; they are sinners, so horrified by their own intents that they are actually grateful to be caught. The scene serves, by such rhetorical devices, to strengthen Henry's claim to the English throne as well as to the territories in France. Opposition to his rule is evil; all persuasive evidences of dynastic rival claims are hidden from our view.

Comedy also contributes to the rhetorical image-making of the hero in *Henry V*. The Boarshead crew is on hand, but decorously more distant from Henry than in the earlier history plays. Only briefly and in disguise, on the night before the battle, does the King encounter Pistol. The name of Bardolph comes to Henry as though in recollection of a distant past, when he hears that Bardolph is about to be executed for stealing from French churches. Henry confirms the sentence: "We would have all such offenders so cut off" (III,vi). Whatever momentary pang Henry may feel, he remains constant to his banishment of Falstaff. And, although Shakespeare pleads for our sympathies in the seriocomic account of Falstaff's death, seen through the childlike naiveté of Mistress Quickly, there is no hope of reconciliation between Henry and his former mates. Pistol, despite his ornamental language, is little better than a boaster, pure coward, and thief. The Boarshead revelers are now the opportunists of war, troublemakers such as are found in every army, engaging rascals deserving to be cudgeled by more honorable men.

Pistol gets his comeuppance from Captain Fluellen, who replaces Falstaff as the chief comic figure both in prominence (his role is second in length to that of Henry) and in proximity to the King. Fluellen is a Welshman, like Harry of Monmouth, and is proud of this kinship. Because Fluellen is loyal and valiant, he is a person worthy to be seen in Henry's company. Yet there is none of the brilliant duel of wits previously linking Hal and Falstaff. Fluellen is a "humorous" character, identified at once by such comically exaggerated features as his Welsh accent and mannerisms of speech, his old-fashioned and somewhat fanatical sense of military propriety, and his devotion to the ancient rules of military discipline. Fluellen is a caricature, subject to mild satirical laughter, and there is a note of condescension in Hal's habit of playing practical jokes on the captain. (Hal makes practical jokes at others' expense as well, such as the soldier named Williams with whom he exchanges gloves.) Unlike Falstaff, Fluellen lacks perspective on his own pomposity. He is a zealot for duty, and one feels Hal is taking unfair advantage to pick on one who is such an easy mark for laughter. We suspect that Hal is "using" people again, bolstering his public image as the king with the common touch, borrowing a little Welsh color for mythmaking purposes. At the same time, Fluellen is steadfast, upright, a credit to his countryman Hal. With his fellow captains from Scotland, Ireland, and England, he demonstrates that Britishers can fight together even if they do antagonize one another with their proud regional customs. Those customs are to be cherished as part of the British character; because Pistol offers gratuitous insult to the Welsh tradition of wearing a leek in the cap on St. Davy's day, he must be thrashed.

As with the comic characters and Hal's political enemies, *Henry V* is rhetorically one-sided in its presentation of the French. Patriotism is a raw emotion, and Henry cannot appeal to it without awakening hostility toward the enemy. (Ironically enough, the great film version of *Henry V* by Laurence Olivier was created during World War II to arouse national feelings more against the Germans than against the French, and with complete success. Any enemy will do in such patriotic moods.) The French are haughty, vastly superior in numbers, envious of one another, contemptuous of their own leadership (especially the Dauphin), treacherous (attacking the boys with the luggage), and craven. Even their joking is characterized by an unattractively bestial kind of bawdry (III,vii). The British—"we few, we happy few"—are tired and outnumbered, but invincible and seemingly protected by God. Henry's order to kill the French prisoners, and his description of the rapes and pillages his soldiers will commit if Harfleur fails to surrender (III,iii), do to be sure raise serious questions about the morality of war under the best of kings; the play may be caustic toward the French nobility, but does not necessarily exonerate the English. Even here, however, we are led to believe that, because the French are so execrably governed, France will suffer less under English rule. Henry takes care that his soldiers do not despoil the French countryside except under conditions of military "necessity." Only in Montjoy, Burgundy, and Katharine of France does Shakespeare offer redeeming portraits of the French character, and in these instances the terms of hierarchical ascendancy seem clear: masculine English dominance, gentle French submissiveness. Katharine becomes "la belle France," depicted in Burgundy's eloquent peacemaking speech as being so much in need of competent management.

Henry woos Katharine with real flair, despite their mutual unstated recognition that their courtship is above all a matter of state in which they must play predetermined roles. The individual within Henry V gives way to the public personality, but he never loses his style. He is ineffably himself, as a wooer or as a soldier. We see him in disguise hobnobbing with common soldiers of his camp on the eve of battle, earnestly discussing with them the morality of war. We see him, with endearing human inconsistency, coveting all the glory of victory over the French, and then adjuring his soldiers to give credit for that victory to God alone. Even if we are at times less attracted to this successful warrior and politician than to the carefree young man of *1 Henry IV,* we can still honor Henry's choice of responsible maturity and see that it is even compassionately self-denying. A king cannot be like other men, and Henry is willing to accept this price of leadership.

The Chorus presents *Henry V* to us as if it were epic as well as drama. Henry is an epic hero, defined in terms of mythic allusions and abstractions. He is compared to Mars, the god of war, with Famine, Sword, and Fire leashed at his heels, crouching for employment. He is the "mirror of all Christian kings," and his followers are "English Mercuries" with winged heels. Personified Expectation sits in the air, promising crowns and crownets to Henry and his followers. Henry's fleet of ships on the English Channel becomes "A city on th' inconstant billows dancing." On the eve of battle, amidst his brothers, friends, and countrymen, Henry warms every heart with "cheerful semblance and sweet majesty" and with his "largess universal, like the sun." He forbids vainglorious pride and gives credit for his victory "Quite from himself to God."

The action the Chorus describes is comparably epic, as it moves from England to France and back again, leaping over times, surveying all levels of society in the English nation, portraying famous military encounters seemingly more suited to epic narration (or to the film) than to the stage. The stage's limitation forms indeed a major burden of the Chorus' argument. He apologizes to the spectators for the "flat unraised spirits" that have dared to bring forth so vast an object "On this unworthy scaffold," in this "cockpit" or "wooden O." The play confines mighty men "In little room," "mangling by starts the full course of their glory."

This apology is no doubt genuine on Shakespeare's part, and calls to mind Ben Jonson's strictures against the use of a few hired actors with rusty swords to dramatize England's great wars of the past. *Henry V* is not a Jonsonian neoclassical play. Yet its limits paradoxically become its greatest achievement. Through the Chorus' repeated appeals to our imaginations as a means of overcoming the limits of our physical surroundings, Shakespeare invites his spectators into his world of art. The play becomes a journey of thought, of making "imaginary puissance." When Shakespeare and his acting company talk of horses, we are to "see them, Printing their proud hoofs i' th' receiving earth." This is not to minimize the importance of the theatrical experience, but indeed quite the opposite, since we are instructed to liberate ourselves through that theatrical experience and to recreate by means of Shakespeare's script an epic vision. Shakespeare's stage, bare of scenery, relying on good actors and the words they speak, becomes through its very flexibility more versatile in creating that vision than the most ornate and mechanically sophisticated of theatres.

The Life of King Henry the Fifth

[*Dramatis Personae*

KING HENRY THE FIFTH.
HUMPHREY DUKE OF GLOUCESTER,
JOHN DUKE OF BEDFORD,
DUKE OF CLARENCE, } *brothers to the King.*
DUKE OF EXETER, *uncle to the King.*
DUKE OF YORK, *cousin to the King.*
EARL OF SALISBURY.
EARL OF WESTMORLAND.
EARL OF WARWICK.
ARCHBISHOP OF CANTERBURY.
BISHOP OF ELY.
EARL OF CAMBRIDGE.
LORD SCROOP.
SIR THOMAS GREY.
SIR THOMAS ERPINGHAM,
GOWER,
FLUELLEN,
MACMORRIS,
JAMY, } *officers in King Henry's army.*
BATES,
COURT,
WILLIAMS, } *soldiers in the same.*
PISTOL.
NYM.
BARDOLPH.
BOY.
HERALD.

CHARLES THE SIXTH, KING OF FRANCE.
LEWIS, THE DAUPHIN.
DUKE OF BURGUNDY.
DUKE OF ORLEANS.
DUKE OF BERRI.
DUKE OF BOURBON.
DUKE OF BEAUMONT.
DUKE OF BRITAINE.
CONSTABLE OF FRANCE.
RAMBURES,
GRANDPRÉ, } *French Lords.*
GOVERNOR OF HARFLEUR.
MONTJOY, *a French Herald.*
AMBASSADORS *to the King of England.*

ISABEL, QUEEN OF FRANCE.
KATHARINE, *daughter to Charles and Isabel.*
ALICE, *a lady attending on her.*
HOSTESS *of a tavern in Eastcheap, formerly* MISTRESS QUICKLY, *and now married to Pistol.*

LORDS, LADIES, OFFICERS, SOLDIERS, CITIZENS, MESSENGERS, *and* ATTENDANTS.

CHORUS.

SCENE: *England; afterwards France.*]

[PROLOGUE]

Enter [Chorus as] Prologue.

[CHORUS]
O for a Muse of fire, that would ascend 1
The brightest heaven of invention! 2
A kingdom for a stage, princes to act,
And monarchs to behold the swelling scene! 4
Then should the warlike Harry, like himself, 5
Assume the port of Mars; and at his heels, 6
Leash'd in like hounds, should famine, sword, and fire
Crouch for employment. But pardon, gentles all,
The flat unraised spirits that hath dar'd 9
On this unworthy scaffold to bring forth 10
So great an object. Can this cockpit hold 11
The vasty fields of France? Or may we cram
Within this wooden O the very casques 13
That did affright the air at Agincourt?
O, pardon! Since a crooked figure may 15
Attest in little place a million; 16
And let us, ciphers to this great account, 17
On your imaginary forces work. 18
Suppose within the girdle of these walls
Are now confin'd two mighty monarchies,
Whose high upreared and abutting fronts 21
The perilous narrow ocean parts asunder. 22
Piece out our imperfections with your thoughts:
Into a thousand parts divide one man,
And make imaginary puissance.
Think, when we talk of horses, that you see them
Printing their proud hoofs i' th' receiving earth.
For 'tis your thoughts that now must deck our kings,
Carry them here and there, jumping o'er times,
Turning th' accomplishment of many years
Into an hour-glass—for the which supply, 31
Admit me Chorus to this history,
Who, Prologue-like, your humble patience pray,
Gently to hear, kindly to judge, our play. *Exit.*

Prologue.
1 Muse of fire (Of the four elements, earth, air, fire, and water, fire is the most sublime and mounting.) **2 invention** poetic imagination **4 swelling** splendid, magnificent **5 like himself** i.e., presented in a fashion worthy of so great a king **6 port** bearing **9 spirits** i.e., actors and playwright **10 scaffold** stage **11 cockpit** (Elizabethan theatres were shaped rather like arenas for animal fighting.) **13 O** (Refers to a round theatre such as the Globe; the play may have been performed at the Curtain.) **casques** helmets **15 crooked figure** cipher or zero (which, added to a number, will multiply its value tenfold) **16 Attest** stand for **17 account** (1) sum total (continuing the metaphor of *crooked figure*) (2) story **18 imaginary forces** forces of imagination **21 fronts** frontiers, i.e., the cliffs of Dover and Calais **22 perilous . . . ocean** i.e., English Channel **31 supply** service

ACT I • SCENE I

Enter the two bishops, [the Archbishop] of Canterbury and [the Bishop of] Ely.

CANTERBURY
My lord, I'll tell you, that self bill is urg'd
Which in th' eleventh year of the last king's reign
Was like, and had indeed against us pass'd,
But that the scambling and unquiet time
Did push it out of farther question.

ELY
But how, my lord, shall we resist it now?

CANTERBURY
It must be thought on. If it pass against us,
We lose the better half of our possession.
For all the temporal lands which men devout
By testament have given to the church
Would they strip from us; being valu'd thus:
As much as would maintain, to the King's honor,
Full fifteen earls and fifteen hundred knights,
Six thousand and two hundred good esquires,
And, to relief of lazars and weak age
Of indigent faint souls past corporal toil,
A hundred almshouses right well supplied;
And to the coffers of the King beside,
A thousand pounds by th' year. Thus runs the bill.

ELY
This would drink deep.

CANTERBURY
'Twould drink the cup and all.

ELY
But what prevention?

CANTERBURY
The King is full of grace and fair regard.

ELY
And a true lover of the holy church.

CANTERBURY
The courses of his youth promis'd it not.
The breath no sooner left his father's body
But that his wildness, mortified in him,
Seem'd to die too; yea, at that very moment
Consideration, like an angel, came
And whipp'd th' offending Adam out of him,
Leaving his body as a paradise
T' envelop and contain celestial spirits.
Never was such a sudden scholar made;
Never came reformation in a flood,
With such a heady currance, scouring faults;
Nor never Hydra-headed willfulness
So soon did lose his seat, and all at once,
As in this king.

ELY
We are blessed in the change.

CANTERBURY
Hear him but reason in divinity,
And, all-admiring, with an inward wish
You would desire the King were made a prelate.
Hear him debate of commonwealth affairs,
You would say it hath been all in all his study.
List his discourse of war, and you shall hear
A fearful battle rend'red you in music.
Turn him to any cause of policy,
The Gordian knot of it he will unloose,
Familiar as his garter, that, when he speaks,
The air, a charter'd libertine, is still,
And the mute wonder lurketh in men's ears
To steal his sweet and honey'd sentences;
So that the art and practic part of life
Must be the mistress to this theoric;
Which is a wonder how his Grace should glean it,
Since his addiction was to courses vain,
His companies unletter'd, rude, and shallow,
His hours fill'd up with riots, banquets, sports,
And never noted in him any study,
Any retirement, any sequestration
From open haunts and popularity.

ELY
The strawberry grows underneath the nettle,
And wholesome berries thrive and ripen best
Neighbor'd by fruit of baser quality;
And so the Prince obscur'd his contemplation
Under the veil of wildness, which, no doubt,
Grew like the summer grass, fastest by night,
Unseen, yet crescive in his faculty.

CANTERBURY
It must be so, for miracles are ceas'd.
And therefore we must needs admit the means
How things are perfected.

ELY
But, my good lord,
How now for mitigation of this bill
Urg'd by the commons? Doth his Majesty
Incline to it, or no?

CANTERBURY
He seems indifferent,
Or rather swaying more upon our part
Than cherishing th' exhibiters against us;
For I have made an offer to his Majesty,
Upon our spiritual convocation
And in regard of causes now in hand,
Which I have open'd to his Grace at large,
As touching France, to give a greater sum
Than ever at one time the clergy yet
Did to his predecessors part withal.

ELY
How did this offer seem receiv'd, my lord?

CANTERBURY
With good acceptance of his Majesty,

I.i. Location: London. An antechamber in the King's palace.
1 self same **3 like** likely (to have passed) **4 scambling** unsettled **9 temporal** used for secular purposes **15 lazars** lepers **26 mortified** killed **28 Consideration** meditation, reflection **29 offending Adam** original sin **34 heady currance** headlong current **35 Hydra-headed** i.e., many-headed. (Alludes to the Lernaean Hydra, a monster of many heads overcome by Hercules.) **36 his seat** its throne

44 rend'red . . . music i.e., eloquently narrated **45 cause of policy** matter of statecraft **46 Gordian knot** (It was foretold that whoever should untie the Gordian knot would rule Asia. Alexander solved the problem by cutting the knot.) **47 Familiar** as offhandedly or routinely. **that** so that **48 charter'd libertine** licensed freeman, able to roam at will **49 the . . . ears** i.e., wonder makes men silent, eagerly listening **50 To . . . sentences** i.e., to hear more of his sweetly profitable wise sayings **51–52 So . . . theoric** so that experience in practical life must have been the teacher by which he acquired his theoretical conception **55 companies** companions **59 open . . . popularity** places of public resort and low company **66 crescive . . . faculty** naturally inclined to grow **67 miracles are ceas'd** (Protestants believed that no miracles occurred after the revelation of Christ.) **68 means** i.e., natural causes **74 exhibiters** those who introduce bills in Parliament **76 Upon** on behalf of. **convocation** formal assembly of the clergy **77 in hand** under consideration **78 open'd** expounded. **at large** in full

Save that there was not time enough to hear,
As I perceiv'd his Grace would fain have done,
The severals and unhidden passages 86
Of his true titles to some certain dukedoms
And generally to the crown and seat of France 88
Deriv'd from Edward, his great-grandfather. 89

ELY
What was th' impediment that broke this off?

CANTERBURY
The French ambassador upon that instant
Crav'd audience; and the hour, I think, is come
To give him hearing. Is it four o'clock?

ELY
It is.

CANTERBURY
Then go we in to know his embassy,
Which I could with a ready guess declare,
Before the Frenchman speak a word of it.

ELY
I'll wait upon you, and I long to hear it. *Exeunt.*

[SCENE II]

Enter the King, Humphrey [Duke of Gloucester], Bedford, Clarence, Warwick, Westmorland, and Exeter [with Attendants].

KING
Where is my gracious Lord of Canterbury?

EXETER
Not here in presence.

KING
Send for him, good uncle.

WESTMORLAND
Shall we call in th' ambassador, my liege?

KING
Not yet, my cousin. We would be resolv'd, 4
Before we hear him, of some things of weight
That task our thoughts, concerning us and France.

Enter two Bishops, [the Archbishop of Canterbury and the Bishop of Ely].

CANTERBURY
God and his angels guard your sacred throne
And make you long become it!

KING
Sure we thank you.
My learned lord, we pray you to proceed,
And justly and religiously unfold
Why the law Salique that they have in France
Or should, or should not, bar us in our claim. 12
And God forbid, my dear and faithful lord,
That you should fashion, wrest, or bow your reading,
Or nicely charge your understanding soul 15
With opening titles miscreate, whose right 16
Suits not in native colors with the truth; 17
For God doth know how many now in health
Shall drop their blood in approbation 19
Of what your reverence shall incite us to.
Therefore take heed how you impawn our person, 21
How you awake our sleeping sword of war.
We charge you, in the name of God, take heed;
For never two such kingdoms did contend
Without much fall of blood, whose guiltless drops
Are every one a woe, a sore complaint 26
'Gainst him whose wrongs gives edge unto the swords 27
That makes such waste in brief mortality. 28
Under this conjuration speak, my lord; 29
For we will hear, note, and believe in heart
That what you speak is in your conscience wash'd
As pure as sin with baptism.

CANTERBURY
Then hear me, gracious sovereign, and you peers,
That owe yourselves, your lives, and services
To this imperial throne. There is no bar
To make against your Highness' claim to France
But this, which they produce from Pharamond: 37
"In terram Salicam mulieres ne succedant,"
"No woman shall succeed in Salique land."
Which Salique land the French unjustly glose 40
To be the realm of France, and Pharamond
The founder of this law and female bar.
Yet their own authors faithfully affirm
That the land Salique is in Germany,
Between the floods of Sala and of Elbe;
Where Charles the Great, having subdu'd the Saxons, 46
There left behind and settled certain French;
Who, holding in disdain the German women
For some dishonest manners of their life, 49
Establish'd then this law: to wit, no female
Should be inheritrix in Salique land;
Which Salique, as I said, 'twixt Elbe and Sala,
Is at this day in Germany call'd Meisen.
Then doth it well appear the Salique law
Was not devised for the realm of France;
Nor did the French possess the Salique land
Until four hundred one and twenty years
After defunction of King Pharamond, 58
Idly suppos'd the founder of this law,
Who died within the year of our redemption
Four hundred twenty-six; and Charles the Great
Subdu'd the Saxons, and did seat the French
Beyond the river Sala, in the year
Eight hundred five. Besides, their writers say,
King Pepin, which deposed Childeric,
Did, as heir general, being descended 66
Of Blithild, which was daughter to King Clothair,
Make claim and title to the crown of France.
Hugh Capet also, who usurp'd the crown

86 severals details. **unhidden passages** obvious lines of descent **88 seat** throne **89 Edward** i.e., Edward III

I.ii. Location: London, the palace. The presence chamber.
4 cousin (Correct form of address from royal family to nobles.) **12 Or** either **15 nicely charge** subtly and foolishly burden **16 opening titles miscreate** expounding spurious claims

17 Suits . . . colors i.e., does not naturally harmonize **19 approbation** support, proof **21 impawn** pledge **26 woe** grievance **27 wrongs** wrongdoings **28 in brief mortality** i.e., among mortal, short-lived men **29 conjuration** solemn adjuration **37 Pharamond** legendary Frankish king **40 glose** explain, interpret **46 Charles the Great** Charlemagne **49 dishonest** unchaste **58 defunction** death **66 heir general** heir through male or female line

Of Charles the Duke of Lorraine, sole heir male
Of the true line and stock of Charles the Great,
To find his title with some shows of truth, 72
Though, in pure truth, it was corrupt and naught,
Convey'd himself as th' heir to th' Lady Lingare, 74
Daughter to Charlemain, who was the son 75
To Lewis the Emperor, and Lewis the son
Of Charles the Great. Also King Lewis the Tenth, 77
Who was sole heir to the usurper Capet,
Could not keep quiet in his conscience,
Wearing the crown of France, till satisfied
That fair Queen Isabel, his grandmother,
Was lineal of the Lady Ermengare, 82
Daughter to Charles the foresaid Duke of Lorraine;
By the which marriage the line of Charles the Great
Was re-united to the crown of France.
So that, as clear as is the summer's sun,
King Pepin's title and Hugh Capet's claim,
King Lewis his satisfaction, all appear 88
To hold in right and title of the female;
So do the Kings of France unto this day.
Howbeit they would hold up this Salique law 91
To bar your Highness claiming from the female,
And rather choose to hide them in a net 93
Than amply to imbar their crooked titles 94
Usurp'd from you and your progenitors.

KING
May I with right and conscience make this claim?

CANTERBURY
The sin upon my head, dread sovereign!
For in the book of Numbers is it writ, 98
When the man dies, let the inheritance
Descend unto the daughter. Gracious lord,
Stand for your own, unwind your bloody flag!
Look back into your mighty ancestors:
Go, my dread lord, to your great-grandsire's tomb,
From whom you claim! Invoke his warlike spirit,
And your great-uncle's, Edward the Black Prince,
Who on the French ground play'd a tragedy, 106
Making defeat on the full power of France,
Whiles his most mighty father on a hill
Stood smiling to behold his lion's whelp
Forage in blood of French nobility. 110
O noble English, that could entertain 111
With half their forces the full pride of France
And let another half stand laughing by,
All out of work and cold for action! 114

ELY
Awake remembrance of these valiant dead,
And with your puissant arm renew their feats!
You are their heir; you sit upon their throne;
The blood and courage that renowned them 118
Runs in your veins; and my thrice-puissant liege
Is in the very May-morn of his youth,
Ripe for exploits and mighty enterprises.

EXETER
Your brother kings and monarchs of the earth
Do all expect that you should rouse yourself,
As did the former lions of your blood.

WESTMORLAND
They know your Grace hath cause, and means, and might;
So hath your Highness! Never King of England 126
Had nobles richer and more loyal subjects,
Whose hearts have left their bodies here in England
And lie pavilion'd in the fields of France. 129

CANTERBURY
O, let their bodies follow, my dear liege,
With blood, and sword, and fire to win your right!
In aid whereof we of the spiritualty 132
Will raise your Highness such a mighty sum
As never did the clergy at one time
Bring in to any of your ancestors.

KING
We must not only arm t' invade the French,
But lay down our proportions to defend 137
Against the Scot, who will make road upon us 138
With all advantages. 139

CANTERBURY
They of those marches, gracious sovereign, 140
Shall be a wall sufficient to defend
Our inland from the pilfering borderers.

KING
We do not mean the coursing snatchers only, 143
But fear the main intendment of the Scot, 144
Who hath been still a giddy neighbor to us. 145
For you shall read that my great-grandfather
Never went with his forces into France
But that the Scot on his unfurnish'd kingdom 148
Came pouring, like the tide into a breach,
With ample and brim fullness of his force,
Galling the gleaned land with hot assays, 151
Girding with grievous siege castles and towns;
That England, being empty of defense,
Hath shook and trembled at th' ill neighborhood. 154

CANTERBURY
She hath been then more fear'd than harm'd, my liege. 155
For hear her but exampled by herself: 156
When all her chivalry hath been in France
And she a mourning widow of her nobles,
She hath herself not only well defended
But taken and impounded as a stray 160
The King of Scots, whom she did send to France 161
To fill King Edward's fame with prisoner kings,

72 find provide **74 Convey'd himself** passed himself off **75 Charlemain** (Holinshed's and Hall's error, followed by Shakespeare, for Charles the Bold.) **77 Lewis the Tenth** (Actually, Louis IX; another error copied from the chronicles.) **82 lineal of** descended from **88 Lewis his satisfaction** Lewis' conviction **91 Howbeit** notwithstanding **93 hide . . . net** i.e., conceal the weakness of their case in a tangle of contradictions **94 amply to imbar** frankly to bar claim to **98 Numbers** (See Numbers 27:8.) **106 tragedy** i.e., the Battle of Crécy, 1346, a major defeat for the French **110 Forage in** prey on **111 entertain** engage, encounter **114 for action** for want of action **118 renowned** brought renown to

126 So so indeed **129 pavilion'd** tented, encamped **132 spiritualty** clergy **137 lay . . . proportions** allocate our forces **138 road** inroad **139 With all advantages** whenever a good opportunity presents itself **140 marches** borderlands (here, in the north) **143 coursing snatchers** mounted raiders **144 intendment** plan, hostile intent **145 still** always. **giddy** unstable, fickle **148 unfurnish'd** unprovided with defense **151 Galling . . . assays** worrying the land stripped of defenders with hot attacks **154 neighborhood** neighborliness **155 fear'd** frightened **156 hear . . . herself** i.e., only listen how she can be instructed by an example from her own history **160 impounded as a stray** (David II of Scotland was captured and imprisoned in 1346 while Edward III was in France.) **161 to France** (Historically, David II was imprisoned in London, not sent to France.)

And make her chronicle as rich with praise
As is the ooze and bottom of the sea
With sunken wrack and sumless treasuries.

ELY
But there's a saying very old and true,
"If that you will France win,
Then with Scotland first begin."
For once the eagle England being in prey,
To her unguarded nest the weasel Scot
Comes sneaking, and so sucks her princely eggs,
Playing the mouse in absence of the cat,
To 'tame and havoc more than she can eat.

EXETER
It follows then the cat must stay at home;
Yet that is but a crush'd necessity,
Since we have locks to safeguard necessaries,
And pretty traps to catch the petty thieves.
While that the armed hand doth fight abroad,
Th' advised head defends itself at home;
For government, though high, and low, and lower,
Put into parts, doth keep in one consent,
Congreeing in a full and natural close,
Like music.

CANTERBURY Therefore doth heaven divide
The state of man in divers functions,
Setting endeavor in continual motion,
To which is fixed, as an aim or butt,
Obedience; for so work the honey-bees,
Creatures that by a rule in nature teach
The act of order to a peopled kingdom.
They have a king, and officers of sorts,
Where some, like magistrates, correct at home;
Others, like merchants, venture trade abroad;
Others, like soldiers, armed in their stings,
Make boot upon the summer's velvet buds,
Which pillage they with merry march bring home
To the tent-royal of their emperor,
Who, busied in his majesty, surveys
The singing masons building roofs of gold,
The civil citizens kneading up the honey,
The poor mechanic porters crowding in
Their heavy burdens at his narrow gate,
The sad-ey'd justice, with his surly hum,
Delivering o'er to executors pale
The lazy yawning drone. I this infer,
That many things, having full reference
To one consent, may work contrariously.
As many arrows, loosed several ways,
Come to one mark; as many ways meet in one
town;
As many fresh streams meet in one salt sea;
As many lines close in the dial's center;
So may a thousand actions, once afoot,
End in one purpose, and be all well borne
Without defeat. Therefore to France, my liege!
Divide your happy England into four,
Whereof take you one quarter into France,
And you withal shall make all Gallia shake.
If we, with thrice such powers left at home,
Cannot defend our own doors from the dog,
Let us be worried, and our nation lose
The name of hardiness and policy.

KING
Call in the messengers sent from the Dauphin.
[*Exeunt some Attendants.*]
Now are we well resolv'd; and, by God's help,
And yours, the noble sinews of our power,
France being ours, we'll bend it to our awe,
Or break it all to pieces. Or there we'll sit,
Ruling in large and ample empery
O'er France and all her almost kingly dukedoms,
Or lay these bones in an unworthy urn,
Tombless, with no remembrance over them.
Either our history shall with full mouth
Speak freely of our acts, or else our grave,
Like Turkish mute, shall have a tongueless mouth,
Not worship'd with a waxen epitaph.

Enter Ambassadors of France [*attended*].

Now are we well prepar'd to know the pleasure
Of our fair cousin Dauphin; for we hear
Your greeting is from him, not from the King.

FIRST AMBASSADOR
May 't please your Majesty to give us leave
Freely to render what we have in charge,
Or shall we sparingly show you far off
The Dauphin's meaning and our embassy?

KING
We are no tyrant, but a Christian king,
Unto whose grace our passion is as subject
As is our wretches fett'red in our prisons.
Therefore with frank and with uncurbed plainness
Tell us the Dauphin's mind.

FIRST AMBASSADOR Thus, then, in few.
Your Highness, lately sending into France,
Did claim some certain dukedoms, in the right
Of your great predecessor, King Edward the Third.
In answer of which claim, the Prince our master
Says that you savor too much of your youth,
And bids you be advis'd there's nought in France
That can be with a nimble galliard won;
You cannot revel into dukedoms there.
He therefore sends you, meeter for your spirit,
This tun of treasure; and, in lieu of this,
Desires you let the dukedoms that you claim
Hear no more of you. This the Dauphin speaks.
[*His attendants present a casket;
Exeter examines its contents.*]

165 sumless inestimable **169 in prey** absent in search of prey **173 'tame** attame, cut into. **havoc** ravage **175 crush'd necessity** forced conclusion **179 advised** wise, prudent **180 though . . . lower** i.e., though composed of three broad social ranks **181 Put into parts** separated into different functions. **one consent** mutual harmony **182 Congreeing** agreeing together. **close** musical cadence **186 aim or butt** i.e., target **194 Make boot** prey **197 majesty** royal office **200 mechanic** engaged in manual labor **202 sad-ey'd** grave-eyed **203 executors** executioners **205–206 having . . . consent** i.e., united by a common understanding **207 loosed several ways** shot from different directions **208 ways** roads **210 close** come together. **dial's** sundial's

216 Gallia France. (Latin name.) **219 worried** torn apart, as by dogs **220 hardiness and policy** bravery and statesmanship **221 Dauphin** heir apparent to the French throne **224 our awe** submission to us **225 Or** either **226 empery** dominion **233 Not . . . epitaph** i.e., with not even so much as a wax (as opposed to bronze) epitaph; one easily effaced **252 galliard** a lively dance **255 tun** cask

KING
What treasure, uncle?
EXETER
Tennis balls, my liege.
KING
We are glad the Dauphin is so pleasant with us.
His present and your pains we thank you for.
When we have match'd our rackets to these balls,
We will, in France, by God's grace, play a set
Shall strike his father's crown into the hazard. 263
Tell him he hath made a match with such a
wrangler 264
That all the courts of France will be disturb'd 265
With chases. And we understand him well, 266
How he comes o'er us with our wilder days, 267
Not measuring what use we made of them.
We never valu'd this poor seat of England, 269
And therefore, living hence, did give ourself 270
To barbarous license; as 'tis ever common
That men are merriest when they are from home. 272
But tell the Dauphin I will keep my state, 273
Be like a king, and show my sail of greatness
When I do rouse me in my throne of France.
For that I have laid by my majesty 276
And plodded like a man for working-days,
But I will rise there with so full a glory
That I will dazzle all the eyes of France,
Yea, strike the Dauphin blind to look on us.
And tell the pleasant Prince this mock of his
Hath turn'd his balls to gun-stones, and his soul 282
Shall stand sore charged for the wasteful vengeance 283
That shall fly with them; for many a thousand
widows
Shall this his mock mock out of their dear husbands;
Mock mothers from their sons, mock castles down;
And some are yet ungotten and unborn
That shall have cause to curse the Dauphin's scorn.
But this lies all within the will of God,
To whom I do appeal, and in whose name
Tell you the Dauphin I am coming on
To venge me as I may, and to put forth
My rightful hand in a well-hallow'd cause.
So get you hence in peace; and tell the Dauphin
His jest will savor but of shallow wit,
When thousands weep more than did laugh at it.—
Convey them with safe conduct.—Fare you well. 297
Exeunt Ambassadors [*and Attendants*].
EXETER
This was a merry message.
KING
We hope to make the sender blush at it.
Therefore, my lords, omit no happy hour 300
That may give furth'rance to our expedition;
For we have now no thought in us but France,
Save those to God, that run before our business.
Therefore let our proportions for these wars 304
Be soon collected, and all things thought upon
That may with reasonable swiftness add
More feathers to our wings; for, God before, 307
We'll chide this Dauphin at his father's door.
Therefore let every man now task his thought, 309
That this fair action may on foot be brought.
Exeunt.

[ACT II • PROLOGUE]

Flourish. Enter Chorus.

[CHORUS]
Now all the youth of England are on fire,
And silken dalliance in the wardrobe lies. 2
Now thrive the armorers, and honor's thought
Reigns solely in the breast of every man.
They sell the pasture now to buy the horse,
Following the mirror of all Christian kings,
With winged heels, as English Mercuries. 7
For now sits Expectation in the air,
And hides a sword, from hilts unto the point 9
With crowns imperial, crowns, and coronets, 10
Promis'd to Harry and his followers.
The French, advis'd by good intelligence
Of this most dreadful preparation,
Shake in their fear and with pale policy 14
Seek to divert the English purposes.
O England! Model to thy inward greatness, 16
Like little body with a mighty heart,
What mightst thou do, that honor would thee do, 18
Were all thy children kind and natural!
But see, thy fault France hath in thee found out,
A nest of hollow bosoms, which he fills
With treacherous crowns; and three corrupted men, 22
One, Richard Earl of Cambridge, and the second,
Henry Lord Scroop of Masham, and the third,
Sir Thomas Grey, knight, of Northumberland,
Have, for the gilt of France—O guilt indeed!— 26
Confirm'd conspiracy with fearful France,
And by their hands this grace of kings must die,
If hell and treason hold their promises,
Ere he take ship for France, and in Southampton.
Linger your patience on, and we'll digest 31
Th' abuse of distance, force a play. 32
The sum is paid, the traitors are agreed,
The King is set from London, and the scene

263 crown (1) coin staked in a game (2) symbol of majesty. **hazard** (1) in tennis of that time, an opening in the wall; hitting the ball into it scored a point (2) jeopardy **264 wrangler** adversary **265 courts** (1) tennis courts (2) royal courts **266 chases** (1) double bounce in tennis, an unsuccessful return (2) pursuits **267 comes o'er us** taunts me. (*Us* is the royal plural.) **269 seat** throne **270 living hence** not frequenting the royal court **272 from** away from **273 keep my state** i.e., fulfill the role of king **276 For that** i.e., for my French kingdom. (Henry says he has not yet revealed his full majesty in laying claim to France.) **282 gun-stones** cannon balls **283 sore charged** sorely burdened with responsibility. **wasteful** destructive **297 Convey** escort **300 omit . . . hour** lose no favorable opportunity

304 proportions levies of men **307 God before** with God leading, helping **309 task** tax, exercise
II. Chorus.
2 silken . . . lies i.e., silken apparel and idle pleasure are packed away **7 Mercuries** (Mercury, classical messenger of the gods, always wears winged heels.) **9 hides a sword** i.e., holds up a sword completely impaled with the prizes of war **10 With . . . coronets** with the crowns of emperors, kings, and nobles **14 pale policy** fear-inspired intrigue **16 Model to** small replica of **18 would** would have **22 crowns** crown pieces, money (as bribe) **26 gilt** gold **31–32 digest . . . distance** overcome the difficulties of representing distance, change of place **32 force a play** fill out the actions of a play in spite of difficulties

Is now transported, gentles, to Southampton.
There is the playhouse now, there must you sit,
And thence to France shall we convey you safe,
And bring you back, charming the narrow seas
To give you gentle pass; for, if we may,
We'll not offend one stomach with our play.
But, till the King come forth, and not till then,
Unto Southampton do we shift our scene. *Exit.*

[SCENE I]

Enter Corporal Nym and Lieutenant Bardolph.

BARDOLPH Well met, Corporal Nym.

NYM Good morrow, Lieutenant Bardolph.

BARDOLPH What, are Ancient Pistol and you friends yet?

NYM For my part, I care not. I say little; but when time shall serve, there shall be smiles—but that shall be as it may. I dare not fight, but I will wink and hold out mine iron. It is a simple one, but what though? It will toast cheese, and it will endure cold as another man's sword will—and there's an end.

BARDOLPH I will bestow a breakfast to make you friends, and we'll be all three sworn brothers to France. Let 't be so, good Corporal Nym.

NYM Faith, I will live so long as I may, that's the certain of it; and when I cannot live any longer, I will do as I may. That is my rest, that is the rendezvous of it.

BARDOLPH It is certain, corporal, that he is married to Nell Quickly, and certainly she did you wrong, for you were troth-plight to her.

NYM I cannot tell. Things must be as they may. Men may sleep, and they may have their throats about them at that time, and some say knives have edges. It must be as it may. Though patience be a tir'd mare, yet she will plod. There must be conclusions. Well, I cannot tell.

Enter Pistol and [*Hostess*] *Quickly.*

BARDOLPH Here comes Ancient Pistol and his wife. Good corporal, be patient here.

NYM How now, mine host Pistol?

PISTOL
Base tike, call'st thou me host?
Now, by this hand, I swear, I scorn the term!
Nor shall my Nell keep lodgers.

HOSTESS No, by my troth, not long; for we cannot lodge and board a dozen or fourteen gentlewomen that live honestly by the prick of their needles, but it will be thought we keep a bawdy house straight. [*Nym and Pistol draw.*] O well a day, Lady, if he be not hewn now, we shall see willful adultery and murder committed.

BARDOLPH Good lieutenant! Good corporal! Offer nothing here.

NYM Pish!

PISTOL
Pish for thee, Iceland dog!
Thou prick-ear'd cur of Iceland!

HOSTESS Good Corporal Nym, show thy valor, and put up your sword.

NYM Will you shog off? I would have you solus.

PISTOL
"Solus," egregious dog? O viper vile!
The "solus" in thy most mervailous face!
The "solus" in thy teeth, and in thy throat,
And in thy hateful lungs, yea, in thy maw, perdy,
And, which is worse, within thy nasty mouth!
I do retort the "solus" in thy bowels;
For I can take, and Pistol's cock is up,
And flashing fire will follow.

NYM I am not Barbason; you cannot conjure me. I have an humor to knock you indifferently well. If you grow foul with me, Pistol, I will scour you with my rapier, as I may, in fair terms. If you would walk off, I would prick your guts a little, in good terms, as I may, and that's the humor of it.

PISTOL
O braggart vile and damned furious wight!
The grave doth gape, and doting death is near.
Therefore exhale!

BARDOLPH Hear me, hear me what I say. He that strikes the first stroke, I'll run him up to the hilts, as I am a soldier. [*Draws.*]

PISTOL
An oath of mickle might, and fury shall abate.
[*Pistol and Nym sheathe their swords.*]
Give me thy fist, thy fore-foot to me give.
Thy spirits are most tall.

NYM I will cut thy throat, one time or other, in fair terms. That is the humor of it.

PISTOL
"Couple a gorge!"
That is the word. I thee defy again.
O hound of Crete, think'st thou my spouse to get?
No; to the spital go,
And from the powd'ring-tub of infamy
Fetch forth the lazar kite of Cressid's kind,

39 pass passage **40 offend one stomach** (1) offend anyone's taste in plays (2) make anyone seasick **41–42 But . . . scene** i.e., the scene will be shifted to Southampton after a scene in London. (These lines sound as though added as an afterthought, to accommodate the inclusion of the comic scene in II.i.)

II.i. Location: London. A street.
3 Ancient ensign, standard-bearer **7 wink** shut the eyes **8 iron** sword **9 endure cold** i.e., doesn't mind being drawn from its sheath **10 there's an end** that's all there is to it **16 rest** last stake (in the gambling game of primero). **rendezvous** last resort **19 troth-plight** betrothed **23–24 Though . . . plod** i.e., patient persistence will ultimately achieve its goal. (Nym hints, as he does elsewhere, at violence toward Pistol.) **24 conclusions** an end to matters. (I.e., the end must come sometime.) **29 tike** cur **34 prick** (with a bawdy double meaning, as also in *Pistol's cock,* l. 53)

36 Lady i.e., by Our Lady. (An oath.) **37 adultery** (Blunder for *battery?*) **39–40 Offer nothing** i.e., do not offer to fight **42 Iceland dog** (Pistol's humor is to use extravagant epithets, like this one, tags from current plays, and scraps of foreign languages.) **44 valor** (She means *calm, forbearance.*) **46 shog off** move along. **solus** alone **48 mervailous** marvelous **50 maw** belly. **perdy** i.e., *par Dieu,* by God **53 take** strike **55 Barbason** (Presumably the name of a fiend. Pistol's preceding speech is a parody of the formula for exorcising spirits.) **57 foul** (1) foulmouthed (2) fouled from firing and in need of scouring **60 that's . . . it** that's my mood **63 exhale** draw (sword) **67 mickle** great **69 tall** valiant **72 Couple a gorge** i.e., *couper la gorge,* cut the throat **74 hound of Crete** (Parallel to *Iceland dog,* l. 42.) **75 spital** hospital **76 powd'ring-tub** (Originally a tub used for salting beef; here, alluding to a method of curing venereal disease by sweating.) **77 lazar . . . kind** i.e., diseased, leprous whore (a *kite* is a bird of prey) like Cressida, the fallen woman, who, in Robert Henryson's *Testament of Cresseid,* is shown as being rejected by Diomede and infected with leprosy

Doll Tearsheet she by name, and her espouse.
I have, and I will hold, the quondam Quickly 79
For the only she; and—pauca! There's enough. 80
Go to.

Enter the Boy.

BOY Mine host Pistol, you must come to my master, and you, hostess. He is very sick, and would to bed. Good Bardolph, put thy face between his sheets, and 84
do the office of a warming-pan. Faith, he's very ill.

BARDOLPH Away, you rogue!

HOSTESS By my troth, he'll yield the crow a pudding 87
one of these days. The King has kill'd his heart. Good 88
husband, come home presently. *Exit* [*with Boy*].

BARDOLPH Come, shall I make you two friends? We must to France together. Why the devil should we keep knives to cut one another's throats?

PISTOL
Let floods o'erswell, and fiends for food howl on!

NYM You'll pay me the eight shillings I won of you at betting?

PISTOL
Base is the slave that pays.

NYM That now I will have. That's the humor of it.

PISTOL
As manhood shall compound. Push home. 98
[*They*] *draw.*

BARDOLPH By this sword, he that makes the first thrust, I'll kill him! By this sword, I will. [*Draws.*]

PISTOL
Sword is an oath, and oaths must have their course.
[*Sheathes his sword.*]

BARDOLPH Corporal Nym, an thou wilt be friends, be friends; an thou wilt not, why, then, be enemies with me too. Prithee, put up.

[NYM I shall have my eight shillings I won of you at betting?]

PISTOL
A noble shalt thou have, and present pay; 107
And liquor likewise will I give to thee,
And friendship shall combine, and brotherhood.
I'll live by Nym, and Nym shall live by me.
Is not this just? For I shall sutler be 111
Unto the camp, and profits will accrue.
Give me thy hand. [*Nym sheathes his sword.*]

NYM I shall have my noble?

PISTOL
In cash most justly paid.

NYM Well, then, that's the humor of 't.

Enter Hostess.

HOSTESS As ever you came of women, come in quickly 117
to Sir John. Ah, poor heart! He is so shak'd of a burning quotidian tertian, that it is most lamentable to be- 119
hold. Sweet men, come to him.

NYM The King hath run bad humors on the knight;
that's the even of it. 122

PISTOL
Nym, thou hast spoke the right.
His heart is fracted and corroborate. 124

NYM The King is a good king, but it must be as it may;
he passes some humors and careers. 126

PISTOL
Let us condole the knight, for, lambkins, we will live. [*Exeunt.*]

[SCENE II]

Enter Exeter, Bedford, and Westmorland.

BEDFORD
'Fore God, his Grace is bold to trust these traitors.

EXETER
They shall be apprehended by and by.

WESTMORLAND
How smooth and even they do bear themselves!
As if allegiance in their bosoms sat,
Crowned with faith and constant loyalty.

BEDFORD
The King hath note of all that they intend,
By interception which they dream not of.

EXETER
Nay, but the man that was his bedfellow, 8
Whom he hath dull'd and cloy'd with gracious favors— 9
That he should, for a foreign purse, so sell
His sovereign's life to death and treachery!

Sound trumpets. Enter the King, Scroop, Cambridge, and Grey, [*Lords, and Attendants*].

KING
Now sits the wind fair, and we will aboard.
My Lord of Cambridge, and my kind Lord of Masham,
And you, my gentle knight, give me your thoughts.
Think you not that the pow'rs we bear with us 15
Will cut their passage through the force of France,
Doing the execution and the act
For which we have in head assembled them? 18

SCROOP
No doubt, my liege, if each man do his best.

KING
I doubt not that, since we are well persuaded
We carry not a heart with us from hence
That grows not in a fair consent with ours, 22
Nor leave not one behind that doth not wish
Success and conquest to attend on us.

CAMBRIDGE
Never was monarch better fear'd and lov'd

79 quondam former **80 pauca** i.e., in brief **84 face** (Bardolph's face was fiery with drinking.) **87 yield . . . pudding** i.e., be hanged on the gallows and eaten by carrion birds **88 his** i.e., Falstaff's **98 As . . . compound** as valor shall settle the matter (in fight) **107 noble . . . pay** i.e., I'll settle for paying you 6 shillings 8 pence ready money **111 sutler** seller of liquor and provisions to the soldiers **117 came** were born **119 quotidian tertian** (Mistress Quickly confuses terms; a *quotidian* fever was one that came daily; a *tertian* fever, one that came on alternate days.)

122 even level truth **124 fracted** broken. **corroborate** (Blunder for *broken to pieces?*) **126 passes** lets pass. **careers** gallops, capers

II.ii. Location: Southampton, a seaport on England's southern coast.
8 bedfellow i.e., constant companion. (Refers to Scroop.) **9 dull'd** tired **15 pow'rs** armed forces **18 in head** as an army **22 grows . . . consent** does not act in harmony

Than is your Majesty. There's not, I think, a subject
That sits in heart-grief and uneasiness
Under the sweet shade of your government.

GREY
True. Those that were your father's enemies
Have steep'd their galls in honey, and do serve you
With hearts create of duty and of zeal.

KING
We therefore have great cause of thankfulness,
And shall forget the office of our hand,
Sooner than quittance of desert and merit
According to the weight and worthiness.

SCROOP
So service shall with steeled sinews toil,
And labor shall refresh itself with hope,
To do your Grace incessant services.

KING
We judge no less. Uncle of Exeter,
Enlarge the man committed yesterday,
That rail'd against our person. We consider
It was excess of wine that set him on,
And on his more advice we pardon him.

SCROOP
That's mercy, but too much security.
Let him be punish'd, sovereign, lest example
Breed, by his sufferance, more of such a kind.

KING
O, let us yet be merciful.

CAMBRIDGE
So may your Highness, and yet punish too.

GREY
Sir,
You show great mercy, if you give him life
After the taste of much correction.

KING
Alas, your too much love and care of me
Are heavy orisons 'gainst this poor wretch!
If little faults, proceeding on distemper,
Shall not be wink'd at, how shall we stretch our eye
When capital crimes, chew'd, swallow'd, and digested,
Appear before us? We'll yet enlarge that man,
Though Cambridge, Scroop, and Grey, in their dear care
And tender preservation of our person,
Would have him punish'd. And now to our French causes.
Who are the late commissioners?

CAMBRIDGE
I one, my lord.
Your Highness bade me ask for it today.

SCROOP
So did you me, my liege.

GREY
And I, my royal sovereign.

KING
Then, Richard Earl of Cambridge, there is yours;
[*Gives them papers.*]
There yours, Lord Scroop of Masham; and, sir knight,
Grey of Northumberland, this same is yours.
Read them, and know I know your worthiness.
My Lord of Westmorland, and uncle Exeter,
We will aboard to night.—Why, how now, gentlemen?
What see you in those papers that you lose
So much complexion?—Look ye how they change!
Their cheeks are paper.—Why, what read you there,
That have so cowarded and chas'd your blood
Out of appearance?

CAMBRIDGE
I do confess my fault,
And do submit me to your Highness' mercy.

GREY, SCROOP
To which we all appeal.

KING
The mercy that was quick in us but late
By your own counsel is suppress'd and kill'd.
You must not dare, for shame, to talk of mercy,
For your own reasons turn into your bosoms,
As dogs upon their masters, worrying you.
See you, my princes and my noble peers,
These English monsters! My Lord of Cambridge here,
You know how apt our love was to accord
To furnish him with all appertinents
Belonging to his honor; and this man
Hath, for a few light crowns, lightly conspir'd
And sworn unto the practices of France
To kill us here in Hampton. To the which
This knight, no less for bounty bound to us
Than Cambridge is, hath likewise sworn. But, O,
What shall I say to thee, Lord Scroop, thou cruel,
Ingrateful, savage, and inhuman creature!
Thou that didst bear the key of all my counsels,
That knew'st the very bottom of my soul,
That almost mightst have coin'd me into gold,
Wouldst thou have practic'd on me for thy use?
May it be possible that foreign hire
Could out of thee extract one spark of evil
That might annoy my finger? 'Tis so strange,
That, though the truth of it stands off as gross
As black and white, my eye will scarcely see it.
Treason and murder ever kept together,
As two yoke-devils sworn to either's purpose,
Working so grossly in a natural cause
That admiration did not hoop at them.
But thou, 'gainst all proportion, didst bring in
Wonder to wait on treason and on murder;

30 galls resentment **31 create** composed **33 office** use, function **34 quittance** requital **40 Enlarge** set free **43 more advice** thinking better of it **44 security** overconfidence **46 sufferance** being pardoned **53 heavy orisons** weighty prayers, pleas **54 proceeding on distemper** resulting from excessive drinking **55 stretch** open wide, not wink **56 chew'd . . . digested** i.e., premeditated **57 yet** in spite of what you say **61 late** recently appointed (to serve while Henry is in France) **63 it** i.e., my commission

76 appearance sight. (Presumably the traitors kneel at this point.) **79 quick** alive **83 worrying** tearing **86 accord** consent **87 appertinents** appurtenances **90 practices** plots **92 This knight** i.e., Grey **99 use** profit (with play on the meaning *interest derived from usury;* Scroop had served as Lord Treasurer) **102 annoy** injure **103 stands . . . gross** appears as obvious **106 yoke-devils** partners in a diabolical cause **107–108 Working . . . them** working together with such obvious fitness, and toward a purpose that suits them so naturally, that they provoked no outcry of wonder. (*Hoop* means *whoop.*) **109 proportion** fitness of things **110 Wonder** astonishment (that Scroop should be a murderer). **wait on** attend, accompany

And whatsoever cunning fiend it was
That wrought upon thee so preposterously
Hath got the voice in hell for excellence.
All other devils that suggest by treasons
Do botch and bungle up damnation
With patches, colors, and with forms being fetch'd
From glist'ring semblances of piety;
But he that temper'd thee bade thee stand up,
Gave thee no instance why thou shouldst do
treason,
Unless to dub thee with the name of traitor.
If that same demon that hath gull'd thee thus
Should with his lion gait walk the whole world,
He might return to vasty Tartar back,
And tell the legions, "I can never win
A soul so easy as that Englishman's."
O, how hast thou with jealousy infected
The sweetness of affiance! Show men dutiful?
Why, so didst thou. Seem they grave and learned?
Why, so didst thou. Come they of noble family?
Why, so didst thou. Seem they religious?
Why, so didst thou. Or are they spare in diet,
Free from gross passion or of mirth or anger,
Constant in spirit, not swerving with the blood,
Garnish'd and deck'd in modest complement,
Not working with the eye without the ear,
And but in purged judgment trusting neither?
Such and so finely bolted didst thou seem.
And thus thy fall hath left a kind of blot
To mark the full-fraught man and best indued
With some suspicion. I will weep for thee;
For this revolt of thine, methinks, is like
Another fall of man. Their faults are open.
Arrest them to the answer of the law;
And God acquit them of their practices!

EXETER I arrest thee of high treason, by the name of Richard Earl of Cambridge.

I arrest thee of high treason, by the name of Henry Lord Scroop of Masham.

I arrest thee of high treason, by the name of Thomas Grey, knight, of Northumberland.

SCROOP
Our purposes God justly hath discover'd,
And I repent my fault more than my death,
Which I beseech your Highness to forgive,
Although my body pay the price of it.

CAMBRIDGE
For me, the gold of France did not seduce,
Although I did admit it as a motive
The sooner to effect what I intended.
But God be thanked for prevention,
Which I in sufferance heartily will rejoice,
Beseeching God and you to pardon me.

GREY
Never did faithful subject more rejoice
At the discovery of most dangerous treason
Than I do at this hour joy o'er myself,
Prevented from a damned enterprise.
My fault, but not my body, pardon, sovereign.

KING
God quit you in his mercy! Hear your sentence.
You have conspir'd against our royal person,
Join'd with an enemy proclaim'd, and from his
coffers
Receiv'd the golden earnest of our death;
Wherein you would have sold your king to
slaughter,
His princes and his peers to servitude,
His subjects to oppression and contempt,
And his whole kingdom into desolation.
Touching our person seek we no revenge,
But we our kingdom's safety must so tender,
Whose ruin you have sought, that to her laws
We do deliver you. Get you therefore hence,
Poor miserable wretches, to your death,
The taste whereof God of his mercy give
You patience to endure, and true repentance
Of all your dear offenses! Bear them hence.
Exeunt [*Cambridge, Scroop, and Grey, guarded*].
Now, lords, for France, the enterprise whereof
Shall be to you, as us, like glorious.
We doubt not of a fair and lucky war,
Since God so graciously hath brought to light
This dangerous treason lurking in our way
To hinder our beginnings. We doubt not now
But every rub is smoothed on our way.
Then forth, dear countrymen! Let us deliver
Our puissance into the hand of God,
Putting it straight in expedition.
Cheerly to sea! The signs of war advance!
No king of England, if not king of France!
Flourish. [*Exeunt.*]

113 voice vote **114 suggest** tempt **115–117 Do . . . piety** i.e., clumsily conceal their damnable temptation by tricking it out in attractive-looking semblances of virtue **118 temper'd** directed (to evil). **stand up** volunteer **119 instance** reason **123 Tartar** Tartarus, the hell of classical mythology **126 jealousy** suspicion **127 affiance** trust. **Show** appear **133 swerving with the blood** sinning through passion **134 deck'd . . . complement** wearing the look of modesty **135 Not . . . ear** i.e., trusting neither eye nor ear alone **136 but . . . judgment** except on the basis of impartial judgment **137 bolted** sifted, refined **139 full-fraught** richly laden (with excellent qualities) **142 open** apparent, obvious **156 did admit it** i.e., allowed it to stand (as a coverup for the real motive) **157 The . . . intended** (Cambridge's real motive, barely hinted at here, was to assist his brother-in-law Edmund Mortimer, fifth Earl of March, to the throne as the standard-bearer of the Yorkist claim against the Lancastrian Henry.)

159 sufferance my suffering **166 quit** acquit **169 golden earnest** advance payment **175 tender** regard, hold dear **181 dear** grievous **183 like** alike, equally **188 But** but that. **rub** obstacle. (A bowling term.) **191 straight in expedition** immediately in action **192 signs** ensigns

[SCENE III]

Enter Pistol, Nym, Bardolph, Boy, and Hostess.

HOSTESS Prithee, honey-sweet husband, let me bring thee to Staines.

PISTOL No; for my manly heart doth earn. Bardolph, be blithe; Nym, rouse thy vaunting veins; Boy, bristle thy courage up; for Falstaff he is dead, and we must earn therefore.

BARDOLPH Would I were with him, wheresome'er he is, either in heaven or in hell!

II.iii. London. Before a tavern (traditionally the Boar's Head Tavern in Eastcheap).
2 Staines town on the road to Southampton **3 earn** grieve

HOSTESS Nay, sure, he's not in hell. He's in Arthur's bosom, if ever man went to Arthur's bosom. 'A made a finer end, and went away an it had been any christom child. 'A parted ev'n just between twelve and one, ev'n at the turning o' th' tide. For after I saw him fumble with the sheets, and play with flowers, and smile upon his finger's end, I knew there was but one way; for his nose was as sharp as a pen, and 'a babbl'd of green fields. "How now, Sir John?" quoth I, "what, man? Be o' good cheer." So 'a cried out, "God, God, God!" three or four times. Now I, to comfort him, bid him 'a should not think of God; I hop'd there was no need to trouble himself with any such thoughts yet. So 'a bade me lay more clothes on his feet. I put my hand into the bed and felt them, and they were as cold as any stone; then I felt to his knees, and so upward and upward, and all was as cold as any stone.

NYM They say he cried out of sack.

HOSTESS Ay, that 'a did.

BARDOLPH And of women.

HOSTESS Nay, that 'a did not.

BOY Yes, that 'a did; and said they were devils incarnate.

HOSTESS 'A could never abide carnation; 'twas a color he never lik'd.

BOY 'A said once the devil would have him about women.

HOSTESS 'A did in some sort, indeed, handle women; but then he was rheumatic, and talk'd of the whore of Babylon.

BOY Do you not remember, 'a saw a flea stick upon Bardolph's nose, and 'a said it was a black soul burning in hell?

BARDOLPH Well, the fuel is gone that maintain'd that fire. That's all the riches I got in his service.

NYM Shall we shog? The King will be gone from Southampton.

PISTOL
Come, let's away. My love, give me thy lips.
[*They kiss.*]
Look to my chattels and my movables.
Let senses rule. The word is "Pitch and Pay."
Trust none;
For oaths are straws, men's faiths are wafer-cakes,
And hold-fast is the only dog, my duck.
Therefore, Caveto be thy counselor.
Go, clear thy crystals. Yoke-fellows in arms,
Let us to France, like horse-leeches, my boys,
To suck, to suck, the very blood to suck!

BOY And that's but unwholesome food, they say.

PISTOL
Touch her soft mouth, and march.

BARDOLPH Farewell, hostess. [*Kissing her.*]

NYM I cannot kiss, that is the humor of it; but, adieu.

PISTOL
Let housewifery appear. Keep close, I thee
command.

HOSTESS Farewell; adieu. *Exeunt.*

[SCENE IV]

Flourish. Enter the French King, the Dauphin, the Dukes of Berri and Britaine, [*the Constable, and others*].

FRENCH KING
Thus comes the English with full power upon us,
And more than carefully it us concerns
To answer royally in our defenses.
Therefore the Dukes of Berri and of Britaine,
Of Brabant and of Orleans, shall make forth,
And you, Prince Dauphin, with all swift dispatch,
To line and new repair our towns of war
With men of courage and with means defendant;
For England his approaches makes as fierce
As waters to the sucking of a gulf.
It fits us then to be as provident
As fear may teach us out of late examples
Left by the fatal and neglected English
Upon our fields.

DAUPHIN My most redoubted father,
It is most meet we arm us 'gainst the foe;
For peace itself should not so dull a kingdom,
Though war nor no known quarrel were in
question,
But that defenses, musters, preparations,
Should be maintain'd, assembled, and collected,
As were a war in expectation.
Therefore, I say 'tis meet we all go forth
To view the sick and feeble parts of France.
And let us do it with no show of fear—
No, with no more than if we heard that England
Were busied with a Whitsun morris-dance.
For, my good liege, she is so idly king'd,
Her scepter so fantastically borne
By a vain, giddy, shallow, humorous youth,
That fear attends her not.

CONSTABLE O peace, Prince Dauphin!
You are too much mistaken in this king.
Question your Grace the late ambassadors,
With what great state he heard their embassy,
How well supplied with noble counselors,

9–10 Arthur's bosom (Malapropism for *Abraham's bosom.*) **11–12 christom** newly christened **16–17 'a babbl'd of green fields** (This line contains Theobald's famous emendation. F has *and a Table of greene fields.* Falstaff would seem to have been reciting the Twenty-third Psalm.) **26 of sack** against sack (a Spanish wine) **36 handle** discuss **37 rheumatic** i.e., feverish, or perhaps an error for "lunatic." (Pronounced "rome-atic," preparing for the allusion to the Whore of Babylon, i.e., the Church of Rome. See also Revelation 17:4–5.) **42 fuel** i.e., liquor, supplied by Falstaff, that has given Bardolph his red face **44 shog** be off **48 Let . . . Pay** i.e., keep your eyes and ears open, and let your motto as hostess be "cash down" **50 wafer-cakes** i.e., easily broken **51 hold-fast** (Cf. the proverb, "Brag is a good dog, but hold-fast is a better.") **52 Caveto** be cautious. (From the Latin imperative of *caveo.*) **53 clear thy crystals** wipe your eyes

60 Let . . . close i.e., be a thrifty housekeeper, and stay at home

II.iv. Location: France. The King's palace.
s.d. Britaine Brittany **7 line** reinforce **10 gulf** whirlpool **12 late** recent **13 fatal and neglected** fatally underestimated **25 Whitsun morris-dance** dance performed during Whitsuntide, in early summer, by persons in fancy costumes **28 humorous** capricious

How modest in exception, and withal
How terrible in constant resolution,
And you shall find his vanities forespent
Were but the outside of the Roman Brutus,
Covering discretion with a coat of folly,
As gardeners do with ordure hide those roots
That shall first spring and be most delicate.

DAUPHIN
Well, 'tis not so, my Lord High Constable;
But though we think it so, it is no matter.
In cases of defense 'tis best to weigh
The enemy more mighty than he seems.
So the proportions of defense are fill'd,
Which of a weak and niggardly projection
Doth, like a miser, spoil his coat with scanting
A little cloth.

FRENCH KING Think we King Harry strong;
And, princes, look you strongly arm to meet him.
The kindred of him hath been flesh'd upon us;
And he is bred out of that bloody strain
That haunted us in our familiar paths.
Witness our too much memorable shame
When Crécy battle fatally was struck,
And all our princes captiv'd by the hand
Of that black name, Edward, Black Prince of Wales;
Whiles that his mountain sire, on mountain standing,
Up in the air, crown'd with the golden sun,
Saw his heroical seed, and smil'd to see him,
Mangle the work of nature and deface
The patterns that by God and by French fathers
Had twenty years been made. This is a stem
Of that victorious stock; and let us fear
The native mightiness and fate of him.

Enter a Messenger.

MESSENGER
Ambassadors from Harry King of England
Do crave admittance to your Majesty.

FRENCH KING
We'll give them present audience. Go, and bring them. *[Exeunt Messenger and certain Lords.]*
You see this chase is hotly followed, friends.

DAUPHIN
Turn head, and stop pursuit; for coward dogs
Most spend their mouths when what they seem to threaten
Runs far before them. Good my sovereign,
Take up the English short, and let them know
Of what a monarchy you are the head.
Self-love, my liege, is not so vile a sin
As self-neglecting.

Enter [Lords, with] Exeter [and train].

FRENCH KING From our brother of England?

EXETER
From him; and thus he greets your Majesty.
He wills you, in the name of God Almighty,
That you divest yourself, and lay apart
The borrowed glories that by gift of heaven,
By law of nature and of nations, 'longs
To him and to his heirs, namely, the crown
And all wide-stretched honors that pertain
By custom and the ordinance of times,
Unto the crown of France. That you may know
'Tis no sinister nor no awkward claim,
Pick'd from the worm-holes of long-vanish'd days,
Nor from the dust of old oblivion rak'd,
He sends you this most memorable line, *[Gives a paper.]*
In every branch truly demonstrative,
Willing you overlook this pedigree.
And when you find him evenly deriv'd
From his most fam'd of famous ancestors,
Edward the Third, he bids you then resign
Your crown and kingdom, indirectly held
From him the native and true challenger.

FRENCH KING
Or else what follows?

EXETER
Bloody constraint; for if you hide the crown
Even in your hearts, there will he rake for it.
Therefore in fierce tempest is he coming,
In thunder and in earthquake, like a Jove,
That, if requiring fail, he will compel;
And bids you, in the bowels of the Lord,
Deliver up the crown, and to take mercy
On the poor souls for whom this hungry war
Opens his vasty jaws; and on your head
Turning the widows' tears, the orphans' cries,
The dead men's blood, the privy maidens' groans,
For husbands, fathers, and betrothed lovers,
That shall be swallowed in this controversy.
This is his claim, his threat'ning, and my message—
Unless the Dauphin be in presence here,
To whom expressly I bring greeting too.

FRENCH KING
For us, we will consider of this further.
Tomorrow shall you bear our full intent
Back to our brother of England.

DAUPHIN For the Dauphin,
I stand here for him. What to him from England?

EXETER
Scorn and defiance, slight regard, contempt,
And any thing that may not misbecome
The mighty sender, doth he prize you at.

34 exception making objections **36 vanities forespent** follies now a thing of the past **37 Brutus** i.e., the elder Brutus, Lucius Junius Brutus, who pretended to be stupid *(brutus)* as a ruse to allay the suspicions of the tyrant Tarquin until the time for overthrow was ripe **45 So . . . fill'd** i.e., thus an adequate and full defense is provided **46 Which . . . projection** i.e., which defense, if it should be provided on a small and miserly scale **50 kindred** i.e., his great-grandfather Edward III and great-uncle Edward the Black Prince. **flesh'd** initiated in the shedding of blood, with foretaste of further success **54 Crécy** French defeat in 1346. **struck** waged **57 mountain sire** i.e., Edward III, born in mountainous Wales, and of sturdy proportions **59 seed** i.e., son **62 twenty years** (i.e., because the warriors thus mangled were born twenty years or so before) **64 fate** what he is destined to do **69 Turn head** stand at bay (a hunting term). **stop** put an end to **70 Most . . . mouths** bay the loudest

78 apart aside **80 'longs** belongs **83 ordinance of times** decrees of tradition **85 sinister** illegitimate **88 line** pedigree **90 Willing you overlook** desiring that you look over **91 evenly** directly **94 indirectly** wrongfully **95 challenger** claimant **101 requiring** requesting **102 bowels** mercy, or innermost being. (Cf. Philippians 1:8.) **107 privy maidens' groans** maidens' secret grievings

Thus says my King: an if your father's Highness
Do not, in grant of all demands at large,
Sweeten the bitter mock you sent his Majesty,
He'll call you to so hot an answer of it
That caves and womby vaultages of France
Shall chide your trespass and return your mock
In second accent of his ordnance.

DAUPHIN

Say, if my father render fair return,
It is against my will; for I desire
Nothing but odds with England. To that end,
As matching to his youth and vanity,
I did present him with the Paris balls.

EXETER

He'll make your Paris Louvre shake for it,
Were it the mistress court of mighty Europe.
And, be assur'd, you'll find a diff'rence,
As we his subjects have in wonder found,
Between the promise of his greener days
And these he masters now. Now he weighs time
Even to the utmost grain. That you shall read
In your own losses, if he stay in France.

FRENCH KING

Tomorrow shall you know our mind at full.
Flourish.

EXETER

Dispatch us with all speed, lest that our King
Come here himself to question our delay;
For he is footed in this land already.

FRENCH KING

You shall be soon dispatch'd with fair conditions.
A night is but small breath and little pause
To answer matters of this consequence. *Exeunt.*

ACT [III • PROLOGUE]

Flourish. Enter Chorus.

[CHORUS]

Thus with imagin'd wing our swift scene flies
In motion of no less celerity
Than that of thought. Suppose that you have seen
The well-appointed King at Hampton pier
Embark his royalty, and his brave fleet
With silken streamers the young Phoebus fanning.
Play with your fancies, and in them behold
Upon the hempen tackle ship-boys climbing;
Hear the shrill whistle which doth order give
To sounds confus'd; behold the threaden sails,
Borne with th' invisible and creeping wind,
Draw the huge bottoms through the furrowed sea,
Breasting the lofty surge. O, do but think
You stand upon the rivage and behold
A city on th' inconstant billows dancing;
For so appears this fleet majestical,
Holding due course to Harfleur. Follow, follow!
Grapple your minds to sternage of this navy,
And leave your England as dead midnight still,
Guarded with grandsires, babies, and old women,
Either past or not arriv'd to pith and puissance;
For who is he, whose chin is but enrich'd
With one appearing hair, that will not follow
These cull'd and choice-drawn cavaliers to France?
Work, work your thoughts, and therein see a siege;
Behold the ordnance on their carriages,
With fatal mouths gaping on girded Harfleur.
Suppose th' ambassador from the French comes back,
Tells Harry that the King doth offer him
Katharine his daughter, and with her, to dowry,
Some petty and unprofitable dukedoms.
The offer likes not; and the nimble gunner
With linstock now the devilish cannon touches,
Alarum, and chambers go off.
And down goes all before them. Still be kind,
And eche out our performance with your mind.
Exit.

[SCENE I]

Enter the King, Exeter, Bedford, and Gloucester. Alarum, [with Soldiers carrying] scaling ladders at Harfleur.

KING

Once more unto the breach, dear friends, once more,
Or close the wall up with our English dead!
In peace there's nothing so becomes a man
As modest stillness and humility.
But when the blast of war blows in our ears,
Then imitate the action of the tiger:
Stiffen the sinews, summon up the blood,
Disguise fair nature with hard-favor'd rage.
Then lend the eye a terrible aspect:
Let it pry through the portage of the head
Like the brass cannon; let the brow o'erwhelm it
As fearfully as doth a galled rock
O'erhang and jutty his confounded base,
Swill'd with the wild and wasteful ocean.
Now set the teeth and stretch the nostril wide,
Hold hard the breath, and bend up every spirit
To his full height. On, on, you noblest English,
Whose blood is fet from fathers of war-proof!

124 womby vaultages deep caverns **126 second accent** echo. **ordnance** cannon **127 fair return** courteous reply **131 Paris balls** tennis balls **132 Louvre** the French royal palace

III. Chorus.
1 imagin'd wing wings of imagination **4 well-appointed** well-equipped **5 brave** handsome **6 the . . . fanning** i.e., fluttering against the rising sun **10 threaden** woven of thread **12 bottoms** hulls of ships **14 rivage** shore

18 to sternage astern **21 pith** strength **27 girded** besieged **32 likes** pleases **33 linstock** staff holding a gunner's match **33 s.d. Alarum** call to arms. **chambers** small cannon (fired off backstage, or "within") **35 eche** eke

III.i. Location: France. Before Harfleur.
s.d. scaling ladders (Presumably these are set up against the façade of the tiring house, backstage, which is perceived to be the walls of Harfleur.) **10 portage** portholes, eyes **11 o'erwhelm** project over **12 galled** washed away, undermined **13 jutty** overhang. **his confounded** its ruined **14 Swill'd** washed. **wasteful** destructive **18 fet** fetched, derived. **of war-proof** proved in war

Fathers that, like so many Alexanders,
Have in these parts from morn till even fought,
And sheath'd their swords for lack of argument.
Dishonor not your mothers; now attest
That those whom you call'd fathers did beget you.
Be copy now to men of grosser blood,
And teach them how to war. And you, good yeomen,
Whose limbs were made in England, show us here
The mettle of your pasture. Let us swear
That you are worth your breeding, which I doubt not,
For there is none of you so mean and base
That hath not noble luster in your eyes.
I see you stand like greyhounds in the slips,
Straining upon the start. The game's afoot!
Follow your spirit, and upon this charge
Cry "God for Harry, England, and Saint George!"
[Exeunt.] Alarum, and chambers go off.

[SCENE II]

Enter Nym, Bardolph, Pistol, and Boy.

BARDOLPH On, on, on, on, on! To the breach, to the breach!

NYM Pray thee, corporal, stay. The knocks are too hot; and, for mine own part, I have not a case of lives. The humor of it is too hot, that is the very plain-song of it.

PISTOL
The plain-song is most just; for humors do abound.
"Knocks go and come; God's vassals drop and die;
And sword and shield,
In bloody field,
Doth win immortal fame."

BOY Would I were in an alehouse in London! I would give all my fame for a pot of ale and safety.

PISTOL
And I:
"If wishes would prevail with me,
My purpose should not fail with me,
But thither would I hie."

BOY
"As duly, but not as truly,
As bird doth sing on bough."

Enter Fluellen.

FLUELLEN Up to the breach, you dogs! Avaunt, you cullions! *[Driving them forward.]*

PISTOL
Be merciful, great duke, to men of mold.
Abate thy rage, abate thy manly rage,
Abate thy rage, great duke!
Good bawcock, bate thy rage! Use lenity, sweet chuck!

NYM These be good humors! Your honor wins bad humors. *Exit [with all but Boy].*

BOY As young as I am, I have observ'd these three swashers. I am boy to them all three, but all they three, though they would serve me, could not be man to me; for indeed three such antics do not amount to a man. For Bardolph, he is white-liver'd and red-fac'd, by the means whereof 'a faces it out, but fights not. For Pistol, he hath a killing tongue and a quiet sword, by the means whereof 'a breaks words, and keeps whole weapons. For Nym, he hath heard that men of few words are the best men, and therefore he scorns to say his prayers, lest 'a should be thought a coward; but his few bad words are match'd with as few good deeds, for 'a never broke any man's head but his own, and that was against a post when he was drunk. They will steal anything, and call it purchase. Bardolph stole a lute-case, bore it twelve leagues, and sold it for three half-pence. Nym and Bardolph are sworn brothers in filching, and in Calais they stole a fire-shovel. I knew by that piece of service the men would carry coals. They would have me as familiar with men's pockets as their gloves or their handkerchers, which makes much against my manhood, if I should take from another's pocket to put into mine, for it is plain pocketing up of wrongs. I must leave them, and seek some better service. Their villainy goes against my weak stomach, and therefore I must cast it up. *Exit.*

Enter Gower [and Fluellen].

GOWER Captain Fluellen, you must come presently to the mines. The Duke of Gloucester would speak with you.

FLUELLEN To the mines? Tell you the Duke, it is not so good to come to the mines; for, look you, the mines is not according to the disciplines of the war. The concavities of it is not sufficient. For, look you, th' athversary, you may discuss unto the Duke, look you, is digt himself four yard under the countermines. By Cheshu, I think 'a will plow up all, if there is not better directions.

GOWER The Duke of Gloucester, to whom the order of the siege is given, is altogether directed by an Irishman, a very valiant gentleman, i' faith.

FLUELLEN It is Captain Macmorris, is it not?

GOWER I think it be.

FLUELLEN By Cheshu, he is an ass, as in the world! I will verify as much in his beard. He has no more directions in the true disciplines of the wars, look you, of the Roman disciplines, than is a puppy-dog.

19 Alexanders (Alexander grieved that there were no new worlds for him to conquer.) **24 copy** models **27 mettle . . . pasture** quality of your breeding. (Literally, *pasture* means "feeding.") **31 slips** leashes **34 Saint George** patron saint of England

III.ii. Location: Before Harfleur, as in the previous scene; the action is essentially continuous.
4 case set **5 plain-song** i.e., simple truth **19 Avaunt** be gone **19–20 cullions** rascals. (Original meaning: *testicles.*) **21 men of mold** mere mortals

24 bawcock fine fellow. (French *beau coq.*) **chuck** (A term of endearment.) **28 swashers** swashbucklers **30 antics** buffoons, zanies **31 white-liver'd** i.e., cowardly. (In extreme fear the blood was thought to sink below the liver, leaving it bloodless.) **32 'a faces it out** i.e., he puts on a brave front **34 breaks words** (1) misuses language and fails to keep his word (2) uses words as weapons **41 purchase** (Thieves' cant for *stolen goods.*) **45–46 carry coals** i.e., submit to insult or degradation **48 makes** i.e., goes **50 pocketing . . . wrongs** (1) putting up with insults (2) receiving stolen goods **51–52 goes . . . stomach** (1) goes against my inclination (2) makes me sick **54 mines** undermining operation in a siege **58 disciplines of the war** science of warfare (about which there were many books from Greek and Roman times down to the Renaissance; Fluellen's humor involves an obsession with this study and a preference for traditional methods) **58–59 concavities** i.e., slope **60 discuss** explain. **digt** digged **61 Cheshu** Jesu, Jesus **62 plow** blow. (In Fluellen's Welsh dialect, "p" is regularly substituted for "b" and "f" for "v.") **70 in his beard** i.e., to his face

Enter Macmorris and Captain Jamy.

GOWER Here 'a comes, and the Scots captain, Captain Jamy, with him.

FLUELLEN Captain Jamy is a marvelous falorous gentleman, that is certain, and of great expedition and knowledge in th' aunchient wars, upon my particular knowledge of his directions. By Cheshu, he will maintain his argument as well as any military man in the world, in the disciplines of the pristine wars of the Romans.

JAMY I say gud day, Captain Fluellen.

FLUELLEN God-den to your worship, good Captain James.

GOWER How now, Captain Macmorris, have you quit the mines? Have the pioners given o'er?

MACMORRIS By Chrish, la, tish ill done! The work ish give over, the trompet sound the retreat. By my hand, I swear, and my father's soul, the work ish ill done; it ish give over. I would have blowed up the town, so Chrish save me, la, in an hour. O, tish ill done, tish ill done! By my hand, tish ill done!

FLUELLEN Captain Macmorris, I beseech you now, will you voutsafe me, look you, a few disputations with you, as partly touching or concerning the disciplines of the war, the Roman wars, in the way of argument, look you, and friendly communication—partly to satisfy my opinion, and partly for the satisfaction, look you, of my mind, as touching the direction of the military discipline, that is the point.

JAMY It sall be vary gud, gud feith, gud captens bath, and I sall quit you with gud leve, as I may pick occasion. That sall I, marry.

MACMORRIS It is no time to discourse, so Chrish save me! The day is hot, and the weather, and the wars, and the King, and the dukes. It is no time to discourse. The town is beseech'd, and the trumpet call us to the breach, and we talk, and, be Chrish, do nothing. 'Tis shame for us all. So God sa' me, 'tis shame to stand still, it is shame, by my hand! And there is throats to be cut, and works to be done, and there ish nothing done, so Chrish sa' me, la!

JAMY By the mess, ere theise eyes of mine take themselves to slomber, ay'll de gud service, or I'll lig i' th' grund for it, ay, or go to death! And I'll pay 't as valorously as I may, that sall I suerly do, that is the breff and the long. Marry, I wad full fain heard some question 'tween you tway.

FLUELLEN Captain Macmorris, I think, look you, under your correction, there is not many of your nation—

MACMORRIS Of my nation? What ish my nation? Ish a villain, and a bastard, and a knave, and a rascal! What ish my nation? Who talks of my nation?

FLUELLEN Look you, if you take the matter otherwise than is meant, Captain Macmorris, peradventure I shall think you do not use me with that affability as in discretion you ought to use me, look you, being as good a man as yourself, both in the disciplines of war, and in the derivation of my birth, and in other particularities.

MACMORRIS I do not know you so good a man as myself. So Chrish save me, I will cut off your head!

GOWER Gentlemen both, you will mistake each other.

JAMY A, that's a foul fault! *A parley [sounded].*

GOWER The town sounds a parley.

FLUELLEN Captain Macmorris, when there is more better opportunity to be required, look you, I will be so bold as to tell you I know the disciplines of war; and there is an end. *Exit [with others].*

[SCENE III]

[Enter the Governor and some Citizens on the walls.] Enter the King [Henry] and all his train before the gates.

KING
How yet resolves the governor of the town?
This is the latest parle we will admit.
Therefore to our best mercy give yourselves,
Or, like to men proud of destruction,
Defy us to our worst; for, as I am a soldier,
A name that in my thoughts becomes me best,
If I begin the batt'ry once again,
I will not leave the half-achieved Harfleur
Till in her ashes she lie buried.
The gates of mercy shall be all shut up,
And the flesh'd soldier, rough and hard of heart,
In liberty of bloody hand shall range
With conscience wide as hell, mowing like grass
Your fresh-fair virgins and your flow'ring infants.
What is it then to me, if impious war,
Array'd in flames like to the prince of fiends,
Do with his smirch'd complexion all fell feats
Enlink'd to waste and desolation?
What is 't to me, when you yourselves are cause,
If your pure maidens fall into the hand
Of hot and forcing violation?
What rein can hold licentious wickedness
When down the hill he holds his fierce career?
We may as bootless spend our vain command
Upon th' enraged soldiers in their spoil
As send precepts to the leviathan
To come ashore. Therefore, you men of Harfleur,
Take pity of your town and of your people,
Whiles yet my soldiers are in my command,
Whiles yet the cool and temperate wind of grace
O'erblows the filthy and contagious clouds

76 expedition readiness (?) **83 God-den** good e'en, good afternoon or evening **86 pioners** sappers, diggers **101 bath** both **102 quit** requite, answer **103 marry** indeed. (Originally, *by the Virgin Mary.*) **107 beseech'd** besieged **113 mess** Mass **114 ay'll de** I'll do. **lig** lie **116 breff** brief **117 heard** have heard **117–118 question** discussion **121 What ish** i.e., what about. **Ish** i.e., (anyone who says anything against my nationality) is

134 s.d. parley trumpet summons to a negotiation **137 required** found

III.iii. Location: Before the gates of Harfleur, as in the previous scene, and immediately afterward. The gates are represented by the tiring house façade. Those who appear *on the walls* are seen in the gallery backstage.
2 latest parle last parley **4 proud of** glorying in **11 flesh'd** made fierce with the taste of blood **17 fell** savage **23 he . . . career** it makes its fierce gallop **24 bootless** fruitlessly **26 precepts** written summons. **leviathan** whale **30 grace** mercy **31 O'erblows** blows away. (Contagion was thought to reside in clouds and mists.)

Of heady murder, spoil, and villainy.
If not, why, in a moment look to see
The blind and bloody soldier with foul hand
Defile the locks of your shrill-shrieking daughters,
Your fathers taken by the silver beards,
And their most reverend heads dash'd to the walls,
Your naked infants spitted upon pikes,
Whiles the mad mothers with their howls confus'd
Do break the clouds, as did the wives of Jewry
At Herod's bloody-hunting slaughtermen.
What say you? Will you yield, and this avoid,
Or, guilty in defense, be thus destroy'd?

GOVERNOR
Our expectation hath this day an end.
The Dauphin, whom of succors we entreated,
Returns us that his powers are yet not ready
To raise so great a siege. Therefore, great King,
We yield our town and lives to thy soft mercy.
Enter our gates, dispose of us and ours,
For we no longer are defensible.

KING
Open your gates. Come, uncle Exeter,
Go you and enter Harfleur; there remain,
And fortify it strongly 'gainst the French.
Use mercy to them all. For us, dear uncle,
The winter coming on and sickness growing
Upon our soldiers, we will retire to Calais.
Tonight in Harfleur will we be your guest;
Tomorrow for the march are we address'd.
Flourish, and enter the town.

[SCENE IV]

Enter Katharine and [Alice,] an old Gentlewoman.

KATHARINE Alice, tu as été en Angleterre, et tu parles bien le langage.

ALICE Un peu, madame.

KATHARINE Je te prie, m'enseignez; il faut que j'apprenne à parler. Comment appelez-vous la main en Anglois?

ALICE La main? Elle est appelée de hand.

KATHARINE De hand. Et les doigts?

ALICE Les doigts? Ma foi, j'oublie les doigts; mais je me souviendrai. Les doigts? Je pense qu'ils sont appelés de fingres; oui, de fingres.

KATHARINE La main, de hand; les doigts, de fingres. Je pense que je suis le bon écolier; j'ai gagné deux mots d'Anglois vîtement. Comment appelez-vous les ongles?

ALICE Les ongles? Nous les appelons de nailes.

KATHARINE De nailes. Écoutez, dites-moi, si je parle bien: de hand, de fingres, et de nailes.

ALICE C'est bien dit, madame; il est fort bon Anglois.

KATHARINE Dites-moi l'Anglois pour le bras.

ALICE De arm, madame.

KATHARINE Et le coude?

ALICE D' elbow.

KATHARINE D' elbow. Je m'en fais la répétition de tous les mots que vous m'avez appris dès à présent.

ALICE Il est trop difficile, madame, comme je pense.

KATHARINE Excusez-moi, Alice; écoutez: d' hand, de fingre, de nailes, d' arma, de bilbow.

ALICE D' elbow, madame.

KATHARINE O Seigneur Dieu, je m'en oublie! D' elbow. Comment appelez-vous le col?

ALICE De nick, madame.

KATHARINE De nick. Et le menton?

ALICE De chin.

KATHARINE De sin. Le col, de nick; le menton, de sin.

ALICE Oui. Sauf votre honneur, en vérité, vous prononcez les mots aussi droit que les natifs d'Angleterre.

KATHARINE Je ne doute point d'apprendre, par la grace de Dieu, et en peu de temps.

ALICE N'avez-vous pas déjà oublié ce que je vous ai enseigné?

KATHARINE Non, je reciterai à vous promptement: d' hand, de fingre, de mailes—

ALICE De nailes, madame.

KATHARINE De nailes, de arm, de ilbow.

ALICE Sauf votre honneur, d' elbow.

KATHARINE Ainsi dis-je; d' elbow, de nick, et de sin. Comment appelez-vous le pied et la robe?

ALICE Le foot, madame, et le count.

KATHARINE Le foot et le count! O Seigneur Dieu! Ils sont les mots de son mauvais, corruptible, gros, et impudique, et non pour les dames d'honneur d'user. Je ne voudrais prononcer ces mots devant les seigneurs de France pour tout le monde. Foh! Le foot et le

32 heady deadly; headstrong **34 blind** i.e., blinded with lust and rage **40 Jewry** Judea **41 Herod's . . . slaughterman** (For the account of Herod's slaughter of the innocent children in his attempt to murder the infant Jesus, see Matthew 2:16–18.) **43 in defense** i.e., by not surrendering **46 Returns** replies to **50 defensible** able to defend ourselves **58 address'd** prepared

III.iv. Location: The French King's palace at Rouen.
Translation:
KATHARINE. Alice, you have been in England and speak the language well.
ALICE. A little, my lady.
KATHARINE. I pray you teach me; I have to learn to speak it. What do you call *la main* in English?
ALICE. *La main?* It is called de hand.
KATHARINE. De hand. And *les doigts?*
ALICE. *Les doigts?* Dear me, I forget *les doigts;* but I shall remember. I think that they are called de fingres; yes, de fingres.
KATHARINE. *La main,* de hand; *les doigts,* de fingres. I think that I am a clever scholar; I have learned two English words in no time. What do you call *les ongles?*
ALICE. *Les ongles?* We call them de nailes.
KATHARINE. De nailes. Listen; tell me whether or not I speak correctly: de hand, de fingres, and de nailes.
ALICE. That is correct, my lady; it is very good English.
KATHARINE. Tell me the English for *le bras.*
ALICE. De arm, my lady.
KATHARINE. And *le coude?*
ALICE. D' elbow.
KATHARINE. D' elbow. I am going to repeat all the words you have taught me so far.
ALICE. It is too hard, my lady, I fear.
KATHARINE. Pardon me, Alice; listen: d' hand, de fingre, de nailes, d' arma, de bilbow.
ALICE. D' elbow, my lady.
KATHARINE. O Lord, I can't remember! D' elbow. What do you call *le col?*
ALICE. De nick, my lady.
KATHARINE. De nick. And *le menton?*
ALICE. De chin.
KATHARINE. De sin. *Le col,* de nick; *le menton,* de sin.
ALICE. Yes. If I may say so, really you pronounce the words just as correctly as native Englishmen.
KATHARINE. I have no doubt that I shall learn, with God's help, in a very short time.
ALICE. Haven't you already forgotten what I have taught you?
KATHARINE. No. I shall recite to you at once: d' hand, de fingre, de mailes—
ALICE. De nailes, my lady.
KATHARINE. De nailes, de arm, de ilbow.
ALICE. By your leave, d' elbow.
KATHARINE. That's what I said; d' elbow, de nick, and de sin. What do you call *le pied* and *la robe?*
ALICE. Le foot, my lady, and le count. [As she pronounces them, *foot* sounds to Katharine like *foutre,* fornicate, and *count* (for *gown*) sounds like French for the female sexual organ, *cunt* in English.]
KATHARINE. Le foot and le count! O Lord! Those are naughty words, wicked, coarse, and immodest, and are not fit to be used by ladies. I wouldn't say those words before French gentlemen for the whole world. Bah! Le foot and le count! Nevertheless, I shall recite my whole lesson once more: d' hand, de fingre, de nailes, de arm, d' elbow, de nick, de sin, de foot, le count.

count! Néanmoins, je réciterai une autre fois ma leçon ensemble: d' hand, de fingre, de nailes, de arm, d' elbow, de nick, de sin, de foot, le count.

ALICE Excellent, madame!

KATHARINE C'est assez pour une fois. Allons-nous à dîner. *Exit [with Alice].* 60

[SCENE V]

Enter the King of France, the Dauphin, [the Duke of Britaine,] the Constable of France, and others.

FRENCH KING
'Tis certain he hath pass'd the river Somme.

CONSTABLE
And if he be not fought withal, my lord,
Let us not live in France; let us quit all
And give our vineyards to a barbarous people.

DAUPHIN
O Dieu vivant! Shall a few sprays of us, 5
The emptying of our fathers' luxury, 6
Our scions, put in wild and savage stock, 7
Spirt up so suddenly into the clouds 8
And overlook their grafters? 9

BRITAINE
Normans, but bastard Normans, Norman bastards!
Mort Dieu, ma vie, if they march along 11
Unfought withal, but I will sell my dukedom,
To buy a slobb'ry and a dirty farm 13
In that nook-shotten isle of Albion. 14

CONSTABLE
Dieu de batailles, where have they this mettle? 15
Is not their climate foggy, raw, and dull,
On whom, as in despite, the sun looks pale,
Killing their fruit with frowns? Can sodden water, 18
A drench for sur-rein'd jades, their barley-broth, 19
Decoct their cold blood to such valiant heat? 20
And shall our quick blood, spirited with wine,
Seem frosty? O, for honor of our land,
Let us not hang like roping icicles 23
Upon our houses' thatch, whiles a more frosty people
Sweat drops of gallant youth in our rich fields!
Poor we call them in their native lords. 26

DAUPHIN
By faith and honor,
Our madams mock at us, and plainly say
Our mettle is bred out, and they will give
Their bodies to the lust of English youth
To new-store France with bastard warriors. 31

ALICE. Excellent, my lady.
KATHARINE. That's enough for one time. Let's go to dinner.

III.v. Location: The French King's palace at Rouen.
5 Dieu vivant living God. **sprays** offshoots, illegitimate stock **6 fathers' luxury** ancestors' lust **7 scions** grafts. **put in** grafted upon **8 Spirt** shoot **9 overlook** rise above. **grafters** trees from which scions are taken **11 Mort Dieu, ma vie** by God's (Christ's) death, my life **13 slobb'ry** slovenly **14 nook-shotten** full of nooks and angles. (Refers to the coast line.) **15 Dieu de batailles** God of battles **18 sodden water** boiled water, i.e., ale **19 drench . . . jades** drink for overridden horses. **barley-broth** ale **20 Decoct** warm up **23 roping** hanging down like a rope **26 Poor . . . lords** i.e., our fields, though rich in themselves, are poor insofar as they are owned by a spiritless people **31 new-store** newly supply

BRITAINE
They bid us to the English dancing-schools 32
And teach lavoltas high and swift corantos, 33
Saying our grace is only in our heels 34
And that we are most lofty runaways.

FRENCH KING
Where is Montjoy the herald? Speed him hence. 36
Let him greet England with our sharp defiance.
Up, princes, and, with spirit of honor edged
More sharper than your swords, hie to the field!
Charles Delabreth, High Constable of France,
You Dukes of Orleans, Bourbon, and of Berri,
Alençon, Brabant, Bar, and Burgundy,
Jaques Chatillion, Rambures, Vaudemont,
Beaumont, Grandpré, Roussi, and Faulconbridge,
Foix, Lestrale, Bouciqualt, and Charolois,
High dukes, great princes, barons, lords, and knights,
For your great seats now quit you of great shames. 47
Bar Harry England, that sweeps through our land
With pennons painted in the blood of Harfleur.
Rush on his host, as doth the melted snow
Upon the valleys, whose low vassal seat
The Alps doth spit and void his rheum upon. 52
Go down upon him, you have power enough,
And in a captive chariot into Rouen
Bring him our prisoner.

CONSTABLE
This becomes the great.
Sorry am I his numbers are so few,
His soldiers sick and famish'd in their march,
For I am sure, when he shall see our army,
He'll drop his heart into the sink of fear 59
And for achievement offer us his ransom. 60

FRENCH KING
Therefore, Lord Constable, haste on Montjoy,
And let him say to England that we send
To know what willing ransom he will give.
Prince Dauphin, you shall stay with us in Rouen.

DAUPHIN
Not so, I do beseech your Majesty.

FRENCH KING
Be patient, for you shall remain with us.
Now forth, Lord Constable and princes all,
And quickly bring us word of England's fall. *Exeunt.*

[SCENE VI]

Enter Captains, English and Welsh: Gower and Fluellen.

GOWER How now, Captain Fluellen? Come you from the bridge? 2

FLUELLEN I assure you, there is very excellent services committed at the bridge.

32 bid us bid us go **33 lavoltas, corantos** fashionable dances **34 in our heels** (1) in dancing gracefully (2) in running away **36 Montjoy** title of the chief herald of France **47 quit you of** redeem yourselves from **52 rheum** i.e., waters **59 sink** pit **60 for achievement** instead of achieving victory

III.vi. Location: The English camp in Picardy.
2 bridge (According to Holinshed, the French were beaten in their attempt to break down the bridge over the Ternois.)

GOWER Is the Duke of Exeter safe?

FLUELLEN The Duke of Exeter is as magnanimous as Agamemnon, and a man that I love and honor with my soul, and my heart, and my duty, and my live, and my living, and my uttermost power. He is not—God be praised and blessed!—any hurt in the world, but keeps the bridge most valiantly, with excellent discipline. There is an aunchient lieutenant there at the pridge, I think in my very conscience he is as valiant a man as Mark Antony, and he is a man of no estimation in the world, but I did see him do as gallant service.

GOWER What do you call him?

FLUELLEN He is call'd Aunchient Pistol.

GOWER I know him not.

Enter Pistol.

FLUELLEN Here is the man.

PISTOL
Captain, I thee beseech to do me favors.
The Duke of Exeter doth love thee well.

FLUELLEN Ay, I praise God, and I have merited some love at his hands.

PISTOL
Bardolph, a soldier, firm and sound of heart,
And of buxom valor, hath, by cruel fate,
And giddy Fortune's furious fickle wheel,
That goddess blind,
That stands upon the rolling restless stone—

FLUELLEN By your patience, Aunchient Pistol. Fortune is painted blind, with a muffler afore her eyes, to signify to you that Fortune is blind; and she is painted also with a wheel, to signify to you, which is the moral of it, that she is turning, and inconstant, and mutability, and variation; and her foot, look you, is fixed upon a spherical stone, which rolls, and rolls, and rolls. In good truth, the poet makes a most excellent description of it. Fortune is an excellent moral.

PISTOL
Fortune is Bardolph's foe, and frowns on him;
For he hath stol'n a pax, and hanged must 'a be—
A damned death!
Let gallows gape for dog; let man go free,
And let not hemp his windpipe suffocate.
But Exeter hath given the doom of death
For pax of little price.
Therefore, go speak—the Duke will hear thy
voice—
And let not Bardolph's vital thread be cut
With edge of penny cord and vile reproach.
Speak, captain, for his life, and I will thee requite.

FLUELLEN Aunchient Pistol, I do partly understand your meaning.

PISTOL
Why then, rejoice therefore.

FLUELLEN Certainly, aunchient, it is not a thing to rejoice at. For if, look you, he were my brother, I would desire the Duke to use his good pleasure, and put him to execution; for discipline ought to be used.

PISTOL
Die and be damn'd! And figo for thy friendship!

FLUELLEN It is well.

PISTOL
The fig of Spain! *Exit.*

FLUELLEN Very good.

GOWER Why, this is an arrant counterfeit rascal! I remember him now; a bawd, a cutpurse.

FLUELLEN I'll assure you, 'a utt'red as prave words at the pridge as you shall see in a summer's day. But it is very well. What he has spoke to me, that is well, I warrant you, when time is serve.

GOWER Why, 'tis a gull, a fool, a rogue, that now and then goes to the wars, to grace himself at his return into London under the form of a soldier. And such fellows are perfect in the great commanders' names, and they will learn you by rote where services were done—at such and such a sconce, at such a breach, at such a convoy; who came off bravely, who was shot, who disgrac'd, what terms the enemy stood on—and this they con perfectly in the phrase of war, which they trick up with new-tun'd oaths. And what a beard of the general's cut and a horrid suit of the camp will do among foaming bottles and ale-wash'd wits is wonderful to be thought on. But you must learn to know such slanders of the age, or else you may be marvelously mistook.

FLUELLEN I tell you what, Captain Gower, I do perceive he is not the man that he would gladly make show to the world he is. If I find a hole in his coat, I will tell him my mind. [*Drum heard.*] Hark you, the King is coming, and I must speak with him from the pridge.

Drum and colors. Enter the King and his poor Soldiers [*and Gloucester*].

God pless your Majesty!

KING How now, Fluellen? Cam'st thou from the bridge?

FLUELLEN Ay, so please your Majesty. The Duke of Exeter has very gallantly maintain'd the pridge. The French is gone off, look you, and there is gallant and most prave passages. Marry, th' athversary was have possession of the pridge, but he is enforced to retire, and the Duke of Exeter is master of the pridge. I can tell your Majesty, the Duke is a prave man.

KING What men have you lost, Fluellen?

FLUELLEN The perdition of th' athversary hath been very great, reasonable great. Marry, for my part, I think the Duke hath lost never a man, but one that is like to be executed for robbing a church, one Bardolph, if your Majesty know the man. His face is all bubukles, and whelks, and knobs, and flames o' fire, and his lips blows at his

7 Agamemnon leader of the Greeks against Troy **8 live** life **12 aunchient lieutenant** (Pistol is elsewhere given the rank of ancient, or ensign.) **14–15 estimation** fame **26 buxom** lively **38 moral** emblem **39 Fortune . . . foe** (Probably alludes to the ballad, "Fortune, my foe!") **40 pax** metal disk with a crucifix stamped on it, kissed by the priest during Mass. (But Holinshed describes an incident in which the object stolen is a *pyx,* the vessel containing the consecrated host.)

57 figo gesture of contempt made by thrusting the thumb between the index and middle finger **67 gull** simpleton **72 sconce** fortification **75 con** learn by heart **77 horrid . . . camp** fierce battle costume **80 slanders of the age** persons who are a disgrace to the times **84 a hole . . . coat** i.e., something discreditable about him by means of which to expose him **86 from the pridge** with news concerning the bridge **93 passages** deeds of arms **98 perdition** losses **102 bubukles** carbuncles. **whelks** boils, pimples

nose, and it is like a coal of fire, sometimes plue and sometimes red; but his nose is executed, and his fire's out.

KING We would have all such offenders so cut off. And we give express charge that, in our marches through the country, there be nothing compell'd from the villages, nothing taken but paid for, none of the French upbraided or abus'd in disdainful language; for when lenity and cruelty play for a kingdom, the gentler gamester
is the soonest winner. 113

Tucket. Enter Montjoy.

MONTJOY You know me by my habit. 114
KING Well then I know thee. What shall I know of thee?
MONTJOY My master's mind.
KING Unfold it.
MONTJOY Thus says my King: Say thou to Harry of En-
gland, though we seem'd dead, we did but sleep. Ad- 119
vantage is a better soldier than rashness. Tell him we 120
could have rebuk'd him at Harfleur, but that we
thought not good to bruise an injury till it were full 122
ripe. Now we speak upon our cue, and our voice is
imperial. England shall repent his folly, see his weak-
ness, and admire our sufferance. Bid him therefore 125
consider of his ransom, which must proportion the
losses we have borne, the subjects we have lost, the
disgrace we have digested; which in weight to re-an- 128
swer, his pettiness would bow under. For our losses, 129
his exchequer is too poor; for th' effusion of our blood,
the muster of his kingdom too faint a number; and for 131
our disgrace, his own person, kneeling at our feet, but
a weak and worthless satisfaction. To this add defi-
ance; and tell him, for conclusion, he hath betray'd his
followers, whose condemnation is pronounc'd. So far
my King and master; so much my office.

KING
What is thy name? I know thy quality. 137
MONTJOY Montjoy.
KING
Thou dost thy office fairly. Turn thee back,
And tell thy King I do not seek him now,
But could be willing to march on to Calais
Without impeachment. For, to say the sooth, 142
Though 'tis no wisdom to confess so much
Unto an enemy of craft and vantage, 144
My people are with sickness much enfeebled,
My numbers lessen'd, and those few I have
Almost no better than so many French,
Who when they were in health, I tell thee, herald,
I thought upon one pair of English legs
Did march three Frenchmen. Yet, forgive me, God,
That I do brag thus! This your air of France
Hath blown that vice in me. I must repent. 152
Go therefore, tell thy master here I am;
My ransom is this frail and worthless trunk,
My army but a weak and sickly guard.
Yet, God before, tell him we will come on,
Though France himself and such another neighbor
Stand in our way. There's for thy labor, Montjoy.
[*Gives a purse.*]
Go, bid thy master well advise himself. 159
If we may pass, we will; if we be hind'red,
We shall your tawny ground with your red blood
Discolor. And so, Montjoy, fare you well.
The sum of all our answer is but this:
We would not seek a battle, as we are,
Nor, as we are, we say we will not shun it.
So tell your master.
MONTJOY
I shall deliver so. Thanks to your Highness. [*Exit.*]
GLOUCESTER
I hope they will not come upon us now.
KING
We are in God's hand, brother, not in theirs.
March to the bridge. It now draws toward night.
Beyond the river we'll encamp ourselves,
And on tomorrow bid them march away. *Exeunt.* 172

[SCENE VII]

Enter the Constable of France, the Lord Rambures, Orleans, Dauphin, with others.

CONSTABLE Tut, I have the best armor of the world. Would it were day!
ORLEANS You have an excellent armor; but let my horse have his due.
CONSTABLE It is the best horse of Europe.
ORLEANS Will it never be morning?
DAUPHIN My Lord of Orleans, and my Lord High Constable, you talk of horse and armor?
ORLEANS You are as well provided of both as any prince in the world.
DAUPHIN What a long night is this! I will not change
my horse with any that treads but on four pasterns. 12
Ça, ha! He bounds from the earth, as if his entrails 13
were hairs; le cheval volant, the Pegasus, chez les na- 14
rines de feu! When I bestride him, I soar, I am a hawk. 15
He trots the air. The earth sings when he touches it.
The basest horn of his hoof is more musical than the 17
pipe of Hermes. 18
ORLEANS He's of the color of the nutmeg.
DAUPHIN And of the heat of the ginger. It is a beast for
Perseus. He is pure air and fire; and the dull elements 21
of earth and water never appear in him, but only in
patient stillness while his rider mounts him. He is in-
deed a horse, and all other jades you may call beasts.

113 s.d. Tucket trumpet signal, fanfare **114 habit** i.e., tabard, herald's coat **119–120 Advantage** circumspection **122 bruise an injury** i.e., squeeze a boil or pimple **125 admire our sufferance** wonder at our patience **128–129 which . . . under** i.e., to compensate for which his means are too slender **131 muster** total population **137 quality** rank and profession **142 impeachment** impediment **144 vantage** superiority in resources **152 blown** brought to bloom

159 advise himself consider **172 bid . . . away** i.e., bid our army march toward Calais

III.vii. Location: The French camp, near Agincourt.
12 pasterns hoofs **13–14 as . . . hairs** i.e., as if here were a tennis ball. (Tennis balls were stuffed with hair.) **14–15 le cheval . . . feu** the flying horse, Pegasus, with nostrils breathing fire **17 basest horn** (1) lowest part (2) hoofbeat **18 pipe of Hermes** (Hermes, messenger of the gods, charmed Argus of the hundred eyes asleep with playing on his pipe.) **21 Perseus** (According to some Greek legends and to Ovid, Perseus rode Pegasus when he rescued Andromeda from the dragon.)

CONSTABLE Indeed, my lord, it is a most absolute and excellent horse.

DAUPHIN It is the prince of palfreys. His neigh is like the bidding of a monarch, and his countenance enforces homage.

ORLEANS No more, cousin.

DAUPHIN Nay, the man hath no wit that cannot, from the rising of the lark to the lodging of the lamb, vary deserv'd praise on my palfrey. It is a theme as fluent as the sea; turn the sands into eloquent tongues, and my horse is argument for them all. 'Tis a subject for a sovereign to reason on, and for a sovereign's sovereign to ride on; and for the world, familiar to us and unknown, to lay apart their particular functions and wonder at him. I once writ a sonnet in his praise and began thus: "Wonder of nature"—

ORLEANS I have heard a sonnet begin so to one's mistress.

DAUPHIN Then did they imitate that which I compos'd to my courser, for my horse is my mistress.

ORLEANS Your mistress bears well.

DAUPHIN Me well, which is the prescript praise and perfection of a good and particular mistress.

CONSTABLE Nay, for methought yesterday your mistress shrewdly shook your back.

DAUPHIN So perhaps did yours.

CONSTABLE Mine was not bridled.

DAUPHIN O then belike she was old and gentle, and you rode, like a kern of Ireland, your French hose off, and in your strait strossers.

CONSTABLE You have good judgment in horsemanship.

DAUPHIN Be warn'd by me, then: they that ride so and ride not warily, fall into foul bogs. I had rather have my horse to my mistress.

CONSTABLE I had as lief have my mistress a jade.

DAUPHIN I tell thee, Constable, my mistress wears his own hair.

CONSTABLE I could make as true a boast as that, if I had a sow to my mistress.

DAUPHIN "Le chien est retourné à son propre vomissement, et la truie lavée au bourbier." Thou mak'st use of anything.

CONSTABLE Yet do I not use my horse for my mistress, or any such proverb so little kin to the purpose.

RAMBURES My Lord Constable, the armor that I saw in your tent tonight, are those stars or suns upon it?

CONSTABLE Stars, my lord.

DAUPHIN Some of them will fall tomorrow, I hope.

CONSTABLE And yet my sky shall not want.

DAUPHIN That may be, for you bear a many superfluously, and 'twere more honor some were away.

CONSTABLE Ev'n as your horse bears your praises, who would trot as well, were some of your brags dismounted.

DAUPHIN Would I were able to load him with his desert! Will it never be day? I will trot tomorrow a mile, and my way shall be pav'd with English faces.

CONSTABLE I will not say so, for fear I should be fac'd out of my way. But I would it were morning, for I would fain be about the ears of the English.

RAMBURES Who will go to hazard with me for twenty prisoners?

CONSTABLE You must first go yourself to hazard, ere you have them.

DAUPHIN 'Tis midnight; I'll go arm myself. *Exit.*

ORLEANS The Dauphin longs for morning.

RAMBURES He longs to eat the English.

CONSTABLE I think he will eat all he kills.

ORLEANS By the white hand of my lady, he's a gallant prince.

CONSTABLE Swear by her foot, that she may tread out the oath.

ORLEANS He is simply the most active gentleman of France.

CONSTABLE Doing is activity, and he will still be doing.

ORLEANS He never did harm, that I heard of.

CONSTABLE Nor will do none tomorrow. He will keep that good name still.

ORLEANS I know him to be valiant.

CONSTABLE I was told that by one that knows him better than you.

ORLEANS What's he?

CONSTABLE Marry, he told me so himself, and he said he car'd not who knew it.

ORLEANS He needs not; it is no hidden virtue in him.

CONSTABLE By my faith, sir, but it is. Never anybody saw it but his lackey. 'Tis a hooded valor, and when it appears, it will bate.

ORLEANS Ill will never said well.

CONSTABLE I will cap that proverb with, "There is flattery in friendship."

ORLEANS And I will take up that with, "Give the devil his due."

CONSTABLE Well plac'd. There stands your friend for the devil. Have at the very eye of that proverb with, "A pox of the devil."

ORLEANS You are the better at proverbs, by how much "A fool's bolt is soon shot."

CONSTABLE You have shot over.

ORLEANS 'Tis not the first time you were overshot.

Enter a Messenger.

MESSENGER My Lord High Constable, the English lie within fifteen hundred paces of your tents.

25 absolute excellent **27 palfreys** saddle-horses **32 lodging** lying down **36 reason** discourse **37–39 for . . . him** for both the known and unknown world to put aside their separate activities and wonder at him (the horse) **44 horse is my mistress** (Here begins a series of bawdy double entendres involving human and animal sexuality: *bears, shook your back, rode, foul bogs, doing,* etc.) **46 prescript** prescribed **47 particular** acknowledging only one master **49 shrewdly** viciously **53 kern** light-armed Irish foot soldier. **French hose** wide breeches **54 strait strossers** tight trousers, i.e., barelegged **58 to** as **64–65 Le chien . . . bourbier** the dog is returned to his own vomit, and the washed sow to the mire. (See II Peter 2:22.) **73 sky** i.e., sky of honor. **want** be lacking (in honor)

82–83 fac'd . . . way braved out of my way, put to shame **85 go to hazard** bet, play at dice. (But the Constable replies in the sense of *encounter danger.*) **95–96 tread . . . oath** (1) fulfill the oath by dancing (2) stamp on, spurn the oath **99 Doing** i.e., acting, pretending. **still** continually **100 did harm** i.e., offended. (But the Constable uses it to mean *hurt any enemy.*) **110–111 Never . . . lackey** i.e., he shows "valor" only in beating his servant **111 hooded valor** (The hawk was kept hooded to prevent it from beating its wings, or "baiting.") **112 bate** (1) beat its wings (2) abate, be downcast **119 Have . . . eye** shoot straight at the mark. (A sporting term appropriate to this verbal contest of "capping proverbs.") **123 shot over** i.e., shot over the mark **124 overshot** i.e., outshot, defeated

CONSTABLE Who hath measur'd the ground?
MESSENGER The Lord Grandpré.
CONSTABLE A valiant and most expert gentleman.
Would it were day! Alas, poor Harry of England! He
longs not for the dawning as we do.
ORLEANS What a wretched and peevish fellow is this
King of England, to mope with his fat-brain'd follow- 133
ers so far out of his knowledge!
CONSTABLE If the English had any apprehension, they 135
would run away.
ORLEANS That they lack; for if their heads had any in-
tellectual armor, they could never wear such heavy
head-pieces.
RAMBURES That island of England breeds very valiant
creatures; their mastiffs are of unmatchable courage.
ORLEANS Foolish curs, that run winking into the mouth 142
of a Russian bear and have their heads crush'd like
rotten apples! You may as well say, that's a valiant flea
that dare eat his breakfast on the lip of a lion.
CONSTABLE Just, just! And the men do sympathize with 146
the mastiffs in robustious and rough coming on, leav-
ing their wits with their wives; and then give them
great meals of beef and iron and steel, they will eat like
wolves and fight like devils.
ORLEANS Ay, but these English are shrewdly out of 151
beef.
CONSTABLE Then shall we find tomorrow they have
only stomachs to eat and none to fight. Now is it time
to arm. Come, shall we about it?
ORLEANS
It is now two o'clock; but, let me see, by ten
We shall have each a hundred Englishmen. *Exeunt.*

ACT [IV • PROLOGUE]

[*Enter*] *Chorus.*

[CHORUS]
Now entertain conjecture of a time
When creeping murmur and the poring dark 2
Fills the wide vessel of the universe.
From camp to camp, through the foul womb of night,
The hum of either army stilly sounds,
That the fix'd sentinels almost receive
The secret whispers of each other's watch.
Fire answers fire, and through their paly flames
Each battle sees the other's umber'd face. 9
Steed threatens steed, in high and boastful neighs
Piercing the night's dull ear; and from the tents
The armorers, accomplishing the knights, 12
With busy hammers closing rivets up,
Give dreadful note of preparation.
The country cocks do crow, the clocks do toll,
And the third hour of drowsy morning name.
Proud of their numbers and secure in soul, 17
The confident and over-lusty French 18
Do the low-rated English play at dice, 19
And chide the cripple tardy-gaited night
Who, like a foul and ugly witch, doth limp
So tediously away. The poor condemned English,
Like sacrifices, by their watchful fires
Sit patiently and inly ruminate
The morning's danger; and their gesture sad, 25
Investing lank-lean cheeks and war-worn coats, 26
Presenteth them unto the gazing moon
So many horrid ghosts. O now, who will behold
The royal captain of this ruin'd band
Walking from watch to watch, from tent to tent,
Let him cry, "Praise and glory on his head!"
For forth he goes and visits all his host,
Bids them good morrow with a modest smile,
And calls them brothers, friends, and countrymen.
Upon his royal face there is no note
How dread an army hath enrounded him. 36
Nor doth he dedicate one jot of color 37
Unto the weary and all-watched night, 38
But freshly looks and overbears attaint 39
With cheerful semblance and sweet majesty;
That every wretch, pining and pale before,
Beholding him, plucks comfort from his looks.
A largess universal like the sun
His liberal eye doth give to every one,
Thawing cold fear, that mean and gentle all 45
Behold, as may unworthiness define, 46
A little touch of Harry in the night.
And so our scene must to the battle fly;
Where—O for pity!—we shall much disgrace
With four or five most vile and ragged foils,
Right ill-dispos'd in brawl ridiculous,
The name of Agincourt. Yet sit and see,
Minding true things by what their mock'ries be. 53
Exit.

[SCENE I]

Enter the King, Bedford, and Gloucester.

KING
Gloucester, 'tis true that we are in great danger;
The greater therefore should our courage be.
Good morrow, brother Bedford. God Almighty!
There is some soul of goodness in things evil,
Would men observingly distill it out;

133 mope wander about **135 apprehension** (1) sense (2) sense of danger **142 winking** shutting their eyes **146 sympathize with** resemble **151 shrewdly out of** devilishly short of

IV. Chorus.
2 poring straining the eyes to see **9 battle** army. **umber'd** shadowed **12 accomplishing** equipping

17 secure overconfident **18 over-lusty** overly merry **19 play** gamble for **25 gesture sad** serious bearing **26 Investing** clothing **36 enrounded** surrounded **37 dedicate** yield up. **color** i.e., bright color of complexion **38 all-watched** spent entirely in wakefulness and waiting **39 overbears attaint** overcomes the effects of weariness and depression **45 mean and gentle** those of low and of high birth **46 as . . . define** as we can express to you only imperfectly **53 Minding** bearing in mind. **mock'ries** inadequate imitations

IV.i. Location: The English camp at Agincourt.

For our bad neighbor makes us early stirrers,
Which is both healthful and good husbandry.
Besides, they are our outward consciences,
And preachers to us all, admonishing
That we should dress us fairly for our end.
Thus may we gather honey from the weed,
And make a moral of the devil himself.

Enter Erpingham.

Good morrow, old Sir Thomas Erpingham.
A good soft pillow for that good white head
Were better than a churlish turf of France.

ERPINGHAM
Not so, my liege. This lodging likes me better,
Since I may say, "Now lie I like a king."

KING
'Tis good for men to love their present pains
Upon example; so the spirit is eased.
And when the mind is quick'ned, out of doubt,
The organs, though defunct and dead before,
Break up their drowsy grave, and newly move
With casted slough and fresh legerity.
Lend me thy cloak, Sir Thomas. [*The King puts on Erpingham's cloak.*] Brothers both,
Commend me to the princes in our camp;
Do my good morrow to them, and anon
Desire them all to my pavilion.

GLOUCESTER
We shall, my liege.

ERPINGHAM
Shall I attend your Grace?

KING
No, my good knight,
Go with my brothers to my lords of England.
I and my bosom must debate a while,
And then I would no other company.

ERPINGHAM
The Lord in heaven bless thee, noble Harry!
Exeunt [*all but King*].

KING
God-a-mercy, old heart! Thou speak'st cheerfully.

Enter Pistol.

PISTOL Che vous lá?

KING A friend.

PISTOL
Discuss unto me; art thou officer?
Or art thou base, common, and popular?

KING I am a gentleman of a company.

PISTOL
Trail'st thou the puissant pike?

KING Even so. What are you?

PISTOL
As good a gentleman as the Emperor.

KING Then you are a better than the King.

PISTOL
The King's a bawcock, and a heart of gold,
A lad of life, an imp of fame,
Of parents good, of fist most valiant.
I kiss his dirty shoe, and from heart-string
I love the lovely bully. What is thy name?

KING Harry le Roy.

PISTOL
Le Roy? A Cornish name. Art thou of Cornish crew?

KING No, I am a Welshman.

PISTOL
Know'st thou Fluellen?

KING Yes.

PISTOL
Tell him, I'll knock his leek about his pate
Upon Saint Davy's day.

KING Do not you wear your dagger in your cap that day, lest he knock that about yours.

PISTOL
Art thou his friend?

KING And his kinsman too.

PISTOL
The figo for thee, then!

KING I thank you. God be with you!

PISTOL
My name is Pistol call'd. *Exit.*

KING It sorts well with your fierceness.
Manet King [*aside*].

Enter Fluellen and Gower.

GOWER Captain Fluellen!

FLUELLEN So, in the name of Jesu Christ, speak fewer. It is the greatest admiration in the universal world, when the true and aunchient prerogatifes and laws of the wars is not kept. If you would take the pains but to examine the wars of Pompey the Great, you shall find, I warrant you, that there is no tiddle taddle nor pibble pabble in Pompey's camp. I warrant you, you shall find the ceremonies of the wars, and the cares of it, and the forms of it, and the sobriety of it, and the modesty of it, to be otherwise.

GOWER Why, the enemy is loud; you hear him all night.

FLUELLEN If the enemy is an ass and a fool and a prating coxcomb, is it meet, think you, that we should also, look you, be an ass and a fool and a prating coxcomb? In your own conscience, now?

GOWER I will speak lower.

FLUELLEN I pray you and beseech you that you will.
Exit [*with Gower*].

KING
Though it appear a little out of fashion,
There is much care and valor in this Welshman.

7 husbandry economy, thrift **10 dress us fairly** prepare ourselves well **15 churlish** niggardly **16 likes** pleases **19 Upon example** following or considering example **22 Break . . . grave** i.e., break out of their lethargy **23 With casted slough** i.e., as though having cast off its old skin, like a snake. **legerity** nimbleness **24 Brothers both** i.e., Bedford and Gloucester **35 Che vous là** i.e., *qui va là;* who goes there, or *qui vous là,* who are you there. (Pistol's imperfect French.) **38 popular** of low birth **40 Trail'st . . . pike** i.e., are you in the infantry?

44 bawcock fine fellow. (From French *beau coq.*) **45 imp of fame** child or scion of renown **51 Welshman** (Henry was born at Monmouth, then considered part of Wales.) **54–55 leek . . . day** (On St. David's Day, March 1, the leek was worn in memory of a Welsh victory over the Saxons, since St. David, the Welsh leader, had commanded his followers to wear leeks in their caps on that occasion.) **60 figo** (A provoking gesture of contempt; see III.vi.57, note.) **63 sorts** suits **66 admiration** wonder **69 Pompey the Great** Roman general defeated by Julius Caesar

Enter three soldiers, John Bates, Alexander Court, and Michael Williams.

COURT Brother John Bates, is not that the morning which breaks yonder?

BATES I think it be. But we have no great cause to desire the approach of day.

WILLIAMS We see yonder the beginning of the day, but I think we shall never see the end of it. Who goes there?

KING A friend.

WILLIAMS Under what captain serve you?

KING Under Sir Thomas Erpingham.

WILLIAMS A good old commander and a most kind gentlemen. I pray you, what thinks he of our estate?

KING Even as men wrack'd upon a sand, that look to be wash'd off the next tide.

BATES He hath not told his thought to the King?

KING No; nor it is not meet he should. For, though I speak it to you, I think the King is but a man, as I am. The violet smells to him as it doth to me; the element shows to him as it doth to me; all his senses have but human conditions. His ceremonies laid by, in his nakedness he appears but a man; and though his affections are higher mounted than ours, yet, when they stoop, they stoop with the like wing. Therefore when he sees reason of fears, as we do, his fears, out of doubt, be of the same relish as ours are. Yet, in reason, no man should possess him with any appearance of fear, lest he, by showing it, should dishearten his army.

BATES He may show what outward courage he will; but I believe, as cold a night as 'tis, he could wish himself in Thames up to the neck; and so I would he were, and I by him, at all adventures, so we were quit here.

KING By my troth, I will speak my conscience of the King: I think he would not wish himself anywhere but where he is.

BATES Then I would he were here alone. So should he be sure to be ransom'd, and a many poor men's lives sav'd.

KING I dare say you love him not so ill to wish him here alone, howsoever you speak this to feel other men's minds. Methinks I could not die anywhere so contented as in the King's company, his cause being just and his quarrel honorable.

WILLIAMS That's more than we know.

BATES Ay, or more than we should seek after; for we know enough, if we know we are the King's subjects. If his cause be wrong, our obedience to the King wipes the crime of it out of us.

WILLIAMS But if the cause be not good, the King himself hath a heavy reckoning to make, when all those legs and arms and heads, chopp'd off in a battle, shall join together at the latter day and cry all, "We died at such a place"—some swearing, some crying for a surgeon, some upon their wives left poor behind them, some upon the debts they owe, some upon their children rawly left. I am afeard there are few die well that die in a battle; for how can they charitably dispose of anything, when blood is their argument? Now, if these men do not die well, it will be a black matter for the King that led them to it; who to disobey were against all proportion of subjection.

KING So, if a son that is by his father sent about merchandise do sinfully miscarry upon the sea, the imputation of his wickedness, by your rule, should be impos'd upon his father that sent him; or if a servant, under his master's command transporting a sum of money, be assail'd by robbers and die in many irreconcil'd iniquities, you may call the business of the master the author of the servant's damnation. But this is not so. The King is not bound to answer the particular endings of his soldiers, the father of his son, nor the master of his servant; for they purpose not their death, when they purpose their services. Besides, there is no king, be his cause never so spotless, if it come to the arbitrement of swords, can try it out with all unspotted soldiers. Some, peradventure, have on them the guilt of premeditated and contriv'd murder; some, of beguiling virgins with the broken seals of perjury; some, making the wars their bulwark, that have before gor'd the gentle bosom of peace with pillage and robbery. Now, if these men have defeated the law and outrun native punishment, though they can outstrip men, they have no wings to fly from God. War is his beadle, war is his vengeance; so that here men are punish'd for before-breach of the King's laws in now the King's quarrel. Where they fear'd the death, they have borne life away; and where they would be safe, they perish. Then if they die unprovided, no more is the King guilty of their damnation than he was before guilty of those impieties for the which they are now visited. Every subject's duty is the King's; but every subject's soul is his own. Therefore should every soldier in the wars do as every sick man in his bed, wash every mote out of his conscience; and dying so, death is to him advantage, or not dying, the time was blessedly lost wherein such preparation was gain'd. And in him that escapes, it were not sin to think that, making God so free an offer, He let him outlive that day to see His greatness and to teach others how they should prepare.

WILLIAMS 'Tis certain, every man that dies ill, the ill upon his own head, the King is not to answer it.

BATES I do not desire he should answer for me; and yet I determine to fight lustily for him.

96 estate condition **102–103 element shows** sky appears **104 conditions** qualities, i.e., limitations. **ceremonies** observances due royalty; royal robes **105–106 affections . . . mounted** desires soar higher. (A falconry metaphor continued in *stoop,* descend, swoop down, and *with the like wing,* similarly.) **109 relish** taste **110 possess him with** induce in him **116 at all adventures** no matter what the risk (since the Thames would be less risky under any circumstances than the impending battle). **quit here** out of this situation

136 latter day last day, Day of Judgment **140 rawly** without provision **144 who** whom **145 proportion of subjection** proper duty of a subject **147 sinfully miscarry** die in his sins **151–152 in . . . iniquities** with his wicked deeds unabsolved **163 bulwark** refuge from punishment (for offenses committed) **165 defeated** broken **166 native** at home **168 beadle** parish officer responsible for punishing petty offenders **169 before-breach** prior violation **170–172 Where . . . perish** i.e., where they feared execution they killed others, and where they looked for safety they die in battle **172–173 unprovided** spiritually unprepared **175 visited** i.e., by punishment **178 mote** small impurity

KING I myself heard the King say he would not be ransom'd.

WILLIAMS Ay, he said so, to make us fight cheerfully; but when our throats are cut, he may be ransom'd, and we ne'er the wiser.

KING If I live to see it, I will never trust his word after.

WILLIAMS You pay him then! That's a perilous shot out of an elder-gun, that a poor and a private displeasure can do against a monarch! You may as well go about to turn the sun to ice with fanning in his face with a peacock's feather. You'll never trust his word after! Come, 'tis a foolish saying.

KING Your reproof is something too round. I should be angry with you, if the time were convenient.

WILLIAMS Let it be a quarrel between us, if you live.

KING I embrace it.

WILLIAMS How shall I know thee again?

KING Give me any gage of thine, and I will wear it in my bonnet. Then, if ever thou dar'st acknowledge it, I will make it my quarrel.

WILLIAMS Here's my glove. Give me another of thine.

KING There.

[*They exchange gloves, and wear them in their caps.*]

WILLIAMS This will I also wear in my cap. If ever thou come to me and say, after tomorrow, "This is my glove," by this hand, I will take thee a box on the ear.

KING If ever I live to see it, I will challenge it.

WILLIAMS Thou dar'st as well be hang'd.

KING Well, I will do it, though I take thee in the King's company.

WILLIAMS Keep thy word. Fare thee well.

BATES Be friends, you English fools, be friends. We have French quarrels enow, if you could tell how to reckon.

KING Indeed, the French may lay twenty French crowns to one they will beat us, for they bear them on their shoulders; but it is no English treason to cut French crowns, and tomorrow the King himself will be a clipper. *Exeunt Soldiers.*

Upon the King! Let us our lives, our souls,
Our debts, our careful wives,
Our children, and our sins lay on the King!
We must bear all. O hard condition,
Twin-born with greatness, subject to the breath
Of every fool, whose sense no more can feel
But his own wringing! What infinite heart's-ease
Must kings neglect, that private men enjoy!
And what have kings, that privates have not too,
Save ceremony, save general ceremony?
And what art thou, thou idol ceremony?
What kind of god art thou, that suffer'st more
Of mortal griefs than do thy worshipers?
What are thy rents? What are thy comings in?
O ceremony, show me but thy worth!
What is thy soul of adoration?
Art thou aught else but place, degree, and form,
Creating awe and fear in other men?
Wherein thou art less happy, being fear'd,
Than they in fearing.
What drink'st thou oft, instead of homage sweet,
But poison'd flattery? O, be sick, great greatness,
And bid thy ceremony give thee cure!
Thinks thou the fiery fever will go out
With titles blown from adulation?
Will it give place to flexure and low bending?
Canst thou, when thou command'st the beggar's knee,
Command the health of it? No, thou proud dream,
That play'st so subtly with a king's repose.
I am a king that find thee, and I know
'Tis not the balm, the scepter, and the ball,
The sword, the mace, the crown imperial,
The intertissued robe of gold and pearl,
The farced title running 'fore the king,
The throne he sits on, nor the tide of pomp
That beats upon the high shore of this world—
No, not all these, thrice-gorgeous ceremony,
Not all these, laid in bed majestical,
Can sleep so soundly as the wretched slave,
Who, with a body fill'd and vacant mind,
Gets him to rest, cramm'd with distressful bread;
Never sees horrid night, the child of hell,
But, like a lackey, from the rise to set
Sweats in the eye of Phoebus, and all night
Sleeps in Elysium; next day after dawn
Doth rise and help Hyperion to his horse,
And follows so the ever-running year
With profitable labor, to his grave.
And, but for ceremony, such a wretch,
Winding up days with toil and nights with sleep,
Had the forehand and vantage of a king.
The slave, a member of the country's peace,
Enjoys it; but in gross brain little wots
What watch the King keeps to maintain the peace,
Whose hours the peasant best advantages.

Enter Erpingham.

ERPINGHAM
My lord, your nobles, jealous of your absence,
Seek through your camp to find you.

KING Good old knight,
Collect them all together at my tent.
I'll be before thee.

ERPINGHAM I shall do 't, my lord. *Exit.*

195 You pay him then i.e., that will really pay him back for his perfidy, won't it. (Said sarcastically.) **196 elder-gun** popgun made from a branch of elder with the pith hollowed out **201 round** direct, brusque **206 gage** pledge **213 take** give, strike **220 enow** enough **222 crowns** (1) coins (2) heads **224 English treason** (It was a treasonable offense to clip or "cut" English coins; it obviously is no offense to slash French heads, and even King Henry will be such a "clipper.") **228 careful** full of cares **231–233 Twin-born . . . wringing** i.e., inseparable from the condition of being born of royal rank, a condition that makes one the subject of the idle gossip of every fool, even those whose sensibilities pay attention to nothing other than the rumbling of their own stomachs **235 privates** private men

242 thy soul of adoration the essential quality that makes you so much admired **243 place** rank **250–251 will . . . adulation** will be extinguished by speeches breathed by flatterers **252 it give place to flexure** it (a fever, illness) yield to bowing **256 find** expose **257 balm** consecrating oil used to anoint a king in his coronation **260 farced** stuffed (with pompous phrases) **267 distressful** earned by hard work **269 lackey** constant attendant **270 Phoebus** the sun god **271 Elysium** in Greek mythology, the abode of the blessed **272 Hyperion** the charioteer of the sun. (The peasant is up before the sun.) **277 forehand** upper hand **278 member** sharer **279 it** i.e., peace. **wots** knows **280 watch** wakeful guard **281 peasant best advantages** most benefit the peasant **282 jealous of** apprehensive because of

KING
O God of battles! Steel my soldiers' hearts,
Possess them not with fear! Take from them now
The sense of reck'ning, if th' opposed numbers
Pluck their hearts from them. Not today, O Lord,
O, not today, think not upon the fault
My father made in compassing the crown!
I Richard's body have interred new,
And on it have bestow'd more contrite tears
Than from it issued forced drops of blood.
Five hundred poor I have in yearly pay,
Who twice a day their wither'd hands hold up
Toward heaven, to pardon blood; and I have built
Two chantries, where the sad and solemn priests
Sing still for Richard's soul. More will I do;
Though all that I can do is nothing worth,
Since that my penitence comes after all,
Imploring pardon.

Enter Gloucester.

GLOUCESTER
My liege!

KING
My brother Gloucester's voice? Ay;
I know thy errand, I will go with thee.
The day, my friends, and all things stay for me.

Exeunt.

[SCENE II]

Enter the Dauphin, Orleans, Rambures, and Beaumont.

ORLEANS
The sun doth gild our armor. Up, my lords!

DAUPHIN Montez à cheval! My horse, varlet lackey! Ha!

ORLEANS O brave spirit!

DAUPHIN Via, les eaux et terre!

ORLEANS Rien puis? L'air et feu?

DAUPHIN Cieux, cousin Orleans.

Enter Constable.

Now, my Lord Constable?

CONSTABLE
Hark, how our steeds for present service neigh!

DAUPHIN
Mount them, and make incision in their hides,
That their hot blood may spin in English eyes,
And dout them with superfluous courage, ha!

RAMBURES
What, will you have them weep our horses' blood?
How shall we, then, behold their natural tears?

Enter Messenger.

MESSENGER
The English are embattled, you French peers.

CONSTABLE
To horse, you gallant princes, straight to horse!
Do but behold yon poor and starved band,
And your fair show shall suck away their souls,
Leaving them but the shales and husks of men.
There is not work enough for all our hands,
Scarce blood enough in all their sickly veins
To give each naked curtle-axe a stain,
That our French gallants shall today draw out,
And sheathe for lack of sport. Let us but blow on them,
The vapor of our valor will o'erturn them.
'Tis positive against all exceptions, lords,
That our superfluous lackeys and our peasants,
Who in unnecessary action swarm
About our squares of battle, were enow
To purge this field of such a hilding foe,
Though we upon this mountain's basis by
Took stand for idle speculation—
But that our honors must not. What's to say?
A very little little let us do,
And all is done. Then let the trumpets sound
The tucket sonance and the note to mount;
For our approach shall so much dare the field
That England shall couch down in fear and yield.

Enter Grandpré.

GRANDPRÉ
Why do you stay so long, my lords of France?
Yond island carrions, desperate of their bones,
Ill-favoredly become the morning field.
Their ragged curtains poorly are let loose,
And our air shakes them passing scornfully.
Big Mars seems bankrupt in their beggar'd host,
And faintly through a rusty beaver peeps.
The horsemen sit like fixed candlesticks,
With torch-staves in their hand, and their poor jades
Lob down their heads, dropping the hides and hips,
The gum down-roping from their pale-dead eyes,
And in their pale dull mouths the gimmal'd bit
Lies foul with chew'd grass, still and motionless;
And their executors, the knavish crows,
Fly o'er them, all impatient for their hour.
Description cannot suit itself in words

288 sense of reck'ning ability to count (the enemy) **290 fault** i.e., the deposition and murder of Richard II **291 compassing** obtaining **292 new** anew **298 chantries** chapels in which masses for the dead were celebrated. **sad** grave **299 still** continually **301 Since that** i.e., as shown by the fact that

IV.ii. Location: The French camp.
2 Montez à cheval to horse **4 Via . . . terre** begone, waters and earth. (The Dauphin imagines himself riding above rivers and solid ground.) **5 Rien . . . feu** nothing more? What about air and fire? (I.e., Why not soar above all four elements, not just water and earth?) **6 Cieux** the heavens. (The Dauphin carries the metaphor one step further to its ultimate height.) **9 incision** i.e., with spurs **10 spin** gush, spatter **11 And . . . courage** i.e., and put out the English eyes with the horses' superfluous blood, the proof of their excessive courage. **dout** put out

14 embattled arranged in battle order **17 fair show** impressive appearance **18 shales** shells **21 curtle-axe** cutlass, short sword **25 exceptions** objections **29 hilding** worthless, base **30 basis** foot. **by** nearby **31 speculation** looking on **35 tucket sonance** trumpet call **36 dare** cause to stare, to be stupified **39 carrions** skeletons, cadavers. **desperate of** without hope of saving **40 Ill-favoredly become** i.e., are an eyesore to **41 curtains** colors, banners **42 passing** exceedingly **43 Mars** the god of war **44 beaver** visor **46 torch-staves** i.e., tapers in place of lances. (The horsemen themselves look like carved candleholders.) **47 Lob** hang down. **dropping** letting droop **48 down-roping** hanging down rope-like **49 gimmal'd** jointed **51 executors** those who will dispose of what remains behind

To demonstrate the life of such a battle,
In life so lifeless as it shows itself.

CONSTABLE
They have said their prayers, and they stay for
death.

DAUPHIN
Shall we go send them dinners and fresh suits,
And give their fasting horses provender,
And after fight with them?

CONSTABLE
I stay but for my guard. On to the field!
I will the banner from a trumpet take,
And use it for my haste. Come, come, away!
The sun is high, and we outwear the day. *Exeunt.*

[SCENE III]

Enter Gloucester, Bedford, Exeter, Erpingham, with all his host, Salisbury, and Westmorland.

GLOUCESTER
Where is the King?

BEDFORD
The King himself is rode to view their battle.

WESTMORLAND
Of fighting men they have full threescore thousand.

EXETER
There's five to one; besides, they all are fresh.

SALISBURY
God's arm strike with us! 'Tis a fearful odds.
God buy you, princes all; I'll to my charge.
If we no more meet till we meet in heaven,
Then, joyfully, my noble Lord of Bedford,
My dear Lord Gloucester, and my good Lord Exeter,
And my kind kinsman, warriors all, adieu!

BEDFORD
Farewell, good Salisbury, and good luck go with
thee!

EXETER
Farewell, kind lord. Fight valiantly today!
And yet I do thee wrong to mind thee of it,
For thou art fram'd of the firm truth of valor.
[*Exit Salisbury.*]

BEDFORD
He is as full of valor as of kindness,
Princely in both.

Enter the King.

WESTMORLAND O that we now had here
But one ten thousand of those men in England
That do no work today!

KING What's he that wishes so?
My cousin Westmorland? No, my fair cousin.
If we are mark'd to die, we are enow
To do our country loss; and if to live,
The fewer men, the greater share of honor.
God's will, I pray thee, wish not one man more.
By Jove, I am not covetous for gold,
Nor care I who doth feed upon my cost;
It yearns me not if men my garments wear;
Such outward things dwell not in my desires.
But if it be a sin to covet honor,
I am the most offending soul alive.
No, faith, my coz, wish not a man from England.
God's peace, I would not lose so great an honor
As one man more, methinks, would share from me
For the best hope I have. O, do not wish one more!
Rather proclaim it, Westmorland, through my host,
That he which hath no stomach to this fight,
Let him depart; his passport shall be made
And crowns for convoy put into his purse.
We would not die in that man's company
That fears his fellowship to die with us.
This day is call'd the feast of Crispian.
He that outlives this day, and comes safe home,
Will stand a-tiptoe when this day is nam'd,
And rouse him at the name of Crispian.
He that shall see this day, and live old age,
Will yearly on the vigil feast his neighbors,
And say, "Tomorrow is Saint Crispian."
Then will he strip his sleeve and show his scars,
[And say, "These wounds I had on Crispin's day."]
Old men forget; yet all shall be forgot,
But he'll remember with advantages
What feats he did that day. Then shall our names,
Familiar in his mouth as household words,
Harry the King, Bedford and Exeter,
Warwick and Talbot, Salisbury and Gloucester,
Be in their flowing cups freshly rememb'red.
This story shall the good man teach his son;
And Crispin Crispian shall ne'er go by,
From this day to the ending of the world,
But we in it shall be remembered—
We few, we happy few, we band of brothers.
For he today that sheds his blood with me
Shall be my brother; be he ne'er so vile,
This day shall gentle his condition.
And gentlemen in England now a-bed
Shall think themselves accurs'd they were not here,
And hold their manhoods cheap whiles any speaks
That fought with us upon Saint Crispin's day.

Enter Salisbury.

SALISBURY
My sovereign lord, bestow yourself with speed.

54 battle army **56 stay for** await **60 guard** (including a standard-bearer) **61 trumpet** trumpeter **63 outwear** waste

IV.iii. Location: The English camp.
2 battle army **6 buy** be with **10 kinsman** i.e., Westmorland, whose son had married Salisbury's daughter **13 mind** remind **14 fram'd** made, built

20–21 enow . . . loss enough loss for our country to suffer **25 upon my cost** at my expense **26 yearns** grieves **30 coz** cousin, kinsman **32 share from me** take from me as his share **37 crowns for convoy** travel money **39 That . . . us** that is afraid to risk his life in my company **40 feast of Crispian** St. Crispin's day, October 25. (Cripinus and Crispianus were martyrs who fled from Rome in the third century; they disguised themselves as shoemakers, and afterward became the patron saints of that craft.) **44 live** live to see **45 vigil** evening before a feast day **49 yet** in time **50 advantages** additions of his own **62 vile** lowly **63 gentle his condition** raise him to the rank of gentleman **68 bestow yourself** take up your battle position

The French are bravely in their battles set,
And will with all expedience charge on us.

KING
All things are ready, if our minds be so.

WESTMORLAND
Perish the man whose mind is backward now!

KING
Thou dost not wish more help from England, coz?

WESTMORLAND
God's will, my liege, would you and I alone,
Without more help, could fight this royal battle!

KING
Why, now thou hast unwish'd five thousand men,
Which likes me better than to wish us one.
You know your places. God be with you all!

Tucket. Enter Montjoy.

MONTJOY
Once more I come to know of thee, King Harry,
If for thy ransom thou wilt now compound,
Before thy most assured overthrow;
For certainly thou art so near the gulf,
Thou needs must be englutted. Besides, in mercy,
The Constable desires thee thou wilt mind
Thy followers of repentance, that their souls
May make a peaceful and a sweet retire
From off these fields, where, wretches, their poor bodies
Must lie and fester.

KING Who hath sent thee now?

MONTJOY
The Constable of France.

KING
I pray thee bear my former answer back:
Bid them achieve me and then sell my bones.
Good God, why should they mock poor fellows thus?
The man that once did sell the lion's skin,
While the beast liv'd, was kill'd with hunting him.
A many of our bodies shall no doubt
Find native graves, upon the which, I trust,
Shall witness live in brass of this day's work.
And those that leave their valiant bones in France,
Dying like men, though buried in your dunghills,
They shall be fam'd; for there the sun shall greet them,
And draw their honors reeking up to heaven,
Leaving their earthly parts to choke your clime,
The smell whereof shall breed a plague in France.
Mark then abounding valor in our English,
That, being dead, like to the bullet's crazing,
Break out into a second course of mischief,
Killing in relapse of mortality.
Let me speak proudly. Tell the Constable
We are but warriors for the working day.
Our gayness and our gilt are all besmirch'd
With rainy marching in the painful field.
There's not a piece of feather in our host—
Good argument, I hope, we will not fly—
And time hath worn us into slovenry.
But, by the mass, our hearts are in the trim!
And my poor soldiers tell me, yet ere night
They'll be in fresher robes, or they will pluck
The gay new coats o'er the French soldiers' heads
And turn them out of service. If they do this—
As, if God please, they shall—my ransom then
Will soon be levied. Herald, save thou thy labor.
Come thou no more for ransom, gentle herald.
They shall have none, I swear, but these my joints,
Which if they have as I will leave 'em them,
Shall yield them little, tell the Constable.

MONTJOY
I shall, King Harry. And so fare thee well.
Thou never shalt hear herald any more. *Exit.*

KING
I fear thou wilt once more come again for a ransom.

Enter York [and kneels].

YORK
My lord, most humbly on my knee I beg
The leading of the vaward.

KING
Take it, brave York. Now, soldiers, march away.
And how thou pleasest, God, dispose the day!
Exeunt.

[SCENE IV]

Alarum. Excursions. Enter Pistol, French Soldier, [and] Boy.

PISTOL Yield, cur!

FRENCH SOLDIER Je pense que vous êtes gentilhomme de bonne qualité.

PISTOL Qualtitie calmie custure me! Art thou a gentleman? What is thy name? Discuss.

FRENCH SOLDIER O Seigneur Dieu!

PISTOL
O, Signieur Dew should be a gentleman.
Perpend my words, O Signieur Dew, and mark:
O Signieur Dew, thou diest on point of fox,
Except, O signieur, thou do give to me
Egregious ransom. *[Threatens him with sword.]*

69 bravely . . . set finely arrayed in their battalions **70 expedience** speed **77 likes** pleases **80 compound** make terms **82 gulf** whirlpool **83 englutted** swallowed up **84 mind** remind **91 achieve** capture **96 native** in their own land (i.e., England) **101 reeking** breathing **105 crazing** grazing, rebounding **107 Killing . . . mortality** killing (their foes) as they (the English) fall back (decompose) into their elements; also, like the bullet, with a deadly rebound

109 for the working day i.e., to do serious work, not take a holiday **117 in fresher robes** i.e., in heavenly garb **119 turn . . . service** i.e., send them away stripped of their finery, like dismissed servants stripped of their livery **121 levied** collected **130 vaward** vanguard

IV.iv. Location: The field of battle.
s.d. Excursions sorties **2–3 Je . . . qualité** I think that you are a gentleman of high rank **4 calmie custure me** (These words are perhaps derived from the refrain of a popular song, supposed to be Irish, "Calen o custure me.") **5 Discuss** speak **6 O Seigneur Dieu** O Lord God **8 Perpend** attend to, consider **9 fox** sword **11 Egregious** huge

FRENCH SOLDIER O, prenez miséricorde! Ayez pitié de moi!

PISTOL
Moy shall not serve. I will have forty moys,
Or I will fetch thy rim out at thy throat
In drops of crimson blood.

FRENCH SOLDIER Est-il impossible d'échapper la force de ton bras?

PISTOL Brass, cur?
Thou damnèd and luxurious mountain goat,
Offer'st me brass?

FRENCH SOLDIER O pardonnez moi!

PISTOL
Say'st thou me so? Is that a ton of moys?
Come hither, boy. Ask me this slave in French
What is his name.

BOY Écoutez: comment êtes-vous appelé?

FRENCH SOLDIER Monsieur le Fer.

BOY He says his name is Master Fer.

PISTOL Master Fer! I'll fer him, and firk him, and ferret him. Discuss the same in French unto him.

BOY I do not know the French for fer, and ferret, and firk.

PISTOL
Bid him prepare, for I will cut his throat.

FRENCH SOLDIER Que dit-il, monsieur?

BOY Il me commande de vous dire que vous faites vous prêt; car ce soldat ici est disposé tout à cette heure de couper votre gorge.

PISTOL
Owy, cuppele gorge, permafoy,
Peasant, unless thou give me crowns, brave crowns,
Or mangled shalt thou be by this my sword.

FRENCH SOLDIER O, je vous supplie, pour l'amour de Dieu, me pardonner! Je suis gentilhomme de bonne maison. Gardez ma vie, et je vous donnerai deux cents écus.

PISTOL
What are his words?

BOY He prays you to save his life. He is a gentleman of a good house, and for his ransom he will give you two hundred crowns.

PISTOL
Tell him my fury shall abate, and I
The crowns will take.

FRENCH SOLDIER Petit monsieur, que dit-il?

BOY Encore qu'il est contre son jurement de pardonner aucun prisonnier, néanmoins, pour les écus que vous l'avez promis, il est content de vous donner la liberté, le franchisement.

FRENCH SOLDIER [*Kneeling*] Sur mes genoux je vous donne mille remercîments; et je m'estime heureux que je suis tombé entre les mains d'un chevalier, je pense, le plus brave, vaillant, et très distingué seigneur d'Angleterre.

PISTOL
Expound unto me, boy.

BOY He gives you, upon his knees, a thousand thanks, and he esteems himself happy that he hath fall'n into the hands of one, as he thinks, the most brave, valorous, and thrice-worthy signieur of England.

PISTOL
As I suck blood, I will some mercy show.
Follow me!

BOY Suivez-vous le grand capitaine. [*Exeunt Pistol and French Soldier.*] I did never know so full a voice issue from so empty a heart! But the saying is true, "The empty vessel makes the greatest sound." Bardolph and Nym had ten times more valor than this roaring devil i' th' old play, that every one may pare his nails with a wooden dagger, and they are both hang'd; and so would this be, if he durst steal anything adventurously. I must stay with the lackeys, with the luggage of our camp. The French might have a good prey of us, if he knew of it, for there is none to guard it but boys. *Exit.*

[SCENE V]

Enter Constable, Orleans, Bourbon, Dauphin, and Rambures.

CONSTABLE O diable!

ORLEANS O seigneur! Le jour est perdu, tout est perdu!

DAUPHIN
Mort Dieu, ma vie! All is confounded, all!
Reproach and everlasting shame
Sits mocking in our plumes. *A short alarum.*
O méchante fortune!
Do not run away.

CONSTABLE Why, all our ranks are broke.

DAUPHIN
O perdurable shame! Let's stab ourselves.
Be these the wretches that we play'd at dice for?

ORLEANS
Is this the king we sent to for his ransom?

BOURBON
Shame and eternal shame, nothing but shame!
Let us die! In once more! Back again!
And he that will not follow Bourbon now,
Let him go hence, and with his cap in hand,

12–13 O . . . moi Oh, have mercy! Take pity on me! **14 Moy** (Pistol, not understanding, takes *moi* for the name of a coin, or a sum of money.) **15 rim** midriff, diaphragm **17–18 Est-il . . . bras** is it impossible to escape the strength of your arm. (But Pistol takes *bras,* arm, for *brass.*) **20 luxurious** lecherous **26 Écoutez . . . appelé** listen: what is your name **29 firk** trounce. **ferret** worry (like a ferret) **34–37 Que . . . gorge** What does he say, sir? *Boy.* He bids me tell you that you must prepare yourself, because this soldier intends to cut your throat immediately **38 Owy** i.e., *oui,* yes. **permafoy** *per ma foi,* by my faith **41–44 O . . . écus** Oh, I pray you, for the love of God, to pardon me. I am a gentleman of a good house; preserve my life, and I shall give you two hundred crowns **51–55 Petit . . . franchisement** What does he say, little sir? *Boy.* Although it is against his oath to pardon any prisoner, nevertheless, for the sake of the crowns you have promised, he is willing to give you your liberty, your freedom

56–60 Sur . . . d'Angleterre On my knees I give you a thousand thanks; and I consider myself happy that I have fallen into the hands of a knight, as I think, the bravest, most valiant, and very distinguished gentleman in England **68 Suivez-vous . . . capitaine** follow the great captain **72 roaring devil** i.e., the devil in the morality play, a comic figure paired with the Vice who traditionally had a wooden dagger

IV.v. Location: The field of battle still.
1 O diable O the devil **2 O . . . perdu** O lord, the day is lost, all is lost **3 Mort Dieu, ma vie** by God's (Christ's) death, my life. **confounded** lost **5 O méchante fortune** malicious fortune **7 perdurable** everlasting

Like a base pandar, hold the chamber-door
Whilst by a slave, no gentler than my dog,
His fairest daughter is contaminated.

CONSTABLE
Disorder, that hath spoil'd us, friend us now!
Let us on heaps go offer up our lives. 18

ORLEANS
We are enow yet living in the field
To smother up the English in our throngs,
If any order might be thought upon.

BOURBON
The devil take order now! I'll to the throng.
Let life be short, else shame will be too long.
Exeunt.

[SCENE VI]

Alarum. Enter the King and his train, [Exeter, and others,] with prisoners.

KING
Well have we done, thrice valiant countrymen!
But all's not done; yet keep the French the field.

EXETER
The Duke of York commends him to your Majesty.

KING
Lives he, good uncle? Thrice within this hour
I saw him down, thrice up again, and fighting.
From helmet to the spur all blood he was.

EXETER
In which array, brave soldier, doth he lie,
Larding the plain; and by his bloody side, 8
Yoke-fellow to his honor-owing wounds, 9
The noble Earl of Suffolk also lies.
Suffolk first died; and York, all haggled over, 11
Comes to him, where in gore he lay insteep'd,
And takes him by the beard, kisses the gashes
That bloodily did yawn upon his face.
He cries aloud, "Tarry, my cousin Suffolk!
My soul shall thine keep company to heaven;
Tarry, sweet soul, for mine, then fly abreast,
As in this glorious and well-foughten field
We kept together in our chivalry!"
Upon these words I came and cheer'd him up.
He smil'd me in the face, raught me his hand, 21
And, with a feeble gripe, says, "Dear my lord,
Commend my service to my sovereign."
So did he turn, and over Suffolk's neck
He threw his wounded arm and kiss'd his lips;
And so, espous'd to death, with blood he seal'd
A testament of noble-ending love.
The pretty and sweet manner of it forc'd
Those waters from me which I would have stopp'd,
But I had not so much of man in me,
And all my mother came into mine eyes 31
And gave me up to tears.

KING
I blame you not;
For, hearing this, I must perforce compound 33
With mistful eyes, or they will issue too. *Alarum.* 34
But, hark, what new alarum is this same?
The French have reinforc'd their scatter'd men.
Then every soldier kill his prisoners! 37
Give the word through. *Exit [with others].*

[SCENE VII]

Enter Fluellen and Gower.

FLUELLEN Kill the poys and the luggage! 'Tis expressly 1
against the law of arms. 'Tis as arrant a piece of knavery, mark you now, as can be offert; in your conscience, now, is it not?

GOWER 'Tis certain there's not a boy left alive; and the cowardly rascals that ran from the battle ha' done this slaughter. Besides, they have burn'd and carried away all that was in the King's tent; wherefore the King, most worthily, hath caus'd every soldier to cut his prisoner's throat. O, 'tis a gallant king!

FLUELLEN Ay, he was porn at Monmouth, Captain 11
Gower. What call you the town's name where Alexander the Pig was born?

GOWER Alexander the Great.

FLUELLEN Why, I pray you, is not "pig" great? The pig, or the great, or the mighty, or the huge, or the magnanimous, are all one reckonings, save the phrase is a little variations.

GOWER I think Alexander the Great was born in Macedon. His father was call'd Philip of Macedon, as I take it.

FLUELLEN I think it is in Macedon where Alexander is porn. I tell you, captain, if you look in the maps of the 'orld, I warrant you sall find, in the comparisons between Macedon and Monmouth, that the situations, look you, is both alike. There is a river in Macedon, and there is also moreover a river at Monmouth. It is call'd Wye at Monmouth, but it is out of my prains what is the name of the other river; but 'tis all one, 'tis alike as my fingers is to my fingers, and there is salmons in both. If you mark Alexander's life well, Harry
of Monmouth's life is come after it indifferent well, for 32
there is figures in all things. Alexander, God knows, 33
and you know, in his rages, and his furies, and his wraths, and his cholers, and his moods, and his displeasures, and his indignations, and also being a little

18 on in

IV.vi. Location: The field of battle still.
8 Larding fattening, enriching (with his blood) **9 honor-owing** honor-owning, honorable **11 haggled over** mangled, hacked **21 raught** reached

31 my mother i.e., the tenderer part of me **33 compound** come to terms **34 issue** i.e., issue forth tears **37 kill his prisoners** (This follows Holinshed, who says that Henry, alarmed by the outcry of the lackeys and boys of the camp, feared a new attack and ordered the prisoners killed as a means of precaution. Gower, IV.vii.9–10, attributes the King's action to revenge.)

IV.vii. Location: The field of battle still.
1 luggage i.e., lackeys guarding the luggage **11 Monmouth** (I.e., in Wales.) **32 is . . . well** resembles it fairly well **33 figures** comparisons, similes

intoxicates in his prains, did, in his ales and his angers, look you, kill his best friend, Cleitus.

GOWER Our King is not like him in that. He never kill'd any of his friends.

FLUELLEN It is not well done, mark you now, to take the tales out of my mouth, ere it is made and finished. I speak but in the figures and comparisons of it. As Alexander kill'd his friend Cleitus, being in his ales and his cups, so also Harry Monmouth, being in his right wits and his good judgments, turn'd away the fat knight with the great belly doublet. He was full of jests, and gipes, and knaveries, and mocks. I have forgot his name.

GOWER Sir John Falstaff.

FLUELLEN That is he. I'll tell you there is good men porn at Monmouth.

GOWER Here comes his Majesty.

Alarum. Enter King Harry, [Warwick, Gloucester, Exeter, and others,] and Bourbon with [other] prisoners. Flourish.

KING
I was not angry since I came to France
Until this instant. Take a trumpet, herald;
Ride thou unto the horsemen on yond hill.
If they will fight with us, bid them come down,
Or void the field. They do offend our sight.
If they'll do neither, we will come to them,
And make them skirr away, as swift as stones
Enforced from the old Assyrian slings.
Besides, we'll cut the throats of those we have,
And not a man of them that we shall take
Shall taste our mercy. Go and tell them so.
[Exit a Herald.]

Enter Montjoy.

EXETER
Here comes the herald of the French, my liege.

GLOUCESTER
His eyes are humbler than they us'd to be.

KING
How now, what means this, herald? Know'st thou not
That I have fin'd these bones of mine for ransom?
Com'st thou again for ransom?

MONTJOY No, great King.
I come to thee for charitable license,
That we may wander o'er this bloody field
To book our dead, and then to bury them;
To sort our nobles from our common men.
For many of our princes—woe the while!—
Lie drown'd and soak'd in mercenary blood;
So do our vulgar drench their peasant limbs
In blood of princes; and their wounded steeds
Fret fetlock deep in gore and with wild rage
Yerk out their armed heels at their dead masters,
Killing them twice. O, give us leave, great King,
To view the field in safety, and dispose
Of their dead bodies!

KING I tell thee truly, herald,
I know not if the day be ours or no,
For yet a many of your horsemen peer
And gallop o'er the field.

MONTJOY The day is yours.

KING
Praised be God, and not our strength, for it!
What is this castle call'd that stands hard by?

MONTJOY
They call it Agincourt.

KING
Then call we this the field of Agincourt,
Fought on the day of Crispin Crispianus.

FLUELLEN Your grandfather of famous memory, an 't please your Majesty, and your great-uncle Edward the Plack Prince of Wales, as I have read in the chronicles, fought a most prave pattle here in France.

KING They did, Fluellen.

FLUELLEN Your Majesty says very true. If your Majesties is rememb'red of it, the Welshmen did good service in a garden where leeks did grow, wearing leeks in their Monmouth caps, which, your Majesty know, to this hour is an honorable badge of the service; and I do believe your Majesty takes no scorn to wear the leek upon Saint Tavy's day.

KING
I wear it for a memorable honor,
For I am Welsh, you know, good countryman.

FLUELLEN All the water in Wye cannot wash your Majesty's Welsh plood out of your pody, I can tell you that. God pless it and preserve it, as long as it pleases his Grace, and his Majesty too!

KING Thanks, good my countryman.

FLUELLEN By Jeshu, I am your Majesty's countryman, I care not who know it. I will confess it to all the 'orld. I need not to be asham'd of your Majesty, prais'd be God, so long as your Majesty is an honest man.

KING
God keep me so!

Enter Williams [with a glove in his cap].

Our heralds go with him.
Bring me just notice of the numbers dead
On both our parts. Call yonder fellow hither.
[Exeunt Heralds and Gower with Montjoy.]

EXETER Soldier, you must come to the King.

KING Soldier, why wear'st thou that glove in thy cap?

WILLIAMS An 't please your Majesty, 'tis the gage of one that I should fight withal, if he be alive.

KING An Englishman?

WILLIAMS An 't please your Majesty, a rascal that swagger'd with me last night, who, if alive and ever dare

38 Cleitus a general and close associate of Alexander, whom Alexander killed in a drinking bout **47 great belly doublet** a man's close-fitting jacket in which the lower part was stuffed out with bombast or padding **48 gipes** japes **55 trumpet** trumpeter **58 void** leave **60 skirr** scurry **61 Enforced** discharged **68 fin'd . . . mine** i.e., agreed to pay as a fine or ransom only these bones of mine and no more **72 book** record **75 mercenary** i.e., of common soldiers, who fought for pay **76 vulgar** commoners

79 Yerk kick **84 peer** appear **91 grandfather** i.e., great-grandfather, Edward III **99 Monmouth caps** round and rimless caps with a tapering crown, commonly worn by the Welsh **115 just** exact

to challenge this glove, I have sworn to take him a box o' th' ear; or if I can see my glove in his cap, which he swore, as he was a soldier, he would wear if alive, I will strike it out soundly.

KING What think you, Captain Fluellen? Is it fit this soldier keep his oath?

FLUELLEN He is a craven and a villain else, an 't please your Majesty, in my conscience.

KING It may be his enemy is a gentleman of great sort, quite from the answer of his degree.

FLUELLEN Though he be as good a gentleman as the devil is, as Lucifer and Belzebub himself, it is necessary, look your Grace, that he keep his vow and his oath. If he be perjur'd, see you now, his reputation is as arrant a villain and a Jack sauce as ever his black shoe trod upon God's ground and His earth, in my conscience, la!

KING Then keep thy vow, sirrah, when thou meet'st the fellow.

WILLIAMS So I will, my liege, as I live.

KING Who serv'st thou under?

WILLIAMS Under Captain Gower, my liege.

FLUELLEN Gower is a good captain, and is good knowledge and literatured in the wars.

KING Call him hither to me, soldier.

WILLIAMS I will, my liege. *Exit.*

KING Here, Fluellen, wear thou this favor for me and stick it in thy cap. [*Gives Fluellen Williams' glove.*] When Alençon and myself were down together, I pluck'd this glove from his helm. If any man challenge this, he is a friend to Alençon, and an enemy to our person. If thou encounter any such, apprehend him, an thou dost me love.

FLUELLEN [*Putting the glove in his cap*] Your Grace doo's me as great honors as can be desir'd in the hearts of his subjects. I would fain see the man, that has but two legs, that shall find himself aggrief'd at this glove, that is all. But I would fain see it once, an please God of his grace that I might see.

KING Know'st thou Gower?

FLUELLEN He is my dear friend, an please you.

KING Pray thee, go seek him, and bring him to my tent.

FLUELLEN I will fetch him. *Exit.*

KING
My Lord of Warwick, and my brother Gloucester,
Follow Fluellen closely at the heels.
The glove which I have given him for a favor
May haply purchase him a box o' th' ear.
It is the soldier's; I by bargain should
Wear it myself. Follow, good cousin Warwick.
If that the soldier strike him, as I judge
By his blunt bearing he will keep his word,
Some sudden mischief may arise of it;
For I do know Fluellen valiant
And touch'd with choler, hot as gunpowder,
And quickly will return an injury.
Follow, and see there be no harm between them.
Go you with me, uncle of Exeter. *Exeunt* [*severally*].

133 quite . . . degree i.e., too high in rank to answer the challenge of one so low **138 Jack sauce** saucy knave **177 touch'd with choler** hot-tempered **178 injury** insult

[SCENE VIII]

Enter Gower and Williams.

WILLIAMS I warrant it is to knight you, captain.

Enter Fluellen.

FLUELLEN God's will and his pleasure, captain, I beseech you now, come apace to the King. There is more good toward you peradventure than is in your knowledge to dream of.

WILLIAMS Sir, know you this glove?

FLUELLEN Know the glove? I know the glove is a glove.

WILLIAMS I know this; and thus I challenge it. *Strikes him.*

FLUELLEN 'Sblood, an arrant traitor as any 's in the universal world, or in France, or in England!

GOWER How now, sir? You villain!

WILLIAMS Do you think I'll be forsworn?

FLUELLEN Stand away, Captain Gower. I will give treason his payment into plows, I warrant you.

WILLIAMS I am no traitor.

FLUELLEN That's a lie in thy throat. I charge you in his Majesty's name, apprehend him. He's a friend of the Duke Alençon's.

Enter Warwick and Gloucester.

WARWICK How now, how now, what's the matter?

FLUELLEN My Lord of Warwick, here is—praised be God for it!—a most contagious treason come to light, look you, as you shall desire in a summer's day.—Here is his Majesty.

Enter King [*Henry*] *and Exeter.*

KING How now, what's the matter?

FLUELLEN My liege, here is a villain and a traitor, that, look your Grace, has struck the glove which your Majesty is take out of the helmet of Alençon.

WILLIAMS My liege, this was my glove; here is the fellow of it. [*Shows his other glove.*] And he that I gave it to in change promis'd to wear it in his cap. I promis'd to strike him, if he did. I met this man with my glove in his cap, and I have been as good as my word.

FLUELLEN Your Majesty hear now, saving your Majesty's manhood, what an arrant, rascally, beggarly, lousy knave it is. I hope your Majesty is pear me testimony and witness, and will avouchment, that this is the glove of Alençon that your Majesty is give me, in your conscience, now.

KING Give me thy glove, soldier. Look, here is the fellow of it. [*Shows his other glove.*]
'Twas I, indeed, thou promised'st to strike,
And thou hast given me most bitter terms.

FLUELLEN An please your Majesty, let his neck answer for it, if there is any martial law in the world.

IV.viii. Location: Before King Henry's Pavilion.
9 'Sblood by His (Christ's) blood **14 his** its **21 contagious** noxious **30 change** exchange **35 is pear** will bear **36 avouchment** avouch **42 terms** words

KING
How canst thou make me satisfaction?

WILLIAMS All offenses, my lord, come from the heart. Never came any from mine that might offend your Majesty.

KING
It was ourself thou didst abuse.

WILLIAMS Your Majesty came not like yourself. You appear'd to me but as a common man—witness the night, your garments, your lowliness. And what your Highness suffer'd under that shape, I beseech you take it for your own fault and not mine; for had you been as I took you for, I made no offense. Therefore, I beseech your Highness, pardon me.

KING
Here, uncle Exeter, fill this glove with crowns,
And give it to this fellow. Keep it, fellow,
And wear it for an honor in thy cap
Till I do challenge it. Give him the crowns.
[*Exeter gives the glove and gold to Williams.*]
And, captain, you must needs be friends with him.

FLUELLEN By this day and this light, the fellow has mettle enough in his belly. Hold, there is twelvepence for you. [*Offers coin.*] And I pray you to serve God, and keep you out of prawls, and prabbles, and quarrels, and dissensions, and, I warrant you, it is the better for you.

WILLIAMS I will none of your money.

FLUELLEN It is with a good will. I can tell you, it will serve you to mend your shoes. Come, wherefore should you be so pashful? Your shoes is not so good. 'Tis a good silling, I warrant you, or I will change it.

Enter [*an English*] *Herald.*

KING
Now, herald, are the dead numb'red?

HERALD
Here is the number of the slaught'red French.
[*Gives a paper.*]

KING
What prisoners of good sort are taken, uncle?

EXETER
Charles Duke of Orleans, nephew to the King,
John Duke of Bourbon, and Lord Bouciqualt.
Of other lords and barons, knights and squires,
Full fifteen hundred, besides common men.

KING
This note doth tell me of ten thousand French
That in the field lie slain. Of princes, in this
number,
And nobles bearing banners, there lie dead
One hundred twenty-six; added to these,
Of knights, esquires, and gallant gentlemen,
Eight thousand and four hundred, of the which
Five hundred were but yesterday dubb'd knights.
So that, in these ten thousand they have lost,
There are but sixteen hundred mercenaries;
The rest are princes, barons, lords, knights, squires,
And gentlemen of blood and quality.
The names of those their nobles that lie dead:
Charles Delabreth, High Constable of France,
Jacques of Chatillion, Admiral of France,
The master of the cross-bows, Lord Rambures,
Great Master of France, the brave Sir Guichard
Dauphin,
John Duke of Alençon, Anthony Duke of Brabant,
The brother to the Duke of Burgundy,
And Edward Duke of Bar; of lusty earls,
Grandpré and Roussi, Faulconbridge and Foix,
Beaumont and Marle, Vaudemont and Lestrale.
Here was a royal fellowship of death!
Where is the number of our English dead?
[*Herald gives him another paper.*]
Edward the Duke of York, the Earl of Suffolk,
Sir Richard Ketly, Davy Gam, esquire;
None else of name, and of all other men
But five and twenty. O God, thy arm was here!
And not to us, but to thy arm alone,
Ascribe we all! When, without stratagem,
But in plain shock and even play of battle,
Was ever known so great and little loss
On one part and on th' other? Take it, God,
For it is none but thine!

EXETER
'Tis wonderful!

KING
Come, go we in procession to the village.
And be it death proclaimed through our host
To boast of this or take that praise from God
Which is his only.

FLUELLEN Is it not lawful, an please your Majesty, to tell how many is kill'd?

KING
Yes, captain; but with this acknowledgment,
That God fought for us.

FLUELLEN Yes, my conscience, he did us great good.

KING
Do we all holy rites.
Let there be sung "Non nobis" and "Te Deum,"
The dead with charity enclos'd in clay,
And then to Calais; and to England then,
Where ne'er from France arriv'd more happy men.
Exeunt.

ACT V • [PROLOGUE]

Enter Chorus.

[CHORUS]
Vouchsafe to those that have not read the story,
That I may prompt them; and of such as have,
I humbly pray them to admit th' excuse
Of time, of numbers, and due course of things,
Which cannot in their huge and proper life

52 lowliness humble mien **75 good sort** high rank **76–112 Charles . . . thine** (The catalogue of the captured and slain is from Holinshed.)

105 name rank, importance **122 Non nobis** i.e., Psalm 115, beginning, "Not unto us, O Lord, not unto us, but unto thy name give glory." **Te Deum** a hymn of thanksgiving, beginning, "We thank thee O God" **125 happy** fortunate

V. Chorus. (Between Acts IV and V there is historically an interval of about five years during which Henry made a second campaign in France that brought the French to terms in the Treaty of Troyes, with which the play ends.)
3 admit th' excuse excuse our handling

Be here presented. Now we bear the King
Toward Calais. Grant him there. There seen,
Heave him away upon your winged thoughts
Athwart the sea. Behold, the English beach
Pales in the flood with men, wives, and boys,
Whose shouts and claps out-voice the deep-mouth'd sea,
Which like a mighty whiffler 'fore the King
Seems to prepare his way. So let him land,
And solemnly see him set on to London.
So swift a pace hath thought that even now
You may imagine him upon Blackheath,
Where that his lords desire him to have borne
His bruised helmet and his bended sword
Before him through the city. He forbids it,
Being free from vainness and self-glorious pride,
Giving full trophy, signal, and ostent
Quite from himself to God. But now behold,
In the quick forge and working-house of thought,
How London doth pour out her citizens!
The Mayor and all his brethren in best sort,
Like to the senators of th' antique Rome,
With the plebeians swarming at their heels,
Go forth and fetch their conqu'ring Caesar in;
As by a lower but loving likelihood,
Were now the general of our gracious Empress,
As in good time he may, from Ireland coming,
Bringing rebellion broached on his sword,
How many would the peaceful city quit
To welcome him! Much more, and much more cause,
Did they this Harry. Now in London place him;
As yet the lamentation of the French
Invites the King of England's stay at home;
The Emperor's coming in behalf of France,
To order peace between them; and omit
All the occurrences, whatever chanc'd,
Till Harry's back-return again to France.
There must we bring him; and myself have play'd
The interim, by rememb'ring you 'tis past.
Then brook abridgment, and your eyes advance,
After your thoughts, straight back again to France.
Exit.

[SCENE I]

Enter Fluellen [*with a leek in his cap*] *and Gower.*

GOWER Nay, that's right. But why wear you your leek today? Saint Davy's day is past.

FLUELLEN There is occasions and causes why and wherefore in all things. I will tell you asse my friend, Captain Gower. The rascally, scald, beggarly, lousy, pragging knave, Pistol, which you and yourself and all the world know to be no petter than a fellow, look you now, of no merits, he is come to me and prings me pread and salt yesterday, look you, and bid me eat my leek. It was in a place where I could not breed no contention with him; but I will be so bold as to wear it in my cap till I see him once again, and then I will tell him a little piece of my desires.

Enter Pistol.

GOWER Why, here he comes, swelling like a turkey-cock.

FLUELLEN 'Tis no matter for his swellings nor his turkey-cocks. God pless you, Aunchient Pistol! You scurvy, lousy knave, God pless you!

PISTOL
Ha, art thou bedlam? Dost thou thirst, base Troyan,
To have me fold up Parca's fatal web?
Hence, I am qualmish at the smell of leek.

FLUELLEN I peseech you heartily, scurvy, lousy knave, at my desires, and my requests, and my petitions, to eat, look you, this leek. [*He offers the leek.*] Because, look you, you do not love it, nor your affections and your appetites and your disgestions doo's not agree with it, I would desire you to eat it.

PISTOL
Not for Cadwallader and all his goats.

FLUELLEN There is one goat for you. (*Strikes him.*) Will you be so good, scald knave, as eat it?

PISTOL
Base Troyan, thou shalt die.

FLUELLEN You say very true, scald knave, when God's will is. I will desire you to live in the mean time, and eat your victuals. Come, there is sauce for it. [*Strikes him.*] You call'd me yesterday mountain-squire, but I will make you today a squire of low degree. I pray you, fall to. If you can mock a leek, you can eat a leek.

GOWER Enough, captain, you have astonish'd him.

FLUELLEN I say, I will make him eat some part of my leek, or I will peat his pate four days. Bite, I pray you; it is good for your green wound and your ploody coxcomb.

PISTOL
Must I bite?

FLUELLEN Yes, certainly, and out of doubt and out of question too, and ambiguities.

PISTOL
By this leek, I will most horribly revenge—
I eat and eat—I swear—

FLUELLEN Eat, I pray you. Will you have some more sauce to your leek? There is not enough leek to swear by.

10 Pales in hems in, surrounds **12 whiffler** an usher heading the procession to clear the way **16 Blackheath** open area just outside London, to the southeast **21 signal** token (of victory). **ostent** external show **25 sort** array **29–34 As . . . him** (Seemingly an allusion to the Earl of Essex, who left London on his Irish expedition on March 27, 1599; he returned unsuccessful and under a cloud on September 28 of the same year. These lines, therefore, were probably written between the dates mentioned.) **29 a . . . likelihood** a less exalted comparison but one that shows much love **30 Empress** i.e., Elizabeth **32 broached** transfixed, spitted **36–37 As . . . home** i.e., the French are so dejected that Henry can stay in England without fear of loss in France **38 Emperor's coming** (The Holy Roman Emperor, Sigismund, came to England on behalf of France in May 1416.) **41 Harry's back-return** i.e., Henry's second campaign, commencing in 1417 **43 rememb'ring** reminding **44 brook** tolerate, excuse

V.i. Location: France. The English camp.

5 scald scurvy **19 bedlam** crazy. **Troyan** i.e., rascal **20 Parca's** (The Parcae, or fates, spun, drew out, and cut the thread of destiny.) **28 Cadwallader** last king of the Welsh. **goats** (Pistol makes the customary taunt that the Welsh were goatherds.) **35 mountain-squire** i.e., a squire owning mountainous, poor land **36 squire of low degree** (Allusion to a popular medieval romance, *The Squire of Low Degree.*) **38 astonish'd** dazed, terrified **41 green** raw **41–42 coxcomb** fool's cap; here, the scalp

PISTOL
Quiet thy cudgel; thou dost see I eat.

FLUELLEN Much good do you, scald knave, heartily. Nay, pray you, throw none away; the skin is good for your broken coxcomb. When you take occasions to see leeks hereafter, I pray you, mock at 'em; that is all.

PISTOL
Good.

FLUELLEN Ay, leeks is good. Hold you, there is a groat to heal your pate. [*Offers a coin.*]

PISTOL
Me a groat?

FLUELLEN Yes, verily and in truth, you shall take it, or I have another leek in my pocket, which you shall eat.

PISTOL
I take thy groat in earnest of revenge.

FLUELLEN If I owe you any thing, I will pay you in cudgels. You shall be a woodmonger, and buy nothing of me but cudgels. God buy you, and keep you, and heal your pate. *Exit.*

PISTOL
All hell shall stir for this.

GOWER Go, go; you are a counterfeit cowardly knave. Will you mock at an ancient tradition, begun upon an honorable respect, and worn as a memorable trophy of predeceas'd valor, and dare not avouch in your deeds any of your words? I have seen you gleeking and galling at this gentleman twice or thrice. You thought, because he could not speak English in the native garb, he could not therefore handle an English cudgel. You find it otherwise; and henceforth let a Welsh correction teach you a good English condition. Fare ye well.
Exit.

PISTOL
Doth Fortune play the huswife with me now?
News have I, that my Doll is dead i' th' spital
Of a malady of France,
And there my rendezvous is quite cut off.
Old I do wax, and from my weary limbs
Honor is cudgel'd. Well, bawd I'll turn,
And something lean to cutpurse of quick hand.
To England will I steal, and there I'll steal;
And patches will I get unto these cudgel'd scars,
And swear I got them in the Gallia wars. *Exit.*

[SCENE II]

Enter, at one door, King Henry, Exeter, Bedford, [*Gloucester,*] *Warwick,* [*Westmorland,*] *and other Lords; at another, Queen Isabel, the* [*French*] *King, the Duke of Burgundy,* [*the Princess Katharine, Alice,*] *and other French.*

KING HENRY
Peace to this meeting, wherefore we are met!
Unto our brother France, and to our sister,
Health and fair time of day; joy and good wishes
To our most fair and princely cousin Katharine;
And, as a branch and member of this royalty,
By whom this great assembly is contriv'd,
We do salute you, Duke of Burgundy;
And, princes French, and peers, health to you all!

FRENCH KING
Right joyous are we to behold your face,
Most worthy brother England. Fairly met!
So are you, princes English, every one.

QUEEN ISABEL
So happy be the issue, brother England,
Of this good day and of this gracious meeting,
As we are now glad to behold your eyes—
Your eyes, which hitherto have borne in them
Against the French that met them in their bent
The fatal balls of murdering basilisks.
The venom of such looks, we fairly hope,
Have lost their quality, and that this day
Shall change all griefs and quarrels into love.

KING HENRY
To cry amen to that, thus we appear.

QUEEN ISABEL
You English princes all, I do salute you.

BURGUNDY
My duty to you both, on equal love,
Great Kings of France and England! That I have labor'd
With all my wits, my pains, and strong endeavors
To bring your most imperial Majesties
Unto this bar and royal interview,
Your mightiness on both parts best can witness.
Since then my office hath so far prevail'd
That, face to face and royal eye to eye,
You have congreeted, let it not disgrace me
If I demand, before this royal view,
What rub or what impediment there is
Why that the naked, poor, and mangled Peace,
Dear nurse of arts, plenties, and joyful births,
Should not in this best garden of the world,
Our fertile France, put up her lovely visage?
Alas, she hath from France too long been chas'd,
And all her husbandry doth lie on heaps,
Corrupting in it own fertility.
Her vine, the merry cheerer of the heart,
Unpruned dies; her hedges even-pleach'd,
Like prisoners wildly overgrown with hair,
Put forth disorder'd twigs; her fallow leas
The darnel, hemlock, and rank fumitory
Doth root upon, while that the coulter rusts
That should deracinate such savagery.
The even mead, that erst brought sweetly forth
The freckled cowslip, burnet, and green clover,
Wanting the scythe, all uncorrected, rank,

57 groat fourpenny coin **70 respect** consideration **71 predeceas'd valor** valor of those now dead **72–73 gleeking and galling** mocking and scoffing **79 huswife** hussy, fickle one **80 Doll** (An error for *Nell;* may indicate an earlier version in which the speaker of these lines was Falstaff.) **spital** hospital **81 malady of France** venereal disease **85 something lean to** incline somewhat to **88 Gallia** French

V.ii. Location: France. A royal palace.

5 royalty royal family **16 in their bent** (1) as they were directed (2) in their glance **17 fatal balls** (1) cannon balls (2) eyeballs. **basilisks** (1) large cannon (2) monsters supposed to kill with their gaze **27 bar** court **31 congreeted** greeted each other **33 rub** obstacle. (A term from bowls.) **37 put up** show **40 it** its **42 even-pleach'd** smoothly intertwined **44 fallow leas** uncultivated open fields **45 darnel . . . fumitory** i.e., weeds that grow in cultivated land **46 coulter** cutting blade in front of the ploughshare **47 deracinate** root out **48 erst** formerly **49 burnet** a herb **50 Wanting** lacking

Conceives by idleness, and nothing teems
But hateful docks, rough thistles, kecksies, burrs,
Losing both beauty and utility.
And all our vineyards, fallows, meads, and hedges,
Defective in their natures, grow to wildness.
Even so our houses and ourselves and children
Have lost, or do not learn for want of time,
The sciences that should become our country,
But grow like savages—as soldiers will
That nothing do but meditate on blood—
To swearing and stern looks, diffus'd attire,
And everything that seems unnatural.
Which to reduce into our former favor
You are assembled, and my speech entreats
That I may know the let why gentle Peace
Should not expel these inconveniences,
And bless us with her former qualities.

KING HENRY
If, Duke of Burgundy, you would the peace,
Whose want gives growth to th' imperfections
Which you have cited, you must buy that peace
With full accord to all our just demands,
Whose tenors and particular effects
You have enschedul'd briefly in your hands.

BURGUNDY
The King hath heard them, to the which as yet
There is no answer made.

KING HENRY Well then, the peace,
Which you before so urg'd, lies in his answer.

FRENCH KING
I have but with a cursitory eye
O'erglanc'd the articles. Pleaseth your Grace
To appoint some of your council presently
To sit with us once more, with better heed
To re-survey them, we will suddenly
Pass our accept and peremptory answer.

KING HENRY
Brother, we shall. Go, uncle Exeter,
And brother Clarence, and you, brother Gloucester,
Warwick, and Huntingdon, go with the King,
And take with you free power to ratify,
Augment, or alter, as your wisdoms best
Shall see advantageable for our dignity,
Anything in or out of our demands,
And we'll consign thereto. Will you, fair sister,
Go with the princes, or stay here with us?

QUEEN ISABEL
Our gracious brother, I will go with them.
Happily a woman's voice may do some good,
When articles too nicely urg'd be stood on.

KING HENRY
Yet leave our cousin Katharine here with us.
She is our capital demand, compris'd
Within the fore-rank of our articles.

QUEEN ISABEL
She hath good leave.

Exeunt omnes. Mane[n]t King [Henry] and Katharine [with Alice].

KING HENRY Fair Katharine, and most fair,
Will you vouchsafe to teach a soldier terms
Such as will enter at a lady's ear
And plead his love-suit to her gentle heart?

KATHARINE Your Majesty shall mock at me. I cannot speak your England.

KING HENRY O fair Katharine, if you will love me soundly with your French heart, I will be glad to hear you confess it brokenly with your English tongue. Do you like me, Kate?

KATHARINE Pardonnez-moi, I cannot tell wat is "like me."

KING HENRY An angel is like you, Kate, and you are like an angel.

KATHARINE Que dit-il? Que je suis semblable à les anges?

ALICE Oui, vraiment, sauf votre Grâce, ainsi dit-il.

KING HENRY I said so, dear Katharine; and I must not blush to affirm it.

KATHARINE O bon Dieu! Les langues des hommes sont pleines de tromperies.

KING HENRY What says she, fair one? That the tongues of men are full of deceits?

ALICE Oui, dat de tongues of de mans is be full of deceits. Dat is de Princess.

KING HENRY The Princess is the better Englishwoman. I' faith, Kate, my wooing is fit for thy understanding. I am glad thou canst speak no better English, for, if thou couldst, thou wouldst find me such a plain king that thou wouldst think I had sold my farm to buy my crown. I know no ways to mince it in love, but directly to say, "I love you." Then if you urge me farther than to say, "do you in faith?" I wear out my suit. Give me your answer, i' faith, do, and so clap hands and a bargain. How say you, lady?

KATHARINE Sauf votre honneur, me understand well.

KING HENRY Marry, if you would put me to verses or to dance for your sake, Kate, why you undid me. For the one, I have neither words nor measure, and for the other, I have no strength in measure, yet a reasonable measure in strength. If I could win a lady at leap-frog, or by vaulting into my saddle with my armor on my back, under the correction of bragging be it spoken, I should quickly leap into a wife. Or if I might buffet for my love, or bound my horse for her favors, I could lay on like a butcher and sit like a jackanapes, never off. But, before God, Kate, I cannot look greenly, nor gasp out my eloquence, nor I have no cunning in protestation—only downright oaths, which I never use till urg'd, nor never break for urging. If thou canst love a fellow of this temper, Kate, whose face is not worth sunburning, that never looks in his glass for love of

51 Conceives gives birth (to weeds) **52 kecksies** dry-stemmed plants, possibly dried hemlock stalks **54 fallows** land plowed and left lying **55 Defective . . . natures** i.e., perverted from their natural function, which is to grow useful plants **61 diffus'd** disordered **63 reduce . . . favor** return to our former good appearance **65 let** hindrance **68 would** wish **72 tenors** general purport. **particular effects** specific details **73 enschedul'd** drawn up in writing **77 cursitory** cursory, hasty **78 Pleaseth** may it please **81 suddenly** speedily **82 Pass . . . answer** deliver an answer acceptable to us and final, decisive **90 consign** agree, subscribe **94 nicely** punctiliously, with insistence on detail. **stood on** insisted on **96 capital** chief

112–114 Que . . . ainsi dit-il What does he say? That I am like the angels? *Alice.* Yes, truly, save your Grace, he says so **123 the better Englishwoman** i.e., she has a true Englishwoman's modesty and mistrust of flattery **130 wear out my suit** expend all my resources as a wooer **131 clap** clasp **136 measure** meter **137 measure** dance **138 measure** amount **141 buffet** box **142 bound** make prance **143 jackanapes** ape, monkey

anything he sees there, let thine eye be thy cook. I speak to thee plain soldier. If thou canst love me for this, take me. If not, to say to thee that I shall die, is true; but for thy love, by the Lord, no. Yet I love thee too. And while thou liv'st, dear Kate, take a fellow of plain and uncoin'd constancy, for he perforce must do thee right, because he hath not the gift to woo in other places. For these fellows of infinite tongue, that can rhyme themselves into ladies' favors, they do always reason themselves out again. What? A speaker is but a prater, a rhyme is but a ballad. A good leg will fall, a straight back will stoop, a black beard will turn white, a curl'd pate will grow bald, a fair face will wither, a full eye will wax hollow; but a good heart, Kate, is the sun and the moon—or rather the sun and not the moon, for it shines bright and never changes, but keeps his course truly. If thou would have such a one, take me. And take me, take a soldier; take a soldier, take a king. And what say'st thou then to my love? Speak, my fair, and fairly, I pray thee.

KATHARINE Is it possible dat I sould love de ennemie of France?

KING HENRY No, it is not possible you should love the enemy of France, Kate; but, in loving me, you should love the friend of France, for I love France so well that I will not part with a village of it. I will have it all mine. And, Kate, when France is mine and I am yours, then yours is France and you are mine.

KATHARINE I cannot tell wat is dat.

KING HENRY No, Kate? I will tell thee in French, which I am sure will hang upon my tongue like a new-married wife about her husband's neck, hardly to be shook off. Je quand sur le possession de France, et quand vous avez le possession de moi—let me see, what then? Saint Denis be my speed!—donc votre est France et vous êtes mienne. It is as easy for me, Kate, to conquer the kingdom as to speak so much more French. I shall never move thee in French, unless it be to laugh at me.

KATHARINE Sauf votre honneur, le François que vous parlez, il est meilleur que l' Anglois lequel je parle.

KING HENRY No, faith, is 't not, Kate. But thy speaking of my tongue, and I thine, most truly-falsely, must needs be granted to be much at one. But, Kate, dost thou understand thus much English: Canst thou love me?

KATHARINE I cannot tell.

KING HENRY Can any of your neighbors tell, Kate? I'll ask them. Come, I know thou lovest me. And at night, when you come into your closet, you'll question this gentlewoman about me; and I know, Kate, you will to her dispraise those parts in me that you love with your heart. But, good Kate, mock me mercifully, the rather, gentle Princess, because I love thee cruelly. If ever thou beest mine, Kate, as I have a saving faith within me tells me thou shalt, I get thee with scambling, and thou must therefore needs prove a good soldier-breeder. Shall not thou and I, between Saint Denis and Saint George, compound a boy, half French, half English, that shall go to Constantinople and take the Turk by the beard? Shall we not? What say'st thou, my fair flower-de-luce?

KATHARINE I do not know dat.

KING HENRY No; 'tis hereafter to know, but now to promise. Do but now promise, Kate, you will endeavor for your French part of such a boy, and for my English moi'ty take the word of a king and a bachelor. How answer you, la plus belle Katharine du monde, mon très cher et devin déesse?

KATHARINE Your Majestee ave fausse French enough to deceive de most sage demoiselle dat is en France.

KING HENRY Now, fie upon my false French! By mine honor, in true English, I love thee, Kate; by which honor I dare not swear thou lovest me, yet my blood begins to flatter me that thou dost, notwithstanding the poor and untempering effect of my visage. Now, beshrew my father's ambition! He was thinking of civil wars when he got me; therefore was I created with a stubborn outside, with an aspect of iron, that, when I come to woo ladies, I fright them. But, in faith, Kate, the elder I wax, the better I shall appear. My comfort is that old age, that ill layer up of beauty, can do no more spoil upon my face. Thou hast me, if thou hast me, at the worst; and thou shalt wear me, if thou wear me, better and better. And therefore tell me, most fair Katharine, will you have me? Put off your maiden blushes; avouch the thoughts of your heart with the looks of an empress; take me by the hand, and say, "Harry of England, I am thine." Which word thou shalt no sooner bless mine ear withal, but I will tell thee aloud, "England is thine, Ireland is thine, France is thine, and Henry Plantagenet is thine"—who, though I speak it before his face, if he be not fellow with the best king, thou shalt find the best king of good fellows. Come, your answer in broken music! For thy voice is music and thy English broken. Therefore, queen of all, Katharine, break thy mind to me in broken English. Wilt thou have me?

KATHARINE Dat is as it sall please de roi mon père.

KING HENRY Nay, it will please him well, Kate. It shall please him, Kate.

KATHARINE Den it sall also content me.

KING HENRY Upon that I kiss your hand, and I call you my queen. [*Attempts to kiss her hand.*]

KATHARINE Laissez, mon seigneur, laissez, laissez! Ma foi, je ne veux point que vous abaissiez votre grandeur en baisant la main d'une—Notre Seigneur!—indigne serviteur. Excusez-moi, je vous supplie, mon très-puissant seigneur.

150 cook (She must dress him with fine qualities as a cook dresses meat.) **155 uncoin'd** not coined for circulation; also, unalloyed, therefore fixed, steady **160 fall** shrink, lose its shapeliness **182–185 Je . . . mienne** (Henry haltingly translates the last sentence in his previous speech.) **184 Saint Denis** patron saint of France **189–190 Sauf . . . parle** save your honor, the French that you speak is better than the English that I speak **199 closet** private chamber

205 scambling scrambling, struggling **211 flower-de-luce** fleur-de-lis, the emblem of France **217–218 la plus . . . déesse** the most beautiful Katharine in the world, my very dear and divine goddess **225 untempering** unsoftening **244 broken music** music in parts **248 de roi mon père** the King my father **254–258 Laissez . . . seigneur** don't, my lord, don't, don't; by my faith, I do not wish to lower your greatness by kissing the hand of an—Our dear Lord!—unworthy servant; excuse me, I beg you, my most powerful lord

KING HENRY Then I will kiss your lips, Kate.

KATHARINE Les dames et demoiselles pour être baisées devant leur noces, il n'est pas la coutume de France.

KING HENRY Madam my interpreter, what says she?

ALICE Dat it is not be de fashion pour les ladies of France—I cannot tell wat is baiser en Anglish.

KING HENRY To kiss.

ALICE Your Majesty entendre bettre que moi.

KING HENRY It is not a fashion for the maids in France to kiss before they are married, would she say?

ALICE Oui, vraiment.

KING HENRY O Kate, nice customs cur'sy to great kings. Dear Kate, you and I cannot be confin'd within the weak list of a country's fashion. We are the makers of manners, Kate; and the liberty that follows our places stops the mouth of all find-faults, as I will do yours, for upholding the nice fashion of your country in denying me a kiss. Therefore, patiently and yielding. [*Kissing her.*] You have witchcraft in your lips, Kate. There is more eloquence in a sugar touch of them than in the tongues of the French council; and they should sooner persuade Harry of England than a general petition of monarchs.—Here comes your father.

Enter the French Power and the English Lords.

BURGUNDY God save your Majesty! My royal cousin, teach you our princess English?

KING HENRY I would have her learn, my fair cousin, how perfectly I love her; and that is good English.

BURGUNDY Is she not apt?

KING HENRY Our tongue is rough, coz, and my condition is not smooth; so that, having neither the voice nor the heart of flattery about me, I cannot so conjure up the spirit of love in her, that he will appear in his true likeness.

BURGUNDY Pardon the frankness of my mirth, if I answer you for that. If you would conjure in her, you must make a circle; if conjure up love in her in his true likeness, he must appear naked and blind. Can you blame her then, being a maid yet ros'd over with the virgin crimson of modesty, if she deny the appearance of a naked blind boy in her naked seeing self? It were, my lord, a hard condition for a maid to consign to.

KING HENRY Yet they do wink and yield, as love is blind and enforces.

BURGUNDY They are then excus'd, my lord, when they see not what they do.

KING HENRY Then, good my lord, teach your cousin to consent winking.

BURGUNDY I will wink on her to consent, my lord, if you will teach her to know my meaning; for maids, well summer'd and warm kept, are like flies at Bartholomew-tide, blind, though they have their eyes, and then they will endure handling, which before would not abide looking on.

KING HENRY This moral ties me over to time and a hot summer; and so I shall catch the fly, your cousin, in the latter end and she must be blind too.

BURGUNDY As love is, my lord, before it loves.

KING HENRY It is so; and you may, some of you, thank love for my blindness, who cannot see many a fair French city for one fair French maid that stands in my way.

FRENCH KING Yes, my lord, you see them perspectively, the cities turn'd into a maid; for they are all girdled with maiden walls that war hath never ent'red.

KING HENRY Shall Kate be my wife?

FRENCH KING So please you.

KING HENRY I am content, so the maiden cities you talk of may wait on her. So the maid that stood in the way for my wish shall show me the way to my will.

FRENCH KING
We have consented to all terms of reason.

KING HENRY
Is 't so, my lords of England?

WESTMORLAND
The King hath granted every article:
His daughter first, and then in sequel all,
According to their firm proposed natures.

EXETER
Only he hath not yet subscribed this:
Where your Majesty demands that the King of France, having any occasion to write for matter of grant, shall name your Highness in this form and with this addition, in French, "Notre très-cher fils Henri, Roi d'Angleterre, Héritier de France"; and thus in Latin, "Praeclarissimus filius noster Henricus, Rex Angliae, et Haeres Franciae."

FRENCH KING
Nor this I have not, brother, so denied
But your request shall make me let it pass.

KING HENRY
I pray you then, in love and dear alliance,
Let that one article rank with the rest,
And thereupon give me your daughter.

FRENCH KING
Take her, fair son, and from her blood raise up
Issue to me, that the contending kingdoms
Of France and England, whose very shores look pale
With envy of each other's happiness,
May cease their hatred, and this dear conjunction
Plant neighborhood and Christian-like accord
In their sweet bosoms, that never war advance
His bleeding sword 'twixt England and fair France.

LORDS Amen!

KING HENRY
Now, welcome, Kate; and bear me witness all,

260–262 Le dames . . . France it is not customary in France for ladies and young girls to be kissed before their marriage **266 entendre . . . moi** understands better than I **269 Oui, vraiment** yes, truly **270 nice** fastidious. **cur'sy** curtsy **272 list** limit, barrier **273 follows our places** attends our (high) rank **287–288 condition** personality **293 conjure in her** (with bawdy double meaning, continued in *circle, hard,* etc.) **299 consign** agree **300 wink** close the eyes **308 summer'd** nurtured **308–309 Bartholomew-tide** August 24 (when flies, bees, etc., are sluggish)

317–319 who . . . my way (i.e., Henry is willing to forego several French cities in exchange for Katharine that he might otherwise take possession of in the negotiations.) **320 perspectively** i.e., distorted by a perspective glass **322 maiden** unbreached **326 wait on her** attend her, go along with her (as part of her dowry) **332 According . . . natures** exactly as specified in the proposals **335 for . . . grant** in official deeds granting title to land and the like **336–337 addition** title **337–338 Notre . . . France** our very dear son Henry, King of England, Heir of France **341 so** so firmly **342 But** but that

That here I kiss her as my sovereign queen. [*Kiss.*]
Flourish.

QUEEN ISABEL
God, the best maker of all marriages,
Combine your hearts in one, your realms in one!
As man and wife, being two, are one in love,
So be there 'twixt your kingdoms such a spousal
That never may ill office, or fell jealousy, 361
Which troubles oft the bed of blessed marriage,
Thrust in between the paction of these kingdoms, 363
To make divorce of their incorporate league;
That English may as French, French Englishmen,
Receive each other. God speak this Amen!

ALL Amen!

KING HENRY
Prepare we for our marriage, on which day,
My Lord of Burgundy, we'll take your oath,
And all the peers', for surety of our leagues.
Then shall I swear to Kate, and you to me;
And may our oaths well kept and prosp'rous be!
Sennet. Exeunt.

[EPILOGUE]

Enter Chorus.

[CHORUS]
Thus far, with rough and all-unable pen,
Our bending author hath pursu'd the story, 2
In little room confining mighty men,
Mangling by starts the full course of their glory. 4
Small time, but in that small most greatly lived
This star of England. Fortune made his sword,
By which the world's best garden he achiev'd, 7
And of it left his son imperial lord.
Henry the Sixth, in infant bands crown'd King 9
Of France and England, did this king succeed;
Whose state so many had the managing,
That they lost France and made his England bleed,
Which oft our stage hath shown; and, for their sake, 13
In your fair minds let this acceptance take. [*Exit.*] 14

361 ill office unfriendly dealings. **fell** cruel **363 paction** alliance, compact

Epilogue.
2 bending i.e., under the weight of his task **4 by starts** in fits and starts, in fragments **7 best garden** i.e., France **9 infant bands** swaddling clothes **13 Which . . . shown** (Refers to the three parts of *King Henry VI.*) **for their sake** i.e., since you liked them **14 this acceptance take** this play meet with your approval

The Famous History of the Life of King Henry the Eighth

However much we may like to think of *The Tempest* (c. 1610–1611) as Shakespeare's farewell to his art, celebrating his retirement to Stratford in 1611 or 1612, his career was in fact not quite finished. He probably wrote all of *The Famous History of the Life of King Henry the Eighth* in 1613, and he evidently collaborated with John Fletcher (and possibly Beaumont) in *The Two Noble Kinsmen* (1613–1616). *Henry VIII* was performed by the King's men at the Globe playhouse on June 29, 1613, as a "new" play, though perhaps it had also been performed earlier that spring at the indoors Blackfriars playhouse. During the Globe performance, small cannon (called "chambers") were discharged to welcome Henry VIII and his fellow-masquers to Wolsey's house (I,iv), accidentally setting fire to the thatch roof and burning the Globe to the ground in less than an hour. (The theatre was subsequently rebuilt.) The letter reporting this incident refers to the play by the title *All Is True,* but its identification with the extant play of *Henry VIII* is virtually certain.

Not everyone has always agreed that the entire play is by Shakespeare, although doubts did not arise until the nineteenth century. Alfred Lord Tennyson was the first to suspect that much of the play is metrically non-Shakespearean. His friend James Spedding took up the suggestion in his study, *Who Wrote Shakespeare's Henry VIII?* His conclusions, based on the assumption that Fletcher's mannered blank verse is generally endstopped and much given to double or "feminine" endings, assigned only I,i-ii, II,iii-iv, III,ii (through line 203), and V,i to Shakespeare, attributing all the rest to Fletcher. These metrical tests have been bolstered by subsequent researchers and augmented by other methods of statistical analysis. The result is perhaps a more elaborate case for joint authorship than for most other plays of doubtful attribution. Some of the stylistic shifts noted by Tennyson are indeed discernible, as for example in the movement from the dense, elliptical grammar and compact images of the first two scenes to the conversational fluency of scenes three and four.

Against these arguments, however, the case for Shakespeare's sole authorship is impressive. Although Shakespeare did apparently collaborate with Fletcher during his last years in *The Two Noble Kinsmen,* that play was excluded from the 1623 Folio whereas *Henry VIII* was included as Shakespeare's final history play. Spedding's hypothesis of joint authorship would rob from Shakespeare several of the play's most famous scenes, such as the farewell speeches of Buckingham, Wolsey, and Queen Katharine, and conversely would credit Fletcher with a dramatic power not shown elsewhere. The "Fletcherian" style may well have been the result of Shakespeare's having known the work of the younger man who became Shakespeare's heir as chief writer for the King's men. Unquestionably, Shakespeare's style did change in his later years under the influence of the Blackfriars audience; the prologue to *Henry VIII* suggests that the play was written with the more exclusive audience of Blackfriars ("The first and happiest hearers of the town") particularly in mind. Even if *Henry VIII* is a different sort of history play from *I Henry IV,* it is stylistically close to Shakespeare's late romances. The shift in texture from scenes i and ii to scenes iii and iv makes good sense dramatically; scene iv, for example, dramatizing an evening party, is suitably conversational, whereas the dense first scene is largely expository. Neither external evidence nor tradition during Shakespeare's day links the play with Fletcher. Scholarly "disintegration" of the text dates only from the nineteenth century, where it should be seen as part of a broader effort to "disintegrate" many other plays and thereby rescue Shakespeare from scenes presumed unworthy of his genius. The very tendency to regard *Henry VIII* as defective and lacking in unity may well have been caused in part by eighteenth- and nineteenth-century productions of the play, which, although frequent and popular, treated the play as a vehicle for famous actors and actresses in the parts of Wolsey and Katharine (Betterton, Kemble, Mrs. Siddons, Kean, and, more recently, Sybil Thorndike, Charles Laughton, Flora Robson), and accordingly cut Act V and sometimes much of Act IV along with other "extraneous" parts. Productions and criticism during the last thirty years, on the other hand, have shown *Henry VIII* to possess an impressive cohesion and to be an integral product of the late years in which Shakespeare centered his attention on romance and tragicomedy. We are safest in assuming that nineteenth-century efforts at disintegration are now happily out of fashion, and that the Folio editors knew what they were doing when they included *Henry VIII.*

What was Shakespeare's purpose in this unexpected return to the English history play? He had set it aside fourteen years earlier, in 1599, bringing to completion in *Henry V* an eight-play saga on England's civil wars of the fifteenth century. Why turn in 1613 to a historical subject so separated in time from that of Shakespeare's earlier interest and potentially so controversial because of its relation to the religious battle between Catholics and Protestants? Earlier generations of critics and playgoers, as we have seen, generally regarded parts of *Henry VIII* as belonging to another author or as the product of Shakespeare's presumed dotage, especially the fifth act with its apparent anticlimax following the deaths of the play's central characters, Wolsey and Katharine. More recent efforts to understand the whole of *Henry VIII* regard it as an experimental work, blending conventional genres (especially history and romance) and stressing masquelike stage effects in the opulent manner of court entertainment. Since its thematic focus is also one of courtly celebration, expressing gratitude for Queen Elizabeth's Protestant rule and her cousin James' succession to the English throne, the play may best be seen as a reworking of the English history play to meet the new mood of 1613. This return to a type of drama long since abandoned by Shakespeare resembles his similar fascination during his late years with the once-forgotten genre of romance.

In some ways, *Henry VIII* is deliberately unlike Shakespeare's earlier history plays, and so should not be judged by their standards. The prologue is at pains to stress that the play will contain no merriment or bawdry, no "fellow In a long motley coat." And indeed the play is unusually lacking in a comic subplot devoted to the antics of engaging commoners. To be sure, the views of the citizens are not ignored, for Queen Katharine champions their hatred of Wolsey's taxes. In the fifth act the people put in a brief appearance, crowding bumptiously forward at the christening of the Princess Elizabeth (V,iv). Even here, however, the tone is one of condescending amusement at their childish eagerness to see their future queen. The common people do not provide choric commentary, as they do in *Richard III* or *Richard II*.

These factors may well reflect the increasing influence of the court on Shakespeare and the King's men. Ever since they became the King's men in 1603, when James I came to the throne, Shakespeare's company had enjoyed a closer relationship with the throne than before. *Measure for Measure* and *Macbeth,* among other of Shakespeare's plays, seem to contain flattering allusions to the new monarch. Moreover, faced with increasing competition from the boys' acting companies, which, since reopening in 1599, had attracted a courtly and sophisticated clientele, Shakespeare's company acquired the lease of Blackfriars in 1608 and henceforth used this "private" theatre as their winter playhouse. Shakespeare's late plays are staged with public, private, and courtly conditions of performance in mind. The late romances show the influence of Inigo Jones' lavish designs for court masques, as in *Cymbeline*'s use of machinery for celestial ascents and descents. *Henry VIII* reflects similar conditions of staging in its masquing scene (I,iv), in the pageantlike trial of Katharine and the baptism of Elizabeth, and in the vision of white-robed figures dancing before the dying Katharine (IV,ii). This affinity to courtly entertainment should not be overstressed, for Shakespeare's company remained a public company throughout his career, and its stage was always fluidly bare of scenery when compared with Jones' ingenious devices and use of scenic perspective. Nonetheless, *Henry VIII* should be viewed as a history play for a somewhat more select audience than that of his earlier histories. The play's ornate compliments to Elizabeth and King James have a courtly flavor. The year 1613 saw the politically important marriage of the Elector Palatinate to James' daughter Elizabeth, who was often flatteringly compared with her namesake Queen Elizabeth; and, although *Henry VIII* is not among the plays known to have been performed for this occasion, the marriage itself would have given added significance to the play's celebration of Tudor and Stuart rule.

Shakespeare's earlier histories also honor as well as examine critically the institution of monarchy, but even here *Henry VIII* provides a different emphasis. Shakespeare's earlier histories had focused on such issues as the education of a prince and on the dilemmas of power a ruler faces. *Henry VIII* is less a study of kingship and more a dramatic expression of gratitude. *Henry VIII* is not a patriotic play in a broadly popular sense. It lacks battles and triumphant oratory. It voices thanksgiving for a particular ruling family. *Henry VIII* is above all the remarkable story of Queen Elizabeth's birth. The story is certainly not without its ironies, for providence works in mysterious ways, and Elizabeth's parents were complex persons. Shakespeare reveals an increasing psychological interest in analysis of motive, as in other late history plays such as Ford's *Perkin Warbeck.* Yet the unifying impulse of the play remains the celebration of the birth of Elizabeth.

This rising action in the play is counterpointed by a series of tragic falls, which indeed seem at first to be the play's chief concern. These falls proceed in remorseless succession—Buckingham, Katharine, Wolsey. In the edifying manner of that staple of medieval tragedy, the "Fall of Princes," these deaths offer useful lessons on statecraft and personal conduct. All these characters stoically exemplify the art of holy dying. One after another, they forgive their enemies and regret such sins as they have committed, and yet they also prophesy that God's retribution will light on offenders' heads. The prevailing mood in the falls of Buckingham and Katharine is one of pity, for both are victims of the ruthless Wolsey.

Cardinal Wolsey is the most interesting character of the three, and best illustrates another convention of medieval tragedy, the Wheel of Fortune. Even as he topples one victim after another, dispatching Surrey to Ireland, wheedling his way into the King's favor, reversing England's foreign policy with bewildering speed from pro-French to pro-Empire and back again, all the while amassing a vast personal fortune and negotiating for supreme power within the Roman church, we sense that he is preparing his own catastrophe. Fortune raises insolent worldly persons of this sort, but an overseeing power is at work and will manifest itself through the King. Wolsey, in a nobly contrite farewell, sees the moral of his fall: had he served God zealously, God would not "Have left me naked to mine enemies" (III,ii). Wolsey knows he has ventured beyond his depth in scheming, "Like little wanton boys that swim on bladders." Shakespeare's appraisal of this controversial man is mixed, partly because his chief source, Holinshed's *Chronicles,* incorporated both anti-Wolseyan diatribes and George Cavendish's appreciative account of Wolsey's last days. Still, the portraiture remains consistent throughout, for Wolsey is always intelligent and munificent (as in his founding of Cardinal College, later Christ Church, at Oxford) even though he employs his talents for worldly ends. His chief wrongdoing is his meddling on behalf of Rome, his finagling to gain the papacy, and most of all his sending of England's wealth overseas for reasons of private gain. Yet even this corrupt behavior has a function in the rising action of the story, for, had not Wolsey schemed against Queen Katharine in his plot to marry King Henry to the French Duchess of Alençon, Katharine might never have fallen to make way for Anne Bullen; and had not Wolsey given a sumptuous party to impress the court with his magnificence (I,iv), Henry might never have met Queen Elizabeth's mother. Wolsey's fate is to introduce Henry to the woman whose rise will mean Wolsey's fall and the birth of a future queen. An overriding cosmic irony converts the worst intents of traitors to beneficent ends.

King Henry and Anne Bullen, who as Elizabeth's parents play the roles essential to England's bright future, are largely unaware of the great destiny they are performing. Henry especially, like Wolsey, is examined with some skepticism. His pious insistence that "conscience" alone banishes him from Katharine's bed elicits a wry observation, *sotto voce,* from the Duke of Suffolk: "No, his conscience Has crept too near another lady" (II,ii). As Henry neglectfully condones Wolsey's abuse of authority and credulously accepts perjured testimony against Buckingham, we catch glimpses of the whimsical tyrant whom history has revealed to us. These criticisms are muted, however, for Henry is after all Elizabeth's father. He is not only exonerated from most wrongdoing, but steps boldly forward at the play's end as champion of religious reform. Anne too is ambivalently treated. In her scene with the Old Lady (II,iii), we are reminded of the all-too-apparent reasons there are for suspecting that Anne is a schemer, a high-class auctioneer of her beauty who knows that Henry will pay handsomely. Yet in her own person Anne refutes these insinuations. All the characters of the play, whether they stand to profit or lose by Anne's marriage, speak admiringly of her beauty and honor. Although her speeches are few, her appearances are sumptuously staged with Anne at the center of a meaningful pageant.

The religious issue is presented with a similar tact and ambiguity, for it too is both controversial and of significance to England's future. Our sympathies are charitably disposed toward Katharine, whose innocent fall is a sad price for England's larger happiness. Shakespeare refuses to associate her with the decaying order of Catholicism, as he might have done. On the other hand, Bishop Gardiner, the villain of Act V, is undeniably a Catholic and persecutor of heretics, a dangerous man whose overthrow by Henry and the Protestant Cranmer signals the beginning of a new era in religion. Though Shakespeare tactfully omits the relationship between Katharine's divorce and the Reformation, his audience would have had little difficulty making the connection in Act V between Cranmer's Protestant victory and the birth of Elizabeth. These two rising actions coalesce and give perspective to the pitiable falls from greatness which have necessarily contributed to a happy and even miraculous conclusion. History and tragicomic romance fulfill a common purpose in *Henry VIII.*

Act V is thus central to the play's thematic concerns, despite the poor opinion in which it was held in the nineteenth century, and despite the apparently episodic way in which it introduces new characters (notably Archbishop Cranmer) and new issues. The ending confirms a pattern seen earlier in the sad stories of Buckingham and especially Wolsey, in which we mortals "outrun By violent swiftness that which we run at, And lose by overrunning" (I,i). Vain human striving after fame overreaches itself and brings itself down. The process is, in *Henry VIII,* not primarily a punishment for villainy, for there are no real villains here, but a curative process by which frail proud men ascend on Fortune's wheel only to discover how illusory are her rewards and how comforting are Fortune's losses that bring us to ourselves. Not a moment of ease does Wolsey enjoy until he is ruined in worldly terms. He assures Thomas Cromwell, at the moment of his fall, that "I know myself now, and I feel within me A peace above all earthly dignities" (III,ii). His fall is thus a happy fall, an instructive one for himself and others: "Mark but my fall, and this that ruin'd me" (III,ii). Even Katharine and her gentleman usher, Griffin, perceive a happiness in Wolsey's decline, not because it satisfies a desire for vengeance but because it offers a comforting precedent of self-discovery through suffering: "His overthrow heap'd happiness upon him, For then, and not till then, he felt himself" (IV,ii). To know oneself in these terms, *nosce teipsum,* is to enjoy the inestimable gift of penance and the laying aside of worldly striving. Cranmer is a suitable protagonist in Act V and substitute for Wolsey as the King's adviser because he cares so little for himself in a worldly sense. He is the instrument of a higher power that, having imposed various trials on members of the court for their individual and collective betterment, at last reveals a meaning in that suffering and a future happiness arising out of man's imperfect attempts to know himself. As Buckingham says earlier (II,i), "Heaven has an end in all."

The play when staged offers a visual contrast between ceremonial pomp and worldly loss leading to renunciation and death. The processions and public events, conveyed by unusually full stage directions, celebrate the ordered arrangement of a hierarchical society. Yet among the most powerful scenes are those of Wolsey bidding farewell to his wealth and power, and Katharine in her isolation and approaching death. The prologue promises to give us noble scenes, "Sad, high, and working, full of state and woe," and in this we are not disappointed. The prologue also promises that the audience "May here find truth too"; and, despite the necessary omission of much bloodshed (Anne Bullen and Sir Thomas More come before us, but without any hint of what is to become of them), the play does give a vivid account of Henry VIII's time. We "see The very persons of our noble story As they were living." Our impression is of great political and religious change, of splendor and richness, above all of the insecurity of worldly felicity under such a king. Theatrically the play is sumptuous, pageant-like; though it chooses not to amuse us with comedy, and eschews battle scenes, it abounds in personages from history. In *Henry VIII* the history play has been adapted to Shakespeare's late world of romance.

The Famous History of the Life of King Henry the Eighth

[*Dramatis Personae*

KING HENRY THE EIGHTH.
CARDINAL WOLSEY.
CARDINAL CAMPEIUS.
CAPUCIUS, *Ambassador from the Emperor Charles V.*
CRANMER, *Archbishop of Canterbury.*
DUKE OF NORFOLK.
DUKE OF BUCKINGHAM.
DUKE OF SUFFOLK.
EARL OF SURREY.
LORD CHAMBERLAIN.
LORD CHANCELLOR.
GARDINER, *King's Secretary, afterwards Bishop of Winchester.*
BISHOP OF LINCOLN.
LORD ABERGAVENNY.
LORD SANDS (*also called* SIR WALTER SANDYS).
SIR HENRY GUILDFORD.
SIR THOMAS LOVELL.
SIR ANTHONY DENNY.
SIR NICHOLAS VAUX.
SECRETARIES *to Wolsey.*
CROMWELL, *Servant to Wolsey.*
GRIFFITH, *Gentleman-usher to Queen Katharine.*
Three GENTLEMEN.
DOCTOR BUTTS, *Physician to the King.*
GARTER KING-AT-ARMS.
SURVEYOR *to the Duke of Buckingham.*
BRANDON, *and a* SERGEANT-AT-ARMS.
DOOR-KEEPER *of the Council-chamber.* PORTER, *and his* MAN.
PAGE *to Gardiner. A* CRIER.

QUEEN KATHARINE, *wife to King Henry, afterwards divorced.*
ANNE BULLEN, *her Maid of Honor, afterwards Queen.*
OLD LADY, *friend to Anne Bullen.*
PATIENCE, *woman to Queen Katharine.*

Several LORDS *and* LADIES *in the Dumb Shows;* WOMEN *attending upon the Queen;* SCRIBES, OFFICERS, GUARDS, *and other* ATTENDANTS. SPIRITS.

SCENE: *London; Westminster; Kimbolton.*]

THE PROLOGUE

I come no more to make you laugh. Things now
That bear a weighty and a serious brow,
Sad, high, and working, full of state and woe, 3
Such noble scenes as draw the eye to flow,
We now present. Those that can pity, here
May, if they think it well, let fall a tear;
The subject will deserve it. Such as give
Their money out of hope they may believe,
May here find truth too. Those that come to see
Only a show or two, and so agree
The play may pass, if they be still and willing,
I'll undertake may see away their shilling
Richly in two short hours. Only they 13
That come to hear a merry bawdy play,
A noise of targets, or to see a fellow 15
In a long motley coat guarded with yellow, 16
Will be deceiv'd. For, gentle hearers, know 17
To rank our chosen truth with such a show
As fool and fight is, beside forfeiting
Our own brains and the opinion that we bring 20
To make that only true we now intend, 21
Will leave us never an understanding friend.
Therefore, for goodness' sake, and as you are known
The first and happiest hearers of the town,
Be sad, as we would make ye. Think ye see 25
The very persons of our noble story
As they were living. Think you see them great,
And follow'd with the general throng and sweat
Of thousand friends; then, in a moment, see
How soon this mightiness meets misery.
And, if you can be merry then, I'll say
A man may weep upon his wedding-day.

ACT I • SCENE I

Enter the Duke of Norfolk at one door; at the other, the Duke of Buckingham and the Lord Abergavenny.

BUCKINGHAM
Good morrow, and well met. How have ye done
Since last we saw in France?

NORFOLK I thank your Grace, 2
Healthful; and ever since a fresh admirer
Of what I saw there.

BUCKINGHAM An untimely ague 4
Stay'd me a prisoner in my chamber when
Those suns of glory, those two lights of men,
Met in the vale of Andren.

NORFOLK 'Twixt Guynes and Arde. 7
I was then present, saw them salute on horseback,
Beheld them when they lighted, how they clung
In their embracement, as they grew together; 10
Which had they, what four thron'd ones could have
weigh'd 11
Such a compounded one?

BUCKINGHAM All the whole time
I was my chamber's prisoner.

NORFOLK Then you lost
The view of earthly glory. Men might say
Till this time pomp was single, but now married
To one above itself. Each following day
Became the next day's master, till the last 17
Made former wonders its. Today the French,
All clinquant, all in gold, like heathen gods, 19
Shone down the English; and, tomorrow, they 20
Made Britain India—every man that stood 21
Show'd like a mine. Their dwarfish pages were
As cherubins, all gilt. The madams too, 23
Not us'd to toil, did almost sweat to bear
The pride upon them, that their very labor 25
Was to them as a painting. Now this masque 26
Was cried incomparable; and th' ensuing night 27
Made it a fool and beggar. The two kings,
Equal in luster, were now best, now worst,
As presence did present them; him in eye, 30
Still him in praise; and, being present both, 31
'Twas said they saw but one, and no discerner
Durst wag his tongue in censure. When these
suns— 33
For so they phrase 'em—by their heralds challeng'd
The noble spirits to arms, they did perform
Beyond thought's compass, that former fabulous
story,
Being now seen possible enough, got credit, 37
That Bevis was believ'd.

BUCKINGHAM O, you go far. 38

NORFOLK
As I belong to worship and affect 39
In honor honesty, the tract of ev'ry thing 40
Would by a good discourser lose some life,
Which action's self was tongue to. All was royal; 42
To the disposing of it nought rebell'd, 43
Order gave each thing view; the office did 44
Distinctly his full function.

BUCKINGHAM Who did guide, 45
I mean, who set the body and the limbs
Of this great sport together, as you guess?

Prologue.
3 Sad . . . working serious, lofty, and exciting the emotions **13 two short hours** (A conventional period of time for a play.) **15 targets** shields **16 motley coat** pied costume of the fool. **guarded** trimmed **17 deceiv'd** disappointed. **know** i.e., it must be acknowledged that **20 opinion** reputation **21 intend** i.e., to play **25 sad** serious

I.i. Location: London. The palace.
2 saw i.e., saw each other **4 what I saw there** (Norfolk's description is of the famous meeting of Henry VIII and Francis I of France in 1520. It was near Calais, at the Field of the Cloth of Gold, so called because of the magnificence of the display.)

7 vale of Andren (The name, more properly *Ardres,* appears as *Andren* in Holinshed.) **10 as** as if **11 Which had they** i.e., if they had grown together. **weigh'd** equaled in weight **17 master** teacher, model **19 clinquant** glittering **20 they** i.e., the English **21 India** i.e., seem as wealthy as the West Indies **23 madams** ladies **25 pride** finery **26 Was . . . painting** i.e., flushed them as though with cosmetics **27 cried** declared **30 As . . . them** i.e., when they appeared **30–31 him . . . praise** i.e., the one in view at the moment received the praise **33 censure** judgment (of one above the other) **37 got credit** gained credibility **38 Bevis** hero of the fourteenth-century romance *Bevis of Hampton* **39 belong to worship** am of noble rank **39–40 affect . . . honesty** i.e., love truth with honorable regard **40 tract** telling; course **42 Which . . . to** i.e., which would be best described by the event itself **43 rebell'd** jarred **44–45 Order . . . function** everything appeared in its proper place, and every official performed his function without confusion

NORFOLK
One, certes, that promises no element 48
In such a business.
BUCKINGHAM I pray you, who, my lord? 49
NORFOLK
All this was ord'red by the good discretion
Of the right reverend Cardinal of York.
BUCKINGHAM
The devil speed him! No man's pie is freed 52
From his ambitious finger. What had he
To do in these fierce vanities? I wonder 54
That such a keech can with his very bulk 55
Take up the rays o' th' beneficial sun
And keep it from the earth.
NORFOLK Surely, sir,
There's in him stuff that puts him to these ends; 58
For, being not propp'd by ancestry, whose grace
Chalks successors their way, nor call'd upon 60
For high feats done to th' crown, neither allied
To eminent assistants, but, spider-like, 62
Out of his self-drawing web, 'a gives us note, 63
The force of his own merit makes his way—
A gift that heaven gives for him, which buys
A place next to the King.
ABERGAVENNY I cannot tell
What heaven hath given him—let some graver eye
Pierce into that—but I can see his pride
Peep through each part of him. Whence has he that?
If not from hell, the devil is a niggard,
Or has given all before, and he begins
A new hell in himself.
BUCKINGHAM Why the devil,
Upon this French going out, took he upon him, 73
Without the privity o' th' King, t' appoint 74
Who should attend on him? He makes up the file 75
Of all the gentry, for the most part such
To whom as great a charge as little honor 77
He meant to lay upon; and his own letter, 78
The honorable board of council out, 79
Must fetch him in he papers.
ABERGAVENNY I do know 80
Kinsmen of mine, three at the least, that have
By this so sicken'd their estates, that never
They shall abound as formerly.
BUCKINGHAM O, many
Have broke their backs with laying manors on 'em 84
For this great journey. What did this vanity 85
But minister communication of 86
A most poor issue?
NORFOLK Grievingly I think 87
The peace between the French and us not values 88
The cost that did conclude it.

BUCKINGHAM Every man,
After the hideous storm that follow'd, was 90
A thing inspir'd, and, not consulting, broke 91
Into a general prophecy: That this tempest,
Dashing the garment of this peace, aboded 93
The sudden breach on 't.
NORFOLK Which is budded out; 94
For France hath flaw'd the league, and hath attach'd 95
Our merchants' goods at Bordeaux.
ABERGAVENNY Is it therefore
Th' ambassador is silenc'd?
NORFOLK Marry, is 't.
ABERGAVENNY
A proper title of a peace; and purchas'd 98
At a superfluous rate!
BUCKINGHAM Why, all this business 99
Our reverend Cardinal carried.
NORFOLK Like it your Grace, 100
The state takes notice of the private difference
Betwixt you and the Cardinal. I advise you—
And take it from a heart that wishes towards you
Honor and plenteous safety—that you read 104
The Cardinal's malice and his potency
Together; to consider further, that 106
What his high hatred would effect wants not 107
A minister in his power. You know his nature, 108
That he's revengeful, and I know his sword
Hath a sharp edge; it's long, and 't may be said
It reaches far, and where 'twill not extend,
Thither he darts it. Bosom up my counsel, 112
You'll find it wholesome. Lo, where comes that rock
That I advise your shunning. 114

Enter Cardinal Wolsey, the purse borne before him, certain of the Guard, and two Secretaries with papers. The Cardinal in his passage fixeth his eye on Buckingham, and Buckingham on him, both full of disdain.

WOLSEY
The Duke of Buckingham's surveyor, ha? 115
Where's his examination?
FIRST SECRETARY Here, so please you. 116
[*Gives paper.*]
WOLSEY
Is he in person ready?
FIRST SECRETARY Ay, please your Grace.
WOLSEY
Well, we shall then know more; and Buckingham
Shall lessen this big look. 119
Exeunt Cardinal and his Train.
BUCKINGHAM
This butcher's cur is venom-mouth'd, and I 120

48–49 One . . . business i.e., one whose mean origin would indicate that he lacked the capacity required for managing business of such a regal nature **52 speed** prosper **54 fierce** extravagant **55 keech** (Literally, fat of a slaughtered animal rolled into a lump; applied to Wolsey as a butcher's son.) **58 stuff . . . him** traits that whet him on **60 Chalks . . . way** indicates the path noble descendants are to follow **62 assistants** high officials of the crown **63 self-drawing** spun out of his own entrails. **'a . . . note** he lets us know **73 going out** expedition, display **74 Without . . . King** without the King's being privy (to his plan) **75 file** list **77–78 To . . . upon** (I.e., the Cardinal imposed charges for defraying the expenses of the costly interview on those noblemen to whom he gave places of little honor.) **78 letter** i.e., summons **79 out** not consulted **80 Must . . . papers** compels the cooperation of every person he cites **84 laying . . . 'em** i.e., pawning estates for wardrobes **85 What . . . vanity** i.e., what did this extravagance accomplish **86–87 minister . . . issue** provide occasion for a conference that had little value, poor results **88 not values** is not worth

90 hideous storm (Holinshed reports such a storm that interrupted the festivities and was taken as a prognostication.) **91 consulting** i.e., each other **93 aboded** foretold **94 on 't** of it **95 flaw'd** broken. **attach'd** seized **98 A proper . . . peace** i.e., a fine business to give the name of peace to **99 superfluous rate** excessive price **100 carried** supervised. **Like it** may it please **104 read** interpret **106 Together** i.e., as equally strong **107–108 wants . . . power** is not without means under his control **112 Bosom up** take to heart and shut up in your bosom **114 s.d. purse** i.e., containing the Great Seal, pertaining to Wolsey as Lord Chancellor **115 surveyor** overseer of a household or estate **116 examination** deposition **119 big** haughty **120 butcher's cur** (Another dig at Wolsey's reputed lowly origin.)

Have not the power to muzzle him; therefore best
Not wake him in his slumber. A beggar's book 122
Outworths a noble's blood.

NORFOLK What, are you chaf'd? 123
Ask God for temp'rance; that's th' appliance only 124
Which your disease requires.

BUCKINGHAM I read in 's looks
Matter against me, and his eye revil'd
Me as his abject object. At this instant
He bores me with some trick. He's gone to th' King; 128
I'll follow and outstare him.

NORFOLK Stay, my lord,
And let your reason with your choler question
What 'tis you go about. To climb steep hills
Requires slow pace at first. Anger is like
A full-hot horse, who, being allow'd his way,
Self-mettle tires him. Not a man in England 134
Can advise me like you. Be to yourself
As you would to your friend.

BUCKINGHAM I'll to the King,
And from a mouth of honor quite cry down
This Ipswich fellow's insolence, or proclaim 138
There's difference in no persons.

NORFOLK Be advis'd; 139
Heat not a furnace for your foe so hot
That it do singe yourself. We may outrun,
By violent swiftness, that which we run at,
And lose by overrunning. Know you not
The fire that mounts the liquor till 't run o'er 144
In seeming to augment it wastes it? Be advis'd.
I say again, there is no English soul
More stronger to direct you than yourself,
If with the sap of reason you would quench,
Or but allay, the fire of passion.

BUCKINGHAM Sir,
I am thankful to you, and I'll go along
By your prescription. But this top-proud fellow,
Whom from the flow of gall I name not, but 152
From sincere motions, by intelligence, 153
And proofs as clear as founts in July when 154
We see each grain of gravel, I do know
To be corrupt and treasonous.

NORFOLK Say not "treasonous."

BUCKINGHAM
To th' King I'll say 't, and make my vouch as strong 157
As shore of rock. Attend. This holy fox,
Or wolf, or both—for he is equal rav'nous
As he is subtle, and as prone to mischief
As able to perform 't—his mind and place
Infecting one another, yea, reciprocally,
Only to show his pomp as well in France
As here at home, suggests the King our master 164
To this last costly treaty, th' interview 165
That swallowed so much treasure and like a glass
Did break i' th' wrenching.

NORFOLK Faith, and so it did. 167

BUCKINGHAM
Pray, give me favor, sir. This cunning Cardinal 168
The articles o' th' combination drew 169
As himself pleas'd; and they were ratified
As he cried "Thus let be," to as much end
As give a crutch to th' dead. But our count-cardinal 172
Has done this, and 'tis well; for worthy Wolsey,
Who cannot err, he did it. Now this follows,
Which, as I take it, is a kind of puppy
To th' old dam, treason: Charles the Emperor, 176
Under pretense to see the Queen his aunt—
For 'twas indeed his color, but he came 178
To whisper Wolsey—here makes visitation;
His fears were that the interview betwixt
England and France might, through their amity,
Breed him some prejudice, for from this league
Peep'd harms that menac'd him; privily
Deals with our Cardinal, and, as I trow,
Which I do well, for I am sure, the Emperor
Paid ere he promis'd, whereby his suit was granted
Ere it was ask'd; but when the way was made
And pav'd with gold, the Emperor thus desir'd
That he would please to alter the King's course, 189
And break the foresaid peace. Let the King know,
As soon he shall by me, that thus the Cardinal
Does buy and sell his honor as he pleases,
And for his own advantage.

NORFOLK I am sorry
To hear this of him, and could wish he were
Something mistaken in 't.

BUCKINGHAM No, not a syllable. 195
I do pronounce him in that very shape
He shall appear in proof. 197

Enter Brandon, a Sergeant-at-arms before him, and two or three of the guard.

BRANDON
Your office, sergeant; execute it.

SERGEANT Sir,
My lord the Duke of Buckingham, and Earl
Of Hereford, Stafford, and Northampton, I
Arrest thee of high treason, in the name
Of our most sovereign King.

BUCKINGHAM Lo, you, my lord,
The net has fall'n upon me! I shall perish
Under device and practice.

BRANDON I am sorry 204
To see you ta'en from liberty, to look on
The business present. 'Tis his Highness' pleasure
You shall to th' Tower.

BUCKINGHAM It will help me nothing
To plead mine innocence, for that dye is on me
Which makes my whit'st part black. The will of heav'n
Be done in this and all things! I obey.
O my Lord Aberga'ny, fare you well!

122 book book-learning **123 chaf'd** angry **124 appliance only** only remedy **128 bores** undermines, cheats **134 Self-mettle** his own ardent spirits **138 Ipswich** (Wolsey's birthplace.) **139 difference** distinctions in rank. **Be advis'd** take care **144 mounts** causes (by boiling) to rise **152 from . . . gall** i.e., from promptings of anger **153 motions** motives. **intelligence** secret information **154 founts** springs **157 vouch** assertion of proof **164 suggests** incites **165 last** latest, recent. **interview** i.e., Field of the Cloth of Gold **167 wrenching** rough handling, rinsing

168 favor attention **169 articles o' th' combination** terms of the peace treaty **172 count-cardinal** i.e., cardinal putting on the airs of an aristocrat **176 Charles** i.e., Charles V, Holy Roman Emperor, nephew of Queen Katharine, who had much to fear from an English-French alliance **178 color** pretext **189 he** i.e., Wolsey **195 Something mistaken** somewhat misunderstood **197 He . . . proof** experience shall prove him **204 device and practice** stratagems and plots

BRANDON
Nay, he must bear you company. [*To Abergavenny.*] The King
Is pleas'd you shall to th' Tower, till you know
How he determines further.

ABERGAVENNY
As the Duke said,
The will of heaven be done, and the King's pleasure
By me obey'd!

BRANDON
Here is a warrant from
The King t' attach Lord Montacute, and the bodies 217
Of the Duke's confessor, John de la Car, 218
One Gilbert Perk, his chancellor—

BUCKINGHAM
So, so; 219
These are the limbs o' th' plot. No more, I hope?

BRANDON
A monk o' th' Chartreux.

BUCKINGHAM
O, Nicholas Hopkins?

BRANDON
He. 221

BUCKINGHAM
My surveyor is false. The o'er-great Cardinal
Hath show'd him gold; my life is spann'd already. 223
I am the shadow of poor Buckingham,
Whose figure even this instant cloud puts on,
By dark'ning my clear sun. My lord, farewell.

Exeunt.

SCENE II

Cornets. Enter King Henry, leaning on the Cardinal's shoulder, the Nobles, and Sir Thomas Lovell; the Cardinal places himself under the King's feet on his right side. [*The Cardinal's Secretary attends him.*]

KING
My life itself, and the best heart of it, 1
Thanks you for this great care. I stood i' th' level 2
Of a full-charg'd confederacy, and give thanks 3
To you that chok'd it. Let be call'd before us
That gentleman of Buckingham's; in person 5
I'll hear him his confessions justify, 6
And point by point the treasons of his master
He shall again relate. 8

A noise within, crying "Room for the Queen!" Enter the Queen [*Katharine*], *usher'd by the Duke of Norfolk, and* [*the Duke of*] *Suffolk. She kneels.* [*The*] *King riseth from his state, takes her up, kisses and placeth her by him.*

KATHARINE
Nay, we must longer kneel. I am a suitor.

KING
Arise, and take place by us. Half your suit
Never name to us; you have half our power.
The other moi'ty, ere you ask, is given; 12
Repeat your will and take it.

KATHARINE
Thank your Majesty. 13
That you would love yourself, and in that love
Not unconsidered leave your honor, nor
The dignity of your office, is the point
Of my petition.

KING
Lady mine, proceed.

KATHARINE
I am solicited, not by a few,
And those of true condition, that your subjects 19
Are in great grievance. There have been commissions 20
Sent down among 'em, which hath flaw'd the heart 21
Of all their loyalties; wherein, although,
My good Lord Cardinal, they vent reproaches
Most bitterly on you, as putter on
Of these exactions, yet the King our master—
Whose honor heaven shield from soil!—even he escapes not
Language unmannerly, yea, such which breaks
The sides of loyalty, and almost appears
In loud rebellion.

NORFOLK
Not almost appears,
It doth appear; for, upon these taxations,
The clothiers all, not able to maintain
The many to them 'longing, have put off 32
The spinsters, carders, fullers, weavers, who, 33
Unfit for other life, compell'd by hunger
And lack of other means, in desperate manner
Daring th' event to th' teeth, are all in uproar, 36
And danger serves among them.

KING
Taxation? 37
Wherein? And what taxation? My Lord Cardinal,
You that are blam'd for it alike with us,
Know you of this taxation?

WOLSEY
Please you, sir,
I know but of a single part in aught
Pertains to th' state, and front but in that file 42
Where others tell steps with me.

KATHARINE
No, my lord? 43
You know no more than others? But you frame 44
Things that are known alike, which are not wholesome 45
To those which would not know them, and yet must 46
Perforce be their acquaintance. These exactions,
Whereof my sovereign would have note, they are 48
Most pestilent to th' hearing; and, to bear 'em,
The back is sacrifice to th' load. They say 50
They are devis'd by you, or else you suffer
Too hard an exclamation.

217 attach arrest **218, 219 John de la Car, Gilbert Perk** (The names are from Holinshed's account: "Maister Iohn de la Car *alias* de la Court, the dukes confessor, and sir Gilbert Perke, priest, the duke's chancellor.") **221 Chartreux** Charterhouse (Carthusian) **223 spann'd** measured

I.ii. Location: London. The council-chamber.
s.d. under . . . feet i.e., at the foot of the royal dais **1 best heart** most essential part **2 level** aim **3 full-charg'd confederacy** fully-prepared conspiracy **5 That . . . Buckingham's** i.e., Buckingham's surveyor (I.i.115), whom Wolsey has induced to testify against his master **6 justify** prove, confirm **8 s.d. state** chair of state, raised seat with a canopy

12 moi'ty half **13 Repeat your will** express your desire **19 condition** disposition (to loyalty) **20 commissions** i.e., writs authorizing a tax levy, and the agents to carry them out **21 flaw'd** damaged, broken **32 to them 'longing** in their employ. **put off** laid off **33 spinsters** spinners. **carders** those who comb wool for impurities. **fullers** those who beat wool to clean it **36 Daring . . . teeth** defiantly challenging the outcome **37 danger . . . them** danger is attendant among them **42–43 front . . . me** take my place merely in the front rank with others who share the responsibility **44–46 You know . . . them** i.e., in a sense you know no more than others; but you devise measures known to all (the council) which are so evil that men would rather not know **48 note** knowledge **50 is sacrifice to** i.e., is bowed down under

KING Still exaction!
The nature of it? In what kind, let's know,
Is this exaction?
KATHARINE I am much too venturous
In tempting of your patience, but am bold'ned
Under your promis'd pardon. The subjects' grief
Comes through commissions, which compels from each
The sixth part of his substance, to be levied
Without delay; and the pretense for this
Is nam'd your wars in France. This makes bold mouths.
Tongues spit their duties out, and cold hearts freeze
Allegiance in them. Their curses now
Live where their prayers did; and it's come to pass
This tractable obedience is a slave
To each incensed will. I would your Highness
Would give it quick consideration, for
There is no primer business.
KING By my life,
This is against our pleasure.
WOLSEY And for me,
I have no further gone in this than by
A single voice, and that not pass'd me but
By learned approbation of the judges. If I am
Traduc'd by ignorant tongues, which neither know
My faculties nor person, yet will be
The chronicles of my doing, let me say
'Tis but the fate of place, and the rough brake
That virtue must go through. We must not stint
Our necessary actions in the fear
To cope malicious censurers, which ever,
As rav'nous fishes, do a vessel follow
That is new-trimm'd, but benefit no further
Than vainly longing. What we oft do best,
By sick interpreters, once weak ones, is
Not ours, or not allow'd; what worst, as oft,
Hitting a grosser quality, is cried up
For our best act. If we shall stand still,
In fear our motion will be mock'd or carp'd at,
We should take root here where we sit, or sit
State-statues only.
KING Things done well,
And with a care, exempt themselves from fear;
Things done without example, in their issue
Are to be fear'd. Have you a precedent
Of this commission? I believe, not any.
We must not rend our subjects from our laws,
And stick them in our will. Sixth part of each?
A trembling contribution! Why, we take
From every tree lop, bark, and part o' th' timber;
And, though we leave it with a root, thus hack'd,
The air will drink the sap. To every county
Where this is question'd send our letters, with
Free pardon to each man that has denied
The force of this commission. Pray look to 't;
I put it to your care.
WOLSEY [*Aside to his Secretary*] A word with you.
Let there be letters writ to every shire,
Of the King's grace and pardon. The grieved commons
Hardly conceive of me; let it be nois'd
That through our intercession this revokement
And pardon comes. I shall anon advise you
Further in the proceeding. *Exit Secretary.*

Enter Surveyor.

KATHARINE
I am sorry that the Duke of Buckingham
Is run in your displeasure.
KING It grieves many.
The gentleman is learn'd, and a most rare speaker,
To nature none more bound; his training such
That he may furnish and instruct great teachers
And never seek for aid out of himself. Yet see,
When these so noble benefits shall prove
Not well dispos'd, the mind growing once corrupt,
They turn to vicious forms, ten times more ugly
Than ever they were fair. This man so complete,
Who was enroll'd 'mongst wonders, and when we,
Almost with ravish'd list'ning, could not find
His hour of speech a minute—he, my lady,
Hath into monstrous habits put the graces
That once were his, and is become as black
As if besmear'd in hell. Sit by us. You shall hear—
This was his gentleman in trust—of him
Things to strike honor sad. Bid him recount
The fore-recited practices, whereof
We cannot feel too little, hear too much.
WOLSEY
Stand forth, and with bold spirit relate what you,
Most like a careful subject, have collected
Out of the Duke of Buckingham.
KING Speak freely.
SURVEYOR
First, it was usual with him—every day
It would infect his speech—that if the King
Should without issue die, he'll carry it so
To make the scepter his. These very words
I've heard him utter to his son-in-law,
Lord Aberga'ny, to whom by oath he menac'd
Revenge upon the Cardinal.
WOLSEY Please your Highness, note
This dangerous conception in this point.
Not friended by his wish to your high person,
His will is most malignant, and it stretches
Beyond you, to your friends.
KATHARINE My learn'd Lord Cardinal,
Deliver all with charity.

52 exclamation reproach **56 grief** grievance **64 tractable** i.e., once docile **64–65 is . . . will** i.e., gives way to angry defiance **67 primer** more urgent **69–70 I have . . . voice** i.e., my part in this was only to cast one vote in the council **73 faculties** qualities **75 place** high office. **brake** thicket **78 To cope** of encountering **80 new-trimm'd** newly fitted out **82 sick interpreters** i.e., those who explain our conduct out of malicious envy. **once** at one time or another **83 Not . . . allow'd** either not credited to us, or disapproved of **84 Hitting . . . quality** being understood, or appreciated, by more vulgar natures. (I.e., the indiscriminate praise achievements less fine because their grosser minds understand them.) **86 In fear** for fear that **90 example** precedent. **issue** consequences **94 stick . . . will** make them the victims of our pleasure **95 trembling** causing to tremble **96 lop** branches

105 Hardly conceive have a bad opinion **110 Is run in** has incurred **112 To . . . bound** none more indebted to nature for talents **114 out of** beyond **118 complete** accomplished **122 habits** garments, i.e., shapes **127 practices** intrigues **130 collected** i.e., learned by spying **134 carry it so** manage affairs so as **140 Not . . . wish** his wish (that the King die childless) being ungratified

KING Speak on.
How grounded he his title to the crown
Upon our fail? To this point hast thou heard him
At any time speak aught?
SURVEYOR He was brought to this
By a vain prophecy of Nicholas Henton.
KING
What was that Henton?
SURVEYOR Sir, a Chartreux friar,
His confessor; who fed him every minute
With words of sovereignty.
KING How know'st thou this?
SURVEYOR
Not long before your Highness sped to France,
The Duke being at the Rose, within the parish
Saint Lawrence Poultney, did of me demand
What was the speech among the Londoners
Concerning the French journey. I replied,
Men fear'd the French would prove perfidious,
To the King's danger. Presently the Duke
Said, 'twas the fear, indeed, and that he doubted
'Twould prove the verity of certain words
Spoke by a holy monk "that oft," says he,
"Hath sent to me, wishing me to permit
John de la Car, my chaplain, a choice hour
To hear from him a matter of some moment;
Whom after under the confession's seal
He solemnly had sworn that what he spoke
My chaplain to no creature living but
To me should utter, with demure confidence
This pausingly ensu'd: 'Neither the King nor 's heirs,
Tell you the Duke, shall prosper. Bid him strive
To gain the love o' th' commonalty; the Duke
Shall govern England.' "
KATHARINE If I know you well,
You were the Duke's surveyor, and lost your office
On the complaint o' th' tenants. Take good heed
You charge not in your spleen a noble person
And spoil your nobler soul. I say, take heed;
Yes, heartily beseech you.
KING Let him on.
Go forward.
SURVEYOR On my soul, I'll speak but truth.
I told my lord the Duke, by th' devil's illusions
The monk might be deceiv'd, and that 'twas
dangerous
For him to ruminate on this so far, until
It forg'd him some design, which, being believ'd,
It was much like to do. He answer'd, "Tush,
It can do me no damage," adding further
That, had the King in his last sickness fail'd,
The Cardinal's and Sir Thomas Lovell's heads
Should have gone off.
KING Ha? What, so rank? Ah ha,
There's mischief in this man. Canst thou say
further?
SURVEYOR
I can, my liege.
KING Proceed.
SURVEYOR Being at Greenwich,
After your Highness had reprov'd the Duke
About Sir William Bulmer—
KING I remember
Of such a time. Being my sworn servant,
The Duke retain'd him his. But on; what hence?
SURVEYOR
"If," quoth he, "I for this had been committed,
As, to the Tower, I thought, I would have play'd
The part my father meant to act upon
Th' usurper Richard, who, being at Salisbury,
Made suit to come in 's presence, which if granted,
As he made semblance of his duty, would
Have put his knife into him."
KING A giant traitor!
WOLSEY
Now, madam, may his Highness live in freedom,
And this man out of prison?
KATHARINE God mend all!
KING
There's something more would out of thee. What
say'st?
SURVEYOR
After "the Duke his father," with "the knife,"
He stretch'd him, and with one hand on his dagger,
Another spread on 's breast, mounting his eyes,
He did discharge a horrible oath, whose tenor
Was, were he evil us'd, he would outgo
His father by as much as a performance
Does an irresolute purpose.
KING There's his period,
To sheathe his knife in us. He is attach'd;
Call him to present trial. If he may
Find mercy in the law, 'tis his; if none,
Let him not seek 't of us. By day and night,
He's traitor to th' height. *Exeunt.*

SCENE III

Enter Lord Chamberlain and Lord Sands.

CHAMBERLAIN
Is 't possible the spells of France should juggle
Men into such strange mysteries?
SANDS New customs,
Though they be never so ridiculous,
Nay, let 'em be unmanly, yet are follow'd.
CHAMBERLAIN
As far as I see, all the good our English
Have got by the late voyage is but merely

143 Deliver tell **145 fail** i.e., dying without an heir **147 Henton** (According to Holinshed, an alias for Nicholas Hopkins; see I.i.221.) **152 the Rose** (A manor house.) **158 doubted** feared, suspected **163 moment** importance **167 demure** grave, solemn **181–182 being . . . do** once believed in, was very likely to cause him mischief **184 fail'd** died

195 my father i.e., the Duke of Buckingham of Richard III's time **198 semblance** pretense **204 stretch'd him** i.e., raised himself to his full height **205 mounting** raising **209 period** aim, goal **210 attach'd** arrested **211 present** immediate

I.iii. Location: London. The palace.
2 mysteries artificial fashions

A fit or two o' th' face; but they are shrewd ones,
For when they hold 'em, you would swear directly
Their very noses had been counselors
To Pepin or Clotharius, they keep state so.

SANDS
They have all new legs, and lame ones. One would
take it,
That never see 'em pace before, the spavin
Or springhalt reign'd among 'em.

CHAMBERLAIN
Death, my lord,
Their clothes are after such a pagan cut to 't,
That, sure, th' have worn out Christendom.

Enter Sir Thomas Lovell.

How now?
What news, Sir Thomas Lovell?

LOVELL
Faith, my lord,
I hear of none but the new proclamation
That's clapp'd upon the court-gate.

CHAMBERLAIN
What is 't for?

LOVELL
The reformation of our travel'd gallants,
That fill the court with quarrels, talk, and tailors.

CHAMBERLAIN
I'm glad 'tis there. Now I would pray our monsieurs
To think an English courtier may be wise,
And never see the Louvre.

LOVELL
They must either,
For so run the conditions, leave those remnants
Of fool and feather that they got in France,
With all their honorable points of ignorance
Pertaining thereunto, as fights and fireworks,
Abusing better men than they can be
Out of a foreign wisdom, renouncing clean
The faith they have in tennis and tall stockings,
Short blist'red breeches, and those types of travel,
And understand again like honest men,
Or pack to their old playfellows. There, I take it,
They may, "cum privilegio," "oui" away
The lag end of their lewdness and be laugh'd at.

SANDS
'Tis time to give 'em physic, their diseases
Are grown so catching.

CHAMBERLAIN
What a loss our ladies
Will have of these trim vanities!

LOVELL
Ay, marry,
There will be woe indeed, lords. The sly whoresons
Have got a speeding trick to lay down ladies;
A French song and a fiddle has no fellow.

SANDS
The devil fiddle 'em! I am glad they are going,
For, sure, there's no converting of 'em. Now
An honest country lord, as I am, beaten
A long time out of play, may bring his plain-song
And have an hour of hearing, and, by 'r lady,
Held current music too.

CHAMBERLAIN
Well said, Lord Sands.
Your colt's tooth is not cast yet?

SANDS
No, my lord,
Nor shall not while I have a stump.

CHAMBERLAIN
Sir Thomas,
Whither were you a-going?

LOVELL
To the Cardinal's.
Your lordship is a guest too.

CHAMBERLAIN
O, 'tis true.
This night he makes a supper, and a great one,
To many lords and ladies. There will be
The beauty of this kingdom, I'll assure you.

LOVELL
That churchman bears a bounteous mind indeed,
A hand as fruitful as the land that feeds us;
His dews fall everywhere.

CHAMBERLAIN
No doubt he's noble;
He had a black mouth that said other of him.

SANDS
He may, my lord. H'as wherewithal in him;
Sparing would show a worse sin than ill doctrine.
Men of his way should be most liberal;
They are set here for examples.

CHAMBERLAIN
True, they are so;
But few now give so great ones. My barge stays;
Your lordship shall along. Come, good Sir Thomas,
We shall be late else, which I would not be,
For I was spoke to, with Sir Henry Guildford
This night to be comptrollers.

SANDS
I am your lordship's.
Exeunt.

SCENE IV

Hautboys. A small table under a state for the Cardinal, a longer table for the guests. Then enter Anne Bullen and divers other Ladies and Gentlemen as guests, at one door; at another door, enter Sir Henry Guildford.

GUILDFORD
Ladies, a general welcome from his Grace
Salutes ye all. This night he dedicates
To fair content and you. None here, he hopes,
In all this noble bevy, has brought with her
One care abroad. He would have all as merry
As, first, good company, good wine, good welcome,
Can make good people.

7 fit . . . face affected ways of screwing up the face into a grimace **10 Pepin, Clotharius** kings of ancient France in the sixth and seventh centuries **11 legs** mannerisms of walking and making obeisances **12 see** saw. **pace** walk. **spavin** disease of horses causing swelling of joints and lameness **13 springhalt** lameness in a horse **14 to 't** moreover, besides **15 th' have . . . Christendom** they have exhausted the repertory of Christian fashions **27 fireworks** i.e., whoring **31 blist'red** puffed. **types** emblems **33 pack** be off **34 cum privilegio** with exclusive right, immunity **34–35 "oui" . . . lewdness** i.e., in French manner pass the last days of their worthless lives **36 physic** medicine **40 speeding** successful. **lay down** seduce, bring to bed of a child **41 fellow** equal

45 play i.e., playing love-games. **plain-song** simple chant or air **47 Held current** regarded as fashionable **48 colt's tooth** i.e., lecherousness of youth. **cast** given up **49 stump** i.e., of a tooth (with a bawdy pun) **58 He . . . mouth** a person must have an evil habit of speech **59 H'as** he has **60 Sparing** frugality. **ill doctrine** heresy **61 way** way of life **63 stays** waits for me **66 spoke to** asked **67 comptrollers** masters of ceremonies

I.iv. Location: Westminster. A hall in York Place.
s.d. state canopy **4 bevy** company

Enter Lord Chamberlain, Lord Sands, and [Sir Thomas] Lovell.

O my lord, y' are tardy.
The very thought of this fair company
Clapp'd wings to me.

CHAMBERLAIN You are young, Sir Harry Guildford.

SANDS
Sir Thomas Lovell, had the Cardinal
But half my lay thoughts in him, some of these
Should find a running banquet ere they rested,
I think would better please 'em. By my life,
They are a sweet society of fair ones.

LOVELL
O, that your lordship were but now confessor
To one or two of these!

SANDS I would I were;
They should find easy penance.

LOVELL Faith, how easy?

SANDS
As easy as a down-bed would afford it.

CHAMBERLAIN
Sweet ladies, will it please you sit? Sir Harry,
Place you that side; I'll take the charge of this.
[*The guests are shown their places at table.*]
His Grace is ent'ring. Nay, you must not freeze;
Two women plac'd together makes cold weather.
My Lord Sands, you are one will keep 'em waking;
Pray, sit between these ladies.

SANDS By my faith,
And thank your lordship. By your leave, sweet ladies.
[*Takes a place between Anne Bullen and another lady.*]
If I chance to talk a little wild, forgive me;
I had it from my father.

ANNE Was he mad, sir?

SANDS
O, very mad, exceeding mad, in love too.
But he would bite none; just as I do now,
He would kiss you twenty with a breath.
[*Kisses her.*]

CHAMBERLAIN
Well said, my lord.
So, now y' are fairly seated. Gentlemen,
The penance lies on you, if these fair ladies
Pass away frowning.

SANDS For my little cure,
Let me alone.

Hautboys. Enter Cardinal Wolsey, and takes his state.

WOLSEY
Y' are welcome, my fair guests. That noble lady
Or gentleman that is not freely merry
Is not my friend. This, to confirm my welcome;
And to you all, good health. [*Drinks.*]

SANDS Your Grace is noble.
Let me have such a bowl may hold my thanks,
And save me so much talking.

WOLSEY My Lord Sands,
I am beholding to you; cheer your neighbors.
Ladies, you are not merry. Gentlemen,
Whose fault is this?

SANDS The red wine first must rise
In their fair cheeks, my lord; then we shall have 'em
Talk us to silence.

ANNE You are a merry gamester,
My Lord Sands.

SANDS Yes, if I make my play.
Here's to your ladyship; and pledge it, madam,
For 'tis to such a thing—

ANNE You cannot show me.

SANDS
I told your Grace they would talk anon.
Drum and trumpet, chambers discharg'd.

WOLSEY What's that?

CHAMBERLAIN
Look out there, some of ye. [*Exit Servant.*]

WOLSEY What warlike voice,
And to what end, is this? Nay, ladies, fear not;
By all the laws of war y' are privileg'd.

Enter a Servant.

CHAMBERLAIN
How now? What is 't?

SERVANT A noble troop of strangers;
For so they seem. Th' have left their barge and landed,
And hither make, as great ambassadors
From foreign princes.

WOLSEY Good Lord Chamberlain,
Go, give 'em welcome; you can speak the French tongue;
And pray receive 'em nobly and conduct 'em
Into our presence, where this heaven of beauty
Shall shine at full upon them. Some attend him.
[*Exit Chamberlain, attended.*]
All rise, and tables remov'd.
You have now a broken banquet, but we'll mend it.
A good digestion to you all! And once more
I show'r a welcome on ye. Welcome all!

Hautboys. Enter King and others, as masquers, habited like shepherds, usher'd by the Lord Chamberlain. They pass directly before the Cardinal, and gracefully salute him.

A noble company! What are their pleasures?

CHAMBERLAIN
Because they speak no English, thus they pray'd

11 lay secular **12 running banquet** hasty meal (with bawdy double meaning, found also perhaps in *lay*, l. 11, *confessor, easy penance*, etc.) **20 Place you** assign places on **23 waking** i.e., lively **30 with a breath** at one breath. **31 said** done **34 cure** (1) remedy (2) cure of souls (continuing the ecclesiastical metaphor of l. 15) **35 s.d. state** chair of state

40 may as may **47 make my play** win my game (of love) **50 s.d. chambers** small pieces of cannon (the firing of which in 1613 probably started the fire that burned down the Globe playhouse) **53 privileg'd** i.e., entitled to immunity in the event of conflict

To tell your Grace that, having heard by fame
Of this so noble and so fair assembly
This night to meet here, they could do no less,
Out of the great respect they bear to beauty,
But leave their flocks, and, under your fair conduct,
Crave leave to view these ladies and entreat
An hour of revels with 'em.

WOLSEY Say, Lord Chamberlain,
They have done my poor house grace, for which I pay 'em
A thousand thanks, and pray 'em take their pleasures.

Choose Ladies; King and Anne Bullen.

KING
The fairest hand I ever touch'd! O beauty,
Till now I never knew thee! *Music. Dance.*

WOLSEY
My lord!

CHAMBERLAIN Your Grace?

WOLSEY Pray, tell 'em thus much from me:
There should be one amongst 'em, by his person
More worthy this place than myself, to whom,
If I but knew him, with my love and duty
I would surrender it.

CHAMBERLAIN I will, my lord.

Whisper [with the Masquers].

WOLSEY
What say they?

CHAMBERLAIN Such a one, they all confess,
There is indeed, which they would have your Grace
Find out, and he will take it.

WOLSEY Let me see, then.
By all your good leaves, gentlemen; here I'll make
My royal choice.

KING [*Unmasking*] Ye have found him, Cardinal.
You hold a fair assembly; you do well, lord.
You are a churchman, or, I'll tell you, Cardinal,
I should judge now unhappily.

WOLSEY I am glad
Your Grace is grown so pleasant.

KING My Lord Chamberlain,
Prithee, come hither. What fair lady's that?

CHAMBERLAIN
An't please your Grace, Sir Thomas Bullen's daughter—
The Viscount Rochford—one of her Highness' women.

KING
By heaven, she is a dainty one.—Sweetheart,
I were unmannerly, to take you out
And not to kiss you. [*Kisses Anne.*] A health, gentlemen!
Let it go round.

WOLSEY
Sir Thomas Lovell, is the banquet ready
I' th' privy chamber?

LOVELL Yes, my lord.

WOLSEY Your Grace,
I fear, with dancing is a little heated.

KING
I fear, too much.

WOLSEY There's fresher air, my lord,
In the next chamber.

KING
Lead in your ladies, ev'ry one.—Sweet partner,
I must not yet forsake you.—Let's be merry,
Good my Lord Cardinal. I have half a dozen healths
To drink to these fair ladies, and a measure
To lead 'em once again; and then let's dream
Who's best in favor. Let the music knock it.

Exeunt with trumpets.

ACT II • SCENE I

Enter two Gentlemen, at several doors.

FIRST GENTLEMAN
Whither away so fast?

SECOND GENTLEMAN O, God save ye!
Ev'n to the hall, to hear what shall become
Of the great Duke of Buckingham.

FIRST GENTLEMAN I'll save you
That labor, sir. All's now done but the ceremony
Of bringing back the prisoner.

SECOND GENTLEMAN Were you there?

FIRST GENTLEMAN
Yes, indeed, was I.

SECOND GENTLEMAN Pray speak what has happen'd.

FIRST GENTLEMAN
You may guess quickly what.

SECOND GENTLEMAN Is he found guilty?

FIRST GENTLEMAN
Yes, truly is he, and condemn'd upon 't.

SECOND GENTLEMAN
I am sorry for 't.

FIRST GENTLEMAN So are a number more.

SECOND GENTLEMAN
But, pray, how pass'd it?

FIRST GENTLEMAN
I'll tell you in a little. The great Duke
Came to the bar; where to his accusations
He pleaded still not guilty and alleg'd
Many sharp reasons to defeat the law.
The King's attorney on the contrary
Urg'd on the examinations, proofs, confessions
Of divers witnesses, which the Duke desir'd
To have brought vivâ voce to his face;
At which appear'd against him his surveyor,
Sir Gilbert Perk his chancellor, and John Car,
Confessor to him, with that devil monk,
Hopkins, that made this mischief.

71 fair conduct kind permission **80 this place** i.e., this chair of state **85 it** i.e., the chair of state **90 unhappily** unfavorably **91 pleasant** merry **96 take you out** lead you out for a dance

107 measure stately dance **109 best in favor** handsomest. **knock it** strike up

II.i. Location: Westminster. A street.
s.d. several different **2 the hall** i.e., Westminster Hall, where the trial was held **10 pass'd it** did it proceed **11 in a little** in brief **16 examinations** depositions **18 vivâ voce** so that their voices can be heard

SECOND GENTLEMAN That was he
That fed him with his prophecies?

FIRST GENTLEMAN The same.
All these accus'd him strongly, which he fain
Would have flung from him, but, indeed, he could not.
And so his peers, upon this evidence,
Have found him guilty of high treason. Much
He spoke, and learnedly, for life; but all
Was either pitied in him or forgotten.

SECOND GENTLEMAN
After all this, how did he bear himself?

FIRST GENTLEMAN
When he was brought again to th' bar, to hear
His knell rung out, his judgment, he was stirr'd
With such an agony he sweat extremely,
And something spoke in choler, ill and hasty.
But he fell to himself again, and sweetly
In all the rest show'd a most noble patience.

SECOND GENTLEMAN
I do not think he fears death.

FIRST GENTLEMAN Sure, he does not;
He never was so womanish. The cause
He may a little grieve at.

SECOND GENTLEMAN Certainly
The Cardinal is the end of this.

FIRST GENTLEMAN 'Tis likely,
By all conjectures: first, Kildare's attainder,
Then deputy of Ireland; who remov'd,
Earl Surrey was sent thither, and in haste too,
Lest he should help his father.

SECOND GENTLEMAN That trick of state
Was a deep envious one.

FIRST GENTLEMAN At his return
No doubt he will requite it. This is noted,
And generally: whoever the King favors,
The Card'nal instantly will find employment,
And far enough from court too.

SECOND GENTLEMAN All the commons
Hate him perniciously, and, o' my conscience,
Wish him ten fathom deep. This Duke as much
They love and dote on; call him bounteous Buckingham,
The mirror of all courtesy—

Enter Buckingham from his arraignment; tipstaves before him; the axe with the edge towards him; halberds on each side; accompanied with Sir Thomas Lovell, Sir Nicholas Vaux, Sir Walter Sands, and common people, etc.

FIRST GENTLEMAN Stay there, sir,
And see the noble ruin'd man you speak of.

SECOND GENTLEMAN
Let's stand close and behold him.

BUCKINGHAM All good people,
You that thus far have come to pity me,
Hear what I say, and then go home and lose me.
I have this day receiv'd a traitor's judgment,
And by that name must die. Yet, heaven bear witness,
And if I have a conscience, let it sink me,
Even as the axe falls, if I be not faithful!
The law I bear no malice for my death;
'T has done, upon the premises, but justice;
But those that sought it I could wish more Christians.
Be what they will, I heartily forgive 'em.
Yet let 'em look they glory not in mischief,
Nor build their evils on the graves of great men,
For then my guiltless blood must cry against 'em.
For further life in this world I ne'er hope,
Nor will I sue, although the King have mercies
More than I dare make faults. You few that lov'd me
And dare be bold to weep for Buckingham,
His noble friends and fellows, whom to leave
Is only bitter to him, only dying,
Go with me, like good angels, to my end;
And, as the long divorce of steel falls on me,
Make of your prayers one sweet sacrifice,
And lift my soul to heaven. Lead on, a' God's name.

LOVELL
I do beseech your Grace, for charity,
If ever any malice in your heart
Were hid against me, now to forgive me frankly.

BUCKINGHAM
Sir Thomas Lovell, I as free forgive you
As I would be forgiven. I forgive all.
There cannot be those numberless offenses
'Gainst me, that I cannot take peace with; no black envy
Shall mark my grave. Commend me to his Grace;
And, if he speak of Buckingham, pray tell him
You met him half in heaven. My vows and prayers
Yet are the King's, and, till my soul forsake,
Shall cry for blessings on him. May he live
Longer than I have time to tell his years!
Ever belov'd and loving may his rule be!
And when old Time shall lead him to his end,
Goodness and he fill up one monument!

LOVELL
To th' water side I must conduct your Grace,
Then give my charge up to Sir Nicholas Vaux,
Who undertakes you to your end.

VAUX Prepare there,
The Duke is coming. See the barge be ready;
And fit it with such furniture as suits
The greatness of his person.

BUCKINGHAM Nay, Sir Nicholas,
Let it alone; my state now will but mock me.
When I came hither, I was Lord High Constable

29 Was . . . forgotten either produced no effect or produced only ineffectual pity **32 judgment** sentence **35 fell to** recovered **40 end** cause **41 Kildare's attainder** i.e., the confiscation of estates and sentencing to death of the Earl of Kildare, Lord Lieutenant of Ireland (whom Wolsey, according to Holinshed, removed to make room for Thomas Howard, Earl of Surrey, son-in-law to Buckingham, and thereby keep Surrey in effective exile) **44 father** i.e., father-in-law **45 envious** malicious **47 generally** by everybody **53 s.d. tipstaves** bailiffs. **halberds** halberdiers, with long-handled weapons. **Walter** ("William" in Holinshed.)

57 lose forget **63 premises** evidence **74 Is . . . dying** alone is bitter to him, he alone dying **77 sacrifice** offering **85 envy** malice **89 forsake** leave my body **91 tell** count **93 Time** age **94 monument** tomb **99 furniture** equipment

And Duke of Buckingham; now, poor Edward Bohun.
Yet I am richer than my base accusers,
That never knew what truth meant. I now seal it; 105
And with that blood will make 'em one day groan for 't.
My noble father, Henry of Buckingham,
Who first rais'd head against usurping Richard, 108
Flying for succor to his servant Banister,
Being distress'd, was by that wretch betray'd,
And without trial fell; God's peace be with him!
Henry the Seventh succeeding, truly pitying
My father's loss, like a most royal prince
Restor'd me to my honors, and, out of ruins,
Made my name once more noble. Now his son,
Henry the Eighth, life, honor, name, and all
That made me happy at one stroke has taken
For ever from the world. I had my trial,
And, must needs say, a noble one; which makes me
A little happier than my wretched father.
Yet thus far we are one in fortunes: both
Fell by our servants, by those men we lov'd most—
A most unnatural and faithless service!
Heaven has an end in all; yet, you that hear me, 124
This from a dying man receive as certain:
Where you are liberal of your loves and counsels
Be sure you be not loose; for those you make friends 127
And give your hearts to, when they once perceive
The least rub in your fortunes, fall away 129
Like water from ye, never found again
But where they mean to sink ye. All good people,
Pray for me! I must now forsake ye. The last hour
Of my long weary life is come upon me.
Farewell! And when you would say something that is sad,
Speak how I fell. I have done; and God forgive me!
Exeunt Duke and Train.

FIRST GENTLEMAN
O, this is full of pity! Sir, it calls,
I fear, too many curses on their heads
That were the authors.

SECOND GENTLEMAN If the Duke be guiltless,
'Tis full of woe. Yet I can give you inkling
Of an ensuing evil, if it fall,
Greater than this.

FIRST GENTLEMAN Good angels keep it from us!
What may it be? You do not doubt my faith, sir? 142

SECOND GENTLEMAN
This secret is so weighty, 'twill require
A strong faith to conceal it.

FIRST GENTLEMAN Let me have it;
I do not talk much.

SECOND GENTLEMAN I am confident; 145
You shall, sir. Did you not of late days hear 146
A buzzing of a separation
Between the King and Katharine?

FIRST GENTLEMAN Yes, but it held not; 148
For when the King once heard it, out of anger
He sent command to the Lord Mayor straight
To stop the rumor, and allay those tongues 151
That durst disperse it.

SECOND GENTLEMAN But that slander, sir,
Is found a truth now; for it grows again
Fresher than e'er it was, and held for certain
The King will venture at it. Either the Cardinal,
Or some about him near, have, out of malice
To the good Queen, possess'd him with a scruple 157
That will undo her. To confirm this too,
Cardinal Campeius is arriv'd, and lately, 159
As all think, for this business.

FIRST GENTLEMAN 'Tis the Cardinal;
And merely to revenge him on the Emperor 161
For not bestowing on him, at his asking,
The archbishopric of Toledo, this is purpos'd.

SECOND GENTLEMAN
I think you have hit the mark. But is 't not cruel
That she should feel the smart of this? The Cardinal
Will have his will, and she must fall.

FIRST GENTLEMAN 'Tis woeful.
We are too open here to argue this; 167
Let's think in private more. *Exeunt.*

SCENE II

Enter Lord Chamberlain, reading this letter.

CHAMBERLAIN "My lord, the horses your lordship sent
for, with all the care I had, I saw well chosen, ridden, 2
and furnish'd. They were young and handsome, and 3
of the best breed in the north. When they were ready
to set out for London, a man of my Lord Cardinal's,
by commission and main power, took 'em from me, 6
with this reason: His master would be serv'd before a
subject, if not before the King; which stopp'd our
mouths, sir."
I fear he will indeed. Well, let him have them.
He will have all, I think.

Enter, to the Lord Chamberlain, the Dukes of Norfolk and Suffolk.

NORFOLK
Well met, my Lord Chamberlain.

CHAMBERLAIN
Good day to both your Graces.

SUFFOLK
How is the King employ'd?

105 seal ratify **108 rais'd head** gathered an army **124 end** aim **127 loose** wanting in restraint **129 rub** impediment. (A term from bowls.) **142 faith** i.e., ability to keep a secret **145 am confident** i.e., trust your discretion **146 shall** i.e., shall hear it

148 held was believed **151 allay** restrain **157 possess'd . . . scruple** put into his mind a doubt. (Katharine had been married to Henry's older brother, Prince Arthur, who died, still in his early teens, a year after the marriage. Such a precontract would normally invalidate a subsequent marriage with any close relative of Arthur's, but Henry's marriage to Katharine had been made possible by a papal dispensation.) **159 Cardinal Campeius** i.e., Cardinal Lorenzo Campeggio, sent from Rome to confer on the legality of the King's marriage **161 Emperor** (The Queen was the aunt of Charles V, Holy Roman Emperor and King of Spain; see I.i.176 and note.) **167 open** public

II.ii. Location: London. The palace.
2 ridden broken in, trained **3 furnish'd** equipped **6 commission** warrant

CHAMBERLAIN I left him private,
Full of sad thoughts and troubles.
NORFOLK What's the cause?
CHAMBERLAIN
It seems the marriage with his brother's wife
Has crept too near his conscience.
SUFFOLK No, his conscience
Has crept too near another lady.
NORFOLK 'Tis so.
This is the Cardinal's doing. The king-cardinal,
That blind priest, like the eldest son of Fortune,
Turns what he list. The King will know him one
day.
SUFFOLK
Pray God he do! He'll never know himself else.
NORFOLK
How holily he works in all his business!
And with what zeal! For, now he has crack'd the
league
Between us and the Emperor, the Queen's great
nephew,
He dives into the King's soul, and there scatters
Dangers, doubts, wringing of the conscience,
Fears, and despairs, and all these for his marriage;
And out of all these to restore the King,
He counsels a divorce, a loss of her
That, like a jewel, has hung twenty years
About his neck, yet never lost her luster;
Of her that loves him with that excellence
That angels love good men with; even of her
That, when the greatest stroke of fortune falls,
Will bless the King. And is not this course pious?
CHAMBERLAIN
Heaven keep me from such counsel! 'Tis most true
These news are everywhere; every tongue speaks
'em,
And every true heart weeps for 't. All that dare
Look into these affairs see this main end,
The French King's sister. Heaven will one day open
The King's eyes, that so long have slept upon
This bold bad man.
SUFFOLK
And free us from his slavery.
NORFOLK We had need pray,
And heartily, for our deliverance,
Or this imperious man will work us all
From princes into pages. All men's honors
Lie like one lump before him, to be fashion'd
Into what pitch he please.
SUFFOLK For me, my lords,
I love him not, nor fear him; there's my creed.
As I am made without him, so I'll stand,
If the King please. His curses and his blessings
Touch me alike, th' are breath I not believe in.
I knew him, and I know him; so I leave him
To him that made him proud, the Pope.
NORFOLK Let's in,
And with some other business put the King
From these sad thoughts that work too much upon
him.
My lord, you'll bear us company?
CHAMBERLAIN Excuse me;
The King has sent me otherwhere. Besides,
You'll find a most unfit time to disturb him.
Health to your lordships.
NORFOLK Thanks, my good Lord Chamberlain.
Exit Lord Chamberlain; and the King draws the curtain and sits reading pensively.
SUFFOLK
How sad he looks! Sure he is much afflicted.
KING
Who's there, ha?
NORFOLK Pray God he be not angry.
KING
Who's there, I say? How dare you thrust yourselves
Into my private meditations?
Who am I? Ha?
NORFOLK
A gracious king that pardons all offenses
Malice ne'er meant. Our breach of duty this way
Is business of estate; in which we come
To know your royal pleasure.
KING Ye are too bold.
Go to! I'll make ye know your times of business.
Is this an hour for temporal affairs, ha?

Enter Wolsey and Campeius, with a commission.

Who's there? My good Lord Cardinal? O my
Wolsey,
The quiet of my wounded conscience,
Thou art a cure fit for a king. [*To Campeius.*] You're
welcome,
Most learned reverend sir, into our kingdom.
Use us and it. [*To Wolsey.*] My good lord, have
great care
I be not found a talker.
WOLSEY Sir, you cannot.
I would your Grace would give us but an hour
Of private conference.
KING [*To Norfolk and Suffolk*] We are busy; go.
NORFOLK [*Aside to Suffolk*]
This priest has no pride in him?
SUFFOLK [*Aside to Norfolk*] Not to speak of.
I would not be so sick though for his place.
But this cannot continue.
NORFOLK [*Aside to Suffolk*] If it do,
I'll venture one; have at him!
SUFFOLK [*Aside to Norfolk*] I another.
Exeunt Norfolk and Suffolk.

15 sad serious **20–21 blind . . . list** (Alludes to Fortune, conventionally depicted as blind and turning her wheel.) **21 list** wishes **41 The . . . sister** i.e., the Duchess of Alençon; see III.ii. 85–86 **42 slept upon** been blind to **48 lump** i.e., lump of clay **49 pitch** height (literally, of a falcon's flight), i.e., degree of dignity. (In a mixed metaphor, the Cardinal is likened to one who reduces all men of rank to one lump which he will refashion into creatures of whatever stature he pleases.) **51 As . . . stand** i.e., inasmuch as my rank was conferred on me by the King, not by Wolsey, I'll stand firm

61 s.d. curtain (The King is probably in a "discovery space" rear stage.) **68 this way** in this respect **69 estate** public weal **78 I . . . talker** i.e., lest my offer of hospitality be only talk, not deeds **82 sick** i.e., sick with pride. **for his place** even for his high office **84 have at him** i.e., thrust at him (Wolsey) in fencing

WOLSEY
Your Grace has given a precedent of wisdom
Above all princes, in committing freely
Your scruple to the voice of Christendom.
Who can be angry now? What envy reach you?
The Spaniard, tied by blood and favor to her,
Must now confess, if they have any goodness,
The trial just and noble. All the clerks,
I mean the learned ones in Christian kingdoms,
Have their free voices. Rome, the nurse of
judgment,
Invited by your noble self, hath sent
One general tongue unto us, this good man,
This just and learned priest, Card'nal Campeius;
Whom once more I present unto your Highness.

KING
And once more in mine arms I bid him welcome,
[Embraces him.]
And thank the holy conclave for their loves.
They have sent me such a man I would have
wish'd for.

CAMPEIUS
Your Grace must needs deserve all strangers' loves,
You are so noble. To you Highness' hand
I tender my commission; by whose virtue,
The Court of Rome commanding, you, my Lord
Cardinal of York, are join'd with me their servant
In the unpartial judging of this business.
[Gives the King a document.]

KING
Two equal men. The Queen shall be acquainted
Forthwith for what you come. Where's Gardiner?

WOLSEY
I know your Majesty has always lov'd her
So dear in heart, not to deny her that
A woman of less place might ask by law:
Scholars allow'd freely to argue for her.

KING
Ay, and the best she shall have; and my favor
To him that does best; God forbid else. Cardinal,
Prithee, call Gardiner to me, my new secretary.
I find him a fit fellow. *[Wolsey goes to the door.]*

Enter Gardiner.

WOLSEY *[Aside to Gardiner]*
Give me your hand. Much joy and favor to you;
You are the King's now.

GARDINER *[Aside to Wolsey]* But to be commanded
For ever by your Grace, whose hand has rais'd me.

KING
Come hither, Gardiner. *Walks and whispers.*

CAMPEIUS
My Lord of York, was not one Doctor Pace
In this man's place before him?

WOLSEY Yes, he was.

CAMPEIUS
Was he not held a learned man?

WOLSEY Yes, surely.

CAMPEIUS
Believe me, there's an ill opinion spread then
Even of yourself, Lord Cardinal.

WOLSEY How? Of me?

CAMPEIUS
They will not stick to say you envied him,
And, fearing he would rise, he was so virtuous,
Kept him a foreign man still, which so griev'd him
That he ran mad and died.

WOLSEY Heav'n's peace be with him!
That's Christian care enough. For living murmurers
There's places of rebuke. He was a fool,
For he would needs be virtuous. That good fellow,
[Indicating Gardiner.]
If I command him, follows my appointment;
I will have none so near else. Learn this, brother,
We live not to be grip'd by meaner persons.

KING *[To Gardiner]*
Deliver this with modesty to th' Queen.
Exit Gardiner.
The most convenient place that I can think of
For such receipt of learning is Blackfriars;
There ye shall meet about this weighty business.
My Wolsey, see it furnish'd. O, my lord,
Would it not grieve an able man to leave
So sweet a bedfellow? But, conscience, conscience!
O, 'tis a tender place, and I must leave her. *Exeunt.*

SCENE III

Enter Anne Bullen and an Old Lady.

ANNE
Not for that neither. Here's the pang that pinches:
His Highness having liv'd so long with her, and she
So good a lady that no tongue could ever
Pronounce dishonor of her—by my life,
She never knew harm-doing—O, now, after
So many courses of the sun enthroned,
Still growing in a majesty and pomp, the which
To leave a thousandfold more bitter than
'Tis sweet at first t' acquire—after this process,
To give her the avaunt! It is a pity
Would move a monster.

OLD LADY Hearts of most hard temper
Melt and lament for her.

ANNE O, God's will, much better
She ne'er had known pomp. Though 't be temporal,

87 voice of Christendom i.e., the Pope, through his representative Campeius, and the clerics and scholars of various continental universities to whom Henry submitted his problem of "conscience" **88 envy** malice **89 The Spaniard** i.e., Charles V and his court **91 clerks** clerics, scholars **93 voices** votes **95 One general tongue** i.e., a spokesman **99 conclave** College of Cardinals **101 strangers'** foreigners' **107 equal** impartial **108 Gardiner** i.e., Stephen Gardiner, Wolsey's secretary; he later became one of the most influential members of the King's council **110 that** that which **111 less place** lower rank

126 stick hesitate. **envied him** i.e., were hostile toward Pace **128 Kept . . . still** kept him constantly abroad on diplomatic missions **130 murmurers** grumblers, troublemakers **133 appointment** bidding **134 none . . . else** i.e., no one besides him so close to the King **135 grip'd** clutched at **136 Deliver** repeat **138 such . . . learning** giving a proper reception to such learned men. **Blackfriars** convent buildings in London surrendered to the crown in Henry VIII's time

II.iii. Location: London. The Queen's apartments in the palace.
13 temporal merely worldly prosperity, not heavenly

Yet, if that quarrel, Fortune, do divorce
It from the bearer, 'tis a sufferance panging
As soul and body's severing.

OLD LADY
Alas, poor lady!
She's a stranger now again.

ANNE
So much the more
Must pity drop upon her. Verily,
I swear, 'tis better to be lowly born,
And range with humble livers in content,
Than to be perk'd up in a glist'ring grief
And wear a golden sorrow.

OLD LADY
Our content
Is our best having.

ANNE
By my troth and maidenhead,
I would not be a queen.

OLD LADY
Beshrew me, I would,
And venture maidenhead for 't; and so would you,
For all this spice of your hypocrisy.
You, that have so fair parts of woman on you,
Have too a woman's heart, which ever yet
Affected eminence, wealth, sovereignty;
Which, to say sooth, are blessings; and which gifts,
Saving your mincing, the capacity
Of your soft cheveril conscience would receive,
If you might please to stretch it.

ANNE
Nay, good troth.

OLD LADY
Yes, troth, and troth. You would not be a queen?

ANNE
No, not for all the riches under heaven.

OLD LADY
'Tis strange. A threepence bow'd would hire me,
Old as I am, to queen it. But, I pray you,
What think you of a duchess? Have you limbs
To bear that load of title?

ANNE
No, in truth.

OLD LADY
Then you are weakly made. Pluck off a little;
I would not be a young count in your way
For more than blushing comes to. If your back
Cannot vouchsafe this burden, 'tis too weak
Ever to get a boy.

ANNE
How you do talk!
I swear again, I would not be a queen
For all the world.

OLD LADY
In faith, for little England
You 'd venture an emballing. I myself
Would for Carnarvonshire, although there 'long'd
No more to th' crown but that. Lo, who comes here?

Enter Lord Chamberlain.

CHAMBERLAIN
Good morrow, ladies. What were 't worth to know
The secret of your conference?

ANNE
My good Lord,
Not your demand; it values not your asking.
Our mistress' sorrows we were pitying.

CHAMBERLAIN
It was a gentle business, and becoming
The action of good woman. There is hope
All will be well.

ANNE
Now, I pray God, amen!

CHAMBERLAIN
You bear a gentle mind, and heav'nly blessings
Follow such creatures. That you may, fair lady,
Perceive I speak sincerely, and high note 's
Ta'en of your many virtues, the King's Majesty
Commends his good opinion of you, and
Does purpose honor to you no less flowing
Than Marchioness of Pembroke; to which title
A thousand pound a year, annual support,
Out of his grace he adds.

ANNE
I do not know
What kind of my obedience I should tender.
More than my all is nothing; nor my prayers
Are not words duly hallowed, nor my wishes
More worth than empty vanities; yet prayers and wishes
Are all I can return. Beseech your lordship,
Vouchsafe to speak my thanks and my obedience,
As from a blushing handmaid, to his Highness;
Whose health and royalty I pray for.

CHAMBERLAIN
Lady,
I shall not fail t' approve the fair conceit
The King hath of you. [*Aside.*] I have perus'd her well;
Beauty and honor in her are so mingled
That they have caught the King. And who knows yet
But from this lady may proceed a gem
To lighten all this isle?—I'll to the King,
And say I spoke with you. *Exit Lord Chamberlain.*

ANNE
My honor'd lord.

OLD LADY
Why, this it is! See, see,
I have been begging sixteen years in court,
Am yet a courtier beggarly, nor could
Come pat betwixt too early and too late
For any suit of pounds; and you, O fate!
A very fresh fish here—fie, fie, fie upon
This compell'd fortune!—have your mouth fill'd up
Before you open it.

ANNE
This is strange to me.

OLD LADY
How tastes it? Is it bitter? Forty pence, no.
There was a lady once, 'tis an old story,
That would not be a queen, that would she not,
For all the mud in Egypt. Have you heard it?

ANNE
Come, you are pleasant.

14 quarrel quarreler, troublemaker **15 panging** causing sorrow **17 stranger** foreigner **20 range** rank. **livers** persons **21 perk'd up** trimmed out **23 having** possession **26 spice** dash, touch **31 Saving your mincing** i.e., your affected coyness notwithstanding **32 cheveril** kid leather. (Used as a type of flexibility.) **36 bow'd** crooked and therefore worthless; with sexual pun on *bawd,* continued in *queen* (quean, whore), *bear, count* (female pudenda), *way, emballing* **40 Pluck off** come lower **43 vouchsafe this burden** i.e., accept this load of honors (with sexual suggestion of bearing a man) **47 emballing** investiture with the ball as a royal emblem (with sexual suggestion) **48 Carnarvonshire** an especially impoverished and barren Welsh county. **'long'd** belonged

52 values not is not worth **74 approve . . . conceit** confirm the good opinion **79 lighten** give light to. (Refers to Queen Elizabeth.) **83 beggarly** i.e., still in need **84 pat** precisely at the opportune time **85 suit of pounds** request for money **87 compell'd** unsought, forced upon one **89 Forty pence, no** i.e., I'll venture a small sum that it isn't bitter to you **92 mud in Egypt** i.e., the wealth of Egypt resulting from its fecund land

OLD LADY With your theme, I could
O'ermount the lark. The Marchioness of Pembroke?
A thousand pounds a year for pure respect?
No other obligation? By my life,
That promises moe thousands. Honor's train
Is longer than his foreskirt. By this time
I know your back will bear a duchess. Say,
Are you not stronger than you were?

ANNE Good lady,
Make yourself mirth with your particular fancy,
And leave me out on 't. Would I had no being
If this salute my blood a jot! It faints me
To think what follows.
The Queen is comfortless, and we forgetful
In our long absence. Pray do not deliver
What here y' have heard to her.

OLD LADY What do you think me? *Exeunt.*

SCENE IV

Trumpets, sennet, and cornets. Enter two Vergers, with short silver wands; next them, two Scribes, in the habit of doctors; after them, the [Arch]bishop of Canterbury alone; after him, the Bishops of Lincoln, Ely, Rochester, and Saint Asaph; next them, with some small distance, follows a Gentleman bearing the purse, with the great seal, and a cardinal's hat; then two Priests, bearing each a silver cross; then a Gentleman Usher bare-headed, accompanied with a Sergeant-at-arms bearing a silver mace; then two Gentlemen bearing two great silver pillars; after them, side by side, the two Cardinals; two Noblemen with the sword and mace. The King takes place under the cloth of state; the two Cardinals sit under him as judges. The Queen takes place some distance from the King. The Bishops place themselves on each side the court, in manner of a consistory; below them, the Scribes. The Lords sit next the Bishops. The rest of the Attendants stand in convenient order about the stage.

WOLSEY
Whilst our commission from Rome is read,
Let silence be commanded.

KING What's the need?
It hath already publicly been read,
And on all sides th' authority allow'd;
You may, then, spare that time.

WOLSEY Be 't so. Proceed.

SCRIBE
Say, Henry King of England, come into the court.

CRIER
Henry King of England, *etc.*

KING
Here.

SCRIBE
Say, Katharine Queen of England, come into the court.

CRIER
Katharine Queen of England, *etc.*

The Queen makes no answer, rises out of her chair, goes about the court, comes to the King, and kneels at his feet; then speaks.

KATHARINE
Sir, I desire you do me right and justice,
And to bestow your pity on me; for
I am a most poor woman, and a stranger,
Born out of your dominions, having here
No judge indifferent, nor no more assurance
Of equal friendship and proceeding. Alas, sir,
In what have I offended you? What cause
Hath my behavior given to your displeasure,
That thus you should proceed to put me off
And take your good grace from me? Heaven witness,
I have been to you a true and humble wife,
At all times to your will conformable,
Ever in fear to kindle your dislike,
Yea, subject to your countenance—glad or sorry
As I saw it inclin'd. When was the hour
I ever contradicted your desire,
Or made it not mine too? Or which of your friends
Have I not strove to love, although I knew
He were mine enemy? What friend of mine
That had to him deriv'd your anger did I
Continue in my liking? Nay, gave notice
He was from thence discharg'd? Sir, call to mind
That I have been your wife, in this obedience,
Upward of twenty years, and have been blest
With many children by you. If, in the course
And process of this time, you can report,
And prove it too, against mine honor aught—
My bond to wedlock, or my love and duty,
Against your sacred person—in God's name,
Turn me away, and let the foul'st contempt
Shut door upon me, and so give me up
To the sharp'st kind of justice. Please you, sir,
The King your father was reputed for
A prince most prudent, of an excellent
And unmatch'd wit and judgment. Ferdinand,
My father, King of Spain, was reckon'd one
The wisest prince that there had reign'd by many
A year before. It is not to be question'd
That they had gather'd a wise council to them
Of every realm, that did debate this business,
Who deem'd our marriage lawful. Wherefore I humbly
Beseech you, sir, to spare me, till I may

93 pleasant merry **97–98 Honor's . . . foreskirt** i.e., honors to come will exceed this present gift, just as an elongated robe trailing behind is longer than the front of a skirt **101 your . . . fancy** your own private imaginings **103 salute** act upon, excite **106 deliver** report

II.iv. Location: London. A hall in Blackfriars.
s.d. sennet trumpet call announcing a procession. **Vergers** those who carry the verge or emblem of office; particularly, attendants on a church dignitary. **habit of doctors** i.e., furred black gowns and flat caps worn by doctors of law. **cloth of state** canopy. **consistory** college of cardinals

15 indifferent impartial **16 equal** fair **30 deriv'd** drawn **35 many children** (The Queen gave birth to five children, only one of whom, later Queen Mary, survived infancy.)

Be by my friends in Spain advis'd, whose counsel
I will implore. If not, i' th' name of God,
Your pleasure be fulfill'd!

WOLSEY
You have here, lady,
And of your choice, these reverend fathers, men
Of singular integrity and learning,
Yea, the elect o' th' land, who are assembled
To plead your cause. It shall be therefore bootless
That longer you desire the court, as well
For your own quiet as to rectify
What is unsettled in the King.

CAMPEIUS
His grace
Hath spoken well and justly. Therefore, madam,
It's fit this royal session do proceed,
And that, without delay, their arguments
Be now produc'd and heard.

KATHARINE
Lord Cardinal,
To you I speak.

WOLSEY
Your pleasure, madam?

KATHARINE
Sir,
I am about to weep; but, thinking that
We are a queen, or long have dream'd so, certain
The daughter of a king, my drops of tears
I'll turn to sparks of fire.

WOLSEY
Be patient yet.

KATHARINE
I will, when you are humble; nay, before,
Or God will punish me. I do believe,
Induc'd by potent circumstances, that
You are mine enemy, and make my challenge
You shall not be my judge. For it is you
Have blown this coal betwixt my lord and me—
Which God's dew quench! Therefore I say again,
I utterly abhor, yea, from my soul
Refuse you for my judge, whom, yet once more,
I hold my most malicious foe, and think not
At all a friend to truth.

WOLSEY
I do profess
You speak not like yourself, who ever yet
Have stood to charity, and display'd th' effects
Of disposition gentle, and of wisdom
O'ertopping woman's pow'r. Madam, you do me wrong.
I have no spleen against you, nor injustice
For you or any. How far I have proceeded,
Or how far further shall, is warranted
By a commission from the consistory,
Yea, the whole consistory of Rome. You charge me
That I have blown this coal. I do deny it.
The King is present. If it be known to him
That I gainsay my deed, how may he wound,
And worthily, my falsehood, yea, as much
As you have done my truth! If he know
That I am free of your report, he knows
I am not of your wrong. Therefore in him
It lies to cure me, and the cure is to
Remove these thoughts from you; the which before
His Highness shall speak in, I do beseech
You, gracious madam, to unthink your speaking
And to say so no more.

KATHARINE
My lord, my lord,
I am a simple woman, much too weak
T' oppose your cunning. Y' are meek and humble-mouth'd;
You sign your place and calling, in full seeming,
With meekness and humility; but your heart
Is cramm'd with arrogancy, spleen, and pride.
You have, by fortune and his Highness' favors,
Gone slightly o'er low steps and now are mounted
Where pow'rs are your retainers, and your words,
Domestics to you, serve your will as 't please
Yourself pronounce their office. I must tell you,
You tender more your person's honor than
Your high profession spiritual; that again
I do refuse you for my judge; and here,
Before you all, appeal unto the Pope,
To bring my whole cause 'fore his Holiness,
And to be judg'd by him.

She curtsies to the King, and offers to depart.

CAMPEIUS
The Queen is obstinate,
Stubborn to justice, apt to accuse it, and
Disdainful to be tried by 't. 'Tis not well.
She's going away.

KING
Call her again.

CRIER
Katharine Queen of England, come into the court.

GENTLEMAN USHER
Madam, you are call'd back.

KATHARINE
What need you note it? Pray you keep your way;
When you are call'd, return. Now, the Lord help!
They vex me past my patience. Pray you, pass on.
I will not tarry; no, nor ever more
Upon this business my appearance make
In any of their courts.

Exeunt Queen, and her Attendants.

KING
Go thy ways, Kate.
That man i' th' world who shall report he has
A better wife, let him in nought be trusted
For speaking false in that. Thou art alone,
If thy rare qualities, sweet gentleness,
Thy meekness saint-like, wife-like government,
Obeying in commanding, and thy parts
Sovereign and pious else, could speak thee out,
The queen of earthly queens. She's noble born;
And, like her true nobility, she has
Carried herself towards me.

WOLSEY
Most gracious sir,

59 bootless profitless **60 That . . . court** that you wish the court inquiry to be prolonged **69 certain** certainly **72 before** i.e., sooner than that (which will never be) **74 Induc'd** persuaded **75 make my challenge** I raise my formal objection (that) **84 stood to** upheld **94 gainsay my deed** deny my acts **97 report** adverse report, accusation **98 am . . . wrong** am innocent of having wronged you

101 in regarding **106 sign** signify, show marks of. **in full seeming** to all appearances **110 slightly** easily **111 pow'rs . . . retainers** i.e., you command the service of people of rank **111–113 your words . . . office** i.e., your clever speeches serve your ends in any way you choose; or, your very words are immediately acted upon **114 tender more** are more concerned for **126 What** why. **keep your way** move on **136 government** behavior **137 parts** qualities **138 speak thee out** declare you as you are

In humblest manner I require your Highness 142
That it shall please you to declare, in hearing
Of all these ears—for where I am robb'd and
bound,
There must I be unloos'd, although not there
At once and fully satisfied—whether ever I 146
Did broach this business to your Highness, or
Laid any scruple in your way, which might
Induce you to the question on 't? Or ever
Have to you, but with thanks to God for such
A royal lady, spake one the least word that might 151
Be to the prejudice of her present state,
Or touch of her good person?

KING My Lord Cardinal, 153
I do excuse you; yea, upon mine honor, 154
I free you from 't. You are not to be taught
That you have many enemies, that know not
Why they are so, but, like to village curs,
Bark when their fellows do. By some of these
The Queen is put in anger. Y' are excus'd.
But will you be more justified? You ever
Have wish'd the sleeping of this business, never
desir'd
It to be stirr'd, but oft have hind'red, oft,
The passages made toward it. On my honor, 163
I speak my good Lord Card'nal to this point, 164
And thus far clear him. Now, what mov'd me to 't,
I will be bold with time and your attention;
Then mark th' inducement. Thus it came; give
heed to 't:
My conscience first receiv'd a tenderness,
Scruple, and prick, on certain speeches utter'd
By th' Bishop of Bayonne, then French ambassador,
Who had been hither sent on the debating
A marriage 'twixt the Duke of Orleans and
Our daughter Mary. I' th' progress of this business,
Ere a determinate resolution, he, 174
I mean the Bishop, did require a respite, 175
Wherein he might the King his lord advertise 176
Whether our daughter were legitimate,
Respecting this our marriage with the dowager, 178
Sometimes our brother's wife. This respite shook 179
The bosom of my conscience, enter'd me,
Yea, with a spitting power, and made to tremble 181
The region of my breast, which forc'd such way
That many maz'd considerings did throng 183
And press'd in with this caution. First, methought
I stood not in the smile of heaven, who had
Commanded nature that my lady's womb,
If it conceiv'd a male child by me, should
Do no more offices of life to 't than
The grave does to th' dead; for her male issue
Or died where they were made, or shortly after 190
This world had air'd them. Hence I took a thought
This was a judgment on me, that my kingdom,
Well worthy the best heir o' th' world, should not
Be gladded in 't by me. Then follows that
I weigh'd the danger which my realms stood in
By this my issue's fail; and that gave to me 196
Many a groaning throe. Thus hulling in 197
The wild sea of my conscience, I did steer
Toward this remedy, whereupon we are
Now present here together; that's to say,
I meant to rectify my conscience—which
I then did feel full sick, and yet not well— 202
By all the reverend fathers of the land
And doctors learn'd. First I began in private
With you, my Lord of Lincoln. You remember
How under my oppression I did reek, 206
When I first mov'd you.

LINCOLN Very well, my liege. 207

KING
I have spoke long. Be pleas'd yourself to say
How far you satisfied me.

LINCOLN So please your Highness,
The question did at first so stagger me,
Bearing a state of mighty moment in 't 211
And consequence of dread, that I committed 212
The daring'st counsel which I had to doubt, 213
And did entreat your Highness to this course
Which you are running here.

KING I then mov'd you,
My Lord of Canterbury, and got your leave
To make this present summons. Unsolicited
I left no reverend person in this court,
But by particular consent proceeded
Under your hands and seals. Therefore, go on, 220
For no dislike i' th' world against the person
Of the good Queen, but the sharp thorny points
Of my alleged reasons, drives this forward.
Prove but our marriage lawful, by my life
And kingly dignity, we are contented
To wear our mortal state to come with her,
Katharine our queen, before the primest creature 227
That's paragon'd o' th' world.

CAMPEIUS So please your Highness, 228
The Queen being absent, 'tis a needful fitness
That we adjourn this court till further day.
Meanwhile must be an earnest motion 231
Made to the Queen, to call back her appeal
She intends unto his Holiness.

KING [*Aside*] I may perceive
These Cardinals trifle with me. I abhor
This dilatory sloth and tricks of Rome.
My learn'd and well-beloved servant, Cranmer,
Prithee, return. With thy approach, I know,
My comfort comes along.—Break up the court!
I say, set on. *Exeunt in manner as they enter'd.*

141 Carried borne, behaved **142 require** request **146 satisfied** given full restitution **151 one the least** a single **153 touch** sullying **154 excuse** exonerate **163 passages** proceedings **164 speak** describe **174 determinate resolution** final decision **175 require** request **176 advertise** inform, confer with **178 dowager** widow **179 Sometimes** formerly **181 spitting** piercing **183 maz'd considerings** conflicting and confused thoughts **190 Or** either

196 By . . . fail by my lacking a son **197 hulling** drifting with sails furled **202 yet** still, even now **206 reek** sweat **207 mov'd** mentioned the business to **211–212 Bearing . . . dread** relating to matters of the greatest consequence to the state and outcome fearful to contemplate **212–213 I committed . . . doubt** i.e., I distrusted the most daring advice I could give **220 Under . . . seals** i.e., with your signed agreement **227 primest** most excellent **228 paragon'd** set forth as a perfect model **231 motion** appeal, request

ACT III • SCENE I

Enter Queen and her Women, as at work.

KATHARINE
Take thy lute, wench. My soul grows sad with troubles;
Sing, and disperse 'em, if thou canst. Leave working. [*One of her women sings to the lute.*]

Song
Orpheus with his lute made trees,
And the mountain tops that freeze,
Bow themselves when he did sing.
To his music plants and flowers
Ever sprung, as sun and showers
There had made a lasting spring.

Every thing that heard him play,
Even the billows of the sea,
Hung their heads, and then lay by.
In sweet music is such art,
Killing care and grief of heart
Fall asleep, or hearing, die.

Enter a Gentleman.

KATHARINE
How now?
GENTLEMAN
An 't please your Grace, the two great Cardinals
Wait in the presence.
KATHARINE Would they speak with me?
GENTLEMAN
They will'd me say so, madam.
KATHARINE Pray their Graces
To come near. [*Gentleman goes to the door.*] What can be their business
With me, a poor weak woman, fall'n from favor?
I do not like their coming. Now I think on 't,
They should be good men; their affairs as righteous.
But all hoods make not monks.

Enter the two Cardinals, Wolsey and Campeius.

WOLSEY Peace to your Highness!
KATHARINE
Your Graces find me here part of a huswife—
I would be all—against the worst may happen.
What are your pleasures with me, reverend lords?
WOLSEY
May it please you, noble madam, to withdraw
Into your private chamber, we shall give you
The full cause of our coming.
KATHARINE Speak it here;
There's nothing I have done yet, o' my conscience,
Deserves a corner. Would all other women
Could speak this with as free a soul as I do!
My lords, I care not, so much I am happy
Above a number, if my actions
Were tried by ev'ry tongue, ev'ry eye saw 'em,
Envy and base opinion set against 'em,
I know my life so even. If your business
Seek me out, and that way I am wife in,
Out with it boldly. Truth loves open dealing.
WOLSEY Tanta est erga te mentis integritas, regina serenissima—
KATHARINE
O, good my lord, no Latin!
I am not such a truant since my coming
As not to know the language I have liv'd in.
A strange tongue makes my cause more strange, suspicious;
Pray, speak in English. Here are some will thank you,
If you speak truth, for their poor mistress' sake;
Believe me, she has had much wrong. Lord Cardinal,
The willing'st sin I ever yet committed
May be absolv'd in English.
WOLSEY Noble lady,
I am sorry my integrity should breed,
And service to his Majesty and you,
So deep suspicion, where all faith was meant.
We come not by the way of accusation,
To taint that honor every good tongue blesses,
Nor to betray you any way to sorrow—
You have too much, good lady—but to know
How you stand minded in the weighty difference
Between the King and you, and to deliver,
Like free and honest men, our just opinions
And comforts to your cause.
CAMPEIUS Most honor'd madam,
My Lord of York, out of his noble nature,
Zeal, and obedience he still bore your Grace,
Forgetting, like a good man, your late censure
Both of his truth and him, which was too far,
Offers, as I do, in a sign of peace,
His service and his counsel.
KATHARINE To betray me.
My lords, I thank you both for your good wills.
Ye speak like honest men; pray God ye prove so!
But how to make ye suddenly an answer
In such a point of weight, so near mine honor—
More near my life, I fear—with my weak wit,
And to such men of gravity and learning,
In truth, I know not. I was set at work
Among my maids, full little, God knows, looking
Either for such men or such business.
For her sake that I have been—for I feel
The last fit of my greatness—good your Graces,

III.i. Location: London. The Queen's apartments.
3 made trees i.e., caused trees to bow **7 as** as if **11 lay by** subsided **13 Killing care** i.e., (that) care which kills **17 presence** presence chamber **22 their affairs** the business they come on **25 I . . . all** i.e., I wish to be a complete housewife, in case I am divorced and forced to live alone. **against** in anticipation of

33 happy fortunate (in virtue) **34 a number** many **36 Envy** malice. **opinion** rumor **37 even** constant, upright **38 Seek . . . in** concerns me regarding my conduct as a wife **40–41 Tanta . . . serenissima** There is toward you such wholeheartedness, most serene queen **45 strange** foreign **49 willing'st** most deliberate **63 still bore** has always borne **65 far** severe **77 For . . . been** for the sake of the queenly person I once was **78 fit** brief space, short spell

Let me have time and counsel for my cause.
Alas, I am a woman, friendless, hopeless!

WOLSEY
Madam, you wrong the King's love with these fears.
Your hopes and friends are infinite.

KATHARINE
In England
But little for my profit. Can you think, lords,
That any Englishman dare give me counsel,
Or be a known friend, 'gainst his Highness' pleasure,
Though he be grown so desperate to be honest,
And live a subject? Nay, forsooth, my friends,
They that must weigh out my afflictions,
They that my trust must grow to, live not here.
They are, as all my other comforts, far hence
In mine own country, lords.

CAMPEIUS
I would your Grace
Would leave your griefs, and take my counsel.

KATHARINE
How, sir?

CAMPEIUS
Put your main cause into the King's protection;
He's loving and most gracious. 'Twill be much
Both for your honor better and your cause;
For if the trial of the law o'ertake ye,
You'll part away disgrac'd.

WOLSEY
He tells you rightly.

KATHARINE
Ye tell me what ye wish for both—my ruin.
Is this your Christian counsel? Out upon ye!
Heaven is above all yet; there sits a judge
That no king can corrupt.

CAMPEIUS
Your rage mistakes us.

KATHARINE
The more shame for ye! Holy men I thought ye,
Upon my soul, two reverend cardinal virtues;
But cardinal sins and hollow hearts I fear ye.
Mend 'em, for shame, my lords! Is this your comfort?
The cordial that ye bring a wretched lady,
A woman lost among ye, laugh'd at, scorn'd?
I will not wish ye half my miseries,
I have more charity. But say I warn'd ye;
Take heed, for heaven's sake take heed, lest at once
The burden of my sorrows fall upon ye.

WOLSEY
Madam, this is a mere distraction.
You turn the good we offer into envy.

KATHARINE
Ye turn me into nothing. Woe upon ye
And all such false professors! Would you have me—
If you have any justice, any pity,
If ye be anything but churchmen's habits—
Put my sick cause into his hands that hates me?
Alas, h'as banish'd me his bed already,
His love, too long ago! I am old, my lords,
And all the fellowship I hold now with him
Is only my obedience. What can happen
To me above this wretchedness? All your studies
Make me a curse like this.

CAMPEIUS
Your fears are worse.

KATHARINE
Have I liv'd thus long—let me speak myself,
Since virtue finds no friends—a wife, a true one?
A woman, I dare say without vainglory,
Never yet branded with suspicion?
Have I with all my full affections
Still met the King? Lov'd him next heav'n? Obey'd him?
Been, out of fondness, superstitious to him?
Almost forgot my prayers to content him?
And am I thus rewarded? 'Tis not well, lords.
Bring me a constant woman to her husband,
One that ne'er dream'd a joy beyond his pleasure;
And to that woman, when she has done most,
Yet will I add an honor, a great patience.

WOLSEY
Madam, you wander from the good we aim at.

KATHARINE
My lord, I dare not make myself so guilty
To give up willingly that noble title
Your master wed me to. Nothing but death
Shall e'er divorce my dignities.

WOLSEY
Pray hear me.

KATHARINE
Would I had never trod this English earth,
Or felt the flatteries that grow upon it!
Ye have angels' faces, but heaven knows your hearts.
What will become of me now, wretched lady?
I am the most unhappy woman living.
[*To her women.*] Alas, poor wenches, where are now your fortunes?
Shipwrack'd upon a kingdom, where no pity,
No friends, no hope, no kindred weep for me,
Almost no grave allow'd me. Like the lily,
That once was mistress of the field and flourish'd,
I'll hang my head and perish.

WOLSEY
If your Grace
Could but be brought to know our ends are honest,
You 'd feel more comfort. Why should we, good lady,
Upon what cause, wrong you? Alas, our places,
The way of our profession is against it;
We are to cure such sorrows, not to sow 'em.
For goodness' sake, consider what you do,
How you may hurt yourself, ay, utterly
Grow from the King's acquaintance, by this carriage.
The hearts of princes kiss obedience,
So much they love it; but to stubborn spirits
They swell and grow as terrible as storms.
I know you have a gentle, noble temper,

86 so desperate i.e., reckless enough as **88 weigh out** compensate for **97 part away** depart **101 mistakes** misjudges **103 cardinal virtues** i.e., justice, temperance, fortitude, and prudence, constituting four of the seven virtues opposing the seven Deadly Sins **104 cardinal sins** i.e., the seven Deadly Sins **110 at once** all at once **112 mere distraction** absolute frenzy **113 envy** malice **117 habits** garments **119 h'as** he has

123–124 All . . . this i.e., I challenge you, in your clerical exertions, to devise a worse fate than I already have **124 worse** i.e., than your wretchedness **125 speak** describe, speak for **130 Still** always **131 superstitious** i.e., to the point of idolatry **161 carriage** conduct

A soul as even as a calm. Pray think us
Those we profess, peacemakers, friends, and
servants.

CAMPEIUS
Madam, you'll find it so. You wrong your virtues
With these weak women's fears. A noble spirit,
As yours was put into you, ever casts
Such doubts, as false coin, from it. The King
loves you;
Beware you lose it not. For us, if you please
To trust us in your business, we are ready
To use our utmost studies in your service.

KATHARINE
Do what ye will, my lords, and pray forgive me;
If I have us'd myself unmannerly,
You know I am a woman, lacking wit
To make a seemly answer to such persons.
Pray do my service to his Majesty.
He has my heart yet, and shall have my prayers
While I shall have my life. Come, reverend fathers,
Bestow your counsels on me. She now begs
That little thought, when she set footing here,
She should have bought her dignities so dear.
Exeunt.

SCENE II

Enter the Duke of Norfolk, Duke of Suffolk, Lord Surrey, and Lord Chamberlain.

NORFOLK
If you will now unite in your complaints,
And force them with a constancy, the Cardinal
Cannot stand under them. If you omit
The offer of this time, I cannot promise
But that you shall sustain moe new disgraces,
With these you bear already.

SURREY I am joyful
To meet the least occasion that may give me
Remembrance of my father-in-law, the Duke,
To be reveng'd on him.

SUFFOLK Which of the peers
Have uncontemn'd gone by him, or at least
Strangely neglected? When did he regard
The stamp of nobleness in any person
Out of himself?

CHAMBERLAIN My lords, you speak your pleasures.
What he deserves of you and me I know;
What we can do to him, though now the time
Gives way to us, I much fear. If you cannot
Bar his access to th' King, never attempt
Anything on him; for he hath a witchcraft
Over the King in 's tongue.

NORFOLK O, fear him not;
His spell in that is out. The King hath found
Matter against him that for ever mars
The honey of his language. No, he's settled,
Not to come off, in his displeasure.

SURREY Sir,
I should be glad to hear such news as this
Once every hour.

NORFOLK Believe it, this is true.
In the divorce his contrary proceedings
Are all unfolded, wherein he appears
As I would wish mine enemy.

SURREY How came
His practices to light?

SUFFOLK Most strangely.

SURREY O, how, how?

SUFFOLK
The Cardinal's letters to the Pope miscarried,
And came to th' eye o' th' King, wherein was read
How that the Cardinal did entreat his Holiness
To stay the judgment o' th' divorce; for if
It did take place, "I do," quoth he, "perceive
My King is tangled in affection to
A creature of the Queen's, Lady Anne Bullen."

SURREY
Has the King this?

SUFFOLK Believe it.

SURREY Will this work?

CHAMBERLAIN
The King in this perceives him, how he coasts
And hedges his own way. But in this point
All his tricks founder, and he brings his physic
After his patient's death. The King already
Hath married the fair lady.

SURREY Would he had!

SUFFOLK
May you be happy in your wish, my lord,
For, I profess, you have it.

SURREY Now, all my joy
Trace the conjunction!

SUFFOLK My amen to 't!

NORFOLK All men's!

SUFFOLK
There's order given for her coronation.
Marry, this is yet but young, and may be left
To some ears unrecounted. But, my lords,
She is a gallant creature, and complete
In mind and feature. I persuade me, from her
Will fall some blessing to this land, which shall
In it be memoriz'd.

SURREY But will the King
Digest this letter of the Cardinal's?
The Lord forbid!

NORFOLK Marry, amen!

SUFFOLK No, no;

170 As . . . you such as was given to you **176 us'd myself** conducted myself **179 do my service** pay my respects

III.ii. Location: London. Antechamber to the King's apartments.
2 force urge **3–4 If . . . time** if you let this opportunity pass **8 father-in-law** i.e., Buckingham. (See II.i.41–44 and note.) **10 uncontemn'd** not held in contempt **13 Out of** excepting **16 Gives way to** favors

20 out finished **23 come off** escape. **his** i.e., the King's **26 contrary** contradictory, divisive **27 unfolded** exposed **36 creature** dependent **38–39 coasts And hedges** goes a roundabout way, as by coast and hedgerow **40 physic** medicine, cure **45 Trace** follow **47 young** recent, new **49 complete** perfect, excellent **52 memoriz'd** caused to be remembered. (Refers prophetically to Elizabeth.) **53 Digest** put up with

There be moe wasps that buzz about his nose
Will make this sting the sooner. Cardinal Campeius
Is stol'n away to Rome, hath ta'en no leave,
Has left the cause o' th' King unhandled, and
Is posted, as the agent of our Cardinal,
To second all his plot. I do assure you
The King cried "Ha!" at this.

CHAMBERLAIN Now, God incense him,
And let him cry "Ha!" louder!

NORFOLK But, my lord,
When returns Cranmer?

SUFFOLK
He is return'd in his opinions, which
Have satisfied the King for his divorce,
Together with all famous colleges
Almost in Christendom. Shortly, I believe,
His second marriage shall be publish'd, and
Her coronation. Katharine no more
Shall be call'd queen, but Princess Dowager
And widow to Prince Arthur.

NORFOLK This same Cranmer's
A worthy fellow, and hath ta'en much pain
In the King's business.

SUFFOLK He has, and we shall see him
For it an archbishop.

NORFOLK So I hear.

SUFFOLK 'Tis so.

Enter Wolsey and Cromwell.

The Cardinal!

NORFOLK Observe, observe, he's moody.

WOLSEY
The packet, Cromwell, gave 't you the King?

CROMWELL
To his own hand, in 's bedchamber.

WOLSEY Look'd he
O' th' inside of the paper?

CROMWELL Presently
He did unseal them, and the first he view'd,
He did it with a serious mind; a heed
Was in his countenance. You he bade
Attend him here this morning.

WOLSEY Is he ready
To come abroad?

CROMWELL I think by this he is.

WOLSEY
Leave me awhile. *Exit Cromwell.*
[*Aside.*] It shall be to the Duchess of Alençon,
The French King's sister; he shall marry her.
Anne Bullen? No; I'll no Anne Bullens for him;
There's more in 't than fair visage. Bullen?
No, we'll no Bullens. Speedily I wish
To hear from Rome. The Marchioness of Pembroke?

NORFOLK
He's discontented.

SUFFOLK May be he hears the King
Does whet his anger to him.

SURREY Sharp enough,
Lord, for thy justice!

WOLSEY [*Aside*]
The late Queen's gentlewoman, a knight's daughter,
To be her mistress' mistress? The Queen's queen?
This candle burns not clear; 'tis I must snuff it,
Then out it goes. What though I know her virtuous
And well deserving? Yet I know her for
A spleeny Lutheran, and not wholesome to
Our cause, that she should lie i' th' bosom of
Our hard-rul'd king. Again, there is sprung up
An heretic, an arch one, Cranmer, one
Hath crawl'd into the favor of the King,
And is his oracle.

NORFOLK He is vex'd at something.

Enter King, reading of a schedule, [*and Lovell. Wolsey stands apart, not observing the King.*]

SURREY
I would 'twere something that would fret the string,
The master-cord on 's heart!

SUFFOLK The King, the King!

KING
What piles of wealth hath he accumulated
To his own portion! And what expense by th' hour
Seems to flow from him! How, i' th' name of thrift,
Does he rake this together?—Now, my lords,
Saw you the Cardinal?

NORFOLK My lord, we have
Stood here observing him. Some strange commotion
Is in his brain. He bites his lip, and starts,
Stops on a sudden, looks upon the ground,
Then lays his finger on his temple; straight
Springs out into fast gait, then stops again,
Strikes his breast hard, and anon he casts
His eye against the moon. In most strange postures
We have seen him set himself.

KING It may well be;
There is a mutiny in 's mind. This morning
Papers of state he sent me to peruse,
As I requir'd; and wot you what I found
There—on my conscience, put unwittingly?
Forsooth, an inventory, thus importing
The several parcels of his plate, his treasure,
Rich stuffs, and ornaments of household, which
I find at such proud rate, that it outspeaks
Possession of a subject.

NORFOLK It's heaven's will.
Some spirit put this paper in the packet,
To bless your eye withal.

KING If we did think
His contemplation were above the earth,
And fix'd on spiritual object, he should still
Dwell in his musings; but I am afraid

59 posted gone in haste **64 in his opinions** having sent ahead his written opinions **83 this** this time

99 spleeny staunch, contentious **101 hard-rul'd** hard to manage **103 Hath** who has **104 s.d. schedule** scroll **105 fret** gnaw through (with a pun on the musical sense of pressing the string of a musical instrument against a "fret" or bar) **106 on 's** of his **125 several parcels** various items **127–128 outspeaks . . . subject** describes possessions exceeding what a subject should have

His thinkings are below the moon, not worth
His serious considering.
King takes his seat; whispers Lovell, who goes to the Cardinal [*Wolsey*].

WOLSEY Heaven forgive me!
Ever God bless your Highness!
KING Good my lord,
You are full of heavenly stuff, and bear the inventory
Of your best graces in your mind, the which
You were now running o'er. You have scarce time
To steal from spiritual leisure a brief span
To keep your earthly audit; sure in that
I deem you an ill husband, and am glad
To have you therein my companion.
WOLSEY Sir,
For holy offices I have a time; a time
To think upon the part of business which
I bear i' th' state; and nature does require
Her times of preservation, which perforce
I, her frail son, amongst my brethren mortal,
Must give my tendance to.
KING You have said well.
WOLSEY
And ever may your Highness yoke together,
As I will lend you cause, my doing well
With my well saying!
KING 'Tis well said again,
And 'tis a kind of good deed to say well;
And yet words are no deeds. My father lov'd you;
He said he did, and with his deed did crown
His word upon you. Since I had my office,
I have kept you next my heart, have not alone
Employ'd you where high profits might come home,
But par'd my present havings, to bestow
My bounties upon you.
WOLSEY [*Aside*] What should this mean?
SURREY [*Aside*]
The Lord increase this business!
KING Have I not made you
The prime man of the state? I pray you tell me
If what I now pronounce you have found true;
And, if you may confess it, say withal
If you are bound to us or no. What say you?
WOLSEY
My sovereign, I confess your royal graces,
Show'r'd on me daily, have been more than could
My studied purposes requite, which went
Beyond all man's endeavors. My endeavors
Have ever come too short of my desires,
Yet fil'd with my abilities. Mine own ends
Have been mine so that evermore they pointed
To th' good of your most sacred person and
The profit of the state. For your great graces
Heap'd upon me, poor undeserver, I
Can nothing render but allegiant thanks,
My pray'rs to heaven for you, my loyalty,
Which ever has and ever shall be growing,
Till death, that winter, kill it.
KING Fairly answer'd;
A loyal and obedient subject is
Therein illustrated. The honor of it
Does pay the act of it, as, i' th' contrary,
The foulness is the punishment. I presume
That, as my hand has open'd bounty to you,
My heart dropp'd love, my pow'r rain'd honor, more
On you than any, so your hand and heart,
Your brain, and every function of your power,
Should, notwithstanding that your bond of duty,
As 'twere in love's particular, be more
To me, your friend, than any.
WOLSEY I do profess
That for your Highness' good I ever labor'd
More than mine own; that am, have, and will be—
Though all the world should crack their duty to you,
And throw it from their soul, though perils did
Abound as thick as thought could make 'em and
Appear in forms more horrid—yet my duty,
As doth a rock against the chiding flood,
Should the approach of this wild river break,
And stand unshaken yours.
KING 'Tis nobly spoken.
Take notice, lords, he has a loyal breast,
For you have seen him open 't. Read o'er this,
[*Giving him papers.*]
And after, this, and then to breakfast with
What appetite you have.
Exit King, frowning upon the Cardinal [*Wolsey*]; *the Nobles throng after him, smiling and whispering.*

WOLSEY What should this mean?
What sudden anger 's this? How have I reap'd it?
He parted frowning from me, as if ruin
Leap'd from his eyes. So looks the chafed lion
Upon the daring huntsman that has gall'd him,
Then makes him nothing. I must read this paper;
I fear, the story of his anger. 'Tis so!
This paper has undone me. 'Tis th' account
Of all that world of wealth I have drawn together
For mine own ends—indeed, to gain the popedom
And fee my friends in Rome. O negligence!
Fit for a fool to fall by. What cross devil
Made me put this main secret in the packet
I sent the King? Is there no way to cure this?
No new device to beat this from his brains?
I know 'twill stir him strongly; yet I know
A way, if it take right, in spite of fortune
Will bring me off again. What's this? "To th' Pope"?
The letter, as I live, with all the business

134 below the moon i.e., in the mortal sphere **142 ill husband** unthrifty manager **149 tendance** attention **159 par'd . . . havings** reduced my own wealth **167–168 more . . . requite** more than I could devise means to repay **171 fil'd** kept pace **172 so that** only to the extent that **176 allegiant** loyal

181 illustrated made evident **181–182 The honor . . . it** (Cf. "Virtue is its own reward.") **188–189 notwithstanding . . . particular** over and above your duty as a subject, as in the case of friends **206 chafed** angry **207 gall'd** wounded **208 makes him nothing** destroys him (the hunter) **214 cross** perverse **215 main** weighty **219 take right** succeed

I writ to 's Holiness. Nay then, farewell!
I have touch'd the highest point of all my greatness,
And, from that full meridian of my glory,
I haste now to my setting. I shall fall
Like a bright exhalation in the evening,
And no man see me more.

Enter to Wolsey the Dukes of Norfolk and Suffolk, the Earl of Surrey, and the Lord Chamberlain.

NORFOLK
Hear the King's pleasure, Cardinal, who commands you
To render up the great seal presently
Into our hands, and to confine yourself
To Asher House, my Lord of Winchester's,
Till you hear further from his Highness.
WOLSEY Stay,
Where's your commission, lords? Words cannot carry
Authority so weighty.
SUFFOLK Who dare cross 'em,
Bearing the King's will from his mouth expressly?
WOLSEY
Till I find more than will or words to do it,
I mean your malice, know, officious lords,
I dare and must deny it. Now I feel
Of what coarse metal ye are molded—envy;
How eagerly ye follow my disgraces
As if it fed ye, and how sleek and wanton
Ye appear in every thing may bring my ruin!
Follow your envious courses, men of malice!
You have Christian warrant for 'em, and no doubt
In time will find their fit rewards. That seal
You ask with such a violence, the King,
Mine and your master, with his own hand gave me;
Bade me enjoy it, with the place and honors,
During my life; and, to confirm his goodness,
Tied it by letters-patents. Now, who'll take it?
SURREY
The King that gave it.
WOLSEY It must be himself, then.
SURREY
Thou art a proud traitor, priest.
WOLSEY Proud lord, thou liest!
Within these forty hours Surrey durst better
Have burnt that tongue than said so.
SURREY Thy ambition,
Thou scarlet sin, robb'd this bewailing land
Of noble Buckingham, my father-in-law.
The heads of all thy brother cardinals,
With thee and all thy best parts bound together,
Weigh'd not a hair of his. Plague of your policy!
You sent me deputy for Ireland,
Far from his succor, from the King, from all
That might have mercy on the fault thou gav'st him;
Whilst your great goodness, out of holy pity,
Absolv'd him with an axe.
WOLSEY This, and all else
This talking lord can lay upon my credit,
I answer is most false. The Duke by law
Found his deserts. How innocent I was
From any private malice in his end,
His noble jury and foul cause can witness.
If I lov'd many words, lord, I should tell you
You have as little honesty as honor,
That in the way of loyalty and truth
Toward the King, my ever royal master,
Dare mate a sounder man than Surrey can be,
And all that love his follies.
SURREY By my soul,
Your long coat, priest, protects you; thou shouldst feel
My sword i' th' life-blood of thee else. My lords,
Can ye endure to hear this arrogance?
And from this fellow? If we live thus tamely,
To be thus jaded by a piece of scarlet,
Farewell nobility! Let his Grace go forward,
And dare us with his cap like larks.
WOLSEY All goodness
Is poison to thy stomach.
SURREY Yes, that goodness
Of gleaning all the land's wealth into one,
Into your own hands, Card'nal, by extortion;
The goodness of your intercepted packets
You writ to th' Pope against the King. Your goodness,
Since you provoke me, shall be most notorious.
My Lord of Norfolk, as you are truly noble,
As you respect the common good, the state
Of our despis'd nobility, our issues,
Who, if he live, will scarce be gentlemen,
Produce the grand sum of his sins, the articles
Collected from his life. I'll startle you
Worse than the sacring bell, when the brown wench
Lay kissing in your arms, Lord Cardinal.
WOLSEY
How much, methinks, I could despise this man,
But that I am bound in charity against it!
NORFOLK
Those articles, my lord, are in the King's hand;
But, thus much, they are foul ones.
WOLSEY So much fairer
And spotless shall mine innocence arise
When the King knows my truth.
SURREY This cannot save you.
I thank my memory, I yet remember
Some of these articles, and out they shall.

226 exhalation i.e., any astronomical phenomenon, such as a meteor or a falling star **234 cross** oppose **239 envy** malice **244 Christian warrant** i.e., the example of other uncharitable Christians **250 letters-patents** formal and public bestowing of rights or powers **255 Thou scarlet sin** (Refers to his cardinal's cassock, described as scarlet; cf. III.i.103–104.) **258 parts** qualities **259 Weigh'd** equaled in weight. **Plague of** a plague on

262 fault . . . him offense you charged him (Buckingham) with **265 lay . . . credit** charge against my good name **272 That** I that **274 mate** rival, vie with **280 jaded** cowed, ridden like a poor horse **282 dare . . . larks** dazzle us with his cardinal's hat as birds with a mirror or a piece of scarlet cloth **291 issues** sons **293 articles** items of the indictment **295 sacring bell** bell rung at the most solemn portions of the mass. (Surrey imagines a scene in which Wolsey is startled in the midst of making love by hearing the mass bell.) **299 hand** possession **300 thus much** (I can say) this much

Now, if you can blush and cry "guilty," Cardinal,
You'll show a little honesty.

WOLSEY Speak on, sir;
I dare your worst objections. If I blush,
It is to see a nobleman want manners.

SURREY
I had rather want those than my head. Have at you!
First, that without the King's assent or knowledge
You wrought to be a legate, by which power
You maim'd the jurisdiction of all bishops.

NORFOLK
Then, that in all you writ to Rome, or else
To foreign princes, "Ego et Rex meus"
Was still inscrib'd, in which you brought the King
To be your servant.

SUFFOLK Then that, without the knowledge
Either of King or Council, when you went
Ambassador to the Emperor, you made bold
To carry into Flanders the great seal.

SURREY
Item, you sent a large commission
To Gregory de Cassado, to conclude,
Without the King's will or the state's allowance,
A league between his Highness and Ferrara.

SUFFOLK
That, out of mere ambition, you have caus'd
Your holy hat to be stamp'd on the King's coin.

SURREY
Then that you have sent innumerable substance—
By what means got, I leave to your own
conscience—
To furnish Rome, and to prepare the ways
You have for dignities, to the mere undoing
Of all the kingdom. Many more there are,
Which, since they are of you, and odious,
I will not taint my mouth with.

CHAMBERLAIN O my lord,
Press not a falling man too far! 'Tis virtue.
His faults lie open to the laws; let them,
Not you, correct him. My heart weeps to see him
So little of his great self.

SURREY I forgive him.

SUFFOLK
Lord Cardinal, the King's further pleasure is—
Because all those things you have done of late
By your power legative within this kingdom
Fall into th' compass of a praemunire—
That therefore such a writ be sued against you,
To forfeit all your goods, lands, tenements,
Chattels, and whatsoever, and to be
Out of the King's protection. This is my charge.

NORFOLK
And so we'll leave you to your meditations
How to live better. For your stubborn answer
About the giving back the great seal to us,
The King shall know it, and, no doubt, shall
thank you.
So fare you well, my little good Lord Cardinal.
Exeunt all but Wolsey.

WOLSEY
So farewell to the little good you bear me.
Farewell? A long farewell, to all my greatness!
This is the state of man: today he puts forth
The tender leaves of hopes; tomorrow blossoms,
And bears his blushing honors thick upon him;
The third day comes a frost, a killing frost,
And when he thinks, good easy man, full surely
His greatness is a-ripening, nips his root,
And then he falls as I do. I have ventur'd,
Like little wanton boys that swim on bladders,
This many summers in a sea of glory,
But far beyond my depth. My high-blown pride
At length broke under me and now has left me,
Weary and old with service, to the mercy
Of a rude stream that must forever hide me.
Vain pomp and glory of this world, I hate ye!
I feel my heart new open'd. O, how wretched
Is that poor man that hangs on princes' favors!
There is, betwixt that smile we would aspire to,
That sweet aspect of princes, and their ruin,
More pangs and fears than wars or women have;
And when he falls, he falls like Lucifer,
Never to hope again.

Enter Cromwell, standing amazed.

Why, how now, Cromwell?

CROMWELL
I have no power to speak, sir.

WOLSEY What, amaz'd
At my misfortunes? Can thy spirit wonder
A great man should decline? Nay, an you weep,
I am fall'n indeed.

CROMWELL How does your Grace?

WOLSEY Why, well;
Never so truly happy, my good Cromwell.
I know myself now, and I feel within me
A peace above all earthly dignities,
A still and quiet conscience. The King has cur'd me,
I humbly thank his Grace; and from these shoulders,
These ruin'd pillars, out of pity, taken
A load would sink a navy—too much honor.
O, 'tis a burden, Cromwell, 'tis a burden
Too heavy for a man that hopes for heaven!

CROMWELL
I am glad your Grace has made that right use of it.

WOLSEY
I hope I have. I am able now, methinks,
Out of a fortitude of soul I feel,

311 wrought connived, worked. **legate** representative of the Pope **314 Ego et Rex meus** my king and I. (Literally, "I and my king"; Norfolk accuses Wolsey of using the phrase in such a way as to make the king his "servant" by naming himself first, but the Latin construction requires that "ego" precede any nouns parallel with it.) **324 mere** sheer **326 innumerable substance** uncountable wealth **328 To furnish Rome** (Implies that Wolsey made gifts to Rome as bribes to obtain his own advancement.) **329 mere** utter **339 legative** as a papal legate **340 Fall . . . praemunire** fall within the penalties for violating a writ of praemunire, i.e., a writ by which one could be charged with appealing to a foreign court (especially a papal court) in an action involving an English subject and hence relevant to the King's court **341 sued** moved, issued

354 blushing glowing **356 easy** easygoing **359 wanton** sportful **364 rude** rough **369 their ruin** the ruin they bring about

To endure more miseries and greater far
Than my weak-hearted enemies dare offer.
What news abroad?

CROMWELL The heaviest and the worst
Is your displeasure with the King.

WOLSEY God bless him!

CROMWELL
The next is, that Sir Thomas More is chosen
Lord Chancellor in your place.

WOLSEY That's somewhat sudden.
But he's a learned man. May he continue
Long in his Highness' favor, and do justice
For truth's sake and his conscience, that his bones,
When he has run his course and sleeps in blessings,
May have a tomb of orphans' tears wept on him!
What more?

CROMWELL That Cranmer is return'd with welcome,
Install'd Lord Archbishop of Canterbury.

WOLSEY
That's news indeed.

CROMWELL Last, that the Lady Anne,
Whom the King hath in secrecy long married,
This day was view'd in open as his queen,
Going to chapel; and the voice is now
Only about her coronation.

WOLSEY
There was the weight that pull'd me down. O
Cromwell,
The King has gone beyond me! All my glories
In that one woman I have lost for ever.
No sun shall ever usher forth mine honors,
Or gild again the noble troops that waited
Upon my smiles. Go, get thee from me, Cromwell!
I am a poor fall'n man, unworthy now
To be thy lord and master. Seek the King;
That sun, I pray, may never set! I have told him
What and how true thou art. He will advance thee;
Some little memory of me will stir him—
I know his noble nature—not to let
Thy hopeful service perish too. Good Cromwell,
Neglect him not; make use now, and provide
For thine own future safety.

CROMWELL O my lord,
Must I, then, leave you? Must I needs forgo
So good, so noble, and so true a master?
Bear witness, all that have not hearts of iron,
With what a sorrow Cromwell leaves his lord.
The King shall have my service; but my pray'rs
For ever and for ever shall be yours.

WOLSEY
Cromwell, I did not think to shed a tear
In all my miseries; but thou hast forc'd me,
Out of thy honest truth, to play the woman.
Let's dry our eyes. And thus far hear me, Cromwell,
And, when I am forgotten, as I shall be,
And sleep in dull cold marble, where no mention
Of me more must be heard of, say I taught thee;
Say, Wolsey, that once trod the ways of glory,
And sounded all the depths and shoals of honor,
Found thee a way, out of his wrack, to rise in,
A sure and safe one, though thy master miss'd it.
Mark but my fall, and that that ruin'd me.
Cromwell, I charge thee, fling away ambition!
By that sin fell the angels; how can man, then,
The image of his Maker, hope to win by it?
Love thyself last; cherish those hearts that hate thee.
Corruption wins not more than honesty.
Still in thy right hand carry gentle peace
To silence envious tongues. Be just, and fear not.
Let all the ends thou aim'st at be thy country's,
Thy God's, and truth's; then if thou fall'st, O
Cromwell,
Thou fall'st a blessed martyr!
Serve the King, and—prithee lead me in.
There take an inventory of all I have,
To the last penny; 'tis the King's. My robe,
And my integrity to heaven, is all
I dare now call mine own. O Cromwell, Cromwell!
Had I but serv'd my God with half the zeal
I serv'd my King, he would not in mine age
Have left me naked to mine enemies.

CROMWELL
Good sir, have patience.

WOLSEY So I have. Farewell
The hopes of court! My hopes in heaven do dwell.
Exeunt.

ACT IV • SCENE I

Enter two Gentlemen, meeting one another.

FIRST GENTLEMAN
Y' are well met once again.

SECOND GENTLEMAN So are you.

FIRST GENTLEMAN
You come to take your stand here, and behold
The Lady Anne pass from her coronation?

SECOND GENTLEMAN
'Tis all my business. At our last encounter,
The Duke of Buckingham came from his trial.

FIRST GENTLEMAN
'Tis very true; but that time offer'd sorrow,
This, general joy.

SECOND GENTLEMAN 'Tis well. The citizens,
I am sure, have shown at full their royal minds—
As, let 'em have their rights, they are ever
forward—
In celebration of this day with shows,
Pageants, and sights of honor.

FIRST GENTLEMAN Never greater,
Nor, I'll assure you, better taken, sir.

399 orphans' i.e., such as would be under the legal guardianship of the Lord Chancellor **405 voice** talk **408 gone beyond** overreached **411 troops** i.e., of retainers **420 make use** take advantage

436 sounded fathomed

IV.i. Location: A street in Westminster.
8 royal minds loyalty to the crown **9 let . . . rights** to give them due credit. **forward** i.e., eager to do **12 taken** received

SECOND GENTLEMAN
May I be bold to ask what that contains,
That paper in your hand?
FIRST GENTLEMAN Yes, 'tis the list
Of those that claim their offices this day
By custom of the coronation.
The Duke of Suffolk is the first, and claims
To be High Steward; next, the Duke of Norfolk,
He to be Earl Marshal. You may read the rest.
[*Offers paper.*]
SECOND GENTLEMAN
I thank you, sir. Had I not known those customs,
I should have been beholding to your paper.
But, I beseech you, what's become of Katharine,
The Princess Dowager? How goes her business?
FIRST GENTLEMAN
That I can tell you too. The Archbishop
Of Canterbury, accompanied with other
Learned and reverend fathers of his order,
Held a late court at Dunstable, six miles off
From Ampthill where the Princess lay, to which
She was often cited by them, but appear'd not;
And, to be short, for not appearance and
The King's late scruple, by the main assent
Of all these learned men she was divorc'd,
And the late marriage made of none effect;
Since which she was remov'd to Kimbolton,
Where she remains now sick.
SECOND GENTLEMAN Alas, good lady!
[*Trumpets.*]
The trumpets sound. Stand close, the Queen is
coming. *Hautboys.*

The Order of the Coronation.

1. *A lively flourish of Trumpets.*
2. *Then, two* Judges.
3. Lord Chancellor, *with purse and mace before him.*
4. Choristers, *singing. Music.*
5. Mayor of London, *bearing the mace. Then* Garter, *in his coat of arms, and on his head he wore a gilt copper crown.*
6. Marquess Dorset, *bearing a scepter of gold, on his head a demi-coronal of gold. With him, the* Earl of Surrey, *bearing the rod of silver with the dove, crowned with an earl's coronet. Collars of SS.*
7. Duke of Suffolk, *in his robe of estate, his coronet on his head, bearing a long white wand, as High Steward. With him, the* Duke of Norfolk, *with the rod of marshalship, a coronet on his head. Collars of SS.*
8. *A canopy borne by four of the* Cinque-ports; *under it, the* Queen *in her robe, in her hair, richly adorned with pearl, crowned. On each side her, the* Bishops of London *and* Winchester.
9. *The old* Duchess of Norfolk, *in a coronal of gold, wrought with flowers, bearing the Queen's train.*
10. *Certain* Ladies *or* Countesses, *with plain circlets of gold without flowers.*
Exeunt, first passing over the stage in order and state, and then a great flourish of trumpets.

SECOND GENTLEMAN
A royal train, believe me. These I know.
Who's that that bears the scepter?
FIRST GENTLEMAN Marquess Dorset,
And that the Earl of Surrey, with the rod.
SECOND GENTLEMAN
A bold brave gentleman. That should be
The Duke of Suffolk?
FIRST GENTLEMAN 'Tis the same: High Steward.
SECOND GENTLEMAN
And that my Lord of Norfolk?
FIRST GENTLEMAN Yes.
SECOND GENTLEMAN [*Looking on the Queen*]
Heaven bless thee!
Thou hast the sweetest face I ever look'd on.
Sir, as I have a soul, she is an angel;
Our King has all the Indies in his arms,
And more and richer, when he strains that lady.
I cannot blame his conscience.
FIRST GENTLEMAN They that bear
The cloth of honor over her are four barons
Of the Cinque-ports.
SECOND GENTLEMAN
Those men are happy, and so are all are near her.
I take it, she that carries up the train
Is that old noble lady, Duchess of Norfolk.
FIRST GENTLEMAN
It is; and all the rest are countesses.
SECOND GENTLEMAN
Their coronets say so. These are stars indeed.
FIRST GENTLEMAN
And sometimes falling ones.
SECOND GENTLEMAN No more of that.
[*Exit procession.*]

Enter a third Gentleman.

FIRST GENTLEMAN
God save you, sir! Where have you been broiling?
THIRD GENTLEMAN
Among the crowd i' th' Abbey, where a finger
Could not be wedg'd in more. I am stifled
With the mere rankness of their joy.
SECOND GENTLEMAN You saw
The ceremony?
THIRD GENTLEMAN That I did.
FIRST GENTLEMAN How was it?
THIRD GENTLEMAN
Well worth the seeing.
SECOND GENTLEMAN Good sir, speak it to us.

27 late recent **28 lay** lodged **29 cited** summoned **31 late** former. **main assent** general agreement **36 close** aside **36 s.d. The Order of the Coronation:** (3) **Lord Chancellor** i.e., Sir Thomas More. (4) **Music** musicians. (5) **Garter** i.e., Garter King-at-Arms. (6) **Collars of SS** golden chains of office made of flat, broad S-shaped links, ornately decorated. (8) **Cinque-ports** barons of the cinque-ports, a group of seaport towns (originally five) situated on the southeast coast of England, in ancient times furnishing the chief parts of the English navy, in return for which they had many privileges and franchises. **in her hair** with hair loosely hanging (customary for brides)

37 train procession **46 strains** embraces **50 all** all who **55 falling** (with a sexual pun) **59 mere rankness** sheer exuberance **61 speak** describe

THIRD GENTLEMAN
As well as I am able. The rich stream
Of lords and ladies, having brought the Queen
To a prepar'd place in the choir, fell off
A distance from her; while her Grace sat down
To rest awhile, some half an hour or so,
In a rich chair of state, opposing freely 67
The beauty of her person to the people—
Believe me, sir, she is the goodliest woman
That ever lay by man—which when the people
Had the full view of, such a noise arose
As the shrouds make at sea in a stiff tempest, 72
As loud, and to as many tunes. Hats, cloaks—
Doublets, I think—flew up; and had their faces
Been loose, this day they had been lost. Such joy
I never saw before. Great-bellied women,
That had not half a week to go, like rams 77
In the old time of war, would shake the press 78
And make 'em reel before 'em. No man living
Could say "This is my wife" there, all were woven
So strangely in one piece.

SECOND GENTLEMAN But what follow'd?

THIRD GENTLEMAN
At length her Grace rose, and with modest paces
Came to the altar, where she kneel'd, and saint-like
Cast her fair eyes to heaven and pray'd devoutly;
Then rose again and bow'd her to the people,
When by the Archbishop of Canterbury
She had all the royal makings of a queen,
As holy oil, Edward Confessor's crown, 88
The rod, and bird of peace, and all such emblems
Laid nobly on her; which perform'd, the choir,
With all the choicest music of the kingdom, 91
Together sung "Te Deum." So she parted, 92
And with the same full state pac'd back again
To York Place, where the feast is held.

FIRST GENTLEMAN Sir,
You must no more call it York Place, that's past;
For, since the Cardinal fell, that title's lost.
'Tis now the King's, and call'd Whitehall.

THIRD GENTLEMAN I know it;
But 'tis so lately alter'd, that the old name
Is fresh about me.

SECOND GENTLEMAN What two reverend bishops
Were those that went on each side of the Queen?

THIRD GENTLEMAN
Stokesly and Gardiner; the one of Winchester, 101
Newly preferr'd from the King's secretary, 102
The other, London.

SECOND GENTLEMAN He of Winchester 103
Is held no great good lover of the Archbishop's,
The virtuous Cranmer.

THIRD GENTLEMAN All the land knows that.
However, yet there is no great breach; when it
comes,
Cranmer will find a friend will not shrink from him. 107

SECOND GENTLEMAN
Who may that be, I pray you?

THIRD GENTLEMAN Thomas Cromwell,
A man in much esteem with th' King, and truly
A worthy friend. The King has made him Master
O' th' Jewel House,
And one, already, of the Privy Council.

SECOND GENTLEMAN
He will deserve more.

THIRD GENTLEMAN Yes, without all doubt.
Come, gentlemen, ye shall go my way, which
Is to th' court, and there ye shall be my guests.
Something I can command. As I walk thither, 116
I'll tell ye more.

BOTH You may command us, sir. *Exeunt.*

SCENE II

Enter Katharine, Dowager, sick, led between Griffith, her gentleman usher, and Patience, her woman.

GRIFFITH
How does your Grace?

KATHARINE O Griffith, sick to death!
My legs, like loaden branches, bow to th' earth,
Willing to leave their burden. Reach a chair. [*Sits.*]
So; now, methinks, I feel a little ease.
Didst thou not tell me, Griffith, as thou led'st me,
That the great child of honor, Cardinal Wolsey,
Was dead?

GRIFFITH Yes, madam; but I think your Grace,
Out of the pain you suffer'd, gave no ear to 't.

KATHARINE
Prithee, good Griffith, tell me how he died.
If well, he stepp'd before me, happily
For my example.

GRIFFITH Well, the voice goes, madam; 11
For after the stout Earl Northumberland
Arrested him at York, and brought him forward,
As a man sorely tainted, to his answer, 14
He fell sick suddenly and grew so ill
He could not sit his mule.

KATHARINE Alas, poor man!

GRIFFITH
At last, with easy roads, he came to Leicester, 17
Lodg'd in the abbey, where the reverend abbot,
With all his covent, honorably receiv'd him; 19
To whom he gave these words, "O, father Abbot,
An old man, broken with the storms of state,
Is come to lay his weary bones among ye;
Give him a little earth for charity!"
So went to bed, where eagerly his sickness

67 opposing presenting in full view **72 shrouds** sail-ropes **77 rams** battering-rams **78 press** crowd **88 As** such as, namely **91 music** i.e., musicians **92 Te Deum** We praise Thee, O God. (A hymn of thanksgiving.) **101–102 Gardiner . . . secretary** (Gardiner, secretary to the King, was made Bishop of Winchester at the fall of Wolsey; he continued to act as secretary for several years.) **103 London** i.e., Bishop of London

107 will not who will not **116 Something . . . command** i.e., I can provide refreshment

IV.ii. Location: Kimbolton Castle in Huntingtonshire. The Queen's apartments.
11 the voice goes i.e., people say **14 sorely tainted** grievously discredited. **answer** i.e., trial **17 roads** stages (of a journey) **19 covent** convent, monastery

Pursu'd him still; and, three nights after this,
About the hour of eight, which he himself
Foretold should be his last, full of repentance,
Continual meditations, tears, and sorrows,
He gave his honors to the world again,
His blessed part to heaven, and slept in peace.

KATHARINE
So may he rest; his faults lie gently on him!
Yet thus far, Griffith, give me leave to speak him,
And yet with charity. He was a man
Of an unbounded stomach, ever ranking
Himself with princes; one that, by suggestion,
Tied all the kingdom. Simony was fair play;
His own opinion was his law. I' th' presence
He would say untruths, and be ever double
Both in his words and meaning. He was never,
But where he meant to ruin, pitiful.
His promises were, as he then was, mighty;
But his performance, as he is now, nothing.
Of his own body he was ill, and gave
The clergy ill example.

GRIFFITH Noble madam,
Men's evil manners live in brass; their virtues
We write in water. May it please your Highness
To hear me speak his good now?

KATHARINE Yes, good Griffith;
I were malicious else.

GRIFFITH This Cardinal,
Though from an humble stock, undoubtedly
Was fashion'd to much honor. From his cradle
He was a scholar, and a ripe and good one,
Exceeding wise, fair-spoken, and persuading;
Lofty and sour to them that lov'd him not,
But to those men that sought him, sweet as summer.
And though he were unsatisfied in getting,
Which was a sin, yet in bestowing, madam,
He was most princely. Ever witness for him
Those twins of learning that he rais'd in you,
Ipswich and Oxford, one of which fell with him,
Unwilling to outlive the good that did it;
The other, though unfinish'd, yet so famous,
So excellent in art, and still so rising,
That Christendom shall ever speak his virtue.
His overthrow heap'd happiness upon him;
For then, and not till then, he felt himself,
And found the blessedness of being little.
And, to add greater honors to his age
Than man could give him, he died fearing God.

KATHARINE
After my death I wish no other herald,
No other speaker of my living actions,
To keep mine honor from corruption,
But such an honest chronicler as Griffith.
Whom I most hated living, thou hast made me,
With thy religious truth and modesty,
Now in his ashes honor. Peace be with him!
Patience, be near me still; and set me lower.
I have not long to trouble thee. Good Griffith,
Cause the musicians play me that sad note
I nam'd my knell, whilst I sit meditating
On that celestial harmony I go to.
Sad and solemn music.

GRIFFITH
She is asleep. Good wench, let's sit down quiet,
For fear we wake her. Softly, gentle Patience.
[*They sit.*]

The vision. Enter, solemnly tripping one after another, six personages, clad in white robes, wearing on their heads garlands of bays, and golden vizards on their faces, branches of bays or palm in their hands. They first congee unto her, then dance; and, at certain changes, the first two hold a spare garland over her head, at which the other four make reverent curtsies. Then the two that held the garland deliver the same to the other next two, who observe the same order in their changes, and holding the garland over her head; which done, they deliver the same garland to the last two, who likewise observe the same order; at which, as it were by inspiration, she makes in her sleep signs of rejoicing, and holdeth up her hands to heaven; and so in their dancing vanish, carrying the garland with them. The music continues.

KATHARINE [*Waking*]
Spirits of peace, where are ye? Are ye all gone,
And leave me here in wretchedness behind ye?

GRIFFITH
Madam, we are here.

KATHARINE It is not you I call for.
Saw ye none enter since I slept?

GRIFFITH None, madam.

KATHARINE
No? Saw you not, even now, a blessed troop
Invite me to a banquet, whose bright faces
Cast thousand beams upon me, like the sun?
They promis'd me eternal happiness,
And brought me garlands, Griffith, which I feel
I am not worthy yet to wear. I shall, assuredly.

GRIFFITH
I am most joyful, madam, such good dreams
Possess your fancy.

KATHARINE Bid the music leave;
They are harsh and heavy to me. *Music ceases.*

PATIENCE [*To Griffith*] Do you note
How much her Grace is alter'd on the sudden?
How long her face is drawn? How pale she looks,
And of an earthy cold? Mark her eyes!

GRIFFITH
She is going, wench. Pray, pray.

PATIENCE Heaven comfort her!

34 stomach ambition **35 suggestion** crafty dealing **36 Tied** fettered, controlled. **Simony** the selling of ecclesiastical offices **37 presence** i.e., of the King **43 ill** i.e., sexually depraved **55 getting** acquiring wealth **58 rais'd in you** built in your cities **59 Ipswich and Oxford** (Wolsey founded a college, no longer extant, at Ipswich, where he was born, and a college at Oxford that is now Christ Church.) **60 good that did** good man that founded **62 art** learning **65 felt** knew **73 Whom** he whom

74 modesty moderation **78 note** tune **82 s.d. The vision: bays** bay leaves. **congee** make a congé, a ceremonious bow. **changes** figures in the dance **94 music leave** musicians cease

Enter a Messenger.

MESSENGER
An 't like your Grace—
KATHARINE You are a saucy fellow.
Deserve we no more reverence?
GRIFFITH You are to blame,
Knowing she will not lose her wonted greatness,
To use so rude behavior. Go to, kneel.
MESSENGER [*Kneeling*]
I humbly do entreat your Highness' pardon;
My haste made me unmannerly. There is staying
A gentleman, sent from the King, to see you.
KATHARINE
Admit him entrance, Griffith. But this fellow
Let me ne'er see again. *Exit Messenger.*

Enter Lord Capucius [*admitted by Griffith*].

If my sight fail not,
You should be Lord Ambassador from the Emperor,
My royal nephew, and your name Capucius.
CAPUCIUS
Madam, the same; your servant.
KATHARINE O, my lord,
The times and titles now are alter'd strangely
With me since first you knew me. But, I pray you,
What is your pleasure with me?
CAPUCIUS Noble lady,
First, mine own service to your Grace; the next,
The King's request that I would visit you,
Who grieves much for your weakness, and by me
Sends you his princely commendations,
And heartily entreats you take good comfort.
KATHARINE
O my good lord, that comfort comes too late;
'Tis like a pardon after execution.
That gentle physic, given in time, had cur'd me;
But now I am past all comforts here but prayers.
How does his Highness?
CAPUCIUS Madam, in good health.
KATHARINE
So may he ever do, and ever flourish,
When I shall dwell with worms, and my poor name
Banish'd the kingdom! Patience, is that letter
I caus'd you write yet sent away?
PATIENCE No, madam.
[*Giving it to Katharine.*]
KATHARINE
Sir, I most humbly pray you to deliver
This to my lord the King.
CAPUCIUS Most willing, madam.
KATHARINE
In which I have commended to his goodness
The model of our chaste loves, his young
daughter—
The dews of heaven fall thick in blessings on her!—
Beseeching him to give her virtuous breeding—
She is young, and of a noble modest nature,
I hope she will deserve well—and a little
To love her for her mother's sake, that lov'd him,
Heaven knows how dearly. My next poor petition
Is that his noble Grace would have some pity
Upon my wretched women, that so long
Have follow'd both my fortunes faithfully;
Of which there is not one, I dare avow,
And now I should not lie, but will deserve,
For virtue and true beauty of the soul,
For honesty and decent carriage,
A right good husband, let him be a noble;
And, sure, those men are happy that shall have 'em.
The last is for my men—they are the poorest,
But poverty could never draw 'em from me—
That they may have their wages duly paid 'em,
And something over to remember me by.
If heaven had pleas'd to have given me longer life
And able means, we had not parted thus.
These are the whole contents. And, good my lord,
By that you love the dearest in this world,
As you wish Christian peace to souls departed,
Stand these poor people's friend, and urge the King
To do me this last right.
CAPUCIUS By heaven, I will,
Or let me lose the fashion of a man!
KATHARINE
I thank you, honest lord. Remember me
In all humility unto his Highness.
Say his long trouble now is passing
Out of this world; tell him, in death I bless'd him,
For so I will. Mine eyes grow dim. Farewell,
My lord. Griffith, farewell. Nay, Patience,
You must not leave me yet. I must to bed;
Call in more women. When I am dead, good wench,
Let me be us'd with honor. Strew me over
With maiden flowers, that all the world may know
I was a chaste wife to my grave. Embalm me,
Then lay me forth. Although unqueen'd, yet like
A queen, and daughter to a king, inter me.
I can no more. *Exeunt, leading Katharine.*

ACT V • SCENE I

Enter Gardiner, Bishop of Winchester, a Page with a torch before him, met by Sir Thomas Lovell.

GARDINER
It's one o'clock, boy, is 't not?
BOY It hath struck.
GARDINER
These should be hours for necessities,
Not for delights; times to repair our nature
With comforting repose, and not for us

100 An 't like if it please **102 lose** forget **105 staying** waiting **122 had** would have **132 model** image. **young daughter** i.e., Mary, the only one of Katharine's many children to live to maturity. She became Queen of England (1553–1558) before her half-sister Elizabeth (1558–1603).

141 both my fortunes i.e., good and ill **143 now** i.e., on my death bed, when true speaking is of utmost spiritual importance **145 honesty . . . carriage** chastity and proper behavior **171 lay me forth** lay me out for burial

V.i. Location: London. A gallery in the palace.

To waste these times. Good hour of night, Sir Thomas!
Whither so late?

LOVELL
Came you from the King, my lord?

GARDINER
I did, Sir Thomas, and left him at primero
With the Duke of Suffolk.

LOVELL
I must to him too,
Before he go to bed. I'll take my leave.

GARDINER
Not yet, Sir Thomas Lovell. What's the matter?
It seems you are in haste. An if there be
No great offense belongs to 't, give your friend
Some touch of your late business. Affairs that walk,
As they say spirits do, at midnight, have
In them a wilder nature than the business
That seeks dispatch by day.

LOVELL
My lord, I love you,
And durst commend a secret to your ear
Much weightier than this work. The Queen's in labor,
They say, in great extremity, and fear'd
She'll with the labor end.

GARDINER
The fruit she goes with
I pray for heartily, that it may find
Good time, and live; but for the stock, Sir Thomas,
I wish it grubb'd up now.

LOVELL
Methinks I could
Cry the amen; and yet my conscience says
She's a good creature, and, sweet lady, does
Deserve our better wishes.

GARDINER
But, sir, sir,
Hear me, Sir Thomas. Y' are a gentleman
Of mine own way. I know you wise, religious;
And, let me tell you, it will ne'er be well—
'Twill not, Sir Thomas Lovell, take 't of me—
Till Cranmer, Cromwell, her two hands, and she,
Sleep in their graves.

LOVELL
Now, sir, you speak of two
The most remark'd i' th' kingdom. As for Cromwell,
Beside that of the Jewel House, is made Master
O' th' Rolls, and the King's secretary; further, sir,
Stands in the gap and trade of moe preferments,
With which the time will load him. Th' Archbishop
Is the King's hand and tongue, and who dare speak
One syllable against him?

GARDINER
Yes, yes, Sir Thomas,
There are that dare, and I myself have ventur'd
To speak my mind of him; and indeed this day,
Sir, I may tell it you, I think I have
Incens'd the lords o' th' council, that he is—
For so I know he is, they know he is—
A most arch heretic, a pestilence
That does infect the land; with which they moved
Have broken with the King, who hath so far
Given ear to our complaint, of his great grace
And princely care foreseeing those fell mischiefs
Our reasons laid before him, hath commanded
Tomorrow morning to the council-board
He be convented. He's a rank weed, Sir Thomas,
And we must root him out. From your affairs
I hinder you too long. Good night, Sir Thomas.

LOVELL
Many good nights, my lord! I rest your servant.
Exeunt Gardiner and Page.

Enter King and Suffolk.

KING
Charles, I will play no more tonight;
My mind's not on 't, you are too hard for me.

SUFFOLK
Sir, I did never win of you before.

KING
But little, Charles,
Nor shall not, when my fancy's on my play.
Now, Lovell, from the Queen what is the news?

LOVELL
I could not personally deliver to her
What you commanded me, but by her woman
I sent your message, who return'd her thanks
In the great'st humbleness, and desir'd your Highness
Most heartily to pray for her.

KING
What say'st thou, ha?
To pray for her? What, is she crying out?

LOVELL
So said her woman, and that her suff'rance made
Almost each pang a death.

KING
Alas, good lady!

SUFFOLK
God safely quit her of her burden, and
With gentle travail, to the gladding of
Your Highness with an heir!

KING
'Tis midnight, Charles.
Prithee, to bed, and in thy pray'rs remember
Th' estate of my poor queen. Leave me alone,
For I must think of that which company
Would not be friendly to.

SUFFOLK
I wish your Highness
A quiet night, and my good mistress will
Remember in my prayers.

KING
Charles, good night.
Exit Suffolk.

Enter Sir Anthony Denny.

Well, sir, what follows?

DENNY
Sir, I have brought my lord the Archbishop,
As you commanded me.

KING
Ha? Canterbury?

DENNY
Ay, my good lord.

KING
'Tis true. Where is he, Denny?

7 primero gambling card game **11 An if** if **13 touch** hint **17 commend** entrust **18 this work** i.e., what I am involved in **22 Good time** good fortune **23 grubb'd up** rooted up **24 Cry the amen** give assent **28 way** religious faith (opposed to Protestant reform) **33 remark'd** under the public eye **34–35 Master . . . Rolls** judge of the court of appeal **36 gap and trade** opening and beaten path. **moe** more **37 time** course of events **43 Incens'd** instigated **46–47 with . . . King** they, moved to anger at the idea, have disclosed it to the King

49 fell terrible, cruel **50 hath** (that) he has **52 convented** summoned **55 rest** remain **68 suff'rance** suffering

DENNY
He attends your Highness' pleasure.

KING
Bring him to us.
[*Exit Denny.*]

LOVELL [*Aside*]
This is about that which the Bishop spake.
I am happily come hither.

Enter Cranmer and Denny.

KING
Avoid the gallery. *(Lovell seems to stay.)* Ha? I have said. Be gone.
What? *Exeunt Lovell and Denny.*

CRANMER [*Aside*] I am fearful. Wherefore frowns he thus?
'Tis his aspect of terror. All's not well.

KING
How now, my lord? You do desire to know
Wherefore I sent for you.

CRANMER [*Kneeling*] It is my duty
T' attend your Highness' pleasure.

KING
Pray you, arise,
My good and gracious Lord of Canterbury.
[*Cranmer rises.*]
Come, you and I must walk a turn together;
I have news to tell you. Come, come, give me your hand.
Ah, my good lord, I grieve at what I speak,
And am right sorry to repeat what follows.
I have, and most unwillingly, of late
Heard many grievous—I do say, my lord,
Grievous—complaints of you; which, being consider'd,
Have mov'd us and our council that you shall
This morning come before us, where I know
You cannot with such freedom purge yourself
But that, till further trial in those charges
Which will require your answer, you must take
Your patience to you, and be well contented
To make your house our Tow'r. You a brother of us,
It fits we thus proceed, or else no witness
Would come against you.

CRANMER [*Kneeling*] I humbly thank your Highness,
And am right glad to catch this good occasion
Most throughly to be winnowed, where my chaff
And corn shall fly asunder. For I know
There's none stands under more calumnious tongues
Than I myself, poor man.

KING
Stand up, good Canterbury!
Thy truth and thy integrity is rooted
In us, thy friend. Give me thy hand, stand up.
[*Cranmer rises.*]
Prithee, let's walk. Now, by my holidame,
What manner of man are you? My lord, I look'd
You would have given me your petition, that
I should have ta'en some pains to bring together
Yourself and your accusers, and to have heard you
Without indurance further.

CRANMER
Most dread liege,
The good I stand on is my truth and honesty.
If they shall fail, I, with mine enemies,
Will triumph o'er my person, which I weigh not,
Being of those virtues vacant. I fear nothing
What can be said against me.

KING
Know you not
How your state stands i' th' world, with the whole world?
Your enemies are many, and not small; their practices
Must bear the same proportion, and not ever
The justice and the truth o' th' question carries
The due o' th' verdict with it. At what ease
Might corrupt minds procure knaves as corrupt
To swear against you? Such things have been done.
You are potently oppos'd, and with a malice
Of as great size. Ween you of better luck,
I mean in perjur'd witness, than your master,
Whose minister you are, whiles here he liv'd
Upon this naughty earth? Go to, go to,
You take a precipice for no leap of danger,
And woo your own destruction.

CRANMER
God and your Majesty
Protect mine innocence, or I fall into
The trap is laid for me.

KING
Be of good cheer;
They shall no more prevail than we give way to.
Keep comfort to you, and this morning see
You do appear before them. If they shall chance,
In charging you with matters, to commit you,
The best persuasions to the contrary
Fail not to use, and with what vehemency
Th' occasion shall instruct you. If entreaties
Will render you no remedy, this ring
Deliver them, and your appeal to us
There make before them. [*Gives ring.*] Look, the good man weeps!
He's honest, on mine honor. God's blest mother,
I swear he is true-hearted, and a soul
None better in my kingdom. Get you gone,
And do as I have bid you. *(Exit Cranmer.)* He has strangled
His language in his tears.

Enter Old Lady, [*Lovell following*].

GENTLEMAN *(Within)* Come back! What mean you?

OLD LADY
I'll not come back. The tidings that I bring
Will make my boldness manners. Now, good angels
Fly o'er thy royal head, and shade thy person
Under their blessed wings!

KING
Now, by thy looks
I guess thy message. Is the Queen deliver'd?
Say, ay, and of a boy.

OLD LADY
Ay, ay, my liege,

84 the Bishop i.e., Gardiner **86 Avoid** vacate **102 freedom** ease and completeness. **purge** excuse, clear **106 brother of us** fellow member of the council **110 throughly** thoroughly **111 corn** grain **112 stands under** is the object of **116 by my holidame** i.e., by Our Lady **117 look'd** expected

121 indurance imprisonment **124–125 which . . . vacant** i.e., which I do not value if it is void of those virtues *(truth* and *honesty)* **128 practices** schemes, plots **129 bear . . . proportion** be correspondingly numerous and mighty **129–131 not . . . it** i.e., the innocence of a person does not always insure his acquittal **131 At what ease** how easily **135 Ween you of** do you expect **136 master** i.e., Christ **138 naughty** wicked **142 is** that is **143 give way to** allow **146 commit** i.e., to prison

And of a lovely boy. The God of heaven
Both now and ever bless her! 'Tis a girl
Promises boys hereafter. Sir, your queen
Desires your visitation, and to be
Acquainted with this stranger. 'Tis as like you
As cherry is to cherry.

KING
Lovell!

LOVELL
Sir?

KING
Give her an hundred marks. I'll to the Queen. 170

Exit King.

OLD LADY
An hundred marks? By this light, I'll ha' more.
An ordinary groom is for such payment. 172
I will have more, or scold it out of him.
Said I for this the girl was like to him?
I'll have more, or else unsay 't; and now,
While 'tis hot, I'll put it to the issue.

Exit Lady [*with Lovell*].

SCENE II

Enter Cranmer, Archbishop of Canterbury,
[*Pursuivants, Pages, etc. attending at the door*].

CRANMER
I hope I am not too late, and yet the gentleman
That was sent to me from the council pray'd me
To make great haste. All fast? What means this? Ho! 3
Who waits there? Sure, you know me?

Enter Keeper.

KEEPER
Yes, my lord;
But yet I cannot help you.

CRANMER
Why?

KEEPER
Your Grace must wait till you be call'd for.

Enter Doctor Butts.

CRANMER
So.

BUTTS [*Aside*]
This is a piece of malice. I am glad
I came this way so happily. The King
Shall understand it presently. *Exit Butts.*

CRANMER [*Aside*]
'Tis Butts,
The King's physician. As he pass'd along,
How earnestly he cast his eyes upon me!
Pray heaven he sound not my disgrace! For certain 13
This is of purpose laid by some that hate me— 14
God turn their hearts! I never sought their malice—
To quench mine honor. They would shame to make
me
Wait else at door, a fellow-counselor,
'Mong boys, grooms, and lackeys. But their
pleasures
Must be fulfill'd, and I attend with patience. 19

Enter the King and Butts at a window above.

BUTTS
I'll show your Grace the strangest sight—

KING
What's that, Butts?

BUTTS
I think your Highness saw this many a day.

KING
Body o' me, where is it?

BUTTS
There, my lord:
The high promotion of his Grace of Canterbury,
Who holds his state at door, 'mongst pursuivants, 24
Pages, and footboys.

KING
Ha? 'Tis he, indeed.
Is this the honor they do one another?
'Tis well there's one above 'em yet. I had thought 27
They had parted so much honesty among 'em— 28
At least, good manners—as not thus to suffer
A man of his place, and so near our favor, 30
To dance attendance on their lordships' pleasures, 31
And at the door too, like a post with packets. 32
By holy Mary, Butts, there's knavery!
Let 'em alone, and draw the curtain close.
We shall hear more anon.

[*They conceal themselves behind the curtain.*
Cranmer remains waiting at the door, below.]

[SCENE III]

A council table brought in with chairs and stools, and placed under the state. Enter Lord Chancellor; places himself at the upper end of the table on the left hand; a seat being left void above him, as for Canterbury's seat. Duke of Suffolk, Duke of Norfolk, Surrey, Lord Chamberlain, Gardiner, seat themselves in order on each side. Cromwell at lower end, as secretary. [*Keeper at the door.*]

CHANCELLOR
Speak to the business, Master Secretary.
Why are we met in council?

CROMWELL
Please your honors,
The chief cause concerns his Grace of Canterbury.

GARDINER
Has he had knowledge of it?

CROMWELL
Yes.

NORFOLK
Who waits there?

170 an hundred marks i.e., about £65 **172 for** suited for

V.ii. Location: London. Adjacent to the council-chamber.
s.d. Pursuivants messengers, subordinates. **at the door** i.e., at a stage door, as though guarding the entrance to the council-chamber **3 fast** locked **13 sound** proclaim **14 laid** contrived as a trap

19 s.d. at a window above (The gallery over the stage, representing a peephole through which the council could be spied upon. The Folio text makes no scene division between this and the following scene, so that the council would assemble under the view and in the hearing of the King; and the main stage, imagined in scene ii to be adjacent to the council-chamber, becomes in scene iii the chamber itself.) **24 holds his state** maintains his dignity **27 one above** (Suggests Henry's role as a godlike figure.) **28 parted** shared **30 place** official position **31 dance attendance** stand waiting around **32 post** messenger. **packets** letters

V.iii. Location: The council-chamber. Scene is continuous with the previous.
s.d. state canopy

KEEPER
Without, my noble lords?
GARDINER
Yes.
KEEPER
My Lord Archbishop,
And has done half an hour, to know your pleasures.
CHANCELLOR
Let him come in.
KEEPER
Your Grace may enter now.
Cranmer approaches the council table.
CHANCELLOR
My good Lord Archbishop, I'm very sorry
To sit here at this present, and behold
That chair stand empty. But we all are men,
In our own natures frail, and capable
Of our flesh—few are angels—out of which frailty
And want of wisdom, you, that best should teach us,
Have misdemean'd yourself, and not a little,
Toward the King first, then his laws, in filling
The whole realm, by your teaching and your chaplains—
For so we are inform'd—with new opinions,
Divers and dangerous; which are heresies,
And, not reform'd, may prove pernicious.
GARDINER
Which reformation must be sudden too,
My noble lords; for those that tame wild horses
Pace 'em not in their hands to make 'em gentle,
But stop their mouths with stubborn bits, and spur 'em,
Till they obey the manage. If we suffer,
Out of our easiness and childish pity
To one man's honor, this contagious sickness,
Farewell all physic! And what follows then?
Commotions, uproars, with a general taint
Of the whole state, as of late days our neighbors,
The upper Germany, can dearly witness,
Yet freshly pitied in our memories.
CRANMER
My good lords, hitherto, in all the progress
Both of my life and office, I have labor'd,
And with no little study, that my teaching
And the strong course of my authority
Might go one way, and safely; and the end
Was ever to do well. Nor is there living—
I speak it with a single heart, my lords—
A man that more detests, more stirs against,
Both in his private conscience and his place,
Defacers of a public peace than I do.
Pray heaven the King may never find a heart
With less allegiance in it! Men that make
Envy and crooked malice nourishment
Dare bite the best. I do beseech your lordships
That in this case of justice, my accusers,
Be what they will, may stand forth face to face,
And freely urge against me.
SUFFOLK
Nay, my lord,
That cannot be. You are a counselor,
And, by that virtue, no man dare accuse you.
GARDINER
My lord, because we have business of more moment,
We will be short with you. 'Tis his Highness' pleasure,
And our consent, for better trial of you,
From hence you be committed to the Tower,
Where, being but a private man again,
You shall know many dare accuse you boldly—
More than, I fear, you are provided for.
CRANMER
Ah, my good Lord of Winchester, I thank you;
You are always my good friend. If your will pass,
I shall both find your lordship judge and juror,
You are so merciful. I see your end;
'Tis my undoing. Love and meekness, lord,
Become a churchman better than ambition.
Win straying souls with modesty again,
Cast none away. That I shall clear myself,
Lay all the weight ye can upon my patience,
I make as little doubt as you do conscience
In doing daily wrongs. I could say more,
But reverence to your calling makes me modest.
GARDINER
My lord, my lord, you are a sectary,
That's the plain truth. Your painted gloss discovers,
To men that understand you, words and weakness.
CROMWELL
My Lord of Winchester, y' are a little,
By your good favor, too sharp; men so noble,
However faulty, yet should find respect
For what they have been. 'Tis a cruelty
To load a falling man.
GARDINER
Good Master Secretary,
I cry your honor mercy; you may, worst
Of all this table, say so.
CROMWELL
Why, my lord?
GARDINER
Do not I know you for a favorer
Of this new sect? Ye are not sound.
CROMWELL
Not sound?
GARDINER
Not sound, I say.
CROMWELL
Would you were half so honest!
Men's prayers then would seek you, not their fears.
GARDINER
I shall remember this bold language.
CROMWELL
Do.
Remember your bold life too.

5 Without outside the door. (Although Cranmer seemingly has never exited, the stage has now become the room into which he has been waiting to be admitted.) **9 present** present time **11–12 capable . . . flesh** susceptible to the weaknesses of the flesh **22 Pace . . . hands** i.e., don't lead them gently **24 manage** training, handling. **suffer** allow **25 easiness** laxness **27 physic** medicine, cure **30 upper Germany** (Refers to the Peasants' Wars, 1524; possibly to the massacre of the Anabaptists in 1535.) **38 single** honest; not given to double-dealing **39 stirs** is active **40 place** official capacity

48 urge make accusation **50 by that virtue** by virtue of that **59 pass** prevail **64 modesty** moderation **66 Lay . . . can** i.e., no matter how hard you press **67–68 I . . . In** I have as little doubt (of my blamelessness) as you have scruples against **70 sectary** follower of a heretical Protestant sect **71 painted gloss discovers** false exterior (in speech and acts) reveals **72 words** i.e., mere words **74 By . . . favor** i.e., begging your pardon **75 find** be accorded **78 I cry . . . mercy** I beg your pardon. **worst** with least reason **81 sound** orthodox

CHANCELLOR This is too much.
Forbear, for shame, my lords.
GARDINER I have done.
CROMWELL And I.
CHANCELLOR
Then thus for you, my lord: it stands agreed,
I take it, by all voices, that forthwith
You be convey'd to th' Tower a prisoner,
There to remain till the King's further pleasure
Be known unto us. Are you all agreed, lords?
ALL
We are.
CRANMER Is there no other way of mercy,
But I must needs to th' Tower, my lords?
GARDINER What other
Would you expect? You are strangely troublesome.
Let some o' th' guard be ready there.

Enter the Guard.

CRANMER For me?
Must I go like a traitor thither?
GARDINER Receive him,
And see him safe i' th' Tower.
CRANMER Stay, good my lords,
I have a little yet to say. Look there, my lords;
[*Shows ring.*]
By virtue of that ring, I take my cause
Out of the gripes of cruel men, and give it
To a most noble judge, the King my master.
CHAMBERLAIN
This is the King's ring.
SURREY 'Tis no counterfeit.
SUFFOLK
'Tis the right ring, by heav'n! I told ye all,
When we first put this dangerous stone a-rolling,
'Twould fall upon ourselves.
NORFOLK Do you think, my lords,
The King will suffer but the little finger
Of this man to be vex'd?
CHANCELLOR 'Tis now too certain.
How much more is his life in value with him!
Would I were fairly out on 't!
CROMWELL My mind gave me,
In seeking tales and informations
Against this man, whose honesty the devil
And his disciples only envy at,
Ye blew the fire that burns ye. Now have at ye!

Enter King, frowning on them; takes his seat.

GARDINER
Dread sovereign, how much are we bound to
heaven
In daily thanks, that gave us such a prince,
Not only good and wise, but most religious;
One that, in all obedience, makes the church
The chief aim of his honor; and, to strengthen
That holy duty, out of dear respect,
His royal self in judgment comes to hear
The cause betwixt her and this great offender.
KING
You were ever good at sudden commendations,
Bishop of Winchester. But know I come not
To hear such flattery now, and in my presence
They are too thin and base to hide offenses.
To me you cannot reach. You play the spaniel,
And think with wagging of your tongue to win me;
But whatsoe'er thou tak'st me for, I'm sure
Thou hast a cruel nature and a bloody.
[*To Cranmer.*] Good man, sit down. [*Cranmer sits.*]
Now let me see the proudest
He, that dares most, but wag his finger at thee.
By all that's holy, he had better starve
Than but once think this place becomes thee not.
SURREY
May it please your Grace—
KING No, sir, it does not please me.
I had thought I had had men of some understanding
And wisdom of my Council; but I find none.
Was it discretion, lords, to let this man,
This good man—few of you deserve that title—
This honest man, wait like a lousy footboy
At chamber door? And one as great as you are?
Why, what a shame was this! Did my commission
Bid ye so far forget yourselves? I gave ye
Power as he was a counselor to try him,
Not as a groom. There's some of ye, I see,
More out of malice than integrity,
Would try him to the utmost, had ye mean,
Which ye shall never have while I live.
CHANCELLOR Thus far,
My most dread sovereign, may it like your Grace
To let my tongue excuse all. What was purpos'd
Concerning his imprisonment was rather,
If there be faith in men, meant for his trial
And fair purgation to the world than malice,
I'm sure, in me.
KING Well, well, my lords, respect him;
Take him, and use him well, he's worthy of it.
I will say thus much for him, if a prince
May be beholding to a subject, I
Am, for his love and service, so to him.
Make me no more ado, but all embrace him.
Be friends, for shame, my lords! [*They all embrace
Cranmer.*] My Lord of Canterbury,
I have a suit which you must not deny me;
That is, a fair young maid that yet wants baptism,
You must be godfather, and answer for her.
CRANMER
The greatest monarch now alive may glory
In such an honor. How may I deserve it,
That am a poor and humble subject to you?

100 gripes clutches **108 in value with** valued by **109 on 't** of it (this trouble). **gave** told

119 dear respect heartfelt piety **122 sudden commendations** unrehearsed compliments **131 He** person **132 starve** die **146 mean** means **148 like** please **152 purgation** clearing of himself

KING
Come, come, my lord, you'd spare your spoons.
  You shall have
Two noble partners with you: the old Duchess of
  Norfolk,
And Lady Marquess Dorset. Will these please you?
Once more, my Lord of Winchester, I charge you,
Embrace and love this man.

GARDINER
                    With a true heart
And brother-love I do it. [*Embraces him.*]

CRANMER
                    And let heaven
Witness how dear I hold this confirmation.

KING
Good man, those joyful tears show thy true heart.
The common voice, I see, is verified
Of thee, which says thus, "Do my Lord of
  Canterbury
A shrewd turn, and he's your friend forever."
Come, lords, we trifle time away; I long
To have this young one made a Christian.
As I have made ye one, lords, one remain;
So I grow stronger, you more honor gain. *Exeunt.*

SCENE [IV]

Noise and tumult within. Enter Porter and his Man.

PORTER You'll leave your noise anon, ye rascals! Do you take the court for Parish Garden? Ye rude slaves, leave your gaping.

ONE *(Within)* Good master porter, I belong to th' larder.

PORTER Belong to th' gallows, and be hang'd, ye rogue! Is this a place to roar in? Fetch me a dozen crab-tree staves, and strong ones; these are but switches to 'em. I'll scratch your heads. You must be seeing christenings? Do you look for ale and cakes here, you rude rascals?

MAN
Pray, sir, be patient. 'Tis as much impossible—
Unless we sweep 'em from the door with cannons—
To scatter 'em, as 'tis to make 'em sleep
On May-day morning, which will never be.
We may as well push against Paul's as stir 'em.

PORTER How got they in, and be hang'd?

MAN
Alas, I know not. How gets the tide in?
As much as one sound cudgel of four foot—
You see the poor remainder—could distribute,
I made no spare, sir.

PORTER
                    You did nothing, sir.

MAN
I am not Samson, nor Sir Guy, nor Colbrand,
To mow 'em down before me; but if I spar'd any
That had a head to hit, either young or old,
He or she, cuckold or cuckold-maker,
Let me ne'er hope to see a chine again;
And that I would not for a cow, God save her!

ONE *(Within)* Do you hear, master porter?

PORTER I shall be with you presently, good master puppy.—Keep the door close, sirrah.

MAN What would you have me do?

PORTER What should you do, but knock 'em down by the dozens? Is this Moorfields to muster in? Or have we some strange Indian with the great tool come to court, the women so besiege us? Bless me, what a fry of fornication is at door! On my Christian conscience, this one christening will beget a thousand; here will be father, godfather, and all together.

MAN The spoons will be the bigger, sir. There is a fellow somewhat near the door, he should be a brazier by his face, for, o' my conscience, twenty of the dog-days now reign in 's nose; all that stand about him are under the line, they need no other penance. That fire-drake did I hit three times on the head, and three times was his nose discharg'd against me; he stands there, like a mortar-piece, to blow us. There was a haberdasher's wife of small wit near him, that rail'd upon me till her pink'd porringer fell off her head, for kindling such a combustion in the state. I miss'd the meteor once, and hit that woman, who cried out "Clubs!" when I might see from far some forty truncheoners draw to her succor, which were the hope o' th' Strand, where she was quarter'd. They fell on; I made good my place. At length they came to th' broom-staff to me. I defied 'em still, when suddenly a file of boys behind 'em, loose shot, deliver'd such a show'r of pebbles that I was fain to draw mine honor in, and let 'em win the work. The devil was amongst 'em, I think, surely.

PORTER These are the youths that thunder at a playhouse, and fight for bitten apples, that no audience but the tribulation of Tower-hill or the limbs of Limehouse, their dear brothers, are able to endure. I have some of 'em in Limbo Patrum, and there they are like to dance these three days, besides the running banquet of two beadles that is to come.

166 you'd . . . spoons (Said jestingly; spoons were a common christening gift.) **176 shrewd** malicious **179 one** united in spirit

V.iv. Location: London. The palace yard.
2 Parish Garden Paris Garden, a bear garden on the Bankside **3 gaping** shouting **4 I . . . larder** i.e., I am a servant of the palace household, in the pantry **7 to 'em** compared to them, i.e., to cudgels made of crab-tree **9 ale and cakes** (Refreshments appropriate to christenings and other festivals.) **14 May-day morning** (Allusion to the custom of rising before dawn on May day for early morning festivities.) **15 Paul's** St. Paul's cathedral

21 Samson Biblical character of great strength. **Sir Guy, Colbrand** (Colbrand was a legendary Danish giant slain by Guy of Warwick in the popular English romance named after its hero.) **25 chine** backbone; hence a joint of beef or other meat **26 for a cow** i.e., for anything (*cow* perhaps being suggested by *chine*) **32 Moorfields** an open space outside London walls, used among other things as a training ground for the militia **33 tool** genitals. (This sentence alludes to the Elizabethan excitement over exhibited Indians.) **34–35 fry of fornication** swarm of would-be fornicators, or of bastards **38 spoons** i.e., as christening presents. (See V.iii.166.) **39 brazier** worker in brass **40–41 dog-days** i.e., midsummer, when Sirius, the Dog Star, rises at about the same time as the sun **42 under the line** on the equator **42–43 fire-drake** fiery dragon **45 mortar-piece** short cannon **47 pink'd porringer** small close-fitting cap ornamented with perforations **49 meteor** i.e., the red-faced brazier **50 Clubs** (The rallying-cry for London apprentices to join in or stop a brawl.) **50–51 truncheoners** men armed with cudgels **52 Strand** a prosperous street of shops and residences. **fell on** made their assault **53 made . . . place** stood my ground **54 broom-staff** i.e., close quarters **55 loose shot** throwers or marksmen not attached to a particular company **57 work** fort **61 tribulation** troublemakers, gang. **limbs** lads; here, rowdies **61–62 Limehouse** a dockyard area east of Tower hill, a rough neighborhood **63 Limbo Patrum** resting place for the pre-Christian patriarchs who had to remain there until the coming of Christ; hence, prison **64–65 running banquet** whipping following imprisonment (like a *banquet* or *dessert* after a meal)

Enter Lord Chamberlain.

CHAMBERLAIN
Mercy o' me, what a multitude are here!
They grow still too; from all parts they are coming,
As if we kept a fair here! Where are these porters,
These lazy knaves? Y' have made a fine hand,
fellows! 69
There's a trim rabble let in. Are all these 70
Your faithful friends o' th' suburbs? We shall have 71
Great store of room, no doubt, left for the ladies,
When they pass back from the christening.

PORTER An 't please your honor,
We are but men; and what so many may do,
Not being torn a-pieces, we have done.
An army cannot rule 'em.

CHAMBERLAIN As I live,
If the King blame me for 't, I'll lay ye all 77
By th' heels, and suddenly, and on your heads 78
Clap round fines for neglect. Y' are lazy knaves, 79
And here ye lie baiting of bombards, when 80
Ye should do service. [*A trumpet.*] Hark, the
trumpets sound.
Th' are come already from the christening.
Go, break among the press, and find a way out 83
To let the troop pass fairly, or I'll find
A Marshalsea shall hold ye play these two months. 85

PORTER
Make way there for the Princess.

MAN You great fellow,
Stand close up, or I'll make your head ache.

PORTER
You i' th' chamblet, get up o' th' rail! 88
I'll peck you o'er the pales else. *Exeunt.* 89

SCENE [V]

Enter trumpets, sounding; then two Aldermen, Lord Mayor, Garter, Cranmer, Duke of Norfolk with his marshal's staff, Duke of Suffolk, two Noblemen bearing great standing-bowls for the christening-gifts; then four Noblemen bearing a canopy, under which the Duchess of Norfolk, godmother, bearing the child richly habited in a mantle, etc., train borne by a Lady; then follows the Marchioness Dorset, the other godmother, and Ladies. The troop pass once about the stage, and Garter speaks.

GARTER Heaven, from thy endless goodness, send prosperous life, long, and ever happy, to the high and mighty Princess of England, Elizabeth!

Flourish. Enter King and Guard.

CRANMER [*Kneeling*]
And to your royal Grace and the good Queen,
My noble partners and myself thus pray
All comfort, joy, in this most gracious lady
Heaven ever laid up to make parents happy
May hourly fall upon ye!

KING
Thank you, good Lord Archbishop.
What is her name?

CRANMER Elizabeth.

KING Stand up, lord.
[*Cranmer rises. The King kisses the child.*]
With this kiss take my blessing. God protect thee,
Into whose hand I give thy life.

CRANMER Amen.

KING
My noble gossips, y' have been too prodigal. 13
I thank ye heartily; so shall this lady,
When she has so much English.

CRANMER Let me speak, sir,
For heaven now bids me; and the words I utter
Let none think flattery, for they'll find 'em truth.
This royal infant—heaven still move about her!— 18
Though in her cradle, yet now promises
Upon this land a thousand thousand blessings,
Which time shall bring to ripeness. She shall be—
But few now living can behold that goodness—
A pattern to all princes living with her,
And all that shall succeed. Saba was never 24
More covetous of wisdom and fair virtue
Than this pure soul shall be. All princely graces,
That mold up such a mighty piece as this is, 27
With all the virtues that attend the good,
Shall still be doubled on her. Truth shall nurse her,
Holy and heavenly thoughts still counsel her.
She shall be lov'd and fear'd. Her own shall bless
her; 31
Her foes shake like a field of beaten corn, 32
And hang their heads with sorrow. Good grows
with her.
In her days every man shall eat in safety
Under his own vine what he plants, and sing
The merry songs of peace to all his neighbors.
God shall be truly known, and those about her
From her shall read the perfect ways of honor, 38
And by those claim their greatness, not by blood. 39
Nor shall this peace sleep with her; but as when 40
The bird of wonder dies, the maiden phoenix, 41
Her ashes new create another heir, 42
As great in admiration as herself, 43
So shall she leave her blessedness to one,
When heaven shall call her from this cloud of
darkness, 45
Who from the sacred ashes of her honor
Shall star-like rise, as great in fame as she was,

69 fine hand fine job. (Said ironically.) **70 trim** fine. (Said ironically.) **71 suburbs** areas outside London walls and hence outside its legal jurisdiction **77–78 lay . . . heels** put you in the stocks or in chains **79 round** heavy **80 baiting of bombards** drinking from leathern bottles **83 press** crowd **85 Marshalsea** prison in Southwark. **hold ye play** keep you engaged **88 chamblet** camlet, a kind of fabric made with goat's hair. (Since no "crowd" is on stage, the Porter may be speaking to his audience here as though it were crowding to see the christening.) **89 peck** pitch. **pales** palings, fence

V.v. Location: London. The palace.

13 gossips godparents **18 still** ever **24 Saba** i.e., the Queen of Sheba, who visited Solomon to discover wisdom from him; see 1 Kings 10:1–10 **27 mighty piece** princely person **31 own** i.e., own people **32 beaten corn** wind-beaten grain **38 read** learn **39 greatness** nobility **40 sleep** i.e., die **41 phoenix** mythical bird believed to rise from its own ashes; a symbol of regeneration **42 heir** i.e., James I **43 great in admiration** greatly wondered at **45 cloud of darkness** i.e., mortal life

And so stand fix'd. Peace, plenty, love, truth, terror,
That were the servants to this chosen infant,
Shall then be his, and like a vine grow to him.
Wherever the bright sun of heaven shall shine,
His honor and the greatness of his name
Shall be, and make new nations. He shall flourish,
And, like a mountain cedar, reach his branches
To all the plains about him. Our children's children
Shall see this, and bless heaven.

KING
Thou speakest wonders.

CRANMER
She shall be, to the happiness of England,
An aged princess; many days shall see her,
And yet no day without a deed to crown it.
Would I had known no more! But she must die,
She must, the saints must have her; yet a virgin,
A most unspotted lily shall she pass
To th' ground, and all the world shall mourn her.

KING
O Lord Archbishop,
Thou hast made me now a man! Never, before
This happy child, did I get anything. 66
This oracle of comfort has so pleas'd me
That when I am in heaven I shall desire
To see what this child does, and praise my Maker.
I thank ye all. To you, my good Lord Mayor,
And you, good brethren, I am much beholding;
I have receiv'd much honor by your presence,
And ye shall find me thankful. Lead the way, lords.
Ye must all see the Queen, and she must thank ye,
She will be sick else. This day, no man think
H'as business at his house; for all shall stay. 76
This little one shall make it holiday. *Exeunt.*

THE EPILOGUE

'Tis ten to one this play can never please
All that are here. Some come to take their ease,
And sleep an act or two; but those, we fear,
W' have frighted with our trumpets; so, 'tis clear,
They'll say 'tis naught; others, to hear the city
Abus'd extremely, and to cry "That's witty!"
Which we have not done neither; that I fear
All the expected good w' are like to hear 8
For this play at this time is only in
The merciful construction of good women,
For such a one we show'd 'em. If they smile,
And say 'twill do, I know, within a while
All the best men are ours; for 'tis ill hap
If they hold when their ladies bid 'em clap. 14

66 get beget; achieve **75 sick** unhappy **76 H'as** (that) he has

Epilogue.
8 expected good anticipated approval, applause **10 construction** interpretation **14 hold** hold back

The Tragedies

Titus Andronicus

Romeo and Juliet

Julius Caesar

Hamlet, Prince of Denmark

Othello, the Moor of Venice

King Lear

Macbeth

Timon of Athens

Antony and Cleopatra

Coriolanus

Titus Andronicus

Titus Andronicus has drawn some unusually harsh criticism. Ben Jonson singled it out, in his Induction to *Bartholomew Fair* (1614), as a play loved by ignorant audiences for its bombastic rhetoric. T. S. Eliot called it "one of the stupidest and most uninspired plays ever written." Others have argued that it was not Shakespeare's at all, or his perfunctory revision of an old play by Marlowe, Kyd, Greene, or Peele, or an early experimental work, or even a burlesque of the revenge play then in vogue. Early it surely was; it appeared in quarto in 1594 as played by Derby's, Pembroke's, and Sussex' men, and could well have been written in 1590 or even before. The allusion in Henslowe's *Diary* for January 24, 1594, to a new production by Sussex' men of "Titus & Ondronicus" could refer to a new play or one newly revised or newly acquired by the company. Shakespeare's *Titus Andronicus* was widely separated in time from the great tragedies; *Romeo and Juliet* is the only other tragedy (excluding the English history plays) of the decade preceding 1599, and it probably followed *Titus Andronicus* by five years or so. Unquestionably *Titus Andronicus* is the least successful of Shakespeare's tragedies, the most deficient in cosmic significance or in affirmation of man's tragic dignity. This judgment compares the play, however, with the greatest dramas of the English language. Probably its most serious critical liability is that it continually reminds us of the later Roman plays and of *Hamlet* and *King Lear.* By any other dramatist the play would not seem so imperfect as it seems when assigned to Shakespeare. *Titus Andronicus* was an early success on stage, and has shown its timeless theatrical appeal in a brilliant production at Stratford-upon-Avon by Sir Laurence Olivier in 1957.

Titus Andronicus is studded with bookish references to classical authors—another likely indication of early date. No other tragedy, perhaps no other Shakespearean play, reveals such direct evidence of youthful learning. Some of its many untranslated Latin phrases are schoolboys' favorites, like the "Integer vitae" of Horace that is immediately recognized by Chiron. "I read it in the grammar long ago," he says (IV,ii). Classical allusions compare the chief characters of the play with Aeneas and Dido Queen of Carthage, Hector, King Priam, and Queen Hecuba of Troy, Ajax and Odysseus among the Greeks, Hercules, Prometheus, Orpheus, Coriolanus, Semiramis the siren Queen of Assyria, Pyramus, Cornelia the mother of the Gracchi, Actaeon, and others. Especially significant are the classical victims of rape and vengeance: Virginia the Roman, killed by her father Virginius to save her from rape; the chaste Lucrece, ravished by Tarquin; Philomel, raped and deprived of her tongue by Tereus, whose name she then reveals by weaving the information into a tapestry; and Procne, her sister and the wife of Tereus, who avenges Philomel by serving Tereus' son Itys to him in a meal.

Ovid's *Metamorphoses* gave Shakespeare his source for many of the legends, especially that of Tereus, Philomel, and Procne. Seneca's *Thyestes* offered him in dramatic form a similar tale of vengeance, in which two sons are slain and served to their parent in a grisly banquet. Shakespeare appears to have used a chapbook called *The History of Titus Andronicus;* the only extant printed copy is from the eighteenth century, but it may give a reliable version of the original. Some scholars believe that one or even two plays about Titus may have existed prior to Shakespeare's, and that we can deduce their contributions to his work by examining two later continental plays derived from them: *Tito Andronico* (German, 1620) and *Aran en Titus* (Dutch, 1641). Possibly one of these earlier plays was the "Titus & Vespacia" entered in Henslowe's *Diary* for April 11, 1592, as acted by Lord Strange's men. Even if Shakespeare used such prose and dramatic sources, however, he also knew well the Ovidian and Senecan originals that had inspired them. Elizabethan revenge tragedy, containing some Senecan influences (though those Senecan elements should not be overstressed), was a strongly formative influence, especially Kyd's *The Spanish Tragedy* (c. 1587). The phenomenal recent stage success of Marlowe left its mark: Titus' killing of his son Mutius recalls *Tamburlaine Part II,* and Aaron's vicelike boasting of wanton villainy recalls *The Jew of Malta.*

As this sizable list of influences suggests, Shakespeare's first tragedy remains close to its models. Although the play anticipates several motifs in the later tragedies—the ingratitude of Rome toward its honored general as in *Coriolanus,* Roman political factionalism as in *Julius Caesar,* infirm old age confronted by human bestiality as in *King Lear*—*Titus Andronicus* is the kind of revenge play one might expect of a gifted young playwright in the early 1590's. The successful models for tragic writing in those years were Kyd and Marlowe; Greene, Peele, and others paid these two the flattery of imitation. So to an extent did Shakespeare. We can best understand *Titus Andronicus* if we view it as a revenge play in the sensational vein of Shakespeare's immediate predecessors, with generous additions of Ovidian pathos. We should not look in *Titus Andronicus* for that humane and compassionate wisdom we expect in mature Shakespearean tragedy; as a revenge play, *Titus Andronicus* focuses on violence and horror, and its mood is one of revulsion. The style too requires some adjustment in our expectations. Owing much to Kyd, Marlowe, and Ovid, it is replete with rhetorical figures and classical allusions in the manner of Shakespeare's Ovidian poems from the early 1590's, *Venus and Adonis* and *The Rape of Lucrece*. Even if its "early" features are manifest, the style works to good dramatic effect in highly wrought scenes, as when Titus pleads for justice to the unresponsive senators (III,i), or lays a trap for Tamora and her sons under the guise of his supposed madness (V,ii). The seeming incongruity of violent action and elaborately refined metaphor, as in Titus' florid lament for Lavinia's mutilation (III,i), is not, as Eugene Waith has shown (*Shakespeare Survey,* 1957), without its purpose, for it evokes pathos on behalf of gruesome suffering in a deliberately Ovidian manner, abstracting and generalizing human torment. As in Ovid, the interest is not in moralizing lessons but in the "transforming power of intense states of emotion."

Violence is an enduring feature of *Titus Andronicus,* and its function must be understood if the play is not to be dismissed as merely hyperbolical in its bloodshed. We are constantly aware of ritual human sacrifice, murder, and maiming, as in Titus' sentencing of Tamora's son Alarbus and his slaying of his own son Mutius, the massacre by Tamora's sons of Bassianus and their ravishing of Lavinia, the subsequent execution of two of Titus' sons wrongfully accused of Bassianus' murder, the cutting off of Titus' hand, the feeding to Tamora of her sons' bodies ground into a fine paste, and still more. Savage mutilation is characteristic of many of these atrocities, especially in the lopping off of hands and tongue. The play's climax is, in the manner of revenge tragedy, a spectacle of blood, with the deaths in rapid succession of Lavinia, Tamora, Titus, and Saturninus. All of these slaughters cause revulsion in some viewers, like T. S. Eliot, but to others the violence reveals a pattern and offers its own ethical stance on vengeance. Although we do not sense in this early play the same controlled perspective on human evil as in *Hamlet,* for example, we see that Shakespeare is intensely aware of the conflict between order and disorder. In the final scenes, Aaron the Moor is caught and sentenced to execution, Tamora and Saturninus are slain, Titus' brother Marcus appeals to Roman justice for vindication on the grounds that his family had no alternative, and Titus' last remaining son Lucius vows as the new emperor to "heal Rome's harms and wipe away her woe" (V,iii). Even if this resolution does not fully satisfy the ethical dilemmas with which the play began, it reveals Shakespeare's disinclination to allow the fulfillment of private vengeance as the play's ultimate concern. Shakespeare is interested throughout in the ethical problems generated by revenge, and the play's relentless horror may be a commentary on the self-defeating nature of a revenge code.

The first part of *Titus Andronicus* functions to give the avenger a motive for his bloody course of action. Ironically, Titus is himself responsible for setting in motion the events that will overwhelm him. His family, the Andronici, are the first to practice vengeance, a fact which diminishes the sympathy they might later have been able to enjoy as victims and exiles. In fact it is Lucius, ultimately to become the restorer of political stability, who first demands the ritual slaying of a captive Goth, Tamora's son Alarbus, to appease the spirits of the Andronici slain in battle. Such a demand is understandable in terms of family honor, but it is also vengeful and pagan. Despite Marcus' injunction to Titus that "Thou art a Roman, be not barbarous," the Roman Andronici do act like barbarian Goths. This irony is complete when the Gothic Queen Tamora and her sons become the spokesmen for godlike mercy. As Tamora's son Chiron bitterly observes, "Was never Scythia half so barbarous."

Equally violent and unnatural is Titus' slaying of his own son, Mutius, for assisting in the abduction of Titus' daughter Lavinia. This tragic error stems, like the first, from Titus' narrow sense of family honor. Titus has unwisely refused the imperial crown, bestowing it instead on the treacherous Saturninus, and has promised Lavinia as bride to the new emperor despite her prior betrothal to Saturninus' virtuous rival, Bassianus. When Titus' sons and Bassianus are driven to the expedient of abducting the lady, Titus cannot endure the shame of his violated promise and so kills Mutius in the ensuing melee. Yet for this sacrifice on behalf of the Emperor, Titus receives only ingratitude and hostility. Moreover, he has taught Tamora and her sons to seek vengeance.

Once the Andronici become the victims of the Goths, they gain in sympathy. They suffer unspeakable atrocities. Hunted down by jeering sadists who amuse themselves through rape and mutilation, the Andronici band together in mutual tribulation and selflessly attempt to ease one another's agony. They discover Rome to be a "wilderness of tigers" in which the law blindly condemns Titus' innocent sons for the murder of Bassianus. Still, Titus has committed the first barbarism, and turns increasingly to barbarism in his desire for vengeance. Because the Andronici are too much like their enemies, the prevailing mood as in most revenge plays is more ironic than tragic. There is no strong sense (despite the capture of Aaron) that moral order is restored along with political order. The Andronici are vindicated, and they have gained some wisdom through suffering, but they are still the avengers who gave the first offense.

Titus Andronicus displays many conventions of the revenge play found earlier in *The Spanish Tragedy*. The avenger, Titus, is a man of high position conscientiously serving the state, like Kyd's Hieronimo, who discovers that the state itself is too corrupt to give him justice in his family wrong. The evildoers are members of the Emperor's family, protected by their royal connection. Private and public interests clash, and public welfare is the loser. The avenger has difficulty proving the identity of the villains, but finds an ingenious way at last (through Lavinia's writing in the sand). Once he becomes the avenger, like Hieronimo, Titus grows as remorseless and canny as his enemies. He becomes a menace to public order, uttering enigmatic threats and blazoning forth the injustices of the state. Wavering on true madness, he also employs madness as a cloak for his Machiavellian intrigues. His plotting succeeds in duping Queen Tamora into allowing him to arrange his gruesome banquet. The drama ends, like *The Spanish Tragedy,* in a kind of play-within-the-play, as Tamora's two sons take the roles of Rape and Murder, Tamora Revenge, and Titus the cook. Playacting turns deadly earnest with a rapid succession of slaughters. Titus and Lavinia, like Hieronimo and Bel-Imperia, do not outlive their act of vengeance.

This conventional pattern embraces revenge as self-justifying. As in *The Spanish Tragedy,* where the choric Revenge controls the action for his own sinister purposes and welcomes the suffering of innocents or the collapse of governments as grist to his mill, *Titus Andronicus* portrays a world in which the avenger can act seemingly only through violence. Even Lavinia and Titus' young grandson endorse plotting and murder. Titus practices cunning toward his enemies, vowing to "o'erreach them in their own devices." Our attention is increasingly drawn to the artistry of the "devices" on both sides. The machinations of Aaron and Tamora demand ingenuity in return. An eye must pay for an eye; the punishment must fit the crime. To be sure, Titus and his family do struggle to understand the moral nature of their universe. "If any power pities wretched tears, To that I call," prays Titus, lifting his mangled hand toward heaven and imploring divine assistance (III,i). Repeatedly the Andronici ask if a divine justice exists, if it cares about savagery among men, and if that justice will assist the defenseless. "O heavens," asks Marcus, "can you hear a good man groan And not relent, or not compassion him?" (IV,i). Marcus seeks the identities of his niece's ravishers, hoping that Lavinia will be able to "display at last What God will have discovered for revenge" (IV,i). Is revenge to be God's or man's? In part at least, Marcus sees himself and his family as agents of divine justice, like Hamlet, though Titus' own errors will also require his own destruction. Yet even these questionings about the cosmos are a part of the revenge tradition, for Hieronimo in *The Spanish Tragedy* implores the gods in similar terms. Titus, for all his pleas to the heavens, is ultimately the avenger in a revenge play. He does not, like Hamlet, submit himself to what he takes to be the will of providence and wait for whatever opportunity heaven will provide. Titus swears an oath of revenge and proceeds with the most gruesome acts imaginable. In his death there is no talk of reconciliation between divine and human will. As the moment of climax approaches, revenge is seen to be a force from hell, from the "infernal regions," while true justice is employed "with Jove in heaven" (IV,ii and iii). Titus is a protagonist suited to a play in which revenge proceeds by its own pitiless rules, in which brutality is the dominant fact of life, and in which violence is the only apparent means of redress. Divine ideas of justice mock man's blind attempts at self-governance without offering reassurance and direction.

As a tragedy of evil, then, *Titus Andronicus* illuminates the nature of that evil more than it attempts to transcend evil through human nobility, as in the later tragedies. This distinctive quality is made especially manifest by the play's outward resemblance to *King Lear.* Titus is old, infirm of judgment, and victimized by his own decision to relinquish power to a person whose villainy he does not comprehend. He is, as Lear says of himself, certainly more sinned against than sinning. Titus approaches madness, and generalizes in his grief about the omnipresence of murder and ingratitude in nature (III,ii). His reflections on human injustice suggest the inversion of appearance and reality ("Grief has so wrought on him He takes false shadows for true substances"), a motif of illusion that reappears in the allegorical play-within-the-play. Queen Tamora reveals an innate viciousness and sexual depravity like that of Goneril and Regan. Aaron the Moor, perhaps the first of Shakespeare's gloating Vicelike villains, resembles Edmund in *King Lear* as well as Richard III, Don John (in *Much Ado about Nothing*), and Iago (in *Othello*). *Titus Andronicus* shows us, in embryonic form and close to their sources, many of Shakespeare's later tragic themes and methods.

Aaron the Moor is the most vital character in this early play. Like the Vice of the morality play or like Marlowe's stage Machiavel, Aaron takes delight in pure evil and displays his cunning for the admiration of the audience. Evil to him is "sport," "wit," "stratagem," and above all "policy" (II,i). His malice encompasses all humanity, and proceeds from no motive other than the sinister pleasure he takes in devising plots. When he is finally captured, Aaron boasts triumphantly of the extent and variety of his cruel accomplishments:

> Even now I curse the day—and yet, I think,
> Few come within the compass of my curse—
> Wherein I did not some notorious ill,
> As kill a man, or else devise his death,
> Ravish a maid, or plot the way to do it,
> Accuse some innocent and forswear myself,
> Set deadly enmity between two friends,
> Make poor men's cattle break their necks,
> Set fire on barns and hay-stacks in the night,
> And bid the owners quench them with their tears.
> Oft have I digg'd up dead men from their graves,
> And set them upright at their dear friends' door,
> Even when their sorrows almost was forgot.

Through its depiction of evil as both comic and diabolical, this portrait gives us a vivid insight into the origins of one type of Shakespearean villain.

The seemingly attractive side to Aaron, his fiercely protective instincts toward his bastard son born of Tamora, is part of the central evil of this play: pride of family turning to violent revenge. His Negroid features, and those of his son, are equated with barbarism, pagan atheism (Aaron scoffs at those who believe in God), and diabolism. Through him, and through Tamora and her kindred, naked evil is rendered with a terrifying brilliance. As a revenge play *Titus Andronicus* is theatrically effective. To be appreciated properly, it should be seen or read in these terms rather than with the expectations we bring to *King Lear.* Shakespeare here presents barbarism and civilization as polar opposites, but allows Titus at last no escape from that barbarism which he himself sets in motion. No tragic self-awareness grows out of Titus' humiliation, as it does in *King Lear,* no regret other than for having relinquished power to Saturninus. Instead of tragic self-awareness we are left with an overpowering impression of man's potential for brutality. This vision is unameliorated. The constant reminder of a better world of justice and compassion merely serves to heighten the play's ironic and futile sense of wasted goodness.

Titus Andronicus

[*Dramatis Personae*

SATURNINUS, *son to the late Emperor of Rome, and afterwards declared Emperor.*
BASSIANUS, *brother to Saturninus; in love with Lavinia.*
TITUS ANDRONICUS, *a noble Roman, general against the Goths.*
MARCUS ANDRONICUS, *tribune of the people, and brother to Titus.*
LUCIUS, QUINTUS, MARTIUS, MUTIUS, *sons to Titus Andronicus.*
YOUNG LUCIUS, *a boy, son to Lucius.*
PUBLIUS, *son to Marcus the Tribune.*
SEMPRONIUS, CAIUS, VALENTINE, *kinsmen to Titus.*
AEMILIUS, *a noble Roman.*
ALARBUS, DEMETRIUS, CHIRON, *sons to Tamora.*
AARON, *a Moor, beloved by Tamora.*
CAPTAIN, TRIBUNE, MESSENGER, *and* CLOWN.

TAMORA, *Queen of the Goths.*
LAVINIA, *daughter to Titus Andronicus.*
NURSE, *and a black* CHILD.

ROMANS, GOTHS, SENATORS, TRIBUNES, OFFICERS, SOLDIERS, *and* ATTENDANTS.

SCENE: *Rome, and the country near it.*]

[ACT I • SCENE I]

[*Flourish.*] *Enter the Tribunes and Senators aloft; and then enter* [*below*] *Saturninus and his Followers at one door, and Bassianus and his Followers* [*at the other,*] *with drums and trumpets.*

SATURNINUS
Noble patricians, patrons of my right,
Defend the justice of my cause with arms;
And, countrymen, my loving followers,
Plead my successive title with your swords.

I.i. Location: Rome. Before the Capitol. The tomb of the Andronici is provided onstage, possibly at a trap door.
s.d. aloft i.e., probably in the gallery rearstage above the tiring house, looking down on the main stage **4 successive title** title to the succession

I am his first-born son, that was the last
That ware the imperial diadem of Rome. 6
Then let my father's honors live in me,
Nor wrong mine age with this indignity. 8

BASSIANUS
Romans, friends, followers, favorers of my right,
If ever Bassianus, Caesar's son,
Were gracious in the eyes of royal Rome,
Keep then this passage to the Capitol, 12
And suffer not dishonor to approach
The imperial seat, to virtue consecrate, 14
To justice, continence, and nobility; 15
But let desert in pure election shine, 16
And, Romans, fight for freedom in your choice.

[Enter] Marcus Andronicus, [aloft,] with the crown.

MARCUS
Princes, that strive by factions and by friends
Ambitiously for rule and empery, 19
Know that the people of Rome, for whom we stand
A special party, have, by common voice, 21
In election for the Roman empery,
Chosen Andronicus, surnamed Pius 23
For many good and great deserts to Rome.
A nobler man, a braver warrior,
Lives not this day within the city walls.
He by the Senate is accited home 27
From weary wars against the barbarous Goths,
That with his sons, a terror to our foes, 29
Hath yok'd a nation strong, train'd up in arms. 30
Ten years are spent since first he undertook
This cause of Rome, and chastised with arms
Our enemies' pride. Five times he hath return'd
Bleeding to Rome, bearing his valiant sons
In coffins from the field, and at this day 35
To the monument of the Andronici,
Done sacrifice of expiation,
And slain the noblest prisoner of the Goths. 38
And now at last, laden with honor's spoils,
Returns the good Andronicus to Rome,
Renowned Titus, flourishing in arms.
Let us entreat, by honor of his name,
Whom worthily you would have now succeed,
And in the Capitol and Senate's right,
Whom you pretend to honor and adore, 45
That you withdraw you and abate your strength,
Dismiss your followers and, as suitors should,
Plead your deserts in peace and humbleness.

SATURNINUS
How fair the tribune speaks to calm my thoughts! 49

BASSIANUS
Marcus Andronicus, so I do affy 50
In thy uprightness and integrity,
And so I love and honor thee and thine,
Thy noble brother Titus and his sons,
And her to whom my thoughts are humbled all,
Gracious Lavinia, Rome's rich ornament,
That I will here dismiss my loving friends,
And to my fortunes and the people's favor
Commit my cause in balance to be weigh'd.
Exeunt Soldiers [of Bassianus].

SATURNINUS
Friends, that have been thus forward in my right,
I thank you all and here dismiss you all,
And to the love and favor of my country
Commit myself, my person, and the cause.
[Exeunt the Soldiers of Saturninus.]
Rome be as just and gracious unto me
As I am confident and kind to thee. 64
Open the gates and let me in.

BASSIANUS
Tribunes, and me, a poor competitor. 66
[Flourish.] They [Saturninus and Bassianus] go up into the Senate House.

Enter a Captain.

CAPTAIN
Romans, make way! The good Andronicus,
Patron of virtue, Rome's best champion,
Successful in the battles that he fights,
With honor and with fortune is return'd
From where he circumscribed with his sword, 71
And brought to yoke, the enemies of Rome.

Sound drums and trumpets, and then enter two of Titus' Sons, [Martius and Mutius]; and then two men bearing a coffin covered with black; then two other Sons [Lucius and Quintus]; then Titus Andronicus; and then Tamora, the Queen of Goths, and her three Sons [Alarbus,] Chiron, and Demetrius, with Aaron the Moor, and others as many as can be. Then set down the coffin, and Titus speaks.

TITUS
Hail, Rome, victorious in thy mourning weeds! 73
Lo, as the bark, that hath discharg'd her fraught, 74
Returns with precious lading to the bay
From whence at first she weigh'd her anchorage, 76
Cometh Andronicus, bound with laurel boughs,
To re-salute his country with his tears,
Tears of true joy for his return to Rome.
Thou great defender of this Capitol, 80
Stand gracious to the rites that we intend!
Romans, of five and twenty valiant sons,
Half of the number that King Priam had, 83
Behold the poor remains, alive and dead!
These that survive let Rome reward with love;
These that I bring unto their latest home, 86
With burial amongst their ancestors. 87

6 ware wore **8 age** seniority **12 Keep** defend **14 consecrate** consecrated **15 continence** restraint **16 pure election** free choice, i.e., of the Roman citizens **19 empery** rule (as emperor) **21 A special party** i.e., a representative group specially chosen **23 Chosen** i.e., nominated **27 accited** summoned **29 That** who, i.e., Titus **30 yok'd** subdued **35–38 and at . . . Goths** [These three and one-half lines, which are inconsistent with ll. 96–149 below, were deleted from the Second and Third Quartos and from the Folio text.] **45 pretend** assert, profess **49 fair** courteously, gently **50 affy** trust

64 confident without suspicion **66 s.d. go up** (The *gates* mentioned in l. 65 are presumably a door in the façade of the tiring house, rearstage, below the gallery. Saturninus and Bassianus presumably exit through this door and ascend inside the tiring house to the gallery or Senate House, where they reappear with the Tribunes and Senators.) **71 circumscribed** restrained **73 weeds** garments **74 fraught** freight, cargo **76 anchorage** i.e., anchors **80 Thou** i.e., Jupiter **83 King Priam** King of Troy at the time of its fall; he had fifty sons **86 latest** final **87 With** i.e., let Rome reward with

Here Goths have given me leave to sheathe my sword.
Titus, unkind and careless of thine own,
Why suffer'st thou thy sons, unburied yet,
To hover on the dreadful shore of Styx?
Make way to lay them by their brethren.
They open the tomb.
There greet in silence, as the dead are wont,
And sleep in peace, slain in your country's wars!
O sacred receptacle of my joys,
Sweet cell of virtue and nobility,
How many sons hast thou of mine in store,
That thou wilt never render to me more!

LUCIUS
Give us the proudest prisoner of the Goths,
That we may hew his limbs, and on a pile
Ad manes fratrum sacrifice his flesh
Before this earthy prison of their bones,
That so the shadows be not unappeas'd,
Nor we disturb'd with prodigies on earth.

TITUS
I give him you, the noblest that survives,
The eldest son of this distressed queen.

TAMORA
Stay, Roman brethren! Gracious conqueror,
Victorious Titus, rue the tears I shed,
A mother's tears in passion for her son;
And if thy sons were ever dear to thee,
O, think my son to be as dear to me!
Sufficeth not that we are brought to Rome
To beautify thy triumphs and return
Captive to thee and to thy Roman yoke,
But must my sons be slaughtered in the streets
For valiant doings in their country's cause?
O, if to fight for king and commonweal
Were piety in thine, it is in these.
Andronicus, stain not thy tomb with blood!
Wilt thou draw near the nature of the gods?
Draw near them then in being merciful.
Sweet mercy is nobility's true badge.
Thrice noble Titus, spare my first-born son.

TITUS
Patient yourself, madam, and pardon me.
These are their brethren, whom your Goths beheld
Alive and dead, and for their brethren slain
Religiously they ask a sacrifice.
To this your son is mark'd, and die he must
T' appease their groaning shadows that are gone.

LUCIUS
Away with him! And make a fire straight,
And with our swords, upon a pile of wood,
Let's hew his limbs till they be clean consum'd.
Exeunt Titus' Sons with Alarbus.

TAMORA
O cruel, irreligious piety!

CHIRON
Was never Scythia half so barbarous.

DEMETRIUS
Oppose not Scythia to ambitious Rome.
Alarbus goes to rest, and we survive
To tremble under Titus' threat'ning look.
Then, madam, stand resolv'd, but hope withal
The self-same gods that arm'd the Queen of Troy
With opportunity of sharp revenge
Upon the Thracian tyrant in his tent
May favor Tamora, the Queen of Goths—
When Goths were Goths and Tamora was queen—
To quit the bloody wrongs upon her foes.

Enter the Sons of Andronicus again [*with their swords bloody*].

LUCIUS
See, lord and father, how we have perform'd
Our Roman rites. Alarbus' limbs are lopp'd,
And entrails feed the sacrificing fire,
Whose smoke, like incense, doth perfume the sky.
Remaineth nought but to inter our brethren,
And with loud 'larums welcome them to Rome.

TITUS
Let it be so; and let Andronicus
Make this his latest farewell to their souls.
Sound trumpets, and lay the coffin in the tomb.
In peace and honor rest you here, my sons;
Rome's readiest champions, repose you here in rest,
Secure from worldly chances and mishaps!
Here lurks no treason, here no envy swells,
Here grow no damned drugs; here are no storms,
No noise, but silence and eternal sleep.
In peace and honor rest you here, my sons!

Enter Lavinia.

LAVINIA
In peace and honor live Lord Titus long;
My noble lord and father, live in fame!
Lo, at this tomb my tributary tears
I render, for my brethren's obsequies,
And at thy feet I kneel, with tears of joy, [*Kneel.*]
Shed on this earth, for thy return to Rome.
O, bless me here with thy victorious hand,
Whose fortunes Rome's best citizens applaud!

TITUS
Kind Rome, that hast thus lovingly reserv'd
The cordial of mine age to glad my heart!
Lavinia, live; outlive thy father's days,
And fame's eternal date, for virtue's praise!
[*She rises.*]
[*Marcus Andronicus speaks from above where he is accompanied by Saturninus, Bassianus, other Tribunes, etc.*]

MARCUS
Long live Lord Titus, my beloved brother,
Gracious triumpher in the eyes of Rome!

89 unkind deficient in natural feeling **91 Styx** river surrounding Hades across which souls might not cross until they had received proper burial **101 Ad manes fratrum** to the departed spirits of (our) brothers **124 Patient** calm **134 Scythia** the district north of the Black Sea; its people were notorious for their savagery

135 Oppose compare **138 withal** together with this **139 Queen of Troy** Hecuba, wife of Priam, who after the fall of Troy was carried to Greece as a slave; here she found occasion to avenge the death of her son Polydorus by killing the two sons of the murderer, Polymnestor, King of Thrace **144 quit** requite **150 'larums** trumpet calls **157 drugs** poisonous plants **162 tributary** paid in tribute **163 obsequies** acts performed in honor of the dead **169 cordial** restorative; or comfort, pleasure

TITUS
Thanks, gentle tribune, noble brother Marcus.

MARCUS
And welcome, nephews, from successful wars,
You that survive, and you that sleep in fame!
Fair lords, your fortunes are alike in all,
That in your country's service drew your swords;
But safer triumph is this funeral pomp
That hath aspir'd to Solon's happiness
And triumphs over chance in honor's bed.
Titus Andronicus, the people of Rome,
Whose friend in justice thou hast ever been,
Send thee by me, their tribune and their trust,
This palliament of white and spotless hue,
And name thee in election for the empire,
With these our late-deceased emperor's sons.
Be candidatus then, and put it on,
And help to set a head on headless Rome.
[*A white cloak is brought to Titus.*]

TITUS
A better head her glorious body fits
Than his that shakes for age and feebleness.
What should I don this robe, and trouble you?
Be chosen with proclamations today,
Tomorrow yield up rule, resign my life,
And set abroad new business for you all?
Rome, I have been thy soldier forty years,
And led my country's strength successfully,
And buried one and twenty valiant sons,
Knighted in field, slain manfully in arms,
In right and service of their noble country.
Give me a staff of honor for mine age,
But not a scepter to control the world.
Upright he held it, lords, that held it last.

MARCUS
Titus, thou shalt obtain and ask the empery.

SATURNINUS
Proud and ambitious tribune, canst thou tell?

TITUS
Patience, Prince Saturninus.

SATURNINUS
Romans, do me right.
Patricians, draw your swords, and sheathe them not
Till Saturninus be Rome's emperor.
Andronicus, would thou were shipp'd to hell,
Rather than rob me of the people's hearts!

LUCIUS
Proud Saturnine, interrupter of the good
That noble-minded Titus means to thee!

TITUS
Content thee, Prince. I will restore to thee
The people's hearts, and wean them from
themselves.

BASSIANUS
Andronicus, I do not flatter thee,
But honor thee, and will do till I die.
My faction if thou strengthen with thy friends,
I will most thankful be; and thanks to men
Of noble minds is honorable meed.

TITUS
People of Rome, and people's tribunes here,
I ask your voices and your suffrages.
Will you bestow them friendly on Andronicus?

TRIBUNES
To gratify the good Andronicus,
And gratulate his safe return to Rome,
The people will accept whom he admits.

TITUS
Tribunes, I thank you, and this suit I make,
That you create our emperor's eldest son,
Lord Saturnine, whose virtues will, I hope,
Reflect on Rome as Titan's rays on earth,
And ripen justice in this commonweal.
Then, if you will elect by my advice,
Crown him, and say "Long live our emperor!"

MARCUS
With voices and applause of every sort,
Patricians and plebeians, we create
Lord Saturninus Rome's great emperor,
And say "Long live our Emperor Saturnine!"
[*A long flourish till they come down.*]

SATURNINUS
Titus Andronicus, for thy favors done
To us in our election this day,
I give thee thanks in part of thy deserts,
And will with deeds requite thy gentleness.
And, for an onset, Titus, to advance
Thy name and honorable family,
Lavinia will I make my empress,
Rome's royal mistress, mistress of my heart,
And in the sacred Pantheon her espouse.
Tell me, Andronicus, doth this motion please thee?

TITUS
It doth, my worthy lord, and in this match
I hold me highly honored of your Grace.
And here in sight of Rome to Saturnine,
King and commander of our commonweal,
The wide world's emperor, do I consecrate
My sword, my chariot, and my prisoners,
Presents well worthy Rome's imperious lord.
Receive them then, the tribute that I owe,
Mine honor's ensigns humbled at thy feet.
[*Lays tributes at Saturninus' feet.*]

SATURNINUS
Thanks, noble Titus, father of my life!
How proud I am of thee and of thy gifts
Rome shall record, and when I do forget
The least of these unspeakable deserts,
Romans, forget your fealty to me.

TITUS [*To Tamora*]
Now, madam, are you prisoner to an emperor,
To him that, for your honor and your state,
Will use you nobly and your followers.

180 aspir'd risen. **Solon's happiness** i.e., the happiness defined by Solon (a Greek sage and lawgiver): that no man may be called happy until after his death **185 palliament** gown or cloak **186 in election** i.e., as a candidate **188 candidatus** (Literally, one clad in white; a candidate.) **192 What** why **195 abroad** i.e., on foot **204 obtain and ask** i.e., obtain simply by asking **205 canst thou tell** i.e., that's what you think **215 from themselves** i.e., from their present intention

220 meed reward **225 gratulate** salute, rejoice in **228 create** i.e., elect **230 Titan's** (Helios, the sun god, was a descendant of the Titans.) **240 in** as **241 gentleness** nobleness **242 onset** beginning **246 Pantheon** Roman temple dedicated to all the gods **247 motion** proposal **249 of** by **254 imperious** imperial **260 unspeakable** inexpressible

SATURNINUS [*Aside*]
A goodly lady, trust me, of the hue
That I would choose, were I to choose anew.—
Clear up, fair queen, that cloudy countenance.
Though change of war hath wrought this change of cheer,
Thou com'st not to be made a scorn in Rome.
Princely shall be thy usage every way.
Rest on my word, and let not discontent
Daunt all your hopes. Madam, he comforts you
Can make you greater than the Queen of Goths.
Lavinia, you are not displeas'd with this?

LAVINIA
Not I, my lord, sith true nobility
Warrants these words in princely courtesy.

SATURNINUS
Thanks, sweet Lavinia. Romans, let us go.
Ransomless here we set our prisoners free.
Proclaim our honors, lords, with trump and drum.
[*Flourish. Saturninus courts Tamora in dumb show.*]

BASSIANUS
Lord Titus, by your leave, this maid is mine.
[*Seizing Lavinia.*]

TITUS
How, sir? Are you in earnest then, my lord?

BASSIANUS
Ay, noble Titus, and resolv'd withal
To do myself this reason and this right.

MARCUS
"Suum cuique" is our Roman justice.
This prince in justice seizeth but his own.

LUCIUS
And that he will, and shall, if Lucius live.

TITUS
Traitors, avaunt! Where is the Emperor's guard?
Treason, my lord! Lavinia is surpris'd!

SATURNINUS
Surpris'd? By whom?

BASSIANUS
By him that justly may
Bear his betroth'd from all the world away.
[*Exeunt Bassianus and Marcus with Lavinia.*]

MUTIUS
Brothers, help to convey her hence away,
And with my sword I'll keep this door safe.
[*Exeunt Lucius, Quintus, and Martius.*]

TITUS [*To Saturninus*]
Follow, my lord, and I'll soon bring her back.

MUTIUS
My lord, you pass not here.

TITUS
What, villain boy?
Barr'st me my way in Rome? [*Stabbing Mutius.*]

MUTIUS
Help, Lucius, help!
[*Dies.*]

[*During the fray, Saturninus, Tamora, Demetrius, Chiron, and Aaron go out and re-enter, above.*]

[*Enter Lucius.*]

LUCIUS
My lord, you are unjust, and more than so,
In wrongful quarrel you have slain your son.

TITUS
Nor thou, nor he, are any sons of mine.
My sons would never so dishonor me.
Traitor, restore Lavinia to the Emperor.

LUCIUS
Dead, if you will; but not to be his wife,
That is another's lawful promis'd love. [*Exit.*]

Enter aloft the Emperor [*Saturninus*] *with Tamora and her two sons and Aaron the Moor.*

SATURNINUS
No, Titus, no; the Emperor needs her not,
Nor her, nor thee, nor any of thy stock.
I'll trust, by leisure, him that mocks me once;
Thee never, nor thy traitorous haughty sons,
Confederates all thus to dishonor me.
Was none in Rome to make a stale
But Saturnine? Full well, Andronicus,
Agree these deeds with that proud brag of thine,
That said'st I begg'd the empire at thy hands.

TITUS
O monstrous! What reproachful words are these?

SATURNINUS
But go thy ways; go, give that changing piece
To him that flourish'd for her with his sword.
A valiant son-in-law thou shalt enjoy,
One fit to bandy with thy lawless sons,
To ruffle in the commonwealth of Rome.

TITUS
These words are razors to my wounded heart.

SATURNINUS
And therefore, lovely Tamora, Queen of Goths,
That like the stately Phoebe 'mongst her nymphs
Dost overshine the gallant'st dames of Rome,
If thou be pleas'd with this my sudden choice,
Behold, I choose thee, Tamora, for my bride,
And will create thee Empress of Rome.
Speak, Queen of Goths, dost thou applaud my choice?
And here I swear by all the Roman gods,
Sith priest and holy water are so near
And tapers burn so bright and everything
In readiness for Hymenaeus stand,
I will not re-salute the streets of Rome,
Or climb my palace, till from forth this place
I lead espous'd my bride along with me.

TAMORA
And here, in sight of heaven, to Rome I swear,
If Saturnine advance the Queen of Goths,
She will a handmaid be to his desires,
A loving nurse, a mother to his youth.

SATURNINUS
Ascend, fair queen, Pantheon. Lords, accompany
Your noble emperor and his lovely bride,
Sent by the heavens for Prince Saturnine,

268 cheer countenance **273 Can** who can **275 sith** since **276 Warrants** justifies **284 Suum cuique** to each his own **287 avaunt** be gone **288 surpris'd** taken

305 by leisure with caution, barely **308 stale** tool, laughingstock **313 piece** wench **316 bandy** brawl **317 ruffle** swagger **320 Phoebe** (One of the names of the moon goddess.) **329 Hymenaeus** god of marriage

Whose wisdom hath her fortune conquered.
There shall we consummate our spousal rites.
Exeunt omnes [*except Titus*].

TITUS
I am not bid to wait upon this bride.
Titus, when wert thou wont to walk alone,
Dishonored thus, and challenged of wrongs?

Enter Marcus and Titus' Sons [*Lucius, Quintus, and Martius*].

MARCUS
O Titus, see, O, see what thou hast done!
In a bad quarrel slain a virtuous son.

TITUS
No, foolish tribune, no; no son of mine,
Nor thou, nor these, confederates in the deed
That hath dishonored all our family.
Unworthy brother, and unworthy sons!

LUCIUS
But let us give him burial, as becomes.
Give Mutius burial with our brethren.

TITUS
Traitors, away! He rests not in this tomb.
This monument five hundred years hath stood,
Which I have sumptuously re-edified.
Here none but soldiers and Rome's servitors
Repose in fame, none basely slain in brawls.
Bury him where you can. He comes not here.

MARCUS
My lord, this is impiety in you.
My nephew Mutius' deeds do plead for him;
He must be buried with his brethren.

MARTIUS
And shall, or him we will accompany.

TITUS
"And shall"? What villain was it spake that word?

MARTIUS
He that would vouch it in any place but here.

TITUS
What, would you bury him in my despite?

MARCUS
No, noble Titus, but entreat of thee
To pardon Mutius and to bury him.

TITUS
Marcus, even thou hast struck upon my crest,
And, with these boys, mine honor thou hast
wounded.
My foes I do repute you every one.
So, trouble me no more, but get you gone.

QUINTUS
He is not with himself. Let us withdraw.

MARTIUS
Not I, till Mutius' bones be buried.
The Brother [*Marcus*] *and the Sons kneel.*

MARCUS
Brother, for in that name doth nature plead—

MARTIUS
Father, and in that name doth nature speak—

TITUS
Speak thou no more, if all the rest will speed.

MARCUS
Renowned Titus, more than half my soul—

LUCIUS
Dear father, soul and substance of us all—

MARCUS
Suffer thy brother Marcus to inter
His noble nephew here in virtue's nest,
That died in honor and Lavinia's cause.
Thou art a Roman. Be not barbarous.
The Greeks upon advice did bury Ajax
That slew himself, and wise Laertes' son
Did graciously plead for his funerals.
Let not young Mutius, then, that was thy joy,
Be barr'd his entrance here.

TITUS
Rise, Marcus, rise.
[*They rise.*]
The dismall'st day is this that e'er I saw,
To be dishonored by my sons in Rome!
Well, bury him, and bury me the next.
They put him in the tomb.

LUCIUS
There lie thy bones, sweet Mutius, with thy friends,
Till we with trophies do adorn thy tomb.
They all kneel.

ALL
No man shed tears for noble Mutius;
He lives in fame that died in virtue's cause.
[*They rise.*]

MARCUS
My lord, to step out of these dreary dumps,
How comes it that the subtle Queen of Goths
Is of a sudden thus advanc'd in Rome?

TITUS
I know not, Marcus, but I know it is;
Whether by device or no, the heavens can tell.
Is she not then beholding to the man
That brought her for this high good turn so far?
[Yes, and will nobly him remunerate.]

[*Flourish.*] *Enter the Emperor* [*Saturninus*], *Tamora, and her two Sons, with* [*Aaron*] *the Moor, at one door. Enter at the other door Bassianus and Lavinia, with others.*

SATURNINUS
So, Bassianus, you have play'd your prize.
God give you joy, sir, of your gallant bride!

BASSIANUS
And you of yours, my lord! I say no more,
Nor wish no less; and so I take my leave.

344 challenged accused **351 becomes** is fitting **356 servitors** armed defenders **364 vouch** maintain **365 in my despite** in despite of me **370 repute** think of **372 not with himself** i.e., distracted

376 if . . . speed if all is to succeed; possibly, if you remaining sons do not wish to be slain like Mutius **379 Suffer** permit **383 advice** deliberation. **Ajax** Greek hero of the Trojan War who went mad because the armor of Achilles was awarded to Odysseus, slew a flock of sheep deludedly thinking them Greeks, and later committed suicide in shame; he was refused burial until *Laertes' son,* l. 384, Odysseus, successfully pleaded for his funeral rites **395 dumps** melancholy **403 play'd your prize** won as in a contest

SATURNINUS
Traitor, if Rome have law or we have power,
Thou and thy faction shall repent this rape.

BASSIANUS
Rape call you it, my lord, to seize my own,
My true-betrothed love and now my wife?
But let the laws of Rome determine all;
Meanwhile am I possess'd of that is mine.

SATURNINUS
'Tis good, sir. You are very short with us;
But, if we live, we'll be as sharp with you.

BASSIANUS
My lord, what I have done, as best I may
Answer I must, and shall do with my life.
Only thus much I give your Grace to know:
By all the duties that I owe to Rome,
This noble gentleman, Lord Titus here,
Is in opinion and in honor wrong'd,
That in the rescue of Lavinia
With his own hand did slay his youngest son,
In zeal to you, and highly mov'd to wrath
To be controll'd in that he frankly gave.
Receive him, then, to favor, Saturnine,
That hath express'd himself in all his deeds
A father and a friend to thee and Rome.

TITUS
Prince Bassianus, leave to plead my deeds.
'Tis thou, and those, that have dishonored me.
Rome and the righteous heavens be my judge
How I have lov'd and honored Saturnine! [*Kneels.*]

TAMORA
My worthy lord, if ever Tamora
Were gracious in those princely eyes of thine,
Then hear me speak indifferently for all;
And at my suit, sweet, pardon what is past.

SATURNINUS
What, madam? Be dishonored openly,
And basely put it up without revenge?

TAMORA
Not so, my lord. The gods of Rome forfend
I should be author to dishonor you!
But on mine honor dare I undertake
For good Lord Titus' innocence in all,
Whose fury not dissembled speaks his griefs.
Then, at my suit, look graciously on him;
Lose not so noble a friend on vain suppose,
Nor with sour looks afflict his gentle heart.
[*Aside to Saturninus.*] My lord, be rul'd by me, be won at last;
Dissemble all your griefs and discontents.
You are but newly planted in your throne;
Lest, then, the people, and patricians too,
Upon a just survey take Titus' part,
And so supplant you for ingratitude,
Which Rome reputes to be a heinous sin,
Yield at entreats; and then let me alone.
I'll find a day to massacre them all
And raze their faction and their family,
The cruel father and his traitorous sons
To whom I sued for my dear son's life,
And make them know what 'tis to let a queen
Kneel in the streets and beg for grace in vain.—
[*Aloud.*] Come, come, sweet Emperor; come, Andronicus;
Take up this good old man, and cheer the heart
That dies in tempest of thy angry frown.

SATURNINUS
Rise, Titus, rise; my Empress hath prevail'd.

TITUS [*Rising*]
I thank your Majesty, and her, my lord.
These words, these looks, infuse new life in me.

TAMORA
Titus, I am incorporate in Rome,
A Roman now adopted happily,
And must advise the Emperor for his good.
This day all quarrels die, Andronicus.
And let it be mine honor, good my lord,
That I have reconcil'd your friends and you.
For you, Prince Bassianus, I have pass'd
My word and promise to the Emperor
That you will be more mild and tractable.
And fear not, lords, and you, Lavinia;
By my advice, all humbled on your knees,
You shall ask pardon of his Majesty. [*They kneel.*]

LUCIUS
We do, and vow to heaven and to his Highness
That what we did was mildly as we might,
Tend'ring our sister's honor and our own.

MARCUS
That, on mine honor, here do I protest.

SATURNINUS
Away, and talk not; trouble us no more.
[*He turns away.*]

TAMORA
Nay, nay, sweet Emperor, we must all be friends.
The tribune and his nephews kneel for grace;
I will not be denied. Sweet heart, look back.

SATURNINUS
Marcus, for thy sake and thy brother's here,
And at my lovely Tamora's entreats,
I do remit these young men's heinous faults.
Stand up. [*They rise.*]
Lavinia, though you left me like a churl,
I found a friend, and sure as death I swore
I would not part a bachelor from the priest.
Come, if the Emperor's court can feast two brides,
You are my guest, Lavinia, and your friends.
This day shall be a love-day, Tamora.

TITUS
Tomorrow, an it please your Majesty
To hunt the panther and the hart with me,

408 rape forcible seizure **412 that** that which **420 opinion** reputation **424 controll'd** opposed, restrained **428 leave to plead** cease pleading **434 indifferently** impartially **437 put it up** put up with it **438 forfend** forbid **439 author** agent **440 undertake** assert **442 speaks his griefs** gives testimonial to his grievances **444 vain suppose** idle supposition

453 at entreats to entreaty. **let me alone** leave it to me **461 Take up** raise from kneeling **480 Tend'ring** having regard for **492 part** depart **495 love-day** day appointed to settle disputes **496 an** if

With horn and hound we'll give your Grace
bonjour. 498

SATURNINUS

Be it so, Titus, and gramercy too. 499

Exeunt. Sound trumpets. Manet [*Aaron the*] *Moor.*

[ACT II • SCENE I]

[*Aaron alone.*]

AARON

Now climbeth Tamora Olympus' top, 1
Safe out of fortune's shot, and sits aloft,
Secure of thunder's crack or lightning flash, 3
Advanc'd above pale envy's threat'ning reach. 4
As when the golden sun salutes the morn,
And, having gilt the ocean with his beams,
Gallops the zodiac in his glistering coach, 7
And overlooks the highest-peering hills,
So Tamora.
Upon her wit doth earthly honor wait,
And virtue stoops and trembles at her frown.
Then, Aaron, arm thy heart, and fit thy thoughts,
To mount aloft with thy imperial mistress,
And mount her pitch, whom thou in triumph long 14
Hast prisoner held, fett'red in amorous chains
And faster bound to Aaron's charming eyes 16
Than is Prometheus tied to Caucasus. 17
Away with slavish weeds and servile thoughts! 18
I will be bright, and shine in pearl and gold,
To wait upon this new-made emperess.
To wait, said I? To wanton with this queen,
This goddess, this Semiramis, this nymph, 22
This siren, that will charm Rome's Saturnine,
And see his shipwrack and his commonweal's.
Holla! What storm is this? 25

Enter Chiron and Demetrius, braving.

DEMETRIUS

Chiron, thy years wants wit, thy wits wants edge, 26
And manners, to intrude where I am grac'd, 27
And may, for aught thou knowest, affected be. 28

CHIRON

Demetrius, thou dost overween in all, 29
And so in this, to bear me down with braves. 30
'Tis not the difference of a year or two
Makes me less gracious or thee more fortunate;
I am as able and as fit as thou
To serve, and to deserve my mistress' grace;
And that my sword upon thee shall approve, 35
And plead my passions for Lavinia's love.

AARON [*Aside*]

Clubs, clubs! These lovers will not keep the peace. 37

DEMETRIUS

Why, boy, although our mother, unadvis'd, 38
Gave you a dancing-rapier by your side, 39
Are you so desperate grown, to threat your friends?
Go to! Have your lath glued within your sheath 41
Till you know better how to handle it.

CHIRON

Meanwhile, sir, with the little skill I have,
Full well shalt thou perceive how much I dare.

DEMETRIUS

Ay, boy, grow ye so brave? *They draw.*

AARON [*Coming forward*] Why, how now, lords?
So near the Emperor's palace dare ye draw,
And maintain such a quarrel openly?
Full well I wot the ground of all this grudge. 48
I would not for a million of gold
The cause were known to them it most concerns,
Nor would your noble mother for much more
Be so dishonored in the court of Rome.
For shame, put up.

DEMETRIUS Not I, till I have sheath'd 53
My rapier in his bosom, and withal
Thrust those reproachful speeches down his throat
That he hath breath'd in my dishonor here.

CHIRON

For that I am prepar'd and full resolv'd.
Foul-spoken coward, that thund'rest with thy
tongue,
And with thy weapon nothing dar'st perform!

AARON

Away, I say!
Now, by the gods that warlike Goths adore,
This petty brabble will undo us all. 62
Why, lords, and think you not how dangerous
It is to jet upon a prince's right? 64
What, is Lavinia then become so loose,
Or Bassianus so degenerate,
That for her love such quarrels may be broach'd 67
Without controlment, justice, or revenge? 68
Young lords, beware! An should the Empress know 69
This discord's ground, the music would not please. 70

CHIRON

I care not, I, knew she and all the world.
I love Lavinia more than all the world.

DEMETRIUS

Youngling, learn thou to make some meaner choice. 73
Lavinia is thine elder brother's hope.

AARON

Why, are ye mad? Or know ye not, in Rome

498 bonjour good morning **499 gramercy** great thanks

II.i. Location: Scene continues. Aaron remains on stage.
1 Olympus home of the Greek gods **3 of** from **4 envy's** hate's, malice's **7 Gallops** i.e., gallops over **14 pitch** height to which a falcon soars before descending on its prey. (The image of *mounting* has sexual connotations also.) **16 charming** exerting a magic spell **17 Prometheus** Titan who stole fire from the chariot of the sun and gave it to man; as punishment, Zeus fastened him to a mountain in the Caucasus and sent a vulture to feast on his liver **18 weeds** garments **22 Semiramis** mythical Queen of Assyria, famous for her cruelty and lust **25 s.d. braving** defying (each other) **26 wants** lack **27 grac'd** honored, favored **28 affected** loved **29 overween** arrogantly presume **30 braves** threats

35 approve prove **37 Clubs, clubs** (A cry summoning the apprentices of London to join in or suppress a riot or rebellion.) **38 unadvis'd** ill-advisedly **39 dancing-rapier** an ornamental weapon **41 lath** counterfeit stage weapon **48 wot** know **53 put up** sheathe your swords **62 brabble** quarrel, brawl **64 jet** encroach **67 broach'd** begun, set flowing **68 controlment** restraint **69 An** if **70 ground** basis (with a pun on the musical meaning *bass upon which a melody is constructed*) **73 meaner** of lower degree

How furious and impatient they be,
And cannot brook competitors in love?
I tell you, lords, you do but plot your deaths
By this device.

CHIRON
Aaron, a thousand deaths
Would I propose to achieve her whom I love.

AARON
To achieve her? How?

DEMETRIUS
Why makes thou it so strange?
She is a woman, therefore may be woo'd;
She is a woman, therefore may be won;
She is Lavinia, therefore must be lov'd.
What, man, more water glideth by the mill
Than wots the miller of, and easy it is
Of a cut loaf to steal a shive, we know.
Though Bassianus be the Emperor's brother,
Better than he have worn Vulcan's badge.

AARON [*Aside*]
Ay, and as good as Saturninus may.

DEMETRIUS
Then why should he despair that knows to court it
With words, fair looks, and liberality?
What, hast not thou full often struck a doe,
And borne her cleanly by the keeper's nose?

AARON
Why, then, it seems some certain snatch or so
Would serve your turns.

CHIRON
Ay, so the turn were serv'd.

DEMETRIUS
Aaron, thou hast hit it.

AARON
Would you had hit it too!
Then should not we be tir'd with this ado.
Why, hark ye, hark ye, and are you such fools
To square for this? Would it offend you, then,
That both should speed?

CHIRON
Faith, not me.

DEMETRIUS
Nor me, so I were one.

AARON
For shame, be friends, and join for that you jar.
'Tis policy and stratagem must do
That you affect; and so must you resolve,
That what you cannot as you would achieve,
You must perforce accomplish as you may.
Take this of me: Lucrece was not more chaste
Than this Lavinia, Bassianus' love.
A speedier course than ling'ring languishment
Must we pursue, and I have found the path.
My lords, a solemn hunting is in hand;
There will the lovely Roman ladies troop.
The forest walks are wide and spacious,
And many unfrequented plots there are
Fitted by kind for rape and villainy.
Single you thither then this dainty doe,
And strike her home by force, if not by words.
This way, or not at all, stand you in hope.
Come, come, our Empress, with her sacred wit
To villainy and vengeance consecrate,
Will we acquaint withal what we intend;
And she shall file our engines with advice,
That will not suffer you to square yourselves,
But to your wishes' height advance you both.
The Emperor's court is like the house of Fame,
The palace full of tongues, of eyes, and ears;
The woods are ruthless, dreadful, deaf, and dull.
There speak, and strike, brave boys, and take your turns;
There serve your lust, shadow'd from heaven's eye,
And revel in Lavinia's treasury.

CHIRON
Thy counsel, lad, smells of no cowardice.

DEMETRIUS
Sit fas aut nefas, till I find the stream
To cool this heat, a charm to calm these fits,
Per Stygia, per manes vehor. *Exeunt.*

[SCENE II]

Enter Titus Andronicus and his three Sons [*and Marcus*], *making a noise with hounds and horns.*

TITUS
The hunt is up, the morn is bright and grey,
The fields are fragrant and the woods are green.
Uncouple here and let us make a bay,
And wake the Emperor and his lovely bride,
And rouse the Prince, and ring a hunter's peal,
That all the court may echo with the noise.
Sons, let it be your charge, as it is ours,
To attend the Emperor's person carefully.
I have been troubled in my sleep this night,
But dawning day new comfort hath inspir'd.

Here a cry of hounds, and wind horns in a peal. Then enter Saturninus, Tamora, Bassianus, Lavinia, Chiron, Demetrius, and their Attendants.

Many good morrows to your Majesty;
Madam, to you as many and as good.
I promised your Grace a hunter's peal.

SATURNINUS
And you have rung it lustily, my lords—
Somewhat too early for new-married ladies.

77 **brook** endure 80 **propose** be ready to meet 81 **strange** surprised 87 **shive** slice 89 **Vulcan's badge** i.e., cuckold's horns, alluding to the public shame to which he was exposed by his wife Venus' intrigue with Mars 91 **knows** knows how 95 **snatch** sudden or quick catch (with a probable bawdy pun) 96 **serve your turns** answer your purposes (with sexual suggestion) 100 **square** quarrel 101 **speed** succeed 102 **so** so long as 103 **join . . . jar** conspire to obtain what you're quarreling over 104 **policy** contrivance, craft 105 **That** that which. **affect** desire 107 **perforce** necessarily 108 **Lucrece** a chaste Roman lady ravished by Tarquin, as told in Shakespeare's poem *The Rape of Lucrece* 110 **languishment** long courtship 112 **solemn** ceremonial 115 **plots** i.e., plots of ground

116 **by kind** by nature 117 **Single** single out (as in hunting) 118 **home** effectually, thoroughly 120 **sacred** i.e., consecrated to villainy 123 **file our engines** sharpen our devices 124 **square yourselves** quarrel with one another 126 **house of Fame** residence of rumor. (Described in Ovid and in Chaucer's *Hous of Fame;* see also Virgil, *Aeneid,* IV. 179–190.) 133 **Sit fas aut nefas** be it right or wrong 135 **Per . . . vehor** I am carried through the Stygian regions, through the realm of the shades. (Adapted from Seneca's *Hippolytus.*)

II.ii. Location: The grounds of the Emperor's palace.
1 **grey** cold, sunless light of early morning 3 **Uncouple** unleash the hounds. **make a bay** keep up a deep, prolonged barking 10 **s.d. cry** deep barking. **wind** blow

BASSIANUS
Lavinia, how say you?
LAVINIA
I say, no;
I have been broad awake two hours and more.
SATURNINUS
Come on, then, horse and chariots let us have,
And to our sport. [*To Tamora.*] Madam, now shall
ye see
Our Roman hunting.
MARCUS
I have dogs, my lord,
Will rouse the proudest panther in the chase,
And climb the highest promontory top.
TITUS
And I have horse will follow where the game
Makes way, and run like swallows o'er the plain.
DEMETRIUS [*To Chiron*]
Chiron, we hunt not, we, with horse nor hound,
But hope to pluck a dainty doe to ground. *Exeunt.*

[SCENE III]

Enter Aaron alone [*with a bag of gold*].

AARON
He that had wit would think that I had none,
To bury so much gold under a tree,
And never after to inherit it.
Let him that thinks of me so abjectly
Know that this gold must coin a stratagem,
Which, cunningly effected, will beget
A very excellent piece of villainy.
And so repose, sweet gold, for their unrest
[*Hides the gold.*]
That have their alms out of the Empress' chest.

Enter Tamora alone to the Moor.

TAMORA
My lovely Aaron, wherefore look'st thou sad,
When everything doth make a gleeful boast?
The birds chant melody on every bush,
The snake lies rolled in the cheerful sun,
The green leaves quiver with the cooling wind
And make a checker'd shadow on the ground.
Under their sweet shade, Aaron, let us sit,
And, whilst the babbling echo mocks the hounds,
Replying shrilly to the well-tun'd horns,
As if a double hunt were heard at once,
Let us sit down and mark their yellowing noise;
And, after conflict such as was suppos'd
The wand'ring prince and Dido once enjoy'd,
When with a happy storm they were surpris'd
And curtain'd with a counsel-keeping cave,
We may, each wreathed in the other's arms,
Our pastimes done, possess a golden slumber;
Whiles hounds and horns and sweet melodious
birds
Be unto us as is a nurse's song
Of lullaby to bring her babe asleep.
AARON
Madam, though Venus govern your desires,
Saturn is dominator over mine.
What signifies my deadly-standing eye,
My silence, and my cloudy melancholy,
My fleece of woolly hair that now uncurls
Even as an adder when she doth unroll
To do some fatal execution?
No, madam, these are no venereal signs.
Vengeance is in my heart, death in my hand,
Blood and revenge are hammering in my head.
Hark, Tamora, the empress of my soul,
Which never hopes more heaven than rests in thee,
This is the day of doom for Bassianus:
His Philomel must lose her tongue today,
Thy sons make pillage of her chastity
And wash their hands in Bassianus' blood.
Seest thou this letter? Take it up, I pray thee,
[*Gives her a letter.*]
And give the King this fatal-plotted scroll.
Now question me no more; we are espied.
Here comes a parcel of our hopeful booty,
Which dreads not yet their lives' destruction.

Enter Bassianus and Lavinia.

TAMORA
Ah, my sweet Moor, sweeter to me than life!
AARON
No more, great Empress, Bassianus comes.
Be cross with him, and I'll go fetch thy sons
To back thy quarrels, whatsoe'er they be. [*Exit.*]
BASSIANUS
Who have we here? Rome's royal Empress,
Unfurnish'd of her well-beseeming troop?
Or is it Dian, habited like her,
Who hath abandoned her holy groves
To see the general hunting in this forest?
TAMORA
Saucy controller of my private steps!
Had I the pow'r that some say Dian had,
Thy temples should be planted presently
With horns, as was Actaeon's, and the hounds
Should drive upon thy new-transformed limbs,
Unmannerly intruder as thou art!
LAVINIA
Under your patience, gentle Empress,

21 chase hunting ground

II.iii. Location: A forest near Rome. A pit is provided in the stage, presumably at a trap door, and near it some representation of an elder tree.
3 inherit possess **5 coin** fabricate **8–9 for . . . chest** i.e., to discomfit those who will find this gold taken from Tamora's treasure chest **11 boast** display **13 rolled** coiled **20 yellowing** baying **22 prince** i.e., Aeneas, who, taking shelter from a storm with Dido in a cave during a hunt, made love to her **23 happy** fortunate **24 counsel-keeping** secret-keeping

31 Saturn . . . mine i.e., Saturn, as the dominant planet in my horoscope, governs my temperament and makes it cold and sullen (unlike Venus' effect, which is amorous) **32 deadly-standing** fixed with a deathly stare **37 venereal** erotic, Venus-like **43 Philomel** (An allusion to the story in Ovid's *Metamorphoses* of Philomela, raped by her brother-in-law, Tereus; cf. II.iv.26 below. He cut out her tongue so that she could not disclose his villainy. She succeeded in weaving the account of her misfortune in a tapestry.) **49 parcel** part. **hopeful** hoped-for **56 Unfurnish'd . . . troop** unprovided with a suitable escort **57 Dian** Diana, huntress and goddess of chastity. (Here used sarcastically.) **habited** dressed **62 presently** immediately **63 Actaeon's** (An allusion to the story of Actaeon, who was transformed into a stag by Diana and killed by his own hounds as punishment for having watched her and her nymphs at their bath.) **66 Under your patience** i.e., begging your pardon for saying so

'Tis thought you have a goodly gift in horning, 67
And to be doubted that your Moor and you 68
Are singled forth to try experiments.
Jove shield your husband from his hounds today!
'Tis pity they should take him for a stag.

BASSIANUS
Believe me, queen, your swarthy Cimmerian 72
Doth make your honor of his body's hue,
Spotted, detested, and abominable.
Why are you sequest'red from all your train,
Dismounted from your snow-white goodly steed,
And wand'red hither to an obscure plot,
Accompanied but with a barbarous Moor,
If foul desire had not conducted you?

LAVINIA
And, being intercepted in your sport,
Great reason that my noble lord be rated 81
For sauciness. I pray you, let us hence,
And let her joy her raven-colored love; 83
This valley fits the purpose passing well.

BASSIANUS
The King my brother shall have notice of this.

LAVINIA
Ay, for these slips have made him noted long. 86
Good king, to be so mightily abus'd! 87

TAMORA
Why have I patience to endure all this?

Enter Chiron and Demetrius.

DEMETRIUS
How now, dear sovereign, and our gracious mother,
Why doth your Highness look so pale and wan?

TAMORA
Have I not reason, think you, to look pale?
These two have 'ticed me hither to this place. 92
A barren detested vale you see it is;
The trees, though summer, yet forlorn and lean,
Overcome with moss and baleful mistletoe;
Here never shines the sun; here nothing breeds,
Unless the nightly owl or fatal raven.
And when they show'd me this abhorred pit,
They told me, here, at dead time of the night,
A thousand fiends, a thousand hissing snakes,
Ten thousand swelling toads, as many urchins, 101
Would make such fearful and confused cries
As any mortal body hearing it
Should straight fall mad, or else die suddenly.
No sooner had they told this hellish tale,
But straight they told me they would bind me here
Unto the body of a dismal yew,
And leave me to this miserable death.
And then they call'd me foul adulteress,
Lascivious Goth, and all the bitterest terms 110
That ever ear did hear to such effect;
And, had you not by wondrous fortune come,
This vengeance on me had they executed.
Revenge it, as you love your mother's life,
Or be ye not henceforth call'd my children.

DEMETRIUS
This is a witness that I am thy son.
Stab him [*Bassianus*].

CHIRON
And this for me, struck home to show my strength.
[*Also stabs Bassianus, who dies.*]

LAVINIA
Ay, come, Semiramis, nay, barbarous Tamora, 118
For no name fits thy nature but thy own!

TAMORA
Give me the poniard; you shall know, my boys,
Your mother's hand shall right your mother's wrong.

DEMETRIUS
Stay, madam, here is more belongs to her.
First thrash the corn, then after burn the straw. 123
This minion stood upon her chastity, 124
Upon her nuptial vow, her loyalty,
And with that painted hope braves your mightiness; 126
And shall she carry this unto her grave?

CHIRON
An if she do, I would I were an eunuch.
Drag hence her husband to some secret hole,
And make his dead trunk pillow to our lust.

TAMORA
But when ye have the honey ye desire,
Let not this wasp outlive, us both to sting. 132

CHIRON
I warrant you, madam, we will make that sure.
Come, mistress, now perforce we will enjoy
That nice-preserved honesty of yours. 135

LAVINIA
O Tamora! Thou bearest a woman's face—

TAMORA
I will not hear her speak. Away with her!

LAVINIA
Sweet lords, entreat her hear me but a word.

DEMETRIUS
Listen, fair madam. Let it be your glory
To see her tears, but be your heart to them
As unrelenting flint to drops of rain.

LAVINIA
When did the tiger's young ones teach the dam?
O, do not learn her wrath; she taught it thee! 143
The milk thou suck'dst from her did turn to marble;
Even at thy teat thou hadst thy tyranny.
Yet every mother breeds not sons alike;
[*To Chiron.*] Do thou entreat her show a woman's
pity.

CHIRON
What, wouldst thou have me prove myself a
bastard?

LAVINIA
'Tis true, the raven doth not hatch a lark.
Yet have I heard—O, could I find it now!—

67 horning cuckolding **68 doubted** suspected, feared **72 Cimmerian** i.e., of black complexion. (The Cimmerii in the *Odyssey* live in perpetual darkness.) **81 rated** berated, chidden **83 joy** enjoy **86 noted** notorious, stigmatized **87 abus'd** deceived **92 'ticed** enticed **101 urchins** hedgehogs **110 Goth** (A quibble; pronounced somewhat like "goat," symbolic of lechery.)

118 Semiramis (See note to II.i.22.) **123 corn** grain **124 minion** hussy, wench. **stood upon** preened herself upon **126 painted** specious, unreal **132 outlive** survive. **sting** i.e., do harm to (us) **135 nice** fastidiously. **honesty** chastity **143 learn** teach

The lion, mov'd with pity, did endure
To have his princely paws par'd all away.
Some say that ravens foster forlorn children,
The whilst their own birds famish in their nests;
O, be to me, though thy hard heart say no,
Nothing so kind, but something pitiful!

TAMORA
I know not what it means. Away with her!

LAVINIA
O, let me teach thee! For my father's sake,
That gave thee life, when well he might have slain thee,
Be not obdurate, open thy deaf ears.

TAMORA
Hadst thou in person ne'er offended me,
Even for his sake am I pitiless.
Remember, boys, I pour'd forth tears in vain
To save your brother from the sacrifice,
But fierce Andronicus would not relent.
Therefore, away with her, and use her as you will—
The worse to her, the better lov'd of me.

LAVINIA
O Tamora, be call'd a gentle queen,
And with thine own hands kill me in this place!
For 'tis not life that I have begg'd so long;
Poor I was slain when Bassianus died.
[*She tugs at Tamora's garments.*]

TAMORA
What begg'st thou, then? Fond woman, let me go.

LAVINIA
'Tis present death I beg, and one thing more
That womanhood denies my tongue to tell:
O, keep me from their worse than killing lust,
And tumble me into some loathsome pit,
Where never man's eye may behold my body!
Do this, and be a charitable murderer.

TAMORA
So should I rob my sweet sons of their fee.
No, let them satisfice their lust on thee.

DEMETRIUS
Away! For thou hast stay'd us here too long.

LAVINIA
No grace, no womanhood? Ah, beastly creature!
The blot and enemy to our general name!
Confusion fall—

CHIRON
Nay, then I'll stop your mouth. Bring thou her husband.
This is the hole where Aaron bid us hide him.
[*Demetrius throws the body of Bassianus into the pit; then exeunt Demetrius and Chiron, dragging off Lavinia.*]

TAMORA
Farewell, my sons. See that you make her sure.
Ne'er let my heart know merry cheer indeed
Till all the Andronici be made away.
Now will I hence to seek my lovely Moor,
And let my spleenful sons this trull deflow'r. [*Exit.*]

Enter Aaron, with two of Titus' Sons [*Quintus and Martius*].

AARON
Come on, my lords, the better foot before.
Straight will I bring you to the loathsome pit
Where I espied the panther fast asleep.

QUINTUS
My sight is very dull, whate'er it bodes.

MARTIUS
And mine, I promise you. Were it not for shame,
Well could I leave our sport to sleep awhile.
[*Falls into the pit.*]

QUINTUS
What, art thou fallen? What subtle hole is this,
Whose mouth is covered with rude-growing briers,
Upon whose leaves are drops of new-shed blood
As fresh as morning dew distill'd on flowers?
A very fatal place it seems to me.
Speak, brother, hast thou hurt thee with the fall?

MARTIUS
O brother, with the dismall'st object hurt
That ever eye with sight made heart lament!

AARON [*Aside*]
Now will I fetch the King to find them here,
That he thereby may have a likely guess
How these were they that made away his brother.
Exit.

MARTIUS
Why dost not comfort me, and help me out
From this unhallowed and blood-stain'd hole?

QUINTUS
I am surprised with an uncouth fear.
A chilling sweat o'er-runs my trembling joints;
My heart suspects more than mine eye can see.

MARTIUS
To prove thou hast a true-divining heart,
Aaron and thou look down into this den,
And see a fearful sight of blood and death.

QUINTUS
Aaron is gone, and my compassionate heart
Will not permit mine eyes once to behold
The thing whereat it trembles by surmise.
O, tell me who it is! For ne'er till now
Was I a child to fear I know not what.

MARTIUS
Lord Bassianus lies beray'd in blood,
All on a heap, like to a slaughtered lamb,
In this detested, dark, blood-drinking pit.

QUINTUS
If it be dark, how dost thou know 'tis he?

MARTIUS
Upon his bloody finger he doth wear
A precious ring, that lightens all this hole,
Which, like a taper in some monument,

152 paws claws **153 forlorn** abandoned (by other birds) **156 Nothing . . . pitiful** i.e., not so kind as the raven, but still showing some pity **172 Fond** foolish **173 present** immediate **174 denies** forbids **180 satisfice** satisfy **183 our general name** i.e., women's reputation **184 Confusion** destruction **187 sure** safe, incapable of revenge **189 made away** murdered

191 spleenful lustful. **trull** whore **211 surprised** overcome. **uncouth** strange **219 by surmise** even to imagine **222 beray'd** defiled **227 ring** (Presumably the carbuncle, which was believed to emit light.)

Doth shine upon the dead man's earthy cheeks,
And shows the ragged entrails of this pit.
So pale did shine the moon on Pyramus
When he by night lay bath'd in maiden blood.
O brother, help me with thy fainting hand—
If fear hath made thee faint, as me it hath—
Out of this fell devouring receptacle,
As hateful as Cocytus' misty mouth.

QUINTUS [*Offering to help*]
Reach me thy hand, that I may help thee out;
Or, wanting strength to do thee so much good,
I may be pluck'd into the swallowing womb
Of this deep pit, poor Bassianus' grave.
I have no strength to pluck thee to the brink.

MARTIUS
Nor I no strength to climb without thy help.

QUINTUS
Thy hand once more; I will not loose again,
Till thou art here aloft, or I below.
Thou canst not come to me—I come to thee.
[*Falls in.*]

Enter the Emperor [*Saturninus*] *and Aaron the Moor.*

SATURNINUS
Along with me! I'll see what hole is here,
And what he is that now is leapt into it.
Say, who art thou that lately didst descend
Into this gaping hollow of the earth?

MARTIUS
The unhappy sons of old Andronicus,
Brought hither in a most unlucky hour,
To find thy brother Bassianus dead.

SATURNINUS
My brother dead! I know thou dost but jest.
He and his lady both are at the lodge
Upon the north side of this pleasant chase;
'Tis not an hour since I left them there.

MARTIUS
We know not where you left them all alive;
But, out, alas! Here have we found him dead.

Enter Tamora, [*Titus*] *Andronicus, and Lucius.*

TAMORA
Where is my lord the King?

SATURNINUS
Here, Tamora, though griev'd with killing grief.

TAMORA
Where is thy brother Bassianus?

SATURNINUS
Now to the bottom dost thou search my wound.
Poor Bassianus here lies murdered.

TAMORA
Then all too late I bring this fatal writ,
The complot of this timeless tragedy;
And wonder greatly that man's face can fold
In pleasing smiles such murderous tyranny.
She giveth Saturnine a letter.

SATURNINUS *(Reads the letter)*
"An if we miss to meet him handsomely,
Sweet huntsman, Bassianus 'tis we mean,
Do thou so much as dig the grave for him.
Thou know'st our meaning. Look for thy reward
Among the nettles at the elder-tree
Which overshades the mouth of that same pit
Where we decreed to bury Bassianus.
Do this, and purchase us thy lasting friends."
O Tamora, was ever heard the like?
This is the pit, and this the elder-tree.
Look, sirs, if you can find the huntsman out
That should have murdered Bassianus here.

AARON [*Finding the gold*]
My gracious lord, here is the bag of gold.

SATURNINUS [*To Titus*]
Two of thy whelps, fell curs of bloody kind,
Have here bereft my brother of his life.—
Sirs, drag them from the pit unto the prison!
There let them bide until we have devis'd
Some never-heard-of torturing pain for them.
[*Martius and Quintus are dragged out of the pit, and Bassianus' body is raised.*]

TAMORA
What, are they in this pit? O wondrous thing!
How easily murder is discovered!

TITUS [*Kneeling*]
High Emperor, upon my feeble knee
I beg this boon, with tears not lightly shed,
That this fell fault of my accursed sons—
Accursed, if the fault be prov'd in them—

SATURNINUS
If it be prov'd? You see it is apparent.
Who found this letter? Tamora, was it you?

TAMORA
Andronicus himself did take it up.

TITUS
I did, my lord, yet let me be their bail.
For, by my fathers' reverend tomb, I vow
They shall be ready at your Highness' will
To answer their suspicion with their lives.

SATURNINUS
Thou shalt not bail them; see thou follow me.
Some bring the murdered body, some the murderers.
Let them not speak a word; the guilt is plain;
For, by my soul, were there worse end than death,
That end upon them should be executed.

TAMORA
Andronicus, I will entreat the King.
Fear not thy sons; they shall do well enough.

TITUS [*Rising*]
Come, Lucius, come; stay not to talk with them.
[*Exeunt bearing the dead body of Bassianus; Martius and Quintus under guard*].

229 earthy clay-colored, pale **230 ragged entrails** i.e., rough interior **231 Pyramus** the lover of Thisbe, who killed himself in the mistaken supposition that she was dead. (See *A Midsummer Night's Dream,* I.ii, III.i, and V.i.) **235 fell** savage **236 Cocytus** one of the rivers of Hades—the river of lamentations **238 wanting** lacking **255 chase** hunting ground **262 search** probe **265 complot** plot. **timeless** untimely **266 fold** hide, enfold

268 handsomely conveniently **279 should** was to **281 kind** nature **292 apparent** evident **296 fathers'** forefathers' **298 their suspicion** the suspicion they are under **305 Fear not** fear not for **306 them** i.e., Martius and Quintus

[SCENE IV]

Enter the Empress' Sons with Lavinia, her hands cut off, and her tongue cut out, and ravish'd.

DEMETRIUS
So, now go tell, an if thy tongue can speak,
Who 'twas that cut thy tongue and ravish'd thee.
CHIRON
Write down thy mind, bewray thy meaning so,
An if thy stumps will let thee play the scribe.
DEMETRIUS
See, how with signs and tokens she can scrowl.
CHIRON
Go home, call for sweet water, wash thy hands.
DEMETRIUS
She hath no tongue to call, nor hands to wash;
And so let's leave her to her silent walks.
CHIRON
An 'twere my cause, I should go hang myself.
DEMETRIUS
If thou hadst hands to help thee knit the cord.
Exeunt [*Chiron and Demetrius*].

Enter Marcus from hunting. [*Lavinia flees from him.*]

MARCUS
Who is this? My niece, that flies away so fast?
Cousin, a word; where is your husband?
[*He see her injuries.*]
If I do dream, would all my wealth would wake me!
If I do wake, some planet strike me down,
That I may slumber an eternal sleep!
Speak, gentle niece, what stern ungentle hands
Hath lopp'd and hew'd and made thy body bare
Of her two branches, those sweet ornaments,
Whose circling shadows kings have sought to sleep in,
And might not gain so great a happiness
As have thy love? Why dost not speak to me?
Alas, a crimson river of warm blood,
Like to a bubbling fountain stirr'd with wind,
Doth rise and fall between thy rosed lips,
Coming and going with thy honey breath.
But, sure, some Tereus hath deflow'red thee,
And, lest thou shouldst detect him, cut thy tongue.
Ah, now thou turn'st away thy face for shame!
And, notwithstanding all this loss of blood,
As from a conduit with three issuing spouts,
Yet do thy cheeks look red as Titan's face
Blushing to be encount'red with a cloud.
Shall I speak for thee? Shall I say 'tis so?
O, that I knew thy heart, and knew the beast,
That I might rail at him, to ease my mind!
Sorrow concealed, like an oven stopp'd,
Doth burn the heart to cinders where it is.
Fair Philomela, why, she but lost her tongue,
And in a tedious sampler sew'd her mind;
But, lovely niece, that mean is cut from thee.
A craftier Tereus, cousin, hast thou met,
And he hath cut those pretty fingers off
That could have better sew'd than Philomel.
O, had the monster seen those lily hands
Tremble, like aspen-leaves, upon a lute,
And make the silken strings delight to kiss them,
He would not then have touch'd them for his life!
Or, had he heard the heavenly harmony
Which that sweet tongue hath made,
He would have dropp'd his knife, and fell asleep
As Cerberus at the Thracian poet's feet.
Come, let us go, and make thy father blind;
For such a sight will blind a father's eye.
One hour's storm will drown the fragrant meads;
What will whole months of tears thy father's eyes?
Do not draw back, for we will mourn with thee.
O, could our mourning ease thy misery! *Exeunt.*

[ACT III • SCENE I]

Enter the Judges and Senators [*and Tribunes*] *with Titus' two Sons bound, passing on the stage to the place of execution, and Titus going before, pleading.*

TITUS
Hear me, grave fathers! Noble tribunes, stay!
For pity of mine age, whose youth was spent
In dangerous wars, whilst you securely slept;
For all my blood in Rome's great quarrel shed,
For all the frosty nights that I have watch'd,
And for these bitter tears, which now you see
Filling the aged wrinkles in my cheeks,
Be pitiful to my condemned sons,
Whose souls is not corrupted as 'tis thought.
For two and twenty sons I never wept,
Because they died in honor's lofty bed.
[*Titus*] *Andronicus lieth down and the Judges pass by him* [*and exeunt with Titus' two sons. Titus weeps.*]
For these, tribunes, in the dust I write
My heart's deep languor and my soul's sad tears.
Let my tears stanch the earth's dry appetite;
My sons' sweet blood will make it shame and blush.
O earth, I will befriend thee more with rain,
That shall distill from these two ancient urns,
Than youthful April shall with all his show'rs.

II.iv. Location: The forest still.
3 bewray reveal **5 scrowl** scrawl **6 sweet** perfumed **9 cause** case **12 Cousin** kinswoman **26 Tereus** i.e., the ravisher of Philomela; see note to II.iii.43 **27 detect** expose **31 Titan's** the sun god's

36 stopp'd closed too long, plugged up **39 tedious sampler** laboriously contrived embroidered cloth or tapestry. (See note to II.iii.43.) **40 mean** means **51 Cerberus . . . feet** (According to legend, Orpheus' sweet singing charmed even Cerberus, three-headed dog guarding the entrance to Hades.)

III.i. Location: Rome. A street.
4 my blood i.e., blood of my sons **5 watch'd** stayed awake **10 two and twenty** (Cf. I.i.82, 198.) **14 stanch** satisfy **15 shame** be ashamed **17 urns** i.e., eyes

In summer's drought I'll drop upon thee still;
In winter with warm tears I'll melt the snow,
And keep eternal springtime on thy face,
So thou refuse to drink my dear sons' blood.

Enter Lucius, with his weapon drawn.

O reverend tribunes! O gentle, aged men!
Unbind my sons, reverse the doom of death;
And let me say, that never wept before,
My tears are now prevailing orators.

LUCIUS
O noble father, you lament in vain.
The tribunes hear you not. No man is by,
And you recount your sorrows to a stone.

TITUS
Ah, Lucius, for thy brothers let me plead.
Grave tribunes, once more I entreat of you—

LUCIUS
My gracious lord, no tribune hears you speak.

TITUS
Why, 'tis no matter, man. If they did hear,
They would not mark me; if they did mark,
They would not pity me, yet plead I must;
And bootless unto them.
Therefore I tell my sorrows to the stones,
Who, though they cannot answer my distress,
Yet in some sort they are better than the tribunes,
For that they will not intercept my tale.
When I do weep, they humbly at my feet
Receive my tears and seem to weep with me;
And, were they but attired in grave weeds,
Rome could afford no tribunes like to these.
A stone is soft as wax, tribunes more hard than stones;
A stone is silent, and offendeth not,
And tribunes with their tongues doom men to death. [*Rises.*]
But wherefore stand'st thou with thy weapon drawn?

LUCIUS
To rescue my two brothers from their death,
For which attempt the judges have pronounc'd
My everlasting doom of banishment.

TITUS
O happy man! They have befriended thee.
Why, foolish Lucius, dost thou not perceive
That Rome is but a wilderness of tigers?
Tigers must prey, and Rome affords no prey
But me and mine. How happy art thou, then,
From these devourers to be banished!
But who comes with our brother Marcus here?

Enter Marcus with Lavinia.

MARCUS
Titus, prepare thy aged eyes to weep,
Or, if not so, thy noble heart to break.
I bring consuming sorrow to thine age.

TITUS
Will it consume me? Let me see it, then.

MARCUS
This was thy daughter.

TITUS
Why, Marcus, so she is.

LUCIUS
Ay me, this object kills me!

TITUS
Faint-hearted boy, arise, and look upon her.
Speak, Lavinia, what accursed hand
Hath made thee handless in thy father's sight?
What fool hath added water to the sea,
Or brought a faggot to bright-burning Troy?
My grief was at the height before thou cam'st,
And now, like Nilus, it disdaineth bounds.
Give me a sword, I'll chop off my hands too,
For they have fought for Rome, and all in vain;
And they have nurs'd this woe, in feeding life;
In bootless prayer have they been held up,
And they have serv'd me to effectless use.
Now all the service I require of them
Is that the one will help to cut the other.
'Tis well, Lavinia, that thou hast no hands;
For hands, to do Rome service, is but vain.

LUCIUS
Speak, gentle sister, who hath martyr'd thee?

MARCUS
O, that delightful engine of her thoughts,
That blabb'd them with such pleasing eloquence,
Is torn from forth that pretty hollow cage,
Where, like a sweet melodious bird, it sung
Sweet varied notes, enchanting every ear!

LUCIUS
O, say thou for her, who hath done this deed?

MARCUS
O, thus I found her, straying in the park,
Seeking to hide herself, as doth the deer
That hath receiv'd some unrecuring wound.

TITUS
It was my deer, and he that wounded her
Hath hurt me more than had he kill'd me dead;
For now I stand as one upon a rock
Environ'd with a wilderness of sea,
Who marks the waxing tide grow wave by wave,
Expecting ever when some envious surge
Will in his brinish bowels swallow him.
This way to death my wretched sons are gone;
Here stands my other son, a banish'd man,
And here my brother, weeping at my woes;
But that which gives my soul the greatest spurn
Is dear Lavinia, dearer than my soul.
Had I but seen thy picture in this plight,
It would have madded me; what shall I do
Now I behold thy lively body so?
Thou hast no hands, to wipe away thy tears,
Nor tongue to tell me who hath martyr'd thee.

19 still continually **22 So** so long as **24 doom** sentence **36 bootless** in vain **40 For that** because. **intercept** interrupt **43 grave weeds** sober garments **44 afford** provide

64 object i.e., object of sight **71 Nilus** the Nile **82 engine** instrument **83 blabb'd** uttered **90 unrecuring** incurable **96 envious** spiteful **97 his** its **101 spurn** stroke, kick **105 lively** living, actual (as contrasted with her picture)

Thy husband he is dead, and for his death
Thy brothers are condemn'd, and dead by this.
Look, Marcus! Ah, son Lucius, look on her!
When I did name her brothers, then fresh tears
Stood on her cheeks, as doth the honey-dew
Upon a gath'red lily almost withered.

MARCUS

Perchance she weeps because they kill'd her husband,
Perchance because she knows them innocent.

TITUS

If they did kill thy husband, then be joyful,
Because the law hath ta'en revenge on them.
No, no, they would not do so foul a deed;
Witness the sorrow that their sister makes.
Gentle Lavinia, let me kiss thy lips,
Or make some sign how I may do thee ease.
Shall thy good uncle, and thy brother Lucius,
And thou, and I, sit round about some fountain,
Looking all downwards, to behold our cheeks
How they are stain'd, like meadows yet not dry,
With miry slime left on them by a flood?
And in the fountain shall we gaze so long
Till the fresh taste be taken from that clearness,
And made a brine-pit with our bitter tears?
Or shall we cut away our hands, like thine?
Or shall we bite our tongues, and in dumb shows
Pass the remainder of our hateful days?
What shall we do? Let us, that have our tongues,
Plot some device of further misery,
To make us wonder'd at in time to come.

LUCIUS

Sweet father, cease your tears; for, at your grief,
See how my wretched sister sobs and weeps.

MARCUS

Patience, dear niece. Good Titus, dry thine eyes.

TITUS

Ah, Marcus, Marcus! Brother, well I wot
Thy napkin cannot drink a tear of mine,
For thou, poor man, hast drown'd it with thine own.

LUCIUS

Ah, my Lavinia, I will wipe thy cheeks.

TITUS

Mark, Marcus, mark! I understand her signs.
Had she a tongue to speak, now would she say
That to her brother which I said to thee:
His napkin, with his true tears all bewet,
Can do no service on her sorrowful cheeks.
O, what a sympathy of woe is this,
As far from help as Limbo is from bliss!

Enter Aaron the Moor alone.

AARON

Titus Andronicus, my lord the Emperor
Sends thee this word: that, if thou love thy sons,
Let Marcus, Lucius, or thyself, old Titus,
Or any one of you, chop off your hand,
And send it to the King. He for the same
Will send thee hither both thy sons alive,
And that shall be the ransom for their fault.

TITUS

O gracious Emperor! O gentle Aaron!
Did ever raven sing so like a lark,
That gives sweet tidings of the sun's uprise?
With all my heart I'll send the Emperor my hand.
Good Aaron, wilt thou help to chop it off?

LUCIUS

Stay, father, for that noble hand of thine,
That hath thrown down so many enemies,
Shall not be sent. My hand will serve the turn.
My youth can better spare my blood than you,
And therefore mine shall save my brothers' lives.

MARCUS

Which of your hands hath not defended Rome,
And rear'd aloft the bloody battle-axe,
Writing destruction on the enemy's castle?
O, none of both but are of high desert.
My hand hath been but idle; let it serve
To ransom my two nephews from their death.
Then have I kept it to a worthy end.

AARON

Nay, come, agree whose hand shall go along,
For fear they die before their pardon come.

MARCUS

My hand shall go.

LUCIUS

By heaven, it shall not go!

TITUS

Sirs, strive no more. Such with'red herbs as these
Are meet for plucking up, and therefore mine.

LUCIUS

Sweet father, if I shall be thought thy son,
Let me redeem my brothers both from death.

MARCUS

And, for our father's sake and mother's care,
Now let me show a brother's love to thee.

TITUS

Agree between you; I will spare my hand.

LUCIUS

Then I'll go fetch an axe.

MARCUS

But I will use the axe. *Exeunt* [*Lucius and Marcus*].

TITUS

Come hither, Aaron. I'll deceive them both.
Lend me thy hand, and I will give thee mine.

AARON [*Aside*]

If that be call'd deceit, I will be honest,
And never, whilst I live, deceive men so;
But I'll deceive you in another sort,
And that you'll say, ere half an hour pass.

He cuts off Titus's hand.

Enter Lucius and Marcus again.

109 by this by now **121 ease** comfort, relief **123 fountain** spring **128 taken** removed, destroyed. **clearness** i.e., of the pure water **139 wot** know **140 napkin** handkerchief **141 drown'd** i.e., saturated **148 sympathy** agreement, conformity **149 Limbo** region bordering hell, where were confined the souls of those barred from heaven through no fault of their own, such as good men who lived before the Christian era

178 meet fit

TITUS
Now stay your strife. What shall be is dispatch'd.
Good Aaron, give his Majesty my hand.
Tell him it was a hand that warded him 194
From thousand dangers. Bid him bury it;
More hath it merited, that let it have.
As for my sons, say I account of them
As jewels purchas'd at an easy price,
And yet dear too, because I bought mine own. 199

AARON
I go, Andronicus, and for thy hand
Look by and by to have thy sons with thee. 201
[*Aside.*] Their heads, I mean. O, how this villainy
Doth fat me with the very thoughts of it! 203
Let fools do good, and fair men call for grace,
Aaron will have his soul black like his face. *Exit.*

TITUS
O, here I lift this one hand up to heaven,
And bow this feeble ruin to the earth. [*Kneels.*]
If any power pities wretched tears,
To that I call! [*To Lavinia, who kneels.*] What,
wouldst thou kneel with me?
Do, then, dear heart, for heaven shall hear our
prayers,
Or with our sighs we'll breathe the welkin dim, 211
And stain the sun with fog, as sometime clouds
When they do hug him in their melting bosoms.

MARCUS
O brother, speak with possibility, 214
And do not break into these deep extremes.

TITUS
Is not my sorrow deep, having no bottom?
Then be my passions bottomless with them!

MARCUS
But yet let reason govern thy lament.

TITUS
If there were reason for these miseries,
Then into limits could I bind my woes.
When heaven doth weep, doth not the earth
o'erflow?
If the winds rage, doth not the sea wax mad,
Threat'ning the welkin with his big-swoll'n face?
And wilt thou have a reason for this coil? 224
I am the sea; hark, how her sighs doth flow!
She is the weeping welkin, I the earth.
Then must my sea be moved with her sighs;
Then must my earth with her continual tears
Become a deluge, overflow'd and drown'd;
For why my bowels cannot hide her woes, 230
But like a drunkard must I vomit them.
Then give me leave, for losers will have leave
To ease their stomachs with their bitter tongues. 233

Enter a Messenger, with two heads and a hand.

MESSENGER
Worthy Andronicus, ill art thou repaid
For that good hand thou sent'st the Emperor.
Here are the heads of thy two noble sons,
And here's thy hand, in scorn to thee sent back—
Thy grief their sports, thy resolution mock'd—
That woe is me to think upon thy woes 239
More than remembrance of my father's death.
[*Sets down the heads and hand, and exit.*]

MARCUS
Now let hot Aetna cool in Sicily, 241
And be my heart an ever-burning hell!
These miseries are more than may be borne.
To weep with them that weep doth ease some deal, 244
But sorrow flouted at is double death.

LUCIUS
Ah, that this sight should make so deep a wound,
And yet detested life not shrink thereat! 247
That ever death should let life bear his name, 248
Where life hath no more interest but to breathe!
[*Lavinia kisses Titus.*]

MARCUS
Alas, poor heart, that kiss is comfortless
As frozen water to a starved snake. 251

TITUS
When will this fearful slumber have an end? 252

MARCUS
Now, farewell, flatt'ry! Die, Andronicus. 253
Thou dost not slumber. See thy two sons' heads,
Thy warlike hand, thy mangled daughter here,
Thy other banish'd son with this dear sight 256
Struck pale and bloodless, and thy brother, I,
Even like a stony image, cold and numb.
Ah, now no more will I control thy griefs!
Rend off thy silver hair, thy other hand
Gnawing with thy teeth, and be this dismal sight
The closing up of our most wretched eyes.
Now is a time to storm; why art thou still?

TITUS Ha, ha, ha!

MARCUS
Why dost thou laugh? It fits not with this hour.

TITUS
Why, I have not another tear to shed.
Besides, this sorrow is an enemy,
And would usurp upon my wat'ry eyes,
And make them blind with tributary tears; 269
Then which way shall I find Revenge's cave?
For these two heads do seem to speak to me,
And threat me I shall never come to bliss
Till all these mischiefs be return'd again
Even in their throats that hath committed them.
Come, let me see what task I have to do.
You heavy people, circle me about, 276
That I may turn me to each one of you,
And swear unto my soul to right your wrongs.
[*They form a circle about Titus,
and he pledges each.*]

194 warded guarded **199 dear** expensive **201 Look** expect **203 fat** fatten, i.e., delight **211 breathe . . . dim** make cloudy the sky with our sighs **214 speak with possibility** speak of things possible **224 coil** noise, fuss **230 For why** because. **bowels** (Supposed to be the seat of compassion.) **233 ease their stomachs** relieve their resentments (with a play on *vomit*)

239 That so that **241 Aetna** volcanic mountain on the island of Sicily (which will, compared to Marcus' burning heart, seem cool) **244 some deal** somewhat **247 shrink** i.e., slip away **248 bear his name** i.e., still be called life **251 starved** i.e., benumbed with cold **252 fearful slumber** i.e., dreadful nightmare **253 flatt'ry** gratifying deception **256 dear** grievous **269 tributary tears** tears exacted as tribute (to sorrow, the usurping enemy) **276 heavy** sorrowing

The vow is made. Come, brother, take a head;
And in this hand the other will I bear.
[*They pick up the two heads, and give the hand to Lavinia.*]
And, Lavinia, thou shalt be employ'd in these arms: 281
Bear thou my hand, sweet wench, between thy teeth.
As for thee, boy, [*To Lucius*] go get thee from my sight;
Thou art an exile, and thou must not stay.
Hie to the Goths and raise an army there.
And, if ye love me, as I think you do,
Let's kiss and part, for we have much to do.
[*Kiss, and*] *exeunt* [*Titus, Marcus, and Lavinia*].

LUCIUS
Farewell, Andronicus, my noble father,
The woefull'st man that ever liv'd in Rome.
Farewell, proud Rome, till Lucius come again!
He loves his pledges dearer than his life. 291
Farewell, Lavinia, my noble sister.
O, would thou wert as thou tofore hast been! 293
But now nor Lucius nor Lavinia lives
But in oblivion and hateful griefs.
If Lucius live, he will requite your wrongs,
And make proud Saturnine and his emperess
Beg at the gates, like Tarquin and his queen. 298
Now will I to the Goths and raise a pow'r 299
To be reveng'd on Rome and Saturnine. *Exit Lucius.*

[SCENE II]

A banquet [*set out*]. *Enter* [*Titus*] *Andronicus, Marcus, Lavinia, and the Boy* [*Young Lucius*].

TITUS
So, so. Now sit, and look you eat no more
Than will preserve just so much strength in us
As will revenge these bitter woes of ours.
Marcus, unknit that sorrow-wreathen knot. 4
Thy niece and I, poor creatures, want our hands, 5
And cannot passionate our tenfold grief 6
With folded arms. This poor right hand of mine
Is left to tyrannize upon my breast,
Who, when my heart, all mad with misery, 9
Beats in this hollow prison of my flesh,
Then thus I thump it down. [*Beats his breast.*]
[*To Lavinia.*] Thou map of woe, that thus dost talk in signs,
When thy poor heart beats with outrageous beating,
Thou canst not strike it thus to make it still.
Wound it with sighing, girl, kill it with groans; 15
Or get some little knife between thy teeth,
And just against thy heart make thou a hole,

281 in these arms (A textual difficulty, perhaps corrupt.) **291 He . . . life** i.e., his vows are more important to him than his life **293 tofore** heretofore, formerly **298 Tarquin** Tarquinius Superbus, seventh king of Rome, who, because his son had raped a Roman lady, Lucretia, was banished and his kingdom overthrown; a republic was then established **299 pow'r** army

III.ii. Location: Rome. Titus' house.
s.d. banquet a light repast, here set out on stage as the scene begins, with appropriate furniture allowing for sitting **4 sorrow-wreathen knot** arms folded in grief **5 want** lack **6 passionate** express passionately **9 Who** which **15 Wound it with sighing** (Each sigh was believed to cost the heart a drop of blood.)

That all the tears that thy poor eyes let fall
May run into that sink, and soaking in 19
Drown the lamenting fool in sea-salt tears. 20

MARCUS
Fie, brother, fie! Teach her not thus to lay
Such violent hands upon her tender life.

TITUS
How now, has sorrow made thee dote already? 23
Why, Marcus, no man should be mad but I.
What violent hands can she lay on her life?
Ah, wherefore dost thou urge the name of hands,
To bid Aeneas tell the tale twice o'er 27
How Troy was burnt and he made miserable?
O, handle not the theme, to talk of hands,
Lest we remember still that we have none.
Fie, fie, how franticly I square my talk, 31
As if we should forget we had no hands,
If Marcus did not name the word of hands!
Come, let's fall to; and, gentle girl, eat this.
Here is no drink? Hark, Marcus, what she says;
I can interpret all her martyr'd signs.
She says she drinks no other drink but tears,
Brew'd with her sorrow, mesh'd upon her cheeks. 38
Speechless complainer, I will learn thy thought;
In thy dumb action will I be as perfect 40
As begging hermits in their holy prayers.
Thou shalt not sigh, nor hold thy stumps to heaven,
Nor wink, nor nod, nor kneel, nor make a sign, 43
But I of these will wrest an alphabet
And by still practice learn to know thy meaning. 45

BOY [*Weeping*]
Good grandsire, leave these bitter deep laments!
Make my aunt merry with some pleasing tale.

MARCUS
Alas, the tender boy, in passion mov'd,
Doth weep to see his grandsire's heaviness.

TITUS
Peace, tender sapling. Thou art made of tears, 50
And tears will quickly melt thy life away.
Marcus strikes the dish with a knife.
What dost thou strike at, Marcus, with thy knife?

MARCUS
At that that I have kill'd, my lord; a fly.

TITUS
Out on thee, murderer! Thou kill'st my heart!
Mine eyes are cloy'd with view of tyranny.
A deed of death done on the innocent
Becomes not Titus' brother. Get thee gone!
I see thou art not for my company.

MARCUS
Alas, my lord, I have but kill'd a fly.

TITUS
"But"? How if that fly had a father and mother?
How would he hang his slender gilded wings,
And buzz lamenting doings in the air! 62
Poor harmless fly,
That, with his pretty buzzing melody,

19 sink receptacle **20 fool** (Here a term of pity or endearment.) **23 dote** be foolish **27 Aeneas** (See *Aeneid,* II.ii.) **31 square** shape, regulate **38 mesh'd** mashed, mixed **40 action** gesture. **perfect** thoroughly acquainted **43 wink** blink the eyes **45 still** continual **62 buzz . . . doings** tell sad stories

Came here to make us merry! And thou hast kill'd him.

MARCUS
Pardon me, sir. It was a black ill-favor'd fly,
Like to the empress' Moor; therefore I kill'd him.

TITUS
O, O, O,
Then pardon me for reprehending thee,
For thou hast done a charitable deed.
Give me thy knife. I will insult on him,
Flattering myself as if it were the Moor
Come hither purposely to poison me.—
There's for thyself, and that's for Tamora!
[*Takes knife and strikes.*]
Ah, sirrah!
Yet, I think, we are not brought so low
But that between us we can kill a fly
That comes in likeness of a coal-black Moor.

MARCUS
Alas, poor man! Grief has so wrought on him,
He takes false shadows for true substances.

TITUS
Come, take away. Lavinia, go with me.
I'll to thy closet, and go read with thee
Sad stories chanced in the times of old.
Come, boy, and go with me. Thy sight is young,
And thou shalt read when mine begin to dazzle.
Exeunt.

[ACT IV • SCENE I]

Enter Lucius' Son, and Lavinia running after him, and the boy flies from her, with his books under his arm. Enter Titus and Marcus.

BOY
Help, grandsire, help! My aunt Lavinia
Follows me everywhere, I know not why.
Good uncle Marcus, see how swift she comes.
Alas, sweet aunt, I know not what you mean.

MARCUS
Stand by me, Lucius; do not fear thine aunt.

TITUS
She loves thee, boy, too well to do thee harm.

BOY
Ay, when my father was in Rome she did.

MARCUS
What means my niece Lavinia by these signs?

TITUS
Fear her not, Lucius, somewhat doth she mean.

MARCUS
See, Lucius, see how much she makes of thee;
Somewhither would she have thee go with her.
Ah, boy, Cornelia never with more care
Read to her sons than she hath read to thee
Sweet poetry and Tully's Orator.
Canst thou not guess wherefore she plies thee thus?

BOY
My lord, I know not, I, nor can I guess,
Unless some fit or frenzy do possess her;
For I have heard my grandsire say full oft,
Extremity of griefs would make men mad,
And I have read that Hecuba of Troy
Ran mad for sorrow. That made me to fear,
Although, my lord, I know my noble aunt
Loves me as dear as e'er my mother did,
And would not, but in fury, fright my youth—
Which made me down to throw my books, and fly,
Causeless, perhaps. But pardon me, sweet aunt;
And, madam, if my uncle Marcus go,
I will most willingly attend your ladyship.

MARCUS
Lucius, I will.
[*Lavinia turns over with her stumps the books which Lucius has let fall.*]

TITUS
How now, Lavinia? Marcus, what means this?
Some book there is that she desires to see.
Which is it, girl, of these? Open them, boy.
But thou art deeper read, and better skill'd;
Come, and take choice of all my library,
And so beguile thy sorrow, till the heavens
Reveal the damn'd contriver of this deed.
Why lifts she up her arms in sequence thus?

MARCUS
I think she means that there were more than one
Confederate in the fact. Ay, more there was;
Or else to heaven she heaves them for revenge.

TITUS
Lucius, what book is that she tosseth so?

BOY
Grandsire, 'tis Ovid's Metamorphosis;
My mother gave it me.

MARCUS
For love of her that's gone,
Perhaps, she cull'd it from among the rest.

TITUS
Soft, so busily she turns the leaves!
Help her.
What would she find? Lavinia, shall I read?
This is the tragic tale of Philomel,
And treats of Tereus' treason and his rape;
And rape, I fear, was root of thy annoy.

MARCUS
See, brother, see, note how she quotes the leaves.

TITUS
Lavinia, wert thou thus surpris'd, sweet girl,
Ravish'd and wrong'd, as Philomela was,
Forc'd in the ruthless, vast, and gloomy woods?
See, see!
Ay, such a place there is, where we did hunt—

71 insult on exult over **72 Flattering . . . if** deluding myself into believing **75 sirrah** (Ordinary term of address to inferiors.) **81 take away** clear the table. (The "banquet" and furniture are removed from the stage as the scene ends.) **82 closet** private room **83 chanced** that occurred **85 dazzle** become dazzled, unable to see

IV.i. Location: Rome. Titus' garden.
12 Cornelia the mother of the Gracchi brothers, the two most famous tribunes in Roman history. (Her success in educating her sons was highly regarded.)

14 Tully's Orator Cicero's treatise on rhetoric, *De Oratore* **20 Hecuba** (See I.i.139.) **24 but in fury** except in madness **37 in sequence** one after the other **39 fact** deed **41 tosseth** turns the pages of **49–50 Philomel, Tereus'** (Cf. II.iii.43, note.) **52 quotes** examines **55 vast** desolate

O, had we never, never hunted there!—
Pattern'd by that the poet here describes,
By nature made for murders and for rapes.

MARCUS
O, why should nature build so foul a den,
Unless the gods delight in tragedies?

TITUS
Give signs, sweet girl, for here are none but friends,
What Roman lord it was durst do the deed;
Or slunk not Saturnine, as Tarquin erst,
That left the camp to sin in Lucrece' bed?

MARCUS
Sit down, sweet niece. Brother, sit down by me.
[They sit.]
Apollo, Pallas, Jove, or Mercury,
Inspire me, that I may this treason find!
My lord, look here. Look here, Lavinia.
He writes his name with his staff, and guides it with feet and mouth.
This sandy plot is plain; guide, if thou canst,
This after me. I have writ my name
Without the help of any hand at all.
Curs'd be that heart that forc'd us to this shift!
Write thou, good niece; and here display, at last,
What God will have discovered for revenge.
Heaven guide thy pen to print thy sorrows plain,
That we may know the traitors and the truth!
She takes the staff in her mouth, and guides it with her stumps, and writes.

TITUS
O, do ye read, my lord, what she hath writ?
"Stuprum. Chiron. Demetrius."

MARCUS
What, what, the lustful sons of Tamora
Performers of this heinous, bloody deed?

TITUS
Magni Dominator poli,
Tam lentus audis scelera? Tam lentus vides?

MARCUS
O, calm thee, gentle lord; although I know
There is enough written upon this earth
To stir a mutiny in the mildest thoughts
And arm the minds of infants to exclaims.
My lord, kneel down with me; Lavinia, kneel;
And kneel, sweet boy, the Roman Hector's hope;
[All kneel.]
And swear with me, as, with the woeful fere
And father of that chaste dishonored dame,
Lord Junius Brutus sware for Lucrece' rape,
That we will prosecute by good advice
Mortal revenge upon these traitorous Goths,
And see their blood, or die with this reproach.
[They rise.]

TITUS
'Tis sure enough, an you knew how.
But if you hunt these bear-whelps, then beware:
The dam will wake an if she wind ye once.
She's with the lion deeply still in league,
And lulls him whilst she playeth on her back,
And when he sleeps will she do what she list.
You are a young huntsman, Marcus; let alone;
And, come, I will go get a leaf of brass,
And with a gad of steel will write these words,
And lay it by. The angry northern wind
Will blow these sands, like Sibyl's leaves, abroad,
And where's our lesson, then? Boy, what say you?

BOY
I say, my lord, that if I were a man,
Their mother's bedchamber should not be safe
For these base bondmen to the yoke of Rome.

MARCUS
Ay, that's my boy! Thy father hath full oft
For his ungrateful country done the like.

BOY
And, uncle, so will I, an if I live.

TITUS
Come, go with me into mine armory.
Lucius, I'll fit thee, and withal my boy
Shalt carry from me to the Empress' sons
Presents that I intend to send them both.
Come, come; thou 'lt do my message, wilt thou not?

BOY
Ay, with my dagger in their bosoms, grandsire.

TITUS
No, boy, not so; I'll teach thee another course.
Lavinia, come. Marcus, look to my house.
Lucius and I'll go brave it at the court;
Ay, marry, will we, sir; and we'll be waited on.
Exeunt [Titus, Lavinia, and Young Lucius].

MARCUS
O heavens, can you hear a good man groan,
And not relent, or not compassion him?
Marcus, attend him in his ecstasy,
That hath more scars of sorrow in his heart
Than foemen's marks upon his batt'red shield,
But yet so just that he will not revenge.
Revenge the heavens for old Andronicus! *Exit.*

[SCENE II]

Enter Aaron, Chiron, and Demetrius, at one door, and at the other door young Lucius and another, with a bundle of weapons and verses writ upon them.

CHIRON
Demetrius, here's the son of Lucius.
He hath some message to deliver us.

59 Pattern'd by on the pattern of **65 erst** once **71 plain** level **72 after me** following my example **74 shift** expedient **76 discovered** revealed, uncovered **80 Stuprum** violation, rape **83–84 Magni . . . vides?** Ruler of the mighty heavens, are you so slow to see and hear the crimes that are committed? (Derived from Seneca, *Hippolytus,* 668–669.) **88 exclaims** exclamations **90 the Roman Hector's hope** i.e., the hope and future of Lucius, whose deeds compare with those of Hector in Troy **91 fere** spouse, husband **93 Brutus** (After Sextus Tarquinius had raped Lucretia—see II.i.108 and Shakespeare's *Rape of Lucrece*—Junius Brutus led the Romans to expel the Tarquin dynasty; see also III.i.298 and *Julius Caesar* II.i.53–54.) **sware** swore **94 advice** deliberation, planning **96 reproach** disgrace, infamy

99 an if if. **wind** scent **102 list** choose, please **104 leaf** sheet **105 gad** stylus, spike **107 Sibyl's leaves** (The Cumaean Sibyl, an inspired woman, wrote her prophecies on leaves which she placed at the entrance to her cave. Those wishing to consult them had to do so before they were scattered by the wind.) **123 brave it** put on a bold front, cut a bold figure **124 marry** (Mild interjection equivalent to "Indeed!"). **be waited on** i.e., demand attention **126 compassion** have compassion for **127 ecstasy** madness **131 Revenge the heavens** may the heavens take revenge

IV.ii. Location: Rome. The Emperor's palace.

AARON
Ay, some mad message from his mad grandfather.
BOY
My lords, with all the humbleness I may,
I greet your honors from Andronicus—
[*Aside.*] And pray the Roman gods confound you
both! 6
DEMETRIUS
Gramercy, lovely Lucius. What's the news? 7
BOY [*Aside*]
That you are both decipher'd, that's the news, 8
For villains mark'd with rape.—May it please you,
My grandsire, well advis'd, hath sent by me 10
The goodliest weapons of his armory
To gratify your honorable youth, 12
The hope of Rome; for so he bid me say.
And so I do, and with his gifts present
Your lordships, that, whenever you have need,
You may be armed and appointed well. 16
[*His attendant presents the bundle.*]
And so I leave you both—[*Aside*] like bloody
villains.
Exit [*with Attendant*].
DEMETRIUS
What's here? A scroll, and written round about?
Let's see:
[*Reads.*] "Integer vitae, scelerisque purus, 20
Non eget Mauri jaculis, nec arcu." 21
CHIRON
O, 'tis a verse in Horace; I know it well.
I read it in the grammar long ago. 23
AARON
Ay, just; a verse in Horace; right, you have it. 24
[*Aside.*] Now, what a thing it is to be an ass!
Here's no sound jest! The old man hath found their
guilt, 26
And sends them weapons wrapp'd about with lines
That wound, beyond their feeling, to the quick. 28
But were our witty Empress well afoot,
She would applaud Andronicus' conceit. 30
But let her rest in her unrest awhile.—
And now, young lords, was 't not a happy star
Led us to Rome, strangers, and more than so,
Captives, to be advanced to this height?
It did me good, before the palace gate
To brave the tribune in his brother's hearing. 36
DEMETRIUS
But me more good, to see so great a lord
Basely insinuate and send us gifts. 38
AARON
Had he not reason, Lord Demetrius?
Did you not use his daughter very friendly?
DEMETRIUS
I would we had a thousand Roman dames
At such a bay, by turn to serve our lust. 42

6 confound destroy **7 Gramercy** many thanks **8 decipher'd** detected **10 well advis'd** having considered carefully **12 gratify** grace **16 appointed** equipped **20–21 Integer . . . arcu** (The opening lines of perhaps the best known of the Odes of Horace, I.22: "He who is spotless in life and free of crime needs not the Moorish bow and arrow.") **23 grammar** i.e., Latin grammar book **24 just** precisely **26 sound** wholesome **28 to the quick** i.e., to the very life **30 conceit** design **36 brave** taunt **38 insinuate** ingratiate himself by flattery **42 At such a bay** cornered thus

CHIRON
A charitable wish and full of love.
AARON
Here lacks but your mother for to say amen.
CHIRON
And that would she for twenty thousand more. 45
DEMETRIUS
Come, let us go, and pray to all the gods
For our beloved mother in her pains. 47
AARON [*Aside*]
Pray to the devils; the gods have given us over.
Trumpets sound [*within*].
DEMETRIUS
Why do the Emperor's trumpets flourish thus?
CHIRON
Belike for joy the Emperor hath a son. 50
DEMETRIUS
Soft, who comes here?

Enter Nurse, with a blackamoor Child [*in her arms*].

NURSE
Good morrow, lords.
O, tell me, did you see Aaron the Moor?
AARON
Well, more or less, or ne'er a whit at all,
Here Aaron is; and what with Aaron now?
NURSE
O gentle Aaron, we are all undone!
Now help, or woe betide thee evermore!
AARON
Why, what a caterwauling dost thou keep!
What dost thou wrap and fumble in thy arms?
NURSE
O, that which I would hide from heaven's eye, 60
Our empress' shame, and stately Rome's disgrace!
She is delivered, lords; she is delivered.
AARON
To whom?
NURSE
I mean she is brought a-bed.
AARON
Well, God give her good rest! What hath he sent
her?
NURSE
A devil.
AARON
Why, then she is the devil's dam; a joyful issue. 67
NURSE
A joyless, dismal, black, and sorrowful issue! 68
Here is the babe, as loathsome as a toad
Amongst the fair-fac'd breeders of our clime.
The Empress sends it thee, thy stamp, thy seal,
And bids thee christen it with thy dagger's point.
AARON
'Zounds, ye whore! Is black so base a hue? 73
Sweet blowse, you are a beauteous blossom, sure. 74

45 more i.e., more *dames* or ladies ravished **47 pains** i.e., labor pains. (Tamora is being delivered of a child sired by Aaron; see l. 29 above.) **50 Belike** probably **67 dam** mother. **issue** result **68 issue** i.e., child **73 'Zounds** by His (Christ's) wounds **74 blowse** red-cheeked wench

DEMETRIUS
Villain, what hast thou done?

AARON
That which thou canst not undo.

CHIRON
Thou hast undone our mother.

AARON
Villain, I have done thy mother.

DEMETRIUS
And therein, hellish dog, thou hast undone her.
Woe to her chance, and damn'd her loathed choice!
Accurs'd the offspring of so foul a fiend!

CHIRON
It shall not live.

AARON
It shall not die.

NURSE
Aaron, it must. The mother wills it so.

AARON
What, must it, nurse? Then let no man but I
Do execution on my flesh and blood.

DEMETRIUS
I'll broach the tadpole on my rapier's point.
Nurse, give it me. My sword shall soon dispatch it.

AARON
Sooner this sword shall plough thy bowels up.
[*Takes the Child from the Nurse, and draws.*]
Stay, murderous villains! Will you kill your brother?
Now, by the burning tapers of the sky
That shone so brightly when this boy was got,
He dies upon my scimitar's sharp point
That touches this my first-born son and heir!
I tell you, younglings, not Enceladus,
With all his threat'ning band of Typhon's brood,
Nor great Alcides, nor the god of war,
Shall seize this prey out of his father's hands.
What, what, ye sanguine, shallow-hearted boys!
Ye white-lim'd walls! Ye alehouse painted signs!
Coal-black is better than another hue,
In that it scorns to bear another hue;
For all the water in the ocean
Can never turn the swan's black legs to white,
Although she lave them hourly in the flood.
Tell the Empress from me, I am of age
To keep mine own, excuse it how she can.

DEMETRIUS
Wilt thou betray thy noble mistress thus?

AARON
My mistress is my mistress; this myself,
The vigor and the picture of my youth.
This before all the world do I prefer;
This maugre all the world will I keep safe,
Or some of you shall smoke for it in Rome.

DEMETRIUS
By this our mother is for ever sham'd.

CHIRON
Rome will despise her for this foul escape.

NURSE
The Emperor, in his rage, will doom her death.

CHIRON
I blush to think upon this ignomy.

AARON
Why, there's the privilege your beauty bears.
Fie, treacherous hue, that will betray with blushing
The close enacts and counsels of the heart!
Here's a young lad fram'd of another leer.
Look how the black slave smiles upon the father,
As who should say, "Old lad, I am thine own."
He is your brother, lords, sensibly fed
Of that self-blood that first gave life to you,
And from that womb where you imprisoned were
He is enfranchised and come to light.
Nay, he is your brother by the surer side,
Although my seal be stamped in his face.

NURSE
Aaron, what shall I say unto the Empress?

DEMETRIUS
Advise thee, Aaron, what is to be done,
And we will all subscribe to thy advice.
Save thou the child, so we may all be safe.

AARON
Then sit we down, and let us all consult.
My son and I will have the wind of you;
Keep there. Now talk at pleasure of your safety.
[*They sit.*]

DEMETRIUS
How many women saw this child of his?

AARON
Why, so, brave lords! When we join in league,
I am a lamb; but if you brave the Moor,
The chafed boar, the mountain lioness,
The ocean swells not so as Aaron storms.
But say, again, how many saw the child?

NURSE
Cornelia the midwife and myself,
And no one else but the delivered Empress.

AARON
The Empress, the midwife, and yourself.
Two may keep counsel when the third's away.
Go to the Empress, tell her this I said. *He kills her.*
Weeke, weeke!—
So cries a pig prepared to the spit.

DEMETRIUS
What mean'st thou, Aaron? Wherefore didst thou this?

AARON
O Lord, sir, 'tis a deed of policy.
Shall she live to betray this guilt of ours,
A long-tongu'd babbling gossip? No, lords, no.
And now be it known to you my full intent.

78 done i.e., made love to **80 chance** luck **87 broach** impale **92 got** begotten **95 Enceladus** one of the Titans, sons of the giant Typhon (cf. I. 96, *Typhon's brood*), all of whom waged war against the gods on Olympus **97 Alcides** i.e., Hercules, a descendant of Alcaeus **99 sanguine** red-cheeked (as distinguished from black-complexioned) **100 white-lim'd** whitewashed **105 lave** wash **112 maugre** in spite of **113 smoke** i.e., suffer

115 escape escapade, outrageous transgression **117 ignomy** ignominy, shame **120 close enacts** secret purposes **121 leer** countenance, complexion **124 sensibly** manifestly to the senses **128 surer** i.e., mother's **132 subscribe** agree **133 so** so long as **135 have . . . you** stay upwind of you (as in hunting, so as not to be scented by the game) **140 chafed** enraged **151 policy** prudent action

Not far, one Muliteus my countryman 155
His wife but yesternight was brought to bed; 156
His child is like to her, fair as you are.
Go pack with him, and give the mother gold, 158
And tell them both the circumstance of all,
And how by this their child shall be advanc'd,
And be received for the Emperor's heir,
And substituted in the place of mine
To calm this tempest whirling in the court;
And let the Emperor dandle him for his own.
Hark ye, lords; you see I have given her physic, 165
[*Pointing to the nurse.*]
And you must needs bestow her funeral. 166
The fields are near, and you are gallant grooms. 167
This done, see that you take no longer days, 168
But send the midwife presently to me.
The midwife and the nurse well made away,
Then let the ladies tattle what they please.

CHIRON
Aaron, I see thou wilt not trust the air
With secrets.

DEMETRIUS For this care of Tamora,
Herself and hers are highly bound to thee.
Exeunt [*Demetrius and Chiron bearing off the Nurse's body*].

AARON
Now to the Goths, as swift as swallow flies,
There to dispose this treasure in mine arms
And secretly to greet the Empress' friends.
Come on, you thick-lipp'd slave, I'll bear you hence,
For it is you that puts us to our shifts. 179
I'll make you feed on berries and on roots,
And feed on curds and whey, and suck the goat,
And cabin in a cave, and bring you up 182
To be a warrior, and command a camp.
Exit [*with the child*].

[SCENE III]

Enter Titus, old Marcus, [*his Son Publius,*] *young Lucius, and other Gentlemen* [*Sempronius, Caius*], *with bows; and Titus bears the arrows with letters on the ends of them.*

TITUS
Come, Marcus, come. Kinsmen, this is the way.
Sir boy, let me see your archery.
Look ye draw home enough, and 'tis there straight. 3
Terras Astraea reliquit; 4
Be you rememb'red, Marcus, she's gone, she's fled. 5
Sirs, take you to your tools. You, cousins, shall
Go sound the ocean, and cast your nets;
Happily you may catch her in the sea. 8
Yet there's as little justice as at land.
No; Publius and Sempronius, you must do it;
'Tis you must dig with mattock and with spade,
And pierce the inmost center of the earth.
Then, when you come to Pluto's region, 13
I pray you deliver him this petition.
Tell him it is for justice and for aid,
And that it comes from old Andronicus,
Shaken with sorrows in ungrateful Rome.
Ah, Rome! Well, well, I made thee miserable
What time I threw the people's suffrages 19
On him that thus doth tyrannize o'er me.
Go, get you gone; and pray be careful all,
And leave you not a man-of-war unsearch'd.
This wicked Emperor may have shipp'd her hence,
And, kinsmen, then we may go pipe for justice. 24

MARCUS
O Publius, is not this a heavy case,
To see thy noble uncle thus distract? 26

PUBLIUS
Therefore, my lords, it highly us concerns
By day and night t' attend him carefully,
And feed his humor kindly as we may, 29
Till time beget some careful remedy.

MARCUS
Kinsmen, his sorrows are past remedy.
Join with the Goths, and with revengeful war
Take wreak on Rome for this ingratitude, 33
And vengeance on the traitor Saturnine.

TITUS
Publius, how now? How now, my masters?
What, have you met with her?

PUBLIUS
No, my good lord, but Pluto sends you word,
If you will have Revenge from hell, you shall.
Marry, for Justice, she is so employ'd, 39
He thinks, with Jove in heaven, or somewhere else,
So that perforce you must needs stay a time.

TITUS
He doth me wrong to feed me with delays.
I'll dive into the burning lake below, 43
And pull her out of Acheron by the heels. 44
Marcus, we are but shrubs, no cedars we,
No big-bon'd men fram'd of the Cyclops' size, 46
But metal, Marcus, steel to the very back,
Yet wrung with wrongs more than our backs can bear.
And, sith there's no justice in earth nor hell, 49
We will solicit heaven and move the gods
To send down Justice for to wreak our wrongs.
Come, to this gear. You are a good archer, Marcus; 52
He gives them the arrows.
"Ad Jovem," that's for you; here, "Ad Apollinem"; 53
"Ad Martem," that's for myself; 54
Here, boy, "to Pallas"; here, "to Mercury"; 55
"To Saturn," Caius, not to Saturnine;

155–156 one . . . wife the wife of a certain Muliteus, a fellow countryman of mine **158 pack** make a deal **165 physic** medicine **166 bestow** provide, furnish **167 grooms** fellows **168 days** time **179 shifts** stratagems, tricks **182 cabin** lodge

IV.iii. Location: Rome. A public place.
3 home to the full extent (of the bow) **4 Terras Astraea reliquit** Astraea (the goddess of justice) has abandoned the earth. (From Ovid, *Metamorphoses,* I.150.) **5 Be you rememb'red** remember **8 Happily** haply, perhaps

13 Pluto's region the underworld **19 What time** when **24 pipe** whistle, i.e., look in vain **26 distract** distracted, crazed **29 humor** mood, whim **33 wreak** vengeance **39 for** as for **43 burning lake** i.e., Phlegethon, the burning river of the underworld **44 Acheron** a river in the underworld **46 Cyclops** one-eyed giants in Homer's *Odyssey* (IX) **49 sith** since **52 gear** business **53–54 Ad Jovem, Ad Apollinem, Ad Martem** to Jove, to Apollo, to Mars **55 Pallas** Minerva, Athena

You were as good to shoot against the wind. 57
To it, boy! Marcus, loose when I bid. 58
Of my word, I have written to effect;
There's not a god left unsolicited.

MARCUS
Kinsmen, shoot all your shafts into the court.
We will afflict the Emperor in his pride.

TITUS
Now, masters, draw. [*They shoot.*] O, well said, Lucius! 63
Good boy, in Virgo's lap; give it Pallas. 64

MARCUS
My lord, I aim a mile beyond the moon;
Your letter is with Jupiter by this.

TITUS Ha, ha!
Publius, Publius, what hast thou done?
See, see, thou hast shot off one of Taurus' horns. 69

MARCUS
This was the sport, my lord: when Publius shot,
The Bull, being gall'd, gave Aries such a knock 71
That down fell both the Ram's horns in the court; 72
And who should find them but the Empress' villain?
She laugh'd, and told the Moor he should not choose
But give them to his master for a present. 75

TITUS
Why, there it goes. God give his lordship joy! 76

Enter the Clown, with a basket, and two pigeons in it.

News, news from heaven! Marcus, the post is come.
Sirrah, what tidings? Have you any letters?
Shall I have justice? What says Jupiter?

CLOWN Ho, the gibbet-maker? He says that he hath 80
taken them down again, for the man must not be hang'd till the next week.

TITUS But what says Jupiter, I ask thee?

CLOWN Alas, sir, I know not Jubiter, I never drank with him in all my life.

TITUS Why, villain, art not thou the carrier?

CLOWN Ay, of my pigeons, sir; nothing else.

TITUS Why, didst thou not come from heaven?

CLOWN From heaven! Alas, sir, I never came there. God forbid I should be so bold to press to heaven in my young days. Why, I am going with my pigeons to the
tribunal plebs, to take up a matter of brawl betwixt my 92
uncle and one of the Emperal's men. 93

MARCUS Why, sir, that is as fit as can be to serve for your oration; and let him deliver the pigeons to the Emperor from you.

TITUS Tell me, can you deliver an oration to the Emperor with a grace?

CLOWN Nay, truly, sir, I could never say grace in all my
life. 100

TITUS
Sirrah, come hither. Make no more ado,
But give your pigeons to the Emperor.
By me thou shalt have justice at his hands.
Hold, hold; meanwhile here's money for thy charges. [*Gives money.*]
Give me pen and ink.
Sirrah, can you with a grace deliver up a supplication?

CLOWN Ay, sir.

TITUS [*Writing and handing him a supplication*] Then here is a supplication for you. And when you come to him, at the first approach you must kneel, then kiss his foot, then deliver up your pigeons, and then look for your reward. I'll be at hand, sir; see you do it
bravely. 113

CLOWN I warrant you, sir, let me alone. 114

TITUS
Sirrah, hast thou a knife? Come let me see it.
[*Takes knife and gives it to Marcus.*]
Here, Marcus, fold it in the oration,
For thou hast made it like an humble suppliant.
And when thou hast given it to the Emperor,
Knock at my door, and tell me what he says.

CLOWN God be with you, sir; I will. *Exit.*

TITUS Come, Marcus, let us go. Publius, follow me. *Exeunt.*

[SCENE IV]

Enter Emperor [*Saturninus*] *and Empress* [*Tamora*] *and her two Sons* [*and others*]. *The Emperor brings the arrows in his hand that Titus shot at him.* [*The Emperor and Empress sit.*]

SATURNINUS
Why, lords, what wrongs are these! Was ever seen
An emperor in Rome thus overborne,
Troubled, confronted thus, and, for the extent 3
Of egall justice, us'd in such contempt? 4
My lords, you know, as know the mightful gods,
However these disturbers of our peace
Buzz in the people's ears, there nought hath pass'd,
But even with law, against the willful sons 8
Of old Andronicus. And what an if
His sorrows have so overwhelm'd his wits,
Shall we be thus afflicted in his wreaks, 11
His fits, his frenzy, and his bitterness?
And now he writes to heaven for his redress.
See, here's to Jove, and this to Mercury,
This to Apollo, this to the god of war—
Sweet scrolls to fly about the streets of Rome!
What's this but libelling against the Senate,
And blazoning our unjustice everywhere? 18

57 You . . . wind you would do as much good shooting against the wind (as you would in appealing to Saturninus) **58 loose** let fly, discharge **63 said** done **64 in Virgo's lap** in the constellation of the Virgin **69, 71 Taurus, Aries** the Bull, the Ram; signs of the zodiac **72 horns** i.e., signs of being a cuckold, bestowed by Aaron on the Emperor **76 s.d. Clown** rustic **80 gibbet-maker** (Comically sounds like "Jupiter.") **92 tribunal plebs** i.e., *tribunus plebis,* tribune of the plebs. **take up** settle amicably **93 Emperal's** (Malapropism for *emperor's.*)

113 bravely handsomely, stylishly **114 let me alone** leave it to me

IV.iv. Location: Rome. Before the palace.
3 extent exercise **4 egall** equal **8 even** conformable **11 wreaks** revengeful acts **18 blazoning** making public

A goodly humor, is it not, my lords?
As who would say, in Rome no justice were.
But if I live, his feigned ecstasies
Shall be no shelter to these outrages;
But he and his shall know that justice lives
In Saturninus' health, whom, if he sleep,
He'll so awake as he in fury shall
Cut off the proud'st conspirator that lives.

TAMORA
My gracious lord, my lovely Saturnine,
Lord of my life, commander of my thoughts,
Calm thee, and bear the faults of Titus' age,
Th' effects of sorrow for his valiant sons,
Whose loss hath pierc'd him deep and scarr'd his heart;
And rather comfort his distressed plight
Than prosecute the meanest or the best
For these contempts. [*Aside.*] Why, thus it shall become
High-witted Tamora to gloze with all.
But, Titus, I have touch'd thee to the quick;
Thy life-blood out, if Aaron now be wise,
Then is all safe, the anchor in the port.

Enter Clown.

How now, good fellow, wouldst thou speak with us?

CLOWN Yea, forsooth, an your mistresship be emperial.

TAMORA Empress I am, but yonder sits the Emperor.

CLOWN 'Tis he. [*Kneels.*] God and Saint Stephen give you godden. I have brought you a letter and a couple of pigeons here. *He* [*Saturninus*] *reads the letter.*

SATURNINUS
Go, take him away, and hang him presently.

CLOWN How much money must I have?

TAMORA Come, sirrah, you must be hang'd.

CLOWN Hang'd! By' Lady, then I have brought up a neck to a fair end. *Exit* [*guarded*].

SATURNINUS
Despiteful and intolerable wrongs!
Shall I endure this monstrous villainy?
I know from whence this same device proceeds.
May this be borne?—as if his traitorous sons,
That died by law for murder of our brother,
Have by my means been butchered wrongfully!
Go, drag the villain hither by the hair;
Nor age nor honor shall shape privilege.
For this proud mock I'll be thy slaughter-man,
Sly frantic wretch, that holp'st to make me great
In hope thyself should govern Rome and me.

Enter nuntius, Aemilius.

What news with thee, Aemilius?

AEMILIUS
Arm, my lords! Rome never had more cause.
The Goths have gathered head, and with a power
Of high-resolved men, bent to the spoil,
They hither march amain, under conduct
Of Lucius, son to old Andronicus,
Who threats, in course of this revenge, to do
As much as ever Coriolanus did.

SATURNINUS
Is warlike Lucius general of the Goths?
These tidings nip me, and I hang the head
As flowers with frost or grass beat down with storms.
Ay, now begins our sorrows to approach.
'Tis he the common people love so much;
Myself hath often heard them say,
When I have walked like a private man,
That Lucius' banishment was wrongfully,
And they have wish'd that Lucius were their emperor.

TAMORA
Why should you fear? Is not your city strong?

SATURNINUS
Ay, but the citizens favor Lucius,
And will revolt from me to succor him.

TAMORA
King, be thy thoughts imperious, like thy name.
Is the sun dimm'd, that gnats do fly in it?
The eagle suffers little birds to sing,
And is not careful what they mean thereby,
Knowing that with the shadow of his wings
He can at pleasure stint their melody;
Even so mayst thou the giddy men of Rome.
Then cheer thy spirit, for know, thou Emperor,
I will enchant the old Andronicus
With words more sweet, and yet more dangerous,
Than baits to fish, or honey-stalks to sheep,
When as the one is wounded with the bait,
The other rotted with delicious feed.

SATURNINUS
But he will not entreat his son for us.

TAMORA
If Tamora entreat him, then he will;
For I can smooth and fill his aged ears
With golden promises; that, were his heart
Almost impregnable, his old ears deaf,
Yet should both ear and heart obey my tongue.
[*To Aemilius.*] Go thou before, to be our ambassador.
Say that the Emperor requests a parley
Of warlike Lucius, and appoint the meeting
Even at his father's house, the old Andronicus.

SATURNINUS
Aemilius, do this message honorably,
And, if he stand on hostage for his safety,
Bid him demand what pledge will please him best.

AEMILIUS
Your bidding shall I do effectually. *Exit.*

19 humor whim, behavior **21 ecstasies** fits of madness **35 gloze** deceive **37 Thy life-blood out** once your life-blood is spilled **43 godden** good evening **48 By' Lady** by Our Lady, the Virgin Mary **57 shape privilege** make for exemption **59 holp'st** helped **60 s.d. nuntius** messenger

63 gathered head raised an armed force **65 amain** forcefully, swiftly **68 Coriolanus** an early Roman hero, turned enemy of Rome, about whom Shakespeare wrote one of his later tragedies **84 careful** full of concern **86 stint** stop **91 honey-stalks** clover **96 smooth** flatter **105 stand** insist **106 demand** request

TAMORA
Now will I to that old Andronicus,
And temper him with all the art I have
To pluck proud Lucius from the warlike Goths.
And now, sweet Emperor, be blithe again,
And bury all thy fear in my devices.

SATURNINUS
Then go successantly, and plead to him. *Exeunt.*

[ACT V • SCENE I]

[Flourish.] Enter Lucius with an army of Goths, with drums and Soldiers.

LUCIUS
Approved warriors, and my faithful friends,
I have received letters from great Rome,
Which signifies what hate they bear their emperor
And how desirous of our sight they are.
Therefore, great lords, be as your titles witness,
Imperious, and impatient of your wrongs,
And wherein Rome hath done you any scath
Let him make treble satisfaction.

FIRST GOTH
Brave slip, sprung from the great Andronicus,
Whose name was once our terror, now our comfort,
Whose high exploits and honorable deeds
Ingrateful Rome requites with foul contempt,
Be bold in us. We'll follow where thou lead'st,
Like stinging bees in hottest summer's day
Led by their master to the flow'red fields,
And be aveng'd on cursed Tamora.

ALL THE GOTHS
And as he saith, so say we all with him.

LUCIUS
I humbly thank him, and I thank you all.
But who comes here, led by a lusty Goth?

Enter a Goth, leading of Aaron with his Child in his arms.

SECOND GOTH
Renowned Lucius, from our troops I stray'd
To gaze upon a ruinous monastery,
And, as I earnestly did fix mine eye
Upon the wasted building, suddenly
I heard a child cry underneath a wall.
I made unto the noise, when soon I heard
The crying babe controll'd with this discourse:
"Peace, tawny slave, half me and half thy dam!
Did not thy hue bewray whose brat thou art,
Had nature lent thee but thy mother's look,
Villain, thou mightst have been an emperor.
But where the bull and cow are both milk-white,
They never do beget a coal-black calf.
Peace, villain, peace!"—even thus he rates the babe—
"For I must bear thee to a trusty Goth,
Who, when he knows thou art the Empress' babe,
Will hold thee dearly for thy mother's sake."
With this, my weapon drawn, I rush'd upon him,
Surpris'd him suddenly, and brought him hither
To use as you think needful of the man.

LUCIUS
O worthy Goth, this is the incarnate devil
That robb'd Andronicus of his good hand!
This is the pearl that pleas'd your Empress' eye,
And here's the base fruit of her burning lust.
Say, wall-ey'd slave, whither wouldst thou convey
This growing image of thy fiend-like face?
Why dost not speak? What, deaf? Not a word?
A halter, soldiers! Hang him on this tree,
And by his side his fruit of bastardy.

AARON
Touch not the boy; he is of royal blood.

LUCIUS
Too like the sire for ever being good.
First hang the child, that he may see it sprawl—
A sight to vex the father's soul withal.
Get me a ladder.
[A ladder brought, which Aaron is made to ascend.]

AARON
Lucius, save the child,
And bear it from me to the Empress.
If thou do this, I'll show thee wondrous things,
That highly may advantage thee to hear.
If thou wilt not, befall what may befall,
I'll speak no more but "Vengeance rot you all!"

LUCIUS
Say on. An if it please me which thou speak'st,
Thy child shall live, and I will see it nourish'd.

AARON
An if it please thee! Why, assure thee, Lucius,
'Twill vex thy soul to hear what I shall speak;
For I must talk of murders, rapes, and massacres,
Acts of black night, abominable deeds,
Complots of mischief, treason, villainies,
Ruthful to hear, yet piteously perform'd.
And this shall all be buried in my death,
Unless thou swear to me my child shall live.

LUCIUS
Tell on thy mind. I say thy child shall live.

AARON
Swear that he shall, and then I will begin.

LUCIUS
Who should I swear by? Thou believest no god.
That granted, how canst thou believe an oath?

AARON
What if I do not? As, indeed, I do not.
Yet, for I know thou art religious
And hast a thing within thee called conscience,
With twenty popish tricks and ceremonies,

109 temper work upon **113 successantly** at once

V.i. Location: Near Rome.
1 Approved put to proof, tried **7 scath** injury **9 slip** offspring, scion **13 bold** confident **21 ruinous** decayed **28 bewray** reveal

33 rates chides **44 wall-ey'd** glaring **45 image** likeness **50 for ever being** ever to be **66 Ruthful** pitiable. **piteously** in a way to excite pity **74 for** because

Which I have seen thee careful to observe,
Therefore I urge thy oath. For that I know
An idiot holds his bauble for a god
And keeps the oath which by that god he swears,
To that I'll urge him. Therefore thou shalt vow
By that same god, what god soe'er it be,
That thou adorest and hast in reverence,
To save my boy, to nourish and bring him up,
Or else I will discover nought to thee.

LUCIUS
Even by my god I swear to thee I will.

AARON
First know thou, I begot him on the Empress.

LUCIUS
O most insatiate and luxurious woman!

AARON
Tut, Lucius, this was but a deed of charity
To that which thou shalt hear of me anon.
'Twas her two sons that murdered Bassianus;
They cut thy sister's tongue and ravish'd her
And cut her hands and trimm'd her as thou sawest.

LUCIUS
O detestable villain! Call'st thou that trimming?

AARON
Why, she was wash'd and cut and trimm'd, and 'twas
Trim sport for them which had the doing of it.

LUCIUS
O barbarous, beastly villains, like thyself!

AARON
Indeed, I was their tutor to instruct them.
That codding spirit had they from their mother,
As sure a card as ever won the set;
That bloody mind, I think, they learn'd of me,
As true a dog as ever fought at head.
Well, let my deeds be witness of my worth.
I train'd thy brethren to that guileful hole
Where the dead corpse of Bassianus lay;
I wrote the letter that thy father found
And hid the gold within that letter mention'd,
Confederate with the Queen and her two sons;
And what not done, that thou hast cause to rue,
Wherein I had no stroke of mischief in it?
I play'd the cheater for thy father's hand,
And, when I had it, drew myself apart
And almost broke my heart with extreme laughter.
I pried me through the crevice of a wall
When, for his hand, he had his two sons' heads,
Beheld his tears, and laugh'd so heartily
That both mine eyes were rainy like to his;
And when I told the Empress of this sport,
She swounded almost at my pleasing tale,
And for my tidings gave me twenty kisses.

FIRST GOTH
What, canst thou say all this, and never blush?

78 For that because **79 bauble** fool's stick **88 luxurious** lecherous **90 To** compared to **99 codding** lustful **100 set** game **102 as . . . head** as ever went for the bear's head (in bearbaiting) **104 train'd** lured **111 cheater** (1) deceiver (2) escheater, one designated to take care of property forfeited to the crown **114 pried me** peered **119 swounded** swooned

AARON
Ay, like a black dog, as the saying is.

LUCIUS
Art thou not sorry for these heinous deeds?

AARON
Ay, that I had not done a thousand more.
Even now I curse the day—and yet, I think,
Few come within the compass of my curse—
Wherein I did not some notorious ill,
As kill a man, or else devise his death,
Ravish a maid, or plot the way to do it,
Accuse some innocent and forswear myself,
Set deadly enmity between two friends,
Make poor men's cattle break their necks,
Set fire on barns and haystalks in the night,
And bid the owners quench them with their tears.
Oft have I digg'd up dead men from their graves,
And set them upright at their dear friends' door,
Even when their sorrows almost was forgot,
And on their skins, as on the bark of trees,
Have with my knife carved in Roman letters,
"Let not your sorrow die, though I am dead."
Tut, I have done a thousand dreadful things
As willingly as one would kill a fly,
And nothing grieves me heartily indeed
But that I cannot do ten thousand more.

LUCIUS
Bring down the devil, for he must not die
So sweet a death as hanging presently.
[*Aaron is brought down.*]

AARON
If there be devils, would I were a devil,
To live and burn in everlasting fire,
So I might have your company in hell
But to torment you with my bitter tongue!

LUCIUS
Sirs, stop his mouth, and let him speak no more.
[*Aaron is gagged.*]

Enter Aemilius.

THIRD GOTH
My lord, there is a messenger from Rome
Desires to be admitted to your presence.

LUCIUS
Let him come near.
Welcome, Aemilius. What's the news from Rome?

AEMILIUS
Lord Lucius, and you princes of the Goths,
The Roman Emperor greets you all by me;
And, for he understands you are in arms,
He craves a parley at your father's house,
Willing you to demand your hostages,
And they shall be immediately deliver'd.

FIRST GOTH
What says our general?

LUCIUS
Aemilius, let the Emperor give his pledges
Unto my father and my uncle Marcus,
And we will come. March away. [*Exeunt.*]

133 haystalks haystacks **158 for** since

[SCENE II]

Enter Tamora and her two Sons, disguised.

TAMORA
Thus, in this strange and sad habiliment,
I will encounter with Andronicus,
And say I am Revenge, sent from below
To join with him and right his heinous wrongs.
Knock at his study, where, they say, he keeps
To ruminate strange plots of dire revenge.
Tell him Revenge is come to join with him,
And work confusion on his enemies.

They knock, and Titus [above] opens his study door.

TITUS
Who doth molest my contemplation?
Is it your trick to make me ope the door
That so my sad decrees may fly away,
And all my study be to no effect?
You are deceiv'd, for what I mean to do
See here in bloody lines I have set down;
And what is written shall be executed.
[*Shows a paper.*]

TAMORA
Titus, I am come to talk with thee.

TITUS
No, not a word. How can I grace my talk,
Wanting a hand to give that accord?
Thou hast the odds of me; therefore no more.

TAMORA
If thou didst know me, thou wouldst talk with me.

TITUS
I am not mad; I know thee well enough.
Witness this wretched stump, witness these crimson lines,
Witness these trenches made by grief and care,
Witness the tiring day and heavy night,
Witness all sorrow, that I know thee well
For our proud Empress, mighty Tamora.
Is not thy coming for my other hand?

TAMORA
Know, thou sad man, I am not Tamora;
She is thy enemy, and I thy friend.
I am Revenge, sent from th' infernal kingdom
To ease the gnawing vulture of thy mind,
By working wreakful vengeance on thy foes.
Come down, and welcome me to this world's light;
Confer with me of murder and of death.
There's not a hollow cave or lurking-place,
No vast obscurity or misty vale,
Where bloody murder or detested rape
Can couch for fear, but I will find them out,
And in their ears tell them my dreadful name,
Revenge, which makes the foul offender quake.

TITUS
Art thou Revenge? And art thou sent to me,
To be a torment to mine enemies?

TAMORA
I am. Therefore come down, and welcome me.

TITUS
Do me some service, ere I come to thee.
Lo, by thy side where Rape and Murder stands;
Now give some surance that thou art Revenge—
Stab them, or tear them on thy chariot-wheels—
And then I'll come and be thy wagoner,
And whirl along with thee about the globe.
Provide thee two proper palfreys, black as jet,
To hale thy vengeful wagon swift away,
And find out murd'rers in their guilty caves;
And when thy car is loaden with their heads,
I will dismount, and by thy wagon-wheel
Trot, like a servile footman, all day long,
Even from Hyperion's rising in the east
Until his very downfall in the sea;
And day by day I'll do this heavy task,
So thou destroy Rapine and Murder there.

TAMORA
These are my ministers, and come with me.

TITUS
Are they thy ministers? What are they call'd?

TAMORA
Rape and Murder, therefore called so
'Cause they take vengeance of such kind of men.

TITUS
Good Lord, how like the Empress' sons they are,
And you, the Empress! But we worldly men
Have miserable, mad, mistaking eyes.
O sweet Revenge, now do I come to thee,
And, if one arm's embracement will content thee,
I will embrace thee in it by and by. [*Exit above.*]

TAMORA
This closing with him fits his lunacy.
Whate'er I forge to feed his brain-sick humors,
Do you uphold and maintain in your speeches,
For now he firmly takes me for Revenge;
And, being credulous in this mad thought,
I'll make him send for Lucius his son,
And, whilst I at a banquet hold him sure,
I'll find some cunning practice out of hand
To scatter and disperse the giddy Goths,
Or, at the least, make them his enemies.
See, here he comes, and I must ply my theme.

[*Enter Titus below.*]

TITUS
Long have I been forlorn, and all for thee.
Welcome, dread Fury, to my woeful house.
Rapine and Murder, you are welcome too.
How like the Empress and her sons you are!
Well are you fitted, had you but a Moor.

V.ii. Location: Rome. The court of Titus' house.
1 sad habiliment somber garments **5 keeps** dwells **11 sad decrees** serious resolves **18 Wanting . . . accord** lacking a hand to provide suitable gesture by way of support **19 odds of** advantage over **23 trenches** i.e., wrinkles **38 couch** lie hidden

46 surance assurance **50 proper** excellent, handsome. **palfreys** horses **53 car** chariot **56 Hyperion's** the sun god's **59 So** provided that **63 of** upon **65 worldly** mortal **70 closing** agreeing **71 forge** invent. **humors** moods, whims **77 practice** plot. **out of hand** on the spur of the moment

Could not all hell afford you such a devil?
For well I wot the Empress never wags 87
But in her company there is a Moor;
And, would you represent our queen aright,
It were convenient you had such a devil. 90
But welcome, as you are. What shall we do?

TAMORA
What wouldst thou have us do, Andronicus?

DEMETRIUS
Show me a murderer, I'll deal with him.

CHIRON
Show me a villain that hath done a rape,
And I am sent to be reveng'd on him.

TAMORA
Show me a thousand that hath done thee wrong,
And I will be revenged on them all.

TITUS [*To one son*]
Look round about the wicked streets of Rome,
And when thou find'st a man that's like thyself,
Good Murder, stab him; he's a murderer.
[*To the other.*] Go thou with him, and when it is
thy hap 101
To find another that is like to thee,
Good Rapine, stab him; he is a ravisher.
[*To Tamora.*] Go thou with them, and in the
Emperor's court
There is a queen, attended by a Moor;
Well shalt thou know her by thine own proportion,
For up and down she doth resemble thee. 107
I pray thee, do on them some violent death;
They have been violent to me and mine.

TAMORA
Well hast thou lesson'd us; this shall we do.
But would it please thee, good Andronicus,
To send for Lucius, thy thrice-valiant son,
Who leads towards Rome a band of warlike Goths,
And bid him come and banquet at thy house,
When he is here, even at thy solemn feast, 115
I will bring in the Empress and her sons,
The Emperor himself, and all thy foes,
And at thy mercy shall they stoop and kneel,
And on them shalt thou ease thy angry heart.
What says Andronicus to this device?

TITUS
Marcus, my brother! 'Tis sad Titus calls.

Enter Marcus.

Go, gentle Marcus, to thy nephew Lucius;
Thou shalt inquire him out among the Goths.
Bid him repair to me, and bring with him 124
Some of the chiefest princes of the Goths.
Bid him encamp his soldiers where they are.
Tell him the Emperor and the Empress too
Feast at my house, and he shall feast with them.
This do thou for my love; and so let him,
As he regards his aged father's life.

MARCUS
This will I do, and soon return again. [*Exit.*]

TAMORA
Now will I hence about thy business,
And take my ministers along with me.

TITUS
Nay, nay, let Rape and Murder stay with me,
Or else I'll call my brother back again,
And cleave to no revenge but Lucius.

TAMORA [*Aside to her sons*]
What say you, boys? Will you abide with him,
Whiles I go tell my lord the Emperor
How I have govern'd our determin'd jest? 139
Yield to his humor, smooth and speak him fair, 140
And tarry with him till I turn again. 141

TITUS [*Aside*]
I know them all, though they suppose me mad,
And will o'erreach them in their own devices—
A pair of cursed hell-hounds and their dam!

DEMETRIUS
Madam, depart at pleasure, leave us here.

TAMORA
Farewell, Andronicus. Revenge now goes
To lay a complot to betray thy foes. 147

TITUS
I know thou dost; and, sweet Revenge, farewell.
[*Exit Tamora.*]

CHIRON
Tell us, old man, how shall we be employ'd?

TITUS
Tut, I have work enough for you to do.
Publius, come hither! Caius, and Valentine!

[*Enter Publius, Caius, and Valentine.*]

PUBLIUS
What is your will?

TITUS
Know you these two?

PUBLIUS
The Empress' sons, I take them, Chiron and
Demetrius.

TITUS
Fie, Publius, fie! Thou art too much deceiv'd.
The one is Murder, and Rape is the other's name;
And therefore bind them, gentle Publius.
Caius and Valentine, lay hands on them.
Oft have you heard me wish for such an hour,
And now I find it; therefore bind them sure, 160
And stop their mouths, if they begin to cry. [*Exit.*]
[*Publius, etc., lay hold on Chiron and Demetrius.*]

CHIRON
Villains, forbear! We are the Empress' sons.

PUBLIUS
And therefore do we what we are commanded.
Stop close their mouths, let them not speak a word.
[*They gag and bind the two sons.*]
Is he sure bound? Look that you bind them fast.

Enter Titus Andronicus with a knife, and Lavinia with a basin.

87 wags moves about **90 were convenient** would be fitting **101 hap** chance **107 up and down** i.e., from top to toe **115 solemn** stately **124 repair** come

139 govern'd . . . jest managed the jest we determined on **140 smooth . . . fair** flatter and humor him **141 turn** return **147 complot** conspiracy

TITUS

Come, come, Lavinia. Look, thy foes are bound.
Sirs, stop their mouths, let them not speak to me,
But let them hear what fearful words I utter.
O villains, Chiron and Demetrius!
Here stands the spring whom you have stain'd with mud,
This goodly summer with your winter mix'd.
You kill'd her husband, and for that vile fault
Two of her brothers were condemn'd to death,
My hand cut off and made a merry jest;
Both her sweet hands, her tongue, and that more dear
Than hands or tongue, her spotless chastity,
Inhuman traitors, you constrain'd and forc'd.
What would you say, if I should let you speak?
Villains, for shame you could not beg for grace.
Hark, wretches, how I mean to martyr you.
This one hand yet is left to cut your throats,
Whiles that Lavinia 'tween her stumps doth hold
The basin that receives your guilty blood.
You know your mother means to feast with me,
And calls herself Revenge, and thinks me mad.
Hark, villains, I will grind your bones to dust
And with your blood and it I'll make a paste,
And of the paste a coffin I will rear 188
And make two pasties of your shameful heads, 189
And bid that strumpet, your unhallowed dam,
Like to the earth swallow her own increase. 191
This is the feast that I have bid her to,
And this the banquet she shall surfeit on;
For worse than Philomel you us'd my daughter,
And worse than Progne I will be reveng'd. 195
And now prepare your throats. Lavinia, come,

He cuts their throats.

Receive the blood, and when that they are dead,
Let me go grind their bones to powder small
And with this hateful liquor temper it; 199
And in that paste let their vile heads be bak'd.
Come, come, be everyone officious 201
To make this banquet, which I wish may prove
More stern and bloody than the Centaurs' feast. 203
So, now bring them in, for I'll play the cook,
And see them ready against their mother comes. 205

Exeunt [bearing the dead bodies].

[SCENE III]

Enter Lucius, Marcus, and the Goths [with Aaron prisoner, and an Attendant bearing his Child].

LUCIUS

Uncle Marcus, since 'tis my father's mind
That I repair to Rome, I am content. 2

FIRST GOTH

And ours with thine, befall what fortune will. 3

LUCIUS

Good uncle, take you in this barbarous Moor,
This ravenous tiger, this accursed devil.
Let him receive no sust'nance. Fetter him,
Till he be brought unto the Empress' face,
For testimony of her foul proceedings.
And see the ambush of our friends be strong;
I fear the Emperor means no good to us.

AARON

Some devil whisper curses in my ear,
And prompt me, that my tongue may utter forth
The venomous malice of my swelling heart!

LUCIUS

Away, inhuman dog, unhallowed slave!
Sirs, help our uncle to convey him in.

[Exeunt Goths, with Aaron.]
Sound trumpets [within].

The trumpets show the Emperor is at hand.

Enter Emperor [Saturninus] and Empress [Tamora], with [Aemilius,] Tribunes, [Senators], and others.

SATURNINUS

What, hath the firmament moe suns than one? 17

LUCIUS

What boots it thee to call thyself a sun? 18

MARCUS

Rome's Emperor, and nephew, break the parle; 19
These quarrels must be quietly debated.
The feast is ready which the careful Titus 21
Hath ordain'd to an honorable end,
For peace, for love, for league, and good to Rome.
Please you therefore draw nigh, and take your places.

SATURNINUS

Marcus, we will.

[A table is brought in. The company sit down.]

Trumpets sounding, enter Titus like a cook, placing the dishes, and Lavinia with a veil over her face, [young Lucius, and others].

TITUS

Welcome, my gracious lord; welcome, dread queen;
Welcome, ye warlike Goths; welcome, Lucius;
And welcome, all. Although the cheer be poor, 28
'Twill fill your stomachs; please you eat of it.

SATURNINUS

Why art thou thus attir'd, Andronicus?

TITUS

Because I would be sure to have all well,
To entertain your Highness and your Empress.

TAMORA

We are beholding to you, good Andronicus.

188 coffin pie crust **189 pasties** meat pie **191 increase** offspring **195 worse than Progne** (An allusion to Procne's revenge on Tereus for raping her sister Philomel; cf. II.iii.43, note. She killed her son Itys and served his flesh to Tereus, his father.) **199 temper** blend, mix **201 officious** busy **203 Centaurs' feast** i.e., the wedding feast of Pirithous and Hippodamia to which the Lapithae invited the Centaurs, fabulous creatures, half men and half horses. (The Centaurs attempted to carry off the women but were slaughtered by their hosts.) **205 against** by the time that

V.iii. Location: Rome. Court of Titus' house.

2 repair return **3 ours with thine** i.e., our intentions are in agreement with yours **17 moe** more **18 boots** avails **19 break the parle** cease the dispute **21 careful** full of sorrows **28 cheer** fare

TITUS
An if your Highness knew my heart, you were.
My lord the Emperor, resolve me this:
Was it well done of rash Virginius
To slay his daughter with his own right hand,
Because she was enforc'd, stain'd, and deflow'r'd?

SATURNINUS
It was, Andronicus.

TITUS
Your reason, mighty lord?

SATURNINUS
Because the girl should not survive her shame,
And by her presence still renew his sorrows.

TITUS
A reason mighty, strong, and effectual;
A pattern, precedent, and lively warrant,
For me, most wretched, to perform the like.
Die, die, Lavinia, and thy shame with thee;
[*Kills Lavinia.*]
And, with thy shame, thy father's sorrow die!

SATURNINUS
What hast thou done, unnatural and unkind?

TITUS
Kill'd her for whom my tears have made me blind.
I am as woeful as Virginius was,
And have a thousand times more cause than he
To do this outrage; and it now is done.

SATURNINUS
What, was she ravish'd? Tell who did the deed.

TITUS
Will 't please you eat? Will 't please your Highness feed?

TAMORA
Why hast thou slain thine only daughter thus?

TITUS
Not I; 'twas Chiron and Demetrius.
They ravish'd her, and cut away her tongue;
And they, 'twas they, that did her all this wrong.

SATURNINUS
Go fetch them hither to us presently.

TITUS
Why, there they are, both baked in this pie,
Whereof their mother daintily hath fed,
Eating the flesh that she herself hath bred.
'Tis true, 'tis true; witness my knife's sharp point.
He stabs the Empress.

SATURNINUS
Die, frantic wretch, for this accursed deed!
[*Kills Titus.*]

LUCIUS
Can the son's eye behold his father bleed?
There's meed for meed, death for a deadly deed!
[*Kills Saturninus. A great tumult.*]

MARCUS
You sad-fac'd men, people and sons of Rome,
By uproars sever'd, as a flight of fowl
Scatter'd by winds and high tempestuous gusts,
O, let me teach you how to knit again
This scattered corn into one mutual sheaf,
These broken limbs again into one body.

AEMILIUS
Let Rome herself be bane unto herself,
And she whom mighty kingdoms cur'sy to,
Like a forlorn and desperate castaway,
Do shameful execution on herself,
But if my frosty signs and chaps of age,
Grave witnesses of true experience,
Cannot induce you to attend my words.
[*To Lucius.*] Speak, Rome's dear friend, as erst our ancestor,
When with his solemn tongue he did discourse
To love-sick Dido's sad attending ear
The story of that baleful burning night
When subtle Greeks surpris'd King Priam's Troy.
Tell us what Sinon hath bewitch'd our ears,
Or who hath brought the fatal engine in
That gives our Troy, our Rome, the civil wound.
My heart is not compact of flint nor steel,
Nor can I utter all our bitter grief,
But floods of tears will drown my oratory,
And break my utt'rance, even in the time
When it should move ye to attend me most,
And force you to commiseration.
Here's Rome's young captain; let him tell the tale,
While I stand by and weep to hear him speak.

LUCIUS
Then, gracious auditory, be it known to you,
That Chiron and the damn'd Demetrius
Were they that murd'red our Emperor's brother,
And they it were that ravished our sister.
For their fell faults our brothers were beheaded;
Our father's tears despis'd, and basely cozen'd
Of that true hand that fought Rome's quarrel out
And sent her enemies unto the grave;
Lastly, myself unkindly banished,
The gates shut on me, and turn'd weeping out
To beg relief among Rome's enemies,
Who drown'd their enmity in my true tears
And op'd their arms to embrace me as a friend.
I am the turned forth, be it known to you,
That have preserv'd her welfare in my blood
And from her bosom took the enemy's point,
Sheathing the steel in my advent'rous body.
Alas, you know I am no vaunter, I;
My scars can witness, dumb although they are,
That my report is just and full of truth.
But, soft, methinks I do digress too much,
Citing my worthless praise. O, pardon me,
For when no friends are by, men praise themselves.

35 resolve answer **36 Virginius** Roman centurion who killed his daughter to save her from rape (rather than killing her afterwards to preserve her honor, as adapted here to accord with Titus' story) **48 unkind** unnatural **66 meed for meed** measure for measure **66 s.d. tumult** (Many editors speculate that Lucius, Marcus, and others go up into the balcony at this point, returning to the main stage at l. 145.)

71 corn grain **73 bane** poison, death **77 But if** if. **frosty signs** i.e., white hair. **chaps** wrinkles **80 erst** formerly, once. **our ancestor** i.e., Aeneas **82 sad** serious **85 Sinon** the crafty Greek who persuaded the Trojans to take the wooden horse (the *fatal engine*) into their city **87 civil** incurred in civil strife **88 compact** composed **100 fell** savage, cruel **101 cozen'd** cheated **104 unkindly** unnaturally **109 turned forth** exile

MARCUS
Now is my turn to speak. Behold the child:
[*Pointing to the Child in the arms of an Attendant.*]
Of this was Tamora delivered;
The issue of an irreligious Moor,
Chief architect and plotter of these woes.
The villain is alive in Titus' house,
And as he is to witness, this is true.
Now judge what cause had Titus to revenge
These wrongs, unspeakable, past patience,
Or more than any living man could bear.
Now have you heard the truth; what say you, Romans?
Have we done aught amiss, show us wherein,
And, from the place where you behold us pleading,
The poor remainder of Andronici
Will, hand in hand, all headlong hurl ourselves,
And on the ragged stones beat forth our souls,
And make a mutual closure of our house.
Speak, Romans, speak; and if you say we shall,
Lo, hand in hand, Lucius and I will fall.

AEMILIUS
Come, come, thou reverend man of Rome,
And bring our Emperor gently in thy hand,
Lucius our Emperor; for well I know
The common voice do cry it shall be so.

ALL
Lucius, all hail, Rome's royal Emperor!

MARCUS [*To Attendants*]
Go, go into old Titus' sorrowful house,
And hither hale that misbelieving Moor
To be adjudg'd some direful slaught'ring death,
As punishment for his most wicked life.
[*Exeunt Attendants.*]

ALL
Lucius, all hail, Rome's gracious governor!

LUCIUS
Thanks, gentle Romans. May I govern so
To heal Rome's harms, and wipe away her woe!
But, gentle people, give me aim awhile,
For nature puts me to a heavy task.
Stand all aloof, but, uncle, draw you near,
To shed obsequious tears upon this trunk.
O, take this warm kiss on thy pale cold lips,
[*Kisses Titus.*]
These sorrowful drops upon thy blood-stain'd face,
The last true duties of thy noble son!

MARCUS
Tear for tear, and loving kiss for kiss,
Thy brother Marcus tenders on thy lips.
[*Kisses Titus.*]
O, were the sum of these that I should pay
Countless and infinite, yet would I pay them!

LUCIUS
Come hither, boy. Come, come, and learn of us
To melt in showers. Thy grandsire lov'd thee well.
Many a time he danc'd thee on his knee,
Sung thee asleep, his loving breast thy pillow;
Many a story hath he told to thee,
And bid thee bear his pretty tales in mind,
And talk of them when he was dead and gone.

MARCUS
How many thousand times hath these poor lips,
When they were living, warm'd themselves on thine!
Oh now, sweet boy, give them their latest kiss.
Bid him farewell; commit him to the grave;
Do them that kindness and take leave of them.

BOY
O grandsire, grandsire! Ev'n with all my heart
Would I were dead, so you did live again!
[*Kisses Titus.*]
O Lord, I cannot speak to him for weeping;
My tears will choke me, if I ope my mouth.

[*Enter Attendants with Aaron.*]

AEMILIUS
You sad Andronici, have done with woes.
Give sentence on this execrable wretch
That hath been breeder of these dire events.

LUCIUS
Set him breast-deep in earth, and famish him;
There let him stand, and rave, and cry for food.
If any one relieves or pities him,
For the offense he dies. This is our doom.
Some stay to see him fast'ned in the earth.

AARON
Ah, why should wrath be mute, and fury dumb?
I am no baby, I, that with base prayers
I should repent the evils I have done.
Ten thousand worse than ever yet I did
Would I perform, if I might have my will.
If one good deed in all my life I did,
I do repent it from my very soul.

LUCIUS
Some loving friends convey the Emperor hence,
And give him burial in his father's grave.
My father and Lavinia shall forthwith
Be closed in our household's monument.
As for that ravenous tiger, Tamora,
No funeral rite, nor man in mourning weed,
No mournful bell shall ring her burial,
But throw her forth to beasts and birds to prey.
Her life was beastly and devoid of pity,
And, being dead, let birds on her take pity.
Exeunt, [*bearing the dead bodies*].

134 closure conclusions, death **149 give me aim** bear with me **152 obsequious** mourning

169 latest last **182 doom** decision, judgment **198 prey** prey upon **200 pity** (The Q1 text closes the play with this line. Q2 and subsequent texts add the following four lines:
See justice done on Aaron, that damn'd Moor,
By whom our heavy haps had their beginning.
Then, afterwards, to order well the state,
That like events may ne'er it ruinate.)

Romeo and Juliet

Though a tragedy, *Romeo and Juliet* is in some ways more closely comparable to Shakespeare's romantic comedies than to his other tragedies. Stylistically belonging to the years 1594–1596, it is in the lyric vein of the sonnets, *A Midsummer Night's Dream,* and *The Merchant of Venice,* all from the mid-1590's. Like them, it uses a variety of rhyme schemes (couplets, quatrians, octets, even sonnets) and revels in punning, flowery Petrarchan metaphor, and wit combat. It is separated in tone and in time from the earliest of the great tragedies, *Julius Caesar* and *Hamlet,* by almost half a decade, and, except for the experimental *Titus Andronicus,* it is Shakespeare's only tragedy (that is not also a "History") in the first decade of his career—a period devoted otherwise to romantic comedy and English history.

Like many comedies, *Romeo and Juliet* is a love story, celebrating the exquisite brief joy of youthful passion. Even its tragic ending stresses the poignancy of that brief beauty, not the bitter futility of love as in *Troilus and Cressida* or *Othello.* The tragic ending of *Romeo and Juliet* underscores the observation made by a vexed lover in *A Midsummer Night's Dream* that "The course of true love never did run smooth" (I,i). True love in *Romeo and Juliet,* as in *A Midsummer Night's Dream,* is destined to be crossed by differences in "blood" or family background, differences in age, the arbitrary choice of family or friends, or other uncontrollable catastrophes such as war, death, and sickness. Love is thus, as in *A Midsummer Night's Dream,* "momentary as a sound, Swift as a shadow, short as any dream," swallowed up by darkness; "So quick bright things come to confusion." A dominant pattern of imagery in *Romeo and Juliet* evokes a corresponding sense of suddenness and violence: fire, gunpowder, hot blood, lightning, the inconstant wind, the storm-tossed or shipwrecked vessel. Love so threatened and fragile is beautiful because it is brief. Tragic outcome therefore affirms the uniqueness and pristine quality of youthful ecstasy. The flowering and fading of a joy "too rich for use, for earth too dear" (I,v), does not condemn the unfeeling world so much as it welcomes the martyrdom of literally dying for love.

As protagonists, Romeo and Juliet lack tragic stature by any classical definition or by the medieval convention of the Fall of Princes. The lovers are not extraordinary except in their passionate attachment to one another. By birth they are respectable citizens rather than nobility. Their dilemma of parental opposition is of the domestic sort often found in comedy. Accordingly, several characters in the play partly resemble the conventional character types of Plautus or Italian neoclassical comedy: the domineering father who insists that his daughter marry according to his choice, the unwelcome rival wooer, the garrulous and bawdy nurse, and of course the lovers. The Italian *novella,* from which Shakespeare ultimately derived his plot, made use of these same types and paid little attention to the classical precept that protagonists in a tragic story ought to be persons of lofty station who are humbled through some inner flaw or *hamartia.* The story evidently began with the motif of the sleeping potion, in the fifth-century Greek romance of *Ephesiaca;* Masuccio of Salerno, in 1476, combined the narrative of the heroine's deathlike trance and seeming burial alive with that of the hero's tragic failure to receive news from the friar that she is still alive. Luigi da Porto, in his *novella* (c. 1530), set the scene at Verona, provided the names of Romeo and Giulietta for the hero and heroine, added the account of their feuding families, the Montecchi and Cappelletti, introduced the killing of Tybalt (Theobaldo), and provided other important details. Luigi's version was followed by Bandello's famous *Novelle* of 1554, which was translated into French by Pierre Boaistuau (1559). The French version became the source for Arthur Brooke's long narrative poem in English, *The Tragicall Historye of Romeus and Juliet* (1562). Brooke mentions having seen a play on the subject, but it is doubtful that Shakespeare either knew or made use of this old play. Brooke's poem was his chief and probably only source. Shakespeare has condensed Brooke's action from nine months to less than a week, greatly expanded the role of Mercutio, and given to the Nurse a warmth and humorous richness not found in the usual Italian duenna or *balia.* He has also tidied up the Friar's immorality and deleted the antipapal tone. Still, Shakespeare retains the romantic (rather than classically tragic) conception of love overwhelmed by external obstacles.

Like the romantic comedies, *Romeo and Juliet* is often funny and bawdy. Samson and Gregory in the first scene are slapstick cowards, hiding behind the law and daring to quarrel only when reinforcements arrive. The Nurse delights us with her earthy recollection of the day she weaned Juliet: the child tasting "the wormwood on the nipple Of my dug," the warm Italian sun, an earthquake, the Nurse's husband telling his lame but often-repeated bawdy joke about women falling on their backs. Mercutio employs his inventive and sardonic humor to twit Romeo for lovesickness and the Nurse for her pomposity. She in turn scolds Peter, and plagues Juliet (who is breathlessly awaiting news from Romeo) with a history of her back ailments. Mercutio and the Nurse are among Shakespeare's bawdiest characters. Their wry and salacious view of love contrasts with the nobly innocent and yet physically passionate love of Romeo and Juliet. Mercutio and the Nurse cannot take part in the play's denouement; one dies, misinterpreting Romeo's appeasement of Tybalt, and the other proves insensitive to Juliet's depth of feeling. Yet the play loses much of its funniness and vitality with the disappearance of these engaging companions.

The lovers too are at first well suited to Shakespearean romantic comedy. When we meet Romeo he is not in love with Juliet at all, despite the play's title, but is mooning over a "hard-hearted wench" (in Mercutio's words) named Rosaline. This "goddess" appropriately never appears in the play; she is almost a disembodied idea in Romeo's mind, a scornful Petrarchan beauty like Phebe in *As You Like It.* Romeo's love for her is tedious and self-pitying, like that of the conventional Petrarchan wooer in a sonnet sequence. Juliet, although not yet fourteen, must change all this by teaching him the nature of true love. She will have none of his shopworn clichés learned in the service of Rosaline, his flowery protestations and swearing by the moon, lest they prove to be love's perjuries. With her innocent candor she insists (like many heroines of the romantic comedies) on dispelling the mask of pretense that lovers too often show one another. "Capulet" and "Montague" are mere labels, not the inner self. Although Juliet would have been more coy, she confesses, had she known that Romeo was overhearing her, she will now "prove more true Than those that have more cunning to be strange." She is more practical than he in assessing danger and making plans. Later she also proves herself remarkably able to bear misfortune.

The comedy of the play's first half is, of course, overshadowed by the certainty of disaster. The opening chorus plainly warns us that the lovers will die. They are "star-cross'd," and speak of themselves as such. Romeo fears "Some consequence yet hanging in the stars" when he reluctantly goes to the Capulets' feast (I,iv); after he has slain Tybalt, he cries "O, I am fortune's fool!" (III,i); and at the news of Juliet's supposed death he proclaims "Then I defy you, stars!" (V,i). Yet in what sense are Romeo and Juliet "star-cross'd"? The concept is deliberately broad in this play, encompassing many factors such as hatred, bumbling, bad luck, and simple lack of awareness.

The first scene presents feuding as a major cause in the tragedy. The quarrel between the two families is so ancient that the original motives are no longer even discussed. Inspired by the "fiery" Tybalt, factionalism pursues its mindless course despite the efforts of the Prince to end it. Although the elders of both families talk of peace, they call for their swords quickly enough when a fray begins. Still, this senseless hatred does not lead to tragedy until its effects are fatally complicated through misunderstanding. With poignant irony, good intentions are repeatedly undermined by lack of knowledge. We can see why Juliet does not tell her family of her secret marriage with a presumably hated Montague, but in fact Capulet has accepted Romeo as a guest in his house, praising him as a "virtuous and well govern'd youth." For all his dictatorial ways, and the manifest advantages he sees in marrying his daughter to an aristocrat, Capulet would never knowingly force his daughter into bigamy. Not knowing, he and his wife can only interpret her refusal to marry Paris as caprice. Count Paris himself is victim of this tragedy of unawareness. He is an eminently suitable wooer for Juliet, rich and nobly born yet considerate, peace-loving, and deeply fond of Juliet (as he shows by his private and sincere grief at her tomb). Certainly he would never intentionally woo a married young woman. Not knowing, he plays the unattractive role of the rival wooer and dies for it. Similarly, Mercutio cannot understand Romeo's seemingly craven behavior toward Tybalt, and so begins the duel that leads to Romeo's banishment. The final scene, with Friar Laurence's retelling of the story, allows us to see the survivors confronted with what they have all unknowingly done.

Chance or "accident" plays a role of equal importance to that of hatred and unawareness. An outbreak of the plague prevents Friar John from conveying Friar Laurence's letter to Romeo at Mantua. Friar Laurence, going hurriedly to the Capulets' tomb, arrives in time for her awakening but some minutes after Romeo has killed Paris and taken poison. Juliet awakens only moments later. The Watch comes just too late to prevent her suicide. As Friar Laurence laments, "what an unkind hour Is guilty of this lamentable chance!" (V,iii). Earlier, Capulet's decision to move the wedding date up one day has crucially affected the timing. Human miscalculation contributes also to the catastrophe: Mercutio is killed under Romeo's arm, and Friar Laurence wonders unhappily if any of his complicated plans "Miscarried by my fault." Even character and human decision play a part in this tragedy, for Romeo should not have dueled with Tybalt no matter what the provocation. To blame the tragedy in Aristotelian fashion on his and Juliet's impulsiveness is, however, an argument that ignores too much of the rest of the play.

Instead, the ending of the play brings a pattern out of the seeming welter of mistakes and animosities. "A greater power than we can contradict Hath thwarted our intents," says Friar Laurence, suggesting that the seeming bad luck of the delayed letter was in fact the intent of a mysterious higher intelligence. Prince Escalus too finds a necessary meaning in tragic event. "See what a scourge is laid upon your hate," he admonishes the Montagues and Capulets, "That heaven finds means to kill your joys with love." Romeo and Juliet are "Poor sacrifices of our enmity." As the Prologue had foretold, their deaths will "bury their parents' strife." The families' feud is a stubborn evil force "which, but their children's end, nought could remove." Order is preciously restored; the price is great, but the sacrifice nonetheless confirms a sense of larger intention in what had appeared to be hatred and misfortune. Throughout the play, love and hate are interrelated opposites, yoked through the rhetorical device of oxymoron or inherent contradiction. Romeo apostrophizes "O brawling love, O loving hate," and Juliet later echoes his words: "My only love sprung from my only hate." This paradox expresses a conflict in man as in the universe itself. "Two such opposed kings encamp them still In man as well as herbs," says Friar Laurence, "grace and rude will." Hatred is a condition of our corrupted wills, of our fall from grace, and it attempts to destroy what is gracious in mankind. In this cosmic strife, love must pay the sacrifice, as Romeo and Juliet do with their lives; but because their deaths are finally perceived as the cost of so much hatred, the two families learn to be chastened by their collective guilt and resolve henceforth to be worthy of the sacrifice.

Structurally, *Romeo and Juliet* gives considerable prominence to the feuding of the two families. Public scenes occur at key points, at beginning, middle, and end (I,i, III,i, and V,iii), and each such scene concerns violence and its consequences. The play begins with a brawl. Tybalt is a baleful presence in I,i and III,i, implacably bent on vengeance. The three public scenes are alike too in that they bring into confrontation the entire families of Capulets and Montagues, who call for swords and demand reprisal from the state for what they themselves have set in motion. Prince Escalus dominates these three public scenes. He must offer judgment in each, giving the families fair warning, then exiling Romeo for Tybalt's death, and finally counseling the families on the meaning of their collective tragedy. He is a spokesman for public order ("Mercy but murders, pardoning those that kill") and is indeed something of a *raisonneur* for the play as a whole; being a Prince, he is above the family conflict though affected by it. On stage, his role is sometimes doubled with that of the Chorus. To him is given the final speech promising both punishment and pardon, and it is he who sums up the paradoxical interdependence of love and hate. Although the morning after the catastrophe brings with it "glooming" and sorrow, it also brings peace. Escalus is spokesman for the restored order through which the families and we are reconciled to what has occurred.

In good part, the public scenes of the play serve to frame the love plot and the increasing isolation of the separated lovers, but these public scenes have a function of their own to the extent that the tragedy has touched and altered everyone. The final tableau is not the kiss of the dying lovers but the handclasp of the reconciled fathers. The long last public ceremonial is important because, although the private catastrophe of the lovers is unalterably complete, recognition occurs only when the whole story is known by all. This recognition is not that of the protagonists, as in the Aristotelian conception of recognition, nor does it accompany the reversal of the love tragedy which has already occurred, in Romeo's banishment and the lovers' deaths. To observe this is not to point out a structural flaw, but rather to stress the dual focus of the tragedy on the lovers and on all Verona. The city itself is a kind of protagonist, suffering through its own violence and coming at last to the sad comfort that wisdom brings.

Romeo and Juliet

[*Dramatis Personae*

ESCALUS, *Prince of Verona.*
PARIS, *a young nobleman, kinsman to the Prince.*
MONTAGUE, } *heads of two houses at variance*
CAPULET, } *with each other.*
An OLD MAN, *cousin to Capulet.*
ROMEO, *son to Montague.*
MERCUTIO, *kinsman to the Prince, and friend to Romeo.*
BENVOLIO, *nephew to Montague, and friend to Romeo.*
TYBALT, *nephew to Capulet's Wife.*
PETRUCHIO, *of the house of Capulet.*
FRIAR LAURENCE, } *Franciscans.*
FRIAR JOHN, }
BALTHASAR, *servant to Romeo.*
SAMSON, }
GREGORY, } *servants to Capulet.*
CLOWN, }
PETER, *servant to Juliet's nurse.*
ABRAHAM, *servant to Montague.*
APOTHECARY.
Three MUSICIANS.
PAGE *to Paris; another* PAGE; *an* OFFICER.

MONTAGUE'S WIFE.
CAPULET'S WIFE.
JULIET, *daughter to Capulet.*
NURSE *to Juliet, called* ANGELICA.

CITIZENS *of Verona; several* MEN *and* WOMEN, *relations to both houses;* MASKERS, GUARDS, WATCHMEN, SERVINGMEN, *and* ATTENDANTS.

CHORUS.

SCENE: *Verona: Mantua.*]

THE PROLOGUE

[*Enter Chorus.*]

CHORUS
Two households, both alike in dignity,
In fair Verona, where we lay our scene,
From ancient grudge break to new mutiny,
Where civil blood makes civil hands unclean.
From forth the fatal loins of these two foes
A pair of star-cross'd lovers take their life;
Whose misadventur'd piteous overthrows
Doth with their death bury their parents' strife.
The fearful passage of their death-mark'd love,
And the continuance of their parents' rage
Which, but their children's end, nought could remove,
Is now the two hours' traffic of our stage;
The which if you with patient ears attend,
What here shall miss, our toil shall strive to mend.
[*Exit.*]

[ACT I • SCENE I]

Enter Samson and Gregory, with swords and bucklers, of the house of Capulet.

SAMSON Gregory, on my word, we'll not carry coals.
GREGORY No, for then we should be colliers.
SAMSON I mean, an we be in choler, we'll draw.
GREGORY Ay, while you live, draw your neck out of collar.
SAMSON I strike quickly, being mov'd.
GREGORY But thou art not quickly mov'd to strike.
SAMSON A dog of the house of Montague moves me.
GREGORY To move is to stir, and to be valiant is to stand. Therefore, if thou art mov'd, thou runn'st away.
SAMSON A dog of that house shall move me to stand. I will take the wall of any man or maid of Montague's.
GREGORY That shows thee a weak slave, for the weakest goes to the wall.
SAMSON 'Tis true; and therefore women, being the weaker vessels, are ever thrust to the wall. Therefore I will push Montague's men from the wall, and thrust his maids to the wall.
GREGORY The quarrel is between our masters and us their men.
SAMSON 'Tis all one. I will show myself a tyrant: when I have fought with the men, I will be civil with the maids—I will cut off their heads.
GREGORY The heads of the maids?
SAMSON Ay, the heads of the maids, or their maidenheads. Take it in what sense thou wilt.
GREGORY They must take it in sense that feel it.
SAMSON Me they shall feel while I am able to stand, and 'tis known I am a pretty piece of flesh.
GREGORY 'Tis well thou art not fish; if thou hadst, thou

Prologue.
3 mutiny strife, discord **4 civil . . . civil** of civic strife . . . citizens' (with a suggestion of *civility*)

6 star-cross'd thwarted by destiny, by adverse stars **9 passage** progress **12 traffic** business **14 miss** i.e., miss the mark

I.i. Location: Verona. A public place.
1 carry coals i.e., endure insults **3 an** if. **choler** anger (produced by one of the four humors). **draw** draw swords **5 collar** i.e., hangman's noose (with pun on *choler*) **6 mov'd** i.e., to anger (with pun in next line) **8 moves** incites **10 stand** i.e., stand one's ground **12 take the wall** i.e., take the cleaner side of the walk nearest the wall, thus forcing others out into the gutter **13–14 the weakest . . . wall** (A proverb expressing the idea that the weakest are always forced to give way.) **16 thrust to the wall** (with bawdy suggestion) **19–20 between . . . men** i.e., between the males of one household and the males of the other household; the women would not fight **26 what sense** whatever meaning **27 They . . . feel it** i.e., it is the maids who must receive by way of physical sensation (*sense*) what I have to offer, because they are the ones who can feel it **28 stand** (With bawdy suggestion, continued in the next few lines in *draw thy tool* and *my naked weapon is out.*) **29–30 flesh . . . fish** (Refers to the proverbial phrase, "neither fish nor flesh.")

hadst been poor John. Draw thy tool. Here comes of the house of Montagues.

Enter two other Servingmen [Abraham and Balthasar].

SAMSON My naked weapon is out. Quarrel, I will back thee.

GREGORY How? Turn thy back and run?

SAMSON Fear me not.

GREGORY No, marry. I fear thee!

SAMSON Let us take the law of our sides; let them begin.

GREGORY I will frown as I pass by, and let them take it as they list.

SAMSON Nay, as they dare. I will bite my thumb at them, which is disgrace to them, if they bear it.

[Samson makes taunting gestures.]

ABRAHAM Do you bite your thumb at us, sir?

SAMSON I do bite my thumb, sir.

ABRAHAM Do you bite your thumb at us, sir?

SAMSON *[Aside to Gregory]* Is the law of our side if I say ay?

GREGORY *[Aside to Samson]* No.

SAMSON No, sir, I do not bite my thumb at you, sir, but I bite my thumb, sir.

GREGORY Do you quarrel, sir?

ABRAHAM Quarrel, sir? No, sir.

SAMSON But if you do, sir, I am for you. I serve as good a man as you.

ABRAHAM No better.

SAMSON Well, sir.

Enter Benvolio.

GREGORY *[To Samson]* Say "better." Here comes one of my master's kinsmen.

SAMSON Yes, better, sir.

ABRAHAM You lie.

SAMSON Draw, if you be men. Gregory, remember thy washing blow. *They fight.*

BENVOLIO
Part, fools!
Put up your swords; you know not what you do.

Enter Tybalt [with sword drawn].

TYBALT
What, art thou drawn among these heartless hinds?
Turn thee, Benvolio, look upon thy death.

BENVOLIO
I do but keep the peace. Put up thy sword,
Or manage it to part these men with me.

TYBALT
What, drawn, and talk of peace? I hate the word,
As I hate hell, all Montagues, and thee.
Have at thee, coward! *[They fight.]*

Enter three or four Citizens with clubs or partisans.

CITIZENS
Clubs, bills, and partisans! Strike! Beat them down!
Down with the Capulets! Down with the
Montagues!

Enter old Capulet in his gown, and his Wife.

CAPULET
What noise is this? Give me my long sword, ho!

CAPULET'S WIFE
A crutch, a crutch! Why call you for a sword?

CAPULET
My sword, I say! Old Montague is come,
And flourishes his blade in spite of me.

Enter old Montague and his Wife.

MONTAGUE
Thou villain Capulet!—Hold me not, let me go.

MONTAGUE'S WIFE
Thou shalt not stir one foot to seek a foe.

Enter Prince Escalus, with his train.

PRINCE
Rebellious subjects, enemies to peace,
Profaners of this neighbor-stained steel—
Will they not hear? What, ho! You men, you beasts,
That quench the fire of your pernicious rage
With purple fountains issuing from your veins,
On pain of torture, from those bloody hands
Throw your mistempered weapons to the ground,
And hear the sentence of your moved prince.
Three civil brawls, bred of an airy word,
By thee, old Capulet, and Montague,
Have thrice disturb'd the quiet of our streets,
And made Verona's ancient citizens
Cast by their grave beseeming ornaments
To wield old partisans, in hands as old,
Cank'red with peace, to part your cank'red hate.
If ever you disturb our streets again,
Your lives shall pay the forfeit of the peace.
For this time, all the rest depart away.
You, Capulet, shall go along with me,
And, Montague, come you this afternoon,
To know our farther pleasure in this case,
To old Free-town, our common judgment-place.
Once more, on pain of death, all men depart.
Exeunt [all but Montague, Montague's Wife, and Benvolio].

MONTAGUE
Who set this ancient quarrel new abroach?
Speak, nephew, were you by when it began?

BENVOLIO
Here were the servants of your adversary,
And yours, close fighting ere I did approach.
I drew to part them. In the instant came

31 poor John hake salted and dried—a poor kind of food **36 Fear** mistrust. (But Gregory deliberately misunderstands in the next line, saying in effect, No indeed, do you think I'd be afraid of you?) **38 take the law of** have the law on **41 list** please **42 bite my thumb** i.e., make an insulting gesture **63 washing** swashing, crushing **66 heartless hinds** cowardly menials **72 Have at thee** i.e., on guard, here I come

73 Clubs rallying cry, summoning apprentices with their clubs. **bills** long-handled spears with hooked blades. **partisans** long-handled spears **78 spite** defiance, despite **82 Profaners . . . steel** i.e., you who profane your weapons by staining them with neighbors' blood **87 mistempered** (1) having been tempered, or hardened, to a wrong use (2) malignant, angry **89 airy** i.e., merely a breath, trivial **93 grave beseeming ornaments** i.e., staffs and other appurtenances suited to wise old age **95 Cank'red . . . cank'red** corroded . . . malignant **102 Free-town** (Brooke's translation in his poem *Romeus and Juliet* of *Villa Franca,* as found in the Italian story.) **104 set . . . abroach** reopened this old quarrel, set it flowing

y Tybalt, with his sword prepar'd,
uch, as he breath'd defiance to my ears,
He swung about his head and cut the winds,
Who nothing hurt withal hiss'd him in scorn.
While we were interchanging thrusts and blows,
Came more and more and fought on part and part,
Till the Prince came, who parted either part.

MONTAGUE'S WIFE
O, where is Romeo? Saw you him today?
Right glad I am he was not at this fray.

BENVOLIO
Madam, an hour before the worship'd sun
Peer'd forth the golden window of the east,
A troubled mind drave me to walk abroad,
Where, underneath the grove of sycamore
That westward rooteth from this city side,
So early walking did I see your son.
Towards him I made, but he was ware of me
And stole into the covert of the wood.
I, measuring his affections by my own,
Which then most sought where most might not be found,
Being one too many by my weary self,
Pursu'd my humor, not pursuing his,
And gladly shunn'd who gladly fled from me.

MONTAGUE
Many a morning hath he there been seen,
With tears augmenting the fresh morning's dew,
Adding to clouds more clouds with his deep sighs;
But all so soon as the all-cheering sun
Should in the farthest east begin to draw
The shady curtains from Aurora's bed,
Away from light steals home my heavy son,
And private in his chamber pens himself,
Shuts up his windows, locks fair daylight out,
And makes himself an artificial night.
Black and portentous must this humor prove,
Unless good counsel may the cause remove.

BENVOLIO
My noble uncle, do you know the cause?

MONTAGUE
I neither know it nor can learn of him.

BENVOLIO
Have you importun'd him by any means?

MONTAGUE
Both by myself and many other friends,
But he, his own affections' counselor,
Is to himself—I will not say how true—
But to himself so secret and so close,
So far from sounding and discovery,
As is the bud bit with an envious worm,
Ere he can spread his sweet leaves to the air
Or dedicate his beauty to the sun.
Could we but learn from whence his sorrows grow,
We would as willingly give cure as know.

Enter Romeo.

BENVOLIO
See where he comes. So please you, step aside.
I'll know his grievance, or be much denied.

MONTAGUE
I would thou wert so happy by thy stay
To hear true shrift. Come, madam, let's away.
Exeunt [Montague and Wife].

BENVOLIO
Good morrow, cousin.

ROMEO
Is the day so young?

BENVOLIO
But new struck nine.

ROMEO
Ay me! Sad hours seem long.
Was that my father that went hence so fast?

BENVOLIO
It was. What sadness lengthens Romeo's hours?

ROMEO
Not having that which, having, makes them short.

BENVOLIO
In love?

ROMEO
Out—

BENVOLIO
Of love?

ROMEO
Out of her favor, where I am in love.

BENVOLIO
Alas, that love, so gentle in his view,
Should be so tyrannous and rough in proof!

ROMEO
Alas, that love, whose view is muffled still,
Should, without eyes, see pathways to his will!
Where shall we dine? O me! What fray was here?
Yet tell me not, for I have heard it all.
Here's much to do with hate, but more with love.
Why, then, O brawling love, O loving hate,
O anything, of nothing first create,
O heavy lightness, serious vanity,
Misshapen chaos of well-seeming forms,
Feather of lead, bright smoke, cold fire, sick health,
Still-waking sleep, that is not what it is!
This love feel I, that feel no love in this.
Dost thou not laugh?

BENVOLIO
No, coz, I rather weep.

ROMEO
Good heart, at what?

BENVOLIO
At thy good heart's oppression.

ROMEO
Why, such is love's transgression.
Griefs of mine own lie heavy in my breast,
Which thou wilt propagate, to have it press'd
With more of thine. This love that thou hast shown
Doth add more grief to too much of mine own.
Love is a smoke made with the fume of sighs;
Being purg'd, a fire sparkling in lovers' eyes;
Being vex'd, a sea nourish'd with lovers' tears.

112 Who nothing which not at all. **withal** therewith **114 on part and part** on one side and the other **122 city** i.e., city's **124 ware** wary, aware **126 affections** wishes, inclination **127 most . . . found** chiefly desired a place where other people would not be present **129 humor** mood, whim **130 who** him who **136 Aurora** goddess of dawn **137 heavy** sad **148 true** trustworthy **149 close** secret **150 sounding** being fathomed (to discover deep or inner secrets) **151 envious** malicious

158 happy fortunate, successful **159 shrift** confession **160 cousin** kinsman **169 his view** its appearance **170 in proof** in reality, in experience **171 view . . . still** sight is blindfolded always **172 to his will** to what he wants **177 create** created **181 Still-waking** continually awake **183 coz** cousin, kinsman **187–188 propagate . . . thine** increase by having it, i.e., my own grief, oppressed or made still heavier with your grief on my account **191 purg'd** i.e., of smoke

What is it else? A madness most discreet,
A choking gall, and a preserving sweet.
Farewell, my coz.

BENVOLIO
Soft! I will go along.
An if you leave me so, you do me wrong.

ROMEO
Tut, I have lost myself; I am not here;
This is not Romeo, he's some other where.

BENVOLIO
Tell me in sadness, who is that you love? 199

ROMEO
What, shall I groan and tell thee?

BENVOLIO
Groan? Why, no, but sadly tell me who.

ROMEO
Bid a sick man in sadness make his will—
A word ill urg'd to one that is so ill!
In sadness, cousin, I do love a woman.

BENVOLIO
I aim'd so near when I suppos'd you lov'd.

ROMEO
A right good mark-man! And she's fair I love. 206

BENVOLIO
A right fair mark, fair coz, is soonest hit. 207

ROMEO
Well, in that hit you miss. She'll not be hit
With Cupid's arrow. She hath Dian's wit, 209
And, in strong proof of chastity well arm'd, 210
From love's weak childish bow she lives unharm'd.
She will not stay the siege of loving terms, 212
Nor bide th' encounter of assailing eyes,
Nor ope her lap to saint-seducing gold.
O, she is rich in beauty, only poor,
That, when she dies, with beauty dies her store. 216

BENVOLIO
Then she hath sworn that she will still live chaste? 217

ROMEO
She hath, and in that sparing makes huge waste, 218
For beauty starv'd with her severity 219
Cuts beauty off from all posterity.
She is too fair, too wise, wisely too fair,
To merit bliss by making me despair. 222
She hath forsworn to love, and in that vow
Do I live dead that live to tell it now.

BENVOLIO
Be rul'd by me, forget to think of her.

ROMEO
O, teach me how I should forget to think!

BENVOLIO
By giving liberty unto thine eyes:
Examine other beauties.

ROMEO
'Tis the way
To call hers, exquisite, in question more. 229
These happy masks that kiss fair ladies' brows,
Being black, puts us in mind they hide the fair.
He that is strucken blind cannot forget
The precious treasure of his eyesight lost.
Show me a mistress that is passing fair, 234
What doth her beauty serve but as a note
Where I may read who pass'd that passing fair?
Farewell. Thou canst not teach me to forget.

BENVOLIO
I'll pay that doctrine, or else die in debt. *Exeunt.* 238

[SCENE II]

Enter Capulet, County Paris, and the Clown [a Servant].

CAPULET
But Montague is bound as well as I,
In penalty alike; and 'tis not hard, I think,
For men so old as we to keep the peace.

PARIS
Of honorable reckoning are you both, 4
And pity 'tis you liv'd at odds so long.
But now, my lord, what say you to my suit?

CAPULET
But saying o'er what I have said before:
My child is yet a stranger in the world;
She hath not seen the change of fourteen years.
Let two more summers wither in their pride,
Ere we may think her ripe to be a bride.

PARIS
Younger than she are happy mothers made.

CAPULET
And too soon marr'd are those so early made.
The earth hath swallowed all my hopes but she;
She's the hopeful lady of my earth. 15
But woo her, gentle Paris, get her heart;
My will to her consent is but a part.
An she agreed, within her scope of choice 18
Lies my consent and fair according voice. 19
This night I hold an old accustom'd feast,
Whereto I have invited many a guest,
Such as I love; and you, among the store,
One more, most welcome, makes my number more.
At my poor house look to behold this night
Earth-treading stars that make dark heaven light.
Such comfort as do lusty young men feel
When well-apparel'd April on the heel
Of limping winter treads, even such delight
Among fresh fennel buds shall you this night 29
Inherit at my house. Hear all, all see,
And like her most whose merit most shall be;
Which on more view of many, mine, being one, 32
May stand in number, though in reck'ning none. 33

199 sadness seriousness. **is that** is it whom **206 fair** beautiful **207 fair mark** clear, distinct target **209 Dian** Diana, huntress and goddess of chastity **210 proof** armor **212 stay** submit to **216 store** wealth. (She will die without children and therefore her beauty will die with her.) **217 still** always **218 sparing** miserliness **219 starv'd** allowed to die **222 To . . . despair** i.e., earning her own salvation through chaste living while driving me to the spiritually dangerous state of despair **229 in question more** even more keenly to mind, into consideration

234 passing surpassingly **238 pay that doctrine** i.e., give that instruction

I.ii. Location: Verona. A street.
s.d. County Count **4 reckoning** estimation, repute **15 the hopeful . . . earth** i.e., my heir and hope for posterity. (*Earth* includes property and lands.) **18 An she** if she be **19 according** agreeing **29 fennel** flowering herb thought to have the power of awakening passion **32–33 Which . . . none** i.e., when you have looked over many ladies, my daughter, being one of them, may be numerically counted among the lot but will count for little in your *reck'ning* or estimation. (Capulet puns on *reck'ning* in the sense of arithmetical calculating, and also on the proverbial saying "one is no number.")

Come, go with me. [*To Servant, giving a paper.*] Go,
sirrah, trudge about 34
Through fair Verona; find those persons out
Whose names are written there, and to them say,
My house and welcome on their pleasure stay.
Exit [*with Paris*].

SERVANT Find them out whose names are written here!
It is written that the shoemaker should meddle with
his yard and the tailor with his last, the fisher with his 40
pencil, and the painter with his nets; but I am sent to 41
find those persons whose names are here writ, and 42
can never find what names the writing person hath 43
here writ. I must to the learned.—In good time! 44

Enter Benvolio and Romeo.

BENVOLIO
Tut, man, one fire burns out another's burning,
One pain is less'ned by another's anguish; 46
Turn giddy, and be holp by backward turning; 47
One desperate grief cures with another's languish.
Take thou some new infection to thy eye,
And the rank poison of the old will die.

ROMEO
Your plaintain leaf is excellent for that. 51

BENVOLIO
For what, I pray thee?

ROMEO
For your broken shin.

BENVOLIO
Why, Romeo, art thou mad?

ROMEO
Not mad, but bound more than a madman is; 54
Shut up in prison, kept without my food,
Whipp'd and tormented and—God-den, good
fellow. 56

SERVANT God gi' god-den. I pray, sir, can you read? 57

ROMEO
Ay, mine own fortune in my misery.

SERVANT Perhaps you have learn'd it without book. 59
But, I pray, can you read anything you see?

ROMEO
Ay, if I know the letters and the language.

SERVANT Ye say honestly. Rest you merry! [*Going.*] 62

ROMEO
Stay, fellow, I can read. *He reads the letter.*
"Signior Martino and his wife and daughters;
County Anselme and his beauteous sisters;
The lady widow of Vitruvio;
Signior Placentio and his lovely nieces;
Mercutio and his brother Valentine;
Mine uncle Capulet, his wife, and daughters;
My fair niece Rosaline, and Livia; 70
Signior Valentio and his cousin Tybalt;
Lucio and the lively Helena."
A fair assembly. Whither should they come?

SERVANT Up.

ROMEO Whither? To supper?

SERVANT To our house.

ROMEO Whose house?

SERVANT My master's.

ROMEO
Indeed, I should have ask'd you that before.

SERVANT Now I'll tell you without asking. My master is
the great rich Capulet; and if you be not of the house
of Montagues, I pray, come and crush a cup of wine. 82
Rest you merry! [*Exit.*]

BENVOLIO
At this same ancient feast of Capulet's 84
Sups the fair Rosaline whom thou so loves,
With all the admired beauties of Verona.
Go thither, and, with unattainted eye 87
Compare her face with some that I shall show,
And I will make thee think thy swan a crow.

ROMEO
When the devout religion of mine eye
Maintains such falsehood, then turn tears to fires;
And these who, often drown'd, could never die, 92
Transparent heretics, be burnt for liars! 93
One fairer than my love? The all-seeing sun
Ne'er saw her match since first the world begun.

BENVOLIO
Tut, you saw her fair, none else being by,
Herself pois'd with herself in either eye; 97
But in that crystal scales let there be weigh'd 98
Your lady's love against some other maid
That I will show you shining at this feast,
And she shall scant show well that now seems best. 101

ROMEO
I'll go along, no such sight to be shown,
But to rejoice in splendor of mine own. [*Exeunt.*]

[SCENE III]

Enter Capulet's Wife and Nurse.

WIFE
Nurse, where's my daughter? Call her forth to me.

NURSE
Now, by my maidenhead at twelve year old,
I bade her come. What, lamb, what, ladybird! 3
God forbid, where's this girl? What, Juliet!

Enter Juliet.

JULIET
How now? Who calls?

NURSE
Your mother.

JULIET
Madam, I am here. What is your will?

34 sirrah (Customary form of address to servants.) **40–41 yard, last, pencil, nets** (The servant humorously assigns these tools of a trade to the wrong person, to suggest how useless it is for him, an illiterate servant, to be given a written instruction.) **yard** yardstick. **last** a shoemaker's form **42–43 find . . . find** locate . . . learn **44 In good time** i.e., here comes help **46 another's anguish** the anguish of another pain **47 holp** helped. **backward** i.e., reverse **51 plantain leaf** herb used for cuts and abrasions, such as a *broken* or bleeding shin. (Romeo undercuts Benvolio's sententiousness by taking his medical metaphor literally, as if curing love were like curing a minor cut.) **54 bound** (The usual treatment for madness.) **56 God-den** good evening. (Used after noon.) **57 gi'** give you **59 without book** by memory. (The Servant takes Romeo's flowery response to his simple question as though it were the title of a literary work; his comment also suggests that one can learn misery without knowing how to read.) **62 Rest you merry** i.e., farewell. (The Servant can see he is getting nowhere.)

82 crush i.e., drink **84 ancient** customary **87 unattainted** uninfected, impartial **92 these** i.e., these my eyes. **drown'd** i.e., in tears **93 Transparent** (1) self-evident (2) clear **97 pois'd** balanced **98 crystal scales** i.e., Romeo's eyes, in which the ladies are to be balanced and compared **101 scant** scarcely

I.iii. Location: Verona. Capulet's house.
3 ladybird i.e., sweetheart; also, loose woman (used endearingly, though perhaps also with the immediate apology, "God forbid")

WIFE
This is the matter.—Nurse, give leave awhile, 8
We must talk in secret.—Nurse, come back again;
I have rememb'red me, thou's hear our counsel. 10
Thou knowest my daughter's of a pretty age.

NURSE
Faith, I can tell her age unto an hour.

WIFE
She's not fourteen.

NURSE
I'll lay fourteen of my teeth—
And yet, to my teen be it spoken, I have but four— 14
She's not fourteen. How long is it now
To Lammas-tide?

WIFE
A fortnight and odd days. 16

NURSE
Even or odd, of all days in the year,
Come Lammas-eve at night shall she be fourteen.
Susan and she—God rest all Christian souls!— 19
Were of an age. Well, Susan is with God;
She was too good for me. But, as I said,
On Lammas-eve at night shall she be fourteen,
That shall she, marry, I remember it well.
'Tis since the earthquake now eleven years,
And she was wean'd—I never shall forget it—
Of all the days of the year, upon that day;
For I had then laid wormwood to my dug, 27
Sitting in the sun under the dove-house wall.
My lord and you were then at Mantua—
Nay, I do bear a brain. But, as I said, 30
When it did taste the wormwood on the nipple
Of my dug and felt it bitter, pretty fool, 32
To see it tetchy and fall out with the dug! 33
"Shake," quoth the dove-house. 'Twas no need, I
trow, 34
To bid me trudge! 35
And since that time it is eleven years,
For then she could stand high-lone; nay, by th'
rood, 37
She could have run and waddled all about.
For even the day before, she broke her brow; 39
And then my husband—God be with his soul!
'A was a merry man—took up the child.
"Yea," quoth he, "dost thou fall upon thy face?
Thou wilt fall backward when thou hast more wit,
Wilt thou not, Jule?" and, by my holidam, 44
The pretty wretch left crying and said "Ay."
To see now how a jest shall come about! 46
I warrant, an I should live a thousand years,
I never should forget it. "Wilt thou not, Jule?" quoth
he,
And, pretty fool, it stinted and said "Ay." 49

WIFE
Enough of this. I pray thee, hold thy peace.

NURSE
Yes, madam. Yet I cannot choose but laugh
To think it should leave crying and say "Ay."
And yet, I warrant, it had upon it brow 53
A bump as big as a young cock'rel's stone— 54
A perilous knock—and it cried bitterly.
"Yea," quoth my husband, "Fall'st upon thy face?
Thou wilt fall backward when thou comest to age,
Wilt thou not, Jule?" It stinted and said "Ay."

JULIET
And stint thou too, I pray thee, nurse, say I. 59

NURSE
Peace, I have done. God mark thee to his grace!
Thou wast the prettiest babe that e'er I nurs'd.
An I might live to see thee married once,
I have my wish.

WIFE
Marry, that "marry" is the very theme
I came to talk of. Tell me, daughter Juliet,
How stands your disposition to be married?

JULIET
It is an honor that I dream not of.

NURSE
An honor? Were not I thine only nurse,
I would say thou hadst suck'd wisdom from thy
teat. 69

WIFE
Well, think of marriage now. Younger than you,
Here in Verona, ladies of esteem,
Are made already mothers. By my count,
I was your mother much upon these years 73
That you are now a maid. Thus then in brief:
The valiant Paris seeks you for his love.

NURSE
A man, young lady! Lady, such a man
As all the world—why, he's a man of wax. 77

WIFE
Verona's summer hath not such a flower.

NURSE
Nay, he's a flower, in faith, a very flower.

WIFE
What say you? Can you love the gentleman?
This night you shall behold him at our feast.
Read o'er the volume of young Paris' face,
And find delight writ there with beauty's pen;
Examine every married lineament 84
And see how one another lends content,
And what obscur'd in this fair volume lies
Find written in the margent of his eyes. 87
This precious book of love, this unbound lover, 88
To beautify him, only lacks a cover. 89
The fish lives in the sea, and 'tis much pride 90
For fair without the fair within to hide. 91
That book in many's eyes doth share the glory, 92
That in gold clasps locks in the golden story; 93
So shall you share all that he doth possess,
By having him, making yourself no less.

8 give leave leave us **10 thou 's** thou shalt **14 teen** sorrow (playing on *teen* and *four* in *fourteen*) **16 Lammas-tide** the days near August 1 **19 Susan** i.e., the Nurse's own child who has evidently died **27 wormwood** (Used to wean the child from the *dug* or teat.) **30 bear a brain** maintain a keen memory **32 fool** (A term of endearment here.) **33 tetchy** fretful **34 "Shake" . . . dove-house** i.e., the dove-house shook. **trow** believe, assure you **35 trudge** i.e., be off quickly **37 high-lone** on her feet, without help. **rood** cross **39 broke her brow** bruised her forehead (by falling) **44 holidam** i.e., "halidom," a relic or holy thing **46 come about** come true **49 stinted** ceased

53 it brow its brow **54 cock'rel's stone** young rooster's testicle **59 say I** (with a pun on *said "Ay"* of previous line) **69 thy teat** i.e., the teat that nourished you **73 much . . . years** at much the same age **77 a man of wax** such as one would picture in wax, i.e., handsome **84 married** harmonized. **lineament** facial feature **87 margent** commentary or marginal gloss **88 unbound** i.e., because not bound in marriage (with a double meaning in the continuing metaphor of an unbound book) **89 cover** i.e., marriage, a wife **90–91 The fish . . . hide** i.e., the fish has its own suitable environment, and by the same token all things in nature should be as attractive to sight as they are intrinsically good within **92–93 That book . . . story** i.e., in many persons' eyes a good story is all the more admirable for being handsomely bound

NURSE
No less? Nay, bigger. Women grow by men.
WIFE
Speak briefly, can you like of Paris' love?
JULIET
I'll look to like, if looking liking move;
But no more deep will I endart mine eye
Than your consent gives strength to make it fly.

Enter Servingman.

SERVANT Madam, the guests are come, supper serv'd up, you call'd, my young lady ask'd for, the nurse curs'd in the pantry, and everything in extremity. I must hence to wait; I beseech you, follow straight.

WIFE
We follow thee. [*Exit Servingman.*] Juliet, the County stays.
NURSE
Go, girl, seek happy nights to happy days. *Exeunt.*

[SCENE IV]

Enter Romeo, Mercutio, Benvolio, with five or six other Maskers; Torch-bearers.

ROMEO
What, shall this speech be spoke for our excuse?
Or shall we on without apology?
BENVOLIO
The date is out of such prolixity.
We'll have no Cupid hoodwink'd with a scarf,
Bearing a Tartar's painted bow of lath,
Scaring the ladies like a crow-keeper;
[Nor no without-book prologue, faintly spoke
After the prompter, for our entrance;]
But, let them measure us by what they will,
We'll measure them a measure, and be gone.
ROMEO
Give me a torch. I am not for this ambling.
Being but heavy, I will bear the light.
MERCUTIO
Nay, gentle Romeo, we must have you dance.
ROMEO
Not I, believe me. You have dancing shoes
With nimble soles; I have a soul of lead
So stakes me to the ground I cannot move.
MERCUTIO
You are a lover; borrow Cupid's wings,
And soar with them above a common bound.
ROMEO
I am too sore enpierced with his shaft
To soar with his light feathers, and so bound
I cannot bound a pitch above dull woe.
Under love's heavy burden do I sink.
MERCUTIO
And, to sink in it, should you burden love—
Too great oppression for a tender thing.
ROMEO
Is love a tender thing? It is too rough,
Too rude, too boist'rous, and it pricks like thorn.
MERCUTIO
If love be rough with you, be rough with love;
Prick love for pricking, and you beat love down.
Give me a case to put my visage in.
[*Puts on a mask.*]
A visor for a visor! What care I
What curious eye doth quote deformities?
Here are the beetle brows shall blush for me.
BENVOLIO
Come, knock and enter; and no sooner in
But every man betake him to his legs.
ROMEO
A torch for me. Let wantons light of heart
Tickle the senseless rushes with their heels,
For I am proverb'd with a grandsire phrase:
I'll be a candle-holder, and look on.
The game was ne'er so fair, and I am done.
MERCUTIO
Tut, dun's the mouse, the constable's own word.
If thou art dun, we'll draw thee from the mire
Of this sir-reverence love, wherein thou stickest
Up to the ears. Come, we burn daylight, ho!
ROMEO
Nay, that's not so.
MERCUTIO I mean, sir, in delay
We waste our lights in vain, like lamps by day.
Take our good meaning, for our judgment sits
Five times in that ere once in our five wits.
ROMEO
And we mean well in going to this mask;
But 'tis no wit to go.
MERCUTIO Why, may one ask?
ROMEO
I dreamt a dream tonight.
MERCUTIO And so did I.

96 bigger i.e., by pregnancy **103 curs'd** i.e., for not helping with the preparations **104 straight** at once **105–106 County stays** Count (Paris) waits for you

I.iv. Location: Verona. A street in the vicinity of Capulet's house.
1 speech (Maskers were customarily preceded by a messenger or "presenter" with a set speech of compliment.) **3 The date . . . prolixity** such windy rhetoric is out of fashion. (Directors sometimes assign this speech to Mercutio.) **4 Cupid** i.e., messenger or "presenter," probably a boy, disguised as Cupid. **hoodwink'd** blindfolded **5 Tartar's . . . bow** (Tartar's bows, shorter and more curved than the English longbow, were thought to have resembled the old Roman bow with which Cupid was pictured.) **lath** flimsy wood **6 crow-keeper** scarecrow **7 without-book** memorized **10 measure . . . measure** perform for them a dance **12 heavy** sad **18 common bound** ordinary leap (in the dancing)

19 sore sorely (with pun on *soar;* see also pun on *soles* and *soul* in l. 15) **20 bound** confined (with pun in l. 21 on the sense of *leap*) **21 pitch** height. (A term from falconry for the highest point of a hawk's flight.) **23 to sink . . . love** i.e., if you should sink in love, you would prove a burden to it **30 visor . . . visor** i.e., a mask for an ugly masklike face **31 quote** take notice of **34 to his legs** i.e., to dancing **36 senseless** lacking sensation. **rushes** (used for floor-covering) **37 grandsire phrase** old proverb **38 candle-holder** i.e., onlooker. (Alludes to the proverb, "A good candle-holder is a good gamester," i.e., he who merely looks on can't get in trouble.) **39 The game . . . done** (Another proverbial notion, that it is wisest to quit when the game is at its best.) **40 dun's the mouse** (A common phrase usually taken to mean "keep still." *Dun,* gray-brown color, plays on *done,* done for. *Dun* also alludes to a Christmas game, "Dun [the grey-brown horse] is in the mire," in which a heavy log representing a horse was hauled out by the players.) **constable's own word** (A constable might caution one to keep still; Mercutio mocks Romeo's caution as lovesickness.) **42 sir-reverence** (A corruption of "save-your-reverence," an apology for an improper expression, which Mercutio supposes "love" to be.) **43 burn daylight** i.e., waste time. (But Romeo quibbles, protesting that it is not literally daytime.) **46–47 Take . . . wits** i.e., try to understand what I intend to say, relying on common sense rather than on the exercise of wit. (The five "wits" or faculties were common sense, imagination, fantasy, judgment, and reason.) **49 wit** wisdom (playing on *wits* in l. 47; *mean* in l. 48 plays on *meaning* in l. 46)

ROMEO
Well, what was yours?

MERCUTIO
That dreamers often lie.

ROMEO
In bed asleep, while they do dream things true.

MERCUTIO
O, then, I see Queen Mab hath been with you.
She is the fairies' midwife, and she comes
In shape no bigger than an agate-stone
On the forefinger of an alderman,
Drawn with a team of little atomies
Over men's noses as they lie asleep.
Her chariot is an empty hazel-nut,
Made by the joiner squirrel or old grub,
Time out o' mind the fairies' coachmakers.
Her wagon-spokes made of long spinners' legs,
The cover of the wings of grasshoppers,
Her traces of the smallest spider web,
Her collars of the moonshine's wat'ry beams,
Her whip of cricket's bone, the lash of film,
Her wagoner a small grey-coated gnat,
Not half so big as a round little worm
Prick'd from the lazy finger of a maid.
And in this state she gallops night by night
Through lovers' brains, and then they dream of love;
O'er courtiers' knees, that dream on cur'sies straight;
O'er lawyers' fingers, who straight dream on fees;
O'er ladies' lips, who straight on kisses dream,
Which oft the angry Mab with blisters plagues,
Because their breaths with sweetmeats tainted are.
Sometime she gallops o'er a courtier's nose,
And then dreams he of smelling out a suit;
And sometime comes she with a tithe-pig's tail
Tickling a parson's nose as 'a lies asleep,
Then dreams he of another benefice.
Sometime she driveth o'er a soldier's neck,
And then dreams he of cutting foreign throats,
Of breaches, ambuscadoes, Spanish blades,
Of healths five-fathom deep; and then anon
Drums in his ear, at which he starts and wakes,
And being thus frighted swears a prayer or two
And sleeps again. This is that very Mab
That plats the manes of horses in the night,
And bakes the elf-locks in foul sluttish hairs,
Which once untangled much misfortune bodes.
This is the hag, when maids lie on their backs,
That presses them and learns them first to bear,
Making them women of good carriage.
This is she—

ROMEO
Peace, peace, Mercutio, peace!
Thou talk'st of nothing.

MERCUTIO
True, I talk of dreams,
Which are the children of an idle brain,
Begot of nothing but vain fantasy,
Which is as thin of substance as the air
And more inconstant than the wind, who woos
Even now the frozen bosom of the north,
And, being anger'd, puffs away from thence,
Turning his side to the dew-dropping south.

BENVOLIO
This wind you talk of blows us from ourselves.
Supper is done, and we shall come too late.

ROMEO
I fear, too early; for my mind misgives
Some consequence yet hanging in the stars
Shall bitterly begin his fearful date
With this night's revels, and expire the term
Of a despised life clos'd in my breast
By some vile forfeit of untimely death.
But He that hath the steerage of my course
Direct my suit! On, lusty gentlemen.

BENVOLIO
Strike, drum.

They march about the stage, and [retire to one side].

[SCENE V]

Servingmen come forth with napkins.

FIRST SERVANT Where's Potpan, that he helps not to take away? He shift a trencher? He scrape a trencher?

SECOND SERVANT When good manners shall lie all in one or two men's hands, and they unwash'd too, 'tis a foul thing.

FIRST SERVANT Away with the joint-stools, remove the court-cupboard, look to the plate. Good thou, save me a piece of marchpane; and, as thou loves me, let the porter let in Susan Grindstone and Nell. [*Exit Second Servant.*] Antony and Potpan!

[*Two Servingmen come forward.*]

THIRD SERVANT Ay, boy, ready.

FIRST SERVANT You are look'd for and call'd for, ask'd for and sought for, in the great chamber.

FOURTH SERVANT We cannot be here and there too. Cheerly, boys; be brisk awhile, and the longer liver take all. *Exeunt.*

Enter [Capulet and family and] all the Guests and Gentlewomen to the Maskers.

CAPULET
Welcome, gentlemen! Ladies that have their toes

53 Queen Mab (Possibly a name of Celtic origin for the Fairy Queen.) **55 agate-stone** (Precious stone often carved with diminutive figures and set in a ring.) **57 atomies** tiny creatures (atoms) **60 joiner** furniture maker **62 spinners'** spiders' **66 film** gossamer thread **68 worm** (Alludes to an ancient superstition that "worms breed in the fingers of the idle.") **70 state** pomp, dignity **72 cur'sies** curtsies, i.e., bows, obeisances. **straight** immediately **78 smelling . . . suit** i.e., finding a petitioner who will pay for the use of his influence at court **79 tithe-pig** pig given to the parson in lieu of money as the parishioner's tithing, or granting of a tenth **81 benefice** ecclesiastical living **84 breaches** opening of gaps in fortifications. **ambuscadoes** ambushes. **Spanish blades** i.e., swords from Toledo, where the best swords were made **85 healths** toasts **89 plats . . . horses** (Alludes to the familiar superstition of "witches' stirrups," tangles in the manes of horses.) **90 elf-locks** tangles. (Thought superstitiously to be the work of elves, who would seek revenge if the elf-locks were untangled.) **93 learns** teaches **94 good carriage** (1) commendable deportment (2) skill in bearing the weight of men in sexual intercourse (3) able subsequently to carry a child

98 vain fantasy empty imagination **108 date** appointed time **109 expire** bring to an end

I.v. Location: The action, continuous from the previous scene, is now imaginatively transferred to a hall in Capulet's house.
2 trencher wooden dish or plate **6 joint-stools** stools with joined corners made by a *joiner* or furniture maker **7 court-cupboard** sideboard. **plate** silverware **8 marchpane** cake made from sugar and almonds, marzipan **15–16 the longer . . . all** (A proverb, "the survivor takes all," here used to advocate seizing the moment of pleasure.)

Unplagu'd with corns will walk a bout with you.
Ah, my mistresses, which of you all
Will now deny to dance? She that makes dainty,
She, I'll swear, hath corns. Am I come near ye now?
Welcome, gentlemen! I have seen the day
That I have worn a visor and could tell
A whispering tale in a fair lady's ear,
Such as would please. 'Tis gone, 'tis gone, 'tis gone.
You are welcome, gentlemen! Come, musicians,
play. *Music plays, and they dance.*
A hall, a hall! Give room, and foot it, girls.
More light, you knaves; and turn the tables up,
And quench the fire, the room is grown too hot.
Ah, sirrah, this unlook'd-for sport comes well.
Nay, sit, nay, sit, good cousin Capulet,
For you and I are past our dancing days.
How long is 't now since last yourself and I
Were in a mask?

SECOND CAPULET By 'r lady, thirty years.

CAPULET
What, man! 'Tis not so much, 'tis not so much:
'Tis since the nuptial of Lucentio,
Come Pentecost as quickly as it will,
Some five and twenty years, and then we mask'd.

SECOND CAPULET
'Tis more, 'tis more. His son is elder, sir;
His son is thirty.

CAPULET Will you tell me that?
His son was but a ward two years ago.

ROMEO [*To a Servant*]
What lady's that which doth enrich the hand
Of yonder knight?

SERVANT
I know not, sir.

ROMEO
O, she doth teach the torches to burn bright!
It seems she hangs upon the cheek of night
As a rich jewel in an Ethiope's ear—
Beauty too rich for use, for earth too dear!
So shows a snowy dove trooping with crows,
As yonder lady o'er her fellows shows.
The measure done, I'll watch her place of stand,
And, touching hers, make blessed my rude hand.
Did my heart love till now? Forswear it, sight!
For I ne'er saw true beauty till this night.

TYBALT
This, by his voice, should be a Montague.
Fetch me my rapier, boy. What dares the slave
Come hither, cover'd with an antic face,
To fleer and scorn at our solemnity?
Now, by the stock and honor of my kin,
To strike him dead I hold it not a sin.

CAPULET
Why, how now, kinsman? Wherefore storm you so?

TYBALT
Uncle, this is a Montague, our foe,
A villain that is hither come in spite,
To scorn at our solemnity this night.

CAPULET
Young Romeo is it?

TYBALT 'Tis he, that villain Romeo.

CAPULET
Content thee, gentle coz, let him alone.
'A bears him like a portly gentleman;
And, to say truth, Verona brags of him
To be a virtuous and well govern'd youth.
I would not for the wealth of all this town
Here in my house do him disparagement.
Therefore be patient, take no note of him.
It is my will, the which if thou respect,
Show a fair presence and put off these frowns,
An ill-beseeming semblance for a feast.

TYBALT
It fits, when such a villain is a guest:
I'll not endure him.

CAPULET He shall be endured.
What, goodman boy? I say he shall. Go to!
Am I the master here, or you? Go to.
You'll not endure him! God shall mend my soul!
You'll make a mutiny among my guests!
You will set cock-a-hoop! You'll be the man!

TYBALT
Why, uncle, 'tis a shame.

CAPULET Go to, go to,
You are a saucy boy. Is 't so, indeed?
This trick may chance to scathe you, I know what.
You must contrary me! Marry, 'tis time.—
Well said, my hearts!—You are a princox, go.
Be quiet, or—More light, more light! —For shame!
I'll make you quiet, what!—Cheerly, my hearts!

TYBALT
Patience perforce with willful choler meeting
Makes my flesh tremble in their different greeting.
I will withdraw. But this intrusion shall,
Now seeming sweet, convert to bitt'rest gall. *Exit.*

ROMEO [*To Juliet*]
If I profane with my unworthiest hand
This holy shrine, the gentle sin is this:
My lips, two blushing pilgrims, ready stand
To smooth that rough touch with a tender kiss.

JULIET
Good pilgrim, you do wrong your hand too much,
Which mannerly devotion shows in this;
For saints have hands that pilgrims' hands do touch,
And palm to palm is holy palmers' kiss.

ROMEO
Have not saints lips, and holy palmers too?

18 walk a bout dance a turn **20 makes dainty** seems coyly reluctant (to dance) **27 A hall** i.e., clear the hall for dancing **28 turn the tables up** (Tables were probably made of hinged leaves and placed on trestles. They were put aside for dancing.) **37 Pentecost** seventh Sunday after Easter (and never as late as mid-July, two weeks before Lammas or August 1 when, according to I.iii.16, the play takes place; a seeming inconsistency) **41 ward** a minor under guardianship **48 dear** precious **49 shows** appears **51 The measure done** when this dance is over **52 rude** rough **56 What** how **57 antic face** fantastic mask **58 fleer** look mockingly. **solemnity** time-honored festivity

67 portly of good deportment **78 goodman boy** (A belittling term for Tybalt; "Goodman" applied to one below the rank of gentleman, but still of some substance, like a wealthy farmer.) **81 mutiny** disturbance **82 You . . . cock-a-hoop** i.e., you want to be cock of the walk. **be the man** play the big man **85 scathe** harm. **what** what I'm doing, or what I'll do **86 'tis time** i.e., it's time you were taught a lesson **87 Well said** well done (said to the dancers). **princox** saucy boy **90 Patience perforce** patience upon compulsion. **willful choler** i.e., passionate anger **91 different greeting** antagonistic opposition **94–107** (These lines are in the form of a Shakespearean sonnet; they are followed by a quatrain.) **95 shrine** i.e., Juliet's hand **99 mannerly** proper **101 palmers** pilgrims who have been to the Holy Land and brought back a palm

JULIET
Ay, pilgrim, lips that they must use in pray'r.
ROMEO
O, then, dear saint, let lips do what hands do!
They pray; grant thou, lest faith turn to despair.
JULIET
Saints do not move, though grant for prayers' sake. 106
ROMEO
Then move not, while my prayer's effect I take.
[*Kiss.*]
Thus from my lips, by thine, my sin is purg'd.
JULIET
Then have my lips the sin that they have took.
ROMEO
Sin from my lips? O trespass sweetly urg'd!
Give me my sin again. [*Kiss again.*]
JULIET
You kiss by th' book. 111
NURSE [*Approaching*]
Madam, your mother craves a word with you.
[*Juliet retires.*]
ROMEO
What is her mother?
NURSE
Marry, bachelor,
Her mother is the lady of the house,
And a good lady, and a wise and virtuous.
I nurs'd her daughter that you talk'd withal.
I tell you, he that can lay hold of her
Shall have the chinks.
ROMEO
Is she a Capulet? 118
O dear account! My life is my foe's debt. 119
BENVOLIO [*Approaching*]
Away, be gone; the sport is at the best.
ROMEO
Ay, so I fear; the more is my unrest.
[*Masquers prepare to leave.*]
CAPULET
Nay, gentlemen, prepare not to be gone;
We have a trifling foolish banquet towards. 123
[*One whispers in his ear.*]
Is it e'en so? Why, then, I thank you all.
I thank you, honest gentlemen; good night.
More torches here! Come on then, let's to bed.
Ah, sirrah, by my fay, it waxes late. 127
I'll to my rest.
[*All proceed to leave but Juliet and Nurse.*]
JULIET
Come hither, nurse. What is yond gentleman?
NURSE
The son and heir of old Tiberio.
JULIET
What's he that now is going out of door?
NURSE
Marry, that, I think, be young Petruchio.
JULIET
What's he that follows here, that would not dance?
NURSE
I know not.

106 move take the initiative. (In the pre-Reformation Church, one might pray to saints to intercede with God.) **grant** they grant **111 again** back again. **by th' book** i.e., by the rule **118 chinks** i.e., plenty of money **119 dear account** heavy reckoning. **my foe's debt** due to my foe, at his mercy **123 foolish banquet towards** insignificant light refreshment in preparation **127 fay** faith

JULIET
Go ask his name. [*Nurse goes.*] If he be married,
My grave is like to be my wedding bed.
NURSE [*Returning*]
His name is Romeo, and a Montague,
The only son of your great enemy.
JULIET
My only love sprung from my only hate!
Too early seen unknown, and known too late!
Prodigious birth of love it is to me 141
That I must love a loathed enemy.
NURSE
What's tis? What's tis?
JULIET
A rhyme I learn'd even now 143
Of one I danc'd withal. *One calls within* "Juliet."
NURSE
Anon, anon! 144
Come, let's away; the strangers all are gone. *Exeunt.*

[ACT II]

[*Enter*] *Chorus.*

CHORUS
Now old desire doth in his death-bed lie,
And young affection gapes to be his heir; 2
That fair for which love groan'd for and would die, 3
With tender Juliet match'd, is now not fair. 4
Now Romeo is belov'd and loves again,
Alike bewitched by the charm of looks; 6
But to his foe suppos'd he must complain, 7
And she steal love's sweet bait from fearful hooks.
Being held a foe, he may not have access
To breathe such vows as lovers use to swear; 10
And she as much in love, her means much less
To meet her new-beloved anywhere.
But passion lends them power, time means, to meet,
Temp'ring extremities with extreme sweet. [*Exit.*]

[SCENE I]

Enter Romeo alone.

ROMEO
Can I go forward when my heart is here?
Turn back, dull earth, and find thy center out. 2
[*Romeo retires.*]

Enter Benvolio with Mercutio.

BENVOLIO
Romeo! My cousin Romeo! Romeo!

141 Prodigious full of omens **143 tis** this. (Dialect pronunciation.) **144 Anon** i.e., we're coming

II. Chorus.
2 gapes yearns, clamors **3 fair** beauty, i.e., Rosaline **4 match'd** compared **6 Alike** i.e., equally with Juliet **7 foe suppos'd** i.e., Juliet, a Capulet; also, his opposite number in the war of love. **complain** offer his love plaint **10 use** are accustomed

II.i. Location: Verona. Outside of Capulet's walled orchard.
2 dull earth i.e., Romeo's body. **center** i.e., Juliet. (The figure of speech is that of man as a microcosm or little world.)

MERCUTIO
He is wise,
And, on my life, hath stol'n him home to bed.
BENVOLIO
He ran this way, and leapt this orchard wall.
Call, good Mercutio.
MERCUTIO Nay, I'll conjure too.
Romeo! Humors! Madman! Passion! Lover!
Appear thou in the likeness of a sigh.
Speak but one rhyme, and I am satisfied;
Cry but "Ay me!" Pronounce but "love" and "dove,"
Speak to my gossip Venus one fair word, 12
One nickname for her purblind son and heir, 13
Young Abraham Cupid, he that shot so true 14
When King Cophetua lov'd the beggar-maid! 15
He heareth not, he stirreth not, he moveth not;
The ape is dead, and I must conjure him. 17
I conjure thee by Rosaline's bright eyes,
By her high forehead and her scarlet lip,
By her fine foot, straight leg, and quivering thigh,
And the demesnes that there adjacent lie, 21
That in thy likeness thou appear to us!
BENVOLIO
An if he hear thee, thou wilt anger him.
MERCUTIO
This cannot anger him. 'Twould anger him
To raise a spirit in his mistress' circle 25
Of some strange nature, letting it there stand 26
Till she had laid it and conjur'd it down; 27
That were some spite. My invocation 28
Is fair and honest; in his mistress' name
I conjure only but to raise up him.
BENVOLIO
Come, he hath hid himself among these trees
To be consorted with the humorous night. 32
Blind is his love and best befits the dark.
MERCUTIO
If love be blind, love cannot hit the mark.
Now will he sit under a medlar tree, 35
And wish his mistress were that kind of fruit
As maids call medlars, when they laugh alone.
O, Romeo, that she were, O, that she were
An open-arse, and thou a pop'rin pear! 39
Romeo, good night. I'll to my truckle-bed; 40
This field-bed is too cold for me to sleep.
Come, shall we go?
BENVOLIO Go, then, for 'tis in vain
To seek him here that means not to be found.
Exit [*with Mercutio*].

12 gossip crony **13 purblind** dim-sighted **14 Young Abraham** i.e., one who is young and yet old, like the Biblical Abraham; Cupid was paradoxically the youngest and oldest of the gods **15 King Cophetua** (In an old ballad, the King falls in love with a beggar-maid and makes her his queen.) **17 ape** (Used as a term of endearment.) **21 demesnes** regions (with bawdy suggestion as to what is adjacent to the thighs; bawdy puns on terms of conjuration continue in *raise, spirit,* i.e., phallus or semen, *circle, stand, laid it, raise up*) **25 circle** (1) conjuring circle (2) vagina **26 strange** belonging to another person (with suggestion of a rival possessing Rosaline sexually) **27 laid it** (1) laid the spirit to rest (2) provided sexual satisfaction leading to cessation of erection **28 spite** injury, vexation **32 consorted** associated. **humorous** moist; also, influenced by humor or mood **35, 39 medlar, pop'rin** (Fruits used as slang terms for the sexual organs, female and male respectively. The medlar was edible only when partly decayed; the poperin pear, taking its name from *Poperinghe* in Flanders, had a phallic shape; the sound of its name is also suggestive.) **39 open-arse** (A name for the *medlar* making explicit the sexual metaphor.) **40 truckle-bed** a bed on casters to be rolled under a standing bed

[SCENE II]

[*Romeo comes forward.*]

ROMEO
He jests at scars that never felt a wound. 1
[*A light appears above, as at Juliet's window.*]
But, soft, what light through yonder window breaks?
It is the east, and Juliet is the sun.
Arise, fair sun, and kill the envious moon,
Who is already sick and pale with grief
That thou her maid art far more fair than she. 6
Be not her maid, since she is envious;
Her vestal livery is but sick and green
And none but fools do wear it; cast it off.
[*Juliet is visible at her window.*]
It is my lady, O, it is my love!
O, that she knew she were!
She speaks, yet she says nothing. What of that?
Her eye discourses; I will answer it.
I am too bold, 'tis not to me she speaks.
Two of the fairest stars in all the heaven,
Having some business, do entreat her eyes
To twinkle in their spheres till they return. 17
What if her eyes were there, they in her head?
The brightness of her cheek would shame those stars,
As daylight doth a lamp; her eyes in heaven
Would through the airy region stream so bright
That birds would sing and think it were not night.
See how she leans her cheek upon her hand!
O, that I were a glove upon that hand,
That I might touch that cheek!
JULIET Ay me!
ROMEO She speaks!
O, speak again, bright angel, for thou art
As glorious to this night, being o'er my head,
As is a winged messenger of heaven
Unto the white-upturned wond'ring eyes 29
Of mortals that fall back to gaze on him
When he bestrides the lazy puffing clouds
And sails upon the bosom of the air.
JULIET
O Romeo, Romeo, wherefore art thou Romeo? 33
Deny thy father and refuse thy name!
Or, if thou wilt not, be but sworn my love,
And I'll no longer be a Capulet.
ROMEO [*Aside*]
Shall I hear more, or shall I speak at this?
JULIET
'Tis but thy name that is my enemy;

II.ii. Location: The action, continuous from the previous scene, is now imaginatively transferred to inside Capulet's orchard. A rhymed couplet links the two scenes. Romeo has been hiding from his friends as though concealed by the orchard wall. He speaks at once, then turns to observe Juliet's window which is probably in the gallery above, rearstage.
1 s.d. A light appears (Some editors assume that Juliet is visible at l. 1.) **6 maid** i.e., votary of Diana, goddess of the moon and patroness of virgins **17 spheres** transparent concentric shells supposed to carry the heavenly bodies with them in their revolution around the earth **29 white-upturned** looking upward so that the whites of the eyes are visible **33 wherefore** why

Thou art thyself, though not a Montague.
What's Montague? It is nor hand, nor foot,
Nor arm, nor face, nor any other part
Belonging to a man. O, be some other name!
What's in a name? That which we call a rose
By any other word would smell as sweet;
So Romeo would, were he not Romeo call'd,
Retain that dear perfection which he owes
Without that title. Romeo, doff thy name,
And for thy name, which is no part of thee,
Take all myself.

ROMEO I take thee at thy word!
Call me but love, and I'll be new baptiz'd;
Henceforth I never will be Romeo.

JULIET
What man art thou that thus bescreen'd in night
So stumblest on my counsel?

ROMEO By a name
I know not how to tell thee who I am.
My name, dear saint, is hateful to myself,
Because it is an enemy to thee;
Had I it written, I would tear the word.

JULIET
My ears have not yet drunk a hundred words
Of thy tongue's uttering, yet I know the sound:
Art thou not Romeo and a Montague?

ROMEO
Neither, fair maid, if either thee dislike.

JULIET
How camest thou hither, tell me, and wherefore?
The orchard walls are high and hard to climb,
And the place death, considering who thou art,
If any of my kinsmen find thee here.

ROMEO
With love's light wings did I o'erperch these walls,
For stony limits cannot hold love out,
And what love can do, that dares love attempt;
Therefore thy kinsmen are no stop to me.

JULIET
If they do see thee, they will murder thee.

ROMEO
Alack, there lies more peril in thine eye
Than twenty of their swords. Look thou but sweet,
And I am proof against their enmity.

JULIET
I would not for the world they saw thee here.

ROMEO
I have night's cloak to hide me from their eyes;
And but thou love me, let them find me here.
My life were better ended by their hate
Than death prorogued, wanting of thy love.

JULIET
By whose direction found'st thou out this place?

ROMEO
By love, that first did prompt me to inquire.
He lent me counsel, and I lent him eyes.
I am no pilot; yet, wert thou as far
As that vast shore wash'd with the farthest sea,
I should adventure for such merchandise.

JULIET
Thou knowest the mask of night is on my face,
Else would a maiden blush bepaint my cheek
For that which thou hast heard me speak tonight.
Fain would I dwell on form, fain, fain deny
What I have spoke; but farewell compliment!
Dost thou love me? I know thou wilt say "Ay,"
And I will take thy word. Yet, if thou swear'st,
Thou mayst prove false. At lovers' perjuries,
They say, Jove laughs. O gentle Romeo,
If thou dost love, pronounce it faithfully.
Or if thou thinkest I am too quickly won,
I'll frown and be perverse and say thee nay,
So thou wilt woo; but else, not for the world.
In truth, fair Montague, I am too fond,
And therefore thou mayst think my behavior light.
But trust me, gentleman, I'll prove more true
Than those that have more coying to be strange.
I should have been more strange, I must confess,
But that thou overheard'st, ere I was ware,
My true-love passion. Therefore pardon me,
And not impute this yielding to light love,
Which the dark night hath so discovered.

ROMEO
Lady, by yonder blessed moon I vow,
That tips with silver all these fruit-tree tops—

JULIET
O, swear not by the moon, th' inconstant moon,
That monthly changes in her circled orb,
Lest that thy love prove likewise variable.

ROMEO
What shall I swear by?

JULIET Do not swear at all;
Or, if thou wilt, swear by thy gracious self,
Which is the god of my idolatry,
And I'll believe thee.

ROMEO If my heart's dear love—

JULIET
Well, do not swear. Although I joy in thee,
I have no joy of this contract tonight.
It is too rash, too unadvis'd, too sudden,
Too like the lightning, which doth cease to be
Ere one can say "It lightens." Sweet, good night!
This bud of love, by summer's ripening breath,
May prove a beauteous flow'r when next we meet.
Good night, good night! As sweet repose and rest
Come to thy heart as that within my breast!

ROMEO
O, wilt thou leave me so unsatisfied?

JULIET
What satisfaction canst thou have tonight?

ROMEO
Th' exchange of thy love's faithful vow for mine.

JULIET
I gave thee mine before thou didst request it;
And yet I would it were to give again.

46 owes owns **53 counsel** secret thought **61 thee dislike** displease you **66 o'erperch** fly over **73 proof** protected **76 but** unless **78 prorogued** postponed. **wanting of** lacking

88 Fain gladly **89 compliment** etiquette, convention **101 coying** coyness. **strange** reserved, aloof, modest **106 discovered** revealed **110 orb** i.e., sphere; see above, l. 17 **117 contract** exchanging of vows

ROMEO
Wouldst thou withdraw it? For what purpose, love?

JULIET
But to be frank, and give it thee again. 131
And yet I wish but for the thing I have.
My bounty is as boundless as the sea,
My love as deep; the more I give to thee,
The more I have, for both are infinite.
[*Nurse calls within.*]
I hear some noise within; dear love, adieu!—
Anon, good nurse!—Sweet Montague, be true.
Stay but a little, I will come again. [*Exit, above.*]

ROMEO
O blessed, blessed night! I am afeard,
Being in night, all this is but a dream,
Too flattering-sweet to be substantial.

[*Enter Juliet, above.*]

JULIET
Three words, dear Romeo, and good night indeed.
If that thy bent of love be honorable, 143
Thy purpose marriage, send me word tomorrow,
By one that I'll procure to come to thee,
Where and what time thou wilt perform the rite;
And all my fortunes at thy foot I'll lay
And follow thee my lord throughout the world.

NURSE [*Within*] Madam!

JULIET
I come, anon.—But if thou meanest not well,
I do beseech thee—

NURSE [*Within*] Madam!

JULIET By and by, I come— 151
To cease thy strife, and leave me to my grief.
Tomorrow will I send.

ROMEO So thrive my soul—

JULIET
A thousand times good night! [*Exit, above.*]

ROMEO
A thousand times the worse, to want thy light.
Love goes toward love as schoolboys from their books,
But love from love, toward school with heavy looks.
[*Starts to leave.*]

Enter Juliet [*above*] *again.*

JULIET
Hist! Romeo, hist! O, for a falc'ner's voice,
To lure this tassel-gentle back again! 159
Bondage is hoarse, and may not speak aloud;
Else would I tear the cave where Echo lies,
And make her airy tongue more hoarse than mine
With repetition of "my Romeo!"

ROMEO
It is my soul that calls upon my name.
How silver-sweet sound lovers' tongues by night,
Like softest music to attending ears!

JULIET
Romeo!

ROMEO My niess?

JULIET What o'clock tomorrow 167
Shall I send to thee?

ROMEO By the hour of nine.

JULIET
I will not fail. 'Tis twenty years till then.—
I have forgot why I did call thee back.

ROMEO
Let me stand here till thou remember it.

JULIET
I shall forget, to have thee still stand there, 172
Rememb'ring how I love thy company.

ROMEO
And I'll still stay, to have thee still forget,
Forgetting any other home but this.

JULIET
'Tis almost morning, I would have thee gone.—
And yet no farther than a wanton's bird, 177
That lets it hop a little from his hand,
Like a poor prisoner in his twisted gyves, 179
And with a silken thread plucks it back again,
So loving-jealous of his liberty. 181

ROMEO
I would I were thy bird.

JULIET Sweet, so would I.
Yet I should kill thee with much cherishing.
Good night, good night! Parting is such sweet sorrow,
That I shall say good night till it be morrow.
[*Exit, above.*]

ROMEO
Sleep dwell upon thine eyes, peace in thy breast!
Would I were sleep and peace, so sweet to rest!
Hence will I to my ghostly friar's close cell, 188
His help to crave, and my dear hap to tell. *Exit.* 189

[SCENE III]

Enter Friar [*Laurence*] *alone, with a basket.*

FRIAR LAURENCE
The grey-ey'd morn smiles on the frowning night,
Check'ring the eastern clouds with streaks of light,
And fleckled darkness like a drunkard reels 3
From forth day's path and Titan's fiery wheels. 4
Now, ere the sun advance his burning eye,
The day to cheer and night's dank dew to dry,
I must up-fill this osier cage of ours 7
With baleful weeds and precious-juiced flowers.
The earth that's nature's mother is her tomb;
What is her burying grave, that is her womb;
And from her womb children of divers kind
We sucking on her natural bosom find,
Many for many virtues excellent,

131 frank liberal, bounteous **143 bent** purpose **151 By and by** immediately **159 tassel-gentle** tercel-gentle, the male of the goshawk

167 niess eyas, fledgling **172 still** always **177 wanton's** spoiled child's **179 gyves** fetters **181 his** its **188 ghostly** spiritual **189 dear hap** good fortune

II.iii. Location: Verona. Near Friar Laurence's cell, perhaps in the monastery garden.
3 fleckled dappled **4 Titan's** (Helios, the sun god, was a descendant of the race of Titans.) **7 osier cage** willow basket

None but for some, and yet all different.
O, mickle is the powerful grace that lies
In plants, herbs, stones, and their true qualities.
For nought so vile that on the earth doth live
But to the earth some special good doth give;
Nor aught so good but, strain'd from that fair use,
Revolts from true birth, stumbling on abuse.
Virtue itself turns vice, being misapplied,
And vice sometime by action dignified.

Enter Romeo.

Within the infant rind of this weak flower
Poison hath residence and medicine power:
For this, being smelt, with that part cheers each
part;
Being tasted, stays all senses with the heart.
Two such opposed kings encamp them still
In man as well as herbs, grace and rude will;
And where the worser is predominant,
Full soon the canker death eats up that plant.

ROMEO
Good morrow, father.

FRIAR LAURENCE Benedicite!
What early tongue so sweet saluteth me?
Young son, it argues a distempered head
So soon to bid good morrow to thy bed.
Care keeps his watch in every old man's eye,
And where care lodges, sleep will never lie;
But where unbruised youth with unstuff'd brain
Doth couch his limbs, there golden sleep doth reign.
Therefore thy earliness doth me assure
Thou art up-rous'd with some distemp'rature;
Or if not so, then here I hit it right,
Our Romeo hath not been in bed tonight.

ROMEO
That last is true; the sweeter rest was mine.

FRIAR LAURENCE
God pardon sin! Wast thou with Rosaline?

ROMEO
With Rosaline, my ghostly father? No.
I have forgot that name, and that name's woe.

FRIAR LAURENCE
That's my good son. But where hast thou been,
then?

ROMEO
I'll tell thee ere thou ask it me again.
I have been feasting with mine enemy,
Where on a sudden one hath wounded me
That's by me wounded. Both our remedies
Within thy help and holy physic lies.
I bear no hatred, blessed man, for, lo,
My intercession likewise steads my foe.

FRIAR LAURENCE
Be plain, good son, and homely in thy drift.
Riddling confession finds but riddling shrift.

ROMEO
Then plainly know my heart's dear love is set
On the fair daughter of rich Capulet.
As mine on hers, so hers is set on mine,
And all combin'd, save what thou must combine
By holy marriage. When and where and how
We met, we woo'd, and made exchange of vow,
I'll tell thee as we pass; but this I pray,
That thou consent to marry us today.

FRIAR LAURENCE
Holy Saint Francis, what a change is here!
Is Rosaline, that thou didst love so dear,
So soon forsaken? Young men's love then lies
Not truly in their hearts, but in their eyes.
Jesu Maria, what a deal of brine
Hath wash'd thy sallow cheeks for Rosaline!
How much salt water thrown away in waste,
To season love, that of it doth not taste!
The sun not yet thy sighs from heaven clears,
Thy old groans yet ringing in mine ancient ears.
Lo, here upon thy cheek the stain doth sit
Of an old tear that is not wash'd off yet.
If e'er thou wast thyself and these woes thine,
Thou and these woes were all for Rosaline.
And art thou chang'd? Pronounce this sentence then:
Women may fall, when there's no strength in men.

ROMEO
Thou chid'st me oft for loving Rosaline.

FRIAR LAURENCE
For doting, not for loving, pupil mine.

ROMEO
And bad'st me bury love.

FRIAR LAURENCE Not in a grave
To lay one in, another out to have.

ROMEO
I pray thee, chide not. She whom I love now
Doth grace for grace and love for love allow.
The other did not so.

FRIAR LAURENCE O, she knew well
Thy love did read by rote, that could not spell.
But come, young waverer, come, go with me,
In one respect I'll thy assistant be;
For this alliance may so happy prove
To turn your households' rancor to pure love.

ROMEO
O, let us hence! I stand on sudden haste.

FRIAR LAURENCE
Wisely and slow. They stumble that run fast.
Exeunt.

[SCENE IV]

Enter Benvolio and Mercutio.

MERCUTIO
Where the dev'l should this Romeo be?
Came he not home tonight?

15 mickle great. **grace** beneficent virtue **25 that part** i.e., the odor **26 stays** halts **30 canker** cankerworm **31 Benedicite** a blessing on you **37 unstuff'd** not overcharged, carefree **52 physic** medicine, healing property **54 intercession** petition. **steads** helps **55 homely** simple **56 shrift** absolution

79 sentence sententious conclusion **86 grace** favor, graciousness **88 did read by rote** i.e., repeated conventional expressions without understanding them **93 stand on** am in need of

II.iv. Location: Verona. A street.
2 tonight last night

BENVOLIO
Not to his father's. I spoke with his man.

MERCUTIO
Why, that same pale hard-hearted wench, that
Rosaline,
Torments him so, that he will sure run mad.

BENVOLIO
Tybalt, the kinsman to old Capulet,
Hath sent a letter to his father's house.

MERCUTIO A challenge, on my life.

BENVOLIO Romeo will answer it.

MERCUTIO Any man that can write may answer a letter.

BENVOLIO Nay, he will answer the letter's master, how he dares, being dar'd.

MERCUTIO Alas poor Romeo! He is already dead; stabb'd with a white wench's black eye; run through the ear with a love-song; the very pin of his heart cleft with the blind bow-boy's butt-shaft. And is he a man to encounter Tybalt?

BENVOLIO Why, what is Tybalt?

MERCUTIO More than prince of cats, I can tell you. O, he's the courageous captain of compliments. He fights as you sing prick-song, keeps time, distance, and proportion; he rests his minim rests, one, two, and the third in your bosom. The very butcher of a silk button, a duellist, a duellist; a gentleman of the very first house, of the first and second cause. Ah, the immortal passado! The punto reverso! The hai!

BENVOLIO The what?

MERCUTIO The pox of such antic, lisping, affecting phantasimes, these new tuners of accent! "By Jesu, a very good blade! A very tall man! A very good whore!" Why, is not this a lamentable thing, grandsire, that we should be thus afflicted with these strange flies, these fashion-mongers, these pardon-me's, who stand so much on the new form that they cannot sit at ease on the old bench? O, their bones, their bones!

Enter Romeo.

BENVOLIO Here comes Romeo, here comes Romeo.

MERCUTIO Without his roe, like a dried herring. O flesh, flesh, how art thou fishified! Now is he for the numbers that Petrarch flow'd in. Laura to his lady was but a kitchen-wench; marry, she had a better love to be-rhyme her; Dido a dowdy; Cleopatra a gypsy; Helen and Hero hildings and harlots; Thisbe a grey eye or so, but not to the purpose. Signior Romeo, bon jour! There's a French salutation to your French slop. You gave us the counterfeit fairly last night.

ROMEO Good morrow to you both. What counterfeit did I give you?

MERCUTIO The slip, sir, the slip. Can you not conceive?

ROMEO Pardon, good Mercutio, my business was great, and in such a case as mine a man may strain courtesy.

MERCUTIO That's as much as to say, such a case as yours constrains a man to bow in the hams.

ROMEO Meaning, to cur'sy.

MERCUTIO Thou hast most kindly hit it.

ROMEO A most courteous exposition.

MERCUTIO Nay, I am the very pink of courtesy.

ROMEO Pink for flower.

MERCUTIO Right.

ROMEO Why, then is my pump well flower'd.

MERCUTIO Sure wit, follow me this jest now till thou hast worn out thy pump, that when the single sole of it is worn, the jest may remain after the wearing solely singular.

ROMEO O single-sol'd jest, solely singular for the singleness!

MERCUTIO Come between us, good Benvolio; my wits faints.

ROMEO Swits and spurs, swits and spurs! Or I'll cry a match.

MERCUTIO Nay, if our wits run the wild-goose chase, I am done, for thou hast more of the wild-goose in one of thy wits than, I am sure, I have in my whole five. Was I with you there for the goose?

ROMEO Thou wast never with me for anything when thou wast not there for the goose.

MERCUTIO I will bite thee by the ear for that jest.

ROMEO Nay, good goose, bite not.

MERCUTIO Thy wit is a very bitter sweeting; it is a most sharp sauce.

ROMEO And is it not, then, well serv'd in to a sweet goose?

MERCUTIO O, here's a wit of cheveril, that stretches from an inch narrow to an ell broad!

ROMEO I stretch it out for that word "broad;" which, added to the goose, proves thee far and wide a broad goose.

MERCUTIO Why, is not this better now than groaning for love? Now art thou sociable, now art thou Romeo; now art thou what thou art, by art as well as by nature. For this driveling love is like a great natural, that runs lolling up and down to hide his bauble in a hole.

9 answer it accept the challenge **15 pin** peg in the center of a target **16 butt-shaft** unbarbed arrow, allotted to children and thus to Cupid **19 prince of cats** (The name of the king of cats in *Reynard the Fox* was Tybalt or Tybert.) **20 captain of compliments** master of ceremony and dueling etiquette **21 prick-song** music written out **21–22 proportion** rhythm **22 minim rests** short rests in musical notation **23 butcher . . . button** i.e., one able to strike a specific button on his adversary's person **24–25 first house** best school of fencing **25 first and second cause** causes according to the code of dueling that would oblige one to seek the satisfaction of one's honor **26 passado** forward thrust. **punto reverso** back-handed stroke. **hai** home thrust **28 The pox of** plague take **28–29 phantasimes** coxcombs, fantastically dressed or mannered **30 tall** valiant **31 grandsire** i.e., one who disapproves the new fashion and prefers old custom **32 flies** parasites **33 pardon me's** i.e., those who affect overly polite manners **34–35 form . . . bench** (*Form* means both *fashion* and *bench*.) **35 bones** French *bon*, good (with play on English *bone*) **37 Without his roe** i.e., looking thin and fatigued (with a pun on the first syllable of Romeo's name; the remaining syllables, *me-oh*, sound like the expression of a melancholy lover) **39 numbers** verses. **Laura** the lady to whom the Italian Renaissance poet Petrarch addressed his love poems. (Other romantic heroines are named in the following passage: Dido, Queen of Carthage; Cleopatra; Helen of Troy; Hero, beloved of Leander; and Thisbe, beloved of Pyramus.) **41 gypsy** Egyptian; whore

42 hildings good-for-nothings **44 French slop** loose trousers of French fashion **45 fairly** handsomely, effectively **48 slip** (Counterfeit coins were called "slips.") **51 case** situation; also, physical condition, hinting here at venereal disease **53 cur'sy** curtsy, make obeisance **54 kindly** naturally; politely **59 pump** shoe. **well flower'd** expertly pinked or perforated in ornamental figures **62–63 solely singular** unique **64 single-sol'd** i.e., thin, contemptible **64–65 singleness** feebleness **68 Swits and spurs** switches and spurs, i.e., keep up the rapid pace of the hunt (in the game of wits) **68–69 cry a match** claim the victory **70 wild-goose chase** a horse race in which the leading rider dares his competitors to follow him wherever he goes **73 Was . . . goose** did I score a point in calling you a goose **75 for the goose** (1) behaving like a goose (2) looking for a prostitute **78 sweeting** a tart-tasting apple **82 cheveril** kid leather, easily stretched **83 ell** (forty-five inches) **85 broad** large, complete; perhaps also wanton **90 natural** idiot **91 lolling** with his tongue hanging out. **bauble** (1) a jester's wand (2) a phallus

BENVOLIO Stop there, stop there.
MERCUTIO Thou desirest me to stop in my tale against 93
the hair. 94
BENVOLIO Thou wouldst else have made thy tale large.
MERCUTIO O, thou art deceiv'd; I would have made it
short, for I was come to the whole depth of my tale,
and meant indeed to occupy the argument no longer.
ROMEO Here's goodly gear! 99

Enter Nurse and her Man [*Peter*].

A sail, a sail!
MERCUTIO Two, two: a shirt and a smock. 101
NURSE Peter!
PETER Anon!
NURSE My fan, Peter.
MERCUTIO Good Peter, to hide her face, for her fan's the
fairer face.
NURSE God ye good morrow, gentlemen.
MERCUTIO God ye good den, fair gentlewoman.
NURSE Is it good den? 109
MERCUTIO 'Tis no less, I tell ye, for the bawdy hand of
the dial is now upon the prick of noon. 111
NURSE Out upon you, what a man are you? 112
ROMEO One, gentlewoman, that God hath made for
himself to mar. 114
NURSE By my troth, it is well said; "for himself to mar,"
quoth 'a? Gentlemen, can any of you tell me where I
may find the young Romeo?
ROMEO I can tell you; but young Romeo will be older
when you have found him than he was when you
sought him. I am the youngest of that name, for fault
of a worse.
NURSE You say well.
MERCUTIO Yea, is the worst well? Very well took, i' 123
faith; wisely, wisely.
NURSE If you be he, sir, I desire some confidence 125
with you.
BENVOLIO She will indite him to some supper. 127
MERCUTIO A bawd, a bawd, a bawd! So ho! 128
ROMEO What hast thou found?
MERCUTIO No hare, sir; unless a hare, sir, in a lenten 130
pie, that is something stale and hoar ere it be spent. 131
[*Sings.*]

An old hare hoar,
And an old hare hoar,
Is very good meat in Lent.
But a hare that is hoar
Is too much for a score, 136
When it hoars ere it be spent.

Romeo, will you come to your father's? We'll to dinner
thither.
ROMEO I will follow you.
MERCUTIO Farewell, ancient lady; farewell, [*Singing*]
"Lady, lady, lady." *Exeunt* [*Mercutio and Benvolio*]. 142
NURSE Marry, farewell! I pray you, sir, what saucy mer- 143
chant was this, that was so full of his ropery? 144
ROMEO A gentleman, nurse, that loves to hear himself
talk, and will speak more in a minute than he will
stand to in a month.
NURSE An 'a speak anything against me, I'll take him 148
down, an 'a were lustier than he is, and twenty such 149
Jacks; and if I cannot, I'll find those that shall. Scurvy 150
knave! I am none of his flirt-gills; I am none of his 151
skains-mates. [*To Peter.*] And thou must stand by too, 152
and suffer every knave to use me at his pleasure!
PETER I saw no man use you at his pleasure. If I had,
my weapon should quickly have been out, I warrant 155
you. I dare draw as soon as another man, if I see oc-
casion in a good quarrel, and the law on my side.
NURSE Now, afore God, I am so vex'd that every part 158
about me quivers. Scurvy knave! Pray you, sir, a 159
word; and as I told you, my young lady bid me in-
quire you out. What she bid me say, I will keep to
myself. But first let me tell ye, if ye should lead her in
a fool's paradise, as they say, it were a very gross kind
of behavior, as they say. For the gentlewoman is
young; and, therefore, if you should deal double with
her, truly it were an ill thing to be off'red to any gen-
tlewoman, and very weak dealing. 167
ROMEO Nurse, commend me to thy lady and mistress.
I protest unto thee— 169
NURSE Good heart, and, i' faith, I will tell her as much.
Lord, Lord, she will be a joyful woman.
ROMEO What wilt thou tell her, nurse? Thou dost not
mark me. 173
NURSE I will tell her, sir, that you do protest, which, as
I take it, is a gentlemanlike offer.
ROMEO
Bid her devise
Some means to come to shrift this afternoon,
And there she shall at Friar Laurence' cell
Be shriv'd and married. Here is for thy pains.
[*Offers money.*]
NURSE No, truly, sir; not a penny.
ROMEO Go to; I say you shall.
NURSE
This afternoon, sir? Well, she shall be there.
ROMEO
And stay, good nurse, behind the abbey wall.
Within this hour my man shall be with thee,
And bring thee cords made like a tackled stair, 185
Which to the high top-gallant of my joy 186

93–94 against the hair against the grain, against my wish (with a bawdy play on *tale, tail;* continued with *large, short, depth, occupy,* etc.) **99 gear** substance, stuff (with sexual inneundo) **101 a shirt . . . smock** i.e., a man and a woman **109 It is good den** is it afternoon already **111 prick** point on the dial of a clock (with bawdy suggestion) **112 Out upon you** (Expression of indignation.) **114 mar** i.e., disfigure morally through sin. (Man, made in God's image, mars that image sinfully.) **123 took** understood **125 confidence** (The Nurse's mistake for *conference.*) **127 indite** (Benvolio's deliberate malapropism for *invite.*) **128 So ho** (Cry of hunter sighting game.) **130 hare** (Slang word for *prostitute;* similarly with *stale* and *meat* in the following lines.) **130–131 lenten pie** a pie that should contain no meat, in observance of Lent **131 hoar** moldy (with pun on *whore*). **spent** consumed **136 for a score** for a reckoning, to pay good money for

142 "Lady, lady, lady" (Refrain from the ballad *Chaste Susanna.*) **143–144 merchant** i.e., fellow **144 ropery** vulgar humor, knavery **148–149 take him down** i.e., cut him down to size (with unintended bawdy suggestion) **150 Jacks** (used as a term of disparagement) **151 flirt-gills** loose women **152 skains-mates** (Perhaps dagger-mates, outlaws, or gangster molls.) **155 weapon** (with bawdy suggestion, perhaps unrecognized by the speaker, as also in *at his pleasure*) **158–159 every part . . . quivers** (More bawdy suggestion, unrecognized by the Nurse.) **167 weak** contemptible **169 protest** vow. (The Nurse may take the word to mean *object, withdraw,* a development she would welcome.) **173 mark** attend to **185 tackled stair** rope ladder **186 top-gallant** highest mast and sail of a ship, the summit

Must be my convoy in the secret night.
Farewell. Be trusty, and I'll quit thy pains.
Farewell. Commend me to thy mistress.
[*Romeo starts to leave.*]

NURSE
Now, God in heaven bless thee! Hark you, sir.

ROMEO
What say'st thou, my dear nurse?

NURSE
Is your man secret? Did you ne'er hear say,
Two may keep counsel, putting one away?

ROMEO
'Warrant thee, my man's as true as steel.

NURSE Well, sir; my mistress is the sweetest lady—Lord, Lord! When 'twas a little prating thing—O, there is a nobleman in town, one Paris, that would fain lay knife aboard; but she, good soul, had as lief see a toad, a very toad, as see him. I anger her sometimes and tell her that Paris is the properer man; but, I'll warrant you, when I say so, she looks as pale as any clout in the versal world. Doth not rosemary and Romeo begin both with a letter?

ROMEO Ay, nurse; what of that? Both with an R.

NURSE Ah, mocker! That's the dog's name; R is for the—No; I know it begins with some other letter—and she hath the prettiest sententious of it, of you and rosemary, that it would do you good to hear it.

ROMEO Commend me to thy lady.

NURSE Ay, a thousand times. [*Exit Romeo.*] Peter!

PETER Anon!

NURSE Before, and apace.

Exeunt.

[SCENE V]

Enter Juliet.

JULIET
The clock struck nine when I did send the nurse;
In half an hour she promised to return.
Perchance she cannot meet him—that's not so.
O, she is lame! Love's heralds should be thoughts,
Which ten times faster glide than the sun's beams,
Driving back shadows over louring hills.
Therefore do nimble-pinion'd doves draw Love,
And therefore hath the wind-swift Cupid wings.
Now is the sun upon the highmost hill
Of this day's journey, and from nine till twelve
Is three long hours, yet she is not come.
Had she affections and warm youthful blood,
She would be as swift in motion as a ball;
My words would bandy her to my sweet love,
And his to me.

187 convoy conveyance, means of passage **188 quit** reward, requite **192 secret** trustworthy **193 keep counsel** keep a secret **200 properer** handsomer **202 clout** rag, cloth. **versal** universal **203 a letter** one and the same letter **205 the dog's name** (The letter *R* was thought to resemble the dog's growl.) **206 No . . . other letter** (The Nurse perhaps thinks that the letter means "arse" and repudiates the association.) **207 sententious** (The Nurse probably means *sentences*, pithy sayings.) **212 Before, and apace** go before me quickly

II.v. Location: Verona. Outside Capulet's house, perhaps in the orchard or garden. **7 Love** i.e., Venus, whose chariot was drawn by swift-winged doves **14 bandy** toss to and fro, as in tennis

But old folks, many feign as they were dead—
Unwieldy, slow, heavy, and pale as lead.

Enter Nurse [and Peter].

O God, she comes!—O honey nurse, what news?
Hast thou met with him? Send thy man away.

NURSE
Peter, stay at the gate. [*Exit Peter.*]

JULIET
Now, good sweet nurse—O Lord, why lookest thou sad?
Though news be sad, yet tell them merrily;
If good, thou shamest the music of sweet news
By playing it to me with so sour a face.

NURSE
I am a-weary, give me leave awhile.
Fie, how my bones ache! What a jaunce have I had!

JULIET
I would thou hadst my bones, and I thy news.
Nay, come, I pray thee, speak; good, good nurse, speak.

NURSE
Jesu, what haste! Can you not stay awhile?
Do you not see that I am out of breath?

JULIET
How art thou out of breath, when thou hast breath
To say to me that thou art out of breath?
The excuse that thou dost make in this delay
Is longer than the tale thou dost excuse.
Is thy news good, or bad? Answer to that;
Say either, and I'll stay the circumstance.
Let me be satisfied, is 't good or bad?

NURSE Well, you have made a simple choice; you know not how to choose a man. Romeo? No, not he. Though his face be better than any man's, yet his leg excels all men's; and for a hand, and a foot, and a body, though they be not to be talk'd on, yet they are past compare. He is not the flower of courtesy, but, I'll warrant him, as gentle as a lamb. Go thy ways, wench; serve God. What, have you din'd at home?

JULIET
No, no; but all this did I know before.
What says he of our marriage? What of that?

NURSE
Lord, how my head aches! What a head have I!
It beats as it would fall in twenty pieces.
My back a t' other side—ah, my back, my back!
Beshrew your heart for sending me about
To catch my death with jauncing up and down!

JULIET
I' faith, I am sorry that thou art not well.
Sweet, sweet, sweet nurse, tell me, what says my love?

NURSE
Your love says, like an honest gentleman,
And a courteous, and a kind, and a handsome,
And, I warrant, a virtuous—Where is your mother?

16 feign as act as though **25 give me leave** let me alone **26 jaunce** jouncing, jolting **29 stay** wait **36 stay the circumstance** await the details **38 simple** foolish **50 a t' other** on the other **51 Beshrew** a curse on (used as a mild oath)

JULIET
Where is my mother? Why, she is within,
Where should she be? How oddly thou repliest!
"Your love says, like an honest gentleman,
Where is your mother?"

NURSE O God's lady dear!
Are you so hot? Marry, come up, I trow; 62
Is this the poultice for my aching bones?
Henceforward do your messages yourself.

JULIET
Here's such a coil! Come, what says Romeo? 65

NURSE
Have you got leave to go to shrift today?

JULIET
I have.

NURSE
Then hie you hence to Friar Laurence' cell;
There stays a husband to make you a wife.
Now comes the wanton blood up in your cheeks;
They'll be in scarlet straight at any news. 71
Hie you to church; I must another way,
To fetch a ladder, by the which your love
Must climb a bird's nest soon when it is dark. 74
I am the drudge, and toil in your delight,
But you shall bear the burden soon at night.
Go. I'll to dinner; hie you to the cell.

JULIET
Hie to high fortune! Honest nurse, farewell.
Exeunt [*severally*].

[SCENE VI]

Enter Friar [*Laurence*] *and Romeo.*

FRIAR LAURENCE
So smile the heavens upon this holy act,
That after hours with sorrow chide us not!

ROMEO
Amen, amen! But come what sorrow can,
It cannot countervail the exchange of joy 4
That one short minute gives me in her sight.
Do thou but close our hands with holy words,
Then love-devouring death do what he dare;
It is enough I may but call her mine.

FRIAR LAURENCE
These violent delights have violent ends
And in their triumph die, like fire and powder,
Which as they kiss consume. The sweetest honey
Is loathsome in his own deliciousness,
And in the taste confounds the appetite. 13
Therefore love moderately. Long love doth so;
Too swift arrives as tardy as too slow.

Enter Juliet.

Here comes the lady. O, so light a foot
Will ne'er wear out the everlasting flint.
A lover may bestride the gossamer 18
That idles in the wanton summer air, 19
And yet not fall; so light is vanity. 20

JULIET
Good even to my ghostly confessor. 21

FRIAR LAURENCE
Romeo shall thank thee, daughter, for us both. 22

JULIET
As much to him, else is his thanks too much. 23

ROMEO
Ah, Juliet, if the measure of thy joy
Be heap'd like mine, and that thy skill be more 25
To blazon it, then sweeten with thy breath 26
This neighbor air, and let rich music's tongue
Unfold the imagin'd happiness that both 28
Receive in either by this dear encounter.

JULIET
Conceit, more rich in matter than in words, 30
Brags of his substance, not of ornament. 31
They are but beggars that can count their worth;
But my true love is grown to such excess
I cannot sum up sum of half my wealth. 34

FRIAR LAURENCE
Come, come with me, and we will make short work;
For, by your leaves, you shall not stay alone
Till holy church incorporate two in one. [*Exeunt.*]

[ACT III • SCENE I]

Enter Mercutio, Benvolio, and Men.

BENVOLIO
I pray thee, good Mercutio, let's retire.
The day is hot, the Capels are abroad, 2
And, if we meet, we shall not scape a brawl;
For now, these hot days, is the mad blood stirring.

MERCUTIO Thou art like one of these fellows that when
he enters the confines of a tavern, claps me his sword
upon the table and says, "God send me no need of
thee!" and by the operation of the second cup draws 8
him on the drawer, when indeed there is no need. 9

BENVOLIO Am I like such a fellow?

MERCUTIO Come, come, thou art as hot a Jack in thy
mood as any in Italy, and as soon mov'd to be moody, 12
and as soon moody to be mov'd.

BENVOLIO And what to?

MERCUTIO Nay, an there were two such, we should
have none shortly, for one would kill the other. Thou!

62 hot impatient. **Marry, come up** (An expression of impatient reproof.) **65 coil** turmoil, fuss **71 in scarlet straight** i.e., blushing immediately **74 bird's nest** i.e., Juliet's room (with suggestion of pubic hair; the bawdry is continued in *bear the burden* two lines later)

II.vi. Location: Verona. Friar Laurence's cell.
4 countervail outweigh, counterbalance **13 confounds** destroys

18 gossamer spider's thread **19 wanton** playful **20 vanity** transitory human love **21 ghostly** spiritual **22 thank thee** i.e., give a kiss in thanks for your greeting **23 As . . . much** i.e., then I give him a greeting also, lest his passionate kiss be too great a thanks for one greeting only **25 that** if **26 blazon** describe, set forth. (A heraldic term.) **28 Unfold** make known. **imagin'd** i.e., unexpressed **30–31 Conceit . . . ornament** true understanding, more enriched by the actual reality (of love) than by mere words, finds more worth in the substance of that reality than in outward show **34 sum up sum** add up the total

III.i. Location: Verona. A public place.
2 Capels Capulets **8–9 draws . . . drawer** draws his sword against the tapster or waiter **9 there is no need** i.e., of his sword **12 moody** angry

Why, thou wilt quarrel with a man that hath a hair more or a hair less in his beard than thou hast. Thou wilt quarrel with a man for cracking nuts, having no other reason but because thou hast hazel eyes. What eye but such an eye would spy out such a quarrel? Thy head is as full of quarrels as an egg is full of meat, and yet thy head hath been beaten as addle as an egg for quarreling. Thou hast quarrel'd with a man for coughing in the street, because he hath waken'd thy dog that hath lain asleep in the sun. Didst thou not fall out with a tailor for wearing his new doublet before Easter? With another, for tying his new shoes with old riband? And yet thou wilt tutor me from quarreling!

BENVOLIO An I were so apt to quarrel as thou art, any man should buy the fee-simple of my life for an hour and a quarter.

MERCUTIO The fee simple! O simple!

Enter Tybalt, Petruchio, and others.

BENVOLIO By my head, here comes the Capulets.

MERCUTIO By my heel, I care not.

TYBALT
Follow me close, for I will speak to them.
Gentlemen, good den. A word with one of you.

MERCUTIO And but one word with one of us? Couple it with something; make it a word and a blow.

TYBALT You shall find me apt enough to that, sir, an you will give me occasion.

MERCUTIO Could you not take some occasion without giving?

TYBALT Mercutio, thou consortest with Romeo.

MERCUTIO Consort? What, dost thou make us minstrels? An thou make minstrels of us, look to hear nothing but discords. Here's my fiddlestick; here's that shall make you dance. 'Zounds, consort!

BENVOLIO
We talk here in the public haunt of men.
Either withdraw unto some private place,
Or reason coldly of your grievances,
Or else depart; here all eyes gaze on us.

MERCUTIO
Men's eyes were made to look, and let them gaze.
I will not budge for no man's pleasure, I.

Enter Romeo.

TYBALT
Well, peace be with you, sir. Here comes my man.

MERCUTIO
But I'll be hang'd, sir, if he wear your livery.
Marry, go before to field, he'll be your follower;
Your worship in that sense may call him "man."

TYBALT
Romeo, the love I bear thee can afford
No better term than this: thou art a villain.

ROMEO
Tybalt, the reason that I have to love thee
Doth much excuse the appertaining rage
To such a greeting. Villain am I none;
Therefore farewell. I see thou knowest me not.

TYBALT
Boy, this shall not excuse the injuries
That thou hast done me; therefore turn and draw.

ROMEO
I do protest I never injur'd thee,
But love thee better than thou canst devise,
Till thou shalt know the reason of my love;
And so, good Capulet—which name I tender
As dearly as mine own—be satisfied.

MERCUTIO
O calm, dishonorable, vile submission!
Alla stoccato carries it away. *[Draws.]*
Tybalt, you rat-catcher, will you walk?

TYBALT
What wouldst thou have with me?

MERCUTIO Good king of cats, nothing but one of your nine lives, that I mean to make bold withal, and, as you shall use me hereafter, dry-beat the rest of the eight. Will you pluck your sword out of his pilcher by the ears? Make haste, lest mine be about your ears ere it be out.

TYBALT I am for you. *[Drawing.]*

ROMEO
Gentle Mercutio, put thy rapier up.

MERCUTIO Come, sir, your passado. *[They fight.]*

ROMEO
Draw, Benvolio, beat down their weapons.
Gentlemen, for shame, forbear this outrage!
Tybalt, Mercutio, the Prince expressly hath
Forbid this bandying in Verona streets.
Hold, Tybalt! Good Mercutio!

[Tybalt under Romeo's arm stabs Mercutio, and flies with his followers.]

MERCUTIO
I am hurt.
A plague o' both your houses! I am sped.
Is he gone, and hath nothing?

BENVOLIO
What, art thou hurt?

MERCUTIO
Ay, ay, a scratch, a scratch; marry, 'tis enough.
Where is my page? Go, villain, fetch a surgeon.
[Exit Page.]

ROMEO
Courage, man, the hurt cannot be much.

MERCUTIO No, 'tis not so deep as a well, nor so wide as a church-door; but 'tis enough, 'twill serve. Ask for me tomorrow, and you shall find me a grave man. I am pepper'd, I warrant, for this world. A plague o' both your houses! 'Zounds, a dog, a rat, a mouse, a cat, to scratch a man to death! A braggart, a rogue, a villain,

22 meat i.e., edible matter **23 addle** addled, confused **27 doublet** man's jacket **31 fee-simple** outright possession **31–32 an hour . . . quarter** i.e., my life would last no longer in such circumstances **44 consortest** (As Mercutio plays with the term, it means [1] accompany in a musical sense [2] attend or wait upon.) **48 'Zounds** i.e., by God's (Christ's) wounds **56 livery** servant's costume. (Mercutio deliberately mistakes Tybalt's phrase *my man* to mean *my servant.*) **57 field** field where a duel might occur

62 excuse . . . rage mollify the angry reaction appropriate **68 devise** understand **70 tender** value **73 Alla stoccato** at the thrust (Italian); i.e., Tybalt, with his fine fencing phrases, *carries it away,* wins the day **74 rat-catcher** (An allusion to Tybalt as king of cats; see II.iv.19.) **77 make bold withal** make free with **78 dry-beat** beat soundly (without drawing blood) **79 his pilcher** its scabbard **84 passado** forward thrust (said derisively) **90 sped** done for **97 grave** (Mercutio thus puns with his last breath.)

that fights by the book of arithmetic! Why the dev'l
came you between us? I was hurt under your arm.

ROMEO
I thought all for the best.

MERCUTIO
Help me into some house, Benvolio,
Or I shall faint. A plague o' both your houses!
They have made worms' meat of me. I have it,
And soundly too. Your houses!
Exit [supported by Benvolio].

ROMEO
This gentleman, the Prince's near ally,
My very friend, hath got this mortal hurt
In my behalf; my reputation stain'd
With Tybalt's slander—Tybalt, that an hour
Hath been my cousin! O sweet Juliet,
Thy beauty hath made me effeminate,
And in my temper soft'ned valor's steel!

Enter Benvolio.

BENVOLIO
O Romeo, Romeo, brave Mercutio is dead!
That gallant spirit hath aspir'd the clouds,
Which too untimely here did scorn the earth.

ROMEO
This day's black fate on moe days doth depend;
This but begins the woe others must end.

[Enter Tybalt.]

BENVOLIO
Here comes the furious Tybalt back again.

ROMEO
He gone in triumph, and Mercutio slain!
Away to heaven, respective lenity,
And fire-ey'd fury be my conduct now!
Now, Tybalt, take the "villain" back again
That late thou gavest me, for Mercutio's soul
Is but a little way above our heads,
Staying for thine to keep him company.
Either thou, or I, or both, must go with him.

TYBALT
Thou, wretched boy, that didst consort him here,
Shalt with him hence.

ROMEO This shall determine that.
They fight; Tybalt falls.

BENVOLIO
Romeo, away, be gone!
The citizens are up, and Tybalt slain.
Stand not amazed. The Prince will doom thee death
If thou art taken. Hence, be gone, away!

ROMEO
O, I am fortune's fool!

BENVOLIO Why dost thou stay?
Exit Romeo.

Enter Citizens.

FIRST CITIZEN
Which way ran he that kill'd Mercutio?
Tybalt, that murderer, which way ran he?

BENVOLIO
There lies that Tybalt.

FIRST CITIZEN Up, sir, go with me;
I charge thee in the Prince's name, obey.

Enter Prince [attended], old Montague, Capulet, their Wives, and all.

PRINCE
Where are the vile beginners of this fray?

BENVOLIO
O noble Prince, I can discover all
The unlucky manage of this fatal brawl.
There lies the man, slain by young Romeo,
That slew thy kinsman, brave Mercutio.

CAPULET'S WIFE
Tybalt, my cousin! O my brother's child!
O Prince! O cousin! Husband! O, the blood is spill'd
Of my dear kinsman! Prince, as thou art true,
For blood of ours, shed blood of Montague.
O cousin, cousin!

PRINCE
Benvolio, who began this bloody fray?

BENVOLIO
Tybalt, here slain, whom Romeo's hand did slay—
Romeo, that spoke him fair, bid him bethink
How nice the quarrel was, and urg'd withal
Your high displeasure. All this, uttered
With gentle breath, calm look, knees humbly bowed,
Could not take truce with the unruly spleen
Of Tybalt deaf to peace, but that he tilts
With piercing steel at bold Mercutio's breast,
Who, all as hot, turns deadly point to point,
And, with a martial scorn, with one hand beats
Cold death aside, and with the other sends
It back to Tybalt, whose dexterity
Retorts it. Romeo he cries aloud,
"Hold, friends! Friends, part!" and, swifter than his tongue,
His agile arm beats down their fatal points,
And 'twixt them rushes; underneath whose arm
An envious thrust from Tybalt hit the life
Of stout Mercutio, and then Tybalt fled;
But by and by comes back to Romeo,
Who had but newly entertain'd revenge,
And to 't they go like lightning, for, ere I
Could draw to part them, was stout Tybalt slain,
And, as he fell, did Romeo turn and fly.
This is the truth, or let Benvolio die.

CAPULET'S WIFE
He is a kinsman to the Montague;
Affection makes him false, he speaks not true.

108 ally kinsman **109 very** true **116 aspir'd** ascended to **118 moe** more. **depend** hang over threateningly **122 respective lenity** considerate gentleness **123 conduct** guide **135 fool** dupe

141 discover reveal **142 manage** conduct **152 fair** civilly **153 nice** trivial **156 take truce** make peace **167 envious** malicious **168 stout** brave **170 entertain'd** harbored thoughts of

Some twenty of them fought in this black strife,
And all those twenty could but kill one life.
I beg for justice, which thou, Prince, must give:
Romeo slew Tybalt, Romeo must not live.

PRINCE
Romeo slew him, he slew Mercutio.
Who now the price of his dear blood doth owe?

MONTAGUE
Not Romeo, Prince, he was Mercutio's friend;
His fault concludes but what the law should end,
The life of Tybalt.

PRINCE
And for that offense
Immediately we do exile him hence.
I have an interest in your heart's proceeding;
My blood for your rude brawls doth lie a-bleeding;
But I'll amerce you with so strong a fine
That you shall all repent the loss of mine.
I will be deaf to pleading and excuses;
Nor tears nor prayers shall purchase out abuses.
Therefore use none. Let Romeo hence in haste,
Else, when he is found, that hour is his last.
Bear hence this body and attend our will.
Mercy but murders, pardoning those that kill.
Exeunt, [some carrying Tybalt's body].

[SCENE II]

Enter Juliet alone.

JULIET
Gallop apace, you fiery-footed steeds,
Towards Phoebus' lodging! Such a wagoner
As Phaethon would whip you to the west,
And bring in cloudy night immediately.
Spread thy close curtain, love-performing night,
That runaways' eyes may wink, and Romeo
Leap to these arms, untalk'd of and unseen.
Lovers can see to do their amorous rites
By their own beauties; or, if love be blind,
It best agrees with night. Come, civil night,
Thou sober-suited matron, all in black,
And learn me how to lose a winning match,
Play'd for a pair of stainless maidenhoods.
Hood my unmann'd blood, bating in my cheeks,
With thy black mantle; till strange love grow bold,
Think true love acted simple modesty.
Come, night; come, Romeo; come, thou day in night;
For thou wilt lie upon the wings of night
Whiter than new snow upon a raven's back.
Come, gentle night, come, loving, black-brow'd night,
Give me my Romeo; and, when he shall die,
Take him and cut him out in little stars,
And he will make the face of heaven so fine
That all the world will be in love with night
And pay no worship to the garish sun.
O, I have bought the mansion of a love,
But not possess'd it, and, though I am sold,
Not yet enjoy'd. So tedious is this day
As is the night before some festival
To an impatient child that hath new robes
And may not wear them. O, here comes my nurse,

Enter Nurse, with cords.

And she brings news; and every tongue that speaks
But Romeo's name speaks heavenly eloquence.
Now, nurse, what news? What hast thou there? The cords
That Romeo bid thee fetch?

NURSE
Ay, ay, the cords.
[*Throws them down.*]

JULIET
Ay me, what news? Why dost thou wring thy hands?

NURSE
Ah, weraday! He's dead, he's dead, he's dead!
We are undone, lady, we are undone!
Alack the day! He's gone, he's kill'd, he's dead!

JULIET
Can heaven be so envious?

NURSE
Romeo can,
Though heaven cannot. O Romeo, Romeo!
Who ever would have thought it? Romeo!

JULIET
What devil art thou, that dost torment me thus?
This torture should be roar'd in dismal hell.
Hath Romeo slain himself? Say thou but "ay,"
And that bare vowel "I" shall poison more
Than the death-darting eye of cockatrice.
I am not I, if there be such an ay,
Or those eyes shut, that makes thee answer "ay."
If he be slain, say "ay"; or if not, "no."
Brief sounds determine of my weal or woe.

NURSE
I saw the wound, I saw it with mine eyes—
God save the mark!—here on his manly breast.
A piteous corse, a bloody piteous corse;
Pale, pale as ashes, all bedaub'd in blood,
All in gore-blood. I swounded at the sight.

JULIET
O, break, my heart! Poor bankrupt, break at once!
To prison, eyes, ne'er look on liberty!
Vile earth, to earth resign; end motion here,

188 My blood i.e., blood of my kinsman **189 amerce** punish by fine **192 purchase out abuses** redeem misdeeds **195 attend our will** be on hand to hear further judgment

III.ii. Location: Verona. Capulet's house.
1 steeds i.e., the horses of the sun god's chariot **2 Phoebus** (Often equated with Helios, the sun god.) **lodging** i.e., in the west, below the horizon **2–3 Such . . . Phaethon** i.e., a rash charioteer like Phaethon, who would quickly bring the day to an end. (Phaethon was son of the sun god, and was allowed to assume the reins of the sun for a day; not being able to restrain the steeds, he had to be slain by the thunderbolt of Zeus.) **6 runaways'** (Refers to the horses of the sun chariot which ran away with Phaethon?) **wink** shut, close **10 civil** circumspect, somberly attired **12 learn** teach **14 Hood** cover. (A term in falconry; the hawk's eyes were covered so that it would not *bate* or beat its wings.) **unmann'd** untamed (in falconry; with a pun on *unmarried*) **15 strange** diffident **16 Think** i.e., and think

37 weraday i.e., welladay, alas **40 envious** malicious **46 "I"** (Pronounced identically with "ay.") **47 cockatrice** i.e., basilisk, a fabulous serpent which could kill by its look **49 those eyes shut** i.e., if Romeo's eyes are shut (in death) **53 God save the mark** (A familiar oath originally intended to avert ill omen.) **54 corse** corpse **56 gore-blood** clotted blood. **swounded** swooned **59 Vile earth** i.e., my body. **resign** surrender, return

And thou and Romeo press one heavy bier!

NURSE
O Tybalt, Tybalt, the best friend I had!
O courteous Tybalt! Honest gentleman!
That ever I should live to see thee dead!

JULIET
What storm is this that blows so contrary?
Is Romeo slaught'red, and is Tybalt dead?
My dearest cousin, and my dearer lord?
Then, dreadful trumpet, sound the general doom! 67
For who is living, if those two are gone?

NURSE
Tybalt is gone, and Romeo banished;
Romeo that kill'd him, he is banished.

JULIET
O God! Did Romeo's hand shed Tybalt's blood?

NURSE
It did, it did. Alas the day it did!

JULIET
O serpent heart, hid with a flow'ring face! 73
Did ever dragon keep so fair a cave? 74
Beautiful tyrant! Fiend angelical!
Dove-feather'd raven! Wolvish-ravening lamb!
Despised substance of divinest show! 77
Just opposite to what thou justly seem'st,
A damned saint, an honorable villain!
O nature, what hadst thou to do in hell
When thou didst bower the spirit of a fiend 81
In mortal paradise of such sweet flesh?
Was ever book containing such vile matter
So fairly bound? O, that deceit should dwell
In such a gorgeous palace!

NURSE
There's no trust,
No faith, no honesty in men; all perjur'd,
All forsworn, all naught, all dissemblers. 87
Ah, where's my man? Give me some aqua vitae. 88
These griefs, these woes, these sorrows make me old.
Shame come to Romeo!

JULIET
Blister'd be thy tongue
For such a wish! He was not born to shame.
Upon his brow shame is asham'd to sit;
For 'tis a throne where honor may be crown'd
Sole monarch of the universal earth.
O, what a beast was I to chide at him!

NURSE
Will you speak well of him that kill'd your cousin?

JULIET
Shall I speak ill of him that is my husband?
Ah, poor my lord, what tongue shall smooth thy name
When I, thy three-hours wife, have mangled it?
But, wherefore, villain, didst thou kill my cousin?
That villain cousin would have kill'd my husband.
Back, foolish tears, back to your native spring;
Your tributary drops belong to woe, 103
Which you, mistaking, offer up to joy.
My husband lives, that Tybalt would have slain,
And Tybalt's dead, that would have slain my husband.
All this is comfort. Wherefore weep I then?
Some word there was, worser than Tybalt's death,
That murd'red me. I would forget it fain,
But, O, it presses to my memory
Like damned guilty deeds to sinners' minds:
"Tybalt is dead, and Romeo—banished."
That "banished," that one word "banished,"
Hath slain ten thousand Tybalts. Tybalt's death
Was woe enough, if it had ended there;
Or, if sour woe delights in fellowship
And needly will be rank'd with other griefs, 117
Why followed not, when she said "Tybalt's dead,"
Thy father, or thy mother, nay, or both,
Which modern lamentation might have moved? 120
But with a rearward following Tybalt's death, 121
"Romeo is banished," to speak that word,
Is father, mother, Tybalt, Romeo, Juliet,
All slain, all dead. "Romeo is banished!"
There is no end, no limit, measure, bound,
In that word's death; no words can that woe sound. 126
Where is my father, and my mother, nurse?

NURSE
Weeping and wailing over Tybalt's corse.
Will you go to them? I will bring you thither.

JULIET
Wash they his wounds with tears? Mine shall be spent,
When theirs are dry, for Romeo's banishment.
Take up those cords. Poor ropes, you are beguil'd,
Both you and I, for Romeo is exil'd.
He made you for a highway to my bed;
But I, a maid, die maiden-widowed.
Come, cords, come, nurse. I'll to my wedding-bed,
And death, not Romeo, take my maidenhead!

NURSE
Hie to your chamber. I'll find Romeo
To comfort you. I wot well where he is. 139
Hark ye, your Romeo will be here at night.
I'll to him; he is hid at Laurence' cell.

JULIET
O, find him! Give this ring to my true knight,
[Gives ring.]
And bid him come to take his last farewell.
Exeunt [severally].

[SCENE III]

Enter Friar [Laurence].

FRIAR LAURENCE
Romeo, come forth; come forth, thou fearful man.

67 trumpet i.e., the last trumpet. **general doom** Day of Judgment **73 flow'ring** i.e., fair, like that of the serpent in the Garden of Eden **74 keep** occupy **77 show** appearance **81 bower** give lodging to **87 naught** worthless, evil **88 aqua vitae** alcoholic spirits **103 Your . . . woe** i.e., you should be shed, offered, on some occasion of real woe

117 needly of necessity **120 modern** ordinary **121 rearward** rear guard **126 sound** (1) fathom (2) express **139 wot** know

III.iii. Location: Verona. Friar Laurence's cell.

Affliction is enamor'd of thy parts, 2
And thou art wedded to calamity.

[Enter] Romeo.

ROMEO
Father, what news? What is the Prince's doom? 4
What sorrow craves acquaintance at my hand,
That I yet know not?

FRIAR LAURENCE Too familiar
Is my dear son with such sour company.
I bring thee tidings of the Prince's doom.

ROMEO
What less than doomsday is the Prince's doom? 9

FRIAR LAURENCE
A gentler judgment vanish'd from his lips: 10
Not body's death, but body's banishment.

ROMEO
Ha, banishment? Be merciful, say "death";
For exile hath more terror in his look,
Much more than death. Do not say "banishment."

FRIAR LAURENCE
Here from Verona art thou banished.
Be patient, for the world is broad and wide.

ROMEO
There is no world without Verona walls, 17
But purgatory, torture, hell itself.
Hence "banished" is banish'd from the world,
And world's exile is death; then "banished"
Is death mis-term'd. Calling death "banished,"
Thou cutt'st my head off with a golden axe,
And smilest upon the stroke that murders me.

FRIAR LAURENCE
O deadly sin! O rude unthankfulness!
Thy fault our law calls death; but the kind Prince,
Taking thy part, hath rush'd aside the law, 26
And turn'd that black word "death" to "banishment."
This is dear mercy, and thou seest it not.

ROMEO
'Tis torture, and not mercy. Heaven is here
Where Juliet lives, and every cat and dog
And little mouse, every unworthy thing,
Live here in heaven and may look on her,
But Romeo may not. More validity, 33
More honorable state, more courtship lives 34
In carrion flies than Romeo. They may seize
On the white wonder of dear Juliet's hand
And steal immortal blessing from her lips,
Who, even in pure and vestal modesty,
Still blush, as thinking their own kisses sin; 39
But Romeo may not, he is banished.
Flies may do this, but I from this must fly:
They are free men, but I am banished.
And sayest thou yet that exile is not death?
Hadst thou no poison mix'd, no sharp-ground knife,
No sudden mean of death, though ne'er so mean, 45
But "banished" to kill me? "Banished"?
O friar, the damned use that word in hell;
Howling attends it. How hast thou the heart,
Being a divine, a ghostly confessor,
A sin-absolver, and my friend profess'd,
To mangle me with that word "banished"?

FRIAR LAURENCE
Thou fond mad man, hear me a little speak. 52

ROMEO
O, thou wilt speak again of banishment.

FRIAR LAURENCE
I'll give thee armor to keep off that word,
Adversity's sweet milk, philosophy,
To comfort thee, though thou art banished.

ROMEO
Yet "banished"? Hang up philosophy!
Unless philosophy can make a Juliet,
Displant a town, reverse a prince's doom,
It helps not, it prevails not. Talk no more.

FRIAR LAURENCE
O, then I see that madmen have no ears.

ROMEO
How should they, when that wise men have no eyes?

FRIAR LAURENCE
Let me dispute with thee of thy estate. 63

ROMEO
Thou canst not speak of that thou dost not feel.
Wert thou as young as I, Juliet thy love,
An hour but married, Tybalt murdered,
Doting like me and like me banished,
Then mightst thou speak, then mightst thou tear thy hair,
And fall upon the ground, as I do now,
Taking the measure of an unmade grave.
[He prostrates himself.]
Knock [within].

FRIAR LAURENCE
Arise; one knocks. Good Romeo, hide thyself.

ROMEO
Not I, unless the breath of heart-sick groans,
Mist-like, infold me from the search of eyes. *Knock.*

FRIAR LAURENCE
Hark, how they knock!—Who's there?—Romeo, arise;
Thou wilt be taken.—Stay awhile!—Stand up;
Knock.
Run to my study.—By and by!—God's will,
What simpleness is this!—I come, I come! *Knock.* 77
Who knocks so hard? Whence come you? What's your will? *[Going to the door.]*

NURSE *[Within]*
Let me come in, and you shall know my errand.
I come from Lady Juliet.

FRIAR LAURENCE Welcome, then.
[Opens the door.]

Enter Nurse.

2 parts qualities **4 doom** judgment **9 doomsday** i.e., death **10 vanish'd** issued (into air) **17 without** outside of **26 rush'd** thrust (aside) **33 validity** value **34 courtship** (1) courtliness (2) occasion for wooing **39 their own kisses** i.e., their touching one another **45 mean . . . mean** means . . . base

52 fond foolish **63 dispute** reason. **estate** situation **77 simpleness** foolishness

NURSE
O holy friar, O, tell me, holy friar,
Where's my lady's lord, where's Romeo?
FRIAR LAURENCE
There on the ground, with his own tears made drunk.
NURSE
O, he is even in my mistress' case,
Just in her case! O woeful sympathy!
Piteous predicament! Even so lies she,
Blubb'ring and weeping, weeping and blubb'ring.
Stand up, stand up; stand, an you be a man.
For Juliet's sake, for her sake, rise and stand!
Why should you fall into so deep an O? 90
ROMEO
Nurse! *[He rises.]*
NURSE
Ah sir, ah sir! Death's the end of all.
ROMEO
Spakest thou of Juliet? How is it with her?
Doth not she think me an old murderer, 94
Now I have stain'd the childhood of our joy
With blood removed but little from her own?
Where is she? And how doth she? And what says
My conceal'd lady to our cancel'd love?
NURSE
O, she says nothing, sir, but weeps and weeps,
And now falls on her bed, and then starts up,
And Tybalt calls, and then on Romeo cries,
And then down falls again.
ROMEO As if that name,
Shot from the deadly level of a gun, 103
Did murder her, as that name's cursed hand
Murder'd her kinsman. O, tell me, friar, tell me,
In what vile part of this anatomy
Doth my name lodge? Tell me, that I may sack 107
The hateful mansion.
[Draws a weapon, but is restrained.]
FRIAR LAURENCE Hold thy desperate hand!
Art thou a man? Thy form cries out thou art;
Thy tears are womanish, thy wild acts denote
The unreasonable fury of a beast.
Unseemly woman in a seeming man,
And ill-beseeming beast in seeming both!
Thou hast amaz'd me. By my holy order,
I thought thy disposition better temper'd.
Hast thou slain Tybalt? Wilt thou slay thyself,
And slay thy lady that in thy life lives,
By doing damned hate upon thyself?
Why railest thou on thy birth, the heaven, and earth,
Since birth, and heaven, and earth, all three do meet 120
In thee at once, which thou at once wouldst lose?
Fie, fie, thou shamest thy shape, thy love, thy wit, 122
Which, like a usurer, abound'st in all, 123
And usest none in that true use indeed
Which should bedeck thy shape, thy love, thy wit.
Thy noble shape is but a form of wax, 126
Digressing from the valor of a man;
Thy dear love sworn but hollow perjury,
Killing that love which thou hast vow'd to cherish;
Thy wit, that ornament to shape and love,
Misshapen in the conduct of them both, 131
Like powder in a skilless soldier's flask 132
Is set afire by thine own ignorance,
And thou dismemb'red with thine own defense. 134
What, rouse thee, man! Thy Juliet is alive,
For whose dear sake thou wast but lately dead;
There art thou happy. Tybalt would kill thee, 137
But thou slewest Tybalt; there art thou happy.
The law that threat'ned death becomes thy friend
And turns it to exile; there art thou happy.
A pack of blessings light upon thy back;
Happiness courts thee in her best array;
But, like a mishaved and sullen wench, 143
Thou pouts upon thy fortune and thy love.
Take heed, take heed, for such die miserable.
Go, get thee to thy love, as was decreed;
Ascend her chamber, hence and comfort her.
But look thou stay not till the watch be set,
For then thou canst not pass to Mantua,
Where thou shalt live till we can find a time
To blaze your marriage, reconcile your friends, 151
Beg pardon of the Prince, and call thee back
With twenty hundred thousand times more joy
Than thou went'st forth in lamentation.
Go before, nurse. Commend me to thy lady,
And bid her hasten all the house to bed,
Which heavy sorrow makes them apt unto.
Romeo is coming.
NURSE
O Lord, I could have stay'd here all the night
To hear good counsel. O, what learning is!
My lord, I'll tell my lady you will come.
ROMEO
Do so, and bid my sweet prepare to chide.
NURSE
Here, sir, a ring she bid me give you, sir.
[Gives ring.]
Hie you, make haste, for it grows very late. *[Exit.]*
ROMEO
How well my comfort is reviv'd by this!
FRIAR LAURENCE
Go hence; good night; and here stands all your state: 166
Either be gone before the watch be set,
Or by the break of day disguis'd from hence.
Sojourn in Mantua. I'll find out your man,
And he shall signify from time to time
Every good hap to you that chances here.
Give me thy hand. 'Tis late. Farewell, good night.
ROMEO
But that a joy past joy calls out on me,
It were a grief, so brief to part with thee.
Farewell. *Exeunt [severally].*

90 an O a fit of groaning **94 old** hardened **103 level** aim **107 sack** destroy **120 heaven, and earth** i.e., soul and body **122 wit** intellect **123 Which** (you) who. **all** all capabilities

126 form of wax waxwork, mere outer form **131 conduct** guidance **132 flask** powder horn **134 defense** that which should defend you, i.e., your *wit* or intellect **137 happy** fortunate **143 mishaved** misbehaved **151 blaze** publish, divulge. **friends** relations **166 here . . . state** your fortune depends on what follows

[SCENE IV]

Enter old Capulet, his Wife, and Paris.

CAPULET
Things have fall'n out, sir, so unluckily,
That we have had no time to move our daughter.
Look you, she lov'd her kinsman Tybalt dearly,
And so did I. Well, we were born to die.
'Tis very late, she'll not come down tonight.
I promise you, but for your company
I would have been a-bed an hour ago.

PARIS
These times of woe afford no times to woo.
Madam, good night. Commend me to your daughter.

WIFE
I will, and know her mind early tomorrow.
Tonight she's mew'd up to her heaviness.

CAPULET
Sir Paris, I will make a desperate tender
Of my child's love. I think she will be rul'd
In all respects by me; nay, more, I doubt it not.
Wife, go you to her ere you go to bed;
Acquaint her here of my son Paris' love.
And bid her, mark you me, on Wednesday next—
But, soft, what day is this?

PARIS
Monday, my lord.

CAPULET
Monday! Ha, ha! Well, Wednesday is too soon,
A' Thursday let it be. A' Thursday, tell her,
She shall be married to this noble earl.
Will you be ready? Do you like this haste?
We'll keep no great ado—a friend or two;
For, hark you, Tybalt being slain so late,
It may be thought we held him carelessly,
Being our kinsman, if we revel much.
Therefore we'll have some half a dozen friends,
And there an end. But what say you to Thursday?

PARIS
My lord, I would that Thursday were tomorrow.

CAPULET
Well, get you gone. A' Thursday be it, then.
Go you to Juliet ere you go to bed;
Prepare her, wife, against this wedding-day.
Farewell, my lord. Light to my chamber, ho!
Afore me, it is so very late,
That we may call it early by and by.
Good night. *Exeunt.*

[SCENE V]

Enter Romeo and Juliet aloft [*at the window*].

JULIET
Wilt thou be gone? It is not yet near day.
It was the nightingale, and not the lark,
That pierc'd the fearful hollow of thine ear;
Nightly she sings on yond pomegranate-tree.
Believe me, love, it was the nightingale.

ROMEO
It was the lark, the herald of the morn,
No nightingale. Look, love, what envious streaks
Do lace the severing clouds in yonder east.
Night's candles are burnt out, and jocund day
Stands tiptoe on the misty mountain tops.
I must be gone and live, or stay and die.

JULIET
Yond light is not daylight, I know it, I.
It is some meteor that the sun exhal'd,
To be to thee this night a torch-bearer,
And light thee on thy way to Mantua.
Therefore stay yet, thou need'st not to be gone.

ROMEO
Let me be ta'en, let me be put to death;
I am content, so thou wilt have it so.
I'll say yon grey is not the morning's eye,
'Tis but the pale reflex of Cynthia's brow;
Nor that is not the lark whose notes do beat
The vaulty heaven so high above our heads.
I have more care to stay than will to go.
Come, death, and welcome! Juliet wills it so.
How is 't, my soul? Let's talk; it is not day.

JULIET
It is, it is. Hie hence, be gone, away!
It is the lark that sings so out of tune,
Straining harsh discords and unpleasing sharps.
Some say the lark makes sweet division;
This doth not so, for she divideth us.
Some say the lark and loathed toad chang'd eyes;
O, now I would they had chang'd voices too,
Since arm from arm that voice doth us affray,
Hunting thee hence with hunt's-up to the day.
O now be gone! More light and light it grows.

ROMEO
More light and light, more dark and dark our woes!

Enter Nurse [*hastily*].

NURSE
Madam!

JULIET
Nurse?

NURSE
Your lady mother is coming to your chamber.
The day is broke; be wary, look about. [*Exit.*]

JULIET
Then window, let day in, and let life out.

ROMEO
Farewell, farewell! One kiss, and I'll descend.
[*They kiss. He climbs down from the window.*]

JULIET
Art thou gone so? Love, lord, ay, husband, friend!

III. iv. Location: Verona. Capulet's house.
6 promise assure **11 mew'd up to** cooped up with. (A falconry term.) **heaviness** sorrow **12 desperate tender** bold offer **20 A'** on **25 held** regarded **32 against** in anticipation of **34 Afore me** i.e., by my life. (A mild oath.)

III.v. Location: Verona. Capulet's orchard with Juliet's chamber window above, and subsequently (l. 68) the interior of Juliet's chamber.

13 exhal'd i.e., has drawn out of the ground. (Meteors were thought to be vapors of luminous gas drawn up by the sun.) **20 Cynthia's** the moon's **28 sharps** notes relatively high in pitch and hence discordant **29 division** variations on a melody, made by dividing each note into notes of briefer duration **31 chang'd** exchanged. (A popular saying, to account for the observation that the lark has ugly eyes and the toad beautiful ones.) **33 arm from arm** from one another's arms. **affray** frighten **34 hunt's up** a song or tune to awaken huntsmen and, later, a newly married couple **43 friend** lover

I must hear from thee every day in the hour,
For in a minute there are many days.
O, by this count I shall be much in years
Ere I again behold my Romeo!

ROMEO [*From below her window*]
Farewell!
I will omit no opportunity
That may convey my greetings, love, to thee.

JULIET
O, think'st thou we shall ever meet again?

ROMEO
I doubt it not; and all these woes shall serve
For sweet discourses in our times to come.

JULIET
O God, I have an ill-divining soul!
Methinks I see thee, now thou art so low,
As one dead in the bottom of a tomb.
Either my eyesight fails, or thou lookest pale.

ROMEO
And trust me, love, in my eye so do you.
Dry sorrow drinks our blood. Adieu, adieu! *Exit.*

JULIET
O Fortune, Fortune! All men call thee fickle.
If thou art fickle, what dost thou with him
That is renown'd for faith? Be fickle, Fortune.
For then, I hope, thou wilt not keep him long,
But send him back.

Enter Mother [*Capulet's Wife*].

WIFE Ho, daughter, are you up?

JULIET
Who is 't that calls? It is my lady mother.
Is she not down so late, or up so early?
What unaccustom'd cause procures her hither?
[*She goeth down from the window.*]

WIFE
Why, how now, Juliet?

JULIET Madam, I am not well.

WIFE
Evermore weeping for your cousin's death?
What, wilt thou wash him from his grave with tears?
An if thou couldst, thou couldst not make him live;
Therefore, have done. Some grief shows much of love,
But much of grief shows still some want of wit.

JULIET
Yet let me weep for such a feeling loss.

WIFE
So shall you feel the loss, but not the friend
Which you weep for.

JULIET Feeling so the loss,
I cannot choose but ever weep the friend.

WIFE
Well, girl, thou weep'st not so much for his death,

54 ill-divining prophesying of evil **59 Dry sorrow** (The heat of the body in sorrow and despair was thought to descend into the bowels and dry up the blood.) **66 down** in bed **67 procures** induces to come. (As indicated by the bracketed stage direction, which is from Q1, Juliet, who has appeared until now at her "window" above the stage, evidently descends quickly to the main stage and joins her mother for the remainder of the scene. The stage, which before was to have been imagined as Capulet's orchard, is now Juliet's chamber. Juliet's mother has entered onto the main stage four lines earlier.) **74 feeling** deeply felt

As that the villain lives which slaughter'd him.

JULIET
What villain, madam?

WIFE That same villain, Romeo.

JULIET [*Aside*]
Villain and he be many miles asunder.—
God pardon him! I do, with all my heart;
And yet no man like he doth grieve my heart.

WIFE
That is because the traitor murderer lives.

JULIET
Ay, madam, from the reach of these my hands.
Would none but I might venge my cousin's death!

WIFE
We will have vengeance for it, fear thou not.
Then weep no more. I'll send to one in Mantua,
Where that same banish'd runagate doth live,
Shall give him such an unaccustom'd dram
That he shall soon keep Tybalt company.
And then, I hope, thou wilt be satisfied.

JULIET
Indeed, I never shall be satisfied
With Romeo till I behold him—dead—
Is my poor heart so for a kinsman vex'd.
Madam, if you could find out but a man
To bear a poison, I would temper it,
That Romeo should, upon receipt thereof,
Soon sleep in quiet. O, how my heart abhors
To hear him nam'd, and cannot come to him
To wreak the love I bore my cousin
Upon his body that hath slaughter'd him!

WIFE
Find thou the means, and I'll find such a man.
But now I'll tell thee joyful tidings, girl.

JULIET
And joy comes well in such a needy time.
What are they, beseech your ladyship?

WIFE
Well, well, thou hast a careful father, child,
One who, to put thee from thy heaviness,
Hath sorted out a sudden day of joy,
That thou expects not, nor I look'd not for.

JULIET
Madam, in happy time, what day is that?

WIFE
Marry, my child, early next Thursday morn,
The gallant, young, and noble gentleman,
The County Paris, at Saint Peter's Church
Shall happily make thee there a joyful bride.

JULIET
Now, by Saint Peter's Church and Peter too,
He shall not make me there a joyful bride!
I wonder at this haste, that I must wed
Ere he that should be husband comes to woo.
I pray you, tell my lord and father, madam,
I will not marry yet; and, when I do, I swear
It shall be Romeo, whom you know I hate,
Rather than Paris. These are news indeed!

83 no man like he (1) no man so much as he (2) like no man he **89 runagate** renegade **97 temper** (1) mix, concoct (2) alloy, dilute **107 careful** full of care (for you) **109 sorted** chosen

WIFE
Here comes your father; tell him so yourself,
And see how he will take it at your hands.

Enter Capulet and Nurse.

CAPULET
When the sun sets, the earth doth drizzle dew;
But for the sunset of my brother's son
It rains downright.
How now, a conduit, girl? What, still in tears? 129
Evermore show'ring? In one little body
Thou counterfeits a bark, a sea, a wind;
For still thy eyes, which I may call the sea,
Do ebb and flow with tears; the bark thy body is,
Sailing in this salt flood; the winds, thy sighs,
Who, raging with thy tears, and they with them,
Without a sudden calm, will overset 136
Thy tempest-tossed body. How now, wife?
Have you delivered to her our decree?

WIFE
Ay, sir, but she will none, she gives you thanks. 139
I would the fool were married to her grave!

CAPULET
Soft, take me with you, take me with you, wife. 141
How? Will she none? Doth she not give us thanks?
Is she not proud? Doth she not count her blest,
Unworthy as she is, that we have wrought 144
So worthy a gentleman to be her bride? 145

JULIET
Not proud you have, but thankful that you have.
Proud can I never be of what I hate,
But thankful even for hate that is meant love.

CAPULET
How, how, how, how, chopp'd logic? What is this? 149
"Proud," and "I thank you," and "I thank you not,"
And yet "not proud." Mistress minion, you, 151
Thank me no thankings, nor proud me no prouds,
But fettle your fine joints 'gainst Thursday next, 153
To go with Paris to Saint Peter's Church,
Or I will drag thee on a hurdle thither. 155
Out, you green-sickness carrion! Out, you baggage! 156
You tallow-face!

WIFE [*To Capulet*] Fie, fie! What, are you mad? 157

JULIET
Good father, I beseech you on my knees,
Hear me with patience but to speak a word.
[*Kneels.*]

CAPULET
Hang thee, young baggage! Disobedient wretch!
I tell thee what: get thee to church a' Thursday,
Or never after look me in the face.
Speak not, reply not, do not answer me!
My fingers itch. Wife, we scarce thought us blest
That God had lent us but this only child;
But now I see this one is one too much,
And that we have a curse in having her.
Out on her, hilding!

NURSE God in heaven bless her! 168
You are to blame, my lord, to rate her so. 169

CAPULET
And why, my Lady Wisdom? Hold your tongue,
Good prudence. Smatter with your gossips, go. 171

NURSE
I speak no treason.

CAPULET O, God-i-god-en! 172

NURSE
May not one speak?

CAPULET Peace, you mumbling fool!
Utter your gravity o'er a gossip's bowl, 174
For here we need it not.

WIFE
You are too hot.

CAPULET God's bread! It makes me mad. 176
Day, night, hour, tide, time, work, play,
Alone, in company, still my care hath been
To have her match'd, and having now provided
A gentleman of noble parentage,
Of fair demesnes, youthful, and nobly lien'd, 181
Stuff'd, as they say, with honorable parts,
Proportion'd as one's thought would wish a man—
And then to have a wretched puling fool, 184
A whining mammet, in her fortune's tender, 185
To answer, "I'll not wed, I cannot love,
I am too young; I pray you, pardon me."
But, an you will not wed, I'll pardon you. 188
Graze where you will, you shall not house with me.
Look to 't, think on 't, I do not use to jest. 190
Thursday is near. Lay hand on heart; advise. 191
An you be mine, I'll give you to my friend;
An you be not, hang, beg, starve, die in the streets,
For, by my soul, I'll ne'er acknowledge thee,
Nor what is mine shall never do thee good.
Trust to 't, bethink you; I'll not be forsworn. *Exit.*

JULIET
Is there no pity sitting in the clouds,
That sees into the bottom of my grief?
O, sweet my mother, cast me not away!
Delay this marriage for a month, a week;
Or, if you do not, make the bridal bed
In that dim monument where Tybalt lies.

WIFE
Talk not to me, for I'll not speak a word.
Do as thou wilt, for I have done with thee. *Exit.*

JULIET
O God!—O nurse, how shall this be prevented?
My husband is on earth, my faith in heaven. 206
How shall that faith return again to earth, 207
Unless that husband send it me from heaven 208
By leaving earth? Comfort me, counsel me. 209
Alack, alack, that heaven should practice stratagems 210

129 conduit water pipe, fountain **136 Without . . . calm** unless they quickly calm themselves **139 will . . . thanks** says "no thank you," she'll have none, no part of it **141 take . . . you** let me understand you **144 wrought** procured **145 bride** bridegroom **149 chopp'd logic** a shallow and sophistical argument, or arguer **151 minion** spoiled darling, minx **153 fettle** make ready. **'gainst** in anticipation of **155 hurdle** a conveyance on which criminals were dragged to execution **156 green-sickness** (An anemic ailment of young unmarried women; it suggests Juliet's paleness.) **baggage** good-for-nothing **157 tallow-face** pale-face

168 hilding worthless person **169 rate** berate, scold **171 Smatter** chatter **172 God-i-god-en** i.e., for God's sake. (Literally, God give you good evening.) **174 gravity** wisdom (said contemptuously) **176 God's bread** i.e., by God's (Christ's) sacrament **181 demesnes** estates. **lien'd** connected by family **184 puling** whining **185 mammet** doll. **in . . . tender** when an offer of good fortune is made to her **188 pardon you** i.e., allow you to depart (said caustically) **190 do not use** am not accustomed **191 advise** consider carefully **206 my faith in heaven** (Juliet refers to her marriage vows.) **207–209 How . . . leaving earth** i.e., how can I remarry unless Romeo dies **210 practice** scheme, contrive

Upon so soft a subject as myself!
What say'st thou? Hast thou not a word of joy?
Some comfort, nurse.

NURSE Faith, here it is.
Romeo is banish'd, and all the world to nothing
That he dares ne'er come back to challenge you;
Or, if he do, it needs must be by stealth.
Then, since the case so stands as now it doth,
I think it best you married with the County.
O, he's a lovely gentleman!
Romeo's a dishclout to him. An eagle, madam,
Hath not so green, so quick, so fair an eye
As Paris hath. Beshrew my very heart,
I think you are happy in this second match,
For it excels your first; or if it did not,
Your first is dead—or 'twere as good he were,
As living here and you no use of him.

JULIET
Speak'st thou from thy heart?

NURSE
And from my soul too; else beshrew them both.

JULIET Amen!

NURSE What?

JULIET
Well, thou hast comforted me marvelous much.
Go in, and tell my lady I am gone,
Having displeas'd my father, to Laurence' cell,
To make confession and to be absolv'd.

NURSE
Marry, I will; and this is wisely done. *[Exit.]*

JULIET
Ancient damnation! O most wicked fiend!
Is it more sin to wish me thus forsworn,
Or to dispraise my lord with that same tongue
Which she hath prais'd him with above compare
So many thousand times? Go, counselor,
Thou and my bosom henceforth shall be twain.
I'll to the friar, to know his remedy.
If all else fail, myself have power to die. *Exit.*

[ACT IV • SCENE I]

Enter Friar [Laurence] and County Paris.

FRIAR LAURENCE
On Thursday, sir? The time is very short.

PARIS
My father Capulet will have it so,
And I am nothing slow to slack his haste.

FRIAR LAURENCE
You say you do not know the lady's mind?
Uneven is the course, I like it not.

PARIS
Immoderately she weeps for Tybalt's death,
And therefore have I little talk'd of love,
For Venus smiles not in a house of tears.
Now, sir, her father counts it dangerous
That she do give her sorrow so much sway,
And in his wisdom hastes our marriage
To stop the inundation of her tears,
Which, too much minded by herself alone,
May be put from her by society.
Now do you know the reason of this haste.

FRIAR LAURENCE *[Aside]*
I would I knew not why it should be slow'd.—
Look, sir, here comes the lady toward my cell.

Enter Juliet.

PARIS
Happily met, my lady and my wife!

JULIET
That may be, sir, when I may be a wife.

PARIS
That may be must be, love, on Thursday next.

JULIET
What must be shall be.

FRIAR LAURENCE That's a certain text.

PARIS
Come you to make confession to this father?

JULIET
To answer that, I should confess to you.

PARIS
Do not deny to him that you love me.

JULIET
I will confess to you that I love him.

PARIS
So will ye, I am sure, that you love me.

JULIET
If I do so, it will be of more price,
Being spoke behind your back, than to your face.

PARIS
Poor soul, thy face is much abus'd with tears.

JULIET
The tears have got small victory by that,
For it was bad enough before their spite.

PARIS
Thou wrong'st it more than tears with that report.

JULIET
That is no slander, sir, which is a truth;
And what I spake, I spake it to my face.

PARIS
Thy face is mine, and thou hast sland'red it.

JULIET
It may be so, for it is not mine own.—
Are you at leisure, holy father, now,
Or shall I come to you at evening mass?

FRIAR LAURENCE
My leisure serves me, pensive daughter, now.
My lord, we must entreat the time alone.

PARIS
God shield I should disturb devotion!
Juliet, on Thursday early will I rouse ye.
Till then, adieu, and keep this holy kiss. *Exit.*

JULIET
O, shut the door! And when thou hast done so,

214 all . . . nothing the odds are overwhelming **215 challenge** lay claim to **226 here** i.e., on earth **236 Ancient damnation** damnable old woman **241 bosom** secret thoughts. **twain** separated

IV.i. Location: Verona. Friar Laurence's cell.
3 nothing not at all

13 minded thought about **41 shield** prevent (that)

Come weep with me—past hope, past cure, past help!

FRIAR LAURENCE
Ah, Juliet, I already know thy grief;
It strains me past the compass of my wits. 47
I hear thou must, and nothing may prorogue it,
On Thursday next be married to this county.

JULIET
Tell me not, friar, that thou hearest of this,
Unless thou tell me how I may prevent it.
If, in thy wisdom, thou canst give no help,
Do thou but call my resolution wise,
And with this knife I'll help it presently. 54
[*Shows a knife.*]
God join'd my heart and Romeo's, thou our hands;
And ere this hand, by thee to Romeo's seal'd,
Shall be the label to another deed, 57
Or my true heart with treacherous revolt
Turn to another, this shall slay them both.
Therefore, out of thy long-experienc'd time, 60
Give me some present counsel, or, behold,
'Twixt my extremes and me this bloody knife 62
Shall play the umpire, arbitrating that
Which the commission of thy years and art 64
Could to no issue of true honor bring.
Be not so long to speak; I long to die,
If what thou speak'st speak not of remedy.

FRIAR LAURENCE
Hold, daughter. I do spy a kind of hope,
Which craves as desperate an execution
As that is desperate which we would prevent.
If, rather than to marry County Paris,
Thou hast the strength of will to slay thyself,
Then is it likely thou wilt undertake
A thing like death to chide away this shame,
That cop'st with Death himself to scape from it; 75
And, if thou darest, I'll give thee remedy.

JULIET
O, bid me leap, rather than marry Paris,
From off the battlements of any tower,
Or walk in thievish ways; or bid me lurk 79
Where serpents are; chain me with roaring bears;
Or hide me nightly in a charnel house, 81
O'er-cover'd quite with dead men's rattling bones,
With reeky shanks and yellow chapless skulls; 83
Or bid me go into a new-made grave
And hide me with a dead man in his tomb—
Things that, to hear them told, have made me tremble—
And I will do it without fear or doubt,
To live an unstain'd wife to my sweet love.

FRIAR LAURENCE
Hold, then. Go home, be merry, give consent
To marry Paris. Wednesday is tomorrow.
Tomorrow night look that thou lie alone;
Let not the nurse lie with thee in thy chamber.
Take thou this vial, being then in bed,
[*Shows her vial.*]
And this distilling liquor drink thou off; 94
When presently through all thy veins shall run
A cold and drowsy humor, for no pulse 96
Shall keep his native progress, but surcease; 97
No warmth, no breath shall testify thou livest;
The roses in thy lips and cheeks shall fade
To wanny ashes, thy eyes' windows fall, 100
Like death, when he shuts up the day of life;
Each part, depriv'd of supple government, 102
Shall, stiff and stark and cold, appear like death.
And in this borrowed likeness of shrunk death
Thou shalt continue two and forty hours,
And then awake as from a pleasant sleep.
Now, when the bridegroom in the morning comes
To rouse thee from thy bed, there art thou dead.
Then, as the manner of our country is,
In thy best robes uncovered on the bier
Thou shalt be borne to that same ancient vault
Where all the kindred of the Capulets lie.
In the mean time, against thou shalt awake, 113
Shall Romeo by my letters know our drift, 114
And hither shall he come; and he and I
Will watch thy waking, and that very night
Shall Romeo bear thee hence to Mantua.
And this shall free thee from this present shame;
If no inconstant toy, nor womanish fear, 119
Abate thy valor in the acting it.

JULIET
Give me, give me! O, tell not me of fear!
[*Takes the vial.*]

FRIAR LAURENCE
Hold, get you gone, be strong and prosperous
In this resolve. I'll send a friar with speed
To Mantua, with my letters to thy lord.

JULIET
Love give me strength, and strength shall help afford.
Farewell, dear father! *Exeunt.*

[SCENE II]

Enter Father Capulet, Mother [*Capulet's Wife*], *Nurse, and Servingmen, two or three.*

CAPULET
So many guests invite as here are writ.
[*Exit First Servant.*]
Sirrah, go hire me twenty cunning cooks.

SECOND SERVANT You shall have none ill, sir, for I'll try 3
if they can lick their fingers.

CAPULET
How canst thou try them so?

47 compass bounds **54 presently** at once **57 label** a strip attached to a deed to carry the seal; hence, confirmation, seal **60 time** age **62 extremes** extreme difficulties **64 commission** authority. **art** skill **75 That cop'st** you who would encounter or negotiate with; or, a thing that would cope **79 thievish ways** roads frequented by thieves **81 charnel house** vault for human bones **83 reeky** reeking, malodorous. **chapless** without the lower jaw

94 distilling infusing **96 humor** fluid, moisture **97 his native** its natural. **surcease** cease **100 wanny** wan, pale **102 supple government** control of motion **113 against** anticipating when **114 drift** plan **119 toy** idle fancy

IV.ii. Location: Verona. Capulet's house.
3 try test

SECOND SERVANT Marry, sir, 'tis an ill cook that cannot lick his own fingers; therefore he that cannot lick his fingers goes not with me.

CAPULET
Go, be gone. [*Exit Second Servant.*]
We shall be much unfurnish'd for this time.
What, is my daughter gone to Friar Laurence?

NURSE
Ay, forsooth.

CAPULET
Well, he may chance to do some good on her.
A peevish self-will'd harlotry it is.

Enter Juliet.

NURSE
See where she comes from shrift with merry look.

CAPULET
How now, my headstrong, where have you been
gadding?

JULIET
Where I have learn'd me to repent the sin
Of disobedient opposition
To you and your behests, and am enjoin'd
By holy Laurence to fall prostrate here, [*She kneels.*]
To beg your pardon. Pardon, I beseech you!
Henceforward I am ever rul'd by you.

CAPULET
Send for the County! Go tell him of this.
I'll have this knot knit up tomorrow morning.

JULIET
I met the youthful lord at Laurence' cell,
And gave him what becomed love I might,
Not stepping o'er the bounds of modesty.

CAPULET
Why, I am glad on 't. This is well. Stand up.
This is as 't should be. Let me see the County;
Ay, marry, go, I say, and fetch him hither.
Now, afore God, this reverend holy friar,
All our whole city is much bound to him.

JULIET
Nurse, will you go with me into my closet,
To help me sort such needful ornaments
As you think fit to furnish me tomorrow?

WIFE
No, not till Thursday. There is time enough.

CAPULET
Go, nurse, go with her. We'll to church tomorrow.
Exeunt [*Juliet and Nurse*].

WIFE
We shall be short in our provision.
'Tis now near night.

CAPULET Tush, I will stir about,
And all things shall be well, I warrant thee, wife.
Go thou to Juliet, help to deck up her.
I'll not to bed tonight; let me alone.
I'll play the huswife for this once.—What, ho!—
They are all forth. Well, I will walk myself
To County Paris, to prepare up him
Against tomorrow. My heart is wondrous light,
Since this same wayward girl is so reclaim'd.
Exeunt.

10 unfurnish'd unprovided **14 A peevish . . . is** i.e., she's a silly good-for-nothing **26 becomed** befitting **33 closet** chamber

[SCENE III]

Enter Juliet and Nurse.

JULIET
Ay, those attires are best. But, gentle nurse,
I pray thee leave me to myself tonight;
For I have need of many orisons
To move the heavens to smile upon my state,
Which, well thou knowest, is cross and full of sin.

Enter Mother [*Capulet's Wife*].

WIFE
What, are you busy, ho? Need you my help?

JULIET
No, madam, we have cull'd such necessaries
As are behooveful for our state tomorrow.
So please you, let me now be left alone,
And let the nurse this night sit up with you,
For, I am sure, you have your hands full all
In this so sudden business.

WIFE Good night.
Get thee to bed, and rest, for thou hast need.
Exeunt [*Lady Capulet and Nurse*].

JULIET
Farewell! God knows when we shall meet again.
I have a faint cold fear thrills through my veins,
That almost freezes up the heat of life.
I'll call them back again to comfort me.
Nurse!—What should she do here?
My dismal scene I needs must act alone.
Come, vial. [*Takes out the vial.*]
What if this mixture do not work at all?
Shall I be married then tomorrow morning?
No, no, this shall forbid it. Lie thou there.
[*Laying down her dagger.*]
What if it be a poison, which the friar
Subtly hath minist'red to have me dead,
Lest in this marriage he should be dishonor'd,
Because he married me before to Romeo?
I fear it is; and yet methinks it should not,
For he hath still been tried a holy man.
How if, when I am laid into the tomb,
I wake before the time that Romeo
Come to redeem me? There's a fearful point!
Shall I not then be stifled in the vault,
To whose foul mouth no healthsome air breathes in,
And there die strangled ere my Romeo comes?
Or, if I live, is it not very like,
The horrible conceit of death and night,

IV.iii. Location: Verona. Capulet's house; Juliet's bed, enclosed by bedcurtains, is thrust out or is otherwise visible.
3 orisons prayers **5 cross** contrary, perverse **8 behooveful** needful. **state** ceremony **15 faint** producing faintness **29 still** always. **tried** proved **36 like** likely **37 conceit** idea

Together with the terror of the place—
As in a vault, an ancient receptacle, 39
Where, for this many hundred years, the bones
Of all my buried ancestors are pack'd;
Where bloody Tybalt, yet but green in earth, 42
Lies fest'ring in his shroud; where, as they say,
At some hours in the night spirits resort—
Alack, alack, is it not like that I,
So early waking, what with loathsome smells,
And shrieks like mandrakes' torn out of the earth, 47
That living mortals, hearing them, run mad—
O, if I wake, shall I not be distraught,
Environed with all these hideous fears, 50
And madly play with my forefathers' joints,
And pluck the mangled Tybalt from his shroud,
And, in this rage, with some great kinsman's bone, 53
As with a club, dash out my desp'rate brains?
O, look! Methinks I see my cousin's ghost
Seeking out Romeo, that did spit his body
Upon a rapier's point. Stay, Tybalt, stay!
Romeo, Romeo, Romeo! Here's drink—I drink to
thee.
[She drinks and falls upon her bed, within the curtains.]

[SCENE IV]

Enter Lady of the House [Capulet's Wife] and Nurse.

WIFE
Hold, take these keys, and fetch more spices, nurse.
NURSE
They call for dates and quinces in the pastry. 2

Enter old Capulet.

CAPULET
Come, stir, stir, stir! The second cock hath crowed,
The curfew-bell hath rung, 'tis three o'clock.
Look to the bak'd meats, good Angelica, 5
Spare not for cost.
NURSE Go, you cot-quean, go, 6
Get you to bed. Faith, you'll be sick tomorrow
For this night's watching. 8
CAPULET
No, not a whit. What, I have watch'd ere now
All night for lesser cause, and ne'er been sick.
WIFE
Ay, you have been a mouse-hunt in your time, 11
But I will watch you from such watching now. 12
Exeunt Lady and Nurse.

CAPULET
A jealous hood, a jealous hood! 13

Enter three or four [Servingmen] with spits and logs, and baskets.

Now, fellow, what is there?
FIRST SERVANT
Things for the cook, sir; but I know not what.
CAPULET
Make haste, make haste. *[Exit First Servingman.]*
Sirrah, fetch drier logs.
Call Peter, he will show thee where they are.
SECOND SERVANT
I have a head, sir, that will find out logs,
And never trouble Peter for the matter.
CAPULET
Mass, and well said; a merry whoreson, ha! 20
Thou shalt be logger-head. *[Exit Servingman.]* Good
faith, 'tis day. 21
The County will be here with music straight,
For so he said he would. I hear him near.
Play music [within].
Nurse! Wife! What, ho! What, nurse, I say!

Enter Nurse.

Go waken Juliet, go and trim her up.
I'll go and chat with Paris. Hie, make haste,
Make haste. The bridegroom he is come already;
Make haste, I say. *[Exit Capulet.]*

[SCENE V]

[The Nurse goes to the bedcurtains.]

NURSE
Mistress! What, mistress! Juliet! Fast, I warrant her,
she. 1
Why, lamb! Why, lady! Fie, you slug-a-bed!
Why, love, I say! Madam! Sweet-heart! Why, bride!
What, not a word? You take your pennyworths
now. 4
Sleep for a week; for the next night, I warrant,
The County Paris hath set up his rest 6
That you shall rest but little. God forgive me,
Marry, and amen! How sound is she asleep!
I needs must wake her. Madam, madam, madam!
Ay, let the County take you in your bed;
He'll fright you up, i' faith. Will it not be?
[Opens the bedcurtains.]
What, dress'd, and in your clothes, and down
again?
I must needs wake you. Lady, lady, lady!
Alas, alas! Help, help! My lady's dead!

39 As namely **42 green** new, freshly **47 mandrakes'** (The root of the mandragora or mandrake resembled the human form; the plant was fabled to utter a shriek when torn from the ground.) **50 fears** objects of fear **53 rage** madness

IV.iv. Location: Scene continues. Juliet's bed remains visible.
2 pastry room in which pastry was made **5 bak'd meats** pies, pastry **6 cot-quean** i.e., a man who acts the housewife. (Literally, a cottage housewife.) **8 watching** being awake **11 mouse-hunt** i.e., hunter of women **12 watch . . . watching** i.e., keep an eye on you to prevent such nighttime activity

13 A jealous hood i.e., you wear the cap of jealousy **20 Mass** by the Mass **21 logger-head** i.e., blockhead, a head for logs

IV.v. Location: Scene continues. Juliet's bed remains visible.
1 Fast fast asleep **4 pennyworths** small portions (of sleep) **6 set up his rest** firmly resolved. (From primero, a card game, where it means "staked his reserve.")

O, weraday, that ever I was born!
Some aqua vitae, ho! My lord! My lady! 16

[Enter Capulet's Wife.]

WIFE
What noise is here?

NURSE
O lamentable day!

WIFE
What is the matter?

NURSE
Look, look! O heavy day!

WIFE
O me, O me! My child, my only life,
Revive, look up, or I will die with thee!
Help, help! Call help.

Enter Father [Capulet].

CAPULET
For shame, bring Juliet forth; her lord is come.

NURSE
She's dead, deceas'd, she's dead; alack the day!

WIFE
Alack the day, she's dead, she's dead, she's dead!

CAPULET
Ha! Let me see her. Out, alas! She's cold.
Her blood is settled, and her joints are stiff;
Life and these lips have long been separated.
Death lies on her like an untimely frost
Upon the sweetest flower of all the field.

NURSE
O lamentable day!

WIFE
O woeful time!

CAPULET
Death, that hath ta'en her hence to make me wail,
Ties up my tongue and will not let me speak.

Enter Friar [Laurence] and the County [Paris, with Musicians].

FRIAR LAURENCE
Come, is the bride ready to go to church?

CAPULET
Ready to go, but never to return.
O son, the night before thy wedding day
Hath Death lain with thy wife. There she lies,
Flower as she was, deflow'red by him.
Death is my son-in-law, Death is my heir;
My daughter he hath wedded. I will die,
And leave him all; life, living, all is Death's.

PARIS
Have I thought long to see this morning's face, 41
And doth it give me such a sight as this?

WIFE
Accurs'd, unhappy, wretched, hateful day! 43
Most miserable hour that e'er time saw
In lasting labor of his pilgrimage! 45
But one, poor one, one poor and loving child,
But one thing to rejoice and solace in,
And cruel Death hath catch'd it from my sight!

NURSE
O woe! O woeful, woeful, woeful day!
Most lamentable day, most woeful day
That ever, ever, I did yet behold!
O day! O day! O day! O hateful day!
Never was seen so black a day as this.
O woeful day, O woeful day!

PARIS
Beguil'd, divorced, wronged, spited, slain!
Most detestable Death, by thee beguil'd,
By cruel cruel thee quite overthrown!
O love! O life! Not life, but love in death!

CAPULET
Despis'd, distressed, hated, martyr'd, kill'd!
Uncomfortable time, why cam'st thou now 60
To murder, murder our solemnity? 61
O child! O child! My soul, and not my child!
Dead art thou! Alack, my child is dead,
And with my child my joys are buried.

FRIAR LAURENCE
Peace, ho, for shame! Confusion's cure lives not 65
In these confusions. Heaven and yourself
Had part in this fair maid; now heaven hath all,
And all the better is it for the maid.
Your part in her you could not keep from death,
But heaven keeps his part in eternal life.
The most you sought was her promotion,
For 'twas your heaven she should be advanc'd;
And weep ye now, seeing she is advanc'd
Above the clouds, as high as heaven itself?
O, in this love, you love your child so ill
That you run mad, seeing that she is well.
She's not well married that lives married long,
But she's best married that dies married young.
Dry up your tears, and stick your rosemary 79
On this fair corse, and, as the custom is,
And in her best array, bear her to church;
For though fond nature bids us all lament, 82
Yet nature's tears are reason's merriment. 83

CAPULET
All things that we ordained festival
Turn from their office to black funeral:
Our instruments to melancholy bells,
Our wedding cheer to a sad burial feast,
Our solemn hymns to sullen dirges change,
Our bridal flowers serve for a buried corse,
And all things change them to the contrary.

FRIAR LAURENCE
Sir, go you in, and, madam, go with him;
And go, Sir Paris. Everyone prepare
To follow this fair corse unto her grave.
The heavens do lour upon you for some ill;
Move them no more by crossing their high will. 95

Exeunt. Manet [Nurse with Musicians].

FIRST MUSICIAN Faith, we may put up our pipes and be gone.

16 aqua vitae strong alcoholic spirits **41 thought long** looked forward to **43 unhappy** fatal **45 lasting** unceasing

60 Uncomfortable comfortless **61 solemnity** ceremony, festivity **65 Confusion's** calamity's **79 rosemary** symbol of immortality and enduring love; therefore used at both funerals and weddings **82 fond nature** foolish human nature **83 nature's . . . merriment** that which causes human nature to weep is an occasion of joy to reason **95 Move** i.e., anger

NURSE
Honest good fellows, ah, put up, put up;
For, well you know, this is a pitiful case. [*Exit.*]

FIRST MUSICIAN Ay, by my troth, the case may be amended.

Enter Peter.

PETER Musicians, O, musicians, "Heart's ease," "Heart's ease." O, an you will have me live, play "Heart's ease."

FIRST MUSICIAN Why "Heart's ease"?

PETER O, musicians, because my heart itself plays "My heart is full." O, play me some merry dump to comfort me.

FIRST MUSICIAN Not a dump we! 'Tis no time to play now.

PETER You will not, then?

FIRST MUSICIAN No.

PETER I will then give it you soundly.

FIRST MUSICIAN What will you give us?

PETER No money, on my faith, but the gleek; I will give you the minstrel.

FIRST MUSICIAN Then will I give you the serving-creature.

PETER Then will I lay the serving-creature's dagger on your pate. [*Shows dagger.*] I will carry no crotchets. I'll re you, I'll fa you. Do you note me?

FIRST MUSICIAN An you re us and fa us, you note us.

SECOND MUSICIAN Pray you, put up your dagger, and put out your wit.

PETER Then have at you with my wit! I will dry-beat you with an iron wit, and put up my iron dagger. Answer me like men:
"When griping griefs the heart doth wound,
[And doleful dumps the mind oppress,]
Then music with her silver sound"—
Why "silver sound"? Why "music with her silver sound"? What say you, Simon Catling?

FIRST MUSICIAN Marry, sir, because silver hath a sweet sound.

PETER Pretty! What say you, Hugh Rebeck?

SECOND MUSICIAN I say "silver sound," because musicians sound for silver.

PETER Pretty too! What say you, James Soundpost?

THIRD MUSICIAN Faith, I know not what to say.

PETER O, I cry you mercy, you are the singer. I will say for you. It is "music with her silver sound," because musicians have no gold for sounding:
"Then music with her silver sound
With speedy help doth lend redress." *Exit.*

FIRST MUSICIAN What a pestilent knave is this same!

SECOND MUSICIAN Hang him, Jack! Come, we'll in here, tarry for the mourners, and stay dinner. *Exeunt.*

[ACT V • SCENE I]

Enter Romeo.

ROMEO
If I may trust the flattering truth of sleep,
My dreams presage some joyful news at hand.
My bosom's lord sits lightly in his throne,
And all this day an unaccustom'd spirit
Lifts me above the ground with cheerful thoughts.
I dreamt my lady came and found me dead—
Strange dream, that gives a dead man leave to think!—
And breath'd such life with kisses in my lips
That I reviv'd and was an emperor.
Ah me, how sweet is love itself possess'd,
When but love's shadows are so rich in joy!

Enter Romeo's Man [*Balthasar, booted*].

News from Verona! How now, Balthasar,
Dost thou not bring me letters from the friar?
How doth my lady? Is my father well?
How fares my Juliet? That I ask again,
For nothing can be ill, if she be well.

BALTHASAR
Then she is well, and nothing can be ill.
Her body sleeps in Capels' monument,
And her immortal part with angels lives.
I saw her laid low in her kindred's vault,
And presently took post to tell it you.
O, pardon me for bringing these ill news,
Since you did leave it for my office, sir.

ROMEO
Is it e'en so? Then I defy you, stars!
Thou knowest my lodging. Get me ink and paper,
And hire post-horses; I will hence tonight.

BALTHASAR
I do beseech you, sir, have patience.
Your looks are pale and wild, and do import
Some misadventure.

ROMEO Tush, thou art deceiv'd.
Leave me, and do the thing I bid thee do.
Hast thou no letters to me from the friar?

BALTHASAR
No, my good lord.

ROMEO No matter. Get thee gone,
And hire those horses. I'll be with thee straight.
Exit [*Balthasar*].
Well, Juliet, I will lie with thee tonight.
Let's see for means. O mischief, thou art swift

100–101 case . . . amended (1) things generally could be much better (2) the instrument case could be repaired **101 s.d. Enter Peter** (Q2 has *Enter Will Kemp,* well-known comic actor and member of Shakespeare's company, for whom Shakespeare evidently intended this role and so named him in the manuscript.) **102, 106–107 "Heart's ease," "My heart is full"** (Popular ballads.) **107 dump** mournful tune or dance **115 gleek** jest, gibe **115–116 give you the minstrel** insultingly term you a minstrel, i.e., vagabond **120 carry no crotchets** (1) endure no whims (2) sing no quarter-notes **121 re, fa** musical notes. **note** (1) heed (2) set to music **124 put out** display **125 dry-beat** thrash (without drawing blood) **128–130 "When . . . sound"** (From Richard Edwards' song "In Commendation of Music," published in *The Paradise of Daintie Devices,* 1576.) **132 Catling** (A catling was a small lutestring made of catgut.) **135 Rebeck** (A rebeck was a fiddle with three strings.) **137 sound** make music **138 Soundpost** (A soundpost is the pillar or peg which supports the sounding board of a stringed instrument.) **140 cry you mercy** beg your pardon **142 have . . . sounding** i.e., are paid only silver for playing

147 stay await

V.i. Location: Mantua. A street.
1 flattering favorable (but potentially illusory) **3 bosom's lord** i.e., heart **21 presently took post** at once started off in haste; or, with posthorses **35 for means** by what means

To enter in the thoughts of desperate men!
I do remember an apothecary—
And hereabouts 'a dwells—which late I noted
In tatt'red weeds, with overwhelming brows,
Culling of simples. Meager were his looks,
Sharp misery had worn him to the bones;
And in his needy shop a tortoise hung,
An alligator stuff'd, and other skins
Of ill-shap'd fishes; and about his shelves
A beggarly account of empty boxes,
Green earthen pots, bladders, and musty seeds,
Remnants of packthread, and old cakes of roses
Were thinly scattered, to make up a show.
Noting this penury, to myself I said,
"An if a man did need a poison now,
Whose sale is present death in Mantua,
Here lives a caitiff wretch would sell it him."
O, this same thought did but forerun my need,
And this same needy man must sell it me.
As I remember, this should be the house.
Being holiday, the beggar's shop is shut.
What, ho! Apothecary!

[Enter Apothecary.]

APOTHECARY Who calls so loud?

ROMEO
Come hither, man. I see that thou art poor.
Hold, there is forty ducats. [*Shows gold.*] Let me have
A dram of poison, such soon-speeding gear
As will disperse itself through all the veins
That the life-weary taker may fall dead,
And that the trunk may be discharg'd of breath
As violently as hasty powder fir'd
Doth hurry from the fatal cannon's womb.

APOTHECARY
Such mortal drugs I have, but Mantua's law
Is death to any he that utters them.

ROMEO
Art thou so bare and full of wretchedness,
And fearest to die? Famine is in thy cheeks,
Need and oppression starveth in thy eyes,
Contempt and beggary hangs upon thy back.
The world is not thy friend, nor the world's law;
The world affords no law to make thee rich.
Then be not poor, but break it, and take this.

APOTHECARY
My poverty, but not my will, consents.

ROMEO
I pay thy poverty, and not thy will.

APOTHECARY
Put this in any liquid thing you will,
And drink it off; and, if you had the strength
Of twenty men, it would dispatch you straight.
[Gives poison, and takes the gold.]

ROMEO
There is thy gold, worse poison to men's souls,
Doing more murder in this loathsome world
Than these poor compounds that thou mayst not sell.
I sell thee poison; thou hast sold me none.
Farewell. Buy food, and get thyself in flesh.
Come, cordial and not poison, go with me
To Juliet's grave, for there must I use thee. *Exeunt.*

[SCENE II]

Enter Friar John to Friar Laurence.

FRIAR JOHN
Holy Franciscan friar! Brother, ho!

Enter [Friar] Laurence.

FRIAR LAURENCE
This same should be the voice of Friar John.
Welcome from Mantua! What says Romeo?
Or, if his mind be writ, give me his letter.

FRIAR JOHN
Going to find a barefoot brother out,
One of our order, to associate me,
Here in this city visiting the sick,
And finding him, the searchers of the town,
Suspecting that we both were in a house
Where the infectious pestilence did reign,
Seal'd up the doors and would not let us forth,
So that my speed to Mantua there was stay'd.

FRIAR LAURENCE
Who bare my letter, then, to Romeo?

FRIAR JOHN
I could not send it—here it is again—
Nor get a messenger to bring it thee,
So fearful were they of infection. *[Gives letter.]*

FRIAR LAURENCE
Unhappy fortune! By my brotherhood,
The letter was not nice but full of charge,
Of dear import, and the neglecting it
May do much danger. Friar John, go hence;
Get me an iron crow, and bring it straight
Unto my cell.

FRIAR JOHN
Brother, I'll go and bring it thee. *Exit.*

FRIAR LAURENCE
Now must I to the monument alone.
Within this three hours will fair Juliet wake.
She will beshrew me much that Romeo
Hath had no notice of these accidents;
But I will write again to Mantua,
And keep her at my cell till Romeo come—
Poor living corse, clos'd in a dead man's tomb! *Exit.*

37 apothecary druggist **39 weeds** clothes. **overwhelming brows** eyebrows jutting out over his eyes **40 simples** medicinal herbs **45 beggarly account** poor array **47 cakes of roses** petals pressed into cakes to be used as perfume **51 present** immediate **52 caitiff** miserable **59 ducats** gold coins **60 soon-speeding gear** quickly effective stuff **66 mortal** deadly **67 any he** anyone. **utters** issues, gives out **70 starveth** are revealed by the starving look

85 cordial restorative for the heart

V.ii. Location: Verona. Friar Laurence's cell.
6 associate accompany **8 searchers of the town** town officials charged with public health (and especially concerned about the *pestilence* or plague) **18 nice** trivial. **charge** importance **19 dear** precious, urgent **21 crow** crowbar **26 beshrew** i.e., reprove **27 accidents** events

[SCENE III]

Enter Paris, and his Page [bearing flowers, perfumed water, and a torch].

PARIS
Give me thy torch, boy. Hence, and stand aloof.
Yet put it out, for I would not be seen.
Under yond yew trees lay thee all along,
Holding thy ear close to the hollow ground.
So shall no foot upon the churchyard tread,
Being loose, unfirm, with digging up of graves,
But thou shalt hear it. Whistle then to me,
As signal that thou hearest something approach.
Give me those flowers. Do as I bid thee, go.

PAGE [*Aside*]
I am almost afraid to stand alone
Here in the churchyard, yet I will adventure.
[*Retires.*]

PARIS
Sweet flower, with flowers thy bridal bed I strew—
[*He strews flowers and sprinkles perfumed water.*]
O woe! Thy canopy is dust and stones—
Which with sweet water nightly I will dew,
Or, wanting that, with tears distill'd by moans.
The obsequies that I for thee will keep
Nightly shall be to strew thy grave and weep.
Whistle Boy.
The boy gives warning something doth approach.
What cursed foot wanders this way tonight,
To cross my obsequies and true love's rite?
What, with a torch? Muffle me, night, awhile.
[*Retires.*]

Enter Romeo and [Balthasar, with a torch, a mattock, and a crowbar].

ROMEO
Give me that mattock and the wrenching iron.
[*Takes the tools.*]
Hold, take this letter. Early in the morning
See thou deliver it to my lord and father.
[*Gives letter and takes torch.*]
Give me the light. Upon thy life I charge thee,
Whate'er thou hearest or seest, stand all aloof,
And do not interrupt me in my course.
Why I descend into this bed of death
Is partly to behold my lady's face,
But chiefly to take thence from her dead finger
A precious ring—a ring that I must use
In dear employment. Therefore hence, be gone.
But if thou, jealous, dost return to pry
In what I farther shall intend to do,
By heaven, I will tear thee joint by joint
And strew this hungry churchyard with thy limbs.
The time and my intents are savage-wild,
More fierce and more inexorable far
Than empty tigers or the roaring sea.

BALTHASAR
I will be gone, sir, and not trouble ye.

ROMEO
So shalt thou show me friendship. Take thou that.
[*Gives him money.*]
Live, and be prosperous; and farewell, good fellow.

BALTHASAR [*Aside*]
For all this same, I'll hide me hereabout.
His looks I fear, and his intents I doubt. [*Retires.*]

ROMEO
Thou detestable maw, thou womb of death,
Gorg'd with the dearest morsel of the earth,
Thus I enforce thy rotten jaws to open,
And, in despite, I'll cram thee with more food!
[*Opens the tomb.*]

PARIS
This is that banish'd haughty Montague
That murd'red my love's cousin, with which grief
It is supposed the fair creature died,
And here is come to do some villainous shame
To the dead bodies. I will apprehend him.
[*Comes forward.*]
Stop thy unhallowed toil, vile Montague!
Can vengeance be pursued further than death?
Condemned villain, I do apprehend thee.
Obey and go with me, for thou must die.

ROMEO
I must indeed, and therefore came I hither.
Good gentle youth, tempt not a desp'rate man.
Fly hence and leave me. Think upon these gone;
Let them affright thee. I beseech thee, youth,
Put not another sin upon my head
By urging me to fury. O, be gone!
By heaven, I love thee better than myself,
For I come hither arm'd against myself.
Stay not, be gone; live, and hereafter say
A madman's mercy bid thee run away.

PARIS
I do defy thy commination,
And apprehend thee for a felon here.

ROMEO
Wilt thou provoke me? Then have at thee, boy!
[*They fight.*]

PAGE
O Lord, they fight! I will go call the watch. [*Exit.*]

PARIS
O, I am slain! [*Falls.*] If thou be merciful,
Open the tomb, lay me with Juliet. [*Dies.*]

ROMEO
In faith, I will. Let me peruse this face.
Mercutio's kinsman, noble County Paris!
What said my man, when my betossed soul
Did not attend him as we rode? I think
He told me Paris should have married Juliet.
Said he not so? Or did I dream it so?

V.iii. Location: Verona. A churchyard and the vault or tomb belonging to the Capulets.
3 all along at full length **6 Being** i.e., the soil being **16 obsequies** ceremonies in memory of the dead **20 cross** interrupt **33 jealous** suspicious

39 empty hungry **44 doubt** suspect **45 womb** belly **60 gone** dead **68 commination** recital of vengeful threatenings (ll. 60–63)

Or am I mad, hearing him talk of Juliet,
To think it was so? O, give me thy hand,
One writ with me in sour misfortune's book!
I'll bury thee in a triumphant grave.
A grave? O, no! A lantern, slaught'red youth, 84
For here lies Juliet, and her beauty makes
This vault a feasting presence full of light. 86
Death, lie thou there, by a dead man interr'd.
[Laying Paris in the tomb.]
How oft when men are at the point of death
Have they been merry, which their keepers call 89
A lightning before death! O, how may I
Call this a lightning? O my love, my wife!
Death, that hath suck'd the honey of thy breath,
Hath had no power yet upon thy beauty.
Thou art not conquer'd; beauty's ensign yet 94
Is crimson in thy lips and in thy cheeks,
And death's pale flag is not advanced there. 96
Tybalt, liest thou there in thy bloody sheet? 97
O, what more favor can I do to thee
Than with that hand that cut thy youth in twain
To sunder his that was thine enemy? 100
Forgive me, cousin! Ah, dear Juliet,
Why art thou yet so fair? Shall I believe
That unsubstantial Death is amorous,
And that the lean abhorred monster keeps
Thee here in dark to be his paramour?
For fear of that, I still will stay with thee, 106
And never from this pallet of dim night 107
Depart again. Here, here will I remain
With worms that are thy chambermaids. O, here
Will I set up my everlasting rest, 110
And shake the yoke of inauspicious stars
From this world-wearied flesh. Eyes, look your last!
Arms, take your last embrace! And, lips, O you
The doors of breath, seal with a righteous kiss
A dateless bargain to engrossing death! 115
[Kisses Juliet.]
Come, bitter conduct, come, unsavory guide, 116
Thou desperate pilot, now at once run on
The dashing rocks thy seasick weary bark!
Here's to my love. *[Drinks.]* O true apothecary!
Thy drugs are quick. Thus with a kiss I die. *[Dies.]*

Enter [at the other end of the churchyard] Friar [Laurence] with lantern, crow, and spade.

FRIAR LAURENCE
Saint Francis be my speed! How oft tonight 121
Have my old feet stumbled at graves! Who's there?

BALTHASAR
Here's one, a friend, and one that knows you well.

FRIAR LAURENCE
Bliss be upon you. Tell me, good my friend,
What torch is yond that vainly lends his light
To grubs and eyeless skulls? As I discern,
It burneth in the Capels' monument.

BALTHASAR
It doth so, holy sir, and there's my master,
One that you love.

FRIAR LAURENCE Who is it?

BALTHASAR Romeo.

FRIAR LAURENCE
How long hath he been there?

BALTHASAR Full half an hour.

FRIAR LAURENCE
Go with me to the vault.

BALTHASAR I dare not, sir.
My master knows not but I am gone hence,
And fearfully did menace me with death
If I did stay to look on his intents.

FRIAR LAURENCE
Stay, then, I'll go alone. Fear comes upon me.
O, much I fear some ill unthrifty thing. 136

BALTHASAR
As I did sleep under this yew-tree here,
I dreamt my master and another fought,
And that my master slew him.

FRIAR LAURENCE *[Advancing to the tomb]* Romeo!
Alack, alack, what blood is this which stains
The stony entrance of this sepulcher?
What mean these masterless and gory swords
To lie discolor'd by this place of peace?
[Enters the tomb.]
Romeo! O, pale! Who else? What, Paris too?
And steep'd in blood? Ah, what an unkind hour 145
Is guilty of this lamentable chance!
The lady stirs. *[Juliet wakes.]*

JULIET
O comfortable friar, where is my lord? 148
I do remember well where I should be,
And there I am. Where is my Romeo? *[Noise within.]*

FRIAR LAURENCE
I hear some noise. Lady, come from that nest
Of death, contagion, and unnatural sleep.
A greater power than we can contradict
Hath thwarted our intents. Come, come away.
Thy husband in thy bosom there lies dead;
And Paris too. Come, I'll dispose of thee
Among a sisterhood of holy nuns.
Stay not to question, for the watch is coming.
Come, go, good Juliet. *[Noise again.]* I dare no
longer stay. *Exit [Friar Laurence].*

JULIET
Go, get thee hence, for I will not away.
What's here? A cup, clos'd in my true love's hand?
Poison, I see, hath been his timeless end. 162
O churl, drunk all, and left no friendly drop
To help me after? I will kiss thy lips;
Happ'ly some poison yet doth hang on them, 165
To make me die with a restorative. *[Kisses him.]*
Thy lips are warm.

FIRST WATCH *[Within]*
Lead, boy. Which way?

84 lantern turret room full of windows **86 feasting presence** presence chamber for feasting **89 keepers** attendants **94 ensign** banner **96 advanced** raised **97 sheet** shroud **100 his** i.e., Romeo's own **106 still** always **107 pallet** platform, i.e., bed. (F reads *Pallace.*) **110 set . . . rest** (See IV.v.6. The meaning is, "make my final determination," with allusion to the idea of repose.) **115 dateless bargain** everlasting contract. **engrossing** monopolizing, taking all; also, drawing up the contract **116 conduct** guide (i.e., the poison) **121 be my speed** prosper me

136 unthrifty unfortunate **145 unkind** unnatural **148 comfortable** comforting **162 timeless** untimely; everlasting **165 Happ'ly** perhaps; or fortunately

JULIET
Yea, noise? Then I'll be brief. O happy dagger! 169
[*Takes Romeo's dagger.*]
This is thy sheath [*Stabs herself.*]; there rust, and let me die. [*Falls on Romeo's body, and dies.*]

Enter [*Paris'*] *Boy and Watch.*

PAGE
This is the place; there, where the torch doth burn.

FIRST WATCH
The ground is bloody. Search about the churchyard.
Go, some of you, whoe'er you find attach. 173
[*Exeunt some.*]
Pitiful sight! Here lies the County slain,
And Juliet bleeding, warm, and newly dead,
Who here hath lain these two days buried.
Go, tell the Prince; run to the Capulets;
Raise up the Montagues; some others search.
[*Exeunt others.*]
We see the ground whereon these woes do lie,
But the true ground of all these piteous woes
We cannot without circumstance descry. 181

Enter [*some of the Watch, with*] *Romeo's Man* [*Balthasar*].

SECOND WATCH
Here's Romeo's man. We found him in the churchyard.

FIRST WATCH
Hold him in safety till the Prince come hither.

Enter Friar [*Laurence*], *and another Watchman* [*with tools*].

THIRD WATCH
Here is a friar, that trembles, sighs, and weeps.
We took this mattock and this spade from him
As he was coming from this churchyard's side.

FIRST WATCH
A great suspicion. Stay the friar too.

Enter the Prince [*and Attendants*].

PRINCE
What misadventure is so early up
That calls our person from our morning rest?

Enter Capels [*Capulet and his Wife, with others*].

CAPULET
What should it be that is so shriek'd abroad?

CAPULET'S WIFE
O, the people in the street cry "Romeo,"
Some "Juliet," and some "Paris," and all run,
With open outcry, toward our monument.

PRINCE
What fear is this which startles in our ears?

FIRST WATCH
Sovereign, here lies the County Paris slain,
And Romeo dead, and Juliet, dead before,
Warm and new kill'd.

PRINCE
Search, seek, and know how this foul murder comes.

FIRST WATCH
Here is a friar, and slaughter'd Romeo's man,
With instruments upon them, fit to open
These dead men's tombs.

CAPULET
O heavens! O wife, look how our daughter bleeds!
This dagger hath mista'en, for, lo, his house 203
Is empty on the back of Montague,
And it mis-sheathed in my daughter's bosom!

CAPULET'S WIFE
O me! This sight of death is as a bell
That warns my old age to a sepulcher.

Enter Montague [*and others*].

PRINCE
Come, Montague, for thou art early up
To see thy son and heir now early down.

MONTAGUE
Alas, my liege, my wife is dead tonight;
Grief of my son's exile hath stopp'd her breath.
What further woe conspires against mine age?

PRINCE
Look, and thou shalt see.

MONTAGUE
O thou untaught! What manners is in this,
To press before thy father to a grave?

PRINCE
Seal up the mouth of outrage for a while, 216
Till we can clear these ambiguities,
And know their spring, their head, their true descent; 218
And then will I be general of your woes, 219
And lead you even to death. Meantime forbear,
And let mischance be slave to patience.
Bring forth the parties of suspicion. 222

FRIAR LAURENCE
I am the greatest, able to do least,
Yet most suspected, as the time and place
Doth make against me, of this direful murder; 225
And here I stand, both to impeach and purge 226
Myself condemned and myself excus'd. 227

PRINCE
Then say at once what thou dost know in this.

FRIAR LAURENCE
I will be brief, for my short date of breath 229
Is not so long as is a tedious tale.
Romeo, there dead, was husband to that Juliet,
And she, there dead, that Romeo's faithful wife.
I married them; and their stol'n marriage-day
Was Tybalt's doomsday, whose untimely death
Banish'd the new-made bridegroom from this city,
For whom, and not for Tybalt, Juliet pin'd.
You, to remove that siege of grief from her,

169 happy opportune **173 attach** arrest, detain **180 ground** basis (playing on the literal meaning in l. 179) **181 circumstance** details

203 his house its scabbard **216 outrage** outcry **218 spring, head** source **219 be . . . woes** be first to express grief **220 to death** i.e., (1) as far as the dead bodies (2) so far in lamentation that we shall seem dead **222 of** under **225 make** conspire, tell **226–227 to . . . excus'd** to accuse myself of what is to be condemned in me, and to exonerate myself where I ought to be excused **229 date of breath** time left to live

Betroth'd and would have married her perforce
To County Paris. Then comes she to me,
And, with wild looks, bid me devise some mean
To rid her from this second marriage,
Or in my cell there would she kill herself.
Then gave I her, so tutor'd by my art,
A sleeping potion, which so took effect
As I intended, for it wrought on her
The form of death. Meantime I writ to Romeo
That he should hither come as this dire night
To help to take her from her borrowed grave,
Being the time the potion's force should cease.
But he which bore my letter, Friar John,
Was stay'd by accident, and yesternight
Return'd my letter back. Then all alone,
At the prefixed hour of her waking,
Came I to take her from her kindred's vault,
Meaning to keep her closely at my cell
Till I conveniently could send to Romeo.
But when I came, some minute ere the time
Of her awakening, here untimely lay
The noble Paris and true Romeo dead.
She wakes, and I entreated her come forth
And bear this work of heaven with patience.
But then a noise did scare me from the tomb,
And she, too desperate, would not go with me,
But, as it seems, did violence on herself.
All this I know, and to the marriage
Her nurse is privy; and, if aught in this
Miscarried by my fault, let my old life
Be sacrific'd, some hour before his time,
Unto the rigor of severest law.

PRINCE
We still have known thee for a holy man.
Where's Romeo's man? What can he say to this?

BALTHASAR
I brought my master news of Juliet's death;
And then in post he came from Mantua
To this same place, to this same monument.
This letter he early bid me give his father,
[*Shows a letter.*]
And threat'ned me with death, going in the vault,
If I departed not and left him there.

PRINCE
Give me the letter; I will look on it.
[*Takes the letter.*]
Where is the County's page, that rais'd the watch?
Sirrah, what made your master in this place?

PAGE
He came with flowers to strew his lady's grave,
And bid me stand aloof, and so I did.
Anon comes one with light to ope the tomb,
And by and by my master drew on him,
And then I ran away to call the watch.

PRINCE
This letter doth make good the friar's words,
Their course of love, the tidings of her death;
And here he writes that he did buy a poison
Of a poor 'pothecary, and therewithal
Came to this vault to die, and lie with Juliet.
Where be these enemies? Capulet, Montague,
See what a scourge is laid upon your hate,
That heaven finds means to kill your joys with love.
And I for winking at your discords too
Have lost a brace of kinsmen. All are punish'd.

CAPULET
O brother Montague, give me thy hand.
This is my daughter's jointure, for no more
Can I demand.

MONTAGUE But I can give thee more,
For I will ray her statue in pure gold,
That whiles Verona by that name is known,
There shall no figure at such rate be set
As that of true and faithful Juliet.

CAPULET
As rich shall Romeo's by his lady's lie;
Poor sacrifices of our enmity!

PRINCE
A glooming peace this morning with it brings;
The sun, for sorrow, will not show his head.
Go hence to have more talk of these sad things.
Some shall be pardon'd, and some punished;
For never was a story of more woe
Than this of Juliet and her Romeo. [*Exeunt.*]

247 as this this very **255 closely** secretly **266 privy** in on the secret **270 still** always **273 post** haste **280 made** did

293 with by means of **294 winking at** shutting my eyes to **295 a brace of** two **297 jointure** marriage portion **299 ray** array, make ready **301 rate** value

Julius Caesar

Julius Caesar stands midway in Shakespeare's dramatic career, at a critical juncture. In some ways it is an epilogue to his English history plays of the 1590's; in other ways it introduces the period of the great tragedies. The play was evidently first performed at the new Globe theatre in the fall of 1599, shortly after *Henry V* (the last of Shakespeare's history plays about medieval England) and around the time of *As You Like It* (one of the last of Shakespeare's happy romantic comedies). It shortly preceded *Hamlet.* It is placed among the tragedies in the Folio of 1623, where it was first published, and is entitled *The Tragedie of Julius Caesar,* but in the table of contents it is listed as *The Life and Death of Julius Caesar* as though it were a history.

Julius Caesar shares with Shakespeare's history plays an absorption in the problems of civil war and popular unrest. Rome, like England, suffers an internal division reflected in the perturbed state of the heavens themselves. The commons, or plebeians, are easily swayed by demagogues. Opportunists prosper in this atmosphere of crisis, although fittingly even they are sometimes undone by their own scheming. Politics seems to require a morality quite apart from that of personal life, posing a tragic dilemma for Brutus as for Richard II or Henry VI. The blending of history and tragedy in *Julius Caesar,* then, is not unlike that found in several English history plays. Rome was a natural subject to which Shakespeare might turn in his continuing depiction of man's political behavior. Roman culture had recently been elevated to new importance by the classical orientation of the Renaissance. As a model of political organization it loomed larger in Elizabethan consciousness than in ours because so few other models were available, and because Greek culture was less accessible in language and tradition. According to a widely accepted mythology, Elizabethans considered themselves descended from the Romans through another Brutus, the great-grandson of Aeneas.

Yet the differences between Roman and English history are as important as the similarities. Rome's choice during her civil wars lay between a senatorial republican form of government and strong single rule. Although the monarchical English might incline to be suspicious of republicanism, they had no experience to compare with it—certainly not their various peasants' revolts such as Jack Cade's rebellion (in *2 Henry VI*). On the other hand, Roman one-man rule as it flourished under Octavius Caesar lacked the English sanctions of divine right and monarchical primogeniture. Rome was, after all, a pagan culture, and Shakespeare carefully preserves this non-Christian frame of reference. The gods are frequently invoked, and appear to respond with prophetic dreams and auguries, but their ultimate intentions are baffling. Man strives blindly; the will of the gods is inscrutable. The outcome of *Julius Caesar* is far different from the restoration of providentially ordained order at the end of *Richard III*. Calm is restored and political authority reestablished, but we are by no means sure that a divine morality has been served. Roman history for Shakespeare is history divested of its divine imperatives and located in a distant political setting, where dispassionate appraisal is less difficult. In Plutarch's *Lives* as translated by Sir Thomas North, Shakespeare discovered a rich opportunity for pursuing the ironies of political life to which he had been increasingly attracted in the English histories. In fact he was drawn throughout his career to Plutarch: to the portrait of Portia in "The Life of Marcus Brutus" not only for Portia in *Julius Caesar* but for Lucrece in *The Rape of Lucrece,* Kate in *1 Henry IV,* and Portia in *The Merchant of Venice;* to "The Life of Theseus" for the Duke of *A Midsummer Night's Dream;* and to various Lives for *Julius Caesar, Coriolanus, Antony and Cleopatra,* and *Timon of Athens.* Freed from the orthodoxies of the Elizabethan world view, Shakespeare turned in the Roman or classical plays toward irony or outright satire (as in *Troilus and Cressida*) and toward the personal tragedy of political dilemma (as in *Coriolanus* and *Julius Caesar*). These are to be the dominant motifs of the Roman or classical plays, as distinguished from both the English histories and the great tragedies of evil in which politics plays a lesser part *(Hamlet, Othello, King Lear, Macbeth).*

Julius Caesar is an ambivalent study of civil conflict. As in *Richard II,* the play is structured around two protagonists rather than one. Caesar and Brutus, men of extraordinary abilities and debilitating weaknesses, are more like one another than either would care to admit. This antithetical balance reflects a dual tradition: the medieval view of Dante and Chaucer condemning Brutus and Cassius as conspirators, and the Renaissance view of Sir Philip Sidney and Ben Jonson condemning Caesar as a tyrant. These opposing views still live on in various twentieth-century productions which seek to enlist the play on the side of conservatism or liberalism. In one famous production by Orson Welles, 1937, Caesar was made out to resemble Benito Mussolini, Italy's fascist dictator. This interpretation reflects what the conspirators themselves believe, as they cry "Liberty! Freedom! Tyranny is dead!" but the play itself will not sustain so one-sided a view. Some more recent productions have favored a balance, as in the film version of the early 1950's by John Houseman and Charles Mankiewicz in which the major roles are evenly distributed among various well-known actors and actresses—John Gielgud as Cassius, Marlon Brando as Antony, James Mason as Brutus, Louis Calhern as Caesar, Greer Garson as Calpurnia, Deborah Kerr as Portia—instead of allowing one actor to dominate the play. Most recent criticism has similarly abandoned the fruitless debate among the Victorians as to whether Brutus or Caesar is the tragic protagonist, in favor of a multiple perspective.

Caesar himself is a study in paradox. He's unquestionably a great general, astute in politics, decisive in his judgments, and sharp in his evaluation of men—as, for example, in his distrust of Cassius with his "lean and hungry look." Yet this mightiest of men, who in Cassius' phrase bestrides the narrow world "like a Colossus," is also deaf in one ear, prone to fevers and epilepsy, unable to compete with Cassius by swimming the Tiber fully armed, and afflicted with a sterile marriage. Physical limitations of this sort are common enough, but in Caesar they are constantly juxtaposed with his aspirations to be above mortal weakness. He dies boasting that he is like the "northern star," constant, unique, "Unshak'd of motion." He professes to fear nothing and yet is notoriously superstitious. He calmly reflects that "death, a necessary end, Will come when it will come," and then arrogantly boasts in the next moment that "danger knows full well That Caesar is more dangerous than he" (II,ii). As his wife puts it, Caesar's "wisdom is consum'd in confidence." He willfully betrays his own best instincts and ignores plain warnings through self-deception. He stops a procession to hear a soothsayer and then dismisses the man as "a dreamer." He commissions his augurers to determine whether he should stay at home on the ides of March, and then persuades himself that acting on their advice would be a sign of weakness. Most fatally, he thinks himself above flattery and so is especially vulnerable to it. So wise and powerful a man as this cannot stop the process of his own fate, because his fate and character are interwoven: he is the victim of his own *hubris.* His insatiable desire for the crown overbalances his judgment; no warnings of the gods can save him. Even his virtues conspire against him, for he regards himself as one who puts public interest ahead of personal affairs, and brushes aside the letter of Artemidorus that would have told him of the conspiracy.

Brutus, for all his opposition to Caesar, is also a paradoxical figure. His strengths are quite unlike those of Caesar, but his weaknesses are surprisingly similar. Brutus is a noble Roman from an ancient family whose glory it has been to defend the personal liberties of Rome, the republican tradition. Brutus' virtues are personal virtues. He enjoys an admirable rapport with his courageous and intelligent wife, and is genuinely kind to his servants. In friendship he is trustworthy. He deplores oaths in the conspiracy because his word is his bond. He finds Caesar's ambition for power distasteful and vulgar; his opposition to Caesar is both idealistic and patrician. Brutus' *hubris* is a pride of family, and on this score he is vulnerable to flattery. As Cassius reminds him, alluding to Brutus' ancestor Lucius Junius Brutus, who founded the Roman Republic in 509 B.C.: "There was a Brutus once that would have brook'd Th' eternal devil to keep his state in Rome As easily as a king" (I,ii). Should not Marcus Brutus be the savior of his country from a return to tyranny? Is not he a more fit leader for Rome than Caesar? " 'Brutus' and 'Caesar.' What should be in that 'Caesar'? Why should that name be sounded more than yours?" Cassius' strategy is to present to Brutus numerous testimonials "all tending to the great opinion That Rome holds of his name." Cassius plays the role of tempter here, but the notion he suggests is not new to Brutus.

Cassius works on Brutus' pride much as, in a parallel and adjoining scene, Decius works on Caesar's ambition (II,i and II,ii). In these two scenes, the protagonists enter alone during the troubled night, call for a servant, receive the conspirators, and dispute the wise caution of their wives. Both men are prone to temptation because of their predisposition toward what is suggested. Brutus has often thought of himself as the indispensable man for the preservation of Rome's liberties. Despite his good breeding and coolly rational manner, he is as dominating a personality as Caesar, as hard to move once his mind is made up. Indeed, the conspiracy founders on Brutus' repeated insistence on having his way. He allows no oaths among the conspirators and will not kill Antony along with Caesar. He permits Antony to speak after him in Caesar's funeral. He vetoes Cicero as a fellow-conspirator. In each instance the other conspirators are unanimously opposed to Brutus' choice but yield to him. Brutus cuts off Cassius' objections before hearing them fully, being accustomed to having his way without dispute. His motives are in part noble and idealistic: Brutus wishes to have the conspirators behave generously and openly, as heroes rather than as henchmen. Yet there is something loftily patrician in his desire to have the fruits of conspiracy without any of the dirty work. His willingness to have Antony speak after him betrays a vain confidence in his own oratory and an unjustified faith in the plebeian mob. Moreover, when Brutus overrides Cassius once more in the decision to fight at Philippi and is proved wrong by the event, no idealistic motive can excuse Brutus' insistence on being obeyed; Cassius is the more experienced soldier. Still, Brutus' fatal limitations as leader of a *coup d'état* are inseparable from his virtues as a private man. The sad truth is that such a noble man is, by his very nature, unsuited for the stern exigencies of assassination and civil war. Brutus is strong-minded about his ideals, but he cannot be ruthless. The means and the end of revolution drift further and further apart. He cannot supply his troops at Philippi because he will not forage among the peasants of the countryside, and will not countenance among his allies the routine corruptions of an army in time of war. Even suicide is distasteful for Brutus, obliging him to embarrass his friends by asking their help. Brutus is too high-minded and genteel a man for the troubled times in which he lives.

The times indeed seem to demand ruthless action of the sort Antony and Octavius are all too ready to provide. The greatest irony of Brutus' fall is that the coup he undertakes for Roman liberty yields only further diminutions of that liberty. The plebeians are not ready for the commonwealth Brutus envisages. From the first they are portrayed as amiable but "saucy" (even in the opinion of their tribunes, Flavius and Marullus). They adulate Caesar at the expense of their previous idol, Pompey. When Brutus successfully appeals for a moment to their changeable loyalties, they cry "Let him be Caesar!" and "Caesar's better parts Shall be crown'd in Brutus" (III,ii). If Brutus were not swayed by this hero-worship, he would have good cause to be disillusioned. To his personal credit he is not the demogogue the plebeians take him for, and so cannot continue to bend them to his will. Cassius, too, for all his villainlike role as tempter to Brutus, his envious motive, and his "Epicurean" skepticism, reveals a finer nature as the play progresses. Inspired perhaps by Brutus' philosophic idealism, Cassius turns philosopher also and accepts defeat in a noble but ineffectual cause. Yet even his death is futile; Cassius is misinformed about the fate of his friend Titinius and so stabs himself just when the battle is going well for the conspirators.

The ultimate victors are Antony and Octavius. Antony, whatever finer nature he may possess, becomes under the stress of circumstance a cunning bargainer with the conspirators and a masterful rhetorician who characterizes himself to the plebeians as a "plain blunt man." In sardonic soliloquy at the end of his funeral oration he observes, "Now let it work. Mischief, thou art afoot, Take thou what course thou wilt" (III,ii). He is, to be sure, stirred by loyalty to Caesar's memory, but to the end of avenging Caesar's death he is prepared to unleash violence at whatever risk to the state. He regards Lepidus contemptuously as a mere "creature" under his command. Antony is older than Octavius, and teaches the younger man about political realities, but an Elizabethan audience would probably savor the irony that Octavius will subsequently beat Antony at his own game. At Philippi, Octavius gives us a glimpse of the peremptory manner for which he is to become famous, like his predecessor. Antony and Octavius together are in any case a fearsome pair, matter-of-factly noting down the names of those who must die, including their own kinsmen. They cut off the bequests left to the populace in Caesar's will, by which Antony had won the hearts of the plebeians (IV,i). Many innocent persons are sacrificed by the new reign of terror, including Cicero and the poet unluckily named Cinna. In such deaths, art and civilization yield to expediency. Rationality gives way to frenzied rhetoric and to a struggle for power in which Rome's republican tradition is buried forever. Such is the achievement of Brutus' noble revolution.

Appropriately for such a depiction of ambivalent political strife, *Julius Caesar* is written chiefly in the oratorical mode. It resembles its near contemporary, *Henry V,* in devoting so much attention to speeches of public persuasion. The famous orations following Caesar's assassination, one by Brutus in the so-called Laconic style (that is, concise and sententious) and one by Antony in the Asiatic style (that is, more florid, anecdotal, and literary), are only the most prominent of many public utterances. In the first scene, Marullus rebukes the plebeians for their disloyalty to Pompey, and for the moment dissuades them from idolizing Caesar. Decius Brutus changes Caesar's presumably unalterable mind about staying home on the ides of March (II,ii). Caesar lectures the Senate on the virtues of constancy. Before Philippi, the contending armies clash with verbal taunts. Octavius ends the play with a tribute to the dead Brutus. In less public scenes, as well, oratory serves to win Brutus over to the conspirators, to urge unavailingly that Brutus confide in his wife, or to warn the unheeding Caesar of his danger. The decline of the conspirators' cause shows in their descent from rational discourse to private bickering (IV,iii). The play gives us a range of rhetorical styles, from the deliberative (having to do with careful consideration of choices) to the forensic (analogous to pleading at law, maintaining one side or the other of a given question), to the epideictic (for display, as in set orations). The imagery, suitably public and rhetorical in its function, is of a fixed star in the firmament, a Colossus bestriding the petty world of men, a tide of fortune in the affairs of men, a statue spouting fountains of blood. The city of Rome is a vivid presence in the play, conveyed at times through Elizabethan anachronisms such as striking clocks, sweaty nightcaps, "tow'rs and windows, yea, . . . chimney-tops," but in an eclectic fusion of native and classical traditions wherein anachronisms become functionally purposeful. Style affords us one more way of considering *Julius Caesar* as a Janus play looking back to Shakespeare's history plays and forward to his tragedies.

A structural pattern to be found in *Julius Caesar,* as noted by John Velz (*Modern Language Review,* 1971), is the undular repetition of rise and fall by which the great men of ancient Rome succeed one another. The process antedates the play itself, for Pompey's faded glory mentioned in Act I is a reminder—or should be a reminder—that man's rise to fortune lasts but a day. We behold Caesar at the point of his greatest triumph and his imminent decline to death. "O mighty Caesar, dost thou lie so low?" asks Antony when he sees the prostrate body of the once most powerful man alive, "Are all thy conquests, glories, triumphs, spoils, Shrunk to this little measure?" (III,i). Brutus and Cassius step forward into prominence only to be supplanted by Antony and Octavius. Antony is unaware, though presumably the audience is aware, that Antony is to fall at the hands of Octavius. The process of incessant change, reinforced by such metaphors as the tide in the affairs of men (already noted), offering its mocking comment on Caesar's self-comparison to the fixed northern star, is not simply a meaningless descent on the grand staircase of history, for Octavius' *Pax Romana* lies at the end of the cycle from republic to empire. Still, that resting-place is beyond the conclusion of this open-ended play. What we see here again and again is a human blindness to history through which a succession of protagonists repeat one another's errors witout intending to do so. Cassius, like Caesar, goes to his death in the face of unpropitious omens which he now partly believes true. The eagles that accompanied Cassius and his army to Philippi desert him as the moment of battle approaches. These omens suggest a balance between character and fate, for, though the leaders of Rome have one by one fallen through their own acts and choices, they have also, it seems, fulfilled a prearranged destiny. Brutus, confronted by the Ghost of Caesar and assured that he will see this "spirit of Caesar" at Philippi, answers resolutely, "Well, I will see thee at Philippi, then" (IV,iii). Defeated in battle as he sensed he would be, Brutus unwillingly takes his life in disregard of the stoic creed that has governed the conduct of his entire life. Cassius dies on his birthday. *Sic transit gloria mundi.*

Julius Caesar

[*Dramatis Personae*

JULIUS CAESAR.
OCTAVIUS CAESAR, MARK ANTONY, M. AEMILIUS LEPIDUS, *triumvirs after the death of Julius Caesar.*
CICERO, PUBLIUS, POPILIUS LENA, *senators.*
MARCUS BRUTUS, CASSIUS, CASCA, TREBONIUS, CAIUS LIGARIUS, DECIUS BRUTUS, METELLUS CIMBER, CINNA, *conspirators against Julius Caesar.*
FLAVIUS *and* MARULLUS, *tribunes.*
ARTEMIDORUS OF CNIDOS, *a teacher of Rhetoric.*
SOOTHSAYER.
CINNA, *a poet.*
Another POET.
LUCILIUS, TITINIUS, MESSALA, YOUNG CATO, VOLUMNIUS, FLAVIUS, *officers under Brutus and Cassius.*
VARRO, CLITUS, CLAUDIUS, DARDANIUS, *soldiers in Brutus' army.*
STRATO, LUCIUS, *servants and slaves to Brutus.*
PINDARUS, *servant and slave to Cassius.*

CALPURNIA, *wife to Caesar.*
PORTIA, *wife to Brutus.*

SENATORS, CITIZENS, GUARDS, ATTENDANTS, *etc.*

SCENE: *Rome; the neighborhood of Sardis; the neighborhood of Philippi.*]

ACT I • SCENE I

Enter Flavius, Marullus, and certain Commoners over the stage.

FLAVIUS
Hence! Home, you idle creatures, get you home!
Is this a holiday? What, know you not,
Being mechanical, you ought not walk 3
Upon a laboring day without the sign 4
Of your profession? Speak, what trade art thou?

CARPENTER Why, sir, a carpenter.

MARULLUS
Where is thy leather apron and thy rule?
What dost thou with thy best apparel on?
You, sir, what trade are you?

COBBLER Truly, sir, in respect of a fine workman, I am 10
but, as you would say, a cobbler. 11

MARULLUS
But what trade art thou? Answer me directly.

COBBLER A trade, sir, that I hope I may use with a safe
conscience, which is indeed sir, a mender of bad soles. 14

FLAVIUS
What trade, thou knave? Thou naughty knave, what trade?

COBBLER Nay, I beseech you, sir, be not out with me. 16
Yet if you be out, sir, I can mend you. 17

FLAVIUS
What mean'st thou by that? Mend me, thou saucy fellow?

COBBLER Why, sir, cobble you.

FLAVIUS
Thou art a cobbler, art thou?

COBBLER Truly, sir, all that I live by is with the awl. I
meddle with no tradesman's matters, nor women's
matters; but withal I am indeed, sir, a surgeon to old 23
shoes. When they are in great danger, I recover them. 24
As proper men as ever trod upon neat's leather have 25
gone upon my handiwork. 26

FLAVIUS
But wherefore art not in thy shop today?
Why dost thou lead these men about the streets?

COBBLER Truly, sir, to wear out their shoes, to get my-
self into more work. But indeed, sir, we make holiday
to see Caesar and to rejoice in his triumph. 31

MARULLUS
Wherefore rejoice? What conquest brings he home?
What tributaries follow him to Rome, 33
To grace in captive bonds his chariot-wheels?
You blocks, you stones, you worse than senseless things!
O you hard hearts, you cruel men of Rome,
Knew you not Pompey? Many a time and oft 37
Have you climb'd up to walls and battlements, 38
To tow'rs and windows, yea, to chimney-tops, 39
Your infants in your arms, and there have sat
The livelong day, with patient expectation,
To see great Pompey pass the streets of Rome. 42
And when you saw his chariot but appear,
Have you not made an universal shout,
That Tiber trembled underneath her banks
To hear the replication of your sounds 46
Made in her concave shores?
And do you now put on your best attire?
And do you now cull out a holiday?
And do you now strew flowers in his way
That comes in triumph over Pompey's blood? 51
Be gone!
Run to your houses, fall upon your knees,
Pray to the gods to intermit the plague 54
That needs must light on this ingratitude.

FLAVIUS
Go, go, good countrymen, and, for this fault,
Assemble all the poor men of your sort;
Draw them to Tiber banks, and weep your tears
Into the channel, till the lowest stream
Do kiss the most exalted shores of all.
Exeunt all the Commoners.
See whe'er their basest metal be not mov'd. 61
They vanish tongue-tied in their guiltiness.
Go you down that way towards the Capitol;
This way will I. Disrobe the images 64
If you do find them deck'd with ceremonies. 65

MARULLUS
May we do so?
You know it is the feast of Lupercal. 67

FLAVIUS
It is no matter. Let no images
Be hung with Caesar's trophies. I'll about,
And drive away the vulgar from the streets. 70
So do you too, where you perceive them thick.
These growing feathers pluck'd from Caesar's wing
Will make him fly an ordinary pitch, 73
Who else would soar above the view of men
And keep us all in servile fearfulness. *Exeunt.*

I.i. Location: Rome. A street.
3 mechanical of the class of artisans **4 sign** garb and implements **10 in . . . workman** (1) as far as skilled work is concerned (2) compared with a skilled workman **11 cobbler** (1) one who works with shoes (2) bungler **14 soles** (with pun on *souls*) **16–17 out** (1) out of temper (2) having worn-out soles **17 mend** (1) reform (2) repair **23 withal** yet (with pun on *with awl*) **24 recover** (1) resole (2) cure **25 proper** handsome. **as . . . leather** as ever wore shoes. (Proverbial.) **neat's leather** cowhide **26 gone** walked **31 triumph** triumphal procession. (Caesar had overthrown the sons of Pompey in Spain at the Battle of Munda, March 17, 45 B.C. The triumph was held that October.) **33 tributaries** captives who will pay ransom (tribute)

37 Pompey (Caesar had overthrown the great soldier and onetime triumvir at the Battle of Pharsalus in 48 B.C., and Pompey had been murdered in Egypt.) **38–39 battlements . . . chimney-tops** (The details are appropriate to an Elizabethan city or town.) **42 great** (Alludes to Pompey's epithet, *Magnus*, great.) **46 replication** echo **51 Pompey's blood** (1) Pompey's offspring (2) the blood of the Pompeys **54 intermit** withhold **61 See . . . mov'd** see how even their ignoble natures can be appealed to. **whe'er** whether. **metal** (1) substance (2) temperament **64 images** statues (of Caesar in royal regalia, set up by his followers) **65 ceremonies** ceremonial trappings of state **67 feast of Lupercal** a feast of purification *(februa,* whence *February)* in honor of Pan, celebrated from ancient times in Rome on February 15 of each year. (Historically, this celebration came some months after Caesar's triumph in October of 45 B.C. The celebrants, called *Luperci,* raced around the Palatine Hill and the Circus carrying thongs of goatskin with which they struck those who came in their way. Women so lashed were supposed to be cured of barrenness; hence Caesar's wish that Antony would strike Calpurnia, I.ii.6–8.) **70 vulgar** commoners, plebeians **73 pitch** highest point in flight. (A term from falconry.)

[SCENE II]

Enter Caesar; Antony, for the course; Calpurnia, Portia, Decius, Cicero, Brutus, Cassius, Casca, a Soothsayer; after them, Marullus and Flavius.

CAESAR
Calpurnia!
CASCA Peace, ho! Caesar speaks.
CAESAR Calpurnia!
CALPURNIA
Here, my lord.
CAESAR
Stand you directly in Antonius' way,
When he doth run his course. Antonius!
ANTONY
Caesar, my lord?
CAESAR
Forget not, in your speed, Antonius,
To touch Calpurnia; for our elders say,
The barren, touched in this holy chase,
Shake off their sterile curse.
ANTONY I shall remember.
When Caesar says, "Do this," it is perform'd.
CAESAR
Set on, and leave no ceremony out. [*Flourish.*]
SOOTHSAYER
Caesar!
CAESAR
Ha? Who calls?
CASCA
Bid every noise be still. Peace yet again!
[*Music ceases.*]
CAESAR
Who is it in the press that calls on me?
I hear a tongue, shriller than all the music,
Cry "Caesar!" Speak. Caesar is turn'd to hear.
SOOTHSAYER
Beware the ides of March.
CAESAR What man is that?
BRUTUS
A soothsayer bids you beware the ides of March.
CAESAR
Set him before me; let me see his face.
CASSIUS
Fellow, come from the throng. [*The soothsayer comes forward.*] Look upon Caesar.
CAESAR
What say'st thou to me now? Speak once again.
SOOTHSAYER
Beware the ides of March.
CAESAR
He is a dreamer. Let us leave him. Pass.
Sennet. Exeunt. Mane[*n*]*t Brutus and Cassius.*

I.ii. Location: A public place or street, perhaps as in the previous scene.
s.d. for the course i.e., stripped for the race, carrying a goatskin thong **15 press** throng **18 ides of March** March 15 **24 s.d. Sennet** trumpet call signaling the arrival or departure of a dignitary

CASSIUS
Will you go see the order of the course?
BRUTUS
Not I.
CASSIUS
I pray you, do.
BRUTUS
I am not gamesome. I do lack some part
Of that quick spirit that is in Antony.
Let me not hinder, Cassius, your desires;
I'll leave you.
CASSIUS
Brutus, I do observe you now of late.
I have not from your eyes that gentleness
And show of love as I was wont to have.
You bear too stubborn and too strange a hand
Over your friend that loves you.
BRUTUS Cassius,
Be not deceiv'd. If I have veil'd my look,
I turn the trouble of my countenance
Merely upon myself. Vexed I am
Of late with passions of some difference,
Conceptions only proper to myself,
Which give some soil, perhaps, to my behaviors.
But let not therefore my good friends be griev'd—
Among which number, Cassius, be you one—
Nor construe any further my neglect,
Than that poor Brutus, with himself at war,
Forgets the shows of love to other men.
CASSIUS
Then, Brutus, I have much mistook your passion,
By means whereof this breast of mine hath buried
Thoughts of great value, worthy cogitations.
Tell me, good Brutus, can you see your face?
BRUTUS
No, Cassius, for the eye sees not itself
But by reflection, by some other things.
CASSIUS
'Tis just.
And it is very much lamented, Brutus,
That you have no such mirrors as will turn
Your hidden worthiness into your eye,
That you might see your shadow. I have heard
Where many of the best respect in Rome,
Except immortal Caesar, speaking of Brutus
And groaning underneath this age's yoke,
Have wish'd that noble Brutus had his eyes.
BRUTUS
Into what dangers would you lead me, Cassius,
That you would have me seek into myself
For that which is not in me?
CASSIUS
Therefore, good Brutus, be prepar'd to hear;
And since you know you cannot see yourself

25 order of the course ritual of the race **28 gamesome** fond of sports, merry **29 quick spirit** liveliness, responsiveness **34 wont** accustomed **35 stubborn** rough. (The metaphor is from horsemanship.) **37 veil'd my look** i.e., been introverted, seemed less friendly **39 Merely** entirely **40 of some difference** conflicting **41 only proper to** relating only to **42 soil** blemish **49–50 By . . . value** i.e., because of which misunderstanding (my assuming you were displeased with me) I have kept to myself important thoughts **54 just** true **58 shadow** image, reflection **59 best respect** highest repute and station

So well as by reflection, I, your glass,
Will modestly discover to yourself 69
That of yourself which you yet know not of.
And be not jealous on me, gentle Brutus. 71
Were I a common laughter, or did use 72
To stale with ordinary oaths my love 73
To every new protester; if you know 74
That I do fawn on men and hug them hard
And after scandal them, or if you know 76
That I profess myself in banqueting 77
To all the rout, then hold me dangerous. 78
Flourish, and shout.

BRUTUS
What means this shouting? I do fear the people
Choose Caesar for their king.

CASSIUS
Ay, do you fear it?
Then must I think you would not have it so.

BRUTUS
I would not, Cassius, yet I love him well.
But wherefore do you hold me here so long?
What is it that you would impart to me?
If it be aught toward the general good,
Set honor in one eye and death i' th' other,
And I will look on both indifferently; 87
For let the gods so speed me as I love 88
The name of honor more than I fear death.

CASSIUS
I know that virtue to be in you, Brutus,
As well as I do know your outward favor. 91
Well, honor is the subject of my story.
I cannot tell what you and other men
Think of this life; but, for my single self,
I had as lief not be as live to be 95
In awe of such a thing as I myself. 96
I was born free as Caesar; so were you.
We both have fed as well, and we can both
Endure the winter's cold as well as he.
For once, upon a raw and gusty day,
The troubled Tiber chafing with her shores,
Caesar said to me, "Dar'st thou, Cassius, now
Leap in with me into this angry flood,
And swim to yonder point?" Upon the word,
Accoutred as I was, I plunged in
And bade him follow; so indeed he did.
The torrent roar'd, and we did buffet it,
With lusty sinews throwing it aside
And stemming it with hearts of controversy; 109
But ere we could arrive the point propos'd,
Caesar cried, "Help me, Cassius, or I sink!"
Ay, as Aeneas, our great ancestor, 112
Did from the flames of Troy upon his shoulder
The old Anchises bear, so from the waves of Tiber
Did I the tired Caesar. And this man
Is now become a god, and Cassius is
A wretched creature and must bend his body
If Caesar carelessly but nod on him.
He had a fever when he was in Spain,
And when the fit was on him, I did mark
How he did shake. 'Tis true, this god did shake.
His coward lips did from their color fly, 122
And that same eye whose bend doth awe the world 123
Did lose his luster. I did hear him groan. 124
Ay, and that tongue of his that bade the Romans
Mark him and write his speeches in their books,
"Alas," it cried, "Give me some drink, Titinius,"
As a sick girl. Ye gods, it doth amaze me
A man of such a feeble temper should 129
So get the start of the majestic world 130
And bear the palm alone. *Shout. Flourish.* 131

BRUTUS
Another general shout?
I do believe that these applauses are
For some new honors that are heap'd on Caesar.

CASSIUS
Why, man, he doth bestride the narrow world
Like a Colossus, and we petty men 136
Walk under his huge legs and peep about
To find ourselves dishonorable graves.
Men at some time are masters of their fates.
The fault, dear Brutus, is not in our stars,
But in ourselves, that we are underlings.
Brutus and Caesar. What should be in that "Caesar"?
Why should that name be sounded more than yours?
Write them together, yours is as fair a name;
Sound them, it doth become the mouth as well;
Weigh them, it is as heavy; conjure with 'em,
"Brutus" will start a spirit as soon as "Caesar." 147
Now, in the names of all the gods at once,
Upon what meat doth this our Caesar feed
That he is grown so great? Age, thou art sham'd!
Rome, thou hast lost the breed of noble bloods!
When went there by an age, since the great flood, 152
But it was fam'd with more than with one man?
When could they say, till now, that talk'd of Rome,
That her wide walks encompass'd but one man?
Now is it Rome indeed and room enough, 156
When there is in it but one only man.
O, you and I have heard our fathers say
There was a Brutus once that would have brook'd 159
Th' eternal devil to keep his state in Rome 160
As easily as a king. 161

BRUTUS
That you do love me, I am nothing jealous. 162

69 modestly without exaggeration **71 jealous on** suspicious of **72 laughter** laughing-stock. **did use** were accustomed **73 stale** cheapen, make common. **ordinary** (1) commonplace (2) customary (3) tavern **74 protester** i.e., one who protests or declares friendship **76 scandal** slander **77 profess myself** make declarations of friendship **78 rout** mob **87 indifferently** impartially **88 speed me** make me prosper **91 favor** appearance **95 as lief not be** just as soon not exist **96 such . . . myself** i.e., a fellow mortal **109 hearts of controversy** hearts fired up by rivalry **112 Aeneas** hero of Virgil's *Aeneid*, the legendary founder of Rome (hence *our great ancestor*), who bore his aged father Anchises out of burning Troy as it was falling to the Greeks

122 color (1) i.e., normal healthy hue (2) military colors, flag. (The lips are personified as deserters.) **123 bend** glance **124 his** its **129 temper** constitution **130 get the start of** outstrip **131 palm** victor's prize **136 Colossus** (A 100-foot-high bronze statue of Helios, the sun god, one of the seven wonders of the ancient world, was commonly supposed to have stood astride the entrance to the harbor of Rhodes.) **147 start** raise **152 flood** i.e., the classical analogue of Noah's flood, one in which all humanity was destroyed except for Deucalion and his wife Pyrrha **156 Rome, room** (Pronounced alike.) **159 Brutus** i.e., Lucius Junius Brutus, who expelled the Tarquins and founded the Roman republic (c. 509 B.C.). **brook'd** tolerated **160 keep his state** i.e., set up his throne **161 As . . . king** as readily as he would tolerate a king **162 nothing jealous** not at all doubtful

What you would work me to, I have some aim.
How I have thought of this, and of these times,
I shall recount hereafter. For this present,
I would not, so with love I might entreat you,
Be any further mov'd. What you have said
I will consider; what you have to say
I will with patience hear, and find a time
Both meet to hear and answer such high things.
Till then, my noble friend, chew upon this:
Brutus had rather be a villager
Than to repute himself a son of Rome
Under these hard conditions as this time
Is like to lay upon us.

CASSIUS
I am glad that my weak words
Have struck but thus much show of fire from
Brutus.

Enter Caesar and his train.

BRUTUS
The games are done and Caesar is returning.

CASSIUS
As they pass by, pluck Casca by the sleeve,
And he will, after his sour fashion, tell you
What hath proceeded worthy note today.

BRUTUS
I will do so. But, look you, Cassius,
The angry spot doth glow on Caesar's brow,
And all the rest look like a chidden train.
Calpurnia's cheek is pale, and Cicero
Looks with such ferret and such fiery eyes
As we have seen him in the Capitol,
Being cross'd in conference by some senators.

CASSIUS
Casca will tell us what the matter is.

CAESAR
Antonius!

ANTONY
Caesar?

CAESAR
Let me have men about me that are fat,
Sleek-headed men, and such as sleep o' nights.
Yond Cassius has a lean and hungry look.
He thinks too much. Such men are dangerous.

ANTONY
Fear him not, Caesar; he's not dangerous.
He is a noble Roman, and well given.

CAESAR
Would he were fatter! But I fear him not.
Yet if my name were liable to fear,
I do not know the man I should avoid
So soon as that spare Cassius. He reads much,
He is a great observer, and he looks
Quite through the deeds of men. He loves no plays,
As thou dost, Antony; he hears no music.
Seldom he smiles, and smiles in such a sort
As if he mock'd himself and scorn'd his spirit
That could be mov'd to smile at anything.
Such men as he be never at heart's ease
Whiles they behold a greater than themselves,
And therefore are they very dangerous.
I rather tell thee what is to be fear'd
Than what I fear; for always I am Caesar.
Come on my right hand, for this ear is deaf,
And tell me truly what thou think'st of him.

Sennet. Exeunt Caesar and his Train. [*Manet Casca.*]

CASCA You pull'd me by the cloak. Would you speak with me?

BRUTUS
Ay, Casca. Tell us what hath chanc'd today,
That Caesar looks so sad.

CASCA Why, you were with him, were you not?

BRUTUS
I should not then ask Casca what had chanc'd.

CASCA Why, there was a crown offer'd him, and being offer'd him, he put it by with the back of his hand, thus; and then the people fell a-shouting.

BRUTUS
What was the second noise for?

CASCA Why, for that too.

CASSIUS
They shouted thrice. What was the last cry for?

CASCA Why, for that too.

BRUTUS
Was the crown offer'd him thrice?

CASCA Ay, marry, was 't, and he put it by thrice, every time gentler than other, and at every putting-by mine honest neighbors shouted.

CASSIUS
Who offer'd him the crown?

CASCA Why, Antony.

BRUTUS
Tell us the manner of it, gentle Casca.

CASCA I can as well be hang'd as tell the manner of it. It was mere foolery; I did not mark it. I saw Mark Antony offer him a crown—yet 'twas not a crown neither, 'twas one of these coronets—and, as I told you, he put it by once; but, for all that, to my thinking, he would fain have had it. Then he offer'd it to him again; then he put it by again; but, to my thinking, he was very loath to lay his fingers off it. And then he offer'd it the third time. He put it the third time by, and still as he refus'd it, the rabblement hooted and clapp'd their chopp'd hands, and threw up their sweaty night-caps, and utter'd such a deal of stinking breath because Caesar refus'd the crown that it had almost chok'd Caesar, for he swounded and fell down at it. And for mine own part I durst not laugh, for fear of opening my lips and receiving the bad air.

CASSIUS
But, soft, I pray you. What, did Caesar swoon?

163 work persuade. **aim** inkling **166 so . . . you** if I might entreat you in the name of friendship **184 train** retinue **186 ferret** ferretlike, i.e., small and red **188 cross'd in conference** opposed in debate **197 given** disposed **203 through** i.e., into the motives of **204 hears no music** (Regarded as a sign of a morose and treacherous character.)

215 cloak (Elizabethan costume; see also *sleeve*, l. 179, and *doublet*, l. 265.) **218 sad** serious **229 marry** i.e., indeed. (Originally, *by the Virgin Mary*.) **231 honest** worthy. (Said contemptuously.) **234 gentle** noble **238 coronets** chaplets, garlands **245 chopp'd** chapped **245–246 night-caps.** (Scornful allusion to the *pilleus*, a felt cap worn by the plebeians on festival days.) **248 swounded** swooned, fainted

CASCA He fell down in the market-place, and foam'd at mouth, and was speechless.

BRUTUS
'Tis very like. He hath the falling sickness.

CASSIUS
No, Caesar hath it not, but you and I,
And honest Casca, we have the falling sickness.

CASCA I know not what you mean by that, but I am sure Caesar fell down. If the tag-rag people did not clap him and hiss him, according as he pleas'd and displeas'd them, as they use to do the players in the theatre, I am no true man.

BRUTUS
What said he when he came unto himself?

CASCA Marry, before he fell down, when he perceiv'd the common herd was glad he refus'd the crown, he pluck'd me ope his doublet and offer'd them his throat to cut. An I had been a man of any occupation, if I would not have taken him at a word, I would I might go to hell among the rogues. And so he fell. When he came to himself again, he said, If he had done or said anything amiss, he desir'd their worships to think it was his infirmity. Three or four wenches, where I stood, cried, "Alas, good soul!" and forgave him with all their hearts. But there's no heed to be taken of them. If Caesar had stabb'd their mothers, they would have done no less.

BRUTUS
And after that, he came thus sad away?

CASCA Ay.

CASSIUS
Did Cicero say anything?

CASCA Ay, he spoke Greek.

CASSIUS
To what effect?

CASCA Nay, an I tell you that, I'll ne'er look you i' th' face again. But those that understood him smil'd at one another and shook their heads; but, for mine own part, it was Greek to me. I could tell you more news too. Marullus and Flavius, for pulling scarfs off Caesar's images, are put to silence. Fare you well. There was more foolery yet, if I could remember it.

CASSIUS Will you sup with me tonight, Casca?

CASCA No, I am promis'd forth.

CASSIUS Will you dine with me tomorrow?

CASCA Ay, if I be alive, and your mind hold, and your dinner worth the eating.

CASSIUS Good. I will expect you.

CASCA Do so. Farewell, both. *Exit.*

BRUTUS
What a blunt fellow is this grown to be!
He was quick mettle when he went to school.

CASSIUS
So is he now in execution
Of any bold or noble enterprise,
However he puts on this tardy form.
This rudeness is a sauce to his good wit,
Which gives men stomach to disgest his words
With better appetite.

BRUTUS
And so it is. For this time I will leave you.
Tomorrow, if you please to speak with me,
I will come home to you; or, if you will,
Come home to me, and I will wait for you.

CASSIUS
I will do so. Till then, think of the world.
Exit Brutus.
Well, Brutus, thou art noble. Yet I see
Thy honorable metal may be wrought
From that it is dispos'd. Therefore it is meet
That noble minds keep ever with their likes;
For who so firm that cannot be seduc'd?
Caesar doth bear me hard, but he loves Brutus.
If I were Brutus now and he were Cassius,
He should not humor me. I will this night,
In several hands, in at his windows, throw,
As if they came from several citizens,
Writings, all tending to the great opinion
That Rome holds of his name, wherein obscurely
Caesar's ambition shall be glanced at.
And after this let Caesar seat him sure,
For we will shake him, or worse days endure. *Exit.*

[SCENE III]

Thunder and lightning. Enter[, meeting,] Casca [with his sword drawn] and Cicero.

CICERO
Good even, Casca. Brought you Caesar home?
Why are you breathless? And why stare you so?

CASCA
Are not you mov'd, when all the sway of earth
Shakes like a thing unfirm? O Cicero,
I have seen tempests when the scolding winds
Have riv'd the knotty oaks, and I have seen
Th' ambitious ocean swell and rage and foam
To be exalted with the threat'ning clouds;
But never till tonight, never till now,
Did I go through a tempest dropping fire.
Either there is a civil strife in heaven,
Or else the world, too saucy with the gods,
Incenses them to send destruction.

CICERO
Why, saw you anything more wonderful?

254 like likely. **falling sickness** epilepsy. (But Cassius takes it to mean *falling into servitude.*) **258 tag-rag** rag-tag, ragged **260 use** are accustomed **265 pluck'd me** i.e., plucked. (*Me* is the ethical dative.) **doublet** Elizabethan upper garment, like a jacket **266 An** if. **man . . . occupation** (1) working man (2) man of action **276 sad** seriously **286 put to silence** dismissed from office. (So reported in Plutarch.) **289 promis'd forth** engaged to dine out **296 quick mettle** of a lively temperament

299 However however much. **tardy form** appearance of sluggishness **300 wit** intellect **301 stomach** appetite, inclination. **disgest** digest **307 the world** i.e., the state of the world **309–310 wrought . . . dispos'd** i.e., turned away from its natural disposition **313 bear me hard** bear me a grudge **315 He** i.e., Brutus. **humor** cajole **316 several hands** different handwriting **321 him sure** himself securely in power

I.iii. Location: A street.
1 Brought escorted **3 sway** established order **6 riv'd** split **8 exalted with** raised to the level of **12 saucy** insolent

CASCA
A common slave—you know him well by sight—
Held up his left hand, which did flame and burn
Like twenty torches join'd, and yet his hand,
Not sensible of fire, remain'd unscorch'd.
Besides—I ha' not since put up my sword—
Against the Capitol I met a lion,
Who glaz'd upon me, and went surly by
Without annoying me. And there were drawn
Upon a heap a hundred ghastly women,
Transformed with their fear, who swore they saw
Men, all in fire, walk up and down the streets.
And yesterday the bird of night did sit
Even at noon-day upon the market-place,
Hooting and shrieking. When these prodigies
Do so conjointly meet, let not men say
"These are their reasons, they are natural,"
For I believe they are portentous things
Unto the climate that they point upon.

CICERO
Indeed, it is a strange-disposed time.
But men may construe things after their fashion,
Clean from the purpose of the things themselves.
Comes Caesar to the Capitol tomorrow?

CASCA
He doth; for he did bid Antonius
Send word to you he would be there tomorrow.

CICERO
Good night then, Casca. This disturbed sky
Is not to walk in.

CASCA
Farewell, Cicero. *Exit Cicero.*

Enter Cassius.

CASSIUS
Who's there?

CASCA
A Roman.

CASSIUS
Casca, by your voice.

CASCA
Your ear is good. Cassius, what night is this!

CASSIUS
A very pleasing night to honest men.

CASCA
Who ever knew the heavens menace so?

CASSIUS
Those that have known the earth so full of faults.
For my part, I have walk'd about the streets,
Submitting me unto the perilous night,
And, thus unbraced, Casca, as you see,
Have bar'd my bosom to the thunder-stone;
And when the cross blue lightning seem'd to open
The breast of heaven, I did present myself
Even in the aim and very flash of it.

CASCA
But wherefore did you so much tempt the heavens?
It is the part of men to fear and tremble,
When the most mighty gods by tokens send
Such dreadful heralds to astonish us.

CASSIUS
You are dull, Casca, and those sparks of life
That should be in a Roman you do want,
Or else you use not. You look pale, and gaze,
And put on fear, and cast yourself in wonder,
To see the strange impatience of the heavens.
But if you would consider the true cause
Why all these fires, why all these gliding ghosts,
Why birds and beasts from quality and kind,
Why old men, fools, and children calculate,
Why all these things change from their ordinance,
Their natures, and preformed faculties,
To monstrous quality—why, you shall find
That heaven hath infus'd them with these spirits
To make them instruments of fear and warning
Unto some monstrous state.
Now could I, Casca, name to thee a man
Most like this dreadful night,
That thunders, lightens, opens graves, and roars
As doth the lion in the Capitol—
A man no mightier than thyself or me
In personal action, yet prodigious grown
And fearful, as these strange eruptions are.

CASCA
'Tis Caesar that you mean, is it not, Cassius?

CASSIUS
Let it be who it is. For Romans now
Have thews and limbs like to their ancestors;
But, woe the while, our fathers' minds are dead,
And we are govern'd with our mothers' spirits.
Our yoke and sufferance show us womanish.

CASCA
Indeed, they say the senators tomorrow
Mean to establish Caesar as a king,
And he shall wear his crown by sea and land,
In every place, save here in Italy.

CASSIUS
I know where I will wear this dagger then;
Cassius from bondage will deliver Cassius.
Therein, ye gods, you make the weak most strong;
Therein, ye gods, you tyrants do defeat.
Nor stony tower, nor walls of beaten brass,
Nor airless dungeon, nor strong links of iron,
Can be retentive to the strength of spirit;
But life, being weary of these worldly bars,
Never lacks power to dismiss itself.
If I know this, know all the world besides,
That part of tyranny that I do bear
I can shake off at pleasure. *Thunder still.*

CASCA
So can I.
So every bondman in his own hand bears
The power to cancel his captivity.

18 Not sensible of not feeling **20 Against** opposite or near **21 glaz'd** stared **22–23 drawn . . . heap** huddled together **23 ghastly** pallid **26 bird of night** owl, a bird of evil omen **28 prodigies** abnormalities, wonders **32 climate** region **34 construe** interpret. (Pronounced *cónster.*) **after their fashion** in their own way **35 Clean . . . purpose** contrary to the actual import or meaning **42 what night** what a night **48 unbraced** with doublet unfastened **49 thunder-stone** thunderbolt **50 cross** forked, jagged **54 part** appropriate role

58 want lack **60 put on** adopt, show signs of **64 from . . . kind** (behaving) contrary to their true nature **65 old men** dotards. **calculate** prophesy **66 ordinance** established nature **67 preformed** innate, congenital **68 monstrous** unnatural **71 monstrous state** government or commonwealth in an unnatural condition **81 thews** sinews, muscles **82 woe the while** alas for the age **84 yoke and sufferance** patience under the yoke **93 Nor** neither **95 be . . . spirit** confine a resolute spirit **96 bars** (1) prison bars (2) burdens (such as tyranny) **98 know . . . besides** let the rest of the world know

CASSIUS

And why should Caesar be a tyrant then?
Poor man, I know he would not be a wolf,
But that he sees the Romans are but sheep;
He were no lion, were not Romans hinds.
Those that with haste will make a mighty fire
Begin it with weak straws. What trash is Rome,
What rubbish and what offal, when it serves
For the base matter to illuminate
So vile a thing as Caesar! But, O grief,
Where hast thou led me? I perhaps speak this
Before a willing bondman; then I know
My answer must be made. But I am arm'd,
And dangers are to me indifferent.

CASCA

You speak to Casca, and to such a man
That is no fleering tell-tale. Hold, my hand.
Be factious for redress of all these griefs,
And I will set this foot of mine as far
As who goes farthest. *[They shake hands.]*

CASSIUS

There's a bargain made.
Now know you, Casca, I have mov'd already
Some certain of the noblest-minded Romans
To undergo with me an enterprise
Of honorable-dangerous consequence;
And I do know, by this, they stay for me
In Pompey's porch. For now, this fearful night,
There is no stir or walking in the streets,
And the complexion of the element
In favor 's like the work we have in hand,
Most bloody, fiery, and most terrible.

Enter Cinna.

CASCA

Stand close awhile, for here comes one in haste.

CASSIUS

'Tis Cinna; I do know him by his gait.
He is a friend.—Cinna, where haste you so?

CINNA

To find out you. Who's that? Metellus Cimber?

CASSIUS

No, it is Casca; one incorporate
To our attempts. Am I not stay'd for, Cinna?

CINNA

I am glad on 't. What a fearful night is this!
There's two or three of us have seen strange sights.

CASSIUS

Am I not stay'd for? Tell me.

CINNA

Yes, you are. O Cassius, if you could
But win the noble Brutus to our party—

CASSIUS

Be you content. Good Cinna, take this paper, *[Gives papers.]*
And look you lay it in the praetor's chair,
Where Brutus may but find it. And throw this
In at his window. Set this up with wax
Upon old Brutus' statue. All this done,
Repair to Pompey's porch, where you shall find us.
Is Decius Brutus and Trebonius there?

CINNA

All but Metellus Cimber; and he's gone
To seek you at your house. Well, I will hie,
And so bestow these papers as you bade me.

CASSIUS

That done, repair to Pompey's theatre.
Exit Cinna.
Come, Casca, you and I will yet ere day
See Brutus at his house. Three parts of him
Is ours already, and the man entire
Upon the next encounter yields him ours.

CASCA

O, he sits high in all the people's hearts;
And that which would appear offense in us,
His countenance, like richest alchemy,
Will change to virtue and to worthiness.

CASSIUS

Him and his worth, and our great need of him,
You have right well conceited. Let us go,
For it is after midnight; and ere day
We will awake him and be sure of him. *Exeunt.*

ACT II • [SCENE I]

Enter Brutus in his orchard.

BRUTUS

What, Lucius, ho!
I cannot, by the progress of the stars,
Give guess how near to day. Lucius, I say!
I would it were my fault to sleep so soundly.
When, Lucius, when? Awake, I say! What, Lucius!

Enter Lucius.

LUCIUS

Call'd you, my lord?

BRUTUS

Get me a taper in my study, Lucius.
When it is lighted, come and call me here.

LUCIUS

I will, my lord. *Exit.*

106 hinds (1) female of the red deer (2) servants, menials **109 offal** rubbish, wood shavings **114 My answer . . . made** I will have to answer (to Caesar) for what I have said. **arm'd** (1) provided with weapons (2) morally fortified **115 indifferent** unimportant **117 fleering** fawning **118 factious** active as a partisan **125 by this** by this time. **stay** wait **126 Pompey's porch** the colonnade of Pompey's great open theatre, dedicated in 55 B.C. Caesar was assassinated there, though Shakespeare has the assassination take place in the Capitol (i.e., the Senate chamber). **128 element** sky **129 favor 's** appearance is **131 close** concealed **135 incorporate** admitted as a member **137 on 't** of it

143 praetor's chair official seat of a praetor, Roman magistrate ranking next below the consul. (Brutus was praetor, one of sixteen.) **144 Where . . . it** where Brutus cannot help finding it **146 old Brutus** (Lucius Junius Brutus; Brutus was reputed to be his descendant.) **154 parts** i.e., quarters **159 countenance** (1) support, approval (2) (honorable) appearance. **alchemy** pseudo-science the chief object of which was the transmutation of metals into gold **162 conceited** conceived, grasped

II.i. Location: Rome. Brutus' orchard, or garden.
7 Get put

BRUTUS
It must be by his death. And, for my part,
I know no personal cause to spurn at him,
But for the general. He would be crown'd.
How that might change his nature, there's the question.
It is the bright day that brings forth the adder,
And that craves wary walking. Crown him that,
And then I grant we put a sting in him
That at his will he may do danger with.
Th' abuse of greatness is when it disjoins
Remorse from power. And, to speak truth of Caesar,
I have not known when his affections sway'd
More than his reason. But 'tis a common proof
That lowliness is young ambition's ladder,
Whereto the climber-upward turns his face;
But when he once attains the upmost round,
He then unto the ladder turns his back,
Looks in the clouds, scorning the base degrees
By which he did ascend. So Caesar may.
Then, lest he may, prevent. And, since the quarrel
Will bear no color for the thing he is,
Fashion it thus: that what he is, augmented,
Would run to these and these extremities.
And therefore think him as a serpent's egg
Which, hatch'd, would, as his kind, grow mischievous,
And kill him in the shell.

Enter Lucius.

LUCIUS
The taper burneth in your closet, sir.
Searching the window for a flint, I found
This paper, thus seal'd up, and I am sure
It did not lie there when I went to bed.
Gives him the letter.

BRUTUS
Get you to bed again. It is not day.
Is not tomorrow, boy, the ides of March?

LUCIUS
I know not, sir.

BRUTUS
Look in the calendar, and bring me word.

LUCIUS
I will, sir. *Exit.*

BRUTUS
The exhalations whizzing in the air
Give so much light that I may read by them.
Opens the letter and reads.
"Brutus, thou sleep'st; awake, and see thyself!
Shall Rome, etc. Speak, strike, redress!
Brutus, thou sleep'st; awake!"
Such instigations have been often dropp'd
Where I have took them up.
"Shall Rome, etc." Thus must I piece it out:
Shall Rome stand under one man's awe? What, Rome?
My ancestors did from the streets of Rome
The Tarquin drive, when he was call'd a king.
"Speak, strike, redress!" Am I entreated
To speak and strike? O Rome, I make thee promise,
If the redress will follow, thou receivest
Thy full petition at the hand of Brutus!

Enter Lucius.

LUCIUS
Sir, March is wasted fifteen days. *Knock within.*

BRUTUS
'Tis good. Go to the gate; somebody knocks.
[Exit Lucius.]
Since Cassius first did whet me against Caesar,
I have not slept.
Between the acting of a dreadful thing
And the first motion, all the interim is
Like a phantasma, or a hideous dream.
The Genius and the mortal instruments
Are then in council; and the state of man,
Like to a little kingdom, suffers then
The nature of an insurrection.

Enter Lucius.

LUCIUS
Sir, 'tis your brother Cassius at the door,
Who doth desire to see you.

BRUTUS
Is he alone?

LUCIUS
No, sir, there are moe with him.

BRUTUS
Do you know them?

LUCIUS
No, sir; their hats are pluck'd about their ears,
And half their faces buried in their cloaks,
That by no means I may discover them
By any mark of favor.

BRUTUS
Let 'em enter. *[Exit Lucius.]*
They are the faction. O conspiracy,
Sham'st thou to show thy dang'rous brow by night,
When evils are most free? O, then by day
Where wilt thou find a cavern dark enough
To mask thy monstrous visage? Seek none, conspiracy!
Hide it in smiles and affability;
For if thou path, thy native semblance on,
Not Erebus itself were dim enough
To hide thee from prevention.

Enter the conspirators, Cassius, Casca, Decius, Cinna, Metellus [Cimber], and Trebonius.

11 spurn kick **12 general** general cause, i.e., common good **15 craves** requires. **that** i.e., king, emperor **19 Remorse** mercy, compassion **20 affections** passions **21 proof** experience **22 lowliness** i.e., pretended humbleness **29 Will . . . is** i.e., can carry no appearance of justice so far as his conduct to date is concerned **33 as his kind** according to his nature **35 closet** private chamber, study **44 exhalations** meteors

57 If . . . follow i.e., if striking Caesar will lead to the reform of grievances **64 motion** proposal **66–67 The Genius . . . council** i.e., the immortal part of man, his rational soul, deliberates or debates with his lower or mortal faculties, his physical and passionate side **67 state of man** i.e., man as a microcosm, a tiny kingdom **70 brother** (Cassius had married a sister of Brutus.) **72 moe** more **75 discover** identify **76 favor** appearance **83 path** proceed, walk about. **thy . . . on** wearing your true appearance **84 Erebus** region of darkness between earth and Hades **85 prevention** detection and being forestalled

CASSIUS
I think we are too bold upon your rest.
Good morrow, Brutus. Do we trouble you?
BRUTUS
I have been up this hour, awake all night.
Know I these men that come along with you?
CASSIUS
Yes, every man of them, and no man here
But honors you; and every one doth wish
You had but that opinion of yourself
Which every noble Roman bears of you.
This is Trebonius.
BRUTUS He is welcome hither.
CASSIUS
This, Decius Brutus.
BRUTUS He is welcome too.
CASSIUS
This, Casca; this, Cinna; and this, Metellus Cimber.
BRUTUS
They are all welcome.
What watchful cares do interpose themselves
Betwixt your eyes and night?
CASSIUS
Shall I entreat a word?
They [*Brutus and Cassius*] *whisper.*
DECIUS
Here lies the east. Doth not the day break here?
CASCA
No.
CINNA
O, pardon, sir, it doth; and yon gray lines
That fret the clouds are messengers of day.
CASCA
You shall confess that you are both deceiv'd.
Here, as I point my sword, the sun arises,
Which is a great way growing on the south,
Weighing the youthful season of the year.
Some two months hence, up higher toward the north
He first presents his fire; and the high east
Stands, as the Capitol, directly here.
BRUTUS
Give me your hands all over, one by one.
CASSIUS
And let us swear our resolution.
BRUTUS
No, not an oath. If not the face of men,
The sufferance of our souls, the time's abuse—
If these be motives weak, break off betimes,
And every man hence to his idle bed;
So let high-sighted tyranny range on,
Till each man drop by lottery. But if these,
As I am sure they do, bear fire enough
To kindle cowards and to steel with valor
The melting spirits of women, then, countrymen,
What need we any spur but our own cause
To prick us to redress? What other bond
Than secret Romans, that have spoke the word,
And will not palter? And what other oath
Than honesty to honesty engag'd
That this shall be, or we will fall for it?
Swear priests and cowards, and men cautelous,
Old feeble carrions, and such suffering souls
That welcome wrongs; unto bad causes swear
Such creatures as men doubt; but do not stain
The even virtue of our enterprise,
Nor th' insuppressive mettle of our spirits,
To think that or our cause or our performance
Did need an oath; when every drop of blood
That every Roman bears, and nobly bears,
Is guilty of a several bastardy
If he do break the smallest particle
Of any promise that hath pass'd from him.
CASSIUS
But what of Cicero? Shall we sound him?
I think he will stand very strong with us.
CASCA
Let us not leave him out.
CINNA No, by no means.
METELLUS
O, let us have him, for his silver hairs
Will purchase us a good opinion
And buy men's voices to commend our deeds.
It shall be said his judgment rul'd our hands;
Our youths and wildness shall no whit appear,
But all be buried in his gravity.
BRUTUS
O, name him not. Let us not break with him;
For he will never follow anything
That other men begin.
CASSIUS Then leave him out.
CASCA
Indeed he is not fit.
DECIUS
Shall no man else be touch'd but only Caesar?
CASSIUS
Decius, well urg'd. I think it is not meet
Mark Antony, so well belov'd of Caesar,
Should outlive Caesar. We shall find of him
A shrewd contriver; and you know, his means,
If he improve them, may well stretch so far
As to annoy us all. Which to prevent,
Let Antony and Caesar fall together.
BRUTUS
Our course will seem too bloody, Caius Cassius,
To cut the head off and then hack the limbs,
Like wrath in death and envy afterwards;

86 upon in intruding upon **104 fret** mark with interlacing lines **107 growing on** toward **108 Weighing** considering, in consequence of **110 high** due **114 face of men** i.e., grave look of all concerned persons in the state **115 sufferance** state of suffering. **time's abuse** corruptions of the present day **116 betimes** at once **117 idle** unused, empty **118 high-sighted** upward-gazing (cf. II.i.26); or haughty, looking down from an Olympian height **119 by lottery** i.e., as the capricious tyrant chances to pick on him. **these** i.e., these injustices just cited

124 prick spur **126 palter** use trickery **127 honesty** personal honor **129 Swear** make swear. **cautelous** deceitful **130 carrions** men who resemble corpses. **suffering** long-suffering **133 even** steadfast, consistent **134 insuppressive** not to be suppressed **135 or . . . or** either . . . or **138 several bastardy** i.e., individual dishonorable act. (A noble Roman failing to keep his promise would be charged with a separate desecration of his birthright for each drop of blood in his body.) **145 purchase** procure (playing on *silver* in l. 144 as money) **150 break with** confide in **157 of** in **159 improve** exploit, make good use of **160 annoy** injure **164 envy** malice

For Antony is but a limb of Caesar.
Let's be sacrificers, but not butchers, Caius.
We all stand up against the spirit of Caesar,
And in the spirit of men there is no blood.
O, that we then could come by Caesar's spirit,
And not dismember Caesar! But, alas,
Caesar must bleed for it. And, gentle friends,
Let's kill him boldly, but not wrathfully;
Let's carve him as a dish fit for the gods,
Not hew him as a carcass fit for hounds.
And let our hearts, as subtle masters do,
Stir up their servants to an act of rage,
And after seem to chide 'em. This shall make
Our purpose necessary, and not envious;
Which so appearing to the common eyes,
We shall be call'd purgers, not murderers.
And for Mark Antony, think not of him;
For he can do no more than Caesar's arm
When Caesar's head is off.

CASSIUS
Yet I fear him,
For in the ingrafted love he bears to Caesar—

BRUTUS
Alas, good Cassius, do not think of him.
If he love Caesar, all that he can do
Is to himself—take thought and die for Caesar.
And that were much he should, for he is given
To sports, to wildness, and much company.

TREBONIUS
There is no fear in him. Let him not die,
For he will live, and laugh at this hereafter.
Clock strikes.

BRUTUS
Peace! Count the clock.

CASSIUS
The clock hath stricken three.

TREBONIUS
'Tis time to part.

CASSIUS
But it is doubtful yet
Whether Caesar will come forth today, or no;
For he is superstitious grown of late,
Quite from the main opinion he held once
Of fantasy, of dreams, and ceremonies.
It may be these apparent prodigies,
The unaccustom'd terror of this night,
And the persuasion of his augurers
May hold him from the Capitol today.

DECIUS
Never fear that. If he be so resolv'd,
I can o'ersway him; for he loves to hear
That unicorns may be betray'd with trees,
And bears with glasses, elephants with holes,
Lions with toils, and men with flatterers;
But when I tell him he hates flatterers,
He says he does, being then most flattered.
Let me work;
For I can give his humor the true bent,
And I will bring him to the Capitol.

CASSIUS
Nay, we will all of us be there to fetch him.

BRUTUS
By the eighth hour. Is that the uttermost?

CINNA
Be that the uttermost, and fail not then.

METELLUS
Caius Ligarius doth bear Caesar hard,
Who rated him for speaking well of Pompey.
I wonder none of you have thought of him.

BRUTUS
Now, good Metellus, go along by him.
He loves me well, and I have given him reasons;
Send him but hither, and I'll fashion him.

CASSIUS
The morning comes upon 's. We'll leave you, Brutus.
And, friends, disperse yourselves; but all remember
What you have said, and show yourselves true Romans.

BRUTUS
Good gentlemen, look fresh and merrily;
Let not our looks put on our purposes,
But bear it as our Roman actors do,
With untir'd spirits and formal constancy.
And so good morrow to you every one.
Exeunt. Manet Brutus.
Boy! Lucius! Fast asleep? It is no matter.
Enjoy the honey-heavy dew of slumber.
Thou hast no figures nor no fantasies
Which busy care draws in the brains of men;
Therefore thou sleep'st so sound.

Enter Portia.

PORTIA
Brutus, my lord!

BRUTUS
Portia, what mean you? Wherefore rise you now?
It is not for your health thus to commit
Your weak condition to the raw cold morning.

PORTIA
Nor for yours neither. Y' have ungently, Brutus,
Stole from my bed. And yesternight, at supper,
You suddenly arose, and walk'd about,
Musing and sighing, with your arms across,
And when I ask'd you what the matter was,
You star'd upon me with ungentle looks.
I urg'd you further; then you scratch'd your head,
And too impatiently stamp'd with your foot.
Yet I insisted, yet you answer'd not,
But, with an angry wafture of your hand,
Gave sign for me to leave you. So I did,

171 gentle noble **176 their servants** i.e., our hands **178 envious** malicious **187 take thought** despond **188 much he should** a good deal for him to do, hence unlikely **190 no fear** nothing to fear **191 s.d. Clock strikes** (A much-commented-upon anachronism; the mechanical clock was not invented until c. 1300.) **196 from the main** contrary to the strong **198 apparent** obvious **204 unicorns . . . trees** i.e., by having the unicorn imprison itself by driving its horn into a tree as it charges at the hunter **205 glasses** mirrors (enabling the hunter to approach the bear while it vainly admires itself in the mirror). **holes** pitfalls **206 toils** nets, snares

210 humor disposition. **true bent** right direction **213 uttermost** latest **215 bear Caesar hard** bear a grudge toward Caesar **216 rated** angrily rebuked **218 by him** by way of his house **219 reasons** i.e., for loving me **220 fashion** shape (to our purposes) **225 put on** display, wear in open view **227 formal constancy** steadfast appearance, decorum **229 Lucius** (Brutus calls to his servant, who is evidently within, asleep, after having admitted the conspirators at l. 85; later, at l. 309, he is still within when Brutus calls to him.) **231 figures** imaginings **240 across** folded **246 wafture** waving

Fearing to strengthen that impatience
Which seem'd too much enkindled, and withal
Hoping it was but an effect of humor,
Which sometime hath his hour with every man.
It will not let you eat, nor talk, nor sleep,
And could it work so much upon your shape
As it hath much prevail'd on your condition,
I should not know you Brutus. Dear my lord,
Make me acquainted with your cause of grief.

BRUTUS
I am not well in health, and that is all.

PORTIA
Brutus is wise, and, were he not in health
He would embrace the means to come by it.

BRUTUS
Why, so I do. Good Portia, go to bed.

PORTIA
Is Brutus sick? And is it physical
To walk unbraced and suck up the humors
Of the dank morning? What, is Brutus sick,
And will he steal out of his wholesome bed
To dare the vile contagion of the night,
And tempt the rheumy and unpurged air
To add unto his sickness? No, my Brutus,
You have some sick offense within your mind,
Which by the right and virtue of my place [*Kneels.*]
I ought to know of. And, upon my knees,
I charm you, by my once-commended beauty,
By all your vows of love, and that great vow
Which did incorporate and make us one,
That you unfold to me, your self, your half,
Why you are heavy, and what men tonight
Have had resort to you; for here have been
Some six or seven, who did hide their faces
Even from darkness.

BRUTUS
Kneel not, gentle Portia.
[*Raises her.*]

PORTIA
I should not need, if you were gentle Brutus.
Within the bond of marriage, tell me, Brutus,
Is it excepted I should know no secrets
That appertain to you? Am I yourself
But, as it were, in sort or limitation,
To keep with you at meals, comfort your bed,
And talk to you sometimes? Dwell I but in the
suburbs
Of your good pleasure? If it be no more,
Portia is Brutus' harlot, not his wife.

BRUTUS
You are my true and honorable wife,
As dear to me as are the ruddy drops
That visit my sad heart.

PORTIA
If this were true, then should I know this secret.
I grant I am a woman, but withal
A woman that Lord Brutus took to wife.
I grant I am a woman, but withal
A woman well-reputed, Cato's daughter.
Think you I am no stronger than my sex,
Being so father'd and so husbanded?
Tell me your counsels, I will not disclose 'em.
I have made strong proof of my constancy,
Giving myself a voluntary wound
Here, in the thigh. Can I bear that with patience,
And not my husband's secrets?

BRUTUS
O ye gods,
Render me worthy of this noble wife!
Knock [*within*].
Hark, hark! One knocks. Portia, go in awhile,
And by and by thy bosom shall partake
The secrets of my heart.
All my engagements I will construe to thee,
All the charactery of my sad brows.
Leave me with haste. *Exit Portia.*
Lucius, who's that knocks?

Enter Lucius and [*Caius*] *Ligarius* [*wearing a kerchief*].

LUCIUS
Here is a sick man that would speak with you.

BRUTUS
Caius Ligarius, that Metellus spake of.
Boy, stand aside. [*Exit Lucius.*] Caius Ligarius, how?

LIGARIUS
Vouchsafe good morrow from a feeble tongue.

BRUTUS
O, what a time have you chose out, brave Caius,
To wear a kerchief! Would you were not sick!

LIGARIUS
I am not sick, if Brutus have in hand
Any exploit worthy the name of honor.

BRUTUS
Such an exploit have I in hand, Ligarius,
Had you a healthful ear to hear of it.

LIGARIUS
By all the gods that Romans bow before,
I here discard my sickness! Soul of Rome!
[*Throws off his kerchief.*]
Brave son, deriv'd from honorable loins!
Thou, like an exorcist, hast conjur'd up
My mortified spirit. Now bid me run,
And I will strive with things impossible,
Yea, get the better of them. What's to do?

BRUTUS
A piece of work that will make sick men whole.

LIGARIUS
But are not some whole that we must make sick?

BRUTUS
That must we also. What it is, my Caius,

249 withal indeed **250 humor** mood **254 condition** inner state of mind **261 physical** healthful **262 humors** damps, mists **266 rheumy** damp. **unpurged** not purified (by the sun) **271 charm** conjure **281 excepted** made an exception that **283 in . . . limitation** only up to a point **285 suburbs** periphery. (In Elizabethan London, prostitutes frequented the suburbs.)

295 Cato's daughter (Cato of Utica was famous for his integrity; he sided with Pompey against Caesar in 48 B.C. and later killed himself rather than submit to Caesar's tyranny. He was Brutus' uncle as well as his father-in-law.) **298 counsels** secrets **307 construe** explain fully **308 charactery** handwriting, i.e., what is figured there **312 how** i.e., how are you **313 Vouchsafe** deign (to accept) **315 To wear a kerchief** i.e., to be ill. (An Elizabethan, not a Roman, practice.) **323 exorcist** conjurer **324 mortified** deadened

I shall unfold to thee as we are going
To whom it must be done.
LIGARIUS Set on your foot, 331
And with a heart new-fir'd I follow you,
To do I know not what; but it sufficeth
That Brutus leads me on. *Thunder.*
BRUTUS Follow me, then. *Exeunt.*

[SCENE II]

Thunder and lightning. Enter Julius Caesar, in his night-gown.

CAESAR
Nor heaven nor earth have been at peace tonight. 1
Thrice hath Calpurnia in her sleep cried out,
"Help, ho, they murder Caesar!" Who's within?

Enter a Servant.

SERVANT
My lord?
CAESAR
Go bid the priests do present sacrifice
And bring me their opinions of success. 6
SERVANT
I will, my lord. *Exit.*

Enter Calpurnia.

CALPURNIA
What mean you, Caesar? Think you to walk forth?
You shall not stir out of your house today.
CAESAR
Caesar shall forth. The things that threaten'd me
Ne'er look'd but on my back. When they shall see
The face of Caesar, they are vanished.
CALPURNIA
Caesar, I never stood on ceremonies, 13
Yet now they fright me. There is one within,
Besides the things that we have heard and seen,
Recounts most horrid sights seen by the watch.
A lioness hath whelped in the streets,
And graves have yawn'd and yielded up their dead;
Fierce fiery warriors fight upon the clouds, 19
In ranks and squadrons and right form of war, 20
Which drizzled blood upon the Capitol;
The noise of battle hurtled in the air, 22
Horses did neigh, and dying men did groan,
And ghosts did shriek and squeal about the streets.
O Caesar, these things are beyond all use, 25
And I do fear them.
CAESAR What can be avoided
Whose end is purpos'd by the mighty gods?
Yet Caesar shall go forth; for these predictions
Are to the world in general as to Caesar.
CALPURNIA
When beggars die, there are no comets seen; 30
The heavens themselves blaze forth the death of princes.
CAESAR
Cowards die many times before their deaths;
The valiant never taste of death but once.
Of all the wonders that I yet have heard,
It seems to me most strange that men should fear,
Seeing that death, a necessary end,
Will come when it will come.

Enter a Servant.

What say the augurers?
SERVANT
They would not have you to stir forth today.
Plucking the entrails of an offering forth,
They could not find a heart within the beast. 40
CAESAR
The gods do this in shame of cowardice.
Caesar should be a beast without a heart,
If he should stay at home today for fear.
No, Caesar shall not. Danger knows full well
That Caesar is more dangerous than he.
We are two lions litter'd in one day,
And I the elder and more terrible;
And Caesar shall go forth.
CALPURNIA Alas, my lord,
Your wisdom is consum'd in confidence. 49
Do not go forth today! Call it my fear
That keeps you in the house, and not your own.
We'll send Mark Antony to the Senate-house,
And he shall say you are not well today.
Let me, upon my knee, prevail in this. *[Kneels.]*
CAESAR
Mark Antony shall say I am not well,
And for thy humor I will stay at home. 56

Enter Decius.

Here's Decius Brutus. He shall tell them so.
DECIUS
Caesar, all hail! Good morrow, worthy Caesar.
I come to fetch you to the Senate-house.
CAESAR
And you are come in very happy time 60
To bear my greeting to the senators
And tell them that I will not come today.
Cannot, is false, and that I dare not, falser;
I will not come today. Tell them so, Decius.
CALPURNIA
Say he is sick.
CAESAR Shall Caesar send a lie?
Have I in conquest stretch'd mine arm so far,
To be afeard to tell graybeards the truth?
Decius, go tell them Caesar will not come.
DECIUS
Most mighty Caesar, let me know some cause,

331 To whom i.e., to him to whom

II.ii. Location: Caesar's house.
s.d. night-gown dressing-gown **1 Nor** neither **6 success** what will follow **13 stood on ceremonies** attached importance to omens **19 fight** did fight **20 right form** regular formation **22 hurtled** clashed **25 use** normal experience

49 consum'd in confidence destroyed by overconfidence **56 humor** whim **60 happy** opportune

Lest I be laugh'd at when I tell them so.

CAESAR

The cause is in my will. I will not come;
That is enough to satisfy the Senate.
But for your private satisfaction,
Because I love you, I will let you know.
Calpurnia here, my wife, stays me at home.
She dreamt tonight she saw my statue,
Which, like a fountain with an hundred spouts,
Did run pure blood; and many lusty Romans
Came smiling, and did bathe their hands in it.
And these does she apply for warnings and portents
And evils imminent, and on her knee
Hath begg'd that I will stay at home today.

DECIUS

This dream is all amiss interpreted;
It was a vision fair and fortunate.
Your statue spouting blood in many pipes,
In which so many smiling Romans bath'd,
Signifies that from you great Rome shall suck
Reviving blood, and that great men shall press
For tinctures, stains, relics, and cognizance.
This by Calpurnia's dream is signified.

CAESAR

And this way have you well expounded it.

DECIUS

I have, when you have heard what I can say;
And know it now. The Senate have concluded
To give this day a crown to mighty Caesar.
If you shall send them word you will not come,
Their minds may change. Besides, it were a mock
Apt to be render'd, for some one to say,
"Break up the Senate till another time
When Caesar's wife shall meet with better dreams."
If Caesar hide himself, shall they not whisper
"Lo, Caesar is afraid"?
Pardon me, Caesar, for my dear dear love
To your proceeding bids me tell you this;
And reason to my love is liable.

CAESAR

How foolish do your fears seem now, Calpurnia!
I am ashamed I did yield to them.
Give me my robe, for I will go.

Enter Brutus, Ligarius, Metellus, Casca, Trebonius, Cinna, and Publius.

And look where Publius is come to fetch me.

PUBLIUS

Good morrow, Caesar.

CAESAR

Welcome, Publius.
What, Brutus, are you stirr'd so early too?
Good morrow, Casca. Caius Ligarius,
Caesar was ne'er so much your enemy
As that same ague which hath made you lean.
What is 't o'clock?

BRUTUS

Caesar, 'tis strucken eight.

CAESAR

I thank you for your pains and courtesy.

Enter Antony.

See, Antony, that revels long o' nights,
Is notwithstanding up. Good morrow, Antony.

ANTONY

So to most noble Caesar.

CAESAR

Bid them prepare within.
I am to blame to be thus waited for.
Now, Cinna. Now, Metellus. What, Trebonius!
I have an hour's talk in store for you;
Remember that you call on me today.
Be near me, that I may remember you.

TREBONIUS

Caesar, I will. [*Aside.*] And so near will I be
That your best friends shall wish I had been further.

CAESAR

Good friends, go in, and taste some wine with me,
And we, like friends, will straightway go together.

BRUTUS [*Aside*]

That every like is not the same, O Caesar,
The heart of Brutus earns to think upon! *Exeunt.*

[SCENE III]

Enter Artemidorus [reading a paper].

ARTEMIDORUS "Caesar, beware of Brutus; take heed of Cassius; come not near Casca; have an eye to Cinna; trust not Trebonius; mark well Metellus Cimber; Decius Brutus loves thee not; thou hast wrong'd Caius Ligarius. There is but one mind in all these men, and it is bent against Caesar. If thou beest not immortal, look about you. Security gives way to conspiracy. The mighty gods defend thee! Thy lover,

Artemidorus."

Here will I stand till Caesar pass along,
And as a suitor will I give him this.
My heart laments that virtue cannot live
Out of the teeth of emulation.
If thou read this, O Caesar, thou mayest live;
If not, the Fates with traitors do contrive. *Exit.*

[SCENE IV]

Enter Portia and Lucius.

PORTIA

I prithee, boy, run to the Senate-house.
Stay not to answer me, but get thee gone.

75 stays detains **76 tonight** last night **78 lusty** lively, merry **80 apply for** interpret as **89 tinctures** handkerchiefs dipped in the blood of martyrs, with healing powers; or colors in a coat of arms. (*Tinctures, stains,* and *relics* are all venerated properties, as though Caesar were a saint.) **cognizance** heraldic emblems worn by a nobleman's followers **96–97 mock . . . render'd** witty remark apt to be made **103 proceeding** advancement **104 reason . . . liable** i.e., love bids me speak frankly, and prudence must bow to my affection for you

119 prepare within i.e., set out a repast of wine in the other room. (Perhaps addressed to Calpurnia.) **129 That . . . same** i.e., that everyone who seems a friend is not actually so. (Proverbial.) **130 earns** grieves

II.iii. Location: A street near the Capitol.
7 Security overconfidence. **gives way** opens a path **8 lover** friend **11 as a suitor** as if I were a petitioner **13 Out . . . emulation** i.e., beyond the reach of grudging envy **15 contrive** conspire

II.iv. Location: Before the house of Brutus.

Why dost thou stay?

LUCIUS
To know my errand, madam.

PORTIA
I would have had thee there and here again
Ere I can tell thee what thou shouldst do there.—
[*Aside.*] O constancy, be strong upon my side,
Set a huge mountain 'tween my heart and tongue!
I have a man's mind, but a woman's might.
How hard it is for women to keep counsel!—
Art thou here yet?

LUCIUS
Madam, what should I do?
Run to the Capitol, and nothing else?
And so return to you, and nothing else?

PORTIA
Yes, bring me word, boy, if thy lord look well,
For he went sickly forth; and take good note
What Caesar doth, what suitors press to him.
Hark, boy, what noise is that?

LUCIUS
I hear none, madam.

PORTIA
Prithee, listen well.
I heard a bustling rumor, like a fray,
And the wind brings it from the Capitol.

LUCIUS
Sooth, madam, I hear nothing.

Enter the Soothsayer.

PORTIA
Come hither, fellow. Which way hast thou been?

SOOTHSAYER
At mine own house, good lady.

PORTIA
What is 't o'clock?

SOOTHSAYER
About the ninth hour, lady.

PORTIA
Is Caesar yet gone to the Capitol?

SOOTHSAYER
Madam, not yet. I go to take my stand,
To see him pass on to the Capitol.

PORTIA
Thou hast some suit to Caesar, hast thou not?

SOOTHSAYER
That I have, lady, if it will please Caesar
To be so good to Caesar as to hear me:
I shall beseech him to befriend himself.

PORTIA
Why, know'st thou any harm's intended towards him?

SOOTHSAYER
None that I know will be, much that I fear may chance.
Good morrow to you. Here the street is narrow.
The throng that follows Caesar at the heels,
Of senators, of praetors, common suitors,
Will crowd a feeble man almost to death.
I'll get me to a place more void, and there
Speak to great Caesar as he comes along. *Exit.*

9 counsel a secret **18 bustling rumor** confused sound **20 Sooth** truly **23 the ninth hour** i.e., 9 a.m. (In Roman reckoning the ninth hour would be 3 p.m.) **37 void** empty, uncrowded

PORTIA
I must go in. Ay me, how weak a thing
The heart of woman is! O Brutus,
The heavens speed thee in thine enterprise!
Sure, the boy heard me.—Brutus hath a suit
That Caesar will not grant.—O, I grow faint.—
Run, Lucius, and commend me to my lord;
Say I am merry. Come to me again,
And bring me word what he doth say to thee.
Exeunt [severally].

ACT III • [SCENE I]

Flourish. Enter Caesar, Brutus, Cassius, Casca, Decius, Metellus [Cimber], Trebonius, Cinna, Antony, Lepidus, Artemidorus, Publius, [Popilius,] and the Soothsayer.

CAESAR [*To the Soothsayer*]
The ides of March are come.

SOOTHSAYER
Ay, Caesar, but not gone.

ARTEMIDORUS
Hail, Caesar! Read this schedule.

DECIUS
Trebonius doth desire you to o'er-read,
At your best leisure, this his humble suit.

ARTEMIDORUS
O Caesar, read mine first, for mine's a suit
That touches Caesar nearer. Read it, great Caesar.

CAESAR
What touches us ourself shall be last serv'd.

ARTEMIDORUS
Delay not, Caesar, read it instantly.

CAESAR
What, is the fellow mad?

PUBLIUS
Sirrah, give place.

CASSIUS
What, urge you your petitions in the street?
Come to the Capitol.

[*Caesar goes to the Capitol, the rest following.*]

POPILIUS [*To Cassius*]
I wish your enterprise today may thrive.

CASSIUS
What enterprise, Popilius?

POPILIUS
Fare you well.
[*Advances to Caesar.*]

BRUTUS
What said Popilius Lena?

CASSIUS
He wish'd today our enterprise might thrive.
I fear our purpose is discovered.

BRUTUS
Look, how he makes to Caesar. Mark him.

III.i. Location: Before the Capitol, and, following l. 12, within the Capitol.
3 schedule document **18 makes to** advances toward

CASSIUS
Casca, be sudden, for we fear prevention.
Brutus, what shall be done? If this be known,
Cassius or Caesar never shall turn back,
For I will slay myself.

BRUTUS Cassius, be constant.
Popilius Lena speaks not of our purposes;
For, look, he smiles, and Caesar doth not change.

CASSIUS
Trebonius knows his time; for, look you, Brutus,
He draws Mark Antony out of the way.
[*Exeunt Antony and Trebonius.*]

DECIUS
Where is Metellus Cimber? Let him go
And presently prefer his suit to Caesar.

BRUTUS
He is address'd. Press near and second him.

CINNA
Casca, you are the first that rears your hand.
[*They press near Caesar.*]

CAESAR
Are we all ready? What is now amiss
That Caesar and his Senate must redress?

METELLUS
Most high, most mighty, and most puissant Caesar,
Metellus Cimber throws before thy seat
An humble heart— [*Kneeling.*]

CAESAR I must prevent thee, Cimber.
These couchings and these lowly courtesies
Might fire the blood of ordinary men,
And turn preordinance and first decree
Into the law of children. Be not fond
To think that Caesar bears such rebel blood
That will be thaw'd from the true quality
With that which melteth fools—I mean, sweet words,
Low-crooked curtsies, and base spaniel fawning.
Thy brother by decree is banished.
If thou dost bend and pray and fawn for him,
I spurn thee like a cur out of my way.
Know, Caesar doth not wrong, nor without cause
Will he be satisfied.

METELLUS
Is there no voice more worthy than my own,
To sound more sweetly in great Caesar's ear
For the repealing of my banish'd brother?

BRUTUS [*Kneeling*]
I kiss thy hand, but not in flattery, Caesar,
Desiring thee that Publius Cimber may
Have an immediate freedom of repeal.

CAESAR
What, Brutus?

CASSIUS [*Kneeling*] Pardon, Caesar! Caesar, pardon!
As low as to thy foot doth Cassius fall,
To beg enfranchisement for Publius Cimber.

CAESAR
I could be well mov'd, if I were as you;
If I could pray to move, prayers would move me.
But I am constant as the northern star,
Of whose true-fix'd and resting quality
There is no fellow in the firmament.
The skies are painted with unnumb'red sparks,
They are all fire and every one doth shine,
But there's but one in all doth hold his place.
So in the world: 'tis furnish'd well with men,
And men are flesh and blood, and apprehensive;
Yet in the number I do know but one
That unassailable holds on his rank,
Unshak'd of motion. And that I am he,
Let me a little show it, even in this—
That I was constant Cimber should be banish'd,
And constant do remain to keep him so.

CINNA
O Caesar—

CAESAR Hence! Wilt thou lift up Olympus?

DECIUS
Great Caesar—

CAESAR Doth not Brutus bootless kneel?

CASCA
Speak, hands, for me!
They stab Caesar, [*Casca first, Brutus last*].

CAESAR
Et tu, Brutè? Then fall, Caesar! *Dies.*

CINNA
Liberty! Freedom! Tyranny is dead!
Run hence, proclaim, cry it about the streets.

CASSIUS
Some to the common pulpits, and cry out
"Liberty, freedom, and enfranchisement!"

BRUTUS
People and senators, be not affrighted.
Fly not; stand still. Ambition's debt is paid.

CASCA
Go to the pulpit, Brutus.

DECIUS
And Cassius too.

BRUTUS Where's Publius?

CINNA
Here, quite confounded with this mutiny.

METELLUS
Stand fast together, lest some friend of Caesar's
Should chance—

BRUTUS
Talk not of standing. Publius, good cheer.
There is no harm intended to your person,
Nor to no Roman else. So tell them, Publius.

CASSIUS
And leave us, Publius, lest that the people,
Rushing on us, should do your age some mischief.

28 presently prefer immediately present **29 address'd** ready **38 preordinance . . . decree** matters already firmly decided **39 law of children** i.e., laws to be changed as children change rules in their games. **fond** foolish **40 rebel** i.e., rebellious against the law and against his own firm nature **41 true quality** i.e., proper firmness and stability **46 spurn** kick **51 repealing** recall **54 freedom of repeal** permission to be recalled **57 enfranchisement** liberation (from the decree of banishment)

59 pray to move make petition (as you do) **61 resting** unmoving **62 fellow** equal **67 apprehensive** capable of reason **69 rank** place in line or file, position **70 Unshak'd of motion** (1) unswayed by petitions (2) with perfectly steady movement **74 Olympus** mountain dwelling of the Greek gods **75 bootless** in vain **77 Et tu, Brutè** and thou, Brutus **80 common pulpits** public rostra **85 Publius** (An old senator, too confused to flee.) **86 mutiny** uprising

BRUTUS
Do so, and let no man abide this deed
But we the doers. [*Exeunt all but the Conspirators.*]

Enter Trebonius.

CASSIUS
Where is Antony?
TREBONIUS Fled to his house amaz'd.
Men, wives, and children stare, cry out, and run
As it were doomsday.
BRUTUS Fates, we will know your pleasures.
That we shall die, we know; 'tis but the time,
And drawing days out, that men stand upon.
CASCA
Why, he that cuts off twenty years of life
Cuts off so many years of fearing death.
BRUTUS
Grant that, and then is death a benefit.
So are we Caesar's friends, that have abridg'd
His time of fearing death. Stoop, Romans, stoop,
And let us bathe our hands in Caesar's blood
Up to the elbows, and besmear our swords.
Then walk we forth, even to the market-place,
And, waving our red weapons o'er our heads,
Let's all cry, "Peace, freedom, and liberty!"
CASSIUS
Stoop, then, and wash. [*They bathe their hands and weapons.*] How many ages hence
Shall this our lofty scene be acted over
In states unborn and accents yet unknown!
BRUTUS
How many times shall Caesar bleed in sport,
That now on Pompey's basis lies along
No worthier than the dust!
CASSIUS
So oft as that shall be,
So often shall the knot of us be call'd
The men that gave their country liberty.
DECIUS
What, shall we forth?
CASSIUS Ay, every man away.
Brutus shall lead, and we will grace his heels
With the most boldest and best hearts of Rome.

Enter a Servant.

BRUTUS
Soft, who comes here? A friend of Antony's.
SERVANT [*Kneeling*]
Thus, Brutus, did my master bid me kneel,
Thus did Mark Antony bid me fall down.
And, being prostrate, thus he bade me say:
Brutus is noble, wise, valiant, and honest;
Caesar was mighty, bold, royal, and loving.
Say I love Brutus, and I honor him;
Say I fear'd Caesar, honor'd him, and lov'd him.
If Brutus will vouchsafe that Antony
May safely come to him, and be resolv'd
How Caesar hath deserv'd to lie in death,
Mark Antony shall not love Caesar dead
So well as Brutus living, but will follow
The fortunes and affairs of noble Brutus
Thorough the hazards of this untrod state
With all true faith. So says my master Antony.
BRUTUS
Thy master is a wise and valiant Roman;
I never thought him worse.
Tell him, so please him come unto this place,
He shall be satisfied and, by my honor,
Depart untouch'd.
SERVANT I'll fetch him presently.
Exit Servant.
BRUTUS
I know that we shall have him well to friend.
CASSIUS
I wish we may. But yet have I a mind
That fears him much; and my misgiving still
Falls shrewdly to the purpose.

Enter Antony.

BRUTUS
But here comes Antony.—Welcome, Mark Antony.
ANTONY
O mighty Caesar! Dost thou lie so low?
Are all thy conquests, glories, triumphs, spoils,
Shrunk to this little measure? Fare thee well.—
I know not, gentlemen, what you intend,
Who else must be let blood, who else is rank;
If I myself, there is no hour so fit
As Caesar's death's hour, nor no instrument
Of half that worth as those your swords, made rich
With the most noble blood of all this world.
I do beseech ye, if you bear me hard,
Now, whilst your purpled hands do reek and smoke,
Fulfill your pleasure. Live a thousand years,
I shall not find myself so apt to die;
No place will please me so, no mean of death,
As here by Caesar, and by you cut off,
The choice and master spirits of this age.
BRUTUS
O Antony, beg not your death of us.
Though now we must appear bloody and cruel,
As, by our hands and this our present act
You see we do, yet see you but our hands
And this the bleeding business they have done.
Our hearts you see not. They are pitiful;
And pity to the general wrong of Rome—
As fire drives out fire, so pity pity—
Hath done this deed on Caesar. For your part,

94 abide (1) stand the consequences of (2) remain here with **96 amaz'd** stunned **100 drawing . . . upon** prolonging their lives, that men attach importance to **115 Pompey's basis** pedestal of Pompey's statue. **along** prostrate **118 knot** group **121 grace** do honor to (by following closely)

132 be resolv'd receive an explanation **137 Thorough** through. **untrod state** new state of affairs **141 so** if it should **144 to friend** for a friend **146 fears** distrusts. **my misgiving still** i.e., such misgiving on my part always or generally **147 Falls . . . purpose** falls ominously close to the mark **153 let blood** bled, i.e., killed. **rank** diseased and in need of bleeding (with pun on *overgrown, too powerful*) **158 bear me hard** bear ill-will to me **159 reek** smoke **160 Live** if I should live **161 apt** ready **162 mean** means **170 pitiful** full of pity **172 pity pity** i.e., pity for the general wrong of Rome drove out pity for Caesar

To you our swords have leaden points, Mark Antony.
Our arms in strength of malice, and our hearts
Of brothers' temper, do receive you in
With all kind love, good thoughts, and reverence.

CASSIUS

Your voice shall be as strong as any man's
In the disposing of new dignities.

BRUTUS

Only be patient till we have appeas'd
The multitude, beside themselves with fear,
And then we will deliver you the cause
Why I, that did love Caesar when I struck him,
Have thus proceeded.

ANTONY I doubt not of your wisdom.
Let each man render me his bloody hand.
First, Marcus Brutus, will I shake with you;
Next, Caius Cassius, do I take your hand;
Now, Decius Brutus, yours; now yours, Metellus;
Yours, Cinna; and, my valiant Casca, yours;
Though last, not least in love, yours, good Trebonius.
Gentlemen all—alas, what shall I say?
My credit now stands on such slippery ground
That one of two bad ways you must conceit me,
Either a coward or a flatterer.
That I did love thee, Caesar, O, 'tis true!
If then thy spirit look upon us now,
Shall it not grieve thee dearer than thy death
To see thy Antony making his peace,
Shaking the bloody fingers of thy foes—
Most noble!—in the presence of thy corse?
Had I as many eyes as thou hast wounds,
Weeping as fast as they stream forth thy blood,
It would become me better than to close
In terms of friendship with thine enemies.
Pardon me, Julius! Here wast thou bay'd, brave hart,
Here didst thou fall, and here thy hunters stand,
Sign'd in thy spoil, and crimson'd in thy lethe.
O world, thou wast the forest to this hart,
And this, indeed, O world, the heart of thee!
How like a deer, strucken by many princes,
Dost thou here lie!

CASSIUS

Mark Antony—

ANTONY Pardon me, Caius Cassius.
The enemies of Caesar shall say this;
Then, in a friend, it is cold modesty.

CASSIUS

I blame you not for praising Caesar so,
But what compact mean you to have with us?
Will you be prick'd in number of our friends,
Or shall we on, and not depend on you?

ANTONY

Therefore I took your hands, but was indeed
Sway'd from the point by looking down on Caesar.
Friends am I with you all, and love you all,
Upon this hope, that you shall give me reasons
Why and wherein Caesar was dangerous.

BRUTUS

Or else were this a savage spectacle.
Our reasons are so full of good regard
That were you, Antony, the son of Caesar,
You should be satisfied.

ANTONY That's all I seek,
And am moreover suitor that I may
Produce his body to the market-place,
And in the pulpit, as becomes a friend,
Speak in the order of his funeral.

BRUTUS

You shall, Mark Antony.

CASSIUS Brutus, a word with you.
[*Aside to Brutus.*] You know not what you do. Do not consent
That Antony speak in his funeral.
Know you how much the people may be mov'd
By that which he will utter?

BRUTUS [*Aside to Cassius*] By your pardon;
I will myself into the pulpit first,
And show the reason of our Caesar's death.
What Antony shall speak, I will protest
He speaks by leave and by permission,
And that we are contented Caesar shall
Have all true rites and lawful ceremonies.
It shall advantage more than do us wrong.

CASSIUS [*Aside to Brutus*]

I know not what may fall; I like it not.

BRUTUS

Mark Antony, here, take you Caesar's body.
You shall not in your funeral speech blame us,
But speak all good you can devise of Caesar,
And say you do 't by our permission.
Else shall you not have any hand at all
About his funeral. And you shall speak
In the same pulpit whereto I am going,
After my speech is ended.

ANTONY Be it so.
I do desire no more.

BRUTUS

Prepare the body then, and follow us.

Exeunt. Manet Antony.

ANTONY

O, pardon me, thou bleeding piece of earth,
That I am meek and gentle with these butchers!
Thou art the ruins of the noblest man
That ever lived in the tide of times.
Woe to the hand that shed this costly blood!
Over thy wounds now do I prophesy—
Which, like dumb mouths, do ope their ruby lips
To beg the voice and utterance of my tongue—
A curse shall light upon the limbs of men;

174 leaden i.e., blunt **175–176 Our . . . temper** i.e., both our arms, though seeming strong in enmity, and our hearts, full of brotherly feeling **179 dignities** offices of state **182 deliver** report to **193 conceit** think, judge **203 close** come to an agreement **205 bay'd** brought to bay. **hart** stag (with pun on *heart*) **207 Sign'd . . . spoil** marked with the tokens of your slaughter. **lethe** river of oblivion in the underworld, here associated with death and blood (perhaps fused with Cocytus, river of blood in the underworld) **213 The enemies** even the enemies **214 modesty** moderation **217 prick'd in number** marked off on a list

225 regard account **231 order** ceremony **239 protest** announce **244 fall** befall, happen **258 tide of times** course of all history **259 costly** (1) valuable (2) fraught with dire consequences

Domestic fury and fierce civil strife
Shall cumber all the parts of Italy;
Blood and destruction shall be so in use
And dreadful objects so familiar
That mothers shall but smile when they behold
Their infants quartered with the hands of war,
All pity chok'd with custom of fell deeds;
And Caesar's spirit, ranging for revenge,
With Ate by his side come hot from hell,
Shall in these confines with a monarch's voice
Cry "Havoc!" and let slip the dogs of war,
That this foul deed shall smell above the earth
With carrion men, groaning for burial.

Enter Octavius' Servant.

You serve Octavius Caesar, do you not?

SERVANT
I do, Mark Antony.

ANTONY
Caesar did write for him to come to Rome.

SERVANT
He did receive his letters, and is coming,
And bid me say to you by word of mouth—
O Caesar!— [*Seeing the body.*]

ANTONY
Thy heart is big. Get thee apart and weep.
Passion, I see, is catching, for mine eyes,
Seeing those beads of sorrow stand in thine,
Began to water. Is thy master coming?

SERVANT
He lies tonight within seven leagues of Rome.

ANTONY
Post back with speed, and tell him what hath chanc'd.
Here is a mourning Rome, a dangerous Rome,
No Rome of safety for Octavius yet;
Hie hence, and tell him so. Yet, stay awhile.
Thou shalt not back till I have borne this corse
Into the market-place. There shall I try,
In my oration, how the people take
The cruel issue of these bloody men,
According to the which thou shalt discourse
To young Octavius of the state of things.
Lend me your hand. *Exeunt* [*with Caesar's body*].

[SCENE II]

Enter Brutus and [*presently*] *goes into the pulpit, and Cassius, with the Plebeians.*

PLEBEIANS
We will be satisfi'd! Let us be satisfi'd!

BRUTUS
Then follow me, and give me audience, friends.
Cassius, go you into the other street,
And part the numbers.
Those that will hear me speak, let 'em stay here;
Those that will follow Cassius, go with him;
And public reasons shall be rendered
Of Caesar's death.

FIRST PLEBEIAN I will hear Brutus speak.

SECOND PLEBEIAN
I will hear Cassius, and compare their reasons,
When severally we hear them rendered.
[*Exit Cassius, with some of the Plebeians.*]

THIRD PLEBEIAN
The noble Brutus is ascended. Silence!

BRUTUS
Be patient till the last.

Romans, countrymen, and lovers, hear me for my cause, and be silent, that you may hear. Believe me for mine honor, and have respect to mine honor, that you may believe. Censure me in your wisdom, and awake your senses, that you may the better judge. If there be any in this assembly, any dear friend of Caesar's, to him I say, that Brutus' love to Caesar was no less than his. If then that friend demand why Brutus rose against Caesar, this is my answer: Not that I lov'd Caesar less, but that I lov'd Rome more. Had you rather Caesar were living and die all slaves, than that Caesar were dead, to live all free men? As Caesar lov'd me, I weep for him; as he was fortunate, I rejoice at it; as he was valiant, I honor him; but, as he was ambitious, I slew him. There is tears for his love; joy for his fortune; honor for his valor; and death for his ambition. Who is here so base that would be a bondman? If any, speak, for him have I offended. Who is here so rude that would not be a Roman? If any, speak, for him have I offended. Who is here so vile that will not love his country? If any, speak, for him have I offended. I pause for a reply.

ALL None, Brutus, none!

BRUTUS Then none have I offended. I have done no more to Caesar than you shall do to Brutus. The question of his death is enroll'd in the Capitol; his glory not extenuated, wherein he was worthy, nor his offenses enforc'd, for which he suffer'd death.

Enter Mark Antony [*and others*] *with Caesar's body.*

Here comes his body, mourn'd by Mark Antony, who, though he had no hand in his death, shall receive the benefit of his dying, a place in the commonwealth, as which of you shall not? With this I depart, that, as I slew my best lover for the good of Rome, I have the same dagger for myself, when it shall please my country to need my death.

265 cumber entangle **267 objects** sights **269 quartered** cut to pieces **270 custom . . . deeds** the familiarity of cruel deeds **271 ranging** roaming up and down in search of prey **272 Ate** goddess of discord and moral chaos **273 confines** regions **274 Havoc** (The signal for sack, pillage, and slaughter.) **let slip** unleash **275 That** so that **287 seven leagues** about 20 miles **291 Hie** hasten **293 try** test **295 issue** deed

III.ii. Location: The Forum.

4 part divide **10 severally** individually, separately **13 lovers** friends. (This speech by Brutus is in what Plutarch calls the Lacedemonian or Spartan style, brief and sententious. Its content is original with Shakespeare.) **16 Censure** judge **17 senses** intellectual powers **30 rude** barbarous **37 shall** i.e., should, if I were to do as Caesar did **37–38 The question . . . enroll'd** the considerations that necessitated his death are recorded **39 extenuated** minimized **40 enforc'd** exaggerated **45 lover** friend

ALL Live, Brutus, live, live!

FIRST PLEBEIAN
Bring him with triumph home unto his house.

SECOND PLEBEIAN
Give him a statue with his ancestors.

THIRD PLEBEIAN
Let him be Caesar.

FOURTH PLEBEIAN Caesar's better parts
Shall be crown'd in Brutus.

FIRST PLEBEIAN
We'll bring him to his house with shouts and clamors.

BRUTUS
My countrymen—

SECOND PLEBEIAN Peace, silence! Brutus speaks.

FIRST PLEBEIAN
Peace, ho!

BRUTUS
Good countrymen, let me depart alone,
And, for my sake, stay here with Antony.
Do grace to Caesar's corpse, and grace his speech
Tending to Caesar's glories, which Mark Antony,
By our permission, is allow'd to make.
I do entreat you, not a man depart,
Save I alone, till Antony have spoke. *Exit.*

FIRST PLEBEIAN
Stay, ho, and let us hear Mark Antony.

THIRD PLEBEIAN
Let him go up into the public chair.
We'll hear him. Noble Antony, go up.

ANTONY
For Brutus' sake, I am beholding to you.
[*Goes into the pulpit.*]

FOURTH PLEBEIAN
What does he say of Brutus?

THIRD PLEBEIAN
He says, for Brutus' sake
He finds himself beholding to us all.

FOURTH PLEBEIAN
'Twere best he speak no harm of Brutus here.

FIRST PLEBEIAN
This Caesar was a tyrant.

THIRD PLEBEIAN Nay, that's certain.
We are blest that Rome is rid of him.

SECOND PLEBEIAN
Peace! Let us hear what Antony can say.

ANTONY
You gentle Romans—

ALL Peace, ho! Let us hear him.

ANTONY
Friends, Romans, countrymen, lend me your ears.
I come to bury Caesar, not to praise him.
The evil that men do lives after them;
The good is oft interred with their bones.
So let it be with Caesar. The noble Brutus
Hath told you Caesar was ambitious.
If it were so, it was a grievous fault,
And grievously hath Caesar answer'd it.
Here, under leave of Brutus and the rest—
For Brutus is an honorable man;
So are they all, all honorable men—
Come I to speak in Caesar's funeral.
He was my friend, faithful and just to me;
But Brutus says he was ambitious,
And Brutus is an honorable man.
He hath brought many captives home to Rome,
Whose ransoms did the general coffers fill.
Did this in Caesar seem ambitious?
When that the poor have cried, Caesar hath wept;
Ambition should be made of sterner stuff.
Yet Brutus says he was ambitious,
And Brutus is an honorable man.
You all did see that on the Lupercal
I thrice presented him a kingly crown,
Which he did thrice refuse. Was this ambition?
Yet Brutus says he was ambitious,
And, sure, he is an honorable man.
I speak not to disprove what Brutus spoke,
But here I am to speak what I do know.
You all did love him once, not without cause.
What cause withholds you then, to mourn for him?
O judgment! Thou art fled to brutish beasts,
And men have lost their reason. Bear with me;
My heart is in the coffin there with Caesar,
And I must pause till it come back to me.
[*He weeps.*]

FIRST PLEBEIAN
Methinks there is much reason in his sayings.

SECOND PLEBEIAN
If thou consider rightly of the matter,
Caesar has had great wrong.

THIRD PLEBEIAN Has he, masters?
I fear there will a worse come in his place.

FOURTH PLEBEIAN
Mark'd ye his words? He would not take the crown;
Therefore 'tis certain he was not ambitious.

FIRST PLEBEIAN
If it be found so, some will dear abide it.

SECOND PLEBEIAN
Poor soul! His eyes are red as fire with weeping.

THIRD PLEBEIAN
There's not a nobler man in Rome than Antony.

FOURTH PLEBEIAN
Now mark him, he begins again to speak.

ANTONY
But yesterday the word of Caesar might
Have stood against the world. Now lies he there,
And none so poor to do him reverence.
O masters! If I were dispos'd to stir
Your hearts and minds to mutiny and rage,
I should do Brutus wrong, and Cassius wrong,

50 Second Plebeian (Not the same person who exited at l. 10; the numbering here is arbitrary.) **58 Do grace** show respect. **grace his speech** i.e., listen courteously to Antony's speech **66 beholding** beholden **75 Friends** (This speech by Antony is thought to illustrate the Asiatic or "florid" style of speaking. In it Shakespeare gathers various hints from Plutarch, Appian, and Dion, but the speech is Shakespeare's invention.)

116 dear abide it pay a heavy penalty for it **122 none . . . reverence** i.e., no one, not even the lowliest person, is below Caesar in fortune now, making obeisance to him **124 mutiny** riot, tumult

Who, you all know, are honorable men.
I will not do them wrong; I rather choose
To wrong the dead, to wrong myself and you,
Than I will wrong such honorable men.
But here's a parchment with the seal of Caesar;
I found it in his closet, 'tis his will. 131
[*Shows the will.*]
Let but the commons hear this testament— 132
Which, pardon me, I do not mean to read—
And they would go and kiss dead Caesar's wounds
And dip their napkins in his sacred blood, 135
Yea, beg a hair of him for memory,
And, dying, mention it within their wills,
Bequeathing it as a rich legacy
Unto their issue.

FOURTH PLEBEIAN
We'll hear the will! Read it, Mark Antony.

ALL
The will, the will! We will hear Caesar's will.

ANTONY
Have patience, gentle friends, I must not read it.
It is not meet you know how Caesar lov'd you. 143
You are not wood, you are not stones, but men;
And, being men, hearing the will of Caesar,
It will inflame you, it will make you mad.
'Tis good you know not that you are his heirs,
For, if you should, O, what would come of it?

FOURTH PLEBEIAN
Read the will! We'll hear it, Antony.
You shall read us the will, Caesar's will.

ANTONY
Will you be patient? Will you stay awhile?
I have o'ershot myself to tell you of it.
I fear I wrong the honorable men
Whose daggers have stabb'd Caesar; I do fear it.

FOURTH PLEBEIAN
They were traitors. Honorable men!

ALL
The will! The testament!

SECOND PLEBEIAN
They were villains, murderers. The will! Read the will!

ANTONY
You will compel me then to read the will?
Then make a ring about the corpse of Caesar,
And let me show you him that made the will.
Shall I descend? And will you give me leave?

ALL
Come down.

SECOND PLEBEIAN
Descend.

THIRD PLEBEIAN You shall have leave.
[*Antony comes down. They gather around Caesar.*]

FOURTH PLEBEIAN A ring; stand round.

FIRST PLEBEIAN
Stand from the hearse, stand from the body. 164

SECOND PLEBEIAN
Room for Antony, most noble Antony.

ANTONY
Nay, press not so upon me. Stand far off. 166

ALL
Stand back! Room! Bear back!

ANTONY
If you have tears, prepare to shed them now.
You all do know this mantle. I remember
The first time ever Caesar put it on;
'Twas on a summer's evening, in his tent,
That day he overcame the Nervii. 172
Look, in this place ran Cassius' dagger through.
See what a rent the envious Casca made. 174
Through this the well-beloved Brutus stabb'd,
And, as he pluck'd his cursed steel away,
Mark how the blood of Caesar followed it,
As rushing out of doors to be resolv'd 178
If Brutus so unkindly knock'd or no; 179
For Brutus, as you know, was Caesar's angel. 180
Judge, O you gods, how dearly Caesar lov'd him!
This was the most unkindest cut of all; 182
For when the noble Caesar saw him stab,
Ingratitude, more strong than traitors' arms,
Quite vanquish'd him. Then burst his mighty heart,
And, in his mantle muffling up his face,
Even at the base of Pompey's statue,
Which all the while ran blood, great Caesar fell.
O, what a fall was there, my countrymen!
Then I, and you, and all of us fell down,
Whilst bloody treason flourish'd over us. 191
O, now you weep, and I perceive you feel
The dint of pity. These are gracious drops. 193
Kind souls, what weep you when you but behold 194
Our Caesar's vesture wounded? Look you here,
Here is himself, marr'd, as you see, with traitors.
[*He lifts Caesar's mantle.*]

FIRST PLEBEIAN O piteous spectacle!

SECOND PLEBEIAN O noble Caesar!

THIRD PLEBEIAN O woeful day!

FOURTH PLEBEIAN O traitors, villains!

FIRST PLEBEIAN O most bloody sight!

SECOND PLEBEIAN We will be reveng'd.

ALL Revenge! About! Seek! Burn! Fire! Kill! Slay! Let not a traitor live! 203

ANTONY
Stay, countrymen.

FIRST PLEBEIAN Peace there! Hear the noble Antony.

SECOND PLEBEIAN We'll hear him, we'll follow him, we'll die with him!

ANTONY
Good friends, sweet friends, let me not stir you up
To such a sudden flood of mutiny.
They that have done this deed are honorable.
What private griefs they have, alas, I know not, 212
That made them do it. They are wise and honorable,

131 closet private chamber **132 commons** common people **135 napkins** handkerchiefs **143 meet** fitting that **164 hearse** bier

166 far farther **172 Nervii** the Belgian tribe whose defeat in 57 B.C. is described in Caesar's *Gallic War,* II.xv–xxviii **174 envious** malicious, spiteful **178 be resolv'd** learn for certain **179 unkindly** cruelly and unnaturally **180 angel** i.e., daimon or genius, second self **182 unkindest** (1) most cruel (2) most unnatural. (The double superlative was grammatically acceptable in Shakespeare's day.) **191 flourish'd** triumphed insolently **193 dint** impression **194 what** why **203 About** to work **212 griefs** grievances

And will no doubt with reasons answer you.
I come not, friends, to steal away your hearts.
I am no orator, as Brutus is,
But, as you know me all, a plain blunt man,
That love my friend; and that they know full well
That gave me public leave to speak of him.
For I have neither wit, nor words, nor worth, 220
Action, nor utterance, nor the power of speech 221
To stir men's blood. I only speak right on.
I tell you that which you yourselves do know,
Show you sweet Caesar's wounds, poor poor dumb mouths,
And bid them speak for me. But were I Brutus,
And Brutus Antony, there were an Antony
Would ruffle up your spirits, and put a tongue 227
In every wound of Caesar that should move
The stones of Rome to rise and mutiny.

ALL
We'll mutiny.

FIRST PLEBEIAN We'll burn the house of Brutus.

THIRD PLEBEIAN
Away, then! Come, seek the conspirators.

ANTONY
Yet hear me, countrymen. Yet hear me speak.

ALL
Peace, ho! Hear Antony. Most noble Antony!

ANTONY
Why, friends, you go to do you know not what.
Wherein hath Caesar thus deserv'd your loves?
Alas, you know not! I must tell you, then,
You have forgot the will I told you of.

ALL
Most true. The will! Let's stay and hear the will.

ANTONY
Here is the will, and under Caesar's seal.
To every Roman citizen he gives,
To every several man, seventy-five drachmas. 241

SECOND PLEBEIAN
Most noble Caesar! We'll revenge his death.

THIRD PLEBEIAN
O royal Caesar!

ANTONY Hear me with patience.

ALL Peace, ho!

ANTONY
Moreover, he hath left you all his walks,
His private arbors and new-planted orchards,
On this side Tiber; he hath left them you,
And to your heirs forever—common pleasures, 248
To walk abroad and recreate yourselves.
Here was a Caesar! When comes such another?

FIRST PLEBEIAN
Never, never! Come, away, away!
We'll burn his body in the holy place,
And with the brands fire the traitors' houses.
Take up the body.

SECOND PLEBEIAN Go fetch fire.

THIRD PLEBEIAN Pluck down benches.

FOURTH PLEBEIAN Pluck down forms, windows, any- 257
thing. *Exeunt Plebeians [with the body].*

ANTONY
Now let it work. Mischief, thou art afoot,
Take thou what course thou wilt!

Enter Servant.

How now, fellow?

SERVANT
Sir, Octavius is already come to Rome.

ANTONY
Where is he?

SERVANT
He and Lepidus are at Caesar's house.

ANTONY
And thither will I straight to visit him.
He comes upon a wish. Fortune is merry, 265
And in this mood will give us anything.

SERVANT
I heard him say, Brutus and Cassius
Are rid like madmen through the gates of Rome. 268

ANTONY
Belike they had some notice of the people, 269
How I had mov'd them. Bring me to Octavius.
Exeunt.

[SCENE III]

Enter Cinna the poet, and after him the Plebeians.

CINNA
I dreamt tonight that I did feast with Caesar, 1
And things unluckily charge my fantasy. 2
I have no will to wander forth of doors,
Yet something leads me forth.

FIRST PLEBEIAN What is your name?

SECOND PLEBEIAN Whither are you going?

THIRD PLEBEIAN Where do you dwell?

FOURTH PLEBEIAN Are you a married man or a bachelor?

SECOND PLEBEIAN Answer every man directly.

FIRST PLEBEIAN Ay, and briefly.

FOURTH PLEBEIAN Ay, and wisely.

THIRD PLEBEIAN Ay, and truly, you were best.

CINNA What is my name? Whither am I going? Where do I dwell? Am I a married man or a bachelor? Then, to answer every man directly and briefly, wisely and truly: wisely I say, I am a bachelor.

SECOND PLEBEIAN That's as much as to say, they are
fools that marry. You'll bear me a bang for that, I fear. 19
Proceed directly.

CINNA Directly, I am going to Caesar's funeral.

220 wit understanding, intelligence. **worth** stature, authority **221 Action** gesture. **utterance** good delivery **227 ruffle up** stir to anger **241 several** individual. **drachmas** coins. (This is a substantial bequest.) **248 common pleasures** public pleasure gardens (in which)

257 forms benches. **windows** i.e., shutters **265 upon a wish** just when wanted. **merry** i.e., favorably disposed **268 Are rid** have ridden **269 Belike** likely enough. **of** about; or from

III.iii. Location: A street.
1 tonight last night **2 unluckily . . . fantasy** oppress my imagination with foreboding **19 bear . . . bang** get a beating from me

FIRST PLEBEIAN As a friend or an enemy?
CINNA As a friend.
SECOND PLEBEIAN That matter is answer'd directly.
FOURTH PLEBEIAN For your dwelling—briefly.
CINNA Briefly, I dwell by the Capitol.
THIRD PLEBEIAN Your name, sir, truly.
CINNA Truly, my name is Cinna.
FIRST PLEBEIAN Tear him to pieces! He's a conspirator!
CINNA I am Cinna the poet, I am Cinna the poet!
FOURTH PLEBEIAN Tear him for his bad verses, tear him for his bad verses!
CINNA I am not Cinna the conspirator.
FOURTH PLEBEIAN It is no matter, his name's Cinna. Pluck but his name out of his heart, and turn him going.
THIRD PLEBEIAN Tear him, tear him! Come, brands, ho! Fire-brands! To Brutus', to Cassius'; burn all! Some to Decius' house, and some to Casca's; some to Ligarius'. Away, go!

Exeunt all the Plebeians, [dragging off Cinna].

ACT IV • [SCENE I]

Enter Antony [with a list], Octavius, and Lepidus.

ANTONY
These many, then, shall die. Their names are
prick'd.
OCTAVIUS
Your brother too must die. Consent you, Lepidus?
LEPIDUS
I do consent—
OCTAVIUS Prick him down, Antony.
LEPIDUS
Upon condition Publius shall not live,
Who is your sister's son, Mark Antony.
ANTONY
He shall not live. Look, with a spot I damn him.
But, Lepidus, go you to Caesar's house.
Fetch the will hither, and we shall determine
How to cut off some charge in legacies.
LEPIDUS
What, shall I find you here?
OCTAVIUS
Or here, or at the Capitol. *Exit Lepidus.*
ANTONY
This is a slight unmeritable man,
Meet to be sent on errands. Is it fit,
The threefold world divided, he should stand
One of the three to share it?
OCTAVIUS So you thought him,
And took his voice who should be prick'd to die
In our black sentence and proscription.
ANTONY
Octavius, I have seen more days than you;
And though we lay these honors on this man,
To ease ourselves of divers sland'rous loads,
He shall but bear them as the ass bears gold,
To groan and sweat under the business,
Either led or driven, as we point the way;
And having brought our treasure where we will,
Then take we down his load, and turn him off,
Like to the empty ass, to shake his ears
And graze in commons.
OCTAVIUS You may do your will;
But he's a tried and valiant soldier.
ANTONY
So is my horse, Octavius, and for that
I do appoint him store of provender.
It is a creature that I teach to fight,
To wind, to stop, to run directly on,
His corporal motion govern'd by my spirit.
And, in some taste, is Lepidus but so.
He must be taught, and train'd, and bid go forth—
A barren-spirited fellow, one that feeds
On objects, arts, and imitations,
Which, out of use and stal'd by other men,
Begin his fashion. Do not talk of him
But as a property. And now, Octavius,
Listen great things. Brutus and Cassius
Are levying powers. We must straight make head.
Therefore let our alliance be combin'd,
Our best friends made, our means stretch'd;
And let us presently go sit in council
How covert matters may be best disclos'd,
And open perils surest answered.
OCTAVIUS
Let us do so, for we are at the stake,
And bay'd about with many enemies;
And some that smile have in their hearts, I fear,
Millions of mischiefs. *Exeunt.*

[SCENE II]

Drum. Enter Brutus, Lucilius, [Lucius,] and the army; Titinius and Pindarus meet them.

BRUTUS Stand, ho!
LUCILIUS Give the word, ho! And stand.

35–36 turn him going send him packing

IV.i. Location: Rome. A table is perhaps set out.
1 prick'd marked down on a list (appropriate to the use of the stylus on waxen tablets or of a pin on paper) **6 spot** mark (on the list). **damn** condemn **8–9 determine . . . legacies** i.e., find a way to reduce the outlay of Caesar's estate, by altering the will **11 Or** either **14 threefold** (I.e., including Europe, Africa, and Asia; alluding also to the triumvirate of Lepidus, Antony, Octavius.)

16 took his voice allowed him to decide (i.e., about Publius) **17 proscription** (Proscription branded a man as an outlaw, confiscated his property, offered a reward for his murder, and forbade his sons and grandsons from holding public office.) **20 divers . . . loads** i.e., some of the slanderous charges that will be leveled against us **26 empty** unloaded **27 commons** public pasture **30 appoint** assign, provide **32 wind** turn. (Horse trainer's term.) **33 corporal** bodily **34 taste** sense **37 On . . . imitations** on curiosities, artificial things, and the following of fashion (?), i.e., copied things merely, taken up secondhand **38 stal'd** made common or cheap **39 Begin his fashion** i.e., these outworn fashions are chosen by him as his fashion **40 property** tool **42 powers** armies. **straight make head** immediately raise an army **43 combin'd** coalesced (i.e., let us work as one) **44 made** mustered. **stretch'd** used to fullest advantage **46 How . . . disclos'd** (to determine) how hidden dangers may best be discovered **47 surest answered** most safely met **48 at the stake** i.e., like a bear in the sport of bearbaiting **49 bay'd about** surrounded as by baying dogs **51 mischiefs** harms, evils

IV.ii. Location: Camp near Sardis, in Asia Minor. Before Brutus' tent.
1–2 Stand . . . stand halt! Pass the word

BRUTUS
What now, Lucilius, is Cassius near?
LUCILIUS
He is at hand, and Pindarus is come
To do you salutation from his master.
BRUTUS
He greets me well. Your master, Pindarus,
In his own change, or by ill officers,
Hath given me some worthy cause to wish
Things done, undone; but, if he be at hand,
I shall be satisfied.
PINDARUS I do not doubt
But that my noble master will appear
Such as he is, full of regard and honor.
BRUTUS
He is not doubted. A word, Lucilius,
How he receiv'd you; let me be resolv'd.
LUCILIUS
With courtesy and with respect enough,
But not with such familiar instances,
Nor with such free and friendly conference,
As he hath us'd of old.
BRUTUS Thou hast describ'd
A hot friend cooling. Ever note, Lucilius,
When love begins to sicken and decay,
It useth an enforced ceremony.
There are no tricks in plain and simple faith.
But hollow men, like horses hot at hand,
Make gallant show and promise of their mettle;
Low march within.
But when they should endure the bloody spur,
They fall their crests, and, like deceitful jades,
Sink in the trial. Comes his army on?
LUCILIUS
They mean this night in Sardis to be quarter'd.
The greater part, the horse in general,
Are come with Cassius.

Enter Cassius and his powers.

BRUTUS Hark, he is arriv'd.
March gently on to meet him.
CASSIUS Stand, ho!
BRUTUS Stand, ho! Speak the word along.
FIRST SOLDIER Stand!
SECOND SOLDIER Stand!
THIRD SOLDIER Stand!
CASSIUS
Most noble brother, you have done me wrong.
BRUTUS
Judge me, you gods! Wrong I mine enemies?
And, if not so, how should I wrong a brother?
CASSIUS
Brutus, this sober form of yours hides wrongs;
And when you do them—
BRUTUS Cassius, be content;
Speak your griefs softly. I do know you well.
Before the eyes of both our armies here,
Which should perceive nothing but love from us,
Let us not wrangle. Bid them move away.
Then in my tent, Cassius, enlarge your griefs,
And I will give you audience.
CASSIUS Pindarus,
Bid our commanders lead their charges off
A little from this ground.
BRUTUS
Lucius, do you the like, and let no man
Come to our tent till we have done our conference.
Let Lucilius and Titinius guard our door.
Exeunt. Mane[n]t Brutus and Cassius.
[*Lucilius and Titinius stand guard at the door.*]

[SCENE III]

CASSIUS
That you have wrong'd me doth appear in this:
You have condemn'd and noted Lucius Pella
For taking bribes here of the Sardians,
Wherein my letters, praying on his side,
Because I knew the man, was slighted off.
BRUTUS
You wrong'd yourself to write in such a case.
CASSIUS
In such a time as this it is not meet
That every nice offense should bear his comment.
BRUTUS
Let me tell you, Cassius, you yourself
Are much condemn'd to have an itching palm,
To sell and mart your offices for gold
To undeservers.
CASSIUS I an itching palm?
You know that you are Brutus that speaks this,
Or, by the gods, this speech were else your last.
BRUTUS
The name of Cassius honors this corruption,
And chastisement doth therefore hide his head.
CASSIUS
Chastisement?
BRUTUS
Remember March, the ides of March remember.
Did not great Julius bleed for justice' sake?
What villain touch'd his body that did stab
And not for justice? What, shall one of us,
That struck the foremost man of all this world
But for supporting robbers, shall we now

6 well i.e., ceremoniously, through Pindarus (who is only a slave; perhaps Brutus is ironic) **7 In . . . officers** whether from an alteration in his feelings toward me, or through the acts of unworthy subordinates **10 be satisfied** have things explained to my satisfaction **12 regard** i.e., consideration of your joint interests **14 resolv'd** informed **16 familiar instances** proofs of intimate friendship **17 conference** conversation **23 hollow** insincere. **hot at hand** restless and full of spirit when held in, at the start **26 fall their crests** let their manes droop (i.e., they hang their heads). **jades** worthless horses **27 Sink** give way, fail **29 the horse in general** all the cavalry **31 gently** mildly, not hostilely **40 sober form** dignified manner

42 griefs grievances **46 enlarge** speak freely **48 charges** troops **52 Lucilius** (The Folio reads *Lucius* here and *Lucilius* in l. 50, but when Shakespeare interpolated a passage in the next scene at ll. 124–166 he evidently intended to have Lucilius guarding the door.)

IV.iii. Location: The scene is continuous. Brutus and Cassius remain on stage, which now represents the interior of Brutus' tent.
2 noted publicly disgraced. **Lucius Pella** a Roman praetor in Sardis **4 letters** i.e., letter **5 slighted off** put slightingly aside **8 nice** trivial. **bear his comment** be made the object of scrutiny **10 condemn'd to have** accused of having **11 mart** traffic in **15 honors** lends the appearance of honor to, countenances **16 chastisement . . . head** i.e., legal authority is afraid to act (because of Cassius' influence) **23 But** only. **robbers** i.e., those who would have robbed Rome of her liberty (?)

Contaminate our fingers with base bribes,
And sell the mighty space of our large honors
For so much trash as may be grasped thus?
I had rather be a dog, and bay the moon,
Than such a Roman.

CASSIUS
Brutus, bait not me!
I'll not endure it. You forget yourself
To hedge me in. I am a soldier, I,
Older in practice, abler than yourself
To make conditions.

BRUTUS
Go to! You are not, Cassius.

CASSIUS
I am.

BRUTUS
I say you are not.

CASSIUS
Urge me no more, I shall forget myself.
Have mind upon your health. Tempt me no farther.

BRUTUS
Away, slight man!

CASSIUS
Is 't possible?

BRUTUS
Hear me, for I will speak.
Must I give way and room to your rash choler?
Shall I be frighted when a madman stares?

CASSIUS
O ye gods, ye gods! Must I endure all this?

BRUTUS
All this? Ay, more. Fret till your proud heart break.
Go show your slaves how choleric you are,
And make your bondmen tremble. Must I budge?
Must I observe you? Must I stand and crouch
Under your testy humor? By the gods,
You shall digest the venom of your spleen
Though it do split you; for, from this day forth,
I'll use you for my mirth, yea, for my laughter,
When you are waspish.

CASSIUS
Is it come to this?

BRUTUS
You say you are a better soldier.
Let it appear so; make your vaunting true,
And it shall please me well. For mine own part,
I shall be glad to learn of noble men.

CASSIUS
You wrong me every way! You wrong me, Brutus.
I said, an elder soldier, not a better.
Did I say "better"?

BRUTUS
If you did, I care not.

CASSIUS
When Caesar liv'd, he durst not thus have mov'd
me.

BRUTUS
Peace, peace! You durst not so have tempted him.

CASSIUS
I durst not?

BRUTUS
No.

CASSIUS
What, durst not tempt him?

BRUTUS
For your life you durst not.

CASSIUS
Do not presume too much upon my love.
I may do that I shall be sorry for.

BRUTUS
You have done that you should be sorry for.
There is no terror, Cassius, in your threats,
For I am arm'd so strong in honesty
That they pass by me as the idle wind,
Which I respect not. I did send to you
For certain sums of gold—which you denied me—
For I can raise no money by vile means.
By heaven, I had rather coin my heart
And drop my blood for drachmas than to wring
From the hard hands of peasants their vile trash
By any indirection. I did send
To you for gold to pay my legions,
Which you denied me. Was that done like Cassius?
Should I have answer'd Caius Cassius so?
When Marcus Brutus grows so covetous
To lock such rascal counters from his friends,
Be ready, gods, with all your thunderbolts;
Dash him to pieces!

CASSIUS
I denied you not.

BRUTUS
You did.

CASSIUS
I did not. He was but a fool that brought
My answer back. Brutus hath riv'd my heart.
A friend should bear his friend's infirmities,
But Brutus makes mine greater than they are.

BRUTUS
I do not, till you practice them on me.

CASSIUS
You love me not.

BRUTUS
I do not like your faults.

CASSIUS
A friendly eye could never see such faults.

BRUTUS
A flatterer's would not, though they do appear
As huge as high Olympus.

CASSIUS
Come, Antony, and young Octavius, come,
Revenge yourselves alone on Cassius,
For Cassius is aweary of the world;
Hated by one he loves, brav'd by his brother,
Check'd like a bondman, all his faults observ'd,
Set in a notebook, learn'd, and conn'd by rote,
To cast into my teeth. O, I could weep
My spirit from mine eyes! There is my dagger,
[*Offers his unsheathed dagger.*]
And here my naked breast; within, a heart
Dearer than Pluto's mine, richer than gold.

25 the mighty . . . honors the greatness of our honorable reputations **26 trash** i.e., money (despised in Brutus' stoic philosophy) **28 bait** harass **32 make conditions** i.e., for the behavior of such men as Lucius Pella and for the appointment of my officers **39 choler** wrathful temperament **40 stares** looks wildly at me **45 observe** pay reverence to **47 digest** swallow. **spleen** i.e., irascibility **54 learn of** learn of the existence of; or, learn from (those who have proved themselves noble) **58 mov'd** angered

69 respect not pay no attention to **75 indirection** devious or unjust means **80 rascal counters** i.e., paltry sums. (*Counters* were uncurrent coins used by shopkeepers as discs in making reckonings.) **85 riv'd** cleft **96 brav'd** defied **97 Check'd** rebuked **102 Pluto** god of the underworld (confused with Plutus, god of riches)

If that thou be'st a Roman, take it forth.
I, that denied thee gold, will give my heart.
Strike, as thou didst at Caesar; for I know,
When thou didst hate him worst, thou lovedst him
better
Than ever thou lovedst Cassius.

BRUTUS Sheathe your dagger.
Be angry when you will, it shall have scope;
Do what you will, dishonor shall be humor.
O Cassius, you are yoked with a lamb
That carries anger as the flint bears fire,
Who, much enforced, shows a hasty spark,
And straight is cold again.

CASSIUS Hath Cassius liv'd
To be but mirth and laughter to his Brutus,
When grief and blood ill-temper'd vexeth him?

BRUTUS
When I spoke that, I was ill-temper'd too.

CASSIUS
Do you confess so much? Give me your hand.

BRUTUS
And my heart too. *[They embrace.]*

CASSIUS O Brutus!

BRUTUS What's the matter?

CASSIUS
Have not you love enough to bear with me,
When that rash humor which my mother gave me
Makes me forgetful?

BRUTUS Yes, Cassius; and, from henceforth,
When you are over-earnest with your Brutus,
He'll think your mother chides, and leave you so.

Enter a Poet [followed by Lucilius and Titinius, who have been standing guard at the door].

POET
Let me go in to see the generals.
There is some grudge between 'em, 'tis not meet
They be alone.

LUCILIUS You shall not come to them.

POET
Nothing but death shall stay me.

CASSIUS
How now? What's the matter?

POET
For shame, you generals! What do you mean?
Love and be friends, as two such men should be;
For I have seen more years, I'm sure, than ye.

CASSIUS
Ha, ha, how vilely doth this cynic rhyme!

BRUTUS
Get you hence, sirrah. Saucy fellow, hence!

CASSIUS
Bear with him, Brutus. 'Tis his fashion.

BRUTUS
I'll know his humor, when he knows his time.
What should the wars do with these jigging fools?
Companion, hence!

CASSIUS Away, away, be gone! *Exit Poet.*

BRUTUS
Lucilius and Titinius, bid the commanders
Prepare to lodge their companies tonight.

CASSIUS
And come yourselves, and bring Messala with you
Immediately to us. *[Exeunt Lucilius and Titinius.]*

BRUTUS *[To Lucius within]* Lucius, a bowl of wine!

CASSIUS
I did not think you could have been so angry.

BRUTUS
O Cassius, I am sick of many griefs.

CASSIUS
Of your philosophy you make no use,
If you give place to accidental evils.

BRUTUS
No man bears sorrow better. Portia is dead.

CASSIUS
Ha? Portia?

BRUTUS
She is dead.

CASSIUS
How scap'd I killing when I cross'd you so?
O insupportable and touching loss!
Upon what sickness?

BRUTUS Impatient of my absence,
And grief that young Octavius with Mark Antony
Have made themselves so strong—for with her
death
That tidings came—with this she fell distract,
And, her attendants absent, swallow'd fire.

CASSIUS
And died so?

BRUTUS Even so.

CASSIUS O ye immortal gods!

Enter Boy [Lucius] with wine and tapers.

BRUTUS
Speak no more of her. Give me a bowl of wine.
In this I bury all unkindness, Cassius. *Drinks.*

CASSIUS
My heart is thirsty for that noble pledge.
Fill, Luicus, till the wine o'erswell the cup;
I cannot drink too much of Brutus' love.
[Drinks. Exit Lucius.]

Enter Titinius and Messala.

BRUTUS
Come in, Titinius! Welcome, good Messala.
Now sit we close about this taper here,
And call in question our necessities. *[They sit.]*

109 dishonor . . . humor i.e., I'll regard your corruption as something to be humored **110 yoked with** allied with (i.e., Brutus compares himself to the lamb) **112 enforced** provoked, struck upon **115 blood ill-temper'd** i.e., disposition imbalanced by the humors of the body **120 that rash humor** i.e., choler, anger **123 leave you so** let it go at that **132 cynic** i.e., rude fellow; also one claiming to be a Cynic philosopher, hence outspoken **135 I'll . . . time** I'll indulge his eccentric behavior when he knows the proper time for it

136 jigging rhyming in jerky doggerel **137 Companion** fellow **145 accidental evils** misfortunes caused by chance (which should be a matter of indifference to a Stoic philosopher like Brutus) **155 swallow'd fire** (According to Plutarch, as translated by Thomas North, Portia "took hot burning coals and cast them in her mouth, and kept her mouth so close that she choked herself.") **161 s.d. Titinius** (Lucilius does not return with Titinius, as he was ordered to do at l. 141, probably because he was not in Shakespeare's original version of this scene.) **164 call in question** examine into

CASSIUS
Portia, art thou gone?
BRUTUS
No more, I pray you.
Messala, I have here received letters
That young Octavius and Mark Antony
Come down upon us with a mighty power,
Bending their expedition toward Philippi.
[Shows letters.]
MESSALA
Myself have letters of the selfsame tenor.
BRUTUS
With what addition?
MESSALA
That by proscription and bills of outlawry
Octavius, Antony, and Lepidus
Have put to death an hundred senators.
BRUTUS
Therein our letters do not well agree;
Mine speak of seventy senators that died
By their proscriptions, Cicero being one.
CASSIUS
Cicero one?
MESSALA
Cicero is dead,
And by that order of proscription.
Had you your letters from your wife, my lord?
BRUTUS
No, Messala.
MESSALA
Nor nothing in your letters writ of her?
BRUTUS
Nothing, Messala.
MESSALA
That, methinks, is strange.
BRUTUS
Why ask you? Hear you aught of her in yours?
MESSALA
No, my lord.
BRUTUS
Now, as you are a Roman, tell me true.
MESSALA
Then like a Roman bear the truth I tell:
For certain she is dead, and by strange manner.
BRUTUS
Why, farewell, Portia. We must die, Messala.
With meditating that she must die once,
I have the patience to endure it now.
MESSALA
Even so great men great losses should endure.
CASSIUS
I have as much of this in art as you,
But yet my nature could not bear it so.
BRUTUS
Well, to our work alive. What do you think
Of marching to Philippi presently?
CASSIUS
I do not think it good.
BRUTUS
Your reason?
CASSIUS
This it is:
'Tis better that the enemy seek us.
So shall he waste his means, weary his soldiers,
Doing himself offense; whilst we, lying still,
Are full of rest, defense, and nimbleness.
BRUTUS
Good reasons must of force give place to better.
The people 'twixt Philippi and this ground
Do stand but in a forc'd affection,
For they have grudg'd us contribution.
The enemy, marching along by them,
By them shall make a fuller number up,
Come on refresh'd, new-added, and encourag'd;
From which advantage shall we cut him off
If at Philippi we do face him there,
These people at our back.
CASSIUS
Hear me, good brother.
BRUTUS
Under your pardon. You must note beside
That we have tried the utmost of our friends,
Our legions are brimfull, our cause is ripe.
The enemy increaseth every day;
We, at the height, are ready to decline.
There is a tide in the affairs of men,
Which, taken at the flood, leads on to fortune;
Omitted, all the voyage of their life
Is bound in shallows and in miseries.
On such a full sea are we now afloat,
And we must take the current when it serves,
Or lose our ventures.
CASSIUS
Then, with your will, go on.
We'll along ourselves, and meet them at Philippi.
BRUTUS
The deep of night is crept upon our talk,
And nature must obey necessity,
Which we will niggard with a little rest.
There is no more to say?
CASSIUS
No more. Good night.
Early tomorrow will we rise, and hence.
BRUTUS
Lucius! *(Enter Lucius.)* My gown. [*Exit Lucius.*]
Farewell, good Messala.
Good night, Titinius. Noble, noble Cassius,
Good night, and good repose.
CASSIUS
O my dear brother!
This was an ill beginning of the night.
Never come such division 'tween our souls!
Let it not, Brutus.

Enter Lucius with the gown.

BRUTUS
Everything is well.
CASSIUS
Good night, my lord.
BRUTUS
Good night, good brother.
TITINIUS, MESSALA
Good night, Lord Brutus.

168 power army **169 expedition** rapid march; military power **172 proscription** (See IV.i.17, note.) **180–194 Had . . . so** (This passage is sometimes regarded as contradictory to and redundant of ll. 142–165. Probably it is the original account of Portia's death; ll. 143–166 are part of a later interpolation.) **190 once** at some time **193 art** i.e., the acquired wisdom of stoical fortitude **195 alive** concerning us as living and dealing with present realities

200 offense harm **208 new-added** reinforced **212 Under your pardon** i.e., excuse me, let me continue **219 Omitted** neglected, missed **223 ventures** investments (of enterprise at sea). **with your will** as you wish **227 niggard** stint (by sleeping only briefly) **230 gown** dressing gown

BRUTUS Farewell, everyone.
Exeunt [all but Brutus and Lucius].
Give me the gown. Where is thy instrument?

LUCIUS
Here in the tent.

BRUTUS What, thou speak'st drowsily?
Poor knave, I blame thee not; thou art o'erwatch'd.
Call Claudius and some other of my men;
I'll have them sleep on cushions in my tent.

LUCIUS
Varro and Claudius!

Enter Varro and Claudius.

VARRO
Calls my lord?

BRUTUS
I pray you, sirs, lie in my tent and sleep.
It may be I shall raise you by and by
On business to my brother Cassius.

VARRO
So please you, we will stand and watch your
pleasure.

BRUTUS
I will not have it so. Lie down, good sirs.
It may be I shall otherwise bethink me.
[Varro and Claudius lie down.]
Look, Lucius, here's the book I sought for so;
I put it in the pocket of my gown.

LUCIUS
I was sure your lordship did not give it me.

BRUTUS
Bear with me, good boy, I am much forgetful.
Canst thou hold up thy heavy eyes awhile,
And touch thy instrument a strain or two?

LUCIUS
Ay, my lord, an 't please you.

BRUTUS It does, my boy.
I trouble thee too much, but thou art willing.

LUCIUS
It is my duty, sir.

BRUTUS
I should not urge thy duty past thy might;
I know young bloods look for a time of rest.

LUCIUS
I have slept, my lord, already.

BRUTUS
It was well done; and thou shalt sleep again;
I will not hold thee long. If I do live,
I will be good to thee.
Music, and a song. [Lucius falls asleep.]
This is a sleepy tune. O murd'rous slumber,
Layest thou thy leaden mace upon my boy,
That plays thee music? Gentle knave, good night;
I will not do thee so much wrong to wake thee.
If thou dost nod, thou break'st thy instrument;
I'll take it from thee. And, good boy, good night.
*[He removes Lucius' instrument,
and begins to read.]*
Let me see, let me see; is not the leaf turn'd down
Where I left reading? Here it is, I think.

Enter the Ghost of Caesar.

How ill this taper burns! Ha! Who comes here?
I think it is the weakness of mine eyes
That shapes this monstrous apparition.
It comes upon me. Art thou any thing?
Art thou some god, some angel, or some devil,
That mak'st my blood cold and my hair to stare?
Speak to me what thou art.

GHOST
Thy evil spirit, Brutus.

BRUTUS Why com'st thou?

GHOST
To tell thee thou shalt see me at Philippi.

BRUTUS
Well; then I shall see thee again?

GHOST
Ay, at Philippi.

BRUTUS
Why, I will see thee at Philippi, then.
[Exit Ghost.]
Now I have taken heart thou vanishest.
Ill spirit, I would hold more talk with thee.
Boy, Lucius! Varro! Claudius! Sirs, awake!
Claudius!

LUCIUS The strings, my lord, are false.

BRUTUS
He thinks he still is at his instrument.
Lucius, awake!

LUCIUS
My lord?

BRUTUS
Didst thou dream, Lucius, that thou so criedst out?

LUCIUS
My lord, I do not know that I did cry.

BRUTUS
Yes, that thou didst. Didst thou see anything?

LUCIUS
Nothing, my lord.

BRUTUS
Sleep again, Lucius. Sirrah Claudius!
[To Varro.] Fellow thou, awake!

VARRO My lord?

CLAUDIUS My lord?
[They get up.]

BRUTUS
Why did you so cry out, sirs, in your sleep?

VARRO, CLAUDIUS
Did we, my lord?

BRUTUS Ay. Saw you anything?

VARRO
No, my lord, I saw nothing.

239 instrument i.e., lute or cithern **241 knave** boy. **o'erwatch'd** tired from lack of sleep **247 raise** rouse **249 watch your pleasure** wakefully await your commands **251 otherwise bethink me** change my mind **262 young bloods** youthful constitutions **267 murd'rous** producing the likeness of death **268 leaden mace** heavy staff of office (used by a sheriff to touch the shoulder of one whom he was arresting)

275 How . . . burns (It is part of the machinery of apparitions that lights burn low and blue.) **280 stare** stand on end **290 false** out of tune

CLAUDIUS Nor I, my lord.

BRUTUS
Go and commend me to my brother Cassius.
Bid him set on his pow'rs betimes before,
And we will follow.

VARRO, CLAUDIUS It shall be done, my lord.

Exeunt.

ACT V • [SCENE I]

Enter Octavius, Antony, and their army.

OCTAVIUS
Now, Antony, our hopes are answered.
You said the enemy would not come down,
But keep the hills and upper regions.
It proves not so. Their battles are at hand;
They mean to warn us at Philippi here,
Answering before we do demand of them.

ANTONY
Tut, I am in their bosoms, and I know
Wherefore they do it. They could be content
To visit other places, and come down
With fearful bravery, thinking by this face
To fasten in our thoughts that they have courage;
But 'tis not so.

Enter a Messenger.

MESSENGER Prepare you, generals.
The enemy comes on in gallant show;
Their bloody sign of battle is hung out,
And something to be done immediately.

ANTONY
Octavius, lead your battle softly on
Upon the left hand of the even field.

OCTAVIUS
Upon the right hand I; keep thou the left.

ANTONY
Why do you cross me in this exigent?

OCTAVIUS
I do not cross you; but I will do so. *March.*

Drum. Enter Brutus, Cassius, and their army; [Lucilius, Titinius, Messala, and others].

BRUTUS
They stand, and would have parley.

CASSIUS
Stand fast, Titinius. We must out and talk.

OCTAVIUS
Mark Antony, shall we give sign of battle?

ANTONY
No, Caesar, we will answer on their charge.
Make forth. The generals would have some words.

OCTAVIUS
Stir not until the signal.

BRUTUS
Words before blows. Is it so, countrymen?

OCTAVIUS
Not that we love words better, as you do.

BRUTUS
Good words are better than bad strokes, Octavius.

ANTONY
In your bad strokes, Brutus, you give good words.
Witness the hole you made in Caesar's heart,
Crying "Long live! Hail, Caesar!"

CASSIUS Antony,
The posture of your blows are yet unknown;
But for your words, they rob the Hybla bees,
And leave them honeyless.

ANTONY
Not stingless too?

BRUTUS O, yes, and soundless too.
For you have stol'n their buzzing, Antony,
And very wisely threat before you sting.

ANTONY
Villains! You did not so, when your vile daggers
Hack'd one another in the sides of Caesar.
You show'd your teeth like apes, and fawn'd like hounds,
And bow'd like bondmen, kissing Caesar's feet,
Whilst damned Casca, like a cur, behind
Struck Caesar on the neck. O you flatterers!

CASSIUS
Flatterers? Now, Brutus, thank yourself!
This tongue had not offended so today
If Cassius might have rul'd.

OCTAVIUS
Come, come, the cause. If arguing make us sweat,
The proof of it will turn to redder drops.
Look, [*He draws.*]
I draw a sword against conspirators.
When think you that the sword goes up again?
Never, till Caesar's three and thirty wounds
Be well aveng'd, or till another Caesar
Have added slaughter to the sword of traitors.

BRUTUS
Caesar, thou canst not die by traitors' hands,
Unless thou bring'st them with thee.

OCTAVIUS So I hope.
I was not born to die on Brutus' sword.

BRUTUS
O, if thou wert the noblest of thy strain,
Young man, thou couldst not die more honorable.

304 set . . . before advance his troops early in the morning, before me

V.i. Location: The plains of Philippi, in Macedonia.
4 battles armies **5 warn** challenge **7 bosoms** secret councils **9 visit other places** i.e., be elsewhere. **come** they come **10 fearful bravery** (1) awesome ostentation (2) a show of bravery to conceal their fear. **face** pretense (of courage) **11 fasten** fix the idea **12 'tis not so** (1) their plan cannot deceive us (2) they have no courage **14 bloody sign** red flag **15 to be** is to be **16 softly** with restraint **19 cross** contradict. **exigent** critical moment **20 do so** i.e., do as I said

24 answer on their charge respond when they attack **25 Make forth** march forward **33 posture** quality **34 for** as for. **Hybla** a mountain and a town in ancient Sicily, famous for honey **39 so** i.e., give warning **41 show'd your teeth** i.e., in smiles **47 rul'd** prevailed (in urging that Antony be killed) **48 the cause** to our business **49 proof** trial **52 up** in its sheath **53 three and thirty** (Plutarch has it three and twenty.) **55 Have . . . to** has also been slaughtered by **56–58 Caesar . . . sword** (Brutus says that if there are any traitors on the battlefield they will perforce be in Octavius' army; Octavius twists Brutus' taunt by pretending that Brutus meant Octavius could not die on Brutus' sword.) **59 strain** lineage

CASSIUS
A peevish schoolboy, worthless of such honor,
Join'd with a masker and a reveler!
ANTONY
Old Cassius still.
OCTAVIUS Come, Antony, away!
Defiance, traitors, hurl we in your teeth.
If you dare fight today, come to the field;
If not, when you have stomachs.
Exeunt Octavius, Antony, and army.
CASSIUS
Why, now, blow wind, swell billow, and swim bark!
The storm is up, and all is on the hazard.
BRUTUS
Ho, Lucilius! Hark, a word with you.
LUCILIUS *(Stands forth)* My lord?
[*Brutus and Lucilius converse apart.*]
CASSIUS
Messala!
MESSALA *(Stands forth)* What says my general?
CASSIUS Messala,
This is my birthday; as this very day
Was Cassius born. Give me thy hand, Messala.
Be thou my witness that against my will,
As Pompey was, am I compell'd to set
Upon one battle all our liberties.
You know that I held Epicurus strong
And his opinion. Now I change my mind,
And partly credit things that do presage.
Coming from Sardis, on our former ensign
Two mighty eagles fell, and there they perch'd,
Gorging and feeding from our soldiers' hands,
Who to Philippi here consorted us.
This morning are they fled away and gone,
And in their steads do ravens, crows, and kites
Fly o'er our heads, and downward look on us,
As we were sickly prey. Their shadows seem
A canopy most fatal, under which
Our army lies, ready to give up the ghost.
MESSALA
Believe not so.
CASSIUS I but believe it partly,
For I am fresh of spirit, and resolv'd
To meet all perils very constantly.
BRUTUS
Even so, Lucilius.
CASSIUS Now, most noble Brutus,
The gods today stand friendly, that we may,
Lovers in peace, lead on our days to age!
But since the affairs of men rest still incertain,
Let's reason with the worst that may befall.
If we do lose this battle, then is this
The very last time we shall speak together.
What are you then determined to do?
BRUTUS
Even by the rule of that philosophy
By which I did blame Cato for the death
Which he did give himself—I know not how,
But I do find it cowardly and vile,
For fear of what might fall, so to prevent
The time of life—arming myself with patience
To stay the providence of some high powers
That govern us below.
CASSIUS Then, if we lose this battle,
You are contented to be led in triumph
Thorough the streets of Rome?
BRUTUS
No, Cassius, no. Think not, thou noble Roman,
That ever Brutus will go bound to Rome;
He bears too great a mind. But this same day
Must end that work the ides of March begun;
And whether we shall meet again I know not.
Therefore our everlasting farewell take.
For ever, and for ever, farewell, Cassius!
If we do meet again, why, we shall smile;
If not, why then this parting was well made.
CASSIUS
For ever, and for ever, farewell, Brutus!
If we do meet again, we'll smile indeed;
If not, 'tis true this parting was well made.
BRUTUS
Why, then, lead on. O, that a man might know
The end of this day's business ere it come!
But it sufficeth that the day will end,
And then the end is known. Come, ho! Away!
Exeunt.

[SCENE II]

Alarum. Enter Brutus and Messala.

BRUTUS
Ride, ride, Messala, ride, and give these bills
Unto the legions on the other side.
[*Gives written orders.*]
Loud alarum.
Let them set on at once; for I perceive
But cold demeanor in Octavius' wing,
And sudden push gives them the overthrow.
Ride, ride, Messala! Let them all come down.
Exeunt.

61 schoolboy (Octavius was 19 at the time of Caesar's assassination.) **62 masker . . . reveler** i.e., Antony, noted for his reveling **66 stomachs** (1) appetites (for fighting) (2) courage **68 on the hazard** at stake **71 as** on **74 Pompey** (The reference is to the battle of Pharsalus, where Pompey was persuaded to fight Caesar against his own judgment.) **set** stake **76 Epicurus** Greek philosopher (341–270 B.C.), whose materialistic philosophy spurned belief in omens or superstitions **78 presage** foretell events **79 former ensign** foremost standard, the legion's *aquila*, a tall standard surmounted by the image of an eagle **80 fell** swooped down **82 consorted** accompanied **86 As** as if **92 Even so, Lucilius** (This phrase ends Brutus' private conversation apart with Lucilius.) **93 The gods** may the gods **94 Lovers** friends **95 still** always **96 reason** reckon

101 Cato i.e., Marcus Porcius Cato, Brutus' father-in-law, who killed himself to avoid submission to Caesar in 46 B.C. (See II.i.295 and note.) **104 fall** befall. **prevent** anticipate the end, cut short **105 time** term, end **106 stay** await

V.ii. Location: Philippi. The field of battle.
s.d. Alarum (This is seemingly an anticipatory stage direction; the battle actually begins with the *Loud alarum* at l. 2.) **1 bills** orders **2 side** wing (i.e., Cassius' wing) **4 cold demeanor** faint-heartedness **6 come down** i.e., from the hills where they have been awaiting the battle; see V.i.2–3.

[SCENE III]

Alarums. Enter Cassius [carrying a standard], and Titinius.

CASSIUS
O, look, Titinius, look, the villains fly!
Myself have to mine own turn'd enemy.
This ensign here of mine was turning back;
I slew the coward, and did take it from him.

TITINIUS
O Cassius, Brutus gave the word too early,
Who, having some advantage on Octavius,
Took it too eagerly. His soldiers fell to spoil,
Whilst we by Antony are all enclos'd.

Enter Pindarus.

PINDARUS
Fly further off, my lord, fly further off!
Mark Antony is in your tents, my lord.
Fly, therefore, noble Cassius, fly far off.

CASSIUS
This hill is far enough. Look, look, Titinius!
Are those my tents where I perceive the fire?

TITINIUS
They are, my lord.

CASSIUS
Titinius, if thou lovest me,
Mount thou my horse, and hide thy spurs in him,
Till he have brought thee up to yonder troops
And here again, that I may rest assur'd
Whether yond troops are friend or enemy.

TITINIUS
I will be here again, even with a thought. *Exit.*

CASSIUS
Go, Pindarus, get higher on that hill.
My sight was ever thick. Regard Titinius,
And tell me what thou not'st about the field.
[*Pindarus goes up.*]
This day I breathed first. Time is come round,
And where I did begin, there shall I end.
My life is run his compass. Sirrah, what news?

PINDARUS *(Above)*
O my lord!

CASSIUS
What news?

PINDARUS [*Above*]
Titinius is enclosed round about
With horsemen, that make to him on the spur;
Yet he spurs on. Now they are almost on him.
Now, Titinius! Now some light. O, he
Lights too. He's ta'en. *(Shout.)* And, hark! They shout for joy.

CASSIUS
Come down, behold no more.
O, coward that I am, to live so long,
To see my best friend ta'en before my face!

Enter Pindarus [from above].

Come hither, sirrah.
In Parthia did I take thee prisoner;
And then I swore thee, saving of thy life,
That whatsoever I did bid thee do,
Thou shouldst attempt it. Come now, keep thine oath.
Now be a freeman, and with this good sword,
That ran through Caesar's bowels, search this bosom.
Stand not to answer. Here, take thou the hilts;
And, when my face is cover'd, as 'tis now,
Guide thou the sword. [*Pindarus does so.*] Caesar, thou art reveng'd,
Even with the sword that kill'd thee. [*Dies.*]

PINDARUS
So, I am free; yet would not so have been,
Durst I have done my will. O Cassius!
Far from this country Pindarus shall run,
Where never Roman shall take note of him. [*Exit.*]

Enter Titinius and Messala.

MESSALA
It is but change, Titinius; for Octavius
Is overthrown by noble Brutus' power,
As Cassius' legions are by Antony.

TITINIUS
These tidings will well comfort Cassius.

MESSALA
Where did you leave him?

TITINIUS
All disconsolate,
With Pindarus his bondman, on this hill.

MESSALA
Is not that he that lies upon the ground?

TITINIUS
He lies not like the living. O my heart!

MESSALA
Is not that he?

TITINIUS
No, this was he, Messala,
But Cassius is no more. O setting sun,
As in thy red rays thou dost sink to night,
So in his red blood Cassius' day is set!
The sun of Rome is set. Our day is gone;
Clouds, dews, and dangers come; our deeds are done!
Mistrust of my success hath done this deed.

MESSALA
Mistrust of good success hath done this deed.
O hateful error, melancholy's child,
Why dost thou show to the apt thoughts of men

V.iii. Location: The field of battle still.
1 the villains i.e., my own troops **2 mine own** my own men **3 ensign** bearer of the standard. (A legion's *aquila* or eagle standard had great moral significance and needed to be guarded.) **7 spoil** looting **19 even . . . thought** as quick as thought **21 thick** imperfect, dim **22 s.d. Pindarus goes up** (Pindarus may exit and ascend behind the scenes to the gallery; at l. 35 he does *enter* in order to return.) **25 compass** circuit, circle (as drawn by a geometer's compass) **29 make . . . spur** approach him riding rapidly **31 light** alight, dismount

37 Parthia (What is now northern Iran.) **38 swore . . . of** made you swear, when I spared **42 search** penetrate **43 Stand** delay **51 change** exchange of advantage, *quid pro quo* **61 to** toward **63 sun** (with pun on *son*) **65 Mistrust** i.e., Cassius' doubt **67 melancholy's child** i.e., chimera bred of a melancholic temperament **68 apt** impressionable

The things that are not? O error, soon conceiv'd,
Thou never com'st unto a happy birth,
But kill'st the mother that engend'red thee!

TITINIUS
What, Pindarus! Where art thou, Pindarus?

MESSALA
Seek him, Titinius, whilst I go to meet
The noble Brutus, thrusting this report
Into his ears. I may say "thrusting" it;
For piercing steel and darts envenomed
Shall be as welcome to the ears of Brutus
As tidings of this sight.

TITINIUS Hie you, Messala,
And I will seek for Pindarus the while.
[Exit Messala.]
Why didst thou send me forth, brave Cassius?
Did I not meet thy friends? And did not they
Put on my brows this wreath of victory,
And bid me give it thee? Didst thou not hear their shouts?
Alas, thou hast misconstrued everything!
But, hold thee, take this garland on thy brow.
[He places a garland on Cassius' brow.]
Thy Brutus bid me give it thee, and I
Will do his bidding. Brutus, come apace,
And see how I regarded Caius Cassius.
By your leave, gods!—This is a Roman's part.
Come, Cassius' sword, and find Titinius' heart.
[Stabs himself and] dies.

Alarum. Enter Brutus, Messala, young Cato, Strato, Volumnius, and Lucilius.

BRUTUS
Where, where, Messala, doth his body lie?

MESSALA
Lo, yonder, and Titinius mourning it.

BRUTUS
Titinius' face is upward.

CATO He is slain.

BRUTUS
O Julius Caesar, thou art mighty yet!
Thy spirit walks abroad, and turns our swords
In our own proper entrails. *Low alarums.*

CATO Brave Titinius!
Look whe'er he have not crown'd dead Cassius!

BRUTUS
Are yet two Romans living such as these?
The last of all the Romans, fare thee well!
It is impossible that ever Rome
Should breed thy fellow. Friends, I owe moe tears
To this dead man than you shall see me pay.
I shall find time, Cassius, I shall find time.
Come, therefore, and to Thasos send his body.
His funerals shall not be in our camp,
Lest it discomfort us. Lucilius, come,
And come, young Cato, let us to the field.
Labeo and Flavius set our battles on.
'Tis three o'clock; and, Romans, yet ere night
We shall try fortune in a second fight. *Exeunt.*

71 the mother i.e., the melancholy person who too readily believed the worst **96 own proper** very own **97 whe'er** whether **104 Thasos** an island off the coast of Thrace, near Philippi **106 discomfort** discourage

108 battles armies **110 s.d. Exeunt** (The bodies of Cassius and Titinius are probably carried off at this point.)

[SCENE IV]

Alarum. Enter Brutus, Messala, [young] Cato, Lucilius, and Flavius.

BRUTUS
Yet, countrymen, O, yet hold up your heads!
[Exit, followed by Messala and Flavius.]

CATO
What bastard doth not? Who will go with me?
I will proclaim my name about the field:
I am the son of Marcus Cato, ho!
A foe to tyrants, and my country's friend.
I am the son of Marcus Cato, ho!

Enter Soldiers and fight.

LUCILIUS
And I am Brutus, Marcus Brutus I!
Brutus, my country's friend! Know me for Brutus!
[Young Cato is slain by Antony's men.]
O young and noble Cato, art thou down?
Why, now thou diest as bravely as Titinius,
And mayst be honor'd, being Cato's son.

FIRST SOLDIER
Yield, or thou diest.

LUCILIUS Only I yield to die.
There is so much that thou wilt kill me straight;
Kill Brutus, and be honor'd in his death.

FIRST SOLDIER
We must not. A noble prisoner!

SECOND SOLDIER
Room, ho! Tell Antony, Brutus is ta'en.

Enter Antony.

FIRST SOLDIER
I'll tell the news. Here comes the general.
Brutus is ta'en, Brutus is ta'en, my lord.

ANTONY
Where is he?

LUCILIUS
Safe, Antony; Brutus is safe enough.
I dare assure thee that no enemy
Shall ever take alive the noble Brutus.
The gods defend him from so great a shame!
When you do find him, or alive or dead,
He will be found like Brutus, like himself.

ANTONY
This is not Brutus, friend, but, I assure you,
A prize no less in worth. Keep this man safe;

V.iv. Location: Scene continues at the field of battle.
2 What . . . not who is so base that he would not do so **12 Only . . . die** i.e., I surrender only to die immediately **13 There . . . straight** i.e., here is money (or perhaps the inducement of honor) if you will kill me at once

Give him all kindness. I had rather have
Such men my friends than enemies. Go on,
And see whe'er Brutus be alive or dead;
And bring us word unto Octavius' tent
How every thing is chanc'd. *Exeunt* [*severally*].

[SCENE V]

Enter Brutus, Dardanius, Clitus, Strato, and Volumnius.

BRUTUS
Come, poor remains of friends, rest on this rock.
[*Sits.*]

CLITUS
Statilius show'd the torchlight, but, my lord,
He came not back. He is or ta'en or slain.

BRUTUS
Sit thee down, Clitus. Slaying is the word.
It is a deed in fashion. Hark thee, Clitus.
[*Whispers.*]

CLITUS
What, I, my lord? No, not for all the world.

BRUTUS
Peace then. No words.

CLITUS
I'll rather kill myself.

BRUTUS
Hark thee, Dardanius. [*Whispers.*]

DARDANIUS
Shall I do such a deed?
[*Dardanius and Clitus move away from Brutus.*]

CLITUS
O Dardanius!

DARDANIUS
O Clitus!

CLITUS
What ill request did Brutus make to thee?

DARDANIUS
To kill him, Clitus. Look, he meditates.

CLITUS
Now is that noble vessel full of grief,
That it runs over even at his eyes.

BRUTUS
Come hither, good Volumnius; list a word.

VOLUMNIUS
What say my lord?

BRUTUS
Why, this, Volumnius:
The ghost of Caesar hath appear'd to me
Two several times by night; at Sardis once,
And, this last night, here in Philippi fields.
I know my hour is come.

VOLUMNIUS
Not so, my lord.

BRUTUS
Nay, I am sure it is, Volumnius.
Thou seest the world, Volumnius, how it goes;
Our enemies have beat us to the pit. *Low alarums.*
It is more worthy to leap in ourselves,
Than tarry till they push us. Good Volumnius,
Thou know'st that we two went to school together.
Even for that our love of old, I prithee,
Hold thou my sword-hilts, whilst I run on it.

VOLUMNIUS
That's not an office for a friend, my lord.
Alarum still.

CLITUS
Fly, fly, my lord! There is no tarrying here.

BRUTUS
Farewell to you; and you; and you, Volumnius.
Strato, thou hast been all this while asleep;
Farewell to thee too, Strato. Countrymen,
My heart doth joy that yet in all my life
I found no man but he was true to me.
I shall have glory by this losing day
More than Octavius and Mark Antony
By this vile conquest shall attain unto.
So fare you well at once; for Brutus' tongue
Hath almost ended his life's history.
Night hangs upon mine eyes; my bones would rest,
That have but labor'd to attain this hour.
Alarum. Cry within, "Fly, fly, fly!"

CLITUS
Fly, my lord, fly!

BRUTUS
Hence, I will follow.
[*Exeunt Clitus, Dardanius, and Volumnius.*]
I prithee, Strato, stay thou by thy lord.
Thou art a fellow of a good respect;
Thy life hath had some smatch of honor in it.
Hold then my sword, and turn away thy face,
While I do run upon it. Wilt thou, Strato?

STRATO
Give me your hand first. Fare you well, my lord.

BRUTUS
Farewell, good Strato. [*Runs on his sword.*]
Caesar, now be still.
I kill'd not thee with half so good a will. *Dies.*

Alarum. Retreat. Enter Antony, Octavius; Messala, Lucilius [*as prisoners*]; *and the army.*

OCTAVIUS
What man is that?

MESSALA
My master's man. Strato, where is thy master?

STRATO
Free from the bondage you are in, Messala.
The conquerors can but make a fire of him,
For Brutus only overcame himself,
And no man else hath honor by his death.

LUCILIUS
So Brutus should be found. I thank thee, Brutus,

32 s.d. Exeunt (The body of young Cato may be carried off at this point; it is not seen by Brutus *et al.* in scene v.)

V.v. Location: The field of battle still.
2 show'd the torchlight (A scout named Statilius has gone to see if Cassius' camp is still occupied; he signals back, but is taken and slain.) **18 several** separate

23 beat driven. **pit** trap for wild animals; also, a grave **27 that our love** that friendship of ours **38 vile** paltry **39 at once** all together **42 That . . . hour** i.e., all their striving has been toward this moment of death **45 respect** reputation **46 some smatch** some flavor, a touch **56 Brutus . . . himself** only Brutus conquered Brutus

That thou hast prov'd Lucilius' saying true.

OCTAVIUS

All that serv'd Brutus, I will entertain them.
Fellow, wilt thou bestow thy time with me?

STRATO

Ay, if Messala will prefer me to you.

OCTAVIUS

Do so, good Messala.

MESSALA

How died my master, Strato?

STRATO

I held the sword, and he did run on it.

MESSALA

Octavius, then take him to follow thee,
That did the latest service to my master.

ANTONY

This was the noblest Roman of them all.
All the conspirators save only he
Did that they did in envy of great Caesar;
He, only in a general honest thought
And common good to all, made one of them.
His life was gentle, and the elements
So mix'd in him that Nature might stand up
And say to all the world, "This was a man!"

OCTAVIUS

According to his virtue let us use him,
With all respect and rites of burial.
Within my tent his bones tonight shall lie,
Most like a soldier, ordered honorably.
So call the field to rest; and let's away,
To part the glories of this happy day. *Exeunt omnes.*

59 saying (See V.iv. 21–25.) **60 entertain** take into service **62 prefer** recommend **67 latest** last **70 that** what. **envy of** malice toward **73 gentle** noble. **elements** (Man as a microcosm was made up of earth, air, fire, and water, whose qualities were mingled in Brutus in due proportions.) **79 ordered** treated, arranged for **80 field** army in the field **81 part** share

Hamlet, Prince of Denmark

A recurring motif in *Hamlet* is of a seemingly healthy exterior concealing inward sickness. Mere pretense of virtue, as Hamlet warns his mother, "will but skin and film the ulcerous place, Whiles rank corruption, mining all within, Infects unseen" (III,iv). Polonius confesses, when he is about to use his daughter as a decoy for Hamlet, that "with devotion's visage And pious action we do sugar o'er The devil himself"; and his observation elicits a more anguished *mea culpa* from Claudius in an aside: "How smart a lash that speech doth give my conscience! The harlot's cheek, beautied with plast'ring art, Is not more ugly to the thing that helps it Than is my deed to my most painted word" (III,i).

This motif of concealed evil and disease continually reminds us that, in both a specific and a broader sense, "Something is rotten in the state of Denmark." The specific source of contamination is a poison: the poison with which Claudius has killed Hamlet Senior, the poison in the players' version of this same murder, and the two poisons (envenomed sword and poisoned drink) with which Claudius and Laertes plot to rid themselves of young Hamlet. More generally, the poison is man's evil nature seeking to destroy his better nature, as in the archetypal murder of Abel by Cain. "O my offense is rank, it smells to heaven," laments Claudius, "It hath the primal curse upon 't, A brother's murder" (III,iii). Hamlet Senior and Claudius typify what is best and worst in man, the sun-god Hyperion compared to a satyr. Claudius is a "serpent" and a "mildew'd ear Blasting his wholesome brother" (III,iv). Too many men, finding this quality in themselves, are perversely drawn in spite of their better qualities to "some vicious mole of nature" in themselves over which they have no control. "Their virtues else—be they as pure as grace, As infinite as man may undergo—Shall in the general censure take corruption From that particular fault." The "dram of evil" pollutes "all the noble substance" (I,iv). Thus poison spreads outward to infect individual men, just as bad men can infect an entire court or nation.

Hamlet, his mind attuned to philosophical matters, is keenly and poetically aware of man's fallen condition. He is, moreover, a shrewd observer of the Danish court, one familiar with its ways and at the same time newly returned from abroad, looking at Denmark with a stranger's eyes. What particularly darkens his view of man, however, is not the general truth of man's corrupted nature but rather Hamlet's knowledge of a dreadful secret. Even before he learns of his father's murder, Hamlet senses that something is more deeply amiss than his mother's overhasty marriage to her deceased husband's brother. This is serious enough, to be sure, for it violates a widely held taboo (parallel to the marriage of a widower to his deceased wife's sister, long regarded as incestuous by the English), and is thus understandably referred to as "incest" by Hamlet and his father's ghost. The appalling spectacle of Gertrude's "wicked speed, to post With such dexterity to incestuous sheets" overwhelms Hamlet with revulsion at carnal appetite and intensifies the emotional crisis any son would go through when forced to contemplate his father's death and mother's remarriage. Still, the Ghost's revelation is of something far worse, something Hamlet has subconsciously feared and suspected. "O my prophetic soul! My uncle!" Now Hamlet has confirming evidence for his intuition that the world itself is "an unweeded garden That grows to seed; things rank and gross in nature Possess it merely" (I,ii).

Something is indeed rotten in the state of Denmark. The monarch on whom the health and safety of the kingdom depends is a murderer. Yet few persons know his secret: Hamlet, Horatio only belatedly, Claudius himself, and ourselves as audience. Many ironies and misunderstandings of the play cannot be understood without a proper awareness of this gap between Hamlet's knowledge and most others' ignorance of the murder. For, according to their own lights, Polonius and the rest behave as courtiers normally behave, obeying and flattering a king whom they acknowledge their legitimate ruler. Hamlet, for his part, is so obsessed with the secret murder that he overreacts to those around him, rejecting overtures of friendship and becoming embittered, callous, brutal, and even violent. His antisocial behavior gives the others good reason to fear him as a menace to the state. Nevertheless, we share with Hamlet a knowledge of the truth, and know that he is right whereas the others are at best unhappily deceived by their own blind complicity in evil.

Rosencrantz and Guildenstern, for instance, are boyhood friends of Hamlet but are now dependent on the favor of King Claudius. Despite their seeming concern for their onetime comrade, and Hamlet's initial pleasure in receiving them, they are faceless courtiers whose very names, like their personalities, are virtually interchangeable. "Thanks, Rosencrantz and gentle Guildenstern," says the King, and "Thanks, Guildenstern and gentle Rosencrantz," echoes the Queen (II,ii). They cannot understand why Hamlet increasingly mocks their overtures of friendship, whereas Hamlet cannot stomach their subservience to the King. The secret murder divides Hamlet from them, since only he knows of it. As the confrontation between Hamlet and Claudius grows more deadly, Rosencrantz and Guildenstern, not knowing the true cause, can only interpret Hamlet's behavior as dangerous madness. The wild display he puts on during the performance of "The Murder of Gonzago," and the killing of Polonius, are evidence of a treasonous threat to the crown, eliciting from them staunch assertions of the divine right of kings. "Most holy and religious fear it is To keep those many many bodies safe That live and feed upon your majesty," professes Guildenstern, and Rosencrantz reiterates the theme: "The cess of majesty Dies not alone; but, like a gulf, doth draw What's near it with it" (III,iii). These sentiments of Elizabethan orthodoxy, which would pass for current in Shakespeare's history plays, are here undercut by a devastating irony, since they are spoken unwittingly in defense of a murderer. This irony pursues Rosencrantz and Guildenstern to their graves, for they are killed performing what they see as their duty to convey Hamlet safely to England. They are as ignorant of Claudius' secret orders for the murder of Hamlet in England as they are of Claudius' real reason for wishing to be rid of his stepson. That Hamlet should ingeniously remove the secret commission from Rosencrantz and Guildenstern's packet and substitute an order for their execution is ironically fitting, even though they are guiltless of having plotted Hamlet's death. "Why, man, they did make love to this employment," says Hamlet to Horatio. "They are not near my conscience; their defeat Does by their own insinuation grow" (V,ii). In other words, they have condemned themselves by interceding officiously in deadly affairs of which they had no comprehension.

Polonius too dies for meddling. It seems a harsh fate, since he wishes no physical harm to Hamlet, and is only trying to ingratiate himself with Claudius. Yet Polonius' complicity in jaded court politics is deeper than his fatuous parental sententiousness might lead one to suppose. His famous advice to his son, often quoted out of context as though it were wise counsel, is in fact a worldly gospel of self-interest and concern for appearances. Like his son Laertes he cynically presumes that Hamlet's affection for Ophelia cannot be serious, since princes are not free to marry ladies of the court; accordingly, Polonius obliges his daughter to return the love letters she so cherishes. Polonius' spies are everywhere, seeking to entrap Polonius' own son in fleshly sin or to discover symptoms of Hamlet's presumed lovesickness. Polonius cuts a ridiculous figure as a prattling busybody, but he has actually helped Claudius to the throne and is an essential instrument of royal policy. His ineffectuality and ignorance of the murder do not really excuse his guilty involvement.

Ophelia is more innocent than her father and brother, and more truly affectionate toward Hamlet. Nevertheless her pitiable story suggests that weak-willed acquiescence is poisoned by the evil to which it surrenders. However passively, Ophelia becomes an instrument through which Claudius attempts to spy on Hamlet. She is much like Gertrude, for the Queen has yielded to Claudius' importunity without ever knowing fully what awful price Claudius has paid for her and for the throne. The resemblance between Ophelia and Gertrude confirms Hamlet's tendency to generalize about feminine weakness—"Frailty, thy name is woman"—and prompts his misogynistic outburst against Ophelia when he concludes she too is spying on him. His rejection of love and friendship (except for Horatio's) seems paranoid in character, and yet is at least partially justified by the fact that so many of the court are in fact conspiring to learn what he is up to.

It is their oversimplification of his dilemma and their facile analyses that vex Hamlet as much as the meddling. When they presume to diagnose his malady, the courtiers actually reveal more about themselves than about Hamlet—something we as readers and viewers might well bear in mind. Rosencrantz and Guildenstern think in political terms reflecting their own ambitious natures, and Hamlet takes mordant delight in leading them on. "Sir, I lack advancement," he mockingly answers Rosencrantz' questioning as to the cause of his distemper. Rosencrantz is immediately taken in: "How can that be, when you have the voice of the King himself for your succession in Denmark?" (III,ii). Actually Hamlet does hold a grudge against Claudius for having "Popp'd in between th' election and my hopes" (V,ii), using the Danish custom of "election" by the chief lords of the realm to deprive young Hamlet of the succession that would normally have been his. Nevertheless, it is a gross oversimplification to suppose that political frustration is the key to Hamlet's sorrow. To speculate thus is more presumptuous than to attempt playing the recorder without having studied that musical instrument. "Why, look you now, how unworthy a thing you would make of me!" Hamlet protests to Rosencrantz and Guildenstern. "You would play upon me; you would seem to know my stops; you would pluck out the heart of my mystery" (III,ii). Yet the worst offender in such distortion of complex truth is Polonius, whose diagnosis of lovesickness appears to have been inspired by recollections of Polonius' own far-off youth. ("Truly in my youth I suffered much extremity for love; very near this," II,ii). Polonius' fatuous complacency in his own powers of analysis—"If circumstances lead me, I will find Where truth is hid, though it were hid indeed Within the center"—reads like a parody of Hamlet's struggle to discover what is true and what is not.

Thus, although Hamlet may seem to react with excessive bitterness toward those who are set to watch over him, the corruption he decries in Denmark is both real and universal. "The time is out of joint," he laments. "O cursed spite That ever I was born to set it right!" (I,v). How is he to proceed in setting things right? Ever since the nineteenth century it has been fashionable to discover reasons for Hamlet's delaying in revenge. The basic Romantic approach is to find a defect, or tragic flaw, in Hamlet himself. In Coleridge's words, Hamlet suffers from "an overbalance in the contemplative faculty," and is "one who vacillates from sensibility and procrastinates from thought, and loses the power of action in the energy of resolve." More recent psychological critics, like Freud's disciple, Ernest Jones, still seek answers to the Romantics' question by explaining Hamlet's failure of will. In Jones' interpretation, Hamlet is the victim of an Oedipal trauma; he has longed unconsciously to possess his mother, and for that very reason cannot bring himself to punish the hated uncle who has supplanted him in his incestuous and forbidden desire. Such interpretations suggest at least that Hamlet continues to serve as a mirror in which analysts who would pluck out the heart of his mystery see an image of themselves—just as Rosencrantz and Guildenstern read politics, and Polonius lovesickness, into Hamlet's distress.

We can ask, however, not only whether the answers to Hamlet's supposed delay are valid but whether the question being asked is itself valid. Is the delay unnecessary or excessive? The question did not even arise until the nineteenth century. Earlier audiences were evidently satisfied that Hamlet must test the Ghost's credibility, since apparitions can tell half-truths to deceive men, and that once Hamlet has confirmed the Ghost's word he proceeds as resolutely as his canny adversary allows. More recent criticism, perhaps reflecting a modern absorption in existentialist philosophy, has proposed that Hamlet's dilemma is not a matter of personal failure but of the absurdity of action itself in a corrupt world. Does what Hamlet is asked to do make any sense, given the bestial nature of man and the impossibility of knowing what is right? In part it is a matter of style: Claudius' Denmark is crassly vulgar, and to combat this vulgarity on its own terms seems to require the sort of bad histrionics Hamlet derides in actors who mouth their lines or tear a passion to tatters. Hamlet's dilemma of action can best be studied in the play by comparing him with various characters who are obliged to act in situations similar to his own, and who respond in meaningfully different ways.

Three young men—Hamlet, Laertes, and Fortinbras—are called upon to avenge their fathers' violent deaths. Ophelia too has lost a father by violent means, and her madness and death are another kind of reaction to such a loss. The responses of Laertes and Fortinbras offer implicit lessons to Hamlet, and in both cases the lesson seems to be the futility of positive and forceful action. Laertes thinks he has received an unambiguous mandate to revenge, since Hamlet has undoubtedly slain Polonius and helped to deprive Ophelia of her sanity. Accordingly Laertes comes back to Denmark in a fury, stirring the rabble with his demagoguery and spouting Senecan rant about dismissing conscience "to the profoundest pit" in his quest for vengeance (IV,v). When Claudius asks what Laertes would do to Hamlet "To show yourself your father's son in deed More than in words," Laertes fires back: "To cut his throat i' th' church!" (IV,vii). This resolution is understandable. The pity is, however, that Laertes has only superficially identified the murderer in the case. He is too easily deceived by Claudius because he has jumped to easy and fallacious conclusions, and so is doomed to become a pawn in Claudius' sly maneuverings. Too late he sees his error and must die for it, begging and receiving Hamlet's forgiveness. Before we accuse Hamlet of thinking too deliberately before acting, we must consider that Laertes has not thought enough.

Fortinbras of Norway, as his name implies ("strong in arms"), is one who believes in decisive action. At the beginning of the play we learn that his father has been slain in battle by old Hamlet, and that Fortinbras has collected an army to win back by force the territory fairly won by the Danes in that encounter. Like Hamlet, young Fortinbras does not succeed his father to the throne, but must now contend with an uncle-king. When this uncle, at Claudius' instigation, forbids Fortinbras to march against the Danes, and rewards him for his restraint with a huge annual income and a commission to fight the Poles instead, Fortinbras sagaciously welcomes the new opportunity. He pockets the money, marches against Poland, and waits for occasion to deliver Denmark as well into his hands. Clearly this is more of a success story than that of Laertes, and Hamlet does after all give his blessing to the "election" of Fortinbras to the Danish throne. Fortinbras is the man of the hour, the representative of a restored political stability. Yet Hamlet's admiration for this man on horseback is qualified by a profound reservation. The spectacle of Fortinbras marching against Poland "to gain a little patch of ground That hath in it no profit but the name" prompts Hamlet to berate himself for inaction, but he cannot ignore the absurdity of the effort. "Two thousand souls and twenty thousand ducats Will not debate the question of this straw." The soldiers will risk their very lives "Even for an egg-shell" (IV,iv). It is only one step from this view of the vanity of ambitious striving to the speculation that great Caesar or Alexander, dead and turned to dust, may one day produce the loam or clay with which to stop the bunghole of a beer barrel. Fortinbras epitomizes the ongoing political order after Hamlet's death, but is that order of any consequence to us after we have imagined with Hamlet the futility of most human endeavor?

To ask such a question is to seek more passive or self-abnegating answers to the riddle of life, and Hamlet is attuned to such inquiries. Even before he learns of his father's murder he contemplates suicide, wishing "that the Everlasting had not fix'd His canon 'gainst self-slaughter" (I,ii). As with the alternative of action, other characters serve as foils to Hamlet, revealing both the attractions and perils of withdrawal. Ophelia is destroyed by meekly acquiescing in others' desires. Whether she commits suicide is uncertain, but the very possibility reminds us that Hamlet has considered and reluctantly rejected this despairing path as forbidden by Christian teaching. He has also playacted at the madness to which Ophelia succumbs. Gertrude identifies herself with Ophelia, and like her has surrendered her will to male aggressiveness. We suspect she knows little of the actual murder but dares not think how deeply she may be implicated. Her death may possibly be a suicide also, one of atonement. A more attractive alternative to decisive action for Hamlet is acting in the theatre, and he is full of advice to the visiting players. The play they perform before Claudius at Hamlet's request and with some lines added by him, a play consciously archaic in style, offers to the Danish court a kind of heightened reflection of itself, a homiletic artifact rendering in conventional terms the taut anxieties and terrors of murder for the sake of ignoble passion. We are not surprised when, in his conversations with the players, Hamlet openly professes his admiration for the way in which art holds "the mirror up to nature, to show virtue her own feature, scorn her own image, and the very age and body of the time his form and pressure" (III,ii). Hamlet admires the dramatist's ability to transmute raw human feeling into tragic art, depicting and ordering reality as Shakespeare's play of *Hamlet* does for us. Yet playacting is also, Hamlet recognizes, a self-indulgent escape for him, a way of unpacking his heart with words, of verbalizing his situation without doing something to remedy it. Acting and talking remind him too much of Polonius, who was an actor in his youth and who continues to be, like Hamlet, an inveterate punster.

Of the passive responses in the play, the stoicism of Horatio is by far the most attractive to Hamlet. "More an antique Roman than a Dane," Horatio is, as Hamlet praises him, immune to flattering or to opportunities for cheap self-advancement. He is "As one, in suff'ring all, that suffers nothing, A man that fortune's buffets and rewards Hast ta'en with equal thanks" (III,ii). Such a person has a sure defense against the worst that life can offer. Hamlet can trust and love Horatio as he can no one else. Yet even here there are limits, for Horatio's skeptical and Roman philosophy cuts him off from a Christian and metaphysical overview. "There are more things in heaven and earth, Horatio, Than are dreamt of in your philosophy" (I,v). After they have beheld together the skulls of Yorick's graveyard, Horatio seemingly does not share with Hamlet the exulting Christian perception that, although human life is indeed vain, providence will reveal a pattern transcending human sorrow.

Hamlet's path must lie somehow between the rash suddenness of Laertes or the canny resoluteness of Fortinbras on the one hand, and the passivity of Ophelia or Gertrude and the stoic resignation of Horatio on the other. He alternates between action and inaction in his attempts to fulfill his mission, finding neither satisfactory. The Ghost has commanded Hamlet to revenge, but has not explained how this is to be done; indeed, Gertrude is to be left passively to heaven and her conscience. If this method will suffice for her (and Christian wisdom taught that such a purgation was as thorough as it was sure), why not for Claudius? If Claudius must be killed, should it be while he is at his sin rather than at his prayers? The play is full of questions, stemming chiefly from the enigmatic commands of the Ghost. "Say, why is this? Wherefore? What should we do?" (I,iv). Hamlet is not incapable of action. He shows unusual strength and cunning on the pirate ship, or in his duel with Laertes ("I shall win at the odds"), or especially in his slaying of Polonius—an action hardly characterized by "thinking too precisely on th' event." Here is forthright action of the sort Laertes espouses. Yet when the corpse behind his mother's arras turns out to be Polonius rather than Claudius, Hamlet knows he has offended heaven. Even if Polonius deserves what he got, Hamlet has made himself into a cruel "scourge" of providence who must himself suffer retribution as well as deal it out. Inconsiderate action has not accomplished what the Ghost commanded.

The Ghost in fact does not appear to speak for providence. His message is of revenge, a pagan concept basic to all primitive societies but at odds with Christian teaching. His wish that Claudius be sent to hell and that Gertrude be more gently treated is not the judgment of an impartial deity but the emotional reaction of a murdered man's restless spirit. This is not to say that Hamlet is being tempted to perform a damnable act, as he fears possible, but that the Ghost's command cannot readily be reconciled with a complex and balanced view of justice. If Hamlet were to spring on Claudius in the fullness of his vice and cut his throat, we would pronounce Hamlet a murderer. What Hamlet believes he has learned instead is that he must become the instrument of providence according to *its* plans, not his own. After his return from England, he senses triumphantly that all will be for the best if he allows an unseen power to decide the time and place for his final act. Under these conditions, rash action will be right. "Prais'd be rashness for it, let us know, Our indiscretion sometime serves us well When our deep plots do pall, and that should teach us There's a divinity that shapes our ends, Rough-hew them how we will" (V,ii). Passivity too is now a proper course, for Hamlet puts himself wholly at the disposal of providence. What had seemed so impossible when Hamlet tried to formulate his own design now proves elementary once he trusts to heaven's justice. Rashness and passivity are perfectly fused. Hamlet is revenged without having to commit premeditated murder, and is relieved of his painful existence without having to commit suicide.

The circumstances of *Hamlet's* catastrophe do indeed accomplish all that Hamlet desires, by a route so circuitous that no man could ever have foreseen or devised it. Polonius' death, as it turns out, was instrumental after all, for it led to Laertes' angry return to Denmark and the challenge to a duel. Every seemingly unrelated event has its place; "There's a special providence in the fall of a sparrow." Repeatedly the characters stress the role of seeming accident leading to just retribution. Horatio sums up a pattern "Of accidental judgments, casual slaughters . . . And, in this upshot, purposes mistook Fall'n on th' inventors' heads." Laertes confesses himself "a woodcock to mine own springe." As Hamlet had said earlier, of Rosencrantz and Guildenstern, " 'tis the sport to have the enginer Hoist with his own petar" (III,iv). Thus, too, Claudius' poisoned cup, intended for Hamlet, kills the Queen for whom Claudius had done such evil.

In its final resolution, *Hamlet* incorporates a broader conception of justice than its revenge formula seemed at first to make possible. Yet in its origins *Hamlet* is a revenge story, and these traditions have left some residual savagery in the play. In the *Historia Danica* of Saxo Grammaticus, 1180–1208, and in the rather free translation of Saxo into French by Belleforest, *Histoires Tragiques* (1576), Hamlet is cunning and bloodily resolute throughout. He kills an eavesdropper without a qualm during the interview with his mother, and exchanges letters on his way to England with characteristic shrewdness. Ultimately he returns to Denmark, sets fire to his uncle's hall, slays its courtly inhabitants, and claims his rightful throne from a grateful people. The Ghost, absent in this account, may well have been supplied by Thomas Kyd, author of *The Spanish Tragedy* (c. 1587) and seemingly of a lost *Hamlet* play in existence by 1589. *The Spanish Tragedy* bears many resemblances to our *Hamlet,* and suggests what the lost *Hamlet* may well have contained: a sensational murder, a Senecan Ghost demanding revenge, the avenger hampered by court intrigue, his resort to a feigned madness, his difficulty in authenticating the ghostly vision. A German version of *Hamlet,* called *Der bestrafte Brudermord* (1710), based seemingly on the older *Hamlet,* includes such details as the play within the play, the sparing of the King at his prayers in order to damn his soul, Ophelia's madness, the fencing match with poisoned swords and poisoned drink, and the final catastrophe of vengeance and death. Similarly, the early pirated first quarto of *Hamlet* (1603) offers some passages seemingly based on the older play by Kyd.

Although this evidence suggests that Shakespeare received most of the material for the plot intact, his transformation of that material was nonetheless immeasurable. To be sure, Kyd's *The Spanish Tragedy* contains many rhetorical passages on the inadequacy of human justice, but the overall effect is still sensational and the outcome is a triumph for the pagan spirit of revenge. So too with the many revenge plays of the 1590's and 1600's which Kyd's dramatic genius had inspired, including Shakespeare's own *Titus Andronicus* (c. 1589–1591). *Hamlet,* written in about 1599–1601 (it is not mentioned by Frances Meres in 1598, and was entered in the Stationers' Register in 1602), is unparalleled in its philosophical richness. Its ending is truly cathartic, for Hamlet dies not as a bloodied avenger but as one who has affirmed the tragic dignity of man. His courage and faith, maintained in the face of great odds, atone for the dismal corruption in which Denmark has festered. His resolutely honest inquiries have taken him beyond the revulsion and doubt that express so eloquently, among other matters, the fearful response of Shakespeare's own generation to a seeming breakdown of established political, theological, and cosmological beliefs. Hamlet finally perceives that "if it be not now, yet it will come," and that "the readiness is all" (V,ii). This discovery, this revelation of necessity and meaning in Hamlet's great reversal of fortune, enables him to confront the tragic circumstance of his life with understanding and heroism, and to demonstrate the triumph of the human spirit even in the moment of his catastrophe.

Hamlet, Prince of Denmark

[*Dramatis Personae*

CLAUDIUS, *King of Denmark.*
HAMLET, *son to the late King Hamlet, and nephew to the present king.*
POLONIUS, *Lord Chamberlain.*
HORATIO, *friend to Hamlet.*
LAERTES, *son to Polonius.*
VOLTIMAND, CORNELIUS, ROSENCRANTZ, GUILDENSTERN, OSRIC, GENTLEMAN, *courtiers.*
PRIEST, *or* DOCTOR OF DIVINITY.
MARCELLUS, BERNARDO, *officers.*
FRANCISCO, *a soldier.*
REYNALDO, *servant to Polonius.*
PLAYERS.
Two CLOWNS, *grave-diggers.*
FORTINBRAS, *Prince of Norway.*
CAPTAIN.
ENGLISH AMBASSADORS.

GERTRUDE, *Queen of Denmark, and mother to Hamlet.*
OPHELIA, *daughter to Polonius.*

LORDS, LADIES, OFFICERS, SOLDIERS, SAILORS, MESSENGERS, *and other* ATTENDANTS.
GHOST *of Hamlet's Father.*

SCENE: *Denmark.*]

[ACT I • SCENE I]

Enter Bernardo and Francisco, two sentinals, [meeting].

BERNARDO
Who's there?
FRANCISCO
Nay, answer me. Stand and unfold yourself. 2
BERNARDO
Long live the King!
FRANCISCO
Bernardo?
BERNARDO
He.
FRANCISCO
You come most carefully upon your hour.
BERNARDO
'Tis now struck twelve. Get thee to bed, Francisco.
FRANCISCO
For this relief much thanks. 'Tis bitter cold,
And I am sick at heart.
BERNARDO
Have you had quiet guard?
FRANCISCO
Not a mouse stirring.
BERNARDO
Well, good night.
If you do meet Horatio and Marcellus,
The rivals of my watch, bid them make haste. 13

Enter Horatio and Marcellus.

FRANCISCO
I think I hear them. Stand, ho! Who is there?
HORATIO
Friends to this ground.
MARCELLUS
And liegemen to the Dane. 15
FRANCISCO
Give you good night.
MARCELLUS
O, farewell, honest soldier. 16
Who hath reliev'd you?
FRANCISCO
Bernardo hath my place.
Give you good night. *Exit Francisco.*
MARCELLUS
Holla! Bernardo!
BERNARDO
Say,
What, is Horatio there?
HORATIO
A piece of him.
BERNARDO
Welcome, Horatio. Welcome, good Marcellus.
HORATIO
What, has this thing appear'd again tonight?
BERNARDO
I have seen nothing.
MARCELLUS
Horatio says 'tis but our fantasy,
And will not let belief take hold of him
Touching this dreaded sight, twice seen of us.
Therefore I have entreated him along
With us to watch the minutes of this night,
That if again this apparition come
He may approve our eyes and speak to it. 29
HORATIO
Tush, tush, 'twill not appear.
BERNARDO
Sit down awhile,
And let us once again assail your ears,
That are so fortified against our story,
What we have two nights seen.
HORATIO
Well, sit we down,
And let us hear Bernardo speak of this.

I.i. Location: Elsinore castle. A guard platform.
2 me (Francisco emphasizes that *he* is the sentry currently on watch.)

13 rivals partners **15 liegemen to the Dane** men sworn to serve the Danish king **16 Give you** God give you **29 approve** corroborate

BERNARDO
Last night of all,
When yond same star that's westward from the pole 36
Had made his course t' illume that part of heaven 37
Where now it burns, Marcellus and myself,
The bell then beating one—

Enter Ghost.

MARCELLUS
Peace, break thee off! Look where it comes again!

BERNARDO
In the same figure, like the King that's dead.

MARCELLUS
Thou art a scholar. Speak to it, Horatio. 42

BERNARDO
Looks 'a not like the King? Mark it, Horatio. 43

HORATIO
Most like. It harrows me with fear and wonder.

BERNARDO
It would be spoke to.

MARCELLUS Speak to it, Horatio. 45

HORATIO
What art thou that usurp'st this time of night,
Together with that fair and warlike form
In which the majesty of buried Denmark 48
Did sometimes march? By heaven I charge thee
speak! 49

MARCELLUS
It is offended.

BERNARDO See, it stalks away.

HORATIO
Stay! Speak, speak! I charge thee, speak! *Exit Ghost.*

MARCELLUS
'Tis gone, and will not answer.

BERNARDO
How now, Horatio? You tremble and look pale.
Is not this something more than fantasy?
What think you on 't?

HORATIO
Before my God, I might not this believe
Without the sensible and true avouch 57
Of mine own eyes.

MARCELLUS Is it not like the King?

HORATIO
As thou art to thyself.
Such was the very armor he had on
When he the ambitious Norway combated. 61
So frown'd he once when, in an angry parle, 62
He smote the sledded Polacks on the ice. 63
'Tis strange.

MARCELLUS
Thus twice before, and jump at this dead hour, 65
With martial stalk hath he gone by our watch.

HORATIO
In what particular thought to work I know not,
But, in the gross and scope of mine opinion, 68
This bodes some strange eruption to our state.

MARCELLUS
Good now, sit down, and tell me, he that knows, 70
Why this same strict and most observant watch
So nightly toils the subject of the land, 72
And why such daily cast of brazen cannon, 73
And foreign mart for implements of war, 74
Why such impress of shipwrights, whose sore task 75
Does not divide the Sunday from the week.
What might be toward, that this sweaty haste 77
Doth make the night joint-laborer with the day?
Who is 't that can inform me?

HORATIO That can I;
At least, the whisper goes so. Our last king,
Whose image even but now appear'd to us,
Was, as you know, by Fortinbras of Norway,
Thereto prick'd on by a most emulate pride, 83
Dar'd to the combat; in which our valiant Hamlet—
For so this side of our known world esteem'd him—
Did slay this Fortinbras; who, by a seal'd compact,
Well ratified by law and heraldry,
Did forfeit, with his life, all those his lands
Which he stood seiz'd of, to the conqueror; 89
Against the which a moi'ty competent 90
Was gaged by our king, which had return'd 91
To the inheritance of Fortinbras
Had he been vanquisher, as, by the same comart 93
And carriage of the article design'd, 94
His fell to Hamlet. Now, sir, young Fortinbras,
Of unimproved mettle hot and full, 96
Hath in the skirts of Norway here and there 97
Shark'd up a list of lawless resolutes 98
For food and diet to some enterprise 99
That hath a stomach in 't, which is no other— 100
As it doth well appear unto our state—
But to recover of us, by strong hand
And terms compulsatory, those foresaid lands
So by his father lost. And this, I take it,
Is the main motive of our preparations,
The source of this our watch, and the chief head 106
Of this post-haste and romage in the land. 107

BERNARDO
I think it be no other but e'en so.
Well may it sort that this portentous figure 109
Comes armed through our watch so like the King
That was and is the question of these wars.

HORATIO
A mote it is to trouble the mind's eye. 112
In the most high and palmy state of Rome, 113
A little ere the mightiest Julius fell,

36 pole polestar **37 his** its **42 scholar** one learned in Latin and able to address spirits **43 'a** he **45 It . . . to** (A ghost could not speak until spoken to.) **48 buried Denmark** the buried king of Denmark **49 sometimes** formerly **57 sensible** confirmed by the senses **61 Norway** King of Norway **62 parle** parley **63 sledded** traveling on sleds. **Polacks** Poles **65 jump** exactly

68 gross and scope general view **70 Good now** (An expression denoting entreaty or expostulation.) **72 toils** causes to toil. **subject** subjects **73 cast** casting **74 mart** buying and selling **75 impress** impressment, conscription **77 toward** in preparation **83 prick'd on** incited. **emulate** ambitious **89 seiz'd** possessed **90 Against the** in return for. **moi'ty competent** sufficient portion **91 gaged** engaged, pledged **93 comart** joint bargain (?) **94 carriage** import, bearing **96 unimproved** not turned to account(?) or untested(?) **97 skirts** outlying regions, outskirts **98 Shark'd up** got together in haphazard fashion. **resolutes** desperadoes **99 food and diet** no pay but their keep **100 stomach** relish of danger **106 head** source **107 romage** bustle, commotion **109 sort** suit **112 mote** speck of dust **113 palmy** flourishing

The graves stood tenantless and the sheeted dead
Did squeak and gibber in the Roman streets;
As stars with trains of fire and dews of blood,
Disasters in the sun; and the moist star
Upon whose influence Neptune's empire stands
Was sick almost to doomsday with eclipse.
And even the like precurse of fear'd events,
As harbingers preceding still the fates
And prologue to the omen coming on,
Have heaven and earth together demonstrated
Unto our climatures and countrymen.

Enter Ghost.

But soft, behold! Lo, where it comes again!
I'll cross it, though it blast me. Stay, illusion!
If thou hast any sound, or use of voice,
Speak to me! *It spreads his arms.*
If there be any good thing to be done
That may to thee do ease and grace to me,
Speak to me!
If thou art privy to thy country's fate,
Which, happily, foreknowing may avoid,
O, speak!
Or if thou hast uphoarded in thy life
Extorted treasure in the womb of earth,
For which, they say, you spirits oft walk in death,
The cock crows.
Speak of it. Stay, and speak! Stop it, Marcellus.

MARCELLUS
Shall I strike at it with my partisan?

HORATIO
Do, if it will not stand. [*They strike at it.*]

BERNARDO
'Tis here!

HORATIO
'Tis here!

MARCELLUS
'Tis gone. [*Exit Ghost.*]
We do it wrong, being so majestical,
To offer it the show of violence;
For it is, as the air, invulnerable,
And our vain blows malicious mockery.

BERNARDO
It was about to speak when the cock crew.

HORATIO
And then it started like a guilty thing
Upon a fearful summons. I have heard,
The cock, that is the trumpet to the morn,
Doth with his lofty and shrill-sounding throat
Awake the god of day, and, at his warning,
Whether in sea or fire, in earth or air,
Th' extravagant and erring spirit hies
To his confine; and of the truth herein
This present object made probation.

MARCELLUS
It faded on the crowing of the cock.
Some say that ever 'gainst that season comes
Wherein our Savior's birth is celebrated,
The bird of dawning singeth all night long,
And then, they say, no spirit dare stir abroad;
The nights are wholesome, then no planets strike,
No fairy takes, nor witch hath power to charm,
So hallowed and so gracious is that time.

HORATIO
So have I heard and do in part believe it.
But, look, the morn, in russet mantle clad,
Walks o'er the dew of yon high eastward hill.
Break we our watch up, and by my advice
Let us impart what we have seen tonight
Unto young Hamlet; for, upon my life,
This spirit, dumb to us, will speak to him.
Do you consent we shall acquaint him with it,
As needful in our loves, fitting our duty?

MARCELLUS
Let's do 't, I pray, and I this morning know
Where we shall find him most conveniently.
Exeunt.

[SCENE II]

Flourish. Enter Claudius, King of Denmark, Gertrude the Queen, Councilors, Polonius and his son Laertes, Hamlet, cum aliis [*including Voltimand and Cornelius*].

KING
Though yet of Hamlet our dear brother's death
The memory be green, and that it us befitted
To bear our hearts in grief and our whole kingdom
To be contracted in one brow of woe,
Yet so far hath discretion fought with nature
That we with wisest sorrow think on him,
Together with remembrance of ourselves.
Therefore our sometime sister, now our queen,
Th' imperial jointress to this warlike state,
Have we, as 'twere with a defeated joy—
With an auspicious and a dropping eye,
With mirth in funeral and with dirge in marriage,
In equal scale weighing delight and dole—
Taken to wife. Nor have we herein barr'd
Your better wisdoms, which have freely gone
With this affair along. For all, our thanks.
Now follows that you know young Fortinbras,
Holding a weak supposal of our worth,
Or thinking by our late dear brother's death
Our state to be disjoint and out of frame,
Colleagued with this dream of his advantage,

115 sheeted shrouded **117 As** (This abrupt transition suggests that matter is possibly omitted between ll. 116 and 117.) **118 Disasters** unfavorable signs or aspects. **moist star** i.e., moon, governing tides **119 Neptune** god of the sea. **stands** depends **120 sick . . . doomsday** (See Matthew 24:29 and Revelation 6:12.) **121 precurse** heralding, foreshadowing **122 harbingers** forerunners. **still** continually **123 omen** calamitous event **125 climatures** regions **127 cross** meet, face directly **134 happily** haply, perchance **140 partisan** long-handled spear **154 extravagant and erring** wandering. (The words have similar meaning.) **156 probation** proof

158 'gainst just before **162 strike** exert evil influence **163 takes** bewitches **164 gracious** full of goodness

I.ii. Location: The castle.
s.d. cum aliis with others **9 jointress** woman possessed of a joint tenancy of an estate **17 know** be informed (that) **18 weak supposal** low estimate **21 Colleagued with** joined to, allied with. **dream . . . advantage** illusory hope of success

He hath not fail'd to pester us with message
Importing the surrender of those lands 23
Lost by his father, with all bands of law, 24
To our most valiant brother. So much for him.
Now for ourself and for this time of meeting.
Thus much the business is: we have here writ
To Norway, uncle of young Fortinbras—
Who, impotent and bed-rid, scarcely hears
Of this his nephew's purpose—to suppress
His further gait herein, in that the levies, 31
The lists, and full proportions are all made 32
Out of his subject; and we here dispatch 33
You, good Cornelius, and you, Voltimand,
For bearers of this greeting to old Norway,
Giving to you no further personal power
To business with the King, more than the scope
Of these delated articles allow. [*Gives a paper.*] 38
Farewell, and let your haste commend your duty.

CORNELIUS, VOLTIMAND
In that, and all things, will we show our duty.

KING
We doubt it nothing. Heartily farewell.
[*Exeunt Voltimand and Cornelius.*]
And now, Laertes, what's the news with you?
You told us of some suit; what is 't, Laertes?
You cannot speak of reason to the Dane 44
And lose your voice. What wouldst thou beg,
Laertes, 45
That shall not be my offer, not thy asking?
The head is not more native to the heart, 47
The hand more instrumental to the mouth, 48
Than is the throne of Denmark to thy father.
What wouldst thou have, Laertes?

LAERTES
My dread lord,
Your leave and favor to return to France,
From whence though willingly I came to Denmark
To show my duty in your coronation,
Yet now I must confess, that duty done,
My thoughts and wishes bend again toward France
And bow them to your gracious leave and pardon. 56

KING
Have you your father's leave? What says Polonius?

POLONIUS
H'ath, my lord, wrung from me my slow leave
By laborsome petition, and at last
Upon his will I seal'd my hard consent. 60
I do beseech you, give him leave to go.

KING
Take thy fair hour, Laertes. Time be thine,
And thy best graces spend it at thy will!
But now, my cousin Hamlet, and my son— 64

HAMLET
A little more than kin, and less than kind. 65

23 Importing pertaining to **24 bands** contracts **31 His** i.e., Fortinbras'. **gait** proceeding **31–33 in that . . . subject** since the levying of troops and supplies is drawn entirely from the King of Norway's own subjects **38 delated** detailed. (Variant of *dilated*.) **44 the Dane** the Danish king **45 lose your voice** waste your speech **47 native** closely connected, related **48 instrumental** serviceable **56 leave and pardon** permission to depart **60 hard** reluctant **64 cousin** any kin not of the immediate family **65 A little . . . kind** i.e., closer than an ordinary nephew (since I am stepson), and yet more separated in natural feeling (with pun on *kind* meaning *affectionate* and *natural, lawful*. This line is often read as an aside, but it need not be.)

KING
How is it that the clouds still hang on you?

HAMLET
Not so, my lord. I am too much in the sun. 67

QUEEN
Good Hamlet, cast thy nighted color off,
And let thine eye look like a friend on Denmark.
Do not forever with thy vailed lids 70
Seek for thy noble father in the dust.
Thou know'st 'tis common, all that lives must die, 72
Passing through nature to eternity.

HAMLET
Ay, madam, it is common.

QUEEN
If it be,
Why seems it so particular with thee?

HAMLET
Seems, madam! Nay, it is. I know not "seems."
'Tis not alone my inky cloak, good mother,
Nor customary suits of solemn black,
Nor windy suspiration of forc'd breath,
No, nor the fruitful river in the eye, 80
Nor the dejected havior of the visage,
Together with all forms, moods, shapes of grief,
That can denote me truly. These indeed seem,
For they are actions that a man might play.
But I have that within which passes show;
These but the trappings and the suits of woe.

KING
'Tis sweet and commendable in your nature,
Hamlet,
To give these mourning duties to your father.
But you must know your father lost a father,
That father lost, lost his, and the survivor bound
In filial obligation for some term
To do obsequious sorrow. But to persever 92
In obstinate condolement is a course 93
Of impious stubbornness. 'Tis unmanly grief.
It shows a will most incorrect to heaven,
A heart unfortified, a mind impatient,
An understanding simple and unschool'd.
For what we know must be and is as common
As any the most vulgar thing to sense, 99
Why should we in our peevish opposition
Take it to heart? Fie, 'tis a fault to heaven,
A fault against the dead, a fault to nature,
To reason most absurd, whose common theme
Is death of fathers, and who still hath cried,
From the first corse till he that died today, 105
"This must be so." We pray you, throw to earth
This unprevailing woe, and think of us 107
As of a father; for let the world take note,
You are the most immediate to our throne, 109
And with no less nobility of love
Than that which dearest father bears his son
Do I impart toward you. For your intent

67 sun i.e., the sunshine of the King's royal favor (with pun on *son*) **70 vailed** downcast **72 common** of universal occurrence. (But Hamlet plays on the sense of *vulgar* in l. 74.) **80 fruitful** abundant **92 obsequious** suited to obsequies or funerals. **persever** persevere **93 condolement** sorrowing **99 As . . . sense** as the most ordinary experience **105 corse** corpse **107 unprevailing** unavailing **109 most immediate** next in succession

In going back to school in Wittenberg,
It is most retrograde to our desire,
And we beseech you bend you to remain
Here in the cheer and comfort of our eye,
Our chiefest courtier, cousin, and our son.

QUEEN
Let not thy mother lose her prayers, Hamlet.
I pray thee, stay with us, go not to Wittenberg.

HAMLET
I shall in all my best obey you, madam.

KING
Why, 'tis a loving and a fair reply.
Be as ourself in Denmark. Madam, come.
This gentle and unforc'd accord of Hamlet
Sits smiling to my heart, in grace whereof
No jocund health that Denmark drinks today
But the great cannon to the clouds shall tell,
And the King's rouse the heaven shall bruit again,
Respeaking earthly thunder. Come away.

Flourish. Exeunt all but Hamlet.

HAMLET
O, that this too too sullied flesh would melt,
Thaw, and resolve itself into a dew!
Or that the Everlasting had not fix'd
His canon 'gainst self-slaughter! O God, God,
How weary, stale, flat, and unprofitable
Seem to me all the uses of this world!
Fie on 't, ah fie! 'Tis an unweeded garden
That grows to seed. Things rank and gross in nature
Possess it merely. That it should come to this!
But two months dead—nay, not so much, not two.
So excellent a king, that was to this
Hyperion to a satyr; so loving to my mother
That he might not beteem the winds of heaven
Visit her face too roughly. Heaven and earth,
Must I remember? Why, she would hang on him
As if increase of appetite had grown
By what it fed on, and yet, within a month—
Let me not think on 't. Frailty, thy name is woman!—
A little month, or ere those shoes were old
With which she followed my poor father's body,
Like Niobe, all tears, why she, even she—
O God, a beast, that wants discourse of reason,
Would have mourn'd longer—married with my uncle,
My father's brother, but no more like my father
Than I to Hercules. Within a month,
Ere yet the salt of most unrighteous tears
Had left the flushing in her galled eyes,
She married. O, most wicked speed, to post
With such dexterity to incestuous sheets!

113 Wittenberg famous German university founded in 1502 **114 retrograde** contrary **115 bend you** incline yourself **125 jocund** merry **127 rouse** draft of liquor. **bruit again** loudly echo **128 thunder** i.e., of trumpet and kettledrum, sounded when the King drinks; see I.iv. 8–12 **129 sullied** defiled. (The early quartos read *sallied,* the Folio *solid.*) **132 canon** law **137 merely** completely **139 to** in comparison to **140 Hyperion** Titan sun-god, father of Helios **141 beteem** allow **149 Niobe** Tantalus' daughter, Queen of Thebes, who boasted that she had more sons and daughters than Leto; for this, Apollo and Artemis, children of Leto, slew her fourteen children. She was turned by Zeus into a stone which continually dropped tears. **150 wants . . . reason** lacks the faculty of reason **155 galled** irritated, inflamed **157 incestuous** (In Shakespeare's day, the marriage of a man like Claudius to his deceased brother's wife was considered incestuous.)

It is not nor it cannot come to good.
But break, my heart, for I must hold my tongue.

Enter Horatio, Marcellus, and Bernardo.

HORATIO
Hail to your lordship!

HAMLET
I am glad to see you well.
Horatio!—or I do forget myself.

HORATIO
The same, my lord, and your poor servant ever.

HAMLET
Sir, my good friend; I'll change that name with you.
And what make you from Wittenberg, Horatio?
Marcellus?

MARCELLUS
My good lord.

HAMLET
I am very glad to see you. [*To Bernardo.*] Good even, sir.—
But what, in faith, make you from Wittenberg?

HORATIO
A truant disposition, good my lord.

HAMLET
I would not hear your enemy say so,
Nor shall you do my ear that violence
To make it truster of your own report
Against yourself. I know you are no truant.
But what is your affair in Elsinore?
We'll teach you to drink deep ere you depart.

HORATIO
My lord, I came to see your father's funeral.

HAMLET
I prithee do not mock me, fellow-student;
I think it was to see my mother's wedding.

HORATIO
Indeed, my lord, it followed hard upon.

HAMLET
Thrift, thrift, Horatio! The funeral bak'd meats
Did coldly furnish forth the marriage tables.
Would I had met my dearest foe in heaven
Or ever I had seen that day, Horatio!
My father!—Methinks I see my father.

HORATIO
Where, my lord?

HAMLET
In my mind's eye, Horatio.

HORATIO
I saw him once. 'A was a goodly king.

HAMLET
'A was a man, take him for all in all,
I shall not look upon his like again.

HORATIO
My lord, I think I saw him yesternight.

HAMLET
Saw? Who?

HORATIO
My lord, the King your father.

HAMLET
The King my father?

163 change exchange (i.e., the name of friend) **164 make** do **179 hard** close **182 dearest** direst **183 Or** ere, before **187 'A** he

HORATIO
Season your admiration for a while
With an attent ear, till I may deliver,
Upon the witness of these gentlemen,
This marvel to you.

HAMLET
For God's love, let me hear!

HORATIO
Two nights together had these gentlemen,
Marcellus and Bernardo, on their watch,
In the dead waste and middle of the night,
Been thus encount'red. A figure like your father,
Armed at point exactly, cap-a-pe,
Appears before them, and with solemn march
Goes slow and stately by them. Thrice he walk'd
By their oppress'd and fear-surprised eyes
Within his truncheon's length, whilst they, distill'd
Almost to jelly with the act of fear,
Stand dumb and speak not to him. This to me
In dreadful secrecy impart they did,
And I with them the third night kept the watch,
Where, as they had delivered, both in time,
Form of the thing, each word made true and good,
The apparition comes. I knew your father;
These hands are not more like.

HAMLET
But where was this?

MARCELLUS
My lord, upon the platform where we watch.

HAMLET
Did you not speak to it?

HORATIO
My lord, I did,
But answer made it none. Yet once methought
It lifted up it head and did address
Itself to motion, like as it would speak;
But even then the morning cock crew loud,
And at the sound it shrunk in haste away,
And vanish'd from our sight.

HAMLET
'Tis very strange.

HORATIO
As I do live, my honor'd lord, 'tis true,
And we did think it writ down in our duty
To let you know of it.

HAMLET
Indeed, indeed, sirs. But this troubles me.
Hold you the watch tonight?

ALL
We do, my lord.

HAMLET
Arm'd, say you?

ALL
Arm'd, my lord.

HAMLET
From top to toe?

ALL
My lord, from head to foot.

HAMLET
Then saw you not his face?

HORATIO
O, yes, my lord, he wore his beaver up.

HAMLET
What, look'd he frowningly?

192 Season your admiration restrain your astonishment **193 attent** attentive **200 at point** completely. **cap-a-pe** from head to foot **204 truncheon** officer's staff **205 act** action, operation **216 it** its **230 beaver** visor on the helmet

HORATIO
A countenance more
In sorrow than in anger.

HAMLET
Pale, or red?

HORATIO
Nay, very pale.

HAMLET
And fix'd his eyes upon you?

HORATIO
Most constantly.

HAMLET
I would I had been there.

HORATIO
It would have much amaz'd you.

HAMLET
Very like, very like. Stay'd it long?

HORATIO
While one with moderate haste might tell a
hundred.

MARCELLUS, BERNARDO
Longer, longer.

HORATIO
Not when I saw 't.

HAMLET
His beard was grizzl'd—no?

HORATIO
It was, as I have seen it in his life,
A sable silver'd.

HAMLET
I will watch tonight.
Perchance 'twill walk again.

HORATIO
I warr'nt it will.

HAMLET
If it assume my noble father's person,
I'll speak to it, though hell itself should gape
And bid me hold my peace. I pray you all,
If you have hitherto conceal'd this sight,
Let it be tenable in your silence still,
And whatsomever else shall hap tonight,
Give it an understanding, but no tongue.
I will requite your loves. So, fare you well.
Upon the platform, 'twixt eleven and twelve,
I'll visit you.

ALL
Our duty to your honor.

HAMLET
Your loves, as mine to you. Farewell.
Exeunt [all but Hamlet].
My father's spirit in arms! All is not well.
I doubt some foul play. Would the night were come!
Till then sit still, my soul. Foul deeds will rise,
Though all the earth o'erwhelm them, to men's eyes.
Exit.

[SCENE III]

Enter Laertes and Ophelia, his Sister.

LAERTES
My necessaries are embark'd. Farewell.
And, sister, as the winds give benefit
And convoy is assistant, do not sleep

237 tell count **241 sable silver'd** black mixed with white **247 tenable** held tightly **255 doubt** suspect

I.iii. Location: Polonius' chambers.
3 convoy is assistant means of conveyance are available

But let me hear from you.
OPHELIA Do you doubt that?
LAERTES
For Hamlet, and the trifling of his favor,
Hold it a fashion and a toy in blood, 6
A violet in the youth of primy nature, 7
Forward, not permanent, sweet, not lasting, 8
The perfume and suppliance of a minute— 9
No more.
OPHELIA No more but so?
LAERTES Think it no more.
For nature crescent does not grow alone 11
In thews and bulk, but, as this temple waxes, 12
The inward service of the mind and soul
Grows wide withal. Perhaps he loves you now, 14
And now no soil nor cautel doth besmirch 15
The virtue of his will; but you must fear, 16
His greatness weigh'd, his will is not his own. 17
[For he himself is subject to his birth.]
He may not, as unvalued persons do,
Carve for himself; for on his choice depends 20
The safety and health of this whole state,
And therefore must his choice be circumscrib'd
Unto the voice and yielding of that body 23
Whereof he is the head. Then if he says he loves you,
It fits your wisdom so far to believe it
As he in his particular act and place
May give his saying deed, which is no further 27
Than the main voice of Denmark goes withal.
Then weigh what loss your honor may sustain
If with too credent ear you list his songs, 30
Or lose your heart, or your chaste treasure open
To his unmast'red importunity.
Fear it, Ophelia, fear it, my dear sister,
And keep you in the rear of your affection,
Out of the shot and danger of desire. 35
The chariest maid is prodigal enough 36
If she unmask her beauty to the moon.
Virtue itself scapes not calumnious strokes.
The canker galls the infants of the spring 39
Too oft before their buttons be disclos'd, 40
And in the morn and liquid dew of youth 41
Contagious blastments are most imminent. 42
Be wary then; best safety lies in fear.
Youth to itself rebels, though none else near.
OPHELIA
I shall the effect of this good lesson keep
As watchman to my heart. But, good my brother,
Do not, as some ungracious pastors do,
Show me the steep and thorny way to heaven,
Whiles, like a puff'd and reckless libertine, 49
Himself the primrose path of dalliance treads,
And recks not his own rede.

Enter Polonius.

LAERTES O, fear me not. 51
I stay too long. But here my father comes.
A double blessing is a double grace; 53
Occasion smiles upon a second leave. 54
POLONIUS
Yet here, Laertes? Aboard, aboard, for shame!
The wind sits in the shoulder of your sail,
And you are stay'd for. There—my blessing with thee!
And these few precepts in thy memory
Look thou character. Give thy thoughts no tongue, 59
Nor any unproportion'd thought his act. 60
Be thou familiar, but by no means vulgar. 61
Those friends thou hast, and their adoption tried, 62
Grapple them to thy soul with hoops of steel,
But do not dull thy palm with entertainment
Of each new-hatch'd, unfledg'd courage. Beware 65
Of entrance to a quarrel, but, being in,
Bear 't that th' opposed may beware of thee. 67
Give every man thy ear, but few thy voice;
Take each man's censure, but reserve thy judgment. 69
Costly thy habit as thy purse can buy,
But not express'd in fancy; rich, not gaudy,
For the apparel oft proclaims the man,
And they in France of the best rank and station
Are of a most select and generous chief in that. 74
Neither a borrower nor a lender be,
For loan oft loses both itself and friend,
And borrowing dulleth edge of husbandry. 77
This above all: to thine own self be true,
And it must follow, as the night the day,
Thou canst not then be false to any man.
Farewell. My blessing season this in thee! 81
LAERTES
Most humbly do I take my leave, my lord.
POLONIUS
The time invests you. Go, your servants tend. 83
LAERTES
Farewell, Ophelia, and remember well
What I have said to you.
OPHELIA
'Tis in my memory lock'd,
And you yourself shall keep the key of it.
LAERTES
Farewell. *Exit Laertes.*
POLONIUS
What is 't, Ophelia, he hath said to you?
OPHELIA
So please you, something touching the Lord Hamlet.
POLONIUS
Marry, well bethought. 91

6 toy in blood passing amorous fancy **7 primy** in its prime, springtime **8 Forward** precocious **9 suppliance** supply, filler **11 crescent** growing, waxing **12 thews** bodily strength. **temple** i.e., body **14 Grows wide withal** grows along with it **15 soil** blemish. **cautel** deceit **16 will** desire **17 greatness weigh'd** high position considered **20 Carve** i.e., choose pleasure **23 voice and yielding** assent, approval **27 deed** effect **30 credent** credulous. **list** listen to **35 shot** range **36 chariest** most scrupulously modest **39 canker galls** cankerworm destroys **40 buttons** buds. **disclos'd** opened **41 liquid dew** i.e., time when dew is fresh **42 blastments** blights **49 puff'd** bloated

51 recks heeds. **rede** counsel **53 double** (I.e., Laertes has already bidden his father good-by.) **54 Occasion** opportunity **59 character** inscribe **60 his** its **61 familiar** sociable. **vulgar** common **62 tried** tested **65 courage** young man of spirit **67 Bear 't that** manage it so that **69 censure** opinion, judgment **74 generous chief** noble eminence (?) **77 husbandry** thrift **81 season** mature **83 invests** besieges. **tend** attend, wait **91 Marry** i.e., by the Virgin Mary. (A mild oath.)

'Tis told me he hath very oft of late
Given private time to you, and you yourself
Have of your audience been most free and
bounteous.
If it be so—as so 'tis put on me,
And that in way of caution—I must tell you
You do not understand yourself so clearly
As it behooves my daughter and your honor.
What is between you? Give me up the truth.

OPHELIA
He hath, my lord, of late made many tenders
Of his affection to me.

POLONIUS
Affection? Pooh! You speak like a green girl,
Unsifted in such perilous circumstance.
Do you believe his tenders, as you call them?

OPHELIA
I do not know, my lord, what I should think.

POLONIUS
Marry, I will teach you. Think yourself a baby
That you have ta'en these tenders for true pay,
Which are not sterling. Tender yourself more dearly,
Or—not to crack the wind of the poor phrase,
Running it thus—you'll tender me a fool.

OPHELIA
My lord, he hath importun'd me with love
In honorable fashion.

POLONIUS
Ay, fashion you may call it. Go to, go to.

OPHELIA
And hath given countenance to his speech, my lord,
With almost all the holy vows of heaven.

POLONIUS
Ay, springes to catch woodcocks. I do know,
When the blood burns, how prodigal the soul
Lends the tongue vows. These blazes, daughter,
Giving more light than heat, extinct in both
Even in their promise, as it is a-making,
You must not take for fire. From this time
Be something scanter of your maiden presence.
Set your entreatments at a higher rate
Than a command to parle. For Lord Hamlet,
Believe so much in him that he is young,
And with a larger tether may he walk
Than may be given you. In few, Ophelia,
Do not believe his vows, for they are brokers,
Not of that dye which their investments show,
But mere implorators of unholy suits,
Breathing like sanctified and pious bawds,
The better to beguile. This is for all:
I would not, in plain terms, from this time forth
Have you so slander any moment leisure
As to give words or talk with the Lord Hamlet.
Look to 't, I charge you. Come your ways.

OPHELIA
I shall obey, my lord. *Exeunt.*

[SCENE IV]

Enter Hamlet, Horatio, and Marcellus.

HAMLET
The air bites shrewdly; it is very cold.

HORATIO
It is a nipping and an eager air.

HAMLET
What hour now?

HORATIO
I think it lacks of twelve.

MARCELLUS
No, it is struck.

HORATIO
Indeed? I heard it not.
It then draws near the season
Wherein the spirit held his wont to walk.
A flourish of trumpets, and two pieces go off [within].
What does this mean, my lord?

HAMLET
The King doth wake tonight and takes his rouse,
Keeps wassail, and the swagg'ring up-spring reels;
And, as he drains his draughts of Rhenish down,
The kettle-drum and trumpet thus bray out
The triumph of his pledge.

HORATIO
Is it a custom?

HAMLET
Ay, marry, is 't,
But to my mind, though I am native here
And to the manner born, it is a custom
More honor'd in the breach than the observance.
This heavy-headed revel east and west
Makes us traduc'd and tax'd of other nations.
They clepe us drunkards, and with swinish phrase
Soil our addition; and indeed it takes
From our achievements, though perform'd at height,
The pith and marrow of our attribute.
So, oft it chances in particular men,
That for some vicious mole of nature in them,
As in their birth—wherein they are not guilty,
Since nature cannot choose his origin—
By the o'ergrowth of some complexion,

95 put on impressed on, told to **100 tenders** offers **103 Unsifted** i.e., untried **107 tenders** (with added meaning here of *promises to pay*) **108 sterling** legal currency. **Tender** hold **109 crack the wind** i.e., run it until it is broken-winded **110 tender me a fool** (1) show yourself to me as a fool (2) show me up as a fool (3) present me with a grandchild. (*Fool* was a term of endearment for a child.) **113 fashion** mere form, pretense **114 countenance** credit, support **116 springes** snares. **woodcocks** birds easily caught; here used to connote gullibility **123 entreatments** negotiations for surrender (a military term) **124 parle** discuss terms with the enemy. (Polonius urges his daughter, in the metaphor of military language, not to meet with Hamlet and consider giving in to him merely because he requests an interview.) **125 so . . . him** this much concerning him **127 In few** briefly **128 brokers** go-betweens, procurers **129 dye** color or sort. **investments** clothes. (I.e., they are not what they seem.) **130 mere implorators** out and out solicitors **131 Breathing** speaking

134 slander bring disgrace or reproach upon

I.iv. Location: The guard platform.
6 s.d. pieces i.e., of ordnance, cannon **8 wake** stay awake and hold revel. **rouse** carouse, drinking bout **9 wassail** carousal. **up-spring** wild German dance **10 Rhenish** Rhine wine **12 triumph . . . pledge** i.e., his feat in draining the wine in a single draught **15 manner** custom (of drinking) **16 More . . . observance** better neglected than followed **17 east and west** i.e., everywhere **18 tax'd of** censured by **19 clepe** call. **with swinish phrase** i.e., by calling us swine **20 addition** reputation **21 at height** outstandingly **24 mole of nature** natural blemish in one's constitution **26 his** its **27 complexion** humor (i.e., one of the four humors or fluids thought to determine temperament)

Oft breaking down the pales and forts of reason,
Or by some habit that too much o'er-leavens
The form of plausive manners, that these men,
Carrying, I say, the stamp of one defect,
Being nature's livery, or fortune's star,
Their virtues else, be they as pure as grace,
As infinite as man may undergo,
Shall in the general censure take corruption
From that particular fault. The dram of eale
Doth all the noble substance of a doubt
To his own scandal.

Enter Ghost.

HORATIO Look, my lord, it comes!

HAMLET
Angels and ministers of grace defend us!
Be thou a spirit of health or goblin damn'd,
Bring with thee airs from heaven or blasts from hell,
Be thy intents wicked or charitable,
Thou com'st in such a questionable shape
That I will speak to thee. I'll call thee Hamlet,
King, father, royal Dane. O, answer me!
Let me not burst in ignorance; but tell
Why thy canoniz'd bones, hearsed in death,
Have burst their cerements; why the sepulcher
Wherein we saw thee quietly interr'd
Hath op'd his ponderous and marble jaws
To cast thee up again. What may this mean,
That thou, dead corse, again in complete steel
Revisits thus the glimpses of the moon,
Making night hideous, and we fools of nature
So horridly to shake our disposition
With thoughts beyond the reaches of our souls?
Say, why is this? Wherefore? What should we do?
[*Ghost*] *beckons* [*Hamlet*].

HORATIO
It beckons you to go away with it,
As if it some impartment did desire
To you alone.

MARCELLUS Look with what courteous action
It waves you to a more removed ground.
But do not go with it.

HORATIO No, by no means.

HAMLET
It will not speak. Then I will follow it.

HORATIO
Do not, my lord!

HAMLET Why, what should be the fear?
I do not set my life at a pin's fee,
And for my soul, what can it do to that,
Being a thing immortal as itself?
It waves me forth again. I'll follow it.

HORATIO
What if it tempt you toward the flood, my lord,
Or to the dreadful summit of the cliff
That beetles o'er his base into the sea,
And there assume some other horrible form
Which might deprive your sovereignty of reason,
And draw you into madness? Think of it.
The very place puts toys of desperation,
Without more motive, into every brain
That looks so many fathoms to the sea
And hears it roar beneath.

HAMLET It waves me still.
Go on, I'll follow thee.

MARCELLUS
You shall not go, my lord.
[*They try to stop him.*]

HAMLET Hold off your hands!

HORATIO
Be rul'd, you shall not go.

HAMLET My fate cries out,
And makes each petty artery in this body
As hardy as the Nemean lion's nerve.
Still am I call'd. Unhand me, gentlemen.
By heaven, I'll make a ghost of him that lets me!
I say, away! Go on, I'll follow thee.
Exeunt Ghost and Hamlet.

HORATIO
He waxes desperate with imagination.

MARCELLUS
Let's follow. 'Tis not fit thus to obey him.

HORATIO
Have after. To what issue will this come?

MARCELLUS
Something is rotten in the state of Denmark.

HORATIO
Heaven will direct it.

MARCELLUS Nay, let's follow him. *Exeunt.*

[SCENE V]

Enter Ghost and Hamlet.

HAMLET
Whither wilt thou lead me? Speak. I'll go no further.

GHOST
Mark me.

HAMLET I will.

GHOST My hour is almost come,
When I to sulph'rous and tormenting flames
Must render up myself.

HAMLET Alas, poor ghost!

28 pales palings, fences (as of a fortification) **29 o'er-leavens** induces a change throughout (as yeast works in dough) **30 plausive** pleasing **32 nature's livery** endowment from nature. **fortune's star** mark placed by fortune **36 dram of eale** small amount of evil (?) **37 of a doubt** (A famous crux, sometimes emended to *oft adout* or *often dout,* i.e., "often erase" or "do out," or to *antidote,* counteract.) **38 To . . . scandal** i.e., to the disgrace of the whole enterprise **40 of health** of spiritual good **43 questionable** inviting question or conversation **47 canoniz'd** buried according to the canons of the church. **hearsed** coffined **48 cerements** grave-clothes **53 glimpses of the moon** i.e., earth by night **54 fools of nature** mere men, limited to natural knowledge **59 impartment** communication **65 fee** value

71 beetles o'er overhangs threateningly. **his** its **73 deprive . . . reason** take away the rule of reason over your mind **75 toys of desperation** fancies of desperate acts, i.e., suicide **81 artery** i.e., sinew **82 Nemean lion** one of the monsters slain by Hercules in his twelve labors. **nerve** sinew **84 lets** hinders **88 issue** outcome **90 it** i.e., the outcome

I.v. Location: The battlements of the castle.

GHOST
Pity me not, but lend thy serious hearing
To what I shall unfold.

HAMLET
Speak. I am bound to hear.

GHOST
So art thou to revenge, when thou shalt hear.

HAMLET
What?

GHOST
I am thy father's spirit,
Doom'd for a certain term to walk the night,
And for the day confin'd to fast in fires,
Till the foul crimes done in my days of nature
Are burnt and purg'd away. But that I am forbid
To tell the secrets of my prison-house,
I could a tale unfold whose lightest word
Would harrow up thy soul, freeze thy young blood,
Make thy two eyes, like stars, start from their
spheres,
Thy knotted and combined locks to part,
And each particular hair to stand an end,
Like quills upon the fearful porpentine.
But this eternal blazon must not be
To ears of flesh and blood. List, list, O, list!
If thou didst ever thy dear father love—

HAMLET
O God!

GHOST
Revenge his foul and most unnatural murder.

HAMLET
Murder?

GHOST
Murder most foul, as in the best it is,
But this most foul, strange, and unnatural.

HAMLET
Haste me to know 't, that I, with wings as swift
As meditation or the thoughts of love,
May sweep to my revenge.

GHOST
I find thee apt;
And duller shouldst thou be than the fat weed
That roots itself in ease on Lethe wharf,
Wouldst thou not stir in this. Now, Hamlet, hear.
'Tis given out that, sleeping in my orchard,
A serpent stung me. So the whole ear of Denmark
Is by a forged process of my death
Rankly abus'd. But know, thou noble youth,
The serpent that did sting thy father's life
Now wears his crown.

HAMLET
O my prophetic soul!
My uncle!

GHOST
Ay, that incestuous, that adulterate beast,
With witchcraft of his wits, with traitorous gifts—
O wicked wit and gifts, that have the power
So to seduce!—won to his shameful lust
The will of my most seeming-virtuous queen.
O Hamlet, what a falling-off was there!
From me, whose love was of that dignity
That it went hand in hand even with the vow
I made to her in marriage, and to decline
Upon a wretch whose natural gifts were poor
To those of mine!
But virtue, as it never will be moved,
Though lewdness court it in a shape of heaven,
So lust, though to a radiant angel link'd,
Will sate itself in a celestial bed,
And prey on garbage.
But, soft, methinks I scent the morning air.
Brief let me be. Sleeping within my orchard,
My custom always of the afternoon,
Upon my secure hour thy uncle stole,
With juice of cursed hebona in a vial,
And in the porches of my ears did pour
The leprous distillment, whose effect
Holds such an enmity with blood of man
That swift as quicksilver it courses through
The natural gates and alleys of the body,
And with a sudden vigor it doth posset
And curd, like eager droppings into milk,
The thin and wholesome blood. So did it mine,
And a most instant tetter bark'd about,
Most lazar-like, with vile and loathsome crust,
All my smooth body.
Thus was I, sleeping, by a brother's hand
Of life, of crown, of queen, at once dispatch'd,
Cut off even in the blossoms of my sin,
Unhous'led, disappointed, unanel'd,
No reck'ning made, but sent to my account
With all my imperfections on my head.
O, horrible! O, horrible, most horrible!
If thou hast nature in thee, bear it not.
Let not the royal bed of Denmark be
A couch for luxury and damned incest.
But, howsomever thou pursues this act,
Taint not thy mind, nor let thy soul contrive
Against thy mother aught. Leave her to heaven
And to those thorns that in her bosom lodge,
To prick and sting her. Fare thee well at once.
The glow-worm shows the matin to be near,
And 'gins to pale his uneffectual fire.
Adieu, adieu, adieu! Remember me. [*Exit.*]

HAMLET
O all you host of heaven! O earth! What else?
And shall I couple hell? O, fie! Hold, hold, my
heart,

12 fast do penance **13 crimes** sins **14 But that** were it not that **18 spheres** i.e., eye-sockets, here compared to the orbits or transparent revolving spheres in which, according to Ptolemaic astronomy, the heavenly bodies were fixed **19 knotted . . . locks** i.e., hair neatly arranged and confined **20 an end** on end **21 fearful porpentine** frightened porcupine **22 eternal blazon** revelation of the secrets of eternity **34 Lethe** the river of forgetfulness in Hades. **wharf** bank **38 forged process** falsified account **39 abus'd** deceived **43 adulterate** adulterous

55 shape of heaven heavenly form **62 secure** confident, unsuspicious **63 hebona** a poison. (The word seems to be a form of *ebony,* though it is perhaps thought to be related to *henbane,* a poison, or to *ebenus,* yew.) **65 leprous** causing leprosy-like disfigurement **69 posset** coagulate, curdle **70 eager** sour, acid **72 tetter** eruption of scabs. **bark'd** covered with a rough covering, like bark on a tree **73 lazar-like** leper-like **76 dispatch'd** suddenly deprived **78 Unhous'led** without having received the sacrament. **disappointed** unready (spiritually) for the last journey. **unanel'd** without having received extreme unction **82 nature** i.e., the promptings of a son **84 luxury** lechery **90 matin** i.e., morning **91 uneffectual fire** cold light **94 couple** add

And you, my sinews, grow not instant old,
But bear me stiffly up. Remember thee!
Ay, thou poor ghost, whiles memory holds a seat
In this distracted globe. Remember thee! 98
Yea, from the table of my memory 99
I'll wipe away all trivial fond records, 100
All saws of books, all forms, all pressures past 101
That youth and observation copied there,
And thy commandment all alone shall live
Within the book and volume of my brain,
Unmix'd with baser matter. Yes, by heaven!
O most pernicious woman!
O villain, villain, smiling, damned villain!
My tables—meet it is I set it down,
That one may smile, and smile, and be a villain.
At least I am sure it may be so in Denmark. 110
[*Writing.*]
So, uncle, there you are. Now to my word;
It is "Adieu, adieu! Remember me."
I have sworn 't.

Enter Horatio and Marcellus.

HORATIO
My lord, my lord!

MARCELLUS Lord Hamlet!

HORATIO Heavens secure him!

HAMLET
So be it!

MARCELLUS
Illo, ho, ho, my lord!

HAMLET
Hillo, ho, ho, boy! Come, bird, come. 117

MARCELLUS
How is 't, my noble lord?

HORATIO What news, my lord?

HAMLET
O, wonderful!

HORATIO
Good my lord, tell it.

HAMLET No, you will reveal it.

HORATIO
Not I, my lord, by heaven.

MARCELLUS Nor I, my lord.

HAMLET
How say you, then, would heart of man once think it?
But you'll be secret?

HORATIO, MARCELLUS Ay, by heaven, my lord.

HAMLET
There's never a villain dwelling in all Denmark
But he's an arrant knave. 125

HORATIO
There needs no ghost, my lord, come from the grave
To tell us this.

HAMLET Why, right, you are in the right.
And so, without more circumstance at all, 128
I hold it fit that we shake hands and part,
You, as your business and desire shall point you—
For every man hath business and desire,
Such as it is—and for my own poor part,
Look you, I'll go pray.

HORATIO
These are but wild and whirling words, my lord.

HAMLET
I am sorry they offend you, heartily;
Yes, faith, heartily.

HORATIO There's no offense, my lord.

HAMLET
Yes, by Saint Patrick, but there is, Horatio, 137
And much offense too. Touching this vision here,
It is an honest ghost, that let me tell you. 139
For your desire to know what is between us,
O'ermaster 't as you may. And now, good friends,
As you are friends, scholars, and soldiers,
Give me one poor request.

HORATIO
What is 't, my lord? We will.

HAMLET
Never make known what you have seen tonight.

HORATIO, MARCELLUS
My lord, we will not.

HAMLET Nay, but swear 't.

HORATIO In faith,
My lord, not I.

MARCELLUS Nor I, my lord, in faith.

HAMLET
Upon my sword. [*Holds out his sword.*]

MARCELLUS We have sworn, my lord, already. 148

HAMLET
Indeed, upon my sword, indeed.
Ghost cries under the stage.

GHOST
Swear.

HAMLET
Ha, ha, boy, say'st thou so? Art thou there, truepenny? 151
Come on, you hear this fellow in the cellarage.
Consent to swear.

HORATIO Propose the oath, my lord.

HAMLET
Never to speak of this that you have seen,
Swear by my sword.

GHOST [*Beneath*]
Swear.

HAMLET
Hic et ubique? Then we'll shift our ground. 157
[*He moves to another spot.*]
Come hither, gentlemen,
And lay your hands again upon my sword.
Swear by my sword
Never to speak of this that you have heard.

GHOST [*Beneath*]
Swear by his sword.

98 globe head **99 table** writing tablet **100 fond** foolish **101 saws** wise sayings. **forms** images. **pressures** impressions stamped **117 Hillo, ho, ho** (A falconer's call to a hawk in air. Hamlet is playing upon Marcellus' *Illo,* i.e., halloo.) **125 arrant** thoroughgoing **128 circumstance** ceremony

137 Saint Patrick (The keeper of Purgatory and patron saint of all blunders and confusion.) **139 honest** i.e., a real ghost and not an evil spirit **148 sword** i.e., the hilt in the form of a cross **151 truepenny** honest old fellow **157 Hic et ubique** here and everywhere. (Latin.)

HAMLET
Well said, old mole! Canst work i' th' earth so fast?
A worthy pioner! Once more remove, good friends. 164
[Moves again.]

HORATIO
O day and night, but this is wondrous strange!

HAMLET
And therefore as a stranger give it welcome.
There are more things in heaven and earth, Horatio,
Than are dreamt of in your philosophy. 168
But come;
Here, as before, never, so help you mercy,
How strange or odd soe'er I bear myself—
As I perchance hereafter shall think meet
To put an antic disposition on— 173
That you, at such times seeing me, never shall,
With arms encumb'red thus, or this headshake, 175
Or by pronouncing of some doubtful phrase,
As "Well, well, we know," or "We could, an if we
would," 177
Or "If we list to speak," or "There be, an if they
might," 178
Or such ambiguous giving out, to note 179
That you know aught of me—this do swear,
So grace and mercy at your most need help you.

GHOST *[Beneath]*
Swear. *[They swear.]*

HAMLET
Rest, rest, perturbed spirit! So, gentlemen,
With all my love I do commend me to you;
And what so poor a man as Hamlet is
May do, t' express his love and friending to you,
God willing, shall not lack. Let us go in together,
And still your fingers on your lips, I pray. 188
The time is out of joint. O cursed spite,
That ever I was born to set it right!
[They wait for him to leave first.]
Nay, come, let's go together. *Exeunt.*

[ACT II • SCENE I]

Enter old Polonius with his man [Reynaldo].

POLONIUS
Give him this money and these notes, Reynaldo.
[Gives money and papers.]

REYNALDO
I will, my lord.

POLONIUS
You shall do marvel's wisely, good Reynaldo, 3
Before you visit him, to make inquire
Of his behavior.

REYNALDO
My lord, I did intend it.

POLONIUS
Marry, well said, very well said. Look you, sir,
Inquire me first what Danskers are in Paris, 7
And how, and who, what means, and where they
keep, 8
What company, at what expense; and finding
By this encompassment and drift of question 10
That they do know my son, come you more nearer 11
Than your particular demands will touch it. 12
Take you, as 'twere, some distant knowledge of
him, 13
As thus, "I know his father and his friends,
And in part him." Do you mark this, Reynaldo?

REYNALDO
Ay, very well, my lord.

POLONIUS
"And in part him, but," you may say, "not well.
But, if 't be he I mean, he's very wild,
Addicted so and so," and there put on him 19
What forgeries you please—marry, none so rank 20
As may dishonor him, take heed of that,
But, sir, such wanton, wild, and usual slips, 22
As are companions noted and most known
To youth and liberty.

REYNALDO
As gaming, my lord.

POLONIUS
Ay, or drinking, fencing, swearing,
Quarreling, drabbing—you may go so far. 26

REYNALDO
My lord, that would dishonor him.

POLONIUS
Faith, no, as you may season it in the charge. 28
You must not put another scandal on him
That he is open to incontinency; 30
That's not my meaning. But breathe his faults so
quaintly 31
That they may seem the taints of liberty, 32
The flash and outbreak of a fiery mind,
A savageness in unreclaimed blood, 34
Of general assault.

REYNALDO
But, my good lord— 35

POLONIUS
Wherefore should you do this?

REYNALDO
Ay, my lord,
I would know that.

POLONIUS
Marry, sir, here's my drift,
And, I believe, it is a fetch of wit. 38
You laying these slight sullies on my son,
As 'twere a thing a little soil'd i' th' working, 40
Mark you,
Your party in converse, him you would sound, 42
Having ever seen in the prenominate crimes 43
The youth you breathe of guilty, be assur'd 44

164 pioner i.e., pioneer, digger, miner **168 your philosophy** i.e., this subject called "natural philosophy" or "science" that people talk about **173 antic** fantastic **175 encumb'red** folded or entwined **177 an if** if **178 list** were inclined **179 giving out** profession of knowledge. **note** give a sign, indicate **188 still** always

II.i. Location: Polonius' chambers.
3 marvel's marvelous(ly)

7 Danskers Danes **8 what means** what wealth (they have). **keep** dwell **10 encompassment** roundabout talking. **drift** gradual approach or course **11–12 come . . . it** i.e., you will find out more this way than by asking pointed questions (*particular demands*) **13 Take** assume, pretend **19 put on** impute to **20 forgeries** invented tales **22 wanton** sportive, unrestrained **26 drabbing** whoring **28 season** temper, soften **30 incontinency** habitual loose behavior **31 quaintly** delicately, ingeniously **32 taints of liberty** faults resulting from freedom **34 unreclaimed** untamed **35 general assault** tendency that assails all unrestrained youth **38 fetch of wit** clever trick **40 soil'd i' th' working** i.e., shopworn **42 converse** conversation. **sound** i.e., sound out **43 Having ever** if he has ever. **prenominate crimes** before-mentioned offenses **44 breathe** speak

He closes with you in this consequence:
"Good sir," or so, or "friend," or "gentleman,"
According to the phrase or the addition
Of man and country.

REYNALDO
Very good, my lord.

POLONIUS
And then, sir, does 'a this—'a does—what was I
about to say?
By the mass, I was about to say something.
Where did I leave?

REYNALDO
At "closes in the consequence."

POLONIUS
At "closes in the consequence," ay, marry.
He closes thus: "I know the gentleman;
I saw him yesterday, or th' other day,
Or then, or then, with such, or such, and, as you
say,
There was 'a gaming, there o'ertook in 's rouse,
There falling out at tennis," or perchance,
"I saw him enter such a house of sale,"
Videlicet, a brothel, or so forth. See you now,
Your bait of falsehood takes this carp of truth;
And thus do we of wisdom and of reach,
With windlasses and with assays of bias,
By indirections find directions out.
So by my former lecture and advice
Shall you my son. You have me, have you not?

REYNALDO
My lord, I have.

POLONIUS
God buy ye; fare ye well.

REYNALDO
Good my lord.

POLONIUS
Observe his inclination in yourself.

REYNALDO
I shall, my lord.

POLONIUS
And let him ply his music.

REYNALDO
Well, my lord.

POLONIUS
Farewell. *Exit Reynaldo.*

Enter Ophelia.

How now, Ophelia, what's the matter?

OPHELIA
O, my lord, my lord, I have been so affrighted!

POLONIUS
With what, i' th' name of God?

OPHELIA
My lord, as I was sewing in my closet,
Lord Hamlet, with his doublet all unbrac'd,
No hat upon his head, his stockings fouled,
Ungart'red, and down-gyved to his ankle,
Pale as his shirt, his knees knocking each other,
And with a look so piteous in purport
As if he had been loosed out of hell
To speak of horrors—he comes before me.

POLONIUS
Mad for thy love?

OPHELIA
My lord, I do not know,
But truly I do fear it.

POLONIUS
What said he?

OPHELIA
He took me by the wrist and held me hard.
Then goes he to the length of all his arm,
And, with his other hand thus o'er his brow,
He falls to such perusal of my face
As 'a would draw it. Long stay'd he so.
At last, a little shaking of mine arm
And thrice his head thus waving up and down,
He rais'd a sigh so piteous and profound
As it did seem to shatter all his bulk
And end his being. That done, he lets me go,
And, with his head over his shoulder turn'd,
He seem'd to find his way without his eyes,
For out o' doors he went without their helps,
And, to the last, bended their light on me.

POLONIUS
Come, go with me. I will go seek the King.
This is the very ecstasy of love,
Whose violent property fordoes itself
And leads the will to desperate undertakings
As oft as any passion under heaven
That does afflict our natures. I am sorry.
What, have you given him any hard words of late?

OPHELIA
No, my good lord, but, as you did command,
I did repel his letters and denied
His access to me.

POLONIUS
That hath made him mad.
I am sorry that with better heed and judgment
I had not quoted him. I fear'd he did but trifle
And meant to wrack thee; but, beshrew my
jealousy!
By heaven, it is as proper to our age
To cast beyond ourselves in our opinions
As it is common for the younger sort
To lack discretion. Come, go we to the King.
This must be known, which, being kept close,
might move
More grief to hide than hate to utter love.
Come. *Exeunt.*

[SCENE II]

Flourish. Enter King and Queen, Rosencrantz, and Guildenstern [with others].

KING
Welcome, dear Rosencrantz and Guildenstern.

45 closes . . . consequence follows your lead in some fashion as follows **47 addition** title **56 o'ertook in 's rouse** overcome by drink **57 falling out** quarreling **59 Videlicet** namely **60 carp** a fish **61 reach** capacity, ability **62 windlasses** i.e., circuitous paths. (Literally, circuits made to head off the game in hunting.) **assays of bias** attempts through indirection (like the curving path of the bowling ball which is biased or weighted to one side) **63 directions** i.e., the way things really are **68 in yourself** in your own person (as well as by asking questions) **70 let him ply** see that he continues to study **74 closet** private chamber **75 doublet** close-fitting jacket. **unbrac'd** unfastened **77 down-gyved** fallen to the ankles (like gyves or fetters)

92 bulk body **99 ecstasy** madness **100 property** nature. **fordoes** destroys **109 quoted** observed **110 beshrew my jealousy** a plague upon my suspicious nature **111 proper . . . age** characteristic of us (old) men **112 cast beyond** overshoot, miscalculate **115 close** secret **115–116 might . . . love** i.e., might cause more grief (to others) by hiding the knowledge of Hamlet's strange behavior to Ophelia than hatred by telling it

II.ii. Location: The castle.

Moreover that we much did long to see you, 2
The need we have to use you did provoke
Our hasty sending. Something have you heard
Of Hamlet's transformation—so call it,
Sith nor th' exterior nor the inward man 6
Resembles that it was. What it should be, 7
More than his father's death, that thus hath put him
So much from th' understanding of himself,
I cannot dream of. I entreat you both
That, being of so young days brought up with him, 11
And sith so neighbor'd to his youth and havior,
That you vouchsafe your rest here in our court 13
Some little time, so by your companies
To draw him on to pleasures, and to gather
So much as from occasion you may glean,
Whether aught to us unknown afflicts him thus,
That, open'd, lies within our remedy. 18

QUEEN
Good gentlemen, he hath much talk'd of you,
And sure I am two men there is not living
To whom he more adheres. If it will please you
To show us so much gentry and good will 22
As to expend your time with us awhile
For the supply and profit of our hope, 24
Your visitation shall receive such thanks
As fits a king's remembrance.

ROSENCRANTZ Both your Majesties
Might, by the sovereign power you have of us,
Put your dread pleasures more into command
Than to entreaty.

GUILDENSTERN But we both obey,
And here give up ourselves in the full bent 30
To lay our service freely at your feet,
To be commanded.

KING
Thanks, Rosencrantz and gentle Guildenstern.

QUEEN
Thanks, Guildenstern and gentle Rosencrantz.
And I beseech you instantly to visit
My too much changed son. Go, some of you,
And bring these gentlemen where Hamlet is.

GUILDENSTERN
Heavens make our presence and our practices
Pleasant and helpful to him!

QUEEN Ay, amen!

Exeunt Rosencrantz and Guildenstern [with some Attendants].

Enter Polonius.

POLONIUS
Th' ambassadors from Norway, my good lord,
Are joyfully return'd.

KING
Thou still hast been the father of good news. 42

POLONIUS
Have I, my lord? I assure my good liege
I hold my duty, as I hold my soul,
Both to my God and to my gracious king;
And I do think, or else this brain of mine
Hunts not the trail of policy so sure
As it hath us'd to do, that I have found
The very cause of Hamlet's lunacy.

KING
O, speak of that! That do I long to hear.

POLONIUS
Give first admittance to th' ambassadors.
My news shall be the fruit to that great feast. 52

KING
Thyself do grace to them, and bring them in.
[Exit Polonius.]
He tells me, my dear Gertrude, he hath found
The head and source of all your son's distemper.

QUEEN
I doubt it is no other but the main, 56
His father's death, and our o'erhasty marriage.

Enter Ambassadors [Voltimand and Cornelius, with Polonius].

KING
Well, we shall sift him.—Welcome, my good friends!
Say, Voltimand, what from our brother Norway?

VOLTIMAND
Most fair return of greetings and desires.
Upon our first, he sent out to suppress 61
His nephew's levies, which to him appear'd
To be a preparation 'gainst the Polack,
But, better look'd into, he truly found
It was against your Highness. Whereat griev'd
That so his sickness, age, and impotence
Was falsely borne in hand, sends out arrests 67
On Fortinbras, which he, in brief, obeys,
Receives rebuke from Norway, and in fine 69
Makes vow before his uncle never more
To give th' assay of arms against your Majesty. 71
Whereon old Norway, overcome with joy,
Gives him three score thousand crowns in annual fee,
And his commission to employ those soldiers,
So levied as before, against the Polack,
With an entreaty, herein further shown,
[Giving a paper.]
That it might please you to give quiet pass
Through your dominions for this enterprise,
On such regards of safety and allowance 79
As therein are set down.

KING It likes us well, 80
And at our more consider'd time we'll read, 81
Answer, and think upon this business.
Meantime we thank you for your well-took labor.
Go to your rest; at night we'll feast together.
Most welcome home! *Exeunt Ambassadors.*

POLONIUS This business is well ended.
My liege, and madam, to expostulate 86
What majesty should be, what duty is,
Why day is day, night night, and time is time,

2 Moreover that besides the fact that **6 Sith** since. **nor . . . nor** neither . . . nor **7 that** what **11 of . . . days** from such early youth **13 vouchsafe your rest** please to stay **18 open'd** revealed **22 gentry** courtesy **24 supply and profit** aid and successful outcome **30 in . . . bent** to the utmost degree of our capacity **42 still** always

52 fruit dessert **56 doubt** fear, suspect. **main** chief point, principal concern **61 Upon our first** at our first words on the business **67 borne in hand** deluded, taken advantage of **69 in fine** in the end **71 assay** trial **79 On . . . allowance** with such pledges of safety and provisos **80 likes** pleases **81 consider'd** suitable for deliberation **86 expostulate** expound

Were nothing but to waste night, day, and time.
Therefore, since brevity is the soul of wit,
And tediousness the limbs and outward flourishes,
I will be brief. Your noble son is mad.
Mad call I it, for, to define true madness,
What is 't but to be nothing else but mad?
But let that go.

QUEEN More matter, with less art.

POLONIUS
Madam, I swear I use no art at all.
That he is mad, 'tis true; 'tis true 'tis pity,
And pity 'tis 'tis true—a foolish figure,
But farewell it, for I will use no art.
Mad let us grant him, then, and now remains
That we find out the cause of this effect,
Or rather say, the cause of this defect,
For this effect defective comes by cause.
Thus it remains, and the remainder thus.
Perpend.
I have a daughter—have while she is mine—
Who, in her duty and obedience, mark,
Hath given me this. Now gather, and surmise.
[*Reads the letter.*] "To the celestial and my soul's idol, the most beautified Ophelia"—
That's an ill phrase, a vile phrase; "beautified" is a vile phrase. But you shall hear. Thus: [*Reads.*]
"In her excellent white bosom, these, etc."

QUEEN
Came this from Hamlet to her?

POLONIUS
Good madam, stay awhile; I will be faithful. [*Reads.*]
"Doubt thou the stars are fire,
Doubt that the sun doth move,
Doubt truth to be a liar,
But never doubt I love.
O dear Ophelia, I am ill at these numbers. I have not art to reckon my groans. But that I love thee best, O most best, believe it. Adieu.
Thine evermore, most dear lady, whilst this machine is to him, Hamlet."
This in obedience hath my daughter shown me,
And, more above, hath his solicitings,
As they fell out by time, by means, and place,
All given to mine ear.

KING But how hath she
Receiv'd his love?

POLONIUS What do you think of me?

KING
As of a man faithful and honorable.

POLONIUS
I would fain prove so. But what might you think,
When I had seen this hot love on the wing—
As I perceiv'd it, I must tell you that,
Before my daughter told me—what might you,
Or my dear Majesty your queen here, think,
If I had play'd the desk or table-book,
Or given my heart a winking, mute and dumb,
Or look'd upon this love with idle sight?
What might you think? No, I went round to work,
And my young mistress thus I did bespeak:
"Lord Hamlet is a prince, out of thy star;
This must not be." And then I prescripts gave her,
That she should lock herself from his resort,
Admit no messengers, receive no tokens.
Which done, she took the fruits of my advice;
And he, repelled—a short tale to make—
Fell into a sadness, then into a fast,
Thence to a watch, thence into a weakness,
Thence to a lightness, and, by this declension,
Into the madness wherein now he raves,
And all we mourn for.

KING
Do you think this?

QUEEN It may be, very like.

POLONIUS
Hath there been such a time—I would fain know that—
That I have positively said "'Tis so,"
When it prov'd otherwise?

KING Not that I know.

POLONIUS [*Pointing to his head and shoulder*]
Take this from this, if this be otherwise.
If circumstances lead me, I will find
Where truth is hid, though it were hid indeed
Within the center.

KING How may we try it further?

POLONIUS
You know, sometimes he walks four hours together
Here in the lobby.

QUEEN So he does indeed.

POLONIUS
At such a time I'll loose my daughter to him.
Be you and I behind an arras then.
Mark the encounter. If he love her not
And be not from his reason fall'n thereon,
Let me be no assistant for a state,
But keep a farm and carters.

KING We will try it.

Enter Hamlet [*reading on a book*].

QUEEN
But look where sadly the poor wretch comes reading.

POLONIUS
Away, I do beseech you both, away.
I'll board him presently.
Exeunt King and Queen [*with Attendants*].
O, give me leave.
How does my good Lord Hamlet?

HAMLET Well, God-a-mercy.

90 wit sound sense or judgment **98 figure** figure of speech **103 For . . . cause** i.e., for this defective behavior, this madness, has a cause **105 Perpend** consider **116 Doubt** suspect, question **120 ill . . . numbers** unskilled at writing verses **121 reckon** (1) count (2) number metrically, scan **124 machine** i.e., body **126 more above** moreover **127 fell out** occurred

136 play'd . . . table-book i.e., remained shut up, concealing the information **137 winking** closing of the eyes **138 with idle sight** complacently or incomprehendingly **139 round** roundly, plainly **140 bespeak** address **141 out of thy star** above your sphere, position **148 watch** state of sleeplessness **149 lightness** lightheadedness. **declension** decline, deterioration **159 center** middle point of the earth (which is also the center of the Ptolemaic universe) **163 arras** hanging, tapestry **165 thereon** on that account **170 board** accost **172 God-a-mercy** i.e., thank you

POLONIUS Do you know me, my lord?
HAMLET Excellent well. You are a fishmonger. 174
POLONIUS Not I, my lord.
HAMLET Then I would you were so honest a man.
POLONIUS Honest, my lord?
HAMLET Ay, sir. To be honest, as this world goes, is to
be one man pick'd out of ten thousand.
POLONIUS That's very true, my lord.
HAMLET For if the sun breed maggots in a dead dog,
being a good kissing carrion—Have you a daughter? 182
POLONIUS I have, my lord.
HAMLET Let her not walk i' th' sun. Conception is a 184
blessing, but as your daughter may conceive, friend,
look to 't.
POLONIUS [*Aside*] How say you by that? Still harping
on my daughter. Yet he knew me not at first; 'a said I
was a fishmonger. 'A is far gone. And truly in my
youth I suff'red much extremity for love, very near
this. I'll speak to him again.—What do you read, my
lord?
HAMLET Words, words, words.
POLONIUS What is the matter, my lord? 194
HAMLET Between who?
POLONIUS I mean, the matter that you read, my lord.
HAMLET Slanders, sir; for the satirical rogue says here
that old men have grey beards, that their faces are wrin-
kled, their eyes purging thick amber and plum-tree 199
gum, and that they have a plentiful lack of wit, to-
gether with most weak hams. All which, sir, though I
most powerfully and potently believe, yet I hold it not
honesty to have it thus set down, for yourself, sir, shall 203
grow old as I am, if like a crab you could go backward.
POLONIUS [*Aside*] Though this be madness, yet there is
method in 't.—Will you walk out of the air, my lord?
HAMLET Into my grave.
POLONIUS Indeed, that's out of the air. [*Aside.*] How
pregnant sometimes his replies are! A happiness that 209
often madness hits on, which reason and sanity could
not so prosperously be deliver'd of. I will leave him, 211
[and suddenly contrive the means of meeting between
him] and my daughter.—My honorable lord, I will
most humbly take my leave of you.
HAMLET You cannot, sir, take from me any thing that I
will more willingly part withal—except my life, except
my life, except my life.

Enter Guildenstern and Rosencrantz.

POLONIUS Fare you well, my lord.
HAMLET These tedious old fools! 219
POLONIUS You go to seek the Lord Hamlet; there he is.
ROSENCRANTZ [*To Polonius*] God save you, sir!
[*Exit Polonius.*]
GUILDENSTERN My honor'd lord!
ROSENCRANTZ My most dear lord!
HAMLET My excellent good friends! How dost thou,
Guildenstern? Ah, Rosencrantz! Good lads, how do
you both?
ROSENCRANTZ
As the indifferent children of the earth. 227
GUILDENSTERN
Happy in that we are not over-happy.
On Fortune's cap we are not the very button.
HAMLET Nor the soles of her shoe?
ROSENCRANTZ Neither, my lord.
HAMLET Then you live about her waist, or in the mid-
dle of her favors?
GUILDENSTERN Faith, her privates we. 234
HAMLET In the secret parts of Fortune? O, most true;
she is a strumpet. What news? 236
ROSENCRANTZ None, my lord, but the world's grown
honest.
HAMLET Then is doomsday near. But your news is not
true. [Let me question more in particular. What have
you, my good friends, deserv'd at the hands of For-
tune that she sends you to prison hither?
GUILDENSTERN Prison, my lord?
HAMLET Denmark's a prison.
ROSENCRANTZ Then is the world one.
HAMLET A goodly one, in which there are many con- 246
fines, wards, and dungeons, Denmark being one o' th' 247
worst.
ROSENCRANTZ We think not so, my lord.
HAMLET Why then 'tis none to you, for there is nothing
either good or bad but thinking makes it so. To me it
is a prison.
ROSENCRANTZ Why then, your ambition makes it one.
'Tis too narrow for your mind.
HAMLET O God, I could be bounded in a nutshell and
count myself a king of infinite space, were it not that
I have bad dreams.
GUILDENSTERN Which dreams indeed are ambition, for
the very substance of the ambitious is merely the 259
shadow of a dream.
HAMLET A dream itself is but a shadow.
ROSENCRANTZ Truly, and I hold ambition of so airy and
light a quality that it is but a shadow's shadow.
HAMLET Then are our beggars bodies, and our mon- 264
archs and outstretch'd heroes the beggars' shadows. 265
Shall we to th' court? For, by my fay, I cannot reason. 266
ROSENCRANTZ, GUILDENSTERN We'll wait upon you. 267
HAMLET No such matter. I will not sort you with the 268
rest of my servants, for, to speak to you like an honest
man, I am most dreadfully attended.] But, in the 270
beaten way of friendship, what make you at Elsinore? 271
ROSENCRANTZ To visit you, my lord, no other occasion.
HAMLET Beggar that I am, I am even poor in thanks;
but I thank you, and sure, dear friends, my thanks are
too dear a halfpenny. Were you not sent for? Is it your 275

174 fishmonger fish merchant. (With connotation of *bawd, procurer?*) **182 good kissing carrion** i.e., a good piece of flesh for kissing, or for the sun to kiss **184 i' th' sun** (with additional implication of the sunshine of princely favors.) **Conception** (1) understanding (2) pregnancy **194 matter** substance. (But Hamlet plays on the sense of *basis for a dispute.*) **199 purging** discharging **203 honesty** decency **209 pregnant** full of meaning. **happiness** felicity of expression **211 prosperously** successfully **219 old fools** i.e., old men like Polonius

227 indifferent ordinary **234 privates** close acquaintances (with sexual pun on *private parts*) **236 strumpet** prostitute. (A common epithet for indescriminate Fortune; see l. 493 below.) **246–247 confines** places of confinement. **247 wards** cells **259 the very . . . ambitious** that seemingly very substantial thing which the ambitious pursue **264 bodies** i.e., solid substances rather than shadows (since beggars are not ambitious) **265 outstretch'd** (1) far-reaching in their ambition (2) elongated as shadows **266 fay** faith **267 wait upon** accompany, attend **268 sort** class, associate **270 dreadfully attended** waited upon in slovenly fashion **271 beaten way** familiar path. **make** do **275 dear a halfpenny** expensive at the price of a halfpenny, i.e., of little worth

own inclining? Is it a free visitation? Come, come, deal justly with me. Come, come; nay, speak.

GUILDENSTERN What should we say, my lord?

HAMLET Why, anything, but to th' purpose. You were sent for; and there is a kind of confession in your looks which your modesties have not craft enough to color. I know the good King and Queen have sent for you.

ROSENCRANTZ To what end, my lord?

HAMLET That you must teach me. But let me conjure you, by the rights of our fellowship, by the consonancy of our youth, by the obligation of our ever-preserv'd love, and by what more dear a better proposer could charge you withal, be even and direct with me, whether you were sent for, or no?

ROSENCRANTZ [*Aside to Guildenstern*] What say you?

HAMLET [*Aside*] Nay, then, I have an eye of you.—If you love me, hold not off.

GUILDENSTERN My lord, we were sent for.

HAMLET I will tell you why; so shall my anticipation prevent your discovery, and your secrecy to the King and Queen molt no feather. I have of late—but wherefore I know not—lost all my mirth, forgone all custom of exercises; and indeed it goes so heavily with my disposition that this goodly frame, the earth, seems to me a sterile promontory; this most excellent canopy, the air, look you, this brave o'erhanging firmament, this majestical roof fretted with golden fire, why, it appeareth nothing to me but a foul and pestilent congregation of vapors. What a piece of work is a man! How noble in reason, how infinite in faculties, in form and moving how express and admirable, in action how like an angel, in apprehension how like a god! The beauty of the world, the paragon of animals! And yet, to me, what is this quintessence of dust? Man delights not me—no, nor woman neither, though by your smiling you seem to say so.

ROSENCRANTZ My lord, there was no such stuff in my thoughts.

HAMLET Why did you laugh then, when I said "man delights not me"?

ROSENCRANTZ To think, my lord, if you delight not in man, what lenten entertainment the players shall receive from you. We coted them on the way, and hither are they coming, to offer you service.

HAMLET He that plays the king shall be welcome; his Majesty shall have tribute of me. The adventurous knight shall use his foil and target, the lover shall not sigh gratis, the humorous man shall end his part in peace, [the clown shall make those laugh whose lungs are tickle o' th' sere], and the lady shall say her mind freely, or the blank verse shall halt for 't. What players are they?

ROSENCRANTZ Even those you were wont to take such delight in, the tragedians of the city.

HAMLET How chances it they travel? Their residence, both in reputation and profit, was better both ways.

ROSENCRANTZ I think their inhibition comes by the means of the late innovation.

HAMLET Do they hold the same estimation they did when I was in the city? Are they so follow'd?

ROSENCRANTZ No, indeed, are they not.

[HAMLET How comes it? Do they grow rusty?

ROSENCRANTZ Nay, their endeavor keeps in the wonted pace. But there is, sir, an aery of children, little eyases, that cry out on the top of question, and are most tyrannically clapp'd for 't. These are now the fashion, and so berattle the common stages—so they call them—that many wearing rapiers are afraid of goose-quills and dare scarce come thither.

HAMLET What, are they children? Who maintains 'em? How are they escoted? Will they pursue the quality no longer than they can sing? Will they not say afterwards, if they should grow themselves to common players—as it is most like, if their means are no better—their writers do them wrong, to make them exclaim against their own succession?

ROSENCRANTZ Faith, there has been much to do on both sides; and the nation holds it no sin to tarre them to controversy. There was, for a while, no money bid for argument unless the poet and the player went to cuffs in the question.

HAMLET Is 't possible?

GUILDENSTERN O, there has been much throwing about of brains.

HAMLET Do the boys carry it away?

ROSENCRANTZ Ay, that they do, my lord—Hercules and his load too.]

HAMLET It is not very strange; for my uncle is King of Denmark, and those that would make mouths at him while my father liv'd, give twenty, forty, fifty, a hundred ducats apiece for his picture in little. 'Sblood, there is something in this more than natural, if philosophy could find it out.

A flourish [*of trumpets within*].

GUILDENSTERN There are the players.

HAMLET Gentlemen, you are welcome to Elsinore. Your hands, come then. Th' appurtenance of welcome is fashion and ceremony. Let me comply with you in this

284 conjure adjure, entreat **285–286 consonancy of our youth** the fact that we are of the same age **287 better proposer** more skillful propounder **288 charge** urge. **even** straight, honest **291 of** on **295 prevent your discovery** forestall your disclosure **296 molt no feather** i.e., not diminish in the least **301 brave** splendid **302 fretted** adorned (with fretwork, as in a vaulted ceiling) **306 express** well-framed (?), exact (?) **309 quintessence** the fifth essence of ancient philosophy, beyond earth, water, air, and fire, supposed to be the substance of the heavenly bodies and to be latent in all things **317 lenten entertainment** meager reception (appropriate to Lent) **318 coted** overtook and passed beyond **322 foil and target** sword and shield **323 humorous man** eccentric character, dominated by one trait or "humor" **325 tickle o' th' sere** easy on the trigger, ready to laugh easily. (*Sere* is part of a gunlock.) **326 halt** limp

330 residence remaining in one place, i.e., in the city **332 inhibition** formal prohibition (from acting plays in the city) **333 innovation** i.e., the new fashion in satirical plays performed by boy actors in the "private" theatres; or possibly a political uprising; or the strict limitations set on the theatre in London in 1600

337–362 How . . . load too (The passage, omitted from the early quartos, alludes to the so-called War of the Theatres, 1599–1602, the rivalry between the children's companies and the adult actors.) **338 wonted** usual **339 aery** nest. **eyases** young hawks **340 cry . . . question** speak shrilly, dominating the controversy (in decrying the public theatres) **340–341 tyrannically** outrageously

342 berattle berate. **common stages** public theatres **343 many wearing rapiers** i.e., many men of fashion, who were afraid to patronize the common players for fear of being satirized by the poets who wrote for the children. **goose-quills** i.e., pens of satirists **346 escoted** maintained. **quality** (acting) profession **346–347 no longer . . . sing** i.e., only until their voices change **348 common** regular, adult **351 succession** i.e., future careers **352 to do** ado **353 tarre** set on (as dogs) **355 argument** plot for a play **355–356 went . . . question** came to blows in the play itself **360 carry it away** i.e., win the day **361–362 Hercules . . . load** (Thought to be an allusion to the sign of the Globe Theatre, which was Hercules bearing the world on his shoulder.) **364 mouths** faces **366 ducats** gold coins. **in little** in miniature **367 'Sblood** by God's (Christ's) blood **372 comply** observe the formalities of courtesy

garb, lest my extent to the players, which, I tell you, must show fairly outwards, should more appear like entertainment than yours. You are welcome. But my uncle-father and aunt-mother are deceiv'd.

GUILDENSTERN In what, my dear lord?

HAMLET I am but mad north-north-west. When the wind is southerly I know a hawk from a handsaw.

Enter Polonius.

POLONIUS Well be with you, gentlemen!

HAMLET Hark you, Guildenstern, and you too; at each ear a hearer. That great baby you see there is not yet out of his swaddling-clouts.

ROSENCRANTZ Happily he is the second time come to them; for they say an old man is twice a child.

HAMLET I will prophesy he comes to tell me of the players; mark it.—You say right, sir, o' Monday morning, 'twas then indeed.

POLONIUS My lord, I have news to tell you.

HAMLET My lord, I have news to tell you. When Roscius was an actor in Rome—

POLONIUS The actors are come hither, my lord.

HAMLET Buzz, buzz!

POLONIUS Upon my honor—

HAMLET Then came each actor on his ass—

POLONIUS The best actors in the world, either for tragedy, comedy, history, pastoral, pastoral-comical, historical-pastoral, tragical-historical, tragical-comical-historical-pastoral, scene individable, or poem unlimited. Seneca cannot be too heavy, nor Plautus too light. For the law of writ and the liberty, these are the only men.

HAMLET O Jephthah, judge of Israel, what a treasure hadst thou!

POLONIUS What a treasure had he, my lord?

HAMLET Why,
"One fair daughter, and no more,
The which he loved passing well."

POLONIUS [*Aside*] Still on my daughter.

HAMLET Am I not i' th' right, old Jephthah?

POLONIUS If you call me Jephthah, my lord, I have a daughter that I love passing well.

HAMLET Nay, that follows not.

POLONIUS What follows, then, my lord?

HAMLET Why,
"As by lot, God wot,"
and then, you know,
"It came to pass, as most like it was"—
the first row of the pious chanson will show you more, for look where my abridgement comes.

Enter the Players.

You are welcome, masters; welcome, all. I am glad to see thee well. Welcome, good friends. O, old friend! Why, thy face is valanc'd since I saw thee last. Com'st thou to beard me in Denmark? What, my young lady and mistress! By 'r lady, your ladyship is nearer to heaven than when I saw you last, by the altitude of a chopine. Pray God your voice, like a piece of uncurrent gold, be not crack'd within the ring. Masters, you are all welcome. We'll e'en to 't like French falconers, fly at anything we see. We'll have a speech straight. Come, give us a taste of your quality; come, a passionate speech.

FIRST PLAYER What speech, my good lord?

HAMLET I heard thee speak me a speech once, but it was never acted, or, if it was, not above once, for the play, I remember, pleas'd not the million; 'twas caviary to the general. But it was—as I receiv'd it, and others, whose judgments in such matters cried in the top of mine—an excellent play, well digested in the scenes, set down with as much modesty as cunning. I remember one said there were no sallets in the lines to make the matter savory, nor no matter in the phrase that might indict the author of affectation, but call'd it an honest method, as wholesome as sweet, and by very much more handsome than fine. One speech in 't I chiefly lov'd: 'twas Aeneas' tale to Dido, and thereabout of it especially when he speaks of Priam's slaughter. If it live in your memory, begin at this line: let me see, let me see—
"The rugged Pyrrhus, like th' Hyrcanian beast"—
'Tis not so. It begins with Pyrrhus:
"The rugged Pyrrhus, he whose sable arms,
Black as his purpose, did the night resemble
When he lay couched in the ominous horse,
Hath now this dread and black complexion smear'd
With heraldry more dismal. Head to foot
Now is he total gules, horridly trick'd
With blood of fathers, mothers, daughters, sons,
Bak'd and impasted with the parching streets,
That lend a tyrannous and a damned light
To their lord's murder. Roasted in wrath and fire,
And thus o'er-sized with coagulate gore,

373 garb i.e., manner. **my extent** i.e., the extent of my showing courtesy **374 show fairly outwards** look cordial to outward appearances **375 entertainment** a (warm) reception **378 north-north-west** i.e., only partly, at times **379 hawk, handsaw** a mattock (or *hack*) and a carpenter's cutting tool respectively; also birds, with a play on *hernshaw* or heron **383 swaddling-clouts** cloths in which to wrap a newborn baby **384 Happily** haply, perhaps **390–391 Roscius** a famous Roman actor who died in 62 B.C. **393 Buzz** (An interjection used to denote stale news.) **399 scene individable** a play observing the unity of place **399–400 poem unlimited** a play disregarding the unities of time and place **400 Seneca** writer of Latin tragedies. **Plautus** writer of Latin comedy **401 law . . . liberty** dramatic composition both according to rules and without rules, i.e., "classical" and "romantic" dramas **403 Jephthah . . . Israel** (Jephthah had to sacrifice his daughter; see Judges 11. Hamlet goes on to quote from a ballad on the theme.) **408 passing** surpassingly **416 wot** knows **418 like** likely, probable

419 row stanza. **chanson** ballad, song **420 my abridgement** something that cuts short my conversation; also, a diversion **423 valenc'd** fringed (with a beard) **424 beard** confront (with obvious pun). **young lady** i.e., boy playing women's parts **427 chopine** thick-soled shoe of Italian fashion **427–428 uncurrent** not passable as lawful coinage **428 crack'd . . . ring** i.e., changed from adolescent to male voice, no longer suitable for women's roles. (Coins featured rings enclosing the sovereign's head; if the coin was cracked within this ring, it was unfit for currency.) **430 straight** at once **436–437 caviary to the general** caviar to the multitude, i.e., a choice dish too elegant for coarse tastes **438–439 cried in the top of** i.e., spoke with greater authority than **440 cunning** skill **441 sallets** salad, i.e., spicy improprieties **443 indict** convict **445 fine** elaborately ornamented, showy **447–448 Priam's slaughter** the slaying of the ruler of Troy, when the Greeks finally took the city **450 Pyrrhus** a Greek hero in the Trojan War, also known as Neoptolemus, son of Achilles. **Hyrcanian beast** i.e., the tiger. (See Virgil, *Aeneid*, IV, 266; compare the whole speech with Marlowe's *Dido Queen of Carthage*, II.i.214 ff.) **452 sable** black (for reasons of camouflage during the episode of the Trojan horse) **454 ominous horse** Trojan horse, by which the Greeks gained access to Troy **456 dismal** ill-omened **457 gules** red (a heraldic term). **trick'd** adorned, decorated **459 impasted** crusted, like a thick paste. **with . . . streets** by the parching heat of the streets (because of the fires everywhere) **461 their lord's** i.e., Priam's **462 o'er-sized** covered as with size or glue

With eyes like carbuncles, the hellish Pyrrhus
Old grandsire Priam seeks."
So proceed you.

POLONIUS 'Fore God, my lord, well spoken, with good
accent and good discretion.

FIRST PLAYER "Anon he finds him
Striking too short at Greeks. His antique sword,
Rebellious to his arm, lies where it falls,
Repugnant to command. Unequal match'd, 471
Pyrrhus at Priam drives, in rage strikes wide,
But with the whiff and wind of his fell sword 473
Th' unnerved father falls. [Then senseless Ilium,] 474
Seeming to feel this blow, with flaming top
Stoops to his base, and with a hideous crash 476
Takes prisoner Pyrrhus' ear. For, lo! His sword,
Which was declining on the milky head
Of reverend Priam, seem'd i' th' air to stick.
So as a painted tyrant Pyrrhus stood, 480
And, like a neutral to his will and matter, 481
Did nothing.
But, as we often see, against some storm, 483
A silence in the heavens, the rack stand still, 484
The bold winds speechless, and the orb below
As hush as death, anon the dreadful thunder
Doth rend the region, so, after Pyrrhus' pause, 487
Aroused vengeance sets him new a-work,
And never did the Cyclops' hammers fall 489
On Mars's armor forg'd for proof eterne 490
With less remorse than Pyrrhus' bleeding sword
Now falls on Priam.
Out, out, thou strumpet Fortune! All you gods,
In general synod, take away her power! 494
Break all the spokes and fellies from her wheel, 495
And bowl the round nave down the hill of heaven, 496
As low as to the fiends!"

POLONIUS This is too long.

HAMLET It shall to the barber's with your beard.—Pri-
thee say on. He's for a jig or a tale of bawdry, or he 500
sleeps. Say on; come to Hecuba. 501

FIRST PLAYER
"But who, ah woe! had seen the mobled queen"— 502

HAMLET "The mobled queen?"

POLONIUS That's good. "Mobled queen" is good.

FIRST PLAYER
"Run barefoot up and down, threat'ning the flames
With bisson rheum, a clout upon that head 506
Where late the diadem stood, and for a robe,
About her lank and all o'er-teemed loins, 508
A blanket, in the alarm of fear caught up—
Who this had seen, with tongue in venom steep'd,
'Gainst Fortune's state would treason have
pronounc'd. 511
But if the gods themselves did see her then
When she saw Pyrrhus make malicious sport
In mincing with his sword her husband's limbs,
The instant burst of clamor that she made,
Unless things mortal move them not at all,
Would have made milch the burning eyes of
heaven, 517
And passion in the gods."

POLONIUS Look whe'er he has not turn'd his color and 519
has tears in 's eyes. Prithee, no more.

HAMLET 'Tis well; I'll have thee speak out the rest of
this soon. Good my lord, will you see the players well
bestow'd? Do you hear, let them be well us'd, for they 523
are the abstract and brief chronicles of the time. After 524
your death you were better have a bad epitaph than
their ill report while you live.

POLONIUS My lord, I will use them according to their
desert.

HAMLET God's bodkin, man, much better! Use every 529
man after his desert, and who shall scape whipping?
Use them after your own honor and dignity. The less
they deserve, the more merit is in your bounty. Take
them in.

POLONIUS Come, sirs.

HAMLET Follow him, friends. We'll hear a play tomor-
row. [*As they start to leave, Hamlet detains the First
Player.*] Dost thou hear me, old friend? Can you play
the Murder of Gonzago?

FIRST PLAYER Ay, my lord.

HAMLET We'll ha 't tomorrow night. You could, for 540
need, study a speech of some dozen or sixteen lines,
which I would set down and insert in 't, could you
not?

FIRST PLAYER Ay, my lord.

HAMLET Very well. Follow that lord, and look you mock
him not.—My good friends, I'll leave you till night.
You are welcome to Elsinore.

Exeunt Polonius and Players.

ROSENCRANTZ Good my lord!

Exeunt [Rosencrantz and Guildenstern].

HAMLET
Ay, so, God buy you.—Now I am alone.
O, what a rogue and peasant slave am I!
Is it not monstrous that this player here,
But in a fiction, in a dream of passion,
Could force his soul so to his own conceit 553
That from her working all his visage wann'd, 554
Tears in his eyes, distraction in his aspect,
A broken voice, and his whole function suiting 556
With forms to his conceit? And all for nothing! 557
For Hecuba!
What's Hecuba to him, or he to Hecuba,
That he should weep for her? What would he do,
Had he the motive and the cue for passion
That I have? He would drown the stage with tears
And cleave the general ear with horrid speech,
Make mad the guilty and appall the free, 564

471 Repugnant disobedient, resistant **473 fell** cruel **474 senseless Ilium** insensate Troy **476 his** its **480 painted** i.e., painted in a picture **481 like . . . matter** i.e., as though poised indecisively between his intention and its fulfillment **483 against** just before **484 rack** mass of clouds **487 region** sky **489 Cyclops** giant armor-makers in the smithy of Vulcan **490 proof eterne** eternal resistance to assault **494 synod** assembly **495 fellies** pieces of wood forming the rim of a wheel **496 nave** hub **500 jig** comic song and dance often given at the end of a play **501 Hecuba** wife of Priam **502 mobled** muffled **506 bisson rheum** blinding tears. **clout** cloth **508 o'er-teemed** worn out with bearing children **511 state** rule, managing. **pronounc'd** proclaimed

517 milch milky, moist with tears **519 whe'er** whether **523 bestow'd** lodged **524 abstract** summary account **529 God's bodkin** by God's (Christ's) little body, *bodykin*. (Not to be confused with *bodkin*, dagger.) **553 conceit** conception **554 wann'd** grew pale **556–557 his whole . . . conceit** his whole being responded with actions to suit his thought **564 free** innocent

Confound the ignorant, and amaze indeed
The very faculties of eyes and ears. Yet I,
A dull and muddy-mettled rascal, peak, 567
Like John-a-dreams, unpregnant of my cause, 568
And can say nothing—no, not for a king
Upon whose property and most dear life 570
A damn'd defeat was made. Am I a coward?
Who calls me villain? Breaks my pate across?
Plucks off my beard, and blows it in my face?
Tweaks me by the nose? Gives me the lie i' th'
throat, 574
As deep as to the lungs? Who does me this?
Ha, 'swounds, I should take it; for it cannot be
But I am pigeon-liver'd, and lack gall 577
To make oppression bitter, or ere this
I should have fatted all the region kites 579
With this slave's offal. Bloody, bawdy villain!
Remorseless, treacherous, lecherous, kindless villain! 581
[O, vengeance!]
Why, what an ass am I! This is most brave,
That I, the son of a dear father murder'd,
Prompted to my revenge by heaven and hell,
Must, like a whore, unpack my heart with words,
And fall a-cursing, like a very drab, 587
A stallion! Fie upon 't, foh! About, my brains! 588
Hum, I have heard
That guilty creatures sitting at a play
Have by the very cunning of the scene
Been struck so to the soul that presently 592
They have proclaim'd their malefactions;
For murder, though it have no tongue, will speak
With most miraculous organ. I'll have these players
Play something like the murder of my father
Before mine uncle. I'll observe his looks;
I'll tent him to the quick. If 'a do blench, 598
I know my course. The spirit that I have seen
May be the devil, and the devil hath power
T' assume a pleasing shape; yea, and perhaps
Out of my weakness and my melancholy,
As he is very potent with such spirits, 603
Abuses me to damn me. I'll have grounds 604
More relative than this. The play's the thing 605
Wherein I'll catch the conscience of the King. *Exit.*

[ACT III • SCENE I]

Enter King, Queen, Polonius, Ophelia, Rosencrantz, Guildenstern, Lords.

KING
And can you, by no drift of conference, 1
Get from him why he puts on this confusion,
Grating so harshly all his days of quiet
With turbulent and dangerous lunacy?

ROSENCRANTZ
He does confess he feels himself distracted,
But from what cause 'a will by no means speak.

GUILDENSTERN
Nor do we find him forward to be sounded, 7
But with a crafty madness keeps aloof
When we would bring him on to some confession
Of his true state.

QUEEN Did he receive you well?

ROSENCRANTZ
Most like a gentleman.

GUILDENSTERN
But with much forcing of his disposition. 12

ROSENCRANTZ
Niggard of question, but of our demands 13
Most free in his reply.

QUEEN Did you assay him 14
To any pastime?

ROSENCRANTZ
Madam, it so fell out that certain players
We o'er-raught on the way. Of these we told him, 17
And there did seem in him a kind of joy
To hear of it. They are here about the court,
And, as I think, they have already order
This night to play before him.

POLONIUS 'Tis most true,
And he beseech'd me to entreat your Majesties
To hear and see the matter.

KING
With all my heart, and it doth much content me
To hear him so inclin'd.
Good gentlemen, give him a further edge, 26
And drive his purpose into these delights.

ROSENCRANTZ
We shall, my lord.
Exeunt Rosencrantz and Guildenstern.

KING Sweet Gertrude, leave us too,
For we have closely sent for Hamlet hither, 29
That he, as 'twere by accident, may here
Affront Ophelia. 31
Her father and myself, [lawful espials,] 32
Will so bestow ourselves that seeing, unseen,
We may of their encounter frankly judge,
And gather by him, as he is behav'd,
If 't be th' affliction of his love or no
That thus he suffers for.

QUEEN I shall obey you.
And for your part, Ophelia, I do wish
That your good beauties be the happy cause
Of Hamlet's wildness. So shall I hope your virtues
Will bring him to his wonted way again,
To both your honors.

OPHELIA Madam, I wish it may.
[*Exit Queen.*]

567 muddy-mettled dull-spirited. **peak** mope, pine **568 John-a-dreams** a sleepy, dreaming idler. **unpregnant of** not quickened by **570 property** i.e., the crown; perhaps also character, quality **574 Gives me the lie** calls me a liar **577 pigeon-liver'd** (The pigeon or dove was popularly supposed to be mild because it secreted no gall.) **579 region kites** kites (birds of prey) of the air, from the vicinity **581 kindless** unnatural **587 drab** prostitute **588 stallion** prostitute (male or female). (Many editors follow F reading of *scullion*.) **About** about it, to work **592 presently** at once **598 tent** probe. **blench** quail, flinch **603 spirits** humors (of melancholy) **604 Abuses** deludes **605 relative** closely related, pertinent

III.i. Location: The castle.
1 drift of conference direction of conversation

7 forward willing. **sounded** i.e., tested deeply **12 disposition** inclination **13 question** conversation **14 assay** try to win **17 o'er-raught** overtook and passed **26 edge** incitement **29 closely** privately **31 Affront** confront, meet **32 espials** spies

POLONIUS
Ophelia, walk you here.—Gracious, so please you, 43
We will bestow ourselves. [*To Ophelia.*] Read on
this book, [*Gives her a book.*]
That show of such an exercise may color 45
Your loneliness. We are oft to blame in this—
'Tis too much prov'd—that with devotion's visage 47
And pious action we do sugar o'er
The devil himself.

KING [*Aside*]
O, 'tis too true!
How smart a lash that speech doth give my
conscience!
The harlot's cheek, beautied with plast'ring art,
Is not more ugly to the thing that helps it 53
Than is my deed to my most painted word.
O heavy burden!

POLONIUS
I hear him coming. Let's withdraw, my lord. 56
[*King and Polonius withdraw.*]

Enter Hamlet. [*Ophelia pretends to read a book.*]

HAMLET
To be, or not to be, that is the question:
Whether 'tis nobler in the mind to suffer
The slings and arrows of outrageous fortune,
Or to take arms against a sea of troubles,
And by opposing end them. To die, to sleep—
No more—and by a sleep to say we end
The heart-ache and the thousand natural shocks
That flesh is heir to. 'Tis a consummation
Devoutly to be wish'd. To die, to sleep;
To sleep, perchance to dream. Ay, there's the rub, 66
For in that sleep of death what dreams may come
When we have shuffled off this mortal coil, 68
Must give us pause. There's the respect 69
That makes calamity of so long life. 70
For who would bear the whips and scorns of time,
Th' oppressor's wrong, the proud man's contumely, 72
The pangs of despis'd love, the law's delay, 73
The insolence of office, and the spurns 74
That patient merit of th' unworthy takes,
When he himself might his quietus make 76
With a bare bodkin? Who would fardels bear, 77
To grunt and sweat under a weary life,
But that the dread of something after death,
The undiscover'd country from whose bourn 80
No traveler returns, puzzles the will,
And makes us rather bear those ills we have
Than fly to others that we know not of?
Thus conscience does make cowards of us all;
And thus the native hue of resolution 85
Is sicklied o'er with the pale cast of thought, 86
And enterprises of great pitch and moment 87
With this regard their currents turn awry, 88
And lose the name of action.—Soft you now,
The fair Ophelia. Nymph, in thy orisons 90
Be all my sins rememb'red.

OPHELIA
Good my lord,
How does your honor for this many a day?

HAMLET
I humbly thank you; well, well, well.

OPHELIA
My lord, I have remembrances of yours,
That I have longed long to re-deliver.
I pray you, now receive them. [*Offers tokens.*]

HAMLET
No, not I, I never gave you aught.

OPHELIA
My honor'd lord, you know right well you did,
And with them words of so sweet breath compos'd
As made the things more rich. Their perfume lost,
Take these again, for to the noble mind
Rich gifts wax poor when givers prove unkind.
There, my lord. [*Gives tokens.*]

HAMLET Ha, ha! Are you honest? 104

OPHELIA My lord?

HAMLET Are you fair? 106

OPHELIA What means your lordship?

HAMLET That if you be honest and fair, your honesty 108
should admit no discourse to your beauty. 109

OPHELIA Could beauty, my lord, have better commerce 110
than with honesty?

HAMLET Ay, truly; for the power of beauty will sooner
transform honesty from what it is to a bawd than the
force of honesty can translate beauty into his likeness.
This was sometime a paradox, but now the time gives 115
it proof. I did love you once.

OPHELIA Indeed, my lord, you made me believe so.

HAMLET You should not have believ'd me, for virtue
cannot so inoculate our old stock but we shall relish of 119
it. I lov'd you not. 120

OPHELIA I was the more deceiv'd.

HAMLET Get thee to a nunn'ry. Why wouldst thou be a
breeder of sinners? I am myself indifferent honest; but 123
yet I could accuse me of such things that it were better
my mother had not borne me: I am very proud, re-
vengeful, ambitious, with more offenses at my beck 126
than I have thoughts to put them in, imagination to
give them shape, or time to act them in. What should
such fellows as I do crawling between earth and
heaven? We are arrant knaves, all; believe none of us.
Go thy ways to a nunn'ry. Where's your father?

OPHELIA At home, my lord.

HAMLET Let the doors be shut upon him, that he may

43 Gracious your Grace (i.e., the King) **45 exercise** act of devotion. (The book she reads is one of devotion.) **color** give a plausible appearance to **47 too much prov'd** too often shown to be true, too often practiced **53 to** compared to. **thing** i.e., the cosmetic **56 s.d. withdraw** (The King and Polonius may retire behind an arras. The stage directions specify that they "enter" again near the end of the scene.) **66 rub** (Literally, an obstacle in the game of bowls.) **68 shuffled** sloughed, cast. **coil** turmoil **69 respect** consideration **70 of . . . life** so long-lived **72 contumely** insolent abuse **73 despis'd** rejected **74 office** officialdom. **spurns** insults **76 quietus** acquittance; here, death **77 bodkin** dagger. **fardels** burdens **80 bourn** boundary **85 native hue** natural color, complexion

86 cast shade of color **87 pitch** height (as of a falcon's flight). **moment** importance **88 regard** respect, consideration. **currents** courses **90 orisons** prayers **104 honest** (1) truthful (2) chaste **106 fair** (1) beautiful (2) just, honorable **108 your honesty** your chastity **109 discourse** familiar dealings **110 commerce** dealings **115 sometime** formerly. **paradox** a view opposite to commonly held opinion. **the time** the present age **119 inoculate** graft, be engrafted to **119–120 but . . . it** i.e., that we do not still have about us a taste of the old stock; i.e., retain our sinfulness **123 indifferent honest** reasonably virtuous **126 beck** command

play the fool nowhere but in 's own house. Farewell.

OPHELIA O, help him, you sweet heavens!

HAMLET If thou dost marry, I'll give thee this plague for
thy dowry: be thou as chaste as ice, as pure as snow,
thou shalt not escape calumny. Get thee to a nunn'ry,
farewell. Or, if thou wilt needs marry, marry a fool,
for wise men know well enough what monsters you 140
make of them. To a nunn'ry, go, and quickly too. Fare- 141
well.

OPHELIA Heavenly powers, restore him!

HAMLET I have heard of your paintings too, well
enough. God hath given you one face, and you make
yourselves another. You jig, you amble, and you 146
lisp, you nickname God's creatures, and make your 147
wantonness your ignorance. Go to, I'll no more on 't; 148
it hath made me mad. I say, we will have no moe
marriage. Those that are married already—all but
one—shall live. The rest shall keep as they are. To a
nunn'ry, go. *Exit.*

OPHELIA
O, what a noble mind is here o'erthrown!
The courtier's, soldier's, scholar's, eye, tongue,
sword,
Th' expectancy and rose of the fair state, 155
The glass of fashion and the mold of form, 156
Th' observ'd of all observers, quite, quite down! 157
And I, of ladies most deject and wretched,
That suck'd the honey of his music vows,
Now see that noble and most sovereign reason,
Like sweet bells jangled, out of time and harsh,
That unmatch'd form and feature of blown youth 162
Blasted with ecstasy. O, woe is me, 163
T' have seen what I have seen, see what I see!

Enter King and Polonius.

KING
Love? His affections do not that way tend;
Nor what he spake, though it lack'd form a little,
Was not like madness. There's something in his
soul,
O'er which his melancholy sits on brood,
And I do doubt the hatch and the disclose 169
Will be some danger; which for to prevent,
I have in quick determination
Thus set it down: he shall with speed to England,
For the demand of our neglected tribute. 173
Haply the seas and countries different
With variable objects shall expel 175
This something-settled matter in his heart, 176
Whereon his brains still beating puts him thus
From fashion of himself. What think you on 't? 178

POLONIUS
It shall do well. But yet do I believe
The origin and commencement of his grief
Sprung from neglected love.—How now, Ophelia?
You need not tell us what Lord Hamlet said;
We heard it all.—My lord, do as you please,
But, if you hold it fit, after the play
Let his queen mother all alone entreat him
To show his grief. Let her be round with him; 186
And I'll be plac'd, so please you, in the ear
Of all their conference. If she find him not,
To England send him, or confine him where
Your wisdom best shall think.

KING It shall be so.
Madness in great ones must not unwatch'd go.
Exeunt.

[SCENE II]

Enter Hamlet and three of the Players.

HAMLET Speak the speech, I pray you, as I pronounc'd
it to you, trippingly on the tongue. But if you mouth
it, as many of our players do, I had as lief the town- 3
crier spoke my lines. Nor do not saw the air too much
with your hand, thus, but use all gently; for in the very
torrent, tempest, and, as I may say, whirlwind of your
passion, you must acquire and beget a temperance
that may give it smoothness. O, it offends me to the
soul to hear a robustious periwig-pated fellow tear a 9
passion to tatters, to very rags, to split the ears of the
groundlings, who for the most part are capable of 11
nothing but inexplicable dumb-shows and noise. I
would have such a fellow whipp'd for o'er-doing Ter- 13
magant. It out-herods Herod. Pray you, avoid it. 14

FIRST PLAYER I warrant your honor.

HAMLET Be not too tame neither, but let your own dis-
cretion be your tutor. Suit the action to the word, the
word to the action, with this special observance, that
you o'erstep not the modesty of nature. For anything
so o'erdone is from the purpose of playing, whose 20
end, both at the first and now, was and is, to hold, as
't were, the mirror up to nature, to show virtue her
feature, scorn her own image, and the very age and
body of the time his form and pressure. Now this 24
overdone, or come tardy off, though it makes the un- 25
skillful laugh, cannot but make the judicious grieve,
the censure of which one must in your allowance 27

140 monsters (An allusion to the horns of a cuckold.) **you** i.e., you women. **141 nunn'ry** (1) convent (2) brothel **146 jig** i.e., dance and sing affectedly and wantonly **147–148 make . . . ignorance** i.e., excuse your affectation on the grounds of your ignorance **155 Th' expectancy . . . state** the hope and ornament of the kingdom made fair (by him) **156 The glass . . . form** the mirror of fashion and the pattern of courtly behavior **157 observ'd . . . observers** i.e., the center of attention and honor in the court **162 blown** blooming **163 ecstasy** madness **169 doubt** fear. **disclose** disclosure **173 For . . . of** to demand **175 variable** various **176 something-settled** somewhat settled **178 From . . . himself** out of his natural manner

186 round blunt

III.ii. Location: The castle.
3 our players (Indefinite use; i.e., *players nowadays*.) **9 robustious** violent, boisterous. **periwig-pated** wearing a wig **11 groundlings** spectators who paid least and stood in the yard of the theatre. **capable of** susceptible of being influenced by **13–14 Termagent** (A god of the Saracens; a character in the St. Nicholas play, where one of his worshipers, leaving him in charge of goods, returns to find them stolen; whereupon he beats the god or idol, which howls vociferously.) **14 Herod** Herod of Jewry. (a character in *The Slaughter of the Innocents* and other cycle plays. The part was played with great noise and fury.) **20 from** contrary to **24 his** its. **pressure** stamp, impressed character **25 come tardy off** inadequately done **27 the censure . . . one** the judgment of even one of whom

o'erweigh a whole theatre of others. O, there be players that I have seen play, and heard others praise, and that highly, not to speak it profanely, that, neither having th' accent of Christians nor the gait of Christian, pagan, nor man, have so strutted and bellow'd that I have thought some of nature's journeymen had made men and not made them well, they imitated humanity so abominably.

FIRST PLAYER I hope we have reform'd that indifferently with us, sir.

HAMLET O, reform it altogether. And let those that play your clowns speak no more than is set down for them; for there be of them that will themselves laugh, to set on some quantity of barren spectators to laugh too, though in the mean time some necessary question of the play be then to be consider'd. That's villainous, and shows a most pitiful ambition in the fool that uses it. Go, make you ready. *[Exeunt Players.]*

Enter Polonius, Guildenstern, and Rosencrantz.

How now, my lord? Will the King hear this piece of work?

POLONIUS And the Queen too, and that presently.

HAMLET Bid the players make haste. *[Exit Polonius.]*
Will you two help to hasten them?

ROSENCRANTZ
Ay, my lord. *Exeunt they two.*

HAMLET What ho, Horatio!

Enter Horatio.

HORATIO
Here, sweet lord, at your service.

HAMLET
Horatio, thou art e'en as just a man
As e'er my conversation cop'd withal.

HORATIO
O, my dear lord—

HAMLET Nay, do not think I flatter;
For what advancement may I hope from thee
That no revenue hast but thy good spirits,
To feed and clothe thee? Why should the poor be flatter'd?
No, let the candied tongue lick absurd pomp,
And crook the pregnant hinges of the knee
Where thrift may follow fawning. Dost thou hear?
Since my dear soul was mistress of her choice
And could of men distinguish her election,
Sh' hath seal'd thee for herself, for thou hast been
As one, in suff'ring all, that suffers nothing,
A man that Fortune's buffets and rewards
Hast ta'en with equal thanks; and blest are those
Whose blood and judgment are so well commeddled
That they are not a pipe for Fortune's finger
To sound what stop she please. Give me that man
That is not passion's slave, and I will wear him
In my heart's core, ay, in my heart of heart,
As I do thee.—Something too much of this.—
There is a play tonight before the King.
One scene of it comes near the circumstance
Which I have told thee of my father's death.
I prithee, when thou seest that act afoot,
Even with the very comment of thy soul
Observe my uncle. If his occulted guilt
Do not itself unkennel in one speech,
It is a damned ghost that we have seen,
And my imaginations are as foul
As Vulcan's stithy. Give him heedful note,
For I mine eyes will rivet to his face,
And after we will both our judgments join
In censure of his seeming.

HORATIO Well, my lord.
If 'a steal aught the whilst this play is playing,
And scape detecting, I will pay the theft.

[Flourish.] Enter trumpets and kettledrums, King, Queen, Polonius, Ophelia, [Rosencrantz, Guildenstern, and other Lords, with Guards carrying torches].

HAMLET They are coming to the play. I must be idle. Get you a place. *[The King, Queen, and courtiers sit.]*

KING How fares our cousin Hamlet?

HAMLET Excellent, i' faith, of the chameleon's dish: I eat the air, promise-cramm'd. You cannot feed capons so.

KING I have nothing with this answer, Hamlet. These words are not mine.

HAMLET No, nor mine now. *[To Polonius.]* My lord, you played once i' th' university, you say?

POLONIUS That did I, my lord; and was accounted a good actor.

HAMLET What did you enact?

POLONIUS I did enact Julius Caesar. I was killed i' th' Capitol; Brutus kill'd me.

HAMLET It was a brute part of him to kill so capital a calf there. Be the players ready?

ROSENCRANTZ Ay, my lord; they stay upon your patience.

QUEEN Come hither, my dear Hamlet, sit by me.

HAMLET No, good mother, here's metal more attractive.

POLONIUS *[To the King]* O, ho, do you mark that?

HAMLET Lady, shall I lie in your lap?
[Lying down at Ophelia's feet.]

OPHELIA No, my lord.

[HAMLET I mean, my head upon your lap?

OPHELIA Ay, my lord.]

HAMLET Do you think I meant country matters?

OPHELIA I think nothing, my lord.

HAMLET That's a fair thought to lie between maids' legs.

OPHELIA What is, my lord?

33 journeymen laborers not yet masters in their trade **36 indifferently** tolerably **40 of them** i.e., some among them **41 barren** i.e., of wit **48 presently** at once **54 my . . . withal** my contact with people provided opportunity for encounter with **59 candied** sugared, flattering **60 pregnant** compliant **61 thrift** profit **68 blood** passion. **commeddled** commingled **70 stop** hole in a wind instrument for controlling the sound

78 very . . . soul i.e., inward and sagacious criticism **79 occulted** hidden **81 damned** in league with Satan **83 stithy** smithy, place of stiths (anvils) **86 censure of his seeming** judgment of his appearance or behavior **92 chameleon's dish** (Chameleons were supposed to feed on air. Hamlet deliberately misinterprets the King's *fares* as *feeds*. By his phrase *eat the air* he also plays on the idea of feeding himself with the promise of succession, of being the *heir*.) **94 have . . . with** make nothing of **95 are not mine** do not respond to what I asked **114 country** (with a bawdy pun)

HAMLET Nothing.

OPHELIA You are merry, my lord.

HAMLET Who, I?

OPHELIA Ay, my lord.

HAMLET O God, your only jig-maker. What should a man do but be merry? For look you how cheerfully my mother looks, and my father died within 's two hours.

OPHELIA Nay, 'tis twice two months, my lord.

HAMLET So long? Nay then, let the devil wear black, for I'll have a suit of sables. O heavens! Die two months ago, and not forgotten yet? Then there's hope a great man's memory may outlive his life half a year. But, by 'r lady, 'a must build churches, then, or else shall 'a suffer not thinking on, with the hobby-horse, whose epitaph is "For, O, for, O, the hobby-horse is forgot."

The trumpets sound. Dumb show follows.

Enter a King and a Queen [very lovingly]; the Queen embracing him, and he her. [She kneels, and makes show of protestation unto him.] He takes her up, and declines his head upon her neck. He lies him down upon a bank of flowers. She, seeing him asleep, leaves him. Anon comes in another man, takes off his crown, kisses it, pours poison in the sleeper's ears, and leaves him. The Queen returns; finds the King dead, makes passionate action. The Poisoner, with some three or four come in again, seem to condole with her. The dead body is carried away. The Poisoner woos the Queen with gifts; she seems harsh awhile, but in the end accepts love.

[*Exeunt.*]

OPHELIA What means this, my lord?

HAMLET Marry, this' miching mallecho; it means mischief.

OPHELIA Belike this show imports the argument of the play.

Enter Prologue.

HAMLET We shall know by this fellow. The players cannot keep counsel; they'll tell all.

OPHELIA Will 'a tell us what this show meant?

HAMLET Ay, or any show that you will show him. Be not you asham'd to show, he'll not shame to tell you what it means.

OPHELIA You are naught, you are naught. I'll mark the play.

PROLOGUE

For us, and for our tragedy,
Here stooping to your clemency,
We beg your hearing patiently. [*Exit.*]

HAMLET Is this a prologue, or the posy of a ring?

OPHELIA 'Tis brief, my lord.

HAMLET As woman's love.

Enter [two Players as] King and Queen.

PLAYER KING

Full thirty times hath Phoebus' cart gone round
Neptune's salt wash and Tellus' orbed ground,
And thirty dozen moons with borrowed sheen
About the world have times twelve thirties been,
Since love our hearts and Hymen did our hands
Unite commutual in most sacred bands.

PLAYER QUEEN

So many journeys may the sun and moon
Make us again count o'er ere love be done!
But, woe is me, you are so sick of late,
So far from cheer and from your former state,
That I distrust you. Yet, though I distrust,
Discomfort you, my lord, it nothing must.
For women's fear and love hold quantity;
In neither aught, or in extremity.
Now, what my love is, proof hath made you know,
And as my love is siz'd, my fear is so.
Where love is great, the littlest doubts are fear;
Where little fears grow great, great love grows there.

PLAYER KING

Faith, I must leave thee, love, and shortly too;
My operant powers their functions leave to do.
And thou shalt live in this fair world behind,
Honor'd, belov'd; and haply one as kind
For husband shalt thou—

PLAYER QUEEN O, confound the rest!
Such love must needs be treason in my breast.
In second husband let me be accurst!
None wed the second but who kill'd the first.

HAMLET Wormwood, wormwood.

PLAYER QUEEN

The instances that second marriage move
Are base respects of thrift, but none of love.
A second time I kill my husband dead,
When second husband kisses me in bed.

PLAYER KING

I do believe you think what now you speak,
But what we do determine oft we break.
Purpose is but the slave to memory,
Of violent birth, but poor validity,
Which now, like fruit unripe, sticks on the tree,
But fall unshaken when they mellow be.
Most necessary 'tis that we forget
To pay ourselves what to ourselves is debt.
What to ourselves in passion we propose,
The passion ending, doth the purpose lose.
The violence of either grief or joy

123 only jig-maker very best composer of jigs (song and dance) **125 within 's** within this **128 suit of sables** garments trimmed with the fur of the sable, and hence suited for a wealthy person, not a mourner (with a pun on *sable*, black) **132 suffer . . . on** undergo oblivion **133 "For . . . forgot"** (Verse of a song occurring also in *Love's Labor's Lost*, III.i.30. The hobby-horse was a character made up to resemble a horse, appearing in the Morris Dance and such May-game sports. This song laments the disappearance of such customs under pressure from the Puritans.) **135 this' miching mallecho** this is sneaking mischief **137 Belike** probably. **argument** plot **140 counsel** secret **142–143 Be not you** if you are not **145 naught** indecent **148 stooping** bowing **150 posy . . . ring** brief motto in verse inscribed in a ring

153 Phoebus' cart the sun god's chariot **154 salt wash** the sea. **Tellus** goddess of the earth, of the *orbed ground* **155 borrowed** i.e., reflected **157 Hymen** god of matrimony **158 commutual** mutually **163 distrust** am anxious about **164 nothing** not at all **165 hold quantity** keep proportion with one another **167 proof** experience **172 operant** active. **leave to do** cease to perform **180 instances** motives. **move** motivate **181 base . . . thrift** ignoble considerations of material prosperity **186 Purpose . . . memory** i.e., our good intentions are subject to forgetfulness **187 validity** strength, durability **190–191 Most . . . debt** i.e., it's inevitable that in time we forget the obligations we have imposed on ourselves

Their own enactures with themselves destroy.
Where joy most revels, grief doth most lament;
Grief joys, joy grieves, on slender accident.
This world is not for aye, nor 'tis not strange
That even our loves should with our fortunes change;
For 'tis a question left us yet to prove,
Whether love lead fortune, or else fortune love.
The great man down, you mark his favorite flies;
The poor advanc'd makes friends of enemies.
And hitherto doth love on fortune tend;
For who not needs shall never lack a friend,
And who in want a hollow friend doth try,
Directly seasons him his enemy.
But, orderly to end where I begun,
Our wills and fates do so contrary run
That our devices still are overthrown;
Our thoughts are ours, their ends none of our own.
So think thou wilt no second husband wed,
But die thy thoughts when thy first lord is dead.

PLAYER QUEEN
Nor earth to me give food, nor heaven light,
Sport and repose lock from me day and night,
To desperation turn my trust and hope,
An anchor's cheer in prison be my scope!
Each opposite that blanks the face of joy
Meet what I would have well and it destroy!
Both here and hence pursue me lasting strife,
If, once a widow, ever I be wife!

HAMLET If she should break it now!

PLAYER KING
'Tis deeply sworn. Sweet, leave me here awhile;
My spirits grow dull, and fain I would beguile
The tedious day with sleep. [*Sleeps.*]

PLAYER QUEEN Sleep rock thy brain,
And never come mischance between us twain! *Exit.*

HAMLET Madam, how like you this play?

QUEEN The lady doth protest too much, methinks.

HAMLET O, but she'll keep her word.

KING Have you heard the argument? Is there no offense in 't?

HAMLET No, no, they do but jest, poison in jest; no offense i' th' world.

KING What do you call the play?

HAMLET "The Mouse-trap." Marry, how? Tropically. This play is the image of a murder done in Vienna. Gonzago is the Duke's name; his wife, Baptista. You shall see anon. 'Tis a knavish piece of work, but what of that? Your Majesty, and we that have free souls, it touches us not. Let the gall'd jade winch, our withers are unwrung.

Enter Lucianus.

This is one Lucianus, nephew to the King.

OPHELIA You are as good as a chorus, my lord.

HAMLET I could interpret between you and your love, if I could see the puppets dallying.

OPHELIA You are keen, my lord, you are keen.

HAMLET It would cost you a groaning to take off mine edge.

OPHELIA Still better, and worse.

HAMLET So you mistake your husbands. Begin, murderer; leave thy damnable faces, and begin. Come, the croaking raven doth bellow for revenge.

LUCIANUS
Thoughts black, hands apt, drugs fit, and time agreeing,
Confederate season, else no creature seeing,
Thou mixture rank, of midnight weeds collected,
With Hecate's ban thrice blasted, thrice infected,
Thy natural magic and dire property
On wholesome life usurp immediately.
[*Pours the poison into the sleeper's ears.*]

HAMLET 'A poisons him i' th' garden for his estate. His name's Gonzago. The story is extant, and written in very choice Italian. You shall see anon how the murderer gets the love of Gonzago's wife.
[*Claudius rises.*]

OPHELIA The King rises.

[HAMLET What, frighted with false fire?]

QUEEN How fares my lord?

POLONIUS Give o'er the play.

KING Give me some light. Away!

POLONIUS Lights, lights, lights!
Exeunt all but Hamlet and Horatio.

HAMLET
"Why, let the strucken deer go weep,
The hart ungalled play.
For some must watch, while some must sleep;
Thus runs the world away."
Would not this, sir, and a forest of feathers—if the rest of my fortunes turn Turk with me—with two Provincial roses on my raz'd shoes, get me a fellowship in a cry of players?

HORATIO Half a share.

HAMLET A whole one, I.
"For thou dost know, O Damon dear,
This realm dismantled was
Of Jove himself, and now reigns here
A very, very—pajock."

195 enactures fulfillments **198 aye** ever **205 who not needs** he who is not in need (of wealth) **206 who in want** he who is in need. **try** test (his generosity) **207 seasons him** ripens him into **210 devices still** intentions continually **211 ends** results **217 anchor's cheer** anchorite's or hermit's fare. **my scope** the extent of my happiness **218 opposite** adverse thing. **blanks** causes to blanch or grow pale **220 hence** in the life hereafter **230 argument** plot **235 Tropically** figuratively. (The Q1 reading, *trapically,* suggests a pun on *trap* in *Mouse-trap.*) **239 free** guiltless **240 gall'd jade** horse whose hide is rubbed by saddle or harness. **winch** wince. **withers** the part between the horse's shoulder blades **241 unwrung** not rubbed sore

243 chorus (In many Elizabethan plays the forthcoming action was explained by an actor known as the "chorus"; at a puppet show the actor who spoke the dialogue was known as an "interpreter," as indicated by the lines following.) **245 dallying** (With sexual suggestion, continued in *keen,* i.e., sexually aroused, *groaning,* i.e., moaning in pregnancy, and *edge,* i.e., sexual desire or impetuosity.) **249 Still . . . worse** more keen-witted and less decorous **250 So** even thus (in marriage). **mistake** mis-take, take erringly, falseheartedly **254 Confederate season** the time and occasion conspiring (to assist the murderer) **256 Hecate's ban** the curse of Hecate, the goddess of witchcraft **264 false fire** the blank discharge of a gun loaded with powder but no shot **269–272 Why . . . away** (Probably from an old ballad, with allusion to the popular belief that a wounded deer retires to weep and die; cf. *As You Like It,* II.i.66.) **270 ungalled** unafflicted **271 watch** remain awake **273 this** i.e., the play. **feathers** (Allusion to the plumes which Elizabethan actors were fond of wearing.) **274 turn Turk with** turn renegade against, go back on **274–275 Provincial roses** rosettes of ribbon like the roses of a part of France **275 raz'd** with ornamental slashing **275–276 fellowship . . . players** partnership in a theatrical company **280 dismantled** stripped, divested **282 pajock** peacock, a bird with a bad reputation. (Here substituted for the obvious rhyme-word *ass.*)

HORATIO You might have rhym'd.

HAMLET O good Horatio, I'll take the ghost's word for a thousand pound. Didst perceive?

HORATIO Very well, my lord.

HAMLET Upon the talk of the pois'ning?

HORATIO I did very well note him.

HAMLET Ah, ha! Come, some music! Come, the recorders!

"For if the King like not the comedy,
Why then, belike, he likes it not, perdy."

Come, some music!

Enter Rosencrantz and Guildenstern.

GUILDENSTERN Good my lord, vouchsafe me a word with you.

HAMLET Sir, a whole history.

GUILDENSTERN The King, sir—

HAMLET Ay, sir, what of him?

GUILDENSTERN Is in his retirement marvelous distemp'red.

HAMLET With drink, sir?

GUILDENSTERN No, my lord, with choler.

HAMLET Your wisdom should show itself more richer to signify this to the doctor, for for me to put him to his purgation would perhaps plunge him into more choler.

GUILDENSTERN Good my lord, put your discourse into some frame and start not so wildly from my affair.

HAMLET I am tame, sir. Pronounce.

GUILDENSTERN The Queen, your mother, in most great affliction of spirit, hath sent me to you.

HAMLET You are welcome.

GUILDENSTERN Nay, good my lord, this courtesy is not of the right breed. If it shall please you to make me a wholesome answer, I will do your mother's commandment; if not, your pardon and my return shall be the end of my business.

HAMLET Sir, I cannot.

ROSENCRANTZ What, my lord?

HAMLET Make you a wholesome answer; my wit's diseas'd. But, sir, such answer as I can make, you shall command, or rather, as you say, my mother. Therefore no more, but to the matter. My mother, you say—

ROSENCRANTZ Then thus she says: your behavior hath struck her into amazement and admiration.

HAMLET O wonderful son, that can so stonish a mother! But is there no sequel at the heels of this mother's admiration? Impart.

ROSENCRANTZ She desires to speak with you in her closet, ere you go to bed.

HAMLET We shall obey, were she ten times our mother. Have you any further trade with us?

ROSENCRANTZ My lord, you once did love me.

HAMLET And do still, by these pickers and stealers.

ROSENCRANTZ Good my lord, what is your cause of distemper? You do surely bar the door upon your own liberty, if you deny your griefs to your friend.

HAMLET Sir, I lack advancement.

ROSENCRANTZ How can that be, when you have the voice of the King himself for your succession in Denmark?

HAMLET Ay, sir, but "While the grass grows"—the proverb is something musty.

Enter the Players with recorders.

O, the recorders! Let me see one. [*He takes a recorder.*] To withdraw with you: why do you go about to recover the wind of me, as if you would drive me into a toil?

GUILDENSTERN O, my lord, if my duty be too bold, my love is too unmannerly.

HAMLET I do not well understand that. Will you play upon this pipe?

GUILDENSTERN My lord, I cannot.

HAMLET I pray you.

GUILDENSTERN Believe me, I cannot.

HAMLET I do beseech you.

GUILDENSTERN I know no touch of it, my lord.

HAMLET It is as easy as lying. Govern these ventages with your fingers and thumb, give it breath with your mouth, and it will discourse most eloquent music. Look you, these are the stops.

GUILDENSTERN But these cannot I command to any utt'rance of harmony; I have not the skill.

HAMLET Why, look you now, how unworthy a thing you make of me! You would play upon me, you would seem to know my stops, you would pluck out the heart of my mystery, you would sound me from my lowest note to the top of my compass, and there is much music, excellent voice, in this little organ, yet cannot you make it speak. 'Sblood, do you think I am easier to be play'd on than a pipe? Call me what instrument you will, though you can fret me, you cannot play upon me.

Enter Polonius.

God bless you, sir!

POLONIUS My lord, the Queen would speak with you, and presently.

HAMLET Do you see yonder cloud that's almost in shape of a camel?

POLONIUS By th' mass, and 'tis like a camel, indeed.

HAMLET Methinks it is like a weasel.

POLONIUS It is back'd like a weasel.

HAMLET Or like a whale?

POLONIUS Very like a whale.

HAMLET Then I will come to my mother by and by. [*Aside.*] They fool me to the top of my bent.—I will come by and by.

289–290 recorders wind instruments of the flute kind **292 perdy** (A corruption of the French *par dieu,* "by God.") **302 choler** i.e., anger. (But Hamlet takes the word in its more basic humors sense of *bilious disorder.*) **308 frame** order **316 pardon** permission to depart **325 admiration** wonder **330 closet** private chamber **334 pickers and stealers** i.e., hands. (So called from the catechism, "to keep my hands from picking and stealing.")

342 "While . . . grows" (The rest of the proverb is "the silly horse starves"; Hamlet may not live long enough to succeed to the kingdom.) **343 something** somewhat **345 withdraw** speak privately **345–346 recover the wind** get to the windward side **346 toil** snare **347–348 if . . . unmannerly** if I am using an unmannerly boldness, it is my love which occasions it **356 ventages** stops of the recorder **366 compass** range (of voice) **367 organ** musical instrument **370 fret** irritate (with a quibble on *fret* meaning the piece of wood, gut, or metal which regulates the fingering on an instrument) **374 presently** at once **382 by and by** immediately **383 fool me** make me play the fool. **top of my bent** limit of my ability or endurance. (Literally, the extent to which a bow may be bent.)

POLONIUS I will say so. *[Exit.]*
HAMLET "By and by" is easily said. Leave me, friends.
[Exeunt all but Hamlet.]
'Tis now the very witching time of night, 387
When churchyards yawn and hell itself breathes out
Contagion to this world. Now could I drink hot blood,
And do such bitter business as the day
Would quake to look on. Soft, now to my mother.
O heart, lose not thy nature! Let not ever
The soul of Nero enter this firm bosom. 393
Let me be cruel, not unnatural;
I will speak daggers to her, but use none.
My tongue and soul in this be hypocrites:
How in my words somever she be shent, 397
To give them seals never, my soul, consent! *Exit.* 398

[SCENE III]

Enter King, Rosencrantz, and Guildenstern.

KING
I like him not, nor stands it safe with us
To let his madness range. Therefore prepare you.
I your commission will forthwith dispatch, 3
And he to England shall along with you.
The terms of our estate may not endure 5
Hazard so near 's as doth hourly grow
Out of his brows.
GUILDENSTERN We will ourselves provide. 7
Most holy and religious fear it is
To keep those many many bodies safe
That live and feed upon your Majesty.
ROSENCRANTZ
The single and peculiar life is bound 11
With all the strength and armor of the mind
To keep itself from noyance, but much more 13
That spirit upon whose weal depends and rests
The lives of many. The cess of majesty 15
Dies not alone, but like a gulf doth draw 16
What's near it with it; or it is a massy wheel
Fix'd on the summit of the highest mount,
To whose huge spokes ten thousand lesser things
Are mortis'd and adjoin'd, which, when it falls,
Each small annexment, petty consequence,
Attends the boist'rous ruin. Never alone 22
Did the King sigh, but with a general groan.
KING
Arm you, I pray you, to this speedy voyage, 24
For we will fetters put about this fear,
Which now goes too free-footed.
ROSENCRANTZ We will haste us.
Exeunt Gentlemen [Rosencrantz and Guildenstern].

Enter Polonius.

POLONIUS
My lord, he's going to his mother's closet.
Behind the arras I'll convey myself 28
To hear the process. I'll warrant she'll tax him home, 29
And, as you said, and wisely was it said,
'Tis meet that some more audience than a mother,
Since nature makes them partial, should o'erhear
The speech, of vantage. Fare you well, my liege. 33
I'll call upon you ere you go to bed,
And tell you what I know.
KING Thanks, dear my lord.
Exit [Polonius].
O, my offense is rank, it smells to heaven;
It hath the primal eldest curse upon 't, 37
A brother's murder. Pray can I not,
Though inclination be as sharp as will. 39
My stronger guilt defeats my strong intent,
And, like a man to double business bound,
I stand in pause where I shall first begin,
And both neglect. What if this cursed hand
Were thicker than itself with brother's blood,
Is there not rain enough in the sweet heavens
To wash it white as snow? Whereto serves mercy 46
But to confront the visage of offense? 47
And what's in prayer but this twofold force,
To be forestalled ere we come to fall, 49
Or pardon'd being down? Then I'll look up;
My fault is past. But, O, what form of prayer
Can serve my turn? "Forgive me my foul murder"?
That cannot be, since I am still possess'd
Of those effects for which I did the murder,
My crown, mine own ambition, and my queen.
May one be pardon'd and retain th' offense?
In the corrupted currents of this world 57
Offense's gilded hand may shove by justice, 58
And oft 'tis seen the wicked prize itself 59
Buys out the law. But 'tis not so above.
There is no shuffling, there the action lies 61
In his true nature, and we ourselves compell'd, 62
Even to the teeth and forehead of our faults, 63
To give in evidence. What then? What rests? 64
Try what repentance can. What can it not?
Yet what can it, when one cannot repent?
O wretched state! O bosom black as death!
O limed soul, that, struggling to be free, 68
Art more engag'd! Help, angels! Make assay. 69
Bow, stubborn knees, and heart with strings of steel,

387 witching time time when spells are cast and evil is abroad **393 Nero** murderer of his mother, Agrippina **397 How . . . somever** however much by my words. **shent** rebuked **398 give them seals** confirm them with deeds

III.iii. Location: The castle.
3 dispatch prepare, cause to be drawn up **5 terms** condition, circumstances. **our estate** my royal position **7 brows** i.e., effronteries, threatening frowns (?) brain (?) **11 single and peculiar** individual and private **13 noyance** harm **15 cess** decease **16 gulf** whirlpool **22 Attends** participates in **24 Arm** prepare

28 arras screen of tapestry placed around the walls of household apartments. (On the Elizabethan stage, the arras was presumably over a door or discovery space in the tiring house façade.) **29 process** proceedings. **tax him home** reprove him severely **33 of vantage** from an advantageous place **37 primal eldest curse** the curse of Cain, the first murderer; he killed his brother Abel **39 Though . . . will** though my desire is as strong as my determination **46–47 Whereto . . . offense** i.e., for what function does mercy serve other than to undo the effects of sin **49 forestalled** prevented (from sinning) **57 currents** courses **58 gilded hand** hand offering gold as a bribe **59 wicked prize** prize won by wickedness **61 shuffling** escape by trickery. **the action lies** the accusation is made manifest, comes up for consideration. (A legal metaphor.) **62 his** its **63 teeth and forehead** face to face, concealing nothing **64 rests** remains **68 limed** caught as with birdlime, a sticky substance used to ensnare birds **69 engag'd** embedded. **assay** trial

Be soft as sinews of the new-born babe!
All may be well.
[*He kneels.*]

Enter Hamlet [*with sword drawn*].

HAMLET
Now might I do it pat, now 'a is a-praying;
And now I'll do 't. And so 'a goes to heaven;
And so am I reveng'd. That would be scann'd:
A villain kills my father, and for that,
I, his sole son, do this same villain send
To heaven.
Why, this is hire and salary, not revenge.
'A took my father grossly, full of bread,
With all his crimes broad blown, as flush as May;
And how his audit stands who knows save heaven?
But in our circumstance and course of thought,
'Tis heavy with him. And am I then reveng'd,
To take him in the purging of his soul,
When he is fit and season'd for his passage?
No!
Up, sword, and know thou a more horrid hent.
[*Puts up his sword.*]
When he is drunk asleep, or in his rage,
Or in th' incestuous pleasure of his bed,
At game a-swearing, or about some act
That has no relish of salvation in 't—
Then trip him, that his heels may kick at heaven,
And that his soul may be as damn'd and black
As hell, whereto it goes. My mother stays.
This physic but prolongs thy sickly days. *Exit.*

KING
My words fly up, my thoughts remain below.
Words without thoughts never to heaven go. *Exit.*

[SCENE IV]

Enter [*Queen*] *Gertrude and Polonius.*

POLONIUS
'A will come straight. Look you lay home to him.
Tell him his pranks have been too broad to bear with,
And that your Grace hath screen'd and stood between
Much heat and him. I'll sconce me even here.
Pray you, be round [with him.

HAMLET *(Within)* Mother, mother, mother!]

QUEEN
I'll warrant you, fear me not.
Withdraw, I hear him coming.
[*Polonius hides behind the arras.*]

Enter Hamlet.

HAMLET
Now, mother, what's the matter?

QUEEN
Hamlet, thou hast thy father much offended.

HAMLET
Mother, you have my father much offended.

QUEEN
Come, come, you answer with an idle tongue.

HAMLET
Go, go, you question with a wicked tongue.

QUEEN
Why, how now, Hamlet?

HAMLET What's the matter now?

QUEEN
Have you forgot me?

HAMLET No, by the rood, not so:
You are the Queen, your husband's brother's wife,
And—would it were not so!—you are my mother.

QUEEN
Nay, then, I'll set those to you that can speak.

HAMLET
Come, come, and sit you down; you shall not budge.
You go not till I set you up a glass
Where you may see the inmost part of you.

QUEEN
What wilt thou do? Thou wilt not murder me?
Help, ho!

POLONIUS [*Behind*] What, ho! Help!

HAMLET [*Drawing*]
How now? A rat? Dead, for a ducat, dead!
[*Makes a pass through the arras.*]

POLONIUS [*Behind*]
O, I am slain! [*Falls and dies.*]

QUEEN O me, what hast thou done?

HAMLET
Nay, I know not. Is it the King?

QUEEN
O, what a rash and bloody deed is this!

HAMLET
A bloody deed—almost as bad, good mother,
As kill a king, and marry with his brother.

QUEEN
As kill a king!

HAMLET Ay, lady, it was my word.
[*Parts the arras and discovers Polonius.*]
Thou wretched, rash, intruding fool, farewell!
I took thee for thy better. Take thy fortune.
Thou find'st to be too busy is some danger.—
Leave wringing of your hands. Peace, sit you down,
And let me wring your heart, for so I shall,
If it be made of penetrable stuff,

73 pat opportunely **75 would be scann'd** needs to be looked into **80 grossly** i.e., not spiritually prepared. **full of bread** i.e., enjoying his worldly pleasures. (See Ezekiel 16:49.) **81 crimes broad blown** sins in full bloom. **flush** lusty **82 audit** account **83 in . . . course** as we see it in our mortal situation **88 know . . . hent** await to be grasped by me on a more horrid occasion **96 physic** purging (by prayer)

III.iv. Location: The Queen's private chamber.
1 lay thrust. (I.e., reprove him soundly.) **2 broad** unrestrained **4 Much heat** i.e., the King's anger. **sconce** ensconce, hide **5 round** blunt

10 thy father i.e., your step-father, Claudius **12 idle** foolish **15 rood** cross

If damned custom have not braz'd it so
That it be proof and bulwark against sense.

QUEEN
What have I done, that thou dar'st wag thy tongue
In noise so rude against me?

HAMLET
Such an art
That blurs the grace and blush of modesty,
Calls virtue hypocrite, takes off the rose
From the fair forehead of an innocent love
And sets a blister there, makes marriage-vows
As false as dicers' oaths. O, such a deed
As from the body of contraction plucks
The very soul, and sweet religion makes
A rhapsody of words. Heaven's face does glow
O'er this solidity and compound mass
With heated visage, as against the doom,
Is thought-sick at the act.

QUEEN
Ay me, what act,
That roars so loud and thunders in the index?

HAMLET
Look here, upon this picture, and on this,
The counterfeit presentment of two brothers.
[*Shows her two likenesses.*]
See, what a grace was seated on this brow:
Hyperion's curls, the front of Jove himself,
An eye like Mars, to threaten and command,
A station like the herald Mercury
New-lighted on a heaven-kissing hill—
A combination and a form indeed,
Where every god did seem to set his seal,
To give the world assurance of a man.
This was your husband. Look you now, what follows:
Here is your husband, like a mildew'd ear,
Blasting his wholesome brother. Have you eyes?
Could you on this fair mountain leave to feed,
And batten on this moor? Ha, have you eyes?
You cannot call it love, for at your age
The heyday in the blood is tame, it's humble,
And waits upon the judgment, and what judgment
Would step from this to this? Sense, sure, you have,
Else could you not have motion, but sure that sense
Is apoplex'd, for madness would not err,
Nor sense to ecstasy was ne'er so thrall'd
But it reserv'd some quantity of choice
To serve in such a difference. What devil was 't
That thus hath cozen'd you at hoodman-blind?
Eyes without feeling, feeling without sight,
Ears without hands or eyes, smelling sans all,
Or but a sickly part of one true sense
Could not so mope.
O shame, where is thy blush? Rebellious hell,
If thou canst mutine in a matron's bones,
To flaming youth let virtue be as wax,
And melt in her own fire. Proclaim no shame
When the compulsive ardor gives the charge,
Since frost itself as actively doth burn,
And reason panders will.

QUEEN
O Hamlet, speak no more!
Thou turn'st mine eyes into my very soul,
And there I see such black and grained spots
As will not leave their tinct.

HAMLET
Nay, but to live
In the rank sweat of an enseamed bed,
Stew'd in corruption, honeying and making love
Over the nasty sty—

QUEEN
O, speak to me no more!
These words, like daggers, enter in my ears.
No more, sweet Hamlet!

HAMLET
A murderer and a villain,
A slave that is not twentieth part the tithe
Of your precedent lord, a vice of kings,
A cutpurse of the empire and the rule,
That from a shelf the precious diadem stole,
And put it in his pocket!

QUEEN
No more!

Enter Ghost [*in his nightgown*].

HAMLET
A king of shreds and patches—
Save me, and hover o'er me with your wings,
You heavenly guards! What would your gracious figure?

QUEEN
Alas, he's mad!

HAMLET
Do you not come your tardy son to chide,
That, laps'd in time and passion, lets go by
Th' important acting of your dread command?
O, say!

GHOST
Do not forget. This visitation
Is but to whet thy almost blunted purpose.
But, look, amazement on thy mother sits.
O, step between her and her fighting soul!
Conceit in weakest bodies strongest works.
Speak to her, Hamlet.

HAMLET
How is it with you, lady?

38 damned custom habitual wickedness. **braz'd** brazened, hardened **39 proof** armor. **sense** feeling **45 sets a blister** i.e., brands as a harlot **47 contraction** the marriage contract **48 religion** i.e., religious vows **49 rhapsody** senseless string **49–52 Heaven's . . . act** heaven's face flushes with anger to look down upon this solid world, this compound mass, with hot face as though the day of doom were near, and is thought-sick at the deed (i.e., Gertrude's marriage) **53 index** table of contents, prelude or preface **55 counterfeit presentment** portrayed representation **57 Hyperion's** the sun god's. **front** brow **59 station** manner of standing **65 ear** i.e., of grain **68 batten** gorge. **moor** barren upland **70 heyday** state of excitement **72 Sense** perception through the five senses (the functions of the middle or sensible soul) **74 apoplex'd** paralyzed. (Hamlet goes on to explain that without such a paralysis of will, mere madness would not so err, nor would the five senses so enthrall themselves to *ecstasy* or lunacy; even such deranged states of mind would be able to make the obvious choice between Hamlet Senior and Claudius.) **78 cozen'd** cheated. **hoodman-blind** blindman's buff **80 sans** without

82 mope be dazed, act aimlessly **84 mutine** mutiny **86–89 Proclaim . . . will** call it no shameful business when the compelling ardor of youth delivers the attack, i.e., commits lechery, since the frost of advanced age burns with as active a fire of lust and reason perverts itself by fomenting lust rather than restraining it **92 grained** dyed in grain, indelible **93 tinct** color **94 enseamed** laden with grease **100 tithe** tenth part **101 precedent** former (i.e., the elder Hamlet). **vice** buffoon. (A reference to the Vice of the morality plays.) **106 shreds and patches** i.e., motley, the traditional costume of the clown or fool **111 laps'd in time and passion** having allowed time to lapse and passion to cool **112 important** importunate, urgent **116 amazement** distraction **118 Conceit** imagination

QUEEN
Alas, how is 't with you,
That you do bend your eye on vacancy,
And with th' incorporal air do hold discourse?
Forth at your eyes your spirits wildly peep,
And, as the sleeping soldiers in th' alarm,
Your bedded hair, like life in excrements,
Start up and stand an end. O gentle son,
Upon the heat and flame of thy distemper
Sprinkle cool patience. Whereon do you look?

HAMLET
On him, on him! Look you how pale he glares!
His form and cause conjoin'd, preaching to stones,
Would make them capable.—Do not look upon me,
Lest with this piteous action you convert
My stern effects. Then what I have to do
Will want true color—tears perchance for blood.

QUEEN
To whom do you speak this?

HAMLET
Do you see nothing there?

QUEEN
Nothing at all; yet all that is I see.

HAMLET
Nor did you nothing hear?

QUEEN
No, nothing but ourselves.

HAMLET
Why, look you there, look how it steals away!
My father, in his habit as he lived!
Look, where he goes, even now, out at the portal!
Exit Ghost.

QUEEN
This is the very coinage of your brain.
This bodiless creation ecstasy
Is very cunning in.

HAMLET
Ecstasy?
My pulse, as yours, doth temperately keep time,
And makes as healthful music. It is not madness
That I have utt'red. Bring me to the test,
And I the matter will reword, which madness
Would gambol from. Mother, for love of grace,
Lay not that flattering unction to your soul
That not your trespass but my madness speaks.
It will but skin and film the ulcerous place,
Whiles rank corruption, mining all within,
Infects unseen. Confess yourself to heaven,
Repent what's past, avoid what is to come,
And do not spread the compost on the weeds
To make them ranker. Forgive me this my virtue;
For in the fatness of these pursy times
Virtue itself of vice must pardon beg,
Yea, curb and woo for leave to do him good.

122 incorporal immaterial **125 bedded** laid in smooth layers. **excrements** outgrowths **126 an** on **130 His . . . conjoin'd** his appearance joined to his cause for speaking **131 capable** receptive **132–133 convert . . . effects** divert me from my stern duty **134 want true color** lack plausibility so that (with a play on the normal sense of *color*) I shall shed tears instead of blood **141 habit** dress **144 ecstasy** madness **151 gambol** skip away **152 unction** ointment **155 mining** working under the surface **158 compost** manure **159 this my virtue** my virtuous talk in reproving you **160 fatness** grossness. **pursy** short-winded, corpulent **162 curb** bow, bend the knee. **leave** permission

QUEEN
O Hamlet, thou hast cleft my heart in twain.

HAMLET
O, throw away the worser part of it,
And live the purer with the other half.
Good night. But go not to my uncle's bed;
Assume a virtue, if you have it not.
That monster, custom, who all sense doth eat,
Of habits devil, is angel yet in this,
That to the use of actions fair and good
He likewise gives a frock or livery
That aptly is put on. Refrain tonight,
And that shall lend a kind of easiness
To the next abstinence; the next more easy;
For use almost can change the stamp of nature,
And either . . . the devil, or throw him out
With wondrous potency. Once more, good night;
And when you are desirous to be bless'd,
I'll blessing beg of you. For this same lord,
[*Pointing to Polonius.*]
I do repent; but heaven hath pleas'd it so
To punish me with this, and this with me,
That I must be their scourge and minister.
I will bestow him, and will answer well
The death I gave him. So, again, good night.
I must be cruel only to be kind.
Thus bad begins and worse remains behind.
One word more, good lady.

QUEEN
What shall I do?

HAMLET
Not this, by no means, that I bid you do:
Let the bloat king tempt you again to bed,
Pinch wanton on your cheek, call you his mouse,
And let him, for a pair of reechy kisses,
Or paddling in your neck with his damn'd fingers,
Make you to ravel all this matter out,
That I essentially am not in madness,
But mad in craft. 'Twere good you let him know,
For who that's but a queen, fair, sober, wise,
Would from a paddock, from a bat, a gib,
Such dear concernings hide? Who would do so?
No, in despite of sense and secrecy,
Unpeg the basket on the house's top,
Let the birds fly, and, like the famous ape,
To try conclusions, in the basket creep
And break your own neck down.

QUEEN
Be thou assur'd, if words be made of breath,
And breath of life, I have no life to breathe
What thou hast said to me.

168 who . . . eat who consumes all proper or natural feeling **169 Of habits devil** devil-like in prompting evil habits **171 livery** an outer appearance, a customary garb (and hence a predisposition easily assumed in time of stress) **175 use** habit **176 And either** (A defective line usually emended by inserting the word *master* after *either,* following Q4 and early editors.) **178 be bless'd** become blessed, i.e., repentant **182 their scourge and minister** i.e., agent of heavenly retribution. (By *scourge,* Hamlet also suggests that he himself will eventually suffer punishment in the process of fulfilling heaven's will.) **183 bestow** stow, dispose of **186 behind** to come **189 bloat** bloated **191 reechy** dirty, filthy **195 good** (Said ironically; also the following 8 lines.) **197 paddock** toad. **gib** tomcat **198 dear concernings** important affairs **200 Unpeg the basket** open the cage, i.e., let out the secret **201 famous ape** (in a story now lost) **202 conclusions** experiments (in which the ape apparently enters a cage from which birds have been released and then tries to fly out of the cage as they have done, falling to his death)

HAMLET
I must to England; you know that?
QUEEN
Alack,
I had forgot. 'Tis so concluded on.
HAMLET
There's letters seal'd, and my two schoolfellows,
Whom I will trust as I will adders fang'd,
They bear the mandate; they must sweep my way, 211
And marshal me to knavery. Let it work.
For 'tis the sport to have the enginer 213
Hoist with his own petar, and 't shall go hard 214
But I will delve one yard below their mines, 215
And blow them at the moon. O, 'tis most sweet,
When in one line two crafts directly meet. 217
This man shall set me packing. 218
I'll lug the guts into the neighbor room.
Mother, good night indeed. This counselor
Is now most still, most secret, and most grave,
Who was in life a foolish prating knave.
Come, sir, to draw toward an end with you. 223
Good night, mother.
Exeunt [severally, Hamlet dragging in Polonius].

[ACT IV • SCENE I]

Enter King and Queen, with Rosencrantz and Guildenstern.

KING
There's matter in these sighs, these profound heaves.
You must translate; 'tis fit we understand them.
Where is your son?
QUEEN
Bestow this place on us a little while.
[Exeunt Rosencrantz and Guildenstern.]
Ah, mine own lord, what have I seen tonight!
KING
What, Gertrude? How does Hamlet?
QUEEN
Mad as the sea and wind, when both contend
Which is the mightier. In his lawless fit,
Behind the arras hearing something stir,
Whips out his rapier, cries, "A rat, a rat!"
And, in this brainish apprehension, kills 11
The unseen good old man.
KING
O heavy deed!
It had been so with us, had we been there.
His liberty is full of threats to all—
To you yourself, to us, to everyone.
Alas, how shall this bloody deed be answer'd?
It will be laid to us, whose providence 17
Should have kept short, restrain'd, and out of haunt 18
This mad young man. But so much was our love
We would not understand what was most fit,
But, like the owner of a foul disease,
To keep it from divulging, let it feed 22
Even on the pith of life. Where is he gone?
QUEEN
To draw apart the body he hath kill'd,
O'er whom his very madness, like some ore 25
Among a mineral of metals base, 26
Shows itself pure: 'a weeps for what is done.
KING
O Gertrude, come away!
The sun no sooner shall the mountains touch
But we will ship him hence; and this vile deed
We must, with all our majesty and skill,
Both countenance and excuse. Ho, Guildenstern!

Enter Rosencrantz and Guildenstern.

Friends both, go join you with some further aid.
Hamlet in madness hath Polonius slain,
And from his mother's closet hath he dragg'd him.
Go seek him out; speak fair, and bring the body
Into the chapel. I pray you, haste in this.
[Exeunt Rosencrantz and Guildenstern.]
Come, Gertrude, we'll call up our wisest friends
And let them know both what we mean to do
And what's untimely done 40
Whose whisper o'er the world's diameter, 41
As level as the cannon to his blank, 42
Transports his pois'ned shot, may miss our name,
And hit the woundless air. O, come away! 44
My soul is full of discord and dismay. *Exeunt.*

[SCENE II]

Enter Hamlet.

HAMLET Safely stow'd.
[ROSENCRANTZ, GUILDENSTERN *(Within)* Hamlet! Lord Hamlet!]
HAMLET But soft, what noise? Who calls on Hamlet? O, here they come.

Enter Rosencrantz and Guildenstern.

ROSENCRANTZ
What have you done, my lord, with the dead body?
HAMLET
Compounded it with dust, whereto 'tis kin.
ROSENCRANTZ
Tell us where 'tis, that we may take it thence
And bear it to the chapel.

211 sweep my way go before me **213 enginer** constructor of military contrivances **214 Hoist with** blown up by. **petar** petard, an explosive used to blow in a door or make a breach **215 mines** tunnels used in warfare to undermine the enemy's emplacements; Hamlet will countermine by going under their mines **217 crafts** acts of guile, plots **218 set me packing** set me to making schemes, and set me to lugging (him), and, also, send me off in a hurry **223 draw . . . end** finish up (with a pun on *draw,* pull)

IV.i. Location: The castle.
11 brainish apprehension headstrong conception

17 providence foresight **18 short** i.e., on a short tether. **out of haunt** secluded **22 divulging** becoming evident **25 ore** vein of gold **26 mineral** mine **40 And . . . done** (A defective line; conjectures as to the missing words include *so, haply, slander* [Capell and others]; *for, haply, slander* [Theobald and others.]) **41 diameter** extent from side to side **42 As level** with as direct aim. **blank** white spot in the center of a target **44 woundless** invulnerable

IV.ii. Location: The castle.

HAMLET Do not believe it.
ROSENCRANTZ Believe what?
HAMLET That I can keep your counsel and not mine
own. Besides, to be demanded of a sponge, what rep- 13
lication should be made by the son of a king? 14
ROSENCRANTZ Take you me for a sponge, my lord?
HAMLET Ay, sir, that soaks up the King's countenance, 16
his rewards, his authorities. But such officers do the
King best service in the end. He keeps them, like an
ape an apple, in the corner of his jaw, first mouth'd,
to be last swallow'd. When he needs what you have
glean'd, it is but squeezing you, and, sponge, you
shall be dry again.
ROSENCRANTZ I understand you not, my lord.
HAMLET I am glad of it. A knavish speech sleeps in a 24
foolish ear.
ROSENCRANTZ My lord, you must tell us where the
body is, and go with us to the King.
HAMLET The body is with the King, but the King is not 28
with the body. The King is a thing— 29
GUILDENSTERN A thing, my lord?
HAMLET Of nothing. Bring me to him. [Hide fox, and 31
all after.] *Exeunt.* 32

[SCENE III]

Enter King, and two or three.

KING
I have sent to seek him, and to find the body.
How dangerous is it that this man goes loose!
Yet must not we put the strong law on him.
He's lov'd of the distracted multitude, 4
Who like not in their judgment, but their eyes,
And where 'tis so, th' offender's scourge is weigh'd, 6
But never the offense. To bear all smooth and even, 7
This sudden sending him away must seem
Deliberate pause. Diseases desperate grown 9
By desperate appliance are reliev'd,
Or not at all.

Enter Rosencrantz, [Guildenstern,] and all the rest.

How now, what hath befall'n?
ROSENCRANTZ
Where the dead body is bestow'd, my lord,
We cannot get from him.
KING But where is he?
ROSENCRANTZ
Without, my lord; guarded, to know your pleasure.
KING
Bring him before us.
ROSENCRANTZ Ho! Bring in the lord.

They enter [with Hamlet].

KING
Now, Hamlet, where's Polonius?
HAMLET At supper.
KING
At supper? Where?
HAMLET Not where he eats, but where 'a is eaten. A
certain convocation of politic worms are e'en at him. 20
Your worm is your only emperor for diet. We fat all 21
creatures else to fat us, and we fat ourselves for mag-
gots. Your fat king and your lean beggar is but
variable service, two dishes, but to one table—that's 24
the end.
KING
Alas, alas!
HAMLET A man may fish with the worm that hath eat 27
of a king, and eat of the fish that hath fed of that
worm.
KING
What dost thou mean by this?
HAMLET Nothing but to show you how a king may go
a progress through the guts of a beggar. 32
KING
Where is Polonius?
HAMLET In heaven. Send thither to see. If your messenger find him not there, seek him i' th' other place yourself. But if indeed you find him not within this month, you shall nose him as you go up the stairs into the lobby.
KING [*To some Attendants*]
Go seek him there.
HAMLET 'A will stay till you come.
[*Exeunt Attendants.*]
KING
Hamlet, this deed, for thine especial safety—
Which we do tender, as we dearly grieve 42
For that which thou hast done—must send thee hence
[With fiery quickness]. Therefore prepare thyself.
The bark is ready, and the wind at help, 45
Th' associates tend, and everything is bent 46
For England.
HAMLET For England!
KING
Ay, Hamlet.
HAMLET Good.
KING
So is it, if thou knew'st our purposes.

13 demanded of questioned by **13–14 replication** reply **16 countenance** favor **24 sleeps in** has no meaning to **28–29 The . . . body** (Perhaps alludes to the legal commonplace of "the king's two bodies," which drew a distinction between the sacred office of kingship and the particular mortal who possessed it at any given time.) **31 Of nothing** of no account **31–32 Hide . . . after** (An old signal cry in the game of hide-and-seek, suggesting that Hamlet now runs away from them.)

IV.iii. Location: The castle.
4 distracted fickle, unstable **6 scourge** punishment. **weigh'd** taken into consideration **7 bear** manage **9 Deliberate pause** carefully considered action

20 politic worms crafty worms (suited to a master spy like Polonius) **21 diet** food, eating (with perhaps a punning reference to the Diet of Worms, a famous *convocation* held in 1521) **24 variable service** different courses of a single meal **27 eat** eaten. (Pronounced *et.*) **32 progress** royal journey of state **42 tender** regard, hold dear. **dearly** intensely **45 bark** sailing vessel **46 tend** wait. **bent** in readiness

HAMLET I see a cherub that sees them. But, come, for
England! Farewell, dear mother.

KING
Thy loving father, Hamlet.

HAMLET My mother. Father and mother is man and
wife, man and wife is one flesh, and so, my mother.
Come, for England! *Exit.*

KING
Follow him at foot; tempt him with speed aboard.
Delay it not; I'll have him hence tonight.
Away! For everything is seal'd and done
That else leans on th' affair. Pray you, make haste.
[*Exeunt all but the King.*]
And, England, if my love thou hold'st at aught—
As my great power thereof may give thee sense,
Since yet thy cicatrice looks raw and red
After the Danish sword, and thy free awe
Pays homage to us—thou mayst not coldly set
Our sovereign process, which imports at full,
By letters congruing to that effect,
The present death of Hamlet. Do it, England,
For like the hectic in my blood he rages,
And thou must cure me. Till I know 'tis done,
Howe'er my haps, my joys were ne'er begun. *Exit.*

[SCENE IV]

Enter Fortinbras with his Army over the stage.

FORTINBRAS
Go, captain, from me greet the Danish king.
Tell him that, by his license, Fortinbras
Craves the conveyance of a promis'd march
Over his kingdom. You know the rendezvous.
If that his Majesty would aught with us,
We shall express our duty in his eye;
And let him know so.

CAPTAIN I will do 't, my lord.

FORTINBRAS
Go softly on. [*Exeunt all but Captain.*]

Enter Hamlet, Rosencrantz, [Guildenstern,] etc.

HAMLET
Good sir, whose powers are these?

CAPTAIN
They are of Norway, sir.

HAMLET
How purpos'd, sir, I pray you?

CAPTAIN
Against some part of Poland.

HAMLET
Who commands them, sir?

CAPTAIN
The nephew to old Norway, Fortinbras.

HAMLET
Goes it against the main of Poland, sir,
Or for some frontier?

CAPTAIN
Truly to speak, and with no addition,
We go to gain a little patch of ground
That hath in it no profit but the name.
To pay five ducats, five, I would not farm it;
Nor will it yield to Norway or the Pole
A ranker rate, should it be sold in fee.

HAMLET
Why, then the Polack never will defend it.

CAPTAIN
Yes, it is already garrison'd.

HAMLET
Two thousand souls and twenty thousand ducats
Will not debate the question of this straw.
This is th' imposthume of much wealth and peace,
That inward breaks, and shows no cause without
Why the man dies. I humbly thank you, sir.

CAPTAIN
God buy you, sir. [*Exit.*]

ROSENCRANTZ Will 't please you go, my lord?

HAMLET
I'll be with you straight. Go a little before.
[*Exeunt all except Hamlet.*]
How all occasions do inform against me,
And spur my dull revenge! What is a man,
If his chief good and market of his time
Be but to sleep and feed? A beast, no more.
Sure he that made us with such large discourse,
Looking before and after, gave us not
That capability and god-like reason
To fust in us unus'd. Now, whether it be
Bestial oblivion, or some craven scruple
Of thinking too precisely on th' event—
A thought which, quarter'd, hath but one part
wisdom
And ever three parts coward—I do not know
Why yet I live to say "This thing's to do,"
Sith I have cause and will and strength and means
To do 't. Examples gross as earth exhort me:
Witness this army of such mass and charge
Led by a delicate and tender prince,
Whose spirit with divine ambition puff'd
Makes mouths at the invisible event,
Exposing what is mortal and unsure
To all that fortune, death, and danger dare,
Even for an egg-shell. Rightly to be great
Is not to stir without great argument,
But greatly to find quarrel in a straw
When honor's at the stake. How stand I then,

52 cherub (Cherubim are angels of knowledge.) **58 at foot** close behind, at heel **61 leans on** bears upon, is related to **62 England** i.e., King of England **64 cicatrice** scar **65 free awe** voluntary show of respect **66 set** esteem **67 process** command **68 congruing** agreeing **69 present** immediate **70 hectic** persistent fever **72 haps** fortunes

IV.iv. Location: The coast of Denmark.
2 license permission **3 conveyance** escort, convoy **6 eye** presence **8 softly** slowly **9 powers** forces

15 main main part **17 addition** exaggeration **20 To pay** i.e., for a yearly rental of. **farm it** take a lease of it **22 ranker** higher. **in fee** fee simple, outright **26 debate . . . straw** settle this trifling matter **27 imposthume** abscess **32 inform against** denounce, betray; take shape against **34 market of** profit of, compensation for **36 discourse** power of reasoning **39 fust** grow moldy **40 oblivion** forgetfulness **41 event** outcome **45 Sith** since **46 gross** obvious **47 charge** expense **50 Makes mouths** makes scornful faces

That have a father kill'd, a mother stain'd,
Excitements of my reason and my blood,
And let all sleep, while, to my shame, I see
The imminent death of twenty thousand men,
That, for a fantasy and trick of fame,
Go to their graves like beds, fight for a plot
Whereon the numbers cannot try the cause,
Which is not tomb enough and continent
To hide the slain? O, from this time forth,
My thoughts be bloody, or be nothing worth! *Exit.*

[SCENE V]

Enter Horatio, [Queen] Gertrude, and a Gentleman.

QUEEN
I will not speak with her.

GENTLEMAN
She is importunate, indeed distract.
Her mood will needs be pitied.

QUEEN
What would she have?

GENTLEMAN
She speaks much of her father, says she hears
There's tricks i' th' world, and hems, and beats her heart,
Spurns enviously at straws, speaks things in doubt
That carry but half sense. Her speech is nothing,
Yet the unshaped use of it doth move
The hearers to collection; they yawn at it,
And botch the words up fit to their own thoughts,
Which, as her winks and nods and gestures yield them,
Indeed would make one think there might be thought,
Though nothing sure, yet much unhappily.

HORATIO
'Twere good she were spoken with, for she may strew
Dangerous conjectures in ill-breeding minds.

QUEEN
Let her come in. *[Exit Gentleman.]*
[*Aside.*] To my sick soul, as sin's true nature is,
Each toy seems prologue to some great amiss.
So full of artless jealousy is guilt,
It spills itself in fearing to be spilt.

Enter Ophelia [distracted].

OPHELIA
Where is the beauteous majesty of Denmark?

QUEEN
How now, Ophelia?

OPHELIA *(She sings)*
"How should I your true love know
From another one?
By his cockle hat and staff,
And his sandal shoon."

QUEEN
Alas, sweet lady, what imports this song?

OPHELIA
Say you? Nay, pray you, mark.
"He is dead and gone, lady, *(Song.)*
He is dead and gone;
At his head a grass-green turf,
At his heels a stone."
O, ho!

QUEEN
Nay, but Ophelia—

OPHELIA
Pray you, mark.
[*Sings.*] "White his shroud as the mountain snow"—

Enter King.

QUEEN
Alas, look here, my lord.

OPHELIA
"Larded all with flowers; *(Song.)*
Which bewept to the ground did not go
With true-love showers."

KING
How do you, pretty lady?

OPHELIA Well, God 'ild you! They say the owl was a baker's daughter. Lord, we know what we are, but know not what we may be. God be at your table!

KING
Conceit upon her father.

OPHELIA Pray let's have no words of this; but when they ask you what it means, say you this:
"Tomorrow is Saint Valentine's day, *(Song.)*
All in the morning betime,
And I a maid at your window,
To be your Valentine.
Then up he rose, and donn'd his clo'es,
And dupp'd the chamber-door,
Let in the maid, that out a maid
Never departed more."

KING
Pretty Ophelia!

OPHELIA Indeed, la, without an oath, I'll make an end on 't:
[*Sings.*] "By Gis and by Saint Charity,
Alack, and fie for shame!
Young men will do 't, if they come to 't;

58 Excitements of promptings by **61 fantasy** fanciful caprice. **trick** trifle **62 plot** i.e., of ground **63 Whereon . . . cause** i.e., on which there is insufficient room for the soldiers needed to engage in a military contest **64 continent** receptacle, container

IV.v. Location: The castle.
5 tricks deceptions. **heart** i.e., breast **6 Spurns . . . straws** kicks spitefully, takes offense at trifles. **in doubt** obscurely **8 unshaped use** distracted manner **9 collection** inference, a guess at some sort of meaning. **yawn** wonder, grasp **10 botch** patch **11 yield** deliver, bring forth (her words) **12 thought** conjectured **15 ill-breeding** prone to suspect the worst **18 toy** trifle. **amiss** calamity **19–20 So . . . spilt** guilt is so full of suspicion that it unskillfully betrays itself in fearing betrayal

25 cockle hat hat with cockleshell stuck in it as a sign that the wearer had been a pilgrim to the shrine of St. James of Compostella in Spain **26 shoon** shoes **38 Larded** decorated **42 God 'ild** God yield or reward. **owl** (Refers to a legend about a baker's daughter who was turned into an owl for refusing Jesus bread.) **45 Conceit** brooding **48 Valentine's** (This song alludes to the belief that the first girl seen by a man on the morning of this day was his valentine or truelove.) **53 dupp'd** opened **59 Gis** Jesus

By Cock, they are to blame.
Quoth she, 'Before you tumbled me,
You promis'd me to wed.' "
He answers:
" 'So would I ha' done, by yonder sun,
An thou hadst not come to my bed.' "

KING
How long hath she been thus?

OPHELIA I hope all will be well. We must be patient, but I cannot choose but weep, to think they would lay him i' th' cold ground. My brother shall know of it; and so I thank you for your good counsel. Come, my coach! Good night, ladies; good night, sweet ladies; good night, good night.

[Exit.]

KING
Follow her close; give her good watch, I pray you.
[Exit Horatio.]
O, this is the poison of deep grief; it springs
All from her father's death—and now behold!
O Gertrude, Gertrude,
When sorrows come, they come not single spies,
But in battalions. First, her father slain;
Next, your son gone, and he most violent author
Of his own just remove; the people muddied,
Thick and unwholesome in their thoughts and whispers,
For good Polonius' death; and we have done but greenly,
In hugger-mugger to inter him; poor Ophelia
Divided from herself and her fair judgment,
Without the which we are pictures, or mere beasts;
Last, and as much containing as all these,
Her brother is in secret come from France,
Feeds on his wonder, keeps himself in clouds,
And wants not buzzers to infect his ear
With pestilent speeches of his father's death,
Wherein necessity, of matter beggar'd,
Will nothing stick our person to arraign
In ear and ear. O my dear Gertrude, this,
Like to a murd'ring-piece, in many places
Gives me superfluous death. *A noise within.*

[QUEEN
Alack, what noise is this?]

KING
Attend!
Where are my Switzers? Let them guard the door.

Enter a Messenger.

What is the matter?

MESSENGER Save yourself, my lord!
The ocean, overpeering of his list,
Eats not the flats with more impiteous haste
Than young Laertes, in a riotous head,
O'erbears your officers. The rabble call him lord,
And, as the world were now but to begin,
Antiquity forgot, custom not known,
The ratifiers and props of every word,
They cry, "Choose we! Laertes shall be king!"
Caps, hands, and tongues applaud it to the clouds,
"Laertes shall be king, Laertes king!" *A noise within.*

QUEEN
How cheerfully on the false trail they cry!
O, this is counter, you false Danish dogs!

Enter Laertes with others.

KING
The doors are broke.

LAERTES
Where is this King? Sirs, stand you all without.

ALL
No, let's come in.

LAERTES I pray you, give me leave.

ALL
We will, we will. *[They retire without the door.]*

LAERTES
I thank you. Keep the door. O thou vile king,
Give me my father!

QUEEN Calmly, good Laertes.
[She tries to hold him back.]

LAERTES
That drop of blood that's calm proclaims me bastard,
Cries cuckold to my father, brands the harlot
Even here, between the chaste unsmirched brow
Of my true mother.

KING What is the cause, Laertes,
That thy rebellion looks so giant-like?
Let him go, Gertrude. Do not fear our person.
There's such divinity doth hedge a king
That treason can but peep to what it would,
Acts little of his will. Tell me, Laertes,
Why thou art thus incens'd. Let him go, Gertrude.
Speak, man.

LAERTES Where is my father?

KING Dead.

QUEEN
But not by him.

KING Let him demand his fill.

LAERTES
How came he dead? I'll not be juggled with.
To hell, allegiance! Vows, to the blackest devil!
Conscience and grace, to the profoundest pit!
I dare damnation. To this point I stand,
That both the worlds I give to negligence,
Let come what comes, only I'll be reveng'd
Most throughly for my father.

62 Cock (A perversion of "God" in oaths.) **79 spies** scouts sent in advance of the main force **82 muddied** stirred up, confused **84 greenly** imprudently, foolishly **85 hugger-mugger** secret haste **90 in clouds** i.e., of suspicion and rumor **91 wants** lacks. **buzzers** gossipers, informers **93 of matter beggar'd** unprovided with facts **94–95 Will . . . ear** will not hesitate to accuse my (royal) person in everybody's ears **96 murd'ring-piece** cannon loaded so as to scatter its shot **100 Switzers** Swiss guards, mercenaries **102 overpeering of his list** overflowing its shore **103 flats** i.e., flatlands near shore. **impiteous** pitiless

104 head armed force **106 as** as if **108 ratifiers and props** (Refer to *antiquity* and *custom.*) **word** promise **113 counter** (A hunting term meaning to follow the trail in a direction opposite to that which the game has taken.) **125 fear our** fear for my **127 can . . . would** can only glance, as from afar off or through a barrier, at what it would intend **128 Acts . . . will** (but) performs little of what it intends **136 both . . . negligence** i.e., both this world and the next are of no consequence to me **138 throughly** thoroughly

KING
Who shall stay you?
LAERTES
My will, not all the world's. 139
And for my means, I'll husband them so well,
They shall go far with little.
KING
Good Laertes,
If you desire to know the certainty
Of your dear father, is 't writ in your revenge
That, swoopstake, you will draw both friend and
foe, 144
Winner and loser?
LAERTES
None but his enemies.
KING
Will you know them then?
LAERTES
To his good friends thus wide I'll ope my arms,
And, like the kind life-rend'ring pelican, 148
Repast them with my blood.
KING
Why, now you speak 149
Like a good child and a true gentleman.
That I am guiltless of your father's death,
And am most sensibly in grief for it, 152
It shall as level to your judgment 'pear 153
As day does to your eye.
A noise within: "Let her come in."
LAERTES
How now, what noise is that?

Enter Ophelia.

O heat, dry up my brains! Tears seven times salt
Burn out the sense and virtue of mine eye! 157
By heaven, thy madness shall be paid with weight 158
Till our scale turn the beam. O rose of May! 159
Dear maid, kind sister, sweet Ophelia!
O heavens, is 't possible a young maid's wits
Should be as mortal as an old man's life?
[Nature is fine in love, and, where 'tis fine, 163
It sends some precious instance of itself 164
After the thing it loves.] 165
OPHELIA
"They bore him barefac'd on the bier; *(Song.)*
[Hey non nonny, nonny, hey nonny,]
And in his grave rain'd many a tear"—
Fare you well, my dove!
LAERTES
Hadst thou thy wits, and didst persuade revenge, 170
It could not move thus.
OPHELIA
You must sing "A-down a-down,
And you call him a-down-a."
O, how the wheel becomes it! It is the false steward 174
that stole his master's daughter.

LAERTES This nothing's more than matter. 176
OPHELIA There's rosemary, that's for remembrance; 177
pray you, love, remember. And there is pansies, that's 178
for thoughts.
LAERTES A document in madness, thoughts and re- 180
membrance fitted.
OPHELIA There's fennel for you, and columbines. 182
There's rue for you, and here's some for me; we may 183
call it herb of grace o' Sundays. You may wear your
rue with a difference. There's a daisy. I would give 185
you some violets, but they wither'd all when my father 186
died. They say 'a made a good end—
[*Sings.*] "For bonny sweet Robin is all my joy."
LAERTES
Thought and afflictions, passion, hell itself, 189
She turns to favor and to prettiness. 190
OPHELIA
"And will 'a not come again? *(Song.)*
And will 'a not come again?
No, no, he is dead.
Go to thy death-bed,
He never will come again.

"His beard was as white as snow,
All flaxen was his poll. 197
He is gone, he is gone,
And we cast away moan.
God 'a' mercy on his soul!"
And of all Christians' souls, I pray god. God buy you.
[*Exit.*]
LAERTES
Do you see this, O God?
KING
Laertes, I must commune with your grief,
Or you deny me right. Go but apart,
Make choice of whom your wisest friends you will,
And they shall hear and judge 'twixt you and me.
If by direct or by collateral hand 207
They find us touch'd, we will our kingdom give, 208
Our crown, our life, and all that we call ours,
To you in satisfaction; but if not,
Be you content to lend your patience to us,
And we shall jointly labor with your soul
To give it due content.
LAERTES
Let this be so.
His means of death, his obscure funeral—
No trophy, sword, nor hatchment o'er his bones, 215
No noble rite nor formal ostentation— 216
Cry to be heard, as 'twere from heaven to earth,
That I must call 't in question.
KING
So you shall;

139 My will . . . world's i.e., I'll stop *(stay)* when my will is accomplished, not for anyone else's **144 swoopstake** (Literally, taking all stakes on the gambling table at once, i.e., indiscriminately; *draw* is also a gambling term.) **148 pelican** (Refers to the belief that the female pelican fed its young with its own blood.) **149 Repast** feed **152 sensibly** feelingly **153 level** plain **157 virtue** faculty, power **158 paid with weight** repaid, avenged equally or more **159 beam** crossbar of a balance **163 fine in** refined by **164 instance** token **165 After . . . loves** i.e., into the grave, along with Polonius **170 persuade** argue cogently for **174 wheel** spinning wheel as accompaniment to the song, or refrain. **false steward** (The story is unknown.)

176 This . . . matter this seeming nonsense is more meaningful than sane utterance **177 rosemary** (Used as a symbol of remembrance both at weddings and at funerals.) **178 pansies** (Emblems of love and courtship; perhaps from French *pensées*, thoughts.) **180 document** instruction, lesson **182 fennel** (Emblem of flattery.) **columbines** (Emblems of unchastity? or ingratitude?) **183 rue** (Emblem of repentance; when mingled with holy water, it was known as *herb of grace*.) **185 with a difference** (Suggests that Ophelia and the Queen have different causes of sorrow and repentance; perhaps with a play on *rue* in the sense of ruth, pity.) **daisy** (Emblem of dissembling, faithlessness.) **186 violets** (Emblems of faithfulness.) **189 Thought** melancholy **190 favor** grace **197 poll** head **207 collateral** indirect **208 us touch'd** me implicated **215 trophy** memorial. **hatchment** tablet displaying the armorial bearings of a deceased person **216 ostentation** ceremony

And where th' offense is, let the great axe fall.
I pray you, go with me. *Exeunt.*

[SCENE VI]

Enter Horatio and others.

HORATIO
What are they that would speak with me?

GENTLEMAN Seafaring men, sir. They say they have letters for you.

HORATIO
Let them come in. [*Exit Gentleman.*]
I do not know from what part of the world
I should be greeted, if not from lord Hamlet.

Enter Sailors.

FIRST SAILOR God bless you sir.

HORATIO
Let him bless thee too.

FIRST SAILOR 'A shall, sir, an 't please him. There's a letter for you, sir—it came from th' ambassador that was bound for England—if your name be Horatio, as I am let to know it is. [*Gives letter.*]

HORATIO [*Reads*] "Horatio, when thou shalt have overlook'd this, give these fellows some means to the King; they have letters for him. Ere we were two days old at sea, a pirate of very warlike appointment gave us chase. Finding ourselves too slow of sail, we put on a compell'd valor, and in the grapple I boarded them. On the instant they got clear of our ship, so I alone became their prisoner. They have dealt with me like thieves of mercy, but they knew what they did: I am to do a good turn for them. Let the King have the letters I have sent, and repair thou to me with as much speed as thou wouldest fly death. I have words to speak in thine ear will make thee dumb; yet are they much too light for the bore of the matter. These good fellows will bring thee where I am. Rosencrantz and Guildenstern hold their course for England. Of them I have much to tell thee. Farewell.
He that thou knowest thine, Hamlet."
Come, I will give you way for these your letters,
And do 't the speedier that you may direct me
To him from whom you brought them. *Exeunt.*

[SCENE VII]

Enter King and Laertes.

KING
Now must your conscience my acquittance seal,
And you must put me in your heart for friend,
Sith you have heard, and with a knowing ear,
That he which hath your noble father slain
Pursued my life.

LAERTES It well appears. But tell me
Why you proceeded not against these feats
So criminal and so capital in nature,
As by your safety, greatness, wisdom, all things else,
You mainly were stirr'd up.

KING O, for two special reasons,
Which may to you, perhaps, seem much unsinew'd,
But yet to me th' are strong. The Queen his mother
Lives almost by his looks, and for myself—
My virtue or my plague, be it either which—
She's so conjunctive to my life and soul
That, as the star moves not but in his sphere,
I could not but by her. The other motive,
Why to a public count I might not go,
Is the great love the general gender bear him,
Who, dipping all his faults in their affection,
Would, like the spring that turneth wood to stone,
Convert his gyves to graces, so that my arrows,
Too slightly timber'd for so loud a wind,
Would have reverted to my bow again
And not where I had aim'd them.

LAERTES
And so have I a noble father lost,
A sister driven into desp'rate terms,
Whose worth, if praises may go back again,
Stood challenger on mount of all the age
For her perfections. But my revenge will come.

KING
Break not your sleeps for that. You must not think
That we are made of stuff so flat and dull
That we can let our beard be shook with danger
And think it pastime. You shortly shall hear more.
I lov'd your father, and we love ourself;
And that, I hope, will teach you to imagine—

Enter a Messenger with letters.

[How now? What news?]

MESSENGER [Letters, my lord, from Hamlet:]
These to your Majesty, this to the Queen.
[*Gives letters.*]

KING
From Hamlet? Who brought them?

MESSENGER
Sailors, my lord, they say; I saw them not.
They were given me by Claudio. He receiv'd them
Of him that brought them.

KING Laertes, you shall hear them.
Leave us. [*Exit Messenger.*]
[*Reads.*] "High and mighty, you shall know I am set naked on your kingdom. Tomorrow shall I beg leave

IV.vi. Location: The castle.
14 means means of access **16 appointment** equipage **21 thieves of mercy** merciful thieves **26 bore** caliber, i.e., importance

IV.vii. Location: The castle.
1 my acquittance seal confirm or acknowledge my innocence

6 feats acts **7 capital** punishable by death **9 mainly** greatly **10 unsinew'd** weak **14 conjunctive** closely united **15 sphere** the hollow sphere in which, according to Ptolemaic astronomy, the planets were supposed to move **17 count** account, reckoning **18 general gender** common people **20 spring** i.e., a spring with such a concentration of lime that it coats a piece of wood with limestone, in effect gilding it **21 gyves** fetters (which, gilded by the people's praise, would look like badges of honor) **22 slightly timber'd** light. **loud** strong **26 terms** state, condition **27 go back** i.e., recall Ophelia's former virtues **28 on mount** set up on high **44 naked** destitute, unarmed, without following

to see your kingly eyes, when I shall, first asking your
pardon thereunto, recount the occasion of my sudden
and more strange return. Hamlet."
What should this mean? Are all the rest come back?
Or is it some abuse, and no such thing?

LAERTES
Know you the hand?

KING
'Tis Hamlet's character. "Naked!"
And in a postscript here, he says "alone."
Can you devise me?

LAERTES
I am lost in it, my lord. But let him come.
It warms the very sickness in my heart
That I shall live and tell him to his teeth,
"Thus didst thou."

KING
If it be so, Laertes—
As how should it be so? How otherwise?—
Will you be rul'd by me?

LAERTES
Ay, my lord,
So you will not o'errule me to a peace.

KING
To thine own peace. If he be now returned,
As checking at his voyage, and that he means
No more to undertake it, I will work him
To an exploit, now ripe in my device,
Under the which he shall not choose but fall;
And for his death no wind of blame shall breathe,
But even his mother shall uncharge the practice
And call it accident.

LAERTES
My lord, I will be rul'd,
The rather if you could devise it so
That I might be the organ.

KING
It falls right.
You have been talk'd of since your travel much,
And that in Hamlet's hearing, for a quality
Wherein, they say, you shine. Your sum of parts
Did not together pluck such envy from him
As did that one, and that, in my regard,
Of the unworthiest siege.

LAERTES
What part is that, my lord?

KING
A very riband in the cap of youth,
Yet needful too, for youth no less becomes
The light and careless livery that it wears
Than settled age his sables and his weeds,
Importing health and graveness. Two months since
Here was a gentleman of Normandy.
I have seen myself, and serv'd against, the French,
And they can well on horseback, but this gallant
Had witchcraft in 't; he grew unto his seat,
And to such wondrous doing brought his horse
As had he been incorps'd and demi-natur'd
With the brave beast. So far he topp'd my thought
That I, in forgery of shapes and tricks,
Come short of what he did.

LAERTES
A Norman was 't?

KING
A Norman.

LAERTES
Upon my life, Lamord.

KING
The very same.

LAERTES
I know him well. He is the brooch indeed
And gem of all the nation.

KING
He made confession of you,
And gave you such a masterly report
For art and exercise in your defense,
And for your rapier most especial,
That he cried out, 'twould be a sight indeed,
If one could match you. The scrimers of their nation,
He swore, had neither motion, guard, nor eye,
If you oppos'd them. Sir, this report of his
Did Hamlet so envenom with his envy
That he could nothing do but wish and beg
Your sudden coming o'er, to play with you.
Now, out of this—

LAERTES
What out of this, my lord?

KING
Laertes, was your father dear to you?
Or are you like the painting of a sorrow,
A face without a heart?

LAERTES
Why ask you this?

KING
Not that I think you did not love your father,
But that I know love is begun by time,
And that I see, in passages of proof,
Time qualifies the spark and fire of it.
There lives within the very flame of love
A kind of wick or snuff that will abate it,
And nothing is at a like goodness still,
For goodness, growing to a plurisy,
Dies in his own too much. That we would do,
We should do when we would; for this "would"
changes
And hath abatements and delays as many
As there are tongues, are hands, are accidents,
And then this "should" is like a spendthrift's sigh,
That hurts by easing. But, to the quick o' th' ulcer:
Hamlet comes back. What would you undertake
To show yourself your father's son in deed
More than in words?

LAERTES
To cut his throat i' th' church.

KING
No place, indeed, should murder sanctuarize;

46 pardon permission **49 abuse** deceit **50 character** handwriting **52 devise** explain to **57 As . . . otherwise** how can this (Hamlet's return) be true? Yet how otherwise than true (since we have the evidence of his letter) **59 So** provided that **61 checking at** i.e., turning aside from (like a falcon leaving the quarry to fly at a chance bird) **66 uncharge the practice** acquit the stratagem of being a plot **69 organ** agent, instrument **72 Your . . . parts** i.e., all your other virtues **75 unworthiest siege** least important rank **80 sables** rich robes furred with sable. **weeds** garments **81 Importing health** indicating prosperity **84 can well** are skilled **87 incorps'd and demi-natur'd** of one body and nearly of one nature (like the centaur)

88 topp'd surpassed **89 forgery** invention **93 brooch** ornament **95 confession** admission of superiority **100 scrimers** fencers **105 play** fence **111 begun by time** i.e., subject to change **112 passages of proof** actual instances **113 qualifies** weakens **115 snuff** the charred part of a candlewick **116 nothing . . . still** nothing remains at a constant level of perfection **117 plurisy** excess, plethora **118 in . . . much** of its own excess. **That** that which **120 abatements** diminutions **121 accidents** occurrences, incidents **122 spendthrift's sigh** (An allusion to the belief that each sigh cost the heart a drop of blood.) **123 hurts by easing** i.e., costs the heart blood even while it affords emotional relief **127 sanctuarize** protect from punishment. (Alludes to the right of sanctuary with which certain religious places were invested.)

Revenge should have no bounds. But, good Laertes,
Will you do this, keep close within your chamber. 129
Hamlet return'd shall know you are come home.
We'll put on those shall praise your excellence 131
And set a double varnish on the fame
The Frenchman gave you, bring you in fine
together, 133
And wager on your heads. He, being remiss, 134
Most generous, and free from all contriving, 135
Will not peruse the foils, so that, with ease,
Or with a little shuffling, you may choose
A sword unbated, and in a pass of practice 138
Requite him for your father.

LAERTES I will do 't.
And for that purpose I'll anoint my sword.
I bought an unction of a mountebank 141
So mortal that, but dip a knife in it,
Where it draws blood no cataplasm so rare, 143
Collected from all simples that have virtue 144
Under the moon, can save the thing from death
That is but scratch'd withal. I'll touch my point
With this contagion, that, if I gall him slightly, 147
It may be death.

KING Let's further think of this,
Weigh what convenience both of time and means
May fit us to our shape. If this should fail, 150
And that our drift look through our bad
performance, 151
'Twere better not assay'd. Therefore this project
Should have a back or second, that might hold
If this did blast in proof. Soft, let me see. 154
We'll make a solemn wager on your cunnings—
I ha 't!
When in your motion you are hot and dry—
As make your bouts more violent to that end— 158
And that he calls for drink, I'll have prepar'd him
A chalice for the nonce, whereon but sipping, 160
If he by chance escape your venom'd stuck, 161
Our purpose may hold there. [*A cry within.*] But
stay, what noise?

Enter Queen.

QUEEN
One woe doth tread upon another's heel,
So fast they follow. Your sister's drown'd, Laertes.

LAERTES
Drown'd! O, where?

QUEEN
There is a willow grows askant the brook, 166
That shows his hoar leaves in the glassy stream; 167
Therewith fantastic garlands did she make
Of crow-flowers, nettles, daisies, and long purples 169
That liberal shepherds give a grosser name, 170
But our cold maids do dead men's fingers call them. 171
There on the pendent boughs her crownet weeds 172
Clamb'ring to hang, an envious sliver broke, 173
When down her weedy trophies and herself 174
Fell in the weeping brook. Her clothes spread wide,
And mermaid-like awhile they bore her up,
Which time she chanted snatches of old lauds, 177
As one incapable of her own distress, 178
Or like a creature native and indued 179
Unto that element. But long it could not be
Till that her garments, heavy with their drink,
Pull'd the poor wretch from her melodious lay
To muddy death.

LAERTES Alas, then she is drown'd?

QUEEN
Drown'd, drown'd.

LAERTES
Too much of water hast thou, poor Ophelia,
And therefore I forbid my tears. But yet
It is our trick; nature her custom holds, 187
Let shame say what it will. [*He weeps.*] When these
are gone, 188
The woman will be out. Adieu, my lord. 189
I have a speech of fire, that fain would blaze,
But that this folly drowns it. *Exit.*

KING Let's follow, Gertrude.
How much I had to do to calm his rage!
Now fear I this will give it start again;
Therefore let's follow. *Exeunt.*

[ACT V • SCENE I]

Enter two Clowns [with spades, etc.]

FIRST CLOWN Is she to be buried in Christian burial when she willfully seeks her own salvation?

SECOND CLOWN I tell thee she is; therefore make her
grave straight. The crowner hath sat on her, and finds 4
it Christian burial.

FIRST CLOWN How can that be, unless she drown'd herself in her own defense?

SECOND CLOWN Why, 'tis found so.

FIRST CLOWN It must be "se offendendo"; it cannot be 9
else. For here lies the point: if I drown myself wittingly,
it argues an act, and an act hath three branches—it is
to act, to do, and to perform. Argal, she drown'd her- 12
self wittingly.

SECOND CLOWN Nay, but hear you, goodman delver—

FIRST CLOWN Give me leave. Here lies the water; good.
Here stands the man; good. If the man go to this wa-
ter, and drown himself, it is, will he, nill he, he goes, 17
mark you that. But if the water come to him and
drown him, he drowns not himself. Argal, he that is
not guilty of his own death shortens not his own life.

SECOND CLOWN But is this law?

129 Will you do this if you wish to do this **131 put on those** instigate those who **133 in fine** finally **134 remiss** negligently unsuspicious **135 generous** noble-minded **138 unbated** not blunted, having no button. **pass of practice** treacherous thrust **141 unction** ointment. **mountebank** quack doctor **143 cataplasm** plaster or poultice **144 simples** herbs **147 gall** graze, wound **150 shape** part we propose to act **151 drift . . . performance** i.e., intention be disclosed by our bungling **154 blast in proof** burst in the test (like a cannon) **158 As** i.e., and you should **160 nonce** occasion **161 stuck** thrust. (From *stoccado*, a fencing term.) **166 askant** aslant **167 hoar** white or grey **169 long purples** early purple orchids **170 liberal** free-spoken **171 cold** chaste

172 crownet made into a chaplet or coronet **173 envious sliver** malicious branch **174 weedy** i.e., of plants **177 lauds** hymns **178 incapable** lacking capacity to apprehend **179 indued** adapted by nature **187 It is our trick** i.e., weeping is our natural way (when sad) **188–189 When . . . out** when my tears are all shed, the woman in me will be expended, satisfied

V.i. Location: A churchyard.
s.d. Clowns rustics **4 straight** straightway, immediately. **crowner** coroner **9 se offendendo** (A comic mistake for *se defendendo*, term used in verdicts of justifiable homicide.) **12 Argal** (Corruption of *ergo*, therefore.) **17 will he** will he not

FIRST CLOWN Ay, marry, is 't—crowner's quest law. 22
SECOND CLOWN Will you ha' the truth on 't? If this had
not been a gentlewoman, she should have been bur-
ied out o' Christian burial.
FIRST CLOWN Why, there thou say'st. And the more 26
pity that great folk should have count'nance in this 27
world to drown or hang themselves, more than their
even-Christen. Come, my spade. There is no ancient 29
gentlemen but gard'ners, ditchers, and grave-makers.
They hold up Adam's profession.
SECOND CLOWN Was he a gentleman?
FIRST CLOWN 'A was the first that ever bore arms.
[SECOND CLOWN Why, he had none.
FIRST CLOWN What, art a heathen? How dost thou un-
derstand the Scripture? The Scripture says "Adam
digg'd." Could he dig without arms?] I'll put another
question to thee. If thou answerest me not to the pur-
pose, confess thyself— 39
SECOND CLOWN Go to.
FIRST CLOWN What is he that builds stronger than ei-
ther the mason, the shipwright, or the carpenter?
SECOND CLOWN The gallows-maker, for that frame out-
lives a thousand tenants.
FIRST CLOWN I like thy wit well, in good faith. The gal-
lows does well; but how does it well? It does well to
those that do ill. Now thou dost ill to say the gallows
is built stronger than the church. Argal, the gallows
may do well to thee. To 't again, come.
SECOND CLOWN "Who builds stronger than a mason, a
shipwright, or a carpenter?"
FIRST CLOWN Ay, tell me that, and unyoke. 52
SECOND CLOWN Marry, now I can tell.
FIRST CLOWN To 't.
SECOND CLOWN Mass, I cannot tell. 55

Enter Hamlet and Horatio [*at a distance*].

FIRST CLOWN Cudgel thy brains no more about it, for
your dull ass will not mend his pace with beating;
and, when you are ask'd this question next, say "a
grave-maker." The houses he makes lasts till dooms-
day. Go, get thee in, and fetch me a stoup of liquor. 60
[*Exit Second Clown. First Clown digs.*]
Song.
"In youth, when I did love, did love, 61
Methought it was very sweet,
To contract—O—the time for—a—my behove, 63
O, methought there—a—was nothing—a—
meet." 64
HAMLET Has this fellow no feeling of his business, that
a sings at grave-making?
HORATIO Custom hath made it in him a property of 67
easiness. 68
HAMLET 'Tis e'en so. The hand of little employment
hath the daintier sense. 70

FIRST CLOWN *Song.*
"But age, with his stealing steps,
Hath claw'd me in his clutch,
And hath shipped me into the land, 73
As if I had never been such."
[*Throws up a skull.*]
HAMLET That skull had a tongue in it, and could sing
once. How the knave jowls it to the ground, as if 76
'twere Cain's jaw-bone, that did the first murder! This
might be the pate of a politician, which this ass now 78
o'erreaches, one that would circumvent God, might 79
it not?
HORATIO It might, my lord.
HAMLET Or of a courtier, which could say "Good mor-
row, sweet lord! How dost thou, sweet lord?" This
might be my Lord Such-a-one, that prais'd my Lord
Such-a-one's horse when 'a meant to beg it, might
it not?
HORATIO Ay, my lord.
HAMLET Why, e'en so, and now my Lady Worm's,
chapless, and knock'd about the mazzard with a sex- 89
ton's spade. Here's fine revolution, an we had the trick 90
to see 't. Did these bones cost no more the breeding, 91
but to play at loggats with them? Mine ache to think 92
on 't.
FIRST CLOWN *Song.*
"A pick-axe, and a spade, a spade,
For and a shrouding sheet; 95
O, a pit of clay for to be made
For such a guest is meet."
[*Throws up another skull.*]
HAMLET There's another. Why may not that be the skull
of a lawyer? Where be his quiddities now, his quilli- 99
ties, his cases, his tenures, and his tricks? Why does 100
he suffer this mad knave now to knock him about the
sconce with a dirty shovel, and will not tell him of his 102
action of battery? Hum! This fellow might be in 's time
a great buyer of land, with his statutes, his recogni- 104
zances, his fines, his double vouchers, his recoveries. 105
[Is this the fine of his fines, and the recovery of his 106
recoveries,] to have his fine pate full of fine dirt? Will 107
his vouchers vouch him no more of his purchases, and
double [ones too], than the length and breadth of a
pair of indentures? The very conveyances of his lands 110
will scarcely lie in this box, and must th' inheritor 111
himself have no more, ha?
HORATIO Not a jot more, my lord.
HAMLET Is not parchment made of sheep-skins?
HORATIO Ay, my lord, and of calf-skins too.

22 quest inquest **26 there thou say'st** i.e., that's right **27 count'nance** privilege **29 even-Christen** fellow Christian **39 confess thyself** (The saying continues, "and be hanged.") **52 unyoke** i.e., after this great effort you may unharness the team of your wits **55 Mass** by the Mass **60 stoup** two-quart measure **61 In . . . love** (This and the two following stanzas, with nonsensical variations, are from a poem attributed to Lord Vaux and printed in *Tottel's Miscellany,* 1557. The *O* and *a* [for "ah"] seemingly are the grunts of the digger.) **63 To contract . . . behove** i.e., to make a betrothal agreement for my benefit (?) **64 meet** suitable, i.e., more suitable **67–68 property of easiness** i.e., something he can do easily and without thinking about it **70 daintier sense** more delicate sense of feeling

73 into the land i.e., toward my grave (?) (But note the lack of rhyme in *steps, land.*) **76 jowls** dashes **78 politician** schemer, plotter **79 o'erreaches** circumvents, gets the better of (with a quibble on the literal sense) **89 chapless** having no lower jaw. **mazzard** i.e., head. (Literally, a drinking vessel.) **90 revolution** change. **an** if **91 the breeding** in the breeding, raising **92 loggats** a game in which pieces of hard wood are thrown to lie as near as possible to a stake **95 For and** and moreover **99 quiddities** subtleties, quibbles. (From Latin *quid,* a thing.) **99–100 quillities** verbal niceties, subtle distinctions. (Variation of *quiddities.*) **100 tenures** the holding of a piece of property or office, or the conditions or period of such holding **102 sconce** head **104–105 statutes, recognizances** legal documents guaranteeing a debt by attaching land and property **105 fines, recoveries** ways of converting entailed estates into "fee simple" or freehold. **double** signed by two signatories. **vouchers** guarantees of the legality of a title to real estate **106–107 fine of his fines . . . fine pate . . . fine dirt** end of his legal maneuvers . . . elegant head . . . minutely sifted dirt **110 pair of indentures** legal document drawn up in duplicate on a single sheet and then cut apart on a zigzag line so that each pair was uniquely matched. (Hamlet may refer to two rows of teeth, or dentures.) **conveyances** deeds **111 this box** ie., the skull. **inheritor** possessor, owner

HAMLET They are sheep and calves which seek out assurance in that. I will speak to this fellow.—Whose grave's this, sirrah?

FIRST CLOWN Mine, sir.

[*Sings.*] "O, a pit of clay for to be made
[For such a guest is meet]."

HAMLET I think it be thine, indeed, for thou liest in 't.

FIRST CLOWN You lie out on 't, sir, and therefore 'tis not yours. For my part, I do not lie in 't, yet it is mine.

HAMLET Thou dost lie in 't, to be in 't and say it is thine. 'Tis for the dead, not for the quick; therefore thou liest.

FIRST CLOWN 'Tis a quick lie, sir; 'twill away again from me to you.

HAMLET What man dost thou dig it for?

FIRST CLOWN For no man, sir.

HAMLET What woman, then?

FIRST CLOWN For none, neither.

HAMLET Who is to be buried in 't?

FIRST CLOWN One that was a woman, sir, but, rest her soul, she's dead.

HAMLET How absolute the knave is! We must speak by the card, or equivocation will undo us. By the Lord, Horatio, this three years I have taken note of it: the age is grown so pick'd that the toe of the peasant comes so near the heel of the courtier, he galls his kibe. How long hast thou been grave-maker?

FIRST CLOWN Of all the days i' th' year, I came to 't that day that our last king Hamlet overcame Fortinbras.

HAMLET How long is that since?

FIRST CLOWN Cannot you tell that? Every fool can tell that. It was that very day that young Hamlet was born—he that is mad, and sent into England.

HAMLET Ay, marry, why was he sent into England?

FIRST CLOWN Why, because 'a was mad. 'A shall recover his wits there, or, if 'a do not, 'tis no great matter there.

HAMLET Why?

FIRST CLOWN 'Twill not be seen in him there. There the men are as mad as he.

HAMLET How came he mad?

FIRST CLOWN Very strangely, they say.

HAMLET How strangely?

FIRST CLOWN Faith, e'en with losing his wits.

HAMLET Upon what ground?

FIRST CLOWN Why, here in Denmark. I have been sexton here, man and boy, thirty years.

HAMLET How long will a man lie i' th' earth ere he rot?

FIRST CLOWN Faith, if 'a be not rotten before 'a die—as we have many pocky corses [now-a-days], that will scarce hold the laying in—'a will last you some eight year or nine year. A tanner will last you nine year.

HAMLET Why he more than another?

FIRST CLOWN Why, sir, his hide is so tann'd with his trade that 'a will keep out water a great while, and your water is a sore decayer of your whoreson dead body. [*Picks up a skull.*] Here's a skull now hath lain you i' th' earth three and twenty years.

HAMLET Whose was it?

FIRST CLOWN A whoreson mad fellow's it was. Whose do you think it was?

HAMLET Nay, I know not.

FIRST CLOWN A pestilence on him for a mad rogue! 'A pour'd a flagon of Rhenish on my head once. This same skull, sir, was Yorick's skull, the King's jester.

HAMLET This?

FIRST CLOWN E'en that.

HAMLET [Let me see.] [*Takes the skull.*] Alas, poor Yorick! I knew him, Horatio, a fellow of infinite jest, of most excellent fancy. He hath borne me on his back a thousand times; and now, how abhorr'd in my imagination it is! My gorge rises at it. Here hung those lips that I have kiss'd I know not how oft. Where be your gibes now? Your gambols, your songs, your flashes of merriment that were wont to set the table on a roar? Not one now, to mock your own grinning? Quite chap-fall'n? Now get you to my lady's chamber, and tell her, let her paint an inch thick, to this favor she must come; make her laugh at that. Prithee, Horatio, tell me one thing.

HORATIO What's that, my lord?

HAMLET Dost thou think Alexander look'd o' this fashion i' th' earth?

HORATIO E'en so.

HAMLET And smelt so? Pah! [*Puts down the skull.*]

HORATIO E'en so, my lord.

HAMLET To what base uses we may return, Horatio! Why may not imagination trace the noble dust of Alexander, till 'a find it stopping a bung-hole?

HORATIO 'Twere to consider too curiously, to consider so.

HAMLET No, faith, not a jot, but to follow him thither with modesty enough, and likelihood to lead it. [As thus]: Alexander died, Alexander was buried, Alexander returneth to dust; the dust is earth; of earth we make loam; and why of that loam, whereto he was converted, might they not stop a beer-barrel?

Imperious Caesar, dead and turn'd to clay,
Might stop a hole to keep the wind away.
O, that that earth which kept the world in awe
Should patch a wall t' expel the winter's flaw!

But soft, but soft awhile! Here comes the King,

Enter King, Queen, Laertes, and the Corse [*of Ophelia, in procession, with Priest, Lords, etc.*].

The Queen, the courtiers. Who is this they follow?
And with such maimed rites? This doth betoken
The corse they follow did with desp'rate hand
Fordo it own life. 'Twas of some estate.
Couch we awhile, and mark.

[*He and Horatio conceal themselves. Ophelia's body is taken to the grave.*]

116–117 assurance in that safety in legal parchments **118 sirrah** term of address to inferiors **126 quick** living **137 absolute** positive, decided **137–138 by the card** by the mariner's card on which the points of the compass were marked, i.e., with precision **138 equivocation** ambiguity in the use of terms **140 pick'd** refined, fastidious **141 galls his kibe** chafes the courtier's chilblain **165 pocky** rotten, diseased. (Literally, with the pox, or syphilis.)

172–173 lain you lain. (*You* is the ethical dative.) **179 Rhenish** Rhine wine **192 chap-fall'n** (1) lacking the lower jaw (2) dejected **193 favor** aspect, appearance **205 curiously** minutely **208 modesty** moderation **211 loam** clay mixture for brickmaking or other clay use **213 Imperious** imperial **216 flaw** gust of wind **221 Fordo it** destroy its. **estate** rank **222 Couch** hide, lurk

LAERTES
What ceremony else?

HAMLET [*To Horatio*]
That is Laertes, a very noble youth. Mark.

LAERTES
What ceremony else?

PRIEST
Her obsequies have been as far enlarg'd
As we have warranty. Her death was doubtful,
And, but that great command o'ersways the order,
She should in ground unsanctified been lodg'd
Till the last trumpet. For charitable prayers,
Shards, flints, and pebbles should be thrown on her.
Yet here she is allow'd her virgin crants,
Her maiden strewments, and the bringing home
Of bell and burial.

LAERTES
Must there no more be done?

PRIEST
No more be done.
We should profane the service of the dead
To sing a requiem and such rest to her
As to peace-parted souls.

LAERTES
Lay her i' th' earth,
And from her fair and unpolluted flesh
May violets spring! I tell thee, churlish priest,
A minist'ring angel shall my sister be
When thou liest howling.

HAMLET [*To Horatio*]
What, the fair Ophelia!

QUEEN [*Scattering flowers*]
Sweets to the sweet! Farewell.
I hop'd thou shouldst have been my Hamlet's wife.
I thought thy bride-bed to have deck'd, sweet maid,
And not have strew'd thy grave.

LAERTES
O, treble woe
Fall ten times treble on that cursed head
Whose wicked deed thy most ingenious sense
Depriv'd thee of! Hold off the earth awhile,
Till I have caught her once more in mine arms.
[*Leaps into the grave and embraces Ophelia.*]
Now pile your dust upon the quick and dead,
Till of this flat a mountain you have made
T' o'ertop old Pelion, or the skyish head
Of blue Olympus.

HAMLET [*Coming forward*]
What is he whose grief
Bears such an emphasis, whose phrase of sorrow
Conjures the wand'ring stars, and makes them stand
Like wonder-wounded hearers? This is I,
Hamlet the Dane.

LAERTES
The devil take thy soul!
[*Grappling with him.*]

HAMLET
Thou pray'st not well.
I prithee, take thy fingers from my throat;
For, though I am not splenitive and rash,
Yet have I in me something dangerous,
Which let thy wisdom fear. Hold off thy hand.

KING
Pluck them asunder.

QUEEN
Hamlet, Hamlet!

ALL
Gentlemen!

HORATIO
Good my lord, be quiet.
[*Hamlet and Horatio are parted.*]

HAMLET
Why, I will fight with him upon this theme
Until my eyelids will no longer wag.

QUEEN
O my son, what theme?

HAMLET
I lov'd Ophelia. Forty thousand brothers
Could not with all their quantity of love
Make up my sum. What wilt thou do for her?

KING
O, he is mad, Laertes.

QUEEN
For love of God, forbear him.

HAMLET
'Swounds, show me what thou't do.
Woo 't weep? Woo 't fight? Woo 't fast? Woo 't tear thyself?
Woo 't drink up eisel? Eat a crocodile?
I'll do 't. Dost thou come here to whine?
To outface me with leaping in her grave?
Be buried quick with her, and so will I.
And, if thou prate of mountains, let them throw
Millions of acres on us, till our ground,
Singeing his pate against the burning zone,
Make Ossa like a wart! Nay, an thou 'lt mouth,
I'll rant as well as thou.

QUEEN
This is mere madness,
And thus awhile the fit will work on him;
Anon, as patient as the female dove
When that her golden couplets are disclos'd,
His silence will sit drooping.

HAMLET
Hear you, sir.
What is the reason that you use me thus?
I lov'd you ever. But it is no matter.
Let Hercules himself do what he may,
The cat will mew, and dog will have his day.

KING
I pray thee, good Horatio, wait upon him.
Exit Hamlet and Horatio.
[*To Laertes.*] Strengthen your patience in our last night's speech;
We'll put the matter to the present push.—
Good Gertrude, set some watch over your son.—
This grave shall have a living monument.
An hour of quiet shortly shall we see;
Till then, in patience our proceeding be. *Exeunt.*

230 For in place of **231 Shards** broken bits of pottery **232 crants** garland **233 strewments** traditional strewing of flowers **233–234 bringing . . . burial** laying to rest of the body in consecrated ground, to the sound of the bell **240 violets** (See IV.v.186 and note.) **248 ingenious sense** mind endowed with finest qualities **253–254 Pelion, Olympus** mountains in the north of Thessaly; see also *Ossa*, below, at l. 283 **256 wand'ring stars** planets **258 the Dane** (This title normally signifies the King; see I.i.15 and note.) **261 splenitive** quick-tempered

274 'Swounds by His (Christ's) wounds **275 Woo't** wilt thou **276 eisel** vinegar **279 quick** alive **282 his pate** its head, i.e., top. **burning zone** sun's orbit **283 Ossa** another mountain in Thessaly. (In their war against the Olympian gods, the giants attempted to heap Ossa, Pelion, and Olympus on one another to scale heaven.) **mouth** i.e., rant **284 mere** utter **287 golden couplets** two baby pigeons, covered with yellow down. **disclos'd** hatched **291–292 Let . . . day** i.e., despite any blustering attempts at interference, every person will sooner or later do what he must do **294 in** i.e., by recalling **295 present push** immediate test **297 living** lasting; also refers (for Laertes' benefit) to the plot against Hamlet

[SCENE II]

Enter Hamlet and Horatio.

HAMLET
So much for this, sir; now shall you see the other. 1
You do remember all the circumstance?
HORATIO
Remember it, my lord!
HAMLET
Sir, in my heart there was a kind of fighting
That would not let me sleep. Methought I lay
Worse than the mutines in the bilboes. Rashly, 6
And prais'd be rashness for it—let us know, 7
Our indiscretion sometime serves us well
When our deep plots do pall, and that should
learn us 9
There's a divinity that shapes our ends,
Rough-hew them how we will—
HORATIO
That is most certain. 11
HAMLET
Up from my cabin,
My sea-gown scarf'd about me, in the dark
Grop'd I to find out them, had my desire,
Finger'd their packet, and in fine withdrew 15
To mine own room again, making so bold,
My fears forgetting manners, to unseal
Their grand commission; where I found, Horatio—
Ah, royal knavery!—an exact command,
Larded with many several sorts of reasons 20
Importing Denmark's health and England's too, 21
With, ho, such bugs and goblins in my life, 22
That, on the supervise, no leisure bated, 23
No, not to stay the grinding of the axe,
My head should be struck off.
HORATIO
Is 't possible?
HAMLET
Here's the commission; read it at more leisure.
[*Gives document.*]
But wilt thou hear now how I did proceed?
HORATIO
I beseech you.
HAMLET
Being thus benetted round with villainies,
Or I could make a prologue to my brains, 30
They had begun the play. I sat me down, 31
Devis'd a new commission, wrote it fair. 32
I once did hold it, as our statists do, 33
A baseness to write fair, and labor'd much 34
How to forget that learning, but, sir, now
It did me yeoman's service. Wilt thou know 36
Th' effect of what I wrote?
HORATIO
Ay, good my lord. 37
HAMLET
An earnest conjuration from the King,
As England was his faithful tributary,
As love between them like the palm might flourish,
As peace should still her wheaten garland wear 41
And stand a comma 'tween their amities, 42
And many such-like as's of great charge, 43
That, on the view and knowing of these contents,
Without debatement further, more or less,
He should those bearers put to sudden death,
Not shriving-time allow'd.
HORATIO
How was this seal'd? 47
HAMLET
Why, even in that was heaven ordinant. 48
I had my father's signet in my purse, 49
Which was the model of that Danish seal;
Folded the writ up in the form of th' other,
Subscrib'd it, gave 't th' impression, plac'd it safely, 52
The changeling never known. Now, the next day 53
Was our sea-fight; and what to this was sequent
Thou knowest already.
HORATIO
So Guildenstern and Rosencrantz go to 't.
HAMLET
[Why, man, they did make love to this
employment.]
They are not near my conscience. Their defeat
Does by their own insinuation grow. 59
'Tis dangerous when the baser nature comes
Between the pass and fell incensed points 61
Of mighty opposites.
HORATIO
Why, what a king is this!
HAMLET
Does it not, think thee, stand me now upon— 63
He that hath kill'd my king and whor'd my mother,
Popp'd in between th' election and my hopes, 65
Thrown out his angle for my proper life, 66
And with such coz'nage—is 't not perfect conscience 67
[To quit him with this arm? And is 't not to be
damn'd 68
To let this canker of our nature come 69
In further evil?
HORATIO
It must be shortly known to him from England
What is the issue of the business there.
HAMLET
It will be short. The interim is mine,
And a man's life 's no more than to say "One." 74
But I am very sorry, good Horatio,
That to Laertes I forgot myself,
For by the image of my cause I see
The portraiture of his. I'll court his favors.
But, sure, the bravery of his grief did put me 79

V.ii. Location: The castle.
1 see the other i.e., hear the other news **6 mutines** mutineers. **bilboes** shackles. **Rashly** on impulse. (This adverb goes with ll. 12ff.) **7 know** acknowledge **9 pall** fail. **learn** teach **11 Rough-hew** shape roughly **15 Finger'd** pilfered, pinched. **in fine** finally, in conclusion **20 Larded** enriched **21 Importing** relating to **22 bugs** bugbears, hobgoblins. **in my life** i.e., to be feared if I were allowed to live **23 supervise** reading. **leisure bated** delay allowed **30–31 Or . . . play** i.e., before I could consciously turn my brain to the matter, it had started working on a plan. (*Or* means *ere.*) **32 fair** in a clear hand **33 statists** statesmen **34 baseness** i.e., lower-class trait **36 yeoman's** i.e., substantial, workmanlike **37 effect** purport

41 wheaten garland (Symbolic of fruitful agriculture, of peace.) **42 comma** (Indicating continuity, link.) **43 as's** (1) the "whereases" of a formal document (2) asses. **charge** (1) import (2) burden **47 shriving-time** time for confession and absolution **48 ordinant** directing **49 signet** small seal **52 Subscrib'd** signed. **impression** i.e., with a wax seal **53 changeling** i.e., the substituted letter. (Literally, a fairy child substituted for a human one.) **59 insinuation** interference **61 pass** thrust. **fell** fierce **63 stand** become incumbent **65 election** (The Danish monarch was "elected" by a small number of high-ranking electors.) **66 angle** fishing line. **proper** very **67 coz'nage** trickery **68 quit** repay **69 canker** ulcer **74 a man's . . . "One"** i.e., to take a man's life requires no more than to count to one as one duels **79 bravery** bravado

Into a tow'ring passion.

HORATIO Peace, who comes here?]

Enter a Courtier [*Osric*].

OSRIC Your lordship is right welcome back to Denmark.

HAMLET I humbly thank you, sir. [*To Horatio.*] Dost know this water-fly?

HORATIO No, my good lord.

HAMLET Thy state is the more gracious, for 'tis a vice to know him. He hath much land, and fertile. Let a beast be lord of beasts, and his crib shall stand at the King's mess. 'Tis a chough, but, as I say, spacious in the possession of dirt.

OSRIC Sweet lord, if your lordship were at leisure, I should impart a thing to you from his Majesty.

HAMLET I will receive it, sir, with all diligence of spirit. Put your bonnet to his right use; 'tis for the head.

OSRIC I thank your lordship, it is very hot.

HAMLET No, believe me, 'tis very cold; the wind is northerly.

OSRIC It is indifferent cold, my lord, indeed.

HAMLET But yet methinks it is very sultry and hot for my complexion.

OSRIC Exceedingly, my lord; it is very sultry, as 'twere—I cannot tell how. My lord, his Majesty bade me signify to you that 'a has laid a great wager on your head. Sir, this is the matter—

HAMLET I beseech you, remember—

[*Hamlet moves him to put on his hat.*]

OSRIC Nay, good my lord; for my ease, in good faith. Sir, here is newly come to court Laertes—believe me, an absolute gentleman, full of most excellent differences, of very soft society and great showing. Indeed, to speak feelingly of him, he is the card or calendar of gentry, for you shall find in him the continent of what part a gentleman would see.

HAMLET Sir, his definement suffers no perdition in you, though, I know, to divide him inventorially would dozy th' arithmetic of memory, and yet but yaw neither in respect of his quick sail. But, in the verity of extolment, I take him to be a soul of great article, and his infusion of such dearth and rareness, as, to make true diction of him, his semblable is his mirror, and who else would trace him, his umbrage, nothing more.

OSRIC Your lordship speaks most infallibly of him.

HAMLET The concernancy, sir? Why do we wrap the gentleman in our more rawer breath?

OSRIC Sir?

HORATIO Is 't not possible to understand in another tongue? You will do 't, sir, really.

HAMLET What imports the nomination of this gentleman?

OSRIC Of Laertes?

HORATIO [*To Hamlet*] His purse is empty already; all 's golden words are spent.

HAMLET Of him, sir.

OSRIC I know you are not ignorant—

HAMLET I would you did, sir; yet, in faith, if you did, it would not much approve me. Well, sir?

OSRIC You are not ignorant of what excellence Laertes is—

HAMLET I dare not confess that, lest I should compare with him in excellence; but to know a man well were to know himself.

OSRIC I mean, sir, for his weapon; but in the imputation laid on him by them, in his meed he's unfellow'd.

HAMLET What's his weapon?

OSRIC Rapier and dagger.

HAMLET That's two of his weapons—but well.

OSRIC The King, sir, hath wager'd with him six Barbary horses, against the which he has impawn'd, as I take it, six French rapiers and poniards, with their assigns, as girdle, hangers, and so. Three of the carriages, in faith, are very dear to fancy, very responsive to the hilts, most delicate carriages, and of very liberal conceit.

HAMLET What call you the carriages?

HORATIO [*To Hamlet*] I knew you must be edified by the margent ere you had done.

OSRIC The carriage, sir, are the hangers.

HAMLET The phrase would be more germane to the matter if we could carry a cannon by our sides; I would it might be hangers till then. But, on: six Barb'ry horses against six French swords, their assigns, and three liberal-conceited carriages; that's the French bet against the Danish. Why is this impawn'd, as you call it?

OSRIC The King, sir, hath laid, sir, that in a dozen passes between yourself and him, he shall not exceed you three hits. He hath laid on twelve for nine, and it would come to immediate trial, if your lordship would vouchsafe the answer.

HAMLET How if I answer no?

OSRIC I mean, my lord, the opposition of your person in trial.

HAMLET Sir, I will walk here in the hall. If it please his Majesty, it is the breathing time of day with me. Let the foils be brought, the gentleman willing, and the King hold his purpose, I will win for him an I can; if

86–88 Let . . . mess i.e., if a man, no matter how beastlike, is as rich in possessions as Osric, he may eat at the King's table **88 chough** chattering jackdaw **97 indifferent** somewhat **99 complexion** temperament **105 for my ease** (A conventional reply declining the invitation to put his hat back on.) **107–108 differences** special qualities **108 soft society** agreeable manners. **great showing** distinguished appearance **109 feelingly** with just perception. **card** chart, map. **calendar** guide **110 gentry** good breeding **110–111 the continent . . . part** one who contains in him all the qualities. (A *continent* is that which contains.) **112 definement** definition. (Hamlet proceeds to mock Osric by using his lofty diction back at him.) **perdition** loss, diminution **113 divide him inventorially** i.e., enumerate his graces **114 dozy** dizzy. **yaw** to move unsteadily. (Said of a ship.) **115 neither** for all that. **in respect of** in comparison with **115–116 in . . . extolment** in true praise (of him) **116 article** moment or importance **117 infusion** essence, character imparted by nature. **dearth and rareness** rarity **117–118 make true diction** speak truly **118 semblable** only true likeness **119 who . . . trace** any other person who would wish to follow. **umbrage** shadow **122 concernancy** import, relevance **123 breath** speech

125–126 to understand . . . tongue i.e., for Osric to understand when someone else speaks in his manner. (Horatio twits Osric for not being able to understand the kind of flowery speech he himself uses when Hamlet speaks in such a vein.) **126 You will do 't** i.e., you can if you try **127 nomination** naming **135 approve** commend **138 compare** i.e., seem to compete **139–140 but . . . himself** i.e., for, to recognize excellence in another man, one must know oneself **141–142 imputation . . . them** reputation given him by others **142 meed** merit. **unfellow'd** unmatched **147 impawn'd** staked, wagered **148 assigns** appurtenances **149 hangers** straps on the sword belt (*girdle*) from which the sword hung. **carriages** (An affected way of saying *hangers;* literally, gun-carriages.) **150 dear to fancy** fancifully designed, tasteful. **responsive** corresponding closely, matching **151 delicate** (i.e., in workmanship) **151–152 liberal conceit** elaborate design **155 margent** margin of a book, place for explanatory notes **163 laid** wagered **164 passes** bouts. (The odds of the betting are hard to explain. Possibly the King bets that Hamlet will win at least five out of twelve, at which point Laertes raises the odds against himself by betting he will win nine.) **172 breathing time** exercise period

not, I will gain nothing but my shame and the odd hits.

OSRIC Shall I deliver you so?

HAMLET To this effect, sir—after what flourish your nature will.

OSRIC I commend my duty to your lordship.

HAMLET Yours, yours. [*Exit Osric.*] He does well to commend it himself; there are no tongues else for 's turn.

HORATIO This lapwing runs away with the shell on his head.

HAMLET 'A did comply, sir, with his dug, before 'a suck'd it. Thus has he—and many more of the same breed that I know the drossy age dotes on—only got the tune of the time and, out of an habit of encounter, a kind of yesty collection, which carries them through and through the most fann'd and winnow'd opinions; and do but blow them to their trial, the bubbles are out.

Enter a Lord.

LORD My lord, his Majesty commended him to you by young Osric, who brings back to him that you attend him in the hall. He sends to know if your pleasure hold to play with Laertes, or that you will take longer time.

HAMLET I am constant to my purposes; they follow the King's pleasure. If his fitness speaks, mine is ready; now or whensoever, provided I be so able as now.

LORD The King and Queen and all are coming down.

HAMLET In happy time.

LORD The Queen desires you to use some gentle entertainment to Laertes before you fall to play.

HAMLET She well instructs me. [*Exit Lord.*]

HORATIO You will lose, my lord.

HAMLET I do not think so. Since he went into France, I have been in continual practice; I shall win at the odds. But thou wouldst not think how ill all's here about my heart; but it is no matter.

HORATIO Nay, good my lord—

HAMLET It is but foolery, but it is such a kind of gain-giving, as would perhaps trouble a woman.

HORATIO If your mind dislike anything, obey it. I will forestall their repair hither, and say you are not fit.

HAMLET Not a whit, we defy augury. There is special providence in the fall of a sparrow. If it be now, 'tis not to come; if it be not to come, it will be now; if it be not now; yet it will come. The readiness is all. Since no man of aught he leaves knows what is 't to leave betimes, let be.

A table prepar'd. [*Enter*] *trumpets, drums, and Officers with cushions; King, Queen,* [*Osric,*] *and all the State; foils, daggers,* [*and wine borne in;*] *and Laertes.*

KING
Come, Hamlet, come, and take this hand from me.
[*The King puts Laertes' hand into Hamlet's.*]

HAMLET
Give me your pardon, sir. I have done you wrong,
But pardon 't, as you are a gentleman.
This presence knows,
And you must needs have heard, how I am punish'd
With a sore distraction. What I have done
That might your nature, honor, and exception
Roughly awake, I here proclaim was madness.
Was 't Hamlet wrong'd Laertes? Never Hamlet.
If Hamlet from himself be ta'en away,
And when he's not himself does wrong Laertes,
Then Hamlet does it not, Hamlet denies it.
Who does it, then? His madness. If 't be so,
Hamlet is of the faction that is wrong'd;
His madness is poor Hamlet's enemy.
[Sir, in this audience,]
Let my disclaiming from a purpos'd evil
Free me so far in your most generous thoughts
That I have shot my arrow o'er the house
And hurt my brother.

LAERTES
I am satisfied in nature,
Whose motive in this case should stir me most
To my revenge. But in my terms of honor
I stand aloof, and will no reconcilement
Till by some elder masters of known honor
I have a voice and precedent of peace
To keep my name ungor'd. But till that time,
I do receive your offer'd love like love,
And will not wrong it.

HAMLET
I embrace it freely,
And will this brothers' wager frankly play.
Give us the foils. Come on.

LAERTES
Come, one for me.

HAMLET
I'll be your foil, Laertes. In mine ignorance
Your skill shall, like a star i' th' darkest night,
Stick fiery off indeed.

LAERTES
You mock me, sir.

HAMLET
No, by this hand.

KING
Give them the foils, young Osric. Cousin Hamlet,
You know the wager?

HAMLET
Very well, my lord.
Your Grace has laid the odds o' th' weaker side.

KING
I do not fear it; I have seen you both.
But since he is better'd, we have therefore odds.

LAERTES
This is too heavy, let me see another.
[*Exchanges his foil for another.*]

184 lapwing (A bird that draws intruders away from its nest and was thought to run about when newly hatched with its head in the shell; a seeming reference to Osric's hat.) **186 comply . . . dug** observe ceremonious formality toward his mother's teat **188 drossy** frivolous **189 tune** temper, mood, manner of speech. **habit of encounter** demeanor of social intercourse **190 yesty** yeasty, frothy. **collection** i.e., of current phrases **191 fann'd and winnow'd** select and refined **192–193 blow . . . out** i.e., put them to the test, and their ignorance is exposed **200 If . . . speaks** i.e., if his readiness answers to the time **203 In happy time** (A phrase of courtesy indicating acceptance.) **204–205 entertainment** greeting **213–214 gain-giving** misgiving **221–222 what . . . betimes** what is the best time to leave it

226 presence royal assembly **229 exception** disapproval **242 in nature** i.e., as to my personal feelings **247 voice** authoritative pronouncement **253 foil** thin metal background which sets a jewel off (with pun on the blunted rapier for fencing) **255 Stick fiery off** stand out brilliantly **261 is better'd** has improved; is the odds-on favorite

HAMLET
This likes me well. These foils have all a length?
[They prepare to play.]

OSRIC
Ay, my good lord.

KING
Set me the stoups of wine upon that table.
If Hamlet give the first or second hit,
Or quit in answer of the third exchange,
Let all the battlements their ordnance fire.
The King shall drink to Hamlet's better breath,
And in the cup an union shall he throw,
Richer than that which four successive kings
In Denmark's crown have worn. Give me the cups,
And let the kettle to the trumpet speak,
The trumpet to the cannoneer without,
The cannons to the heavens, the heaven to earth,
"Now the King drinks to Hamlet." Come, begin.
Trumpets the while.
And you, the judges, bear a wary eye.

HAMLET
Come on sir.

LAERTES
Come, my lord. *[They play. Hamlet scores a hit.]*

HAMLET
One.

LAERTES
No.

HAMLET
Judgment.

OSRIC A hit, a very palpable hit.
Drum, trumpets, and shot. Flourish.
A piece goes off.

LAERTES
Well, again.

KING
Stay, give me drink. Hamlet, this pearl is thine.
[He throws a pearl in Hamlet's cup,
and drinks.]
Here's to thy health. Give him the cup.

HAMLET
I'll play this bout first; set it by awhile.
Come. *[They play.]* Another hit; what say you?

LAERTES
A touch, a touch, I do confess 't.

KING
Our son shall win.

QUEEN He's fat, and scant of breath.
Here, Hamlet, take my napkin, rub thy brows.
The Queen carouses to thy fortune, Hamlet.

HAMLET
Good madam!

KING
Gertrude, do not drink.

QUEEN
I will, my lord; I pray you pardon me. *[Drinks.]*

KING *[Aside]*
It is the pois'ned cup. It is too late.

HAMLET
I dare not drink yet, madam; by and by.

QUEEN
Come, let me wipe thy face.

LAERTES *[To King]*
My lord, I'll hit him now.

KING I do not think 't.

LAERTES *[Aside]*
And yet it is almost against my conscience.

HAMLET
Come, for the third, Laertes. You do but dally.
I pray you, pass with your best violence;
I am afeard you make a wanton of me.

LAERTES
Say you so? Come on. *[They play.]*

OSRIC
Nothing, neither way.

LAERTES
Have at you now!
[Laertes wounds Hamlet; then, in scuffling,
they change rapiers, and Hamlet wounds Laertes.]

KING Part them! They are incens'd.

HAMLET
Nay, come, again. *[The Queen falls.]*

OSRIC Look to the Queen there, ho!

HORATIO
They bleed on both sides. How is it, my lord?

OSRIC
How is 't, Laertes?

LAERTES
Why, as a woodcock to mine own springe, Osric;
I am justly kill'd with mine own treachery.

HAMLET
How does the Queen?

KING She swoons to see them bleed.

QUEEN
No, no, the drink, the drink—O my dear Hamlet—
The drink, the drink! I am pois'ned. *[Dies.]*

HAMLET
O villainy! Ho, let the door be lock'd!
Treachery! Seek it out. *[Laertes falls.]*

LAERTES
It is here, Hamlet. Hamlet, thou art slain.
No med'cine in the world can do thee good;
In thee there is not half an hour's life.
The treacherous instrument is in thy hand,
Unbated and envenom'd. The foul practice
Hath turn'd itself on me. Lo, here I lie,
Never to rise again. Thy mother's pois'ned.
I can no more. The King, the King's to blame.

HAMLET
The point envenom'd too? Then, venom, to thy
work. *[Stabs the King.]*

ALL
Treason! Treason!

KING
O, yet defend me, friends; I am but hurt.

267 quit repay (with a hit) **270 union** pearl. (So called, according to Pliny's *Natural History*, IX, because pearls are *unique*, never identical.) **273 kettle** kettledrum **289 fat** not physically fit, out of training **290 napkin** handkerchief **291 carouses** drinks a toast

302 make . . . me i.e., treat me like a spoiled child, holding back to give me an advantage **305 s.d. in scuffling, they change rapiers** (This stage direction occurs in F. According to a widespread stage tradition, Hamlet receives a scratch, realizes that Laertes' sword is unbated, and accordingly forces an exchange.) **309 woodcock** a bird, a type of stupidity or as a decoy. **springe** trap, snare **320 Unbated** not blunted with a button

HAMLET
Here, thou incestuous, murd'rous, damned Dane,
[*He forces the King to drink the poisoned cup.*]
Drink off this potion. Is thy union here? 328
Follow my mother. [*King dies.*]

LAERTES
He is justly serv'd.
It is a poison temper'd by himself. 330
Exchange forgiveness with me, noble Hamlet.
Mine and my father's death come not upon thee,
Nor thine on me! [*Dies.*]

HAMLET
Heaven make thee free of it! I follow thee.
I am dead, Horatio. Wretched Queen, adieu!
You that look pale and tremble at this chance,
That are but mutes or audience to this act, 337
Had I but time—as this fell sergeant, Death, 338
Is strict in his arrest—O, I could tell you—
But let it be. Horatio, I am dead;
Thou livest. Report me and my cause aright
To the unsatisfied.

HORATIO
Never believe it.
I am more an antique Roman than a Dane. 343
Here's yet some liquor left.
[*He attempts to drink from the poisoned cup. Hamlet prevents him.*]

HAMLET
As th' art a man,
Give me the cup! Let go! By heaven, I'll ha 't.
O God, Horatio, what a wounded name,
Things standing thus unknown, shall I leave behind me!
If thou didst ever hold me in thy heart,
Absent thee from felicity awhile,
And in this harsh world draw thy breath in pain
To tell my story.
A march afar off [*and a volley within*].
What warlike noise is this?

OSRIC
Young Fortinbras, with conquest come from Poland,
To the ambassadors of England gives
This warlike volley.

HAMLET
O, I die, Horatio!
The potent poison quite o'ercrows my spirit. 355
I cannot live to hear the news from England,
But I do prophesy th' election lights
On Fortinbras. He has my dying voice. 358
So tell him, with th' occurrents more and less 359
Which have solicited—the rest is silence. [*Dies.*] 360

HORATIO
Now cracks a noble heart. Good night, sweet prince;
And flights of angels sing thee to thy rest!
[*March within.*]
Why does the drum come hither?

Enter Fortinbras, with the [*English*] *Ambassadors* [*with drum, colors, and attendants*].

FORTINBRAS
Where is this sight?

HORATIO
What is it you would see?
If aught of woe or wonder, cease your search.

FORTINBRAS
This quarry cries on havoc. O proud Death, 366
What feast is toward in thine eternal cell, 367
That thou so many princes at a shot
So bloodily hast struck?

FIRST AMBASSADOR
The sight is dismal;
And our affairs from England come too late.
The ears are senseless that should give us hearing,
To tell him his commandment is fulfill'd,
That Rosencrantz and Guildenstern are dead.
Where should we have our thanks?

HORATIO
Not from his mouth, 374
Had it th' ability of life to thank you.
He never gave commandment for their death.
But since, so jump upon this bloody question, 377
You from the Polack wars, and you from England,
Are here arriv'd, give order that these bodies
High on a stage be placed to the view, 380
And let me speak to th' yet unknowing world
How these things came about. So shall you hear
Of carnal, bloody, and unnatural acts,
Of accidental judgments, casual slaughters, 384
Of deaths put on by cunning and forc'd cause, 385
And, in this upshot, purposes mistook
Fall'n on th' inventors' heads. All this can I
Truly deliver.

FORTINBRAS
Let us haste to hear it,
And call the noblest to the audience.
For me, with sorrow I embrace my fortune.
I have some rights of memory in this kingdom, 391
Which now to claim my vantage doth invite me. 392

HORATIO
Of that I shall have also cause to speak,
And from his mouth whose voice will draw on more. 394
But let this same be presently perform'd, 395
Even while men's minds are wild, lest more mischance
On plots and errors happen.

FORTINBRAS
Let four captains 397
Bear Hamlet, like a soldier, to the stage,
For he was likely, had he been put on, 399
To have prov'd most royal; and, for his passage, 400
The soldiers' music and the rite of war
Speak loudly for him.
Take up the bodies. Such a sight as this
Becomes the field, but here shows much amiss. 404
Go, bid the soldiers shoot.
Exeunt [*marching, bearing off the dead bodies; a peal of ordnance is shot off*].

328 union pearl. (See l. 270; with grim puns on the word's other meanings: marriage, shared death?) **330 temper'd** mixed **337 mutes** silent observers **338 fell** cruel. **sergeant** sheriff's officer **343 Roman** (It was the Roman custom to follow masters in death.) **355 o'ercrows** triumphs over **358 voice** vote **359 occurrents** events, incidents **360 solicited** moved, urged

366 quarry heap of dead. **cries on havoc** proclaims a general slaughter **367 toward** in preparation **374 his** i.e., Claudius' **377 jump** precisely. **question** dispute **380 stage** platform **384 judgments** retributions. **casual** occurring by chance **385 put on** instigated **391 of memory** traditional, remembered **392 vantage** i.e., presence at this opportune moment **394 voice . . . more** vote will influence still others **395 presently** immediately **397 On** on the basis of **399 put on** i.e., invested in royal office, and so put to the test **400 passage** death **404 field** i.e., of battle

Othello, the Moor of Venice

Othello differs in several respects from the other three major Shakespearean tragedies with which it is usually ranked. Written seemingly about the time of its performance at court by the King's men on November 1, 1604, after *Hamlet* (c. 1599–1601) and before *King Lear* (c. 1605) and *Macbeth* (c. 1606–1607), *Othello* shares with these other plays a fascination with evil in its most virulent and universal aspect. These plays study the devastating effects of ambitious pride, ingratitude, wrath, jealousy, and vengeful hate—the deadly sins of the spirit—with only a passing interest in the political strife to which Shakespeare's Roman or classical tragedies are generally devoted. Of the four, *Othello* is the most concentrated upon one particular evil. The action concerns sexual jealousy, and, although human sinfulness is such that jealousy ceaselessly touches on other forms of depravity, the center of interest always returns in *Othello* to the destruction of a love through jealousy. *Othello* is a tragic portrait of a marriage. The protagonist is not a king or prince, as in the tragedies already mentioned, but a general recently married. There are no supernatural visitations as in *Hamlet* and *Macbeth*. Ideas of divine justice, while essential to *Othello*'s portrayal of a battle between good and evil for the allegiance of the protagonist, do not encompass the wide sweep of *King Lear;* nor do we find here the same broad indictment of humanity. Social order is not seriously shaken by Othello's tragedy. The fair-minded Duke of Venice remains firmly in control, and his deputy Lodovico oversees a just conclusion on Cyprus.

By the same token, *Othello* does not offer the remorseless questioning about man's relationship to the cosmos that we find in *King Lear, Hamlet,* and *Macbeth*. The battle of good and evil is of course cosmic, but in *Othello* that battle is realized through a taut narrative of jealousy and murder. One cluster of images is domestic and animal, having to do with goats, monkeys, wolves, baboons, guinea hens, wildcats, spiders, flies, asses, dogs, copulating horses and sheep, serpents, and toads; other images, more wide-ranging in scope, include green-eyed monsters, devils, blackness, poisons, money-purses, tarnished jewels, music untuned, and light extinguished. The story is immediate and direct, retaining the sensational atmosphere of its Italian prose source by Giovanni Baptista Giraldi Cinthio, in his *Hecatommithi* of 1565 (translated into French in 1584). Events move even more swiftly than in Cinthio, for Shakespeare has compressed the story into two or three nights and days (albeit with an intervening sea journey and with an elastic use of stage time to allow for the maturing of long-term plans, as when we learn that Iago has begged Emilia "a hundred times" to steal Desdemona's handkerchief, or that Iago has accused Cassio of making love to Desdemona "a thousand times"). *Othello* does not have a fully developed double plot as in *King Lear* or a comparatively large group of characters serving as foils to the protagonist as in *Hamlet*. *Othello*'s cast is small and the plot is concentrated to an unusual degree on Othello, Desdemona, and Iago. What *Othello* may lose in breadth it gains in dramatic intensity.

Daringly, Shakespeare opens this tragedy of love not with a direct and sympathetic portrayal of the lovers themselves, but with a scene of vicious insinuation about their marriage. The images employed by Iago to describe the coupling of Othello and Desdemona are revoltingly animalistic, sodomistic. "Even now, now, very now, an old black ram Is tupping your white ewe," he taunts Desdemona's father Brabantio. ("Tupping" is a word used specifically for the copulating of sheep.) "You'll have your daughter cover'd with a Barbary horse; you'll have your nephews neigh to you"; "Your daughter and the Moor are now making the beast with two backs"; "the devil will make a grandsire of you." This degraded view reduces the marriage to one of utter carnality, with repeated emphasis on the word "gross": Desdemona has yielded "to the gross clasps of a lascivious Moor," and has made "a gross revolt" against her family and society. Iago's second theme, one that is habitual with him, is money. "What, ho, Brabantio! Thieves, thieves! Look to your house, your daughter, and your bags!" The implication is of a sinister bond between thievery in sex and thievery in gold. Sex and money are both commodities to be protected by watchful fathers against libidinous and opportunistic children.

We as audience make plentiful allowance for Iago's bias in all this, since he has admitted to Roderigo his knavery and resentment of Othello. Even so, the carnal vision of love we confront is calculatedly disturbing, because it seems so equated with a pejorative image of blackness. Othello is unquestionably a black man, referred to disparagingly by his detractors as the "thick-lips," with a "sooty bosom"; Elizabethan usage applied the term "Moor" to Africans without attempting to distinguish between Arabian and Negroid peoples. From the ugly start of the play, Othello and Desdemona have to prove the worth of their love in the face of preset attitudes against miscegenation. Brabantio takes refuge in the thought that Othello must have bewitched Desdemona. His basic assumption—one to be echoed later by Iago and by Othello himself—is that miscegenation is unnatural by definition. In confronting and accusing Othello he repeatedly appeals "to all things of sense" (that is, to common sense) and asks if it is not "gross in sense" (self-evident) that Othello has practiced magic on her, since nothing else could prompt human nature so to leave its natural path. "For nature so preposterously to err, Being not deficient, blind, or lame of sense, Sans witchcraft could not" (I,ii–iii). We as audience do not endorse Brabantio's view, and recognize in him the type of imperious father who conventionally opposes romantic love. It is sadly ironic that he should now prefer Roderigo as a son-in-law, evidently concluding that any white Venetian would be preferable to the prince of blacks. Still, Brabantio has been hospitable to the Moor and trusting of his daughter. He is a sorrowful rather than ridiculous figure, and the charge he levels at the married pair, however much based on *a priori* assumptions of what is "natural" in human behavior, remains to be answered.

After all, we find ourselves wondering, what did attract Othello and Desdemona to one another? Even though he certainly did not use witchcraft, may Othello not have employed a subtler kind of enchantment in the exotic character of his travels among "the Cannibals that each other eat, The Anthropophagi, and men whose heads Do grow beneath their shoulders" (I,iii)? These "passing strange" events fascinate Desdemona as they do everyone including the Duke of Venice ("I think this tale would win my daughter too"). Othello has not practiced unfairly on her—"This only is the witchcraft I have us'd." Yet may he not represent for Desdemona a radical novelty, being a man at once less devious and more mysterious than the dissolute Venetian swaggerers like Roderigo who follow her about? Was her deceiving of her father by means of the elopement a protest, an escape from conventionality? Why has she been attracted to a man so much older than herself? For his part, Othello gives the impression of being inexperienced with women, at least of Desdemona's rank and complexion, and is both intrigued and flattered by her attentions. "She lov'd me for the dangers I had pass'd, And I lov'd her that she did pity them." Desdemona fulfills a place in Othello's view of himself. Does she also represent status for him in Venetian society, where he has been employed as a military commander but treated nonetheless as something of an alien?

These subtle but impertinent ways of doubting the motivations of Othello and Desdemona are thrust upon us by the play's opening, and are later crucial to Iago's strategy of breeding mistrust. Just as importantly, however, these insinuations are refuted by Othello and especially by Desdemona. Whatever others may think, she never gives any slightest indication of regarding her husband as different or exotic because he is black and old. In fact the images of blackness and age are significantly reversed during the play's early scenes. Othello's blackness, like that of the natives dwelling in heathen lands, could betoken to Elizabethan audiences an innocent proneness to accept Christianity, and Othello is one who has already embraced Christian faith. His first appearance on stage, when he confronts a party of torch-bearing men coming to arrest him and bids his followers sheathe their swords, is sufficiently reminiscent of Christ's arrest in the Garden of Gethsemane to convey a fleeting comparison between Othello and the Christian God whose charity and forbearance he seeks to emulate. Othello's blackness is no doubt used as an emblem of fallen man, but so are we all fallen. His age similarly strengthens our impression of his wisdom, restraint, leadership. Any suggestions of comic sexual infidelity in the marriage of an old man and an attractive young bride are confuted by what we see in Desdemona's chaste yet sensual regard for the good man she has chosen.

Desdemona is utterly fond of Othello, admiring, and faithful. We believe her when she says that she does not even know what it means to be unfaithful; the word "whore" is not in her vocabulary. She is defenseless against the charges brought against her because she does not even comprehend them, cannot believe that anyone would imagine such things. Her love, both erotic and chaste, is of that transcendent wholesomeness common to several late Shakespearean heroines such as Cordelia in *King Lear* and Hermione in *The Winter's Tale,* whose names are synonymous with grace. Her "preferring" Othello to her father, like Cordelia's placing her duty to a husband before that to a father, is not ungrateful but natural and proper. And Othello, however much he may regard Desdemona as an extention of himself (he calls her "my fair warrior"), does cherish Desdemona as she deserves. "I cannot speak enough of this content," he exclaims when he rejoins her on Cyprus. "It stops me here; it is too much of joy" (II,i). The very passionate intensity of his love prepares the way for his tragedy, for he knows only too well that "when I love thee not, Chaos is come again" (III,iii). Iago speaks truly when he observes that Othello "Is of a constant, loving, noble nature" (II,i). Othello's tragedy is not that he is easily duped, but that his strong faith can be destroyed at such terrible cost. Othello never forgets how much he is losing. The threat to his love is not an initial lack of wholesomeness, but rather the insidious assumption that Desdemona cannot love him because such a love is unnatural. The fear of being unlovable exists in Othello's mind, but the human instrument of this vicious gospel is Iago.

Iago belongs to a select group of villains in Shakespeare who, while plausibly motivated in human terms, also take delight in evil for its own sake: Aaron the Moor in *Titus Andronicus,* Richard III, Don John in *Much Ado,* Iago, Edmund in *King Lear.* They are not, like Macbeth or like Claudius in *Hamlet,* men driven by ambition to commit crimes they clearly recognize as wrong. Although Edmund does belatedly try to make amends, these villains are essentially conscienceless, sinister, and amused at their own cunning. As Bernard Spivack observes (in *Shakespeare and the Allegory of Evil*), they are related to one another by a stage metaphor of personified evil derived from the Vice of the morality play. Like that engaging tempter of Mankind, they take the audience into their confidence, boast in soliloquy of their cleverness, exult in the triumph of evil, and improvise plans with daring and resourcefulness. They are all superb actors, deceiving virtually every character on stage until late in the action with their protean and hypocritical display. They take pleasure in this "sport" and amaze us by their virtuosity. The role is essentially comic, although it is the grim and ironic comedy of vice. We know that we are to condemn morally even while we applaud the skill.

The tradition of vice comedy may best explain a puzzling feature of Iago, noted long ago and memorably phrased by Coleridge as "the motive hunting of a motiveless malignity." Iago does offer plausible motives for what he does. Despite his resemblance to the morality Vice, he is no allegorized abstraction but an ensign in the army, a junior field officer who hates being outranked by a theoretician or staff officer. As an old-school professional he also resents that he has not been promoted on the basis of seniority, the "old gradation." Even his efforts at using influence with Othello have come to naught, and Iago can scarcely be blamed for supposing that Cassio's friendship with Othello has won him special favor. Thus Iago has reason to plot against Cassio as well as Othello. Nevertheless a further dimension is needed to explain the gloating, the utter lack of moral reflection, the concentration on destroying Desdemona (who has not wronged Iago), the absorption in ingenious methods of plotting, the finesse and the style. Probably the tradition of the stage Machiavel, as in Marlowe's *Jew of Malta,* adds an ingredient; this tradition was readily assimilated with that of the Vice.

Iago's machinations yield him both "sport" and "profit" (I,iii); that is, he enjoys his evil-doing, although he is also driven by a motive. This Vice-like behavior in human garb creates a restless sense of a dark metaphysical reality lying behind his visible exterior. Even his stated motives do not always make sense. When in an outburst of hatred he soliloquizes that "I hate the Moor; And it is thought abroad, that 'twixt my sheets H' as done my office," Iago goes on to concede the unlikelihood of this charge. "I know not if 't be true; But I, for mere suspicion in that kind, Will do as if for surety" (I,iii). The charge is so absurd, in fact, that we have to look into Iago himself for the origin of this jealous paranoia. The answer may be partly emblematic: as the embodiment and genius of sexual jealousy, Iago suffers with ironic appropriateness from the evil he preaches, and without external cause. Emilia understands that jealousy is not a rational affliction but a self-induced disease of the mind. Jealous persons, she tells Desdemona, "are not ever jealous for the cause, But jealous for they are jealous: 'tis a monster Begot upon itself, born on itself" (III,iv). Iago's own testimonial bears this out, for his jealousy is at once wholly irrational and agonizingly self-destructive. "I do suspect the lusty Moor Hath leap'd into my seat; the thought whereof Doth, like a poisonous mineral, gnaw my inwards" (II,i). In light of this nightmare, we can see that even his seemingly plausible resentment of Cassio's promotion is jealous envy.

Othello comes at last to regard Iago as a "demi-devil" who has tempted Othello to damn himself "beneath all depth in hell"; Lodovico speaks of Iago in the closing lines of the play as a "hellish villain"; and Iago himself boasts that "When devils will the blackest sins put on, They do suggest at first with heavenly shows, As I do now" (II,iii). Iago thus bears some affinity to both Vice and devil, suggesting his relationship both to Othello's inner temptation and to a preexistent evil force in the universe itself. Conversely, Desdemona is in Emilia's words an "angel," purely chaste; "So come my soul to bliss, as I speak true" (V,ii). When Desdemona lands on Cyprus, she is greeted in words that echo the *Ave Maria:* "Hail to thee, lady! And the grace of heaven . . . Enwheel thee round!" (II,i). These images introduce metaphorically a conflict of good and evil in which Othello, typical of fallen man, has chosen evil and destroyed the good at the prompting of a diabolical counselor. Again we see the heritage of the morality play, especially of the later morality in which the Mankind figure was sometimes damned rather than saved. Even so, to allegorize *Othello* is to obscure and misread its clash of human passion. The theological issue of salvation or damnation is not relevant in dramatic terms; the play is not a homily on the dangers of jealousy. The metaphysical dimensions of a homiletic tradition are transmuted into human drama. Acknowledging these limitations, we can notwithstanding see a spiritual analogy in Iago's devillike method of undoing his victims.

His trick resembles that of the similarly mischief-making Don John in *Much Ado:* an optical illusion by which the blameless heroine is impugned as an adulteress. The concealed Othello must watch Cassio boasting of sexual triumphs, and believe he is talking about Desdemona. Like the devil, Iago is given power over men's frail senses, especially the eyes. He can create illusions to induce Othello to see what Iago wants him to see, as Don John does with Claudio, but Othello's acceptance of the lie must be his own responsibility, a failure of his corrupted will. Iago practices on Othello with an *a priori* logic used before on Brabantio and Roderigo, urging the proneness of all mortals to sin and the unnaturalness of a black-white marriage. All women have appetites; Desdemona is a woman; hence Desdemona has appetites. "The wine she drinks is made of grapes," he scoffs to Roderigo. "If she had been bless'd, she would never have lov'd the Moor" (II,i). She is a Venetian, and "In Venice they do let heaven see the pranks They dare not show their husbands" (III,iii). Therefore she too is a hypocrite; "she did deceive her father." Most of all, it stands to reason that she must long for a man of her own race. As Iago succeeds in getting Othello to ponder: "And yet, how nature erring from itself . . ." This proposition that Nature teaches all persons, including Desdemona, to seek a harmonious matching of "clime, complexion, and degree" strikes a responsive chord in Othello, since he knows that he is black and alien. "Haply, for I am black And have not those soft parts of conversation That chamberers have . . ." Then, too, he is sensitive that he is considerably older than she, "declin'd Into the vale of years" (III,iii), "the young affects In me defunct" (I,iii). And so, if one must conclude from the preceding that Desdemona will seek a lover, the only question is who. "This granted—as it is a most pregnant and unforc'd position—who stands so eminent in the degree of this fortune as Cassio does?" (II,i). Once Othello has accepted this syllogistic sequence of proofs, specious not through any lapse in logic but because the axiomatic assumptions about human nature are degraded and do not apply to Desdemona, Othello has arrived at an unshakable conclusion to which all subsequent evidence must be forced as "a foregone conclusion." "Villain, be sure thou prove my love a whore," he commissions Iago (III,iii). Desdemona's innocent pleading for Cassio only makes things look worse. Cassio's reputed muttering while asleep, like the handkerchief seen in his possession or his giddy talk about his mistress Bianca, "speaks against her [Desdemona] with the other proofs."

How has Othello fallen so far in so short a time? His bliss with Desdemona as they are rejoined on Cyprus knows no limit. These two persons represent married love at its very best, erotic and spiritual, she enhancing his manliness, he cherishing her beauty and virtue. His blackness and age are positive images in him, despite earlier insinuations to the contrary. He is a man of public worthiness, of command, of self-assurance. Desdemona is the most domestic of Shakespeare's tragic heroines, even while she is also representative of so much that is transcendent. Husband and wife are bound happily in one of Shakespeare's few detailed portraits of serious commitment in marriage. What then gives way? We look at Iago for one important insight, but ultimately the cause must be in Othello himself. Arthur Kirsch has argued persuasively (in *Modern Language Review,* 1978) that Othello's most grave failing is an insufficient regard for himself. Jealousy stems from a profound suspicion that others cannot love us because we do not deem ourselves lovable. Othello has loved Desdemona as an extension of himself, and in his moments of greatest contentedness his marriage is sustained by an idealized vision of himself serving as the object of his exalted romantic passion. When he destroys Desdemona, as he realizes with a terrible clarity, Othello destroys himself; the act is a prelude to his actual suicide. Iago's means of temptation, then, is to persuade Othello to regard himself with the eyes of Venice, to accept the view that Othello is himself alien and that any woman who loves him does so perversely. In Othello's tainted state of mind, Desdemona's very sexuality becomes an unbearable threat to him, her warmth and devotion a "proof" of disloyalty. Othello's most tortured speeches (III,iv and IV,ii) reveal the extent to which he equates the seemingly betraying woman he has so depended on for happiness with his own mother, who gave Othello's father a handkerchief and threatened him with loss of her love if he should lose it. Othello has briefly learned and then forgotten the precious art of harmonizing erotic passion and spiritual love, and, as these two great aims of love are driven apart in him, he comes to loathe and fear the sexuality that puts him so much in mind of his physical frailty and dependence on woman. The horror and pity of *Othello* rests above all in the spectacle of a love that was once so whole and noble made filthy by self-hatred.

The increasing surrender of Othello's judgment to passion can be measured in three successive trial scenes in the play: the entirely fair trial of Othello himself by the Venetian senate concerning the elopement, Othello's trial of Cassio for drinking and rioting (when, ominously, Othello's "blood begins my safer guides to rule"), and finally the prejudged sentencing of Desdemona without any opportunity for her to defend herself. In a corollary decline, Othello falls from the Christian compassion of the opening scenes (he customarily confesses to heaven "the vices of my blood," I,iii) to the pagan savagery of his vengeful and ritualistic execution of his wife. "My heart is turned to stone" (IV,i), he vows, and at the play's end he grievingly characterizes himself as a "base Indian" who "threw a pearl away Richer than all his tribe." (The First Folio reading of "Iudean" or "Judean" refers perhaps to Judas Iscariot or to Herod; most editors prefer the quarto reading of "Indian.") Iago knows that he must persuade Othello to sentence and execute Desdemona himself, for only by active commitment to evil will Othello damn himself. In nothing does Iago so resemble the devil as in his wish to see Othello destroy the innocence and goodness on which his happiness depends.

The fate of some of the lesser characters echoes that of Othello, for Iago's evil intent is to "enmesh them all" (II,iii). Cassio in particular is, like Othello, an attractive man with a single but fatally vulnerable weakness, in his case fleshly appetite for wine and women. For him, alternately idolizing and depreciating women as he does, the gap between spiritual and sensual love remains vast, but he is essentially goodnatured and trustworthy. His seemingly genial flaws lead to disaster because they put him at the mercy of a remorseless enemy. Iago is, with fitting irony, the apostle of absolute self-control: "Our bodies are our gardens, to the which our wills are gardeners" (I,iii). Thus, Cassio's tragedy is anything but a straightforward homily on the virtues of temperance. Similarly, Bianca is undone not through any simple cause-and-effect punishment of her sexual conduct—she is, after all, fond of Cassio and loyal to him, even if he will not marry her—but because Iago is able to turn appearances against her. With his usual appeal to *a priori* logic, he builds a case that she and Cassio are in cahoots: "I do suspect this trash To be a party in this injury . . . This is the fruit of whoring" (V,i). Roderigo is another of Iago's victims, a contemptible one, led by the nose because he too has surrendered reason to passion. Emilia cannot escape Iago's evil influence, and steals the handkerchief for him despite knowing its value for Desdemona. Flaws are magnified into disasters by a remorseless evil intelligence. Men must be ceaselessly circumspect; a good reputation is sooner lost than recovered. Emilia is a conventionally decent enough woman—she would be faithless in marriage, she tells Desdemona, only for a very high price—and yet her one small compromise with her conscience contributes to the murder of her mistress. Like Othello she offers atonement too late, by denouncing her husband. Desdemona is the only person in the play too good to be struck down through some inner flaw, which may explain why Iago is committed above all else to seeing that she be destroyed.

As a tragic hero, Othello obtains self-knowledge at a terrible price. He knows finally that what he has destroyed was ineffably good. The discovery is too late for him to make amends, and he dies by his own hand as atonement. Despite the loss, however, his reaffirmation of faith in Desdemona's goodness undoes what the devillike Iago had most hoped to achieve: the separation of Othello from a belief in goodness. In this important sense, Othello's self-knowledge is cathartic and a compensation for the terrible price he has paid. The very existence of a person as good as Desdemona gives the lie to Iago's creed that everyone has his price. She is the sacrificial victim who must die for Othello's loss of faith, and, by dying, rekindle that faith. She cannot restore him to himself, for self-hatred has done its ugly work, but she is the means by which he understands at last the chimerical and wantonly destructive nature of his jealousy. His greatness appears in his acknowledgment of this truth, and in the heroic struggle with which he has confronted an inner darkness we all share.

Othello, the Moor of Venice

The Names of the Actors

OTHELLO, *the Moor.*
BRABANTIO, [*a senator,*] *father to Desdemona.*
CASSIO, *an honorable lieutenant* [*to Othello*].
IAGO, [*Othello's ancient,*] *a villain.*
RODERIGO, *a gull'd gentleman.*
DUKE OF VENICE.
SENATORS [*of Venice*].
MONTANO, *Governor of Cyprus.*
LODOVICO *and* GRATIANO, [*kinsmen to Brabantio,*] *two noble Venetians.*
CLOWN.

DESDEMONA, [*daughter to Brabantio and*] *wife to Othello.*
EMILIA, *wife to Iago.*
BIANCA, *a courtezan* [*and mistress to Cassio*].

GENTLEMEN *of Cyprus,* SAILORS, [MESSENGER, HERALD, OFFICERS, MUSICIANS, *and* ATTENDANTS.]

[SCENE: *Venice; a sea-port in Cyprus.*]

ACT I • SCENE I

Enter Roderigo and Iago.

RODERIGO
Tush, never tell me! I take it much unkindly 1
That thou, Iago, who hast had my purse
As if the strings were thine, shouldst know of this. 3

IAGO
'Sblood, but you'll not hear me. 4
If ever I did dream of such a matter,
Abhor me.

RODERIGO
Thou told'st me thou didst hold him in thy hate.

IAGO
Despise me
If I do not. Three great ones of the city,
In personal suit to make me his lieutenant,
Off-capp'd to him; and, by the faith of man, 11

I.i. Location: Venice. A street.
1 never tell me don't talk to me **3 this** i.e., Desdemona's elopement **4 'Sblood** i.e., by God's (Christ's) blood **11 him** i.e., Othello

I know my price, I am worth no worse a place.
But he, as loving his own pride and purposes,
Evades them with a bombast circumstance 14
Horribly stuff'd with epithets of war,
[And, in conclusion,]
Nonsuits my mediators; for, "Certes," says he, 17
"I have already chose my officer."
And what was he?
Forsooth, a great arithmetician, 20
One Michael Cassio, a Florentine,
A fellow almost damn'd in a fair wife, 22
That never set a squadron in the field,
Nor the division of a battle knows 24
More than a spinster—unless the bookish theoric, 25
Wherein the toged consuls can propose 26
As masterly as he. Mere prattle without practice
Is all his soldiership. But he, sir, had th' election;
And I, of whom his eyes had seen the proof 29
At Rhodes, at Cyprus, and on other grounds
Christian and heathen, must be belee'd and calm'd 31
By debitor and creditor. This counter-caster, 32
He, in good time, must his lieutenant be, 33
And I—God bless the mark!—his Moorship's
ancient. 34

RODERIGO
By heaven, I rather would have been his hangman.

IAGO
Why, there's no remedy. 'Tis the curse of service;
Preferment goes by letter and affection, 37
And not by old gradation, where each second 38
Stood heir to th' first. Now, sir, be judge yourself
Whether I in any just term am affin'd 40
To love the Moor.

RODERIGO
I would not follow him then.

IAGO
O, sir, content you;
I follow him to serve my turn upon him.
We cannot all be masters, nor all masters
Cannot be truly follow'd. You shall mark
Many a duteous and knee-crooking knave
That, doting on his own obsequious bondage,
Wears out his time, much like his master's ass,
For nought but provender, and, when he's old,
cashier'd. 49
Whip me such honest knaves. Others there are
Who, trimm'd in forms and visages of duty, 51
Keep yet their hearts attending on themselves,
And, throwing but shows of service on their lords,
Do well thrive by them, and when they have lin'd
their coats
Do themselves homage. These fellows have some
soul;
And such a one do I profess myself. For, sir,
It is as sure as you are Roderigo,
Were I the Moor, I would not be Iago.
In following him, I follow but myself—
Heaven is my judge, not I for love and duty,
But seeming so, for my peculiar end. 61
For when my outward action doth demonstrate
The native act and figure of my heart
In compliment extern, 'tis not long after 64
But I will wear my heart upon my sleeve
For daws to peck at. I am not what I am.

RODERIGO
What a full fortune does the thick-lips owe, 67
If he can carry 't thus!

IAGO
Call up her father.
Rouse him, make after him, poison his delight,
Proclaim him in the streets; incense her kinsmen,
And, though he in a fertile climate dwell, 71
Plague him with flies. Though that his joy be joy, 72
Yet throw such changes of vexation on 't 73
As it may lose some color. 74

RODERIGO
Here is her father's house. I'll call aloud.

IAGO
Do, with like timorous accent and dire yell 76
As when, by night and negligence, the fire
Is spied in populous cities.

RODERIGO
What, ho, Brabantio! Signior Brabantio, ho!

IAGO
Awake! What, ho, Brabantio! Thieves, thieves!
Look to your house, your daughter, and your bags!
Thieves, thieves!

Brabantio [appears] above [at a window].

BRABANTIO
What is the reason of this terrible summons?
What is the matter there?

RODERIGO
Signior, is all your family within?

IAGO
Are your doors lock'd?

BRABANTIO
Why, wherefore ask you this?

IAGO
'Zounds, sir, y' are robb'd. For shame, put on your
gown!
Your heart is burst, you have lost half your soul.
Even now, now, very now, an old black ram
Is tupping your white ewe. Arise, arise! 90
Awake the snorting citizens with the bell, 91
Or else the devil will make a grandsire of you.
Arise, I say!

14 bombast circumstance wordy evasion. (*Bombast* is cotton padding.) **17 Nonsuits** rejects **20 arithmetician** i.e., a man whose military knowledge is merely theoretical, based on books of tactics **22 A . . . wife** (Cassio does not seem to be married, but his counterpart in Shakespeare's source did have a wife. See also IV.i.129.) **24 division of a battle** disposition of a military unit **25 theoric** theory **26 toged** wearing the toga. **propose** discuss **29 his** i.e., Othello's **31 belee'd and calm'd** left to leeward without wind, becalmed. (A sailing metaphor.) **32 debitor and creditor** (A name for a system of bookkeeping, here used as a contemptuous nickname for Cassio.) **counter-caster** i.e., bookkeeper, one who tallies with *counters* or metal disks. (Said contemptuously.) **33 in good time** i.e., forsooth **34 ancient** standard-bearer, ensign **37 affection** favoritism **38 old gradation** seniority, the traditional way **40 term** respect. **affin'd** bound **49 cashier'd** dismissed from service **51 trimm'd** accoutered, fitted out

61 peculiar particular, personal **64 compliment extern** outward show (conforming in this case to the inner workings and intention of the heart) **67 thick-lips** (Elizabethans often applied the term "Moor" to Negroes.) **owe** own **71–72 though . . . flies** i.e., disrupt his seeming prosperity and happiness with a grievous vexation (since even the best-situated life is not immune to misery) **72 Though . . . be joy** i.e., although he seems fortunate and happy. (Repeats the idea of l. 71.) **73 changes of vexation** vexing changes **74 color** appearance (of happiness) **76 timorous** frightening **90 tupping** copulating with. (Said of sheep.) **91 snorting** snoring

BRABANTIO What, have you lost your wits?

RODERIGO

Most reverend signior, do you know my voice?

BRABANTIO

Not I. What are you?

RODERIGO

My name is Roderigo.

BRABANTIO The worser welcome.

I have charg'd thee not to haunt about my doors.
In honest plainness thou hast heard me say
My daughter is not for thee; and now, in madness,
Being full of supper and distemp'ring draughts,
Upon malicious bravery, dost thou come 101
To start my quiet. 102

RODERIGO

Sir, sir, sir—

BRABANTIO But thou must needs be sure

My spirits and my place have in their power
To make this bitter to thee.

RODERIGO Patience, good sir.

BRABANTIO

What tell'st thou me of robbing? This is Venice;
My house is not a grange.

RODERIGO Most grave Brabantio, 107

In simple and pure soul I come to you.

IAGO 'Zounds, sir, you are one of those that will not
serve God if the devil bid you. Because we come to do
you service and you think we are ruffians, you'll have
your daughter cover'd with a Barbary horse; you'll
have your nephews neigh to you; you'll have coursers 113
for cousins and gennets for germans. 114

BRABANTIO

What profane wretch art thou?

IAGO I am one, sir, that comes to tell you your daughter
and the Moor are now making the beast with two
backs.

BRABANTIO

Thou art a villain.

IAGO You are—a senator.

BRABANTIO

This thou shalt answer. I know thee, Roderigo.

RODERIGO

Sir, I will answer anything. But, I beseech you,
If 't be your pleasure and most wise consent,
As partly I find it is, that your fair daughter,
At this odd-even and dull watch o' th' night, 124
Transported with no worse nor better guard
But with a knave of common hire, a gondolier,
To the gross clasps of a lascivious Moor—
If this be known to you and your allowance, 128
We then have done you bold and saucy wrongs;
But if you know not this, my manners tell me
We have your wrong rebuke. Do not believe
That, from the sense of all civility, 132
I thus would play and trifle with your reverence.
Your daughter, if you have not given her leave,
I say again, hath made a gross revolt,
Tying her duty, beauty, wit, and fortunes
In an extravagant and wheeling stranger 137
Of here and everywhere. Straight satisfy yourself. 138
If she be in her chamber or your house,
Let loose on me the justice of the state
For thus deluding you.

BRABANTIO

Strike on the tinder, ho! 142
Give me a taper! Call up all my people!
This accident is not unlike my dream. 144
Belief of it oppresses me already.
Light, I say, light! *Exit* [*above*].

IAGO Farewell, for I must leave you.

It seems not meet, nor wholesome to my place,
To be producted—as, if I stay, I shall— 148
Against the Moor. For I do know the state,
However this may gall him with some check, 150
Cannot with safety cast him, for he's embark'd 151
With such loud reason to the Cyprus wars,
Which even now stands in act, that, for their souls, 153
Another of his fathom they have none, 154
To lead their business; in which regard,
Though I do hate him as I do hell-pains,
Yet, for necessity of present life,
I must show out a flag and sign of love,
Which is indeed but sign. That you shall surely find
him,
Lead to the Sagittary the raised search, 160
And there will I be with him. So, farewell. *Exit.* 161

Enter [*below*] *Brabantio* [*in his nightgown*] *with Servants and torches.*

BRABANTIO

It is too true an evil. Gone she is;
And what's to come of my despised time 163
Is nought but bitterness. Now, Roderigo,
Where didst thou see her? —O unhappy girl!—
With the Moor, say'st thou?—Who would be a
father!—
How didst thou know 'twas she?—O, she
deceives me
Past thought!—What said she to you?—Get moe
tapers. 168
Raise all my kindred.—Are they married, think
you?

RODERIGO

Truly, I think they are.

BRABANTIO

O heaven! How got she out? O treason of the blood!
Fathers, from hence trust not your daughters' minds
By what you see them act. Is there not charms
By which the property of youth and maidhood 174

101 Upon malicious bravery because of a malicious desire to defy me **102 start** disrupt **107 grange** isolated farmhouse **113 nephews** i.e., grandsons. **coursers** powerful horses **114 gennets** small Spanish horses. **germans** near relatives **124 odd-even** between one day and the next, i.e., about midnight **128 allowance** permission **132 from** contrary to

137 extravagant expatriate, wandering far from home. **wheeling** roving about, vagabond **138 Straight** straightway **142 tinder** charred linen ignited by a spark from flint and steel, used to light torches or *tapers* (ll. 143, 168) **144 accident** occurrence, event **148 producted** produced (as a witness) **150 gall** rub; oppress. **check** rebuke **151 cast** dismiss **153 stands in act** are going on **154 fathom** i.e., ability, depth of experience **160 Sagittary** (An inn where Othello and Desdemona are staying.) **161 s.d. nightgown** dressing gown **163 time** i.e., remainder of life **168 moe** more **174 property** special quality, nature

May be abus'd? Have you not read, Roderigo,
Of some such thing?

RODERIGO Yes, sir, I have indeed.

BRABANTIO
Call up my brother.—O, would you had had her!—
Some one way, some another.—Do you know
Where we may apprehend her and the Moor?

RODERIGO
I think I can discover him, if you please
To get good guard and go along with me.

BRABANTIO
Pray you, lead on. At every house I'll call;
I may command at most.—Get weapons, ho!
And raise some special officers of night.—
On, good Roderigo; I will deserve your pains.

Exeunt.

SCENE II

Enter Othello, Iago, Attendants with torches.

IAGO
Though in the trade of war I have slain men,
Yet do I hold it very stuff o' th' conscience
To do no contriv'd murder. I lack iniquity
Sometime to do me service. Nine or ten times
I had thought t' have yerk'd him here under the ribs.

OTHELLO
'Tis better as it is.

IAGO Nay, but he prated,
And spoke such scurvy and provoking terms
Against your honor
That, with the little godliness I have,
I did full hard forbear him. But, I pray you, sir,
Are you fast married? Be assur'd of this,
That the magnifico is much belov'd,
And hath in his effect a voice potential
As double as the Duke's. He will divorce you,
Or put upon you what restraint and grievance
The law, with all his might to enforce it on,
Will give him cable.

OTHELLO Let him do his spite.
My services which I have done the signiory
Shall out-tongue his complaints. 'Tis yet to know—
Which, when I know that boasting is an honor,
I shall promulgate—I fetch my life and being
From men of royal siege, and my demerits
May speak unbonneted to as proud a fortune
As this that I have reach'd. For know, Iago,
But that I love the gentle Desdemona,
I would not my unhoused free condition
Put into circumscription and confine
For the sea's worth. But, look, what lights come yond?

Enter Cassio [and certain Officers] with torches.

IAGO
Those are the raised father and his friends.
You were best go in.

OTHELLO Not I; I must be found.
My parts, my title, and my perfect soul
Shall manifest me rightly. Is it they?

IAGO
By Janus, I think no.

OTHELLO
The servants of the Duke? And my lieutenant?
The goodness of the night upon you, friends!
What is the news?

CASSIO The Duke does greet you, general,
And he requires your haste-post-haste appearance,
Even on the instant.

OTHELLO What is the matter, think you?

CASSIO
Something from Cyprus, as I may divine.
It is a business of some heat. The galleys
Have sent a dozen sequent messengers
This very night at one another's heels,
And many of the consuls, rais'd and met,
Are at the Duke's already. You have been hotly call'd for;
When, being not at your lodging to be found,
The Senate hath sent about three several quests
To search you out.

OTHELLO 'Tis well I am found by you.
I will but spend a word here in the house,
And go with you. *[Exit.]*

CASSIO Ancient, what makes he here?

IAGO
Faith, he tonight hath boarded a land carrack.
If it prove lawful prize, he's made forever.

CASSIO
I do not understand.

IAGO He's married.

CASSIO To who?

[Enter Othello.]

IAGO
Marry, to—Come, captain, will you go?

OTHELLO
Have with you.

CASSIO
Here comes another troop to seek for you.

Enter Brabantio, Roderigo, with Officers and torches.

185 deserve show gratitude for

I.ii. Location: Venice. Another street.
5 yerk'd stabbed **10 full hard** scarcely **12 magnifico** Venetian grandee, i.e., Brabantio **13 in his effect** at his command. **potential** powerful **14 double** doubly powerful **17 cable** i.e., scope **18 signiory** Venetian government **19 yet to know** not yet widely known **22 siege** i.e., rank. (Literally, a *seat* used by a person of distinction.) **demerits** deserts **23 unbonneted** without removing the hat, i.e., on equal terms (? *Bonneted* can mean "with hat off.")

26 unhoused unconfined, undomesticated **31 My . . . soul** my merits, my position or reputation, and my unflawed conscience **33 Janus** Roman god of beginnings **41 sequent** successive **43 consuls** senators **46 several** separate **49 makes** does **50 carrack** large merchant ship **54 Have with you** i.e., let's go

IAGO
It is Brabantio. General, be advis'd.
He comes to bad intent.
OTHELLO
Holla! Stand there!
RODERIGO
Signior, it is the Moor.
BRABANTIO
Down with him, thief!
[*They draw on both sides.*]
IAGO
You, Roderigo! Come, sir, I am for you.
OTHELLO
Keep up your bright swords, for the dew will rust
them. 60
Good signior, you shall more command with years
Than with your weapons.
BRABANTIO
O thou foul thief, where hast thou stow'd my
daughter?
Damn'd as thou art, thou hast enchanted her!
For I'll refer me to all things of sense, 65
If she in chains of magic were not bound
Whether a maid so tender, fair, and happy,
So opposite to marriage that she shunn'd
The wealthy curled darlings of our nation,
Would ever have, t' incur a general mock,
Run from her guardage to the sooty bosom 71
Of such a thing as thou—to fear, not to delight.
Judge me the world, if 'tis not gross in sense 73
That thou hast practic'd on her with foul charms,
Abus'd her delicate youth with drugs or minerals
That weakens motion. I'll have 't disputed on; 76
'Tis probable, and palpable to thinking.
I therefore apprehend and do attach thee 78
For an abuser of the world, a practicer
Of arts inhibited and out of warrant. 80
Lay hold upon him! If he do resist,
Subdue him at his peril.
OTHELLO
Hold your hands,
Both you of my inclining, and the rest. 83
Were it my cue to fight, I should have known it
Without a prompter. Whither will you that I go
To answer this your charge?
BRABANTIO
To prison, till fit time
Of law and course of direct session 88
Call thee to answer.
OTHELLO
What if I do obey?
How may the Duke be therewith satisfied,
Whose messengers are here about my side
Upon some present business of the state
To bring me to him?
FIRST OFFICER
'Tis true, most worthy signior.
The Duke's in council, and your noble self,
I am sure, is sent for.
BRABANTIO
How? The Duke in council?
In this time of the night? Bring him away.
Mine's not an idle cause. The Duke himself, 97
Or any of my brothers of the state,
Cannot but feel this wrong as 'twere their own;
For if such actions may have passage free,
Bond-slaves and pagans shall our statesmen be.
Exeunt.

SCENE III

Enter Duke [*and*] *Senators* [*and sit at a table, with lights*], *and Officers.* [*The Duke and Senators are reading dispatches.*]

DUKE
There is no composition in these news 1
That gives them credit.
FIRST SENATOR
Indeed, they are disproportioned. 3
My letters say a hundred and seven galleys.
DUKE
And mine, a hundred forty.
SECOND SENATOR
And mine, two hundred.
But though they jump not on a just account— 6
As in these cases, where the aim reports, 7
'Tis oft with difference—yet do they all confirm
A Turkish fleet, and bearing up to Cyprus.
DUKE
Nay, it is possible enough to judgment.
I do not so secure me in the error 11
But the main article I do approve 12
In fearful sense.
SAILOR *(Within)* What ho, what ho, what ho!

Enter Sailor.

FIRST OFFICER
A messenger from the galleys.
DUKE
Now, what's the business?
SAILOR
The Turkish preparation makes for Rhodes.
So was I bid report here to the state
By Signior Angelo. [*Exit Sailor.*]
DUKE
How say you by this change?
FIRST SENATOR
This cannot be
By no assay of reason. 'Tis a pageant 19
To keep us in false gaze. When we consider 20
Th' importancy of Cyprus to the Turk,
And let ourselves again but understand
That, as it more concerns the Turk than Rhodes,
So may he with more facile question bear it, 24
For that it stands not in such warlike brace, 25

60 Keep up i.e., sheathe **65 things of sense** commonsense understandings, or, creatures possessing common sense **71 guardage** guardianship **73 gross in sense** obvious **76 weakens motion** impair the vital faculties. **disputed on** argued in court by professional counsel, discussed by experts **78 attach** arrest **80 inhibited** prohibited. **out of warrant** illegal **83 inclining** following, party **88 course of direct session** regular legal proceedings

97 idle trifling

I.iii. Location: Venice. A council-chamber.
1 composition consistency **3 disproportioned** inconsistent **6 jump** agree. **just** exact **7 aim** conjecture **11–12 I do not . . . approve** I do not take such (false) comfort in the discrepancies that I fail to perceive the main point, i.e., that the Turkish fleet is threatening **19 assay** test **20 in false gaze** looking the wrong way **24 So . . . it** provided he (the Turk) can more easily capture it (Cyprus) **25 brace** state of defense

But altogether lacks th' abilities
That Rhodes is dress'd in—if we make thought of this,
We must not think the Turk is so unskillful
To leave that latest which concerns him first, 29
Neglecting an attempt of ease and gain
To wake and wage a danger profitless. 31

DUKE
Nay, in all confidence, he's not for Rhodes.

FIRST OFFICER
Here is more news.

Enter a Messenger.

MESSENGER
The Ottomites, reverend and gracious,
Steering with due course toward the isle of Rhodes,
Have there injointed them with an after fleet. 36

FIRST SENATOR
Ay, so I thought. How many, as you guess?

MESSENGER
Of thirty sail; and now they do re-stem 38
Their backward course, bearing with frank appearance 39
Their purposes toward Cyprus. Signior Montano,
Your trusty and most valiant servitor,
With his free duty recommends you thus, 42
And prays you to believe him. [*Exit Messenger.*]

DUKE
'Tis certain, then, for Cyprus.
Marcus Luccicos, is not he in town?

FIRST SENATOR
He's now in Florence.

DUKE
Write from us to him, post-post-haste.
Dispatch.

FIRST SENATOR
Here comes Brabantio and the valiant Moor.

Enter Brabantio, Othello, Cassio, Iago, Roderigo, and Officers.

DUKE
Valiant Othello, we must straight employ you 50
Against the general enemy Ottoman.
[*To Brabantio.*] I did not see you; welcome, gentle signior.
We lack'd your counsel and your help tonight.

BRABANTIO
So did I yours. Good your Grace, pardon me;
Neither my place nor aught I heard of business
Hath rais'd me from my bed, nor doth the general care
Take hold on me, for my particular grief
Is of so flood-gate and o'erbearing nature
That it engluts and swallows other sorrows 59
And it is still itself.

DUKE
Why, what's the matter?

BRABANTIO
My daughter! O, my daughter!

DUKE AND SENATORS
Dead?

BRABANTIO
Ay, to me.
She is abus'd, stol'n from me, and corrupted 62
By spells and medicines bought of mountebanks;
For nature so preposterously to err,
Being not deficient, blind, or lame of sense, 65
Sans witchcraft could not. 66

DUKE
Whoe'er he be that in this foul proceeding
Hath thus beguil'd your daughter of herself,
And you of her, the bloody book of law
You shall yourself read in the bitter letter
After your own sense—yea, though our proper son 71
Stood in your action.

BRABANTIO
Humbly I thank your Grace. 72
Here is the man, this Moor, whom now, it seems
Your special mandate for the state-affairs
Hath hither brought.

ALL
We are very sorry for 't.

DUKE [*To Othello*]
What, in your own part, can you say to this?

BRABANTIO
Nothing, but this is so.

OTHELLO
Most potent, grave, and reverend signiors,
My very noble and approv'd good masters, 79
That I have ta'en away this old man's daughter,
It is most true; true, I have married her.
The very head and front of my offending 82
Hath this extent, no more. Rude am I in my speech, 83
And little bless'd with the soft phrase of peace;
For since these arms of mine had seven years' pith, 85
Till now some nine moons wasted, they have us'd 86
Their dearest action in the tented field;
And little of this great world can I speak
More than pertains to feats of broil and battle,
And therefore little shall I grace my cause
In speaking for myself. Yet, by your gracious patience,
I will a round unvarnish'd tale deliver 92
Of my whole course of love—what drugs, what charms,
What conjuration, and what mighty magic,
For such proceeding I am charg'd withal,
I won his daughter.

BRABANTIO
A maiden never bold;
Of spirit so still and quiet that her motion 97
Blush'd at herself; and she, in spite of nature, 98
Of years, of country, credit, everything, 99
To fall in love with what she fear'd to look on!
It is a judgment maim'd and most imperfect
That will confess perfection so could err 102
Against all rules of nature, and must be driven

29 latest last **31 wage** risk **36 injointed them** joined themselves. **after** second **38 re-stem** steer again **39 frank appearance** i.e., undisguised intent **42 free duty** freely given and loyal service. **recommends** commends himself and reports to **59 engluts** engulfs

62 abus'd deceived **65 deficient** defective **66 Sans** without **71 After . . . sense** according to your own interpretation. **our proper** my own **72 Stood . . . action** were under your accusation **79 approv'd** proved **82 front** forehead, face **83 Rude** unpolished **85 pith** strength, vigor. (I.e., since I was seven.) **86 Till . . . wasted** until some nine months ago (during which time Othello has evidently not been on active duty, but in Venice) **92 round** plain **97–98 her . . . herself** her very emotions prompted her to blush, to discover such feelings in herself **99 credit** virtuous reputation **102 confess** concede (that)

To find out practices of cunning hell
Why this should be. I therefore vouch again
That with some mixtures pow'rful o'er the blood,
Or with some dram conjur'd to this effect,
He wrought upon her.

DUKE
To vouch this is no proof,
Without more wider and more overt test
Than these thin habits and poor likelihoods
Of modern seeming do prefer against him.

FIRST SENATOR
But, Othello, speak.
Did you by indirect and forced courses
Subdue and poison this young maid's affections?
Or came it by request and such fair question
As soul to soul affordeth?

OTHELLO
I do beseech you,
Send for the lady to the Sagittary,
And let her speak of me before her father.
If you do find me foul in her report,
The trust, the office I do hold of you,
Not only take away, but let your sentence
Even fall upon my life.

DUKE
Fetch Desdemona hither.

OTHELLO
Ancient, conduct them; you best know the place.
[Exeunt Iago and Attendants.]
And, till she come, as truly as to heaven
I do confess the vices of my blood,
So justly to your grave ears I'll present
How I did thrive in this fair lady's love,
And she in mine.

DUKE
Say it, Othello.

OTHELLO
Her father lov'd me, oft invited me;
Still question'd me the story of my life,
From year to year—the battles, sieges, fortunes,
That I have pass'd.
I ran it through, even from my boyish days
To th' very moment that he bade me tell it,
Wherein I spoke of most disastrous chances,
Of moving accidents by flood and field,
Of hair-breadth scapes i' th' imminent deadly breach,
Of being taken by the insolent foe
And sold to slavery, of my redemption thence,
And portance in my travels' history,
Wherein of antres vast and deserts idle,
Rough quarries, rocks, and hills whose heads touch heaven,
It was my hint to speak—such was my process—
And of the Cannibals that each other eat,
The Anthropophagi, and men whose heads
Do grow beneath their shoulders. This to hear
Would Desdemona seriously incline;
But still the house-affairs would draw her thence,
Which ever as she could with haste dispatch
She 'd come again, and with a greedy ear
Devour up my discourse. Which I, observing,
Took once a pliant hour, and found good means
To draw from her a prayer of earnest heart
That I would all my pilgrimage dilate,
Whereof by parcels she had something heard,
But not intentively. I did consent,
And often did beguile her of her tears,
When I did speak of some distressful stroke
That my youth suffer'd. My story being done,
She gave me for my pains a world of sighs.
She swore, in faith, 'twas strange, 'twas passing strange,
'Twas pitiful, 'twas wondrous pitiful.
She wish'd she had not heard it, yet she wish'd
That heaven had made her such a man. She thank'd me,
And bade me, if I had a friend that lov'd her,
I should but teach him how to tell my story,
And that would woo her. Upon this hint I spake.
She lov'd me for the dangers I had pass'd,
And I lov'd her that she did pity them.
This only is the witchcraft I have us'd.
Here comes the lady. Let her witness it.

Enter Desdemona, Iago, [and] Attendants.

DUKE
I think this tale would win my daughter too.
Good Brabantio,
Take up this mangled matter at the best.
Men do their broken weapons rather use
Than their bare hands.

BRABANTIO
I pray you, hear her speak.
If she confess that she was half the wooer,
Destruction on my head if my bad blame
Light on the man! Come hither, gentle mistress.
Do you perceive in all this noble company
Where most you owe obedience?

DESDEMONA
My noble father,
I do perceive here a divided duty.
To you I am bound for life and education;
My life and education both do learn me
How to respect you. You are the lord of duty;
I am hitherto your daughter. But here's my husband,
And so much duty as my mother show'd
To you, preferring you before her father,
So much I challenge that I may profess
Due to the Moor my lord.

BRABANTIO
God be with you! I have done.
Please it your Grace, on to the state affairs.
I had rather to adopt a child than get it.
Come hither, Moor. *[He joins the hands of Othello and Desdemona.]*
I here do give thee that with all my heart

104 practices plots **105 vouch** assert **106 blood** passions **110 habits** garments, i.e., appearances **111 modern seeming** commonplace assumption. **prefer** bring forth **115 question** conversation **125 blood** passions **131 Still** continually **137 accidents** happenings **138 imminent . . . breach** death-threatening gap made in a fortification **141 portance** conduct **142 antres** caverns. **idle** barren, unprofitable **144 hint** occasion, opportunity **146 Anthropophagi** man-eaters. (A term from Pliny's *Natural History*.)

153 pliant well-suiting **155 dilate** relate in detail **157 intentively** with full attention **168 hint** opportunity **184 education** upbringing **185 learn** teach **190 challenge** claim **194 get** beget

Which, but thou hast already, with all my heart
I would keep from thee. For your sake, jewel, 198
I am glad at soul I have no other child;
For thy escape would teach me tyranny,
To hang clogs on them.—I have done, my lord.

DUKE
Let me speak like yourself, and lay a sentence, 202
Which, as a grise or step, may help these lovers 203
[Into your favor.]
When remedies are past, the griefs are ended
By seeing the worst, which late on hopes depended.
To mourn a mischief that is past and gone
Is the next way to draw new mischief on. 208
What cannot be preserv'd when fortune takes, 209
Patience her injury a mock'ry makes. 210
The robb'd that smiles steals something from the thief;
He robs himself that spends a bootless grief. 212

BRABANTIO
So let the Turk of Cyprus us beguile;
We lose it not, so long as we can smile.
He bears the sentence well that nothing bears 215
But the free comfort which from thence he hears, 216
But he bears both the sentence and the sorrow 217
That, to pay grief, must of poor patience borrow. 218
These sentences, to sugar or to gall,
Being strong on both sides, are equivocal.
But words are words. I never yet did hear
That the bruis'd heart was pierced through the ear.
I humbly beseech you, proceed to th' affairs of state.

DUKE The Turk with a most mighty preparation makes
for Cyprus. Othello, the fortitude of the place is best 225
known to you; and though we have there a substitute 226
of most allow'd sufficiency, yet opinion, a sovereign 227
mistress of effects, throws a more safer voice on you. 228
You must therefore be content to slubber the gloss of 229
your new fortunes with this more stubborn and
boist'rous expedition.

OTHELLO
The tyrant custom, most grave senators,
Hath made the flinty and steel couch of war
My thrice-driven bed of down. I do agnize 234
A natural and prompt alacrity
I find in hardness, and do undertake 236
These present wars against the Ottomites.
Most humbly therefore bending to your state, 238
I crave fit disposition for my wife,
Due reference of place and exhibition, 240
With such accommodation and besort 241
As levels with her breeding.

DUKE If you please, 242
Be 't at her father's.

BRABANTIO I will not have it so.

OTHELLO
Nor I.

DESDEMONA Nor I. I would not there reside,
To put my father in impatient thoughts
By being in his eye. Most gracious Duke,
To my unfolding lend your prosperous ear, 247
And let me find a charter in your voice 248
T' assist my simpleness.

DUKE
What would you, Desdemona?

DESDEMONA
That I did love the Moor to live with him,
My downright violence and storm of fortunes
May trumpet to the world. My heart's subdu'd
Even to the very quality of my lord.
I saw Othello's visage in his mind,
And to his honors and his valiant parts 256
Did I my soul and fortunes consecrate.
So that, dear lords, if I be left behind,
A moth of peace, and he go to the war,
The rites for why I love him are bereft me,
And I a heavy interim shall support
By his dear absence. Let me go with him.

OTHELLO
Let her have your voice.
Vouch with me, heaven, I therefore beg it not
To please the palate of my appetite,
Nor to comply with heat—the young affects 266
In me defunct—and proper satisfaction, 267
But to be free and bounteous to her mind.
And heaven defend your good souls, that you think
I will your serious and great business scant
When she is with me. No, when light-wing'd toys
Of feather'd Cupid seel with wanton dullness 272
My speculative and offic'd instruments, 273
That my disports corrupt and taint my business, 274
Let huswives make a skillet of my helm,
And all indign and base adversities 276
Make head against my estimation! 277

DUKE
Be it as you shall privately determine,
Either for her stay or going. Th' affair cries haste,
And speed must answer it.

FIRST SENATOR
You must away tonight.

OTHELLO With all my heart.

DUKE
At nine i' th' morning here we'll meet again.
Othello, leave some officer behind,
And he shall our commission bring to you,

198 For your sake on your account **202 like yourself** i.e., as you would, in your proper temper. **sentence** maxim (also at l. 219) **203 grise** step **208 next** nearest **209 What** whatever **210 Patience . . . makes** patience laughs at the injury inflicted by fortune (and thus eases the pain) **212 bootless** incurable **215–218 He bears . . . borrow** i.e., a person well bears out your maxim who takes with him only the philosophic consolation it teaches him, a comfort free from sorrow; but anyone whose grief bankrupts his poor patience is left with your saying and his sorrow too. (*Bears the sentence* also plays on the meaning of *receiving judicial sentence.*) **225 fortitude** strength **226 substitute** deputy **227 allow'd** acknowledged **227–228 opinion . . . on you** general opinion, an important determiner of affairs, chooses you as the best man **229 slubber** soil, sully **234 thrice-driven** thrice sifted, winnowed. **agnize** know in myself, acknowledge **236 hardness** hardship **238 bending . . . state** bowing or kneeling to your authority **240 reference . . . exhibition** provision of place to live and allowance of money **241 accommodation** apparel. **besort** attendance

242 levels equals, suits **247 prosperous** propitious **248 charter** privilege **256 parts** qualities **266 heat** sexual passion. **young affects** passions of youth, desires **267 proper** personal **272 seel** i.e., make blind (as in falconry, by sewing up the eyes of the hawk during training) **273 speculative . . . instruments** i.e., perceptive faculties used in the performance of duty **274 That** so that. **disports** pastimes. **taint** impair **276 indign** unworthy, shameful **277 Make head** raise an army. **estimation** reputation

With such things else of quality and respect
As doth import you.

OTHELLO So please your Grace, my ancient; 286
A man he is of honesty and trust.
To his conveyance I assign my wife,
With what else needful your good Grace shall think
To be sent after me.

DUKE Let it be so.
Good night to everyone. [*To Brabantio.*] And, noble signior,
If virtue no delighted beauty lack, 292
Your son-in-law is far more fair than black.

FIRST SENATOR
Adieu, brave Moor. Use Desdemona well.

BRABANTIO
Look to her, Moor, if thou hast eyes to see.
She has deceiv'd her father, and may thee.
Exeunt [*Duke, Senators, Officers, etc.*].

OTHELLO
My life upon her faith! Honest Iago,
My Desdemona must I leave to thee.
I prithee, let thy wife attend on her,
And bring them after in the best advantage. 300
Come, Desdemona. I have but an hour
Of love, of worldly matters and direction,
To spend with thee. We must obey the time.
Exit [*with Desdemona*].

RODERIGO Iago—

IAGO What say'st thou, noble heart?

RODERIGO What will I do, think'st thou?

IAGO Why, go to bed and sleep.

RODERIGO I will incontinently drown myself. 308

IAGO If thou dost, I shall never love thee after. Why, thou silly gentleman?

RODERIGO It is silliness to live when to live is torment; and then have we a prescription to die when death is our physician.

IAGO O villainous! I have look'd upon the world for four times seven years, and, since I could distinguish betwixt a benefit and an injury, I never found man that knew how to love himself. Ere I would say I would drown myself for the love of a guinea-hen, I would change my humanity with a baboon.

RODERIGO What should I do? I confess it is my shame
to be so fond, but it is not in my virtue to amend it. 321

IAGO Virtue? A fig! 'Tis in ourselves that we are thus or
thus. Our bodies are our gardens, to the which our
wills are gardeners; so that if we will plant nettles or
sow lettuce, set hyssop and weed up thyme, supply it 325
with one gender of herbs or distract it with many, ei- 326
ther to have it sterile with idleness or manur'd with 327
industry—why, the power and corrigible authority of 328
this lies in our wills. If the balance of our lives had not
one scale of reason to poise another of sensuality, the 330
blood and baseness of our natures would conduct us
to most prepost'rous conclusions. But we have reason
to cool our raging motions, our carnal stings, our un- 333
bitted lusts, whereof I take this that you call love to be 334
a sect or scion. 335

RODERIGO It cannot be.

IAGO It is merely a lust of the blood and a permission
of the will. Come, be a man. Drown thyself? Drown
cats and blind puppies. I have profess'd me thy friend,
and I confess me knit to thy deserving with cables of
perdurable toughness. I could never better stead thee 341
than now. Put money in thy purse. Follow thou the
wars; defeat thy favor with an usurp'd beard. I say, 343
put money in thy purse. It cannot be long that Des-
demona should continue her love to the Moor—put
money in thy purse—nor he his to her. It was a vio-
lent commencement in her, and thou shalt see an an- 347
swerable sequestration—put but money in thy purse. 348
These Moors are changeable in their wills—fill thy 349
purse with money. The food that to him now is as
luscious as locusts shall be to him shortly as bitter as 351
coloquintida. She must change for youth; when she is 352
sated with his body, she will find the error of her
choice. She must have change, she must. Therefore
put money in thy purse. If thou wilt needs damn thy-
self, do it a more delicate way than drowning. Make 356
all the money thou canst. If sanctimony and a frail vow
betwixt an erring barbarian and a super-subtle Vene- 358
tian be not too hard for my wits and all the tribe of
hell, thou shalt enjoy her. Therefore make money. A
pox of drowning thyself! It is clean out of the way.
Seek thou rather to be hang'd in compassing thy joy
than to be drown'd and go without her.

RODERIGO Wilt thou be fast to my hopes, if I depend on 364
the issue?

IAGO Thou art sure of me—go, make money. I have
told thee often, and I retell thee again and again, I hate
the Moor. My cause is hearted; thine hath no less rea- 368
son. Let us be conjunctive in our revenge against him; 369
if thou canst cuckold him, thou dost thyself a pleasure,
me a sport. There are many events in the womb of
time which will be deliver'd. Traverse, go, provide thy 372
money. We will have more of this tomorrow. Adieu.

RODERIGO Where shall we meet i' th' morning?

IAGO At my lodging.

RODERIGO I'll be with thee betimes. [*Starts to leave.*]

IAGO Go to, farewell.—Do you hear, Roderigo?

[RODERIGO What say you?

IAGO No more of drowning, do you hear?

RODERIGO I am chang'd.

IAGO Go to, farewell. Put money enough in your purse.]

RODERIGO I'll sell all my land. *Exit.*

IAGO
Thus do I ever make my fool my purse;
For I mine own gain'd knowledge should profane,

286 import concern **292 delighted** capable of delighting **300 in . . . advantage** at the most favorable opportunity **308 incontinently** immediately **321 fond** infatuated. **virtue** strength, nature **325 hyssop** a herb of the mint family **326 gender** kind **327 idleness** want of cultivation **328 corrigible authority** power to correct **330 poise** counterbalance

333 motions appetites **333–334 unbitted** uncontrolled **335 sect or scion** cutting or offshoot **341 perdurable** very durable. **stead** assist **343 defeat thy favor** disguise and disfigure your face **347–348 answerable sequestration** a corresponding separation or estrangement **349 wills** carnal appetites **351 locusts** fruit of the carob tree (see Matthew 3:4), or perhaps honeysuckle **352 coloquintida** colocynth or bitter apple, a purgative **356 Make** raise, collect **358 erring** wandering, vagabond, unsteady **364 fast** true **368 hearted** fixed in the heart **369 conjunctive** united **372 Traverse** go forward. (A military term.)

If I would time expend with such a snipe 386
But for my sport and profit. I hate the Moor;
And it is thought abroad that 'twixt my sheets
H'as done my office. I know not if 't be true;
But I, for mere suspicion in that kind,
Will do as if for surety. He holds me well;
The better shall my purpose work on him.
Cassio's a proper man. Let me see now: 393
To get his place and to plume up my will 394
In double knavery—How, how?—Let's see:
After some time, to abuse Othello's ears
That he is too familiar with his wife. 397
He hath a person and a smooth dispose 398
To be suspected, fram'd to make women false.
The Moor is of a free and open nature, 400
That thinks men honest that but seem to be so,
And will as tenderly be led by th' nose
As asses are.
I have 't. It is engend'red. Hell and night
Must bring this monstrous birth to the world's light.
[*Exit.*]

ACT II • SCENE I

Enter Montano and two Gentlemen.

MONTANO
What from the cape can you discern at sea?

FIRST GENTLEMAN
Nothing at all. It is a high-wrought flood.
I cannot, 'twixt the heaven and the main, 3
Descry a sail.

MONTANO
Methinks the wind hath spoke aloud at land;
A fuller blast ne'er shook our battlements.
If it hath ruffian'd so upon the sea, 7
What ribs of oak, when mountains melt on them, 8
Can hold the mortise? What shall we hear of this? 9

SECOND GENTLEMAN
A segregation of the Turkish fleet. 10
For do but stand upon the foaming shore,
The chidden billow seems to pelt the clouds;
The wind-shak'd surge, with high and monstrous mane,
Seems to cast water on the burning Bear 14
And quench the guards of th' ever-fixed pole.
I never did like molestation view 16
On the enchafed flood. 17

MONTANO
If that the Turkish fleet
Be not enshelter'd and embay'd, they are drown'd;
It is impossible to bear it out.

Enter a [Third] Gentleman.

THIRD GENTLEMAN
News, lads! Our wars are done.
The desperate tempest hath so bang'd the Turks
That their designment halts. A noble ship of Venice 23
Hath seen a grievous wrack and sufferance 24
On most part of their fleet.

MONTANO
How? Is this true?

THIRD GENTLEMAN The ship is here put in,
A Veronesa; Michael Cassio, 27
Lieutenant to the warlike Moor Othello,
Is come on shore; the Moor himself at sea,
And is in full commission here for Cyprus.

MONTANO
I am glad on 't; 'tis a worthy governor.

THIRD GENTLEMAN
But this same Cassio, though he speak of comfort
Touching the Turkish loss, yet he looks sadly,
And prays the Moor be safe; for they were parted
With foul and violent tempest.

MONTANO Pray heaven he be;
For I have serv'd him, and the man commands
Like a full soldier. Let's to the seaside, ho! 37
As well to see the vessel that's come in
As to throw out our eyes for brave Othello,
Even till we make the main and th' aerial blue
An indistinct regard.

THIRD GENTLEMAN Come, let's do so; 41
For every minute is expectancy
Of more arrivance. 43

Enter Cassio.

CASSIO
Thanks, you the valiant of this warlike isle,
That so approve the Moor! O, let the heavens
Give him defense against the elements,
For I have lost him on a dangerous sea.

MONTANO
Is he well shipp'd?

CASSIO
His bark is stoutly timber'd, and his pilot
Of very expert and approv'd allowance; 50
Therefore my hopes, not surfeited to death, 51
Stand in bold cure.
[*A cry*] *within:* "A sail, a sail, a sail!" 52

[*Enter a Messenger.*]

CASSIO
What noise?

MESSENGER
The town is empty; on the brow o' th' sea
Stand ranks of people, and they cry "A sail!"

386 snipe woodcock, i.e., fool **393 proper** handsome **394 plume up** glorify, gratify **397 he** i.e., Cassio **398 dispose** manner, bearing **400 free** frank, generous. **open** unsuspicious

II.i. Location: A seaport in Cyprus. An open place near the quay.
3 main ocean (also at l. 40) **7 ruffian'd** raged **8 mountains** i.e., of water **9 hold the mortise** hold their joints together. (A *mortise* is the socket hollowed out in fitting timbers.) **10 segregation** dispersion **14 burning Bear** i.e., the constellation Ursa Major or the Big Bear or Dipper, close to the north pole star (and hence regarded as the *guards of th' ever-fixed pole* in the next line) **16 like molestation** comparable uproar **17 enchafed** angry

23 designment enterprise **24 sufferance** disaster **27 Veronesa** Veronese ship **37 full** perfect **41 An indistinct regard** i.e., indistinguishable in our view **43 arrivance** arrival **50 allowance** reputation **51 surfeited to death** i.e., overextended, worn thin through repeated application or delayed fulfillment **52 in bold cure** in strong hopes of fulfillment

CASSIO
My hopes do shape him for the governor.
[*A shot within.*]

SECOND GENTLEMAN
They do discharge their shot of courtesy;
Our friends at least.

CASSIO
I pray you, sir, go forth,
And give us truth who 'tis that is arriv'd.

SECOND GENTLEMAN
I shall. *Exit.*

MONTANO
But, good lieutenant, is your general wiv'd?

CASSIO
Most fortunately. He hath achiev'd a maid
That paragons description and wild fame,
One that excels the quirks of blazoning pens,
And in th' essential vesture of creation
Does tire the ingener.

Enter [*Second*] *Gentleman.*

How now? Who has put in?

SECOND GENTLEMAN
'Tis one Iago, ancient to the general.

CASSIO
H'as had most favorable and happy speed.
Tempests themselves, high seas, and howling winds,
The gutter'd rocks and congregated sands—
Traitors ensteep'd to clog the guiltless keel—
As having sense of beauty, do omit
Their mortal natures, letting go safely by
The divine Desdemona.

MONTANO
What is she?

CASSIO
She that I spake of, our great captain's captain,
Left in the conduct of the bold Iago,
Whose footing here anticipates our thoughts
A se'nnight's speed. Great Jove, Othello guard,
And swell his sail with thine own pow'rful breath,
That he may bless this bay with his tall ship,
Make love's quick pants in Desdemona's arms,
Give renew'd fire to our extincted spirits,
[And bring all Cyprus comfort!]

Enter Desdemona, Iago, Roderigo, and Emilia, [*with Attendants*].

O, behold,
The riches of the ship is come on shore! [*Kneels.*]
You men of Cyprus, let her have your knees.
Hail to thee, lady! And the grace of heaven,
Before, behind thee, and on every hand,
Enwheel thee round! [*He rises.*]

DESDEMONA
I thank you, valiant Cassio.
What tidings can you tell me of my lord?

CASSIO
He is not yet arriv'd, nor know I aught
But that he's well and will be shortly here.

DESDEMONA
O, but I fear—How lost you company?

CASSIO
The great contention of the sea and skies
Parted our fellowship.
(*Within*) "A sail, a sail!" [*A shot.*]
But hark. A sail!

SECOND GENTLEMAN
They give their greeting to the citadel.
This likewise is a friend.

CASSIO
See for the news.
[*Exit Second Gentleman.*]
Good ancient, you are welcome. [*To Emilia.*]
Welcome, mistress.
Let it not gall your patience, good Iago,
That I extend my manners; 'tis my breeding
That gives me this bold show of courtesy.
[*Kissing her.*]

IAGO
Sir, would she give you so much of her lips
As of her tongue she oft bestows on me,
You would have enough.

DESDEMONA
Alas, she has no speech!

IAGO
In faith, too much.
I find it still, when I have list to sleep.
Marry, before your ladyship, I grant,
She puts her tongue a little in her heart,
And chides with thinking.

EMILIA
You have little cause to say so.

IAGO
Come on, come on; you are pictures out of doors,
Bells in your parlors, wildcats in your kitchens,
Saints in your injuries, devils being offended,
Players in your huswifery, and huswives in your beds.

DESDEMONA
O, fie upon thee, slanderer!

IAGO
Nay, it is true, or else I am a Turk.
You rise to play, and go to bed to work.

EMILIA
You shall not write my praise.

IAGO
No, let me not.

DESDEMONA
What wouldst thou write of me, if thou shouldst praise me?

IAGO
O gentle lady, do not put me to 't,
For I am nothing if not critical.

DESDEMONA
Come on, assay.—There's one gone to the harbor?

63 paragons surpasses **64 quirks** witty conceits. **blazoning** setting forth as though in heraldic language **65–66 in . . . ingener** in her real beauty (she) outdoes anyone who would inventively praise her **66 put in** i.e., to harbor **70 gutter'd** jagged, trenched **71 ensteep'd** lying under water **73 mortal** deadly **77 footing** landing **78 se'nnight's** week's

99 extend show **108 with thinking** i.e., in her thoughts only **109 pictures out of doors** i.e., painted surfaces, all cosmetics **110 Bells. . . kitchens** i.e., making pleasant conversation to your guests and angry shouts at your servants **111 Saints** martyrs **112 huswifery** housekeeping. **huswives** hussies. (I.e., women are "busy" in bed.) **119 critical** censorious **120 assay** try

IAGO
Ay, madam.

DESDEMONA
I am not merry; but I do beguile
The thing I am, by seeming otherwise.—
Come, how wouldst thou praise me?

IAGO
I am about it; but indeed my invention
Comes from my pate as birdlime does from frieze,
It plucks out brains and all. But my Muse labors,
And thus she is deliver'd:
If she be fair and wise, fairness and wit,
The one's for use, the other useth it.

DESDEMONA
Well prais'd! How if she be black and witty?

IAGO
If she be black, and thereto have a wit,
She'll find a white that shall her blackness fit.

DESDEMONA
Worse and worse.

EMILIA How if fair and foolish?

IAGO
She never yet was foolish that was fair,
For even her folly help'd her to an heir.

DESDEMONA These are old fond paradoxes to make fools laugh i' th' alehouse. What miserable praise hast thou for her that's foul and foolish?

IAGO
There's none so foul and foolish thereunto,
But does foul pranks which fair and wise ones do.

DESDEMONA O heavy ignorance! Thou praisest the worst best. But what praise couldst thou bestow on a deserving woman indeed, one that, in the authority of her merit, did justly put on the vouch of very malice itself?

IAGO
She that was ever fair, and never proud,
Had tongue at will, and yet was never loud,
Never lack'd gold, and yet went never gay,
Fled from her wish, and yet said, "Now I may,"
She that being ang'red, her revenge being nigh,
Bade her wrong stay, and her displeasure fly,
She that in wisdom never was so frail
To change the cod's head for the salmon's tail,
She that could think, and ne'er disclose her mind,
See suitors following, and not look behind,
She was a wight, if ever such wight were—

DESDEMONA To do what?

IAGO
To suckle fools and chronicle small beer.

DESDEMONA O most lame and impotent conclusion! Do not learn of him, Emilia, though he be thy husband. How say you, Cassio? Is he not a most profane and liberal counselor?

CASSIO He speaks home, madam. You may relish him more in the soldier than in the scholar.

[Cassio and Desdemona stand together, conversing intimately.]

IAGO *[Aside]* He takes her by the palm. Ay, well said, whisper. With as little a web as this will I ensnare as great a fly as Cassio. Ay, smile upon her, do; I will gyve thee in thine own courtship. You say true; 'tis so, indeed. If such tricks as these strip you out of your lieutenantry, it had been better you had not kiss'd your three fingers so oft, which now again you are most apt to play the sir in. Very good; well kiss'd! An excellent courtesy! 'Tis so, indeed. Yet again your fingers to your lips? Would they were clyster-pipes for your sake! *[Trumpet within.]*
The Moor! I know his trumpet.

CASSIO
'Tis truly so.

DESDEMONA Let's meet him and receive him.

CASSIO
Lo, where he comes!

Enter Othello and Attendants.

OTHELLO
O my fair warrior!

DESDEMONA My dear Othello!

OTHELLO
It gives me wonder great as my content
To see you here before me. O my soul's joy!
If after every tempest come such calms
May the winds blow till they have waken'd death!
And let the laboring bark climb hills of seas
Olympus-high, and duck again as low
As hell's from heaven! If it were now to die,
'Twere now to be most happy; for, I fear,
My soul hath her content so absolute
That not another comfort like to this
Succeeds in unknown fate.

DESDEMONA The heavens forbid
But that our loves and comforts should increase,
Even as our days do grow!

OTHELLO
Amen to that, sweet powers!
I cannot speak enough of this content;
It stops me here; it is too much of joy.
And this, and this, the greatest discords be
[Kissing her.]
That e'er our hearts shall make!

IAGO *[Aside]*
O, you are well tun'd now!
But I'll set down the pegs that make this music,

126 birdlime sticky substance used to catch small birds. **frieze** coarse woolen cloth **130 The one's . . . it** i.e., her cleverness will make use of her beauty **131 black** dark complexioned **133 white** a fair person (with word-play on *wight*, a person). **fit** (with sexual suggestion of mating) **136 folly** (with added meaning of *lechery, wantonness*). **to an heir** i.e., to bear a child **137 fond** foolish **139 foul** ugly **145 put . . . vouch** compel the approval **149 gay** extravagantly clothed **150 Fled . . . may** avoided temptation where the choice was hers **152 Bade . . . stay** i.e., resolved to put up with her injury patiently **154 To . . . tail** i.e., to exchange something cheap and nutritious for something expensive but worthless (? with perhaps a sexual suggestion of exchanging wisdom for carnality) **159 suckle fools** breastfeed babies. **chronicle small beer** i.e., keep petty household accounts

163 liberal licentious, free-spoken **164 home** i.e., without reserve **169 gyve** fetter, shackle. **courtship** courtesy, show of courtly manners **173 the sir** i.e., the fine gentleman **175 clyster-pipes** tubes used for enemas **191 Succeeds . . . fate** i.e., can follow in the unknown future **200 set down** loosen (and hence untune the instrument)

As honest as I am.

OTHELLO Come, let us to the castle.
News, friends! Our wars are done, the Turks are drown'd.
How does my old acquaintance of this isle?—
Honey, you shall be well desir'd in Cyprus; 204
I have found great love amongst them. O my sweet,
I prattle out of fashion, and I dote
In mine own comforts. I prithee, good Iago,
Go to the bay and disembark my coffers.
Bring thou the master to the citadel; 209
He is a good one, and his worthiness
Does challenge much respect. Come, Desdemona, 211
Once more, well met at Cyprus.

Exeunt Othello and Desdemona [*and all but Iago and Roderigo*].

IAGO [*To an Attendant*] Do thou meet me presently at
the harbor. [*To Roderigo.*] Come hither. If thou be'st
valiant—as, they say, base men being in love have
then a nobility in their natures more than is native to
them—list me. The lieutenant tonight watches on the
court of guard. First, I must tell thee this: Desdemona 218
is directly in love with him.

RODERIGO With him? Why, 'tis not possible.

IAGO Lay thy finger thus, and let thy soul be instructed. 221
Mark me with what violence she first lov'd the Moor,
but for bragging and telling her fantastical lies. And
will she love him still for prating? Let not thy discreet
heart think it. Her eye must be fed; and what delight
shall she have to look on the devil? When the blood is
made dull with the act of sport, there should be, again
to inflame it and to give satiety a fresh appetite, love-
liness in favor, sympathy in years, manners, and
beauties—all which the Moor is defective in. Now, for
want of these requir'd conveniences, her delicate ten- 231
derness will find itself abus'd, begin to heave the 232
gorge, disrelish and abhor the Moor. Very nature will 233
instruct her in it and compel her to some second
choice. Now, sir, this granted—as it is a most preg- 235
nant and unforc'd position—who stands so eminent 236
in the degree of this fortune as Cassio does? A knave
very voluble; no further conscionable than in putting 238
on the mere form of civil and humane seeming, for the 239
better compassing of his salt and most hidden loose 240
affection? Why, none, why, none. A slipper and subtle 241
knave, a finder of occasions, that has an eye can stamp 242
and counterfeit advantages, though true advantage
never present itself; a devilish knave. Besides, the
knave is handsome, young, and hath all those requi-
sites in him that folly and green minds look after. A
pestilent complete knave, and the woman hath found
him already.

RODERIGO I cannot believe that in her; she's full of most bless'd condition.

IAGO Bless'd fig's-end! The wine she drinks is made of grapes. If she had been bless'd, she would never have lov'd the Moor. Bless'd pudding! Didst thou not see her paddle with the palm of his hand? Didst not mark that?

RODERIGO Yes, that I did; but that was but courtesy.

IAGO Lechery, by this hand. An index and obscure pro- 257
logue to the history of lust and foul thoughts. They
met so near with their lips that their breaths embrac'd
together. Villainous thoughts, Roderigo! When these
mutualities so marshal the way, hard at hand comes 261
the master and main exercise, th' incorporate conclu- 262
sion. Pish! But, sir, be you rul'd by me. I have brought
you from Venice. Watch you tonight; for the com-
mand, I'll lay 't upon you. Cassio knows you not. I'll
not be far from you. Do you find some occasion to
anger Cassio, either by speaking too loud, or tainting 267
his discipline, or from what other course you please,
which the time shall more favorably minister.

RODERIGO Well.

IAGO Sir, he's rash and very sudden in choler, and hap- 271
pily may strike at you. Provoke him, that he may; for 272
even out of that will I cause these of Cyprus to mutiny,
whose qualification shall come into no true taste again 274
but by the displanting of Cassio. So shall you have a
shorter journey to your desires by the means I shall
then have to prefer them; and the impediment most 277
profitably remov'd, without the which there were no
expectation of our prosperity.

RODERIGO I will do this, if I can bring it to any opportunity.

IAGO I warrant thee. Meet me by and by at the citadel. 282
I must fetch his necessaries ashore. Farewell.

RODERIGO Adieu. *Exit.*

IAGO
That Cassio loves her, I do well believe 't;
That she loves him, 'tis apt and of great credit. 286
The Moor, howbeit that I endure him not,
Is of a constant, loving, noble nature,
And I dare think he'll prove to Desdemona
A most dear husband. Now, I do love her too,
Not out of absolute lust, though peradventure
I stand accountant for as great a sin, 292
But partly led to diet my revenge, 293
For that I do suspect the lusty Moor
Hath leap'd into my seat; the thought whereof
Doth, like a poisonous mineral, gnaw my inwards;
And nothing can or shall content my soul
Till I am even'd with him, wife for wife,
Or failing so, yet that I put the Moor
At least into a jealousy so strong
That judgment cannot cure. Which thing to do,
If this poor trash of Venice, whom I trash 302
For his quick hunting, stand the putting on, 303

204 desir'd welcomed **209 master** ship's captain **211 challenge** lay claim to, deserve **218 court of guard** guardhouse. (Cassio is in charge of the watch.) **221 thus** i.e., on your lips **231 conveniences** compatibilities **232–233 heave the gorge** experience nausea **235–236 pregnant** evident, readily believable **238 conscionable** conscientious, conscience-bound **239 humane** polite, courteous **240 salt** licentious **241 slipper** slippery **242 an eye can stamp** an eye that can coin, create

257 index table of contents **261 mutualities** exchanges, intimacies **262 incorporate** carnal **267 tainting** disparaging **271 choler** wrath **271–272 happily** haply, perchance **274 qualification** appeasement. **true taste** acceptable state **277 prefer** advance **282 by and by** immediately **286 apt** probable. **credit** credibility **292 accountant** accountable **293 diet** feed **302 I trash** I hold in check. (A hunting term, meaning to put weights on a hunting dog in order to slow him down.) **303 For** to make more eager. **stand . . . on** responds properly when I incite him to quarrel

I'll have our Michael Cassio on the hip, 304
Abuse him to the Moor in the rank garb— 305
For I fear Cassio with my night-cap too— 306
Make the Moor thank me, love me, and reward me
For making him egregiously an ass
And practicing upon his peace and quiet 309
Even to madness. 'Tis here, but yet confus'd.
Knavery's plain face is never seen till us'd. *Exit.*

SCENE II

Enter Othello's Herald with a proclamation.

HERALD It is Othello's pleasure, our noble and valiant general, that, upon certain tidings now arriv'd, im-
porting the mere perdition of the Turkish fleet, every 3
man put himself into triumph; some to dance, some to make bonfires, each man to what sport and revels his addiction leads him. For, besides these beneficial news, it is the celebration of his nuptial. So much was
his pleasure should be proclaim'd. All offices are open, 8
and there is full liberty of feasting from this present hour of five till the bell have told eleven. Heaven bless the isle of Cyprus and our noble general Othello! *Exit.*

[SCENE III]

Enter Othello, Desdemona, Cassio, and Attendants.

OTHELLO
Good Michael, look you to the guard tonight.
Let's teach ourselves that honorable stop, 2
Not to outsport discretion.

CASSIO
Iago hath direction what to do;
But, notwithstanding, with my personal eye
Will I look to 't.

OTHELLO Iago is most honest.
Michael, good night. Tomorrow with your earliest
Let me have speech with you. [*To Desdemona.*]
Come, my dear love,
The purchase made, the fruits are to ensue;
That profit's yet to come 'tween me and you.—
Good night.
Exit [Othello, with Desdemona and Attendants].

Enter Iago.

CASSIO Welcome, Iago. We must to the watch.

IAGO Not this hour, lieutenant; 'tis not yet ten o' th'
clock. Our general cast us thus early for the love of his 14
Desdemona; who let us not therefore blame. He hath not yet made wanton the night with her, and she is sport for Jove.

CASSIO She's a most exquisite lady.

IAGO And, I'll warrant her, full of game.

CASSIO Indeed, she's a most fresh and delicate creature.

IAGO What an eye she has! Methinks it sounds a parley 21
to provocation.

CASSIO An inviting eye; and yet methinks right modest.

IAGO And when she speaks, is it not an alarum to love? 24

CASSIO She is indeed perfection.

IAGO Well, happiness to their sheets! Come, lieutenant,
I have a stoup of wine, and here without are a brace 27
of Cyprus gallants that would fain have a measure to the health of black Othello.

CASSIO Not tonight, good Iago. I have very poor and unhappy brains for drinking. I could well wish courtesy would invent some other custom of entertainment.

IAGO O, they are our friends. But one cup! I'll drink for you.

CASSIO I have drunk but one cup tonight, and that was
craftily qualified too, and behold what innovation it 37
makes here. I am unfortunate in the infirmity, and 38
dare not task my weakness with any more.

IAGO What, man? 'Tis a night of revels. The gallants desire it.

CASSIO Where are they?

IAGO Here at the door. I pray you, call them in.

CASSIO I'll do 't; but it dislikes me. *Exit.*

IAGO
If I can fasten but one cup upon him,
With that which he hath drunk tonight already,
He'll be as full of quarrel and offense
As my young mistress' dog. Now, my sick fool
Roderigo,
Whom love hath turn'd almost the wrong side out,
To Desdemona hath tonight carous'd
Potations pottle-deep; and he's to watch. 51
Three lads of Cyprus, noble swelling spirits,
That hold their honors in a wary distance, 53
The very elements of this warlike isle, 54
Have I tonight fluster'd with flowing cups,
And they watch too. Now, 'mongst this flock of
drunkards 56
Am I to put our Cassio in some action
That may offend the isle.—But here they come.

Enter Cassio, Montano, and Gentlemen; [servants following with wine].

If consequence do but approve my dream, 59
My boat sails freely, both with wind and stream.

304 on the hip at my mercy, where I can throw him. (A wrestling term.) **305 rank garb** coarse manner, gross fashion **306 with my night-cap** i.e., as a rival in my bed, as one who gives me cuckold's horns **309 practicing upon** plotting against

II.ii. Location: Cyprus. A street.
3 mere perdition complete destruction **8 offices** rooms where food and drink are kept

II.iii. Location: Cyprus. The citadel.
2 stop restraint

14 cast dismissed **21 sounds a parley** calls for a conference, issues an invitation **24 alarum** signal calling men to arms (continuing the military metaphor of *parley,* l. 21) **27 stoup** measure of liquor, two quarts **37 qualified** diluted. **innovation** disturbance, insurrection **38 here** i.e., in Cassio's head **51 pottle-deep** to the bottom of the tankard **53 hold . . . distance** i.e., are extremely sensitive of their honor **54 very elements** true representatives **56 watch** are members of the guard **59 If . . . dream** if subsequent events will only confirm my scheme

CASSIO 'Fore God, they have given me a rouse already.

MONTANO Good faith, a little one; not past a pint, as I am a soldier.

IAGO Some wine, ho!

[*Sings.*] "And let me the canakin clink, clink;
And let me the canakin clink.
A soldier's a man,
O, man's life's but a span;
Why, then, let a soldier drink."

Some wine, boys!

CASSIO 'Fore God, an excellent song.

IAGO I learn'd it in England, where indeed they are most potent in potting. Your Dane, your German, and your swag-bellied Hollander—Drink, ho!—are nothing to your English.

CASSIO Is your Englishman so exquisite in his drinking?

IAGO Why, he drinks you, with facility, your Dane dead drunk; he sweats not to overthrow your Almain; he gives your Hollander a vomit ere the next pottle can be fill'd.

CASSIO To the health of our general!

MONTANO I am for it, lieutenant; and I'll do you justice.

IAGO O sweet England! [*Sings.*]

"King Stephen was and-a worthy peer,
His breeches cost him but a crown;
He held them sixpence all too dear,
With that he call'd the tailor lown.

He was a wight of high renown,
And thou art but of low degree.
'Tis pride that pulls the country down;
Then take thy auld cloak about thee."

Some wine, ho!

CASSIO 'Fore God, this is a more exquisite song than the other.

IAGO Will you hear 't again?

CASSIO No; for I hold him to be unworthy of his place that does those things. Well, God's above all; and there be souls must be sav'd, and there be souls must not be sav'd.

IAGO It's true, good lieutenant.

CASSIO For mine own part—no offense to the general, nor any man of quality—I hope to be sav'd.

IAGO And so do I too, lieutenant.

CASSIO Ay, but, by your leave, not before me; the lieutenant is to be sav'd before the ancient. Let's have no more of this; let's to our affairs.—God forgive us our sins!—Gentlemen, let's look to our business. Do not think, gentlemen, I am drunk. This is my ancient; this is my right hand, and this is my left. I am not drunk now; I can stand well enough, and speak well enough.

ALL Excellent well.

CASSIO Why, very well then; you must not think then that I am drunk. *Exit.*

MONTANO
To th' platform, masters. Come, let's set the watch.

IAGO
You see this fellow that is gone before.
He's a soldier fit to stand by Caesar
And give direction; and do but see his vice.
'Tis to his virtue a just equinox,
The one as long as th' other. 'Tis pity of him.
I fear the trust Othello puts him in,
On some odd time of his infirmity,
Will shake this island.

MONTANO But is he often thus?

IAGO
'Tis evermore the prologue to his sleep.
He'll watch the horologe a double set,
If drink rock not his cradle.

MONTANO It were well
The general were put in mind of it.
Perhaps he sees it not, or his good nature
Prizes the virtue that appears in Cassio
And looks not on his evils. Is not this true?

Enter Roderigo.

IAGO [*Aside to him*]
How now, Roderigo?
I pray you, after the lieutenant; go. [*Exit Roderigo.*]

MONTANO
And 'tis great pity that the noble Moor
Should hazard such a place as his own second
With one of an ingraft infirmity.
It were an honest action to say so
To the Moor.

IAGO Not I, for this fair island.
I do love Cassio well, and would do much
To cure him of this evil. [*Cry within:* Help! Help!]
But, hark! What noise?

Enter Cassio, pursuing Roderigo.

CASSIO 'Zounds, you rogue! You rascal!

MONTANO What's the matter, lieutenant?

CASSIO A knave teach me my duty? I'll beat the knave into a twiggen bottle.

RODERIGO Beat me?

CASSIO Dost thou prate, rogue? [*Striking Roderigo.*]

MONTANO Nay, good lieutenant; [*Staying him.*] I pray you, sir, hold your hand.

CASSIO Let me go, sir, or I'll knock you o'er the mazzard.

MONTANO Come, come, you're drunk.

CASSIO Drunk? [*They fight.*]

IAGO [*Aside to Roderigo*]
Away, I say; go out, and cry a mutiny.
[*Exit Roderigo.*]
Nay, good lieutenant—God's will, gentlemen—
Help, ho!—Lieutenant—sir—Montano—sir—

61 rouse full draft of liquor **65 canakin** small drinking vessel **78 Almain** German **82 I'll . . . justice** i.e., I'll drink as much as you **87 lown** lout, rascal **90 pride** i.e., extravagance in dress **91 auld** old

118 just equinox exact counterpart. (*Equinox* is an equal length of days and nights.) **124 watch . . . set** stay awake twice around the clock or *horologe* **133 second** i.e., second in command **134 ingraft** ingrafted, inveterate **142 twiggen** wicker-covered **147–148 mazzard** i.e., head. (Literally, a drinking vessel.)

Help, masters!—Here's a goodly watch indeed!
[*Bell rings.*]
Who's that which rings the bell?—Diablo, ho!
The town will rise. God's will, lieutenant, hold!
You'll be asham'd for ever.

Enter Othello and Attendants.

OTHELLO
What is the matter here?

MONTANO
'Zounds, I bleed still;
I am hurt to th' death. He dies! [*Thrusts at Cassio.*]

OTHELLO
Hold for your lives!

IAGO
Hold, ho! Lieutenant—sir—Montano—gentlemen—
Have you forgot all sense of place and duty?
Hold! The general speaks to you. Hold, for shame!

OTHELLO
Why, how now, ho! From whence ariseth this?
Are we turn'd Turks, and to ourselves do that
Which heaven hath forbid the Ottomites?
For Christian shame, put by this barbarous brawl!
He that stirs next to carve for his own rage
Holds his soul light; he dies upon his motion.
Silence that dreadful bell. It frights the isle
From her propriety. What is the matter, masters?
Honest Iago, that looks dead with grieving,
Speak. Who began this? On thy love, I charge thee.

IAGO
I do not know. Friends all, but now, even now,
In quarter, and in terms like bride and groom
Devesting them for bed; and then, but now—
As if some planet had unwitted men—
Swords out, and tilting one at other's breast,
In opposition bloody. I cannot speak
Any beginning to this peevish odds;
And would in action glorious I had lost
Those legs that brought me to a part of it!

OTHELLO
How comes it, Michael, you are thus forgot?

CASSIO
I pray you, pardon me; I cannot speak.

OTHELLO
Worthy Montano, you were wont to be civil;
The gravity and stillness of your youth
The world hath noted, and your name is great
In mouths of wisest censure. What's the matter
That you unlace your reputation thus,
And spend your rich opinion for the name
Of a night-brawler? Give me answer to it.

MONTANO
Worthy Othello, I am hurt to danger.
Your officer, Iago, can inform you—
While I spare speech, which something now
offends me—
Of all that I do know; nor know I aught
By me that's said or done amiss this night,
Unless self-charity be sometimes a vice,
And to defend ourselves it be a sin
When violence assails us.

OTHELLO
Now, by heaven,
My blood begins my safer guides to rule,
And passion, having my best judgment collied,
Assays to lead the way. If I once stir,
Or do but lift this arm, the best of you
Shall sink in my rebuke. Give me to know
How this foul rout began, who set it on;
And he that is approv'd in this offense,
Though he had twinn'd with me, both at a birth,
Shall lose me. What? In a town of war,
Yet wild, the people's hearts brimful of fear,
To manage private and domestic quarrel?
In night, and on the court and guard of safety?
'Tis monstrous. Iago, who began 't?

MONTANO
If partially affin'd, or leagu'd in office,
Thou dost deliver more or less than truth,
Thou art no soldier.

IAGO
Touch me not so near.
I had rather have this tongue cut from my mouth
Than it should do offense to Michael Cassio;
Yet, I persuade myself, to speak the truth
Shall nothing wrong him. Thus it is, general.
Montano and myself being in speech,
There comes a fellow crying out for help,
And Cassio following him with determin'd sword
To execute upon him. Sir, this gentleman
[*Indicating Montano.*]
Steps in to Cassio, and entreats his pause.
Myself the crying fellow did pursue,
Lest by his clamor—as it so fell out—
The town might fall in fright. He, swift of foot,
Outran my purpose; and I return'd the rather
For that I heard the clink and fall of swords,
And Cassio high in oath; which till tonight
I ne'er might say before. When I came back—
For this was brief—I found them close together,
At blow and thrust, even as again they were
When you yourself did part them.
More of this matter cannot I report.
But men are men; the best sometimes forget.
Though Cassio did some little wrong to him,
As men in rage strike those that wish them best,
Yet surely Cassio, I believe, receiv'd
From him that fled some strange indignity,
Which patience could not pass.

OTHELLO
I know, Iago,
Thy honesty and love doth mince this matter,
Making it light to Cassio. Cassio, I love thee;
But never more be officer of mine.

Enter Desdemona, attended.

155 Diablo the devil **156 rise** grow riotous **165 forbid** i.e., by destroying their fleet, so that the Venetians need not fight them **167 carve for** i.e., indulge, satisfy **170 propriety** proper state or condition **174 In quarter** in good military order, within bounds **179 peevish odds** childish quarrel **187 censure** judgment **188 unlace** undo, degrade **189 opinion** reputation **193 something** somewhat. **offends** pains

199 blood passion (of anger). **guides** i.e., reason **200 collied** darkened **201 Assays** undertakes **204 rout** riot **205 approv'd in** found guilty of **209 manage** undertake **210 court and guard** i.e., the main guardhouse or headquarters **212 partially affin'd** made partial by some personal relationship **222 execute** give effect to (his anger) **227 rather** sooner **240 pass** pass over, overlook

Look, if my gentle love be not rais'd up.
I'll make thee an example.

DESDEMONA
What is the matter, dear?

OTHELLO
All's well now, sweeting;
Come away to bed. [*To Montano.*] Sir, for your hurts,
Myself will be your surgeon.—Lead him off.
[*Montano is led off.*]
Iago, look with care about the town,
And silence those whom this vile brawl distracted.
Come, Desdemona. 'Tis the soldiers' life
To have their balmy slumbers wak'd with strife.
Exit [*with all but Iago and Cassio*].

IAGO What, are you hurt, lieutenant?

CASSIO Ay, past all surgery.

IAGO Marry, God forbid!

CASSIO Reputation, reputation, reputation! O, I have lost my reputation! I have lost the immortal part of myself, and what remains is bestial. My reputation, Iago, my reputation!

IAGO As I am an honest man, I thought you had receiv'd some bodily wound; there is more sense in that than in reputation. Reputation is an idle and most false imposition; oft got without merit, and lost without deserving. You have lost no reputation at all, unless you repute yourself such a loser. What, man, there are ways to recover the general again. You are but now cast in his mood, a punishment more in policy than in malice, even so as one would beat his offenseless dog to affright an imperious lion. Sue to him again, and he's yours.

CASSIO I will rather sue to be despis'd than to deceive so good a commander with so slight, so drunken, and so indiscreet an officer. Drunk? And speak parrot? And squabble? Swagger? Swear? And discourse fustian with one's own shadow? O thou invisible spirit of wine, if thou hast no name to be known by, let us call thee devil!

IAGO What was he that you follow'd with your sword? What had he done to you?

CASSIO I know not.

IAGO Is 't possible?

CASSIO I remember a mass of things, but nothing distinctly; a quarrel, but nothing wherefore. O God, that men should put an enemy in their mouths to steal away their brains! That we should, with joy, pleasance, revel, and applause, transform ourselves into beasts!

IAGO Why, but you are now well enough. How came you thus recover'd?

CASSIO It hath pleas'd the devil drunkenness to give place to the devil wrath. One unperfectness shows me another, to make me frankly despise myself.

IAGO Come, you are too severe a moraler. As the time, the place, and the condition of this country stands, I could heartily wish this had not befall'n; but since it is as it is, mend it for your own good.

CASSIO I will ask him for my place again; he shall tell me I am a drunkard! Had I as many mouths as Hydra, such an answer would stop them all. To be now a sensible man, by and by a fool, and presently a beast! O strange! Every inordinate cup is unbless'd, and the ingredient is a devil.

IAGO Come, come, good wine is a good familiar creature, if it be well us'd. Exclaim no more against it. And, good lieutenant, I think you think I love you.

CASSIO I have well approv'd it, sir. I drunk!

IAGO You or any man living may be drunk at a time, man. I'll tell you what you shall do. Our general's wife is now the general—I may say so in this respect, for that he hath devoted and given up himself to the contemplation, mark, and denotement of her parts and graces. Confess yourself freely to her; importune her help to put you in your place again. She is of so free, so kind, so apt, so bless'd a disposition, she holds it a vice in her goodness not to do more than she is requested. This broken joint between you and her husband entreat her to splinter; and, my fortunes against any lay worth naming, this crack of your love shall grow stronger than it was before.

CASSIO You advise me well.

IAGO I protest, in the sincerity of love and honest kindness.

CASSIO I think it freely; and betimes in the morning I will beseech the virtuous Desdemona to undertake for me. I am desperate of my fortunes if they check me here.

IAGO You are in the right. Good night, lieutenant; I must to the watch.

CASSIO Good night, honest Iago. *Exit Cassio.*

IAGO
And what's he then that says I play the villain?
When this advice is free I give and honest,
Probal to thinking, and indeed the course
To win the Moor again? For 'tis most easy
Th' inclining Desdemona to subdue
In any honest suit; she's fram'd as fruitful
As the free elements. And then for her
To win the Moor—were 't to renounce his baptism,
All seals and symbols of redeemed sin—
His soul is so enfetter'd to her love
That she may make, unmake, do what she list,
Even as her appetite shall play the god
With his weak function. How am I then a villain
To counsel Cassio to this parallel course,
Directly to his good? Divinity of hell!
When devils will the blackest sins put on,
They do suggest at first with heavenly shows,

263 imposition thing artificially imposed and of no real value **266 recover** regain favor with **267 cast in his mood** dismissed in a moment of anger **273 speak parrot** talk nonsense, rant. (*Discourse fustian*, ll. 274–275, has the same meaning.)

298 Hydra the Lernaean Hydra, a monster with many heads, slain by Hercules as the second of his twelve labors **306 approv'd** proved **311 mark, and denotement.** (Both words mean *observation.*) **parts** qualities **313 free** generous **317 splinter** bind with splints **318 lay** stake, wager **325 check** repulse **332 Probal** probable **334 inclining** favorably disposed. **subdue** persuade **335 fruitful** generous **336 free elements** i.e., earth, air, fire, and water, which sustain life (?) **343 parallel** corresponding to these facts and to his best interest **344 Divinity of hell** inverted theology of hell (which seduces the soul to its damnation) **345 put on** further, instigate **346 suggest** tempt

As I do now. For whiles this honest fool
Plies Desdemona to repair his fortunes,
And she for him pleads strongly to the Moor,
I'll pour this pestilence into his ear,
That she repeals him for her body's lust; 351
And by how much she strives to do him good,
She shall undo her credit with the Moor.
So will I turn her virtue into pitch,
And out of her own goodness make the net
That shall enmesh them all.

Enter Roderigo.

How now, Roderigo?

RODERIGO I do follow here in the chase, not like a
hound that hunts, but one that fills up the cry. My 358
money is almost spent; I have been tonight exceed-
ingly well cudgel'd; and I think the issue will be, I
shall have so much experience for my pains, and so,
with no money at all and a little more wit, return again
to Venice.

IAGO
How poor are they that have not patience!
What wound did ever heal but by degrees?
Thou know'st we work by wit, and not by
witchcraft;
And wit depends on dilatory time.
Does 't not go well? Cassio hath beaten thee,
And thou, by that small hurt, hast cashier'd Cassio. 369
Though other things grow fair against the sun,
Yet fruits that blossom first will first be ripe.
Content thyself awhile. By the mass, 'tis morning!
Pleasure and action make the hours seem short.
Retire thee; go where thou art billeted.
Away, I say! Thou shalt know more hereafter.
Nay, get thee gone. *Exit Roderigo.*
Two things are to be done.
My wife must move for Cassio to her mistress;
I'll set her on;
Myself the while to draw the Moor apart,
And bring him jump when he may Cassio find 380
Soliciting his wife. Ay, that's the way!
Dull not device by coldness and delay. *Exit.*

ACT III • SCENE I

Enter Cassio [and] Musicians.

CASSIO
Masters, play here, I will content your pains; 1
Something that's brief; and bid "Good morrow,
general." *[They play.]*

[Enter] Clown.

CLOWN Why, masters, have your instruments been in
Naples, that they speak i' th' nose thus? 4

FIRST MUSICIAN How, sir, how?

CLOWN Are these, I pray you, wind instruments?

FIRST MUSICIAN Ay, marry, are they, sir.

CLOWN O, thereby hangs a tail.

FIRST MUSICIAN Whereby hangs a tale, sir?

CLOWN Marry, sir, by many a wind instrument that I 10
know. But, masters, here's money for you. *[Gives
money.]* And the general so likes your music that he
desires you, for love's sake, to make no more noise
with it.

FIRST MUSICIAN Well, sir, we will not.

CLOWN If you have any music that may not be heard,
to 't again; but, as they say, to hear music the general
does not greatly care.

FIRST MUSICIAN We have none such, sir.

CLOWN Then put up your pipes in your bag, for I'll
away. Go, vanish into air, away! *Exeunt Musicians.*

CASSIO Dost thou hear, mine honest friend?

CLOWN No, I hear not your honest friend; I hear you.

CASSIO Prithee, keep up thy quillets. There's a poor 24
piece of gold for thee. *[Gives money.]* If the gentle-
woman that attends the general's wife be stirring, tell
her there's one Cassio entreats her a little favor of
speech. Wilt thou do this?

CLOWN She is stirring, sir. If she will stir hither, I shall
seem to notify unto her.

CASSIO
[Do, good my friend.] *Exit Clown.*

Enter Iago.

In happy time, Iago. 31

IAGO
You have not been a-bed, then?

CASSIO
Why, no; the day had broke
Before we parted. I have made bold, Iago,
To send in to your wife. My suit to her
Is that she will to virtuous Desdemona
Procure me some access.

IAGO
I'll send her to you presently;
And I'll devise a mean to draw the Moor
Out of the way, that your converse and business
May be more free.

CASSIO
I humbly thank you for 't. *Exit [Iago].*
I never knew
A Florentine more kind and honest. 43

Enter Emilia.

EMILIA
Good morrow, good lieutenant. I am sorry
For your displeasure; but all will sure be well.
The general and his wife are talking of it,
And she speaks for you stoutly. The Moor replies
That he you hurt is of great fame in Cyprus
And great affinity, and that in wholesome wisdom 49

351 repeals him i.e., attempts to get him restored **358 cry** pack **369 cashier'd** dismissed from service **380 jump** precisely

III.i. Location: Before the chamber of Othello and Desdemona.
1 content reward **4 speak i' th' nose** (1) sound nasal (2) sound like one whose nose has been attacked by syphilis. (Naples was popularly supposed to have a high incidence of venereal disease.)

10 wind instrument (The term, together with *tail* in l. 8, suggests a joke on flatulence.) **24 quillets** quibbles, puns **31 In happy time** i.e., well met **43 Florentine** i.e., even a fellow-Florentine. (Iago is a Venetian, Cassio a Florentine.) **49 affinity** kindred, family connnection

He might not but refuse you; but he protests he
  loves you
And needs no other suitor but his likings
[To take the safest occasion by the front]
To bring you in again.

CASSIO
Yet, I beseech you,
If you think fit, or that it may be done,
Give me advantage of some brief discourse
With Desdemon alone.

EMILIA
Pray you, come in.
I will bestow you where you shall have time
To speak your bosom freely.

CASSIO
I am much bound to you. [*Exeunt.*]

SCENE II

Enter Othello, Iago, and Gentlemen.

OTHELLO
These letters give, Iago, to the pilot, [*Gives letters.*]
And by him do my duties to the Senate.
That done, I will be walking on the works;
Repair there to me.

IAGO
Well, my good lord, I'll do 't.

OTHELLO
This fortification, gentlemen, shall we see 't?

GENTLEMEN
We'll wait upon your lordship. *Exeunt.*

SCENE III

Enter Desdemona, Cassio, and Emilia.

DESDEMONA
Be thou assur'd, good Cassio, I will do
All my abilities in thy behalf.

EMILIA
Good madam, do. I warrant it grieves my husband
As if the case were his.

DESDEMONA
O, that's an honest fellow. Do not doubt, Cassio,
But I will have my lord and you again
As friendly as you were.

CASSIO
Bounteous madam,
Whatever shall become of Michael Cassio,
He's never anything but your true servant.

DESDEMONA
I know 't; I thank you. You do love my lord;
You have known him long; and be you well assur'd
He shall in strangeness stand no farther off
Than in a politic distance.

CASSIO
Ay, but, lady,
That policy may either last so long,
Or feed upon such nice and waterish diet,
Or breed itself so out of circumstance,
That, I being absent and my place supplied,
My general will forget my love and service.

DESDEMONA
Do not doubt that; before Emilia here
I give thee warrant of thy place. Assure thee,
If I do vow a friendship, I'll perform it
To the last article. My lord shall never rest.
I'll watch him tame and talk him out of patience;
His bed shall seem a school, his board a shrift;
I'll intermingle everything he does
With Cassio's suit. Therefore be merry, Cassio,
For thy solicitor shall rather die
Than give thy cause away.

Enter Othello and Iago [*at a distance*].

EMILIA
Madam, here comes my lord.

CASSIO
Madam, I'll take my leave.

DESDEMONA
Why, stay, and hear me speak.

CASSIO
Madam, not now. I am very ill at ease,
Unfit for mine own purposes.

DESDEMONA
Well, do your discretion. *Exit Cassio.*

IAGO
Ha? I like not that.

OTHELLO
What dost thou say?

IAGO
Nothing, my lord; or if—I know not what.

OTHELLO
Was not that Cassio parted from my wife?

IAGO
Cassio, my lord? No, sure, I cannot think it,
That he would steal away so guilty-like,
Seeing you coming.

OTHELLO
I do believe 'twas he.

DESDEMONA
How now, my lord?
I have been talking with a suitor here,
A man that languishes in your displeasure.

OTHELLO
Who is 't you mean?

DESDEMONA
Why, your lieutenant, Cassio. Good my lord,
If I have any grace or power to move you,
His present reconciliation take;
For if he be not one that truly loves you,
That errs in ignorance and not in cunning,
I have no judgment in an honest face.
I prithee, call him back.

52 occasion . . . front opportunity by the forelock **58 bosom** inmost thoughts

III.ii. Location: The citadel.
3 works breastworks, fortifications

III.iii. Location: The garden of the citadel.
12 strangeness aloofness

13 politic required by wise policy **15 Or . . . diet** or sustain itself at length upon a trivial and meager means of support **16 circumstance** chance events **19 doubt** fear **23 watch him tame** tame him by keeping him from sleeping. (A term from falconry.) **out of patience** past his endurance **24 shrift** confessional **47 present** immediate

OTHELLO
Went he hence now?
DESDEMONA Yes, faith, so humbled
That he hath left part of his grief with me
To suffer with him. Good love, call him back.
OTHELLO
Not now, sweet Desdemon; some other time.
DESDEMONA
But shall 't be shortly?
OTHELLO The sooner, sweet, for you.
DESDEMONA
Shall 't be tonight at supper?
OTHELLO No, not tonight.
DESDEMONA
Tomorrow dinner, then?
OTHELLO I shall not dine at home;
I meet the captains at the citadel.
DESDEMONA
Why, then, tomorrow night, or Tuesday morn,
On Tuesday noon, or night, on Wednesday morn.
I prithee, name the time, but let it not
Exceed three days. In faith, he's penitent;
And yet his trespass, in our common reason—
Save that, they say, the wars must make example
Out of her best—is not almost a fault
T' incur a private check. When shall he come?
Tell me, Othello. I wonder in my soul
What you would ask me, that I should deny,
Or stand so mamm'ring on. What? Michael Cassio,
That came a-wooing with you, and so many a time,
When I have spoke of you dispraisingly,
Hath ta'en your part—to have so much to do
To bring him in! By'r Lady, I could do much—
OTHELLO
Prithee, no more. Let him come when he will;
I will deny thee nothing.
DESDEMONA
Why, this is not a boon;
'Tis as I should entreat you wear your gloves,
Or feed on nourishing dishes, or keep you warm,
Or sue to you to do a peculiar profit
To your own person. Nay, when I have a suit
Wherein I mean to touch your love indeed,
It shall be full of poise and difficult weight,
And fearful to be granted.
OTHELLO
I will deny thee nothing.
Whereon, I do beseech thee, grant me this,
To leave me but a little to myself.
DESDEMONA
Shall I deny you? No. Farewell, my lord.
OTHELLO
Farewell, my Desdemona. I'll come to thee straight.
DESDEMONA
Emilia, come.—Be as your fancies teach you;
Whate'er you be, I am obedient. *Exit [with Emilia].*
OTHELLO
Excellent wretch! Perdition catch my soul
But I do love thee! And when I love thee not,
Chaos is come again.
IAGO
My noble lord—
OTHELLO What dost thou say, Iago?
IAGO
Did Michael Cassio, when you woo'd my lady,
Know of your love?
OTHELLO
He did, from first to last. Why dost thou ask?
IAGO
But for a satisfaction of my thought;
No further harm.
OTHELLO Why of thy thought, Iago?
IAGO
I did not think he had been acquainted with her.
OTHELLO
O, yes, and went between us very oft.
IAGO
Indeed?
OTHELLO
Indeed? Ay, indeed. Discern'st thou aught in that?
Is he not honest?
IAGO
Honest, my lord?
OTHELLO
Honest. Ay, honest.
IAGO
My lord, for aught I know.
OTHELLO
What dost thou think?
IAGO
Think, my lord?
OTHELLO
Think, my lord? By heaven, he echoes me,
As if there were some monster in his thought
Too hideous to be shown. Thou dost mean
something.
I heard thee say even now, thou lik'st not that,
When Cassio left my wife. What didst not like?
And when I told thee he was of my counsel
In my whole course of wooing, thou criedst
"Indeed!"
And didst contract and purse thy brow together,
As if thou then hadst shut up in thy brain
Some horrible conceit. If thou dost love me,
Show me thy thought.
IAGO
My lord, you know I love you.
OTHELLO I think thou dost;
And, for I know thou 'rt full of love and honesty,
And weigh'st thy words before thou giv'st them
breath,
Therefore these stops of thine fright me the more;

64 common reason everyday judgments **65–66 Save . . . best** were it not that, as the saying goes, military discipline requires making an example of the very best men. (*Her* refers to *wars* as a singular concept.) **66 not almost** scarcely **67 a private check** even a private reprimand **70 mamm'ring on** wavering about **74 bring him in** restore him to favor **80 peculiar** particular, personal **83 poise** weight, heaviness; or equipoise, delicate balance involving hard choice

92 wretch (A term of affectionate endearment.) **93 But I do** if I do not **120 conceit** fancy

For such things in a false disloyal knave
Are tricks of custom, but in a man that's just
They're close dilations, working from the heart
That passion cannot rule.

IAGO
For Michael Cassio,
I dare be sworn I think that he is honest.

OTHELLO
I think so too.

IAGO
Men should be what they seem;
Or those that be not, would they might seem none!

OTHELLO
Certain, men should be what they seem.

IAGO
Why, then, I think Cassio's an honest man.

OTHELLO
Nay, yet there's more in this.
I prithee speak to me as to thy thinkings,
As thou dost ruminate, and give thy worst of
thoughts
The worst of words.

IAGO
Good my lord, pardon me.
Though I am bound to every act of duty,
I am not bound to that all slaves are free to.
Utter my thoughts? Why, say they are vile and false,
As where's that palace whereinto foul things
Sometimes intrude not? Who has a breast so pure
But some uncleanly apprehensions
Keep leets and law-days and in sessions sit
With meditations lawful?

OTHELLO
Thou dost conspire against thy friend, Iago,
If thou but think'st him wrong'd, and mak'st his ear
A stranger to thy thoughts.

IAGO
I do beseech you—
Though I perchance am vicious in my guess,
As, I confess, it is my nature's plague
To spy into abuses, and oft my jealousy
Shapes faults that are not—that your wisdom yet,
From one that so imperfectly conceits,
Would take no notice, nor build yourself a trouble
Out of his scattering and unsure observance.
It were not for your quiet nor your good,
Nor for my manhood, honesty, or wisdom,
To let you know my thoughts.

OTHELLO
What dost thou mean?

IAGO
Good name in man and woman, dear my lord,
Is the immediate jewel of their souls.
Who steals my purse steals trash; 'tis something,
nothing;
'Twas mine, 'tis his, and has been slave to
thousands;
But he that filches from me my good name
Robs me of that which not enriches him
And makes me poor indeed.

OTHELLO
By heaven, I'll know thy thoughts.

IAGO
You cannot, if my heart were in your hand;
Nor shall not, whilst 'tis in my custody.

OTHELLO
Ha?

IAGO O, beware, my lord, of jealousy!
It is the green-ey'd monster which doth mock
The meat it feeds on. That cuckold lives in bliss
Who, certain of his fate, loves not his wronger;
But, O, what damned minutes tells he o'er
Who dotes, yet doubts, suspects, yet strongly loves!

OTHELLO
O misery!

IAGO
Poor and content is rich, and rich enough,
But riches fineless is as poor as winter
To him that ever fears he shall be poor.
Good God, the souls of all my tribe defend
From jealousy!

OTHELLO
Why, why is this?
Think'st thou I'd make a life of jealousy,
To follow still the changes of the moon
With fresh suspicions? No! To be once in doubt
Is once to be resolv'd. Exchange me for a goat
When I shall turn the business of my soul
To such exsufflicate and blown surmises,
Matching thy inference. 'Tis not to make me jealous
To say my wife is fair, feeds well, loves company,
Is free of speech, sings, plays, and dances well;
Where virtue is, these are more virtuous.
Nor from mine own weak merits will I draw
The smallest fear or doubt of her revolt,
For she had eyes, and chose me. No, Iago,
I'll see before I doubt; when I doubt, prove;
And on the proof, there is no more but this—
Away at once with love or jealousy!

IAGO
I am glad of this, for now I shall have reason
To show the love and duty that I bear you
With franker spirit. Therefore, as I am bound,
Receive it from me. I speak not yet of proof.
Look to your wife; observe her well with Cassio.
Wear your eye thus, not jealous nor secure.
I would not have your free and noble nature,
Out of self-bounty, be abus'd. Look to 't.
I know our country disposition well;
In Venice they do let God see the pranks
They dare not show their husbands; their best
conscience
Is not to leave 't undone, but keep 't unknown.

OTHELLO
Dost thou say so?

128 close dilations secret or involuntary expressions **129 passion cannot rule** i.e., are too passionately strong to be restrained **140 that** that which. **free to** i.e., free with respect to **145 leets and law-days** sessions of the courts **146 With** along with. **lawful** innocent **147 thy friend** i.e., Othello **150 vicious** wrong **152 jealousy** suspicion of evil **154 one** i.e., myself, Iago. **conceits** judges, conjectures

173 his wronger i.e., his faithless wife **178 fineless** boundless **188 exsufflicate and blown** inflated and flyblown. (*Exsufflicate* may also mean *spat out,* hence, loathsome, disgusting.) **194 doubt . . . revolt** fear of her unfaithfulness **204 not** neither. **secure** free from uneasiness **206 self-bounty** inherent or natural goodness

IAGO
She did deceive her father, marrying you;
And when she seem'd to shake and fear your looks,
She lov'd them most.

OTHELLO
And so she did.

IAGO
Why, go to then!
She that, so young, could give out such a seeming
To seel her father's eyes up close as oak—
He thought 'twas witchcraft—but I am much to blame;
I humbly do beseech you of your pardon
For too much loving you.

OTHELLO
I am bound to thee forever.

IAGO
I see this hath a little dash'd your spirits.

OTHELLO
Not a jot, not a jot.

IAGO
I' faith, I fear it has.
I hope you will consider what is spoke
Comes from my love. But I do see y' are mov'd.
I am to pray you not to strain my speech
To grosser issues nor to larger reach
Than to suspicion.

OTHELLO
I will not.

IAGO
Should you do so, my lord,
My speech should fall into such vile success
As my thoughts aim'd not. Cassio's my worthy friend—
My lord, I see y' are mov'd.

OTHELLO
No, not much mov'd.
I do not think but Desdemona's honest.

IAGO
Long live she so! And long live you to think so!

OTHELLO
And yet, how nature erring from itself—

IAGO
Ay, there's the point! As—to be bold with you—
Not to affect many proposed matches
Of her own clime, complexion, and degree,
Whereto we see in all things nature tends—
Foh! One may smell in such a will most rank,
Foul disproportion, thoughts unnatural.
But pardon me; I do not in position
Distinctly speak of her; though I may fear
Her will, recoiling to her better judgment,
May fall to match you with her country forms,
And happily repent.

OTHELLO
Farewell, farewell!
If more thou dost perceive, let me know more;
Set on thy wife to observe. Leave me, Iago.

IAGO [*Going*]
My lord, I take my leave.

OTHELLO
Why did I marry? This honest creature doubtless
Sees and knows more, much more, than he unfolds.

IAGO [*Returning*]
My Lord, I would I might entreat your honor
To scan this thing no farther; leave it to time.
Although 'tis fit that Cassio have his place—
For, sure, he fills it up with great ability—
Yet, if you please to hold him off awhile,
You shall by that perceive him and his means.
Note if your lady strain his entertainment
With any strong or vehement importunity;
Much will be seen in that. In the mean time,
Let me be thought too busy in my fears—
As worthy cause I have to fear I am—
And hold her free, I do beseech your honor.

OTHELLO
Fear not my government.

IAGO
I once more take my leave.
Exit.

OTHELLO
This fellow's of exceeding honesty,
And knows all qualities, with a learned spirit,
Of human dealings. If I do prove her haggard,
Though that her jesses were my dear heartstrings,
I 'd whistle her off, and let her down the wind
To prey at fortune. Haply, for I am black
And have not those soft parts of conversation
That chamberers have, or for I am declin'd
Into the vale of years—yet that's not much—
She's gone. I am abus'd, and my relief
Must be to loathe her. O curse of marriage,
That we can call these delicate creatures ours,
And not their appetites! I had rather be a toad,
And live upon the vapor of a dungeon,
Than keep a corner in the thing I love
For others' uses. Yet, 'tis the plague of great ones;
Prerogativ'd are they less than the base.
'Tis destiny unshunnable, like death.
Even then this forked plague is fated to us
When we do quicken. Look where she comes.

Enter Desdemona and Emilia.

If she be false, O, then heaven mocks itself!
I'll not believe 't.

DESDEMONA
How now, my dear Othello?
Your dinner, and the generous islanders
By you invited, do attend your presence.

OTHELLO
I am to blame.

DESDEMONA
Why do you speak so faintly?
Are you not well?

214 go to (An expression of impatience.) **215 seeming** false appearance **216 seel** blind. (A term from falconry.) **oak** (A close-grained wood.) **226 issues** significances. **reach** meaning, scope **232 honest** chaste **236 affect** prefer, desire **239 will** sensuality, appetite **240 disproportion** abnormality **241 position** argument **243 recoiling** reverting **244 fall . . . forms** undertake to compare you with Venetian norms of handsomeness **245 happily repent** haply repent her marriage

257 strain his entertainment urge his reinstatement **262 hold her free** regard her as innocent **263 government** self-control, conduct **265 qualities** natures, types **266 haggard** a wild female hawk **267 jesses** straps fastened around the legs of a trained hawk **269 at fortune** at random. **for** because **271 chamberers** gallants **280 Prerogativ'd** privileged (to have honest wives) **282 forked** (An allusion to the horns of the cuckold.) **283 quicken** receive life. (*Quicken* may also mean to swarm with maggots as the body festers, as in IV.ii.67, in which case ll. 282–283 suggest that *even then,* in death, we are cuckolded by *forked* worms.) **286 generous** noble

OTHELLO
I have a pain upon my forehead here.
DESDEMONA
Faith, that's with watching; 'twill away again. 291
[*Offers her handkerchief.*]
Let me but bind it hard, within this hour
It will be well.
OTHELLO Your napkin is too little. 293
Let it alone. Come, I'll go in with you.
[*He puts the handkerchief from him; and it drops.*]
DESDEMONA
I am very sorry that you are not well.
Exit [*with Othello*].
EMILIA [*Picking up the handkerchief*]
I am glad I have found this napkin.
This was her first remembrance from the Moor.
My wayward husband hath a hundred times
Woo'd me to steal it; but she so loves the token,
For he conjur'd her she should ever keep it,
That she reserves it evermore about her
To kiss and talk to. I'll have the work ta'en out, 302
And give 't Iago. What he will do with it
Heaven knows, not I;
I nothing but to please his fantasy. 305

Enter Iago.

IAGO
How now? What do you here alone?
EMILIA
Do not you chide. I have a thing for you.
IAGO
A thing for me? It is a common thing— 308
EMILIA Ha?
IAGO
To have a foolish wife.
EMILIA
O, is that all? What will you give me now
For that same handkerchief?
IAGO What handkerchief?
EMILIA
What handkerchief?
Why, that the Moor first gave to Desdemona;
That which so often you did bid me steal.
IAGO
Hast stol'n it from her?
EMILIA
No, faith; she let it drop by negligence,
And, to th' advantage, I, being here, took 't up. 318
Look, here 'tis.
IAGO A good wench! Give it me.
EMILIA
What will you do with 't, that you have been so
earnest
To have me filch it?
IAGO [*Snatching it*] Why, what is that to you?
EMILIA
If it be not for some purpose of import,
Give 't me again. Poor lady, she'll run mad
When she shall lack it.
IAGO Be not acknown on 't; 324
I have use for it. Go, leave me.
Exit Emilia.
I will in Cassio's lodging lose this napkin,
And let him find it. Trifles light as air
Are to the jealous confirmations strong
As proofs of holy writ. This may do something.
The Moor already changes with my poison.
Dangerous conceits are, in their natures, poisons, 331
Which at the first are scarce found to distaste,
But with a little act upon the blood 333
Burn like the mines of sulphur.

Enter Othello.

I did say so.
Look where he comes! Not poppy, nor mandragora, 335
Nor all the drowsy syrups of the world,
Shall ever medicine thee to that sweet sleep
Which thou ow'dst yesterday.
OTHELLO Ha, ha, false to me?
IAGO
Why, how now, general? No more of that.
OTHELLO
Avaunt! Be gone! Thou hast set me on the rack.
I swear 'tis better to be much abus'd
Than but to know 't a little.
IAGO How now, my lord?
OTHELLO
What sense had I of her stol'n hours of lust?
I saw 't not, thought it not, it harm'd not me.
I slept the next night well, fed well, was free and
merry; 345
I found not Cassio's kisses on her lips.
He that is robb'd, not wanting what is stol'n, 347
Let him not know 't, and he's not robb'd at all.
IAGO
I am sorry to hear this.
OTHELLO
I had been happy if the general camp,
Pioners and all, had tasted her sweet body, 351
So I had nothing known. O, now, forever
Farewell the tranquil mind! Farewell content!
Farewell the plumed troop, and the big wars 354
That makes ambition virtue! O, farewell!
Farewell the neighing steed, and the shrill trump,
The spirit-stirring drum, th' ear-piercing fife,
The royal banner, and all quality,
Pride, pomp, and circumstance of glorious war! 359
And, O you mortal engines, whose rude throats 360
Th' immortal Jove's dread clamors counterfeit,

291 watching working late **293 napkin** handkerchief **302 work ta'en out** design of the embroidery copied **305 fantasy** whim **308 common thing** (with bawdy suggestion) **318 to th' advantage** taking the opportunity

324 Be . . . on 't do not confess knowledge of it **331 conceits** fancies, ideas **333 act** action, working **335 mandragora** an opiate made of the mandrake root **345 free** carefree **347 wanting** missing **351 Pioners** diggers of mines, the lowest grade of soldiers **354 big** stately **359 Pride** rich display. **circumstance** pageantry **360 mortal engines** i.e., cannon

Farewell! Othello's occupation's gone.

IAGO

Is 't possible, my lord?

OTHELLO

Villain, be sure thou prove my love a whore!
Be sure of it. Give me the ocular proof,
Or, by the worth of mine eternal soul,
Thou hadst been better have been born a dog
Than answer my wak'd wrath!

IAGO

Is 't come to this?

OTHELLO

Make me to see 't, or, at the least, so prove it
That the probation bear no hinge nor loop
To hang a doubt on; or woe upon thy life!

IAGO

My noble lord—

OTHELLO

If thou dost slander her and torture me,
Never pray more; abandon all remorse;
On horror's head horrors accumulate;
Do deeds to make heaven weep, all earth amaz'd;
For nothing canst thou to damnation add
Greater than that.

IAGO

O grace! O heaven forgive me!
Are you a man? Have you a soul or sense?
God buy you; take mine office. O wretched fool,
That liv'st to make thine honesty a vice!
O monstrous world! Take note, take note, O world,
To be direct and honest is not safe.
I thank you for this profit, and from hence
I'll love no friend, sith love breeds such offense.

OTHELLO

Nay, stay. Thou shouldst be honest.

IAGO

I should be wise, for honesty's a fool
And loses that it works for.

OTHELLO

By the world,
I think my wife be honest and think she is not;
I think that thou art just and think thou art not.
I'll have some proof. Her name, that was as fresh
As Dian's visage, is now begrim'd and black
As mine own face. If there be cords, or knives,
Poison, or fire, or suffocating streams,
I'll not endure it. Would I were satisfied!

IAGO

I see, sir, you are eaten up with passion.
I do repent me that I put it to you.
You would be satisfied?

OTHELLO

Would? Nay, and I will.

IAGO

And may; but how? How satisfied, my lord?
Would you, the supervisor, grossly gape on?
Behold her topp'd?

OTHELLO

Death and damnation! O!

IAGO

It were a tedious difficulty, I think,
To bring them to that prospect; damn them then,
If ever mortal eyes do see them bolster
More than their own. What then? How then?
What shall I say? Where's satisfaction?
It is impossible you should see this,
Were they as prime as goats, as hot as monkeys,
As salt as wolves in pride, and fools as gross
As ignorance made drunk. But yet, I say,
If imputation and strong circumstances
Which lead directly to the door of truth
Will give you satisfaction, you might have 't.

OTHELLO

Give me a living reason she's disloyal.

IAGO

I do not like the office.
But sith I am ent'red in this cause so far,
Prick'd to 't by foolish honesty and love,
I will go on. I lay with Cassio lately;
And, being troubled with a raging tooth,
I could not sleep. There are a kind of men
So loose of soul that in their sleeps will mutter
Their affairs. One of this kind is Cassio.
In sleep I heard him say, "Sweet Desdemona,
Let us be wary, let us hide our loves!"
And then, sir, would he gripe and wring my hand,
Cry, "O sweet creature!" and then kiss me hard,
As if he pluck'd up kisses by the roots
That grew upon my lips; then laid his leg
Over my thigh, and sigh'd, and kiss'd, and then
Cried, "Cursed fate that gave thee to the Moor!"

OTHELLO

O monstrous! Monstrous!

IAGO

Nay, this was but his dream.

OTHELLO

But this denoted a foregone conclusion.
'Tis a shrewd doubt, though it be but a dream.

IAGO

And this may help to thicken other proofs
That do demonstrate thinly.

OTHELLO

I'll tear her all to pieces.

IAGO

Nay, but be wise. Yet we see nothing done;
She may be honest yet. Tell me but this,
Have you not sometimes seen a handkerchief
Spotted with strawberries in your wife's hand?

OTHELLO

I gave her such a one; 'twas my first gift.

IAGO

I know not that; but such a handkerchief—
I am sure it was your wife's—did I today
See Cassio wipe his beard with.

OTHELLO

If it be that—

IAGO

If it be that, or any that was hers,
It speaks against her with the other proofs.

OTHELLO

O, that the slave had forty thousand lives!

370 probation proof **374 remorse** pity **375 horrors accumulate** add still more horrors **380 God buy you** i.e., goodbye **381 vice** failing **384 profit** profitable instruction. **hence** henceforth **385 sith** since **386 Thou shouldst be** it appears that you are. (But Iago replies in the sense of *ought to be*.) **392 Dian** Diana, goddess of the moon and of chastity **400 supervisor** onlooker

403 damn i.e., to condemn **404–405 If . . . own** only if some human eyes other than their own do see them lie together **408 prime** lustful **409 salt** wanton, sensual. **pride** heat **432 foregone conclusion** concluded experience or action **433 shrewd doubt** suspicious circumstance

One is too poor, too weak for my revenge.
Now do I see 'tis true. Look here, Iago,
All my fond love thus do I blow to heaven.
'Tis gone.
Arise, black vengeance, from the hollow hell!
Yield up, O love, thy crown and hearted throne 452
To tyrannous hate! Swell, bosom, with thy fraught, 453
For 'tis of aspics' tongues!

IAGO
Yet be content. 454

OTHELLO
O, blood, blood, blood!

IAGO
Patience, I say. Your mind perhaps may change.

OTHELLO
Never, Iago. Like to the Pontic Sea, 457
Whose icy current and compulsive course
Nev'r feels retiring ebb, but keeps due on
To the Propontic and the Hellespont, 460
Even so my bloody thoughts, with violent pace,
Shall nev'r look back, nev'r ebb to humble love,
Till that a capable and wide revenge 463
Swallow them up. Now, by yond marble heaven, 464
[*Kneels.*] In the due reverence of a sacred vow
I here engage my words.

IAGO
Do not rise yet.
[*Kneels.*] Witness, you ever-burning lights above,
You elements that clip us round about, 468
Witness that here Iago doth give up
The execution of his wit, hands, heart, 470
To wrong'd Othello's service! Let him command,
And to obey shall be in me remorse, 472
What bloody business ever. [*They rise.*]

OTHELLO
I greet thy love,
Not with vain thanks, but with acceptance bounteous,
And will upon the instant put thee to 't.
Within these three days let me hear thee say
That Cassio's not alive.

IAGO
My friend is dead;
'Tis done at your request. But let her live.

OTHELLO
Damn her, lewd minx! O, damn her, damn her!
Come, go with me apart. I will withdraw 480
To furnish me with some swift means of death
For the fair devil. Now art thou my lieutenant.

IAGO
I am your own for ever. *Exeunt.*

SCENE IV

Enter Desdemona, Emilia, and Clown.

DESDEMONA Do you know, sirrah, where Lieutenant Cassio lies? 2

CLOWN I dare not say he lies anywhere.

DESDEMONA Why, man?

CLOWN He's a soldier, and for one to say a soldier lies, 'tis stabbing.

DESDEMONA Go to. Where lodges he?

CLOWN To tell you where he lodges is to tell you where I lie.

DESDEMONA Can anything be made of this?

CLOWN I know not where he lodges, and for me to devise a lodging and say he lies here, or he lies there, were to lie in mine own throat.

DESDEMONA Can you inquire him out, and be edified by report?

CLOWN I will catechize the world for him; that is, make questions, and by them answer.

DESDEMONA Seek him, bid him come hither. Tell him I
have mov'd my lord on his behalf, and hope all will be 19
well.

CLOWN To do this is within the compass of man's wit, and therefore I will attempt the doing it. *Exit Clown.*

DESDEMONA
Where should I lose that handkerchief, Emilia?

EMILIA
I know not, madam.

DESDEMONA
Believe me, I had rather have lost my purse
Full of crusadoes; and, but my noble Moor 26
Is true of mind, and made of no such baseness
As jealous creatures are, it were enough
To put him to ill thinking.

EMILIA
Is he not jealous?

DESDEMONA
Who, he? I think the sun where he was born
Drew all such humors from him.

EMILIA
Look where he comes. 31

Enter Othello.

DESDEMONA
I will not leave him now till Cassio
Be call'd to him.—How is 't with you, my lord?

OTHELLO
Well, my good lady. [*Aside.*] O, hardness to dissemble!—
How do you, Desdemona?

DESDEMONA
Well, my good lord.

OTHELLO
Give me your hand. [*She gives her hand.*] This hand is moist, my lady.

DESDEMONA
It yet hath felt no age nor known no sorrow.

OTHELLO
This argues fruitfulness and liberal heart.
Hot, hot, and moist. This hand of yours requires
A sequester from liberty, fasting and prayer, 40
Much castigation, exercise devout;
For here's a young and sweating devil here
That commonly rebels. 'Tis a good hand,
A frank one.

452 hearted fixed in the heart **453 fraught** freight, burden **454 aspics'** venomous serpents' **457 Pontic Sea** Black Sea **460 Propontic** body of water between the Bosporus and Hellespont **463 capable** comprehensive **464 marble** i.e., gleaming like marble **468 clip** encompass **470 execution** exercise, action. **wit** mind **472 remorse** pity (for Othello's wrongs)

III.iv. Location: Before the citadel.
2 lies lodges. (But the Clown makes the obvious pun.)

19 mov'd petitioned **26 crusadoes** Portuguese gold coins **31 humors** (Refers to the four bodily fluids thought to determine temperament.) **40 sequester** separation, sequestration

DESDEMONA You may, indeed, say so;
For 'twas that hand that gave away my heart.

OTHELLO
A liberal hand! The hearts of old gave hands;
But our new heraldry is hands, not hearts.

DESDEMONA
I cannot speak of this. Come now, your promise.

OTHELLO
What promise, chuck?

DESDEMONA
I have sent to bid Cassio come speak with you.

OTHELLO
I have a salt and sorry rheum offends me;
Lend me thy handkerchief.

DESDEMONA
Here, my lord. [*She gives a handkerchief.*]

OTHELLO
That which I gave you.

DESDEMONA I have it not about me.

OTHELLO
Not?

DESDEMONA
No, faith, my lord.

OTHELLO
That's a fault. That handkerchief
Did an Egyptian to my mother give;
She was a charmer, and could almost read
The thoughts of people. She told her, while she kept it,
'Twould make her amiable and subdue my father
Entirely to her love, but if she lost it
Or made a gift of it, my father's eye
Should hold her loathed and his spirits should hunt
After new fancies. She, dying, gave it me,
And bid me, when my fate would have me wiv'd,
To give it her. I did so; and take heed on 't;
Make it a darling like your precious eye.
To lose 't or give 't away were such perdition
As nothing else could match.

DESDEMONA Is 't possible?

OTHELLO
'Tis true. There's magic in the web of it.
A sibyl, that had numb'red in the world
The sun to course two hundred compasses,
In her prophetic fury sew'd the work;
The worms were hallowed that did breed the silk;
And it was dy'd in mummy which the skillful
Conserv'd of maidens' hearts.

DESDEMONA I' faith! Is 't true?

OTHELLO
Most veritable. Therefore look to 't well.

DESDEMONA
Then would to God that I had never seen 't!

OTHELLO
Ha? Wherefore?

DESDEMONA
Why do you speak so startingly and rash?

OTHELLO
Is 't lost? Is 't gone? Speak, is 't out o' th' way?

DESDEMONA
Heaven bless us!

OTHELLO
Say you?

DESDEMONA
It is not lost; but what an if it were?

OTHELLO
How?

DESDEMONA
I say, it is not lost.

OTHELLO Fetch 't, let me see 't.

DESDEMONA
Why, so I can, sir, but I will not now.
This is a trick to put me from my suit.
Pray you, let Cassio be receiv'd again.

OTHELLO
Fetch me the handkerchief! My mind misgives.

DESDEMONA
Come, come;
You'll never meet a more sufficient man.

OTHELLO
The handkerchief!

[DESDEMONA I pray, talk me of Cassio.

OTHELLO
The handkerchief!]

DESDEMONA A man that all his time
Hath founded his good fortunes on your love,
Shar'd dangers with you—

OTHELLO
The handkerchief!

DESDEMONA I' faith, you are to blame.

OTHELLO
'Zounds! *Exit Othello.*

EMILIA
Is not this man jealous?

DESDEMONA
I nev'r saw this before.
Sure, there's some wonder in this handkerchief.
I am most unhappy in the loss of it.

EMILIA
'Tis not a year or two shows us a man.
They are all but stomachs, and we all but food;
They eat us hungerly, and when they are full
They belch us.

Enter Iago and Cassio.

Look you, Cassio and my husband.

IAGO
There is no other way; 'tis she must do 't.
And, lo, the happiness! Go, and importune her.

DESDEMONA
How now, good Cassio? What's the news with you?

47 But . . . hearts i.e., in our decadent times the joining of hands is no longer a badge to signify the giving of hearts **51 salt . . . rheum** distressful head cold or watering of the eyes **59 charmer** sorceress **61 amiable** desirable **69 perdition** loss **73 compasses** annual circlings. (The *sibyl,* or prophetess, was 200 years old.) **76 mummy** medicinal or magical preparation drained from mummified bodies **77 Conserv'd of** prepared or preserved out of

95 all his time throughout his career **104 'Tis . . . man** i.e., you can't really know a man even in a year or two of experience (?) or, real men come along seldom (?) **105 but** nothing but **109 the happiness** in happy time, fortunately met

CASSIO
Madam, my former suit. I do beseech you
That by your virtuous means I may again
Exist, and be a member of his love
Whom I with all the office of my heart
Entirely honor. I would not be delay'd.
If my offense be of such mortal kind
That nor my service past nor present sorrows,
Nor purpos'd merit in futurity,
Can ransom me into his love again,
But to know so must be my benefit;
So shall I clothe me in a forc'd content,
And shut myself up in some other course,
To fortune's alms.

DESDEMONA Alas, thrice-gentle Cassio,
My advocation is not now in tune.
My lord is not my lord; nor should I know him,
Were he in favor as in humor alter'd.
So help me every spirit sanctified,
As I have spoken for you all my best
And stood within the blank of his displeasure
For my free speech! You must awhile be patient.
What I can do I will, and more I will
Than for myself I dare. Let that suffice you.

IAGO
Is my lord angry?

EMILIA He went hence but now,
And certainly in strange unquietness.

IAGO
Can he be angry? I have seen the cannon,
When it hath blown his ranks into the air,
And, like the devil, from his very arm
Puff'd his own brother—and is he angry?
Something of moment then. I will go meet him.
There's matter in 't indeed, if he be angry.

DESDEMONA
I prithee, do so. *Exit* [*Iago*].
Something, sure, of state,
Either from Venice, or some unhatch'd practice
Made demonstrable here in Cyprus to him,
Hath puddled his clear spirit; and in such cases
Men's natures wrangle with inferior things,
Though great ones are their object. 'Tis even so;
For let our finger ache, and it endues
Our other healthful members even to a sense
Of pain. Nay, we must think men are not gods,
Nor of them look for such observancy
As fits the bridal. Beshrew me much, Emilia,
I was, unhandsome warrior as I am,
Arraigning his unkindness with my soul;
But now I find I had suborn'd the witness,
And he's indicted falsely.

EMILIA Pray heaven it be
State matters, as you think, and no conception,
Nor no jealous toy, concerning you.

DESDEMONA
Alas the day! I never gave him cause.

EMILIA
But jealous souls will not be answer'd so;
They are not ever jealous for the cause,
But jealous for they're jealous. It is a monster
Begot upon itself, born on itself.

DESDEMONA
Heaven keep that monster from Othello's mind!

EMILIA
Lady, amen.

DESDEMONA
I will go seek him. Cassio, walk here about.
If I do find him fit, I'll move your suit
And seek to effect it to my uttermost.

CASSIO
I humbly thank your ladyship.
Exit [*Desdemona with Emilia*].

Enter Bianca.

BIANCA
Save you, friend Cassio!

CASSIO What make you from home?
How is 't with you, my most fair Bianca?
I' faith, sweet love, I was coming to your house.

BIANCA
And I was going to your lodging, Cassio.
What, keep a week away? Seven days and nights?
Eight score eight hours? And lovers' absent hours,
More tedious than the dial eight score times?
O weary reck'ning!

CASSIO Pardon me, Bianca.
I have this while with leaden thoughts been press'd;
But I shall, in a more continuate time,
Strike off this score of absence. Sweet Bianca,
[*Giving her Desdemona's handkerchief.*]
Take me this work out.

BIANCA O Cassio, whence came this?
This is some token from a newer friend.
To the felt absence now I feel a cause.
Is 't come to this? Well, well.

CASSIO Go to, woman!
Throw your vile guesses in the devil's teeth,
From whence you have them. You are jealous now
That this is from some mistress, some remembrance.
No, by my faith, Bianca.

BIANCA Why, whose is it?

CASSIO
I know not, neither. I found it in my chamber.
I like the work well; ere it be demanded—
As like enough it will—I would have it copied.
Take it, and do 't, and leave me for this time.

BIANCA
Leave you? Wherefore?

CASSIO
I do attend here on the general,

116 mortal fatal **117 nor . . . nor** neither . . . nor **120 But . . . benefit** merely to know that my case is hopeless must be all I can expect **123 To fortune's alms** throwing myself on the mercy of fortune **124 advocation** advocacy **126 favor** appearance **129 blank** white spot in the center of a target, i.e., directly in the line of fire **142 unhatch'd practice** as yet unexecuted plot **144 puddled** muddied **147 endues** brings to the same condition **150 observancy** attentiveness **151 bridal** wedding (when a bridegroom is newly attentive to his bride) **152 unhandsome** insufficient, unskillful **153 with** before the bar of

157 toy fancy **161 for** because **162 Begot upon itself** generated solely from itself **169 make** do **178 continuate** uninterrupted **179 Strike . . . score** settle this account **180 Take . . . out** copy this embroidery for me

And think it no addition, nor my wish,
To have him see me woman'd.

BIANCA
Why, I pray you?

CASSIO Not that I love you not.

BIANCA
But that you do not love me.
I pray you, bring me on the way a little,
And say if I shall see you soon at night.

CASSIO
'Tis but a little way that I can bring you,
For I attend here; but I'll see you soon.

BIANCA
'Tis very good. I must be circumstanc'd.
Exeunt omnes.

ACT IV • SCENE I

Enter Othello and Iago.

IAGO
Will you think so?

OTHELLO Think so, Iago?

IAGO What,
To kiss in private?

OTHELLO An unauthoriz'd kiss!

IAGO
Or to be naked with her friend in bed
An hour or more, not meaning any harm?

OTHELLO
Naked in bed, Iago, and not mean harm?
It is hypocrisy against the devil.
They that mean virtuously, and yet do so,
The devil their virtue tempts, and they tempt heaven.

IAGO
If they do nothing, 'tis a venial slip.
But if I give my wife a handkerchief—

OTHELLO
What then?

IAGO
Why, then, 'tis hers, my lord; and, being hers,
She may, I think, bestow 't on any man.

OTHELLO
She is protectress of her honor too.
May she give that?

IAGO
Her honor is an essence that's not seen;
They have it very oft that have it not.
But, for the handkerchief—

OTHELLO
By heaven, I would most gladly have forgot it.
Thou said'st—O, it comes o'er my memory,
As doth the raven o'er the infectious house,
Boding to all—he had my handkerchief.

IAGO
Ay, what of that?

OTHELLO That's not so good now.

IAGO What
If I had said I had seen him do you wrong?
Or heard him say—as knaves be such abroad,
Who having, by their own importunate suit,
Or voluntary dotage of some mistress,
Convinced or supplied them, cannot choose
But they must blab—

OTHELLO Hath he said anything?

IAGO
He hath, my lord; but be you well assur'd,
No more than he'll unswear.

OTHELLO What hath he said?

IAGO
Faith, that he did—I know not what he did.

OTHELLO
What? What?

IAGO
Lie—

OTHELLO With her?

IAGO With her, on her; what you will.

OTHELLO Lie with her? Lie on her? We say lie on her, when they belie her. Lie with her! 'Zounds, that's fulsome.—Handkerchief—confessions—handkerchief! —To confess, and be hang'd for his labor—first, to be hang'd, and then to confess.—I tremble at it. Nature would not invest herself in such shadowing passion without some instruction. It is not words that shakes me thus. Pish! Noses, ears, and lips.—Is 't possible?—Confess—handkerchief!—O devil!
Falls in a trance.

IAGO
Work on,
My medicine, work! Thus credulous fools are caught;
And many worthy and chaste dames even thus,
All guiltless, meet reproach.—What, ho! My lord!
My lord, I say! Othello!

Enter Cassio.

How now, Cassio?

CASSIO
What's the matter?

IAGO
My lord is fall'n into an epilepsy.
This is his second fit; he had one yesterday.

CASSIO
Rub him about the temples.

IAGO [No, forbear;]
The lethargy must have his quiet course.
If not, he foams at mouth, and by and by
Breaks out to savage madness. Look, he stirs.

194 addition i.e., addition to my reputation **202 be circumstanc'd** be governed by circumstance, yield to your conditions

IV.i. Location: Before the citadel.
17 They have it i.e., they enjoy a reputation for it **21 raven . . . house** (Allusion to the belief that the raven hovered over a house of sickness or infection, such as one visited by the plague.)

25 abroad around about **28 Convinced or supplied** seduced or gratified **39–41 Nature . . . instruction** i.e., without some foundation in fact, nature would not have dressed herself in such an overwhelming passion that comes over me now and fills my mind with images; or, in such a life-like fantasy as Cassio had in his dream of lying with Desdemona **53 lethargy** coma. **his** its

Do you withdraw yourself a little while,
He will recover straight. When he is gone,
I would on great occasion speak with you.
[Exit Cassio.]
How is it, general? Have you not hurt your head?

OTHELLO
Dost thou mock me?

IAGO I mock you not, by heaven. 60
Would you would bear your fortune like a man!

OTHELLO
A horned man's a monster and a beast.

IAGO
There's many a beast then in a populous city,
And many a civil monster. 64

OTHELLO
Did he confess it?

IAGO Good sir, be a man.
Think every bearded fellow that's but yok'd 66
May draw with you. There's millions now alive 67
That nightly lie in those unproper beds 68
Which they dare swear peculiar; your case is better. 69
O, 'tis the spite of hell, the fiend's arch-mock,
To lip a wanton in a secure couch, 71
And to suppose her chaste! No, let me know;
And knowing what I am, I know what she shall be.

OTHELLO
O, thou art wise. 'Tis certain.

IAGO
Stand you awhile apart;
Confine yourself but in a patient list. 76
Whilst you were here o'erwhelmed with your grief—
A passion most unsuiting such a man—
Cassio came hither. I shifted him away,
And laid good 'scuses upon your ecstasy, 80
Bade him anon return and here speak with me,
The which he promis'd. Do but encave yourself 82
And mark the fleers, the gibes, and notable scorns, 83
That dwell in every region of his face;
For I will make him tell the tale anew,
Where, how, how oft, how long ago, and when
He hath, and is again to cope your wife. 87
I say, but mark his gesture. Marry, patience!
Or I shall say y' are all in all in spleen, 89
And nothing of a man.

OTHELLO Dost thou hear, Iago?
I will be found most cunning in my patience;
But—dost thou hear?—most bloody.

IAGO That's not amiss;
But yet keep time in all. Will you withdraw?
[Othello retires.]
Now will I question Cassio of Bianca,
A huswife that by selling her desires 95
Buys herself bread and clothes. It is a creature
That dotes on Cassio, as 'tis the strumpet's plague
To beguile many and be beguil'd by one.
He, when he hears of her, cannot refrain
From the excess of laughter. Here he comes.

Enter Cassio.

As he shall smile, Othello shall go mad;
And his unbookish jealousy must conster 102
Poor Cassio's smiles, gestures, and light behavior
Quite in the wrong.—How do you now, lieutenant?

CASSIO
The worser that you give me the addition 105
Whose want even kills me.

IAGO
Ply Desdemona well, and you are sure on 't.
[Speaking lower.] Now, if this suit lay in Bianca's power,
How quickly should you speed!

CASSIO *[Laughing]* Alas, poor caitiff! 109

OTHELLO
Look, how he laughs already!

IAGO
I never knew woman love man so.

CASSIO
Alas, poor rogue! I think, i' faith, she loves me.

OTHELLO
Now he denies it faintly, and laughs it out.

IAGO
Do you hear, Cassio?

OTHELLO Now he importunes him
To tell it o'er. Go to! Well said, well said.

IAGO
She gives it out that you shall marry her.
Do you intend it?

CASSIO Ha, ha, ha!

OTHELLO
Do you triumph, Roman? Do you triumph? 119

CASSIO I marry her? What? A customer? Prithee, bear 120
some charity to my wit; do not think it so unwholesome. Ha, ha, ha!

OTHELLO So, so, so, so! They laugh that win. 123

IAGO Faith, the cry goes that you shall marry her.

CASSIO Prithee, say true.

IAGO I am a very villain else.

OTHELLO Have you scor'd me? Well. 127

CASSIO This is the monkey's own giving out. She is persuaded I will marry her, out of her own love and flattery, not out of my promise.

OTHELLO Iago beckons me; now he begins the story. 131

CASSIO She was here even now; she haunts me in every
place. I was the other day talking on the seabank with
certain Venetians, and thither comes the bauble, and, 134
by this hand, she falls me thus about my neck—
[He embraces Iago.]

OTHELLO Crying, "O dear Cassio!" as it were; his gesture imports it.

CASSIO So hangs, and lolls, and weeps upon me; so shakes, and pulls me. Ha, ha, ha!

60 mock (Othello takes Iago's question about hurting his head to be a mocking reference to the cuckold's horns.) **64 civil** i.e., dwelling in a city **66 yok'd** i.e., married **67 draw with you** pull as you do like oxen who are yoked, i.e., share your fate as cuckold **68 unproper** not exclusively their own **69 peculiar** private, their own. **better** i.e., because you know the truth **71 secure** free from suspicion **76 in . . . list** within the bounds of patience **80 ecstasy** trance **82 encave** conceal **83 fleers** sneers **87 cope** encounter with **89 all in all in spleen** utterly governed by passionate impulses **95 huswife** hussy

102 unbookish uninstructed. **conster** construe **105 addition** title **109 caitiff** wretch **119 Roman** (The Romans were noted for their *triumphs* or triumphal processions.) **120 customer** i.e., prostitute **123 They . . . win** i.e., they that laugh last laugh best **127 scor'd me** scored off me, beaten me, made up my reckoning **131 beckons** signals **134 bauble** plaything

OTHELLO Now he tells how she pluck'd him to my chamber. O, I see that nose of yours, but not that dog I shall throw it to.

CASSIO Well, I must leave her company.

IAGO Before me, look where she comes.

Enter Bianca [with Othello's handkerchief].

CASSIO 'Tis such another fitchew! Marry, a perfum'd one.—What do you mean by this haunting of me?

BIANCA Let the devil and his dam haunt you! What did you mean by that same handkerchief you gave me even now? I was a fine fool to take it. I must take out the work? A likely piece of work, that you should find it in your chamber, and know not who left it there! This is some minx's token, and I must take out the work? There; give it your hobby-horse. [*Gives him the handkerchief.*] Wheresoever you had it, I'll take out no work on 't.

CASSIO How now, my sweet Bianca? How now? How now?

OTHELLO By heaven, that should be my handkerchief!

BIANCA If you'll come to supper tonight, you may; if you will not, come when you are next prepar'd for. *Exit.*

IAGO After her, after her.

CASSIO Faith, I must; she'll rail in the streets else.

IAGO Will you sup there?

CASSIO Faith, I intend so.

IAGO Well, I may chance to see you, for I would very fain speak with you.

CASSIO Prithee, come. Will you?

IAGO Go to; say no more. [*Exit Cassio.*]

OTHELLO [*Advancing*] How shall I murder him, Iago?

IAGO Did you perceive how he laugh'd at his vice?

OTHELLO O Iago!

IAGO And did you see the handkerchief?

OTHELLO Was that mine?

IAGO Yours, by this hand. And to see how he prizes the foolish woman your wife! She gave it him, and he hath giv'n it his whore.

OTHELLO I would have him nine years a-killing. A fine woman! A fair woman! A sweet woman!

IAGO Nay, you must forget that.

OTHELLO Ay, let her rot, and perish, and be damn'd tonight; for she shall not live. No, my heart is turn'd to stone; I strike it, and it hurts my hand. O, the world hath not a sweeter creature! She might lie by an emperor's side and command him tasks.

IAGO Nay, that's not your way.

OTHELLO Hang her! I do but say what she is. So delicate with her needle! An admirable musician! O, she will sing the savageness out of a bear. Of so high and plenteous wit and invention!

IAGO She's the worse for all this.

OTHELLO O, a thousand, a thousand times! And then, of so gentle a condition!

IAGO Ay, too gentle.

OTHELLO Nay, that's certain. But yet the pity of it, Iago! O Iago, the pity of it, Iago!

IAGO If you are so fond over her iniquity, give her patent to offend; for, if it touch not you, it comes near nobody.

OTHELLO I will chop her into messes. Cuckold me?

IAGO O, 'tis foul in her.

OTHELLO With mine officer?

IAGO That's fouler.

OTHELLO Get me some poison, Iago; this night. I'll not expostulate with her, lest her body and beauty unprovide my mind again. This night, Iago.

IAGO Do it not with poison. Strangle her in her bed, even the bed she hath contaminated.

OTHELLO Good, good! The justice of it pleases. Very good.

IAGO And for Cassio, let me be his undertaker. You shall hear more by midnight.

OTHELLO
Excellent good. [*A trumpet within.*]
What trumpet is that same?

IAGO
I warrant something from Venice.

Enter Lodovico, Desdemona, and Attendants.

'Tis Lodovico. This comes from the Duke.
See, your wife's with him.

LODOVICO
God save you, worthy general!

OTHELLO
With all my heart, sir.

LODOVICO
The Duke and the senators of Venice greet you.
[*Gives him a letter.*]

OTHELLO
I kiss the instrument of their pleasures.
[*Opens the letter, and reads.*]

DESDEMONA
And what's the news, good cousin Lodovico?

IAGO
I am very glad to see you, Signior;
Welcome to Cyprus.

LODOVICO
I thank you. How does Lieutenant Cassio?

IAGO
Lives, sir.

DESDEMONA
Cousin, there's fall'n between him and my lord
An unkind breach; but you shall make all well.

OTHELLO
Are you sure of that?

DESDEMONA
My lord?

OTHELLO [*Reads*]
"This fail you not to do, as you will—"

LODOVICO
He did not call; he's busy in the paper.
Is there division 'twixt my lord and Cassio?

144 Before me i.e., on my soul **145 fitchew** polecat (because of her strong perfume; also, slang word for a prostitute) **153 hobby-horse** harlot **185 your way** i.e., the way you should think of her

196 fond foolish **196–197 patent** license **199 messes** portions of food, i.e., bits **204–205 unprovide** weaken, unfit **210 be his undertaker** undertake to dispatch him

DESDEMONA
A most unhappy one. I would do much
T' atone them, for the love I bear to Cassio.
OTHELLO
Fire and brimstone!
DESDEMONA
My lord?
OTHELLO
Are you wise?
DESDEMONA
What, is he angry?
LODOVICO May be the letter mov'd him;
For, as I think, they do command him home,
Deputing Cassio in his government.
DESDEMONA
By my troth, I am glad on 't.
OTHELLO Indeed?
DESDEMONA My lord?
OTHELLO
I am glad to see you mad.
DESDEMONA Why, sweet Othello—
OTHELLO [*Striking her*]
Devil!
DESDEMONA
I have not deserv'd this.
LODOVICO
My lord, this would not be believ'd in Venice,
Though I should swear I saw 't. 'Tis very much.
Make her amends; she weeps.
OTHELLO O devil, devil!
If that the earth could teem with woman's tears,
Each drop she falls would prove a crocodile.
Out of my sight!
DESDEMONA I will not stay to offend you.
[*Going.*]
LODOVICO
Truly, an obedient lady.
I do beseech your lordship, call her back.
OTHELLO
Mistress!
DESDEMONA My lord?
OTHELLO What would you with her, sir?
LODOVICO
Who, I, my lord?
OTHELLO
Ay, you did wish that I would make her turn.
Sir, she can turn, and turn, and yet go on
And turn again; and she can weep, sir, weep;
And she's obedient, as you say, obedient,
Very obedient.—Proceed you in your tears.—
Concerning this, sir—O well-painted passion!—
I am commanded home.—Get you away;
I'll send for you anon.—Sir, I obey the mandate,
And will return to Venice.—Hence, avaunt!
[*Exit Desdemona.*]
Cassio shall have my place. And, sir, tonight
I do entreat that we may sup together.
You are welcome, sir, to Cyprus.—Goats and
monkeys! *Exit.*
LODOVICO
Is this the noble Moor whom our full Senate
Call all in all sufficient? Is this the nature
Whom passion could not shake? Whose solid virtue
The shot of accident, nor dart of chance,
Could neither graze nor pierce?
IAGO He is much chang'd.
LODOVICO
Are his wits safe? Is he not light of brain?
IAGO
He's that he is; I may not breathe my censure
What he might be. If what he might he is not,
I would to heaven he were!
LODOVICO What, strike his wife?
IAGO
Faith, that was not so well; yet would I knew
That stroke would prove the worst!
LODOVICO Is it his use?
Or did the letters work upon his blood,
And new-create this fault?
IAGO Alas, alas!
It is not honesty in me to speak
What I have seen and known. You shall
observe him,
And his own courses will denote him so
That I may save my speech. Do but go after,
And mark how he continues.
LODOVICO
I am sorry that I am deceiv'd in him. *Exeunt.*

SCENE II

Enter Othello and Emilia.

OTHELLO
You have seen nothing then?
EMILIA
Nor ever heard, nor ever did suspect.
OTHELLO
Yes, you have seen Cassio and she together.
EMILIA
But then I saw no harm, and then I heard
Each syllable that breath made up between them.
OTHELLO
What, did they never whisper?
EMILIA Never, my lord.
OTHELLO
Nor send you out o' th' way?
EMILIA
Never.
OTHELLO
To fetch her fan, her gloves, her mask, nor nothing?

232 atone reconcile **238 government** office **246 teem** breed, be impregnated **247 fall** lets fall. **crocodile** (Crocodiles were supposed to weep hypocritical tears for their victims.)

271–273 I may . . . were i.e., I dare not venture an opinion as to whether he's of unsound mind, as you suggest; but if he isn't, then it might be better to wish he were in fact insane, since only that could excuse his wild behavior **275 use** custom

IV.ii. Location: The citadel.

EMILIA
Never, my lord.

OTHELLO
That's strange.

EMILIA
I durst, my lord, to wager she is honest,
Lay down my soul at stake. If you think other,
Remove your thought; it doth abuse your bosom.
If any wretch have put this in your head,
Let heaven requite it with the serpent's curse!
For if she be not honest, chaste, and true,
There's no man happy; the purest of their wives
Is foul as slander.

OTHELLO
Bid her come hither. Go.
Exit Emilia.
She says enough; yet she's a simple bawd
That cannot say as much. This is a subtle whore,
A closet lock and key of villainous secrets.
And yet she'll kneel and pray; I have seen her do 't.

Enter Desdemona and Emilia.

DESDEMONA
My lord, what is your will?

OTHELLO
Pray you, chuck, come hither.

DESDEMONA
What is your pleasure?

OTHELLO
Let me see your eyes;
Look in my face.

DESDEMONA
What horrible fancy's this?

OTHELLO [*To Emilia*]
Some of your function, mistress;
Leave procreants alone and shut the door;
Cough, or cry "hem," if anybody come.
Your mystery, your mystery! Nay, dispatch.
Exit Emilia.

DESDEMONA [*Kneeling*]
Upon my knees, what doth your speech import?
I understand a fury in your words,
[But not the words.]

OTHELLO
Why, what art thou?

DESDEMONA
Your wife, my lord; your true
And loyal wife.

OTHELLO
Come, swear it, damn thyself,
Lest, being like one of heaven, the devils themselves
Should fear to seize thee. Therefore be double damn'd;
Swear thou art honest.

DESDEMONA
Heaven doth truly know it.

OTHELLO
Heaven truly knows that thou art false as hell.

DESDEMONA
To whom, my lord? With whom? How am I false?

OTHELLO [*Weeping*]
Ah, Desdemon! Away, away, away!

16 serpent's curse the curse pronounced by God on the serpent for deceiving Eve, just as some man has done to Othello and Desdemona. (See Genesis 3:14.) **20–21 she's . . . much** i.e., any procuress or go-between who couldn't make up as convincing a story as Emilia's would have to be pretty stupid **22 closet lock and key** complete storeroom **27 Some . . . function** i.e., practice your chosen profession, that of bawd (by guarding the door) **28 procreants** mating couples **30 mystery** trade, occupation **36 being . . . heaven** looking like an angel

DESDEMONA
Alas the heavy day! Why do you weep?
Am I the motive of these tears, my lord?
If happily you my father do suspect
An instrument of this your calling back,
Lay not your blame on me. If you have lost him,
Why, I have lost him too.

OTHELLO
Had it pleas'd heaven
To try me with affliction, had they rain'd
All kinds of sores and shames on my bare head,
Steep'd me in poverty to the very lips,
Given to captivity me and my utmost hopes,
I should have found in some place of my soul
A drop of patience. But, alas, to make me
A fixed figure for the time of scorn
To point his slow unmoving finger at!
Yet could I bear that too, well, very well.
But there where I have garner'd up my heart,
Where either I must live or bear no life,
The fountain from the which my current runs
Or else dries up—to be discarded thence!
Or keep it as a cistern for foul toads
To knot and gender in! Turn thy complexion there,
Patience, thou young and rose-lipp'd cherubin—
Ay, there look grim as hell!

DESDEMONA
I hope my noble lord esteems me honest.

OTHELLO
O, ay; as summer flies are in the shambles,
That quicken even with blowing. O thou weed,
Who art so lovely fair and smell'st so sweet
That the sense aches at thee, would thou hadst ne'er been born!

DESDEMONA
Alas, what ignorant sin have I committed?

OTHELLO
Was this fair paper, this most goodly book,
Made to write "whore" upon? What committed?
Committed? O thou public commoner!
I should make very forges of my cheeks,
That would to cinders burn up modesty,
Did I but speak thy deeds. What committed?
Heaven stops the nose at it and the moon winks,
The bawdy wind that kisses all it meets
Is hush'd within the hollow mine of earth,
And will not hear 't. What committed?
[Impudent strumpet!]

DESDEMONA
By heaven, you do me wrong.

OTHELLO
Are not you a strumpet?

DESDEMONA
No, as I am a Christian.
If to preserve this vessel for my lord
From any other foul unlawful touch

48 they i.e., heavenly powers **54 time of scorn** i.e., scornful world **55 his** its. **slow unmoving finger** finger which rises slowly to the point and then stops, forever fixed and immobile in its pointing **62 knot** i.e., couple. **gender** engender. **Turn . . . there** change your color, grow pale, at such a sight **63–64 Patience . . . hell** (I.e., even Patience, that rose-lipped cherub, will look grim and pale at this spectacle.) **66 shambles** slaughterhouse **67 quicken** come to life. **with blowing** i.e., with the puffing up of something rotten in which maggots are breeding **73 commoner** prostitute **77 winks** closes her eyes **83 vessel** i.e., body

Be not to be a strumpet, I am none.

OTHELLO
What, not a whore?

DESDEMONA No, as I shall be sav'd.

OTHELLO
Is 't possible?

DESDEMONA
O, heaven forgive us!

OTHELLO I cry you mercy, then.
I took you for that cunning whore of Venice
That married with Othello. [*Calling out.*] You,
mistress,
That have the office opposite to Saint Peter,
And keep the gate of hell!

Enter Emilia.

You, you, ay, you!
We have done our course. There's money for your
pains. [*Gives money.*]
I pray you, turn the key and keep our counsel. *Exit.*

EMILIA
Alas, what does this gentleman conceive?
How do you, madam? How do you, my good lady?

DESDEMONA
Faith, half asleep.

EMILIA
Good madam, what's the matter with my lord?

DESDEMONA
With who?

EMILIA
Why, with my lord, madam.

DESDEMONA
Who is thy lord?

EMILIA He that is yours, sweet lady.

DESDEMONA
I have none. Do not talk to me, Emilia;
I cannot weep; nor answers have I none,
But what should go by water. Prithee tonight
Lay on my bed my wedding sheets, remember;
And call thy husband hither.

EMILIA
Here's a change indeed! *Exit.*

DESDEMONA
'Tis meet I should be us'd so, very meet.
How have I been behav'd, that he might stick
The small'st opinion on my least misuse?

Enter Iago and Emilia.

IAGO
What is your pleasure, madam? How is 't with you?

DESDEMONA
I cannot tell. Those that do teach young babes
Do it with gentle means and easy tasks.
He might have chid me so; for, in good faith,
I am a child to chiding.

IAGO
What is the matter, lady?

EMILIA
Alas, Iago, my lord hath so bewhor'd her,
Thrown such despite and heavy terms upon her,
That true hearts cannot bear it.

DESDEMONA
Am I that name, Iago?

IAGO What name, fair lady?

DESDEMONA
Such as she said my lord did say I was.

EMILIA
He call'd her whore. A beggar in his drink
Could not have laid such terms upon his callet.

IAGO
Why did he so?

DESDEMONA [*Weeping*]
I do not know; I am sure I am none such.

IAGO
Do not weep, do not weep. Alas the day!

EMILIA
Hath she forsook so many noble matches,
Her father and her country and her friends,
To be call'd whore? Would it not make one weep?

DESDEMONA
It is my wretched fortune.

IAGO Beshrew him for 't!
How comes this trick upon him?

DESDEMONA Nay, heaven doth know.

EMILIA
I will be hang'd if some eternal villain,
Some busy and insinuating rogue,
Some cogging, cozening slave, to get some office,
Have not devis'd this slander. I will be hang'd else.

IAGO
Fie, there is no such man; it is impossible.

DESDEMONA
If any such there be, heaven pardon him!

EMILIA
A halter pardon him! And hell gnaw his bones!
Why should he call her whore? Who keeps her
company?
What place? What time? What form? What
likelihood?
The Moor's abus'd by some most villainous knave,
Some base notorious knave, some scurvy fellow.
O heaven, that such companions thou'dst unfold,
And put in every honest hand a whip
To lash the rascals naked through the world
Even from the east to th' west!

IAGO Speak within door.

EMILIA
O, fie upon them! Some such squire he was
That turn'd your wit the seamy side without,
And made you to suspect me with the Moor.

IAGO
You are a fool; go to.

DESDEMONA Alas, Iago,
What shall I do to win my lord again?

88 cry you mercy beg your pardon **97 half asleep** i.e., dazed **104 go by water** be expressed by tears **110 opinion** censure. **least misuse** slightest misconduct

123 callet whore **131 trick** strange behavior **134 cogging** cheating. **cozening** defrauding **140 form** circumstance **143 companions** fellows. **unfold** expose **146 within door** i.e., not so loud

Good friend, go to him; for, by this light of heaven,
I know not how I lost him. Here I kneel. [*Kneels.*]
If e'er my will did trespass 'gainst his love,
Either in discourse of thought or actual deed,
Or that mine eyes, mine ears, or any sense
Delighted them in any other form;
Or that I do not yet, and ever did,
And ever will—though he do shake me off
To beggarly divorcement—love him dearly,
Comfort forswear me! Unkindness may do much;
And his unkindness may defeat my life,
But never taint my love. I cannot say "whore."
It does abhor me now I speak the word;
To do the act that might the addition earn
Not the world's mass of vanity could make me.

IAGO
I pray you, be content. 'Tis but his humor.
The business of the state does him offense,
[And he does chide with you.]

DESDEMONA
If 'twere no other—

IAGO
It is but so, I warrant.
[*Trumpets within.*]
Hark, how these instruments summon to supper!
The messengers of Venice stays the meat.
Go in, and weep not. All things shall be well.
Exeunt Desdemona and Emilia.

Enter Roderigo.

How now, Roderigo?

RODERIGO I do not find that thou deal'st justly with me.

IAGO What in the contrary?

RODERIGO Every day thou daff'st me with some device, Iago, and rather, as it seems to me now, keep'st from me all conveniency than suppliest me with the least advantage of hope. I will indeed no longer endure it, nor am I yet persuaded to put up in peace what already I have foolishly suff'red.

IAGO Will you hear me, Roderigo?

RODERIGO Faith, I have heard too much, for your words and performances are no kin together.

IAGO You charge me most unjustly.

RODERIGO With nought but truth. I have wasted myself out of my means. The jewels you have had from me to deliver to Desdemona would half have corrupted a votarist. You have told me she hath receiv'd them and return'd me expectations and comforts of sudden respect and acquaintance, but I find none.

IAGO Well, go to; very well.

RODERIGO Very well! Go to! I cannot go to, man, nor 'tis not very well. By this hand, I think it is scurvy, and begin to find myself fopp'd in it.

IAGO Very well.

RODERIGO I tell you 'tis not very well. I will make myself known to Desdemona. If she will return me my jewels, I will give over my suit and repent my unlawful solicitation; if not, assure yourself I will seek satisfaction of you.

IAGO You have said now.

RODERIGO Ay, and said nothing but what I protest intendment of doing.

IAGO Why, now I see there's mettle in thee, and even from this instant do build on thee a better opinion than ever before. Give me thy hand, Roderigo. Thou hast taken against me a most just exception; but yet I protest I have dealt most directly in thy affair.

RODERIGO It hath not appear'd.

IAGO I grant indeed it hath not appear'd, and your suspicion is not without wit and judgment. But, Roderigo, if thou hast that in thee indeed which I have greater reason to believe now than ever, I mean purpose, courage, and valor, this night show it. If thou the next night following enjoy not Desdemona, take me from this world with treachery and devise engines for my life.

RODERIGO Well, what is it? Is it within reason and compass?

IAGO Sir, there is especial commission come from Venice to depute Cassio in Othello's place.

RODERIGO Is that true? Why, then Othello and Desdemona return again to Venice.

IAGO O, no; he goes into Mauritania and taketh away with him the fair Desdemona, unless his abode be ling'red here by some accident; wherein none can be so determinate as the removing of Cassio.

RODERIGO How do you mean, removing him?

IAGO Why, by making him uncapable of Othello's place; knocking out his brains.

RODERIGO And that you would have me to do?

IAGO Ay, if you dare do yourself a profit and a right. He sups tonight with a harlotry, and thither will I go to him. He knows not yet of his honorable fortune. If you will watch his going thence, which I will fashion to fall out between twelve and one, you may take him at your pleasure. I will be near to second your attempt, and he shall fall between us. Come, stand not amaz'd at it, but go along with me; I will show you such a necessity in his death that you shall think yourself bound to put it on him. It is now high supper-time, and the night grows to waste. About it.

RODERIGO I will hear further reason for this.

IAGO And you shall be satisfied. *Exeunt.*

SCENE III

Enter Othello, Lodovico, Desdemona, Emilia, and Attendants.

LODOVICO
I do beseech you, sir, trouble yourself no further.

162 defeat destroy **165 addition** title **172 stays the meat** are waiting to dine **177 thou daff'st me** you put me off with an excuse **179 conveniency** advantage, opportunity **181 put up** submit to, tolerate **189–190 votarist** nun **191–192 sudden respect** immediate consideration **196 fopp'd** fooled, duped

218–219 engines for plots against **229 determinate** effective **235 harlotry** courtesan

IV.iii. Location: The citadel.

OTHELLO
O, pardon me; 'twill do me good to walk.

LODOVICO
Madam, good night. I humbly thank your ladyship.

DESDEMONA
Your honor is most welcome.

OTHELLO
Will you walk, sir?
O, Desdemona!

DESDEMONA
My lord?

OTHELLO Get you to bed on th' instant; I will be return'd forthwith. Dismiss your attendant there. Look 't be done.

DESDEMONA
I will, my lord.
Exit [Othello, with Lodovico and Attendants].

EMILIA How goes it now? He looks gentler than he did.

DESDEMONA
He says he will return incontinent,
And hath commanded me to go to bed,
And bade me to dismiss you.

EMILIA Dismiss me?

DESDEMONA
It was his bidding; therefore, good Emilia,
Give me my nightly wearing, and adieu.
We must not now displease him.

EMILIA I would you had never seen him!

DESDEMONA
So would not I. My love doth so approve him,
That even his stubbornness, his checks, his frowns—
Prithee unpin me—have grace and favor in them.
[Emilia prepares Desdemona for bed.]

EMILIA I have laid those sheets you bade me on the bed.

DESDEMONA
All's one. Good faith, how foolish are our minds!
If I do die before thee, prithee shroud me
In one of those same sheets.

EMILIA
Come, come, you talk.

DESDEMONA
My mother had a maid call'd Barbary.
She was in love, and he she lov'd prov'd mad
And did forsake her. She had a song of "Willow,"
An old thing 'twas, but it express'd her fortune,
And she died singing it. That song tonight
Will not go from my mind; I have much to do
But to go hang my head all at one side
And sing it like poor Barbary. Prithee, dispatch.

EMILIA Shall I go fetch your nightgown?

DESDEMONA
No, unpin me here.
This Lodovico is a proper man.

EMILIA A very handsome man.

DESDEMONA
He speaks well.

EMILIA I know a lady in Venice would have walk'd barefoot to Palestine for a touch of his nether lip.

DESDEMONA *[Singing]*
"The poor soul sat sighing by a sycamore tree,
Sing all a green willow;
Her hand on her bosom, her head on her knee,
Sing willow, willow, willow.
The fresh streams ran by her, and murmur'd her moans;
Sing willow, willow, willow;
Her salt tears fell from her, and soft'ned the stones"—
Lay by these.
[Singing.] "Sing willow, willow, willow"—
Prithee, hie thee; he'll come anon.
[Singing.] "Sing all a green willow must be my garland.
Let nobody blame him; his scorn I approve"—
Nay, that's not next.—Hark! Who is 't that knocks?

EMILIA It's the wind.

DESDEMONA *[Singing]*
"I call'd my love false love; but what said he then?
Sing willow, willow, willow;
If I court moe women, you'll couch with moe men"—
So, get thee gone; good night. Mine eyes do itch;
Doth that bode weeping?

EMILIA
'Tis neither here nor there.

DESDEMONA
I have heard it said so. O, these men, these men!
Dost thou in conscience think—tell me, Emilia—
That there be women do abuse their husbands
In such gross kind?

EMILIA
There be some such, no question.

DESDEMONA
Wouldst thou do such a deed for all the world?

EMILIA
Why, would not you?

DESDEMONA
No, by this heavenly light!

EMILIA
Nor I neither by this heavenly light;
I might do 't as well i' th' dark.

DESDEMONA
Wouldst thou do such a deed for all the world?

EMILIA
The world's a huge thing. It is a great price
For a small vice.

DESDEMONA
Good troth, I think thou wouldst not.

EMILIA By my troth, I think I should; and undo 't when I had done. Marry, I would not do such a thing for a joint-ring, nor for measures of lawn, nor for gowns, petticoats, nor caps, nor any petty exhibition; but, for all the whole world—'ud's pity, who would not make her husband a cuckold to make him a monarch? I should venture purgatory for 't.

12 incontinent immediately **21 stubbornness** roughness. **checks** rebukes **29 mad** wild, i.e., faithless **33–34 I . . . hang** I can scarcely keep myself from hanging

52 hie thee hurry **76 joint-ring** a ring made in separate halves. **lawn** fine linen **77 exhibition** gift **78 'ud's** i.e., God's

DESDEMONA
Beshrew me if I would do such a wrong
For the whole world.

EMILIA Why, the wrong is but a wrong i' th' world; and having the world for your labor, 'tis a wrong in your own world, and you might quickly make it right.

DESDEMONA
I do not think there is any such woman.

EMILIA Yes, a dozen; and as many to th' vantage as 87
would store the world they play'd for. 88
But I do think it is their husbands' faults
If wives do fall. Say that they slack their duties,
And pour our treasures into foreign laps, 91
Or else break out in peevish jealousies,
Throwing restraint upon us? Or say they strike us,
Or scant our former having in despite? 94
Why, we have galls, and though we have some
  grace, 95
Yet have we some revenge. Let husbands know
Their wives have sense like them. They see, and
  smell, 97
And have their palates both for sweet and sour,
As husbands have. What is it that they do
When they change us for others? Is it sport?
I think it is. And doth affection breed it?
I think it doth. Is 't frailty that thus errs?
It is so too. And have not we affections,
Desires for sport, and frailty, as men have?
Then let them use us well; else let them know,
The ills we do, their ills instruct us so.

DESDEMONA
Good night, good night. God me such uses send, 107
Not to pick bad from bad, but by bad mend! 108
Exeunt.

ACT V • SCENE I

Enter Iago and Roderigo.

IAGO
Here stand behind this bulk; straight will he come. 1
Wear thy good rapier bare, and put it home.
Quick, quick! Fear nothing; I'll be at thy elbow.
It makes us, or it mars us; think on that,
And fix most firm thy resolution.

RODERIGO
Be near at hand; I may miscarry in 't.

IAGO
Here, at thy hand. Be bold, and take thy stand.
[*Iago stands aside. Roderigo conceals himself.*]

RODERIGO
I have no great devotion to the deed;
And yet he hath given me satisfying reasons.
'Tis but a man gone. Forth, my sword! He dies.
[*Draws.*]

IAGO
I have rubb'd this young quat almost to the sense, 11
And he grows angry. Now, whether he kill Cassio,
Or Cassio him, or each do kill the other,
Every way makes my gain. Live Roderigo,
He calls me to a restitution large
Of gold and jewels that I bobb'd from him 16
As gifts to Desdemona.
It must not be. If Cassio do remain,
He hath a daily beauty in his life
That makes me ugly; and besides, the Moor
May unfold me to him; there stand I in much peril.
No, he must die. Be 't so. I hear him coming.

Enter Cassio.

RODERIGO [*Coming forth*]
I know his gait, 'tis he.—Villain, thou diest!
[*Makes a pass at Cassio.*]

CASSIO
That thrust had been mine enemy indeed,
But that my coat is better than thou know'st. 25
I will make proof of thine.
[*Draws, and wounds Roderigo.*]

RODERIGO O, I am slain! [*Falls.*]

[*Iago from behind wounds Cassio in the leg, and exit.*]

CASSIO
I am maim'd forever. Help, ho! Murder! Murder!

Enter Othello.

OTHELLO
The voice of Cassio! Iago keeps his word.

RODERIGO
O, villain that I am!

OTHELLO It is even so.

CASSIO
O, help, ho! Light! A surgeon!

OTHELLO
'Tis he. O brave Iago, honest and just,
That hast such noble sense of thy friend's wrong!
Thou teachest me. Minion, your dear lies dead, 33
And your unblest fate hies. Strumpet, I come. 34
Forth of my heart those charms, thine eyes, are
  blotted;
Thy bed, lust-stain'd, shall with lust's blood be
  spotted. *Exit Othello.*

Enter Lodovico and Gratiano.

CASSIO
What, ho! No watch? No passage? Murder! Murder! 37

GRATIANO
'Tis some mischance; the voice is very direful.

87 to th' vantage in addition, to boot **88 store** populate **91 pour . . . laps** i.e., are unfaithful, give what is rightfully ours (semen) to other women **94 scant . . . despite** reduce our allowance to spite us **95 have galls** i.e., are capable of resenting injury and insult **97 sense** physical sense **107 uses** habit, practice **108 Not . . . mend** i.e., not to learn bad conduct from other's badness (as Emilia has suggested women learn from men), but to mend my ways by perceiving what badness is, making spiritual benefit out of evil and adversity

V.i. Location: A street in Cyprus.
1 bulk framework projecting from the front of a shop

11 quat pimple, pustule. **to the sense** to the quick **16 bobb'd** filched cunningly **25 coat** garment of mail (under his outer clothing) **33 Minion** hussy (i.e., Desdemona) **34 hies** hastens on **37 passage** people passing

CASSIO
O, help!

LODOVICO
Hark!

RODERIGO
O wretched villain!

LODOVICO
Two or three groan. 'Tis heavy night;
These may be counterfeits. Let's think 't unsafe
To come in to the cry without more help.
[*They remain near the entrance.*]

RODERIGO
Nobody come? Then shall I bleed to death.

Enter Iago [*in his shirtsleeves, with a light*].

LODOVICO
Hark!

GRATIANO
Here's one comes in his shirt, with light and
weapons.

IAGO
Who's there? Whose noise is this that cries on
murder?

LODOVICO
We do not know.

IAGO
Did not you hear a cry?

CASSIO
Here, here! For heaven sake, help me!

IAGO
What's the matter?
[*He moves toward Cassio.*]

GRATIANO [*To Lodovico*]
This is Othello's ancient, as I take it.

LODOVICO [*To Gratiano*]
The same indeed; a very valiant fellow.

IAGO
What are you here that cry so grievously?

CASSIO
Iago? O, I am spoil'd, undone by villains!
Give me some help.

IAGO
O me, lieutenant! What villains have done this?

CASSIO
I think that one of them is hereabout,
And cannot make away.

IAGO
O treacherous villains!
[*To Lodovico and Gratiano.*] What are you there?
Come in, and give some help. [*They advance.*]

RODERIGO
O, help me there!

CASSIO
That's one of them.

IAGO
O murd'rous slave! O villain!
[*Stabs Roderigo.*]

RODERIGO
O damn'd Iago! O inhuman dog!

IAGO
Kill men i' th' dark?—Where be these bloody
thieves?—
How silent is this town!—Ho! Murder, murder!—
[*To Lodovico and Gratiano.*] What may you be? Are
you of good or evil?

LODOVICO
As you shall prove us, praise us.

IAGO
Signior Lodovico?

LODOVICO
He, sir.

IAGO
I cry you mercy. Here's Cassio hurt by villains.

GRATIANO
Cassio?

IAGO
How is 't, brother?

CASSIO
My leg is cut in two.

IAGO
Marry, heaven forbid!
Light, gentlemen! I'll bind it with my shirt.
[*He hands them the light, and tends to Cassio's wound.*]

Enter Bianca.

BIANCA
What is the matter, ho? Who is 't that cried?

IAGO
Who is 't that cried?

BIANCA
O my dear Cassio! My sweet Cassio!
O Cassio, Cassio, Cassio!

IAGO
O notable strumpet! Cassio, may you suspect
Who they should be that have thus mangled you?

CASSIO
No.

GRATIANO
I am sorry to find you thus. I have been to
seek you.

IAGO
Lend me a garter. [*Applies a tourniquet.*] So.—O, for
a chair,
To bear him easily hence!

BIANCA
Alas, he faints! O Cassio, Cassio, Cassio!

IAGO
Gentlemen all, I do suspect this trash
To be a party in this injury.—
Patience awhile, good Cassio.—Come, come;
Lend me a light. [*Shines the light on Roderigo.*]
Know we this face or no?
Alas, my friend and my dear countryman
Roderigo! No.—Yes, sure.—O heaven! Roderigo!

GRATIANO
What, of Venice?

IAGO
Even he, sir. Did you know him?

GRATIANO
Know him? Ay.

42 heavy thick, dark **48 cries on** cries out **58 make** get **59 What** who. (Also at l. 65.)

82 chair litter

IAGO
Signior Gratiano? I cry your gentle pardon.
These bloody accidents must excuse my manners
That so neglected you.

GRATIANO
I am glad to see you.

IAGO
How do you, Cassio? O, a chair, a chair!

GRATIANO
Roderigo!

IAGO
He, he, 'tis he. [*A litter brought in.*] O, that's well said; the chair.
Some good man bear him carefully from hence;
I'll fetch the general's surgeon. [*To Bianca.*] For you, mistress,
Save you your labor.—He that lies slain here, Cassio,
Was my dear friend. What malice was between you?

CASSIO
None in the world; nor do I know the man.

IAGO [*To Bianca*]
What, look you pale?—O, bear him out o' th' air.
[*Cassio and Roderigo are borne off.*]
Stay you, good gentlemen.—Look you pale, mistress?—
Do you perceive the gastness of her eye?—
Nay, if you stare, we shall hear more anon.—
Behold her well; I pray you, look upon her.
Do you see, gentlemen? Nay, guiltiness will speak,
Though tongues were out of use.

[*Enter Emilia.*]

EMILIA
'Las, what's the matter? What's the matter, husband?

IAGO
Cassio hath here been set on in the dark
By Roderigo and fellows that are scap'd.
He's almost slain, and Roderigo dead.

EMILIA
Alas, good gentleman! Alas, good Cassio!

IAGO
This is the fruits of whoring. Prithee, Emilia,
Go know of Cassio where he supp'd tonight.
[*To Bianca.*] What, do you shake at that?

BIANCA
He supp'd at my house; but I therefore shake not.

IAGO
O, did he so? I charge you go with me.

EMILIA
O, fie upon thee, strumpet!

BIANCA
I am no strumpet, but of life as honest
As you that thus abuse me.

EMILIA
As I? Foh! Fie upon thee!

IAGO
Kind gentlemen, let's go see poor Cassio dress'd.
Come, mistress, you must tell 's another tale.
Emilia, run you to the citadel,
And tell my lord and lady what hath happ'd.—
Will you go on afore? [*Aside.*] This is the night
That either makes me or fordoes me quite. *Exeunt.*

SCENE II

Enter Othello [*with a light*], *and Desdemona in her bed.*

OTHELLO
It is the cause, it is the cause, my soul.
Let me not name it to you, you chaste stars!
It is the cause. Yet I'll not shed her blood,
Nor scar that whiter skin of hers than snow,
And smooth as monumental alabaster.
Yet she must die, else she'll betray more men.
Put out the light, and then put out the light.
If I quench thee, thou flaming minister,
I can again thy former light restore,
Should I repent me; but once put out thy light,
Thou cunning'st pattern of excelling nature,
I know not where is that Promethean heat
That can thy light relume. When I have pluck'd the rose,
I cannot give it vital growth again,
It needs must wither. I'll smell thee on the tree.
[*Kissing her.*]
O balmy breath, that dost almost persuade
Justice to break her sword! One more, one more.
Be thus when thou art dead, and I will kill thee,
And love thee after. One more, and that's the last.
So sweet was ne'er so fatal. I must weep,
But they are cruel tears. This sorrow's heavenly;
It strikes where it doth love. She wakes.

DESDEMONA
Who's there? Othello?

OTHELLO
Ay, Desdemona.

DESDEMONA
Will you come to bed, my lord?

OTHELLO
Have you pray'd tonight, Desdemon?

DESDEMONA
Ay, my lord.

OTHELLO
If you bethink yourself of any crime
Unreconcil'd as yet to heaven and grace,
Solicit for it straight.

DESDEMONA
Alack, my lord, what may you mean by that?

OTHELLO
Well, do it, and be brief; I will walk by.
I would not kill thy unprepared spirit.

98 well said well done **106 gastness** terror

129 fordoes undoes, ruins

V.ii. Location: A bedchamber in the citadel.
s.d. in her bed (The bed is presumably "thrust out" on stage as the scene begins.) **1 cause** i.e., cause of justice, the offense itself, which Othello must correct as an agent of justice **12 Promethean heat** divine fire. (Alluding to the theft of fire from heaven by Prometheus.) **13 relume** rekindle

No, heaven forfend! I would not kill thy soul.

DESDEMONA
Talk you of killing?

OTHELLO Ay, I do.

DESDEMONA Then heaven
Have mercy on me!

OTHELLO Amen, with all my heart!

DESDEMONA
If you say so, I hope you will not kill me.

OTHELLO Hum!

DESDEMONA
And yet I fear you; for you're fatal then
When your eyes roll so. Why I should fear I know not,
Since guiltiness I know not; but yet I feel I fear.

OTHELLO
Think on thy sins.

DESDEMONA They are loves I bear to you.

OTHELLO
Ay, and for that thou diest.

DESDEMONA
That death's unnatural that kills for loving.
Alas, why gnaw you so your nether lip?
Some bloody passion shakes your very frame.
These are portents; but yet I hope, I hope,
They do not point on me.

OTHELLO Peace, and be still!

DESDEMONA
I will so. What's the matter?

OTHELLO
That handkerchief which I so lov'd and gave thee
Thou gav'st to Cassio.

DESDEMONA No, by my life and soul!
Send for the man, and ask him.

OTHELLO
Sweet soul, take heed, take heed of perjury.
Thou art on thy deathbed.

DESDEMONA
Ay, but not yet to die.

OTHELLO Yes, presently.
Therefore confess thee freely of thy sin;
For to deny each article with oath
Cannot remove nor choke the strong conception
That I do groan withal. Thou art to die.

DESDEMONA
Then Lord have mercy on me!

OTHELLO I say, amen.

DESDEMONA
And have you mercy too! I never did
Offend you in my life; never lov'd Cassio
But with such general warranty of heaven
As I might love. I never gave him token.

OTHELLO
By heaven, I saw my handkerchief in 's hand.
O perjur'd woman! Thou dost stone my heart,
And makes me call what I intend to do
A murder, which I thought a sacrifice.
I saw the handkerchief.

DESDEMONA He found it then;
I never gave it him. Send for him hither;
Let him confess a truth.

OTHELLO He hath confess'd.

DESDEMONA
What, my lord?

OTHELLO
That he hath us'd thee.

DESDEMONA How? Unlawfully?

OTHELLO Ay.

DESDEMONA
He will not say so.

OTHELLO No, his mouth is stopp'd;
Honest Iago hath ta'en order for 't.

DESDEMONA
O, my fear interprets. What, is he dead?

OTHELLO
Had all his hairs been lives, my great revenge
Had stomach for them all.

DESDEMONA
Alas, he is betray'd and I undone! [*Weeps.*]

OTHELLO
Out, strumpet! Weep'st thou for him to my face?

DESDEMONA
O, banish me, my lord, but kill me not!

OTHELLO
Down, strumpet!

DESDEMONA
Kill me tomorrow; let me live tonight!

OTHELLO
Nay, if you strive—

DESDEMONA
But half an hour!

OTHELLO Being done, there is no pause.

DESDEMONA
But while I say one prayer!

OTHELLO It is too late.
Smothers her.

EMILIA *(At the door)*
My lord, my lord! What, ho! My lord, my lord!

OTHELLO
What noise is this? Not dead? Not yet quite dead?
I that am cruel am yet merciful;
I would not have thee linger in thy pain.
[*He dispatches her.*]
So, so.

EMILIA *(Within)*
What, ho! My lord, my lord!

OTHELLO
Who's there?

EMILIA [*Within*]
O, good my lord, I would speak a word with you!

OTHELLO
Yes, 'tis Emilia.—By and by.—She's dead.
'Tis like she comes to speak of Cassio's death.—
The noise was here. Ha! No more moving?
Still as the grave. Shall she come in? Were 't good?—

58 conception belief (of your guilt) **66 stone** turn to stone, harden

75 ta'en order taken measures **85 Being done** i.e., since justice has begun its relentless course

I think she stirs again. No. What's best to do?
If she come in, she'll sure speak to my wife.
My wife! My wife! What wife? I have no wife.
O, insupportable! O heavy hour!
Methinks it should be now a huge eclipse
Of sun and moon, and that th' affrighted globe
Should yawn at alteration.

EMILIA [*Within*] I do beseech you
That I may speak with you, O, good my lord!

OTHELLO
I had forgot thee. O, come in, Emilia.—
Soft; by and by. Let me the curtains draw.—
[*Closes bed-curtains and opens door.*]
Where art thou?

Enter Emilia.

What's the matter with thee now?

EMILIA
O, my good lord, yonder's foul murders done!

OTHELLO
What, now?

EMILIA
But now, my lord.

OTHELLO
It is the very error of the moon;
She comes more nearer earth than she was wont,
And makes men mad.

EMILIA
Cassio, my lord, hath kill'd a young Venetian
Call'd Roderigo.

OTHELLO Roderigo kill'd?
And Cassio kill'd?

EMILIA No, Cassio is not kill'd.

OTHELLO
Not Cassio kill'd? Then murder's out of tune,
And sweet revenge grows harsh.

DESDEMONA
O, falsely, falsely murder'd!

EMILIA
O lord, what cry is that?

OTHELLO
That? What?

EMILIA
Out, and alas, that was my lady's voice.
[*She opens the bed-curtains.*]
Help, help, ho, help! O lady, speak again!
Sweet Desdemona! O sweet mistress, speak!

DESDEMONA
A guiltless death I die.

EMILIA
O, who hath done this deed?

DESDEMONA
Nobody; I myself. Farewell.
Commend me to my kind lord. O, farewell! [*Dies.*]

OTHELLO
Why, how should she be murd'red?

EMILIA Alas, who knows?

OTHELLO
You heard her say herself, it was not I.

EMILIA
She said so. I must needs report the truth.

OTHELLO
She's like a liar gone to burning hell!
'Twas I that kill'd her.

EMILIA O, the more angel she,
And you the blacker devil!

OTHELLO
She turn'd to folly, and she was a whore.

EMILIA
Thou dost belie her, and thou art a devil.

OTHELLO
She was false as water.

EMILIA Thou art rash as fire, to say
That she was false. O, she was heavenly true!

OTHELLO
Cassio did top her; ask thy husband else.
O, I were damn'd beneath all depth in hell
But that I did proceed upon just grounds
To this extremity. Thy husband knew it all.

EMILIA
My husband?

OTHELLO
Thy husband.

EMILIA
That she was false to wedlock?

OTHELLO
Ay, with Cassio. Nay, had she been true,
If heaven would make me such another world
Of one entire and perfect chrysolite,
I 'd not have sold her for it.

EMILIA
My husband?

OTHELLO
Ay, 'twas he that told me on her first.
An honest man he is, and hates the slime
That sticks on filthy deeds.

EMILIA
My husband?

OTHELLO
What needs this iterance, woman? I say thy
husband.

EMILIA
O mistress, villainy hath made mocks with love!
My husband say she was false?

OTHELLO He, woman;
I say thy husband. Dost understand the word?
My friend, thy husband, honest, honest Iago.

EMILIA
If he say so, may his pernicious soul
Rot half a grain a day! He lies to th' heart.
She was too fond of her most filthy bargain.

OTHELLO
Ha? [*He draws.*]

105 yawn gape in amazement, i.e., move in an earthquake. (According to Pliny, earthquakes often happen during eclipses.) **113 error** aberration, irregularity

150 chrysolite precious topaz **157 iterance** iteration, repetition **158 made mocks with** derided, made sport of

EMILIA
Do thy worst!
This deed of thine is no more worthy heaven
Than thou wast worthy her.

OTHELLO
Peace, you were best.

EMILIA
Thou hast not half that pow'r to do me harm
As I have to be hurt. O gull! O dolt!
As ignorant as dirt! Thou hast done a deed—
I care not for thy sword; I'll make thee known,
Though I lost twenty lives.—Help! Help, ho, help!
The Moor hath kill'd my mistress! Murder, murder!

Enter Montano, Gratiano, and Iago [*with others*].

MONTANO
What is the matter? How now, general?

EMILIA
O, are you come, Iago? You have done well,
That men must lay their murders on your neck.

GRATIANO
What is the matter?

EMILIA
Disprove this villain, if thou be'st a man.
He says thou told'st him that his wife was false.
I know thou didst not; thou 'rt not such a villain.
Speak, for my heart is full.

IAGO
I told him what I thought, and told no more
Than what he found himself was apt and true.

EMILIA
But did you ever tell him she was false?

IAGO
I did.

EMILIA
You told a lie, an odious, damned lie!
Upon my soul, a lie, a wicked lie.
She false with Cassio? Did you say with Cassio?

IAGO
With Cassio, mistress. Go to, charm your tongue.

EMILIA
I will not charm my tongue; I am bound to speak.
My mistress here lies murdered in her bed—

ALL
O heavens forfend!

EMILIA
And your reports have set the murder on.

OTHELLO
Nay, stare not, masters. It is true indeed.

GRATIANO
'Tis a strange truth.

MONTANO
O monstrous act!

EMILIA
Villainy, villainy, villainy!
I think upon 't—I think I smell 't! O villainy!
I thought so then—I'll kill myself for grief—
O villainy, villainy!

IAGO
What, are you mad? I charge you, get you home.

EMILIA
Good gentlemen, let me have leave to speak.
'Tis proper I obey him, but not now.
Perchance, Iago, I will ne'er go home.

OTHELLO
O! O! O! [*He falls on the bed.*]

EMILIA
Nay, lay thee down and roar;
For thou hast kill'd the sweetest innocent
That e'er did lift up eye.

OTHELLO [*Rising*]
O, she was foul!
I scarce did know you, uncle. There lies your niece,
Whose breath, indeed, these hands have newly stopp'd.
I know this act shows horrible and grim.

GRATIANO
Poor Desdemon! I am glad thy father's dead.
Thy match was mortal to him, and pure grief
Shore his old thread in twain. Did he live now,
This sight would make him do a desperate turn,
Yea, curse his better angel from his side,
And fall to reprobance.

OTHELLO
'Tis pitiful; but yet Iago knows
That she with Cassio hath the act of shame
A thousand times committed. Cassio confess'd it;
And she did gratify his amorous works
With that recognizance and pledge of love
Which I first gave her. I saw it in his hand;
It was a handkerchief, an antique token
My father gave my mother.

EMILIA
O God! O heavenly God!

IAGO
'Zounds, hold your peace.

EMILIA
'Twill out, 'twill out! I peace?
No, I will speak as liberal as the north.
Let heaven and men and devils, let them all,
All, all, cry shame against me, yet I'll speak.

IAGO
Be wise, and get you home.

EMILIA
I will not.
[*Iago offers to stab Emilia.*]

GRATIANO
Fie!
Your sword upon a woman?

EMILIA
O thou dull Moor! That handkerchief thou speak'st of
I found by fortune and did give my husband;
For often, with a solemn earnestness,
More than indeed belong'd to such a trifle,
He begg'd of me to steal it.

IAGO
Villainous whore!

EMILIA
She give it Cassio? No, alas! I found it,
And I did give 't my husband.

170 to be hurt i.e., to endure hurt **190 charm** keep silent (as though by a magic spell) **199 then** (I.e., probably at IV.ii.132–146.)

210 shows looks **213 Shore** sheared, cut **216 reprobance** damnation **221 recognizance** token **227 liberal as the north** freely as the north wind (blows)

IAGO Filth, thou liest!

EMILIA
By heaven, I do not, I do not, gentlemen.
O murd'rous coxcomb, what should such a fool
Do with so good a wife?

OTHELLO
Are there no stones in heaven
But what serves for the thunder?—Precious villain!
[He runs at Iago; Montano disarms Othello. Iago, from behind, stabs Emilia, and exit.]

GRATIANO
The woman falls! Sure he hath kill'd his wife.

EMILIA
Ay, ay. O, lay me by my mistress' side.

GRATIANO
He's gone, but his wife's kill'd.

MONTANO
'Tis a notorious villain. Take you this weapon,
Which I have here recover'd from the Moor.
Come, guard the door without; let him not pass,
But kill him rather. I'll after that same villain,
For 'tis a damned slave.
Exit [with all but Othello and Emilia, who has been laid by Desdemona's side].

OTHELLO
I am not valiant neither,
But every puny whipster gets my sword.
But why should honor outlive honesty?
Let it go all.

EMILIA What did thy song bode, lady?
Hark, canst thou hear me? I will play the swan,
And die in music. [*Sings.*] "Willow, willow,
willow."
Moor, she was chaste. She lov'd thee, cruel Moor;
So come my soul to bliss, as I speak true.
So speaking as I think, alas, I die.
[Dies.]

OTHELLO
I have another weapon in this chamber;
It is a sword of Spain, the ice-brook's temper—
O, here it is. [*Finds a sword.*] Uncle, I must come
forth.

GRATIANO [*Within*]
If thou attempt it, it will cost thee dear.
Thou hast no weapon, and perforce must suffer.

OTHELLO
Look in upon me then and speak with me,
Or, naked as I am, I will assault thee.

[Enter Gratiano.]

GRATIANO
What is the matter?

OTHELLO Behold, I have a weapon;
A better never did itself sustain
Upon a soldier's thigh. I have seen the day
That, with this little arm and this good sword,
I have made my way through more impediments
Than twenty times your stop. But, O vain boast!
Who can control his fate? 'Tis not so now.
Be not afraid, though you do see me weapon'd;
Here is my journey's end, here is my butt
And very sea-mark of my utmost sail.
[Gratiano steps back.]
Do you go back dismay'd? 'Tis a lost fear;
Man but a rush against Othello's breast,
And he retires. Where should Othello go?
[He turns to Desdemona.]
Now, how dost thou look now? O ill-starr'd wench!
Pale as thy smock! When we shall meet at compt,
This look of thine will hurl my soul from heaven,
And fiends will snatch at it. Cold, cold, my girl?
Even like thy chastity. O cursed, cursed slave!
Whip me, ye devils,
From the possession of this heavenly sight!
Blow me about in winds! Roast me in sulphur!
Wash me in steep-down gulfs of liquid fire!
O Desdemon! Dead, Desdemon! Dead! Oh! Oh!

Enter Lodovico, Cassio [carried in a litter], Montano, and Iago [prisoner], with Officers.

LODOVICO
Where is this rash and most unfortunate man?

OTHELLO
That's he that was Othello. Here I am.

LODOVICO
Where is that viper? Bring the villain forth.
[Iago is led forward.]

OTHELLO
I look down towards his feet; but that's a fable.
If that thou be'st a devil, I cannot kill thee.
[Wounds Iago.]

LODOVICO
Wrench his sword from him.
[Othello is disarmed.]

IAGO I bleed, sir, but not kill'd.

OTHELLO
I am not sorry neither. I 'd have thee live;
For, in my sense, 'tis happiness to die.

LODOVICO
O thou Othello, that was once so good,
Fall'n in the practice of a damned slave,
What shall be said to thee?

OTHELLO Why, anything.
An honorable murderer, if you will;
For nought I did in hate, but all in honor.

LODOVICO
This wretch hath part confess'd his villainy.
Did you and he consent in Cassio's death?

OTHELLO
Ay.

CASSIO
Dear general, I never gave you cause.

OTHELLO
I do believe it, and I ask your pardon.

240 coxcomb fool. (Addressed to Othello.) **242 stones** bolts, such as those used for thunderbolts **253 whipster** contemptible fellow **254 honor** i.e., the bravery for which one enjoys a soldier's reputation. **honesty** true integrity **262 the ice-brook's temper** tempered in ice-cold water **267 naked** unarmed

273 stop power (to stop) **276 butt** goal, limit. (An archery term.) **277 sea-mark** beacon (marking his destination or limit) **278 lost** wasted, unneeded **279 Man . . . rush** wield no more than a reed **282 compt** account, judgment day **294 towards his feet** i.e., to see if they are cloven like a devil's **300 practice** plotting

Will you, I pray, demand that demi-devil
Why he hath thus ensnar'd my soul and body?

IAGO
Demand me nothing. What you know, you know.
From this time forth I never will speak word.

LODOVICO
What, not to pray?

GRATIANO Torments will ope your lips.

OTHELLO
Well, thou dost best.

LODOVICO
Sir, you shall understand what hath befall'n,
Which, as I think, you know not. Here is a letter
Found in the pocket of the slain Roderigo;
And here another. [*Produces letters.*] The one of them imports
The death of Cassio to be undertook
By Roderigo.

OTHELLO
O villain!

CASSIO Most heathenish and most gross!

LODOVICO
Now here's another discontented paper,
Found in his pocket too. [*Shows another paper.*] And this, it seems,
Roderigo meant t' have sent this damned villain;
But that belike Iago in the nick
Came in and satisfied him.

OTHELLO
O thou pernicious caitiff!—
How came you, Cassio, by that handkerchief
That was my wife's?

CASSIO I found it in my chamber;
And he himself confess'd but even now
That there he dropp'd it for a special purpose
Which wrought to his desire.

OTHELLO O fool, fool, fool!

CASSIO
There is besides, in Roderigo's letter,
How he upbraids Iago, that he made him
Brave me upon the watch, whereon it came
That I was cast; and even but now he spake,
After long seeming dead, Iago hurt him,
Iago set him on.

LODOVICO
You must forsake this room and go with us.
Your power and your command is taken off,
And Cassio rules in Cyprus. For this slave,
If there be any cunning cruelty
That can torment him much and hold him long,
It shall be his. You shall close prisoner rest,
Till that the nature of your fault be known
To the Venetian state. Come, bring away.

OTHELLO
Soft you; a word or two before you go.
I have done the state some service, and they know 't.
No more of that. I pray you, in your letters,
When you shall these unlucky deeds relate,
Speak of me as I am; nothing extenuate,
Nor set down aught in malice. Then must you speak
Of one that lov'd not wisely but too well;
Of one not easily jealous, but, being wrought,
Perplex'd in the extreme; of one whose hand,
Like the base Indian, threw a pearl away
Richer than all his tribe; of one whose subdu'd eyes,
Albeit unused to the melting mood,
Drops tears as fast as the Arabian trees
Their medicinable gum. Set you down this;
And say besides, that in Aleppo once,
Where a malignant and a turban'd Turk
Beat a Venetian and traduc'd the state,
I took by th' throat the circumcised dog,
And smote him, thus. [*Stabs himself.*]

LODOVICO
O bloody period!

GRATIANO All that is spoke is marr'd.

OTHELLO
I kiss'd thee ere I kill'd thee. No way but this,
Killing myself, to die upon a kiss.
[*Falls on the bed, and*] *dies.*

CASSIO
This did I fear, but thought he had no weapon;
For he was great of heart.

LODOVICO [*To Iago*] O Spartan dog,
More fell than anguish, hunger, or the sea!
Look on the tragic loading of this bed;
This is thy work. The object poisons sight;
Let it be hid. Gratiano, keep the house,
[*The bed-curtains are drawn.*]
And seize upon the fortunes of the Moor,
For they succeed on you. To you, Lord Governor,
Remains the censure of this hellish villain,
The time, the place, the torture. O, enforce it!
Myself will straight aboard, and to the state
This heavy act with heavy heart relate. *Exeunt.*

335 Brave defy **336 cast** dismissed

356 Indian (This reading from Q1 pictures an ignorant savage who cannot recognize the value of a precious jewel. The F reading, *Iudean* or *Judean,* i.e., infidel or disbeliever, may refer to Herod, who slew Miriamne in a fit of jealousy, or to Judas Iscariot, the betrayer of Christ.) **357 subdu'd** i.e., by grief **366 period** termination, conclusion **370 Spartan dog** (Spartan dogs were noted for their savagery and silence.) **371 fell** cruel **374 Let it be hid** i.e., draw the bed-curtains. (No stage direction specifies that the dead are to be carried off stage at the end of the play.)

King Lear

In *King Lear,* Shakespeare pushes to its limit the hypothesis of a malign or at least indifferent universe in which man's life is meaningless and brutal. Few plays other than *Hamlet* and *Macbeth* approach *King Lear* in evoking the wretchedness of human existence, and even they cannot match the devastating spectacle of Gloucester blinded or Cordelia dead in Lear's arms. The responses of the chief characters are correspondingly searing. "Is man no more than this?" rages Lear. "Unaccommodated man is no more but such a poor, bare, forked animal as thou art" (III,iv). Life he calls a "great stage of fools," an endless torment: "the first time that we smell the air, We wawl and cry" (IV,vi). Gloucester's despair takes the form of accusing the gods of gleeful malice toward man: "As flies to wanton boys are we to th' gods, They kill us for their sport" (IV,i). Gloucester's ministering son Edgar can offer him no greater consolation than stoic resolve: "Men must endure Their going hence, even as their coming hither. Ripeness is all" (V,ii). These statements need not be read as choric expressions of "meaning" for the play as a whole, but they do attest to the depth of suffering. In no other Shakespearean play does injustice appear to triumph so ferociously, for so long, and with such impunity. Will the heavens countenance this reign of injustice on earth? Retribution is late in coming and is not certainly the work of the heavens themselves. For, at the last, we must confront the wanton death of the innocent Cordelia, a death no longer willed even by the villain who arranged her execution. "Is this the promis'd end?" asks Kent, stressing the unparalleled horror of the catastrophe.

Throughout its earlier history, the ancient story of King Lear had always ended happily. In the popular folktale of Cinderella, to which the legend of Lear's daughters bears a significant resemblance, the youngest and virtuous daughter triumphs over her two older wicked sisters and is married to her princely wooer. Geoffrey of Monmouth's *Historia Regum Britanniae* (c. 1136), the earliest known version of the Lear story, records that after Lear is overthrown by his sons-in-law (more than by his daughters), he is restored to his throne by the intervention of the French King and is allowed to enjoy his kingdom and Cordelia's love until his natural death. (Cordelia, as his successor, is later dethroned and murdered by her wicked nephews, but that is another story.) Sixteenth-century Tudor versions of the Lear story with which Shakespeare was familiar—John Higgins' account in *The First parte of the Mirour for Magistrates* (1574), Holinshed's *Chronicles* (1587), Spenser's *The Faerie Queene,* II,x,27–32, and a play called *The True Chronicle History of King Leir* (by 1594, published 1605)—all retain the happy ending. The tragic pattern may have been suggested instead by Shakespeare's probable source for the Gloucester-Edgar-Edmund plot, Sir Philip Sidney's *Arcadia,* II,10, in which the Paphlagonian King is the victim of filial ingratitude and deceit.

Yet even Shakespeare's authority was not sufficient to put down the craving for a happy resolution. Nahum Tate's adaptation (1681), which banished the Fool as indecorous for a tragedy and united Edgar and Cordelia in marriage, placing Lear once again on his throne, held the English stage for about 150 years. David Garrick restored some of Shakespeare's lines, and Edmund Kean restored the tragic ending, but it was not until 1838 that *King Lear* was again performed more or less as he wrote it. Dr. Johnson evidently spoke for most eighteenth-century audiences when he confessed that he could not bring himself to read Shakespeare's text. Cordelia's slaughter violated that age's longing for "poetic justice." Her death implied a wanton universe and so counseled philosophic despair. Today, Shakespeare's relentless honesty and refusal to accept easy answers convince us that he was right to defy the conventions of his source, though no doubt we too distort the play in our way in order to pander to our supposed toughness of vision. For all its unforgettable excellence and persuasiveness, Peter Brook's film version of *King Lear* (1970) is avowedly modern in perspective and employs rearrangements and cuts not wholly unlike those of Tate though opposite in their thrust.

Shakespeare evidently wrote *King Lear* some time before it was performed at court in December of 1606, probably in 1605 and certainly no earlier than 1603–1604; Edgar's speeches as Tom o' Bedlam contain references to Samuel Harsnett's *Declaration of Egregious Popishe Impostures* which was registered for publication in March of 1603. Thus *King Lear* was probably written between *Othello* (c. 1603–1604) and *Macbeth* (c. 1606–1607), when Shakespeare was at the height of his tragic power.

When we look at the play in formal terms, we are apt to be struck first by its complex double plot. Nowhere else in Shakespearean tragedy do we find anything approaching the rich orchestration of the double plotting in *King Lear.* The links and parallels between the two plots are established on a narrative level early in the play and continue to the end. King Lear misjudges his children and disinherits his loving daughter Cordelia in favor of her duplicitous sisters, whereas Gloucester falls prey to Edmund's deceptions and disinherits his loyal son Edgar; Lear is turned out into the storm by his false daughters while Gloucester is branded as a traitor by Edmund and deprived of his eyesight; Lear in his madness realizes his fault against Cordelia while the blind Gloucester "sees" at last the truth about Edgar; both fathers are cared for by their loving children and are belatedly reconciled to them, but die brokenhearted. As recent criticism has noted, these narrative parallels are not especially significant in themselves; we are moved not by the mere repetition of event but by the enlargement of tragic vision that results from the counterpointing of two such actions. When we see juxtaposed to one another two scenes of trial, Lear's mad arraignment of the absent Goneril and Regan and then the cruel imposition of the mere "form of justice" on the pinioned Gloucester (III,vi and vii), we begin to measure the extent to which justice and injustice are inverted by cruelty. When at last the two old men come together, during the storm scenes and especially at Dover, the sad comfort they derive from sharing the wreckage of their lives calls forth piercing eloquence against the stench of mortality (IV,vi). The sight is "most pitiful in the meanest wretch, Past speaking of in a king."

The play's double structure suggests another duality central to *King Lear:* an opposition of parable and realism, of "divided and distinguished worlds" bound together for instructive contrast. (These terms are Maynard Mack's, in his *King Lear in Our Time.*) To a remarkable degree, this play derives its story from folklore and legend, with many of the wondrous and implausible circumstances of popular romance. A prose rendition might almost begin, "Once upon a time there was a king who had three daughters. . . ." Yet Shakespeare arouses romantic expectation only to crush it by aborting the conventional happy ending, setting up a dramatic tension between an idealized world of make-believe and the actual world of disappointed hopes. We are aware of artifice and convention, and yet are deeply moved by the "truth" of suffering, love, and hatred. The characters pull us two ways at once; we regard them as types with universalized characteristics, a king and father, his cruel daughters, his loving daughter, and the like, and yet we scrutinize them for psychological motivation because they seem so real and individual.

This duality appears in both the central and the secondary characters. The King of France is in part a hero out of romance, one who makes selfless choices and rescues the heroine Cordelia from her distress; yet we are equally obliged to appraise his motive in the context of a bitter struggle for power. Why does he leave the English court "in choler," and why does he return to England with an army? Is it only to aid his wife and her beleagured father, or is he negotiating for military advantage? Certainly a French invasion of England on behalf of Lear complicates the issues of loyalty for the well-meaning Duke of Albany. The dual focus of the play invites conflicting interpretation. Similarly, Edgar is presented to us on the one hand as the traduced victim in a starkly pessimistic story, dominated by Edgar's rationalistic brother who scoffs at religion and undertakes to manipulate those around him for personal gain; on the other hand, Edgar's story grows increasingly improbable as he undertakes a series of disguises and emerges finally as an anonymous champion of chivalry, challenging his brother in the lists like a knight-errant out of Arthurian romance. Edgar's motives are hard to follow. Is he the hero of a fabulous story whose disguises and contriving of illusions for his father are an accepted part of that storytelling tradition, or is he, in more realistic terms, a man whose disguises are a defensive mask and whose elaborate contrivances defeat themselves? Edmund, his brother, is no less complex. On stage today he is usually interpreted as smooth and plausible, well-motivated by his father's condescending attitude and by the arbitrariness of the law that has excluded him from legitimacy and inheritance. Yet parable elevates Edmund into something monstrous. He becomes an embodiment of gleeful villainy, like Iago in *Othello,* malignantly evil simply because the evil that is in the universe must find a human form through which to express itself. Edmund's belated attempt to do some good adds to our difficulties in appraising his character, but the restless power of the dual conception supplies a vitality not to be found alone in fable or in realistic literature.

What we see then in Edmund and others is the union of the universal and the particular, making *King Lear* at once parable and compellingly real. The parable or folktale element is prominent at the beginning of the play, and focuses attention on the archetypal situations with which the story is concerned: rivalry between siblings, fear of parental rejection, and, at the same time, parental fear of children's ingratitude. The "unrealistic" contrast between Cordelia and her wicked sisters, or between Edgar and Edmund, is something we accept as a convention of storytelling because it expresses vividly the psychic truth of rivalry between brothers and sisters. We identify with Cordelia and Edgar as virtuous children whose worth is misunderstood, and who are losing to wicked siblings the contest for parental approval. (In folklore the rejecting parent is usually a stepparent, to signify our conviction that he or she is not a true parent at all.) Similarly, we accept as a meaningful convention of storytelling the equally "unrealistic" device by which Lear tests the love of his daughters. Like any parent, he wishes to be loved and appreciated in return for the kindnesses he has performed. The tension between fathers and their marriageable daughters is a recurrent pattern in Shakespeare's late plays, as in *Othello* (where Brabantio accuses Desdemona of deceiving and deserting him), in *Pericles, Cymbeline,* and *The Winter's Tale,* and in *The Tempest* where the pattern is best resolved. In *King Lear,* Shakespeare explores the inherently explosive situation of an imperious father, who, having provided for his children and grown old, assumes he has a right to expect that those children will express their gratitude by looking after him.

The difficulty is that the parable of Lear and his children

presents two contrasting viewpoints, that of the unappreciated child and that of the unwanted aging parent. Tragic misunderstanding is inevitable and outweighs the question of assessing blame. From Lear's point of view, Cordelia's silence is a truculent scanting of obedience. What he has devised is, after all, only a prearranged formality, with Cordelia to receive the richest third of England. Cannot such a ceremony be answered with the conventional hyperbole of courtly language, to which the King's ear is attuned? Don't parents have a right to be verbally reassured of their children's love? How can children be so laconic about such a precious matter? For her part, however, Cordelia senses that Lear is demanding love as payment for his parental kindliness, *quid pro quo*. True love ought rather to be selfless, as the King of France tells Burgundy: "Love's not love When it is mingled with regards that stands Aloof from th' entire point." Is Cordelia being asked to prefer Lear before her own husband-to-be? Is this the price she must pay for her upbringing? Lear's ego seems fully capable of demanding this sacrifice from his daughters, especially from his favorite, Cordelia; he has given them his whole kingdom, now let them care for him as befits his royal rank and patriarchal role. The "second childishness" of old age brings with it a self-centered longing to monopolize the lives of his children and to be a child again. Besides, as king, Lear has long grown accustomed to flattery and absolute obedience. Goneril and Regan are content to flatter and promise obedience, knowing they will turn him out once he has relinquished his authority. Cordelia refuses to lie in this fashion, but she also will not yield to Lear's implicit request for her undivided affection. Part of her must be loyal to her own husband and her children, in the natural cycle of the generations. "When I shall wed, That lord whose hand must take my plight shall carry Half my love with him, half my care and duty." Marriage will not prevent her from obeying, loving, and honoring her father as is fit, but will establish a new priority. To Lear, as to other fathers contemplating a daughter's marriage in late Shakespearean plays, this savors of desertion.

Lear is sadly deficient in self-knowledge. As Regan drily observes, "he hath ever but slenderly known himself," and has grown ever more changeable and imperious with age. By dividing his kingdom in three, ostensibly so that "future strife May be prevented now," he instead sets in motion a civil war and French invasion. His intention of putting aside his regal authority while still retaining "The name, and all th' additions to a king," perhaps betrays a lack of comprehension of the realities of power, although Lear may also have plausible political reasons for what he does in view of the restive ambitions of Cornwall, Albany, and Burgundy. In any case, he hearkens to poisoned flattery but interprets well-intended criticism, whether from Cordelia or Kent, as treason. These failures in no sense justify what Lear's ungrateful children do to him; as he later says, just before going mad, "I am a man More sinn'd against than sinning" (III,ii). His failures are, however, tokens of his worldly insolence from which he must fall. The process is a painful one, but since it brings self-discovery it is not without its compensations. Indeed a central paradox of the play is that by no other way could Lear have learned what human suffering and need are all about.

Lear's Fool is instrumental in elucidating this paradox. The Fool offers Lear advice in palatable form as mere foolery or entertainment, and thus obtains a hearing when Kent and Cordelia have been angrily dismissed. Beneath his seemingly innocent jibes, however, are plain warnings of the looming disaster Lear blindly refuses to acknowledge. The Fool knows, as indeed any fool could tell, that Goneril and Regan are remorseless and unnatural. The real fool, therefore, is Lear himself, for having placed himself in their power. In a metaphor of which the Renaissance was fond—as in Erasmus' *In Praise of Folly*, Cervantes' *Don Quixote*, and Shakespeare's own earlier *As You Like It* and *Twelfth Night*—folly and wisdom exchange places. By a similar inversion of logic, the Fool offers his coxcomb to Kent for siding with Lear in his exile, "for taking one's part that's out of favor" (I,iv). Worldly wisdom is to serve those whose fortunes are on the rise, as does the obsequious and servile Oswald. Indeed, the sinister progress of the first half of the play seems to confirm the Fool's contention that kindness and love are a sure way to exile and poverty. "Let go thy hold when a great wheel runs down a hill, lest it break thy neck with following; but the great one that goes upward, let him draw thee after" (II,iv). Yet the Fool resolves to ignore his own cynical advice; "I would have none but knaves follow it, since a fool gives it." Beneath his mocking, the Fool expresses the deeper truth that it is better to be a "fool" and suffer than to win on the world's terms. The greatest fools truly are those who prosper through cruelty and become hardened in sin. As the Fool puts it, deriving a seemingly contrary lesson from Lear's rejection of Cordelia: "Why, this fellow has banish'd two on 's daughters, and did the third a blessing against his will" (I,iv).

These paradoxes find a parallel in Christian teaching, although the play is nominally pagan in setting. (The lack of explicit Christian reference may be in part the result of a recent Parliamentary order banning references to "God" on stage as blasphemous.) Christianity does not hold a monopoly on the idea that one must lose the world to win a better world, but its expressions of that idea were plentifully available to Shakespeare: "Blessed are the meek, for they shall inherit the earth" (the Sermon on the Mount); "Go and sell that thou hast, and give to the poor, and thou shalt have treasure in heaven" (Matthew 19:21); "He hath put down the mighty from their seats, and exalted them of low degree" (Luke 1:52). Cordelia's vision of true love is of this exalted spiritual order. She is, as the King of France extols her, "most rich, being poor; Most choice, forsaken; and most lov'd, despis'd" (I,i). This is the sense in which Lear has bestowed on her an unintended blessing, by exiling her from a worldly prosperity that is inherently pernicious. Now, with poetic fitness, Lear must learn the same lesson himself. He does so, paradoxically, at the very moment he goes mad, parting ways with the conventional truths of the corrupted world. "My wits begin to turn," he says, and then speaks his first kind words to the Fool, who is his companion in the storm. Lear senses companionship with a fellow mortal who is cold and outcast as he is. In his madness he perceives both the worth of this insight and the need for suffering to attain it: "The art of our necessities is strange, That can make vile things precious" (III,ii). Misery teaches Lear things he never could know as king about other "Poor naked wretches" who "bide the pelting of this pitiless storm." How are such poor persons to be fed and clothed? "O, I have ta'en Too little care of this! Take physic, pomp; Expose thyself to feel what wretches feel, That thou mayst shake the superflux to them, And show the heavens more just" (III,iv). This vision of perfect justice is visionary and utopian, utterly mad in fact, but it is also spiritual wisdom dearly bought.

Gloucester learns a similar truth and expresses it in much the same way. Like Lear he has driven into exile a virtuous child and has placed himself in the power of the wicked. Enlightenment comes only through suffering. Just as Lear achieves spiritual wisdom when he goes mad, Gloucester achieves spiritual vision when he is physically blinded. His eyes having been ground out by the heel of Cornwall's boot, Gloucester asks for Edmund only to learn that Edmund has betrayed him for siding with Lear in the approaching civil war. Gloucester's response, however, is not to accuse Edmund of treachery but to beg forgiveness of the wronged Edgar. No longer does Gloucester need eyes to see this truth; "I stumbled when I saw." Although the discovery is shattering, Gloucester perceives, as does Lear, that adversity is paradoxically of some benefit since prosperity had previously caused him to be so spiritually blind. "Full oft 'tis seen, Our means secure us, and our mere defects Prove our commodities." And this realization leads him, as it does Lear, to express a longing for utopian social justice in which arrogant men will be humbled and the poor raised up by redistributed wealth. "Heavens, deal so still! Let the superfluous and lust-dieted man, That slaves your ordinance, that will not see Because he does not feel, feel your pow'r quickly; So distribution should undo excess, And each man have enough" (IV,i).

To say that Lear and Gloucester learn something precious is not, however, to deny that they are also devastated and broken by their savage humiliation. Indeed, Gloucester is driven to a despairing attempt at suicide, and Lear remains obsessed with the rotten stench of his own mortality, "bound Upon a wheel of fire" (IV,vii). Every value, every decency that we like to associate with civilization is grotesquely inverted during the storm scenes. Justice, for example, is portrayed in two sharply contrasting scenes: the mere "form of justice" by which Cornwall condemns Gloucester for treason (III,vii), and the earnestly play-acted trial by which the mad Lear arraigns Goneril and Regan of filial ingratitude (III,vi). The appearance and the reality of justice have exchanged places, as have folly and wisdom or blindness and seeing. The trial of Gloucester is outwardly correct, for Cornwall possesses the legal authority to try his subjects, and at least goes through the motions of interrogating his prisoner. The outcome is, however, cruelly predetermined. In the playacting trial concurrently taking place in a wretched hovel, the outward appearance of justice is pathetically absurd. Here justice on earth is personified by a madman (Lear), Edgar disguised as another madman (Tom o' Bedlam), and a Fool, the latter two addressed by Lear as "Thou robed man of justice" and "thou, his yoke-fellow of equity." They are caught up in a pastime of illusion, using a footstool to represent Lear's ungrateful daughters. Yet true justice is here and not inside the manor house.

Similar contrasts invert the values of loyalty, obedience, and family bonds. Edmund becomes, in the language of the villains, the "loyal" son whose loyalty is demonstrated by turning on his own "traitorous" father. Cornwall becomes a new father to Edmund ("thou shalt find a dearer father in my love"). Conversely, a servant who tries to restrain Cornwall from blinding Gloucester is, in Regan's eyes, monstrously insubordinate. "A peasant stand up thus!" Personal and sexual relationships betray signs of the universal malaise. The explicitly sexual ties in the play, notably those of Goneril, Regan, and Edmund, are grossly carnal and lead to jealousy and murder, while in Cordelia's wifely role the sensual is underplayed. The relationships we cherish—those of Cordelia, Kent, the Fool, and Gloucester to King Lear and Edgar to Gloucester—are filial or are characterized by loyal service, both pointedly nonsexual. Nowhere do we find an embodiment of love that is both sensual and spiritual, as in Desdemona in *Othello* or Hermione in *The Winter's Tale*. The Fool's and Tom o' Bedlam's (i.e., Edgar's) gibes about codpieces and plackets (III,iv) anticipate Lear's towering indictment of carnality in which fear of woman's insatiable appetite and revulsion at what she resembles "Down from the waist" ("There is the sulphurous pit, Burning, scalding, stench, consumption. Fie, fie, fie! Pah, pah!") combine with a destructive self-hatred (IV,vi).

All these inversions and polarizations are subsumed in the inversion of the word "natural." Edmund is the "natural" son of Gloucester, meaning literally that he is illegitimate. Figuratively he therefore represents a violation of traditional moral order. In appearance he is smooth and plausible, but in reality he is an archdeceiver like the Vice in the morality play, a superb actor who boasts to the audience in soliloquy of his protean villainy. (See the Introduction to *Othello* for a comparison with Iago.) "Nature" is his goddess, and by this he means something like a naturalistic universe in which the race goes to the swiftest and in which conscience, morality, and religion are empty myths. Whereas Lear invokes Nature as a goddess who will punish ungrateful daughters and defend rejected fathers (I,iv), and whereas Gloucester believes in a cosmic correspondence between eclipses of the moon or sun and mutinous discords among men (I,ii), Edmund scoffs at all such metaphysical speculations. He spurns, in other words, the Boethian conception of a divine harmony uniting the cosmos and man, with man at the Ptolemaic center of the universe. As a rationalist, Edmund echoes Jacobean challenges of the older world order in politics and religion as well as in science. He is a Machiavellian, atheist, Epicurean, everything inimical to traditional Elizabethan order. To him, "natural" means precisely what Lear and Gloucester call "unnatural."

His creed provides the play with its supreme test. Which definition of "natural" is true? Do the heavens exist, and will they let Edmund and his cohorts get away with their evil? The question is frequently asked, but the answers are ambiguous. "If you do love old men," Lear implores the gods, "if your sweet sway Allow obedience, if you yourselves are old, Make it your cause" (II,iv). His exhortations mount into frenzied rant, until finally the heavens do send down a terrible storm—on Lear himself. Witnesses agree that the absence of divine order in the universe would have the gravest consequences. "If that the heavens do not their visible spirits Send quickly down to tame these vile offenses," says Albany of Lear's ordeal, "It will come, Humanity must perforce prey on itself, Like monsters of the deep" (IV,ii). And Cornwall's servants have perceived earlier the dire implications of their masters' evil deeds. "I'll never care what wickedness I do, If this man come to good," says one, and his fellow agrees: "If she [Regan] live long, And in the end meet the old course of death, Women will all turn monsters" (III,vii). Yet these servants do in fact obey their own best instincts, turning on Cornwall and ministering to Gloucester despite danger to themselves. Similarly, Albany abandons his mild attempts at conciliation and uses his power for good. The crimes of the villains are punished, and Albany sees divine cause in this. Just as plausibly, however, one can postulate an innate decency in humankind that has at last asserted itself, revulsed by what it has seen. In part, too, villainy destroys itself, for Edmund's insatiable ambition extends past Cornwall to the English throne, and Goneril and Regan would willingly kill one another to be Edmund's queen. Even in Cordelia's capture and death we can find affirmation of the human spirit, for her ability to forgive and cherish her father, and Edgar's comparable ministering to Gloucester, give the lie to Edmund's "natural" or amoral view of humanity. Certain it is that whatever force oversees the restoration of at least some semblance of justice cannot or will not prevent the death of Cordelia. The last tableau is a vision of doomsday, with Cordelia strangled, Lear dying of heartbreak though perhaps clinging to the illusion that his daughter still lives, the "gor'd state" in such disarray that we cannot be sure what restoration can occur. Indeed, the political question of order is dwarfed by the enormity of Lear's disaster. No one wishes longer life for the King: "He hates him That would upon the rack of this tough world Stretch him out longer." He is dead; "The wonder is he hath endur'd so long." Lear's view of life's terrible corruption, pronounced in his madness, seems confirmed in his end, but so is his greatness of heart confirmed. Overwhelmed as we are by the testimonial before us of mankind's vicious capacity for self-destruction, we are stirred too by the ability in some men and women to confront their fearful destiny with probity and with patient adherence to what they believe to be good.

King Lear

[*Dramatis Personae*

LEAR, *King of Britain.*
KING OF FRANCE.
DUKE OF BURGUNDY.
DUKE OF CORNWALL, *husband to Regan.*
DUKE OF ALBANY, *husband to Goneril.*
EARL OF KENT.
EARL OF GLOUCESTER.
EDGAR, *son to Gloucester.*
EDMUND, *bastard son to Gloucester.*
CURAN, *a courtier.*
OLD MAN, *tenant to Gloucester.*
DOCTOR.
FOOL.
OSWALD, *steward to Goneril.*
CAPTAIN *employed by Edmund.*
GENTLEMAN.
HERALD.
SERVANTS *to Cornwall.*

GONERIL, REGAN, CORDELIA, } *daughters to Lear.*

KNIGHTS *of Lear's train,* CAPTAINS, MESSENGERS, SOLDIERS, *and* ATTENDANTS.

SCENE: *Britain.*]

ACT I • SCENE I

Enter Kent, Gloucester, and Edmund.

KENT I thought the King had more affected the Duke of 1
Albany than Cornwall. 2
GLOUCESTER It did always seem so to us; but now, in
the division of the kingdom, it appears not which of
the dukes he values most, for equalities are so weigh'd 5
that curiosity in neither can make choice of either's 6
moi'ty. 7
KENT Is not this your son, my lord?
GLOUCESTER His breeding, sir, hath been at my charge. 9
I have so often blush'd to acknowledge him, that now
I am braz'd to 't. 11
KENT I cannot conceive you. 12
GLOUCESTER Sir, this young fellow's mother could;
whereupon she grew round-womb'd, and had, in-
deed, sir, a son for her cradle ere she had a husband
for her bed. Do you smell a fault?
KENT I cannot wish the fault undone, the issue of it
being so proper. 18
GLOUCESTER But I have a son, sir, by order of law, some
year elder than this, who yet is no dearer in my ac- 20
count. Though this knave came something saucily to 21
the world before he was sent for, yet was his mother
fair; there was good sport at his making, and the
whoreson must be acknowledg'd. Do you know this 24
noble gentleman, Edmund?
EDMUND No, my lord.
GLOUCESTER My lord of Kent. Remember him hereafter
as my honorable friend.
EDMUND My services to your lordship.
KENT I must love you, and sue to know you better.
EDMUND Sir, I shall study deserving.
GLOUCESTER He hath been out nine years, and away he 32
shall again. The King is coming. 33

Sennet. Enter King Lear, Cornwall, Albany, Goneril, Regan, Cordelia, and Attendants.

LEAR
Attend the lords of France and Burgundy,
Gloucester.
GLOUCESTER
I shall, my lord. *Exit [with Edmund].*
LEAR
Meantime we shall express our darker purpose. 36
Give me the map there. [*Takes a map.*] Know that
we have divided
In three our kingdom; and 'tis our fast intent 38
To shake all cares and business from our age,
Conferring them on younger strengths, while we
Unburden'd crawl toward death. Our son of
Cornwall,
And you, our no less loving son of Albany,
We have this hour a constant will to publish 43
Our daughters' several dowers, that future strife 44
May be prevented now. The princes, France and
Burgundy,
Great rivals in our youngest daughter's love,
Long in our court have made their amorous sojourn,
And here are to be answer'd. Tell me, my
daughters—
Since now we will divest us both of rule,
Interest of territory, cares of state— 50
Which of you shall we say doth love us most,
That we our largest bounty may extend
Where nature doth with merit challenge? Goneril, 53
Our eldest-born, speak first.

I.i. Location: King Lear's palace.
1 more affected better liked **2 Albany** i.e., Scotland **5–7 equalities . . . moi'ty** the shares balance so equally that close scrutiny cannot find advantage in either's portion **9 breeding** raising, care. **charge** expense **11 braz'd** hardened **12 conceive** understand. (But Gloucester puns in the sense of *become pregnant.*)

18 proper handsome **20–21 account** estimation **21 something** somewhat **24 whoreson** low fellow; suggesting bastardy, but (like *knave* above) used with affectionate condescension **32 out** i.e., abroad, absent **33 s.d. Sennet** trumpet signal heralding a procession **36 darker purpose** undeclared intention **38 fast** firm **43 constant . . . publish** firm resolve to proclaim **44 several** individual **50 Interest** possession **53 Where . . . challenge** where both natural affection and merit claim it as due

GONERIL
Sir, I love you more than word can wield the matter;
Dearer than eyesight, space, and liberty,
Beyond what can be valued, rich or rare,
No less than life, with grace, health, beauty, honor;
As much as child e'er lov'd, or father found;
A love that makes breath poor, and speech unable.
Beyond all manner of so much I love you.

CORDELIA [*Aside*]
What shall Cordelia speak? Love, and be silent.

LEAR [*Indicating on map*]
Of all these bounds, even from this line to this,
With shadowy forests and with champains rich'd,
With plenteous rivers and wide-skirted meads,
We make thee lady. To thine and Albany's issue
Be this perpetual.—What says our second daughter,
Our dearest Regan, wife of Cornwall? Speak.

REGAN
I am made of that self mettle as my sister,
And prize me at her worth. In my true heart
I find she names my very deed of love;
Only she comes too short, that I profess
Myself an enemy to all other joys
Which the most precious square of sense possesses,
And find I am alone felicitate
In your dear Highness' love.

CORDELIA [*Aside*] Then poor Cordelia!
And yet not so, since I am sure my love's
More ponderous than my tongue.

LEAR
To thee and thine hereditary ever
Remain this ample third of our fair kingdom,
No less in space, validity, and pleasure
Than that conferr'd on Goneril.—Now, our joy,
Although our last and least, to whose young love
The vines of France and milk of Burgundy
Strive to be interess'd, what can you say to draw
A third more opulent than your sisters'? Speak.

CORDELIA
Nothing, my lord.

LEAR
Nothing?

CORDELIA
Nothing.

LEAR
Nothing will come of nothing. Speak again.

CORDELIA
Unhappy that I am, I cannot heave
My heart into my mouth. I love your Majesty
According to my bond, no more nor less.

LEAR
How, how, Cordelia? Mend your speech a little,
Lest you may mar your fortunes.

CORDELIA Good my lord,
You have begot me, bred me, lov'd me. I
Return those duties back as are right fit,
Obey you, love you, and most honor you.
Why have my sisters husbands, if they say
They love you all? Happily, when I shall wed,
That lord whose hand must take my plight shall carry
Half my love with him, half my care and duty.
Sure I shall never marry like my sisters,
[To love my father all.]

LEAR
But goes thy heart with this?

CORDELIA Ay, my good lord.

LEAR
So young, and so untender?

CORDELIA
So young, my lord, and true.

LEAR
Let it be so; thy truth, then, be thy dow'r!
For, by the sacred radiance of the sun,
The mysteries of Hecate and the night,
By all the operation of the orbs
From whom we do exist and cease to be,
Here I disclaim all my paternal care,
Propinquity and property of blood,
And as a stranger to my heart and me
Hold thee, from this, forever. The barbarous Scythian,
Or he that makes his generation messes
To gorge his appetite, shall to my bosom
Be as well neighbor'd, pitied, and reliev'd,
As thou my sometime daughter.

KENT Good my liege—

LEAR
Peace, Kent!
Come not between the dragon and his wrath.
I lov'd her most, and thought to set my rest
On her kind nursery. [*To Cordelia.*] Hence, and avoid my sight!—
So be my grave my peace, as here I give
Her father's heart from her! Call France. Who stirs?
Call Burgundy. Cornwall and Albany,
With my two daughters' dow'rs digest the third;
Let pride, which she calls plainness, marry her.
I do invest you jointly with my power,
Preeminence, and all the large effects
That troop with majesty. Ourself, by monthly course,
With reservation of an hundred knights,
By you to be sustain'd, shall our abode
Make with you by due turns. Only we shall retain
The name, and all th' addition to a king.
The sway, revenue, execution of the rest,
Beloved sons, be yours; which to confirm,

60 breath . . . unable language cheap and speech inadequate **64 champains rich'd** fertile plains **69 self** same **70 prize . . . worth** value myself as her equal (in love for you) **71 names . . . love** describes my love in very deed **72 that** in that **74 most . . . possesses** most sensitive measurement is capable of recording **75 felicitate** made happy **78 ponderous** weighty **81 validity** value **83 least** youngest **84 vines** vineyards. **milk** pastures (?) **85 interess'd** affiliated **93 bond** filial obligation

97 right fit proper and fitting **100 Happily** haply, perhaps **101 plight** pledge **110 Hecate** goddess of witchcraft **111 operation** influence. **orbs** heavenly bodies **114 Propinquity . . . blood** intimacy and close kinship **116 this** this time forth. **Scythian** (Scythians were famous in antiquity for savagery.) **117 makes . . . messes** makes meals of his children **120 sometime** former **123 set my rest** repose myself. (A phrase from a game of cards meaning "to stake all.") **124 nursery** nursing, care **125 So . . . peace, as** let me rest peacefully in my grave, only as **131 effects** outward shows **132 Ourself** I. (The royal "we.") **136 addition** honors and prerogatives

This coronet part between you.
KENT Royal Lear, 139
Whom I have ever honor'd as my king,
Lov'd as my father, as my master follow'd,
As my great patron thought on in my prayers—
LEAR
The bow is bent and drawn, make from the shaft. 143
KENT
Let it fall rather, though the fork invade 144
The region of my heart. Be Kent unmannerly,
When Lear is mad. What wouldst thou do, old man?
Think'st thou that duty shall have dread to speak
When power to flattery bows?
To plainness honor's bound, 149
When majesty falls to folly. Reserve thy state, 150
And in thy best consideration check
This hideous rashness. Answer my life my
judgment, 152
Thy youngest daughter does not love thee least,
Nor are those empty-hearted whose low sounds
Reverb no hollowness.
LEAR Kent, on thy life, no more. 155
KENT
My life I never held but as a pawn 156
To wage against thine enemies; nor fear to lose it, 157
Thy safety being motive.
LEAR Out of my sight!
KENT
See better, Lear, and let me still remain
The true blank of thine eye. 160
LEAR
Now, by Apollo—
KENT Now, by Apollo, King,
Thou swear'st thy gods in vain.
LEAR O, vassal! Miscreant! 162
[*Laying his hand on his sword.*]
ALBANY, CORNWALL
Dear sir, forbear.
KENT
Kill thy physician, and thy fee bestow
Upon the foul disease. Revoke thy gift,
Or, whilst I can vent clamor from my throat,
I'll tell thee thou dost evil.
LEAR
Hear me, recreant, on thine allegiance, hear me! 168
That thou hast sought to make us break our vows, 169
Which we durst never yet, and with strain'd pride 170
To come betwixt our sentence and our power, 171
Which nor our nature nor our place can bear, 172
Our potency made good, take thy reward. 173
Five days we do allot thee, for provision
To shield thee from disasters of the world,
And on the sixth to turn thy hated back
Upon our kingdom. If, on the tenth day following,
Thy banish'd trunk be found in our dominions, 178
The moment is thy death. Away! By Jupiter,
This shall not be revok'd.
KENT
Fare thee well, King. Sith thus thou wilt appear, 181
Freedom lives hence, and banishment is here.
[*To Cordelia.*] The gods to their dear shelter take
thee, maid,
That justly think'st and hast most rightly said!
[*To Regan and Goneril.*] And your large speeches
may your deeds approve, 185
That good effects may spring from words of love.
Thus Kent, O princes, bids you all adieu.
He'll shape his old course in a country new. *Exit.* 188

Flourish. Enter Gloucester, with France and Burgundy; Attendants.

GLOUCESTER
Here's France and Burgundy, my noble lord.
LEAR
My lord of Burgundy,
We first address toward you, who with this king
Hath rival'd for our daughter. What, in the least,
Will you require in present dower with her,
Or cease your quest of love?
BURGUNDY Most royal Majesty,
I crave no more than hath your Highness offer'd,
Nor will you tender less.
LEAR Right noble Burgundy, 196
When she was dear to us, we did hold her so;
But now her price is fallen. Sir, there she stands.
If aught within that little seeming substance, 199
Or all of it, with our displeasure piec'd, 200
And nothing more, may fitly like your Grace, 201
She's there, and she is yours.
BURGUNDY I know no answer.
LEAR
Will you, with those infirmities she owes, 203
Unfriended, new-adopted to our hate,
Dow'r'd with our curse, and stranger'd with our
oath, 205
Take her, or leave her?
BURGUNDY Pardon me, royal sir;
Election makes not up in such conditions. 207
LEAR
Then leave her, sir; for, by the pow'r that made me,
I tell you all her wealth. [*To France.*] For you, great
King,
I would not from your love make such a stray 210
To match you where I hate; therefore beseech you
T' avert your liking a more worthier way 212

139 coronet i.e., the symbol of regal authority, perhaps a chaplet or garland **143 make from** get out of the way of **144 fall** strike. **fork** barbed head of an arrow **149 To . . . bound** allegiance demands frankness **150 Reserve thy state** retain your royal authority **152 Answer . . . judgment** I wager my life on my judgment that **155 Reverb no hollowness** i.e., do not reverberate like a hollow drum, insincerely **156 pawn** stake, chess piece **157 wage** wager, hazard in warfare **160 blank** white center of the target **162 vassal** i.e., wretch. **Miscreant** (Literally, infidel; hence, villain, rascal.) **168 recreant** traitor **169 That** in that, since **170 strain'd** excessive **171 To . . . power** i.e., to block my power to give sentence **172 Which . . . place** which neither my personal inclination nor my office as king **173 Our . . . good** my potency now being validated

178 trunk body **181 Sith** since **185 your . . . approve** may your deeds confirm your speeches with their vast claims **188 shape . . . course** follow his traditional ways **196 tender** offer **199 seeming** specious, insincere **200 piec'd** added, joined **201 like** please **203 owes** owns **205 stranger'd with** made a stranger by **207 Election . . . conditions** no choice is possible under such conditions **210 make such a stray** stray so far **212 avert your liking** turn your affections

Than on a wretch whom nature is asham'd
Almost t' acknowledge hers.

FRANCE This is most strange,
That she, whom even but now was your best object,
The argument of your praise, balm of your age, 216
The best, the dearest, should in this trice of time
Commit a thing so monstrous, to dismantle
So many folds of favor. Sure, her offense
Must be of such unnatural degree
That monsters it, or your fore-vouch'd affection 221
Fall into taint, which to believe of her 222
Must be a faith that reason without miracle
Should never plant in me. 224

CORDELIA
I yet beseech your Majesty—
If for I want that glib and oily art 226
To speak and purpose not, since what I well intend, 227
I'll do 't before I speak—that you make known
It is no vicious blot, murder, or foulness,
No unchaste action, or dishonored step,
That hath depriv'd me of your grace and favor,
But even for want of that for which I am richer—
A still-soliciting eye, and such a tongue 233
That I am glad I have not, though not to have it
Hath lost me in your liking.

LEAR Better thou hadst
Not been born than not t' have pleas'd me better.

FRANCE
Is it but this—a tardiness in nature
Which often leaves the history unspoke
That it intends to do? My lord of Burgundy,
What say you to the lady? Love's not love
When it is mingled with regards that stands 241
Aloof from th' entire point. Will you have her? 242
She is herself a dowry.

BURGUNDY Royal King,
Give but that portion which yourself propos'd,
And here I take Cordelia by the hand,
Duchess of Burgundy.

LEAR
Nothing. I have sworn; I am firm.

BURGUNDY
I am sorry, then, you have so lost a father
That you must lose a husband.

CORDELIA Peace be with Burgundy!
Since that respects of fortune are his love, 250
I shall not be his wife.

FRANCE
Fairest Cordelia, that art most rich being poor,
Most choice forsaken, and most lov'd despis'd,
Thee and thy virtues here I seize upon,
Be it lawful I take up what's cast away.
[Takes her hand.]
Gods, gods! 'Tis strange that from their cold'st neglect
My love should kindle to inflam'd respect. 257
Thy dow'rless daughter, King, thrown to my chance,
Is queen of us, of ours, and our fair France.
Not all the dukes of wat'rish Burgundy 260
Can buy this unpriz'd precious maid of me. 261
Bid them farewell, Cordelia, though unkind.
Thou losest here, a better where to find. 263

LEAR
Thou hast her, France. Let her be thine, for we
Have no such daughter, nor shall ever see
That face of hers again. [*To Cordelia.*] Therefore be gone
Without our grace, our love, our benison. 267
Come, noble Burgundy.
Flourish. Exeunt [all but France, Goneril, Regan, and Cordelia].

FRANCE
Bid farewell to your sisters.

CORDELIA
The jewels of our father, with wash'd eyes 270
Cordelia leaves you. I know you what you are,
And like a sister am most loath to call 272
Your faults as they are nam'd. Love well our father. 273
To your professed bosoms I commit him. 274
But yet, alas, stood I within his grace,
I would prefer him to a better place. 276
So, farewell to you both.

REGAN
Prescribe not us our duty.

GONERIL Let your study
Be to content your lord, who hath receiv'd you
At fortune's alms. You have obedience scanted, 280
And well are worth the want that you have wanted. 281

CORDELIA
Time shall unfold what plighted cunning hides, 282
Who covers faults, at last shame them derides. 283
Well may you prosper!

FRANCE Come, my fair Cordelia.
Exeunt France and Cordelia.

GONERIL Sister, it is not little I have to say of what most nearly appertains to us both. I think our father will hence tonight.

REGAN That's most certain, and with you; next month with us.

GONERIL You see how full of changes his age is; the observation we have made of it hath not been little. He always lov'd our sister most; and with what poor judgment he hath now cast her off appears too grossly. 293

REGAN 'Tis the infirmity of his age, yet he hath ever but slenderly known himself.

GONERIL The best and soundest of his time hath been 296
but rash; then must we look from his age to receive 297

216 argument theme **221 monsters** makes monstrous. **or** ere, before. **fore-vouch'd** hitherto affirmed **222 taint** decay **224 Should** could **226 for I want** because I lack **227 purpose not** not intend to do what I say **233 still-soliciting** ever-begging **241–242 regards . . . point** irrelevant considerations **250 respects of fortune** concern for wealth and position

257 inflam'd respect ardent affection **260 wat'rish** (1) well-watered with rivers (2) feeble, fickle **261 unpriz'd** not appreciated (with perhaps a sense also of *priceless*) **263 here** this place. **where** place elsewhere **267 benison** blessing **270 wash'd** tear-washed **272 like a sister** i.e., because I am your sister **273 as . . . nam'd** by their true names **274 professed bosoms** publicly avowed love **276 prefer** raise, promote **280 At . . . alms** as a pittance or dole from fortune **281 well . . . wanted** well deserve the lack of affection which you yourself have shown. (*Want* may also refer to her dowry.) **282 plighted** pleated, enfolded **283 Who . . . derides** i.e., time may conceal faults for a while, but at last they are shamefully exposed and derided **293 grossly** obviously **296–297 The best . . . rash** i.e., even in the prime of his life, he was stormy and unpredictable

not alone the imperfections of long-ingraff'd condi- 298
tion, but therewithal the unruly waywardness that in- 299
firm and choleric years bring with them.

REGAN Such unconstant starts are we like to have from 301
him as this of Kent's banishment.

GONERIL There is further compliment of leave-taking 303
between France and him. Pray you, let us hit together; 304
if our father carry authority with such disposition as
he bears, this last surrender of his will but offend us. 306

REGAN We shall further think of it.

GONERIL We must do something, and i' th' heat. 308

Exeunt.

SCENE II

Enter Bastard [Edmund, with a letter].

EDMUND
Thou, nature, art my goddess; to thy law 1
My services are bound. Wherefore should I
Stand in the plague of custom, and permit 3
The curiosity of nations to deprive me, 4
For that I am some twelve or fourteen moonshines 5
Lag of a brother? Why bastard? Wherefore base? 6
When my dimensions are as well compact, 7
My mind as generous, and my shape as true, 8
As honest madam's issue? Why brand they us 9
With base? With baseness? Bastardy? Base, base?
Who, in the lusty stealth of nature, take 11
More composition and fierce quality 12
Than doth within a dull, stale, tired bed
Go to th' creating a whole tribe of fops
Got 'tween asleep and wake? Well, then, 15
Legitimate Edgar, I must have your land.
Our father's love is to the bastard Edmund
As to th' legitimate. Fine word, "legitimate"!
Well, my legitimate, if this letter speed 19
And my invention thrive, Edmund the base 20
Shall top th' legitimate. I grow, I prosper.
Now, gods, stand up for bastards!

Enter Gloucester.

GLOUCESTER
Kent banish'd thus? And France in choler parted?
And the King gone tonight? Prescrib'd his pow'r, 24
Confin'd to exhibition? All this done 25
Upon the gad! Edmund, how now? What news? 26

EDMUND [*Putting up the letter*]
So please your lordship, none.

GLOUCESTER Why so earnestly seek you to put up that letter?

EDMUND I know no news, my lord.

GLOUCESTER What paper were you reading?

EDMUND Nothing, my lord.

GLOUCESTER No? What needed, then, that terrible dis- 33
patch of it into your pocket? The quality of nothing
hath not such need to hide itself. Let's see. Come, if it
be nothing, I shall not need spectacles.

EDMUND I beseech you, sir, pardon me. It is a letter
from my brother, that I have not all o'er-read; and for
so much as I have perus'd, I find it not fit for your
o'erlooking. 40

GLOUCESTER Give me the letter, sir.

EDMUND I shall offend, either to detain or give it. The
contents, as in part I understand them, are to blame. 43

GLOUCESTER Let's see, let's see. [*Edmund gives letter.*]

EDMUND I hope, for my brother's justification, he wrote
this but as an essay or taste of my virtue. 46

GLOUCESTER *(Reads)* "This policy and reverence of age 47
makes the world bitter to the best of our times; keeps 48
our fortunes from us till our oldness cannot relish
them. I begin to find an idle and fond bondage in the 50
oppression of aged tyranny, who sways, not as it hath 51
power, but as it is suffer'd. Come to me, that of this I 52
may speak more. If our father would sleep till I wak'd
him, you should enjoy half his revenue forever, and
live the belov'd of your brother,
Edgar."
Hum! Conspiracy!—"Sleep till I wak'd him, you
should enjoy half his revenue." My son Edgar! Had he
a hand to write this? A heart and brain to breed it
in?—When came you to this? Who brought it? 59

EDMUND It was not brought me, my lord; there's the
cunning of it. I found it thrown in at the casement of 61
my closet. 62

GLOUCESTER You know the character to be your 63
brother's?

EDMUND If the matter were good, my lord, I durst 65
swear it were his; but, in respect of that, I would fain 66
think it were not.

GLOUCESTER It is his.

EDMUND It is his hand, my lord; but I hope his heart is not in the contents.

GLOUCESTER Has he never before sounded you in this business?

EDMUND Never, my lord. But I have heard him oft
maintain it to be fit that, sons at perfect age and fathers 74
declin'd, the father should be as ward to the son, and 75
the son manage his revenue.

GLOUCESTER O villain, villain! His very opinion in the 77

298–299 long-engraff'd condition long-implanted habit **299 therewithal** added thereto **301 unconstant starts** impulsive acts. **like** likely **303 compliment** ceremony **304 hit** agree **306 last surrender** latest abdication. **offend** harm, injure **308 i' th' heat** i.e., while the iron is hot

I.ii. Location: The Earl of Gloucester's house.
1 nature i.e., the material world, governed solely by mechanistic amoral forces **3 Stand . . . custom** submit to the vexatious injustice of convention **4 curiosity** fastidious distinctions. **nations** societies **5 For that** because. **moonshines** months **6 Lag of** younger than **7 compact** knit together, fitted **8 generous** noble, refined **9 honest** chaste **11–12 take . . . quality** acquire greater completeness and energetic force **15 Got** begotten **19 speed** succeed **20 invention thrive** scheme prosper **24 Prescrib'd** limited **25 exhibition** an allowance, pension **26 Upon the gad** suddenly, as if pricked by a gad or spur

33 terrible terrified **40 o'erlooking** perusal **43 to blame** blameworthy **46 essay or taste** i.e., assay, test **47 policy and reverence of** i.e., policy of reverencing **48 the best . . . times** the best years of our lives, i.e., our youth **50 idle** useless. **fond** foolish **51 who sways** which rules **52 suffer'd** permitted (by the young, who could seize power if they wished) **59 to this** upon this (letter) **61 casement** window **62 closet** private room **63 character** handwriting **65 matter** contents **66 in . . . that** considering what the contents are. **fain** gladly **74 perfect age** full maturity **75 declin'd** having become feeble **77 villain** i.e., vile wretch, diabolical schemer

letter! Abhorred villain! Unnatural, detested, brutish villain! Worse than brutish! Go, sirrah, seek him; I'll apprehend him. Abominable villain! Where is he?

EDMUND I do not well know, my lord. If it shall please you to suspend your indignation against my brother till you can derive from him better testimony of his intent, you should run a certain course; where, if you violently proceed against him, mistaking his purpose, it would make a great gap in your own honor, and shake in pieces the heart of his obedience. I dare pawn down my life for him that he hath writ this to feel my affection to your honor, and to no other pretense of danger.

GLOUCESTER Think you so?

EDMUND If your honor judge it meet, I will place you where you shall hear us confer of this, and by an auricular assurance have your satisfaction, and that without any further delay than this very evening.

GLOUCESTER He cannot be such a monster—

[EDMUND Nor is not, sure.

GLOUCESTER To his father, that so tenderly and entirely loves him. Heaven and earth!] Edmund, seek him out; wind me into him, I pray you. Frame the business after your own wisdom. I would unstate myself, to be in a due resolution.

EDMUND I will seek him, sir, presently, convey the business as I shall find means, and acquaint you withal.

GLOUCESTER These late eclipses in the sun and moon portend no good to us. Though the wisdom of nature can reason it thus and thus, yet nature finds itself scourg'd by the sequent effects. Love cools, friendship falls off, brothers divide; in cities, mutinies; in countries, discord; in palaces, treason; and the bond crack'd 'twixt son and father. This villain of mine comes under the prediction; there's son against father. The King falls from bias of nature; there's father against child. We have seen the best of our time. Machinations, hollowness, treachery, and all ruinous disorders follow us disquietly to our graves. Find out this villain, Edmund. It shall lose thee nothing; do it carefully. And the noble and true-hearted Kent banish'd! His offense, honesty! 'Tis strange. *Exit.*

EDMUND This is the excellent foppery of the world, that when we are sick in fortune—often the surfeits of our own behavior—we make guilty of our disasters the sun, the moon, and stars, as if we were villains on necessity, fools by heavenly compulsion, knaves, thieves, and treachers by spherical predominance, drunkards, liars, and adulterers by an enforc'd obedience of planetary influence, and all that we are evil in, by a divine thrusting on. An admirable evasion of whoremaster man, to lay his goatish disposition on the charge of a star! My father compounded with my mother under the Dragon's Tail, and my nativity was under Ursa Major, so that it follows I am rough and lecherous. Fut, I should have been that I am, had the maidenliest star in the firmament twinkled on my bastardizing. Edgar—

Enter Edgar.

and pat he comes like the catastrophe of the old comedy. My cue is villainous melancholy, with a sigh like Tom o' Bedlam.—O, these eclipses do portend these divisions! Fa, sol, la, mi.

EDGAR How now, brother Edmund, what serious contemplation are you in?

EDMUND I am thinking, brother, of a prediction I read this other day, what should follow these eclipses.

EDGAR Do you busy yourself with that?

EDMUND I promise you, the effects he writes of succeed unhappily, [as of unnaturalness between the child and the parent, death, dearth, dissolutions of ancient amities, divisions in state, menaces and maledictions against king and nobles, needless diffidences, banishment of friends, dissipation of cohorts, nuptial breaches, and I know not what.

EDGAR How long have you been a sectary astronomical?

EDMUND Come, come,] when saw you my father last?

EDGAR The night gone by.

EDMUND Spake you with him?

EDGAR Ay, two hours together.

EDMUND Parted you in good terms? Found you no displeasure in him by word nor countenance?

EDGAR None at all.

EDMUND Bethink yourself wherein you may have offended him; and at my entreaty forbear his presence until some little time hath qualified the heat of his displeasure, which at this instant so rageth in him that with the mischief of your person it would scarcely allay.

EDGAR Some villain hath done me wrong.

EDMUND That's my fear. I pray you, have a continent forbearance till the speed of his rage goes slower; and, as I say, retire with me to my lodging, from whence I will fitly bring you to hear my lord speak. Pray ye, go; there's my key. [*Gives key.*] If you do stir abroad, go arm'd.

EDGAR Arm'd, brother?

EDMUND Brother, I advise you to the best. I am no honest man if there be any good meaning toward you. I have told you what I have seen and heard; but faintly, nothing like the image and horror of it. Pray you, away.

78 Abhorred abhorrent. **detested** detestable **84 certain** safe. **where** whereas **88 feel** feel out **89–90 pretense of danger** dangerous purpose **100 wind me into him** insinuate yourself into his confidence. (*Me* is the ethical dative.) **Frame** arrange **101–102 unstate . . . resolution** suffer loss of all to know the truth **103 presently** immediately. **convey** manage **106 late** recent **107 wisdom of nature** natural science **109 sequent effects** i.e., devastating consequences **114 bias of nature** natural inclination **121 foppery** foolishness **126 treachers** traitors. **spherical predominance** astrological determinism **130 goatish** lecherous

131–132 compounded . . . Dragon's Tail had sex with my mother under the constellation Draco **133 Ursa Major** the big bear **137 catastrophe** conclusion, resolution (of a play) **139 Tom o' Bedlam** a lunatic patient of Bethlehem Hospital in London turned out to beg for his bread **146–147 succeed unhappily** follow unluckily **150 needless diffidences** groundless distrust of others **151 dissipation of cohorts** falling away of supporters **153–154 sectary astronomical** believer in astrology **164 qualified** moderated **166 mischief . . . person** harmful effect of your presence **167 allay** be allayed **169–170 have . . . forbearance** keep a wary distance **172 fitly** at a fit time **179 image and horror** horrid reality

EDGAR Shall I hear from you anon?

EDMUND
I do serve you in this business. *Exit* [*Edgar*].
A credulous father and a brother noble,
Whose nature is so far from doing harms
That he suspects none; on whose foolish honesty
My practices ride easy. I see the business.
Let me, if not by birth, have lands by wit.
All with me's meet that I can fashion fit. *Exit.*

SCENE III

Enter Goneril, and [*Oswald, her*] *steward.*

GONERIL Did my father strike my gentleman for chiding of his fool?

OSWALD Ay, madam.

GONERIL
By day and night he wrongs me! Every hour
He flashes into one gross crime or other,
That sets us all at odds. I'll not endure it.
His knights grow riotous, and himself upbraids us
On every trifle. When he returns from hunting,
I will not speak with him; say I am sick.
If you come slack of former services,
You shall do well; the fault of it I'll answer.
[*Horns within.*]

OSWALD He's coming, madam; I hear him.

GONERIL
Put on what weary negligence you please,
You and your fellows. I'd have it come to question.
If he distaste it, let him to my sister,
Whose mind and mine, I know, in that are one,
[Not to be overrul'd. Idle old man,
That still would manage those authorities
That he hath given away! Now, by my life,
Old fools are babes again, and must be us'd
With checks as flatteries, when they are seen abus'd.]
Remember what I have said.

OSWALD Well, madam.

GONERIL
And let his knights have colder looks among you.
What grows of it, no matter. Advise your fellows so.
[I would breed from hence occasions, and I shall,
That I may speak.] I'll write straight to my sister
To hold my course. Prepare for dinner. *Exeunt.*

186 practices plots **187 wit** intelligence **188 meet** justifiable. **fit** i.e., to my purpose

I.iii. Location: The Duke of Albany's palace.
5 crime offense **10 come slack** fall short **15 distaste** dislike **17 Idle** foolish **18 manage those authorities** i.e., assert those prerogatives **21 With . . . abus'd** with rebukes instead of flattery, when they (old men) act unselfknowingly (as Lear does) **26–27 I would . . . speak** I wish to create from these incidents the opportunity to speak out

SCENE IV

Enter Kent [*disguised*].

KENT
If but as well I other accents borrow,
That can my speech defuse, my good intent
May carry through itself to that full issue
For which I raz'd my likeness. Now, banish'd Kent,
If thou canst serve where thou dost stand condemn'd,
So may it come, thy master, whom thou lov'st,
Shall find thee full of labors.

Horns within. Enter Lear, [*Knights,*] *and Attendants.*

LEAR Let me not stay a jot for dinner; go get it ready. [*Exit an Attendant.*] How now, what art thou?

KENT A man, sir.

LEAR What dost thou profess? What wouldst thou with us?

KENT I do profess to be no less than I seem, to serve him truly that will put me in trust, to love him that is honest, to converse with him that is wise and says little, to fear judgment, to fight when I cannot choose, and to eat no fish.

LEAR What art thou?

KENT A very honest-hearted fellow, and as poor as the King.

LEAR If thou be'st as poor for a subject as he's for a king, thou art poor enough. What wouldst thou?

KENT Service.

LEAR Who wouldst thou serve?

KENT You.

LEAR Dost thou know me, fellow?

KENT No, sir; but you have that in your countenance which I would fain call master.

LEAR What's that?

KENT Authority.

LEAR What services canst thou do?

KENT I can keep honest counsel, ride, run, mar a curious tale in telling it, and deliver a plain message bluntly. That which ordinary men are fit for, I am qualified in, and the best of me is diligence.

LEAR How old art thou?

KENT Not so young, sir, to love a woman for singing, nor so old to dote on her for any thing. I have years on my back forty eight.

LEAR Follow me; thou shalt serve me. If I like thee no worse after dinner, I will not part from thee yet. Din-

I.iv. Location: The Duke of Albany's palace still. The sense of time is virtually continuous.
1 as well i.e., as well as I have disguised myself by means of costume **2 defuse** disguise **3 carry . . . issue** succeed to that perfect result **4 raz'd my likeness** erased my outward appearance (perhaps shaving beard?) **8 stay** wait **11 What . . . profess** what is your special calling. (But Kent puns in his answer on *profess* meaning to *claim.*) **15 converse** associate **16 judgment** i.e., God's judgment. **choose** i.e., choose but to fight **17 eat no fish** i.e., eat a manly diet (?) **32 keep honest counsel** respect confidences **32–33 curious** ornate, elaborate

ner, ho, dinner! Where's my knave? My fool? Go you
and call my fool hither. [*Exit an Attendant.*]

Enter Steward [*Oswald*].

You, you, sirrah, where's my daughter?
OSWALD So please you— *Exit.*
LEAR What says the fellow there? Call the clotpoll back. 46
[*Exit a Knight.*] Where's my fool, ho? I think the
world's asleep.

[*Enter Knight.*]

How now? Where's that mongrel?
KNIGHT He says, my lord, your daughter is not well.
LEAR Why came not the slave back to me when I call'd
him?
KNIGHT Sir, he answer'd me in the roundest manner, 53
he would not.
LEAR He would not?
KNIGHT My lord, I know not what the matter is, but, to
my judgment, your Highness is not entertain'd with
that ceremonious affection as you were wont. There's
a great abatement of kindness appears as well in the
general dependents as in the Duke himself also and
your daughter.
LEAR Ha? Say'st thou so?
KNIGHT I beseech you, pardon me, my lord, if I be mis-
taken, for my duty cannot be silent when I think your
Highness wrong'd.
LEAR Thou but remembr'est me of mine own concep- 66
tion. I have perceiv'd a most faint neglect of late, 67
which I have rather blam'd as mine own jealous curi- 68
osity than as a very pretense and purpose of unkind- 69
ness. I will look further into 't. But where's my fool? I
have not seen him this two days.
KNIGHT Since my young lady's going into France, sir,
the fool hath much pin'd away.
LEAR No more of that; I have noted it well. Go you and
tell my daughter I would speak with her. [*Exit an At-
tendant.*] Go you call hither my fool.
[*Exit an Attendant.*]

Enter Steward [*Oswald*].

O, you, sir, you, come you hither, sir. Who am I, sir?
OSWALD My lady's father.
LEAR "My lady's father"? My lord's knave! You whore-
son dog, you slave, you cur!
OSWALD I am none of these, my lord, I beseech your
pardon.
LEAR Do you bandy looks with me, you rascal? 83
[*Striking him.*]
OSWALD I'll not be strucken, my lord.
KENT Nor tripp'd neither, you base football player. 85
[*Tripping up his heels.*]
LEAR I thank thee, fellow. Thou serv'st me, and I'll love
thee.

KENT Come, sir, arise, away! I'll teach you differences. 88
Away, away! If you will measure your lubber's length
again, tarry; but away! Go to. Have you wisdom? So.
[*Pushes Oswald out.*]
LEAR Now, my friendly knave, I thank thee. There's
earnest of thy service. [*Gives Kent money.*] 92

Enter Fool.

FOOL Let me hire him too. Here's my coxcomb. 93
[*Offering Kent his cap.*]
LEAR How now, my pretty knave, how dost thou?
FOOL Sirrah, you were best take my coxcomb.
KENT Why, fool?
FOOL Why? For taking one's part that's out of favor.
Nay, an thou canst not smile as the wind sits, thou 'lt 98
catch cold shortly. There, take my coxcomb. Why, this
fellow has banish'd two on 's daughters, and did the 100
third a blessing against his will; if thou follow him, thou 101
must needs wear my coxcomb.—How now, nuncle? 102
Would I had two coxcombs and two daughters.
LEAR Why, my boy?
FOOL If I gave them all my living, I'd keep my cox- 105
combs myself. There's mine; beg another of thy
daughters.
LEAR Take heed, sirrah; the whip.
FOOL Truth's a dog must to kennel; he must be
whipp'd out, when the Lady Brach may stand by th' 110
fire and stink.
LEAR A pestilent gall to me! 112
FOOL Sirrah, I'll teach thee a speech.
LEAR Do.
FOOL Mark it, nuncle:
Have more than thou showest,
Speak less than thou knowest,
Lend less than thou owest, 118
Ride more than thou goest, 119
Learn more than thou trowest, 120
Set less than thou throwest; 121
Leave thy drink and thy whore,
And keep in-a-door, 123
And thou shalt have more 124
Than two tens to a score. 125
KENT This is nothing, fool.
FOOL Then 'tis like the breath of an unfee'd lawyer; you 127
gave me nothing for 't. Can you make no use of noth-
ing, nuncle?
LEAR Why, no, boy; nothing can be made out of
nothing.
FOOL [*To Kent*] Prithee, tell him, so much the rent of his 132
land comes to. He will not believe a fool.
LEAR A bitter fool! 134

46 clotpoll blockhead **53 roundest** bluntest **66 rememb'rest** remind **67 faint** half-hearted **68–69 jealous curiosity** overscrupulous regard for minutiae **69 very pretense** true intention **83 bandy** volley, exchange (as in tennis) **85 football** (A raucous street game played by the lower classes.)

88 differences distinctions in rank **92 earnest** partial advance payment **93 coxcomb** fool's cap, crested with a red comb **98 smile . . . sits** i.e., play along with those in power **100 banish'd** (I.e., paradoxically, by giving Goneril and Regan his kingdom, Lear has lost them, given them power over him.) **101 blessing** i.e., bestowing Cordelia on France **102 nuncle** (Contraction of "mine uncle.") **105 living** property **110 Brach** hound bitch (here suggesting flattery) **112 gall** irritation **118 owest** own **119 goest** i.e., on foot **120 Learn** i.e., listen to. **trowest** believe **121 Set . . . throwest** stake less at dice than you have a chance to throw, i.e., don't bet all you can **123 in-a-door** indoors, at home **124–125 shalt . . . score** i.e., will do better than break even (since a *score* equals two tens, or 20) **127 breath** speech, counsel **132 rent** (Lear has no land, hence no rent.) **134 bitter** satirical

FOOL Dost thou know the difference, my boy, between
a bitter fool and a sweet one?

LEAR No, lad; teach me.

FOOL
[That lord that counsel'd thee
To give away thy land,
Come place him here by me,
Do thou for him stand.
The sweet and bitter fool
Will presently appear;
The one in motley here, 144
The other found out there.

LEAR Dost thou call me fool, boy?

FOOL All thy other titles thou hast given away; that
thou wast born with.

KENT This is not altogether fool, my lord.

FOOL No, faith, lords and great men will not let me; if 150
I had a monopoly out, they would have part on 't. And 151
ladies too, they will not let me have all the fool to my-
self; they'll be snatching.] Nuncle, give me an egg, and
I'll give thee two crowns.

LEAR What two crowns shall they be?

FOOL Why, after I have cut the egg i' th' middle and eat
up the meat, the two crowns of the egg. When thou
clovest thy crown i' th' middle and gav'st away both
parts, thou bor'st thine ass on thy back o'er the dirt. 159
Thou hadst little wit in thy bald crown when thou
gav'st thy golden one away. If I speak like myself in 161
this, let him be whipp'd that first finds it so. 162
[*Sings.*] "Fools had ne'er less grace in a year, 163
For wise men are grown foppish, 164
And know not how their wits to wear, 165
Their manners are so apish."

LEAR When were you wont to be so full of songs,
sirrah?

FOOL I have us'd it, nuncle, e'er since thou mad'st thy 169
daughters thy mothers; for when thou gav'st them the
rod, and put'st down thine own breeches,
[*Sings.*] "Then they for sudden joy did weep,
And I for sorrow sung,
That such a king should play bo-peep, 174
And go the fools among."
Prithee, nuncle, keep a schoolmaster that can teach thy
fool to lie. I would fain learn to lie.

LEAR An you lie, sirrah, we'll have you whipp'd.

FOOL I marvel what kin thou and thy daughters are.
They'll have me whipp'd for speaking true, thou 'lt
have me whipp'd for lying; and sometimes I am
whipp'd for holding my peace. I had rather be any
kind o' thing than a fool, and yet I would not be thee,
nuncle; thou hast par'd thy wit o' both sides, and left
nothing i' th' middle. Here comes one o' the parings.

Enter Goneril.

LEAR
How now, daughter? What makes that frontlet on? 186
You are too much of late i' th' frown.

FOOL Thou wast a pretty fellow when thou hadst no
need to care for her frowning; now thou art an O with- 189
out a figure. I am better than thou art now; I am a fool, 190
thou art nothing. [*To Goneril.*] Yes, forsooth, I will
hold my tongue; so your face bids me, though you say
nothing.
Mum, mum,
He that keeps nor crust nor crumb, 195
Weary of all, shall want some. 196
[*Pointing to Lear.*] That's a sheal'd peascod. 197

GONERIL
Not only, sir, this your all-licens'd fool, 198
But other of your insolent retinue
Do hourly carp and quarrel, breaking forth
In rank and not-to-be-endured riots. Sir,
I had thought, by making this well known unto
you,
To have found a safe redress, but now grow fearful, 203
By what yourself too late have spoke and done, 204
That you protect this course and put it on 205
By your allowance; which if you should, the fault 206
Would not scape censure, nor the redresses sleep, 207
Which, in the tender of a wholesome weal, 208
Might in their working do you that offense
Which else were shame, that then necessity 210
Will call discreet proceeding.

FOOL For, you know, nuncle, 211
"The hedge-sparrow fed the cuckoo so long 212
That it had it head bit off by it young." 213
So, out went the candle, and we were left darkling. 214

LEAR
Are you our daughter?

GONERIL
I would you would make use of your good wisdom,
Whereof I know you are fraught, and put away 217
These dispositions which of late transport you
From what you rightly are.

FOOL May not an ass know when the cart draws the
horse? Whoop, Jug! I love thee. 221

LEAR
Does any here know me? This is not Lear.
Does Lear walk thus? Speak thus? Where are his
eyes?
Either his notion weakens, his discernings 224
Are lethargied—Ha! Waking? 'Tis not so. 225
Who is it that can tell me who I am?

144 motley the particolored dress of the professional fool. (The Fool identifies himself as the sweet fool, Lear as the bitter fool who counseled himself to give away his kingdom.) **150 No . . . let me** i.e., great persons at court will not let me monopolize folly; I am not *altogether fool* in the sense of being *all the fool there is* **151 a monopoly out** a corner on the market. (The granting of monopolies was a common abuse under King James and Queen Elizabeth.) **on 't** of it **159 bor'st . . . dirt** i.e., bore the ass instead of letting the ass bear you **161 like myself** i.e., like a fool **162 whipp'd** i.e., as a fool. **finds it so** discovers from his experience that it is true (as Lear is now discovering) **163 Fools . . . year** fools have never enjoyed less favor; i.e., they are made obsolete by the folly of supposed wise men **164 foppish** foolish, vain **165 wear** use **169 us'd** practiced **174 bo-peep** a child's game

186 frontlet a band worn on the forehead; here, frown **189–190 O without a figure** cipher of no value unless preceded by a digit **195 crumb** the bread inside the crust **196 want** lack **197 sheal'd peascod** shelled pea pod **198 all-licens'd** authorized to speak or act freely **203 safe** certain **204 too late** all too recently **205 put it on** encourage it **206 allowance** approval **207 redresses sleep** punishments (for the riotous conduct of Lear's attendants) lie dormant **208 tender . . . weal** care for preservation of the peace of the state **210 else were** in other circumstances would be regarded as. **then necessity** the necessity of the times **211 discreet** prudent **212 cuckoo** a bird which lays its eggs in other birds' nests **213 it head** its head. **it young** i.e., the young cuckoo **214 darkling** in the dark **217 fraught** freighted, laden **221 Jug** i.e., Joan. (The origin of this phrase is uncertain.) **224 notion** intellectual power **224–225 discernings Are lethargied** faculties are asleep **225 Waking** i.e., am I really awake

FOOL Lear's shadow.
[LEAR
I would learn that; for, by the marks of sovereignty, 228
Knowledge, and reason, I should be false persuaded
I had daughters.
FOOL Which they will make an obedient father.] 231
LEAR
Your name, fair gentlewoman?
GONERIL
This admiration, sir, is much o' th' savor 233
Of other your new pranks. I do beseech you
To understand my purposes aright.
As you are old and reverend, should be wise. 236
Here do you keep a hundred knights and squires,
Men so disorder'd, so debosh'd and bold, 238
That this our court, infected with their manners,
Shows like a riotous inn. Epicurism and lust 240
Makes it more like a tavern or a brothel
Than a grac'd palace. The shame itself doth speak 242
For instant remedy. Be then desir'd
By her, that else will take the thing she begs,
A little to disquantity your train, 245
And the remainders that shall still depend 246
To be such men as may besort your age, 247
Which know themselves and you.
LEAR Darkness and devils!
Saddle my horses; call my train together.
Degenerate bastard! I'll not trouble thee.
Yet have I left a daughter.
GONERIL
You strike my people, and your disorder'd rabble
Make servants of their betters.

Enter Albany.

LEAR
Woe, that too late repents! [O, sir, are you come?] 254
Is it your will? Speak, sir.—Prepare my horses.—
Ingratitude, thou marble-hearted fiend,
More hideous when thou show'st thee in a child
Than the sea-monster!
ALBANY
Pray, sir, be patient.
LEAR [*To Goneril*] Detested kite, thou liest! 259
My train are men of choice and rarest parts, 260
That all particulars of duty know,
And in the most exact regard support 262
The worships of their name. O most small fault, 263
How ugly didst thou in Cordelia show!
Which, like an engine, wrench'd my frame of nature 265
From the fix'd place; drew from my heart all love,
And added to the gall. O Lear, Lear, Lear!
Beat at this gate, that let thy folly in [*Striking his head*]
And thy dear judgment out! Go, go, my people.
[*Exeunt Knights and Kent.*]
ALBANY
My lord, I am guiltless as I am ignorant
Of what hath moved you.
LEAR It may be so, my lord.
Hear, Nature, hear; dear goddess, hear!
Suspend thy purpose, if thou didst intend
To make this creature fruitful!
Into her womb convey sterility;
Dry up in her the organs of increase,
And from her derogate body never spring 277
A babe to honor her! If she must teem, 278
Create her child of spleen, that it may live
And be a thwart disnatur'd torment to her! 280
Let it stamp wrinkles in her brow of youth,
With cadent tears fret channels in her cheeks, 282
Turn all her mother's pains and benefits 283
To laughter and contempt, that she may feel
How sharper than a serpent's tooth it is
To have a thankless child! Away, away! *Exit.*
ALBANY
Now, gods that we adore, whereof comes this?
GONERIL
Never afflict yourself to know more of it,
But let his disposition have that scope
As dotage gives it. 290

Enter Lear.

LEAR
What, fifty of my followers at a clap?
Within a fortnight?
ALBANY What's the matter, sir?
LEAR
I'll tell thee. [*To Goneril.*] Life and death! I am asham'd
That thou hast power to shake my manhood thus,
That these hot tears, which break from me perforce,
Should make thee worth them. Blasts and fogs upon thee!
Th' untented woundings of a father's curse 297
Pierce every sense about thee! Old fond eyes, 298
Beweep this cause again, I'll pluck ye out, 299
And cast you, with the waters that you loose, 300
To temper clay. [Yea, is 't come to this?] 301
Ha! Let it be so. I have another daughter,
Who, I am sure, is kind and comfortable. 303
When she shall hear this of thee, with her nails
She'll flay thy wolvish visage. Thou shalt find
That I'll resume the shape which thou dost think
I have cast off for ever.
Exit [*Lear, with Kent, and Attendants*].
GONERIL Do you mark that?
ALBANY
I cannot be so partial, Goneril,

228 marks of sovereignty outward and visible evidence that I am king **231 Which** whom **233 admiration** (guise of) wonderment **236 should** i.e., you should **238 debosh'd** debauched **240 Epicurism** luxury **242 grac'd** honorable **245 disquantity your train** diminish the number of your attendants **246 the remainders . . . depend** those who remain to attend you **247 besort** befit **254 Woe, that** woe to the person who **259 kite** bird of prey **260 parts** qualities **262 in . . . regard** with extreme care **263 worships** honors, reputations **265 engine** powerful mechanical contrivance, able to wrench Lear's *frame of nature* or natural self from his *fix'd place* or foundation like a building being torn from its foundation

277 derogate debased **278 teem** increase the species **280 thwart disnatur'd** obstinate perverse **282 cadent** falling **283 mother's** motherly. **benefits** kind offerings **290 As** which **297 untented** too deep to be probed and cleansed **298 fond** foolish **299 Beweep** if you weep for **300 loose** let loose **301 temper** soften **303 comfortable** willing to comfort

To the great love I bear you—

GONERIL
Pray you, content.—What, Oswald, ho!
[*To the Fool.*] You, sir, more knave than fool, after your master.

FOOL Nuncle Lear, nuncle Lear, tarry, take the fool with thee.

A fox, when one has caught her,
And such a daughter,
Should sure to the slaughter,
If my cap would buy a halter.
So the fool follows after. *Exit.*

GONERIL
This man hath had good counsel—a hundred knights!
'Tis politic and safe to let him keep 320
At point a hundred knights—yes, that on every dream, 321
Each buzz, each fancy, each complaint, dislike, 322
He may enguard his dotage with their pow'rs
And hold our lives in mercy.—Oswald, I say! 324

ALBANY
Well, you may fear too far. 325

GONERIL
Safer than trust too far.
Let me still take away the harms I fear, 327
Not fear still to be taken. I know his heart. 328
What he hath utter'd I have writ my sister.
If she sustain him and his hundred knights,
When I have show'd th' unfitness—

Enter Steward [Oswald].

How now, Oswald?
What, have you writ that letter to my sister?

OSWALD Ay, madam.

GONERIL
Take you some company, and away to horse.
Inform her full of my particular fear,
And thereto add such reasons of your own
As may compact it more. Get you gone, 337
And hasten your return. [*Exit Oswald.*] No, no, my lord,
This milky gentleness and course of yours 339
Though I condemn not, yet, under pardon, 340
You are much more attask'd for want of wisdom 341
Than prais'd for harmful mildness. 342

ALBANY
How far your eyes may pierce I cannot tell. 343
Striving to better, oft we mar what's well.

GONERIL
Nay, then—

ALBANY
Well, well; th' event. *Exeunt.* 346

320 politic prudent (Said ironically.) **321 At point** under arms **322 buzz** idle rumor **324 in mercy** at his mercy **325 fear too far** overestimate the danger **327 take away** remove **327, 328 still** always **328 taken** overtaken (by the *harms*) **337 compact** confirm **339 milky . . . course** humane and gentle way **340 under pardon** if you'll excuse my saying so **341 attask'd** taken to task for, blamed **342 harmful mildness** mildness that causes harm **343 pierce** i.e., see into matters **346 th' event** i.e., time will show

SCENE V

Enter Lear, Kent [disguised as Caius], and Fool.

LEAR Go you before to Gloucester with these letters. 1
[*Gives letter.*] Acquaint my daughter no further with anything you know than comes from her demand out of the letter. If your diligence be not speedy, I shall be there afore you.

KENT I will not sleep, my lord, till I have deliver'd your letter. *Exit.*

FOOL If a man's brains were in 's heels, were 't not in danger of kibes? 9

LEAR Ay, boy.

FOOL Then, I prithee, be merry; thy wit shall not go slip-shod. 12

LEAR Ha, ha, ha!

FOOL Shalt see thy other daughter will use thee kindly; 14
for though she's as like this as a crab's like an apple, 15
yet I can tell what I can tell.

LEAR What canst tell, boy?

FOOL She will taste as like this as a crab does to a crab. Thou canst tell why one's nose stands i' th' middle on 's face? 20

LEAR No.

FOOL Why, to keep one's eyes of either side 's nose, that what a man cannot smell out he may spy into.

LEAR I did her wrong. 24

FOOL Canst tell how an oyster makes his shell?

LEAR No.

FOOL Nor I neither; but I can tell why a snail has a house.

LEAR Why?

FOOL Why, to put 's head in; not to give it away to his daughters, and leave his horns without a case. 31

LEAR I will forget my nature. So kind a father!—Be my horses ready?

FOOL Thy asses are gone about 'em. The reason why 34
the seven stars are no moe than seven is a pretty 35
reason.

LEAR Because they are not eight.

FOOL Yes, indeed. Thou wouldst make a good fool.

LEAR To take 't again perforce! Monster ingratitude! 39

FOOL If thou wert my fool, nuncle, I 'd have thee beaten for being old before thy time.

LEAR How's that?

FOOL Thou shouldst not have been old till thou hadst been wise.

LEAR
O, let me not be mad, not mad, sweet heaven!
Keep me in temper; I would not be mad!

[Enter Gentleman.]

I.v. Location: Before Albany's palace.
1 Gloucester i.e., the place in Gloucestershire. **these letters** this letter **9 kibes** chilblains **12 slip-shod** in slippers, worn because of chilblains. (There are no brains, thinks the Fool, in Lear's heels when they are on their way to visit Regan.) **14 Shalt** thou shalt. **kindly** (1) according to filial nature. (Said ironically.) (2) according to her own nature **15 crab** crab apple **20 on 's** of his **24 her** i.e., Cordelia **31 horns** (Suggests cuckold's horns, as though Lear were figuratively not the father of Goneril and Regan.) **34 Thy . . . 'em** i.e., your servants (who labor like asses) have gone about readying the horses **35 seven stars** Pleiades **39 again** back again

How now, are the horses ready?

GENTLEMAN Ready, my lord.

LEAR Come, boy.

FOOL
She that's a maid now, and laughs at my departure,
Shall not be a maid long, unless things be cut shorter.

Exeunt.

ACT II • SCENE I

Enter Bastard [Edmund] and Curan, severally.

EDMUND Save thee, Curan.

CURAN And you, sir. I have been with your father, and given him notice that the Duke of Cornwall and Regan his duchess will be here with him this night.

EDMUND How comes that?

CURAN Nay, I know not. You have heard of the news abroad—I mean the whisper'd ones, for they are yet but ear-kissing arguments?

EDMUND Not I. Pray you, what are they?

CURAN Have you heard of no likely wars toward, 'twixt the Dukes of Cornwall and Albany?

EDMUND Not a word.

CURAN You may do, then, in time. Fare you well, sir.

Exit.

EDMUND
The Duke be here tonight? The better! Best!
This weaves itself perforce into my business.
My father hath set guard to take my brother,
And I have one thing, of a queasy question,
Which I must act. Briefness and fortune, work!
Brother, a word. Descend. Brother, I say!

Enter Edgar.

My father watches. O sir, fly this place!
Intelligence is given where you are hid.
You have now the good advantage of the night.
Have you not spoken 'gainst the Duke of Cornwall?
He's coming hither, now, i' th' night, i' th' haste,
And Regan with him. Have you nothing said
Upon his party 'gainst the Duke of Albany?
Advise yourself.

EDGAR I am sure on 't, not a word.

EDMUND
I hear my father coming. Pardon me;
In cunning I must draw my sword upon you.
Draw, seem to defend yourself; now quit you well.— [*They draw.*]
Yield! Come before my father!—Light, ho, here!—
Fly, brother.—Torches, torches!—So, farewell.

Exit Edgar.

Some blood drawn on me would beget opinion [*Wounds his arm.*]
Of my more fierce endeavor. I have seen drunkards
Do more than this in sport.—Father, father!
Stop, stop! No help?

Enter Gloucester, and Servants with torches.

GLOUCESTER
Now, Edmund, where's the villain?

EDMUND
Here stood he in the dark, his sharp sword out,
Mumbling of wicked charms, conjuring the moon
To stand auspicious mistress.

GLOUCESTER But where is he?

EDMUND
Look, sir, I bleed.

GLOUCESTER Where is the villain, Edmund?

EDMUND
Fled this way, sir. When by no means he could—

GLOUCESTER
Pursue him, ho! Go after. [*Exeunt some Servants.*] By no means what?

EDMUND
Persuade me to the murder of your lordship,
But that I told him the revenging gods
'Gainst parricides did all the thunder bend,
Spoke with how manifold and strong a bond
The child was bound to th' father; sir, in fine,
Seeing how loathly opposite I stood
To his unnatural purpose, in fell motion
With his prepared sword he charges home
My unprovided body, latch'd mine arm;
And when he saw my best alarum'd spirits,
Bold in the quarrel's right, rous'd to th' encounter,
Or whether gasted by the noise I made,
Full suddenly he fled.

GLOUCESTER Let him fly far.
Not in this land shall he remain uncaught;
And found—dispatch. The noble Duke my master,
My worthy arch and patron, comes tonight.
By his authority I will proclaim it
That he which finds him shall deserve our thanks,
Bringing the murderous coward to the stake;
He that conceals him, death.

EDMUND
When I dissuaded him from his intent,
And found him pight to do it, with curst speech
I threaten'd to discover him. He replied,
"Thou unpossessing bastard, dost thou think,
If I would stand against thee, would the reposal
Of any trust, virtue, or worth in thee
Make thy words faith'd? No. What I should deny—
As this I would, ay, though thou didst produce
My very character—I 'd turn it all
To thy suggestion, plot, and damned practice;

51 things i.e., penises. **cut shorter** (A bawdy joke addressed to the audience.)

II.i. Location: The Earl of Gloucester's house.
s.d. severally separately **1 Save** God save **8 ear-kissing arguments** lightly whispered topics **10 toward** impending **17 queasy question** hazardous or ticklish nature **18 Briefness and fortune** expeditious dispatch and good luck **26 Upon his party 'gainst** i.e., reflecting on his feud with **27 Advise yourself** think it over carefully **30 quit you** acquit yourself

46 bend aim **48 in fine** in conclusion **49 loathly opposite** loathingly opposed **50 fell motion** deadly thrust **52 unprovided** unarmed. **latch'd** nicked, lanced **53 best alarum'd** thoroughly aroused to action as by a trumpet **54 quarrel's right** justice of the cause **55 gasted** frightened **58 dispatch** i.e., that will be the end for him **59 arch** chief **65 pight** determined. **curst** angry **66 discover** expose **67 unpossessing** unable to inherit, beggarly **68 reposal** placing **70 faith'd** believed **72 character** written testimony **73 suggestion** instigation. **practice** plot

And thou must make a dullard of the world, 74
If they not thought the profits of my death 75
Were very pregnant and potential spirits 76
To make thee seek it."

GLOUCESTER O strange and fast'ned villain! 77
Would he deny his letter, said he?
[I never got him.] *Tucket within.* 79
Hark, the Duke's trumpets! I know not why he comes.
All ports I'll bar; the villain shall not scape; 81
The Duke must grant me that. Besides, his picture
I will send far and near, that all the kingdom
May have due note of him; and of my land,
Loyal and natural boy, I'll work the means
To make thee capable. 86

Enter Cornwall, Regan, and Attendants.

CORNWALL
How now, my noble friend? Since I came hither,
Which I can call but now, I have heard strange news.

REGAN
If it be true, all vengeance comes too short
Which can pursue th' offender. How dost, my lord?

GLOUCESTER
O, madam, my old heart is crack'd, it's crack'd!

REGAN
What, did my father's godson seek your life?
He whom my father nam'd? Your Edgar?

GLOUCESTER
O, lady, lady, shame would have it hid!

REGAN
Was he not companion with the riotous knights
That tended upon my father?

GLOUCESTER
I know not, madam. 'Tis too bad, too bad.

EDMUND
Yes, madam, he was of that consort. 98

REGAN
No marvel, then, though he were ill affected.
'Tis they have put him on the old man's death, 100
To have th' expense and waste of his revenues. 101
I have this present evening from my sister
Been well inform'd of them, and with such cautions,
That if they come to sojourn at my house,
I'll not be there.

CORNWALL Nor I, assure thee, Regan.
Edmund, I hear that you have shown your father
A child-like office.

EDMUND It was my duty, sir. 107

GLOUCESTER
He did bewray his practice, and receiv'd 108
This hurt you see, striving to apprehend him.

CORNWALL
Is he pursued?

GLOUCESTER
Ay, my good lord.

CORNWALL
If he be taken, he shall never more
Be fear'd of doing harm. Make your own purpose, 113
How in my strength you please. For you, Edmund, 114
Whose virtue and obedience doth this instant
So much commend itself, you shall be ours.
Natures of such deep trust we shall much need;
You we first seize on.

EDMUND I shall serve you, sir,
Truly, however else.

GLOUCESTER
For him I thank your Grace.

CORNWALL
You know not why we came to visit you—

REGAN
Thus out of season, threading dark-ey'd night.
Occasions, noble Gloucester, of some prize, 123
Wherein we must have use of your advice.
Our father he hath writ, so hath our sister,
Of differences, which I best thought it fit 126
To answer from our home; the several messengers 127
From hence attend dispatch. Our good old friend, 128
Lay comforts to your bosom, and bestow
Your needful counsel to our businesses, 130
Which craves the instant use.

GLOUCESTER I serve you, madam. 131
Your Graces are right welcome.

Exeunt. Flourish.

SCENE II

Enter Kent [disguised as Caius] and Steward [Oswald], severally.

OSWALD Good dawning to thee, friend. Art of this 1
house?

KENT Ay.

OSWALD Where may we set our horses?

KENT I' th' mire.

OSWALD Prithee, if thou lov'st me, tell me. 6

KENT I love thee not.

OSWALD Why, then, I care not for thee.

KENT If I had thee in Lipsbury pinfold, I would make 9
thee care for me.

OSWALD Why dost thou use me thus? I know thee not.

KENT Fellow, I know thee.

OSWALD What dost thou know me for?

KENT A knave, a rascal, an eater of broken meats; 14
a base, proud, shallow, beggarly, three-suited, 15

74 make . . . world think everyone idiotic **75 not thought** did not think. **of my death** i.e, that Edmund would gain through Edgar's death **76 pregnant . . . spirits** fertile and potent tempters **77 fast'ned** confirmed **79 got** begot **79 s.d. Tucket** series of notes on the trumpet, here indicating Cornwall's arrival **81 ports** gateways **86 capable** legally able to become the inheritor **98 consort** set, company **100 put him on** incited him to **101 expense and waste** squandering **107 child-like** filial **108 bewray his practice** expose his (Edgar's) plot

113–114 Make . . . please form your plans, making free use of my authority **114 For** as for **123 prize** significance **126 differences** quarrels **127 from** away from **128 attend dispatch** wait to be dispatched **130 needful** necessary **131 instant use** immediate attention

II.ii. Location: Before Gloucester's house.
1 dawning (It is not yet day.) **6 if thou lov'st me** i.e., if you bear good will toward me. (But Kent deliberately takes the phrase in its literal, not courtly, sense.) **9 Lipsbury pinfold** i.e., within the pinfold of the lips, between my teeth. (A *pinfold* is a pound for stray animals.) **14 broken meats** scraps of food **15 three-suited** (Three suits a year were allowed to servants.)

hundred-pound, filthy, worsted-stocking knave; a lily-liver'd, action-taking, whoreson, glass-gazing, superservicable, finical rogue; one-trunk-inheriting slave; one that wouldst be a bawd in way of good service, and art nothing but the composition of a knave, beggar, coward, pander, and the son and heir of a mongrel bitch; one whom I will beat into clamorous whining, if thou deny'st the least syllable of thy addition.

OSWALD Why, what a monstrous fellow art thou, thus to rail on one that is neither known of thee nor knows thee!

KENT What a brazen-fac'd varlet art thou, to deny thou knowest me! Is it two days since I tripp'd up thy heels and beat thee before the King? Draw, you rogue, for, though it be night, yet the moon shines. I'll make a sop o' th' moonshine of you. You whoreson cullionly barber-monger, draw! [*Draws his sword.*]

OSWALD Away! I have nothing to do with thee.

KENT Draw, you rascal! You come with letters against the King, and take Vanity the puppet's part against the royalty of her father. Draw, you rogue, or I'll so carbonado your shanks. Draw, you rascal! Come your ways.

OSWALD Help, ho! Murder! Help!

KENT Strike, you slave! Stand, rogue, stand, you neat slave, strike! [*Beats him.*]

OSWALD Help, ho! Murder! Murder!

Enter Bastard [*Edmund, with his rapier drawn*], *Cornwall, Regan, Gloucester, Servants.*

EDMUND How now, what's the matter? Part!

KENT With you, goodman boy, if you please! Come, I'll flesh ye. Come on, young master.

GLOUCESTER Weapons? Arms? What's the matter here?

CORNWALL Keep peace, upon your lives! [*Kent and Oswald are parted.*] He dies that strikes again. What is the matter?

REGAN The messengers from our sister and the King.

CORNWALL What is your difference? Speak.

OSWALD I am scarce in breath, my lord.

KENT No marvel, you have so bestirr'd your valor. You cowardly rascal, nature disclaims in thee. A tailor made thee.

CORNWALL Thou art a strange fellow. A tailor make a man?

KENT A tailor, sir. A stone-cutter or a painter could not have made him so ill, though they had been but two years o' th' trade.

CORNWALL Speak yet, how grew your quarrel?

OSWALD This ancient ruffian, sir, whose life I have spar'd at suit of his gray beard—

KENT Thou whoreson zed! Thou unnecessary letter! My lord, if you will give me leave, I will tread this unbolted villain into mortar, and daub the wall of a jakes with him. Spare my gray beard, you wagtail?

CORNWALL Peace, sirrah!
You beastly knave, know you no reverence?

KENT
Yes, sir; but anger hath a privilege.

CORNWALL
Why art thou angry?

KENT
That such a slave as this should wear a sword,
Who wears no honesty. Such smiling rogues as these,
Like rats, oft bite the holy cords a-twain
Which are too intrinse t' unloose; smooth every passion
That in the natures of their lords rebel,
Bring oil to fire, snow to their colder moods;
Renege, affirm, and turn their halcyon beaks
With every gale and vary of their masters,
Knowing nought, like dogs, but following.
A plague upon your epileptic visage!
Smile you my speeches, as I were a fool?
Goose, if I had you upon Sarum plain,
I 'd drive ye cackling home to Camelot.

CORNWALL
What, art thou mad, old fellow?

GLOUCESTER
How fell you out? Say that.

KENT
No contraries hold more antipathy
Than I and such a knave.

CORNWALL
Why dost thou call him knave? What is his fault?

KENT
His countenance likes me not.

CORNWALL
No more, perchance, does mine, nor his, nor hers.

KENT
Sir, 'tis my occupation to be plain:
I have seen better faces in my time
Than stands on any shoulder that I see
Before me at this instant.

CORNWALL This is some fellow
Who, having been prais'd for bluntness, doth affect
A saucy roughness, and constrains the garb
Quite from his nature. He cannot flatter, he,

16 hundred-pound (Possible allusion to the minimum property qualification for the status of gentleman.) **worsted-stocking** i.e., too poor and menial to wear silk stockings **17 action-taking** settling quarrels by resort to law instead of arms, cowardly. **glass-gazing** fond of looking in the mirror **18 superservicable** officious. **finical** foppish, fastidious. **one-trunk-inheriting** possessing effects sufficient for one trunk only **19–20 bawd . . . service** i.e., pimp or pander as a way of providing good service **20 composition** composite **23–24 addition** titles **32 sop o' th' moonshine** something so perforated that it will soak up moonshine as a sop (floating piece of toast) soaks up liquor **32–33 cullionly barber-monger** base frequenter of barber shops, fop. (*Cullion* originally meant *testicle.*) **36 Vanity . . . part** i.e., the part of Goneril (here personified as a character in a morality play) **38 carbonado** cut crosswise like meat for broiling **38–39 Come your ways** come on **41 neat** (1) foppish (2) calf-like. (*Neat* means "horned cattle.") **44 matter** i.e., trouble. (But Kent takes the meaning *cause for quarrel.*) **45 goodman boy** (A contemptuous epithet.) **46 flesh** initiate into combat **55 disclaims in** disowns

65 zed the letter *z*, regarded as unnecessary and often not included in dictionaries **66–67 unbolted** unsifted; hence, coarse **67 daub** plaster. **jakes** privy **68 wagtail** i.e., bird wagging its tailfeathers in pert obsequiousness **75 holy cords** sacred bonds of affection and order **76 intrinse** intricate, tightly knotted. **smooth** flatter, humor **79 Renege** deny. **halcyon beaks** (The halcyon or kingfisher, if hung up, would supposedly turn its beak against the wind.) **80 gale and vary** variation in the wind **82 epileptic** i.e., pale with fright and distorted with a grin (?) **83 Smile you** do you smile at. **as** as if **84 Sarum** Salisbury **85 Camelot** legendary seat of King Arthur and his Round Table, said to have been at Cadbury and at Winchester and hence in the general vicinity of Salisbury and Gloucester **91 likes** pleases **98–99 constrains . . . nature** i.e., distorts plainness to the point of caricature, away from its true purpose

An honest mind and plain, he must speak truth!
An they will take it, so; if not, he's plain.
These kind of knaves I know, which in this plainness
Harbor more craft and more corrupter ends
Than twenty silly ducking observants
That stretch their duties nicely.

KENT
Sir, in good faith, in sincere verity,
Under th' allowance of your great aspect,
Whose influence, like the wreath of radiant fire
On flick'ring Phoebus' front—

CORNWALL
What mean'st by this?

KENT To go out of my dialect, which you discommend so much. I know, sir, I am no flatterer. He that beguil'd you in a plain accent was a plain knave, which for my part I will not be, though I should win your displeasure to entreat me to 't.

CORNWALL
What was th' offense you gave him?

OSWALD
I never gave him any.
It pleas'd the King his master very late
To strike at me, upon his misconstruction;
When he, compact, and flattering his displeasure,
Tripp'd me behind; being down, insulted, rail'd,
And put upon him such a deal of man
That worthied him, got praises of the King
For him attempting who was self-subdu'd,
And, in the fleshment of this dread exploit,
Drew on me here again.

KENT
None of these rogues and cowards
But Ajax is their fool.

CORNWALL
Fetch forth the stocks!
You stubborn ancient knave, you reverent braggart,
We'll teach you—

KENT
Sir, I am too old to learn.
Call not your stocks for me. I serve the King,
On whose employment I was sent to you.
You shall do small respect, show too bold malice
Against the grace and person of my master,
Stocking his messenger.

CORNWALL
Fetch forth the stocks! As I have life and honor,
There shall he sit till noon.

REGAN
Till noon? Till night, my lord; and all night too.

KENT
Why, madam, if I were your father's dog,
You should not use me so.

REGAN
Sir, being his knave, I will.

CORNWALL
This is a fellow of the self-same color
Our sister speaks of. Come, bring away the stocks!
Stocks brought out.

GLOUCESTER
Let me beseech your Grace not to do so.
[His fault is much, and the good King his master
Will check him for 't. Your purpos'd low correction
Is such as basest and contemned'st wretches
For pilf'rings and most common trespasses
Are punish'd with.] The King must take it ill
That he, so slightly valued in his messenger,
Should have him thus restrain'd.

CORNWALL
I'll answer that.

REGAN
My sister may receive it much more worse
To have her gentleman abus'd, assaulted,
[For following her affairs. Put in his legs.]
[*Kent is put in the stocks.*]
Come, my lord, away.
Exit [*with all but Gloucester and Kent*].

GLOUCESTER
I am sorry for thee, friend. 'Tis the Duke's pleasure,
Whose disposition, all the world well knows,
Will not be rubb'd nor stopp'd. I'll entreat for thee.

KENT
Pray, do not, sir. I have watch'd and travel'd hard.
Some time I shall sleep out, the rest I'll whistle.
A good man's fortune may grow out at heels.
Give you good morrow!

GLOUCESTER
The Duke's to blame in this. 'Twill be ill taken.
Exit.

KENT
Good King, that must approve the common saw,
Thou out of heaven's benediction com'st
To the warm sun!
Approach, thou beacon to this under globe,
That by thy comfortable beams I may
Peruse this letter. Nothing almost sees miracles
But misery. [*Examines letter.*] I know 'tis from Cordelia,
Who hath most fortunately been inform'd
Of my obscured course; and shall find time
From this enormous state, seeking to give
Losses their remedies. All weary and o'erwatch'd,

104 ducking observants bowing, obsequious courtiers **105 nicely** punctiliously **106 Sir, in good faith,** etc. (Kent assumes the wordy mannerisms of courtly flattery.) **107 allowance** approval. **aspect** (1) countenance (2) astrological position **108 influence** astrological might **109 Phoebus' front** i.e., the sun's forehead **111–112 He . . . accent** i.e., the man who used plain speech to you craftily (see ll. 102–105) and thereby taught you to suspect plain speakers of deceit **112–114 which . . . . me to 't** i.e., I will no longer use plain speech, despite the incentive of incurring your displeasure by doing so. (Kent prefers to displease Cornwall, since Cornwall is pleased only by flatterers, and Kent has assumed until now that plain speech was the best way to offend; but he now argues mockingly that he can no longer speak plainly since his honest utterance will be interpreted as duplicity.) **117 late** recently **118 misconstruction** misunderstanding (me) **119 he** i.e., Kent. **compact** joined, united with the King **121 put . . . man** acted like such a hero **122 worthied** won reputation for **123 For . . . self-subdu'd** for assailing one (i.e., myself) who chose not to resist **124 fleshment** excitement resulting from a first success **126–127 None . . . fool** i.e., you never find any rogues and cowards of this sort who do not outdo the blustering Ajax in their boasting **128 reverent** reverend (because old) **133 grace** sovereignty

142 away along **145 check** rebuke, correct **157 rubb'd** hindered, obstructed. (A term from bowls.) **158 watch'd** gone sleepless **160 A . . . heels** i.e., even good men suffer decline in fortune at times **161 Give you** i.e., God give you **163 approve** prove true. **saw** proverb (i.e., "To run out of God's blessing into the warm sun," meaning "to go from better to worse") **166 beacon . . . globe** the moon (see ll. 31 and 176) **167 comfortable** useful, aiding **168–169 Nothing . . . misery** i.e., scarcely anything can make one appreciate miracles like being in a state of misery **171 obscured** disguised. **shall** she shall **171–173 and . . . remedies** (This incoherent passage is either textually corrupt or fragments from the letter Kent is reading.) **172 From** i.e., to provide relief from (?) **enormous state** monstrous state of affairs, enormity **173 Losses** reversals of fortune. **o'erwatch'd** exhausted with staying awake

Take vantage, heavy eyes, not to behold
This shameful lodging.
Fortune, good night. Smile once more; turn thy
wheel! *[Sleeps.]*

[SCENE III]

Enter Edgar.

EDGAR
I heard myself proclaim'd,
And by the happy hollow of a tree
Escap'd the hunt. No port is free, no place
That guard and most unusual vigilance
Does not attend my taking. Whiles I may scape,
I will preserve myself, and am bethought
To take the basest and most poorest shape
That ever penury, in contempt of man,
Brought near to beast. My face I'll grime with filth,
Blanket my loins, elf all my hairs in knots,
And with presented nakedness outface
The winds and persecutions of the sky.
The country gives me proof and precedent
Of Bedlam beggars, who, with roaring voices,
Strike in their numb'd and mortified arms
Pins, wooden pricks, nails, sprigs of rosemary;
And with this horrible object, from low farms,
Poor pelting villages, sheep-cotes, and mills,
Sometimes with lunatic bans, sometime with
prayers,
Enforce their charity. Poor Turlygod! Poor Tom!
That's something yet. Edgar I nothing am. *Exit.*

[SCENE IV]

Enter Lear, Fool, and Gentleman.

LEAR
'Tis strange that they should so depart from home,
And not send back my messenger.
GENTLEMAN As I learn'd,
The night before there was no purpose in them
Of this remove.
KENT Hail to thee, noble master!
LEAR Ha?
Mak'st thou this shame thy pastime?
KENT No, my lord.
FOOL Ha, ha, he wears cruel garters. Horses are tied by the heads, dogs and bears by th' neck, monkeys by th' loins, and men by th' legs. When a man's over-lusty at legs, then he wears wooden nether-stocks.
LEAR
What's he that hath so much thy place mistook
To set thee here?
KENT It is both he and she;
Your son and daughter.
LEAR
No.
KENT
Yes.
LEAR
No, I say.
KENT
I say, yea.
[LEAR
No, no, they would not.
KENT
Yes, they have.]
LEAR
By Jupiter, I swear no.
KENT
By Juno, I swear ay.
LEAR They durst not do 't!
They could not, would not do 't. 'Tis worse than
murder
To do upon respect such violent outrage.
Resolve me, with all modest haste, which way
Thou mightst deserve, or they impose, this usage,
Coming from us.
KENT My lord, when at their home
I did commend your Highness' letters to them,
Ere I was risen from the place that show'd
My duty kneeling, came there a reeking post,
Stew'd in his haste, half breathless, panting forth
From Goneril his mistress salutations;
Deliver'd letters, spite of intermission,
Which presently they read; on whose contents
They summon'd up their meiny, straight took horse,
Commanded me to follow and attend
The leisure of their answer, gave me cold looks;
And meeting here the other messenger,
Whose welcome, I perceiv'd, had poison'd mine—
Being the very fellow which of late
Display'd so saucily against your Highness—
Having more man than wit about me, drew.
He rais'd the house with loud and coward cries.
Your son and daughter found this trespass worth
The shame which here it suffers.
FOOL Winter's not gone yet, if the wild-geese fly
that way.
Fathers that wear rags
Do make their children blind,

174 vantage advantage (of sleep) **175 lodging** i.e., the stocks **176 wheel** (Since Kent is at the bottom of Fortune's wheel, any turning will improve his situation.)

II.iii. Location: Scene continues. Kent is dozing in the stocks.
2 happy luckily found **5 attend** watch, wait for **6 bethought** resolved **10 elf** tangle into elf-locks **11 presented** i.e., this display of **13 proof** example **14 Bedlam** (See note to I.ii.139.) **15 Strike** stick. **mortified** deadened **16 wooden pricks** skewers **17 object** spectacle. **low** lowly **18 pelting** paltry **19 bans** curses **20 Turlygod** (Meaning unknown.) **21 Edgar** i.e., as Edgar

II.iv. Location: Scene continues before Gloucester's house. Kent still dozing in the stocks.
4 remove change of residence **7 cruel** (Q: *crewell*, a double meaning [1] unkind [2] crewel, a thin yarn of which garters were made.)

9–10 over-lusty at legs given to running away **10 nether-stocks** stockings **23 upon respect** i.e., against my delegates (who deserve respect) **24 Resolve** enlighten. **modest** moderate **26 their home** (Kent and Oswald went first to Cornwall's palace after leaving Albany's palace.) **27 commend** deliver **29 reeking** steaming (with heat of travel) **30 Stew'd** i.e., thoroughly heated **32 spite of intermission** in disregard of interrupting me **33 presently** instantly **34 meiny** retinue of servants, household **40 Display'd so saucily** behaved so insolently **41 man** manhood **45–46 Winter . . . way** i.e., the signs still point to continued and worsening fortune **48 blind** i.e., indifferent to their father's needs

But fathers that bear bags
Shall see their children kind.
Fortune, that arrant whore,
Ne'er turns the key to th' poor.
But, for all this, thou shalt have as many dolors for thy daughters as thou canst tell in a year.

LEAR
O, how this mother swells up toward my heart!
Hysterica passio, down, thou climbing sorrow,
Thy element's below!—Where is this daughter?

KENT
With the Earl, sir, here within.

LEAR
Follow me not; stay here. *Exit.*

GENTLEMAN
Made you no more offense but what you speak of?

KENT
None.
How chance the King comes with so small a number?

FOOL An thou hadst been set i' th' stocks for that question, thou'dst well deserv'd it.

KENT Why, fool?

FOOL We'll set thee to school to an ant, to teach thee there's no laboring i' th' winter. All that follow their noses are led by their eyes but blind men, and there's not a nose among twenty but can smell him that's stinking. Let go thy hold when a great wheel runs down a hill, lest it break thy neck with following; but the great one that goes upward, let him draw thee after. When a wise man gives thee better counsel, give me mine again. I would have none but knaves follow it, since a fool gives it.

That sir which serves and seeks for gain,
And follows but for form,
Will pack when it begins to rain,
And leave thee in the storm.
But I will tarry; the fool will stay,
And let the wise man fly.
The knave turns fool that runs away;
The fool no knave, perdy.

Enter Lear and Gloucester.

KENT Where learn'd you this, fool?

FOOL Not i' th' stocks, fool.

LEAR
Deny to speak with me? They are sick? They are weary?
They have travel'd all the night? Mere fetches,
The images of revolt and flying off.
Fetch me a better answer.

GLOUCESTER My dear lord,
You know the fiery quality of the Duke,
How unremovable and fix'd he is
In his own course.

LEAR
Vengeance! Plague! Death! Confusion!
Fiery? What quality? Why, Gloucester, Gloucester,
I 'd speak with the Duke of Cornwall and his wife.

GLOUCESTER
Well, my good lord, I have inform'd them so.

LEAR
Inform'd them? Dost thou understand me, man?

GLOUCESTER
Ay, my good lord.

LEAR
The King would speak with Cornwall. The dear father
Would with his daughter speak, commands, tends, service.
Are they inform'd of this? My breath and blood!
Fiery? The fiery Duke? Tell the hot Duke that—
No, but not yet. May be he is not well.
Infirmity doth still neglect all office
Whereto our health is bound; we are not ourselves
When nature, being oppress'd, commands the mind
To suffer with the body. I'll forbear,
And am fallen out with my more headier will,
To take the indispos'd and sickly fit
For the sound man. [*Looks at Kent.*] Death on my state! Wherefore
Should he sit here? This act persuades me
That this remotion of the Duke and her
Is practice only. Give me my servant forth.
Go tell the Duke and 's wife I 'd speak with them,
Now, presently. Bid them come forth and hear me,
Or at their chamber-door I'll beat the drum
Till it cry sleep to death.

GLOUCESTER
I would have all well betwixt you. *Exit.*

LEAR
O me, my heart, my rising heart! But down!

FOOL Cry to it, nuncle, as the cockney did to the eels when she put 'em i' th' paste alive. She knapp'd 'em o' th' coxcombs with a stick, and cried "Down, wantons, down!" 'Twas her brother that, in pure kindness to his horse, butter'd his hay.

Enter Cornwall, Regan, Gloucester, [and] Servants.

LEAR
Good morrow to you both.

CORNWALL Hail to your Grace!
Kent here set at liberty.

REGAN
I am glad to see your Highness.

49 bags i.e., of gold **52 turns the key** i.e., opens the door **53 dolors** griefs (with pun on *dollars*, English word for an Austrian or Spanish coin) **54 tell** (1) relate (2) count **55, 56 mother, Hysterica passio** i.e., hysteria, giving the sensation of choking or suffocating **57 element's** proper place is. (Hysteria was thought to be produced by vapors ascending from the abdomen.) **62 chance** chances it **66–67 We'll . . . winter** i.e., just as the ant knows not to labor in the winter, the wise man knows not to labor for one whose fortunes are fallen **67–70 All . . . stinking** i.e., one who is out of favor can be easily detected (he smells of misfortune), and so is easily avoided by timeservers **78 pack** be off **82 The knave . . . away** i.e., deserting one's master is the greatest folly **83 perdy** *par Dieu* (French), by God **87 fetches** pretexts, dodges **88 images** signs. **flying off** desertion

100 tends attends, waits for **104–105 all . . . bound** duties which in good health we are bound to perform **108–109 am . . . take** now disapprove of my more impetuous will in taking **110 state** royal authority **112 remotion** removal, inaccessibility **113 practice** deception **117 cry sleep to death** i.e., hound sleep to death **120 cockney** i.e., a Londoner, ignorant of ways of cooking eels **121 paste** pastry pie. **knapp'd** rapped **122 coxcombs** heads **122–123 wantons** playful creatures, promiscuous things **123–124 'Twas . . . hay** (Another city ignorance; the act is well-intended, but horses do not like greasy hay.)

LEAR
Regan, I think you are. I know what reason
I have to think so. If thou shouldst not be glad,
I would divorce me from thy mother's tomb,
Sepulchring an adultress. [*To Kent.*] O, are you free?
Some other time for that.—Beloved Regan,
Thy sister's naught. O Regan, she hath tied
Sharp-tooth'd unkindness, like a vulture, here.
[*Points to his heart.*]
I can scarce speak to thee. Thou 'lt not believe
With how deprav'd a quality—O Regan!

REGAN
I pray you, sir, take patience. I have hope
You less know how to value her desert
Than she to scant her duty.

LEAR
Say, how is that?

REGAN
I cannot think my sister in the least
Would fail her obligation. If, sir, perchance
She have restrain'd the riots of your followers,
'Tis on such ground, and to such wholesome end,
As clears her from all blame.

LEAR
My curses on her!

REGAN
O, sir, you are old;
Nature in you stands on the very verge
Of his confine. You should be rul'd and led
By some discretion that discerns your state
Better than you yourself. Therefore, I pray you
That to our sister you do make return;
Say you have wrong'd her.

LEAR
Ask her forgiveness?
Do you but mark how this becomes the house:
"Dear daughter, I confess that I am old; [*Kneels.*]
Age is unnecessary. On my knees I beg
That you'll vouchsafe me raiment, bed, and food."

REGAN
Good sir, no more. These are unsightly tricks.
Return you to my sister.

LEAR [*Rising*]
Never, Regan.
She hath abated me of half my train,
Look'd black upon me, struck me with her tongue,
Most serpent-like, upon the very heart.
All the stor'd vengeances of heaven fall
On her ingrateful top! Strike her young bones,
You taking airs, with lameness!

CORNWALL
Fie, sir, fie!

LEAR
You nimble lightnings, dart your blinding flames
Into her scornful eyes! Infect her beauty,
You fen-suck'd fogs, drawn by the pow'rful sun,
To fall and blister!

REGAN
O the blest gods! So will you wish on me,
When the rash mood is on.

LEAR
No, Regan, thou shalt never have my curse.
Thy tender-hefted nature shall not give
Thee o'er to harshness. Her eyes are fierce, but thine
Do comfort and not burn. 'Tis not in thee
To grudge my pleasures, to cut off my train,
To bandy hasty words, to scant my sizes,
And in conclusion to oppose the bolt
Against my coming in. Thou better know'st
The offices of nature, bond of childhood,
Effects of courtesy, dues of gratitude.
Thy half o' th' kingdom hast thou not forgot,
Wherein I thee endow'd.

REGAN
Good sir, to th' purpose.

LEAR
Who put my man i' th' stocks? *Tucket within.*

CORNWALL
What trumpet's that?

REGAN
I know 't, my sister's. This approves her letter,
That she would soon be here.

Enter Steward [Oswald].

Is your lady come?

LEAR
This is a slave, whose easy-borrowed pride
Dwells in the fickle grace of her he follows.
Out, varlet, from my sight!

CORNWALL
What means your Grace?

LEAR
Who stock'd my servant? Regan, I have good hope
Thou didst not know on 't.

Enter Goneril.

Who comes here? O heavens,
If you do love old men, if your sweet sway
Allow obedience, if you yourselves are old,
Make it your cause; send down, and take my part!
[*To Goneril.*] Art not asham'd to look upon this
beard? [*Goneril and Regan join hands.*]
O Regan, will you take her by the hand?

GONERIL
Why not by th' hand, sir? How have I offended?
All's not offense that indiscretion finds
And dotage terms so.

LEAR
O sides, you are too tough!
Will you yet hold? How came my man i' th' stocks?

CORNWALL
I set him there, sir; but his own disorders
Deserv'd much less advancement.

LEAR
You? Did you?

REGAN
I pray you, father, being weak, seem so.
If, till the expiration of your month,
You will return and sojourn with my sister,
Dismissing half your train, come then to me.
I am now from home, and out of that provision
Which shall be needful for your entertainment.

129 divorce me i.e., refuse to be buried beside **130 Sepulchring** i.e., since it would surely contain the dead body of **132 naught** wicked **135 quality** disposition **145–146 Nature . . . confine** i.e., your life has almost completed its alotted scope **147 discretion** discreet person. **discerns your state** understands your situation **151 becomes the house** suits domestic decorum **161 ingrateful top** ungrateful head **162 taking** infectious **165 fen-suck'd** (It was supposed that the sun sucked up poisons from fens or marshes.) **166 fall** strike

170 tender-hefted gently disposed **174 scant my sizes** diminish my allowances **175 oppose the bolt** lock the door **177 offices of nature** natural duties **178 Effects** actions **180 purpose** point **182 approves** confirms **184 easy-borrowed** i.e., acquired with little collateral, weak commitment **185 grace** favor **186 varlet** worthless fellow **190 Allow** approve, sanction

LEAR
Return to her, and fifty men dismiss'd?
No! Rather I abjure all roofs, and choose
To wage against the enmity o' th' air, 208
To be a comrade with the wolf and owl—
Necessity's sharp pinch. Return with her?
Why, the hot-blooded France, that dowerless took 211
Our youngest born, I could as well be brought
To knee his throne, and, squire-like, pension beg 213
To keep base life afoot. Return with her?
Persuade me rather to be slave and sumpter 215
To this detested groom. [*Points to Oswald.*]
GONERIL
At your choice, sir.
LEAR
I prithee, daughter, do not make me mad.
I will not trouble thee, my child; farewell.
We'll no more meet, no more see one another.
But yet thou art my flesh, my blood, my daughter;
Or rather a disease that's in my flesh,
Which I must needs call mine. Thou art a boil,
A plague-sore, or embossed carbuncle 223
In my corrupted blood. But I'll not chide thee;
Let shame come when it will, I do not call it. 225
I do not bid the thunder-bearer shoot, 226
Nor tell tales of thee to high-judging Jove. 227
Mend when thou canst, be better at thy leisure;
I can be patient. I can stay with Regan,
I and my hundred knights.
REGAN
Not altogether so.
I look'd not for you yet, nor am provided
For your fit welcome. Give ear, sir, to my sister;
For those that mingle reason with your passion 234
Must be content to think you old, and so—
But she knows what she does.
LEAR
Is this well spoken?
REGAN
I dare avouch it, sir. What, fifty followers? 237
Is it not well? What should you need of more?
Yea, or so many, sith that both charge and danger 239
Speak 'gainst so great a number? How, in one
house,
Should many people under two commands
Hold amity? 'Tis hard, almost impossible.
GONERIL
Why might not you, my lord, receive attendance
From those that she calls servants or from mine?
REGAN
Why not, my lord? If then they chanc'd to slack ye, 245
We could control them. If you will come to me—
For now I spy a danger—I entreat you
To bring but five and twenty. To no more
Will I give place or notice. 249
LEAR
I gave you all—
REGAN
And in good time you gave it.
LEAR
Made you my guardians, my depositaries, 251
But kept a reservation to be followed 252
With such a number. What, must I come to you
With five and twenty? Regan, said you so?
REGAN
And speak 't again, my lord; no more with me.
LEAR
Those wicked creatures yet do look well-favor'd
When others are more wicked; not being the worst
Stands in some rank of praise. [*To Goneril.*] I'll go
with thee. 258
Thy fifty yet doth double five-and-twenty,
And thou art twice her love.
GONERIL
Hear me, my lord:
What need you five and twenty, ten, or five,
To follow in a house where twice so many
Have a command to tend you?
REGAN
What need one?
LEAR
O, reason not the need! Our basest beggars 264
Are in the poorest thing superfluous. 265
Allow not nature more than nature needs, 266
Man's life is cheap as beast's. Thou art a lady;
If only to go warm were gorgeous, 268
Why, nature needs not what thou gorgeous wear'st, 269
Which scarcely keeps thee warm. But, for true
need— 270
You heavens, give me that patience, patience I need!
You see me here, you gods, a poor old man,
As full of grief as age, wretched in both.
If it be you that stirs these daughters' hearts
Against their father, fool me not so much 275
To bear it tamely; touch me with noble anger, 276
And let not women's weapons, water-drops,
Stain my man's cheeks! No, you unnatural hags,
I will have such revenges on you both,
That all the world shall—I will do such things—
What they are, yet I know not, but they shall be
The terrors of the earth. You think I'll weep;
No, I'll not weep. *Storm and tempest.*
I have full cause of weeping; but this heart
Shall break into a hundred thousand flaws 285
Or ere I'll weep. O fool, I shall go mad! 286
Exeunt [*Lear, Gloucester, Kent, and Fool*].
CORNWALL
Let us withdraw; 'twill be a storm.
REGAN
This house is little. The old man and 's people
Cannot be well bestow'd. 289
GONERIL
'Tis his own blame hath put himself from rest, 290
And must needs taste his folly. 291

208 wage wage war **211 hot-blooded** choleric. (Cf. I.ii.23.) **213 knee** fall on my knees before **215 sumpter** pack horse; hence, drudge **223 embossed** swollen, tumid **225 call** summon **226 thunder-bearer** i.e., Jove **227 high-judging** judging from on high **234 mingle . . . passion** consider your passionate behavior reasonably **237 avouch** vouch for **239 sith that** since. **charge** expense **245 slack** neglect **249 notice** recognition, acknowledgment

251 depositaries trustees **252 kept a reservation** reserved a right **258 Stands . . . praise** achieves, by necessity, some relative deserving of praise **264 reason not** do not dispassionately analyze **265 Are . . . superfluous** have some wretched possession they can dispense with **266 Allow not** if you do not allow. **needs** i.e., to survive **268–270 If . . . warm** i.e., if fashions in clothes were determined only by the need for warmth, this natural standard wouldn't justify the rich robes you wear to be gorgeous—which don't serve well for warmth in any case **275–276 fool . . . To** do not make me so foolish as to **285 flaws** fragments **286 Or ere** before **289 bestow'd** lodged **290 blame** fault. **from rest** i.e., out of the house; also, lacking peace of mind **291 taste** experience

REGAN
For his particular, I'll receive him gladly, 292
But not one follower.
GONERIL
So am I purpos'd. Where is my Lord of Gloucester?
CORNWALL
Follow'd the old man forth.

Enter Gloucester.

He is return'd.
GLOUCESTER
The King is in high rage.
CORNWALL Whither is he going?
GLOUCESTER
He calls to horse, but will I know not whither.
CORNWALL
'Tis best to give him way; he leads himself.
GONERIL
My lord, entreat him by no means to stay.
GLOUCESTER
Alack, the night comes on, and the high winds
Do sorely ruffle; for many miles about 301
There's scarce a bush.
REGAN O, sir, to willful men
The injuries that they themselves procure
Must be their schoolmasters. Shut up your doors.
He is attended with a desperate train,
And what they may incense him to, being apt 306
To have his ear abus'd, wisdom bids fear. 307
CORNWALL
Shut up your doors, my lord; 'tis a wild night.
My Regan counsels well. Come out o' th' storm.
Exeunt.

ACT III • SCENE I

Storm still. Enter Kent [disguised as Caius] and a Gentleman, severally.

KENT
Who's there, besides foul weather?
GENTLEMAN
One minded like the weather, most unquietly.
KENT
I know you. Where's the King?
GENTLEMAN
Contending with the fretful elements;
Bids the wind blow the earth into the sea,
Or swell the curled waters 'bove the main, 6
That things might change or cease; [tears his white hair,
Which the impetuous blasts, with eyeless rage,
Catch in their fury, and make nothing of; 9
Strives in his little world of man to outscorn 10
The to-and-fro-conflicting wind and rain.
This night, wherein the cub-drawn bear would couch, 12
The lion and the belly-pinched wolf
Keep their fur dry, unbonneted he runs,
And bids what will take all.]
KENT But who is with him? 15
GENTLEMAN
None but the fool, who labors to outjest
His heart-struck injuries.
KENT Sir, I do know you,
And dare, upon the warrant of my note, 18
Commend a dear thing to you. There is division, 19
Although as yet the face of it is cover'd
With mutual cunning, 'twixt Albany and Cornwall;
Who have—as who have not, that their great stars 22
Thron'd and set high?—servants, who seem no less, 23
Which are to France the spies and speculations 24
Intelligent of our state. What hath been seen, 25
Either in snuffs and packings of the Dukes, 26
Or the hard rein which both of them hath borne
Against the old kind King, or something deeper,
Whereof perchance these are but furnishings— 29
[But, true it is, from France there comes a power 30
Into this scattered kingdom, who already, 31
Wise in our negligence, have secret feet 32
In some of our best ports, and are at point 33
To show their open banner. Now to you:
If on my credit you dare build so far 35
To make your speed to Dover, you shall find
Some that will thank you, making just report
Of how unnatural and bemadding sorrow
The King hath cause to plain. 39
I am a gentleman of blood and breeding,
And, from some knowledge and assurance, offer
This office to you.] 42
GENTLEMAN
I will talk further with you.
KENT No, do not.
For confirmation that I am much more
Than my out-wall, open this purse, and take 45
What it contains. [*Gives purse and ring.*] If you shall see Cordelia—
As fear not but you shall—show her this ring,
And she will tell you who that fellow is 48
That yet you do not know. Fie on this storm!
I will go seek the King.
GENTLEMAN
Give me your hand. Have you no more to say?
KENT
Few words, but, to effect, more than all yet: 52
That when we have found the King—in which your pain 53
That way, I'll this—he that first lights on him 54
Holla the other. *Exeunt [severally].*

292 For his particular as for him individually **301 ruffle** bluster **306–307 being . . . abus'd** (he) being inclined to hearken to wild counsel

III.i. Location: An open place in Gloucestershire.
6 main mainland **9 make nothing of** treat disrespectfully **10 little world of man** i.e., the microcosm, which is an epitome of the macrocosm or universe

12 cub-drawn famished, with udders sucked dry (and hence ravenous). **couch** lie close in its den **15 take all** (A cry of desperate defiance, said by a gambler in staking his last.) **18 upon . . . note** on the strength of what I know (about you) **19 Commend . . . thing** entrust a precious undertaking **22 that** whom. **stars** destinies **23 no less** i.e., no other than servants **24 speculations** scouts, spies **25 Intelligent of** supplying intelligence pertinent to **26 snuffs** quarrels. **packings** intrigues **29 furnishings** outward shows **30 power** armed force **31 scattered** divided **32 Wise in** taking advantage of. **feet** i.e., troops **33 at point** ready **35 credit** trustworthiness **39 plain** complain **42 office** service **45 out-wall** exterior appearance **48 fellow** i.e., Kent **52 to effect** to the purpose **53–54 pain That way** laborious quest (take you) that way

SCENE II

Storm still. Enter Lear and Fool.

LEAR
Blow, winds, and crack your cheeks! Rage, blow!
You cataracts and hurricanoes, spout 2
Till you have drench'd our steeples, drown'd the
cocks! 3
You sulph'rous and thought-executing fires, 4
Vaunt-couriers of oak-cleaving thunderbolts, 5
Singe my white head! And thou, all-shaking
thunder,
Strike flat the thick rotundity o' th' world!
Crack nature's molds, all germains spill at once, 8
That makes ingrateful man!

FOOL O nuncle, court holy-water in a dry house is bet- 10
ter than this rain-water out o' door. Good nuncle, in,
ask thy daughters' blessing. Here's a night pities
neither wise men nor fools.

LEAR
Rumble thy bellyful! Spit, fire! Spout, rain!
Nor rain, wind, thunder, fire, are my daughters.
I tax not you, you elements, with unkindness; 16
I never gave you kingdom, call'd you children,
You owe me no subscription. Then let fall 18
Your horrible pleasure. Here I stand, your slave,
A poor, infirm, weak, and despis'd old man.
But yet I call you servile ministers,
That will with two pernicious daughters join
Your high-engender'd battles 'gainst a head 23
So old and white as this. O, ho! 'Tis foul!

FOOL He that has a house to put 's head in has a good
head-piece.
The codpiece that will house 27
Before the head has any,
The head and he shall louse;
So beggars marry many.
The man that makes his toe
What he his heart should make
Shall of a corn cry woe,
And turn his sleep to wake.
For there was never yet fair woman but she made 35
mouths in a glass. 36

LEAR
No, I will be the pattern of all patience;
I will say nothing.

Enter Kent, [disguised as Caius].

KENT
Who's there?

FOOL Marry, here's grace and a codpiece; that's a wise
man and a fool.

KENT
Alas, sir, are you here? Things that love night
Love not such nights as these. The wrathful skies
Gallow the very wanderers of the dark, 44
And make them keep their caves. Since I was man, 45
Such sheets of fire, such bursts of horrid thunder,
Such groans of roaring wind and rain, I never
Remember to have heard. Man's nature cannot carry 48
Th' affliction nor the fear.

LEAR Let the great gods,
That keep this dreadful pudder o'er our heads, 50
Find out their enemies now. Tremble, thou wretch, 51
That hast within thee undivulged crimes,
Unwhipp'd of justice! Hide thee, thou bloody hand,
Thou perjur'd, and thou simular of virtue 54
That art incestuous! Caitiff, to pieces shake, 55
That under covert and convenient seeming 56
Has practic'd on man's life! Close pent-up guilts, 57
Rive your concealing continents, and cry 58
These dreadful summoners grace! I am a man 59
More sinn'd against than sinning.

KENT Alack, bare-headed?
Gracious my lord, hard by here is a hovel;
Some friendship will it lend you 'gainst the tempest.
Repose you there, while I to this hard house—
More harder than the stones whereof 'tis rais'd,
Which even but now, demanding after you, 65
Denied me to come in—return, and force
Their scanted courtesy.

LEAR My wits begin to turn. 67
Come on, my boy. How dost, my boy? Art cold?
I am cold myself. Where is this straw, my fellow?
The art of our necessities is strange,
That can make vile things precious. Come, your
hovel.
Poor fool and knave, I have one part in my heart
That's sorry yet for thee.

FOOL
[Sings]
"He that has and a little tiny wit—
With heigh-ho, the wind and the rain—
Must make content with his fortunes fit,
Though the rain it raineth every day."

LEAR
True, boy. Come, bring us to this hovel.
Exit [with Kent].

FOOL This is a brave night to cool a courtezan. I'll speak 79
a prophecy ere I go:
When priests are more in word than matter; 81
When brewers mar their malt with water; 82
When nobles are their tailors' tutors; 83
No heretics burn'd, but wenches' suitors; 84

III.ii. Location: An open place, as before.
2 hurricanoes waterspouts **3 drench'd** drowned. **cocks** weathercocks **4 thought-executing** acting with the quickness of thought **5 Vaunt-couriers** forerunners **8 nature's molds** the molds in which Nature makes men. **germains** germs, seeds. **spill** destroy **10 court holy-water** flattery **16 tax** accuse **18 subscription** allegiance **23 high-engender'd battles** battalions created by the heavens **27–34 The codpiece . . . wake** i.e., a man who cohabits sexually but improvidentially can expect penury; and one who elevates what is base above what is noble (as Lear has done with his daughters) can expect misery and wakeful tossing also **35–36 made . . . glass** practiced making attractive faces in a mirror

44 Gallow frighten **45 keep** occupy, remain inside **48 carry** endure **50 pudder** pother, turmoil **51 Find . . . now** i.e., expose criminals (by their display of fear) **54 simular** pretender **55 Caitiff** wretch **56 seeming** hypocrisy **57 practic'd on** plotted against. **Close** secret **58 Rive** split. **continents** covering, containers **58–59 cry . . . grace** pray for mercy at the hands of the officers of divine justice. (A *summoner* was the police officer of an ecclesiastical court.) **65 Which** i.e., the occupants of the house. **demanding** I inquiring **67 scanted** stinted **79 brave** fine **81 more . . . matter** better in speech than in substance or Gospel truth. (This and the next three lines satirize the present state of affairs.) **82 mar** adulterate **83 are . . . tutors** i.e., know more than their tailors about fashion **84 burn'd** (I.e., heretics in love catch venereal disease.)

Then shall the realm of Albion 85
Come to great confusion.
When every case in law is right; 87
No squire in debt, nor no poor knight;
When slanders do not live in tongues;
Nor cutpurses come not to throngs;
When usurers tell their gold i' th' field, 91
And bawds and whores do churches build;
Then comes the time, who lives to see 't,
That going shall be us'd with feet. 94
This prophecy Merlin shall make, for I live before his 95
time. *Exit.*

SCENE III

Enter Gloucester and Edmund [with lights].

GLOUCESTER Alack, alack, Edmund, I like not this un-
natural dealing. When I desir'd their leave that I might
pity him, they took from me the use of mine own 3
house, charg'd me on pain of perpetual displeasure
neither to speak of him, entreat for him, or any way
sustain him.

EDMUND
Most savage and unnatural!

GLOUCESTER Go to; say you nothing. There is division
between the Dukes, and a worse matter than that. I
have receiv'd a letter this night; 'tis dangerous to be
spoken; I have lock'd the letter in my closet. These in- 11
juries the King now bears will be reveng'd home; 12
there is part of a power already footed. We must in- 13
cline to the King. I will look him and privily relieve 14
him. Go you and maintain talk with the Duke, that
my charity be not of him perceiv'd. If he ask for me, I
am ill and gone to bed. If I die for it, as no less is
threat'ned me, the King my old master must be re-
liev'd. There is strange things toward, Edmund; pray 19
you be careful. *Exit.*

EDMUND
This courtesy forbid thee shall the Duke 21
Instantly know, and of that letter too.
This seems a fair deserving, and must draw me 23
That which my father loses—no less than all.
The younger rises when the old doth fall. *Exit.*

SCENE IV

Enter Lear, Kent [disguised as Caius], and Fool.

KENT
Here is the place, my lord. Good my lord, enter.
The tyranny of the open night's too rough
For nature to endure. *Storm still.*

LEAR Let me alone.

KENT
Good my lord, enter here.

LEAR Wilt break my heart? 4

KENT
I had rather break mine own. Good my lord, enter.

LEAR
Thou think'st 'tis much that this contentious storm
Invades us to the skin. So 'tis to thee,
But where the greater malady is fix'd, 8
The lesser is scarce felt. Thou'dst shun a bear,
But if thy flight lay toward the roaring sea,
Thou'dst meet the bear i' th' mouth. When the
mind's free, 11
The body's delicate. The tempest in my mind
Doth from my senses take all feeling else
Save what beats there. Filial ingratitude!
Is it not as this mouth should tear this hand 15
For lifting food to 't? But I will punish home. 16
No, I will weep no more. In such a night
To shut me out? Pour on; I will endure.
In such a night as this? O Regan, Goneril,
Your old kind father, whose frank heart gave all— 20
O, that way madness lies; let me shun that!
No more of that.

KENT Good my lord, enter here.

LEAR
Prithee, go in thyself; seek thine own ease.
This tempest will not give me leave to ponder
On things would hurt me more. But I'll go in.
[To the Fool.] In, boy; go first. You houseless
poverty—
Nay, get thee in. I'll pray, and then I'll sleep.
Exit [Fool into the hovel].
Poor naked wretches, wheresoe'er you are,
That bide the pelting of this pitiless storm, 29
How shall your houseless heads and unfed sides,
Your loop'd and window'd raggedness, defend you 31
From seasons such as these? O, I have ta'en
Too little care of this! Take physic, pomp; 33
Expose thyself to feel what wretches feel,
That thou mayst shake the superflux to them, 35
And show the heavens more just.

EDGAR *[Within]* Fathom and half, fathom and half! 37
Poor Tom!

Enter Fool [from the hovel].

FOOL Come not in here, nuncle, here's a spirit. Help
me, help me!

KENT
Give me thy hand. Who's there?

FOOL A spirit, a spirit! He says his name's poor Tom.

85 realm of Albion kingdom of England **87 right** just. (This and the next five lines offer a utopian vision of justice and charity that will never be realized in this corrupted world.) **91 tell** count. **i' th' field** i.e., openly, without fear **94 going . . . feet** walking will be done on foot **95 Merlin** (A great wizard of the court of King Arthur, who came before Lear.)

III.iii. Location: Gloucester's house.
3 pity have mercy on **11 closet** private chamber **12 home** thoroughly **13 power** armed force. **footed** landed **13–14 incline to** side with **14 look** look for **19 toward** impending **21 courtesy forbid thee** kindness (to Lear) which you were forbidden to show **23 fair deserving** meritorious action

III.iv. Location: An open place. Before a hovel.

4 break my heart i.e., cause me anguish by relieving my physical wants and thus forcing me to confront again my *greater malady* (l. 8) **8 fix'd** lodged, implanted **11 i' th' mouth** i.e., head-on. **free** free of anxiety **15 as** as if **16 home** fully **20 frank** liberal **29 bide** endure **31 loop'd and window'd** full of openings like windows and loopholes **33 Take physic, pomp** cure yourself, O distempered great ones **35 superflux** superfluity (with suggestion of *flux, bodily discharge,* introduced by *physic, purgative,* in l. 33) **37 Fathom and half** (A sailor's cry while taking soundings, hence appropriate to a deluge.)

KENT
What art thou that dost grumble there i' th' straw?
Come forth.

Enter Edgar [disguised as a madman].

EDGAR Away! The foul fiend follows me! Through the sharp hawthorn blows the cold wind. Hum! Go to thy bed, and warm thee.

LEAR
Didst thou give all to thy daughters?
And art thou come to this?

EDGAR Who gives anything to poor Tom? Whom the foul fiend hath led through fire and through flame, through ford and whirlpool, o'er bog and quagmire; that hath laid knives under his pillow, and halters in his pew, set ratsbane by his porridge, made him proud of heart, to ride on a bay trotting-horse over four-inch'd bridges, to course his own shadow for a traitor. Bless thy five wits! Tom's a-cold—O, do de, do de, do de. Bless thee from whirlwinds, star-blasting, and taking! Do poor Tom some charity, whom the foul fiend vexes. There could I have him now—and there—and there again, and there. *Storm still.*

LEAR
Has his daughters brought him to this pass?
Couldst thou save nothing? Wouldst thou give 'em all?

FOOL Nay, he reserv'd a blanket, else we had been all sham'd.

LEAR
Now, all the plagues that in the pendulous air
Hang fated o'er men's faults light on thy daughters!

KENT
He hath no daughters, sir.

LEAR
Death, traitor! Nothing could have subdu'd nature
To such a lowness but his unkind daughters.
Is it the fashion, that discarded fathers
Should have thus little mercy on their flesh?
Judicious punishment! 'Twas this flesh begot
Those pelican daughters.

EDGAR Pillicock sat on Pillicock-hill. Alow, alow, loo, loo!

FOOL This cold night will turn us all to fools and madmen.

EDGAR Take heed o' th' foul fiend. Obey thy parents; keep thy word's justice; swear not; commit not with man's sworn spouse; set not thy sweet heart on proud array. Tom's a-cold.

LEAR What hast thou been?

EDGAR A servingman, proud in heart and mind; that curl'd my hair; wore gloves in my cap; serv'd the lust of my mistress' heart, and did the act of darkness with her; swore as many oaths as I spake words, and broke them in the sweet face of heaven. One that slept in the contriving of lust, and wak'd to do it. Wine lov'd I deeply, dice dearly; and in woman out-paramour'd the Turk. False of heart, light of ear, bloody of hand; hog in sloth, fox in stealth, wolf in greediness, dog in madness, lion in prey. Let not the creaking of shoes nor the rustling of silks betray thy poor heart to woman. Keep thy foot out of brothels, thy hand out of plackets, thy pen from lenders' books, and defy the foul fiend. Still through the hawthorn blows the cold wind; says suum, mun, nonny. Dolphin my boy, boy, sessa! Let him trot by. *Storm still.*

LEAR Thou wert better in a grave than to answer with thy uncover'd body this extremity of the skies. Is man no more than this? Consider him well. Thou ow'st the worm no silk, the beast no hide, the sheep no wool, the cat no perfume. Ha! Here's three on 's are sophisticated. Thou art the thing itself; unaccommodated man is no more but such a poor, bare, forked animal as thou art. Off, off, you lendings! Come, unbutton here. *[Tearing off his clothes.]*

FOOL Prithee, nuncle, be contented; 'tis a naughty night to swim in. Now a little fire in a wild field were like an old lecher's heart—a small spark, all the rest on 's body cold.

Enter Gloucester, with a torch.

Look, here comes a walking fire.

EDGAR This is the foul Flibbertigibbet! He begins at curfew, and walks till the first cock; he gives the web and the pin, squints the eye, and makes the hare-lip; mildews the white wheat, and hurts the poor creature of earth.

Swithold footed thrice the 'old;
He met the night-mare, and her nine-fold;
Bid her alight,
And her troth plight,
And, aroint thee, witch, aroint thee!

KENT
How fares your Grace?

LEAR
What's he?

KENT
Who's there? What is 't you seek?

GLOUCESTER
What are you there? Your names?

EDGAR Poor Tom, that eats the swimming frog, the toad, the tadpole, the wall-newt and the water; that in the fury of his heart, when the foul fiend rages, eats

45–46 Through . . . wind (A line from a ballad.) **53–54 knives, halters, ratsbane** (Tempting means to commit suicide and hence be damned.) **55–56 over four-inch'd bridges** i.e., taking mad risks on narrow bridges with the devil's assistance **56 course** chase. **for** as **58–59 star-blasting** being blighted by influence of the stars **59 taking** pestilence; or witchcraft **62 pass** miserable plight **64 reserv'd a blanket** kept a wrap (for his nakedness) **66 pendulous** suspended **72 have . . . flesh** i.e., punish themselves, as Edgar has done **74 pelican** greedy. (Young pelicans supposedly fed on the blood of their mothers' breasts.) **75 Pillicock** (From an old rhyme, suggested by the sound of *pelican. Pillicock* in nursery rhyme seems to have been a euphemism for penis, *Pillicock-hill* for the Mount of Venus.) **80 commit not** i.e., do not commit adultery **85 gloves** i.e., his mistress' favors

90–91 out-paramour'd the Turk outdid the Sultan in keeping mistresses **91 light of ear** foolishly credulous; frivolous **93 prey** preying **96 plackets** slits in skirts or petticoats. **thy pen . . . books** i.e., do not sign a contract for a loan **98 suum . . . nonny** (Imitative of the wind?) **Dolphin my boy** (A slang phrase, or bit of song?) **102 ow'st** have borrowed from **104 cat** civet cat **104–105 sophisticated** clad in the trappings of civilized life; adulterated **110 wild** barren, uncultivated **114 Flibbertigibbet** (A devil from Elizabethan folklore whose name appears in Samuel Harsnett's *Declaration* of 1603 and elsewhere.) **115 first cock** midnight **115–116 web and the pin** cataract of the eye **117 white** ripening **119 Swithold** St. Withold, a famous Anglo-Saxon exorcist. **footed . . . 'old** thrice traversed the wold (tract of hilly upland) **120 night-mare** demon. **nine-fold** nine offspring (with possible pun on *fold, foal*) **122 her troth plight** give her promise (to do no harm) **123 aroint thee** begone **129 water** i.e., water-newt

cow-dung for sallets; swallows the old rat and the ditch-dog; drinks the green mantle of the standing pool; who is whipp'd from tithing to tithing, and stock-punish'd and imprison'd; who hath had three suits to his back, six shirts to his body,

Horse to ride, and weapon to wear;
But mice and rats, and such small deer,
Have been Tom's food for seven long year.

Beware my follower. Peace, Smulkin, peace, thou fiend!

GLOUCESTER
What, hath your Grace no better company?

EDGAR The prince of darkness is a gentleman. Modo he's call'd, and Mahu.

GLOUCESTER
Our flesh and blood, my lord, is grown so vile
That it doth hate what gets it.

EDGAR Poor Tom's a-cold.

GLOUCESTER
Go in with me. My duty cannot suffer
T' obey in all your daughters' hard commands.
Though their injunction be to bar my doors
And let this tyrannous night take hold upon you,
Yet have I ventured to come seek you out,
And bring you where both fire and food is ready.

LEAR
First let me talk with this philosopher.
What is the cause of thunder?

KENT
Good my lord, take his offer; go into th' house.

LEAR
I'll talk a word with this same learned Theban.
What is your study?

EDGAR How to prevent the fiend, and to kill vermin.

LEAR
Let me ask you one word in private.

KENT [*To Gloucester*]
Importune him once more to go, my lord.
His wits begin t' unsettle.

GLOUCESTER Canst thou blame him?
Storm still.
His daughters seek his death. Ah, that good Kent!
He said it would be thus, poor banish'd man.
Thou sayest the King grows mad; I'll tell thee, friend,
I am almost mad myself. I had a son,
Now outlaw'd from my blood; he sought my life,
But lately, very late. I lov'd him, friend,
No father his son dearer. True to tell thee,
The grief hath craz'd my wits. What a night 's this!—
I do beseech your Grace—

LEAR
O, cry you mercy, sir.
Noble philosopher, your company.

EDGAR Tom's a-cold.

GLOUCESTER [*To Edgar*]
In, fellow, there, into th' hovel. Keep thee warm.

LEAR [*Starting toward the hovel*]
Come, let's in all.

KENT This way, my lord.

LEAR With him!
I will keep still with my philosopher.

KENT [*To Gloucester*]
Good my lord, soothe him; let him take the fellow.

GLOUCESTER [*To Kent*]
Take him you on.

KENT [*To Edgar*]
Sirrah, come on; go along with us.

LEAR
Come, good Athenian.

GLOUCESTER
No words, no words! Hush.

EDGAR
Child Rowland to the dark tower came;
His word was still, "Fie, foh, and fum,
I smell the blood of a British man." *Exeunt.*

131 **sallets** salads 132 **ditch-dog** i.e., dead dog in a ditch. **mantle** scum 133 **tithing to tithing** i.e., one ward or parish to another 134 **stock-punish'd** placed in the stocks 137 **deer** animals 139, 141–142 **Smulkin, Modo, Mahu** (Shakespeare found these Elizabethan devils in Samuel Harsnett's *Declaration.*) 144 **gets** begets 146 **suffer** permit me 155 **Theban** i.e., one deeply versed in "philosophy" or natural science 156 **study** special competence 157 **prevent** thwart 165 **outlaw'd . . . blood** exiled from kinship with me 170 **cry you mercy** I beg your pardon

177 **Take . . . on** i.e., take Edgar along with you 179 **Athenian** i.e., philosopher 181 **Child Rowland,** etc. (Fragments of a ballad about the hero of the Charlemagne legends. A *child* is a candidate for knighthood.) 182 **still** always

SCENE V

Enter Cornwall and Edmund [with a letter].

CORNWALL I will have my revenge ere I depart his house.

EDMUND How, my lord, I may be censur'd, that nature thus gives way to loyalty, something fears me to think of.

CORNWALL I now perceive it was not altogether your brother's evil disposition made him seek his death, but a provoking merit, set a-work by a reproveable badness in himself.

EDMUND How malicious is my fortune, that I must repent to be just! This is the letter which he spoke of, which approves him an intelligent party to the advantages of France. O heavens! That this treason were not, or not I the detector!

CORNWALL Go with me to the Duchess.

EDMUND If the matter of this paper be certain, you have mighty business in hand.

CORNWALL True or false, it hath made thee Earl of Gloucester. Seek out where thy father is, that he may be ready for our apprehension.

EDMUND [*Aside*] If I find him comforting the King, it will stuff his suspicion more fully.—I will persevere in my course of loyalty, though the conflict be sore between that and my blood.

CORNWALL I will lay trust upon thee; and thou shalt find a dearer father in my love. *Exeunt.*

III.v. Location: Gloucester's house.
4 **something fears** somewhat frightens 7 **his** i.e., his father's 8–9 **a provoking . . . himself** i.e., an evil propensity in Edgar himself, incited also by the badness of Gloucester which deserved punishment 12 **approves** proves 12–13 **an intelligent . . . advantages** a spy in the service 21 **him** i.e., Gloucester 22 **his** i.e., Cornwall's 24 **blood** family loyalty, filial instincts

SCENE VI

Enter Kent [disguised as Caius] and Gloucester.

GLOUCESTER Here is better than the open air; take it thankfully. I will piece out the comfort with what addition I can. I will not be long from you.

KENT All the pow'r of his wits have given way to his impatience. The gods reward your kindness!

Exit [Gloucester]

Enter Lear, Edgar [as Mad Tom], and Fool.

EDGAR Frateretto calls me, and tells me Nero is an angler in the lake of darkness. Pray, innocent, and beware the foul fiend.

FOOL Prithee, nuncle, tell me whether a madman be a gentleman or a yeoman?

LEAR
A king, a king!

FOOL No, he's a yeoman that has a gentleman to his son; for he's a mad yeoman that sees his son a gentleman before him.

LEAR
To have a thousand with red burning spits
Come hizzing in upon 'em—

[EDGAR The foul fiend bites my back.

FOOL He's mad that trusts in the tameness of a wolf, a horse's health, a boy's love, or a whore's oath.

LEAR
It shall be done; I will arraign them straight.
[*To Edgar.*] Come, sit thou here, most learned justice;
[*To the Fool.*] Thou, sapient sir, sit here. Now, you she-foxes!

EDGAR Look where he stands and glares! Want'st thou eyes at trial, madam?
[*Sings*] Come o'er the bourn, Bessy, to me—

FOOL [*Sings*]
Her boat hath a leak,
And she must not speak
Why she dares not come over to thee.

EDGAR The foul fiend haunts poor Tom in the voice of a nightingale. Hoppedance cries in Tom's belly for two white herring. Croak not, black angel; I have no food for thee.

KENT
How do you, sir? Stand you not so amaz'd.
Will you lie down and rest upon the cushions?

LEAR
I'll see their trial first. Bring in their evidence.
[*To Edgar.*] Thou robed man of justice, take thy place;
[*To the Fool.*] And thou, his yoke-fellow of equity,
Bench by his side. [*To Kent.*] You are o' th' commission,
Sit you too. [*They sit.*]

EDGAR Let us deal justly. [*Sings.*]
Sleepest or wakest thou, jolly shepherd?
Thy sheep be in the corn;
And for one blast of thy minikin mouth,
Thy sheep shall take no harm.
Purr the cat is gray.

LEAR Arraign her first; 'tis Goneril, I here take my oath before this honorable assembly, kick'd the poor King her father.

FOOL Come hither, mistress. Is your name Goneril?

LEAR She cannot deny it.

FOOL Cry you mercy, I took you for a joint-stool.

LEAR
And here's another, whose warp'd looks proclaim
What store her heart is made on. Stop her there!
Arms, arms, sword, fire! Corruption in the place!
False justicer, why hast thou let her scape?]

EDGAR Bless thy five wits!

KENT
O pity! Sir, where is the patience now
That you so oft have boasted to retain?

EDGAR [*Aside*]
My tears begin to take his part so much
They mar my counterfeiting.

LEAR
The little dogs and all,
Tray, Blanch, and Sweet-heart, see, they bark at me.

EDGAR Tom will throw his head at them. Avaunt, you curs!
Be thy mouth or black or white,
Tooth that poisons if it bite;
Mastiff, greyhound, mongrel grim,
Hound or spaniel, brach or lym,
Or bobtail tike or trundle-tail,
Tom will make him weep and wail;
For, with throwing thus my head,
Dogs leapt the hatch, and all are fled.
Do de, de, de. Sessa! Come, march to wakes and fairs and market-towns. Poor Tom, thy horn is dry.

LEAR Then let them anatomize Regan; see what breeds about her heart. Is there any cause in nature that make these hard hearts? [*To Edgar.*] You, sir, I entertain for one of my hundred; only I do not like the fashion of your garments. You will say they are Persian; but let them be chang'd.

III.vi. Location: Within a building on Gloucester's estate, near or adjoining his house; or part of the house itself. See III.iv.146–154. Cushions are provided, and a stool.

5 impatience rage **6 Frateretto** (Another of the fiends from Harsnett.) **6–7 Nero is an angler** (See Chaucer's "Monk's Tale," ll. 485–486; in Rabelais, ii. 30, Nero is described as a fiddler and Trajan an angler in the underworld.) **7 innocent** simpleton, fool (i.e., the Fool) **16 hizzing** hissing **23 he** (Probably one of Edgar's devils.) **23–24 Want'st . . . trial** do you lack spectators at your trial (?) **25 Come . . . me** (First line of a ballad by William Birche, 1558. A *bourn* is a *burn* or brook. The Fool makes a ribald reply, in which the *leaky boat* suggests her easy virtue.) **30 Hoppedance** (Harsnett mentions "Hobberdidance.") **31 white** unsmoked (contrasted with *black devil*). **Croak** (Refers to the rumbling in Edgar's stomach denoting hunger.) **33 amaz'd** bewildered

35 their evidence the witnesses against them **37 yoke-fellow of equity** partner in the law **38 o' th' commission** one commissioned to be a justice **42 corn** grain field **43 minikin** dainty, pretty **45 Purr the cat** (A devil from Harsnett; see III.iv.114, note.) **51 joint-stool** low stool made by a *joiner,* or maker of furniture with joined parts. (Proverbially this phrase meant "I beg your pardon for failing to notice you." The reference is also presumably to a real stool on stage.) **53 store** material **54 Corruption in the place** i.e., there is iniquity or bribery in this court **63 throw his head at** i.e., threaten **68 brach** hound bitch. **lym** bloodhound **69 bobtail** short-tailed small dog, cur. **trundle-tail** long-tailed dog **72 hatch** lower half of a divided door **73 Sessa** i.e., away. **wakes** (Here, parish festivals.) **74 horn** i.e., horn bottle used by beggars to beg for drinks **79 Persian** i.e., gorgeous intricate attire

KENT
Now, good my lord, lie here and rest awhile.

LEAR [*Lying on cushions*] Make no noise, make no noise; draw the curtains. So, so. We'll go to supper i' th' morning. [*Sleeps.*]

FOOL And I'll go to bed at noon.

Enter Gloucester.

GLOUCESTER
Come hither, friend. Where is the King my master?

KENT
Here, sir; but trouble him not, his wits are gone.

GLOUCESTER
Good friend, I prithee, take him in thy arms.
I have o'erheard a plot of death upon him.
There is a litter ready; lay him in 't,
And drive toward Dover, friend, where thou shalt meet
Both welcome and protection. Take up thy master.
If thou shouldst dally half an hour, his life,
With thine and all that offer to defend him,
Stand in assured loss. Take up, take up,
And follow me, that will to some provision
Give thee quick conduct.

[KENT Oppressed nature sleeps.
This rest might yet have balm'd thy broken sinews,
Which, if convenience will not allow,
Stand in hard cure. [*To the Fool.*] Come, help to bear thy master;
Thou must not stay behind.] [*They pick up Lear.*]

GLOUCESTER Come, come, away.
Exeunt [*all but Edgar*].

[EDGAR
When we our betters see bearing our woes,
We scarcely think our miseries our foes.
Who alone suffers suffers most i' th' mind,
Leaving free things and happy shows behind;
But then the mind much sufferance doth o'erskip,
When grief hath mates, and bearing fellowship.
How light and portable my pain seems now,
When that which makes me bend makes the King bow.
He childed as I fathered! Tom, away!
Mark the high noises, and thyself bewray
When false opinion, whose wrong thoughts defile thee,
In thy just proof repeals and reconciles thee.
What will hap more tonight, safe scape the King!
Lurk, lurk.] [*Exit.*]

83 curtains bed-curtains. (They presumably exist only in Lear's mad imagination.) **95 Stand . . . loss** will assuredly be lost **96 provision** supplies; or, means of providing for safety **97 conduct** guidance **98 balm'd** cured, healed. **sinews** nerves **99 convenience** fortunate circumstances **100 Stand . . . cure** will be hard to cure **102 our woes** woes like ours **103 our foes** i.e., hostile toward us alone (since we see how human suffering afflicts even the great) **104 Who . . . mind** i.e., he who suffers alone suffers mental agonies greater than those who perceive they have companions in misery **105 free** carefree. **shows** scenes **106 sufferance** suffering **107 bearing fellowship** tribulation (has) company **108 portable** bearable, endurable **111 Mark . . . noises** i.e., observe what is being said about those in high places, or about great events. **bewray** reveal **113 In . . . thee** upon your being proved innocent recalls you and restores you to favor **114 What . . . King** whatever else happens tonight, may the King escape safely

SCENE VII

Enter Cornwall, Regan, Goneril, Bastard [*Edmund*], *and Servants.*

CORNWALL [*To Goneril*] Post speedily to my lord your husband; show him this letter. [*Gives letter.*] The army of France is landed.—Seek out the traitor Gloucester.
[*Exeunt some of the Servants.*]

REGAN Hang him instantly.

GONERIL Pluck out his eyes.

CORNWALL Leave him to my displeasure. Edmund, keep you our sister company; the revenges we are bound to take upon your traitorous father are not fit for your beholding. Advise the Duke, where you are going, to a most festinate preparation; we are bound to the like. Our posts shall be swift and intelligent betwixt us. Farewell, dear sister; farewell, my Lord of Gloucester.

Enter Steward [*Oswald*].

How now? Where's the King?

OSWALD
My Lord of Gloucester hath convey'd him hence.
Some five or six and thirty of his knights,
Hot questrists after him, met him at gate,
Who, with some other of the lord's dependants,
Are gone with him toward Dover, where they boast
To have well-armed friends.

CORNWALL
Get horses for your mistress.
[*Exit Oswald.*]

GONERIL
Farewell, sweet lord, and sister.

CORNWALL
Edmund, farewell. *Exit* [*Goneril with Edmund*].
Go seek the traitor Gloucester,
Pinion him like a thief, bring him before us.
[*Exeunt other Servants.*]
Though well we may not pass upon his life
Without the form of justice, yet our power
Shall do a court'sy to our wrath, which men
May blame, but not control.

Enter Gloucester, and Servants [*leading him*].

Who's there? The traitor?

REGAN
Ingrateful fox! 'Tis he.

CORNWALL
Bind fast his corky arms.

III.vii. Location: Gloucester's house.
7 sister i.e., sister-in-law, Goneril **9 the Duke** i.e., Albany **10 festinate** hasty **11 posts** messengers. **intelligent** serviceable in bearing information, knowledgeable **12–13 my . . . Gloucester** i.e., Edmund, the recipient now of his father's forfeited estate and title. (Two lines later, Oswald uses the same title to refer to Edmund's father.) **16–17 his, him** i.e., Lear's, Lear **17 questrists** searchers **18 the lord's** i.e., Gloucester's **25 pass upon** pass sentence upon **30 corky** withered with age

GLOUCESTER
What means your Graces? Good my friends, consider
You are my guests. Do me no foul play, friends.

CORNWALL
Bind him, I say. [*Servants bind him.*]

REGAN
Hard, hard. O filthy traitor!

GLOUCESTER
Unmerciful lady as you are, I'm none.

CORNWALL
To this chair bind him. Villain, thou shalt find— [*Regan plucks his beard.*]

GLOUCESTER
By the kind gods, 'tis most ignobly done
To pluck me by the beard.

REGAN
So white, and such a traitor?

GLOUCESTER
Naughty lady,
These hairs which thou dost ravish from my chin
Will quicken, and accuse thee. I am your host.
With robbers' hands my hospitable favors
You should not ruffle thus. What will you do?

CORNWALL
Come, sir, what letters had you late from France?

REGAN
Be simple-answer'd, for we know the truth.

CORNWALL
And what confederacy have you with the traitors
Late footed in the kingdom?

REGAN
To whose hands
You have sent the lunatic King. Speak.

GLOUCESTER
I have a letter guessingly set down,
Which came from one that's of a neutral heart,
And not from one oppos'd.

CORNWALL
Cunning.

REGAN
And false.

CORNWALL
Where hast thou sent the King?

GLOUCESTER
To Dover.

REGAN
Wherefore to Dover? Wast thou not charg'd at peril—

CORNWALL
Wherefore to Dover? Let him answer that.

GLOUCESTER
I am tied to th' stake, and I must stand the course.

REGAN
Wherefore to Dover?

GLOUCESTER
Because I would not see thy cruel nails
Pluck out his poor old eyes; nor thy fierce sister
In his anointed flesh stick boarish fangs.
The sea, with such a storm as his bare head
In hell-black night endur'd, would have buoy'd up
And quench'd the stelled fires;
Yet, poor old heart, he holp the heavens to rain.
If wolves had at thy gate howl'd that stern time,
Thou shouldst have said, "Good porter, turn the key."
All cruels else subscribe. But I shall see
The winged vengeance overtake such children.

CORNWALL
See 't shalt thou never. Fellows, hold the chair.
Upon these eyes of thine I'll set my foot.

GLOUCESTER
He that will think to live till he be old,
Give me some help! O cruel! O you gods!
[*Servants hold the chair as Cornwall grinds out one of Gloucester's eyes with his boot.*]

REGAN
One side will mock another; th' other too.

CORNWALL
If you see vengeance—

FIRST SERVANT
Hold your hand, my lord!
I have serv'd you ever since I was a child;
But better service have I never done you
Than now to bid you hold.

REGAN
How now, you dog?

FIRST SERVANT
If you did wear a beard upon your chin,
I'd shake it on this quarrel. What do you mean?

CORNWALL
My villain? [*They draw and fight.*]

FIRST SERVANT
Nay, then, come on, and take the chance of anger.
[*Cornwall is wounded.*]

REGAN
Give me thy sword. A peasant stand up thus?
[*Takes a sword, and runs at him behind.*]
Kills him.

FIRST SERVANT
O, I am slain! My lord, you have one eye left
To see some mischief on him. O! [*Dies.*]

CORNWALL
Lest it see more, prevent it. Out, vile jelly!
[*He puts out Gloucester's other eye.*]
Where is thy luster now?

GLOUCESTER
All dark and comfortless. Where's my son Edmund?
Edmund, enkindle all the sparks of nature,
To quit this horrid act.

REGAN
Out, treacherous villain!
Thou call'st on him that hates thee. It was he
That made the overture of thy treasons to us;
Who is too good to pity thee.

GLOUCESTER
O my follies! Then Edgar was abus'd.
Kind gods, forgive me that, and prosper him!

38 white i.e., white-haired, venerable. **Naughty** wicked **40 quicken** come to life **41 my hospitable favors** the features of me, your host **42 ruffle** tear or snatch at **43 late** lately **44 simple-answer'd** straightforward in your answers **46 footed** landed **48 guessingly set down** which was tentatively stated **53 charg'd at peril** commanded on peril of your life **55 tied to th' stake** i.e., like a bear to be baited with dogs. **the course** the dogs' attack

61 buoy'd lifted itself **62 stelled fires** stars **63 holp** helped **65 turn the key** i.e., let them in **66 All . . . subscribe** all other cruel creatures would show forgiveness except you **70 will think** hopes **78 I'd . . . quarrel** i.e., I'd pull your beard in vehement defiance in this cause. **What do you mean** i.e., what are you thinking of **79 villain** servant, bondman **83 mischief** injury **87 nature** i.e., filial love **88 quit** requite **90 overture** disclosure **92 abus'd** wronged

REGAN
Go thrust him out at gates, and let him smell
His way to Dover. *Exit [one] with Gloucester.* How
is 't, my lord? How look you? 95
CORNWALL
I have receiv'd a hurt. Follow me, lady.—
Turn out that eyeless villain; throw this slave
Upon the dunghill.—Regan, I bleed apace.
Untimely comes this hurt. Give me your arm.
Exeunt [Cornwall, led by Regan].
[SECOND SERVANT
I'll never care what wickedness I do,
If this man come to good.
THIRD SERVANT If she live long,
And in the end meet the old course of death, 102
Women will all turn monsters.
SECOND SERVANT
Let's follow the old Earl, and get the Bedlam
To lead him where he would. His roguish madness 105
Allows itself to anything. 106
THIRD SERVANT
Go thou. I'll fetch some flax and whites of eggs
To apply to his bleeding face. Now, heaven help
him!] *Exeunt [severally].* 108

ACT IV • SCENE I

Enter Edgar [disguised as Mad Tom].

EDGAR
Yet better thus, and known to be contemn'd, 1
Than still contemn'd and flatter'd. To be worst,
The lowest and most dejected thing of fortune, 3
Stands still in esperance, lives not in fear. 4
The lamentable change is from the best; 5
The worst returns to laughter. Welcome, then, 6
Thou unsubstantial air that I embrace!
The wretch that thou hast blown unto the worst
Owes nothing to thy blasts.

Enter Gloucester, and an Old Man [leading him].

But who comes here? 9
My father, poorly led? World, world, O world!
But that thy strange mutations make us hate thee, 11
Life would not yield to age. 12
OLD MAN
O, my good lord, I have been your tenant,
And your father's tenant, these fourscore years.
GLOUCESTER
Away, get thee away! Good friend, be gone.
Thy comforts can do me no good at all; 16
Thee they may hurt.
OLD MAN You cannot see your way.
GLOUCESTER
I have no way, and therefore want no eyes;
I stumbled when I saw. Full oft 'tis seen
Our means secure us, and our mere defects 20
Prove our commodities. O dear son Edgar, 21
The food of thy abused father's wrath! 22
Might I but live to see thee in my touch, 23
I 'd say I had eyes again!
OLD MAN How now? Who's there?
EDGAR [*Aside*]
O gods! Who is 't can say "I am at the worst"?
I am worse than e'er I was.
OLD MAN 'Tis poor mad Tom.
EDGAR [*Aside*]
And worse I may be yet. The worst is not
So long as we can say "This is the worst."
OLD MAN
Fellow, where goest?
GLOUCESTER Is it a beggar-man?
OLD MAN
Madman and beggar too.
GLOUCESTER
He has some reason, else he could not beg. 31
I' th' last night's storm I such a fellow saw,
Which made me think a man a worm. My son
Came then into my mind, and yet my mind
Was then scarce friends with him. I have heard
more since.
As flies to wanton boys are we to th' gods, 36
They kill us for their sport.
EDGAR [*Aside*] How should this be?
Bad is the trade that must play fool to sorrow,
Ang'ring itself and others.—Bless thee, master! 39
GLOUCESTER
Is that the naked fellow?
OLD MAN Ay, my lord.
GLOUCESTER
Then prithee get thee gone. If for my sake
Thou wilt o'ertake us hence a mile or twain 42
I' th' way toward Dover, do it for ancient love, 43
And bring some covering for this naked soul,
Which I'll entreat to lead me.
OLD MAN Alack, sir, he is mad.
GLOUCESTER
'Tis the time's plague, when madmen lead the
blind. 46
Do as I bid thee, or rather do thy pleasure;
Above the rest, be gone.
OLD MAN
I'll bring him the best 'parel that I have,
Come on 't what will. *Exit.*

95 How look you how is it with you **102 old** customary, natural **105–106 His . . . anything** i.e., his being a madman and derelict allows him to do anything **108 s.d. Exeunt** (At some point after ll. 97–98 the body of the slain First Servant must be removed.)

IV.i. Location: An open place.
1 contemn'd despised **3 dejected . . . of** debased or humbled by **4 esperance** hope **5–6 The lamentable . . . laughter** i.e., any change from the best is grievous, just as any change from the worst is an occasion for joy **9 Owes nothing** can pay no more **11–12 But . . . age** i.e., if it were not for your hateful inconstancy, we would never be reconciled to old age and death

16 comforts kindnesses **20 Our means secure us** our prosperity makes us overconfident. **mere defects** sheer afflictions **21 commodities** benefits **22 abused** deceived **23 in** i.e., by means of **31 reason** power of reason **36 wanton** playful **39 Ang'ring** offending, distressing **42 o'ertake us** catch up to us (after you have found clothing for Tom o' Bedlam) **43 ancient love** i.e., the mutually trusting relationship of tenant and master that Gloucester and the Old Man have long enjoyed **46 times' plague** i.e., spreading sickness of our present state

GLOUCESTER
Sirrah, naked fellow—

EDGAR
Poor Tom's a-cold. [*Aside.*] I cannot daub it further.

GLOUCESTER
Come hither, fellow.

EDGAR [*Aside*]
And yet I must.—Bless thy sweet eyes, they bleed.

GLOUCESTER
Know'st thou the way to Dover?

EDGAR Both stile and gate, horse-way and foot-path. Poor Tom hath been scar'd out of his good wits. Bless thee, good man's son, from the foul fiend! [Five fiends have been in poor Tom at once: of lust, as Obidicut; Hobbididance, prince of dumbness; Mahu, of stealing; Modo, of murder; Flibbertigibbet, of mopping and mowing, who since possesses chambermaids and waiting-women. So, bless thee, master!]

GLOUCESTER
Here, take this purse, thou whom the heavens' plagues [*Gives purse.*]
Have humbled to all strokes. That I am wretched
Makes thee the happier. Heavens, deal so still!
Let the superfluous and lust-dieted man,
That slaves your ordinance, that will not see
Because he does not feel, feel your pow'r quickly;
So distribution should undo excess,
And each man have enough. Dost thou know Dover?

EDGAR Ay, master.

GLOUCESTER
There is a cliff, whose high and bending head
Looks fearfully in the confined deep.
Bring me but to the very brim of it,
And I'll repair the misery thou dost bear
With something rich about me. From that place
I shall no leading need.

EDGAR
Give me thy arm.
Poor Tom shall lead thee. *Exeunt.*

SCENE II

Enter Goneril [and] Bastard [Edmund].

GONERIL
Welcome, my lord. I marvel our mild husband
Not met us on the way.

[Enter] Steward [Oswald].

Now, where's your master?

OSWALD
Madam, within, but never man so chang'd.
I told him of the army that was landed;
He smil'd at it. I told him you were coming;
His answer was "The worse." Of Gloucester's treachery,
And of the loyal service of his son,
When I inform'd him, then he call'd me sot,
And told me I had turn'd the wrong side out.
What most he should dislike seems pleasant to him;
What like, offensive.

GONERIL [*To Edmund*] Then shall you go no further.
It is the cowish terror of his spirit,
That dares not undertake. He'll not feel wrongs
Which tie him to an answer. Our wishes on the way
May prove effects. Back, Edmund, to my brother;
Hasten his musters and conduct his pow'rs.
I must change names at home, and give the distaff
Into my husband's hands. This trusty servant
Shall pass between us. Ere long you are like to hear,
If you dare venture in your own behalf,
A mistress's command. Wear this; spare speech.
[*Gives a favor.*]
Decline your head. [*Kisses him.*] This kiss, if it durst speak,
Would stretch thy spirits up into the air.
Conceive, and fare thee well.

EDMUND
Yours in the ranks of death. *Exit.*

GONERIL
My most dear Gloucester!
O, the difference of man and man!
To thee a woman's services are due;
My fool usurps my body.

OSWALD
Madam, here comes my lord. [*Exit.*]

Enter Albany.

GONERIL
I have been worth the whistle.

ALBANY
O Goneril,
You are not worth the dust which the rude wind
Blows in your face. [I fear your disposition;
That nature which contemns its origin
Cannot be bordered certain in itself.
She that herself will sliver and disbranch
From her material sap, perforce must wither
And come to deadly use.

GONERIL
No more; the text is foolish.

ALBANY
Wisdom and goodness to the vile seem vile;
Filths savor but themselves. What have you done?
Tigers, not daughters, what have you perform'd?

52 daub it further i.e., keep up this pretense **59–61 Obidicut . . . Flibbertigibbet** (Fiends borrowed, as before in III.iv.139–142, from Harsnett.) **61–62 mopping and mowing** making grimaces and mouths **67 superfluous** having a superfluity. **lust-dieted** feeding luxuriously **68 slaves your ordinance** i.e., makes the laws of heaven his slaves **73 bending** overhanging **74 in . . . deep** i.e., to the sea below, where it is confined by its shores

IV.ii. Location: Before the Duke of Albany's palace.
1 Welcome (Goneril, who has just arrived home from Gloucestershire escorted by Edmund, bids him brief welcome before he must return.) **2 Not met** has not met

8 sot fool **12 cowish** cowardly **13 undertake** venture **14 tie . . . answer** oblige him to respond, to fight. **Our . . . way** i.e., our wishes expressed by me to you on the way that you might supplant Albany **15 prove effects** come to pass. **brother** i.e., brother-in-law, Cornwall **16 musters** assembling of troops. **pow'rs** armed forces **17 change names** i.e., exchange the roles of master and mistress of the household. **distaff** spinning-staff, symbolizing the wife's role **24 Conceive** understand, take my meaning (with sexual double entendre, continuing from *stretch thy spirits* in the previous line) **28 My fool . . . body** i.e., my husband forcibly occupies my body **30 worth the whistle** i.e., worth the attentions of men. (Alludes to the proverb, "It is a poor dog that is not worth the whistling.") **32 fear your disposition** mistrust your nature **34 bordered certain** safely restrained, kept within bounds **35 sliver** tear off **36 material sap** nourishing substance **40 savor but themselves** i.e., hunger only for that which is filthy

A father, and a gracious aged man,
Whose reverence even the head-lugg'd bear would lick, 43
Most barbarous, most degenerate, have you madded. 44
Could my good brother suffer you to do it?
A man, a prince, by him so benefited!
If that the heavens do not their visible spirits 47
Send quickly down to tame these vile offenses,
It will come,
Humanity must perforce prey on itself,
Like monsters of the deep.]

GONERIL Milk-liver'd man, 51
That bear'st a cheek for blows, a head for wrongs,
Who hast not in thy brows an eye discerning 53
Thine honor from thy suffering, [that not know'st 54
Fools do those villains pity who are punish'd 55
Ere they have done their mischief. Where's thy drum? 56
France spreads his banners in our noiseless land, 57
With plumed helm thy state begins to threat, 58
Whilst thou, a moral fool, sits still and cries 59
"Alack, why does he so?"]

ALBANY See thyself, devil! 60
Proper deformity seems not in the fiend 61
So horrid as in woman.

GONERIL O vain fool!

[ALBANY
Thou changed and self-cover'd thing, for shame, 63
Be-monster not thy feature. Were 't my fitness 64
To let these hands obey my blood, 65
They are apt enough to dislocate and tear
Thy flesh and bones. Howe'er thou art a fiend,
A woman's shape doth shield thee.

GONERIL
Marry, your manhood, mew!] 69

Enter a Messenger.

[ALBANY
What news?]

MESSENGER
O, my good lord, the Duke of Cornwall's dead,
Slain by his servant, going to put out
The other eye of Gloucester.

ALBANY Gloucester's eyes!

MESSENGER
A servant that he bred, thrill'd with remorse, 74
Oppos'd against the act, bending his sword 75
To his great master, who, thereat enrag'd, 76
Flew on him, and amongst them fell'd him dead, 77
But not without that harmful stroke which since
Hath pluck'd him after.

ALBANY This shows you are above, 79
You justicers, that these our nether crimes 80
So speedily can venge! But, O poor Gloucester!
Lost he his other eye?

MESSENGER Both, both, my lord.—
This letter, madam, craves a speedy answer;
'Tis from your sister. *[Gives her a letter.]*

GONERIL *[Aside]* One way I like this well; 84
But being widow, and my Gloucester with her,
May all the building in my fancy pluck 86
Upon my hateful life. Another way, 87
The news is not so tart.—I'll read, and answer. 88
[Exit.]

ALBANY
Where was his son when they did take his eyes?

MESSENGER
Come with my lady hither.

ALBANY He is not here.

MESSENGER
No, my good lord; I met him back again. 91

ALBANY
Knows he the wickedness?

MESSENGER
Ay, my good lord. 'Twas he inform'd against him,
And quit the house on purpose that their punishment
Might have the freer course.

ALBANY Gloucester, I live
To thank thee for the love thou show'dst the King,
And to revenge thine eyes. Come hither, friend.
Tell me what more thou know'st. *Exeunt.*

SCENE [III]

[Enter Kent and a Gentleman.

KENT Why the King of France is so suddenly gone back know you no reason?

GENTLEMAN Something he left imperfect in the state, 3
which since his coming forth is thought of, which im- 4
ports to the kingdom so much fear and danger that his 5
personal return was most requir'd and necessary.

KENT
Who hath he left behind him general?

GENTLEMAN
The Marshal of France, Monsieur La Far.

KENT Did your letters pierce the Queen to any demonstration of grief?

43 head-lugg'd dragged by the head and infuriated **44 madded** driven mad **47 visible** made visible **51 Milk-liver'd** i.e., cowardly **53–54 discerning . . . suffering** able to tell the difference between an insult to your honor and something you should tolerate **55 Fools** i.e., only fools. (Goneril goes on to say that only fools are so tenderhearted as to worry about injustices to potential troublemakers, like Lear and Gloucester, instead of applauding measures taken to insure order.) **56 thy drum** i.e., your military preparations **57 noiseless** peaceful, having none of the bustle of war **58 thy state . . . threat** i.e., France begins to threaten your kingdom **59 moral** moralizing **60 why does he so** i.e., why does the King of France invade England **61 Proper deformity** i.e., the deformity appropriate to the fiend **63 changed** transformed. **self-cover'd** having the true nature concealed **64 Be-monster . . . feature** i.e., do not, however evil you are, take on the outward form of a monster or fiend. **my fitness** suitable for me **65 blood** passion **69 mew** (An exclamation of disgust; or, *mew up,* restrain as one restrains a falcon.) **74 bred** nurtured, trained. **thrill'd with remorse** deeply moved with pity **75–76 bending . . . To** directing his sword against

77 amongst them together with the others (?) in their midst (?) out of their number (?) **79 after** along (to death) **80 nether** i.e., committed here below, on earth **84 One way** i.e., because Edmund is now Duke of Gloucester and Cornwall, a dangerous rival for the throne, is dead **86–87 May . . . life** i.e., may pull down my imagined happiness (of possessing the entire kingdom with Edmund) and make hateful my life **88 tart** bitter, sour **91 back** going back

IV.iii. Location: The French camp near Dover.
3 imperfect in the state unsettled in state affairs **4–5 imports** portends

GENTLEMAN
Ay, sir. She took them, read them in my presence,
And now and then an ample tear trill'd down 12
Her delicate cheek. It seem'd she was a queen
Over her passion, who, most rebel-like,
Sought to be king o'er her.

KENT
O, then it moved her?

GENTLEMAN
Not to a rage. Patience and sorrow strove
Who should express her goodliest. You have seen
Sunshine and rain at once. Her smiles and tears
Were like a better way; those happy smilets 19
That play'd on her ripe lip seem'd not to know
What guests were in her eyes, which parted thence
As pearls from diamonds dropp'd. In brief,
Sorrow would be a rarity most beloved,
If all could so become it. 24

KENT
Made she no verbal question?

GENTLEMAN
Faith, once or twice she heav'd the name of "father" 26
Pantingly forth, as if it press'd her heart;
Cried "Sisters, sisters! Shame of ladies, sisters!
Kent! Father! Sisters! What, i' th' storm, i' th' night?
Let pity not be believ'd!" There she shook 30
The holy water from her heavenly eyes,
And, clamor-moistened, then away she started 32
To deal with grief alone.

KENT
It is the stars,
The stars above us, govern our conditions, 34
Else one self mate and make could not beget 35
Such different issues. You spoke not with her since? 36

GENTLEMAN
No.

KENT
Was this before the King return'd?

GENTLEMAN
No, since.

KENT
Well, sir, the poor distressed Lear 's i' th' town,
Who sometime, in his better tune, remembers 40
What we are come about, and by no means
Will yield to see his daughter.

GENTLEMAN
Why, good sir?

KENT
A sovereign shame so elbows him—his own
unkindness, 43
That stripp'd her from his benediction, turn'd her
To foreign casualties, gave her dear rights 45
To his dog-hearted daughters—these things sting
His mind so venomously, that burning shame
Detains him from Cordelia.

GENTLEMAN
Alack, poor gentleman!

KENT
Of Albany's and Cornwall's powers you heard not?

GENTLEMAN
'Tis so, they are afoot.

KENT
Well, sir, I'll bring you to our master Lear,
And leave you to attend him. Some dear cause 53
Will in concealment wrap me up awhile;
When I am known aright, you shall not grieve
Lending me this acquaintance. I pray you go
Along with me. *Exeunt.*]

SCENE [IV]

Enter, with drum and colors, Cordelia, Doctor, and Soldiers.

CORDELIA
Alack, 'tis he! Why, he was met even now
As mad as the vex'd sea, singing aloud,
Crown'd with rank fumiter and furrow-weeds, 3
With hardocks, hemlock, nettles, cuckoo-flow'rs, 4
Darnel, and all the idle weeds that grow 5
In our sustaining corn. A century send forth! 6
Search every acre in the high-grown field,
And bring him to our eye. [*Exit an Officer.*] What
can man's wisdom 8
In the restoring his bereaved sense?
He that helps him take all my outward worth. 10

DOCTOR
There is means, madam.
Our foster-nurse of nature is repose,
The which he lacks. That to provoke in him 13
Are many simples operative, whose power 14
Will close the eye of anguish.

CORDELIA
All blest secrets,
All you unpublish'd virtues of the earth, 16
Spring with my tears! Be aidant and remediate 17
In the good man's distress! Seek, seek for him,
Lest his ungovern'd rage dissolve the life
That wants the means to lead it.

Enter Messenger.

MESSENGER
News, madam. 20
The British pow'rs are marching hitherward.

CORDELIA
'Tis known before. Our preparation stands
In expectation of them. O dear father,
It is thy business that I go about;
Therefore great France
My mourning and importun'd tears hath pitied. 26

12 trill'd trickled **19 like a better way** better than that, though similar **24 If . . . it** i.e., if all persons were as attractive in sorrow as she **26 heav'd** breathed out **30 believ'd** i.e., believed to be extant **32 clamor-moistened** i.e., her outcry of grief assuaged by tears. **started** i.e., went **34 conditions** characters **35 Else . . . make** otherwise, one couple (husband and wife) **36 issues** offspring **40 better tune** more composed state **43 sovereign** overruling. **elbows** i.e., prods his memory **45 foreign casualties** chances of fortune abroad

53 dear cause important purpose

IV.iv. Location: The French camp.
3 fumiter i.e., fumitory, a weed or herb **4 hardocks** i.e., burdocks or hoardocks, white-leaved **5 Darnel** (A weed of the grass kind.) **idle** worthless **6 sustaining** giving sustenance. **corn** grain. **century** troop of 100 men **8 What . . . wisdom** whatever can man's knowledge accomplish **10 outward** material **13 That to provoke** to induce that **14 simples** medicinal plants. **operative** effective **16 unpublish'd virtues** little-known benign herbs **17 Spring** grow. **aidant and remediate** helpful and remedial **20 wants** lacks. **means** i.e., his reason **26 importun'd** importunate

No blown ambition doth our arms incite,
But love, dear love, and our ag'd father's right.
Soon may I hear and see him! *Exeunt.*

SCENE [V]

Enter Regan and Steward [*Oswald*].

REGAN
But are my brother's pow'rs set forth?
OSWALD
Ay, madam.
REGAN
Himself in person there?
OSWALD
Madam, with much ado.
Your sister is the better soldier.
REGAN
Lord Edmund spake not with your lord at home?
OSWALD
No, madam.
REGAN
What might import my sister's letter to him?
OSWALD
I know not, lady.
REGAN
Faith, he is posted hence on serious matter.
It was great ignorance, Gloucester's eyes being out,
To let him live. Where he arrives he moves
All hearts against us. Edmund, I think, is gone,
In pity of his misery, to dispatch
His nighted life; moreover, to descry
The strength o' th' enemy.
OSWALD
I must needs after him, madam, with my letter.
REGAN
Our troops set forth tomorrow. Stay with us;
The ways are dangerous.
OSWALD I may not, madam.
My lady charg'd my duty in this business.
REGAN
Why should she write to Edmund? Might not you
Transport her purposes by word? Belike
Something—I know not what. I'll love thee much,
Let me unseal the letter.
OSWALD Madam, I had rather—
REGAN
I know your lady does not love her husband,
I am sure of that; and at her late being here
She gave strange oeillades and most speaking looks
To noble Edmund. I know you are of her bosom.
OSWALD
I, madam?

27 blown puffed up with pride

IV.v. Location: Gloucester's house.
8 import bear as its purport, express **10 is posted** has hurried **11 ignorance** error **15 nighted** benighted, blinded **20 charg'd** ordered strictly **22 Belike** it may be **26 late** recently **27 oeillades** amorous glances **28 of her bosom** in her confidence

REGAN
I speak in understanding; y' are, I know 't.
Therefore I do advise you, take this note:
My lord is dead; Edmund and I have talk'd,
And more convenient is he for my hand
Than for your lady's. You may gather more.
If you do find him, pray you, give him this;
And when your mistress hears thus much from you,
I pray, desire her call her wisdom to her.
So, fare you well.
If you do chance to hear of that blind traitor,
Preferment falls on him that cuts him off.
OSWALD
Would I could meet him, madam! I should show
What party I do follow.
REGAN Fare thee well.
Exeunt [*severally*].

SCENE [VI]

Enter Gloucester [*being led*], *and Edgar* [*dressed like a peasant*].

GLOUCESTER
When shall I come to th' top of that same hill?
EDGAR
You do climb up it now. Look how we labor.
GLOUCESTER
Methinks the ground is even.
EDGAR Horrible steep.
Hark, do you hear the sea?
GLOUCESTER No, truly.
EDGAR
Why, then, your other senses grow imperfect
By your eyes' anguish.
GLOUCESTER So may it be, indeed.
Methinks thy voice is alter'd, and thou speak'st
In better phrase and matter than thou didst.
EDGAR
Y' are much deceiv'd. In nothing am I chang'd
But in my garments.
GLOUCESTER Methinks y' are better spoken.
EDGAR
Come on, sir, here's the place. Stand still. How fearful
And dizzy 'tis, to cast one's eyes so low!
The crows and choughs that wing the midway air
Show scarce so gross as beetles. Half way down
Hangs one that gathers samphire, dreadful trade!
Methinks he seems no bigger than his head.
The fishermen that walk upon the beach
Appear like mice; and yond tall anchoring bark,
Diminish'd to her cock; her cock, a buoy

31 take this note i.e., mark this advice **34 gather more** i.e., infer what I am trying to suggest **35 this** i.e., this information **37 call . . . to her** recall her to her senses **40 Preferment** advancement

IV.vi. Location: Open place near Dover.
13 choughs jackdaws. **midway** halfway down **14 gross** large **15 samphire** (A herb used for pickles.) **19 Diminish'd . . . cock** reduced to the size of her cockboat, small ship's boat

Almost too small for sight. The murmuring surge,
That on th' unnumb'red idle pebbles chafes, 21
Cannot be heard so high. I'll look no more,
Lest my brain turn, and the deficient sight 23
Topple down headlong.

GLOUCESTER Set me where you stand. 24

EDGAR
Give me your hand. You are now within a foot
Of th' extreme verge. For all beneath the moon
Would I not leap upright.

GLOUCESTER Let go my hand. 27
Here, friend, 's another purse; in it a jewel
Well worth a poor man's taking. Fairies and gods
Prosper it with thee! [*Gives purse.*] Go thou further off.
Bid me farewell, and let me hear thee going.

EDGAR [*Moving away*]
Now fare ye well, good sir.

GLOUCESTER With all my heart.

EDGAR [*Aside*]
Why I do trifle thus with his despair
Is done to cure it.

GLOUCESTER [*Kneeling*] O you mighty gods!
This world I do renounce, and in your sights
Shake patiently my great affliction off.
If I could bear it longer, and not fall
To quarrel with your great opposeless wills, 38
My snuff and loathed part of nature should 39
Burn itself out. If Edgar live, O, bless him!
Now, fellow, fare thee well. [*He falls forward.*]

EDGAR Gone, sir. Farewell.—
And yet I know not how conceit may rob 42
The treasury of life, when life itself
Yields to the theft. Had he been where he thought, 44
By this, had thought been past. Alive or dead?—
Ho, you sir! Friend! Hear you, sir! Speak!—
Thus might he pass indeed; yet he revives.— 47
What are you, sir?

GLOUCESTER Away, and let me die. 48

EDGAR
Hadst thou been aught but gossamer, feathers, air,
So many fathom down precipitating,
Thou 'dst shiver'd like an egg; but thou dost breathe,
Hast heavy substance, bleed'st not, speak'st, art sound.
Ten masts at each make not the altitude 53
Which thou hast perpendicularly fell.
Thy life's a miracle. Speak yet again.

GLOUCESTER
But have I fall'n, or no?

EDGAR
From the dread summit of this chalky bourn. 57
Look up a-height; the shrill-gorg'd lark so far 58
Cannot be seen or heard. Do but look up.

GLOUCESTER
Alack, I have no eyes.
Is wretchedness depriv'd that benefit
To end itself by death? 'Twas yet some comfort
When misery could beguile the tyrant's rage, 63
And frustrate his proud will.

EDGAR Give me your arm.
[*Lifts him up.*]
Up—so. How is 't? Feel you your legs? You stand.

GLOUCESTER
Too well, too well.

EDGAR This is above all strangeness.
Upon the crown o' th' cliff, what thing was that
Which parted from you?

GLOUCESTER A poor unfortunate beggar.

EDGAR
As I stood here below, methought his eyes
Were two full moons; he had a thousand noses,
Horns whelk'd and waved like the enridged sea. 71
It was some fiend. Therefore, thou happy father, 72
Think that the clearest gods, who make them honors 73
Of men's impossibilities, have preserved thee. 74

GLOUCESTER
I do remember now. Henceforth I'll bear
Affliction till it do cry out itself
"Enough, enough," and die. That thing you speak of,
I took it for a man; often 'twould say
"The fiend, the fiend." He led me to that place.

EDGAR
Bear free and patient thoughts.

Enter Lear [*mad, bedecked with weeds*].

But who comes here? 80
The safer sense will ne'er accommodate 81
His master thus.

LEAR No, they cannot touch me for coining; I am the King himself. 83

EDGAR
O thou side-piercing sight!

LEAR Nature's above art in that respect. There's your 86
press-money. That fellow handles his bow like a crow- 87
keeper; draw me a clothier's yard. Look, look, a 88
mouse! Peace, peace; this piece of toasted cheese will
do 't. There's my gauntlet; I'll prove it on a giant. Bring 90
up the brown bills. O, well flown, bird! I' th' clout, i' 91
th' clout—hewgh! Give the word. 92

21 unnumb'red innumerable **23–24 the deficient sight Topple** my failing sight topple me **27 upright** i.e., up and down, much less forward **38 To quarrel with** into rebellion against. **opposeless** irresistible **39 snuff** i.e., useless residue. (Literally, the smoking wick of a candle.) **of nature** i.e., of my life **42 conceit** imagination **44 Yields** consents **47 pass** die **48 What** who. (Edgar now speaks in a new voice, differing from that of "poor Tom" and also from the "alter'd" voice he used at the start of this scene; see ll. 7–10.) **53 at each** end to end **57 bourn** limit, boundary

58 a-height on high. **shrill-gorg'd** shrill-throated **63 beguile** outwit **71 whelk'd** twisted, convoluted. **enridged** furrowed (by the wind) **72 happy father** lucky old man **73 clearest** purest, most righteous **73–74 who . . . impossibilities** who win our awe and reverence by doing things impossible to men **80 free** i.e., free from despair **81 The safer sense** a sane mind. **accommodate** furnish, dress **83 touch** arrest, prosecute. **coining** minting coins. (A royal prerogative; the King wants money for his imaginary soldiers, ll. 86–87.) **86 Nature's . . . respect** i.e., a king, graced with divine right like Nature herself, is above the forger who learns his craft by art or skill (?) **87 press-money** enlistment bonus **87–88 crow-keeper** laborer hired to scare away the crows **88 me** for me. **clothier's yard** arrow the length of a cloth yard **90 do 't** i.e., capture the mouse, an imagined enemy. **gauntlet** armored glove thrown down as a challenge. **prove it on** maintain it against **91 brown bills** soldiers carrying pikes (painted brown), or the pikes themselves. **well flown, bird** (Lear uses the language of hawking to describe the flight of an arrow.) **92 clout** target, bull's eye. **word** password

EDGAR Sweet marjoram.
LEAR Pass.
GLOUCESTER
I know that voice.
LEAR Ha! Goneril, with a white beard? They flatter'd me like a dog, and told me I had white hairs in my beard ere the black ones were there. To say "ay" and "no" to everything that I said! "Ay," and "no" too, was no good divinity. When the rain came to wet me once, and the wind to make me chatter, when the thunder would not peace at my bidding, there I found 'em, there I smelt 'em out. Go to, they are not men o' their words. They told me I was everything. 'Tis a lie, I am not ague-proof.
GLOUCESTER
The trick of that voice I do well remember.
Is 't not the King?
LEAR Ay, every inch a king.
When I do stare, see how the subject quakes.
I pardon that man's life. What was thy cause?
Adultery?
Thou shalt not die. Die for adultery? No.
The wren goes to 't, and the small gilded fly
Does lecher in my sight.
Let copulation thrive; for Gloucester's bastard son
Was kinder to his father than my daughters
Got 'tween the lawful sheets.
To 't, luxury, pell-mell, for I lack soldiers.
Behold yond simp'ring dame,
Whose face between her forks presages snow,
That minces virtue, and does shake the head
To hear of pleasure's name;
The fitchew, nor the soiled horse, goes to 't
With a more riotous appetite.
Down from the waist they are Centaurs,
Though women all above.
But to the girdle do the gods inherit,
Beneath is all the fiends'.
There's hell, there's darkness, there is the sulphurous pit,
Burning, scalding, stench, consumption. Fie, fie, fie!
Pah, pah! Give me an ounce of civet, good apothecary, sweeten my imagination. There's money for thee.
GLOUCESTER
O, let me kiss that hand!
LEAR Let me wipe it first; it smells of mortality.
GLOUCESTER
O ruin'd piece of nature! This great world
Shall so wear out to nought. Dost thou know me?
LEAR I remember thine eyes well enough. Dost thou squiny at me? No, do thy worst, blind Cupid; I'll not love. Read thou this challenge; mark but the penning of it.
GLOUCESTER
Were all thy letters suns, I could not see.
EDGAR [*Aside*]
I would not take this from report; it is,
And my heart breaks at it.
LEAR Read.
GLOUCESTER
What, with the case of eyes?
LEAR O, ho, are you there with me? No eyes in your head, nor no money in your purse? Your eyes are in a heavy case, your purse in a light; yet you see how this world goes.
GLOUCESTER
I see it feelingly.
LEAR What, art mad? A man may see how this world goes with no eyes. Look with thine ears. See how yond justice rails upon yond simple thief. Hark in thine ear: change places, and, handy-dandy, which is the justice, which is the thief? Thou hast seen a farmer's dog bark at a beggar?
GLOUCESTER
Ay, sir.
LEAR And the creature run from the cur? There thou mightst behold the great image of authority; a dog's obey'd in office.
Thou rascal beadle, hold thy bloody hand!
Why dost thou lash that whore? Strip thy own back;
Thou hotly lusts to use her in that kind
For which thou whipp'st her. The usurer hangs the cozener.
Through tatter'd clothes small vices do appear;
Robes and furr'd gowns hide all. Plate sin with gold,
And the strong lance of justice hurtless breaks;
Arm it in rags, a pigmy's straw does pierce it.
None does offend, none, I say, none! I'll able 'em.
Take that of me, my friend, who have the power
To seal th' accuser's lips. Get thee glass eyes,
And, like a scurvy politician, seem
To see the things thou dost not. Now, now, now, now!
Pull off my boots. Harder, harder! So.
EDGAR [*Aside*]
O, matter and impertinency mix'd!
Reason in madness!
LEAR
If thou wilt weep my fortunes, take my eyes.
I know thee well enough; thy name is Gloucester.
Thou must be patient. We came crying hither.
Thou know'st, the first time that we smell the air
We wawl and cry. I will preach to thee. Mark.
GLOUCESTER
Alack, alack the day!
LEAR
When we are born, we cry that we are come

93 Sweet marjoram (A herb used to cure madness.) **97 like a dog** i.e., as a dog fawns **97–98 had . . . beard** i.e., had wisdom **98–99 To . . . "no"** i.e., to agree **100 no good divinity** not good theology, contrary to biblical teaching. (See II Cor. 1:18 and James 5:12.) **102–103 found 'em** found them out **106 trick** peculiar characteristic **109 cause** offense **117 luxury** lechery **119 Whose . . . snow** whose frosty countenance seems to suggest frigidity between her legs **120 minces** affects, mimics **121 pleasure's name** i.e., any talk of sexual pleasure **122 fitchew** polecat. **soiled horse** horse turned out to grass **124 Centaurs** incontinent monsters, half man, half horse **126 But** only. **girdle** waist. **inherit** possess **130 civet** musk perfume **134 piece** masterpiece. **This great world** i.e., the macrocosm, of which man, the masterpiece of nature, is the microcosm **135 so** similarly **137 squiny** squint

141 take believe, credit **144 case** mere sockets **145 are . . . me** is that your situation **147 heavy case** sad plight (with pun on *case* in l. 144) **149 feelingly** (1) by touch (2) keenly, painfully **153 handy-dandy** take your choice of hands (as in a well-known child's game) **157 creature** poor fellow **158–159 a dog's . . . office** i.e., even currish power commands submission **160 beadle** parish officer, responsible for giving whippings **162 kind** way **163 The usurer** i.e., a judge guilty of lending money at usurious rates. **cozener** petty cheater **166 hurtless breaks** splinters harmlessly **168 able** give warrant to **169 that** i.e., a guarantee of immunity **170 glass eyes** spectacles (?) **171 politician** opportunist **174 matter and impertinency** sense and nonsense

To this great stage of fools.—This' a good block. 183
It were a delicate stratagem to shoe 184
A troop of horse with felt. I'll put 't in proof, 185
And when I have stol'n upon these son-in-laws,
Then, kill, kill, kill, kill, kill, kill!

Enter a Gentleman [with Attendants].

GENTLEMAN
O, here he is. Lay hand upon him.—Sir,
Your most dear daughter—

LEAR
No rescue? What, a prisoner? I am even
The natural fool of fortune. Use me well; 191
You shall have ransom. Let me have surgeons;
I am cut to th' brains.

GENTLEMAN You shall have anything. 193

LEAR
No seconds? All myself? 194
Why, this would make a man a man of salt 195
To use his eyes for garden water-pots,
[Ay, and laying autumn's dust.

GENTLEMAN Good sir—]

LEAR
I will die bravely, like a smug bridegroom. What? 198
I will be jovial. Come, come, I am a king,
Masters, know you that?

GENTLEMAN
You are a royal one, and we obey you.

LEAR Then there's life in 't. Come, an you get it, you 202
shall get it by running. Sa, sa, sa, sa. 203
Exit [running; Attendants follow].

GENTLEMAN
A sight most pitiful in the meanest wretch,
Past speaking of in a king! Thou hast one daughter
Who redeems nature from the general curse 206
Which twain have brought her to.

EDGAR
Hail, gentle sir.

GENTLEMAN Sir, speed you. What's your will? 208

EDGAR
Do you hear aught, sir, of a battle toward? 209

GENTLEMAN
Most sure and vulgar. Everyone hears that 210
Which can distinguish sound.

EDGAR But, by your favor, 211
How near's the other army?

GENTLEMAN
Near and on speedy foot. The main descry 213
Stands on the hourly thought. 214

EDGAR
I thank you, sir; that's all.

GENTLEMAN
Though that the Queen on special cause is here, 216
Her army is mov'd on.

EDGAR I thank you, sir.
Exit [Gentleman].

GLOUCESTER
You ever-gentle gods, take my breath from me;
Let not my worser spirit tempt me again 219
To die before you please!

EDGAR Well pray you, father.

GLOUCESTER
Now, good sir, what are you? 221

EDGAR
A most poor man, made tame to fortune's blows,
Who, by the art of known and feeling sorrows, 223
Am pregnant to good pity. Give me your hand, 224
I'll lead you to some biding. *[Offers his arm.]*

GLOUCESTER Hearty thanks. 225
The bounty and the benison of heaven 226
To boot, and boot!

Enter Steward [Oswald].

OSWALD A proclaim'd prize! Most happy! 227
[Draws sword.]
That eyeless head of thine was first fram'd flesh 228
To raise my fortunes. Thou old unhappy traitor,
Briefly thyself remember. The sword is out 230
That must destroy thee.

GLOUCESTER Now let thy friendly hand
Put strength enough to 't. *[Edgar interposes.]*

OSWALD Wherefore, bold peasant,
Dar'st thou support a publish'd traitor? Hence, 233
Lest that th' infection of his fortune take
Like hold on thee. Let go his arm.

EDGAR 'Chill not let go, zir, without vurther 'casion. 236

OSWALD
Let go, slave, or thou diest!

EDGAR Good gentleman, go your gait, and let poor volk 238
pass. An 'chud ha' bin zwagger'd out of my life, 239
'twould not ha' bin zo long as 'tis by a vortnight. Nay,
come not near th' old man; keep out, 'che vor ye, or 241
Ise try whether your costard or my ballow be the 242
harder. 'Chill be plain with you.

OSWALD
Out, dunghill! *[They fight.]*

EDGAR 'Chill pick your teeth, zir. Come, no matter vor
your foins. *[Edgar fells him with his cudgel.]* 246

OSWALD
Slave, thou hast slain me. Villain, take my purse.
If ever thou wilt thrive, bury my body,
And give the letters which thou find'st about me 249
To Edmund Earl of Gloucester; seek him out
Upon the English party. O, untimely death! 251
Death! *[Dies.]*

183 This' this is. **block** felt hat (?) (Lear may refer to the weeds strewn in his hair, which he removes as though doffing a hat before preaching a sermon.) **184 delicate** subtle **185 in proof** to the test **191 natural fool** born plaything **193 cut** wounded **194 seconds** supporters **195 of salt** of salt tears **198 smug** trimly dressed. (*Bridegroom* continues the punning sexual suggestion of *die bravely,* have sex successfully.) **202 life** i.e., hope still **203 Sa . . . sa** (A hunting cry.) **206 general curse** universal damnation **208 speed** God speed **209 toward** imminent **210 vulgar** in everyone's mouth, generally known **211 Which** who **213–214 The main . . . thought** the full view of the main body is expected every hour **216 on special cause** for a special reason, i.e., to minister to Lear

219 worser spirit bad angel **221 what** who. (Again, Edgar alters his voice to personate a new stranger assisting Gloucester. See l. 48, above, and note.) **223 feeling** heartfelt, deep **224 pregnant** prone **225 biding** abiding place **226–227 The bounty . . . and boot** i.e., in addition to my thanks, I wish you the bounty of heaven **227 proclaim'd prize** one with a price on his head. **happy** fortunate **228 fram'd flesh** born **230 thyself remember** i.e., confess your sins **233 publish'd** proclaimed **236 'Chill** I will. (Literally, a contraction of *Ich will.* Edgar adopts Somerset dialect, a stage convention regularly used for peasants.) **238 go your gait** go your own way **239 An 'chud** if I could. **zwagger'd** swaggered, bluffed **241 'che vor ye** I warrant you **242 Ise** I shall. **costard** head. (Literally, an apple.) **ballow** cudgel **246 foins** thrusts **249 letters** letter. **about me** upon my person **251 party** side

EDGAR
I know thee well: a serviceable villain,
As duteous to the vices of thy mistress
As badness would desire.

GLOUCESTER
What, is he dead?

EDGAR
Sit you down, father; rest you. [*Gloucester sits.*]
Let's see these pockets; the letters that he speaks of
May be my friends. He's dead; I am only sorry
He had no other deathsman. Let us see.
[*Finds letter, and opens it.*]
Leave, gentle wax, and, manners, blame us not.
To know our enemies' minds, we rip their hearts;
Their papers is more lawful. *(Reads the letter.)*

"Let our reciprocal vows be remember'd. You have many opportunities to cut him off; if your will want not, time and place will be fruitfully offer'd. There is nothing done, if he return the conqueror. Then am I the prisoner, and his bed my jail, from the loath'd warmth whereof deliver me, and supply the place for your labor.

"Your—wife, so I would say—
"Affectionate servant, Goneril."

O indistinguish'd space of woman's will!
A plot upon her virtuous husband's life,
And the exchange my brother! Here, in the sands,
Thee I'll rake up, the post unsanctified
Of murderous lechers; and in the mature time
With this ungracious paper strike the sight
Of the death-practic'd Duke. For him 'tis well
That of thy death and business I can tell.

GLOUCESTER
The King is mad. How stiff is my vile sense,
That I stand up, and have ingenious feeling
Of my huge sorrows! Better I were distract;
So should my thoughts be sever'd from my griefs,
And woes by wrong imaginations lose
The knowledge of themselves. *Drum afar off.*

EDGAR
Give me your hand.
Far off, methinks, I hear the beaten drum.
Come, father, I'll bestow you with a friend. *Exeunt.*

SCENE VII

Enter Cordelia, Kent [dressed still in his disguise costume, Doctor,] and Gentleman.

CORDELIA
O thou good Kent, how shall I live and work
To match thy goodness? My life will be too short,
And every measure fail me.

KENT
To be acknowledg'd, madam, is o'erpaid.
All my reports go with the modest truth,
Nor more nor clipp'd, but so.

CORDELIA
Be better suited.
These weeds are memories of those worser hours;
I prithee, put them off.

KENT
Pardon, dear madam;
Yet to be known shortens my made intent.
My boon I make it that you know me not
Till time and I think meet.

CORDELIA
Then be 't so, my good lord. [*To the Doctor.*] How does the King?

DOCTOR
Madam, sleeps still.

CORDELIA
O you kind gods,
Cure this great breach in his abused nature!
Th' untun'd and jarring senses, O, wind up
Of this child-changed father!

DOCTOR
So please your Majesty
That we may wake the King? He hath slept long.

CORDELIA
Be govern'd by your knowledge, and proceed
I' th' sway of your own will. Is he array'd?

Enter Lear in a chair carried by Servants.

GENTLEMAN
Ay, madam; in the heaviness of sleep
We put fresh garments on him.

DOCTOR
Be by, good madam, when we do awake him.
I doubt not of his temperance.

[CORDELIA
Very well. [*Music.*]

DOCTOR
Please you, draw near.—Louder the music there!]

CORDELIA
O my dear father! Restoration hang
Thy medicine on my lips, and let this kiss
Repair those violent harms that my two sisters
Have in thy reverence made! [*Kisses him.*]

KENT
Kind and dear princess!

CORDELIA
Had you not been their father, these white flakes
Did challenge pity of them. Was this a face
To be oppos'd against the warring winds?
[To stand against the deep dread-bolted thunder?
In the most terrible and nimble stroke
Of quick cross lightning? To watch—poor perdu!—
With this thin helm?] Mine enemy's dog,
Though he had bit me, should have stood that night
Against my fire; and wast thou fain, poor father,

253 serviceable officious **259 deathsman** executioner **260 Leave** by your leave. **wax** wax seal on the letter **264–265 want not** is not lacking **272 indistinguish'd . . . will** incalculable range of woman's appetite **275 rake up** cover up. **post unsanctified** unholy messenger **276 in . . . time** when the time is ripe **277 ungracious** wicked. **strike** blast **278 death-practic'd** whose death is plotted **280 stiff** obstinate. **sense** consciousness, sanity **281 ingenious** conscious **282 distract** distracted, crazy **284 wrong imaginations** delusions **287 bestow** lodge. (At the scene's end, Edgar leads off Gloucester; presumably he also disposes of Oswald's body, which must be removed from the stage or somehow concealed.)

IV.vii. Location: A tent in the French camp.

5 go conform **6 Nor . . . clipp'd** i.e., neither more nor less. **suited** dressed **7 weeds** garments. **memories** remembrances **9 Yet . . . intent** i.e., to reveal my true identity now would alter my carefully made plan **10 My . . . it** the reward I seek is **11 meet** appropriate **16 wind up** tune (as by winding the slackened string of an instrument) **17 child-changed** changed (in mind) by children's cruelty **21 I' th' sway** under the direction **31 Had you** even if you had. **flakes** locks of hair **32 Did challenge** would have demanded **34 dread-bolted** furnished with the dreadful thunderstone **36 perdu** soldier placed in a position of peculiar danger **37 helm** helmet, i.e., his scanty hair

To hovel thee with swine, and rogues forlorn,
In short and musty straw? Alack, alack!
'Tis wonder that thy life and wits at once
Had not concluded all.—He wakes; speak to him.

DOCTOR
Madam, do you; 'tis fittest.

CORDELIA
How does my royal lord? How fares your Majesty?

LEAR
You do me wrong to take me out o' th' grave.
Thou art a soul in bliss; but I am bound
Upon a wheel of fire, that mine own tears
Do scald like molten lead.

CORDELIA Sir, do you know me?

LEAR
You are a spirit, I know. When did you die?

CORDELIA
Still, still, far wide!

DOCTOR
He's scarce awake. Let him alone awhile.

LEAR
Where have I been? Where am I? Fair daylight?
I am mightily abus'd. I should e'en die with pity
To see another thus. I know not what to say.
I will not swear these are my hands. Let's see;
I feel this pin prick. Would I were assur'd
Of my condition!

CORDELIA O, look upon me, sir,
And hold your hand in benediction o'er me.
[*He attempts to kneel.*]
You must not kneel.

LEAR
Pray, do not mock me.
I am a very foolish fond old man,
Fourscore and upward, not an hour more nor less;
And, to deal plainly,
I fear I am not in my perfect mind.
Methinks I should know you, and know this man,
Yet I am doubtful; for I am mainly ignorant
What place this is, and all the skill I have
Remembers not these garments, nor I know not
Where I did lodge last night. Do not laugh at me;
For, as I am a man, I think this lady
To be my child Cordelia.

CORDELIA [*Weeping*] And so I am, I am.

LEAR
Be your tears wet? Yes, faith. I pray weep not.
If you have poison for me, I will drink it.
I know you do not love me; for your sisters
Have, as I do remember, done me wrong.
You have some cause, they have not.

CORDELIA No cause, no cause.

LEAR
Am I in France?

KENT In your own kingdom, sir.

LEAR
Do not abuse me.

DOCTOR
Be comforted, good madam. The great rage,
You see, is kill'd in him, [and yet it is danger
To make him even o'er the time he has lost.]
Desire him to go in. Trouble him no more
Till further settling.

CORDELIA
Will 't please your Highness walk?

LEAR
You must bear with me.
Pray you now, forget and forgive.
I am old and foolish.
Exeunt [*all but Kent and Gentleman*].

[GENTLEMAN Holds it true, sir, that the Duke of Cornwall was so slain?

KENT Most certain, sir.

GENTLEMAN Who is conductor of his people?

KENT As 'tis said, the bastard son of Gloucester.

GENTLEMAN They say Edgar, his banish'd son, is with the Earl of Kent in Germany.

KENT Report is changeable. 'Tis time to look about; the powers of the kingdom approach apace.

GENTLEMAN The arbitrement is like to be bloody. Fare you well, sir. [*Exit.*]

KENT
My point and period will be throughly wrought,
Or well or ill, as this day's battle's fought. [*Exit.*]]

ACT V • SCENE I

Enter, with drum and colors, Edmund, Regan, Gentlemen, and Soldiers.

EDMUND
Know of the Duke if his last purpose hold,
Or whether since he is advis'd by aught
To change the course. He's full of alteration
And self-reproving. Bring his constant pleasure.
[*To a Gentleman, who goes out.*]

REGAN
Our sister's man is certainly miscarried.

EDMUND
'Tis to be doubted, madam.

REGAN Now, sweet lord,
You know the goodness I intend upon you.
Tell me, but truly—but then speak the truth—
Do you not love my sister?

EDMUND In honor'd love.

REGAN
But have you never found my brother's way
To the forfended place?

43 concluded all come to an end altogether **48 wheel of fire** (A hellish torment for the eternally damned.) **54 abus'd** confused **67 mainly** perfectly **79 abuse** deceive

82 even o'er fill in, go over in his mind **84 settling** composing of his mind **97 powers** armies **98 arbitrement** decision by arms **100 My . . . wrought** i.e., the conclusion of my destiny will be thoroughly brought about **101 Or** either. **as** according as

V.i. Location: The British camp near Dover.
1 Know inquire. **last purpose hold** most recent intention (to fight) remain firm **2 since** since then. **advis'd** persuaded **4 constant pleasure** settled decision **5 miscarried** lost, perished **6 doubted** feared **7 intend** intend to confer **9 honor'd** honorable **11 forfended** forbidden

[EDMUND
That thought abuses you.

REGAN
I am doubtful that you have been conjunct
And bosom'd with her, as far as we call hers.]

EDMUND
No, by mine honor, madam.

REGAN
I never shall endure her. Dear my lord,
Be not familiar with her.

EDMUND
Fear me not.—She and the Duke her husband!

Enter, with drum and colors, Albany, Goneril, [and] Soldiers.

[GONERIL [*Aside*]
I had rather lose the battle than that sister
Should loosen him and me.]

ALBANY
Our very loving sister, well be-met.
Sir, this I heard: the King is come to his daughter,
With others whom the rigor of our state
Forc'd to cry out. [Where I could not be honest,
I never yet was valiant. For this business,
It touches us as France invades our land,
Not bolds the King, with others whom, I fear,
Most just and heavy causes make oppose.

EDMUND
Sir, you speak nobly.]

REGAN Why is this reason'd?

GONERIL
Combine together 'gainst the enemy;
For these domestic and particular broils
Are not the question here.

ALBANY Let's then determine
With th' ancient of war on our proceeding.

[EDMUND
I shall attend you presently at your tent.]

REGAN
Sister, you'll go with us?

GONERIL
No.

REGAN
'Tis most convenient. Pray go with us.

GONERIL [*Aside*]
O, ho, I know the riddle.—I will go.

[*As they are going out,*] *enter Edgar* [*disguised*].

EDGAR [*To Albany*]
If e'er your Grace had speech with man so poor,
Hear me one word.

ALBANY [*To his troops*] I'll overtake you.—Speak.
Exeunt both the armies.

EDGAR
Before you fight the battle, ope this letter.
[*Gives letter.*]
If you have victory, let the trumpet sound
For him that brought it. Wretched though I seem,
I can produce a champion that will prove
What is avouched there. If you miscarry,
Your business of the world hath so an end,
And machination ceases. Fortune love you!

ALBANY
Stay till I have read the letter.

EDGAR
I was forbid it.
When time shall serve, let but the herald cry,
And I'll appear again.

ALBANY
Why, fare thee well. I will o'erlook thy paper.
Exit [*Edgar*].

Enter Edmund.

EDMUND
The enemy's in view; draw up your powers.
Here is the guess of their true strength and forces
By diligent discovery; but your haste
Is now urg'd on you.

ALBANY We will greet the time. *Exit.*

EDMUND
To both these sisters have I sworn my love;
Each jealous of the other, as the stung
Are of the adder. Which of them shall I take?
Both? One? Or neither? Neither can be enjoy'd,
If both remain alive. To take the widow
Exasperates, makes mad her sister Goneril;
And hardly shall I carry out my side,
Her husband being alive. Now then, we'll use
His countenance for the battle, which being done,
Let her who would be rid of him devise
His speedy taking off. As for the mercy
Which he intends to Lear and to Cordelia,
The battle done, and they within our power,
Shall never see his pardon; for my state
Stands on me to defend, not to debate.
Exit.

SCENE II

Alarum within. Enter, with drum and colors, Lear, Cordelia, and Soldiers, over the stage; and exeunt.

Enter Edgar and Gloucester.

EDGAR
Here, father, take the shadow of this tree
For your good host; pray that the right may thrive.

12 abuses degrades, wrongs **13–14 I am . . . hers** I suspect that you have been joined together in the fullest manner **17 familiar** intimate **24 honest** honorable **26 touches us as** concerns us insofar as **27 Not . . . others** not because France encourages the King and others **28 heavy causes** weighty reasons. **make oppose** compel to fight (against us) **29 reason'd** argued **31 particular broils** private quarrels **33 ancient of war** veteran officers **37 convenient** proper, befitting **38 know the riddle** i.e., understand Regan's enigmatic demand that Goneril accompany her, which is that Regan wants to keep Goneril from Edmund

42 sound sound a summons **45 miscarry** perish, come to destruction **47 machination** plotting (against your life) **52 o'erlook** peruse **54 guess** estimate **55 discovery** reconnoitering **56 greet the time** meet the occasion **58 jealous** suspicious **63 carry out my side** fulfill my ambition, and satisfy her (Goneril) **65 countenance** backing, authority of his name **70 Shall** they shall **70–71 my state . . . debate** my position depends upon maintenance by force, not by talk

V.ii. Location: A field between the two camps.

If ever I return to you again,
I'll bring you comfort.

GLOUCESTER
Grace go with you, sir!

Exit [Edgar].

Alarum and retreat within. Enter Edgar.

EDGAR
Away, old man, give me thy hand, away!
King Lear hath lost, he and his daughter ta'en.
Give me thy hand; come on.

GLOUCESTER
No further, sir; a man may rot even here.

EDGAR
What, in ill thoughts again? Men must endure
Their going hence, even as their coming hither;
Ripeness is all. Come on.

GLOUCESTER
And that's true too. 11

Exeunt.

SCENE III

Enter, in conquest, with drum and colors, Edmund; Lear and Cordelia, as prisoners; Soldiers, Captain, [etc.].

EDMUND
Some officers take them away. Good guard,
Until their greater pleasures first be known 2
That are to censure them.

CORDELIA
We are not the first 3
Who, with best meaning, have incurr'd the worst. 4
For thee, oppressed king, I am cast down;
Myself could else out-frown false fortune's frown.
Shall we not see these daughters and these sisters?

LEAR
No, no, no, no! Come, let's away to prison.
We two alone will sing like birds i' th' cage.
When thou dost ask me blessing, I'll kneel down,
And ask of thee forgiveness. So we'll live,
And pray, and sing, and tell old tales, and laugh
At gilded butterflies, and hear poor rogues 13
Talk of court news; and we'll talk with them too—
Who loses and who wins; who's in, who's out—
And take upon 's the mystery of things,
As if we were God's spies; and we'll wear out, 17
In a wall'd prison, packs and sects of great ones, 18
That ebb and flow by th' moon.

EDMUND
Take them away. 19

LEAR
Upon such sacrifices, my Cordelia,
The gods themselves throw incense. Have I caught
thee? 21
He that parts us shall bring a brand from heaven, 22
And fire us hence like foxes. Wipe thine eyes; 23
The good-years shall devour them, flesh and fell, 24
Ere they shall make us weep! We'll see 'em starv'd
first.
Come.

Exit [with Cordelia, guarded].

EDMUND
Come hither, captain; hark.
Take thou this note [*Gives a paper.*]; go follow them
to prison.
One step I have advanc'd thee; if thou dost
As this instructs thee, thou dost make thy way
To noble fortunes. Know thou this, that men
Are as the time is. To be tender-minded
Does not become a sword. Thy great employment 33
Will not bear question; either say thou 'lt do 't, 34
Or thrive by other means.

CAPTAIN
I'll do 't, my lord.

EDMUND
About it; and write happy when th' hast done. 36
Mark, I say, instantly, and carry it so
As I have set it down.

[CAPTAIN
I cannot draw a cart, nor eat dried oats;
If it be man's work, I'll do 't.]

Exit Captain.

Flourish. Enter Albany, Goneril, Regan, [another Captain, and] Soldiers.

ALBANY
Sir, you have show'd today your valiant strain,
And fortune led you well. You have the captives
Who were the opposites of this day's strife; 43
I do require them of you, so to use them
As we shall find their merits and our safety
May equally determine.

EDMUND
Sir, I thought it fit
To send the old and miserable King
To some retention [and appointed guard], 49
Whose age had charms in it, whose title more,
To pluck the common bosom on his side, 51
And turn our impress'd lances in our eyes 52
Which do command them. With him I sent the
Queen, 53
My reason all the same; and they are ready
Tomorrow, or at further space, t' appear 55
Where you shall hold your session. [At this time
We sweat and bleed; the friend hath lost his friend;

11 Ripeness i.e., fulfillment of one's allotted years and readiness for death when it comes

V.iii. Location: The British camp.
2 their greater pleasures i.e., the wishes of those in command **3 censure** judge **4 meaning** intentions **13 gilded butterflies** i.e., gaily dressed courtiers and other ephemeral types **17 God's spies** i.e., detached observers surveying the deeds of mankind from an eternal vantage point. **wear out** outlast **18–19 packs . . . moon** i.e., followers and cliques attached to persons of high station, whose fortunes change erratically and constantly

21 throw incense participate as celebrants **22–23 He . . . foxes** i.e., anyone seeking to part us will have to employ a heavenly firebrand to drive us out of our prison refuge as foxes are driven out of their holes by fire and smoke. (Suggests that only death will part them). **24 good-years** (Apparently a word connoting evil or conceivably the passage of time.) **flesh and fell** flesh and skin, completely **33 become a sword** i.e., suit a warrior **34 bear question** admit of discussion **36 write happy** call yourself fortunate **43 opposites** enemies **49 retention** confinement **51 common bosom** affection of the multitude **52 turn . . . eyes** i.e., turn against us the weapons of those very troops whom we impressed into service **53 Which** we who **55 space** interval of time

And the best quarrels, in the heat, are curs'd
By those that feel their sharpness.
The question of Cordelia and her father
Requires a fitter place.]

ALBANY Sir, by your patience,
I hold you but a subject of this war,
Not as a brother.

REGAN That's as we list to grace him.
Methinks our pleasure might have been demanded
Ere you had spoke so far. He led our powers,
Bore the commission of my place and person;
The which immediacy may well stand up
And call itself your brother.

GONERIL Not so hot.
In his own grace he doth exalt himself
More than in your addition.

REGAN In my rights,
By me invested, he compeers the best.

GONERIL
That were the most if he should husband you.

REGAN
Jesters do oft prove prophets.

GONERIL Holla, holla!
That eye that told you so look'd but a-squint.

REGAN
Lady, I am not well, else I should answer
From a full-flowing stomach. General,
Take thou my soldiers, prisoners, patrimony;
Dispose of them, of me; the walls is thine.
Witness the world that I create thee here
My lord and master.

GONERIL Mean you to enjoy him?

ALBANY
The let-alone lies not in your good will.

EDMUND
Nor in thine, lord.

ALBANY Half-blooded fellow, yes.

REGAN [*To Edmund*]
Let the drum strike, and prove my title thine.

ALBANY
Stay yet; hear reason. Edmund, I arrest thee
On capital treason; and, in thy attaint,
This gilded serpent. [*Points to Goneril.*] For your claim, fair sister,
I bar it in the interest of my wife;
'Tis she is sub-contracted to this lord,
And I, her husband, contradict your banns.
If you will marry, make your loves to me,
My lady is bespoke.

GONERIL An interlude!

ALBANY
Thou art arm'd, Gloucester. Let the trumpet sound.
If none appear to prove upon thy person
Thy heinous, manifest, and many treasons,
There is my pledge. [*Throws down a glove.*] I'll make it on thy heart,
Ere I taste bread, thou art in nothing less
Than I have here proclaim'd thee.

REGAN Sick, O, sick!

GONERIL [*Aside*]
If not, I'll ne'er trust medicine.

EDMUND
There's my exchange. [*Throws down a glove.*] What in the world he is
That names me traitor, villain-like he lies.
Call by the trumpet. He that dares approach,
On him, on you—who not?—I will maintain
My truth and honor firmly.

ALBANY
A herald, ho!

[EDMUND A herald, ho, a herald!]

ALBANY
Trust to thy single virtue; for thy soldiers,
All levied in my name, have in my name
Took their discharge.

REGAN My sickness grows upon me.

ALBANY
She is not well. Convey her to my tent.
[*Exit Regan, led.*]

Enter a Herald.

Come hither, herald. Let the trumpet sound,
And read out this. [*Gives paper.*]

[CAPTAIN Sound, trumpet!] *A trumpet sounds.*

HERALD *(Reads)* "If any man of quality or degree within the lists of the army will maintain upon Edmund, supposed Earl of Gloucester, that he is a manifold traitor, let him appear by the third sound of the trumpet. He is bold in his defense."

[EDMUND Sound!] *First trumpet.*

HERALD Again! *Second trumpet.*

HERALD Again! *Third trumpet.*
Trumpet answers within.

Enter Edgar [at the third sound], armed [with a trumpeter before him].

ALBANY
Ask him his purposes, why he appears
Upon this call o' th' trumpet.

HERALD What are you?
Your name, your quality? And why you answer
This present summons?

EDGAR Know my name is lost,
By treason's tooth bare-gnawn and canker-bit.
Yet am I noble as the adversary
I come to cope.

ALBANY Which is that adversary?

EDGAR
What's he that speaks for Edmund Earl of Gloucester?

58 quarrels causes **59 sharpness** keenness, painful consequences **62 subject of** subordinate in **63 list** please **64 pleasure** wish. **demanded** asked about **67 immediacy** nearness of connection **70 your addition** the titles you confer **71 compeers** is equal with **72 That . . . most** that investiture would be most complete **76 full-flowing stomach** full tide of angry rejoinder **77 patrimony** inheritance **78 the walls is thine** i.e., the citadel of my heart surrenders completely to you **81 let-alone** preventing, denying **82 Half-blooded** only partly of noble blood **83 Let . . . strike** i.e., let there be a public announcement (?) a battle (?) **85 in thy attaint** i.e., as partner in your corruption **89 banns** public announcement of a proposed marriage **91 interlude** play; i.e., you are being melodramatic

95 make prove **96 in nothing less** in no respect less guilty **98 medicine** i.e., poison **99 What** whoever **105 single virtue** unaided prowess **112 degree** rank **121 What** who **124 canker-bit** eaten as by the caterpillar **126 cope** encounter

EDMUND
Himself. What say'st thou to him?
EDGAR
Draw thy sword,
That, if my speech offend a noble heart,
Thy arm may do thee justice. Here is mine.
[*Draws.*]
Behold, it is my privilege,
The privilege of mine honors,
My oath, and my profession. I protest,
Maugre thy strength, place, youth, and eminence,
Despite thy victor sword and fire-new fortune,
Thy valor, and thy heart, thou art a traitor—
False to thy gods, thy brother, and thy father,
Conspirant 'gainst this high-illustrious prince,
And, from th' extremest upward of thy head
To the descent and dust below thy foot
A most toad-spotted traitor. Say thou "No,"
This sword, this arm, and my best spirits, are bent
To prove upon thy heart, whereto I speak,
Thou liest.
EDMUND
In wisdom I should ask thy name;
But, since thy outside looks so fair and warlike,
And that thy tongue some say of breeding breathes,
What safe and nicely I might well delay
By rule of knighthood I disdain and spurn.
Back do I toss these treasons to thy head,
With the hell-hated lie o'erwhelm thy heart,
Which—for they yet glance by and scarcely bruise—
This sword of mine shall give them instant way,
Where they shall rest forever. Trumpets, speak!
[*He draws.*] *Alarums. Fight.* [*Edmund falls.*]
ALBANY
Save him, save him!
GONERIL
This is practice, Gloucester.
By th' law of war thou wast not bound to answer
An unknown opposite. Thou art not vanquish'd,
But cozen'd and beguil'd.
ALBANY
Shut your mouth, dame,
Or with this paper shall I stop it.—Hold, sir.—
[*To Goneril.*] Thou worse than any name, read thine own evil.
[*Shows her the letter.*]
No tearing, lady; I perceive you know it.
GONERIL
Say if I do, the laws are mine, not thine.
Who can arraign me for 't?
ALBANY
Most monstrous! O!
Know'st thou this paper?
GONERIL
Ask me not what I know.
Exit.
ALBANY
Go after her. She's desperate; govern her.
[*Exit an Officer.*]
EDMUND
What you have charg'd me with, that have I done,
And more, much more. The time will bring it out.
'Tis past, and so am I. But what art thou
That hast this fortune on me? If thou 'rt noble,
I do forgive thee.
EDGAR
Let's exchange charity.
I am no less in blood than thou art, Edmund;
If more, the more th' hast wrong'd me.
My name is Edgar, and thy father's son.
The gods are just, and of our pleasant vices
Make instruments to plague us.
The dark and vicious place where thee he got
Cost him his eyes.
EDMUND
Th' hast spoken right, 'tis true.
The wheel is come full circle; I am here.
ALBANY
Methought thy very gait did prophesy
A royal nobleness. I must embrace thee.
[*They embrace.*]
Let sorrow split my heart, if ever I
Did hate thee or thy father!
EDGAR
Worthy prince, I know 't.
ALBANY
Where have you hid yourself?
How have you known the miseries of your father?
EDGAR
By nursing them, my lord. List a brief tale,
And when 'tis told, O, that my heart would burst!
The bloody proclamation to escape
That follow'd me so near—O, our lives' sweetness,
That we the pain of death would hourly die
Rather than die at once!—taught me to shift
Into a madman's rags, t' assume a semblance
That very dogs disdain'd; and in this habit
Met I my father with his bleeding rings,
Their precious stones new lost; became his guide,
Led him, begg'd for him, sav'd him from despair;
Never—O fault!—reveal'd myself unto him
Until some half-hour past, when I was arm'd.
Not sure, though hoping, of this good success,
I ask'd his blessing, and from first to last
Told him our pilgrimage. But his flaw'd heart—
Alack, too weak the conflict to support—
'Twixt two extremes of passion, joy and grief,
Burst smilingly.
EDMUND
This speech of yours hath mov'd me,
And shall perchance do good. But speak you on;
You look as you had something more to say.
ALBANY
If there be more, more woeful, hold it in,
For I am almost ready to dissolve,
Hearing of this.
[EDGAR
This would have seem'd a period
To such as love not sorrow; but another,
To amplify too much, would make much more,
And top extremity. Whilst I

132 of mine honors i.e., of my knighthood **133 profession** i.e., knighthood **134 Maugre** in spite of **135 fire-new** newly minted **136 heart** courage **139 upward** top **140 descent** lowest extreme **141 toad-spotted** venomous, or having spots of infamy **144 wisdom** prudence **146 say** flavor, indication **147 safe and nicely** prudently and punctiliously **149 treasons . . . head** i.e., accusations of treason in your teeth **150 hell-hated** hated as hell is hated **151 for** since. **yet** as yet **152 give . . . way** i.e., provide them an immediate pathway to your heart **154 Save** spare. **practice** trickery; or (said sardonically) astute management **157 cozen'd** tricked **164 govern** restrain

168 fortune on victory over **173 pleasant** pleasurable **175 got** begot **177 wheel** i.e., wheel of fortune. **here** i.e., at its bottom **187 The . . . escape** in order to escape the death-threatening proclamation **193 rings** sockets **200 flaw'd** cracked **208 a period** the limit **209–211 but . . . extremity** i.e., another sorrowful circumstance, adding to what is already too much, would increase it and exceed the limit

Was big in clamor, came there in a man
Who, having seen me in my worst estate,
Shunn'd my abhorr'd society; but then, finding
Who 'twas that so endur'd, with his strong arms
He fastened on my neck, and bellowed out
As he'd burst heaven; threw him on my father;
Told the most piteous tale of Lear and him
That ever ear receiv'd, which in recounting
His grief grew puissant, and the strings of life
Began to crack. Twice then the trumpets sounded,
And there I left him tranc'd.

ALBANY
But who was this?

EDGAR
Kent, sir, the banish'd Kent, who in disguise
Follow'd his enemy king, and did him service
Improper for a slave.]

Enter a Gentleman [with a bloody knife].

GENTLEMAN
Help, help, O, help!

EDGAR
What kind of help?

ALBANY
Speak, man.

EDGAR
What means this bloody knife?

GENTLEMAN
'Tis hot, it smokes.
It came even from the heart of—O, she's dead!

ALBANY
Who dead? Speak, man.

GENTLEMAN
Your lady, sir, your lady; and her sister
By her is poison'd; she confesses it.

EDMUND
I was contracted to them both. All three
Now marry in an instant.

EDGAR
Here comes Kent.

Enter Kent.

ALBANY
Produce the bodies, be they alive or dead.
[Exit Gentleman.]
This judgment of the heavens, that makes us tremble,
Touches us not with pity.—O, is this he?
The time will not allow the compliment
Which very manners urges.

KENT
I am come
To bid my king and master aye good night.
Is he not here?

ALBANY
Great thing of us forgot!
Speak, Edmund, where's the King? And where's Cordelia?
Goneril's and Regan's bodies [are] brought out.
See'st thou this object, Kent?

KENT
Alack, why thus?

EDMUND
Yet Edmund was belov'd.
The one the other poison'd for my sake,
And after slew herself.

ALBANY
Even so. Cover their faces.

EDMUND
I pant for life. Some good I mean to do,
Despite of mine own nature. Quickly send,
Be brief in it, to th' castle, for my writ
Is on the life of Lear and on Cordelia.
Nay, send in time.

ALBANY
Run, run, O, run!

EDGAR
To who, my lord? Who has the office? Send
Thy token of reprieve.

EDMUND
Well thought on. Take my sword,
Give it the captain.

EDGAR
Haste thee, for thy life.
[Exit Officer with Edmund's sword.]

EDMUND
He hath commission from thy wife and me
To hang Cordelia in the prison, and
To lay the blame upon her own despair,
That she fordid herself.

ALBANY
The gods defend her! Bear him hence awhile.
[Edmund is borne off.]

Enter Lear, with Cordelia in his arms; [Gentleman, Captain, and others following].

LEAR
Howl, howl, howl! O, you are men of stones!
Had I your tongues and eyes, I 'd use them so
That heaven's vault should crack. She's gone for ever!
I know when one is dead, and when one lives;
She's dead as earth. Lend me a looking-glass;
If that her breath will mist or stain the stone,
Why, then she lives.

KENT
Is this the promis'd end?

EDGAR
Or image of that horror?

ALBANY
Fall, and cease!

LEAR
This feather stirs; she lives! If it be so,
It is a chance which does redeem all sorrows
That ever I have felt.

KENT *[Kneeling]*
O my good master!

LEAR
Prithee, away.

EDGAR
'Tis noble Kent, your friend.

LEAR
A plague upon you, murderers, traitors all!
I might have sav'd her; now she's gone forever!
Cordelia, Cordelia! Stay a little. Ha!
What is 't thou say'st? Her voice was ever soft,

212 big in clamor loud in my lamenting **220 puissant** powerful **222 tranc'd** entranced, senseless **227 smokes** steams **237 compliment** ceremony **238 very manners urges** mere decency requires **242 object** sight **243 Yet** despite everything

252 office commission **259 fordid** destroyed **266 stone** crystal or polished stone of which the mirror is made **267 promis'd end** i.e., Last Judgment **268 image** duplicate. **Fall, and cease** i.e., let heavens fall and all things cease

Gentle, and low, an excellent thing in woman.
I kill'd the slave that was a-hanging thee.

CAPTAIN
'Tis true, my lords, he did.

LEAR
Did I not, fellow?
I have seen the day, with my good biting falchion
I would have made them skip. I am old now,
And these same crosses spoil me. Who are you?
Mine eyes are not o' th' best; I'll tell you straight.

KENT
If Fortune brag of two she lov'd and hated,
One of them we behold.

LEAR
This is a dull sight. Are you not Kent?

KENT
The same,
Your servant Kent. Where is your servant Caius?

LEAR
He's a good fellow, I can tell you that;
He'll strike, and quickly too. He's dead and rotten.

KENT
No, my good lord, I am the very man—

LEAR
I'll see that straight.

KENT
That from your first of difference and decay
Have follow'd your sad steps—

LEAR
You are welcome hither.

KENT
Nor no man else. All's cheerless, dark, and deadly.
Your eldest daughters have fordone themselves,
And desperately are dead.

LEAR
Ay, so I think.

ALBANY
He knows not what he says, and vain is it
That we present us to him.

EDGAR
Very bootless.

Enter a Messenger.

MESSENGER
Edmund is dead, my lord.

ALBANY
That's but a trifle here.
You lords and noble friends, know our intent.
What comfort to this great decay may come
Shall be applied. For us, we will resign,
During the life of this old majesty,
To him our absolute power. [*To Edgar and Kent.*]
You, to your rights,
With boot, and such addition as your honors
Have more than merited. All friends shall taste
The wages of their virtue, and all foes
The cup of their deservings. O, see, see!

280 falchion light sword **282 crosses spoil me** adversities take away my strength **283 I'll . . . straight** I'll recognize you in a moment **284 two** i.e., Lear, and a hypothetical individual whose misfortunes are without parallel. **lov'd and hated** i.e., first raised and then lowered **286 This . . . sight** i.e., my vision is clouding **287 Caius** (Kent's disguise name.) **291 see that straight** attend to that soon; or, comprehend that soon **292 first of difference** beginning of your change for the worst **294 Nor . . . else** no, not I nor anyone else **295 fordone** destroyed **296 desperately** in despair **302 What . . . come** i.e., whatever means of comforting this ruined king may present themselves **306 boot** advantage, good measure. **addition** titles, further distinctions

LEAR
And my poor fool is hang'd! No, no, no life?
Why should a dog, a horse, a rat, have life,
And thou no breath at all? Thou'lt come no more,
Never, never, never, never, never!
Pray you, undo this button. Thank you, sir.
Do you see this? Look on her, look, her lips,
Look there, look there! *He dies.*

EDGAR
He faints. My lord, my lord!

KENT
Break, heart, I prithee, break!

EDGAR
Look up, my lord.

KENT
Vex not his ghost. O, let him pass! He hates him
That would upon the rack of this tough world
Stretch him out longer.

EDGAR
He is gone, indeed.

KENT
The wonder is he hath endur'd so long.
He but usurp'd his life.

ALBANY
Bear them from hence. Our present business
Is general woe. [*To Kent and Edgar.*] Friends of my soul, you twain
Rule in this realm, and the gor'd state sustain.

KENT
I have a journey, sir, shortly to go;
My master calls me, I must not say no.

EDGAR
The weight of this sad time we must obey,
Speak what we feel, not what we ought to say.
The oldest hath borne most; we that are young
Shall never see so much, nor live so long.
Exeunt, with a dead march.

310 poor fool i.e., Cordelia. (*Fool* is here a term of endearment.) **319 rack** torture rack (with suggestion, in F and Q spelling *wracke*, of shipwreck, disaster) **331 s.d. Exeunt** (Presumably the dead bodies are borne out in procession.)

Macbeth

Macbeth is perhaps the last in a series of four great Shakespearean tragedies concerned with spiritual evil, as distinguished from political strife. The play was certainly in existence by April 20, 1611, when Simon Forman saw it at the Globe, but the style and some rather tenuous topical clues suggest a date around 1606–1607: King James' accession to the English throne in 1603, his reassertion of the power of the royal touch to cure the "King's evil" in 1604–1605 (see IV,iii), the trial of the Gunpowder Plot conspirators (to which the Porter may allude in his remarks about "equivocators") in March of 1606, and a seeming reference in a play called *The Puritan,* published in 1607, to Banquo's ghost sitting "at the upper end of the table." As the possible culmination, then, of an analysis of evil begun with *Hamlet* (c. 1599–1601) and extending through *Othello* (c. 1603–1604) and *King Lear* (c. 1605), *Macbeth* offers a terse and gloomy vision of a particular man's encounter with the powers of darkness. However much Macbeth may possess freedom of will and be personally responsible for his fate, his tragic doom seems relentlessly unavoidable.

To an extent not found in the other tragedies, the issue is stated in terms of salvation versus damnation. Macbeth knows before he acts that Duncan's virtues "Will plead like angels, trumpet-tongu'd, against The deep damnation of his taking-off" (I,vii). After the murder, he is equally aware that he has "Put rancors in the vessel of my peace . . . and mine eternal jewel Given to the common enemy of man" (III,i). His enemies later describe him as a devil and a "hell-hound." He is, like Marlowe's Doctor Faustus before him, one who has knowingly sold his soul for gain. And although as a mortal he still has time to repent his crimes, horrible as they are, Macbeth cannot find the words to be penitent. "Wherefore could not I pronounce 'Amen'?" he implores his wife after they have committed the murder. "I had most need of blessing, and 'Amen' Stuck in my throat" (II,ii). Macbeth's own answer seems to be that he has committed himself so inexorably to evil that he cannot turn back. Sentence has been pronounced: "Glamis hath murder'd sleep, and therefore Cawdor Shall sleep no more; Macbeth shall sleep no more."

Macbeth is not a conventional morality play (even less so than *Doctor Faustus*), and is not concerned primarily with preaching against sinfulness or demonstrating that Macbeth is finally damned for what he does. A homiletic tradition has been transformed into an intensely human study of the psychological effects of evil on a particular man and, to a lesser extent, on his wife. That homiletic tradition nevertheless provides as its legacy a spiritual and cosmic framework for understanding how evil operates. A perverse ambition seemingly inborn in Macbeth himself is abetted by dark forces dwelling in the universe, waiting to catch him off guard. Among Shakespeare's tragedies, indeed, *Macbeth* is remarkable for its focus on evil in the protagonist, and on his relationship to the sinister forces tempting him. In no other Shakespearean play do we identify to such an extent with the evildoer himself. *Richard III* also focuses on an evil protagonist, but in that play we are distanced by the gloating and are not partakers in the introspective soliloquies of a man confronting his own ambition. Macbeth is more like us. We share Macbeth's inclination toward brutality, as well as his humane resistance of that urge. We witness and struggle to understand his downfall through two phases: the soul-struggle leading up to the crime, and the despairing aftermath with its vain quest for security through continued violence. Evil is thus presented in two aspects, first as insidious suggestion leading us on toward an illusory promise of gain, and then as frenzied addiction to the hated thing by which we are possessed.

In the first phase, up to the crime, we wonder to what extent the powers of darkness are a determining factor in what Macbeth does. Can he avoid the fate the witches proclaim? Evidently he and Lady Macbeth have previously considered murdering Duncan; the witches appear after the thought, not before. Lady Macbeth reminds her wavering husband that he was the first to "break this enterprise" to her, on some previous occasion when "Nor time nor place Did then adhere, and yet you would make both" (I,vii). Elizabethans would understand that evil spirits such as witches appear when summoned, whether by our conscious or unconscious minds. Macbeth is ripe for their insinuations. A mind free of taint would see no sinister invitation in their prophecy of greatness to come. And in a saner moment Macbeth knows that his restless desire to interfere with destiny is arrogant and useless. "If chance will have me king, why, chance may crown me, Without my stir" (I,iii). Banquo, his companion, serves as his dramatic opposite by consistently displaying the correct attitude toward the witches. "Speak then to me," he addresses them, "who neither beg nor fear Your favors nor your hate." Like Horatio in *Hamlet,* Banquo is strongly resistant, though not without an agonizing night of moral struggle, to the blandishments of fortune as well as to its buffets. Indeed, promises of success are often more ruinous than setbacks—as in the seemingly paradoxical instance of the farmer, cited by Macbeth's Porter, who "hang'd himself on the expectation of plenty." It is by showing Macbeth that he is two-thirds of his way to the throne that the witches tempt him to seize the last third at whatever cost. "Glamis, and Thane of Cawdor! The greatest is behind."

Banquo comprehends the nature of temptation. "To win us to our harm," he observes, "The instruments of darkness tell us truths, Win us with honest trifles, to betray 's In deepest consequence." The devil can speak true, and his strategy is to invite us into a trap we help prepare. Without our active consent in evil (as Othello also learns) we cannot fall. Yet in what sense are the witches trifling with Macbeth, or prevaricating? When they address him as one "that shalt be king hereafter," they are stating a certainty, for they can "look into the seeds of time, And say which grain will grow and which will not," as Banquo says. They know that Banquo will be "Lesser than Macbeth, and greater, Not so happy, yet much happier," since Banquo will beget a race of kings and Macbeth will not. How then do they know that Macbeth will be king? If we consider the hypothetical question, what if Macbeth does *not* murder Duncan, we can perceive the very center of the relationship between character and fate; for the only valid answer is that the question remains hypothetical, Macbeth *does* kill Duncan, the witches are right in their prediction. It is idle to speculate that providence would have found another way to make Macbeth king, for the witches' prophecy is self-fulfilling in the very way they foresee. Character is fate; they know Macbeth's fatal weakness, and know they can "enkindle" him to seize the crown by laying irresistible temptations before him. This does not mean that they predetermine his choice, but rather that Macbeth's choice is predictable and therefore unavoidable, even though not preordained. He has free choice, but that choice will in fact go only one way—as with Adam and Eve in Milton's *Paradise Lost,* and in the medieval exegetical tradition from which it was derived.

The powers of evil cannot predetermine Macbeth's choice, but they can influence the external conditions affecting that choice. By a series of apparently circumstantial events, calculatedly timed, they can repeatedly assail him just when he is about to rally to the call of conscience. The witches, armed with supernatural knowledge, inform Macbeth he is to be the Thane of Cawdor shortly before the King's ambassadors confirm the new title. Duncan chooses this very night to lodge under Macbeth's roof. And just when Macbeth resolves to abandon even this unparalleled opportunity, his wife intervenes on the side of the witches. Macbeth commits the murder in part to keep his word to her and prove he is no coward (like Donwald, the slayer of King Duff in one of Shakespeare's chief sources from Holinshed's *Chronicles*). Not only the opportunities presented to Macbeth but the obstacles put in his way are cannily timed to overwhelm his conscience. When King Duncan announces that his son Malcolm is now Prince of Cumberland and official heir to the throne (I,iv), the unintended threat to Macbeth arouses him from a mood of gratitude and acceptance to one of hostility. These are mitigating circumstances in our judgment of Macbeth, and even though they cannot excuse him they certainly increase our sympathetic identification.

We are moved too by the poetic intensity of Macbeth's moral vision. His soliloquies are memorable as poetry, not merely because Shakespeare wrote them but because Macbeth is a sensitively aware man. The horror, indeed, of his crime is that his cultivated self is revulsed by what he cannot prevent himself from doing. He understands with a terrible clarity not only the moral wrong of what he is about to do, but also the inescapably destructive consequences for himself. He is as reluctant as we to see the crime committed, and yet he goes to it in a sad and rational deliberation rather than in a self-blinding fury. There is no seeming loss of perspective, and yet there is total alienation of the act from the doer's moral consciousness. The arguments for and against murdering Duncan, as Macbeth perceptively appraises them—and more characteristically *sees* them in his picturing imagination—are overwhelmingly opposed to the deed. Duncan is his king and his guest, both sacred obligations. The King is virtuous and able. He has shown every favor to Macbeth, thereby removing any sane motive for striving after further promotion. Furthermore, all human history shows that murders of this sort "return To plague th' inventor" (I,vii). Finally, judgment in "the life to come" remains to be considered. On the other side of the ledger is nothing but Macbeth's "Vaulting ambition, which o'erleaps itself"—an empty, motiveless refusal to be content with his present good fortune since there is more that beckons. Who could weigh the issues so dispassionately and still choose the wrong? The answer apparently is that we could, for Macbeth strikes us as typically human both in his understanding and in his perverse ambition.

Macbeth's clarity of vision is contrasted with that of his wife. He is always seeing visions or hearing voices—a dagger in the air, the ghost of Banquo, a voice crying "Sleep no more!"—and she is always denying them. "The sleeping and the dead Are but as pictures," she insists. He knows that "all great Neptune's ocean" cannot wash the blood from his hands; "No, this my hand will rather The multitudinous seas incarnadine, Making the green one red." To Lady Macbeth, contrastingly, "A little water clears us of this deed. How easy is it, then!" (II,ii). Macbeth knows that the murder of Duncan is but the beginning: "We have scorch'd the snake, not kill'd it." Lady Macbeth would prefer to believe that "What's done is done" (III,ii). Paradoxically, she is the one who must finally endure visions of the most agonizing sort, sleepwalking in her madness and trying to rub away the "damned spot" that before seemed so easy to remove. This relationship between Macbeth and Lady Macbeth owes much to traditions contrasting male and female, including the archetypal relationship of Adam and Eve. The man is the more rational of the two but knowingly shares his wife's sin through uxorious fondness for her. She has failed to foresee the long-range consequences of sinful ambition and so becomes a temptress to her husband. The fall of man takes place in an incongruous atmosphere of domestic intimacy and mutual concern; Lady Macbeth is motivated by ambition for her husband in much the same way that he sins to win her approbation.

The fatal disharmony flawing this domestic accord is conveyed through images of sexual inversion. Lady Macbeth prepares for her ordeal with the incantation, "Come, you spirits That tend on mortal thoughts, unsex me here . . . Come to my woman's breasts, And take my milk for gall" (I,v). When she accuses her husband of unmanly cowardice, and vows she would dash out the brains of her own infant for such effeminacy as he has displayed, he extols her with "Bring forth men-children only; For thy undaunted mettle should compose Nothing but males" (I,vii). She takes the initiative, devising and then carrying out the plan to drug Duncan's chamberguards with wine. This assumption of the dominant male role by the woman would again bring to the Elizabethan mind numerous medieval parallels deploring the ascendancy of passion over reason: Eve choosing for Adam, Noah's wife taking command of the ark, the Wife of Bath dominating her husbands, Venus emasculating Mars, and others.

In *Macbeth,* sexual inversion also draws a parallel between Lady Macbeth and the witches or weird sisters, the bearded women. Their unnaturalness betokens disorder in nature, for they can sail in a sieve, and "look not like th' inhabitants o' th' earth, And yet are on 't" (I,iii). Habitually they speak in paradoxes: "When the battle's lost and won," "Fair is foul, and foul is fair." Shakespeare probably drew on numerous sources to depict them: Holinshed's *Chronicles* (in which he conflated two accounts, one of Duncan and Macbeth, and the other of King Duff slain by Donwald with the help of his wife), King James' writings on witchcraft, Harsnett's *Declaration of Egregious Popishe Impostures* (used also for *King Lear*), and the accounts of the Scottish witch trials published around 1590. In the last, particularly, Shakespeare could have found mention of witches raising storms and sailing in sieves to endanger vessels at sea, performing threefold rituals blaspheming the Trinity, and brewing witches' broth. Holinshed's *Chronicles* refer to the weird sisters as "goddesses of destinie," associating them with the three fates, Clotho, Lachesis, and Atropos, who spin, pull, and cut the thread of life. In *Macbeth* the sisters' power to control fortune is curtailed, and they are portrayed as witches according to popular contemporary understanding rather than goddesses of destiny; nonetheless, witches were thought to be servants of the Devil (Banquo wonders if the Devil can speak true in their utterances, I,iii), and through them Macbeth has made an ominous pact with evil itself. The popularity of witchlore tempted Shakespeare's company to expand the witches' scenes with spectacle of song and dance, and the Folio text we have evidently contains interpolations derived in part from Middleton's *The Witch* (see especially III,v and part of IV,i containing mention of Middleton's songs "Come away" and "Black spirits"). Nevertheless, Shakespeare's original theme of a disharmony in nature remains clearly visible.

Patterns of imagery throughout the play point to the same disorder in nature and in man. The murder of Duncan, like that of Julius Caesar, is accompanied by signs of the heavens' anger. Various observers report that chimneys blow down during the unruly night, that owls clamor and attack falcons, that the earth shakes, and that Duncan's horses devour each other. (Some of these prodigies are from Holinshed.) Owls appear repeatedly in the imagery, along with other creatures associated with nighttime and horror: the wolf, serpents, scorpions, bats, toads, beetles, crows, rooks. Darkness itself assumes tangible and menacing shapes of hidden stars or extinguished candles, a thick blanket shrouded "in the dunnest smoke of hell," an entombment of the earth in place of "living light," a scarf to hoodwink the eye of "pitiful day," and a bloody and invisible hand to tear to pieces the lives of virtuous men. Sleep is transformed from "great nature's second course" and a "nourisher" of life that "knits up the ravel'd sleave of care" (II,ii) into "death's counterfeit" and a living hell for Lady Macbeth. Life becomes sterile for Macbeth, a denial of harvest, the lees or dregs of the wine and "the sear, the yellow leaf." In a theatrical metaphor life becomes for him unreal, "a walking shadow, a poor player That struts and frets his hour upon the stage And then is heard no more" (V,v). This theme of empty illusion carries over into the recurring image of borrowed or ill-fitting garments that belie the wearer. For Macbeth is an actor, a hypocrite, whose "False face must hide what the false heart doth know" (I,vii) and who must "look like the innocent flower, But be the serpent under 't" (I,v). Even the show of grief is an assumed mask whereby evildoers deceive the virtuous, so much so that Malcolm, Donalbain, and Macduff learn to conceal their true feeling rather than be thought to "show an unfelt sorrow."

Blood is not only a literal sign of disorder but an emblem of Macbeth's remorseless butchery, a "damned spot" on the conscience, and a promise of divine vengeance: "It will have blood; they say, blood will have blood" (III,iv). The emphasis on corrupted blood also suggests disease, in which Macbeth's tyranny is a sickness to his country as well as to himself. Scotland bleeds (IV,iii), needing a physician; Macduff and his allies call themselves "the med'cine of the sickly weal" (V,ii). Lady Macbeth's disease is incurable, beyond the practice of a doctor, something spiritually corrupt wherein "the patient Must minister to himself." Conversely, the English King Edward is renowned for his divine gift of curing the "king's evil," or scrofula.

Throughout, the defenders of righteousness are associated with positive images of natural order. Duncan rewards his subjects by saying, "I have begun to plant thee, and will labor To make thee full of growing" (I,iv). His arrival at

Inverness Castle is heralded by signs of summer, sweet air, and "the temple-haunting martlet" (I,vi). He is a fatherly figure, so much so that even Lady Macbeth balks at an act so like parricide. Macduff too is a father and husband whose family is butchered. Banquo is above all a patriarchal figure, ancestor of the royal line governing Scotland and England at the time the play was written. These harmonies are restorative. Scotland's peace is violated for a time, and in that bloody interim "to do harm Is often laudable, to do good sometime Accounted dangerous folly" (IV,ii), but we sense in *Macbeth* (more than in *King Lear*) an enduring stability to which the country will return. Even the witches' riddling prophecies, "the equivocation of the fiend" luring Macbeth into further atrocities with the vain promise of security, anticipate a divinely inspired retribution. Man's fall is unavoidable, but the concern of providence is no less sure.

Macbeth

[*Dramatis Personae*

DUNCAN, *King of Scotland.*
MALCOLM, DONALBAIN, } *his sons.*
MACBETH, BANQUO, } *generals of the King's army.*
MACDUFF, LENNOX, ROSS, MENTEITH, ANGUS, CAITHNESS, } *noblemen of Scotland.*
FLEANCE, *son to Banquo.*
SIWARD, *Earl of Northumberland, general of the English forces.*
YOUNG SIWARD, *his son.*
SEYTON, *an officer attending on Macbeth.*
BOY, *son to Macduff.*
ENGLISH DOCTOR.
SCOTTISH DOCTOR.
CAPTAIN.
SOLDIER.
PORTER.
OLD MAN.
Three MURDERERS.

LADY MACBETH.
LADY MACDUFF.
GENTLEWOMAN *attending on Lady Macbeth.*

HECATE.
Three WITCHES.
APPARITIONS.

LORDS, GENTLEMEN, OFFICERS, SOLDIERS, ATTENDANTS, *and* MESSENGERS.

SCENE: *Scotland; England.*]

ACT I • SCENE I

Thunder and lightning. Enter three Witches.

FIRST WITCH
When shall we three meet again?
In thunder, lightning, or in rain? 2
SECOND WITCH
When the hurlyburly's done, 3
When the battle's lost and won.

I.i. Location: An open place.
2 In thunder . . . rain (Witches were thought able to choose and localize the storms about them.) **3 hurlyburly** tumult

THIRD WITCH
That will be ere the set of sun.
FIRST WITCH
Where the place?
SECOND WITCH Upon the heath.
THIRD WITCH
There to meet with Macbeth.
FIRST WITCH
I come, Graymalkin!
SECOND WITCH
Paddock calls.
THIRD WITCH
Anon.
ALL
Fair is foul, and foul is fair.
Hover through the fog and filthy air. *Exeunt.*

SCENE II

Alarum within. Enter King [Duncan], Malcolm, Donalbain, Lennox, with Attendants, meeting a bleeding Captain.

DUNCAN
What bloody man is that? He can report,
As seemeth by his plight, of the revolt
The newest state.
MALCOLM
This is the sergeant
Who like a good and hardy soldier fought
'Gainst my captivity. Hail, brave friend!
Say to the King the knowledge of the broil
As thou didst leave it.
CAPTAIN
Doubtful it stood,
As two spent swimmers, that do cling together
And choke their art. The merciless Macdonwald—
Worthy to be a rebel, for to that
The multiplying villainies of nature
Do swarm upon him—from the Western Isles
Of kerns and gallowglasses is supplied;
And Fortune, on his damned quarrel smiling,
Show'd like a rebel's whore. But all's too weak;
For brave Macbeth—well he deserves that name—
Disdaining Fortune, with his brandish'd steel,
Which smok'd with bloody execution,
Like valor's minion carved out his passage
Till he fac'd the slave;
Which nev'r shook hands, nor bade farewell to him,
Till he unseam'd him from the nave to th' chops,
And fix'd his head upon our battlements.
DUNCAN
O valiant cousin, worthy gentleman!
CAPTAIN
As whence the sun 'gins his reflection
Shipwracking storms and direful thunders break,
So from that spring whence comfort seem'd to come
Discomfort swells. Mark, King of Scotland, mark.
No sooner justice had, with valor arm'd,
Compell'd these skipping kerns to trust their heels
But the Norweyan lord, surveying vantage,
With furbish'd arms and new supplies of men
Began a fresh assault.
DUNCAN
Dismay'd not this our captains, Macbeth and
Banquo?
CAPTAIN
Yes, as sparrows eagles, or the hare the lion.
If I say sooth, I must report they were
As cannons overcharg'd with double cracks,
So they doubly redoubled strokes upon the foe.
Except they meant to bathe in reeking wounds,
Or memorize another Golgotha,
I cannot tell. But I am faint,
My gashes cry for help.
DUNCAN
So well thy words become thee as thy wounds;
They smack of honor both. Go get him surgeons.
[Exit Captain, attended.]

Enter Ross and Angus.

Who comes here?
MALCOLM The worthy Thane of Ross.
LENNOX
What a haste looks through his eyes!
So should he look that seems to speak things
strange.
ROSS
God save the King!
DUNCAN
Whence cam'st thou, worthy thane?
ROSS From Fife, great King,
Where the Norweyan banners flout the sky
And fan our people cold.
Norway himself, with terrible numbers,
Assisted by that most disloyal traitor
The Thane of Cawdor, began a dismal conflict,
Till that Bellona's bridegroom, lapp'd in proof,
Confronted him with self-comparisons,
Point against point, rebellious arm 'gainst arm,
Curbing his lavish spirit; and, to conclude,
The victory fell on us.
DUNCAN Great happiness!
ROSS
That now

8 Graymalkin i.e., gray cat, name of the witch's familiar spirit **9 Paddock** toad; also a familiar **10 Anon** at once

I.ii. Location: A camp near Forres.
s.d. Alarum trumpet call to arms **4 sergeant** i.e., staff officer. (There may be no inconsistency with his rank of "captain" in the stage direction and speech prefixes in F.) **7 broil** battle **10 spent** tired out **11 choke their art** render their skill useless **12 to that** to that end or purpose **14 Western Isles** islands to the west of Scotland, the Hebrides and perhaps Ireland **15 Of kerns** with light-armed Irish foot soldiers. **gallowglasses** retainers of Irish chiefs, armed with axes **17 Show'd** appeared **21 minion** darling **23 Which** who, i.e., Macbeth. **shook hands** i.e., in bidding farewell **24 nave** navel. **chops** jaws

26 cousin kinsman **27 As whence** just as from the place where. **'gins his reflection** begins its turning back (from its southward progression during winter) **28 break** break forth, emanate **33 surveying vantage** seeing an opportunity **39 cracks** charges of explosive **40 So** so that **41 Except** unless **42 memorize** make memorable or famous. **Golgotha** "place of a skull," where Christ was crucified. (Mark 15:22.) **47 Thane** Scottish title of honor, roughly equivalent to *Earl* **49 seems to** seems about to **52 flout** mock, insult **56 dismal** ominous **57 Till . . . proof** i.e., until Macbeth, clad in well-tested armor. (Bellona was the Roman goddess of war.) **58 self-comparisons** i.e., matching counter-thrusts **60 lavish** insolent, unrestrained

Sweno, the Norways' king, craves composition;
Nor would we deign him burial of his men
Till he disbursed at Saint Colme's inch
Ten thousand dollars to our general use.

DUNCAN
No more that Thane of Cawdor shall deceive
Our bosom interest. Go pronounce his present
death,
And with his former title greet Macbeth.

ROSS
I'll see it done.

DUNCAN
What he hath lost noble Macbeth hath won.
Exeunt.

SCENE III

Thunder. Enter the three Witches.

FIRST WITCH
Where hast thou been, sister?

SECOND WITCH
Killing swine.

THIRD WITCH
Sister, where thou?

FIRST WITCH
A sailor's wife had chestnuts in her lap,
And munch'd, and munch'd, and munch'd. "Give
me," quoth I.
"Aroint thee, witch!" the rump-fed ronyon cries.
Her husband's to Aleppo gone, master o' th' Tiger;
But in a sieve I'll thither sail,
And, like a rat without a tail,
I'll do, I'll do, and I'll do.

SECOND WITCH
I'll give thee a wind.

FIRST WITCH
Th' art kind.

THIRD WITCH
And I another.

FIRST WITCH
I myself have all the other,
And the very ports they blow,
All the quarters that they know
I' th' shipman's card.
I'll drain him dry as hay.
Sleep shall neither night nor day
Hang upon his penthouse lid.
He shall live a man forbid.
Weary sev'nights nine times nine
Shall he dwindle, peak, and pine.
Though his bark cannot be lost,
Yet it shall be tempest-tost.
Look what I have.

SECOND WITCH
Show me, show me.

FIRST WITCH
Here I have a pilot's thumb,
Wrack'd as homeward he did come. *Drum within.*

THIRD WITCH
A drum, a drum!
Macbeth doth come.

ALL [*Dancing in a circle*]
The weird sisters, hand in hand,
Posters of the sea and land,
Thus do go about, about,
Thrice to thine, and thrice to mine,
And thrice again, to make up nine.
Peace! The charm's wound up.

Enter Macbeth and Banquo.

MACBETH
So foul and fair a day I have not seen.

BANQUO
How far is 't call'd to Forres?—What are these
So wither'd and so wild in their attire,
That look not like th' inhabitants o' th' earth,
And yet are on 't? Live you? Or are you aught
That man may question? You seem to understand me,
By each at once her choppy finger laying
Upon her skinny lips. You should be women,
And yet your beards forbid me to interpret
That you are so.

MACBETH
Speak, if you can. What are you?

FIRST WITCH
All hail, Macbeth! Hail to thee, Thane of Glamis!

SECOND WITCH
All hail, Macbeth! Hail to thee, Thane of Cawdor!

THIRD WITCH
All hail, Macbeth, that shalt be king hereafter!

BANQUO
Good sir, why do you start, and seem to fear
Things that do sound so fair?—I' th' name of truth,
Are ye fantastical, or that indeed
Which outwardly ye show? My noble partner
You greet with present grace and great prediction
Of noble having and of royal hope,
That he seems rapt withal. To me you speak not.
If you can look into the seeds of time,
And say which grain will grow and which will not,
Speak then to me, who neither beg nor fear
Your favors nor your hate.

FIRST WITCH Hail!

SECOND WITCH Hail!

THIRD WITCH Hail!

FIRST WITCH
Lesser than Macbeth, and greater.

SECOND WITCH
Not so happy, yet much happier.

63 Norways' Norwegians'. **composition** agreement, treaty of peace **65 Saint Colme's inch** Inchcolm, the Isle of St. Columba in the Firth of Forth **66 dollars** Spanish or Dutch coins **68 bosom** close and affectionate

I.iii. Location: A heath near Forres.
6 Aroint thee avaunt, begone. **rump-fed** fed on refuse, or fat-rumped. **ronyon** mangy creature, scabby woman **7 Tiger** (A ship's name.) **9 without a tail** (A *familiar* or transformed witch was thought to be recognizable by some bodily defect. The missing tail here, suggestive of a generative defect and hence of futility, introduces a sexual pun on *do,* l. 10.) **15 they blow** i.e., to or from which the winds blow. (The witches can control a ship's destination this way.) **17 shipman's card** compass card, or a chart **20 penthouse lid** i.e., eyelid (which projects out over the eye like a *penthouse* or slope-roofed structure) **21 forbid** accursed **22 sev'nights** weeks **23 peak** grow peaked or thin

32 weird connected with fate **33 Posters of** swift travelers over **44 choppy** chapped **53 fantastical** creatures of fantasy or imagination **54 show** appear **55 grace** honor **57 rapt** carried away (by thought) **66 happy** fortunate

THIRD WITCH
Thou shalt get kings, though thou be none. 67
So all hail, Macbeth and Banquo!

FIRST WITCH
Banquo and Macbeth, all hail!

MACBETH
Stay, you imperfect speakers, tell me more! 70
By Sinel's death I know I am Thane of Glamis, 71
But how of Cawdor? The Thane of Cawdor lives,
A prosperous gentleman; and to be king
Stands not within the prospect of belief,
No more than to be Cawdor. Say from whence
You owe this strange intelligence? Or why 76
Upon this blasted heath you stop our way
With such prophetic greeting? Speak, I charge you.
Witches vanish.

BANQUO
The earth hath bubbles, as the water has,
And these are of them. Whither are they vanish'd?

MACBETH
Into the air; and what seem'd corporal melted 81
As breath into the wind. Would they had stay'd!

BANQUO
Were such things here as we do speak about?
Or have we eaten on the insane root 84
That takes the reason prisoner?

MACBETH
Your children shall be kings.

BANQUO
You shall be king.

MACBETH
And Thane of Cawdor too. Went it not so?

BANQUO
To th' selfsame tune and words.—Who's here?

Enter Ross and Angus.

ROSS
The King hath happily receiv'd, Macbeth,
The news of thy success; and when he reads 90
Thy personal venture in the rebels' fight,
His wonders and his praises do contend 92
Which should be thine or his. Silenc'd with that, 93
In viewing o'er the rest o' th' selfsame day,
He finds thee in the stout Norweyan ranks,
Nothing afeard of what thyself didst make, 96
Strange images of death. As thick as tale 97
Came post with post, and every one did bear 98
Thy praises in his kingdom's great defense,
And pour'd them down before him.

ANGUS
We are sent
To give thee from our royal master thanks,
Only to herald thee into his sight,
Not pay thee.

ROSS
And, for an earnest of a greater honor, 104
He bade me, from him, call thee Thane of Cawdor;
In which addition, hail, most worthy thane! 106
For it is thine.

BANQUO
What, can the devil speak true?

MACBETH
The Thane of Cawdor lives. Why do you dress me
In borrowed robes?

ANGUS
Who was the thane lives yet, 109
But under heavy judgment bears that life
Which he deserves to lose. Whether he was
combin'd 111
With those of Norway, or did line the rebel 112
With hidden help and vantage, or that with both
He labor'd in his country's wrack, I know not; 114
But treasons capital, confess'd and prov'd, 115
Have overthrown him.

MACBETH [*Aside*]
Glamis, and Thane of Cawdor!
The greatest is behind. [*To Ross and Angus.*] Thanks
for your pains. 117
[*Aside to Banquo.*] Do you not hope your children
shall be kings,
When those that gave the Thane of Cawdor to me
Promis'd no less to them?

BANQUO [*To Macbeth*]
That, trusted home, 120
Might yet enkindle you unto the crown,
Besides the Thane of Cawdor. But 'tis strange;
And oftentimes, to win us to our harm,
The instruments of Darkness tell us truths, 124
Win us with honest trifles, to betray 's
In deepest consequence.— 126
Cousins, a word, I pray you.
[*He converses apart with Ross and Angus.*]

MACBETH [*Aside*]
Two truths are told, 127
As happy prologues to the swelling act 128
Of the imperial theme.—I thank you, gentlemen.
[*Aside.*] This supernatural soliciting 130
Cannot be ill, cannot be good. If ill,
Why hath it given me earnest of success,
Commencing in a truth? I am Thane of Cawdor.
If good, why do I yield to that suggestion
Whose horrid image doth unfix my hair
And make my seated heart knock at my ribs,
Against the use of nature? Present fears 137
Are less than horrible imaginings.
My thought, whose murder yet is but fantastical, 139
Shakes so my single state of man that function 140
Is smother'd in surmise, and nothing is 141
But what is not.

BANQUO
Look how our partner's rapt. 142

MACBETH [*Aside*]
If chance will have me king, why, chance may
crown me
Without my stir.

BANQUO
New honors come upon him, 144
Like our strange garments, cleave not to their mold 145
But with the aid of use.

67 get beget **70 imperfect** incomplete **71 Sinel's** (Sinel was Macbeth's father.) **76 owe** own, possess. **strange** (1) unusual (2) unnatural, frighteningly alien to human experience (as often elsewhere in this play) **81 corporal** bodily **84 insane root** root causing insanity; variously identified **90 reads** i.e., considers **92–93 His . . . that** i.e., your wondrous deeds so outdo any praise he could offer that he is silenced **96 Nothing** not at all **97–98 As . . . with post** as fast as can be recounted came messenger after messenger **104 earnest** token payment **106 addition** title

109 Who he who **111 combin'd** confederate **112 line** strengthen. **the rebel** i.e., Macdonwald **114 in** i.e., to bring about **115 capital** deserving death **117 behind** to come **120 home** all the way **124 Darkness** (Indicates the demonic beyond the witches.) **126 In deepest consequence** in the profoundly important sequel **127 Cousins** i.e., fellow lords **128 swelling act** stately drama **130 soliciting** tempting **137 fears** things feared **139 whose** in which. **but fantastical** merely imagined **140 single . . . man** weak human condition. **function** normal power of action **141 surmise** speculation, imaginings **141–142 nothing . . . not** only unreal imaginings have (for me) any reality **144 stir** bestirring (myself). **come** i.e., which have come **145 strange** unaccustomed (with an ironical glance at *alien*). **their mold** i.e., the shape of the person within them

MACBETH [*Aside*] Come what come may,
Time and the hour runs through the roughest day.

BANQUO
Worthy Macbeth, we stay upon your leisure.

MACBETH
Give me your favor. My dull brain was wrought
With things forgotten. Kind gentlemen, your pains
Are regist'red where every day I turn
The leaf to read them. Let us toward the King.
[*Aside to Banquo.*] Think upon what hath chanc'd, and, at more time,
The interim having weigh'd it, let us speak
Our free hearts each to other.

BANQUO [*To Macbeth*] Very gladly.

MACBETH [*To Banquo*]
Till then, enough.—Come, friends. *Exeunt.*

SCENE IV

Flourish. Enter King [Duncan], Lennox, Malcolm, Donalbain, and Attendants.

DUNCAN
Is execution done on Cawdor? Are not
Those in commission yet return'd?

MALCOLM My liege,
They are not yet come back. But I have spoke
With one that saw him die, who did report
That very frankly he confess'd his treasons,
Implor'd your Highness' pardon, and set forth
A deep repentance. Nothing in his life
Became him like the leaving it. He died
As one that had been studied in his death
To throw away the dearest thing he ow'd,
As 'twere a careless trifle.

DUNCAN There's no art
To find the mind's construction in the face.
He was a gentleman on whom I built
An absolute trust.

Enter Macbeth, Banquo, Ross, and Angus.

O worthiest cousin!
The sin of my ingratitude even now
Was heavy on me. Thou art so far before
That swiftest wing of recompense is slow
To overtake thee. Would thou hadst less deserv'd,
That the proportion both of thanks and payment
Might have been mine! Only I have left to say,
More is thy due than more than all can pay.

MACBETH
The service and the loyalty I owe,
In doing it, pays itself. Your Highness' part
Is to receive our duties; and our duties
Are to your throne and state children and servants,
Which do but what they should, by doing everything
Safe toward your love and honor.

DUNCAN Welcome hither!
I have begun to plant thee, and will labor
To make thee full of growing. Noble Banquo,
That hast no less deserv'd, nor must be known
No less to have done so, let me infold thee
And hold thee to my heart.

BANQUO There if I grow,
The harvest is your own.

DUNCAN My plenteous joys,
Wanton in fullness, seek to hide themselves
In drops of sorrow.—Sons, kinsmen, thanes,
And you whose places are the nearest, know
We will establish our estate upon
Our eldest, Malcolm, whom we name hereafter
The Prince of Cumberland; which honor must
Not unaccompanied invest him only,
But signs of nobleness, like stars, shall shine
On all deservers. From hence to Inverness,
And bind us further to you.

MACBETH
The rest is labor which is not us'd for you.
I'll be myself the harbinger and make joyful
The hearing of my wife with your approach;
So humbly take my leave.

DUNCAN My worthy Cawdor!

MACBETH [*Aside*]
The Prince of Cumberland! That is a step
On which I must fall down, or else o'erleap,
For in my way it lies. Stars, hide your fires;
Let not light see my black and deep desires.
The eye wink at the hand; yet let that be
Which the eye fears, when it is done, to see. *Exit.*

DUNCAN
True, worthy Banquo. He is full so valiant,
And in his commendations I am fed;
It is a banquet to me. Let's after him,
Whose care is gone before to bid us welcome.
It is a peerless kinsman. *Flourish. Exeunt.*

SCENE V

Enter Macbeth's Wife, alone, with a letter.

LADY MACBETH [*Reads*] "They met me in the day of success; and I have learn'd by the perfect'st report they have more in them than mortal knowledge. When I

148 stay wait **149 favor** pardon **151 regist'red** recorded (in my memory) **153 at more time** at a time of greater leisure **155 Our free hearts** our hearts freely

I.iv. Location: Forres. The palace.
2 in commission having warrant (to see to the execution of Cawdor) **10 ow'd** owned **11 careless** uncared for **16 before** ahead (in deserving) **19–20 That . . . mine** i.e., that I might have thanked and rewarded you in ample proportion to your worth

25 Are . . . servants i.e., are like children and servants in relation to your throne and dignity, existing only to serve you **27 Safe toward** to safeguard **34 Wanton** unrestrained **37 establish our estate** fix the succession of our state **40 Not . . . only** i.e., not be bestowed on Malcolm alone; other deserving nobles are to share honors **42 Inverness** the seat or location of Macbeth's castle, Dunsinane **43 bind . . . you** i.e., put me further in your (Macbeth's) obligation by your hospitality **44 The . . . you** i.e., even repose, when not devoted to your service, becomes tedious and wearisome **45 harbinger** forerunner, messenger **50 in my way it lies** (Prince of Cumberland was the title of the heir apparent to Duncan's throne. The monarchy was not hereditary, and Macbeth had a right to believe that he himself might be chosen as Duncan's successor; he here questions whether he will interfere with the course of events.) **52 wink . . . hand** blind itself to the hand's deed

I.v. Location: Inverness. Macbeth's castle.
2 perfect'st most accurate

burnt in desire to question them further, they made themselves air, into which they vanish'd. Whiles I stood rapt in the wonder of it, came missives from the King, who all-hail'd me 'Thane of Cawdor,' by which title, before, these weird sisters saluted me, and referr'd me to the coming on of time with 'Hail, king that shalt be!' This have I thought good to deliver thee, my dearest partner of greatness, that thou mightst not lose the dues of rejoicing by being ignorant of what greatness is promis'd thee. Lay it to thy heart, and farewell."

Glamis thou art, and Cawdor, and shalt be
What thou art promis'd. Yet do I fear thy nature;
It is too full o' th' milk of human kindness
To catch the nearest way. Thou wouldst be great,
Art not without ambition, but without
The illness should attend it. What thou wouldst highly,
That wouldst thou holily; wouldst not play false,
And yet wouldst wrongly win. Thou'dst have, great Glamis,
That which cries "Thus thou must do," if thou have it;
And that which rather thou dost fear to do
Than wishest should be undone. Hie thee hither,
That I may pour my spirits in thine ear,
And chastise with the valor of my tongue
All that impedes thee from the golden round,
Which fate and metaphysical aid doth seem
To have thee crown'd withal.

Enter Messenger.

What is your tidings?

MESSENGER
The King comes here tonight.

LADY MACBETH
Thou 'rt mad to say it!
Is not thy master with him? Who, were 't so,
Would have inform'd for preparation.

MESSENGER
So please you, it is true. Our thane is coming.
One of my fellows had the speed of him,
Who, almost dead for breath, had scarcely more
Than would make up his message.

LADY MACBETH
Give him tending;
He brings great news. *Exit Messenger.*
The raven himself is hoarse
That croaks the fatal entrance of Duncan
Under my battlements. Come, you spirits
That tend on mortal thoughts, unsex me here,
And fill me from the crown to the toe top-full
Of direst cruelty! Make thick my blood;
Stop up th' access and passage to remorse,
That no compunctious visitings of nature
Shake my fell purpose, nor keep peace between
Th' effect and it! Come to my woman's breasts,
And take my milk for gall, you murd'ring ministers,
Wherever in your sightless substances
You wait on nature's mischief! Come, thick night,
And pall thee in the dunnest smoke of hell,
That my keen knife see not the wound it makes,
Nor heaven peep through the blanket of the dark,
To cry "Hold, hold!"

Enter Macbeth.

Great Glamis! Worthy Cawdor!
Greater than both, by the all-hail hereafter!
Thy letters have transported me beyond
This ignorant present, and I feel now
The future in the instant.

MACBETH
My dearest love,
Duncan comes here tonight.

LADY MACBETH
And when goes hence?

MACBETH
Tomorrow, as he purposes.

LADY MACBETH
O, never
Shall sun that morrow see!
Your face, my thane, is as a book where men
May read strange matters. To beguile the time,
Look like the time; bear welcome in your eye,
Your hand, your tongue. Look like th' innocent flower,
But be the serpent under 't. He that's coming
Must be provided for; and you shall put
This night's great business into my dispatch,
Which shall to all our nights and days to come
Give solely sovereign sway and masterdom.

MACBETH
We will speak further.

LADY MACBETH
Only look up clear.
To alter favor ever is to fear.
Leave all the rest to me. *Exeunt.*

SCENE VI

Hautboys and torches. Enter King [Duncan], Malcolm, Donalbain, Banquo, Lennox, Macduff, Ross, Angus, and Attendants.

DUNCAN
This castle hath a pleasant seat. The air
Nimbly and sweetly recommends itself
Unto our gentle senses.

BANQUO
This guest of summer,
The temple-haunting martlet, does approve,
By his lov'd mansionry, that the heaven's breath
Smells wooingly here. No jutty, frieze,
Buttress, nor coign of vantage, but this bird

6 missives messengers **10 deliver** inform **20 illness** evil (which) **24–25 And that . . . undone** i.e., your fears to achieve what you desire exceed your wish to see the thing accomplished **28 round** crown **29 metaphysical** supernatural **33 inform'd for preparation** i.e., sent me word so that I might get things ready **35 had . . . of** outstripped **41 tend . . . thoughts** attend on, act as the instruments of deadly or murderous thoughts **44 remorse** pity **45 nature** natural feelings **46 fell** fierce, cruel. **keep peace** intervene

48 for gall in exchange for gall. **ministers** agents **49 sightless** invisible **50 wait on** attend, assist **51 pall** envelop. **dunnest** darkest **56 letters have** i.e., letter has **63 beguile the time** i.e., deceive all observers **68 dispatch** management **71 look up clear** give the appearance of being untroubled **72 To . . . fear** to show a troubled countenance is to arouse suspicion

I.vi. Location: Before Macbeth's castle.
s.d. Hautboys oboes **1 seat** site **3 gentle** (1) noble (2) delicate (applied to the air) **4 temple-haunting** nesting in churches. **martlet** house martin. **approve** prove **5 mansionry** nest-building **6 jutty** projection of wall or building **7 coign of vantage** convenient corner, i.e., for nesting

Hath made his pendent bed and procreant cradle. 8
Where they most breed and haunt, I have observ'd
The air is delicate.

Enter Lady [Macbeth].

DUNCAN See, see, our honor'd hostess!
The love that follows us sometime is our trouble, 11
Which still we thank as love. Herein I teach you 12
How you shall bid God 'ild us for your pains, 13
And thank us for your trouble.

LADY MACBETH All our service
In every point twice done, and then done double,
Were poor and single business to contend 16
Against those honors deep and broad wherewith 17
Your Majesty loads our house. For those of old, 18
And the late dignities heap'd up to them, 19
We rest your hermits.

DUNCAN Where's the Thane of Cawdor? 20
We cours'd him at the heels, and had a purpose 21
To be his purveyor; but he rides well, 22
And his great love, sharp as his spur, hath holp him 23
To his home before us. Fair and noble hostess,
We are your guest tonight.

LADY MACBETH Your servants ever
Have theirs, themselves, and what is theirs, in
compt, 26
To make their audit at your Highness' pleasure,
Still to return your own.

DUNCAN Give me your hand. 28
Conduct me to mine host; we love him highly,
And shall continue our graces towards him.
By your leave, hostess. *Exeunt.*

SCENE VII

Hautboys. Torches. Enter a Sewer, and divers Servants with dishes and service, [and pass] over the stage. Then enter Macbeth.

MACBETH
If it were done when 'tis done, then 'twere well
It were done quickly. If th' assassination
Could trammel up the consequence, and catch 3
With his surcease success, that but this blow 4
Might be the be-all and the end-all—here, 5
But here, upon this bank and shoal of time,
We'd jump the life to come. But in these cases 7

8 procreant for breeding **11–12 The love . . . love** i.e., the love that sometimes forces itself inconveniently upon us we still appreciate, since it is meant as love. (Duncan is graciously suggesting that his visit is a bother, but, he hopes, a welcome one.) **13 bid . . . pains** ask God to reward me for the trouble I'm giving you. (This is said in the same gently jocose spirit as ll. 11–12.) **16 single** small, inconsiderable **16–17 contend Against** vie with **18 those of old** i.e., honors formerly bestowed on us **19 late** recent. **to** beside, in addition to **20 rest** remain. **hermits** i.e., those who will pray for you like hermits or beadsmen **21 cours'd** followed (as in a hunt) **22 purveyor** an officer sent ahead to provide for entertainment; here, forerunner **23 holp** helped **26 Have theirs** i.e., have their servants. **what is theirs** their wealth, possessions. **in compt** in trust, under obligation (to serve the King) **28 Still** always. **return your own** i.e., merely render back what is yours, since we hold it in trust from you

I.vii. Location: Macbeth's castle; an inner courtyard.
s.d. Sewer chief waiter, butler **3 trammel . . . consequence** entangle in a net and prevent the resulting events **4 surcease** cessation (of the assassination and of Duncan's life). **success** what succeeds, follows **5 here** in this world **7 jump** risk. (But imaging the physical act is characteristic of Macbeth; cf. l. 27.)

We still have judgment here, that we but teach 8
Bloody instructions, which, being taught, return 9
To plague th' inventor. This even-handed justice
Commends th' ingredience of our poison'd chalice 11
To our own lips. He's here in double trust:
First, as I am his kinsman and his subject,
Strong both against the deed; then, as his host,
Who should against his murderer shut the door,
Not bear the knife myself. Besides, this Duncan
Hath borne his faculties so meek, hath been 17
So clear in his great office, that his virtues 18
Will plead like angels, trumpet-tongu'd, against
The deep damnation of his taking-off; 20
And pity, like a naked new-born babe,
Striding the blast, or heaven's cherubin, hors'd
Upon the sightless couriers of the air, 23
Shall blow the horrid deed in every eye,
That tears shall drown the wind. I have no spur 25
To prick the sides of my intent, but only
Vaulting ambition, which o'erleaps itself
And falls on th' other— 28

Enter Lady [Macbeth].

How now, what news?

LADY MACBETH
He has almost supp'd. Why have you left the
chamber?

MACBETH
Hath he ask'd for me?

LADY MACBETH Know you not he has?

MACBETH
We will proceed no further in this business.
He hath honor'd me of late, and I have bought 33
Golden opinions from all sorts of people,
Which would be worn now in their newest gloss,
Not cast aside so soon.

LADY MACBETH Was the hope drunk
Wherein you dress'd yourself? Hath it slept since?
And wakes it now, to look so green and pale 38
At what it did so freely? From this time
Such I account thy love. Art thou afeard
To be the same in thine own act and valor
As thou art in desire? Wouldst thou have that
Which thou esteem'st the ornament of life,
And live a coward in thine own esteem,
Letting "I dare not" wait upon "I would,"
Like the poor cat i' th' adage?

MACBETH Prithee, peace! 46
I dare do all that may become a man;
Who dares do more is none.

LADY MACBETH What beast was 't, then,
That made you break this enterprise to me? 49
When you durst do it, then you were a man;
And, to be more than what you were, you would
Be so much more the man. Nor time nor place

8 still have judgment are invariably punished. **that** in that **9 instructions** lessons **11 ingredience** contents of a mixture **17 faculties** powers of office **18 clear** free of taint **20 taking-off** murder **23 sightless couriers** invisible steeds or runners, i.e., the winds **25 shall drown the wind** i.e., will be as heavy as a downpour of rain, which is thought to still the wind **28 other** other side. (The image is of a horseman vaulting into his saddle and ignominiously falling on the opposite side.) **33 bought** acquired **38 green** sickly **46 adage** (I.e., "The cat would eat fish, and would not wet her feet.") **49 break** broach

Did then adhere, and yet you would make both. 53
They have made themselves, and that their
fitness now 54
Does unmake you. I have given suck, and know
How tender 'tis to love the babe that milks me;
I would, while it was smiling in my face,
Have pluck'd my nipple from his boneless gums
And dash'd the brains out, had I so sworn as you
Have done to this.

MACBETH
If we should fail?

LADY MACBETH
We fail?
But screw your courage to the sticking place, 61
And we'll not fail. When Duncan is asleep—
Whereto the rather shall his day's hard journey
Soundly invite him—his two chamberlains
Will I with wine and wassail so convince 65
That memory, the warder of the brain, 66
Shall be a fume, and the receipt of reason 67
A limbeck only. When in swinish sleep 68
Their drenched natures lies as in a death,
What cannot you and I perform upon
Th' unguarded Duncan? What not put upon
His spongy officers, who shall bear the guilt 72
Of our great quell?

MACBETH
Bring forth men-children only! 73
For thy undaunted mettle should compose 74
Nothing but males. Will it not be receiv'd, 75
When we have mark'd with blood those sleepy two
Of his own chamber, and us'd their very daggers,
That they have done 't?

LADY MACBETH
Who dares receive it other, 78
As we shall make our griefs and clamor roar
Upon his death?

MACBETH
I am settled, and bend up
Each corporal agent to this terrible feat.
Away, and mock the time with fairest show. 82
False face must hide what the false heart doth know.
Exeunt.

ACT II • SCENE I

Enter Banquo, and Fleance, with a torch before him.

BANQUO
How goes the night, boy?

FLEANCE
The moon is down; I have not heard the clock.

BANQUO
And she goes down at twelve.

FLEANCE
I take 't, 'tis later, sir.

BANQUO
Hold, take my sword. [*Gives him his sword.*] There's
husbandry in heaven; 4
Their candles are all out. Take thee that too.
[*Gives him his belt and dagger.*]
A heavy summons lies like lead upon me, 6
And yet I would not sleep. Merciful Powers, 7
Restrain in me the cursed thoughts that nature
Gives way to in repose!

Enter Macbeth, and a Servant with a torch.

Give me my sword.
[*Takes sword.*]
Who's there?

MACBETH
A friend.

BANQUO
What, sir, not yet at rest? The King's a-bed.
He hath been in unusual pleasure, and
Sent forth great largess to your offices. 14
This diamond he greets your wife withal,
By the name of most kind hostess, and shut up 16
In measureless content. [*Gives diamond.*]

MACBETH
Being unprepar'd, 17
Our will became the servant to defect, 18
Which else should free have wrought. 19

BANQUO
All's well.
I dreamt last night of the three weird sisters.
To you they have show'd some truth.

MACBETH
I think not of them.
Yet, when we can entreat an hour to serve,
We would spend it in some words upon that
business,
If you would grant the time.

BANQUO
At your kind'st leisure.

MACBETH
If you shall cleave to my consent, when 'tis, 26
It shall make honor for you.

BANQUO
So I lose none 27
In seeking to augment it, but still keep
My bosom franchis'd and allegiance clear, 29
I shall be counsel'd.

MACBETH
Good repose the while! 30

BANQUO
Thanks, sir. The like to you.
Exit Banquo [*with Fleance*].

MACBETH
Go bid thy mistress, when my drink is ready,
She strike upon the bell. Get thee to bed.
Exit [*Servant*].
Is this a dagger which I see before me,

53 adhere agree, suit **54 that their fitness** their very suitability **61 But** only. **sticking place** the notch into which is fitted the string of a cross-bow cranked taut for shooting **65 wassail** carousal, drink. **convince** overpower **66–68 warder . . . only** (The brain was thought to be divided into three ventricles, imagination in front, memory at the back, and between them the seat of reason. The fumes of wine, arising from the stomach, would deaden memory and judgment.) **67 receipt** receptacle, ventricle **68 limbeck** alembic, still **72 spongy** soaked, drunken **73 quell** murder **74 mettle** substance, quality **75 receiv'd** i.e., as truth **78 other** otherwise **82 mock** deceive

II.i. Location: Inner courtyard of Macbeth's castle. Time is virtually continuous from the previous scene.

4 husbandry economy **6 summons** i.e., to sleep **7 Powers** order of angels deputed by God to resist demons **14 largess** gifts, gratuities. **offices** quarters where the household work was done **16–17 shut up In** concluded what he had to say with expressions of; or, perhaps, he professes himself enclosed in **18 Our . . . defect** our good will (to entertain the King handsomely) was limited by our meager means (at such short notice) **19 free** freely, unrestrainedly **26 cleave . . . 'tis** give me your support when the time comes **27 So** provided **29 franchis'd** free (from guilt). **clear** unstained **30 counsel'd** receptive to suggestion

The handle toward my hand? Come, let me clutch thee.
I have thee not, and yet I see thee still.
Art thou not, fatal vision, sensible
To feeling as to sight? Or art thou but
A dagger of the mind, a false creation,
Proceeding from the heat-oppressed brain?
I see thee yet, in form as palpable
As this which now I draw. *[Draws dagger.]*
Thou marshall'st me the way that I was going,
And such an instrument I was to use.
Mine eyes are made the fools o' th' other senses,
Or else worth all the rest. I see thee still,
And on thy blade and dudgeon gouts of blood, 47
Which was not so before. There's no such thing.
It is the bloody business which informs 49
Thus to mine eyes. Now o'er the one half-world
Nature seems dead, and wicked dreams abuse 51
The curtain'd sleep; witchcraft celebrates
Pale Hecate's off'rings, and wither'd murder, 53
Alarum'd by his sentinel, the wolf, 54
Whose howl's his watch, thus with his stealthy pace, 55
With Tarquin's ravishing strides, towards his design 56
Moves like a ghost. Thou sure and firm-set earth,
Hear not my steps, which way they walk, for fear
Thy very stones prate of my whereabout,
And take the present horror from the time, 60
Which now suits with it. Whiles I threat, he lives; 61
Words to the heat of deeds too cold breath gives.
A bell rings.
I go, and it is done; the bell invites me.
Hear it not, Duncan, for it is a knell
That summons thee to heaven or to hell. *Exit.*

SCENE II

Enter Lady [Macbeth].

LADY MACBETH
That which hath made them drunk hath made me bold;
What hath quench'd them hath given me fire. Hark! Peace!
It was the owl that shriek'd, the fatal bellman, 3
Which gives the stern'st good-night. He is about it. 4
The doors are open; and the surfeited grooms 5
Do mock their charge with snores. I have drugg'd their possets, 6
That death and nature do contend about them
Whether they live or die.
MACBETH *[Within]* Who's there? What, ho!
LADY MACBETH
Alack, I am afraid they have awak'd,
And 'tis not done. Th' attempt and not the deed
Confounds us. Hark! I laid their daggers ready; 11
He could not miss 'em. Had he not resembled
My father as he slept, I had done 't.

Enter Macbeth, [bearing bloody daggers].

My husband!
MACBETH
I have done the deed. Didst thou not hear a noise?
LADY MACBETH
I heard the owl scream and the crickets cry.
Did not you speak?
MACBETH When?
LADY MACBETH Now.
MACBETH As I descended?
LADY MACBETH
Ay.
MACBETH Hark! Who lies i' th' second chamber?
LADY MACBETH
Donalbain.
MACBETH This is a sorry sight. *[Looks at his hands.]*
LADY MACBETH
A foolish thought, to say a sorry sight.
MACBETH
There's one did laugh in 's sleep, and one cried "Murder!"
That they did wake each other. I stood and heard them.
But they did say their prayers, and address'd them 22
Again to sleep.
LADY MACBETH There are two lodg'd together.
MACBETH
One cried "God bless us!" and "Amen!" the other,
As they had seen me with these hangman's hands. 25
List'ning their fear, I could not say "Amen,"
When they did say "God bless us!"
LADY MACBETH
Consider it not so deeply.
MACBETH
But wherefore could not I pronounce "Amen"?
I had most need of blessing, and "Amen"
Stuck in my throat.
LADY MACBETH These deeds must not be thought 31
After these ways; so, it will make us mad.
MACBETH
Methought I heard a voice cry "Sleep no more!
Macbeth does murder sleep," the innocent sleep,

47 dudgeon hilt of a dagger. **gouts** drops **49 informs** creates forms or impressions **51 abuse** deceive **53 Hecate's** (Hecate was the goddess of witchcraft.) **54 Alarum'd** given the signal to action **55 watch** i.e., a cry like the hourly call of the night watchman **56 Tarquin's** (Tarquin was a Roman tyrant who ravished Lucrece.) **60–61 And take . . . with it** and thus imitate and augment the horror which is so suited to this evil hour (?) or, remove the present horror, the murder, by crying out and revealing Macbeth's intent (?)

II.ii. Location: Scene continues.
3 bellman town-crier, night-watch **4 stern'st good-night** i.e., notice to condemned criminals that they are to be executed in the morning **5 grooms** servants

6 possets hot milk poured on ale or wine and spiced, a bedtime drink common at the time **11 Confounds** ruins **22 address'd them** settled themselves **25 As** as if. **hangman's hands** bloody hands (because the hangman would draw and quarter the condemned, and also executed with an axe) **31 thought** thought upon

Sleep that knits up the ravel'd sleave of care,
The death of each day's life, sore labor's bath,
Balm of hurt minds, great nature's second course,
Chief nourisher in life's feast—

LADY MACBETH What do you mean?

MACBETH
Still it cried "Sleep no more!" to all the house;
"Glamis hath murder'd sleep, and therefore Cawdor
Shall sleep no more; Macbeth shall sleep no more."

LADY MACBETH
Who was it that thus cried? Why, worthy thane,
You do unbend your noble strength, to think
So brainsickly of things. Go get some water,
And wash this filthy witness from your hand.
Why did you bring these daggers from the place?
They must lie there. Go carry them, and smear
The sleepy grooms with blood.

MACBETH I'll go no more.
I am afraid to think what I have done;
Look on 't again I dare not.

LADY MACBETH Infirm of purpose!
Give me the daggers. The sleeping and the dead
Are but as pictures. 'Tis the eye of childhood
That fears a painted devil. If he do bleed,
I'll gild the faces of the grooms withal,
For it must seem their guilt.

[Takes daggers, and] Exit. Knock within.

MACBETH Whence is that knocking?
How is 't with me, when every noise appalls me?
What hands are here? Ha! They pluck out mine
eyes.
Will all great Neptune's ocean wash this blood
Clean from my hand? No, this my hand will rather
The multitudinous seas incarnadine,
Making the green one red.

Enter Lady [Macbeth].

LADY MACBETH
My hands are of your color; but I shame
To wear a heart so white. *(Knock.)* I hear a knocking
At the south entry. Retire we to our chamber.
A little water clears us of this deed.
How easy is it, then! Your constancy
Hath left you unattended. *(Knock.)* Hark! More
knocking.
Get on your nightgown, lest occasion calls us
And show us to be watchers. Be not lost
So poorly in your thoughts.

MACBETH
To know my deed, 'twere best not know myself.
Knock.
Wake Duncan with thy knocking! I would thou
couldst! *Exeunt.*

35 ravel'd sleave tangled skein **37 second course** (Ordinary feasts had two courses, of which the second was the *chief nourisher;* here, sleep is seen as following eating in a restorative process.) **43 unbend** slacken **54 gild** (Gold was ordinarily spoken of as red.) **60 incarnadine** make red **61 one red** one all-pervading red **66–67 Your . . . unattended** your firmness has deserted you **68 nightgown** dressing gown **69 watchers** those who have remained awake **70 poorly** dejectedly **71 To . . . myself** i.e., it were better to be lost in my thoughts than to have consciousness of my deed

SCENE III

Knocking within. Enter a Porter.

PORTER Here's a knocking indeed! If a man were porter of hell gate, he should have old turning the key. *(Knock.)* Knock, knock, knock! Who's there, i' th' name of Beelzebub? Here's a farmer that hang'd himself on th' expectation of plenty. Come in time! Have napkins enow about you; here you'll sweat for 't. *(Knock.)* Knock, knock! Who's there, in th' other devil's name? Faith, here's an equivocator, that could swear in both the scales against either scale; who committed treason enough for God's sake, yet could not equivocate to heaven. O, come in, equivocator. *(Knock.)* Knock, knock, knock! Who's there? Faith, here's an English tailor come hither for stealing out of a French hose. Come in, tailor. Here you may roast your goose. *(Knock.)* Knock, knock! Never at quiet! What are you? But this place is too cold for hell. I'll devil-porter it no further. I had thought to have let in some of all professions that go the primrose way to th' everlasting bonfire. *(Knock.)* Anon, anon! [*Opens the gate.*] I pray you, remember the porter.

Enter Macduff and Lennox.

MACDUFF
Was it so late, friend, ere you went to bed,
That you do lie so late?

PORTER Faith, sir, we were carousing till the second cock; and drink, sir, is a great provoker of three things.

MACDUFF What three things does drink especially provoke?

PORTER Marry, sir, nose-painting, sleep, and urine. Lechery, sir, it provokes, and unprovokes; it provokes the desire, but it takes away the performance. Therefore much drink may be said to be an equivocator with lechery: it makes him, and it mars him; it sets him on, and it takes him off; it persuades him, and disheartens him; makes him stand to, and not stand to; in conclusion, equivocates him in a sleep, and, giving him the lie, leaves him.

MACDUFF I believe drink gave thee the lie last night.

PORTER That it did, sir, i' the very throat on me; but I requited him for his lie; and, I think, being too strong

II.iii. Location: Scene continues. The knocking at the door has already been heard in II.ii. It is not necessary to assume literally, however, that Macbeth and Lady Macbeth have been talking near the *south entry* (II.ii.64) where the knocking is heard.
2 old i.e., plenty of **4–5 Here's . . . plenty** i.e., here's a farmer who has hoarded in anticipation of a scarcity, and will be justly punished by a crop surplus and low prices **5 Come in time** i.e., you have come in good time **6 napkins** handkerchiefs. **enow** enough **8 equivocator** (This is regarded by many editors as an allusion to the trial of the Jesuit Henry Garnet for treason in the spring of 1606, and to the doctrine of equivocation said to have been presented in his defense; according to this doctrine a lie was not a lie if the utterer had in his mind a different meaning in which the utterance was true.) **14 French hose** very narrow breeches and therefore hard for the tailor to steal cloth from when he made them; or, very loose-fitting breeches, in which case the tailor would easily be tempted to skimp on the cloth supplied him for their manufacture **14–15 roast your goose** heat your tailor's smoothing iron (with an obvious pun) **23–24 second cock** i.e., 3 a.m., when the cock was thought to crow a second time **27 Marry** (Originally, an oath by the Virgin Mary.) **nose-painting** i.e., reddening of the nose through drink **36 gave thee the lie** (1) called you a liar (2) made you unable to stand, and put you to sleep

for him, though he took up my legs sometime, yet I made a shift to cast him.

MACDUFF Is thy master stirring?

Enter Macbeth.

Our knocking has awak'd him. Here he comes.

LENNOX
Good morrow, noble sir.

MACBETH Good morrow, both.

MACDUFF
Is the King stirring, worthy thane?

MACBETH Not yet.

MACDUFF
He did command me to call timely on him.
I have almost slipp'd the hour.

MACBETH I'll bring you to him.

MACDUFF
I know this is a joyful trouble to you;
But yet 'tis one.

MACBETH
The labor we delight in physics pain.
This is the door.

MACDUFF I'll make so bold to call,
For 'tis my limited service. *Exit Macduff.*

LENNOX
Goes the King hence today?

MACBETH
He does; he did appoint so.

LENNOX
The night has been unruly. Where we lay,
Our chimneys were blown down, and, as they say,
Lamentings heard i' th' air; strange screams of death,
And prophesying, with accents terrible
Of dire combustion and confus'd events
New hatch'd to th' woeful time. The obscure bird
Clamor'd the livelong night. Some say the earth
Was feverous and did shake.

MACBETH 'Twas a rough night.

LENNOX
My young remembrance cannot parallel
A fellow to it.

Enter Macduff.

MACDUFF
O horror, horror, horror! Tongue nor heart
Cannot conceive nor name thee!

MACBETH AND LENNOX What's the matter?

MACDUFF
Confusion now hath made his masterpiece!
Most sacrilegious murder hath broke ope
The Lord's anointed temple, and stole thence
The life o' th' building!

MACBETH What is 't you say? The life?

LENNOX
Mean you his Majesty?

MACDUFF
Approach the chamber, and destroy your sight
With a new Gorgon. Do not bid me speak;
See, and then speak yourselves.

Exeunt Macbeth and Lennox.

Awake, awake!
Ring the alarum-bell. Murder and treason!
Banquo and Donalbain! Malcolm! Awake!
Shake off this downy sleep, death's counterfeit,
And look on death itself! Up, up, and see
The great doom's image! Malcolm! Banquo!
As from your graves rise up, and walk like sprites,
To countenance this horror! Ring the bell. *Bell rings.*

Enter Lady [Macbeth].

LADY MACBETH
What's the business,
That such a hideous trumpet calls to parley
The sleepers of the house? Speak, speak!

MACDUFF
O gentle lady,
'Tis not for you to hear what I can speak.
The repetition, in a woman's ear,
Would murder as it fell.

Enter Banquo.

O Banquo, Banquo,
Our royal master's murder'd!

LADY MACBETH Woe, alas!
What, in our house?

BANQUO Too cruel anywhere.
Dear Duff, I prithee, contradict thyself
And say it is not so.

Enter Macbeth, Lennox, and Ross.

MACBETH
Had I but died an hour before this chance,
I had liv'd a blessed time; for, from this instant,
There's nothing serious in mortality;
All is but toys. Renown and grace is dead;
The wine of life is drawn, and the mere lees
Is left this vault to brag of.

Enter Malcolm and Donalbain.

DONALBAIN
What is amiss?

MACBETH You are, and do not know 't.
The spring, the head, the fountain of your blood
Is stopp'd; the very source of it is stopp'd.

MACDUFF
Your royal father's murder'd.

MALCOLM O, by whom?

LENNOX
Those of his chamber, as it seem'd, had done 't.
Their hands and faces were all badg'd with blood;

40 cast (1) throw as in wrestling (2) vomit **45 timely** betimes, early **46 slipp'd** let slip **49 physics pain** i.e., cures that labor of its troublesome aspect **51 limited** appointed **58 combustion** tumult **59 obscure bird** owl, the bird of darkness **66 Confusion** destruction

72 Gorgon one of three monsters with hideous faces (Medusa was a Gorgon) whose look turned the beholders to stone **78 great doom's image** replica of Doomsday **80 countenance** (1) be in keeping with (2) see **86 repetition** recital, report **92 chance** occurrence (the murder of Duncan) **94 serious in mortality** worthwhile in mortal life **95 toys** trifles **96 lees** dregs **97 vault** (1) wine-vault (2) earth, with its vaulted sky **103 badg'd** marked as with a badge or emblem

So were their daggers, which unwip'd we found
Upon their pillows. They star'd and were distracted.
No man's life was to be trusted with them.

MACBETH
O, yet I do repent me of my fury,
That I did kill them.

MACDUFF
Wherefore did you so?

MACBETH
Who can be wise, amaz'd, temp'rate and furious,
Loyal and neutral, in a moment? No man.
Th' expedition of my violent love 111
Outrun the pauser, reason. Here lay Duncan,
His silver skin lac'd with his golden blood, 113
And his gash'd stabs look'd like a breach in nature
For ruin's wasteful entrance; there, the murderers,
Steep'd in the colors of their trade, their daggers
Unmannerly breech'd with gore. Who could refrain, 117
That had a heart to love, and in that heart
Courage to make 's love known?

LADY MACBETH
Help me hence, ho! 119

MACDUFF
Look to the lady.

MALCOLM [*Aside to Donalbain*]
Why do we hold our tongues,
That most may claim this argument for ours? 121

DONALBAIN [*Aside to Malcolm*]
What should be spoken here, where our fate,
Hid in an auger-hole, may rush and seize us? 123
Let's away;
Our tears are not yet brew'd.

MALCOLM [*Aside to Donalbain*]
Nor our strong sorrow
Upon the foot of motion.

BANQUO
Look to the lady. 126
[*Lady Macbeth is carried out.*]
And when we have our naked frailties hid, 127
That suffer in exposure, let us meet
And question this most bloody piece of work, 129
To know it further. Fears and scruples shake us. 130
In the great hand of God I stand, and thence 131
Against the undivulg'd pretense I fight 132
Of treasonous malice.

MACDUFF
And so do I.

ALL
So all. 133

MACBETH
Let's briefly put on manly readiness, 134
And meet i' th' hall together.

ALL
Well contented.

Exeunt [*all but Malcolm and Donalbain*].

MALCOLM
What will you do? Let's not consort with them. 136
To show an unfelt sorrow is an office
Which the false man does easy. I'll to England.

DONALBAIN
To Ireland, I. Our separated fortune
Shall keep us both the safer. Where we are,
There's daggers in men's smiles; the near in blood, 141
The nearer bloody.

MALCOLM
This murderous shaft that's shot 142
Hath not yet lighted, and our safest way 143
Is to avoid the aim. Therefore, to horse,
And let us not be dainty of leave-taking,
But shift away. There's warrant in that theft 146
Which steals itself, when there's no mercy left.

Exeunt.

SCENE IV

Enter Ross with an old Man.

OLD MAN
Threescore and ten I can remember well,
Within the volume of which time I have seen
Hours dreadful and things strange, but this sore night
Hath trifled former knowings.

ROSS
Ha, good father, 4
Thou seest the heavens, as troubled with man's act,
Threatens his bloody stage. By th' clock 'tis day,
And yet dark night strangles the traveling lamp. 7
Is 't night's predominance, or the day's shame, 8
That darkness does the face of earth entomb,
When living light should kiss it?

OLD MAN
'Tis unnatural,
Even like the deed that's done. On Tuesday last,
A falcon, tow'ring in her pride of place, 12
Was by a mousing owl hawk'd at and kill'd. 13

ROSS
And Duncan's horses—a thing most strange and certain—
Beauteous and swift, the minions of their race, 15
Turn'd wild in nature, broke their stalls, flung out,
Contending 'gainst obedience, as they would
Make war with mankind.

OLD MAN
'Tis said they eat each other. 18

ROSS
They did so, to th' amazement of mine eyes
That look'd upon 't.

Enter Macduff.

Here comes the good Macduff.
How goes the world, sir, now?

MACDUFF
Why, see you not?

ROSS
Is 't known who did this more than bloody deed?

111 expedition haste **113 golden** (See II.ii.54, note.) **117 breech'd with gore** covered to the hilts with gore (as with breeches) **119 make 's love known** make manifest his love **121 argument** topic, business **123 in an auger-hole** i.e., in some hiding place, in ambush **126 Upon . . . motion** yet in motion **127 frailties hid** (1) bodies clothed (2) emotions controlled **129 question** discuss **130 scruples** doubts **131–133 thence . . . malice** i.e., with God's help I will fight against the as-yet-unknown purpose which prompted this treason **134 briefly** quickly. **manly readiness** men's clothing, or armor **136 consort** keep company, associate

141 near nearer **142 The nearer bloody** i.e., the greater the danger of being murdered **143 lighted** alighted, descended **146 shift away** disappear by stealth. **warrant** justification

II.iv. Location: Outside Macbeth's castle of Inverness.
4 trifled former knowings made trivial all former experiences **7 traveling lamp** i.e., sun **8 predominance** ascendancy, superior influence (as of a heavenly body) **12 tow'ring** soaring. (A term in falconry.) **place** pitch, highest point in the falcon's flight **13 mousing** i.e., ordinarily preying on mice **15 minions** darlings **18 eat** ate. (Pronounced *et.*)

MACDUFF
Those that Macbeth hath slain.

ROSS
Alas, the day,
What good could they pretend?

MACDUFF
They were suborn'd.
Malcolm and Donalbain, the King's two sons,
Are stol'n away and fled, which puts upon them
Suspicion of the deed.

ROSS
'Gainst nature still!
Thriftless ambition, that will ravin up
Thine own life's means! Then 'tis most like
The sovereignty will fall upon Macbeth.

MACDUFF
He is already nam'd, and gone to Scone
To be invested.

ROSS
Where is Duncan's body?

MACDUFF
Carried to Colmekill,
The sacred storehouse of his predecessors
And guardian of their bones.

ROSS
Will you to Scone?

MACDUFF
No, cousin, I'll to Fife.

ROSS
Well, I will thither.

MACDUFF
Well, may you see things well done there. Adieu,
Lest our old robes sit easier than our new!

ROSS
Farewell, father.

OLD MAN
God's benison go with you, and with those
That would make good of bad, and friends of foes!
Exeunt omnes.

ACT III • SCENE I

Enter Banquo.

BANQUO
Thou hast it now—King, Cawdor, Glamis, all,
As the weird women promis'd, and, I fear,
Thou play'dst most foully for 't. Yet it was said
It should not stand in thy posterity,
But that myself should be the root and father
Of many kings. If there come truth from them—
As upon thee, Macbeth, their speeches shine—
Why, by the verities on thee made good,
May they not be my oracles as well,
And set me up in hope? But hush, no more.

Sennet sounded. Enter Macbeth, as King, Lady [Macbeth], Lennox, Ross, Lords, and Attendants.

MACBETH
Here's our chief guest.

LADY MACBETH
If he had been forgotten,
It had been as a gap in our great feast,
And all-thing unbecoming.

MACBETH
Tonight we hold a solemn supper, sir,
And I'll request your presence.

BANQUO
Let your Highness
Command upon me, to the which my duties
Are with a most indissoluble tie
For ever knit.

MACBETH
Ride you this afternoon?

BANQUO
Ay, my good lord.

MACBETH
We should have else desir'd your good advice,
Which still hath been both grave and prosperous,
In this day's council; but we'll take tomorrow.
Is 't far you ride?

BANQUO
As far, my lord, as will fill up the time
'Twixt this and supper. Go not my horse the better,
I must become a borrower of the night
For a dark hour or twain.

MACBETH
Fail not our feast.

BANQUO
My lord, I will not.

MACBETH
We hear our bloody cousins are bestow'd
In England and in Ireland, not confessing
Their cruel parricide, filling their hearers
With strange invention. But of that tomorrow,
When therewithal we shall have cause of state
Craving us jointly. Hie you to horse. Adieu,
Till you return at night. Goes Fleance with you?

BANQUO
Ay, my good lord. Our time does call upon 's.

MACBETH
I wish your horses swift and sure of foot;
And so I do commend you to their backs.
Farewell. *Exit Banquo.*
Let every man be master of his time
Till seven at night. To make society
The sweeter welcome, we will keep ourself
Till supper-time alone. While then, God be
with you!
Exeunt Lords [with Lady Macbeth and others. Manet Macbeth, and a Servant.]
Sirrah, a word with you. Attend those men
Our pleasure?

SERVANT
They are, my lord, without the palace gate.

MACBETH
Bring them before us. *Exit Servant.*
To be thus is nothing,

24 pretend hope for. **suborn'd** bribed, hired **28 Thriftless** wasteful. **ravin up** devour ravenously **31 nam'd** elected. (See I.iv.50, note.) **Scone** ancient royal city of Scotland near Perth **33 Colmekill** Icolmkill, i.e., Cell of St. Columba, the barren islet of Iona in the Western Islands, a sacred spot where the kings were buried; here called a *storehouse* **36 Fife** (Of which Macduff is Thane.) **40 benison** blessing

III.i. Location: Forres. The palace.
7 shine are brilliantly manifest **10 s.d. Sennet** trumpet call

13 all-thing in every way **14 solemn** ceremonious **21 still** always. **prosperous** profitable **25 Go . . . better** i.e., unless my horse makes better time than I expect **29 bestow'd** lodged **32 invention** falsehood **33–34 cause . . . jointly** questions of state occupying our joint attention **43 While** till **47 thus** i.e., king

But to be safely thus.—Our fears in Banquo
Stick deep, and in his royalty of nature
Reigns that which would be fear'd. 'Tis much he dares;
And to that dauntless temper of his mind
He hath a wisdom that doth guide his valor
To act in safety. There is none but he
Whose being I do fear; and under him
My Genius is rebuk'd, as it is said
Mark Antony's was by Caesar. He chid the sisters
When first they put the name of king upon me,
And bade them speak to him. Then, prophet-like,
They hail'd him father to a line of kings.
Upon my head they plac'd a fruitless crown,
And put a barren scepter in my gripe,
Thence to be wrench'd with an unlineal hand,
No son of mine succeeding. If 't be so,
For Banquo's issue have I fil'd my mind;
For them the gracious Duncan have I murder'd,
Put rancors in the vessel of my peace
Only for them, and mine eternal jewel
Given to the common enemy of man
To make them kings, the seeds of Banquo kings!
Rather than so, come fate into the list,
And champion me to th' utterance!—Who's there?

Enter Servant and two Murderers.

Now go to the door, and stay there till we call.
Exit Servant.
Was it not yesterday we spoke together?

MURDERERS
It was, so please your Highness.

MACBETH
Well then, now
Have you consider'd of my speeches? Know
That it was he in the times past which held you
So under fortune, which you thought had been
Our innocent self. This I made good to you
In our last conference, pass'd in probation with you
How you were borne in hand, how cross'd, the instruments,
Who wrought with them, and all things else that might
To half a soul and to a notion craz'd
Say, "Thus did Banquo."

FIRST MURDERER
You made it known to us.

MACBETH
I did so, and went further, which is now
Our point of second meeting. Do you find
Your patience so predominant in your nature
That you can let this go? Are you so gospel'd
To pray for this good man and for his issue,
Whose heavy hand hath bow'd you to the grave
And beggar'd yours forever?

FIRST MURDERER
We are men, my liege.

MACBETH
Ay, in the catalogue ye go for men,
As hounds and greyhounds, mongrels, spaniels, curs,
Shoughs, water-rugs, and demi-wolves are clept
All by the name of dogs. The valued file
Distinguishes the swift, the slow, the subtle,
The housekeeper, the hunter, every one
According to the gift which bounteous nature
Hath in him clos'd, whereby he does receive
Particular addition, from the bill
That writes them all alike; and so of men.
Now, if you have a station in the file,
Not i' th' worst rank of manhood, say 't;
And I will put that business in your bosoms
Whose execution takes your enemy off,
Grapples you to the heart and love of us,
Who wear our health but sickly in his life,
Which in his death were perfect.

SECOND MURDERER
I am one, my liege,
Whom the vile blows and buffets of the world
Hath so incens'd that I am reckless what
I do to spite the world.

FIRST MURDERER
And I another
So weary with disasters, tugg'd with fortune,
That I would set my life on any chance
To mend it or be rid on 't.

MACBETH
Both of you
Know Banquo was your enemy.

BOTH MURDERERS
True, my lord.

MACBETH
So is he mine, and in such bloody distance
That every minute of his being thrusts
Against my near'st of life. And though I could
With barefac'd power sweep him from my sight
And bid my will avouch it, yet I must not,
For certain friends that are both his and mine,
Whose loves I may not drop, but wail his fall
Who I myself struck down. And thence it is
That I to your assistance do make love,
Masking the business from the common eye
For sundry weighty reasons.

SECOND MURDERER
We shall, my lord,
Perform what you command us.

FIRST MURDERER
Though our lives—

MACBETH
Your spirits shine through you. Within this hour at most
I will advise you where to plant yourselves,
Acquaint you with the perfect spy o' th' time,

48 But unless. **in** concerning **50 would be** deserves to be **51 to** added to **55 Genius** guardian spirit **56 Caesar** Octavius Caesar **61 gripe** grasp **62 with** by **64 fil'd** defiled **66 rancors** malignant enemies (here visualized as a poison added to a vessel full of wholesome drink) **67 eternal jewel** i.e., soul **68 common . . . man** i.e., devil **70 list** lists, place of combat **71 champion me** fight with me in single combat. **to th' utterance** to the last extremity (French, *à l'outrance*) **77 under** out of favor with **79 in probation** in proof, i.e., in detail **80 borne in hand** deceived by false promises. **cross'd** thwarted. **instruments** agents **82 To half a soul** even to a half-wit. **notion** mind **87 gospel'd** imbued with the gospel spirit

93 Shoughs a kind of shaggy dog. **water-rugs** long-haired water dogs. **demi-wolves** a crossbreed with the wolf. **clept** called **94 valued file** list classified according to value **96 housekeeper** watchdog **98 in him clos'd** endowed him with **99–100 Particular . . . alike** particular qualification apart from the catalog that lists them all indiscriminately **111 tugg'd with** pulled about by (as in wrestling) **112 set** risk, stake **115 distance** hostility, enmity **117 near'st of life** most vital part, the heart **119 avouch** warrant **120 For** because of **121 wail** i.e., I must lament **129 perfect spy o' th' time** knowledge or espial of the exact time (?)

The moment on 't, for 't must be done tonight,
And something from the palace; always thought
That I require a clearness. And with him—
To leave no rubs nor botches in the work—
Fleance his son, that keeps him company,
Whose absence is no less material to me
Than is his father's, must embrace the fate
Of that dark hour. Resolve yourselves apart.
I'll come to you anon.

BOTH MURDERERS
We are resolv'd, my lord.

MACBETH
I'll call upon you straight. Abide within.
Exeunt [*Murderers*].
It is concluded. Banquo, thy soul's flight,
If it find heaven, must find it out tonight. [*Exit.*]

SCENE II

Enter Macbeth's Lady and a Servant.

LADY MACBETH
Is Banquo gone from court?

SERVANT
Ay, madam, but returns again tonight.

LADY MACBETH
Say to the King I would attend his leisure
For a few words.

SERVANT
Madam, I will. *Exit.*

LADY MACBETH
Nought's had, all's spent,
Where our desire is got without content.
'Tis safer to be that which we destroy
Than by destruction dwell in doubtful joy.

Enter Macbeth.

How now, my lord? Why do you keep alone,
Of sorriest fancies your companions making,
Using those thoughts which should indeed have died
With them they think on? Things without all remedy
Should be without regard. What's done is done.

MACBETH
We have scorch'd the snake, not kill'd it.
She'll close and be herself, whilst our poor malice
Remains in danger of her former tooth.
But let the frame of things disjoint, both the worlds suffer,
Ere we will eat our meal in fear and sleep
In the affliction of these terrible dreams
That shake us nightly. Better be with the dead,
Whom we, to gain our peace, have sent to peace,
Than on the torture of the mind to lie
In restless ecstasy. Duncan is in his grave;
After life's fitful fever he sleeps well.
Treason has done his worst; nor steel, nor poison,
Malice domestic, foreign levy, nothing,
Can touch him further.

LADY MACBETH
Come on;
Gentle my lord, sleek o'er your rugged looks,
Be bright and jovial among your guests tonight.

MACBETH
So shall I, love, and so, I pray, be you.
Let your remembrance apply to Banquo;
Present him eminence, both with eye and tongue—
Unsafe the while, that we
Must lave our honors in these flattering streams,
And make our faces vizards to our hearts,
Disguising what they are.

LADY MACBETH
You must leave this.

MACBETH
O, full of scorpions is my mind, dear wife!
Thou know'st that Banquo, and his Fleance, lives.

LADY MACBETH
But in them nature's copy's not eterne.

MACBETH
There's comfort yet; they are assailable.
Then be thou jocund. Ere the bat hath flown
His cloister'd flight, ere to black Hecate's summons
The shard-borne beetle with his drowsy hums
Hath rung night's yawning peal, there shall be done
A deed of dreadful note.

LADY MACBETH
What's to be done?

MACBETH
Be innocent of the knowledge, dearest chuck,
Till thou applaud the deed. Come, seeling night,
Scarf up the tender eye of pitiful day,
And with thy bloody and invisible hand
Cancel and tear to pieces that great bond
Which keeps me pale! Light thickens, and the crow
Makes wing to th' rooky wood;
Good things of day begin to droop and drowse,
Whiles night's black agents to their preys do rouse.
Thou marvel'st at my words, but hold thee still;
Things bad begun make strong themselves by ill.
So, prithee, go with me. *Exeunt.*

131 something from some distance removed from. **thought** being borne in mind **132 clearness** freedom from suspicion **133 rubs** defects, rough spots **137 Resolve yourselves apart** make up your minds in private conference

III.ii. Location: The palace.
11 sorriest most despicable or wretched **14 without regard** not pondered upon **15 scorch'd** slashed, cut **16 close** heal. **poor malice** feeble hostility **17 her former tooth** her fang, just as before **18 let . . . suffer** let the universe itself fall apart, both heaven and earth perish

22 peace . . . peace content through satisfaction of desire . . . eternal rest **23 torture** rack **24 ecstasy** frenzy **27 Malice domestic** civil war. **foreign levy** levying of foreign troops (against Scotland) **30 Gentle . . . looks** my noble lord, smooth over your rough looks **33 apply** be shown **34 eminence** favor **35–36 Unsafe . . . streams** i.e., we are unsafe at present, and so must put on a show of flattering cordiality to make our reputation look clean; or, we are unsafe so long as we must flatter thus. (*Lave* means *wash.*) **37 vizards** masks **41 nature's copy** lease of life (i.e., by copyhold or lease subject to cancellation); also, the individual man made from Nature's mold. **eterne** perpetual **45 shard-borne** borne on shards, or horny wing cases **46 yawning** drowsy **48 chuck** (A term of endearment.) **49 seeling** eye-closing. (Night is pictured here as a falconer sewing up the eyes of day lest it should struggle against the deed that is to be done.) **50 Scarf up** blindfold **52 bond** i.e., Banquo's lease of life **54 rooky** full of rooks

SCENE III

Enter three Murderers.

FIRST MURDERER
But who did bid thee join with us?
THIRD MURDERER Macbeth.
SECOND MURDERER
He needs not our mistrust, since he delivers 2
Our offices and what we have to do 3
To the direction just.
FIRST MURDERER Then stand with us. 4
The west yet glimmers with some streaks of day.
Now spurs the lated traveler apace 6
To gain the timely inn, and near approaches
The subject of our watch.
THIRD MURDERER
Hark, I hear horses.
BANQUO *(Within)*
Give us a light there, ho!
SECOND MURDERER
Then 'tis he. The rest
That are within the note of expectation 12
Already are i' th' court.
FIRST MURDERER
His horses go about.
THIRD MURDERER
Almost a mile; but he does usually,
So all men do, from hence to th' palace gate
Make it their walk.

Enter Banquo and Fleance, with a torch.

SECOND MURDERER
A light, a light!
THIRD MURDERER
'Tis he.
FIRST MURDERER
Stand to 't.
BANQUO
It will be rain tonight.
FIRST MURDERER Let it come down.
[*They set upon Banquo.*]
BANQUO
O, treachery! Fly, good Fleance, fly, fly, fly!
Thou mayst revenge.—O slave!
[*Dies. Fleance escapes.*]
THIRD MURDERER
Who did strike out the light?
FIRST MURDERER Was 't not the way? 24
THIRD MURDERER
There's but one down; the son is fled.
SECOND MURDERER
We have lost best half of our affair.
FIRST MURDERER
Well, let's away, and say how much is done. 27
Exeunt.

III.iii. Location: A park near the palace.
2–3 He . . . offices we need not mistrust this man, since he states exactly our duties (as told us by Macbeth) **4 To** according to. **just** exactly. (That is, one can tell he comes from Macbeth, since he has identical instructions.) **6 lated** belated **12 note of expectation** list of those expected **24 way** i.e., thing to do **27 s.d. Exeunt** (Presumably the murderers drag the body of Banquo offstage as they go.)

SCENE IV

Banquet prepar'd. Enter Macbeth, Lady [Macbeth], Ross, Lennox, Lords, and Attendants.

MACBETH
You know your own degrees; sit down. At first 1
And last the hearty welcome. [*They sit.*]
LORDS Thanks to your Majesty. 2
MACBETH
Ourself will mingle with society,
And play the humble host.
Our hostess keeps her state, but in best time 5
We will require her welcome. 6
LADY MACBETH
Pronounce it for me, sir, to all our friends,
For my heart speaks they are welcome.

Enter First Murderer [at the door].

MACBETH
See, they encounter thee with their hearts' thanks. 9
Both sides are even. Here I'll sit i' th' midst. [*Sits.*]
Be large in mirth; anon we'll drink a measure 11
The table round.—[*Rises and goes to the door.*]
There's blood upon thy face.
MURDERER
'Tis Banquo's then.
MACBETH
'Tis better thee without than he within. 14
Is he dispatch'd?
MURDERER
My lord, his throat is cut; that I did for him.
MACBETH
Thou art the best o' th' cut-throats. Yet he's good
That did the like for Fleance; if thou didst it,
Thou art the nonpareil.
MURDERER Most royal sir,
Fleance is scap'd.
MACBETH
Then comes my fit again. I had else been perfect,
Whole as the marble, founded as the rock, 22
As broad and general as the casing air. 23
But now I am cabin'd, cribb'd, confin'd, bound in 24
To saucy doubts and fears. But Banquo's safe? 25
MURDERER
Ay, my good lord. Safe in a ditch he bides,
With twenty trenched gashes on his head,

III.iv. Location: A hall in the palace.
1 degrees ranks (as a determinant of seating) **1–2 At . . . last** at the beginning and the end (of the feast), once for all **5 keeps her state** remains in her chair of state **6 require** request **9 encounter** respond to **11 large** unrestrained **14 'Tis . . . within** it is better for you to have it on you than he to have it within him **22 founded** firmly established **23 broad and general** unconfined. **casing** encasing, enveloping **24 cribb'd** shut in **25 saucy** sharp, impudent

The least a death to nature.

MACBETH Thanks for that.
There the grown serpent lies; the worm that's fled
Hath nature that in time will venom breed,
No teeth for th' present. Get thee gone. Tomorrow
We'll hear ourselves again. *Exit Murderer.*

LADY MACBETH My royal lord,
You do not give the cheer. The feast is sold
That is not often vouch'd, while 'tis a-making,
'Tis given with welcome. To feed were best at home;
From thence, the sauce to meat is ceremony.
Meeting were bare without it.

Enter the Ghost of Banquo, and sits in Macbeth's place.

MACBETH Sweet remembrancer!
Now, good digestion wait on appetite,
And health on both!

LENNOX May 't please your Highness sit.

MACBETH
Here had we now our country's honor roof'd,
Were the grac'd person of our Banquo present,
Who may I rather challenge for unkindness
Than pity for mischance.

ROSS His absence, sir,
Lays blame upon his promise. Please 't your Highness
To grace us with your royal company?

MACBETH [*Seeing his place occupied*]
The table's full.

LENNOX Here is a place reserv'd, sir.

MACBETH
Where?

LENNOX
Here, my good lord. What is 't that moves your Highness?

MACBETH
Which of you have done this?

LORDS What, my good lord?

MACBETH
Thou canst not say I did it. Never shake
Thy gory locks at me.

ROSS
Gentlemen rise. His Highness is not well.
[*They start to rise.*]

LADY MACBETH
Sit, worthy friends. My lord is often thus,
And hath been from his youth. Pray you keep seat.
The fit is momentary; upon a thought
He will again be well. If much you note him,
You shall offend him and extend his passion.
Feed, and regard him not.—[*She confers apart with Macbeth.*] Are you a man?

MACBETH
Ay, and a bold one, that dare look on that
Which might appall the devil.

LADY MACBETH O proper stuff!
This is the very painting of your fear.
This is the air-drawn dagger which, you said,
Led you to Duncan. O, these flaws and starts,
Impostors to true fear, would well become
A woman's story at a winter's fire,
Authoriz'd by her grandam. Shame itself!
Why do you make such faces? When all's done,
You look but on a stool.

MACBETH Prithee, see there!
Behold! Look! Lo, how say you?
Why, what care I? If thou canst nod, speak too.
If charnel-houses and our graves must send
Those that we bury back, our monuments
Shall be the maws of kites. [*Exit Ghost.*]

LADY MACBETH
What, quite unmann'd in folly?

MACBETH
If I stand here, I saw him.

LADY MACBETH Fie, for shame!

MACBETH
Blood hath been shed ere now, i' th' olden time,
Ere humane statute purg'd the gentle weal;
Ay, and since too, murders have been perform'd
Too terrible for the ear. The time has been
That, when the brains were out, the man would die,
And there an end; but now they rise again
With twenty mortal murders on their crowns,
And push us from our stools. This is more strange
Than such a murder is.

LADY MACBETH My worthy lord,
Your noble friends do lack you.

MACBETH [*Approaching the table*] I do forget.
Do not muse at me, my most worthy friends;
I have a strange infirmity, which is nothing
To those that know me. Come, love and health to all!
Then I'll sit down. Give me some wine. Fill full.
[*He is given wine.*]

Enter Ghost.

I drink to th' general joy o' th' whole table,
And to our dear friend Banquo, whom we miss.
Would he were here! To all, and him, we thirst,
And all to all.

LORDS Our duties, and the pledge.
[*They drink.*]

MACBETH [*Seeing Ghost*]
Avaunt, and quit my sight! Let the earth hide thee!
Thy bones are marrowless, thy blood is cold;

29 worm small serpent **32 hear ourselves** confer **33–35 is sold . . . welcome** i.e., seems grudgingly given, as if in return for money, unless it is often accompanied with assurances of welcome while it is in progress **35 To feed . . . home** i.e., mere eating is best done at home **36 From thence** i.e., away from home, dining in company. **meat** food **37 Meeting were bare** gatherings of friends would be unadorned **38 wait on** attend **40 roof'd** under one roof **41 grac'd** gracious **42 Who may I** whom I hope I may. **challenge for** reprove for **55 upon a thought** in a moment **57 extend** prolong

60 O proper stuff O nonsense **62 air-drawn** made of thin air, or floating disembodied in space **63 flaws** gusts, outbursts **64 to** compared with **66 Authoriz'd** vouched for **72–73 our . . . kites** i.e., our only tombs will be the stomachs of birds of prey (since burying will be ineffectual) **77 humane** (This spelling, interchangeable with *human*, carries both meanings: "appertaining to mankind" and "befitting man.") **purg'd . . . weal** cleansed the commonwealth of violence and made it gentle **82 mortal murders** deadly wounds. **crowns** heads **92 thirst** desire to drink **93 all to all** all good wishes to all; or, let all drink to everyone else

Thou hast no speculation in those eyes 96
Which thou dost glare with!

LADY MACBETH
Think of this, good peers,
But as a thing of custom. 'Tis no other;
Only it spoils the pleasure of the time.

MACBETH
What man dare, I dare.
Approach thou like the rugged Russian bear,
The arm'd rhinoceros, or th' Hyrcan tiger; 102
Take any shape but that, and my firm nerves 103
Shall never tremble. Or be alive again,
And dare me to the desert with thy sword; 105
If trembling I inhabit then, protest me 106
The baby of a girl. Hence, horrible shadow! 107
Unreal mock'ry, hence!
[Exit Ghost.]
Why, so; being gone,
I am a man again. Pray you, sit still.

LADY MACBETH
You have displac'd the mirth, broke the good meeting,
With most admir'd disorder.

MACBETH
Can such things be, 111
And overcome us like a summer's cloud, 112
Without our special wonder? You make me strange 113
Even to the disposition that I owe, 114
When now I think you can behold such sights,
And keep the natural ruby of your cheeks,
When mine is blanch'd with fear.

ROSS
What sights, my lord?

LADY MACBETH
I pray you, speak not. He grows worse and worse;
Question enrages him. At once, good night. 119
Stand not upon the order of your going,
But go at once.

LENNOX
Good night; and better health
Attend his Majesty!

LADY MACBETH
A kind good night to all!
Exeunt Lords [and attendants].

MACBETH
It will have blood, they say; blood will have blood.
Stones have been known to move and trees to speak;
Augures and understood relations have 125
By maggot-pies and choughs and rooks brought forth 126
The secret'st man of blood. What is the night? 127

LADY MACBETH
Almost at odds with morning, which is which.

MACBETH
How say'st thou, that Macduff denies his person
At our great bidding?

LADY MACBETH
Did you send to him, sir?

MACBETH
I hear it by the way; but I will send. 131
There's not a one of them but in his house
I keep a servant fee'd. I will tomorrow, 133
And betimes I will, to the weird sisters. 134
More shall they speak; for now I am bent to know,
By the worst means, the worst. For mine own good,
All causes shall give way. I am in blood
Stepp'd in so far that, should I wade no more,
Returning were as tedious as go o'er.
Strange things I have in head, that will to hand,
Which must be acted ere they may be scann'd. 141

LADY MACBETH
You lack the season of all natures, sleep. 142

MACBETH
Come, we'll to sleep. My strange and self-abuse 143
Is the initiate fear that wants hard use. 144
We are yet but young in deed. *Exeunt.*

SCENE V

Thunder. Enter the three Witches, meeting Hecate.

FIRST WITCH
Why, how now, Hecate! You look angerly.

HECATE
Have I not reason, beldams as you are, 2
Saucy and overbold? How did you dare
To trade and traffic with Macbeth
In riddles and affairs of death;
And I, the mistress of your charms,
The close contriver of all harms, 7
Was never call'd to bear my part,
Or show the glory of our art?
And, which is worse, all you have done
Hath been but for a wayward son,
Spiteful and wrathful, who, as others do,
Loves for his own ends, not for you.
But make amends now. Get you gone,
And at the pit of Acheron 15
Meet me i' th' morning. Thither he
Will come to know his destiny.
Your vessels and your spells provide,
Your charms and every thing beside.
I am for th' air. This night I'll spend
Unto a dismal and a fatal end.
Great business must be wrought ere noon.
Upon the corner of the moon
There hangs a vap'rous drop profound; 24
I'll catch it ere it come to ground,
And that, distill'd by magic sleights,

96 speculation power of sight **102 Hyrcan** of Hyrcania, in ancient times a region near the Caspian Sea **103 nerves** sinews **105 the desert** some solitary place **106 If . . . then** i.e., if then I tremble **107 The baby of a girl** a baby girl, or, girl's doll **111 admir'd** wondered at **112 overcome** come over **113–114 You make . . . owe** you cause me to feel I do not know my own nature (which I had presumed to be that of a brave man) **119 Question** talk **125 Augures** auguries. **understood relations** comprehended reports or utterances **126 By . . . choughs** by means of magpies and jackdaws. **brought forth** revealed **127 man of blood** murderer

131 by the way casually **133 fee'd** i.e., paid to spy **134 betimes** early **141 ere . . . scann'd** i.e., even before thinking about them carefully, at once **142 season** seasoning, preservative **143 strange and self-abuse** strange self-delusion **144 initiate fear** fear experienced by a novice. **wants hard use** lacks toughening experience

III.v. Location: A heath. (This scene is probably by another author.)
2 beldams hags **7 close** secret **15 Acheron** the river of sorrows in Hades **24 profound** i.e., heavily pendent, ready to drop off

Shall raise such artificial sprites 27
As by the strength of their illusion
Shall draw him on to his confusion.
He shall spurn fate, scorn death, and bear
His hopes 'bove wisdom, grace, and fear.
And you all know, security 32
Is mortals' chiefest enemy. *Music and a song.*
Hark! I am call'd. My little spirit, see,
Sits in a foggy cloud, and stays for me. [*Exit.*] 35
Sing within, "Come away, come away," *etc.*

FIRST WITCH
Come, let's make haste; she'll soon be back again.
Exeunt.

SCENE VI

Enter Lennox and another Lord.

LENNOX
My former speeches have but hit your thoughts, 1
Which can interpret farther. Only I say 2
Things have been strangely borne. The gracious
Duncan 3
Was pitied of Macbeth; marry, he was dead. 4
And the right valiant Banquo walk'd too late,
Whom you may say, if 't please you, Fleance kill'd,
For Fleance fled. Men must not walk too late.
Who cannot want the thought how monstrous 8
It was for Malcolm and for Donalbain
To kill their gracious father? Damned fact!
How it did grieve Macbeth! Did he not straight
In pious rage the two delinquents tear
That were the slaves of drink and thralls of sleep? 13
Was not that nobly done? Ay, and wisely too;
For 'twould have anger'd any heart alive
To hear the men deny 't. So that I say
He has borne all things well; and I do think
That had he Duncan's sons under his key—
As, an 't please heaven, he shall not—they should
find
What 'twere to kill a father; so should Fleance.
But peace! For from broad words and 'cause he fail'd 21
His presence at the tyrant's feast, I hear
Macduff lives in disgrace. Sir, can you tell
Where he bestows himself?

LORD
The son of Duncan,
From whom this tyrant holds the due of birth, 25
Lives in the English court, and is receiv'd
Of the most pious Edward with such grace 27
That the malevolence of fortune nothing
Takes from his high respect. Thither Macduff 29
Is gone to pray the holy king upon his aid 30
To wake Northumberland and warlike Siward,
That by the help of these—with Him above
To ratify the work—we may again
Give to our tables meat, sleep to our nights,
Free from our feasts and banquets bloody knives, 35
Do faithful homage and receive free honors— 36
All which we pine for now. And this report
Hath so exasperate the King that he 38
Prepares for some attempt of war.

LENNOX
Sent he to Macduff?

LORD
He did; and with an absolute "Sir, not I," 41
The cloudy messenger turns me his back, 42
And hums, as who should say, "You'll rue the time
That clogs me with this answer."

LENNOX
And that well might 44
Advise him to a caution, t' hold what distance 45
His wisdom can provide. Some holy angel 46
Fly to the court of England and unfold
His message ere he come, that a swift blessing
May soon return to this our suffering country 49
Under a hand accurs'd! 50

LORD
I'll send my prayers with him. *Exeunt.*

ACT IV • SCENE I

Thunder. Enter the three Witches.

FIRST WITCH
Thrice the brinded cat hath mew'd. 1

SECOND WITCH
Thrice, and once the hedge-pig whin'd. 2

THIRD WITCH
Harpier cries, "'Tis time, 'tis time." 3

FIRST WITCH
Round about the cauldron go;
In the poison'd entrails throw.
Toad, that under cold stone
Days and nights has thirty one 7
Swelt'red venom sleeping got. 8
Boil thou first i' th' charmed pot.

ALL [*As they dance round the cauldron*]
Double, double, toil and trouble;
Fire burn, and cauldron bubble.

27 artificial produced by magical arts **35 security** overconfidence **35 s.d. Come away** etc. (The song occurs in Thomas Middleton's *The Witch*.)

III.vi. Location: Somewhere in Scotland.
1 My former speeches what I've just said. **hit** coincided with **2 interpret farther** draw further conclusions **3 borne** carried on **4 of** by. **marry . . . dead** i.e., to be sure, this pity occurred after Duncan died, not before **8 cannot . . . thought** can help thinking **13 thralls** slaves **21 from broad words** on account of plain speech **25 holds . . . birth** witholds the birthright (i.e., the Scottish crown) **27 Of** by. **Edward** Edward the Confessor

29 his high respect high respect paid to him. (I.e., being out of fortune has not lessened the dignity with which Malcolm is received in England.) **30 upon his aid** i.e., in aid of Malcolm **35 Free . . . banquets** free our feasts and banquets from **36 free** freely bestowed; or, pertaining to freemen **38 exasperate the King** i.e., exasperated Macbeth **41 with . . . I** i.e., when Macduff answered the messenger curtly with a refusal **42 cloudy** angry. **turns me** i.e., turns. (*Me* is the ethical dative.) **44 clogs** encumbers, loads **45–46 Advise . . . provide** warn him (Macduff) to keep what safe distance he can (from Macbeth) **49–50 suffering country Under** country suffering under

IV.i. Location: A cavern (see III.v.15). In the middle, a boiling cauldron (provided presumably by means of the trap door; see IV.i.106. The trap door must also be used in this scene for the apparitions.)
1 brinded marked by streaks (as by fire), brindled **2 hedge-pig** hedgehog **3 Harpier** (The name of a familiar spirit; probably derived from *harpy*.) **7–8 Days . . . got** for thirty-one days and nights has exuded venom formed during sleep

SECOND WITCH
Fillet of a fenny snake, 12
In the cauldron boil and bake;
Eye of newt and toe of frog,
Wool of bat and tongue of dog,
Adder's fork and blindworm's sting, 16
Lizard's leg and howlet's wing, 17
For a charm of pow'rful trouble,
Like a hell-broth boil and bubble.

ALL
Double, double, toil and trouble;
Fire burn and cauldron bubble.

THIRD WITCH
Scale of dragon, tooth of wolf,
Witches' mummy, maw and gulf 23
Of the ravin'd salt-sea shark, 24
Root of hemlock digg'd i' th' dark,
Liver of blaspheming Jew,
Gall of goat, and slips of yew
Sliver'd in the moon's eclipse, 28
Nose of Turk and Tartar's lips,
Finger of birth-strangled babe
Ditch-deliver'd by a drab, 31
Make the gruel thick and slab. 32
Add thereto a tiger's chaudron, 33
For th' ingredients of our cauldron.

ALL
Double, double, toil and trouble;
Fire burn and cauldron bubble.

SECOND WITCH
Cool it with a baboon's blood,
Then the charm is firm and good.

Enter Hecate to the other three Witches.

HECATE
O, well done! I commend your pains, 39
And everyone shall share i' th' gains.
And now about the cauldron sing,
Like elves and fairies in a ring,
Enchanting all that you put in. 43

Music and a song: "Black spirits," etc.
[*Hecate retires.*]

SECOND WITCH
By the pricking of my thumbs,
Something wicked this way comes.
Open, locks,
Whoever knocks!

Enter Macbeth.

MACBETH
How now, you secret, black, and midnight hags!
What is 't you do?

ALL
A deed without a name.

MACBETH
I conjure you, by that which you profess,
Howe'er you come to know it, answer me.
Though you untie the winds and let them fight
Against the churches, though the yesty waves 53
Confound and swallow navigation up, 54
Though bladed corn be lodg'd and trees blown down, 55
Though castles topple on their warders' heads,
Though palaces and pyramids do slope 57
Their heads to their foundations, though the treasure
Of nature's germains tumble all together, 59
Even till destruction sicken, answer me 60
To what I ask you.

FIRST WITCH
Speak.

SECOND WITCH
Demand.

THIRD WITCH
We'll answer.

FIRST WITCH
Say if th' hadst rather hear it from our mouths,
Or from our masters?

MACBETH
Call 'em. Let me see 'em.

FIRST WITCH
Pour in sow's blood, that hath eaten
Her nine farrow; grease that's sweaten 65
From the murderer's gibbet throw
Into the flame.

ALL
Come high or low,
Thyself and office deftly show! 68

Thunder. First Apparition, an armed Head.

MACBETH
Tell me, thou unknown power—

FIRST WITCH
He knows thy thought.
Hear his speech, but say thou nought.

FIRST APPARITION
Macbeth! Macbeth! Macbeth! Beware Macduff,
Beware the Thane of Fife. Dismiss me. Enough. 72
He descends.

MACBETH
Whate'er thou art, for thy good caution, thanks;
Thou hast harp'd my fear aright. But one word more— 74

FIRST WITCH
He will not be commanded. Here's another,
More potent than the first. 76

Thunder. Second Apparition, a bloody Child.

SECOND APPARITION
Macbeth! Macbeth! Macbeth!

MACBETH
Had I three ears, I'd hear thee.

12 Fillet slice. **fenny** inhabiting fens or swamps **16 fork** forked tongue. **blindworm** a harmless lizard **17 howlet's** owl's **23 mummy** mummified flesh made into a magical potion. **maw and gulf** stomach and gullet **24 ravin'd** ravenous **28 Sliver'd** broken off (as a branch) **31 drab** harlot **32 slab** viscous, thick **33 chaudron** entrails **39–43 O . . . in** (These lines are universally regarded as non-Shakespearean.) **43 s.d. Black spirits** etc. (This song is found in Middleton's *The Witch*.)

53 yesty yeasty, foamy **54 Confound** destroy **55 bladed** in the ear. **corn** (General name for wheat and other grains.) **lodg'd** thrown down, laid **57 slope** bend **59 nature's germains** seed or elements from which all nature operates **60 sicken** be surfeited **65 nine farrow** litter of nine. **sweaten** sweated **68 office** function **68 s.d. armed Head** (Perhaps symbolizes the head of Macbeth cut off by Macduff and presented by him to Malcolm; or the rebellion of Macduff.) **72 s.d. He descends** (I.e., by means of the trap door.) **74 harp'd** hit, touched (as in touching a harp to make it sound) **76 s.d. bloody Child** (Symbolizes Macduff untimely ripped from his mother's womb; see V.viii.15–16.)

SECOND APPARITION
Be bloody, bold, and resolute; laugh to scorn
The pow'r of man, for none of woman born
Shall harm Macbeth. *Descends.*

MACBETH
Then live, Macduff; what need I fear of thee?
But yet I'll make assurance double sure,
And take a bond of fate. Thou shalt not live,
That I may tell pale-hearted fear it lies,
And sleep in spite of thunder.

Thunder. Third Apparition, a Child crowned, with a tree in his hand.

What is this
That rises like the issue of a king,
And wears upon his baby-brow the round
And top of sovereignty?

ALL Listen, but speak not to 't.

THIRD APPARITION
Be lion-mettled, proud, and take no care
Who chafes, who frets, or where conspirers are.
Macbeth shall never vanquish'd be until
Great Birnam wood to high Dunsinane hill
Shall come against him. *Descends.*

MACBETH That will never be.
Who can impress the forest, bid the tree
Unfix his earth-bound root? Sweet bodements, good!
Rebellious dead, rise never till the wood
Of Birnam rise, and our high-plac'd Macbeth
Shall live the lease of nature, pay his breath
To time and mortal custom. Yet my heart
Throbs to know one thing. Tell me, if your art
Can tell so much: shall Banquo's issue ever
Reign in this kingdom?

ALL Seek to know no more.

MACBETH
I will be satisfied. Deny me this,
And an eternal curse fall on you! Let me know.
Why sinks that cauldron? And what noise is this?
[*The cauldron descends.*] *Hautboys.*

FIRST WITCH Show!

SECOND WITCH Show!

THIRD WITCH Show!

ALL
Show his eyes, and grieve his heart;
Come like shadows, so depart!

A show of Eight Kings and Banquo last; [*the eighth King*] *with a glass in his hand.*

MACBETH
Thou art too like the spirit of Banquo. Down!
Thy crown does sear mine eyeballs. And thy hair,
Thou other gold-bound brow, is like the first.
A third is like the former. Filthy hags,
Why do you show me this? A fourth? Start, eyes!
What, will the line stretch out to th' crack of doom?
Another yet? A seventh? I'll see no more.
And yet the eighth appears, who bears a glass
Which shows me many more; and some I see
That twofold balls and treble scepters carry.
Horrible sight! Now, I see, 'tis true,
For the blood-bolter'd Banquo smiles upon me,
And points at them for his. [*Apparitions vanish.*]
What, is this so?

FIRST WITCH
Ay, sir, all this is so. But why
Stands Macbeth thus amazedly?
Come, sisters, cheer we up his sprites,
And show the best of our delights.
I'll charm the air to give a sound,
While you perform your antic round,
That this great king may kindly say
Our duties did his welcome pay.
Music. The Witches dance, and vanish.

MACBETH
Where are they? Gone? Let this pernicious hour
Stand aye accursed in the calendar!
Come in, without there!

Enter Lennox.

LENNOX What's your Grace's will?

MACBETH
Saw you the weird sisters?

LENNOX No, my lord.

MACBETH
Came they not by you?

LENNOX No, indeed, my lord.

MACBETH
Infected be the air whereon they ride,
And damn'd all those that trust them! I did hear
The galloping of horse. Who was 't came by?

LENNOX
'Tis two or three, my lord, that bring you word
Macduff is fled to England.

MACBETH Fled to England!

LENNOX
Ay, my good lord.

MACBETH
Time, thou anticipat'st my dread exploits.
The flighty purpose never is o'ertook
Unless the deed go with it. From this moment
The very firstlings of my heart shall be
The firstlings of my hand. And even now,
To crown my thoughts with acts, be it thought and done:
The castle of Macduff I will surprise,

84 take a bond of get a guarantee from (i.e., by killing Macduff, to make doubly sure he can do no harm) **86 s.d. Child . . . hand** (Symbolizes Malcolm, the royal child; the tree anticipates the cutting of boughs in Birnam Wood, V.iv.) **88–89 round And top** crown **95 impress** press into service, like soldiers **96 bodements** prophecies **97 Rebellious dead** i.e., Banquo and his lineage (?) **99 lease of nature** natural period, full life-span **100 mortal custom** death, the common lot of men **106 noise** music **111 s.d. glass** (magic) mirror **114 other** i.e., second

116 Start bulge from their sockets **121 twofold balls** (A probable reference to the double coronation of James at Scone and Westminster, as King of England and Scotland.) **treble scepters** (Probably refers to James' assumed title as King of Great Britain, France, and Ireland.) **123 blood-bolter'd** having his hair matted with blood **125–132 Ay . . . pay** (These lines are held to be spurious.) **130 antic round** grotesque dance in a circle **132 pay** repay **144 thou anticipat'st** you forestall. (I.e., by allowing time to pass without my acting, I have lost an opportunity.) **145 flighty** fleeting **146 Unless . . . it** unless the execution of the deed accompanies the conception of it immediately **147–148 The very . . . hand** i.e., my impulses will be acted on immediately

Seize upon Fife, give to th' edge o' th' sword
His wife, his babes, and all unfortunate souls
That trace him in his line. No boasting like a fool;
This deed I'll do before this purpose cool.
But no more sights!—Where are these gentlemen?
Come, bring me where they are. *Exeunt.*

SCENE II

Enter Macduff's Wife, her Son, and Ross.

LADY MACDUFF
What had he done, to make him fly the land?

ROSS
You must have patience, madam.

LADY MACDUFF He had none.
His flight was madness. When our actions do not,
Our fears do make us traitors.

ROSS You know not
Whether it was his wisdom or his fear.

LADY MACDUFF
Wisdom? To leave his wife, to leave his babes,
His mansion and his titles in a place
From whence himself does fly? He loves us not,
He wants the natural touch; for the poor wren,
The most diminutive of birds, will fight,
Her young ones in her nest, against the owl.
All is the fear and nothing is the love,
As little is the wisdom, where the flight
So runs against all reason.

ROSS My dearest coz,
I pray you, school yourself. But for your husband,
He is noble, wise, judicious, and best knows
The fits o' th' season. I dare not speak much further,
But cruel are the times when we are traitors
And do not know ourselves, when we hold rumor
From what we fear, yet know not what we fear,
But float upon a wild and violent sea
Each way and move. I take my leave of you;
Shall not be long but I'll be here again.
Things at the worst will cease, or else climb upward
To what they were before. My pretty cousin,
Blessing upon you!

LADY MACDUFF
Father'd he is, and yet he's fatherless.

ROSS
I am so much a fool, should I stay longer,
It would be my disgrace and your discomfort.
I take my leave at once. *Exit Ross.*

LADY MACDUFF
Sirrah, your father's dead;
And what will you do now? How will you live?

SON
As birds do, mother.

LADY MACDUFF What, with worms and flies?

SON
With what I get, I mean; and so do they.

LADY MACDUFF
Poor bird! Thou'dst never fear the net nor lime,
The pitfall nor the gin.

SON
Why should I, mother? Poor birds they are not
set for.
My father is not dead, for all your saying.

LADY MACDUFF
Yes, he is dead. How wilt thou do for a father?

SON Nay, how will you do for a husband?

LADY MACDUFF Why, I can buy me twenty at any market.

SON Then you'll buy 'em to sell again.

LADY MACDUFF
Thou speak'st with all thy wit; and yet, i' faith,
With wit enough for thee.

SON Was my father a traitor, mother?

LADY MACDUFF Ay, that he was.

SON What is a traitor?

LADY MACDUFF Why, one that swears and lies.

SON And be all traitors that do so?

LADY MACDUFF Every one that does so is a traitor, and must be hang'd.

SON And must they all be hang'd that swear and lie?

LADY MACDUFF Every one.

SON Who must hang them?

LADY MACDUFF Why, the honest men.

SON Then the liars and swearers are fools, for there are liars and swearers enow to beat the honest men and hang up them.

LADY MACDUFF Now, God help thee, poor monkey! But how wilt thou do for a father?

SON If he were dead, you'd weep for him; if you would not, it were a good sign that I should quickly have a new father.

LADY MACDUFF Poor prattler, how thou talk'st!

Enter a Messenger.

MESSENGER
Bless you, fair dame! I am not to you known,
Though in your state of honor I am perfect.
I doubt some danger does approach you nearly.
If you will take a homely man's advice,
Be not found here. Hence with your little ones!
To fright you thus, methinks, I am too savage;
To do worse to you were fell cruelty,
Which is too nigh your person. Heaven preserve
you!
I dare abide no longer. *Exit Messenger.*

LADY MACDUFF Whither should I fly?

153 trace follow. **line** family succession

IV.ii. Location: Fife. Macduff's castle.
3–4 When . . . traitors i.e., even when we have committed no treasonous act, our fears of being suspected traitors make us act as if we were **9 wants** lacks. **touch** affection, feeling **14 coz** kinswoman **17 fits o' th' season** violent disorders of the time **18–19 are traitors . . . ourselves** i.e., are accused of treason without knowing why **19–20 hold . . . fear** i.e., believe every fearful rumor without knowing how real the danger is **22 Each . . . move** (Possibly an incomplete sentence; it conveys the idea of being tossed this way and that.) **23 Shall** it shall **29 It . . . discomfort** i.e., I should weep and embarrass us both

35 lime birdlime **36 gin** snare **37 they** i.e., the snares **58 enow** enough **67 in . . . honor** with your honorable state. **perfect** perfectly acquainted **68 doubt** fear **69 homely** plain **72 To do worse** i.e., actually to harm you. **fell** savage **73 Which . . . person** i.e., which savage cruelty is all too near at hand

I have done no harm. But I remember now
I am in this earthly world, where to do harm
Is often laudable, to do good sometime
Accounted dangerous folly. Why then, alas,
Do I put up that womanly defense
To say I have done no harm?

Enter Murderers.

What are these faces?

FIRST MURDERER
Where is your husband?

LADY MACDUFF
I hope in no place so unsanctified
Where such as thou mayst find him.

FIRST MURDERER He's a traitor.

SON
Thou liest, thou shag-ear'd villain!

FIRST MURDERER What, you egg? 84
[*Stabs him.*]
Young fry of treachery!

SON He has kill'd me, mother. 85
Run away, I pray you! [*Dies.*] 86

Exit [*Lady Macduff*] *crying* "Murder!"
[*followed by Murderers*].

SCENE III

Enter Malcolm and Macduff.

MALCOLM
Let us seek out some desolate shade, and there
Weep our sad bosoms empty.

MACDUFF Let us rather
Hold fast the mortal sword, and like good men 3
Bestride our down-fall'n birthdom. Each new morn 4
New widows howl, new orphans cry, new sorrows
Strike heaven on the face, that it resounds
As if it felt with Scotland and yell'd out
Like syllable of dolor.

MALCOLM What I believe, I'll wail; 8
What know, believe; and what I can redress, 9
As I shall find the time to friend, I will. 10
What you have spoke, it may be so perchance.
This tyrant, whose sole name blisters our tongues, 12
Was once thought honest. You have lov'd him well;
He hath not touch'd you yet. I am young; but
something 14
You may deserve of him through me, and wisdom 15
To offer up a weak, poor, innocent lamb
T' appease an angry god.

MACDUFF
I am not treacherous.

MALCOLM But Macbeth is.
A good and virtuous nature may recoil 19
In an imperial charge. But I shall crave your pardon. 20
That which you are, my thoughts cannot transpose. 21
Angels are bright still, though the brightest fell. 22
Though all things foul would wear the brows of
grace, 23
Yet grace must still look so.

MACDUFF I have lost my hopes. 24

MALCOLM
Perchance even there where I did find my doubts. 25
Why in that rawness left you wife and child, 26
Those precious motives, those strong knots of love, 27
Without leave-taking? I pray you,
Let not my jealousies be your dishonors, 29
But mine own safeties. You may be rightly just, 30
Whatever I shall think.

MACDUFF Bleed, bleed, poor country!
Great tyranny, lay thou thy basis sure, 32
For goodness dare not check thee; wear thou thy
wrongs, 33
The title is affeer'd! Fare thee well, lord. 34
I would not be the villain that thou think'st
For the whole space that's in the tyrant's grasp,
And the rich East to boot.

MALCOLM Be not offended.
I speak not as in absolute fear of you.
I think our country sinks beneath the yoke;
It weeps, it bleeds, and each new day a gash
Is added to her wounds. I think withal
There would be hands uplifted in my right;
And here from gracious England have I offer 43
Of goodly thousands. But, for all this,
When I shall tread upon the tyrant's head,
Or wear it on my sword, yet my poor country
Shall have more vices than it had before,
More suffer, and more sundry ways than ever, 48
By him that shall succeed.

MACDUFF What should he be? 49

MALCOLM
It is myself I mean, in whom I know
All the particulars of vice so grafted 51
That, when they shall be open'd, black Macbeth 52
Will seem as pure as snow, and the poor state
Esteem him as a lamb, being compar'd
With my confineless harms.

MACDUFF Not in the legions 55
Of horrid hell can come a devil more damn'd

84 shag-ear'd i.e., shaggy-haired **85 fry** spawn, progeny **86 s.d. Exit** (The child's body must be removed from the stage; probably it is dragged off by the murderers.)

IV.iii. Location: England. Before King Edward the Confessor's palace.
3 mortal deadly **4 Bestride** stand over in defense. **birthdom** fatherland **8 Like . . . dolor** a similar cry of pain **8–9 What . . . believe** i.e., what I believe to be amiss in Scotland I will grieve for, and anything I am certain to be true I will believe. (But one must be cautious in these duplicitous times.) **10 to friend** opportune **12 sole** mere **14 He . . . yet** i.e., the fact that Macbeth hasn't hurt you yet makes me suspicious of your loyalties. **young** i.e., inexperienced **14–15 something . . . me** i.e., you may win favor with Macbeth by delivering me to him **15 wisdom** i.e., it would be worldly-wise

19 recoil fall away, degenerate **20 In . . . charge** under pressure from royal command **21 transpose** alter **22 the brightest** i.e., Lucifer **23 wear the brows of** i.e., disguise themselves to resemble **24 so** i.e., like grace. **hopes** i.e., hopes of Malcolm's assistance in the cause against Macbeth **25 doubts** i.e., fears such as that Macduff may covertly be on Macbeth's side **26 rawness** unprotected condition. (Malcolm suggests that Macduff's leaving his family unprotected could be construed as more evidence of his not having anything to fear from Macbeth.) **27 motives** incentives to offer strong protection **29–30 Let . . . safeties** i.e., may it be true that my suspicions of your lack of honor are founded only in my own wariness **32 basis** foundation **33 wrongs** wrongfully gained powers **34 affeer'd** confirmed, certified **43 England** i.e., the King of England **48 more sundry** in more various **49 What** who **51 particulars** varieties **52 open'd** unfolded **55 my confineless harms** the boundless injuries I shall inflict

In evils to top Macbeth.
MALCOLM I grant him bloody,
Luxurious, avaricious, false, deceitful,
Sudden, malicious, smacking of every sin
That has a name. But there's no bottom, none,
In my voluptuousness. Your wives, your daughters,
Your matrons, and your maids could not fill up
The cistern of my lust, and my desire
All continent impediments would o'erbear
That did oppose my will. Better Macbeth
Than such an one to reign.
MACDUFF Boundless intemperance
In nature is a tyranny; it hath been
Th' untimely emptying of the happy throne
And fall of many kings. But fear not yet
To take upon you what is yours. You may
Convey your pleasures in a spacious plenty,
And yet seem cold, the time you may so hoodwink.
We have willing dames enough. There cannot be
That vulture in you to devour so many
As will to greatness dedicate themselves,
Finding it so inclin'd.
MALCOLM With this there grows
In my most ill-compos'd affection such
A stanchless avarice that, were I king,
I should cut off the nobles for their lands,
Desire his jewels, and this other's house,
And my more-having would be as a sauce
To make me hunger more, that I should forge
Quarrels unjust against the good and loyal,
Destroying them for wealth.
MACDUFF This avarice
Sticks deeper, grows with more pernicious root
Than summer-seeming lust, and it hath been
The sword of our slain kings. Yet do not fear;
Scotland hath foisons to fill up your will
Of your mere own. All these are portable,
With other graces weigh'd.
MALCOLM
But I have none. The king-becoming graces,
As justice, verity, temp'rance, stableness,
Bounty, perseverance, mercy, lowliness,
Devotion, patience, courage, fortitude,
I have no relish of them, but abound
In the division of each several crime,
Acting it many ways. Nay, had I pow'r, I should
Pour the sweet milk of concord into hell,
Uproar the universal peace, confound
All unity on earth.
MACDUFF O Scotland, Scotland!
MALCOLM
If such a one be fit to govern, speak.
I am as I have spoken.
MACDUFF Fit to govern?
No, not to live. O nation miserable,
With an untitled tyrant bloody-sceptred,
When shalt thou see thy wholesome days again,
Since that the truest issue of thy throne
By his own interdiction stands accurs'd,
And does blaspheme his breed? Thy royal father
Was a most sainted king; the queen that bore thee,
Oft'ner upon her knees than on her feet,
Died every day she liv'd. Fare thee well!
These evils thou repeat'st upon thyself
Hath banish'd me from Scotland. O my breast,
Thy hope ends here!
MALCOLM Macduff, this noble passion,
Child of integrity, hath from my soul
Wip'd the black scruples, reconcil'd my thoughts
To thy good truth and honor. Devilish Macbeth
By many of these trains hath sought to win me
Into his power, and modest wisdom plucks me
From over-credulous haste. But God above
Deal between thee and me! For even now
I put myself to thy direction, and
Unspeak mine own detraction, here abjure
The taints and blames I laid upon myself,
For strangers to my nature. I am yet
Unknown to woman, never was forsworn,
Scarcely have coveted what was mine own,
At no time broke my faith, would not betray
The devil to his fellow, and delight
No less in truth than life. My first false speaking
Was this upon myself. What I am truly
Is thine and my poor country's to command—
Whither indeed, before thy here-approach,
Old Siward, with ten thousand warlike men
Already at a point was setting forth.
Now we'll together; and the chance of goodness
Be like our warranted quarrel! Why are you silent?
MACDUFF
Such welcome and unwelcome things at once
'Tis hard to reconcile.

Enter a Doctor.

MALCOLM
Well, more anon.—Comes the King forth, I pray
you?
DOCTOR
Ay, sir. There are a crew of wretched souls
That stay his cure. Their malady convinces
The great assay of art; but at his touch—
Such sanctity hath heaven given his hand—
They presently amend.
MALCOLM I thank you, doctor.
Exit [*Doctor*].

58 Luxurious lecherous **59 Sudden** violent, passionate **64 continent** restraining, containing **67 nature** man's nature **69 yet** nevertheless **71 Convey** manage with secrecy **72 the time . . . hoodwink** you may so deceive the age **77 ill-compos'd affection** evil disposition **78 stanchless** insatiable **86 summer-seeming** i.e., passing away with youth, transitory **87 sword** i.e., cause of overthrow **88 foisons** resources, plenty **89 Of . . . own** i.e., in your own royal estates alone. **portable** bearable **93 lowliness** humility **95 relish** flavor or trace **96 division** subdivisions, various possible forms. **several** separate

104 untitled lacking rightful title, usurping **107 interdiction** debarring of self **108 blaspheme** slander, defame. **breed** breeding **111 Died . . . liv'd** i.e., lived a life of daily mortification **118 trains** plots, artifices **119 modest . . . me** wise prudence holds me back **125 For** as **135 at a point** ready, prepared **136 goodness** success **137 Be . . . quarrel** be equal to the justice of our cause **142 stay** wait for. **convinces** conquers **143 assay of art** efforts of medical skill

MACDUFF
What's the disease he means?

MALCOLM
'Tis call'd the evil.
A most miraculous work in this good king,
Which often, since my here-remain in England,
I have seen him do. How he solicits heaven,
Himself best knows; but strangely-visited people,
All swoll'n and ulcerous, pitiful to the eye,
The mere despair of surgery, he cures,
Hanging a golden stamp about their necks,
Put on with holy prayers; and 'tis spoken,
To the succeeding royalty he leaves
The healing benediction. With this strange virtue,
He hath a heavenly gift of prophecy,
And sundry blessings hang about his throne,
That speak him full of grace.

Enter Ross.

MACDUFF
See who comes here.

MALCOLM
My countryman; but yet I know him not.

MACDUFF
My ever-gentle cousin, welcome hither.

MALCOLM
I know him now. Good God betimes remove
The means that makes us strangers!

ROSS
Sir, amen.

MACDUFF
Stands Scotland where it did?

ROSS
Alas, poor country,
Almost afraid to know itself. It cannot
Be call'd our mother, but our grave; where nothing,
But who knows nothing, is once seen to smile;
Where sighs and groans and shrieks that rend the air
Are made, not mark'd; where violent sorrow seems
A modern ecstasy. The dead man's knell
Is there scarce ask'd for who, and good men's lives
Expire before the flowers in their caps,
Dying or ere they sicken.

MACDUFF
O, relation
Too nice, and yet too true!

MALCOLM
What's the newest grief?

ROSS
That of an hour's age doth hiss the speaker;
Each minute teems a new one.

MACDUFF
How does my wife?

ROSS
Why, well.

MACDUFF
And all my children?

ROSS
Well too.

MACDUFF
The tyrant has not batter'd at their peace?

ROSS
No, they were well at peace when I did leave 'em.

MACDUFF
Be not a niggard of your speech. How goes 't?

ROSS
When I came hither to transport the tidings,
Which I have heavily borne, there ran a rumor
Of many worthy fellows that were out,
Which was to my belief witness'd the rather
For that I saw the tyrant's power afoot.
Now is the time of help; your eye in Scotland
Would create soldiers, make our women fight,
To doff their dire distresses.

MALCOLM
Be 't their comfort
We are coming thither. Gracious England hath
Lent us good Siward and ten thousand men;
An older and a better soldier none
That Christendom gives out.

ROSS
Would I could answer
This comfort with the like! But I have words
That would be howl'd out in the desert air,
Where hearing should not latch them.

MACDUFF
What concern they?
The general cause? Or is it a fee-grief
Due to some single breast?

ROSS
No mind that's honest
But in it shares some woe, though the main part
Pertains to you alone.

MACDUFF
If it be mine,
Keep it not from me, quickly let me have it.

ROSS
Let not your ears despise my tongue forever,
Which shall possess them with the heaviest sound
That ever yet they heard.

MACDUFF
Humh! I guess at it.

ROSS
Your castle is surpris'd, your wife and babes
Savagely slaughter'd. To relate the manner
Were, on the quarry of these murder'd deer,
To add the death of you.

MALCOLM
Merciful heaven!
What, man, ne'er pull your hat upon your brows;
Give sorrow words. The grief that does not speak
Whispers the o'er-fraught heart and bids it break.

MACDUFF
My children too?

ROSS
Wife, children, servants, all
That could be found.

MACDUFF
And I must be from thence!
My wife kill'd too?

ROSS
I have said.

MALCOLM
Be comforted.
Let's make us med'cines of our great revenge
To cure this deadly grief.

MACDUFF
He has no children. All my pretty ones?

146 evil i.e., scrofula, supposedly cured by the royal touch; James I claimed this power **150 strangely-visited** afflicted by strange diseases **152 mere** utter **153 stamp** minted coin **166 nothing** nobody **167 But who** except him who. **once** ever **169 mark'd** noticed **170 modern ecstasy** commonplace emotion **173 or ere** before. **relation** report **174 nice** minutely accurate **175 hiss** cause to be hissed (for repeating stale news) **176 teems** teems with, yields

182 heavily sadly **183 out** in arms **184 witness'd the rather** made the more believable **185 power** army **188 doff** put off, get rid of **192 gives out** tells of, proclaims **195 latch** catch (the sound of) **196 fee-grief** a grief with an individual owner, having absolute ownership **206 quarry** heap of slaughtered deer at a hunt **210 Whispers** whispers to. **o'er-fraught** overburdened **216 He has no children** i.e., no father would do such a thing (?) or, he (Malcolm) speaks comfort without knowing what such a loss feels like (?)

Did you say all? O hell-kite! All?
What, all my pretty chickens and their dam
At one fell swoop?

MALCOLM
Dispute it like a man.

MACDUFF
I shall do so;
But I must also feel it as a man.
I cannot but remember such things were,
That were most precious to me. Did heaven look on,
And would not take their part? Sinful Macduff,
They were all struck for thee! Naught that I am,
Not for their own demerits, but for mine,
Fell slaughter on their souls. Heaven rest them now!

MALCOLM
Be this the whetstone of your sword. Let grief
Convert to anger; blunt not the heart, enrage it.

MACDUFF
O, I could play the woman with mine eyes
And braggart with my tongue! But, gentle heavens,
Cut short all intermission. Front to front
Bring thou this fiend of Scotland and myself;
Within my sword's length set him. If he scape,
Heaven forgive him too!

MALCOLM
This tune goes manly.
Come, go we to the King. Our power is ready;
Our lack is nothing but our leave. Macbeth
Is ripe for shaking, and the pow'rs above
Put on their instruments. Receive what cheer
you may.
The night is long that never finds the day. *Exeunt.*

ACT V • SCENE I

Enter a Doctor of Physic and a Waiting-Gentlewoman.

DOCTOR I have two nights watch'd with you, but can perceive no truth in your report. When was it she last walk'd?

GENTLEWOMAN Since his Majesty went into the field, I have seen her rise from her bed, throw her nightgown upon her, unlock her closet, take forth paper, fold it, write upon 't, read it, afterwards seal it, and again return to bed; yet all this while in a most fast sleep.

DOCTOR A great perturbation in nature, to receive at once the benefit of sleep, and do the effects of watching! In this slumb'ry agitation, besides her walking and other actual performances, what, at any time, have you heard her say?

GENTLEWOMAN That, sir, which I will not report after her.

DOCTOR You may to me, and 'tis most meet you should.

GENTLEWOMAN Neither to you nor anyone, having no witness to confirm my speech.

Enter Lady [Macbeth], with a taper.

Lo you, here she comes! This is her very guise; and, upon my life, fast asleep. Observe her; stand close.

[They stand aside.]

DOCTOR How came she by that light?

GENTLEWOMAN Why, it stood by her. She has light by her continually; 'tis her command.

DOCTOR You see her eyes are open.

GENTLEWOMAN Ay, but their sense are shut.

DOCTOR What is it she does now? Look how she rubs her hands.

GENTLEWOMAN It is an accustom'd action with her, to seem thus washing her hands. I have known her continue in this a quarter of an hour.

LADY MACBETH Yet here's a spot.

DOCTOR Hark, she speaks. I will set down what comes from her, to satisfy my remembrance the more strongly.

LADY MACBETH Out, damned spot! Out, I say! One—two—why, then 'tis time to do 't. Hell is murky.—Fie, my lord, fie, a soldier, and afeard? What need we fear who knows it, when none can call our pow'r to account? Yet who would have thought the old man to have had so much blood in him.

DOCTOR Do you mark that?

LADY MACBETH The Thane of Fife had a wife. Where is she now?—What, will these hands ne'er be clean?—No more o' that, my lord, no more o' that; you mar all with this starting.

DOCTOR Go to, go to; you have known what you should not.

GENTLEWOMAN She has spoke what she should not, I am sure of that. Heaven knows what she has known.

LADY MACBETH Here's the smell of the blood still. All the perfumes of Arabia will not sweeten this little hand. Oh, oh, oh!

DOCTOR What a sigh is there! The heart is sorely charg'd.

GENTLEWOMAN I would not have such a heart in my bosom for the dignity of the whole body.

DOCTOR Well, well, well.

GENTLEWOMAN Pray God it be, sir.

DOCTOR This disease is beyond my practice. Yet I have known those which have walk'd in their sleep who have died holily in their beds.

LADY MACBETH Wash your hands, put on your nightgown; look not so pale! I tell you yet again, Banquo's buried; he cannot come out on 's grave.

DOCTOR Even so?

LADY MACBETH To bed, to bed! There's knocking at the gate. Come, come, come, come, give me your hand. What's done cannot be undone. To bed, to bed, to bed! *Exit Lady.*

DOCTOR Will she go now to bed?

220 Dispute it i.e., fight on the issue; or, be a man, don't give in to grief **229 Convert** change **232 intermission** delay, interval. **Front to front** face to face **237 Our . . . leave** we need only to take our leave (of the English King) **239 Put . . . instruments** set us on as their agents; or, arm themselves

V.i. Location: Dunsinane. Macbeth's castle.
5 closet chest or desk **9–10 effects of watching** deeds characteristic of waking

19 close concealed **44 starting** startled movements **52–53 sorely charg'd** heavily burdened **63 on 's** of his

GENTLEWOMAN Directly.

DOCTOR
Foul whisp'rings are abroad. Unnatural deeds
Do breed unnatural troubles. Infected minds
To their deaf pillows will discharge their secrets.
More needs she the divine than the physician.
God, God forgive us all! Look after her;
Remove from her the means of all annoyance,
And still keep eyes upon her. So, good night.
My mind she has mated, and amaz'd my sight.
I think, but dare not speak.

GENTLEWOMAN Good night, good doctor.
Exeunt.

SCENE II

Drum and colors. Enter Menteith, Caithness, Angus, Lennox, [and] Soldiers.

MENTEITH
The English pow'r is near, led on by Malcolm,
His uncle Siward, and the good Macduff.
Revenges burn in them; for their dear causes
Would to the bleeding and the grim alarm
Excite the mortified man.

ANGUS Near Birnam wood
Shall we well meet them; that way are they coming.

CAITHNESS
Who knows if Donalbain be with his brother?

LENNOX
For certain, sir, he is not. I have a file
Of all the gentry. There is Siward's son,
And many unrough youths that even now
Protest their first of manhood.

MENTEITH What does the tyrant?

CAITHNESS
Great Dunsinane he strongly fortifies.
Some say he's mad, others that lesser hate him
Do call it valiant fury; but for certain
He cannot buckle his distemper'd cause
Within the belt of rule.

ANGUS Now does he feel
His secret murders sticking on his hands.
Now minutely revolts upbraid his faith-breach;
Those he commands move only in command,
Nothing in love. Now does he feel his title
Hang loose about him, like a giant's robe
Upon a dwarfish thief.

MENTEITH Who then shall blame
His pester'd senses to recoil and start,
When all that is within him does condemn
Itself for being there?

CAITHNESS Well, march we on
To give obedience where 'tis truly ow'd.
Meet we the med'cine of the sickly weal,
And with him pour we in our country's purge
Each drop of us.

LENNOX Or so much as it needs,
To dew the sovereign flower and drown the weeds.
Make we our march towards Birnam.
Exeunt, marching.

SCENE III

Enter Macbeth, Doctor, and Attendants.

MACBETH
Bring me no more reports. Let them fly all!
Till Birnam wood remove to Dunsinane,
I cannot taint with fear. What's the boy Malcolm?
Was he not born of woman? The spirits that know
All mortal consequences have pronounc'd me thus:
"Fear not, Macbeth; no man that's born of woman
Shall e'er have power upon thee." Then fly, false thanes,
And mingle with the English epicures!
The mind I sway by and the heart I bear
Shall never sag with doubt nor shake with fear.

Enter Servant.

The devil damn thee black, thou cream-fac'd loon!
Where got'st thou that goose look?

SERVANT
There is ten thousand—

MACBETH Geese, villain?

SERVANT Soldiers, sir.

MACBETH
Go prick thy face, and over-red thy fear,
Thou lily-liver'd boy. What soldiers, patch?
Death of thy soul! Those linen cheeks of thine
Are counselors to fear. What soldiers, whey-face?

SERVANT
The English force, so please you.

MACBETH
Take thy face hence. [*Exit Servant.*] Seyton!—I am sick at heart
When I behold—Seyton, I say!—This push
Will cheer me ever, or disseat me now.
I have liv'd long enough. My way of life
Is fall'n into the sear, the yellow leaf,
And that which should accompany old age,
As honor, love, obedience, troops of friends,
I must not look to have; but, in their stead,

76 annoyance i.e., harming herself **78 mated** bewildered, stupified

V.ii. Location: The country near Dunsinane.
4 bleeding bloody. **alarm** call to battle **5 Excite . . . man** awaken the dead **6 well** no doubt **8 file** list, roster **10 unrough** beardless **11 Protest** assert publicly **15 distemper'd** disease-swollen, dropsical **18 minutely** every minute **23 pester'd** troubled, tormented

27 med'cine i.e., Malcolm **30 dew** bedew, water

V.iii. Location: Dunsinane. Macbeth's castle.
1 them i.e., the thanes **3 taint** become imbued with **5 mortal consequences** what befalls man **8 epicures** luxury-loving persons **9 sway** direct myself **11 loon** stupid fellow **14 over-red** redden over. (The servant's blood has all retired into his lower abdomen on account of his fear, so that he is very pale and there is no blood in his liver, where his courage should have resided—hence, *lily-liver'd* l. 15.) **15 patch** domestic fool **16 of thy** on your **17 Are . . . fear** i.e., teach others to fear **20 behold** (Macbeth does not finish this thought.) **push** onset, struggle **23 sear** dry and withered

Curses, not loud but deep, mouth-honor, breath,
Which the poor heart would fain deny, and
dare not.
Seyton!

Enter Seyton.

SEYTON
What's your gracious pleasure?

MACBETH
What news more?

SEYTON
All is confirm'd, my lord, which was reported.

MACBETH
I'll fight till from my bones my flesh be hack'd.
Give me my armor.

SEYTON
'Tis not needed yet.

MACBETH
I'll put it on.
Send out moe horses, skirr the country round;
Hang those that talk of fear. Give me mine armor.
How does your patient, doctor?

DOCTOR
Not so sick, my lord,
As she is troubled with thick-coming fancies,
That keep her from her rest.

MACBETH
Cure her of that.
Canst thou not minister to a mind diseas'd,
Pluck from the memory a rooted sorrow,
Raze out the written troubles of the brain
And with some sweet oblivious antidote
Cleanse the stuff'd bosom of that perilous stuff
Which weighs upon the heart?

DOCTOR
Therein the patient
Must minister to himself.

MACBETH
Throw physic to the dogs; I'll none of it.
Come, put mine armor on; give me my staff.
[*Attendants arm him.*]
Seyton, send out. Doctor, the thanes fly from me.—
Come, sir, dispatch.—If thou couldst, doctor, cast
The water of my land, find her disease,
And purge it to a sound and pristine health,
I would applaud thee to the very echo,
That should applaud again.—Pull 't off, I say.—
What rhubarb, senna, or what purgative drug
Would scour these English hence? Hear'st thou of
them?

DOCTOR
Ay, my good lord. Your royal preparation
Makes us hear something.

MACBETH
Bring it after me.—
I will not be afraid of death and bane,
Till Birnam forest come to Dunsinane.
Exeunt [*all but the doctor*].

DOCTOR
Were I from Dunsinane away and clear,
Profit again should hardly draw me here. [*Exit.*]

35 moe more. **skirr** scour **43 Raze** erase. **written troubles of** troubles written on **44 oblivious** causing forgetfulness **48 physic** medicine **49 staff** lance **51 dispatch** hurry. **cast** diagnose **52 water** i.e., urine, used in diagnosis **55 Pull 't off** (Refers to some part of the armor not properly put on.) **56 senna** a purgative drug **59 it** i.e., the armor not yet put on Macbeth

SCENE IV

Drum and colors. Enter Malcolm, Siward, Macduff, Siward's Son, Menteith, Caithness, Angus, [*Lennox, Ross,*] *and Soldiers, marching.*

MALCOLM
Cousins, I hope the days are near at hand
That chambers will be safe.

MENTEITH
We doubt it nothing.

SIWARD
What wood is this before us?

MENTEITH
The wood of Birnam.

MALCOLM
Let every soldier hew him down a bough
And bear 't before him. Thereby shall we shadow
The numbers of our host, and make discovery
Err in report of us.

SOLDIERS
It shall be done.

SIWARD
We learn no other but the confident tyrant
Keeps still in Dunsinane, and will endure
Our setting down before 't.

MALCOLM
'Tis his main hope;
For where there is advantage to be given,
Both more and less have given him the revolt,
And none serve with him but constrained things
Whose hearts are absent too.

MACDUFF
Let our just censures
Attend the true event, and put we on
Industrious soldiership.

SIWARD
The time approaches
That will with due decision make us know
What we shall say we have and what we owe.
Thoughts speculative their unsure hopes relate,
But certain issue strokes must arbitrate—
Towards which advance the war. *Exeunt, marching.*

SCENE V

Enter Macbeth, Seyton, and Soldiers, with drum and colors.

MACBETH
Hang out our banners on the outward walls.
The cry is still "They come!" Our castle's strength
Will laugh a siege to scorn. Here let them lie
Till famine and the ague eat them up.
Were they not forc'd with those that should be ours,
We might have met them dareful, beard to beard,

V.iv. Location: Country near Birnam Wood.
2 chambers . . . safe i.e., we may sleep safely in our bedchambers. **nothing** not at all **6 discovery** scouting reports **10 setting down before** laying siege to **11 advantage** opportunity **12 more and less** high and low **14–15 Let . . . event** i.e., let us postpone judgment until we have taken the action we must take **18 owe** own **19–20 Thoughts . . . arbitrate** i.e., speculating can only convey our sense of hope; blows must decide the actual outcome **21 war** army

V.v. Location: Dunsinane. Macbeth's castle.
5 forc'd reinforced **6 dareful** boldly

And beat them backward home.
A cry within of women.
What is that noise?

SEYTON
It is the cry of women, my good lord. [*Exit.*]

MACBETH
I have almost forgot the taste of fears.
The time has been my senses would have cool'd
To hear a night-shriek, and my fell of hair
Would at a dismal treatise rouse and stir
As life were in 't. I have supp'd full with horrors;
Direness, familiar to my slaughterous thoughts,
Cannot once start me.

[*Enter Seyton.*]

Wherefore was that cry?

SEYTON
The Queen, my lord, is dead.

MACBETH
She should have died hereafter;
There would have been a time for such a word.
Tomorrow, and tomorrow, and tomorrow
Creeps in this petty pace from day to day
To the last syllable of recorded time,
And all our yesterdays have lighted fools
The way to dusty death. Out, out, brief candle!
Life's but a walking shadow, a poor player
That struts and frets his hour upon the stage
And then is heard no more. It is a tale
Told by an idiot, full of sound and fury,
Signifying nothing.

Enter a Messenger.

Thou com'st to use thy tongue; thy story quickly.

MESSENGER
Gracious my lord,
I should report that which I say I saw,
But know not how to do 't.

MACBETH Well, say, sir.

MESSENGER
As I did stand my watch upon the hill,
I look'd toward Birnam, and anon, methought,
The wood began to move.

MACBETH Liar and slave!

MESSENGER
Let me endure your wrath, if 't be not so.
Within this three mile may you see it coming;
I say, a moving grove.

MACBETH If thou speak'st false,
Upon the next tree shall thou hang alive,
Till famine cling thee. If thy speech be sooth,
I care not if thou dost for me as much.
I pull in resolution, and begin
To doubt th' equivocation of the fiend
That lies like truth. "Fear not, till Birnam wood
Do come to Dunsinane," and now a wood
Comes toward Dunsinane. Arm, arm, and out!
If this which he avouches does appear,
There is nor flying hence nor tarrying here.
I 'gin to be aweary of the sun,
And wish th' estate o' th' world were now undone.
Ring the alarum-bell! Blow, wind! Come, wrack!
At least we'll die with harness on our back. *Exeunt.*

SCENE VI

Drum and colors. Enter Malcolm, Siward, Macduff, and their Army, with boughs.

MALCOLM
Now near enough. Your leavy screens throw down,
And show like those you are. You, worthy uncle,
Shall with my cousin, your right noble son,
Lead our first battle. Worthy Macduff and we
Shall take upon 's what else remains to do,
According to our order.

SIWARD Fare you well.
Do we but find the tyrant's power tonight,
Let us be beaten, if we cannot fight.

MACDUFF
Make all our trumpets speak! Give them all breath,
Those clamorous harbingers of blood and death.
Exeunt. Alarums continued.

SCENE VII

Enter Macbeth.

MACBETH
They have tied me to a stake. I cannot fly,
But bear-like I must fight the course. What's he
That was not born of woman? Such a one
Am I to fear, or none.

Enter young Siward.

YOUNG SIWARD
What is thy name?

MACBETH Thou'lt be afraid to hear it.

YOUNG SIWARD
No, though thou call'st thyself a hotter name
Than any is in hell.

MACBETH My name's Macbeth.

YOUNG SIWARD
The devil himself could not pronounce a title

10 cool'd felt the chill of terror **11 my fell of hair** the hair of my scalp **12 dismal treatise** sinister story **15 start me** make me start **17 She . . . hereafter** she would have died some day; or, she should have died at some more appropriate time freed from the relentless pressures of the moment **19–28 Tomorrow . . . nothing** (For biblical echoes in this speech, see Psalms 18:28, 22:15, 90:9; Job 8:9, 14:1–2, 18:6.) **40 cling** cause to shrivel. **sooth** truth **42 pull in** check, restrain

51 wrack ruin **52 harness** armor

V.vi. Location: Dunsinane. Before Macbeth's castle.
2 show appear **4 battle** battalion **6 order** plan of battle **7 power** army

V.vii. Location: Before Macbeth's castle; the battle action is continuous here.
2 course bout or round of bearbaiting, in which the bear was tied to a stake and dogs were set upon him

More hateful to mine ear.

MACBETH
No, nor more fearful.

YOUNG SIWARD
Thou liest, abhorred tyrant! With my sword
I'll prove the lie thou speak'st. 11
Fight, and young Siward slain.

MACBETH
Thou wast born of woman.
But swords I smile at, weapons laugh to scorn,
Brandish'd by man that's of a woman born. *Exit.*

Alarums. Enter Macduff.

MACDUFF
That way the noise is. Tyrant, show thy face!
If thou be'st slain and with no stroke of mine,
My wife and children's ghosts will haunt me still.
I cannot strike at wretched kerns, whose arms 17
Are hir'd to bear their staves. Either thou, Macbeth, 18
Or else my sword with an unbattered edge
I sheathe again undeeded. There thou shouldst be;
By this great clatter, one of greatest note
Seems bruited. Let me find him, Fortune, 22
And more I beg not. *Exit. Alarums.*

Enter Malcolm and Siward.

SIWARD
This way, my lord. The castle's gently rend'red. 24
The tyrant's people on both sides do fight;
The noble thanes do bravely in the war.
The day almost itself professes yours,
And little is to do.

MALCOLM
We have met with foes
That strike beside us.

SIWARD
Enter, sir, the castle. 29
Exeunt. Alarum.

[SCENE VIII]

Enter Macbeth.

MACBETH
Why should I play the Roman fool, and die 1
On mine own sword? Whiles I see lives, the gashes 2
Do better upon them.

Enter Macduff.

MACDUFF
Turn, hell-hound, turn!

MACBETH
Of all men else I have avoided thee.
But get thee back! My soul is too much charg'd
With blood of thine already.

MACDUFF
I have no words.
My voice is in my sword, thou bloodier villain
Than terms can give thee out! *Fight. Alarum.*

MACBETH
Thou losest labor. 8
As easy mayst thou the intrenchant air 9
With thy keen sword impress as make me bleed. 10
Let fall thy blade on vulnerable crests;
I bear a charmed life, which must not yield
To one of woman born.

MACDUFF
Despair thy charm; 13
And let the angel whom thou still hast serv'd 14
Tell thee, Macduff was from his mother's womb
Untimely ripp'd.

MACBETH
Accursed be that tongue that tells me so,
For it hath cow'd my better part of man! 18
And be these juggling fiends no more believ'd,
That palter with us in a double sense, 20
That keep the word of promise to our ear,
And break it to our hope. I'll not fight with thee.

MACDUFF
Then yield thee, coward,
And live to be the show and gaze o' th' time!
We'll have thee, as our rarer monsters are,
Painted upon a pole, and underwrit, 26
"Here may you see the tyrant."

MACBETH
I will not yield,
To kiss the ground before young Malcolm's feet,
And to be baited with the rabble's curse.
Though Birnam wood be come to Dunsinane,
And thou oppos'd, being of no woman born,
Yet I will try the last. Before my body
I throw my warlike shield. Lay on, Macduff,
And damn'd be him that first cries "Hold, enough!" 34
Exeunt, fighting. Alarums.

Enter fighting, and Macbeth slain. [Exit Macduff with Macbeth's body.] Retreat, and flourish. Enter, with drum and colors, Malcolm, Siward, Ross, Thanes, and Soldiers.

MALCOLM
I would the friends we miss were safe arriv'd.

SIWARD
Some must go off; and yet, by these I see, 36
So great a day as this is cheaply bought.

MALCOLM
Macduff is missing, and your noble son.

ROSS
Your son, my lord, has paid a soldier's debt.
He only liv'd but till he was a man,
The which no sooner had his prowess confirm'd
In the unshrinking station where he fought, 42
But like a man he died.

SIWARD
Then he is dead?

11 s.d. young Siward slain (In some unspecified way, young Siward's body must be removed from the stage; his own father enters at l. 23 and perceives nothing amiss, and in V.viii.38 young Siward is reported "missing" in action. Perhaps Macbeth drags off the body, or perhaps it is removed by soldiers during the alarums.) **17 kerns** (Properly, Irish foot soldiers; here applied contemptuously to the rank and file.) **18 staves** spears **22 bruited** noised abroad, announced **24 rend'red** surrendered **29 strike beside us** fight on our side

V.viii. Location: Before Macbeth's castle, as the battle continues; after l. 34, within the castle.
1 Roman fool i.e., suicide, like Brutus, Mark Antony, and others **2 Whiles . . . lives** i.e., as long as I see any enemy living

8 give thee out name you, describe you **9 intrenchant** invulnerable, indivisible **10 impress** make an impression on **13 Despair** despair of **14 angel** evil angel, Macbeth's genius **18 better . . . man** i.e., courage **20 palter . . . sense** equivocate with us **26 Painted . . . pole** i.e., painted on a board suspended on a pole **34 s.d. Enter, with drum and colors, etc.** (The remainder of the play takes place in Macbeth's castle, and properly should be marked as a separate scene.) **36 go off** die. **by these** to judge by these (assembled) **42 unshrinking station** post from which he did not shrink

ROSS
Ay, and brought off the field. Your cause of sorrow
Must not be measur'd by his worth, for then
It hath no end.

SIWARD Had he his hurts before?

ROSS
Ay, on the front.

SIWARD Why then, God's soldier be he!
Had I as many sons as I have hairs,
I would not wish them to a fairer death.
And so, his knell is knoll'd.

MALCOLM He's worth more sorrow,
And that I'll spend for him.

SIWARD He's worth no more.
They say he parted well, and paid his score,
And so, God be with him! Here comes newer
comfort.

Enter Macduff, with Macbeth's head.

MACDUFF
Hail, King! For so thou art. Behold where stands
Th' usurper's cursed head. The time is free. 55
I see thee compass'd with thy kingdom's pearl, 56
That speak my salutation in their minds,
Whose voices I desire aloud with mine:
Hail, King of Scotland!

ALL
Hail, King of Scotland! *Flourish.*

MALCOLM
We shall not spend a large expense of time
Before we reckon with your several loves, 62
And make us even with you. My thanes and
kinsmen, 63
Henceforth be earls, the first that ever Scotland
In such an honor nam'd. What's more to do,
Which would be planted newly with the time, 66
As calling home our exil'd friends abroad
That fled the snares of watchful tyranny,
Producing forth the cruel ministers 69
Of this dead butcher and his fiend-like queen,
Who, as 'tis thought, by self and violent hands 71
Took off her life—this, and what needful else
That calls upon us, by the grace of Grace,
We will perform in measure, time, and place.
So, thanks to all at once and to each one,
Whom we invite to see us crown'd at Scone.
Flourish. Exeunt omnes.

55 free released from tyranny **56 compass'd . . . pearl** surrounded by the nobles of your kingdom (literally, the pearls encircling a crown) **62 reckon** come to a reckoning **63 make . . . you** i.e., repay your worthiness **66 would . . . time** i.e., should be established at the commencement of this new era **69 Producing forth** bringing forward to trial **71 self and violent** her own violent

Timon of Athens

Timon of Athens is Shakespeare's most relentless study in misanthropy. It expresses with *King Lear* a moral outrage at human depravity, but refuses to soften anger with compassionate tears. The protagonist learns little other than bitterness from his encounters with avarice and ingratitude. In its mordant vision of human folly, *Timon of Athens* resembles a number of other Roman or classical plays. As in *Julius Caesar, Titus Andronicus, Coriolanus,* and *Troilus and Cressida,* the dominant mood is one of enervation and futility. Political conflicts end in stalemate or a victory for opportunists; the populace and their leaders are fickle and craven; private virtues of noble men must yield to crass considerations of statecraft. Banishment or self-exile is too often the reward of those who have given their lives to public service. Shakespeare's misanthropic vision in *Timon of Athens* is, then, integral to his portrayal of man's political and social nature in the ancient classical world. This is a world to which Shakespeare turned often during his writing career, especially during the period from about 1601 to 1608 when he was engaged primarily in writing tragedies. As a group, the Roman and classical plays tend to differ from the great tragedies of evil *(Hamlet, Othello, King Lear, Macbeth)* in that the classical plays naturally make less use of a Christian perspective and focus instead on a sardonic and dispiriting view of life's tragic absurdity. Even in *Antony and Cleopatra,* where Shakespeare offers us an ennobling dream of greatness to offset the worldly failure of his protagonists, the arena of human conflict remains pitiless and disillusioning. *Timon of Athens* offers no compensatory vision; it is bleak to the end, unwavering in its denial.

Timon of Athens appears to have been written between 1605 and 1608, and is often grouped with *King Lear* (c. 1605) on grounds of stylistic and thematic similarity. For its chief source it uses Thomas North's translation of Plutarch's *Lives of the Noble Grecians and Romans,* a source also for *Julius Caesar, Antony and Cleopatra, Coriolanus,* and parts of other plays. *Timon of Athens* also makes use, through intermediary versions, of the dialogue called *Timon,* or *The Misanthrope,* by the Greek satirist Lucian. The play may not have been produced; the text, not printed until the 1623 Folio, appears to have been taken from the author's unfinished manuscript, with contradictory uncanceled lines (see Timon's will, V,iv,70–73), unresolved discrepancies as to the amount of money Timon gives or requests, and passages of half-versified prose. Whatever the exact date and circumstance of composition, the play certainly belongs to the period of Shakespeare's most unsparing portrayal of human villainy and corruption.

Like *Troilus and Cressida, Timon of Athens* defies the conventional categories of tragedy, comedy, and history. In terms of Northrop Frye's *Anatomy of Criticism,* the play stands chiefly between tragedy and satire: that is, its mythic connotations are those of dying and sterility, as at the end of the cycle of the seasons, rather than those of renewal and growth. The play is tragic in portraying a fall from greatness, satiric in exposing an unfeeling society. Satire is potentially comic as well, and we are invited to laugh sardonically at the hypocrisies of Timon's fair-weather friends. The play is also a history, drawn from historical sources, as its Folio title, *The Life of Timon of Athens,* suggests. We ought to see or read it with the expectations not simply of tragedy but also of satire and ironic history.

As a genre, in fact, the play most resembles those works which the Painter and the Poet wish to offer Timon himself: a "moral painting" and a "satire against the softness of prosperity" (I,i and V,i). Such a genre is deliberately old-fashioned, reminiscent of medieval morality plays and of the "hybrid" morality plays of the 1570's and '80's like Thomas Lupton's *All for Money* (c. 1577) or Thomas Lodge and Robert Greene's *A Looking Glass for London and England* (1587–1591), which inveigh against usury and the neglect of military heroes. John Marston's later quasi-morality, *Histriomastix* (c. 1599), proclaims the decline of civilization through worldly insolence. Ben Jonson's *Volpone* (1605–1606), though "comical" rather than "tragical" in its satire, similarly castigates human greed. The *Parnassus* trilogy (1598–1603) indulges in a massive venting of spleen against a Philistine culture. *Timon of Athens* follows this tradition of social satire, derived from both English and classical models. Like most satire of the 1600's, both dramatic and nondramatic, it is crabbed in style, features a railing protagonist, and denounces through exaggerated caricature an ugly array of types representing a broad social spectrum. Choice of the satiric morality play as a generic model accords well with the play's acerbic view of decadence and "softness."

Human greed, with which *Timon of Athens* is so occupied, lends itself readily to satiric treatment. Avarice does not seem terrifying at first, like the spiritual sins of envy or prideful ambition as portrayed in *Othello* and *Macbeth;* instead, it is disgusting, ludicrous, and incredibly tenacious. Avarice is after all one of the Deadly Sins, and is often referred to in medieval commentary as the privotal Sin, the *radix malorum* or root of all evils. Although less vivid in its manifestation than pride or envy, greed is insidious and all-embracing. We see these qualities in Timon's friends. Those who sponge off him and then desert him are quick to return when he is rumored to have found gold in his exile. Greed is also self-deceiving. Many are the excuses offered for failing to come to Timon's aid: one friend rates Timon as a bad credit risk, another happens to be short of ready cash at the moment, a third insists that Timon's generosity to him wasn't as great as people suppose, and so on. No wonder Timon feels he must, like Volpone and Mosca, devise for such hypocrites a suitable comeuppance, consisting of a farewell banquet in which their crass expectations are rewarded with a mocking litany of curses and a dinner of water and stones.

Appropriately for this satirical depiction of human greed, the characters are virtually all types or social abstractions in a generic portrayal of avarice. Several represent the crafts and professions, and are abstractly labeled as such: the Poet, the Painter, the Jeweler, the Merchant. Others are "flattering lords" or "false friends" or "thieves." Seldom in Shakespeare do we find so many characters without proper names. They are depersonalized, and we are distanced from them. Apemantus is another type, a "churlish philosopher," recognizable in all his appearances by this one feature; we learn little about him other than that he professes to scoff at worldliness with a scabrous wit derived in part from legends about Diogenes the Cynic philosopher and other devotees of an extravagantly simple mode of life. (*Troilus and Cressida* makes similar use of the type in Thersites.) Timon himself becomes a type in his conversion to misanthropy, "infected," as Apemantus says, by "A poor unmanly melancholy sprung From change of fortune" (IV,iii). Apemantus' remark appeals to a view of personality as governed by "humors" or dominant traits such as melancholy or irascibility, which are generated by imbalance in the body of the four "humors," blood, phlegm, bile, and black bile. Images of disease, prominent throughout the play, are often derived from such "humorous" imbalances. The imagery also associates character types, as in *Volpone,* with various beasts: the lion, the fox, the ass, the wolf, the bear, and most of all the dog. By means of such techniques, Shakespeare portrays those whom Timon comes to despise with a seemingly intentional onesidedness; the caricatures of avarice are vivid and amusing with little allowance for subtlety or change. The plot too is, by Shakespeare's standard, unusually lacking in complication: Timon discovers the ingratitude and graspingness of his fellow man and retires from a world he can no longer tolerate, breathing upon it his dying curse. The dramatic tension of this uneventful story lies instead in Timon's own tortured spiritual saga, in the painful process of realization, in the revulsion, the refusal to compromise, the spurning even of honest friendship, the bitter renunciation and longing for oblivion. Alcibiades, too, is a complex character, offering as he does the alternatives of vengeful action against an ungrateful world or of successful conciliation; the debate between Alcibiades and Timon is an essential part of Timon's working toward total rejection of hope. The true drama is thus inner, and is increasingly contrasted with a static and superficial society toward which we are asked to feel revulsion and finally indifference.

There are no villains in *Timon of Athens,* only weak and foolish men. What is depressing about greed, in fact, is its insidious normality. Those who desert Timon have many prudent arguments on their side. After all, his original generosity is excessive and reckless. If his friends take advantage of him, they can at least say they have tried to warn him. Even a fool can see what lies in store. Much of Timon's wealth goes into drunken and gluttonous debauchery, into "feasts, pomps, and vainglories." Timon does not know how to use prosperity wisely, and even his loyal servants deplore the "riot." He is deaf to the friendly counsel of his steward, Flavius. For one who is so openhanded, Timon is surprisingly churlish with his creditors. And is he not presumptuous to assume that his friends will come to his aid when such vast sums are needed? Are they to be blamed for not emulating his prodigal decline into poverty? Clearly Timon expects too much. We readily though sadly perceive, as do all Timon's friends, that commerce is a god worshiped by all; need he be so shocked at this? As bystanders, we share with Timon's choric servants the certainty that his large requests for help will be refused. And yet, no matter how stupid or blind Timon may be, the desertion of him is still monstrous. Timon differs from us chiefly in being an idealist, in expecting that men will repay kindness with gratitude. We know, as do Timon's sympathetic servants, that most men are not like that.

Timon thus tears himself apart in a rage at what we consider the way of the world. We find his misanthropy intemperate, and yet we cannot help being moved by his sweeping indictment of man's pettiness and inhumanity. Timon's furor carries him beyond satire. He is, like Lear, all the more clear-sighted for being near to madness. Wisdom and folly exchange places, as Apemantus' friend the Fool has already pointed out (II,ii). In Timon's mad vision beggars and lords are interchangeable, distinguished only by wealth and position. Love of gold, he sees, inverts everything decent in human life, making "black white, foul fair, Wrong right, base noble, old young, coward valiant" (IV,iii). Thieves and whores are at least more honest than their counterparts in everyday life, the respectable citizens of Athens and their wives, and so Timon mockingly rewards the thieves and insults the hypocrites. His curse embraces the cosmos as well as humanity, inverting all semblance of hierarchical order: obedience must turn to rebellion, fidelity to incontinence, virginity to lasciviousness. "Degrees, observances, customs, and laws" must "Decline to your confounding contraries" (IV,i). Clothing and cosmetics must be stripped away, as in *King Lear,* so that man's monstrosity may be revealed for what it truly is.

Three persons, Apemantus, Alcibiades, and Flavius, serve as chief foils to Timon in his estrangement from humanity. Apemantus the cynic, who first taught Timon to rail at greed, now counsels him to find stoic contentment in renunciation of desire, or, conversely, to thrive as a flatterer by preying on those who have undone him (IV,iii). Alcibiades, the military commander banished by an ungrateful Athenian senate for presuming to beg the life of one who had rashly shed blood in a quarrel, offers Timon the means to active revenge against his enemies; subsequently, he offers Athens the olive branch with the sword, making "war breed peace," in an accommodating move that is important for the conclusion of the play and its final mitigating tone. Timon, although resembling both men as railer and as victim of ingratitude, rejects their counsels as too politic, too worldly. His stand is unflinching, absolute, so lacking in compromise that his sole choice can be to curse, die, and hope for oblivion. Only Flavius, his steward, offers brief consolation. Flavius comes to him, like Kent to King Lear, offering love and service in exile. Flavius even speaks in paradoxes reminiscent of *King Lear,* calling Timon "My dearest lord, bless'd to be most accurs'd, Rich only to be wretched" (IV,ii). These are precious words, showing that humanity is not utterly irredeemable. Still, this consolation is evidently too late to offset the nightmarish truth that Timon has learned. Timon experiences little of the compassionate love that comes to Lear in his madness, but he at least faces the bleakness of human existence with unbending honesty.

Timon of Athens

The Actors' Names

TIMON OF ATHENS.
LUCIUS *and* LUCULLUS, } *two flattering lords.*
SEMPRONIUS, *another flattering lord.*
VENTIDIUS, *one of Timon's false friends.*
APEMANTUS, *a churlish philosopher.*
ALCIBIADES, *an Athenian captain.*
[FLAVIUS, *steward to Timon.*]
POET, PAINTER, JEWELER, [*and*] MERCHANT.
FLAMINIUS, *one of Timon's servants.*
[LUCILIUS, *another.*]
SERVILIUS, *another.*
CAPHIS, PHILOTUS, TITUS, HORTENSIUS, [*And* others,] } *several servants to usurers* [*Timon's creditors*].
[*A* PAGE. *A* FOOL. *Three* STRANGERS.]
[PHRYNIA, TIMANDRA,} *mistresses to Alcibiades.*]

CUPID [*and*] *certain* MASKERS [*as Amazons*].
Certain SENATORS [*and other* LORDS, OFFICERS, *and* SOLDIERS], *certain* THIEVES [*or* BANDETTI], *with divers other* SERVANTS *and* ATTENDANTS.

[SCENE: *Athens, and the neighboring woods.*]

ACT I • SCENE I

Enter Poet, Painter, Jeweler, and Merchant, at several doors. [*The Poet and Painter form one group, the Jeweler and Merchant another.*]

POET
Good day, sir.
PAINTER
I am glad y' are well.
POET
I have not seen you long. How goes the world?
PAINTER
It wears, sir, as it grows.
POET
Ay, that 's well known.
But what particular rarity? What strange,
Which manifold record not matches? See,

I.i. Location: Athens. Timon's house.
3 long for a long time **4 wears** decays. **grows** ages **5 rarity** unusual occurrence **6 Which . . . matches** i.e., which all recorded history cannot equal

Magic of bounty! All these spirits thy power
Hath conjur'd to attend. I know the merchant.

PAINTER
I know them both; th' other's a jeweler.

MERCHANT [*To Jeweler*]
O, 'tis a worthy lord.

JEWELER
Nay, that's most fix'd.

MERCHANT
A most incomparable man, breath'd, as it were,
To an untirable and continuate goodness.
He passes.

JEWELER
I have a jewel here—

MERCHANT
O, pray, let's see 't. For the Lord Timon, sir?

JEWELER
If he will touch the estimate. But for that—

POET [*Reciting to himself*]
"When we for recompense have prais'd the vile,
It stains the glory in that happy verse
Which aptly sings the good."

MERCHANT [*Looking at the jewel*] 'Tis a good form.

JEWELER
And rich. Here is a water, look ye.

PAINTER [*To Poet*]
You are rapt, sir, in some work, some dedication
To the great lord.

POET
A thing slipp'd idly from me.
Our poesy is as a gum, which oozes
From whence 'tis nourish'd. The fire i' th' flint
Shows not till it be struck; our gentle flame
Provokes itself and like the current flies
Each bound it chafes. What have you there?

PAINTER
A picture, sir. When comes your book forth?

POET
Upon the heels of my presentment, sir.
Let's see your piece. [*Examines the painting.*]

PAINTER
'Tis a good piece.

POET
So 'tis. This comes off well and excellent.

PAINTER
Indifferent.

POET
Admirable! How this grace
Speaks his own standing! What a mental power
This eye shoots forth! How big imagination
Moves in this lip! To th' dumbness of the gesture
One might interpret.

PAINTER
It is a pretty mocking of the life.
Here is a touch; is 't good?

POET
I will say of it,
It tutors nature. Artificial strife
Lives in these touches, livelier than life.

Enter certain Senators [*and pass over*].

PAINTER
How this lord is followed!

POET
The senators of Athens. Happy men!

PAINTER
Look, moe!

POET
You see this confluence, this great flood of visitors.
[*He shows his poem.*]
I have, in this rough work, shap'd out a man
Whom this beneath world doth embrace and hug
With amplest entertainment. My free drift
Halts not particularly, but moves itself
In a wide sea of wax; no level'd malice
Infects one comma in the course I hold,
But flies an eagle flight, bold and forth on,
Leaving no tract behind.

PAINTER
How shall I understand you?

POET
I will unbolt to you.
You see how all conditions, how all minds,
As well of glib and slipp'ry creatures as
Of grave and austere quality, tender down
Their services to Lord Timon. His large fortune
Upon his good and gracious nature hanging
Subdues and properties to his love and tendance
All sorts of hearts; yea, from the glass-fac'd flatterer
To Apemantus, that few things loves better
Than to abhor himself—even he drops down
The knee before him and returns in peace
Most rich in Timon's nod.

PAINTER
I saw them speak together.

POET
Sir, I have upon a high and pleasant hill
Feign'd Fortune to be thron'd. The base o' th' mount
Is rank'd with all deserts, all kind of natures,
That labor on the bosom of this sphere
To propagate their states. Amongst them all,
Whose eyes are on this sovereign lady fix'd,
One do I personate of Lord Timon's frame,
Whom Fortune with her ivory hand wafts to her,
Whose present grace to present slaves and servants

7 Magic of bounty i.e., the remarkable attractive power of generosity **10 worthy lord** i.e., Timon. **fix'd** certain **11 breath'd** inspired; or trained through exercise **12 continuate** habitual **13 passes** surpasses **16 touch the estimate** offer or meet the price **18 happy** felicitous, matching truthful praise to a worthy object **19 form** shape, appearance. (Refers to the jewel.) **20 water** luster **21 dedication** (Such works were customarily dedicated to great noblemen.) **26 Provokes itself** i.e., is self-generating **26–27 flies . . . chafes** seeks escape from the riverbanks that confine it **29 Upon . . . presentment** as soon as I have presented it (to Lord Timon, in hopes of obtaining his patronage) **33 Indifferent** i.e., not bad. **this grace** i.e., of the person in the picture **34 Speaks . . . standing** conveys the dignity of its subject **35 big** largely **36–37 To . . . interpret** i.e., the very gestures depicted are eloquent **38 mocking** mirroring

40 Artificial strife the striving of art to surpass nature **44 moe** more **47 beneath world** i.e., the world itself, beneath the sphere of the moon **48 drift** design **49 Halts not particularly** doesn't concern itself with anyone individually **49–50 moves . . . wax** i.e., moves freely about. (*Sea of wax* may allude to writing on a wax tablet with a stylus.) **50 level'd** aimed, as a gun is aimed at a particular object **51 comma** i.e., detail **53 tract** track, trace **55 unbolt** unlock, disclose **56 conditions** ranks, temperaments **58 tender down** tender, offer **61 properties** appropriates. **tendance** tending on him (also in l. 85) **62 glass-fac'd** showing in his look, as by reflection, the looks of his patron **65 returns** departs **69 Feign'd** imagined, supposed **70 rank'd . . . deserts** filled with the ranks of all degrees of merit **72 propagate** enlarge. **states** fortunes **74 personate** represent **76–77 Whose . . . rivals** i.e., Fortune, whose gracious favor transforms his (Timon's) rivals immediately into slaves and servants

Translates his rivals.
PAINTER 'Tis conceiv'd to scope. 77
This throne, this Fortune, and this hill, methinks,
With one man beckon'd from the rest below,
Bowing his head against the steepy mount
To climb his happiness, would be well express'd 81
In our condition.
POET Nay, sir, but hear me on. 82
All those which were his fellows but of late—
Some better than his value—on the moment 84
Follow his strides, his lobbies fill with tendance,
Rain sacrificial whisperings in his ear,
Make sacred even his stirrup, and through him 87
Drink the free air.
PAINTER Ay, marry, what of these? 88
POET
When Fortune in her shift and change of mood
Spurns down her late beloved, all his dependents
Which labor'd after him to the mountain's top
Even on their knees and hands, let him slip down,
Not one accompanying his declining foot.
PAINTER
'Tis common.
A thousand moral paintings I can show 95
That shall demonstrate these quick blows of Fortune's
More pregnantly than words. Yet you do well
To show Lord Timon that mean eyes have seen 98
The foot above the head. 99

Trumpets sound. Enter Lord Timon, addressing himself courteously to every suitor; [*a Messenger from Ventidius talking with him; Lucilius and other servants following*].

TIMON
Imprison'd is he, say you?
MESSENGER
Ay, my good lord. Five talents is his debt, 101
His means most short, his creditors most strait. 102
Your honorable letter he desires
To those have shut him up; which failing 104
Periods his comfort.
TIMON Noble Ventidius! Well, 105
I am not of that feather to shake off
My friend when he must need me. I do know him
A gentleman that well deserves a help,
Which he shall have. I'll pay the debt, and free him.
MESSENGER
Your lordship ever binds him. 110
TIMON
Commend me to him. I will send his ransom;
And being enfranchis'd, bid him come to me.
'Tis not enough to help the feeble up,
But to support him after. Fare you well. 114
MESSENGER
All happiness to your honor! *Exit.*

Enter an old Athenian.

OLD ATHENIAN
Lord Timon, hear me speak.
TIMON Freely, good father.
OLD ATHENIAN
Thou hast a servant nam'd Lucilius.
TIMON
I have so. What of him?
OLD ATHENIAN
Most noble Timon, call the man before thee.
TIMON
Attends he here, or no? Lucilius!
LUCILIUS [*Coming forward*]
Here, at your lordship's service.
OLD ATHENIAN
This fellow here, Lord Timon, this thy creature, 122
By night frequents my house. I am a man
That from my first have been inclin'd to thrift,
And my estate deserves an heir more rais'd 125
Than one which holds a trencher.
TIMON Well; what further? 126
OLD ATHENIAN
One only daughter have I, no kin else,
On whom I may confer what I have got.
The maid is fair, o' th' youngest for a bride,
And I have bred her at my dearest cost
In qualities of the best. This man of thine
Attempts her love. I prithee, noble lord, 132
Join with me to forbid him her resort; 133
Myself have spoke in vain.
TIMON
The man is honest.
OLD ATHENIAN Therefore he will be, Timon. 135
His honesty rewards him in itself;
It must not bear my daughter. 137
TIMON
Does she love him?
OLD ATHENIAN She is young and apt. 138
Our own precedent passions do instruct us
What levity's in youth.
TIMON [*To Lucilius*] Love you the maid?
LUCILIUS
Ay, my good lord, and she accepts of it.
OLD ATHENIAN
If in her marriage my consent is missing,
I call the gods to witness, I will choose
Mine heir from forth the beggars of the world,
And dispossess her all. 145

77 to scope to the purpose **81 his happiness** i.e., to his good fortune **81–82 would . . . condition** would find a striking parallel in the human condition **84 better . . . value** his superiors **87 stirrup** i.e., as they help him to his horse **87–88 through . . . air** seem to breathe the free air only through his bounty **95 moral paintings** allegorical depictions **98 mean eyes** i.e., men of low degree **99 The foot . . . head** i.e., highest fortune tumbling headlong downward by the turn of Fortune's wheel **101 talents** units of money today worth $2000 or more. (But Shakespeare was evidently uncertain about the *talent's* value as he wrote this play. *Talents* is also a Biblical term; see, for example, Matthew 25:14–29.) **102 strait** severe, exacting **104 those** those who **104–105 which failing Periods** the lack of which puts an end to **110 binds him** i.e., to grateful obligation

114 But i.e., but one must continue **122 creature** dependent, hanger-on **125 more rais'd** of higher social position **126 holds a trencher** i.e., serves at table, handling wooden dishes **132 Attempts** tries to win **133 her resort** access to her **135 Therefore he will be** i.e., he will be if we forbid him to see my daughter **137 bear my daughter** take my daughter as a burden too great for his honesty **138 apt** easily wooed, impressionable **145 all** wholly

TIMON
How shall she be endow'd,
If she be mated with an equal husband? 147

OLD ATHENIAN
Three talents on the present; in future, all.

TIMON
This gentleman of mine hath serv'd me long;
To build his fortune I will strain a little,
For 'tis a bond in men. Give him thy daughter. 151
What you bestow, in him I'll counterpoise,
And make him weigh with her.

OLD ATHENIAN Most noble lord, 153
Pawn me to this your honor, she is his. 154

TIMON
My hand to thee; mine honor on my promise.

LUCILIUS
Humbly I thank your lordship. Never may
That state or fortune fall into my keeping 157
Which is not ow'd to you!

Exit [Lucilius with Old Athenian].

POET [*Presenting his poem*]
Vouchsafe my labor, and long live your lordship!

TIMON
I thank you; you shall hear from me anon.
Go not away. What have you there, my friend?

PAINTER
A piece of painting, which I do beseech
Your lordship to accept. [*Presents painting.*]

TIMON Painting is welcome.
The painting is almost the natural man; 164
For since dishonor traffics with man's nature, 165
He is but outside; these pencil'd figures are 166
Even such as they give out. I like your work, 167
And you shall find I like it. Wait attendance
Till you hear further from me.

PAINTER The gods preserve ye!

TIMON
Well fare you, gentleman. Give me your hand;
We must needs dine together.—Sir, your jewel
Hath suffer'd under praise.

JEWELER What, my lord, dispraise? 172

TIMON
A mere satiety of commendations. 173
If I should pay you for 't as 'tis extoll'd,
It would unclew me quite.

JEWELER My lord, 'tis rated 175
As those which sell would give; but you well know 176
Things of like value differing in the owners
Are prized by their masters. Believe 't, dear lord, 178
You mend the jewel by the wearing it.

[*Presents jewel.*]

TIMON
Well mock'd.

MERCHANT
No, my good lord, he speaks the common tongue,
Which all men speak with him.

Enter Apemantus.

TIMON
Look who comes here. Will you be chid?

JEWELER
We'll bear, with your lordship. 184

MERCHANT
He'll spare none.

TIMON
Good morrow to thee, gentle Apemantus!

APEMANTUS
Till I be gentle, stay thou for thy good morrow— 187
When thou art Timon's dog, and these knaves
honest. 188

TIMON
Why dost thou call them knaves? Thou know'st
them not.

APEMANTUS Are they not Athenians?

TIMON Yes.

APEMANTUS Then I repent not. 192

JEWELER You know me, Apemantus?

APEMANTUS Thou know'st I do. I call'd thee by thy 194
name. 195

TIMON Thou art proud, Apemantus.

APEMANTUS Of nothing so much as that I am not like Timon.

TIMON Whither art going?

APEMANTUS To knock out an honest Athenian's brains.

TIMON That's a deed thou'lt die for.

APEMANTUS Right, if doing nothing be death by 202
th' law.

TIMON How lik'st thou this picture, Apemantus?

APEMANTUS The best, for the innocence. 205

TIMON Wrought he not well that painted it?

APEMANTUS He wrought better that made the painter; and yet he's but a filthy piece of work.

PAINTER Y' are a dog. 209

APEMANTUS Thy mother's of my generation. What's 210
she, if I be a dog?

TIMON Wilt dine with me, Apemantus?

APEMANTUS No; I eat not lords. 213

TIMON An thou shouldst, thou'dst anger ladies.

APEMANTUS O, they eat lords. So they come by great bellies.

TIMON That's a lascivious apprehension. 217

APEMANTUS So thou apprehend'st it; take it for thy labor.

TIMON How dost thou like this jewel, Apemantus?

APEMANTUS Not so well as plain-dealing, which will
not cost a man a doit. 222

147 equal husband one of equal estate **151 bond** obligation **153 weigh with her** be equal to her in estate **154 Pawn . . . honor** if you'll pledge your word of honor to do as you have said **157 That** i.e., any **164 the natural man** man as he truly is, not what he pretends to be **165 traffics** deals (improperly) **166 He is but outside** i.e., he becomes a mere outward appearance. **pencil'd** painted **167 give out** appear **172 suffer'd under praise** been overwhelmed by praise, making its sale less easy. (But the Jeweler misunderstands.) **173 mere** utter **175 unclew** unwind, i.e., ruin **176 As . . . give** at a price which merchants would pay, i.e., at cost **178 prized . . . masters** valued as their owners are respected; i.e., the gem will increase in value because Timon will wear it

184 We'll . . . lordship i.e., we'll put up with it if your lordship can **187–188 Till . . . honest** i.e., you must wait for my "good morrow" until I have become free of satirical sharpness and until men are free of the faults I criticize, as animals are **192 repent not** don't regret what I said **194–195 thy name** i.e., knave **202 doing nothing** i.e., since there are no honest Athenians, I will be doing nothing **205 innocence** innocuous character, inability to do harm (as real life can) **209 dog** (*Cynic* is derived from the Greek for "dog.") **210 generation** species **213 eat not lords** do not consume the substance of great men. (But in his next speech Apemantus gives the phrase a sexual meaning.) **217 apprehension** (1) interpretation (2) seizure **222 doit** half a farthing, coin of slight value

TIMON What dost thou think 'tis worth?

APEMANTUS Not worth my thinking.—How now, poet?

POET How now, philosopher?

APEMANTUS Thou liest.

POET Art not one?

APEMANTUS Yes.

POET Then I lie not.

APEMANTUS Art not a poet?

POET Yes.

APEMANTUS Then thou liest. Look in thy last work, 233
where thou hast feigned him a worthy fellow.

POET That's not feigned; he is so.

APEMANTUS Yes, he is worthy of thee, and to pay thee for thy labor. He that loves to be flatter'd is worthy o' th' flatterer. Heavens, that I were a lord!

TIMON What wouldst do then, Apemantus?

APEMANTUS E'en as Apemantus does now: hate a lord with my heart.

TIMON What, thyself?

APEMANTUS Ay.

TIMON Wherefore?

APEMANTUS That I had no angry wit to be a lord.—Art 245
not thou a merchant?

MERCHANT Ay, Apemantus.

APEMANTUS Traffic confound thee, if the gods will not! 248

MERCHANT If traffic do it, the gods do it.

APEMANTUS Traffic's thy god; and thy god confound thee!

Trumpet sounds. Enter a Messenger.

TIMON
What trumpet's that?

MESSENGER
'Tis Alcibiades, and some twenty horse,
All of companionship. 254

TIMON
Pray, entertain them; give them guide to us.
[Exeunt some Attendants.]
You must needs dine with me. Go not you hence
Till I have thank'd you. When dinner's done,
Show me this piece. I am joyful of your sights. 258

Enter Alcibiades, with the rest.

Most welcome, sir!

APEMANTUS So, so there! Aches contract
And starve your supple joints! That there should be
Small love amongest these sweet knaves, and all
This courtesy! The strain of man's bred out 262
Into baboon and monkey.

ALCIBIADES
Sir, you have sav'd my longing, and I feed 264
Most hungerly on your sight.

TIMON Right welcome, sir!
Ere we depart, we'll share a bounteous time 266
In different pleasures. Pray you, let us in. 267
Exeunt [all except Apemantus].

Enter two Lords.

FIRST LORD What time o' day is 't, Apemantus?

APEMANTUS Time to be honest.

FIRST LORD That time serves still. 270

APEMANTUS The most accursed thou, that still omitt'st it. 271

SECOND LORD Thou art going to Lord Timon's feast?

APEMANTUS Ay, to see meat fill knaves and wine heat fools.

SECOND LORD Fare thee well, fare thee well.

APEMANTUS Thou art a fool to bid me farewell twice.

SECOND LORD Why, Apemantus?

APEMANTUS Shouldst have kept one to thyself, for I mean to give thee none.

FIRST LORD Hang thyself!

APEMANTUS No, I will do nothing at thy bidding. Make thy requests to thy friend.

SECOND LORD Away, unpeaceable dog, or I'll spurn thee 283
hence!

APEMANTUS I will fly, like a dog, the heels o' th' ass.
[Exit.]

FIRST LORD
He's opposite to humanity. Come, shall we in,
And taste Lord Timon's bounty? He outgoes
The very heart of kindness.

SECOND LORD
He pours it out. Plutus, the god of gold,
Is but his steward. No meed but he repays 290
Sevenfold above itself; no gift to him
But breeds the giver a return exceeding
All use of quittance.

FIRST LORD The noblest mind he carries 293
That ever govern'd man.

SECOND LORD
Long may he live in fortunes! Shall we in?

FIRST LORD
I'll keep you company. *Exeunt.*

[SCENE II]

Hautboys playing loud music. A great banquet serv'd in [Flavius and others attending]; and then enter Lord Timon, the States, the Athenian Lords, [Alcibiades, and] Ventidius (which Timon redeemed from prison). Then comes, dropping after all, Apemantus, discontentedly, like himself.

VENTIDIUS
Most honored Timon,
It hath pleas'd the gods to remember my
father's age,

233 Then thou liest (because poets are supposed to feign) **245 That . . . lord** i.e., that in becoming a lord I had forfeited the angry wit that only an independent philosopher can enjoy **248 Traffic confound** may business or trade ruin **254 of companionship** belonging to the same party **258 of your sights** to see you **262 bred out** degenerated **264 sav'd** anticipated and prevented **266 depart** part company

267 different various. **in** enter **270 still** always **271 most** i.e., more. **omitt'st** fail to seize upon **283 spurn** kick **290 meed** merit; or gift **293 use of quittance** usual rates of repayment with interest

I.ii. Location: A banqueting-room in Timon's house.
s.d. Hautboys oboes. **States** i.e., rulers of the state, senators

And call him to long peace.
He is gone happy, and has left me rich.
Then, as in grateful virtue I am bound
To your free heart, I do return those talents, 6
Doubled with thanks and service, from whose help
I deriv'd liberty. [*Offers money.*]

TIMON
O, by no means,
Honest Ventidius. You mistake my love.
I gave it freely ever; and there's none
Can truly say he gives, if he receives. 12
If our betters play at that game, we must not dare 13
To imitate them; faults that are rich are fair. 14

VENTIDIUS
A noble spirit!
[*They all stand ceremoniously looking on Timon.*]

TIMON
Nay, my lords, ceremony was but devis'd at first
To set a gloss on faint deeds, hollow welcomes, 17
Recanting goodness, sorry ere 'tis shown;
But where there is true friendship, there needs none.
Pray, sit. More welcome are ye to my fortunes
Than my fortunes to me. [*They sit.*]

FIRST LORD
My lord, we always have confess'd it. 22

APEMANTUS
Ho, ho, confess'd it? Hang'd it, have you not?

TIMON
O, Apemantus, you are welcome.

APEMANTUS
No,
You shall not make me welcome.
I come to have thee thrust me out of doors.

TIMON
Fie, th' art a churl. Y' have got a humor there 27
Does not become a man; 'tis much to blame. 28
They say, my lords, "Ira furor brevis est," but yond 29
man is ever angry. Go, let him have a table by himself,
for he does neither affect company, nor is he fit for 't, 31
indeed.

APEMANTUS Let me stay at thine apperil, Timon. I come 33
to observe; I give thee warning on 't.

TIMON I take no heed of thee. Th' art an Athenian,
therefore welcome. I myself would have no power; 36
prithee, let my meat make thee silent.

APEMANTUS I scorn thy meat; 'twould choke me, for I 38
should ne'er flatter thee. O you gods, what a number 39
of men eats Timon, and he sees 'em not! It grieves me
to see so many dip their meat in one man's blood; and 41
all the madness is, he cheers them up too. 42
I wonder men dare trust themselves with men.
Methinks they should invite them without knives; 44
Good for their meat, and safer for their lives. 45
There's much example for 't. The fellow that sits next
him now, parts bread with him, pledges the breath of
him in a divided draught, is the readiest man to kill 48
him. 'T has been prov'd. If I were a huge man, I 49
should fear to drink at meals,
Lest they should spy my windpipe's dangerous notes. 51
Great men should drink with harness on their throats. 52

TIMON [*To a Lord who drinks to him*]
My lord, in heart! And let the health go round. 53

SECOND LORD
Let it flow this way, my good lord.

APEMANTUS Flow this way? A brave fellow! He keeps
his tides well. Those healths will make thee and thy 56
state look ill, Timon.
Here's that which is too weak to be a sinner,
Honest water, which ne'er left man i' th' mire.
This and my food are equals; there's no odds.
Feasts are too proud to give thanks to the gods. 61

Apemantus' grace.

Immortal gods, I crave no pelf;
I pray for no man but myself.
Grant I may never prove so fond 64
To trust man on his oath or bond,
Or a harlot, for her weeping,
Or a dog, that seems a-sleeping,
Or a keeper with my freedom, 68
Or my friends, if I should need 'em.
Amen. So fall to 't.
Rich men sin, and I eat root. [*Eats and drinks.*]

Much good dich thy good heart, Apemantus! 72

TIMON Captain Alcibiades, your heart's in the field
now.

ALCIBIADES My heart is ever at your service, my lord.

TIMON You had rather be at a breakfast of enemies than 76
a dinner of friends. 77

ALCIBIADES So they were bleeding new, my lord, 78
there's no meat like 'em; I could wish my best friend
at such a feast.

APEMANTUS Would all those flatterers were thine ene-
mies then, that then thou mightst kill 'em—and bid
me to 'em!

FIRST LORD Might we but have that happiness, my lord,
that you would once use our hearts, whereby we 85
might express some part of our zeals, we should think
ourselves forever perfect. 87

TIMON O, no doubt, my good friends, but the gods
themselves have provided that I shall have much help

6 free generous **12 gives . . . receives** (Cf. Acts 20:35: "It is more blessed to give than to receive.") **13 betters** superiors. **at that game** i.e., taking in wealth while seeming to be generous **14 that are rich** i.e., in those who are rich. **fair** i.e., excused by their wealth **17 set a gloss on** give a speciously fair appearance to **22 confess'd** declared. (But Apemantus replies with a jesting allusion to the saying, "Confess and be hang'd.") **it** i.e., Timon's goodness **27 humor** disposition **28 Does** which does **29 Ira furor brevis est** wrath is a brief madness. (Horace's *Epistles*, I.ii.62.) **31 affect** like **33 thine apperil** your peril, risk **36 no power** i.e., to silence you **38–39 for I . . . thee** (Apemantus implies that Timon's food is to reward flatterers; Apemantus, being none, would choke on it.) **41 one man's blood** (Possible allusion to the Last Supper.) **42 all . . . too** the most mad aspect of his behavior is that he encourages them

44 without knives (Refers to the Renaissance custom of guests bringing their own knives.) **45 Good . . . meat** i.e., without knives, the guests would eat less food **48 divided draught** a cup which they share **49 huge** great in rank and wealth **51 windpipe's . . . notes** indications on my throat of where my windpipe is (and hence where it might be slit) as the head is thrown back **52 harness** armor **53 in heart** heartily **56 tides** times, seasons (with quibbling reference to *flow* of tides) **61 Feasts** i.e., partakers of fine feasts **64 fond** foolish **68 keeper** jailer **72 dich** may it do. (Originally a contraction of "d' it ye" in the phrase "much good do it you.") **76 of** consisting of **77 of** among **78 So** provided that **85 use our hearts** make trial of our love **87 forever perfect** completely happy from you. How had you been my friends else? Why have you that charitable title from thousands, did not you chiefly belong to my heart? I have told more of you to myself than you can with modesty speak in your own behalf; and thus far I confirm you. O you gods, think I, what need we have any friends, if we should ne'er have need of 'em? They were the most needless creatures living, should we ne'er have use for 'em, and would most resemble sweet instruments hung up in cases, that keeps their sounds to themselves. Why, I have often wish'd myself poorer, that I might come nearer to you. We are born to do benefits; and what better or properer can we call our own than the riches of our friends? O, what a precious comfort 'tis to have so many, like brothers, commanding one another's fortunes! O joy's e'en made away ere 't can be born! Mine eyes cannot hold out water, methinks. To forget their faults, I drink to you.

[He weeps, and drinks a toast.]

APEMANTUS Thou weep'st to make them drink, Timon.

SECOND LORD
Joy had the like conception in our eyes
And at that instant like a babe sprung up.

APEMANTUS
Ho, ho! I laugh to think that babe a bastard.

THIRD LORD
I promise you, my lord, you mov'd me much.

APEMANTUS Much! *Sound tucket [within].*

TIMON
What means that trump?

Enter Servant.

How now?

SERVANT Please you, my lord, there are certain ladies most desirous of admittance.

TIMON Ladies? What are their wills?

SERVANT There comes with them a forerunner, my lord, which bears that office to signify their pleasures.

TIMON I pray, let them be admitted.

[Exit Servant.]

Enter Cupid.

CUPID
Hail to thee, worthy Timon, and to all
That of his bounties taste! The five best senses
Acknowledge thee their patron, and come freely
To gratulate thy plenteous bosom. Th' ear,
Taste, touch, and smell, pleas'd from thy table rise;
They only now come but to feast thine eyes.

TIMON
They're welcome all; let 'em have kind admittance.
Music, make their welcome! *[Exit Cupid.]*

FIRST LORD
You see, my lord, how ample y' are belov'd.

[Music.] Enter Cupid, with a mask of Ladies [as] Amazons, with lutes in their hands, dancing and playing.

APEMANTUS
Hoyday!
What a sweep of vanity comes this way!
They dance? They are mad women.
Like madness is the glory of this life,
As this pomp shows to a little oil and root.
We make ourselves fools to disport ourselves,
And spend our flatteries to drink those men
Upon whose age we void it up again
With poisonous spite and envy.
Who lives that's not depraved or depraves?
Who dies, that bears not one spurn to their graves
Of their friends' gift?
I should fear those that dance before me now
Would one day stamp upon me. 'T has been done;
Men shut their doors against a setting sun.

The Lords rise from table, with much adoring of Timon; and to show their loves, each singles out an Amazon, and all dance, men with women, a lofty strain or two to the hautboys, and cease.

TIMON
You have done our pleasures much grace, fair ladies,
Set a fair fashion on our entertainment,
Which was not half so beautiful and kind.
You have added worth unto 't and luster,
And entertain'd me with mine own device.
I am to thank you for 't.

FIRST LADY
My lord, you take us even at the best.

APEMANTUS Faith, for the worst is filthy, and would not hold taking, I doubt me.

TIMON
Ladies, there is an idle banquet attends you.
Please you to dispose yourselves.

ALL LADIES
Most thankfully, my lord.

Exeunt [Cupid and Ladies].

TIMON
Flavius.

FLAVIUS
My lord?

TIMON The little casket bring me hither.

FLAVIUS
Yes, my lord. *[Aside.]* More jewels yet?
There is no crossing him in 's humor;
Else I should tell him well, i' faith, I should,
When all's spent, he'd be cross'd then, an he could.

91 charitable title beloved name. **from** from among **92 told** (1) recited (2) counted **94 confirm you** endorse your claim to be my worthy friends **105 made away** destroyed, i.e., turned to tears **106 born** i.e., expressed **111 bastard** i.e., illegitimate, without genuine source. (Refers to the guests' tears.) **119 which** who. **office** function. **pleasures** wishes **124 gratulate** greet, salute. **plenteous bosom** generous heart **126 They** i.e., the maskers

133 Like similar, equal. **glory** vainglory **134 As . . . root** i.e., in the same way as this splendid feast appears when compared with the mere necessities of life **136–138 And . . . envy** and lavish our flatteries in order to drink the healths of those upon whom, when old, we cast up our surfeit in poisonous spite and malice **139 depraved** vilified, slandered **141 gift** giving **147 was not** i.e., before your arrival was not **149 with . . . device** (The mask appears to have been designed by Timon to surprise his guests; or, he acknowledges that it was designed especially for him.) **150 am to** am under obligation to **151 take . . . best** i.e., praise us most generously **152–153 would . . . taking** i.e., (1) would not warrant notice (2) is too rotten with venereal disease **153 doubt me** fear **154 idle** trifling, slight **155 dispose yourselves** take your places **160 humor** frame of mind **161 well** plainly **162 cross'd** (1) wishing to have his debts canceled (2) thwarted (as in l. 160)

'Tis pity bounty had not eyes behind,
That man might ne'er be wretched for his mind.
Exit.

FIRST LORD
Where be our men?

SERVANT
Here, my lord, in readiness.

SECOND LORD
Our horses!

Enter Flavius [*with the casket*].

TIMON O my friends, I have one word
To say to you. Look you, my good lord,
I must entreat you honor me so much
As to advance this jewel; accept it and wear it,
Kind my lord. [*Offers jewel.*]

FIRST LORD
I am so far already in your gifts—

ALL
So are we all.

Enter a Servant.

SERVANT
My lord, there are certain nobles of the Senate
Newly alighted, and come to visit you.

TIMON
They are fairly welcome. [*Exit Servant.*]

FLAVIUS I beseech your honor,
Vouchsafe me a word; it does concern you near.

TIMON
Near? Why then, another time I'll hear thee.
I prithee, let's be provided to show them
entertainment.

FLAVIUS [*Aside*]
I scarce know how.

Enter another Servant.

SECOND SERVANT
May it please your honor, Lord Lucius,
Out of his free love, hath presented to you
Four milk-white horses, trapp'd in silver.

TIMON
I shall accept them fairly; let the presents
Be worthily entertain'd. [*Exit Servant.*]

Enter a third Servant.

How now? What news?

THIRD SERVANT Please you, my lord, that honorable gentleman, Lord Lucullus, entreats your company tomorrow to hunt with him, and has sent your honor two brace of greyhounds.

TIMON
I'll hunt with him; and let them be receiv'd,
Not without fair reward. [*Exit Servant.*]

FLAVIUS [*Aside*] What will this come to?
He commands us to provide, and give great gifts,
And all out of an empty coffer;
Nor will he know his purse, or yield me this,
To show him what a beggar his heart is,
Being of no power to make his wishes good.
His promises fly so beyond his state
That what he speaks is all in debt; he owes
For ev'ry word. He is so kind that he now
Pays interest for 't; his land's put to their books.
Well, would I were gently put out of office
Before I were forc'd out!
Happier is he that has no friend to feed
Than such that do e'en enemies exceed.
I bleed inwardly for my lord. *Exit.*

TIMON You do yourselves
Much wrong, you bate too much of your own
merits.
Here, my lord, a trifle of our love. [*Offers gift.*]

SECOND LORD
With more than common thanks I will receive it.

THIRD LORD
O, he's the very soul of bounty!

TIMON And now I remember, my lord, you gave good words the other day of a bay courser I rode on. 'Tis yours, because you lik'd it.

THIRD LORD
O, I beseech you, pardon me, my lord, in that.

TIMON
You may take my word, my lord: I know no man
Can justly praise but what he does affect.
I weigh my friends' affection with mine own.
I'll tell you true, I'll call to you.

ALL LORDS
O, none so welcome.

TIMON
I take all and your several visitations
So kind to heart, 'tis not enough to give.
Methinks I could deal kingdoms to my friends,
And ne'er be weary. Alcibiades,
Thou art a soldier, therefore seldom rich.
It comes in charity to thee; for all thy living
Is 'mongst the dead, and all the lands thou hast
Lie in a pitch'd field.

ALCIBIADES
Ay, defil'd land, my lord.

FIRST LORD
We are so virtuously bound—

TIMON
And so am I to you.

SECOND LORD
So infinitely endear'd—

TIMON
All to you. Lights, more lights!

164 for his mind on account of his generous inclinations **170 advance** make more worthy; i.e., by possessing it **183 trapp'd in silver** in silver-mounted trappings

194 yield me this grant me opportunity **196 Being of** i.e., the desires of his heart having **197 state** estate **200 put . . . books** i.e., mortgaged to those whom he has befriended with gifts **204 Than . . . exceed** i.e., than so-called "friends" who, by consuming his wealth, outdo his enemies in ruining him **206 bate . . . of** belittle too much **213 pardon . . . that** i.e., forgive my mentioning the horse **215 but . . . affect** a thing unless he likes and desires it **216 weigh . . . with** give equal weight to . . . as compared with **217 call to** call on; or, perhaps, appeal to in time of need **219 all . . . several** your joint and individual **224 It . . . thee** i.e., giving to you is an act of real charity. **living** (1) existence (2) property, wealth **226 pitch'd field** battlefield. **227 defil'd** (1) with a quibble on pitch'd; cf. *Ecclesiasticus* 13:1: "He that toucheth pitch shall be defiled" (2) arrayed with files or rows of soldiers **231 All to you** i.e., the obligation is entirely mine; or, all mine is yours

FIRST LORD
The best of happiness, honor, and fortunes
Keep with you, Lord Timon!

TIMON
Ready for his friends.

Exeunt lords [and all but Apemantus and Timon].

APEMANTUS
What a coil's here!
Serving of becks and jutting-out of bums!
I doubt whether their legs be worth the sums
That are given for 'em. Friendship's full of dregs.
Methinks false hearts should never have sound legs.
Thus honest fools lay out their wealth on curt'sies.

TIMON
Now, Apemantus, if thou wert not sullen,
I would be good to thee.

APEMANTUS No, I'll nothing; for if I should be brib'd too, there would be none left to rail upon thee, and then thou wouldst sin the faster. Thou giv'st so long, Timon, I fear me thou wilt give away thyself in paper shortly. What needs these feasts, pomps, and vain-glories?

TIMON Nay, an you begin to rail on society once, I am sworn not to give regard to you. Farewell, and come with better music. *Exit.*

APEMANTUS So.
Thou wilt not hear me now; thou shalt not then.
I'll lock thy heaven from thee.
O, that men's ears should be
To counsel deaf, but not to flattery! *Exit.*

[ACT II • SCENE I]

Enter a Senator [with papers in his hand].

SENATOR
And late, five thousand. To Varro and to Isidore
He owes nine thousand, besides my former sum,
Which makes it five and twenty. Still in motion
Of raging waste? It cannot hold; it will not.
If I want gold, steal but a beggar's dog
And give it Timon, why, the dog coins gold.
If I would sell my horse, and buy twenty moe
Better than he, why, give my horse to Timon,
Ask nothing, give it him, it foals me straight
And able horses. No porter at his gate,
But rather one that smiles and still invites
All that pass by. It cannot hold; no reason
Can sound his state in safety. Caphis, ho!
Caphis, I say!

Enter Caphis.

CAPHIS Here, sir. What is your pleasure?

SENATOR
Get on your cloak, and haste you to Lord Timon.
Importune him for my moneys. Be not ceas'd
With slight denial, nor then silenc'd when
"Commend me to your master" and the cap
Plays in the right hand, thus, but tell him
My uses cry to me; I must serve my turn
Out of mine own. His days and times are past,
And my reliances on his fracted dates
Have smit my credit. I love and honor him,
But must not break my back to heal his finger.
Immediate are my needs, and my relief
Must not be toss'd and turn'd to me in words,
But find supply immediate, Get you gone.
Put on a most importunate aspect,
A visage of demand; for I do fear,
When every feather sticks in his own wing,
Lord Timon will be left a naked gull,
Which flashes now a phoenix. Get you gone.

CAPHIS
I go, sir.

SENATOR
Ay, go, sir. Take the bonds along with you,
And have the dates in compt.

CAPHIS I will, sir.

SENATOR Go. *Exeunt.*

[SCENE II]

Enter Steward [Flavius] with many bills in his hand.

FLAVIUS
No care, no stop! So senseless of expense,
That he will neither know how to maintain it,
Nor cease his flow of riot; takes no account
How things go from him, nor resumes no care
Of what is to continue. Never mind
Was to be so unwise, to be so kind.
What shall be done? He will not hear, till feel.
I must be round with him, now he comes from
hunting.
Fie, fie, fie, fie!

Enter Caphis [and the Servants of] Isidore and Varro.

CAPHIS
Good even, Varro. What, you come for money?

VARRO'S SERVANT
Is 't not your business too?

235 coil fuss **236 Serving of becks** bowing **237 legs** (1) limbs (2) bows, curtsies **239 have sound legs** i.e., be disguised by the outwardly healthy appearance of sound legs able to make bows **246 paper** bonds, promises to pay **254 thy heaven** i.e., my saving advice

II.i. Location: Athens. A Senator's house.
1 late lately **4 hold** hold out, last **5 steal but** I need only steal **9 foals me straight** at once yields me foals, i.e., more horses (as gifts) **10 And able horses** i.e., and what's more they are full-grown horses, not literally foals. **porter** i.e., one who sternly denies entrance **13 sound . . . safety** i.e., by sounding its depth find it to be safe

16 ceas'd silenced **20 uses** needs **21 days and times** i.e., dates for repayment of his loans **22 fracted** broken (by failure to meet payments on notes due) **23 smit** smitten, hurt **26 toss'd and turn'd** i.e., bandied back as in tennis **30 When . . . wing** i.e., when everything is in the hands of its rightful possessor **31 gull** (1) unfledged bird (2) dupe **32 phoenix** mythical bird, one of a kind, i.e., rare and precious creature **35 in compt** reckoned

II.ii. Location: Athens. Before Timon's house.
4–5 resumes . . . continue makes no provision for continuing **5–6 Never . . . kind** never was there a mind so unwise in being so kind **7 till feel** until he suffers feelingly **8 round** plainspoken

CAPHIS
It is; and yours too, Isidore?
ISIDORE'S SERVANT It is so.
CAPHIS
Would we were all discharg'd!
VARRO'S SERVANT
I fear it.
CAPHIS
Here comes the lord.

Enter Timon and his train [with Alcibiades].

TIMON
So soon as dinner's done, we'll forth again,
My Alcibiades.—With me? What is your will?
CAPHIS [*Presenting a bill*]
My lord, here is a note of certain dues.
TIMON
Dues? Whence are you?
CAPHIS Of Athens here, my lord.
TIMON
Go to my steward.
CAPHIS
Please it your lordship, he hath put me off
To the succession of new days this month.
My master is awak'd by great occasion
To call upon his own, and humbly prays you
That with your other noble parts you'll suit
In giving him his right.
TIMON Mine honest friend,
I prithee but repair to me next morning.
CAPHIS
Nay, good my lord—
TIMON Contain thyself, good friend.
VARRO'S SERVANT
One Varro's servant, my good lord—
ISIDORE'S SERVANT
From Isidore; he humbly prays your speedy payment.
CAPHIS
If you did know, my lord, my master's wants—
VARRO'S SERVANT
'Twas due on forfeiture, my lord, six weeks and past.
ISIDORE'S SERVANT
Your steward puts me off, my lord, and I
Am sent expressly to your lordship.
TIMON
Give me breath.—
I do beseech you, good my lords, keep on;
I'll wait upon you instantly.
[*Exeunt Alcibiades and Lords.*]
[*To Flavius.*] Come hither. Pray you,
How goes the world, that I am thus encount'red
With clamorous demands of debt, broken bonds,
And the detention of long-since-due debts,
Against my honor?
FLAVIUS Please you, gentlemen,
The time is unagreeable to this business.
Your importunacy cease till after dinner,
That I may make his lordship understand
Wherefore you are not paid.
TIMON
Do so, my friends. See them well entertain'd.
[*Exit.*]
FLAVIUS
Pray draw near. *Exit.*

Enter Apemantus and Fool.

CAPHIS Stay, stay, here comes the fool with Apemantus. Let's ha' some sport with 'em.
VARRO'S SERVANT Hang him, he'll abuse us.
ISIDORE'S SERVANT A plague upon him, dog!
VARRO'S SERVANT How dost, fool?
APEMANTUS Dost dialogue with thy shadow?
VARRO'S SERVANT I speak not to thee.
APEMANTUS No, 'tis to thyself. [*To the Fool.*] Come away.
ISIDORE'S SERVANT [*To Varro's Servant*] There's the fool hangs on your back already.
APEMANTUS No, thou stand'st single, th' art not on him yet.
CAPHIS Where's the fool now?
APEMANTUS He last ask'd the question. Poor rogues and usurer's men, bawds between gold and want!
ALL SERVANTS What are we, Apemantus?
APEMANTUS Asses.
ALL SERVANTS Why?
APEMANTUS That you ask me what you are, and do not know yourselves. Speak to 'em, fool.
FOOL How do you, gentlemen?
ALL SERVANTS Gramercies, good fool. How does your mistress?
FOOL She's e'en setting on water to scald such chickens as you are. Would we could see you at Corinth!
APEMANTUS Good! Gramercy.

Enter Page.

FOOL Look you, here comes my mistress' page.
PAGE [*To the Fool*] Why, how now, captain? What do you in this wise company? How dost thou, Apemantus?
APEMANTUS Would I had a rod in my mouth, that I might answer thee profitably.
PAGE Prithee, Apemantus, read me the superscription of these letters. I know not which is which.
[*Shows letters.*]
APEMANTUS Canst not read?
PAGE No.

13 discharg'd paid **14 fear it** i.e., am apprehensive about our being paid **22 To . . . month** from one day to another all month **25 with . . . parts** in conformity to your otherwise noble nature **27 repair** come **32 on forfeiture** on penalty of forfeit if not paid on the date prescribed **36 keep on** go ahead without me **37 wait . . . instantly** be with you in a moment **40 detention** withholding payment

47 draw near come this way. (Said to the creditors' servants, who, however, decide to remain.) **55 'tis to thyself** i.e., you (Varro's servant) speak to yourself when you say "fool" **57–58 There's . . . already** i.e., you (Varro's servant) have been labeled fool already. (See l. 55.) **59–60 No . . . yet** i.e., no, you (Isidore's servant), a fool, are standing by yourself, you're not on the back of Varro's servant yet **61 Where's . . . now** i.e., whose back is labeled fool now **62 He** he who (i.e., Caphis, who has now been called a fool like the others) **70 Gramercies** many thanks **72 She's . . . scald** (Allusion to the sweating-tub treatment for venereal disease, a disease which causes loss of hair just as a chicken loses its feathers through scalding.) **73 Corinth** a city noted for its brothels; hence, a brothel or the district for such houses **79 rod** stick (to use for a beating) **81 superscription** address

APEMANTUS There will little learning die then, that day thou art hang'd. This is to Lord Timon, this to Alcibiades. Go; thou wast born a bastard, and thou 't die a bawd.

PAGE Thou wast whelp'd a dog, and thou shalt famish a dog's death. Answer not; I am gone. *Exit.*

APEMANTUS E'en so thou outrunn'st grace. Fool, I will go with you to Lord Timon's.

FOOL Will you leave me there?

APEMANTUS If Timon stay at home. You three serve three usurers?

ALL SERVANTS Ay; would they serv'd us!

APEMANTUS So would I—as good a trick as ever hangman serv'd thief.

FOOL Are you three usurers' men?

ALL SERVANTS Ay, fool.

FOOL I think no usurer but has a fool to his servant; my mistress is one, and I am her fool. When men come to borrow of your masters, they approach sadly, and go away merry; but they enter my mistress' house merrily, and go away sadly. The reason of this?

VARRO'S SERVANT I could render one.

APEMANTUS Do it then, that we may account thee a whoremaster and a knave; which notwithstanding, thou shalt be no less esteem'd.

VARRO'S SERVANT What is a whoremaster, fool?

FOOL A fool in good clothes, and something like thee. 'Tis a spirit; sometime 't appears like a lord, sometime like a lawyer, sometime like a philosopher, with two stones moe than 's artificial one. He is very often like a knight; and, generally, in all shapes that man goes up and down in from fourscore to thirteen, this spirit walks in.

VARRO'S SERVANT Thou art not altogether a fool.

FOOL Nor thou altogether a wise man. As much foolery as I have, so much wit thou lack'st.

APEMANTUS That answer might have become Apemantus.

ALL SERVANTS Aside, aside; here comes Lord Timon. [*They stand aside.*]

Enter Timon and Steward [*Flavius*].

APEMANTUS Come with me, fool, come.

FOOL I do not always follow lover, elder brother, and woman; sometime the philosopher.

[*Exeunt Apemantus and Fool.*]

FLAVIUS [*To Servants*]
Pray you walk near. I'll speak with you anon.
Exeunt [*Servants*].

TIMON
You make me marvel wherefore ere this time
Had you not fully laid my state before me,
That I might so have rated my expense
As I had leave of means.

FLAVIUS You would not hear me,
At many leisures I propos'd.

TIMON Go to!
Perchance some single vantages you took,
When my indisposition put you back,
And that unaptness made your minister
Thus to excuse yourself.

FLAVIUS O my good lord,
At many times I brought in my accounts,
Laid them before you. You would throw them off,
And say you found them in mine honesty.
When, for some trifling present, you have bid me
Return so much, I have shook my head and wept;
Yea, 'gainst th' authority of manners, pray'd you
To hold your hand more close. I did endure
Not seldom, nor no slight checks, when I have
Prompted you in the ebb of your estate
And your great flow of debts. My lov'd lord,
Though you hear now too late, yet now's a time;
The greatest of your having lacks a half
To pay your present debts.

TIMON
Let all my land be sold.

FLAVIUS
'Tis all engag'd, some forfeited and gone,
And what remains will hardly stop the mouth
Of present dues. The future comes apace;
What shall defend the interim? And at length
How goes our reck'ning?

TIMON
To Lacedaemon did my land extend.

FLAVIUS
O my good lord, the world is but a word.
Were it all yours to give it in a breath,
How quickly were it gone!

TIMON You tell me true.

FLAVIUS
If you suspect my husbandry or falsehood,
Call me before th' exactest auditors
And set me on the proof. So the gods bless me,
When all our offices have been oppress'd
With riotous feeders, when our vaults have wept
With drunken spilth of wine, when every room
Hath blaz'd with lights and bray'd with minstrelsy,
I have retir'd me to a wasteful cock,
And set mine eyes at flow. [*Weeps.*]

TIMON Prithee no more.

FLAVIUS
Heavens, have I said, the bounty of this lord!
How many prodigal bits have slaves and peasants
This night englutted! Who is not Timon's?

89 famish die **91 thou outrunn'st grace** you run away from profitable teaching **94 If . . . home** i.e., while Timon remains at home, a fool is there **106 one** (Implies that the Fool's mistress' house is a bawdy house, where men come merrily but leave diseased and poorer.) **112 spirit** i.e., one that can assume various shapes **114 stones** testicles. **than 's** than his, the philosopher's. **artificial one** i.e., the philosopher's stone, supposed to change other metals into gold **125–126 lover . . . woman** i.e., various sorts of persons whom the Fool might serve; an *elder brother* is the oldest son, one who will inherit property **130 rated** i.e., estimated and regulated

131 As . . . means as my means permitted **133 single vantages** occasional opportunities **135–136 that . . . yourself** i.e., my disinclination to listen on those occasions served as your excuse thereafter for remaining silent. (*Made your minister* means *became your agent or means.*) **139 found . . . honesty** i.e., found warrant for believing the books properly kept in knowing me to be honest **141 Return so much** give as in repayment a large gift **144 checks** rebukes **145 in** in regard to **147 yet . . . time** i.e., late as it is, it is necessary that you be made acquainted with it **148 The greatest . . . having** your total wealth at a most optimistic reckoning **151 engag'd** mortgaged **156 Lacedaemon** Sparta **160 husbandry** management, stewardship. **or** (Perhaps an error for *of.*) **163 offices** rooms, especially the kitchen and pantries **165 spilth** spilling **167 retir'd . . . cock** withdrawn to sit beside the wastefully flowing faucet of a barrel **170 bits** morsels **171 is not** i.e., does not profess himself to be

What heart, head, sword, force, means, but is Lord Timon's?
Great Timon, noble, worthy, royal Timon!
Ah, when the means are gone that buy this praise,
The breath is gone whereof this praise is made.
Feast-won, fast-lost; one cloud of winter show'rs,
These flies are couch'd.

TIMON Come, sermon me no further.
No villainous bounty yet hath pass'd my heart;
Unwisely, not ignobly, have I given.
Why dost thou weep? Canst thou the conscience lack
To think I shall lack friends? Secure thy heart;
If I would broach the vessels of my love,
And try the argument of hearts by borrowing,
Men and men's fortunes could I frankly use
As I can bid thee speak.

FLAVIUS
Assurance bless your thoughts!

TIMON
And in some sort these wants of mine are crown'd,
That I account them blessings; for by these
Shall I try friends. You shall perceive how you
Mistake my fortunes; I am wealthy in my friends.
Within there! Flaminius! Servilius!

Enter three servants [Flaminius, Servilius, and another].

SERVANTS My lord? My lord?

TIMON I will dispatch you severally: [*To Servilius*] you to Lord Lucius; [*To Flaminius*] to Lord Lucullus you— I hunted with his honor today; [*To the other*] you to Sempronius. Commend me to their loves, and, I am proud, say, that my occasions have found time to use 'em toward a supply of money. Let the request be fifty talents.

FLAMINIUS As you have said, my lord.
[*Exeunt Servants.*]

FLAVIUS [*Aside*] Lord Lucius and Lucullus? Humh!

TIMON
Go you, sir, to the senators—
Of whom, even to the state's best health, I have
Deserv'd this hearing—bid 'em send o' th' instant
A thousand talents to me.

FLAVIUS I have been bold—
For that I knew it the most general way—
To them to use your signet and your name,
But they do shake their heads, and I am here
No richer in return.

TIMON Is 't true? Can 't be?

FLAVIUS
They answer, in a joint and corporate voice,
That now they are at fall, want treasure, cannot
Do what they would, are sorry; you are honorable,
But yet they could have wish'd—they know not—
Something hath been amiss—a noble nature
May catch a wrench—would all were well—'tis pity—
And so, intending other serious matters,
After distasteful looks and these hard fractions,
With certain half-caps and cold-moving nods
They froze me into silence.

TIMON You gods, reward them!
Prithee, man, look cheerly. These old fellows
Have their ingratitude in them hereditary.
Their blood is cak'd, 'tis cold, it seldom flows;
'Tis lack of kindly warmth they are not kind;
And nature, as it grows again toward earth,
Is fashion'd for the journey, dull and heavy.
Go to Ventidius. Prithee, be not sad,
Thou art true and honest; ingeniously I speak,
No blame belongs to thee. Ventidius lately
Buried his father, by whose death he's stepp'd
Into a great estate. When he was poor,
Imprison'd, and in scarcity of friends,
I clear'd him with five talents. Greet him from me.
Bid him suppose some good necessity
Touches his friend, which craves to be rememb'red
With those five talents. That had, give 't these fellows
To whom 'tis instant due. Nev'r speak or think
That Timon's fortunes 'mong his friends can sink.

FLAVIUS
I would I could not think it.
That thought is bounty's foe;
Being free itself, it thinks all others so. *Exeunt.*

[ACT III • SCENE I]

Flaminius waiting to speak with a Lord, [Lucullus,] from his Master; enters a Servant to him.

SERVANT I have told my lord of you; he is coming down to you.

FLAMINIUS I thank you, sir.

Enter Lucullus.

SERVANT Here's my lord.

LUCULLUS [*Aside*] One of Lord Timon's men? A gift, I warrant. Why, this hits right; I dreamt of a silver basin and ewer tonight.—Flaminius, honest Flaminius, you are very respectively welcome, sir.—Fill me some wine. [*Exit Servant.*] And how does that honorable, complete, free-hearted gentleman of Athens, thy very bountiful good lord and master?

176 fast-lost (1) lost in time of fast (2) lost quickly and for good **177 are couch'd** hide themselves (to avoid Timon's requests for help) **180 conscience** faith, or judgment **181 Secure** set at ease **182 broach** tap, open **183 try . . . hearts** test protestations of love **184 frankly** as freely **186 Assurance . . . thoughts** may your hopes prove well founded **187 crown'd** given a special dignity **188 That** so that **193 severally** separately **203 to . . . health** i.e., for my services in behalf of the state's welfare. (Cf. IV.iii.93–96, where Alcibiades refers to Timon's sword and fortune offered in the defense of Athens.) **206 general** comprehensive, or customary (?) **207 signet** signet ring and seal, token of authority **211 at fall** at low ebb. **want** lack

215 catch a wrench be wrenched away from its true bent **216 intending** turning their attention to, or pretending (?) **217 fractions** broken sentences **218 half-caps** i.e., curt salutations **223 'Tis . . . kind** it is lack of natural warmth which makes them not generous (with pun on *kind,* natural, of humankind) **224 earth** i.e., the grave **227 ingeniously** frankly **230–232 When he was poor,** etc. (These lines echo Matthew 25:34–37 when Jesus discusses the Last Judgment.) **235 That had** when you have that **239 That . . . foe** i.e., the naive assumption that friends will remain true in hard times is the undoing of the bounteous impulse **240 Being free itself** being generous itself

III.i. Location: Athens. Lucullus' house.
6 hits right accords perfectly **7 tonight** last night **8 respectively** particularly

FLAMINIUS His health is well, sir.

LUCULLUS I am right glad that his health is well, sir. And what hast thou there under thy cloak, pretty Flaminius?

FLAMINIUS Faith, nothing but an empty box, sir, which, in my lord's behalf, I come to entreat your honor to supply; who, having great and instant occasion to use fifty talents, hath sent to your lordship to furnish him, nothing doubting your present assistance therein.

LUCULLUS La, la, la la! "Nothing doubting," says he? Alas, good lord! A noble gentleman 'tis, if he would not keep so good a house. Many a time and often I ha' din'd with him, and told him on 't, and come again to supper to him of purpose to have him spend less, and yet he would embrace no counsel, take no warning by my coming. Every man has his fault, and honesty is his. I ha' told him on 't, but I could ne'er get him from 't.

Enter Servant, with wine.

SERVANT Please your lordship, here is the wine.

LUCULLUS Flaminius, I have noted thee always wise. Here's to thee. [*Offers a toast.*]

FLAMINIUS Your lordship speaks your pleasure.

LUCULLUS I have observ'd thee always for a towardly prompt spirit—give thee thy due—and one that knows what belongs to reason; and canst use the time well, if the time use thee well. Good parts in thee! [*To Servant.*] Get you gone, sirrah. [*Exit Servant.*] Draw nearer, honest Flaminius. Thy lord 's a bountiful gentleman; but thou art wise, and thou know'st well enough, although thou com'st to me, that this is no time to lend money, especially upon bare friendship, without security. Here's three solidares for thee. [*Gives him a tip.*] Good boy, wink at me, and say thou saw'st me not. Fare thee well.

FLAMINIUS

Is 't possible the world should so much differ,
And we alive that liv'd? Fly, damned baseness,
To him that worships thee! [*Throw the money back.*]

LUCULLUS Ha? Now I see thou art a fool, and fit for thy master. *Exit Lucullus.*

FLAMINIUS

May these add to the number that may scald thee!
Let molten coin be thy damnation,
Thou disease of a friend, and not himself!
Has friendship such a faint and milky heart
It turns in less than two nights? O you gods!
I feel my master's passion. This slave unto his honor
Has my lord's meat in him.
Why should it thrive and turn to nutriment
When he is turn'd to poison?
O, may diseases only work upon 't!
And, when he's sick to death, let not that part of
nature
Which my lord paid for be of any power
To expel sickness, but prolong his hour! *Exit.*

[SCENE II]

Enter Lucius, with three Strangers.

LUCIUS Who, the Lord Timon? He is my very good friend, and an honorable gentleman.

FIRST STRANGER We know him for no less, though we are but strangers to him. But I can tell you one thing, my lord, and which I hear from common rumors: now Lord Timon's happy hours are done and past, and his estate shrinks from him.

LUCIUS Fie, no, do not believe it! He cannot want for money.

SECOND STRANGER But believe you this, my lord, that not long ago one of his men was with the Lord Lucullus to borrow so many talents, nay, urg'd extremely for 't, and show'd what necessity belong'd to 't, and yet was denied.

LUCIUS How?

SECOND STRANGER I tell you, denied, my lord.

LUCIUS What a strange case was that! Now, before the gods, I am asham'd on 't. Denied that honorable man? There was very little honor show'd in 't. For my own part, I must needs confess, I have receiv'd some small kindnesses from him, as money, plate, jewels, and such-like trifles, nothing comparing to his; yet had he mistook him and sent to me, I should ne'er have denied his occasion so many talents.

Enter Servilius.

SERVILIUS See, by good hap, yonder's my lord; I have sweat to see his honor. My honor'd lord— [*To Lucius.*]

LUCIUS Servilius? You are kindly met, sir. Fare thee well. Commend me to thy honorable virtuous lord, my very exquisite friend. [*Starts to go.*]

SERVILIUS May it please your honor, my lord hath sent—

LUCIUS Ha? What has he sent? I am so much endear'd to that lord; he's ever sending. How shall I thank him, think'st thou? And what has he sent now?

SERVILIUS H'as only sent his present occasion now, my lord, requesting your lordship to supply his instant use with so many talents.

LUCIUS

I know his lordship is but merry with me;
He cannot want fifty—five hundred—talents.

18 supply fill **20 nothing** not at all **24 keep . . . house** be so lavish in his entertaining **25 on 't** of it **26 of** on **28 honesty** liberality **34 Your . . . pleasure** it pleases your lordship to say so **35–36 towardly prompt** quick to meet another's thoughts, well-disposed **44 solidares** small coins. (A term invented by Shakespeare, evidently.) **45 wink** shut the eyes **47–48 so . . . liv'd** i.e., change so much in our lifetime **53 Let . . . damnation** i.e., may you be killed and sent to hell by having molten metal poured down your throat **56 It turns** that it sours like milk (with quibble on the idea of *turn* as in turncoat) **57 feel . . . passion** i.e., feel angry on my master's behalf, share his anger **58 meat** i.e., food of a feast

III.ii. Location: Athens. A public place.
22 his i.e., Lucullus' receiving of generosity **23 mistook . . . me** i.e., mistakenly sent to me, who owe him less **25 hap** fortune **25–26 I have sweat** i.e., I have been hurrying **29 exquisite** sought after **35 H'as** he has **39 He cannot . . . talents** (Probably an indication of Shakespeare's uncertainty over the value of this currency; see also *so many* above in ll. 12, 24, and 37.)

SERVILIUS
But in the mean time he wants less, my lord.
If his occasion were not virtuous, 41
I should not urge it half so faithfully.

LUCIUS
Dost thou speak seriously, Servilius?

SERVILIUS
Upon my soul, 'tis true, sir.

LUCIUS What a wicked beast was I to disfurnish myself 45
against such a good time, when I might ha' shown 46
myself honorable! How unluckily it happ'ned that I
should purchase the day before for a little part, and 48
undo a great deal of honor! Servilius, now before the
gods, I am not able to do—the more beast, I say—I
was sending to use Lord Timon myself, these gentle- 51
men can witness; but I would not, for the wealth of
Athens, I had done 't now. Commend me bountifully
to his good lordship, and I hope his honor will con- 54
ceive the fairest of me, because I have no power to be 55
kind. And tell him this from me, I count it one of my
greatest afflictions, say, that I cannot pleasure such an
honorable gentleman. Good Servilius, will you be-
friend me so far as to use mine own words to him?

SERVILIUS Yes, sir, I shall.

LUCIUS
I'll look you out a good turn, Servilius. 61
Exit Servilius.
True, as you said, Timon is shrunk indeed;
And he that's once denied will hardly speed. 63
Exit.

FIRST STRANGER
Do you observe this, Hostilius?

SECOND STRANGER
Ay, too well.

FIRST STRANGER
Why, this is the world's soul, 66
And just of the same piece
Is every flatterer's sport. Who can call him his
friend,
That dips in the same dish? For, in my knowing,
Timon has been this lord's father, 70
And kept his credit with his purse, 71
Supported his estate; nay, Timon's money
Has paid his men their wages. He ne'er drinks
But Timon's silver treads upon his lip,
And yet—O, see the monstrousness of man
When he looks out in an ungrateful shape!— 76
He does deny him, in respect of his, 77
What charitable men afford to beggars.

THIRD STRANGER
Religion groans at it.

FIRST STRANGER For mine own part,
I never tasted Timon in my life, 80
Nor came any of his bounties over me
To mark me for his friend; yet I protest,
For his right noble mind, illustrious virtue,
And honorable carriage, 84
Had his necessity made use of me,
I would have put my wealth into donation 86
And the best half should have return'd to him,
So much I love his heart. But I perceive
Men must learn now with pity to dispense;
For policy sits above conscience. *Exeunt.*

[SCENE III]

Enter a third Servant [of Timon's] with Sempronius, another of Timon's Friends.

SEMPRONIUS
Must he needs trouble me in 't—hum!—'bove all
others?
He might have tried Lord Lucius or Lucullus;
And now Ventidius is wealthy too,
Whom he redeem'd from prison. All these
Owe their estates unto him.

SERVANT
My lord,
They have all been touch'd and found base metal, 7
For they have all denied him.

SEMPRONIUS
How? Have they denied him?
Has Ventidius and Lucullus denied him?
And does he send to me? Three? Humh!
It shows but little love or judgment in him.
Must I be his last refuge? His friends, like
physicians,
Thrive, give him over. Must I take th' cure
upon me? 14
H'as much disgrac'd me in 't; I'm angry at him,
That might have known my place. I see no sense
for 't
But his occasions might have woo'd me first; 17
For, in my conscience, I was the first man
That e'er received gift from him,
And does he think so backwardly of me now
That I'll requite it last? No!
So it may prove an argument of laughter 22
To th' rest, and 'mongst lords I be thought a fool.
I'd rather than the worth of thrice the sum
H'ad sent to me first, but for my mind's sake; 25
I'd such a courage to do him good. But now return, 26
And with their faint reply this answer join:
Who bates mine honor shall not know my coin. 28
Exit.

41 were not virtuous were due to a fault instead of a virtue, i.e., generosity **45 disfurnish** unprovide (with money) **46 against . . . time** to deal with such an excellent opportunity **48 for . . . part** something of little use to myself and my reputation (?) **51 use** i.e., as a source of borrowing **54–55 conceive the fairest** think the best **55 because** i.e., even though **61 look you out** seek occasion to do you **63 speed** prosper **66 soul** real essence, vital principle **70 father** i.e., patron **71 kept his** i.e., maintained Lucius'. **his purse** i.e., Timon's wealth **76 looks out** appears **77 in . . . his** considering his (Lucius') possessions **80 tasted Timon** i.e., sampled Timon's liberality

84 carriage conduct **86 put . . . donation** i.e., regarded all my wealth as a gift from him

III.iii. Location: Athens. Sempronius' house.
7 touch'd (Metaphor derived from testing metals with a touchstone to see if they are gold.) **14 Thrive . . . over** i.e., thrive on his wealth, but now give him up as beyond help **17 But his occasions** i.e., but that he, in his need **22 argument of** subject for **25 H'ad** he had **26 courage** desire **28 Who bates** whoever abates, detracts from

SERVANT Excellent! Your lordship's a goodly villain.
The devil knew not what he did when he made man
politic; he cross'd himself by 't, and I cannot think but, 31
in the end, the villainies of man will set him clear. 32
How fairly this lord strives to appear foul! Takes vir- 33
tuous copies to be wicked, like those that under hot 34
ardent zeal would set whole realms on fire. 35
Of such a nature is his politic love.
This was my lord's best hope; now all are fled,
Save only the gods. Now his friends are dead,
Doors, that were ne'er acquainted with their wards 39
Many a bounteous year, must be employ'd
Now to guard sure their master. 41
And this is all a liberal course allows; 42
Who cannot keep his wealth must keep his house. 43
Exit.

[SCENE IV]

Enter [two of] Varro's Men, meeting [Titus and] others, all [being servants of] Timon's creditors, to wait for his coming out. Then enter Lucius' [Servant] and Hortensius.

VARRO'S FIRST SERVANT
Well met; good morrow, Titus and Hortensius.
TITUS
The like to you, kind Varro.
HORTENSIUS Lucius!
What, do we meet together?
LUCIUS' SERVANT Ay, and I think
One business does command us all;
For mine is money.
TITUS So is theirs and ours.

Enter Philotus.

LUCIUS' SERVANT
And, sir, Philotus too!
PHILOTUS Good day at once. 6
LUCIUS' SERVANT
Welcome, good brother.
What do you think the hour?
PHILOTUS Laboring for nine.
LUCIUS' SERVANT
So much?
PHILOTUS Is not my lord seen yet?
LUCIUS' SERVANT Not yet.
PHILOTUS
I wonder on 't; he was wont to shine at seven.
LUCIUS' SERVANT
Ay, but the days are wax'd shorter with him.
You must consider that a prodigal course
Is like the sun's,
But not, like his, recoverable. I fear 14
'Tis deepest winter in Lord Timon's purse;
That is, one may reach deep enough, and yet
Find little.
PHILOTUS I am of your fear for that.
TITUS
I'll show you how t' observe a strange event.
Your lord sends now for money?
HORTENSIUS Most true, he does.
TITUS
And he wears jewels now of Timon's gift,
For which I wait for money. 21
HORTENSIUS
It is against my heart.
LUCIUS' SERVANT
Mark how strange it shows:
Timon in this should pay more than he owes,
And e'en as if your lord should wear rich jewels 25
And send for money for 'em. 26
HORTENSIUS
I'm weary of this charge, the gods can witness. 27
I know my lord hath spent of Timon's wealth,
And now ingratitude makes it worse than stealth. 29
VARRO'S FIRST SERVANT
Yes, mine's three thousand crowns. What's yours?
LUCIUS' SERVANT
Five thousand mine.
VARRO'S FIRST SERVANT
'Tis much deep, and it should seem by th' sum
Your master's confidence was above mine, 33
Else surely his had equal'd. 34

Enter Flaminius.

TITUS One of Lord Timon's men.
LUCIUS' SERVANT Flaminius? Sir, a word. Pray, is my lord ready to come forth?
FLAMINIUS No, indeed, he is not.
TITUS We attend his lordship. Pray signify so much.
FLAMINIUS I need not tell him that. He knows you are too diligent. *[Exit.]*

Enter Steward [Flavius] in a cloak, muffled.

LUCIUS' SERVANT
Ha! Is not that his steward muffled so?
He goes away in a cloud. Call him, call him. 43
TITUS Do you hear, sir?
VARRO'S SECOND SERVANT By your leave, sir—
FLAVIUS
What do ye ask of me, my friend?
TITUS
We wait for certain money here, sir.
FLAVIUS Ay,
If money were as certain as your waiting,
'Twere sure enough.
Why then preferr'd you not your sums and bills, 50

31 cross'd foiled (by making man his rival in treachery) **32 set him clear** i.e., make even the devil look innocent **33–35 Takes . . . fire** i.e., how this lord models himself on the virtuous for wicked purposes, like religious bigots who for zealous purposes would burn down whole kingdoms **39 wards** bolts, locks **41 guard sure** i.e., protect from arrest for debt **42 liberal** generous **43 keep . . . keep** preserve . . . stay inside

III.iv. Location: Athens. Timon's house.
6 at once to one and all

14 But . . . recoverable i.e., the sun will return from its wintery path, but Timon cannot recover (since his funds are not *recoverable*) **21 For . . . money** i.e., while I wait for the money used to buy those jewels **25–26 e'en . . . for 'em** i.e., it's just as though your master should both wear the jewels Timon gave him and simultaneously demand the money that paid for those jewels **27 charge** commission **29 stealth** theft **33 mine** my master's **34 his had equal'd** i.e., my master's loan would have equaled in amount your master's **43 in a cloud** (1) muffled (2) in a surly humor **50 preferr'd** presented

When your false masters eat of my lord's meat?
Then they could smile and fawn upon his debts,
And take down th' int'rest into their glutt'nous maws.
You do yourselves but wrong to stir me up;
Let me pass quietly.
Believe 't, my lord and I have made an end;
I have no more to reckon, he to spend.

LUCIUS' SERVANT
Ay, but this answer will not serve.

FLAVIUS
If 'twill not serve, 'tis not so base as you;
For you serve knaves. [*Exit.*]

VARRO'S FIRST SERVANT How? What does his cashier'd worship mutter?

VARRO'S SECOND SERVANT No matter what; he's poor, and that's revenge enough. Who can speak broader than he that has no house to put his head in? Such may rail against great buildings.

Enter Servilius.

TITUS O, here's Servilius. Now we shall know some answer.

SERVILIUS If I might beseech you, gentlemen, to repair some other hour, I should derive much from 't. For take 't of my soul, my lord leans wondrously to discontent. His comfortable temper has forsook him; he's much out of health, and keeps his chamber.

LUCIUS' SERVANT
Many do keep their chambers are not sick;
And, if it be so far beyond his health,
Methinks he should the sooner pay his debts,
And make a clear way to the gods.

SERVILIUS Good gods!

TITUS
We cannot take this for answer, sir.

FLAMINIUS *(Within)*
Servilius, help! My lord, my lord!

Enter Timon, in a rage.

TIMON
What, are my doors oppos'd against my passage?
Have I been ever free, and must my house
Be my retentive enemy, my jail?
The place which I have feasted, does it now,
Like all mankind, show me an iron heart?

LUCIUS' SERVANT Put in now, Titus.

TITUS My lord, here is my bill.

LUCIUS' SERVANT Here's mine.

HORTENSIUS And mine, my lord.

BOTH VARRO'S SERVANTS And ours, my lord.

PHILOTUS All our bills.

TIMON
Knock me down with 'em! Cleave me to the girdle!

LUCIUS' SERVANT Alas, my lord—

TIMON
Cut my heart in sums!

TITUS Mine, fifty talents.

TIMON
Tell out my blood!

LUCIUS' SERVANT Five thousand crowns, my lord.

TIMON
Five thousand drops pays that. What yours?
And yours?

VARRO'S FIRST SERVANT My lord—

VARRO'S SECOND SERVANT My lord—

TIMON
Tear me, take me, and the gods fall upon you!
Exit Timon.

HORTENSIUS Faith, I perceive our masters may throw their caps at their money. These debts may well be call'd desperate ones, for a madman owes 'em.
Exeunt.

Enter Timon [and Flavius].

TIMON
They have e'en put my breath from me, the slaves.
Creditors? Devils!

FLAVIUS
My dear lord—

TIMON
What if it should be so?

FLAVIUS
My lord—

TIMON
I'll have it so. My steward!

FLAVIUS Here, my lord.

TIMON
So fitly? Go, bid all my friends again,
Lucius, Lucullus, and Sempronius—all.
I'll once more feast the rascals.

FLAVIUS O my lord,
You only speak from your distracted soul;
There's not so much left to furnish out
A moderate table.

TIMON
Be it not in thy care. Go,
I charge thee, invite them all. Let in the tide
Of knaves once more. My cook and I'll provide.
Exeunt.

[SCENE V]

Enter three Senators at one door, Alcibiades meeting them, with Attendants.

FIRST SENATOR
My lord, you have my voice to 't.
The fault's bloody;
'Tis necessary he should die.

51 eat ate. (Pronounced *et*.) **53 th' int'rest** i.e., the food and drink they consumed as though it were interest on the loans **56 made an end** severed our relationship **61 cashier'd** dismissed **64 broader** (1) more freely (2) more in the open, abroad **65–66 Such . . . buildings** i.e., just as a houseless man may criticize great building, so a masterless servant may rail at those in service **69 repair** return **74 are** who are **75 if . . . health** if his condition is so far from good health **77 make . . . gods** i.e., pay all his debts and so get ready to die **91 Knock, Cleave** (Timon puns on *bills* as weapons.)

95 Tell out count out by the drop **102–103 throw . . . at** i.e., give up hope of recovering **108 What . . . so** i.e., suppose I give it a try. (Timon has thought of the mock banquet he will serve in III.vi.)

III.v. Location: Athens. The Senate-house.
1 voice to 't vote in favor of it (the death sentence under consideration)

Nothing emboldens sin so much as mercy.

SECOND SENATOR
Most true; the law shall bruise 'em.

ALCIBIADES
Honor, health, and compassion to the Senate!

FIRST SENATOR
Now, captain?

ALCIBIADES
I am an humble suitor to your virtues;
For pity is the virtue of the law,
And none but tyrants use it cruelly.
It pleases time and fortune to lie heavy
Upon a friend of mine, who, in hot blood,
Hath stepp'd into the law, which is past depth
To those that, without heed, do plunge into 't.
He is a man, setting his fate aside,
Of comely virtues;
Nor did he soil the fact with cowardice—
An honor in him which buys out his fault—
But with a noble fury and fair spirit,
Seeing his reputation touch'd to death,
He did oppose his foe;
And with such sober and unnoted passion
He did behave his anger, ere 'twas spent,
As if he had but prov'd an argument.

FIRST SENATOR
You undergo too strict a paradox,
Striving to make an ugly deed look fair.
Your words have took such pains as if they labor'd
To bring manslaughter into form and set quarreling
Upon the head of valor—which indeed
Is valor misbegot, and came into the world
When sects and factions were newly born.
He's truly valiant that can wisely suffer
The worst that man can breathe,
And make his wrongs his outsides,
To wear them like his raiment, carelessly,
And ne'er prefer his injuries to his heart,
To bring it into danger.
If wrongs be evils and enforce us kill,
What folly 'tis, to hazard life for ill!

ALCIBIADES
My lord—

FIRST SENATOR You cannot make gross sins look clear.
To revenge is no valor, but to bear.

ALCIBIADES
My lords, then, under favor, pardon me,
If I speak like a captain.
Why do fond men expose themselves to battle,
And not endure all threats? Sleep upon 't,
And let the foes quietly cut their throats
Without repugnancy? If there be
Such valor in the bearing, what make we
Abroad? Why then, women are more valiant
That stay at home, if bearing carry it,
And the ass more captain than the lion, the felon
Loaden with irons wiser than the judge,
If wisdom be in suffering. O my lords,
As you are great, be pitifully good.
Who cannot condemn rashness in cold blood?
To kill, I grant, is sin's extremest gust;
But, in defense, by mercy, 'tis most just.
To be in anger is impiety;
But who is man that is not angry?
Weigh but the crime with this.

SECOND SENATOR
You breathe in vain.

ALCIBIADES In vain? His service done
At Lacedaemon and Byzantium
Were a sufficient briber for his life.

FIRST SENATOR
What's that?

ALCIBIADES
Why, I say, my lords, h'as done fair service,
And slain in fight many of your enemies.
How full of valor did he bear himself
In the last conflict, and made plenteous wounds!

SECOND SENATOR
He has made too much plenty with 'em.
He's a sworn rioter; he has a sin that often
Drowns him, and takes his valor prisoner.
If there were no foes, that were enough
To overcome him. In that beastly fury
He has been known to commit outrages
And cherish factions. 'Tis inferr'd to us
His days are foul and his drink dangerous.

FIRST SENATOR
He dies.

ALCIBIADES Hard fate! He might have died in war.
My lords, if not for any parts in him—
Though his right arm might purchase his own time
And be in debt to none—yet, more to move you,
Take my deserts to his, and join 'em both;
And, for I know your reverend ages love
Security, I'll pawn my victories, all
My honors, to you, upon his good returns.
If by this crime he owes the law his life,
Why, let the war receive 't in valiant gore;
For law is strict, and war is nothing more.

FIRST SENATOR
We are for law. He dies; urge it no more,
On height of our displeasure. Friend or brother,

5 'em i.e., all offenders **6 compassion to the Senate** i.e., may the Senate have compassion **13 stepp'd into** incurred the penalties of **13–14 past depth To** over the heads of **15 setting . . . aside** excluding his ill-fated action **17 fact** deed **18 buys out** redeems **20 touch'd to death** fatally threatened **22 unnoted** so well under control as to be unobservable **23 behave** control **25 undergo** undertake **28 bring . . . form** make manslaughter appear orderly, or according to form **28–29 set . . . of** make quarreling the highest kind of, or subdivision of **29 which** i.e., quarreling, duelling **34 his outsides** merely external circumstance **35 carelessly** without anxiety **36 prefer** present **39 'tis** this is, i.e., this code that obliges one to repay evil with violence. **for ill** in a bad cause **40 clear** innocent **41 to bear** i.e., bearing insults calmly is true valor **42 under favor** by your leave **44 fond** foolish **45 Sleep** i.e., why do they not sleep **47 repugnancy** resistance

48 the bearing i.e., putting up with insults. **make** do **49 Abroad** away from home **50 bearing** putting up with insults (with a pun on *childbearing* and perhaps on *supporting the man in sexual intercourse*) **54 pitifully good** good by showing mercy **56 sin's extremest gust** the relish of extremest sin. (*Gust* means outburst, indulgence.) **57 by mercy** by a merciful interpretation of law **59 not** i.e., never **69 made . . . 'em** i.e., used them as an excuse for an excess of riotous pleasure (playing on *plenty, plenteous*) **70 sworn rioter** inveterate debauchee. **sin** i.e., drunkenness **72 If** even if. **foes** accusers **75 cherish factions** support plots, insubordinations. **inferr'd** alleged **78 parts** admirable traits **79 his right . . . time** i.e., his ability in war should obtain his freedom and let him live out his natural life **82 for** because **83 Security** (1) safety (2) collateral for a loan (using a financial metaphor found also in *purchase, pawn, good returns,* etc.) **84 upon . . . returns** as a pledge that he will make a good return on your investment in him, i.e., fight bravely in war **86 let . . . gore** i.e., let him pay his debt by dying as a soldier **89 On . . . our** on pain of our highest

He forfeits his own blood that spills another.

ALCIBIADES
Must it be so? It must not be. My lords,
I do beseech you, know me.

SECOND SENATOR
How?

ALCIBIADES
Call me to your remembrances.

THIRD SENATOR
What?

ALCIBIADES
I cannot think but your age has forgot me;
It could not else be I should prove so base
To sue and be denied such common grace.
My wounds ache at you.

FIRST SENATOR Do you dare our anger?
'Tis in few words, but spacious in effect:
We banish thee forever.

ALCIBIADES Banish me?
Banish your dotage, banish usury,
That makes the Senate ugly.

FIRST SENATOR
If, after two days' shine, Athens contain thee,
Attend our weightier judgment.
And, not to swell our spirit,
He shall be executed presently. *Exeunt* [*Senators*].

ALCIBIADES
Now the gods keep you old enough
That you may live
Only in bone, that none may look on you!
I'm worse than mad. I have kept back their foes,
While they have told their money and let out
Their coin upon large interest, I myself
Rich only in large hurts. All those for this?
Is this the balsam that the usuring Senate
Pours into captains' wounds? Banishment!
It comes not ill; I hate not to be banish'd.
It is a cause worthy my spleen and fury,
That I may strike at Athens. I'll cheer up
My discontented troops, and lay for hearts.
'Tis honor with most lands to be at odds.
Soldiers should brook as little wrongs as gods. *Exit.*

[SCENE VI]

[*Music. Tables and seats set out; Servants attending.*] *Enter divers Friends* [*of Timon*] *at several doors.*

FIRST LORD The good time of day to you, sir.

SECOND LORD I also wish it to you. I think this honorable lord did but try us this other day.

FIRST LORD Upon that were my thoughts tiring, when we encount'red. I hope it is not so low with him as he made it seem in the trial of his several friends.

SECOND LORD It should not be, by the persuasion of his new feasting.

FIRST LORD I should think so. He hath sent me an earnest inviting, which many my near occasions did urge me to put off; but he hath conjur'd me beyond them, and I must needs appear.

SECOND LORD In like manner was I in debt to my importunate business, but he would not hear my excuse. I am sorry, when he sent to borrow of me, that my provision was out.

FIRST LORD I am sick of that grief too, as I understand how all things go.

SECOND LORD Every man here 's so. What would he have borrow'd of you?

FIRST LORD A thousand pieces.

SECOND LORD A thousand pieces?

FIRST LORD What of you?

SECOND LORD He sent to me, sir—Here he comes.

Enter Timon and Attendants.

TIMON With all my heart, gentlemen both; and how fare you?

FIRST LORD Ever at the best, hearing well of your lordship.

SECOND LORD The swallow follows not summer more willing than we your lordship.

TIMON [*Aside*] Nor more willingly leaves winter; such summer-birds are men.—Gentlemen, our dinner will not recompense this long stay. Feast your ears with the music awhile, if they will fare so harshly o' th' trumpet's sound; we shall to 't presently.

FIRST LORD I hope it remains not unkindly with your lordship that I return'd you an empty messenger.

TIMON O, sir, let it not trouble you.

SECOND LORD My noble lord—

TIMON Ah, my good friend, what cheer?

The banquet brought in.

SECOND LORD My most honorable lord, I am e'en sick of shame that, when your lordship this other day sent to me, I was so unfortunate a beggar.

TIMON Think not on 't, sir.

SECOND LORD If you had sent but two hours before—

TIMON Let it not cumber your better remembrance.—Come, bring in all together.

SECOND LORD All cover'd dishes!

FIRST LORD Royal cheer, I warrant you.

THIRD LORD Doubt not that, if money and the season can yield it.

FIRST LORD How do you? What's the news?

THIRD LORD Alcibiades is banish'd. Hear you of it?

FIRST AND SECOND LORD Alcibiades banish'd?

THIRD LORD 'Tis so, be sure of it.

FIRST LORD How? How?

90 another i.e., another's **98 To sue** as to request **100 spacious in effect** of great import (with quibble on the spacious world to which Alcibiades is banished) **105 Attend . . . judgment** expect our more severe sentence **106 spirit** anger **110 Only in bone** i.e., mere skeletons **112 told** reckoned **115 balsam** a medicine **120 lay for hearts** endeavor to win their affection **121 'Tis . . . odds** it's honorable to be at variance with a country (and its political leaders) in most instances **122 brook . . . gods** endure insults as little as the gods do

III.vi. Location: Athens. A banqueting-room in Timon's house.
4 tiring preying, feeding, i.e., busily engaged

7 persuasion evidence **10 many . . . occasions** my many urgent necessities or business **11 conjur'd . . . them** summoned me so urgently as to overcome my previous commitments **13 in debt to** obligated to **34 they . . . o'** they (your ears) will deign to feast on such rough fare as **43 so . . . beggar** so unfortunate as to be out of ready reserves **46 cumber . . . remembrance** trouble your happier thoughts, memories **48 cover'd** (Implies particularly elegant fare.)

SECOND LORD I pray you, upon what?
TIMON My worthy friends, will you draw near?
THIRD LORD I'll tell you more anon. Here's a noble feast toward.
SECOND LORD This is the old man still.
THIRD LORD Will 't hold? Will 't hold?
SECOND LORD It does; but time will—and so—
THIRD LORD I do conceive.
TIMON Each man to his stool, with that spur as he would to the lip of his mistress. Your diet shall be in all places alike. Make not a city feast of it, to let the meat cool ere we can agree upon the first place; sit, sit. [*They sit.*] The gods require our thanks.

You great benefactors, sprinkle our society with thankfulness. For your own gifts, make yourselves prais'd; but reserve still to give, lest your deities be despis'd. Lend to each man enough, that one need not lend to another; for, were your godheads to borrow of men, men would forsake the gods. Make the meat be belov'd more than the man that gives it. Let no assembly of twenty be without a score of villains. If there sit twelve women at the table, let a dozen of them be—as they are. The rest of your fees, O gods—the senators of Athens, together with the common lag of people—what is amiss in them, you gods, make suitable for destruction. For these my present friends, as they are to me nothing, so in nothing bless them, and to nothing are they welcome.

Uncover, dogs, and lap!
[*The dishes are uncovered and seen to be full of warm water.*]
SOME SPEAK What does his lordship mean?
SOME OTHER I know not.
TIMON
May you a better feast never behold,
You knot of mouth-friends! Smoke and luke-warm water
Is your perfection. This is Timon's last,
Who, stuck and spangled with your flatteries,
Washes it off, and sprinkles in your faces
Your reeking villainy.
[*Throwing the water in their faces.*]
Live loath'd and long,
Most smiling, smooth, detested parasites,
Courteous destroyers, affable wolves, meek bears,
You fools of fortune, trencher-friends, time's flies,
Cap-and-knee slaves, vapors, and minute-jacks!
Of man and beast the infinite malady
Crust you quite o'er! What, dost thou go?
Soft! Take thy physic first—thou too—and thou;
Stay, I will lend thee money, borrow none.
[*Throws the dishes at them, and drives them out.*]
What, all in motion? Henceforth be no feast
Whereat a villain's not a welcome guest.
Burn, house! Sink, Athens! Henceforth hated be
Of Timon, man, and all humanity! *Exit.*

Enter the Senators, with other Lords, [*returning*].

FIRST LORD How now, my lords?
SECOND LORD Know you the quality of Lord Timon's fury?
THIRD LORD Push! Did you see my cap?
FOURTH LORD I have lost my gown.
FIRST LORD He's but a mad lord, and nought but humors sways him. He gave me a jewel th' other day, and now he has beat it out of my hat. Did you see my jewel? [*They search for their belongings.*]
THIRD LORD Did you see my cap?
SECOND LORD Here 'tis.
FOURTH LORD Here lies my gown.
FIRST LORD Let's make no stay.
SECOND LORD Lord Timon's mad.
THIRD LORD I feel 't upon my bones.
FOURTH LORD One day he gives us diamonds, next day stones. *Exeunt the Senators* [*etc.*].

[ACT IV • SCENE I]

Enter Timon.

TIMON
Let me look back upon thee. O thou wall,
That girdles in those wolves, dive in the earth,
And fence not Athens! Matrons, turn incontinent!
Obedience fail in children! Slaves and fools,
Pluck the grave wrinkled Senate from the bench,
And minister in their steads! To general filths
Convert o' th' instant, green virginity!
Do 't in your parents' eyes! Bankrupts, hold fast;
Rather than render back, out with your knives,
And cut your trusters' throats! Bound servants, steal!
Large-handed robbers your grave masters are,
And pill by law. Maid, to thy master's bed;
Thy mistress is o' th' brothel! Son of sixteen,
Pluck the lin'd crutch from thy old limping sire,
With it beat out his brains! Piety, and fear,
Religion to the gods, peace, justice, truth,
Domestic awe, night-rest, and neighborhood,
Instruction, manners, mysteries, and trades,
Degrees, observances, customs, and laws,

57 what what ground **60 toward** imminent **61 old** same as before **62 hold** last **63 will** i.e., will tell **64 conceive** understand **67 city feast** formal occasion, with seating by rank **68 first place** place of honor **72 reserve still** always hold back something **79 fees** i.e., what is held in fee from you, your gifts or benefactions (?) or, those who hold their lives in fee from you (?) **80 lag** dregs, lowest class **82 For** as for **89 mouth-friends** i.e., those who have fed off Timon and flattered him. **Smoke** i.e., steam, "hot air" **90 Is your perfection** suits you perfectly **91 stuck and spangled** bespattered and decorated **96 time's flies** fair-weather insects **97 Cap-and-knee slaves** men obsequious with their caps and curtsies. **vapors** substanceless creatures. **minute-jacks** mannikins which strike a bell on the outside of a clock; hence, time-servers **98 the infinite malady** every loathsome disease

100 physic medicine **107 quality** occasion **109 Push** pshaw **111–112 humors** caprice

IV.i. Location: Outside the walls of Athens.
3 fence (1) enclose (2) defend **6 general filths** common prostitutes **7 green** young **10 Bound** indentured **11 Large-handed** rapacious **12 pill** pillage **14 lin'd** stuffed, padded **15 fear** religious awe **16 Religion to** veneration of **17 Domestic awe** respect for the seniors of a household. **neighborhood** neighborliness **18 mysteries** crafts

Decline to your confounding contraries,
And yet confusion live! Plagues, incident to men, 21
Your potent and infectious fevers heap
On Athens, ripe for stroke! Thou cold sciatica, 23
Cripple our senators, that their limbs may halt 24
As lamely as their manners! Lust and liberty 25
Creep in the minds and marrows of our youth,
That 'gainst the stream of virtue they may strive, 27
And drown themselves in riot! Itches, blains,
Sow all th' Athenian bosoms, and their crop
Be general leprosy! Breath infect breath,
That their society, as their friendship, may 31
Be merely poison! Nothing I'll bear from thee 32
But nakedness, thou detestable town!
[He strips off his garments.]
Take thou that too, with multiplying bans! 34
Timon will to the woods, where he shall find
Th' unkindest beast more kinder than mankind.
The gods confound—hear me, you good gods all—
Th' Athenians both within and out that wall!
And grant, as Timon grows, his hate may grow
To the whole race of mankind, high and low!
Amen. *Exit.*

[SCENE II]

Enter Steward [Flavius], with two or three Servants.

FIRST SERVANT
Hear you, master steward, where's our master?
Are we undone, cast off, nothing remaining?

FLAVIUS
Alack, my fellows, what should I say to you?
Let me be recorded by the righteous gods,
I am as poor as you.

FIRST SERVANT
Such a house broke?
So noble a master fall'n? All gone, and not
One friend to take his fortune by the arm,
And go along with him?

SECOND SERVANT
As we do turn our backs
From our companion thrown into his grave,
So his familiars to his buried fortunes 11
Slink all away, leave their false vows with him,
Like empty purses pick'd; and his poor self,
A dedicated beggar to the air, 14
With his disease of all-shunn'd poverty,
Walks, like contempt, alone. More of our fellows. 16

Enter other Servants.

FLAVIUS
All broken implements of a ruin'd house.

THIRD SERVANT
Yet do our hearts wear Timon's livery;
That see I by our faces. We are fellows still,
Serving alike in sorrow. Leak'd is our bark, 20
And we, poor mates, stand on the dying deck, 21
Hearing the surges threat. We must all part
Into this sea of air.

FLAVIUS
Good fellows all,
The latest of my wealth I'll share amongst you. 24
Wherever we shall meet, for Timon's sake,
Let's yet be fellows. Let's shake our heads, and say,
As 'twere a knell unto our master's fortunes,
"We have seen better days." Let each take some;
[Gives them money.]
Nay, put out all your hands. Not one word more.
Thus part we rich in sorrow, parting poor.
[Servants] embrace, and part several ways.
O, the fierce wretchedness that glory brings us!
Who would not wish to be from wealth exempt,
Since riches point to misery and contempt?
Who would be so mock'd with glory, or to live
But in a dream of friendship,
To have his pomp and all what state compounds 36
But only painted, like his varnish'd friends? 37
Poor honest lord, brought low by his own heart,
Undone by goodness! Strange, unusual blood, 39
When man's worst sin is he does too much good!
Who then dares to be half so kind again?
For bounty, that makes gods, do still mar men.
My dearest lord, blest to be most accurs'd, 43
Rich only to be wretched, thy great fortunes
Are made thy chief afflictions. Alas, kind lord!
He's flung in rage from this ingrateful seat
Of monstrous friends, nor has he with him to 47
Supply his life, or that which can command it. 48
I'll follow and inquire him out.
I'll ever serve his mind with my best will; 50
Whilst I have gold, I'll be his steward still. *Exit.*

[SCENE III]

Enter Timon, in the woods [with a spade].

TIMON
O blessed breeding sun, draw from the earth
Rotten humidity; below thy sister's orb 2
Infect the air! Twinn'd brothers of one womb,
Whose procreation, residence, and birth
Scarce is dividant, touch them with several fortunes, 5

21 yet i.e., in the face of all other destruction **23 sciatica** nerve pain in hip and leg **24 halt** limp **25 liberty** licentiousness **27 stream** current **31 society** associating with one another **32 merely** entirely **34 bans** curses

IV.ii. Location: Athens. Timon's house.
11 his familiars . . . fortunes those familiar with him when he was fortunate, now perceiving his ruin **14 dedicated . . . air** beggar having nothing and nowhere to go **16 like contempt** as if he were contempt itself

20 bark sailing vessel **21 mates** (1) fellows (2) mates of a vessel. **dying** i.e., sinking **24 latest** last remnant **36 what state compounds** that which constitutes dignity and splendor **37 But only** nothing more than **39 blood** nature **43 to be** only to be **47–48 has . . . life** he has nothing to maintain himself **48 that . . . it** i.e., money **50 serve his mind** execute his wishes

IV.iii. Location: Woods and cave, near the seashore; in front of Timon's cave.
2 Rotten humidity damp-causing rot. **thy sister's** i.e., the moon's **5 dividant** separate, divisible. **touch** test. **several** different

The greater scorns the lesser. Not nature, 6
To whom all sores lay siege, can bear great fortune 7
But by contempt of nature. 8
Raise me this beggar, and deny 't that lord; 9
The senator shall bear contempt hereditary, 10
The beggar native honor. 11
It is the pasture lards the rother's sides, 12
The want that makes him lean. Who dares, who dares 13
In purity of manhood stand upright
And say "This man's a flatterer"? If one be,
So are they all; for every grize of fortune 16
Is smooth'd by that below. The learned pate 17
Ducks to the golden fool. All's obliquy; 18
There's nothing level in our cursed natures 19
But direct villainy. Therefore, be abhorr'd
All feasts, societies, and throngs of men!
His semblable, yea, himself, Timon disdains. 22
Destruction fang mankind! Earth, yield me roots! 23
[*Digs.*]
Who seeks for better of thee, sauce his palate
With thy most operant poison! [*Finds gold.*] What is here? 25
Gold? Yellow, glittering, precious gold?
No gods, I am no idle votarist. 27
Roots, you clear heavens! Thus much of this will make
Black white, foul fair, wrong right,
Base noble, old young, coward valiant.
Ha, you gods! Why this? What this, you gods? Why, this
Will lug your priests and servants from your sides,
Pluck stout men's pillows from below their heads. 33
This yellow slave
Will knit and break religions, bless th' accurs'd,
Make the hoar leprosy ador'd, place thieves 36
And give them title, knee, and approbation 37
With senators on the bench. This is it
That makes the wappen'd widow wed again; 39
She, whom the spital-house and ulcerous sores 40
Would cast the gorge at, this embalms and spices 41
To th' April day again. Come, damned earth, 42
Thou common whore of mankind, that puts odds 43
Among the rout of nations, I will make thee 44
Do thy right nature. *(March afar off.)* Ha? A drum? Th' art quick, 45
But yet I'll bury thee. Thou 'lt go, strong thief, 46
When gouty keepers of thee cannot stand.
[*Buries gold.*]
Nay, stay thou out for earnest. [*Keeps some gold.*] 48

Enter Alcibiades, with drum and fife, in warlike manner; and Phrynia and Timandra.

ALCIBIADES
What art thou there? Speak.

TIMON
A beast, as thou art. The canker gnaw thy heart
For showing me again the eyes of man!

ALCIBIADES
What is thy name? Is man so hateful to thee,
That art thyself a man?

TIMON
I am Misanthropos, and hate mankind. 54
For thy part, I do wish thou wert a dog,
That I might love thee something.

ALCIBIADES I know thee well, 56
But in thy fortunes am unlearn'd and strange. 57

TIMON
I know thee too; and more than that I know thee
I not desire to know. Follow thy drum;
With man's blood paint the ground, gules, gules. 60
Religious canons, civil laws are cruel;
Then what should war be? This fell whore of thine 62
Hath in her more destruction than thy sword,
For all her cherubin look.

PHRYNIA Thy lips rot off! 64

TIMON
I will not kiss thee; then the rot returns
To thine own lips again.

ALCIBIADES
How came the noble Timon to this change?

TIMON
As the moon does, by wanting light to give. 68
But then renew I could not, like the moon;
There were no suns to borrow of.

ALCIBIADES Noble Timon,
What friendship may I do thee?

TIMON None, but to
Maintain my opinion.

ALCIBIADES What is it, Timon?

TIMON Promise me friendship, but perform none. If 73
thou wilt not promise, the gods plague thee, for thou 74
art a man! If thou dost perform, confound thee, for 75
thou art a man! 76

ALCIBIADES
I have heard in some sort of thy miseries. 77

TIMON
Thou saw'st them when I had prosperity.

ALCIBIADES
I see them now; then was a blessed time.

TIMON
As thine is now, held with a brace of harlots.

6 The and the result is that the **6–8 Not . . . nature** i.e., human nature, which suffers so many afflictions, cannot bear good fortune without scorning fellow creatures who are less fortunate **9 Raise me** raise. (*Me* is the ethical dative.) **10 bear contempt hereditary** receive contempt as though he were born low **11 native honor** (will receive) honor as though born great **12 lards** that fattens. **rother's** ox's **12–13 It is . . . lean** i.e., some are raised to prosperity and honor, others not **16 grize** step **17 smooth'd** assiduously prepared **18 Ducks** bows obsequiously. **golden** rich. **All's obliquy** i.e., all's deviating from the right **19 level** direct. (The contrary to *obliquy*.) **22 His semblable** i.e., his own kind, his own image **23 fang** seize **25 operant** active, potent **27 no idle votarist** no trifler in my vows **33 Pluck . . . heads** i.e., expedite the death of healthy men **36 hoar** white-skinned. **place** give recognized status and high office to **37 knee** the bended deferential knee **39 wappen'd** worn out **40 spital-house** house for the diseased (cf. hospital) **41 cast the gorge** vomit **41–42 this . . . again** i.e., money causes the diseased old woman to embalm herself with cosmetics to look April-like and marriageable **42 damned earth** i.e., gold **43–44 puts . . . nations** causes strife among various peoples **45 Do . . . nature** i.e., cause strife, according to your true nature. **quick** (1) swift to act (2) alive **46 go** walk

48 earnest token money **54 Misanthropos** hater of mankind **56 something** somewhat, a little **57 unlearn'd and strange** uninformed and ignorant **60 gules** (Heraldic name for "red.") **62 fell** deadly **64 cherubin** angelic **68 wanting** lacking **73–76 If . . . a man** i.e., may the gods plague you for being a man whether you perform your promises or don't even make promises **77 I . . . sort** i.e., I have heard something

TIMANDRA
Is this th' Athenian minion, whom the world 81
Voic'd so regardfully?

TIMON
Art thou Timandra? 82

TIMANDRA
Yes.

TIMON
Be a whore still. They love thee not that use thee;
Give them diseases, leaving with thee their lust.
Make use of thy salt hours. Season the slaves 86
For tubs and baths; bring down rose-cheek'd youth 87
To the tub-fast and the diet.

TIMANDRA
Hang thee, monster!

ALCIBIADES
Pardon him, sweet Timandra, for his wits
Are drown'd and lost in his calamities.
I have but little gold of late, brave Timon,
The want whereof doth daily make revolt
In my penurious band. I have heard, and griev'd, 93
How cursed Athens, mindless of thy worth,
Forgetting thy great deeds, when neighbor states,
But for thy sword and fortune, trod upon them—

TIMON
I prithee beat thy drum and get thee gone.

ALCIBIADES
I am thy friend and pity thee, dear Timon.

TIMON
How dost thou pity him whom thou dost trouble?
I had rather be alone.

ALCIBIADES
Why, fare thee well. Here is some gold for thee.
[*Offers gold.*]

TIMON
Keep it, I cannot eat it.

ALCIBIADES
When I have laid proud Athens on a heap—

TIMON
Warr'st thou 'gainst Athens?

ALCIBIADES
Ay, Timon, and have cause.

TIMON
The gods confound them all in thy conquest,
And thee after, when thou hast conquer'd!

ALCIBIADES
Why me, Timon?

TIMON
That by killing of villains
Thou wast born to conquer my country.
Put up thy gold. Go on—here's gold—go on;
[*Offers gold.*]
Be as a planetary plague, when Jove 111
Will o'er some high-vic'd city hang his poison 112
In the sick air. Let not thy sword skip one.
Pity not honor'd age for his white beard;
He is an usurer. Strike me the counterfeit matron; 115
It is her habit only that is honest, 116
Herself's a bawd. Let not the virgin's cheek
Make soft thy trenchant sword; for those milk paps, 118
That through the window-bars bore at men's eyes, 119
Are not within the leaf of pity writ, 120
But set them down horrible traitors. Spare not the babe,
Whose dimpled smiles from fools exhaust their mercy; 122
Think it a bastard, whom the oracle
Hath doubtfully pronounc'd thy throat shall cut, 124
And mince it sans remorse. Swear against objects; 125
Put armor on thine ears and on thine eyes,
Whose proof nor yells of mothers, maids, nor babes, 127
Nor sight of priests in holy vestments bleeding,
Shall pierce a jot. There's gold to pay thy soldiers.
Make large confusion; and, thy fury spent, 130
Confounded be thyself! Speak not, be gone.

ALCIBIADES
Hast thou gold yet? I'll take the gold thou givest me,
Not all thy counsel. [*Takes gold.*]

TIMON
Dost thou, or dost thou not, heaven's curse upon thee! 134

PHRYNIA AND TIMANDRA
Give us some gold, good Timon. Hast thou more?

TIMON
Enough to make a whore forswear her trade,
And to make whores, a bawd. Hold up, you sluts, 137
Your aprons mountant. You are not oathable, 138
Although I know you'll swear, terribly swear,
Into strong shudders and to heavenly agues,
Th' immortal gods that hear you. Spare your oaths;
I'll trust to your conditions. Be whores still; 142
And he whose pious breath seeks to convert you,
Be strong in whore, allure him, burn him up;
Let your close fire predominate his smoke, 145
And be no turncoats. Yet may your pains six months 146
Be quite contrary. And thatch your poor thin roofs 147
With burdens of the dead—some that were hang'd, 148
No matter; wear them, betray with them. Whore still; 149
Paint till a horse may mire upon your face. 150
A pox of wrinkles! [*Gives gold.*]

PHRYNIA AND TIMANDRA
Well, more gold. What then? 151
Believe 't that we'll do anything for gold.

81 Athenian minion darling of Athens **82 Voic'd** spoke of. **regardfully** respectfully **86 salt** lecherous **87 tubs and baths** (Allusion to the treatments for venereal diseases, as also in *tub-fast* and *diet* in the next line.) **93 penurious** poverty-stricken **111 planetary plague** (Allusion to the belief in the malignant influence of planets.) **112 high-vic'd** extremely vicious **115 counterfeit** pretending respectability **116 habit** costume, outward appearance. **honest** chaste

118 trenchant sharp **119 window-bars** i.e., lattice-work of her bodice (?) **120 Are . . . writ** i.e., are not written down on the list of those to whom pity is to be shown **122 exhaust** draw forth **124 doubtfully** ambiguously. **thy . . . cut** will cut your throat. (However, the phrase can also be ambiguously reversed.) **125 mince** slash, cut in small pieces. **sans** without. **Swear against objects** bind yourself by oath against objections (to your cruelty) **127 Whose proof** the tested strength of which armor. **nor yells** neither the yells **130 large confusion** wholesale destruction **134 Dost . . . not** whether you do or not **137 to . . . bawd** i.e., to make a bawd retire from turning women into whores **138 mountant** (A heraldic coinage, with sexual suggestion; see also *erection* in l. 166.) **oathable** to be believed on your oath **142 your conditions** what you are, your characters **145 Let . . . smoke** i.e., let your secret and disease-carrying passion overcome his pious professions **146–147 Yet . . . contrary** i.e., may you suffer intense pain for six months (?) (Perhaps *six months* is simply an arbitrary figure, or alludes to the early symptoms of syphilis.) **147–148 thatch . . . dead** i.e., cover your balding heads (caused by venereal disease) with wigs made of the hair of corpses **149 betray with them** i.e., use these wigs to create false beauty to betray more men **150 mire upon** bog down in **151 A pox of wrinkles** i.e., may you be plagued with wrinkles

TIMON
Consumptions sow 153
In hollow bones of man; strike their sharp shins,
And mar men's spurring. Crack the lawyer's voice, 155
That he may never more false title plead,
Nor sound his quillets shrilly. Hoar the flamen, 157
That scolds against the quality of flesh, 158
And not believes himself. Down with the nose, 159
Down with it flat; take the bridge quite away
Of him that, his particular to foresee, 161
Smells from the general weal. Make curl'd-pate ruffians bald, 162
And let the unscarr'd braggarts of the war
Derive some pain from you. Plague all,
That your activity may defeat and quell
The source of all erection. There's more gold. 166
[*Gives gold.*]
Do you damn others, and let this damn you,
And ditches grave you all! 168

PHRYNIA AND TIMANDRA
More counsel with more money, bounteous Timon.

TIMON
More whore, more mischief first; I have given you earnest. 170

ALCIBIADES
Strike up the drum towards Athens! Farewell, Timon.
If I thrive well, I'll visit thee again.

TIMON
If I hope well, I'll never see thee more.

ALCIBIADES
I never did thee harm.

TIMON
Yes, thou spok'st well of me.

ALCIBIADES
Call'st thou that harm?

TIMON
Men daily find it. Get thee away, and take 176
Thy beagles with thee.

ALCIBIADES
We but offend him. Strike! 177
[*Drum beats.*] *Exeunt* [*Alcibiades, Phrynia, and Timandra*].

TIMON
That nature, being sick of man's unkindness,
Should yet be hungry! Common mother, thou
[*Digs.*]
Whose womb unmeasurable and infinite breast
Teems and feeds all; whose self-same mettle, 181
Whereof thy proud child, arrogant man, is puff'd,
Engenders the black toad and adder blue,
The gilded newt and eyeless venom'd worm, 184
With all th' abhorred births below crisp heaven
Whereon Hyperion's quick'ning fire doth shine: 186
Yield him who all thy human sons do hate, 187
From forth thy plenteous bosom, one poor root!
Ensear thy fertile and conceptious womb, 189
Let it no more bring out ingrateful man!
Go great with tigers, dragons, wolves, and bears; 191
Teem with new monsters, whom thy upward face 192
Hath to the marbled mansion all above
Never presented! [*Finds a root.*] O, a root! Dear thanks!—
Dry up thy marrows, vines, and plough-torn leas, 195
Whereof ingrateful man, with liquorish draughts 196
And morsels unctuous, greases his pure mind,
That from it all consideration slips— 198

Enter Apemantus.

More man? Plague, plague!

APEMANTUS
I was directed hither. Men report
Thou dost affect my manners, and dost use them. 201

TIMON
'Tis, then, because thou dost not keep a dog,
Whom I would imitate. Consumption catch thee! 203

APEMANTUS
This is in thee a nature but infected, 204
A poor unmanly melancholy sprung
From change of fortune. Why this spade? This place?
This slave-like habit and these looks of care?
Thy flatterers yet wear silk, drink wine, lie soft,
Hug their diseas'd perfumes, and have forgot 209
That ever Timon was. Shame not these woods
By putting on the cunning of a carper. 211
Be thou a flatterer now, and seek to thrive
By that which has undone thee. Hinge thy knee,
And let his very breath whom thou'lt observe 214
Blow off thy cap; praise his most vicious strain,
And call it excellent. Thou wast told thus; 216
Thou gav'st thine ears, like tapsters that bade welcome, 217
To knaves and all approachers. 'Tis most just
That thou turn rascal; hadst thou wealth again,
Rascals should have 't. Do not assume my likeness.

TIMON
Were I like thee, I'd throw away myself.

APEMANTUS
Thou hast cast away thyself, being like thyself;
A madman so long, now a fool. What, think'st 223
That the bleak air, thy boisterous chamberlain, 224
Will put thy shirt on warm? Will these moss'd trees, 225
That have outliv'd the eagle, page thy heels 226

153 Consumptions sow plant wasting diseases such as syphilis **155 spurring** i.e., riding of women (metaphorically compared to horse riding) **157 quillets** quibbles. **Hoar the flamen** whiten (with leprosy) the priest (with a pun on *hoar, whore*) **158 quality of flesh** fleshly desire **159 Down . . . nose** (An effect of syphilis.) **161 his . . . foresee** in order to look out for his own interests **162 Smells . . . weal** (1) loses the scent of the common good (2) stinks above the common crowd **166 erection** advancement (with bawdy pun) **168 grave** enclose in the grave (with a pun on *ditches* and *damming* continued from l. 167) **170 whore** whoring. **earnest** earnest money, token payment **176 find it** i.e., find it harmful to be well spoken well of **177 beagles** i.e., beagle hounds, fawning followers—the prostitutes **181 mettle** spirit, essence (with pun on *metal;* the words were virtually interchangeable) **184 eyeless venom'd worm** the blindworm (wrongly supposed poisonous)

186 Hyperion's i.e., the sun's. **quick'ning** life-giving **187 who . . . hate** who hates all your human offspring **189 Ensear** dry up. **conceptious** fertile **191 Go great** be pregnant **192 upward face** i.e., surface, looking skyward **195 plough-torn leas** ploughed-up pastureland **196 liquorish** sweet, alcoholic **198 consideration** reflection, rationality; regard for others, or for other things than sensual **201 affect** put on **203 would** i.e., would in that case **204 but infected** i.e., not inborn and philosophical but induced by misery and hence shallow **209 perfumes** perfumed mistresses **211 putting . . . carper** assuming the manner and profession of a cynic **214 observe** bow obsequiously before **216 Thou . . . thus** i.e., you were flattered in exactly this manner **217 like tapsters** i.e., like barkeeps who welcome all comers indiscriminately **223–225 think'st . . . warm** (Alludes to the practice of having a servant warm one's garment by the fire.) **226 page thy heels** i.e., follow you obediently

And skip when thou point'st out? Will the cold
  brook,
Candied with ice, caudle thy morning taste
To cure thy o'ernight's surfeit? Call the creatures
Whose naked natures live in all the spite
Of wreakful heaven, whose bare unhoused trunks,
To the conflicting elements expos'd,
Answer mere nature; bid them flatter thee.
O, thou shalt find—

TIMON
A fool of thee. Depart.

APEMANTUS
I love thee better now than e'er I did.

TIMON
I hate thee worse.

APEMANTUS
Why?

TIMON
Thou flatter'st misery.

APEMANTUS
I flatter not, but say thou art a caitiff.

TIMON
Why dost thou seek me out?

APEMANTUS
To vex thee.

TIMON
Always a villain's office or a fool's.
Dost please thyself in 't?

APEMANTUS
Ay.

TIMON
What, a knave too?

APEMANTUS
If thou didst put this sour-cold habit on
To castigate thy pride, 'twere well, but thou
Dost it enforcedly. Thou 'dst courtier be again,
Wert thou not beggar. Willing misery
Outlives incertain pomp, is crown'd before:
The one is filling still, never complete;
The other, at high wish. Best state, contentless,
Hath a distracted and most wretched being,
Worse than the worst, content.
Thou shouldst desire to die, being miserable.

TIMON
Not by his breath that is more miserable.
Thou art a slave, whom Fortune's tender arm
With favor never clasp'd, but bred a dog.
Hadst thou, like us from our first swath, proceeded
The sweet degrees that this brief world affords
To such as may the passive drugs of it
Freely command, thou wouldst have plung'd thyself
In general riot, melted down thy youth
In different beds of lust, and never learn'd
The icy precepts of respect, but followed
The sug'red game before thee. But myself,
Who had the world as my confectionary,
The mouths, the tongues, the eyes, and hearts
  of men
At duty, more than I could frame employment;
That numberless upon me stuck as leaves
Do on the oak, have with one winter's brush
Fell from their boughs and left me open, bare
For every storm that blows—I to bear this,
That never knew but better, is some burden.
Thy nature did commence in sufferance, time
Hath made thee hard in 't. Why shouldst thou hate
  men?
They never flatter'd thee. What hast thou given?
If thou wilt curse, thy father, that poor rag,
Must be thy subject, who in spite put stuff
To some she beggar and compounded thee
Poor rogue hereditary. Hence, be gone!
If thou hadst not been born the worst of men,
Thou hadst been a knave and flatterer.

APEMANTUS
Art thou proud yet?

TIMON
Ay, that I am not thee.

APEMANTUS
I, that I was no prodigal.

TIMON
I, that I am one now.
Were all the wealth I have shut up in thee,
I'd give thee leave to hang it. Get thee gone.
That the whole life of Athens were in this!
Thus would I eat it. [*Eats a root.*]

APEMANTUS
Here, I will mend thy feast.
[*Offers him food.*]

TIMON
First mend my company, take away thyself.

APEMANTUS
So I shall mend mine own, by th' lack of thine.

TIMON
'Tis not well mended so, it is but botch'd;
If not, I would it were.

APEMANTUS
What wouldst thou have to Athens?

TIMON
Thee thither in a whirlwind. If thou wilt,
Tell them there I have gold; look, so I have.
[*Shows his gold.*]

APEMANTUS
Here is no use for gold.

TIMON
The best and truest;
For here it sleeps, and does no hired harm.

APEMANTUS Where liest o' nights, Timon?

TIMON Under that's above me.
Where feed'st thou o' days, Apemantus?

APEMANTUS Where my stomach finds meat; or, rather,
where I eat it.

TIMON Would poison were obedient and knew my
mind!

227 skip . . . out jump to fulfill your command **228 Candied** crystalline. **caudle . . . taste** i.e., provide you with a caudle, a hot spiced drink **230 in** exposed to **231 wreakful** revengeful **233 Answer** cope with, contend with. **mere** stark, unrelieved **234 of** in **237 caitiff** wretch **245–246 Willing . . . before** deliberately chosen poverty outlasts the life of insecure ceremony and wealth, and is sooner crowned with spiritual reward **247 is filling still** is never satisfied **248 at high wish** as content as it desires **248–250 Best . . . content** being at the height of prosperity without contentment means a wretched existence, worse than being at the bottom of prosperity with contentment **252 Not . . . miserable** i.e., not when he who speaks (Apemantus) is more to be pitied than I **254 bred** i.e., one whom Fortune bred **255 swath** swaddling clothes. **proceeded** passed through (like a student taking an academic degree) **257 drugs** drudges **260 different** various **262 sug'red game** sweet-tasting quarry. (Cf. l. 228.)

265 At duty subservient to my wishes. **frame** provide with **266 stuck** having stuck **267 winter's brush** gust of wintry wind **268 Fell** fallen **269 I . . . this** that I should bear this **271 sufferance** suffering, poverty **278 worst** lowest in station **284 hang it** i.e., hang yourself **289 botch'd** badly mended (since you remain in your own company) **290 If . . . were** i.e., even so, I wish you were out of my company (?) **291 What . . . have** what would you have me convey. (But Timon caustically jests in a more literal sense of the phrase.) **297 that 's** that which is

APEMANTUS Where wouldst thou send it?

TIMON To sauce thy dishes.

APEMANTUS The middle of humanity thou never knewest, but the extremity of both ends. When thou wast in thy gilt and thy perfume, they mock'd thee for too much curiosity; in thy rags thou know'st none, but art despis'd for the contrary. There's a medlar for thee, eat it. [*Gives a fruit.*]

TIMON On what I hate I feed not.

APEMANTUS Dost hate a medlar?

TIMON Ay, though it look like thee.

APEMANTUS An th' hadst hated meddlers sooner, thou shouldst have lov'd thyself better now. What man didst thou ever know unthrift that was belov'd after his means?

TIMON Who, without those means thou talk'st of, didst thou ever know belov'd?

APEMANTUS Myself.

TIMON I understand thee. Thou hadst some means to keep a dog.

APEMANTUS What things in the world canst thou nearest compare to thy flatterers?

TIMON Women nearest; but men—men are the things themselves. What wouldst thou do with the world, Apemantus, if it lay in thy power?

APEMANTUS Give it the beasts, to be rid of the men.

TIMON Wouldst thou have thyself fall in the confusion of men, and remain a beast with the beasts?

APEMANTUS Ay, Timon.

TIMON A beastly ambition, which the gods grant thee t' attain to! If thou wert the lion, the fox would beguile thee; if thou wert the lamb, the fox would eat thee; if thou wert the fox, the lion would suspect thee, when peradventure thou wert accus'd by the ass; if thou wert the ass, thy dullness would torment thee, and still thou liv'dst but as a breakfast to the wolf; if thou wert the wolf, thy greediness would afflict thee, and oft thou shouldst hazard thy life for thy dinner; wert thou the unicorn, pride and wrath would confound thee and make thine own self the conquest of thy fury; wert thou a bear, thou wouldst be kill'd by the horse; wert thou a horse, thou wouldst be seiz'd by the leopard; wert thou a leopard, thou wert germane to the lion and the spots of thy kindred were jurors on thy life; all thy safety were remotion and thy defense absence. What beast couldst thou be, that were not subject to a beast? And what a beast art thou already, that seest not thy loss in transformation!

APEMANTUS If thou couldst please me with speaking to me, thou mightst have hit upon it here. The commonwealth of Athens is become a forest of beasts.

TIMON How has the ass broke the wall, that thou art out of the city?

APEMANTUS Yonder comes a poet and a painter. The plague of company light upon thee! I will fear to catch it, and give way. When I know not what else to do, I'll see thee again.

TIMON When there is nothing living but thee, thou shalt be welcome. I had rather be a beggar's dog than Apemantus.

APEMANTUS
Thou art the cap of all the fools alive.

TIMON
Would thou wert clean enough to spit upon!

APEMANTUS
A plague on thee! Thou art too bad to curse.

TIMON
All villains that do stand by thee are pure.

APEMANTUS
There is no leprosy but what thou speak'st.

TIMON
If I name thee.
I'll beat thee, but I should infect my hands.

APEMANTUS
I would my tongue could rot them off!

TIMON
Away, thou issue of a mangy dog!
Choler does kill me that thou art alive;
I swoon to see thee.

APEMANTUS Would thou wouldst burst!

TIMON Away,
Thou tedious rogue! I am sorry I shall lose
A stone by thee. [*Throws a stone at him.*]

APEMANTUS Beast!

TIMON Slave!

APEMANTUS Toad!

TIMON
Rogue, rogue, rogue!
I am sick of this false world, and will love nought
But even the mere necessities upon 't.
Then, Timon, presently prepare thy grave.
Lie where the light foam of the sea may beat
Thy grave-stone daily. Make thine epitaph,
That death in me at others' lives may laugh.
[*To the gold.*] O thou sweet king-killer, and dear divorce
'Twixt natural son and sire! Thou bright defiler
Of Hymen's purest bed! Thou valiant Mars!
Thou ever young, fresh, lov'd, and delicate wooer,
Whose blush doth thaw the consecrated snow
That lies on Dian's lap! Thou visible god,
That sold'rest close impossibilities,
And mak'st them kiss; that speak'st with every tongue
To every purpose! O thou touch of hearts!
Think thy slave man rebels, and by thy virtue

308 curiosity fastidiousness, refinement **309 medlar** fruit like a small brown-skinned apple, eaten when nearly decayed; used here, as often, for the sake of a quibble on *meddler* **313 like thee** i.e., in a state of decay, or as one who meddles **316–317 after his means** (1) after his wealth was gone (2) according to his means **321–322 Thou . . . dog** i.e., even in your poverty you were able to keep a dog, and it loved you (since all creatures love only in return for favors) **329–330 in . . . men** i.e., in the destruction of mankind you've just wished for **338 liv'dst** wouldst live **341 unicorn** (A legendary creature, supposedly caught by being goaded into charging a tree and embedding its horn in the tree trunk.) **345 germane** akin, related **346 the spots . . . life** i.e., the crimes of those closely related to you would bring down a sentence of death upon you (with a pun on *spots* meaning *leopard's spots* and *stains, crimes*) **346–347 all . . . remotion** your only safety would consist in your constantly going from place to place **350 in transformation** in being changed into a beast

356 Yonder . . . painter (In fact, they do not appear until V.i; this line may give evidence of an incompletely revised manuscript.) **358 give way** (I will) leave **363 cap** acme, summit **366 by** compared to **369 I'll** I would **381 even** only **387 natural** i.e., born in the course of nature **388 Hymen** god of marriage. **Mars** i.e., as the adulterous lover of Venus **390 blush** i.e., reddish glow of gold **391 Dian** Diana, goddess of the hunt and patroness of chastity **392 close** tightly together. **impossibilities** things incapable of being united **394 touch** touchstone **395 virtue** power

Set them into confounding odds, that beasts
May have the world in empire!

APEMANTUS Would 'twere so!
But not till I am dead. I'll say th' hast gold;
Thou wilt be throng'd to shortly.

TIMON Throng'd to?

APEMANTUS Ay.

TIMON
Thy back, I prithee.

APEMANTUS Live, and love thy misery.

TIMON
Long live so, and so die. I am quit.

APEMANTUS
Moe things like men! Eat, Timon, and abhor them.
Exit Apemantus.

Enter the Banditti.

FIRST BANDIT Where should he have this gold? It is some poor fragment, some slender ort of his remainder. The mere want of gold, and the falling-from of his friends, drove him into this melancholy.

SECOND BANDIT It is nois'd he hath a mass of treasure.

THIRD BANDIT Let us make the assay upon him. If he care not for 't, he will supply us easily; if he covetously reserve it, how shall 's get it?

SECOND BANDIT True; for he bears it not about him, 'tis hid.

FIRST BANDIT Is not this he?

BANDITTI Where?

SECOND BANDIT 'Tis his description.

THIRD BANDIT He; I know him.

BANDITTI Save thee, Timon.

TIMON Now, thieves?

BANDITTI
Soldiers, not thieves.

TIMON Both too; and women's sons.

BANDITTI
We are not thieves, but men that much do want.

TIMON
Your greatest want is, you want much of meat.
Why should you want? Behold, the earth hath roots;
Within this mile break forth a hundred springs;
The oaks bear mast, the briers scarlet hips;
The bounteous huswife, nature, on each bush
Lays her full mess before you. What? Why want?

FIRST BANDIT
We cannot live on grass, on berries, water,
As beasts and birds and fishes.

TIMON
Nor on the beasts themselves, the birds, and fishes;
You must eat men. Yet thanks I must you con
That you are thieves profess'd, that you work not
In holier shapes; for there is boundless theft
In limited professions. Rascal thieves, [*Gives gold.*]
Here's gold. Go, suck the subtle blood o' th' grape,
Till the high fever seethe your blood to froth,
And so scape hanging. Trust not the physician;
His antidotes are poison, and he slays
Moe than you rob. Take wealth and lives together.
Do, villains, do, since you protest to do 't,
Like workmen. I'll example you with thievery:
The sun's a thief, and with his great attraction
Robs the vast sea; the moon's an arrant thief,
And her pale fire she snatches from the sun;
The sea's a thief, whose liquid surge resolves
The moon into salt tears; the earth's a thief,
That feeds and breeds by a composture stol'n
From gen'ral excrement. Each thing's a thief.
The laws, your curb and whip, in their rough power
Has uncheck'd theft. Love not yourselves. Away!
Rob one another. There's more gold. Cut throats.
All that you meet are thieves. To Athens go,
Break open shops; nothing can you steal
But thieves do lose it. Steal less for this I give you,
And gold confound you howsoe'er! Amen.

THIRD BANDIT H'as almost charm'd me from my profession, by persuading me to it.

FIRST BANDIT 'Tis in the malice of mankind that he thus advises us, not to have us thrive in our mystery.

SECOND BANDIT I'll believe him as an enemy, and give over my trade.

FIRST BANDIT Let us first see peace in Athens. There is no time so miserable but a man may be true.
Exeunt Thieves.

Enter the Steward [Flavius] to Timon.

FLAVIUS
O you gods!
Is yond despis'd and ruinous man my lord?
Full of decay and failing? O monument
And wonder of good deeds evilly bestow'd!
What an alteration of honor has desp'rate want
made!
What viler thing upon the earth than friends,
Who can bring noblest minds to basest ends!
How rarely does it meet with this time's guise,
When man was wish'd to love his enemies!
Grant I may ever love, and rather woo
Those that would mischief me than those that do!—
H'as caught me in his eye. I will present
My honest grief unto him, and, as my lord,
Still serve him with my life.—My dearest master!

TIMON
Away! What art thou?

FLAVIUS Have you forgot me, sir?

396 Set . . . odds set men at self-destroying conflict with one another **401 quit** rid (of Apemantus) **402 Moe** more **403 should he have** can he have obtained **404 ort** fragment **405 mere** utter **408 assay** trial, test (as one would test gold ore for its content) **410 shall 's** shall we **417 Save** God save **420 want** (1) lack (2) desire **421 Your . . . meat** i.e., your greatest deficiency is that you crave such rich food (as Timon goes on to explain) **424 mast** i.e., acorns and fruit of similar trees. **hips** fruit of the rosebush **426 mess** food, meal **430 thanks . . . con** I must offer you thanks **433 limited** regulated, legal (with a play on *boundless*, l. 432, as the opposite of *limited*)

434 subtle treacherous in its influence **435 seethe** boil **436 scape hanging** i.e., avoid death by law by dying of excess drinking, using a natural substance **439 protest** profess **440 example you with** give you instances of **444 resolves** melts, dissolves. (Alludes to the belief that the moon drew moisture from the air and deposited it in the sea, thus creating the effect of tides.) **446 composture** compost, manure **453–454 Steal . . . howsoe'er** if you steal less because of my giving you this gold, may gold destroy you no matter what happens **457 the malice of** i.e., his hating of **458 mystery** trade **459 as** as I would **461–462 Let . . . true** i.e., let's not rush into reformation, at least not until there is peace in Athens; besides, there will always be time to repent **464 ruinous** brought to ruin **470–471 How . . . enemies** i.e., how suitable in this degenerate age, and how rarely heeded, is the teaching that man should love his enemies **472–473 rather . . . do** i.e., in loving my enemies may I rather encounter those who only intend to harm me rather than those who do real harm; may my enemies not prevail

TIMON
Why dost ask that? I have forgot all men.
Then, if thou grant'st th' art a man, I have forgot thee.

FLAVIUS
An honest poor servant of yours.

TIMON
Then I know thee not.
I never had honest man about me, I; all
I kept were knaves, to serve in meat to villains.

FLAVIUS
The gods are witness,
Nev'r did poor steward wear a truer grief
For his undone lord than mine eyes for you.
[*Weeps.*]

TIMON
What, dost thou weep? Come nearer. Then I love thee,
Because thou art a woman, and disclaim'st
Flinty mankind, whose eyes do never give
But thorough lust and laughter. Pity's sleeping.
Strange times, that weep with laughing, not with weeping!

FLAVIUS
I beg of you to know me, good my lord,
T' accept my grief, and whilst this poor wealth lasts
To entertain me as your steward still.
[*Offers money.*]

TIMON
Had I a steward
So true, so just, and now so comfortable?
It almost turns my dangerous nature mild.
Let me behold thy face. Surely, this man
Was born of woman.
Forgive my general and exceptless rashness,
You perpetual-sober gods! I do proclaim
One honest man—mistake me not, but one;
No more, I pray—and he's a steward.
How fain would I have hated all mankind!
And thou redeem'st thyself. But all, save thee,
I fell with curses.
Methinks thou art more honest now than wise,
For, by oppressing and betraying me,
Thou mightst have sooner got another service;
For many so arrive at second masters,
Upon their first lord's neck. But tell me true—
For I must ever doubt, though ne'er so sure—
Is not thy kindness subtle, covetous,
If not a usuring kindness, and, as rich men deal gifts,
Expecting in return twenty for one?

FLAVIUS
No, my most worthy master, in whose breast
Doubt and suspect, alas, are plac'd too late.
You should have fear'd false times when you did feast.
Suspect still comes where an estate is least.
That which I show, heaven knows, is merely love,
Duty, and zeal to your unmatched mind,
Care of your food and living; and believe it,
My most honor'd lord,
For any benefit that points to me,
Either in hope or present, I'd exchange
For this one wish, that you had power and wealth
To requite me by making rich yourself.

TIMON
Look thee, 'tis so! Thou singly honest man,
Here, take. [*Offers gold.*] The gods out of my misery
Has sent thee treasure. Go, live rich and happy,
But thus condition'd: thou shalt build from men;
Hate all, curse all, show charity to none,
But let the famish'd flesh slide from the bone
Ere thou relieve the beggar. Give to dogs
What thou deniest to men. Let prisons swallow 'em,
Debts wither 'em to nothing; be men like blasted woods,
And may diseases lick up their false bloods!
And so farewell and thrive.

FLAVIUS
O, let me stay
And comfort you, my master.

TIMON
If thou hat'st curses,
Stay not; fly, whilst thou art blest and free.
Ne'er see thou man, and let me ne'er see thee.
Exit [*Flavius; Timon retires to his cave*].

[ACT V • SCENE I]

Enter Poet and Painter. [*Timon watches them from his cave.*]

PAINTER As I took note of the place, it cannot be far where he abides.

POET What's to be thought of him? Does the rumor hold for true, that he's so full of gold?

PAINTER Certain. Alcibiades reports it; Phrynia and Timandra had gold of him. He likewise enrich'd poor straggling soldiers with great quantity. 'Tis said he gave unto his steward a mighty sum.

POET Then this breaking of his has been but a try for his friends?

PAINTER Nothing else. You shall see him a palm in Athens again, and flourish with the highest. Therefore 'tis not amiss we tender our loves to him in this suppos'd distress of his. It will show honestly in us, and is very likely to load our purposes with what they travail for, if it be a just and true report that goes of his having.

POET What have you now to present unto him?

PAINTER Nothing at this time but my visitation. Only I will promise him an excellent piece.

483 serve in meat serve food **489 give** give forth tears **490 thorough** through **494 entertain** receive, employ **496 comfortable** comforting **500 exceptless** making no exception **517 suspect** suspicion **519 still** always

520 merely purely **524 points to me** appears in prospect for me **525 in hope** in the future **528 singly** (1) uniquely (2) earnestly **531 thus condition'd** upon this condition. **from** away from **536 blasted** withered

V.i. Location: The woods. Before Timon's cave. The scene is virtually continuous; Timon may well remain visible to the audience.
9 breaking bankruptcy. **try** test **14 show honestly** appear to be seemly or worthy **15 load our purposes** i.e., crown our efforts. **travail** labor **16 having** wealth

POET I must serve him so too, tell him of an intent that's
coming toward him.

PAINTER Good as the best. Promising is the very air o'
th' time; it opens the eyes of expectation. Performance
is ever the duller for his act; and, but in the plainer 24
and simpler kind of people, the deed of saying is quite 25
out of use. To promise is most courtly and fashionable;
performance is a kind of will or testament which ar-
gues a great sickness in his judgment that makes it.

Enter Timon from his cave.

TIMON [*Aside*] Excellent workman! Thou canst not
paint a man so bad as is thyself.

POET I am thinking what I shall say I have provided for
him. It must be a personating of himself; a satire 32
against the softness of prosperity, with a discovery of 33
the infinite flatteries that follow youth and opulency.

TIMON [*Aside*] Must thou needs stand for a villain in 35
thine own work? Wilt thou whip thine own faults in
other men? Do so, I have gold for thee.

POET
Nay, let's seek him.
Then do we sin against our own estate 39
When we may profit meet, and come too late.

PAINTER
True;
When the day serves, before black-corner'd night, 42
Find what thou want'st by free and offer'd light. 43
Come.

TIMON [*Aside*]
I'll meet you at the turn. What a god's gold, 45
That he is worship'd in a baser temple
Than where swine feed!
'Tis thou that rigg'st the bark and plough'st the foam,
Settlest admired reverence in a slave. 49
To thee be worship, and thy saints for aye
Be crown'd with plagues, that thee alone obey!
Fit I meet them. [*Comes forward.*] 52

POET
Hail, worthy Timon!

PAINTER Our late noble master!

TIMON
Have I once liv'd to see two honest men? 54

POET
Sir,
Having often of your open bounty tasted,
Hearing you were retir'd, your friends fall'n off,
Whose thankless natures—O abhorred spirits!—
Not all the whips of heaven are large enough—
What, to you,
Whose star-like nobleness gave life and influence 61
To their whole being? I am rapt and cannot cover 62
The monstrous bulk of this ingratitude
With any size of words.

TIMON
Let it go naked, men may see 't the better.
You that are honest, by being what you are
Make them best seen and known.

PAINTER He and myself 67
Have travail'd in the great show'r of your gifts,
And sweetly felt it.

TIMON Ay, you are honest men.

PAINTER
We are hither come to offer you our service.

TIMON
Most honest men! Why, how shall I requite you?
Can you eat roots, and drink cold water? No.

BOTH
What we can do, we'll do, to do you service.

TIMON
Y' are honest men. Y' have heard that I have gold;
I am sure you have. Speak truth; y' are honest men.

PAINTER
So it is said, my noble lord; but therefore 76
Came not my friend nor I.

TIMON
Good honest men! Thou draw'st a counterfeit 78
Best in all Athens. Th' art, indeed, the best;
Thou counterfeit'st most lively.

PAINTER So, so, my lord. 80

TIMON
E'en so, sir, as I say. [*To the Poet.*] And, for thy fiction, 81
Why, thy verse swells with stuff so fine and smooth 82
That thou art even natural in thine art. 83
But, for all this, my honest-natur'd friends,
I must needs say you have a little fault;
Marry, 'tis not monstrous in you, neither wish I
You take much pains to mend.

BOTH Beseech your honor
To make it known to us.

TIMON You'll take it ill.

BOTH
Most thankfully, my lord.

TIMON Will you, indeed?

BOTH
Doubt it not, worthy lord.

TIMON
There's never a one of you but trusts a knave 91
That mightily deceives you.

BOTH Do we, my lord?

TIMON
Ay, and you hear him cog, see him dissemble, 93
Know his gross patchery, love him, feed him, 94
Keep in your bosom; yet remain assur'd
That he's a made-up villain. 96

24 for his act for its being completed. **but in** excepting among **25 deed of saying** actions fulfilling words or promises **32 personating of himself** i.e., representation of his case **33 discovery** disclosure **35 stand for** serve as a model for **39 estate** worldly well-being **42 black-corner'd night** night which darkens as in corners **43 free and offer'd light** the light of day, freely offered to all **45 at the turn** i.e., trick for trick in a cheating game **49 admired . . . slave** wondering awe in a slave for his master **52 Fit** it is fit that **54 once** actually **61 Whose . . . influence** i.e., whose nobility of character was of such power as to influence men's destinies. (An astrological metaphor.) **62 rapt** i.e., overwhelmed

67 them i.e., the ungrateful men you condemn, or ungrateful acts **76 therefore** for that reason **78 counterfeit** picture, likeness (with quibble on the idea of *fraudulence*) **80 So, so** passably **81 fiction** any creative writing; here, poetry (with connotation of *lying*) **82 swells . . . smooth** (1) is elegantly styled and adorned (2) is a vainglorious concoction of specious fabrication **83 thou . . . art** (1) your art is able to triumph over nature in verisimilitude (2) you're a born fool and a liar in your art **91 There's . . . but** i.e., each of you **93 cog** cheat **94 patchery** knavery **96 made-up** utter, complete

PAINTER
I know none such, my lord.
POET
Nor I.
TIMON
Look you, I love you well; I'll give you gold,
Rid me these villains from your companies.
Hang them or stab them, drown them in a draught,
Confound them by some course, and come to me,
I'll give you gold enough.
BOTH
Name them, my lord, let's know them.
TIMON
You that way and you this, but two in company;
Each man apart, all single and alone,
Yet an arch-villain keeps him company.
[*To one.*] If where thou art two villains shall not be,
Come not near him. [*To the other.*] If thou wouldst not reside
But where one villain is, then him abandon.—
Hence, pack! There's gold; you came for gold, ye slaves.
[*To one.*] You have work'd for me; there's payment. Hence!
[*To the other.*] You are an alchemist; make gold of that.
Out, rascal dogs!
Exeunt [*both, beaten out by Timon, who retires to his cave*].

Enter Steward [*Flavius*] *and two Senators.*

FLAVIUS
It is vain that you would speak with Timon;
For he is set so only to himself
That nothing but himself which looks like man
Is friendly with him.
FIRST SENATOR Bring us to his cave.
It is our part and promise to th' Athenians
To speak with Timon.
SECOND SENATOR At all times alike
Men are not still the same. 'Twas time and griefs
That fram'd him thus. Time, with his fairer hand,
Offering the fortunes of his former days,
The former man may make him. Bring us to him,
And chance it as it may.
FLAVIUS Here is his cave.—
Peace and content be here! Lord Timon! Timon!
Look out, and speak to friends. Th' Athenians,
By two of their most reverend Senate, greet thee.
Speak to them, noble Timon.

Enter Timon out of his cave.

TIMON
Thou sun that comforts, burn! Speak and be hang'd!
For each true word, a blister, and each false
Be as a cauterizing to the root o' th' tongue,
Consuming it with speaking!
FIRST SENATOR Worthy Timon—
TIMON
Of none but such as you, and you of Timon.
FIRST SENATOR
The senators of Athens greet thee, Timon.
TIMON
I thank them; and would send them back the plague,
Could I but catch it for them.
FIRST SENATOR O, forget
What we are sorry for ourselves in thee.
The senators with one consent of love
Entreat thee back to Athens, who have thought
On special dignities which vacant lie
For thy best use and wearing.
SECOND SENATOR They confess
Toward thee forgetfulness too general gross;
Which now the public body, which doth seldom
Play the recanter, feeling in itself
A lack of Timon's aid, hath sense withal
Of it own fail, restraining aid to Timon,
And send forth us to make their sorrowed render,
Together with a recompense more fruitful
Than their offense can weigh down by the dram;
Ay, even such heaps and sums of love and wealth
As shall to thee blot out what wrongs were theirs
And write in thee the figures of their love,
Ever to read them thine.
TIMON You witch me in it;
Surprise me to the very brink of tears.
Lend me a fool's heart and a woman's eyes,
And I'll beweep these comforts, worthy senators.
FIRST SENATOR
Therefore, so please thee to return with us
And of our Athens, thine and ours, to take
The captainship, thou shalt be met with thanks,
Allow'd with absolute power, and thy good name
Live with authority; so soon we shall drive back
Of Alcibiades th' approaches wild,
Who, like a boar too savage, doth root up
His country's peace.
SECOND SENATOR And shakes his threat'ning sword
Against the walls of Athens.
FIRST SENATOR Therefore, Timon—
TIMON
Well, sir, I will; therefore, I will, sir; thus:
If Alcibiades kill my countrymen,
Let Alcibiades know this of Timon,

100 Rid me if you'll rid **101 draught** privy, cesspool **102 Confound** destroy **105 You . . . company** (Timon riddlingly suggests that if the two of them stand apart from one another with no one else around, each has an arch-villain—himself—to keep him company.) **108 shall not be** are not to be **109 him** i.e., the other one. **thou** (Timon addresses this other one.) **111 pack** be off **112 there's payment** i.e., a beating or a thrown stone **113 that** i.e., a beating or a thrown stone **115 vain** in vain **116 set . . . himself** so self-absorbed **118 friendly with** congenial to **119 our . . . promise** the part we have promised to undertake **121 still** always **124 The former . . . him** may turn him into his former self

134 Of . . . Timon i.e., we are worthy of nothing better than one another, being men **138 What . . . thee** those wrongs which we regret having done you **139 consent** unanimous voice **143 general gross** evident to everyone **146 Timon's aid** aid to Timon **147 it** its. **restraining** in witholding **148 render** rendering, i.e., of their apologies **150 can . . . dram** can outweigh under the most scrupulous measurement **152 theirs** of their making **153 figures** (1) representations (2) numbers written in a ledger **154 Ever . . . thine** i.e., to provide a perpetual record of the Athenians' love for you. **witch** bewitch **158 so** if it **161 Allow'd** vested **162 Live with** continue to exercise

That Timon cares not. But if he sack fair Athens,
And take our goodly aged men by th' beards,
Giving our holy virgins to the stain
Of contumelious, beastly, mad-brain'd war, 173
Then let him know, and tell him Timon speaks it,
In pity of our aged and our youth,
I cannot choose but tell him that I care not,
And let him take 't at worst—for their knives care not, 177
While you have throats to answer. For myself, 178
There's not a whittle in th' unruly camp 179
But I do prize it at my love before 180
The reverend'st throat in Athens. So I leave you
To the protection of the prosperous gods, 182
As thieves to keepers.

FLAVIUS
Stay not, all's in vain. 183

TIMON
Why, I was writing of my epitaph;
It will be seen tomorrow. My long sickness
Of health and living now begins to mend,
And nothing brings me all things. Go, live still; 187
Be Alcibiades your plague, you his,
And last so long enough!

FIRST SENATOR
We speak in vain.

TIMON
But yet I love my country, and am not
One that rejoices in the common wrack,
As common bruit doth put it.

FIRST SENATOR
That's well spoke. 192

TIMON
Commend me to my loving countrymen—

FIRST SENATOR
These words become your lips as they pass thorough them.

SECOND SENATOR
And enter in our ears like great triumphers
In their applauding gates.

TIMON
Commend me to them,
And tell them that, to ease them of their griefs,
Their fears of hostile strokes, their aches, losses,
Their pangs of love, with other incident throes
That nature's fragile vessel doth sustain
In life's uncertain voyage, I will some kindness do them:
I'll teach them to prevent wild Alcibiades' wrath. 202

FIRST SENATOR
I like this well; he will return again.

TIMON
I have a tree, which grows here in my close, 204
That mine own use invites me to cut down,
And shortly must I fell it. Tell my friends,
Tell Athens, in the sequence of degree
From high to low throughout, that whoso please
To stop affliction, let him take his haste,
Come hither, ere my tree hath felt the axe,
And hang himself. I pray you, do my greeting.

FLAVIUS
Trouble him no further; thus you still shall find him.

TIMON
Come not to me again. But say to Athens,
Timon hath made his everlasting mansion
Upon the beached verge of the salt flood, 215
Who once a day with his embossed froth 216
The turbulent surge shall cover. Thither come,
And let my grave-stone be your oracle. 218
Lips, let sour words go by and language end!
What is amiss, plague and infection mend!
Graves only be men's works and death their gain!
Sun, hide thy beams! Timon hath done his reign.
Exit Timon [into his cave].

FIRST SENATOR
His discontents are unremovably
Coupled to nature. 224

SECOND SENATOR
Our hope in him is dead. Let us return,
And strain what other means is left unto us
In our dear peril.

FIRST SENATOR
It requires swift foot. *Exeunt.* 227

[SCENE II]

Enter two other Senators with a Messenger.

THIRD SENATOR
Thou hast painfully discover'd; are his files 1
As full as thy report?

MESSENGER
I have spoke the least. 2
Besides, his expedition promises 3
Present approach.

FOURTH SENATOR
We stand much hazard, if they bring not Timon. 5

MESSENGER
I met a courier, one mine ancient friend,
Whom, though in general part we were oppos'd, 7
Yet our old love made a particular force, 8
And made us speak like friends. This man was riding
From Alcibiades to Timon's cave
With letters of entreaty, which imported 11
His fellowship i' th' cause against your city, 12
In part for his sake mov'd.

Enter the other Senators [from Timon].

THIRD SENATOR
Here come our brothers. 13

173 contumelious insolent **177 take 't at worst** interpret what I say in the worst manner possible; or, (let Alcibiades' troops) do their worst destruction **178 answer** suffer the consequences **179 whittle** small clasp-knife **180 at** in **182 prosperous** causing prosperity **183 keepers** jailers **187 nothing** oblivion, death **192 bruit** rumor **202 prevent** frustrate, forestall (with a quibble on *anticipate*) **204 close** enclosure

215 verge . . . flood boundary or margin of the sea. (See V.iv.66.) **216 Who** whom or which, i.e., Timon or his grave, his "everlasting mansion" (l. 214), both of which the foaming tide will cover daily. **embossed** foaming **218 oracle** source of wisdom **224 Coupled to nature** integrally part of him **227 dear** costly

V.ii. Location: Before the walls of Athens.
1 painfully discover'd revealed unsettling news (?) or reconnoitered with painstaking effort (?). **files** military ranks **2 spoke the least** given the lowest estimate **3 expedition** speed **5 they** i.e., the senators who were sent to Timon **7 in general part** on public issues **8 particular** personal **11 imported** (1) concerned, had to do with (2) importuned **12 fellowship** partnership **13 In . . . mov'd** undertaken partly on his (Timon's) behalf

FIRST SENATOR
No talk of Timon, nothing of him expect.
The enemies' drum is heard, and fearful scouring
Doth choke the air with dust. In, and prepare.
Ours is the fall, I fear; our foes the snare. *Exeunt.*

[SCENE III]

Enter a Soldier in the woods, seeking Timon.

SOLDIER
By all description this should be the place.
Who's here? Speak, ho! No answer! What is this?
[*He finds a rude tomb.*]
"Timon is dead, who hath outstretch'd his span.
Some beast read this; there does not live a man."
Dead, sure; and this his grave. What's on this tomb
I cannot read; the character I'll take with wax.
[*Makes a wax impression.*]
Our captain hath in every figure skill,
An ag'd interpreter, though young in days.
Before proud Athens he's set down by this,
Whose fall the mark of his ambition is. *Exit.*

[SCENE IV]

Trumpets sound. Enter Alcibiades with his powers before Athens.

ALCIBIADES
Sound to this coward and lascivious town
Our terrible approach. *Sounds a parley.*

The Senators appear on the walls.

Till now you have gone on and fill'd the time
With all licentious measure, making your wills
The scope of justice; till now myself and such
As slept within the shadow of your power
Have wander'd with our travers'd arms, and breath'd
Our sufferance vainly. Now the time is flush,
When crouching marrow in the bearer strong
Cries of itself, "No more!" Now breathless wrong
Shall sit and pant in your great chairs of ease,
And pursy insolence shall break his wind
With fear and horrid flight.

FIRST SENATOR Noble and young,
When thy first griefs were but a mere conceit,
Ere thou hadst power or we had cause of fear,
We sent to thee, to give thy rages balm,
To wipe out our ingratitude with loves
Above their quantity.

SECOND SENATOR So did we woo
Transformed Timon to our city's love
By humble message and by promis'd means.
We were not all unkind, nor all deserve
The common stroke of war.

FIRST SENATOR These walls of ours
Were not erected by their hands from whom
You have receiv'd your griefs; nor are they such
That these great tow'rs, trophies, and schools should fall
For private faults in them.

SECOND SENATOR Nor are they living
Who were the motives that you first went out.
Shame, that they wanted cunning, in excess
Hath broke their hearts. March, noble lord,
Into our city with thy banners spread.
By decimation, and a tithed death—
If thy revenges hunger for that food
Which nature loathes—take thou the destin'd tenth,
And by the hazard of the spotted die
Let die the spotted.

FIRST SENATOR All have not offended;
For those that were, it is not square to take
On those that are, revenges. Crimes, like lands,
Are not inherited. Then, dear countryman,
Bring in thy ranks, but leave without thy rage;
Spare thy Athenian cradle and those kin
Which in the bluster of thy wrath must fall
With those that have offended. Like a shepherd
Approach the fold and cull th' infected forth,
But kill not all together.

SECOND SENATOR What thou wilt,
Thou rather shalt enforce it with thy smile
Than hew to 't with thy sword.

FIRST SENATOR Set but thy foot
Against our rampir'd gates, and they shall ope,
So thou wilt send thy gentle heart before
To say thou 'lt enter friendly.

SECOND SENATOR Throw thy glove,
Or any token of thine honor else,
That thou wilt use the wars as thy redress
And not as our confusion, all thy powers
Shall make their harbor in our town till we

15 scouring hurrying along

V.iii. Location: The woods. Seemingly near Timon's cave, but also at the edge of the sea; see V.i.214–217 and V.iv. 66. A rude tomb is seen.
4 Some . . . man i.e., whoever reads this will be a beast, since all men are beasts **6 I cannot read** (Suggests there is another inscription in a strange language, or that this scene shows signs of incomplete revision and hence apparent inconsistency.) **the . . . wax** I'll take an impression of the inscription in wax **7 every figure** all kinds of writing **10 mark** goal

V.iv. Location: Before the walls of Athens. Appearances *on the walls* are probably located in the gallery, above, to the rear of the stage.
2 s.d. parley trumpet call to a negotiation **4–5 making . . . justice** equating justice with your wills **7 travers'd arms** arms inactive or folded. (A term in military drill.) **7–8 breath'd Our sufferance** voiced our sufferings **8 flush** at flood, ripe **9 crouching marrow** latent resolution and might **10 breathless wrong** wrongdoers who are frightened into breathlessness

12 pursy short-winded **13 horrid** terrified **14 griefs** grievances. **conceit** fancy, imagined scheme of action **17–18 loves . . . quantity** offers of friendship exceeding the quantity of your grievances **25 trophies** monuments **26 them** i.e., those from whom you have received your injuries **27 motives . . . out** instigators that prompted your banishment **28 Shame . . . excess** i.e., an excess of shame for their lack of cunning in statecraft **31 decimation, tithed death** selection of every tenth to die. (The two phrases mean the same thing.) **34 die** (Singular of *dice;* with a play on the verb *die.*) **35 the spotted** the corrupt, wicked (with a play on the spots on the dice) **36 square** just **37–38 like . . not** are not, like lands **39 without** outside **47 rampir'd** barricaded **48 So** if only **49 Throw** if you will throw **52 confusion** overthrow

Have seal'd thy full desire.
ALCIBIADES Then there's my glove. 54
[*Throws down glove.*]
Descend, and open your uncharged ports. 55
Those enemies of Timon's and mine own
Whom you yourselves shall set out for reproof
Fall, and no more; and, to atone your fears 58
With my more noble meaning, not a man 59
Shall pass his quarter, or offend the stream 60
Of regular justice in your city's bounds
But shall be render'd to your public laws
At heaviest answer.
BOTH 'Tis most nobly spoken. 63
ALCIBIADES
Descend, and keep your words. 64
[*The Senators descend, and open the gates.*]

Enter [*Soldier as*] *a Messenger* [*with a wax tablet*].

SOLDIER
My noble general, Timon is dead,
Entomb'd upon the very hem o' th' sea;
And on his grave-stone this insculpture, which
With wax I brought away, whose soft impression
Interprets for my poor ignorance.
ALCIBIADES *(Reads the epitaph)*
"Here lies a wretched corse, of wretched soul bereft. 70
Seek not my name. A plague consume you wicked caitiffs left!
Here lie I, Timon, who, alive, all living men did hate.
Pass by and curse thy fill, but pass and stay not here thy gait." 73
These well express in thee thy latter spirits.
Though thou abhorr'dst in us our human griefs,
Scorn'dst our brains' flow and those our droplets which 76
From niggard nature fall, yet rich conceit 77
Taught thee to make vast Neptune weep for aye
On thy low grave, on faults forgiven. Dead
Is noble Timon, of whose memory
Hereafter more. Bring me into your city,
And I will use the olive with my sword, 82
Make war breed peace, make peace stint war, make each 83
Prescribe to other as each other's leech. 84
Let our drums strike. *Exeunt.*

54 seal'd satisfied **55 uncharged ports** unattacked gates **58 atone** appease, make "at one" **59 man** i.e., soldier of mine **60 pass his quarter** leave his assigned duty area **63 At heaviest answer** to receive severest punishment **64 s.d. open the gates** (Presumably, the *gates* are a door in the tiring house façade representing here the *walls* of Athens; the gallery above is *on the walls*.) **70–73 Here . . . gait** (Of these two inscriptions, both found in Plutarch, Shakespeare would presumably have deleted one, since they contradict one another.) **76 brains' flow** i.e., tears **77 conceit** imagination, fancy **82 olive, sword** (Symbols of peace and war.) **83 stint** stop **84 leech** physician

Antony and Cleopatra

Shakespeare probably wrote *Antony and Cleopatra* in 1606 or 1607; it was registered for publication on May 20, 1608, and apparently influenced a revision of Samuel Daniel's *Cleopatra* that was published "newly altered" in 1607. *Antony and Cleopatra* was thus roughly contemporary with *King Lear* and *Macbeth.* Yet the contrast between those dark tragedies of evil and this Roman tragedy of love and political struggle is immense. Unlike *Macbeth,* with its taut focus on a murderer and his wife, *Antony and Cleopatra* moves back and forth across the Mediterranean in its epic sweep of characters and events, weaving together the fates of Pompey, Octavius Caesar, Octavia, and Lepidus with those of the protagonists. *King Lear* gives proper names to fourteen characters, *Macbeth* to eighteen, *Antony and Cleopatra* to thirty-one. The Roman play requires no less than forty-two separate scenes, of which most occur in what modern editors label Acts III and IV—although no play is less suited to the classical rigors of five-act structure, and these divisions are not found in the reliable Folio text of 1623. Indeed, it is as though Shakespeare resolved at the height of his career to show that he could dispense entirely with the classical "rules," which had never taken serious hold of the English popular stage in any case. The flouting of the unities is so extreme that John Dryden, in his *All for Love or The World Well Lost* (1678), undertook not so much to revise Shakespeare as to start afresh on the same subject. Dryden's play is restricted to the last few hours of the protagonists' lives, at Cleopatra's tomb in Alexandria, with a severely limited cast of characters and much of the narrative revealed through recollection. Although a substantial achievement in its own right, *All for Love* surely reveals that Shakespeare knew what he was doing, for Dryden has excised a good deal of the panorama, the excitement, the "infinite variety."

Shakespeare departs also from the somber tone of his tragedies of evil. He creates instead a world that bears affinities both to the other Roman plays, characterized by ambivalent political conflict, and to the comedies and late romances, characterized by imaginative reconciliation. As protagonists, Antony and Cleopatra lack tragic stature, or so it first appears: she is a tawny gypsy temptress and he a "strumpet's fool," a once-great general now bound in "strong Egyptian fetters" and lost in "dotage." Several scenes, especially those set in Egypt, are comic and delightfully bawdy: Charmian learning her fortune from the soothsayer, Cleopatra practicing her charms in vain to keep Antony from leaving Egypt or raunchily daydreaming of being Antony's horse "to bear the weight of Antony" (I,v), Cleopatra flying into a magnificent rage at the news of Antony's marriage to Octavia and then consoling herself with catty reflections on Octavia's reported low voice and shortness of stature ("I think so, Charmian. Dull of tongue, and dwarfish," III,iii). In its comic texture the play somewhat resembles *Romeo and Juliet,* an earlier play about a younger pair of lovers, although there the bawdry is used chiefly to characterize the lovers' companions and confidantes, whereas in *Antony and Cleopatra* it is central to our vision of Cleopatra especially. In any case, the later play is a tragedy about lovers who, despite their quarrels and uncertainties and betrayals of self, are reconciled in a vision of the greatness of their love. In its depiction of two contrasting worlds, also, *Antony and Cleopatra* recalls the movement of several earlier comedies from the realistic world of political conniving to a dream world of the romantic and the unexpected. We can endorse neither world fully in *Antony and Cleopatra,* and accordingly the vision of life presented is often ambivalent and ironic as much as it is tragic. The contrast of values separating Egypt and Rome underscores the paradox of man's quest for seemingly irreconcilable goals. The ending is neither a triumph nor a defeat for the lovers, but something of both. If Antony and Cleopatra seem in one way too small to be tragic protagonists, in another way they seem too large, creating imaginative visions of themselves and their union that escape the realm of tragedy altogether. Our interest is less on the way in which the protagonists come to understand some meaningful relationship between their character and the fate required of them by a tragic universe, than on the almost comic way in which the absurdity of worldly striving, both Egyptian and Roman, is transfigured in the world of the imagination.

The Roman point of view opens the play, and never entirely loses its force. At first it may seem superior to that of Egypt. Demetrius and Philo, disinterested choric figures even though they are also Roman soldiers, lament the decline of Antony into Circean enslavement. Their tragic concept is of the Fall of Princes, all the more soberly edifying because of the height from which Antony has toppled. "You shall see in him The triple pillar of the world transform'd Into a strumpet's fool." Egypt is enchanting but clearly enervating—a bizarre assemblage of soothsayers, eunuchs, and waiting-gentlewomen who wish to be "married to three kings in a forenoon, and widow them all." Their mirth is all bawdry, tinged with practices like transvestitism that Roman custom views as licentious. Prevailing images are of procreation in various shapes, sleep (mandragora, Lethe), the oriental opulence of Cleopatra's barge (a golden poop, purple sails, silver oars, divers-colored fans), Epicurean feasting, and drinking. As Enobarbus says, "Mine, and most of our fortunes, tonight, shall be—drunk to bed" (I,ii).

Antony, for all his reckless defiance of Rome, agrees in his more reflective moments with what Demetrius and Philo have said. "A Roman thought hath struck him," Cleopatra observantly remarks, and Antony has indeed determined that "I must from this enchanting queen break off" (I,ii). His later return to Cleopatra is at least in part a surrender, a betrayal of his marriage vows to Octavia and his political assurances to Caesar. In the ensuing battles, Antony submits himself dangerously to Cleopatra's governance, and this inversion of dominance in sexual roles is emblematic of a deeper disorder within Antony. As Enobarbus concludes bitterly, Antony "would make his will Lord of his reason," and so has subverted his "judgment" (III,xiii) to passion.

From the beginning, Cleopatra has sought dominance over Antony in the war of the sexes. When Antony first came to her on the River Cydnus, we learn, he was so overcome in all his senses that he was "barber'd ten time o'er," (II,ii). Cleopatra boasts that she "angled" for Antony on that occasion, catching him the way fishermen "betray" fish, and that when she had "drunk him to his bed" she "put my tires and mantles on him, whilst I wore his sword Philippan" (II,v). Caesar, affronted by such transvestite debauchery, charges that Antony "is not more manlike Than Cleopatra, nor the queen of Ptolemy More womanly than he" (I,iv). During the battle scenes, Antony's followers complain that "Photinus an eunuch" and Cleopatra's maids manage the war: "So our leader's led, And we are women's men" (III,vii). Antony confesses too late that they were right. He becomes a "doting mallard," one whose heart is "tied by th' strings" to Cleopatra's rudder when her ships retreat in the first naval engagement (III,xi). In the mythic images used to raise their relationship to heroic proportions, Antony is like Mars to Cleopatra's Venus (I,v), both in a positive and negative sense. The image has positive connotations of the way in which, as Milton puts it, the "two great sexes animate the world," the masterful soldier and his attractive consort complementing one another in a right relationship of martial prowess and beauty, bravery and love, reason and will; but to the Renaissance the myth of Mars and Venus could also be read in a destructive sense as well, as an adulterous relationship in which reason is subverted to appetite. In another mythic comparison, Antony is like Hercules, not in his prime but with the shirt of Nessus on his back—a poisoned shirt given Hercules by his wife in a mistaken hope of thereby assuring his love for her (IV,xii). Antony's soldiers understandably believe that the god Hercules has deserted his reputed descendant and onetime champion (IV,iii).

Despite Antony's shameful violation of manhood, honor, attention to duty, self-knowledge, and all that Rome stands for, however, the end of his story is anything but a one-sided endorsement for the Roman point of view. The actual Rome, disfigured by political conniving, falls far short of the ideal. Antony has a point when he protests that "Kingdoms are clay" (I,i). Alliances are unstable and are governed by mere political expediency. At first, Antony's wife Fulvia and his brother Lucius have fought one another until forced to unite against the greater threat of Octavius Caesar. Similarly, Antony and Caesar come together only because Pompey has become dangerously powerful at sea and has won the favor of the fickle mob, "Our slippery people." This *detente* is not meant to last. As Enobarbus bluntly puts it, "if you borrow one another's love for the instant, you may, when you hear no more words of Pompey, return it again" (II,ii). Enobarbus is rebuked for his unstatesmanlike tone, but no one denies the validity of what he says. In this cynical negotiation, Octavia is a pawn between husband and brother, shabbily treated by both. Caesar coldly bargains away the happiness of the one person whom he is able to love; Antony, although hating false promises and resolving to be loyal to Octavia, knows within himself that it won't work. To make matters worse for the fair-minded Antony, he has received great favors from Pompey which he must now uncharitably repudiate in the interests of politics. Pompey does not miss the opportunity to remind Antony of his ingratitude, but the prevailing mood is not so much of bitterness as of ironic futility. Old friendships must be sacrificed; no one seems wholly to blame, no one can stop the game. Pompey is as much in the wrong as anyone, and as powerless. Despite his idealistic hope of rescuing Rome from political infighting, he has had to ally himself with pirates who offer him sinister temptations. He could be "lord of all the world" if he would only murder on occasion, but Pompey is destined to be trapped between lofty ends and ignoble means. Lepidus is still another dismaying victim of political callousness, used condescendingly by Caesar and permitted to drink himself into oblivion, until he is cashiered on a trumped-up charge and imprisoned for life.

Octavius Caesar embodies most of all the ironic limits of political ambition. He has avoided enslavement to passion at the very real cost of enslaving himself to his public career as general, triumvir, and future emperor. His ideal warrior is one who, driven by military necessity, would "drink The stale [urine] of horses, and the gilded puddle Which beasts would cough at" (I,iv). As a general he is Antony's opposite in every way. He attacks only when he has the advantage, and places those who have deserted Antony in his own front lines so "That Antony may seem to spend his fury Upon himself" (IV,vi). He controls his supplies cannily, believing it a "waste" to feast his army (IV,i). He of course declines Antony's offers of single combat. Antony meantime recklessly accepts Caesar's challenge to fight at sea, feasts debauchingly in one "gaudy night" after another, and generously refuses to blame or penalize those who leave him. His sending Enobarbus' belongings after him into Caesar's camp convinces that honest soldier he has made a fatal error; for, however imprudent Antony's chivalry may be, it is unquestionably noble and great-hearted. Caesar is a superb general and political genius, but he is also a military automaton, a logistical reckoner, a Machiavel. In his personal life he is no less austere and puritanical. He deplores loosening his tongue with alcohol. About women he is deeply cynical, believing that "want will perjure The ne'er-touch'd vestal" (III,xii). Between him and Cleopatra there is a profound antipathy, based in part on his revulsion at her earlier affair with his namesake and predecessor, Julius Caesar (III,vi). Cleopatra may entertain briefly the notion of trying to seduce this new Caesar (III,xiii), for like Charmian she loves long life "better than figs," but if so she soon discovers that she and Caesar are not compatible. All that he represents she must instead grandly repudiate, choosing death and an eternity with Antony as her way to "call great Caesar ass Unpolicied" (V,ii).

Cleopatra's greatness is elusive, all the more enthralling because so mysterious. She rises above her counterpart in Shakespeare's source, Plutarch's *Lives,* where she is an impressive queenly woman but still essentially a temptress causing the lamentable fall of the hero. Shakespeare's Cleopatra is that, but is also something indefinable that can be gotten at only through paradox. Her very character is the essence of contradiction: she knows how "to chide, to laugh, to weep," to be sullen or violent, like a skillful actor keeping Antony continually off guard. Dispassionately examined, she is a woman no longer young who abuses messengers like an oriental despot, who lies about her wealth when captured by Caesar (what is she planning to do with that wealth, anyway?), and who may take her own life only when she realizes that the alternative is public shame and captivity. Yet we are not invited to see her dispassionately. Her charm is eternal, and so are the myths surrounding that charm. Observers evoking her splendor do not describe her person directly, but rather her effects and surroundings: Enobarbus says simply that "For her own person, It beggar'd all description," and goes on to catalogue her cloth-of-gold pavilion and her mermaid-like attendants. Most of all, she is paradox: she makes defect perfection, age cannot wither her, and "vilest things Become themselves in her, that the holy priests Bless her when she is riggish" (II,ii). She is both a whore and the Lucretian Venus, both sluttish and holy. In her, "fancy" exceeds "nature"; the fertility of her Egypt overflows the measure, exceeding the sterility of Rome as her own imaginative fertility exceeds reality itself. When she protests that she will not go to Rome to behold herself in a wretched play and thus see "Some squeaking Cleopatra boy my greatness I' th' posture of a whore" (V,ii), we realize that Shakespeare is calling attention to his own art as well, pointing out how Elizabethan boy actors on a bare stage can transform reality into a dream that we believe. Cleopatra's mystery is like that of poetry itself. The "real" world pales into insignificance of a "little O, the earth," something "no better than a sty," full of illusory shadows that "mock our eyes with air"; and Caesar's triumph vanishes with it. In its place, Antony and Cleopatra raise up a vision of themselves as lovers who, through art, have indeed become eternal. Together they will overpicture Venus and Mars, and will be so renowned that "Dido and her Aeneas shall want troops, And all the haunt be ours" (IV,xiv). Antony is no longer dying Hercules but the god of Cleopatra's dream whose "legs bestrid the ocean; his rear'd arm Crested the world; his voice was propertied As all the tuned spheres" (V,ii). Through Cleopatra's vision we realize how all the characteristics that made Antony at once so noble and so sure to fall before Caesar—his generosity amounting to imprudence, his spontaneity, his impatience with the ordinary, his staking his all on love when he hears of Cleopatra's supposed death—have not deserted him. His death serves to reaffirm the magnificence of the very qualities that have brought him down. His essential nobility is confirmed, even if it must be defined in non-Roman ways. He and Cleopatra share the "immortal longings" for which she goes willingly to her death, dressed in her "best attires" like a queen; for neither lover will accept anything less than greatness.

Antony and Cleopatra

[*Dramatis Personae*

MARK ANTONY, OCTAVIUS CAESAR, M. AEMILIUS LEPIDUS, *triumvirs.*
SEXTUS POMPEIUS
DOMITIUS ENOBARBUS, VENTIDIUS, EROS, SCARUS, DERCETAS, DEMETRIUS, PHILO, *friends to Antony.*
MAECENAS, AGRIPPA, DOLABELLA, PROCULEIUS, THIDIAS, GALLUS, *friends to Caesar.*
MENAS, MENECRATES, VARRIUS, *friends to Pompey.*
TAURUS, *lieutenant-general to Caesar.*
CANIDIUS, *lieutenant-general to Antony.*
SILIUS, *an Officer in Ventidius' army.*
A SCHOOLMASTER, *Ambassador from Antony to Caesar.*
ALEXAS, MARDIAN, *A Eunuch,* SELEUCUS, DIOMEDES, *attendants on Cleopatra.*
A SOOTHSAYER.
A CLOWN.

CLEOPATRA, *Queen of Egypt.*
OCTAVIA, *sister to Caesar and wife to Antony.*
CHARMIAN, IRAS, *attendants on Cleopatra.*

OFFICERS, SOLDIERS, MESSENGERS, *and other* ATTENDANTS.

SCENE: *In several parts of the Roman Empire.*]

ACT I • SCENE I

Enter Demetrius and Philo.

PHILO
Nay, but this dotage of our general's
O'erflows the measure. Those his goodly eyes,
That o'er the files and musters of the war
Have glow'd like plated Mars, now bend, now turn
The office and devotion of their view
Upon a tawny front. His captain's heart,
Which in the scuffles of great fights hath burst
The buckles on his breast, reneges all temper,
And is become the bellows and the fan
To cool a gipsy's lust.

Flourish. Enter Antony, Cleopatra, her Ladies, the train, with Eunuchs fanning her.

Look where they come.
Take but good note, and you shall see in him
The triple pillar of the world transform'd
Into a strumpet's fool. Behold and see.

CLEOPATRA
If it be love indeed, tell me how much.

ANTONY
There's beggary in the love that can be reckon'd.

CLEOPATRA
I'll set a bourn how far to be belov'd.

ANTONY
Then must thou needs find out new heaven, new earth.

Enter a Messenger.

MESSENGER
News, my good lord, from Rome.

ANTONY
Grates me! The sum.

CLEOPATRA
Nay, hear them, Antony.
Fulvia perchance is angry; or, who knows
If the scarce-bearded Caesar have not sent
His pow'rful mandate to you, "Do this, or this;
Take in that kingdom, and enfranchise that;
Perform 't, or else we damn thee."

ANTONY
How, my love?

CLEOPATRA
Perchance? Nay, and most like.
You must not stay here longer, your dismission
Is come from Caesar; therefore hear it, Antony.
Where's Fulvia's process? Caesar's, I would say? Both?
Call in the messengers. As I am Egypt's queen,

I.i. Location: Alexandria. Cleopatra's palace.
1 dotage foolish affection, sometimes associated with old age **4 plated** clothed in armor **5 office** function **6 tawny front** dark face. (Literally, forehead.) **8 reneges** renounces. **temper** moderation **10 gipsy's** (Gipsies were widely believed to have come from Egypt, and to be lustful and cunning.) **12 triple** one of three. (Alludes to the Triumvirate of Antony, Lepidus, and Octavius Caesar; also to tripartite division of the world into Asia, Africa, and Europe.) **16 bourn** boundary, limit **19 Grates me** it annoys me. **The sum** i.e., be brief. **them** i.e., the news **20 Fulvia** Antony's wife **23 Take in** conquer. **enfranchise** set free **25 like** likely **26 dismission** dismissal **28 process** formal command

Thou blushest, Antony, and that blood of thine
Is Caesar's homager; else so thy cheek pays shame 31
When shrill-tongu'd Fulvia scolds. The messengers!

ANTONY
Let Rome in Tiber melt, and the wide arch
Of the rang'd empire fall! Here is my space. 34
Kingdoms are clay; our dungy earth alike
Feeds beast as man. The nobleness of life
Is to do thus; when such a mutual pair 37
And such a twain can do 't, in which I bind,
On pain of punishment, the world to weet 39
We stand up peerless.

CLEOPATRA
Excellent falsehood!
Why did he marry Fulvia, and not love her?
I'll seem the fool I am not. Antony 43
Will be himself.

ANTONY But stirr'd by Cleopatra. 44
Now, for the love of Love and her soft hours,
Let's not confound the time with conference harsh. 46
There's not a minute of our lives should stretch 47
Without some pleasure now. What sport tonight?

CLEOPATRA
Hear the ambassadors.

ANTONY Fie, wrangling queen!
Whom everything becomes—to chide, to laugh,
To weep; whose every passion fully strives
To make itself, in thee, fair and admir'd!
No messenger but thine; and all alone
Tonight we'll wander through the streets and note
The qualities of people. Come, my queen;
Last night you did desire it.—Speak not to us.
Exeunt [Antony and Cleopatra] with the train.

DEMETRIUS
Is Caesar with Antonius priz'd so slight? 57

PHILO
Sir, sometimes when he is not Antony
He comes too short of that great property 59
Which still should go with Antony.

DEMETRIUS I am full sorry
That he approves the common liar, who 61
Thus speaks of him at Rome; but I will hope
Of better deeds tomorrow. Rest you happy! *Exeunt.*

[SCENE II]

Enter Enobarbus, Lamprius, a Soothsayer, Rannius, Lucillius, Charmian, Iras, Mardian the Eunuch, and Alexas.

CHARMIAN Lord Alexas, sweet Alexas, most anything
Alexas, almost most absolute Alexas, where's the 2
soothsayer that you prais'd so to th' Queen? O, that I
knew this husband, which, you say, must charge his 4
horns with garlands! 5

ALEXAS Soothsayer!

SOOTHSAYER
Your will?

CHARMIAN
Is this the man? Is 't you, sir, that know things?

SOOTHSAYER
In nature's infinite book of secrecy
A little I can read.

ALEXAS Show him your hand.

ENOBARBUS [*To Servants within*]
Bring in the banquet quickly; wine enough 12
Cleopatra's health to drink.

CHARMIAN [*Giving hand to Soothsayer*] Good sir, give me good fortune.

SOOTHSAYER
I make not, but foresee.

CHARMIAN Pray, then, foresee me one.

SOOTHSAYER
You shall be yet far fairer than you are.

CHARMIAN He means in flesh. 19

IRAS No, you shall paint when you are old. 20

CHARMIAN Wrinkles forbid!

ALEXAS Vex not his prescience; be attentive.

CHARMIAN Hush!

SOOTHSAYER
You shall be more beloving than beloved.

CHARMIAN I had rather heat my liver with drinking. 25

ALEXAS Nay, hear him.

CHARMIAN Good now, some excellent fortune! Let me
be married to three kings in a forenoon, and widow
them all. Let me have a child at fifty, to whom Herod 29
of Jewry may do homage. Find me to marry me with 30
Octavius Caesar, and companion me with my mis- 31
tress.

SOOTHSAYER
You shall outlive the lady whom you serve.

CHARMIAN O excellent, I love long life better than figs. 34

SOOTHSAYER
You have seen and prov'd a fairer former fortune 35
Than that which is to approach.

CHARMIAN Then belike my children shall have no 37
names. Prithee, how many boys and wenches must I 38
have?

SOOTHSAYER
If every of your wishes had a womb,
And fertile every wish, a million.

CHARMIAN Out, fool! I forgive thee for a witch. 42

ALEXAS You think none but your sheets are privy to 43
your wishes.

31 homager vassal, one who does homage **34 rang'd** ordered, or possibly, extended **37 thus** (May indicate an embrace; or Antony may refer more generally to their way of life.) **39 weet** know **43 I'll . . . not** i.e., I'll pretend to be gullible and believe Antony (?) **44 be himself** i.e., be the fool he is (?) **stirr'd** moved **46 confound** ruin, waste **47 should** that should. **stretch** (Suggests that time can be stretched or extended.) **57 priz'd** valued **59 property** quality, distinction **61 approves** corroborates

I.ii. Location: Alexandria. Cleopatra's palace.
s.d. Lamprius etc. (Lamprius may possibly be the soothsayer, but Rannius and Lucillius have no speaking parts here and do not appear again in the play. Mardian is mute here but does speak in later scenes.) **2 absolute** perfect

4–5 must . . . garlands i.e., must decorate his cuckold's horns with a garland of flowers, like a sacrificial beast. (Cuckolded men were derisively thought of as growing horns, as a badge of their infamy.) **12 banquet** light repast, dessert **19 in flesh** i.e., by putting on weight **20 paint** i.e., use makeup **25 heat . . . drinking** i.e., heat my liver with wine rather than with unrequited love. (The liver was believed to be the seat of sexual desire.) **29–30 Herod of Jewry** i.e., even the blustering tyrant who massacred the children of Judea **31 companion me with** provide as my attendant; or, give me equal fortune with **34 better than figs** (Probably a proverbial expression; with phallic suggestion.) **35 prov'd** experienced **37 belike** probably **37–38 have no names** be illegitimate **38 wenches** girls **42 Out . . . witch** (Charmian jokingly says that since soothsayers, like fools, are allowed to speak freely without penalty, she will not charge him with the crime of wizardry.) **43 privy to** in on the secret of

CHARMIAN Nay, come, tell Iras hers.

ALEXAS We'll know all our fortunes.

ENOBARBUS Mine, and most of our fortunes tonight, shall be—drunk to bed.

IRAS [*Giving hand to Soothsayer*] There's a palm presages chastity, if nothing else.

CHARMIAN E'en as the o'erflowing Nilus presageth famine.

IRAS Go, you wild bedfellow, you cannot soothsay.

CHARMIAN Nay, if an oily palm be not a fruitful prognostication, I cannot scratch mine ear. Prithee, tell her but a worky-day fortune.

SOOTHSAYER
Your fortunes are alike.

IRAS But how, but how? Give me particulars.

SOOTHSAYER
I have said.

IRAS Am I not an inch of fortune better than she?

CHARMIAN Well, if you were but an inch of fortune better than I, where would you choose it?

IRAS Not in my husband's nose.

CHARMIAN Our worser thoughts heavens mend! Alexas—come, his fortune, his fortune! O, let him marry a woman that cannot go, sweet Isis, I beseech thee! And let her die too, and give him a worse! And let worse follow worse, till the worst of all follow him laughing to his grave, fifty-fold a cuckold! Good Isis, hear me this prayer, though thou deny me a matter of more weight. Good Isis, I beseech thee!

IRAS Amen. Dear goddess, hear that prayer of the people! For, as it is a heart-breaking to see a handsome man loose-wiv'd, so it is a deadly sorrow to behold a foul knave uncuckolded. Therefore, dear Isis, keep decorum, and fortune him accordingly!

CHARMIAN Amen.

ALEXAS Lo, now, if it lay in their hands to make me a cuckold, they would make themselves whores but they'd do 't!

Enter Cleopatra.

ENOBARBUS
Hush! Here comes Antony.

CHARMIAN Not he; the Queen.

CLEOPATRA
Saw you my lord?

ENOBARBUS No, lady.

CLEOPATRA Was he not here?

CHARMIAN
No, madam.

CLEOPATRA
He was dispos'd to mirth, but on the sudden
A Roman thought hath struck him. Enobarbus!

ENOBARBUS
Madam?

CLEOPATRA
Seek him, and bring him hither. Where's Alexas?

ALEXAS
Here, at your service. My lord approaches.

Enter Antony with a Messenger [and Attendants].

CLEOPATRA
We will not look upon him. Go with us.

Exeunt [all but Antony, Messenger, and Attendants].

MESSENGER
Fulvia thy wife first came into the field.

ANTONY
Against my brother Lucius?

MESSENGER
Ay.
But soon that war had end, and the time's state
Made friends of them, jointing their force 'gainst Caesar,
Whose better issue in the war, from Italy,
Upon the first encounter, drave them.

ANTONY
Well, what worst?

MESSENGER
The nature of bad news infects the teller.

ANTONY
When it concerns the fool or coward. On.
Things that are past are done with me. 'Tis thus:
Who tells me true, though in his tale lie death,
I hear him as he flatter'd.

MESSENGER Labienus—
This is stiff news—hath with his Parthian force
Extended Asia; from Euphrates
His conquering banner shook, from Syria
To Lydia and to Ionia,
Whilst—

ANTONY Antony, thou wouldst say.

MESSENGER O, my lord!

ANTONY
Speak to me home, mince not the general tongue.
Name Cleopatra as she is call'd in Rome;
Rail thou in Fulvia's phrase, and taunt my faults
With such full license as both truth and malice
Have power to utter. O, then we bring forth weeds
When our quick minds lie still, and our ills told us
Is as our earing. Fare thee well awhile.

MESSENGER
At your noble pleasure. *Exit Messenger.*

ANTONY
From Sicyon, ho, the news? Speak there!

FIRST ATTENDANT
The man from Sicyon—is there such an one?

51–52 E'en . . . famine (Charmian speaks ironically; the overflowing Nile presaged abundance. See II.vii. 18–24.) **54 oily palm** sweaty or moist palm (indication of a sensual disposition) **54–55 fruitful prognostication** omen of fertility **56 worky-day** ordinary **61, 63 inch, nose** (with suggestion that Iras would prefer her husband to be sexually well-endowed) **66 cannot go** cannot make love satisfactorily, or cannot bear children. **Isis** Egyptian goddess usually identified with fertility and the moon **75 foul** ugly **75–76 keep decorum** deal suitably with the case

93 time's state circumstances prevailing at the moment **94 jointing** uniting **95 better issue** success **102 as** as if. **Labienus** (Brutus and Cassius [see *Julius Caesar*] had sent Quintus Labienus to Orodes, King of Parthia, to seek aid against Antony and Octavius Caesar; with a force thus obtained, he is now overrunning the Roman provinces in the Middle East.) **104 Extended** seized upon. (A legal phrase.) **108 Speak . . . tongue** speak bluntly; don't minimize the common report **113 quick** alive, inventive **113–114 our ills . . . earing** hearing our faults told to us improves us, as plowing *(earing)* improves land by rooting out the weeds

SECOND ATTENDANT
He stays upon your will.
ANTONY
Let him appear.—
These strong Egyptian fetters I must break,
Or lose myself in dotage.

Enter another Messenger, with a letter.

What are you?
SECOND MESSENGER
Fulvia thy wife is dead.
ANTONY
Where died she?
SECOND MESSENGER
In Sicyon.
Her length of sickness, with what else more serious
Importeth thee to know, this bears. [*Gives a letter.*]
ANTONY
Forbear me.
[*Exit Second Messenger.*]
There's a great spirit gone! Thus did I desire it.
What our contempts doth often hurl from us,
We wish it ours again. The present pleasure,
By revolution low'ring, does become
The opposite of itself. She's good, being gone;
The hand could pluck her back that shov'd her on.
I must from this enchanting queen break off.
Ten thousand harms, more than the ills I know,
My idleness doth hatch.

Enter Enobarbus.

How now, Enobarbus!
ENOBARBUS What's your pleasure, sir?
ANTONY
I must with haste from hence.
ENOBARBUS Why, then, we kill all our women. We see how mortal an unkindness is to them; if they suffer our departure, death's the word.
ANTONY
I must be gone.
ENOBARBUS Under a compelling occasion, let women die. It were pity to cast them away for nothing, though between them and a great cause they should be esteem'd nothing. Cleopatra, catching but the least noise of this, dies instantly; I have seen her die twenty times upon far poorer moment. I do think there is mettle in death, which commits some loving act upon her, she hath such a celerity in dying.
ANTONY
She is cunning past man's thought.
ENOBARBUS Alack, sir, no; her passions are made of nothing but the finest part of pure love. We cannot call her winds and waters sighs and tears; they are greater storms and tempests than almanacs can report. This cannot be cunning in her; if it be, she makes a show'r of rain as well as Jove.
ANTONY
Would I had never seen her!
ENOBARBUS O, sir, you had then left unseen a wonderful piece of work, which not to have been blest withal would have discredited your travel.
ANTONY Fulvia is dead.
ENOBARBUS Sir?
ANTONY Fulvia is dead.
ENOBARBUS Fulvia?
ANTONY Dead.
ENOBARBUS Why, sir, give the gods a thankful sacrifice. When it pleaseth their deities to take the wife of a man from him, it shows to man the tailors of the earth; comforting therein, that when old robes are worn out, there are members to make new. If there were no more women but Fulvia, then had you indeed a cut, and the case to be lamented. This grief is crown'd with consolation; your old smock brings forth a new petticoat, and indeed the tears live in an onion that should water this sorrow.
ANTONY
The business she hath broached in the state
Cannot endure my absence.
ENOBARBUS And the business you have broach'd here cannot be without you, especially that of Cleopatra's, which wholly depends on your abode.
ANTONY
No more light answers. Let our officers
Have notice what we purpose. I shall break
The cause of our expedience to the Queen,
And get her leave to part. For not alone
The death of Fulvia, with more urgent touches,
Do strongly speak to us; but the letters too
Of many our contriving friends in Rome
Petition us at home. Sextus Pompeius
Hath given the dare to Caesar, and commands
The empire of the sea. Our slippery people,
Whose love is never link'd to the deserver
Till his deserts are past, begin to throw
Pompey the Great and all his dignities
Upon his son, who, high in name and power,
Higher than both in blood and life, stands up
For the main soldier; whose quality, going on,
The sides o' th' world may danger. Much is
breeding,
Which, like the courser's hair, hath yet but life,

118 stays upon awaits **123 Sicyon** ancient city in Greece (where Antony left Fulvia) **125 Importeth** concerns. **Forbear** leave **129 By revolution low'ring** losing value by the revolution of Fortune's wheel and the changing of our opinions **131 could** would be willing to **132 enchanting** having the power of a witch **146 poorer moment** lesser cause. **mettle** i.e., sexual vigor. (Enobarbus puns on *die* in the sense of completing the sex act.)

167 the tailors (The gods are tailors in Enobarbus' figure because they fashion a new wife to replace a worn out one just as tailors fashion a new garment. *Members* has a bawdy suggestion, pursued in ll. 170–171 and 177 in *cut, case, business,* and *broach'd; cut* and *case* suggest the female sexual organs; *broach'd* suggests something that is stabbed, pricked, opened.) **175 broached** opened up. (But see previous note.) **179 abode** staying **181 break** i.e., break the news of **182 expedience** haste **183 leave** permission **184 urgent touches** pressing matters **186 Of . . . friends** from many friends working in our interest **187 at home** i.e., to come home. **Sextus Pompeius** son of Pompey the Great, who, though outlawed, had been able to exploit the division between Antony and Octavius and thereby gain command of Sicily and the sea; he appears in Act II **189 slippery** fickle **191 throw** bestow **192 Pompey the Great** i.e., the title of "the Great" **194 blood and life** mettle and vitality **194–195 stands . . . soldier** is achieving position as, or claims to be, the leading military leader **195 quality** character and position. **going on** i.e., if this keeps on **196 The sides . . . danger** may endanger the frame of the world **197 like . . . hair** (Allusion to the popular belief that a horse-hair put into water would turn to a snake.)

And not a serpent's poison. Say our pleasure
To such whose place is under us, require
Our quick remove from hence.
ENOBARBUS I shall do 't. *[Exeunt.]*

[SCENE III]

Enter Cleopatra, Charmian, Alexas, and Iras.

CLEOPATRA
Where is he?
CHARMIAN I did not see him since. 1
CLEOPATRA
See where he is, who's with him, what he does.
I did not send you. If you find him sad, 3
Say I am dancing; if in mirth, report
That I am sudden sick. Quick, and return.
[Exit Alexas or Attendant.]
CHARMIAN
Madam, methinks, if you did love him dearly,
You do not hold the method to enforce
The like from him.
CLEOPATRA What should I do, I do not? 8
CHARMIAN
In each thing give him way, cross him in nothing.
CLEOPATRA
Thou teachest like a fool; the way to lose him.
CHARMIAN
Tempt him not so too far. I wish, forbear. 11
In time we hate that which we often fear.

Enter Antony.

But here comes Antony.
CLEOPATRA I am sick and sullen.
ANTONY
I am sorry to give breathing to my purpose— 14
CLEOPATRA
Help me away, dear Charmian; I shall fall.
It cannot be thus long, the sides of nature 16
Will not sustain it.
ANTONY Now, my dearest queen—
CLEOPATRA
Pray you stand farther from me.
ANTONY What's the matter?
CLEOPATRA
I know by that same eye there's some good news.
What, says the married woman you may go? 20
Would she had never given you leave to come!
Let her not say 'tis I that keep you here.
I have no power upon you; hers you are.
ANTONY
The gods best know—
CLEOPATRA O, never was there queen
So mightily betray'd! Yet at the first
I saw the treasons planted.
ANTONY Cleopatra—
CLEOPATRA
Why should I think you can be mine, and true,
Though you in swearing shake the throned gods,
Who have been false to Fulvia? Riotous madness, 29
To be entangled with those mouth-made vows,
Which break themselves in swearing!
ANTONY Most sweet queen— 31
CLEOPATRA
Nay, pray you, seek no color for your going, 32
But bid farewell, and go. When you sued staying, 33
Then was the time for words. No going then;
Eternity was in our lips and eyes, 35
Bliss in our brows' bent; none our parts so poor 36
But was a race of heaven. They are so still, 37
Or thou, the greatest soldier of the world,
Art turn'd the greatest liar.
ANTONY How now, lady?
CLEOPATRA
I would I had thy inches; thou shouldst know 40
There were a heart in Egypt.
ANTONY Hear me, Queen: 41
The strong necessity of time commands
Our services awhile, but my full heart
Remains in use with you. Our Italy 44
Shines o'er with civil swords; Sextus Pompeius 45
Makes his approaches to the port of Rome;
Equality of two domestic powers 47
Breed scrupulous faction; the hated, grown to strength, 48
Are newly grown to love; the condemn'd Pompey, 49
Rich in his father's honor, creeps apace
Into the hearts of such as have not thrived
Upon the present state, whose numbers threaten; 52
And quietness, grown sick of rest, would purge 53
By any desperate change. My more particular, 54
And that which most with you should safe my going, 55
Is Fulvia's death.
CLEOPATRA
Though age from folly could not give me freedom,
It does from childishness. Can Fulvia die?
ANTONY
She's dead, my queen.
Look here, and at thy sovereign leisure read
The garboils she awak'd. At the last, best, 61
See when and where she died.
[Offers letters.]

I.iii. Location: Alexandria. Cleopatra's palace.
1 since lately **3 I did . . . you** i.e., do not let anyone know I sent you. **sad** serious **8 I do not** that I am not doing **11 Tempt** try. **I wish** I wish you would **14 breathing** utterance **16 sides of nature** i.e., human body, frame **20 the married woman** i.e., Fulvia

29 Who you who **31 in swearing** even while they are being sworn **32 color** pretext **33 sued staying** begged to stay **35 our** i.e., my. (The royal plural.) **36 bent** arch, curve **37 race of heaven** of heavenly origin; or possibly, of the flavor of heaven **40 inches** (1) height (2) manly strength **41 a heart in Egypt** i.e., a mighty courage in the Queen of Egypt **44 in use with you** for your use **45 civil swords** i.e., weapons of civil war **47 Equality . . . powers** i.e., the equal splitting of domestic power between two, Caesar and Antony **48 scrupulous** carping, concerned with trifles **49 Are . . . love** have recently come into favor **52 state** government (i.e., of the triumvirate). **whose** i.e., those supporting Pompey **53 purge** cleanse or purify itself to be rid of sickness. (Peace, long continued, seems diseased and requires the purging effect of war.) **54 particular** personal concern **55 safe** make safe **61 garboils** disturbances, commotions. **best** i.e., best of all

CLEOPATRA O most false love!
Where be the sacred vials thou shouldst fill
With sorrowful water? Now I see, I see,
In Fulvia's death how mine receiv'd shall be.

ANTONY
Quarrel no more, but be prepar'd to know
The purposes I bear, which are, or cease,
As you shall give th' advice. By the fire
That quickens Nilus' slime, I go from hence
Thy soldier, servant, making peace or war
As thou affects.

CLEOPATRA Cut my lace, Charmian, come!
But let it be; I am quickly ill, and well,
So Antony loves.

ANTONY My precious queen, forbear,
And give true evidence to his love which stands
An honorable trial.

CLEOPATRA So Fulvia told me.
I prithee, turn aside and weep for her;
Then bid adieu to me, and say the tears
Belong to Egypt. Good now, play one scene
Of excellent dissembling, and let it look
Like perfect honor.

ANTONY You'll heat my blood; no more.

CLEOPATRA
You can do better yet; but this is meetly.

ANTONY
Now, by my sword—

CLEOPATRA And target. Still he mends.
But this is not the best. Look, prithee, Charmian,
How this Herculean Roman does become
The carriage of his chafe.

ANTONY
I'll leave you, lady.

CLEOPATRA Courteous lord, one word.
Sir, you and I must part, but that's not it;
Sir, you and I have lov'd, but there's not it;
That you know well. Something it is I would—
O, my oblivion is a very Antony,
And I am all forgotten.

ANTONY But that your royalty
Holds idleness your subject, I should take you
For idleness itself.

CLEOPATRA 'Tis sweating labor
To bear such idleness so near the heart
As Cleopatra this. But, sir, forgive me,
Since my becomings kill me when they do not
Eye well to you. Your honor calls you hence;
Therefore be deaf to my unpitied folly,
And all the gods go with you! Upon your sword
Sit laurel victory, and smooth success
Be strew'd before your feet!

ANTONY Let us go. Come;
Our separation so abides and flies
That thou, residing here, goes yet with me,
And I, hence fleeting, here remain with thee.
Away! *Exeunt.*

[SCENE IV]

Enter Octavius [*Caesar*], *reading a letter, Lepidus, and their train.*

CAESAR
You may see, Lepidus, and henceforth know,
It is not Caesar's natural vice to hate
Our great competitor. From Alexandria
This is the news: he fishes, drinks, and wastes
The lamps of night in revel; is not more manlike
Than Cleopatra, nor the queen of Ptolemy
More womanly than he; hardly gave audience, or
Vouchsaf'd to think he had partners. You shall find there
A man who is th' abstract of all faults
That all men follow.

LEPIDUS I must not think there are
Evils enow to darken all his goodness.
His faults in him seem as the spots of heaven,
More fiery by night's blackness; hereditary,
Rather than purchas'd; what he cannot change,
Than what he chooses.

CAESAR
You are too indulgent. Let's grant it is not
Amiss to tumble on the bed of Ptolemy,
To give a kingdom for a mirth, to sit
And keep the turn of tippling with a slave,
To reel the streets at noon, and stand the buffet
With knaves that smell of sweat. Say this becomes him—
As his composure must be rare indeed
Whom these things cannot blemish—yet must Antony
No way excuse his foils, when we do bear
So great weight in his lightness. If he fill'd
His vacancy with his voluptuousness,
Full surfeits and the dryness of his bones
Call on him for 't. But to confound such time

63 sacred vials (Alludes to the supposed Roman custom of putting bottles filled with tears in the tombs of the departed.) **67 which are** which will proceed **68 fire** i.e., sun **69 quickens** brings to life. **Nilus' slime** the mud left by the overflow of the Nile **71 thou affects** you desire. **lace** cord or laces fastening the bodice **73 So** provided that; or, possibly, *in the same way, with changes as sudden as my own* **74 evidence** witness (?) **stands** will sustain **75 told** has taught (by her example of being quickly forgotten by Antony) **78 Belong to Egypt** are shed for the Queen of Egypt **81 meetly** i.e., fairly good **82 target** shield. **mends** improves (in his "scene Of excellent dissembling") **84–85 How . . . chafe** i.e., how Antony, who claims descent from Hercules, plays the role of his enraged ancestor well. (Hercules had become a stock figure of the enraged hero or tyrant.) **chafe** rage **90 my . . . Antony** my forgetful memory is like Antony (who is now leaving and thus forgetting me) **91 I . . . forgotten** (1) I have forgotten what I was going to say (2) I am entirely forgotten (by Antony) **91–92 But . . . subject** if your trifling banter were not subject to your control, used by you to serve your royal purposes **94 such idleness** such apparently trifling banter **96 my becomings** those qualities that become me (i.e., are attractive in me or are suitable to my present position); perhaps also, the various roles that I become **97 Eye** appear

I.iv. Location: Rome.
3 competitor partner **6 Ptolemy** (Cleopatra's royal brother, to whom she had been married according to Egyptian custom.) **7 gave audience** i.e., received messengers **9 abstract** epitome **11 enow** enough **12 spots** i.e., stars **14 purchas'd** acquired **18 mirth** jest, diversion **19 keep . . . of** take turns **20 stand the buffet** exchange blows **22 As his composure** considering that a man's composition or temperament **24 foils** blemishes **24–25 when . . . lightness** when we have to carry the heavy burden imposed by his levity **26 His vacancy** his leisure time **27–28 Full . . . for 't** i.e., the physical disabilities resulting from such voluptuousness (such as venereal disease) will call him to account **28 confound** ruin, waste

That drums him from his sport and speaks as loud
As his own state and ours, 'tis to be chid
As we rate boys, who, being mature in knowledge,
Pawn their experience to their present pleasure,
And so rebel to judgment.

Enter a Messenger.

LEPIDUS Here's more news.

MESSENGER
Thy biddings have been done, and every hour,
Most noble Caesar, shalt thou have report
How 'tis abroad. Pompey is strong at sea,
And it appears he is belov'd of those
That only have fear'd Caesar. To the ports
The discontents repair, and men's reports
Give him much wrong'd.

CAESAR I should have known no less.
It hath been taught us from the primal state
That he which is was wish'd until he were;
And the ebb'd man, ne'er lov'd till ne'er worth love,
Comes dear'd by being lack'd. This common body,
Like to a vagabond flag upon the stream,
Goes to and back, lackeying the varying tide,
To rot itself with motion.

MESSENGER
Caesar, I bring thee word
Menecrates and Menas, famous pirates,
Make the sea serve them, which they ear and
wound
With keels of every kind. Many hot inroads
They make in Italy; the borders maritime
Lack blood to think on 't, and flush youth revolt.
No vessel can peep forth but 'tis as soon
Taken as seen; for Pompey's name strikes more
Than could his war resisted.

CAESAR Antony,
Leave thy lascivious wassails. When thou once
Was beaten from Modena, where thou slew'st
Hirtius and Pansa, consuls, at thy heel
Did famine follow, whom thou fought'st against,
Though daintily brought up, with patience more
Than savages could suffer. Thou didst drink
The stale of horses, and the gilded puddle
Which beasts would cough at. Thy palate then did
deign
The roughest berry on the rudest hedge.
Yea, like the stag, when snow the pasture sheets,
The barks of trees thou brows'd. On the Alps
It is reported thou didst eat strange flesh,
Which some did die to look on. And all this—
It wounds thine honor that I speak it now—
Was borne so like a soldier that thy cheek
So much as lank'd not.

LEPIDUS
'Tis pity of him.

CAESAR
Let his shames quickly
Drive him to Rome. 'Tis time we twain
Did show ourselves i' th' field, and to that end
Assemble we immediate council. Pompey
Thrives in our idleness.

LEPIDUS Tomorrow, Caesar,
I shall be furnish'd to inform you rightly
Both what by sea and land I can be able
To front this present time.

CAESAR Till which encounter,
It is my business too. Farewell.

LEPIDUS
Farewell, my lord. What you shall know meantime
Of stirs abroad, I shall beseech you, sir,
To let me be partaker.

CAESAR
Doubt not, sir; I knew it for my bond.

Exeunt [severally].

29 drums summons (as with a military signal) **29–30 speaks . . . ours** i.e., summons him urgently in view of his precarious political position and ours as well **31 rate** berate. **mature in knowledge** old enough to know what their duty is **33 to judgment** against better judgment **38 That . . . Caesar** i.e., that have obeyed Caesar only through fear **39 discontents** discontented. (See I.iii. 48–52.) **40 Give him** represent him as **41 from . . . state** since the first government; or possibly, since the earliest state of being **42 That . . . were** that the man in power was desired (by the populace) until he obtained power **43 ebb'd** decayed in fortune. **ne'er . . . love** not loved until he was unworthy of love, i.e., until he lost power **44 Comes dear'd** becomes loved, gains value in men's eyes. **common body** populace **45 flag** iris **46 lackeying** following in servile fashion like a lackey **50 ear** plow **53 Lack blood** turn pale. **flush** vigorous; flushed, ruddy (contrasted with "Lack blood") **55–56 strikes . . . resisted** inflicts more damage than his forces could against our resistance **57 wassails** carousals **60 whom** i.e., famine **63 stale** urine. **gilded** covered with red or yellow slime **64 deign** condescend to accept

72 lank'd became thin **80 be able** be capable of mustering **81 front** confront, deal with **86 bond** bounden duty

[SCENE V]

Enter Cleopatra, Charmian, Iras, and Mardian.

CLEOPATRA
Charmian!

CHARMIAN
Madam?

CLEOPATRA
Ha, ha! Give me to drink mandragora.

CHARMIAN
Why, madam?

CLEOPATRA
That I might sleep out this great gap of time
My Antony is away.

CHARMIAN
You think of him too much.

CLEOPATRA
O, 'tis treason!

CHARMIAN Madam, I trust, not so.

CLEOPATRA
Thou, eunuch Mardian!

MARDIAN What's your Highness' pleasure?

CLEOPATRA
Not now to hear thee sing. I take no pleasure
In aught an eunuch has. 'Tis well for thee
That, being unseminar'd, thy freer thoughts
May not fly forth of Egypt. Hast thou affections?

I.v. Location: Egypt. Cleopatra's palace.
3 mandragora juice of the mandrake (a narcotic) **12 unseminar'd** castrated **13 fly forth of Egypt** i.e., try to leave her as Antony has done

MARDIAN
Yes, gracious madam.
CLEOPATRA
Indeed?
MARDIAN
Not in deed, madam, for I can do nothing
But what indeed is honest to be done.
Yet have I fierce affections, and think
What Venus did with Mars.
CLEOPATRA O Charmian,
Where think'st thou he is now? Stands he, or sits he?
Or does he walk? Or is he on his horse?
O happy horse, to bear the weight of Antony!
Do bravely, horse! For wot'st thou whom thou mov'st?
The demi-Atlas of this earth, the arm
And burgonet of men. He's speaking now,
Or murmuring, "Where's my serpent of old Nile?"
For so he calls me. Now I feed myself
With most delicious poison. Think on me,
That am with Phoebus' amorous pinches black,
And wrinkled deep in time. Broad-fronted Caesar,
When thou wast here above the ground, I was
A morsel for a monarch. And great Pompey
Would stand and make his eyes grow in my brow;
There would he anchor his aspect and die
With looking on his life.

Enter Alexas.

ALEXAS
Sovereign of Egypt, hail!
CLEOPATRA
How much unlike art thou Mark Antony!
Yet, coming from him, that great med'cine hath
With his tinct gilded thee.
How goes it with my brave Mark Antony?
ALEXAS
Last thing he did, dear Queen,
He kiss'd—the last of many doubled kisses—
This orient pearl. [*Gives pearl.*] His speech sticks in my heart.
CLEOPATRA
Mine ear must pluck it thence.
ALEXAS "Good friend," quoth he,
"Say the firm Roman to great Egypt sends
This treasure of an oyster; at whose foot,
To mend the petty present, I will piece
Her opulent throne with kingdoms. All the east,
Say thou, shall call her mistress." So he nodded,
And soberly did mount an arm-gaunt steed,
Who neigh'd so high that what I would have spoke
Was beastly dumb'd by him.
CLEOPATRA
What, was he sad or merry?
ALEXAS
Like to the time o' th' year between the extremes
Of hot and cold, he was nor sad nor merry.
CLEOPATRA
O well-divided disposition! Note him,
Note him, good Charmian, 'tis the man; but note him.
He was not sad, for he would shine on those
That make their looks by his; he was not merry,
Which seem'd to tell them his remembrance lay
In Egypt with his joy; but between both.
O heavenly mingle! Be'st thou sad or merry,
The violence of either thee becomes,
So does it no man else.—Met'st thou my posts?
ALEXAS
Ay, madam, twenty several messengers.
Why do you send so thick?
CLEOPATRA Who's born that day
When I forget to send to Antony
Shall die a beggar. Ink and paper, Charmian.
Welcome, my good Alexas. Did I, Charmian,
Ever love Caesar so?
CHARMIAN O that brave Caesar!
CLEOPATRA
Be chok'd with such another emphasis!
Say, "the brave Antony."
CHARMIAN The valiant Caesar!
CLEOPATRA
By Isis, I will give thee bloody teeth,
If thou with Caesar paragon again
My man of men.
CHARMIAN By your most gracious pardon,
I sing but after you.
CLEOPATRA My salad days,
When I was green in judgment; cold in blood,
To say as I said then! But, come, away,
Get me ink and paper.
He shall have every day a several greeting,
Or I'll unpeople Egypt. *Exeunt.*

[ACT II • SCENE I]

Enter Pompey, Menecrates, and Menas, in warlike manner.

POMPEY
If the great gods be just, they shall assist
The deeds of justest men.
MENECRATES Know, worthy Pompey,
That what they do delay, they not deny.
POMPEY
Whiles we are suitors to their throne, decays

23 wot'st thou do you know **24 demi-Atlas** one who (together with Caesar) supports the weight of the whole world, as Atlas did. (Cleopatra disregards Lepidus as a triumvir.) **25 burgonet** light helmet or steel cap; i.e., a protector of men **29 Phoebus'** the sun's **30 Broad-fronted** with broad forehead. **Caesar** i.e., Julius Caesar **34 aspect** look, gaze **38 great med'cine** supposed substance by which alchemists hoped to turn all baser metals into gold **39 his tinct** its alchemical potency; also, its color **43 orient** shining, bright. (The best pearls were from the East or Orient.) **45 firm** constant, true **47 piece** augment **50 arm-gaunt** gaunt from warlike service; or possibly, gaunt of limb, or hungry for battle **52 dumb'd** drowned out, made inaudible

57 the man i.e., perfectly characteristic of him **59 make . . . his** model their appearance on his look, or, are dependent on his appearance for their moods **64 posts** messengers **65 several** separate, distinct **74 paragon** match or compare

II.i. Location: Pompey's camp.

The thing we sue for.
MENECRATES We, ignorant of ourselves,
Beg often our own harms, which the wise pow'rs
Deny us for our good; so find we profit
By losing of our prayers.
POMPEY I shall do well.
The people love me, and the sea is mine;
My powers are crescent, and my auguring hope
Says it will come to th' full. Mark Antony
In Egypt sits at dinner, and will make
No wars without doors. Caesar gets money where
He loses hearts. Lepidus flatters both,
Of both is flatter'd; but he neither loves,
Nor either cares for him.
MENAS Caesar and Lepidus
Are in the field. A mighty strength they carry.
POMPEY
Where have you this? 'Tis false.
MENAS From Silvius, sir.
POMPEY
He dreams. I know they are in Rome together
Looking for Antony. But all the charms of love,
Salt Cleopatra, soften thy wan'd lip!
Let witchcraft join with beauty, lust with both!
Tie up the libertine in a field of feasts,
Keep his brain fuming; Epicurean cooks
Sharpen with cloyless sauce his appetite,
That sleep and feeding may prorogue his honor
Even till a Lethe'd dullness!

Enter Varrius.

How now, Varrius?
VARRIUS
This is most certain that I shall deliver:
Mark Antony is every hour in Rome
Expected. Since he went from Egypt 'tis
A space for further travel.
POMPEY
I could have given less matter
A better ear. Menas, I did not think
This amorous surfeiter would have donn'd his helm
For such a petty war. His soldiership
Is twice the other twain. But let us rear
The higher our opinion, that our stirring
Can from the lap of Egypt's widow pluck
The ne'er-lust-wearied Antony.
MENAS I cannot hope
Caesar and Antony shall well greet together.
His wife that's dead did trespasses to Caesar;
His brother warr'd upon him, although, I think,
Not mov'd by Antony.
POMPEY I know not, Menas,
How lesser enmities may give way to greater.
Were 't not that we stand up against them all,
'Twere pregnant they should square between themselves,
For they have entertained cause enough
To draw their swords. But how the fear of us
May cement their divisions and bind up
The petty difference, we yet not know.
Be 't as our gods will have 't! It only stands
Our lives upon to use our strongest hands.
Come, Menas. *Exeunt.*

[SCENE II]

Enter Enobarbus and Lepidus.

LEPIDUS
Good Enobarbus, 'tis a worthy deed,
And shall become you well, to entreat your captain
To soft and gentle speech.
ENOBARBUS I shall entreat him
To answer like himself. If Caesar move him,
Let Antony look over Caesar's head
And speak as loud as Mars. By Jupiter,
Were I the wearer of Antonius' beard,
I would not shave 't today.
LEPIDUS
'Tis not a time for private stomaching.
ENOBARBUS
Every time serves for the matter that is then born in 't.
LEPIDUS
But small to greater matters must give way.
ENOBARBUS
Not if the small come first.
LEPIDUS Your speech is passion;
But pray you stir no embers up. Here comes
The noble Antony.

Enter Antony and Ventidius.

ENOBARBUS And yonder, Caesar.

Enter Caesar, Maecenas, and Agrippa.

ANTONY
If we compose well here, to Parthia.
Hark, Ventidius.
CAESAR
I do not know, Maecenas, ask Agrippa.
LEPIDUS
Noble friends,
That which combin'd us was most great, and let not
A leaner action rend us. What's amiss,
May it be gently heard. When we debate
Our trivial difference loud, we do commit

10 crescent on the increase. **auguring** prophesying **11 it** i.e., Pompey's powers or fortune (seen as a crescent moon, becoming full) **13 without doors** outdoors, i.e., in the battlefield, rather than in the bedroom **20 Looking for** awaiting **21 Salt** lustful. **wan'd** faded, withered **23 Tie . . . feasts** i.e., tether him like an animal in a rich pasture **25 cloyless** which will not satiate **26 prorogue** defer the operation of **27 Lethe'd** oblivious. (From the river of the underworld whose waters cause forgetfulness in those who drink.) **31 space . . . travel** time enough for an even longer journey **32 less** less important **37 opinion** i.e., of ourselves **38 Egypt's widow** i.e., Cleopatra, widow of the young King Ptolemy **39 hope** expect **40 well greet** greet one another kindly **42 brother** i.e., Lucius Antonius. (See I.ii. 93 ff.)

46 pregnant likely. **square** quarrel **47 entertained** maintained **51–52 It . . . hands** our very lives depend upon our using our greatest strength

II.ii. Location: Rome. Furniture is put out on which Antony and Caesar are to sit.
4 like himself i.e., in a way befitting his greatness. **move him** i.e., to anger **8 I . . . shav 't** i.e., I would continue to wear it and thereby dare Caesar to pluck it (in a symbolic gesture for starting a fight) **9 stomaching** resentment **15 compose** come to an agreement **20 leaner** lesser, more trivial. **rend** divide

Murder in healing wounds. Then, noble partners,
The rather for I earnestly beseech,
Touch you the sourest points with sweetest terms,
Nor curstness grow to th' matter.

ANTONY 'Tis spoken well.
Were we before our armies, and to fight,
I should do thus. *Flourish.*

CAESAR
Welcome to Rome.

ANTONY
Thank you.

CAESAR
Sit.

ANTONY
Sit, sir.

CAESAR
Nay, then. [*They sit.*]

ANTONY
I learn you take things ill which are not so,
Or being, concern you not.

CAESAR I must be laugh'd at
If, or for nothing or a little, I
Should say myself offended, and with you
Chiefly i' th' world; more laugh'd at, that I should
Once name you derogately, when to sound your name
It not concern'd me.

ANTONY
My being in Egypt, Caesar, what was 't to you?

CAESAR
No more than my residing here at Rome
Might be to you in Egypt. Yet if you there
Did practice on my state, your being in Egypt
Might be my question.

ANTONY How intend you, practic'd?

CAESAR
You may be pleas'd to catch at mine intent
By what did here befall me. Your wife and brother
Made wars upon me, and their contestation
Was theme for you—you were the word of war.

ANTONY
You do mistake your business. My brother never
Did urge me in his act. I did inquire it,
And have my learning from some true reports
That drew their swords with you. Did he not rather
Discredit my authority with yours,
And make the wars alike against my stomach,
Having alike your cause? Of this my letters
Before did satisfy you. If you'll patch a quarrel,
As matter whole you have to make it with,
It must not be with this.

CAESAR You praise yourself
By laying defects of judgment to me; but
You patch'd up your excuses.

ANTONY Not so, not so;
I know you could not lack, I am certain on 't,
Very necessity of this thought, that I,
Your partner in the cause 'gainst which he fought,
Could not with graceful eyes attend those wars
Which fronted mine own peace. As for my wife,
I would you had her spirit in such another;
The third o' th' world is yours, which with a snaffle
You may pace easy, but not such a wife.

ENOBARBUS Would we had all such wives, that the men might go to wars with the women!

ANTONY
So much uncurbable, her garboils, Caesar,
Made out of her impatience—which not wanted
Shrewdness of policy too—I grieving grant
Did you too much disquiet. For that you must
But say I could not help it.

CAESAR I wrote to you
When rioting in Alexandria; you
Did pocket up my letters, and with taunts
Did gibe my missive out of audience.

ANTONY Sir,
He fell upon me ere admitted, then;
Three kings I had newly feasted, and did want
Of what I was i' th' morning. But next day
I told him of myself, which was as much
As to have ask'd him pardon. Let this fellow
Be nothing of our strife; if we contend,
Out of our question wipe him.

CAESAR You have broken
The article of your oath, which you shall never
Have tongue to charge me with.

LEPIDUS
Soft, Caesar!

ANTONY
No, Lepidus, let him speak.
The honor is sacred which he talks on now,
Supposing that I lack'd it. But, on, Caesar;
The article of my oath—

CAESAR
To lend me arms and aid when I requir'd them,
The which you both denied.

ANTONY Neglected, rather;
And then when poisoned hours had bound me up
From mine own knowledge. As nearly as I may,
I'll play the penitent to you; but mine honesty
Shall not make poor my greatness, nor my power
Work without it. Truth is, that Fulvia,
To have me out of Egypt, made wars here;
For which myself, the ignorant motive, do

23 healing i.e., attempting to heal **24 The rather for** all the more because **26 Nor . . . grow** nor let ill humor be added **35 being** being so, i.e., even if they are amiss **36 or . . . or** either . . . or **39 derogately** disparagingly **44 practice on my state** plot against my position **45 question** business **49 Was . . . war** provided you with a theme, had you for its theme (or perhaps, operated in your behalf); your name was the watchword, i.e., the central cause, of that conflict **51 urge . . . act** claim that he was fighting in my behalf. **inquire** inquire into **52 reports** reporters **53 drew . . . you** i.e., fought in your army **54 Discredit** injure. **with** along with **55 stomach** i.e., desire **56 Having . . . cause** i.e., I having just as much reason as you to deplore Lucius' action **57–59 If . . . this** if you insist on manufacturing a quarrel out of shreds and patches, even though you have substantial material to make it with, you've chosen a weak matter to use

64 he i.e., Lucius **65 with . . . attend** regard favorably **66 fronted** confronted, opposed **68 snaffle** bridle bit **69 pace** put through its paces, manage **72–75 So . . . disquiet** I unhappily concede that her unmanageable commotions, caused by her impatience but not lacking in keenness of stratagem, did too much to disquiet you, Caesar **79 missive** messenger **81–82 want . . . morning** in the morning (being hung over) I fell short of my true self **83 of myself** i.e., of my having had a lot to drink **86 question** contention **97 From . . . knowledge** from knowing myself **98–100 mine . . . it** my honesty (in admitting my overindulgence) will not go so far as to dishonor my greatness, nor, conversely, will my great power function without honesty

So far ask pardon as befits mine honor
To stoop in such a case.

LEPIDUS 'Tis noble spoken.

MAECENAS
If it might please you, to enforce no further
The griefs between ye; to forget them quite
Were to remember that the present need
Speaks to atone you.

LEPIDUS Worthily spoken, Maecenas.

ENOBARBUS Or, if you borrow one another's love for the instant, you may, when you hear no more words of Pompey, return it again. You shall have time to wrangle in when you have nothing else to do.

ANTONY
Thou art a soldier only. Speak no more.

ENOBARBUS That truth should be silent I had almost forgot.

ANTONY
You wrong this presence. Therefore speak no more.

ENOBARBUS Go to, then; your considerate stone.

CAESAR
I do not much dislike the matter, but
The manner of his speech; for 't cannot be
We shall remain in friendship, our conditions
So diff'ring in their acts. Yet, if I knew
What hoop should hold us stanch, from edge to
edge
O' th' world I would pursue it.

AGRIPPA Give me leave, Caesar—

CAESAR
Speak, Agrippa.

AGRIPPA
Thou hast a sister by the mother's side,
Admir'd Octavia. Great Mark Antony
Is now a widower.

CAESAR Say not so, Agrippa.
If Cleopatra heard you, your reproof
Were well deserv'd of rashness.

ANTONY
I am not married, Caesar. Let me hear
Agrippa further speak.

AGRIPPA
To hold you in perpetual amity,
To make you brothers, and to knit your hearts
With an unslipping knot, take Antony
Octavia to his wife, whose beauty claims
No worse a husband than the best of men,
Whose virtue and whose general graces speak
That which none else can utter. By this marriage
All little jealousies, which now seem great,
And all great fears, which now import their dangers,
Would then be nothing. Truths would be tales,
Where now half tales be truths. Her love to both
Would each to other, and all loves to both,
Draw after her. Pardon what I have spoke,
For 'tis a studied, not a present thought,
By duty ruminated.

ANTONY
Will Caesar speak?

CAESAR
Not till he hears how Antony is touch'd
With what is spoke already.

ANTONY
What power is in Agrippa,
If I would say, "Agrippa, be it so,"
To make this good?

CAESAR The power of Caesar, and
His power unto Octavia.

ANTONY May I never
To this good purpose, that so fairly shows,
Dream of impediment! Let me have thy hand.
Further this act of grace, and from this hour
The heart of brothers govern in our loves
And sway our great designs!

CAESAR There's my hand.
[They clasp hands.]
A sister I bequeath you, whom no brother
Did ever love so dearly. Let her live
To join our kingdoms and our hearts, and never
Fly off our loves again!

LEPIDUS Happily, amen!

ANTONY
I did not think to draw my sword 'gainst Pompey,
For he hath laid strange courtesies and great
Of late upon me. I must thank him only,
Lest my remembrance suffer ill report;
At heel of that, defy him.

LEPIDUS Time calls upon 's.
Of us must Pompey presently be sought,
Or else he seeks out us.

ANTONY
Where lies he?

CAESAR
About the mount Mesena.

ANTONY What is his strength
By land?

CAESAR Great and increasing; but by sea
He is an absolute master.

ANTONY So is the fame.
Would we had spoke together! Haste we for it.
Yet, ere we put ourselves in arms, dispatch we
The business we have talk'd of.

CAESAR With most gladness,
And do invite you to my sister's view,
Whither straight I'll lead you.

ANTONY Let us, Lepidus,
Not lack your company.

LEPIDUS Noble Antony,
Not sickness should detain me.

108 atone reconcile **116 presence** company **117 your considerate stone** i.e., I shall continue to think (consider), but be as silent as a stone **120 conditions** temperaments, dispositions **129 of rashness** because of your rashness (in overlooking Cleopatra's claim to Antony) **139 jealousies** misunderstandings, suspicions **140 import** carry with them **141–142 Truths . . . truths** true reports (no matter how distressing) would then be taken for mere rumors, whereas at present half-true reports are taken for the whole truth

154 fairly shows looks so promising **161–162 never . . . again** may our amity never desert us again **164 strange** remarkable **166 remembrance** readiness to remember or acknowledge favors done **167 At heel of** immediately after **168 Of** by. **presently** at once **171 Mesena** i.e., Misenum, in southern Italy (not in Sicily, where II.i. perhaps takes place) **173 fame** report **177 my sister's view** to see my sister

Flourish. Exeunt. Mane[n]t Enobarbus, Agrippa, Maecenas.

MAECENAS Welcome from Egypt, sir.
ENOBARBUS Half the heart of Caesar, worthy Maecenas!
My honorable friend, Agrippa!
AGRIPPA Good Enobarbus!
MAECENAS We have cause to be glad that matters are so well disgested. You stay'd well by 't in Egypt.
ENOBARBUS Ay, sir, we did sleep day out of countenance, and made the night light with drinking.
MAECENAS Eight wild boars roasted whole at a breakfast, and but twelve persons there; is this true?
ENOBARBUS This was but as a fly by an eagle. We had much more monstrous matter of feast, which worthily deserv'd noting.
MAECENAS She's a most triumphant lady, if report be square to her.
ENOBARBUS When she first met Mark Antony, she purs'd up his heart, upon the river of Cydnus.
AGRIPPA There she appear'd indeed; or my reporter devis'd well for her.
ENOBARBUS
I will tell you.
The barge she sat in, like a burnish'd throne,
Burnt on the water. The poop was beaten gold;
Purple the sails, and so perfumed that
The winds were love-sick with them; the oars were silver,
Which to the tune of flutes kept stroke, and made
The water which they beat to follow faster,
As amorous of their strokes. For her own person,
It beggar'd all description: she did lie
In her pavilion—cloth-of-gold of tissue—
O'er-picturing that Venus where we see
The fancy outwork nature. On each side her
Stood pretty dimpled boys, like smiling Cupids,
With divers-color'd fans, whose wind did seem
To glow the delicate cheeks which they did cool,
And what they undid did.
AGRIPPA O, rare for Antony!
ENOBARBUS
Her gentlewomen, like the Nereides,
So many mermaids, tended her i' th' eyes,
And made their bends adornings. At the helm
A seeming mermaid steers. The silken tackle
Swell with the touches of those flower-soft hands,
That yarely frame the office. From the barge
A strange invisible perfume hits the sense
Of the adjacent wharfs. The city cast
Her people out upon her; and Antony,
Enthron'd i' th' market-place, did sit alone,
Whistling to th' air, which, but for vacancy,
Had gone to gaze on Cleopatra too,
And made a gap in nature.
AGRIPPA Rare Egyptian!
ENOBARBUS
Upon her landing, Antony sent to her,
Invited her to supper. She replied,
It should be better he became her guest;
Which she entreated. Our courteous Antony,
Whom ne'er the word of "No" woman heard speak,
Being barber'd ten times o'er, goes to the feast,
And for his ordinary pays his heart
For what his eyes eat only.
AGRIPPA Royal wench!
She made great Caesar lay his sword to bed;
He plough'd her, and she cropp'd.
ENOBARBUS I saw her once
Hop forty paces through the public street;
And having lost her breath, she spoke, and panted,
That she did make defect perfection
And breathless pow'r breathe forth.
MAECENAS
Now Antony must leave her utterly.
ENOBARBUS
Never; he will not.
Age cannot wither her, nor custom stale
Her infinite variety. Other women cloy
The appetites they feed, but she makes hungry
Where most she satisfies; for vilest things
Become themselves in her, that the holy priests
Bless her when she is riggish.
MAECENAS
If beauty, wisdom, modesty, can settle
The heart of Antony, Octavia is
A blessed lottery to him.
AGRIPPA Let us go.
Good Enobarbus, make yourself my guest
Whilst you abide here.
ENOBARBUS Humbly, sir, I thank you.
Exeunt.

[SCENE III]

Enter Antony, Caesar, Octavia between them, [and Attendants].

ANTONY
The world and my great office will sometimes
Divide me from your bosom.
OCTAVIA All which time
Before the gods my knee shall bow my prayers
To them for you.
ANTONY Good night, sir. My Octavia,
Read not my blemishes in the world's report.

182 Half the heart i.e., one of Caesar's two closest advisers, along with Agrippa; or, simply, a very close friend of Caesar's **186 disgested** digested, disposed. **stay'd well by 't** kept at it **187–188 we . . . countenance** we insulted day by sleeping right through it **188 light** giddy and frivolous (with pun on the commoner meaning of *bright*) **191 by** beside, compared with **195 square** just **197 purs'd up** pocketed up, put in her purse **198–199 devis'd** invented **207 As** as if **209 cloth-of-gold of tissue** cloth made of gold thread and silk woven together **211 fancy** imagination **214 glow** cause to glow **216 Nereides** sea nymphs **217 i' th' eyes** in her sight (?) in the sight of those watching (?) **218 made . . . adornings** made their graceful bowings beautiful, as in a work of art **221 yarely frame** nimbly perform

226 but for vacancy except that it would have created a vacuum **235 ordinary** meal, supper (such as one might obtain at a public table in a tavern) **236 eat** ate. (Pronounced *et.*) **237 Caesar** i.e., Julius Caesar, by whom Cleopatra had a son named Caesarion **238 cropp'd** bore fruit (a son) **249 Become themselves** are becoming, attractive **250 riggish** lustful **253 lottery** prize, gift of fortune

II.iii. Location: Rome.

I have not kept my square, but that to come 6
Shall all be done by th' rule. Good night, dear lady.
Good night, sir.

CAESAR
Good night. *Exit [with Octavia].*

Enter Soothsayer.

ANTONY
Now, sirrah; you do wish yourself in Egypt?

SOOTHSAYER
Would I had never come from thence, nor you
thither.

ANTONY
If you can, your reason?

SOOTHSAYER
I see it in my motion, have it not in my tongue; 13
But yet hie you to Egypt again.

ANTONY
Say to me,
Whose fortunes shall rise higher, Caesar's or mine?

SOOTHSAYER
Caesar's.
Therefore, O Antony, stay not by his side.
Thy daemon, that thy spirit which keeps thee, is 19
Noble, courageous, high, unmatchable,
Where Caesar's is not; but near him thy angel
Becomes a fear, as being o'erpow'r'd. Therefore 22
Make space enough between you.

ANTONY
Speak this no more.

SOOTHSAYER
To none but thee; no more but when to thee.
If thou dost play with him at any game,
Thou art sure to lose; and of that natural luck 26
He beats thee 'gainst the odds. Thy luster thickens 27
When he shines by. I say again, thy spirit
Is all afraid to govern thee near him;
But, he away, 'tis noble.

ANTONY
Get thee gone.
Say to Ventidius I would speak with him.
Exit [Soothsayer].
He shall to Parthia.—Be it art or hap, 32
He hath spoken true. The very dice obey him,
And in our sports my better cunning faints 34
Under his chance. If we draw lots, he speeds; 35
His cocks do win the battle still of mine, 36
When it is all to nought; and his quails ever 37
Beat mine, inhoop'd, at odds. I will to Egypt; 38
And though I make this marriage for my peace,
I' th' east my pleasure lies.

Enter Ventidius.

O, come, Ventidius,
You must to Parthia. Your commission's ready;
Follow me, and receive 't. *Exeunt.*

6 kept my square kept to a straight course (as guided by a carpenter's square; with pun on *rule, ruler* in next line) **13 in my motion** intuitively, by inward prompting **19 daemon** guardian spirit **22 Becomes a fear** i.e., becomes afraid and stops guarding you (see ll. 28–29) **26 of** by **27 thickens** grows dim **32 art or hap** skill or luck **34 cunning** skill **35 chance** luck. **speeds** wins **36 still** always **37 When . . . nought** when the odds are everything to nothing (in my favor) **38 inhoop'd** (The birds were enclosed in hoops to make them fight.)

[SCENE IV]

Enter Lepidus, Maecenas, and Agrippa.

LEPIDUS
Trouble yourselves no further. Pray you hasten
Your generals after.

AGRIPPA
Sir, Mark Antony
Will e'en but kiss Octavia, and we'll follow.

LEPIDUS
Till I shall see you in your soldier's dress,
Which will become you both, farewell.

MAECENAS
We shall,
As I conceive the journey, be at the Mount 6
Before you, Lepidus.

LEPIDUS
Your way is shorter;
My purposes do draw me much about. 8
You'll win two days upon me.

MAECENAS, AGRIPPA
Sir, good success!

LEPIDUS
Farewell. *Exeunt.*

[SCENE V]

Enter Cleopatra, Charmian, Iras, and Alexas.

CLEOPATRA
Give me some music; music, moody food
Of us that trade in love.

ALL
The music, ho!

Enter Mardian the Eunuch.

CLEOPATRA
Let it alone. Let's to billiards. Come, Charmian.

CHARMIAN
My arm is sore; best play with Mardian.

CLEOPATRA
As well a woman with an eunuch play'd
As with a woman. Come, you'll play with me, sir?

MARDIAN
As well as I can, madam.

CLEOPATRA
And when good will is show'd, though 't come too
short, 8
The actor may plead pardon. I'll none now.
Give me mine angle; we'll to th' river. There, 10
My music playing far off, I will betray
Tawny-finn'd fishes. My bended hook shall pierce
Their slimy jaws, and, as I draw them up,
I'll think them every one an Antony,
And say "Ah, ha! Y' are caught."

CHARMIAN
'Twas merry when
You wager'd on your angling, when your diver

II.iv. Location: Rome. A street.
6 the Mount i.e., Mount Misenum **8 about** roundabout

II.v. Location: Alexandria. Cleopatra's palace.
8 too short (A bawdy joke on Mardian's being castrated; *will* suggests *sexual desire, come* suggests *reach orgasm*.) **10 angle** rod and line

Did hang a salt fish on his hook, which he 17
With fervency drew up.

CLEOPATRA That time—O times!—
I laugh'd him out of patience; and that night
I laugh'd him into patience. And next morn,
Ere the ninth hour, I drunk him to his bed,
Then put my tires and mantles on him, whilst 22
I wore his sword Philippan.

Enter a Messenger.

O, from Italy! 23
Ram thou thy fruitful tidings in mine ears,
That long time have been barren.

MESSENGER Madam, madam—

CLEOPATRA
Antonio's dead! If thou say so, villain,
Thou kill'st thy mistress; but well and free,
If thou so yield him, there is gold, and here
My bluest veins to kiss—a hand that kings
Have lipp'd, and trembled kissing.
[*Offers him gold, and her hand to kiss.*]

MESSENGER
First, madam, he is well.

CLEOPATRA
Why, there's more gold. But, sirrah, mark, we use
To say the dead are well. Bring it to that, 33
The gold I give thee will I melt and pour
Down thy ill-uttering throat.

MESSENGER
Good madam, hear me.

CLEOPATRA Well, go to, I will.
But there's no goodness in thy face, if Antony
Be free and healthful—so tart a favor 38
To trumpet such good tidings! If not well,
Thou shouldst come like a Fury crown'd with snakes,
Not like a formal man.

MESSENGER Will 't please you hear me? 41

CLEOPATRA
I have a mind to strike thee ere thou speak'st.
Yet, if thou say Antony lives, is well,
Or friends with Caesar, or not captive to him,
I'll set thee in a shower of gold, and hail
Rich pearls upon thee.

MESSENGER Madam, he's well.

CLEOPATRA Well said.

MESSENGER
And friends with Caesar.

CLEOPATRA Th' art an honest man.

MESSENGER
Caesar and he are greater friends than ever.

CLEOPATRA
Make thee a fortune from me.

MESSENGER But yet, madam—

CLEOPATRA
I do not like "But yet," it does allay 50
The good precedence; fie upon "But yet"! 51
"But yet" is as a jailer to bring forth
Some monstrous malefactor. Prithee, friend,
Pour out the pack of matter to mine ear,
The good and bad together. He's friends with Caesar,
In state of health thou say'st, and thou say'st free.

MESSENGER
Free, madam? No, I made no such report.
He's bound unto Octavia.

CLEOPATRA For what good turn?

MESSENGER
For the best turn i' th' bed.

CLEOPATRA I am pale, Charmian.

MESSENGER
Madam, he's married to Octavia.

CLEOPATRA
The most infectious pestilence upon thee!
Strikes him down.

MESSENGER
Good madam, patience.

CLEOPATRA What say you? Hence,
Strikes him.
Horrible villain, or I'll spurn thine eyes 63
Like balls before me! I'll unhair thy head! 64
She hales him up and down.
Thou shalt be whipp'd with wire, and stew'd in brine,
Smarting in ling'ring pickle!

MESSENGER Gracious madam, 66
I that do bring the news made not the match.

CLEOPATRA
Say 'tis not so, a province I will give thee,
And make thy fortunes proud. The blow thou hadst
Shall make thy peace for moving me to rage,
And I will boot thee with what gift beside 71
Thy modesty can beg.

MESSENGER He's married, madam.

CLEOPATRA
Rogue, thou hast liv'd too long! *Draw a knife.*

MESSENGER Nay, then I'll run.
What mean you, madam? I have made no fault.
Exit.

CHARMIAN
Good madam, keep yourself within yourself.
The man is innocent.

CLEOPATRA
Some innocents scape not the thunderbolt.
Melt Egypt into Nile! And kindly creatures
Turn all to serpents! Call the slave again.
Though I am mad, I will not bite him. Call!

CHARMIAN
He is afeard to come.

CLEOPATRA I will not hurt him.
[*The Messenger is sent for.*]
These hands do lack nobility, that they strike
A meaner than myself, since I myself
Have given myself the cause.

Enter the Messenger again.

17 salt dried, preserved in salt **22 tires** headdresses, or perhaps attire **23 Philippan** (Named for Antony's victory over Brutus and Cassius at Philippi.) **33 well** i.e., well off **38 tart a favor** sour a face **41 like . . . man** in ordinary human form **50–51 allay . . . precedence** annul the good news that preceded it

63 spurn kick **64 s.d. hales** drags **66 pickle** pickling solution **71 boot thee with** give you into the bargain, or make amends with

Come hither, sir. 84
Though it be honest, it is never good
To bring bad news. Give to a gracious message
An host of tongues, but let ill tidings tell
Themselves when they be felt.

MESSENGER
I have done my duty. 88

CLEOPATRA
Is he married?
I cannot hate thee worser than I do
If thou again say "Yes."

MESSENGER
He's married, madam.

CLEOPATRA
The gods confound thee! Dost thou hold there still? 92

MESSENGER
Should I lie, madam?

CLEOPATRA
O, I would thou didst,
So half my Egypt were submerg'd and made 94
A cistern for scal'd snakes! Go, get thee hence!
Hadst thou Narcissus in thy face, to me 96
Thou wouldst appear most ugly. He is married?

MESSENGER
I crave your Highness' pardon.

CLEOPATRA
He is married?

MESSENGER
Take no offense that I would not offend you; 99
To punish me for what you make me do
Seems much unequal. He's married to Octavia. 101

CLEOPATRA
O, that his fault should make a knave of thee, 102
That art not what th' art sure of! Get thee hence. 103
The merchandise which thou hast brought from Rome
Are all too dear for me. Lie they upon thy hand, 105
And be undone by 'em! *[Exit Messenger.]*

CHARMIAN
Good your Highness, patience. 106

CLEOPATRA
In praising Antony, I have disprais'd Caesar.

CHARMIAN
Many times, madam.

CLEOPATRA
I am paid for 't now. Lead me from hence;
I faint. O Iras, Charmian! 'Tis no matter.
Go to the fellow, good Alexas. Bid him
Report the feature of Octavia, her years,
Her inclination; let him not leave out 113
The color of her hair. Bring me word quickly.
[Exit Alexas.]
Let him for ever go!—Let him not, Charmian! 115
Though he be painted one way like a Gorgon, 116
The other way's a Mars. *[To Mardian.]* Bid you Alexas 117
Bring me word how tall she is.—Pity me, Charmian,
But do not speak to me. Lead me to my chamber.
Exeunt.

[SCENE VI]

Flourish. Enter Pompey [and Menas] at one door, with drum and trumpet; at another, Caesar, Lepidus, Antony, Enobarbus, Maecenas, Agrippa, with Soldiers marching.

POMPEY
Your hostages I have, so have you mine;
And we shall talk before we fight.

CAESAR
Most meet 2
That first we come to words; and therefore have we
Our written purposes before us sent,
Which, if thou hast considered, let us know
If 'twill tie up thy discontented sword
And carry back to Sicily much tall youth 7
That else must perish here.

POMPEY
To you all three,
The senators alone of this great world,
Chief factors for the gods, I do not know 10
Wherefore my father should revengers want, 11
Having a son and friends, since Julius Caesar, 12
Who at Philippi the good Brutus ghosted, 13
There saw you laboring for him. What was 't 14
That mov'd pale Cassius to conspire? And what
Made all-honor'd, honest, Roman Brutus,
With the arm'd rest, courtiers of beauteous freedom,
To drench the Capitol, but that they would
Have one man but a man? And that is it 19
Hath made me rig my navy, at whose burden
The anger'd ocean foams, with which I meant
To scourge th' ingratitude that despiteful Rome
Cast on my noble father.

CAESAR
Take your time.

ANTONY
Thou canst not fear us, Pompey, with thy sails; 24
We'll speak with thee at sea. At land, thou know'st 25
How much we do o'ercount thee.

POMPEY
At land indeed 26
Thou dost o'ercount me of my father's house;
But, since the cuckoo builds not for himself, 28
Remain in 't as thou mayst.

84 the cause i.e., by loving Antony **88 when . . . felt** i.e., when they occur, making themselves known by the occurrence **92 confound** destroy **94 So** even if **96 Narcissus** beautiful youth of Greek mythology who fell in love with his own reflected image **99 Take . . . offend you** don't be offended that I hesitate to offend you (by telling bad news); or, don't interpret as offense what is not meant to offend **101 much unequal** most unjust **102–103 O, that . . . sure of** i.e., it's too bad that Antony's fault puts you in the wrong, you who shouldn't be equated with the bad news you report as true **105–106 Lie . . . undone** may they remain in your possession unsold, and may you be bankrupt, financially ruined. (I.e., may you never profit from your bad tidings.) **113 inclination** disposition **115 him** i.e., Antony **116–117 Though . . . Mars** (Alludes to a type of picture known as a perspective, which shows different objects when looked at from different angles of vision.) **116 Gorgon** a female monster with serpents in its hair; its head was capable of turning to stone anything that met its gaze

II.vi. Location: Near Misenum, in southern Italy near modern Naples. (But II.i. perhaps took place in Messina, Sicily.)
2 meet suitable **7 tall** brave **10 factors** agents **10–14 I do . . . for him** (Julius Caesar defeated Pompey's father, Pompey the Great, and was subsequently assassinated by Brutus and Cassius among others. Caesar's ghost appeared to Brutus at Philippi, where the combined forces of Antony, Octavius, and Lepidus defeated Brutus and Cassius. [See *Julius Caesar*.] Since Antony, Octavius, and Lepidus thus defeated the avengers of Pompey the Great's death, Pompey the Great's sons and friends should become his avengers by continuing to war on Antony, Octavius, and Lepidus.) **11 want** lack **13 ghosted** haunted **19 Have . . . a man** (The republican conspirators acted to keep Julius Caesar from accepting the crown.) **24 fear** frighten **25 speak with** confront **26 o'ercount** outnumber. (But Pompey's use of the word in the next line implies that Antony has cheated him. Plutarch informs us that Antony bought the elder Pompey's house at auction and later refused to pay for it.) **28 cuckoo** a bird that builds no nest for itself but lays its eggs in other birds' nests. (Perhaps suggests also that Antony is a cuckold-maker.)

LEPIDUS Be pleas'd to tell us—
For this is from the present—how you take
The offers we have sent you.
CAESAR There's the point.
ANTONY
Which do not be entreated to, but weigh
What it is worth embrac'd.
CAESAR And what may follow,
To try a larger fortune.
POMPEY You have made me offer
Of Sicily, Sardinia; and I must
Rid all the sea of pirates; then, to send
Measures of wheat to Rome. This 'greed upon,
To part with unhack'd edges, and bear back
Our targes undinted.
CAESAR, ANTONY, LEPIDUS That's our offer.
POMPEY Know then
I came before you here a man prepar'd
To take this offer, but Mark Antony
Put me to some impatience. Though I lose
The praise of it by telling, you must know,
When Caesar and your brother were at blows,
Your mother came to Sicily and did find
Her welcome friendly.
ANTONY I have heard it, Pompey;
And am well studied for a liberal thanks
Which I do owe you.
POMPEY Let me have your hand.
I did not think, sir, to have met you here.
ANTONY
The beds i' th' east are soft; and thanks to you,
That call'd me timelier than my purpose hither;
For I have gain'd by 't.
CAESAR Since I saw you last,
There's a change upon you.
POMPEY Well, I know not
What counts harsh fortune casts upon my face,
But in my bosom shall she never come
To make my heart her vassal.
LEPIDUS Well met here.
POMPEY
I hope so, Lepidus. Thus we are agreed.
I crave our composition may be written,
And seal'd between us.
CAESAR That's the next to do.
POMPEY
We'll feast each other ere we part; and let's
Draw lots who shall begin.
ANTONY That will I, Pompey.
POMPEY
No, Antony, take the lot;
But, first or last, your fine Egyptian cookery
Shall have the fame. I have heard that Julius Caesar
Grew fat with feasting there.
ANTONY
You have heard much.
POMPEY I have fair meanings, sir.
ANTONY
And fair words to them.
POMPEY Then so much have I heard.
And, I have heard, Apollodorus carried—
ENOBARBUS
No more of that. He did so.
POMPEY What, I pray you?
ENOBARBUS
A certain queen to Caesar in a mattress.
POMPEY
I know thee now. How far'st thou, soldier?
ENOBARBUS Well;
And well am like to do; for I perceive
Four feasts are toward.
POMPEY Let me shake thy hand;
I never hated thee. I have seen thee fight,
When I have envied thy behavior.
ENOBARBUS Sir,
I never lov'd you much, but I ha' prais'd ye
When you have well deserv'd ten times as much
As I have said you did.
POMPEY Enjoy thy plainness,
It nothing ill becomes thee.
Aboard my galley I invite you all.
Will you lead, lords?
CAESAR, ANTONY, LEPIDUS Show 's the way, sir.
POMPEY Come.
Exeunt. Mane [n]t Enobarbus and Menas.
MENAS [*Aside*] Thy father, Pompey, would ne'er have made this treaty.—You and I have known, sir.
ENOBARBUS At sea, I think.
MENAS We have, sir.
ENOBARBUS You have done well by water.
MENAS And you by land.
ENOBARBUS I will praise any man that will praise me, though it cannot be denied what I have done by land.
MENAS Nor what I have done by water.
ENOBARBUS Yes, something you can deny for your own safety: you have been a great thief by sea.
MENAS And you by land.
ENOBARBUS There I deny my land service. But give me your hand, Menas. If our eyes had authority, here they might take two thieves kissing.
MENAS All men's faces are true, whatsome'er their hands are.
ENOBARBUS But there is never a fair woman has a true face.
MENAS No slander; they steal hearts.
ENOBARBUS We came hither to fight with you.
MENAS For my part, I am sorry it is turn'd to a drinking.

29 as thou mayst as long as you can, or since you can **30 from the present** digressing from the business at hand **32 do . . . to** i.e., do not accept merely because we ask **33 embrac'd** if accepted by you **34 To . . . fortune** i.e., if you decide to risk war with the triumvirs; or, if you join with us to share a greater fortune **38 edges** swords **39 targes** shields **47 well studied for** well prepared to deliver **51 timelier** earlier **54 counts** tally marks. (From the practice of casting accounts or reckonings by means of marks or notches on tallies.) **58 composition** agreement **62 take the lot** draw lots with the rest of us

67 Then . . . heard i.e., I am not implying more about Antony in Egypt than my words honestly mean **68–70 Apollodorus . . . mattress** (Alludes to a tale told by Plutarch according to which Cleopatra had herself rolled up in a mattress and carried secretly by Apollodorus to meet Julius Caesar.) **73 toward** coming up **79 nothing . . . thee** suits you not at all badly **83 known** known each other **94 There** in respect to that **95 authority** i.e., to make arrests, like a constable **96 take** arrest. **two thieves kissing** (1) our two thieving hands shaking (2) two thieves greeting one another **99 true** honest (because women use cosmetic art to conceal defects) **101 No slander** i.e., you speak true (since women in their own way are thieves also)

Pompey doth this day laugh away his fortune.

ENOBARBUS If he do, sure, he cannot weep 't back again.

MENAS Y' have said, sir. We look'd not for Mark Antony here. Pray you, is he married to Cleopatra?

ENOBARBUS Caesar's sister is called Octavia.

MENAS True, sir; she was the wife of Caius Marcellus.

ENOBARBUS But she is now the wife of Marcus Antonius.

MENAS Pray ye, sir?

ENOBARBUS 'Tis true.

MENAS Then is Caesar and he forever knit together.

ENOBARBUS If I were bound to divine of this unity, I would not prophesy so.

MENAS I think the policy of that purpose made more in the marriage than the love of the parties.

ENOBARBUS I think so too. But you shall find the band that seems to tie their friendship together will be the very strangler of their amity. Octavia is of a holy, cold, and still conversation.

MENAS Who would not have his wife so?

ENOBARBUS Not he that himself is not so, which is Mark Antony. He will to his Egyptian dish again. Then shall the sighs of Octavia blow the fire up in Caesar, and, as I said before, that which is the strength of their amity shall prove the immediate author of their variance. Antony will use his affection where it is; he married but his occasion here.

MENAS And thus it may be. Come, sir, will you aboard? I have a health for you.

ENOBARBUS I shall take it, sir. We have us'd our throats in Egypt.

MENAS Come, let's away. *Exeunt.*

[SCENE VII]

Music plays. Enter two or three Servants with a banquet.

FIRST SERVANT Here they'll be, man. Some o' their plants are ill-rooted already; the least wind i' th' world will blow them down.

SECOND SERVANT Lepidus is high-color'd.

FIRST SERVANT They have made him drink alms-drink.

SECOND SERVANT As they pinch one another by the disposition, he cries out "No more," reconciles them to his entreaty, and himself to th' drink.

FIRST SERVANT But it raises the greater war between him and his discretion.

SECOND SERVANT Why, this it is to have a name in great men's fellowship. I had as lief have a reed that will do me no service as a partisan I could not heave.

FIRST SERVANT To be call'd into a huge sphere, and not to be seen to move in 't, are the holes where eyes should be, which pitifully disaster the cheeks.

A sennet sounded. Enter Caesar, Antony, Pompey, Lepidus, Agrippa, Maecenas, Enobarbus, Menas, with other captains.

ANTONY [*To Caesar*]
Thus do they, sir: they take the flow o' th' Nile
By certain scales i' th' pyramid. They know,
By th' height, the lowness, or the mean, if dearth
Or foison follow. The higher Nilus swells,
The more it promises; as it ebbs, the seedsman
Upon the slime and ooze scatters his grain,
And shortly comes to harvest.

LEPIDUS Y' have strange serpents there.

ANTONY Ay, Lepidus.

LEPIDUS Your serpent of Egypt is bred now of your mud by the operation of your sun. So is your crocodile.

ANTONY They are so.

POMPEY Sit—and some wine! A health to Lepidus! [*They sit, and drink.*]

LEPIDUS I am not so well as I should be, but I'll ne'er out.

ENOBARBUS Not till you have slept; I fear me you'll be in till then.

LEPIDUS Nay, certainly, I have heard the Ptolemies' pyramises are very goodly things; without contradiction, I have heard that.

MENAS [*Aside to Pompey*]
Pompey, a word.

POMPEY [*To Menas*] Say in mine ear. What is 't?

MENAS *(Whispers in 's ear)*
Forsake thy seat, I do beseech thee, captain,
And hear me speak a word.

POMPEY [*To Menas*]
Forbear me till anon.—This wine for Lepidus!

LEPIDUS What manner o' thing is your crocodile?

ANTONY It is shap'd, sir, like itself, and it is as broad as it hath breadth. It is just so high as it is, and moves with it own organs. It lives by that which nourisheth it, and, the elements once out of it, it transmigrates.

LEPIDUS What color is it of?

ANTONY Of it own color too.

LEPIDUS 'Tis a strange serpent.

ANTONY 'Tis so. And the tears of it are wet.

CAESAR Will this description satisfy him?

ANTONY With the health that Pompey gives him, else he is a very epicure. [*Menas whispers again.*]

113 Pray ye are you in earnest **116 divine of** prophesy about **118 made more** played more of a role **123 conversation** demeanor **130–131 his . . . is** his passion where it is, i.e., in Egypt **131 his occasion** what his interests demanded

II.vii. Location: On board Pompey's galley, off Misenum in southern Italy. A table and stools are brought on.

s.d. banquet a course of the feast, probably dessert **2 plants** soles of the feet (with pun on usual sense) **5 alms-drink** drink given or taken in charity (?), i.e., to further the business of reconciliation (as indicated in the following speech) **6–7 pinch . . . disposition** chafe one another, fall to bickering as prompted by their contrasting temperaments. (Lepidus stops them but has to join them in fresh rounds of drink.)

13 partisan long-bladed spear. (Here, metaphorically, too large a weapon for Lepidus to wield.) **14–16 To . . . cheeks** to be summoned by fortune to greatness and yet not be able to fulfill the role greatly is like having eye sockets with no eyes in them, a defect which will disfigure *(disaster)* the cheeks. (The underlying image is of a heavenly body that cannot move properly in its sphere, causing *disaster,* meaning both disfigurement and the evil effects of unfavorable aspect of a planet.) **17 take** measure **18 scales** graduated markings **20 foison** plenty **26 Your serpent** i.e., this serpent that people talk about. (The colloquial indefinite *your.*) **31–32 I'll ne'er out** i.e., I'll never refuse a toast, never quit **34 in** in drink, in your cups **36 pyramises** (Lepidus' drunken error for *pyramides,* plural of *pyramis* or *pyramid.*) **45 it own** its own **46 elements** vital elements **50 tears** (Alludes to the ancient belief that the crocodile wept insincere "crocodile tears" over its victim before devouring it.)

POMPEY [*Aside to Menas*]
Go hang, sir, hang! Tell me of that? Away!
Do as I bid you.—Where's this cup I call'd for?

MENAS [*Aside to Pompey*]
If for the sake of merit thou wilt hear me,
Rise from thy stool.

POMPEY [*To Menas*] I think th' art mad. [*Rises, and they walk aside.*] The matter?

MENAS
I have ever held my cap off to thy fortunes.

POMPEY
Thou hast serv'd me with much faith. What's else to say?—
Be jolly, lords.

ANTONY These quicksands, Lepidus,
Keep off them, for you sink.

MENAS
Wilt thou be lord of all the world?

POMPEY What say'st thou?

MENAS
Wilt thou be lord of the whole world? That's twice.

POMPEY
How should that be?

MENAS But entertain it, and,
Though thou think me poor, I am the man
Will give thee all the world.

POMPEY Hast thou drunk well?

MENAS
No, Pompey, I have kept me from the cup.
Thou art, if thou dar'st be, the earthly Jove.
Whate'er the ocean pales, or sky inclips,
Is thine, if thou wilt ha 't.

POMPEY Show me which way.

MENAS
These three world-sharers, these competitors,
Are in thy vessel. Let me cut the cable,
And, when we are put off, fall to their throats.
All there is thine.

POMPEY Ah, this thou shouldst have done,
And not have spoke on 't! In me 'tis villainy,
In thee 't had been good service. Thou must know,
'Tis not my profit that does lead mine honor;
Mine honor, it. Repent that e'er thy tongue
Hath so betray'd thine act. Being done unknown,
I should have found it afterwards well done,
But must condemn it now. Desist, and drink.
[*He returns to the feast.*]

MENAS [*Aside*]
For this,
I'll never follow thy pall'd fortunes more.
Who seeks, and will not take when once 'tis offer'd,
Shall never find it more.

POMPEY This health to Lepidus!

ANTONY
Bear him ashore. I'll pledge it for him, Pompey.

ENOBARBUS
Here's to thee, Menas! [*They drink.*]

MENAS Enobarbus, welcome!

POMPEY
Fill till the cup be hid.

ENOBARBUS
There's a strong fellow, Menas.
[*Pointing to the Attendant who carries off Lepidus.*]

MENAS Why?

ENOBARBUS 'A bears
The third part of the world, man; see'st not?

MENAS
The third part, then, is drunk. Would it were all,
That it might go on wheels!

ENOBARBUS
Drink thou; increase the reels.

MENAS
Come.

POMPEY
This is not yet an Alexandrian feast.

ANTONY
It ripens towards it. Strike the vessels, ho!
Here's to Caesar!

CAESAR I could well forbear 't.
It's monstrous labor when I wash my brain
And it grows fouler.

ANTONY Be a child o' th' time.

CAESAR
Possess it, I'll make answer.
But I had rather fast from all four days
Than drink so much in one.

ENOBARBUS [*To Antony*] Ha, my brave emperor!
Shall we dance now the Egyptian Bacchanals,
And celebrate our drink?

POMPEY
Let's ha 't, good soldier.

ANTONY Come, let's all take hands,
Till that the conquering wine hath steep'd our sense
In soft and delicate Lethe.

ENOBARBUS All take hands.
Make battery to our ears with the loud music;
The while I'll place you; then the boy shall sing.
The holding every man shall bear as loud
As his strong sides can volley.
Music plays. Enobarbus places them hand in hand.

The Song.

Come, thou monarch of the vine,
Plumpy Bacchus with pink eyne!
In thy fats our cares be drown'd,
With thy grapes our hairs be crown'd.
Cup us, till the world go round,
Cup us, till the world go round!

56 merit i.e., my merits as a loyal follower, or the merit of my ideas **58 held . . . off** i.e., been a respectful and faithful servant **64 But entertain it** only accept the possibility **69 pales** impales, fences in. **inclips** embraces **71 competitors** partners (with secondary sense of *rivals*) **78 Mine honor, it** i.e., my honor comes before my personal profit. **Repent** regret **83 pall'd** decayed, darkened **84 Who** he who **86 pledge it** i.e., drink the toast (since Lepidus is too far gone to drink)

92 go on wheels go fast or easily. (Proverbial.) **93 reels** (1) revels (2) reeling and whirling of drunkenness **96 Strike the vessels** broach the casks **100 Possess it** drink it off. **make answer** drink in return **103 Bacchanals** drunken dance to Bacchus, god of wine **107 Lethe** i.e., forgetfulness. (Literally, the river of oblivion in Hades.) **110 holding** refrain. **bear** carry, sing **113 pink eyne** (i.e., from drinking) **114 fats** vats, vessels

CAESAR
What would you more? Pompey, good night. Good brother,
Let me request you off. Our graver business 119
Frowns at this levity. Gentle lords, let's part;
You see we have burnt our cheeks. Strong Enobarb
Is weaker than the wine, and mine own tongue
Splits what it speaks. The wild disguise hath almost 123
Antick'd us all. What needs more words? Good night. 124
Good Antony, your hand.

POMPEY
I'll try you on the shore. 126

ANTONY
And shall, sir. Give 's your hand.

POMPEY
O Antony, you have my father's house.
But what? We are friends. Come, down into the boat.

ENOBARBUS
Take heed you fall not.
[Exeunt all but Enobarbus and Menas.]
Menas, I'll not on shore.

MENAS
No, to my cabin.
These drums, these trumpets, flutes, what?
Let Neptune hear we bid a loud farewell
To these great fellows. Sound and be hang'd, sound out! *Sound a flourish, with drums.*

ENOBARBUS
Hoo! says 'a. There's my cap.

MENAS
Ho! Noble captain, come. *Exeunt.*

[ACT III • SCENE I]

Enter Ventidius as it were in triumph [with Silius, and other Romans, Officers, and Soldiers], the dead body of Pacorus borne before him.

VENTIDIUS
Now, darting Parthia, art thou struck, and now 1
Pleas'd fortune does of Marcus Crassus' death 2
Make me revenger. Bear the King's son's body
Before our army. Thy Pacorus, Orodes, 4
Pays this for Marcus Crassus.

SILIUS
Noble Ventidius,
Whilst yet with Parthian blood thy sword is warm,
The fugitive Parthians follow. Spur through Media,
Mesopotamia, and the shelters whither
The routed fly; so thy grand captain, Antony,
Shall set thee on triumphant chariots and
Put garlands on thy head.

VENTIDIUS
O Silius, Silius,
I have done enough. A lower place, note well, 12
May make too great an act. For learn this, Silius:
Better to leave undone, than by our deed
Acquire too high a fame when him we serve's away.
Caesar and Antony have ever won
More in their officer than person. Sossius,
One of my place in Syria, his lieutenant, 18
For quick accumulation of renown,
Which he achiev'd by th' minute, lost his favor. 20
Who does i' th' wars more than his captain can
Becomes his captain's captain; and ambition,
The soldier's virtue, rather makes choice of loss 23
Than gain which darkens him. 24
I could do more to do Antonius good,
But 'twould offend him; and in his offense 26
Should my performance perish.

SILIUS
Thou hast, Ventidius,
That without the which a soldier and his sword 28
Grants scarce distinction. Thou wilt write to Antony? 29

VENTIDIUS
I'll humbly signify what in his name,
That magical word of war, we have effected—
How with his banners and his well-paid ranks
The ne'er-yet-beaten horse of Parthia 33
We have jaded out o' th' field.

SILIUS
Where is he now? 34

VENTIDIUS
He purposeth to Athens, whither, with what haste
The weight we must convey with 's will permit, 36
We shall appear before him.—On, there; pass along! *Exeunt.*

[SCENE II]

Enter Agrippa at one door, Enobarbus at another.

AGRIPPA
What, are the brothers parted? 1

ENOBARBUS
They have dispatch'd with Pompey, he is gone; 2
The other three are sealing. Octavia weeps 3
To part from Rome; Caesar is sad; and Lepidus,
Since Pompey's feast, as Menas says, is troubled

119 off to come away **123 disguise** i.e., drunkenness as a disguise **124 Antick'd** made buffoons or fools of **126 try you** i.e., take you on in a drinking contest

III.i. Location: A plain in Syria.
1 darting (The Parthians were famous for archery and for the Parthian dart which they discharged as they fled.) **Parthia** i.e., Orodes, King of Parthia **2 Crassus' death** (Crassus, member of the first triumvirate with Pompey the Great and Julius Caesar, was overthrown and treacherously murdered by Orodes in 53 B.C.) **4 Pacorus, Orodes** (Pacorus was the son of Orodes.)

12 A lower place i.e., one of lower rank **18 of my place** of the same rank as I. **his lieutenant** i.e., the commanding officer acting for Antony **20 by th' minute** minute by minute, steadily **23 makes choice of** chooses **24 darkens him** deprives his superior of renown **26 offense** taking offense **28–29 That . . . distinction** i.e., discretion, without the which a soldier can scarcely be distinguished from the sword he uses **33 horse** cavalry **34 jaded** driven exhausted like jades, inferior horses **36 with 's** with us

III.ii. Location: Rome.
1 parted departed **2 dispatch'd** concluded the business **3 sealing** affixing seals to their agreements, settling matters

With the green sickness.
AGRIPPA 'Tis a noble Lepidus. 6
ENOBARBUS
A very fine one. O, how he loves Caesar!
AGRIPPA
Nay, but how dearly he adores Mark Antony!
ENOBARBUS
Caesar? Why, he's the Jupiter of men.
AGRIPPA
What's Antony? The god of Jupiter.
ENOBARBUS
Spake you of Caesar? How, the nonpareil!
AGRIPPA
O Antony! O thou Arabian bird! 12
ENOBARBUS
Would you praise Caesar, say "Caesar," go no
further.
AGRIPPA
Indeed, he plied them both with excellent praises.
ENOBARBUS
But he loves Caesar best; yet he loves Antony.
Hoo! Hearts, tongues, figures, scribes, bards, poets,
cannot
Think, speak, cast, write, sing, number, hoo! 17
His love to Antony. But as for Caesar,
Kneel down, kneel down, and wonder.
AGRIPPA Both he loves.
ENOBARBUS
They are his shards, and he their beetle. [*Trumpets
within.*] So; 20
This is to horse. Adieu, noble Agrippa.
AGRIPPA
Good fortune, worthy soldier, and farewell.

Enter Caesar, Antony, Lepidus, and Octavia.

ANTONY
No further, sir. 23
CAESAR
You take from me a great part of myself;
Use me well in 't. Sister, prove such a wife
As my thoughts make thee, and as my farthest band 26
Shall pass on thy approof. Most noble Antony, 27
Let not the piece of virtue, which is set 28
Betwixt us as the cement of our love,
To keep it builded, be the ram to batter
The fortress of it; for better might we
Have lov'd without this mean, if on both parts 32
This be not cherish'd.
ANTONY Make me not offended
In your distrust.
CAESAR I have said.
ANTONY You shall not find,
Though you be therein curious, the least cause 35
For what you seem to fear. So the gods keep you,
And make the hearts of Romans serve your ends!
We will here part.
CAESAR
Farewell, my dearest sister, fare thee well.
The elements be kind to thee, and make
Thy spirits all of comfort! Fare thee well.
OCTAVIA
My noble brother! [*Weeps.*]
ANTONY
The April's in her eyes; it is love's spring,
And these the showers to bring it on. Be cheerful.
OCTAVIA
Sir, look well to my husband's house; and— 45
CAESAR
What, Octavia?
OCTAVIA I'll tell you in your ear.
[*Whispers to Caesar.*]
ANTONY
Her tongue will not obey her heart, nor can 47
Her heart inform her tongue—the swan's down-
feather, 48
That stands upon the swell at full of tide, 49
And neither way inclines. 50
ENOBARBUS [*Aside to Agrippa*]
Will Caesar weep?
AGRIPPA [*Aside to Enobarbus*] He has a cloud in 's face.
ENOBARBUS [*Aside to Agrippa*]
He were the worse for that, were he a horse; 52
So is he, being a man.
AGRIPPA [*Aside to Enobarbus*] Why, Enobarbus,
When Antony found Julius Caesar dead,
He cried almost to roaring; and he wept
When at Philippi he found Brutus slain.
ENOBARBUS [*Aside to Agrippa*]
That year, indeed, he was troubled with a rheum; 57
What willingly he did confound he wail'd, 58
Believe 't, till I wept too.
CAESAR No, sweet Octavia,
You shall hear from me still; the time shall not 60
Outgo my thinking on you.
ANTONY Come, sir, come, 61
I'll wrestle with you in my strength of love.
Look, here I have you [*Embracing him*]; thus I let
you go,
And give you to the gods.
CAESAR Adieu; be happy!
LEPIDUS
Let all the number of the stars give light
To thy fair way!
CAESAR Farewell, farewell! *Kisses Octavia.*
ANTONY Farewell!
Trumpets sound. Exeunt [severally].

6 green sickness a kind of anemia supposed to affect young women, especially those afflicted with love-longing. (Used ironically here to refer to Lepidus' hangover and to his love for Antony and Caesar.) **12 Arabian bird** i.e., the fabled phoenix. (Only one existed at a time; it recreated itself by arising from its ashes.) **17 cast** calculate. **number** write verses **20 shards** wings or wing-cases; i.e., protectors, patrons **23 No further** i.e., you need not go on urging your point; or, you need accompany me no further **26–27 as . . . approof** such that my utmost bond shall be justified in certifying what you will prove to be **28 piece** masterpiece **32 mean** intermediary, or means **35 curious** overly inquisitive

45 husband's house (Octavia is a widow; see III.iii.29.) **47–50 Her . . . inclines** i.e., her conflicting emotions make her unable to speak aloud, like a swan's down-feather floating at full tide, moving neither up nor down stream **52 He . . . horse** (Alludes to the belief that a horse without any light coloring on its face was apt to be bad-tempered.) **57 rheum** i.e., running at the eyes. (Used of any discharge of mucus from the head.) **58 confound** destroy. **wail'd** bewailed **60 still** regularly **60–61 the time . . . you** time itself will not outlast my thinking of you

[SCENE III]

Enter Cleopatra, Charmian, Iras, and Alexas.

CLEOPATRA
Where is the fellow?
ALEXAS
Half afeard to come.
CLEOPATRA
Go to, go to.

Enter the Messenger as before.

Come hither, sir.
ALEXAS
Good Majesty,
Herod of Jewry dare not look upon you
But when you are well pleas'd.
CLEOPATRA
That Herod's head
I'll have; but how, when Antony is gone
Through whom I might command it? Come thou
near.
MESSENGER
Most gracious Majesty!
CLEOPATRA
Didst thou behold Octavia?
MESSENGER
Ay, dread Queen.
CLEOPATRA
Where?
MESSENGER
Madam, in Rome;
I look'd her in the face, and saw her led
Between her brother and Mark Antony.
CLEOPATRA
Is she as tall as me?
MESSENGER
She is not, madam.
CLEOPATRA
Didst hear her speak? Is she shrill-tongu'd or low?
MESSENGER
Madam, I heard her speak. She is low-voic'd.
CLEOPATRA
That's not so good. He cannot like her long.
CHARMIAN
Like her! O Isis! 'Tis impossible.
CLEOPATRA
I think so, Charmian. Dull of tongue, and dwarfish.
What majesty is in her gait? Remember,
If e'er thou look'dst on majesty.
MESSENGER
She creeps.
Her motion and her station are as one;
She shows a body rather than a life,
A statue than a breather.
CLEOPATRA
Is this certain?
MESSENGER
Or I have no observance.
CHARMIAN
Three in Egypt
Cannot make better note.
CLEOPATRA
He's very knowing;
I do perceive 't. There's nothing in her yet.
The fellow has good judgment.
CHARMIAN
Excellent.
CLEOPATRA
Guess at her years, I prithee.
MESSENGER
Madam,
She was a widow—
CLEOPATRA
Widow? Charmian, hark.
MESSENGER
And I do think she's thirty.
CLEOPATRA
Bear'st thou her face in mind? Is 't long or round?
MESSENGER
Round even to faultiness.
CLEOPATRA
For the most part, too, they are foolish that are so.
Her hair, what color?
MESSENGER
Brown, madam; and her forehead
As low as she would wish it.
CLEOPATRA
There's gold for thee. [*Gives money.*]
Thou must not take my former sharpness ill.
I will employ thee back again; I find thee
Most fit for business. Go make thee ready;
Our letters are prepar'd. [*Exit Messenger.*]
CHARMIAN
A proper man.
CLEOPATRA
Indeed, he is so. I repent me much
That so I harried him. Why, methinks, by him,
This creature's no such thing.
CHARMIAN
Nothing, madam.
CLEOPATRA
The man hath seen some majesty, and should know.
CHARMIAN
Hath he seen majesty? Isis else defend,
And serving you so long!
CLEOPATRA
I have one thing more to ask him yet, good
Charmian—
But 'tis no matter, thou shalt bring him to me
Where I will write. All may be well enough.
CHARMIAN
I warrant you, madam. *Exeunt.*

III.iii. Location: Alexandria. Cleopatra's palace.
2 Go to (An expression of impatience.) **3 Herod of Jewry** i.e., even the famous tyrant who slaughtered the children. (See I.ii.29–30.) **20 motion** moving. **station** standing **21 shows** appears as **22 breather** living being

36 As . . . it i.e., as low as could be. (A colloquial way of suggesting she is ugly; high foreheads were thought more beautiful.) **43 harried** maltreated. **by** according to **44 no such thing** nothing much **46 else defend** forbid otherwise. (An interjection.) **51 warrant** assure

[SCENE IV]

Enter Antony and Octavia.

ANTONY
Nay, nay, Octavia, not only that—
That were excusable, that, and thousands more
Of semblable import—but he hath wag'd

III.iv. Location: Athens. Antony's quarters.
3 semblable similar

New wars 'gainst Pompey; made his will, and
read it 4
To public ear;
Spoke scantly of me; when perforce he could not
But pay me terms of honor, cold and sickly
He vented them, most narrow measure lent me; 8
When the best hint was given him, he not took 't, 9
Or did it from his teeth.

OCTAVIA
O my good lord, 10
Believe not all, or, if you must believe,
Stomach not all. A more unhappy lady, 12
If this division chance, ne'er stood between, 13
Praying for both parts.
The good gods will mock me presently,
When I shall pray, "O, bless my lord and husband!"
Undo that prayer, by crying out as loud,
"O, bless my brother!" Husband win, win brother,
Prays, and destroys the prayer; no midway
'Twixt these extremes at all.

ANTONY
Gentle Octavia,
Let your best love draw to that point which seeks 21
Best to preserve it. If I lose mine honor, 22
I lose myself; better I were not yours
Than yours so branchless. But, as you requested, 24
Yourself shall go between 's. The mean time, lady,
I'll raise the preparation of a war 26
Shall stain your brother. Make your soonest haste; 27
So your desires are yours.

OCTAVIA
Thanks to my lord. 28
The Jove of power make me most weak, most weak,
Your reconciler! Wars 'twixt you twain would be
As if the world should cleave, and that slain men
Should solder up the rift.

ANTONY
When it appears to you where this begins, 33
Turn your displeasure that way, for our faults 34
Can never be so equal that your love
Can equally move with them. Provide your going; 36
Choose your own company, and command what
cost
Your heart has mind to. *Exeunt.*

[SCENE V]

Enter Enobarbus and Eros, [meeting].

ENOBARBUS How now, friend Eros?
EROS There's strange news come, sir.
ENOBARBUS What, man?
EROS Caesar and Lepidus have made wars upon Pompey.
ENOBARBUS This is old. What is the success? 6
EROS Caesar, having made use of him in the wars 7
'gainst Pompey, presently denied him rivality, would 8
not let him partake in the glory of the action; and, not
resting here, accuses him of letters he had formerly 10
wrote to Pompey; upon his own appeal, seizes him. 11
So the poor third is up, till death enlarge his confine. 12

ENOBARBUS
Then, world, thou hast a pair of chaps, no more; 13
And throw between them all the food thou hast,
They'll grind the one the other. Where's Antony?

EROS
He's walking in the garden—thus, and spurns 16
The rush that lies before him; cries, "Fool Lepidus!" 17
And threats the throat of that his officer 18
That murd'red Pompey.

ENOBARBUS
Our great navy's rigg'd. 19

EROS
For Italy and Caesar. More, Domitius; 20
My lord desires you presently. My news
I might have told hereafter.

ENOBARBUS
'Twill be naught;
But let it be. Bring me to Antony.

EROS
Come, sir. *Exeunt.*

[SCENE VI]

Enter Agrippa, Maecenas, and Caesar.

CAESAR
Contemning Rome, he has done all this, and more 1
In Alexandria. Here's the manner of 't:
I' th' market-place, on a tribunal silver'd, 3
Cleopatra and himself in chairs of gold
Were publicly enthron'd. At the feet sat
Caesarion, whom they call my father's son, 6
And all the unlawful issue that their lust
Since then hath made between them. Unto her
He gave the stablishment of Egypt, made her 9
Of lower Syria, Cyprus, Lydia,
Absolute queen.

MAECENAS
This in the public eye?

CAESAR
I' th' common show-place, where they exercise.
His sons he there proclaim'd the kings of kings:
Great Media, Parthia, and Armenia,
He gave to Alexander; to Ptolemy he assign'd
Syria, Cilicia, and Phoenicia. She

4 read it (to win the populace by showing them what benefits they might expect from him) **8 vented** gave vent to, expressed. **narrow measure** small credit **9 hint** occasion (to praise Antony) **10 from his teeth** i.e., from his mouth, not from the heart **12 Stomach** resent **13 chance** occur **21–22 Let . . . it** let your warmest love be given to that one of us who seeks to preserve it (your love) best **24 branchless** pruned (of honor) **26–27 I'll . . . brother** I'll raise an army which will deprive your brother of his luster **28 So . . . yours** i.e., thus you have obtained your desire (to go). (Or, *so* may mean *as long as*.) **33 where this begins** who started this quarrel **34 our** i.e., Caesar's and mine **36 Provide** make arrangements for

III.v. Location: Athens. Antony's quarters.

6 success sequel, result **7 him** i.e., Lepidus **8 rivality** rights of a partner. (Caesar and Lepidus have newly gone to war against Pompey and have defeated him.) **10 resting here** i.e., stopping with this insult **11 his own appeal** Caesar's own accusation **12 up** shut up (in prison) **13 pair of chaps** two jaws. **no more** i.e., no more than one pair, no third partner **16 thus** (Eros imitates Antony's angry walk.) **spurns** kicks **17 rush** strewn rushes **18 that his officer** that officer of his (Antony's) **19 Pompey** (After his defeat by Caesar and Lepidus, Pompey was murdered—perhaps, according to history, on Antony's orders; but here Antony blames his officer for killing Pompey because he might have been a useful ally against Caesar.) **20 More** I have more to say

III.vi. Location: Rome.

1 Contemning disdaining **3 tribunal** seat of state, dais **6 my father's** i.e., Julius Caesar's. (Julius Caesar had adopted his nephew Octavius as his son.) **9 stablishment** settled possession

In th' habiliments of the goddess Isis
That day appear'd, and oft before gave audience,
As 'tis reported, so.

MAECENAS Let Rome be thus
Inform'd.

AGRIPPA Who, queasy with his insolence
Already, will their good thoughts call from him.

CAESAR
The people knows it, and have now receiv'd
His accusations.

AGRIPPA Who does he accuse?

CAESAR
Caesar, and that, having in Sicily
Sextus Pompeius spoil'd, we had not rated him
His part o' th' isle. Then does he say he lent me
Some shipping unrestor'd. Lastly, he frets
That Lepidus of the triumvirate
Should be depos'd; and, being, that we detain
All his revenue.

AGRIPPA Sir, this should be answer'd.

CAESAR
'Tis done already, and the messenger gone.
I have told him Lepidus was grown too cruel,
That he his high authority abus'd,
And did deserve his change. For what I have
conquer'd,
I grant him part; but then in his Armenia,
And other of his conquer'd kingdoms, I
Demand the like.

MAECENAS He'll never yield to that.

CAESAR
Nor must not then be yielded to in this.

Enter Octavia with her train.

OCTAVIA
Hail, Caesar, and my lord! Hail, most dear Caesar!

CAESAR
That ever I should call thee castaway!

OCTAVIA
You have not call'd me so, nor have you cause.

CAESAR
Why have you stol'n upon us thus? You come not
Like Caesar's sister. The wife of Antony
Should have an army for an usher, and
The neighs of horse to tell of her approach
Long ere she did appear. The trees by th' way
Should have borne men, and expectation fainted,
Longing for what it had not. Nay, the dust
Should have ascended to the roof of heaven,
Rais'd by your populous troops. But you are come
A market-maid to Rome; and have prevented
The ostentation of our love, which, left unshown,
Is often left unlov'd. We should have met you
By sea and land, supplying every stage
With an augmented greeting.

OCTAVIA Good my lord,
To come thus was I not constrain'd, but did it
On my free will. My lord, Mark Antony,
Hearing that you prepar'd for war, acquainted
My grieved ear withal; whereon, I begg'd
His pardon for return.

CAESAR Which soon he granted,
Being an abstract 'tween his lust and him.

OCTAVIA
Do not say so, my lord.

CAESAR I have eyes upon him,
And his affairs come to me on the wind.
Where is he now?

OCTAVIA
My lord, in Athens.

CAESAR
No, my most wronged sister. Cleopatra
Hath nodded him to her. He hath given his empire
Up to a whore, who now are levying
The kings o' th' earth for war. He hath assembled
Bocchus, the King of Libya; Archelaus,
Of Cappadocia; Philadelphos, King
Of Paphlagonia; the Thracian king, Adallas;
King Malchus of Arabia; King of Pont;
Herod of Jewry; Mithridates, King
Of Comagene; Polemon and Amyntas,
The Kings of Mede and Lycaonia,
With a more larger list of scepters.

OCTAVIA
Ay me, most wretched,
That have my heart parted betwixt two friends
That does afflict each other!

CAESAR Welcome hither.
Your letters did withhold our breaking forth,
Till we perceiv'd both how you were wrong led
And we in negligent danger. Cheer your heart.
Be you not troubled with the time, which drives
O'er your content these strong necessities,
But let determin'd things to destiny
Hold unbewail'd their way. Welcome to Rome;
Nothing more dear to me. You are abus'd
Beyond the mark of thought; and the high gods,
To do you justice, makes his ministers
Of us and those that love you. Best of comfort,
And ever welcome to us.

AGRIPPA Welcome, lady.

MAECENAS
Welcome, dear madam.
Each heart in Rome does love and pity you.
Only th' adulterous Antony, most large
In his abominations, turns you off,
And gives his potent regiment to a trull,
That noises it against us.

OCTAVIA Is it so, sir?

20 queasy disgusted. (Refers to the Roman people.) **25 spoil'd** despoiled, plundered. **rated** allotted **26 th' isle** i.e., Sicily **27 unrestor'd** i.e., that I did not return to him **28 of** from **29 being** i.e., having been deposed **51 prevented** forestalled (by your too-early arrival) **52 ostentation** ceremonial display **52–53 which . . . unlov'd** i.e., a love that is not given proper outward display often remains unexercised and dwindles into neglect. (Also, Caesar wants the display of love to be seen publicly.)

60 pardon permission **61 Being an abstract** i.e., your departure being the abstracting or removal of an impediment (?) or, you being a compendium of all standing in the way (?) **68 who** i.e., and they **81 withhold** restrain **83 negligent danger** danger through negligence **86 to destiny** to their destined conclusion **89 mark** reach **89–91 the high . . . Of us** i.e., the high gods (here a single concept) make us their ministers of justice in your cause **95 large** unrestrained **97 regiment** government, rule. **trull** prostitute **98 noises it** is clamorous

CAESAR
Most certain. Sister, welcome. Pray you
Be ever known to patience. My dear'st sister! *Exeunt.*

[SCENE VII]

Enter Cleopatra and Enobarbus.

CLEOPATRA
I will be even with thee, doubt it not.
ENOBARBUS
But why, why, why?
CLEOPATRA
Thou hast forspoke my being in these wars,
And say'st it is not fit.
ENOBARBUS Well, is it, is it?
CLEOPATRA
If not denounc'd against us, why should not we
Be there in person?
ENOBARBUS [*Aside*] Well, I could reply.
If we should serve with horse and mares together,
The horse were merely lost; the mares would bear
A soldier and his horse.
CLEOPATRA What is 't you say?
ENOBARBUS
Your presence needs must puzzle Antony,
Take from his heart, take from his brain, from 's time,
What should not then be spar'd. He is already
Traduc'd for levity, and 'tis said in Rome
That Photinus an eunuch and your maids
Manage this war.
CLEOPATRA Sink Rome, and their tongues rot
That speak against us! A charge we bear i' th' war,
And, as the president of my kingdom, will
Appear there for a man. Speak not against it;
I will not stay behind.

Enter Antony and Canidius.

ENOBARBUS Nay, I have done.
Here comes the Emperor.
ANTONY Is it not strange, Canidius,
That from Tarentum and Brundusium
He could so quickly cut the Ionian sea,
And take in Toryne?—You have heard on 't, sweet?
CLEOPATRA
Celerity is never more admir'd
Than by the negligent.
ANTONY A good rebuke,
Which might have well becom'd the best of men,
To taunt at slackness. Canidius, we will fight
With him by sea.
CLEOPATRA By sea, what else?
CANIDIUS Why will
My lord do so?
ANTONY For that he dares us to 't.
ENOBARBUS
So hath my lord dar'd him to single fight.
CANIDIUS
Ay, and to wage this battle at Pharsalia,
Where Caesar fought with Pompey. But these offers,
Which serve not for his vantage, he shakes off,
And so should you.
ENOBARBUS Your ships are not well mann'd;
Your mariners are muleters, reapers, people
Ingross'd by swift impress. In Caesar's fleet
Are those that often have 'gainst Pompey fought;
Their ships are yare, yours, heavy. No disgrace
Shall fall you for refusing him at sea,
Being prepar'd for land.
ANTONY By sea, by sea.
ENOBARBUS
Most worthy sir, you therein throw away
The absolute soldiership you have by land,
Distract your army, which doth most consist
Of war-mark'd footmen, leave unexecuted
Your own renowned knowledge, quite forego
The way which promises assurance, and
Give up yourself merely to chance and hazard,
From firm security.
ANTONY I'll fight at sea.
CLEOPATRA
I have sixty sails, Caesar none better.
ANTONY
Our overplus of shipping will we burn,
And, with the rest full-mann'd, from th' head of Actium
Beat th' approaching Caesar. But if we fail,
We then can do 't at land.

Enter a Messenger.

Thy business?
MESSENGER
The news is true, my lord, he is descried;
Caesar has taken Toryne.
ANTONY
Can he be there in person? 'Tis impossible;
Strange that his power should be. Canidius,
Our nineteen legions thou shalt hold by land,
And our twelve thousand horse. We'll to our ship.
Away, my Thetis!

Enter a Soldier.

How now, worthy soldier?
SOLDIER
O noble Emperor, do not fight by sea;
Trust not to rotten planks. Do you misdoubt
This sword and these my wounds? Let th' Egyptians

III.vii. Location: Near Actium, on the northwestern coast of Greece. Antony's camp.
3 forspoke spoken against **5 If . . . us** i.e., even if the war were not declared against me (which it is) **8 merely** utterly **16 charge** responsibility **22 Ionian** (Often applied to the Aegean, but here the Adriatic. Tarentum and Brundusium or Brundisium are in the "heel" of Italy, across the Adriatic from Actium and Toryne.) **23 take in** conquer

29 For that because **35 muleters** mule-drivers, peasants **36 Ingross'd** collected wholesale. **impress** impressment, conscription **38 yare** quick, maneuverable **39 fall** befall **43 Distract** divide, divert, confuse the purpose of **57 his power** i.e., his army, let alone himself **60 Thetis** sea goddess, the mother of Achilles

And the Phoenicians go a-ducking; we
Have us'd to conquer standing on the earth,
And fighting foot to foot.

ANTONY
Well, well; away!
Exeunt Antony, Cleopatra, and Enobarbus.

SOLDIER
By Hercules, I think I am i' th' right.

CANIDIUS
Soldier, thou art; but his whole action grows
Not in the power on 't. So our leader's led,
And we are women's men.

SOLDIER
You keep by land
The legions and the horse whole, do you not?

CANIDIUS
Marcus Octavius, Marcus Justeius,
Publicola, and Caelius are for sea;
But we keep whole by land. This speed of Caesar's
Carries beyond belief.

SOLDIER
While he was yet in Rome,
His power went out in such distractions as
Beguil'd all spies.

CANIDIUS
Who's his lieutenant, hear you?

SOLDIER
They say, one Taurus.

CANIDIUS
Well I know the man.

Enter a Messenger.

MESSENGER
The Emperor calls Canidius.

CANIDIUS
With news the time's with labor, and throws forth
Each minute some. *Exeunt.*

[SCENE VIII]

Enter Caesar [and Taurus] with his army, marching.

CAESAR
Taurus!

TAURUS
My lord?

CAESAR
Strike not by land; keep whole. Provoke not battle
Till we have done at sea. Do not exceed
The prescript of this scroll. [*Gives scroll.*] Our
fortune lies
Upon this jump. *Exit [with army].*

68–69 his . . . on 't his whole action develops away from the source of the potential or inherent power **75 Carries beyond** surpasses (like an arrow in archery) **77 distractions** detachments, divisions **81–82 With news . . . some** more news is born each minute. **throws forth** gives birth

III.viii. Location: A field near Actium, as before.
5 prescript orders **6 jump** chance, hazard

[SCENE IX]

Enter Antony and Enobarbus.

ANTONY
Set we our squadrons on yond side o' th' hill,
In eye of Caesar's battle, from which place
We may the number of the ships behold,
And so proceed accordingly. *Exit [with Enobarbus].*

[SCENE X]

Canidius marcheth with his land army one way over the stage; and Taurus, the lieutenant of Caesar, the other way. After their going in is heard the noise of a sea-fight.

Alarum. Enter Enobarbus.

ENOBARBUS
Naught, naught, all naught! I can behold no longer.
Th' Antoniad, the Egyptian admiral,
With all their sixty, fly and turn the rudder.
To see 't mine eyes are blasted.

Enter Scarus.

SCARUS
Gods and goddesses,
All the whole synod of them!

ENOBARBUS
What's thy passion?

SCARUS
The greater cantle of the world is lost
With very ignorance; we have kiss'd away
Kingdoms and provinces.

ENOBARBUS
How appears the fight?

SCARUS
On our side like the token'd pestilence,
Where death is sure. Yon ribaudred nag of Egypt—
Whom leprosy o'ertake!—i' th' midst o' th' fight,
When vantage like a pair of twins appear'd,
Both as the same, or rather ours the elder,
The breese upon her, like a cow in June,
Hoists sails and flies.

ENOBARBUS
That I beheld.
Mine eyes did sicken at the sight, and could not
Endure a further view.

SCARUS
She once being loof'd,
The noble ruin of her magic, Antony,
Claps on his sea-wing and, like a doting mallard,

III.ix. Location: A field near Actium, as before.
2 battle battle line

III.x. Location: A field near Actium, as before.
2 admiral flagship **5 synod** assembly **6 cantle** corner; hence, piece or part **9 token'd pestilence** (Certain red spots appeared on the bodies of the plague-smitten, called tokens.) **10 ribaudred** foul, obscene **12–13 When . . . same** i.e., when the advantage was equal on either side **13 elder** i.e., more advanced, more likely to inherit **14 breese** gadfly (with pun on *breeze*) **18 loof'd** luffed, with ship's head brought close to the wind (with a pun on *aloofed,* becoming distant) **20 Claps . . . sea-wing** i.e., hoists sail, preparing for flight like a water-bird. **mallard** drake

Leaving the fight in height, flies after her.
I never saw an action of such shame.
Experience, manhood, honor, ne'er before
Did violate so itself.

ENOBARBUS Alack, alack!

Enter Canidius.

CANIDIUS
Our fortune on the sea is out of breath,
And sinks most lamentably. Had our general
Been what he knew himself, it had gone well.
O, he has given example for our flight,
Most grossly, by his own!

ENOBARBUS Ay, are you thereabouts? 29
Why, then, good night indeed.

CANIDIUS
Toward Peloponnesus are they fled. 31

SCARUS
'Tis easy to 't; and there I will attend 32
What further comes.

CANIDIUS To Caesar will I render
My legions and my horse. Six kings already
Show me the way of yielding.

ENOBARBUS I'll yet follow
The wounded chance of Antony, though my reason 36
Sits in the wind against me. [*Exeunt severally.*] 37

[SCENE XI]

Enter Antony with Attendants.

ANTONY
Hark! The land bids me tread no more upon 't;
It is asham'd to bear me. Friends, come hither.
I am so lated in the world that I 3
Have lost my way forever. I have a ship
Laden with gold. Take that, divide it; fly,
And make your peace with Caesar.

ALL Fly? Not we.

ANTONY
I have fled myself, and have instructed cowards
To run and show their shoulders. Friends, be gone. 8
I have myself resolv'd upon a course
Which has no need of you. Be gone.
My treasure's in the harbor, take it. O,
I follow'd that I blush to look upon! 12
My very hairs do mutiny, for the white
Reprove the brown for rashness, and they them 14
For fear and doting. Friends, be gone. You shall
Have letters from me to some friends that will
Sweep your way for you. Pray you, look not sad, 17
Nor make replies of loathness; take the hint 18
Which my despair proclaims. Let that be left 19
Which leaves itself. To the sea-side straightway; 20
I will possess you of that ship and treasure.
Leave me, I pray, a little; pray you now,
Nay, do so; for, indeed, I have lost command, 23
Therefore I pray you. I'll see you by and by. 24
Sits down.

Enter Cleopatra led by Charmian, [Iras,] and Eros.

EROS
Nay, gentle madam, to him, comfort him.

IRAS
Do, most dear Queen.

CHARMIAN
Do? Why, what else?

CLEOPATRA
Let me sit down. O Juno!

ANTONY
No, no, no, no, no.

EROS
See you here, sir?

ANTONY
O fie, fie, fie!

CHARMIAN
Madam!

IRAS
Madam, O good Empress!

EROS
Sir, sir!—

ANTONY
Yes, my lord, yes. He at Philippi kept 35
His sword e'en like a dancer, while I struck 36
The lean and wrinkled Cassius; and 'twas I
That the mad Brutus ended. He alone 38
Dealt on lieutenantry, and no practice had 39
In the brave squares of war; yet now—No matter. 40

CLEOPATRA
Ah, stand by.

EROS The Queen, my lord, the Queen.

IRAS
Go to him, madam, speak to him.
He 's unqualitied with very shame. 43

CLEOPATRA
Well then, sustain me. O!

EROS
Most noble sir, arise, the Queen approaches.
Her head's declin'd, and death will seize her, but 46
Your comfort makes the rescue.

ANTONY
I have offended reputation,
A most unnoble swerving.

EROS Sir, the Queen.

29 thereabouts i.e., of that mind, thinking of desertion **31 Peloponnesus** southern Greece (from which Antony then crosses the Mediterranean to Egypt) **32 to 't** to get to it **36 wounded chance** broken fortunes **37 Sits . . . me** i.e., is in opposition to me

III.xi. Location: Alexandria. Cleopatra's palace. (Historically, events such as dispatching the Schoolmaster to Caesar took place in Egypt; however, the dramatic impression of this scene is that it occurs soon after the battle.)
3 lated belated, like a traveler still journeying when night falls **8 shoulders** i.e., backs **12 that** that which **14 they them** i.e., the brown hairs reprove the white **17 Sweep your way** clear your way (to Caesar)

18 loathness unwillingness **19 that** i.e., Antony and his cause **20 leaves** is untrue to, deserts **23 lost command** (1) lost command of myself (2) lost command of my troops and my right to command **24 pray** entreat **35 He** i.e., Octavius. **kept** kept in its sheath **36 e'en . . . dancer** i.e., as though for ornament only, in a dance **38 ended** i.e., defeated. (Not *killed;* Brutus and Cassius committed suicide.) **39 Dealt on lieutenantry** let his subordinates do the fighting **40 brave squares** splendid squadrons, bodies of troops drawn up in square formation **43 unqualitied** dispossessed of his own quality, i.e., not himself **46 but** unless

ANTONY
O, whither hast thou led me, Egypt? See
How I convey my shame out of thine eyes
By looking back what I have left behind
'Stroy'd in dishonor.
CLEOPATRA O my lord, my lord,
Forgive my fearful sails! I little thought
You would have followed.
ANTONY Egypt, thou knew'st too well
My heart was to thy rudder tied by th' strings,
And thou shouldst tow me after. O'er my spirit
Thy full supremacy thou knew'st, and that
Thy beck might from the bidding of the gods
Command me.
CLEOPATRA O, my pardon!
ANTONY Now I must
To the young man send humble treaties, dodge
And palter in the shifts of lowness, who
With half the bulk o' th' world play'd as I pleas'd,
Making and marring fortunes. You did know
How much you were my conqueror, and that
My sword, made weak by my affection, would
Obey it on all cause.
CLEOPATRA Pardon, pardon!
ANTONY
Fall not a tear, I say; one of them rates
All that is won and lost. Give me a kiss. [*Kiss.*]
Even this repays me.—We sent our schoolmaster;
Is 'a come back?—Love, I am full of lead.—
Some wine, within there, and our viands! Fortune
knows
We scorn her most when most she offers blows.
Exeunt.

[SCENE XII]

Enter Caesar, Agrippa, [Thidias,] and Dolabella, with others.

CAESAR
Let him appear that's come from Antony.
Know you him?
DOLABELLA Caesar, 'tis his schoolmaster;
An argument that he is pluck'd, when hither
He sends so poor a pinion of his wing,
Which had superfluous kings for messengers
Not many moons gone by.

Enter Ambassador from Antony.

CAESAR Approach, and speak.
AMBASSADOR
Such as I am, I come from Antony.
I was of late as petty to his ends
As is the morn-dew on the myrtle-leaf
To his grand sea.
CAESAR Be 't so. Declare thine office.
AMBASSADOR
Lord of his fortunes he salutes thee, and
Requires to live in Egypt; which not granted,
He lessens his requests, and to thee sues
To let him breathe between the heavens and earth,
A private man in Athens. This for him.
Next, Cleopatra does confess thy greatness,
Submits her to thy might, and of thee craves
The circle of the Ptolemies for her heirs,
Now hazarded to thy grace.
CAESAR For Antony,
I have no ears to his request. The Queen
Of audience nor desire shall fail, so she
From Egypt drive her all-disgraced friend,
Or take his life there. This if she perform,
She shall not sue unheard. So to them both.
AMBASSADOR
Fortune pursue thee!
CAESAR Bring him through the bands.
[*Exit Ambassador.*]
[*To Thidias*] To try thy eloquence, now 'tis time.
Dispatch.
From Antony win Cleopatra; promise,
And in our name, what she requires; add more,
From thine invention, offers. Women are not
In their best fortunes strong, but want will perjure
The ne'er-touch'd vestal. Try thy cunning, Thidias;
Make thine own edict for thy pains, which we
Will answer as a law.
THIDIAS Caesar, I go.
CAESAR
Observe how Antony becomes his flaw,
And what thou think'st his very action speaks
In every power that moves.
THIDIAS Caesar, I shall. *Exeunt.*

[SCENE XIII]

Enter Cleopatra, Enobarbus, Charmian, and Iras.

CLEOPATRA
What shall we do, Enobarbus?
ENOBARBUS Think, and die.
CLEOPATRA
Is Antony or we in fault for this?
ENOBARBUS
Antony only, that would make his will

50–53 See . . . dishonor i.e., see how I avert my eyes in shame from yours as though looking back on the ruin of my fortunes and honor **61 treaties** entreaties, propositions for settlement **62 palter** use trickery. **shifts of lowness** pitiful evasions used by those lacking power **66 affection** passion **68 Fall** let fall. **rates** equals **70 schoolmaster** (Identified historically as Euphronius, tutor to Antony's children by Cleopatra.)

III.xii. Location: Egypt. Caesar's camp.
4 pinion i.e., pinion-feather, outer feather **5 Which** who

8 petty insignificant compared **10 To . . . sea** compared to its, the dew-drop's, great source, the sea **12 Requires** asks **14 breathe** i.e., live **18 circle** crown **19 hazarded . . . grace** dependent on your favor **21 Of audience** neither of hearing. **so** provided that **25 bands** troops **30 In . . . fortunes** even when at the height of their fortune **32 Make . . . edict** decree your own reward **34 becomes his flaw** bears his misfortune and disgrace (perhaps also suggesting *is transformed into his weakness,* or *makes his fall becoming*) **35 speaks** signifies **36 power that moves** faculty or passion that manifests itself

III.xiii. Location: Alexandria. Cleopatra's palace.
1 Think i.e., take thought on our grievous situation **3 will** desire (especially sexual)

Lord of his reason. What though you fled
From that great face of war, whose several ranges
Frighted each other? Why should he follow?
The itch of his affection should not then
Have nick'd his captainship, at such a point,
When half to half the world oppos'd, he being
The mered question. 'Twas a shame no less
Than was his loss, to course your flying flags,
And leave his navy gazing.

CLEOPATRA Prithee, peace.

Enter the Ambassador with Antony.

ANTONY
Is that his answer?

AMBASSADOR
Ay, my lord.

ANTONY
The Queen shall then have courtesy, so she
Will yield us up.

AMBASSADOR He says so.

ANTONY Let her know 't.
To the boy Caesar send this grizzled head,
And he will fill thy wishes to the brim
With principalities.

CLEOPATRA That head, my lord?

ANTONY
To him again. Tell him he wears the rose
Of youth upon him, from which the world should
note
Something particular. His coin, ships, legions,
May be a coward's, whose ministers would prevail
Under the service of a child as soon
As i' th' command of Caesar. I dare him therefore
To lay his gay comparisons apart,
And answer me declin'd, sword against sword,
Ourselves alone. I'll write it. Follow me.
[*Exeunt Antony and Ambassador.*]

ENOBARBUS [*Aside*]
Yes, like enough, high-battled Caesar will
Unstate his happiness, and be stag'd to th' show
Against a sworder! I see men's judgments are
A parcel of their fortunes, and things outward
Do draw the inward quality after them,
To suffer all alike. That he should dream,
Knowing all measures, the full Caesar will
Answer his emptiness! Caesar, thou hast subdu'd
His judgment too.

Enter a Servant.

SERVANT A messenger from Caesar.

CLEOPATRA
What, no more ceremony? See, my women!
Against the blown rose may they stop their nose
That kneel'd unto the buds.—Admit him, sir.
[*Exit Servant.*]

ENOBARBUS [*Aside*]
Mine honesty and I begin to square.
The loyalty well held to fools does make
Our faith mere folly; yet he that can endure
To follow with allegiance a fall'n lord
Does conquer him that did his master conquer,
And earns a place i' th' story.

Enter Thidias.

CLEOPATRA Caesar's will?

THIDIAS
Hear it apart.

CLEOPATRA None but friends. Say boldly.

THIDIAS
So, haply, are they friends to Antony.

ENOBARBUS
He needs as many, sir, as Caesar has,
Or needs not us. If Caesar please, our master
Will leap to be his friend; for us, you know
Whose he is we are, and that is Caesar's.

THIDIAS So.
Thus then, thou most renown'd: Caesar entreats
Not to consider in what case thou stand'st
Further than he is Caesar.

CLEOPATRA Go on: right royal.

THIDIAS
He knows that you embrace not Antony
As you did love, but as you fear'd him.

CLEOPATRA O!

THIDIAS
The scars upon your honor, therefore, he
Does pity, as constrained blemishes,
Not as deserv'd.

CLEOPATRA He is a god, and knows
What is most right. Mine honor was not yielded,
But conquer'd merely.

ENOBARBUS [*Aside*] To be sure of that,
I will ask Antony. Sir, sir, thou art so leaky
That we must leave thee to thy sinking, for
Thy dearest quit thee. *Exit Enobarbus.*

THIDIAS Shall I say to Caesar
What you require of him? For he partly begs
To be desir'd to give. It much would please him
That of his fortunes you should make a staff
To lean upon; but it would warm his spirits
To hear from me you had left Antony,
And put yourself under his shroud,
The universal landlord.

CLEOPATRA What's your name?

5 ranges ranks, lines (of ships) **8 nick'd** cut short or damaged (from being nicked), or (from gaming) got the better of, since a *nick* was a winning throw in a game of chance **10 mered question** sole ground of quarrel **11 course** pursue (as in hunting) **15 so** provided **22 Something particular** some achievement or exploit of his own **26 gay comparisons** i.e., the wealth and splendor just mentioned (as compared with Antony's poverty); or, the comparisons between them that Caesar makes on the basis of his wealth and power **27 declin'd** i.e., in fortune and in years **29 high-battled** provided with or raised up by noble armies **30 Unstate** depose. **happiness** good fortune. **stag'd** exhibited publicly **31 sworder** one fighting with a sword **32 A parcel of** of a piece with **33 quality** nature **34 To . . . alike** i.e., so that they deteriorate simultaneously **35 Knowing all measures** i.e., knowing how things are weighed in the world

39 blown overblown, starting to decay **41 honesty** (with meaning also of *honor*). **square** quarrel **45 Does . . . conquer** i.e., achieves a moral victory surpassing in honor the military victory of the winner **48 haply** perhaps **49–50 He . . . us** i.e., Antony would need as many followers as Caesar to be a threat to him; otherwise, as things stand, we few would be of no use to him in opposing Caesar and thus are not dangerous **52 Whose . . . Caesar's** i.e., we are Antony's friends, and he is Caesar's, so that we too are Caesar's **54–55 Not . . . Caesar** i.e., not to worry about your situation other than to consider that you are dealing with Caesar, the embodiment of magnanimity **66 require** ask **71 shroud** shelter, protection

THIDIAS
My name is Thidias.
CLEOPATRA Most kind messenger,
Say to great Caesar this in deputation:
I kiss his conqu'ring hand. Tell him I am prompt
To lay my crown at 's feet, and there to kneel.
Tell him, from his all-obeying breath I hear
The doom of Egypt.
THIDIAS 'Tis your noblest course.
Wisdom and fortune combating together,
If that the former dare but what it can,
No chance may shake it. Give me grace to lay
My duty on your hand. [*Kisses her hand.*]
CLEOPATRA
Your Caesar's father oft,
When he hath mus'd of taking kingdoms in,
Bestow'd his lips on that unworthy place,
As it rain'd kisses.

Enter Antony and Enobarbus.

ANTONY Favors? By Jove that thunders!
What art thou, fellow?
THIDIAS One that but performs
The bidding of the fullest man, and worthiest
To have command obey'd.
ENOBARBUS [*Aside*] You will be whipp'd.
ANTONY [*Calling for Servants*]
Approach, there!—Ah, you kite!—Now, gods and devils!
Authority melts from me. Of late, when I cried "Ho!"
Like boys unto a muss, kings would start forth
And cry, "Your will?"—Have you no ears?—I am
Antony yet.

Enter a Servant [*followed by others*].

Take hence this Jack, and whip him.
ENOBARBUS [*Aside*]
'Tis better playing with a lion's whelp
Than with an old one dying.
ANTONY Moon and stars!
Whip him. Were 't twenty of the greatest tributaries
That do acknowledge Caesar, should I find them
So saucy with the hand of she here—what's her name,
Since she was Cleopatra? Whip him, fellows,
Till, like a boy, you see him cringe his face,
And whine aloud for mercy. Take him hence.
THIDIAS
Mark Antony—
ANTONY Tug him away! Being whipp'd,
Bring him again. This Jack of Caesar's shall
Bear us an errand to him.
Exeunt [*Servants*] *with Thidias.*
You were half blasted ere I knew you. Ha?
Have I my pillow left unpress'd in Rome,
Forborne the getting of a lawful race,
And by a gem of women, to be abus'd
By one that looks on feeders?
CLEOPATRA Good my lord—
ANTONY
You have been a boggler ever.
But when we in our viciousness grow hard—
O misery on 't!—the wise gods seel our eyes,
In our own filth drop our clear judgments, make us
Adore our errors, laugh at 's while we strut
To our confusion.
CLEOPATRA O, is 't come to this?
ANTONY
I found you as a morsel cold upon
Dead Caesar's trencher; nay, you were a fragment
Of Cneius Pompey's, besides what hotter hours,
Unregist'red in vulgar fame, you have
Luxuriously pick'd out. For I am sure,
Though you can guess what temperance should be,
You know not what it is.
CLEOPATRA Wherefore is this?
ANTONY
To let a fellow that will take rewards
And say "God quit you!" be familiar with
My playfellow, your hand, this kingly seal
And plighter of high hearts! O, that I were
Upon the hill of Basan, to outroar
The horned herd! For I have savage cause,
And to proclaim it civilly were like
A halter'd neck which does the hangman thank
For being yare about him.

Enter a Servant with Thidias.

Is he whipp'd?
SERVANT
Soundly, my lord.
ANTONY Cried he? And begg'd 'a pardon?
SERVANT
He did ask favor.
ANTONY
If that thy father live, let him repent
Thou wast not made his daughter; and be thou sorry
To follow Caesar in his triumph, since
Thou hast been whipp'd for following him. Henceforth
The white hand of a lady fever thee,
Shake thou to look on 't. Get thee back to Caesar,
Tell him thy entertainment. Look thou say
He makes me angry with him; for he seems
Proud and disdainful, harping on what I am,
Not what he knew I was. He makes me angry,
And at this time most easy 'tis to do 't,

74 in deputation by you as deputy **77 all-obeying** obeyed by all **78 doom of** judgment on, fate of **80 If . . . can** if wisdom dares to do only what it can do (i.e., not the impossible) **86 As** as if **90 kite** a rapacious bird of prey that feeds on ignoble objects. (Said of Cleopatra.) **92 muss** game in which small objects are thrown down to be scrambled for **94 Jack** fellow. (Contemptuous.) **106 blasted** withered, blighted

109 abus'd deceived, betrayed **110 feeders** servants **111 boggler** waverer, shifty person. (Often used of shying horses.) **113 seel** blind. (A term in falconry for sewing shut the eyes of wild hawks in order to tame them.) **118 trencher** wooden plate. **fragment** leftover **120 vulgar fame** common gossip **121 Luxuriously** lustfully **125 quit** reward. (*God quit you* is said obsequiously to acknowledge a tip.) **128 hill of Basan** (Allusion to the strong bulls of Bashan, Psalms 22:12 and 68:15. Antony imagines himself as the greatest horned beast, i.e., cuckold, of that herd.) **132 yare** ready, quick **141 entertainment** reception

When my good stars, that were my former guides,
Have empty left their orbs, and shot their fires
Into th' abysm of hell. If he mislike
My speech and what is done, tell him he has
Hipparchus, my enfranched bondman, whom
He may at pleasure whip, or hang, or torture,
As he shall like, to quit me. Urge it thou.
Hence with thy stripes, begone! *Exit Thidias.*

CLEOPATRA
Have you done yet?

ANTONY
Alack, our terrene moon
Is now eclips'd, and it portends alone
The fall of Antony!

CLEOPATRA
I must stay his time.

ANTONY
To flatter Caesar, would you mingle eyes
With one that ties his points?

CLEOPATRA
Not know me yet?

ANTONY
Cold-hearted toward me?

CLEOPATRA
Ah, dear, if I be so,
From my cold heart let heaven engender hail,
And poison it in the source, and the first stone
Drop in my neck; as it determines, so
Dissolve my life! The next Caesarion smite,
Till by degrees the memory of my womb,
Together with my brave Egyptians all,
By the discandying of this pelleted storm,
Lie graveless, till the flies and gnats of Nile
Have buried them for prey!

ANTONY
I am satisfied.
Caesar sits down in Alexandria, where
I will oppose his fate. Our force by land
Hath nobly held; our sever'd navy too
Have knit again, and fleet, threat'ning most sea-like.
Where hast thou been, my heart? Dost thou hear, lady?
If from the field I shall return once more
To kiss these lips, I will appear in blood;
I and my sword will earn our chronicle.
There's hope in 't yet.

CLEOPATRA
That's my brave lord!

ANTONY
I will be treble-sinew'd, hearted, breath'd,
And fight maliciously. For when mine hours
Were nice and lucky, men did ransom lives
Of me for jests; but now I'll set my teeth,
And send to darkness all that stop me. Come,
Let's have one other gaudy night. Call to me
All my sad captains, fill our bowls once more;
Let's mock the midnight bell.

CLEOPATRA
It is my birthday.
I had thought t' have held it poor; but, since my lord
Is Antony again, I will be Cleopatra.

ANTONY
We will yet do well.

CLEOPATRA
Call all his noble captains to my lord.

ANTONY
Do so, we'll speak to them, and tonight I'll force
The wine peep through their scars. Come on, my queen,
There's sap in 't yet. The next time I do fight,
I'll make Death love me, for I will contend
Even with his pestilent scythe.
Exeunt [*all but Enobarbus*].

ENOBARBUS
Now he'll outstare the lightning. To be furious
Is to be frighted out of fear, and in that mood
The dove will peck the estridge; and I see still
A diminution in our captain's brain
Restores his heart. When valor preys on reason,
It eats the sword it fights with. I will seek
Some way to leave him. *Exit.*

147 orbs spheres **150 Hipparchus** (According to Plutarch, the man was a deserter to Caesar's side.) **enfranched** enfranchised, freed **152 quit** requite, pay back **154 terrene** earthly. **moon** (with an allusion to Cleopatra; she is associated with the moon in V.ii. 240–241) **156 stay his time** i.e., be patient until his fury has subsided **158 his** Caesar's. **points** laces by which articles of clothing were secured **162 determines** comes to an end, dissolves (see l. 166) **164 memory of my womb** i.e., my offspring **166 discandying** melting. **pelleted** falling in pellets **169 sits down in** lays siege to **170 oppose his fate** confront his fortune **172 fleet** float **173 heart** courage **175 in blood** (1) bloody from battle (2) full-spirited **176 chronicle** place in history **181 nice** delicate, fastidious, able to appreciate chivalrous niceties **181–182 men . . . jests** i.e., I allowed enemies to be ransomed for trifles or as a magnanimous gesture **183 to darkness** i.e., to death, the underworld **184 gaudy** festive

198 estridge kind of hawk

[ACT IV • SCENE I]

Enter Caesar, Agrippa, and Maecenas, with his army; Caesar reading a letter.

CAESAR
He calls me boy, and chides as he had power
To beat me out of Egypt. My messenger
He hath whipp'd with rods; dares me to personal combat,
Caesar to Antony. Let the old ruffian know
I have many other ways to die; meantime
Laugh at his challenge.

MAECENAS
Caesar must think,
When one so great begins to rage, he's hunted
Even to falling. Give him no breath, but now
Make boot of his distraction. Never anger
Made good guard for itself.

CAESAR
Let our best heads
Know that tomorrow the last of many battles
We mean to fight. Within our files there are,
Of those that serv'd Mark Antony but late,
Enough to fetch him in. See it done,
And feast the army; we have store to do 't,
And they have earn'd the waste. Poor Antony!
Exeunt.

IV.i. Location: Before Alexandria. Caesar's camp.
9 breath breathing space **10 boot** advantage **11 heads** commanding officers **13 files** (as in *rank and file*) **15 fetch him in** surround, capture him

[SCENE II]

Enter Antony, Cleopatra, Enobarbus, Charmian, Iras, Alexas, with others.

ANTONY
He will not fight with me, Domitius?
ENOBARBUS
No.
ANTONY
Why should he not?
ENOBARBUS
He thinks, being twenty times of better fortune,
He is twenty men to one.
ANTONY Tomorrow, soldier,
By sea and land I'll fight. Or I will live, 6
Or bathe my dying honor in the blood
Shall make it live again. Woo 't thou fight well? 8
ENOBARBUS
I'll strike, and cry "Take all."
ANTONY Well said; come on. 9
Call forth my household servants. Let's tonight
Be bounteous at our meal.

Enter three or four Servitors.

Give me thy hand,
Thou hast been rightly honest—so hast thou—
Thou—and thou—and thou. You have serv'd me well,
And kings have been your fellows.
CLEOPATRA [*Aside to Enobarbus*] What means this? 14
ENOBARBUS [*Aside to Cleopatra*]
'Tis one of those odd tricks which sorrow shoots
Out of the mind.
ANTONY And thou art honest too.
I wish I could be made so many men, 17
And all of you clapp'd up together in 18
An Antony, that I might do you service
So good as you have done.
ALL The gods forbid!
ANTONY
Well, my good fellows, wait on me tonight.
Scant not my cups, and make as much of me
As when mine empire was your fellow too, 23
And suffer'd my command.
CLEOPATRA [*Aside to Enobarbus*] What does he mean? 24
ENOBARBUS [*Aside to Cleopatra*]
To make his followers weep.
ANTONY Tend me tonight;
May be it is the period of your duty. 26
Haply you shall not see me more; or if,
A mangled shadow. Perchance tomorrow
You'll serve another master. I look on you
As one that takes his leave. Mine honest friends,
I turn you not away, but, like a master
Married to your good service, stay till death.
Tend me tonight two hours, I ask no more,
And the gods yield you for 't!
ENOBARBUS What mean you, sir, 34
To give them this discomfort? Look, they weep,
And I, an ass, am onion-ey'd. For shame,
Transform us not to women.
ANTONY Ho, ho, ho!
Now the witch take me, if I meant it thus! 38
Grace grow where those drops fall! My hearty friends, 39
You take me in too dolorous a sense,
For I spake to you for your comfort, did desire you
To burn this night with torches. Know, my hearts,
I hope well of tomorrow, and will lead you
Where rather I'll expect victorious life
Than death and honor. Let's to supper, come,
And drown consideration. *Exeunt.* 46

[SCENE III]

Enter a company of Soldiers.

FIRST SOLDIER
Brother, good night. Tomorrow is the day
SECOND SOLDIER
It will determine one way. Fare you well.
Heard you of nothing strange about the streets?
FIRST SOLDIER
Nothing. What news?
SECOND SOLDIER
Belike 'tis but a rumor. Good night to you.
FIRST SOLDIER
Well, sir, good night.

They meet other Soldiers.

SECOND SOLDIER
Soldiers, have careful watch.
THIRD SOLDIER
And you. Good night, good night.
They place themselves in every corner of the stage.
FOURTH SOLDIER
Here we. And if tomorrow
Our navy thrive, I have an absolute hope
Our landmen will stand up.
THIRD SOLDIER
'Tis a brave army, and full of purpose. 12
Music of the hautboys is under the stage.
SECOND SOLDIER
Peace! What noise?
FIRST SOLDIER
List, list!

IV.ii. Location: Alexandria. Cleopatra's palace.
6 Or either **8 Shall** which shall. **Woo' t** wilt **9 Take all** i.e., winner take all **14 fellows** i.e., fellow servants of me **17 made . . . men** divided into as many men as you are **18 clapp'd up** combined **23 fellow** i.e., fellow servant **24 suffer'd** acknowledged, submitted to **26 period** end

34 yield reward **38 the witch take me** may I be bewitched **39 Grace grow** (1) may rue or herb of grace grow (2) may gracious fortune flourish **46 consideration** thinking, brooding

IV.iii. Location: Alexandria. Before the palace.
12 s.d. hautboys oboes

SECOND SOLDIER
Hark!

FIRST SOLDIER
Music i' th' air.

THIRD SOLDIER
Under the earth.

FOURTH SOLDIER
It signs well, does it not?

THIRD SOLDIER
No.

FIRST SOLDIER
Peace, I say! What should this mean?

SECOND SOLDIER
'Tis the god Hercules, whom Antony lov'd,
Now leaves him.

FIRST SOLDIER
Walk; let's see if other watchmen
Do hear what we do. [*They advance to another post.*]

SECOND SOLDIER
How now, masters?

ALL (*Speak together*)
How now? How now? Do you hear this?

FIRST SOLDIER
Ay; is 't not strange?

THIRD SOLDIER
Do you hear, masters? Do you hear?

FIRST SOLDIER
Follow the noise so far as we have quarter;
Let's see how it will give off.

ALL
Content. 'Tis strange.
Exeunt.

[SCENE IV]

Enter Antony and Cleopatra, with [*Charmian and*] *others* [*attending*].

ANTONY
Eros! Mine armor, Eros!

CLEOPATRA
Sleep a little.

ANTONY
No, my chuck. Eros, come; mine armor, Eros!

Enter Eros [*with armor*].

Come, good fellow, put thine iron on.
If fortune be not ours today, it is
Because we brave her. Come.

CLEOPATRA
Nay, I'll help too.
What's this for? [*She helps to arm him.*]

ANTONY
Ah, let be, let be! Thou art
The armorer of my heart. False, false; this, this.

CLEOPATRA
Sooth, la, I'll help. Thus it must be.

ANTONY
Well, well,
We shall thrive now. Seest thou, my good fellow?
Go put on thy defenses.

EROS
Briefly, sir.

CLEOPATRA
Is not this buckled well?

ANTONY
Rarely, rarely.
He that unbuckles this, till we do please
To daff 't for our repose, shall hear a storm.
Thou fumblest, Eros; and my queen's a squire
More tight at this than thou. Dispatch. O love,
That thou couldst see my wars today, and knew'st
The royal occupation! Thou shouldst see
A workman in 't.

Enter an armed Soldier.

Good morrow to thee; welcome.
Thou look'st like him that knows a warlike charge.
To business that we love we rise betime,
And go to 't with delight.

SOLDIER
A thousand, sir,
Early though 't be, have on their riveted trim,
And at the port expect you. *Shout. Trumpets flourish.*

Enter Captains and Soldiers.

CAPTAIN
The morn is fair. Good morrow, general.

ALL
Good morrow, general.

ANTONY
'Tis well blown, lads.
This morning, like the spirit of a youth
That means to be of note, begins betimes.
So, so; come, give me that. This way. Well said.
Fare thee well, dame, whate'er becomes of me.
This is a soldier's kiss. Rebukable [*Kisses her.*]
And worthy shameful check it were, to stand
On more mechanic compliment. I'll leave thee
Now, like a man of steel. You that will fight,
Follow me close; I'll bring you to 't. Adieu.
Exeunt [*Antony, Eros, Captains, and Soldiers*].

CHARMIAN
Please you, retire to your chamber.

CLEOPATRA
Lead me.
He goes forth gallantly. That he and Caesar might
Determine this great war in single fight!
Then, Antony—but now—Well, on. *Exeunt.*

[SCENE V]

Trumpets sound. Enter Antony and Eros; [*a Soldier meeting them*].

SOLDIER
The gods make this a happy day to Antony!

ANTONY
Would thou and those thy scars had once prevail'd

18 signs well is a good sign **28 as we have quarter** as our watch post extends **29 give off** cease

IV.iv. Location: Alexandria. The palace.
2 chuck (A term of endearment.) **3 thine iron** i.e., my armor that you have there. (Or perhaps he is telling Eros to arm.) **5 brave** defy **7 False** wrong

10 defenses armor **11 Rarely** excellently **13 daff 't** doff it, take it off **15 tight** deft, skillful. **Dispatch** finish up **19 charge** duty, responsibility **20 betime** betimes, early **22 riveted trim** i.e., armor **23 port** gate **25 'Tis well blown** i.e., the morning begins well; or, refers to trumpets in l. 23 **28 said** done **31 check** reproof **31–32 stand On** be particular about, insist on **32 mechanic** dwelling on technicalities; vulgar. **compliment** exchange of courtesies

IV.v. Location: Alexandria. Antony's camp.
2 once formerly

To make me fight at land!

SOLDIER
Hadst thou done so,
The kings that have revolted, and the soldier
That has this morning left thee, would have still
Follow'd thy heels.

ANTONY
Who's gone this morning?

SOLDIER
Who?
One ever near thee. Call for Enobarbus,
He shall not hear thee, or from Caesar's camp
Say "I am none of thine."

ANTONY
What sayest thou?

SOLDIER
Sir,
He is with Caesar.

EROS
Sir, his chests and treasure
He has not with him.

ANTONY
Is he gone?

SOLDIER
Most certain.

ANTONY
Go, Eros, send his treasure after; do it.
Detain no jot, I charge thee. Write to him—
I will subscribe—gentle adieus and greetings; 14
Say that I wish he never find more cause
To change a master. O, my fortunes have
Corrupted honest men! Dispatch.—Enobarbus!
Exit [*with Eros and Soldier*].

[SCENE VI]

Flourish. Enter Agrippa, Caesar, with Enobarbus, and Dolabella.

CAESAR
Go forth, Agrippa, and begin the fight.
Our will is Antony be took alive;
Make it so known.

AGRIPPA
Caesar, I shall. [*Exit.*]

CAESAR
The time of universal peace is near. 5
Prove this a prosp'rous day, the three-nook'd world 6
Shall bear the olive freely.

Enter a Messenger.

MESSENGER
Antony
Is come into the field.

CAESAR
Go charge Agrippa
Plant those that have revolted in the vant, 9
That Antony may seem to spend his fury
Upon himself. *Exeunt* [*all but Enobarbus*].

ENOBARBUS
Alexas did revolt, and went to Jewry on
Affairs of Antony; there did dissuade 13
Great Herod to incline himself to Caesar,
And leave his master Antony. For this pains
Caesar hath hang'd him. Canidius and the rest
That fell away have entertainment, but 17
No honorable trust. I have done ill,
Of which I do accuse myself so sorely
That I will joy no more.

Enter a Soldier of Caesar's.

SOLDIER
Enobarbus, Antony
Hath after thee sent all thy treasure, with
His bounty overplus. The messenger
Came on my guard, and at thy tent is now 23
Unloading of his mules.

ENOBARBUS
I give it you.

SOLDIER
Mock not, Enobarbus.
I tell you true. Best you saf'd the bringer 26
Out of the host; I must attend mine office, 27
Or would have done 't myself. Your emperor
Continues still a Jove. *Exit.*

ENOBARBUS
I am alone the villain of the earth,
And feel I am so most. O Antony, 31
Thou mine of bounty, how wouldst thou have paid
My better service, when my turpitude
Thou dost so crown with gold! This blows my heart. 34
If swift thought break it not, a swifter mean 35
Shall outstrike thought; but thought will do 't, I feel. 36
I fight against thee? No, I will go seek
Some ditch wherein to die. The foul'st best fits
My latter part of life. *Exit.*

[SCENE VII]

Alarum. Drums and trumpets. Enter Agrippa [*and others*].

AGRIPPA
Retire, we have engag'd ourselves too far.
Caesar himself has work, and our oppression 2
Exceeds what we expected. *Exit* [*with soldiers*].

Alarums. Enter Antony, and Scarus wounded.

SCARUS
O my brave Emperor, this is fought indeed!
Had we done so at first, we had droven them home
With clouts about their heads.

ANTONY
Thou bleed'st apace. 6

SCARUS
I had a wound here that was like a T,
But now 'tis made an H. [*Sound retreat*] *far off.*

ANTONY
They do retire. 8

14 subscribe sign

IV.vi. Location: Alexandria. Caesar's camp.
5 The . . . near (The Renaissance identified Octavius Caesar, or the Emperor Augustus as he was subsequently titled, with this *Pax Romana,* peace under the Roman Empire.) **6 three-nook'd** three-cornered. (Refers to Asia, Europe, and Africa.) **9 vant** vanguard, front lines **13 dissuade** i.e., from following Antony

17 entertainment employment, maintenance **23 on my guard** while I was standing guard **26 Best you saf'd** it would be best for you to provide safe-conduct for **27 host** army **31 And . . . most** and am the one who feels it most **34 blows** causes to swell to the bursting point **35 mean** i.e., suicide **36 do 't** i.e., break my heart

IV.vii. Location: Field of battle between the camps.
2 our oppression the heavy attacks against us **6 clouts** bandages, or blows and knocks **8 H** i.e., the bottom of the *T* has been cut across to make an H lying on its side. (There is a pun on *ache,* pronounced *aitch.*)

SCARUS
We'll beat 'em into bench-holes. I have yet 9
Room for six scotches more. 10

Enter Eros.

EROS
They are beaten, sir, and our advantage serves
For a fair victory.

SCARUS Let us score their backs,
And snatch 'em up, as we take hares, behind!
'Tis sport to maul a runner.

ANTONY I will reward thee
Once for thy spritely comfort, and tenfold
For thy good valor. Come thee on.

SCARUS
I'll halt after. *Exeunt.* 17

[SCENE VIII]

Alarum. Enter Antony again in a march; Scarus, with others.

ANTONY
We have beat him to his camp. Run one before,
And let the Queen know of our gests. Tomorrow, 2
Before the sun shall see 's, we'll spill the blood
That has today escap'd. I thank you all,
For doughty-handed are you, and have fought
Not as you serv'd the cause, but as 't had been 6
Each man's like mine; you have shown all Hectors. 7
Enter the city, clip your wives, your friends, 8
Tell them your feats, whilst they with joyful tears
Wash the congealment from your wounds, and kiss
The honor'd gashes whole.

Enter Cleopatra [attended].

[*To Scarus.*] Give me thy hand;
To this great fairy I'll commend thy acts, 12
Make her thanks bless thee. [*To Cleopatra.*] O thou
day o' th' world, 13
Chain mine arm'd neck; leap thou, attire and all,
Through proof of harness to my heart, and there 15
Ride on the pants triumphing! [*They embrace.*]

CLEOPATRA Lord of lords! 16
O infinite virtue, com'st thou smiling from 17
The world's great snare uncaught?

ANTONY My nightingale,
We have beat them to their beds. What, girl!
Though grey
Do something mingle with our younger brown, yet
ha' we
A brain that nourishes our nerves, and can 21
Get goal for goal of youth. Behold this man; 22
Commend unto his lips thy favoring hand.—
Kiss it, my warrior. [*Scarus kisses Cleopatra's hand.*]—He hath fought today
As if a god, in hate of mankind, had
Destroy'd in such a shape.

CLEOPATRA I'll give thee, friend,
An armor all of gold; it was a king's.

ANTONY
He has deserv'd it, were it carbuncled 28
Like holy Phoebus' car. Give me thy hand. 29
Through Alexandria make a jolly march;
Bear our hack'd targets like the men that owe them. 31
Had our great palace the capacity
To camp this host, we all would sup together,
And drink carouses to the next day's fate,
Which promises royal peril. Trumpeters,
With brazen din blast you the city's ear,
Make mingle with our rattling taborines,
That heaven and earth may strike their sounds
together,
Applauding our approach. [*Trumpets sound.*] *Exeunt.*

[SCENE IX]

Enter a Sentry and his company. Enobarbus follows.

SENTRY
If we be not reliev'd within this hour,
We must return to th' court of guard. The night 2
Is shiny, and they say we shall embattle 3
By th' second hour i' th' morn.

FIRST WATCH
This last day was a shrewd one to 's. 5

ENOBARBUS
O, bear me witness, night—

SECOND WATCH
What man is this?

FIRST WATCH
Stand close, and list him. 8

ENOBARBUS
Be witness to me, O thou blessed moon,
When men revolted shall upon record
Bear hateful memory, poor Enobarbus did
Before thy face repent!

SENTRY
Enobarbus?

SECOND WATCH
Peace! Hark further.

ENOBARBUS
O sovereign mistress of true melancholy, 15

9 bench-holes the holes of privies, i.e., any desperate place to hide **10 scotches** cuts **17 halt** limp

IV.viii. Location: Before Alexandria. The action is virtually continuous.
2 gests deeds **6 as . . . as 't** as if . . . as if it **7 shown** shown yourselves **8 clip** embrace **12 fairy** i.e., fairy queen (?) **13 day** i.e., sun; or, span, time of existence (? i.e., the world exists through her) **15 proof of harness** proof-armor, tested armor **16 pants** heartbeats **17 virtue** valor **21 nerves** sinews, tendons

22 Get . . . of i.e., stay competitively equal with. **this man** i.e., Scarus **28 carbuncled** set with carbuncles **29 Phoebus' car** the chariot of the sun **31 targets** shields. **like** as becomes. **owe** own

IV.ix. Location: Caesar's camp.
2 court of guard guardroom **3 embattle** fall in for the combat **5 shrewd** malignant **8 close** concealed **15 mistress . . . melancholy** i.e., the moon, so addressed because of her supposed influence in causing lunacy

The poisonous damp of night disponge upon me, 16
That life, a very rebel to my will,
May hang no longer on me. Throw my heart
Against the flint and hardness of my fault,
Which, being dried with grief, will break to powder, 20
And finish all foul thoughts. O Antony,
Nobler than my revolt is infamous,
Forgive me in thine own particular, 23
But let the world rank me in register
A master-leaver and a fugitive.
O Antony! O Antony! [*Dies.*]

FIRST WATCH
Let's speak to him.

SENTRY
Let's hear him, for the things he speaks
May concern Caesar.

SECOND WATCH Let's do so. But he sleeps.

SENTRY
Swoons rather, for so bad a prayer as his
Was never yet for sleep.

FIRST WATCH Go we to him.

SECOND WATCH
Awake, sir, awake. Speak to us.

FIRST WATCH
Hear you, sir?

SENTRY The hand of death hath raught him. 33
(*Drums afar off.*)
Hark, the drums demurely wake the sleepers. 34
Let us bear him to th' court of guard; he is of note.
Our hour is fully out.

SECOND WATCH
Come on, then; he may recover yet.
Exeunt [*with the body*].

[SCENE X]

Enter Antony and Scarus, with their Army.

ANTONY
Their preparation is today by sea;
We please them not by land.

SCARUS For both, my lord.

ANTONY
I would they'd fight i' th' fire or i' th' air;
We'd fight there too. But this it is: our foot 4
Upon the hills adjoining to the city
Shall stay with us—order for sea is given;
They have put forth the haven— 7
Where their appointment we may best discover, 8
And look on their endeavor. *Exeunt.*

[SCENE XI]

Enter Caesar, and his Army.

CAESAR
But being charg'd, we will be still by land, 1
Which, as I take 't, we shall; for his best force
Is forth to man his galleys. To the vales,
And hold our best advantage. *Exeunt.*

[SCENE XII]

Enter Antony and Scarus.

ANTONY
Yet they are not join'd. Where yond pine does stand,
I shall discover all. I'll bring thee word
Straight how 'tis like to go. *Exit.*

SCARUS Swallows have built
In Cleopatra's sails their nests. The augurers
Say they know not, they cannot tell, look grimly,
And dare not speak their knowledge. Antony
Is valiant, and dejected, and by starts
His fretted fortunes give him hope and fear 8
Of what he has, and has not.
Alarum afar off, as at a sea-fight.

Enter Antony.

ANTONY All is lost!
This foul Egyptian hath betrayed me.
My fleet hath yielded to the foe, and yonder
They cast their caps up and carouse together
Like friends long lost. Triple-turn'd whore! 'Tis thou 13
Hast sold me to this novice, and my heart
Makes only wars on thee. Bid them all fly;
For when I am reveng'd upon my charm, 16
I have done all. Bid them all fly; begone.
[*Exit Scarus.*]
O sun, thy uprise shall I see no more.
Fortune and Antony part here; even here
Do we shake hands. All come to this? The hearts
That spaniel'd me at heels, to whom I gave 21
Their wishes, do discandy, melt their sweets 22
On blossoming Caesar; and this pine is bark'd, 23
That overtopp'd them all. Betray'd I am.
O this false soul of Egypt! This grave charm, 25
Whose eye beck'd forth my wars, and call'd them home, 26
Whose bosom was my crownet, my chief end, 27

16 disponge pour down (as from a squeezed sponge) **20 Which** i.e., the heart. **dried with grief** (Elizabethans thought that the spirits of a man in Enobarbus' state of mind would descend into his bowels, leaving his heart dry.) **23 in . . . particular** in your own person **33 raught** reached **34 demurely** with subdued sound

IV.x. Location: The field of battle.
4 foot foot soldiers **7 forth** forth from **8 appointment** disposition of forces

IV.xi. Location: The field of battle.
1 But being unless we are. **still** inactive

IV.xii. Location: The field of battle.
8 fretted worn away **13 Triple-turn'd** three times faithless (to Julius Caesar, Cneius Pompey, and now Antony) **16 charm** practicer of charms or spells **21 spaniel'd** fawned upon like a spaniel **22 discandy** melt, dissolve **23 bark'd** stripped of its bark and thus killed **25 This grave charm** i.e., this sorceress who has heavy or fatal spells **26 beck'd** beckoned **27 crownet** coronet. **end** aim

Like a right gipsy, hath at fast and loose
Beguil'd me to the very heart of loss.
What, Eros, Eros!

Enter Cleopatra.

Ah, thou spell! Avaunt!

CLEOPATRA
Why is my lord enrag'd against his love?

ANTONY
Vanish, or I shall give thee thy deserving,
And blemish Caesar's triumph. Let him take thee,
And hoist thee up to the shouting plebeians!
Follow his chariot, like the greatest spot
Of all thy sex; most monster-like, be shown
For poor'st diminutives, for dolts, and let
Patient Octavia plough thy visage up
With her prepared nails. *Exit Cleopatra.*
'Tis well th' art gone,
If it be well to live; but better 'twere
Thou fell'st into my fury, for one death
Might have prevented many. Eros, ho!
The shirt of Nessus is upon me. Teach me,
Alcides, thou mine ancestor, thy rage.
Let me lodge Lichas on the horns o' th' moon,
And with those hands, that grasp'd the heaviest club,
Subdue my worthiest self. The witch shall die.
To the young Roman boy she hath sold me, and I fall
Under this plot. She dies for 't. Eros, ho! *Exit.*

[SCENE XIII]

Enter Cleopatra, Charmian, Iras, [*and*] *Mardian.*

CLEOPATRA
Help me, my women! O, he's more mad
Than Telamon for his shield; the boar of Thessaly
Was never so emboss'd.

CHARMIAN To th' monument!
There lock yourself, and send him word you are dead.
The soul and body rive not more in parting
Than greatness going off.

CLEOPATRA To th' monument!
Mardian, go tell him I have slain myself;

28 right veritable. **fast and loose** a cheating game **30 spell** enchantment, spell-maker (?) **Avaunt** be gone **33 triumph** triumphal procession (in Rome) **35 spot** blemish, disgrace **36 shown** exhibited **37 diminutives** undersized creatures, i.e., the populace **42 many** i.e., many experiences like death through shame, fear, etc. (?) or many other killings through Antony's rage (?) **43–45 Nessus, Alcides, Lichas** (When Hercules or *Alcides* had fatally wounded the centaur *Nessus* for trying to rape Hercules' wife Deianira, Nessus vengefully gave his blood-soaked shirt to Deianira as a supposed love-charm for her husband. The poison gave Hercules such agony that he cast his page *Lichas* into the air.)

IV.xiii. Location: Alexandria. Near Cleopatra's palace (? This scene appears to follow scene xii closely. The sense of location is very fluid, and it is not clear where the end of xii takes place.)
2 Telamon Ajax Telamon, who after the capture of Troy went mad and slew himself when he was not awarded the shield and armor of Achilles. **boar of Thessaly** the boar sent by Diana or Artemis to ravage the fields of Calydon, and slain by Meleager **3 emboss'd** foaming at the mouth from rage. **monument** tomb built in anticipation of Cleopatra's death **5 rive** split, sever **6 going off** i.e., bidding farewell to its glory

Say, that the last I spoke was "Antony,"
And word it, prithee, piteously. Hence, Mardian,
And bring me how he takes my death. To th' monument! *Exeunt.*

[SCENE XIV]

Enter Antony and Eros.

ANTONY
Eros, thou yet behold'st me?

EROS Ay, noble lord.

ANTONY
Sometime we see a cloud that's dragonish,
A vapor sometime like a bear or lion,
A tower'd citadel, a pendant rock,
A forked mountain, or blue promontory
With trees upon 't that nod unto the world
And mock our eyes with air. Thou hast seen these signs,
They are black vesper's pageants.

EROS Ay, my lord.

ANTONY
That which is now a horse, even with a thought
The rack dislimns, and makes it indistinct,
As water is in water.

EROS It does, my lord.

ANTONY
My good knave Eros, now thy captain is
Even such a body. Here I am Antony,
Yet cannot hold this visible shape, my knave.
I made these wars for Egypt, and the Queen,
Whose heart I thought I had, for she had mine—
Which whilst it was mine had annex'd unto 't
A million moe, now lost—she, Eros, has
Pack'd cards with Caesar, and false-play'd my glory
Unto an enemy's triumph.
Nay, weep not, gentle Eros; there is left us
Ourselves to end ourselves.

Enter Mardian.

O, thy vile lady!
She has robb'd me of my sword.

MARDIAN No, Antony,
My mistress lov'd thee, and her fortunes mingled
With thine entirely.

ANTONY Hence, saucy eunuch; peace!
She hath betray'd me and shall die the death.

MARDIAN
Death of one person can be paid but once,
And that she has discharg'd. What thou wouldst do
Is done unto thy hand. The last she spake
Was "Antony, most noble Antony!"

IV.xiv. Location: Alexandria. Near Cleopatra's palace (? See location of scene xiii; again, the sense of time is immediate and the place fluid.)
8 black vesper's pageants i.e., shows heralding the approach of night **10 rack** floating vapor or cloud. **dislimns** effaces **12 knave** boy **18 moe** more **19 Pack'd cards** i.e., stacked the deck. **false-play'd** falsely played away **20 triumph** (1) victory (2) trump card **23 sword** i.e., prowess as a soldier, masculinity **27 of** by **29 unto thy hand** for you

Then in the midst a tearing groan did break
The name of Antony; it was divided
Between her heart and lips. She rend'red life,
Thy name so buried in her.

ANTONY Dead, then?

MARDIAN Dead.

ANTONY
Unarm, Eros. The long day's task is done,
And we must sleep. [*To Mardian.*] That thou
depart'st hence safe
Does pay thy labor richly; go. *Exit Mardian.*
Off, pluck off! [*Eros unarms him.*]
The sevenfold shield of Ajax cannot keep
The battery from my heart. O, cleave, my sides!
Heart, once be stronger than thy continent,
Crack thy frail case! Apace, Eros, apace.
No more a soldier. Bruised pieces, go;
You have been nobly borne.—From me awhile.
Exit Eros.
I will o'ertake thee, Cleopatra, and
Weep for my pardon. So it must be, for now
All length is torture; since the torch is out,
Lie down, and stray no farther. Now all labor
Mars what it does; yea, very force entangles
Itself with strength. Seal then, and all is done.
Eros!—I come, my queen.—Eros!—Stay for me.
Where souls do couch on flowers, we'll hand in
hand,
And with our sprightly port make the ghosts gaze.
Dido and her Aeneas shall want troops,
And all the haunt be ours.—Come, Eros, Eros!

Enter Eros.

EROS
What would my lord?

ANTONY Since Cleopatra died
I have liv'd in such dishonor that the gods
Detest my baseness. I, that with my sword
Quarter'd the world, and o'er green Neptune's back
With ships made cities, condemn myself to lack
The courage of a woman—less noble mind
Than she which by her death our Caesar tells
"I am conqueror of myself." Thou art sworn, Eros,
That, when the exigent should come, which now
Is come indeed, when I should see behind me
Th' inevitable prosecution of
Disgrace and horror, that, on my command,
Thou then wouldst kill me. Do 't, the time is come.
Thou strik'st not me, 'tis Caesar thou defeat'st.
Put color in thy cheek.

EROS The gods withhold me!
Shall I do that which all the Parthian darts,
Though enemy, lost aim and could not?

ANTONY Eros,
Wouldst thou be window'd in great Rome and see
Thy master thus with pleach'd arms, bending down
His corrigible neck, his face subdu'd
To penetrative shame, whilst the wheel'd seat
Of fortunate Caesar, drawn before him, branded
His baseness that ensu'd?

EROS I would not see 't.

ANTONY
Come, then; for with a wound I must be cur'd.
Draw that thy honest sword, which thou hast worn
Most useful for thy country.

EROS O, sir, pardon me!

ANTONY
When I did make thee free, swor'st thou not then
To do this when I bade thee? Do it at once;
Or thy precedent services are all
But accidents unpurpos'd. Draw, and come.

EROS
Turn from me, then, that noble countenance,
Wherein the worship of the whole world lies.

ANTONY
Lo thee! [*Turns from him.*]

EROS
My sword is drawn.

ANTONY Then let it do at once
That thing why thou hast drawn it.

EROS My dear master,
My captain, and my emperor, let me say,
Before I strike this bloody stroke, farewell.

ANTONY
'Tis said, man; and farewell.

EROS
Farewell, great chief. Shall I strike now?

ANTONY Now, Eros.

EROS (*Kills himself*)
Why, there then! Thus I do escape the sorrow
Of Antony's death.

ANTONY Thrice-nobler than myself!
Thou teachest me, O valiant Eros, what
I should, and thou couldst not. My queen and Eros
Have by their brave instruction got upon me
A nobleness in record. But I will be
A bridegroom in my death, and run into 't
As to a lover's bed. Come, then; and, Eros,
Thy master dies thy scholar. To do thus
[*Falls on his sword.*]
I learn'd of thee. How, not dead? Not dead?
The guard, ho! O, dispatch me!

Enter [Dercetas and] a [Company of the] Guard.

FIRST GUARD What's the noise?

32–33 it . . . lips i.e., she half-groaned Antony's name and then her heart groaned as she died **33 rend'red** gave up **38 sevenfold** with seven thicknesses. (The shield of Ajax was of brass reinforced with seven thicknesses of oxhide.) **39 battery** battering, bombardment **40 thy continent** that which contains you **46 length** length of life **49 with strength** i.e., with its own strength. **Seal** finish the business (as in sealing a letter) **51 couch** lie (here, in the Elysian fields) **52 port** bearing **53 Dido . . . troops** i.e., Antony and Cleopatra will be the most distinguished lovers in the Elysian fields, outshining even the Queen of Carthage and her famous lover. (In the *Aeneid,* Aeneas deserts Dido in order to found Rome, putting public good ahead of private passion as Antony does not. Dido scorns Aeneas when they meet in the underworld; Antony imagines them in the Elysian fields.) **want troops** lack followers **59 With . . . cities** i.e., assembled flotillas as dense and populous as cities. **to lack** for lacking **63 exigent** exigency, compelling need **65 prosecution** pursuit

72 window'd placed in a window to look on **73 pleach'd** folded **74 corrigible** submissive to correction **75 penetrative** penetrating **76–77 branded . . . ensu'd** rendered conspicuous as by a brand the shame of him that followed **83 precedent** former **84 accidents unpurpos'd** events leading to no purpose **98–99 got . . . record** won a noble place in history before I have

ANTONY
I have done my work ill, friends. O, make an end
Of what I have begun.
SECOND GUARD The star is fall'n.
FIRST GUARD
And time is at his period.
ALL Alas, and woe!
ANTONY
Let him that loves me strike me dead.
FIRST GUARD Not I.
SECOND GUARD
Nor I.
THIRD GUARD
Nor anyone. *Exeunt [Guard].*
DERCETAS
Thy death and fortunes bid thy followers fly.
This sword but shown to Caesar, with this tidings,
Shall enter me with him. [*Takes up Antony's sword.*]

Enter Diomedes.

DIOMEDES Where's Antony?
DERCETAS
There, Diomed, there.
DIOMEDES
Lives he? Wilt thou not answer, man?
[*Exit Dercetas.*]
ANTONY
Art thout here, Diomed? Draw thy sword, and give me
Sufficing strokes for death.
DIOMEDES Most absolute lord,
My mistress Cleopatra sent me to thee.
ANTONY
When did she send thee?
DIOMEDES Now, my lord.
ANTONY Where is she?
DIOMEDES
Lock'd in her monument. She had a prophesying fear
Of what hath come to pass. For when she saw—
Which never shall be found—you did suspect
She had dispos'd with Caesar, and that your rage
Would not be purg'd, she sent you word she was dead;
But, fearing since how it might work, hath sent
Me to proclaim the truth, and I am come,
I dread, too late.
ANTONY
Too late, good Diomed. Call my guard, I prithee.
DIOMEDES
What, ho, the Emperor's guard! The guard, what, ho!
Come, your lord calls!

Enter four or five of the Guard of Antony.

ANTONY
Bear me, good friends, where Cleopatra bides;
'Tis the last service that I shall command you.
FIRST GUARD
Woe, woe are we, sir, you may not live to wear
All your true followers out.
ALL Most heavy day!
ANTONY
Nay, good my fellows, do not please sharp fate
To grace it with your sorrows. Bid that welcome
Which comes to punish us, and we punish it,
Seeming to bear it lightly. Take me up.
I have led you oft; carry me now, good friends,
And have my thanks for all. *Exeunt, bearing Antony.*

[SCENE XV]

Enter Cleopatra, and her maids aloft, with Charmian and Iras.

CLEOPATRA
O Charmian, I will never go from hence.
CHARMIAN
Be comforted, dear madam.
CLEOPATRA No, I will not.
All strange and terrible events are welcome,
But comforts we despise; our size of sorrow,
Proportion'd to our cause, must be as great
As that which makes it.

Enter [below] Diomedes.

How now, is he dead?
DIOMEDES
His death's upon him, but not dead.
Look out o' th' other side your monument;
His guard have brought him thither.

Enter [below] Antony, and the Guard [bearing him].

CLEOPATRA
O sun,
Burn the great sphere thou mov'st in! Darkling stand
The varying shore o' th' world. O Antony,
Antony, Antony! Help, Charmian, help, Iras, help;
Help, friends below. Let's draw him hither.
ANTONY Peace!
Not Caesar's valor hath o'erthrown Antony,
But Antony's hath triumph'd on itself.
CLEOPATRA
So it should be, that none but Antony
Should conquer Antony; but woe 'tis so!
ANTONY
I am dying, Egypt, dying; only
I here importune death awhile, until
Of many thousand kisses the poor last
I lay upon thy lips.
CLEOPATRA I dare not, dear—

107 his period its end **113 enter . . . him** admit me to his service, put me in his good graces **123 dispos'd with** come to terms with

136 To grace by gracing or honoring

IV.xv. Location: Alexandria. Cleopatra's monument.
11 Darkling in darkness **20 importune** i.e., beg a delay of **22 I dare not** i.e., come down to Antony

Dear my lord, pardon—I dare not,
Lest I be taken. Not th' imperious show
Of the full-fortun'd Caesar ever shall
Be brooch'd with me; if knife, drugs, serpents, have
Edge, sting, or operation, I am safe.
Your wife Octavia, with her modest eyes
And still conclusion, shall acquire no honor
Demuring upon me. But come, come, Antony—
Help me, my women—we must draw thee up.
Assist, good friends.

ANTONY
O, quick, or I am gone.

CLEOPATRA
Here's sport indeed! How heavy weighs my lord!
Our strength is all gone into heaviness,
That makes the weight. Had I great Juno's power,
The strong-wing'd Mercury should fetch thee up,
And set thee by Jove's side. Yet come a little—
Wishers were ever fools—O, come, come, come;

They heave Antony aloft to Cleopatra.

And welcome, welcome! Die when thou hast liv'd,
Quicken with kissing. Had my lips that power,
Thus would I wear them out. [*Kisses him.*]

ALL
A heavy sight!

ANTONY
I am dying, Egypt, dying.
Give me some wine, and let me speak a little.

CLEOPATRA
No, let me speak; and let me rail so high,
That the false huswife Fortune break her wheel,
Provok'd by my offense.

ANTONY
One word, sweet Queen:
Of Caesar seek your honor, with your safety. O!

CLEOPATRA
They do not go together.

ANTONY
Gentle, hear me.
None about Caesar trust but Proculeius.

CLEOPATRA
My resolution and my hands I'll trust;
None about Caesar.

ANTONY
The miserable change now at my end
Lament nor sorrow at. But please your thoughts
In feeding them with those my former fortunes
Wherein I liv'd, the greatest prince o' th' world,
The noblest, and do now not basely die,
Not cowardly put off my helmet to
My countryman—a Roman by a Roman
Valiantly vanquish'd. Now my spirit is going;
I can no more.

CLEOPATRA
Noblest of men, woo 't die?
Hast thou no care of me? Shall I abide
In this dull world, which in thy absence is
No better than a sty? O, see, my women,

[*Antony dies.*]

The crown o' th' earth doth melt. My lord!
O, wither'd is the garland of the war,
The soldier's pole is fall'n! Young boys and girls
Are level now with men; the odds is gone,
And there is nothing left remarkable
Beneath the visiting moon. [*Faints.*]

CHARMIAN
O, quietness, lady!

IRAS
She's dead too, our sovereign.

CHARMIAN
Lady!

IRAS
Madam!

CHARMIAN
O madam, madam, madam!

IRAS
Royal Egypt, Empress!

CHARMIAN
Peace, peace, Iras!

CLEOPATRA [*Reviving*]
No more but e'en a woman, and commanded
By such poor passion as the maid that milks
And does the meanest chares. It were for me
To throw my scepter at the injurious gods,
To tell them that this world did equal theirs
Till they had stol'n our jewel. All's but naught;
Patience is sottish, and impatience does
Become a dog that's mad. Then is it sin
To rush into the secret house of death,
Ere death dare come to us? How do you, women?
What, what, good cheer! Why, how now,
Charmian!
My noble girls! Ah, women, women, look,
Our lamp is spent, it's out! Good sirs, take heart.
We'll bury him; and then, what's brave, what's
noble,
Let's do 't after the high Roman fashion,
And make death proud to take us. Come, away.
This case of that huge spirit now is cold.
Ah, women, women! Come; we have no friend
But resolution, and the briefest end.

Exeunt, [those above] bearing off Antony's body.

[ACT V • SCENE I]

Enter Caesar, Agrippa, Dolabella, Maecenas, [Gallus, Proculeius,] with his council of war.

CAESAR
Go to him, Dolabella, bid him yield;
Being so frustrate, tell him he mocks
The pauses that he makes.

DOLABELLA
Caesar, I shall. [*Exit.*]

Enter Dercetas, with the sword of Antony.

24 imperious show imperial triumphal procession **26 brooch'd** adorned (as with a brooch) **29 still conclusion** silent aim or judgment **30 Demuring** looking demurely **34 heaviness** (1) sadness (2) weight **38 Wishers . . . fools** i.e., we wish for unattainable things **40 Quicken** revive **45 huswife** hussy, wanton **46 offense** offensive speech **60 woo 't** wilt thou

66 pole polestar, on which men orient themselves (?) banner or standard (?) **67 odds** distinctive quality or measure, or perhaps the quality distinguishing one thing from another **75 chares** chores, drudgery. **were** would be fitting **79–80 Patience . . . mad** i.e., patience is for fools, and impatience is for the mad; both are useless here **85 Good sirs** (Addressed to the women.)

V.i. Location: Alexandria. Caesar's camp.
2 frustrate helpless, baffled **2–3 mocks . . . makes** makes himself ridiculous by his delays (in yielding)

CAESAR
Wherefore is that? And what art thou that dar'st
Appear thus to us?

DERCETAS I am call'd Dercetas.
Mark Antony I serv'd, who best was worthy
Best to be serv'd. Whilst he stood up and spoke,
He was my master, and I wore my life
To spend upon his haters. If thou please
To take me to thee, as I was to him
I'll be to Caesar; if thou pleasest not,
I yield thee up my life.

CAESAR What is 't thou say'st?

DERCETAS
I say, O Caesar, Antony is dead.

CAESAR
The breaking of so great a thing should make
A greater crack. The round world
Should have shook lions into civil streets,
And citizens to their dens. The death of Antony
Is not a single doom; in the name lay
A moi'ty of the world.

DERCETAS He is dead, Caesar,
Not by a public minister of justice,
Nor by a hired knife, but that self hand
Which writ his honor in the acts it did
Hath, with the courage which the heart did lend it,
Splitted the heart. This is his sword;
I robb'd his wound of it. Behold it stain'd
With his most noble blood. [*Offers sword.*]

CAESAR Look you, sad friends;
The gods rebuke me, but it is tidings
To wash the eyes of kings.

AGRIPPA And strange it is
That nature must compel us to lament
Our most persisted deeds.

MAECENAS His taints and honors
Wag'd equal with him.

AGRIPPA A rarer spirit never
Did steer humanity; but you, gods, will give us
Some faults to make us men. Caesar is touch'd.

MAECENAS
When such a spacious mirror's set before him,
He needs must see himself.

CAESAR O Antony,
I have followed thee to this; but we do launch
Diseases in our bodies. I must perforce
Have shown to thee such a declining day,
Or look on thine; we could not stall together
In the whole world. But yet let me lament,
With tears as sovereign as the blood of hearts,
That thou, my brother, my competitor
In top of all design, my mate in empire,
Friend and companion in the front of war,
The arm of mine own body, and the heart
Where mine his thoughts did kindle—that our stars,
Unreconcilable, should divide
Our equalness to this. Hear me, good friends—

Enter an Egyptian.

But I will tell you at some meeter season.
The business of this man looks out of him;
We'll hear him what he says.—Whence are you?

EGYPTIAN
A poor Egyptian yet. The Queen my mistress,
Confin'd in all she has, her monument,
Of thy intents desires instruction,
That she preparedly may frame herself
To th' way she's forc'd to.

CAESAR Bid her have good heart.
She soon shall know of us, by some of ours,
How honorable and how kindly we
Determine for her; for Caesar cannot live
To be ungentle.

EGYPTIAN So the gods preserve thee! *Exit.*

CAESAR
Come hither, Proculeius. Go and say
We purpose her no shame. Give her what comforts
The quality of her passion shall require,
Lest, in her greatness, by some mortal stroke
She do defeat us; for her life in Rome
Would be eternal in our triumph. Go,
And with your speediest bring us what she says,
And how you find of her.

PROCULEIUS Caesar, I shall.
Exit Proculeius.

CAESAR
Gallus, go you along. [*Exit Gallus.*] Where's
Dolabella,
To second Proculeius?

ALL Dolabella!

CAESAR
Let him alone, for I remember now
How he's employ'd. He shall in time be ready.
Go with me to my tent, where you shall see
How hardly I was drawn into this war,
How calm and gentle I proceeded still
In all my writings. Go with me, and see
What I can show in this. *Exeunt.*

[SCENE II]

Enter Cleopatra, Charmian, Iras, and Mardian.

CLEOPATRA
My desolation does begin to make

15 crack (1) cracking apart (2) loud report **16 civil** city **17 their** i.e., the lions'. (Nature should be inverted.) **19 moi'ty** half **21 self** same **27 but it is** if it be not **30 persisted** persistently desired or pursued **31 Wag'd equal with** battled equally in **36 followed** pursued **36–37 but . . . bodies** i.e., I pursued you as men seek to cure diseases for their health's sake. (In introducing the extended medical metaphor of ll. 36–46, *launch* means *lance.*) **38 shown to thee** i.e., suffered myself at your hands **39 stall** dwell **41 as sovereign . . . hearts** as precious or efficacious as hearts' blood. (Caesar weeps rather than using bleeding as a cure; *bleeding* suggests both a medical remedy and death by the sword.) **42 competitor** associate, partner (and rival) **43 In . . . design** at the head of every grand enterprise

44 front forehead, face **45–46 the heart . . . kindle** i.e., (Antony was) the brave heart where my heart kindled its *(his)* thoughts of courage **49 meeter season** more suitable time **50 looks . . . him** reveals itself in his eyes **52 A . . . yet** i.e. (I come from) Egyptian Cleopatra, still reduced in circumstance (and awaiting your will) **57 ours** my people **65 life in Rome** presence in Rome alive **66 eternal in our triumph** an eternal glory in our triumphal procession **74 hardly** reluctantly

V.ii. Location: Alexandria. Cleopatra's monument.

A better life. 'Tis paltry to be Caesar;
Not being Fortune, he's but Fortune's knave,
A minister of her will. And it is great
To do that thing that ends all other deeds,
Which shackles accidents and bolts up change,
Which sleeps, and never palates more the dung,
The beggar's nurse and Caesar's.

Enter [to the gates of the monument] Proculeius.

PROCULEIUS
Caesar sends greeting to the Queen of Egypt,
And bids thee study on what fair demands
Thou mean'st to have him grant thee.
CLEOPATRA What's thy name?
PROCULEIUS
My name is Proculeius.
CLEOPATRA Antony
Did tell me of you, bade me trust you; but
I do not greatly care to be deceiv'd,
That have no use for trusting. If your master
Would have a queen his beggar, you must tell him
That majesty, to keep decorum, must
No less beg than a kingdom. If he please
To give me conquer'd Egypt for my son,
He gives me so much of mine own as I
Will kneel to him with thanks.
PROCULEIUS Be of good cheer;
Y' are fall'n into a princely hand, fear nothing.
Make your full reference freely to my lord,
Who is so full of grace that it flows over
On all that need. Let me report to him
Your sweet dependency, and you shall find
A conqueror that will pray in aid for kindness
Where he for grace is kneel'd to.
CLEOPATRA Pray you tell him
I am his fortune's vassal, and I send him
The greatness he has got. I hourly learn
A doctrine of obedience, and would gladly
Look him i' th' face.
PROCULEIUS This I'll report, dear lady.
Have comfort, for I know your plight is pitied
Of him that caus'd it.
[Here some of the Guard come behind Cleopatra and seize her.]
You see how easily she may be surpris'd.
[*To the Guard.*] Guard her till Caesar come.
IRAS Royal Queen!
CHARMIAN
O Cleopatra! Thou art taken, Queen.
CLEOPATRA
Quick, quick, good hands. [*Drawing a dagger.*]
PROCULEIUS Hold, worthy lady, hold!
[*Seizes and disarms her.*]
Do not yourself such wrong, who are in this
Reliev'd, but not betray'd.
CLEOPATRA What, of death too,
That rids our dogs of languish?
PROCULEIUS Cleopatra,
Do not abuse my master's bounty by
Th' undoing of yourself. Let the world see
His nobleness well acted, which your death
Will never let come forth.
CLEOPATRA Where art thou, death?
Come hither, come! Come, come, and take a queen
Worth many babes and beggars!
PROCULEIUS O, temperance, lady!
CLEOPATRA
Sir, I will eat no meat, I'll not drink, sir;
If idle talk will once be necessary,
I'll not sleep neither. This mortal house I'll ruin,
Do Caesar what he can. Know, sir, that I
Will not wait pinion'd at your master's court,
Nor once be chastis'd with the sober eye
Of dull Octavia. Shall they hoist me up
And show me to the shouting varletry
Of censuring Rome? Rather a ditch in Egypt
Be gentle grave unto me! Rather on Nilus' mud
Lay me stark naked, and let the water-flies
Blow me into abhorring! Rather make
My country's high pyramides my gibbet,
And hang me up in chains!
PROCULEIUS You do extend
These thoughts of horror further than you shall
Find cause in Caesar.

Enter Dolabella.

DOLABELLA Proculeius,
What thou hast done thy master Caesar knows,
And he hath sent for thee. For the Queen,
I'll take her to my guard.
PROCULEIUS So, Dolabella,
It shall content me best. Be gentle to her.
[*To Cleopatra.*] To Caesar I will speak what you shall please,
If you'll employ me to him.
CLEOPATRA Say, I would die.
Exit Proculeius [with Soldiers].
DOLABELLA
Most noble Empress, you have heard of me?
CLEOPATRA
I cannot tell.
DOLABELLA Assuredly you know me.
CLEOPATRA
No matter, sir, what I have heard or known.
You laugh when boys or women tell their dreams;
Is 't not your trick?
DOLABELLA I understand not, madam.
CLEOPATRA
I dreamt there was an Emperor Antony.

3 knave servant **5–8 To do . . . Caesar's** i.e., to commit suicide, which subdues accident and change and by which we sleep in death, relishing no more the dungy earth that sustains both Caesar and the beggar. (*Bolts up* means *fetters* or *locks up.*) **14 care** wish **23 Make . . . reference** refer your case **27 pray in aid** beg your assistance. (A legal term meaning "to call in the assistance of an outside person.") **for kindness** i.e., in thinking of ways to be kind **29–30 I send . . . got** i.e., I acknowledge his superiority over all he has won, including myself

40 Reliev'd rescued **41 languish** lingering disease **44 acted** accomplished **47 babes and beggars** i.e., those whom death takes easily and often **49 If . . . necessary** even if on occasion I must resort to idle talk (to keep myself awake) **52 wait** attend, as a slave. **pinion'd** like a bird with clipped wings, unable to fly **55 varletry** rabble **59 Blow . . . abhorring** cause me to swell abhorrently with maggots **74 trick** manner, way

O, such another sleep, that I might see
But such another man!

DOLABELLA
If it might please ye—

CLEOPATRA
His face was as the heav'ns, and therein stuck
A sun and moon, which kept their course, and lighted
The little O, th' earth.

DOLABELLA
Most sovereign creature—

CLEOPATRA
His legs bestrid the ocean, his rear'd arm
Crested the world, his voice was propertied 82
As all the tuned spheres, and that to friends; 83
But when he meant to quail and shake the orb, 84
He was as rattling thunder. For his bounty,
There was no winter in 't; an autumn it was
That grew the more by reaping. His delights 87
Were dolphin-like; they show'd his back above 88
The element they liv'd in. In his livery 89
Walk'd crowns and crownets; realms and islands were 90
As plates dropp'd from his pocket.

DOLABELLA
Cleopatra— 91

CLEOPATRA
Think you there was, or might be, such a man
As this I dreamt of?

DOLABELLA
Gentle madam, no.

CLEOPATRA
You lie, up to the hearing of the gods.
But, if there be nor ever were one such, 95
It's past the size of dreaming. Nature wants stuff 96
To vie strange forms with fancy; yet t' imagine 97
An Antony were nature's piece 'gainst fancy, 98
Condemning shadows quite.

DOLABELLA
Hear me, good madam. 99
Your loss is as yourself, great; and you bear it
As answering to the weight. Would I might never 101
O'ertake pursu'd success, but I do feel, 102
By the rebound of yours, a grief that smites
My very heart at root.

CLEOPATRA
I thank you, sir.
Know you what Caesar means to do with me?

DOLABELLA
I am loath to tell you what I would you knew.

CLEOPATRA
Nay, pray you, sir.—

DOLABELLA
Though he be honorable—

CLEOPATRA
He'll lead me, then, in triumph?

DOLABELLA
Madam, he will, I know 't. *Flourish.*

Enter Proculeius, Caesar, Gallus, Maecenas, [Seleucus,] and others of his train.

ALL
Make way there! Caesar! *110*

CAESAR
Which is the Queen of Egypt?

DOLABELLA
It is the Emperor, madam. *Cleopatra kneels.*

CAESAR
Arise, you shall not kneel.
I pray you, rise; rise, Egypt.

CLEOPATRA
Sir, the gods
Will have it thus; my master and my lord
I must obey.

CAESAR
Take to you no hard thoughts.
The record of what injuries you did us,
Though written in our flesh, we shall remember
As things but done by chance.

CLEOPATRA
Sole sir o' th' world,
I cannot project mine own cause so well 120
To make it clear, but do confess I have
Been laden with like frailties which before
Have often sham'd our sex.

CAESAR
Cleopatra, know
We will extenuate rather than enforce. 124
If you apply yourself to our intents, 125
Which towards you are most gentle, you shall find
A benefit in this change; but if you seek
To lay on me a cruelty, by taking 128
Antony's course, you shall bereave yourself
Of my good purposes, and put your children
To that destruction which I'll guard them from
If thereon you rely. I'll take my leave.

CLEOPATRA
And may, through all the world; 'tis yours, and we,
Your scutcheons and your signs of conquest, shall 134
Hang in what place you please. Here, my good lord.
[Gives him a scroll.]

CAESAR
You shall advise me in all for Cleopatra. 136

CLEOPATRA
This is the brief of money, plate, and jewels 137
I am possess'd of. 'Tis exactly valued,
Not petty things admitted. Where's Seleucus? 139

SELEUCUS
Here, madam.

CLEOPATRA
This is my treasurer. Let him speak, my lord,
Upon his peril, that I have reserv'd
To myself nothing. Speak the truth, Seleucus.

SELEUCUS
Madam, I had rather seel my lips 144
Than to my peril speak that which is not.

CLEOPATRA
What have I kept back?

82 Crested formed a crest for; surmounted (like a raised arm in heraldry) **82–83 propertied . . . friends** endowed with qualities which, when he spoke to friends, recalled the harmony of the heavenly bodies in their spheres **84 quail** make quail, overawe. **orb** world **87–89 His . . . in** i.e., his pleasures were both of the ordinary and rising out of it, just as a dolphin rises out of the element in which it lives, the sea **89–90 In . . . crownets** i.e., among his retainers (those who would wear his livery) were kings and princes **91 plates** coins **95 nor ever were** or if there never existed **96 It's . . . dreaming** no dream can come up to it, my image of him **96–97 Nature . . . fancy** nature lacks material to equal the remarkable forms produced by fancy or imagination **97–99 yet . . . quite** i.e., yet the very act of imagining an Antony would itself be a work of nature, in fact would be nature's masterpeice in the competition with fancy **101–102 Would . . . do** i.e., may I never succeed at what I desire if I do not

120 project set forth **124 enforce** lay stress upon and punish (them) **125 If . . . intents** if you comply with my plans **128 lay . . . cruelty** make me appear a tyrant **134 scutcheons** shields showing armorial bearings; hence, shields hung up as monuments of victory **136 in all for Cleopatra** i.e., in all matters pertaining to yourself **137 brief** list **139 Not . . . admitted** petty things omitted **144 seel** sew up (like a falcon's eyes)

SELEUCUS
Enough to purchase what you have made known.
CAESAR
Nay, blush not Cleopatra; I approve
Your wisdom in the deed.
CLEOPATRA See, Caesar! O, behold,
How pomp is followed! Mine will now be yours;
And, should we shift estates, yours would be mine.
The ingratitude of this Seleucus does
Even make me wild. O slave, of no more trust
Than love that's hir'd! [*Seleucus retreats from her.*]
What, goest thou back? Thou shalt
Go back, I warrant thee; but I'll catch thine eyes,
Though they had wings. Slave, soulless villain, dog!
O rarely base!
CAESAR Good Queen, let us entreat you.
CLEOPATRA
O Caesar, what a wounding shame is this,
That thou, vouchsafing here to visit me,
Doing the honor of thy lordliness
To one so meek, that mine own servant should
Parcel the sum of my disgraces by
Addition of his envy! Say, good Caesar,
That I some lady trifles have reserv'd,
Immoment toys, things of such dignity
As we greet modern friends withal; and say
Some nobler token I have kept apart
For Livia and Octavia, to induce
Their mediation. Must I be unfolded
With one that I have bred? The gods! It smites me
Beneath the fall I have. [*To Seleucus.*] Prithee, go hence,
Or I shall show the cinders of my spirits
Through th' ashes of my chance. Wert thou a man,
Thou wouldst have mercy on me.
CAESAR
Forbear, Seleucus. [*Seleucus withdraws.*]
CLEOPATRA
Be it known that we, the greatest, are misthought
For things that others do; and, when we fall,
We answer others' merits in our name,
Are therefore to be pitied.
CAESAR Cleopatra,
Not what you have reserv'd, nor what acknowledg'd,
Put we i' th' roll of conquest. Still be 't yours,
Bestow it at your pleasure, and believe
Caesar's no merchant to make prize with you
Of things that merchants sold. Therefore be cheer'd;
Make not your thoughts your prisons. No, dear Queen,
For we intend so to dispose you as
Yourself shall give us counsel. Feed, and sleep.
Our care and pity is so much upon you
That we remain your friend; and so, adieu.
CLEOPATRA
My master, and my lord!
CAESAR Not so. Adieu.
Flourish. Exeunt Caesar and his train.
CLEOPATRA
He words me, girls, he words me, that I should not
Be noble to myself. But hark thee, Charmian.
[*Whispers to Charmian.*]
IRAS
Finish, good lady; the bright day is done,
And we are for the dark.
CLEOPATRA Hie thee again.
I have spoke already, and it is provided;
Go put it to the haste.
CHARMIAN Madam, I will.

Enter Dolabella.

DOLABELLA
Where's the Queen?
CHARMIAN Behold, sir. [*Exit.*]
CLEOPATRA Dolabella!
DOLABELLA
Madam, as thereto sworn by your command,
Which my love makes religion to obey,
I tell you this: Caesar through Syria
Intends his journey, and within three days
You with your children will he send before.
Make your best use of this. I have perform'd
Your pleasure and my promise.
CLEOPATRA Dolabella,
I shall remain your debtor.
DOLABELLA I your servant.
Adieu, good Queen; I must attend on Caesar.
CLEOPATRA
Farewell, and thanks. Exit [*Dolabella*].
Now, Iras, what think'st thou?
Thou, an Egyptian puppet, shall be shown
In Rome, as well as I. Mechanic slaves
With greasy aprons, rules, and hammers, shall
Uplift us to the view. In their thick breaths,
Rank of gross diet, shall we be enclouded,
And forc'd to drink their vapor.
IRAS The gods forbid!
CLEOPATRA
Nay, 'tis most certain, Iras. Saucy lictors
Will catch at us, like strumpets, and scald rhymers
Ballad us out o' tune. The quick comedians
Extemporally will stage us, and present
Our Alexandrian revels; Antony
Shall be brought drunken forth, and I shall see
Some squeaking Cleopatra boy my greatness
I' th' posture of a whore.
IRAS O the good gods!

150 Mine my followers **151 shift estates** reverse fortunes, exchange places **162 Parcel** particularize **163 envy** malice **164 lady** ladylike, feminine **165 Immoment toys** trifles of no moment or importance **166 modern** common **168 Livia** Caesar's wife **169–170 unfolded With** exposed by **172 cinders** smoldering hot coals **173 chance** (fallen) fortune **175 Forbear** withdraw **176 misthought** misjudged **178 We . . . name** we are accountable in our name for the deserts (misdeeds) of others **183 make prize** haggle **185 Make . . . prisons** i.e., don't imprison yourself in your thoughts by misconceiving of your situation **186 dispose** dispose of

212 Rank . . . diet reeking of coarse food **213 drink** drink in, breathe deeply **214 lictors** minor officials in attendance on Roman magistrates **215 scald** scurvy **220 boy** (Allusion to the practice of having women's parts acted by boys on the Elizabethan stage.)

CLEOPATRA
Nay, that's certain.

IRAS
I'll never see 't; for, I am sure, my nails
Are stronger than mine eyes.

CLEOPATRA
Why, that's the way
To fool their preparation, and to conquer
Their most absurd intents.

Enter Charmian.

Now, Charmian!
Show me, my women, like a queen. Go fetch
My best attires. I am again for Cydnus,
To meet Mark Antony. Sirrah Iras, go. [*Exit Iras.*]
Now, noble Charmian, we'll dispatch indeed,
And, when thou hast done this chare, I'll give thee leave
To play till doomsday. Bring our crown and all.
A noise within
Wherefore's this noise?

Enter a Guardsman.

GUARDSMAN
Here is a rural fellow
That will not be denied your Highness' presence.
He brings you figs.

CLEOPATRA
Let him come in. *Exit Guardsman.*
What poor an instrument
May do a noble deed! He brings me liberty.
My resolution's plac'd, and I have nothing
Of woman in me. Now from head to foot
I am marble-constant; now the fleeting moon
No planet is of mine.

Enter Guardsman, and Clown [*bringing in a basket*].

GUARDSMAN
This is the man.

CLEOPATRA
Avoid, and leave him. *Exit Guardsman.*
Hast thou the pretty worm of Nilus there,
That kills and pains not?

CLOWN Truly, I have him, but I would not be the party that should desire you to touch him, for his biting is immortal; those that do die of it do seldom or never recover.

CLEOPATRA
Remember'st thou any that have died on 't?

CLOWN Very many, men and women too. I heard of one of them no longer than yesterday, a very honest woman—but something given to lie, as a woman should not do but in the way of honesty—how she died of the biting of it, what pain she felt. Truly, she makes a very good report o' th' worm; but he that will believe all that they say shall never be sav'd by half that they do. But this is most falliable, the worm's an odd worm.

CLEOPATRA
Get thee hence; farewell.

CLOWN I wish you all joy of the worm.

CLEOPATRA
Farewell.

CLOWN You must think this, look you, that the worm will do his kind.

CLEOPATRA
Ay, ay; farewell.

CLOWN Look you, the worm is not to be trusted but in the keeping of wise people; for indeed there is no goodness in the worm.

CLEOPATRA
Take thou no care; it shall be heeded.

CLOWN Very good. Give it nothing, I pray you, for it is not worth the feeding.

CLEOPATRA
Will it eat me?

CLOWN You must not think I am so simple but I know the devil himself will not eat a woman. I know that a woman is a dish for the gods, if the devil dress her not. But, truly, these same whoreson devils do the gods great harm in their women; for in every ten that they make, the devils mar five.

CLEOPATRA
Well, get thee gone; farewell.

CLOWN Yes, forsooth. I wish you joy o' th' worm.
Exit.

[*Enter Iras with royal attire.*]

CLEOPATRA
Give me my robe, put on my crown; I have
Immortal longings in me. Now no more
The juice of Egypt's grape shall moist this lip.
[*The women dress her.*]
Yare, yare, good Iras; quick. Methinks I hear
Antony call; I see him rouse himself
To praise my noble act. I hear him mock
The luck of Caesar, which the gods give men
To excuse their after wrath. Husband, I come!
Now to that name my courage prove my title!
I am fire and air; my other elements
I give to baser life. So; have you done?
Come then, and take the last warmth of my lips.
Farewell, kind Charmian; Iras, long farewell.
[*Kisses them. Iras falls and dies.*]
Have I the aspic in my lips? Dost fall?
If thou and nature can so gently part,
The stroke of death is as a lover's pinch,
Which hurts, and is desir'd. Dost thou lie still?
If thus thou vanishest, thou tell'st the world
It is not worth leave-taking.

CHARMIAN
Dissolve, thick cloud, and rain, that I may say
The gods themselves do weep!

CLEOPATRA
This proves me base.
If she first meet the curled Antony,

231 chare task, chore. (Charmian may exit after this speech to fetch the crown.) **238 plac'd** fixed **241 s.d. Clown** rustic **242 Avoid** withdraw **243 worm** snake, serpent **247 immortal** (Blunder for "mortal.") **252 to lie** (with sexual second meaning hinted at also in *honest,* i.e., chaste, *die,* i.e., reach orgasm, and *worm*) **257 falliable** (Blunder for "infallible.")

263 his kind its natural function **274 dress** prepare, as in cooking **283 Yare** quick **287 their after wrath** i.e., the wrath of the gods visited on those who have been fortunate **289 other elements** i.e., earth and water, the heavier elements **293 aspic** asp **301 curled** freshly barbered

He'll make demand of her, and spend that kiss
Which is my heaven to have. Come, thou mortal
wretch,
[*To an asp, which she applies to her breast.*]
With thy sharp teeth this knot intrinsicate
Of life at once untie. Poor venomous fool,
Be angry, and dispatch. O, couldst thou speak,
That I might hear thee call great Caesar ass
Unpolicied!

CHARMIAN O eastern star!

CLEOPATRA Peace, peace!
Dost thou not see my baby at my breast,
That sucks the nurse asleep?

CHARMIAN O, break! O, break!

CLEOPATRA
As sweet as balm, as soft as air, as gentle—
O Antony!—Nay, I will take thee too.
[*Applying another asp to her arm.*]
What should I stay— *Dies.*

CHARMIAN
In this wild world? So, fare thee well.
Now boast thee, death, in thy possession lies
A lass unparallel'd. Downy windows, close;
And golden Phoebus never be beheld
Of eyes again so royal! Your crown's awry;
I'll mend it, and then play—

Enter the Guard, rustling in.

FIRST GUARD
Where's the Queen?

CHARMIAN Speak softly, wake her not.

FIRST GUARD
Caesar hath sent—

CHARMIAN Too slow a messenger.
[*Applies an asp.*]
O, come apace, dispatch! I partly feel thee.

FIRST GUARD
Approach, ho! All's not well. Caesar's beguil'd.

SECOND GUARD
There's Dolabella sent from Caesar; call him.

FIRST GUARD
What work is here! Charmian, is this well done?

CHARMIAN
It is well done, and fitting for a princess
Descended of so many royal kings.
Ah, soldier! *Charmian dies.*

Enter Dolabella.

DOLABELLA
How goes it here?

SECOND GUARD All dead.

DOLABELLA Caesar, thy thoughts
Touch their effects in this. Thyself art coming
To see perform'd the dreaded act which thou
So sought'st to hinder.

Enter Caesar and all his train, marching.

ALL A way there, a way for Caesar!

DOLABELLA
O sir, you are too sure an augurer;
That you did fear is done.

CAESAR Bravest at the last,
She level'd at our purposes, and, being royal,
Took her own way. The manner of their deaths?
I do not see them bleed.

DOLABELLA Who was last with them?

FIRST GUARD
A simple countryman, that brought her figs.
This was his basket.

CAESAR Poison'd, then.

FIRST GUARD O Caesar,
This Charmian liv'd but now; she stood and spake.
I found her trimming up the diadem
On her dead mistress; tremblingly she stood
And on the sudden dropp'd.

CAESAR O noble weakness!
If they had swallow'd poison, 'twould appear
By external swelling; but she looks like sleep,
As she would catch another Antony
In her strong toil of grace.

DOLABELLA Here, on her breast,
There is a vent of blood and something blown;
The like is on her arm.

FIRST GUARD
This is an aspic's trail, and these fig-leaves
Have slime upon them, such as th' aspic leaves
Upon the caves of Nile.

CAESAR Most probable
That so she died; for her physician tells me
She hath pursu'd conclusions infinite
Of easy ways to die. Take up her bed,
And bear her women from the monument.
She shall be buried by her Antony.
No grave upon the earth shall clip in it
A pair so famous. High events as these
Strike those that make them; and their story is
No less in pity than his glory which
Brought them to be lamented. Our army shall
In solemn show attend this funeral,
And then to Rome. Come, Dolabella, see
High order in this great solemnity.
Exeunt omnes, [*bearing the dead bodies*].

302 He'll . . . kiss i.e., he will question her about me and kiss her for giving him information **303 mortal** deadly. **wretch** (An affectionate term of abuse.) **304 intrinsicate** intricate **308 Unpolicied** outwitted **313 What** why **323 beguil'd** cheated, tricked **330 Touch their effects** meet with realization

335 level'd at aimed at, guessed **347 toil** net **348 vent** discharge. **blown** swollen **354 conclusions** experiments **358 clip** embrace, clasp **360 Strike . . . them** touch with sorrow those who brought about these acts

Coriolanus

Coriolanus may be Shakespeare's last tragedy. Even though external evidence is scarce as to its actual date, the style suggests a time around 1608. If so, Shakespeare's final statement on man's tragic destiny is disillusioned, wry, almost anticlimactic, in the vein of his Roman and classical tragedies rather than of his great tragedies of evil *(Hamlet, Othello, King Lear, Macbeth).* Shakespeare based *Coriolanus* on Plutarch's *Lives of the Noble Grecians and Romans,* in the translation by Sir Thomas North. As in the presumably earlier Plutarchan plays, *Julius Caesar, Timon of Athens,* and *Antony and Cleopatra,* and in the non-Plutarchan *Titus Andronicus* and *Troilus and Cressida,* Shakespeare's ancient political world is one of constant upheaval. In the clash of ideologies, the plebeian mob turns giddily from one idol to the next, and strong men rise briefly only to be supplanted by a rival. The result of unceasing change is political stalemate. The great men of the ancient world seem fascinatingly alive to us, but they also seem blind to their own limitations, fatally proud, and hemmed in by circumstance. Their virtues and their defects are inseparable and indeed often identical, for private virtues serve these tragic heroes poorly in the amoral and pitiless arena of politics. Their natures cannot easily be moved from a predilection for catastrophe, and so their downfall proceeds inexorably from what Aristotle, writing of Greek tragedy, termed a flaw, or *hamartia,* in their characters. The ending, ironic rather than cathartic in its effect, leaves us with an impression of tragic waste.

Coriolanus admirably captures this conflict dividing personal nobility from political reality. The play returns to a political problem studied before in *Julius Caesar:* the rivalry in ancient Rome between democratic and aristocratic rule. *Coriolanus,* although written later than *Julius Caesar,* analyzes an earlier period of Roman history. In *Coriolanus* we witness the birth of republicanism in its distinctively Roman form, a blend of aristocratic and democratic elements; in *Julius Caesar* we see the demise of this delicately balanced regime. Shakespeare views both events with ironic detachment.

Republicanism was potentially a matter of controversy on the Jacobean stage, insofar as spectators might draw analogies between it and parliamentary efforts to curb the power of the English throne. The differences are real, of course, especially in *Julius Caesar,* where Caesar's claim to absolute rule has no sanction of divine right and Brutus' republicanism is ineffably genteel rather than populist. *Coriolanus,* however, hits closer to home. Here the plebeians are profoundly dissatisfied with aristocratic rule. Popular unrest over famine and high prices leads to rioting and the expression of democratic sentiments such as were heard and feared by the authorities in England. Riots over scarcity of grain occurred in Northamptonshire, Warwickshire, and Leicestershire during the summer of 1607. King James I, who had come to the throne in 1603, took a dim view of Puritan efforts to democratize church government and of corresponding challenges in Parliament on behalf of the common law. From the vantage point of ancient Rome, distant in time and place, *Coriolanus* appraises the conflict in terms that bear no precise relation to Jacobean England and yet have a timeless relevance. Without taking sides, the play dwells on the ambiguity of the struggle and on the indecisive, self-defeating results ironically achieved by both parties.

As in *Julius Caesar,* men on both sides are passionately sincere but driven to shortsighted extremism. The tribunes insist on behalf of the mob that the peoples' voice is to be the ultimate law of Rome. Coriolanus, in angry response, sees the mob and its elected tribunes as the enemies of hierarchical prerogative, threatening the very existence of the state. Which view is correct? Is the peoples' voice a brave force of resistance against aristocratic hauteur and class privilege, as exemplified by Coriolanus, or is the tribunes' program a grab for power by demagogues willing to risk anarchy and to weaken Rome's military might? Shakespeare seems to offer no unequivocal answer. Like Plutarch, he explores the weaknesses and strengths of both parties. He uses a dramatic structure, as in *Julius Caesar,* of sustained ambiguity. If any conclusion emerges, it is that violent political struggle leads only to an undoing of those civilized institutions which moderate men, caught in the middle, strive vainly to preserve.

The citizens play a dominant role in *Coriolanus.* The action begins, as in *Julius Caesar,* with a mob scene, setting a tone of ominous instability. The mob is too easily swayed. Lacking any consistent political philosophy of its own, it will follow whatever charismatic orator catches its fancy. It despises Coriolanus one moment and adulates him the next. Its own members agree that the mob is a "many-headed multitude," directionless, irresponsible. Other characters besides Coriolanus protest the offensive stench of the crowd, "stinking" breaths, "reechy" necks, "stinking greasy caps," and unclean teeth. The Roman citizens are a "herd," "apron-men," "garlic-eaters," curs, hares, foxes, geese, a "cockle of rebellion, insolence, sedition." This deliberately repulsive portrayal merely intensifies what is true in the other Roman plays and in the English history plays as well. Nowhere in Shakespeare does mob action lead to anything constructive or even politically acceptable. At the same time the mob does not bear chief responsibility for disaster either, in *Coriolanus* or elsewhere in Shakespeare. Individually its members are good-natured, slow to be aroused, quick to forget injury, too credulous indeed for their own good. In *Coriolanus,* they have to be prompted again and again by the tribunes to press forward with their resentment. Many citizens, left to themselves, are wise and patient. They are a neutral force, dangerous only when whipped up to collective frenzy by demagogic persuasion.

Much blame would seem to fall then on the tribunes, and indeed the play's moderating and choral spokesmen such as Menenius are deeply mistrustful of Junius Brutus and Sicinius Velutus. These tribunes are willing to risk mob violence to achieve their ends, especially when they urge the "rabble of Plebeians" to "bustle about Coriolanus" (III,i). Ignoring Menenius' pleas that "This is the way to kindle, not to quench," and that "Confusion's near," the tribunes deliberately goad Coriolanus to anger. Their strategy is to foment clamor, and "with a din confus'd Enforce the present execution," shouting down reason with hysteria (III,iii). They carefully stage each confrontation with Coriolanus, rehearsing the citizens in what they are to do, cannily timing their provocations. They talk like conspirators. Shakespeare's audience, accustomed to governmental warnings against mob violence, would probably have understood the menace posed by the tribunes, and would have savored the irony that Rome is weakened rather than strengthened by their machinations.

Still, Shakespeare's portrayal of the tribunes is remarkably sympathetic. They honestly fear that Coriolanus seeks "one sole throne Without assistance" (IV,vi), and that as consul he will do everything he can to suppress the peoples' liberties. This is no idle fear; Coriolanus' own friends merely counsel him to attack the tribunes after he has achieved power, not before. Although the tribunes do arouse the people to actions they would not otherwise take, the tribunes believe they are doing so in the people's best interests, providing leadership for a constituency that has hitherto lacked a voice. They believe in a government "by the consent of all" that can hold aristocratic insolence in check through the "lawful censure" of the commons. "What is the city but the people?" (III,i). Moreover, they are not revolutionaries by temperament and abandon mob tactics once they have made their point. Their achievements mock them when Rome proves defenseless against the return of Coriolanus, but even here they can argue with some reason that Rome would have achieved peace had it not been for Coriolanus' lawless vengeance.

Perhaps then Coriolanus must bear the responsibility for provoking democratic extremism through his contempt of the citizenry. From his first appearance, he antagonizes us as well as the populace with his curt, insulting manner. He addresses the people as "dissentious rogues" itching with scabby diseases, and dismisses them as "curs" who are "beneath abhorring." His hatred amounts to revulsion, and we fear he is all too ready to employ his sword on "thousands of these quarter'd slaves." When denied the consulship by the tribunes, in fact, he draws his sword in the marketplace, relishing the opportunity for a military solution. His tendency to forget names betrays a coldness. Although he professes not to speak merely in anger, he is too easily baited by the tribunes, too quick to speak his mind. Even those who admire his virtues concede that "to seem to affect the malice and displeasure of the people is as bad as that which he dislikes, to flatter them for their love" (II,ii). Coriolanus is glad to hear of the impending Volscian attack on Rome, for he prefers war to peace and sees conscription as a way of channeling revolutionary energies against an outward foe. He professes love of his country, but because his attachment is to an exclusively patrician order he is ready to turn traitor against a Rome that gives a political voice to the plebeians he so abhors.

Nevertheless, the portrayal of Coriolanus, as of the tribunes, is delicately balanced. We admire Coriolanus' hatred of hypocrisy. He is scrupulously honest, refusing all spoils of war except those to which his fellow soldiers are entitled. Despite his pride in family and name, he genuinely dislikes to hear himself praised. Though he disdains to lead cowardly citizen-soldiers, and shines most in single deeds of valor rather than in generalship, he is inspiring and even popular among valiant soldiers like himself. He is generous in praising the achievements of his colleagues. Even in matters of state he shows resoluteness and integrity. He has a consistent political philosophy, one bolstered by Menenius' comparison of the state to a body in which the members must harmoniously interact (I,i). Jacobean spectators would recognize in this analogy the orthodox appeal to order and degree they heard regularly from pulpit and throne. Coriolanus firmly believes that the established prerogatives of the aristocracy are Rome's only safe bulwark against chaos. By granting power to the tribunes, in his view, the senate has sealed its doom. He sees the people as their own worst enemies, insatiable and irrational in their demands, unable to comprehend the subtleties of government, instinctively envious of their betters. Such base mortals require subjection to their masters, though they cannot be expected to realize this themselves. Coriolanus knows that his views are out of fashion, and that the current trend is to appease popular demands with compromise, but he can see no end to the compromises that will be needed once the tribunes have established their prerogatives. He prefers a battle to the death, and welcomes the danger to himself. If his courage and consistency are "too absolute," if he is "too noble for the world," he would prefer to believe that the fault lies in that world rather than in him.

Between the extremes of democratic and aristocratic rule, the middle position of compromise offers many attractions. Menenius sanely desires to see "On both sides more respect," and pleads with those who would be "truly your country's friend" to "temp'rately proceed to what you would Thus violently redress" (III,i). Although his sympathies are patrician, he acknowledges the tribunes' power as a political reality which must be dealt with. He finds fault with Coriolanus for not having "temporiz'd." Menenius is a bluff, honest fellow who directs our sympathies, like the equally outspoken Enobarbus in *Antony and Cleopatra*. Yet compromise always has its ridiculous aspect. Menenius increasingly assumes the self-contradictory and sardonically amusing role of the appeaser, like York of *Richard II,* urging actions that are repugnant to him personally. At the last, after having denounced the tribunes for betraying Rome, he must go as their ambassador to beg mercy of Coriolanus. When Aufidius' guardsmen scoff at him for having been turned away by Coriolanus, Menenius is beyond caring for their taunts. He does in fact hold to a consistent principle, the survival of his beloved city at whatever cost to his pride. He and Rome blunder pragmatically through, though not without loss of dignity.

Coriolanus' mother Volumnia is caught in an even more ironic dilemma. She of course shares her son's aristocratic pride, having taught him a code of death before dishonor. The emotional bond between mother and son is extraordinarily, even distressingly, close. She speaks of him metaphorically as her husband, and of his warlike prowess as a vicarious substitute for "the embracements of his bed" (I,iii). Throughout, Coriolanus' deeds of war are love-offerings to his mother. Every citizen of Rome knows that whatever Coriolanus has done for his country he also did "to please his mother" (I,i). The conflict arises from her desire to have him famous not only in war but in politics. Here she must, like Menenius, espouse the compromise and "policy" that they all hate. She and Menenius stage Coriolanus' public appearances with as much care as the tribunes rehearse their plebeians. They "prompt" Coriolanus to "perform a part" for which he has no aptitude (III,ii); as he later says, capitulating to his mother for the last time, "Like a dull actor now, I have forgot my part, and I am out" (V,iii). This integrity has its admirable side, but brings disaster to Volumnia's plans. She is defeated by the very pride she has engendered in him, and he is defeated by her overriding ambition for him. To win her praise he must put away his true disposition, becoming effeminate and emasculated like a "harlot" or "an eunuch." To satisfy her quest for fame he must give up his attack on Rome, perjure himself to Aufidius, and die a condemned traitor to the Volscian state. Volumnia's crushing love for her son proves ironically fatal to everything they have cherished.

Coriolanus' relationship to Aufidius is one of love as well as hate, and it too poses a fatal conflict. Despite their rivalry to the death, these two military heroes are singularly attracted to one another. Coriolanus confesses "I sin in envying his nobility," and considers Aufidius "a lion That I am proud to hunt" (I,i). Coriolanus' fate is to love his enemy and hate his birthplace. Aufidius, in turn, greets Coriolanus with more joy "Than when I first my wedded mistress saw Bestride my threshold" (IV,v). Yet Aufidius has always resented Coriolanus' superiority in battle, and has planned to overcome him by fair means or foul. In their brief military alliance, Coriolanus proves too attractive a rival, overshadowing the achievements of Aufidius. For these reasons Aufidius secretly exults in Coriolanus' fatal dilemma, since the Volscian general prefers vengeance to victory over Rome. In a final disillusioning scene he stages one more public outcry against Coriolanus, goading him into a proud rage, and then with his fellow conspirators ingloriously performs an execution "whereat valor will weep." Aufidius' virtues, like those of Coriolanus, have been betrayed by his worst instincts. Throughout, the Volscians have been cunning enemies, lying in wait for Rome to tear herself apart. The laws governing the relations between states are brutally competitive, characterized by the "slippery turns" of fortune that ironically bring together former enemies as allies and then turn them against one another. In this world of sudden reversals, Coriolanus' last act is something he could never have foreseen: saving the Roman state and its tribunes from a destruction he himself had wished on it. As Coriolanus wrily observes of his own destiny, "The gods look down, and this unnatural scene They laugh at."

Coriolanus

[*Dramatis Personae*

CAIUS MARCIUS, *afterwards* CAIUS MARCIUS CORIOLANUS.
TITUS LARTIUS, COMINIUS, } *generals against the Volscians.*
MENENIUS AGRIPPA, *friend to Coriolanus.*
SICINIUS VELUTUS, JUNIUS BRUTUS, } *tribunes of the people.*
Young MARCIUS, *son to Coriolanus.*
Roman HERALD.
NICANOR, *a Roman.*
TULLUS AUFIDIUS, *general of the Volscians.*
LIEUTENANT *to Aufidius.*
CONSPIRATORS *with Aufidius.*
ADRIAN, *a Volscian.*
CITIZEN *of Antium.*
Two Volscian GUARDS.

VOLUMNIA, *mother to Coriolanus.*
VIRGILIA, *wife to Coriolanus.*
VALERIA, *friend to Virgilia.*
GENTLEWOMAN, *attending on Virgilia.*

Roman and Volscian SENATORS, PATRICIANS, AEDILES, LICTORS, SOLDIERS, CITIZENS, MESSENGERS, SERVANTS *to Aufidius, and other* ATTENDANTS.

SCENE: *Rome and the neighborhood; Corioles and the neighborhood; Antium.*]

ACT I • SCENE I

Enter a company of mutinous Citizens, with staves, clubs, and other weapons.

FIRST CITIZEN Before we proceed any further, hear me speak.

ALL Speak, speak.

FIRST CITIZEN You are all resolv'd rather to die than to famish?

ALL Resolv'd, resolv'd.

FIRST CITIZEN First, you know Caius Marcius is chief enemy to the people.

ALL We know 't, we know 't.

FIRST CITIZEN Let us kill him, and we'll have corn at our own price. Is 't a verdict?

ALL No more talking on 't; let it be done. Away, away!

SECOND CITIZEN One word, good citizens.

FIRST CITIZEN We are accounted poor citizens, the patricians good. What authority surfeits on would relieve us. If they would yield us but the superfluity, while it were wholesome, we might guess they reliev'd us humanely; but they think we are too dear. The leanness that afflicts us, the object of our misery, is as an inventory to particularize their abundance; our sufferance is a gain to them. Let us revenge this with our pikes, ere we become rakes; for the gods know I speak this in hunger for bread, not in thirst for revenge.

SECOND CITIZEN Would you proceed especially against Caius Marcius?

ALL Against him first. He's a very dog to the commonalty.

SECOND CITIZEN Consider you what services he has done for his country?

FIRST CITIZEN Very well; and could be content to give him good report for 't, but that he pays himself with being proud.

SECOND CITIZEN Nay, but speak not maliciously.

FIRST CITIZEN I say unto you, what he hath done famously, he did it to that end. Though soft-conscienc'd men can be content to say it was for his country, he did it to please his mother, and to be partly proud, which he is, even to the altitude of his virtue.

SECOND CITIZEN What he cannot help in his nature, you account a vice in him. You must in no way say he is covetous.

FIRST CITIZEN If I must not, I need not be barren of accusations; he hath faults, with surplus, to tire in repetition. *(Shouts within.)* What shouts are these? The other side o' th' city is risen. Why stay we prating here? To th' Capitol!

ALL Come, come.

FIRST CITIZEN Soft, who comes here?

Enter Menenius Agrippa.

SECOND CITIZEN Worthy Menenius Agrippa, one that hath always lov'd the people.

FIRST CITIZEN He's one honest enough. Would all the rest were so!

MENENIUS
What work's, my countrymen, in hand? Where go you
With bats and clubs? The matter? Speak, I pray you.

FIRST CITIZEN Our business is not unknown to th' Senate. They have had inkling this fortnight what we intend to do, which now we'll show 'em in deeds. They say poor suitors have strong breaths; they shall know we have strong arms too.

MENENIUS
Why, masters, my good friends, mine honest neighbors,

I.i. Location: Rome. A street.
10 corn grain, such as wheat or barley **11 Is 't a verdict** are we agreed **12 on 't** of it, about it

15 good i.e., noble, well-to-do **18 too dear** costing more than we are worth (but also, paradoxically, "a gain"; see l. 21) **19 object** sight **19–20 is as . . . abundance** serves as a catalogue or inventory to point out in detail (by means of contrast) how rich they are **20 sufferance** suffering **21 pikes** spears, lances; pitchforks (playing on *rakes*, l. 22) **22 rakes** i.e., as lean as rakes **34–35 famously** achieving fame **35 to that end** i.e., in order to become famous **37 to be partly proud** partly out of pride **38 even . . . virtue** i.e., he is as proud as he is brave **42 If** even if **46 Capitol** Temple of Jupiter on Capitoline Hill; used here to stand for the Senate building **48 Soft** stay, stop **54 bats** stout staves **58 suitors** petitioners

Will you undo yourselves?
FIRST CITIZEN We cannot, sir, we are undone already.
MENENIUS
I tell you, friends, most charitable care
Have the patricians of you. For your wants,
Your suffering in this dearth, you may as well
Strike at the heaven with your staves as lift them
Against the Roman state, whose course will on
The way it takes, cracking ten thousand curbs
Of more strong link asunder than can ever
Appear in your impediment. For the dearth,
The gods, not the patricians, make it, and
Your knees to them, not arms, must help. Alack,
You are transported by calamity
Thither where more attends you, and you slander
The helms o' th' state, who care for you like fathers,
When you curse them as enemies.

FIRST CITIZEN Care for us? True, indeed! They ne'er car'd for us yet. Suffer us to famish, and their store-houses cramm'd with grain; make edicts for usury, to support usurers; repeal daily any wholesome act establish'd against the rich, and provide more piercing statutes daily to chain up and restrain the poor. If the wars eat us not up, they will; and there's all the love they bear us.

MENENIUS
Either you must
Confess yourselves wondrous malicious,
Or be accus'd of folly. I shall tell you
A pretty tale. It may be you have heard it,
But, since it serves my purpose, I will venture
To stale 't a little more.

FIRST CITIZEN Well, I'll hear it, sir; yet you must not think to fob off our disgrace with a tale. But, an 't please you, deliver.

MENENIUS
There was a time when all the body's members
Rebell'd against the belly, thus accus'd it:
That only like a gulf it did remain
I' th' midst o' th' body, idle and unactive,
Still cupboarding the viand, never bearing
Like labor with the rest, where th' other instruments
Did see and hear, devise, instruct, walk, feel,
And, mutually participate, did minister
Unto the appetite and affection common
Of the whole body. The belly answer'd—
FIRST CITIZEN Well, sir, what answer made the belly?
MENENIUS
Sir, I shall tell you. With a kind of smile,
Which ne'er came from the lungs, but even thus—
For, look you, I may make the belly smile
As well as speak—it tauntingly replied
To th' discontented members, the mutinous parts
That envied his receipt; even so most fitly
As you malign our senators for that
They are not such as you.
FIRST CITIZEN
Your belly's answer? What?
The kingly-crowned head, the vigilant eye,
The counselor heart, the arm our soldier,
Our steed the leg, the tongue our trumpeter,
With other muniments and petty helps
In this our fabric, if that they—
MENENIUS What then?
'Fore me, this fellow speaks! What then? What then?
FIRST CITIZEN
Should by the cormorant belly be restrain'd,
Who is the sink o' th' body—
MENENIUS Well, what then?
FIRST CITIZEN
The former agents, if they did complain,
What could the belly answer?
MENENIUS I will tell you;
If you'll bestow a small—of what you have little—
Patience awhile, you'st hear the belly's answer.
FIRST CITIZEN
Y' are long about it.
MENENIUS Note me this, good friend;
Your most grave belly was deliberate,
Not rash like his accusers, and thus answered:
"True is it, my incorporate friends," quoth he,
"That I receive the general food at first
Which you do live upon; and fit it is,
Because I am the store-house and the shop
Of the whole body. But, if you do remember,
I send it through the rivers of your blood,
Even to the court, the heart, to th' seat o' th' brain;
And, through the cranks and offices of man,
The strongest nerves and small inferior veins
From me receive that natural competency
Whereby they live. And though that all at once"—
You, my good friends, this says the belly,
mark me—
FIRST CITIZEN
Ay, sir, well, well.
MENENIUS "Though all at once cannot
See what I do deliver out to each,
Yet I can make my audit up, that all
From me do back receive the flour of all,
And leave me but the bran." What say you to 't?
FIRST CITIZEN
It was an answer. How apply you this?
MENENIUS
The senators of Rome are this good belly,
And you the mutinous members. For examine
Their counsels and their cares, disgest things rightly
Touching the weal o' th' common, you shall find
No public benefit which you receive

64 For as for **65 dearth** famine **67 on** continue on **68 cracking** breaking **70 in your impediment** in any hindrance you may be able to offer **73 transported** carried out of control **74 attends** awaits **75 helms** helmsmen **90 stale 't** make it stale by repeating it **92 fob . . . disgrace** set aside by a trick our feeling of suffering hardship. **an 't** if it **93 deliver** tell your tale **98 Still** always. **cupboarding** stowing away **99 Like** equal. **where** whereas. **instruments** organs **101 participate** participating, taking part **102 affection** inclination **106 lungs** i.e., supposed organ of laughter **110 his receipt** what it received

111 for that because **117 muniments** furnishing, or defenses **118 fabric** body formed by the conjunction of various parts **119 'Fore me** (An oath.) **120 cormorant** ravenous, rapacious **121 sink** cesspool **125 you'st** you shall **126 Y' are** you are **127 Your** i.e., this **129 incorporate** belonging to one body **136 cranks** winding passages. **offices** service rooms of a household; kitchen, etc. **137 nerves** sinews **138 natural competency** sufficiency for the purposes of nature **149 disgest** digest **150 weal o' th' common** public welfare

But it proceeds or comes from them to you
And no way from yourselves. What do you think,
You, the great toe of this assembly?

FIRST CITIZEN
I the great toe? Why the great toe?

MENENIUS
For that, being one o' th' lowest, basest, poorest,
Of this most wise rebellion, thou go'st foremost.
Thou rascal, that art worst in blood to run,
Lead'st first to win some vantage.
But make you ready your stiff bats and clubs.
Rome and her rats are at the point of battle;
The one side must have bale.

Enter Caius Marcius.

Hail, noble Marcius!

MARCIUS
Thanks. What's the matter, you dissentious rogues,
That, rubbing the poor itch of your opinion,
Make yourselves scabs?

FIRST CITIZEN We have ever your good word.

MARCIUS
He that will give good words to thee will flatter
Beneath abhorring. What would you have, you curs,
That like nor peace nor war? The one affrights you,
The other makes you proud. He that trusts to you,
Where he should find you lions, finds you hares;
Where foxes, geese. You are no surer, no,
Than is the coal of fire upon the ice,
Or hailstone in the sun. Your virtue is
To make him worthy whose offense subdues him
And curse that justice did it. Who deserves greatness
Deserves your hate; and your affections are
A sick man's appetite, who desires most that
Which would increase his evil. He that depends
Upon your favors swims with fins of lead
And hews down oaks with rushes. Hang ye! Trust ye?
With every minute you do change a mind,
And call him noble that was now your hate,
Him vile that was your garland. What's the matter,
That in these several places of the city
You cry against the noble Senate, who,
Under the gods, keep you in awe, which else
Would feed on one another?—What's their seeking?

MENENIUS
For corn at their own rates, whereof, they say,
The city is well stor'd.

MARCIUS Hang 'em! They say?
They'll sit by th' fire, and presume to know
What's done i' th' Capitol; who's like to rise,
Who thrives and who declines; side factions, and give out
Conjectural marriages, making parties strong
And feebling such as stand not in their liking
Below their cobbled shoes. They say there's grain enough?
Would the nobility lay aside their ruth
And let me use my sword, I'd make a quarry
With thousands of these quarter'd slaves, as high
As I could pick my lance.

MENENIUS
Nay, these are almost thoroughly persuaded;
For though abundantly they lack discretion,
Yet are they passing cowardly. But, I beseech you,
What says the other troop?

MARCIUS
They are dissolv'd. Hang 'em!
They said they were an-hungry; sigh'd forth proverbs,
That hunger broke stone walls, that dogs must eat,
That meat was made for mouths, that the gods sent not
Corn for the rich men only. With these shreds
They vented their complainings, which being answer'd,
And a petition granted them—a strange one,
To break the heart of generosity
And make bold power look pale—they threw their caps
As they would hang them on the horns o' th' moon,
Shouting their emulation.

MENENIUS What is granted them?

MARCIUS
Five tribunes to defend their vulgar wisdoms,
Of their own choice. One's Junius Brutus,
Sicinius Velutus, and I know not—'Sdeath!
The rabble should have first unroof'd the city
Ere so prevail'd with me. It will in time
Win upon power, and throw forth greater themes
For insurrection's arguing.

MENENIUS This is strange.

MARCIUS
Go, get you home, you fragments!

Enter a Messenger, hastily.

MESSENGER
Where's Caius Marcius?

MARCIUS Here. What's the matter?

MESSENGER
The news is, sir, the Volsces are in arms.

MARCIUS
I am glad on 't. Then we shall ha' means to vent
Our musty superfluity.—See, our best elders.

158 rascal lean deer not worth the hunting. (Hence the modern meaning.) **in blood** in vigor, condition. (A hunting term.) **160 stiff bats** stout cudgels **162 The one . . . bale** one side or the other must get the worst of it, receive injury **163 dissentious** rebellious **165 scabs** (1) scurvy fellows, rascals (2) sores **168 nor . . . nor** neither . . . nor. **The one** i.e., war **169 The other** i.e., peace **174–175 To make . . . it** to glorify that person whose wrongdoing has subjected him to punishment and curse the justice which punishes him **176 your affections are** i.e., being loved by you is **182 now** just now **183 garland** object of highest honor and praise **186 which** who. **else** otherwise **187 seeking** demand

192 side take sides with. **give out** report **193 marriages** i.e., political alliances. **making parties strong** asserting certain parties to be strong **194 feebling** declaring to be weak **195 cobbled** mended **196 ruth** tenderheartedness **197 quarry** heap of slain **198 quarter'd** cut into quarters, slaughtered like criminals **199 pick** pitch **202 passing** exceedingly **205 an-hungry** hungry **206 dogs** i.e., even dogs **207 meat** food **208 shreds** bits, scraps (of wisdom) **211 generosity** the nobles **214 emulation** envy of superiors **215 tribunes** official representatives of the people's interests **217 'Sdeath** i.e., by God's death. (An oath.) **220 Win upon** gain advantage over **221 For insurrection's arguing** to be fought over by uprisings **225 vent** get rid of

Enter Sicinius Velutus, Junius Brutus, Cominius, Titus Lartius, with other Senators.

FIRST SENATOR
Marcius, 'tis true that you have lately told us;
The Volsces are in arms.
MARCIUS They have a leader,
Tullus Aufidius, that will put you to 't. 229
I sin in envying his nobility;
And, were I anything but what I am,
I would wish me only he.
COMINIUS You have fought together? 232
MARCIUS
Were half to half the world by th' ears and he 233
Upon my party, I'd revolt, to make 234
Only my wars with him. He is a lion 235
That I am proud to hunt.
FIRST SENATOR Then, worthy Marcius,
Attend upon Cominius to these wars.
COMINIUS
It is your former promise.
MARCIUS Sir, it is,
And I am constant. Titus Lartius, thou 239
Shalt see me once more strike at Tullus' face.
What, art thou stiff? Stand'st out?
LARTIUS No, Caius Marcius, 241
I'll lean upon one crutch and fight with t' other,
Ere stay behind this business.
MENENIUS O, true-bred!
FIRST SENATOR
Your company to th' Capitol, where, I know,
Our greatest friends attend us.
LARTIUS [*To Cominius*] Lead you on.
[*To Marcius.*] Follow Cominius. We must follow you;
Right worthy you priority.
COMINIUS Noble Marcius! 247
FIRST SENATOR [*To the Citizens*]
Hence to your homes, be gone!
MARCIUS Nay, let them follow.
The Volsces have much corn; take these rats thither
To gnaw their garners. Worshipful mutiners, 250
Your valor puts well forth. Pray follow. 251
Exeunt. Citizens steal away.
Mane[n]t Sicinius and Brutus.

SICINIUS
Was ever man so proud as is this Marcius?
BRUTUS
He has no equal.
SICINIUS
When we were chosen tribunes for the people—
BRUTUS
Mark'd you his lip and eyes?
SICINIUS Nay, but his taunts.
BRUTUS
Being mov'd, he will not spare to gird the gods. 256
SICINIUS
Be-mock the modest moon. 257
BRUTUS
The present wars devour him! He is grown
Too proud to be so valiant.
SICINIUS Such a nature, 259
Tickled with good success, disdains the shadow 260
Which he treads on at noon. But I do wonder
His insolence can brook to be commanded 262
Under Cominius.
BRUTUS Fame, at the which he aims,
In whom already he's well grac'd, cannot 264
Better be held nor more attain'd than by
A place below the first; for what miscarries 266
Shall be the general's fault, though he perform
To th' utmost of a man, and giddy censure 268
Will then cry out of Marcius, "O, if he
Had borne the business!"
SICINIUS Besides, if things go well,
Opinion that so sticks on Marcius shall
Of his demerits rob Cominius.
BRUTUS Come. 272
Half all Cominius' honors are to Marcius, 273
Though Marcius earn'd them not, and all his faults
To Marcius shall be honors, though indeed
In aught he merit not.
SICINIUS Let's hence, and hear
How the dispatch is made, and in what fashion, 277
More than his singularity, he goes 278
Upon this present action.
BRUTUS Let's along. *Exeunt.*

[SCENE II]

Enter Tullus Aufidius with Senators of Corioles.

FIRST SENATOR
So, your opinion is, Aufidius,
That they of Rome are ent'red in our counsels 2
And know how we proceed.
AUFIDIUS Is it not yours?
What ever have been thought on in this state
That could be brought to bodily act ere Rome
Had circumvention? 'Tis not four days gone 6
Since I heard thence. These are the words—I think
I have the letter here. Yes, here it is. [*Finds letter.*]
[*Reads.*] "They have press'd a power, but it is not known 9
Whether for east or west. The dearth is great,

229 to 't i.e., to the test **232 together** against one another **233 by th' ears** at variance (with the other half) **234 Upon my party** on my side **235 with** against **239 constant** true to my promise **241 stiff** resistant, reluctant. (But Lartius answers as though the word had meant *stiff with age.*) **Stand'st out** do you refuse to engage **247 Right . . . priority** you well deserve to take precedence **250 Worshipful mutiners** worthy mutineers. (Said with mock politeness.) **251 puts well forth** begins to bud, shows a fair promise. (Said ironically.)

256 gird gird at, scoff at **257 modest** i.e., as representing Diana, goddess of chastity **259 to be** of being **260 Tickled with** flattered by **262 brook** endure **264 whom** which **266 miscarries** goes wrong **268 giddy censure** thoughtless popular opinion **272 demerits** merits, deserts **273 are to** belong to **273 dispatch** execution of the business **278 More . . . singularity** i.e., apart from his special peculiarities

I.ii. Location: Corioles (or Corioli), southeast of Rome. The Senate house.
2 ent'red in acquainted with **6 circumvention** i.e., warning enabling them to circumvent **9 press'd a power** raised an army

The people mutinous; and, it is rumor'd,
Cominius, Marcius your old enemy,
Who is of Rome worse hated than of you,
And Titus Lartius, a most valiant Roman,
These three lead on this preparation
Whither 'tis bent. Most likely 'tis for you.
Consider of it."

FIRST SENATOR Our army's in the field.
We never yet made doubt but Rome was ready
To answer us.

AUFIDIUS Nor did you think it folly
To keep your great pretenses veil'd till when
They needs must show themselves, which in the hatching,
It seem'd, appear'd to Rome. By the discovery
We shall be short'ned in our aim, which was
To take in many towns ere almost Rome
Should know we were afoot.

SECOND SENATOR Noble Aufidius,
Take your commission, hie you to your bands;
Let us alone to guard Corioles.
If they set down before 's, for the remove
Bring up your army; but, I think, you'll find
Th' have not prepar'd for us.

AUFIDIUS O, doubt not that;
I speak from certainties. Nay more,
Some parcels of their power are forth already,
And only hitherward. I leave your honors.
If we and Caius Marcius chance to meet,
'Tis sworn between us we shall ever strike
Till one can do no more.

ALL The gods assist you!

AUFIDIUS
And keep your honors safe!

FIRST SENATOR Farewell.

SECOND SENATOR Farewell.

ALL
Farewell. *Exeunt omnes.*

[SCENE III]

Enter Volumnia and Virgilia, mother and wife to Marcius. They set them down on two low stools, and sew.

VOLUMNIA I pray you, daughter, sing, or express yourself in a more comfortable sort. If my son were my husband, I should freelier rejoice in that absence wherein he won honor than in the embracements of his bed where he would show most love. When yet he was but tender-bodied and the only son of my womb, when youth with comeliness pluck'd all gaze his way, when for a day of kings' entreaties a mother should not sell him an hour from her beholding, I, considering how honor would become such a person, that it was no better than picture-like to hang by th' wall, if renown made it not stir, was pleas'd to let him seek danger where he was like to find fame. To a cruel war I sent him, from whence he return'd, his brows bound with oak. I tell thee, daughter, I sprang not more in joy at first hearing he was a man-child than now in first seeing he had prov'd himself a man.

VIRGILIA But had he died in the business, madam, how then?

VOLUMNIA Then his good report should have been my son; I therein would have found issue. Hear me profess sincerely: had I a dozen sons, each in my love alike and none less dear than thine and my good Marcius, I had rather had eleven die nobly for their country than one voluptuously surfeit out of action.

Enter a Gentlewoman.

GENTLEWOMAN
Madam, the Lady Valeria is come to visit you.

VIRGILIA
Beseech you, give me leave to retire myself.

VOLUMNIA
Indeed, you shall not.
Methinks I hear hither your husband's drum;
See him pluck Aufidius down by th' hair;
As children from a bear, the Volsces shunning him.
Methinks I see him stamp thus, and call thus:
"Come on, you cowards! You were got in fear,
Though you were born in Rome." His bloody brow
With his mail'd hand then wiping, forth he goes,
Like to a harvest-man that's task'd to mow
Or all or lose his hire.

VIRGILIA
His bloody brow? O Jupiter, no blood!

VOLUMNIA
Away, you fool! It more becomes a man
Than gilt his trophy. The breasts of Hecuba,
When she did suckle Hector, look'd not lovelier
Than Hector's forehead when it spit forth blood
At Grecian sword, contemning. Tell Valeria
We are fit to bid her welcome. *Exit Gentlewoman.*

VIRGILIA
Heavens bless my lord from fell Aufidius!

VOLUMNIA
He'll beat Aufidius' head below his knee
And tread upon his neck.

Enter Valeria, with an Usher and a Gentlewoman.

VALERIA My ladies both, good day to you.

VOLUMNIA Sweet madam.

VIRGILIA I am glad to see your ladyship.

13 of by **16 Whither 'tis bent** against whatever destination it is intended **20 pretenses** intentions **22 appear'd** became evident **23 be short'ned** fall short **24 take in** capture **26 bands** companies of soldiers **28 set down before 's** lay siege to us. **remove** raising of the siege **30 prepar'd for us** i.e., laid plans to besiege us **32 parcels** parts **35 ever strike** keep on exchanging blows

I.iii. Location: Rome. Marcius' house.
2 comfortable sort cheerful manner **7 all gaze** the gaze of all

15 bound with oak i.e., as a badge to signify that he had saved the life of a Roman citizen. (The *cruel war* was that against the Latins and Tarquin the Proud; see II.i.148–149 and note.) **29 hither** i.e., penetrating hither **33 got** begot **36 task'd** set the task **37 Or** either **40 Than . . . trophy** i.e., than gilding sets off his monument. **Hecuba** Queen of Troy, mother of Hector and many other sons **43 contemning** scorning (the Grecian sword) **45 bless** protect. **fell** cruel

VALERIA How do you both? You are manifest housekeepers. What are you sewing here? A fine spot, in good faith. How does your little son?

VIRGILIA I thank your ladyship; well, good madam.

VOLUMNIA He had rather see the swords and hear a drum than look upon his schoolmaster.

VALERIA O' my word, the father's son. I'll swear 'tis a very pretty boy. O' my troth, I look'd upon him o' Wednesday half an hour together. H'as such a confirm'd countenance! I saw him run after a gilded butterfly, and when he caught it, he let it go again, and after it again, and over and over he comes, and up again; catch'd it again. Or whether his fall enrag'd him, or how 'twas, he did so set his teeth and tear it—O, I warrant, how he mammock'd it!

VOLUMNIA One on 's father's moods.

VALERIA Indeed, la, 'tis a noble child.

VIRGILIA A crack, madam.

VALERIA Come, lay aside your stitchery. I must have you play the idle huswife with me this afternoon.

VIRGILIA No, good madam, I will not out of doors.

VALERIA Not out of doors?

VOLUMNIA She shall, she shall.

VIRGILIA Indeed, no, by your patience. I'll not over the threshold till my lord return from the wars.

VALERIA Fie, you confine yourself most unreasonably. Come, you must go visit the good lady that lies in.

VIRGILIA I will wish her speedy strength, and visit her with my prayers; but I cannot go thither.

VOLUMNIA Why, I pray you?

VIRGILIA 'Tis not to save labor, nor that I want love.

VALERIA You would be another Penelope. Yet, they say, all the yarn she spun in Ulysses' absence did but fill Ithaca full of moths. Come; I would your cambric were sensible as your finger, that you might leave pricking it for pity. Come, you shall go with us.

VIRGILIA No, good madam, pardon me; indeed, I will not forth.

VALERIA In truth, la, go with me, and I'll tell you excellent news of your husband.

VIRGILIA O, good madam, there can be none yet.

VALERIA Verily, I do not jest with you. There came news from him last night.

VIRGILIA Indeed, madam?

VALERIA In earnest, it's true; I heard a senator speak it. Thus it is: the Volsces have an army forth, against whom Cominius the general is gone, with one part of our Roman power. Your lord and Titus Lartius are set down before their city Corioles. They nothing doubt prevailing and to make it brief wars. This is true, on mine honor; and so, I pray, go with us.

VIRGILIA Give me excuse, good madam. I will obey you in everything hereafter.

VOLUMNIA Let her alone, lady. As she is now, she will but disease our better mirth.

VALERIA In troth, I think she would. Fare you well, then. Come, good sweet lady. Prithee, Virgilia, turn thy solemness out o' door, and go along with us.

VIRGILIA No, at a word, madam; indeed, I must not. I wish you much mirth.

VALERIA Well, then, farewell. *Exeunt Ladies.*

[SCENE IV]

Enter Marcius, Titus Lartius, with drum and colors, with Captains and Soldiers, as before the city [*of*] *Corioles. To them a Messenger.*

MARCIUS
Yonder comes news. A wager they have met.

LARTIUS
My horse to yours, no.

MARCIUS
'Tis done.

LARTIUS
Agreed.

MARCIUS
Say, has our general met the enemy?

MESSENGER
They lie in view, but have not spoke as yet.

LARTIUS
So, the good horse is mine.

MARCIUS
I'll buy him of you.

LARTIUS
No, I'll nor sell nor give him. Lend you him I will
For half a hundred years. Summon the town.

MARCIUS
How far off lie these armies?

MESSENGER
Within this mile and half.

MARCIUS
Then shall we hear their 'larum, and they ours.
Now, Mars, I prithee, make us quick in work,
That we with smoking swords may march from
hence
To help our fielded friends! Come, blow thy blast.

They sound a parley. Enter two Senators with others on the walls of Corioles.

Tullus Aufidius, is he within your walls?

FIRST SENATOR
No, nor a man that fears you less than he,
That's lesser than a little. (*Drum afar off.*) Hark! Our
drums
Are bringing forth our youth. We'll break our walls
Rather than they shall pound us up. Our gates,
Which yet seem shut, we have but pinn'd with
rushes;

51–52 manifest housekeepers clearly being stay-at-homes today **52 sewing** embroidering. **spot** pattern, figure **59 H' as** he has **59–60 confirm'd** resolute **65 mammock'd** tore into fragments **66 on 's** of his **68 crack** pert little imp **77 lies in** is expecting a child **81 want** am deficient in **82 You would be** i.e., one might take you for. **Penelope** faithful wife of Ulysses in Homer's *Odyssey*, who delayed her suitors by insisting she must finish the weaving which she then unraveled every night **84 cambric** fine white linen **85 sensible** sensitive **99 nothing** not at all **105 disease . . . mirth** trouble our mirth which would be greater without her

109 at a word finally

I.iv. Location: Before Corioles.
2 My horse to yours i.e., I'll bet my horse against yours that they, Cominius' Roman force and the Volscian army under Aufidius, 1½ miles away, have not met in battle **4 in view** i.e., of one another. **spoke** i.e., encountered **7 Summon the town** i.e., by trumpet, to parley **10 'larum** call to arms **12 smoking** steaming **13 fielded** in the field of battle **13 s.d. on the walls** i.e., in the gallery backstage. (Throughout this scene, the tiring-house façade represents the *walls* of Corioles, and a door in that façade represents the *gates*.) **16 lesser than a little** virtually not at all **18 pound** shut up as in a pound

They'll open of themselves. *(Alarum far off.)* Hark
you, far off!
There is Aufidius. List what work he makes
Amongst your cloven army.

MARCIUS
O, they are at it!

LARTIUS
Their noise be our instruction. Ladders, ho!

Enter the army of the Volsces [from the city].

MARCIUS
They fear us not, but issue forth their city.
Now put your shields before your hearts, and fight
With hearts more proof than shields. Advance,
brave Titus!
They do disdain us much beyond our thoughts,
Which makes me sweat with wrath. Come on, my
fellows!
He that retires, I'll take him for a Volsce,
And he shall feel mine edge.

Alarum. The Romans are beat back to their trenches [and thus exeunt].
Enter Marcius, cursing, [with Soldiers].

MARCIUS
All the contagion of the south light on you,
You shames of Rome! You herd of—Boils and
plagues
Plaster you o'er, that you may be abhorr'd
Farther than seen, and one infect another
Against the wind a mile! You souls of geese,
That bear the shapes of men, how have you run
From slaves that apes would beat! Pluto and hell!
All hurt behind! Backs red, and faces pale
With flight and agued fear! Mend and charge home,
Or, by the fires of heaven, I'll leave the foe
And make my wars on you. Look to 't. Come on!
If you'll stand fast, we'll beat them to their wives,
As they us to our trenches. Follow 's!

Another alarum; [the Volsces fly back into the city,] and Marcius follows them to [the] gates.

So, now the gates are ope. Now prove good
seconds!
'Tis for the followers fortune widens them,
Not for the fliers. Mark me, and do the like.
Enter the gates and is shut in.

FIRST SOLDIER
Fool-hardiness; not I.

SECOND SOLDIER
Nor I.

FIRST SOLDIER
See,
They have shut him in.

ALL
To th' pot, I warrant him.
Alarum continues.

Enter Titus Lartius.

LARTIUS
What is become of Marcius?

ALL
Slain, sir, doubtless.

FIRST SOLDIER
Following the fliers at the very heels,
With them he enters; who, upon the sudden,
Clapp'd to their gates. He is himself alone,
To answer all the city.

LARTIUS
O noble fellow!
Who sensibly outdares his senseless sword,
And, when it bows, stand'st up. Thou art left,
Marcius.
A carbuncle entire, as big as thou art,
Were not so rich a jewel. Thou wast a soldier
Even to Cato's wish, not fierce and terrible
Only in strokes, but, with thy grim looks and
The thunder-like percussion of thy sounds,
Thou mad'st thine enemies shake, as if the world
Were feverous and did tremble.

Enter Marcius, bleeding, [from the city], assaulted by the enemy.

FIRST SOLDIER
Look, sir.

LARTIUS
O, 'tis Marcius!
Let's fetch him off, or make remain alike.
They fight, and all enter the city.

[SCENE V]

Enter certain Romans, with spoils.

FIRST ROMAN
This will I carry to Rome.

SECOND ROMAN
And I this.

THIRD ROMAN
A murrain on 't! I took this for silver.
Exeunt. Alarum continues still afar off.

Enter Marcius and Titus [Lartius] with a trumpet.

MARCIUS
See here these movers that do prize their hours
At a crack'd drachma! Cushions, leaden spoons,
Irons of a doit, doublets that hangmen would
Bury with those that wore them, these base slaves,
Ere yet the fight be done, pack up. Down with
them!
And hark, what noise the general makes! To him!
There is the man of my soul's hate, Aufidius,
Piercing our Romans. Then, valiant Titus, take

22 cloven split in two, divided **23 our instruction** a lesson to us **26 proof** impenetrable **30 edge** sword **31 south** south wind (as a supposed source of contagion) **35 Against . . . mile** i.e., so great that it will carry a mile against the wind **39 agued** trembling as though with an ague or fever. **Mend** (1) do better, reform your battle ranks (2) recover from fever. **home** to the utmost **44 seconds** supporters **45 followers** pursuers **46 the fliers** those pursued **48 To th' pot** i.e., to certain destruction

52 Clapp'd to shut **54–55 Who . . . up** who, though endowed with feeling, dares more than his insensible sword; it might bend to fear, he would not **55 left** alone, unique; perhaps also, abandoned **58 Cato** Marcus Cato the Censor (234–149 B.C.), celebrated in Plutarch as a staunch soldier and exponent of Roman ethics **65 make remain alike** remain to share his fate

I.v. Location: Corioles. A street. The siege of Corioles continues.
2 murrain plague **2 s.d. trumpet** trumpeter **3 movers** active persons. (Here used ironically.) **prize their hours** value their time **4 drachma** small Greek coin **5 of a doit** worth a coin of small value **5–6 hangmen . . . them** i.e., hangmen, entitled to the clothes of persons put to death, would not have these **8 the general** i.e., Cominius, fighting Aufidius nearby

Convenient numbers to make good the city,
Whilst I, with those that have the spirit, will haste
To help Cominius.

LARTIUS
Worthy sir, thou bleed'st.
Thy exercise hath been too violent
For a second course of fight.

MARCIUS
Sir, praise me not;
My work hath yet not warm'd me. Fare you well.
The blood I drop is rather physical
Than dangerous to me. To Aufidius thus
I will appear, and fight.

LARTIUS
Now the fair goddess Fortune
Fall deep in love with thee, and her great charms
Misguide thy opposers' swords! Bold gentleman,
Prosperity be thy page!

MARCIUS
Thy friend no less
Than those she placeth highest! So, farewell.

LARTIUS
Thou worthiest Marcius! [*Exit Marcius.*]
Go sound thy trumpet in the market-place.
Call thither all the officers o' th' town,
Where they shall know our mind. Away! *Exeunt.*

[SCENE VI]

Enter Cominius, as it were in retire, with Soldiers.

COMINIUS
Breathe you, my friends. Well fought! We are come off
Like Romans, neither foolish in our stands
Nor cowardly in retire. Believe me, sirs,
We shall be charg'd again. Whiles we have struck,
By interims and conveying gusts we have heard
The charges of our friends. The Roman gods,
Lead their successes as we wish our own,
That both our powers, with smiling fronts encount'ring,
May give you thankful sacrifice.

Enter a Messenger.

Thy news?

MESSENGER
The citizens of Corioles have issued,
And given to Lartius and to Marcius battle.
I saw our party to their trenches driven,
And then I came away.

COMINIUS
Though thou speakest truth,
Methinks thou speak'st not well. How long is 't since?

MESSENGER
Above an hour, my lord.

COMINIUS
'Tis not a mile; briefly we heard their drums.
How couldst thou in a mile confound an hour,
And bring thy news so late?

MESSENGER
Spies of the Volsces
Held me in chase, that I was forc'd to wheel
Three or four miles about; else had I, sir,
Half an hour since brought my report.

Enter Marcius.

COMINIUS
Who's yonder,
That does appear as he were flay'd? O gods!
He has the stamp of Marcius, and I have
Before-time seen him thus.

MARCIUS
Come I too late?

COMINIUS
The shepherd knows not thunder from a tabor
More than I know the sound of Marcius' tongue
From every meaner man.

MARCIUS
Come I too late?

COMINIUS
Ay, if you come not in the blood of others,
But mantled in your own.

MARCIUS
O, let me clip ye
In arms as sound as when I woo'd, in heart
As merry as when our nuptial day was done,
And tapers burnt to bedward! [*They embrace.*]

COMINIUS
Flower of warriors, how is 't with Titus Lartius?

MARCIUS
As with a man busied about decrees:
Condemning some to death, and some to exile;
Ransoming him, or pitying, threat'ning th' other;
Holding Corioles in the name of Rome,
Even like a fawning greyhound in the leash,
To let him slip at will.

COMINIUS
Where is that slave
Which told me they had beat you to your trenches?
Where is he? Call him hither.

MARCIUS
Let him alone;
He did inform the truth. But for our gentlemen,
The common file—a plague! Tribunes for them!—
The mouse ne'er shunn'd the cat as they did budge
From rascals worse than they.

COMINIUS
But how prevail'd you?

MARCIUS
Will the time serve to tell? I do not think.
Where is the enemy? Are you lords o' th' field?
If not, why cease you till you are so?

COMINIUS
Marcius, we have at disadvantage fought,
And did retire to win our purpose.

MARCIUS
How lies their battle? Know you on which side
They have plac'd their men of trust?

11 make good hold, secure **15 course** bout, or course in a banquet. **praise me not** don't praise me yet **17 physical** curative **21 charms** spells **23 be thy page** i.e., attend on you. **Thy . . . less** i.e., may she be no less your friend **24 those** i.e., friend to those

I.vi. Location: Near the camp of Cominius. The fighting near Corioles, heard until now at a short distance, is at a lull.
1 Breathe rest. **are come off** have left the field of battle **2 foolish** foolhardy **5 By . . . gusts** at intervals and borne to us on the wind **6 friends** i.e., the besiegers of Corioles. **The Roman** ye Roman **8 powers** armies. **fronts** (1) foreheads, brows (2) front lines **10 issued** issued forth

16 briefly recently **17 confound** consume **19 that** so that **22 as** as if **25 knows** distinguishes (also in l. 26). **tabor** small drum **27 meaner** less noble **28–29 Ay . . . own** i.e., if you yourself are bleeding all that blood, you are presumably too weak to help, but if it is enemies' blood, you are in time to shed more **29 clip** embrace **32 tapers . . . bedward** i.e., indicated the approach of bedtime, or showed the way to bed **36 Ransoming him** releasing one man for ransom money. **pitying** releasing without ransom **39 let him slip** unleash him **43 common file** ordinary soldiers, plebeians **44 budge** flinch **50 to . . . purpose** i.e., to regroup **51 battle** army, battle line

COMINIUS
As I guess, Marcius,
Their bands i' th' vaward are the Antiates,
Of their best trust; o'er them Aufidius,
Their very heart of hope.

MARCIUS
I do beseech you,
By all the battles wherein we have fought,
By th' blood we have shed together, by th' vows we have made
To endure friends, that you directly set me
Against Aufidius and his Antiates,
And that you not delay the present, but,
Filling the air with swords advanc'd and darts,
We prove this very hour.

COMINIUS
Though I could wish
You were conducted to a gentle bath
And balms applied to you, yet dare I never
Deny your asking. Take your choice of those
That best can aid your action.

MARCIUS
Those are they
That most are willing. If any such be here—
As it were sin to doubt—that love this painting
Wherein you see me smear'd; if any fear
Lesser his person than an ill report;
If any think brave death outweighs bad life,
And that his country's dearer than himself;
Let him alone, or so many so minded,
Wave thus, to express his disposition,
And follow Marcius.

They all shout and wave their swords, take him up in their arms, and cast up their caps.

O, me alone! Make you a sword of me?
If these shows be not outward, which of you
But is four Volsces? None of you but is
Able to bear against the great Aufidius
A shield as hard as his. A certain number,
Though thanks to all, must I select from all;
The rest shall bear the business in some other fight,
As cause will be obey'd. Please you to march,
And four shall quickly draw out my command,
Which men are best inclin'd.

COMINIUS
March on, my fellows!
Make good this ostentation, and you shall
Divide in all with us. *Exeunt.*

[SCENE VII]

Titus Lartius, having set a guard upon Corioles, going with drum and trumpet toward Cominius and Caius Marcius, enters [from the city] with a Lieutenant, other Soldiers, and a Scout.

LARTIUS
So, let the ports be guarded. Keep your duties,
As I have set them down. If I do send, dispatch
Those centuries to our aid; the rest will serve
For a short holding. If we lose the field,
We cannot keep the town.

LIEUTENANT
Fear not our care, sir.

LARTIUS
Hence, and shut your gates upon 's.
Our guider, come; to th' Roman camp conduct us.
Exeunt [severally, the Lieutenant returning into the city].

[SCENE VIII]

Alarum as in battle. Enter Marcius and Aufidius at several doors.

MARCIUS
I'll fight with none but thee; for I do hate thee
Worse than a promise-breaker.

AUFIDIUS
We hate alike.
Not Afric owns a serpent I abhor
More than thy fame and envy. Fix thy foot.

MARCIUS
Let the first budger die the other's slave,
And the gods doom him after!

AUFIDIUS
If I fly, Marcius, holloa me like a hare.

MARCIUS
Within these three hours, Tullus,
Alone I fought in your Corioles walls,
And made what work I pleas'd. 'Tis not my blood
Wherein thou seest me mask'd. For thy revenge
Wrench up thy power to th' highest.

AUFIDIUS
Wert thou the Hector
That was the whip of your bragg'd progeny,
Thou shouldst not scape me here.

Here they fight, and certain Volsces come in the aid of Aufidius. Marcius fights till they be driven in breathless.

Officious, and not valiant, you have sham'd me
In your condemned seconds. *[Exeunt.]*

[SCENE IX]

Flourish. Alarum. A retreat is sounded. Enter, at one door, Cominius with the Romans; at another door Marcius, with his arm in a scarf.

COMINIUS
If I should tell thee o'er this thy day's work,
Thou 't not believe thy deeds. But I'll report it

53 vaward vanguard. **Antiates** inhabitants of Antium **58 endure** continue **62 prove** test **68 painting** i.e., blood **70 Lesser . . . report** less for his safety than for his reputation **77 outward** external, deceptive **83 As . . . obey'd** as necessity shall require **86 ostentation** showing

I.vii. Location: Before the gates of Corioles. The military action near Corioles continues.
1 ports gates

3 centuries companies of a hundred **4 short holding** i.e., brief occupation of the city

I.viii. Location: A field of battle near the Roman camp. The military action near Corioles continues.
s.d. several different **4 fame and envy** hateful reputation **7 holloa** cry in pursuit of **13 the whip . . . progeny** the champion among your boasted (Trojan) ancestors. (Alludes to the supposed descent of the Romans from the Trojans via Aeneas.) **16 condemned seconds** futile and despised efforts at assistance

I.ix. Location: Scene continues. The Roman camp. The military action near Corioles continues.
2 Thou 't thou wouldst

Where senators shall mingle tears with smiles,
Where great patricians shall attend and shrug,
I' th' end admire; where ladies shall be frighted,
And, gladly quak'd, hear more; where the dull
tribunes,
That with the fusty plebeians hate thine honors,
Shall say against their hearts, "We thank the gods
Our Rome hath such a soldier."
Yet cam'st thou to a morsel of this feast,
Having fully din'd before.

Enter Titus [Lartius] with his power, from the pursuit.

LARTIUS O general,
Here is the steed, we the caparison.
Hadst thou beheld—

MARCIUS Pray now, no more. My mother,
Who has a charter to extol her blood,
When she does praise me grieves me. I have done
As you have done—that's what I can;
Induc'd as you have been—that's for my country.
He that has but effected his good will
Hath overta'en mine act.

COMINIUS You shall not be
The grave of your deserving. Rome must know
The value of her own. 'Twere a concealment
Worse than a theft, no less than a traducement,
To hide your doings, and to silence that
Which, to the spire and top of praises vouch'd,
Would seem but modest. Therefore, I beseech you—
In sign of what you are, not to reward
What you have done—before our army hear me.

MARCIUS
I have some wounds upon me, and they smart
To hear themselves rememb'red.

COMINIUS Should they not,
Well might they fester 'gainst ingratitude,
And tent themselves with death. Of all the horses,
Whereof we have ta'en good and good store, of all
The treasure in this field achiev'd and city,
We render you the tenth, to be ta'en forth,
Before the common distribution, at
Your only choice.

MARCIUS I thank you, general,
But cannot make my heart consent to take
A bribe to pay my sword. I do refuse it,
And stand upon my common part with those
That have beheld the doing. *A long flourish.*
They all cry "Marcius! Marcius!"
cast up their caps and lances.
Cominius and Lartius stand bare.

May these same instruments, which you profane,
Never sound more! When drums and trumpets shall
I' th' field prove flatterers, let courts and cities be
Made all of false-fac'd soothing! When steel grows
Soft as the parasite's silk, let him be made
An overture for th' wars. No more, I say!
For that I have not wash'd my nose that bled,
Or foil'd some debile wretch—which without note
Here's many else have done—you shout me forth
In acclamations hyperbolical,
As if I lov'd my little should be dieted
In praises sauc'd with lies.

COMINIUS Too modest are you,
More cruel to your good report than grateful
To us that give you truly. By your patience,
If 'gainst yourself you be incens'd, we'll put you,
Like one that means his proper harm, in manacles,
Then reason safely with you. Therefore be it known,
As to us, to all the world, that Caius Marcius
Wears this war's garland, in token of the which
My noble steed, known to the camp, I give him,
With all his trim belonging; and from this time,
For what he did before Corioles, call him,
With all th' applause and clamor of the host,
Caius Marcius Coriolanus! Bear
Th' addition nobly ever!
Flourish. Trumpets sound, and drums.

ALL
Caius Marcius Coriolanus!

CORIOLANUS
I will go wash;
And when my face is fair, you shall perceive
Whether I blush or no. Howbeit, I thank you.
I mean to stride your steed, and at all times
To undercrest your good addition
To th' fairness of my power.

COMINIUS So, to our tent,
Where, ere we do repose us, we will write
To Rome of our success. You, Titus Lartius,
Must to Corioles back. Send us to Rome
The best, with whom we may articulate
For their own good and ours.

LARTIUS I shall, my lord.

CORIOLANUS
The gods begin to mock me. I, that now
Refus'd most princely gifts, am bound to beg
Of my lord general.

COMINIUS Take 't, 'tis yours. What is 't?

CORIOLANUS
I sometime lay here in Corioles
At a poor man's house; he us'd me kindly.
He cried to me; I saw him prisoner;
But then Aufidius was within my view,
And wrath o'erwhelm'd my pity. I request you
To give my poor host freedom.

6 gladly quak'd glad to be frightened **7 fusty** moldy, ill-smelling **8 against their hearts** unwillingly **10 to . . . feast** i.e., only to a small portion of all you fed on **12 steed** i.e., Marcius. **caparison** mere trappings of a steed **14 charter . . . blood** right to praise her child **18 effected** manifested in action. **will** intention **19–20 You . . . deserving** you shall not conceal your merit (by your modesty) **22 traducement** calumny, slander **24 vouch'd** affirmed, proclaimed **25 modest** moderate, barely sufficient (in relation to all you did) **26 sign** token merely. **reward** amply compensate **29 not** i.e., not be praised **31 tent** cure by probing. (I.e., the wounds would find no help other than death.) **32 good and good store** excellent ones and plenty of them

44 soothing flattery **44–46 When . . . wars** i.e., when steel armor grows soft with peace, like the silks of flatterers, let it (this softened steel) be made an overture to war, an invitation to invasion by foreign enemies (? Various emendations proposed.) **47 For that** because **48 foil'd** have overthrown. **debile** weak. **note** notice taken **51 my little** that the little I have done. **dieted** fed **52 In** on, by **54 give** report **56 means . . . harm** intends to injure himself **61 his trim belonging** the equipment that goes with him **71 undercrest** adopt and support, bear up (as a heraldic crest). **addition** title **72 fairness of my power** best of my ability **76 best** i.e., best in blood among the Volscians. **articulate** come to terms (about the return of Corioles to the Volscians) **81 sometime lay** once lodged **83 cried** cried out (at the time of the battle just ended)

COMINIUS O, well begg'd!
Were he the butcher of my son, he should
Be free as is the wind. Deliver him, Titus.

LARTIUS
Marcius, his name?

CORIOLANUS By Jupiter, forgot!
I am weary; yea, my memory is tir'd.
Have we no wine here?

COMINIUS Go we to our tent.
The blood upon your visage dries; 'tis time
It should be look'd to. Come. *Exeunt.*

[SCENE X]

A flourish. Cornets. Enter Tullus Aufidius, bloody, with two or three Soldiers.

AUFIDIUS
The town is ta'en!

FIRST SOLDIER
'Twill be deliver'd back on good condition.

AUFIDIUS
Condition?
I would I were a Roman; for I cannot,
Being a Volsce, be that I am. Condition?
What good condition can a treaty find
I' th' part that is at mercy? Five times, Marcius,
I have fought with thee; so often hast thou beat me,
And wouldst do so, I think, should we encounter
As often as we eat. By th' elements,
If e'er again I meet him beard to beard,
He's mine, or I am his. Mine emulation
Hath not that honor in 't it had; for where
I thought to crush him in an equal force,
True sword to sword, I'll potch at him some way
Or wrath or craft may get him.

FIRST SOLDIER He's the devil.

AUFIDIUS
Bolder, though not so subtle. My valor's poison'd
With only suff'ring stain by him; for him
Shall fly out of itself. Nor sleep nor sanctuary,
Being naked, sick, nor fane nor Capitol,
The prayers of priests nor times of sacrifice,
Embarquements all of fury, shall lift up
Their rotten privilege and custom 'gainst
My hate to Marcius. Where I find him, were it
At home, upon my brother's guard, even there,
Against the hospitable canon, would I
Wash my fierce hand in 's heart. Go you to th' city;
Learn how 'tis held, and what they are that must
Be hostages for Rome.

FIRST SOLDIER Will not you go?

AUFIDIUS
I am attended at the cyprus grove. I pray you—
'Tis south the city mills—bring me word thither
How the world goes, that to the pace of it
I may spur on my journey.

FIRST SOLDIER I shall, sir.
[*Exeunt severally.*]

I.x. Location: The camp of the Volsces, after the battle.
2 condition terms **5 be . . . am** i.e., be honorable, proud **7 I' . . . mercy** for the side that lies at the mercy of the winner **12 emulation** rivalry **13 where** whereas **15 potch** thrust **16 Or . . . craft** in which either wrath or craft **18 stain** tarnishment, eclipse **19 Shall . . . itself** (my valor) shall deviate from its own natural course. **Nor sleep** i.e., neither to find him asleep **20 naked** unarmed. **fane** temple, shrine **22 Embarquements** embargoes, restraints **25 upon** under **26 hospitable canon** law of hospitality **28–29 what . . . Rome** who they are that are to be taken to Rome as hostages during the negotiations about the return of Corioles to the Volscians; see I.ix.76

30 attended waited for

ACT II • [SCENE I]

Enter Menenius with the two Tribunes of the people, Sicinius and Brutus.

MENENIUS The augurer tells me we shall have news tonight.

BRUTUS Good or bad?

MENENIUS Not according to the prayer of the people, for they love not Marcius.

SICINIUS Nature teaches beasts to know their friends.

MENENIUS Pray you, who does the wolf love?

SICINIUS The lamb.

MENENIUS Ay, to devour him, as the hungry plebeians would the noble Marcius.

BRUTUS He's a lamb indeed, that baas like a bear.

MENENIUS He's a bear indeed, that lives like a lamb. You two are old men; tell me one thing that I shall ask you.

BOTH Well, sir.

MENENIUS In what enormity is Marcius poor in, that you two have not in abundance?

BRUTUS He's poor in no one fault, but stor'd with all.

SICINIUS Especially in pride.

BRUTUS And topping all others in boasting.

MENENIUS This is strange now. Do you two know how you are censur'd here in the city, I mean of us o' th' right-hand file? Do you?

BOTH Why, how are we censur'd?

MENENIUS Because you talk of pride now—will you not be angry?

BOTH Well, well, sir, well.

MENENIUS Why, 'tis no great matter; for a very little thief of occasion will rob you of a great deal of patience. Give your dispositions the reins, and be angry at your pleasures—at the least, if you take it as a pleasure to you in being so. You blame Marcius for being proud?

BRUTUS We do it not alone, sir.

MENENIUS I know you can do very little alone; for your helps are many, or else your actions would grow wondrous single. Your abilities are too infant-like for doing much alone. You talk of pride. O that you could turn your eyes toward the napes of your necks, and make but an interior survey of your good selves! O that you could!

II.i. Location: Rome. A public place.
23 right-hand file i.e., party of aristocrats **28–29 very . . . occasion** very slight occasion acting like a thief **37 single** poor, feeble

BOTH What then, sir?

MENENIUS Why then you should discover a brace of unmeriting, proud, violent, testy magistrates, alias fools, as any in Rome.

SICINIUS Menenius, you are known well enough too.

MENENIUS I am known to be a humorous patrician, and one that loves a cup of hot wine with not a drop of allaying Tiber in 't; said to be something imperfect in favoring the first complaint; hasty and tinder-like upon too trivial motion; one that converses more with the buttock of the night than with the forehead of the morning. What I think I utter, and spend my malice in my breath. Meeting two such wealsmen as you are—I cannot call you Lycurguses—if the drink you give me touch my palate adversely, I make a crooked face at it. I cannot say your worships have deliver'd the matter well, when I find the ass in compound with the major part of your syllables; and though I must be content to bear with those that say you are reverend grave men, yet they lie deadly that tell you you have good faces. If you see this in the map of my microcosm, follows it that I am known well enough too? What harm can your bisson conspectuities glean out of this character, if I be known well enough too?

BRUTUS Come, sir, come, we know you well enough.

MENENIUS You know neither me, yourselves, nor anything. You are ambitious for poor knaves' caps and legs. You wear out a good wholesome forenoon in hearing a cause between an orange-wife and a forset-seller, and then rejourn the controversy of threepence to a second day of audience. When you are hearing a matter between party and party, if you chance to be pinch'd with the colic, you make faces like mummers; set up the bloody flag against all patience; and, in roaring for a chamber-pot, dismiss the controversy bleeding, the more entangled by your hearing. All the peace you make in their cause is calling both the parties knaves. You are a pair of strange ones.

BRUTUS Come, come, you are well understood to be a perfecter giber for the table than a necessary bencher in the Capitol.

MENENIUS Our very priests must become mockers, if they shall encounter such ridiculous subjects as you are. When you speak best unto the purpose, it is not worth the wagging of your beards; and your beards deserve not so honorable a grave as to stuff a botcher's cushion, or to be entomb'd in an ass's pack-saddle. Yet you must be saying Marcius is proud; who, in a cheap estimation, is worth all your predecessors since Deucalion, though peradventure some of the best of 'em were hereditary hangmen. God-den to your worships. More of your conversation would infect my brain, being the herdsmen of the beastly plebeians. I will be bold to take my leave of you.

Brutus and Sicinius [*go*] *aside.*

Enter Volumnia, Virgilia, and Valeria.

How now, my as fair as noble ladies—and the moon, were she earthly, no nobler—whither do you follow your eyes so fast?

VOLUMNIA Honorable Menenius, my boy Marcius approaches. For the love of Juno, let's go.

MENENIUS Ha? Marcius coming home!

VOLUMNIA Ay, worthy Menenius, and with most prosperous approbation.

MENENIUS Take my cap, Jupiter, and I thank thee. [*Tosses his cap.*] Hoo! Marcius coming home?

VALERIA, VIRGILIA Nay, 'tis true.

VOLUMNIA Look, here's a letter from him. [*Shows a letter.*] The state hath another, his wife another; and, I think, there's one at home for you.

MENENIUS I will make my very house reel tonight. A letter for me?

VIRGILIA Yes, certain, there's a letter for you; I saw 't.

MENENIUS A letter for me? It gives me an estate of seven years' health, in which time I will make a lip at the physician. The most sovereign prescription in Galen is but empiricutic, and, to this preservative, of no better report than a horse-drench. Is he not wounded? He was wont to come home wounded.

VIRGILIA O, no, no, no.

VOLUMNIA O, he is wounded, I thank the gods for 't.

MENENIUS So do I too, if it be not too much. Brings 'a victory in his pocket? The wounds become him.

VOLUMNIA On 's brows. Menenius, he comes the third time home with the oaken garland.

MENENIUS Has he disciplin'd Aufidius soundly?

VOLUMNIA Titus Lartius writes they fought together, but Aufidius got off.

MENENIUS And 'twas time for him too, I'll warrant him that. An he had stay'd by him, I would not have been so fidius'd for all the chests in Corioles, and the gold that's in them. Is the Senate possess'd of this?

VOLUMNIA Good ladies, let's go.—Yes, yes, yes; the Senate has letters from the general, wherein he gives my son the whole name of the war. He hath in this action outdone his former deeds doubly.

VALERIA In troth, there's wondrous things spoke of him.

47 humorous whimsical, governed by humors **49 allaying Tiber** water which dilutes **49–50 something . . . complaint** somewhat influenced by the first version of a dispute that reaches my ears **51 motion** cause **51–53 one . . . morning** i.e., one who is better acquainted with the late hours of the night than with the early hours of the morning **54 wealsmen** statesmen **55 Lycurguses** (Said ironically; Lycurgus was the famous Spartan lawgiver.) **55–56 drink you give me** (with a suggestion also of *things you tell me*) **57 deliver'd** reported **58–59 I find . . . syllables** i.e., I find assininity in nearly everything you say (with a pun on *ass in compound* meaning legal phases ending in *-as*, like *whereas*) **62 this** i.e., all that I have freely admitted. **the map of my microcosm** my face, or chart of my little world (as opposed to the macrocosm or great world) **63 known . . . too** (Menenius mocks their phrase, l. 46, and its implication that they "see through" him.) **64 bisson conspectuities** blind faculty of sight **65 character** character sketch **68–69 caps and legs** doffing caps and making obeisances to indicate servility **70 orange-wife** woman who sells oranges and other fruit **70–71 forset-seller** one who sells taps for drawing liquor from barrels **71 rejourn** adjourn, postpone **74 mummers** masqueraders, performers in dumb shows **75 set . . . flag** declare violent war **76–77 bleeding** unhealed, unsettled **77–79 peace . . . knaves** (Perhaps a reference to the song "Hold thy peace, thou knave"; see *Twelfth Night,* II.iii.63–70.) **81–82 perfecter . . . Capitol** i.e., better at dinner-table jesting than at sitting in the Senate as a counselor **87 botcher** one who patches old clothes or boots

91 Deucalion the Noah of classical story, survivor of a great flood **92 hereditary hangmen** men serving as executioners (a very low social station) generation after generation. **God-den** good evening **102–103 prosperous approbation** success and good reputation **114 make a lip** make a contemptuous face, mock **115 sovereign** efficacious. **Galen** Greek physician and authority on medicine (born considerably after the time of Coriolanus) **116 empiricutic** empirical, quacklike. **to** compared to **117 horse-drench** dose of medicine for horses **121 'a** he **129 An** if **130 fidius'd** (Menenius' coined word meaning "treated as Aufidius deserves, beaten.") **131 possess'd** informed **134 name** credit, reputation

MENENIUS Wondrous? Ay, I warrant you, and not
without his true purchasing.
VIRGILIA The gods grant them true!
VOLUMNIA True? Pow, waw. 141
MENENIUS True? I'll be sworn they are true. Where is
he wounded? [*To the Tribunes.*] God save your good
worships! Marcius is coming home. He has more
cause to be proud.—Where is he wounded?
VOLUMNIA I' th' shoulder and i' th' left arm. There will
be large cicatrices to show the people, when he shall 147
stand for his place. He receiv'd in the repulse of Tar- 148
quin seven hurts i' th' body. 149
MENENIUS One i' th' neck, and two i' th' thigh—there's
nine that I know.
VOLUMNIA He had, before this last expedition, twenty-
five wounds upon him.
MENENIUS Now it's twenty-seven—every gash was an
enemy's grave. *(A shout and flourish.)* Hark, the trum-
pets.
VOLUMNIA These are the ushers of Marcius. Before him
he carries noise, and behind him he leaves tears.
Death, that dark spirit, in 's nervy arm doth lie, 159
Which, being advanc'd, declines, and then men die. 160

A sennet. Trumpets sound. Enter Cominius the general, and Titus Lartius; between them, Coriolanus, crowned with an oaken garland; with Captains and Soldiers, and a Herald.

HERALD
Know, Rome, that all alone Marcius did fight
Within Corioles gates, where he hath won,
With fame, a name to Caius Marcius; these 163
In honor follows Coriolanus.
Welcome to Rome, renowned Coriolanus!
Sound. Flourish.
ALL
Welcome to Rome, renowned Coriolanus!
CORIOLANUS
No more of this; it does offend my heart.
Pray now, no more.
COMINIUS Look, sir, your mother!
CORIOLANUS O,
You have, I know, petition'd all the gods
For my prosperity! *Kneels.*
VOLUMNIA Nay, my good soldier, up.
My gentle Marcius, worthy Caius, and
By deed-achieving honor newly nam'd— 172
What is it? Coriolanus must I call thee?—
But, O, thy wife!
CORIOLANUS [*Rising*] My gracious silence, hail!
Wouldst thou have laugh'd had I come coffin'd
home,
That weep'st to see me triumph? Ah, my dear,
Such eyes the widows in Corioles wear,
And mothers that lack sons.
MENENIUS Now, the gods crown thee!
CORIOLANUS
And live you yet? [*To Valeria.*] O my sweet lady,
pardon.
VOLUMNIA
I know not where to turn. O, welcome home!
[*To Cominius.*] And welcome, general! And y' are
welcome all.
MENENIUS
A hundred thousand welcomes! I could weep
And I could laugh, I am light and heavy. Welcome. 183
A curse begin at very root on 's heart 184
That is not glad to see thee! You are three
That Rome should dote on; yet, by the faith of men,
We have some old crab-trees here at home that
will not 187
Be grafted to your relish. Yet welcome, warriors! 188
We call a nettle but a nettle, and 189
The faults of fools but folly.
COMINIUS Ever right. 190
CORIOLANUS
Menenius ever, ever. 191
HERALD
Give way there, and go on!
CORIOLANUS [*To Volumnia and Virgilia*]
Your hand, and yours.
Ere in our own house I do shade my head,
The good patricians must be visited,
From whom I have receiv'd not only greetings,
But with them change of honors.
VOLUMNIA I have liv'd 196
To see inherited my very wishes 197
And the buildings of my fancy. Only
There's one thing wanting, which I doubt not but
Our Rome will cast upon thee.
CORIOLANUS Know, good mother,
I had rather be their servant in my way
Than sway with them in theirs.
COMINIUS On, to the Capitol! 202
Flourish. Cornets. Exeunt in state, as before.
Brutus and Sicinius [*come forward*].
BRUTUS
All tongues speak of him, and the bleared sights 203
Are spectacled to see him. Your prattling nurse 204
Into a rapture lets her baby cry 205
While she chats him; the kitchen malkin pins 206
Her richest lockram 'bout her reechy neck, 207
Clamb'ring the walls to eye him; stalls, bulks,
windows 208
Are smother'd up, leads fill'd, and ridges hors'd 209

141 Pow, waw i.e., pish **147 cicatrices** scars **148 stand for his place** i.e., seek the consulship **148–149 repulse of Tarquin** (Plutarch reports that Marcius fought his first battle against King Tarquin the Proud in 499 B.C. on the occasion of Tarquin's last attempt to regain the kingdom; see I.iii.13–15 and note, and II.ii.88 ff.) **159 nervy** sinewy **160 advanc'd** raised. **declines** descends **163 With** in addition to. **to** added to **172 deed-achieving** achieved by deeds

183 light and heavy merry and sad **184 on 's** of his **187 old crab-trees** i.e., sour-natured old men (such as the Tribunes) **188 grafted to your relish** implanted with a liking for you **189–190 We . . . folly** i.e., some unpleasant things cannot be changed and must be acknowledged for what they are **191 Menenius ever** same old Menenius **196 change of honors** promotion **197 inherited** realized **202 sway** bear rule **203–204 bleared . . . spectacled** people with dimmed vision put on spectacles **205 rapture** fit **206 chats him** i.e., gossips about Coriolanus. **malkin** untidy servantmaid **207 lockram** coarse linen fabric. **reechy** dirty, filthy **208 bulks** structures projecting from the front of a shop **209 leads** leaded roofs. **ridges** roof-tops. **hors'd** bestridden (as a horse)

With variable complexions, all agreeing
In earnestness to see him. Seld-shown flamens
Do press among the popular throngs, and puff
To win a vulgar station. Our veil'd dames
Commit the war of white and damask in
Their nicely-gauded cheeks to th' wanton spoil
Of Phoebus' burning kisses—such a pother
As if that whatsoever god who leads him
Were slily crept into his human powers
And gave him graceful posture.

SICINIUS On the sudden,
I warrant him consul.

BRUTUS Then our office may,
During his power, go sleep.

SICINIUS
He cannot temp'rately transport his honors
From where he should begin and end, but will
Lose those he hath won.

BRUTUS In that there's comfort.

SICINIUS Doubt not
The commoners, for whom we stand, but they
Upon their ancient malice will forget
With the least cause these his new honors, which
That he will give them make I as little question
As he is proud to do 't.

BRUTUS I heard him swear,
Were he to stand for consul, never would he
Appear i' th' market-place nor on him put
The napless vesture of humility;
Nor, showing, as the manner is, his wounds
To th' people, beg their stinking breaths.

SICINIUS 'Tis right.

BRUTUS
It was his word. O, he would miss it rather
Than carry it but by the suit of the gentry to him
And the desire of the nobles.

SICINIUS I wish no better
Than have him hold that purpose and to put it
In execution.

BRUTUS 'Tis most like he will.

SICINIUS
It shall be to him then as our good wills,
A sure destruction.

BRUTUS So it must fall out
To him, or our authorities, for an end.
We must suggest the people in what hatred
He still hath held them; that to 's power he would
Have made them mules, silenc'd their pleaders, and
Dispropertied their freedoms, holding them,
In human action and capacity,
Of no more soul nor fitness for the world
Than camels in their war, who have their provand
Only for bearing burdens, and sore blows
For sinking under them.

SICINIUS This—as you say, suggested
At some time when his soaring insolence
Shall touch the people, which time shall not want
If he be put upon 't, and that's as easy
As to set dogs on sheep—will be his fire
To kindle their dry stubble; and their blaze
Shall darken him for ever.

Enter a Messenger.

BRUTUS What's the matter?

MESSENGER
You are sent for to the Capitol. 'Tis thought
That Marcius shall be consul.
I have seen the dumb men throng to see him, and
The blind to hear him speak. Matrons flung gloves,
Ladies and maids their scarfs and handkerchers,
Upon him as he pass'd. The nobles bended,
As to Jove's statue, and the commons made
A shower and thunder with their caps and shouts.
I never saw the like.

BRUTUS Let's to the Capitol,
And carry with us ears and eyes for th' time,
But hearts for the event.

SICINIUS Have with you. *Exeunt.*

[SCENE II]

Enter two Officers, to lay cushions, as it were in the Capitol.

FIRST OFFICER Come, come, they are almost here. How many stand for consulships?

SECOND OFFICER Three, they say; but 'tis thought of everyone Coriolanus will carry it.

FIRST OFFICER That's a brave fellow; but he's vengeance proud, and loves not the common people.

SECOND OFFICER Faith, there hath been many great men that have flatter'd the people who ne'er lov'd them; and there be many that they have lov'd, they know not wherefore; so that, if they love they know not why, they hate upon no better a ground. Therefore, for Coriolanus neither to care whether they love or hate him manifests the true knowledge he has in their disposition, and out of his noble carelessness lets them plainly see 't.

FIRST OFFICER If he did not care whether he had their love or no, he wav'd indifferently 'twixt doing them neither good nor harm; but he seeks their hate with greater devotion than they can render it him, and

210 variable various. **complexions** types **211 Seld-shown** seldom seen. **flamens** priests (of ancient Rome) **212 popular** plebeian, vulgar. **puff** pant, exert themselves **213 vulgar station** place in the crowd **214 damask** red **215 nicely-gauded** daintily adorned or made up **216 Phoebus'** i.e., the sun's. **pother** hubbub **222–223 He . . . end** i.e., he cannot, as a temperate man could, carry his honors throughout his course **226 Upon . . . malice** because of their long-standing hostility **227 With . . . cause** upon the slightest provocation. **which** i.e., which provocation **228 make . . . question** I have as little doubt **229 As** as that **232 napless** threadbare **234 breaths** i.e., votes **235 it** i.e., the consulship **236 carry it but** win it otherwise than **239 like** likely **240 as . . . wills** as we would have it **242 authorities** offices. **for an end** ultimately **243 suggest** insinuate to **244 still** always. **to 's power** to the extent of his power **245 mules** i.e., beasts of burden. **pleaders** i.e., the tribunes **246 Dispropertied** alienated, deprived (them) of

249 provand provender, food **253 want** be lacking **254 put upon 't** urged, incited to it **255 his fire** i.e., the spark that kindles his hatred **267 time** present situation **268 hearts . . . event** i.e., deeper desires and purposes for what is to follow

II.ii. Location: Rome. The Capitol.
3 of by **5 vengeance** terribly **13 in** of **17 wav'd indifferently** would waver impartially

leaves nothing undone that may fully discover him their opposite. Now, to seem to affect the malice and displeasure of the people is as bad as that which he dislikes, to flatter them for their love.

SECOND OFFICER He hath deserv'd worthily of his country; and his ascent is not by such easy degrees as those who, having been supple and courteous to the people, bonneted, without any further deed to have them at all into their estimation and report. But he hath so planted his honors in their eyes and his actions in their hearts that for their tongues to be silent and not confess so much were a kind of ingrateful injury; to report otherwise were a malice that, giving itself the lie, would pluck reproof and rebuke from every ear that heard it.

FIRST OFFICER No more of him; he's a worthy man. Make way, they are coming.

A sennet. Enter the Patricians and the Tribunes of the people, Lictors before them; Coriolanus, Menenius, Cominius the Consul. Sicinius and Brutus take their places by themselves. Coriolanus stands.

MENENIUS
Having determin'd of the Volsces and
To send for Titus Lartius, it remains,
As the main point of this our after-meeting,
To gratify his noble service that
Hath thus stood for his country. Therefore, please you,
Most reverend and grave elders, to desire
The present consul, and last general
In our well-found successes, to report
A little of that worthy work perform'd
By Caius Marcius Coriolanus, whom
We met here both to thank and to remember
With honors like himself. [*Coriolanus sits.*]

FIRST SENATOR Speak, good Cominius.
Leave nothing out for length, and make us think
Rather our state's defective for requital
Than we to stretch it out. [*To the Tribunes.*] Masters o' th' people,
We do request your kindest ears, and after,
Your loving motion toward the common body,
To yield what passes here.

SICINIUS We are convented
Upon a pleasing treaty, and have hearts
Inclinable to honor and advance
The theme of our assembly.

BRUTUS Which the rather
We shall be blest to do, if he remember
A kinder value of the people than
He hath hereto priz'd them at.

MENENIUS That's off, that's off!
I would you rather had been silent. Please you
To hear Cominius speak?

BRUTUS Most willingly;
But yet my caution was more pertinent
Than the rebuke you give it.

MENENIUS He loves your people;
But tie him not to be their bedfellow.
Worthy Cominius, speak.
Coriolanus rises and offers to go away.
Nay, keep your place.

FIRST SENATOR
Sit, Coriolanus. Never shame to hear
What you have nobly done.

CORIOLANUS Your honors' pardon.
I had rather have my wounds to heal again
Than hear say how I got them.

BRUTUS Sir, I hope
My words disbench'd you not?

CORIOLANUS No, sir. Yet oft,
When blows have made me stay, I fled from words.
You sooth'd not, therefore hurt not; but your people,
I love them as they weigh.—

MENENIUS Pray now, sit down.

CORIOLANUS
I had rather have one scratch my head i' th' sun
When the alarum were struck than idly sit
To hear my nothings monster'd. *Exit Coriolanus.*

MENENIUS Masters of the people,
Your multiplying spawn how can he flatter—
That's thousand to one good one—when you now see
He had rather venture all his limbs for honor
Than one on 's ears to hear it?—Proceed, Cominius.

COMINIUS
I shall lack voice. The deeds of Coriolanus
Should not be utter'd feebly. It is held
That valor is the chiefest virtue, and
Most dignifies the haver; if it be,
The man I speak of cannot in the world
Be singly counterpois'd. At sixteen years,
When Tarquin made a head for Rome, he fought
Beyond the mark of others. Our then dictator,
Whom with all praise I point at, saw him fight,
When with his Amazonian chin he drove
The bristled lips before him. He bestrid
An o'erpress'd Roman, and i' th' consul's view
Slew three opposers. Tarquin's self he met,
And struck him on his knee. In that day's feats,
When he might act the woman in the scene,

20–21 discover . . . opposite reveal him to be their adversary **21 affect** seek out, desire **27 bonneted** took their hats off. **have them** make their way **32–33 giving . . . lie** manifesting its own falsehood **36 s.d. Lictors** officials attendant upon Roman magistrates **37 determin'd of** i.e., reached a decision concerning the terms for returning Corioles, etc. **40 gratify** reward, requite **43 last** late **44 well-found** fortunately met with **48 like himself** i.e., worthy of his greatness **50–51 Rather . . . out** that our state is defective in the very means to reward adequately rather than that we are defective in intention to extend what reward we have at our disposal **53 loving . . . body** friendly intervention with the common people **54 yield** grant. **passes** is voted. **convented** summoned, convened **55 Upon** in order to consider. **treaty** proposal **57 rather** sooner **58 blest** happy **59 kinder value** more favorable estimation

60 off jarring, not pertinent **71 disbench'd you not** did not make you leave your seat **73 sooth'd** flattered **74 as they weigh** according to their deserts **75–76 have . . . struck** i.e., engage in idle pleasure when the battle signal is sounded **77 monster'd** pointed out as wonderful **79 That's . . . one** in which there are a thousand bad ones to one good one; or, a thousand bad ones contrasted to the noble Coriolanus **81 on's** of his. **it** i.e., praise of his honor **87 singly counterpois'd** equaled by any other single one **88 made . . . for** raised a force to attack (and reconquer) **89 mark** ability, reach. **dictator** leader constitutionally given absolute authority to deal with a specific emergency such as a war **91 Amazonian** i.e., beardless (like the female warriors, the Amazons) **92 bestrid** stood over in battle, protected **93 o'erpress'd** overwhelmed **95 on** to **96 he . . . scene** i.e., he was young enough not to have been blamed for cowardice (with perhaps an allusion to boys playing women's roles in the theatre)

He prov'd best man i' th' field, and for his meed 97
Was brow-bound with the oak. His pupil age
Man-ent'red thus, he waxed like a sea, 99
And in the brunt of seventeen battles since
He lurch'd all swords of the garland. For this last, 101
Before and in Corioles, let me say,
I cannot speak him home. He stopp'd the fliers, 103
And by his rare example made the coward
Turn terror into sport. As weeds before
A vessel under sail, so men obey'd
And fell below his stem. His sword, death's stamp, 107
Where it did mark, it took; from face to foot 108
He was a thing of blood, whose every motion
Was tim'd with dying cries. Alone he ent'red 110
The mortal gate o' th' city, which he painted 111
With shunless destiny; aidless came off, 112
And with a sudden reinforcement struck
Corioles like a planet. Now all's his, 114
When by and by the din of war gan pierce 115
His ready sense; then straight his doubled spirit 116
Requick'ned what in flesh was fatigate, 117
And to the battle came he, where he did
Run reeking o'er the lives of men, as if 119
'Twere a perpetual spoil; and till we call'd 120
Both field and city ours, he never stood 121
To ease his breast with panting.

MENENIUS Worthy man!

FIRST SENATOR
He cannot but with measure fit the honors 123
Which we devise him.

COMINIUS Our spoils he kick'd at,
And look'd upon things precious as they were
The common muck of the world. He covets less
Than misery itself would give, rewards 127
His deeds with doing them, and is content 128
To spend the time to end it.

MENENIUS He's right noble. 129
Let him be call'd for.

FIRST SENATOR Call Coriolanus.

OFFICER
He doth appear.

Enter Coriolanus.

MENENIUS
The Senate, Coriolanus, are well pleas'd
To make thee consul.

CORIOLANUS I do owe them still 133
My life and services.

MENENIUS It then remains
That you do speak to the people.

CORIOLANUS I do beseech you,
Let me o'erleap that custom; for I cannot
Put on the gown, stand naked, and entreat them 137
For my wounds' sake to give their suffrage.
Please you
That I may pass this doing.

SICINIUS Sir, the people 139
Must have their voices; neither will they bate 140
One jot of ceremony.

MENENIUS Put them not to 't. 141
Pray you, go fit you to the custom and
Take to you, as your predecessors have,
Your honor with your form.

CORIOLANUS It is a part 144
That I shall blush in acting, and might well
Be taken from the people.

BRUTUS [*To Sicinius*] Mark you that?

CORIOLANUS
To brag unto them, "Thus I did, and thus!"
Show them th' unaching scars which I should hide,
As if I had receiv'd them for the hire
Of their breath only!

MENENIUS Do not stand upon 't. 150
We recommend to you, tribunes of the people, 151
Our purpose to them, and to our noble consul
Wish we all joy and honor.

SENATORS
To Coriolanus come all joy and honor!

Flourish cornets. Then exeunt. Mane[*n*]*t Sicinius and Brutus.*

BRUTUS
You see how he intends to use the people.

SICINIUS
May they perceive 's intent! He will require them 156
As if he did contemn what he requested 157
Should be in them to give.

BRUTUS Come, we'll inform them
Of our proceedings here. On th' market-place
I know they do attend us. [*Exeunt.*]

[SCENE III]

Enter seven or eight Citizens.

FIRST CITIZEN Once if he do require our voices, we ought not to deny him. 1

SECOND CITIZEN We may, sir, if we will.

THIRD CITIZEN We have power in ourselves to do it, but it is a power that we have no power to do; for if he show us his wounds and tell us his deeds, we are to put our tongues into those wounds and speak for them; so, if he tell us his noble deeds, we must also tell him our noble acceptance of them. Ingratitude is

97 meed reward **99 Man-ent'red** entered into manhood **101 lurch'd** robbed, cheated **103 speak him home** praise him adequately **107 stem** main timber of the prow of a ship **108 took** took possession, slew **110 Was tim'd** kept time, was accompanied **111 mortal** deadly. **painted** i.e., stained **112 shunless destiny** i.e., the blood of those who could not escape their doom **114 like a planet** (Refers to the power of striking or blasting, believed in astrology to belong to the planets.) **115 gan** began to **116 ready sense** i.e., alert sense of hearing. **straight** at once **117 Requick'ned** revivified. **fatigate** fatigued **119 reeking** steaming (with enemies' blood) **120 perpetual spoil** endless slaughter **121 stood** stopped **123 with measure** becomingly **127 misery** poverty **128–129 is content . . . end it** is satisfied to be repaid for his time spent with the pleasure of having spent his time thus **133 still** ever

137 naked exposed **139 pass** disregard, omit **140 voices** votes. **bate** abate, do without **141 Put . . . to 't** i.e., do not force the issue **144 with your form** i.e., with the accompanying conventionalities **150 stand upon 't** make a point of it **151 recommend** commit, consign **156 require** ask, request **157 contemn** scorn (that)

II.iii. Location: Rome. The Forum.
1 Once if if in fact

monstrous, and for the multitude to be ingrateful were to make a monster of the multitude; of the which we, being members, should bring ourselves to be monstrous members.

FIRST CITIZEN And to make us no better thought of, a little help will serve; for once we stood up about the corn, he himself stuck not to call us the many-headed multitude.

THIRD CITIZEN We have been call'd so of many; not that our heads are some brown, some black, some abram, some bald, but that our wits are so diversely color'd; and truly I think if all our wits were to issue out of one skull, they would fly east, west, north, south, and their consent of one direct way should be at once to all the points o' th' compass.

SECOND CITIZEN Think you so? Which way do you judge my wit would fly?

THIRD CITIZEN Nay, your wit will not so soon out as another man's will; 'tis strongly wedg'd up in a blockhead; but if it were at liberty, 'twould, sure, southward.

SECOND CITIZEN Why that way?

THIRD CITIZEN To lose itself in a fog, where being three parts melted away with rotten dews, the fourth would return for conscience' sake, to help to get thee a wife.

SECOND CITIZEN You are never without your tricks. You may, you may.

THIRD CITIZEN Are you all resolv'd to give your voices? But that's no matter, the greater part carries it. I say, if he would incline to the people, there was never a worthier man.

Enter Coriolanus in a gown of humility, with Menenius.

Here he comes, and in the gown of humility. Mark his behavior. We are not to stay all together, but to come by him where he stands, by ones, by twos, and by threes. He's to make his requests by particulars, wherein every one of us has a single honor, in giving him our own voices with our own tongues. Therefore follow me, and I'll direct you how you shall go by him.

ALL Content, content. *[Exeunt citizens.]*

MENENIUS
O sir, you are not right. Have you not known
The worthiest men have done 't?

CORIOLANUS What must I say?
"I pray, sir"—Plague upon 't! I cannot bring
My tongue to such a pace. "Look, sir, my wounds!
I got them in my country's service, when
Some certain of your brethren roar'd and ran
From th' noise of our own drums."

MENENIUS O me, the gods!
You must not speak of that. You must desire them
To think upon you.

CORIOLANUS Think upon me? Hang 'em!
I would they would forget me, like the virtues
Which our divines lose by 'em.

MENENIUS You'll mar all.
I'll leave you. Pray you speak to 'em, I pray you,
In wholesome manner. *Exit.*

Enter three of the Citizens.

CORIOLANUS Bid them wash their faces
And keep their teeth clean. So, here comes a
brace.—
You know the cause, sir, of my standing here.

THIRD CITIZEN
We do, sir; tell us what hath brought you to 't.

CORIOLANUS Mine own desert.

SECOND CITIZEN Your own desert?

CORIOLANUS Ay, but not mine own desire.

THIRD CITIZEN How, not your own desire?

CORIOLANUS No, sir, 'twas never my desire yet to trouble the poor with begging.

THIRD CITIZEN You must think, if we give you anything, we hope to gain by you.

CORIOLANUS Well then, I pray, your price o' th' consulship?

FIRST CITIZEN The price is to ask it kindly.

CORIOLANUS Kindly, sir, I pray, let me ha 't. I have wounds to show you, which shall be yours in private. Your good voice, sir; what say you?

SECOND CITIZEN You shall ha 't, worthy sir.

CORIOLANUS A match, sir. There's in all two worthy voices begg'd. I have your alms. Adieu.

THIRD CITIZEN But this is something odd.

SECOND CITIZEN An 'twere to give again—but 'tis no matter. *Exeunt [the three Citizens].*

Enter two other Citizens.

CORIOLANUS Pray you now, if it may stand with the tune of your voices that I may be consul, I have here the customary gown.

FOURTH CITIZEN You have deserv'd nobly of your country, and you have not deserv'd nobly.

CORIOLANUS Your enigma?

FOURTH CITIZEN You have been a scourge to her enemies, you have been a rod to her friends; you have not indeed lov'd the common people.

CORIOLANUS You should account me the more virtuous that I have not been common in my love. I will, sir, flatter my sworn brother, the people, to earn a dearer estimation of them; 'tis a condition they account gentle. And since the wisdom of their choice is rather to have my hat than my heart, I will practice the insinuating nod and be off to them most counterfeitly; that is, sir, I will counterfeit the bewitchment of some popular man and give it bountiful to the desirers. Therefore, beseech you, I may be consul.

14–15 a little . . . serve a small amount will suffice **15 once** when **16 stuck not** did not hesitate **18 of** by. **that** because **19 abram** auburn **23 consent of** agreement upon **29–30 southward** (The south wind was believed to bring pestilence.) **33 rotten** unwholesome **35–36 You may** i.e., go on, say what you like **38 greater part** majority **44 by particulars** to individuals, one by one **45 single** separate, individual

59 lose by 'em vainly seek to instill in them (by preaching) **62 brace** pair. (Used contemptuously here.) **77 yours** available for your inspection **80 match** deal, bargain **85 stand with** be consistent with **90 enigma** riddle **96–97 dearer . . . them** higher esteem on their part **97 condition** quality **100 be off** doff my hat. **counterfeitly** hypocritically **101 bewitchment** sorcery, bewitching powers **101–102 popular man** demagogue **102 bountiful** bountifully

FIFTH CITIZEN We hope to find you our friend; and therefore give you our voices heartily.

FOURTH CITIZEN You have receiv'd many wounds for your country.

CORIOLANUS I will not seal your knowledge with showing them. I will make much of your voices, and so trouble you no farther.

BOTH CITIZENS The gods give you joy, sir, heartily!

[*Exeunt Citizens.*]

CORIOLANUS
Most sweet voices!
Better it is to die, better to starve,
Than crave the hire which first we do deserve.
Why in this woolvish toge should I stand here,
To beg of Hob and Dick, that does appear,
Their needless vouches? Custom calls me to 't.
What custom wills, in all things should we do 't,
The dust on antique time would lie unswept,
And mountainous error be too highly heap'd
For truth to o'erpeer. Rather than fool it so,
Let the high office and the honor go
To one that would do thus. I am half through;
The one part suffer'd, the other will I do.

Enter three Citizens more.

Here come moe voices.—
Your voices! For your voices I have fought;
Watch'd for your voices; for your voices bear
Of wounds two dozen odd; battles thrice six
I have seen and heard of; for your voices have
Done many things, some less, some more. Your
voices!
Indeed, I would be consul.

SIXTH CITIZEN He has done nobly, and cannot go without any honest man's voice.

SEVENTH CITIZEN Therefore let him be consul. The gods give him joy, and make him good friend to the people!

ALL Amen, amen. God save thee, noble consul!

[*Exeunt Citizens.*]

CORIOLANUS
Worthy voices!

Enter Menenius, with Brutus and Sicinius.

MENENIUS
You have stood your limitation, and the tribunes
Endue you with the people's voice. Remains
That, in th' official marks invested, you
Anon do meet the Senate.

CORIOLANUS
Is this done?

SICINIUS
The custom of request you have discharg'd.
The people do admit you, and are summon'd
To meet anon, upon your approbation.

CORIOLANUS
Where? At the Senate-house?

SICINIUS
There, Coriolanus.

CORIOLANUS
May I change these garments?

SICINIUS
You may, sir.

CORIOLANUS
That I'll straight do; and, knowing myself again,
Repair to th' Senate-house.

MENENIUS
I'll keep you company. Will you along?

BRUTUS
We stay here for the people.

SICINIUS
Fare you well.

Exeunt Coriolanus and Menenius.

He has it now, and by his looks methinks
'Tis warm at 's heart.

BRUTUS
With a proud heart he wore
His humble weeds. Will you dismiss the people?

Enter the Plebeians.

SICINIUS
How now, my masters, have you chose this man?

FIRST CITIZEN
He has our voices, sir.

BRUTUS
We pray the gods he may deserve your loves.

SECOND CITIZEN
Amen, sir. To my poor unworthy notice,
He mock'd us when he begg'd our voices.

THIRD CITIZEN
Certainly he flouted us downright.

FIRST CITIZEN
No, 'tis his kind of speech. He did not mock us.

SECOND CITIZEN
Not one amongst us, save yourself, but says
He us'd us scornfully. He should have show'd us
His marks of merit, wounds receiv'd for 's country.

SICINIUS
Why, so he did, I am sure.

ALL
No, no; no man saw 'em.

THIRD CITIZEN
He said he had wounds, which he could show in
private;
And with his hat, thus waving it in scorn,
"I would be consul," says he. "Aged custom,
But by your voices, will not so permit me;
Your voices therefore." When we granted that,
Here was "I thank you for your voices. Thank you.
Your most sweet voices! Now you have left your
voices,
I have no further with you." Was not this mockery?

SICINIUS
Why either were you ignorant to see 't,
Or, seeing it, of such childish friendliness

108 seal confirm **114 crave . . . deserve** beg the reward or wages we have already earned **115 woolvish toge** wolf's toga (like a wolf in sheep's clothing ?), or woolen toga (?) **116 Hob and Dick** (Typical names for rustics.) **that does appear** as they come forward **117 vouches** confirmations of approval **118 in . . . do 't** if we should obey custom indiscriminately **121 o'erpeer** overtop, be visible over. **fool it** play the fool **125 moe voices** more votes **127 Watch'd** kept watch (in camp) **139 limitation** allotted time **140 Endue** endow. **Remains** it remains **141 official marks** insignia

145 upon your approbation to confirm your having been elected **175 ignorant** too dull

To yield your voices?
BRUTUS Could you not have told him
As you were lesson'd? When he had no power,
But was a petty servant to the state,
He was your enemy, ever spake against
Your liberties and the charters that you bear
I' th' body of the weal; and now, arriving
A place of potency and sway o' th' state,
If he should still malignantly remain
Fast foe to th' plebii, your voices might
Be curses to yourselves. You should have said
That as his worthy deeds did claim no less
Than what he stood for, so his gracious nature
Would think upon you for your voices and
Translate his malice towards you into love,
Standing your friendly lord.
SICINIUS Thus to have said,
As you were fore-advis'd, had touch'd his spirit
And tried his inclination; from him pluck'd
Either his gracious promise, which you might,
As cause had call'd you up, have held him to;
Or else it would have gall'd his surly nature,
Which easily endures not article
Tying him to aught; so putting him to rage,
You should have ta'en th' advantage of his choler
And pass'd him unelected.
BRUTUS Did you perceive
He did solicit you in free contempt
When he did need your loves, and do you think
That his contempt shall not be bruising to you
When he hath power to crush? Why, had your bodies
No heart among you? Or had you tongues to cry
Against the rectorship of judgment?
SICINIUS Have you
Ere now denied the asker? And now again,
Of him that did not ask but mock, bestow
Your sued-for tongues?
THIRD CITIZEN
He's not confirm'd; we may deny him yet.
SECOND CITIZEN
And will deny him.
I'll have five hundred voices of that sound.
FIRST CITIZEN
I twice five hundred, and their friends to piece 'em.
BRUTUS
Get you hence instantly, and tell those friends
They have chose a consul that will from them take
Their liberties, make them of no more voice
Than dogs that are as often beat for barking
As therefore kept to do so.
SICINIUS Let them assemble,
And on a safer judgment all revoke
Your ignorant election. Enforce his pride,
And his old hate unto you. Besides, forget not
With what contempt he wore the humble weed,
How in his suit he scorn'd you; but your loves,
Thinking upon his services, took from you
Th' apprehension of his present portance,
Which most gibingly, ungravely, he did fashion
After the inveterate hate he bears you.
BRUTUS Lay
A fault on us, your tribunes, that we labor'd,
No impediment between, but that you must
Cast your election on him.
SICINIUS Say, you chose him
More after our commandment than as guided
By your own true affections, and that your minds,
Preoccupied with what you rather must do
Than what you should, made you against the grain
To voice him consul. Lay the fault on us.
BRUTUS
Ay, spare us not. Say we read lectures to you,
How youngly he began to serve his country,
How long continued, and what stock he springs of,
The noble house o' th' Marcians, from whence came
That Ancus Marcius, Numa's daughter's son,
Who after great Hostilius here was king;
Of the same house Publius and Quintus were,
That our best water brought by conduits hither;
[And Censorinus, that was so surnam'd,]
And nobly named so, twice being censor,
Was his great ancestor.
SICINIUS One thus descended,
That hath beside well in his person wrought
To be set high in place, we did commend
To your remembrances; but you have found,
Scaling his present bearing with his past,
That he's your fixed enemy, and revoke
Your sudden approbation.
BRUTUS Say, you ne'er had done 't—
Harp on that still—but by our putting on;
And presently, when you have drawn your number,
Repair to th' Capitol.
ALL We will so. Almost all
Repent in their election. *Exeunt Plebeians.*
BRUTUS Let them go on.
This mutiny were better put in hazard
Than stay, past doubt, for greater.
If, as his nature is, he fall in rage
With their refusal, both observe and answer
The vantage of his anger.
SICINIUS To th' Capitol, come.
We will be there before the stream o' th' people;
And this shall seem, as partly 'tis, their own,
Which we have goaded onward. *Exeunt.*

181 charters privileges **182 body of the weal** commonwealth. **arriving** attaining **185 plebii** plebeians **188 what . . . for** i.e., the office he was seeking **189 Would think upon** should esteem **192 had touch'd** would have tested (as gold and silver were tested with the touchstone) **195 call'd you up** aroused you (during his consulship) **197 article** stipulated condition **199 choler** anger **201 free** frank **205 heart** i.e., as a seat of courage. **to cry** only to rebel **206 rectorship** guidance. **judgment** common sense **206–207 Have . . . asker** haven't you on previous occasions denied one asking for your support **208 Of** upon **213 piece** add to, reinforce

220 Enforce lay stress upon **225 apprehension** perceiving. **portance** behavior **227 After** in accord with **229 No impediment between** without admitting any impediment **240 Numa** legendary successor of Romulus as King of Rome **243 conduits** aqueducts **244 And . . . surnam'd** (This bracketed line has been supplied by editors from Plutarch.) **250 Scaling** estimating, weighing **253 putting on** urging **254 drawn** assembled, collected **256 in** of **257 put in hazard** risked **258 for greater** for a greater risk (later on) **260–261 answer The vantage** make use

ACT III • [SCENE I]

Cornets. Enter Coriolanus, Menenius, all the Gentry, Cominius, Titus Lartius, and other Senators.

CORIOLANUS
Tullus Aufidius then had made new head?
LARTIUS
He had, my lord; and that it was which caus'd
Our swifter composition.
CORIOLANUS
So then the Volsces stand but as at first,
Ready, when time shall prompt them, to make road
Upon 's again.
COMINIUS They are worn, Lord Consul, so,
That we shall hardly in our ages see
Their banners wave again.
CORIOLANUS Saw you Aufidius?
LARTIUS
On safeguard he came to me, and did curse
Against the Volsces, for they had so vilely
Yielded the town. He is retir'd to Antium.
CORIOLANUS
Spoke he of me?
LARTIUS He did, my lord.
CORIOLANUS How? What?
LARTIUS
How often he had met you, sword to sword;
That of all things upon the earth he hated
Your person most; that he would pawn his fortunes
To hopeless restitution, so he might
Be call'd your vanquisher.
CORIOLANUS At Antium lives he?
LARTIUS
At Antium.
CORIOLANUS
I wish I had a cause to seek him there,
To oppose his hatred fully. Welcome home.

Enter Sicinius and Brutus.

Behold, these are the tribunes of the people,
The tongues o' th' common mouth. I do despise them,
For they do prank them in authority,
Against all noble sufferance.
SICINIUS [*Advancing*] Pass no further.
CORIOLANUS
Ha? What is that?
BRUTUS
It will be dangerous to go on. No further.
CORIOLANUS
What makes this change?
MENENIUS
The matter?
COMINIUS
Hath he not pass'd the noble and the common?
BRUTUS
Cominius, no.
CORIOLANUS Have I had children's voices?
FIRST SENATOR
Tribunes, give way; he shall to th' market-place.
BRUTUS
The people are incens'd against him.
SICINIUS Stop,
Or all will fall in broil.
CORIOLANUS Are these your herd?
Must these have voices, that can yield them now
And straight disclaim their tongues? What are your offices?
You being their mouths, why rule you not their teeth?
Have you not set them on?
MENENIUS Be calm, be calm.
CORIOLANUS
It is a purpos'd thing, and grows by plot,
To curb the will of the nobility.
Suffer 't, and live with such as cannot rule
Nor ever will be rul'd.
BRUTUS Call 't not a plot.
The people cry you mock'd them and, of late,
When corn was given them gratis, you repin'd;
Scandal'd the suppliants for the people, call'd them
Time-pleasers, flatterers, foes to nobleness.
CORIOLANUS
Why, this was known before.
BRUTUS Not to them all.
CORIOLANUS
Have you inform'd them sithence?
BRUTUS How? I inform them?
COMINIUS
You are like to do such business.
BRUTUS
Not unlike, each way, to better yours.
CORIOLANUS
Why then should I be consul? By yond clouds,
Let me deserve so ill as you, and make me
Your fellow tribune.
SICINIUS You show too much of that
For which the people stir. If you will pass
To where you are bound, you must inquire your way,
Which you are out of, with a gentler spirit,
Or never be so noble as a consul,
Nor yoke with him for tribune.
MENENIUS Let's be calm.
COMINIUS
The people are abus'd, set on. This palt'ring

III.i. Location: Rome. A street.
1 made new head raised another army **3 composition** coming to terms (about the return of Corioles to the Volscians) **5 road** inroad, attack **6 worn** i.e., militarily weakened **9 safeguard** safe-conduct **10 for** because **16 To . . . restitution** beyond hope of redemption **23 prank them** dress themselves up **24 Against . . . sufferance** beyond the power of nobility to tolerate

40 live i.e., you will have to live **43 repin'd** expressed regret **44 Scandal'd** defamed **47 sithence** since **49 Not . . . yours** not unlikely to prove, in any case, a better way than yours **52 that** i.e., that quality **53 stir** are aroused, angry **53–54 If . . . bound** i.e., if you wish to attain the consulship **55 are out of** have strayed from **57 yoke** be joined **58 abus'd** deceived. **set on** incited. **palt'ring** equivocation, ruse

Becomes not Rome, nor has Coriolanus
Deserv'd this so dishonor'd rub, laid falsely
I' th' plain way of his merit.

CORIOLANUS Tell me of corn!
This was my speech, and I will speak 't again—

MENENIUS
Not now, not now.

FIRST SENATOR
Not in this heat, sir, now.

CORIOLANUS Now, as I live,
I will. My nobler friends, I crave their pardons.
For the mutable, rank-scented meiny, let them
Regard me as I do not flatter, and
Therein behold themselves. I say again,
In soothing them, we nourish 'gainst our Senate
The cockle of rebellion, insolence, sedition,
Which we ourselves have plough'd for, sow'd, and scatter'd,
By mingling them with us, the honor'd number,
Who lack not virtue, no, nor power, but that
Which they have given to beggars.

MENENIUS Well, no more.

FIRST SENATOR
No more words, we beseech you.

CORIOLANUS How? No more?
As for my country I have shed my blood,
Not fearing outward force, so shall my lungs
Coin words till their decay against those measles
Which we disdain should tetter us, yet sought
The very way to catch them.

BRUTUS You speak o' th' people
As if you were a god to punish, not
A man of their infirmity.

SICINIUS 'Twere well
We let the people know 't.

MENENIUS What, what? His choler?

CORIOLANUS
Choler?
Were I as patient as the midnight sleep,
By Jove, 'twould be my mind!

SICINIUS It is a mind
That shall remain a poison where it is,
Not poison any further.

CORIOLANUS Shall remain?
Hear you this Triton of the minnows? Mark you
His absolute "shall"?

COMINIUS 'Twas from the canon.

CORIOLANUS "Shall"?
O good but most unwise patricians! Why,
You grave but reckless senators, have you thus
Given Hydra here to choose an officer,
That with his peremptory "shall," being but
The horn and noise o' th' monster's, wants not spirit
To say he'll turn your current in a ditch,
And make your channel his? If he have power,
Then vail your ignorance; if none, awake
Your dangerous lenity. If you are learn'd,
Be not as common fools; if you are not,
Let them have cushions by you. You are plebeians,
If they be senators; and they are no less
When, both your voices blended, the great'st taste
Most palates theirs. They choose their magistrate,
And such a one as he, who puts his "shall,"
His popular "shall," against a graver bench
Than ever frown'd in Greece. By Jove himself,
It makes the consuls base! And my soul aches
To know, when two authorities are up,
Neither supreme, how soon confusion
May enter 'twixt the gap of both and take
The one by th' other.

COMINIUS Well, on to th' market-place.

CORIOLANUS
Whoever gave that counsel, to give forth
The corn o' th' storehouse gratis, as 'twas us'd
Sometime in Greece—

MENENIUS Well, well, no more of that.

CORIOLANUS
Though there the people had more absolute pow'r,
I say they nourish'd disobedience, fed
The ruin of the state.

BRUTUS Why shall the people give
One that speaks thus their voice?

CORIOLANUS I'll give my reasons,
More worthier than their voices. They know the corn
Was not our recompense, resting well assur'd
They ne'er did service for 't. Being press'd to th' war,
Even when the navel of the state was touch'd,
They would not thread the gates. This kind of service
Did not deserve corn gratis. Being i' th' war,
Their mutinies and revolts, wherein they show'd
Most valor, spoke not for them. Th' accusation
Which they have often made against the Senate,
All cause unborn, could never be the native
Of our so frank donation. Well, what then?
How shall this bosom multiplied digest
The Senate's courtesy? Let deeds express
What's like to be their words: "We did request it;
We are the greater poll, and in true fear
They gave us our demands." Thus we debase

60 dishonor'd dishonoring. **rub** obstacle (as in the game of bowls) **66–68 For . . . themselves** as for the changeable, foul-smelling multitude, let them see themselves in the unflattering truth I show to them **70 cockle** weed **78 till their decay** i.e., until my lungs are no more. **measles** loathsome disease spots **79 tetter** infect with tetter (skin eruption). **sought** have sought **89 Triton of the minnows** i.e., god of the little fish. (Triton was Neptune's son and trumpeter.) **90 from the canon** not according to proper form, exceeding the authority granted the Tribunes **93 Given** permitted. **Hydra** many-headed monster slain by Hercules; here, the mob

95 horn and noise noisy horn. (See allusion to Triton above.) **96 turn** divert. **in** into **98 vail your ignorance** bow down to him in your ignorant yielding **98–99 awake . . . lenity** arouse yourselves from your dangerous mildness **101 cushions** i.e., seats in the Senate **102–104 and . . . theirs** and they are to all intents and purposes senators if, when their voices are mingled with yours, the resulting action savors of them rather than of you **106 popular** on behalf of the populace. **graver bench** more august deliberative body **107 frown'd** looked austere in judgment. **Greece** (famous for its law-giving institutions) **109 up** established, in action **111 gap of both** space between the two. **take** destroy **112 by** by means of **114 us'd** practiced **121 our recompense** reward from us **122 press'd** enlisted **123 navel** vital center **124 thread** pass through **129 All cause unborn** unjustifiably. **native** natural source or origin **130 frank** freely granted **131 bosom multiplied** many-bosomed multitude. **digest** i.e., consider, regard (with also the literal sense of eating the grain) **134 greater poll** majority

The nature of our seats and make the rabble
Call our cares fears; which will in time
Break ope the locks o' th' Senate, and bring in
The crows to peck the eagles.

MENENIUS
Come, enough.

BRUTUS
Enough, with over-measure.

CORIOLANUS
No, take more!
What may be sworn by, both divine and human,
Seal what I end withal! This double worship,
Where one part does disdain with cause, the other
Insult without all reason, where gentry, title, wisdom,
Cannot conclude but by the yea and no
Of general ignorance—it must omit
Real necessities, and give way the while
To unstable slightness. Purpose so barr'd, it follows
Nothing is done to purpose. Therefore, beseech you—
You that will be less fearful than discreet,
That love the fundamental part of state
More than you doubt the change on 't, that prefer
A noble life before a long, and wish
To jump a body with a dangerous physic
That's sure of death without it—at once pluck out
The multitudinous tongue; let them not lick
The sweet which is their poison. Your dishonor
Mangles true judgment, and bereaves the state
Of that integrity which should become 't,
Not having the power to do the good it would,
For th' ill which doth control 't.

BRUTUS
H'as said enough.

SICINIUS
H'as spoken like a traitor, and shall answer
As traitors do.

CORIOLANUS
Thou wretch, despite o'erwhelm thee!
What should the people do with these bald tribunes?
On whom depending, their obedience fails
To th' greater bench. In a rebellion,
When what's not meet, but what must be, was law,
Then were they chosen. In a better hour,
Let what is meet be said it must be meet,
And throw their power i' th' dust.

BRUTUS
Manifest treason!

SICINIUS
This a consul? No!

BRUTUS
The aediles, ho!

Enter an Aedile.

Let him be apprehended.

141 What whatever **142 Seal** confirm. **double worship** divided authority **145 conclude** come to a final conclusion **148 Purpose so barr'd** planning being thus obstructed **150 less . . . discreet** less actuated by fear than by foresight **151–152 That . . . on 't** i.e., that love the essentials of our government more than you fear revolutionary attempts to change it **154 jump** risk (treating). **physic** cure **157 sweet . . . poison** i.e., power which in their hands will undo them as well as Rome **161 For** because of. **ill** i.e., tribunal, popular power. **H'as** he has **163 despite** scorn **164 bald** petty **166 greater bench** i.e., senators collectively **167 what's . . . be** unfitting but unavoidable necessity **169 Let . . . be meet** i.e., let us openly say what's right is right **172 aediles** officers attached to the tribunes

SICINIUS
Go, call the people [*Exit Aedile*], in whose name myself
Attach thee as a traitorous innovator,
A foe to th' public weal. Obey, I charge thee,
And follow to thine answer.

CORIOLANUS
Hence, old goat!

ALL PATRICIANS
We'll surety him.

COMINIUS
Ag'd sir, hands off.

CORIOLANUS
Hence, rotten thing! Or I shall shake thy bones
Out of thy garments.

SICINIUS
Help, ye citizens!

Enter a rabble of Plebeians, with the Aediles.

MENENIUS
On both sides more respect.

SICINIUS
Here's he that would
Take from you all your power.

BRUTUS
Seize him, aediles!

ALL PLEBEIANS
Down with him! Down with him!

SECOND SENATOR
Weapons, weapons, weapons!

They all bustle about Coriolanus.

ALL
Tribunes!—Patricians!—Citizens!—What, ho!—
Sicinius!—Brutus!—Coriolanus!—Citizens!—
Peace, peace, peace!—Stay, hold, peace!

MENENIUS
What is about to be? I am out of breath;
Confusion's near; I cannot speak. You, tribunes
To th' people! Coriolanus, patience!
Speak, good Sicinius.

SICINIUS
Hear me, people; peace!

ALL PLEBEIANS
Let's hear our tribune. Peace! Speak, speak, speak.

SICINIUS
You are at point to lose your liberties.
Marcius would have all from you; Marcius,
Whom late you have nam'd for consul.

MENENIUS
Fie, fie, fie!
This is the way to kindle, not to quench.

FIRST SENATOR
To unbuild the city and to lay all flat.

SICINIUS
What is the city but the people?

ALL PLEBEIANS
True,
The people are the city.

BRUTUS
By the consent of all, we were establish'd
The people's magistrates.

ALL PLEBEIANS
You so remain.

MENENIUS
And so are like to do.

174 Attach arrest **176 answer** defense, answer to a charge **177 surety** go bail for **192 at point to lose** on the point of losing

COMINIUS
That is the way to lay the city flat,
To bring the roof to the foundation,
And bury all, which yet distinctly ranges,
In heaps and piles of ruin.
SICINIUS This deserves death.
BRUTUS
Or let us stand to our authority,
Or let us lose it. We do here pronounce,
Upon the part o' th' people, in whose power
We were elected theirs, Marcius is worthy
Of present death.
SICINIUS Therefore lay hold of him!
Bear him to th' rock Tarpeian, and from thence
Into destruction cast him.
BRUTUS Aediles, seize him!
ALL PLEBEIANS
Yield, Marcius, yield!
MENENIUS Hear me one word.
Beseech you, tribunes, hear me but a word.
AEDILES
Peace, peace!
MENENIUS [*To Brutus*]
Be that you seem, truly your country's friend,
And temp'rately proceed to what you would
Thus violently redress.
BRUTUS Sir, those cold ways,
That seem like prudent helps, are very poisonous
Where the disease is violent.—Lay hands
upon him,
And bear him to the rock.
Coriolanus draws his sword.
CORIOLANUS No, I'll die here.
There's some among you have beheld me fighting.
Come, try upon yourselves what you have seen me.
MENENIUS
Down with that sword! Tribunes, withdraw awhile.
BRUTUS
Lay hands upon him.
MENENIUS Help Marcius, help!
You that be noble, help him, young and old!
ALL PLEBEIANS
Down with him, down with him!
In this mutiny, the Tribunes, the Aediles, and the People are beat in.
MENENIUS [*To Coriolanus*]
Go, get you to your house; be gone, away!
All will be naught else.
SECOND SENATOR Get you gone.
CORIOLANUS Stand fast!
We have as many friends as enemies.
MENENIUS
Shall it be put to that?
FIRST SENATOR The gods forbid!
I prithee, noble friend, home to thy house;
Leave us to cure this cause.
MENENIUS
For 'tis a sore upon us
You cannot tent yourself. Be gone, beseech you.
COMINIUS
Come, sir, along with us.
CORIOLANUS
I would they were barbarians, as they are,
Though in Rome litter'd; not Romans, as they
are not,
Though calved i' th' porch o' th' Capitol!
MENENIUS Be gone!
Put not your worthy rage into your tongue.
One time will owe another.
CORIOLANUS On fair ground
I could beat forty of them.
MENENIUS I could myself
Take up a brace o' th' best of them; yea, the two
tribunes.
COMINIUS
But now 'tis odds beyond arithmetic,
And manhood is call'd foolery when it stands
Against a falling fabric. Will you hence
Before the tag return, whose rage doth rend
Like interrupted waters and o'erbear
What they are us'd to bear?
MENENIUS Pray you, be gone.
I'll try whether my old wit be in request
With those that have but little. This must be patch'd
With cloth of any color.
COMINIUS Nay, come away.
Exeunt Coriolanus and Cominius [with others].
A PATRICIAN
This man has marr'd his fortune.
MENENIUS
His nature is too noble for the world.
He would not flatter Neptune for his trident,
Or Jove for 's power to thunder. His heart's his
mouth.
What his breast forges, that his tongue must vent;
And, being angry, does forget that ever
He heard the name of death. *A noise within.*
Here's goodly work!
A PATRICIAN
I would they were a-bed!
MENENIUS
I would they were in Tiber! What the vengeance!
Could he not speak 'em fair?

Enter Brutus and Sicinius, with the rabble again.

SICINIUS Where is this viper
That would depopulate the city and
Be every man himself?
MENENIUS You worthy tribunes—
SICINIUS
He shall be thrown down the Tarpeian rock
With rigorous hands. He hath resisted law,

204 distinctly ranges stretches out in proper order **211 rock Tarpeian** famous precipice on the Capitoline Hill in ancient Rome from which persons condemned for offenses against the state were thrown down **229 naught else** lost or ruined otherwise

235 tent treat (by probing a wound), cure **241 One . . . another** i.e., this occasion of the people's rebelling will be made up for on another occasion **243 Take up** cope with **246 fabric** building **247 tag** rabble **248 interrupted waters** waves breaking over their banks **250 request** demand **251–252 patch'd . . . color** i.e., mended in any way possible **262 'em fair** to them courteously

And therefore law shall scorn him further trial
Than the severity of the public power
Which he so sets at nought.

FIRST CITIZEN He shall well know
The noble tribunes are the people's mouths,
And we their hands.

ALL PLEBEIANS
He shall, sure on 't.

MENENIUS
Sir, sir—

SICINIUS
Peace!

MENENIUS
Do not cry havoc, where you should but hunt 275
With modest warrant.

SICINIUS Sir, how comes 't that you 276
Have holp to make this rescue?

MENENIUS Hear me speak! 277
As I do know the consul's worthiness,
So can I name his faults.

SICINIUS Consul? What consul?

MENENIUS
The consul Coriolanus.

BRUTUS He consul!

ALL PLEBEIANS
No, no, no, no, no.

MENENIUS
If, by the tribunes' leave, and yours, good people,
I may be heard, I would crave a word or two,
The which shall turn you to no further harm
Than so much loss of time.

SICINIUS Speak briefly then,
For we are peremptory to dispatch 286
This viperous traitor. To eject him hence
Were but one danger, and to keep him here
Our certain death; therefore it is decreed
He dies tonight.

MENENIUS Now the good gods forbid
That our renowned Rome, whose gratitude
Towards her deserved children is enroll'd
In Jove's own book, like an unnatural dam 293
Should now eat up her own!

SICINIUS
He's a disease that must be cut away.

MENENIUS
O, he's a limb that has but a disease;
Mortal, to cut it off; to cure it, easy. 297
What has he done to Rome that's worthy death?
Killing our enemies, the blood he hath lost—
Which, I dare vouch, is more than that he hath,
By many an ounce—he dropp'd it for his country;
And what is left, to lose it by his country
Were to us all that do 't and suffer it
A brand to th' end o' th' world.

SICINIUS This is clean kam. 304

BRUTUS
Merely awry. When he did love his country, 305
It honor'd him.

MENENIUS The service of the foot,
Being once gangren'd, is not then respected
For what before it was.

BRUTUS We'll hear no more.
Pursue him to his house and pluck him thence,
Lest his infection, being of catching nature,
Spread further.

MENENIUS
One word more, one word.
This tiger-footed rage, when it shall find
The harm of unscann'd swiftness, will too late 314
Tie leaden pounds to 's heels. Proceed by process, 315
Lest parties, as he is belov'd, break out, 316
And sack great Rome with Romans.

BRUTUS If it were so—

SICINIUS
What do ye talk? 318
Have we not had a taste of his obedience?
Our aediles smote? Ourselves resisted? Come.

MENENIUS
Consider this: he has been bred i' th' wars
Since 'a could draw a sword, and is ill school'd
In bolted language; meal and bran together 323
He throws without distinction. Give me leave,
I'll go to him, and undertake to bring him
Where he shall answer, by a lawful form,
In peace, to his utmost peril.

FIRST SENATOR Noble tribunes,
It is the humane way. The other course
Will prove too bloody, and the end of it
Unknown to the beginning.

SICINIUS Noble Menenius, 330
Be you then as the people's officer.
Masters, lay down your weapons.

BRUTUS Go not home.

SICINIUS
Meet on the market-place. We'll attend you there,
Where, if you bring not Marcius, we'll proceed
In our first way.

MENENIUS
I'll bring him to you.
[*To the Senators.*] Let me desire your company. He
must come,
Or what is worst will follow.

FIRST SENATOR Pray you, let's to him.

Exeunt omnes.

[SCENE II]

Enter Coriolanus with Nobles.

CORIOLANUS
Let them pull all about mine ears, present me
Death on the wheel or at wild horses' heels, 2

275 cry havoc give the order for general slaughter **276 modest** moderate **277 holp** helped **286 peremptory** determined **293 dam** mother **297 Mortal** fatal **304 brand** i.e., of infamy. **clean kam** quite perverse, wrong **305 Merely** completely

314 unscann'd unconsidered **315 pounds** weights. **process** legal method **316 parties** factions **318 What** why **323 bolted** sifted, refined

III.ii. Location: Rome. Coriolanus' house.
2 wheel instrument of torture and death by which the victim's limbs were broken

Or pile ten hills on the Tarpeian rock,
That the precipitation might down stretch
Below the beam of sight, yet will I still
Be thus to them.

NOBLE
You do the nobler.

CORIOLANUS
I muse my mother
Does not approve me further, who was wont
To call them woolen vassals, things created
To buy and sell with groats, to show bare heads
In congregations, to yawn, be still, and wonder,
When one but of my ordinance stood up
To speak of peace or war.

Enter Volumnia.

I talk of you.
Why did you wish me milder? Would you have me
False to my nature? Rather say I play
The man I am.

VOLUMNIA
O, sir, sir, sir,
I would have had you put your power well on,
Before you had worn it out.

CORIOLANUS
Let go.

VOLUMNIA
You might have been enough the man you are,
With striving less to be so. Lesser had been
The thwartings of your dispositions, if
You had not show'd them how ye were dispos'd
Ere they lack'd power to cross you.

CORIOLANUS
Let them hang!

VOLUMNIA
Ay, and burn too.

Enter Menenius with the Senators.

MENENIUS
Come, come, you have been too rough, something
too rough;
You must return and mend it.

FIRST SENATOR
There's no remedy,
Unless, by not so doing, our good city
Cleave in the midst, and perish.

VOLUMNIA
Pray be counsel'd.
I have a heart as little apt as yours,
But yet a brain that leads my use of anger
To better vantage.

MENENIUS
Well said, noble woman!
Before he should thus stoop to th' herd, but that
The violent fit o' th' time craves it as physic
For the whole state, I would put mine armor on,
Which I can scarcely bear.

CORIOLANUS
What must I do?

MENENIUS
Return to th' tribunes.

CORIOLANUS
Well, what then? What then?

MENENIUS
Repent what you have spoke.

CORIOLANUS
For them? I cannot do it to the gods;
Must I then do 't to them?

VOLUMNIA
You are too absolute;
Though therein you can never be too noble,
But when extremities speak. I have heard you say
Honor and policy, like unsever'd friends,
I' th' war do grow together. Grant that, and tell me
In peace what each of them by th' other lose
That they combine not there.

CORIOLANUS
Tush, tush!

MENENIUS
A good demand.

VOLUMNIA
If it be honor in your wars to seem
The same you are not, which, for your best ends,
You adopt your policy, how is it less or worse
That it shall hold companionship in peace
With honor, as in war, since that to both
It stands in like request?

CORIOLANUS
Why force you this?

VOLUMNIA
Because that now it lies you on to speak
To th' people, not by your own instruction,
Nor by th' matter which your heart prompts you,
But with such words that are but roted in
Your tongue, though but bastards and syllables
Of no allowance to your bosom's truth.
Now, this no more dishonors you at all
Than to take in a town with gentle words,
Which else would put you to your fortune and
The hazard of much blood.
I would dissemble with my nature where
My fortunes and my friends at stake requir'd
I should do so in honor. I am in this
Your wife, your son, these senators, the nobles;
And you will rather show our general louts
How you can frown, than spend a fawn upon 'em
For the inheritance of their loves and safeguard
Of what that want might ruin.

MENENIUS
Noble lady!—
Come, go with us; speak fair. You may salve so,
Not what is dangerous present, but the loss
Of what is past.

VOLUMNIA
I prithee now, my son,
Go to them, with this bonnet in thy hand,
And thus far having stretch'd it—here be with
them—
Thy knee bussing the stones; for in such business
Action is eloquence, and the eyes of th' ignorant
More learned than the ears; waving thy head,
Which often thus correcting thy stout heart,

4 precipitation precipitousness **5 beam** range **7 muse** wonder that **9 woolen** coarsely clad **10 groats** fourpenny pieces **11 yawn** i.e., gape with amazement **12 ordinance** rank **20 Let go** enough **25 Ere . . . you** i.e., until you became consul and were beyond their control **31 apt** compliant **34 but** were it not **35 craves** demands. **physic** medicine

43 But . . . speak except when necessity requires **44 policy** the proper consideration of stratagem and craft. **unsever'd** inseparable **53 It . . . request** it is equally needed. **force** urge **54 lies you on** is your duty **57 are but roted in** have been learned by heart in **59 Of . . . to** unsanctioned by **61 take in** capture **62 fortune** i.e., of war **66–67 I am . . . wife** in this I represent your wife **68 general** common, vulgar **69 fawn** flattering appeal **70 inheritance** obtaining **71 that want** i.e., the lack of their loves **73–74 Not . . . past** not only the present danger but what has been lost already **76 And . . . them** i.e., and go to them holding your hat out thus—do it this way for them. (She gestures.) **77 bussing** kissing **79 learned** i.e., receptive. **waving** bowing up and down **80 correcting** chastening. **stout** proud

Now humble as the ripest mulberry
That will not hold the handling. Or say to them
Thou art their soldier, and, being bred in broils,
Hast not the soft way which, thou dost confess,
Were fit for thee to use as they to claim,
In asking their good loves, but thou wilt frame
Thyself, forsooth, hereafter theirs, so far
As thou hast power and person.

MENENIUS
This but done,
Even as she speaks, why, their hearts were yours;
For they have pardons, being ask'd, as free
As words to little purpose.

VOLUMNIA
Prithee now,
Go, and be rul'd; although I know thou hadst rather
Follow thine enemy in a fiery gulf
Than flatter him in a bower.

Enter Cominius.

Here is Cominius.

COMINIUS
I have been i' th' market-place; and, sir, 'tis fit
You make strong party, or defend yourself
By calmness or by absence. All's in anger.

MENENIUS
Only fair speech.

COMINIUS
I think 'twill serve, if he
Can thereto frame his spirit.

VOLUMNIA
He must, and will.
Prithee now say you will, and go about it.

CORIOLANUS
Must I go show them my unbarb'd sconce? Must I
With my base tongue give to my noble heart
A lie that it must bear? Well, I will do 't.
Yet, were there but this single plot to lose,
This mold of Marcius, they to dust should grind it
And throw 't against the wind. To th' market-place!
You have put me now to such a part which never
I shall discharge to th' life.

COMINIUS
Come, come, we'll prompt you.

VOLUMNIA
I prithee now, sweet son, as thou hast said
My praises made thee first a soldier, so,
To have my praise for this, perform a part
Thou hast not done before.

CORIOLANUS
Well, I must do 't.
Away, my disposition, and possess me
Some harlot's spirit! My throat of war be turn'd,
Which quired with my drum, into a pipe
Small as an eunuch, or the virgin voice
That babies lulls asleep! The smiles of knaves
Tent in my cheeks, and schoolboys' tears take up
The glasses of my sight! A beggar's tongue
Make motion through my lips, and my arm'd knees,
Who bow'd but in my stirrup, bend like his
That hath receiv'd an alms! I will not do 't,
Lest I surcease to honor mine own truth
And by my body's action teach my mind
A most inherent baseness.

VOLUMNIA
At thy choice, then.
To beg of thee, it is my more dishonor
Than thou of them. Come all to ruin. Let
Thy mother rather feel thy pride than fear
Thy dangerous stoutness, for I mock at death
With as big heart as thou. Do as thou list.
Thy valiantness was mine, thou suck'dst it from me,
But owe thy pride thyself.

CORIOLANUS
Pray, be content.
Mother, I am going to the market-place;
Chide me no more. I'll mountebank their loves,
Cog their hearts from them, and come home belov'd
Of all the trades in Rome. Look, I am going.
Commend me to my wife. I'll return consul,
Or never trust to what my tongue can do
I' th' way of flattery further.

VOLUMNIA
Do your will.
Exit Volumnia.

COMINIUS
Away! The tribunes do attend you. Arm yourself
To answer mildly; for they are prepar'd
With accusations, as I hear, more strong
Than are upon you yet.

CORIOLANUS
The word is "mildly." Pray you let us go.
Let them accuse me by invention, I
Will answer in mine honor.

MENENIUS
Ay, but mildly.

CORIOLANUS
Well, mildly be it then. Mildly! *Exeunt.*

[SCENE III]

Enter Sicinius and Brutus.

BRUTUS
In this point charge him home, that he affects
Tyrannical power. If he evade us there,
Enforce him with his envy to the people,
And that the spoil got on the Antiates
Was ne'er distributed.

Enter an Aedile.

What, will he come?

AEDILE
He's coming.

BRUTUS
How accompanied?

81–82 Now . . . handling i.e., now is as soft and malleable as overripe fruit **85 fit** as fit. **as they** as for them **87 theirs** to suit their wish **89 Even** exactly. **were** would be **90 as free** i.e., which they will grant as freely **93 in** into **94 bower** arbor, or lady's boudoir **96 make strong party** support your side strongly **101 unbarb'd sconce** unhelmeted head **104 this single plot** this piece of earth only, i.e., my own person **105 mold** bodily form **108 discharge to th' life** perform convincingly **114 harlot's** rascal's **115 quired** harmonized, sang in chorus **117 babies lulls** lulls dolls **118 Tent** lodge, set up camp. **take up** fill up, occupy **119 glasses** eyeballs

123 surcease cease **129 Thy dangerous stoutness** the dangers resulting from your obstinate pride **132 owe** own **134 mountebank** win over as with the tricks of a quack medicine salesman **135 Cog** cheat **140 attend** await **144 word** watch-word **145 by invention** by inventing charges against me **146 in** in accordance with

III.iii. Location: Rome. The Forum.
1 charge him home press charges against him all the way. **affects** aspires to **3 Enforce . . . to** urge against him his inveterate malice toward **4 on** from

AEDILE
With old Menenius, and those senators
That always favor'd him.

SICINIUS Have you a catalogue
Of all the voices that we have procur'd
Set down by th' poll?

AEDILE I have; 'tis ready.

SICINIUS
Have you collected them by tribes?

AEDILE I have.

SICINIUS
Assemble presently the people hither;
And when they hear me say "It shall be so
I' th' right and strength o' th' commons," be it either
For death, for fine, or banishment, then let them,
If I say fine, cry "Fine!"; if death, cry "Death!";
Insisting on the old prerogative
And power i' th' truth o' th' cause.

AEDILE I shall inform them.

BRUTUS
And when such time they have begun to cry,
Let them not cease, but with a din confus'd
Enforce the present execution
Of what we chance to sentence.

AEDILE Very well.

SICINIUS
Make them be strong, and ready for this hint
When we shall hap to give 't them.

BRUTUS Go about it.
[Exit Aedile.]
Put him to choler straight. He hath been us'd
Ever to conquer, and to have his worth
Of contradiction. Being once chaf'd, he cannot
Be rein'd again to temperance. Then he speaks
What's in his heart; and that is there which looks
With us to break his neck.

Enter Coriolanus, Menenius, and Cominius, with others [Senators and Patricians].

SICINIUS Well, here he comes.

MENENIUS
Calmly, I do beseech you.

CORIOLANUS
Ay, as an ostler, that for th' poorest piece
Will bear the knave by th' volume.—Th' honor'd gods
Keep Rome in safety, and the chairs of justice
Supplied with worthy men! Plant love among 's!
Throng our large temples with the shows of peace,
And not our streets with war!

FIRST SENATOR Amen, amen.

MENENIUS
A noble wish.

Enter the Aedile, with the Plebeians.

SICINIUS
Draw near, ye people.

AEDILE
List to your tribunes. Audience! Peace, I say!

CORIOLANUS
First, hear me speak.

BOTH TRIBUNES
Well, say. Peace, ho!

CORIOLANUS
Shall I be charg'd no further than this present?
Must all determine here?

SICINIUS I do demand
If you submit you to the people's voices,
Allow their officers, and are content
To suffer lawful censure for such faults
As shall be prov'd upon you?

CORIOLANUS I am content.

MENENIUS
Lo, citizens, he says he is content.
The warlike service he has done, consider; think
Upon the wounds his body bears, which show
Like graves i' th' holy churchyard.

CORIOLANUS Scratches with briers,
Scars to move laughter only.

MENENIUS Consider further,
That when he speaks not like a citizen,
You find him like a soldier. Do not take
His rougher accents for malicious sounds,
But, as I say, such as become a soldier,
Rather than envy you.

COMINIUS Well, well, no more.

CORIOLANUS
What is the matter
That, being pass'd for consul with full voice,
I am so dishonor'd that the very hour
You take it off again?

SICINIUS Answer to us.

CORIOLANUS
Say, then. 'Tis true, I ought so.

SICINIUS
We charge you that you have contriv'd to take
From Rome all season'd office and to wind
Yourself into a power tyrannical,
For which you are a traitor to the people.

CORIOLANUS
How? Traitor?

MENENIUS Nay, temperately; your promise.

CORIOLANUS
The fires i' th' lowest hell fold in the people!
Call me their traitor! Thou injurious tribune!
Within thine eyes sat twenty thousand deaths,
In thy hands clutch'd as many millions, in
Thy lying tongue both numbers, I would say
"Thou liest" unto thee with a voice as free
As I do pray the gods.

SICINIUS Mark you this, people?

10 by th' poll by individual names **11 tribes** divisions of the Roman populace **18 truth** justice. **cause** case **19 cry** cry out, shout **25 choler** anger. **straight** straightway. **us'd** accustomed **26 worth** i.e., full quota or portion **27 contradiction** prerogative of answering back **29 looks** promises, tends **30 With us** from our point of view, in terms of our interest **32 ostler** hostler, caretaker of horses. **piece** coin, piece of money **33 bear . . . by th' volume** endure being called knave to any extent **36 shows** ceremonies

40 Audience listen, give heed **43 this present** this present occasion **44 determine** come to an end, be concluded. **demand** ask **46 Allow** acknowledge **58 Rather . . . you** rather than such as show malice toward you **62 Answer to us** i.e., we'll do the asking, not you **63 so** to do so **65 season'd** established **69 fold in** enclose, encircle **71–73 Within . . . numbers** (Understand "although" before each of the three clauses.)

ALL PLEBEIANS
To th' rock, to th' rock with him!
SICINIUS
Peace!
We need not put new matter to his charge.
What you have seen him do and heard him speak,
Beating your officers, cursing yourselves,
Opposing laws with strokes, and here defying
Those whose great power must try him—even this,
So criminal and in such capital kind,
Deserves th' extremest death.
BRUTUS
But since he hath
Serv'd well for Rome—
CORIOLANUS
What do you prate of service?
BRUTUS
I talk of that, that know it.
CORIOLANUS
You?
MENENIUS
Is this the promise that you made your mother?
COMINIUS
Know, I pray you—
CORIOLANUS
I'll know no further.
Let them pronounce the steep Tarpeian death,
Vagabond exile, flaying, pent to linger
But with a grain a day, I would not buy
Their mercy at the price of one fair word,
Nor check my courage for what they can give,
To have 't with saying "Good morrow."
SICINIUS
For that he has,
As much as in him lies, from time to time
Envied against the people, seeking means
To pluck away their power, as now at last
Given hostile strokes, and that not in the presence
Of dreaded justice, but on the ministers
That doth distribute it; in the name o' th' people
And in the power of us the tribunes, we,
Ev'n from this instant, banish him our city,
In peril of precipitation
From off the rock Tarpeian, never more
To enter our Rome gates. I' th' people's name,
I say it shall be so.
ALL PLEBEIANS
It shall be so, it shall be so! Let him away!
He's banish'd, and it shall be so!
COMINIUS
Hear me, my masters, and my common friends—
SICINIUS
He's sentenc'd; no more hearing.
COMINIUS
Let me speak.
I have been consul, and can show for Rome
Her enemies' marks upon me. I do love
My country's good with a respect more tender,
More holy and profound, than mine own life,
My dear wife's estimate, her womb's increase,
And treasure of my loins. Then if I would
Speak that—
SICINIUS
We know your drift. Speak what?
BRUTUS
There's no more to be said, but he is banish'd
As enemy to the people and his country.
It shall be so.
ALL PLEBEIANS
It shall be so, it shall be so!
CORIOLANUS
You common cry of curs, whose breath I hate
As reek o' th' rotten fens, whose loves I prize
As the dead carcasses of unburied men
That do corrupt my air, I banish you!
And here remain with your uncertainty!
Let every feeble rumor shake your hearts!
Your enemies, with nodding of their plumes,
Fan you into despair! Have the power still
To banish your defenders, till at length
Your ignorance, which finds not till it feels,
Making but reservation of yourselves,
Still your own foes, deliver you as most
Abated captives to some nation
That won you without blows! Despising,
For you, the city, thus I turn my back.
There is a world elsewhere.
Exeunt Coriolanus, Cominius,
[Menenius, Senators, and Patricians].
AEDILE
The people's enemy is gone, is gone!
ALL PLEBEIANS
Our enemy is banish'd! He is gone! Hoo! Hoo!
They all shout, and throw up their caps.
SICINIUS
Go, see him out at gates, and follow him,
As he hath follow'd you, with all despite;
Give him deserv'd vexation. Let a guard
Attend us through the city.
ALL PLEBEIANS
Come, come; let's see him out at gates! Come.
The gods preserve our noble tribunes! Come.
Exeunt.

ACT IV • [SCENE I]

Enter Coriolanus, Volumnia, Virgilia, Menenius, Cominius, with the young Nobility of Rome.

CORIOLANUS
Come, leave your tears; a brief farewell. The beast
With many heads butts me away. Nay, mother,
Where is your ancient courage? You were us'd

82 capital death-deserving **91–92 pent . . . day** imprisoned to starve with but a small particle of food a day **94 check** restrain **95 To have 't** if I might have it. **with saying** merely by saying. **For that** because **96 in him lies** he could **97 Envied against** showed malice toward **98 as** i.e., and inasmuch as (he has) **99 not** not merely **116 estimate** reputation

124 cry pack **128 remain** may you remain. **uncertainty** inconstancy, fickleness; also, insecurity (as explained in the following lines) **133 finds . . . feels** learns only through experience **134 Making . . . yourselves** seeking only to preserve yourselves **136 Abated** humbled **138 For** because of

IV.i. Location: Rome.
3 ancient former

To say extremities was the trier of spirits;
That common chances common men could bear;
That when the sea was calm all boats alike
Show'd mastership in floating; fortune's blows 7
When most struck home, being gentle wounded
craves 8
A noble cunning. You were us'd to load me 9
With precepts that would make invincible
The heart that conn'd them. 11

VIRGILIA
O heavens! O heavens!

CORIOLANUS
Nay, I prithee, woman—

VOLUMNIA
Now the red pestilence strike all trades in Rome, 13
And occupations perish!

CORIOLANUS
What, what, what! 14
I shall be lov'd when I am lack'd. Nay, mother, 15
Resume that spirit when you were wont to say,
If you had been the wife of Hercules,
Six of his labors you'd have done, and sav'd
Your husband so much sweat. Cominius,
Droop not; adieu. Farewell, my wife, my mother.
I'll do well yet. Thou old and true Menenius,
Thy tears are salter than a younger man's,
And venomous to thine eyes. My sometime general,
I have seen thee stern, and thou hast oft beheld
Heart-hard'ning spectacles; tell these sad women
'Tis fond to wail inevitable strokes, 26
As 'tis to laugh at 'em. My mother, you wot well 27
My hazards still have been your solace; and 28
Believe 't not lightly—though I go alone,
Like to a lonely dragon, that his fen 30
Makes fear'd and talk'd of more than seen—
your son
Will or exceed the common or be caught 32
With cautelous baits and practice.

VOLUMNIA
My first son, 33
Whither wilt thou go? Take good Cominius
With thee awhile. Determine on some course,
More than a wild exposture to each chance 36
That starts i' th' way before thee.

CORIOLANUS
O the gods! 37

COMINIUS
I'll follow thee a month, devise with thee 38
Where thou shalt rest, that thou mayst hear of us
And we of thee; so if the time thrust forth
A cause for thy repeal, we shall not send 41
O'er the vast world to seek a single man,
And lose advantage, which doth ever cool 43
I' th' absence of the needer.

CORIOLANUS
Fare ye well.
Thou hast years upon thee, and thou art too full
Of the wars' surfeits to go rove with one 46
That's yet unbruis'd. Bring me but out at gate. 47
Come, my sweet wife, my dearest mother, and
My friends of noble touch, when I am forth, 49
Bid me farewell, and smile. I pray you, come.
While I remain above the ground, you shall
Hear from me still, and never of me aught
But what is like me formerly.

MENENIUS
That's worthily
As any ear can hear. Come, let's not weep.
If I could shake off but one seven years
From these old arms and legs, by the good gods,
I'd with thee every foot.

CORIOLANUS
Give me thy hand.
Come. *Exeunt.*

7–9 fortune's . . . cunning i.e., when fortune strikes her hardest blows, to bear one's afflictions like a true gentleman requires great wisdom and nobility **11 conn'd** studied, memorized **13 red pestilence** (Red spots presaged death to those stricken with the plague.) **14 occupations** trades, handicrafts **15 lack'd** missed **26 fond** foolish **27 wot** know **28 still** always **30 fen** lurking place, marsh **32 or . . . common** either exceed the ordinary deeds of men **33 cautelous** crafty, deceitful. **practice** treacherous methods **36 exposture** exposure **37 starts** breaks from cover, darts across your path **38 follow** go with **41 repeal** recall from banishment **43 advantage** opportunity **46 wars' surfeits** wearing effects of military service

47 Bring conduct **49 noble touch** approved nobility. (From the use of the touchstone with precious metals.)

[SCENE II]

Enter the two Tribunes, Sicinius and Brutus, with the Aedile.

SICINIUS
Bid them all home. He's gone, and we'll no further.
The nobility are vex'd, whom we see have sided
In his behalf.

BRUTUS
Now we have shown our power,
Let us seem humbler after it is done
Than when it was a-doing.

SICINIUS
Bid them home.
Say their great enemy is gone, and they
Stand in their ancient strength.

BRUTUS
Dismiss them home. 7
[*Exit Aedile.*]
Here comes his mother.

Enter Volumnia, Virgilia, and Menenius.

SICINIUS
Let's not meet her.

BRUTUS
Why?

SICINIUS
They say she's mad.

BRUTUS
They have ta'en note of us. Keep on your way.
[*They start to leave.*]

VOLUMNIA
O, y' are well met. Th' hoarded plague o' th' gods 11
Requite your love!

MENENIUS
Peace, peace; be not so loud.

VOLUMNIA
If that I could for weeping, you should hear—
Nay, and you shall hear some. Will you be gone?

VIRGILIA
You shall stay too. I would I had the power 15

IV.ii. Location: Rome. A street.
7 ancient former **11 hoarded** stored up **15 You shall stay too** (Sometimes read as if addressed to the second of the two Tribunes, but it may mean *you shall too stay*, i.e., whether you want to or not. See l. 23.)

To say so to my husband.

SICINIUS
Are you mankind?

VOLUMNIA
Ay, fool, is that a shame? Note but this fool.
Was not a man my father? Hadst thou foxship
To banish him that struck more blows for Rome
Than thou hast spoken words?

SICINIUS
O blessed heavens!

VOLUMNIA
Moe noble blows than ever thou wise words,
And for Rome's good. I'll tell thee what—yet go.
Nay, but thou shalt stay too. I would my son
Were in Arabia, and thy tribe before him,
His good sword in his hand.

SICINIUS
What then?

VIRGILIA
What then?
He'd make an end of thy posterity.

VOLUMNIA
Bastards and all.
Good man, the wounds that he does bear for Rome!

MENENIUS
Come, come, peace.

SICINIUS
I would he had continued to his country
As he began, and not unknit himself
The noble knot he made.

BRUTUS
I would he had.

VOLUMNIA
"I would he had"? 'Twas you incens'd the rabble.
Cats, that can judge as fitly of his worth
As I can of those mysteries which heaven
Will not have earth to know!

BRUTUS
Pray let's go.

VOLUMNIA
Now, pray, sir, get you gone.
You have done a brave deed. Ere you go, hear this:
As far as doth the Capitol exceed
The meanest house in Rome, so far my son—
This lady's husband here, this, do you see?
Whom you have banish'd—does exceed you all.

BRUTUS
Well, well, we'll leave you.

SICINIUS
Why stay we to be baited
With one that wants her wits? *Exeunt Tribunes.*

VOLUMNIA
Take my prayers with you.
I would the gods had nothing else to do
But to confirm my curses! Could I meet 'em
But once a day, it would unclog my heart
Of what lies heavy to 't.

MENENIUS
You have told them home;
And, by my troth, you have cause. You'll sup
with me?

VOLUMNIA
Anger's my meat; I sup upon myself,
And so shall starve with feeding. Come, let's go.
[*To Virgilia.*] Leave this faint puling and lament
as I do,
In anger, Juno-like. Come, come, come.

MENENIUS
Fie, fie, fie! *Exeunt.*

[SCENE III]

Enter a Roman and a Volsce [*meeting*].

ROMAN I know you well, sir, and you know me. Your name, I think, is Adrian.

VOLSCE It is so, sir. Truly, I have forgot you.

ROMAN I am a Roman; and my services are, as you are, against 'em. Know you me yet?

VOLSCE Nicanor, no?

ROMAN The same, sir.

VOLSCE You had more beard when I last saw you; but your favor is well appear'd by your tongue. What's the news in Rome? I have a note from the Volscian state to find you out there. You have well sav'd me a day's journey.

ROMAN There hath been in Rome strange insurrections; the people against the senators, patricians, and nobles.

VOLSCE Hath been? Is it ended, then? Our state thinks not so. They are in a most warlike preparation, and hope to come upon them in the heat of their division.

ROMAN The main blaze of it is past, but a small thing would make it flame again; for the nobles receive so to heart the banishment of that worthy Coriolanus that they are in a ripe aptness to take all power from the people and to pluck from them their tribunes forever. This lies glowing, I can tell you, and is almost mature for the violent breaking out.

VOLSCE Coriolanus banish'd?

ROMAN Banish'd, sir.

VOLSCE You will be welcome with this intelligence, Nicanor.

ROMAN The day serves well for them now. I have heard it said, the fittest time to corrupt a man's wife is when she's fall'n out with her husband. Your noble Tullus Aufidius will appear well in these wars, his great opposer, Coriolanus, being now in no request of his country.

VOLSCE He cannot choose. I am most fortunate, thus accidentally to encounter you. You have ended my business, and I will merrily accompany you home.

ROMAN I shall, between this and supper, tell you most strange things from Rome, all tending to the good of their adversaries. Have you an army ready, say you?

VOLSCE A most royal one: the centurions and their charges, distinctly billeted, already in th' entertainment, and to be on foot at an hour's warning.

ROMAN I am joyful to hear of their readiness, and am the man, I think, that shall set them in present action.

16 mankind masculine (i.e., railing like a man), or infuriated. (Volumnia responds as though it meant *of the human race.*) **18 foxship** craftiness **21 Moe** more **24 Arabia** i.e., a deserted spot, with no place to hide **43–44 baited With** harassed by **48 to 't** upon it. **told them home** berated them thoroughly **52 puling** whimpering

IV.iii. Location: A road between Rome and Antium.
9 your tongue your voice is recognizable **29 them** i.e., the Volscians **33 in no request of** unvalued by **35 choose** do otherwise (than appear well) **38 this** this present time **41 centurions** officers each in command of a hundred men or "century" **42 distinctly billeted** separately enrolled **42–43 in th' entertainment** readied for combat

So, sir, heartily well met, and most glad of your company.

VOLSCE You take my part from me, sir; I have the most 48
cause to be glad of yours.

ROMAN Well, let us go together. *Exeunt.*

[SCENE IV]

Enter Coriolanus in mean apparel, disguis'd and muffled.

CORIOLANUS
A goodly city is this Antium. City,
'Tis I that made thy widows. Many an heir
Of these fair edifices 'fore my wars 3
Have I heard groan and drop. Then know me not,
Lest that thy wives with spits and boys with stones
In puny battle slay me.

Enter a Citizen.

Save you, sir. 6

CITIZEN
And you.

CORIOLANUS Direct me, if it be your will,
Where great Aufidius lies. Is he in Antium? 8

CITIZEN
He is, and feasts the nobles of the state
At his house this night.

CORIOLANUS
Which is his house, beseech you?

CITIZEN
This, here before you.

CORIOLANUS Thank you, sir. Farewell.
Exit Citizen.

O world, thy slippery turns! Friends now fast sworn,
Whose double bosoms seems to wear one heart,
Whose hours, whose bed, whose meal and exercise
Are still together, who twin, as 'twere, in love 16
Unseparable, shall within this hour,
On a dissension of a doit, break out 18
To bitterest enmity; so, fellest foes, 19
Whose passions and whose plots have broke their sleep
To take the one the other, by some chance, 21
Some trick not worth an egg, shall grow dear friends 22
And interjoin their issues. So with me: 23
My birth-place hate I, and my love's upon
This enemy town. I'll enter. If he slay me,
He does fair justice; if he give me way, 26
I'll do his country service. *Exit.*

48 my part i.e., the words I should say

IV.iv. Location: Antium. Before Aufidius' house.
3 'fore my wars before my onslaught **6 puny** petty. **Save** God save **8 lies** dwells **16 still** ever **18 dissension of a doit** i.e., paltry dispute. (A *doit* is a small coin.) **19 fellest** fiercest **21 To . . . other** by which the one tries to get the better of the other **22 trick** trifle **23 issues** children (by marriage ?); fortunes (?) **26 give me way** accede to my request

[SCENE V]

Music plays. Enter a Servingman.

FIRST SERVANT Wine, wine, wine! What service is here? I think our fellows are asleep. *[Exit.]*

Enter another Servingman.

SECOND SERVANT Where's Cotus? My master calls for him. Cotus! *Exit.*

Enter Coriolanus.

CORIOLANUS
A goodly house. The feast smells well, but I
Appear not like a guest.

Enter the First Servingman.

FIRST SERVANT What would you have, friend? Whence are you? Here's no place for you. Pray go to the door. *Exit.*

CORIOLANUS
I have deserv'd no better entertainment, 9
In being Coriolanus.

Enter Second Servant.

SECOND SERVANT Whence are you, sir? Has the porter his eyes in his head, that he gives entrance to such
companions? Pray get you out. 13

CORIOLANUS Away!

SECOND SERVANT Away? Get you away.

CORIOLANUS Now th' art troublesome.

SECOND SERVANT Are you so brave? I'll have you talk'd with anon.

Enter Third Servingman. The First, [entering,] meets him.

THIRD SERVANT What fellow's this?

FIRST SERVANT A strange one as ever I look'd on. I cannot get him out o' th' house. Prithee call my master to him. *[Exit.]*

THIRD SERVANT What have you to do here, fellow? Pray
you avoid the house. 24

CORIOLANUS Let me but stand; I will not hurt your hearth.

THIRD SERVANT What are you?

CORIOLANUS A gentleman.

THIRD SERVANT A marv'lous poor one.

CORIOLANUS True, so I am.

THIRD SERVANT Pray you, poor gentleman, take up some other station; here's no place for you. Pray you avoid. Come.

CORIOLANUS Follow your function, go, and batten on 34
cold bits. *Pushes him away from him.*

THIRD SERVANT What, you will not? Prithee tell my master what a strange guest he has here.

IV.v. Location: Antium. The house of Aufidius. The sense of time here is virtually continuous; the stage is imaginatively transformed from the outside to the inside of Aufidius' house.
9 entertainment reception **13 companions** rascals, base persons **24 avoid** leave **34 Follow your function** go back to your ordinary business. **batten** grow fat

SECOND SERVANT And I shall. *Exit Second Servingman.*
THIRD SERVANT Where dwell'st thou?
CORIOLANUS Under the canopy.
THIRD SERVANT Under the canopy?
CORIOLANUS Ay.
THIRD SERVANT Where's that?
CORIOLANUS I' th' city of kites and crows.
THIRD SERVANT I' th' city of kites and crows? What an ass it is! Then thou dwell'st with daws too?
CORIOLANUS No, I serve not thy master.
THIRD SERVANT How, sir? Do you meddle with my master?
CORIOLANUS Ay, 'tis an honester service than to meddle with thy mistress.
Thou prat'st, and prat'st. Serve with thy trencher.
Hence! *Beats him away.* [*Exit Third Servingman.*]

Enter Aufidius with the [*Second*] *Servingman.*

AUFIDIUS
Where is this fellow?
SECOND SERVANT Here, sir. I 'd have beaten him like a dog, but for disturbing the lords within.
[*He and First Servant stand aside.*]
AUFIDIUS
Whence com'st thou? What wouldst thou? Thy name?
Why speak'st not? Speak, man. What's thy name?
CORIOLANUS [*Unmuffling*]
If, Tullus,
Not yet thou know'st me, and, seeing me, dost not
Think me for the man I am, necessity
Commands me name myself.
AUFIDIUS What is thy name?
CORIOLANUS
A name unmusical to the Volscians' ears,
And harsh in sound to thine.
AUFIDIUS Say, what's thy name?
Thou hast a grim appearance, and thy face
Bears a command in 't; though thy tackle's torn,
Thou show'st a noble vessel. What's thy name?
CORIOLANUS
Prepare thy brow to frown. Know'st thou me yet?
AUFIDIUS
I know thee not. Thy name?
CORIOLANUS
My name is Caius Marcius, who hath done
To thee particularly and to all the Volsces
Great hurt and mischief; thereto witness may
My surname, Coriolanus. The painful service,
The extreme dangers, and the drops of blood
Shed for my thankless country are requited
But with that surname—a good memory,
And witness of the malice and displeasure
Which thou shouldst bear me. Only that name remains.
The cruelty and envy of the people,
Permitted by our dastard nobles, who
Have all forsook me, hath devour'd the rest,
And suffer'd me by th' voice of slaves to be
Whoop'd out of Rome. Now this extremity
Hath brought me to thy hearth; not out of hope—
Mistake me not—to save my life, for if
I had fear'd death, of all the men i' th' world
I would have 'voided thee; but in mere spite,
To be full quit of those my banishers,
Stand I before thee here. Then if thou hast
A heart of wreak in thee, that wilt revenge
Thine own particular wrongs, and stop those maims
Of shame seen through thy country, speed thee straight,
And make my misery serve thy turn. So use it
That my revengeful services may prove
As benefits to thee, for I will fight
Against my cank'red country with the spleen
Of all the under fiends. But if so be
Thou dar'st not this and that to prove more fortunes
Th' art tir'd, then, in a word, I also am
Longer to live most weary, and present
My throat to thee and to thy ancient malice;
Which not to cut would show thee but a fool,
Since I have ever followed thee with hate,
Drawn tuns of blood out of thy country's breast,
And cannot live but to thy shame, unless
It be to do thee service.
AUFIDIUS O Marcius, Marcius!
Each word thou hast spoke hath weeded from my heart
A root of ancient envy. If Jupiter
Should from yond cloud speak divine things,
And say "'Tis true," I'd not believe them more
Than thee, all-noble Marcius. Let me twine
Mine arms about that body, whereagainst
My grained ash an hundred times hath broke,
And scarr'd the moon with splinters. [*They embrace.*] Here I clip
The anvil of my sword, and do contest
As hotly and as nobly with thy love
As ever in ambitious strength I did
Contend against thy valor. Know thou first,
I lov'd the maid I married; never man
Sigh'd truer breath. But that I see thee here,
Thou noble thing, more dances my rapt heart
Than when I first my wedded mistress saw
Bestride my threshold. Why, thou Mars, I tell thee,
We have a power on foot; and I had purpose
Once more to hew thy target from thy brawn,
Or lose mine arm for 't. Thou hast beat me out
Twelve several times, and I have nightly since
Dreamt of encounters 'twixt thyself and me;

41 canopy i.e., of heaven **44 kites and crows** i.e., birds of prey **46 daws** jackdaws. (Types of foolishness.) **48 meddle** concern yourself with. (But Coriolanus answers in the sense of *have sexual intercourse with.*) **52 trencher** wooden plate **67 show'st** appear to be **76 memory** reminder

83 Whoop'd driven with hoots **87 mere** utter **88 full quit of** fully evened with **90 wreak** vengeance **91–92 maims Of shame** dishonoring injuries **92 through** throughout **96 cank'red** infected with evils (as from the action of the cankerworm) **97 under fiends** fiends of the underworld **98 prove more fortunes** try your fortunes further **104 tuns** large barrels **113 grained ash** spear with ashen shaft **114 clip** embrace **115 anvil** i.e., Coriolanus, on whom Aufidius' sword has beaten as on an anvil **121 dances** makes to dance. **rapt** enraptured **124 power on foot** force in the field **125 target** shield. **brawn** i.e., muscular arm **126 out** thoroughly **127 several** distinct

We have been down together in my sleep,
Unbuckling helms, fisting each other's throat, 130
And wak'd half dead with nothing. Worthy Marcius, 131
Had we no other quarrel else to Rome but that
Thou art thence banish'd, we would muster all
From twelve to seventy, and, pouring war 134
Into the bowels of ungrateful Rome,
Like a bold flood o'erbeat. O, come, go in, 136
And take our friendly senators by th' hands,
Who now are here, taking their leaves of me,
Who am prepar'd against your territories,
Though not for Rome itself.

CORIOLANUS You bless me, gods!

AUFIDIUS
Therefore, most absolute sir, if thou wilt have 141
The leading of thine own revenges, take
Th' one half of my commission; and set down— 143
As best thou art experienc'd, since thou know'st
Thy country's strength and weakness—thine own ways,
Whether to knock against the gates of Rome,
Or rudely visit them in parts remote,
To fright them ere destroy. But come in.
Let me commend thee first to those that shall
Say yea to thy desires. A thousand welcomes!
And more a friend than e'er an enemy;
Yet, Marcius, that was much. Your hand. Most welcome! *Exeunt [Coriolanus and Aufidius].*

Two of the Servingmen [come forward].

FIRST SERVANT Here's a strange alteration!

SECOND SERVANT By my hand, I had thought to have
strucken him with a cudgel; and yet my mind gave me 155
his clothes made a false report of him.

FIRST SERVANT What an arm he has! He turn'd me
about with his finger and his thumb, as one would set 158
up a top. 159

SECOND SERVANT Nay, I knew by his face that there was something in him. He had, sir, a kind of face, methought—I cannot tell how to term it.

FIRST SERVANT He had so, looking as it were—Would I were hang'd, but I thought there was more in him than I could think.

SECOND SERVANT So did I, I'll be sworn. He is simply the rarest man i' th' world.

FIRST SERVANT I think he is. But a greater soldier than
he, you wot one. 169

SECOND SERVANT Who, my master?

FIRST SERVANT Nay, it's no matter for that. 171

SECOND SERVANT Worth six on him.

FIRST SERVANT Nay, not so neither. But I take him to be 173
the greater soldier.

SECOND SERVANT Faith, look you, one cannot tell how to say that. For the defense of a town, our general is excellent.

FIRST SERVANT Ay, and for an assault too.

Enter the Third Servingman.

THIRD SERVANT O slaves, I can tell you news—news, you rascals!

BOTH [FIRST AND SECOND SERVANTS] What, what, what? Let's partake.

THIRD SERVANT I would not be a Roman, of all nations;
I had as lieve be a condemn'd man. 184

BOTH [FIRST AND SECOND SERVANTS] Wherefore? Wherefore?

THIRD SERVANT Why, here's he that was wont to thwack our general, Caius Marcius.

FIRST SERVANT Why do you say "thwack our general"?

THIRD SERVANT I do not say "thwack our general," but he was always good enough for him.

SECOND SERVANT Come, we are fellows and friends. He was ever too hard for him; I have heard him say so himself.

FIRST SERVANT He was too hard for him, directly to say
the troth on 't, before Corioles, he scotch'd him and 196
notch'd him like a carbonado. 197

SECOND SERVANT An he had been cannibally given, he 198
might have boil'd and eaten him too.

FIRST SERVANT But, more of thy news.

THIRD SERVANT Why, he is so made on here within as 201
if he were son and heir to Mars; set at upper end o' th'
table; no question ask'd him by any of the senators
but they stand bald before him. Our general himself 204
makes a mistress of him, sanctifies himself with 's 205
hand, and turns up the white o' th' eye to his discourse. 206
But the bottom of the news is, our general is cut i' th' 207
middle and but one half of what he was yesterday; for
the other has half, by the entreaty and grant of the
whole table. He'll go, he says, and sowl the porter of 210
Rome gates by th' ears. He will mow all down before
him, and leave his passage poll'd. 212

SECOND SERVANT And he's as like to do 't as any man I can imagine.

THIRD SERVANT Do 't? He will do 't! For look you, sir,
he has as many friends as enemies; which friends, sir,
as it were, durst not, look you, sir, show themselves,
as we term it, his friends whilst he's in directitude. 218

FIRST SERVANT Directitude? What's that?

THIRD SERVANT But when they shall see, sir, his crest
up again, and the man in blood, they will out of their 221
burrows like conies after rain, and revel all with him. 222

FIRST SERVANT But when goes this forward?

THIRD SERVANT Tomorrow, today, presently. You shall
have the drum struck up this afternoon. 'Tis, as it
were, a parcel of their feast, and to be executed ere 226
they wipe their lips.

SECOND SERVANT Why, then we shall have a stirring world again. This peace is nothing but to rust iron, increase tailors, and breed ballad-makers.

130 fisting clutching **131 wak'd** (I have) awakened **134 twelve** i.e., aged twelve **136 o'erbeat** overflow, surge over **141 absolute** perfect **143 commission** command. **set down** determine upon **155 gave** told **158–159 set up** set going **169 you wot one** you know one who is greater, i.e., Aufidius **171 Nay . . . that** i.e., never mind about names **173 him** i.e., Aufidius. (Some commentators argue that *him* is Coriolanus; the Servants tend to contradict themselves in their newfound admiration for Coriolanus and their loyalty toward their own general.)

184 as lieve as soon **196 scotch'd** scored, gashed **197 carbonado** meat scored across for broiling **198 An** if **201 made on** made much of **204 but** unless. **bald** bareheaded **205–206 sanctifies . . . hand** touches his (Coriolanus') hand as though it were a holy relic **207 bottom** last item **210 sowl** drag **212 poll'd** stripped (as one would strip branches or foliage) **218 directitude** (A blunder for something like *discretitude* or *discredit.*) **221 in blood** in full vigor. (Usually said of hounds.) **222 conies** rabbits **226 parcel** part

FIRST SERVANT Let me have war, say I. It exceeds peace as far as day does night. It's spritely walking, audible, and full of vent. Peace is a very apoplexy, lethargy, mull'd, deaf, sleepy, insensible, a getter of more bastard children than war's a destroyer of men.

SECOND SERVANT 'Tis so; and as wars, in some sort, may be said to be a ravisher, so it cannot be denied but peace is a great maker of cuckolds.

FIRST SERVANT Ay, and it makes men hate one another.

THIRD SERVANT Reason: because they then less need one another. The wars for my money! I hope to see Romans as cheap as Volscians.—They are rising, they are rising.

BOTH [FIRST AND SECOND SERVANTS] In, in, in, in!

Exeunt.

[SCENE VI]

Enter the two Tribunes, Sicinius and Brutus.

SICINIUS
We hear not of him, neither need we fear him.
His remedies are tame: the present peace
And quietness of the people, which before
Were in wild hurry. Here do we make his friends
Blush that the world goes well, who rather had,
Though they themselves did suffer by 't, behold
Dissentious numbers pest'ring streets than see
Our tradesmen singing in their shops and going
About their functions friendly.

BRUTUS
We stood to 't in good time.

Enter Menenius.

Is this Menenius?

SICINIUS
'Tis he, 'tis he. O, he is grown most kind of late.—
Hail, sir!

MENENIUS
Hail to you both!

SICINIUS
Your Coriolanus is not much miss'd
But with his friends. The commonwealth doth stand,
And so would do, were he more angry at it.

MENENIUS
All's well; and might have been much better, if
He could have temporiz'd.

SICINIUS
Where is he, hear you?

MENENIUS
Nay, I hear nothing.
His mother and his wife hear nothing from him.

Enter three or four Citizens.

ALL CITIZENS
The gods preserve you both!

SICINIUS
Good-e'en, our neighbors.

BRUTUS
Good-e'en to you all, good-e'en to you all.

FIRST CITIZEN
Ourselves, our wives, and children, on our knees,
Are bound to pray for you both.

SICINIUS
Live, and thrive!

BRUTUS
Farewell, kind neighbors! We wish'd Coriolanus
Had lov'd you as we did.

ALL CITIZENS
Now the gods keep you!

BOTH TRIBUNES
Farewell, farewell. *Exeunt Citizens.*

SICINIUS
This is a happier and more comely time
Than when these fellows ran about the streets,
Crying confusion.

BRUTUS
Caius Marcius was
A worthy officer i' th' war, but insolent,
O'ercome with pride, ambitious, past all thinking
Self-loving.

SICINIUS
And affecting one sole throne, without assistance.

MENENIUS
I think not so.

SICINIUS
We should by this, to all our lamentation,
If he had gone forth consul, found it so.

BRUTUS
The gods have well prevented it, and Rome
Sits safe and still without him.

Enter an Aedile.

AEDILE
Worthy tribunes,
There is a slave, whom we have put in prison,
Reports the Volsces with two several powers
Are ent'red in the Roman territories,
And with the deepest malice of the war
Destroy what lies before 'em.

MENENIUS
'Tis Aufidius,
Who, hearing of our Marcius' banishment,
Thrusts forth his horns again into the world,
Which were inshell'd when Marcius stood for Rome,
And durst not once peep out.

SICINIUS
Come, what talk you of Marcius?

BRUTUS
Go see this rumorer whipp'd. It cannot be
The Volsces dare break with us.

MENENIUS
Cannot be?
We have record that very well it can,
And three examples of the like hath been
Within my age. But reason with the fellow,

232 audible keen of hearing **233 vent** activity, vitality. **apoplexy** paralysis **234 mull'd** insipid, drowsy. **getter** begetter **242 rising** i.e., rising from table

IV.vi. Location: Rome. A public place.
2 His . . . tame the remedies needed to expel Coriolanus, i.e., the peoples' protests, are tame **7 pest'ring** crowding **10 stood to 't** i.e., stood up against Coriolanus **15 But with** except among

28 comely gracious **34 assistance** partnership (in rule) **36 this** this time **41 several powers** separate armed forces **46 Thrusts . . . again** (i.e., like a snail) **47 inshell'd** i.e., in the shell like a snail's horns **49 what** why **54 reason** discuss

Before you punish him, where he heard this,
Lest you shall chance to whip your information
And beat the messenger who bids beware
Of what is to be dreaded.

SICINIUS
Tell not me.
I know this cannot be.

BRUTUS
Not possible.

Enter a Messenger.

MESSENGER
The nobles in great earnestness are going
All to the Senate-house. Some news is come
That turns their countenances.

SICINIUS
'Tis this slave—
Go whip him 'fore the people's eyes—his raising,
Nothing but his report.

MESSENGER
Yes, worthy sir,
The slave's report is seconded; and more,
More fearful, is deliver'd.

SICINIUS
What more fearful?

MESSENGER
It is spoke freely out of many mouths—
How probable I do not know—that Marcius,
Join'd with Aufidius, leads a power 'gainst Rome,
And vows revenge as spacious as between
The young'st and oldest thing.

SICINIUS
This is most likely!

BRUTUS
Rais'd only that the weaker sort may wish
Good Marcius home again.

SICINIUS
The very trick on 't.

MENENIUS
This is unlikely. He and Aufidius can
No more atone than violent'st contrariety.

Enter [a Second] Messenger.

SECOND MESSENGER
You are sent for to the Senate.
A fearful army, led by Caius Marcius
Associated with Aufidius, rages
Upon our territories, and have already
O'erborne their way, consum'd with fire, and took
What lay before them.

Enter Cominius.

COMINIUS
O, you have made good work!

MENENIUS
What news? What news?

COMINIUS
You have holp to ravish your own daughters and
To melt the city leads upon your pates,
To see your wives dishonor'd to your noses—

MENENIUS
What's the news? What's the news?

COMINIUS
Your temples burned in their cement, and
Your franchises, whereon you stood, confin'd
Into an auger's bore.

MENENIUS
Pray now, your news?—
You have made fair work, I fear me.—Pray, your news?
If Marcius should be join'd wi' th' Volscians—

COMINIUS
If?
He is their god. He leads them like a thing
Made by some other deity than nature,
That shapes man better; and they follow him
Against us brats with no less confidence
Than boys pursuing summer butterflies,
Or butchers killing flies.

MENENIUS
You have made good work,
You and your apron-men; you that stood so much
Upon the voice of occupation and
The breath of garlic-eaters!

COMINIUS
He'll shake
Your Rome about your ears.

MENENIUS
As Hercules
Did shake down mellow fruit. You have made fair work!

BRUTUS
But is this true, sir?

COMINIUS
Ay; and you'll look pale
Before you find it other. All the regions
Do smilingly revolt; and who resists
Are mock'd for valiant ignorance,
And perish constant fools. Who is 't can blame him?
Your enemies and his find something in him.

MENENIUS
We are all undone, unless
The noble man have mercy.

COMINIUS
Who shall ask it?
The tribunes cannot do 't for shame; the people
Deserve such pity of him as the wolf
Does of the shepherds. For his best friends, if they
Should say "Be good to Rome," they charg'd him even
As those should do that had deserv'd his hate,
And therein show'd like enemies.

MENENIUS
'Tis true.
If he were putting to my house the brand
That should consume it, I have not the face
To say, "Beseech you, cease." You have made fair hands,
You and your crafts! You have crafted fair!

COMINIUS
You have brought
A trembling upon Rome, such as was never
S' incapable of help.

62 turns changes **62–63 slave . . . his raising** slave's incitement for which let him be publicly whipped **66 deliver'd** reported **70–71 as spacious . . . thing** comprehensive enough to embrace every living person **72 Rais'd** invented, stirred up. (See *raising*, l. 63 above.) **75 atone** come to a reconciliation **80 O'erborne their way** carried all before them **84 leads** roofs of lead **85 to** before

87 in their cement i.e., to their foundations **88 franchises** political rights. **stood** insisted **89 auger's bore** hole drilled by an auger, i.e., narrow space **95 brats** mere children **98 apron-men** artisans (who wore aprons) **99 voice of occupation** votes of the laboring men **101–102 Hercules . . . fruit** (Hercules' eleventh labor was to carry off the golden apples of the Hesperides.) **104 other** otherwise **105 who** whoever **107 constant** loyal **108 Your . . . him** i.e., both your enemies, the patricians, and his enemies, the Volscians, find cause to ally with him **113 For** as for **114 they . . . even** they would be enjoining him just **116 show'd** would appear **119 made fair hands** done fine work. (Said ironically.) **120 crafted fair** (1) cleverly advanced the interests of the crafts or occupations (2) shown your expert craft or cunning

BOTH TRIBUNES Say not we brought it.

MENENIUS
How? Was 't we? We lov'd him, but, like beasts
And cowardly nobles, gave way unto your clusters, 124
Who did hoot him out o' th' city.

COMINIUS But I fear
They'll roar him in again. Tullus Aufidius, 126
The second name of men, obeys his points 127
As if he were his officer. Desperation
Is all the policy, strength, and defense
That Rome can make against them.

Enter a troop of Citizens.

MENENIUS Here come the clusters.
And is Audifius with him? You are they
That made the air unwholesome, when you cast
Your stinking greasy caps in hooting at
Coriolanus' exile. Now he's coming,
And not a hair upon a soldier's head
Which will not prove a whip. As many coxcombs 136
As you threw caps up will he tumble down,
And pay you for your voices. 'Tis no matter;
If he could burn us all into one coal,
We have deserv'd it.

ALL CITIZENS
Faith, we hear fearful news.

FIRST CITIZEN For mine own part,
When I said, banish him, I said, 'twas pity.

SECOND CITIZEN And so did I.

THIRD CITIZEN And so did I; and, to say the truth, so
did very many of us. That we did, we did for the best; 145
and though we willingly consented to his banishment,
yet it was against our will.

COMINIUS
Y' are goodly things, you voices!

MENENIUS You have made good work,
You and your cry! Shall 's to the Capitol? 149

COMINIUS
O, ay, what else?

Exeunt both [*Cominius and Menenius*].

SICINIUS
Go, masters, get you home, be not dismay'd.
These are a side that would be glad to have 152
This true which they so seem to fear. Go home,
And show no sign of fear.

FIRST CITIZEN The gods be good to us! Come, masters,
let 's home. I ever said we were i' th' wrong when we
banish'd him.

SECOND CITIZEN So did we all. But, come, let 's home.

Exeunt Citizens.

BRUTUS
I do not like this news.

SICINIUS
Nor I.

BRUTUS
Let 's to the Capitol. Would half my wealth
Would buy this for a lie!

SICINIUS Pray, let 's go.

Exeunt Tribunes.

[SCENE VII]

Enter Aufidius with his Lieutenant.

AUFIDIUS
Do they still fly to th' Roman?

LIEUTENANT
I do not know what witchcraft's in him, but
Your soldiers use him as the grace 'fore meat,
Their talk at table, and their thanks at end;
And you are dark'ned in this action, sir, 5
Even by your own.

AUFIDIUS I cannot help it now, 6
Unless by using means I lame the foot 7
Of our design. He bears himself more proudlier,
Even to my person, than I thought he would
When first I did embrace him. Yet his nature
In that's no changeling, and I must excuse
What cannot be amended.

LIEUTENANT Yet I wish, sir—
I mean for your particular—you had not 13
Join'd in commission with him, but either had
borne
The action of yourself, or else to him
Had left it solely.

AUFIDIUS
I understand thee well; and be thou sure,
When he shall come to his account, he knows not
What I can urge against him. Although it seems,
And so he thinks, and is no less apparent
To th' vulgar eye, that he bears all things fairly,
And shows good husbandry for the Volscian state, 22
Fights dragon-like, and does achieve as soon
As draw his sword; yet he hath left undone
That which shall break his neck or hazard mine,
Whene'er we come to our account.

LIEUTENANT
Sir, I beseech you, think you he'll carry Rome?

AUFIDIUS
All places yields to him ere he sits down, 28
And the nobility of Rome are his;
The senators and patricians love him too.
The tribunes are no soldiers; and their people
Will be as rash in the repeal as hasty 32
To expel him thence. I think he'll be to Rome
As is the osprey to the fish, who takes it 34
By sovereignty of nature. First he was
A noble servant to them, but he could not

124 clusters mobs **126 roar . . . again** i.e., roar with pain when he returns **127 second . . . men** second greatest name among men. **his points** Coriolanus' instructions **136 coxcombs** fool's heads **145 That** what **149 cry** pack. **Shall 's** i.e., shall we go **152 side** party, faction

IV.vii. Location: A camp, at a small distance from Rome.
5 you . . . action your glory is dimmed in this undertaking **6 your own** i.e., your followers, or your own action **7 using means** resorting to means by which **13 for your particular** regarding your self-interest **22 husbandry** management **28 sits down** besieges **32 repeal** recall from exile **34 osprey** fish hawk, said to have had the power to fascinate fishes

Carry his honors even. Whether 'twas pride,
Which out of daily fortune ever taints
The happy man; whether defect of judgment,
To fail in the disposing of those chances
Which he was lord of; or whether nature,
Not to be other than one thing, not moving
From th' casque to th' cushion, but commanding peace
Even with the same austerity and garb
As he controll'd the war; but one of these—
As he hath spices of them all, not all,
For I dare so far free him—made him fear'd,
So hated, and so banish'd. But he has a merit
To choke it in the utt'rance. So our virtues
Lie in th' interpretation of the time;
And power, unto itself most commendable,
Hath not a tomb so evident as a chair
T' extol what it hath done.
One fire drives out one fire; one nail, one nail;
Rights by rights falter, strengths by strengths do fail.
Come, let 's away. When, Caius, Rome is thine,
Thou art poor'st of all; then shortly art thou mine.
Exeunt.

ACT V • [SCENE I]

Enter Menenius, Cominius; Sicinius, Brutus, the two Tribunes; with others.

MENENIUS
No, I'll not go. You hear what he hath said
Which was sometime his general, who loved him
In a most dear particular. He call'd me father;
But what o' that? Go you that banish'd him;
A mile before his tent fall down, and knee
The way into his mercy. Nay, if he coy'd
To hear Cominius speak, I'll keep at home.

COMINIUS
He would not seem to know me.

MENENIUS
Do you hear?

COMINIUS
Yet one time he did call me by my name.
I urg'd our old acquaintance, and the drops
That we have bled together. Coriolanus
He would not answer to; forbade all names.
He was a kind of nothing, titleless,
Till he had forg'd himself a name o' th' fire
Of burning Rome.

MENENIUS
Why, so; you have made good work!
A pair of tribunes that have rack'd for Rome,
To make coals cheap! A noble memory!

COMINIUS
I minded him how royal 'twas to pardon
When it was less expected. He replied,
It was a bare petition of a state
To one whom they had punish'd.

MENENIUS
Very well.
Could he say less?

COMINIUS
I offer'd to awaken his regard
For 's private friends. His answer to me was,
He could not stay to pick them in a pile
Of noisome musty chaff. He said 'twas folly,
For one poor grain or two, to leave unburnt
And still to nose th' offense.

MENENIUS
For one poor grain or two!
I am one of those! His mother, wife, his child,
And this brave fellow too, we are the grains.
You are the musty chaff, and you are smelt
Above the moon. We must be burnt for you.

SICINIUS
Nay, pray, be patient. If you refuse your aid
In this so never-needed help, yet do not
Upbraid 's with our distress. But, sure, if you
Would be your country's pleader, your good tongue,
More than the instant army we can make,
Might stop our countryman.

MENENIUS
No, I'll not meddle.

SICINIUS
Pray you, go to him.

MENENIUS
What should I do?

BRUTUS
Only make trial what your love can do
For Rome, towards Marcius.

MENENIUS
Well, and say that Marcius return me,
As Cominius is return'd, unheard, what then?
But as a discontented friend, grief-shot
With his unkindness? Say 't be so?

SICINIUS
Yet your good will
Must have that thanks from Rome, after the measure
As you intended well.

MENENIUS
I'll undertake 't.
I think he'll hear me. Yet, to bite his lip
And hum at good Cominius much unhearts me.
He was not taken well; he had not din'd.
The veins unfill'd, our blood is cold, and then

37 Carry . . . even bear his honors temperately **38 daily fortune** continuous success. **taints** corrupts **39 happy** fortunate **40 disposing** clever using **41 nature** (his) character **43 casque** helmet (as symbolic of the warrior). **cushion** i.e., seat for a senator **44 austerity and garb** austere behavior **46 spices** tastes, traces **47 free** free from blame **48–49 he . . . utt'rance** i.e., his merit is of the perverse sort that undoes the praise it should receive; it *chokes* itself by its very *utt'rance.* (Also interpreted as meaning, "He has so many counterbalancing good points that the words stick in my throat.") **50 the time** i.e., our contemporaries **51–53 power . . . done** i.e., however worthy the exercise of power may be in itself, if popular opinion so determines it may be left with no suitable memorial to praise it. (*Chair* is variously interpreted as a public rostrum, a magistrate's chair, or a simple wooden chair, a mere nothing as a memorial; perhaps the idea is that power has only its own *chair of office* to be remembered by.) **55 by rights falter** i.e., are made to seem less by other rights. (The point is that great deeds, eclipsed by the subsequent deeds of others, are soon forgotten.)

V.i. Location: Rome. A public place.
1 he i.e., Cominius **2 Which** who. **sometime** formerly. **3 He** i.e., Coriolanus **5 knee** crawl on knee **6 coy'd** showed reluctance, disdained

16 rack'd striven. (The F spelling, *wrack'd,* suggests a pun on *brought ruin.*) **18 minded** reminded **20 bare** mere, paltry **23 offer'd** attempted **25 stay . . . them** take time to pick them out **26 noisome** evil-smelling **28 nose th' offense** smell the offensive stuff **35 In . . . help** in this strait where help is needed as never before **38 instant army** army we can raise at this instant **49–50 after . . . As** in proportion that **53 taken well** approached at the right time

We pout upon the morning, are unapt
To give or to forgive; but when we have stuff'd
These pipes and these conveyances of our blood
With wine and feeding, we have suppler souls
Than in our priest-like fasts. Therefore I'll watch him
Till he be dieted to my request,
And then I'll set upon him.

BRUTUS
You know the very road into his kindness,
And cannot lose your way.

MENENIUS Good faith, I'll prove him,
Speed how it will. I shall ere long have knowledge
Of my success. *Exit.*

COMINIUS He'll never hear him.

SICINIUS Not?

COMINIUS
I tell you, he does sit in gold, his eye
Red as 'twould burn Rome; and his injury
The jailer to his pity. I kneel'd before him;
'Twas very faintly he said "Rise"; dismiss'd me
Thus, with his speechless hand. What he would do
He sent in writing after me; what he would not,
Bound with an oath to yield to his conditions;
So that all hope is vain
Unless his noble mother, and his wife,
Who, as I hear, mean to solicit him
For mercy to his country. Therefore, let 's hence,
And with our fair entreaties haste them on. *Exeunt.*

[SCENE II]

Enter Menenius to the Watch or Guard.

FIRST WATCH
Stay! Whence are you?

SECOND WATCH
Stand, and go back.

MENENIUS
You guard like men; 'tis well. But, by your leave,
I am an officer of state, and come
To speak with Coriolanus.

FIRST WATCH
From whence?

MENENIUS
From Rome.

FIRST WATCH
You may not pass, you must return. Our general
Will no more hear from thence.

SECOND WATCH
You'll see your Rome embrac'd with fire before
You'll speak with Coriolanus.

MENENIUS Good my friends,
If you have heard your general talk of Rome,
And of his friends there, it is lots to blanks
My name hath touch'd your ears. It is Menenius.

FIRST WATCH
Be it so; go back. The virtue of your name
Is not here passable.

MENENIUS I tell thee, fellow,
Thy general is my lover. I have been
The book of his good acts, whence men have read
His fame unparallel'd, happ'ly amplified;
For I have ever verified my friends,
Of whom he's chief, with all the size that verity
Would without lapsing suffer. Nay, sometimes,
Like to a bowl upon a subtle ground,
I have tumbled past the throw, and in his praise
Have almost stamp'd the leasing. Therefore, fellow,
I must have leave to pass.

FIRST WATCH Faith, sir, if you had told as many lies in his behalf as you have utter'd words in your own, you should not pass here; no, though it were as virtuous to lie as to live chastely. Therefore go back.

MENENIUS Prithee, fellow, remember my name is Menenius, always factionary on the party of your general.

SECOND WATCH Howsoever you have been his liar, as you say you have, I am one that, telling true under him, must say you cannot pass. Therefore go back.

MENENIUS Has he din'd, canst thou tell? For I would not speak with him till after dinner.

FIRST WATCH You are a Roman, are you?

MENENIUS I am, as thy general is.

FIRST WATCH Then you should hate Rome, as he does. Can you, when you have push'd out your gates the very defender of them, and, in a violent popular ignorance, given your enemy your shield, think to front his revenges with the easy groans of old women, the virginal palms of your daughters, or with the palsied intercession of such a decay'd dotant as you seem to be? Can you think to blow out the intended fire your city is ready to flame in, with such weak breath as this? No, you are deceiv'd; therefore, back to Rome, and prepare for your execution. You are condemn'd; our general has sworn you out of reprieve and pardon.

MENENIUS Sirrah, if thy captain knew I were here, he would use me with estimation.

FIRST WATCH Come, my captain knows you not.

MENENIUS I mean, thy general.

FIRST WATCH My general cares not for you. Back, I say, go, lest I let forth your half-pint of blood. Back! That's the utmost of your having. Back!

MENENIUS Nay, but, fellow, fellow,—

60 dieted to fed properly so as to be in a mood for **63 prove** attempt **64 Speed** succeed **65 success** outcome **66 in gold** in a golden chair. (Gold was considered red of hue, like blood.) **69 faintly** coldly, indifferently **71–72 what . . . conditions** i.e., what terrible actions he would not take against Rome if we bound ourselves under oath to agree to his terms. (See V.iii.14.) **74 Unless** unless in, except from

V.ii. Location: The Volscian camp before Rome.

13 lots to blanks prize-winning tickets compared to valueless ones, i.e., all the world to nothing **15 virtue** strength **16 passable** current (like a coin), and able to provide passage **17 lover** friend **19 happ'ly** haply, perhaps **20 verified** testified to the worth of **21 size** amplification **22 lapsing** erring, distorting. **suffer** allow **23 bowl** ball used in bowls. **subtle** deceptively irregular **24 throw** distance aimed at **25 stamp'd the leasing** given currency to lying, i.e., overstated praise of him **27 if** even if **30 chastely** honestly **32 factionary** active as a partisan **35–36 telling . . . him** telling the truth in his service **43–44 violent popular ignorance** folly of mob violence **44 shield** defender, i.e., Coriolanus. **front** meet **45 easy groans** i.e., groans that are easily provoked **46 virginal . . . daughters** uplifted hands of your virgin daughters **47 dotant** dotard **52 out of** beyond the reach of **54 use** treat. **estimation** esteem **59 utmost of your having** all you are going to get

Enter Coriolanus with Aufidius.

CORIOLANUS What's the matter?

MENENIUS Now, you companion, I'll say an errand for 62
you. You shall know now that I am in estimation; you
shall perceive that a Jack guardant cannot office me 64
from my son Coriolanus. Guess, but by my entertain- 65
ment with him, if thou standest not i' th' state of hang- 66
ing, or of some death more long in spectatorship and 67
crueller in suffering; behold now presently, and
swoon for what's to come upon thee. [*To Coriolanus.*]
The glorious gods sit in hourly synod about thy partic-
ular prosperity, and love thee no worse than thy old
father Menenius does! O my son, my son! Thou art
preparing fire for us; look thee, here's water to quench
it. I was hardly mov'd to come to thee; but being as-
sur'd none but myself could move thee, I have been
blown out of your gates with sighs, and conjure thee
to pardon Rome and thy petitionary countrymen. The
good gods assuage thy wrath, and turn the dregs of it
upon this varlet here—this, who, like a block, hath 79
denied my access to thee.

CORIOLANUS Away!

MENENIUS How? Away?

CORIOLANUS
Wife, mother, child, I know not. My affairs
Are servanted to others. Though I owe 84
My revenge properly, my remission lies 85
In Volscian breasts. That we have been familiar, 86
Ingrate forgetfulness shall poison, rather 87
Than pity note how much. Therefore be gone. 88
Mine ears against your suits are stronger than
Your gates against my force. Yet, for I lov'd thee, 90
Take this along; I writ it for thy sake, [*Gives a letter.*]
And would have sent it. Another word, Menenius,
I will not hear thee speak. This man, Aufidius,
Was my belov'd in Rome; yet thou behold'st!

AUFIDIUS
You keep a constant temper. 95
Exeunt. Mane[*n*]*t the Guard and Menenius.*

FIRST WATCH Now, sir, is your name Menenius?

SECOND WATCH 'Tis a spell, you see, of much power.
You know the way home again.

FIRST WATCH Do you hear how we are shent for keep- 99
ing your greatness back?

SECOND WATCH What cause, do you think, I have to
swoon?

MENENIUS I neither care for th' world nor your general.
For such things as you, I can scarce think there's any, 104
y' are so slight. He that hath a will to die by himself 105
fears it not from another. Let your general do his
worst. For you, be that you are, long; and your misery 107
increase with your age! I say to you, as I was said to,
"Away!" *Exit.*

62 say an errand deliver a message **64 Jack guardant** knave on guard duty. **office** officiously keep **65–66 entertainment with** reception by **67 spectatorship** watching **79 block** (1) impediment (2) blockhead **84 servanted** subjected. **owe** own, possess **85 properly** as my own. **remission** power to forgive **86–88 That . . . much** i.e., though we have been close, I will allow ungrateful forgetfulness (prompted by Rome's ingratitude) to poison the memory of our friendship rather than allowing my pity to recall how much we meant to each other **90 for** because **95 constant temper** firm mind **99 shent** blamed **104 For** as for. (Also at l. 107.) **105 die by himself** destroy himself **107 that** what. **long** long-lived (and tediously so)

FIRST WATCH A noble fellow, I warrant him.

SECOND WATCH The worthy fellow is our general. He's
the rock, the oak not to be wind-shaken. *Exit Watch.*

[SCENE III]

Enter Coriolanus and Aufidius [*with others*].

CORIOLANUS
We will before the walls of Rome tomorrow
Set down our host. My partner in this action,
You must report to th' Volscian lords how plainly 3
I have borne this business.

AUFIDIUS Only their ends
You have respected; stopp'd your ears against
The general suit of Rome; never admitted
A private whisper, no, not with such friends
That thought them sure of you.

CORIOLANUS This last old man,
Whom with a crack'd heart I have sent to Rome,
Lov'd me above the measure of a father,
Nay, godded me indeed. Their latest refuge 11
Was to send him; for whose old love I have,
Though I show'd sourly to him, once more offer'd 13
The first conditions, which they did refuse
And cannot now accept. To grace him only
That thought he could do more, a very little
I have yielded to. Fresh embassies and suits,
Nor from the state nor private friends, hereafter 18
Will I lend ear to. (*Shout within.*) Ha? What shout is
this?
Shall I be tempted to infringe my vow
In the same time 'tis made? I will not.

Enter [*in mourning attire*] *Virgilia, Volumnia, Valeria, young Marcius, with Attendants.*

My wife comes foremost; then the honor'd mold 22
Wherein this trunk was fram'd, and in her hand 23
The grandchild to her blood. But, out, affection!
All bond and privilege of nature, break!
Let it be virtuous to be obstinate.
What is that curt'sy worth? Or those doves' eyes,
Which can make gods forsworn? I melt, and am not
Of stronger earth than others. My mother bows,
As if Olympus to a molehill should
In supplication nod; and my young boy
Hath an aspect of intercession, which 32
Great nature cries, "Deny not." Let the Volsces
Plough Rome and harrow Italy, I'll never
Be such a gosling to obey instinct, but stand
As if a man were author of himself
And knew no other kin.

VIRGILIA My lord and husband!

V.iii. Location: The Volscian camp. The tent of Coriolanus.
3 plainly openly **11 godded** deified. **latest** last **13 show'd** acted **18 Nor** neither **22 mold** form, body (of my mother) **23 this trunk** my body **32 aspect** look

CORIOLANUS
These eyes are not the same I wore in Rome.

VIRGILIA
The sorrow that delivers us thus chang'd
Makes you think so.

CORIOLANUS Like a dull actor now,
I have forgot my part, and I am out,
Even to a full disgrace. Best of my flesh,
Forgive my tyranny; but do not say
For that, "Forgive our Romans." O, a kiss
Long as my exile, sweet as my revenge! [*Kiss.*]
Now, by the jealous queen of heaven, that kiss
I carried from thee, dear; and my true lip
Hath virgin'd it e'er since. You gods! I prate,
And the most noble mother of the world
Leave unsaluted. Sink, my knee, i' th' earth; *Kneels.*
Of thy deep duty more impression show
Than that of common sons.

VOLUMNIA O, stand up blest!
Whilst with no softer cushion than the flint
I kneel before thee, and unproperly
Show duty, as mistaken all this while
Between the child and parent. [*Kneels.*]

CORIOLANUS What's this?
Your knees to me? To your corrected son?
[*Raises her.*]
Then let the pebbles on the hungry beach
Fillip the stars! Then let the mutinous winds
Strike the proud cedars 'gainst the fiery sun,
Murd'ring impossibility, to make
What cannot be, slight work.

VOLUMNIA Thou art my warrior;
I holp to frame thee. Do you know this lady?

CORIOLANUS
The noble sister of Publicola,
The moon of Rome, chaste as the icicle
That's curdied by the frost from purest snow
And hangs on Dian's temple—dear Valeria!

VOLUMNIA
This is a poor epitome of yours,
Which by th' interpretation of full time
May show like all yourself.

CORIOLANUS [*To his son*] The god of soldiers,
With the consent of supreme Jove, inform
Thy thoughts with nobleness, that thou mayst prove
To shame unvulnerable, and stick i' th' wars
Like a great sea-mark, standing every flaw,
And saving those that eye thee!

VOLUMNIA Your knee, sirrah.
[*Young Marcius kneels.*]

CORIOLANUS
That's my brave boy!

VOLUMNIA
Even he, your wife, this lady, and myself,
Are suitors to you.

CORIOLANUS I beseech you, peace.
Or, if you'd ask, remember this before:
The thing I have forsworn to grant may never
Be held by you denials. Do not bid me
Dismiss my soldiers, or capitulate
Again with Rome's mechanics. Tell me not
Wherein I seem unnatural; desire not
T' allay my rages and revenges with
Your colder reasons.

VOLUMNIA O, no more, no more!
You have said you will not grant us anything;
For we have nothing else to ask but that
Which you deny already. Yet we will ask,
That, if you fail in our request, the blame
May hang upon your hardness. Therefore hear us.

CORIOLANUS
Aufidius, and you Volsces, mark; for we'll
Hear nought from Rome in private. [*Sits.*] Your
request?

VOLUMNIA
Should we be silent and not speak, our raiment
And state of bodies would bewray what life
We have led since thy exile. Think with thyself
How more unfortunate than all living women
Are we come hither; since that thy sight, which
should
Make our eyes flow with joy, hearts dance with
comforts,
Constrains them weep and shake with fear and
sorrow,
Making the mother, wife, and child to see
The son, the husband, and the father tearing
His country's bowels out. And to poor we
Thine enmity's most capital. Thou barr'st us
Our prayers to the gods, which is a comfort
That all but we enjoy; for how can we,
Alas, how can we for our country pray,
Whereto we are bound, together with thy victory,
Whereto we are bound? Alack, or we must lose
The country, our dear nurse, or else thy person,
Our comfort in the country. We must find
An evident calamity, though we had
Our wish, which side should win; for either thou
Must as a foreign recreant be led
With manacles through our streets, or else
Triumphantly tread on thy country's ruin,
And bear the palm for having bravely shed
Thy wife and children's blood. For myself, son,
I purpose not to wait on fortune till
These wars determine. If I cannot persuade thee
Rather to show a noble grace to both parts
Than seek the end of one, thou shalt no sooner
March to assault thy country than to tread—

38–40 These . . . so (Coriolanus says, "I see with different eyes from those I wore in Rome." Virgilia replies, taking his words literally, "Our sorrow has changed us past recognition.") **41 I am out** I am at a loss for words **43 tyranny** cruelty **46 jealous . . . heaven** i.e., Juno, patroness of marriage **48 prate** talk idly **54 unproperly** unnaturally; uncharacteristically **58 hungry** unfertile, barren **59 Fillip** flip, strike **61 Murd'ring** i.e., removing **62 slight work** an easy task **63 holp** helped **65 moon of Rome** (Allusion to Diana, goddess of chastity and associated with the moon.) **66 curdied** congealed **68 poor epitome** (Refers to the son of Coriolanus.) **69 by . . . time** when time shall have revealed and fulfilled all **70 show** look **71 inform** inspire **73 stick** stand out **74 sea-mark** reference object used by mariners in navigating. **standing** withstanding. **flaw** gust of wind **75 eye thee** i.e., guide themselves by you, use you as a *sea-mark*

80–81 The thing . . . denials i.e., it would be unjust to regard me as refusing to grant what I have sworn not to grant and hence no longer have the power of granting **82 capitulate** come to terms **83 mechanics** tradesmen **94 Should we** even if we should **95 bewray** reveal **104 capital** fatal **109 or** either **112 evident** certain **114 recreant** traitor **117 palm** i.e., emblem of victory **120 determine** come to an end, settle matters **121 parts** sides

Trust to 't, thou shalt not—on thy mother's womb
That brought thee to this world.

VIRGILIA Ay, and mine,
That brought you forth this boy, to keep your name
Living to time.

YOUNG MARCIUS 'A shall not tread on me;
I'll run away till I am bigger, but then I'll fight.

CORIOLANUS
Not of a woman's tenderness to be
Requires nor child nor woman's face to see.
I have sat too long. [*He rises.*]

VOLUMNIA Nay, go not from us thus.
If it were so that our request did tend
To save the Romans, thereby to destroy
The Volsces whom you serve, you might
condemn us
As poisonous of your honor. No, our suit
Is that you reconcile them, while the Volsces
May say, "This mercy we have show'd," the
Romans,
"This we receiv'd," and each in either side
Give the all-hail to thee, and cry, "Be blest
For making up this peace!" Thou know'st, great son,
The end of war's uncertain, but this certain,
That, if thou conquer Rome, the benefit
Which thou shalt thereby reap is such a name
Whose repetition will be dogg'd with curses,
Whose chronicle thus writ: "The man was noble,
But with his last attempt he wip'd it out,
Destroy'd his country, and his name remains
To th' ensuing age abhorr'd." Speak to me, son.
Thou hast affected the fine strains of honor,
To imitate the graces of the gods;
To tear with thunder the wide cheeks o' th' air,
And yet to charge thy sulphur with a bolt
That should but rive an oak. Why dost not speak?
Think'st thou it honorable for a nobleman
Still to remember wrongs? Daughter, speak you;
He cares not for your weeping. Speak thou, boy;
Perhaps thy childishness will move him more
Than can our reasons. There's no man in the world
More bound to 's mother, yet here he lets me prate
Like one i' th' stocks.—Thou hast never in thy life
Show'd thy dear mother any courtesy,
When she, poor hen, fond of no second brood,
Has cluck'd thee to the wars and safely home,
Loaden with honor. Say my request's unjust,
And spurn me back; but if it be not so,
Thou art not honest, and the gods will plague thee
That thou restrain'st from me the duty which
To a mother's part belongs.—He turns away.
Down, ladies! Let us shame him with our knees.
To his surname Coriolanus 'longs more pride
Than pity to our prayers. Down! [*They kneel.*]
An end;
This is the last. So we will home to Rome,
And die among our neighbors.—Nay, behold 's!
This boy, that cannot tell what he would have,
But kneels and holds up hands for fellowship,
Does reason our petition with more strength
Than thou hast to deny 't.—Come, let us go.
This fellow had a Volscian to his mother;
His wife is in Corioles, and his child [*They rise.*]
Like him by chance.—Yet give us our dispatch.
I am hush'd until our city be afire,
And then I'll speak a little.
[*He*] *holds her by the hand, silent.*

CORIOLANUS O mother, mother!
What have you done? Behold, the heavens do ope,
The gods look down, and this unnatural scene
They laugh at. O my mother, mother! O!
You have won a happy victory to Rome;
But for your son—believe it, O, believe it!—
Most dangerously you have with him prevail'd,
If not most mortal to him. But, let it come.—
Aufidius, though I cannot make true wars,
I'll frame convenient peace. Now, good Aufidius,
Were you in my stead, would you have heard
A mother less? Or granted less, Aufidius?

AUFIDIUS
I was mov'd withal.

CORIOLANUS I dare be sworn you were.
And, sir, it is no little thing to make
Mine eyes to sweat compassion. But, good sir,
What peace you'll make, advise me. For my part,
I'll not to Rome, I'll back with you; and pray you,
Stand to me in this cause. O mother! Wife!

AUFIDIUS [*Aside*]
I am glad thou hast set thy mercy and thy honor
At difference in thee. Out of that I'll work
Myself a former fortune.
[*The Ladies make signs to Coriolanus.*]

CORIOLANUS [*To Volumnia, etc.*] Ay, by and by;
But we will drink together; and you shall bear
A better witness back than words, which we,
On like conditions, will have counter-seal'd.
Come, enter with us. Ladies, you deserve
To have a temple built you. All the swords
In Italy, and her confederate arms,
Could not have made this peace. *Exeunt.*

[SCENE IV]

Enter Menenius and Sicinius.

MENENIUS See you yond coign o' th' Capitol, yond cornerstone?

124 Trust . . . not (Read this parenthetical phrase after *sooner* in l. 122.) **129–130 Not . . . see** if a man is not to yield to a womanly tenderness, he must not look upon any child's or woman's face **146 attempt** undertaking. **it** i.e., the nobility **149 affected** sought, cherished **152 charge** load. **sulphur** lightning **153 but rive an oak** i.e., do no undeserved harm to men; Coriolanus wishes like Jupiter to be mighty but wise in his use of power **156 cares not for** is unmoved by **159–160 prate . . . stocks** i.e., talk uselessly like a prisoner who has been publicly humiliated **162 When** whereas. **fond** desirous **163 cluck'd** marshaled as a hen her brood **166 honest** honorable, just **170 'longs** belongs

174 This boy i.e., Coriolanus' son **175 for fellowship** merely to keep us company **176 reason** argue for **178 to** for **180 dispatch** dismissal, leave to go **191 convenient** fitting, proper **196 sweat compassion** i.e., weep with pity **199 Stand to** stand by **202 former fortune** fortune great as formerly **204 better witness** i.e., formal document of peace **205 On . . . seal'd** having agreed to the same conditions, will both have sealed and guaranteed **208 her confederate arms** the weapons of her allies

V.iv. Location: Rome. A public place.
1 coign corner

SICINIUS Why, what of that?
MENENIUS If it be possible for you to displace it with
your little finger, there is some hope the ladies of
Rome, especially his mother, may prevail with him.
But I say there is no hope in 't; our throats are
sentenc'd and stay upon execution. 8
SICINIUS Is 't possible that so short a time can alter the
condition of a man?
MENENIUS There is differency between a grub and a
butterfly, yet your butterfly was a grub. This Marcius
is grown from man to dragon. He has wings; he's
more than a creeping thing.
SICINIUS He lov'd his mother dearly.
MENENIUS So did he me; and he no more remembers
his mother now than an eight-year-old horse. The tart-
ness of his face sours ripe grapes. When he walks, he
moves like an engine, and the ground shrinks before 19
his treading. He is able to pierce a corslet with his eye; 20
talks like a knell, and his hum is a battery. He sits in 21
his state, as a thing made for Alexander. What he bids 22
be done is finish'd with his bidding. He wants noth- 23
ing of a god but eternity and a heaven to throne in. 24
SICINIUS Yes, mercy, if you report him truly. 25
MENENIUS I paint him in the character. Mark what 26
mercy his mother shall bring from him. There is no
more mercy in him than there is milk in a male tiger;
that shall our poor city find. And all this is long of you. 29
SICINIUS The gods be good unto us!
MENENIUS No, in such a case the gods will not be good
unto us. When we banish'd him, we respected not
them; and, he returning to break our necks, they re-
spect not us.

Enter a Messenger.

MESSENGER
Sir, if you'd save your life, fly to your house!
The plebeians have got your fellow-tribune
And hale him up and down, all swearing, if
The Roman ladies bring not comfort home,
They'll give him death by inches.

Enter another Messenger.

SICINIUS What's the news?
SECOND MESSENGER
Good news, good news! The ladies have prevail'd,
The Volscians are dislodg'd, and Marcius gone. 41
A merrier day did never yet greet Rome,
No, not th' expulsion of the Tarquins. 43
SICINIUS
Friend, art thou certain this is true?
Is 't most certain?
SECOND MESSENGER
As certain as I know the sun is fire.
Where have you lurk'd, that you make doubt of it?
Ne'er through an arch so hurried the blown tide 48
As the recomforted through th' gates. Why,
hark you! 49
Trumpets, hautboys, drums beat, all together.
The trumpets, sackbuts, psalteries, and fifes, 50
Tabors and cymbals, and the shouting Romans, 51
Make the sun dance. Hark you! *A shout within.*
MENENIUS This is good news.
I will go meet the ladies. This Volumnia
Is worth of consuls, senators, patricians,
A city full; of tribunes, such as you,
A sea and land full. You have pray'd well today.
This morning for ten thousand of your throats
I'd not have given a doit. Hark, how they joy! 58
Sound still, with the shouts.
SICINIUS
First, the gods bless you for your tidings!
Next, accept my thankfulness.
SECOND MESSENGER
Sir, we have all great cause to give great thanks.
SICINIUS
They are near the city?
SECOND MESSENGER
Almost at point to enter.
SICINIUS
We'll meet them, and help the joy.
Exeunt.

[SCENE V]

Enter two Senators with Ladies [Volumnia, Virgilia, Valeria] passing over the stage, with other Lords.

FIRST SENATOR
Behold our patroness, the life of Rome!
Call all your tribes together, praise the gods,
And make triumphant fires! Strew flowers before
them!
Unshout the noise that banish'd Marcius; 4
Repeal him with the welcome of his mother. 5
Cry, "Welcome, ladies, welcome!"
ALL
Welcome, ladies, welcome!
A flourish with drums and trumpets. [*Exeunt.*]

[SCENE VI]

Enter Tullus Aufidius, with Attendants.

AUFIDIUS
Go tell the lords o' th' city I am here.

8 stay upon await **19 engine** heavy instrument of war such as a battering-ram **20 corslet** body armor **21 battery** assault by artillery **22 state** chair of state. **as . . . Alexander** as though he were a statue of Alexander the Great (who lived after Coriolanus) **23 finish'd . . . bidding** i.e., as good as done once he orders it. **wants** lacks **24 throne** be enthroned **25 mercy** i.e., he lacks mercy **26 in the character** to the life **29 long of** owing to **41 dislodg'd** gone from their camp **43 expulsion of the Tarquins** i.e., the expulsion of Rome's last kings and beginning of the Republic

48 arch i.e., arch of a bridge, such as London bridge. **blown** swollen **49 s.d. hautboys** oboes **50 sackbuts** early trombones. **psalteries** stringed instruments played by plucking the strings **51 Tabors** small drums **58 doit** very small coin

V.v. Location: Rome. A street near the gate. The time is virtually continuous from the previous scene.
4 Unshout recall, or cancel by more shouting **5 Repeal** recall

V.vi. Location: Corioles. A public place.

Deliver them this paper. [*Gives paper.*] Having read
it,
Bid them repair to th' market-place, where I,
Even in theirs and in the commons' ears,
Will vouch the truth of it. Him I accuse 5
The city ports by this hath enter'd and 6
Intends t' appear before the people, hoping
To purge himself with words. Dispatch.
[*Exeunt Attendants.*]

Enter three or four Conspirators of Aufidius' faction.

Most welcome!

FIRST CONSPIRATOR
How is it with our general?

AUFIDIUS
Even so
As with a man by his own alms empoison'd,
And with his charity slain.

SECOND CONSPIRATOR
Most noble sir, 11
If you do hold the same intent wherein
You wish'd us parties, we'll deliver you 13
Of your great danger.

AUFIDIUS
Sir, I cannot tell.
We must proceed as we do find the people.

THIRD CONSPIRATOR
The people will remain uncertain whilst
'Twixt you there's difference; but the fall of either
Makes the survivor heir of all.

AUFIDIUS
I know it;
And my pretext to strike at him admits 19
A good construction. I rais'd him, and I pawn'd 20
Mine honor for his truth; who, being so heighten'd,
He watered his new plants with dews of flattery,
Seducing so my friends; and to this end
He bow'd his nature, never known before
But to be rough, unswayable, and free.

THIRD CONSPIRATOR
Sir, his stoutness 26
When he did stand for consul, which he lost
By lack of stooping—

AUFIDIUS
That I would have spoke of. 28
Being banish'd for 't, he came unto my hearth,
Presented to my knife his throat. I took him;
Made him joint-servant with me; gave him way 31
In all his own desires; nay, let him choose
Out of my files, his projects to accomplish, 33
My best and freshest men; serv'd his designments
In mine own person; holp to reap the fame
Which he did end all his; and took some pride 36
To do myself this wrong—till at the last
I seem'd his follower, not partner, and
He wag'd me with his countenance, as if 39
I had been mercenary.

FIRST CONSPIRATOR
So he did, my lord.
The army marvel'd at it, and, in the last,
When he had carried Rome and that we look'd 42
For no less spoil than glory—

AUFIDIUS
There was it
For which my sinews shall be stretch'd upon him. 44
At a few drops of women's rheum, which are 45
As cheap as lies, he sold the blood and labor
Of our great action. Therefore shall he die,
And I'll renew me in his fall. But, hark!
Drums and trumpets sounds, with great shouts of the People.

FIRST CONSPIRATOR
Your native town you enter'd like a post, 49
And had no welcomes home; but he returns,
Splitting the air with noise.

SECOND CONSPIRATOR
And patient fools,
Whose children he hath slain, their base throats tear
With giving him glory.

THIRD CONSPIRATOR
Therefore, at your vantage, 53
Ere he express himself, or move the people
With what he would say, let him feel your sword,
Which we will second. When he lies along, 56
After your way his tale pronounc'd shall bury 57
His reasons with his body.

AUFIDIUS
Say no more. 58
Here come the lords.

Enter the Lords of the city.

ALL LORDS
You are most welcome home.

AUFIDIUS
I have not deserv'd it.
But, worthy lords, have you with heed perus'd
What I have written to you?

ALL LORDS
We have.

FIRST LORD
And grieve to hear 't.
What faults he made before the last, I think 65
Might have found easy fines; but there to end 66
Where he was to begin, and give away
The benefit of our levies, answering us 68
With our own charge, making a treaty where 69
There was a yielding—this admits no excuse. 70

AUFIDIUS
He approaches. You shall hear him.

Enter Coriolanus, marching with drum and colors; the Commoners being with him.

CORIOLANUS
Hail, lords! I am return'd your soldier,
No more infected with my country's love
Than when I parted hence, but still subsisting
Under your great command. You are to know
That prosperously I have attempted, and 76
With bloody passage led your wars even to

5 Him he whom **6 ports** gates. **by this** by this time **11 with his** by his own **13 parties** as allies, partners **19 pretext** intention, motive **20 construction** interpretation **26 stoutness** obstinacy **28 That . . . of** I was about to mention that **31 joint-servant** partner **33 files** ranks, troops **36 end all his** gather in as all his own **39 wag'd** remunerated. **countenance** patronage, favor

42 carried virtually overcome, or might have overcome **44 my . . . upon** I shall exert all my strength against **45 rheum** i.e., tears **49 post** messenger **53 at your vantage** seizing your opportune moment **56 lies along** lies low **57 After . . . pronounc'd** your own version of the story **58 reasons** justifications **65 made** committed **66 fines** penalties **68 levies** expenses incurred in raising an army **68–69 answering . . . charge** rewarding us with our own expenses **70 yielding** i.e., complete victory for us **76 prosperously . . . attempted** my warlike enterprise has been prosperous

The gates of Rome. Our spoils we have brought
home
Doth more than counterpoise a full third part
The charges of the action. We have made peace
With no less honor to the Antiates
Than shame to th' Romans; and we here deliver,
Subscrib'd by th' consuls and patricians,
Together with the seal o' th' Senate, what
We have compounded on.
[*Offers document.*]

AUFIDIUS
Read it not, noble lords,
But tell the traitor, in the highest degree
He hath abus'd your powers.

CORIOLANUS
"Traitor"? How now?

AUFIDIUS
Ay, traitor, Marcius!

CORIOLANUS
"Marcius"?

AUFIDIUS
Ay, Marcius, Caius Marcius! Dost thou think
I'll grace thee with that robbery, thy stol'n name
Coriolanus, in Corioles?
You lords and heads o' th' state, perfidiously
He has betray'd your business, and given up,
For certain drops of salt, your city Rome—
I say "your city,"—to his wife and mother,
Breaking his oath and resolution like
A twist of rotten silk, never admitting
Counsel o' th' war, but at his nurse's tears
He whin'd and roar'd away your victory,
That pages blush'd at him and men of heart
Look'd wond'ring each at other.

CORIOLANUS
Hear'st thou, Mars?

AUFIDIUS
Name not the god, thou boy of tears!

CORIOLANUS
Ha?

AUFIDIUS
No more.

CORIOLANUS
Measureless liar, thou hast made my heart
Too great for what contains it. "Boy"? O slave!
Pardon me, lords, 'tis the first time that ever
I was forc'd to scold. Your judgments, my grave
lords,
Must give this cur the lie; and his own notion—
Who wears my stripes impress'd upon him, that
Must bear my beating to his grave—shall join
To thrust the lie unto him.

FIRST LORD
Peace, both, and hear me speak.

CORIOLANUS
Cut me to pieces, Volsces. Men and lads,
Stain all your edges on me. "Boy"? False hound!
If you have writ your annals true, 'tis there
That, like an eagle in a dove-cote, I
Flutter'd your Volscians in Corioles.
Alone I did it. "Boy"!

AUFIDIUS
Why, noble lords,
Will you be put in mind of his blind fortune,
Which was your shame, by this unholy braggart,
'Fore your own eyes and ears?

ALL CONSPIRATORS
Let him die for 't.

ALL PEOPLE Tear him to pieces!—Do it presently! He killed my son!—My daughter!—He kill'd my cousin Marcus!—He kill'd my father!

SECOND LORD
Peace, ho! No outrage! Peace!
The man is noble, and his fame folds in
This orb o' th' earth. His last offenses to us
Shall have judicious hearing. Stand, Aufidius,
And trouble not the peace.

CORIOLANUS
O that I had him,
With six Aufidiuses, or more, his tribe,
To use my lawful sword!

AUFIDIUS
Insolent villain!

ALL CONSPIRATORS Kill, kill, kill, kill, kill him!

Draw the Conspirators, and kill Marcius, who falls. Aufidius stands on him.

LORDS Hold, hold, hold, hold!

AUFIDIUS
My noble masters, hear me speak.

FIRST LORD
O Tullus!

SECOND LORD
Thou hast done a deed whereat valor will weep.

THIRD LORD
Tread not upon him. Masters all, be quiet;
Put up your swords.

AUFIDIUS
My lords, when you shall know—as in this rage,
Provok'd by him, you cannot—the great danger
Which this man's life did owe you, you'll rejoice
That he is thus cut off. Please it your honors
To call me to your Senate, I'll deliver
Myself your loyal servant, or endure
Your heaviest censure.

FIRST LORD
Bear from hence his body,
And mourn you for him. Let him be regarded
As the most noble corse that ever herald
Did follow to his urn.

SECOND LORD
His own impatience
Takes from Aufidius a great part of blame.
Let's make the best of it.

AUFIDIUS
My rage is gone,
And I am struck with sorrow. Take him up.
Help, three o' th' chiefest soldiers; I'll be one.
Beat thou the drum that it speak mournfully;
Trail your steel pikes. Though in this city he
Hath widow'd and unchilded many a one,
Which to this hour bewail the injury,
Yet he shall have a noble memory.
Assist.

Exeunt, bearing the body of Marcius. A dead march sounded.

79 Doth . . . part outweigh by a full third **83 Subscrib'd** signed **85 compounded** agreed **101 heart** courage **107 Too . . . it** swollen with rage so that my breast cannot contain it **110 notion** understanding, mind **116 edges** swords **117 there** recorded there

121 blind fortune gift of Fortune, the blind goddess; mere good luck **128 folds in** overspreads, enwraps **130 judicious** judicial. **Stand** stop **142 Which . . . owe you** which while this man lived was owing to you, would sooner or later have befallen you **144 deliver** show, demonstrate **153 be one** i.e., be the fourth **158 memory** memorial

The Romances

Pericles

Cymbeline

The Winter's Tale

The Tempest

Pericles

Pericles is a deceptively simple play. Although it was popular in its own time, and in recent years has proved to be successful and deeply moving on stage, the play may seem naive and trivial on the printed page. Its apparent lack of "depth" seems especially striking when we compare it with its contemporaries *King Lear, Macbeth, Timon of Athens,* and *Antony and Cleopatra.* It purports to be the work of a medieval poet, John Gower, who as chorus-figure apologizes to his sophisticated Jacobean audience ("born in these latter times When wit's more ripe") for the "lame feet of my rhyme" and the quaintness of his ditty. The narrative offers a series of sea voyages, separations, hairbreadth escapes, and reunions. Thrilling circumstances abound: Pericles fleeing the wrath of Antiochus, his wife Thaisa giving birth to Marina on board ship in the midst of a gigantic storm, and Marina later being rescued by pirates from a would-be murderer only to be sold by her new captors to a house of prostitution. Time leaps forward in sequential segments from Pericles' own youth to that of his daughter Marina. The action takes place in lands remote, shifting constantly back and forth among six eastern Mediterranean localities: Antioch, Tyre, Tharsus, Pentapolis, Ephesus, and Mytilene. Conventional devices of plot include the expounding of riddles, the discovery of incest at court, the exposure of infants to the hostile elements, the miraculous restoration of life after seeming death, the appearance of the gods in a vision, and recognition of long-lost loved ones by means of signs or tokens.

These are the attributes of popular romance, a distinctly old-fashioned genre in 1606–1608 when *Pericles* was apparently written. Robert Greene had composed prose romances of this sort in the 1580's and early 1590's, including *Pandosto,* Shakespeare's source for *The Winter's Tale.* Sir Philip Sidney's *Arcadia* had endowed romance with noble eloquence and literary fashionableness, but that too was in the late 1580's. One source for *Pericles* itself, a prose history of Apollonius of Tyre by Laurence Twine, was registered for publication in 1576, although no edition exists before that of 1594 or 1595. Earlier accounts of Apollonius (as the hero was originally named), going back to Greek romance, include a ninth-century *Historia Apollonii Regis Tyri,* Godfrey of Viterbo's *Pantheon* (c. 1186), John Gower's *Confessio Amantis* (c. 1383–1393) and the *Gesta Romanorum.* Why did Shakespeare's company refurbish such an outmoded romantic story in 1606–1608?

The puzzle is aggravated by questions of authorship and textual reliability. The editors of the First Folio did not include *Pericles* in the canon of Shakespeare's plays. Perhaps they experienced copyright difficulties or could not lay their hands on the prompt-book, but it is also possible they either suspected or knew that Shakespeare was not sole author. Printed editions were available to them: the first quarto of 1609 and the subsequent quartos of 1609, 1611, and 1619, each based on the preceding edition. The first quarto was, however, a bad text with occasionally glaring contradictions. In Act I, scene ii, for example, Pericles' lords wish him a safe journey when no one has yet spoken of his departure, and Helicanus rebukes these same lords for flattery even though they have not said anything remotely sycophantic. Other scenes present similar difficulties, especially in the first two acts. The characters do not always seem consistent: Cleon is condemned in Act V for having tried to murder Marina, even though our earlier impression of him is of a man who is genuinely horrified at his wife's villainy. He weakly bends to the will of Dionyza but is no murderer. Such inconsistencies and errors, and the naiveté of the whole, have generally led to three hypotheses: that Shakespeare worked with a collaborator such as Thomas Heywood or George Wilkins, that he revised an older play and left the first two acts pretty much as they were, or that he wrote the entire play which was then "pirated" by two unemployed actors whose portions differed markedly in accuracy.

To complicate matters still further, a prose version of the story called *The Painfull Aduentures of Pericles* by George Wilkins appeared in 1608, purporting to be "the true History of the Play of Pericles"—that is, to be a prose account of a dramatic performance. This redaction is indeed close at times to the play we have, but at other times it departs widely. The departures of the later work are sometimes explained with the hypothesis that Wilkins based his account on an older play, one to which Wilkins might have contributed himself; another and more current opinion favors the notion that Wilkins took what he needed from the play we have, borrowing also from Twine's prose version or from his own imagination. Apparently, then, *Pericles* was such a popular stage success that it inspired Wilkins' *Painfull Aduentures* in 1608, a new reprint in 1607 of Twine's *Patterne of Painefull Aduentures* on which the play itself had been partly based, and a botched surreptitious quarto edition of the play in 1609. Shakespeare's sole authorship must remain in doubt, although the incongruities, especially in the first two acts, are sometimes explained as the result of faulty memorial reporting and compositorial error. On stage, to be sure, even the first two acts make fine dramatic sense, establishing motifs and situations that are essential to the rest of the play, so that the overall impression in the theatre is of cohesion.

The naiveté of *Pericles* is probably deliberate. Its romantic motifs continue on into that group of plays known generally as the late romances: *Cymbeline* (c. 1608–1610),

The Winter's Tale (c. 1610–1611), and *The Tempest* (c. 1610–1611). Nor are these motifs entirely new in *Pericles:* the "problem" comedies *All's Well that Ends Well* and *Measure for Measure* use a tragicomic structure in which miraculous cures or providential interventions triumph over the semblance of death. *Pericles* occupies an integral place, then, in the development of Shakespearean comedy during the "tragic" period. To that development it offers a new emphasis on the simplicity of folk legend. Of the four late romances, *Pericles,* the earliest, is also the nearest in tone to romance of the 1580's. The play seems to have constituted a revival of that old genre, and was so immensely popular that it did much to establish the vogue of tragicomedy exploited by Beaumont and Fletcher.

The Chorus, old Gower, gives to the episodic materials of the play a unified point of view. He speaks with the authority of one who has told the story before, even though his *Confessio Amantis* (c. 1383–1393) was probably not Shakespeare's immediate source. Gower adopts a kind of Chaucerian persona, appealing to "what mine authors say" and apologizing for his rude simplicity. Like the chorus of *Henry V,* he repeatedly urges his auditors to transcend the limitations of his naive art, using the power of imagination to bridge gaps in time and to suppose the stage a storm-tossed ship or the city of Antioch. His appearances divide the action into seven episodic segments, surely a more authentic structure than the five "acts" conventionally employed by later editions. He offers moral appraisals of his various characters, often before we have had a chance to see them, contrasting the good with the bad. Most importantly, he presides as a sort of benign deity over the changing fortunes of his characters, assuring us that as narrator he will not allow the virtuous to come to grief or the wicked to escape punishment. He thus paces our expectations and provides a comic reassurance appropriate to romance. He promises to "show you those in trouble's reign, Losing a mite, a mountain gain." To the virtuous he will ultimately give his "benison." Under his direction, the vacillations of fortune take on a predictable rhythm, whereby the rewards of virtuous conduct may be delayed but cannot eventually fail. Pericles, he tells us, will suffer adversity "Till fortune, tir'd with doing bad, Threw him ashore, to give him glad" (II, Chorus). This pattern is repeated several times.

The characters often remind us of characters from a fairy story, outwardly stereotyped and one-dimensional, divided for the most part into contrasting types of villainy and virtue, and yet suggesting beneath their conventional surfaces the conflicts in family relationships that are essential to the fairy story. Incest is a recurrent motif, from its most blunt and evil manifestation in the court of Antiochus to more subtle inversions and variations in the relationships of Simonides and his daughter Thaisa, and, most centrally, of Pericles and his daughter Marina. The interest in fathers and daughters, and in the difficulties fathers have in coming to terms with their daughters' marrying young men, continues to fascinate Shakespeare from *Othello* and *King Lear* into all of his late romances. The mystery of incest is stated in terms of a riddle at the start of *Pericles,* and the moving dramatic conclusion in which the hero is reunited at last with his daughter seems to represent at some level a resolution of conflict between father and daughter. Pericles and Marina have "found" one another and themselves, literally in the narrative sense and also in some deeper psychic and spiritual way.

The characters expressing this and other conflicts are repeatedly paired opposite to one another as contrasting "foils," illustrating a type of human depravity and its ideal opposite. One such contrast is that of tyranny and true monarchy. For example, both Antiochus and Simonides seem to welcome the various suitors who flock to their courts, seeking the hand in marriage of the two kings' daughters. Antiochus does so deceitfully, however, since he is his daughter's incestuous lover. Pericles learns in Antioch the danger of perceiving too much about the private affairs of a suspicious and vengeful tyrant like Antiochus. Simonides is, on the other hand, a true prince, beloved by the simplest of his subjects, generous, lacking in envy, courteous to strangers, and more impressed with inner substance than with outward show. He approves of Pericles as a son-in-law, though (like Prospero in *The Tempest*) he imposes artificial restraints on the lovers to make their eventual triumph of love seem all the more sweet. Antiochus and his daughter are eventually shriveled up by a fire from heaven, whereas Simonides and Thaisa earn the just rewards of gracious hospitality. Another opposing pair of characters, Thaliard and Helicanus, are conventionally typed as false and true courtiers. Thaliard, ordered by Antiochus to murder Pericles, is evasive and self-serving; Helicanus, when offered the opportunity to supplant Pericles as ruler of Tyre, loyally awaits his master's return.

Pericles is apparently conceived in these same conventional terms as a prince of chivalry, young, brave, admirable both as a romantic wooer and as a resolute adventurer. His visit to the city of Tharsus, which has recently been toppled from wealth to poverty, shows him practicing the generosity that befits his lofty rank and innately noble qualities. Even when fortune strips him of his finery, his princely bearing is evident to discerning observers like King Simonides and Thaisa. Pericles thus differs outwardly from the flawed tragicomic protagonists more often found in the late romances, such as Posthumus in *Cymbeline* and Leontes in *The Winter's Tale,* who bring grief upon themselves and must suffer agonizing contrition before gaining an unexpected second chance. Pericles seems to be virtually without fault, a hero of romance rather than of tragedy. His soliloquies and eloquent speeches are not darkly introspective and psychological, like Leontes'. Although he grieves in sackcloth and ashes, he does so for undeserved misfortune rather than for his own follies. The play accordingly has little to say about man's perverse instinct for self-destruction. Yet critics have been unable to agree as to whether Pericles is simply a good man buffeted by misfortune or a man somehow perplexed by inner conflict. Are there unresolved wishes in his relationships to Thaisa and Marina that link him to the manifestly flawed protagonists of *Cymbeline* and *The Winter's Tale?* What is it that causes his excessive despair in his grief, and his withdrawal into absolute silence? At any rate, on the surface his story is one of undeserved misfortune leading at last to happy reunion and an end of his trials. He learns a more affirmative and patient response from his courageous daughter Marina, whereupon his trials have run their necessary course. Even his learning such a lesson is of less importance than the sublime sense of mystery and joy that accompanies his reunion with Marina.

In several ways, Marina is a typical heroine of Shakespeare's late romances. Her name, like that of Perdita in *The Winter's Tale,* signifies loss and recovery. Marina is the gift of the sea, that mysterious power of fortune in *Pericles* which takes with one hand even while it gives with the other. Just as the sea tosses Pericles on the coast of Pentapolis and then returns to him the suit of armor in which he will joust for the love of fair Thaisa, so in another storm at sea Thaisa apparently dies giving birth to Marina. The child is a "fresh new seafarer" on the troubled voyage of life. The sea parts her from her mother and father and leads to the misunderstandings whereby Marina is supposed dead, but the sea also eventually deposits Pericles on the coast of Mytilene where he finds his long-lost daughter. Like Perdita, Marina is associated with flowers and with Tellus, a divinity of the earth. The inscription on her monument, when she is supposed dead, speaks of elemental strife between the sea and the shore caused by her death, in which the angry sea gods "Make raging battery upon shores of flint" (IV,iv). She is a princess from folk legend, like Snow White or like Imogen in *Cymbeline,* who must flee the envious wrath of a witchlike stepmother and queen. Her true mother, Thaisa, another princess in a folk tale, is washed ashore in a treasure-filled chest, smelling sweetly and betokening some miraculous change of fortune.

Most important, Marina is one who can preach conversion to the sinful and cure distempered souls. She recovers her husband-to-be, Lysimachus, from the brothels of Mytilene, and even converts pimps and prostitutes by her innocent faith. As one with a strange power to bring new life to dead hope, she resembles a number of mysterious artist-figures and magicians in the late romances. One such is Cerimon, who restores life to Thaisa. Like him, or like Paulina in *The Winter's Tale,* whose devices are "lawful" though seemingly magical, Marina offers cures that can be rationally explained and yet appear to be miraculous. To Pericles, her ministrations seem "the rarest dream that e'er dull sleep Did mock sad fools withal" (V,i). Yet what she has taught him, by her own example, is simple patience; she has suffered even more than he, but nevertheless knows how to endure, how to "look Like Patience gazing on kings' graves and smiling Extremity out of act."

Through her we understand finally why providence has allowed so much misfortune to afflict the virtuous: only by such testing can men learn to conquer time and death. Time will always remain "the king of men; He's both their parent, and he is their grave, And gives them what he will, not what they crave" (II,iii). Nevertheless, providence can turn the accidents of time and fortune to good purpose for those who are Joblike in their patient faith. Even pirates unknowingly take part in a divine plan, rescuing Marina from the clutches of the evil Dionyza. As Gower puts it, those who are "assail'd with fortune fierce and keen" are also "Led on by heaven, and crown'd with joy at last" (Epilogue). To Pericles, such a delayed reward is ample compensation for his sorrows, almost indeed an unbearable joy. "No more, you gods!" he movingly pleads, "Your present kindness Makes my past miseries sports."

Pericles

[*Dramatis Personae*

ANTIOCHUS, *King of Antioch.*
PERICLES, *Prince of Tyre.*
HELICANUS, } *two lords of Tyre.*
ESCANES, }
SIMONIDES, *King of Pentapolis.*
CLEON, *Governor of Tharsus.*
LYSIMACHUS, *Governor of Mytilene.*
CERIMON, *a lord of Ephesus.*
THALIARD, *a lord of Antioch.*
PHILEMON, *servant to Cerimon.*
LEONINE, *servant to Dionyza.*
MARSHAL.
PANDAR.
BOULT, *his servant.*
Another SERVANT.

DAUGHTER *of Antiochus.*
DIONYZA, *wife to Cleon.*
THAISA, *daughter to Simonides.*
MARINA, *daughter to Pericles and Thaisa.*
LYCHORIDA, *nurse to Marina.*
BAWD.

LORDS, LADIES, KNIGHTS, GENTLEMEN, SAILORS, PIRATES, FISHERMEN, *and* MESSENGERS.

The goddess DIANA.

GOWER, *as Chorus.*

SCENE: *In various eastern Mediterranean countries.*]

[ACT I]

Enter Gower [before the palace of Antioch, on the walls of which can be seen a row of impaled heads].

GOWER
To sing a song that old was sung, 1
From ashes ancient Gower is come, 2
Assuming man's infirmities, 3
To glad your ear and please your eyes.
It hath been sung at festivals,
On ember-eves and holy-ales; 6
And lords and ladies in their lives
Have read it for restoratives.
The purchase is to make men glorious; 9
Et bonum quo antiquius, eo melius. 10
If you, born in these latter times,
When wit's more ripe, accept my rhymes,
And that to hear an old man sing 13
May to your wishes pleasure bring,
I life would wish, and that I might
Waste it for you, like taper-light. 16
This Antioch, then; Antiochus the Great 17
Built up this city for his chiefest seat,
The fairest in all Syria—
I tell you what mine authors say.
This king unto him took a peer, 21
Who died and left a female heir,
So buxom, blithe, and full of face 23
As heaven had lent her all his grace; 24
With whom the father liking took,
And her to incest did provoke.
Bad child, worse father, to entice his own
To evil should be done by none! 28
But custom what they did begin 29
Was with long use account'd no sin.
The beauty of this sinful dame
Made many princes thither frame, 32
To seek her as a bedfellow,
In marriage-pleasures playfellow;
Which to prevent he made a law,
To keep her still, and men in awe, 36
That whoso ask'd her for his wife,
His riddle told not, lost his life. 38
So for her many a wight did die, 39
As yon grim looks do testify.
[*Points to the heads of the unsuccessful suitors, displayed on the walls.*]
What now ensues, to the judgment of your eye
I give, my cause who best can justify. *Exit.* 42

[SCENE I]

Enter Antiochus, Prince Pericles, and followers.

ANTIOCHUS
Young Prince of Tyre, you have at large receiv'd 1
The danger of the task you undertake.
PERICLES
I have, Antiochus, and, with a soul

Pericles (guide)
I. Chorus. (Gower is seen to be standing before the palace of Antioch, where scene i will take place.)
1 old of old **2 ancient Gower** the fourteenth-century poet John Gower, who related the adventures of Apollonius of Tyre (of which *Pericles* is a version) in his *Confessio Amantis* **3 Assuming man's infirmities** taking on a mortal body

6 ember-eves evenings before the ember days—the periodic fast days which coincide with the four changes of the seasons. **holy-ales** i.e., church ales or festivals **9 purchase** profit **10 Et . . . melius** a good thing is better for being older. (Latin.) **13 And that** i.e., and if **16 Waste** spend **17 This** i.e., this is **21 peer** consort **23 buxom** cheerful, lively. **full of face** beautiful **24 As** as if. **his** its **28 should** that should **29 custom** continued practice (of) **32 frame** direct their steps **36 still** always, forever. **and men** and to keep men **38 His riddle told not** but left his (Antiochus') riddle unsolved **39 wight** person **42 who** i.e., your eye. **justify** witness

I.i. Location: Antioch. The palace, as before.
1 at large receiv'd heard in detail

Embold'ned with the glory of her praise,
Think death no hazard in this enterprise.

ANTIOCHUS

Music!
Bring in our daughter, clothed like a bride,
For th' embracements even of Jove himself;
At whose conception, till Lucina reign'd,
Nature this dowry gave: to glad her presence,
The senate-house of planets all did sit,
To knit in her their best perfections.

[Music.] Enter Antiochus' Daughter.

PERICLES

See where she comes, apparel'd like the spring,
Graces her subjects, and her thoughts the king
Of every virtue gives renown to men!
Her face the book of praises, where is read
Nothing but curious pleasures, as from thence
Sorrow were ever ras'd, and testy wrath
Could never be her mild companion.
You gods that made me man, and sway in love,
That have inflam'd desire in my breast
To taste the fruit of yon celestial tree
Or die in the adventure, be my helps,
As I am son and servant to your will,
To compass such a boundless happiness!

ANTIOCHUS

Prince Pericles—

PERICLES

That would be son to great Antiochus.

ANTIOCHUS

Before thee stands this fair Hesperides,
With golden fruit, but dangerous to be touch'd;
For death-like dragons here affright thee hard.
Her face, like heaven, enticeth thee to view
Her countless glory, which desert must gain;
And which, without desert, because thine eye
Presumes to reach, all the whole heap must die.
Yon sometimes famous princes, like thyself,
[Points to the heads on the walls.]
Drawn by report, advent'rous by desire,
Tell thee, with speechless tongues and semblance pale,
That without covering, save yon field of stars,
Here they stand martyrs, slain in Cupid's wars;
And with dead cheeks advise thee to desist
For going on death's net, whom none resist.

PERICLES

Antiochus, I thank thee, who hath taught
My frail mortality to know itself,
And by those fearful objects to prepare
This body, like to them, to what I must;
For death remembered should be like a mirror,
Who tells us life's but breath, to trust it error.
I'll make my will then, and, as sick men do
Who know the world, see heaven, but, feeling woe,
Gripe not at earthly joys as erst they did.
So I bequeath a happy peace to you
And all good men, as every prince should do;
My riches to the earth from whence they came;
[To the Princess.] But my unspotted fire of love to you.
Thus ready for the way of life or death,
I wait the sharpest blow, Antiochus.

ANTIOCHUS

Scorning advice, read the conclusion, then;
Which read and not expounded, 'tis decreed,
As these before thee, thou thyself shalt bleed.

DAUGHTER

Of all 'say'd yet, mayst thou prove prosperous!
Of all 'say'd yet, I wish thee happiness!

PERICLES

Like a bold champion, I assume the lists,
Nor ask advice of any other thought
But faithfulness and courage. *[He reads] the riddle.*

I am no viper, yet I feed
On mother's flesh which did me breed.
I sought a husband, in which labor
I found that kindness in a father.
He's father, son, and husband mild;
I mother, wife, and yet his child.
How they may be, and yet in two,
As you will live, resolve it you.

[Aside.] Sharp physic is the last! But, O you powers
That gives heaven countless eyes to view men's acts,
Why cloud they not their sights perpetually,
If this be true, which makes me pale to read it?
Fair glass of light, I lov'd you, and could still,
Were not this glorious casket stor'd with ill.
But I must tell you, now my thoughts revolt;
For he's no man on whom perfections wait
That, knowing sin within, will touch the gate.
You are a fair viol, and your sense the strings;
Who, finger'd to make man his lawful music,
Would draw heaven down, and all the gods, to hearken;
But being play'd upon before your time,
Hell only danceth at so harsh a chime.
Good sooth, I care not for you.

ANTIOCHUS

Prince Pericles, touch not, upon thy life,

9 At . . . reign'd i.e., from her conception until her birth. (Lucina was goddess of childbirth in her capacity as goddess of light.) **10–12 Nature . . . perfections** i.e., Nature bestowed on her, to make her presence gladsome, a favorable aspect of all the planets so that all perfect qualities would be combined in her **15 gives** that gives **16 book of praises** collection of praiseworthy qualities **17 curious** exquisite. **as** as if **18 ever ras'd** forever erased **19 her mild companion** companion of her mildness **20 sway** rule **23 adventure** attempt **25 compass** encompass, achieve **28 Hesperides** (Correctly speaking, nymphs who guarded Juno's golden fruit. The name was frequently applied to the garden where these fruits grew. Here it applies to the Princess, beyond price but dangerous to seek.) **30 death-like dragons** (Alludes to the dragon which also guarded the garden of the Hesperides.) **34 heap** i.e., body of Pericles **35 sometimes** once, formerly **41 For going on** from entering

45 must must someday be **50 Gripe** grip, clutch. **erst** formerly **57 conclusion** problem, riddle **60, 61 'say'd** who have assayed, attempted **62 champion** combatant. **assume the lists** i.e., undertake the combat, enter the tournament ground **65–66 I am . . . breed** (Seager, *Shakespeare's Natural History*, p. 331, quotes from Bartholomew, Trevisa's translation: "Viper is a manner kind of serpents that is full venomous, and hath that name for she bringeth forth brood by strength; for when her womb draweth to the time of whelping, the whelps abideth not convenable time nor kind passing, but gnaweth and fretteth the sides of their mother, and they come so into this world with strength and with the death of the mother.") **68 kindness** (1) affection (2) kinship **71 two** i.e., two people **73 Sharp . . . last** i.e., it is bitter medicine *(physic)* to stake my life on solving this riddle **74 eyes** i.e., the stars **77 glass** mirror (i.e., the Princess, fair in appearance only) **80 on . . . wait** with perfections as his attendants **82 sense** senses **86 only** alone **87 Good sooth** in truth **88 touch not** (Antiochus evidently believes Pericles is about to touch the Princess's hand or some such forbidden thing.)

For that's an article within our law,
As dangerous as the rest. Your time's expir'd.
Either expound now, or receive your sentence.

PERICLES
Great King,
Few love to hear the sins they love to act;
'Twould braid yourself too near for me to tell it. 94
Who has a book of all that monarchs do, 95
He's more secure to keep it shut than shown.
For vice repeated is like the wand'ring wind, 97
Blows dust in others' eyes, to spread itself; 98
And yet the end of all is bought thus dear, 99
The breath is gone, and the sore eyes see clear 100
To stop the air would hurt them. The blind mole
casts 101
Copp'd hills towards heaven, to tell the earth is
throng'd 102
By man's oppression, and the poor worm doth die
for 't. 103
Kings are earth's gods; in vice their law's their will;
And if Jove stray, who dares say Jove doth ill?
It is enough you know; and it is fit, 106
What being more known grows worse, to
smother it. 107
All love the womb that their first being bred;
Then give my tongue like leave to love my head. 109

ANTIOCHUS [*Aside*]
Heaven, that I had thy head! He has found the
meaning.
But I will gloze with him.—Young prince of Tyre, 111
Though by the tenor of our strict edict,
Your exposition misinterpreting, 113
We might proceed to cancel of your days,
Yet hope, succeeding from so fair a tree 115
As your fair self, doth tune us otherwise.
Forty days longer we do respite you,
If by which time our secret be undone,
This mercy shows we'll joy in such a son.
And until then your entertain shall be 120
As doth befit our honor and your worth.
[*Exeunt.*] *Manet Pericles solus.*

PERICLES
How courtesy would seem to cover sin, 122
When what is done is like an hypocrite,
The which is good in nothing but in sight! 124
If it be true that I interpret false,
Then were it certain you were not so bad
As with foul incest to abuse your soul;
Where now you're both a father and a son,
By your untimely claspings with your child,
Which pleasures fits a husband, not a father,
And she an eater of her mother's flesh,
By the defiling of her parent's bed;
And both like serpents are, who, though they feed
On sweetest flowers, yet they poison breed.
Antioch, farewell, for wisdom sees those men 135
Blush not in actions blacker than the night
Will 'schew no course to keep them from the light. 137
One sin, I know, another doth provoke;
Murder's as near to lust as flame to smoke.
Poison and treason are the hands of sin,
Ay, and the targets, to put off the shame. 141
Then, lest my life be cropp'd to keep you clear,
By flight I'll shun the danger which I fear. *Exit.*

Enter Antiochus.

ANTIOCHUS
He hath found the meaning,
For which we mean to have his head.
He must not live to trumpet forth my infamy,
Nor tell the world Antiochus doth sin
In such a loathed manner;
And therefore instantly this prince must die,
For by his fall my honor must keep high.
Who attends us there?

Enter Thaliard.

THALIARD
Doth your Highness call?

ANTIOCHUS
Thaliard, you are of our chamber, Thaliard, 153
And our mind partakes her private actions 154
To your secrecy; and for your faithfulness
We will advance you. Thaliard, behold,
[*Gives poison and money.*]
Here's poison and here's gold. We hate the Prince
Of Tyre, and thou must kill him. It fits thee not
To ask the reason why, because we bid it.
Say, is it done?

THALIARD My lord, 'tis done.

ANTIOCHUS Enough.

Enter a Messenger.

Let your breath cool yourself, telling your haste. 161

MESSENGER
My lord, Prince Pericles is fled. [*Exit.*]

ANTIOCHUS [*To Thaliard*] As thou wilt live, fly after,
and like an arrow shot from a well-experienc'd archer
hits the mark his eye doth level at, so thou never re- 165
turn unless thou say Prince Pericles is dead.

THALIARD My lord, if I can get him within my pistol's length, I'll make him sure enough. So farewell to your Highness.

ANTIOCHUS
Thaliard, adieu! [*Exit Thaliard.*] Till Pericles be dead,
My heart can lend no succor to my head. [*Exit.*]

94 braid . . . near upbraid you too directly **95 Who** he who **97 repeated** talked about **98 Blows . . . itself** i.e., which in spreading itself blows dust in offenders' eyes **99 thus dear** at this high price **100–101 The breath . . . them** i.e., the speaker has lost his breath, whereas the offenders can see well enough, despite the irritating dust, to stop the breath of those who have attempted to indict them **102 Copp'd** peaked. **throng'd** beset **103 worm** i.e., creature **106 you know** i.e., that you know that I know your riddle **107 What . . . it** to cover up a deed that is only worsened by revelation **109 like leave** similar permission **111 gloze** talk smoothly and speciously **113 Your . . . misinterpreting** since your exposition interprets wrongly **115 succeeding** proceeding **120 entertain** entertainment, reception **122 would seem** speciously endeavors **124 sight** appearance

135 sees those men sees that those men who **137 'schew** eschew **141 targets** shields. **put off** deflect **153 of our chamber** my chamberlain **154 partakes** imparts **161 Let . . . haste** i.e., cool your hot haste with the breath of your explanation for it **165 level** aim

[SCENE II]

Enter Pericles with his Lords.

PERICLES
Let none disturb us. [*The Lords stay at the door.*]
Why should this change of thoughts,
The sad companion, dull-ey'd melancholy,
Be my so us'd a guest as not an hour
In the day's glorious walk or peaceful night,
The tomb where grief should sleep, can breed me quiet?
Here pleasures court mine eyes, and mine eyes shun them,
And danger, which I fear'd, is at Antioch,
Whose arm seems far too short to hit me here.
Yet neither pleasure's art can joy my spirits,
Nor yet the other's distance comfort me.
Then it is thus: the passions of the mind,
That have their first conception by misdread,
Have after-nourishment and life by care;
And what was first but fear what might be done
Grows elder now, and cares it be not done.
And so with me: the great Antiochus,
'Gainst whom I am too little to contend,
Since he's so great can make his will his act,
Will think me speaking, though I swear to silence;
Nor boots it me to say I honor him,
If he suspect I may dishonor him.
And what may make him blush in being known,
He'll stop the course by which it might be known.
With hostile forces he'll o'erspread the land,
And with th' ostent of war will look so huge,
Amazement shall drive courage from the state,
Our men be vanquish'd ere they do resist,
And subjects punish'd that ne'er thought offense;
Which care of them, not pity of myself—
Who am no more but as the tops of trees
Which fence the roots they grow by and defend them—
Makes both my body pine and soul to languish,
And punish that before that he would punish.

Enter [Helicanus and] all the Lords to Pericles.

FIRST LORD
Joy and all comfort in your sacred breast!

SECOND LORD
And keep your mind, till you return to us,
Peaceful and comfortable!

HELICANUS
Peace, peace, and give experience tongue.
They do abuse the King that flatter him.
For flattery is the bellows blows up sin;
The thing the which is flattered, but a spark
To which that blast gives heat and stronger glowing;
Whereas reproof, obedient and in order,
Fits kings as they are men, for they may err.
When Signior Sooth here does proclaim peace,
He flatters you, makes war upon your life.
Prince, pardon me, or strike me, if you please;
I cannot be much lower than my knees. [*Kneels.*]

PERICLES
All leave us else; but let your cares o'erlook
What shipping and what lading's in our haven,
And then return to us. [*Exeunt Lords.*] Helicanus, thou
Hast moved us. What seest thou in our looks?

HELICANUS
An angry brow, dread lord.

PERICLES
If there be such a dart in princes' frowns,
How durst thy tongue move anger to our face?

HELICANUS
How dares the plants look up to heaven,
From whence they have their nourishment?

PERICLES
Thou knowest I have power to take thy life from thee.

HELICANUS
I have ground the axe myself;
Do you but strike the blow.

PERICLES
Rise, prithee, rise. [*He rises.*] Sit down. Thou art no flatterer,
I thank thee for 't; and heaven forbid
That kings should let their ears hear their faults hid!
Fit counselor and servant for a prince,
Who by thy wisdom makes a prince thy servant,
What wouldst thou have me do?

HELICANUS
To bear with patience such griefs
As you yourself do lay upon yourself.

PERICLES
Thou speak'st like a physician, Helicanus,
That ministers a potion unto me
That thou wouldst tremble to receive thyself.
Attend me, then: I went to Antioch,
Where, as thou know'st, against the face of death
I sought the purchase of a glorious beauty
From whence an issue I might propagate,
Are arms to princes, and bring joys to subjects.
Her face was to mine eye beyond all wonder;
The rest—hark in thine ear—as black as incest,
Which by my knowledge found, the sinful father
Seem'd not to strike, but smooth. But thou know'st this,

I.ii. Location: Tyre. The palace.
1 us i.e., me. **change of thoughts** altered disposition of mind **3 us'd** familiar. **as** that **4 walk** i.e., traversing of the sun **12 misdread** fear **13 care** anxiety **15 cares** takes care **18 so great can** so powerful that he can **20 boots** avails **25 ostent** display **26 Amazement** (that) dismay, consternation **31 fence** shield, shelter **33 punish . . . he** punishes me beforehand (through fear) whom he (Antiochus) **35 till you return to us** (Here the lords of Tyre appear to know of Pericles' departure. In the next scene we find that he left *unlicens'd of their loves,* i.e., without their knowledge. The prose narratives which recount the same story state that his departure was accomplished secretly. This is one of the several inconsistencies of this rather garbled text.) **37 give experience tongue** let the experienced speak

39 blows up that inflames, heats **40 the which** which **44 When** while. **Signior Sooth** Sir Flattery, one who flatters. (Though, puzzlingly, no one in this scene has in fact flattered Pericles.) **48 else** i.e., except Helicanus. **o'erlook** supervise **49 lading's** cargo is **62 hear . . . hid** hear words that gloss over their faults **75 Are** which are, or such as are. (The antecedent is in the plural idea of *issue,* i.e., sons.) **arms** weapons, defense **79 smooth** gloss over

'Tis time to fear when tyrants seem to kiss.
Which fear so grew in me, I hither fled,
Under the covering of a careful night,
Who seem'd my good protector; and, being here,
Bethought me what was past, what might succeed.
I knew him tyrannous, and tyrants' fears
Decrease not, but grow faster than the years;
And should he doubt 't, as no doubt he doth,
That I should open to the list'ning air
How many worthy princes' bloods were shed
To keep his bed of blackness unlaid ope,
To lop that doubt, he'll fill this land with arms,
And make pretense of wrong that I have done him;
When all, for mine, if I may call offense,
Must feel war's blow, who spares not innocence;
Which love to all, of which thyself art one,
Who now reprov'st me for 't—

HELICANUS Alas, sir!

PERICLES
Drew sleep out of mine eyes, blood from my cheeks,
Musings into my mind, with thousand doubts
How I might stop this tempest ere it came;
And finding little comfort to relieve them,
I thought it princely charity to grieve for them.

HELICANUS
Well, my lord, since you have given me leave to speak,
Freely will I speak. Antiochus you fear,
And justly too, I think, you fear the tyrant,
Who either by public war or private treason
Will take away your life.
Therefore, my lord, go travel for a while,
Till that his rage and anger be forgot,
Or till the Destinies do cut his thread of life.
Your rule direct to any; if to me,
Day serves not light more faithful than I'll be.

PERICLES
I do not doubt thy faith;
But should he wrong my liberties in my absence?

HELICANUS
We'll mingle our bloods together in the earth,
From whence we had our being and our birth.

PERICLES
Tyre, I now look from thee then, and to Tharsus
Intend my travel, where I'll hear from thee,
And by whose letters I'll dispose myself.
The care I had and have of subjects' good
On thee I lay, whose wisdom's strength can bear it.
I'll take thy word for faith, not ask thine oath.
Who shuns not to break one will sure crack both.
But in our orbs we'll live so round and safe,
That time of both this truth shall ne'er convince,
Thou show'dst a subject's shine, I a true prince'.
Exeunt.

[SCENE III]

Enter Thaliard solus.

THALIARD So, this is Tyre, and this the court. Here must I kill King Pericles; an if I do it not, I am sure to be hang'd at home. 'Tis dangerous. Well, I perceive he was a wise fellow and had good discretion that, being bid to ask what he would of the King, desir'd he might know none of his secrets. Now do I see he had some reason for 't; for if a king bid a man be a villain, he's bound by the indenture of his oath to be one. Husht! Here comes the lords of Tyre.

Enter Helicanus [and] Escanes, with other Lords [of Tyre].

HELICANUS
You shall not need, my fellow peers of Tyre,
Further to question me of your king's departure.
His seal'd commission, left in trust with me,
Does speak sufficiently he's gone to travel.

THALIARD *[Aside]* How? The King gone?

HELICANUS
If further yet you will be satisfied,
Why, as it were unlicens'd of your loves,
He would depart, I'll give some light unto you.
Being at Antioch—

THALIARD *[Aside]* What from Antioch?

HELICANUS
Royal Antiochus—on what cause I know not—
Took some displeasure at him, at least he judg'd so;
And doubting lest he had err'd or sinn'd,
To show his sorrow, he'd correct himself;
So puts himself unto the shipman's toil,
With whom each minute threatens life or death.

THALIARD *[Aside]*
Well, I perceive
I shall not be hang'd now, although I would;
But since he's gone, the King's ears it must please
He scap'd the land, to perish at the seas.
I'll present myself.—Peace to the lords of Tyre!

HELICANUS
Lord Thaliard from Antiochus is welcome.

THALIARD
From him I come
With message unto princely Pericles;
But since my landing I have understood
Your lord has betook himself to unknown travels;
Now my message must return from whence it came.

HELICANUS
We have no reason to desire it,
Commended to our master, not to us.

82 careful protecting **87 doubt 't** suspect it **88 open** reveal **90 unlaid ope** unrevealed **93 all . . . offense** all (my subjects) for my offense—if I may call it offense **94 who** which **110 direct** delegate **113 should he** what if he (Antiochus) should. **liberties** royal rights and prerogatives **114 mingle . . . earth** i.e., die fighting him **123 orbs** orbits, spheres. **round** with probity. (A line appears to be lost here, rhyming with *safe*.) **124 time . . . convince** time will never confute this truth regarding us two **125 shine** brightness (as of true gold). **prince'** prince's

I.iii. Location: Tyre. The palace.
2 an if if **3–6 he . . . secrets** (So the poet Philippides asked of Lysimachus; mentioned by Plutarch and Barnabe Riche.) **8 indenture** terms by which a servant is bound to his master **12 seal'd** bearing the royal seal **16 unlicens'd . . . loves** without your loving assent. (Cf. I.ii.35, note.) **21 doubting lest** fearing that **23 toil** travail, hence dangers **26 although I would** even though I wished to be **36 desire it** i.e., wish to know the message's contents **37 Commended** directed as it is

Yet, ere you shall depart, this we desire,
As friends to Antioch, we may feast in Tyre.
Exeunt.

[SCENE IV]

Enter Cleon, the governor of Tharsus, with [Dionyza] his Wife, and others.

CLEON
My Dionyza, shall we rest us here,
And by relating tales of others' griefs
See if 'twill teach us to forget our own?

DIONYZA
That were to blow at fire in hope to quench it;
For who digs hills because they do aspire
Throws down one mountain to cast up a higher.
O my distressed lord, even such our griefs are;
Here they are but felt, and seen with mischief's eyes,
But like to groves, being topp'd, they higher rise.

CLEON
O Dionyza,
Who wanteth food and will not say he wants it,
Or can conceal his hunger till he famish?
Our tongues and sorrows do sound deep our woes
Into the air; our eyes do weep, till lungs
Fetch breath that may proclaim them louder, that,
If heaven slumber while their creatures want,
They may awake their helps to comfort them.
I'll then discourse our woes, felt several years,
And wanting breath to speak help me with tears.

DIONYZA
I'll do my best, sir.

CLEON
This Tharsus, o'er which I have the government,
A city on whom Plenty held full hand,
For Riches strew'd herself even in her streets;
Whose towers bore heads so high they kiss'd the clouds,
And strangers ne'er beheld but wond'red at;
Whose men and dames so jetted and adorn'd,
Like one another's glass to trim them by;
Their tables were stor'd full, to glad the sight,
And not so much to feed on as delight;
All poverty was scorn'd, and pride so great,
The name of help grew odious to repeat.

DIONYZA
O, 'tis too true.

CLEON
But see what heaven can do by this our change:
These mouths who, but of late, earth, sea, and air
Were all too little to content and please,
Although they gave their creatures in abundance,
As houses are defil'd for want of use,
They are now starv'd for want of exercise.
Those palates who, not yet two summers younger,
Must have inventions to delight the taste,
Would now be glad of bread, and beg for it.
Those mothers who, to nousle up their babes,
Thought nought too curious, are ready now
To eat those little darlings whom they lov'd.
So sharp are hunger's teeth that man and wife
Draw lots who first shall die to lengthen life.
Here stands a lord, and there a lady weeping;
Here many sink, yet those which see them fall
Have scarce strength left to give them burial.
Is not this true?

DIONYZA
Our cheeks and hollow eyes do witness it.

CLEON
O, let those cities that of Plenty's cup
And her prosperities so largely taste,
With their superfluous riots, hear these tears!
The misery of Tharsus may be theirs.

Enter a Lord.

LORD
Where's the Lord Governor?

CLEON
Here.
Speak out thy sorrows which thou bring'st in haste,
For comfort is too far for us to expect.

LORD
We have descried, upon our neighboring shore,
A portly sail of ships make hitherward.

CLEON
I thought as much.
One sorrow never comes but brings an heir
That may succeed as his inheritor;
And so in ours, some neighboring nation,
Taking advantage of our misery,
Hath stuff'd these hollow vessels with their power
To beat us down, the which are down already,
And make a conquest of unhappy me,
Whereas no glory's got to overcome.

LORD
That's the least fear; for, by the semblance
Of their white flags display'd, they bring us peace,
And come to us as favorers, not as foes.

CLEON
Thou speak'st like him 's untutor'd to repeat:
Who makes the fairest show means most deceit.

I.iv. Location: Tharsus. The Governor's house.
5 who digs whoever digs up, removes. **aspire** mount up **8 Here . . . eyes** i.e., our misfortunes seem bad enough in our present downcast state. **mischief's** calamity's **9 topp'd** cut back **11 wanteth** lacks **15 them** i.e., *woes* (l. 13) **19 wanting** i.e., when I lack. **help me** i.e., you help me **23 Riches** (A singular concept, probably derived from the French *richesse,* equivalent to "plenty"; the image is that of the cornucopia being held aloft over the city.) **her** i.e., the city's **26 jetted** strutted **27 glass . . . by** mirror by which to adorn themselves, or to mirror each others' finery **31 The name . . . repeat** i.e., that it became odious even to mention the very possibility of asking for help

33 see . . . change see by our change in fortune what heaven can do **40 inventions** novelties **42 nousle** nursle, cherish, nurture **43 nought too curious** nothing too choice (for their babes) **46 lengthen life** i.e., provide food for the other to cannibalize **54 superfluous riots** prodigal living. **tears** i.e., sounds of weeping **61 portly** majestic, stately **70 Whereas . . . overcome** a conquest which brings no glory **71 the least fear** i.e., something to be feared least **74 him 's untutored** one untaught **75 Who** he who

But bring they what they will and what they can,
What need we fear?
The ground's the lowest, and we are half way there.
Go tell their general we attend him here,
To know for what he comes, and whence he comes,
And what he craves.

LORD
I go, my lord. [*Exit.*]

CLEON
Welcome is peace, if he on peace consist; 83
If wars, we are unable to resist.

Enter Pericles with Attendants.

PERICLES
Lord Governor, for so we hear you are,
Let not our ships and number of our men
Be like a beacon fir'd t' amaze your eyes.
We have heard your miseries as far as Tyre,
And seen the desolation of your streets;
Nor come we to add sorrow to your tears,
But to relieve them of their heavy load;
And these our ships you happily may think 92
Are like the Troyan horse was stuff'd within 93
With bloody veins, expecting overthrow, 94
Are stor'd with corn to make your needy bread, 95
And give them life whom hunger starv'd half dead.

ALL
The gods of Greece protect you!
And we'll pray for you. [*They kneel.*]

PERICLES.
Arise, I pray you, rise.
We do not look for reverence, but for love,
And harborage for ourself, our ships, and men.

CLEON
The which when any shall not gratify,
Or pay you with unthankfulness in thought,
Be it our wives, our children, or ourselves,
The curse of heaven and men succeed their evils! 105
Till when—the which I hope shall ne'er be seen—
Your Grace is welcome to our town and us.

PERICLES
Which welcome we'll accept; feast here awhile,
Until our stars that frown lend us a smile. *Exeunt.*

[ACT II]

Enter Gower.

GOWER
Here have you seen a mighty king
His child, I wis, to incest bring; 2
A better prince and benign lord,
That will prove aweful both in deed and word. 4
Be quiet then as men should be,
Till he hath pass'd necessity. 6
I'll show you those in trouble's reign, 7
Losing a mite, a mountain gain.
The good in conversation, 9
To whom I give my benison, 10
Is still at Tharsus, where each man
Thinks all is writ he speken can; 12
And, to remember what he does, 13
Build his statue to make him glorious.
But tidings to the contrary 15
Are brought your eyes; what need speak I?

Dumb Show.

Enter at one door Pericles talking with Cleon; all the train with them. Enter at another door a Gentleman, with a letter to Pericles; Pericles shows the letter to Cleon; Pericles gives the Messenger a reward, and knights him. Exit Pericles at one door, and Cleon at another.

Good Helicane, that stay'd at home—
Not to eat honey like a drone
From others' labors, for though he strive 19
To killen bad, keep good alive,
And to fulfill his prince' desire—
Sends word of all that haps in Tyre:
How Thaliard came full bent with sin 23
And hid intent to murder him, 24
And that in Tharsus was not best
Longer for him to make his rest.
He, doing so, put forth to seas, 27
Where when men been there's seldom ease; 28
For now the wind begins to blow;
Thunder above and deeps below
Makes such unquiet, that the ship
Should house him safe is wrack'd and split, 32
And he, good prince, having all lost,
By waves from coast to coast is toss'd.
All perishen of man, of pelf, 35
Ne aught escapend but himself; 36
Till fortune, tir'd with doing bad,
Threw him ashore, to give him glad. 38
And here he comes. What shall be next,
Pardon old Gower—this longs the text. [*Exit.*] 40

[SCENE I]

Enter Pericles, wet.

PERICLES
Yet cease your ire, you angry stars of heaven!

83 on peace consist stand on peace **92 you happily** which you perchance **93 was** which was **94 bloody veins** i.e., bloodthirsty Greek warriors. **expecting overthrow** (Perhaps modifies *you* in l. 92.) **95 corn** grain. **your needy bread** desperately needed bread, or bread for your needy people **105 succeed** follow as a consequence of

II. Chorus.
2 I wis iwis, certainly **4 aweful** deserving of awe, respect

6 necessity those hardships imposed by fate **7 those** i.e., those who **9 The good in conversation** the good man (Pericles) in matters of conduct **10 benison** blessing **12 writ** holy writ. **he speken can** which he (Pericles) speaks. (An archaic affectation.) **13 remember** commemorate **15 to the contrary** adverse **19 for** (Difficult to explain as the text stands; some editors emend to *forth,* others omit.) **23 bent with** intent upon **24 hid** hidden **27 so** i.e., as advised **28 been** are **32 Should** which should **35 pelf** goods, property **36 Ne aught escapend** nothing escaping **38 glad** gladness **40 this . . . text** i.e., that ends my speech. *(Longs* means *belongs to.)*

II.i. Location: Pentapolis. The seaside.

Wind, rain, and thunder, remember, earthly man
Is but a substance that must yield to you;
And I, as fits my nature, do obey you.
Alas, the seas hath cast me on the rocks,
Wash'd me from shore to shore, and left me breath
Nothing to think on but ensuing death.
Let it suffice the greatness of your powers
To have bereft a prince of all his fortunes;
And having thrown him from your wat'ry grave,
Here to have death in peace is all he'll crave.

Enter three Fishermen.

FIRST FISHERMAN What, ho, Pilch!

SECOND FISHERMAN Ha, come and bring away the nets!

FIRST FISHERMAN What, Patch-breech, I say!

THIRD FISHERMAN What say you, master?

FIRST FISHERMAN Look how thou stirr'st now! Come away, or I'll fetch th' with a wanion.

THIRD FISHERMAN Faith, master, I am thinking of the poor men that were cast away before us even now.

FIRST FISHERMAN Alas, poor souls, it griev'd my heart to hear what pitiful cries they made to us to help them, when, well-a-day, we could scarce help ourselves.

THIRD FISHERMAN Nay, master, said not I as much when I saw the porpoise how he bounc'd and tumbled? They say they're half fish, half flesh. A plague on them, they ne'er come but I look to be wash'd. Master, I marvel how the fishes live in the sea.

FIRST FISHERMAN Why, as men do a-land; the great ones eat up the little ones. I can compare our rich misers to nothing so fitly as to a whale; 'a plays and tumbles, driving the poor fry before him, and at last devours them all at a mouthful. Such whales have I heard on o' th' land, who never leave gaping till they swallow'd the whole parish, church, steeple, bells, and all.

PERICLES [*Aside*] A pretty moral.

THIRD FISHERMAN But, master, if I had been the sexton, I would have been that day in the belfry.

SECOND FISHERMAN Why, man?

THIRD FISHERMAN Because he should have swallow'd me too; and when I had been in his belly, I would have kept such a jangling of the bells that he should never have left, till he cast bells, steeple, church, and parish up again. But if the good King Simonides were of my mind—

PERICLES [*Aside*] Simonides?

THIRD FISHERMAN We would purge the land of these drones, that rob the bee of her honey.

PERICLES [*Aside*]
How from the finny subject of the sea
These fishers tell the infirmities of men,
And from their wat'ry empire recollect
All that may men approve or men detect!—
Peace be at your labor, honest fishermen.

SECOND FISHERMAN Honest, good fellow, what's that? If it be a day fits you, search out of the calendar, and nobody look after it.

PERICLES
May see the sea hath cast upon your coast—

SECOND FISHERMAN What a drunken knave was the sea to cast thee in our way!

PERICLES
A man whom both the waters and the wind,
In that vast tennis-court, hath made the ball
For them to play upon, entreats you pity him.
He asks of you that never us'd to beg.

FIRST FISHERMAN No, friend, cannot you beg? Here's them in our country of Greece gets more with begging than we can do with working.

SECOND FISHERMAN Canst thou catch any fishes, then?

PERICLES I never practic'd it.

SECOND FISHERMAN Nay, then thou wilt starve, sure; for here's nothing to be got now-a-days, unless thou canst fish for 't.

PERICLES
What I have been I have forgot to know,
But what I am, want teaches me to think on:
A man throng'd up with cold; my veins are chill,
And have no more of life than may suffice
To give my tongue that heat to ask your help;
Which if you shall refuse, when I am dead,
For that I am a man, pray you see me buried.

FIRST FISHERMAN Die keth 'a? Now gods forbid 't, an I have a gown here; come, put it on, keep thee warm. [*Gives garment; Pericles puts it on.*] Now, afore me, a handsome fellow! Come, thou shalt go home, and we'll have flesh for holidays, fish for fasting-days, and moreo'er puddings and flap-jacks, and thou shalt be welcome.

PERICLES I thank you, sir.

SECOND FISHERMAN Hark you, my friend. You said you could not beg?

PERICLES I did but crave.

SECOND FISHERMAN But crave? Then I'll turn craver too, and so I shall scape whipping.

PERICLES Why, are your beggars whipp'd, then?

SECOND FISHERMAN O, not all, my friend, not all; for if all your beggars were whipp'd, I would wish no better office than to be beadle. But, master, I'll go draw up the net. [*Exit with Third Fisherman.*]

PERICLES [*Aside*]
How well this honest mirth becomes their labor!

FIRST FISHERMAN Hark you, sir, do you know where ye are?

PERICLES Not well.

FIRST FISHERMAN Why, I'll tell you. This is called Pentápolis, and our king the good Simonides.

12, 14 Pilch, Patch-breech (Names derived from the clothes they presumably wear; *Pilch,* a leather garment.) **13 bring away** bring here, bring along **16 Look . . . now** i.e., get a move on **17 fetch th'** deal you a blow. **wanion** vengeance **19 before us** before our eyes **22 well-a-day** alas **24 porpoise** (These actions of porpoises were recognized prognostications of stormy weather.) **26 wash'd** i.e., wetted by a storm **32–33 heard on** heard of **42 cast** vomited **48 subject** i.e., residents **50 recollect** gather up **51 may . . . detect** men may find true or uncover

52–55 Peace . . . after it (Most commentators think something lost here, perhaps a line in which Pericles bids the fishermen good day; if so, the Second Fisherman's reply could mean, "if the day fits your wretched condition, scratch it out of the calendar and let no one miss it.") **56 May** you may **58 cast** (punning on *vomit,* as suggested by *drunken;* see l. 42) **73 throng'd up** overwhelmed **78 keth 'a** quoth he. **an** if, so long as **80 afore me** (A mild oath.) **83 puddings** sausages **88 crave** request **90 scape whipping** i.e., escape the punishment for begging (as required by Elizabethan law) **94 beadle** parish official responsible for administering corporal punishment

PERICLES The good Simonides, do you call him?
FIRST FISHERMAN Ay, sir, and he deserves so to be call'd
for his peaceable reign and good government.
PERICLES He is a happy king, since he gains from his
subjects the name of good by his government. How
far is his court distant from this shore?
FIRST FISHERMAN Marry, sir, half a day's journey. And
I'll tell you, he hath a fair daughter, and tomorrow is
her birthday; and there are princes and knights come
from all parts of the world to just and tourney for her 111
love.
PERICLES Were my fortunes equal to my desires, I could
wish to make one there. 114
FIRST FISHERMAN O, sir, things must be as they may;
and what a man cannot get, he may lawfully deal for
his wife's soul. 117

Enter the two [other] Fishermen, drawing up a net.

SECOND FISHERMAN Help, master, help! Here's a fish
hangs in the net, like a poor man's right in the law;
'twill hardly come out. Ha! Bots on 't, 'tis come at last, 120
and 'tis turn'd to a rusty armor.
[Hauls in Pericles' armor.]

PERICLES
An armor, friends? I pray you, let me see it.
Thanks, fortune, yet, that, after all my crosses, 123
Thou givest me somewhat to repair myself;
And though it was mine own, part of my heritage, 125
Which my dead father did bequeath to me,
With this strict charge, even as he left his life,
"Keep it, my Pericles; it hath been a shield
'Twixt me and death,"—and pointed to this brace— 129
"For that it sav'd me, keep it; in like necessity—
The which the gods protect thee from!—may defend
thee."
It kept where I kept, I so dearly lov'd it; 132
Till the rough seas, that spares not any man,
Took it in rage, though calm'd have given 't again.
I thank thee for 't. My shipwrack now's no ill,
Since I have here my father gave in his will. 136
FIRST FISHERMAN What mean you, sir?
PERICLES
To beg of you, kind friends, this coat of worth, 138
For it was sometime target to a king; 139
I know it by this mark. He lov'd me dearly,
And for his sake I wish the having of it;
And that you'd guide me to your sovereign's court,
Where with it I may appear a gentleman;
And if that ever my low fortune's better,
I'll pay your bounties; till then rest your debtor. 145
FIRST FISHERMAN Why, wilt thou tourney for the lady?
PERICLES
I'll show the virtue I have borne in arms.

FIRST FISHERMAN Why, do 'e take it, and the gods give
thee good on 't! *[Pericles puts it on.]*
SECOND FISHERMAN Ay, but hark you, my friend; 'twas
we that made up this garment through the rough
seams of the waters. There are certain condolements, 152
certain vails. I hope, sir, if you thrive, you'll remember 153
from whence you had them. 154
PERICLES
Believe 't, I will.
By your furtherance I am cloth'd in steel;
And, spite of all the rapture of the sea, 157
This jewel holds his building on my arm. 158
Unto thy value I will mount myself 159
Upon a courser, whose delightful steps
Shall make the gazer joy to see him tread.
Only, my friend, I yet am unprovided
Of a pair of bases. 163
SECOND FISHERMAN We'll sure provide. Thou shalt have
my best gown to make thee a pair; and I'll bring thee
to the court myself.
PERICLES
Then honor be but a goal to my will,
This day I'll rise, or else add ill to ill. *[Exeunt.]*

[SCENE II]

Enter [King] Simonides, with attendance, and Thaisa, [and take their places].

SIMONIDES
Are the knights ready to begin the triumph? 1
FIRST LORD
They are, my liege,
And stay your coming to present themselves. 3
SIMONIDES
Return them we are ready; and our daughter here, 4
In honor of whose birth these triumphs are,
Sits here, like beauty's child, whom nature gat 6
For men to see, and seeing wonder at. *[Exit a Lord.]*
THAISA
It pleaseth you, my royal father, to express
My commendations great, whose merit's less.
SIMONIDES
It's fit it should be so, for princes are
A model which heaven makes like to itself.
As jewels lose their glory if neglected,
So princes their renowns if not respected. 13
'Tis now your honor, daughter, to entertain 14
The labor of each knight in his device. 15
THAISA
Which, to preserve mine honor, I'll perform.

111 just joust **114 make one** be among those **117 his wife's soul** (A difficult line; the text may be imperfect here.) **120 Bots on 't** i.e., plague take it. (*Bots* is a disease of horses.) **123 crosses** thwartings, misfortunes **125 And though** even though **129 brace** mailed arm protector **132 kept** lodged **136 my father** what my father **138 coat** i.e., armor, coat of mail **139 target** shield, i.e., protector **145 pay** repay. **bounties** acts of generosity

152 condolements (Probably confused with dole.) **153 vails** perquisites, tips **154 them** i.e., the pieces of armor **157 rapture** plundering **158 holds his building** occupies its proper place (and will provide a means to buy a courser) **159 thy** i.e., the jewel's **163 bases** pleated skirts attached to the doublet and reaching from the waist to the knee

II.ii. Location: Pentapolis. A public way leading to the lists. A pavilion by the side of it for the reception of the King, Princess, Lords, etc.
1 triumph festive entertainment **3 stay** await **4 Return** reply to **6 gat** begot **13 respected** taken account of **14 honor** i.e., honorable duty. **entertain** receive, review **15 device** emblem with motto on the knights' shields

The first Knight passes by [and his Squire presents his shield to the Princess].

SIMONIDES
Who is the first that doth prefer himself? 17

THAISA
A knight of Sparta, my renowned father,
And the device he bears upon his shield
Is a black Ethiope reaching at the sun;
The word, "Lux tua vita mihi." 21

SIMONIDES
He loves you well that holds his life of you.
The Second Knight [passes over].
Who is the second that presents himself?

THAISA
A prince of Macedon, my royal father,
And the device he bears upon his shield
Is an arm'd knight that's conquer'd by a lady;
The motto thus, in Spanish, "Piu por dulzura que por fuerza." *Third Knight [passes over].* 27

SIMONIDES
And what's the third?

THAISA
The third of Antioch,
And his device, a wreath of chivalry;
The word, "Me pompae provexit apex." 30
Fourth Knight [passes over].

SIMONIDES
What is the fourth?

THAISA
A burning torch that's turned upside down;
The word, "Quod me alit, me extinguit." 33

SIMONIDES
Which shows that beauty hath his power and will, 34
Which can as well inflame as it can kill.
Fifth Knight [passes over].

THAISA
The fifth, an hand environed with clouds,
Holding out gold that's by the touchstone tried; 37
The motto thus, "Sic spectanda fides." 38
Sixth Knight, [Pericles, passes over; he himself presents his device to Thaisa].

SIMONIDES
And what's
The sixth and last, the which the knight himself
With such a graceful courtesy delivered?

THAISA
He seems to be a stranger; but his present is 42
A withered branch, that's only green at top;
The motto, "In hac spe vivo." 44

SIMONIDES
A pretty moral;
From the dejected state wherein he is,
He hopes by you his fortunes yet may flourish.

FIRST LORD
He had need mean better than his outward show 48
Can any way speak in his just commend; 49
For by his rusty outside he appears
To have practic'd more the whipstock than the lance. 51

SECOND LORD
He well may be a stranger, for he comes
To an honor'd triumph strangely furnish'd.

THIRD LORD
And on set purpose let his armor rust
Until this day, to scour it in the dust.

SIMONIDES
Opinion's but a fool, that makes us scan 56
The outward habit by the inward man.
But stay, the knights are coming. We will withdraw
Into the gallery. *[Exeunt.]*
Great shouts [within], and all cry "The mean knight!"

[SCENE III]

[A banquet prepared.] Enter the King [Simonides, Thaisa, Marshal, Ladies, Lords, Attendants], and Knights from tilting, [in armor].

SIMONIDES
Knights,
To say you're welcome were superfluous.
To place upon the volume of your deeds,
As in a title-page, your worth in arms,
Were more than you expect, or more than's fit,
Since every worth in show commends itself. 6
Prepare for mirth, for mirth becomes a feast. 7
You are princes and my guests.

THAISA
But you, my knight and guest, 9
To whom this wreath of victory I give,
And crown you king of this day's happiness.
[Crowns Pericles with wreath.]

PERICLES
'Tis more by fortune, lady, than by merit.

SIMONIDES
Call it by what you will, the day is yours;
And here, I hope, is none that envies it.
In framing an artist, art hath thus decreed, 15
To make some good, but others to exceed;
And you are her labor'd scholar. Come, queen o' th' feast— 17
For, daughter, so you are—here take your place.
[To the Marshal.] Marshal, the rest, as they deserve their grace. 19

KNIGHTS
We are honor'd much by good Simonides.
[They take their places.]

17 prefer present **21 Lux . . . mihi** your light is my life. (Latin; also at ll.30,33, 38, 44.) **27 Piu . . . fuerza** more by gentleness than by force **30 Me . . . apex** the highest summit of honor has led me on **33 Quod . . . extinguit** who feeds my flame puts out my light **34 his** its **37 touchstone** flint used to test gold for purity **38 Sic spectanda fides** thus is faith to be tried **42 present** presented device **44 In . . . vivo** in this hope I live **48 mean** means, riches **49 commend** commendation

51 whipstock i.e., as if he were accustomed to driving work horses **56 Opinion** judgment of a person's worth

II.iii. Location: Pentapolis. The palace.
6 show action, deeds **7 becomes** suits **9 you** you are **15 framing** making **17 her labor'd scholar** the one on whom art has bestowed the most pains **19 the rest** i.e., place the rest of the company

SIMONIDES
Your presence glads our days. Honor we love;
For who hates honor hates the gods above.
MARSHAL [*To Pericles*]
Sir, yonder is your place.
PERICLES
Some other is more fit.
FIRST KNIGHT
Contend not, sir, for we are gentlemen
Have neither in our hearts nor outward eyes
Envied the great, nor shall the low despise.
PERICLES
You are right courteous knights.
SIMONIDES
Sit, sir, sit. [*They sit.*]
[*Aside.*] By Jove, I wonder, that is king of thoughts,
These cates resist me, he not thought upon.
THAISA [*Aside*]
By Juno, that is queen of marriage,
All viands that I eat do seem unsavory,
Wishing him my meat. [*To Simonides.*] Sure, he's a
gallant gentleman.
SIMONIDES [*To Thaisa*]
He's but a country gentleman.
H'as done no more than other knights have done;
H'as broken a staff or so; so let it pass.
THAISA [*Aside*]
To me he seems like diamond to glass.
PERICLES [*Aside*]
Yon king's to me like to my father's picture,
Which tells me in that glory once he was;
Had princes sit like stars about his throne,
And he the sun for them to reverence;
None that beheld him but, like lesser lights,
Did vail their crowns to his supremacy;
Where now his son's like a glow-worm in the night,
The which hath fire in darkness, none in light.
Whereby I see that Time's the king of men,
He's both their parent, and he is their grave,
And gives them what he will, not what they crave.
SIMONIDES
What, are you merry, knights?
KNIGHTS
Who can be other in this royal presence?
SIMONIDES
Here, with a cup that's stor'd unto the brim—
As you do love, fill to your mistress' lips—
We drink this health to you. [*Drinks a toast.*]
KNIGHTS We thank your Grace.
SIMONIDES
Yet pause awhile.
Yon knight doth sit too melancholy,
As if the entertainment in our court
Had not a show might countervail his worth.
Note it not you, Thaisa?
THAISA
What is 't to me, my father?
SIMONIDES
O, attend, my daughter.
Princes in this should live like gods above,
Who freely give to everyone that come
To honor them;
And princes not doing so are like to gnats,
Which make a sound, but kill'd are wond'red at.
Therefore to make his entrance more sweet,
Here, say we drink this standing-bowl of wine
to him. [*Drinks a toast.*]
THAISA
Alas, my father, it befits not me
Unto a stranger knight to be so bold.
He may my proffer take for an offense,
Since men take women's gifts for impudence.
SIMONIDES
How?
Do as I bid you, or you'll move me else.
THAISA [*Aside*]
Now, by the gods, he could not please me better.
SIMONIDES
And furthermore tell him we desire to know of him
Of whence he is, his name and parentage.
THAISA [*Going to Pericles*]
The King my father, sir, has drunk to you—
PERICLES
I thank him.
THAISA
Wishing it so much blood unto your life.
PERICLES
I thank both him and you, and pledge him freely.
THAISA
And further, he desires to know of you
Of whence you are, your name and parentage.
PERICLES
A gentleman of Tyre, my name, Pericles,
My education been in arts and arms;
Who, looking for adventures in the world,
Was by the rough seas reft of ships and men,
And after shipwrack driven upon this shore.
THAISA [*Returning to King*]
He thanks your Grace; names himself Pericles,
A gentleman of Tyre,
Who only by misfortune of the seas
Bereft of ships and men, cast on this shore.
SIMONIDES
Now, by the gods, I pity his misfortune,
And will awake him from his melancholy.—
Come, gentlemen, we sit too long on trifles,
And waste the time which looks for other revels.
Even in your armors, as you are address'd,
Will well become a soldier's dance.
I will not have excuse with saying this;
Loud music is too harsh for ladies' heads,
Since they love men in arms as well as beds.
They dance.
So this was well ask'd, 'twas so well perform'd.

26 Have who have **30–31 By Jove . . . upon** by Jove, who rules over human thoughts, I marvel that these delicacies do not seem appealing to me, he (Pericles) not considered or provided for as a guest **36, 37 H'as** he has **38 to** compared with **40 that** similar, like **44 vail** remove submissively **58 might countervail** which could equal

66 are wond'red at i.e., cause amazement at the loud noise such small insects could make while living **74 move** anger **87 reft** bereft **97 address'd** accoutered **98 Will** you will **99 have . . . this** allow any excuses to what I've said **100 Loud music** i.e., noise of armor (?) **102 So . . . ask'd** as this was opportunely asked

Come, sir, [*Presents Thaisa to Pericles.*]
Here's a lady that wants breathing too.
And I have heard you knights of Tyre
Are excellent in making ladies trip,
And that their measures are as excellent.

PERICLES
In those that practice them they are, my lord.

SIMONIDES
O, that's as much as you would be denied
Of your fair courtesy. *They dance.*
Unclasp, unclasp!
Thanks, gentlemen, to all; all have done well,
[*To Pericles.*] But you the best.—Pages and lights, to conduct
These knights unto their several lodgings! [*To Pericles.*] Yours, sir,
We have given order to be next our own.

PERICLES
I am at your Grace's pleasure.

SIMONIDES
Princes, it is too late to talk of love,
And that's the mark I know you level at.
Therefore each one betake him to his rest.
Tomorrow all for speeding do their best. [*Exeunt.*]

[SCENE IV]

Enter Helicanus and Escanes.

HELICANUS
No, Escanes, know this of me,
Antiochus from incest liv'd not free;
For which, the most high gods not minding longer
To withhold the vengeance that they had in store,
Due to this heinous capital offense,
Even in the height and pride of all his glory,
When he was seated in a chariot of
An inestimable value, and his daughter with him,
A fire from heaven came and shrivel'd up
Those bodies, even to loathing; for they so stunk
That all those eyes ador'd them ere their fall
Scorn now their hand should give them burial.

ESCANES
'Twas very strange.

HELICANUS
And yet but justice; for though
This king were great, his greatness was no guard
To bar heaven's shaft, but sin had his reward.

ESCANES
'Tis very true.

Enter two or three Lords.

FIRST LORD
See, not a man in private conference
Or council has respect with him but he.

SECOND LORD
It shall no longer grieve without reproof.

THIRD LORD
And curs'd be he that will not second it.

FIRST LORD
Follow me, then.—Lord Helicane, a word.

HELICANUS
With me? And welcome. Happy day, my lords.

FIRST LORD
Know that our griefs are risen to the top,
And now at length they overflow their banks.

HELICANUS
Your griefs? For what? Wrong not your prince you love.

FIRST LORD
Wrong not yourself, then, noble Helicane;
But if the Prince do live, let us salute him,
Or know what ground's made happy by his breath.
If in the world he live, we'll seek him out;
If in his grave he rest, we'll find him there;
And be resolved he lives to govern us,
Or dead, give 's cause to mourn his funeral,
And leave us to our free election.

SECOND LORD
Whose death's indeed the strongest in our censure;
And knowing this kingdom is without a head—
Like goodly buildings left without a roof
Soon fall to ruin—your noble self,
That best know how to rule and how to reign,
We thus submit unto, our sovereign.

ALL
Live, noble Helicane!

HELICANUS
Try honor's cause, forbear your suffrages.
If that you love Prince Pericles, forbear.
Take I your wish, I leap into the seas,
Where's hourly trouble for a minute's ease.
A twelvemonth longer let me entreat you
To forbear the absence of your king,
If in which time expir'd he not return,
I shall with aged patience bear your yoke.
But if I cannot win you to this love,
Go search like nobles, like noble subjects,
And in your search spend your adventurous worth;
Whom if you find, and win unto return,
You shall like diamonds sit about his crown.

FIRST LORD
To wisdom he's a fool that will not yield;
And since Lord Helicane enjoineth us,
We with our travels will endeavor.

HELICANUS
Then you love us, we you, and we'll clasp hands.
When peers thus knit, a kingdom ever stands. [*Exeunt.*]

104 breathing exercise **106 trip** dance lightly (with a suggestion of go *astray*) **107 measures** stately, formal dances (with sexual suggestion) **109–110 that's . . . courtesy** that's the equivalent of your denial of your accomplishment **117 level** aim **119 speeding** succeeding (as wooers)

II.iv. Location: Tyre. The Governor's house.
3 minding intending **11 ador'd** which adored

18 respect influence. **he** i.e., Escanes **19 grieve without reproof** cause grievance without (our) protest **31 resolved** satisfied, assured **34 Whose . . . censure** in our judgment he is most likely dead **41 Try . . . suffrages** i.e., follow the honorable course, refrain from choosing me in your "free election" (l. 33) **43 Take . . . wish** if I should act on your wish

[SCENE V]

Enter the King [*Simonides*] *reading of a letter, at one door; the Knights meet him.*

FIRST KNIGHT
Good morrow to the good Simonides.
SIMONIDES
Knights, from my daughter this I let you know,
That for this twelvemonth she'll not undertake
A married life.
Her reason to herself is only known,
Which from her by no means can I get.
SECOND KNIGHT
May we not get access to her, my lord?
SIMONIDES
Faith, by no means. She hath so strictly tied
Her to her chamber that 'tis impossible.
One twelve moons more she'll wear Diana's livery. 10
This by the eye of Cynthia hath she vowed, 11
And on her virgin honor will not break it.
THIRD KNIGHT
Loath to bid farewell, we take our leaves.
[*Exeunt Knights.*]
SIMONIDES
So,
They are well dispatch'd. Now to my daughter's letter.
She tells me here she'll wed the stranger knight,
Or never more to view nor day nor light. 17
'Tis well, mistress. Your choice agrees with mine;
I like that well. Nay, how absolute she's in 't, 19
Not minding whether I dislike or no!
Well, I do commend her choice,
And will no longer have it be delay'd.
Soft, here he comes. I must dissemble it.

Enter Pericles.

PERICLES
All fortune to the good Simonides!
SIMONIDES
To you as much! Sir, I am beholding to you
For your sweet music this last night. I do
Protest my ears were never better fed
With such delightful pleasing harmony.
PERICLES
It is your Grace's pleasure to commend,
Not my desert.
SIMONIDES Sir, you are music's master. 30
PERICLES
The worst of all her scholars, my good lord.
SIMONIDES
Let me ask you one thing:
What do you think of my daughter, sir?
PERICLES
A most virtuous princess.
SIMONIDES
And she is fair too, is she not?
PERICLES
As a fair day in summer, wondrous fair.
SIMONIDES
Sir, my daughter thinks very well of you;
Ay, so well that you must be her master,
And she will be your scholar. Therefore look to it.
PERICLES
I am unworthy for her schoolmaster.
SIMONIDES
She thinks not so. Peruse this writing else. 41
[*Gives letter.*]
PERICLES [*Aside*]
What's here?
A letter, that she loves the knight of Tyre!
'Tis the King's subtlety to have my life.—
O, seek not to entrap me, gracious lord,
A stranger and distressed gentleman,
That never aim'd so high to love your daughter, 47
But bent all offices to honor her. 48
SIMONIDES
Thou hast bewitch'd my daughter, and thou art
A villain.
PERICLES
By the gods, I have not!
Never did thought of mine levy offense, 52
Nor never did my actions yet commence
A deed might gain her love or your displeasure. 54
SIMONIDES
Traitor, thou liest!
PERICLES Traitor?
SIMONIDES Ay, traitor.
PERICLES
Even in his throat—unless it be the King—
That calls me traitor, I return the lie.
SIMONIDES [*Aside*]
Now, by the gods, I do applaud his courage.
PERICLES
My actions are as noble as my thoughts,
That never relish'd of a base descent. 60
I came unto your court for honor's cause,
And not to be a rebel to her state; 62
And he that otherwise accounts of me,
This sword shall prove he's honor's enemy.
SIMONIDES
No?
Here comes my daughter, she can witness it.

Enter Thaisa.

PERICLES
Then, as you are as virtuous as fair,
Resolve your angry father, if my tongue 68

II.v. Location: Pentapolis. The palace.
10 wear Diana's livery continue to serve Diana, goddess of chastity **11 Cynthia** the moon goddess, equated with Diana **17 nor day nor** either day or. (A double negative.) **19 absolute** unconditional, positive

41 else i.e., if you don't believe me **47 to** as to **48 bent all offices** devoted all my service **52 levy** raise, collect, receive; or perhaps level, aim at (?) **54 might** which might **60 relish'd of** showed any trace of **62 her** i.e., honor's **68 Resolve** satisfy, explain to

Did e'er solicit, or my hand subscribe
To any syllable that made love to you.

THAISA
Why, sir, say if you had, who takes offense
At that would make me glad?

SIMONIDES
Yea, mistress, are you so peremptory?
(Aside.) I am glad on 't with all my heart.—
I'll tame you; I'll bring you in subjection!
Will you, not having my consent,
Bestow your love and your affections
Upon a stranger? *(Aside.)* Who, for aught I know,
May be, nor can I think the contrary,
As great in blood as I myself.—
Therefore hear you, mistress: either frame
Your will to mine—and you, sir, hear you—
Either be rul'd by me, or I'll make you—
Man and wife.
Nay, come, your hands and lips must seal it too.
And being join'd, I'll thus your hopes destroy;
And for further grief—God give you joy!
What, are you both pleased?

THAISA
Yes, if you love me, sir.

PERICLES
Even as my life my blood that fosters it.

SIMONIDES
What, are you both agreed?

BOTH
Yes, if 't please your Majesty.

SIMONIDES
It pleaseth me so well that I will see you wed;
And then with what haste you can get you to bed.
Exeunt.

[ACT III]

Enter Gower.

GOWER
Now sleep yslaked hath the rout;
No din but snores the house about,
Made louder by the o'er-fed breast
Of this most pompous marriage-feast.
The cat, with eyne of burning coal,
Now couches from the mouse's hole;
And crickets sing at the oven's mouth,
Are the blither for their drouth.
Hymen hath brought the bride to bed,
Where, by the loss of maidenhead,
A babe is molded. Be attent,
And time that is so briefly spent
With your fine fancies quaintly eche.
What's dumb in show I'll plain with speech.

[Dumb Show.]

Enter Pericles and Simonides, at one door, with Attendants; a Messenger meets them, kneels, and gives Pericles a letter. Pericles shows it Simonides; the Lords kneel to him [*Pericles*]. *Then enter Thaisa with child, with Lychorida a nurse. The King shows her the letter; she rejoices. She and Pericles take leave of her father, and depart* [*with Lychorida and their Attendants. Then exeunt Simonides and the rest.*]

By many a dern and painful perch
Of Pericles the careful search,
By the four opposing coigns
Which the world together joins,
Is made with all due diligence
That horse and sail and high expense
Can stead the quest. At last from Tyre,
Fame answering the most strange inquire,
To th' court of King Simonides
Are letters brought, the tenor these:
Antiochus and his daughter dead,
The men of Tyrus on the head
Of Helicanus would set on
The crown of Tyre, but he will none.
The mutiny he there hastes t' oppress;
Says to 'em, if King Pericles
Come not home in twice six moons,
He, obedient to their dooms,
Will take the crown. The sum of this,
Brought hither to Pentapolis,
Y-ravished the regions round,
And everyone with claps can sound,
"Our heir-apparent is a king!
Who dreamt, who thought of such a thing?"
Brief, he must hence depart to Tyre.
His queen, with child, makes her desire—
Which who shall cross?—along to go.
Omit we all their dole and woe.
Lychorida, her nurse, she takes,
And so to sea. Their vessel shakes
On Neptune's billow; half the flood
Hath their keel cut. But fortune, mov'd,
Varies again; the grisled north
Disgorges such a tempest forth,
That, as a duck for life that dives,
So up and down the poor ship drives.
The lady shrieks, and well-a-near
Does fall in travail with her fear;
And what ensues in this fell storm
Shall for itself itself perform.

72 that that which **81 frame** accommodate, shape **90 my life** i.e., my life loves

III. Chorus.
1 yslaked laid to rest. **rout** whole crowd, assembly **4 pompous** ceremonial, splendid **5 eyne** eyes **6 from** i.e., near **8 Are . . . drouth** (and) are the happier for their dryness **9 Hymen** god of marriage **11 attent** attentive

13 quaintly eche cleverly eke out **14 plain** make plain **15 dern** dark, drear. **perch** measure of land **17 coigns** corners, compass points **21 stead** assist **22 Fame . . . inquire** rumor answering inquiry into the most remote areas **32 dooms** judgments **35 Y-ravished** delighted **36 can sound** began to proclaim **45–46 half . . . cut** i.e., their vessel has completed half the voyage **47 grisled** fearful, horrible **51 well-a-near** (A cry of lamentation.) **52 travail** labor **53 fell** fierce

I nill relate, action may 55
Conveniently the rest convey,
Which might not what by me is told. 57
In your imagination hold
This stage the ship, upon whose deck
The sea-toss'd Pericles appears to speak. [*Exit.*]

[SCENE I]

Enter Pericles, a-shipboard.

PERICLES
Thou god of this great vast, rebuke these surges, 1
Which wash both heaven and hell; and thou, that hast
Upon the winds command, bind them in brass,
Having call'd them from the deep! O, still
Thy deaf'ning, dreadful thunders; gently quench
Thy nimble, sulphurous flashes!—O, how, Lychorida,
How does my queen?—Thou storm, venomously
Wilt thou spit all thyself? The seaman's whistle
Is as a whisper in the ears of death,
Unheard.—Lychorida!—Lucina, O
Divinest patroness, and midwife gentle
To those that cry by night, convey thy deity
Aboard our dancing boat; make swift the pangs
Of my queen's travails!

Enter Lychorida [with an Infant].

Now, Lychorida!

LYCHORIDA
Here is a thing too young for such a place,
Who, if it had conceit, would die, as I 16
Am like to do. Take in your arms this piece
Of your dead queen.

PERICLES How? How, Lychorida?

LYCHORIDA
Patience, good sir; do not assist the storm. 19
Here's all that is left living of your queen,
A little daughter. For the sake of it,
Be manly, and take comfort. [*Gives him the child.*]

PERICLES O you gods!
Why do you make us love your goodly gifts,
And snatch them straight away? We here below
Recall not what we give, and therein may 25
Use honor with you.

LYCHORIDA Patience, good sir, 26
Even for this charge.

PERICLES Now, mild may be thy life! 27
For a more blustrous birth had never babe.
Quiet and gentle thy conditions! For 29
Thou art the rudeliest welcome to this world
That ever was prince's child. Happy what follows!
Thou hast as chiding a nativity
As fire, air, water, earth, and heaven can make,
To herald thee from the womb. Even at the first 34
Thy loss is more than can thy portage quit 35
With all thou canst find here. Now, the good gods 36
Throw their best eyes upon 't! 37

Enter two Sailors.

FIRST SAILOR What courage, sir? God save you!

PERICLES
Courage enough. I do not fear the flaw; 39
It hath done to me the worst. Yet, for the love
Of this poor infant, this fresh new seafarer,
I would it would be quiet.

FIRST SAILOR Slack the bolins there!—Thou wilt not, wilt thou? Blow, and split thyself. 43

SECOND SAILOR But sea-room, an the brine and cloudy billow kiss the moon, I care not. 45

FIRST SAILOR Sir, your queen must overboard. The sea works high, the wind is loud, and will not lie till the ship be clear'd of the dead.

PERICLES
That's your superstition.

FIRST SAILOR Pardon us, sir. With us at sea it hath been still observ'd, and we are strong in custom. Therefore 52 briefly yield 'er, for she must overboard straight. 53

PERICLES
As you think meet. Most wretched queen!

LYCHORIDA
Here she lies, sir. 55

PERICLES
A terrible childbed hast thou had, my dear;
No light, no fire. Th' unfriendly elements
Forgot thee utterly, nor have I time
To give thee hallow'd to thy grave, but straight
Must cast thee, scarcely coffin'd, in the ooze;
Where, for a monument upon thy bones, 61
And e'er-remaining lamps, the belching whale 62
And humming water must o'erwhelm thy corpse,
Lying with simple shells. O Lychorida,
Bid Nestor bring me spices, ink and paper,
My casket and my jewels; and bid Nicander
Bring me the satin coffin. Lay the babe
Upon the pillow. Hie thee, whiles I say
A priestly farewell to her. Suddenly, woman. 69
[*Exit Lychorida.*]

SECOND SAILOR Sir, we have a chest beneath the hatches, caulk'd and bitum'd ready. 71

PERICLES
I thank thee. Mariner, say what coast is this?

55 nill will not **57 Which . . . told** which action could not dramatize easily the story I've just told

III.i. Location: A ship at sea.
1 vast expanse (of sea) **16 conceit** understanding (of its precarious position) **19 assist** i.e., with your sighs and tears **25 Recall** take back. **therein** in that respect **26 Use honor** share, are entitled to, equal honor **27 for this charge** for the sake of this infant, this responsibility **29 conditions** circumstances

34–36 Even . . . here your loss at birth (of your mother) exceeds anything that your life can offer by way of compensation. (*Portage* is the cargo one has aboard at the start of a voyage, i.e., one's natural endowments.) **37 best eyes** most auspicious looks **39 flaw** gust, storm **43 bolins** bowlines **45 But sea-room** so long as we have room enough to maneuver. **an** if **52 still** always **53 briefly** quickly **55 Here she lies** (Perhaps the sailors have brought the Queen's body on stage, but it may be that Pericles apostrophizes her in her absence in ll. 56–64. Line 55 could mean, "Here is what is left of the Queen, here is her daughter.") **61 for** in place of **62 e'er-remaining** ever-burning. **belching** blowing **69 s.d. Exit Lychorida** (Evidently she takes the babe with her.) **71 bitum'd** caulked with pitch

SECOND SAILOR We are near Tharsus.

PERICLES
Thither, gentle mariner,
Alter thy course for Tyre. When canst thou reach it?

SECOND SAILOR By break of day, if the wind cease.

PERICLES
O, make for Tharsus!
There will I visit Cleon, for the babe
Cannot hold out to Tyrus. There I'll leave it
At careful nursing. Go thy ways, good mariner.
I'll bring the body presently. *Exeunt.*

[SCENE II]

Enter Lord Cerimon, with a Servant [and some Persons who have been shipwrecked].

CERIMON
Philemon, ho!

Enter Philemon.

PHILEMON
Doth my lord call?

CERIMON
Get fire and meat for these poor men.
[*Exit Philemon.*]
'T has been a turbulent and stormy night.

SERVANT
I have been in many; but such a night as this,
Till now, I ne'er endured.

CERIMON
Your master will be dead ere you return;
There's nothing can be minist'red to nature
That can recover him. [*To another.*] Give this to the pothecary,
And tell me how it works. [*Exeunt all but Cerimon.*]

Enter two Gentlemen.

FIRST GENTLEMAN
Good morrow.

SECOND GENTLEMAN
Good morrow to your lordship.

CERIMON
Gentlemen, why do you stir so early?

FIRST GENTLEMAN
Sir,
Our lodgings, standing bleak upon the sea,
Shook as the earth did quake;
The very principals did seem to rend,
And all to topple. Pure surprise and fear
Made me to quit the house.

SECOND GENTLEMAN
That is the cause we trouble you so early;
'Tis not our husbandry.

CERIMON
O, you say well.

FIRST GENTLEMAN
But I much marvel that your lordship, having
Rich tire about you, should at these early hours
Shake off the golden slumber of repose.
'Tis most strange
Nature should be so conversant with pain,
Being thereto not compell'd.

CERIMON
I hold it ever
Virtue and cunning were endowments greater
Than nobleness and riches. Careless heirs
May the two latter darken and expend,
But immortality attends the former,
Making a man a god. 'Tis known I ever
Have studied physic, through which secret art,
By turning o'er authorities, I have,
Together with my practice, made familiar
To me and to my aid the blest infusions
That dwells in vegetives, in metals, stones;
And can speak of the disturbances
That nature works, and of her cures; which doth give me
A more content in course of true delight
Than to be thirsty after tottering honor,
Or tie my treasure up in silken bags,
To please the fool and death.

SECOND GENTLEMAN
Your honor has through Ephesus pour'd forth
Your charity, and hundreds call themselves
Your creatures, who by you have been restor'd;
And not your knowledge, your personal pain, but even
Your purse, still open, hath built Lord Cerimon
Such strong renown as time shall never—

Enter two or three [Servants] with a chest.

FIRST SERVANT
So; lift there.

CERIMON What's that?

FIRST SERVANT Sir, even now
Did the sea toss up upon our shore this chest.
'Tis of some wrack.

CERIMON Set 't down, let's look upon 't.

SECOND GENTLEMAN
'Tis like a coffin, sir.

CERIMON Whate'er it be,
'Tis wondrous heavy. Wrench it open straight.
If the sea's stomach be o'ercharg'd with gold,

75 Alter . . . Tyre change your course, which has been for Tyre **81 presently** immediately **81 s.d. Exeunt** (If Thaisa's body was brought on stage before l. 55 it must presumably be carried off now.)

III.ii. Location: Ephesus. Cerimon's house.
3 meat food **9 recover** restore. **pothecary** druggist **16 as** as if **17 principals** main timbers of houses

21 husbandry thrifty management, zeal for rising early **24 tire** furnishings **27 pain** toil **29 hold it ever** have always believed that **30 cunning** knowledge, skill **32 expend** squander **35 physic** medicine **36 turning o'er authorities** turning the pages of learned texts **38 my aid** i.e., Philemon and other assistants. **infusions** medicinal properties **39 vegetives** herbs, plants **42 more** greater. **course** pursuit **48 Your creatures** i.e., people created anew because of your restoratives **49 not** not only

'Tis a good constraint of fortune it belches upon us.

SECOND GENTLEMAN
'Tis so, my lord.

CERIMON
How close 'tis caulk'd and bitumed!
Did the sea cast it up?

FIRST SERVANT
I never saw so huge a billow, sir,
As toss'd it upon shore.

CERIMON
Wrench it open.
Soft! It smells most sweetly in my sense.

SECOND GENTLEMAN
A delicate odor.

CERIMON
As ever hit my nostril. So, up with it.
[They open the chest.]
O you most potent gods! What's here? A corse?

SECOND GENTLEMAN
Most strange!

CERIMON
Shrouded in cloth of state, balmed and entreasured
With full bags of spices! A passport too!
Apollo, perfect me in the characters! *[Reads from a scroll.]*
"Here I give to understand,
If e'er this coffin drives a-land,
I, King Pericles, have lost
This queen, worth all our mundane cost.
Who finds her, give her burying;
She was the daughter of a king.
Besides this treasure for a fee,
The gods requite his charity!"
If thou livest, Pericles, thou hast a heart
That even cracks for woe! This chanc'd tonight.

SECOND GENTLEMAN
Most likely, sir.

CERIMON
Nay, certainly tonight,
For look how fresh she looks! They were too rough
That threw her in the sea. Make a fire within.
Fetch hither all my boxes in my closet.
[Exit a Servant.]
Death may usurp on nature many hours,
And yet the fire of life kindle again
The o'erpress'd spirits. I heard of an Egyptian
That had nine hours lien dead,
Who was by good appliance recovered.

Enter one with [boxes,] napkins, and fire.

Well said, well said! The fire and cloths.
The rough and woeful music that we have,
Cause it to sound, beseech you. *[Music.]*
The viol once more. How thou stirr'st, thou block!
The music there!—I pray you, give her air.
Gentlemen, this queen will live. Nature awakes;
A warmth breathes out of her. She hath not been
Entranc'd above five hours. See how she gins
To blow into life's flower again!

FIRST GENTLEMAN
The heavens,
Through you, increase our wonder and sets up
Your fame for ever.

CERIMON
She is alive! Behold,
Her eyelids, cases to those heavenly jewels
Which Pericles hath lost, begin to part
Their fringes of bright gold. The diamonds
Of a most praised water doth appear,
To make the world twice rich. Live, and make
Us weep to hear your fate, fair creature,
Rare as you seem to be. *She moves.*

THAISA
O dear Diana,
Where am I? Where's my lord? What world is this?

SECOND GENTLEMAN
Is not this strange?

FIRST GENTLEMAN
Most rare.

CERIMON
Hush, my gentle neighbors!
Lend me your hands. To the next chamber bear her.
Get linen. Now this matter must be look'd to,
For her relapse is mortal. Come, come!
And Aesculapius guide us!
They carry her away. Exeunt omnes.

[SCENE III]

Enter Pericles at Tharsus, with Cleon and Dionyza [and Lychorida with Marina in her arms].

PERICLES
Most honor'd Cleon, I must needs be gone.
My twelve months are expir'd, and Tyrus stands
In a litigious peace. You and your lady
Take from my heart all thankfulness! The gods
Make up the rest upon you!

CLEON
Your shafts of fortune, though they hurt you mortally,
Yet glance full woundingly on us.

DIONYZA
O your sweet queen! That the strict fates had pleas'd
You had brought her hither, to have bless'd mine eyes with her!

PERICLES
We cannot but obey the powers above us.
Could I rage and roar as doth the sea
She lies in, yet the end must be as 'tis.
My gentle babe Marina,
Whom, for she was born at sea, I have named so,
Here I charge your charity withal,
Leaving her the infant of your care,

58 constraint of act controlled by, compulsion **66 corse** corpse **70 perfect . . . characters** enable me to read the writing **74 mundane cost** worldly wealth **80 tonight** last night **82 rough** i.e., hasty **90 Well said** well done **93 How thou stirr'st** i.e., how slow you are **97 Entranc'd** unconscious

98 blow bloom **104 water** luster and clearness. (Used of precious stones.) **114 is mortal** would be fatal **115 Aesculapius** god of healing

III.iii. Location: Tharsus. Cleon's (the Governor's) house.
3 litigious disturbed by disputes (especially legal) **4 Take** receive **5 upon** to **14 for** since

Beseeching you to give her princely training,
That she may be manner'd as she is born.

CLEON
Fear not, my lord, but think
Your Grace, that fed my country with your corn,
For which the people's prayers still fall upon you,
Must in your child be thought on. If neglection
Should therein make me vile, the common body, 23
By you reliev'd, would force me to my duty.
But if to that my nature need a spur,
The gods revenge it upon me and mine
To the end of generation!

PERICLES I believe you. 27
Your honor and your goodness teach me to 't
Without your vows. Till she be married, madam,
By bright Diana, whom we honor, all
Unscissor'd shall this hair of mine remain,
Though I show ill in 't. So I take my leave.
Good madam, make me blessed in your care
In bringing up my child.

DIONYZA I have one myself,
Who shall not be more dear to my respect
Than yours, my lord.

PERICLES Madam, my thanks and prayers.

CLEON
We'll bring your Grace e'en to the edge o' th' shore,
Then give you up to the mask'd Neptune and 38
The gentlest winds of heaven.

PERICLES
I will embrace your offer. Come, dearest madam.
O, no tears, Lychorida, no tears.
Look to your little mistress, on whose grace
You may depend hereafter. Come, my lord.
[Exeunt.]

[SCENE IV]

Enter Cerimon and Thaisa.

CERIMON
Madam, this letter, and some certain jewels,
Lay with you in your coffer, which are
At your command. Know you the character? 3
[Shows her the letter.]

THAISA
It is my lord's. That I was shipp'd at sea,
I well remember, even on my eaning time; 5
But whether there delivered, by the holy gods,
I cannot rightly say. But since King Pericles,
My wedded lord, I ne'er shall see again,
A vestal livery will I take me to, 9
And never more have joy.

CERIMON
Madam, if this you purpose as ye speak,
Diana's temple is not distant far,
Where you may abide till your date expire. 13
Moreover, if you please, a niece of mine
Shall there attend you.

THAISA
My recompense is thanks, that's all;
Yet my good will is great, though the gift small.
Exeunt.

[ACT IV]

Enter Gower.

GOWER
Imagine Pericles arriv'd at Tyre,
Welcom'd and settled to his own desire.
His woeful queen we leave at Ephesus,
Unto Diana there's a votaress. 4
Now to Marina bend your mind,
Whom our fast-growing scene must find
At Tharsus, and by Cleon train'd
In music's letters, who hath gain'd 8
Of education all the grace,
Which makes her both the heart and place 10
Of general wonder. But, alack, 11
That monster Envy, oft the wrack
Of earned praise, Marina's life
Seeks to take off by treason's knife. 14
And in this kind hath our Cleon 15
One daughter, and a wench full grown,
Even ripe for marriage-rite. This maid
Hight Philoten, and it is said 18
For certain in our story, she
Would ever with Marina be.
Be 't when she weav'd the sleided silk 21
With fingers long, small, white as milk; 22
Or when she would with sharp needle wound
The cambric, which she made more sound
By hurting it; or when to th' lute
She sung, and made the night-bird mute, 26
That still records with moan; or when 27
She would with rich and constant pen 28
Vail to her mistress Dian; still 29
This Philoten contends in skill
With absolute Marina. So 31
With the dove of Paphos might the crow 32
Vie feathers white. Marina gets 33
All praises, which are paid as debts, 34
And not as given. This so darks 35
In Philoten all graceful marks,

23 common body common people **27 of generation** i.e., of my descendants **38 mask'd Neptune** i.e., the sea wearing a festive face, as though wearing a mask at a revels (?) or with its strength hidden (?)

III.iv. Location: Ephesus. Cerimon's house.
3 character handwriting **5 eaning time** time of delivery **9 vestal livery** garments of chastity

13 date term of life

IV. Chorus.
4 there's there as **8 music's letters** the study of music **10–11 both . . . wonder** the focal point of the admiration of all **14 treason's** treachery's **15 kind** manner **18 Hight** is called **21 sleided** divided into filaments **22 small** slender **26 night-bird** nightingale with its sad song (*moan*, l. 27) **27 still records** always sings **28 constant** fixedly loyal **29 Vail** do homage **31 absolute** free from any imperfection **32 Paphos** city sacred to Venus **33 Vie feathers white** challenge in whiteness of plumage **34 as debts** as owed to her **35 given** i.e., gratuitous gifts. **darks** darkens, obscures

That Cleon's wife, with envy rare,
A present murderer does prepare
For good Marina, that her daughter
Might stand peerless by this slaughter.
The sooner her vile thoughts to stead,
Lychorida, our nurse, is dead;
And cursed Dionyza hath
The pregnant instrument of wrath
Prest for this blow. The unborn event
I do commend to your content;
Only I carry winged time
Post on the lame feet of my rhyme,
Which never could I so convey
Unless your thoughts went on my way.
Dionyza does appear,
With Leonine, a murderer. *Exit.*

[SCENE I]

Enter Dionyza with Leonine.

DIONYZA
Thy oath remember; thou hast sworn to do 't.
'Tis but a blow, which never shall be known.
Thou canst not do a thing in the world so soon
To yield thee so much profit. Let not conscience,
Which is but cold, inflaming love i' thy bosom,
Inflame too nicely; nor let pity, which
Even women have cast off, melt thee, but be
A soldier to thy purpose.

LEONINE
I will do 't, but yet she is a goodly creature.

DIONYZA
The fitter, then, the gods should have her.
Here she comes weeping for her only mistress'
death.
Thou art resolv'd?

LEONINE
I am resolv'd.

Enter Marina, with a basket of flowers.

MARINA
No, I will rob Tellus of her weed,
To strew thy green with flowers. The yellows, blues,
The purple violets, and marigolds,
Shall as a carpet hang upon thy grave
While summer days doth last. Ay me! Poor maid,
Born in a tempest, when my mother died,
This world to me is a lasting storm,
Whirring me from my friends.

DIONYZA
How now, Marina? Why do you keep alone?
How chance my daughter is not with you?
Do not consume your blood with sorrowing;
Have you a nurse of me. Lord, how your favor's
Chang'd with this unprofitable woe!
Come, give me your flowers, ere the sea mar it.
Walk with Leonine; the air is quick there,
And it pierces and sharpens the stomach. Come,
Leonine, take her by the arm, walk with her.

MARINA
No, I pray you;
I'll not bereave you of your servant.

DIONYZA
Come, come,
I love the King your father, and yourself,
With more than foreign heart. We every day
Expect him here. When he shall come and find
Our paragon to all reports thus blasted,
He will repent the breadth of his great voyage,
Blame both my lord and me that we have taken
No care to your best courses. Go, I pray you,
Walk, and be cheerful once again. Reserve
That excellent complexion, which did steal
The eyes of young and old. Care not for me;
I can go home alone.

MARINA
Well, I will go;
But yet I have no desire to it.

DIONYZA
Come, come, I know 'tis good for you.
Walk half an hour, Leonine, at the least.
Remember what I have said.

LEONINE
I warrant you, madam.

DIONYZA
I'll leave you, my sweet lady, for a while.
Pray walk softly, do not heat your blood.
What, I must have a care of you.

MARINA
My thanks, sweet madam. *[Exit Dionyza.]*
Is this wind westerly that blows?

LEONINE
Southwest.

MARINA
When I was born, the wind was north.

LEONINE
Was 't so?

MARINA
My father, as nurse says, did never fear,
But cried "Good seamen!" to the sailors,
Galling his kingly hands, haling ropes;
And, clasping to the mast, endured a sea
That almost burst the deck.

LEONINE
When was this?

MARINA
When I was born.
Never was waves nor wind more violent;
And from the ladder-tackle washes off
A canvas-climber. "Ha!" says one, "wolt out?"

37 rare keen **41 stead** assist **44 pregnant** willing, ready **45 Prest** prepared **46 content** pleasure (in watching) **48 Post** swiftly

IV.i. Location: Tharsus. An open place near the seashore.
6 too nicely over scrupulously **11 only mistress'** i.e., Lychorida's. *(Only* means *one and only.)* **14 Tellus** goddess of the earth. **weed** garment (here, flowers) **15 green** i.e., grave

24 with sorrowing i.e., with sighs, thought to cost the heart its blood **25 Have . . . me** i.e., take me as your nurse. **favor** face, appearance **27 it** i.e., the bouquet (? An often-emended line.) **28 quick** fresh, invigorating **29 stomach** appetite **35 more . . . heart** i.e., as though related **37 Our . . . blasted** the person whom all regard as a paragon of beauty thus withered **41 Reserve** preserve **57 Galling** chafing, blistering. **haling** hauling on **64 wolt out** so you want to get out. (Addressed perhaps as a cruel jest to the *canvas-climber* or sailor in the rigging who is washed overboard.)

And with a dropping industry they skip
From stem to stern. The boatswain whistles, and
The master calls, and trebles their confusion.

LEONINE
Come, say your prayers.

MARINA
What mean you?

LEONINE
If you require a little space for prayer,
I grant it. Pray, but be not tedious,
For the gods are quick of ear, and I am sworn
To do my work with haste.

MARINA
Why will you kill me?

LEONINE
To satisfy my lady.

MARINA
Why would she have me kill'd?
Now, as I can remember, by my troth,
I never did her hurt in all my life.
I never spake bad word, nor did ill turn
To any living creature. Believe me, la,
I never kill'd a mouse, nor hurt a fly.
I trod upon a worm against my will,
But I wept for 't. How have I offended,
Wherein my death might yield her any profit,
Or my life imply her any danger?

LEONINE
My commission
Is not to reason of the deed, but do 't.

MARINA
You will not do 't for all the world, I hope.
You are well favored, and your looks foreshow
You have a gentle heart. I saw you lately,
When you caught hurt in parting two that fought;
Good sooth, it show'd well in you. Do so now.
Your lady seeks my life; come you between,
And save poor me, the weaker.

LEONINE
I am sworn, and will dispatch. *[He seizes her.]*

Enter Pirates.

FIRST PIRATE Hold, villain! *[Leonine runs away.]*

SECOND PIRATE A prize, a prize!

THIRD PIRATE Half-part, mates, half-part. Come, let's have her aboard suddenly.

Exeunt [Pirates with Marina].

Enter Leonine.

LEONINE
These roguing thieves serve the great pirate Valdes,
And they have seiz'd Marina. Let her go.
There's no hope she will return. I'll swear she's dead
And thrown into the sea. But I'll see further;
Perhaps they will but please themselves upon her,
Not carry her aboard. If she remain,
Whom they have ravish'd must by me be slain. *Exit.*

65 with . . . industry dripping wet as they labored **76 as** as far as **88 well favored** pleasant-looking. **foreshow** proclaim **90 caught hurt** received an injury **97 Half-part** shares

[SCENE II]

Enter the three Bawds [Pandar, Bawd, and Boult].

PANDAR Boult!

BOULT Sir?

PANDAR Search the market narrowly. Mytilene is full of gallants. We lost too much money this mart by being too wenchless.

BAWD We were never so much out of creatures. We have but poor three, and they can do no more than they can do; and they with continual action are even as good as rotten.

PANDAR Therefore let's have fresh ones, whate'er we pay for them. If there be not a conscience to be us'd in every trade, we shall never prosper.

BAWD Thou say'st true. 'Tis not our bringing up of poor bastards—as, I think, I have brought up some eleven—

BOULT Ay, to eleven; and brought them down again. But shall I search the market?

BAWD What else, man? The stuff we have, a strong wind will blow it to pieces, they are so pitifully sodden.

PANDAR Thou sayest true; there's two unwholesome, o' conscience. The poor Transylvanian is dead that lay with the little baggage.

BOULT Ay, she quickly poop'd him; she made him roast-meat for worms. But I'll go search the market. *Exit.*

PANDAR Three or four thousand chequins were as pretty a proportion to live quietly, and so give over.

BAWD Why to give over, I pray you? Is it a shame to get when we are old?

PANDAR O, our credit comes not in like the commodity, nor the commodity wages not with the danger. Therefore, if in our youths we could pick up some pretty estate, 'twere not amiss to keep our door hatch'd. Besides, the sore terms we stand upon with the gods will be strong with us for giving o'er.

BAWD Come, other sorts offend as well as we.

PANDAR As well as we? Ay, and better too; we offend worse. Neither is our profession any trade; it's no calling. But here comes Boult.

Enter Boult, with the Pirates and Marina.

BOULT Come your ways, my masters. You say she's a virgin?

FIRST PIRATE O, sir, we doubt it not.

IV.ii. Location: Mytilene. A brothel.
s.d. Bawds (Used for either sex.) **4 this mart** at the last market time **11 If . . . us'd** i.e., if one does not conscientiously offer good quality **13–14 'Tis . . . bastards** i.e., raising bastard children doesn't bring us enough wealth. (As Boult points out, the children are raised only to be introduced into prostitution.) **16 to eleven** to the age of eleven. **brought . . . again** i.e., lowered them into debauchery **20 sodden** boiled (by being treated in the sweating tub for venereal disease) **21 unwholesome** diseased. **o'** on my **23 baggage** whore **24 poop'd** i.e., infected with venereal disease **26 chequins** gold coins **27 proportion to** portion or fortune on which **28 give over** give up business. **get** earn money **30 credit** reputation. **commodity** profit **31 wages not** does not keep pace **33 keep . . . hatch'd** keep the lower halfdoor (the hatch) closed, i.e., closed to customers **35 strong** strong inducement **36 sorts** kinds of people

BOULT Master, I have gone through for this piece you see. If you like her, so; if not, I have lost my earnest.

BAWD Boult, has she any qualities?

BOULT She has a good face, speaks well, and has excellent good clothes. There's no farther necessity of qualities can make her be refus'd.

BAWD What's her price, Boult?

BOULT I cannot be bated one doit of a thousand pieces.

PANDAR Well, follow me, my masters, you shall have your money presently. Wife, take her in; instruct her what she has to do, that she may not be raw in her entertainment. [*Exeunt Pandar and Pirates.*]

BAWD Boult, take you the marks of her, the color of her hair, complexion, height, her age, with warrant of her virginity; and cry, "He that will give most shall have her first." Such a maidenhead were no cheap thing, if men were as they have been. Get this done as I command you.

BOULT Performance shall follow. *Exit.*

MARINA
Alack that Leonine was so slack, so slow!
He should have struck, not spoke; or that these pirates,
Not enough barbarous, had not o'erboard thrown me
For to seek my mother!

BAWD Why lament you, pretty one?

MARINA That I am pretty.

BAWD Come, the gods have done their part in you.

MARINA I accuse them not.

BAWD You are light into my hands, where you are like to live.

MARINA
The more my fault
To scape his hands where I was like to die.

BAWD Ay, and you shall live in pleasure.

MARINA No.

BAWD Yes, indeed shall you, and taste gentlemen of all fashions. You shall fare well; you shall have the difference of all complexions. What do you stop your ears?

MARINA Are you a woman?

BAWD What would you have me be, an I be not a woman?

MARINA An honest woman, or not a woman.

BAWD Marry, whip the gosling! I think I shall have something to do with you. Come, you're a young foolish sapling, and must be bow'd as I would have you.

MARINA The gods defend me!

BAWD If it please the gods to defend you by men, then men must comfort you, men must feed you, men stir you up. Boult's return'd.

[*Enter Boult.*]

Now, sir, hast thou cried her through the market?

BOULT I have cried her almost to the number of her hairs; I have drawn her picture with my voice.

BAWD And I prithee tell me, how dost thou find the inclination of the people, especially of the younger sort?

BOULT Faith, they listen'd to me as they would have hearken'd to their father's testament. There was a Spaniard's mouth wat'red an he went to bed to her very description.

BAWD We shall have him here tomorrow with his best ruff on.

BOULT Tonight, tonight. But, mistress, do you know the French knight that cowers i' the hams?

BAWD Who, Monsieur Verolles?

BOULT Ay, he. He offer'd to cut a caper at the proclamation; but he made a groan at it, and swore he would see her tomorrow.

BAWD Well, well, as for him, he brought his disease hither; here he does but repair it. I know he will come in our shadow, to scatter his crowns in the sun.

BOULT Well, if we had of every nation a traveler, we should lodge them with this sign.

BAWD [*To Marina*] Pray you, come hither awhile. You have fortunes coming upon you. Mark me: you must seem to do that fearfully which you commit willingly, despise profit where you have most gain. To weep that you live as ye do makes pity in your lovers; seldom but that pity begets you a good opinion, and that opinion a mere profit.

MARINA I understand you not.

BOULT O, take her home, mistress, take her home! These blushes of hers must be quench'd with some present practice.

BAWD Thou sayest true, i' faith, so they must; for your bride goes to that with shame which is her way to go with warrant.

BOULT Faith, some do, and some do not. But, mistress, if I have bargain'd for the joint—

BAWD Thou mayst cut a morsel off the spit.

BOULT I may so.

BAWD Who should deny it? Come, young one, I like the manner of your garments well.

BOULT Ay, by my faith, they shall not be chang'd yet.

BAWD Boult, spend thou that in the town. [*Gives money.*] Report what a sojourner we have; you'll lose nothing by custom. When nature fram'd this piece, she meant thee a good turn; therefore say what a paragon she is, and thou hast the harvest out of thine own report.

BOULT I warrant you, mistress, thunder shall not so awake the beds of eels as my giving out her beauty stirs up the lewdly-inclin'd. I'll bring home some tonight.

43 gone through made a deal **44 earnest** earnest money, down payment **50 be bated** get the price lowered (? Or perhaps *I* should read *It.*) **doit** small coin. **of** less than **70 are light** have chanced to light. **like** likely **71 live** remain **72 fault** misfortune **77–78 difference** variety **78 What** why **80 an** if **82 honest** chaste **83 whip the gosling** i.e., the devil take this goose of a girl **84 something to do** i.e., my hands full **90 cried** proclaimed, advertised

97 testament will **98 an** as if **103 cowers i' the hams** i.e., shows a weakness typical of venereal disease **105 offer'd** tried **109 repair** (1) return with (2) mend, renew **110 in our shadow** i.e., under our roof. **crowns in the sun** i.e., gold coins (?) (*French crown* plays on the idea of a bald head resulting from venereal disease.) **112 lodge . . . sign** i.e., attract them to lodge here by means of Marina's picture, metaphorically hung out as though it were a shop sign **116 despise** and must seem to despise **119 mere** utter, absolute **121 take her home** talk plainly, i.e., be direct with her; or, take her inside **124–125 your bride** even your bride **126 with warrant** with lawful sanction **128 joint** roast of meat **137 by custom** by increasing our trade (since you'll get a cut) **142 bed of eels** (Seager, *Natural History*, p. 98, quotes *Hortus Sanitatus:* the eel "is disturbed by the sound of thunder." Used here with possible bawdy connotation.)

BAWD Come your ways; follow me.

MARINA

If fires be hot, knives sharp, or waters deep,
Untied I still my virgin knot will keep.
Diana aid my purpose!

BAWD What have we to do with Diana? Pray you, will you go with us? *Exeunt.*

[SCENE III]

Enter Cleon and Dionyza.

DIONYZA

Why, are you foolish? Can it be undone?

CLEON

O Dionyza, such a piece of slaughter
The sun and moon ne'er look'd upon!

DIONYZA

I think you'll turn a child again.

CLEON

Were I chief lord of all this spacious world,
I'd give it to undo the deed. O lady, 6
Much less in blood than virtue, yet a princess
To equal any single crown o' th' earth
I' th' justice of compare! O villain Leonine! 9
Whom thou hast pois'ned too.
If thou hadst drunk to him, 't had been a kindness 11
Becoming well thy fact. What canst thou say 12
When noble Pericles shall demand his child?

DIONYZA

That she is dead. Nurses are not the fates,
To foster it, nor ever to preserve. 15
She died at night; I'll say so. Who can cross it?
Unless you play the pious innocent,
And for an honest attribute cry out 18
"She died by foul play."

CLEON O, go to. Well, well, 19
Of all the faults beneath the heavens, the gods
Do like this worst.

DIONYZA Be one of those that thinks
The petty wrens of Tharsus will fly hence
And open this to Pericles. I do shame 23
To think of what a noble strain you are,
And of how coward a spirit.

CLEON To such proceeding
Whoever but his approbation added, 26
Though not his prime consent, he did not flow 27
From honorable sources.

DIONYZA Be it so, then. 28
Yet none does know, but you, how she came dead,
Nor none can know, Leonine being gone.
She did distain my child, and stood between 31
Her and her fortunes. None would look on her,
But cast their gazes on Marina's face,
Whilst ours was blurted at and held a mawkin 34
Not worth the time of day. It pierc'd me thorough;
And though you call my course unnatural,
You not your child well loving, yet I find
It greets me as an enterprise of kindness 38
Perform'd to your sole daughter.

CLEON

Heavens forgive it!

DIONYZA And as for Pericles,
What should he say? We wept after her hearse,
And yet we mourn. Her monument
Is almost finished, and her epitaphs
In glitt'ring golden characters express
A general praise to her, and care in us
At whose expense 'tis done.

CLEON Thou art like the harpy, 46
Which, to betray, dost, with thine angel's face,
Seize with thine eagle's talents. 48

DIONYZA

Ye're like one that superstitiously
Do swear to th' gods that winter kills the flies. 50
But yet I know you'll do as I advise. [*Exeunt.*]

IV.iii. Location: Tharsus. Cleon's (the Governor's) house.
6 lady i.e., Marina **9 I' . . . compare** if justly compared **11 drunk to him** i.e., drunk his health from the poisoned cup **12 fact** deed **15 To . . . preserve** i.e., to nurture life or preserve it forever (?) (The text may be corrupt.) **18 attribute** reputation **19 go to** (A term of reproach or anger.) **23 open** reveal. (Birds were anciently thought to reveal murders.) **26 but** merely **27 prime** original. **flow** i.e., proceed, come **28 honorable sources** noble family. (See *noble strain* in l. 24.) **31 distain** tarnish by comparison

34 blurted at treated with scorn. **mawkin** malkin, slut **38 greets** manifests itself to **46 harpy** monstrous bird with the face of a woman **48 talents** talons **50 Do . . . flies** i.e., you blame the death of flies on winter, thus exculpating yourself before the gods (? A line variously interpreted, but seemingly Dionyza accuses her husband of superstitiously and hypocritically washing his hands of the dirty business by which his own daughter has been helped; see ll. 36–39.)

[SCENE IV]

[*Enter Gower, before the monument of Marina at Tharsus.*]

GOWER

Thus time we waste, and long leagues make short; 1
Sail seas in cockles, have and wish but for 't; 2
Making, to take your imagination, 3
From bourn to bourn, region to region.
By you being pardoned, we commit no crime
To use one language in each several clime
Where our scenes seem to live. I do beseech you
To learn of me, who stand i' th' gaps to teach you, 8
The stages of our story. Pericles
Is now again thwarting the wayward seas, 10
Attended on by many a lord and knight,
To see his daughter, all his life's delight.
Old Helicanus goes along. Behind
Is left to govern it, you bear in mind, 14
Old Escanes, whom Helicanus late
Advanc'd in time to great and high estate.
Well-sailing ships and bounteous winds have brought

IV.iv. Location: Tharsus.
1 waste i.e., pass quickly over **2 cockles** cockleshells, i.e., as supernatural creatures do (alluding to the imaginary crossing of the seas between scenes of the play). **have . . . for 't** have something if we but wish it **3 Making** journeying. **to take** by taking (?) to please, captivate (?) **8 stand i' th' gaps** bridge the gaps (of time and space between scenes) **10 thwarting** crossing. **wayward** unruly **14 it** i.e., Tyre

This King to Tharsus—think his pilot thought;
So with his steerage shall your thoughts grow on—
To fetch his daughter home, who first is gone.
Like motes and shadows see them move awhile;
Your ears unto your eyes I'll reconcile.

[Dumb Show.]

Enter Pericles, at one door, with all his train; Cleon and Dionyza, at the other. Cleon shows Pericles the tomb; whereat Pericles makes lamentation, puts on sackcloth, and in a mighty passion departs. [*Then exeunt Cleon and Dionyza.*]

See how belief may suffer by foul show!
This borrowed passion stands for true old woe;
And Pericles, in sorrow all devour'd,
With sighs shot through, and biggest tears o'ershow'r'd,
Leaves Tharsus and again embarks. He swears
Never to wash his face, nor cut his hairs;
He puts on sackcloth, and to sea. He bears
A tempest, which his mortal vessel tears,
And yet he rides it out. Now please you wit
The epitaph is for Marina writ
By wicked Dionyza.
[*Reads the inscription on Marina's monument.*]
"The fairest, sweetest, and best lies here,
Who withered in her spring of year.
She was of Tyrus the King's daughter,
On whom foul death hath made this slaughter.
Marina was she call'd, and at her birth,
Thetis, being proud, swallow'd some part o' th' earth.
Therefore the earth, fearing to be o'erflowed,
Hath Thetis' birth-child on the heavens bestowed;
Wherefore she does, and swears she'll never stint,
Make raging battery upon shores of flint."

No visor does become black villainy
So well as soft and tender flattery.
Let Pericles believe his daughter's dead,
And bear his courses to be ordered
By Lady Fortune, while our scene must play
His daughter's woe and heavy well-a-day
In her unholy service. Patience, then,
And think you now are all in Mytilene. *Exit.*

[SCENE V]

Enter [*from the brothel*] *two Gentlemen.*

FIRST GENTLEMAN Did you ever hear the like?

SECOND GENTLEMAN No, nor never shall do in such a place as this, she being once gone.

FIRST GENTLEMAN But to have divinity preach'd there! Did you ever dream of such a thing?

SECOND GENTLEMAN No, no. Come, I am for no more bawdy houses. Shall 's go hear the vestals sing?

FIRST GENTLEMAN I'll do any thing now that is virtuous, but I am out of the road of rutting for ever. *Exeunt.*

[SCENE VI]

Enter three Bawds [*Pandar, Bawd, and Boult*].

PANDAR Well, I had rather than twice the worth of her she had ne'er come here.

BAWD Fie, fie upon her! She's able to freeze the god Priapus, and undo a whole generation. We must either get her ravish'd, or be rid of her. When she should do for clients her fitment, and do me the kindness of our profession, she has me her quirks, her reasons, her master reasons, her prayers, her knees, that she would make a puritan of the devil if he should cheapen a kiss of her.

BOULT Faith, I must ravish her, or she'll disfurnish us of all our cavalleria, and make our swearers priests.

PANDAR Now, the pox upon her green-sickness for me!

BAWD Faith, there's no way to be rid on 't but by the way to the pox. Here comes the Lord Lysimachus disguis'd.

BOULT We should have both lord and lown, if the peevish baggage would but give way to customers.

Enter Lysimachus.

LYSIMACHUS How now? How a dozen of virginities?

BAWD Now, the gods to-bless your honor!

BOULT I am glad to see your honor in good health.

LYSIMACHUS You may so; 'tis the better for you that your resorters stand upon sound legs. How now? Wholesome iniquity have you, that a man may deal withal and defy the surgeon?

BAWD We have here one, sir, if she would—but there never came her like in Mytilene.

LYSIMACHUS If she'd do the deeds of darkness, thou wouldst say.

BAWD Your honor knows what 'tis to say well enough.

LYSIMACHUS Well, call forth, call forth.

BOULT For flesh and blood, sir, white and red, you shall see a rose; and she were a rose indeed, if she had but—

LYSIMACHUS What, prithee?

BOULT O, sir, I can be modest.

18 think . . . thought imagine that he is being piloted by swift thoughts **19 his steerage** the steering of his ship **20 first** already **23 foul show** foul dissembling **24 borrowed** dissembled (by Dionyza and Cleon) **30 mortal vessel** human body, life (which suffers from mental anguish) **31 wit** know **32 is** which is **39 Thetis** a sea-nymph, often confused (as here) with Tethys, a Titaness and consort of Oceanus **42 she** i.e., Thetis. **stint** cease **43 Make . . . flint** continuously beats upon rocky shores **47–48 bear . . . Fortune** direct his passage as fortune orders

IV.v. Location: Mytilene. The brothel.

7 Shall 's shall we **9 rutting** sexual indulgence

IV.vi. Location: The brothel, as before.

4 Priapus god of fertility and lechery. **undo . . . generation** (1) prevent the engendering of the next generation (2) prevent the pleasures of the present generation **6 fitment** sexual duty. **do me** do. (*Me* is the ethical dative; see also *has me* in next line.) **10 cheapen** bargain for **12 cavalleria** cavaliers. **our swearers** our sworn (i.e., faithful) customers, or our profane customers (?) **13 green-sickness** i.e., moody obstinacy or squeamishness, like that caused by anemia in young women **15 pox** syphilis. (In l. 13, *pox* is used in an oath, i.e., *the plague upon her.*) **17 lown** low fellow **19 How a** what price for **20 to-bless** bless completely **23 resorters** those who resort to your place, customers **24 Wholesome iniquity** (1) healthy prostitutes (2) salutary sin **25 surgeon** barber-surgeon (to treat syphilis) **30 what 'tis to say** what I'm trying to say

LYSIMACHUS That dignifies the renown of a bawd, no 37
less than it gives a good report to a number to be 38
chaste. [*Exit Boult.*] 39

BAWD Here comes that which grows to the stalk; never pluck'd yet, I can assure you.

[*Enter Boult with Marina.*]

Is she not a fair creature?

LYSIMACHUS Faith, she would serve after a long voyage at sea. Well, there's for you. [*Gives money.*] Leave us.

BAWD I beseech your honor, give me leave a word, and I'll have done presently.

LYSIMACHUS I beseech you, do.

BAWD [*Aside to Marina*] First, I would have you note, 48
this is an honorable man.

MARINA I desire to find him so, that I may worthily
note him. 51

BAWD Next, he's the Governor of this country, and a
man whom I am bound to. 53

MARINA If he govern the country, you are bound to 54
him indeed; but how honorable he is in that, I know not.

BAWD Pray you, without any more virginal fencing, will you use him kindly? He will line your apron with gold.

MARINA What he will do graciously, I will thankfully receive.

LYSIMACHUS Ha' you done?

BAWD My lord, she's not pac'd yet. You must take 63
some pains to work her to your manage. Come, we 64
will leave his honor and her together. Go thy ways.

[*Exeunt Bawd, Pandar, and Boult.*]

LYSIMACHUS Now, pretty one, how long have you been at this trade?

MARINA What trade, sir?

LYSIMACHUS Why, I cannot name 't but I shall offend.

MARINA I cannot be offended with my trade. Please you to name it.

LYSIMACHUS How long have you been of this profession?

MARINA E'er since I can remember.

LYSIMACHUS Did you go to 't so young? Were you a
gamester at five, or at seven? 76

MARINA Earlier too, sir, if now I be one.

LYSIMACHUS Why, the house you dwell in proclaims you to be a creature of sale.

MARINA Do you know this house to be a place of such resort, and will come into 't? I hear say you're of honorable parts, and are the Governor of this place.

LYSIMACHUS Why, hath your principal made known unto you who I am?

MARINA Who is my principal?

LYSIMACHUS Why, your herb-woman, she that sets seeds and roots of shame and iniquity. O, you have heard something of my power, and so stand aloof for more serious wooing. But I protest to thee, pretty one,
my authority shall not see thee, or else look friendly 90
upon thee. Come, bring me to some private place. Come, come.

MARINA
If you were born to honor, show it now;
If put upon you, make the judgment good 94
That thought you worthy of it.

LYSIMACHUS
How's this? How's this? Some more; be sage.

MARINA For me,
That am a maid, though most ungentle fortune
Have plac'd me in this sty, where, since I came,
Diseases have been sold dearer than physic—
That the gods
Would set me free from this unhallowed place,
Though they did change me to the meanest bird 102
That flies i' th' purer air!

LYSIMACHUS I did not think
Thou couldst have spoke so well; ne'er dreamt thou couldst.
Had I brought hither a corrupted mind,
Thy speech had altered it. Hold, here's gold for thee. 106
Persevere in that clear way thou goest,
And the gods strengthen thee! [*Gives gold.*]

MARINA
The good gods preserve you!

LYSIMACHUS
For me, be you thoughten 110
That I came with no ill intent; for to me
The very doors and windows savor vilely.
Fare thee well. Thou art a piece of virtue, and
I doubt not but thy training hath been noble.
Hold, here's more gold for thee. [*Gives gold.*]
A curse upon him, die he like a thief,
That robs thee of thy goodness! If thou dost
Hear from me, it shall be for thy good.

[*Enter Boult.*]

BOULT I beseech your honor, one piece for me.

LYSIMACHUS
Avaunt, thou damned door-keeper!
Your house, but for this virgin that doth prop it,
Would sink and overwhelm you. Away! [*Exit.*]

BOULT How's this? We must take another course with
you. If your peevish chastity, which is not worth a
breakfast in the cheapest country under the cope, shall 125
undo a whole household, let me be gelded like a spaniel. Come your ways.

MARINA Whither would you have me?

BOULT I must have your maidenhead taken off, or the
common hangman shall execute it. Come your ways. 130
We'll have no more gentlemen driven away. Come your ways, I say.

Enter Bawd.

BAWD How now, what's the matter?

37–39 That . . . chaste i.e., modesty in speech gives good reputation to a bawd, as well as attesting to the chastity of many women who deserve no such reputation **48, 51 note** (1) observe (2) set down as having a certain character, in this case a good character **53, 54 bound** (1) obligated (2) subject **63, 64 pac'd, manage.** (Terms used in training horses.) **76 gamester** wanton woman

90 my authority . . . thee i.e., I'll wink at your offenses, not enforce the laws against prostitutes **94 If put upon** i.e., if your high position was conferred after birth, not through inheritance **102 meanest** lowest **106 had** would have **110 be you thoughten** assure yourself **125 cope** firmament

BOULT Worse and worse, mistress. She has here spoken holy words to the Lord Lysimachus.

BAWD O abominable!

BOULT She makes our profession as it were to stink afore the face of the gods.

BAWD Marry, hang her up forever!

BOULT The nobleman would have dealt with her like a nobleman, and she sent him away as cold as a snowball, saying his prayers too.

BAWD Boult, take her away; use her at thy pleasure. Crack the glass of her virginity, and make the rest malleable.

BOULT An if she were a thornier piece of ground than she is, she shall be plough'd.

MARINA Hark, hark, you gods!

BAWD She conjures. Away with her! Would she had never come within my doors! Marry, hang you! She's born to undo us. Will you not go the way of womenkind? Marry, come up, my dish of chastity with rosemary and bays! *[Exit.]*

BOULT Come, mistress, come your ways with me.

MARINA Whither wilt thou have me?

BOULT To take from you the jewel you hold so dear.

MARINA Prithee, tell me one thing first.

BOULT Come now, your one thing.

MARINA
What canst thou wish thine enemy to be?

BOULT Why, I could wish him to be my master, or rather, my mistress.

MARINA
Neither of these are so bad as thou art,
Since they do better thee in their command.
Thou hold'st a place for which the pained'st fiend
Of hell would not in reputation change.
Thou art the damned doorkeeper to every
Coistrel that comes inquiring for his Tib.
To the choleric fisting of every rogue
Thy ear is liable; thy food is such
As hath been belch'd on by infected lungs.

BOULT What would you have me do? Go to the wars, would you? Where a man may serve seven years for the loss of a leg, and have not money enough in the end to buy him a wooden one?

MARINA
Do anything but this thou doest. Empty
Old receptacles, or common shores, of filth;
Serve by indenture to the common hangman.
Any of these ways are yet better than this;
For what thou professest, a baboon, could he speak,
Would own a name too dear. That the gods
Would safely deliver me from this place!
Here, here's gold for thee. *[Gives gold.]*
If that thy master would gain by me,
Proclaim that I can sing, weave, sew, and dance,
With other virtues, which I'll keep from boast,
And will undertake all these to teach.
I doubt not but this populous city will
Yield many scholars.

BOULT But can you teach all this you speak of?

MARINA
Prove that I cannot, take me home again,
And prostitute me to the basest groom
That doth frequent your house.

BOULT Well, I will see what I can do for thee. If I can place thee, I will.

MARINA
But amongst honest women.

BOULT Faith, my acquaintance lies little amongst them. But since my master and mistress hath bought you, there's no going but by their consent. Therefore I will make them acquainted with your purpose, and I doubt not but I shall find them tractable enough. Come, I'll do for thee what I can; come your ways.
Exeunt.

146 An if even if **152 Marry, come up** i.e., hoity-toity **152–153 rosemary and bays** (Customary garnishes for certain foods; the Bawd means that Marina's chastity is beyond the ordinary.) **159 What . . . to be** i.e., what is the worst possible evil you could wish upon your enemy **160–161 my master . . . mistress** i.e., like my master in wickedness, or even more, like my mistress **163 do . . . command** i.e., have you at command and so can order you to do their evil (?) **167 Coistrel** knave. **Tib** common woman **168 choleric fisting** angry blows **172 for** i.e., to end up with **176 shores** sewers **180 own . . . dear** consider himself too good for that

188 scholars pupils

[ACT V]

Enter Gower.

GOWER
Marina thus the brothel scapes, and chances
Into an honest house, our story says.
She sings like one immortal, and she dances
As goddess-like to her admired lays.
Deep clerks she dumbs; and with her neele
composes
Nature's own shape, of bud, bird, branch, or berry,
That even her art sisters the natural roses;
Her inkle, silk, twin with the rubied cherry;
That pupils lacks she none of noble race,
Who pour their bounty on her; and her gain
She gives the cursed bawd. Here we her place,
And to her father turn our thoughts again,
Where we left him, on the sea. We there him lost,
Where, driven before the winds, he is arriv'd
Here where his daughter dwells; and on this coast
Suppose him now at anchor. The city striv'd
God Neptune's annual feast to keep, from whence
Lysimachus our Tyrian ship espies,
His banners sable, trimm'd with rich expense,
And to him in his barge with fervor hies.
In your supposing once more put your sight;
Of heavy Pericles think this his bark,
Where what is done in action, more, if might,
Shall be discover'd; please you, sit and hark. *Exit.*

V. Chorus.
4 lays songs **5 Deep . . . dumbs** she silences profound scholars. **neele** needle **7 That** so that. **sisters** equals in appearance **8 inkle** kind of tape; also linen or yarn from which it is made. **twin with** resemble closely **19, 20 His, him** its, it **21 supposing** imagination **22 heavy** sorrowful **23 if might** if it were possible **24 discover'd** revealed, shown

[SCENE I]

Enter Helicanus. To him two Sailors, [*one belonging to the Tyrian vessel, the other to a barge of Mytilene that is evidently alongside, out of view*].

TYRIAN SAILOR [*To the Sailor of Mytilene*]
Where is Lord Helicanus? He can resolve you.
O, here he is.
Sir, there is a barge put off from Mytilene,
And in it is Lysimachus the governor,
Who craves to come aboard. What is your will?

HELICANUS
That he have his. Call up some gentlemen.

TYRIAN SAILOR
Ho, gentlemen! My lord calls.

Enter two or three Gentlemen.

FIRST GENTLEMAN
Doth your lordship call?

HELICANUS
Gentlemen,
There is some of worth would come aboard.
I pray, greet him fairly.
[*The Gentlemen and the two Sailors go to greet Lysimachus.*]

Enter [*as from the barge*] *Lysimachus,* [*escorted*].

TYRIAN SAILOR [*To Lysimachus*]
Sir,
This is the man that can, in aught you would,
Resolve you.

LYSIMACHUS
Hail, reverend sir! The gods preserve you!

HELICANUS
And you, to outlive the age I am,
And die as I would do.

LYSIMACHUS
You wish me well.
Being on shore, honoring of Neptune's triumphs,
Seeing this goodly vessel ride before us,
I made to it, to know of whence you are.

HELICANUS
First, what is your place?

LYSIMACHUS
I am the Governor of this place you lie before.

HELICANUS
Sir,
Our vessel is of Tyre, in it the King,
A man who for this three months hath not spoken
To anyone, nor taken sustenance
But to prorogue his grief.

LYSIMACHUS
Upon what ground is his distemperature?

HELICANUS
'Twould be too tedious to repeat,
But the main grief springs from the loss
Of a beloved daughter and a wife.

LYSIMACHUS
May we not see him?

HELICANUS
You may,
But bootless is your sight. He will not speak
To any.

LYSIMACHUS
Yet let me obtain my wish.

HELICANUS
Behold him. [*Pericles is discovered to view.*] This was a goodly person,
Till the disaster that, one mortal night,
Drove him to this.

LYSIMACHUS
Sir King, all hail! The gods preserve you!
Hail, royal sir!

HELICANUS
It is in vain; he will not speak to you.

FIRST LORD
Sir,
We have a maid in Mytilene, I durst wager,
Would win some words of him.

LYSIMACHUS
'Tis well bethought.
She questionless, with her sweet harmony
And other chosen attractions, would allure,
And make a batt'ry through his deafen'd parts,
Which now are midway stopp'd.
She is all happy as the fairest of all,
And, with her fellow maids, is now upon
The leafy shelter that abuts against
The island's side. [*Whispers to a Lord, who goes off to bring Marina.*]

HELICANUS
Sure, all effectless; yet nothing we'll omit
That bears recovery's name. But, since your kindness
We have stretch'd thus far, let us beseech you
That for our gold we may provision have,
Wherein we are not destitute for want,
But weary for the staleness.

LYSIMACHUS
O, sir, a courtesy
Which if we should deny, the most just gods
For every graff would send a caterpillar,
And so inflict our province. Yet once more
Let me entreat to know at large the cause
Of your king's sorrow.

HELICANUS
Sit, sir, I will recount it to you.—
But, see, I am prevented.

[*Enter, as though from the barge, Lord, with Marina, and a young Lady.*]

LYSIMACHUS
O, here's the lady that I sent for.

V.i. Location: On board Pericles' ship, off Mytilene. A pavilion for Pericles is provided on stage, with a curtain before it, perhaps by means of a "discovery space"; Pericles, reclining within, is "discovered" to view at l. 37 by the drawing back of the curtain.
1 resolve answer, satisfy **10 some of worth** some nobleman (who) **18 honoring . . . triumphs** celebrating a festival in honor of Neptune **21 place** office **27 prorogue** prolong

34 bootless fruitless **47 chosen** choice **48 make . . . parts** force an entrance through his deafened sense of hearing **54 effectless** useless **55 bears recovery's name** deserves the name of cure **59 for** because of **61 graff** scion, shoot **62 inflict** afflict **63 at large** in detail

Welcome, fair one!—Is 't not a goodly presence?

HELICANUS

She's a gallant lady.

LYSIMACHUS

She's such a one that, were I well assur'd
Came of a gentle kind and noble stock,
I'd wish no better choice, and think me rarely wed.
Fair one, all goodness that consists in beauty,
Expect even here, where is a kingly patient,
If that thy prosperous and artificial feat
Can draw him but to answer thee in aught,
Thy sacred physic shall receive such pay
As thy desires can wish.

MARINA

Sir, I will use
My utmost skill in his recovery, provided
That none but I and my companion maid
Be suffered to come near him.

LYSIMACHUS

Come, let us leave her;
And the gods make her prosperous!
[*They stand aside.*] *The song* [*by Marina*].

LYSIMACHUS [*Advancing*]

Mark'd he your music?

MARINA

No, nor look'd on us.

LYSIMACHUS [*To Helicanus*]

See, she will speak to him.

MARINA [*To Pericles*]

Hail, sir! My lord, lend ear.

PERICLES

Hum, ha! [*Pushes her away.*]

MARINA

I am a maid, my lord, that ne'er before
Invited eyes, but have been gazed on
Like a comet. She speaks,
My lord, that, may be, hath endured a grief
Might equal yours, if both were justly weigh'd.
Though wayward fortune did malign my state,
My derivation was from ancestors
Who stood equivalent with mighty kings;
But time hath rooted out my parentage,
And to the world and awkward casualties
Bound me in servitude. [*Aside.*] I will desist;
But there is something glows upon my cheek,
And whispers in mine ear, "Go not till he speak."

PERICLES

My fortunes—parentage—good parentage—
To equal mine!—Was it not thus? What say you?

MARINA

I said, my lord, if you did know my parentage,
You would not do me violence.

PERICLES

I do think so. Pray you, turn your eyes upon me.
You're like something that—What countrywoman?
Here of these shores?

MARINA

No, nor of any shores.
Yet I was mortally brought forth, and am
No other than I appear.

PERICLES

I am great with woe, and shall deliver weeping.
My dearest wife was like this maid, and such a one
My daughter might have been. My queen's square
brows;
Her stature to an inch; as wand-like straight;
As silver-voic'd; her eyes as jewel-like
And cas'd as richly; in pace another Juno;
Who starves the ears she feeds, and makes them
hungry,
The more she gives them speech. Where do you
live?

MARINA

Where I am but a stranger. From the deck
You may discern the place.

PERICLES

Where were you bred? And how achiev'd you these
Endowments which you make more rich to owe?

MARINA

If I should tell my history, it would seem
Like lies disdain'd in the reporting.

PERICLES

Prithee speak.
Falseness cannot come from thee, for thou lookest
Modest as Justice, and thou seemest a palace
For the crown'd Truth to dwell in. I will believe
thee,
And make my senses credit thy relation
To points that seem impossible, for thou lookest
Like one I loved indeed. What were thy friends?
Didst thou not say, when I did push thee back—
Which was when I perceiv'd thee—that thou cam'st
From good descending?

MARINA

So indeed I did.

PERICLES

Report thy parentage. I think thou said'st
Thou hadst been toss'd from wrong to injury,
And that thou thought'st thy griefs might equal
mine,
If both were opened.

MARINA

Some such thing
I said, and said no more but what my thoughts
Did warrant me was likely.

PERICLES

Tell thy story;
If thine, considered, prove the thousand part
Of my endurance, thou art a man, and I
Have suffered like a girl. Yet thou dost look
Like Patience gazing on kings' graves, and smiling
Extremity out of act. What were thy friends?
How lost thou them? Thy name, my most kind
virgin?
Recount, I do beseech thee. Come, sit by me.

MARINA

My name is Marina.

PERICLES

O, I am mock'd,
And thou by some incensed god sent hither
To make the world to laugh at me.

71 gentle kind noble kindred **72 rarely** excellently **73 all . . . beauty** i.e., you, Marina, possessed of all good that beauty can contain. (An often emended phrase.) **75 prosperous** producing favorable results. **artificial** skillful
88 Invited eyes asked to be looked at **96 awkward** adverse. **casualties** misfortunes **107 mortally** of human parentage

109 great (1) pregnant (2) heavy. **deliver** (1) give birth (2) speak **114 cas'd** enclosed, framed **120 to owe** by possessing **122 in the reporting** even as I spoke them **126 credit** believe. **relation** account **128 friends** relatives **138 thousand** thousandth **139 my endurance** what I have endured **141–142 smiling . . . act** disarming with a smile the worst that fortune can do

MARINA
Patience, good sir, or here I'll cease.
PERICLES
Nay, I'll be patient. Thou little know'st how thou
Dost startle me to call thyself Marina.
MARINA
The name
Was given me by one that had some power,
My father, and a king.
PERICLES How, a king's daughter?
And call'd Marina?
MARINA You said you would believe me;
But, not to be a troubler of your peace,
I will end here.
PERICLES But are you flesh and blood?
Have you a working pulse, and are no fairy?
Motion? Well, speak on. Where were you born?
And wherefore call'd Marina?
MARINA Call'd Marina
For I was born at sea.
PERICLES At sea! What mother?
MARINA
My mother was the daughter of a king,
Who died the minute I was born,
As my good nurse Lychorida hath oft
Delivered weeping.
PERICLES O, stop there a little!
This is the rarest dream that e'er dull sleep
Did mock sad fools withal. This cannot be
My daughter—buried!—Well, where were you
bred?
I'll hear you more, to th' bottom of your story,
And never interrupt you.
MARINA
You scorn. Believe me, 'twere best I did give o'er.
PERICLES
I will believe you by the syllable
Of what you shall deliver. Yet, give me leave:
How came you in these parts? Where were you
bred?
MARINA
The King my father did in Tharsus leave me,
Till cruel Cleon, with his wicked wife,
Did seek to murder me; and having woo'd
A villain to attempt it, who having drawn to do 't,
A crew of pirates came and rescued me;
Brought me to Mytilene. But, good sir,
Whither will you have me? Why do you weep? It
may be
You think me an impostor. No, good faith;
I am the daughter to King Pericles,
If good King Pericles be.
PERICLES
Ho, Helicanus!
HELICANUS
Calls my lord?
PERICLES
Thou art a grave and noble counselor,
Most wise in general. Tell me, if thou canst,
What this maid is, or what is like to be,
That thus hath made me weep?
HELICANUS I know not, but
Here's the Regent, sir, of Mytilene
Speaks nobly of her.
LYSIMACHUS She never would tell
Her parentage; being demanded that,
She would sit still and weep.
PERICLES
O Helicanus, strike me, honor'd sir,
Give me a gash, put me to present pain,
Lest this great sea of joys rushing upon me
O'erbear the shores of my mortality,
And drown me with their sweetness. O, come
hither,
Thou that beget'st him that did thee beget;
Thou that wast born at sea, buried at Tharsus,
And found at sea again! O Helicanus,
Down on thy knees, thank the holy gods as loud
As thunder threatens us. This is Marina.
What was thy mother's name? Tell me but that,
For truth can never be confirm'd enough,
Though doubts did ever sleep.
MARINA First, sir, I pray,
What is your title?
PERICLES I am Pericles of Tyre.
But tell me now my drown'd queen's name, as in
The rest you said thou hast been godlike perfect,
The heir of kingdoms, and another like
To Pericles thy father.
MARINA
Is it no more to be your daughter than
To say my mother's name was Thaisa?
Thaisa was my mother, who did end
The minute I began.
PERICLES
Now, blessing on thee! Rise, th' art my child.
Give me fresh garments. Mine own Helicanus,
She is not dead at Tharsus, as she should have
been,
By savage Cleon. She shall tell thee all,
When thou shalt kneel, and justify in knowledge
She is thy very princess.—Who is this?
HELICANUS
Sir, 'tis the Governor of Mytilene,
Who, hearing of your melancholy state,
Did come to see you.
PERICLES
I embrace you.
Give me my robes. I am wild in my beholding.
O heavens bless my girl! But, hark, what music?
Tell Helicanus, my Marina, tell him
O'er, point by point, for yet he seems to dote,
How sure you are my daughter. But, what music?
HELICANUS
My lord, I hear none.

159 Motion i.e., you have motion; or, you are no puppet (?) **165 Delivered** recited, told **181 Whither . . . me** where are you leading me in this interrogation **184 be** live

213 Is it no more is nothing more required **219 should have been** was thought to have been; or was intended to have been **221 When** whereupon. **justify in knowledge** be made certain (that) **227 wild . . . beholding** unkempt, savage in appearance **230 dote** be in a daze

PERICLES
None?
The music of the spheres! List, my Marina.
LYSIMACHUS
It is not good to cross him; give him way.
PERICLES
Rarest sounds! Do ye not hear?
LYSIMACHUS
Music, my lord? I hear.
PERICLES Most heavenly music!
It nips me unto list'ning, and thick slumber 237
Hangs upon mine eyes. Let me rest. *[Sleeps.]*
LYSIMACHUS
A pillow for his head.
So, leave him all. Well, my companion friends,
If this but answer to my just belief, 241
I'll well remember you. *[Exeunt all but Pericles.]* 242

Diana [*appears to Pericles as in a vision*].

DIANA
My temple stands in Ephesus. Hie thee thither,
And do upon mine altar sacrifice.
There, when my maiden priests are met together
Before the people all,
Reveal how thou at sea didst lose thy wife.
To mourn thy crosses, with thy daughter's, call 248
And give them repetition to the life. 249
Or perform my bidding, or thou livest in woe; 250
Do 't, and happy, by my silver bow!
Awake, and tell thy dream. *[Disappears.]*
PERICLES
Celestial Dian, goddess argentine, 253
I will obey thee. Helicanus!

[Enter Helicanus, Lysimachus, and Marina.]

HELICANUS Sir?
PERICLES
My purpose was for Tharsus, there to strike
The inhospitable Cleon, but I am
For other service first. Toward Ephesus
Turn our blown sails; eftsoons I'll tell thee why. 258
[*To Lysimachus.*] Shall we refresh us, sir, upon your shore,
And give you gold for such provision
As our intents will need?
LYSIMACHUS
Sir,
With all my heart; and, when you come ashore,
I have another suit.
PERICLES You shall prevail,
Were it to woo my daughter; for it seems
You have been noble towards her.
LYSIMACHUS
Sir, lend me your arm.
PERICLES
Come, my Marina. *Exeunt.*

237 nips me arrests my attention **241 but . . . belief** only turn out as I expect it to **242 remember** reward **248 crosses** misfortunes. **call** lift your voice **249 give . . . life** repeat them point for point **250 Or** either **253 argentine** silvery in appearance (as appropriate to the moon goddess) **258 eftsoons** shortly

[SCENE II]

[Enter Gower, before the temple of Diana of Ephesus; Thaisa standing near the altar, as high priestess; a number of Virgins on each side; Cerimon and other inhabitants of Ephesus attending.]

GOWER
Now our sands are almost run;
More a little, and then dumb.
This, my last boon, give me,
For such kindness must relieve me:
That you aptly will suppose
What pageantry, what feats, what shows,
What minstrelsy, and pretty din,
The Regent made in Mytilin
To greet the King. So he thrived
That he is promis'd to be wived
To fair Marina, but in no wise
Till he had done his sacrifice, 12
As Dian bade; whereto being bound,
The interim, pray you, all confound. 14
In feather'd briefness sails are fill'd, 15
And wishes fall out as they're will'd.
At Ephesus the temple see,
Our King and all his company.
That he can hither come so soon
Is by your fancies' thankful doom. *[Exit.]* 20

[SCENE III]

[Enter Pericles, with his train; Lysimachus, Helicanus, Marina, and a Lady.]

PERICLES
Hail, Dian! To perform thy just command,
I here confess myself the King of Tyre,
Who, frighted from my country, did wed
At Pentapolis the fair Thaisa.
At sea in childbed died she, but brought forth
A maid-child call'd Marina, who, O goddess,
Wears yet thy silver livery. She at Tharsus
Was nurs'd with Cleon, who at fourteen years
He sought to murder; but her better stars
Brought her to Mytilene, 'gainst whose shore
Riding, her fortunes brought the maid aboard us, 11
Where, by her own most clear remembrance, she
Made known herself my daughter.
THAISA Voice and favor! 13
You are, you are—O royal Pericles! *[Faints.]*
PERICLES
What means the nun? She dies! Help, gentlemen!
CERIMON
Noble sir,

V.ii. Location: The temple of Diana at Ephesus.
12 he i.e., Pericles **14 confound** destroy, omit **15 feather'd** winged **20 thankful doom** judgment to which thanks is due

V.iii. Location: Scene continues; the temple, as before.
11 Riding (we) riding at anchor **13 favor** face, appearance

If you have told Diana's altar true,
This is your wife.

PERICLES Reverend appearer, no;
I threw her overboard with these very arms.

CERIMON
Upon this coast, I warrant you.

PERICLES 'Tis most certain.

CERIMON
Look to the lady; O, she's but overjoy'd.
Early in blustering morn this lady was
Thrown upon this shore. I op'd the coffin,
Found there rich jewels; recovered her, and plac'd her
Here in Diana's temple.

PERICLES May we see them?

CERIMON
Great sir, they shall be brought you to my house,
Whither I invite you. Look, Thaisa is
Recovered.

THAISA [*Rising*]
O, let me look!
If he be none of mine, my sanctity
Will to my sense bend no licentious ear,
But curb it, spite of seeing. O, my lord,
Are you not Pericles? Like him you spake,
Like him you are. Did you not name a tempest,
A birth, and death?

PERICLES The voice of dead Thaisa!

THAISA
That Thaisa am I, supposed dead
And drown'd.

PERICLES
Immortal Dian!

THAISA Now I know you better.
When we with tears parted Pentapolis,
The King my father gave you such a ring.
[*Points to his ring.*]

PERICLES
This, this! No more, you gods! Your present kindness
Makes my past miseries sports. You shall do well
That on the touching of her lips I may
Melt and no more be seen. O, come, be buried
A second time within these arms! [*They embrace.*]

MARINA [*Kneeling*] My heart
Leaps to be gone into my mother's bosom.

PERICLES
Look who kneels here! Flesh of thy flesh, Thaisa,
Thy burden at the sea, and call'd Marina
For she was yielded there.

THAISA Blest, and mine own!
[*They embrace.*]

HELICANUS
Hail, madam, and my queen!

THAISA I know you not.

PERICLES
You have heard me say, when I did fly from Tyre,
I left behind an ancient substitute.
Can you remember what I call'd the man?
I have nam'd him oft.

THAISA
'Twas Helicanus then.

PERICLES Still confirmation!
Embrace him, dear Thaisa, this is he.
[*They embrace.*]
Now do I long to hear how you were found,
How possibly preserved, and who to thank,
Besides the gods, for this great miracle.

THAISA
Lord Cerimon, my lord; this man,
Through whom the gods have shown their power, that can
From first to last resolve you.

PERICLES Reverend sir,
The gods can have no mortal officer
More like a god than you. Will you deliver
How this dead queen re-lives?

CERIMON I will, my lord.
Beseech you, first go with me to my house,
Where shall be shown you all was found with her;
How she came plac'd here in the temple;
No needful thing omitted.

PERICLES
Pure Dian, I bless thee for thy vision, and
Will offer night-oblations to thee. Thaisa,
This prince, the fair-betrothed of your daughter,
Shall marry her at Pentapolis. And now
This ornament
Makes me look dismal will I clip to form;
And what this fourteen years no razor touch'd,
To grace thy marriage-day, I'll beautify.

THAISA
Lord Cerimon hath letters of good credit, sir,
My father's dead.

PERICLES
Heavens make a star of him! Yet there, my queen,
We'll celebrate their nuptials, and ourselves
Will in that kingdom spend our following days.
Our son and daughter shall in Tyrus reign.
Lord Cerimon, we do our longing stay
To hear the rest untold. Sir, lead 's the way.
[*Exeunt.*]

[*Enter Gower.*]

GOWER
In Antiochus and his daughter you have heard
Of monstrous lust the due and just reward.
In Pericles, his queen and daughter, seen,
Although assail'd with fortune fierce and keen,
Virtue preserv'd from fell destruction's blast,
Led on by heaven, and crown'd with joy at last.

30–32 If . . . seeing if he is not my husband, my holy way of life will lend no credence to my physical sense of sight, but will curb my longings (for marriage, my lost life of domestic pleasure) despite what I see before me **39 parted** departed from **40 s.d. Points to his ring** (Possibly Pericles included this ring among the jewels he laid in Thaisa's casket; or she may recognize it on his finger now.) **43 That** if **49 yielded** born

58 possibly by what possible means **62 resolve you** satisfy your curiosity **63 mortal officer** human agent **64 deliver** recount **71 night-oblations** nightly sacrifices **74 ornament** i.e., hair and beard **75 Makes** which makes **78 of good credit** trustworthy **80 there** i.e., in Pentapolis **84 do . . . stay** merely postpone the completion of our desires

In Helicanus may you well descry
A figure of truth, of faith, of loyalty.
In reverend Cerimon there well appears
The worth that learned charity aye wears.
For wicked Cleon and his wife, when fame
Had spread his cursed deed, the honor'd name
Of Pericles, to rage the city turn,
That him and his they in his palace burn;
The gods for murder seemed so content
To punish—although not done, but meant.
So, on your patience evermore attending,
New joy wait on you! Here our play has ending.
[*Exit.*]

Cymbeline

The genre of *Cymbeline* can be suggested by such critical terms as romance, tragicomedy, and the comedy of forgiveness. As in *Pericles, The Winter's Tale,* and other late plays, Shakespeare turns to the improbable fictions of romance: a stepmother-queen skilled in poisons and envious of her fair and virtuous stepdaughter (as in *Snow White*), lost sons recognized by the inevitable birthmark, the reunion of many persons long separated by exile and wandering, the intervention of the gods by means of a riddling and inane prophecy. These are the distinguishing features of English romance in the 1580's, a titillating vogue exploited by Robert Greene and other professional writers of the period. From two romantic plays of the 1580's—*Sir Clyomon and Sir Clamydes* and *The Rare Triumphs of Love and Fortune*—Shakespeare may in fact have drawn source material. Why did he turn to such old-fashioned models in 1608–1610? The choice has puzzled many critics, and has prompted them to speak condescendingly of Shakespeare's dotage or to assign parts of the play (notably the descent of Jupiter) to some other dramatist.

Shakespeare nevertheless courted the improbabilities, even the deliberate absurdities, of romance with a serious artistic purpose. In part he was responding to a new literary fashion, evident especially in the private theatres, for a tragicomedy of refined sensibility—a literary fashion that produced Beaumont and Fletcher's *Philaster.* This play of about 1609 features, like *Cymbeline,* a rapidly moving and ingeniously woven plot of separation and reunion, a king's daughter betrothed by her father to a churl and then wrongly accused of infidelity, a young maiden in male disguise, and other comparable details. Whether *Cymbeline* preceded or followed *Philaster* is a matter difficult to determine, since *Cymbeline* can be dated only approximately in 1608–1610 on grounds of style; but in any case Shakespeare's fascination with romance goes back at least to *All's Well that Ends Well* (c. 1601–1604) and *Pericles* (c. 1606–1608). His experiments in the genre must be viewed as innovative and unique. Despite the affinities to Fletcherian tragicomedy, Shakespeare never indulges in the cloying sensationalism, the exaggerated heightening of exotic emotion, and (except in *The Winter's Tale*) the trickery of concealing essential information from the audience, such as we find in works of Beaumont and Fletcher. Shakespeare's interest in romantic improbability is related to the serious motif of redemption, of an unexpected and undeserved second chance for erring mankind.

The tragic possibilities are manifold. Cymbeline, like Lear (another king from British mythic history in Holinshed's *Chronicles*), tyrannically repulses a virtuous daughter and rewards the vicious members of his family with predictably unhappy consequences. Posthumus Leonatus, like Othello, commands the death of his beloved mistress because he believes a groundless but cunningly presented accusation of her infidelity; finally, concluding too late that he has destroyed the only person capable of giving order to his life, he despairingly longs for death. Whereas in a similar situation Lear and Othello suffer the tragic consequences of their choice, however, Cymbeline and Posthumus are spared. Some benign force, integral to the world of this play, prevents fallible men from pursuing their misguided intentions to the point of irreversible injury. Posthumus relies for his vengeance on the virtuous Pisanio, who cannot bring himself to slay Imogen. The Queen's box of "poison," given ultimately to Imogen by the well-meaning but duped Pisanio, is only a sleeping potion concocted by that kindly manipulator behind the scenes, Doctor Cornelius. These fortunate avoidances of disaster recall other such narrow escapes in *Much Ado about Nothing, All's Well that Ends Well,* and *Measure for Measure*. They also anticipate similar events in *The Winter's Tale*.

Because *Cymbeline* begins with dilemmas like those of *King Lear* and *Othello,* the prevailing tone is at first serious. (The editors of the 1623 Folio printed the play among the tragedies.) The King's behavior toward Imogen and her virtuous but humbly ranked lover Posthumus is tyrannical. Disinterested observers condemn the wicked Queen's dominance over Cymbeline, and laugh up their sleeves at the Queen's cowardly and ridiculous son Cloten. A good man like Belarius suffers lifelong banishment from the envious court and spends his exile dwelling in caves. Many conventional features of romantic narrative—wandering and return, loss and rediscovery, apparent death and rebirth—are set in motion by the need to escape from a court dominated by the wicked Queen. One by one, honest persons of the play—Posthumus, Imogen, Pisanio—leave society in disfavor to be reunited in the wild landscape of Belarius and his foster sons. Italy is no better a place than the English court. Its evil genius is Iachimo, apostle of animal appetite, duplicity, and a cynical indifference to human values.

Despite the prevailing tragic mood at first, however, there are promises of brighter prospects. Posthumus' birth is attended by wondrous circumstances that would appear to single him out for an extraordinary career. In the first scene, moreover, we learn that the King's only two sons were stolen from their nursery in their infancy—an obvious hint that they will turn up sooner or later. Cloten, too, strikes us as a ludicrous suitor for Imogen, the type of buffoonish rival appropriate to a love comedy. Because he is witless, superficial, and preoccupied with clothes, he deserves to be exposed and ridiculed. Even his death is grotesquely comic. He acts as a foil or caricature to Posthumus, in whose clothes he is erroneously taken by Imogen to be her dead husband; the outward resemblance of the two men suggests to us that Posthumus has not been unlike Cloten when he has suspected Imogen of betraying him and has vowed revenge. Cloten's death signals an end to Posthumus' disposition to be fooled by appearances.

The initial somber mood, with its threat of tragic outcome, is further lightened by the juxtaposition of sorrow and hope. When Arviragus and Guiderius mourn the "death" of Imogen with an exquisite song on the vanity of human striving, we respond to the appropriateness of the sentiment and yet qualify our sorrow with our consoling knowledge that she has really taken a sleeping potion. Similarly, when Posthumus jests eloquently about death with his jailer, and prepares to find his only freedom in surcease, we cannot ignore Jupiter's assurance of eventual redress in the action immediately preceding. As in *Measure for Measure,* suffering and regret are framed in the benign context of a providential design that the audience alone can fully appreciate.

Tragicomedy threatens and consoles at the same time. The chief source of anxiety is Posthumus' renunciation of Imogen. The sensationalism of the plot derives in part from the use of the "wager" motif found in several Italianate *novelle,* such as the ninth tale of the second day in Boccaccio's *Decameron.* The psychological portrait of Posthumus' wavering and fall, like that of Othello or Leontes, is intense and ugly, fraught with grotesque images of sexual coupling. As with Othello and Leontes, Posthumus is threatened by his wife's sexuality, and is unable to respond securely to her offered love that is appropriately sensual and spiritual. He is comfortable only when he thinks of her as sexually restrained even in her marriage bed, praying forbearance of her husband with "A pudency so rosy the sweet view on 't Might well have warm'd old Saturn" (II,v). He is aroused by virginal unresponsiveness, repelled by too great a responsiveness. Such unbalanced expectations leave him prone to insinuations that women practice deception. Once Imogen has been made to appear carnal to him, she becomes monstrous and insatiable in his imagination. He conjures up the imagined sexual triumph of Iachimo in animalistic terms: "Perchance he spoke not, but, Like a full-acorn'd boar, a German one, Cried 'O!' and mounted." Like Othello, he insists on being proved a cuckold; once he has experienced jealousy, he can expect only one conclusion. He longs "to tear her limb-meal," and like Lear he would violently destroy "the woman's part in me." Such perversity in a man who is in most respects noble threatens disaster and demands either a tragic ending or the unexpected second chance of tragicomedy. Posthumus receives that second chance, but meantime he has raised a familiarly Shakespearean question about his responsibility for his fall. How could he have avoided accusing Imogen falsely?

Powerful forces militate against Posthumus. Iachimo is a plausible villain, in the vein of Don John *(Much Ado about Nothing),* Iago, and Edmund. Like them he plots to arouse envy and dissension in others, by means of appearance falsely presented to the senses. We can readily perceive motive in him as a quarrelsome and lecherous man, and yet he also puts us in mind of an all-encompassing evil that delights in mischief. His contention is that every woman has her price (and every man, too). When he discovers in Imogen a wholesomeness that will not yield to his insinuations, he seeks to destroy her as a dangerous refutation of his low premise about human nature. He states the confrontation between them in cosmic terms: "Though this a heavenly angel, hell is here" (II,ii). He does not, to be sure, boast gleefully to the audience, or dominate the play as Iago does; moreover, he himself experiences the beneficent change brought about by the play's happy ending, and speaks in praise of Imogen's virtue. As befits a tragicomedy, he is more sinister than potent, almost at times a travesty of a tragic villain. Nevertheless, in his scenes of villainy his function is that of a diabolical tempter working through man's frail senses. His use of the ring as evidence recalls the handkerchief in *Othello.* Iachimo creates a minutely circumstantial inference of Imogen's transgression, and lets Posthumus' inclination to believe the worst do the rest.

Like Othello, then, Posthumus must bear the blame for loss of faith. The tempter can prevail upon his senses, but man's own wavering heart chooses evil. Trustworthy observers perceive Posthumus' fallacy and indicate the correct response; as Philario says, "This is not strong enough to be believ'd Of one persuaded well of" (II,iv). True faith urges that, being what she is, Imogen could not do the thing alleged. She is, like Helena and Desdemona before her, a virtuous woman who responds to her undeserved tribulations with forbearance (though even her patience has a limit, and she too is capable of overreacting and misjudging). She overbalances faithlessness with her forgiveness. Her perseverance in virtue confounds Iachimo's thesis and rescues Posthumus from his worst self. Iachimo and she are spiritual contestants for the allegiance of Posthumus' faith. She triumphs not through Posthumus' choice (which is for evil) but through her own unassailable goodness. Belatedly, too, Posthumus makes amends that are necessary if we are to accept him as the restored hero. He forgives Imogen even before he knows of her innocence, seeks death as an atonement, and moves by degrees through sin to regret, confession of guilt, and penance. His peasant costume in Act V signals the resignation of worldly desire he must achieve to be worthy of an almost miraculous second chance. As fallen man he can never truly deserve that mercy, but he can strive at least to atone for what he has done.

The story of King Cymbeline's long-lost sons is similarly tragicomic, and is even more explicitly indebted to the conventions of romance with its motifs of banishment, wandering, and eventual recognition and reunion. The sylvan setting of this romantic narrative lends to the second half of the play a primal vigor and mystery (as also in *The Winter's Tale*). Arviragus and Guiderius remind us of medieval legends about Parzival: that is, like Parzival they are young princes raised in a wilderness, lacking courtly training and yet possessing an "invisible instinct" that prompts them to assert their royal blood. Ignoring their foster father's warnings about the ingratitude and decadence of the courtly society he has abandoned, the princes long to prove themselves in deeds of chivalry. They are a rejuvenating force in this play, bringing together the ideals of medieval knighthood and the unsullied strength of their sylvan world. Cloten, that effete semblance of a courtier and their foil in every respect, is appropriately killed by these agents of "divine Nature." They cherish Imogen as one of their own, and grieve for her seeming death with the vivid immediacy of those who have lived with nature. Her seeming death and reawakening is for them something like the restorative cycle of the seasons, bringing a renewal of natural vigor that nicely complements the spiritual grace she embodies for Posthumus. Her name to them is appropriately "Fidele." Old Belarius' reconciliation with Cymbeline signals an end to political injustice, still another consequence of man's fallen condition for which grace must be provided.

The story of the war between Britain and Rome, derived in part from Holinshed, contributes also to the process of spiritual rebirth. The war sets in motion a series of apparently unrelated events, including the return to Britain of Posthumus and Iachimo, without which the play's happy conclusion would be impossible. Although the war itself is destructive and is supported chiefly by Cloten and the Queen (whose patriotic speeches show us just how hollow a thing patriotism can be), the war does lead ultimately to new life for Britain as well as for the romantic lovers. Sudden turns in the battle, especially when an old man and two boys defend a narrow lane against an army, are seen as marvels directed by some higher power. In the benign aftermath of peace, the King, no longer misled by evil counselors, finds reconciliation with his daughter and her husband as well as with Rome. The final scene, in which the seeming accidents of fortune are unraveled, is a structural tour de force of comic discovery. Shakespeare thus creates a world of the play in which seeming accident is benign. His spokesman as *deus ex machina* (literally illustrating that term, for Jupiter "descends" from the stage roof by means of some mechanical device) is Jupiter. The scene of this divine intervention (V,iv) is so blatantly unrealistic that, as we have seen, many critics have wished to exonerate Shakespeare of having written it; but this very unreality is the keynote of the play's ending. Jupiter places the suffering we have witnessed in a larger perspective: "Whom best I love I cross; to make my gift, The more delay'd, delighted. Be content." In the tragicomic view, suffering is merely a manifestation of a design to test and strengthen us, engineered and supervised by a loving deity. The test affirms Imogen's strength, shows Posthumus a reason to cherish what he would otherwise destroy, and even reclaims the evil agent by whom the test had been administered.

Cymbeline

[Dramatis Personae

CYMBELINE, *King of Britain.*
CLOTEN, *son to the Queen by a former husband.*
POSTHUMUS LEONATUS, *a gentleman, husband to Imogen.*
BELARIUS, *a banished lord, disguised under the name of Morgan.*
GUIDERIUS, ARVIRAGUS, *sons to Cymbeline, disguised under the names of Polydore and Cadwal, supposed sons to Morgan.*
PHILARIO, *friend to Posthumus,* IACHIMO, *friend to Philario,* *Italians.*
CAIUS LUCIUS, *general of the Roman forces.*
PISANIO, *servant to Posthumus.*
CORNELIUS, *a physician.*
PHILARMONUS, *a soothsayer.*
ROMAN CAPTAIN.
Two BRITISH CAPTAINS.
FRENCHMAN, *friend to Philario.*
Two LORDS *of Cymbeline's court.*
Two GENTLEMEN *of the same.*
Two JAILERS.

QUEEN, *wife to Cymbeline.*
IMOGEN, *daughter to Cymbeline by a former queen.*
HELEN, *a lady attending on Imogen.*

LORDS, LADIES, ROMAN SENATORS, TRIBUNES, DUTCHMAN, SPANIARD, MUSICIANS, OFFICERS, CAPTAINS, SOLDIERS, MESSENGERS, *and other* ATTENDANTS.

APPARITIONS.

SCENE: *Britain; Italy.]*

ACT I • SCENE I

Enter two Gentlemen.

FIRST GENTLEMAN
You do not meet a man but frowns. Our bloods
No more obey the heavens than our courtiers'
Still seem as does the King's.
SECOND GENTLEMAN But what's the matter?

I.i. Location: Britain. The grounds of Cymbeline's palace.
1–3 Our . . . King's i.e., just as man's moods and dispositions obey the influence of the heavenly bodies, our courtiers' demeanors and looks follow those of the King

FIRST GENTLEMAN
His daughter, and the heir of 's kingdom, whom
He purpos'd to his wife's sole son—a widow
That late he married—hath referr'd herself
Unto a poor but worthy gentleman. She's wedded,
Her husband banish'd, she imprison'd. All
Is outward sorrow, though I think the King
Be touch'd at very heart.

SECOND GENTLEMAN None but the King?

FIRST GENTLEMAN
He that hath lost her too; so is the Queen,
That most desir'd the match. But not a courtier,
Although they wear their faces to the bent
Of the King's looks, hath a heart that is not
Glad at the thing they scowl at.

SECOND GENTLEMAN And why so?

FIRST GENTLEMAN
He that hath miss'd the Princess is a thing
Too bad for bad report, and he that hath her—
I mean, that married her, alack, good man!
And therefore banish'd—is a creature such
As, to seek through the regions of the earth
For one his like, there would be something failing
In him that should compare. I do not think
So fair an outward and such stuff within
Endows a man but he.

SECOND GENTLEMAN You speak him far.

FIRST GENTLEMAN
I do extend him, sir, within himself,
Crush him together rather than unfold
His measure duly.

SECOND GENTLEMAN What's his name and birth?

FIRST GENTLEMAN
I cannot delve him to the root. His father
Was call'd Sicilius, who did join his honor
Against the Romans with Cassibelan,
But had his titles by Tenantius whom
He serv'd with glory and admir'd success,
So gain'd the sur-addition Leonatus;
And had, besides this gentleman in question,
Two other sons, who in the wars o' th' time
Died with their swords in hand; for which their
  father,
Then old and fond of issue, took such sorrow
That he quit being, and his gentle lady,
Big of this gentleman our theme, deceas'd
As he was born. The King he takes the babe
To his protection, calls him Posthumus Leonatus,
Breeds him and makes him of his bedchamber,
Puts to him all the learnings that his time
Could make him the receiver of, which he took,
As we do air, fast as 'twas minist'red,
And in 's spring became a harvest, liv'd in court—
Which rare it is to do—most prais'd, most lov'd,
A sample to the youngest, to th' more mature
A glass that feated them, and to the graver
A child that guided dotards. To his mistress,
For whom he now is banish'd, her own price
Proclaims how she esteem'd him; and his virtue
By her election may be truly read
What kind of man he is.

SECOND GENTLEMAN I honor him
Even out of your report. But, pray you, tell me,
Is she sole child to th' King?

FIRST GENTLEMAN His only child.
He had two sons; if this be worth your hearing,
Mark it: the eldest of them at three years old,
I' th' swathing-clothes the other, from their nursery
Were stol'n, and to this hour no guess in knowledge
Which way they went.

SECOND GENTLEMAN
How long is this ago?

FIRST GENTLEMAN Some twenty years.

SECOND GENTLEMAN
That a king's children should be so convey'd,
So slackly guarded, and the search so slow,
That could not trace them!

FIRST GENTLEMAN Howso'er 'tis strange,
Or that the negligence may well be laugh'd at,
Yet is it true, sir.

SECOND GENTLEMAN I do well believe you.

FIRST GENTLEMAN
We must forbear. Here comes the gentleman,
The Queen, and Princess. *Exeunt.*

Enter the Queen, Posthumus, and Imogen.

QUEEN
No, be assur'd you shall not find me, daughter,
After the slander of most stepmothers,
Evil-ey'd unto you. You're my prisoner, but
Your jailer shall deliver you the keys
That lock up your restaint. For you, Posthumus,
So soon as I can win th' offended King,
I will be known your advocate. Marry, yet
The fire of rage is in him, and 'twere good
You lean'd unto his sentence with what patience
Your wisdom may inform you.

POSTHUMUS Please your Highness,
I will from hence today.

QUEEN You know the peril.
I'll fetch a turn about the garden, pitying
The pangs of barr'd affections, though the King
Hath charg'd you should not speak together. *Exit.*

IMOGEN O
Dissembling courtesy! How fine this tyrant
Can tickle where she wounds! My dearest husband,
I something fear my father's wrath, but nothing—

5 purpos'd to intended for **6 late** lately. **referr'd** given (in marriage) **9 outward** mere pretense of (as explained in ll. 9–22) **13 bent** inclination **22 him . . . compare** anyone chosen for comparison **24 speak him far** go far in praising him **25 I . . . himself** I stretch his virtues within the limits of what he actually is **29 join his honor** give his honorable assistance **30 Cassibelan** Cymbeline's uncle; see III.i.5. (According to Holinshed, Cassibelan was Cymbeline's great-uncle, being younger brother and successor to King Lud.) **31 Tenantius** Cymbeline's father, son of King Lud. (In Holinshed, Tenantius is Cassibelan's nephew.) **33 sur-additiion** additional title, surname **37 fond of issue** devoted to his children **38 quit being** left existence, died **39 Big . . . theme** i.e., pregnant with Posthumus **40 King he** i.e., King **42 of his bedchamber** one of his intimate retinue **43 time** age

48 sample example **49 glass . . . them** mirror that reflected their best features **51 her own price** the price she willingly paid (of her father's hostility) **53 election** choice **59 swathing** swaddling **60 guess in knowledge** credible conjecture **63 convey'd** carried off **71 After the slander** according to what is slanderously told **76 Marry** i.e., indeed. (Originally, by the Virgin Mary.) **78 lean'd unto** deferred to **79 inform** instill in **86 something** somewhat. **nothing** not in the least

Always reserv'd my holy duty—what
His rage can do on me. You must be gone,
And I shall here abide the hourly shot
Of angry eyes, not comforted to live,
But that there is this jewel in the world
That I may see again.

POSTHUMUS My queen, my mistress!
O lady, weep no more, lest I give cause
To be suspected of more tenderness
Than doth become a man. I will remain
The loyal'st husband that did e'er plight troth.
My residence in Rome at one Philario's,
Who to my father was a friend, to me
Known but by letter; thither write, my queen,
And with mine eyes I'll drink the words you send,
Though ink be made of gall.

Enter Queen.

QUEEN Be brief, I pray you.
If the King come, I shall incur I know not
How much of his displeasure. [*Aside.*] Yet I'll
move him
To walk this way. I never do him wrong
But he does buy my injuries, to be friends;
Pays dear for my offenses. [*Exit.*]

POSTHUMUS
Should we be taking leave
As long a term as yet we have to live,
The loathness to depart would grow. Adieu!

IMOGEN
Nay, stay a little!
Were you but riding forth to air yourself,
Such parting were too petty. Look here, love;
This diamond was my mother's. Take it, heart,
But keep it till you woo another wife
When Imogen is dead.
[*Gives ring, or puts it on his finger.*]

POSTHUMUS How, how? Another?
You gentle gods, give me but this I have,
And cere up my embracements from a next
With bonds of death! Remain, remain thou here
While sense can keep it on. And, sweetest, fairest,
As I my poor self did exchange for you,
To your so infinite loss, so in our trifles
I still win of you. For my sake wear this.
It is a manacle of love; I'll place it
Upon this fairest prisoner.
[*Puts a bracelet upon her arm.*]

IMOGEN O the gods!
When shall we see again?

Enter Cymbeline and Lords.

POSTHUMUS Alack, the King!

CYMBELINE
Thou basest thing, avoid hence, from my sight!
If after this command thou fraught the court
With thy unworthiness, thou diest. Away!
Thou 'rt poison to my blood.

POSTHUMUS The gods protect you,
And bless the good remainders of the court!
I am gone. *Exit.*

IMOGEN There cannot be a pinch in death
More sharp than this is.

CYMBELINE O disloyal thing,
That shouldst repair my youth, thou heap'st
A year's age on me.

IMOGEN I beseech you, sir,
Harm not yourself with your vexation.
I am senseless of your wrath; a touch more rare
Subdues all pangs, all fears.

CYMBELINE Past grace? Obedience?

IMOGEN
Past hope, and in despair; that way, past grace.

CYMBELINE
That mightst have had the sole son of my queen!

IMOGEN
O blessed, that I might not! I chose an eagle,
And did avoid a puttock.

CYMBELINE
Thou took'st a beggar; wouldst have made my
throne
A seat for baseness.

IMOGEN No, I rather added
A luster to it.

CYMBELINE O thou vile one!

IMOGEN Sir,
It is your fault that I have lov'd Posthumus.
You bred him as my playfellow, and he is
A man worth any woman, overbuys me
Almost the sum he pays.

CYMBELINE What, art thou mad?

IMOGEN
Almost, sir. Heaven restore me! Would I were
A neatherd's daughter, and my Leonatus
Our neighbor shepherd's son!

Enter Queen.

CYMBELINE Thou foolish thing!—
[*To Queen.*] They were again together. You have
done
Not after our command. Away with her,
And pen her up.

QUEEN Beseech your patience.—Peace,
Dear lady daughter, peace!—Sweet sovereign,
Leave us to ourselves, and make yourself some
comfort
Out of your best advice.

CYMBELINE Nay, let her languish
A drop of blood a day, and, being aged,

87 reserv'd excepted. **duty** i.e., duty of a daughter to her father **90 comforted to live** finding comfort in life **104–105 I . . . friends** i.e., whenever I wrong him, he mistakes those injuries for kindnesses **117 cere up** cover with wax, as the linen of a shroud **118 Remain** (Said to the ring.) **119 sense** sensory feeling **125 see** see each other **127 fraught** burden

130 remainders of those who remain at **134 repair** restore **137 senseless of** insensible to. **a touch** a feeling (of love for Posthumus and pain at his banishment) **142 puttock** kite, bird of prey **148–149 overbuys . . . pays** pays more for me than I am worth by almost as much as the price he pays (which is himself) **149 mad** insane. (But Imogen uses the word to mean *mad with grief;* cf. her pun on *grace* in l. 139.) **151 neatherd's** cowherd's **155 Beseech** I beseech **158 best advice** most mature reflection **159 drop of blood** (Sighs were supposed to deprive the heart of a drop of blood.)

Die of this folly! *Exit* [*with Lords*].

QUEEN Fie, you must give way.

Enter Pisanio.

Here is your servant. How now, sir? What news?

PISANIO
My lord your son drew on my master.

QUEEN Ha?
No harm, I trust, is done?

PISANIO There might have been,
But that my master rather play'd than fought
And had no help of anger. They were parted
By gentlemen at hand.

QUEEN I am very glad on 't.

IMOGEN
Your son's my father's friend; he takes his part.
To draw upon an exile. O brave sir!
I would they were in Afric both together,
Myself by with a needle that I might prick
The goer-back. Why came you from your master?

PISANIO
On his command. He would not suffer me
To bring him to the haven; left these notes
Of what commands I should be subject to,
When 't pleas'd you to employ me.

QUEEN This hath been
Your faithful servant. I dare lay mine honor
He will remain so.

PISANIO I humbly thank your Highness.

QUEEN
Pray, walk awhile.

IMOGEN [*To Pisanio*] About some half-hour hence,
Pray you, speak with me. You shall at least
Go see my lord aboard. For this time leave me.
Exeunt.

SCENE [II]

Enter Cloten and two Lords.

FIRST LORD Sir, I would advise you to shift a shirt; the violence of action hath made you reek as a sacrifice. Where air comes out, air comes in; there's none abroad so wholesome as that you vent.

CLOTEN If my shirt were bloody, then to shift it. Have I hurt him?

SECOND LORD [*Aside*] No, faith, not so much as his patience.

FIRST LORD Hurt him? His body's a passable carcass, if he be not hurt; it is a throughfare for steel, if it be not hurt.

SECOND LORD [*Aside*] His steel was in debt; it went o' th' backside the town.

CLOTEN The villain would not stand me.

SECOND LORD [*Aside*] No, but he fled forward still, toward your face.

FIRST LORD Stand you? You have land enough of your own, but he added to your having, gave you some ground.

SECOND LORD [*Aside*] As many inches as you have oceans. Puppies!

CLOTEN I would they had not come between us.

SECOND LORD [*Aside*] So would I, till you had measur'd how long a fool you were upon the ground.

CLOTEN And that she should love this fellow and refuse me!

SECOND LORD [*Aside*] If it be a sin to make a true election, she is damn'd.

FIRST LORD Sir, as I told you always, her beauty and her brain go not together. She's a good sign, but I have seen small reflection of her wit.

SECOND LORD [*Aside*] She shines not upon fools, lest the reflection should hurt her.

CLOTEN Come, I'll to my chamber. Would there had been some hurt done!

SECOND LORD [*Aside*] I wish not so, unless it had been the fall of an ass, which is no great hurt.

CLOTEN You'll go with us?

FIRST LORD I'll attend your lordship.

CLOTEN Nay, come, let's go together.

SECOND LORD Well, my lord. *Exeunt.*

SCENE [III]

Enter Imogen and Pisanio.

IMOGEN
I would thou grew'st unto the shores o' th' haven,
And questioned'st every sail. If he should write
And I not have it, 'twere a paper lost
As offer'd mercy is. What was the last
That he spake to thee?

PISANIO It was his queen, his queen!

IMOGEN
Then wav'd his handkerchief?

PISANIO And kiss'd it, madam.

IMOGEN
Senseless linen, happier therein than I!
And that was all?

PISANIO No, madam; for so long
As he could make me with this eye or ear

162 My . . . master i.e., Cloten drew his sword on Posthumus **165 had . . . anger** was not whetted on by anger **169 in Afric** i.e., in some deserted spot **176 lay** wager

I.ii. Location: Britain. The grounds of Cymbeline's palace, as before. The time is virtually continuous; Cloten still sweats from his duel (I.i.162).
1 shift change **4 abroad** outside you. (The outside air coming in is here said to cause the odor of perspiration.) **9 passable** (1) penetrable (2) tolerable **10 throughfare** thoroughfare

12–13 His . . . town i.e., Cloten's rapier avoided the fight in a cowardly fashion, as a debtor hides in back streets **14 stand me** stand up to me **15 still** continually **18–19 gave . . . ground** fell back before your advance (with pun on literal meaning) **21 Puppies** arrogant, vain people **27–28 election** choice. (A theological expression.) **30 sign** semblance, appearance

I.iii. Location: Britain. Cymbeline's palace.
3–4 'twere . . . is i.e., the loss of such a letter would be as unfortunate as a pardon offered but failing to arrive before the execution, or as God's mercy similarly having no effect **7 Senseless** without feeling

Distinguish him from others, he did keep
The deck, with glove, or hat, or handkerchief
Still waving, as the fits and stirs of 's mind
Could best express how slow his soul sail'd on,
How swift his ship.

IMOGEN Thou shouldst have made him
As little as a crow, or less, ere left
To after-eye him.

PISANIO Madam, so I did.

IMOGEN
I would have broke mine eye-strings, crack'd
them, but
To look upon him, till the diminution
Of space had pointed him sharp as my needle—
Nay, followed him till he had melted from
The smallness of a gnat to air, and then
Have turn'd mine eye and wept. But, good Pisanio,
When shall we hear from him?

PISANIO Be assur'd, madam,
With his next vantage.

IMOGEN
I did not take my leave of him, but had
Most pretty things to say. Ere I could tell him
How I would think on him at certain hours
Such thoughts and such; or I could make him swear
The shes of Italy should not betray
Mine interest and his honor; or have charg'd him
At the sixth hour of morn, at noon, at midnight,
T' encounter me with orisons, for then
I am in heaven for him; or ere I could
Give him that parting kiss which I had set
Betwixt two charming words, comes in my father,
And like the tyrannous breathing of the north
Shakes all our buds from growing.

Enter a Lady.

LADY The Queen, madam,
Desires your Highness' company.

IMOGEN
Those things I bid you do, get them dispatch'd.
I will attend the Queen.

PISANIO Madam, I shall. *Exeunt.*

SCENE [IV]

Enter Philario, Iachimo, a Frenchman, a Dutchman, and a Spaniard.

IACHIMO Believe it, sir, I have seen him in Britain. He was then of a crescent note, expected to prove so worthy as since he hath been allow'd the name of. But I could then have look'd on him without the help of admiration, though the catalogue of his endowments had been tabled by his side and I to peruse him by items.

PHILARIO You speak of him when he was less furnish'd than now he is with that which makes him both without and within.

FRENCHMAN I have seen him in France. We had very many there could behold the sun with as firm eyes as he.

IACHIMO This matter of marrying his king's daughter, wherein he must be weigh'd rather by her value than his own, words him, I doubt not, a great deal from the matter.

FRENCHMAN And then his banishment.

IACHIMO Ay, and the approbation of those that weep this lamentable divorce under her colors are wonderfully to extend him, be it but to fortify her judgment, which else an easy battery might lay flat, for taking a beggar without less quality. But how comes it he is to sojourn with you? How creeps acquaintance?

PHILARIO His father and I were soldiers together, to whom I have been often bound for no less than my life.

Enter Posthumus.

Here comes the Briton. Let him be so entertain'd amongst you as suits, with gentlemen of your knowing, to a stranger of his quality.—I beseech you all, be better known to this gentleman, whom I commend to you as a noble friend of mine. How worthy he is I will leave to appear hereafter, rather than story him in his own hearing.

FRENCHMAN Sir, we have known together in Orleans.

POSTHUMUS Since when I have been debtor to you for courtesies, which I will be ever to pay and yet pay still.

FRENCHMAN Sir, you o'er-rate my poor kindness. I was glad I did atone my countryman and you. It had been pity you should have been put together with so mortal a purpose as then each bore, upon importance of so slight and trivial a nature.

POSTHUMUS By your pardon, sir, I was then a young traveler; rather shunn'd to go even with what I heard than in my every action to be guided by others' experiences. But upon my mended judgment—if I offend not to say it is mended—my quarrel was not altogether slight.

FRENCHMAN Faith, yes, to be put to the arbitrement of swords, and by such two that would by all likelihood have confounded one the other, or have fall'n both.

IACHIMO Can we, with manners, ask what was the difference?

15–16 ere . . . him before you left off following him with your gaze **17 but** merely **24 next vantage** first opportunity **32 encounter** join. **orisons** prayers **33 in heaven** i.e., praying **35 charming** having magical potency **36 north** north wind

I.iv. Rome. Philario's house. Perhaps a feast is in progress; see V.v.157.
2 crescent note growing reputation of importance **5 admiration** wonder. (i.e., Iachimo was not dazzled by Posthumus.)

6 tabled set down in a list **9–10 makes . . . within** establishes him as regards both his fortune and his character **12 behold the sun** i.e., like an eagle, a royal bird supposedly able to stare at the sun unblinkingly **16–17 words . . . matter** causes him to be described in accounts that go beyond the truth **20 divorce** i.e., separation through banishment. **under her colors** i.e., in Imogen's party, influenced by her **21 extend him** praise him beyond his merit **22–23 which . . . quality** i.e., which judgment of hers would otherwise be vulnerable to attack for having chosen a beggar lacking the qualities they ascribe to him **24 How creeps acquaintance** how has he crept into your favor **29–30 knowing** knowledge, *savoir faire* **30 stranger** foreigner. **quality** rank **33 story** give an account of **35 known together** been acquainted **39 atone** set at one, reconcile **40 put together** i.e., in a duel. **mortal** deadly **41 importance** matter, occasion **44 shunn'd to go even** declined to agree **46 upon** even upon. **mended** improved **51 confounded** destroyed

FRENCHMAN Safely, I think; 'twas a contention in public, which may, without contradiction, suffer the report. It was much like an argument that fell out last night, where each of us fell in praise of our country mistresses; this gentleman at that time vouching—and upon warrant of bloody affirmation—his to be more fair, virtuous, wise, chaste, constant, qualified and less attemptable than any the rarest of our ladies in France.

IACHIMO That lady is not now living, or this gentleman's opinion by this worn out.

POSTHUMUS She holds her virtue still and I my mind.

IACHIMO You must not so far prefer her 'fore ours of Italy.

POSTHUMUS Being so far provok'd as I was in France, I would abate her nothing, though I profess myself her adorer, not her friend.

IACHIMO As fair and as good—a kind of hand-in-hand comparison—had been something too fair and too good for any lady in Britain. If she went before others I have seen, as that diamond of yours outlusters many I have beheld, I could not but believe she excell'd many. But I have not seen the most precious diamond that is, nor you the lady.

POSTHUMUS I prais'd her as I rated her. So do I my stone.

IACHIMO What do you esteem it at?

POSTHUMUS More than the world enjoys.

IACHIMO Either your unparagon'd mistress is dead, or she's outpriz'd by a trifle.

POSTHUMUS You are mistaken. The one may be sold or given, or if there were wealth enough for the purchase, or merit for the gift. The other is not a thing for sale, and only the gift of the gods.

IACHIMO Which the gods have given you?

POSTHUMUS Which, by their graces, I will keep.

IACHIMO You may wear her in title yours; but, you know, strange fowl light upon neighboring ponds. Your ring may be stol'n too. So your brace of unprizable estimations, the one is but frail and the other casual. A cunning thief, or a that way accomplish'd courtier, would hazard the winning both of first and last.

POSTHUMUS Your Italy contains none so accomplish'd a courtier to convince the honor of my mistress, if, in the holding or loss of that, you term her frail. I do nothing doubt you have store of thieves; notwithstanding, I fear not my ring.

PHILARIO Let us leave here, gentlemen.

POSTHUMUS Sir, with all my heart. This worthy signior, I thank him, makes no stranger of me; we are familiar at first.

IACHIMO With five times so much conversation, I should get ground of your fair mistress, make her go back, even to the yielding, had I admittance and opportunity to friend.

POSTHUMUS No, no.

IACHIMO I dare thereupon pawn the moi'ty of my estate to your ring, which in my opinion o'ervalues it something. But I make my wager rather against your confidence than her reputation; and, to bar your offense herein too, I durst attempt it against any lady in the world.

POSTHUMUS You are a great deal abus'd in too bold a persuasion, and I doubt not you sustain what y' are worthy of by your attempt.

IACHIMO What's that?

POSTHUMUS A repulse—though your attempt, as you call it, deserve more: a punishment too.

PHILARIO Gentlemen, enough of this. It came in too suddenly; let it die as it was born, and, I pray you, be better acquainted.

IACHIMO Would I had put my estate and my neighbor's on the approbation of what I have spoke!

POSTHUMUS What lady would you choose to assail?

IACHIMO Yours, whom in constancy you think stands so safe. I will lay you ten thousand ducats to your ring, that, commend me to the court where your lady is, with no more advantage than the opportunity of a second conference, and I will bring from thence that honor of hers which you imagine so reserv'd.

POSTHUMUS I will wage against your gold, gold to it. My ring I hold dear as my finger; 'tis part of it.

IACHIMO You are a friend, and therein the wiser. If you buy ladies' flesh at a million a dram, you cannot preserve it from tainting. But I see you have some religion in you, that you fear.

POSTHUMUS This is but a custom in your tongue; you bear a graver purpose, I hope.

IACHIMO I am the master of my speeches, and would undergo what's spoken, I swear.

POSTHUMUS Will you? I shall but lend my diamond till your return. Let there be covenants drawn between 's. My mistress exceeds in goodness the hugeness of your unworthy thinking. I dare you to this match; here's my ring. [*He wagers his ring.*]

PHILARIO I will have it no lay.

IACHIMO By the gods, it is one. If I bring you no sufficient testimony that I have enjoy'd the dearest bodily part of your mistress, my ten thousand ducats are yours; so is your diamond too. If I come off, and leave her in such honor as you have trust in, she your jewel, this your jewel, and my gold are yours—provided I have your commendation for my more free entertainment.

55–56 without . . . report without objection be reported or told **57–58 our country mistresses** the lady each of us loves in his native land **59 bloody affirmation** affirming the truth with his blood **60 qualified** having fine qualities **61 attemptable** open to attempts on her virtue **63 by this** by now **64 mind** opinion **68 abate her nothing** lower her estimate not at all **69 friend** lover **70–71 hand-in-hand comparison** comparison claiming equality **72 went before** were superior to **73 diamond** i.e., the ring Imogen gave Posthumus **84 or if** if either **89 wear . . . yours** possess her in name, claim title to her **90–91 ponds, ring** (with bawdy suggestion) **91–92 your . . . estimations** the pair of objects (ring and lady) that you esteem beyond value **92–93 casual** susceptible to accident (such as theft) **93 that way** i.e., in seducing women **96 to convince** as to overcome **98 nothing** not at all **100 leave** leave off, cease

105–106 go back succumb, give way **107 to friend** as my friend **109 moi'ty** half **110–111 something** somewhat **115–116 abus'd . . . persuasion** deceived by too bold an opinion **116 sustain** will sustain, receive **124 put** wagered **125 approbation** attestation, confirmation **129 commend me** if you provide me a letter of introduction **133 wage** lay as a wager. **to it** in equal amount **135 You . . . wiser** i.e., you know her too well, being her lover, to bet your ring on her **138 that** since **142 undergo** undertake **147 s.d. wagers his ring** (Possibly Posthumus hands the ring to Iachimo or to Philario as official of the wager, or perhaps he still keeps it himself; see II.iv.108.) **148 I . . . lay** I will not let it be a wager **155 commendation** introduction (to Imogen) **155–156 entertainment** welcome

POSTHUMUS I embrace these conditions. Let us have articles betwixt us. Only, thus far you shall answer: if you make your voyage upon her and give me directly to understand you have prevail'd, I am no further your enemy; she is not worth our debate. If she remain unseduc'd, you not making it appear otherwise, for your ill opinion and th' assault you have made to her chastity you shall answer me with your sword.

IACHIMO Your hand; a covenant. [*They shake hands.*] We will have these things set down by lawful counsel, and straight away for Britain, lest the bargain should catch cold and starve. I will fetch my gold and have our two wagers recorded.

POSTHUMUS Agreed. [*Exeunt Posthumus and Iachimo.*]

FRENCHMAN Will this hold, think you?

PHILARIO Signior Iachimo will not from it. Pray let us follow 'em. *Exeunt.*

SCENE [V]

Enter Queen, Ladies, and Cornelius.

QUEEN
Whiles yet the dew's on ground, gather those
flowers;
Make haste. Who has the note of them?

FIRST LADY I, madam.

QUEEN
Dispatch. *Exeunt Ladies.*
Now, master doctor, have you brought those drugs?

CORNELIUS
Pleaseth your Highness, ay. Here they are, madam.
[*Presents a small box.*]
But I beseech your Grace, without offense—
My conscience bids me ask—wherefore you have
Commanded of me these most poisonous
compounds,
Which are the movers of a languishing death,
But though slow, deadly?

QUEEN I wonder, doctor,
Thou ask'st me such a question. Have I not been
Thy pupil long? Hast thou not learn'd me how
To make perfumes? Distill? Preserve? Yea, so
That our great King himself doth woo me oft
For my confections? Having thus far proceeded—
Unless thou think'st me devilish—is 't not meet
That I did amplify my judgment in
Other conclusions? I will try the forces
Of these thy compounds on such creatures as
We count not worth the hanging—but none
human—
To try the vigor of them and apply
Allayments to their act, and by them gather
Their several virtues and effects.

CORNELIUS Your Highness
Shall from this practice but make hard your heart.
Besides, the seeing these effects will be
Both noisome and infectious.

QUEEN O, content thee.

Enter Pisanio.

[*Aside.*] Here comes a flattering rascal; upon him
Will I first work. He's for his master,
And enemy to my son.—How now, Pisanio?
Doctor, your service for this time is ended;
Take your own way.

CORNELIUS [*Aside*] I do suspect you, madam;
But you shall do no harm.

QUEEN [*To Pisanio*] Hark thee, a word.

CORNELIUS [*Aside*]
I do not like her. She doth think she has
Strange ling'ring poisons. I do know her spirit,
And will not trust one of her malice with
A drug of such damn'd nature. Those she has
Will stupify and dull the sense awhile,
Which first, perchance, she'll prove on cats and
dogs,
Then afterward up higher; but there is
No danger in what show of death it makes,
More than the locking-up the spirits a time,
To be more fresh, reviving. She is fool'd
With a most false effect; and I the truer,
So to be false with her.

QUEEN
No further service, doctor,
Until I send for thee.

CORNELIUS
I humbly take my leave. *Exit.*

QUEEN
Weeps she still, say'st thou? Dost thou think in time
She will not quench and let instructions enter
Where folly now possesses? Do thou work.
When thou shalt bring me word she loves my son,
I'll tell thee on the instant thou art then
As great as is thy master; greater, for
His fortunes all lie speechless and his name
Is at last gasp. Return he cannot, nor
Continue where he is. To shift his being
Is to exchange one misery with another,
And every day that comes comes to decay
A day's work in him. What shalt thou expect
To be depender on a thing that leans,
Who cannot be new built, nor has no friends,
So much as but to prop him? [*The Queen drops the
box: Pisanio takes it up.*] Thou tak'st up
Thou know'st not what; but take it for thy labor.
It is a thing I made, which hath the King
Five times redeem'd from death. I do not know
What is more cordial. Nay, I prithee, take it;

I.v. Location: Britain. Cymbeline's palace.
2 note list **5 Pleaseth** may it please **5 s.d. Presents a small box** (Perhaps Cornelius hesitates before actually giving it to her; she may snatch it from him.) **12 learn'd** taught **15 confections** compounds (of drugs) **18 conclusions** experiments **22 Allayments** antidotes. **act** action. **them** i.e., the experiments. **gather** collect a record of

26 noisome noxious, foul-smelling. **content thee** do not trouble yourself **38 prove** test **43 truer** more honest **49 quench** become cool **56 shift his being** change his abode **58–59 And . . . him** i.e., and every new day destroys the possibility of fruitful action **60 leans** is about to fall **66 cordial** restorative (literally, to the heart)

It is an earnest of a farther good
That I mean to thee. Tell thy mistress how
The case stands with her; do 't as from thyself.
Think what a chance thou changest on, but think
Thou hast thy mistress still—to boot, my son,
Who shall take notice of thee. I'll move the King
To any shape of thy preferment such
As thou 'lt desire; and then myself, I chiefly,
That set thee on to this desert, am bound
To load thy merit richly. Call my women.
Think on my words. *Exit Pisanio.*
A sly and constant knave,
Not to be shak'd; the agent for his master,
And the remembrancer of her to hold
The hand-fast to her lord. I have given him that
Which, if he take, shall quite unpeople her
Of liegers for her sweet, and which she after,
Except she bend her humor, shall be assur'd
To taste of too.

Enter Pisanio, and Ladies [with flowers].

So, so. Well done, well done.
The violets, cowslips, and the primroses
Bear to my closet. Fare thee well, Pisanio;
Think on my words. *Exeunt Queen and Ladies.*

PISANIO
And shall do.
But when to my good lord I prove untrue,
I'll choke myself. There's all I'll do for you. *Exit.*

SCENE [VI]

Enter Imogen alone.

IMOGEN
A father cruel, and a step-dame false,
A foolish suitor to a wedded lady
That hath her husband banish'd. O, that husband!
My supreme crown of grief, and those repeated
Vexations of it! Had I been thief-stol'n,
As my two brothers, happy! But most miserable
Is the desire that's glorious. Blessed be those,
How mean soe'er, that have their honest wills,
Which seasons comfort.—Who may this be? Fie!

Enter Pisanio and Iachimo.

PISANIO
Madam, a noble gentleman of Rome,
Comes from my lord with letters.

IACHIMO
Change you, madam;
The worthy Leonatus is in safety
And greets your Highness dearly.
[Presents a letter or letters.]

IMOGEN
Thanks, good sir.
You're kindly welcome.

IACHIMO *[Aside]*
All of her that is out of door most rich!
If she be furnish'd with a mind so rare,
She is alone th' Arabian bird, and I
Have lost the wager. Boldness be my friend!
Arm me, audacity, from head to foot!
Or, like the Parthian, I shall flying fight—
Rather, directly fly.

IMOGEN *(Reads)* "He is one of the noblest note, to whose kindnesses I am most infinitely tied. Reflect upon him accordingly, as you value your trust—
Leonatus."

So far I read aloud.
But even the very middle of my heart
Is warm'd by th' rest, and takes it thankfully.
You are as welcome, worthy sir, as I
Have words to bid you, and shall find it so
In all that I can do.

IACHIMO
Thanks, fairest lady.
What, are men mad? Hath nature given them eyes
To see this vaulted arch and the rich crop
Of sea and land, which can distinguish 'twixt
The fiery orbs above and the twinn'd stones
Upon the number'd beach, and can we not
Partition make with spectacles so precious
'Twixt fair and foul?

IMOGEN
What makes your admiration?

IACHIMO
It cannot be i' th' eye, for apes and monkeys
'Twixt two such shes would chatter this way and
Contemn with mows the other; nor i' th' judgment,
For idiots in this case of favor would
Be wisely definite; nor i' th' appetite;
Sluttery, to such neat excellence oppos'd,
Should make desire vomit emptiness,
Not so allur'd to feed.

IMOGEN
What is the matter, trow?

IACHIMO
The cloyed will—
That satiate yet unsatisfied desire, that tub
Both fill'd and running—ravening first the lamb,
Longs after for the garbage.

IMOGEN
What, dear sir,
Thus raps you? Are you well?

IACHIMO
Thanks, madam, well. *[To Pisanio.]* Beseech you, sir,

70 chance . . . on opportunity you here discover to change service **75 desert** deserving action **78 shak'd** shaken (in his loyalty) **79 remembrancer of her** one who reminds her **80 hand-fest** marriage contract **81 unpeople her** deprive her of the services **82 liegers** ambassadors. **her sweet** i.e., Posthumus **83 Except . . . humor** unless she change her mind (about not accepting Cloten) **86 closet** private chamber

I.vi. Location: Britain. Cymbeline's palace.
3 That . . . banish'd whose husband is banished **4 repeated** already enumerated **7 the desire that's glorious** i.e., the person who desires too much happiness **8 mean** lowly. **honest wills** simple desires **9 seasons** adds relish to **11 Comes** who comes. **Change you** i.e., cheer up, don't be sad

15 out of door external **17 Arabian bird** i.e., phoenix, therefore unique **20 Parthian** (The Parthians were proverbial in ancient times for discharging a flight of arrows as they fled.) **22 note** reputation **23 Reflect** bestow attention **33 vaulted arch** sky. **crop** harvest, produce **35 twinn'd** exactly alike **36 number'd** abounding (in stones) **37 Partition** distinction. **with . . . precious** i.e., with such precious sights as Imogen **38 admiration** wonder **40 chatter this way** i.e., indicate approval of Imogen **41 Contemn** show scorn. **mows** grimaces, wry faces **42 in . . . favor** in question concerning a face of such grace and beauty **43 Be wisely definite** choose wisely **44 Sluttery** sluttishness. **neat** elegant. **oppos'd** contrasted **45 make . . . emptiness** make desire refuse to satisfy itself and turn away in self-disgust **46 so allur'd** attracted by this, i.e., by sluttishness **47 trow** (An expletive, meaning something like *for goodness' sake.*) **will** lustful appetite **49 running** emptying itself. **ravening** devouring greedily **51 raps** transports, makes rapt

Desire my man's abode where I did leave him.
He's strange and peevish.

PISANIO
I was going, sir,
To give him welcome. *Exit.*

IMOGEN
Continues well my lord? His health, beseech you?

IACHIMO
Well, madam.

IMOGEN
Is he dispos'd to mirth? I hope he is.

IACHIMO
Exceeding pleasant; none a stranger there
So merry and so gamesome. He is call'd
The Britain reveler.

IMOGEN
When he was here,
He did incline to sadness, and oft-times
Not knowing why.

IACHIMO
I never saw him sad.
There is a Frenchman his companion, one
An eminent monsieur that, it seems, much loves
A Gallian girl at home. He furnaces
The thick sighs from him, whiles the jolly Briton—
Your lord, I mean—laughs from 's free lungs, cries "O,
Can my sides hold, to think that man, who knows
By history, report, or his own proof,
What woman is, yea, what she cannot choose
But must be, will 's free hours languish
For assured bondage?"

IMOGEN
Will my lord say so?

IACHIMO
Ay, madam, with his eyes in flood with laughter.
It is a recreation to be by
And hear him mock the Frenchman. But, heavens know,
Some men are much to blame.

IMOGEN
Not he, I hope.

IACHIMO
Not he; but yet heaven's bounty towards him might
Be us'd more thankfully. In himself, 'tis much;
In you, which I account his, beyond all talents.
Whilst I am bound to wonder, I am bound
To pity too.

IMOGEN
What do you pity, sir?

IACHIMO
Two creatures heartily.

IMOGEN
Am I one, sir?
You look on me. What wrack discern you in me
Deserves your pity?

IACHIMO
Lamentable! What,
To hide me from the radiant sun and solace
I' th' dungeon by a snuff?

IMOGEN
I pray you, sir,
Deliver with more openness your answers
To my demands. Why do you pity me?

IACHIMO
That others do—
I was about to say—enjoy your—But
It is an office of the gods to venge it,
Not mine to speak on 't.

IMOGEN
You do seem to know
Something of me, or what concerns me. Pray you—
Since doubting things go ill often hurts more
Than to be sure they do; for certainties
Either are past remedies, or, timely knowing,
The remedy then born—discover to me
What both you spur and stop.

IACHIMO
Had I this cheek
To bathe my lips upon; this hand, whose touch,
Whose every touch, would force the feeler's soul
To th' oath of loyalty; this object, which
Takes prisoner the wild motion of mine eye,
Fixing it only here; should I, damn'd then,
Slaver with lips as common as the stairs
That mount the Capitol; join gripes with hands
Made hard with hourly falsehood—falsehood, as
With labor; then by-peeping in an eye
Base and illustrous as the smoky light
That's fed with stinking tallow; it were fit
That all the plagues of hell should at one time
Encounter such revolt.

IMOGEN
My lord, I fear,
Has forgot Britain.

IACHIMO
And himself. Not I,
Inclin'd to this intelligence, pronounce
The beggary of his change; but 'tis your graces
That from my mutest conscience to my tongue
Charms this report out.

IMOGEN
Let me hear no more.

IACHIMO
O dearest soul, your cause doth strike my heart
With pity that doth make me sick. A lady
So fair, and fasten'd to an empery
Would make the great'st King double—to be partner'd
With tomboys hir'd with that self exhibition
Which your own coffers yield; with diseas'd ventures
That play with all infirmities for gold
Which rottenness can lend nature; such boil'd stuff
As well might poison poison! Be reveng'd;
Or she that bore you was no queen, and you
Recoil from your great stock.

IMOGEN
Reveng'd?

53 Desire . . . abode bid my servant remain **54 strange and peevish** a stranger and easily upset **62 sadness** seriousness **66 Gallian** Gallic, French. **furnaces** gives forth like a furnace **70 proof** experience **72 languish** give up to languishing **78 bounty** generosity (in bestowing on him his own qualities, and Imogen) **79 In . . . much** i.e., as for his own qualities, heaven has been generous **80 In you** i.e., as for heaven's generosity in giving him you. **talents** natural endowments, or wealth **86 hide me** i.e., hide. **solace** take delight **87 snuff** smoking candlewick

95 doubting fearing that **97 timely knowing** if one knows in time **98 then born** i.e., is then born. **discover** reveal **99 What . . . stop** i.e., what you simultaneously urge toward disclosure and then conceal **106 gripes** claspings **107–108 as With labor** as if made hard by labor **108 by-peeping** giving sidelong glances **109 illustrous** not lustrous **112 Encounter** meet (with punishment). **revolt** inconstancy **113–114 Not . . . pronounce** not through any inclination to disclose this information do I report **116 mutest conscience** most silent inner knowledge **120 empery** empire (i.e., her graces and possessions) **121 Would** which would. **double** as having twice the majesty **121–122 partner'd With** put on a level with, made to share rights with **122 tomboys** wantons. **self** very same. **exhibition** allowance (of money) **123 ventures** commercial women **124–125 That . . . nature** who for money chance all the infirmities of mind and body that rottenness (venereal disease) can lend to human nature. (*Lend*, because we can be said only to "borrow" infirmities until we die.) **125 boil'd stuff** i.e., women treated by "sweating" for venereal disease **128 Recoil** fall away, degenerate

How should I be reveng'd? If this be true—
As I have such a heart that both mine ears
Must not in haste abuse—if it be true,
How should I be reveng'd?

IACHIMO Should he make me
Live, like Diana's priest, betwixt cold sheets, 134
Whiles he is vaulting variable ramps, 135
In your despite, upon your purse? Revenge it. 136
I dedicate myself to your sweet pleasure,
More noble than that runagate to your bed, 138
And will continue fast to your affection, 139
Still close as sure.

IMOGEN What, ho, Pisanio! 140

IACHIMO
Let me my service tender on your lips.

IMOGEN
Away! I do condemn mine ears that have
So long attended thee. If thou wert honorable, 143
Thou wouldst have told this tale for virtue, not
For such an end thou seek'st—as base as strange.
Thou wrong'st a gentleman who is as far
From thy report as thou from honor, and
Solicits here a lady that disdains
Thee and the devil alike. What ho, Pisanio!
The King my father shall be made acquainted
Of thy assault. If he shall think it fit
A saucy stranger in his court to mart 152
As in a Romish stew and to expound 153
His beastly mind to us, he hath a court
He little cares for and a daughter who
He not respects at all. What, ho, Pisanio!

IACHIMO
O happy Leonatus! I may say
The credit that thy lady hath of thee 158
Deserves thy trust, and thy most perfect goodness
Her assur'd credit. Blessed live you long,
A lady to the worthiest sir that ever
Country call'd his, and you his mistress, only 162
For the most worthiest fit! Give me your pardon.
I have spoke this to know if your affiance 164
Were deeply rooted, and shall make your lord,
That which he is, new o'er; and he is one 166
The truest manner'd, such a holy witch 167
That he enchants societies into him. 168
Half all men's hearts are his.

IMOGEN You make amends.

IACHIMO
He sits 'mongst men like a descended god.
He hath a kind of honor sets him off,
More than a mortal seeming. Be not angry,
Most mighty Princess, that I have adventur'd
To try your taking of a false report, which hath
Honor'd with confirmation your great judgment
In the election of a sir so rare, 176
Which you know cannot err. The love I bear him 177
Made me to fan you thus, but the gods made you, 178
Unlike all others, chaffless. Pray, your pardon. 179

IMOGEN
All's well, sir. Take my pow'r i' th' court for yours.

IACHIMO
My humble thanks. I had almost forgot
T' entreat your Grace but in a small request,
And yet of moment too, for it concerns
Your lord, myself, and other noble friends
Are partners in the business.

IMOGEN Pray, what is 't? 185

IACHIMO
Some dozen Romans of us and your lord—
The best feather of our wing—have mingled sums
To buy a present for the Emperor;
Which I, the factor for the rest, have done 189
In France. 'Tis plate of rare device, and jewels
Of rich and exquisite form, their values great,
And I am something curious, being strange, 192
To have them in safe stowage. May it please you
To take them in protection?

IMOGEN Willingly;
And pawn mine honor for their safety. Since
My lord hath interest in them, I will keep them
In my bedchamber.

IACHIMO They are in a trunk,
Attended by my men. I will make bold
To send them to you, only for this night;
I must aboard tomorrow.

IMOGEN O, no, no.

IACHIMO
Yes, I beseech; or I shall short my word 201
By length'ning my return. From Gallia
I cross'd the seas on purpose and on promise
To see your Grace.

IMOGEN I thank you for your pains.
But not away tomorrow!

IACHIMO O, I must, madam.
Therefore I shall beseech you, if you please
To greet your lord with writing, do 't tonight.
I have outstood my time, which is material 208
To th' tender of our present.

IMOGEN I will write. 209
Send your trunk to me; it shall safe be kept,
And truly yielded you. You're very welcome. *Exeunt.*

ACT II • SCENE I

Enter Cloten and the two Lords.

CLOTEN Was there ever man had such luck? When I kiss'd the jack, upon an up-cast to be hit away! I had 2

134 priest i.e., priestess **135 vaulting . . . ramps** mounting various prostitutes **136 In your despite** in contempt for you **138 runagate** renegade **139 fast** firm **140 close** secret **143 attended** listened to **152 to mart** should bargain **153 stew** house of prostitution **158 credit . . . of** faith . . . in **162 call'd his** called its own **164 affiance** fidelity **166 new o'er** refreshed and renewed, made over again **166–167 one The** uniquely, above all others **167 witch** charmer, fascinating person **168 societies into** whole groups of people to **176 election** choice **177 Which** who

178 fan test. (A metaphor from winnowing of grain.) **179 chaffless** without chaff, i.e., perfect **185 Are** who are **189 factor** agent **192 something curious** somewhat anxious. **strange** a foreigner **201 short my word** impair my promise **208 outstood** outstayed **209 tender of our present** offering of our gift

II.i. Location: Britain. The grounds of Cymbeline's palace.
2 kiss'd the jack touched and lay near the small bowl used as target in the game of bowls. **up-cast** i.e., subsequent throw in the game of bowls

a hundred pound on 't. And then a whoreson jackanapes must take me up for swearing, as if I borrow'd mine oaths of him and might not spend them at my pleasure.

FIRST LORD What got he by that? You have broke his pate with your bowl.

SECOND LORD [*Aside*] If his wit had been like him that broke it, it would have run all out.

CLOTEN When a gentleman is dispos'd to swear, it is not for any standers-by to curtal his oaths, ha?

SECOND LORD No, my lord; [*Aside*] nor crop the ears of them.

CLOTEN Whoreson dog! I gave him satisfaction? Would he had been one of my rank!

SECOND LORD [*Aside*] To have smell'd like a fool.

CLOTEN I am not vex'd more at anything in th' earth. A pox on 't! I had rather not be so noble as I am. They dare not fight with me because of the Queen my mother. Every Jack-slave hath his bellyful of fighting, and I must go up and down like a cock that nobody can match.

SECOND LORD [*Aside*] You are cock and capon too, and you crow, cock, with your comb on.

CLOTEN Sayest thou?

SECOND LORD It is not fit your lordship should undertake every companion that you give offense to.

CLOTEN No, I know that, but it is fit I should commit offense to my inferiors.

SECOND LORD Ay, it is fit for your lordship only.

CLOTEN Why, so I say.

FIRST LORD Did you hear of a stranger that's come to court tonight?

CLOTEN A stranger, and I not know on 't?

SECOND LORD [*Aside*] He's a strange fellow himself, and knows it not.

FIRST LORD There's an Italian come, and, 'tis thought, one of Leonatus' friends.

CLOTEN Leonatus? A banish'd rascal; and he's another, whatsoever he be. Who told you of this stranger?

FIRST LORD One of your lordship's pages.

CLOTEN Is it fit I went to look upon him? Is there no derogation in 't?

SECOND LORD You cannot derogate, my lord.

CLOTEN Not easily, I think.

SECOND LORD [*Aside*] You are a fool granted; therefore your issues, being foolish, do not derogate.

CLOTEN Come, I'll go see this Italian. What I have lost today at bowls I'll win tonight of him. Come, go.

SECOND LORD I'll attend your lordship.

Exeunt [*Cloten and First Lord*].

That such a crafty devil as is his mother
Should yield the world this ass! A woman that
Bears all down with her brain, and this her son
Cannot take two from twenty, for his heart,
And leave eighteen. Alas, poor Princess,
Thou divine Imogen, what thou endur'st,
Betwixt a father by thy step-dame govern'd,
A mother hourly coining plots, a wooer
More hateful than the foul expulsion is
Of thy dear husband, than that horrid act
Of the divorce he'd make! The heavens hold firm
The walls of thy dear honor, keep unshak'd
That temple, thy fair mind, that thou mayst stand
T' enjoy thy banish'd lord and this great land! *Exit.*

SCENE II

Enter Imogen in her bed, and a Lady [*attending*].

IMOGEN
Who's there? My woman Helen?

LADY
Please you, madam.

IMOGEN
What hour is it?

LADY
Almost midnight, madam.

IMOGEN
I have read three hours then. Mine eyes are weak.
[*Gives her the book.*]
Fold down the leaf where I have left. To bed.
Take not away the taper, leave it burning;
And if thou canst awake by four o' th' clock,
I prithee, call me. Sleep hath seiz'd me wholly.
[*Exit Lady, leaving the book beside the bed.*]
To your protection I commend me, gods.
From fairies and the tempters of the night
Guard me, beseech ye.
Sleeps. Iachimo [*comes*] *from the trunk.*

IACHIMO
The crickets sing, and man's o'er-labor'd sense
Repairs itself by rest. Our Tarquin thus
Did softly press the rushes ere he waken'd
The chastity he wounded. Cytherea,
How bravely thou becom'st thy bed, fresh lily,
And whiter than the sheets! That I might touch!
But kiss, one kiss! Rubies unparagon'd,
How dearly they do 't! 'Tis her breathing that
Perfumes the chamber thus. The flame o' th' taper
Bows toward her, and would under-peep her lids,
To see th' enclosed lights, now canopied
Under these windows, white and azure lac'd
With blue of heaven's own tinct. But my design,

3–4 whoreson jackanapes wretched ape, coxcomb **4 take me up** take me to task **12 curtal** shorten, curtail, as one might bob the tail of a curtal dog; hence, *crop the ears* (of the *oaths*) in the next speech **15 gave** was to give **16 rank** social class. (But the Second Lord takes it in the sense of *rankness of smell.*) **21 Jack-slave** lowborn fellow **24 capon** castrated rooster (used quibblingly for *capon*, i.e., with fool's cap or coxcomb) **26 Sayest thou** what do you say **27–28 undertake** engage with, give satisfaction to **28 companion** fellow **29–30 commit offense to** attack, initiate action against (with unintended sense of *defecate upon*) **44 derogation** action unbecoming my position **45 cannot derogate** (1) cannot do anything undignified (2) have no dignity to lose **48 issues** offspring, i.e., deeds, actions

54 Bears all down triumphs over everyone **55 for his heart** for the life of him

II.ii. Location: Britain. Imogen's bedchamber in Cymbeline's palace.
s.d. in her bed (On the Elizabethan stage a bed presumably would be "thrust out" at this point, and the trunk carried on containing Iachimo—unless he uses the trap door or other such device. Imogen has a book; a lighted candle is provided.) **9 fairies** i.e., evil spirits **12 Our Tarquin** the Roman Sextus Tarquinius who raped Lucrece **13 press the rushes** (Elizabethan floors were strewn with rushes.) **14 Cytherea** Venus **15 bravely** handsomely **18 do 't** i.e., kiss one another **22 windows** i.e., eyelids **23 tinct** color, hue

To note the chamber. I will write all down:
[*Writes.*]
Such and such pictures; there the window; such
Th' adornment of her bed; the arras, figures,
Why, such and such; and the contents o' th' story.
Ah, but some natural notes about her body,
Above ten thousand meaner moveables
Would testify, t' enrich mine inventory.
O sleep, thou ape of death, lie dull upon her,
And be her sense but as a monument,
Thus in a chapel lying! Come off, come off;
[*Takes off her bracelet.*]
As slippery as the Gordian knot was hard!
'Tis mine; and this will witness outwardly,
As strongly as the conscience does within,
To th' madding of her lord. On her left breast
A mole cinque-spotted, like the crimson drops
I' th' bottom of a cowslip. Here's a voucher,
Stronger than ever law could make. This secret
Will force him think I have pick'd the lock and ta'en
The treasure of her honor. No more. To what end?
Why should I write this down that's riveted,
Screw'd to my memory? She hath been reading late
The tale of Tereus; here the leaf's turn'd down
Where Philomel gave up. I have enough.
To th' trunk again, and shut the spring of it.
Swift, swift, you dragons of the night, that dawning
May bare the raven's eye! I lodge in fear;
Though this a heavenly angel, hell is here.
Clock strikes.
One, two, three. Time, time!
[*Goes into the trunk.*] *Exeunt.*

SCENE III

Enter Cloten and Lords.

FIRST LORD Your lordship is the most patient man in loss, the most coldest that ever turn'd up ace.

CLOTEN It would make any man cold to lose.

FIRST LORD But not every man patient after the noble temper of your lordship. You are most hot and furious when you win.

CLOTEN Winning will put any man into courage. If I could get this foolish Imogen, I should have gold enough. It's almost morning, is 't not?

FIRST LORD Day, my lord.

CLOTEN I would this music would come. I am advis'd to give her music o' mornings; they say it will penetrate.

Enter Musicians.

Come on; tune. If you can penetrate her with your fingering, so; we'll try with tongue too. If none will do, let her remain, but I'll never give o'er. First, a very excellent good-conceited thing; after, a wonderful sweet air, with admirable rich words to it—and then let her consider.

Song.

Hark, hark, the lark at heaven's gate sings,
  And Phoebus 'gins arise,
His steeds to water at those springs
  On chalic'd flow'rs that lies;
And winking Mary-buds begin
  To ope their golden eyes.
With everything that pretty is,
  My lady sweet, arise,
    Arise, arise!

CLOTEN So, get you gone. If this penetrate, I will consider your music the better; if it do not, it is a vice in her ears, which horsehairs and calves'-guts, nor the voice of unpav'd eunuch to boot, can never amend.
[*Exeunt Musicians.*]

Enter Cymbeline and Queen.

SECOND LORD Here comes the King.

CLOTEN I am glad I was up so late, for that's the reason I was up so early. He cannot choose but take this service I have done fatherly.—Good morrow to your Majesty and to my gracious mother.

CYMBELINE
Attend you here the door of our stern daughter?
Will she not forth?

CLOTEN I have assail'd her with musics, but she vouchsafes no notice.

CYMBELINE
The exile of her minion is too new;
She hath not yet forgot him. Some more time
Must wear the print of his remembrance on 't,
And then she's yours.

QUEEN
You are most bound to th' King,
Who lets go by no vantages that may
Prefer you to his daughter. Frame yourself
To orderly solicits, and be friended
With aptness of the season; make denials
Increase your services; so seem as if
You were inspir'd to do those duties which
You tender to her; that you in all obey her,

26 arras hangings of tapestry. **figures** carvings **27 story** subject set forth in embroidery on the tapestry (?) **28 notes** marks **29 meaner moveables** less important furnishings **31 dull** heavy **32 monument** horizontal effigy on a tomb **34 Gordian knot** (According to prophecy, whoever untied the knot binding the yoke to the pole of the chariot of Gordius, peasant King of Phrygia, should be king of all Asia. Alexander severed the knot with his sword.) **36 conscience** consciousness **37 madding** maddening **38 cinque-spotted** with five spots **45 Tereus** mythical king of Thrace, who raped Philomela, sister of his wife, Procne. (He had Philomela's tongue cut out so that she could not tell the story, but she wove it into a tapestry.) **49 raven's eye** (The raven was supposed to wake at early dawn.) **51 s.d. Exeunt** (Presumably the bed, and trunk with Iachimo inside, are carried off stage, unless Iachimo exits by trap door or other means as a way of reentering the "trunk.")

II.iii. Location: Britain. An antechamber adjoining Imogen's apartments. The sense of time is nearly continuous, since it is early morn.
2 most coldest coolest, most deliberate. **turn'd up ace** made the losing throw at dice (with a pun on *ass*) **3 cold** gloomy, dispirited

12–13 penetrate (1) affect (2) penetrate her sexually; see also ll. 72, 77, and notes) **15 so** it is well **17 good-conceited** imaginatively invented **21 Phoebus** i.e., the sun god with his chariot and horses **24 winking Mary-buds** closed buds of marigolds **29–30 consider** reward (?) value (?) **31 horsehairs and calves'-guts** bowstrings and fiddlestrings **32 unpav'd** unstoned, castrated **36 fatherly** as a father **42 minion** darling **48 Prefer** recommend. **Frame** conform, prepare **49 solicits** solicitings, importunings **49–50 be . . . season** make timely use of your best opportunity

Save when command to your dismission tends, 54
And therein you are senseless.

CLOTEN
Senseless? Not so. 55

[Enter a Messenger.]

MESSENGER
So like you, sir, ambassadors from Rome; 56
The one is Caius Lucius.

CYMBELINE
A worthy fellow,
Albeit he comes on angry purpose now;
But that's no fault of his. We must receive him
According to the honor of his sender;
And towards himself, his goodness forespent on us, 61
We must extend our notice. Our dear son,
When you have given good morning to your
mistress,
Attend the Queen and us. We shall have need
T' employ you towards this Roman. Come, our
queen. *Exeunt [all but Cloten].*

CLOTEN
If she be up, I'll speak with her; if not,
Let her lie still and dream. By your leave, ho!
I know her women are about her. What
If I do line one of their hands? 'Tis gold 69
Which buys admittance—oft it doth—yea, and
makes
Diana's rangers false themselves, yield up 71
Their deer to th' stand o' th' stealer; and 'tis gold 72
Which makes the true man kill'd and saves the thief,
Nay, sometime hangs both thief and true man.
What
Can it not do and undo? I will make
One of her women lawyer to me, for
I yet not understand the case myself. 77
By your leave. *Knocks.*

Enter a Lady.

LADY
Who's there that knocks?

CLOTEN
A gentleman.

LADY
No more?

CLOTEN
Yes, and a gentlewoman's son.

LADY
That's more
Than some, whose tailors are as dear as yours, 81
Can justly boast of. What's your lordship's pleasure?

CLOTEN
Your lady's person. Is she ready?

LADY
Ay, 83
To keep her chamber.

CLOTEN
There is gold for you;
Sell me your good report. *[Offers money.]* 85

LADY
How? My good name? Or to report of you
What I shall think is good?—The Princess!

Enter Imogen.

CLOTEN
Good morrow, fairest; sister, your sweet hand.
[Exit Lady.]

IMOGEN
Good morrow, sir. You lay out too much pains
For purchasing but trouble. The thanks I give
Is telling you that I am poor of thanks
And scarce can spare them.

CLOTEN
Still, I swear I love you.

IMOGEN
If you but said so, 'twere as deep with me. 93
If you swear still, your recompense is still
That I regard it not.

CLOTEN
This is no answer.

IMOGEN
But that you shall not say I yield being silent, 96
I would not speak. I pray you, spare me. Faith,
I shall unfold equal discourtesy
To your best kindness. One of your great knowing 99
Should learn, being taught, forbearance.

CLOTEN
To leave you in your madness, 'twere my sin.
I will not.

IMOGEN
Fools are not mad folks.

CLOTEN
Do you call me fool? 103

IMOGEN
As I am mad, I do. 104
If you'll be patient, I'll no more be mad;
That cures us both. I am much sorry, sir,
You put me to forget a lady's manners,
By being so verbal; and learn now, for all, 108
That I, which know my heart, do here pronounce,
By th' very truth of it, I care not for you,
And am so near the lack of charity
To accuse myself I hate you—which I had rather 112
You felt than make 't my boast.

CLOTEN
You sin against 113
Obedience, which you owe your father. For 114
The contract you pretend with that base wretch,
One bred of alms and foster'd with cold dishes,
With scraps o' th' court, it is no contract, none.
And though it be allow'd in meaner parties— 118
Yet who than he more mean?—to knit their souls,
On whom there is no more dependency 120
But brats and beggary, in self-figur'd knot, 121
Yet you are curb'd from that enlargement by 122
The consequence o' th' crown, and must not foil 123

54 dismission dismissal, rejection **55 senseless** insensible (to her commands; but Cloten understands the word as meaning *stupid*) **56 So like you** if you please **61 his goodness forespent** (because of) his goodness previously bestowed **69 line** i.e., with gold **71 rangers** gamekeepers, i.e., nymphs (vowed to chastity). **false** turn false **72 stand** (1) station of huntsman waiting for game (2) erection **77 understand the case** know how to conduct my suit (with pun on *stand* again, l. 72, and on *case* meaning *vagina*) **81 dear** costly **83 ready** dressed. (But the Lady quibbles in another sense.) **85 good report** favorable speech. (But the Lady quibbles on the sense of *reputation, good name.*)

93 deep binding, efficacious **96 But . . . silent** if it were not for the fact that you might interpret my silence as giving consent **99 knowing** knowledge, discernment. (Said with tactful irony.) **103 Fools . . . folks** i.e., if I'm mad, as you say, at least I'm not a fool like you (?) **104 As** insofar as **108 By . . . verbal** (If the phrase refers to Cloten, the meaning of *verbal* is "verbose"; if to Imogen, "plain-spoken.") **112 I hate you** of hating you **113 felt** i.e., perceived without my having to say it **114 For** as for **118 meaner parties** persons of lower social rank **120 On whom** from whose marriage. **dependency** consequence **121 But** i.e., than. **self-figur'd** self-contracted **122 enlargement** liberty **123 consequence** succession. **foil** defile, foul

The precious note of it with a base slave, 124
A hilding for a livery, a squire's cloth, 125
A pantler—not so eminent.

IMOGEN Profane fellow! 126
Wert thou the son of Jupiter and no more
But what thou art besides, thou wert too base
To be his groom. Thou wert dignified enough, 129
Even to the point of envy, if 'twere made 130
Comparative for your virtues, to be styl'd 131
The under-hangman of his kingdom, and hated
For being preferr'd so well.

CLOTEN The south-fog rot him! 133

IMOGEN
He never can meet more mischance than come
To be but nam'd of thee. His mean'st garment 135
That ever hath but clipp'd his body is dearer 136
In my respect than all the hairs above thee, 137
Were they all made such men.—How now, Pisanio!

Enter Pisanio.

CLOTEN
"His garment!" Now the devil—

IMOGEN
To Dorothy my woman hie thee presently.

CLOTEN
"His garment!"

IMOGEN I am sprited with a fool, 141
Frighted, and ang'red worse. Go bid my woman
Search for a jewel that too casually
Hath left mine arm. It was thy master's. 'Shrew me 144
If I would lose it for a revenue
Of any king's in Europe. I do think
I saw 't this morning; confident I am
Last night 'twas on mine arm; I kiss'd it.
I hope it be not gone to tell my lord
That I kiss aught but he.

PISANIO 'Twill not be lost.

IMOGEN
I hope so. Go and search. [*Exit Pisanio.*]

CLOTEN You have abus'd me.
"His meanest garment!"

IMOGEN Ay, I said so, sir.
If you will make 't an action, call witness to 't. 153

CLOTEN
I will inform your father.

IMOGEN Your mother too.
She's my good lady, and will conceive, I hope, 155
But the worst of me. So, I leave you, sir,
To th' worst of discontent. *Exit.*

CLOTEN I'll be reveng'd.
"His meanest garment!" Well. *Exit.*

SCENE IV

Enter Posthumus and Philario.

POSTHUMUS
Fear it not, sir. I would I were so sure
To win the King as I am bold her honor 2
Will remain hers.

PHILARIO What means do you make to him? 3

POSTHUMUS
Not any, but abide the change of time,
Quake in the present winter's state, and wish
That warmer days would come. In these fear'd
hopes 6
I barely gratify your love; they failing, 7
I must die much your debtor.

PHILARIO
Your very goodness and your company
O'erpays all I can do. By this, your King 10
Hath heard of great Augustus; Caius Lucius
Will do 's commission throughly. And I think
He'll grant the tribute, send th' arrearages, 13
Or look upon our Romans, whose remembrance 14
Is yet fresh in their grief.

POSTHUMUS I do believe, 15
Statist though I am none, nor like to be, 16
That this will prove a war; and you shall hear
The legions now in Gallia sooner landed
In our not-fearing Britain than have tidings
Of any penny tribute paid. Our countrymen
Are men more order'd than when Julius Caesar 21
Smil'd at their lack of skill, but found their courage
Worthy his frowning at. Their discipline,
Now mingled with their courages, will make known
To their approvers they are people such 25
That mend upon the world.

Enter Iachimo.

PHILARIO See! Iachimo! 26

POSTHUMUS
The swiftest harts have posted you by land, 27
And winds of all the corners kiss'd your sails, 28
To make your vessel nimble.

PHILARIO Welcome, sir.

POSTHUMUS
I hope the briefness of your answer made 30
The speediness of your return.

IACHIMO Your lady
Is one of the fairest that I have look'd upon.

POSTHUMUS
And therewithal the best, or let her beauty
Look thorough a casement to allure false hearts

124 note distinction **125 hilding for a livery** good-for-nothing fellow fit only for wearing a servant's uniform. **cloth** dress, livery **126 pantler** pantry-servant. **not** not even **129 wert dignified** would be elevated in dignity **130–131 if . . . virtues** i.e., if you were given a position corresponding to your innate qualities **133 preferr'd** advanced. **south-fog** (The south wind was supposed to be laden with poisonous vapors and diseases.) **135 of** by **136 clipp'd** embraced **137 respect** regard. **above thee** on your head **141 sprited with** haunted by **144 'Shrew me** beshrew me **153 action** action at law **155 good lady** i.e., patroness. (Said ironically.) **conceive** believe, think

II.iv. Location: Rome. Philario's house.
2 bold confident **3 means** approach. **him** i.e., the King **6 fear'd** mixed with fear **7 gratify** repay **10 this** this time **13 He'll** i.e., Cymbeline will. **arrearages** arrears, parts of the tribute due but unpaid **14 Or look** before he will look (?) or else look(?) **15 their** i.e., the Britons', or, caused by the Romans **16 Statist** statesman **21 more order'd** better disciplined and governed **25 their approvers** those who test their courage **26 mend . . . world** improve their reputation **27 harts** deer. (Proverbially swift runners.) **posted** sped **28 corners** quarters **30 your answer** the answer you were given

And be false with them.
IACHIMO Here are letters for you.
[*Gives letter.*]
POSTHUMUS
Their tenor good, I trust.
IACHIMO 'Tis very like.
PHILARIO
Was Caius Lucius in the Britain court
When you were there?
IACHIMO He was expected then,
But not approach'd.
POSTHUMUS
All is well yet.
Sparkles this stone as it was wont, or is 't not
Too dull for your good wearing? [*Indicates ring.*]
IACHIMO If I have lost it, 42
I should have lost the worth of it in gold.
I'll make a journey twice as far, t' enjoy
A second night of such sweet shortness which
Was mine in Britain, for the ring is won.
POSTHUMUS
The stone's too hard to come by.
IACHIMO Not a whit,
Your lady being so easy.
POSTHUMUS Make not, sir,
Your loss your sport. I hope you know that we
Must not continue friends.
IACHIMO Good sir, we must,
If you keep covenant. Had I not brought
The knowledge of your mistress home, I grant 52
We were to question farther; but I now 53
Profess myself the winner of her honor,
Together with your ring, and not the wronger
Of her or you, having proceeded but
By both your wills.
POSTHUMUS If you can make 't apparent
That you have tasted her in bed, my hand
And ring is yours; if not, the foul opinion
You had of her pure honor gains or loses
Your sword or mine, or masterless leave both 61
To who shall find them.
IACHIMO Sir, my circumstances, 62
Being so near the truth as I will make them,
Must first induce you to believe; whose strength
I will confirm with oath, which I doubt not
You'll give me leave to spare, when you shall find 66
You need it not.
POSTHUMUS Proceed.
IACHIMO First, her bedchamber—
Where, I confess, I slept not, but profess
Had that was well worth watching—it was hang'd 69
With tapestry of silk and silver; the story
Proud Cleopatra, when she met her Roman,
And Cydnus swell'd above the banks, or for 72
The press of boats or pride. A piece of work
So bravely done, so rich, that it did strive 74
In workmanship and value, which I wonder'd 75
Could be so rarely and exactly wrought,
Since the true life on 't was—
POSTHUMUS This is true;
And this you might have heard of here, by me,
Or by some other.
IACHIMO More particulars
Must justify my knowledge.
POSTHUMUS So they must,
Or do your honor injury.
IACHIMO The chimney
Is south the chamber, and the chimney-piece 82
Chaste Dian bathing. Never saw I figures
So likely to report themselves. The cutter 84
Was as another nature, dumb; outwent her, 85
Motion and breath left out.
POSTHUMUS This is a thing 86
Which you might from relation likewise reap, 87
Being, as it is, much spoke of.
IACHIMO The roof o' th' chamber
With golden cherubins is fretted. Her andirons— 89
I had forgot them—were two winking Cupids 90
Of silver, each on one foot standing, nicely
Depending on their brands.
POSTHUMUS This is her honor! 92
Let it be granted you have seen all this—and praise
Be given to your remembrance—the description
Of what is in her chamber nothing saves 95
The wager you have laid.
IACHIMO Then, if you can
Be pale, I beg but leave to air this jewel. See!
[*Shows the bracelet.*]
And now 'tis up again. It must be married 98
To that your diamond; I'll keep them.
POSTHUMUS Jove!
Once more let me behold it. Is it that
Which I left with her?
IACHIMO Sir—I thank her—that.
She stripp'd it from her arm; I see her yet;
Her pretty action did outsell her gift, 103
And yet enrich'd it too. She gave it me,
And said she priz'd it once.
POSTHUMUS
May be she pluck'd it off
To send it me.
IACHIMO She writes so to you, doth she?
POSTHUMUS
O, no, no, no! 'Tis true. Here, take this too;
[*Gives the ring.*]
It is a basilisk unto mine eye, 109
Kills me to look on 't. Let there be no honor
Where there is beauty; truth, where semblance; love,

42 s.d. Indicates ring (The ring possibly is in the custody of Philario as official of the wager; although Posthumus appears to have it himself at l. 108, he may then take it from Philario and give it to Iachimo.) **52 knowledge** i.e., carnal knowledge **53 question** dispute, i.e., settle matters by a duel. **61 leave** may it leave **62 circumstances** detailed observations **66 spare** leave out **69 that** that which. **watching** remaining awake (for) **72 Cydnus** a river in Cilicia, or modern-day southern Turkey, the scene of the meeting of Antony and Cleopatra. (See *Antony and Cleopatra,* II.ii.201–243.) **or for** either because of

74 bravely handsomely **75 value** i.e., costly materials **82 chimney-piece** sculptured mantelpiece **84 So . . . themselves** so like what they purported to represent **84–85 cutter . . . dumb** sculptor rivaled nature in creative power, though creating works unable to speak. **her** i.e., nature **86 left out** excepted **87 relation** hearsay, second hand **89 fretted** adorned with carved or embossed work in decorative patterns **90 winking** i.e., blind **92 Depending** leaning. **brands** torches **95 nothing** not at all **98 up** put up, pocketed **103 outsell** exceed in value **109 basilisk** fabulous serpent or dragon whose look was fatal

Where there's another man. The vows of women
Of no more bondage be to where they are made
Than they are to their virtues, which is nothing.
O, above measure false!

PHILARIO
Have patience, sir,
And take your ring again; 'tis not yet won.
It may be probable she lost it; or
Who knows if one her women, being corrupted,
Hath stol'n it from her?

POSTHUMUS
Very true,
And so, I hope, he came by 't. Back my ring!
[Takes back the ring.]
Render to me some corporal sign about her,
More evident than this; for this was stol'n.

IACHIMO
By Jupiter, I had it from her arm.

POSTHUMUS
Hark you, he swears; by Jupiter he swears.
'Tis true—nay, keep the ring—'tis true. I am sure
She would not lose it. Her attendants are
All sworn and honorable. They induc'd to steal it?
And by a stranger? No, he hath enjoy'd her.
The cognizance of her incontinency
Is this. She hath bought the name of whore thus dearly.
There, take thy hire, and all the fiends of hell
Divide themselves between you! *[Gives ring again.]*

PHILARIO
Sir, be patient.
This is not strong enough to be believ'd
Of one persuaded well of.

POSTHUMUS
Never talk on 't;
She hath been colted by him.

IACHIMO
If you seek
For further satisfying, under her breast—
Worthy the pressing—lies a mole, right proud
Of that most delicate lodging. By my life,
I kiss'd it, and it gave me present hunger
To feed again, though full. You do remember
This stain upon her?

POSTHUMUS
Ay, and it doth confirm
Another stain, as big as hell can hold,
Were there no more but it.

IACHIMO
Will you hear more?

POSTHUMUS
Spare your arithmetic; never count the turns.
Once, and a million!

IACHIMO
I'll be sworn—

POSTHUMUS
No swearing.
If you will swear you have not done 't, you lie,
And I will kill thee if thou dost deny
Thou'st made me cuckold.

IACHIMO
I'll deny nothing.

POSTHUMUS
O, that I had her here, to tear her limb-meal!
I will go there and do 't, i' th' court, before
Her father. I'll do something— *Exit.*

PHILARIO
Quite besides
The government of patience! You have won.
Let's follow him, and pervert the present wrath
He hath against himself.

IACHIMO
With all my heart. *Exeunt.*

[SCENE V]

Enter Posthumus.

POSTHUMUS
Is there no way for men to be but women
Must be half-workers? We are all bastards,
And that most venerable man which I
Did call my father was I know not where
When I was stamp'd. Some coiner with his tools
Made me a counterfeit; yet my mother seem'd
The Dian of that time. So doth my wife
The nonpareil of this. O, vengeance, vengeance!
Me of my lawful pleasure she restrain'd
And pray'd me oft forbearance; did it with
A pudency so rosy the sweet view on 't
Might well have warm'd old Saturn, that I thought her
As chaste as unsunn'd snow. O, all the devils!
This yellow Iachimo, in an hour, was 't not?
Or less? At first? Perchance he spoke not, but,
Like a full-acorn'd boar, a German one,
Cried "O!" and mounted; found no opposition
But what he look'd for should oppose and she
Should from encounter guard. Could I find out
The woman's part in me! For there's no motion
That tends to vice in man but I affirm
It is the woman's part. Be it lying, note it,
The woman's; flattering, hers; deceiving, hers;
Lust and rank thoughts, hers, hers; revenges, hers;
Ambitions, covetings, change of prides, disdain,
Nice longing, slanders, mutability,
All faults that have a name, nay, that hell knows,
Why, hers, in part or all, but rather all.
For even to vice
They are not constant, but are changing still
One vice but of a minute old for one
Not half so old as that. I'll write against them,
Detest them, curse them. Yet 'tis greater skill
In a true hate to pray they have their will;
The very devils cannot plague them better. *Exit.*

112 The vows i.e., let the vows **113 bondage** obligation. **where** i.e., the men to whom **118 one her** one of her **130 cognizance** mark or token by which a thing is recognized, as a servant is identified by his livery and identifying mark **135 persuaded well of** well thought of **136 colted** enjoyed sexually **150 limb-meal** limb from limb

152 besides beyond **154 pervert** divert

II.v. Location: Philario's house, as before.
1 be exist **8 nonpareil** one that has no equal **11 pudency** modesty **14 yellow** sallow **16 full-acorn'd** full of acorns, favorite food of boars. (In German, *eichel*, acorn, also means *penis* because of its glans-like shape.) **20 motion** impulse **25 change of prides** varying vanities (in dress, etc.) **26 Nice** fastidious, wanton. **mutability** inconstancy **32 write against** denounce **33 skill** reason

ACT III • SCENE I

Enter in state, Cymbeline, Queen, Cloten, and Lords at one door, and at another, Caius Lucius and Attendants.

CYMBELINE
Now say, what would Augustus Caesar with us?
LUCIUS
When Julius Caesar, whose remembrance yet
Lives in men's eyes, and will to ears and tongues
Be theme and hearing ever, was in this Britain
And conquer'd it, Cassibelan, thine uncle—
Famous in Caesar's praises no whit less
Than in his feats deserving it—for him
And his succession granted Rome a tribute,
Yearly three thousand pounds, which by thee lately
Is left untender'd.
QUEEN And, to kill the marvel,
Shall be so ever.
CLOTEN There be many Caesars,
Ere such another Julius. Britain's a world
By itself, and we will nothing pay
For wearing our own noses.
QUEEN That opportunity
Which then they had to take from 's, to resume
We have again. Remember, sir, my liege,
The kings your ancestors, together with
The natural bravery of your isle, which stands
As Neptune's park, ribb'd and paled in
With rocks unscalable and roaring waters,
With sands that will not bear your enemies' boats,
But suck them up to th' topmast. A kind of conquest
Caesar made here, but made not here his brag
Of "Came and saw and overcame." With shame—
The first that ever touch'd him—he was carried
From off our coast, twice beaten; and his shipping,
Poor ignorant baubles, on our terrible seas,
Like egg-shells mov'd upon their surges, crack'd
As easily 'gainst our rocks. For joy whereof
The fam'd Cassibelan, who was once at point—
O giglot fortune!—to master Caesar's sword,
Made Lud's town with rejoicing fires bright
And Britons strut with courage.

CLOTEN Come, there's no more tribute to be paid. Our kingdom is stronger than it was at that time; and, as I said, there is no moe such Caesars. Other of them may have crook'd noses, but to owe such straight arms, none.

CYMBELINE
Son, let your mother end.

CLOTEN We have yet many among us can gripe as hard as Cassibelan. I do not say I am one; but I have a hand. Why tribute? Why should we pay tribute? If Caesar can hide the sun from us with a blanket, or put the moon in his pocket, we will pay him tribute for light; else, sir, no more tribute, pray you now.

CYMBELINE
You must know,
Till the injurious Romans did extort
This tribute from us, we were free. Caesar's ambition,
Which swell'd so much that it did almost stretch
The sides o' th' world, against all color here
Did put the yoke upon 's; which to shake off
Becomes a warlike people, whom we reckon
Ourselves to be. We do say then to Caesar,
Our ancestor was that Mulmutius which
Ordain'd our laws, whose use the sword of Caesar
Hath too much mangled, whose repair and franchise
Shall, by the power we hold, be our good deed,
Though Rome be therefore angry. Mulmutius made our laws,
Who was the first of Britain which did put
His brows within a golden crown and call'd
Himself a king.
LUCIUS I am sorry, Cymbeline,
That I am to pronounce Augustus Caesar—
Caesar, that hath moe kings his servants than
Thyself domestic officers—thine enemy.
Receive it from me, then: war and confusion
In Caesar's name pronounce I 'gainst thee. Look
For fury not to be resisted. Thus defied,
I thank thee for myself.
CYMBELINE Thou art welcome, Caius.
Thy Caesar knighted me; my youth I spent
Much under him. Of him I gather'd honor,
Which he to seek of me again, perforce,
Behooves me keep at utterance. I am perfect
That the Pannonians and Dalmatians for
Their liberties are now in arms, a precedent
Which not to read would show the Britons cold.
So Caesar shall not find them.
LUCIUS Let proof speak.

CLOTEN His Majesty bids you welcome. Make pastime with us a day or two, or longer. If you seek us afterwards in other terms, you shall find us in our saltwater girdle. If you beat us out of it, it is yours; if you fall in the adventure, our crows shall fare the better for you, and there's an end.

LUCIUS
So, sir.
CYMBELINE
I know your master's pleasure and he mine.
All the remain is "Welcome!" *Exeunt.*

III.i. Location: Britain. Cymbeline's palace.
10 kill the marvel end the surprise (by making nonpayment a regular practice) **15–16 to resume . . . again** we now have the opportunity to take it back **19 ribb'd** enclosed. **paled** fenced **27 ignorant** silly, unskilled **30 Cassibelan** (The incident referred to is recorded of Nennius, brother of Cassibelan, in Holinshed.) **30–31 at point . . . to master** on the point . . . of mastering **31 giglot** lewd, wanton **32 Lud's town** London (supposedly named after King Lud, Cymbeline's grandfather) **36 moe** more **37 owe** own

40 gripe grasp (a sword) **47 injurious** insolent **50 against all color** in defiance of all rightful claim **56 whose . . . franchise** the repair and free exercise of which laws **67 Thus defied** you having been thus defied **71 he to seek** since he seeks it **72 keep at utterance** defend to the last extremity. **perfect** well aware **75 cold** lacking spirit **85 remain** remainder (to be said)

SCENE II

Enter Pisanio, reading of a letter.

PISANIO
How? Of adultery? Wherefore write you not
What monsters her accuse? Leonatus,
O master, what a strange infection
Is fall'n into thy ear! What false Italian,
As poisonous-tongu'd as handed, hath prevail'd
On thy too ready hearing? Disloyal? No.
She's punish'd for her truth, and undergoes,
More goddess-like than wife-like, such assaults
As would take in some virtue. O my master,
Thy mind to her is now as low as were
Thy fortunes. How? That I should murder her,
Upon the love and truth and vows which I
Have made to thy command? I, her? Her blood?
If it be so to do good service, never
Let me be counted serviceable. How look I,
That I should seem to lack humanity
So much as this fact comes to? [*Reads.*] "Do 't. The letter
That I have sent her, by her own command
Shall give thee opportunity." O damn'd paper,
Black as the ink that's on thee! Senseless bauble,
Art thou a feodary for this act, and look'st
So virgin-like without? Lo, here she comes.

Enter Imogen.

I am ignorant in what I am commanded.

IMOGEN
How now, Pisanio?

PISANIO
Madam, here is a letter from my lord.

IMOGEN [*Taking the Letter*]
Who, thy lord? That is my lord Leonatus?
O, learn'd indeed were that astronomer
That knew the stars as I his characters;
He'd lay the future open. You good gods,
Let what is here contain'd relish of love,
Of my lord's health, of his content—yet not
That we two are asunder; let that grieve him;
Some griefs are med'cinable; that is one of them,
For it doth physic love—of his content
All but in that! Good wax, thy leave. [*She breaks the seal.*] Blest be
You bees that make these locks of counsel! Lovers
And men in dangerous bonds pray not alike;
Though forfeiters you cast in prison, yet
You clasp young Cupid's tables. Good news, gods!
[*Reads.*] "Justice, and your father's wrath, should he take me in his dominion, could not be so cruel to me as you, O the dearest of creatures, would even renew me with your eyes. Take notice that I am in Cambria, at Milford-Haven. What your own love will out of this advise you, follow. So he wishes you all happiness that remains loyal to his vow, and your increasing in love. Leonatus Posthumus."
O, for a horse with wings! Hear'st thou, Pisanio?
He is at Milford-Haven. Read, and tell me
How far 'tis thither. If one of mean affairs
May plod it in a week, why may not I
Glide thither in a day? Then, true Pisanio,
Who long'st like me to see thy lord, who long'st—
O, let me bate—but not like me, yet long'st,
But in a fainter kind—O, not like me,
For mine's beyond beyond; say, and speak thick—
Love's counselor should fill the bores of hearing,
To th' smothering of the sense—how far it is
To this same blessed Milford. And by th' way
Tell me how Wales was made so happy as
T' inherit such a haven. But first of all,
How we may steal from hence, and for the gap
That we shall make in time from our hence-going
And our return, to excuse. But first, how get hence?
Why should excuse be born or ere begot?
We'll talk of that hereafter. Prithee speak,
How many score of miles may we well rid
'Twixt hour and hour?

PISANIO
One score 'twixt sun and sun,
Madam, 's enough for you—and too much too.

IMOGEN
Why, one that rode to 's execution, man,
Could never go so slow. I have heard of riding wagers,
Where horses have been nimbler than the sands
That run i' th' clock's behalf. But this is fool'ry.
Go bid my woman feign a sickness, say
She'll home to her father; and provide me presently
A riding-suit, no costlier than would fit
A franklin's huswife.

PISANIO
Madam, you're best consider.

IMOGEN
I see before me, man. Nor here, nor here,
Nor what ensues, but have a fog in them,
That I cannot look through. Away, I prithee!
Do as I bid thee. There's no more to say.
Accessible is none but Milford way.

Exeunt [severally].

III.ii. Location: Britain. Cymbeline's palace.
7 truth fidelity. **undergoes** i.e., withstands **9 take in** cause to yield **10 to** compared to **17 fact** deed **20 Senseless bauble** trifle incapable of feeling **21 feodary** accomplice **23 am ignorant** will pretend not to know **27 astronomer** astrologer **28 characters** handwriting **30 relish** taste **31 not** i.e., not content **33 med'cinable** curative, health-giving **34 physic** make healthy, strong **36 locks of counsel** waxen seals enclosing confidential matters **37 in dangerous bonds** under contracts risking penalties (which are similarly sealed with wax)

38 forfeiters those who forfeit their bonds **39 clasp** seal (with wax). **tables** writing tablets, used here for love letters **42 as** but that. (The letter, however, is studiously ambiguous, and suggests also that no one can be so cruel as she.) **43 Cambria** Wales **50 mean affairs** ordinary business **54 bate** reduce in amount, modify **56 thick** many words quickly **58 To . . . sense** i.e., to the point of overwhelming the sense of hearing **65 or ere begot** i.e., even before the need for it arises **67 rid** cover, consume **71 riding** racing **73 i' . . . behalf** i.e., doing the service of a clock or an hourglass **77 franklin's** yeoman's. (A franklin was a farmer who owned his own land but was not of noble birth.) **you're best** you had better **78 Nor . . . here** (The actor gestures: not to this side, not to that.) **79 ensues** happens later (Imogen can only look directly ahead to Milford-Haven, nowhere else and not beyond.)

SCENE III

Enter [from the cave] Belarius; Guiderius, and Arviragus [following].

BELARIUS
A goodly day not to keep house, with such
Whose roof 's as low as ours! Stoop, boys; this gate
Instructs you how t' adore the heavens and bows you
To a morning's holy office. The gates of monarchs
Are arch'd so high that giants may jet through
And keep their impious turbans on, without
Good morrow to the sun. Hail, thou fair heaven!
We house i' th' rock, yet use thee not so hardly
As prouder livers do.

GUIDERIUS
Hail, heaven!

ARVIRAGUS
Hail, heaven!

BELARIUS
Now for our mountain sport. Up to yond hill;
Your legs are young. I'll tread these flats. Consider,
When you above perceive me like a crow,
That it is place which lessens and sets off,
And you may then revolve what tales I have told you
Of courts, of princes, of the tricks in war.
This service is not service, so being done,
But being so allow'd. To apprehend thus
Draws us a profit from all things we see;
And often, to our comfort, shall we find
The sharded beetle in a safer hold
Than is the full-wing'd eagle. O, this life
Is nobler than attending for a check,
Richer than doing nothing for a bauble,
Prouder than rustling in unpaid-for silk;
Such gain the cap of him that makes him fine,
Yet keeps his book uncross'd. No life to ours.

GUIDERIUS
Out of your proof you speak. We poor unfledg'd
Have never wing'd from view o' th' nest, nor know not
What air's from home. Hap'ly this life is best,
If quiet life be best, sweeter to you
That have a sharper known, well corresponding
With your stiff age; but unto us it is
A cell of ignorance, traveling abed,
A prison, or a debtor that not dares
To stride a limit.

ARVIRAGUS
What should we speak of
When we are old as you? When we shall hear
The rain and wind beat dark December, how,
In this our pinching cave, shall we discourse
The freezing hours away? We have seen nothing.
We are beastly, subtle as the fox for prey,
Like warlike as the wolf for what we eat;
Our valor is to chase what flies. Our cage
We make a choir, as doth the prison'd bird,
And sing our bondage freely.

BELARIUS
How you speak!
Did you but know the city's usuries
And felt them knowingly; the art o' th' court,
As hard to leave as keep; whose top to climb
Is certain falling, or so slipp'ry that
The fear's as bad as falling; the toil o' th' war,
A pain that only seems to seek out danger
I' th' name of fame and honor, which dies i' th' search
And hath as oft a sland'rous epitaph
As record of fair act; nay, many times,
Doth ill deserve by doing well; what's worse,
Must curtsy at the censure. O boys, this story
The world may read in me. My body's mark'd
With Roman swords, and my report was once
First with the best of note. Cymbeline lov'd me,
And when a soldier was the theme, my name
Was not far off. Then was I as a tree
Whose boughs did bend with fruit. But in one night,
A storm or robbery, call it what you will,
Shook down my mellow hangings, nay, my leaves,
And left me bare to weather.

GUIDERIUS
Uncertain favor!

BELARIUS
My fault being nothing—as I have told you oft—
But that two villains, whose false oaths prevail'd
Before my perfect honor, swore to Cymbeline
I was confederate with the Romans. So
Follow'd my banishment, and this twenty years
This rock and these demesnes have been my world,
Where I have liv'd at honest freedom, paid
More pious debts to heaven than in all
The fore-end of my time. But up to th' mountains!
This is not hunters' language. He that strikes
The venison first shall be the lord o' th' feast;
To him the other two shall minister,
And we will fear no poison, which attends
In place of greater state. I'll meet you in the valleys.
Exeunt [Guiderius and Arviragus].
How hard it is to hide the sparks of nature!
These boys know little they are sons to th' King,
Nor Cymbeline dreams that they are alive.
They think they are mine; and though train'd up thus meanly
I' th' cave wherein they bow, their thoughts do hit
The roofs of palaces, and nature prompts them
In simple and low things to prince it much
Beyond the trick of others. This Polydore,
The heir of Cymbeline and Britain, who

III.iii. Location: Wales. Before the cave of Belarius.
1 keep house stay at home **3 bows you** makes you bow **4 holy office** i.e., morning prayer **5 jet** walk pompously, strut **12 like a crow** appearing through distance as small as a crow **13 place** position. **sets off** enhances **16–17 This . . . allow'd** i.e., any act of service at court is valued not for itself, but is valued by the lord as proof of his greatness in acknowledging or accepting such tokens of submission **20 sharded** covered with shards or the sheaths of insects' wings. **hold** stronghold **22 attending . . . check** doing service (at court) only to be rewarded with a rebuke **24 unpaid-for** for which the wearer is in debt to his tailor **25 gain . . . fine** win the respectful greeting of him who dresses elegantly, or of his tailor **26 keeps . . . uncross'd** does nothing to cancel his record of debts. **to** compared to **27 proof** experience **29 What . . . home** what the air is like away from home. **Hap'ly** perhaps **33 abed** i.e., in imagination only, in dreams **35 stride a limit** overpass a bound (where he will be liable for arrest)

41 Like alike, equally **50 pain** labor **54 deserve** earn **58 note** distinction, importance **63 hangings** hanging fruit **70 demesnes** domains, regions **73 fore-end** earlier part **85 prince it** play the prince **86 trick** manner

The King his father call'd Guiderius—Jove!
When on my three-foot stool I sit and tell
The warlike feats I have done, his spirits fly out
Into my story; say, "Thus mine enemy fell,
And thus I set my foot on 's neck," even then
The princely blood flows in his cheek, he sweats,
Strains his young nerves and puts himself in posture 94
That acts my words. The younger brother, Cadwal,
Once Arviragus, in as like a figure 96
Strikes life into my speech and shows much more
His own conceiving. [*Sounds of hunting are heard.*]—
Hark, the game is rous'd!—
O Cymbeline, heaven and my conscience knows
Thou didst unjustly banish me; whereon,
At three and two years old, I stole these babes,
Thinking to bar thee of succession, as
Thou refts me of my lands. Euriphile,
Thou wast their nurse; they took thee for their mother,
And every day do honor to her grave.
Myself, Belarius, that am Morgan call'd,
They take for natural father.—The game is up. 107
Exit.

SCENE IV

Enter Pisanio and Imogen.

IMOGEN
Thou told'st me, when we came from horse, the place 1
Was near at hand. Ne'er long'd my mother so
To see me first, as I have now. Pisanio, man, 3
Where is Posthumus? What is in thy mind,
That makes thee stare thus? Wherefore breaks that sigh
From th' inward of thee? One but painted thus
Would be interpreted a thing perplex'd
Beyond self-explication. Put thyself
Into a havior of less fear, ere wildness 9
Vanquish my staider senses. What's the matter?
[*He offers her a letter.*]
Why tender'st thou that paper to me, with
A look untender? If 't be summer news,
Smile to 't before; if winterly, thou need'st
But keep that count'nance still. My husband's hand?
That drug-damn'd Italy hath outcraftied him, 15
And he's at some hard point. Speak, man. Thy tongue
May take off some extremity, which to read 17
Would be even mortal to me.

PISANIO
Please you, read,
And you shall find me, wretched man, a thing
The most disdain'd of fortune.

IMOGEN (*Reads*) "Thy mistress, Pisanio, hath play'd the strumpet in my bed; the testimonies whereof lies bleeding in me. I speak not out of weak surmises, but from proof as strong as my grief and as certain as I expect my revenge. That part thou, Pisanio, must act for me, if thy faith be not tainted with the breach of hers. Let thine own hands take away her life. I shall give thee opportunity at Milford-Haven—she hath my letter for the purpose—where, if thou fear to strike and to make me certain it is done, thou art the pander to her dishonor and equally to me disloyal."

PISANIO
What shall I need to draw my sword? The paper
Hath cut her throat already. No, 'tis slander,
Whose edge is sharper than the sword, whose tongue
Outvenoms all the worms of Nile, whose breath 35
Rides on the posting winds and doth belie 36
All corners of the world. Kings, queens, and states, 37
Maids, matrons, nay, the secrets of the grave
This viperous slander enters.—What cheer, madam?

IMOGEN
False to his bed? What is it to be false?
To lie in watch there and to think on him? 41
To weep 'twixt clock and clock? If sleep charge nature, 42
To break it with a fearful dream of him 43
And cry myself awake? That's false to 's bed, is it?

PISANIO
Alas, good lady!

IMOGEN
I false? Thy conscience witness! Iachimo,
Thou didst accuse him of incontinency.
Thou then look'dst like a villain; now methinks
Thy favor's good enough. Some jay of Italy, 49
Whose mother was her painting, hath betray'd him. 50
Poor I am stale, a garment out of fashion,
And, for I am richer than to hang by th' walls, 52
I must be ripp'd. To pieces with me! O,
Men's vows are women's traitors! All good seeming,
By thy revolt, O husband, shall be thought 55
Put on for villainy; not born where 't grows, 56
But worn a bait for ladies.

PISANIO
Good madam, hear me.

IMOGEN
True honest men being heard, like false Aeneas, 58
Were in his time thought false, and Sinon's weeping 59
Did scandal many a holy tear, took pity 60
From most true wretchedness. So thou, Posthumus, 61
Wilt lay the leaven on all proper men; 62
Goodly and gallant shall be false and perjur'd 63
From thy great fail.—Come, fellow, be thou honest; 64

94 nerves sinews **96 in . . . figure** acting his part equally well **107 up** roused

III.iv. Location: Wales. Country near Milford-Haven.
1 came from horse dismounted **3 have** i.e., have longing to see Posthumus **9 of less fear** less frightening **15 drug-damn'd** condemned for its drugs and poisons. **outcraftied** outwitted **17 take . . . extremity** reduce somewhat the shock

35 worms serpents **36 posting** hastening. **belie** spread lies throughout **37 states** statesmen **41 in watch** awake **42 'twixt . . . clock** from hour to hour. **charge nature** i.e., overcome wakefulness **43 fearful dream of him** dream fearful about his safety **49 favor's** countenance is. **jay** i.e., flashy or light woman **50 Whose . . . painting** i.e., who owed her beauty to cosmetics **52 for . . . than** because I am too fine **55 revolt** inconstancy **56 born** i.e., innate **58 Aeneas** (Thought of as the pattern of faithless love because of his desertion of Dido.) **59 Sinon** Greek who by his guile persuaded the Trojans to introduce within the walls of Troy the wooden horse filled with armed men **60 scandal** bring scandal to, discredit **60–61 took pity From** prevented the bestowing of well-deserved pity upon **62 lay . . . men** take credit away from all well-deserving men (just as sour *leaven* causes dough to ferment and spoil) **63 be** i.e., be thought **64 fail** fault, offense

Do thou thy master's bidding. When thou
see'st him,
A little witness my obedience. Look, 66
[Draws sword and offers it to him.]
I draw the sword myself. Take it, and hit
The innocent mansion of my love, my heart.
Fear not; 'tis empty of all things but grief.
Thy master is not there, who was indeed
The riches of it. Do his bidding, strike.
Thou mayst be valiant in a better cause,
But now thou seem'st a coward.

PISANIO
Hence, vile instrument!
[He rejects the sword.]
Thou shalt not damn my hand.

IMOGEN
Why, I must die;
And if I do not by thy hand, thou art
No servant of thy master's. Against self-slaughter
There is a prohibition so divine
That cravens my weak hand. Come, here's my heart. 78
Something's afore 't. Soft, soft! We'll no defense; 79
Obedient as the scabbard. What is here? *[Takes letters from her bodice.]* 80
The scriptures of the loyal Leonatus, 81
All turn'd to heresy? Away, away,
Corrupters of my faith! *[Throws away letters.]* You
shall no more
Be stomachers to my heart. Thus may poor fools 84
Believe false teachers. Though those that are betray'd
Do feel the treason sharply, yet the traitor
Stands in worse case of woe.
And thou, Posthumus, thou that didst set up 88
My disobedience 'gainst the King my father
And make me put into contempt the suits
Of princely fellows, shalt hereafter find
It is no act of common passage, but 92
A strain of rareness; and I grieve myself 93
To think, when thou shalt be disedg'd by her 94
That now thou tirest on, how thy memory 95
Will then be pang'd by me. Prithee, dispatch. 96
The lamb entreats the butcher. Where's thy knife?
Thou art too slow to do thy master's bidding,
When I desire it too.

PISANIO
O gracious lady,
Since I receiv'd command to do this business
I have not slept one wink.

IMOGEN
Do 't, and to bed then.

PISANIO
I'll wake mine eyeballs blind first.

IMOGEN
Wherefore then 102
Didst undertake it? Why hast thou abus'd
So many miles with a pretense? This place?
Mine action and thine own? Our horses' labor?
The time inviting thee? The perturb'd court,
For my being absent? Whereunto I never
Purpose return. Why hast thou gone so far,
To be unbent when thou hast ta'en thy stand, 109
Th' elected deer before thee?

PISANIO
But to win time 110
To lose so bad employment, in the which 111
I have consider'd of a course. Good lady,
Hear me with a patience.

IMOGEN
Talk thy tongue weary, speak.
I have heard I am a strumpet, and mine ear,
Therein false struck, can take no greater wound, 115
Nor tent to bottom that. But speak.

PISANIO
Then, madam, 116
I thought you would not back again.

IMOGEN
Most like, 117
Bringing me here to kill me.

PISANIO
Not so, neither.
But if I were as wise as honest, then
My purpose would prove well. It cannot be
But that my master is abus'd. Some villain, 121
Ay, and singular in his art, hath done 122
You both this cursed injury.

IMOGEN
Some Roman courtezan.

PISANIO
No, on my life.
I'll give but notice you are dead, and send him
Some bloody sign of it, for 'tis commanded
I should do so. You shall be miss'd at court,
And that will well confirm it.

IMOGEN
Why, good fellow,
What shall I do the while? Where bide? How live?
Or in my life what comfort, when I am
Dead to my husband?

PISANIO
If you'll back to th' court—

IMOGEN
No court, no father, nor no more ado
With that harsh, noble, simple nothing,
That Cloten, whose love-suit hath been to me
As fearful as a siege.

PISANIO
If not at court,
Then not in Britain must you bide.

IMOGEN
Where then?
Hath Britain all the sun that shines? Day, night,
Are they not but in Britain? I' th' world's volume
Our Britain seems as of it, but not in 't; 139
In a great pool a swan's nest. Prithee think
There's livers out of Britain.

PISANIO
I am most glad 141
You think of other place. Th' ambassador,
Lucius the Roman, comes to Milford-Haven
Tomorrow. Now, if you could wear a mind
Dark as your fortune is, and but disguise 145
That which, t' appear itself, must not yet be 146
But by self-danger, you should tread a course
Pretty and full of view; yea, happily, near 148

66 A little witness testify somewhat to **78 cravens** renders cowardly **79 Something's** i.e., Posthumus' letter is **80 Obedient** i.e., as willing to receive the sword **81 scriptures** writings, letters (with a pun on *Holy Scriptures*) **84 stomachers** ornamental coverings for the breast **88 set up** incite, encourage **92–93 It . . . rareness** that my choice (of you) was no act of a common sort but a rare trait **94 disedg'd** surfeited **95 thou tirest on** you tear or devour (as a bird of prey) **96 pang'd** pained, tortured **102 wake . . . blind** remain awake until I go blind

109 unbent with unbent bow (and thus refusing to shoot) **110 elected** chosen **111 which** i.e., which time **115 take** receive **116 tent . . . that** probe that wound to the bottom **117 back** go back (to court). **like** likely **121 abus'd** deceived **122 singular** unexcelled **139 as . . . in 't** i.e., as part of it but a small and relatively insignificant part, on the periphery **141 livers** persons living **145 Dark** obscure, mean **146 That** i.e., the fact that you are a woman. **appear itself** reveal itself for what it truly is **148 Pretty . . . view** advantageous and promising. **happily** haply, perhaps

The residence of Posthumus, so nigh at least
That, though his actions were not visible, yet
Report should render him hourly to your ear
As truly as he moves.

IMOGEN
O, for such means!
Though peril to my modesty, not death on 't,
I would adventure.

PISANIO
Well, then, here's the point.
You must forget to be a woman, change
Command into obedience, fear and niceness—
The handmaids of all women, or, more truly,
Woman it pretty self—into a waggish courage;
Ready in gibes, quick-answer'd, saucy, and
As quarrelous as the weasel. Nay, you must
Forget that rarest treasure of your cheek,
Exposing it—but, O, the harder heart!
Alack, no remedy—to the greedy touch
Of common-kissing Titan, and forget
Your laborsome and dainty trims, wherein
You made great Juno angry.

IMOGEN
Nay, be brief.
I see into thy end, and am almost
A man already.

PISANIO
First, make yourself but like one.
Forethinking this, I have already fit—
'Tis in my cloak-bag—doublet, hat, hose, all
That answer to them. Would you in their serving,
And with what imitation you can borrow
From youth of such a season, 'fore noble Lucius
Present yourself, desire his service, tell him
Wherein you're happy—which will make him
know,
If that his head have ear in music—doubtless
With joy he will embrace you, for he's honorable,
And, doubling that, most holy. Your means abroad,
You have me, rich; and I will never fail
Beginning nor supplyment. [*Gives her cloak-bag.*]

IMOGEN
Thou art all the comfort
The gods will diet me with. Prithee away.
There's more to be consider'd; but we'll even
All that good time will give us. This attempt
I am soldier to, and will abide it with
A prince's courage. Away, I prithee.

PISANIO
Well, madam, we must take a short farewell,
Lest, being miss'd, I be suspected of
Your carriage from the court. My noble mistress,
Here is a box; I had it from the Queen. [*Gives box.*]
What's in 't is precious. If you are sick at sea,
Or stomach-qualm'd at land, a dram of this
Will drive away distemper. To some shade,
And fit you to your manhood. May the gods
Direct you to the best!

IMOGEN
Amen. I thank thee.
Exeunt [severally].

SCENE V

Enter Cymbeline, Queen, Cloten, Lucius, [Attendants,] and Lords.

CYMBELINE
Thus far, and so farewell.

LUCIUS
Thanks, royal sir.
My Emperor hath wrote I must from hence;
And am right sorry that I must report ye
My master's enemy.

CYMBELINE
Our subjects, sir,
Will not endure his yoke; and for ourself
To show less sovereignty than they must needs
Appear unkinglike.

LUCIUS
So, sir. I desire of you
A conduct overland to Milford-Haven.
Madam, all joy befall your Grace, and you!

CYMBELINE
My lords, you are appointed for that office;
The due of honor in no point omit.
So farewell, noble Lucius.

LUCIUS
Your hand, my lord.

CLOTEN
Receive it friendly; but from this time forth
I wear it as your enemy.

LUCIUS
Sir, the event
Is yet to name the winner. Fare you well.

CYMBELINE
Leave not the worthy Lucius, good my lords,
Till he have cross'd the Severn. Happiness!
Exeunt Lucius etc.

QUEEN
He goes hence frowning, but it honors us
That we have given him cause.

CLOTEN
'Tis all the better;
Your valiant Britons have their wishes in it.

CYMBELINE
Lucius hath wrote already to the Emperor
How it goes here. It fits us therefore ripely
Our chariots and our horsemen be in readiness.
The pow'rs that he already hath in Gallia
Will soon be drawn to head, from whence he moves
His war for Britain.

QUEEN
'Tis not sleepy business,
But must be look'd to speedily and strongly.

CYMBELINE
Our expectation that it would be thus
Hath made us forward. But, my gentle queen,

156 Command i.e., as befitting one of royal birth. **niceness** fastidiousness, reserve **158 it** its. **waggish** roguish, masculine **160 quarrelous** quarrelsome **162 harder** too hard **164 common-kissing** kissing everybody and everything. **Titan** god of the sun **165 laborsome . . . trims** elaborate and dainty apparel **166 angry** i.e., jealous **169 Forethinking** foreseeing, anticipating. **fit** ready **171 answer to** go along with. **in their serving** assisted by them **173 of . . . season** i.e., of such an age as you will represent **174 his service** employment in his service **175 happy** gifted, skillful. **make him know** convince him **176 If . . . music** i.e., if he has an ear for music, since he then cannot fail to appreciate your voice **177 embrace** take you in (to his service) **178 Your means abroad** as to your means while you are abroad **182 even** keep even with, profit by **184 soldier to** enlisted to, devoted to **188 Your carriage** having removed you

III.v. Location: Cymbeline's palace.
8 conduct safe-conduct, escort **10 office** duty (as escorts of Lucius) **14 event** outcome **22 fits** befits. **ripely** speedily **25 drawn to head** brought together, levied **29 forward** well prepared

Where is our daughter? She hath not appear'd
Before the Roman, nor to us hath tender'd
The duty of the day. She looks us like 32
A thing more made of malice than of duty.
We have noted it. Call her before us, for
We have been too slight in sufferance.
[*Exit an Attendant.*]

QUEEN
Royal sir, 35
Since the exile of Posthumus, most retir'd
Hath her life been; the cure whereof, my lord,
'Tis time must do. Beseech your Majesty,
Forbear sharp speeches to her. She's a lady
So tender of rebukes that words are strokes,
And strokes death to her.

Enter [*Attendant as*] *Messenger.*

CYMBELINE
Where is she, sir? How
Can her contempt be answer'd?

ATTENDANT
Please you, sir, 42
Her chambers are all lock'd, and there's no answer
That will be given to th' loud of noise we make. 44

QUEEN
My lord, when last I went to visit her,
She pray'd me to excuse her keeping close, 46
Whereto constrain'd by her infirmity
She should that duty leave unpaid to you 48
Which daily she was bound to proffer. This
She wish'd me to make known, but our great court 50
Made me to blame in memory.

CYMBELINE
Her doors lock'd?
Not seen of late? Grant, heavens, that which I fear
Prove false! *Exit.*

QUEEN
Son, I say, follow the King.

CLOTEN
That man of hers, Pisanio, her old servant,
I have not seen these two days.

QUEEN
Go, look after.
Exit [*Cloten*].
Pisanio, thou that stand'st so for Posthumus! 56
He hath a drug of mine; I pray his absence
Proceed by swallowing that, for he believes 58
It is a thing most precious. But for her,
Where is she gone? Haply despair hath seiz'd her,
Or, wing'd with fervor of her love, she's flown
To her desir'd Posthumus. Gone she is
To death or to dishonor, and my end
Can make good use of either. She being down,
I have the placing of the British crown.

Enter Cloten.

How now, my son?

CLOTEN
'Tis certain she is fled.
Go in and cheer the King. He rages; none
Dare come about him.

QUEEN
All the better. May
This night forestall him of the coming day! 69
Exit Queen.

CLOTEN
I love and hate her, for she's fair and royal, 70
And that she hath all courtly parts more exquisite 71
Than lady, ladies, woman. From every one
The best she hath, and she, of all compounded,
Outsells them all. I love her therefore, but 74
Disdaining me and throwing favors on
The low Posthumus slanders so her judgment
That what's else rare is chok'd; and in that point
I will conclude to hate her, nay, indeed,
To be reveng'd upon her. For when fools shall—

Enter Pisanio. [*He attempts to avoid Cloten.*]

Who is here? What, are you packing, sirrah? 80
Come hither. Ah, you precious pander! Villain,
Where is thy lady? In a word, or else
Thou art straightway with the fiends.
[*Threatens him with his sword.*]

PISANIO
O, good my lord!

CLOTEN
Where is thy lady? Or, by Jupiter,
I will not ask again. Close villain, 85
I'll have this secret from thy heart, or rip
Thy heart to find it. Is she with Posthumus?
From whose so many weights of baseness cannot
A dram of worth be drawn.

PISANIO
Alas, my lord,
How can she be with him? When was she miss'd?
He is in Rome.

CLOTEN
Where is she, sir? Come nearer. 91
No farther halting. Satisfy me home 92
What is become of her.

PISANIO
O, my all-worthy lord!

CLOTEN
All-worthy villain!
Discover where thy mistress is at once, 95
At the next word. No more of "worthy lord"!
Speak, or thy silence on the instant is
Thy condemnation and thy death.

PISANIO
Then, sir,
This paper is the history of my knowledge
Touching her flight. [*Presents a letter.*]

CLOTEN
Let's see 't. I will pursue her
Even to Augustus' throne.

PISANIO [*Aside*]
Or this, or perish. 101
She's far enough, and what he learns by this
May prove his travel, not her danger.

CLOTEN
Humh!

PISANIO [*Aside*]
I'll write to my lord she's dead. O Imogen,
Safe mayst thou wander, safe return again!

CLOTEN
Sirrah, is this letter true?

32 looks us seems to us (?) looks at us (?) **35 slight in sufferance** permissive toward it **42 answer'd** accounted for **44 loud** loudness **46 close** in private **48 She . . . leave** she found herself obliged to leave that duty **50 great court** important courtly business **56 stand'st so for** strongly support **58 by** from

69 forestall deprive (i.e., bring about his death) **70 for** because **71 that** because. **parts** endowments, graces **74 Outsells** outvalues, excels **80 packing** plotting **85 Close** secretive **91 Come nearer** answer more to the point **92 home** completely **95 Discover** disclose **101 Or** either

PISANIO Sir, as I think.

CLOTEN It is Posthumus' hand, I know 't. Sirrah, if thou wouldst not be a villain, but do me true service, undergo those employments wherein I should have cause to use thee with a serious industry—that is, what villainy soe'er I bid thee do, to perform it directly and truly—I would think thee an honest man. Thou shouldst neither want my means for thy relief nor my voice for thy preferment.

PISANIO Well, my good lord.

CLOTEN Wilt thou serve me? For since patiently and constantly thou hast stuck to the bare fortune of that beggar Posthumus, thou canst not, in the course of gratitude, but be a diligent follower of mine. Wilt thou serve me?

PISANIO Sir, I will.

CLOTEN Give me thy hand; here's my purse. [*Gives money.*] Hast any of thy late master's garments in thy possession?

PISANIO I have, my lord, at my lodging, the same suit he wore when he took leave of my lady and mistress.

CLOTEN The first service thou dost me, fetch that suit hither. Let it be thy first service; go.

PISANIO I shall, my lord. *Exit.*

CLOTEN Meet thee at Milford-Haven!—I forgot to ask him one thing; I'll remember 't anon.—Even there, thou villain Posthumus, will I kill thee. I would these garments were come. She said upon a time—the bitterness of it I now belch from my heart—that she held the very garment of Posthumus in more respect than my noble and natural person, together with the adornment of my qualities. With that suit upon my back will I ravish her; first kill him, and in her eyes. There shall she see my valor, which will then be a torment to
her contempt. He on the ground, my speech of insult- 141
ment ended on his dead body, and when my lust hath 142
din'd—which, as I say, to vex her I will execute in the
clothes that she so prais'd—to the court I'll knock her
back, foot her home again. She hath despis'd me re- 145
joicingly, and I'll be merry in my revenge.

Enter Pisanio [with the clothes].

Be those the garments?

PISANIO Ay, my noble lord.

CLOTEN How long is 't since she went to Milford-Haven?

PISANIO She can scarce be there yet.

CLOTEN Bring this apparel to my chamber; that is the second thing that I have commanded thee. The third is that thou wilt be a voluntary mute to my design. Be but duteous, and true preferment shall tender itself to thee. My revenge is now at Milford. Would I had wings to follow it! Come, and be true. *Exit.*

PISANIO

Thou bid'st me to my loss, for true to thee
Were to prove false, which I will never be,
To him that is most true. To Milford go,
And find not her whom thou pursuest. Flow, flow,
You heavenly blessings, on her! This fool's speed
Be cross'd with slowness; labor be his meed! *Exit.* 163

SCENE VI

Enter Imogen alone [in boy's clothes].

IMOGEN

I see a man's life is a tedious one.
I have tir'd myself, and for two nights together
Have made the ground my bed. I should be sick,
But that my resolution helps me. Milford,
When from the mountain top Pisanio show'd thee,
Thou wast within a ken. O Jove, I think 6
Foundations fly the wretched—such, I mean, 7
Where they should be reliev'd. Two beggars told me
I could not miss my way. Will poor folks lie,
That have afflictions on them, knowing 'tis
A punishment or trial? Yes; no wonder, 11
When rich ones scarce tell true. To lapse in fullness 12
Is sorer than to lie for need, and falsehood 13
Is worse in kings than beggars. My dear lord!
Thou art one o' th' false ones. Now I think on thee,
My hunger's gone; but even before I was 16
At point to sink for food. [*Sees cave.*] But what is this? 17
Here is a path to 't. 'Tis some savage hold. 18
I were best not call; I dare not call. Yet famine,
Ere clean it o'erthrow nature, makes it valiant. 20
Plenty and peace breeds cowards; hardness ever 21
Of hardiness is mother. Ho! Who's here?
If anything that's civil, speak; if savage,
Take or lend. Ho! No answer? Then I'll enter. 24
Best draw my sword; an if mine enemy
But fear the sword like me, he'll scarcely look on 't.
Such a foe, good heavens! 27

[*Draws sword, and*] *exit* [*into the cave*].

Enter Belarius, Guiderius, and Arviragus.

BELARIUS

You, Polydore, have prov'd best woodman and 28
Are master of the feast. Cadwal and I
Will play the cook and servant; 'tis our match. 30
The sweat of industry would dry and die
But for the end it works to. Come, our stomachs
Will make what's homely savory; weariness 33
Can snore upon the flint, when resty sloth 34
Finds the down pillow hard. Now peace be here,

141–142 insultment contemptuous triumph **145 foot** kick

163 cross'd thwarted. **meed** reward

III.vi. Location: Wales. Before the cave of Belarius.
6 within a ken within sight **7 Foundations** (1) fixed places (2) charitable institutions **11 trial** test of virtue **12 lapse in fullness** lie and commit other sins in a state of prosperity **13 sorer** worse, more wicked **16 but even before** just now **17 for** for lack of **18 hold** stronghold, fastness **20 clean** altogether **21 hardness** hardship **24 Take or lend** take my life or give me food **27 Such . . . heavens** i.e., may the heavens grant me a foe as timid as myself **28 woodman** woodsman, huntsman **30 match** agreement, bargain **33 homely** plain **34 resty** sluggish, indolent

Poor house, that keep'st thyself!

GUIDERIUS
I am throughly weary.

ARVIRAGUS
I am weak with toil, yet strong in appetite.

GUIDERIUS
There is cold meat i' th' cave; we'll browse on that,
Whilst what we have kill'd be cook'd.

BELARIUS [*Looking into the cave*]
Stay, come not in.
But that it eats our victuals, I should think
Here were a fairy.

GUIDERIUS
What's the matter, sir?

BELARIUS
By Jupiter, an angel! Or, if not,
An earthly paragon! Behold divineness
No elder than a boy!

Enter Imogen.

IMOGEN
Good masters, harm me not.
Before I enter'd here, I call'd, and thought
To have begg'd or bought what I have took. Good troth,
I have stol'n nought, nor would not, though I had found
Gold strew'd i' th' floor. Here's money for my meat.
[*Offers money.*]
I would have left it on the board so soon
As I had made my meal, and parted
With pray'rs for the provider.

GUIDERIUS
Money, youth?

ARVIRAGUS
All gold and silver rather turn to dirt,
As 'tis no better reckon'd but of those
Who worship dirty gods.

IMOGEN
I see you're angry.
Know, if you kill me for my fault, I should
Have died had I not made it.

BELARIUS
Whither bound?

IMOGEN
To Milford-Haven.

BELARIUS
What's your name?

IMOGEN
Fidele, sir. I have a kinsman who
Is bound for Italy; he embark'd at Milford;
To whom being going, almost spent with hunger,
I am fall'n in this offense.

BELARIUS
Prithee, fair youth,
Think us no churls, nor measure our good minds
By this rude place we live in. Well encounter'd!
'Tis almost night; you shall have better cheer
Ere you depart, and thanks to stay and eat it.
Boys, bid him welcome.

GUIDERIUS
Were you a woman, youth,
I should woo hard but be your groom in honesty.
I bid for you as I do buy.

ARVIRAGUS
I'll make 't my comfort
He is a man; I'll love him as my brother.
And such a welcome as I 'd give to him
After long absence, such is yours. Most welcome!
Be sprightly, for you fall 'mongst friends.

IMOGEN
'Mongst friends,
If brothers. [*Aside.*] Would it had been so, that they
Had been my father's sons! Then had my prize
Been less, and so more equal ballasting
To thee, Posthumus.

BELARIUS
He wrings at some distress.

GUIDERIUS
Would I could free 't!

ARVIRAGUS
Or I, whate'er it be,
What pain it cost, what danger. Gods!

BELARIUS
Hark, boys.
[*Whispers to them.*]

IMOGEN [*To herself*]
Great men,
That had a court no bigger than this cave,
That did attend themselves and had the virtue
Which their own conscience seal'd them, laying by
That nothing-gift of differing multitudes,
Could not outpeer these twain. Pardon me, gods!
I 'd change my sex to be companion with them,
Since Leonatus's false.

BELARIUS
It shall be so.
Boys, we'll go dress our hunt. Fair youth, come in.
Discourse is heavy, fasting; when we have supp'd,
We'll mannerly demand thee of thy story,
So far as thou wilt speak it.

GUIDERIUS
Pray draw near.

ARVIRAGUS
The night to th' owl and morn to th' lark less welcome.

IMOGEN
Thanks, sir.

ARVIRAGUS
I pray draw near. *Exeunt.*

SCENE [VII]

Enter two Roman Senators and Tribunes.

FIRST SENATOR
This is the tenor of the Emperor's writ:
That since the common men are now in action
'Gainst the Pannonians and Dalmatians,
And that the legions now in Gallia are
Full weak to undertake our wars against

36 keep'st thyself i.e., is untended, empty. **throughly** thoroughly **38 browse** nibble **54 of** by **57 made** committed **63 in** into **69 but be** i.e., but I'd be **70 I bid . . . buy** i.e., I bid for you as one who would have you, one who values you (?)

73 him i.e., my brother **77 prize** (1) value (i.e., she would not have been heir to the throne) (2) captured sea vessel **78 ballasting** cargo of a sea vessel giving it stability **79 wrings** writhes **84 attend** wait on **85 conscience seal'd** self-knowledge assured **85–86 laying . . . multitudes** disregarding the valueless gift of adulation from the fickle populace **87 outpeer** excel **90 hunt** game taken in the hunt

III.vii. Location: Rome. A public place.

The fall'n-off Britons, that we do incite
The gentry to this business. He creates
Lucius proconsul, and to you the tribunes,
For this immediate levy, he commands
His absolute commission. Long live Caesar!

FIRST TRIBUNE
Is Lucius general of the forces?

SECOND SENATOR Ay.

FIRST TRIBUNE
Remaining now in Gallia?

FIRST SENATOR With those legions
Which I have spoke of, whereunto your levy
Must be supplyant. The words of your commission
Will tie you to the numbers and the time
Of their dispatch.

FIRST TRIBUNE We will discharge our duty.
Exeunt.

ACT IV • SCENE I

Enter Cloten alone, [dressed in Posthumus' garments].

CLOTEN I am near to th' place where they should meet, if Pisanio have mapp'd it truly. How fit his garments serve me! Why should his mistress, who was made by him that made the tailor, not be fit too? The rather—saving reverence of the word—for 'tis said a woman's fitness comes by fits. Therein I must play the workman. I dare speak it to myself, for it is not vain-glory for a man and his glass to confer in his own chamber—I mean, the lines of my body are as well drawn as his; no less young, more strong, not beneath him in fortunes, beyond him in the advantage of the time, above him in birth, alike conversant in general services, and more remarkable in single oppositions. Yet this imperceiverant thing loves him in my despite. What mortality is! Posthumus, thy head, which now is growing upon thy shoulders, shall within this hour be off, thy mistress enforc'd, thy garments cut to pieces before her face; and all this done, spurn her home to her father, who may happily be a little angry for my so rough usage; but my mother, having power of his testiness, shall turn all into my commendations. My horse is tied up safe. Out, sword, and to a sore purpose! [*Draws.*] Fortune, put them into my hand! This is the very description of their meeting-place, and the fellow dares not deceive me. [*Exit.*]

6 fall'n-off revolted **9 commands** commands to be given, entrusts **10 absolute commission** unlimited authority **14 supplyant** reinforcing, auxiliary **15 tie you to** specify for you

IV.i. Location: Wales. Near the cave of Belarius.
5 saving reverence asking pardon (i.e., for the indecent pun on *fit*). **for** because **6 fitness** i.e., sexual inclination. **fits** i.e., fits and starts **11–12 advantage of the time** superiority in social opportunity **12–13 alike . . . services** equally versed in military matters **13 single oppositions** single combat **14 imperceiverant** dull of perception **15 What mortality is** what a thing life is **19 happily** haply, perchance **20–21 power of** power over

SCENE II

Enter Belarius, Guiderius, Arviragus, and Imogen from the cave.

BELARIUS [*To Imogen*]
You are not well. Remain here in the cave;
We'll come to you after hunting.

ARVIRAGUS [*To Imogen*] Brother, stay here.
Are we not brothers?

IMOGEN So man and man should be,
But clay and clay differs in dignity,
Whose dust is both alike. I am very sick.

GUIDERIUS
Go you to hunting; I'll abide with him.

IMOGEN
So sick I am not, yet I am not well;
But not so citizen a wanton as
To seem to die ere sick. So please you, leave me;
Stick to your journal course. The breach of custom
Is breach of all. I am ill, but your being by me
Cannot amend me; society is no comfort
To one not sociable. I am not very sick,
Since I can reason of it. Pray you, trust me here—
I'll rob none but myself—and let me die,
Stealing so poorly.

GUIDERIUS I love thee—I have spoke it—
How much the quantity, the weight as much,
As I do love my father.

BELARIUS What? How? How?

ARVIRAGUS
If it be sin to say so, sir, I yoke me
In my good brother's fault. I know not why
I love this youth; and I have heard you say,
Love's reason 's without reason. The bier at door,
And a demand who is 't shall die, I 'd say
"My father, not this youth."

BELARIUS [*Aside*] O noble strain!
O worthiness of nature! Breed of greatness!
Cowards father cowards and base things sire base;
Nature hath meal and bran, contempt and grace.
I'm not their father; yet who this should be
Doth miracle itself, lov'd before me.—
'Tis the ninth hour o' th' morn.

ARVIRAGUS Brother, farewell.

IMOGEN
I wish ye sport.

ARVIRAGUS You health. [*To Belarius.*] So please you, sir.

IMOGEN [*Aside*]
These are kind creatures. Gods, what lies I have heard!
Our courtiers say all's savage but at court.
Experience, O, thou disprov'st report!

IV.ii. Location: Before the cave of Belarius.
4 clay and clay different persons. **dignity** social position, rank **5 dust** remains after death **8 citizen** effeminate, city-bred. **wanton** spoiled or pampered person **10 journal** daily **16 so poorly** i.e., only from myself **17 How much** however much **22 reason 's** reason is **28–29 who . . . before me** it is miraculous that this youth, whoever he is, should be loved in preference to me **31 You** i.e., I wish you

Th' imperious seas breeds monsters; for the dish,
Poor tributary rivers as sweet fish.
I am sick still, heartsick. Pisanio,
I'll now taste of thy drug. [*Swallows some.*]

GUIDERIUS
I could not stir him.
He said he was gentle, but unfortunate;
Dishonestly afflicted, but yet honest.

ARVIRAGUS
Thus did he answer me, yet said hereafter
I might know more.

BELARIUS
To th' field, to th' field!
We'll leave you for this time. Go in and rest.

ARVIRAGUS
We'll not be long away.

BELARIUS
Pray be not sick,
For you must be our huswife.

IMOGEN
Well or ill,
I am bound to you. *Exit* [*to the cave*].

BELARIUS
And shalt be ever.
This youth, howe'er distress'd, appears he hath had
Good ancestors.

ARVIRAGUS
How angel-like he sings!

GUIDERIUS
But his neat cookery! He cut our roots in characters,
And sauc'd our broths, as Juno had been sick
And he her dieter.

ARVIRAGUS
Nobly he yokes
A smiling with a sigh, as if the sigh
Was that it was for not being such a smile;
The smile mocking the sigh, that it would fly
From so divine a temple to commix
With winds that sailors rail at.

GUIDERIUS
I do note
That grief and patience, rooted in them both,
Mingle their spurs together.

ARVIRAGUS
Grow, patience,
And let the stinking elder, grief, untwine
His perishing root with the increasing vine!

BELARIUS
It is great morning. Come, away!—Who's there?

Enter Cloten, [*not seeing them at first*].

CLOTEN
I cannot find those runagates. That villain
Hath mock'd me. I am faint.

BELARIUS
"Those runagates"?
Means he not us? I partly know him. 'Tis
Cloten, the son o' th' Queen. I fear some ambush.
I saw him not these many years, and yet
I know 'tis he. We are held as outlaws. Hence!

GUIDERIUS
He is but one. You and my brother search
What companies are near. Pray you, away.
Let me alone with him.
[*Exeunt Belarius and Arviragus.*]

CLOTEN
Soft, what are you
That fly me thus? Some villain mountaineers?
I have heard of such. What slave art thou?

GUIDERIUS
A thing
More slavish did I ne'er than answering
A slave without a knock.

CLOTEN
Thou art a robber,
A law-breaker, a villain. Yield thee, thief.

GUIDERIUS
To who? To thee? What art thou? Have not I
An arm as big as thine? A heart as big?
Thy words, I grant, are bigger, for I wear not
My dagger in my mouth. Say what thou art,
Why I should yield to thee?

CLOTEN
Thou villain base,
Know'st me not by my clothes?

GUIDERIUS
No, nor thy tailor, rascal,
Who is thy grandfather. He made those clothes,
Which, as it seems, make thee.

CLOTEN
Thou precious varlet,
My tailor made them not.

GUIDERIUS
Hence, then, and thank
The man that gave them thee. Thou art some fool;
I am loath to beat thee.

CLOTEN
Thou injurious thief,
Hear but my name, and tremble.

GUIDERIUS
What's thy name?

CLOTEN
Cloten, thou villain.

GUIDERIUS
Cloten, thou double villain, be thy name,
I cannot tremble at it. Were it Toad, or Adder,
Spider,
'Twould move me sooner.

CLOTEN
To thy further fear,
Nay, to thy mere confusion, thou shalt know
I am son to th' Queen.

GUIDERIUS
I am sorry for 't; not seeming
So worthy as thy birth.

CLOTEN
Art not afeard?

GUIDERIUS
Those that I reverence, those I fear—the wise;
At fools I laugh, not fear them.

CLOTEN
Die the death!
When I have slain thee with my proper hand,
I'll follow those that even now fled hence,
And on the gates of Lud's-town set your heads.
Yield, rustic mountaineer! *Fight, and exeunt.*

Enter Belarius and Arviragus.

BELARIUS
No company's abroad?

ARVIRAGUS
None in the world. You did mistake him, sure.

35 imperious imperial **36 as sweet fish** i.e., breed as sweet fish (for eating) as the sea **38 stir** i.e., to tell about himself **39 gentle** well born **50 characters** letters, designs **51 as** as if **54 that** what **58 them** i.e., the smile and the sigh **59 spurs** roots **60 elder** elder tree (on which Judas is supposed to have hanged himself). **untwine** cease to twine **61 perishing** baleful. **with . . . vine** (1) i.e., with patience (2) i.e., as patience increases **62 great morning** broad day **68 held** regarded **70 companies** companions

82 Know'st . . . clothes (Cloten is dressed as one from the court.) **87 injurious** insulting, malicious **93 mere** utter **98 proper** own

BELARIUS
I cannot tell. Long is it since I saw him,
But time hath nothing blurr'd those lines of favor 105
Which then he wore. The snatches in his voice, 106
And burst of speaking, were as his. I am absolute 107
'Twas very Cloten.
ARVIRAGUS In this place we left them. 108
I wish my brother make good time with him, 109
You say he is so fell.
BELARIUS Being scarce made up, 110
I mean, to man, he had not apprehension 111
Of roaring terrors; for defect of judgment 112
Is oft the cause of fear.

Enter Guiderius [with Cloten's head].

But see, thy brother. 113
GUIDERIUS
This Cloten was a fool, an empty purse;
There was no money in 't. Not Hercules
Could have knock'd out his brains, for he had none.
Yet I not doing this, the fool had borne
My head as I do his.
BELARIUS What hast thou done?
GUIDERIUS
I am perfect what: cut off one Cloten's head, 119
Son to the Queen, after his own report;
Who call'd me traitor, mountaineer, and swore
With his own single hand he 'd take us in,
Displace our heads where—thank the gods!—they grow,
And set them on Lud's-town.
BELARIUS We are all undone.
GUIDERIUS
Why, worthy father, what have we to lose,
But that he swore to take, our lives? The law 126
Protects not us. Then why should we be tender 127
To let an arrogant piece of flesh threat us,
Play judge and executioner all himself,
For we do fear the law? What company 130
Discover you abroad?
BELARIUS No single soul
Can we set eye on, but in all safe reason
He must have some attendants. Though his humor 133
Was nothing but mutation—ay, and that 134
From one bad thing to worse—not frenzy,
Not absolute madness could so far have rav'd
To bring him here alone. Although perhaps
It may be heard at court that such as we
Cave here, hunt here, are outlaws, and in time
May make some stronger head, the which he hearing— 140
As it is like him—might break out and swear 141
He 'd fetch us in, yet is 't not probable 142
To come alone, either he so undertaking 143
Or they so suffering. Then on good ground we fear, 144
If we do fear this body hath a tail
More perilous than the head.
ARVIRAGUS Let ordinance 146
Come as the gods foresay it. Howsoe'er,
My brother hath done well.
BELARIUS I had no mind
To hunt this day. The boy Fidele's sickness
Did make my way long forth.
GUIDERIUS With his own sword, 150
Which he did wave against my throat, I have ta'en
His head from him. I'll throw 't into the creek
Behind our rock, and let it to the sea
And tell the fishes he's the Queen's son, Cloten.
That's all I reck. *Exit.*
BELARIUS I fear 'twill be reveng'd. 155
Would, Polydore, thou hadst not done 't, though valor
Becomes thee well enough.
ARVIRAGUS Would I had done 't,
So the revenge alone pursu'd me! Polydore, 158
I love thee brotherly, but envy much
Thou hast robb'd me of this deed. I would revenges, 160
That possible strength might meet, would seek us through 161
And put us to our answer.
BELARIUS Well, 'tis done. 162
We'll hunt no more today, nor seek for danger
Where there's no profit. I prithee, to our rock;
You and Fidele play the cooks. I'll stay
Till hasty Polydore return, and bring him
To dinner presently.
ARVIRAGUS Poor sick Fidele!
I'll willingly to him. To gain his color 168
I 'd let a parish of such Clotens blood, 169
And praise myself for charity. *Exit.*
BELARIUS O thou goddess,
Thou divine Nature, thou thyself thou blazon'st 171
In these two princely boys! They are as gentle
As zephyrs blowing below the violet,
Not wagging his sweet head; and yet as rough,
Their royal blood enchaf'd, as the rud'st wind 175
That by the top doth take the mountain pine
And make him stoop to th' vale. 'Tis wonder
That an invisible instinct should frame them 178
To royalty unlearn'd, honor untaught,
Civility not seen from other, valor
That wildly grows in them but yields a crop
As if it had been sow'd. Yet still it's strange
What Cloten's being here to us portends,
Or what his death will bring us.

Enter Guiderius.

105 nothing not at all. **lines of favor** facial lines **106 snatches** hesitations **107 absolute** positive **108 very Cloten** Cloten himself **109 make good time** acquit himself well **110 fell** fierce **110–113 Being . . . fear** i.e., even in his youth, when he was scarcely a man, he had no proper conception of fear, having no wits at all, unlike those in whom defective judgment causes fear (?) **119 perfect** well aware **126 that** that which **127 tender** quick, keen **130 For** because **133 humor** disposition **134 mutation** changeability **140 head** armed force **141 break out** burst out (in speech) **142 fetch us in** capture us

143 To come that he would come **144 suffering** permitting **146 ordinance** what is ordained **150 make . . . forth** make my wanderings (from the cave) seem long **155 reck** care **158 So** so that. **pursu'd** would have pursued **160 would** wish that **161 That . . . meet** i.e., all that our available strength might encounter in combat. **seek us through** find us out, come upon us **162 put . . . answer** force us to retaliate **168 gain his color** restore the color (to his cheeks) **169 let . . . blood** i.e., drain the blood from a parish full of such Clotens **171 thou . . . blazon'st** you proudly display yourself **175 enchaf'd** heated (with anger) **178 frame** shape, direct

GUIDERIUS Where's my brother?
I have sent Cloten's clotpoll down the stream 185
In embassy to his mother. His body 's hostage 186
For his return. *Solemn music.*
BELARIUS My ingenious instrument! 187
Hark, Polydore, it sounds. But what occasion
Hath Cadwal now to give it motion? Hark!
GUIDERIUS
Is he at home?
BELARIUS He went hence even now.
GUIDERIUS
What does he mean? Since death of my dear'st mother
It did not speak before. All solemn things
Should answer solemn accidents. The matter? 193
Triumphs for nothing and lamenting toys 194
Is jollity for apes and grief for boys.
Is Cadwal mad?

Enter Arviragus, with Imogen, [*as*] *dead, bearing her in his arms.*

BELARIUS Look, here he comes,
And brings the dire occasion in his arms
Of what we blame him for.
ARVIRAGUS The bird is dead
That we have made so much on. I had rather 199
Have skipp'd from sixteen years of age to sixty,
To have turn'd my leaping-time into a crutch,
Than have seen this.
GUIDERIUS O sweetest, fairest lily!
My brother wears thee not the one half so well
As when thou grew'st thyself.
BELARIUS O melancholy,
Who ever yet could sound thy bottom, find 205
The ooze, to show what coast thy sluggish crare 206
Might eas'liest harbor in? Thou blessed thing, 207
Jove knows what man thou mightst have made; but I, 208
Thou diedst, a most rare boy, of melancholy.
How found you him?
ARVIRAGUS Stark, as you see, 210
Thus smiling, as some fly had tickled slumber, 211
Not as death's dart, being laugh'd at; his right cheek 212
Reposing on a cushion.
GUIDERIUS Where?
ARVIRAGUS O' th' floor;
His arms thus leagu'd. I thought he slept, and put 214
My clouted brogues from off my feet, whose rudeness 215
Answer'd my steps too loud.
GUIDERIUS Why, he but sleeps.
If he be gone, he'll make his grave a bed;
With female fairies will his tomb be haunted,
And worms will not come to thee.
ARVIRAGUS With fairest flowers
Whilst summer lasts and I live here, Fidele,
I'll sweeten thy sad grave. Thou shalt not lack
The flower that's like thy face, pale primrose, nor
The azur'd harebell, like thy veins, no, nor
The leaf of eglantine, whom, not to slander,
Out-sweet'ned not thy breath. The ruddock would, 225
With charitable bill—O bill, sore shaming
Those rich-left heirs that let their fathers lie
Without a monument!—bring thee all this,
Yea, and furr'd moss besides. When flow'rs are none,
To winter-ground thy corse—
GUIDERIUS Prithee, have done, 230
And do not play in wench-like words with that 231
Which is so serious. Let us bury him,
And not protract with admiration what 233
Is now due debt. To th' grave!
ARVIRAGUS Say, where shall 's lay him? 234
GUIDERIUS
By good Euriphile, our mother.
ARVIRAGUS Be 't so.
And let us, Polydore, though now our voices
Have got the mannish crack, sing him to th' ground,
As once to our mother; use like note and words,
Save that Euriphile must be Fidele.
GUIDERIUS
Cadwal,
I cannot sing. I'll weep, and word it with thee;
For notes of sorrow out of tune are worse
Than priests and fanes that lie.
ARVIRAGUS We'll speak it, then. 243
BELARIUS
Great griefs, I see, med'cine the less; for Cloten
Is quite forgot. He was a queen's son, boys,
And, though he came our enemy, remember
He was paid for that. Though mean and mighty, rotting
Together, have one dust, yet reverence,
That angel of the world, doth make distinction
Of place 'tween high and low. Our foe was princely,
And, though you took his life, as being our foe,
Yet bury him as a prince.
GUIDERIUS Pray you fetch him hither.
Thersites' body is as good as Ajax', 253
When neither are alive.
ARVIRAGUS If you'll go fetch him,
We'll say our song the whilst. Brother, begin.
[*Exit Belarius.*]
GUIDERIUS
Nay, Cadwal, we must lay his head to th' east; 256
My father hath a reason for 't.
ARVIRAGUS 'Tis true.
GUIDERIUS
Come on then, and remove him.
[*Thy lay out Imogen with her head to the east.*]

185 clotpoll blockhead, head **186 body 's** body is **187 ingenious** skillfully made (?) **193 answer** correspond to. **accidents** events **194 lamenting toys** grief over trifles (such as Cloten's death) **199 on** of **205 sound thy bottom** measure your depth **206 crare** skiff, small boat **207 thing** i.e., Fidele **208 but** i.e., but I know that **210 Stark** stiff **211 as** as if **212 as . . . laughed at** as though laughing at death's dart, i.e., not as though aware of death **214 leagu'd** folded **215 clouted brogues** hobnailed boots

225 ruddock robin redbreast **230 winter-ground** cover so as to protect from frost **231 wench-like** womanish **233 admiration** wonder **234 shall 's** shall we **243 fanes** temples **253 Thersites' . . . Ajax'** (Thersites was the base scoffer in the *Iliad;* Ajax, a Greek hero.) **256 lay . . . east** (Opposite to the Christian custom.)

ARVIRAGUS So Begin.

Song.

GUIDERIUS
Fear no more the heat o' th' sun,
Nor the furious winter's rages;
Thou thy worldly task hast done,
Home art gone, and ta'en thy wages.
Golden lads and girls all must,
As chimney-sweepers, come to dust.

ARVIRAGUS
Fear no more the frown o' th' great;
Thou art past the tyrant's stroke.
Care no more to clothe and eat;
To thee the reed is as the oak.
The scepter, learning, physic, must
All follow this, and come to dust.

GUIDERIUS
Fear no more the lightning-flash,
ARVIRAGUS
Nor th' all-dreaded thunder-stone.
GUIDERIUS
Fear not slander, censure rash;
ARVIRAGUS
Thou hast finish'd joy and moan.
BOTH
All lovers young, all lovers must
Consign to thee, and come to dust.
GUIDERIUS
No exorciser harm thee!
ARVIRAGUS
Nor no witchcraft charm thee!
GUIDERIUS
Ghost unlaid forbear thee!
ARVIRAGUS
Nothing ill come near thee!
BOTH
Quiet consummation have,
And renowned be thy grave!

Enter Belarius, with the [*headless*] *body of Cloten.*

GUIDERIUS
We have done our obsequies. Come, lay him down.
[*Cloten is laid next to Imogen.*]
BELARIUS
Here's a few flow'rs; but 'bout midnight, more.
[*They strew flowers.*]
The herbs that have on them cold dew o' th' night
Are strewings fitt'st for graves. Upon their faces.
You were as flow'rs, now wither'd; even so
These herblets shall, which we upon you strew.
Come on, away; apart upon our knees.
The ground that gave them first has them again.
Their pleasures here are past, so is their pain.
Exeunt [*Belarius, Guiderius, and Arviragus*].

IMOGEN (*Awakes*)
Yes, sir, to Milford-Haven; which is the way?
I thank you. By yond bush? Pray, how far thither?
'Ods pittikins! Can it be six mile yet?
I have gone all night. Faith, I'll lie down and sleep.
But soft, no bedfellow? [*Sees or touches Cloten's body.*] O gods and goddesses!
These flow'rs are like the pleasures of the world;
This bloody man, the care on 't. I hope I dream;
For so I thought I was a cave-keeper,
And cook to honest creatures. But 'tis not so;
'Twas but a bolt of nothing, shot at nothing,
Which the brain makes of fumes. Our very eyes
Are sometimes like our judgments, blind. Good faith,
I tremble still with fear; but if there be
Yet left in heaven as small a drop of pity
As a wren's eye, fear'd gods, a part of it!
The dream's here still. Even when I wake, it is
Without me, as within me; not imagin'd, felt.
A headless man? The garments of Posthumus?
I know the shape of 's leg; this is his hand,
His foot Mercurial, his Martial thigh,
The brawns of Hercules; but his Jovial face—
Murder in heaven? How? 'Tis gone. Pisanio,
All curses madded Hecuba gave the Greeks,
And mine to boot, be darted on thee! Thou,
Conspir'd with that irregulous devil, Cloten,
Hath here cut off my lord. To write and read
Be henceforth treacherous! Damn'd Pisanio
Hath with his forged letters—damn'd Pisanio—
From this most bravest vessel of the world
Struck the main-top! O Posthumus! Alas,
Where is thy head? Where's that? Ay me, where's that?
Pisanio might have kill'd thee at the heart,
And left this head on. How should this be, Pisanio?
'Tis he and Cloten. Malice and lucre in them
Have laid this woe here. O, 'tis pregnant, pregnant!
The drug he gave me, which he said was precious
And cordial to me, have I not found it
Murd'rous to th' senses? That confirms it home.
This is Pisanio's deed, and Cloten. O!
Give color to my pale cheek with thy blood,
That we the horrider may seem to those
Which chance to find us. O, my lord, my lord!
[*Falls on the body.*]

Enter Lucius, Captains, and a Soothsayer.

CAPTAIN
To them the legions garrison'd in Gallia,
After your will, have cross'd the sea, attending

268 reed, oak (Contrasting symbols of fragility and mightiness.) **269 physic** medical learning **272 thunder-stone** (the supposed solid body accompanying a stroke of lightning) **276 Consign to** co-sign with, share a similar fate with **277 exorciser** conjurer **281 consummation** end, death **286 Upon their faces** i.e., strew flowers on the dead persons' faces

294 'Ods pittikins God's pity. (A diminutive oath.) **295 gone** walked **299 cave-keeper** one who dwells in a cave **301 bolt** arrow **302 fumes** vapors engendered of humors which, according to current theory, rose up into the brain and, by affecting imagination in the forechamber of the brain, caused dreams **306 wren's eye** i.e., a very small eye, rendering a small teardrop **311 Mercurial** nimble and swift like the foot of Mercury. **Martial** powerful for war like that of Mars **312 brawns** muscles. **Jovial** Jove-like **314 madded** maddened. **Hecuba** wife of Priam, King of Troy **316 Conspir'd** conspiring. **irregulous** lawless **321 main-top** top of mainmast, i.e., head **325 lucre** greed **326 pregnant** i.e., evident **328 cordial** restorative to the heart **329 home** utterly **330 Cloten** i.e., Cloten's **334 To them** i.e., in addition to the forces we've already mentioned **335 After** according to

You here at Milford-Haven with your ships.
They are in readiness.

LUCIUS
But what from Rome?

CAPTAIN
The Senate hath stirr'd up the confiners
And gentlemen of Italy, most willing spirits,
That promise noble service, and they come
Under the conduct of bold Iachimo,
Sienna's brother.

LUCIUS
When expect you them?

CAPTAIN
With the next benefit o' th' wind.

LUCIUS
This forwardness
Makes our hopes fair. Command our present numbers
Be muster'd; bid the captains look to 't. Now, sir,
What have you dream'd of late of this war's purpose?

SOOTHSAYER
Last night the very gods show'd me a vision—
I fast and pray'd for their intelligence—thus:
I saw Jove's bird, the Roman eagle, wing'd
From the spongy south to this part of the west,
There vanish'd in the sunbeams, which portends—
Unless my sins abuse my divination—
Success to th' Roman host.

LUCIUS
Dream often so,
And never false. [*Sees Cloten and Imogen.*] Soft, ho, what trunk is here
Without his top? The ruin speaks that sometime
It was a worthy building. How? A page?
Or dead, or sleeping on him? But dead rather;
For nature doth abhor to make his bed
With the defunct, or sleep upon the dead.
Let's see the boy's face.

CAPTAIN
He's alive, my lord.

LUCIUS
He'll then instruct us of this body. Young one,
Inform us of thy fortunes, for it seems
They crave to be demanded. Who is this
Thou mak'st thy bloody pillow? Or who was he
That, otherwise than noble nature did,
Hath alter'd that good picture? What's thy interest
Is this sad wrack? How came 't? Who is 't?
What art thou?

IMOGEN
I am nothing; or if not,
Nothing to be were better. This was my master,
A very valiant Briton and a good,
That here by mountaineers lies slain. Alas,
There is no more such masters. I may wander
From east to occident, cry out for service,
Try many, all good, serve truly, never
Find such another master.

LUCIUS
'Lack, good youth!
Thou mov'st no less with thy complaining than
Thy master in bleeding. Say his name, good friend.

IMOGEN
Richard du Champ. [*Aside.*] If I do lie and do
No harm by it, though the gods hear, I hope
They'll pardon it.—Say you, sir?

LUCIUS
Thy name?

IMOGEN
Fidele, sir.

LUCIUS
Thou dost approve thyself the very same;
Thy name well fits thy faith, thy faith thy name.
Wilt take thy chance with me? I will not say
Thou shalt be so well master'd, but be sure
No less belov'd. The Roman Emperor's letters,
Sent by a consul to me, should not sooner
Than thine own worth prefer thee. Go with me.

IMOGEN
I'll follow, sir. But first, an 't please the gods,
I'll hide my master from the flies, as deep
As these poor pickaxes can dig; and when
With wild wood-leaves and weeds I ha' strew'd his grave,
And on it said a century of prayers,
Such as I can, twice o'er, I'll weep and sigh,
And leaving so his service, follow you,
So please you entertain me.

LUCIUS
Ay, good youth,
And rather father thee than master thee.
My friends,
The boy hath taught us manly duties. Let us
Find out the prettiest daisied plot we can,
And make him with our pikes and partisans
A grave. Come, arm him. Boy, he's preferr'd
By thee to us, and he shall be interr'd
As soldiers can. Be cheerful; wipe thine eyes.
Some falls are means the happier to arise.
Exeunt, [*bearing Cloten's body*].

338 **confiners** inhabitants 342 **Sienna's** the Duke of Sienna's 348 **fast** fasted 350 **spongy** damp 352 **abuse** falsify 357 **Or** either 365 **otherwise . . . did** i.e., unlike the noble way that nature causes death 376 **mov'st** i.e., to pity

381 **approve** prove. **the very same** (*Fidele* means *faithful.*) 387 **prefer** recommend 390 **pickaxes** i.e., fingers 392 **century** hundred 395 **entertain** employ 400 **partisans** long-handled weapons, halberds 401 **arm him** help him up

SCENE III

Enter Cymbeline, Lords, [*Attendants,*] *and Pisanio.*

CYMBELINE
Again; and bring me word how 'tis with her.
[*Exit an Attendant.*]
A fever with the absence of her son,
A madness, of which her life's in danger. Heavens,
How deeply you at once do touch me! Imogen,
The great part of my comfort, gone; my queen
Upon a desperate bed, and in a time
When fearful wars point at me; her son gone,
So needful for this present! It strikes me, past
The hope of comfort. But for thee, fellow,
Who needs must know of her departure and
Dost seem so ignorant, we'll enforce it from thee
By a sharp torture.

PISANIO
Sir, my life is yours;
I humbly set it at your will. But for my mistress,
I nothing know where she remains, why gone,

IV.iii. Location: Britain. Cymbeline's palace.
2 **with** brought on by 11 **seem** pretend to be

Nor when she purposes return. Beseech your
Highness,
Hold me your loyal servant.

FIRST LORD
Good my liege, 16
The day that she was missing he was here.
I dare be bound he's true, and shall perform
All parts of his subjection loyally. For Cloten, 19
There wants no diligence in seeking him, 20
And will, no doubt, be found.

CYMBELINE
The time is troublesome.
[*To Pisanio.*] We'll slip you for a season, but our
jealousy 22
Does yet depend.

FIRST LORD
So please your Majesty, 23
The Roman legions, all from Gallia drawn,
Are landed on your coast, with a supply
Of Roman gentlemen, by the Senate sent.

CYMBELINE
Now for the counsel of my son and queen!
I am amaz'd with matter.

FIRST LORD
Good my liege, 28
Your preparation can affront no less 29
Than what you hear of. Come more, for more you're
ready. 30
The want is but to put those pow'rs in motion 31
That long to move.

CYMBELINE
I thank you. Let's withdraw,
And meet the time as it seeks us. We fear not
What can from Italy annoy us, but 34
We grieve at chances here. Away! 35
Exeunt [*all but Pisanio*].

PISANIO
I heard no letter from my master since
I wrote him Imogen was slain. 'Tis strange.
Nor hear I from my mistress, who did promise
To yield me often tidings. Neither know I
What is betid to Cloten, but remain 40
Perplex'd in all. The heavens still must work.
Wherein I am false I am honest; not true, to be true.
These present wars shall find I love my country,
Even to the note o' th' King, or I'll fall in them. 44
All other doubts, by time let them be clear'd;
Fortune brings in some boats that are not steer'd.
Exit.

SCENE IV

Enter Belarius, Guiderius, and Arviragus.

GUIDERIUS
The noise is round about us.

BELARIUS
Let us from it.

ARVIRAGUS
What pleasure, sir, find we in life, to lock it
From action and adventure?

GUIDERIUS
Nay, what hope
Have we in hiding us? This way, the Romans 4
Must or for Britons slay us, or receive us 5
For barbarous and unnatural revolts 6
During their use, and slay us after.

BELARIUS
Sons, 7
We'll higher to the mountains, there secure us.
To the King's party there's no going. Newness
Of Cloten's death—we being not known, not
muster'd
Among the bands—may drive us to a render 11
Where we have liv'd, and so extort from 's that
Which we have done, whose answer would be
death 13
Drawn on with torture.

GUIDERIUS
This is, sir, a doubt 14
In such a time nothing becoming you, 15
Nor satisfying us.

ARVIRAGUS
It is not likely
That when they hear the Roman horses neigh,
Behold their quarter'd fires, have both their eyes 18
And ears so cloy'd importantly as now, 19
That they will waste their time upon our note, 20
To know from whence we are.

BELARIUS
O, I am known
Of many in the army. Many years,
Though Cloten then but young, you see, not
wore him
From my remembrance. And besides, the King
Hath not deserv'd my service nor your loves,
Who find in my exile the want of breeding, 26
The certainty of this hard life; aye hopeless 27
To have the courtesy your cradle promis'd, 28
But to be still hot summer's tanlings and 29
The shrinking slaves of winter.

GUIDERIUS
Than be so
Better to cease to be. Pray, sir, to th' army.
I and my brother are not known; yourself
So out of thought, and thereto so o'ergrown, 33
Cannot be question'd.

ARVIRAGUS
By this sun that shines,
I'll thither. What thing is 't that I never 35
Did see man die, scarce ever look'd on blood
But that of coward hares, hot goats, and venison! 37
Never bestrid a horse, save one that had
A rider like myself, who ne'er wore rowel 39
Nor iron on his heel! I am asham'd
To look upon the holy sun, to have
The benefit of his blest beams, remaining
So long a poor unknown.

GUIDERIUS
By heavens, I'll go.

16 Hold regard **19 subjection** duty **20 wants** is lacking **22 slip you** let you go. **jealousy** suspicion **23 depend** impend, threaten **28 amaz'd with matter** confused by the pressure of affairs **29 preparation** military force already mustered **29–30 affront . . . Than** confront in combat as large (an army) as **30 Come more** if more (enemy) come **31 want is but** sole thing needed is **34 annoy** injure **35 chances** accidents (the Queen's illness, etc.) **40 betid** happened **44 note** knowledge, recognition

IV.iv. Location: Wales. Before the cave of Belarius.

4 This way i.e., by this course of conduct **5 Must or** must either **6 revolts** deserters, rebels **7 During their use** while they are making use of us **11 bands** army rolls. **render** rendering of an account, relation **13 answer** consequence **14 Drawn on with** preceded and lengthened by **15 nothing** not at all **18 quarter'd fires** camp fires **19 cloy'd importantly** filled with urgent business **20 our note** noting us **26–28 Who . . . promis'd** you who find in exile with me want of breeding and the certain results of this hard life, perpetually without hope of ever finding the refinement promised you by your high birth **29 tanlings** those tanned by the sun **33 thereto** in addition. **o'ergrown** i.e., with hair and beard; or, replaced in their thoughts **35 What thing** i.e., what a disgraceful thing **37 hot** lecherous **39 rowel** wheel of a spur

If you will bless me, sir, and give me leave,
I'll take the better care, but if you will not,
The hazard therefore due fall on me by
The hands of Romans!

ARVIRAGUS So say I. Amen.

BELARIUS
No reason I, since of your lives you set
So slight a valuation, should reserve
My crack'd one to more care. Have with you, boys!
If in your country wars you chance to die,
That is my bed too, lads, and there I'll lie.
Lead, lead. [*Aside.*] The time seems long; their blood thinks scorn
Till it fly out and show them princes born. *Exeunt.*

ACT V • SCENE I

Enter Posthumus alone [*in Italian dress, with a bloody handkerchief*].

POSTHUMUS
Yea, bloody cloth, I'll keep thee, for I wish'd
Thou shouldst be color'd thus. You married ones,
If each of you should take this course, how many
Must murder wives much better than themselves
For wrying but a little! O Pisanio!
Every good servant does not all commands;
No bond but to do just ones. Gods, if you
Should have ta'en vengeance on my faults, I never
Had liv'd to put on this; so had you sav'd
The noble Imogen to repent, and struck
Me, wretch more worth your vengeance. But, alack,
You snatch some hence for little faults; that's love,
To have them fall no more; you some permit
To second ills with ills, each elder worse,
And make them dread it, to the doers' thrift.
But Imogen is your own. Do your best wills,
And make me blest to obey! I am brought hither
Among th' Italian gentry, and to fight
Against my lady's kingdom. 'Tis enough
That, Britain, I have kill'd thy mistress; peace,
I'll give no wound to thee. Therefore, good heavens,
Hear patiently my purpose: I'll disrobe me
Of these Italian weeds and suit myself
As does a Britain peasant; so I'll fight
Against the part I come with; so I'll die
For thee, O Imogen, even for whom my life
Is every breath a death; and thus, unknown,
Pitied nor hated, to the face of peril
Myself I'll dedicate. Let me make men know
More valor in me than my habits show.
Gods, put the strength o' th' Leonati in me!
To shame the guise o' th' world, I will begin
The fashion, less without and more within. *Exit.*

SCENE II

Enter Lucius, Iachimo, and the Roman Army at one door, and the Britain army at another, Leonatus Posthumus following, like a poor soldier. They march over and go out. Then enter again, in skirmish, Iachimo and Posthumus; he vanquisheth and disarmeth Iachimo, and then leaves him.

IACHIMO
The heaviness and guilt within my bosom
Takes off my manhood. I have belied a lady,
The Princess of this country, and the air on 't
Revengingly enfeebles me; or could this carl,
A very drudge of nature's, have subdu'd me
In my profession? Knighthoods and honors, borne
As I wear mine, are titles but of scorn.
If that thy gentry, Britain, go before
This lout as he exceeds our lords, the odds
Is that we scarce are men and you are gods. *Exit.*

The battle continues; the Britons fly; Cymbeline is taken. Then enter, to his rescue, Belarius, Guiderius, and Arviragus.

BELARIUS
Stand, stand! We have th' advantage of the ground;
The lane is guarded. Nothing routs us but
The villainy of our fears.

GUIDERIUS, ARVIRAGUS Stand, stand, and fight!

Enter Posthumus, and seconds the Britons. They rescue Cymbeline, and exeunt. Then enter Lucius, Iachimo, and Imogen.

LUCIUS
Away, boy, from the troops, and save thyself;
For friends kill friends, and the disorder's such
As war were hoodwink'd.

IACHIMO 'Tis their fresh supplies.

LUCIUS
It is a day turn'd strangely. Or betimes
Let's reinforce, or fly. *Exeunt.*

SCENE III

Enter Posthumus [*dressed as a British peasant still*], *and a Britain Lord.*

LORD
Cam'st thou from where they made the stand?

POSTHUMUS I did;
Though you, it seems, come from the fliers.

LORD I did.

46 hazard therefore due i.e., danger resulting from disobedience and lack of parental blessing **50 crack'd** i.e., with age. **Have with you** i.e., come on, then **51 country** country's

V.i. Location: Britain. The Roman camp.
5 wrying swerving from the right course **7 bond but** obligation except **9 put on** incite, encourage (?) burden myself with (?) **12–13 that's . . . more** that is a loving act, since it makes them sin no more **14 second** follow up. **elder** subsequent (sin) **15 make . . . thrift** i.e., make those evil-doers repent their deeds, to their ultimate spiritual profit **23 suit** clothe **25 part** party, side **28 Pitied** neither pitied **30 habits** clothes

32 guise custom **33 fashion, less without** the fashion of relying less on outward show

V.ii. Location: Britain. Field of battle between the British and Roman camps.
3 on 't of it **4 carl** churl, peasant **8 go before** excel **16 As** as if. **hoodwink'd** blindfolded **17 Or betimes** either swiftly

V.iii. Location: The field of battle, as before.

POSTHUMUS

No blame be to you, sir, for all was lost,
But that the heavens fought. The King himself
Of his wings destitute, the army broken,
And but the backs of Britons seen, all flying
Through a strait lane; the enemy full-hearted,
Lolling the tongue with slaught'ring, having work
More plentiful than tools to do 't, struck down
Some mortally, some slightly touch'd, some falling
Merely through fear, that the strait pass was
damm'd
With dead men hurt behind, and cowards living
To die with length'ned shame.

LORD

Where was this lane?

POSTHUMUS

Close by the battle, ditch'd, and wall'd with turf;
Which gave advantage to an ancient soldier,
An honest one, I warrant, who deserv'd
So long a breeding as his white beard came to,
In doing this for 's country. Athwart the lane,
He, with two striplings—lads more like to run
The country base than to commit such slaughter,
With faces fit for masks, or rather fairer
Than those for preservation cas'd, or shame—
Made good the passage, cried to those that fled,
"Our Britain's harts die flying, not our men.
To darkness fleet souls that fly backwards. Stand!
Or we are Romans and will give you that
Like beasts which you shun beastly, and may save
But to look back in frown. Stand, stand!" These
three,
Three thousand confident, in act as many—
For three performers are the file when all
The rest do nothing—with this word "Stand,
stand,"
Accommodated by the place, more charming
With their own nobleness, which could have turn'd
A distaff to a lance, gilded pale looks,
Part shame, part spirit renew'd, that some, turn'd
coward
But by example—O, a sin in war,
Damn'd in the first beginners!—gan to look
The way that they did, and to grin like lions
Upon the pikes o' th' hunters. Then began
A stop i' th' chaser, a retire, anon
A rout, confusion thick. Forthwith they fly
Chickens, the way which they stoop'd eagles; slaves,
The strides they victors made. And now our
cowards,
Like fragments in hard voyages, became
The life o' th' need. Having found the back door
open
Of the unguarded hearts, heavens, how they
wound!
Some slain before, some dying, some their friends
O'er-borne i' th' former wave. Ten chas'd by one
Are now each one the slaughter-man of twenty.
Those that would die or ere resist are grown
The mortal bugs o' th' field.

LORD

This was strange chance:
A narrow lane, an old man, and two boys!

POSTHUMUS

Nay, do not wonder at it. You are made
Rather to wonder at the things you hear
Than to work any. Will you rhyme upon 't,
And vent it for a mock'ry? Here is one:
"Two boys, an old man twice a boy, a lane,
Preserv'd the Britons, was the Romans' bane."

LORD

Nay, be not angry, sir.

POSTHUMUS

'Lack, to what end?
Who dares not stand his foe, I'll be his friend;
For if he'll do as he is made to do,
I know he'll quickly fly my friendship too.
You have put me into rhyme.

LORD

Farewell. You're angry.
Exit.

POSTHUMUS

Still going? This is a lord! O noble misery,
To be i' th' field, and ask "what news?" of me!
Today how many would have given their honors
To have sav'd their carcasses! Took heel to do 't,
And yet died too! I, in mine own woe charm'd,
Could not find Death where I did hear him groan,
Nor feel him where he struck. Being an ugly
monster,
'Tis strange he hides him in fresh cups, soft beds,
Sweet words; or hath moe ministers than we
That draw his knives i' th' war. Well, I will
find him;
For being now a favorer to the Briton,
[*Removing his British garb.*]
No more a Briton, I have resum'd again
The part I came in. Fight I will no more,
But yield me to the veriest hind that shall
Once touch my shoulder. Great the slaughter is
Here made by th' Roman; great the answer be
Britons must take. For me, my ransom's death.
On either side I come to spend my breath,
Which neither here I'll keep nor bear again,
But end it by some means for Imogen.

Enter two [*British*] *Captains and Soldiers.*

7 strait narrow. **full-hearted** full of courage and confidence **8 Lolling** letting hang out **12 behind** from the rear (while running away) **17 breeding** life, support **20 base** prisoner's base, a game in which rapid running is the means to victory **21 fit for masks** delicate enough to deserve sheltering from the elements **22 those . . . shame** i.e., ladies' faces masked *(cas'd)* either for protection against the elements or for modesty **25 fleet** hasten **26 are Romans** i.e., will act like Romans. **that** i.e., death blows **27 beastly** like cowards. **save** prevent **28 But . . . frown** only by looking back in defiance **30 file** i.e., entire force (as in *rank and file*) **32 Accommodated** provided with advantage. **more charming** working their spell on others (to turn and fight) **33 turn'd** transformed **34 A distaff to a lance** i.e., a housewife into a soldier. **gilded** imparted a flush of color to **35 Part . . . renew'd** (moved them so that) shame revived some, courage others **37 first beginners** i.e., those who first set an example of cowardice. **gan** began **38 they** i.e., Belarius and his two "sons." **grin** bare the teeth **40 chaser** pursuer **41 Forthwith** immediately **42 Chickens** i.e., like chickens. **the way . . . eagles** along the very path which just before they had swooped over like eagles **42–43 slaves . . . made** retracing, like slaves, the steps they took as victors **44 fragments** scraps, fragments of food

45 The life o' th' need support for life in time of necessity. **back door** i.e., vulnerable soft spot of the Romans **47 Some . . . dying** i.e., some Britons formerly listed as dead or wounded in action. **their friends** i.e., the friends of those cowards already discussed **48 Ten . . . one** i.e., ten Britons, formerly retreating before one Roman **50 or ere** rather than **51 mortal bugs** deadly bugbears, terrors **55 work any** perform any such wonders yourself **56 vent** air, circulate **59 'Lack** alack **60 Who** whoever. **stand** stand against **61 made** inclined **64 going** fleeing. **noble misery** false nobility **68 charm'd** i.e., made invulnerable **74 being . . . favorer to** i.e., since Death now favors **75 No . . . Briton** I remaining no longer a Briton **76 The part. . . in** i.e., my Roman guise (in which my capture and execution seems assured) **77 hind** peasant **78 touch my shoulder** i.e., place me under arrest **79 answer** retaliation **81 spend my breath** give up my life

FIRST CAPTAIN
Great Jupiter be prais'd! Lucius is taken.
'Tis thought the old man and his sons were angels.

SECOND CAPTAIN
There was a fourth man, in a silly habit,
That gave th' affront with them.

FIRST CAPTAIN So 'tis reported,
But none of 'em can be found. Stand! Who's there?

POSTHUMUS
A Roman,
Who had not now been drooping here, if seconds
Had answer'd him.

SECOND CAPTAIN Lay hands on him; a dog!
A leg of Rome shall not return to tell
What crows have peck'd them here. He brags his service
As if he were of note. Bring him to th' King.

Enter Cymbeline, Belarius, Guiderius, Arviragus, Pisanio, [Soldiers, Attendants,] and Roman Captives. The Captains present Posthumus to Cymbeline, who delivers him over to a Jailer. [*Then exeunt omnes.*]

SCENE IV

Enter Posthumus [in chains] and [two] Jailer[s].

FIRST JAILER
You shall not now be stol'n, you have locks upon you;
So graze as you find pasture.

SECOND JAILER Ay, or a stomach.
[*Exeunt Jailers.*]

POSTHUMUS
Most welcome, bondage! For thou art a way,
I think, to liberty. Yet am I better
Than one that's sick o' th' gout, since he had rather
Groan so in perpetuity than be cur'd
By th' sure physician, Death, who is the key
T' unbar these locks. My conscience, thou art fetter'd
More than my shanks and wrists. You good gods, give me
The penitent instrument to pick that bolt,
Then, free for ever! Is 't enough I am sorry?
So children temporal fathers do appease;
Gods are more full of mercy. Must I repent?
I cannot do it better than in gyves,
Desir'd more than constrain'd. To satisfy,
If of my freedom 'tis the main part, take
No stricter render of me than my all.
I know you are more clement than vile men,
Who of their broken debtors take a third,
A sixth, a tenth, letting them thrive again
On their abatement. That's not my desire.
For Imogen's dear life take mine; and though
'Tis not so dear, yet 'tis a life; you coin'd it.
'Tween man and man they weigh not every stamp;
Though light, take pieces for the figure's sake;
You rather mine, being yours. And so, great pow'rs,
If you will take this audit, take this life,
And cancel these cold bonds. O Imogen!
I'll speak to thee in silence. [*Sleeps.*]

Solemn music. Enter, as in an apparition, Sicilius Leonatus, father to Posthumus, an old man, attired like a warrior; leading in his hand an ancient Matron, his wife, and mother to Posthumus, with music before them. Then, after other music, follows the two young Leonati, brothers to Posthumus, with wounds as they died in the wars. They circle Posthumus round, as he lies sleeping.

SICILIUS
No more, thou Thunder-master, show
Thy spite on mortal flies.
With Mars fall out, with Juno chide,
That thy adulteries
Rates and revenges.
Hath my poor boy done aught but well,
Whose face I never saw?
I died whilst in the womb he stay'd
Attending nature's law;
Whose father then, as men report
Thou orphans' father art,
Thou shouldst have been, and shielded him
From this earth-vexing smart.

MOTHER
Lucina lent not me her aid,
But took me in my throes,
That from me was Posthumus ripp'd,
Came crying 'mongst his foes,
A thing of pity!

SICILIUS
Great nature, like his ancestry,
Molded the stuff so fair,
That he deserv'd the praise o' th' world,
As great Sicilius' heir.

FIRST BROTHER
When once he was mature for man,
In Britain where was he
That could stand up his parallel,
Or fruitful object be
In eye of Imogen, that best
Could deem his dignity?

86 silly simple, rustic **87 affront** attack **90 seconds** supporters **91 answer'd him** followed his lead

V.iv. Location: A British prison or stockade.
10 penitent . . . bolt i.e., penitence to unlock the fetters encumbering my conscience **14 gyves** fetters **15 constrain'd** forced (upon me). **satisfy** make atonement **16 If . . . part** i.e., if such atonement is essential to freeing my conscience **17 stricter render** sterner repayment

19 broken bankrupt **21 abatement** diminished principal **24 'Tween . . . stamp** in commercial transactions men don't weigh every coin (*stamp*) exactly **25 Though . . . sake** even if some coins may be under the exact weight, men accept them for the sake of the image stamped thereon, i.e., the image of the King **26 You . . . yours** i.e., you should all the more readily take my life, even though I am a light (worthless) coin, since I am stamped in your image **27 take this audit** accept this accounting **28 bonds** (1) fetters, both literal and figurative (2) legal contracts **30 Thunder-master** i.e., Jupiter **34 Rates** scolds **38 Attending nature's law** i.e., awaiting the completion of his term in the womb **42 earth-vexing smart** suffering to which all life is prone **43 Lucina** goddess of childbirth **49 stuff** substance **52 mature for man** grown to manhood **53 he** any man **57 deem** judge

MOTHER

With marriage wherefore was he mock'd,
To be exil'd, and thrown
From Leonati seat, and cast
From her his dearest one,
Sweet Imogen?

SICILIUS

Why did you suffer Iachimo,
Slight thing of Italy,
To taint his nobler heart and brain
With needless jealousy,
And to become the geck and scorn
O' th' other's villainy?

SECOND BROTHER

For this from stiller seats we came,
Our parents and us twain,
That striking in our country's cause
Fell bravely and were slain,
Our fealty and Tenantius' right
With honor to maintain.

FIRST BROTHER

Like hardiment Posthumus hath
To Cymbeline perform'd.
Then, Jupiter, thou king of gods,
Why hast thou thus adjourn'd
The graces for his merits due,
Being all to dolors turn'd?

SICILIUS

Thy crystal window ope; look out.
No longer exercise
Upon a valiant race thy harsh
And potent injuries.

MOTHER

Since, Jupiter, our son is good,
Take off his miseries.

SICILIUS

Peep through thy marble mansion. Help,
Or we poor ghosts will cry
To th' shining synod of the rest
Against thy deity.

BROTHERS

Help, Jupiter, or we appeal,
And from thy justice fly.

Jupiter descends in thunder and lightning, sitting upon an eagle. He throws a thunderbolt. The Ghosts fall on their knees.

JUPITER

No more, you petty spirits of region low,
Offend our hearing. Hush! How dare you ghosts
Accuse the Thunderer, whose bolt, you know,
Sky-planted, batters all rebelling coasts?
Poor shadows of Elysium, hence, and rest
Upon your never-withering banks of flow'rs.
Be not with mortal accidents oppress'd.
No care of yours it is; you know 'tis ours.
Whom best I love I cross; to make my gift,
The more delay'd, delighted. Be content.
Your low-laid son our godhead will uplift.
His comforts thrive, his trials well are spent.
Our Jovial star reign'd at his birth, and in
Our temple was he married. Rise, and fade.
He shall be lord of lady Imogen,
And happier much by his affliction made.
This tablet lay upon his breast, wherein
Our pleasure his full fortune doth confine.
[*He delivers a tablet.*]
And so, away! No farther with your din
Express impatience, lest you stir up mine.
Mount, eagle, to my palace crystalline. *Ascends.*

SICILIUS

He came in thunder; his celestial breath
Was sulphurous to smell. The holy eagle
Stoop'd, as to foot us. His ascension is
More sweet than our blest fields. His royal bird
Prunes the immortal wing and cloys his beak,
As when his god is pleas'd.

ALL

Thanks, Jupiter!

SICILIUS

The marble pavement closes, he is enter'd
His radiant roof. Away! And, to be blest,
Let us with care perform his great behest.
[*The Ghosts place the tablet on Posthumus' breast, and*] *vanish.*

POSTHUMUS [*Waking*]

Sleep, thou hast been a grandsire, and begot
A father to me; and thou hast created
A mother and two brothers. But, O scorn,
Gone! They went hence so soon as they were born.
And so I am awake. Poor wretches that depend
On greatness' favor dream as I have done,
Wake and find nothing. But, alas, I swerve!
[*He sees the tablet.*]
Many dream not to find, neither deserve,
And yet are steep'd in favors; so am I,
That have this golden chance and know not why.
What fairies haunt this ground? A book? O rare one!
Be not, as is our fangled world, a garment
Nobler than that it covers! Let thy effects
So follow, to be most unlike our courtiers,
As good as promise.

(Reads.) "When as a lion's whelp shall, to himself unknown, without seeking find, and be embrac'd by a piece of tender air; and when from a stately cedar shall be lopp'd branches, which, being dead many years, shall after revive, be jointed to the old stock, and freshly grow; then shall Posthumus end his miseries, Britain be fortunate and flourish in peace and plenty."

'Tis still a dream, or else such stuff as madmen
Tongue and brain not; either both or nothing,
Or senseless speaking, or a speaking such
As sense cannot untie. Be what it is,

64 Slight worthless **67 geck** dupe **69 stiller seats** quieter abodes (i.e., the Elysian fields) **71 That** who **73 Tenantius'** Cymbeline's father's **75 Like hardiment** similar bold exploits **78 adjourn'd** deferred **89 synod of the rest** assembly of the gods **96 Sky-planted** growing out of the sky **99 accidents** events

102 delighted delighted in **104 spent** ended **105 Jovial star** the planet Jupiter, the happiest of all planets to be born under **110 confine** precisely state **116 Stoop'd** swooped down. **foot** seize (in his talons) **118 Prunes** preens. **cloys** claws, strokes with the claw **120 marble pavement** heavens (above the Elizabethan stage; cf. *marble mansion* in l. 87) **125 scorn** mockery **129 swerve** mistake, go astray **130 to find** of finding **133 book** i.e., the tablet or scroll. **rare** excellent **134 fangled** characterized by fripperies or gaudiness **136 to** so as **138 When as** when **146 Tongue** speak. **brain** understand **147 Or** either

The action of my life is like it, which
I'll keep, if but for sympathy.

Enter [First] Jailer.

FIRST JAILER Come, sir, are you ready for death?

POSTHUMUS Over-roasted rather; ready long ago.

FIRST JAILER Hanging is the word, sir. If you be ready for that, you are well cook'd.

POSTHUMUS So, if I prove a good repast to the spectators, the dish pays the shot.

FIRST JAILER A heavy reckoning for you, sir. But the comfort is, you shall be call'd to no more payments, fear no more tavern-bills, which are often the sadness of parting, as the procuring of mirth. You come in faint for want of meat, depart reeling with too much drink; sorry that you have paid too much, and sorry that you are paid too much; purse and brain both empty; the brain the heavier for being too light, the purse too light, being drawn of heaviness. O, of this contradiction you shall now be quit. O, the charity of a penny cord! It sums up thousands in a trice. You have no true debitor and creditor but it; of what's past, is, and to come, the discharge. Your neck, sir, is pen, book, and counters; so the acquittance follows.

POSTHUMUS I am merrier to die than thou art to live.

FIRST JAILER Indeed, sir, he that sleeps feels not the toothache. But a man that were to sleep your sleep, and a hangman to help him to bed, I think he would change places with his officer; for, look you, sir, you know not which way you shall go.

POSTHUMUS Yes, indeed do I, fellow.

FIRST JAILER Your death has eyes in 's head then; I have not seen him so pictur'd. You must either be directed by some that take upon them to know, or to take upon yourself that which I am sure you do not know, or jump the after inquiry on your own peril. And how you shall speed in your journey's end, I think you'll never return to tell one.

POSTHUMUS I tell thee, fellow, there are none want eyes to direct them the way I am going, but such as wink and will not use them.

FIRST JAILER What an infinite mock is this, that a man should have the best use of eyes to see the way of blindness! I am sure hanging's the way of winking.

Enter a Messenger.

MESSENGER Knock off his manacles; bring your prisoner to the King.

POSTHUMUS Thou bring'st good news; I am call'd to be made free. *[He is freed from his irons.]*

FIRST JAILER I'll be hang'd then.

POSTHUMUS Thou shalt be then freer than a jailer; no bolts for the dead. *Exeunt [all but the First Jailer].*

FIRST JAILER Unless a man would marry a gallows and beget young gibbets, I never saw one so prone. Yet, on my conscience, there are verier knaves desire to live, for all he be a Roman; and there be some of them too that die against their wills. So should I, if I were one. I would we were all of one mind, and one mind good. O, there were desolation of jailers and gallowses! I speak against my present profit, but my wish hath a preferment in 't. *[Exit.]*

150 sympathy i.e., resemblance (between my life and this mystery) **153 Hanging** (1) hanging up like cooking meat (2) being hanged as a criminal **156 the dish . . . shot** (1) the food is worth the tavern reckoning (2) my death settles my account **159 often** as often **163 are paid** are subjugated (by excessive drink) **165 drawn** tapped, emptied **168 debitor and creditor** accounting book **169 discharge** payment **170 counters** metal disks used for calculating **175 officer** i.e., the hangman **180 take upon them** undertake, profess **182 jump** gamble on **183 speed** succeed **186 wink** close the eyes

199 prone ready, eager **200–203** i.e., **there . . . one** he's not such a bad fellow, even if he is a Roman; worse men than he desire to live when they're to be executed, as I would in such a plight **206 preferment** i.e., a preference for us all to live in a better world

SCENE V

Enter Cymbeline, Belarius, Guiderius, Arviragus, Pisanio, [Officers, Attendants,] and Lords.

CYMBELINE
Stand by my side, you whom the gods have made
Preservers of my throne. Woe is my heart
That the poor soldier that so richly fought,
Whose rags sham'd gilded arms, whose naked breast
Stepp'd before targes of proof, cannot be found.
He shall be happy that can find him, if
Our grace can make him so.

BELARIUS I never saw
Such noble fury in so poor a thing,
Such precious deeds in one that promis'd nought
But beggary and poor looks.

CYMBELINE No tidings of him?

PISANIO
He hath been search'd among the dead and living,
But no trace of him.

CYMBELINE To my grief, I am
The heir of his reward, *[To Belarius, Guiderius, and Arviragus]* which I will add
To you, the liver, heart, and brain of Britain,
By whom I grant she lives. 'Tis now the time
To ask of whence you are. Report it.

BELARIUS Sir,
In Cambria are we born, and gentlemen.
Further to boast were neither true nor modest,
Unless I add we are honest.

CYMBELINE Bow your knees.
[They kneel.]
Arise my knights o' th' battle. *[They arise.]* I create you
Companions to our person, and will fit you
With dignities becoming your estates.

Enter Cornelius and Ladies.

There's business in these faces. Why so sadly
Greet you our victory? You look like Romans,

V.v. Location: Britain. Cymbeline's tent in the British camp.
5 targes of proof shields hardened to withstand tests **20 knights o' th' battle** knights created on the battlefield **22 estates** i.e., new status

And not o' th' court of Britain.
CORNELIUS Hail, great King!
To sour your happiness, I must report
The Queen is dead.
CYMBELINE Who worse than a physician
Would this report become? But I consider
By med'cine life may be prolong'd, yet death
Will seize the doctor too. How ended she?
CORNELIUS
With horror, madly dying, like her life,
Which, being cruel to the world, concluded
Most cruel to herself. What she confess'd
I will report, so please you. These her women
Can trip me, if I err, who with wet cheeks 35
Were present when she finish'd.
CYMBELINE Prithee say.
CORNELIUS
First, she confess'd she never lov'd you, only
Affected greatness got by you, not you; 38
Married your royalty, was wife to your place,
Abhorr'd your person.
CYMBELINE She alone knew this;
And, but she spoke it dying, I would not 41
Believe her lips in opening it. Proceed. 42
CORNELIUS
Your daughter, whom she bore in hand to love 43
With such integrity, she did confess
Was as a scorpion to her sight, whose life,
But that her flight prevented it, she had
Ta'en off by poison.
CYMBELINE O most delicate fiend! 47
Who is 't can read a woman? Is there more?
CORNELIUS
More, sir, and worse. She did confess she had
For you a mortal mineral, which, being took, 50
Should by the minute feed on life and, ling'ring, 51
By inches waste you. In which time she purpos'd,
By watching, weeping, tendance, kissing, to 53
O'ercome you with her show and, in time,
When she had fitted you with her craft, to work 55
Her son into th' adoption of the crown; 56
But, failing of her end by his strange absence,
Grew shameless desperate; open'd, in despite 58
Of heaven and men, her purposes; repented 59
The evils she hatch'd were not effected; so
Despairing died.
CYMBELINE Heard you all this, her women?
LADIES
We did, so please your Highness.
CYMBELINE
Mine eyes
Were not in fault, for she was beautiful;
Mine ears, that heard her flattery; nor my heart,
That thought her like her seeming. It had been
vicious 66
To have mistrusted her. Yet, O my daughter,
That it was folly in me thou mayst say,
And prove it in thy feeling. Heaven mend all! 69

Enter Lucius, Iachimo, [the Soothsayer,] and other Roman Prisoners, [guarded; Posthumus] Leonatus behind, and Imogen.

Thou com'st not, Caius, now for tribute. That
The Britons have raz'd out, though with the loss 71
Of many a bold one, whose kinsmen have made
suit
That their good souls may be appeas'd with
slaughter
Of you their captives, which ourself have granted.
So think of your estate. 75
LUCIUS
Consider, sir, the chance of war. The day
Was yours by accident; had it gone with us,
We should not, when the blood was cool, have
threaten'd
Our prisoners with the sword. But since the gods
Will have it thus, that nothing but our lives
May be call'd ransom, let it come. Sufficeth
A Roman with a Roman's heart can suffer.
Augustus lives to think on 't; and so much
For my peculiar care. This one thing only 84
I will entreat: my boy, a Briton born,
Let him be ransom'd. Never master had
A page so kind, so duteous, diligent,
So tender over his occasions, true, 88
So feat, so nurse-like. Let his virtue join 89
With my request, which I'll make bold your
Highness
Cannot deny. He hath done no Briton harm,
Though he have serv'd a Roman. Save him, sir,
And spare no blood beside.
CYMBELINE I have surely seen him; 93
His favor is familiar to me. Boy, 94
Thou hast look'd thyself into my grace, 95
And art mine own. I know not why, wherefore,
To say "Live, boy." Ne'er thank thy master. Live,
And ask of Cymbeline what boon thou wilt,
Fitting my bounty and thy state, I'll give it;
Yea, though thou do demand a prisoner,
The noblest ta'en.
IMOGEN I humbly thank your Highness.
LUCIUS
I do not bid thee beg my life, good lad;
And yet I know thou wilt.
IMOGEN No, no, alack,
There's other work in hand. I see a thing 104
Bitter to me as death. Your life, good master,
Must shuffle for itself.
LUCIUS The boy disdains me,

35 trip refute, contradict **38 Affected** desired **41 but** were it not that **42 opening** revealing **43 bore in hand** pretended **47 Ta'en off** ended. **delicate** subtle **50 mortal mineral** deadly poison **51 by the minute** minute by minute **53 tendance** attentiveness **55 fitted** shaped to her wish **56 adoption** right of an adopted heir **58 open'd** revealed **59 repented** regretted **66 vicious** wrong

69 prove experience. **feeling** i.e., suffering **71 raz'd out** erased **75 estate** spiritual estate (in preparation for your death) **84 my peculiar care** my concern for myself **88 occasions** particular wants or requirements **89 feat** adroit, neat **93 And** even if (you) **94 favor** face **95 look'd . . . grace** won my favor by your appearance **104 thing** i.e., the ring on Iachimo's finger

He leaves me, scorns me. Briefly die their joys
That place them on the truth of girls and boys.
Why stands he so perplex'd?

CYMBELINE
What wouldst thou, boy?
I love thee more and more. Think more and more
What's best to ask. Know'st him thou look'st on? Speak,
Wilt have him live? Is he thy kin? Thy friend?

IMOGEN
He is a Roman, no more kin to me
Than I to your Highness; who, being born your vassal,
Am something nearer.

CYMBELINE
Wherefore ey'st him so?

IMOGEN
I'll tell you, sir, in private, if you please
To give me hearing.

CYMBELINE
Ay, with all my heart,
And lend my best attention. What's thy name?

IMOGEN
Fidele, sir.

CYMBELINE
Thou 'rt my good youth, my page;
I'll be thy master. Walk with me; speak freely.
[*Cymbeline and Imogen converse apart.*]

BELARIUS
Is not this boy reviv'd from death?

ARVIRAGUS
One sand another
Not more resembles that sweet rosy lad
Who died, and was Fidele. What think you?

GUIDERIUS
The same dead thing alive.

BELARIUS
Peace, peace! See further. He eyes us not; forbear.
Creatures may be alike. Were 't he, I am sure
He would have spoke to us.

GUIDERIUS
But we saw him dead.

BELARIUS
Be silent; let's see further.

PISANIO [*Aside*]
It is my mistress.
Since she is living, let the time run on
To good or bad.
[*Cymbeline and Imogen come forward.*]

CYMBELINE
Come, stand thou by our side;
Make thy demand aloud. [*To Iachimo.*] Sir, step you forth;
Give answer to this boy, and do it freely,
Or, by our greatness and the grace of it,
Which is our honor, bitter torture shall
Winnow the truth from falsehood.—On, speak to him.

IMOGEN
My boon is that this gentleman may render
Of whom he had this ring.
[*Points to the ring Iachimo wears.*]

POSTHUMUS [*Aside*]
What's that to him?

CYMBELINE
That diamond upon your finger, say
How came it yours?

IACHIMO
Thou 'lt torture me to leave unspoken that
Which, to be spoke, would torture thee.

CYMBELINE
How? Me?

IACHIMO
I am glad to be constrain'd to utter that
Which torments me to conceal. By villainy
I got this ring. 'Twas Leonatus' jewel,
Whom thou didst banish; and—which more may grieve thee,
As it doth me—a nobler sir ne'er liv'd
'Twixt sky and ground. Wilt thou hear more, my lord?

CYMBELINE
All that belongs to this.

IACHIMO
That paragon, thy daughter,
For whom my heart drops blood, and my false spirits
Quail to remember—Give me leave; I faint.

CYMBELINE
My daughter? What of her? Renew thy strength.
I had rather thou shouldst live while nature will
Than die ere I hear more. Strive, man, and speak.

IACHIMO
Upon a time—unhappy was the clock
That struck the hour!—it was in Rome—accurs'd
The mansion where!—'twas at a feast—O, would
Our viands had been poison'd, or at least
Those which I heav'd to head!—the good Posthumus—
What should I say? He was too good to be
Where ill men were, and was the best of all
Amongst the rar'st of good ones—sitting sadly,
Hearing us praise our loves of Italy
For beauty that made barren the swell'd boast
Of him that best could speak; for feature, laming
The shrine of Venus or straight-pight Minerva,
Postures beyond brief nature, for condition,
A shop of all the qualities that man
Loves woman for, besides that hook of wiving,
Fairness which strikes the eye—

CYMBELINE
I stand on fire.
Come to the matter.

IACHIMO
All too soon I shall,
Unless thou wouldst grieve quickly. This Posthumus,
Most like a noble lord in love and one
That had a royal lover, took his hint,
And, not dispraising whom we prais'd—therein
He was as calm as virtue—he began
His mistress' picture; which by his tongue being made,
And then a mind put in 't, either our brags
Were crack'd of kitchen trulls, or his description

107–108 Briefly . . . That swiftly die the joys of those who **108 truth** fidelity

141 to leave for leaving **153 live . . . will** continue to live as long as nature permits **159 heav'd to head** raised to lips **164 made . . . boast** rendered ineffectual even the exaggerated boasting **165–166 for . . . Venus** (praising them) for figure, making the image of Venus seem crippled in comparison **166 straight-pight** erect **167 Postures . . . nature** forms beyond the capacity of human nature, immortal. **for condition** (praising them) for temper of mind **168 shop** storehouse **169 hook of wiving** incentive to matrimony **179 crack'd of** boasted in praise of. **kitchen trulls** kitchen maids

Prov'd us unspeaking sots.
CYMBELINE Nay, nay, to th' purpose.
IACHIMO
Your daughter's chastity—there it begins.
He spake of her, as Dian had hot dreams,
And she alone were cold; whereat I, wretch,
Made scruple of his praise, and wager'd with him
Pieces of gold 'gainst this which then he wore
Upon his honor'd finger, to attain
In suit the place of 's bed and win this ring
By hers and mine adultery. He, true knight,
No lesser of her honor confident
Than I did truly find her, stakes this ring;
And would so, had it been a carbuncle
Of Phoebus' wheel, and might so safely, had it
Been all the worth of 's car. Away to Britain
Post I in this design. Well may you, sir,
Remember me at court, where I was taught
Of your chaste daughter the wide difference
'Twixt amorous and villainous. Being thus quench'd
Of hope, not longing, mine Italian brain
'Gan in your duller Britain operate
Most vilely; for my vantage, excellent.
And, to be brief, my practice so prevail'd
That I return'd with simular proof enough
To make the noble Leonatus mad,
By wounding his belief in her renown
With tokens thus, and thus; averring notes
Of chamber-hanging, pictures, this her bracelet—
[*Shows the bracelet.*]
Oh cunning, how I got it!—nay, some marks
Of secret on her person, that he could not
But think her bond of chastity quite crack'd,
I having ta'en the forfeit. Whereupon—
Methinks, I see him now—
POSTHUMUS Ay, so thou dost,
Italian fiend! Ay me, most credulous fool,
Egregious murderer, thief, any thing
That's due to all the villains past, in being,
To come! O, give me cord, or knife, or poison,
Some upright justicer! Thou, King, send out
For torturers ingenious! It is I
That all th' abhorred things o' th' earth amend
By being worse than they. I am Posthumus,
That kill'd thy daughter—villain-like, I lie—
That caus'd a lesser villain than myself,
A sacrilegious thief, to do 't. The temple
Of virtue was she; yea, and she herself.
Spit, and throw stones, cast mire upon me, set
The dogs o' th' street to bay me! Every villain
Be call'd Posthumus Leonatus, and
Be villainy less than 'twas! O Imogen!
My queen, my life, my wife! O Imogen,
Imogen, Imogen!
IMOGEN Peace, my lord. Hear, hear—
POSTHUMUS
Shall 's have a play of this? Thou scornful page,
There lie thy part. [*Strikes her; she falls.*]
PISANIO O, gentlemen, help!
[*Goes to her assistance.*]
Mine and your mistress! O, my lord Posthumus,
You ne'er kill'd Imogen till now. Help, help!
Mine honor'd lady!
CYMBELINE Does the world go round?
POSTHUMUS
How comes these staggers on me?
PISANIO Wake, my mistress!
CYMBELINE
If this be so, the gods do mean to strike me
To death with mortal joy.
PISANIO How fares my mistress?
IMOGEN
O, get thee from my sight!
Thou gav'st me poison. Dangerous fellow, hence!
Breathe not where princes are.
CYMBELINE The tune of Imogen!
PISANIO
Lady,
The gods throw stones of sulphur on me, if
That box I gave you was not thought by me
A precious thing. I had it from the Queen.
CYMBELINE
New matter still?
IMOGEN It poison'd me.
CORNELIUS O gods!
I left out one thing which the Queen confess'd,
Which must approve thee honest. "If Pisanio
Have," said she, "given his mistress that confection
Which I gave him for cordial, she is serv'd
As I would serve a rat."
CYMBELINE What's this, Cornelius?
CORNELIUS
The Queen, sir, very oft importun'd me
To temper poisons for her, still pretending
The satisfaction of her knowledge only
In killing creatures vile, as cats and dogs,
Of no esteem. I, dreading that her purpose
Was of more danger, did compound for her
A certain stuff which, being ta'en, would cease
The present pow'r of life, but in short time
All offices of nature should again
Do their due functions. Have you ta'en of it?
IMOGEN
Most like I did, for I was dead.
BELARIUS My boys,
There was our error.
GUIDERIUS This is, sure, Fidele.
IMOGEN
Why did you throw your wedded lady from you?
[*Embraces him.*]
Think that you are upon a rock, and now

180 unspeaking sots inarticulate blockheads **182 as** as if **191 would so** would have done so **192 Phoebus' wheel** i.e., wheel of the sun-god's chariot **194 Post** hasten **196 Of** by **198 not longing** though not of my desire **199 duller** i.e., slower-minded (supposedly caused by the northern climate) **200 vantage** profit **201 practice** scheming **202 simular** simulated, or pretended **204 renown** good name **205 averring** avouching, citing **210 the forfeit** i.e., what was forfeited by the breaking of her bond of chaste loyalty **218 That . . . amend** who make all loathsome things seem better in comparison **223 she herself** i.e., virtue herself

230 Shall 's shall we **235 staggers** dizziness, bewilderment **240 tune** voice **242 stones of sulpher** thunderbolts **247 approve** prove **248 confection** composition of drugs **252 temper** mix **257 cease** cause to cease **264 rock** i.e., solid ground (?) (Some editors conjecture *lock,* a wrestling embrace.)

Throw me again.

POSTHUMUS Hang there like fruit, my soul,
Till the tree die!

CYMBELINE How now, my flesh, my child?
What, mak'st thou me a dullard in this act?
Wilt thou not speak to me?

IMOGEN [*Kneeling*] Your blessing, sir.

BELARIUS [*To Guiderius and Arviragus*]
Though you did love this youth, I blame ye not;
You had a motive for 't.

CYMBELINE My tears that fall
Prove holy water on thee! Imogen,
Thy mother's dead.

IMOGEN I am sorry for 't, my lord.

CYMBELINE
O, she was naught; and long of her it was 273
That we meet here so strangely. But her son
Is gone, we know not how nor where.

PISANIO My lord,
Now fear is from me, I'll speak troth. Lord Cloten, 276
Upon my lady's missing, came to me
With his sword drawn, foam'd at the mouth, and swore,
If I discover'd not which way she was gone, 279
It was my instant death. By accident
I had a feigned letter of my master's
Then in my pocket, which directed him
To seek her on the mountains near to Milford;
Where, in a frenzy, in my master's garments,
Which he enforc'd from me, away he posts
With unchaste purpose and with oath to violate
My lady's honor. What became of him
I further know not.

GUIDERIUS Let me end the story:
I slew him there.

CYMBELINE Marry, the gods forfend! 289
I would not thy good deeds should from my lips 290
Pluck a hard sentence. Prithee, valiant youth,
Deny 't again.

GUIDERIUS I have spoke it, and I did it. 292

CYMBELINE
He was a prince.

GUIDERIUS
A most incivil one. The wrongs he did me
Were nothing prince-like, for he did provoke me
With language that would make me spurn the sea
If it could so roar to me. I cut off 's head,
And am right glad he is not standing here
To tell this tale of mine.

CYMBELINE I am sorrow for thee. 299
By thine own tongue thou art condemn'd, and must
Endure our law. Thou 'rt dead.

IMOGEN That headless man
I thought had been my lord.

CYMBELINE Bind the offender,
And take him from our presence.
[*Guards start to bind him.*]

BELARIUS Stay, sir King.
This man is better than the man he slew,
As well descended as thyself, and hath
More of thee merited than a band of Clotens
Had ever scar for. [*To the Guard.*] Let his arms alone; 307
They were not born for bondage.

CYMBELINE Why, old soldier,
Wilt thou undo the worth thou art unpaid for
By tasting of our wrath? How of descent
As good as we?

ARVIRAGUS In that he spake too far.

CYMBELINE
And thou shalt die for 't.

BELARIUS We will die all three
But I will prove that two on 's are as good 313
As I have given out him. My sons, I must 314
For mine own part unfold a dangerous speech,
Though, haply, well for you.

ARVIRAGUS Your danger's ours.

GUIDERIUS
And our good his.

BELARIUS Have at it then, by leave. 317
Thou hadst, great King, a subject who
Was call'd Belarius.

CYMBELINE What of him? He is
A banish'd traitor.

BELARIUS He it is that hath
Assum'd this age; indeed a banish'd man, 321
I know not how a traitor.

CYMBELINE Take him hence!
The whole world shall not save him.

BELARIUS Not too hot.
First pay me for the nursing of thy sons,
And let it be confiscate all, so soon
As I have receiv'd it.

CYMBELINE Nursing of my sons?

BELARIUS
I am too blunt and saucy. Here's my knee. [*Kneels.*]
Ere I arise, I will prefer my sons; 328
Then spare not the old father. Mighty sir,
These two young gentlemen, that call me father
And think they are my sons, are none of mine;
They are the issue of your loins, my liege,
And blood of your begetting.

CYMBELINE How? My issue?

BELARIUS
So sure as you your father's. I, old Morgan,
Am that Belarius whom you sometime banish'd.
Your pleasure was my mere offense, my punishment 336
Itself, and all my treason; that I suffer'd
Was all the harm I did. These gentle princes—
For such and so they are—these twenty years
Have I train'd up; those arts they have as I
Could put into them. My breeding was, sir, as
Your Highness knows. Their nurse, Euriphile,
Whom for the theft I wedded, stole these children

273 naught wicked. **long of** on account of **276 troth** truth **279 discover'd** disclosed **289 forfend** forbid **290 thy good deeds** i.e., you, who fought so valiantly against the Romans **292 again** i.e., in speaking again **299 tell . . . mine** i.e., tell of cutting off my head

307 scar i.e., battle scar **313 But I will** unless I do not. **on 's** of us **314 given out** reported **317 Have at it** i.e., here goes. **by leave** with your permission **321 Assum'd** reached, attained **328 prefer** promote **336 Your . . . offense** i.e., what it pleased you to denounce me for was all the offense I committed

Upon my banishment. I mov'd her to 't,
Having receiv'd the punishment before
For that which I did then. Beaten for loyalty
Excited me to treason. Their dear loss,
The more of you 'twas felt, the more it shap'd
Unto my end of stealing them. But, gracious sir,
Here are your sons again, and I must lose
Two of the sweet'st companions in the world.
The benediction of these covering heavens
Fall on their heads like dew! For they are worthy
To inlay heaven with stars.

CYMBELINE Thou weep'st, and speak'st.
The service that you three have done is more
Unlike than this thou tell'st. I lost my children;
If these be they, I know not how to wish
A pair of worthier sons.

BELARIUS Be pleas'd awhile.
This gentleman, whom I call Polydore,
Most worthy prince, as yours, is true Guiderius;
This gentleman, my Cadwal, Arviragus,
Your younger princely son. He, sir, was lapp'd
In a most curious mantle, wrought by th' hand
Of his queen mother, which for more probation
I can with ease produce.

CYMBELINE Guiderius had
Upon his neck a mole, a sanguine star;
It was a mark of wonder.

BELARIUS This is he,
Who hath upon him still that natural stamp.
It was wise nature's end in the donation
To be his evidence now.

CYMBELINE O, what, am I
A mother to the birth of three? Ne'er mother
Rejoic'd deliverance more. Blest pray you be,
That, after this strange starting from your orbs,
You may reign in them now! O Imogen,
Thou hast lost by this a kingdom.

IMOGEN No, my lord;
I have got two worlds by 't. O my gentle brothers,
Have we thus met? O, never say hereafter
But I am truest speaker. You call'd me brother,
When I was but your sister; I you brothers,
When ye were so indeed.

CYMBELINE Did you e'er meet?

ARVIRAGUS
Ay, my good lord.

GUIDERIUS And at first meeting lov'd;
Continu'd so, until we thought he died.

CORNELIUS
By the Queen's dram she swallow'd.

CYMBELINE O rare instinct!
When shall I hear all through? This fierce
abridgement
Hath to it circumstantial branches, which
Distinction should be rich in. Where, how liv'd you?
And when came you to serve our Roman captive?
How parted with your brothers? How first met
them?
Why fled you from the court? And whither? These,
And your three motives to the battle, with
I know not how much more, should be demanded,
And all the other by-dependencies,
From chance to chance; but nor the time nor place
Will serve our long interrogatories. See,
Posthumus anchors upon Imogen,
And she, like harmless lightning, throws her eye
On him, her brothers, me, her master, hitting
Each object with a joy; the counterchange
Is severally in all. Let's quit this ground,
And smoke the temple with our sacrifices.
[*To Belarius.*] Thou art my brother; so we'll hold
thee ever.

IMOGEN [*To Belarius*]
You are my father too, and did relieve me
To see this gracious season.

CYMBELINE All o'erjoy'd,
Save these in bonds. Let them be joyful too,
For they shall taste our comfort.

IMOGEN [*To Lucius*] My good master,
I will yet do you service.

LUCIUS Happy be you!

CYMBELINE
The forlorn soldier, that so nobly fought,
He would have well becom'd this place, and grac'd
The thankings of a king.

POSTHUMUS I am, sir,
The soldier that did company these three
In poor beseeming; 'twas a fitment for
The purpose I then follow'd. That I was he,
Speak, Iachimo. I had you down and might
Have made you finish.

IACHIMO [*Kneeling*] I am down again;
But now my heavy conscience sinks my knee,
As then your force did. Take that life, beseech you,
Which I so often owe; but your ring first;
And here the bracelet of the truest princess
That ever swore her faith. [*Gives ring and bracelet.*]

POSTHUMUS Kneel not to me.
The pow'r that I have on you is to spare you;
The malice towards you to forgive you. Live,
And deal with others better. [*Iachimo rises.*]

CYMBELINE Nobly doom'd!
We'll learn our freeness of a son-in-law;
Pardon's the word to all.

ARVIRAGUS [*To Posthumus*] You holp us, sir,
As you did mean indeed to be our brother;
Joy'd are we that you are.

346 Beaten being beaten **348 of** by **348–349 shap'd . . . of** contributed to my purpose in **356 Unlike** unlikely, incredible **362 lapp'd** enfolded **363 curious** artfully made **364 probation** proof **366 sanguine** blood-red **369 end** aim, purpose **370 his evidence** evidence of his identity **371–372 Ne'er . . . more** never did deliverance (in childbed) more rejoice a mother **373 starting . . . orbs** shooting from your orbits, i.e., leaving your places at court **374 reign** i.e., both as royal persons and as planets with influence **384 fierce abridgement** unduly compressed account

385–386 circumstantial . . . in i.e., details and ramifications to be distinguished in all their abundance **390 your three motives** the motives of you three **392 by-dependencies** attendant circumstances **393 chance to chance** event to event **398–399 the counterchange . . . all** the exchange (of happy glances) involves each of us to everyone else **400 smoke** fill with incense **407 forlorn** lost, missing **411 beseeming** appearance. **fitment** makeshift disguise **414 made you finish** put an end to you **415 sinks** causes to sink **417 often** many times over **422 doom'd** decreed, judged **423 freeness** liberality, generosity

POSTHUMUS
Your servant, princes. Good my lord of Rome,
Call forth your soothsayer. As I slept, methought
Great Jupiter, upon his eagle back'd,
Appear'd to me, with other spritely shows 430
Of mine own kindred. When I wak'd, I found
This label on my bosom [*Shows tablet*], whose containing 432
Is so from sense in hardness, that I can 433
Make no collection of it. Let him show 434
His skill in the construction.

LUCIUS
Philarmonus! 435

SOOTHSAYER
Here, my good lord.

LUCIUS
Read, and declare the meaning.

SOOTHSAYER (*Reads*) "When as a lion's whelp shall, to himself unknown, without seeking find, and be embrac'd by a piece of tender air; and when from a stately cedar shall be lopp'd branches, which, being dead many years, shall after revive, be jointed to the old stock, and freshly grow; then shall Posthumus end his miseries, Britain be fortunate and flourish in peace and plenty."
Thou, Leonatus, art the lion's whelp;
The fit and apt construction of thy name,
Being Leo-natus, doth import so much. 447
[*To Cymbeline.*] The piece of tender air, thy virtuous daughter,
Which we call "mollis aer," and "mollis aer" 449
We term it "mulier"; which "mulier" I divine
Is this most constant wife; who, even now,
Answering the letter of the oracle, [*To Posthumus.*] 452
Unknown to you, unsought, were clipp'd about 453
With this most tender air.

CYMBELINE
This hath some seeming. 454

SOOTHSAYER
The lofty cedar, royal Cymbeline,
Personates thee, and thy lopp'd branches point
Thy two sons forth; who, by Belarius stol'n,
For many years thought dead, are now reviv'd,
To the majestic cedar join'd, whose issue
Promises Britain peace and plenty.

CYMBELINE
Well,
My peace we will begin. And, Caius Lucius,
Although the victor, we submit to Caesar,
And to the Roman empire, promising
To pay our wonted tribute, from the which
We were dissuaded by our wicked queen,
Whom heavens, in justice, both on her and hers, 466
Have laid most heavy hand.

SOOTHSAYER
The fingers of the pow'rs above do tune
The harmony of this peace. The vision
Which I made known to Lucius, ere the stroke
Of this yet scarce-cold battle, at this instant
Is full accomplish'd; for the Roman eagle,
From south to west on wing soaring aloft,
Lessen'd herself, and in the beams o' th' sun
So vanish'd; which foreshow'd our princely eagle,
Th' imperial Caesar, should again unite
His favor with the radiant Cymbeline,
Which shines here in the west.

CYMBELINE
Laud we the gods, 478
And let our crooked smokes climb to their nostrils 479
From our blest altars. Publish we this peace
To all our subjects. Set we forward. Let
A Roman and a British ensign wave
Friendly together. So through Lud's-town march,
And in the temple of great Jupiter
Our peace we'll ratify, seal it with feasts.
Set on there! Never was a war did cease, 486
Ere bloody hands were wash'd, with such a peace.
Exeunt.

430 spritely ghostly, in the form of spirits. **shows** appearances **432 label** tablet, paper **432–433 whose . . . hardness** whose meaning is so remote from sense in its difficulty **434 collection of** inference or deduction from **435 construction** construing of it **447 Leo-natus** one born of the lion **449 mollis aer** tender air. (A fanciful derivation of Latin *mulier,* woman.) **452 Answering** corresponding with **453 were clipp'd about** i.e., you were embraced **454 seeming** plausibility **466 Whom** on whom. **hers** i.e., Cloten

478 Laud praise **479 crooked** curling, twining **486 Set on there** forward march

The Winter's Tale

The Winter's Tale (c. 1610–1611), with its almost symmetrical division into two halves of bleak tragedy and comic romance, illustrates perhaps more clearly than any other Shakespearean play the genre of tragicomedy. To be sure, all the late romances feature journeys of separation, apparent deaths, and tearful reconciliations. Marina and Thaisa in *Pericles,* Imogen in *Cymbeline,* and Ferdinand in *The Tempest,* all supposed irrecoverably lost, are brought back to life by apparently miraculous devices. Of the four late romances, however, *The Winter's Tale* uses the most formal structure to evoke the antithesis of tragedy and romance. It is sharply divided into contrasting halves by a gap of sixteen years. The tragic first half takes place almost entirely in Sicilia, whereas the action of the second half is limited for the most part to Bohemia. At the court of Sicilia we see tyrannical jealousy producing a spiritual climate of "winter In storm perpetual"; in Bohemia we witness a pastoral landscape and a sheepshearing evoking "the sweet o' the year," "When daffodils begin to peer."

Although this motif of a renewing journey from jaded court to idealized countryside reminds us of *As You Like It* and other early comedies, we sense in the late romances and especially in *The Winter's Tale* a new preoccupation with man's tragic folly. The vision of human depravity is world-weary and pessimistic, as though infected by the gloomy spirit of the great tragedies. And because man is so bent on destroying himself, the restoration is at once more urgently needed and more miraculous than in the "festive" world of early comedy. Renewal is mythically associated with the seasonal cycle from winter to summer.

King Leontes' tragedy seems at first irreversible and terrifying, like that of Shakespeare's greatest tragic protagonists. He suffers from irrational jealousy, as does Othello, and attempts to destroy the person on whom all his happiness depends. Unlike Othello, however, Leontes needs no diabolical tempter such as Iago to poison his mind against Queen Hermione. Leontes is undone by his own fantasies. No differences in race or age can explain Leontes' fears of estrangement from Hermione. She is not imprudent in her conduct, like her counterpart in Robert Greene's *Pandosto* (1588), the prose romance from which Shakespeare drew his narrative. Although Hermione is graciously fond of Leontes' dear friend Polixenes, and urges him to stay longer in Sicilia, she does so only with a hospitable warmth demanded by the occasion and encouraged by her husband. In every way, then, Shakespeare strips away from Leontes the motive and the occasion for plausible doubting of his wife. All observers in the Sicilian court are incredulous and shocked at the King's accusations. Even so, Leontes is neither an unsympathetic nor an unbelievable character. Like Othello, Leontes cherishes his wife and perceives with a horrifying intensity what a fearful cost he must pay for his suspicions. Not only his marriage, but his lifelong friendship with Polixenes, his sense of pride in his children, and his enjoyment of his subjects' warm regard, all must be sacrificed to a single overwhelming compulsion.

Whatever may be the psychological cause of this obsession, it manifests itself as a revulsion against all sexual behavior. Like mad Lear, Leontes imagines lechery to be the unavoidable fact of the cosmos and of the human condition, the lowest common denominator to which all persons (including Hermione) must stoop. He is persuaded that "It is a bawdy planet," in which cuckolded man has "his pond fish'd by his next neighbor, by Sir Smile, his neighbor" (I,ii). Leontes' tortured soliloquies are laden with sexual images, of unattended "gates" letting in and out the enemy "with bag and baggage," and of a "dagger" that must be "muzzl'd Lest it should bite its master." As in *King Lear,* order is inverted to disorder, sanity to madness, legitimacy to illegitimacy. Sexual misconduct is emblematic of a universal malaise: "Why, then the world and all that's in 't is nothing, The covering sky is nothing, Bohemia nothing, My wife is nothing." Other characters too see the trial of Hermione as a testing of humanity's worth: if Hermione prove false, Antigonus promises, he will treat his own wife as a stable-horse and will "geld" his three daughters (II,i). Prevailing images are of spiders, venom, infection, sterility, and the "dungy" earth.

Cosmic order is never really challenged, however. Leontes' fantasies of universal disorder are chimerical. His wife is in fact chaste, Polixenes true, and the King's courtiers loyal. Camillo refuses to carry out Leontes' order to murder Polixenes, not only because he knows murder to be wrong but because history offers not one example of a man "that had struck anointed kings And flourish'd after" (I,ii). The cosmos of this play is one in which crimes are invariably and swiftly punished. The Delphic oracle vindicates Hermione and gives Leontes stern warning. When Leontes persists in his madness, his son Mamillius' death follows as an immediate consequence. As Leontes at once perceives, "Apollo's angry, and the heavens themselves Do strike at my injustice" (III,ii). Leontes paradoxically welcomes the lengthy contrition he must undergo, for it confirms a pattern in the universe of just cause and effect. Although as tragic protagonist he has discovered the truth about Hermione moments too late, and so must pay richly for his error, Leontes has at least recovered faith in Hermione's transcendent goodness. His nightmare now over, he accepts and embraces suffering as a necessary atonement.

The transition to romance is therefore anticipated to an extent by the play's first half, even though the tone of the last two acts is strikingly different. Old Father Time comes on stage as Chorus, like Gower in *Pericles,* to remind us of the conscious artifice of the dramatist. He can "o'erthrow law" and carry us over sixteen years as if we had merely dreamed out the interim. Shakespeare flaunts the improbability of his story by giving Bohemia a seacoast (much to the distress of Ben Jonson), and by employing animals on stage in a fanciful way *("Exit pursued by a bear").* The narrative uses many typical devices of romance: a babe abandoned to the elements, a princess brought up by shepherds, a prince disguised as a swain, a sea voyage, and a recognition scene. Love is threatened not by the internal psychic obstacle of jealousy, but by the external obstacles of parental opposition and a seeming disparity of social rank between the lovers. Comedy easily finds solutions for such difficulties by the unraveling of illusion. This comic world also properly includes clownish shepherds, coy shepherdesses, and Autolycus, the roguish pedlar, whose songs help set the mood of jollity and whose machinations contribute in an unforeseen manner to the working out of the love plot.

The conventional romantic ending is infused, however, with a sadness and a mystery that take the play well beyond what is usual in comedy. In Shakespeare's most notable departure from his source, Greene's *Pandosto,* Hermione is brought back to life. All observers view this event, and the rediscovery of Perdita, as grossly implausible, "so like an old tale that the verity of it is in strong suspicion" (V,ii). The play's very title, *The Winter's Tale,* reinforces this sense of naive improbability. Why does Shakespeare stress this riddling paradox of an unbelievable reality, and why does he deliberately mislead his audience into believing that Hermione has in fact died (III,iii), using a kind of theatrical trickery found in no other Shakespearean play? The answer may well be that, in Paulina's words, we must awake our faith, accepting a narrative of death and return to life that cannot ultimately be comprehended by reason. On the rational level we are told that Hermione has been kept in hiding for sixteen years, in order to bring Leontes' contrition to fulfillment. Such an explanation seems psychologically incomprehensible, however, for it casts both Hermione and her keeper Paulina in the role of sadistic punishers of the King. Instead we are drawn toward an emblematic interpretation, bearing in mind that it is more an evocative hint than a complete truth. Throughout the play, Hermione has been repeatedly associated with "Grace" and with the goddess Proserpina, whose return from the underworld, after "Three crabbed months had sour'd themselves to death" (I,ii), signals the coming of spring. Perdita, also associated with Proserpina (IV,iv), is welcomed by her father "As is the spring to th' earth" (V,i). Paulina has a similarly emblematic role, that of Conscience, patiently guiding the King to a divinely appointed renewal of his joy. Paulina speaks of herself as an artist-figure, like Prospero in *The Tempest,* performing wonders of illusion though she rejects the assistance of wicked powers. These emblematic hints do not rob the story of its human drama, but they do lend a transcendent significance to Leontes' bittersweet story of sinful error, affliction, and an unexpected second happiness.

The Winter's Tale

The Names of the Actors

LEONTES, *King of Sicilia.*
MAMILLIUS, *young prince of Sicilia.*
CAMILLO, ANTIGONUS, CLEOMENES, DION, *four Lords of Sicilia.*
POLIXENES, *King of Bohemia.*
FLORIZEL, *Prince of Bohemia.*
ARCHIDAMUS, *a lord of Bohemia.*
Old SHEPHERD, *reputed father of Perdita.*
CLOWN, *his son.*
AUTOLYCUS, *a rogue.*
[*A* MARINER.]
[*A* JAILER.]

HERMIONE, *queen to Leontes.*
PERDITA, *daughter to Leontes and Hermione.*
PAULINA, *wife to Antigonus.*
EMILIA, *a lady* [*attending on Hermione*].

[MOPSA, DORCAS, *Shepherdesses.*]

Other LORDS *and* GENTLEMEN, [LADIES, OFFICERS,] *and* SERVANTS, SHEPHERDS, *and* SHEPHERDESSES.

[TIME, *as Chorus.*]

[SCENE: *Sicilia, and Bohemia.*]

ACT I • SCENE I

Enter Camillo and Archidamus.

ARCHIDAMUS If you shall chance, Camillo, to visit Bohemia, on the like occasion whereon my services are now on foot, you shall see, as I have said, great difference betwixt our Bohemia and your Sicilia.

CAMILLO I think, this coming summer, the King of Sicilia means to pay Bohemia the visitation which he justly owes him.

ARCHIDAMUS Wherein our entertainment shall shame us. We will be justified in our loves; for indeed—

CAMILLO Beseech you—

ARCHIDAMUS Verily, I speak it in the freedom of my knowledge. We cannot with such magnificence—in so rare—I know not what to say. We will give you sleepy drinks, that your senses, unintelligent of our insufficience, may, though they cannot praise us, as little accuse us.

CAMILLO You pay a great deal too dear for what's given freely.

ARCHIDAMUS Believe me, I speak as my understanding instructs me and as mine honesty puts it to utterance.

CAMILLO Sicilia cannot show himself over-kind to Bohemia. They were train'd together in their childhoods; and there rooted betwixt them then such an affection which cannot choose but branch now. Since their more mature dignities and royal necessities made separation of their society, their encounters, though not personal, hath been royally attorney'd with interchange of gifts, letters, loving embassies, that they have seem'd to be together though absent, shook hands as over a vast, and embrac'd as it were from the ends of oppos'd winds. The heavens continue their loves!

ARCHIDAMUS I think there is not in the world either malice or matter to alter it. You have an unspeakable comfort of your young prince Mamillius. It is a gentleman of the greatest promise that ever came into my note.

CAMILLO I very well agree with you in the hopes of him. It is a gallant child, one that indeed physics the subject, makes old hearts fresh. They that went on crutches ere he was born desire yet their life to see him a man.

ARCHIDAMUS Would they else be content to die?

CAMILLO Yes, if there were no other excuse why they should desire to live.

ARCHIDAMUS If the King had no son, they would desire to live on crutches till he had one. *Exeunt.*

I.i. Location: Sicilia. Leontes' palace.
8–9 Wherein . . . loves i.e., in which visit our attempts to entertain you will shame us by falling short, yet we will make up for it by our affection
14 unintelligent unaware **24 branch** put forth new growth, flourish (also perhaps with opposite and unconscious suggestion of *divide*) **27 attorney'd** carried out by deputy **30 vast** boundless space **35 of** in the person of **37 note** observation **39–40 physics the subject** acts as a medicine to the people

SCENE II

Enter Leontes, Hermione, Mamillius, Polixenes, Camillo, [*and Attendants*].

POLIXENES
Nine changes of the wat'ry star hath been
The shepherd's note since we have left our throne
Without a burden. Time as long again
Would be fill'd up, my brother, with our thanks,
And yet we should, for perpetuity,
Go hence in debt. And therefore, like a cipher,
Yet standing in rich place, I multiply

I.ii. Location: The same.
1 wat'ry star moon **2 note** observation. **we** i.e., I. (The royal "we.") **3 burden** i.e., occupant **5 for perpetuity** forever **6–7 like . . . place** like a zero at the end of a number, multiplying its quantity

With one "We thank you" many thousands moe
That go before it.

LEONTES
Stay your thanks a while,
And pay them when you part.

POLIXENES
Sir, that's tomorrow.
I am question'd by my fears of what may chance
Or breed upon our absence, that may blow
No sneaping winds at home, to make us say
"This is put forth too truly." Besides, I have stay'd
To tire your royalty.

LEONTES
We are tougher, brother,
Than you can put us to 't.

POLIXENES
No longer stay.

LEONTES
One sev'n-night longer.

POLIXENES
Very sooth, tomorrow.

LEONTES
We'll part the time between 's then, and in that
I'll no gainsaying.

POLIXENES
Press me not, beseech you, so.
There is no tongue that moves, none, none i' th'
world,
So soon as yours could win me. So it should now,
Were there necessity in your request, although
'Twere needful I denied it. My affairs
Do even drag me homeward, which to hinder
Were in your love a whip to me, my stay
To you a charge and trouble. To save both,
Farewell, our brother.

LEONTES
Tongue-tied our Queen? Speak you.

HERMIONE
I had thought, sir, to have held my peace until
You had drawn oaths from him not to stay. You, sir,
Charge him too coldly. Tell him you are sure
All in Bohemia's well; this satisfaction
The by-gone day proclaim'd. Say this to him,
He's beat from his best ward.

LEONTES
Well said, Hermione.

HERMIONE
To tell he longs to see his son were strong.
But let him say so then, and let him go;
But let him swear so, and he shall not stay,
We'll thwack him hence with distaffs.
Yet of your royal presence I'll adventure
The borrow of a week. When at Bohemia
You take my lord, I'll give him my commission
To let him there a month behind the gest
Prefix'd for 's parting. Yet, good deed, Leontes,
I love thee not a jar o' th' clock behind
What lady she her lord. You'll stay?

POLIXENES
No, madam.

HERMIONE
Nay, but you will?

POLIXENES
I may not, verily.

HERMIONE
Verily?
You put me off with limber vows; but I,
Though you would seek t' unsphere the stars with
oaths,
Should yet say, "Sir, no going." Verily,
You shall not go. A lady's "Verily" is
As potent as a lord's. Will you go yet?
Force me to keep you as a prisoner,
Not like a guest, so you shall pay your fees
When you depart and save your thanks. How
say you?
My prisoner, or my guest? By your dread "Verily,"
One of them you shall be.

POLIXENES
Your guest, then, madam.
To be your prisoner should import offending,
Which is for me less easy to commit
Than you to punish.

HERMIONE
Not your jailer, then,
But your kind hostess. Come, I'll question you
Of my lord's tricks and yours when you were boys.
You were pretty lordings then?

POLIXENES
We were, fair Queen,
Two lads that thought there was no more behind
But such a day tomorrow as today,
And to be boy eternal.

HERMIONE
Was not my lord
The verier wag o' th' two?

POLIXENES
We were as twinn'd lambs that did frisk i' th' sun,
And bleat the one at th' other. What we chang'd
Was innocence for innocence; we knew not
The doctrine of ill-doing, nor dream'd
That any did. Had we pursu'd that life,
And our weak spirits ne'er been higher rear'd
With stronger blood, we should have answer'd
heaven
Boldly "not guilty," the imposition clear'd
Hereditary ours.

HERMIONE
By this we gather
You have tripp'd since.

POLIXENES
O my most sacred lady,
Temptations have since then been born to 's, for
In those unfledg'd days was my wife a girl;
Your precious self had then not cross'd the eyes
Of my young playfellow.

HERMIONE
Grace to boot!
Of this make no conclusion, lest you say
Your queen and I are devils. Yet go on.
Th' offenses we have made you do we'll answer,
If you first sinn'd with us and that with us
You did continue fault and that you slipp'd not

8 moe more **11–14 I am . . . truly** i.e., I am anxious what may happen in Bohemia, either by chance or bred directly out of my absence; I am anxious lest biting or envious winds may be abroad that will cause me to say my fears were all too plausible **16 Than . . . to 't** than anything you can do to try me **18 part the time** split the difference, i.e., divide a week in two **19 I'll no gainsaying** I will have no refusal **25 Were . . . whip** would be to make your fondness for me a punishment **26 charge** expense, burden **31–32 this . . . proclaim'd** yesterday brought news to satisfy on that score (that all is well in Bohemia) **33 ward** defense **38 adventure** risk (because, as she explains, she'll undertake to repay each week with a month) **39 borrow** borrowing **40 take** capture; receive **41 let him** let him stay. **gest** time allotted for a halt **42 good deed** i.e., in truth **43 jar** tick **44 What lady she** any lady

47 limber limp **53 fees** payments often demanded by jailers of prisoners at the time of their release **57 import offending** imply my having offended **63 behind** to come **66 The verier wag** truly the more mischievous **68 chang'd** exchanged **73 stronger blood** i.e., mature sexual passions **74–75 the imposition . . . ours** freed from original sin **80 Grace to boot** i.e., Heaven help me **85 fault** offense

With any but with us.
LEONTES Is he won yet?
HERMIONE
He'll stay, my lord.
LEONTES At my request he would not.
Hermione, my dearest, thou never spok'st
To better purpose.
HERMIONE Never?
LEONTES Never but once.
HERMIONE
What? Have I twice said well? When was 't before?
I prithee tell me. Cram 's with praise, and make 's
As fat as tame things. One good deed dying
tongueless
Slaughters a thousand waiting upon that.
Our praises are our wages. You may ride 's
With one soft kiss a thousand furlongs ere
With spur we heat an acre. But to th' goal:
My last good deed was to entreat his stay.
What was my first? It has an elder sister,
Or I mistake you. O, would her name were Grace!
But once before I spoke to th' purpose. When?
Nay, let me have 't; I long.
LEONTES Why, that was when
Three crabbed months had sour'd themselves to
death
Ere I could make thee open thy white hand
And clap thyself my love. Then didst thou utter
"I am yours for ever."
HERMIONE 'Tis grace indeed.
Why, lo you now, I have spoke to th' purpose twice:
The one for ever earn'd a royal husband,
Th' other for some while a friend.
[*Gives her hand to Polixenes.*]
LEONTES [*Aside*] Too hot, too hot!
To mingle friendship far is mingling bloods.
I have tremor cordis on me. My heart dances,
But not for joy, not joy. This entertainment
May a free face put on, derive a liberty
From heartiness, from bounty, fertile bosom,
And well become the agent. 'T may, I grant.
But to be paddling palms and pinching fingers,
As now they are, and making practic'd smiles,
As in a looking-glass, and then to sigh, as 'twere
The mort o' th' deer; O, that is entertainment
My bosom likes not, nor my brows!—Mamillius,
Art thou my boy?
MAMILLIUS Ay, my good lord.
LEONTES I' fecks!
Why, that's my bawcock. What, hast smutch'd thy
nose?
They say it is a copy out of mine. Come, captain,
We must be neat; not neat, but cleanly, captain.
And yet the steer, the heifer, and the calf
Are all call'd neat.—Still virginalling
Upon his palm?—How now, you wanton calf?
Art thou my calf?
MAMILLIUS Yes, if you will, my lord.
LEONTES
Thou want'st a rough pash and the shoots that I
have,
To be full like me; yet they say we are
Almost as like as eggs. Women say so,
That will say anything. But were they false
As o'er-dy'd blacks, as wind, as waters, false
As dice are to be wish'd by one that fixes
No bourn 'twixt his and mine, yet were it true
To say this boy were like me. Come, sir page,
Look on me with your welkin eye. Sweet villain!
Most dear'st! My collop! Can thy dam?—
may 't be?—
Affection, thy intention stabs the center.
Thou dost make possible things not so held,
Communicat'st with dreams—how can this be?—
With what's unreal thou coactive art,
And fellow'st nothing. Then 'tis very credent
Thou mayst co-join with something; and thou dost,
And that beyond commission, and I find it,
And that to the infection of my brains
And hard'ning of my brows.
POLIXENES What means Sicilia?
HERMIONE
He something seems unsettled.
POLIXENES How, my lord?
What cheer? How is 't with you, best brother?
HERMIONE You look
As if you held a brow of much distraction.
Are you mov'd, my lord?
LEONTES No, in good earnest.
How sometimes nature will betray its folly,
Its tenderness, and make itself a pastime
To harder bosoms! Looking on the lines
Of my boy's face, methoughts I did recoil
Twenty-three years, and saw myself unbreech'd,
In my green velvet coat, my dagger muzzled
Lest it should bite its master and so prove,
As ornaments oft do, too dangerous.
How like, methought, I then was to this kernel,
This squash, this gentleman. Mine honest friend,
Will you take eggs for money?
MAMILLIUS
No, my lord, I'll fight.

92 tongueless unpraised, unsung **93 Slaughters . . . that** i.e., will inhibit many other good deeds, since they are encouraged by praise **96 heat** traverse as in a race. **to th' goal** to come to the point **104 clap** clasp hands, plight troth **110 tremor cordis** fluttering of the heart **111 entertainment** i.e., of Polixenes by Hermione **112 free face** innocent appearance **113 fertile bosom** i.e., generous affection **114 well . . . agent** look well in her (Hermione) who does these things **118 mort** note sounded on a horn at the death of the hunted deer **119 brows** (Alludes to cuckolds' horns, the supposed badge of men whose wives are unfaithful.) **120 I' fecks** in faith **121 bawcock** i.e., fine fellow. (French *beau coq.*)

123 not . . . cleanly (Leontes changes the word because *neat* also means "cattle" and hence reminds him of cuckolds' horns.) **125 virginalling** touching hands, as in playing on the virginals, a keyed instrument **128 rough pash** shaggy head. **shoots** horns. (Another allusion to cuckolds' horns.) **129 full** fully **132 o'er-dy'd blacks** black garments that have been weakened by too much dye, or dyed in another color **134 bourn** boundary **136 welkin** sky-blue **137 collop** small piece of meat; i.e., of my own flesh. **dam** mother **138–143 Affection . . . something** Strong passion, your intense power pierces to the very center, the soul of man. You deal in matters normally considered fantastic; you partake of the nature of dreams. How can this be? You collaborate with unreality, and create imagined fantasies. It's likely, then, that such imaginings may also become real. **144 commission** what is lawful **147 something** somewhat **152 pastime** occasion for amusement **154 methoughts** it seemed to me. **recoil** i.e., go back in memory **160 squash** unripe peascod or pea pod. **honest** worthy **161 take eggs for money** i.e., be imposed upon. (Proverbial.)

LEONTES
You will? Why, happy man be 's dole! My brother,
Are you so fond of your young prince as we
Do seem to be of ours?

POLIXENES
If at home, sir,
He's all my exercise, my mirth, my matter,
Now my sworn friend and then mine enemy,
My parasite, my soldier, statesman, all.
He makes a July's day short as December,
And with his varying childness cures in me
Thoughts that would thick my blood.

LEONTES
So stands this squire
Offic'd with me. We two will walk, my lord,
And leave you to your graver steps. Hermione,
How thou lov'st us, show in our brother's welcome.
Let what is dear in Sicily be cheap.
Next to thyself and my young rover, he's
Apparent to my heart.

HERMIONE
If you would seek us,
We are yours i' th' garden. Shall 's attend you there?

LEONTES
To your own bents dispose you. You'll be found,
Be you beneath the sky. [*Aside.*] I am angling now,
Though you perceive me not how I give line.
Go to, go to!
How she holds up the neb, the bill to him,
And arms her with the boldness of a wife
To her allowing husband!
[*Exeunt Polixenes, Hermione, and Attendants.*]
Gone already!
Inch-thick, knee-deep, o'er head and ears a
fork'd one!
Go, play, boy, play. Thy mother plays, and I
Play too, but so disgrac'd a part, whose issue
Will hiss me to my grave. Contempt and clamor
Will be my knell. Go, play, boy, play. There have
been,
Or I am much deceiv'd, cuckolds ere now;
And many a man there is, even at this present,
Now while I speak this, holds his wife by th' arm,
That little thinks she has been sluic'd in 's absence
And his pond fish'd by his next neighbor, by
Sir Smile, his neighbor. Nay, there's comfort in 't
Whiles other men have gates and those gates
open'd,
As mine, against their will. Should all despair
That have revolted wives, the tenth of mankind
Would hang themselves. Physic for 't there's none.
It is a bawdy planet, that will strike
Where 'tis predominant; and 'tis powerful, think it,
From east, west, north and south. Be it concluded,
No barricado for a belly. Know 't,
It will let in and out the enemy
With bag and baggage. Many thousand on 's
Have the disease, and feel 't not. How now, boy?

MAMILLIUS
I am like you, they say.

LEONTES
Why, that's some comfort.
What, Camillo there?

CAMILLO
Ay, my good lord.

LEONTES
Go play, Mamillius; thou 'rt an honest man.
[*Exit Mamillius.*]
Camillo, this great sir will yet stay longer.

CAMILLO
You had much ado to make his anchor hold.
When you cast out, it still came home.

LEONTES
Didst note it?

CAMILLO
He would not stay at your petitions, made
His business more material.

LEONTES
Didst perceive it?
[*Aside.*] They're here with me already, whisp'ring,
rounding
"Sicilia is a so-forth." 'Tis far gone,
When I shall gust it last.—How came 't, Camillo,
That he did stay?

CAMILLO
At the good Queen's entreaty.

LEONTES
At the Queen's be 't. "Good" should be pertinent;
But, so it is, it is not. Was this taken
By any understanding pate but thine?
For thy conceit is soaking, will draw in
More than the common blocks. Not noted, is 't,
But of the finer natures? By some severals
Of head-piece extraordinary? Lower messes
Perchance are to this business purblind? Say.

CAMILLO
Business, my lord? I think most understand
Bohemia stays here longer.

LEONTES
Ha?

CAMILLO
Stays here longer.

LEONTES
Ay, but why?

CAMILLO
To satisfy your Highness and the entreaties
Of our most gracious mistress.

LEONTES
Satisfy?
Th' entreaties of your mistress? Satisfy?
Let that suffice. I have trusted thee, Camillo,
With all the nearest things to my heart, as well
My chamber-councils, wherein, priest-like, thou
Hast cleans'd my bosom. I from thee departed
Thy penitent reform'd. But we have been
Deceiv'd in thy integrity, deceiv'd
In that which seems so.

CAMILLO
Be it forbid, my lord!

163 happy . . . dole may good fortune be his lot. (Proverbial.) **166 matter** concern **170 childness** childlike ways **171 thick my blood** (Melancholy thoughts were supposed to thicken the blood.) **172 Offic'd** placed in particular function **177 Apparent** heir apparent **178 Shall 's** shall we **179 To . . . dispose you** act according to your inclinations **183 neb** beak, i.e., nose, face **184 arms her with** assumes **185 allowing** approving **186 fork'd** horned **187 play** play games. **plays** i.e., in a sexual liaison **188 Play** play a role. **issue** outcome (with a pun on the sense of *offspring* and *exit*, i.e., death) **200 Physic** medicine **201 It** i.e., the cause of unchastity. **strike** blast, destroy by a malign influence **202 predominant** in the ascendant. (Said of a planet.)

206 on 's of us **213 still** continually **215 material** important **216 They're . . . already** people are already on to my secret. **rounding** whispering, gossiping **218 gust** taste, i.e., hear of **220 pertinent** i.e., appropriately applied **221 so** as. **taken** perceived **223 conceit** understanding. **soaking** i.e., very receptive **224 blocks** blockheads **225 severals** individuals **226 Lower messes** those who sit lower at table, i.e., inferior men **227 purblind** totally blind **232 Satisfy** (Leontes takes the word in a sexual sense.) **236 chamber-councils** private affair **240 Be it forbid** i.e., God forbid I should do such a thing

LEONTES
To bide upon 't, thou art not honest; or,
If thou inclin'st that way, thou art a coward,
Which hoxes honesty behind, restraining
From course requir'd; or else thou must be counted
A servant grafted in my serious trust
And therein negligent; or else a fool
That seest a game play'd home, the rich stake drawn,
And tak'st it all for jest.

CAMILLO My gracious lord,
I may be negligent, foolish, and fearful;
In every one of these no man is free,
But that his negligence, his folly, fear,
Among the infinite doings of the world,
Sometime puts forth. In your affairs, my lord,
If ever I were willful-negligent,
It was my folly; if industriously
I play'd the fool, it was my negligence,
Not weighing well the end; if ever fearful
To do a thing, where I the issue doubted,
Whereof the execution did cry out
Against the non-performance, 'twas a fear
Which oft infects the wisest. These, my lord,
Are such allow'd infirmities that honesty
Is never free of. But, beseech your Grace,
Be plainer with me; let me know my trespass
By its own visage. If I then deny it,
'Tis none of mine.

LEONTES Ha' not you seen, Camillo—
But that's past doubt, you have, or your eye-glass
Is thicker than a cuckold's horn—or heard—
For to a vision so apparent rumor
Cannot be mute—or thought —for cogitation
Resides not in that man that does not think—
My wife is slippery? If thou wilt confess,
Or else be impudently negative,
To have nor eyes nor ears nor thought, then say
My wife's a hobby-horse, deserves a name
As rank as any flax-wench that puts to
Before her troth-plight. Say 't and justify 't.

CAMILLO
I would not be a stander-by to hear
My sovereign mistress clouded so, without
My present vengeance taken. 'Shrew my heart,
You never spoke what did become you less
Than this, which to reiterate were sin
As deep as that, though true.

LEONTES Is whispering nothing?
Is leaning cheek to cheek? Is meeting noses?
Kissing with inside lip? Stopping the career
Of laughter with a sigh—a note infallible
Of breaking honesty? Horsing foot on foot?
Skulking in corners? Wishing clocks more swift?
Hours, minutes? Noon, midnight? And all eyes
Blind with the pin and web but theirs, theirs only,
That would unseen be wicked? Is this nothing?
Why, then the world and all that's in 't is nothing,
The covering sky is nothing, Bohemia nothing,
My wife is nothing, nor nothing have these nothings,
If this be nothing.

CAMILLO Good my lord, be cur'd
Of this diseas'd opinion, and betimes,
For 'tis most dangerous.

LEONTES Say it be, 'tis true.

CAMILLO
No, no, my lord.

LEONTES It is. You lie, you lie!
I say thou liest, Camillo, and I hate thee,
Pronounce thee a gross lout, a mindless slave,
Or else a hovering temporizer, that
Canst with thine eyes at once see good and evil,
Inclining to them both. Were my wife's liver
Infected as her life, she would not live
The running of one glass.

CAMILLO Who does infect her?

LEONTES
Why, he that wears her like her medal, hanging
About his neck, Bohemia—who, if I
Had servants true about me, that bare eyes
To see alike mine honor as their profits,
Their own particular thrifts, they would do that
Which should undo more doing. Ay, and thou,
His cupbearer—whom I from meaner form
Have bench'd and rear'd to worship, who mayst see
Plainly as heaven sees earth and earth sees heaven,
How I am gall'd—mightst bespice a cup,
To give mine enemy a lasting wink;
Which draught to me were cordial.

CAMILLO Sir, my lord,
I could do this, and that with no rash potion,
But with a ling'ring dram that should not work
Maliciously like poison. But I cannot
Believe this crack to be in my dread mistress,
So sovereignly being honorable.
I have lov'd thee—

LEONTES Make that thy question, and go rot!
Dost think I am so muddy, so unsettled,
To appoint myself in this vexation, sully
The purity and whiteness of my sheets—

241 bide dwell, insist. **upon 't** i.e., on your integrity. **or** either **242 inclin'st that way** i.e., prefer being honest under ordinary circumstances **243 Which hoxes** who hamstrings **244 From course requir'd** i.e., from the direction honest inquiry must take to find the truth **245 grafted . . . trust** taken into my complete confidence. (*Grafted* means *deeply embedded,* like a graft.) **247 home** i.e., for keeps, in earnest. **drawn** won **253 puts forth** appears **255 industriously** willfully **256 play'd the fool** i.e., took some matter lightly **258 issue** outcome. **doubted** feared **259–260 Whereof . . . non-performance** in which the necessity of completing the task justly rebuked my non-performance **262 allow'd** acknowledged. **that** as **265 visage** face, i.e., plain appearance **267 eye-glass** lens of the eye **269 vision** thing visible **271 think** i.e., think so **273 Or else** the only possible alternative to which is to **275 hobby-horse** wanton woman **276 flax-wench** common slut. **puts to** engages in sex **280 present** immediate. **'Shrew** beshrew, curse **282–283 which . . . true** i.e., to repeat which accusation would be to sin as deeply as her supposed adultery, even if it were true (which it isn't)

285 career full gallop **287 honesty** chastity. **Horsing** setting, placing (and then moving the feet up and down together) **290 pin and web** cataract of the eye. (I.e., the lovers wish to think themselves unobserved.) **296 betimes** quickly **297 Say it be** i.e., even if it is dangerous **301 hovering** wavering **304 Infected as her life** as full of disease as is her moral conduct **305 glass** hourglass **308 bare** bore **310 thrifts** gains **312 meaner form** humbler station **313 bench'd** placed on the bench of authority. **worship** dignity, honor **315 gall'd** rubbed, chafed **316 lasting wink** everlasting closing of the eyes (in death) **317 were cordial** would be restorative **318 rash** quick-acting **321 dread** worthy of awe **322 sovereignly** supremely **323 Make . . . rot** i.e., if you're going to raise questions like that, may you rot in hell **324 muddy** muddle-headed

Which to preserve is sleep, which being spotted
Is goads, thorns, nettles, tails of wasps—
Give scandal to the blood o' th' Prince my son,
Who I do think is mine and love as mine,
Without ripe moving to 't? Would I do this? 331
Could man so blench?

CAMILLO
I must believe you, sir. 332
I do, and will fetch off Bohemia for 't; 333
Provided that, when he's remov'd, your Highness
Will take again your queen as yours at first,
Even for your son's sake, and thereby for sealing 336
The injury of tongues in courts and kingdoms
Known and allied to yours.

LEONTES
Thou dost advise me
Even so as I mine own course have set down.
I'll give no blemish to her honor, none.

CAMILLO
My lord,
Go then, and with a countenance as clear
As friendship wears at feasts, keep with Bohemia 343
And with your queen. I am his cupbearer.
If from me he have wholesome beverage,
Account me not your servant.

LEONTES
This is all.
Do 't and thou hast the one half of my heart;
Do 't not, thou split'st thine own.

CAMILLO
I'll do 't, my lord.

LEONTES
I will seem friendly, as thou hast advis'd me. *Exit.*

CAMILLO
O miserable lady! But, for me,
What case stand I in? I must be the poisoner
Of good Polixenes; and my ground to do 't
Is the obedience to a master, one
Who in rebellion with himself will have
All that are his so too. To do this deed, 355
Promotion follows. If I could find example 356
Of thousands that had struck anointed kings
And flourish'd after, I'd not do 't; but since 358
Nor brass nor stone nor parchment bears not one, 359
Let villainy itself forswear 't. I must
Forsake the court. To do 't, or no, is certain 361
To me a break-neck. Happy star reign now! 362
Here comes Bohemia.

Enter Polixenes.

POLIXENES
This is strange. Methinks
My favor here begins to warp. Not speak? 364
Good day, Camillo.

CAMILLO
Hail, most royal sir!

POLIXENES
What is the news i' th' court?

CAMILLO
None rare, my lord. 366

POLIXENES
The King hath on him such a countenance
As he had lost some province and a region 368
Lov'd as he loves himself. Even now I met him
With customary compliment, when he,
Wafting his eyes to th' contrary and falling 371
A lip of much contempt, speeds from me, and
So leaves me to consider what is breeding 373
That changeth thus his manners.

CAMILLO
I dare not know, my lord.

POLIXENES
How, dare not? Do not? Do you know, and
dare not? 376
Be intelligent to me. 'Tis thereabouts, 377
For to yourself, what you do know, you must, 378
And cannot say you dare not. Good Camillo, 379
Your chang'd complexions are to me a mirror
Which shows me mine chang'd too; for I must be
A party in this alteration, finding 382
Myself thus alter'd with 't.

CAMILLO
There is a sickness
Which puts some of us in distemper, but
I cannot name the disease; and it is caught
Of you that yet are well.

POLIXENES
How? Caught of me?
Make me not sighted like the basilisk. 387
I have look'd on thousands, who have sped the
better 388
By my regard, but kill'd none so. Camillo, 389
As you are certainly a gentleman, thereto 390
Clerk-like experienc'd, which no less adorns 391
Our gentry than our parents' noble names, 392
In whose success we are gentle, I beseech you, 393
If you know aught which does behoove my
knowledge
Thereof to be inform'd, imprison 't not
In ignorant concealment.

CAMILLO
I may not answer. 396

POLIXENES
A sickness caught of me, and yet I well?
I must be answer'd. Dost thou hear, Camillo?
I conjure thee, by all the parts of man 399
Which honor does acknowledge, whereof the least
Is not this suit of mine, that thou declare
What incidency thou dost guess of harm 402
Is creeping toward me; how far off, how near;
Which way to be prevented, if to be; 404
If not, how best to bear it.

CAMILLO
Sir, I will tell you,
Since I am charg'd in honor and by him

331 ripe ample, urgent **332 blench** swerve (from sensible conduct) **333 fetch off** do away with; or, with deliberate ambiguity, rescue (as also in *remov'd* in the next line) **336 sealing** silencing **343 keep** remain in company **355 All . . . too** i.e., all who follow him similarly in rebellion against his best self and obedience to his worst self **356 If** even if **358–359 but . . . one** i.e., but since recorded history shows no instances of men who have killed a king and prospered afterwards **361 To do 't, or no** i.e., either to kill Polixenes or not to kill him **362 break-neck** destruction, ruin. **Happy** propitious, favorable **364 warp** change, grow askew (as wood warps). **Not speak** (Leontes has just passed by Polixenes without speaking.) **366 rare** noteworthy

368 As as if **371 Wafting . . . contrary** averting his eyes. **falling** letting fall **373 breeding** hatching **376 Do not** i.e., or do you mean you don't know **377 intelligent** intelligible. **'Tis thereabouts** it must be something of this sort, i.e., that you know and dare not tell **378–379 For . . . dare not** i.e, for in your heart, whatever it is you know, you must in fact know, and can't claim it's a matter of not daring to know **382 A party . . . alteration** involved some way in this change of affairs **387 sighted** provided with a gaze. **basilisk** a fabled serpent whose gaze was fatal **388 sped** prospered **389 regard** look **390 thereto** in addition to which **391 Clerk-like** like an educated man **392 gentry** gentleman-like condition **393 whose success** succession from whom. **gentle** wellborn **396 ignorant concealment** concealment that would keep me ignorant, or that would proceed from pretended ignorance on your part **399 parts** obligations **402 incidency** likelihood **404 if to be** if it can be (prevented)

That I think honorable. Therefore mark my counsel,
Which must be ev'n as swiftly followed as
I mean to utter it, or both yourself and me
Cry lost, and so good night!

POLIXENES On, good Camillo.

CAMILLO
I am appointed him to murder you.

POLIXENES
By whom, Camillo?

CAMILLO By the King.

POLIXENES For what?

CAMILLO
He thinks, nay, with all confidence he swears,
As he had seen 't or been an instrument
To vice you to 't, that you have touch'd his queen
Forbiddenly.

POLIXENES O, then my best blood turn
To an infected jelly, and my name
Be yok'd with his that did betray the Best!
Turn then my freshest reputation to
A savor that may strike the dullest nostril
Where I arrive, and my approach be shunn'd,
Nay, hated too, worse than the great'st infection
That e'er was heard or read!

CAMILLO Swear his thought over
By each particular star in heaven and
By all their influences, you may as well
Forbid the sea for to obey the moon
As or by oath remove or counsel shake
The fabric of his folly, whose foundation
Is pil'd upon his faith and will continue
The standing of his body.

POLIXENES How should this grow?

CAMILLO
I know not. But I am sure 'tis safer to
Avoid what 's grown than question how 'tis born.
If therefore you dare trust my honesty,
That lies enclosed in this trunk which you
Shall bear along impawn'd, away tonight!
Your followers I will whisper to the business,
And will by twos and threes at several posterns
Clear them o' th' city. For myself, I'll put
My fortunes to your service, which are here
By this discovery lost. Be not uncertain,
For, by the honor of my parents, I
Have utt'red truth, which if you seek to prove,
I dare not stand by; nor shall you be safer
Than one condemn'd by the King's own mouth,
  thereon
His execution sworn.

POLIXENES I do believe thee;
I saw his heart in 's face. Give me thy hand.
Be pilot to me, and thy places shall
Still neighbor mine. My ships are ready and
My people did expect my hence departure
Two days ago. This jealousy
Is for a precious creature. As she's rare,
Must it be great; and as his person's mighty,
Must it be violent; and as he does conceive
He is dishonor'd by a man which ever
Profess'd to him, why, his revenges must
In that be made more bitter. Fear o'ershades me.
Good expedition be my friend, and comfort
The gracious queen, part of his theme, but nothing
Of his ill-ta'en suspicion! Come, Camillo;
I will respect thee as a father if
Thou bear'st my life off hence. Let us avoid.

CAMILLO
It is in mine authority to command
The keys of all the posterns. Please your Highness
To take the urgent hour. Come, sir, away. *Exeunt.*

ACT II • SCENE I

Enter Hermione, Mamillius, [and] Ladies.

HERMIONE
Take the boy to you. He so troubles me,
'Tis past enduring.

FIRST LADY [*Taking Mamillius from the Queen*]
Come, my gracious lord,
Shall I be your playfellow?

MAMILLIUS
No, I'll none of you.

FIRST LADY Why, my sweet lord?

MAMILLIUS
You'll kiss me hard and speak to me as if
I were a baby still.—I love you better.

SECOND LADY
And why so, my lord?

MAMILLIUS Not for because
Your brows are blacker; yet black brows, they say,
Become some women best, so that there be not
Too much hair there, but in a semicircle,
Or a half-moon made with a pen.

SECOND LADY Who taught' this?

MAMILLIUS
I learn'd it out of women's faces. Pray now
What color are your eyebrows?

FIRST LADY Blue, my lord.

MAMILLIUS
Nay, that's a mock. I have seen a lady's nose
That has been blue, but not her eyebrows.

FIRST LADY Hark ye,
The Queen your mother rounds apace. We shall
Present our services to a fine new prince
One of these days, and then you'd wanton with us,
If we would have you.

410 good night i.e., this is the end **411 him** by him (Leontes); or, the one **415 vice** impel, tempt. (The *Vice* was a tempter in the morality play.) **418 his . . . Best** (A reference to Judas.) **423 Swear . . . over** deny his suspicion with oaths **427 or . . . or** either . . . or **430 standing** life, existence. **How . . . grow** i.e., how could this suspicion have arisen **434 trunk** body **435 impawn'd** i.e., as a pledge of good faith **436 whisper to** secretly inform of and urge **437 posterns** rear gates **440 discovery** revelation, disclosure **442 prove** test **443 stand by** affirm publicly; stay **447–448 thy . . . mine** your official position will always be near to me

455 Profess'd openly professed friendship **457–459 Good . . . suspicion** may my hasty departure prove my best course, and ease the predicament of the gracious Queen, who is the object of the King's suspicions but who is guiltless of them **461 avoid** depart

II.i. Location: Sicilia. Leontes' palace.
11 taught' taught you **14 mock** (1) taunt (2) counterfeit **18 wanton** sport, play

SECOND LADY She is spread of late
Into a goodly bulk. Good time encounter her!
HERMIONE [*Calling to her women*]
What wisdom stirs amongst you? Come, sir, now
I am for you again. Pray you, sit by us,
And tell 's a tale.
MAMILLIUS Merry or sad shall 't be?
HERMIONE
As merry as you will.
MAMILLIUS
A sad tale's best for winter. I have one
Of sprites and goblins.
HERMIONE Let's have that, good sir.
Come on, sit down. Come on, and do your best
To fright me with your sprites; you're pow'rful at it.
MAMILLIUS
There was a man—
HERMIONE Nay, come, sit down; then on.
[*Mamillius sits.*]
MAMILLIUS
Dwelt by a churchyard. I will tell it softly;
Yond crickets shall not hear it.
HERMIONE
Come on, then, and give 't me in mine ear.

[*Enter*] *Leontes, Antigonus, Lords,* [*and others*].

LEONTES
Was he met there? His train? Camillo with him?
FIRST LORD
Behind the tuft of pines I met them; never
Saw I men scour so on their way. I ey'd them
Even to their ships.
LEONTES How blest am I
In my just censure, in my true opinion!
Alack, for lesser knowledge! How accurs'd
In being so blest! There may be in the cup
A spider steep'd, and one may drink, depart,
And yet partake no venom, for his knowledge
Is not infected; but if one present
Th' abhorr'd ingredient to his eye, make known
How he hath drunk, he cracks his gorge, his sides,
With violent hefts. I have drunk, and seen the
spider.
Camillo was his help in this, his pander.
There is a plot against my life, my crown.
All's true that is mistrusted. That false villain
Whom I employ'd was pre-employ'd by him.
He has discover'd my design, and I
Remain a pinch'd thing, yea, a very trick
For them to play at will. How came the posterns
So easily open?
FIRST LORD By his great authority,
Which often hath no less prevail'd than so
On your command.
LEONTES
I know 't too well.
Give me the boy. I am glad you did not nurse him.
Though he does bear some signs of me, yet you
Have too much blood in him.
HERMIONE What is this? Sport?
LEONTES
Bear the boy hence; he shall not come about her.
Away with him! And let her sport herself
With that she's big with, for 'tis Polixenes
Has made thee swell thus. [*Mamillius is led out.*]
HERMIONE But I'd say he had not,
And I'll be sworn you would believe my saying,
Howe'er you lean to th' nayward.
LEONTES You, my lords,
Look on her, mark her well; be but about
To say "She is a goodly lady," and
The justice of your hearts will thereto add
"'Tis pity she's not honest, honorable."
Praise her but for this her without-door form,
Which on my faith deserves high speech, and
straight
The shrug, the hum, or ha, these petty brands
That calumny doth use—O, I am out,
That mercy does, for calumny will sear
Virtue itself—these shrugs, these hums, and ha's,
When you have said she's goodly, come between
Ere you can say she's honest. But be 't known,
From him that has most cause to grieve it should be,
She's an adulteress.
HERMIONE Should a villain say so,
The most replenish'd villain in the world,
He were as much more villain. You, my lord,
Do but mistake.
LEONTES You have mistook, my lady,
Polixenes for Leontes. O thou thing!
Which I'll not call a creature of thy place,
Lest barbarism, making me the precedent,
Should a like language use to all degrees
And mannerly distinguishment leave out
Betwixt the prince and beggar. I have said
She's an adulteress; I have said with whom.
More, she's a traitor, and Camillo is
A federary with her, and one that knows
What she should shame to know herself
But with her most vile principal, that she's
A bed-swerver, even as bad as those
That vulgars give bold'st titles, ay, and privy
To this their late escape.
HERMIONE No, by my life,
Privy to none of this. How will this grieve you,
When you shall come to clearer knowledge, that
You thus have publish'd me! Gentle my lord,
You scarce can right me throughly then to say
You did mistake.
LEONTES No; if I mistake

31 crickets i.e., the court ladies, tittering and laughing **35 scour** scurry **37 censure** judgment **38 Alack . . . knowledge** i.e., would that what I know weren't true **45 hefts** heavings, retchings **48 mistrusted** suspected **50 discover'd** disclosed **51 pinch'd** tortured, ridiculous

59 Sport a joke **63 I'd** I need only **65 nayward** negative, opposite **70 without-door** outward, external **71 straight** straightway, at once **72 brands** i.e., signs, expressions **73 out** wrong, in error **74 does** uses. (Leontes' point is that no one commits calumny by suggesting with a shrug that Hermione is unchaste; calumny attacks *virtue itself,* whereas Hermione has only the false appearance of virtue.) **76 come between** interrupt **80 replenish'd** full, complete **84 Which . . . place** on whom I'll not bestow the honorable name of your position **87 mannerly distinguishment** polite distinctions **91 federary** confederate, accomplice **93 principal** partner **95 vulgars . . . titles** common people call by the rudest names. **privy** in on the secret **99 publish'd** proclaimed **100 throughly** thoroughly

In those foundations which I build upon,
The center is not big enough to bear 103
A schoolboy's top. Away with her, to prison!
He who shall speak for her is afar off guilty 105
But that he speaks.

HERMIONE There's some ill planet reigns. 106
I must be patient till the heavens look
With an aspect more favorable. Good my lords,
I am not prone to weeping, as our sex
Commonly are, the want of which vain dew
Perchance shall dry your pities; but I have
That honorable grief lodg'd here which burns
Worse than tears drown. Beseech you all, my lords,
With thoughts so qualified as your charities 114
Shall best instruct you, measure me; and so 115
The King's will be perform'd!

LEONTES Shall I be heard? 116

HERMIONE
Who is 't that goes with me? Beseech your
 Highness
My women may be with me, for you see
My plight requires it. Do not weep, good fools; 119
There is no cause. When you shall know your
 mistress
Has deserv'd prison, then abound in tears
As I come out. This action I now go on
Is for my better grace. Adieu, my lord.
I never wish'd to see you sorry; now
I trust I shall. My women, come; you have leave.

LEONTES
Go, do our bidding; hence!
[*Exit Queen, guarded, with Ladies.*]

FIRST LORD
Beseech your Highness, call the Queen again.

ANTIGONUS
Be certain what you do, sir, lest your justice
Prove violence, in the which three great ones suffer,
Yourself, your queen, your son.

FIRST LORD For her, my lord,
I dare my life lay down and will do 't, sir,
Please you t' accept it, that the Queen is spotless
I' th' eyes of heaven and to you—I mean,
In this which you accuse her.

ANTIGONUS If it prove
She's otherwise, I'll keep my stables where 135
I lodge my wife. I'll go in couples with her; 136
Than when I feel and see her no farther trust her.
For every inch of woman in the world,
Ay, every dram of woman's flesh is false,
If she be.

LEONTES Hold your peaces.

FIRST LORD Good my lord—

ANTIGONUS
It is for you we speak, not for ourselves.
You are abus'd, and by some putter-on
That will be damn'd for 't. Would I knew the villain,
I would land-damn him. Be she honor-flaw'd, 144
I have three daughters—the eldest is eleven,
The second and the third, nine, and some five— 146
If this prove true, they'll pay for 't. By mine honor,
I'll geld 'em all; fourteen they shall not see
To bring false generations. They are co-heirs, 149
And I had rather glib myself than they 150
Should not produce fair issue.

LEONTES Cease; no more.
You smell this business with a sense as cold
As is a dead man's nose; but I do see 't and feel 't,
As you feel doing thus [*Grasps Antigonus' arm.*]—
 and see withal
The instruments that feel.

ANTIGONUS If it be so, 155
We need no grave to bury honesty;
There's not a grain of it the face to sweeten
Of the whole dungy earth.

LEONTES What? Lack I credit? 158

FIRST LORD
I had rather you did lack than I, my lord,
Upon this ground; and more it would content me 160
To have her honor true than your suspicion,
Be blam'd for 't how you might.

LEONTES Why, what need we 162
Commune with you of this, but rather follow
Our forceful instigation? Our prerogative 164
Calls not your counsels, but our natural goodness 165
Imparts this; which if you—or stupified 166
Or seeming so in skill—cannot or will not 167
Relish a truth like us, inform yourselves 168
We need no more of your advice. The matter,
The loss, the gain, the ord'ring on 't, is all 170
Properly ours.

ANTIGONUS And I wish, my liege,
You had only in your silent judgment tried it,
Without more overture.

LEONTES How could that be? 173
Either thou art most ignorant by age, 174
Or thou wert born a fool. Camillo's flight,
Added to their familiarity—
Which was as gross as ever touch'd conjecture, 177
That lack'd sight only, nought for approbation 178
But only seeing, all other circumstances
Made up to th' deed—doth push on this
 proceeding. 180
Yet, for a greater confirmation—
For in an act of this importance 'twere
Most piteous to be wild—I have dispatch'd in post 183
To sacred Delphos, to Apollo's temple,
Cleomenes and Dion, whom you know
Of stuff'd sufficiency. Now from the oracle 186

103 center earth **105 afar off** indirectly **106 But . . . speaks** merely by speaking **114 qualified** tempered **115 measure** judge **116 heard** i.e., obeyed **119 fools** (Here, a term of endearment.) **135–136 I'll . . . wife** (A difficult passage, suggesting perhaps that Antigonus will treat his wife as he treats his horses, guarding her suspiciously.) **136 in couples** i.e., like two hounds hunting together **142 abus'd** deceived. **putter-on** instigator

144 land-damn (Meaning uncertain.) **146 some** about **149 false generations** illegitimate children **150 glib** castrate, geld **155 instruments** i.e., Leontes' fingers **158 credit** credibility **160 Upon this ground** in this matter **162 we** I. (The royal "we.") **164 instigation** incentive **164–166 Our prerogative . . . this** my royal prerogative is under no obligation to consult you, but rather out of natural generosity I inform you of the matter **166 or** either **167 Or . . . skill** or pretending to be stupified out of cunning **168 Relish** savor, appreciate **170 on 't** of it **173 overture** public disclosure **174 by age** through the folly of old age **177 as gross . . . conjecture** as palpably evident as any conjecture ever touched upon and verified **178 approbation** proof **180 Made up** added up. **push on** urge onward **183 wild** rash. **post** haste **186 stuff'd sufficiency** abundant in fine qualities

They will bring all, whose spiritual counsel had
Shall stop or spur me. Have I done well?

FIRST LORD
Well done, my lord.

LEONTES
Though I am satisfied and need no more
Than what I know, yet shall the oracle
Give rest to th' minds of others, such as he
Whose ignorant credulity will not
Come up to th' truth. So have we thought it good
From our free person she should be confin'd,
Lest that the treachery of the two fled hence
Be left her to perform. Come, follow us.
We are to speak in public, for this business
Will raise us all.

ANTIGONUS [*Aside*] To laughter, as I take it,
If the good truth were known. *Exeunt.*

SCENE II

Enter Paulina, a Gentleman [*and Attendants*].

PAULINA
The keeper of the prison, call to him;
Let him have knowledge who I am. [*Gentleman goes to the door.*] Good lady,
No court in Europe is too good for thee;
What dost thou then in prison?

[*Enter*] *Jailer.*

Now, good sir,
You know me, do you not?

JAILER For a worthy lady
And one who much I honor.

PAULINA Pray you then,
Conduct me to the Queen.

JAILER I may not, madam.
To the contrary I have express commandment.

PAULINA
Here's ado, to lock up honesty and honor from
Th' access of gentle visitors! Is 't lawful, pray you,
To see her women? Any of them? Emilia?

JAILER
So please you, madam,
To put apart these your attendants, I
Shall bring Emilia forth.

PAULINA I pray now, call her.—
Withdraw yourselves.

[*Gentleman and attendants withdraw.*]

JAILER
And, madam,
I must be present at your conference.

PAULINA
Well, be 't so, prithee. [*Exit Jailer.*]

Here's such ado to make no stain a stain
As passes coloring.

[*Enter Jailer, with*] *Emilia.*

Dear gentlewoman,
How fares our gracious lady?

EMILIA
As well as one so great and so forlorn
May hold together. On her frights and griefs,
Which never tender lady hath borne greater,
She is something before her time deliver'd.

PAULINA
A boy?

EMILIA A daughter, and a goodly babe,
Lusty and like to live. The Queen receives
Much comfort in 't, says, "My poor prisoner,
I am innocent as you."

PAULINA I dare be sworn.
These dangerous unsafe lunes i' th' King, beshrew them!
He must be told on 't, and he shall. The office
Becomes a woman best; I'll take 't upon me.
If I prove honey-mouth'd, let my tongue blister
And never to my red-look'd anger be
The trumpet any more. Pray you, Emilia,
Commend my best obedience to the Queen.
If she dares trust me with her little babe,
I'll show 't the King and undertake to be
Her advocate to th' loud'st. We do not know
How he may soften at the sight o' th' child.
The silence often of pure innocence
Persuades when speaking fails.

EMILIA Most worthy madam,
Your honor and your goodness is so evident
That your free undertaking cannot miss
A thriving issue. There is no lady living
So meet for this great errand. Please your ladyship
To visit the next room, I'll presently
Acquaint the Queen of your most noble offer,
Who but today hammer'd of this design,
But durst not tempt a minister of honor,
Lest she should be denied.

PAULINA Tell her, Emilia,
I'll use that tongue I have. If wit flow from 't
As boldness from my bosom, let 't not be doubted
I shall do good.

EMILIA Now be you blest for it!
I'll to the Queen.—Please you, come something nearer.

JAILER
Madam, if 't please the Queen to send the babe,
I know not what I shall incur to pass it,
Having no warrant.

PAULINA You need not fear it, sir.
This child was prisoner to the womb, and is

187 had having been obtained **192 he** any person **194 Come up to** face **195 From** away from. **free** accessible **199 raise** rouse
II.ii. Location: Sicilia. A prison.

20 passes coloring surpasses any justification (with a pun on *coloring* in the sense of *stain* in the previous line) **23 On** in consequence of **25 something** somewhat **27 Lusty** vigorous. **like** likely **30 lunes** fits of lunacy **32 Becomes** suits **34 red-look'd** red-faced **39 to th' loud'st** as loudly as I can **44 free** generous **45 thriving issue** successful outcome **47 presently** at once **49 hammer'd of** formulated, conceived **50 tempt** solicit (to serve as ambassador in such a case)

By law and process of great nature thence 60
Freed and enfranchis'd, not a party to
The anger of the King nor guilty of,
If any be, the trespass of the Queen.

JAILER
I do believe it.

PAULINA
Do not you fear. Upon mine honor, I
Will stand betwixt you and danger. *Exeunt.*

SCENE III

Enter Leontes; Servants [keeping the door].

LEONTES
Nor night nor day no rest. It is but weakness
To bear the matter thus, mere weakness. If
The cause were not in being—part o' th' cause, 3
She th' adulteress; for the harlot king 4
Is quite beyond mine arm, out of the blank 5
And level of my brain, plot-proof; but she 6
I can hook to me—say that she were gone,
Given to the fire, a moi'ty of my rest 8
Might come to me again.—Who's there?

FIRST SERVANT [*Coming forward*] My lord?

LEONTES
How does the boy?

FIRST SERVANT
He took good rest tonight; 'tis hop'd 11
His sickness is discharg'd.

LEONTES To see his nobleness!
Conceiving the dishonor of his mother,
He straight declin'd, droop'd, took it deeply,
Fasten'd and fix'd the shame on 't in himself, 15
Threw off his spirit, his appetite, his sleep,
And downright languish'd.—Leave me solely. Go 17
See how he fares. [*Exit Servant.*] Fie, fie! No
thought of him. 18
The very thought of my revenges that way
Recoil upon me—in himself too mighty,
And in his parties, his alliance. Let him be,
Until a time may serve. For present vengeance,
Take it on her. Camillo and Polixenes
Laugh at me, make their pastime at my sorrow.
They should not laugh if I could reach them, nor
Shall she within my power.

Enter Paulina [with a baby]; Antigonus and Lords [trying to hold her back].

FIRST LORD You must not enter.

PAULINA
Nay, rather, good my lords, be second to me. 27
Fear you his tyrannous passion more, alas,
Than the Queen's life? A gracious innocent soul,
More free than he is jealous.

ANTIGONUS That's enough. 30

SECOND SERVANT
Madam, he hath not slept tonight, commanded
None should come at him.

PAULINA Not so hot, good sir.
I come to bring him sleep. 'Tis such as you,
That creep like shadows by him and do sigh
At each his needless heavings, such as you
Nourish the cause of his awaking. I 36
Do come with words as medicinal as true,
Honest as either, to purge him of that humor 38
That presses him from sleep.

LEONTES What noise there, ho?

PAULINA
No noise, my lord, but needful conference
About some gossips for your Highness.

LEONTES How? 41
Away with that audacious lady! Antigonus,
I charg'd thee that she should not come about me.
I knew she would.

ANTIGONUS I told her so, my lord,
On your displeasure's peril and on mine,
She should not visit you.

LEONTES What, canst not rule her?

PAULINA
From all dishonesty he can. In this,
Unless he take the course that you have done—
Commit me for committing honor—trust it, 49
He shall not rule me.

ANTIGONUS La you now, you hear!
When she will take the rein I let her run,
But she'll not stumble.

PAULINA Good my liege, I come—
And, I beseech you hear me, who professes
Myself your loyal servant, your physician,
Your most obedient counselor, yet that dares
Less appear so in comforting your evils, 56
Than such as most seem yours—I say, I come 57
From your good queen.

LEONTES
Good queen?

PAULINA
Good queen, my lord, good queen, I say good
queen,
And would by combat make her good, so were I 61
A man, the worst about you.

LEONTES Force her hence. 62

PAULINA
Let him that makes but trifles of his eyes
First hand me. On mine own accord I'll off;
But first I'll do my errand. The good queen,
For she is good, hath brought you forth a
daughter—

II.iii. Location: Sicilia. Leontes' palace.
3 in being alive **4 harlot** lewd. (Originally applied to either sex.) **5 blank** the center of a target; here, aim **6 level** aim **8 Given to the fire** burned at the stake (as a traitor conspiring against the king). **moi'ty** portion **11 tonight** last night **15 on 't** of it **17 solely** alone **18 him** i.e., Polixenes **27 be second to** aid, second

30 free innocent **36 awaking** inability to sleep **38 humor** distemper **41 gossips** godparents for the baby **49 Commit** i.e., to prison **56–57 comforting . . . yours** encouraging your evil courses, than those flatterers who seem to be your most loyal servants **61 by combat** by trial by combat **62 worst** least manly, or lowest in rank

Here 'tis—commends it to your blessing.
[*Lays down the baby.*]

LEONTES
Out!
A mankind witch! Hence with her, out o' door!
A most intelligencing bawd!

PAULINA
Not so.
I am as ignorant in that as you
In so entitling me, and no less honest
Than you are mad; which is enough, I'll warrant,
As this world goes, to pass for honest.

LEONTES
Traitors!
Will you not push her out? [*To Antigonus.*] Give her the bastard.
Thou dotard, thou art woman-tir'd, unroosted
By thy dame Partlet here. Take up the bastard!
Take 't up, I say. Give 't to thy crone.

PAULINA
Forever
Unvenerable be thy hands, if thou
Tak'st up the Princess by that forced baseness
Which he has put upon 't!

LEONTES
He dreads his wife.

PAULINA
So I would you did; then 'twere past all doubt
You'd call your children yours.

LEONTES
A nest of traitors!

ANTIGONUS
I am none, by this good light.

PAULINA
Nor I, nor any
But one that's here, and that's himself; for he
The sacred honor of himself, his queen's,
His hopeful son's, his babe's, betrays to slander,
Whose sting is sharper than the sword's; and will not—
For, as the case now stands, it is a curse
He cannot be compell'd to 't—once remove
The root of his opinion, which is rotten
As ever oak or stone was sound.

LEONTES
A callet
Of boundless tongue, who late hath beat her husband
And now baits me! This brat is none of mine;
It is the issue of Polixenes.
Hence with it, and together with the dam
Commit them to the fire!

PAULINA
It is yours;
And, might we lay th' old proverb to your charge,
So like you, 'tis the worse. Behold, my lords,
Although the print be little, the whole matter
And copy of the father—eye, nose, lip,
The trick of 's frown, his forehead, nay, the valley,
The pretty dimples of his chin and cheek, his smiles,
The very mold and frame of hand, nail, finger.
And thou, good goddess Nature, which hast made it
So like to him that got it, if thou hast
The ordering of the mind too, 'mongst all colors
No yellow in 't, lest she suspect, as he does,
Her children not her husband's!

LEONTES
A gross hag!
And, lozel, thou art worthy to be hang'd,
That wilt not stay her tongue.

ANTIGONUS
Hang all the husbands
That cannot do that feat, you'll leave yourself
Hardly one subject.

LEONTES
Once more, take her hence.

PAULINA
A most unworthy and unnatural lord
Can do no more.

LEONTES
I'll ha' thee burnt.

PAULINA
I care not.
It is an heretic that makes the fire,
Not she which burns in 't. I'll not call you tyrant;
But this most cruel usage of your queen,
Not able to produce more accusation
Than your own weak-hing'd fancy, something savors
Of tyranny, and will ignoble make you,
Yea, scandalous to the world.

LEONTES
On your allegiance,
Out of the chamber with her! Were I a tyrant,
Where were her life? She durst not call me so
If she did know me one. Away with her!

PAULINA
I pray you, do not push me; I'll be gone.
Look to your babe, my lord; 'tis yours. Jove send her
A better guiding spirit! What needs these hands?
You, that are thus so tender o'er his follies,
Will never do him good, not one of you.
So, so. Farewell; we are gone. *Exit.*

LEONTES
Thou, traitor, hast set on thy wife to this.
My child? Away with 't! Even thou, that hast
A heart so tender o'er it, take it hence
And see it instantly consum'd with fire;
Even thou and none but thou. Take it up straight.
Within this hour bring me word 'tis done,
And by good testimony, or I'll seize thy life,
With what thou else call'st thine. If thou refuse
And wilt encounter with my wrath, say so;
The bastard brains with these my proper hands
Shall I dash out. Go, take it to the fire,
For thou set'st on thy wife.

ANTIGONUS
I did not, sir.
These lords, my noble fellows, if they please,
Can clear me in 't.

LORDS
We can. My royal liege,
He is not guilty of her coming hither.

LEONTES
You're liars all.

68 mankind masculine **69 intelligencing** acting as go-between and spy (for the Queen and Polixenes) **75 woman-tir'd** henpecked. (From *tire* in falconry, meaning "tear with the beak.") **unroosted** driven from perch **76 Partlet** or Pertilote, a common name for a hen (as in *Reynard the Fox* and in Chaucer's "Nun's Priest's Tale") **79 forced baseness** false attribution of illegitimacy **91 callet** scold **101 valley** cleft of the chin (?) **105 got** begot

107 yellow i.e., the color of jealousy **109 lozel** worthless person, scoundrel (i.e., Antigonus) **110 stay** restrain **115–116 It is . . . in 't** i.e., only a heretic can be burned guiltily; an innocent person may be burned, but that fact alone doesn't make her guilty **123 Where . . . life** i.e., how could she escape execution at my command **127 What . . . hands** i.e., what need is there to push me **140 proper** own

FIRST LORD
Beseech your Highness, give us better credit.
We have always truly serv'd you, and beseech'
So to esteem of us; and on our knees we beg,
As recompense of our dear services
Past and to come, that you do change this purpose,
Which being so horrible, so bloody, must
Lead on to some foul issue. We all kneel.

LEONTES
I am a feather for each wind that blows.
Shall I live on to see this bastard kneel
And call me father? Better burn it now
Than curse it then. But be it; let it live.
It shall not neither. [*To Antigonus.*] You, sir, come you hither;
You that have been so tenderly officious
With Lady Margery, your midwife there,
To save this bastard's life—for 'tis a bastard,
So sure as this beard's grey—what will you adventure
To save this brat's life?

ANTIGONUS Anything, my lord,
That my ability may undergo
And nobleness impose. At least thus much:
I'll pawn the little blood which I have left
To save the innocent—anything possible.

LEONTES [*Holding his sword*]
It shall be possible. Swear by this sword
Thou wilt perform my bidding.

ANTIGONUS I will, my lord.

LEONTES
Mark and perform it, see'st thou; for the fail
Of any point in 't shall not only be
Death to thyself but to thy lewd-tongu'd wife,
Whom for this time we pardon. We enjoin thee,
As thou art liege-man to us, that thou carry
This female bastard hence and that thou bear it
To some remote and desert place quite out
Of our dominions, and that there thou leave it,
Without more mercy, to it own protection
And favor of the climate. As by strange fortune
It came to us, I do in justice charge thee,
On thy soul's peril and thy body's torture,
That thou commend it strangely to some place
Where chance may nurse or end it. Take it up.

ANTIGONUS [*Taking up the baby*]
I swear to do this, though a present death
Had been more merciful. Come on, poor babe.
Some powerful spirit instruct the kites and ravens
To be thy nurses! Wolves and bears, they say,
Casting their savageness aside, have done
Like offices of pity. Sir, be prosperous
In more than this deed does require! And blessing
Against this cruelty fight on thy side,
Poor thing, condemn'd to loss! *Exit* [*with the baby*].

LEONTES No, I'll not rear
Another's issue.

148 beseech' beseech you **160 Margery** (A derisive term, evidently equivalent to *Partlet* in l. 76.) **170 fail** failure **178 it** its **182 commend . . . place** commit it to some foreign place **190 more** i.e., more ways, more extent (?) **require** deserve **192 loss** destruction

Enter a Servant.

SERVANT Please your Highness, posts
From those you sent to th' oracle are come
An hour since. Cleomenes and Dion,
Being well arriv'd from Delphos, are both landed,
Hasting to th' court.

FIRST LORD So please you, sir, their speed
Hath been beyond account.

LEONTES Twenty-three days
They have been absent. 'Tis good speed, foretells
The great Apollo suddenly will have
The truth of this appear. Prepare you, lords,
Summon a session, that we may arraign
Our most disloyal lady; for, as she hath
Been publicly accus'd, so shall she have
A just and open trial. While she lives
My heart will be a burden to me. Leave me,
And think upon my bidding. *Exeunt* [*severally*].

ACT III • SCENE I

Enter Cleomenes and Dion.

CLEOMENES
The climate's delicate, the air most sweet,
Fertile the isle, the temple much surpassing
The common praise it bears.

DION I shall report,
For most it caught me, the celestial habits—
Methinks I so should term them—and the reverence
Of the grave wearers. O, the sacrifice!
How ceremonious, solemn, and unearthly
It was i' th' off'ring!

CLEOMENES But of all, the burst
And the ear-deaf'ning voice o' th' oracle,
Kin to Jove's thunder, so surpris'd my sense
That I was nothing.

DION If th' event o' th' journey
Prove as successful to the Queen—O be 't so!—
As it hath been to us rare, pleasant, speedy,
The time is worth the use on 't.

CLEOMENES Great Apollo
Turn all to th' best! These proclamations,
So forcing faults upon Hermione,
I little like.

DION The violent carriage of it
Will clear or end the business. When the oracle,
Thus by Apollo's great divine seal'd up,
Shall the contents discover, something rare
Even then will rush to knowledge. Go. Fresh horses!
And gracious be the issue! *Exeunt.*

193 posts messengers **198 beyond account** i.e., unprecedented **200 suddenly** at once **202 session** trial

III.i. Location: Sicilia. On the way to Leontes' palace.
2 isle (Shakespeare follows Greene's *Pandosto* in fictitiously placing Delphi on an island.) **11 event** outcome **14 worth . . . on 't** well employed **17 carriage** execution, management **19 divine** priest **20 discover** reveal

SCENE II

Enter Leontes, Lords, [and] Officers.

LEONTES
This sessions, to our great grief we pronounce,
Even pushes 'gainst our heart—the party tried
The daughter of a king, our wife, and one
Of us too much belov'd. Let us be clear'd
Of being tyrannous, since we so openly
Proceed in justice, which shall have due course,
Even to the guilt or the purgation.
Produce the prisoner.

OFFICER
It is his Highness' pleasure that the Queen
Appear in person here in court. Silence!

[Enter] Hermione, as to her trial, [Paulina, and] Ladies.

LEONTES
Read the indictment.

OFFICER *[Reads]* "Hermione, Queen to the worthy Leontes, King of Sicilia, thou art here accus'd and arraign'd of high treason, in committing adultery with Polixenes, King of Bohemia, and conspiring with Camillo to take away the life of our sovereign lord the King, thy royal husband; the pretense whereof being by circumstances partly laid open, thou, Hermione, contrary to the faith and allegiance of a true subject, didst counsel and aid them, for their better safety, to fly away by night."

HERMIONE
Since what I am to say must be but that
Which contradicts my accusation, and
The testimony on my part no other
But what comes from myself, it shall scarce boot me
To say "not guilty." Mine integrity,
Being counted falsehood, shall, as I express it,
Be so receiv'd. But thus: if pow'rs divine
Behold our human actions, as they do,
I doubt not then but innocence shall make
False accusation blush, and tyranny
Tremble at patience. You, my lord, best know,
Who least will seem to do so, my past life
Hath been as continent, as chaste, as true,
As I am now unhappy; which is more
Than history can pattern, though devis'd
And play'd to take spectators. For behold me—
A fellow of the royal bed, which owe
A moi'ty of the throne, a great king's daughter,
The mother to a hopeful prince—here standing
To prate and talk for life and honor 'fore
Who please to come and hear. For life, I prize it
As I weigh grief, which I would spare. For honor,
'Tis a derivative from me to mine,
And only that I stand for. I appeal
To your own conscience, sir, before Polixenes
Came to your court, how I was in your grace,
How merited to be so; since he came,
With what encounter so uncurrent I
Have strain'd t' appear thus; if one jot beyond
The bound of honor, or in act or will
That way inclining, hard'ned be the hearts
Of all that hear me, and my near'st of kin
Cry fie upon my grave!

LEONTES
I ne'er heard yet
That any of these bolder vices wanted
Less impudence to gainsay what they did
Than to perform it first.

HERMIONE
That's true enough,
Though 'tis a saying, sir, not due to me.

LEONTES
You will not own it.

HERMIONE
More than mistress of
Which comes to me in name of fault, I must not
At all acknowledge. For Polixenes,
With whom I am accus'd, I do confess
I lov'd him as in honor he requir'd;
With such a kind of love as might become
A lady like me; with a love even such,
So and no other, as yourself commanded;
Which not to have done I think had been in me
Both disobedience and ingratitude
To you and toward your friend, whose love had spoke,
Even since it could speak, from an infant, freely
That it was yours. Now, for conspiracy,
I know not how it tastes, though it be dish'd
For me to try how. All I know of it
Is that Camillo was an honest man;
And why he left your court, the gods themselves,
Wotting no more than I, are ignorant.

LEONTES
You knew of his departure, as you know
What you have underta'en to do in 's absence.

HERMIONE
Sir,
You speak a language that I understand not.
My life stands in the level of your dreams,
Which I'll lay down.

LEONTES
Your actions are my dreams;
You had a bastard by Polixenes,
And I but dream'd it. As you were past all shame—
Those of your fact are so—so past all truth,

III.ii. Location: Sicilia. A place of justice, probably at court. **4 Of** by **7 purgation** clearing from the accusation **17 pretense** purpose, design **25 boot** avail **36 pattern** show a similar example for **37 take** please, charm **38 which owe** who own **39 moi'ty** share

42 Who please whoever chooses **42–45 For . . . stand for** as for life, I value it as I value grief, and I would willingly dismiss it; as for honor, it is transmitted from me to my descendants, and that only I maintain **49–50 With . . . thus** (I ask) by what behavior so improper I have exceeded bounds so that I appear thus (in disgrace and on trial) **55–56 wanted Less** were more lacking in **58 due** applicable **59–61 More . . . acknowledge** I will not acknowledge that I am answerable for more than what may be called ordinary human faults. (I.e., Hermione is not guilty of the *bolder vices* of l. 55.) **63 requir'd** deserved **72 dish'd** served up **76 Wotting** i.e., supposing they knew **81 level** aim, range **82 Your . . . dreams** i.e., you have performed what I have fantasized, and what you have done preys on my mind **85 Those of your fact** all those who do what you did

Which to deny concerns more than avails; for as
Thy brat hath been cast out, like to itself,
No father owning it—which is, indeed,
More criminal in thee than it—so thou
Shalt feel our justice, in whose easiest passage
Look for no less than death.

HERMIONE Sir, spare your threats.
The bug which you would fright me with I seek.
To me can life be no commodity.
The crown and comfort of my life, your favor,
I do give lost; for I do feel it gone,
But know not how it went. My second joy
And first-fruits of my body, from his presence
I am barr'd, like one infectious. My third comfort,
Starr'd most unluckily, is from my breast,
The innocent milk in it most innocent mouth,
Hal'd out to murder; myself on every post
Proclaim'd a strumpet; with immodest hatred
The child-bed privilege denied, which 'longs
To women of all fashion; lastly, hurried
Here to this place, i' th' open air, before
I have got strength of limit. Now, my liege,
Tell me what blessings I have here alive,
That I should fear to die? Therefore proceed.
But yet hear this; mistake me not. No life,
I prize it not a straw. But for mine honor,
Which I would free, if I shall be condemn'd
Upon surmises, all proofs sleeping else
But what your jealousies awake, I tell you
'Tis rigor and not law. Your honors all,
I do refer me to the oracle.
Apollo be my judge!

FIRST LORD This your request
Is altogether just. Therefore bring forth,
And in Apollo's name, his oracle.
[*Exeunt certain Officers.*]

HERMIONE
The Emperor of Russia was my father.
O that he were alive, and here beholding
His daughter's trial! That he did but see
The flatness of my misery, yet with eyes
Of pity, not revenge!

[*Enter Officers, with*] Cleomenes [*and*] Dion.

OFFICER [*Holding a sword*]
You here shall swear upon this sword of justice,
That you, Cleomenes and Dion, have
Been both at Delphos, and from thence have brought
This seal'd-up oracle, by the hand deliver'd
Of great Apollo's priest, and that since then
You have not dar'd to break the holy seal
Nor read the secrets in 't.

CLEOMENES, DION All this we swear.

86 concerns . . . avails may seem an understandable concern on your part but will not help **87 like to itself** as it ought to be (since it has no father) **90–91 in whose . . . death** i.e., which will impose the death sentence at least, perhaps torture also **92 bug** bugbear, bogey, imaginary object of terror **93 commodity** asset **95 give** reckon as **99 Starr'd** fated **100 it** its **102 immodest** immoderate **103 'longs** belongs **104 fashion** rank **106 got . . . limit** i.e., regained my strength after having borne a child **109 No life** i.e., I do not ask for life **114 rigor** tyranny **122 flatness** absoluteness

LEONTES
Break up the seals and read.

OFFICER [*Reads*] "Hermione is chaste, Polixenes blameless, Camillo a true subject, Leontes a jealous tyrant, his innocent babe truly begotten, and the King shall live without an heir, if that which is lost be not found."

LORDS
Now blessed be the great Apollo!

HERMIONE Praised!

LEONTES
Hast thou read truth?

OFFICER Ay, my lord, even so
As it is here set down.

LEONTES
There is no truth at all i' th' oracle.
The sessions shall proceed. This is mere falsehood.

[*Enter Servant.*]

SERVANT
My lord the King, the King!

LEONTES What is the business?

SERVANT
O sir, I shall be hated to report it!
The Prince your son, with mere conceit and fear
Of the Queen's speed, is gone.

LEONTES How? Gone?

SERVANT Is dead.

LEONTES
Apollo's angry, and the heavens themselves
Do strike at my injustice. [*Hermione swoons.*] How now there?

PAULINA
This news is mortal to the Queen. Look down
And see what death is doing.

LEONTES Take her hence.
Her heart is but o'ercharg'd; she will recover.
I have too much believ'd mine own suspicion.
Beseech you, tenderly apply to her
Some remedies for life.
[*Exeunt Paulina and Ladies, with Hermione.*]
Apollo, pardon
My great profaneness 'gainst thine oracle!
I'll reconcile me to Polixenes,
New woo my queen, recall the good Camillo,
Whom I proclaim a man of truth, of mercy;
For, being transported by my jealousies
To bloody thoughts and to revenge, I chose
Camillo for the minister to poison
My friend Polixenes; which had been done,
But that the good mind of Camillo tardied
My swift command, though I with death and with
Reward did threaten and encourage him,
Not doing it and being done. He, most humane
And fill'd with honor, to my kingly guest
Unclasp'd my practice, quit his fortunes here,
Which you knew great, and to the hazard

131 up open **144 conceit and fear** i.e., anxious concern **145 speed** success **165 Not . . . done** i.e., death if he did not do it, and reward if he did **167 Unclasp'd my practice** disclosed my plot

Of all incertainties himself commended,
No richer than his honor. How he glisters
Through my rust! And how his piety
Does my deeds make the blacker!
[*Enter Paulina.*]

PAULINA Woe the while!
O, cut my lace, lest my heart, cracking it,
Break too!

FIRST LORD What fit is this, good lady?

PAULINA
What studied torments, tyrant, hast for me?
What wheels? Racks? Fires? What flaying? Boiling
In leads or oils? What old or newer torture
Must I receive, whose every word deserves
To taste of thy most worst? Thy tyranny,
Together working with thy jealousies,
Fancies too weak for boys, too green and idle
For girls of nine, O, think what they have done,
And then run mad indeed, stark mad! For all
Thy by-gone fooleries were but spices of it.
That thou betray'dst Polixenes, 'twas nothing;
That did but show thee, of a fool, inconstant
And damnable ingrateful. Nor was 't much
Thou wouldst have poison'd good Camillo's honor,
To have him kill a king—poor trespasses,
More monstrous standing by; whereof I reckon
The casting forth to crows thy baby-daughter
To be or none or little, though a devil
Would have shed water out of fire ere done 't.
Nor is 't directly laid to thee, the death
Of the young Prince, whose honorable thoughts,
Thoughts high for one so tender, cleft the heart
That could conceive a gross and foolish sire
Blemish'd his gracious dam. This is not, no,
Laid to thy answer. But the last—O lords,
When I have said, cry "Woe!"—the Queen, the Queen,
The sweet'st, dear'st creature's dead, and vengeance for 't
Not dropp'd down yet.

FIRST LORD The higher pow'rs forbid!

PAULINA
I say she's dead; I'll swear 't. If word nor oath
Prevail not, go and see. If you can bring
Tincture or luster in her lip, her eye,
Heat outwardly or breath within, I'll serve you
As I would do the gods. But, O thou tyrant!
Do not repent these things, for they are heavier
Than all thy woes can stir. Therefore betake thee
To nothing but despair. A thousand knees
Ten thousand years together, naked, fasting,
Upon a barren mountain, and still winter
In storm perpetual, could not move the gods
To look that way thou wert.

LEONTES Go on, go on.
Thou canst not speak too much; I have deserv'd
All tongues to talk their bitt'rest.

FIRST LORD Say no more.
Howe'er the business goes, you have made fault
I' th' boldness of your speech.

PAULINA I am sorry for 't.
All faults I make, when I shall come to know them,
I do repent. Alas, I have show'd too much
The rashness of a woman; he is touch'd
To th' noble heart. What's gone and what's past help
Should be past grief. Do not receive affliction
At my petition; I beseech you, rather
Let me be punish'd, that have minded you
Of what you should forget. Now, good my liege,
Sir, royal sir, forgive a foolish woman.
The love I bore your queen—lo, fool again!—
I'll speak of her no more, nor of your children;
I'll not remember you of my own lord,
Who is lost too. Take your patience to you,
And I'll say nothing.

LEONTES Thou didst speak but well
When most the truth, which I receive much better
Than to be pitied of thee. Prithee, bring me
To the dead bodies of my queen and son.
One grave shall be for both. Upon them shall
The causes of their death appear, unto
Our shame perpetual. Once a day I'll visit
The chapel where they lie, and tears shed there
Shall be my recreation. So long as nature
Will bear up with this exercise, so long
I daily vow to use it. Come and lead me
To these sorrows. *Exeunt.*

SCENE III

Enter Antigonus [*and*] *a Mariner,* [*with a*] *Babe.*

ANTIGONUS
Thou art perfect then, our ship hath touch'd upon
The deserts of Bohemia?

MARINER Ay, my lord, and fear
We have landed in ill time. The skies look grimly
And threaten present blusters. In my conscience,
The heavens with that we have in hand are angry
And frown upon 's.

ANTIGONUS
Their sacred wills be done! Go, get aboard;
Look to thy bark. I'll not be long before
I call upon thee.

MARINER Make your best haste, and go not
Too far i' th' land. 'Tis like to be loud weather.
Besides, this place is famous for the creatures

169 commended entrusted **170 No richer than** with no riches except. **glisters** shines **184 spices** foretastes, samples **186 of** for **189 poor** slight **190 More . . . by** when more monstrous sins are at hand for comparison **193 shed . . . fire** wept from his fiery eyes **196 tender** young **209 woes can stir** penance can remove **214 To look . . . wert** to regard you

225 minded reminded **230 remember** remind **231 Take . . . you** be patient

III.iii. Location: Bohemia. The seacoast.
1 perfect certain **2 deserts of Bohemia** i.e., deserted region on the coast. (Shakespeare follows Greene's *Pandosto* in giving Bohemia a seacoast.) **4 present** immediate. **conscience** opinion

Of prey that keep upon 't.
ANTIGONUS Go thou away.
I'll follow instantly.
MARINER I am glad at heart
To be so rid o' th' business. [*Exit.*]
ANTIGONUS Come, poor babe.
I have heard, but not believ'd, the spirits o' th' dead
May walk again. If such thing be, thy mother
Appear'd to me last night, for ne'er was dream
So like a waking. To me comes a creature,
Sometimes her head on one side, some another;
I never saw a vessel of like sorrow,
So fill'd and so becoming. In pure white robes,
Like very sanctity, she did approach
My cabin where I lay; thrice bow'd before me,
And, gasping to begin some speech, her eyes
Became two spouts. The fury spent, anon
Did this break from her: "Good Antigonus,
Since fate, against thy better disposition,
Hath made thy person for the thrower-out
Of my poor babe, according to thine oath,
Places remote enough are in Bohemia;
There weep and leave it crying. And, for the babe
Is counted lost forever, Perdita,
I prithee, call 't. For this ungentle business,
Put on thee by my lord, thou ne'er shalt see
Thy wife Paulina more." And so, with shrieks,
She melted into air. Affrighted much,
I did in time collect myself and thought
This was so and no slumber. Dreams are toys;
Yet for this once, yea, superstitiously,
I will be squar'd by this. I do believe
Hermione hath suffer'd death, and that
Apollo would, this being indeed the issue
Of King Polixenes, it should here be laid,
Either for life or death, upon the earth
Of its right father. Blossom, speed thee well!
[*He lays down the baby.*]
There lie, and there thy character; there these,
[*Places a scroll and bundle beside the baby.*]
Which may, if fortune please, both breed thee, pretty,
And still rest thine. [*Thunder.*] The storm begins. Poor wretch,
That for thy mother's fault art thus expos'd
To loss and what may follow! Weep I cannot,
But my heart bleeds; and most accurs'd am I
To be by oath enjoin'd to this. Farewell!
The day frowns more and more. Thou 'rt like to have
A lullaby too rough. I never saw
The heavens so dim by day. A savage clamor!
Well may I get aboard! This is the chase.
I am gone forever. *Exit, pursued by a bear.*

[*Enter a*] *Shepherd.*

SHEPHERD I would there were no age between ten and three-and-twenty, or that youth would sleep out the rest; for there is nothing in the between but getting wenches with child, wronging the ancientry, stealing, fighting—Hark you now! Would any but these boil'd brains of nineteen and two-and-twenty hunt this weather? They have scar'd away two of my best sheep, which I fear the wolf will sooner find than the master. If anywhere I have them, 'tis by the seaside, browsing of ivy. Good luck, an 't be thy will! What have we here? Mercy on 's, a barne, a very pretty barne! A boy or a child, I wonder? A pretty one, a very pretty one. Sure, some scape. Though I am not bookish, yet I can read waiting-gentlewoman in the scape. This has been some stair-work, some trunk-work, some behind-door-work. They were warmer that got this than the poor thing is here. I'll take it up for pity. Yet I'll tarry till my son come; he halloo'd but even now. Whoa, ho, hoa!

Enter Clown.

CLOWN Hilloa, loa!

SHEPHERD What, art so near? If thou 'lt see a thing to talk on when thou art dead and rotten, come hither. What ail'st thou, man?

CLOWN I have seen two such sights, by sea and by land! But I am not to say it is a sea, for it is now the sky; betwixt the firmament and it you cannot thrust a bodkin's point.

SHEPHERD Why, boy, how is it?

CLOWN I would you did but see how it chafes, how it rages, how it takes up the shore! But that's not to the point. O, the most piteous cry of the poor souls! Sometimes to see 'em, and not to see 'em; now the ship boring the moon with her mainmast, and anon swallow'd with yest and froth, as you 'd thrust a cork into a hogshead. And then for the land-service, to see how the bear tore out his shoulder-bone; how he cried to me for help and said his name was Antigonus, a nobleman. But to make an end of the ship, to see how the sea flap-dragon'd it; but, first, how the poor souls roar'd, and the sea mock'd them; and how the poor gentleman roar'd and the bear mock'd him, both roaring louder than the sea or weather.

SHEPHERD Name of mercy, when was this, boy?

CLOWN Now, now. I have not wink'd since I saw these sights. The men are not yet cold under water, nor the bear half din'd on the gentleman. He's at it now.

SHEPHERD Would I had been by, to have help'd the old man!

CLOWN I would you had been by the ship side, to have help'd her. There your charity would have lack'd footing.

SHEPHERD Heavy matters, heavy matters! But look thee

12 keep upon 't inhabit it **21 So . . . becoming** i.e., so filled with sorrow and so attractive thus **31 for** because **32 Perdita** i.e., the lost girl **33 ungentle** ignoble **38 toys** trifles **40 squar'd** directed in my course **46 character** writing, written account (i.e., the same which subsequently will serve to identify Perdita). **these** i.e., the gold and jewels found by the shepherd, also later used to identify her **47 breed** keep, support. **pretty** pretty one **48 rest** remain. (I.e., may a residue remain.)

61 ancientry old people **62–63 boil'd brains** hotheaded youths **68 barne** bairn, child **69 child** i.e., female infant **70 scape** sexual escapade **72 stair-work, trunk-work** i.e., sexual liaisons under or behind the stairs or using a trunk for concealment **73 got** begot **76 s.d. Clown** country fellow, rustic **84 bodkin's** needle's. (A *bodkin* can also be a dagger, awl, etc.) **87 takes up** contends with, rebukes **91 yest** yeast, foam **92 land-service** (1) dish of food served on land (2) military service on land (as distinguished from naval service); here, the doings on land **96 flap-dragon'd** swallowed as one would a flapdragon, i.e., a raisin or the like snatched up out of burning brandy in the game of snapdragon

here, boy. Now bless thyself. Thou mett'st with things dying, I with things new-born. Here's a sight for thee; look thee, a bearing-cloth for a squire's child! Look thee here; take up, take up, boy; open 't. So, let's see. It was told me I should be rich by the fairies. This is some changeling. Open 't. What's within, boy?

[*The Clown opens the bundle.*]

CLOWN You're a made old man. If the sins of your youth are forgiven you, you're well to live. Gold, all gold!

SHEPHERD This is fairy gold, boy, and 'twill prove so. Up with 't, keep it close. Home, home, the next way. We are lucky, boy, and to be so still requires nothing but secrecy. Let my sheep go. Come, good boy, the next way home.

CLOWN Go you the next way with your findings. I'll go see if the bear be gone from the gentleman and how much he hath eaten. They are never curst but when they are hungry. If there be any of him left, I'll bury it.

SHEPHERD That's a good deed. If thou mayest discern by that which is left of him what he is, fetch me to th' sight of him.

CLOWN Marry, will I; and you shall help to put him i' th' ground.

SHEPHERD 'Tis a lucky day, boy, and we'll do good deeds on 't. *Exeunt.*

ACT IV • SCENE I

Enter Time, the Chorus.

TIME

I, that please some, try all, both joy and terror
Of good and bad, that makes and unfolds error,
Now take upon me, in the name of Time,
To use my wings. Impute it not a crime
To me or my swift passage, that I slide
O'er sixteen years and leave the growth untried
Of that wide gap, since it is in my pow'r
To o'erthrow law and in one self-born hour
To plant and o'erwhelm custom. Let me pass
The same I am, ere ancient'st order was
Or what is now receiv'd. I witness to
The times that brought them in; so shall I do
To th' freshest things now reigning, and make stale
The glistering of this present, as my tale
Now seems to it. Your patience this allowing,
I turn my glass and give my scene such growing
As you had slept between. Leontes leaving—
Th' effects of his fond jealousies so grieving
That he shuts up himself—imagine me,
Gentle spectators, that I now may be
In fair Bohemia. And remember well,
I mention'd a son o' th' King's, which Florizel
I now name to you; and with speed so pace
To speak of Perdita, now grown in grace
Equal with wond'ring. What of her ensues
I list not prophesy; but let Time's news
Be known when 'tis brought forth. A shepherd's
daughter,
And what to her adheres, which follows after,
Is th' argument of Time. Of this allow,
If ever you have spent time worse ere now;
If never, yet that Time himself doth say
He wishes earnestly you never may. *Exit.*

SCENE II

Enter Polixenes and Camillo.

POLIXENES I pray thee, good Camillo, be no more importunate. 'Tis a sickness denying thee anything, a death to grant this.

CAMILLO It is fifteen years since I saw my country. Though I have for the most part been air'd abroad, I desire to lay my bones there. Besides, the penitent King, my master, hath sent for me, to whose feeling sorrows I might be some allay—or I o'erween to think so—which is another spur to my departure.

POLIXENES As thou lov'st me, Camillo, wipe not out the rest of thy services by leaving me now. The need I have of thee thine own goodness hath made. Better not to have had thee than thus to want thee. Thou, having made me businesses which none without thee can sufficiently manage, must either stay to execute them thyself or take away with thee the very services thou hast done; which if I have not enough consider'd—as too much I cannot—to be more thankful to thee shall be my study, and my profit therein the heaping friendships. Of that fatal country, Sicilia, prithee speak no more, whose very naming punishes me with the remembrance of that penitent, as thou call'st him, and reconcil'd king, my brother, whose loss of his most precious queen and children are even now to be afresh lamented. Say to me, when saw'st thou the Prince Florizel, my son? Kings are no less unhappy, their issue not being gracious, than they are in losing them when they have approv'd their virtues.

CAMILLO Sir, it is three days since I saw the Prince. What his happier affairs may be are to me unknown; but I have missingly noted he is of late much retir'd from court, and is less frequent to his princely exercises than formerly he hath appear'd.

POLIXENES I have consider'd so much, Camillo, and with some care, so far that I have eyes under my service which look upon his removedness; from whom I

112 bearing-cloth rich cloth or mantle in which a child was carried to its baptism **115 changeling** child left or taken by fairies **117 well to live** well to do **120 close** secret. **next** nearest **121 still** always **126 curst** mean, fierce

IV.i.
1 try test **6 growth untried** developments unexplored **8 self-born** selfsame **10–11 ere . . . receiv'd** i.e., from the beginnings of time to the present **12 them** i.e., law and custom **14 glistering** glistening freshness **15 seems to it** seems (stale) when compared with the present **16 glass** hourglass **18 fond** foolish

23 pace proceed **25 Equal with wond'ring** as great as the wonder people feel in seeing her **26 list not** do not wish to **28 to her adheres** concerns her **29 argument** subject of a story **31 yet that** i.e., yet allow that

IV.ii. Location: Bohemia. Polixenes' palace.
5 been air'd abroad lived in foreign lands **8 allay** means of abatement. **o'erween** am presumptuous **13 want** lack **18 consider'd** i.e., rewarded **20 heaping friendships** heaping up of (your) kind services and our mutual affection **27 their . . . gracious** if their children behave ungraciously **28 approv'd** proved **31 missingly** i.e., noting the Prince's absence **35–36 eyes . . . removedness** spies who keep an eye on him in his absence

have this intelligence, that he is seldom from the house of a most homely shepherd—a man, they say, that from very nothing, and beyond the imagination of his neighbors, is grown into an unspeakable estate.

CAMILLO I have heard, sir, of such a man, who hath a daughter of most rare note. The report of her is extended more than can be thought to begin from such a cottage.

POLIXENES That's likewise part of my intelligence; but, I fear, the angle that plucks our son thither. Thou shalt accompany us to the place, where we will, not appearing what we are, have some question with the shepherd; from whose simplicity I think it not uneasy to get the cause of my son's resort thither. Prithee, be my present partner in this business, and lay aside the thoughts of Sicilia.

CAMILLO I willingly obey your command.

POLIXENES My best Camillo! We must disguise ourselves.

Exit [with Camillo].

SCENE III

Enter Autolycus, singing.

AUTOLYCUS
When daffodils begin to peer,
With heigh, the doxy over the dale!
Why, then comes in the sweet o' the year;
For the red blood reigns in the winter's pale.

The white sheet bleaching on the hedge,
With heigh, the sweet birds, O, how they sing!
Doth set my pugging tooth on edge;
For a quart of ale is a dish for a king.

The lark, that tirra-lyra chants,
With heigh, with heigh, the thrush and the jay!
Are summer songs for me and my aunts,
While we lie tumbling in the hay.

I have serv'd Prince Florizel and in my time wore three-pile; but now I am out of service.

But shall I go mourn for that, my dear?
The pale moon shines by night;
And when I wander here and there,
I then do most go right.

If tinkers may have leave to live,
And bear the sow-skin budget,
Then my account I well may give,
And in the stocks avouch it.

My traffic is sheets; when the kite builds, look to lesser linen. My father nam'd me Autolycus, who being, as I am, litter'd under Mercury, was likewise a snapper-up of unconsider'd trifles. With die and drab I purchas'd this caparison, and my revenue is the silly cheat. Gallows and knock are too powerful on the highway; beating and hanging are terrors to me. For the life to come, I sleep out the thought of it. A prize, a prize!

Enter Clown.

CLOWN Let me see: every 'leven wether tods; every tod yields pound and odd shilling; fifteen hundred shorn, what comes the wool to?

AUTOLYCUS [*Aside*] If the springe hold, the cock's mine.

CLOWN I cannot do 't without counters. Let me see; what am I to buy for our sheep-shearing feast? Three pound of sugar, five pound of currants, rice—what will this sister of mine do with rice? But my father hath made her mistress of the feast, and she lays it on. She hath made me four and twenty nosegays for the shearers—three-man-song-men all, and very good ones, but they are most of them means and bases; but one Puritan amongst them, and he sings psalms to hornpipes. I must have saffron to color the warden pies; mace; dates?—none, that's out of my note; nutmegs, seven; a race or two of ginger, but that I may beg; four pound of prunes, and as many of raisins o' th' sun.

AUTOLYCUS O that ever I was born! [*Grovels on the ground.*]

CLOWN I' th' name of me—

AUTOLYCUS O, help me, help me! Pluck but off these rags; and then, death, death!

CLOWN Alack, poor soul! Thou hast need of more rags to lay on thee, rather than have these off.

AUTOLYCUS O sir, the loathsomeness of them offends me more than the stripes I have receiv'd, which are mighty ones and millions.

CLOWN Alas, poor man! A million of beating may come to a great matter.

AUTOLYCUS I am robb'd, sir, and beaten; my money and apparel ta'en from me, and these detestable things put upon me.

CLOWN What, by a horseman, or a footman?

AUTOLYCUS A footman, sweet sir, a footman.

CLOWN Indeed, he should be a footman by the garments he has left with thee. If this be a horseman's coat, it hath seen very hot service. Lend me thy hand, I'll help thee. Come, lend me thy hand. [*Helps him up.*]

AUTOLYCUS O, good sir, tenderly, O!

38 homely simple **40 unspeakable** i.e., beyond description **46 angle** baited fishhook

IV.iii. Location: Bohemia. A road near the Shepherd's cottage.
2 doxy beggar's mistress **4 pale** (1) paleness (2) enclosure, i.e., region of authority (3) withdrawal. (The image is of red blood restoring vitality to a pale complexion.) **7 pugging** thievish **11 aunts** i.e., whores **14 three-pile** velvet having very rich pile or nap **20 budget** bag **22 in . . . avouch it** i.e., give evidence of my trade by sitting in the stocks, where tinkers and vagabonds often end up

23 kite (The kite, a bird of prey, was supposed to carry off small pieces of linen with which to construct its nest, whereas Autolycus makes off with larger linen or sheets hung out to dry.) **24 Autolycus** (Like his namesake, Ulysses' grandfather, the son of Mercury, this Autolycus is an expert thief.) **25 litter'd under Mercury** (1) sired by Mercury, the god of thieves (2) born when the planet Mercury was in the ascendant **26–28 With . . . cheat** i.e., gambling and women have brought me to the wearing of these tattered rags, and my source of income is in cheating simpletons **28 knock** beating **29 For** as for **30 prize** booty **32 every . . . tods** every eleven sheep yield a *tod*, i.e., a bulk of wool weighing twenty-eight pounds **35 springe** snare. **cock** woodcock. (A proverbially stupid bird.) **36 counters** metal disks used in reckoning **42 three-man-song-men** singers of catches or rounds for three voices **43 means** tenors **44–45 hornpipes** merry dance tunes **45 warden** made of the warden pear **46 out of my note** not on my list **47 race** root **48 o' th' sun** dried in the sun **63 footman** man on foot. (But in l. 65 the Clown uses the word to mean *attendant* who might have poor clothes.)

CLOWN Alas, poor soul!

AUTOLYCUS O, good sir, softly, good sir! I fear, sir, my shoulder-blade is out.

CLOWN How now? Canst stand?

AUTOLYCUS [*Picking his pocket*] Softly, dear sir; good sir, softly. You ha' done me a charitable office.

CLOWN Dost lack any money? I have a little money for thee.

AUTOLYCUS No, good sweet sir; no, I beseech you, sir. I have a kinsman not past three quarters of a mile hence, unto whom I was going; I shall there have money, or anything I want. Offer me no money, I pray you; that kills my heart.

CLOWN What manner of fellow was he that robb'd you?

AUTOLYCUS A fellow, sir, that I have known to go about with troll-my-dames. I knew him once a servant of the Prince. I cannot tell, good sir, for which of his virtues it was, but he was certainly whipp'd out of the court.

CLOWN His vices, you would say. There's no virtue whipp'd out of the court. They cherish it to make it stay there; and yet it will no more but abide.

AUTOLYCUS Vices, I would say, sir. I know this man well. He hath been since an ape-bearer, then a process-server, a bailiff. Then he compass'd a motion of the Prodigal Son, and married a tinker's wife within a mile where my land and living lies, and, having flown over many knavish professions, he settled only in rogue. Some call him Autolycus.

CLOWN Out upon him! Prig, for my life, prig! He haunts wakes, fairs, and bear-baitings.

AUTOLYCUS Very true, sir; he, sir, he. That's the rogue that put me into this apparel.

CLOWN Not a more cowardly rogue in all Bohemia. If you had but look'd big and spit at him, he 'd have run.

AUTOLYCUS I must confess to you, sir, I am no fighter. I am false of heart that way, and that he knew, I warrant him.

CLOWN How do you now?

AUTOLYCUS Sweet sir, much better than I was; I can stand and walk. I will even take my leave of you, and pace softly towards my kinsman's.

CLOWN Shall I bring thee on the way?

AUTOLYCUS No, good-fac'd sir; no, sweet sir.

CLOWN Then fare thee well. I must go buy spices for our sheep-shearing. *Exit.*

AUTOLYCUS Prosper you, sweet sir! Your purse is not hot enough to purchase your spice. I'll be with you at your sheep-shearing too. If I make not this cheat bring out another, and the shearers prove sheep, let me be unroll'd and my name put in the book of virtue!

Song.

Jog on, jog on, the foot-path way,
And merrily hent the stile-a;
A merry heart goes all the day,
Your sad tires in a mile-a. *Exit.*

85 **troll-my-dames** a game in which the object was to "troll" balls through arches set on a board, usually played by ladies **90 abide** make a temporary stay **92 ape-bearer** one who carries a monkey about for exhibition **93 compass'd a motion** got possession of or devised a puppet-show **98 Prig** thief **99 wakes** village festivals. (A *wake* is also a vigil for a dead person or similar ceremony.) **118–119 cheat bring out** swindle lead to **120 unroll'd** taken off the roll (of rogues and vagabonds) **122 hent** take hold of (as a means of leaping over)

SCENE IV

Enter Florizel [*in shepherd's garb, and*] *Perdita* [*in holiday attire*].

FLORIZEL
These your unusual weeds to each part of you
Does give a life; no shepherdess, but Flora
Peering in April's front. This your sheep-shearing
Is as a meeting of the petty gods,
And you the queen on 't.

PERDITA Sir, my gracious lord,
To chide at your extremes it not becomes me.
O, pardon, that I name them! Your high self,
The gracious mark o' th' land, you have obscur'd
With a swain's wearing, and me, poor lowly maid,
Most goddess-like prank'd up. But that our feasts
In every mess have folly, and the feeders
Digest it with a custom, I should blush
To see you so attir'd, sworn, I think,
To show myself a glass.

FLORIZEL I bless the time
When my good falcon made her flight across
Thy father's ground.

PERDITA Now Jove afford you cause!
To me the difference forges dread; your greatness
Hath not been us'd to fear. Even now I tremble
To think your father, by some accident,
Should pass this way as you did. O, the Fates!
How would he look, to see his work so noble
Vilely bound up? What would he say? Or how
Should I, in these my borrowed flaunts, behold
The sternness of his presence?

FLORIZEL Apprehend
Nothing but jollity. The gods themselves,
Humbling their deities to love, have taken
The shapes of beasts upon them. Jupiter
Became a bull, and bellow'd; the green Neptune
A ram, and bleated; and the fire-rob'd god,
Golden Apollo, a poor humble swain,
As I seem now. Their transformations
Were never for a piece of beauty rarer,
Nor in a way so chaste, since my desires
Run not before mine honor, nor my lusts
Burn hotter than my faith.

PERDITA O, but, sir,
Your resolution cannot hold, when 'tis
Oppos'd, as it must be, by th' pow'r of the King.
One of these two must be necessities,
Which then will speak, that you must change this purpose,

IV.iv. Location: Bohemia. The Shepherd's cottage. (See ll. 181–182, 187, etc.)
1 unusual weeds special, holiday attire **2 Flora** goddess of flowers **3 Peering . . . front** peeping forth in early April **6 extremes** extravagant statements **8 mark** example, pattern **9 wearing** garb **10 prank'd up** bedecked **11 In every mess** at every table, in each group **12 Digest** swallow, i.e., accept. **with a custom** from habit **13–14 sworn . . . glass** intended, I think, to show me myself as in a mirror. (Some editors emend *sworn* to *swoon*.) **17 difference** i.e., of rank. **forges** i.e., creates **22 bound up** i.e., covered in lowly outer garments. (The metaphor is from bookbinding.) **23 flaunts** finery **27–30 Jupiter . . . swain** (Jupiter in the guise of a bull wooed Europa, Neptune disguised as a ram wooed Theopane, and Apollo took the guise of a humble shepherd to enable Admetus to woo Alcestis.) **33 in a way** i.e., pursuing a purpose

Or I my life.

FLORIZEL Thou dearest Perdita,
With these forc'd thoughts, I prithee, darken not
The mirth o' th' feast. Or I'll be thine, my fair,
Or not my father's. For I cannot be
Mine own, not anything to any, if
I be not thine. To this I am most constant,
Though destiny say no. Be merry, gentle!
Strangle such thoughts as these with any thing
That you behold the while. Your guests are coming.
Lift up your countenance, as it were the day
Of celebration of that nuptial which
We two have sworn shall come.

PERDITA O lady Fortune,
Stand you auspicious!

FLORIZEL See, your guests approach.
Address yourself to entertain them sprightly,
And let's be red with mirth.

[Enter] *Shepherd, Clown; Polixenes, Camillo* *[disguised]*; *Mopsa, Dorcas; Servants.*

SHEPHERD
Fie, daughter! When my old wife liv'd, upon
This day she was both pantler, butler, cook,
Both dame and servant; welcom'd all, serv'd all;
Would sing her song and dance her turn; now here,
At upper end o' th' table, now i' th' middle;
On his shoulder, and his; her face o' fire
With labor, and the thing she took to quench it
She would to each one sip. You are retir'd,
As if you were a feasted one and not
The hostess of the meeting. Pray you, bid
These unknown friends to 's welcome, for it is
A way to make us better friends, more known.
Come, quench your blushes and present yourself
That which you are, mistress o' th' feast. Come on,
And bid us welcome to your sheep-shearing,
As your good flock shall prosper.

PERDITA [*To Polixenes*] Sir, welcome.
It is my father's will I should take on me
The hostess-ship o' th' day. [*To Camillo.*] You're welcome, sir.
Give me those flow'rs there, Dorcas. Reverend sirs,
For you there's rosemary and rue; these keep
Seeming and savor all the winter long.
Grace and remembrance be to you both,
And welcome to our shearing! [*Giving them flowers.*]

POLIXENES Shepherdess—
A fair one are you—well you fit our ages
With flow'rs of winter.

PERDITA Sir, the year growing ancient,
Not yet on summer's death, nor on the birth
Of trembling winter, the fairest flow'rs o' th' season
Are our carnations and streak'd gillyvors,
Which some call nature's bastards. Of that kind
Our rustic garden's barren, and I care not
To get slips of them.

POLIXENES Wherefore, gentle maiden,
Do you neglect them?

PERDITA For I have heard it said
There is an art which in their piedness shares
With great creating nature.

POLIXENES Say there be;
Yet nature is made better by no mean
But nature makes that mean. So, over that art
Which you say adds to nature, is an art
That nature makes. You see, sweet maid, we marry
A gentler scion to the wildest stock,
And make conceive a bark of baser kind
By bud of nobler race. This is an art
Which does mend nature, change it rather, but
The art itself is nature.

PERDITA So it is.

POLIXENES
Then make your garden rich in gillyvors,
And do not call them bastards.

PERDITA I'll not put
The dibble in earth to set one slip of them,
No more than, were I painted, I would wish
This youth should say 'twere well, and only therefore
Desire to breed by me. Here's flow'rs for you: [*Giving flowers.*]
Hot lavender, mints, savory, marjoram;
The marigold, that goes to bed wi' th' sun
And with him rises weeping. These are flow'rs
Of middle summer, and I think they are given
To men of middle age. Y' are very welcome.

CAMILLO
I should leave grazing, were I of your flock,
And only live by gazing.

PERDITA Out, alas!
You'd be so lean, that blasts of January
Would blow you through and through. [*To Florizel.*] Now, my fair'st friend,
I would I had some flow'rs o' th' spring that might
Become your time of day; [*To Shepherdesses*] and yours, and yours,
That wear upon your virgin branches yet
Your maidenheads growing. O Proserpina,
For the flow'rs now that, frighted, thou let'st fall
From Dis's wagon! Daffodils,
That come before the swallow dares, and take
The winds of March with beauty; violets dim,
But sweeter than the lids of Juno's eyes
Or Cytherea's breath; pale primroses,
That die unmarried, ere they can behold
Bright Phoebus in his strength—a malady
Most incident to maids; bold oxlips and
The crown imperial; lillies of all kinds,
The flow'r-de-luce being one. O, these I lack,
To make you garlands of, and my sweet friend,

41 forc'd farfetched, unnatural **42 Or** either **49 as** as if **53 Address** prepare **56 pantler** pantry servant **60 On his . . . his** at one man's . . . another's **75 Seeming** outward appearance, color **76 Grace and remembrance** (Equated respectively with rue and rosemary.) **79 the year . . . ancient** i.e., when autumn arrives **82 gillyvors** gillyflowers, a kind of carnation or pink **83 nature's bastards** i.e., the result of artificial breeding. (See ll. 86–88.)

86 For because **87 art** i.e., of cross-breeding. **piedness** particolor appearance **89 mean** means **100 dibble** tool for making holes in which to implant seed **104 Hot** eager, ardent, aromatic (?) **116 Proserpina** daughter of Ceres, stolen away by Pluto *(Dis)* and taken to Hades when, according to Ovid, she was gathering flowers in her garden **119 take** charm **122 Cytherea's** Venus' **124 Phoebus** the sun god **126 crown imperial** a flower from the Levant, cultivated in English gardens **127 flow'r-de-luce** *fleur-de-lis*

To strew him o'er and o'er!

FLORIZEL What, like a corse? 129

PERDITA
No, like a bank for love to lie and play on,
Not like a corse; or if, not to be buried,
But quick and in mine arms. Come, take your
flow'rs. [*Gives flowers.*] 132
Methinks I play as I have seen them do
In Whitsun pastorals. Sure this robe of mine 134
Does change my disposition.

FLORIZEL What you do
Still betters what is done. When you speak, sweet,
I'd have you do it ever. When you sing,
I'd have you buy and sell so, so give alms,
Pray so; and, for the ord'ring your affairs,
To sing them too. When you do dance, I wish you
A wave o' th' sea, that you might ever do
Nothing but that; move still, still so,
And own no other function. Each your doing, 143
So singular in each particular,
Crowns what you are doing in the present deeds,
That all your acts are queens.

PERDITA O Doricles, 146
Your praises are too large. But that your youth,
And the true blood which peeps fairly through 't,
Do plainly give you out an unstain'd shepherd,
With wisdom I might fear, my Doricles,
You woo'd me the false way.

FLORIZEL I think you have
As little skill to fear as I have purpose 152
To put you to 't. But come, our dance, I pray.
Your hand, my Perdita. So turtles pair 154
That never mean to part.

PERDITA I'll swear for 'em.
[*They speak apart.*]

POLIXENES [*To Camillo*]
This is the prettiest low-born lass that ever
Ran on the green-sward. Nothing she does or seems
But smacks of something greater than herself,
Too noble for this place.

CAMILLO He tells her something
That makes her blood look on 't. Good sooth, she is 160
The queen of curds and cream.

CLOWN Come on, strike up!

DORCAS
Mopsa must be your mistress. Marry, garlic,
To mend her kissing with!

MOPSA Now, in good time! 163

CLOWN
Not a word, a word. We stand upon our manners.
Come, strike up!
[*Music.*] *Here a dance of Shepherds and Shepherdesses.*

POLIXENES
Pray, good shepherd, what fair swain is this
Which dances with your daughter?

SHEPHERD
They call him Doricles, and boasts himself
To have a worthy feeding. But I have it 169
Upon his own report and I believe it;
He looks like sooth. He says he loves my daughter. 171
I think so too, for never gaz'd the moon
Upon the water as he'll stand and read
As 'twere my daughter's eyes; and, to be plain,
I think there is not half a kiss to choose
Who loves another best.

POLIXENES She dances featly. 176

SHEPHERD
So she does anything, though I report it
That should be silent. If young Doricles
Do light upon her, she shall bring him that 179
Which he not dreams of.

Enter Servant.

SERVANT O master, if you did but hear the pedlar at the
door, you would never dance again after a tabor and 182
pipe; no, the bagpipe could not move you. He sings
several tunes faster than you'll tell money; he utters 184
them as he had eaten ballads and all men's ears grew
to his tunes.

CLOWN He could never come better; he shall come in. 187
I love a ballad but even too well, if it be doleful matter
merrily set down, or a very pleasant thing indeed and
sung lamentably.

SERVANT He hath songs for man or woman, of all sizes;
no milliner can so fit his customers with gloves. He
has the prettiest love-songs for maids; so without
bawdry, which is strange; with such delicate burdens 194
of dildos and fadings, "jump her and thump her"; and 195
where some stretch-mouth'd rascal would, as it were, 196
mean mischief and break a foul gap into the matter, 197
he makes the maid to answer, "Whoop, do me no
harm, good man"; puts him off, slights him, with
"Whoop, do me no harm, good man."

POLIXENES This is a brave fellow. 201

CLOWN Believe me, thou talkest of an admirable con- 202
ceited fellow. Has he any unbraided wares? 203

SERVANT He hath ribbons of all the colors i' th' rain-
bow; points more than all the lawyers in Bohemia can 205
learnedly handle, though they come to him by th'
gross; inkles, caddisses, cambrics, lawns. Why, he 207
sings 'em over as they were gods or goddesses; you
would think a smock were a she-angel, he so chants to
the sleeve-hand and the work about the square on 't. 210

CLOWN Prithee bring him in, and let him approach
singing.

PERDITA Forewarn him that he use no scurrilous words
in 's tunes. [*Servant goes to the door.*]

129 corse corpse **132 quick** alive **134 Whitsun pastorals** plays and English morris dances often performed at Whitsuntide, seven Sundays after Easter **143 Each your doing** each thing you do and how you do it **146 Doricles** (Florizel's disguise name.) **152 skill** reason **154 turtles** turtledoves, as symbols of faithful love **160 makes . . . on 't** makes her blush **163 kissing** i.e., bad breath. **in good time** (An expression of indignation.)

169 feeding pasturage, lands **171 like sooth** truthful **176 another** the other. **featly** gracefully **179 light upon** choose **182 tabor** small drum **184 tell** count **187 better** at a better time **194 burdens** refrains **195 dildos and fadings** words used as part of the refrains of ballads (but with bawdy double meaning unperceived by the servant, as also in *jump her, thump her, do me no harm,* etc.) **196 stretch-mouth'd** wide-mouthed, foul-mouthed **197 gap** gross and obscene insertion **201 brave** excellent **202–203 conceited** witty, clever **203 unbraided** untarnished, undamaged **205 points** (1) laces for fastening clothes (2) headings in an argument **207 inkles** linen tape. **caddisses** worsted tape used for garters **210 sleeve-hand** wristband. **square on 't** embroidered bosom or yoke of the garment

CLOWN You have of these pedlars that have more in them than you'd think, sister.

PERDITA Ay, good brother, or go about to think.

Enter Autolycus, singing.

AUTOLYCUS

Lawn as white as driven snow,
Cyprus black as e'er was crow,
Gloves as sweet as damask roses,
Masks for faces and for noses,
Bugle bracelet, necklace amber,
Perfume for a lady's chamber,
Golden quoifs and stomachers,
For my lads to give their dears,
Pins and poking-sticks of steel,
What maids lack from head to heel.
Come buy of me, come; come buy, come buy.
Buy, lads, or else your lasses cry.
Come buy.

CLOWN If I were not in love with Mopsa, thou shouldst take no money of me; but being enthrall'd as I am, it will also be the bondage of certain ribbons and gloves.

MOPSA I was promis'd them against the feast, but they come not too late now.

DORCAS He hath promis'd you more than that, or there be liars.

MOPSA He hath paid you all he promis'd you. May be he has paid you more, which will shame you to give him again.

CLOWN Is there no manners left among maids? Will they wear their plackets where they should bear their faces? Is there not milking-time, when you are going to bed, or kiln-hole, to whistle off these secrets, but you must be tittle-tattling before all our guests? 'Tis well they are whisp'ring. Clamor your tongues, and not a word more.

MOPSA I have done. Come, you promis'd me a tawdry-lace and a pair of sweet gloves.

CLOWN Have I not told thee how I was cozen'd by the way and lost all my money?

AUTOLYCUS And indeed, sir, there are cozeners abroad; therefore it behooves men to be wary.

CLOWN Fear not thou, man, thou shalt lose nothing here.

AUTOLYCUS I hope so, sir, for I have about me many parcels of charge.

CLOWN What hast here? Ballads?

MOPSA Pray now, buy some. I love a ballad in print, a life, for then we are sure they are true.

AUTOLYCUS Here's one to a very doleful tune, how a usurer's wife was brought to bed of twenty money-bags at a burden, and how she long'd to eat adders' heads and toads carbonado'd.

MOPSA Is it true, think you?

AUTOLYCUS Very true, and but a month old.

DORCAS Bless me from marrying a usurer!

AUTOLYCUS Here's the midwife's name to 't, one Mistress Tale-porter, and five or six honest wives that were present. Why should I carry lies abroad?

MOPSA Pray you now, buy it.

CLOWN Come on, lay it by, and let's first see moe ballads. We'll buy the other things anon.

AUTOLYCUS Here's another ballad of a fish, that appear'd upon the coast on Wednesday the fourscore of April, forty thousand fathom above water, and sung this ballad against the hard hearts of maids. It was thought she was a woman and was turn'd into a cold fish for she would not exchange flesh with one that lov'd her. The ballad is very pitiful and as true.

DORCAS Is it true too, think you?

AUTOLYCUS Five justices' hands at it, and witnesses more than my pack will hold.

CLOWN Lay it by too. Another.

AUTOLYCUS This is a merry ballad, but a very pretty one.

MOPSA Let's have some merry ones.

AUTOLYCUS Why, this is a passing merry one and goes to the tune of "Two maids wooing a man." There's scarce a maid westward but she sings it. 'Tis in request, I can tell you.

MOPSA We can both sing it. If thou'lt bear a part, thou shalt hear; 'tis in three parts.

DORCAS We had the tune on 't a month ago.

AUTOLYCUS I can bear my part; you must know 'tis my occupation; have at it with you.

Song.

AUTOLYCUS

Get you hence, for I must go
Where it fits not you to know.

DORCAS

Whither?

MOPSA O, whither?

DORCAS Whither?

MOPSA

It becomes thy oath full well,
Thou to me thy secrets tell.

DORCAS

Me too; let me go thither.

MOPSA

Or thou goest to th' grange or mill.

DORCAS

If to either, thou dost ill.

AUTOLYCUS

Neither.

DORCAS What, neither?

AUTOLYCUS Neither.

DORCAS

Thou hast sworn my love to be.

215 You . . . pedlars you'll find pedlars **217 go about** intend **217 s.d. Enter Autolycus** (Apparently he is wearing a false beard; later in this scene he removes it to impersonate a courtier to the Clown and Shepherd.) **219 Cyprus** crepe **220 sweet** i.e., perfumed **222 Bugle bracelet** bracelet of black glossy beads **224 quoifs** close-fitting caps. **stomachers** embroidered fronts for ladies' dresses **226 poking-sticks** rods used for ironing and stiffening the plaits of ruffs **234 against** in anticipation of, before **239 paid you** i.e., made you pregnant **242 plackets** slits in petticoats **244 kiln-hole** fireplace. **whistle off** turn loose (as one would a falcon) **246 Clamor** silence **248–249 tawdry-lace** cheap and showy lace, or neckerchief. (So called from St. Audrey's Fair.) **250 cozen'd** cheated **257 parcels of charge** valuable items **259–260 a life** on my life **263 at a burden** in one childbirth

264 carbonado'd scored across and grilled **269 Tale-porter** i.e., tale-bearer, gossip **275 fourscore** eightieth (!) **276 forty thousand fathom** 240,000 feet **303 grange** farm

MOPSA
Thou hast sworn it more to me.
Then whither goest? Say, whither?

CLOWN We'll have this song out anon by ourselves. My father and the gentlemen are in sad talk, and we'll not trouble them. Come, bring away thy pack after me. Wenches, I'll buy for you both. Pedlar, let's have the first choice. Follow me, girls.
[*Exit with Dorcas and Mopsa.*]

AUTOLYCUS And you shall pay well for 'em.
[*Follows singing.*]

Song.

Will you buy any tape,
Or lace for your cape,
My dainty duck, my dear-a?
Any silk, any thread,
And toys for your head,
Of the new'st and fin'st, fin'st wear-a?
Come to the pedlar;
Money's a medler,
That doth utter all men's ware-a. *Exit.*

[*Enter Servant.*]

SERVANT Master, there is three carters, three shepherds, three neatherds, three swineherds, that have made themselves all men of hair. They call themselves Saltiers, and they have a dance which the wenches say is a gallimaufry of gambols, because they are not in 't; but they themselves are o' th' mind, if it be not too rough for some that know little but bowling, it will please plentifully.

SHEPHERD Away! We'll none on 't. Here has been too much homely foolery already.—I know, sir, we weary you.

POLIXENES You weary those that refresh us. Pray, let's see these four threes of herdsmen.

SERVANT One three of them, by their own report, sir, hath danc'd before the King; and not the worst of the three but jumps twelve foot and a half by th' squier.

SHEPHERD Leave your prating. Since these good men are pleas'd, let them come in; but quickly now.

SERVANT Why, they stay at door, sir.
[*Goes to the door.*]

Here a dance of twelve Satyrs.

POLIXENES
O, father, you'll know more of that hereafter.
[*To Camillo.*] Is it not too far gone? 'Tis time to part them.
He's simple and tells much. [*To Florizel.*] How now, fair shepherd?
Your heart is full of something that does take
Your mind from feasting. Sooth, when I was young
And handed love as you do, I was wont
To load my she with knacks. I would have ransack'd
The pedlar's silken treasury and have pour'd it
To her acceptance; you have let him go
And nothing marted with him. If your lass
Interpretation should abuse and call this
Your lack of love or bounty, you were straited
For a reply, at least if you make a care
Of happy holding her.

FLORIZEL Old sir, I know
She prizes not such trifles as these are.
The gifts she looks from me are pack'd and lock'd
Up in my heart, which I have given already,
But not deliver'd. [*To Perdita.*] O, hear me breathe my life
Before this ancient sir, who, it should seem,
Hath sometime lov'd! I take thy hand, this hand,
As soft as dove's down and as white as it,
Or Ethiopian's tooth, or the fann'd snow that's bolted
By th' northern blasts twice o'er. [*Taking her hand.*]

POLIXENES What follows this?
How prettily th' young swain seems to wash
The hand was fair before! I have put you out.
But to your protestation; let me hear
What you profess.

FLORIZEL Do, and be witness to 't.

POLIXENES
And this my neighbor too?

FLORIZEL And he, and more
Than he, and men—the earth, the heavens, and all:
That, were I crown'd the most imperial monarch,
Thereof most worthy, were I the fairest youth
That ever made eye swerve, had force and knowledge
More than was ever man's, I would not prize them
Without her love; for her employ them all;
Commend them and condemn them to her service
Or to their own perdition.

POLIXENES Fairly offer'd.

CAMILLO
This shows a sound affection.

SHEPHERD But, my daughter,
Say you the like to him?

PERDITA I cannot speak
So well, nothing so well; no, nor mean better.
By th' pattern of mine own thoughts I cut out
The purity of his.

SHEPHERD Take hands, a bargain!
And, friends unknown, you shall bear witness to 't:
I give my daughter to him, and will make
Her portion equal his.

FLORIZEL O, that must be
I' th' virtue of your daughter. One being dead,

310 sad serious **319 toys** trifles **323 utter** put on the market **325 neatherds** cowherds **326 of hair** dressed in skins **327 Saltiers** i.e., Satyrs **328 gallimaufry** jumble **330 bowling** (A more gentle sport than the vigorous satyr dancing.) **337 three** threesome **339 squier** square, foot rule

348 handed handled, dealt in **352 nothing marted with** bought nothing from **353 Interpretation should abuse** should interpret wrongly **354 were straited** would be hard pressed **356 happy holding her** keeping her happy **358 looks** looks for **360 breathe my life** i.e., pronounce eternal vows **364 fann'd** blown. **bolted** sifted **367 was** which was. **out** i.e., from your speech **377–378 Commend . . . perdition** either commend them to her service, or, failing that, condemn them to deserved destruction

I shall have more than you can dream of yet;
Enough then for your wonder. But, come on,
Contract us 'fore these witnesses.

SHEPHERD
Come, your hand;
And, daughter, yours.

POLIXENES
Soft, swain, awhile, beseech you.
Have you a father?

FLORIZEL
I have, but what of him?

POLIXENES
Knows he of this?

FLORIZEL
He neither does nor shall.

POLIXENES
Methinks a father
Is at the nuptial of his son a guest
That best becomes the table. Pray you once more,
Is not your father grown incapable
Of reasonable affairs? Is he not stupid
With age and alt'ring rheums? Can he speak? Hear?
Know man from man? Dispute his own estate?
Lies he not bed-rid, and again does nothing
But what he did being childish?

FLORIZEL
No, good sir,
He has his health and ampler strength indeed
Than most have of his age.

POLIXENES
By my white beard,
You offer him, if this be so, a wrong
Something unfilial. Reason my son
Should choose himself a wife, but as good reason
The father, all whose joy is nothing else
But fair posterity, should hold some counsel
In such a business.

FLORIZEL
I yield all this;
But for some other reasons, my grave sir,
Which 'tis not fit you know, I not acquaint
My father of this business.

POLIXENES
Let him know 't.

FLORIZEL
He shall not.

POLIXENES
Prithee, let him.

FLORIZEL
No, he must not.

SHEPHERD
Let him, my son. He shall not need to grieve
At knowing of thy choice.

FLORIZEL
Come, come, he must not.
Mark our contract.

POLIXENES
Mark your divorce, young sir,
[*Discovers himself.*]
Whom son I dare not call. Thou art too base
To be acknowledg'd. Thou a scepter's heir,
That thus affects a sheephook?—Thou old traitor,
I am sorry that by hanging thee I can
But shorten thy life one week.—And thou, fresh piece
Of excellent witchcraft, who of force must know
The royal fool thou cop'st with—

SHEPHERD
O, my heart!

POLIXENES
I'll have thy beauty scratch'd with briers, and made
More homely than thy state.—For thee, fond boy,
If I may ever know thou dost but sigh
That thou no more shalt see this knack, as never
I mean thou shalt, we'll bar thee from succession,
Not hold thee of our blood, no, not our kin,
Farre than Deucalion off. Mark thou my words.
Follow us to the court.—Thou churl, for this time,
Though full of our displeasure, yet we free thee
From the dead blow of it.—And you, enchantment,
Worthy enough a herdsman—yea, him too,
That makes himself, but for our honor therein,
Unworthy thee—if ever henceforth thou
These rural latches to his entrance open,
Or hoop his body more with thy embraces,
I will devise a death as cruel for thee
As thou art tender to 't. *Exit.*

PERDITA
Even here undone!
I was not much afeard; for once or twice
I was about to speak and tell him plainly
The selfsame sun that shines upon his court
Hides not his visage from our cottage, but
Looks on alike. Will 't please you, sir, be gone?
I told you what would come of this. Beseech you,
Of your own state take care. This dream of mine—
Being now awake, I'll queen it no inch farther,
But milk my ewes and weep.

CAMILLO
Why, how now, father?
Speak ere thou diest.

SHEPHERD
I cannot speak, nor think,
Nor dare to know that which I know. [*To Florizel.*] O sir,
You have undone a man of fourscore three,
That thought to fill his grave in quiet, yea,
To die upon the bed my father died,
To lie close by his honest bones; but now
Some hangman must put on my shroud and lay me
Where no priest shovels in dust. [*To Perdita.*] O cursed wretch,
That knew'st this was the Prince, and wouldst adventure
To mingle faith with him! Undone! Undone!
If I might die within this hour, I have liv'd
To die when I desire. *Exit.*

FLORIZEL
Why look you so upon me?
I am but sorry, not afeard; delay'd,
But nothing alt'red. What I was, I am,
More straining on for plucking back, not following
My leash unwillingly.

CAMILLO
Gracious my lord,
You know your father's temper. At this time
He will allow no speech, which I do guess
You do not purpose to him; and as hardly

399 alt'ring rheums weakening diseases **400 Dispute** discuss. **estate** condition **406 Something** somewhat. **Reason** it is reasonable that **410 yield** concede **420 affects** desires, shows inclination for **423 of force** of necessity **424 thou cop'st** you deal

426 fond foolish **428 knack** trifle, schemer **431 Farre . . . off** farther off in kinship than Deucalion (the Noah of classical mythology) **432 churl** i.e., the Shepherd **434 dead** deadly. **enchantment** i.e., Perdita **435 year, him** i.e., worthy of him (Florizel) **446 alike** indifferently **455 died** i.e., died on **466 More . . . back** i.e., like a hound on the leash, all the more eager to go forward for having been restrained

Will he endure your sight as yet, I fear.
Then, till the fury of his Highness settle,
Come not before him.

FLORIZEL
I not purpose it.
I think Camillo?

CAMILLO
Even he, my lord.

PERDITA
How often have I told you 'twould be thus!
How often said, my dignity would last
But till 'twere known!

FLORIZEL
It cannot fail but by
The violation of my faith; and then
Let nature crush the sides o' th' earth together
And mar the seeds within! Lift up thy looks.
From my succession wipe me, father; I
Am heir to my affection.

CAMILLO
Be advis'd.

FLORIZEL
I am, and by my fancy. If my reason
Will thereto be obedient, I have reason;
If not, my senses, better pleas'd with madness,
Do bid it welcome.

CAMILLO
This is desperate, sir.

FLORIZEL
So call it, but it does fulfill my vow;
I needs must think it honesty. Camillo,
Not for Bohemia, nor the pomp that may
Be thereat glean'd, for all the sun sees or
The close earth wombs or the profound seas hides
In unknown fathoms, will I break my oath
To this my fair belov'd. Therefore, I pray you,
As you have ever been my father's honor'd friend,
When he shall miss me—as, in faith, I mean not
To see him any more—cast your good counsels
Upon his passion. Let myself and fortune
Tug for the time to come. This you may know
And so deliver: I am put to sea
With her who here I cannot hold on shore;
And most opportune to our need I have
A vessel rides fast by, but not prepar'd
For this design. What course I mean to hold
Shall nothing benefit your knowledge, nor
Concern me the reporting.

CAMILLO
O my lord,
I would your spirit were easier for advice,
Or stronger for your need.

FLORIZEL
Hark, Perdita.
[*Drawing her aside.*]
[*To Camillo.*] I'll hear you by and by.

CAMILLO [*To himself*]
He's irremovable,
Resolv'd for flight. Now were I happy if
His going I could frame to serve my turn,
Save him from danger, do him love and honor,
Purchase the sight again of dear Sicilia
And that unhappy king, my master, whom
I so much thirst to see.

FLORIZEL
Now, good Camillo,
I am so fraught with curious business that
I leave out ceremony.

CAMILLO
Sir, I think
You have heard of my poor services, i' th' love
That I have borne your father?

FLORIZEL
Very nobly
Have you deserv'd. It is my father's music
To speak your deeds, not little of his care
To have them recompens'd as thought on.

CAMILLO
Well, my lord,
If you may please to think I love the King
And through him what 's nearest to him, which is
Your gracious self, embrace but my direction,
If your more ponderous and settled project
May suffer alteration. On mine honor,
I'll point you where you shall have such receiving
As shall become your Highness, where you may
Enjoy your mistress, for the whom, I see,
There's no disjunction to be made, but by—
As heavens forfend!—your ruin; marry her,
And, with my best endeavors in your absence,
Your discontenting father strive to qualify
And bring him up to liking.

FLORIZEL
How, Camillo,
May this, almost a miracle, be done,
That I may call thee something more than man,
And after that trust to thee?

CAMILLO
Have you thought on
A place whereto you'll go?

FLORIZEL
Not any yet.
But as th' unthought-on accident is guilty
To what we wildly do, so we profess
Ourselves to be the slaves of chance and flies
Of every wind that blows.

CAMILLO
Then list to me.
This follows, if you will not change your purpose
But undergo this flight: make for Sicilia,
And there present yourself and your fair princess,
For so I see she must be, 'fore Leontes.
She shall be habited as it becomes
The partner of your bed. Methinks I see
Leontes opening his free arms and weeping
His welcomes forth; asks thee there, son, forgiveness,
As 'twere i' th' father's person; kisses the hands
Of your fresh princess; o'er and o'er divides him
'Twixt his unkindness and his kindness; th' one
He chides to hell, and bids the other grow
Faster than thought or time.

FLORIZEL
Worthy Camillo,
What color for my visitation shall I
Hold up before him?

480 mar the seeds within i.e., destroy the sources of life on earth **482 Be advis'd** think carefully, be receptive to wise advice **483 fancy** love **491 wombs** encloses, conceals **498 Tug** contend **499 deliver** report **500 who** whom **504–505 Shall . . . reporting** would not behoove you to know nor me to report **510 frame** shape

515 curious demanding care **521 as thought on** in proportion to his high estimate of them **525 ponderous** serious and carefully deliberated **526 suffer** permit **533 discontenting** discontented, displeased. **qualify** appease, pacify **534 bring . . . liking** raise him to the pitch of approval **539–540 as . . . wildly do** just as the unexpected happening (of our being discovered by the King) is responsible for what we rashly do at this point **552–553 divides . . . kindness** divides his speech between his former unkindness (which he condemns) and his present intention of kindness **555 Faster** firmer; also, more swiftly **556 color** excuse, pretext

CAMILLO Sent by the King your father
To greet him and to give him comforts. Sir,
The manner of your bearing towards him, with
What you, as from your father, shall deliver,
Things known betwixt us three, I'll write you down,
The which shall point you forth at every sitting 562
What you must say, that he shall not perceive
But that you have your father's bosom there
And speak his very heart.

FLORIZEL I am bound to you.
There is some sap in this.

CAMILLO A course more promising
Than a wild dedication of yourselves
To unpath'd waters, undream'd shores, most certain
To miseries enough; no hope to help you,
But as you shake off one to take another;
Nothing so certain as your anchors, who
Do their best office if they can but stay you
Where you'll be loath to be. Besides, you know
Prosperity's the very bond of love,
Whose fresh complexion and whose heart together
Affliction alters.

PERDITA One of these is true:
I think affliction may subdue the cheek, 577
But not take in the mind.

CAMILLO Yea, say you so? 578
There shall not at your father's house these seven
years 579
Be born another such.

FLORIZEL My good Camillo,
She's as forward of her breeding as 581
She is i' th' rear 'our birth. 582

CAMILLO
I cannot say 'tis pity
She lacks instructions, for she seems a mistress 584
To most that teach.

PERDITA Your pardon, sir; for this
I'll blush you thanks.

FLORIZEL My prettiest Perdita!
But O, the thorns we stand upon! Camillo,
Preserver of my father, now of me,
The medicine of our house, how shall we do?
We are not furnish'd like Bohemia's son,
Nor shall appear in Sicilia.

CAMILLO My lord, 591
Fear none of this. I think you know my fortunes
Do all lie there. It shall be so my care
To have you royally appointed as if 594
The scene you play were mine. For instance, sir,
That you may know you shall not want, one word.
[*They talk aside.*]

Enter Autolycus.

AUTOLYCUS Ha, ha, what a fool Honesty is! And Trust,
his sworn brother, a very simple gentleman! I have
sold all my trumpery; not a counterfeit stone, not a
ribbon, glass, pomander, brooch, table-book, ballad, 600
knife, tape, glove, shoe-tie, bracelet, horn-ring, to
keep my pack from fasting. They throng who should 602
buy first, as if my trinkets had been hallow'd and
brought a benediction to the buyer; by which means
I saw whose purse was best in picture, and what I 605
saw, to my good use I rememb'red. My clown, who
wants but something to be a reasonable man, grew so 607
in love with the wenches' song, that he would not stir
his pettitoes till he had both tune and words, which 609
so drew the rest of the herd to me that all their other
senses stuck in ears. You might have pinch'd a 611
placket, it was senseless; 'twas nothing to geld a cod- 612
piece of a purse; I could have fil'd keys off that hung 613
in chains. No hearing, no feeling, but my sir's song, 614
and admiring the nothing of it. So that in this time of
lethargy I pick'd and cut most of their festival purses;
and had not the old man come in with whoo-bub 617
against his daughter and the King's son and scar'd my
choughs from the chaff, I had not left a purse alive in 619
the whole army.

[*Camillo, Florizel, and Perdita come forward.*]

CAMILLO
Nay, but my letters, by this means being there
So soon as you arrive, shall clear that doubt.

FLORIZEL
And those that you'll procure from King Leontes—

CAMILLO
Shall satisfy your father.

PERDITA Happy be you!
All that you speak shows fair.

CAMILLO [*Seeing Autolycus*] Who have we here?
We'll make an instrument of this, omit
Nothing may give us aid.

AUTOLYCUS If they have overheard me now, why, hanging.

CAMILLO How now, good fellow? Why shak'st thou so?
Fear not, man, here's no harm intended to thee.

AUTOLYCUS I am a poor fellow, sir.

CAMILLO Why, be so still; here's nobody will steal that
from thee. Yet for the outside of thy poverty we must 634
make an exchange. Therefore discase thee instantly— 635
thou must think there's a necessity in 't—and change
garments with this gentleman. Though the penny- 637
worth on his side be the worst, yet hold thee, there's 638
some boot. [*Gives money.*] 639

AUTOLYCUS I am a poor fellow, sir. [*Aside.*] I know ye well enough.

CAMILLO Nay, prithee, dispatch. The gentleman is half 642
flay'd already. 643

AUTOLYCUS Are you in earnest, sir? [*Aside.*] I smell the trick on 't.

562 point you forth indicate to you. **sitting** conference **577 subdue the cheek** i.e., with tears and pale complexion **578 take in** overcome **579 your father's** (Said to Florizel, and meaning Polixenes' palace?) **these seven years** i.e., for a long time to come **581 forward . . . breeding** in advance of her lowly rearing **582 'our** of our, of my **584 instructions** formal schooling **591 appear** appear as such **594 appointed** equipped, outfitted

600 pomander ball composed of perfume. **table-book** notebook **602 from fasting** i.e., from being empty **605 best in picture** i.e., best to look at, most promising **607 wants but something** lacks one thing only (i.e., intelligence) **609 pettitoes** pig's toes; here, toes **611 stuck in ears** were occupied with their ears **612 placket** (Literally, slit in a petticoat.) **senseless** insensible **612–613 geld a codpiece** cut loose from the pouch worn at the front of a man's breeches **614 my sir's** i.e., the Clown's **617 whoo-bub** hubbub **619 choughs** jackdaws **634 outside of thy poverty** i.e., your ragged clothing **635 discase** undress **637–638 pennyworth** i.e., value of the bargain **639 some boot** something in addition **642 dispatch** hurry **643 flay'd** skinned, i.e., undressed

FLORIZEL Dispatch, I prithee.

AUTOLYCUS Indeed, I have had earnest, but I cannot with conscience take it.

CAMILLO Unbuckle, unbuckle,

[*Florizel and Autolycus exchange garments.*]

Fortunate mistress—let my prophecy
Come home to ye!—you must retire yourself
Into some covert. Take your sweetheart's hat
And pluck it o'er your brows, muffle your face,
Dismantle you, and, as you can, disliken
The truth of your own seeming, that you may—
For I do fear eyes over—to shipboard
Get undescried.

PERDITA I see the play so lies
That I must bear a part.

CAMILLO No remedy.
Have you done there?

FLORIZEL Should I now meet my father,
He would not call me son.

CAMILLO
Nay, you shall have no hat. [*Gives it to Perdita.*]
Come, lady, come. Farewell, my friend.

AUTOLYCUS Adieu, sir.

FLORIZEL
O Perdita, what have we twain forgot?
Pray you, a word.

CAMILLO [*Aside*]
What I do next shall be to tell the King
Of this escape and whither they are bound;
Wherein my hope is I shall so prevail
To force him after; in whose company
I shall review Sicilia, for whose sight
I have a woman's longing.

FLORIZEL Fortune speed us!
Thus we set on, Camillo, to th' sea-side.

CAMILLO
The swifter speed the better.

Exit [*with Florizel and Perdita*].

AUTOLYCUS I understand the business, I hear it. To have an open ear, a quick eye, and a nimble hand, is necessary for a cutpurse; a good nose is requisite also, to smell out work for th' other senses. I see this is the time that the unjust man doth thrive. What an exchange had this been without boot! What a boot is here with this exchange! Sure the gods do this year connive at us, and we may do anything extempore. The Prince himself is about a piece of iniquity, stealing away from his father with his clog at his heels. If I thought it were a piece of honesty to acquaint the King withal, I would not do 't. I hold it the more knavery to conceal it; and therein am I constant to my profession.

Enter Clown and Shepherd [*carrying a bundle and a box*].

Aside, aside! Here is more matter for a hot brain. Every lane's end, every shop, church, session, hanging, yields a careful man work.

CLOWN See, see, what a man you are now! There is no other way but to tell the King she's a changeling and none of your flesh and blood.

SHEPHERD Nay, but hear me.

CLOWN Nay, but hear me.

SHEPHERD Go to, then.

CLOWN She being none of your flesh and blood, your flesh and blood has not offended the King, and so your flesh and blood is not to be punish'd by him. Show those things you found about her, those secret things, all but what she has with her. This being done, let the law go whistle, I warrant you.

SHEPHERD I will tell the King all, every word, yea, and his son's pranks too; who, I may say, is no honest man, neither to his father nor to me, to go about to make me the King's brother-in-law.

CLOWN Indeed, brother-in-law was the farthest off you could have been to him, and then your blood had been the dearer by I know how much an ounce.

AUTOLYCUS [*Aside*] Very wisely, puppies!

SHEPHERD Well, let us to the King. There is that in this fardel will make him scratch his beard.

AUTOLYCUS [*Aside*] I know not what impediment this complaint may be to the flight of my master.

CLOWN Pray heartily he be at' palace.

AUTOLYCUS [*Aside*] Though I am not naturally honest, I am so sometimes by chance. Let me pocket up my pedlar's excrement. [*Takes off his false beard.*] How now, rustics, whither are you bound?

SHEPHERD To th' palace, an it like your worship.

AUTOLYCUS Your affairs there, what, with whom, the condition of that fardel, the place of your dwelling, your names, your ages, of what having, breeding, and anything that is fitting to be known, discover.

CLOWN We are but plain fellows, sir.

AUTOLYCUS A lie; you are rough and hairy. Let me have no lying. It becomes none but tradesmen, and they often give us soldiers the lie, but we pay them for it with stamp'd coin, not stabbing steel; therefore they do not give us the lie.

CLOWN Your worship had like to have given us one, if you had not taken yourself with the manner.

SHEPHERD Are you a courtier, an 't like you, sir?

AUTOLYCUS Whether it like me or no, I am a courtier. Seest thou not the air of the court in these enfoldings? Hath not my gait in it the measure of the court? Receives not thy nose court-odor from me? Reflect I not on thy baseness court-contempt? Think'st thou, for that I insinuate, or toaze from thee thy business, I am

647 earnest advance payment (playing on *in earnest* in l. 644) **650–651 let . . . to ye** i.e., let my prophecy that Perdita will be fortunate be fulfilled for her **652 covert** secret place **654 as you can** as much as you can **654–655 disliken . . . seeming** disguise your outward appearance **656 eyes over** spying eyes **670 review** see again **679 without** i.e., even without **681 connive at** look indulgently at **683 clog** encumbrance (i.e., Perdita)

688 session court session **691 changeling** child left by the fairies **704 go about** make it his object **711 fardel** bundle **714 at'** at the **717 excrement** hair, beard **719 like** please **722 having** property **723 discover** reveal **724 plain** simple. (But Autolycus plays on the meaning *smooth.*) **727 give . . . lie** i.e., cheat us. (But *giving the lie* also means to accuse a person to his face of lying, an affront which a soldier would repay with *stabbing steel.*) **729 give** (Autolycus punningly observes that since soldiers pay tradesmen for their wares, the tradesmen cannot be said to have *given* the lie, and so a duel is avoided.) **730 had like** was about **731 taken . . . manner** i.e., caught yourself in the act, stopped short. (The Clown observes that Autolycus has once again avoided the "giving of the lie" and its consequences in a duel by his clever equivocation. Cf. Touchstone in *As You Like It*, V.iv.) **734 enfoldings** clothes **738 toaze** tease, draw out, comb out

therefore no courtier? I am courtier cap-a-pe, and one that will either push on or pluck back thy business there. Whereupon I command thee to open thy affair.

SHEPHERD My business, sir, is to the King.

AUTOLYCUS What advocate hast thou to him?

SHEPHERD I know not, an 't like you.

CLOWN [*To Shepherd*] Advocate's the court-word for a pheasant. Say you have none.

SHEPHERD None, sir; I have no pheasant, cock nor hen.

AUTOLYCUS How blessed are we that are not simple men! Yet nature might have made me as these are, therefore I will not disdain.

CLOWN [*To Shepherd*] This cannot be but a great courtier.

SHEPHERD His garments are rich, but he wears them not handsomely.

CLOWN He seems to be the more noble in being fantastical. A great man, I'll warrant; I know by the picking on 's teeth.

AUTOLYCUS The fardel there? What's i' th' fardel? Wherefore that box?

SHEPHERD Sir, there lies such secrets in this fardel and box, which none must know but the King; and which he shall know within this hour, if I may come to th' speech of him.

AUTOLYCUS Age, thou hast lost thy labor.

SHEPHERD Why, sir?

AUTOLYCUS The King is not at the palace. He is gone aboard a new ship to purge melancholy and air himself; for, if thou be'st capable of things serious, thou must know the King is full of grief.

SHEPHERD So 'tis said, sir; about his son, that should have married a shepherd's daughter.

AUTOLYCUS If that shepherd be not in handfast, let him fly. The curses he shall have, the tortures he shall feel, will break the back of man, the heart of monster.

CLOWN Think you so, sir?

AUTOLYCUS Not he alone shall suffer what wit can make heavy and vengeance bitter; but those that are germane to him, though remov'd fifty times, shall all come under the hangman, which, though it be great pity, yet it is necessary. An old sheep-whistling rogue, a ram-tender, to offer to have his daughter come into grace? Some say he shall be ston'd; but that death is too soft for him, say I. Draw our throne into a sheep-cote? All deaths are too few, the sharpest too easy.

CLOWN Has the old man e'er a son, sir, do you hear, an 't like you, sir?

AUTOLYCUS He has a son, who shall be flay'd alive; then 'nointed over with honey, set on the head of a wasp's nest; then stand till he be three quarters and a dram dead; then recover'd again with aqua-vitae or some other hot infusion; then, raw as he is, and in the hottest day prognostication proclaims, shall he be set against a brick wall, the sun looking with a southward eye upon him, where he is to behold him with flies blown to death. But what talk we of these traitorly rascals, whose miseries are to be smil'd at, their offenses being so capital? Tell me, for you seem to be honest plain men, what you have to the King. Being something gently consider'd, I'll bring you where he is aboard, tender your persons to his presence, whisper him in your behalfs; and if it be in man besides the King to effect your suits, here is man shall do it.

CLOWN [*To Shepherd*] He seems to be of great authority. Close with him, give him gold; and though authority be a stubborn bear, yet he is oft led by the nose with gold. Show the inside of your purse to the outside of his hand, and no more ado. Remember "ston'd," and "flay'd alive."

SHEPHERD An 't please you, sir, to undertake the business for us, here is that gold I have. [*Offers money.*] I'll make it as much more and leave this young man in pawn till I bring it you.

AUTOLYCUS After I have done what I promis'd?

SHEPHERD Ay, sir.

AUTOLYCUS Well, give me the moi'ty. [*Takes money.*] Are you a party in this business?

CLOWN In some sort, sir; but, though my case be a pitiful one, I hope I shall not be flay'd out of it.

AUTOLYCUS O, that's the case of the shepherd's son. Hang him, he'll be made an example.

CLOWN Comfort, good comfort! We must to the King and show our strange sights. He must know 'tis none of your daughter nor my sister; we are gone else. Sir, I will give you as much as this old man does when the business is perform'd, and remain, as he says, your pawn till it be brought you.

AUTOLYCUS I will trust you. Walk before toward the sea-side; go on the right hand. I will but look upon the hedge and follow you.

CLOWN We are bless'd in this man, as I may say, even bless'd.

SHEPHERD Let's before as he bids us. He was provided to do us good. *Exeunt* [*Shepherd and Clown*].

AUTOLYCUS If I had a mind to be honest, I see Fortune would not suffer me; she drops booties in my mouth. I am courted now with a double occasion, gold and a means to do the Prince my master good; which who knows how that may turn back to my advancement? I will bring these two moles, these blind ones, aboard him. If he think it fit to shore them again and that the complaint they have to the King concerns him nothing, let him call me rogue for being so far officious, for I am proof against that title and what shame else belongs to 't. To him will I present them; there may be matter in it. [*Exit.*]

739 cap-a-pe from head to foot **741 open** reveal **746 pheasant** (The rustics suppose that Autolycus has asked them what gift they propose to present, as a bribe.) **756–757 picking on 's teeth** (A stylish affectation in Shakespeare's time.) **764 Age** old man **768 be'st capable of** know anything about **772 handfast** custody (with a play on *betrothal*) **777–778 germane** related **789 a dram** i.e., a small amount, a fraction **790 aqua-vitae** brandy **792 prognostication** forecasting (in the almanac)

795 blown swollen **798–799 Being . . . considered** i.e., being a gentleman of some influence; or, if I receive a gentlemanly consideration, a bribe **800 tender your persons** introduce you **804 Close with him** accept his offer **815 moi'ty** half **817, 819 case** (1) cause (2) skin **823 gone else** undone otherwise **828–829 look . . . hedge** i.e., relieve myself **839–840 aboard him** i.e., to him (Prince Florizel) aboard his ship **840 shore** put ashore

ACT V • SCENE I

Enter Leontes, Cleomenes, Dion, Paulina, [*and*] *Servants.*

CLEOMENES
Sir, you have done enough, and have perform'd
A saint-like sorrow. No fault could you make
Which you have not redeem'd—indeed, paid down
More penitence than done trespass. At the last,
Do as the heavens have done, forget your evil;
With them forgive yourself.

LEONTES
Whilst I remember
Her and her virtues, I cannot forget
My blemishes in them, and so still think of
The wrong I did myself, which was so much
That heirless it hath made my kingdom and
Destroy'd the sweet'st companion that e'er man
Bred his hopes out of.

PAULINA
True, too true, my lord.
If, one by one, you wedded all the world,
Or from the all that are took something good
To make a perfect woman, she you kill'd
Would be unparallel'd.

LEONTES
I think so. Kill'd?
She I kill'd? I did so, but thou strik'st me
Sorely, to say I did. It is as bitter
Upon thy tongue as in my thought. Now, good now,
Say so but seldom.

CLEOMENES
Not at all, good lady.
You might have spoken a thousand things that would
Have done the time more benefit and grac'd
Your kindness better.

PAULINA
You are one of those
Would have him wed again.

DION
If you would not so,
You pity not the state nor the remembrance
Of his most sovereign name, consider little
What dangers by his Highness' fail of issue
May drop upon his kingdom and devour
Incertain lookers-on. What were more holy
Than to rejoice the former queen is well?
What holier than, for royalty's repair,
For present comfort and for future good,
To bless the bed of majesty again
With a sweet fellow to 't?

PAULINA
There is none worthy,
Respecting her that's gone. Besides, the gods
Will have fulfill'd their secret purposes;
For has not the divine Apollo said,
Is 't not the tenor of his oracle,
That King Leontes shall not have an heir
Till his lost child be found? Which that it shall
Is all as monstrous to our human reason
As my Antigonus to break his grave
And come again to me, who, on my life,
Did perish with the infant. 'Tis your counsel
My lord should to the heavens be contrary,
Oppose against their wills. [*To Leontes.*] Care not for issue;
The crown will find an heir. Great Alexander
Left his to th' worthiest; so his successor
Was like to be the best.

LEONTES
Good Paulina,
Who hast the memory of Hermione,
I know, in honor, O, that ever I
Had squar'd me to thy counsel! Then even now
I might have look'd upon my queen's full eyes,
Have taken treasure from her lips—

PAULINA
And left them
More rich for what they yielded.

LEONTES
Thou speak'st truth.
No more such wives; therefore, no wife! One worse,
And better us'd, would make her sainted spirit
Again possess her corpse, and on this stage,
Where we're offenders now, appear soul-vex'd,
And begin, "Why to me?"

PAULINA
Had she such power,
She had just cause.

LEONTES
She had, and would incense me
To murder her I married.

PAULINA
I should so.
Were I the ghost that walk'd, I'd bid you mark
Her eye, and tell me for what dull part in 't
You chose her; then I'd shriek, that even your ears
Should rift to hear me, and the words that follow'd
Should be, "Remember mine."

LEONTES
Stars, stars,
And all eyes else dead coals! Fear thou no wife;
I'll have no wife, Paulina.

PAULINA
Will you swear
Never to marry but by my free leave?

LEONTES
Never, Paulina, so be bless'd my spirit!

PAULINA
Then, good my lords, bear witness to his oath.

CLEOMENES
You tempt him overmuch.

PAULINA
Unless another,
As like Hermione as is her picture,
Affront his eye.

CLEOMENES
Good madam—

PAULINA
I have done.
Yet, if my lord will marry—if you will, sir,
No remedy, but you will—give me the office
To choose you a queen. She shall not be so young
As was your former, but she shall be such

V.i. Location: Sicilia. Leontes' palace.
19 good now i.e., if you please **25 remembrance** perpetuation (through bearing a child and heir) **27 fail** failure **29 Incertain** not knowing what to think or do (about the royal succession) **30 well** happy, at rest (in heaven) **35 Respecting** in comparison with

48 Left . . . worthiest (When Alexander the Great died in 323 B.C., his son Alexander was yet unborn, necessitating the choice of an heir.) **52 squar'd me** adjusted or regulated myself **58 possess her corpse** i.e., return to earth *(this stage)* in her human shape **60 Why to me** i.e., why this offense to me **66 rift** rive, split **73 tempt** bear down on **75 Affront** confront

As, walk'd your first queen's ghost, it should take joy
To see her in your arms.

LEONTES
My true Paulina,
We shall not marry till thou bid'st us.

PAULINA
That
Shall be when your first queen's again in breath;
Never till then.

Enter a Servant.

SERVANT
One that gives out himself Prince Florizel,
Son of Polixenes, with his princess, she
The fairest I have yet beheld, desires access
To your high presence.

LEONTES
What with him? He comes not
Like to his father's greatness. His approach,
So out of circumstance and sudden, tells us
'Tis not a visitation fram'd, but forc'd
By need and accident. What train?

SERVANT
But few,
And those but mean.

LEONTES
His princess, say you, with him?

SERVANT
Ay, the most peerless piece of earth, I think,
That e'er the sun shone bright on.

PAULINA
O Hermione,
As every present time doth boast itself
Above a better gone, so must thy grave
Give way to what's seen now! Sir, you yourself
Have said and writ so, but your writing now
Is colder than that theme, "She had not been,
Nor was not to be equal'd"—thus your verse
Flow'd with her beauty once. 'Tis shrewdly ebb'd,
To say you have seen a better.

SERVANT
Pardon, madam.
The one I have almost forgot—your pardon—
The other, when she has obtain'd your eye,
Will have your tongue too. This is a creature,
Would she begin a sect, might quench the zeal
Of all professors else, make proselytes
Of who she but bid follow.

PAULINA
How? Not women?

SERVANT
Women will love her, that she is a woman
More worth than any man; men, that she is
The rarest of all women.

LEONTES
Go, Cleomenes;
Yourself, assisted with your honor'd friends,
Bring them to our embracement.
Exit [Cleomenes and others].
Still, 'tis strange
He thus should steal upon us.

PAULINA
Had our Prince,
Jewel of children, seen this hour, he had pair'd
Well with this lord. There was not full a month
Between their births.

91 fram'd planned **92 train** retinue **93 mean** lowly **104 shrewdly** damagingly **108 professors else** believers in other sects or deities

LEONTES
Prithee, no more, cease. Thou know'st
He dies to me again when talk'd of. Sure,
When I shall see this gentleman, thy speeches
Will bring me to consider that which may
Unfurnish me of reason. They are come.

Enter Florizel, Perdita, Cleomenes, and others.

Your mother was most true to wedlock, Prince,
For she did print your royal father off,
Conceiving you. Were I but twenty-one,
Your father's image is so hit in you,
His very air, that I should call you brother,
As I did him, and speak of something wildly
By us perform'd before. Most dearly welcome!
And your fair princess—goddess! O, alas!
I lost a couple, that 'twixt heaven and earth
Might thus have stood begetting wonder as
You, gracious couple, do. And then I lost—
All mine own folly—the society,
Amity too, of your brave father, whom,
Though bearing misery, I desire my life
Once more to look on him.

FLORIZEL
By his command
Have I here touch'd Sicilia and from him
Give you all greetings that a king, at friend,
Can send his brother; and, but infirmity
Which waits upon worn times hath something seiz'd
His wish'd ability, he had himself
The lands and waters 'twixt your throne and his
Measur'd to look upon you, whom he loves—
He bade me say so—more than all the scepters
And those that bear them living.

LEONTES
O my brother,
Good gentleman! The wrongs I have done thee stir
Afresh within me, and these thy offices,
So rarely kind, are as interpreters
Of my behind-hand slackness. Welcome hither,
As is the spring to th' earth. And hath he too
Expos'd this paragon to th' fearful usage,
At least ungentle, of the dreadful Neptune,
To greet a man not worth her pains, much less
Th' adventure of her person?

FLORIZEL
Good my lord,
She came from Libya.

LEONTES
Where the warlike Smalus,
That noble honor'd lord, is fear'd and lov'd?

FLORIZEL
Most royal sir, from thence, from him, whose daughter
His tears proclaim'd his, parting with her. Thence,
A prosperous south-wind friendly, we have cross'd,
To execute the charge my father gave me
For visiting your Highness. My best train

123 Unfurnish deprive, divest **127 hit** exactly reproduced **137 my life** i.e., to live long enough **140 at friend** in friendship **141 but** were it not that **142 waits . . . times** attends old age. **something** to some extent **142–143 seiz'd . . . ability** taken away his ability (to travel) as he wishes **145 Measur'd** traversed **147 those . . . living** those living kings who bear scepters **149 offices** messages of good will, courteous attentions **156 adventure** hazard

I have from your Sicilian shores dismiss'd,
Who for Bohemia bend, to signify
Not only my success in Libya, sir,
But my arrival and my wife's in safety,
Here, where we are.

LEONTES The blessed gods
Purge all infection from our air whilst you
Do climate here! You have a holy father, 170
A graceful gentleman, against whose person, 171
So sacred as it is, I have done sin,
For which the heavens, taking angry note,
Have left me issueless; and your father's bless'd,
As he from heaven merits it, with you,
Worthy his goodness. What might I have been,
Might I a son and daughter now have look'd on,
Such goodly things as you?

Enter a Lord.

LORD Most noble sir,
That which I shall report will bear no credit,
Were not the proof so nigh. Please you, great sir,
Bohemia greets you from himself by me;
Desires you to attach his son, who has— 182
His dignity and duty both cast off—
Fled from his father, from his hopes, and with
A shepherd's daughter.

LEONTES Where's Bohemia? Speak.

LORD
Here in your city; I now came from him.
I speak amazedly, and it becomes 187
My marvel and my message. To your court 188
Whiles he was hast'ning, in the chase, it seems,
Of this fair couple, meets he on the way
The father of this seeming lady and
Her brother, having both their country quitted
With this young prince.

FLORIZEL Camillo has betray'd me,
Whose honor and whose honesty till now
Endur'd all weathers.

LORD Lay 't so to his charge. 195
He's with the King your father.

LEONTES Who? Camillo?

LORD
Camillo, sir. I spake with him, who now
Has these poor men in question. Never saw I 198
Wretches so quake. They kneel, they kiss the earth,
Forswear themselves as often as they speak.
Bohemia stops his ears, and threatens them
With divers deaths in death.

PERDITA O my poor father!
The heaven sets spies upon us, will not have
Our contract celebrated.

LEONTES You are married?

FLORIZEL
We are not, sir, nor are we like to be.
The stars, I see, will kiss the valleys first;
The odds for high and low's alike.

LEONTES My lord, 207
Is this the daughter of a king?

FLORIZEL She is,
When once she is my wife.

LEONTES
That "once," I see by your good father's speed,
Will come on very slowly. I am sorry,
Most sorry, you have broken from his liking
Where you were tied in duty, and as sorry
Your choice is not so rich in worth as beauty, 214
That you might well enjoy her.

FLORIZEL Dear, look up.
Though Fortune, visible an enemy,
Should chase us with my father, pow'r no jot
Hath she to change our loves. Beseech you, sir,
Remember since you ow'd no more to time 219
Than I do now. With thought of such affections, 220
Step forth mine advocate. At your request
My father will grant precious things as trifles.

LEONTES
Would he do so, I'd beg your precious mistress,
Which he counts but a trifle.

PAULINA Sir, my liege,
Your eye hath too much youth in 't. Not a month
'Fore your queen died, she was more worth such gazes
Than what you look on now.

LEONTES I thought of her,
Even in these looks I made. [*To Florizel.*] But your petition
Is yet unanswer'd. I will to your father.
Your honor not o'erthrown by your desires, 230
I am friend to them and you. Upon which errand
I now go toward him; therefore follow me
And mark what way I make. Come, good my lord. 233
Exeunt.

SCENE II

Enter Autolycus and a Gentleman.

AUTOLYCUS Beseech you, sir, were you present at this relation? 2

FIRST GENTLEMAN I was by at the opening of the fardel, heard the old shepherd deliver the manner how he 4
found it; whereupon, after a little amazedness, we were all commanded out of the chamber; only this methought I heard the shepherd say, he found the child.

170 climate dwell, reside (in this clime) **171 graceful** full of grace, gracious **182 attach** arrest **187–188 I . . . message** i.e., I speak perplexedly as befits my perplexity and my astonishing news **195 Lay . . . charge** i.e., confront him with it directly **198 in question** under interrogation

207 The odds . . . alike i.e., Fortune is the same for the high and low (?) **214 worth** rank **219–220 since . . . now** when you were no older than I am now **230 Your . . . desires** i.e., if your chaste honor has not been overcome by sexual desire; or, if what you want in this match is compatible with your royal honor **233 way** progress

V.ii. Location: Sicilia. Before Leontes' palace.
2 relation narrative, account **4 deliver** report

AUTOLYCUS I would most gladly know the issue of it.

FIRST GENTLEMAN I make a broken delivery of the business; but the changes I perceiv'd in the King and Camillo were very notes of admiration. They seem'd almost, with staring on one another, to tear the cases of their eyes. There was speech in their dumbness, language in their very gesture; they look'd as they had heard of a world ransom'd, or one destroy'd. A notable passion of wonder appear'd in them; but the wisest beholder, that knew no more but seeing, could not say if th' importance were joy or sorrow; but in the extremity of the one it must needs be.

Enter another Gentleman.

Here comes a gentleman that happily knows more. The news, Rogero?

SECOND GENTLEMAN Nothing but bonfires. The oracle is fulfill'd; the King's daughter is found. Such a deal of wonder is broken out within this hour that ballad-makers cannot be able to express it.

Enter another Gentleman.

Here comes the Lady Paulina's steward; he can deliver you more. How goes it now, sir? This news which is call'd true is so like an old tale that the verity of it is in strong suspicion. Has the King found his heir?

THIRD GENTLEMAN Most true, if ever truth were pregnant by circumstance. That which you hear you'll swear you see, there is such unity in the proofs. The mantle of Queen Hermione's, her jewel about the neck of it, the letters of Antigonus found with it which they know to be his character, the majesty of the creature in resemblance of the mother, the affection of nobleness which nature shows above her breeding, and many other evidences proclaim her with all certainty to be the King's daughter. Did you see the meeting of the two kings?

SECOND GENTLEMAN No.

THIRD GENTLEMAN Then have you lost a sight which was to be seen, cannot be spoken of. There might you have beheld one joy crown another, so and in such manner that it seem'd Sorrow wept to take leave of them, for their joy waded in tears. There was casting up of eyes, holding up of hands, with countenance of such distraction that they were to be known by garment, not by favor. Our King, being ready to leap out of himself for joy of his found daughter, as if that joy were now become a loss, cries, "O, thy mother, thy mother!" then asks Bohemia forgiveness; then embraces his son-in-law; then again worries he his daughter with clipping her; now he thanks the old shepherd, which stands by like a weather-bitten conduit of many kings' reigns. I never heard of such another encounter, which lames report to follow it and undoes description to do it.

SECOND GENTLEMAN What, pray you, became of Antigonus, that carried hence the child?

THIRD GENTLEMAN Like an old tale still, which will have matter to rehearse, though credit be asleep and not an ear open. He was torn to pieces with a bear. This avouches the shepherd's son, who has not only his innocence, which seems much, to justify him, but a handkerchief and rings of his that Paulina knows.

FIRST GENTLEMAN What became of his bark and his followers?

THIRD GENTLEMAN Wrack'd the same instant of their master's death and in the view of the shepherd; so that all the instruments which aided to expose the child were even then lost when it was found. But O, the noble combat that 'twixt joy and sorrow was fought in Paulina! She had one eye declin'd for the loss of her husband, another elevated that the oracle was fulfill'd. She lifted the Princess from the earth, and so locks her in embracing, as if she would pin her to her heart that she might no more be in danger of losing.

FIRST GENTLEMAN The dignity of this act was worth the audience of kings and princes, for by such was it acted.

THIRD GENTLEMAN One of the prettiest touches of all, and that which angled for mine eyes, caught the water though not the fish, was when, at the relation of the Queen's death, with the manner how she came to 't bravely confess'd and lamented by the King, how attentiveness wounded his daughter; till, from one sign of dolor to another, she did, with an "Alas," I would fain say, bleed tears, for I am sure my heart wept blood. Who was most marble there chang'd color; some swounded, all sorrow'd. If all the world could have seen 't, the woe had been universal.

FIRST GENTLEMAN Are they return'd to the court?

THIRD GENTLEMAN No. The Princess hearing of her mother's statue, which is in the keeping of Paulina—a piece many years in doing and now newly perform'd by that rare Italian master, Julio Romano, who, had he himself eternity and could put breath into his work, would beguile Nature of her custom, so perfectly he is her ape; he so near to Hermione hath done Hermione that they say one would speak to her and stand in hope of answer—thither with all greediness of affection are they gone, and there they intend to sup.

SECOND GENTLEMAN I thought she had some great matter there in hand, for she hath privately twice or thrice a day, ever since the death of Hermione, visited that remov'd house. Shall we thither and with our company piece the rejoicing?

FIRST GENTLEMAN Who would be thence that has the

10 broken disjointed, fragmented **12 notes of admiration** exclamations of wonder **13–14 cases of their eyes** eyelids **18 no . . . seeing** nothing except what he could see **19 importance** import, meaning **20 of the one** of one or the other **21 happily** haply, perhaps **31–32 pregnant by circumstance** made apparent by detailed evidence **36 character** handwriting **37 affection of** natural disposition to **48 countenance** bearing, demeanor **50 favor** features **55 clipping** embracing **56–57 conduit** fountain (weeping tears)

59 undoes . . . it i.e., surpasses the power of language to describe it **63 credit** belief **64 with** by **66 innocence** simplemindedness (such that he would seem unable to invent such a story) **67 his** i.e., Antigonus' **97 perform'd** completed **98 Julio Romano** Italian painter and sculptor of the sixteenth century (and an anachronism in this play) **100 beguile** deprive, cheat. **custom** trade **101 ape** imitator **103–104 greediness of affection** eagerness born of love **104 sup** i.e., feed their hungry eyes (?) or perhaps, have a commemorative banquet (?) **109 piece** add to, augment

benefit of access? Every wink of an eye some new grace will be born. Our absence makes us unthrifty to our knowledge. Let's along. *Exeunt* [*Gentlemen*].

AUTOLYCUS Now, had I not the dash of my former life in me, would preferment drop on my head. I brought the old man and his son aboard the Prince, told him I heard them talk of a fardel and I know not what. But he at that time, overfond of the shepherd's daughter, so he then took her to be, who began to be much sea-sick, and himself little better, extremity of weather continuing, this mystery remain'd undiscover'd. But 'tis all one to me; for had I been the finder out of this secret, it would not have relish'd among my other discredits.

Enter Shepherd and Clown, [*dressed in finery*].

Here come those I have done good to against my will, and already appearing in the blossoms of their fortune.

SHEPHERD Come, boy. I am past moe children, but thy sons and daughters will be all gentlemen born.

CLOWN You are well met, sir. You denied to fight with me this other day, because I was no gentleman born. See you these clothes? Say you see them not and think me still no gentleman born. You were best say these robes are not gentlemen born. Give me the lie, do, and try whether I am not now a gentleman born.

AUTOLYCUS I know you are now, sir, a gentleman born.

CLOWN Ay, and have been so any time these four hours.

SHEPHERD And so have I, boy.

CLOWN So you have. But I was a gentleman born before my father; for the King's son took me by the hand, and call'd me brother; and then the two kings call'd my father brother; and then the Prince my brother and the Princess my sister call'd my father father; and so we wept, and there was the first gentleman-like tears that ever we shed.

SHEPHERD We may live, son, to shed many more.

CLOWN Ay, or else 'twere hard luck, being in so preposterous estate as we are.

AUTOLYCUS I humbly beseech you, sir, to pardon me all the faults I have committed to your worship and to give me your good report to the Prince my master.

SHEPHERD Prithee, son, do; for we must be gentle, now we are gentlemen.

CLOWN Thou wilt amend thy life?

AUTOLYCUS Ay, an it like your good worship.

CLOWN Give me thy hand. I will swear to the Prince thou art as honest a true fellow as any is in Bohemia.

SHEPHERD You may say it, but not swear it.

CLOWN Not swear it, now I am a gentleman? Let boors and franklins say it, I'll swear it.

SHEPHERD How if it be false, son?

CLOWN If it be ne'er so false, a true gentleman may swear it in the behalf of his friend. And I'll swear to the Prince thou art a tall fellow of thy hands and that thou wilt not be drunk; but I know thou art no tall fellow of thy hands and that thou wilt be drunk. But I'll swear it, and I would thou wouldst be a tall fellow of thy hands.

AUTOLYCUS I will prove so, sir, to my power.

CLOWN Ay, by any means prove a tall fellow. If I do not wonder how thou dar'st venture to be drunk, not being a tall fellow, trust me not. Hark! The kings and the princes, our kindred, are going to see the Queen's picture. Come, follow us. We'll be thy good masters. *Exeunt.*

SCENE III

Enter Leontes, Polixenes, Florizel, Perdita, Camillo, Paulina, Lords, etc.

LEONTES
O grave and good Paulina, the great comfort
That I have had of thee!

PAULINA What, sovereign sir,
I did not well, I meant well. All my services
You have paid home. But that you have vouchsaf'd,
With your crown'd brother and these your contracted
Heirs of your kingdoms, my poor house to visit,
It is a surplus of your grace, which never
My life may last to answer.

LEONTES O Paulina,
We honor you with trouble. But we came
To see the statue of our Queen. Your gallery
Have we pass'd through, not without much content
In many singularities; but we saw not
That which my daughter came to look upon,
The statue of her mother.

PAULINA As she liv'd peerless,
So her dead likeness, I do well believe,
Excels whatever yet you look'd upon
Or hand of man hath done. Therefore I keep it
Lonely, apart. But here it is. Prepare
To see the life as lively mock'd as ever
Still sleep mock'd death. Behold, and say 'tis well.
[*Paulina draws a curtain, and discovers*]
Hermione [*standing*] *like a statue.*
I like your silence; it the more shows off
Your wonder. But yet speak; first, you, my liege.
Comes it not something near?

LEONTES Her natural posture!
Chide me, dear stone, that I may say indeed
Thou art Hermione; or rather, thou art she
In thy not chiding, for she was as tender
As infancy and grace. But yet, Paulina,

112 unthrifty to passing up an opportunity to increase **123 relish'd** tasted well, suited **148–149 preposterous** (Blunder for *prosperous*.) **160 boors** peasants **161 franklins** farmers who owned their own small farms

165 tall . . . hands brave fellow **170 my power** the best of my ability **175 picture** i.e., likeness, painted statue

V.iii. Location: Sicilia. Paulina's house.
4 home fully **8 answer** repay adequately **12 singularities** rarities, curiosities

Hermione was not as much wrinkled, nothing
So aged as this seems.

POLIXENES
O, not by much.

PAULINA
So much the more our carver's excellence,
Which lets go by some sixteen years and makes her
As she liv'd now.

LEONTES
As now she might have done,
So much to my good comfort, as it is
Now piercing to my soul. O, thus she stood,
Even with such life of majesty, warm life,
As now it coldly stands, when first I woo'd her!
I am asham'd. Does not the stone rebuke me
For being more stone than it? O royal piece,
There's magic in thy majesty, which has
My evils conjur'd to remembrance and
From thy admiring daughter took the spirits,
Standing like stone with thee.

PERDITA
And give me leave,
And do not say 'tis superstition, that
I kneel and then implore her blessing. Lady,
[*Kneeling.*]
Dear Queen, that ended when I but began,
Give me that hand of yours to kiss.

PAULINA
O, patience!
The statue is but newly fix'd, the color's
Not dry.

CAMILLO
My lord, your sorrow was too sore laid on
Which sixteen winters cannot blow away,
So many summers dry. Scarce any joy
Did ever so long live; no sorrow
But kill'd itself much sooner.

POLIXENES
Dear my brother,
Let him that was the cause of this have pow'r
To take off so much grief from you as he
Will piece up in himself.

PAULINA
Indeed, my lord,
If I had thought the sight of my poor image
Would thus have wrought you—for the stone is mine—
I'd not have show'd it.

LEONTES
Do not draw the curtain.

PAULINA
No longer shall you gaze on 't, lest your fancy
May think anon it moves.

LEONTES
Let be, let be.
Would I were dead, but that, methinks, already—
What was he that did make it? See, my lord,
Would you not deem it breath'd? And that those veins
Did verily bear blood?

POLIXENES
Masterly done.
The very life seems warm upon her lip.

LEONTES
The fixture of her eye has motion in 't,
As we are mock'd with art.

PAULINA
I'll draw the curtain.
My lord's almost so far transported that
He'll think anon it lives.

LEONTES
O sweet Paulina,
Make me to think so twenty years together!
No settled senses of the world can match
The pleasure of that madness. Let 't alone.

PAULINA
I am sorry, sir, I have thus far stirr'd you; but
I could afflict you farther.

LEONTES
Do, Paulina;
For this affliction has a taste as sweet
As any cordial comfort. Still, methinks,
There is an air comes from her. What fine chisel
Could ever yet cut breath? Let no man mock me,
For I will kiss her.

PAULINA
Good my lord, forbear.
The ruddiness upon her lip is wet;
You'll mar it if you kiss it, stain your own
With oily painting. Shall I draw the curtain?

LEONTES
No, not these twenty years.

PERDITA
So long could I
Stand by, a looker on.

PAULINA
Either forbear,
Quit presently the chapel, or resolve you
For more amazement. If you can behold it,
I'll make the statue move indeed, descend
And take you by the hand. But then you'll think—
Which I protest against—I am assisted
By wicked powers.

LEONTES
What you can make her do,
I am content to look on, what to speak,
I am content to hear; for 'tis as easy
To make her speak as move.

PAULINA
It is requir'd
You do awake your faith. Then all stand still.
On; those that think it is unlawful business
I am about, let them depart.

LEONTES
Proceed.
No foot shall stir.

PAULINA
Music, awake her; strike! [*Music.*]
'Tis time; descend; be stone no more; approach;
Strike all that look upon with marvel. Come,
I'll fill your grave up. Stir, nay, come away,
Bequeath to death your numbness, for from him
Dear life redeems you. You perceive she stirs.
[*Hermione comes down.*]
Start not; her actions shall be holy as
You hear my spell is lawful. Do not shun her
Until you see her die again, for then
You kill her double. Nay, present your hand.
When she was young you woo'd her; now in age
Is she become the suitor? [*Leontes touches her.*]

LEONTES
O, she's warm!
If this be magic, let it be an art
Lawful as eating.

38 piece work of art **41 admiring** filled with wonder. **spirits** vital spirits **51 So . . . dry** i.e., and sixteen summers cannot dry up **54 him** i.e., myself (as an innocent cause, but still a cause) **56 piece up in himself** take upon himself **58 wrought** affected **67 The fixture . . . in 't** i.e., her eye, though motionless, gives the appearance of motion

68 As . . . art in such a way that we are fooled by artistic illusion **72 settled** sane, calm **102 him** i.e., death **106 then** in that case **107 double** a second time

POLIXENES She embraces him.

CAMILLO

She hangs about his neck.
If she pertain to life, let her speak too.

POLIXENES

Ay, and make it manifest where she has liv'd,
Or how stol'n from the dead.

PAULINA That she is living,
Were it but told you, should be hooted at
Like an old tale; but it appears she lives,
Though yet she speak not. Mark a little while.
Please you to interpose, fair madam. Kneel
And pray your mother's blessing. Turn, good lady;
Our Perdita is found.

HERMIONE You gods, look down
And from your sacred vials pour your graces
Upon my daughter's head! Tell me, mine own,
Where hast thou been preserv'd? Where liv'd? How found
Thy father's court? For thou shalt hear that I,
Knowing by Paulina that the oracle
Gave hope thou wast in being, have preserv'd
Myself to see the issue.

PAULINA

There's time enough for that;
Least they desire upon this push to trouble
Your joys with like relation. Go together,
You precious winners all; your exultation
Partake to everyone. I, an old turtle,
Will wing me to some wither'd bough and there
My mate, that's never to be found again,
Lament till I am lost.

LEONTES O, peace, Paulina!
Thou shouldst a husband take by my consent,
As I by thine a wife. This is a match,
And made between 's by vows. Thou hast found mine;
But how, is to be question'd, for I saw her,
As I thought, dead, and have in vain said many
A prayer upon her grave. I'll not seek far—
For him, I partly know his mind—to find thee
An honorable husband. Come, Camillo,
And take her by the hand, whose worth and honesty
Is richly noted and here justified
By us, a pair of kings. Let's from this place.
[*To Hermione.*] What? Look upon my brother. Both your pardons,
That e'er I put between your holy looks
My ill suspicion. This' your son-in-law
And son unto the King, whom, heavens directing,
Is troth-plight to your daughter. Good Paulina,
Lead us from hence, where we may leisurely
Each one demand and answer to his part
Perform'd in this wide gap of time since first
We were dissever'd. Hastily lead away. *Exeunt.*

130–131 Least . . . relation the last thing they desire at this dramatic moment is to interrupt your joys with a narrative of that sort **133 Partake to** share with, communicate. **turtle** turtledove **146 justified** avouched **150 This'** this is

The Tempest

Shakespeare creates in *The Tempest* an idealized world of imagination, a place of magical rejuvenation like the forests of *A Midsummer Night's Dream* and *As You Like It.* The journey to Shakespeare's island is to a visionary realm, where everything is controlled by the artist. Yet the journey is no escape from reality, for the island shows men what they are and ought to be. Even its location juxtaposes "real" world with idealized landscape: like Plato's New Atlantis or Thomas More's Utopia, Shakespeare's island is to be found both somewhere and nowhere. On the narrative level it is located in the Mediterranean Sea. Yet there are overtones of the New World, the Western Hemisphere, where Thomas More had situated his island of Utopia. Ariel fetches dew at Prospero's command from the "Bermoothes," or Bermudas (I,ii). Caliban when prostrate reminds Trinculo of a "dead Indian" who might be displayed before gullible crowds eager to see such a prodigious creature from across the seas; and Caliban's god Setebos was, according to Richard Eden's account of Magellan's circumnavigation of the globe, worshiped by South American natives. An inspiration for Shakespeare's story (for which no direct literary source is known) may well have been various accounts of an actual shipwreck in the Bermudas of the *Sea Venture,* in 1609, carrying settlers to the new Virginian colony. Shakespeare borrowed details from Sylvester Jourdain's *A Discovery of the Barmudas, otherwise called the Isle of Divels,* published in 1610, and from William Strachey's *A true Reportory of the Wracke and Redemption . . . from the Ilands of the Bermudas,* which Shakespeare must have seen in manuscript since it was not published until after his death. He wrote the play shortly after reading these works, for *The Tempest* was acted at court in 1611. He may also have known or heard of various accounts of Magellan's circumnavigation of the world in 1519–1522 (including Richard Eden's shortened English version of an Italian narrative by Antonio Pigafetta), Francis Fletcher's journal of Sir Francis Drake's circumnavigation in 1577–1580, Richard Rich's *Newes from Virginia* (1610), and still other potential sources of information. Shakespeare's fascination with the Western Hemisphere gave him not the "actual" location of his story, which remains Mediterranean, but a state of mind associated with newness and hope. Miranda sees on the island a "new world" in which mankind appears "brave"; and, although her wonder must be tempered by Prospero's rejoinder ("'Tis new to thee") and by Aldous Huxley's ironic use of her phrase (in his satirical novel, *Brave New World*), the island still endures as a restorative vision. Even though we experience it fleetingly, as in a dream, this nonexistent realm assumes a permanence enjoyed by all great works of art.

Prospero rules as the artist-king over this imaginary world, conjuring up trials to test men's intentions and visions to promote their renewed faith in goodness. To the island come an assortment of men who, because they require varied ordeals, are separated by Prospero and Ariel into three groups: King Alonso and those accompanying him; Alonso's son Ferdinand; and Stephano and Trinculo. Prospero's authority over them, though strong, has limits. As Duke of Milan he was bookishly inattentive to political matters and thus vulnerable to the Machiavellian conniving of his younger brother Antonio. Only in this world apart, the artist's world, do his powers derived from learning find their proper sphere. Because he cannot control the world beyond his isle, he must wait for "strange, bountiful Fortune (Now my dear lady)" to bring his enemies near his shore. He eschews, moreover, the black arts of diabolism. His is a "white" magic, devoted ultimately to merciful ends: rescuing Ariel from the spell of the witch Sycorax, curbing the appetite of Caliban, spying on Antonio and Sebastian in the role of Conscience. He uses Fortune's gift of delivering his enemies into his hands to forgive and restore them, not to be revenged. Such a use of power imitates the divine, though Prospero is no god. His chief power, learned from books and exercised through Ariel, is to control the elements so as to create illusion—of separation, of death, of the gods' blessing. Yet since he is a man, even this power is an immense burden. Prospero has much to learn, like those whom he controls; he must overcome the vengeful impulse he experiences toward those who have wronged him, and he must conquer the longing any father feels to hold on to his daughter when she is desired by a younger man. He does these things through his art, devising games and shows in which his angry self-pity and jealousy are transmuted into play-acting scenes of divine warning and forgiveness toward his enemies and watchful parental austerity toward Miranda and Ferdinand. Prospero's responsibilities cause him to behave magisterially and to be resented by the spirits of the isle. Even Ariel longs to be free, and it is with genuine relief as well as melancholy that Prospero finally lays aside his demanding role as creative moral intelligence.

Alonso and his court party variously illustrate the unregenerate world left behind in Naples and Milan. We first see them on shipboard, panicky and desperate, their titles and finery mocked by roaring waves. Futile ambition seems destined for a watery demise. Yet death by water in this play is a transfiguration rather than an end, a mystical rebirth as in the regenerative cycle of the seasons from winter to summer. Ariel suggests as much in his song about a drowned father: "Those are pearls that were his eyes. Nothing of him that doth fade But doth suffer a sea-change Into something rich and strange" (I,ii). Still, this miracle is not apparent at first to men caught in the illusion of death. As in T. S. Eliot's *The Waste Land,* which repeatedly alludes to *The Tempest,* self-blinded men fear a disaster that is ironically the prelude to reawakening.

Prospero creates an illusion of loss to test his enemies and to make them reveal their true selves. Only Gonzalo, no enemy at all but one who long ago aided Prospero and Miranda when they were banished from Milan, responds affirmatively. He alone notices that his garments and those of his shipwrecked companions have miraculously been left unharmed by the salt water. His ideal commonwealth (II,i), which Shakespeare drew in part from an essay by Montaigne, postulates a natural goodness in man and makes no allowance for the dark propensities of Caliban, but at least Gonzalo's cheerfulness is in refreshing contrast to the jaded sneers of some of his companions. Sebastian and Antonio react to the magic isle, as to Gonzalo's commonwealth, by cynically refusing to believe in miracles. Confident that they are unobserved, they seize the opportunity of Alonso's sleeping to plot a murder and political coup. This attempt is not only despicable but madly ludicrous, for they are all shipwrecked and no longer have kingdoms over which to quarrel. Even more ironically, Sebastian and Antonio, despite their insolent belief in their self-sufficiency, are being observed. The villains must be taught that an unseen power keeps track of their misdeeds. They may revert to type when returned to their usual habitat, but even they are at last briefly moved to a faith in the unseen (III,iii). Alonso, more worthy than they though burdened too with sin, responds to his situation with guilt and despair, for he assumes that his son Ferdinand's death is the just punishment of the gods for Alonso's part in the earlier overthrow of Prospero. Alonso must be led, by Prospero's curative illusions, through the purgative experience of contrition to the reward he thinks impossible and undeserved: reunion with his lost son.

Alonso is thus, like Posthumus in *Cymbeline* or Leontes in *The Winter's Tale,* a tragicomic figure—sinful, contrite, forgiven. Alonso's son Ferdinand must also undergo ordeals and visions devised by Prospero to test his worth, but more on the level of romantic comedy. Ferdinand is young, innocent, and hopeful, well-matched to Miranda. Prospero obviously approves from the start of his prospective son-in-law. Yet even Prospero, needing to prepare himself for a life in which Miranda will no longer be solely his, is not ready to lay aside at least the comic fiction of parental opposition. He invents difficulties, imposes tasks of logbearing (like those assigned Caliban) and issues stern warnings against premarital lust. In the comic mode, parents are expected to cross their children in matters of the heart. As a teacher of youth, moreover, Prospero is convinced by long experience that prizes too easily won are too lightly esteemed. Manifold are the temptations urging Ferdinand to surrender to the "natural" rhythms of the isle, and to fulfill his desire like Caliban. In place of ceremonies conducted in civilized societies by the church, Prospero must create the illusion of ceremony by his art. The marriage of Ferdinand and Miranda accordingly unites the best of both worlds: the natural innocence of the island, which teaches them to avoid corruptions of civilization at its worst, and the higher law of nature achieved through moral wisdom at its best. To this marriage, the goddesses Iris, Ceres, and Juno bring promises of bounteous harvest, "refreshing show'rs," celestial harmony, and a springtime brought back to the earth by Proserpina's return from Hades (IV,i). In Ferdinand and Miranda, "nurture" is wedded to "nature." This bond unites spirit and flesh, legitimizing erotic pleasure by incorporating it within a cosmic moral order.

At the lowest level of this same cosmic and moral framework are Stephano and Trinculo. Their comic scenes juxtapose them with Caliban, for he represents untutored nature whereas they represent unnatural depths to which men brought up in civilized society can fall. In this they resemble Sebastian and Antonio, who have learned in supposedly civilized Italy arts of intrigue and political murder. The antics of Stephano and Trinculo burlesque the conduct of their presumed betters, thereby exposing to ridicule the self-deceptions of ambitious men. The clowns desire to exploit the natural wonders of the isle by taking Caliban back to civilization to be shown in carnivals, or by plying him with strong drink and whetting his resentment against authority. These plottings are in vain, however, for like Sebastian and Antonio the clowns are being watched. The clowns teach Caliban to cry out for "freedom," by which they mean license to do as one pleases, but are foiled by Ariel as comic nemesis. Because they are degenerate buffoons, their exposure is appropriately humiliating and satirical.

In contrast with them, Caliban is almost a sympathetic character. His sensitivity to natural beauty, as in his descriptions of the "nimble marmoset" or the dreaming music he so often hears (II,ii and III,ii), is entirely appropriate to this child of nature. He is, to be sure, the child of a witch, and is called many harsh names such as "Abhorred slave" and "a born devil, on whose nature Nurture can never stick." Yet he protests with some justification that the island was his in the first place, and that Prospero and Miranda are interlopers. His very existence calls radically into question the value of civilization, which has shown itself capable of limitless depravity. What profit has Caliban derived from learning Prospero's language other than, as he puts it, to "know how to curse"? With instinctive cunning he senses that books are his chief enemy, and plots to destroy them first in his attempt at rebellion. The unspoiled natural world does indeed offer to civilized man a unique perspective on himself. Ultimately, however, Shakespeare's play celebrates man's highest achievement in the union of the island with the civilized world, as in the marriage of Ferdinand

and Miranda. Even Caliban may be at last reconciled to this solution. Prospero speaks of him as a "thing of darkness I Acknowledge mine," and Caliban vows to "be wise hereafter And seek for grace" (V,i). This synthesis suggests that the natural man within us is more contented, better understood, and more truly free when harmonized with reason.

Caliban is a part of humanity, Ariel is not. Ariel can comprehend what compassion and forgiveness would be like, "were I human," and can take good-natured part in Prospero's designs to castigate or reform his fellow man, but Ariel longs to be free in quite another sense from that meant by Caliban. Ariel takes no part in the final integration of human society. This spirit belongs to a magic world of song, music, and illusion which the artist borrows for his use but which exists eternally outside of him. Like the elements of air, earth, fire, and water in which it mysteriously dwells, this spirit is morally neutral but incredibly vital. From it the artist achieves powers of imagination, enabling him to bedim the noontide sun or call forth the dead from their graves. These visions are illusory in the profound sense that all life is illusory, an "insubstantial pageant" melted into thin air. Prospero the artist cherishes his own humanity, as a promise of surcease from his labors. Yet the artifact created by the artist endures, existing apart from time and place as does Ariel: "Then to the elements Be free, and fare thou well!" No doubt it is a romantic fiction to associate the dramatist Shakespeare with Prospero's farewell to his art, but it is an almost irresistible idea because we are so moved by the sense of completion and yet humility, the exultation and yet the calm.

The Tempest

Names of the Actors

ALONSO, *King of Naples.*
SEBASTIAN, *his brother.*
PROSPERO, *the right Duke of Milan.*
ANTONIO, *his brother, the usurping Duke of Milan.*
FERDINAND, *son to the King of Naples.*
GONZALO, *an honest old Counselor.*
ADRIAN *and* FRANCISCO, *Lords.*
CALIBAN, *a savage and deformed Slave.*
TRINCULO, *a Jester.*
STEPHANO, *a drunken Butler.*
MASTER *of a Ship.*
BOATSWAIN.
MARINERS.

MIRANDA, *daughter to Prospero.*

ARIEL, *an airy Spirit.*
IRIS, CERES, JUNO, NYMPHS, REAPERS, *[presented by] Spirits.*

[Other SPIRITS *attending on Prospero.]*

THE SCENE: *An uninhabited island.*

ACT I • SCENE I

A tempestuous noise of thunder and lightning heard. Enter a Ship-Master and a Boatswain.

MASTER Boatswain!
BOATSWAIN Here, master. What cheer?
MASTER Good, speak to th' mariners. Fall to 't, yarely, 3
or we run ourselves aground. Bestir, bestir. *Exit.*

Enter Mariners.

BOATSWAIN Heigh, my hearts! Cheerly, cheerly, my
hearts! Yare, yare! Take in the topsail. Tend to th' mas- 6
ter's whistle.—Blow till thou burst thy wind, if room 7
enough! 8

I.i. Location: On a ship at sea.
3 Good i.e., it's good you've come; or, my good fellow. **yarely** nimbly **6 Tend** attend **7 Blow** (Addressed to the wind.) **7–8 if room enough** as long as we have sea-room enough

Enter Alonso, Sebastian, Antonio, Ferdinand, Gonzalo, and others.

ALONSO Good boatswain, have care. Where's the master? Play the men.

BOATSWAIN I pray now, keep below.

ANTONIO Where is the master, bos'n?

BOATSWAIN Do you not hear him? You mar our labor. Keep your cabins; you do assist the storm.

GONZALO Nay, good, be patient.

BOATSWAIN When the sea is. Hence! What cares these roarers for the name of king? To cabin! Silence! Trouble us not.

GONZALO Good, yet remember whom thou hast aboard.

BOATSWAIN None that I more love than myself. You are a counselor; if you can command these elements to silence, and work the peace of the present, we will not hand a rope more. Use your authority. If you cannot, give thanks you have liv'd so long, and make yourself ready in your cabin for the mischance of the hour, if it so hap.—Cheerly, good hearts!—Out of our way, I say. *Exit.*

GONZALO I have great comfort from this fellow. Methinks he hath no drowning mark upon him; his complexion is perfect gallows. Stand fast, good Fate, to his hanging! Make the rope of his destiny our cable, for our own doth little advantage. If he be not born to be hang'd, our case is miserable. *Exeunt.*

Enter Boatswain.

BOATSWAIN Down with the topmast! Yare! Lower, lower! Bring her to try with main-course. *(A cry within.)* A plague upon this howling! They are louder than the weather or our office.

Enter Sebastian, Antonio, and Gonzalo.

Yet again? What do you here? Shall we give o'er and drown? Have you a mind to sink?

SEBASTIAN A pox o' your throat, you bawling, blasphemous, incharitable dog!

BOATSWAIN Work you then.

ANTONIO Hang, cur! Hang, you whoreson, insolent noisemaker! We are less afraid to be drown'd than thou art.

GONZALO I'll warrant him for drowning, though the ship were no stronger than a nutshell and as leaky as an unstanch'd wench.

BOATSWAIN Lay her a-hold, a-hold! Set her two courses off to sea again! Lay her off!

Enter Mariners wet.

MARINERS All lost! To prayers, to prayers! All lost! [*Exeunt.*]

BOATSWAIN What, must our mouths be cold?

GONZALO
The King and Prince at prayers! Let's assist them,
For our case is as theirs.

SEBASTIAN I am out of patience.

ANTONIO
We are merely cheated of our lives by drunkards.
This wide-chopp'd rascal! Would thou mightst lie drowning
The washing of ten tides!

GONZALO He'll be hang'd yet,
Though every drop of water swear against it
And gape at wid'st to glut him.
(A confused noise within:) "Mercy on us!"—
"We split, we split!"—"Farewell my wife and children!"—
"Farewell, brother!"—"We split, we split, we split!"
[*Exit Boatswain.*]

ANTONIO
Let's all sink wi' th' King.

SEBASTIAN
Let's take leave of him. *Exit* [*with Antonio*].

GONZALO Now would I give a thousand furlongs of sea for an acre of barren ground, long heath, brown furze, anything. The wills above be done! But I would fain die a dry death. *Exit.*

SCENE II

Enter Prospero [*in his magic robes*] *and Miranda.*

MIRANDA
If by your art, my dearest father, you have
Put the wild waters in this roar, allay them.
The sky, it seems, would pour down stinking pitch,
But that the sea, mounting to th' welkin's cheek,
Dashes the fire out. O, I have suffered
With those that I saw suffer! A brave vessel,
Who had, no doubt, some noble creature in her,
Dash'd all to pieces. O, the cry did knock
Against my very heart! Poor souls, they perish'd.
Had I been any god of power, I would
Have sunk the sea within the earth or ere
It should the good ship so have swallow'd and
The fraughting souls within her.

PROSPERO Be collected.
No more amazement. Tell your piteous heart

10 Play the men act like men (?) ply, urge the men to exert themselves (?) **17 roarers** waves or winds, or both; spoken to as though they were "bullies" or "blusterers" **24 hand** handle **30–31 complexion . . . gallows** appearance shows he was born to be hanged (and therefore, according to the proverb, in no danger of drowning) **33 our . . . advantage** i.e., our own cable is of little benefit **36 Bring . . . course** sail her close to the wind by means of the mainsail **38 our office** i.e., the noise we make at our work **47 warrant him for drowning** guarantee that he will never be drowned **49 unstanch'd** insatiable, loose, unrestrained **50 a-hold** a-hull, close to the wind. **courses** sails, i.e., foresail as well as mainsail, set in an attempt to get the ship back out into open water

53 must . . . cold i.e., let us heat up our mouths with liquor **56 merely** quite **57 wide-chopp'd** with mouth wide open **57–58 lie . . . tides** (Pirates were hanged on the shore and left until three tides had come in.) **60 glut** swallow **66 heath** uncultivated ground; heather. **furze** a weed growing on waste land

I.ii. Location: The island. Before Prospero's cell.
4 welkin's cheek sky's face **6 brave** gallant, splendid **11 or ere** before **13 fraughting** forming the cargo. **collected** calm, composed **14 amazement** consternation

There's no harm done.

MIRANDA O, woe the day!

PROSPERO No harm.
I have done nothing but in care of thee,
Of thee, my dear one, thee, my daughter, who
Art ignorant of what thou art, nought knowing
Of whence I am, nor that I am more better
Than Prospero, master of a full poor cell,
And thy no greater father.

MIRANDA More to know
Did never meddle with my thoughts.

PROSPERO 'Tis time
I should inform thee farther. Lend thy hand,
And pluck my magic garment from me. So,
[*Lays down his magic robe and staff.*]
Lie there, my art. Wipe thou thine eyes; have comfort.
The direful spectacle of the wrack, which touch'd
The very virtue of compassion in thee,
I have with such provision in mine art
So safely ordered that there is no soul—
No, not so much perdition as an hair
Betid to any creature in the vessel
Which thou heard'st cry, which thou saw'st sink. Sit down;
For thou must now know farther.

MIRANDA You have often
Begun to tell me what I am, but stopp'd
And left me to a bootless inquisition,
Concluding, "Stay, not yet."

PROSPERO The hour's now come;
The very minute bids thee ope thine ear.
Obey and be attentive. Canst thou remember
A time before we came unto this cell?
I do not think thou canst, for then thou wast not
Out three years old.

MIRANDA Certainly, sir, I can.

PROSPERO
By what? By any other house or person?
Of anything the image, tell me, that
Hath kept with thy remembrance.

MIRANDA 'Tis far off,
And rather like a dream than an assurance
That my remembrance warrants. Had I not
Four or five women once that tended me?

PROSPERO
Thou hadst, and more, Miranda. But how is it
That this lives in thy mind? What seest thou else
In the dark backward and abysm of time?
If thou rememb'rest aught ere thou cam'st here,
How thou cam'st here thou mayst.

MIRANDA But that I do not.

PROSPERO
Twelve year since, Miranda, twelve year since,
Thy father was the Duke of Milan and
A prince of power.

MIRANDA Sir, are not you my father?

PROSPERO
Thy mother was a piece of virtue, and
She said thou wast my daughter; and thy father
Was Duke of Milan; and thou his only heir
And princess no worse issued.

MIRANDA O the heavens!
What foul play had we, that we came from thence?
Or blessed was 't we did?

PROSPERO Both, both, my girl.
By foul play, as thou say'st, were we heav'd thence,
But blessedly holp hither.

MIRANDA O, my heart bleeds
To think o' th' teen that I have turn'd you to,
Which is from my remembrance! Please you, farther.

PROSPERO
My brother and thy uncle, call'd Antonio—
I pray thee mark me—that a brother should
Be so perfidious!—he whom next thyself
Of all the world I lov'd, and to him put
The manage of my state, as at that time
Through all the signories it was the first
And Prospero the prime duke, being so reputed
In dignity, and for the liberal arts
Without a parallel; those being all my study,
The government I cast upon my brother
And to my state grew stranger, being transported
And rapt in secret studies. Thy false uncle—
Dost thou attend me?

MIRANDA Sir, most heedfully.

PROSPERO
Being once perfected how to grant suits,
How to deny them, who t' advance and who
To trash for overtopping, new created
The creatures that were mine, I say, or chang'd 'em,
Or else new form'd 'em; having both the key
Of officer and office, set all hearts i' th' state
To what tune pleas'd his ear, that now he was
The ivy which had hid my princely trunk,
And suck'd my verdure out on 't. Thou attend'st not.

MIRANDA
O, good sir, I do.

PROSPERO I pray thee mark me.
I, thus neglecting worldly ends, all dedicated
To closeness and the bettering of my mind
With that which, but by being so retir'd,
O'er-priz'd all popular rate, in my false brother
Awak'd an evil nature; and my trust,
Like a good parent, did beget of him
A falsehood in its contrary as great
As my trust was, which had indeed no limit,
A confidence sans bound. He being thus lorded,
Not only with what my revenue yielded,

20 full very **30 perdition** loss **31 Betid** happened **35 bootless inquisition** profitless inquiry **41 Out** fully **45–46 assurance . . . warrants** certainty that my memory guarantees

56 piece masterpiece, exemplar **59 issued** born, descended **63 holp** helped **64 teen . . . to** trouble I've caused you to remember, or put you to **65 from** out of **71 signories** i.e., city-states of northern Italy **79 perfected** grown skillful **81 trash** check a hound by tying a weight to its neck. **overtopping** running too far ahead of the pack; or, growing too tall **82 creatures** dependents. **or** either **83 key** (1) key for unlocking (2) tool for tuning stringed instruments **90 closeness** retirement, seclusion **91–92 but . . . rate** except that it was done in retirement, (would have) surpassed in value all popular estimate **94 good parent** (Alludes to the proverb that good parents often bear bad children; see also l. 120.) **97 sans** without. **lorded** raised to lordship, with power and wealth

But what my power might else exact—like one
Who having into truth, by telling of it, 100
Made such a sinner of his memory 101
To credit his own lie—he did believe 102
He was indeed the Duke, out o' th' substitution, 103
And executing th' outward face of royalty, 104
With all prerogative. Hence his ambition growing—
Dost thou hear?

MIRANDA Your tale, sir, would cure deafness.

PROSPERO
To have no screen between this part he play'd
And him he play'd it for, he needs will be 108
Absolute Milan. Me, poor man, my library 109
Was dukedom large enough. Of temporal royalties 110
He thinks me now incapable; confederates— 111
So dry he was for sway—wi' th' King of Naples 112
To give him annual tribute, do him homage, 113
Subject his coronet to his crown, and bend 114
The dukedom yet unbow'd—alas, poor Milan!—
To most ignoble stooping.

MIRANDA O the heavens!

PROSPERO
Mark his condition and th' event, then tell me 117
If this might be a brother.

MIRANDA I should sin
To think but nobly of my grandmother.
Good wombs have borne bad sons.

PROSPERO Now the condition.
This King of Naples, being an enemy
To me inveterate, hearkens my brother's suit,
Which was that he, in lieu o' th' premises 123
Of homage and I know not how much tribute,
Should presently extirpate me and mine 125
Out of the dukedom and confer fair Milan
With all the honors on my brother. Whereon,
A treacherous army levied, one midnight
Fated to th' purpose, did Antonio open
The gates of Milan, and, i' th' dead of darkness,
The ministers for th' purpose hurried thence
Me and thy crying self.

MIRANDA Alack, for pity!
I, not rememb'ring how I cried out then,
Will cry it o'er again. It is a hint 134
That wrings mine eyes to 't.

PROSPERO Hear a little further,
And then I'll bring thee to the present business
Which now's upon 's, without the which this story
Were most impertinent.

MIRANDA Wherefore did they not 138
That hour destroy us?

PROSPERO Well demanded, wench.
My tale provokes that question. Dear, they durst
not,
So dear the love my people bore me, nor set
A mark so bloody on the business, but
With colors fairer painted their foul ends.
In few, they hurried us aboard a bark, 144
Bore us some leagues to sea, where they prepar'd
A rotten carcass of a butt, not rigg'd, 146
Nor tackle, sail, nor mast; the very rats
Instinctively have quit it. There they hoist us,
To cry to th' sea that roar'd to us, to sigh
To th' winds whose pity, sighing back again,
Did us but loving wrong.

MIRANDA Alack, what trouble 151
Was I then to you!

PROSPERO O, a cherubin
Thou wast that did preserve me. Thou didst smile,
Infused with a fortitude from heaven,
When I have deck'd the sea with drops full salt, 155
Under my burden groan'd, which rais'd in me 156
An undergoing stomach, to bear up 157
Against what should ensue.

MIRANDA
How came we ashore?

PROSPERO By Providence divine.
Some food we had, and some fresh water, that
A noble Neapolitan, Gonzalo,
Out of his charity, who being then appointed
Master of this design, did give us, with
Rich garments, linens, stuffs, and necessaries,
Which since have steaded much. So, of his
gentleness, 165
Knowing I lov'd my books, he furnish'd me
From mine own library with volumes that
I prize above my dukedom.

MIRANDA Would I might
But ever see that man!

PROSPERO Now I arise.
[*Resumes his magic robes.*]
Sit still, and hear the last of our sea-sorrow.
Here in this island we arriv'd; and here
Have I, thy schoolmaster, made thee more profit 172
Than other princess' can that have more time 173
For vainer hours and tutors not so careful.

MIRANDA
Heavens thank you for 't! And now, I pray you, sir,
For still 'tis beating in my mind, your reason
For raising this sea-storm?

PROSPERO Know thus far forth.
By accident most strange, bountiful Fortune,
Now my dear lady, hath mine enemies
Brought to this shore; and by my prescience
I find my zenith doth depend upon 181
A most auspicious star, whose influence 182
If now I court not but omit, my fortunes
Will ever after droop. Here cease more questions.
Thou art inclin'd to sleep; 'tis a good dullness,
And give it way. I know thou canst not choose.
[*Miranda sleeps.*]

100–102 Who . . . lie i.e., who, by repeatedly telling the lie (that he was indeed Duke of Milan), made his memory such a confirmed sinner against truth that he began to believe his own lie **103 out o'** as a result of **104 And . . . royalty** and (as a result of) his carrying out all the ceremonial functions of royalty **108 him** i.e., himself **109 Absolute Milan** unconditional Duke of Milan **110 temporal royalties** practical prerogatives and responsibilities of a sovereign **111 confederates** conspires, allies himself **112 dry** thirsty **113 him** i.e., the King of Naples **114 his . . . his** Antonio's . . . the King of Naples' **117 condition** pact. **event** outcome **123 in . . . premises** in return for the stipulation **125 presently extirpate** at once remove **134 hint** occasion **138 impertinent** irrelevant

144 few few words **146 butt** cask, tub **151 loving wrong** (I.e., the winds pitied Prospero and Miranda though of necessity they blew them from shore.) **155 deck'd** covered (with salt tears); adorned **156 which** i.e., the smile **157 undergoing stomach** courage to go on **165 steaded much** been of much use **172 more profit** profit more **173 princess'** princesses **181 zenith** height of fortune. (Astrological term.) **182 influence** astrological power

Come away, servant, come! I am ready now. 187
Approach, my Ariel, come.

Enter Ariel.

ARIEL
All hail, great master! Grave sir, hail! I come
To answer thy best pleasure; be 't to fly,
To swim, to dive into the fire, to ride
On the curl'd clouds. To thy strong bidding, task 192
Ariel and all his quality.

PROSPERO
Hast thou, spirit, 193
Perform'd to point the tempest that I bade thee? 194

ARIEL
To every article.
I boarded the King's ship; now on the beak, 196
Now in the waist, the deck, in every cabin, 197
I flam'd amazement. Sometime I'd divide, 198
And burn in many places; on the topmast,
The yards, and boresprit, would I flame distinctly, 200
Then meet and join. Jove's lightnings, the precursors
O' th' dreadful thunder-claps, more momentary
And sight-outrunning were not; the fire and cracks
Of sulphurous roaring the most mighty Neptune
Seem to besiege and make his bold waves tremble,
Yea, his dread trident shake.

PROSPERO
My brave spirit!
Who was so firm, so constant, that this coil 207
Would not infect his reason?

ARIEL
Not a soul
But felt a fever of the mad and play'd 209
Some tricks of desperation. All but mariners
Plung'd in the foaming brine and quit the vessel;
Then all afire with me, the King's son, Ferdinand,
With hair up-staring—then like reeds, not hair— 213
Was the first man that leapt; cried, "Hell is empty,
And all the devils are here."

PROSPERO
Why, that's my spirit!
But was not this nigh shore?

ARIEL
Close by, my master.

PROSPERO
But are they, Ariel, safe?

ARIEL
Not a hair perish'd.
On their sustaining garments not a blemish, 218
But fresher than before; and, as thou bad'st me,
In troops I have dispers'd them 'bout the isle.
The King's son have I landed by himself,
Whom I left cooling of the air with sighs
In an odd angle of the isle and sitting, 223
His arms in this sad knot. [*Folds his arms.*]

PROSPERO
Of the King's ship, 224
The mariners, say how thou hast dispos'd,
And all the rest o' th' fleet.

ARIEL
Safely in harbor

187 Come away come **192 task** make demands upon **193 quality** (1) fellow-spirits (2) abilities **194 to point** to the smallest detail **196 beak** prow **197 waist** midships. **deck** poopdeck at the stern **198 flam'd amazement** struck terror in the guise of fire, i.e., St. Elmo's fire **200 boresprit** bowsprit. **distinctly** in different places **207 coil** tumult **209 of the mad** i.e., such as madmen feel **213 up-staring** standing on end **218 sustaining garments** garments that buoyed them up in the sea **223 angle** corner **224 sad knot** (Folded arms are indicative of melancholy.)

Is the King's ship; in the deep nook, where once 227
Thou call'dst me up at midnight to fetch dew
From the still-vex'd Bermoothes, there she's hid; 229
The mariners all under hatches stow'd,
Who, with a charm join'd to their suff'red labor, 231
I have left asleep; and for the rest o' th' fleet,
Which I dispers'd, they all have met again
And are upon the Mediterranean flote 234
Bound sadly home for Naples,
Supposing that they saw the King's ship wrack'd
And his great person perish.

PROSPERO
Ariel, thy charge
Exactly is perform'd. But there's more work.
What is the time o' th' day?

ARIEL
Past the mid season. 239

PROSPERO
At least two glasses. The time 'twixt six and now 240
Must by us both be spent most preciously.

ARIEL
Is there more toil? Since thou dost give me pains,
Let me remember thee what thou hast promis'd, 243
Which is not yet perform'd me.

PROSPERO
How now? Moody?
What is 't thou canst demand?

ARIEL
My liberty.

PROSPERO
Before the time be out? No more!

ARIEL
I prithee,
Remember I have done thee worthy service,
Told thee no lies, made thee no mistakings, serv'd
Without or grudge or grumblings. Thou didst promise
To bate me a full year.

PROSPERO
Dost thou forget 250
From what a torment I did free thee?

ARIEL
No.

PROSPERO
Thou dost, and think'st it much to tread the ooze
Of the salt deep,
To run upon the sharp wind of the north,
To do me business in the veins o' th' earth
When it is bak'd with frost.

ARIEL
I do not, sir.

PROSPERO
Thou liest, malignant thing! Hast thou forgot
The foul witch Sycorax, who with age and envy 258
Was grown into a hoop? Hast thou forgot her?

ARIEL
No, sir.

PROSPERO
Thou hast. Where was she born? Speak. Tell me.

ARIEL
Sir, in Argier.

PROSPERO
O, was she so? I must 262
Once in a month recount what thou hast been,
Which thou forget'st. This damn'd witch Sycorax,
For mischiefs manifold and sorceries terrible

227 nook bay **229 still-vex'd Bermoothes** ever stormy Bermudas. (Perhaps refers to the then-recent Bermuda shipwreck; see Play Introduction.) **231 with . . . labor** by means of a spell added to all the labor they have undergone **234 flote** sea **239 mid season** noon **240 glasses** i.e., hourglasses **243 remember** remind **250 bate** remit, deduct **258 envy** malice **262 Argier** Algiers

To enter human hearing, from Argier,
Thou know'st, was banish'd; for one thing she did
They would not take her life. Is not this true?

ARIEL
Ay, sir.

PROSPERO
This blue-ey'd hag was hither brought with child
And here was left by th' sailors. Thou, my slave,
As thou report'st thyself, was then her servant;
And, for thou wast a spirit too delicate
To act her earthy and abhorr'd commands,
Refusing her grand hests, she did confine thee,
By help of her more potent ministers,
And in her most unmitigable rage,
Into a cloven pine, within which rift
Imprison'd thou didst painfully remain
A dozen years; within which space she died
And left thee there, where thou did'st vent thy
groans
As fast as mill-wheels strike. Then was this island—
Save for the son that she did litter here,
A freckled whelp hag-born—not honor'd with
A human shape.

ARIEL Yes, Caliban her son.

PROSPERO
Dull thing, I say so; he, that Caliban
Whom now I keep in service. Thou best know'st
What torment I did find thee in; thy groans
Did make wolves howl and penetrate the breasts
Of ever angry bears. It was a torment
To lay upon the damn'd, which Sycorax
Could not again undo. It was mine art,
When I arriv'd and heard thee, that made gape
The pine and let thee out.

ARIEL I thank thee, master.

PROSPERO
If thou more murmur'st, I will rend an oak
And peg thee in his knotty entrails till
Thou hast howl'd away twelve winters.

ARIEL Pardon, master;
I will be correspondent to command
And do my spriting gently.

PROSPERO
Do so, and after two days
I will discharge thee.

ARIEL That's my noble master!
What shall I do? Say what? What shall I do?

PROSPERO
Go make thyself like a nymph o' th' sea. Be subject
To no sight but thine and mine, invisible
To every eyeball else. Go take this shape
And hither come in 't. Go, hence with diligence!
Exit [*Ariel*].
Awake, dear heart, awake! Thou hast slept well;
Awake!

MIRANDA The strangeness of your story put
Heaviness in me.

PROSPERO Shake it off. Come on;
We'll visit Caliban my slave, who never
Yields us kind answer.

MIRANDA 'Tis a villain, sir,
I do not love to look on.

PROSPERO But, as 'tis,
We cannot miss him. He does make our fire,
Fetch in our wood, and serves in offices
That profit us. What, ho! Slave! Caliban!
Thou earth, thou! Speak.

CALIBAN (*Within*) There's wood enough within.

PROSPERO
Come forth, I say! There's other business for thee.
Come, thou tortoise! When?

Enter Ariel like a water-nymph.

Fine apparition! My quaint Ariel,
Hark in thine ear. [*Whispers.*]

ARIEL My lord, it shall be done. *Exit.*

PROSPERO
Thou poisonous slave, got by the devil himself
Upon thy wicked dam, come forth!

Enter Caliban.

CALIBAN
As wicked dew as e'er my mother brush'd
With raven's feather from unwholesome fen
Drop on you both! A south-west blow on ye
And blister you all o'er!

PROSPERO
For this, be sure, tonight thou shalt have cramps,
Side-stitches that shall pen thy breath up; urchins
Shall, for that vast of night that they may work,
All exercise on thee. Thou shalt be pinch'd
As thick as honeycomb, each pinch more stinging
Than bees that made 'em.

CALIBAN I must eat my dinner.
This island's mine, by Sycorax my mother,
Which thou tak'st from me. When thou cam'st first,
Thou strok'st me and made much of me, wouldst
give me
Water with berries in 't, and teach me how
To name the bigger light, and how the less,
That burn by day and night; and then I lov'd thee
And show'd thee all the qualities o' th' isle,
The fresh springs, brine-pits, barren place and
fertile.
Curs'd be I that did so! All the charms
Of Sycorax, toads, beetles, bats, light on you!
For I am all the subjects that you have,
Which first was mine own king; and here you
sty me
In this hard rock, whiles you do keep from me
The rest o' th' island.

PROSPERO Thou most lying slave,

267 one . . . did (Perhaps a reference to her pregnancy, for which her life would be spared.) **270 blue-ey'd** with dark circles under the eyes **273 for** because **275 hests** commands **296 his** its **298 correspondent** responsive, submissive

313 miss do without **319 quaint** ingenious **323 wicked** mischievous, harmful **325 south-west** i.e., wind thought to bring disease **328 urchins** hedgehogs; here, suggesting goblins in the guise of hedgehogs **329 vast** lengthy, desolate time. **that . . . work** (Malignant spirits were thought to be restricted to the hours of darkness.)

Whom stripes may move, not kindness! I have us'd thee,
Filth as thou art, with humane care, and lodg'd thee
In mine own cell, till thou didst seek to violate
The honor of my child.

CALIBAN
O ho, O ho! Would 't had been done!
Thou didst prevent me; I had peopled else
This isle with Calibans.

MIRANDA Abhorred slave,
Which any print of goodness wilt not take,
Being capable of all ill! I pitied thee,
Took pains to make thee speak, taught thee each hour
One thing or other. When thou didst not, savage,
Know thine own meaning, but wouldst gabble like
A thing most brutish, I endow'd thy purposes
With words that made them known. But thy vile race,
Though thou didst learn, had that in 't which good natures
Could not abide to be with; therefore wast thou
Deservedly confin'd into this rock,
Who hadst deserv'd more than a prison.

CALIBAN
You taught me language, and my profit on 't
Is, I know how to curse. The red plague rid you
For learning me your language!

PROSPERO Hag-seed, hence!
Fetch us in fuel; and be quick, thou 'rt best,
To answer other business. Shrug'st thou, malice?
If thou neglect'st or dost unwillingly
What I command, I'll rack thee with old cramps,
Fill all thy bones with aches, make thee roar
That beasts shall tremble at thy din.

CALIBAN No, pray thee.
[*Aside.*] I must obey. His art is of such pow'r,
It would control my dam's god, Setebos,
And make a vassal of him.

PROSPERO So, slave, hence!
Exit Caliban.

Enter Ferdinand; and Ariel, invisible, playing and singing. [*Ferdinand does not see Prospero and Miranda.*]

Ariel's Song.
Come unto these yellow sands,
And then take hands.
Curtsied when you have and kiss'd,
The wild waves whist,
Foot it featly here and there;
And, sweet sprites, the burden bear.
Hark, hark!
Burden, dispersedly [*within*]. Bow-wow.
The watch-dogs bark.
[*Burden, dispersedly within.*] Bow-wow.
Hark, hark! I hear
The strain of strutting chanticleer
Cry, Cock-a-diddle-dow.

FERDINAND
Where should this music be? I' th' air or th' earth?
It sounds no more; and, sure, it waits upon
Some god o' th' island. Sitting on a bank,
Weeping again the King my father's wrack,
This music crept by me upon the waters,
Allaying both their fury and my passion
With its sweet air. Thence I have follow'd it,
Or it hath drawn me rather. But 'tis gone.
No, it begins again.

Ariel's Song.
Full fathom five thy father lies;
Of his bones are coral made;
Those are pearls that were his eyes.
Nothing of him that doth fade
But doth suffer a sea-change
Into something rich and strange.
Sea-nymphs hourly ring his knell:
Burden [*within*]. Ding-dong.
Hark, now I hear them—Ding-dong, bell.

FERDINAND
The ditty does remember my drown'd father.
This is no mortal business, nor no sound
That the earth owes. I hear it now above me.

PROSPERO
The fringed curtains of thine eye advance
And say what thou seest yond.

MIRANDA What is 't? A spirit?
Lord, how it looks about! Believe me, sir,
It carries a brave form. But 'tis a spirit.

PROSPERO
No, wench, it eats and sleeps and hath such senses
As we have, such. This gallant which thou seest
Was in the wrack; and, but he's something stain'd
With grief, that's beauty's canker, thou mightst call him
A goodly person. He hath lost his fellows
And strays about to find 'em.

MIRANDA I might call him
A thing divine, for nothing natural
I ever saw so noble.

PROSPERO [*Aside*] It goes on, I see,
As my soul prompts it. Spirit, fine spirit, I'll free thee
Within two days for this.

FERDINAND [*Seeing Miranda*] Most sure, the goddess
On whom these airs attend!—Vouchsafe my pray'r
May know if you remain upon this island,
And that you will some good instruction give
How I may bear me here. My prime request,
Which I do last pronounce, is, O you wonder!

347 stripes lashes **353–364 Abhorred . . . prison** (Sometimes assigned by editors to Prospero.) **359 purposes** meanings, desires **360 race** natural disposition; species, nature **366 red plague** bubonic plague. **rid** destroy **367 learning** teaching. **Hag-seed** offspring of a female demon **368 thou'rt best** you'd be well advised **371 old** such as old people suffer; or, plenty of **372 aches** (Pronounced "aitches.") **380 whist** being hushed **381 featly** nimbly **382 burden** refrain, undersong **384 dispersedly** i.e., from all directions

408 remember commemorate **410 owes** owns **411 advance** raise **414 brave** excellent **417 but** except that. **something stain'd** somewhat disfigured **418 canker** cankerworm (feeding on buds and leaves) **422 It goes on** i.e., my plan works **426 remain** dwell **428 bear me** conduct myself. **prime** chief

If you be maid or no?
MIRANDA No wonder, sir,
But certainly a maid.
FERDINAND My language? Heavens!
I am the best of them that speak this speech, 432
Were I but where 'tis spoken.
PROSPERO [*Coming forward*] How? The best?
What wert thou, if the King of Naples heard thee?
FERDINAND
A single thing, as I am now, that wonders 435
To hear thee speak of Naples. He does hear me; 436
And that he does I weep. Myself am Naples, 437
Who with mine eyes, never since at ebb, beheld
The King my father wrack'd.
MIRANDA Alack, for mercy!
FERDINAND
Yes, faith, and all his lords, the Duke of Milan
And his brave son being twain.
PROSPERO [*Aside*] The Duke of Milan 441
And his more braver daughter could control thee, 442
If now 'twere fit to do 't. At the first sight
They have chang'd eyes. Delicate Ariel, 444
I'll set thee free for this. [*To Ferdinand.*] A word, good sir.
I fear you have done yourself some wrong. A word! 446
MIRANDA [*Aside*]
Why speaks my father so ungently? This
Is the third man that e'er I saw, the first
That e'er I sigh'd for. Pity move my father
To be inclin'd my way!
FERDINAND O, if a virgin,
And your affection not gone forth, I'll make you
The Queen of Naples.
PROSPERO Soft, sir! One word more.
[*Aside.*] They are both in either's pow'rs; but this swift business
I must uneasy make, lest too light winning 454
Make the prize light. [*To Ferdinand.*] One word more: I charge thee 455
That thou attend me. Thou dost here usurp
The name thou ow'st not, and hast put thyself 457
Upon this island as a spy, to win it
From me, the lord on 't.
FERDINAND No, as I am a man.
MIRANDA
There's nothing ill can dwell in such a temple.
If the ill spirit have so fair a house,
Good things will strive to dwell with 't.
PROSPERO Follow me.—
Speak not you for him; he's a traitor.—Come,
I'll manacle thy neck and feet together.
Sea-water shalt thou drink; thy food shall be
The fresh-brook mussels, wither'd roots, and husks
Wherein the acorn cradled. Follow.
FERDINAND No.
I will resist such entertainment till 468
Mine enemy has more pow'r.
He draws, and is charmed from moving.
MIRANDA O dear father,
Make not too rash a trial of him, for
He's gentle, and not fearful.
PROSPERO What, I say, 471
My foot my tutor?—Put thy sword up, traitor, 472
Who mak'st a show but dar'st not strike, thy conscience
Is so possess'd with guilt. Come, from thy ward, 474
For I can here disarm thee with this stick
And make thy weapon drop.
[*Brandishes his staff.*]
MIRANDA [*Trying to hinder him*] Beseech you, father.
PROSPERO
Hence! Hang not on my garments.
MIRANDA Sir, have pity!
I'll be his surety.
PROSPERO Silence! One word more
Shall make me chide thee, if not hate thee. What,
An advocate for an impostor? Hush!
Thou think'st there is no more such shapes as he,
Having seen but him and Caliban. Foolish wench,
To th' most of men this is a Caliban 483
And they to him are angels.
MIRANDA My affections
Are then most humble; I have no ambition
To see a goodlier man.
PROSPERO [*To Ferdinand*] Come on, obey.
Thy nerves are in their infancy again 487
And have no vigor in them.
FERDINAND So they are.
My spirits, as in a dream, are all bound up.
My father's loss, the weakness which I feel,
The wrack of all my friends, nor this man's threats
To whom I am subdu'd, are but light to me,
Might I but through my prison once a day
Behold this maid. All corners else o' th' earth
Let liberty make use of; space enough
Have I in such a prison.
PROSPERO [*Aside*] It works. [*To Ferdinand.*] Come on.—
Thou hast done well, fine Ariel! [*To Ferdinand.*] Follow me.
[*To Ariel.*] Hark what thou else shalt do me.
MIRANDA [*To Ferdinand*] Be of comfort. 498
My father's of a better nature, sir,
Than he appears by speech. This is unwonted
Which now came from him.
PROSPERO [*To Ariel*] Thou shalt be as free
As mountain winds; but then exactly do
All points of my command.
ARIEL To th' syllable.
PROSPERO [*To Ferdinand*]
Come, follow. [*To Miranda.*] Speak not for him.
Exeunt.

432 best i.e., in birth **435 single** (1) solitary (2) feeble **436–437 He . . . weep** i.e., this man to whom I speak (Prospero) hears me as I hear him, proving to me I am indeed alive, not dreaming, and am in the sad plight I imagined (?) **437 Naples** the King of Naples (also in l. 436) **441 son** (The only reference in the play to a son of Antonio.) **442 control** confute **444 chang'd eyes** exchanged amorous glances **446 done . . . wrong** i.e., spoken falsely **454 uneasy** difficult **454–455 light . . . light** easy . . . cheap **457 ow'st** ownest

468 entertainment treatment **471 gentle** wellborn. **fearful** cowardly **472 foot** subordinate. (Miranda, the foot, presumes to instruct Prospero, the head.) **474 ward** defensive posture (in fencing) **483 To** compared to **487 nerves** sinews **498 me** for me

ACT II • SCENE I

Enter Alonso, Sebastian, Antonio, Gonzalo, Adrian, Francisco, and others.

GONZALO
Beseech you, sir, be merry. You have cause,
So have we all, of joy, for our escape
Is much beyond our loss. Our hint of woe
Is common; every day some sailor's wife,
The masters of some merchant, and the merchant,
Have just our theme of woe; but for the miracle,
I mean our preservation, few in millions
Can speak like us. Then wisely, good sir, weigh
Our sorrow with our comfort.

ALONSO Prithee, peace.

SEBASTIAN [*To Antonio*] He receives comfort like cold porridge.

ANTONIO [*To Sebastian*] The visitor will not give him o'er so.

SEBASTIAN Look, he's winding up the watch of his wit; by and by it will strike.

GONZALO Sir—

SEBASTIAN [*To Antonio*] One. Tell.

GONZALO
When every grief is entertain'd that's offer'd,
Comes to th' entertainer—

SEBASTIAN A dollar.

GONZALO Dolor comes to him, indeed. You have spoken truer than you purpos'd.

SEBASTIAN You have taken it wiselier than I meant you should.

GONZALO Therefore, my lord—

ANTONIO Fie, what a spendthrift is he of his tongue!

ALONSO I prithee, spare.

GONZALO Well, I have done. But yet—

SEBASTIAN He will be talking.

ANTONIO Which, of he or Adrian, for a good wager, first begins to crow?

SEBASTIAN The old cock.

ANTONIO The cock'rel.

SEBASTIAN Done. The wager?

ANTONIO A laughter.

SEBASTIAN A match!

ADRIAN Though this island seem to be desert—

SEBASTIAN Ha, ha, ha!

ANTONIO So, you're paid.

ADRIAN Uninhabitable and almost inaccessible—

SEBASTIAN Yet—

ADRIAN Yet—

ANTONIO He could not miss 't.

ADRIAN It must needs be of subtle, tender, and delicate temperance.

ANTONIO Temperance was a delicate wench.

SEBASTIAN Ay, and a subtle, as he most learnedly deliver'd.

ADRIAN The air breathes upon us here most sweetly.

SEBASTIAN As if it had lungs, and rotten ones.

ANTONIO Or as 'twere perfum'd by a fen.

GONZALO Here is everything advantageous to life.

ANTONIO True, save means to live.

SEBASTIAN Of that there's none, or little.

GONZALO How lush and lusty the grass looks! How green!

ANTONIO The ground indeed is tawny.

SEBASTIAN With an eye of green in 't.

ANTONIO He misses not much.

SEBASTIAN No; he doth but mistake the truth totally.

GONZALO But the rarity of it is—which is indeed almost beyond credit—

SEBASTIAN As many vouch'd rarities are.

GONZALO That our garments, being, as they were, drench'd in the sea, hold notwithstanding their freshness and glosses, being rather new-dyed than stain'd with salt water.

ANTONIO If but one of his pockets could speak, would it not say he lies?

SEBASTIAN Ay, or very falsely pocket up his report.

GONZALO Methinks our garments are now as fresh as when we put them on first in Afric, at the marriage of the King's fair daughter Claribel to the King of Tunis.

SEBASTIAN 'Twas a sweet marriage, and we prosper well in our return.

ADRIAN Tunis was never grac'd before with such a paragon to their queen.

GONZALO Not since widow Dido's time.

ANTONIO Widow! A pox o' that! How came that widow in? Widow Dido!

SEBASTIAN What if he had said "widower Aeneas" too? Good Lord, how you take it!

ADRIAN "Widow Dido" said you? You make me study of that. She was of Carthage, not of Tunis.

GONZALO This Tunis, sir, was Carthage.

ADRIAN Carthage?

GONZALO I assure you, Carthage.

ANTONIO His word is more than the miraculous harp.

SEBASTIAN He hath rais'd the wall and houses too.

II.i. Location: Another part of the island.
3 hint of occasion for **5 masters . . . the merchant** officers of some merchant vessel and the merchant himself, the owner **11 porridge** (with a pun on *peace* and *pease*, a usual ingredient of porridge) **12 visitor** one taking nourishment and comfort to the sick, i.e., Gonzalo **12–13 give him o'er** abandon him **17 Tell** keep count **18–19 When . . . entertainer** when every sorrow that presents itself is accepted without resistance, there comes to the recipient **20 dollar** widely-circulated coin, the German *Thaler* and the Spanish *piece of eight*. (Sebastian puns on *entertainer* in the sense of *innkeeper;* to Gonzalo, *dollar* suggests *dolor,* grief.) **30–31 Which . . . crow** which of the two, Gonzalo or Adrian, do you bet will speak (crow) first **32 old cock** i.e., Gonzalo **33 cock'rel** i.e., Adrian **35 laughter** (1) burst of laughter (2) sitting of eggs. (When Adrian, the *cock'rel,* begins to speak two lines later, Sebastian loses the bet. Some editors alter the speech prefixes in ll. 38–39 so that Antonio enjoys his laugh as the prize for winning, but possibly Sebastian pays for losing with a laugh.) **36 A match** a bargain; agreed

43 miss 't (1) avoid saying "Yet" (2) miss the island **45 temperance** climate **46 Temperance** a girl's name. **delicate** (Here it means *given to pleasure, voluptuous;* in l. 44, *pleasant.* Antonio is evidently suggesting that "tender, and delicate temperance" sounds like a Puritan phrase, which Antonio then mocks by applying the words to a woman rather than an island. He began this bawdy comparison with a double entendre on *inaccessible,* l. 40.) **47 subtle** (Here it means *tricky;* in l. 44, *delicate.*) **47–48 deliver'd** uttered. (Sebastian joins in the Puritan baiting of Antonio with his use of the pious cant phrase "learnedly deliver'd.") **55 lusty** healthy **57 tawny** dull brown, yellowish **58 eye** tinge, or spot (perhaps with reference to Gonzalo's eye or judgment) **63 vouch'd** certified **68 pockets** i.e., because they are muddy **70 pocket up** receive unprotestingly, fail to respond to a challenge **77 to** for **78 widow Dido** Queen of Carthage, deserted by Aeneas. (She was in fact a widow when Aeneas, a widower, met her, but Antonio may be amused at the term "widow" to describe a woman deserted by her lover.) **88 miraculous harp** (Alludes to Amphion's harp with which he raised the walls of Thebes; Gonzalo has exceeded that deed by creating a modern Carthage—walls *and houses*—mistakenly on the site of Tunis.)

ANTONIO What impossible matter will he make easy next?
SEBASTIAN I think he will carry this island home in his pocket and give it his son for an apple.
ANTONIO And, sowing the kernels of it in the sea, bring forth more islands.
GONZALO Ay. 96
ANTONIO Why, in good time. 97
GONZALO [*To Alonso*] Sir, we were talking that our garments seem now as fresh as when we were at Tunis at the marriage of your daughter, who is now queen.
ANTONIO And the rarest that e'er came there. 101
SEBASTIAN Bate, I beseech you, widow Dido. 102
ANTONIO O, widow Dido? Ay, widow Dido.
GONZALO Is not, sir, my doublet as fresh as the first day I wore it? I mean, in a sort. 105
ANTONIO That "sort" was well fish'd for.
GONZALO When I wore it at your daughter's marriage?
ALONSO
You cram these words into mine ears against
The stomach of my sense. Would I had never 109
Married my daughter there! For, coming thence, 110
My son is lost and, in my rate, she too, 111
Who is so far from Italy removed
I ne'er again shall see her. O thou mine heir
Of Naples and of Milan, what strange fish
Hath made his meal on thee?
FRANCISCO Sir, he may live.
I saw him beat the surges under him,
And ride upon their backs. He trod the water,
Whose enmity he flung aside, and breasted
The surge most swoll'n that met him. His bold head
'Bove the contentious waves he kept, and oared
Himself with his good arms in lusty stroke 121
To th' shore, that o'er his wave-worn basis bowed, 122
As stooping to relieve him. I not doubt 123
He came alive to land.
ALONSO No, no, he's gone.
SEBASTIAN
Sir, you may thank yourself for this great loss,
That would not bless our Europe with your daughter,
But rather loose her to an African,
Where she at least is banish'd from your eye,
Who hath cause to wet the grief on 't.
ALONSO Prithee, peace. 129
SEBASTIAN
You were kneel'd to and importun'd otherwise
By all of us, and the fair soul herself 131
Weigh'd between loathness and obedience, at 132
Which end o' th' beam should bow. We have lost your son, 133
I fear, for ever. Milan and Naples have
Moe widows in them of this business' making 135
Than we bring men to comfort them.
The fault's your own.
ALONSO
So is the dear'st o' th' loss.
GONZALO My lord Sebastian, 138
The truth you speak doth lack some gentleness,
And time to speak it in. You rub the sore, 140
When you should bring the plaster.
SEBASTIAN Very well.
ANTONIO
And most chirurgeonly. 142
GONZALO
It is foul weather in us all, good sir,
When you are cloudy.
SEBASTIAN [*To Antonio*] Foul weather?
ANTONIO [*To Sebastian*] Very foul.
GONZALO
Had I plantation of this isle, my lord— 145
ANTONIO
He'd sow 't with nettle-seed.
SEBASTIAN Or docks, or mallows. 146
GONZALO
And were the king on 't, what would I do?
SEBASTIAN
Scape being drunk for want of wine.
GONZALO
I' th' commonwealth I would by contraries 149
Execute all things; for no kind of traffic 150
Would I admit; no name of magistrate;
Letters should not be known; riches, poverty, 152
And use of service, none; contract, succession, 153
Bourn, bound of land, tilth, vineyard, none; 154
No use of metal, corn, or wine, or oil; 155
No occupation; all men idle, all,
And women too, but innocent and pure;
No sovereignty—
SEBASTIAN Yet he would be king on 't.
ANTONIO The latter end of his commonwealth forgets the beginning.
GONZALO
All things in common nature should produce
Without sweat or endeavor. Treason, felony,
Sword, pike, knife, gun, or need of any engine, 163
Would I not have; but nature should bring forth,
Of it own kind, all foison, all abundance, 165
To feed my innocent people.
SEBASTIAN No marrying 'mong his subjects?
ANTONIO None, man; all idle—whores and knaves.
GONZALO
I would with such perfection govern, sir,
T' excel the golden age.
SEBASTIAN Save his Majesty! 170

96 Ay (Gonzalo may be reasserting his point about Carthage, or he may be responding ironically to Antonio who in turn answers sarcastically.) **97 in good time** (An expression of ironical acquiescence or amazement; i.e., *sure, right away*) **101 rarest** most remarkable, beautiful **102 Bate** abate, except, leave out. (I.e., don't forget Dido; or, let's have no more talk of Dido.) **105 in a sort** in a way **109 stomach** appetite **110 Married** given in marriage **111 rate** estimation, consideration **121 lusty** vigorous **122 that . . . bowed** that hung out over its wave-worn foot **123 As** as if **129 Who** which, i.e., the eye **131–133 the fair . . . bow** i.e., Claribel herself was poised uncertain between unwillingness to marry and obedience to her father as to which end of the scale should sink, which should prevail

135 Moe more **138 dear'st** heaviest, most costly **140 time** appropriate time **142 chirurgeonly** like a skilled surgeon. (Antonio mocks Gonzalo's medical analogy of a *plaster* applied curatively to a wound.) **145 plantation** colonization (with subsequent wordplay on the literal meaning) **146 docks, mallows** (Various weeds.) **149 by contraries** by what is directly opposite to usual custom **150 traffic** trade **152 Letters** learning **153 use of service** custom of employing servants. **succession** holding of property by right of inheritance **154 Bourn** boundaries. **bound of land** landmarks. **tilth** tillage of soil **155 corn** grain **163 engine** instrument of warfare **165 it** its. **foison** plenty **170 Save** God save

ANTONIO
Long live Gonzalo!
GONZALO And—do you mark me, sir?
ALONSO
Prithee, no more. Thou dost talk nothing to me.
GONZALO I do well believe your Highness, and did it to minister occasion to these gentlemen, who are of such sensible and nimble lungs that they always use to laugh at nothing.
ANTONIO 'Twas you we laugh'd at.
GONZALO Who in this kind of merry fooling am nothing to you; so you may continue and laugh at nothing still.
ANTONIO What a blow was there given!
SEBASTIAN An it had not fall'n flat-long.
GONZALO You are gentlemen of brave mettle; you would lift the moon out of her sphere, if she would continue in it five weeks without changing.

Enter Ariel [invisible] playing solemn music.

SEBASTIAN We would so, and then go a-batfowling.
ANTONIO Nay, good my lord, be not angry.
GONZALO No, I warrant, you, I will not adventure my discretion so weakly. Will you laugh me asleep? For I am very heavy.
ANTONIO Go sleep, and hear us.
[All sleep except Alonso, Sebastian, and Antonio.]
ALONSO
What, all so soon asleep? I wish mine eyes
Would, with themselves, shut up my thoughts. I find
They are inclin'd to do so.
SEBASTIAN Please you, sir,
Do not omit the heavy offer of it.
It seldom visits sorrow; when it doth,
It is a comforter.
ANTONIO We two, my lord,
Will guard your person while you take your rest,
And watch your safety.
ALONSO Thank you. Wondrous heavy.
[Alonso sleeps. Exit Ariel.]
SEBASTIAN
What a strange drowsiness possesses them!
ANTONIO
It is the quality o' th' climate.
SEBASTIAN Why
Doth it not then our eyelids sink? I find not
Myself dispos'd to sleep.
ANTONIO Nor I; my spirits are nimble.
They fell together all, as by consent;
They dropp'd, as by a thunder-stroke. What might,
Worthy Sebastian? O, what might—? No more—
And yet methinks I see it in thy face,
What thou shouldst be. Th' occasion speaks thee, and
My strong imagination sees a crown
Dropping upon thy head.
SEBASTIAN What, art thou waking?
ANTONIO
Do you not hear me speak?
SEBASTIAN I do; and surely
It is a sleepy language and thou speak'st
Out of thy sleep. What is it thou didst say?
This is a strange repose, to be asleep
With eyes wide open—standing, speaking, moving—
And yet so fast asleep.
ANTONIO Noble Sebastian,
Thou let'st thy fortune sleep—die, rather; wink'st
Whiles thou art waking.
SEBASTIAN Thou dost snore distinctly;
There's meaning in thy snores.
ANTONIO
I am more serious than my custom. You
Must be so too, if heed me; which to do
Trebles thee o'er.
SEBASTIAN Well, I am standing water.
ANTONIO
I'll teach you how to flow.
SEBASTIAN Do so. To ebb
Hereditary sloth instructs me.
ANTONIO O,
If you but knew how you the purpose cherish
Whiles thus you mock it! How, in stripping it,
You more invest it! Ebbing men, indeed,
Most often do so near the bottom run
By their own fear or sloth.
SEBASTIAN Prithee say on.
The setting of thine eye and cheek proclaim
A matter from thee, and a birth indeed
Which throes thee much to yield.
ANTONIO Thus, sir:
Although this lord of weak remembrance, this,
Who shall be of as little memory
When he is earth'd, hath here almost persuaded—
For he's a spirit of persuasion, only
Professes to persuade—the King his son's alive,
'Tis as impossible that he's undrown'd
As he that sleeps here swims.
SEBASTIAN I have no hope
That he's undrown'd.
ANTONIO O, out of that "no hope"
What great hope have you! No hope that way is
Another way so high a hope that even

174 minister occasion furnish opportunity **175 sensible** sensitive **182 An** if. **flat-long** with the flat of the sword, i.e., ineffectually. (Cf. *fallen flat.*) **186 a-batfowling** hunting birds at night with lantern and stick; also, gulling a simpleton. (Gonzalo is the simpleton, or fowl, and Sebastian will use the moon as his lantern.) **188–189 adventure . . . weakly** risk my reputation for discretion for so trivial a cause (by getting angry at these sarcastic fellows) **190 heavy** sleepy **191 Go . . . us** let our laughing send you to sleep, or, go to sleep and hear us laugh at you **195 omit** neglect. **heavy** drowsy

208 speaks calls upon; or, pronounces, proclaims (Sebastian as usurper of Alonso's crown) **217 wink'st** shut your eyes **222 Trebles thee o'er** makes you three times as great and rich. **standing water** water which neither ebbs nor flows, at a standstill, indecisive **224 Hereditary sloth** natural laziness **225 purpose** i.e., of being king. **cherish** i.e., make dear, enrich **227 invest** clothe. (Antonio's paradox is that by sceptically stripping away illusions Sebastian can see the essence of a situation and the opportunity it presents, or that by disclaiming and deriding his purpose Sebastian shows how he values it.) **228 the bottom** i.e., on which unadventurous men may go aground and miss the tide of fortune **230 setting** set expression (of earnestness) **231 matter** matter of importance **232 throes** causes pain, as in giving birth **233 this lord** i.e., Gonzalo. **remembrance** (1) power of remembering (2) being remembered after his death **235 earth'd** buried **236–237 only . . . persuade** i.e., whose whole function (as a privy councilor) is to persuade **241 that way** i.e., in regard to Ferdinand's being saved

Ambition cannot pierce a wink beyond,
But doubt discovery there. Will you grant with me
That Ferdinand is drown'd?

SEBASTIAN He's gone.

ANTONIO Then, tell me,
Who's the next heir of Naples?

SEBASTIAN Claribel.

ANTONIO
She that is Queen of Tunis; she that dwells
Ten leagues beyond man's life; she that from Naples
Can have no note, unless the sun were post—
The man i' th' moon's too slow—till new-born chins
Be rough and razorable; she that from whom
We all were sea-swallow'd, though some cast again,
And by that destiny to perform an act
Whereof what's past is prologue, what to come
In yours and my discharge.

SEBASTIAN
What stuff is this? How say you?
'Tis true, my brother's daughter's Queen of Tunis;
So is she heir of Naples; 'twixt which regions
There is some space.

ANTONIO A space whose ev'ry cubit
Seems to cry out, "How shall that Claribel
Measure us back to Naples? Keep in Tunis,
And let Sebastian wake." Say this were death
That now hath seiz'd them; why, they were no worse
Than now they are. There be that can rule Naples
As well as he that sleeps; lords that can prate
As amply and unnecessarily
As this Gonzalo; I myself could make
A chough of as deep chat. O, that you bore
The mind that I do! What a sleep were this
For your advancement! Do you understand me?

SEBASTIAN
Methinks I do.

ANTONIO And how does your content
Tender your own good fortune?

SEBASTIAN I remember
You did supplant your brother Prospero.

ANTONIO True.
And look how well my garments sit upon me,
Much feater than before. My brother's servants
Were then my fellows; now they are my men.

SEBASTIAN
But, for your conscience?

ANTONIO
Ay, sir, where lies that? If 'twere a kibe,
'Twould put me to my slipper; but I feel not
This deity in my bosom. Twenty consciences,
That stand 'twixt me and Milan, candied be they

243–244 Ambition . . . there ambition itself cannot see any further than that hope (of the crown), but is unsure of itself in seeing even so far, is dazzled by daring to think so high **248 Ten . . . life** i.e., it would take more than a lifetime to get there **249 note** news, intimation. **post** messenger **251 from** on our voyage from **252 cast** were disgorged (with a pun on *casting* of parts for a play) **255 discharge** performance **261 Measure us** i.e., traverse the cubits, find her way **262 wake** i.e., to his good fortune **267–268 I . . . chat** I could teach a jackdaw to talk as wisely, or, be such a garrulous talker myself **271 content** desire, inclination **272 Tender** regard, look after **275 feater** more becomingly, fittingly **278 kibe** chilblain, sore on the heel **279 put me to** oblige me to wear **281 Milan** the dukedom of Milan. **candied** frozen, congealed in crystalline form

And melt ere they molest! Here lies your brother,
No better than the earth he lies upon,
If he were that which now he's like—that's dead,
Whom I, with this obedient steel, three inches of it,
Can lay to bed forever; whiles you, doing thus,
To the perpetual wink for aye might put
This ancient morsel, this Sir Prudence, who
Should not upbraid our course. For all the rest,
They'll take suggestion as a cat laps milk;
They'll tell the clock to any business that
We say befits the hour.

SEBASTIAN Thy case, dear friend,
Shall be my precedent. As thou got'st Milan,
I'll come by Naples. Draw thy sword. One stroke
Shall free thee from the tribute which thou payest,
And I the king shall love thee.

ANTONIO Draw together;
And when I rear my hand, do you the like,
To fall it on Gonzalo. [*They draw.*]

SEBASTIAN O, but one word.
[*They talk apart.*]

Enter Ariel [*invisible*], *with music and song.*

ARIEL
My master through his art foresees the danger
That you, his friend, are in, and sends me forth—
For else his project dies—to keep them living.
Sings in Gonzalo's ear.

While you here do snoring lie,
Open-ey'd conspiracy
His time doth take.
If of life you keep a care,
Shake off slumber, and beware.
Awake, awake!

ANTONIO
Then let us both be sudden.

GONZALO [*Waking*]
Now, good angels preserve the King!
[*The others wake.*]

ALONSO
Why, how now, ho, awake? Why are you drawn?
Wherefore this ghastly looking?

GONZALO What's the matter?

SEBASTIAN
Whiles we stood here securing your repose,
Even now, we heard a hollow burst of bellowing
Like bulls, or rather lions. Did 't not wake you?
It struck mine ear most terribly.

ALONSO I heard nothing.

ANTONIO
O, 'twas a din to fright a monster's ear,
To make an earthquake! Sure it was the roar
Of a whole herd of lions.

ALONSO
Heard you this, Gonzalo?

287 wink sleep, closing of eyes **291 tell the clock** i.e., answer appropriately, chime **295 tribute** (See I.ii.113–124) **304 time** opportunity **312 securing** standing guard over

GONZALO
Upon mine honor, sir, I heard a humming,
And that a strange one too, which did awake me.
I shak'd you, sir, and cried. As mine eyes open'd,
I saw their weapons drawn. There was a noise,
That's verily. 'Tis best we stand upon our guard,
Or that we quit this place. Let's draw our weapons.

ALONSO
Lead off this ground, and let's make further search
For my poor son.

GONZALO Heavens keep him from these beasts!
For he is, sure, i' th' island.

ALONSO Lead away.

ARIEL [*Aside*]
Prospero my lord shall know what I have done.
So, King, go safely on to seek thy son.
Exeunt [*severally*].

SCENE II

Enter Caliban with a burden of wood. A noise of thunder heard.

CALIBAN
All the infections that the sun sucks up
From bogs, fens, flats, on Prosper fall and make him
By inch-meal a disease! His spirits hear me, 3
And yet I needs must curse. But they'll nor pinch, 4
Fright me with urchin-shows, pitch me i' th' mire, 5
Nor lead me, like a firebrand, in the dark 6
Out of my way, unless he bid 'em; but
For every trifle are they set upon me;
Sometime like apes that mow and chatter at me 9
And after bite me, then like hedgehogs which
Lie tumbling in my barefoot way and mount
Their pricks at my footfall; sometime am I
All wound with adders who with cloven tongues
Do hiss me into madness.

Enter Trinculo.

Lo, now, lo!
Here comes a spirit of his, and to torment me
For bringing wood in slowly. I'll fall flat;
Perchance he will not mind me. [*Lies down.*] 17

TRINCULO Here's neither bush nor shrub, to bear off 18
any weather at all, and another storm brewing; I hear
it sing i' th' wind. Yond same black cloud, yond huge
one, looks like a foul bombard that would shed his 21
liquor. If it should thunder as it did before, I know not
where to hide my head. Yond same cloud cannot
choose but fall by pailfuls. [*Sees Caliban.*] What have
we here? A man or a fish? Dead or alive? A fish, he
smells like a fish; a very ancient and fish-like smell; a
kind of not of the newest Poor-John. A strange fish! 27
Were I in England now, as once I was, and had but
this fish painted, not a holiday fool there but would 29
give a piece of silver. There would this monster make 30
a man; any strange beast there makes a man. When 31
they will not give a doit to relieve a lame beggar, they 32
will lay out ten to see a dead Indian. Legg'd like a
man! And his fins like arms! Warm, o' my troth! I do
now let loose my opinion, hold it no longer: this is no
fish, but an islander, that hath lately suffer'd by a
thunderbolt. [*Thunder.*] Alas, the storm is come again!
My best way is to creep under his gaberdine; there is 38
no other shelter hereabout. Misery acquaints a man
with strange bedfellows. I will here shroud till the 40
dregs of the storm be past. 41
[*Creeps under Caliban's garment.*]

Enter Stephano, singing, [*a bottle in his hand*].

STEPHANO
"I shall no more to sea, to sea,
Here shall I die ashore—"
This is a very scurvy tune to sing at a man's funeral.
Well, here's my comfort. *Drinks.*
(Sings.)
"The master, the swabber, the boatswain and I,
The gunner and his mate
Lov'd Mall, Meg, and Marian, and Margery,
But none of us car'd for Kate;
For she had a tongue with a tang,
Would cry to a sailor, 'Go hang!'
She lov'd not the savor of tar nor of pitch,
Yet a tailor might scratch her where'er she did itch.
Then to sea, boys, and let her go hang!"
This is a scurvy tune too; but here's my comfort.
Drinks.

CALIBAN Do not torment me! Oh!

STEPHANO What's the matter? Have we devils here? Do
you put tricks upon 's with savages and men of Ind, 58
ha? I have not scap'd drowning to be afeard now of
your four legs; for it hath been said, "As proper a man 60
as ever went on four legs cannot make him give 61
ground"; and it shall be said so again while Stephano
breathes at' nostrils. 63

CALIBAN This spirit torments me! Oh!

STEPHANO This is some monster of the isle with four
legs, who hath got, as I take it, an ague. Where the
devil should he learn our language? I will give him
some relief, if it be but for that. If I can recover him 68
and keep him tame and get to Naples with him, he's
a present for any emperor that ever trod on neat's- 70
leather. 71

CALIBAN Do not torment me, prithee. I'll bring my wood home faster.

II.ii. Location: Another part of the island.
3 By inch-meal inch by inch **4 nor** neither **5 urchin-shows** apparitions shaped like hedgehogs **6 like a firebrand** in the guise of a will-o'-the-wisp **9 mow** make faces **17 mind** notice **18 bear off** keep off **21 foul bombard** dirty leathern bottle. **his** its

27 Poor-John salted hake, type of poor fare **29 painted** i.e., painted on a sign set up outside a booth or tent at a fair **30–31 make a man** make one's fortune **32 doit** small coin **38 gaberdine** cloak, loose upper garment **40 shroud** take shelter **41 dregs** i.e., last remains **58 Ind** India **60 proper** handsome **61 four legs** (The conventional phrase would supply *two legs.*) **63 at'** at the **68 for that** i.e., for knowing our language. **recover** restore **70–71 neat's-leather** cowhide

STEPHANO He's in his fit now and does not talk after the wisest. He shall taste of my bottle; if he have never drunk wine afore, it will go near to remove his fit. If I can recover him and keep him tame, I will not take too much for him; he shall pay for him that hath him, and that soundly.

CALIBAN
Thou dost me yet but little hurt;
Thou wilt anon, I know it by thy trembling.
Now Prosper works upon thee.

STEPHANO Come on your ways; open your mouth; here is that which will give language to you, cat. Open your mouth; this will shake your shaking, I can tell you, and that soundly. [*Gives Caliban drink.*] You cannot tell who's your friend. Open your chaps again.

TRINCULO I should know that voice. It should be—but he is drown'd; and these are devils. O defend me!

STEPHANO Four legs and two voices; a most delicate monster! His forward voice now is to speak well of his friend; his backward voice is to utter foul speeches and to detract. If all the wine in my bottle will recover him, I will help his ague. Come. [*Gives drink.*] Amen! I will pour some in thy other mouth.

TRINCULO Stephano!

STEPHANO Doth thy other mouth call me? Mercy, mercy! This is a devil, and no monster. I will leave him; I have no long spoon.

TRINCULO Stephano! If thou beest Stephano, touch me and speak to me; for I am Trinculo—be not afeard—thy good friend Trinculo.

STEPHANO If thou beest Trinculo, come forth. I'll pull thee by the lesser legs. If any be Trinculo's legs, these are they. [*Pulls him out.*] Thou art very Trinculo indeed! How cam'st thou to be the siege of this mooncalf? Can he vent Trinculos?

TRINCULO I took him to be kill'd with a thunder-stroke. But art thou not drown'd, Stephano? I hope now thou art not drown'd. Is the storm overblown? I hid me under the dead moon-calf's gaberdine for fear of the storm. And art thou living, Stephano? O Stephano, two Neapolitans scap'd!

STEPHANO Prithee, do not turn me about; my stomach is not constant.

CALIBAN
These be fine things, an if they be not sprites.
That's a brave god and bears celestial liquor.
I will kneel to him.

STEPHANO How didst thou scape? How cam'st thou hither? Swear by this bottle how thou cam'st hither. I escap'd upon a butt of sack which the sailors heav'd o'erboard—by this bottle, which I made of the bark of a tree with mine own hands since I was cast ashore.

CALIBAN [*Kneeling*] I'll swear upon that bottle to be thy true subject, for the liquor is not earthly.

STEPHANO Here; swear then how thou escap'dst.

TRINCULO Swum ashore, man, like a duck. I can swim like a duck, I'll be sworn.

STEPHANO Here, kiss the book. Though thou canst swim like a duck, thou art made like a goose. [*Gives drink.*]

TRINCULO O Stephano, hast any more of this?

STEPHANO The whole butt, man. My cellar is in a rock by the sea-side where my wine is hid. How now, moon-calf? How does thine ague?

CALIBAN
Hast thou not dropp'd from heaven?

STEPHANO Out o' th' moon, I do assure thee. I was the man i' th' moon when time was.

CALIBAN
I have seen thee in her and I do adore thee.
My mistress show'd me thee and thy dog and thy
bush.

STEPHANO Come, swear to that; kiss the book. I will furnish it anon with new contents. Swear. [*Gives drink.*]

TRINCULO By this good light, this is a very shallow monster! I afeard of him? A very weak monster! The man i' th' moon? A most poor credulous monster! Well drawn, monster, in good sooth!

CALIBAN
I'll show thee every fertile inch o' th' island;
And I will kiss thy foot. I prithee, be my god.

TRINCULO By this light, a most perfidious and drunken monster! When 's god's asleep, he'll rob his bottle.

CALIBAN
I'll kiss thy foot. I'll swear myself thy subject.

STEPHANO Come on then; down, and swear. [*Caliban kneels.*]

TRINCULO I shall laugh myself to death at this puppy-headed monster. A most scurvy monster! I could find in my heart to beat him—

STEPHANO Come, kiss.

TRINCULO But that the poor monster's in drink. An abominable monster!

CALIBAN
I'll show thee the best springs; I'll pluck thee berries;
I'll fish for thee and get thee wood enough.
A plague upon the tyrant that I serve!
I'll bear him no more sticks, but follow thee,
Thou wondrous man.

TRINCULO A most ridiculous monster, to make a wonder of a poor drunkard!

CALIBAN
I prithee, let me bring thee where crabs grow;
And I with my long nails will dig thee pig-nuts,
Show thee a jay's nest, and instruct thee how
To snare the nimble marmoset. I'll bring thee
To clust'ring filberts, and sometimes I'll get thee
Young scamels from the rock. Wilt thou go with me?

77–78 I will . . . much i.e., no sum can be too much **78 hath** possesses, receives **84–85 cat . . . mouth** (Allusion to the proverb, "Good liquor will make a cat speak.") **87 chaps** jaws **99 long spoon** (Allusion to the proverb, "He that sups with the devil has need of a long spoon.") **106 siege** excrement **106–107 moon-calf** monster, abortion. (Supposed to be caused by the influence of the moon.) **107 vent** emit **115 not constant** unsteady **116 an if** if **117 brave** fine, magnificent **121 butt of sack** barrel of Canary wine

129 book i.e., bottle **137 when time was** once upon a time **138–139 dog . . . bush** (The man in the moon was popularly imagined to have with him a dog and a bush of thorn.) **142 By . . . light** by God's light, by this good light from heaven **144–145 Well drawn** well pulled (on the bottle) **165 crabs** crab apples **166 pig-nuts** peanuts **168 marmoset** small monkey **170 scamels** (Possibly "seamews," mentioned in Strachey's letter, or shellfish; or perhaps from *squamelle,* furnished with little scales. (Contemporary French and Italian travel accounts report that the natives of Patagonia in South American ate small fish described as *fort scameux* and *squame.*)

STEPHANO I prithee now, lead the way without any more talking. Trinculo, the King and all our company else being drown'd, we will inherit here. Here! Bear 173
my bottle. Fellow Trinculo, we'll fill him by and by again.

CALIBAN *(Sings drunkenly)*
Farewell, master; farewell, farewell!

TRINCULO A howling monster; a drunken monster!

CALIBAN
No more dams I'll make for fish,
Nor fetch in firing
At requiring,
Nor scrape trenchering, nor wash dish. 181
'Ban, 'Ban, Ca–Caliban
Has a new master, get a new man.
Freedom, high-day! High-day, freedom! Freedom, 184
high-day, freedom!

STEPHANO O brave monster! Lead the way. *Exeunt.*

ACT III • SCENE I

Enter Ferdinand, bearing a log.

FERDINAND
There be some sports are painful, and their labor
Delight in them sets off; some kinds of baseness 2
Are nobly undergone; and most poor matters
Point to rich ends. This my mean task
Would be as heavy to me as odious, but
The mistress which I serve quickens what's dead 6
And makes my labors pleasures. O, she is
Ten times more gentle than her father's crabbed,
And he's compos'd of harshness. I must remove
Some thousands of these logs and pile them up,
Upon a sore injunction. My sweet mistress 11
Weeps when she sees me work, and says such baseness
Had never like executor. I forget;
But these sweet thoughts do even refresh my labors,
Most busy lest, when I do it.

Enter Miranda; and Prospero [at a distance, unseen].

MIRANDA Alas, now, pray you, 15
Work not so hard. I would the lightning had
Burnt up those logs that you are enjoin'd to pile!
Pray, set it down and rest you. When this burns,
'Twill weep for having wearied you. My father
Is hard at study; pray now, rest yourself. 20
He's safe for these three hours.

FERDINAND O most dear mistress,
The sun will set before I shall discharge
What I must strive to do.

MIRANDA If you'll sit down,
I'll bear your logs the while. Pray give me that.
I'll carry it to the pile.

FERDINAND No, precious creature,
I had rather crack my sinews, break my back,
Than you should such dishonor undergo
While I sit lazy by.

MIRANDA It would become me
As well as it does you; and I should do it
With much more ease, for my good will is to it,
And yours it is against.

PROSPERO [*Aside*] Poor worm, thou art infected!
This visitation shows it.

MIRANDA You look wearily. 32

FERDINAND
No, noble mistress, 'tis fresh morning with me
When you are by at night. I do beseech you—
Chiefly that I might set it in my prayers—
What is your name?

MIRANDA Miranda.—O my father,
I have broke your hest to say so.

FERDINAND Admir'd Miranda! 37
Indeed the top of admiration! Worth
What's dearest to the world! Full many a lady
I have ey'd with best regard, and many a time
Th' harmony of their tongues hath into bondage
Brought my too diligent ear. For several virtues
Have I lik'd several women, never any
With so full soul but some defect in her
Did quarrel with the noblest grace she ow'd 45
And put it to the foil. But you, O you, 46
So perfect and so peerless, are created
Of every creature's best!

MIRANDA I do not know
One of my sex; no woman's face remember,
Save, from my glass, mine own. Nor have I seen
More that I may call men than you, good friend,
And my dear father. How features are abroad,
I am skilless of; but, by my modesty, 53
The jewel in my dower, I would not wish
Any companion in the world but you,
Nor can imagination form a shape,
Besides yourself, to like of. But I prattle
Something too wildly, and my father's precepts
I therein do forget.

FERDINAND I am in my condition
A prince, Miranda; I do think, a king—
I would, not so!—and would no more endure
This wooden slavery than to suffer
The flesh-fly blow my mouth. Hear my soul speak: 63
The very instant that I saw you, did
My heart fly to your service; there resides,
To make me slave to it; and for your sake
Am I this patient log-man.

MIRANDA Do you love me?

FERDINAND
O heaven, O earth, bear witness to this sound,

173 inherit take possession **181 trenchering** trenchers, wooden plates **184 high-day** holiday (?)

III.i. Location: Before Prospero's cell.
2 sets off makes seem greater by contrast **6 quickens** gives life to **11 sore injunction** severe command **15 Most . . . it** i.e., least troubled by my labor when I think of her (?). (The line may be in need of emendation.)

32 visitation (1) visit (2) visitation of the plague, i.e., infection of love **37 hest** command **45 ow'd** owned **46 put . . . foil** (1) overthrew it (as in wrestling) (2) served as a "foil" or contrast to set it off **53 skilless** ignorant **63 blow** befoul with fly-eggs

And crown what I profess with kind event
If I speak true! If hollowly, invert
What best is boded me to mischief! I
Beyond all limit of what else i' th' world
Do love, prize, honor you.

MIRANDA [*Weeping*] I am a fool
To weep at what I am glad of.

PROSPERO [*Aside*] Fair encounter
Of two most rare affections! Heavens rain grace
On that which breeds between 'em!

FERDINAND Wherefore weep you?

MIRANDA
At mine unworthiness, that dare not offer
What I desire to give, and much less take
What I shall die to want. But this is trifling,
And all the more it seeks to hide itself
The bigger bulk it shows. Hence, bashful cunning,
And prompt me, plain and holy innocence!
I am your wife, if you will marry me;
If not, I'll die your maid. To be your fellow
You may deny me, but I'll be your servant,
Whether you will or no.

FERDINAND My mistress, dearest,
And I thus humble ever.

MIRANDA
My husband, then?

FERDINAND Ay, with a heart as willing
As bondage e'er of freedom. Here's my hand.

MIRANDA
And mine, with my heart in 't. And now farewell
Till half an hour hence.

FERDINAND A thousand thousand!

Exeunt [*Ferdinand and Miranda severally*].

PROSPERO
So glad of this as they I cannot be,
Who are surpris'd with all; but my rejoicing
At nothing can be more. I'll to my book,
For yet ere supper-time must I perform
Much business appertaining. *Exit.*

SCENE II

Enter Caliban, Stephano, and Trinculo.

STEPHANO Tell not me. When the butt is out, we will drink water, not a drop before. Therefore bear up, and board 'em. Servant-monster, drink to me.

TRINCULO Servant-monster? The folly of this island! They say there's but five upon this isle; we are three of them. If th' other two be brain'd like us, the state totters.

STEPHANO Drink, servant-monster, when I bid thee. Thy eyes are almost set in thy head. [*Gives drink.*]

TRINCULO Where should they be set else? He were a brave monster indeed if they were set in his tail.

STEPHANO My man-monster hath drown'd his tongue in sack. For my part, the sea cannot drown me; I swam, ere I could recover the shore, five and thirty leagues off and on. By this light, thou shalt be my lieutenant, monster, or my standard.

TRINCULO Your lieutenant, if you list; he's no standard.

STEPHANO We'll not run, Monsieur Monster.

TRINCULO Nor go neither, but you'll lie like dogs and yet say nothing neither.

STEPHANO Moon-calf, speak once in thy life, if thou beest a good moon-calf.

CALIBAN
How does thy honor? Let me lick thy shoe.
I'll not serve him; he is not valiant.

TRINCULO Thou liest, most ignorant monster, I am in case to justle a constable. Why, thou debosh'd fish thou, was there ever man a coward that hath drunk so much sack as I today? Wilt thou tell a monstrous lie, being but half a fish and half a monster?

CALIBAN
Lo, how he mocks me! Wilt thou let him, my lord?

TRINCULO "Lord," quoth he? That a monster should be such a natural!

CALIBAN
Lo, lo, again! Bite him to death, I prithee.

STEPHANO Trinculo, keep a good tongue in your head. If you prove a mutineer—the next tree! The poor monster's my subject and he shall not suffer indignity.

CALIBAN
I thank my noble lord. Wilt thou be pleas'd
To hearken once again to the suit I made to thee?

STEPHANO Marry, will I. Kneel and repeat it; I will stand, and so shall Trinculo. [*Caliban kneels.*]

Enter Ariel, invisible.

CALIBAN
As I told thee before, I am subject to a tyrant,
A sorcerer, that by his cunning hath
Cheated me of the island.

ARIEL
Thou liest.

CALIBAN Thou liest, thou jesting monkey, thou!
I would my valiant master would destroy thee.
I do not lie.

STEPHANO Trinculo, if you trouble him any more in 's tale, by this hand, I will supplant some of your teeth.

TRINCULO Why, I said nothing.

STEPHANO Mum, then, and no more.—Proceed.

CALIBAN
I say, by sorcery he got this isle;
From me he got it. If thy greatness will
Revenge it on him—for I know thou dar'st,

69 kind event favorable outcome **70 hollowly** insincerely, falsely **71 boded** destined for **79 want** lack **84 fellow** mate, equal

III.ii. Location: Another part of the island.
1 out empty **2–3 bear . . . 'em** (Stephano uses the terminology of maneuvering at sea and boarding a vessel under attack as a way of urging an assault on the liquor supply.) **9 set** fixed in a drunken stare; or sunk, like the sun

11 brave fine, splendid **14 recover** arrive at **16 standard** standard-bearer, ancient, i.e., ensign (as distinguished from *lieutenant,* l. 17) **17 list** prefer. **no standard** i.e., not able to stand up **18 run** (1) retreat (2) urinate (taking Trinculo's *standard,* l. 17, in the old sense of *conduit*) **19 go** walk. **lie** (1) tell lies (2) lie prostrate (3) excrete **26 case . . . constable** i.e., in fit condition, made valiant by drink, to taunt or challenge the police. **debosh'd** debauched **32 natural** (1) idiot (2) natural as opposed to unnatural, monster-like **35 the next tree** i.e., you'll hang **39 Marry** i.e., indeed. (Originally an oath by the Virgin Mary.)

But this thing dare not—
STEPHANO That's most certain.
CALIBAN
Thou shalt be lord of it, and I'll serve thee.
STEPHANO How now shall this be compass'd? Canst thou bring me to the party?
CALIBAN
Yea, yea, my lord. I'll yield him thee asleep,
Where thou mayst knock a nail into his head.
ARIEL
Thou liest; thou canst not.
CALIBAN
What a pied ninny's this! Thou scurvy patch!
I do beseech thy greatness, give him blows
And take his bottle from him. When that's gone
He shall drink nought but brine, for I'll not show him
Where the quick freshes are.
STEPHANO Trinculo, run into no further danger. Interrupt the monster one word further, and, by this hand, I'll turn my mercy out o' doors and make a stock-fish of thee.
TRINCULO Why, what did I? I did nothing. I'll go farther off.
STEPHANO Didst thou not say he lied?
ARIEL
Thou liest.
STEPHANO Do I so? Take thou that. [*Beats Trinculo.*] As you like this, give me the lie another time.
TRINCULO I did not give the lie. Out o' your wits and hearing too? A pox o' your bottle! This can sack and drinking do. A murrain on your monster, and the devil take your fingers!
CALIBAN Ha, ha, ha!
STEPHANO Now, forward with your tale. [*To Trinculo.*] Prithee, stand further off.
CALIBAN
Beat him enough. After a little time
I'll beat him too.
STEPHANO Stand farther.—Come, proceed.
CALIBAN
Why, as I told thee, 'tis a custom with him
I' th' afternoon to sleep. There thou mayst brain him,
Having first seiz'd his books, or with a log
Batter his skull, or paunch him with a stake,
Or cut his wezand with thy knife. Remember
First to possess his books; for without them
He's but a sot, as I am, nor hath not
One spirit to command. They all do hate him
As rootedly as I. Burn but his books.
He has brave utensils—for so he calls them—
Which, when he has a house, he'll deck withal.
And that most deeply to consider is
The beauty of his daughter. He himself
Calls her a nonpareil. I never saw a woman,
But only Sycorax my dam and she;
But she as far surpasseth Sycorax
As great'st does least.
STEPHANO Is it so brave a lass?
CALIBAN
Ay, lord; she will become thy bed, I warrant,
And bring thee forth brave brood.
STEPHANO Monster, I will kill this man. His daughter and I will be king and queen—save our Graces!—and Trinculo and thyself shall be viceroys. Dost thou like the plot, Trinculo?
TRINCULO Excellent.
STEPHANO Give me thy hand. I am sorry I beat thee; but, while thou liv'st, keep a good tongue in thy head.
CALIBAN
Within this half hour will he be asleep.
Wilt thou destroy him then?
STEPHANO Ay, on mine honor.
ARIEL [*Aside*]
This will I tell my master.
CALIBAN
Thou mak'st me merry; I am full of pleasure.
Let us be jocund. Will you troll the catch
You taught me but while-ere?
STEPHANO At thy request, monster, I will do reason, any reason. Come on, Trinculo, let us sing. *Sings.*
"Flout 'em and scout 'em
And scout 'em and flout 'em!
Thought is free."
CALIBAN
That's not the tune.
Ariel plays the tune on a tabor and pipe.
STEPHANO What is this same?
TRINCULO This is the tune of our catch, play'd by the picture of Nobody.
STEPHANO If thou beest a man, show thyself in thy likeness. If thou beest a devil, take 't as thou list.
TRINCULO O, forgive me my sins!
STEPHANO He that dies pays all debts. I defy thee. Mercy upon us!
CALIBAN
Art thou afeard?
STEPHANO No, monster, not I.
CALIBAN
Be not afeard. The isle is full of noises,
Sounds and sweet airs, that give delight and hurt not.
Sometimes a thousand twangling instruments
Will hum about mine ears, and sometime voices
That, if I then had wak'd after long sleep,
Will make me sleep again; and then, in dreaming,
The clouds methought would open and show riches
Ready to drop upon me, that, when I wak'd,
I cried to dream again.
STEPHANO This will prove a brave kingdom to me, where I shall have my music for nothing.
CALIBAN
When Prospero is destroy'd.

54 this thing i.e., Trinculo **62 pied ninny** fool in motley. **patch** fool **66 quick freshes** running springs **69 stock-fish** dried cod beaten before cooking **76 give me the lie** call me a liar to my face **79 murrain** plague. (Literally, a cattle disease.) **90 paunch** stab in the belly **91 wezand** windpipe **93 sot** fool **96 brave utensils** fine furnishings

119 troll the catch sing the round **120 while-ere** a short time ago **123 scout** deride **126 s.d. tabor** small drum **129 picture of Nobody** (Refers to a familiar figure with head, arms, and legs, but no trunk.) **131 take 't . . . list** i.e., take my defiance as you please, as best you can

STEPHANO That shall be by and by. I remember the story.

TRINCULO The sound is going away. Let's follow it, and after do our work.

STEPHANO Lead, monster; we'll follow. I would I could see this taborer; he lays it on.

TRINCULO Wilt come? I'll follow, Stephano.

Exeunt [following Ariel's music].

SCENE III

Enter Alonso, Sebastian, Antonio, Gonzalo, Adrian, Francisco, etc.

GONZALO
By 'r lakin, I can go no further, sir;
My old bones aches. Here's a maze trod indeed
Through forth-rights and meanders! By your patience,
I needs must rest me.

ALONSO Old lord, I cannot blame thee,
Who am myself attach'd with weariness,
To th' dulling of my spirits. Sit down, and rest.
Even here I will put off my hope and keep it
No longer for my flatterer. He is drown'd
Whom thus we stray to find, and the sea mocks
Our frustrate search on land. Well, let him go.
[Alonso and Gonzalo sit.]

ANTONIO [*Aside to Sebastian*]
I am right glad that he's so out of hope.
Do not, for one repulse, forego the purpose
That you resolv'd t' effect.

SEBASTIAN [*To Antonio*] The next advantage
Will we take throughly.

ANTONIO [*To Sebastian*] Let it be tonight,
For, now they are oppress'd with travail, they
Will not, nor cannot, use such vigilance
As when they are fresh.

SEBASTIAN [*To Antonio*] I say tonight. No more.
Solemn and strange music; and Prospero on the top, invisible.

ALONSO
What harmony is this? My good friends, hark!

GONZALO
Marvelous sweet music!

Enter several strange Shapes, bringing in a banquet, and dance about it with gentle actions of salutations; and, inviting the King, etc., to eat, they depart.

ALONSO
Give us kind keepers, heavens! What were these?

SEBASTIAN
A living drollery. Now I will believe
That there are unicorns, that in Arabia
There is one tree, the phoenix' throne, one phoenix
At this hour reigning there.

ANTONIO I'll believe both;
And what does else want credit, come to me,
And I'll be sworn 'tis true. Travelers ne'er did lie,
Though fools at home condemn 'em.

GONZALO If in Naples
I should report this now, would they believe me
If I should say I saw such islanders?
For, certes, these are people of the island,
Who, though they are of monstrous shape, yet, note,
Their manners are more gentle, kind, than of
Our human generation you shall find
Many, nay, almost any.

PROSPERO [*Aside*] Honest lord,
Thou hast said well; for some of you there present
Are worse than devils.

ALONSO I cannot too much muse
Such shapes, such gesture, and such sound, expressing,
Although they want the use of tongue, a kind
Of excellent dumb discourse.

PROSPERO [*Aside*] Praise in departing.

FRANCISCO
They vanish'd strangely.

SEBASTIAN No matter, since
They have left their viands behind; for we have stomachs.
Will 't please you taste of what is here?

ALONSO Not I.

GONZALO
Faith, sir, you need not fear. When we were boys,
Who would believe that there were mountaineers
Dew-lapp'd like bulls, whose throats had hanging at 'em
Wallets of flesh? Or that there were such men
Whose heads stood in their breasts? Which now we find
Each putter-out of five for one will bring us
Good warrant of.

ALONSO I will stand to and feed,
Although my last—no matter, since I feel
The best is past. Brother, my lord the Duke,
Stand to and do as we. *[They approach the table.]*

Thunder and lightning. Enter Ariel, like a harpy; claps his wings upon the table; and, with a quaint device, the banquet vanishes.

ARIEL
You are three men of sin, whom Destiny,
That hath to instrument this lower world

III.iii. Location: Another part of the island.
1 By'r lakin by our Ladykin, by our Lady **3 forth-rights and meanders** paths straight and crooked **5 attach'd** seized **12 for** because of **14 throughly** thoroughly **17 s.d. on the top** at some high point of the tiring-house or the theatre **20 kind keepers** guardian angels **21 drollery** puppet show

25 want credit lack credence **30 certes** certainly **36 muse** wonder at **39 Praise in departing** i.e., save your praise until the end of the performance **45 Dew-lapp'd** having a dewlap, or fold of skin hanging from the neck, like cattle **47 in their breasts** (I.e., like the Anthropophagi described in *Othello* I.iii.146.) **48 putter-out . . . one** one who invests money, or gambles on the risks of travel on the condition that, if he returns safely, he is to receive five times the amount deposited; hence, any traveler **49 stand to** fall to; take the risk **52 s.d. harpy** a fabulous monster with a woman's face and vulture's body, supposed to be a minister of divine vengeance. **quaint device** ingenious stage contrivance. **banquet vanishes** i.e., the food vanishes; the table remains until l. 82 **54 to** i.e., as its

And what is in 't, the never-surfeited sea
Hath caus'd to belch up you, and on this island
Where man doth not inhabit—you 'mongst men
Being most unfit to live. I have made you mad;
And even with such-like valor men hang and drown
Their proper selves.

[Alonso, Sebastian, and Antonio draw their swords.]

You fools! I and my fellows
Are ministers of Fate. The elements,
Of whom your swords are temper'd, may as well
Wound the loud winds, or with bemock'd-at stabs
Kill the still-closing waters, as diminish
One dowle that's in my plume. My fellow-ministers
Are like invulnerable. If you could hurt,
Your swords are now too massy for your strengths
And will not be uplifted. But remember—
For that's my business to you—that you three
From Milan did supplant good Prospero;
Expos'd unto the sea, which hath requit it,
Him and his innocent child; for which foul deed
The pow'rs, delaying, not forgetting, have
Incens'd the seas and shores, yea, all the creatures,
Against your peace. Thee of thy son, Alonso,
They have bereft; and do pronounce by me
Ling'ring perdition, worse than any death
Can be at once, shall step by step attend
You and your ways; whose wraths to guard you from—
Which here, in this most desolate isle, else falls
Upon your heads—is nothing but heart's sorrow
And a clear life ensuing.

He vanishes in thunder; then, to soft music, enter the Shapes again, and dance, with mocks and mows, and carrying out the table.

PROSPERO
Bravely the figure of this harpy hast thou
Perform'd, my Ariel; a grace it had devouring.
Of my instruction hast thou nothing bated
In what thou hadst to say. So, with good life
And observation strange, my meaner ministers
Their several kinds have done. My high charms work,
And these mine enemies are all knit up
In their distractions. They now are in my pow'r;
And in these fits I leave them, while I visit
Young Ferdinand, whom they suppose is drown'd,
And his and mine lov'd darling. *[Exit above.]*

GONZALO
I' th' name of something holy, sir, why stand you
In this strange stare?

ALONSO
O, it is monstrous, monstrous!
Methought the billows spoke and told me of it;
The winds did sing it to me, and the thunder,
That deep and dreadful organ-pipe, pronounc'd
The name of Prosper; it did bass my trespass.
Therefore my son i' th' ooze is bedded, and
I'll seek him deeper than e'er plummet sounded
And with him there lie mudded. *Exit.*

SEBASTIAN
But one fiend at a time,
I'll fight their legions o'er.

ANTONIO
I'll be thy second.
Exeunt [Sebastian and Antonio].

GONZALO
All three of them are desperate. Their great guilt,
Like poison given to work a great time after,
Now 'gins to bite the spirits. I do beseech you,
That are of suppler joints, follow them swiftly
And hinder them from what this ecstasy
May now provoke them to.

ADRIAN
Follow, I pray you.
Exeunt omnes.

ACT IV • SCENE I

Enter Prospero, Ferdinand, and Miranda.

PROSPERO
If I have too austerely punish'd you,
Your compensation makes amends, for I
Have given you here a third of mine own life,
Or that for which I live; who once again
I tender to thy hand. All thy vexations
Were but my trials of thy love, and thou
Hast strangely stood the test. Here, afore Heaven,
I ratify this my rich gift. O Ferdinand,
Do not smile at me that I boast her off,
For thou shalt find she will outstrip all praise
And make it halt behind her.

FERDINAND
I do believe it
Against an oracle.

PROSPERO
Then, as my gift and thine own acquisition
Worthily purchas'd, take my daughter. But
If thou dost break her virgin-knot before
All sanctimonious ceremonies may
With full and holy rite be minist'red,
No sweet aspersion shall the heavens let fall
To make this contract grow; but barren hate,
Sour-ey'd disdain, and discord shall bestrew
The union of your bed with weeds so loathly
That you shall hate it both. Therefore take heed,

59 such-like valor i.e., the reckless valor derived from madness **60 proper** own **62 whom** which **64 still-closing** always closing again when parted **65 dowle** soft, fine feather **66 like** likewise, similarly. **If** even if **71 requit** requited, avenged **79 whose** (Refers to the heavenly powers.) **81 is nothing** there is no way **82 clear** unspotted, innocent **82 s.d. mocks and mows** mocking gestures and grimaces **83 Bravely** finely, dashingly **84 a grace . . . devouring** i.e., you gracefully caused the banquet to disappear as if you had consumed it (with puns on *grace* meaning "gracefulness" and "a blessing on the meal," and on *devouring* meaning "a literal eating" and "an all-consuming or ravishing grace") **85 bated** abated, diminished **86 good life** faithful reproduction **87 observation strange** exceptional attention to detail. **meaner** i.e., subordinate to Ariel **88 several kinds** individual parts **94 why** (Gonzalo was not addressed in Ariel's speech to the "three men of sin," l. 53, and is not as they are in a maddened state; see ll. 105–107.)

95 it i.e., my sin **99 bass my trespass** proclaim my trespass like a bass note in music **104 o'er** one after another

IV.i. Location: Before Prospero's cell.
3 a third i.e., Miranda, into whose education Prospero has put a third of his life (?) or who represents a large part of what he cares about, along with his dukedom and his learned study (?) **7 strangely** extraordinarily **9 boast her off** i.e., praise her so **11 halt** limp **12 Against an oracle** i.e., even if an oracle should declare otherwise **16 sanctimonious** sacred **18 aspersion** dew, shower

As Hymen's lamps shall light you.

FERDINAND As I hope
For quiet days, fair issue, and long life,
With such love as 'tis now, the murkiest den,
The most opportune place, the strong'st suggestion
Our worser genius can, shall never melt
Mine honor into lust, to take away
The edge of that day's celebration
When I shall think or Phoebus' steeds are founder'd
Or Night kept chain'd below.

PROSPERO Fairly spoke.
Sit then and talk with her; she is thine own.
[Ferdinand and Miranda sit.]
What, Ariel! My industrious servant, Ariel!

Enter Ariel.

ARIEL
What would my potent master? Here I am.

PROSPERO
Thou and thy meaner fellows your last service
Did worthily perform; and I must use you
In such another trick. Go bring the rabble,
O'er whom I give thee pow'r, here to this place.
Incite them to quick motion, for I must
Bestow upon the eyes of this young couple
Some vanity of mine art. It is my promise,
And they expect it from me.

ARIEL Presently?

PROSPERO
Ay, with a twink.

ARIEL
Before you can say "come" and "go,"
And breathe twice and cry "so, so,"
Each one, tripping on his toe,
Will be here with mop and mow.
Do you love me, master? No?

PROSPERO
Dearly, my delicate Ariel. Do not approach
Till thou dost hear me call.

ARIEL Well, I conceive. *Exit.*

PROSPERO
Look thou be true; do not give dalliance
Too much the rein. The strongest oaths are straw
To th' fire i' th' blood. Be more abstemious,
Or else good night your vow!

FERDINAND I warrant you, sir;
The white cold virgin snow upon my heart
Abates the ardor of my liver.

PROSPERO Well.
Now come, my Ariel! Bring a corollary,
Rather than want a spirit. Appear, and pertly!
No tongue! All eyes! Be silent. *Soft music.*

Enter Iris.

IRIS
Ceres, most bounteous lady, thy rich leas
Of wheat, rye, barley, vetches, oats, and pease;
Thy turfy mountains, where live nibbling sheep,
And flat meads thatch'd with stover, them to keep;
Thy banks with pioned and twilled brims,
Which spongy April at thy hest betrims,
To make cold nymphs chaste crowns; and thy broom-groves,
Whose shadow the dismissed bachelor loves,
Being lass-lorn; thy pole-clipt vineyard;
And thy sea-marge, sterile and rocky-hard,
Where thou thyself dost air—the queen o' th' sky,
Whose wat'ry arch and messenger am I,
Bids thee leave these, and with her sovereign grace,
Juno descends [slowly in her car].
Here on this grass-plot, in this very place,
To come and sport. Her peacocks fly amain.
Approach, rich Ceres, her to entertain.

Enter Ceres.

CERES
Hail, many-color'd messenger, that ne'er
Dost disobey the wife of Jupiter,
Who with thy saffron wings upon my flow'rs
Diffusest honey-drops, refreshing show'rs,
And with each end of thy blue bow dost crown
My bosky acres and my unshrubb'd down,
Rich scarf to my proud earth; why hath thy Queen
Summon'd me hither, to this short-grass'd green?

IRIS
A contract of true love to celebrate,
And some donation freely to estate
On the bless'd lovers.

CERES Tell me, heavenly bow,
If Venus or her son, as thou dost know,
Do now attend the Queen? Since they did plot
The means that dusky Dis my daughter got,
Her and her blind boy's scandal'd company
I have forsworn.

IRIS Of her society
Be not afraid. I met her deity
Cutting the clouds towards Paphos, and her son
Dove-drawn with her. Here thought they to have done
Some wanton charm upon this man and maid,
Whose vows are, that no bed-right shall be paid
Till Hymen's torch be lighted; but in vain;
Mars's hot minion is return'd again;
Her waspish-headed son has broke his arrows,

23 Hymen's (Hymen was the Greek and Roman god of marriage.) **27 worser genius** evil genius, or evil attendant spirit **30 or** either. **founder'd** broken down, made lame. (I.e., Ferdinand will wait impatiently for the bridal night.) **37 rabble** band, i.e., the *meaner fellows* of l. 35 **41 vanity** illusion **47 mop and mow** gestures and grimaces **50 conceive** understand **56 liver** (as the presumed seat of the passions) **57 corollary** surplus, extra supply **58 want** lack. **pertly** briskly **59 s.d. Iris** goddess of the rainbow, and Juno's messenger

60 Ceres goddess of the generative power of nature. **leas** meadows **61 vetches** plants for forage, fodder **63 stover** winter fodder for cattle **64 pioned and twilled** undercut by the swift current and protected by roots and branches woven into a mat (?) **66 broom-groves** clumps of broom, gorse, yellow-flowered shrub **67 dismissed bachelor** rejected male lover **68 pole-clipt** hedged in with poles; or pruned **70 queen o' th' sky** i.e., Juno **71 wat'ry arch** rainbow **72 s.d. Juno descends** i.e., starts her descent from the "heavens" above the stage (?) **74 peacocks** birds sacred to Juno, and used to pull her chariot. **amain** with full speed **75 entertain** receive **81 bosky** wooded. **down** upland **85 estate** bestow **87 son** i.e., Cupid **89 Dis . . . got** (Pluto, or *Dis,* god of the infernal regions, carried off Persephone, daughter of Ceres, to be his bride in Hades.) **90 Her** i.e., Venus. **scandal'd** scandalous **92 her deity** i.e., her highness **93 Paphos** place on the island of Cyprus, sacred to Venus **98 Mars' hot minion** i.e., Venus, the beloved of Mars **99 waspish-headed** fiery, hotheaded, peevish

Swears he will shoot no more, but play with sparrows
And be a boy right out.

[*Juno alights.*]

CERES Highest Queen of state,
Great Juno, comes; I know her by her gait.

JUNO
How does my bounteous sister? Go with me
To bless this twain, that they may prosperous be
And honor'd in their issue. *They sing:*

JUNO
Honor, riches, marriage-blessing,
Long continuance, and increasing,
Hourly joys be still upon you!
Juno sings her blessings on you.

CERES
Earth's increase, foison plenty,
Barns and garners never empty,
Vines with clust'ring bunches growing,
Plants with goodly burden bowing;

Spring come to you at the farthest
In the very end of harvest!
Scarcity and want shall shun you;
Ceres' blessing so is on you.

FERDINAND
This is a most majestic vision, and
Harmonious charmingly. May I be bold
To think these spirits?

PROSPERO Spirits, which by mine art
I have from their confines call'd to enact
My present fancies.

FERDINAND Let me live here ever;
So rare a wond'red father and a wife
Makes this place Paradise.

Juno and Ceres whisper, and send Iris on employment.

PROSPERO Sweet now, silence!
Juno and Ceres whisper seriously;
There's something else to do. Hush and be mute,
Or else our spell is marr'd.

IRIS
You nymphs, call'd Naiads, of the windring brooks,
With your sedg'd crowns and ever-harmless looks,
Leave your crisp channels, and on this green land
Answer your summons; Juno does command.
Come, temperate nymphs, and help to celebrate
A contract of true love; be not too late.

Enter certain Nymphs.

You sunburnt sicklemen, of August weary,
Come hither from the furrow and be merry.
Make holiday; your rye-straw hats put on
And these fresh nymphs encounter every one
In country footing.

Enter certain Reapers, properly habited. They join with the Nymphs in a graceful dance, towards the end whereof Prospero starts suddenly, and speaks; after which, to a strange, hollow, and confused noise, they heavily vanish.

PROSPERO [*Aside*]
I had forgot that foul conspiracy
Of the beast Caliban and his confederates
Against my life. The minute of their plot
Is almost come. [*To the Spirits.*] Well done! Avoid; no more!

FERDINAND
This is strange. Your father's in some passion
That works him strongly.

MIRANDA Never till this day
Saw I him touch'd with anger so distemper'd.

PROSPERO
You do look, my son, in a mov'd sort,
As if you were dismay'd. Be cheerful, sir.
Our revels now are ended. These our actors,
As I foretold you, were all spirits and
Are melted into air, into thin air;
And, like the baseless fabric of this vision,
The cloud-capp'd tow'rs, the gorgeous palaces,
The solemn temples, the great globe itself,
Yea, all which it inherit, shall dissolve
And, like this insubstantial pageant faded,
Leave not a rack behind. We are such stuff
As dreams are made on, and our little life
Is rounded with a sleep. Sir, I am vex'd.
Bear with my weakness; my old brain is troubled.
Be not disturb'd with my infirmity.
If you be pleas'd, retire into my cell
And there repose. A turn or two I'll walk
To still my beating mind.

FERDINAND, MIRANDA We wish your peace.
Exeunt.

PROSPERO
Come with a thought! I thank thee, Ariel. Come.

Enter Ariel.

ARIEL
Thy thoughts I cleave to. What's thy pleasure?

PROSPERO Spirit,
We must prepare to meet with Caliban.

ARIEL
Ay, my commander. When I presented Ceres,
I thought to have told thee of it, but I fear'd
Lest I might anger thee.

PROSPERO
Say again, where didst thou leave these varlets?

ARIEL
I told you, sir, they were red-hot with drinking,
So full of valor that they smote the air
For breathing in their faces; beat the ground
For kissing of their feet; yet always bending

100 sparrows (Supposed lustful, and sacred to Venus.) **101 right out** outright **110 foison plenty** plentiful harvest **111 garners** granaries **123 wond'red** wonder-performing, wondrous. **wife** (Sometimes emended to *wise*.) **128 windring** wandering, winding (?) **130 crisp** curled, rippled **132 temperate** chaste **138 country footing** country dancing

138 s.d. heavily slowly, dejectedly **142 Avoid** depart, withdraw **146 mov'd sort** troubled state, condition **148 revels** entertainments, pageants **151 baseless** without substance **154 which it inherit** who occupy it **156 rack** wisp of cloud **157 on** of **164 with a thought** i.e., on the instant, or summoned by my thought, no sooner thought on than here **167 presented** acted the part of, or introduced

Towards their project. Then I beat my tabor,
At which, like unback'd colts, they prick'd their ears,
Advanc'd their eyelids, lifted up their noses
As they smelt music. So I charm'd their ears
That calf-like they my lowing follow'd through
Tooth'd briers, sharp furzes, pricking goss, and thorns,
Which ent'red their frail shins. At last I left them
I' th' filthy-mantled pool beyond your cell,
There dancing up to th' chins, that the foul lake
O'erstunk their feet.

PROSPERO This was well done, my bird.
Thy shape invisible retain thou still.
The trumpery in my house, go bring it hither,
For stale to catch these thieves.

ARIEL I go, I go. *Exit.*

PROSPERO
A devil, a born devil, on whose nature
Nurture can never stick; on whom my pains,
Humanely taken, all, all lost, quite lost!
And as with age his body uglier grows,
So his mind cankers. I will plague them all,
Even to roaring.

Enter Ariel, loaden with glistering apparel, etc.

Come, hang them on this line.

[*Ariel hangs up the showy finery; Prospero and Ariel remain, invisible.*] *Enter Caliban, Stephano, and Trinculo, all wet.*

CALIBAN
Pray you, tread softly, that the blind mole may not
Hear a foot fall. We now are near his cell.

STEPHANO Monster, your fairy, which you say is a harmless fairy, has done little better than play'd the Jack with us.

TRINCULO Monster, I do smell all horse-piss, at which my nose is in great indignation.

STEPHANO So is mine. Do you hear, monster? If I should take a displeasure against you, look you—

TRINCULO Thou wert but a lost monster.

CALIBAN
Good my lord, give me thy favor still.
Be patient, for the prize I'll bring thee to
Shall hoodwink this mischance. Therefore speak softly.
All's hush'd as midnight yet.

TRINCULO Ay, but to lose our bottles in the pool—

STEPHANO There is not only disgrace and dishonor in that, monster, but an infinite loss.

TRINCULO That's more to me than my wetting. Yet this is your harmless fairy, monster!

STEPHANO I will fetch off my bottle, though I be o'er ears for my labor.

CALIBAN
Prithee, my King, be quiet. See'st thou here,
This is the mouth o' th' cell. No noise, and enter.
Do that good mischief which may make this island
Thine own for ever, and I, thy Caliban,
For aye thy foot-licker.

STEPHANO Give me thy hand. I do begin to have bloody thoughts.

TRINCULO [*Seeing the finery*] O King Stephano! O peer! O worthy Stephano! Look what a wardrobe here is for thee!

CALIBAN
Let it alone, thou fool! It is but trash.

TRINCULO O, ho, monster! We know what belongs to a frippery. O King Stephano! [*Takes a gown.*]

STEPHANO Put off that gown, Trinculo. By this hand, I'll have that gown.

TRINCULO Thy Grace shall have it.

CALIBAN
The dropsy drown this fool! What do you mean
To dote thus on such luggage? Let's alone
And do the murder first. If he awake,
From toe to crown he'll fill our skins with pinches,
Make us strange stuff.

STEPHANO Be you quiet, monster. Mistress line, is not this my jerkin? [*Takes it down.*] Now is the jerkin under the line. Now, jerkin, you are like to lose your hair and prove a bald jerkin.

TRINCULO Do, do! We steal by line and level, an 't like your Grace.

STEPHANO I thank thee for that jest. Here's a garment for 't. [*Gives a garment.*] Wit shall not go unrewarded while I am king of this country. "Steal by line and level" is an excellent pass of pate. There's another garment for 't.

TRINCULO Monster, come, put some lime upon your fingers, and away with the rest.

CALIBAN
I will have none on 't. We shall lose our time,
And all be turn'd to barnacles, or to apes
With foreheads villainous low.

STEPHANO Monster, lay to your fingers. Help to bear this away where my hogshead of wine is, or I'll turn you out of my kingdom. Go to, carry this.

TRINCULO And this.

STEPHANO Ay, and this.
[*They collect more and more garments.*]

A noise of hunters heard. Enter divers Spirits, in shape of dogs and hounds, hunting them about, Prospero and Ariel setting them on.

176 unback'd unbroken, unridden **177 Advanc'd** lifted up **180 goss** gorse, a prickly shrub **182 filthy-mantled** covered with a slimy coating **186 trumpery** cheap goods, the *glistering apparel* mentioned in the following stage direction **187 stale** (1) decoy (2) out of fashion garments (with possible further suggestions of *fit for a stale* or prostitute, *stale* meaning "horse-piss," l. 199, and *steal,* pronounced like *stale*) **192 cankers** festers, grows malignant **193 line** lime tree or linden **198 Jack** (1) knave (2) will-o-the wisp **206 hoodwink** cover up, make you not see. (A hawking term.)

222 King . . . peer (Alludes to the old ballad beginning, "King Stephen was a worthy peer.") **227 frippery** place where cast-off clothes are sold **232 luggage** cumbersome trash **237 jerkin** jacket made of leather **237–238 under the line** under the lime tree (with punning sense of being south of the equinoctial line or equator; sailors to the southern regions were popularly supposed to lose their hair from scurvy or other diseases. Stephano also quibbles bawdily on losing hair through syphilis, and in *Mistress* and *jerkin.*) **240 by line and level** i.e., by means of plumb-line and carpenter's level, methodically (with pun on *line,* "lime tree," l. 238, and *steal,* pronounced *stale,* i.e., prostitute, continuing Stephano's bawdy quibble). **an 't like** if it please **245 pass of pate** sally of wit **247 lime** birdlime, sticky substance (to give Caliban sticky fingers) **250 barnacles** barnacle geese, formerly supposed to be hatched from seashells attached to trees and to fall thence into the water; here evidently used, like *apes,* as types of simpletons **251 villainous** miserably

PROSPERO Hey, Mountain, hey!
ARIEL Silver! There it goes, Silver!
PROSPERO Fury, Fury! There, Tyrant, there! Hark! Hark!
[Caliban, Stephano, and Trinculo are driven out.]
Go charge my goblins that they grind their joints
With dry convulsions, shorten up their sinews 261
With aged cramps, and more pinch-spotted make
them 262
Than pard or cat o' mountain.
ARIEL Hark, they roar! 263
PROSPERO
Let them be hunted soundly. At this hour
Lies at my mercy all mine enemies.
Shortly shall all my labors end, and thou
Shalt have the air at freedom. For a little
Follow, and do me service. *Exeunt.*

ACT V • SCENE I

Enter Prospero in his magic robes, [with his staff,] and Ariel.

PROSPERO
Now does my project gather to a head.
My charms crack not, my spirits obey, and Time
Goes upright with his carriage. How's the day? 3
ARIEL
On the sixth hour; at which time, my lord,
You said our work should cease.
PROSPERO I did say so,
When first I rais'd the tempest. Say, my spirit,
How fares the King and 's followers?
ARIEL Confin'd together
In the same fashion as you gave in charge,
Just as you left them; all prisoners, sir,
In the line-grove which weather-fends your cell. 10
They cannot budge till your release. The King, 11
His brother, and yours, abide all three distracted,
And the remainder mourning over them,
Brimful of sorrow and dismay; but chiefly
Him that you term'd, sir, "The good old lord,
Gonzalo."
His tears runs down his beard like winter's drops
From eaves of reeds. Your charm so strongly works
'em 17
That if you now beheld them, your affections
Would become tender.
PROSPERO Dost thou think so, spirit?
ARIEL
Mine would, sir, were I human.
PROSPERO And mine shall.
Hast thou, which art but air, a touch, a feeling
Of their afflictions, and shall not myself,
One of their kind, that relish all as sharply, 23
Passion as they, be kindlier mov'd than thou art? 24
Though with their high wrongs I am struck to th'
quick,
Yet with my nobler reason 'gainst my fury
Do I take part. The rarer action is 27
In virtue than in vengeance. They being penitent,
The sole drift of my purpose doth extend
Not a frown further. Go release them, Ariel.
My charms I'll break, their senses I'll restore,
And they shall be themselves.
ARIEL I'll fetch them, sir.
Exit.
[Prospero traces a charmed circle with his staff.]
PROSPERO
Ye elves of hills, brooks, standing lakes, and groves, 33
And ye that on the sands with printless foot
Do chase the ebbing Neptune, and do fly him
When he comes back; you demi-puppets that 36
By moonshine do the green sour ringlets make, 37
Whereof the ewe not bites; and you whose pastime
Is to make midnight mushrooms, that rejoice
To hear the solemn curfew; by whose aid,
Weak masters though ye be, I have bedimm'd
The noontide sun, call'd forth the mutinous winds,
And 'twixt the green sea and the azur'd vault
Set roaring war; to the dread rattling thunder 44
Have I given fire, and rifted Jove's stout oak 45
With his own bolt; the strong-bas'd promontory
Have I made shake, and by the spurs pluck'd up 47
The pine and cedar; graves at my command
Have wak'd their sleepers, op'd, and let 'em forth
By my so potent art. But this rough magic
I here abjure, and, when I have requir'd 51
Some heavenly music, which even now I do,
To work mine end upon their senses that
This airy charm is for, I'll break my staff,
Bury it certain fathoms in the earth,
And deeper than did ever plummet sound
I'll drown my book. *Solemn music.*

Here enters Ariel before; then Alonso, with a frantic gesture, attended by Gonzalo; Sebastian and Antonio in like manner, attended by Adrian and Francisco. They all enter the circle which Prospero had made, and there stand charm'd; which Prospero observing, speaks:

A solemn air, and the best comforter 58
To an unsettled fancy, cure thy brains,
Now useless, boil'd within thy skull! There stand,
For you are spell-stopp'd.
Holy Gonzalo, honorable man,
Mine eyes, ev'n sociable to the show of thine, 63

261 dry associated with age, arthritic (?) **convulsions** cramps **262 aged** characteristic of old age **263 pard** panther or leopard. **cat o' mountain** wildcat

V.i. Location: Before Prospero's cell.
3 his carriage its burden. (I.e., Time is unstopped, runs smoothly.) **10 line-grove** grove of lime trees. **weather-fends** protects from the weather **11 your release** you release them **17 eaves of reeds** thatched roofs

23 relish all experience quite **24 Passion** experience deep feeling **27 rarer** nobler **33–50 Ye . . . art** (This famous passage is an embellished paraphrase of Golding's translation of Ovid's *Metamorphoses*, vii.197–219.) **36 demi-puppets** puppets of half-size, i.e., elves and fairies **37 green sour ringlets** fairy rings, circles in grass (actually produced by mushrooms) **44–45 to . . . fire** I have discharged the dread rattling thunderbolt **45 rifted** riven, split **47 spurs** roots **51 requir'd** requested **58 and** i.e., which is **63 sociable** sympathetic. **show** appearance

Fall fellowly drops. The charm dissolves apace,
And as the morning steals upon the night,
Melting the darkness, so their rising senses
Begin to chase the ignorant fumes that mantle
Their clearer reason. O good Gonzalo,
My true preserver, and a loyal sir
To him thou follow'st! I will pay thy graces
Home both in word and deed. Most cruelly
Didst thou, Alonso, use me and my daughter.
Thy brother was a furtherer in the act.
Thou art pinch'd for 't now, Sebastian. Flesh and blood,
You, brother mine, that entertain'd ambition,
Expell'd remorse and nature, who, with Sebastian,
Whose inward pinches therefore are most strong,
Would here have kill'd your king, I do forgive thee,
Unnatural though thou art.—Their understanding
Begins to swell, and the approaching tide
Will shortly fill the reasonable shore
That now lies foul and muddy. Not one of them
That yet looks on me, or would know me. Ariel,
Fetch me the hat and rapier in my cell.
[Ariel goes to the cell and returns immediately.]
I will discase me, and myself present
As I was sometime Milan. Quickly, spirit;
Thou shalt ere long be free.

Ariel sings and helps to attire him.

ARIEL

Where the bee sucks, there suck I;
In a cowslip's bell I lie;
There I couch when owls do cry.
On the bat's back I do fly
After summer merrily.
Merrily, merrily shall I live now
Under the blossom that hangs on the bough.

PROSPERO

Why, that's my dainty Ariel! I shall miss thee;
But yet thou shalt have freedom. So, so, so.
To the King's ship, invisible as thou art!
There shalt thou find the mariners asleep
Under the hatches. The master and the boatswain
Being awake, enforce them to this place,
And presently, I prithee.

ARIEL

I drink the air before me, and return
Or ere your pulse twice beat. *Exit.*

GONZALO

All torment, trouble, wonder, and amazement
Inhabits here. Some heavenly power guide us
Out of this fearful country!

PROSPERO Behold, sir King,
The wronged Duke of Milan, Prospero.
For more assurance that a living prince
Does now speak to thee, I embrace thy body;
And to thee and thy company I bid
A hearty welcome. *[Embraces him.]*

ALONSO Whe'er thou be'st he or no,
Or some enchanted trifle to abuse me,
As late I have been, I not know. Thy pulse
Beats as of flesh and blood; and, since I saw thee,
Th' affliction of my mind amends, with which,
I fear, a madness held me. This must crave,
An if this be at all, a most strange story.
Thy dukedom I resign, and do entreat
Thou pardon me my wrongs. But how should Prospero
Be living and be here?

PROSPERO *[To Gonzalo]* First, noble friend,
Let me embrace thine age, whose honor cannot
Be measur'd or confin'd. *[Embraces him.]*

GONZALO Whether this be
Or be not, I'll not swear.

PROSPERO You do yet taste
Some subtleties o' th' isle, that will not let you
Believe things certain. Welcome, my friends all!
[Aside to Sebastian and Antonio.] But you, my brace of lords, were I so minded,
I here could pluck his Highness' frown upon you
And justify you traitors. At this time
I will tell no tales.

SEBASTIAN The devil speaks in him.

PROSPERO No.
For you, most wicked sir, whom to call brother
Would even infect my mouth, I do forgive
Thy rankest fault—all of them; and require
My dukedom of thee, which perforce I know
Thou must restore.

ALONSO If thou be'st Prospero,
Give us particulars of thy preservation,
How thou hast met us here, who three hours since
Were wrack'd upon this shore; where I have lost—
How sharp the point of this remembrance is!—
My dear son Ferdinand.

PROSPERO I am woe for 't, sir.

ALONSO

Irreparable is the loss, and Patience
Says it is past her cure.

PROSPERO I rather think
You have not sought her help, of whose soft grace
For the like loss I have her sovereign aid
And rest myself content.

ALONSO You the like loss?

PROSPERO

As great to me as late; and, supportable
To make the dear loss, have I means much weaker
Than you may call to comfort you, for I
Have lost my daughter.

ALONSO

A daughter?
O heavens, that they were living both in Naples,

64 Fall let fall **70 pay thy graces** reward your favors **71 Home** fully **76 remorse** pity. **nature** natural feeling **85 discase** disrobe **86 As . . . Milan** in my former appearance as Duke of Milan **96 So, so, so** (Expresses approval of Ariel's help as valet.)

112 trifle trick of magic. **abuse** deceive **116 crave** require **117 An . . . all** if this is actually happening **118 Thy . . . resign** (Alonso made arrangement with Antonio at the time of Prospero's banishment for Milan to pay tribute to Naples; see I.ii.113–127.) **124 subtleties** illusions, magical powers **128 justify you** prove you to be **139 woe** sorry **145 late** recent

The king and queen there! That they were, I wish
Myself were mudded in that oozy bed
Where my son lies. When did you lose your
daughter?

PROSPERO

In this last tempest. I perceive these lords
At this encounter do so much admire
That they devour their reason and scarce think
Their eyes do offices of truth, their words
Are natural breath. But, howsoev'r you have
Been justled from your senses, know for certain
That I am Prospero and that very duke
Which was thrust forth of Milan, who most
strangely
Upon this shore, where you were wrack'd, was
landed,
To be the lord on 't. No more yet of this,
For 'tis a chronicle of day by day,
Not a relation for a breakfast nor
Befitting this first meeting. Welcome, sir;
This cell's my court. Here have I few attendants
And subjects none abroad. Pray you look in.
My dukedom since you have given me again,
I will requite you with as good a thing,
At least bring forth a wonder, to content ye
As much as me my dukedom.

Here Prospero discovers Ferdinand and Miranda, playing at chess.

MIRANDA

Sweet lord, you play me false.

FERDINAND

No, my dearest love,
I would not for the world.

MIRANDA

Yes, for a score of kingdoms you should wrangle,
And I would call it fair play.

ALONSO

If this prove
A vision of the island, one dear son
Shall I twice lose.

SEBASTIAN

A most high miracle!

FERDINAND

Though the seas threaten, they are merciful;
I have curs'd them without cause. [*Kneels.*]

ALONSO

Now all the blessings
Of a glad father compass thee about!
Arise, and say how thou cam'st here.

MIRANDA

O, wonder!
How many goodly creatures are there here!
How beauteous mankind is! O brave new world,
That has such people in 't!

PROSPERO

'Tis new to thee.

155 admire wonder **156–158 scarce . . . breath** scarcely believe that their eyes inform them accurately what they see or that their words are naturally spoken **172 s.d. discovers** i.e., by opening a curtain, presumably rear-stage **176–177 Yes . . . play** i.e., yes, even if we were playing for twenty kingdoms, something less than the whole world, you would still contend mightily against me and play me false, and I would let you do it as though it were fair play; or, if you were to play not just for stakes but literally for kingdoms, my accusation of false play would be out of order in that your "wrangling" would be proper **185 brave** splendid, gorgeously appareled, handsome

ALONSO

What is this maid with whom thou wast at play?
Your eld'st acquaintance cannot be three hours.
Is she the goddess that hath sever'd us,
And brought us thus together?

FERDINAND

Sir, she is mortal;
But by immortal Providence she's mine.
I chose her when I could not ask my father
For his advice, nor thought I had one. She
Is daughter to this famous Duke of Milan,
Of whom so often I have heard renown,
But never saw before; of whom I have
Receiv'd a second life; and second father
This lady makes him to me.

ALONSO

I am hers.
But, O, how oddly will it sound that I
Must ask my child forgiveness!

PROSPERO

There, sir, stop.
Let us not burden our remembrances with
A heaviness that's gone.

GONZALO

I have inly wept
Or should have spoke ere this. Look down, you
gods,
And on this couple drop a blessed crown!
For it is you that have chalk'd forth the way
Which brought us hither.

ALONSO

I say Amen, Gonzalo!

GONZALO

Was Milan thrust from Milan, that his issue
Should become kings of Naples? O, rejoice
Beyond a common joy, and set it down
With gold on lasting pillars: In one voyage
Did Claribel her husband find at Tunis,
And Ferdinand, her brother, found a wife
Where he himself was lost; Prospero his dukedom
In a poor isle; and all of us ourselves
When no man was his own.

ALONSO [*To Ferdinand and Miranda*]

Give me your hands.
Let grief and sorrow still embrace his heart
That doth not wish you joy!

GONZALO

Be it so! Amen!

Enter Ariel, with the Master and Boatswain amazedly following.

O, look, sir, look, sir! Here is more of us.
I prophesied, if a gallows were on land,
This fellow could not drown. Now, blasphemy,
That swear'st grace o'erboard, not an oath on shore?
Hast thou no mouth by land? What is the news?

BOATSWAIN

The best news is that we have safely found
Our King and company; the next, our ship—
Which, but three glasses since, we gave out split—
Is tight and yare and bravely rigg'd as when
We first put out to sea.

188 eld'st longest **207 Was Milan** was the Duke of Milan **216 still** always. **his** that man's **217 That** who **225 glasses** i.e., hours. **gave out** reported **226 yare** ready

ARIEL [*Aside to Prospero*] Sir, all this service
Have I done since I went.
PROSPERO [*Aside to Ariel*] My tricksy spirit!
ALONSO
These are not natural events; they strengthen
From strange to stranger. Say, how came you hither?
BOATSWAIN
If I did think, sir, I were well awake,
I'd strive to tell you. We were dead of sleep,
And—how we know not—all clapp'd under hatches;
Where but even now with strange and several noises
Of roaring, shrieking, howling, jingling chains,
And moe diversity of sounds, all horrible,
We were awak'd; straightway, at liberty;
Where we, in all her trim, freshly beheld
Our royal, good, and gallant ship, our master
Cap'ring to eye her. On a trice, so please you,
Even in a dream, were we divided from them
And were brought moping hither.
ARIEL [*Aside to Prospero*] Was 't well done?
PROSPERO [*Aside to Ariel*]
Bravely, my diligence. Thou shalt be free.
ALONSO
This is as strange a maze as e'er men trod,
And there is in this business more than nature
Was ever conduct of. Some oracle
Must rectify our knowledge.
PROSPERO Sir, my liege,
Do not infest your mind with beating on
The strangeness of this business. At pick'd leisure,
Which shall be shortly, single I'll resolve you,
Which to you shall seem probable, of every
These happen'd accidents; till when, be cheerful
And think of each thing well. [*Aside to Ariel.*] Come hither, spirit.
Set Caliban and his companions free;
Untie the spell. [*Exit Ariel.*] How fares my gracious sir?
There are yet missing of your company
Some few odd lads that you remember not.

Enter Ariel, driving in Caliban, Stephano, and Trinculo, in their stol'n apparel.

STEPHANO Every man shift for all the rest, and let no man take care for himself; for all is but fortune. Coragio, bully-monster, coragio!
TRINCULO If these be true spies which I wear in my head, here's a goodly sight.
CALIBAN
O Setebos, these be brave spirits indeed!
How fine my master is! I am afraid
He will chastise me.
SEBASTIAN
Ha, ha!
What things are these, my lord Antonio?
Will money buy 'em?
ANTONIO Very like. One of them
Is a plain fish, and no doubt marketable.
PROSPERO
Mark but the badges of these men, my lords,
Then say if they be true. This misshapen knave,
His mother was a witch, and one so strong
That could control the moon, make flows and ebbs,
And deal in her command without her power.
These three have robb'd me; and this demi-devil—
For he's a bastard one—had plotted with them
To take my life. Two of these fellows you
Must know and own; this thing of darkness I
Acknowledge mine.
CALIBAN I shall be pinch'd to death.
ALONSO
Is not this Stephano, my drunken butler?
SEBASTIAN
He is drunk now. Where had he wine?
ALONSO
And Trinculo is reeling ripe. Where should they
Find this grand liquor that hath gilded 'em?
How cam'st thou in this pickle?
TRINCULO I have been in such a pickle since I saw you last that, I fear me, will never out of my bones. I shall not fear fly-blowing.
SEBASTIAN
Why, how now, Stephano?
STEPHANO O, touch me not! I am not Stephano, but a cramp.
PROSPERO
You'd be king o' the isle, sirrah?
STEPHANO I should have been a sore one then.
ALONSO [*Pointing to Caliban*]
This is a strange thing as e'er I look'd on.
PROSPERO
He is as disproportion'd in his manners
As in his shape. Go, sirrah, to my cell;
Take with you your companions. As you look
To have my pardon, trim it handsomely.
CALIBAN
Ay, that I will; and I'll be wise hereafter
And seek for grace. What a thrice-double ass
Was I to take this drunkard for a god
And worship this dull fool!
PROSPERO Go to; away!
ALONSO
Hence, and bestow your luggage where you found it.
SEBASTIAN
Or stole it, rather.
[*Exeunt Caliban, Stephano, and Trinculo.*]
PROSPERO
Sir, I invite your Highness and your train

240 Cap'ring to eye dancing for joy to see **242 moping** in a daze **246 conduct** guide, leader **248 infest** harass, disturb **249 pick'd** chosen, convenient **250 single** i.e., by my own human powers **252 accidents** occurrences **259–260 Coragio** courage **260 bully-monster** gallant monster. (Ironical.) **264 fine** splendidly attired

270 badges emblems of cloth or silver worn on the arms of retainers. (Prospero refers here to the stolen clothes as emblems of their villainy.) **271 true** honest **274 deal . . . power** wield the moon's power, either without her authority or beyond her influence **278 own** recognize, admit as belonging to you **283 gilded** (1) flushed, made drunk (2) covered with gilt (suggesting the horse-urine) **284 pickle** (1) fix, predicament (2) pickling brine (in this case, horse urine) **287 fly-blowing** i.e., being fouled by fly-eggs (from which he is saved by being pickled) **291 sirrah** (Standard form of address to an inferior.) **292 sore** (1) tyrannical (2) wracked by pain

To my poor cell, where you shall take your rest
For this one night; which, part of it, I'll waste 306
With such discourse as, I not doubt, shall make it
Go quick away—the story of my life,
And the particular accidents gone by 309
Since I came to this isle. And in the morn
I'll bring you to your ship, and so to Naples,
Where I have hope to see the nuptial
Of these our dear-belov'd solemnized;
And thence retire me to my Milan, where
Every third thought shall be my grave.

ALONSO I long
To hear the story of your life, which must
Take the ear strangely.

PROSPERO I'll deliver all; 317
And promise you calm seas, auspicious gales,
And sail so expeditious that shall catch
Your royal fleet far off. [*Aside to Ariel.*] My Ariel,
chick,
That is thy charge. Then to the elements
Be free, and fare thou well!—Please you, draw near. 322
Exeunt omnes.

EPILOGUE

Spoken by PROSPERO.

Now my charms are all o'erthrown,
And what strength I have 's mine own,
Which is most faint. Now, 'tis true,
I must be here confin'd by you,
Or sent to Naples. Let me not,
Since I have my dukedom got
And pardon'd the deceiver, dwell
In this bare island by your spell,
But release me from my bands 9
With the help of your good hands. 10
Gentle breath of yours my sails
Must fill, or else my project fails,
Which was to please. Now I want 13
Spirits to enforce, art to enchant,
And my ending is despair,
Unless I be reliev'd by prayer, 16
Which pierces so that it assaults 17
Mercy itself and frees all faults. 18
As you from crimes would pardon'd be, 19
Let your indulgence set me free. *Exit.*

306 waste spend **309 accidents** occurrences **317 Take** take effect upon, enchant. **deliver** declare, relate **322 draw near** i.e., enter my cell

Epilogue.
9 bands bonds **10 hands** i.e., applause (the noise of which would break the spell of silence) **13 want** lack **16 prayer** i.e., Prospero's petition to the audience **17 assaults** rightfully gains the attention of **18 frees** obtains forgiveness of **19 crimes** sins

The Poems

Venus and Adonis

Like most of his contemporaries, Shakespeare apparently did not regard the writing of plays as an elegant literary pursuit. He must have known that he was good at it, and he certainly became famous in his day as a playwright, but he took no pains over the publication of his plays. We have no literary prefaces for them, no indication that Shakespeare saw them through the press. Writing for the theatre was rather like writing for the movies today, a profitable and even glamorous venture but subliterary. When Ben Jonson brought out his collected *Works* (mostly plays) during his lifetime, he was jeered at for pretention.

The writing of sonnets and other "serious" poetry, on the other hand, was conventionally a bid for true literary fame. Shakespeare's prefatory epistle to his *Venus and Adonis* betrays an eagerness for recognition. Deferentially he seeks the sponsorship of the Earl of Southampton, in hopes of cachet as well as financial support. He speaks of *Venus and Adonis* as "the first heir of my invention," as though he had written no plays earlier, and promises Southampton a "graver labor" to appear shortly. *Venus and Adonis* in 1593 and *The Rape of Lucrece* in 1594 were in fact Shakespeare's first publications. Both were carefully and correctly printed. They were probably composed between June of 1592 and May of 1594, a period when the theatres were closed because of the plague. Shakespeare's belief in their importance to his literary career is confirmed by the reports of his contemporaries. Richard Barnfield singled them out as the works most likely to assure a place for Shakespeare in "fames immortall Booke." Francis Meres exclaimed in 1598 that "the sweete wittie soule of *Ouid* liues in mellifluous & hony-tongued *Shakespeare,* witnes his *Venus* and *Adonis,* his *Lucrece,* his sugred Sonnets among his priuate friends, &c." Gabriel Harvey, although preferring *Lucrece* and *Hamlet* as more pleasing to "the wiser sort," conceded that "the younger sort takes much delight in Shakespeares Venus, & Adonis." John Weever and still others add further testimonials to the extraordinary reputation of Shakespeare's nondramatic poems.

As Gabriel Harvey's puritanical comment on *Venus and Adonis* suggests, this poem was regarded as amatory and even risqué. It mirrored a current vogue for Ovidian erotic poetry, as exemplified by Thomas Lodge's *Scilla's Metamorphosis,* 1589 (in which an amorous nymph courts a reluctant young man), and by Christopher Marlowe's *Hero and Leander.* This latter poem, left unfinished at Marlowe's death in 1593 and published in 1598 with a continuation by George Chapman, was evidently circulated in manuscript as were so many poems of this sophisticated sort (including Shakespeare's sonnets). Shakespeare may well have been influenced by Marlowe's tone of wryly comic detachment and sensuous grace. He may also have read Michael Drayton's *Endimion and Phoebe* (published 1595 but written earlier), in which the erotic tradition is somewhat idealized into moral allegory. Most importantly, however, Shakespeare knew his Ovid, both firsthand and in Golding's English translation (1567). He appears to have combined three mythical tales from the *Metamorphoses.* The narrative outline is to be found in Venus' pursuit of Adonis (Book X), but the bashful reluctance of the young man is more reminiscent of Hermaphroditus (Book IV) and Narcissus (Book III). Hermaphroditus pleads youth as his reason for wishing to escape the clutches of the water-nymph Salmacis, and so is transformed with her into a single body containing both sexes; Narcissus evades the nymph Echo out of self-infatuation. Shakespeare has thus drawn a composite portrait of male coyness, a subject he was to explore further in the sonnets. Such a theme was suited to a nobleman of Southampton's youth and prospects. In tone it was also well suited to the aristocratic and intellectual set who read such poetry. Shakespeare here aimed at a more refined audience than that for which he wrote plays, though his theatrical audience was generally intelligent and well to do. The ornate qualities of *Venus and Adonis* should be judged in the fashionable context of a sophisticated audience.

The poem is, among other things, a tour de force of stylized poetic techniques. The story itself is relatively insignificant, and the characters are static. For two-thirds of the poem, very little happens other than a series of amorous claspings from which Adonis feebly attempts to extricate himself. Even his subsequent fight with the boar and his violent death are occasions for rhetorical pathos rather than for vivid narrative description. The story is essentially a frame. Similarly, we must not expect psychological insight or meaningful self-discovery. The conventions of amatory verse do not encourage a serious interest in character. Venus and Adonis are mouthpieces for contrasting attitudes toward love. They debate a favorite courtly topic in the style of John Lyly. Both appeal to conventional wisdom and speak in *sententiae,* or aphoristic pronouncements. Venus, for example, warning Adonis of the need for caution in pursuing the boar, opines that "Danger deviseth shifts, wit waits on fear" (690). Adonis, pleading his unreadiness for love, cites commonplace analogies: "No fisher but the ungrown fry forbears. The mellow plum doth fall, the green sticks fast" (526–527). In substance, their arguments are equally conventional. Venus urges a *carpe diem* philosophy of seizing the moment of pleasure. "Make use of time, let not advantage slip; Beauty within itself should not be wasted" (129–130). She bolsters her claim with an appeal to the "law of nature," according to which all living things are obliged to reproduce themselves; only by begetting can man conquer time and death. Yet however close this position may be to a major theme of the sonnets, it does not go unchallenged. Adonis charges plausibly that Venus is only rationalizing her lust: "O strange excuse, When reason is the bawd to lust's abuse!" (791–792). His plea for more time in which to mature and prove his manliness is commendable, however much we may smile at his inability to be aroused by Venus' blandishments. Thus, neither contestant wins the argument. Venus is proved right in her fear that Adonis will be killed by the boar he hunts, but Adonis' rejection of idle lust for manly activity affirms a conventional truth. The debate is in a sense an ingeniously elaborate literary exercise, yet it also allows for reflection on contrasting views of love as sensual and spiritual, absurd and magnificent, funny and serious.

The narrator's persona is central to the ambivalence in the debate. He too speaks in *sententiae,* and his aphorisms appear to sympathize with both contestants. At times, he affirms the irresistible force of love: "What though the rose have prickles, yet 'tis plucked" (574). At other times, he laughs at Venus for her vacillation of mood: "Thy weal and woe are both of them extremes; Despair and hope makes thee ridiculous" (987–988). Like Ovid's usual persona, the speaker here is both intrigued and amused by love, compelled to heed its power and yet aware of the absurdities. The result is a characteristic Ovidian blend of irony and pathos. The irony is especially evident in the delightful comic touches which undermine the potential seriousness of the action: Venus like an Amazon pulling Adonis off his mount and tucking him under one arm, pouting and blushing; Adonis' horse chasing away after a mare in heat, leaving Adonis to fend for himself; Venus fainting at the thought of the boar and pulling Adonis right on top of her, "in the very lists of love, Her champion mounted for the hot encounter" (595–596). These devices "distance" us from the action and create an atmosphere of elegant entertainment. Yet the poem is also suffused with the rich pathos of sensuous emotion. The sensuousness would cloy without the ironic humor, whereas the humor would seem frivolous without the pathos.

The poem hints at moral allegory, in the manner of Ovidian mythologizing. Venus represents herself as the goddess not only of erotic passion but of eternal love conquering time and death. Because Adonis perversely spurns this ideal, Venus concludes that human beauty must perish and that man's happiness must be subject to mischance. Yet this reading is only one part of the argument, and is contradicted by an opposing suggestion that Adonis is the rational principle attempting unsuccessfully to govern man's lust (the boar, and Adonis' unbridled horse). These contradictions, which derive from the structure of the poem as a debate, and also from Renaissance neo-Platonism, confirm our impression that the allegory is not the true "meaning" of the poem but is part of an ambiguous view of love as both exalted and earthly, a mystery that we will never comprehend in single terms. The allegory elevates the seriousness, adding poetic dignity to what might otherwise appear to be an unabashedly erotic poem. We should not minimize the sexual teasing, or fail to acknowledge our own erotic pleasure in it. Venus' repeated encounters with Adonis take the form of ingeniously varied positions, ending in coital embrace although without consummation. Adonis' passive role invites the male reader to fantasize himself in Adonis' place, being seduced by the goddess of beauty. The famous passage comparing Venus' body to a deer park with "pleasant fountains," "sweet bottom-grass," and "round rising hillocks" (229–240) is graphic through the use of double entendre without being pornographic. The poem is equally explicit in its "banquet" of the five senses (433–450). This is the "naughty" Ovid of the *Ars Amatoria*.

Shakespeare's poem is an embroidery of poetic flourishes, of "conceits" or ingeniously wrought similes, of artfully constructed digressions such as the narrative of Adonis' horse, and of color symbolism. Images are usually drawn from nature (eagles, birds caught in nets, wolves, berries) or connote burning, blazing, and shining (torches, jewels). The dominant colors are red and white, usually paired antithetically: the red of the rising sun or Adonis' blushing face or Mars' ensign, the white of an alabaster hand or fresh bed linen or "ashy-pale" anger. Ironically, too, the boar's frothy-white mouth is stained with red, and Adonis' red blood blemishes his "wonted lily white." Adonis' flower, the anemone, is reddish-purple and white. A similarly balanced antithesis pervades the play's rhetorical figures, as in the symmetrical repetition of words in grammatically parallel phrases *(parison),* or in phrases of equal length *(isocolon),* or in inverted order *(antimetabole),* or at the beginning and ending of a line *(epanalepsis),* and so on. These pyrotechnics may at first seem mechanical, but they too have a place in a work of art that celebrates both the erotic and the spiritual in love. Decoration has its function and is not mere embellishment for its own sake.

Venus and Adonis

"Vilia miretur vulgus; mihi flavus Apollo Pocula Castalia plena ministret aqua."

To the RIGHT HONORABLE HENRY WRIOTHESLEY, *Earl of Southampton, and Baron of Titchfield.*

RIGHT HONORABLE

I know not how I shall offend in dedicating my unpolish'd lines to your lordship, nor how the world will censure me for choosing so strong a prop to support so weak a burden; only if your honor seem but pleas'd, I account myself highly prais'd, and vow to take advantage of all idle hours, till I have honor'd you with some graver labor. But if the first heir of my invention prove deform'd, I shall be sorry it had so noble a godfather, and never after ear so barren a land, for fear it yield me still so bad a harvest. I leave it to your honorable survey, and your honor to your heart's content; which I wish may always answer your own wish and the world's hopeful expectation.

Your honor's in all duty,

William Shakespeare.

Even as the sun with purple-color'd face
Had ta'en his last leave of the weeping morn,
Rose-cheek'd Adonis hied him to the chase.
Hunting he lov'd, but love he laugh'd to scorn.
Sick-thoughted Venus makes amain unto him,
And like a bold-fac'd suitor 'gins to woo him.

"Thrice-fairer than myself," thus she began,
"The field's chief flower, sweet above compare,
Stain to all nymphs, more lovely than a man,
More white and red than doves or roses are,
Nature that made thee, with herself at strife,
Saith that the world hath ending with thy life.

"Vouchsafe, thou wonder, to alight thy steed,
And rein his proud head to the saddle-bow.
If thou wilt deign this favor, for thy meed
A thousand honey secrets shalt thou know.
Here come and sit, where never serpent hisses,
And being set, I'll smother thee with kisses;

"And yet not cloy thy lips with loath'd satiety,
But rather famish them amid their plenty,
Making them red and pale with fresh variety—
Ten kisses short as one, one long as twenty.
A summer's day will seem an hour but short,
Being wasted in such time-beguiling sport."

With this she seizeth on his sweating palm,
The precedent of pith and livelihood,
And, trembling in her passion, calls it balm,
Earth's sovereign salve, to do a goddess good.
Being so enrag'd, desire doth lend her force
Courageously to pluck him from his horse.

Over one arm the lusty courser's rein,
Under her other was the tender boy,
Who blush'd and pouted in a dull disdain,
With leaden appetite, unapt to toy;
She red and hot as coals of glowing fire,
He red for shame, but frosty in desire.

The studded bridle on a ragged bough
Nimbly she fastens. O, how quick is love!
The steed is stalled up, and even now
To tie the rider she begins to prove.
Backward she push'd him, as she would be thrust,
And govern'd him in strength, though not in lust.

So soon was she along as he was down,
Each leaning on their elbows and their hips.
Now doth she stroke his cheek, now doth he frown,
And 'gins to chide, but soon she stops his lips,
And kissing speaks, with lustful language broken,
"If thou wilt chide, thy lips shall never open."

He burns with bashful shame; she with her tears
Doth quench the maiden burning of his cheeks.
Then with her windy sighs and golden hairs
To fan and blow them dry again she seeks.
He saith she is immodest, blames her miss;
What follows more, she murders with a kiss.

Motto: **Vilia miretur,** etc. Let the base vulgar admire trash; may golden-haired Apollo serve me goblets filled from the Castalian spring. (Ovid, *Amores,* I.xv.35–36).
Dedication: **Henry Wriothesley, Earl of Southampton** (A popular and brilliant young gentleman of nineteen years, already prominent at court. Subsequent dedications by Shakespeare and others indicate that he was a genuinely devoted patron of literature throughout his life.)
the first . . . invention (This phrase has been variously interpreted to mean Shakespeare's first written work, his first printed work, his first "invented" work in the sense that the plots of his plays were unoriginal, his first work independent of collaborators, or his first "literary" work, since plays were unliterary in the Elizabethan sense. The second and last are the most probable.)
ear plough, cultivate
2 the weeping morn i.e., the goddess of the dawn, Aurora, weeping to be left by the sun god. (*Weeping* suggests the dew of morning.) **3 hied him** betook himself, hastened **5 Sick-thoughted** lovesick. **makes amain** hastens **9 Stain to** eclipsing (in beauty)

11–12 Nature . . . life i.e., nature strove to surpass herself in making her masterpiece, Adonis, and says if you die the world will cease. (The story of Adonis' death, and of the anemone that springs from his blood, is a vegetation myth.) **15 meed** reward **24 wasted** spent **25 sweating** i.e., indicative of youth; not dried with age **26 precedent** sign, promise. **pith and livelihood** sexual strength and vitality **28 sovereign** efficacious **29 enrag'd** ardent **34 unapt to toy** undisposed to dally amorously **39 stalled** fastened, secured (as in a stall) **40 prove** try **43 along** lying at his side **53 miss** offense, misconduct

Even as an empty eagle, sharp by fast,
Tires with her beak on feathers, flesh, and bone,
Shaking her wings, devouring all in haste,
Till either gorge be stuff'd or prey be gone,
  Even so she kiss'd his brow, his cheek, his chin,
  And where she ends she doth anew begin.

Forc'd to content, but never to obey,
Panting he lies and breatheth in her face.
She feedeth on the steam as on a prey,
And calls it heavenly moisture, air of grace,
  Wishing her cheeks were gardens full of flowers,
  So they were dew'd with such distilling showers.

Look how a bird lies tangled in a net,
So fast'ned in her arms Adonis lies;
Pure shame and aw'd resistance made him fret,
Which bred more beauty in his angry eyes.
  Rain added to a river that is rank
  Perforce will force it overflow the bank.

Still she entreats, and prettily entreats,
For to a pretty ear she tunes her tale.
Still is he sullen, still he lours and frets,
'Twixt crimson shame and anger ashy-pale.
  Being red, she loves him best; and being white,
  Her best is better'd with a more delight.

Look how he can, she cannot choose but love;
And by her fair immortal hand she swears
From his soft bosom never to remove,
Till he take truce with her contending tears,
  Which long have rain'd, making her cheeks all
    wet;
  And one sweet kiss shall pay this countless debt.

Upon this promise did he raise his chin,
Like a dive-dapper peering through a wave,
Who, being look'd on, ducks as quickly in.
So offers he to give what she did crave;
  But when her lips were ready for his pay,
  He winks, and turns his lips another way.

Never did passenger in summer's heat
More thirst for drink than she for this good turn.
Her help she sees, but help she cannot get;
She bathes in water, yet her fire must burn.
  "O, pity," gan she cry, "flint-hearted boy!
  'Tis but a kiss I beg. Why art thou coy?

"I have been wooed, as I entreat thee now,
Even by the stern and direful god of war,
Whose sinewy neck in battle ne'er did bow,
Who conquers where he comes in every jar;
  Yet hath he been my captive and my slave,
  And begg'd for that which thou unask'd shalt
    have.

"Over my altars hath he hung his lance,
His batt'red shield, his uncontrolled crest,
And for my sake hath learn'd to sport and dance,
To toy, to wanton, dally, smile, and jest,
  Scorning his churlish drum and ensign red,
  Making my arms his field, his tent my bed.

"Thus he that overrul'd I overswayed,
Leading him prisoner in a red-rose chain.
Strong-temper'd steel his stronger strength obeyed,
Yet was he servile to my coy disdain.
  O, be not proud, nor brag not of thy might,
  For mast'ring her that foil'd the god of fight!

"Touch but my lips with those fair lips of thine—
Though mine be not so fair, yet are they red—
The kiss shall be thine own as well as mine.
What seest thou in the ground? Hold up thy head.
  Look in mine eyeballs, there thy beauty lies;
  Then why not lips on lips, since eyes in eyes?

"Art thou asham'd to kiss? Then wink again,
And I will wink; so shall the day seem night.
Love keeps his revels where there are but twain;
Be bold to play, our sport is not in sight.
  These blue-vein'd violets whereon we lean
  Never can blab, nor know not what we mean.

"The tender spring upon thy tempting lip
Shows thee unripe, yet mayst thou well be tasted.
Make use of time, let not advantage slip;
Beauty within itself should not be wasted.
  Fair flowers that are not gath'red in their prime
  Rot and consume themselves in little time.

"Were I hard-favor'd, foul, or wrinkled-old,
Ill-nurtur'd, crooked, churlish, harsh in voice,
O'erworn, despised, rheumatic, and cold,
Thick-sighted, barren, lean, and lacking juice,
  Then mightst thou pause, for then I were not for
    thee;
  But having no defects, why dost abhor me?

"Thou canst not see one wrinkle in my brow;
Mine eyes are grey and bright and quick in turning;
My beauty as the spring doth yearly grow,
My flesh is soft and plump, my marrow burning;
  My smooth moist hand, were it with thy hand
    felt,
  Would in thy palm dissolve, or seem to melt.

55 sharp by fast hungry as a result of fasting **56 Tires** tears, feeds ravenously **61 content** acquiesce **66 So** provided that. **distilling** gently falling, in fine droplets **67 Look how** just as **69 aw'd** daunted, overborne **71 rank** full to overflowing **78 more** greater **82 take truce** come to terms **84 countless** beyond reckoning **86 dive-dapper** dabchick, a common English water bird **90 winks** shuts his eyes (and winces) **91 passenger** wayfarer **100 jar** fight

104 uncontrolled unconquered, unbowed. **crest** i.e., of helmet **121 wink** close the eyes **124 not in sight** i.e., observed by no one **126 mean** intend **127 spring** growth. (I.e., a coming beard.) **129 advantage** opportunity **130 Beauty . . . wasted** beauty should not be wasted by being kept to itself **133 hard-favor'd** ugly. **foul** ugly **135 O'erworn** worn by time **136 Thick-sighted** dim-eyed **140 grey** i.e., blue **141 as . . . grow** i.e., is perennially renewed, like spring

"Bid me discourse, I will enchant thine ear,
Or, like a fairy, trip upon the green, 146
Or, like a nymph, with long disheveled hair,
Dance on the sands, and yet no footing seen. 148
Love is a spirit all compact of fire, 149
Not gross to sink, but light, and will aspire. 150

"Witness this primrose bank whereon I lie;
These forceless flowers like sturdy trees support me. 152
Two strengthless doves will draw me through the sky,
From morn till night, even where I list to sport me. 154
Is love so light, sweet boy, and may it be
That thou shouldst think it heavy unto thee?

"Is thine own heart to thine own face affected? 157
Can thy right hand seize love upon thy left? 158
Then woo thyself, be of thyself rejected,
Steal thine own freedom and complain on theft.
Narcissus so himself himself forsook, 161
And died to kiss his shadow in the brook.

"Torches are made to light, jewels to wear,
Dainties to taste, fresh beauty for the use,
Herbs for their smell, and sappy plants to bear. 165
Things growing to themselves are growth's abuse. 166
Seeds spring from seeds and beauty breedeth beauty.
Thou wast begot; to get it is thy duty. 168

"Upon the earth's increase why shouldst thou feed,
Unless the earth with thy increase be fed?
By law of nature thou art bound to breed,
That thine may live when thou thyself art dead;
And so, in spite of death, thou dost survive,
In that thy likeness still is left alive."

By this the love-sick queen began to sweat, 175
For where they lay the shadow had forsook them,
And Titan, tired in the midday heat, 177
With burning eye did hotly overlook them, 178
Wishing Adonis had his team to guide, 179
So he were like him, and by Venus' side. 180

And now Adonis, with a lazy sprite, 181
And with a heavy, dark, disliking eye,
His louring brows o'erwhelming his fair sight, 183
Like misty vapors when they blot the sky,
Souring his cheeks, cries, "Fie, no more of love! 185
The sun doth burn my face; I must remove."

"Ay me," quoth Venus, "young, and so unkind?
What bare excuses mak'st thou to be gone!
I'll sigh celestial breath, whose gentle wind
Shall cool the heat of this descending sun.
I'll make a shadow for thee of my hairs;
If they burn too, I'll quench them with my tears.

"The sun that shines from heaven shines but warm,
And, lo, I lie between that sun and thee.
The heat I have from thence doth little harm;
Thine eye darts forth the fire that burneth me,
And were I not immortal, life were done 197
Between this heavenly and earthly sun.

"Art thou obdurate, flinty, hard as steel?
Nay, more than flint, for stone at rain relenteth. 200
Art thou a woman's son, and canst not feel
What 'tis to love, how want of love tormenteth?
O, had thy mother borne so hard a mind,
She had not brought forth thee, but died unkind. 204

"What am I, that thou shouldst contemn me this? 205
Or what great danger dwells upon my suit? 206
What were thy lips the worse for one poor kiss? 207
Speak, fair, but speak fair words, or else be mute.
Give me one kiss, I'll give it thee again,
And one for int'rest, if thou wilt have twain.

"Fie, lifeless picture, cold and senseless stone,
Well-painted idol, image dull and dead,
Statue contenting but the eye alone,
Thing like a man, but of no woman bred!
Thou art no man, though of a man's complexion,
For men will kiss even by their own direction." 216

This said, impatience chokes her pleading tongue,
And swelling passion doth provoke a pause.
Red cheeks and fiery eyes blaze forth her wrong; 219
Being judge in love, she cannot right her cause. 220
And now she weeps, and now she fain would speak,
And now her sobs do her intendments break. 222

Sometime she shakes her head and then his hand,
Now gazeth she on him, now on the ground;
Sometime her arms infold him like a band.
She would, he will not in her arms be bound;
And when from thence he struggles to be gone,
She locks her lily fingers one in one.

"Fondling," she saith, "since I have hemm'd thee here 229
Within the circuit of this ivory pale, 230
I'll be a park, and thou shalt be my deer. 231
Feed where thou wilt, on mountain or in dale;
Graze on my lips; and if those hills be dry,
Stray lower, where the pleasant fountains lie.

146 trip dance **148 footing** footprint **149 compact** composed **150 aspire** rise **152 forceless** frail **154 list** desire **157 affected** drawn by affection **158 upon thy left** i.e., by clasping the left hand **161 Narcissus** a beautiful youth in classical mythology who, leaning over a pool to drink, fell in love with his reflection and stayed there until he died. He was afterwards changed into a flower. (Ovid, *Metamorphoses,* III.339–510.) **165 sappy plants** fruit trees **166 to themselves** i.e., solely for their own use **168 get** beget, procreate **175 By this** by this time **177 Titan** the sun god. **tired** attired **178 overlook** look upon **179 his team** i.e., Titan's team of horses **180 So he** provided that he, Titan **181 lazy sprite** dull spirit **183 o'erwhelming** overhanging, so as to cover. **sight** eyes **185 Souring his cheeks** scowling

197 done undone, finished **200 relenteth** wears slowly away **204 unkind** unnaturally unrelenting **205 contemn** refuse scornfully. **this** i.e., this request **206 dwells upon** attends **207 What** in what way **216 direction** inclination **219 blaze forth** proclaim (with a metaphorical sense of *seeming to burn*) **220 Being . . . cause** i.e., although goddess of love, Venus cannot prevail in her own case **222 intendments** intention to speak **229 Fondling** foolish one **230 pale** fence (i.e., her arms; the sexual topography is continued in *fountains, bottom-grass, hillocks, brakes,* etc.) **231 park** deer preserve

"Within this limit is relief enough,
Sweet bottom-grass and high delightful plain,
Round rising hillocks, brakes obscure and rough,
To shelter thee from tempest and from rain.
Then be my deer, since I am such a park;
No dog shall rouse thee, though a thousand bark."

At this Adonis smiles as in disdain,
That in each cheek appears a pretty dimple.
Love made those hollows, if himself were slain,
He might be buried in a tomb so simple,
Foreknowing well, if there he came to lie,
Why, there Love liv'd and there he could not die.

These lovely caves, these round enchanting pits,
Open'd their mouths to swallow Venus' liking.
Being mad before, how doth she now for wits?
Struck dead at first, what needs a second striking?
Poor queen of love, in thine own law forlorn,
To love a cheek that smiles at thee in scorn!

Now which way shall she turn? What shall she say?
Her words are done, her woes the more increasing;
The time is spent, her object will away,
And from her twining arms doth urge releasing.
"Pity," she cries, "some favor, some remorse!"
Away he springs and hasteth to his horse.

But, lo, from forth a copse that neighbors by,
A breeding jennet, lusty, young, and proud,
Adonis' trampling courser doth espy,
And forth she rushes, snorts, and neighs aloud.
The strong-neck'd steed, being tied unto a tree,
Breaketh his rein, and to her straight goes he.

Imperiously he leaps, he neighs, he bounds,
And now his woven girths he breaks asunder.
The bearing earth with his hard hoof he wounds,
Whose hollow womb resounds like heaven's thunder.
The iron bit he crusheth 'tween his teeth,
Controlling what he was controlled with.

His ears up-prick'd, his braided hanging mane
Upon his compass'd crest now stand on end;
His nostrils drink the air, and forth again,
As from a furnace, vapors doth he send.
His eye, which scornfully glisters like fire,
Shows his hot courage and his high desire.

Sometime he trots, as if he told the steps,
With gentle majesty and modest pride;
Anon he rears upright, curvets, and leaps,
As who should say "Lo, thus my strength is tried,
And this I do to captivate the eye
Of the fair breeder that is standing by."

What recketh he his rider's angry stir,
His flattering "Holla," or his "Stand, I say"?
What cares he now for curb or pricking spur?
For rich caparisons or trappings gay?
He sees his love, and nothing else he sees,
For nothing else with his proud sight agrees.

Look when a painter would surpass the life,
In limning out a well-proportioned steed,
His art with nature's workmanship at strife,
As if the dead the living should exceed,
So did this horse excel a common one
In shape, in courage, color, pace, and bone.

Round-hoof'd, short-jointed, fetlocks shag and long,
Broad breast, full eye, small head, and nostril wide,
High crest, short ears, straight legs and passing strong,
Thin mane, thick tail, broad buttock, tender hide:
Look what a horse should have he did not lack,
Save a proud rider on so proud a back.

Sometime he scuds far off and there he stares;
Anon he starts at stirring of a feather;
To bid the wind a base he now prepares,
And whe'er he run or fly they know not whether;
For through his mane and tail the high wind sings,
Fanning the hairs, who wave like feath'red wings.

He looks upon his love and neighs unto her;
She answers him as if she knew his mind.
Being proud, as females are, to see him woo her,
She puts on outward strangeness, seems unkind,
Spurns at his love and scorns the heat he feels,
Beating his kind embracements with her heels.

Then, like a melancholy malcontent,
He vails his tail that, like a falling plume,
Cool shadow to his melting buttock lent;
He stamps and bites the poor flies in his fume.
His love, perceiving how he was enrag'd,
Grew kinder, and his fury was assuag'd.

His testy master goeth about to take him,
When, lo, the unback'd breeder, full of fear,
Jealous of catching, swiftly doth forsake him,
With her the horse, and left Adonis there.
As they were mad, unto the wood they hie them,
Out-stripping crows that strive to overfly them.

235 limit boundary. **relief** (1) pasture (2) sexual pleasure **236 bottom-grass** valley-grass (with an allusion to pubic hair) **237 brakes** thickets (again with sexual suggestion) **239 deer** (with conventional pun on *dear*) **240 rouse** cause to start from cover **242 That** so that **243 if** so that if **248 liking** desire **249 how . . . wits** i.e., how may she keep her sanity now **251 in . . . forlorn** condemned to suffer under your own rule of love **257 remorse** compassion **260 jennet** small Spanish mare **267 bearing** receiving **272 compass'd** arched. **crest** ridge of the neck **276 courage** passion **277 told** numbered

283 stir bustle **284 flattering** cajoling. **Holla** stop **289 Look when** just as when **290 limning out** portraying, drawing **294 bone** frame **295 shag** shaggy **297 crest** ridge of the neck **299 Look what** whatever **303 bid the wind a base** challenge the wind to a contest. (From the children's game of prisoner's base.) **304 whe'er** whether. **whether** which of the two **310 outward strangeness** seeming coldness **314 vails** lowers **316 fume** anger **319 testy** irritated. **goeth about** makes an effort **320 unback'd** unbroken, riderless **321 Jealous of catching** fearful of being caught **322 horse** i.e., stallion **323 As** as if **324 overfly them** fly faster than they can run, or keep pace with them in flight

All swoll'n with chafing, down Adonis sits,
Banning his boist'rous and unruly beast;
And now the happy season once more fits
That love-sick Love by pleading may be blest;
For lovers say, the heart hath treble wrong
When it is barr'd the aidance of the tongue.

An oven that is stopp'd, or river stay'd,
Burneth more hotly, swelleth with more rage;
So of concealed sorrow may be said.
Free vent of words love's fire doth assuage;
But when the heart's attorney once is mute,
The client breaks, as desperate in his suit.

He sees her coming, and begins to glow,
Even as a dying coal revives with wind,
And with his bonnet hides his angry brow,
Looks on the dull earth with disturbed mind,
Taking no notice that she is so nigh,
For all askance he holds her in his eye.

O, what a sight it was, wistly to view
How she came stealing to the wayward boy!
To note the fighting conflict of her hue,
How white and red each other did destroy!
But now her cheek was pale, and by and by
It flash'd forth fire, as lightning from the sky.

Now was she just before him as he sat,
And like a lowly lover down she kneels;
With one fair hand she heaveth up his hat,
Her other tender hand his fair cheek feels.
His tend'rer cheek receives her soft hand's print,
As apt as new-fall'n snow takes any dint.

O, what a war of looks was then between them!
Her eyes petitioners to his eyes suing,
His eyes saw her eyes as they had not seen them;
Her eyes woo'd still, his eyes disdain'd the wooing;
And all this dumb play had his acts made plain
With tears, which, chorus-like, her eyes did rain.

Full gently now she takes him by the hand,
A lily prison'd in a jail of snow,
Or ivory in an alabaster band,
So white a friend engirts so white a foe.
This beauteous combat, willful and unwilling,
Show'd like two silver doves that sit a-billing.

Once more the engine of her thoughts began:
"O fairest mover on this mortal round,
Would thou wert as I am, and I a man,
My heart all whole as thine, thy heart my wound!
For one sweet look thy help I would assure thee,
Though nothing but my body's bane would cure thee."

"Give me my hand," saith he, "why dost thou feel it?"
"Give me my heart," saith she, "and thou shalt have it.
O, give it me, lest thy hard heart do steel it,
And being steel'd, soft sighs can never grave it.
Then love's deep groans I never shall regard,
Because Adonis' heart hath made mine hard."

"For shame," he cries, "let go, and let me go!
My day's delight is past, my horse is gone,
And 'tis your fault I am bereft him so.
I pray you hence, and leave me here alone;
For all my mind, my thought, my busy care,
Is how to get my palfrey from the mare."

Thus she replies: "Thy palfrey, as he should,
Welcomes the warm approach of sweet desire.
Affection is a coal that must be cool'd,
Else, suffer'd, it will set the heart on fire.
The sea hath bounds, but deep desire hath none;
Therefore no marvel though thy horse be gone.

"How like a jade he stood, tied to the tree,
Servilely master'd with a leathern rein!
But when he saw his love, his youth's fair fee,
He held such petty bondage in disdain,
Throwing the base thong from his bending crest,
Enfranchising his mouth, his back, his breast.

"Who sees his true-love in her naked bed,
Teaching the sheets a whiter hue than white,
But when his glutton eye so full hath fed,
His other agents aim at like delight?
Who is so faint that dares not be so bold
To touch the fire, the weather being cold?

"Let me excuse thy courser, gentle boy;
And learn of him, I heartily beseech thee,
To take advantage on presented joy.
Though I were dumb, yet his proceedings teach thee.
O, learn to love; the lesson is but plain,
And once made perfect, never lost again."

"I know not love," quoth he, "nor will not know it,
Unless it be a boar, and then I chase it;
'Tis much to borrow, and I will not owe it;
My love to love is love but to disgrace it;
For I have heard it is a life in death,
That laughs and weeps, and all but with a breath.

325 chafing showing anger **326 Banning** cursing **330 aidance** help **331 stopp'd** stopped up. **stay'd** hindered, dammed **335 heart's attorney** i.e., the tongue **336 breaks** (1) goes bankrupt (2) breaks asunder, as the heart is said to break in rejected love **343 wistly** earnestly, attentively **347 But now** a short time ago **354 dint** impression **357 as** as if **359 dumb play** dumb show. **his** its **360 With** by. **chorus-like** i.e., providing a choric interpretation to the dumb show **367 engine of her thoughts** i.e., her tongue **368 mortal round** earth **370 thy heart my wound** your heart wounded by me as mine is by you

371 thy help . . . thee I would promise to help you **372 bane** ruin, death **373 Give me** i.e., let go **375 steel** turn to steel **376 grave** engrave, make an impression on **387 Affection** passion **388 suffer'd** permitted to continue **393 fair fee** due reward **397 in . . . bed** i.e., naked in her bed **400 agents** organs, senses **408 made perfect** learned completely **411 borrow** assume as an obligation. **owe** have to repay **412 My . . . disgrace it** my only inclination toward love is a desire to render it contemptible **414 all . . . breath** all in the same breath

"Who wears a garment shapeless and unfinish'd?
Who plucks the bud before one leaf put forth?
If springing things be any jot diminish'd, 417
They wither in their prime, prove nothing worth.
The colt that's back'd and burden'd being young 419
Loseth his pride and never waxeth strong.

"You hurt my hand with wringing. Let us part,
And leave this idle theme, this bootless chat. 422
Remove your siege from my unyielding heart;
To love's alarms it will not ope the gate. 424
Dismiss your vows, your feigned tears, your flatt'ry;
For where a heart is hard they make no batt'ry." 426

"What, canst thou talk?" quoth she, "hast thou a tongue?
O, would thou hadst not, or I had no hearing!
Thy mermaid's voice hath done me double wrong; 429
I had my load before, now press'd with bearing: 430
Melodious discord, heavenly tune harsh sounding,
Ear's deep sweet music, and heart's deep sore wounding.

"Had I no eyes but ears, my ears would love
That inward beauty and invisible; 434
Or were I deaf, thy outward parts would move 435
Each part in me that were but sensible. 436
Though neither eyes nor ears, to hear nor see,
Yet should I be in love by touching thee.

"Say that the sense of feeling were bereft me,
And that I could not see, nor hear, nor touch,
And nothing but the very smell were left me,
Yet would my love to thee be still as much;
For from the stillitory of thy face excelling 443
Comes breath perfum'd that breedeth love by smelling.

"But, O, what banquet wert thou to the taste,
Being nurse and feeder of the other four!
Would they not wish the feast might ever last,
And bid Suspicion double-lock the door, 448
Lest Jealousy, that sour unwelcome guest,
Should, by his stealing in, disturb the feast?"

Once more the ruby-color'd portal open'd,
Which to his speech did honey passage yield, 452
Like a red morn, that ever yet betoken'd
Wrack to the seaman, tempest to the field, 454
Sorrow to shepherds, woe unto the birds,
Gusts and foul flaws to herdmen and to herds. 456

This ill presage advisedly she marketh. 457
Even as the wind is hush'd before it raineth,
Or as the wolf doth grin before he barketh, 459
Or as the berry breaks before it staineth,
Or like the deadly bullet of a gun,
His meaning struck her ere his words begun.

And at his look she flatly falleth down,
For looks kill love and love by looks reviveth;
A smile recures the wounding of a frown. 465
But blessed bankrupt, that by love so thriveth!
The silly boy, believing she is dead, 467
Claps her pale cheek, till clapping makes it red;

And all amaz'd brake off his late intent,
For sharply he did think to reprehend her,
Which cunning Love did wittily prevent.
Fair fall the wit that can so well defend her! 472
For on the grass she lies as she were slain,
Till his breath breatheth life in her again.

He wrings her nose, he strikes her on the cheeks,
He bends her fingers, holds her pulses hard,
He chafes her lips; a thousand ways he seeks
To mend the hurt that his unkindness marr'd.
He kisses her; and she, by her good will,
Will never rise, so he will kiss her still. 480

The night of sorrow now is turn'd to day.
Her two blue windows faintly she upheaveth,
Like the fair sun, when in his fresh array
He cheers the morn and all the earth relieveth;
And as the bright sun glorifies the sky,
So is her face illumin'd with her eye,

Whose beams upon his hairless face are fix'd,
As if from thence they borrow'd all their shine.
Were never four such lamps together mix'd,
Had not his clouded with his brow's repine; 490
But hers, which through the crystal tears gave light,
Shone like the moon in water seen by night.

"O, where am I?" quoth she, "in earth or heaven,
Or in the ocean drench'd, or in the fire?
What hour is this? Or morn or weary even?
Do I delight to die, or life desire?
But now I liv'd, and life was death's annoy; 497
But now I died, and death was lively joy. 498

"O, thou didst kill me; kill me once again!
Thy eyes' shrewd tutor, that hard heart of thine, 500
Hath taught them scornful tricks and such disdain
That they have murd'red this poor heart of mine;
And these mine eyes, true leaders to their queen, 503
But for thy piteous lips no more had seen.

417 springing sprouting, immature **419 back'd** broken in **422 bootless** profitless **424 alarms** signals of attack **426 batt'ry** breach in a fortified wall **429 mermaid's** siren's **430 press'd** oppressed, weighted down (making her previous burden of his coy beauty now unbearable) **434 That . . . invisible** i.e., the unseen beauty of your voice **435 outward parts** i.e., tangible body **436 sensible** susceptible to sensual impressions **443 stillitory** alembic, a still. **excelling** exceedingly fair **448 Suspicion** caution **452 honey** sweet **454 Wrack** shipwreck **456 flaws** gusts of wind

457 advisedly attentively **459 grin** bare its teeth **465 recures** restores **467 silly** naive **472 Fair fall** good luck befall **480 so** provided that. **still** continually **490 repine** repining, dissatisfaction **497 death's annoy** i.e., as wretched as death **498 lively joy** i.e., as joyous as life **500 shrewd** sharp, harsh **503 queen** i.e., the heart

"Long may they kiss each other, for this cure!
O, never let their crimson liveries wear!
And as they last, their verdure still endure,
To drive infection from the dangerous year!
  That the star-gazers, having writ on death,
  May say, the plague is banish'd by thy breath.

"Pure lips, sweet seals in my soft lips imprinted,
What bargains may I make, still to be sealing?
To sell myself I can be well contented,
So thou wilt buy and pay and use good dealing,
  Which purchase if thou make, for fear of slips
  Set thy seal manual on my wax-red lips.

"A thousand kisses buys my heart from me;
And pay them at thy leisure, one by one.
What is ten hundred touches unto thee?
Are they not quickly told and quickly gone?
  Say for non-payment that the debt should double,
  Is twenty hundred kisses such a trouble?"

"Fair queen," quoth he, "if any love you owe me,
Measure my strangeness with my unripe years.
Before I know myself, seek not to know me.
No fisher but the ungrown fry forbears.
  The mellow plum doth fall, the green sticks fast,
  Or being early pluck'd is sour to taste.

"Look the world's comforter, with weary gait,
His day's hot task hath ended in the west;
The owl, night's herald, shrieks, 'tis very late;
The sheep are gone to fold, birds to their nest,
  And coal-black clouds that shadow heaven's light
  Do summon us to part and bid good night.

"Now let me say 'Good night,' and so say you;
If you will say so, you shall have a kiss."
"Good night," quoth she, and, ere he says "Adieu,"
The honey fee of parting tend'red is.
  Her arms do lend his neck a sweet embrace;
  Incorporate then they seem; face grows to face;

Till, breathless, he disjoin'd, and backward drew
The heavenly moisture, that sweet coral mouth,
Whose precious taste her thirsty lips well knew,
Whereon they surfeit, yet complain on drouth.
  He with her plenty press'd, she faint with dearth,
  Their lips together glued, fall to the earth.

Now quick desire hath caught the yielding prey,
And glutton-like she feeds, yet never filleth;
Her lips are conquerors, his lips obey,
Paying what ransom the insulter willeth,
  Whose vulture thought doth pitch the price so high
  That she will draw his lips' rich treasure dry.

And having felt the sweetness of the spoil,
With blindfold fury she begins to forage;
Her face doth reek and smoke, her blood doth boil,
And careless lust stirs up a desperate courage,
  Planting oblivion, beating reason back,
  Forgetting shame's pure blush and honor's wrack.

Hot, faint, and weary, with her hard embracing,
Like a wild bird being tam'd with too much handling,
Or as the fleet-foot roe that's tir'd with chasing,
Or like the froward infant still'd with dandling,
  He now obeys, and now no more resisteth,
  While she takes all she can, not all she listeth.

What wax so frozen but dissolves with temp'ring,
And yields at last to very light impression?
Things out of hope are compass'd oft with vent'ring,
Chiefly in love, whose leave exceeds commission.
  Affection faints not like a pale-fac'd coward,
  But then woos best when most his choice is froward.

When he did frown, O, had she then gave over,
Such nectar from his lips she had not suck'd.
Foul words and frowns must not repel a lover.
What though the rose have prickles, yet 'tis pluck'd.
  Were beauty under twenty locks kept fast,
  Yet love breaks through and picks them all at last.

For pity now she can no more detains him;
The poor fool prays her that he may depart.
She is resolv'd no longer to restrain him,
Bids him farewell, and look well to her heart,
  The which, by Cupid's bow she doth protest,
  He carries thence incaged in his breast.

"Sweet boy," she says, "this night I'll waste in sorrow,
For my sick heart commands mine eyes to watch.
Tell me, Love's master, shall we meet tomorrow?
Say, shall we, shall we? Wilt thou make the match?"
  He tells her no, tomorrow he intends
  To hunt the boar with certain of his friends.

"The boar!" quoth she, whereat a sudden pale,
Like lawn being spread upon the blushing rose,
Usurps her cheek. She trembles at his tale
And on his neck her yoking arms she throws.
  She sinketh down, still hanging by his neck,
  He on her belly falls, she on her back.

505 for in payment for **506 wear** wear out **507 verdure** fresh fragrance. (Alludes to the belief in the wholesome effects of certain herbs in the presence of the sick.) **509 writ on death** predicted (by means of astrology) an epidemic of plague **512 still to be sealing** (1) to continue kissing always (2) to seal a bargain **514 So** provided that **515 slips** errors or fraudulent payment (which Venus suggests they avoid by means of a *seal-manual* or seal placed on the contract of their love) **519 touches** i.e., kisses **520 told** counted **523 owe** bear **524 Measure . . . with** i.e., explain my reserve by **526 No . . . forbears** there is no fisherman who does not throw back immature fish **529 Look** see how. **world's comforter** i.e., sun **540 Incorporate** united into one body **545 press'd** oppressed **550 insulter** boasting conqueror

551 vulture i.e., ravenous **555 reek** i.e., steam **556 careless** heedless **557 Planting oblivion** implanting or causing forgetfulness of all that she ought to remember **558 wrack** ruin **562 froward** fretful **564 listeth** desires **565 temp'ring** heating and working with the fingers **567 out of** beyond. **compass'd** encompassed, accomplished **568 leave exceeds commission** liberties go beyond due warrant **569 Affection** passion. **faints not** does not relent or fall back **570 choice is froward** chosen one is stubborn, obstinate **573 Foul** hostile, disagreeable **578 fool** (An affectionate term.) **583 waste** spend **584 watch** stay awake **589 pale** pallor **590 lawn** fine linen

Now is she in the very lists of love, 595
Her champion mounted for the hot encounter.
All is imaginary she doth prove, 597
He will not manage her, although he mount her; 598
That worse than Tantalus' is her annoy, 599
To clip Elysium and to lack her joy. 600

Even as poor birds, deceiv'd with painted grapes, 601
Do surfeit by the eye and pine the maw, 602
Even so she languisheth in her mishaps,
As those poor birds that helpless berries saw. 604
The warm effects which she in him finds missing 605
She seeks to kindle with continual kissing.

But all in vain; good queen, it will not be.
She hath assay'd as much as may be prov'd. 608
Her pleading hath deserv'd a greater fee;
She's Love, she loves, and yet she is not lov'd.
"Fie, fie," he says, "you crush me, let me go!
You have no reason to withhold me so."

"Thou hadst been gone," quoth she, "sweet boy, ere this,
But that thou told'st me thou wouldst hunt the boar.
O, be advis'd! Thou know'st not what it is
With javelin's point a churlish swine to gore,
Whose tushes never sheath'd he whetteth still, 617
Like to a mortal butcher bent to kill. 618

"On his bow-back he hath a battle set 619
Of bristly pikes, that ever threat his foes;
His eyes, like glow-worms, shine when he doth fret;
His snout digs sepulchers where'er he goes;
Being mov'd, he strikes whate'er is in his way, 623
And whom he strikes his crooked tushes slay.

"His brawny sides, with hairy bristles armed,
Are better proof than thy spear's point can enter; 626
His short thick neck cannot be easily harmed;
Being ireful, on the lion he will venter. 628
The thorny brambles and embracing bushes,
As fearful of him, part, through whom he rushes. 630

"Alas, he nought esteems that face of thine,
To which Love's eyes pays tributary gazes,
Nor thy soft hands, sweet lips, and crystal eyne, 633
Whose full perfection all the world amazes;
But having thee at vantage—wondrous dread!—
Would root these beauties as he roots the mead. 636

"O, let him keep his loathsome cabin still! 637
Beauty hath nought to do with such foul fiends.
Come not within his danger by thy will; 639
They that thrive well take counsel of their friends.
When thou didst name the boar, not to dissemble,
I fear'd thy fortune, and my joints did tremble. 642

"Didst thou not mark my face? Was it not white?
Sawest thou not signs of fear lurk in mine eye?
Grew I not faint, and fell I not downright? 645
Within my bosom, whereon thou dost lie,
My boding heart pants, beats, and takes no rest,
But, like an earthquake, shakes thee on my breast.

"For where Love reigns, disturbing Jealousy 649
Doth call himself Affection's sentinel,
Gives false alarms, suggesteth mutiny, 651
And in a peaceful hour doth cry 'Kill, kill!'
Distemp'ring gentle Love in his desire, 653
As air and water do abate the fire.

"This sour informer, this bate-breeding spy, 655
This canker that eats up Love's tender spring, 656
This carry-tale, dissentious Jealousy,
That sometime true news, sometime false doth bring,
Knocks at my heart and whispers in mine ear
That if I love thee, I thy death should fear;

"And more than so, presenteth to mine eye
The picture of an angry-chafing boar,
Under whose sharp fangs on his back doth lie
An image like thyself, all stain'd with gore,
Whose blood upon the fresh flowers being shed
Doth make them droop with grief and hang the head.

"What should I do, seeing thee so indeed, 667
That tremble at th' imagination? 668
The thought of it doth make my faint heart bleed,
And fear doth teach it divination.
I prophesy thy death, my living sorrow,
If thou encounter with the boar tomorrow.

"But if thou needs wilt hunt, be rul'd by me;
Uncouple at the timorous flying hare, 674
Or at the fox which lives by subtlety,
Or at the roe which no encounter dare.
Pursue these fearful creatures o'er the downs,
And on thy well-breath'd horse keep with thy hounds. 678

"And when thou hast on foot the purblind hare, 679
Mark the poor wretch, to overshoot his troubles 680
How he outruns the wind and with what care
He cranks and crosses with a thousand doubles. 682

595 lists tournament field (with erotic suggestion) **597 she doth prove** that she experiences **598 manage** control, ride (as one manages a horse) **599 Tantalus'** a son of Zeus who was punished by perpetual hunger and thirst with food and drink always in sight yet untouchable **600 clip** embrace. **Elysium** blissful afterlife in classical mythology **601 birds . . . grapes** (Allusion to Zeuxis, a Greek painter of the fifth century B.C., so skillful an artist that birds were said to peck at his picture of a bunch of grapes.) **602 pine the maw** starve the stomach **604 helpless** affording no sustinence **605 effects** response **608 assay'd** tried. **prov'd** tried **617 tushes** tusks. **still** continually **618 mortal** deadly **619 battle** i.e., martial array **623 mov'd** angered **626 proof** armor **628 venter** venture **630 As** as if **633 eyne** eyes **636 root** root up **637 keep** occupy. **cabin** den

639 danger i.e., zone of danger. **by thy will** intentionally **642 fear'd** feared for **645 downright** forthwith **649 Jealousy** apprehension **651 suggesteth mutiny** incites dissension **653 Distem'pring** quenching **655 bate-breeding** strife-breeding **656 canker** cankerworm. **spring** young shoot of a plant **667–668 seeing . . . imagination** if I should actually see you dead, when merely imagining it makes me tremble **674 Uncouple** unleash the hounds **678 well-breath'd** sound in wind **679 on foot** in chase. **purblind** dimsighted **680 overshoot** run beyond **682 cranks** turns

The many musets through the which he goes
Are like a labyrinth to amaze his foes.

"Sometime he runs among a flock of sheep,
To make the cunning hounds mistake their smell,
And sometime where earth-delving conies keep,
To stop the loud pursuers in their yell,
And sometime sorteth with a herd of deer.
Danger deviseth shifts, wit waits on fear.

"For there his smell with others being mingled,
The hot scent-snuffing hounds are driven to doubt,
Ceasing their clamorous cry till they have singled
With much ado the cold fault cleanly out.
Then do they spend their mouths; echo replies,
As if another chase were in the skies.

"By this, poor Wat, far off upon a hill,
Stands on his hinder legs with list'ning ear,
To hearken if his foes pursue him still.
Anon their loud alarums he doth hear,
And now his grief may be compared well
To one sore sick that hears the passing bell.

"Then shalt thou see the dew-bedabbled wretch
Turn, and return, indenting with the way;
Each envious brier his weary legs do scratch,
Each shadow makes him stop, each murmur stay;
For misery is trodden on by many,
And, being low, never reliev'd by any.

"Lie quietly, and hear a little more.
Nay, do not struggle, for thou shalt not rise.
To make thee hate the hunting of the boar,
Unlike myself thou hear'st me moralize,
Applying this to that, and so to so;
For love can comment upon every woe.

"Where did I leave?" "No matter where," quoth he,
"Leave me, and then the story aptly ends;
The night is spent." "Why, what of that?" quoth she.
"I am," quoth he, "expected of my friends,
And now 'tis dark, and going I shall fall."
"In night," quoth she, "desire sees best of all.

"But if thou fall, O, then imagine this,
The earth, in love with thee, thy footing trips,
And all is but to rob thee of a kiss.
Rich preys make true men thieves; so do thy lips
Make modest Dian cloudy and forlorn,
Lest she should steal a kiss and die forsworn.

"Now of this dark night I perceive the reason:
Cynthia for shame obscures her silver shine,
Till forging Nature be condemn'd of treason,
For stealing molds from heaven that were divine,
Wherein she fram'd thee, in high heaven's despite,
To shame the sun by day and her by night.

"And therefore hath she brib'd the Destinies
To cross the curious workmanship of nature,
To mingle beauty with infirmities,
And pure perfection with impure defeature,
Making it subject to the tyranny
Of mad mischances and much misery;

"As burning fevers, agues pale and faint,
Life-poisoning pestilence and frenzies wood,
The marrow-eating sickness, whose attaint
Disorder breeds by heating of the blood;
Surfeits, imposthumes, grief, and damn'd despair
Swear Nature's death for framing thee so fair.

"And not the least of all these maladies
But in one minute's fight brings beauty under.
Both favor, savor, hue, and qualities,
Whereat th' impartial gazer late did wonder,
Are on the sudden wasted, thaw'd, and done,
As mountain snow melts with the midday sun.

"Therefore, despite of fruitless chastity,
Love-lacking vestals and self-loving nuns,
That on the earth would breed a scarcity
And barren dearth of daughters and of sons,
Be prodigal. The lamp that burns by night
Dries up his oil to lend the world his light.

"What is thy body but a swallowing grave,
Seeming to bury that posterity
Which by the rights of time thou needs must have,
If thou destroy them not in dark obscurity?
If so, the world will hold thee in disdain,
Sith in thy pride so fair a hope is slain.

"So in thyself thyself art made away,
A mischief worse than civil home-bred strife,
Or theirs whose desperate hands themselves do slay,
Or butcher sire that reaves his son of life.
Foul cank'ring rust the hidden treasure frets,
But gold that's put to use more gold begets."

"Nay, then," quoth Adon, "you will fall again
Into your idle over-handled theme.
The kiss I gave you is bestow'd in vain,
And all in vain you strive against the stream;
For, by this black-fac'd night, desire's foul nurse,
Your treatise makes me like you worse and worse.

"If love have lent you twenty thousand tongues,
And every tongue more moving than your own,

683 musets gaps in hedge or fence **684 amaze** bewilder **687 conies** rabbits. **keep** dwell **688 yell** cry **689 sorteth** consorts, mingles **690 shifts** tricks. **wit waits** intelligence attends **694 cold fault** cold or lost scent **695 spend their mouths** give the cry on spotting the game **697 Wat** (A common name applied to the hare.) **702 passing bell** funeral bell **704 indenting** zigzagging **705 envious** malicious **724 preys** spoils. **true** honest **725 Dian** Diana, goddess of the moon, chastity, and the hunt. **cloudy** obscured with clouds; sorrowful **726 forsworn** i.e., having broken her vow as the goddess of chastity **727 of** for **728 Cynthia** i.e., Diana, the moon **729 forging** counterfeiting

731 she i.e., Nature **732 her** i.e., the moon **734 cross** thwart. **curious** ingenious **736 defeature** disfigurement **740 wood** mad **741 attaint** infection **743 imposthumes** abscesses **744 Swear . . . fair** (all these diseases) swear to kill Nature because she formed you so beautiful **747 favor** beauty of feature **748 impartial** i.e., uninfluenced by love **762 Sith** since **766 reaves** bereaves **767 cank'ring** consuming (like the cankerworm). **frets** eats away **774 treatise** discourse

Bewitching like the wanton mermaids' songs,
Yet from mine ear the tempting tune is blown;
    For know, my heart stands armed in mine ear,
    And will not let a false sound enter there,

"Lest the deceiving harmony should run
Into the quiet closure of my breast;
And then my little heart were quite undone,
In his bedchamber to be barr'd of rest.
    No, lady, no; my heart longs not to groan,
    But soundly sleeps, while now it sleeps alone.

"What have you urg'd that I cannot reprove?
The path is smooth that leadeth on to danger.
I hate not love, but your device in love,
That lends embracements unto every stranger.
    You do it for increase. O strange excuse,
    When reason is the bawd to lust's abuse!

"Call it not love, for Love to heaven is fled,
Since sweating Lust on earth usurp'd his name,
Under whose simple semblance he hath fed
Upon fresh beauty, blotting it with blame;
    Which the hot tyrant stains and soon bereaves,
    As caterpillars do the tender leaves.

"Love comforteth like sunshine after rain,
But Lust's effect is tempest after sun;
Love's gentle spring doth always fresh remain,
Lust's winter comes ere summer half be done.
    Love surfeits not, Lust like a glutton dies;
    Love is all truth, Lust full of forged lies.

"More I could tell, but more I dare not say;
The text is old, the orator too green.
Therefore, in sadness, now I will away.
My face is full of shame, my heart of teen;
    Mine ears, that to your wanton talk attended,
    Do burn themselves for having so offended."

With this, he breaketh from the sweet embrace
Of those fair arms which bound him to her breast,
And homeward through the dark laund runs apace,
Leaves Love upon her back deeply distress'd.
    Look how a bright star shooteth from the sky,
    So glides he in the night from Venus' eye;

Which after him she darts, as one on shore
Gazing upon a late-embarked friend,
Till the wild waves will have him seen no more,
Whose ridges with the meeting clouds contend.
    So did the merciless and pitchy night
    Fold in the object that did feed her sight.

Whereat amaz'd, as one that unaware
Hath dropp'd a precious jewel in the flood,
Or stonish'd as night-wand'rers often are,
Their light blown out in some mistrustful wood,
    Even so confounded in the dark she lay,
    Having lost the fair discovery of her way.

And now she beats her heart, whereat it groans,
That all the neighbor caves, as seeming troubled,
Make verbal repetition of her moans.
Passion on passion deeply is redoubled:
    "Ay me!" she cries, and twenty times "Woe,
      woe!"
    And twenty echoes twenty times cry so.

She marking them begins a wailing note
And sings extemporally a woeful ditty
How love makes young men thrall and old men dote,
How love is wise in folly, foolish witty.
    Her heavy anthem still concludes in woe,
    And still the choir of echoes answer so.

Her song was tedious and outwore the night,
For lovers' hours are long, though seeming short.
If pleas'd themselves, others, they think, delight
In such-like circumstance, with such-like sport.
    Their copious stories, oftentimes begun,
    End without audience and are never done.

For who hath she to spend the night withal
But idle sounds resembling parasits,
Like shrill-tongu'd tapsters answering every call,
Soothing the humor of fantastic wits?
    She says "'Tis so," they answer all "'Tis so,"
    And would say after her, if she said "No."

Lo here the gentle lark, weary of rest,
From his moist cabinet mounts up on high,
And wakes the morning, from whose silver breast
The sun ariseth in his majesty,
    Who doth the world so gloriously behold
    That cedar-tops and hills seem burnish'd gold.

Venus salutes him with this fair good morrow:
"O thou clear god, and patron of all light,
From whom each lamp and shining star doth borrow
The beauteous influence that makes him bright,
    There lives a son that suck'd an earthly mother,
    May lend thee light, as thou dost lend to other."

This said, she hasteth to a myrtle grove,
Musing the morning is so much o'erworn,
And yet she hears no tidings of her love.
She hearkens for his hounds and for his horn.
    Anon she hears them chant it lustily,
    And all in haste she coasteth to the cry.

And as she runs, the bushes in the way
Some catch her by the neck, some kiss her face,
Some twine about her thigh to make her stay.

782 closure enclosure **787 reprove** refute **789 device** cunning, deceitful conduct **795 whose** i.e., Love's. **simple semblance** guileless appearance. **he** i.e., Lust **796 blotting** soiling **797 bereaves** spoils **806 green** young, unpracticed **807 in sadness** seriously, truly **808 teen** grief, vexation **813 laund** glade **823 amaz'd** dazed, confused **825 stonish'd** dismayed

826 mistrustful causing apprehension **832 Passion** lamentation **837 thrall** captive **848 parasits** parasites, flattering attendants **850 Soothing . . . wits** i.e., complying with the whim of capricious tavern customers **854 moist cabinet** dewy dwelling, nest **863 a son** i.e., Adonis **870 coasteth to** makes progress toward

She wildly breaketh from their strict embrace,
Like a milch doe, whose swelling dugs do ache,
Hasting to feed her fawn hid in some brake.

By this, she hears the hounds are at a bay,
Whereat she starts, like one that spies an adder
Wreath'd up in fatal folds just in his way,
The fear whereof doth make him shake and shudder;
Even so the timorous yelping of the hounds
Appalls her senses and her spirit confounds.

For now she knows it is no gentle chase,
But the blunt boar, rough bear, or lion proud,
Because the cry remaineth in one place,
Where fearfully the dogs exclaim aloud.
Finding their enemy to be so curst,
They all strain curt'sy who shall cope him first.

This dismal cry rings sadly in her ear,
Through which it enters to surprise her heart,
Who, overcome by doubt and bloodless fear,
With cold-pale weakness numbs each feeling part.
Like soldiers, when their captain once doth yield,
They basely fly and dare not stay the field.

Thus stands she in a trembling ecstasy,
Till, cheering up her senses all dismay'd,
She tells them 'tis a causeless fantasy,
And childish error, that they are afraid;
Bids them leave quaking, bids them fear no more—
And with that word she spied the hunted boar,

Whose frothy mouth, bepainted all with red,
Like milk and blood being mingled both together,
A second fear through all her sinews spread,
Which madly hurries her she knows not whither.
This way she runs, and now she will no further,
But back retires to rate the boar for murther.

A thousand spleens bear her a thousand ways;
She treads the path that she untreads again;
Her more than haste is mated with delays,
Like the proceedings of a drunken brain,
Full of respects, yet nought at all respecting,
In hand with all things, nought at all effecting.

Here kennel'd in a brake she finds a hound,
And asks the weary caitiff for his master,
And there another licking of his wound,
'Gainst venom'd sores the only sovereign plaster;
And here she meets another sadly scowling,
To whom she speaks, and he replies with howling.

When he hath ceas'd his ill-resounding noise,
Another flap-mouth'd mourner, black and grim,
Against the welkin volleys out his voice;
Another and another answer him,
Clapping their proud tails to the ground below,
Shaking their scratch'd ears, bleeding as they go.

Look how the world's poor people are amazed
At apparitions, signs, and prodigies,
Whereon with fearful eyes they long have gazed,
Infusing them with dreadful prophecies;
So she at these sad signs draws up her breath
And, sighing it again, exclaims on Death.

"Hard-favor'd tyrant, ugly, meager, lean,
Hateful divorce of love!"—thus chides she Death—
"Grim-grinning ghost, earth's worm, what dost thou mean
To stifle beauty and to steal his breath,
Who, when he liv'd, his breath and beauty set
Gloss on the rose, smell to the violet?

"If he be dead—O no, it cannot be,
Seeing his beauty, thou shouldst strike at it!
O yes, it may; thou hast no eyes to see,
But hatefully at random dost thou hit.
Thy mark is feeble age, but thy false dart
Mistakes that aim and cleaves an infant's heart.

"Hadst thou but bid beware, then he had spoke,
And, hearing him, thy power had lost his power.
The Destinies will curse thee for this stroke;
They bid thee crop a weed, thou pluck'st a flower.
Love's golden arrow at him should have fled,
And not Death's ebon dart, to strike him dead.

"Dost thou drink tears, that thou provok'st such weeping?
What may a heavy groan advantage thee?
Why hast thou cast into eternel sleeping
Those eyes that taught all other eyes to see?
Now Nature cares not for thy mortal vigor,
Since her best work is ruin'd with thy rigor."

Here overcome, as one full of despair,
She vail'd her eyelids, who, like sluices, stopp'd
The crystal tide that from her two cheeks fair
In the sweet channel of her bosom dropp'd;
But through the flood-gates breaks the silver rain,
And with his strong course opens them again.

O, how her eyes and tears did lend and borrow!
Her eye seen in the tears, tears in her eye,
Both crystals, where they view'd each other's sorrow,
Sorrow that friendly sighs sought still to dry;

877 at a bay i.e., faced by their quarry **887 curst** savage **888 strain curt'sy** are punctiliously polite, stand upon ceremony; i.e., they hold back. **cope** cope with **889 dismal** foreboding ill **890 surprise** assail suddenly **892 feeling part** organ of sense **895 ecstasy** agitated state **906 rate** berate **907 spleens** impulses **908 untreads** retraces **909 mated** confounded, checked **911 respects** designs, considerations. **nought at all respecting** i.e., heedless **912 In hand with** busy about **913 kennel'd** hiding as if in its kennel **914 caitiff** wretch **916 only sovereign plaster** best all-curing application

920 flap-mouth'd having broad, hanging lips **921 welkin** sky **925 Look how** just as **928 Infusing them with** attributing to them. **prophecies** prophetic qualities **930 exclaims on** denounces **932 divorce** terminator **933 worm** i.e., cankerworm, consumer of flowers **935 set** gave **941 mark** target **944 his** its **948 ebon** ebony, black **953 cares . . . vigor** does not fear your deadly power **956 vail'd** lowered. **who** which. **stopp'd** stopped up **961 lend and borrow** i.e., reflect each other **963 crystals** i.e., mirrors **964 friendly** i.e., consoling

But like a stormy day, now wind, now rain,
Sighs dry her cheeks, tears make them wet again.

Variable passions throng her constant woe,
As striving who should best become her grief. 968
All entertain'd, each passion labors so 969
That every present sorrow seemeth chief,
But none is best; then join they all together,
Like many clouds consulting for foul weather. 972

By this, far off she hears some huntsman hallow; 973
A nurse's song ne'er pleas'd her babe so well.
The dire imagination she did follow
This sound of hope doth labor to expel;
For now reviving joy bids her rejoice,
And flatters her it is Adonis' voice.

Whereat her tears began to turn their tide, 979
Being prison'd in her eye like pearls in glass;
Yet sometimes falls an orient drop beside, 981
Which her cheek melts, as scorning it should pass,
To wash the foul face of the sluttish ground,
Who is but drunken when she seemeth drown'd.

O hard-believing love, how strange it seems
Not to believe, and yet too credulous!
Thy weal and woe are both of them extremes.
Despair and hope makes thee ridiculous:
The one doth flatter thee in thoughts unlikely, 989
In likely thoughts the other kills thee quickly.

Now she unweaves the web that she hath wrought;
Adonis lives, and Death is not to blame;
It was not she that call'd him all to naught. 993
Now she adds honors to his hateful name:
She clepes him king of graves and grave for kings, 995
Imperious supreme of all mortal things. 996

"No, no," quoth she, "sweet Death, I did but jest.
Yet pardon me, I felt a kind of fear
When as I met the boar, that bloody beast, 999
Which knows no pity, but is still severe. 1000
Then, gentle shadow—truth I must confess— 1001
I rail'd on thee, fearing my love's decesse. 1002

"'Tis not my fault; the boar provok'd my tongue.
Be wreak'd on him, invisible commander. 1004
'Tis he, foul creature, that hath done thee wrong;
I did but act, he's author of thy slander. 1006
Grief hath two tongues, and never woman yet 1007
Could rule them both without ten women's wit."

Thus hoping that Adonis is alive,
Her rash suspect she doth extenuate; 1010
And that his beauty may the better thrive,
With Death she humbly doth insinuate; 1012
Tells him of trophies, statues, tombs, and stories 1013
His victories, his triumphs, and his glories.

"O Jove," quoth she, "how much a fool was I
To be of such a weak and silly mind
To wail his death who lives and must not die
Till mutual overthrow of mortal kind! 1018
For, he being dead, with him is beauty slain,
And, beauty dead, black chaos comes again.

"Fie, fie, fond love, thou art as full of fear 1021
As one with treasure laden, hemm'd with thieves;
Trifles, unwitnessed with eye or ear, 1023
Thy coward heart with false bethinking grieves." 1024
Even at this word she hears a merry horn,
Whereat she leaps that was but late forlorn. 1026

As falcon to the lure, away she flies—
The grass stoops not, she treads on it so light—
And in her haste unfortunately spies
The foul boar's conquest on her fair delight;
Which seen, her eyes, as murd'red with the view,
Like stars asham'd of day, themselves withdrew; 1032

Or, as the snail, whose tender horns being hit,
Shrinks backward in his shelly cave with pain,
And there, all smoth'red up, in shade doth sit,
Long after fearing to creep forth again;
So, at his bloody view, her eyes are fled
Into the deep dark cabins of her head,

Where they resign their office and their light
To the disposing of her troubled brain,
Who bids them still consort with ugly night 1041
And never wound the heart with looks again— 1042
Who, like a king perplexed in his throne, 1043
By their suggestion gives a deadly groan. 1044

Whereat each tributary subject quakes, 1045
As when the wind, imprison'd in the ground, 1046
Struggling for passage, earth's foundation shakes,
Which with cold terror doth men's minds confound.
This mutiny each part doth so surprise 1049
That from their dark beds once more leap her eyes;

And, being open'd, threw unwilling light
Upon the wide wound that the boar had trench'd
In his soft flank, whose wonted lily white
With purple tears, that his wound wept, was drench'd.
No flow'r was nigh, no grass, herb, leaf, or weed,
But stole his blood and seem'd with him to bleed.

968 who which **969 entertain'd** admitted **972 consulting for** cooperating to produce **973 hallow** halloo **979 turn their tide** ebb **981 orient** shining **989 The one** i.e., hope **993 all to naught** wholly evil **995 clepes** names, calls **996 Imperious supreme** imperial ruler **999 When as** when **1000 still severe** incessantly ruthless **1001 shadow** specter **1002 decesse** decease **1004 wreak'd** avenged **1006 act** i.e., act as agent **1007 two tongues** i.e., true sorrow, and angry condemnation of its cause (?) **1010 rash suspect** too hasty suspicion (of Death)

1012 insinuate ingratiate herself **1013 stories** narrates, relates **1018 mutual** i.e., universal **1021 fond** foolish **1023–1024 Trifles . . . grieves** mere trifles, not actually seen by eye or heard by ear, grieve your cowardly heart with false imaginings **1026 leaps** i.e., leaps for joy. **late** lately **1032 asham'd of** made ashamed by **1041 still consort** always remain **1042 with looks** by looking **1043 Who** which, i.e., the heart **1044 By their suggestion** incited by the eyes **1045 tributary subject** i.e., subordinate part of the body **1046 wind . . . ground** (The common Elizabethan explanation of earthquakes; cf. *1 Henry IV*, III.i.30.) **1049 surprise** attack suddenly

This solemn sympathy poor Venus noteth.
Over one shoulder doth she hang her head.
Dumbly she passions, franticly she doteth; 1059
She thinks he could not die, he is not dead.
Her voice is stopp'd, her joints forget to bow;
Her eyes are mad that they have wept till now. 1062

Upon his hurt she looks so steadfastly,
That her sight dazzling makes the wound seem three; 1064
And then she reprehends her mangling eye,
That makes more gashes where no breach should be.
His face seems twain, each several limb is doubled;
For oft the eye mistakes, the brain being troubled.

"My tongue cannot express my grief for one,
And yet," quoth she, "behold two Adons dead!
My sighs are blown away, my salt tears gone,
Mine eyes are turn'd to fire, my heart to lead.
Heavy heart's lead, melt at mine eyes' red fire!
So shall I die by drops of hot desire.

"Alas, poor world, what treasure hast thou lost!
What face remains alive that's worth the viewing?
Whose tongue is music now? What canst thou boast
Of things long since, or anything ensuing? 1078
The flowers are sweet, their colors fresh and trim;
But true-sweet beauty liv'd and died with him.

"Bonnet nor veil henceforth no creature wear!
Nor sun nor wind will ever strive to kiss you.
Having no fair to lose, you need not fear; 1083
The sun doth scorn you and the wind doth hiss you.
But when Adonis liv'd, sun and sharp air
Lurk'd like two thieves, to rob him of his fair.

"And therefore would he put his bonnet on,
Under whose brim the gaudy sun would peep;
The wind would blow it off and, being gone,
Play with his locks. Then would Adonis weep;
And straight, in pity of his tender years,
They both would strive who first should dry his tears.

"To see his face the lion walk'd along
Behind some hedge, because he would not fear him; 1094
To recreate himself when he hath song, 1095
The tiger would be tame and gently hear him;
If he had spoke, the wolf would leave his prey
And never fright the silly lamb that day. 1098

"When he beheld his shadow in the brook,
The fishes spread on it their golden gills;
When he was by, the birds such pleasure took
That some would sing, some other in their bills
Would bring him mulberries and ripe-red cherries;
He fed them with his sight, they him with berries.

"But this foul, grim, and urchin-snouted boar, 1105
Whose downward eye still looketh for a grave, 1106
Ne'er saw the beauteous livery that he wore— 1107
Witness the entertainment that he gave. 1108
If he did see his face, why then I know
He thought to kiss him, and hath kill'd him so.

"'Tis true, 'tis true! Thus was Adonis slain:
He ran upon the boar with his sharp spear,
Who did not whet his teeth at him again,
But by a kiss thought to persuade him there; 1114
And, nuzzling in his flank, the loving swine
Sheath'd unaware the tusk in his soft groin.

"Had I been tooth'd like him, I must confess,
With kissing him I should have kill'd him first;
But he is dead, and never did he bless
My youth with his—the more am I accurst."
With this, she falleth in the place she stood,
And stains her face with his congealed blood.

She looks upon his lips, and they are pale;
She takes him by the hand, and that is cold;
She whispers in his ears a heavy tale,
As if they heard the woeful words she told;
She lifts the coffer-lids that close his eyes,
Where, lo, two lamps, burnt out, in darkness lies;

Two glasses, where herself herself beheld
A thousand times, and now no more reflect,
Their virtue lost, wherein they late excell'd, 1131
And every beauty robb'd of his effect.
"Wonder of time," quoth she, "this is my spite, 1133
That, thou being dead, the day should yet be light.

"Since thou art dead, lo, here I prophesy:
Sorrow on love hereafter shall attend.
It shall be waited on with jealousy, 1137
Find sweet beginning, but unsavory end,
Ne'er settled equally, but high or low,
That all love's pleasure shall not match his woe.

"It shall be fickle, false, and full of fraud,
Bud and be blasted in a breathing while; 1142
The bottom poison, and the top o'erstraw'd 1143
With sweets that shall the truest sight beguile.
The strongest body shall it make most weak,
Strike the wise dumb and teach the fool to speak.

1059 passions shows grief **1062 till now** before now **1064 dazzling** dazzling itself **1078 Of . . . ensuing** past or to come **1083 fair** beauty **1094 would not fear** did not wish to frighten **1095 To recreate . . . song** whenever he sang for his own recreation **1098 silly** innocent

1105 urchin-snouted having a snout like a hedgehog **1106 still** continually **1107 livery** i.e., outside appearance **1108 entertainment** treatment **1114 persuade** win over, or persuade to stay **1131 virtue** power (to shine) **1133 spite** torment, vexation **1137 with** by **1142 blasted** blighted. **breathing while** short time **1143 o'erstraw'd** strewn over

"It shall be sparing and too full of riot, 1147
Teaching decrepit age to tread the measures; 1148
The staring ruffian shall it keep in quiet, 1149
Pluck down the rich, enrich the poor with treasures;
  It shall be raging mad and silly mild,
  Make the young old, the old become a child.

"It shall suspect where is no cause of fear;
It shall not fear where it should most mistrust;
It shall be merciful and too severe,
And most deceiving when it seems most just;
  Perverse it shall be where it shows most toward, 1157
  Put fear to valor, courage to the coward.

"It shall be cause of war and dire events,
And set dissension 'twixt the son and sire,
Subject and servile to all discontents, 1161
As dry combustious matter is to fire.
  Sith in his prime Death doth my love destroy,
  They that love best their loves shall not enjoy."

By this, the boy that by her side lay kill'd
Was melted like a vapor from her sight,
And in his blood that on the ground lay spill'd
A purple flower sprung up, check'red with white,
  Resembling well his pale cheeks and the blood
  Which in round drops upon their whiteness
    stood.

She bows her head, the new-sprung flower to smell,
Comparing it to her Adonis' breath,
And says within her bosom it shall dwell,
Since he himself is reft from her by death.
  She crops the stalk, and in the breach appears
  Green dropping sap, which she compares to tears.

"Poor flow'r," quoth she, "this was thy father's guise— 1177
Sweet issue of a more sweet-smelling sire—
For every little grief to wet his eyes;
To grow unto himself was his desire,
  And so 'tis thine; but know, it is as good
  To wither in my breast as in his blood.

"Here was thy father's bed, here in my breast;
Thou art the next of blood, and 'tis thy right.
Lo, in this hollow cradle take thy rest;
My throbbing heart shall rock thee day and night.
  There shall not be one minute in an hour
  Wherein I will not kiss my sweet love's flow'r."

Thus weary of the world, away she hies
And yokes her silver doves, by whose swift aid
Their mistress mounted through the empty skies
In her light chariot quickly is convey'd,
  Holding their course to Paphos, where their
    queen 1193
  Means to immure herself and not be seen.

1147 sparing . . . riot i.e., both niggardly and excessive **1148 tread the measures** dance. (An inappropriate action for the old.) **1149 staring** looking savage, glaring **1157 toward** tractable **1161 Subject . . . discontents** (love will be) both the cause and the unwilling slave of every kind of dissension **1177 guise** manner, way **1193 Paphos** Venus' dwelling in Cyprus

The Rape of Lucrece

The Rape of Lucrece is a companion poem to *Venus and Adonis.* The two were published about a year apart, in 1593 and 1594, both printed by Richard Field. Both are dedicated to the young Earl of Southampton, Henry Wriothesley, whose confidence and friendship Shakespeare appears to have gained during the interim between the two poems; the dedicatory preface to *The Rape of Lucrece* sounds more assured and grateful for acceptance. Stylistically the two poems are of a piece, alike reliant on Petrarchan ornament and rhetorical showmanship, alike steeped in Ovidian pathos. Yet they are complementary rather than similar in attitude and subject. *The Rape of Lucrece* appears to be the "graver labor" promised to Southampton in the dedication of the earlier poem, a planned sequel in which love would be subjected to a darker treatment. *Venus and Adonis* is chiefly about sensual pleasure whereas *The Rape of Lucrece* is about heroic chastity. The first poem is amatory, erotic, and amusing despite its sad end; the second is moral, declamatory, and lugubrious. As Gabriel Harvey observed (c. 1598–1601), "The younger sort takes much delight in Shakespeares Venus, & Adonis: but his Lucrece, & his tragedie of Hamlet, Prince of Denmarke, haue it in them, to please the wiser sort."

Harvey's pairing of this poem with *Hamlet* suggests that, to Harvey at least, Shakespeare aspires to sublime effects in *Lucrece.* For his verse pattern Shakespeare chooses the seven-line rhyme royal stanza, traditionally used for tragic expression as in Chaucer's *Troilus and Criseyde* and several of the more didactic *Canterbury Tales,* in Lydgate's *The Fall of Princes* and its continuation in *A Myrroure for Magistrates,* in Samuel Daniel's *The Complaint of Rosamond,* and others. Although Shakespeare turns to Ovid once again as his chief source, he chooses a tale of ravishment, suicide, and vengeance rather than of titillating amatory pursuit. The story of Lucrece had gained wide currency in the ancient and medieval worlds as an *exemplum* of chaste conduct in women. Shakespeare seems to have known Livy's *History of Rome* (Book I, chaps. 57–59), though he relied primarily on Ovid's *Fasti* (II, 721–852). Among later versions he may have known Chaucer's *The Legend of Good Women* and a translation of Livy in Painter's *Palace of Pleasure* (1566). He encountered other "complaints" in *A Myrroure for Magistrates* and in Daniel's *The Complaint of Rosamond,* and it is to this well-established genre that *Lucrece* belongs. The poem had the desired effect of enhancing Shakespeare's reputation for elegant poetry; it was reprinted five times during his lifetime and was frequently admired by his contemporaries. *Venus and Adonis* was, to be sure, more popular still (it was reprinted nine times during Shakespeare's lifetime), but no one in Shakespeare's day seems to have regarded *Lucrece* as anything other than a noble work.

To recapture today some of that earlier enthusiasm for the poem, we must recognize its conventions and not expect it to be other than what it professes to be. As in *Venus and Adonis,* plot and character are secondary. Although the story outlined in "The Argument" is potentially sensational and swift-moving, Shakespeare deliberately cuts away most of the action. We do not see Lucius Tarquinius' murder of his father-in-law and tyrannical seizure of Rome, or Collatinus' rash boasting of his wife Lucrece's virtue in the presence of the King's lustful son Sextus Tarquinius. Nor, at the conclusion of the story, do we learn much about the revenging of Lucrece's rape. Shakespeare's focus is on the attitudes of the two protagonists immediately before and after the ravishment. Even here, despite opportunities for psychological probing, Shakespeare's real interest is not in the characters themselves so much as in the social ramifications of their actions. As Coppélia Kahn has shown (in *Shakespeare Studies IX*), the rape serves as a means of examining the nature of marriage in a patriarchal society where competition for ownership and struggles for power characterize men's attitudes toward politics and sex. Using Rome as a familiar mirror for English customs, Shakespeare presents Lucrece as a heroine acting to uphold the institution of marriage. It is she who acquires the stain through being violated, and she who must pay the cost of wifely duty in marriage. Like a number of Shakespeare's later heroines, such as Imogen in *Cymbeline,* Lucrece is portrayed as beautiful but not alluring, restrained even in her marriage bed. She arranges her death so as to make the most of its social implications.

Shakespeare casts his narrative in the form of a series of rhetorical disputations, each a set piece presented as a debate or as a formal declamation. The debates are built around familiar antitheses: honor versus lust, rude will versus conscience, "affection" versus reason, nobility versus baseness, and so on. Many of the images are similarly arranged in contrasting pairs: dove and owl, daylight and darkness, clear and cloudy weather, white and red. Tarquin debates with himself the reasons for and against rape; Lucrece tries to persuade him of the depravity of his course; Lucrece ponders suicide. These debates generate in turn a number of rhetorical apostrophes to marital fidelity (22–28), to the ideal of kingship as a moral example to others (610–637), to Night (764–812), to Opportunity

(876–924), and to Time (925–1022). Another rhetorical formula, perhaps the most successful in the poem, is the use of structural digression. The most notable describes a painting of Troy with obvious relevance to Lucrece's sad fate: Troy is a city destroyed by a rape, Paris achieves his selfish pleasure at the expense of the public good, Sinon wins his sinister victory through deceitful appearance.

Throughout, the poem's ornament strives after heightened and elaborate effects. The comparisons, or "conceits" as the Elizabethans called them, are intentionally contrived and reliant on ingenious word play. Shakespeare puns on the word "will," for example, as he does in the Sonnets, where he takes advantage of his own first name being Will (see Sonnet 135), or in *Venus and Adonis* (see 365). In *The Rape of Lucrece,* the word is central to Shakespeare's depiction of Tarquin, as we see the ravisher holding a disputation "between frozen conscience and hot-burning will" (247), forcing the locks "between her chamber and his will" (302), feeding ravenously "in his will his willful eye" (417), and the like. These and other passages often frame the word in a polarity of *will* and *heart,* and range over numerous meanings that include inclination, desire, appetite, sexual lust, request or command, volition, pleasure, permission, good will, spontaneity. The fact that the word rhymes with *kill* and *ill* adds to its usefulness. Another kind of "conceit" found throughout *The Rape of Lucrece* is the extended military metaphor of a city under siege. Tarquin's heart beats an alarum, Lucrece's breasts are "round turrets" made pale by the assault (432–441), and, in her subsequent death, she is likened to a "late-sack'd island" surrounded by rivers of her own blood (1740). Elsewhere she is a house that has been pillaged, "Her mansion battered by the enemy" (1170–1171). Classical allusions are of course common, notably to the story of the rape of Philomel (1079, 1128, etc.). Rhetorical devices of antithesis are displayed with the same ornate versatility as in *Venus and Adonis.* In a poem on a serious subject, these devices may seem overly contrived to us. We should nevertheless recognize them as conventional in the genre to which *The Rape of Lucrece* belongs. We find a similar blending of the sensuous and the moral in the sometimes grotesque conceits of the Catholic poet Robert Southwell (d. 1595), and in the later baroque paradoxes of Richard Crashaw (d. 1649). Among Shakespeare's dramatic works, *Titus Andronicus* seems closest to *The Rape of Lucrece* in its pathos, refined sensationalism, and use of classical allusion and specifically in the character of Lavinia whose misfortunes and chaste dignity so much resemble those of Lucrece.

The Rape of Lucrece

To the RIGHT HONORABLE HENRY WRIOTHESLEY,
Earl of Southampton, and Baron of Titchfield.

The love I dedicate to your lordship is without end;
whereof this pamphlet, without beginning, is but a su- 2
perfluous moi'ty. The warrant I have of your honor- 3
able disposition, not the worth of my untutor'd lines,
makes it assur'd of acceptance. What I have done is
yours; what I have to do is yours; being part in all I 6
have, devoted yours. Were my worth greater, my duty 7
would show greater; meantime, as it is, it is bound to
your lordship, to whom I wish long life, still length'ned
with all happiness.

Your lordship's in all duty,

William Shakespeare.

The Argument

Lucius Tarquinius, for his excessive pride surnam'd
Superbus, after he had caus'd his own father-in-law 2
Servius Tullius to be cruelly murd'red, and, contrary
to the Roman laws and customs, not requiring or 4
staying for the people's suffrages, had possess'd
himself of the kingdom, went, accompanied with
his sons and other noblemen of Rome, to besiege
Ardea. During which siege the principal men of the
army meeting one evening at the tent of Sextus Tar-
quinius, the King's son, in their discourses after
supper everyone commended the virtues of his own
wife; among whom Collatinus extoll'd the incom-
parable chastity of his wife Lucretia. In that pleasant
humor they all posted to Rome; and intending, by
their secret and sudden arrival, to make trial of that
which everyone had before avouch'd, only Colla-
tinus finds his wife, though it were late in the night,
spinning amongst her maids; the other ladies were
all found dancing and reveling, or in several dis- 19
ports. Whereupon the noblemen yielded Collatinus 20
the victory, and his wife the fame. At that time Sextus Tarquinius being inflam'd with Lucrece' beauty, yet smothering his passions for the present, departed with the rest back to the camp; from whence

Dedication.
2 without beginning i.e., beginning *in medias res,* in the middle of the action **3 moi'ty** part. **warrant** assurance **6–7 being . . . have** since you are part of everything I have done and have to do

The Argument.
2 Superbus "the Proud" **4 requiring** requesting **19–20 several disports** various pastimes

he shortly after privily withdrew himself, and was, according to his estate, royally entertain'd and lodg'd by Lucrece at Collatium. The same night he treacherously stealeth into her chamber, violently ravish'd her, and early in the morning speedeth away. Lucrece, in this lamentable plight, hastily dispatcheth messengers, one to Rome for her father, another to the camp for Collatine. They came, the one accompanied with Junius Brutus, the other with Publius Valerius; and finding Lucrece attir'd in mourning habit, demanded the cause of her sorrow. She, first taking an oath of them for her revenge, reveal'd the actor, and whole manner of his dealing, and withal suddenly stabb'd herself. Which done, with one consent they all vow'd to root out the whole hated family of the Tarquins; and bearing the dead body to Rome, Brutus acquainted the people with the doer and manner of the vile deed, with a bitter invective against the tyranny of the King, wherewith the people were so mov'd, that with one consent and a general acclamation the Tarquins were all exil'd, and the state government chang'd from kings to consuls.

From the besieged Ardea all in post,
Borne by the trustless wings of false desire,
Lust-breathed Tarquin leaves the Roman host,
And to Collatium bears the lightless fire
Which, in pale embers hid, lurks to aspire
And girdle with embracing flames the waist
Of Collatine's fair love, Lucrece the chaste.

Hap'ly that name of "chaste" unhap'ly set
This bateless edge on his keen appetite;
When Collatine unwisely did not let
To praise the clear unmatched red and white
Which triumph'd in that sky of his delight,
Where mortal stars, as bright as heaven's beauties,
With pure aspects did him peculiar duties.

For he the night before, in Tarquin's tent,
Unlock'd the treasure of his happy state;
What priceless wealth the heavens had him lent
In the possession of his beauteous mate;
Reck'ning his fortune at such high proud rate
That kings might be espoused to more fame,
But king nor peer to such a peerless dame.

O happiness enjoy'd but of a few!
And, if possess'd, as soon decay'd and done
As is the morning's silver melting dew
Against the golden splendor of the sun!
An expir'd date, cancel'd ere well begun.
Honor and beauty, in the owner's arms,
Are weakly fortress'd from a world of harms.

26 estate rank

1 Ardea a city twenty-four miles south of Rome. **post** haste **2 trustless** treacherous **3 Lust-breathed** excited by lust **4 Collatium** a city about ten miles east of Rome. **lightless** i.e., smoldering invisibly **5 aspire** rise, i.e., break into flames **8 Hap'ly** perchance. **unhap'ly** (1) unhappily (2) by mischance **9 bateless** not to be blunted **10 let** forbear **12 sky** i.e., Lucrece's face **13 mortal stars** i.e., Lucrece's eyes **14 aspects** (1) looks (2) astrologically favorable position. **peculiar** exclusively for him **23 done** done with **26 date** period of time

Beauty itself doth of itself persuade
The eyes of men without an orator;
What needeth then apologies be made
To set forth that which is so singular?
Or why is Collatine the publisher
Of that rich jewel he should keep unknown
From thievish ears, because it is his own?

Perchance his boast of Lucrece' sov'reignty
Suggested this proud issue of a king;
For by our ears our hearts oft tainted be.
Perchance that envy of so rich a thing,
Braving compare, disdainfully did sting
His high-pitch'd thoughts, that meaner men should vaunt
That golden hap which their superiors want.

But some untimely thought did instigate
His all too timeless speed, if none of those.
His honor, his affairs, his friends, his state,
Neglected all, with swift intent he goes
To quench the coal which in his liver glows.
O rash false heat, wrapp'd in repentant cold,
Thy hasty spring still blasts, and ne'er grows old!

When at Collatium this false lord arrived,
Well was he welcom'd by the Roman dame,
Within whose face beauty and virtue strived
Which of them both should underprop her fame.
When virtue bragg'd, beauty would blush for shame;
When beauty boasted blushes, in despite
Virtue would stain that o'er with silver white.

But beauty, in that white entituled
From Venus' doves, doth challenge that fair field.
Then virtue claims from beauty beauty's red,
Which virtue gave the golden age to gild
Their silver cheeks, and call'd it then their shield,
Teaching them thus to use it in the fight,
When shame assail'd, the red should fence the white.

This heraldry in Lucrece' face was seen,
Argued by beauty's red and virtue's white.
Of either's color was the other queen,
Proving from world's minority their right.
Yet their ambition makes them still to fight,
The sovereignty of either being so great
That oft they interchange each other's seat.

This silent war of lilies and of roses,
Which Tarquin view'd in her fair face's field,
In their pure ranks his traitor eye encloses,

29 of by **37 Suggested** tempted. **issue** offspring, son (i.e., Tarquin) **40 Braving compare** defying comparison **41 meaner** less nobly born **42 hap** fortune. **want** lack **44 timeless** unseemly, unseasonable **45 state** position **47 liver** (Regarded as the seat of the passions.) **49 blasts** is blighted (by cold winds) **57 entituled** entitled, having a claim **58 challenge** claim. **field** (1) battlefield (2) the surface of the shield, where the armorial device is displayed **60 gild** i.e., cover with a blush of modesty. (Gold and red were often considered interchangeable as colors.) **63 fence** defend **65 Argued** disputed, and demonstrated **67 world's minority** the long-ago *golden age*, mentioned in l. 60. (I.e., their right is as old as the doves of Venus and the first blush.) **73 encloses** surrounds, overwhelms

Where, lest between them both it should be kill'd,
The coward captive vanquished doth yield
To those two armies that would let him go,
Rather than triumph in so false a foe.

Now thinks he that her husband's shallow tongue,
The niggard prodigal that prais'd her so, 79
In that high task hath done her beauty wrong,
Which far exceeds his barren skill to show.
Therefore that praise which Collatine doth owe 82
Enchanted Tarquin answers with surmise, 83
In silent wonder of still-gazing eyes.

This earthly saint, adored by this devil,
Little suspecteth the false worshiper,
For unstain'd thoughts do seldom dream on evil;
Birds never lim'd no secret bushes fear. 88
So guiltless she securely gives good cheer 89
And reverend welcome to her princely guest,
Whose inward ill no outward harm express'd.

For that he color'd with his high estate, 92
Hiding base sin in plaits of majesty, 93
That nothing in him seem'd inordinate 94
Save sometime too much wonder of his eye,
Which, having all, all could not satisfy;
But, poorly rich, so wanteth in his store, 97
That, cloy'd with much, he pineth still for more.

But she, that never cop'd with stranger eyes, 99
Could pick no meaning from their parling looks, 100
Nor read the subtle-shining secrecies
Writ in the glassy margents of such books. 102
She touch'd no unknown baits, nor fear'd no hooks;
Nor could she moralize his wanton sight, 104
More than his eyes were open'd to the light. 105

He stories to her ears her husband's fame, 106
Won in the fields of fruitful Italy,
And decks with praises Collatine's high name,
Made glorious by his manly chivalry
With bruised arms and wreaths of victory. 110
Her joy with heav'd-up hand she doth express,
And, wordless, so greets heaven for his success.

Far from the purpose of his coming thither,
He makes excuses for his being there.
No cloudy show of stormy blust'ring weather
Doth yet in his fair welkin once appear, 116
Till sable Night, mother of dread and fear,
Upon the world dim darkness doth display,
And in her vaulty prison stows the day.

For then is Tarquin brought unto his bed,
Intending weariness with heavy sprite; 121
For, after supper, long he questioned 122
With modest Lucrece, and wore out the night.
Now leaden slumber with life's strength doth fight,
And everyone to rest themselves betake,
Save thieves, and cares, and troubled minds, that wake.

As one of which doth Tarquin lie revolving
The sundry dangers of his will's obtaining;
Yet ever to obtain his will resolving,
Though weak-built hopes persuade him to abstaining.
Despair to gain doth traffic oft for gaining; 131
And when great treasure is the meed proposed, 132
Though death be adjunct, there's no death supposed. 133

Those that much covet are with gain so fond, 134
That what they have not, that which they possess 135
They scatter and unloose it from their bond, 136
And so, by hoping more, they have but less;
Or, gaining more, the profit of excess 138
Is but to surfeit, and such griefs sustain 139
That they prove bankrupt in this poor rich gain.

The aim of all is but to nurse the life
With honor, wealth, and ease, in waning age;
And in this aim there is such thwarting strife 143
That one for all, or all for one, we gage: 144
As life for honor in fell battle's rage, 145
Honor for wealth; and oft that wealth doth cost
The death of all, and all together lost.

So that in vent'ring ill we leave to be 148
The things we are for that which we expect; 149
And this ambitious foul infirmity, 150
In having much, torments us with defect 151
Of that we have. So then we do neglect
The thing we have, and, all for want of wit, 153
Make something nothing by augmenting it.

Such hazard now must doting Tarquin make,
Pawning his honor to obtain his lust,
And for himself himself he must forsake. 157
Then where is truth, if there be no self-trust?
When shall he think to find a stranger just,
When he himself himself confounds, betrays
To sland'rous tongues and wretched hateful days.?

Now stole upon the time the dead of night,
When heavy sleep had clos'd up mortal eyes.
No comfortable star did lend his light, 164

79 niggard prodigal unwisely lavish yet coming too short in praise **82 doth owe** i.e., must still render, having fallen short on previous occasions **83 answers** renders. **surmise** visual contemplation **88 lim'd** snared with birdlime, a sticky substance placed on branches **89 securely** unsuspiciously **92 that he color'd** i.e., he disguised his harmful intent **93 plaits** cunning folds, concealments **94 That** so that **97 so . . . store** feels such a craving despite the abundance **99 stranger eyes** eyes of a stranger **100 parling** speaking, conferring **102 glassy . . . books** (Refers to the custom of printing explanatory comments in book margins; cf. *Romeo and Juliet,* I.iii.87.) **104 moralize** interpret. **sight** looking **105 than** than that **106 stories** relates **110 bruised arms** armor battered in combat **116 welkin** sky, i.e., appearance, face

121 Intending pretending. **sprite** spirit **122 questioned** conversed **131 Despair . . . gaining** despair of success again and again changes place with a will to succeed **132 meed** reward **133 adjunct** adjoined, resultant. **supposed** thought of **134 fond** infatuated **135 what** for what **136 bond** possession **138 profit of excess** advantage of having more than enough **139 such griefs sustain** i.e., to sustain such griefs as accompany surfeit **143 And** yet **144 gage** pledge, risk **145 fell** fierce **148 leave to be** cease being **149 expect** i.e., hope to be **150 infirmity** i.e., covetousness **151 In having much** though we have much. **defect** the imagined deficiency **153 wit** common sense **157 for . . . forsake** he must forsake his honorable self to satisfy his lustful self **164 comfortable** cheering, benevolent. **his** its

No noise but owls' and wolves' death-boding cries.
Now serves the season that they may surprise
The silly lambs. Pure thoughts are dead and still, 167
While lust and murder wakes to stain and kill.

And now this lustful lord leapt from his bed,
Throwing his mantle rudely o'er his arm;
Is madly toss'd between desire and dread;
Th' one sweetly flatters, th' other feareth harm;
But honest fear, bewitch'd with lust's foul charm
Doth too too oft betake him to retire, 174
Beaten away by brain-sick rude desire.

His falchion on a flint he softly smiteth, 176
That from the cold stone sparks of fire do fly;
Whereat a waxen torch forthwith he lighteth,
Which must be lodestar to his lustful eye; 179
And to the flame thus speaks advisedly: 180
"As from this cold flint I enforc'd this fire,
So Lucrece must I force to my desire."

Here pale with fear he doth premeditate
The dangers of his loathsome enterprise,
And in his inward mind he doth debate
What following sorrow may on this arise.
Then looking scornfully, he doth despise
His naked armor of still-slaughtered lust, 188
And justly thus controls his thoughts unjust:

"Fair torch, burn out thy light, and lend it not
To darken her whose light excelleth thine;
And die, unhallowed thoughts, before you blot
With your uncleanness that which is divine.
Offer pure incense to so pure a shrine.
Let fair humanity abhor the deed
That spots and stains love's modest snow-white
weed. 196

"O shame to knighthood and to shining arms!
O foul dishonor to my household's grave! 198
O impious act, including all foul harms! 199
A martial man to be soft fancy's slave! 200
True valor still a true respect should have; 201
Then my digression is so vile, so base, 202
That it will live engraven in my face.

"Yea, though I die, the scandal will survive,
And be an eyesore in my golden coat; 205
Some loathsome dash the herald will contrive 206
To cipher me how fondly I did dote; 207
That my posterity, sham'd with the note, 208
Shall curse my bones, and hold it for no sin
To wish that I their father had not been.

167 silly helpless, defenseless **174 betake . . . retire** i.e., (honest fear) retires in confusion **176 falchion** curved sword **179 lodestar** the guiding pole star **180 advisedly** deliberately **188 His . . . lust** his poor defense against his own lust which is continually being slaughtered, i.e., temporarily satiated, but never killed; or, his insatiable and vulnerable lust which will be his only poor armor once he has committed the rape **196 weed** garment (i.e., chastity) **198 my household's grave** memorial tomb of my forebears **199 including** encompassing **200 fancy's** love's, infatuation's **201 true respect** i.e., proper consideration for virtue **202 digression** falling away (from honor) **205 coat** coat of arms **206 dash** bar, stroke (devised by the heralds to indicate something dishonorable in the pedigree) **207 cipher** express in characters, indicate. **fondly** foolishly **208 note** stigma, the heraldic bar (l. 206)

"What win I, if I gain the thing I seek?
A dream, a breath, a froth of fleeting joy.
Who buys a minute's mirth to wail a week?
Or sells eternity to get a toy? 214
For one sweet grape who will the vine destroy?
Or what fond beggar, but to touch the crown,
Would with the scepter straight be strucken
down?

"If Collatinus dream of my intent,
Will he not wake, and in a desp'rate rage
Post hither, this vile purpose to prevent?
This siege that hath engirt his marriage,
This blur to youth, this sorrow to the sage,
This dying virtue, this surviving shame,
Whose crime will bear an ever-during blame?

"O, what excuse can my invention make
When thou shalt charge me with so black a deed?
Will not my tongue be mute, my frail joints shake,
Mine eyes forego their light, my false heart bleed?
The guilt being great, the fear doth still exceed;
And extreme fear can neither fight nor fly,
But coward-like with trembling terror die.

"Had Collatinus kill'd my son or sire,
Or lain in ambush to betray my life,
Or were he not my dear friend, this desire
Might have excuse to work upon his wife,
As in revenge or quittal of such strife; 236
But as he is my kinsman, my dear friend,
The shame and fault finds no excuse nor end.

"Shameful it is; ay, if the fact be known, 239
Hateful it is. There is no hate in loving.
I'll beg her love. But she is not her own. 241
The worst is but denial and reproving.
My will is strong, past reason's weak removing.
Who fears a sentence or an old man's saw 244
Shall by a painted cloth be kept in awe." 245

Thus, graceless, holds he disputation
'Tween frozen conscience and hot-burning will,
And with good thoughts makes dispensation, 248
Urging the worser sense for vantage still,
Which in a moment doth confound and kill
All pure effects, and doth so far proceed 251
That what is vile shows like a virtuous deed.

Quoth he, "She took me kindly by the hand,
And gaz'd for tidings in my eager eyes,
Fearing some hard news from the warlike band,
Where her beloved Collatinus lies.
O, how her fear did make her color rise!
First red as roses that on lawn we lay, 258
Then white as lawn, the roses took away.

214 toy trifle **236 quittal** requital **239 fact** deed **241 she . . . own** i.e., she is not entirely independent, since she has duties to her husband **244 Who** whoever. **sentence** moral sentiment. **saw** saying, proverb **245 painted cloth** wall hanging in which moral tales and maxims were sometimes depicted. (Cf. ll. 1366–1456, where such a painted cloth is described.) **248 makes dispensation** dispenses, sets aside **251 effects** impulses **258 lawn** fine white linen

"And how her hand, in my hand being lock'd,
Forc'd it to tremble with her loyal fear!
Which struck her sad, and then it faster rock'd,
Until her husband's welfare she did hear;
Wherat she smiled with so sweet a cheer
  That had Narcissus seen her as she stood, 265
  Self-love had never drown'd him in the flood.

"Why hunt I then for color or excuses? 267
All orators are dumb when beauty pleadeth;
Poor wretches have remorse in poor abuses; 269
Love thrives not in the heart that shadows dreadeth. 270
Affection is my captain, and he leadeth; 271
  And when his gaudy banner is display'd,
  The coward fights and will not be dismay'd. 273

"Then, childish fear, avaunt! Debating, die!
Respect and reason, wait on wrinkled age! 275
My heart shall never countermand mine eye. 276
Sad pause and deep regard beseems the sage; 277
My part is youth, and beats these from the stage.
  Desire my pilot is, beauty my prize;
  Then who fears sinking where such treasure lies?"

As corn o'ergrown by weeds, so heedful fear 281
Is almost chok'd by unresisted lust.
Away he steals with open list'ning ear,
Full of foul hope and full of fond mistrust,
Both which, as servitors to the unjust,
  So cross him with their opposite persuasion 286
  That now he vows a league, and now invasion. 287

Within his thought her heavenly image sits,
And in the self-same seat sits Collatine.
That eye which looks on her confounds his wits; 290
That eye which him beholds, as more divine, 291
Unto a view so false will not incline,
  But with a pure appeal seeks to the heart, 293
  Which once corrupted takes the worser part;

And therein heartens up his servile powers, 295
Who, flatt'red by their leader's jocund show, 296
Stuff up his lust, as minutes fill up hours;
And as their captain, so their pride doth grow,
Paying more slavish tribute than they owe.
  By reprobate desire thus madly led,
  The Roman lord marcheth to Lucrece' bed.

The locks between her chamber and his will,
Each one by him enforc'd retires his ward; 303
But, as they open, they all rate his ill, 304
Which drives the creeping thief to some regard. 305
The threshold grates the door to have him heard;
  Night-wand'ring weasels shriek to see him there; 307
  They fright him, yet he still pursues his fear. 308

As each unwilling portal yields him way,
Through little vents and crannies of the place
The wind wars with his torch to make him stay,
And blows the smoke of it into his face,
Extinguishing his conduct in this case; 313
  But his hot heart, which fond desire doth
    scorch,
  Puffs forth another wind that fires the
    torch.

And being lighted, by the light he spies
Lucretia's glove, wherein her needle sticks.
He takes it from the rushes where it lies, 318
And griping it, the needle his finger pricks, 319
As who should say, "This glove to wanton tricks
  Is not inur'd. Return again in haste;
  Thou see'st our mistress' ornaments are
    chaste."

But all these poor forbiddings could not stay him; 323
He in the worst sense consters their denial. 324
The doors, the wind, the glove, that did delay
  him,
He takes for accidental things of trial, 326
Or as those bars which stop the hourly dial, 327
  Who with a ling'ring stay his course doth
    let, 328
  Till every minute pays the hour his debt.

"So, so," quoth he, "these lets attend the time, 330
Like little frosts that sometime threat the spring,
To add a more rejoicing to the prime, 332
And give the sneaped birds more cause to sing. 333
Pain pays the income of each precious thing; 334
  Huge rocks, high winds, strong pirates,
    shelves and sands 335
  The merchant fears, ere rich at home he
    lands."

Now is he come unto the chamber door,
That shuts him from the heaven of his thought,
Which with a yielding latch, and with no more,
Hath barr'd him from the blessed thing he sought.
So from himself impiety hath wrought, 341
  That for his prey to pray he doth begin,
  As if the heavens should countenance his sin.

But in the midst of his unfruitful prayer,
Having solicited th' eternal power

265 Narcissus youth who fell in love with his own reflection in the water **267 color** pretext **269 Poor . . . abuses** i.e., only lowborn cowardly men feel remorse for their paltry misdeeds **270 shadows** i.e., the chimeras of conscience **271 Affection** passion **273 The coward** i.e., even the coward **75 Respect** circumspection. **wait on** attend, accompany **276 heart** (Here, *moral sense*; cf. ll. 293 ff., where the heart is corrupted.) **277 Sad** serious, reflective **281 corn** grain **286 cross** thwart **287 league** treaty (of peace) **290 confounds his wits** i.e., overwhelms reason with lust **291 as more divine** i.e., as representing reason **293 seeks** applies **295 servile powers** base passions, appetites. (The image is the common one of the faculties as an army: the heart as captain of the sensible soul commands all the affections to serve his life. Cf. l. 433f., below.) **296 jocund** sprightly **303 retires his ward** draws back its guard, i.e., the locking bolt **304 rate his ill** chide his evil (by creaking) **305 regard** caution

307 weasels (Weasels were sometimes kept in houses as rat catchers.) **308 his fear** i.e., the cause of his fear **313 conduct** conductor, i.e., his torch **318 rushes** reeds used as floor covering **319 griping** grasping **323 stay** restrain **324 consters** construes **326 accidental . . . trial** i.e., accidents that test his resolve, not portents **327 bars . . . dial** minute-marks on a clock face at which the minute hand seems to pause slightly **328 Who** which. **his** its. **let** hinder **330 these . . . time** i.e., these pauses (at the minute-marks) are essential to the telling of the time, mark its passage for us **332 more** greater. **prime** spring **333 sneaped** nipped or pinched with cold **334 pays . . . of** is the price of obtaining **335 shelves** sandbars **341 So . . . wrought** impiety has so wrested him away from his true nature

That his foul thoughts might compass his fair fair, 346
And they would stand auspicious to the hour, 347
Even there he starts. Quoth he, "I must deflow'r. 348
The powers to whom I pray abhor this fact; 349
How can they then assist me in the act?

"Then Love and Fortune be my gods, my guide!
My will is back'd with resolution.
Thoughts are but dreams till their effects be tried;
The blackest sin is clear'd with absolution;
Against love's fire fear's frost hath dissolution.
The eye of heaven is out, and misty night 356
Covers the shame that follows sweet delight."

This said, his guilty hand pluck'd up the latch,
And with his knee the door he opens wide.
The dove sleeps fast that this night-owl will catch.
Thus treason works ere traitors be espied.
Who sees the lurking serpent steps aside; 362
But she, sound sleeping, fearing no such thing,
Lies at the mercy of his mortal sting.

Into the chamber wickedly he stalks,
And gazeth on her yet unstained bed.
The curtains being close, about he walks,
Rolling his greedy eyeballs in his head.
By their high treason is his heart misled,
Which gives the watch-word to his hand full soon
To draw the cloud that hides the silver moon. 371

Look as the fair and fiery-pointed sun, 372
Rushing from forth a cloud, bereaves our sight,
Even so, the curtain drawn, his eyes begun
To wink, being blinded with a greater light. 375
Whether it is that she reflects so bright,
That dazzleth them, or else some shame supposed;
But blind they are, and keep themselves enclosed.

O, had they in that darksome prison died!
Then had they seen the period of their ill. 380
Then Collatine again, by Lucrece' side,
In his clear bed might have reposed still. 382
But they must ope, this blessed league to kill,
And holy-thoughted Lucrece to their sight
Must sell her joy, her life, her world's delight.

Her lily hand her rosy cheek lies under,
Coz'ning the pillow of a lawful kiss, 387
Who, therefore angry, seems to part in sunder,
Swelling on either side to want his bliss; 389
Between whose hills her head entombed is;
Where, like a virtuous monument, she lies,
To be admir'd of lewd unhallowed eyes.

Without the bed her other fair hand was, 393
On the green coverlet, whose perfect white
Show'd like an April daisy on the grass,
With pearly sweat resembling dew of night.
Her eyes, like marigolds, had sheath'd their light,
And canopied in darkness sweetly lay,
Till they might open to adorn the day.

Her hair, like golden threads, play'd with her breath—
O modest wantons, wanton modesty!
Showing life's triumph in the map of death, 402
And death's dim look in life's mortality. 403
Each in her sleep themselves so beautify,
As if between them twain there were no strife,
But that life liv'd in death, and death in life.

Her breasts like ivory globes circled with blue,
A pair of maiden worlds unconquered,
Save of their lord no bearing yoke they knew,
And him by oath they truly honored.
These worlds in Tarquin new ambition bred,
Who, like a foul usurper, went about
From this fair throne to heave the owner out.

What could he see but mightily he noted?
What did he note but strongly he desired?
What he beheld, on that he firmly doted,
And in his will his willful eye he tired. 417
With more than admiration he admired
Her azure veins, her alabaster skin,
Her coral lips, her snow-white dimpled chin.

As the grim lion fawneth o'er his prey,
Sharp hunger by the conquest satisfied,
So o'er this sleeping soul doth Tarquin stay,
His rage of lust by gazing qualified— 424
Slack'd, not suppress'd, for standing by her side,
His eye, which late this mutiny restrains, 426
Unto a greater uproar tempts his veins.

And they, like straggling slaves for pillage fighting, 428
Obdurate vassals fell exploits effecting, 429
In bloody death and ravishment delighting,
Nor children's tears nor mothers' groans respecting,
Swell in their pride, the onset still expecting. 432
Anon his beating heart, alarum striking,
Gives the hot charge and bids them do their liking.

His drumming heart cheers up his burning eye,
His eye commends the leading to his hand; 436
His hand, as proud of such a dignity,
Smoking with pride, march'd on to make his stand
On her bare breast, the heart of all her land;

346 compass encompass, possess. **fair fair** virtuous fair one **347 they** i.e., that they, the eternal powers of heaven **348 starts** i.e., is startled, taken aback **349 fact** deed **356 out** extinguished **362 Who** whoever **371 draw the cloud** i.e., draw back the bedcurtains **372 Look as** just as **375 wink** shut **380 period** end **382 clear** pure, innocent **387 Coz'ning** cheating **389 to want his** i.e., protesting the lack of its

393 Without on the outside of **402 the map of death** i.e., sleep. (*Map* means *image, picture.*) **403 life's mortality** life's least-living aspect, i.e., sleep **417 will** lust. **tired** (1) exhausted (2) glutted, fed ravenously. (A term from falconry.) **424 qualified** softened, abated **426 late** lately, a moment ago **428 slaves** i.e., baseborn soldiers **429 fell** fierce. **effecting** i.e., on the verge of carrying out **432 pride** lust. **still** continually **436 commends** entrusts, commissions

Whose ranks of blue veins, as his hand did scale, 440
Left their round turrets destitute and pale.

They, must'ring to the quiet cabinet 442
Where their dear governess and lady lies,
Do tell her she is dreadfully beset,
And fright her with confusion of their cries.
She, much amaz'd, breaks ope her lock'd-up eyes,
Who, peeping forth this tumult to behold,
Are by his flaming torch dimm'd and controll'd. 448

Imagine her as one in dead of night
From forth dull sleep by dreadful fancy waking,
That thinks she hath beheld some ghastly sprite,
Whose grim aspect sets every joint a-shaking.
What terror 'tis! But she, in worser taking, 453
From sleep disturbed, heedfully doth view
The sight which makes supposed terror true.

Wrapp'd and confounded in a thousand fears,
Like to a new-kill'd bird she trembling lies.
She dares not look; yet, winking, there appears 458
Quick-shifting antics, ugly in her eyes. 459
Such shadows are the weak brain's forgeries,
Who, angry that the eyes fly from their lights, 461
In darkness daunts them with more dreadful sights.

His hand, that yet remains upon her breast—
Rude ram, to batter such an ivory wall!— 464
May feel her heart—poor citizen!—distress'd,
Wounding itself to death, rise up and fall,
Beating her bulk, that his hand shakes withal. 467
This moves in him more rage and lesser pity
To make the breach and enter this sweet city.

First, like a trumpet, doth his tongue begin
To sound a parley to his heartless foe, 471
Who o'er the white sheet peers her whiter chin,
The reason of this rash alarm to know,
Which he by dumb demeanor seeks to show; 474
But she with vehement prayers urgeth still 475
Under what color he commits this ill. 476

Thus he replies: "The color in thy face, 477
That even for anger makes the lily pale,
And the red rose blush at her own disgrace,
Shall plead for me and tell my loving tale.
Under that color am I come to scale 481
Thy never-conquered fort; the fault is thine,
For those thine eyes betray thee unto mine.

"Thus I forestall thee, if thou mean to chide:
Thy beauty hath ensnar'd thee to this night,
Where thou with patience must my will abide—
My will that marks thee for my earth's delight,
Which I to conquer sought with all my might.
But as reproof and reason beat it dead, 489
By thy bright beauty was it newly bred.

"I see what crosses my attempt will bring; 491
I know what thorns the growing rose defends;
I think the honey guarded with a sting; 493
All this beforehand counsel comprehends.
But will is deaf and hears no heedful friends;
Only he hath an eye to gaze on beauty,
And dotes on what he looks, 'gainst law or duty. 497

"I have debated, even in my soul,
What wrong, what shame, what sorrow I shall breed;
But nothing can affection's course control, 500
Or stop the headlong fury of his speed.
I know repentant tears ensue the deed,
Reproach, disdain, and deadly enmity;
Yet strive I to embrace mine infamy."

This said, he shakes aloft his Roman blade,
Which, like a falcon tow'ring in the skies,
Coucheth the fowl below with his wings' shade, 507
Whose crooked beak threats if he mount he dies. 508
So under his insulting falchion lies 509
Harmless Lucretia, marking what he tells
With trembling fear, as fowl hear falcons' bells. 511

"Lucrece," quoth he, "this night I must enjoy thee.
If thou deny, then force must work my way,
For in thy bed I purpose to destroy thee.
That done, some worthless slave of thine I'll slay,
To kill thine honor with thy life's decay;
And in thy dead arms do I mean to place him,
Swearing I slew him, seeing thee embrace him.

"So thy surviving husband shall remain
The scornful mark of every open eye, 520
Thy kinsmen hang their heads at this disdain,
Thy issue blurr'd with nameless bastardy;
And thou, the author of their obloquy,
Shalt have thy trepass cited up in rhymes,
And sung by children in succeeding times.

"But if thou yield, I rest thy secret friend. 526
The fault unknown is as a thought unacted;
A little harm done to a great good end
For lawful policy remains enacted. 529
The poisonous simple sometime is compacted 530
In a pure compound; being so applied,
His venom in effect is purified.

440 scale ascend (as in military attack) **442 must'ring** gathering. **cabinet** i.e., heart **448 controll'd** overpowered **453 taking** state of agitation **458 winking** closing the eyes **459 antics** phantoms, fantastic appearances, shapes **461 fly . . . lights** i.e., refuse to send out the beams which enable the eyes to see **464 ram** battering ram **467 bulk** i.e., chest, breast. **that** so that **471 parley** a summoning of the defenders to a negotiation. **heartless** spiritless, wanting courage **474 dumb demeanor** dumbshow **475 urgeth** cries out to know **476 color** pretext **477 color** hue (punning on the previous line) **481 color** banner (punning on l. 476)

489 as as soon as **491 crosses** vexations **493 think the honey** know the honey to be **497 looks** sees **500 affection's** passion's **507 Coucheth** causes to couch, i.e., remain concealed **508 Whose** i.e., the falcon's. **he** i.e., the fowl **509 insulting** exulting in triumph **511 bells** (Falcons had bells attached to their feet.) **526 rest** remain. **friend** lover **529 For . . . enacted** is accepted as a legal expedient **530 simple** ingredient, drug. **compacted** mixed

"Then, for thy husband and thy children's sake,
Tender my suit. Bequeath not to their lot
The shame that from them no device can take,
The blemish that will never be forgot,
Worse than a slavish wipe or birth-hour's blot.
For marks descried in men's nativity
Are nature's faults, not their own infamy."

Here with a cockatrice' dead-killing eye
He rouseth up himself and makes a pause,
While she, the picture of pure piety,
Like a white hind under the gripe's sharp claws,
Pleads, in a wilderness where are no laws,
To the rough beast that knows no gentle right,
Nor aught obeys but his foul appetite.

But when a black-fac'd cloud the world doth threat,
In his dim mist th' aspiring mountains hiding,
From earth's dark womb some gentle gust doth get,
Which blows these pitchy vapors from their biding,
Hind'ring their present fall by this dividing;
So his unhallowed haste her words delays,
And moody Pluto winks while Orpheus plays.

Yet, foul night-waking cat, he doth but dally,
While in his hold-fast foot the weak mouse panteth.
Her sad behavior feeds his vulture folly,
A swallowing gulf that even in plenty wanteth.
His ear her prayers admits, but his heart granteth
No penetrable entrance to her plaining;
Tears harden lust, though marble wear with raining.

Her pity-pleading eyes are sadly fixed
In the remorseless wrinkles of his face;
Her modest eloquence with sighs is mixed,
Which to her oratory adds more grace.
She puts the period often from his place,
And midst the sentence so her accent breaks
That twice she doth begin ere once she speaks.

She conjures him by high almighty Jove,
By knighthood, gentry, and sweet friendship's oath,
By her untimely tears, her husband's love,
By holy human law, and common troth,
By heaven and earth, and all the power of both,
That to his borrowed bed he make retire
And stoop to honor, not to foul desire.

Quoth she, "Reward not hospitality
With such black payment as thou hast pretended.
Mud not the fountain that gave drink to thee;
Mar not the thing that cannot be amended.
End thy ill aim before thy shoot be ended;
He is no woodman that doth bend his bow
To strike a poor unseasonable doe.

"My husband is thy friend; for his sake spare me.
Thyself art mighty; for thine own sake leave me.
Myself a weakling; do not then ensnare me.
Thou look'st not like deceit; do not deceive me.
My sighs, like whirlwinds, labor hence to heave thee.
If ever man were mov'd with woman's moans,
Be moved with my tears, my sighs, my groans;

"All which together, like a troubled ocean,
Beat at thy rocky and wrack-threat'ning heart,
To soften it with their continual motion;
For stones dissolv'd to water do convert.
O, if no harder than a stone thou art,
Melt at my tears, and be compassionate!
Soft pity enters at an iron gate.

"In Tarquin's likeness I did entertain thee.
Hast thou put on his shape to do him shame?
To all the host of heaven I complain me,
Thou wrong'st his honor, wound'st his princely name.
Thou art not what thou seem'st; and if the same,
Thou seem'st not what thou art, a god, a king;
For kings like gods should govern everything.

"How will thy shame be seeded in thine age,
When thus thy vices bud before thy spring?
If in thy hope thou dar'st do such outrage,
What dar'st thou not when once thou art a king?
O, be rememb'red, no outrageous thing
From vassal actors can be wip'd away;
Then kings' misdeeds cannot be hid in clay.

"This deed will make thee only lov'd for fear,
But happy monarchs still are fear'd for love.
With foul offenders thou perforce must bear,
When they in thee the like offenses prove.
If but for fear of this, thy will remove;
For princes are the glass, the school, the book,
Where subjects' eyes do learn, do read, do look.

"And wilt thou be the school where Lust shall learn?
Must he in thee read lectures of such shame?
Wilt thou be glass wherein it shall discern
Authority for sin, warrant for blame,

534 Tender regard **535 device** heraldic motto **537 slavish wipe** brand with which slaves were marked. **birth-hour's blot** unsightly birthmark **540 cockatrice** the basilisk, said to be hatched by a serpent from a cock's egg and to kill by its breath and the rays it emitted from its eyes **543 gripe's** vulture's, or griffin's **545 gentle right** the right that should be given to the weak and noble. (*Gentle* means both *weak* and *nobly born*.) **549 doth get** comes into being **550 their biding** where they hang **551 their present fall** i.e., the imminent onset of the storm **552 So . . . delays** thus her words delay his unhallowed haste **553 Orpheus** husband of Eurydice who went to the underworld for her and charmed Pluto, ruler of the underworld, with his playing the lyre **556 vulture folly** ravenous lewdness and madness **557 gulf** maw, belly. **wanteth** craves insatiably **559 plaining** complaining **562 wrinkles** i.e., frowns **565 his place** its place (in the sentence; i.e., she speaks in broken phrases) **569 gentry** nobleness of birth and breeding **573 borrowed** lent him for the night **574 stoop** (Plays on the meanings *subject oneself, debase oneself,* and *stoop to the lure or prey* like a falcon.)

576 pretended proposed **578 amended** returned to its former purity **579 shoot** shooting, hunting **580 woodman** huntsman **581 unseasonable** in foal or not yet bearing **592 stones . . . convert** i.e., stones are worn away in time by water **603 be seeded** ripen **605 in thy hope** i.e., while you are yet only heir to the kingdom **607 be rememb'red** bear in mind **608 vassal actors** i.e., vassals or ordinary subjects who commit crimes **609 in clay** i.e., even in death **614 thy will remove** dissuade your lust **615 glass** mirror and paradigm

To privilege dishonor in thy name? 621
Thou back'st reproach against long-living laud, 622
And mak'st fair reputation but a bawd.

"Hast thou command? By him that gave it thee,
From a pure heart command thy rebel will.
Draw not thy sword to guard iniquity,
For it was lent thee all that brood to kill.
Thy princely office how canst thou fulfill,
When, pattern'd by thy fault, foul Sin may say
He learn'd to sin, and thou didst teach the way?

"Think but how vile a spectacle it were
To view thy present trespass in another.
Men's faults do seldom to themselves appear;
Their own transgressions partially they smother. 634
This guilt would seem death-worthy in thy brother.
O, how are they wrapp'd in with infamies
That from their own misdeeds askance their eyes! 637

"To thee, to thee, my heav'd-up hands appeal,
Not to seducing lust, thy rash relier. 639
I sue for exil'd majesty's repeal; 640
Let him return, and flatt'ring thoughts retire.
His true respect will prison false desire, 642
And wipe the dim mist from thy doting eyne, 643
That thou shalt see thy state and pity mine."

"Have done," quoth he, "my uncontrolled tide
Turns not, but swells the higher by this let. 646
Small lights are soon blown out, huge fires abide,
And with the wind in greater fury fret.
The petty streams that pay a daily debt
To their salt sovereign, with their fresh falls' haste 650
Add to his flow, but alter not his taste."

"Thou art," quoth she, "a sea, a sovereign king;
And, lo, there falls into thy boundless flood
Black lust, dishonor, shame, misgoverning,
Who seek to stain the ocean of thy blood.
If all these petty ills shall change thy good,
Thy sea within a puddle's womb is hearsed, 657
And not the puddle in thy sea dispersed.

"So shall these slaves be king, and thou their slave;
Thou nobly base, they basely dignified; 660
Thou their fair life, and they thy fouler grave;
Thou loathed in their shame, they in thy pride.
The lesser thing should not the greater hide;
The cedar stoops not to the base shrub's foot,
But low shrubs wither at the cedar's root.

"So let thy thoughts, low vassals to thy state"—
"No more," quoth he, "by heaven, I will not hear thee.
Yield to my love; if not, enforced hate, 668
Instead of love's coy touch, shall rudely tear thee.
That done, despitefully I mean to bear thee
Unto the base bed of some rascal groom,
To be thy partner in this shameful doom."

This said, he sets his foot upon the light,
For light and lust are deadly enemies;
Shame folded up in blind concealing night,
When most unseen, then most doth tyrannize.
The wolf hath seiz'd his prey, the poor lamb cries;
Till with her own white fleece her voice controll'd 678
Entombs her outcry in her lips' sweet fold. 679

For with the nightly linen that she wears
He pens her piteous clamors in her head,
Cooling his hot face in the chastest tears
That ever modest eyes with sorrow shed.
O, that prone lust should stain so pure a bed! 684
The spots whereof could weeping purify, 685
Her tears should drop on them perpetually.

But she hath lost a dearer thing than life,
And he hath won what he would lose again.
This forced league doth force a further strife;
This momentary joy breeds months of pain;
This hot desire converts to cold disdain.
Pure Chastity is rifled of her store,
And Lust, the thief, far poorer than before.

Look as the full-fed hound or gorged hawk, 694
Unapt for tender smell or speedy flight, 695
Make slow pursuit, or altogether balk 696
The prey wherein by nature they delight;
So surfeit-taking Tarquin fares this night.
His taste delicious, in digestion souring,
Devours his will, that liv'd by foul devouring.

O, deeper sin than bottomless conceit 701
Can comprehend in still imagination!
Drunken Desire must vomit his receipt 703
Ere he can see his own abomination.
While Lust is in his pride, no exclamation 705
Can curb his heat or rein his rash desire,
Till like a jade Self-will himself doth tire. 707

And then with lank and lean discolor'd cheek,
With heavy eye, knit brow, and strengthless pace,
Feeble Desire, all recreant, poor, and meek, 710
Like to a bankrupt beggar wails his case.
The flesh being proud, Desire doth fight with Grace,
For there it revels, and when that decays,
The guilty rebel for remission prays.

621 privilege license **622 Thou back'st** you support. **laud** praise **634 partially** showing partiality toward themselves **637 askance** avert **639 thy rash relier** on which you rashly rely **640 repeal** recall from exile **642 His true respect** true respect for him; or, his true judgment. **prison** imprison **643 eyne** eyes **646 let** hindrance **650 salt sovereign** i.e., the sea **657 hearsed** buried, coffined

668 enforced hate (I.e., you will force me to hate you.) **678–679 Till . . . fold** until, overmastering her voice with her own night-wear, he buries her outcry as though in the fold of her sweet lips. (*Fold* refers to her folded or compressed lips and to a sheepfold; hence *pens* in l. 681.) **684 prone** eager, headlong **685 could weeping** if weeping could **694 Look as** just as **695 tender smell** delicate scent **696 balk** turn away from **701 bottomless conceit** limitless imagination **703 his receipt** what it has swallowed **705 exclamation** protest **707 jade** untrained or unbroken horse **710 recreant** craven, cowed

So fares it with this faultful lord of Rome,
Who this accomplishment so hotly chased;
For now against himself he sounds this doom, 717
That through the length of times he stands disgraced.
Besides, his soul's fair temple is defaced,
To whose weak ruins muster troops of cares,
To ask the spotted princess how she fares. 721

She says her subjects with foul insurrection 722
Have batter'd down her consecrated wall,
And by their mortal fault brought in subjection 724
Her immortality, and made her thrall
To living death and pain perpetual,
Which in her prescience she controlled still, 727
But her foresight could not forestall their will. 728

Ev'n in this thought through the dark night he stealeth,
A captive victor that hath lost in gain, 730
Bearing away the wound that nothing healeth,
The scar that will, despite of cure, remain,
Leaving his spoil perplex'd in greater pain. 733
She bears the load of lust he left behind,
And he the burden of a guilty mind.

He like a thievish dog creeps sadly thence;
She like a wearied lamb lies panting there.
He scowls and hates himself for his offense;
She, desperate, with her nails her flesh doth tear.
He faintly flies, sweating with guilty fear;
She stays, exclaiming on the direful night; 741
He runs, and chides his vanish'd, loath'd delight.

He thence departs a heavy convertite; 743
She there remains a hopeless castaway.
He in his speed looks for the morning light;
She prays she never may behold the day.
"For day," quoth she, "night's scapes doth open lay, 747
And my true eyes have never practic'd how
To cloak offenses with a cunning brow.

"They think not but that every eye can see
The same disgrace which they themselves behold;
And therefore would they still in darkness be,
To have their unseen sin remain untold;
For they their guilt with weeping will unfold, 754
And grave, like water that doth eat in steel, 755
Upon my cheeks what helpless shame I feel."

Here she exclaims against repose and rest,
And bids her eyes hereafter still be blind.
She wakes her heart by beating on her breast,
And bids it leap from thence, where it may find
Some purer chest to close so pure a mind. 761
Frantic with grief thus breathes she forth her spite
Against the unseen secrecy of night:

"O comfort-killing Night, image of hell,
Dim register and notary of shame, 765
Black stage for tragedies and murders fell,
Vast sin-concealing chaos, nurse of blame! 767
Blind muffled bawd, dark harbor for defame, 768
Grim cave of death, whisp'ring conspirator
With close-tongu'd treason and the ravisher!

"O hateful, vaporous, and foggy Night,
Since thou art guilty of my cureless crime,
Muster thy mists to meet the eastern light,
Make war against proportion'd course of time; 774
Or if thou wilt permit the sun to climb
His wonted height, yet ere he go to bed
Knit poisonous clouds about his golden head.

"With rotten damps ravish the morning air;
Let their exhal'd unwholesome breaths make sick
The life of purity, the supreme fair, 780
Ere he arrive his weary noon-tide prick; 781
And let thy musty vapors march so thick
That in their smoky ranks his smoth'red light
May set at noon and make perpetual night.

"Were Tarquin Night, as he is but Night's child,
The silver-shining queen he would distain; 786
Her twinkling handmaids too, by him defil'd, 787
Through Night's black bosom should not peep again.
So should I have co-partners in my pain;
And fellowship in woe doth woe assuage,
As palmers' chat makes short their pilgrimage; 791

"Where now I have no one to blush with me, 792
To cross their arms and hang their heads with mine,
To mask their brows and hide their infamy;
But I alone alone must sit and pine,
Seasoning the earth with show'rs of silver brine,
Mingling my talk with tears, my grief with groans,
Poor wasting monuments of lasting moans. 798

"O Night, thou furnace of foul-reeking smoke!
Let not the jealous Day behold that face
Which underneath thy black all-hiding cloak
Immodestly lies martyr'd with disgrace. 802
Keep still possession of thy gloomy place,
That all the faults which in thy reign are made
May likewise be sepulcher'd in thy shade.

"Make me not object to the tell-tale Day. 806
The light will show, character'd in my brow, 807

717 doom judgment **721 spotted princess** i.e., his contaminated soul, of whom the *temple,* l. 719, is the body **722 subjects** i.e., the senses **724 mortal** deadly **727–728 Which . . . will** i.e., she could foresee the inevitable coming of pain and death but could do nothing to prevent it **730 captive victor** i.e., Tarquin, who has triumphed over Lucrece and thus gained perpetual durance in sin **733 spoil** prey, i.e., Lucrece **741 exclaiming on** denouncing **743 heavy convertite** sad penitent **747 scapes** transgressions **754 unfold** reveal **755 grave** engrave. **water** i.e., aqua fortis, nitric acid **761 close** enclose

765 notary recorder **767 blame** evil **768 defame** infamy **774 proportion'd** i.e., orderly in the regulated interchange of day and night **780 life** lifegiving essence. **supreme fair** i.e., the sun **781 prick** mark (as on a dial) **786 queen** i.e., moon. **distain** stain, soil **787 handmaids** i.e., stars **791 palmers'** pilgrims' **792 Where** whereas **798 monuments** tokens, momentos **802 martyr'd** i.e., disfigured **806 object** a thing perceived, object of gossip **807 character'd** inscribed

The story of sweet chastity's decay,
The impious breach of holy wedlock vow.
Yea, the illiterate, that know not how
To cipher what is writ in learned books,
Will quote my loathsome trespass in my looks.

"The nurse, to still her child, will tell my story,
And fright her crying babe with Tarquin's name;
The orator, to deck his oratory,
Will couple my reproach to Tarquin's shame;
Feast-finding minstrels, tuning my defame,
Will tie the hearers to attend each line,
How Tarquin wronged me, I Collatine.

"Let my good name, that senseless reputation,
For Collatine's dear love be kept unspotted.
If that be made a theme for disputation,
The branches of another root are rotted,
And undeserv'd reproach to him allotted
That is as clear from this attaint of mine
As I, ere this, was pure to Collatine.

"O unseen shame, invisible disgrace!
O unfelt sore, crest-wounding, private scar!
Reproach is stamp'd in Collatinus' face,
And Tarquin's eye may read the mot afar,
How he in peace is wounded, not in war.
Alas, how many bear such shameful blows,
Which not themselves, but he that gives them knows!

"If, Collatine, thine honor lay in me,
From me by strong assault it is bereft:
My honey lost, and I, a drone-like bee,
Have no perfection of my summer left,
But robb'd and ransack'd by injurious theft.
In thy weak hive a wand'ring wasp hath crept,
And suck'd the honey which thy chaste bee kept.

"Yet am I guilty of thy honor's wrack;
Yet for thy honor did I entertain him.
Coming from thee, I could not put him back,
For it had been dishonor to disdain him.
Besides, of weariness he did complain him,
And talk'd of virtue. O unlook'd-for evil,
When virtue is profan'd in such a devil!

"Why should the worm intrude the maiden bud?
Or hateful cuckoos hatch in sparrows' nests?
Or toads infect fair founts with venom mud?
Or tyrant folly lurk in gentle breasts?
Or kings be breakers of their own behests?
But no perfection is so absolute,
That some impurity doth not pollute.

"The aged man that coffers up his gold
Is plagu'd with cramps and gouts and painful fits,
And scarce hath eyes his treasure to behold,
But like still-pining Tantalus he sits,
And useless barns the harvest of his wits,
Having no other pleasure of his gain
But torment that it cannot cure his pain.

"So then he hath it when he cannot use it,
And leaves it to be mast'red by his young,
Who in their pride do presently abuse it.
Their father was too weak, and they too strong,
To hold their cursed-blessed fortune long.
The sweets we wish for turn to loathed sours
Even in the moment that we call them ours.

"Unruly blasts wait on the tender spring;
Unwholesome weeds take root with precious flow'rs;
The adder hisses where the sweet birds sing;
What virtue breeds iniquity devours.
We have no good that we can say is ours,
But ill-annexed Opportunity
Or kills his life or else his quality.

"O Opportunity, thy guilt is great!
'Tis thou that execut'st the traitor's treason;
Thou sets the wolf where he the lamb may get;
Whoever plots the sin, thou 'point'st the season.
'Tis thou that spurn'st at right, at law, at reason;
And in thy shady cell, where none may spy him,
Sits Sin, to seize the souls that wander by him.

"Thou makest the vestal violate her oath;
Thou blowest the fire when temperance is thaw'd;
Thou smother'st honesty, thou murd'rest troth.
Thou foul abettor, thou notorious bawd,
Thou plantest scandal and displacest laud.
Thou ravisher, thou traitor, thou false thief,
Thy honey turns to gall, thy joy to grief!

"Thy secret pleasure turns to open shame,
Thy private feasting to a public fast,
Thy smoothing titles to a ragged name,
Thy sug'red tongue to bitter wormwood taste.
Thy violent vanities can never last.
How comes it then, vile Opportunity,
Being so bad, such numbers seek for thee?

"When wilt thou be the humble suppliant's friend,
And bring him where his suit may be obtained?
When wilt thou sort an hour great strifes to end?

811 cipher decipher, read **812 quote** note, observe **817 Feast-finding** searching out feasts at which to sing **820 senseless** impalpable **828 crest-wounding** disgraceful to the crest, or device above the shield in one's coat of arms **830 mot** motto **837 Have . . . left** have nothing left of the honey I perfected in the summer

858 still-pining continually starving. **Tantalus** a son of Zeus who was punished by perpetual hunger and thirst with unreachable food and drink always in sight. (Renaissance commentators on Ovid glossed Tantalus as a usurer; hence the image of ll. 859 ff.) **859 barns** stores, as in a barn **874 ill-annexed** joined to the good for an evil purpose **875 Or . . . quality** either destroys that good thing or else destroys its nature that makes it good **879 'point'st** appointest **885 honesty** chastity. **troth** honesty **887 laud** praise **892 smoothing** flattering **899 sort** choose, appoint

Or free that soul which wretchedness hath chained?
Give physic to the sick, ease to the pained?
The poor, lame, blind, halt, creep, cry out for thee,
But they ne'er meet with Opportunity.

"The patient dies while the physician sleeps;
The orphan pines while the oppressor feeds;
Justice is feasting while the widow weeps;
Advice is sporting while infection breeds.
Thou grant'st no time for charitable deeds.
Wrath, envy, treason, rape, and murder's rages,
Thy heinous hours wait on them as their pages.

"When Truth and Virtue have to do with thee,
A thousand crosses keep them from thy aid.
They buy thy help; but Sin ne'er gives a fee,
He gratis comes; and thou art well apaid
As well to hear as grant what he hath said.
My Collatine would else have come to me
When Tarquin did, but he was stay'd by thee.

"Guilty thou art of murder and of theft,
Guilty of perjury and subornation,
Guilty of treason, forgery, and shift,
Guilty of incest, that abomination—
An accessary by thine inclination
To all sins past and all that are to come,
From the creation to the general doom.

"Misshapen Time, copesmate of ugly Night,
Swift subtle post, carrier of grisly care,
Eater of youth, false slave to false delight,
Base watch of woes, sin's pack-horse, virtue's snare!
Thou nursest all, and murd'rest all that are.
O, hear me then, injurious, shifting Time!
Be guilty of my death, since of my crime.

"Why hath thy servant Opportunity
Betray'd the hours thou gav'st me to repose,
Cancel'd my fortunes, and enchained me
To endless date of never-ending woes?
Time's office is to fine the hate of foes,
To eat up errors by opinion bred,
Not spend the dowry of a lawful bed.

"Time's glory is to calm contending kings,
To unmask falsehood and bring truth to light,
To stamp the seal of time in aged things,
To wake the morn and sentinel the night,
To wrong the wronger till he render right,
To ruinate proud buildings with thy hours,
And smear with dust their glitt'ring golden tow'rs;

"To fill with worm-holes stately monuments,
To feed oblivion with decay of things,
To blot old books and alter their contents,
To pluck the quills from ancient ravens' wings,
To dry the old oak's sap and cherish springs,
To spoil antiquities of hammer'd steel,
And turn the giddy round of Fortune's wheel;

"To show the beldam daughters of her daughter,
To make the child a man, the man a child,
To slay the tiger that doth live by slaughter,
To tame the unicorn and lion wild,
To mock the subtle in themselves beguil'd,
To cheer the ploughman with increaseful crops,
And waste huge stones with little water-drops.

"Why work'st thou mischief in thy pilgrimage,
Unless thou couldst return to make amends?
One poor retiring minute in an age
Would purchase thee a thousand thousand friends,
Lending him wit that to bad debtors lends.
O, this dread night, wouldst thou one hour come back,
I could prevent this storm and shun thy wrack!

"Thou ceaseless lackey to Eternity,
With some mischance cross Tarquin in his flight!
Devise extremes beyond extremity
To make him curse this cursed crimeful night.
Let ghastly shadows his lewd eyes affright,
And the dire thought of his committed evil
Shape every bush a hideous shapeless devil.

"Disturb his hours of rest with restless trances,
Afflict him in his bed with bedrid groans;
Let there bechance him pitiful mischances,
To make him moan, but pity not his moans.
Stone him with hard'ned hearts harder than stones,
And let mild women to him lose their mildness,
Wilder to him than tigers in their wildness.

"Let him have time to tear his curled hair,
Let him have time against himself to rave,
Let him have time of Time's help to despair,
Let him have time to live a loathed slave,
Let him have time a beggar's orts to crave,
And time to see one that by alms doth live
Disdain to him disdained scraps to give.

"Let him have time to see his friends his foes,
And merry fools to mock at him resort;
Let him have time to mark how slow time goes
In time of sorrow, and how swift and short
His time of folly and his time of sport;
And ever let his unrecalling crime
Have time to wail th' abusing of his time.

905 pines starves **907 Advice** i.e., medical advice. **sporting** taking idle pleasure **912 crosses** hindrances **914 apaid** satisfied **915 As . . . as** both to hear and **920 shift** fraud **924 general doom** Doomsday, Day of Judgment **925 copesmate** companion **926 post** messenger **928 watch** crier, one who announces woes **935 date** duration **936 fine** put an end to **937 opinion** popular rumor

948 blot erase, obliterate **949 To pluck . . . wings** i.e., to end even the existence of long-lived ravens **950 springs** new growth, shoots **953 beldam** old woman **954 a child** i.e., in the second childishness of old age **957 subtle . . . beguil'd** crafty who are foiled by their own cleverness **958 increaseful** fruitful **959 waste** wear away **962 retiring** returning (thereby allowing men an opportunity to undo some evil) **964 wit** i.e., an opportunity to reconsider **967 ceaseless lackey** omnipresent attendant **968 cross** thwart **974 trances** visions, fits **985 orts** refuse, fragments of food **993 unrecalling** that may not be recalled

"O Time, thou tutor both to good and bad,
Teach me to curse him that thou taught'st this ill!
At his own shadow let the thief run mad,
Himself himself seek every hour to kill!
Such wretched hands such wretched blood should spill;
For who so base would such an office have
As sland'rous deathsman to so base a slave? 1001

"The baser is he, coming from a king,
To shame his hope with deeds degenerate. 1003
The mightier man, the mightier is the thing
That makes him honor'd, or begets him hate;
For greatest scandal waits on greatest state.
The moon being clouded presently is miss'd,
But little stars may hide them when they list.

"The crow may bathe his coal-black wings in mire,
And unperceiv'd fly with the filth away,
But if the like the snow-white swan desire,
The stain upon his silver down will stay.
Poor grooms are sightless night, kings glorious day. 1013
Gnats are unnoted wheresoe'er they fly,
But eagles gaz'd upon with every eye.

"Out, idle words, servants to shallow fools,
Unprofitable sounds, weak arbitrators!
Busy yourselves in skill-contending schools; 1018
Debate where leisure serves with dull debaters;
To trembling clients be you mediators.
For me, I force not argument a straw, 1021
Since that my case is past the help of law.

"In vain I rail at Opportunity,
At Time, at Tarquin, and uncheerful Night;
In vain I cavil with mine infamy, 1025
In vain I spurn at my confirm'd despite. 1026
This helpless smoke of words doth me no right. 1027
The remedy indeed to do me good
Is to let forth my foul-defiled blood.

"Poor hand, why quiver'st thou at this decree?
Honor thyself to rid me of this shame;
For if I die, my honor lives in thee,
But if I live, thou liv'st in my defame.
Since thou couldst not defend thy loyal dame,
And wast afeard to scratch her wicked foe,
Kill both thyself and her for yielding so."

This said, from her be-tumbled couch she starteth,
To find some desp'rate instrument of death;
But this no slaughterhouse no tool imparteth 1039
To make more vent for passage of her breath,
Which, thronging through her lips, so vanisheth
As smoke from Aetna, that in air consumes,
Or that which from discharged cannon fumes.

"In vain," quoth she, "I live, and seek in vain
Some happy mean to end a hapless life.
I fear'd by Tarquin's falchion to be slain, 1046
Yet for the self-same purpose seek a knife;
But when I fear'd I was a loyal wife.
So am I now.—O no, that cannot be!
Of that true type hath Tarquin rifled me. 1050

"O, that is gone for which I sought to live,
And therefore now I need not fear to die.
To clear this spot by death, at least I give
A badge of fame to slander's livery, 1054
A dying life to living infamy.
Poor helpless help, the treasure stol'n away,
To burn the guiltless casket where it lay!

"Well, well, dear Collatine, thou shalt not know
The stained taste of violated troth;
I will not wrong thy true affection so
To flatter thee with an infringed oath; 1061
This bastard graff shall never come to growth. 1062
He shall not boast who did thy stock pollute
That thou art doting father of his fruit.

"Nor shall he smile at thee in secret thought,
Nor laugh with his companions at thy state,
But thou shalt know thy int'rest was not bought 1067
Basely with gold, but stol'n from forth thy gate.
For me, I am the mistress of my fate,
And with my trespass never will dispense 1070
Till life to death acquit my forc'd offense. 1071

"I will not poison thee with my attaint,
Nor fold my fault in cleanly coin'd excuses; 1073
My sable ground of sin I will not paint, 1074
To hide the truth of this false night's abuses.
My tongue shall utter all; mine eyes, like sluices,
As from a mountain-spring that feeds a dale,
Shall gush pure streams to purge my impure tale."

By this, lamenting Philomel had ended 1079
The well-tun'd warble of her nightly sorrow,
And solemn night with slow sad gait descended
To ugly hell; when, lo, the blushing morrow
Lends light to all fair eyes that light will borrow; 1083
But cloudy Lucrece shames herself to see, 1084
And therefore still in night would cloist'red be.

Revealing day through every cranny spies,
And seems to point her out where she sits weeping,

1001 sland'rous despised, contemptible **1003 his hope** the hope men had of him as heir to the crown **1013 sightless** making things invisible; pitch dark **1018 in . . . schools** i.e., among scholars who perennially debate with words **1021 force** value. **a straw** i.e., a straw's worth **1025 cavil with** raise objections to **1026 confirm'd despite** unavoidable injury **1027 helpless** affording no help **1039 no slaughterhouse** being no slaughterhouse. **imparteth** provides

1046 falchion curved sword **1050 type** stamp; example **1054 fame** good reputation. **livery** clothing or uniform worn by those in service, bearing a *badge* on the sleeve to indicate in whose service the livery is worn. (Lucrece says that the livery of shame will be partially redeemed by the badge of an honorable death.) **1061 flatter** deceive **1062 graff** graft, scion **1067 int'rest** claim, property **1070 dispense** [*with*] condone by dispensation **1071 acquit** atone for **1073 cleanly coin'd** cleverly counterfeited **1074 sable ground** dark surface on a heraldic device **1079 Philomel** woman raped by her brother-in-law, Tereus, who cut out her tongue so that she could not disclose his villainy; she was changed into a nightingale **1083 borrow** i.e., make use of that which heaven lends **1084 shames** is ashamed

To whom she sobbing speaks: "O eye of eyes,
Why pry'st thou through my window? Leave thy peeping.
Mock with thy tickling beams eyes that are sleeping.
Brand not my forehead with thy piercing light,
For day hath nought to do what's done by night." 1092

Thus cavils she with every thing she sees.
True grief is fond and testy as a child, 1094
Who wayward once, his mood with nought agrees. 1095
Old woes, not infant sorrows, bear them mild; 1096
Continuance tames the one, the other wild,
Like an unpractic'd swimmer plunging still,
With too much labor drowns for want of skill.

So she, deep-drenched in a sea of care,
Holds disputation with each thing she views,
And to herself all sorrow doth compare;
No object but her passion's strength renews,
And as one shifts, another straight ensues. 1104
Sometime her grief is dumb and hath no words,
Sometime 'tis mad and too much talk affords.

The little birds that tune their morning's joy
Make her moans mad with their sweet melody,
For mirth doth search the bottom of annoy; 1109
Sad souls are slain in merry company.
Grief best is pleas'd with grief's society.
True sorrow then is feelingly suffic'd 1112
When with like semblance it is sympathiz'd. 1113

'Tis double death to drown in ken of shore; 1114
He ten times pines that pines beholding food;
To see the salve doth make the wound ache more;
Great grief grieves most at that would do it good; 1117
Deep woes roll forward like a gentle flood,
Who, being stopp'd, the bounding banks o'erflows;
Grief dallied with nor law nor limit knows. 1120

"You mocking birds," quoth she, "your tunes entomb
Within your hollow-swelling feathered breasts,
And in my hearing be you mute and dumb.
My restless discord loves no stops nor rests; 1124
A woeful hostess brooks not merry guests. 1125
Relish your nimble notes to pleasing ears; 1126
Distress likes dumps when time is kept with tears. 1127

"Come, Philomel, that sing'st of ravishment,
Make thy sad grove in my dishevel'd hair.
As the dank earth weeps at thy languishment,
So I at each sad strain will strain a tear,. 1131
And with deep groans the diapason bear; 1132
For burden-wise I'll hum on Tarquin still, 1133
While thou on Tereus descants better skill. 1134

"And whiles against a thorn thou bear'st thy part 1135
To keep thy sharp woes waking, wretched I,
To imitate thee well, against my heart
Will fix a sharp knife to affright mine eye,
Who, if it wink, shall thereon fall and die. 1139
These means, as frets upon an instrument, 1140
Shall tune our heart-strings to true languishment.

"And for, poor bird, thou sing'st not in the day, 1142
As shaming any eye should thee behold, 1143
Some dark deep desert, seated from the way, 1144
That knows not parching heat nor freezing cold,
Will we find out; and there we will unfold
To creatures stern sad tunes, to change their kinds. 1147
Since men prove beasts, let beasts bear gentle minds."

As the poor frighted deer, that stands at gaze, 1149
Wildly determining which way to fly,
Or one encompass'd with a winding maze,
That cannot tread the way out readily,
So with herself is she in mutiny,
To live or die which of the twain were better,
When life is sham'd and death reproach's debtor. 1155

"To kill myself," quoth she, "alack, what were it,
But with my body my poor soul's pollution? 1157
They that lose half with greater patience bear it
Than they whose whole is swallowed in confusion. 1159
That mother tries a merciless conclusion 1160
Who, having two sweet babes, when death takes one,
Will slay the other and be nurse to none.

"My body or my soul, which was the dearer,
When the one pure, the other made divine?
Whose love of either to myself was nearer, 1165
When both were kept for heaven and Collatine?
Ay me! The bark pill'd from the lofty pine, 1167
His leaves will wither and his sap decay;
So must my soul, her bark being pill'd away.

1092 to do to do with **1094 fond** foolish **1095 wayward once** i.e., once in a peevish mood **1096 them** themselves. **mild** mildly, calmly **1104 shifts** moves, yields place **1109 search** probe. **annoy** grief, injury **1112 suffic'd** contented **1113 sympathiz'd** matched **1114 ken** sight **1117 would** which wishes to **1120 dallied** trifled. **nor . . . nor** neither . . . nor **1124 restless** agitated (with a pun on the musical sense of having no *stops* or *rests*, i.e., being ceaseless, without pause) **1125 brooks** enjoys **1126 Relish** (1) warble, make attractive (2) elaborate with musical ornamentation. **pleasing** capable of being pleased **1127 dumps** mournful songs **1131 strain** (1) melody (2) force, squeeze

1132 diapason bass accompaniment an octave below the melody **1133 burden-wise** in the manner of an undersong or bass (with a play on *burden* meaning *sorrow*) **1134 descants better skill** i.e., sing a musical elaboration in the upper register with better skill (than my bass accompaniment) **1135 against a thorn** (According to popular belief, the nightingale perched deliberately with a thorn against her breast to keep herself awake.) **1139 Who** which, i.e., her heart. **if it wink** i.e., if her eye should close in sleep **1140 frets** bars placed on the fingerboards of stringed instruments to regulate the fingering (with a pun on *frets* meaning *vexations*) **1142 for** because. **sing'st not in the day** (One of the common errors of the time; nightingales sing both by day and by night.) **1143 As shaming** as though being ashamed **1144 desert** deserted place. **seated from** situated away from **1147 kinds** natures **1149 at gaze** transfixed, bewildered **1155 death reproach's debtor** i.e., death by suicide would incur reproach **1157 But . . . pollution** but to add my poor soul's pollution (through suicide) to that of my body (through the rape) **1159 confusion** ruin **1160 conclusion** experiment **1165 Whose . . . either** love of which of the two **1167 pill'd** peeled, stripped off

"Her house is sack'd, her quiet interrupted,
Her mansion batter'd by the enemy,
Her sacred temple spotted, spoil'd, corrupted,
Grossly engirt with daring infamy.
Then let it not be call'd impiety
If in this blemish'd fort I make some hole 1175
Through which I may convey this troubled soul. 1176

"Yet die I will not till my Collatine
Have heard the cause of my untimely death,
That he may vow, in that sad hour of mine,
Revenge on him that made me stop my breath.
My stained blood to Tarquin I'll bequeath,
Which by him tainted shall for him be spent,
And as his due writ in my testament. 1183

"My honor I'll bequeath unto the knife
That wounds my body so dishonored.
'Tis honor to deprive dishonor'd life, 1186
The one will live, the other being dead.
So of shame's ashes shall my fame be bred,
For in my death I murder shameful scorn;
My shame so dead, mine honor is new born.

"Dear lord of that dear jewel I have lost,
What legacy shall I bequeath to thee?
My resolution, love, shall be thy boast,
By whose example thou reveng'd mayst be.
How Tarquin must be us'd, read it in me:
Myself, thy friend, will kill myself, thy foe,
And for my sake serve thou false Tarquin so.

"This brief abridgment of my will I make:
My soul and body to the skies and ground;
My resolution, husband, do thou take;
Mine honor be the knife's that makes my wound;
My shame be his that did my fame confound;
And all my fame that lives disbursed be
To those that live, and think no shame of me.

"Thou, Collatine, shalt oversee this will.
How was I overseen that thou shalt see it! 1206
My blood shall wash the slander of mine ill;
My life's foul deed, my life's fair end shall free it.
Faint not, faint heart, but stoutly say "So be it."
Yield to my hand; my hand shall conquer thee.
Thou dead, both die, and both shall victors be."

This plot of death when sadly she had laid,
And wip'd the brinish pearl from her bright eyes,
With untun'd tongue she hoarsely calls her maid, 1214
Whose swift obedience to her mistress hies;
For fleet-wing'd duty with thought's feathers flies.
Poor Lucrece' cheeks unto her maid seem so
As winter meads when sun doth melt their snow.

Her mistress she doth give demure good morrow,
With soft-slow tongue, true mark of modesty,
And sorts a sad look to her lady's sorrow, 1221
For why her face wore sorrow's livery; 1222
But durst not ask of her audaciously
Why her two suns were cloud-eclipsed so,
Nor why her fair cheeks over-wash'd with woe.

But as the earth doth weep, the sun being set,
Each flow'r moist'ned like a melting eye,
Even so the maid with swelling drops gan wet
Her circled eyne, enforc'd by sympathy 1229
Of those fair suns set in her mistress' sky,
Who in a salt-wav'd ocean quench their light,
Which makes the maid weep like the dewy night.

A pretty while these pretty creatures stand, 1233
Like ivory conduits coral cisterns filling. 1234
One justly weeps, the other takes in hand 1235
No cause, but company, of her drops spilling. 1236
Their gentle sex to weep are often willing,
Grieving themselves to guess at others' smarts, 1238
And then they drown their eyes or break their hearts.

For men have marble, women waxen, minds, 1240
And therefore are they form'd as marble will. 1241
The weak oppress'd, th' impression of strange kinds 1242
Is form'd in them by force, by fraud, or skill.
Then call them not the authors of their ill,
No more than wax shall be accounted evil
Wherein is stamp'd the semblance of a devil.

Their smoothness, like a goodly champaign plain, 1247
Lays open all the little worms that creep; 1248
In men, as in a rough-grown grove, remain
Cave-keeping evils that obscurely sleep. 1250
Through crystal walls each little mote will peep.
Though men can cover crimes with bold stern looks,
Poor women's faces are their own faults' books.

No man inveigh against the withered flow'r,
But chide rough winter that the flow'r hath kill'd.
Not that devour'd, but that which doth devour,
Is worthy blame. O, let it not be hild 1257
Poor women's faults, that they are so fulfill'd 1258
With men's abuses. Those proud lords, to blame,
Make weak-made women tenants to their shame.

The precedent whereof in Lucrece view, 1261
Assail'd by night with circumstances strong
Of present death, and shame that might ensue

1175 fort i.e., body **1176 convey** let out **1183 testament** last will and testament **1186 deprive** take away **1206 overseen** deluded, taken advantage of (with quibble on *oversee,* (l. 1205, i.e., attend to as an executor of an estate) **1214 untun'd** discordant

1221 sorts adapts **1222 For why** because **1229 circled** rounded. **eyne** eyes **1233 pretty** considerable **1234 conduits** (Alludes to conduit spouts and fountains shaped in the form of human figures; the women's eyes run like conduits.) **1235 takes in hand** acknowledges, entertains **1236 No . . . spilling** i.e., no cause for the shedding of teardrops other than to keep her mistress company **1238 to guess at** i.e., merely when they conjecture **1240 waxen** i.e., soft, impressionable **1241 will** wills, wishes **1242 strange kinds** natures unlike their own **1247 champaign** level, open **1248 Lays open** reveals. **worms** reptiles, i.e., blemishes **1250 Cave-keeping** remaining concealed in caves **1257 hild** held **1258 fulfill'd** filled **1261 precedent** proof, example

By that her death, to do her husband wrong.
Such danger to resistance did belong
  That dying fear through all her body spread; 1266
  And who cannot abuse a body dead?

By this, mild patience bid fair Lucrece speak 1268
To the poor counterfeit of her complaining: 1269
"My girl," quoth she, "on what occasion break
Those tears from thee, that down thy cheeks are
  raining?
If thou dost weep for grief of my sustaining, 1272
  Know, gentle wench, it small avails my mood.
  If tears could help, mine own would do me good.

"But tell me, girl, when went"—and there she stay'd
Till after a deep groan—"Tarquin from hence?"
"Madam, ere I was up," replied the maid,
"The more to blame my sluggard negligence.
Yet with the fault I thus far can dispense: 1279
  Myself was stirring ere the break of day,
  And, ere I rose, was Tarquin gone away.

"But, lady, if your maid may be so bold,
She would request to know your heaviness." 1283
"O, peace!" quoth Lucrece. "If it should be told,
The repetition cannot make it less;
For more it is than I can well express,
  And that deep torture may be call'd a hell
  When more is felt than one hath power to tell.

"Go, get me hither paper, ink, and pen.
Yet save that labor, for I have them here.
What should I say? One of my husband's men
Bid thou be ready, by and by, to bear
A letter to my lord, my love, my dear.
  Bid him with speed prepare to carry it;
  The cause craves haste, and it will soon be writ."

Her maid is gone, and she prepares to write,
First hovering o'er the paper with her quill.
Conceit and grief an eager combat fight; 1298
What wit sets down is blotted straight with will; 1299
This is too curious-good, this blunt and ill. 1300
  Much like a press of people at a door
  Throng her inventions, which shall go before.

At last she thus begins: "Thou worthy lord
Of that unworthy wife that greeteth thee,
Health to thy person! Next vouchsafe t' afford—
If ever, love, thy Lucrece thou wilt see—
Some present speed to come and visit me.
  So, I commend me from our house in grief.
  My woes are tedious, though my words are
    brief." 1309

Here folds she up the tenor of her woe,
Her certain sorrow writ uncertainly. 1311
By this short schedule Collatine may know 1312
Her grief, but not her grief's true quality.
She dares not thereof make discovery,
  Lest he should hold it her own gross abuse,
  Ere she with blood had stain'd her stain'd excuse. 1316

Besides, the life and feeling of her passion
She hoards, to spend when he is by to hear her,
When sighs and groans and tears may grace the
  fashion
Of her disgrace, the better so to clear her
From that suspicion which the world might bear her.
  To shun this blot, she would not blot the letter 1322
  With words, till action might become them better.

To see sad sights moves more than hear them told,
For then the eye interprets to the ear
The heavy motion that it doth behold, 1326
When every part a part of woe doth bear. 1327
'Tis but a part of sorrow that we hear.
  Deep sounds make lesser noise than shallow
    fords, 1329
  And sorrow ebbs, being blown with wind of
    words.

Her letter now is seal'd, and on it writ,
"At Ardea to my lord with more than haste."
The post attends, and she delivers it, 1333
Charging the sour-fac'd groom to hie as fast
As lagging fowls before the northern blast. 1335
  Speed more than speed but dull and slow she
    deems;
  Extremity still urgeth such extremes.

The homely villain cur'sies to her low; 1338
And, blushing on her, with a steadfast eye
Receives the scroll without or yea or no,
And forth with bashful innocence doth hie.
But they whose guilt within their bosoms lie
  Imagine every eye beholds their blame;
  For Lucrece thought he blush'd to see her shame,

When, seely groom, God wot, it was defect 1345
Of spirit, life, and bold audacity.
Such harmless creatures have a true respect 1347
To talk in deeds, while others saucily
Promise more speed, but do it leisurely.
  Even so this pattern of the worn-out age 1350
  Pawn'd honest looks, but laid no words to gage. 1351

His kindled duty kindled her mistrust, 1352
That two red fires in both their faces blazed.

1266 dying i.e., paralyzing **1268 By this** by this time **1269 counterfeit** likeness, imitation **1272 of my sustaining** borne by me **1279 dispense** give dispensation, excuse **1283 know** i.e., know the reason for **1298 Conceit** thought (of what she will write) **1299 wit** intellect. **blotted** canceled. **will** passion, feeling **1300 curious** fastidiously, studiedly **1309 tedious** prolonged, painful

1311 uncertainly i.e., not in precise detail, vaguely **1312 schedule** document, summary **1316 her stain'd excuse** i.e., the explanation of her shame **1322 blot . . . blot** stain . . . mar **1326 heavy motion** sad action **1327 every part** i.e., of the body **1329 Deep sounds** deep waters (with pun on *sounds* and *noise*) **1333 post** messenger **1335 lagging** falling behind in migratory flight **1338 villain** servant. **cur'sies** curtsies, bows **1345 seely** simple **1347 respect** care **1350 pattern . . . age** i.e., example of faithful service in the good old days **1351 Pawn'd** offered as security. **to gage** as guarantee **1352 mistrust** i.e., fear of her shame being known

She thought he blush'd as knowing Tarquin's lust,
And, blushing with him, wistly on him gazed; 1355
Her earnest eye did make him more amazed. 1356
The more she saw the blood his cheeks replenish,
The more she thought he spied in her some blemish.

But long she thinks till he return again, 1359
And yet the duteous vassal scarce is gone.
The weary time she cannot entertain, 1361
For now 'tis stale to sigh, to weep, and groan.
So woe hath wearied woe, moan tired moan,
That she her plaints a little while doth stay, 1364
Pausing for means to mourn some newer way.

At last she calls to mind where hangs a piece
Of skillful painting, made for Priam's Troy, 1367
Before the which is drawn the power of Greece, 1368
For Helen's rape the city to destroy,
Threat'ning cloud-kissing Ilion with annoy, 1370
Which the conceited painter drew so proud, 1371
As heaven, it seem'd, to kiss the turrets bow'd.

A thousand lamentable objects there,
In scorn of nature, art gave lifeless life. 1374
Many a dry drop seem'd a weeping tear,
Shed for the slaught'red husband by the wife.
The red blood reek'd, to show the painter's strife; 1377
And dying eyes gleam'd forth their ashy lights,
Like dying coals burnt out in tedious nights.

There might you see the laboring pioner 1380
Begrim'd with sweat, and smeared all with dust;
And from the tow'rs of Troy there would appear
The very eyes of men through loopholes thrust,
Gazing upon the Greeks with little lust. 1384
Such sweet observance in this work was had 1385
That one might see those far-off eyes look sad.

In great commanders grace and majesty
You might behold, triumphing in their faces;
In youth, quick bearing and dexterity; 1389
And here and there the painter interlaces
Pale cowards, marching on with trembling paces,
Which heartless peasants did so well resemble 1392
That one would swear he saw them quake and tremble.

In Ajax and Ulysses, O, what art
Of physiognomy might one behold!
The face of either cipher'd either's heart; 1396
Their face their manners most expressly told.
In Ajax' eyes blunt rage and rigor roll'd,
But the mild glance that sly Ulysses lent
Show'd deep regard and smiling government. 1400

There pleading might you see grave Nestor stand,
As 'twere encouraging the Greeks to fight,
Making such sober action with his hand
That it beguil'd attention, charm'd the sight.
In speech, it seem'd, his beard, all silver white,
Wagg'd up and down, and from his lips did fly
Thin winding breath, which purl'd up to the sky. 1407

About him were a press of gaping faces,
Which seem'd to swallow up his sound advice,
All jointly list'ning, but with several graces, 1410
As if some mermaid did their ears entice,
Some high, some low, the painter was so nice. 1412
The scalps of many, almost hid behind, 1413
To jump up higher seem'd, to mock the mind. 1414

Here one man's hand lean'd on another's head,
His nose being shadowed by his neighbor's ear;
Here one being throng'd bears back, all boll'n and red; 1417
Another smother'd seems to pelt and swear; 1418
And in their rage such signs of rage they bear,
As, but for loss of Nestor's golden words 1420
It seem'd they would debate with angry swords.

For much imaginary work was there,
Conceit deceitful, so compact, so kind, 1423
That for Achilles' image stood his spear,
Grip'd in an armed hand; himself, behind,
Was left unseen, save to the eye of mind.
A hand, a foot, a face, a leg, a head,
Stood for the whole to be imagined.

And from the walls of strong-besieged Troy
When their brave hope, bold Hector, march'd to field,
Stood many Troyan mothers, sharing joy
To see their youthful sons bright weapons wield;
And to their hope they such odd action yield, 1433
That through their light joy seemed to appear,
Like bright things stain'd, a kind of heavy fear.

And from the strond of Dardan, where they fought, 1436
To Simois' reedy banks the red blood ran, 1437
Whose waves to imitate the battle sought
With swelling ridges; and their ranks began
To break upon the galled shore, and than 1440
Retire again, till, meeting greater ranks,
They join and shoot their foam at Simois' banks.

1355 wistly attentively **1356 amazed** embarrassed **1359 long she thinks** she thinks it long **1361 entertain** occupy **1364 stay** halt **1367 made for** depicting **1368 drawn** drawn up, arrayed. **power** army **1370 cloud-kissing Ilion** i.e., lofty-towered Troy. **annoy** harm **1371 conceited** ingenious **1374 In scorn of** i.e., defiantly rivaling. **lifeless** inanimate **1377 strife** rivalry, i.e., with Nature **1380 pioner** digger, miner **1384 lust** pleasure, delight **1385 sweet observance** i.e., verisimilitude created with loving attention to detail **1389 quick** lively **1392 heartless** cowardly **1396 cipher'd** showed, expressed

1400 deep . . . government profound wisdom and the complacency arising from passions being under the command of reason **1407 purl'd** curled **1410 with several graces** i.e., in differing attitudes **1412 Some . . . low** some tall, some short. **nice** accurate, particular **1413 scalps** heads of hair **1414 To jump . . . mind** i.e., (those in the back of the crowd) gave the illusion of seeming to jump up higher in order to hear Nestor; or, possibly, mockingly tempted the spectator to lift himself higher, as though to be able to see figures hidden behind those in front **1417 throng'd** crowded. **bears** pushes. **boll'n** swollen up **1418 pelt** scold **1420 but . . . words** i.e., were it not that they would thereby miss Nestor's speech **1423 Conceit** contrivance, techniques. **compact** economical. **kind** natural **1433 they . . . yield** they add such actions and emotions at odds with the joy **1436 strond** strand, shore **1437 Simois** river near Troy **1440 galled** eroded. **than** then

To this well-painted piece is Lucrece come,
To find a face where all distress is stell'd. 1444
Many she sees where cares have carved some,
But none where all distress and dolor dwell'd,
Till she despairing Hecuba beheld,
Staring on Priam's wounds with her old eyes,
Which bleeding under Pyrrhus' proud foot lies.

In her the painter had anatomiz'd 1450
Time's ruin, beauty's wrack, and grim care's reign.
Her cheeks with chops and wrinkles were disguis'd; 1452
Of what she was no semblance did remain.
Her blue blood, chang'd to black in every vein,
Wanting the spring that those shrunk pipes had fed,
Show'd life imprison'd in a body dead.

On this sad shadow Lucrece spends her eyes,
And shapes her sorrow to the beldam's woes,
Who nothing wants to answer her but cries, 1459
And bitter words to ban her cruel foes. 1460
The painter was no god to lend her those;
And therefore Lucrece swears he did her wrong,
To give her so much grief and not a tongue.

"Poor instrument," quoth she, "without a sound,
I'll tune thy woes with my lamenting tongue,
And drop sweet balm in Priam's painted wound,
And rail on Pyrrhus that hath done him wrong,
And with my tears quench Troy that burns so long,
And with my knife scratch out the angry eyes
Of all the Greeks that are thine enemies.

"Show me the strumpet that began this stir,
That with my nails her beauty I may tear.
Thy heat of lust, fond Paris, did incur 1473
This load of wrath that burning Troy doth bear.
Thy eye kindled the fire that burneth here,
And here in Troy, for trespass of thine eye,
The sire, the son, the dame, and daughter die.

"Why should the private pleasure of some one
Become the public plague of many moe? 1479
Let sin, alone committed, light alone
Upon his head that hath transgressed so;
Let guiltless souls be freed from guilty woe.
For one's offense why should so many fall,
To plague a private sin in general? 1484

"Lo, here weeps Hecuba, here Priam dies,
Here manly Hector faints, here Troilus swounds, 1486
Here friend by friend in bloody channel lies, 1487
And friend to friend gives unadvised wounds, 1488
And one man's lust these many lives confounds.
Had doting Priam check'd his son's desire,
Troy had been bright with fame and not with fire."

Here feelingly she weeps Troy's painted woes,
For sorrow, like a heavy-hanging bell,
Once set on ringing, with his own weight goes; 1494
Then little strength rings out the doleful knell.
So Lucrece, set a-work, sad tales doth tell
To pencil'd pensiveness and color'd sorrow; 1497
She lends them words, and she their looks doth borrow.

She throws her eyes about the painting round,
And who she finds forlorn she doth lament.
At last she sees a wretched image bound, 1501
That piteous looks to Phrygian shepherds lent. 1502
His face, though full of cares, yet show'd content;
Onward to Troy with the blunt swains he goes,
So mild that patience seem'd to scorn his woes. 1505

In him the painter labor'd with his skill
To hide deceit, and give the harmless show 1507
An humble gait, calm looks, eyes wailing still, 1508
A brow unbent, that seem'd to welcome woe,
Cheeks neither red nor pale, but mingled so
That blushing red no guilty instance gave, 1511
Nor ashy pale the fear that false hearts have.

But, like a constant and confirmed devil,
He entertain'd a show so seeming just, 1514
And therein so ensconc'd his secret evil,
That jealousy itself could not mistrust 1516
False-creeping craft and perjury should thrust
Into so bright a day such black-fac'd storms,
Or blot with hell-born sin such saint-like forms.

The well-skill'd workman this mild image drew
For perjur'd Sinon, whose enchanting story 1521
The credulous old Priam after slew;
Whose words like wildfire burnt the shining glory 1523
Of rich-built Ilion, that the skies were sorry,
And little stars shot from their fixed places,
When their glass fell wherein they view'd their faces. 1526

This picture she advisedly perus'd, 1527
And chid the painter for his wondrous skill,
Saying, some shape in Sinon's was abus'd; 1529
So fair a form lodg'd not a mind so ill.
And still on him she gaz'd, and gazing still,

1444 stell'd portrayed, engraved **1450 anatomiz'd** laid open, dissected **1452 chops** chaps, cracks and lines in the skin. **disguis'd** disfigured **1459 wants** lacks **1460 ban** curse **1473 fond** doting **1479 moe** more **1484 in general** publicly. (I.e., to punish the general public for an individual's sin.) **1486 swounds** swoons **1487 channel** gutter **1488 unadvised wounds** wounds they never intended for each other

1494 his its **1497 pencil'd** painted. **color'd** painted **1501 image** i.e., of Sinon, betrayer of Troy. **bound** onward bound **1502 piteous . . . lent** i.e., drew pitying looks from Phrygian shepherds. (I.e., Sinon deceived humble Trojans into pitying him as a deserter from the Greeks, thereby persuading them to admit the wooden horse.) **1505 patience** i.e., his patience. **scorn** make light of **1507 harmless show** outwardly harmless appearance **1508 still** continually **1511 guilty instance** symptom of guilt **1514 entertain'd a show** kept up an appearance **1516 jealousy** suspicion. **mistrust** suspect **1521 enchanting** bewitching **1523 wildfire** a highly inflammable mixture of tar, sulphur, grease, etc., used in war **1526 glass** mirror (i.e., rich-built Troy) **1527 advisedly** studiously **1529 some shape** i.e., the figure of some other person. **abus'd** slanderously portrayed

Such signs of truth in his plain face she spied
That she concludes the picture was belied.

"It cannot be," quoth she, "that so much guile"—
She would have said "can lurk in such a look";
But Tarquin's shape came in her mind the while,
And from her tongue "can lurk" from "cannot" took.
"It cannot be" she in that sense forsook,
And turn'd it thus, "It cannot be, I find,
But such a face should bear a wicked mind.

"For even as subtle Sinon here is painted,
So sober-sad, so weary, and so mild,
As if with grief or travail he had fainted,
To me came Tarquin armed, so beguil'd
With outward honesty, but yet defil'd
With inward vice. As Priam him did cherish,
So did I Tarquin; so my Troy did perish.

"Look, look, how list'ning Priam wets his eyes,
To see those borrowed tears that Sinon sheeds!
Priam, why art thou old and yet not wise?
For every tear he falls a Troyan bleeds.
His eye drops fire, no water thence proceeds;
Those round clear pearls of his, that move thy
pity,
Are balls of quenchless fire to burn thy city.

"Such devils steal effects from lightless hell,
For Sinon in his fire doth quake with cold,
And in that cold hot-burning fire doth dwell.
These contraries such unity do hold
Only to flatter fools and make them bold.
So Priam's trust false Sinon's tears doth flatter,
That he finds means to burn his Troy with
water."

Here, all enrag'd, such passion her assails,
That patience is quite beaten from her breast.
She tears the senseless Sinon with her nails,
Comparing him to that unhappy guest
Whose deed hath made herself herself detest.
At last she smilingly with this gives o'er;
"Fool, fool!" quoth she, "his wounds will not be
sore."

Thus ebbs and flows the current of her sorrow,
And time doth weary time with her complaining.
She looks for night, and then she longs for morrow,
And both she thinks too long with her remaining.
Short time seems long in sorrow's sharp sustaining;
Though woe be heavy, yet it seldom sleeps,
And they that watch see time how slow it creeps;

Which all this time hath overslipp'd her thought,
That she with painted images hath spent,
Being from the feeling of her own grief brought
By deep surmise of others' detriment,
Losing her woes in shows of discontent.
It easeth some, though none it ever cured,
To think their dolor others have endured.

But now the mindful messenger, come back,
Brings home his lord and other company,
Who finds his Lucrece clad in mourning black,
And round about her tear-distained eye
Blue circles stream'd, like rainbows in the sky.
These water-galls in her dim element
Foretell new-storms to those already spent.

Which when her sad-beholding husband saw,
Amazedly in her sad face he stares.
Her eyes, though sod in tears, look'd red and raw,
Her lively color kill'd with deadly cares.
He hath no power to ask her how she fares;
Both stood, like old acquaintance in a trance,
Met far from home, wond'ring each other's
chance.

At last he takes her by the bloodless hand,
And thus begins: "What uncouth ill event
Hath thee befall'n, that thou dost trembling stand?
Sweet love, what spite hath thy fair color spent?
Why art thou thus attir'd in discontent?
Unmask, dear dear, this moody heaviness,
And tell thy grief, that we may give redress."

Three times with sighs she gives her sorrow fire,
Ere once she can discharge one word of woe.
At length address'd to answer his desire,
She modestly prepares to let them know
Her honor is ta'en prisoner by the foe,
While Collatine and his consorted lords
With sad attention long to hear her words.

And now this pale swan in her wat'ry nest
Begins the sad dirge of her certain ending:
"Few words," quoth she, "shall fit the trespass best,
Where no excuse can give the fault amending.
In me moe woes than words are now depending,
And my laments would be drawn out too long,
To tell them all with one poor tired tongue.

"Then be this all the task it hath to say:
Dear husband, in the interest of thy bed
A stranger came, and on that pillow lay

1544 armed equipped, accoutered. **beguil'd** disguised **1549 borrowed** counterfeited. **sheeds** sheds **1551 he** i.e., Sinon. **falls** lets fall **1555 Such devils** (The ability to weep without real tears—*effects*—was attributed to devils.) **1558–1561 These . . . water** i.e., this illusory coinciding of contraries, hot and cold, is designed to encourage and embolden fools, just as Sinon hoodwinks Priam into a false sense of security; thus false Sinon's tears lull Priam into misplaced trust, so that Sinon finds means to burn Priam's Troy by use of false tears. (*Fools*, l. 1559, can perhaps refer to Priam or to Sinon, and much of the grammar is ingeniously reversible.) **1564 senseless** inanimate; unfeeling **1565 unhappy** causing unhappiness **1574 heavy** exhausting; sorrowful **1575 watch** stay awake

1578 brought made mindful **1579 surmise** contemplation **1580 shows of discontent** representations of sorrow, i.e., the painted scene of Troy's woe **1583 mindful** diligent **1586 tear-distained** tear-stained **1588 water-galls** fragments of rainbow, secondary rainbows (foretelling stormy weather). **element** sky, i.e., face or eye **1589 to** besides **1592 sod** sodden, steeped **1596 wond'ring . . . chance** wondering about each other's fortune; or, each wondering at the chance that had brought him to the other **1598 uncouth** strange **1600 spite** injury **1604–1605 Three . . . woe** (The metaphor is that of discharging firearms by means of a match.) **1606 address'd** prepared **1609 consorted** companion **1610 sad** serious **1611 swan** (Alludes to the belief that the swan, ordinarily without a song, sang beautifully at its own death.) **1619 in the interest** claiming possession

Where thou wast wont to rest thy weary head;
And what wrong else may be imagined
By foul enforcement might be done to me,
From that, alas, thy Lucrece is not free.

"For in the dreadful dead of dark midnight,
With shining falchion in my chamber came
A creeping creature, with a flaming light,
And softly cried 'Awake, thou Roman dame,
And entertain my love! Else lasting shame
On thee and thine this night I will inflict,
If thou my love's desire do contradict.

" 'For some hard-favor'd groom of thine,' quoth he, 1632
'Unless thou yoke thy liking to my will,
I'll murder straight, and then I'll slaughter thee
And swear I found you where you did fulfill
The loathsome act of lust, and so did kill
The lechers in their deed. This act will be
My fame and thy perpetual infamy.'

"With this, I did begin to start and cry;
And then against my heart he set his sword, 1640
Swearing, unless I took all patiently,
I should not live to speak another word;
So should my shame still rest upon record,
And never be forgot in mighty Rome
Th' adulterate death of Lucrece and her groom.

"Mine enemy was strong, my poor self weak,
And far the weaker with so strong a fear.
My bloody judge forbod my tongue to speak; 1648
No rightful plea might plead for justice there.
His scarlet lust came evidence to swear 1650
That my poor beauty had purloin'd his eyes;
And when the judge is robb'd the prisoner dies.

"O, teach me how to make mine own excuse!
Or at the least this refuge let me find:
Though my gross blood be stain'd with this abuse,
Immaculate and spotless is my mind.
That was not forc'd, that never was inclin'd
To accessary yieldings, but still pure 1658
Doth in her poison'd closet yet endure." 1659

Lo, here, the hopeless merchant of this loss, 1660
With head declin'd, and voice damm'd up with woe,
With sad set eyes, and wreathed arms across,
From lips new waxen pale begins to blow 1663
The grief away that stops his answer so.
But, wretched as he is, he strives in vain;
What he breathes out his breath drinks up again.

As through an arch the violent roaring tide 1667
Outruns the eye that doth behold his haste,
Yet in the eddy boundeth in his pride

1632 hard-favor'd rough-faced **1648 forbod** forbade **1650 came evidence** supplied evidence **1658 accessary yieldings** i.e., as an accessory to crime **1659 poison'd closet** i.e., violated body **1660 merchant of this loss** i.e., owner who has sustained this loss, Collatine **1663 new waxen** newly turned **1667 arch** i.e., of a bridge, such as London bridge or Clopton bridge

Back to the strait that forc'd him on so fast—
In rage sent out, recall'd in rage, being past—
Even so his sighs, his sorrows, make a saw, 1672
To push grief on, and back the same grief draw.

Which speechless woe of his poor she attendeth,
And his untimely frenzy thus awaketh: 1675
"Dear lord, thy sorrow to my sorrow lendeth
Another power; no flood by raining slaketh. 1677
My woe too sensible thy passion maketh 1678
More feeling-painful. Let it then suffice 1679
To drown one woe, one pair of weeping eyes.

"And for my sake, when I might charm thee so, 1681
For she that was thy Lucrece, now attend me:
Be suddenly revenged on my foe,
Thine, mine, his own. Suppose thou dost defend me
From what is past. The help that thou shalt lend me
Comes all too late, yet let the traitor die;
For sparing justice feeds iniquity. 1687

"But ere I name him, you fair lords," quoth she,
Speaking to those that came with Collatine,
"Shall plight your honorable faiths to me,
With swift pursuit to venge this wrong of mine;
For 'tis a meritorious fair design
To chase injustice with revengeful arms.
Knights, by their oaths, should right poor ladies' harms."

At this request, with noble disposition
Each present lord began to promise aid,
As bound in knighthood to her imposition, 1697
Longing to hear the hateful foe bewray'd. 1698
But she, that yet her sad task hath not said, 1699
The protestation stops. "O, speak," quoth she,
"How may this forced stain be wip'd from me?

"What is the quality of my offense, 1702
Being constrain'd with dreadful circumstance?
May my pure mind with the foul act dispense, 1704
My low-declined honor to advance? 1705
May any terms acquit me from this chance? 1706
The poisoned fountain clears itself again,
And why not I from this compelled stain?"

With this, they all at once began to say,
Her body's stain her mind untainted clears;
While with a joyless smile she turns away
The face, that map which deep impression bears
Of hard misfortune, carv'd in it with tears.
"No, no," quoth she, "no dame, hereafter living,
By my excuse shall claim excuse's giving." 1715

1672 saw i.e., sawlike back-and-forth motion **1675 And . . . awaketh** and awakens him from his ill-timed distraction **1677 Another power** added strength **1678–1679 My . . . painful** your passionate grief makes my woe, already too keenly felt, even more painfully perceived **1681 so** i.e., in the person of my former self, still unravished **1687 sparing** too lenient. **feeds iniquity** encourages wrongdoing **1697 imposition** injunction **1698 bewray'd** revealed, named **1699 her . . . said** had not yet finished her sad task of speaking **1702 quality** nature **1704 with . . . dispense** be able to free itself from the foul deed **1705 advance** raise up **1706 terms** mitigating grounds **1715 By . . . giving** will be able to claim the right to offer (give) an excuse using my excuse as her precedent

Here with a sigh, as if her heart would break,
She throws forth Tarquin's name: "He, he," she says,
But more than "he" her poor tongue could not speak;
Till after many accents and delays,
Untimely breathings, sick and short assays,
She utters this, "He, he, fair lords, 'tis he,
That guides this hand to give this wound to me."

Even here she sheathed in her harmless breast
A harmful knife, that thence her soul unsheathed.
That blow did bail it from the deep unrest
Of that polluted prison where it breathed.
Her contrite sighs unto the clouds bequeathed
Her winged sprite, and through her wounds doth fly
Life's lasting date from cancel'd destiny.

Stone-still, astonish'd with this deadly deed,
Stood Collatine and all his lordly crew,
Till Lucrece' father, that beholds her bleed,
Himself on her self-slaught'red body threw,
And from the purple fountain Brutus drew
The murd'rous knife, and, as it left the place,
Her blood, in poor revenge, held it in chase;

And bubbling from her breast, it doth divide
In two slow rivers, that the crimson blood
Circles her body in on every side,
Who, like a late-sack'd island, vastly stood
Bare and unpeopled in this fearful flood.
Some of her blood still pure and red remain'd,
And some look'd black, and that false Tarquin stain'd.

About the mourning and congealed face
Of that black blood a wat'ry rigol goes,
Which seems to weep upon the tainted place;
And ever since, as pitying Lucrece' woes,
Corrupted blood some watery token shows,
And blood untainted still doth red abide,
Blushing at that which is so putrified.

"Daughter, dear daughter," old Lucretius cries,
"That life was mine which thou hast here deprived.
If in the child the father's image lies,
Where shall I live now Lucrece is unlived?
Thou wast not to this end from me derived.
If children pre-decease progenitors,
We are their offspring, and they none of ours.

"Poor broken glass, I often did behold
In thy sweet semblance my old age new born;
But now that fair fresh mirror dim and old
Shows me a bare-bon'd death by time outworn.
O, from thy checks my image thou hast torn,
And shiver'd all the beauty of my glass,
That I no more can see what once I was!

"O Time, cease thou thy course and last no longer,
If they surcease to be that should survive.
Shall rotten Death make conquest of the stronger
And leave the falt'ring feeble souls alive?
The old bees die, the young possess their hive.
Then live, sweet Lucrece, live again and see
Thy father die, and not thy father thee!"

By this, starts Collatine as from a dream,
And bids Lucretius give his sorrow place;
And then in key-cold Lucrece' bleeding stream
He falls, and bathes the pale fear in his face,
And counterfeits to die with her a space;
Till manly shame bids him possess his breath
And live to be revenged on her death.

The deep vexation of his inward soul
Hath serv'd a dumb arrest upon his tongue,
Who, mad that sorrow should his use control,
Or keep him from heart-easing words so long,
Begins to talk; but through his lips do throng
Weak words, so thick come in his poor heart's aid,
That no man could distinguish what he said.

Yet sometime "Tarquin" was pronounced plain,
But through his teeth, as if the name he tore.
This windy tempest, till it blow up rain,
Held back his sorrow's tide, to make it more.
At last it rains, and busy winds give o'er;
Then son and father weep with equal strife
Who should weep most, for daughter or for wife.

The one doth call her his, the other his,
Yet neither may possess the claim they lay.
The father says "She's mine." "O, mine she is,"
Replies her husband. "Do not take away
My sorrow's interest. Let no mourner say
He weeps for her, for she was only mine,
And only must be wail'd by Collatine."

"O," quoth Lucretius, "I did give that life
Which she too early and too late hath spill'd."
"Woe, woe," quoth Collatine, "She was my wife,
I owed her, and 'tis mine that she hath kill'd."
"My daughter" and "my wife" with clamors fill'd
The dispers'd air, who, holding Lucrece' life,
Answer'd their cries, "my daughter" and "my wife."

Brutus, who pluck'd the knife from Lucrece' side,
Seeing such emulation in their woe,

1725 bail pay for its release **1729 Life's . . . destiny** i.e., the life which now has a perpetual existence, its subjugation to corporeal existence having been canceled **1734 Brutus** Lucius Junius Brutus, whose brother had been killed by the father of the Tarquin in this poem **1740 late-sack'd** recently pillaged. **vastly** having been desolated **1745 rigol** rim of serum **1758 glass** mirror (i.e., Lucrece, the image of her father) **1761 death** death's head, skull

1766 surcease cease **1773 give . . . place** yield him precedence in sorrowing **1774 key-cold** i.e., cold as steel **1775 pale fear** fearful pallor **1776 a space** for a period of time **1780 dumb arrest** injunction to be silent **1784 thick** thickly, fast **1797 interest** claim to possession **1801 late** recently **1803 owed** owned

Began to clothe his wit in state and pride, 1809
Burying in Lucrece' wound his folly's show. 1810
He with the Romans was esteemed so
As seely jeering idiots are with kings, 1812
For sportive words and utt'ring foolish things.

But now he throws that shallow habit by, 1814
Wherein deep policy did him disguise, 1815
And arm'd his long-hid wits advisedly
To check the tears in Collatinus' eyes.
"Thou wronged lord of Rome," quoth he, "arise!
Let my unsounded self, suppos'd a fool, 1819
Now set thy long-experienc'd wit to school.

"Why, Collatine, is woe the cure for woe?
Do wounds help wounds, or grief help grievous deeds?
Is it revenge to give thyself a blow
For his foul act by whom thy fair wife bleeds?
Such childish humor from weak minds proceeds.
Thy wretched wife mistook the matter so,
To slay herself, that should have slain her foe.

"Courageous Roman, do not steep thy heart
In such relenting dew of lamentations,
But kneel with me and help to bear thy part
To rouse our Roman gods with invocations,
That they will suffer these abominations,
Since Rome herself in them doth stand disgraced,
By our strong arms from forth her fair streets chased. 1834

"Now, by the Capitol that we adore,
And by this chaste blood so unjustly stained,
By heaven's fair sun that breeds the fat earth's store, 1837
By all our country rights in Rome maintained, 1838
And by chaste Lucrece' soul that late complained
Her wrongs to us, and by this bloody knife,
We will revenge the death of this true wife."

This said, he struck his hand upon his breast,
And kiss'd the fatal knife, to end his vow;
And to his protestation urg'd the rest,
Who, wond'ring at him, did his words allow. 1845
Then jointly to the ground their knees they bow,
And that deep vow which Brutus made before,
He doth again repeat, and that they swore.

When they had sworn to this advised doom, 1849
They did conclude to bear dead Lucrece thence,
To show her bleeding body thorough Rome, 1851
And so to publish Tarquin's foul offense; 1852
Which being done with speedy diligence,
The Romans plausibly did give consent 1854
To Tarquin's everlasting banishment.

1809 state dignity **1810 folly's show** pretense of folly. (Brutus feigned madness to escape the fate of his brother; see l. 1734.) **1812 seely jeering idiots** i.e., innocent court jesters **1814 habit** cloak and disposition **1815 policy** cunning **1819 unsounded** unplumbed, unexplored **1834 chased** i.e., to be chased away **1837 fat** fertile **1838 country rights** rights we have as a people **1845 allow** approve **1849 advised doom** considered judgment **1851 thorough** throughout **1852 publish** make public **1854 plausibly** with applause

The Passionate Pilgrim

Shakespeare became so popular in his own day that his name was inevitably used by publishers to sell books. Most of the poems in *The Passionate Pilgrim,* offered to the public in 1599 as entirely by Shakespeare, are either careless versions of his earlier work or poems of other Elizabethan writers passed off as his. Although the printer, William Jaggard, was later to be instrumental in publishing the First Folio, his work on this octavo collection seems to have been unauthorized and unscrupulous. He brought out what appears to be a second edition in 1599, setting up his text from an earlier edition of which two leaves (containing two poems) still exist in a Folger Library copy. When Jaggard printed another edition in 1612, adding materials from Thomas Heywood's *Troia Britanica* (1609), Heywood complained that both he and Shakespeare had been annoyed by the piracy.

The contents of the volume hardly inspire confidence. Of the twenty or twenty-one poems (number 14 appears as one poem in the original text but is sometimes divided by modern editors), five are indisputably Shakespeare's but are not newly composed for the volume. Poems 1 and 2 are sonnets 138 and 144; 3, 5, and 16 are from Act IV of *Love's Labor's Lost* (published 1598). Poem 11 is a sonnet from Bartholomew Griffin's *Fidessa More Chaste than Kind* (1596), and 4, 6, and 9 are so closely related to it in subject and style that they seem part of a sequence. The obvious resemblance in all four to Shakespeare's *Venus and Adonis* is probably a tribute to that poem's popularity rather than an indication of Shakespeare's authorship of these sonnets. Poems 8 and 20 first appeared in *Poems in Divers Humors,* 1598, by Richard Barnfield. The second of these was reprinted in another popular anthology, *England's Helicon* (1600), in which poem 17 also appears and is attributed to the author of 20, that is, to Barnfield. (Poem 17 was first published in Thomas Weelkes' *Madrigals,* 1597.) *England's Helicon* also printed a version of poem 19, attributing this famous lyric to "Chr. Marlowe," although its Reply (signed "Ignoto") was later said to be by Sir Walter Ralegh.

These attributions, most of them fairly reliable, leave only 7, 10, 12, 13, 14, 15, and 18 as possible new works by Shakespeare. Because of the volume's unreliability, and because most of these unattributed verses are mediocre, no good reason exists to credit any of them to Shakespeare. If one poem is to be singled out for praise, the usual choice is 12. Even here we find no unequivocal sign of Shakespeare's genius.

The Passionate Pilgrim

[1]

When my love swears that she is made of truth,
I do believe her, though I know she lies, 2
That she might think me some untutor'd youth,
Unskillful in the world's false forgeries.
Thus vainly thinking that she thinks me young,
Although I know my years be past the best,
I smiling credit her false-speaking tongue,
Outfacing faults in love with love's ill rest. 8
But wherefore says my love that she is young?
And wherefore say not I that I am old?
O, love's best habit is a soothing tongue, 11
And age, in love, loves not to have years told. 12
Therefore I'll lie with love, and love with me,
Since that our faults in love thus smother'd be.

[2]

Two loves I have, of comfort and despair,
That like two spirits do suggest me still: 2
My better angel is a man right fair,
My worser spirit a woman color'd ill. 4
To win me soon to hell, my female evil
Tempteth my better angel from my side,
And would corrupt my saint to be a devil,
Wooing his purity with her fair pride.
And whether that my angel be turn'd fiend,
Suspect I may, yet not directly tell;
For being both to me, both to each friend, 11
I guess one angel in another's hell. 12
The truth I shall not know, but live in doubt,
Till my bad angel fire my good one out. 14

[3]

Did not the heavenly rhetoric of thine eye,
'Gainst whom the world could not hold argument,
Persuade my heart to this false perjury?
Vows for thee broke deserve not punishment.
A woman I forswore; but I will prove,
Thou being a goddess, I forswore not thee;
My vow was earthly, thou a heavenly love;
Thy grace being gain'd cures all disgrace in me.
My vow was breath, and breath a vapor is;
Then thou, fair sun, that on this earth doth shine,
Exhale this vapor vow; in thee it is; 11
If broken, then it is no fault of mine.
If by me broke, what fool is not so wise 13
To break an oath to win a paradise?

[4]

Sweet Cytherea, sitting by a brook 1
With young Adonis, lovely, fresh, and green, 2
Did court the lad with many a lovely look, 3
Such looks as none could look but beauty's queen.
She told him stories to delight his ear;
She show'd him favors to allure his eye;
To win his heart, she touch'd him here and there—
Touches so soft still conquer chastity.
But whether unripe years did want conceit, 9
Or he refus'd to take her figur'd proffer, 10
The tender nibbler would not touch the bait,
But smile and jest at every gentle offer.
Then fell she on her back, fair queen, and toward. 13
He rose and ran away; ah, fool too froward! 14

[5]

If love make me forsworn, how shall I swear to love?
O never faith could hold, if not to beauty vowed!
Though to myself forsworn, to thee I'll constant prove;
Those thoughts, to me like oaks, to thee like osiers bowed. 4
Study his bias leaves, and makes his book thine eyes, 5
Where all those pleasures live that art can comprehend. 6
If knowledge be the mark, to know thee shall suffice;
Well learned is that tongue that well can thee commend,
All ignorant that soul that sees thee without wonder;
Which is to me some praise, that I thy parts admire.
Thine eye Jove's lightning seems, thy voice his dreadful thunder,
Which, not to anger bent, is music and sweet fire.
Celestial as thou art, O do not love that wrong,
To sing heaven's praise with such an earthly tongue. 14

[6]

Scarce had the sun dried up the dewy morn,
And scarce the herd gone to the hedge for shade,
When Cytherea, all in love forlorn,
A longing tarriance for Adonis made 4
Under an osier growing by a brook,

1 • A slightly varying version of Sonnet 138.
2 believe i.e., pretend to believe **8 Outfacing** (modifies *I*). **ill rest** lack of stability. (Sonnet 138 has an entirely different line; the line here is not satisfactorily explained.) **11 habit** demeanor (with, however, a suggestion of *garb,* i.e., something put on). **soothing** flattering **12 told** counted

2 • A variant of Sonnet 144.
2 suggest urge, offer counsel. **still** continually **4 ill** i.e., dark of complexion **11 For . . . friend** being both friends to me and also to each other **12 I . . . hell** I suspect that she (the evil angel) has him in her power (i.e., her sexual embracement) **14 fire . . . out** drive out my good angel (with the suggestion of "communicate a venereal disease")

3 • Cf. *Love's Labor's Lost,* IV.iii.56–69.

11 Exhale draw up, as the sun draws vapor from the earth **13 so wise** so wise as, wise enough

4 •
1 Cytherea Venus **2 Adonis** (See the poem *Venus and Adonis.*) **green** young **3 lovely** amorous **9 want conceit** lack understanding **10 figur'd** indicated by gesture **13 toward** willing **14 froward** perverse, resisting

5 • Cf. *Love's Labor's Lost,* IV.ii.104–117.
4 osiers willows **5 Study . . . leaves** the student abandons his habitual inclination (to learning) **6 art** learning **14 To sing** (In *Love's Labor's Lost,* this reads "That sings," which gives a clearer sense, though in either case the line is difficult.)

6 • (This sonnet, following Ovid, deals with Adonis bathing in a brook; cf. *The Taming of the Shrew,* Induction, ii.50–53.)
4 tarriance tarrying

A brook where Adon us'd to cool his spleen.
Hot was the day, she hotter that did look
For his approach, that often there had been.
Anon he comes, and throws his mantle by,
And stood stark naked on the brook's green brim.
The sun look'd on the world with glorious eye,
Yet not so wistly as this queen on him.
He, spying her, bounc'd in, whereas he stood:
"O Jove," quoth she, "why was not I a flood!"

[7]

Fair is my love, but not so fair as fickle;
Mild as a dove, but neither true nor trusty;
Brighter than glass, and yet, as glass is, brittle;
Softer than wax, and yet, as iron, rusty.
A lily pale, with damask dye to grace her,
None fairer, nor none falser to deface her.

Her lips to mine how often hath she joined,
Between each kiss her oaths of true love swearing!
How many tales to please me hath she coined,
Dreading my love, the loss whereof still fearing!
Yet in the midst of all her pure protestings,
Her faith, her oaths, her tears, and all were jestings.

She burnt with love, as straw with fire flameth;
She burnt out love, as soon as straw outburneth;
She fram'd the love, and yet she foil'd the framing;
She bade love last, and yet she fell a-turning.
Was this a lover, or a lecher whether?
Bad in the best, though excellent in neither.

[8]

If music and sweet poetry agree,
As they must needs, the sister and the brother,
Then must the love be great 'twixt thee and me,
Because thou lov'st the one, and I the other.
Dowland to thee is dear, whose heavenly touch
Upon the lute doth ravish human sense;
Spenser to me, whose deep conceit is such
As, passing all conceit, needs no defense.
Thou lov'st to hear the sweet melodious sound
That Phoebus' lute, the queen of music, makes;
And I in deep delight am chiefly drown'd
Whenas himself to singing he betakes.
One god is god of both, as poets feign;
One knight loves both, and both in thee remain.

6 spleen heat **12 wistly** eagerly, intently **13 whereas** where

7 •
5 damask pale red (as with the red of a damask rose) **6 nor . . . her** nor, to her discredit, is any woman falser **10 Dreading** i.e., dreading to lose. **still** continually **15 fram'd** created, built. **foil'd** undid **16 a-turning** i.e., to other men **17 whether** which of the two **18 Bad . . . neither** worse at being a lover but not excellent as a lecher either (?) or, even what she did best, she did badly and she was not excellent as either lover or lecher (?)

8 • A sonnet by Barnfield.
3 'twixt thee and me i.e., between Barnfield and R.L., to whom he addressed the poem **5 Dowland** John Dowland (1563?–1626?), lutanist and composer **7 Spenser** Edmund Spenser, author of *The Faerie Queene* **7–8 conceit . . . conceit** imaginative conception . . . play of fancy **10 Phoebus** Apollo, god of music and poetry. (The Renaissance often thought of his *lute* rather than his *lyre*.) **12 Whenas** when. **himself** i.e., Phoebus (?) **14 One knight** (Possibly Sir George Carey, K.G., to whom Dowland dedicated his first book of airs.)

[9]

Fair was the morn when the fair queen of love,
* * * * *
Paler for sorrow than her milk-white dove,
For Adon's sake, a youngster proud and wild,
Her stand she takes upon a steep-up hill.
Anon Adonis comes with horn and hounds;
She, silly queen, with more than love's good will,
Forbade the boy he should not pass those grounds.
"Once," quoth she, "Did I see a fair sweet youth
Here in these brakes deep-wounded with a boar,
Deep in the thigh, a spectacle of ruth!
See, in my thigh," quoth she, "here was the sore."
She showed hers; he saw more wounds than one,
And blushing fled, and left her all alone.

[10]

Sweet rose, fair flower, untimely pluck'd, soon vaded,
Pluck'd in the bud, and vaded in the spring!
Bright orient pearl, alack, too timely shaded!
Fair creature, kill'd too soon by death's sharp sting!
Like a green plum that hangs upon a tree,
And falls, through wind, before the fall should be.

I weep for thee, and yet no cause I have,
For why thou lefts me nothing in thy will;
And yet thou lefts me more than I did crave,
For why I craved nothing of thee still.
O yes, dear friend, I pardon crave of thee,
Thy discontent thou didst bequeath to me.

[11]

Venus, with young Adonis sitting by her
Under a myrtle shade, began to woo him.
She told the youngling how god Mars did try her,
And as he fell to her, so fell she to him.
"Even thus," quoth she, "the warlike god embrac'd me,"
And then she clipp'd Adonis in her arms;
"Even thus," quoth she, "the warlike god unlac'd me,"
As if the boy should use like loving charms;
"Even thus," quoth she, "he seized on my lips,"
And with her lips on his did act the seizure;
And as she fetched breath, away he skips,
And would not take her meaning nor her pleasure.
Ah, that I had my lady at this bay,
To kiss and clip me till I run away!

[12]

Crabbed age and youth cannot live together.
Youth is full of pleasance, age is full of care;

9 • (The second line, rhyming with *wild*, is apparently missing.)
5 steep-up steeply rising **7 silly** pitiable. **with . . . will** with more passionate intentions than simply good will **13 wounds** (with a sexual double entendre)

10 •
1 vaded faded **3 timely** soon, early **8 For why** because. **lefts** left'st

11 •
6 clipp'd embraced **13 at this bay** cornered, at a stand. (A term from hunting.)

12 •
2 pleasance gaiety, merriment

Youth like summer morn, age like winter weather;
Youth like summer brave, age like winter bare. 4
Youth is full of sport, age's breath is short;
Youth is nimble, age is lame;
Youth is hot and bold, age is weak and cold;
Youth is wild, and age is tame.
Age, I do abhor thee; youth, I do adore thee.
O, my love, my love is young!
Age, I do defy thee. O, sweet shepherd, hie thee, 11
For methinks thou stays too long. 12

[13]

Beauty is but a vain and doubtful good,
A shining gloss that vadeth suddenly,
A flower that dies when first it gins to bud,
A brittle glass that's broken presently—
A doubtful good, a gloss, a glass, a flower,
Lost, vaded, broken, dead within an hour.

And as goods lost are seld or never found, 7
As vaded gloss no rubbing will refresh,
As flowers dead lie withered on the ground,
As broken glass no cement can redress,
So beauty blemish'd once, forever lost,
In spite of physic, painting, pain, and cost. 12

[14]

Good night, good rest. Ah, neither be my share!
She bade good night that kept my rest away,
And daff'd me to a cabin hang'd with care, 3
To descant on the doubts of my decay. 4
"Farewell," quoth she, "and come again tomorrow."
Fare well I could not, for I supp'd with sorrow. 6

Yet at my parting sweetly did she smile,
In scorn or friendship, nill I conster whether. 8
'T may be she joy'd to jest at my exile,
'T may be again to make me wander thither.
"Wander," a word for shadows like myself,
As take the pain, but cannot pluck the pelf. 12

Lord, how mine eyes throw gazes to the east!
My heart doth charge the watch; the morning rise 14
Doth cite each moving sense from idle rest. 15
Not daring trust the office of mine eyes,
While Philomela sits and sings, I sit and mark, 17
And wish her lays were tuned like the lark; 18

For she doth welcome daylight with her ditty,
And drives away dark dreaming night.
The night so pack'd, I post unto my pretty; 21
Heart hath his hope, and eyes their wished sight;
Sorrow chang'd to solace, and solace mix'd with sorrow;
For why, she sigh'd and bade me come tomorrow.

Were I with her, the night would post too soon, 25
But now are minutes added to the hours; 26
To spite me now, each minute seems a moon; 27
Yet not for me, shine sun to succor flowers! 28
Pack night, peep day; good day, of night now borrow;
Short night tonight, and length thyself tomorrow. 30

4 brave elegantly dressed **11 hie thee** hasten **12 stays** delay

13 •
7 seld seldom **12 physic** medicine. **pain** labor

14 •
3 daff'd put aside, turned away. **cabin** small room. **hang'd** furnished (as with wall hangings or tapestries) **4 descant** compose variations, make musical variations. **doubts** fears **6 Fare** (punning on the sense of *eat*) **8 nill . . . whether** I won't undertake to say which of the two **12 As** who, such as. **pelf** reward **14 My . . . watch** (Variously interpreted: my heart does charge my eyes to watch the morning rise; or does accuse the watch for marking the time so slowly; or does give notice to the watchman to proclaim the dawn.) **15 cite** summon **17 Philomela** i.e., the nightingale **18 like the lark** i.e., to the dawn

21 pack'd disposed of, departed. **post** hasten **25 post** hasten onward **26 added to** i.e., made to seem as lengthy as **27 moon** month **28 Yet not for me** if not for me, at least **30 Short . . . tomorrow** day, make tonight short and lengthen your day tomorrow

SONNETS TO SUNDRY NOTES OF MUSIC

[15]

It was a lording's daughter, the fairest one of three, 1
That liked of her master as well as well might be, 2
Till looking on an Englishman, the fair'st that eye could see,
Her fancy fell a-turning.
Long was the combat doubtful that love with love did fight,
To leave the master loveless, or kill the gallant knight; 6
To put in practice either, alas, it was a spite
Unto the silly damsel! 8
But one must be refused; more mickle was the pain 9
That nothing could be used to turn them both to gain, 10
For of the two the trusty knight was wounded with disdain.
Alas, she could not help it!
Thus art with arms contending was victor of the day, 13
Which by a gift of learning did bear the maid away;
Then, lullaby, the learned man hath got the lady gay,
For now my song is ended.

[16]

On a day—alack the day!—
Love, whose month was ever May,
Spied a blossom passing fair,
Playing in the wanton air. 4

15 •
1 lording's lord's **2 master** teacher, tutor **6 kill** i.e., by rejecting him. **knight** i.e., the Englishman (l. 3) **8 silly** pitiable **9 mickle** great **10 used** done **13 art** learning

16 • Cf. *Love's Labor's Lost*, IV.iii.97–116.
4 wanton frolicsome, sportive

Through the velvet leaves the wind,
All unseen, gan passage find;
That the lover, sick to death, 7
Wish'd himself the heaven's breath.
"Air," quoth he, "thy cheeks may blow;
Air, would I might triumph so!
But, alas! My hand hath sworn
Ne'er to pluck thee from thy thorn;
Vow, alack, for youth unmeet,
Youth, so apt to pluck a sweet!
Thou for whom Jove would swear
Juno but an Ethiope were,
And deny himself for Jove,
Turning mortal for thy love."

[17]

My flocks feed not, my ewes breed not,
My rams speed not, all is amiss; 2
Love is dying, faith's defying,
Heart's denying, causer of this.
All my merry jigs are quite forgot,
All my lady's love is lost, God wot.
Where her faith was firmly fix'd in love,
There a nay is plac'd without remove.
One silly cross wrought all my loss. 9
O frowning Fortune, cursed fickle dame!
For now I see inconstancy
More in women than in men remain.

In black mourn I, all fears scorn I,
Love hath forlorn me, living in thrall. 14
Heart is bleeding, all help needing,
O cruel speeding, fraughted with gall. 16
My shepherd's pipe can sound no deal; 17
My wether's bell rings doleful knell;
My curtal dog, that wont to have play'd, 19
Plays not at all, but seems afraid;
With sighs so deep procures to weep, 21
In howling wise, to see my doleful plight.
How sighs resound through heartless ground, 23
Like a thousand vanquish'd men in bloody fight! 24

Clear wells spring not, sweet birds sing not, 25
Green plants bring not forth their dye; 26
Herds stand weeping, flocks all sleeping,
Nymphs back peeping fearfully.
All our pleasure known to us poor swains,
All our merry meetings on the plains,
All our evening sport from us is fled,
All our love is lost, for Love is dead.
Farewell, sweet lass, thy like ne'er was
For a sweet content, the cause of all my moan.
Poor Corydon must live alone;
Other help for him I see that there is none.

[18]

When as thine eye hath chose the dame,
And stall'd the deer that thou shouldst strike, 2
Let reason rule things worthy blame, 3
As well as fancy partial might. 4
Take counsel of some wiser head,
Neither too young nor yet unwed.

And when thou com'st thy tale to tell,
Smooth not thy tongue with filed talk, 8
Lest she some subtle practice smell—
A cripple soon can find a halt— 10
But plainly say thou lov'st her well,
And set her person forth to sale. 12

And to her will frame all thy ways;
Spare not to spend, and chiefly there
Where thy desert may merit praise,
By ringing in thy lady's ear.
The strongest castle, tower, and town,
The golden bullet beats it down.

Serve always with assured trust,
And in thy suit be humble true; 20
Unless thy lady prove unjust,
Press never thou to choose anew.
When time shall serve, be thou not slack
To proffer, though she put thee back.

What though her frowning brows be bent,
Her cloudy looks will calm ere night,
And then too late she will repent
That thus dissembled her delight;
And twice desire, ere it be day,
That which with scorn she put away.

What though she strive to try her strength,
And ban and brawl, and say thee nay, 32
Her feeble force will yield at length,
When craft hath taught her thus to say:
"Had women been so strong as men,
In faith, you had not had it then."

The wiles and guiles that women work,
Dissembled with an outward show,
The tricks and toys that in them lurk,
The cock that treads them shall not know.
Have you not heard it said full oft,
A woman's nay doth stand for nought?

Think women still to strive with men, 43
To sin and never for to saint. 44
There is no heaven; be holy then, 45

7 That so that

17 • (First published in a collection of madrigals by Thomas Weelkes; reprinted in *England's Helicon* [1600] as "The Unknown Shepherd's Complaint.")
2 speed prosper **9 cross** misfortune **14 forlorn me** made me forlorn **16 speeding** faring, succeeding. **fraughted** loaded, burdened **17 no deal** not at all **19 curtal** dock-tailed **21 procures** manages so as **23 heartless** desolate **24 vanquish'd men in** men vanquished in **25 wells** springs **26 their dye** i.e., their usual green color

18 •
2 stall'd got within range of. **deer** (with customary pun on *dear*) **3–4 Let . . . might** i.e., use wise counsel as your guide in this seduction, surely as apt a guide as infatuation (?) **8 filed talk** studied or polished language **10 A cripple . . . halt** i.e., she, expert in smooth talk, can soon find out a flatterer, just as a cripple can soon detect another cripple **12 And set . . . sale** and praise her qualities like a merchant praising wares **32 ban** curse **43 Think** expect **44 saint** play the saint **45 There** i.e., in women

When time with age shall them attaint.
Were kisses all the joys in bed,
One woman would another wed.

But, soft, enough! Too much, I fear,
Lest that my mistress hear my song;
She will not stick to round me on th' ear,
To teach my tongue to be so long.
Yet will she blush, here be it said,
To hear her secrets so bewray'd.

[19]

Live with me and be my love,
And we will all the pleasures prove
That hills and valleys, dales and fields,
And all the craggy mountains yield.

There will we sit upon the rocks,
And see the shepherds feed their flocks,
By shallow rivers, by whose falls
Melodious birds sing madrigals.

There will I make thee a bed of roses,
With a thousand fragrant posies,
A cap of flowers, and a kirtle
Embroider'd all with leaves of myrtle.

A belt of straw and ivy buds,
With coral clasps and amber studs;
And if these pleasures may thee move,
Then live with me and be my love.

Love's Answer

If that the world and love were young,
And truth in every shepherd's tongue,
These pretty pleasures might me move
To live with thee and be thy love.

[20]

As it fell upon a day
In the merry month of May,
Sitting in a pleasant shade
Which a grove of myrtles made,
Beasts did leap, and birds did sing,
Trees did grow, and plants did spring;
Everything did banish moan,
Save the nightingale alone.
She, poor bird, as all forlorn,
Lean'd her breast up-till a thorn,
And there sung the dolefull'st ditty,
That to hear it was great pity.
"Fie, fie, fie," now would she cry;
"Tereu, tereu!" by and by;
That to hear her so complain,
Scarce I could from tears refrain;
For her griefs, so lively shown,
Made me think upon mine own.
Ah, thought I, thou mourn'st in vain!
None takes pity on thy pain.
Senseless trees they cannot hear thee;
Ruthless beasts they will not cheer thee.
King Pandion he is dead;
All thy friends are lapp'd in lead;
All thy fellow birds do sing,
Careless of thy sorrowing.
[Even so, poor bird, like thee,
None alive will pity me.]
Whilst as fickle Fortune smil'd,
Thou and I were both beguil'd.
Everyone that flatters thee
Is no friend in misery.
Words are easy, like the wind;
Faithful friends are hard to find.
Every man will be thy friend
Whilst thou hast wherewith to spend;
But if store of crowns be scant,
No man will supply thy want.
If that one be prodigal,
Bountiful they will him call,
And with such-like flattering,
"Pity but he were a king!"
If he be addict to vice,
Quickly him they will entice;
If to women he be bent,
They have at commandement.
But if Fortune once do frown,
Then farewell his great renown;
They that fawn'd on him before
Use his company no more.
He that is thy friend indeed,
He will help thee in thy need.
If thou sorrow, he will weep;
If thou wake, he cannot sleep;
Thus of every grief in heart
He with thee doth bear a part.
These are certain signs to know
Faithful friend from flatt'ring foe.

51 stick . . . ear hesitate to take me to task **54 bewray'd** revealed

19 • (The first publication of Marlowe's lyric, which appeared also in *England's Helicon,* 1600, with the accompanying poem, "The Nymph's Reply to the Shepherd," attributed to Sir Walter Ralegh.)
2 prove experience

20 • (From Richard Barnfield's *Poems in Divers Humors,* 1598.)
10 up-till up against

23 King Pandion King of Athens, father of Philomela (who was ravished by Tereus and transformed into a nightingale) and Progne. (See Ovid, *Metamorphoses,* VI.424–676.) **42 but he were** that he is not **46 They have** i.e., they have women **54 wake** are wakeful

The Phoenix and Turtle

"The Phoenix and Turtle" first appeared in a collection of poems called *Loves Martyr: Or, Rosalins Complaint* by Robert Chester (1601). This quarto volume offered various poetic exercises about the Phoenix and the Turtle "by the best and chiefest of our moderne writers." The poem assigned to Shakespeare has been universally accepted as his, and is one of his most remarkable productions. With a deceptively simple diction, in gracefully pure tetrameter quatrains and triplets, the poem effortlessly evokes the transcendental ideal of a love existing eternally beyond death. The occasion is an assembly of birds to observe the funeral rites of the Phoenix and the Turtle. The Phoenix, legendary bird of resurrection from her own ashes, once more finds life through death in the company of the Turtledove, emblem of pure constancy in affection. Their spiritual union becomes a mystical oneness in whose presence Reason stands virtually speechless. Baffled human discourse must resort to paradox in order to explain how two beings become one essence, "Hearts remote yet not asunder." Mathematics and logic are "confounded" by this joining of two spirits into a "concordant one." This paradox of oneness echoes scholastic theology and its expounding of the doctrine of the Trinity, although, somewhat in the manner of John Donne's poetry, this allusion is more a part of the poem's serious wit than its symbolic meaning. The poignant brevity of this vision is rendered all the more mysterious by our not knowing what if any human tragedy may have prompted this metaphysical affirmation.

The Phoenix and Turtle

Let the bird of loudest lay,
On the sole Arabian tree,
Herald sad and trumpet be,
To whose sound chaste wings obey.

But thou shrieking harbinger,
Foul precurrer of the fiend,
Augur of the fever's end,
To this troop come thou not near.

From this session interdict
Every fowl of tyrant wing,
Save the eagle, feath'red king;
Keep the obsequy so strict.

Let the priest in surplice white,
That defunctive music can,
Be the death-divining swan,
Lest the requiem lack his right.

And thou treble-dated crow,
That thy sable gender mak'st
With the breath thou giv'st and tak'st,
'Mongst our mourners shalt thou go.

Here the anthem doth commence.
Love and constancy is dead;
Phoenix and the turtle fled
In a mutual flame from hence.

So they loved, as love in twain
Had the essence but in one,
Two distincts, division none;
Number there in love was slain.

Hearts remote, yet not asunder;
Distance, and no space was seen
'Twixt this turtle and his queen;
But in them it were a wonder.

Title: **Phoenix** mythical bird that was thought to be consumed in flame and reborn in its own ashes, symbol of immortality. **Turtle** turtledove, symbol of constancy in love
1 bird . . . lay the bird (possibly the nightingale) of loudest song **2 sole Arabian tree** (The phoenix was thought to build its nest in a unique tree in Arabia.) **3 sad** solemn. **trumpet** trumpeter **4 obey** are obedient **5 shrieking harbinger** i.e., screech owl **6 precurrer** forerunner **7 Augur . . . end** i.e., prognosticator of death **10 fowl . . . wing** bird of prey **14 defunctive** funereal. **can** knows, has skill in **15 death-divining swan** (Alludes to the belief that the swan foresees its own death and sings when it is about to die.) **16 his right** its proper ceremony **17 treble-dated** i.e., living thrice as long as the normal span of life **18–19 That . . . tak'st** (Cf. *Hortus Sanitatis*, Bk. III, sec. 34, in Seager's *Natural History in Shakespeare's Time:* "They [ravens] are said to conceive and to lay eggs at the bill. The young become black on the seventh day.") **25 So . . . as** they so loved that **27 distincts** separate or individual persons or things **28 Number . . . slain** i.e., their love, being of one essence, paradoxically renders the very concept of number meaningless; "one is no number" **32 But . . . wonder** this phenomenon, had it been seen anywhere but in them, would have seemed amazing

So between them love did shine, 33
That the turtle saw his right 34
Flaming in the phoenix' sight; 35
Either was the other's mine. 36

Property was thus appalled, 37
That the self was not the same; 38
Single nature's double name
Neither two nor one was called.

Reason, in itself confounded, 41
Saw division grow together, 42
To themselves yet either neither, 43
Simple were so well compounded, 44

That it cried, "How true a twain 45
Seemeth this concordant one!
Love hath reason, reason none, 47
If what parts can so remain." 48

Whereupon it made this threne 49
To the phoenix and the dove,
Co-supremes and stars of love,
As chorus to their tragic scene.

THRENOS

Beauty, truth, and rarity,
Grace in all simplicity,
Here enclos'd in cinders lie.

Death is now the phoenix' nest,
And the turtle's loyal breast
To eternity doth rest,

Leaving no posterity;
'Twas not their infirmity, 60
It was married chastity. 61

Truth may seem, but cannot be; 62
Beauty brag, but 'tis not she;
Truth and beauty buried be.

To this urn let those repair
That are either true or fair;
For these dead birds sigh a prayer.

33 So in such a way **34 right** true nature, what pertained uniquely and rightly to him **35 sight** eyes **36 mine** i.e., very own **37–38 Property . . . same** i.e., the very idea of a peculiar or essential quality was thus confounded by the paradoxical revelation here that each lover's identity was merged into the other's and was no longer itself **41–44 Reason . . . compounded** I.e., pure reason had seen these unlike and, according to its insight, quite incompatible essences, unite together. In the union neither had an entirely separate identity, because *simple,* that is, simples or elementary elements, were so perfectly compounded or united. **45 it** i.e., Reason **47–48 Love . . . remain** i.e., Love, which ordinarily lacks reason, is reasonable, and reason itself lacks reason, if two that can be disunited or parted nevertheless remain thus in union **49 threne** lamentation, funeral song *(Threnos)* **60–61 'Twas . . . chastity** i.e., it was not a defect in them to leave no posterity, but an emblem of their mystical eternal trothplight **62 seem** appear to exist. (I.e., fidelity and beauty as known to mortal perception are only illusory, for their ideal incarnation now lies buried with the Phoenix and Turtle.)

A Lover's Complaint

Thomas Thorpe published "A Lover's Complaint" in his 1609 quarto of Shakespeare's *Sonnets,* ascribing the poem to "William Shake-speare" in its title heading (sig. K[v]). The ascription must not be given too much weight, for Thorpe evidently did not have Shakespeare's authorization to publish the sonnets and may possibly have added the last two sonnets from some other source. Yet Thorpe's edition remains the only objective evidence we have, and its authority has never been convincingly refuted. The modern tendency to dismiss "A Lover's Complaint" as unworthy of Shakespeare's genius rests on subjective judgment and on stylistic "tests" that are too often proved unreliable. The poem was never ascribed to anyone else during Shakespeare's lifetime. On balance, the evidence is in favor of his authorship, though the issue will continue to remain in doubt.

The poem's genre, the "complaint" of a forsaken maiden, is conventional, along with the pastoral setting, the catalogue of the fickle lover's features, and the sententious warnings against blind passion. The poem did not add to Shakespeare's contemporary reputation. Still, it cannot safely be assigned to any other Elizabethan poet. Nor does it read like a mere effusion of Shakespeare's youth. Though written in *The Rape of Lucrece*'s seven-line rhyme royal stanza, the poem eschews Ovidian and Petrarchan conceit for an occasional richness and complexity of metaphor.

A Lover's Complaint

From off a hill whose concave womb re-worded 1
A plaintful story from a sist'ring vale, 2
My spirits t' attend this double voice accorded, 3
And down I laid to list the sad-tun'd tale;
Ere long espied a fickle maid full pale, 5
Tearing of papers, breaking rings a-twain, 6
Storming her world with sorrow's wind and rain.

Upon her head a platted hive of straw, 8
Which fortified her visage from the sun,
Whereon the thought might think sometime it saw 10
The carcass of a beauty spent and done.
Time had not scythed all that youth begun,
Nor youth all quit; but, spite of heaven's fell rage, 13
Some beauty peep'd through lattice of sear'd age. 14

Oft did she heave her napkin to her eyne, 15
Which on it had conceited characters, 16
Laund'ring the silken figures in the brine
That seasoned woe had pelleted in tears, 18
And often reading what contents it bears;
As often shrieking undistinguish'd woe, 20
In clamors of all size, both high and low.

Sometimes her level'd eyes their carriage ride, 22
As they did batt'ry to the spheres intend; 23
Sometime diverted their poor balls are tied
To th' orbed earth; sometimes they do extend
Their view right on; anon their gazes lend
To every place at once, and, nowhere fix'd,
The mind and sight distractedly commix'd.

Her hair, nor loose nor tied in formal plat, 29
Proclaim'd in her a careless hand of pride; 30
For some, untuck'd, descended her sheav'd hat, 31
Hanging her pale and pined cheek beside;
Some in her threaden fillet still did bide, 33
And true to bondage would not break from thence,
Though slackly braided in loose negligence.

A thousand favors from a maund she drew 36
Of amber, crystal, and of beaded jet,
Which one by one she in a river threw,
Upon whose weeping margent she was set, 39
Like usury, applying wet to wet, 40

1 re-worded re-echoed **2 sist'ring** neighboring **3 accorded** inclined, consented **5 fickle** i.e., perturbed **6 papers** i.e., love letters **8 platted hive** i.e., woven hat **10 the thought** the mind; that which thinks **13 fell** deadly, cruel **14 sear'd** dried up **15 heave** lift. **napkin** handkerchief. **eyne** eyes **16 conceited characters** fanciful or emblematic devices **18 seasoned** (1) matured (2) salted. **pelleted** formed into small globules **20 undistinguish'd woe** incoherent cries of grief **22 her . . . ride** i.e., her eyes, directed and aimed like a cannon, swiveled about as on a gun carriage **23 As . . . intend** as if they did intend to direct their fire against the heavens **29 in formal plat** neatly braided **30 careless . . . pride** hand careless of appearances **31 sheav'd** straw **33 threaden fillet** i.e., ribbon binding her hair **36 favors** love tokens. **maund** woven basket with handles **39 weeping margent** moist bank **40 usury** i.e., applying money to money

Or monarch's hands that lets not bounty fall
Where want cries some, but where excess begs all.

Of folded schedules had she many a one,
Which she perus'd, sigh'd, tore, and gave the flood;
Crack'd many a ring of posied gold and bone,
Bidding them find their sepulchers in mud;
Found yet moe letters sadly penn'd in blood,
With sleided silk feat and affectedly
Enswath'd and seal'd to curious secrecy.

These often bath'd she in her fluxive eyes,
And often kiss'd, and often 'gan to tear;
Cried "O false blood, thou register of lies,
What unapproved witness dost thou bear!
Ink would have seem'd more black and damned here!"
This said, in top of rage the lines she rents,
Big discontent so breaking their contents.

A reverend man that graz'd his cattle nigh—
Sometime a blusterer, that the ruffle knew
Of court, of city, and had let go by
The swiftest hours, observed as they flew—
Towards this afflicted fancy fastly drew,
And, privileg'd by age, desires to know
In brief the grounds and motives of her woe.

So slides he down upon his grained bat,
And comely-distant sits he by her side,
When he again desires her, being sat,
Her grievance with his hearing to divide.
If that from him there may be aught applied
Which may her suffering ecstasy assuage,
'Tis promis'd in the charity of age.

"Father," she says, "though in me you behold
The injury of many a blasting hour,
Let it not tell your judgment I am old;
Not age, but sorrow, over me hath power.
I might as yet have been a spreading flower,
Fresh to myself, if I had self-applied
Love to myself and to no love beside.

"But, woe is me! Too early I attended
A youthful suit—it was to gain my grace—
Of one by nature's outwards so commended
That maidens' eyes stuck over all his face.
Love lack'd a dwelling, and made him her place;
And when in his fair parts she did abide,
She was new lodg'd and newly deified.

"His browny locks did hang in crooked curls,
And every light occasion of the wind
Upon his lips their silken parcels hurls.
What's sweet to do, to do will aptly find;
Each eye that saw him did enchant the mind,
For on his visage was in little drawn
What largeness thinks in Paradise was sawn.

"Small show of man was yet upon his chin;
His phoenix down began but to appear
Like unshorn velvet on that termless skin
Whose bare outbragg'd the web it seem'd to wear.
Yet show'd his visage by that cost more dear;
And nice affections wavering stood in doubt
If best were as it was, or best without.

"His qualities were beauteous as his form,
For maiden-tongu'd he was, and thereof free;
Yet, if men mov'd him, was he such a storm
As oft 'twixt May and April is to see,
When winds breathe sweet, unruly though they be.
His rudeness so with his authoriz'd youth
Did livery falseness in a pride of truth.

"Well could he ride, and often men would say,
'That horse his mettle from his rider takes.
Proud of subjection, noble by the sway,
What rounds, what bounds, what course, what stop
he makes!'
And controversy hence a question takes,
Whether the horse by him became his deed,
Or he his manage by th' well-doing steed.

"But quickly on this side the verdict went:
His real habitude gave life and grace
To appertainings and to ornament,
Accomplish'd in himself, not in his case.
All aids, themselves made fairer by their place,
Came for additions, yet their purpos'd trim
Piec'd not his grace, but were all grac'd by him.

"So on the tip of his subduing tongue
All kind of arguments and question deep,
All replication prompt, and reason strong,
For his advantage still did wake and sleep.
To make the weeper laugh, the laugher weep,
He had the dialect and different skill,
Catching all passions in his craft of will,

43 schedules papers containing writing, i.e., letters **44 gave the flood** threw in the stream **45 posied** inscribed with a motto **47 moe** more **48 sleided** raveled, separated into threads. **feat** featly, adroitly. **affectedly** lovingly **49 curious** careful, delicate **50 fluxive** flowing **52 register** recorder **53 unapproved** unconfirmed, false **57 reverend** i.e., suggesting old age **58 Sometime** at one time. **blusterer** boisterous fellow. **ruffle** commotion, bustle **60 swiftest hours** i.e., time of youth **61 fancy** i.e., the person in love **64 So . . . bat** and so he lowers himself by means of his club or staff that is worn and showing the grain **65 comely-distant** at a decorous distance **67 divide** share **69 ecstasy** fit (of grief) **72 blasting** blighting, withering **78 attended** heeded **79 grace** favor

88 to do will . . . find i.e., will find a doer or an occasion **90 in little** in miniature **91 What . . . sawn** what one supposes was seen in full scale in Paradise **93 phoenix** i.e., suggesting his unique perfection (since only one phoenix, a mythical bird, exists at one time) **94 termless** youthful **95 bare outbragg'd** bareness surpassed. **web** i.e., covering, the downy beard **96 cost** (1) expense (2) rich covering; i.e., his face seemed lovelier from its rich or silken covering. **dear** (1) costly (2) lovely **97 nice affections** carefully discriminating tastes **98 without** i.e., lacking the downy beard **100 maiden-tongu'd** modest of speech. **free** innocent **101 mov'd** i.e., to anger **102 to see** to be seen **104–105 His . . . truth** his roughness, privileged by his youth, thereby did dress falseness in a magnificent garment or concealment of truth **108 noble by the sway** made noble by the way he's controlled **109 stop** sudden check in a horse's "career" or trial gallop at full speed **110 takes** takes up, considers **111–112 Whether . . . steed** whether it was owing to his horsemanship that his horse acted so becomingly or whether he seemed such a good rider because he had so good a horse **114 habitude** constitution, temperament **116 case** conditions and circumstances, e.g., the possession of so good a horse **118 Came for additions** came in for consideration as additional graces. **purpos'd trim** intended function as adornment **119 Piec'd** mended, augmented **122 replication** reply **123 still** continually. **wake and sleep** i.e., work in varying moods, now actively, now insinuatingly **125 dialect** manner of expression. **different** varied, readily adaptable **126 craft of will** skill in persuasion

"That he did in the general bosom reign
Of young, of old, and sexes both enchanted,
To dwell with him in thoughts, or to remain
In personal duty, following where he haunted.
Consents bewitch'd, ere he desire, have granted,
And dialogu'd for him what he would say,
Ask'd their own wills, and made their wills obey.

"Many there were that did his picture get
To serve their eyes, and in it put their mind,
Like fools that in th' imagination set
The goodly objects which abroad they find
Of lands and mansions, theirs in thought assign'd,
And laboring in moe pleasures to bestow them
Than the true gouty landlord which doth owe them;

"So many have, that never touch'd his hand,
Sweetly suppos'd them mistress of his heart.
My woeful self, that did in freedom stand,
And was my own fee-simple, not in part,
What with his art in youth, and youth in art,
Threw my affections in his charmed power,
Reserv'd the stalk and gave him all my flower.

"Yet did I not, as some my equals did,
Demand of him, nor being desired yielded;
Finding myself in honor so forbid,
With safest distance I mine honor shielded.
Experience for me many bulwarks builded
Of proofs new-bleeding, which remain'd the foil
Of this false jewel, and his amorous spoil.

"But, ah, who ever shunn'd by precedent
The destin'd ill she must herself assay?
Or forc'd examples, 'gainst her own content,
To put the by-past perils in her way?
Counsel may stop awhile what will not stay;
For when we rage, advice is often seen
By blunting us to make our wits more keen.

"Nor gives it satisfaction to our blood
That we must curb it upon others' proof,
To be forbod the sweets that seems so good
For fear of harms that preach in our behoof.
O appetite, from judgment stand aloof!
The one a palate hath that needs will taste,
Though Reason weep and cry, 'It is thy last.'

127 general bosom hearts of all **130 haunted** frequented **131–133 Consents . . . obey** i.e., women have consented to his will before he even asked them, and have made up his love speeches to them for him, and have made themselves obey their own desires **135 in it . . . mind** let their minds become engrossed with it **137 objects** i.e., of sight **138 theirs . . . assign'd** imagining those possessions to be their own **139 laboring . . . them** striving to derive more pleasure from them **140 owe** own **141 So many** thus many persons, many women **142 them** themselves **144 was . . . part** i.e., had total control of my own destiny, not partial control, as of land held in freehold **146 charmed power** power to charm or cast a spell **148 my equals** i.e., of those equal to me in age and station **149 Demand . . . yielded** i.e., ask him to take me, or yield myself to him the moment he desired me to **152–153 Experience . . . new-bleeding** i.e., the experience of those recently undone in love by him provided me with many defenses. **foil** dark background used to show off the brilliance of a jewel **154 this false jewel** i.e., the young man **156 assay** learn by experience **157 forc'd** proffered, urged. **content** i.e., presumed happiness in love **158 To . . . way** to raise as objections (to her own love happiness) the past perils (of others) **159 stay** remain stopped forever **160 rage** i.e., in passion **161 By . . . keen** i.e., in attempting to stop us, merely making us all the more ingenious and eager **162 blood** passion **163 proof** experience **164 forbod** forbidden **165 preach in our behoof** i.e., offer us good advice, to our benefit

"For further I could say 'This man's untrue,'
And knew the patterns of his foul beguiling;
Heard where his plants in others' orchards grew,
Saw how deceits were gilded in his smiling;
Knew vows were ever brokers to defiling;
Thought characters and words merely but art,
And bastards of his foul adulterate heart.

"And long upon these terms I held my city,
Till thus he gan besiege me: 'Gentle maid,
Have of my suffering youth some feeling pity,
And be not of my holy vows afraid.
That's to ye sworn to none was ever said;
For feasts of love I have been call'd unto,
Till now did ne'er invite, nor never woo.

" 'All my offenses that abroad you see
Are errors of the blood, none of the mind.
Love made them not. With acture they may be,
Where neither party is nor true nor kind.
They sought their shame that so their shame did find;
And so much less of shame in me remains
By how much of me their reproach contains.

" 'Among the many that mine eyes have seen,
Not one whose flame my heart so much as warmed,
Or my affection put to th' smallest teen,
Or any of my leisures ever charmed.
Harm have I done to them, but ne'er was harmed;
Kept hearts in liveries, but mine own was free,
And reign'd, commanding in his monarchy.

" 'Look here what tributes wounded fancies sent me,
Of pallid pearls and rubies red as blood,
Figuring that they their passions likewise lent me
Of grief and blushes, aptly understood
In bloodless white and the encrimson'd mood—
Effects of terror and dear modesty,
Encamp'd in hearts but fighting outwardly.

" 'And, lo, behold these talents of their hair,
With twisted metal amorously impleach'd,
I have receiv'd from many a several fair,
Their kind acceptance weepingly beseech'd,
With th' annexions of fair gems enrich'd,
And deep-brain'd sonnets that did amplify
Each stone's dear nature, worth, and quality.

" 'The diamond—why, 'twas beautiful and hard,
Whereto his invis'd properties did tend;
The deep-green em'rald, in whose fresh regard

170 knew . . . beguiling I had examples of his treachery before me **171 plants** i.e., children illegitimately begotten. **orchards** gardens **173 brokers** panders **174 characters and words** i.e., the written and spoken word. **art** artifice **180 That's** that which is **181–182 For . . . woo** I have been invited to other feasts of love before now, but never until now did I do the inviting and the wooing **185–186 With . . . kind** they may be physically performed where neither partner is faithful or truly in love **188–189 And . . . contains** the more they reproach me, the less shame I in fact deserve **192 teen** sorrow **195 in liveries** in the uniform of a person in service, i.e., almost enslaved **199 Figuring** symbolizing **201 mood** i.e., blushes **202 Effects** the signs or results **204 talents** treasures, riches **205 impleach'd** intertwined **206 a several fair** different ladies **207 The kind . . . beseech'd** who have besought me with their tears to accept their gifts kindly **208 annexions** additions **209 deep-brain'd** intricate. **amplify** enlarge upon, go into detail about **212 his invis'd** its invisible (?) **did tend** were good for **213 regard** aspect, sight

Weak sights their sickly radiance do amend;
The heaven-hu'd sapphire and the opal blend
With objects manifold—each several stone,
With wit well blazon'd, smil'd or made some moan.

" 'Lo, all these trophies of affections hot,
Of pensiv'd and subdu'd desires the tender,
Nature hath charg'd me that I hoard them not,
But yield them up where I myself must render,
That is, to you, my origin and ender;
For these, of force, must your oblations be,
Since I their altar, you enpatron me.

" 'O, then, advance of yours that phraseless hand,
Whose white weighs down the airy scale of praise!
Take all these similes to your own command,
Hallowed with sighs that burning lungs did raise;
What me, your minister, for you obeys,
Works under you; and to your audit comes
Their distract parcels in combined sums.

" 'Lo, this device was sent me from a nun,
Or sister sanctified, of holiest note,
Which late her noble suit in court did shun,
Whose rarest havings made the blossoms dote;
For she was sought by spirits of richest coat,
But kept cold distance, and did thence remove
To spend her living in eternal love.

" 'But, O my sweet, what labor is 't to leave
The thing we have not, mast'ring what not strives,
Playing the place which did no form receive,
Playing patient sports in unconstrained gyves?
She that her fame so to herself contrives,
The scars of battle scapeth by the flight,
And makes her absence valiant, not her might.

" 'O, pardon me, in that my boast is true.
The accident which brought me to her eye
Upon the moment did her force subdue,
And now she would the caged cloister fly.
Religious love put out religion's eye.
Not to be tempted, would she be inur'd,
And now to tempt all liberty procur'd.

" 'How mighty then you are, O, hear me tell!
The broken bosoms that to me belong
Have emptied all their fountains in my well,
And mine I pour your ocean all among.
I strong o'er them, and you o'er me being strong,
Must for your victory us all congest,
As compound love to physic your cold breast.

" 'My parts had pow'r to charm a sacred nun,
Who, disciplin'd, ay, dieted in grace,
Believ'd her eyes when they t' assail begun,
All vows and consecrations giving place.
O most potential love! Vow, bond, nor space,
In thee hath neither sting, knot, nor confine,
For thou art all, and all things else are thine.

" 'When thou impressest, what are precepts worth
Of stale example? When thou wilt inflame,
How coldly those impediments stand forth
Of wealth, of filial fear, law, kindred, fame!
Love's arms are peace, 'gainst rule, 'gainst sense,
'gainst shame,
And sweetens, in the suff'ring pangs it bears,
The aloes of all forces, shocks, and fears.

" 'Now all these hearts that do on mine depend,
Feeling it break, with bleeding groans they pine,
And supplicant their sighs to you extend
To leave the batt'ry that you make 'gainst mine,
Lending soft audience to my sweet design,
And credent soul to that strong-bonded oath
That shall prefer and undertake my troth.'

"This said, his wat'ry eyes he did dismount,
Whose sights till then were level'd on my face;
Each cheek a river running from a fount
With brinish current downward flow'd apace.
O, how the channel to the stream gave grace!
Who glaz'd with crystal gate the glowing roses
That flame through water which their hue encloses.

"O father, what a hell of witchcraft lies
In the small orb of one particular tear!
But with the inundation of the eyes
What rocky heart to water will not wear?
What breast so cold that is not warmed here?
O cleft effect! Cold modesty, hot wrath,
Both fire from hence and chill extincture hath.

214 radiance power of vision **215–216 blend . . . manifold** blended with many colors (?) or, blended with (or that blends with) many objects presented to the sight (?) or, affect a number of objects beneficently (?) **217 blazon'd** proclaimed, described (in the accompanying sonnets) **218 affections** passions **219 pensiv'd** saddened. **tender** offering **222 ender** end, conclusion **224 Since . . . me** since I am the altar (on which these gifts are offered), and you are my patron saint (to whom the altar is dedicated) **225 phraseless** which no words can describe **226 weighs . . . praise** i.e., outweighs in the scales any praise that can be offered to it in airy words **227 similes** i.e., love tokens or gems accompanied by sonnets **229 What . . . obeys** whatever obeys me, your minister or agent, acting on your authority **230 audit** accounting **231 distract** separate **234–235 Which . . . dote** who recently rejected the suit of a nobleman (or noblemen) wooing her at court, whose exceptional endowments made the other young women to dote **236 coat** coat of arms, i.e., descent **238 eternal love** love of the eternal God. (I.e., she became a nun.) **239–242 what . . . gyves** i.e., what a hard thing it is to give up something we haven't tried yet, mastering an emotion such as love that offers no resistance, paling or fencing in the heart upon which no lover has yet made any impression, patiently pretending to endure restraints (as in a convent) which in fact impose no restraint and which one is not obliged to endure. (*Playing* in l. 241 is possibly an error for *Paling,* i.e., enclosing or fencing in.) **243 fame . . . contrives** devises for herself a reputation (for renouncing love) **245 makes . . . might** i.e., shows valor only in avoiding temptation, not in confronting it directly **250 Religious . . . eye** i.e., love of me put out love of the divine **251–252 Not . . . procur'd** before, she wished to be shut up from temptation, but now she sought liberty to venture everything

254 bosoms i.e., hearts **257 strong** victorious **258 for** because of. **congest** gather together **259 physic** cure **260 parts** qualities **261 dieted** nourished, controlled **262 assail** i.e., assail her heart **264–265 Vow . . . confine** against you vows have no strength, bonds have no binding force, and space is no barrier or impediment **267 thou impressest** you make an impression on a heart, or conscript it into your service **271 are . . . shame** prevails with its sweet concord in the teeth of reason, good sense, and decorum **273 aloes** i.e., bitterness **275 break** i.e., break in disappointment at the threat of rejection by the woman now addressed **276 supplicant** as supplicants **280 prefer** advance. **undertake** guarantee **281 dismount** lower (as with an artillery piece) **282 level'd on** aimed at **286 Who** which, i.e., the stream of tears. **gate** i.e., a protective layer **288 father** i.e., the old man to whom she is talking **293 cleft** twofold. **wrath** passion (the wrath of love) **294 extincture** extinguishing

"For, lo, his passion, but an art of craft,
Even there resolv'd my reason into tears;
There my white stole of chastity I daff'd,
Shook off my sober guards and civil fears;
Appear to him, as he to me appears,
All melting; though our drops this diff'rence bore,
His poison'd me, and mine did him restore.

"In him a plenitude of subtle matter,
Applied to cautels, all strange forms receives,
Of burning blushes, or of weeping water,
Or swounding paleness; and he takes and leaves,
In either's aptness, as it best deceives,
To blush at speeches rank, to weep at woes,
Or to turn white and swoon at tragic shows;

"That not a heart which in his level came
Could scape the hail of his all-hurting aim,
Showing fair nature is both kind and tame;
And, veil'd in them, did win whom he would maim.
Against the thing he sought he would exclaim;
When he most burnt in heart-wish'd luxury,
He preach'd pure maid, and prais'd cold chastity.

"Thus merely with the garment of a Grace
The naked and concealed fiend he cover'd,
That th' unexperient gave the tempter place,
Which like a cherubin above them hover'd.
Who, young and simple, would not be so lover'd?
Ay me! I fell, and yet do question make
What I should do again for such a sake.

"O, that infected moisture of his eye,
O, that false fire which in his cheek so glow'd,
O, that forc'd thunder from his heart did fly,
O, that sad breath his spongy lungs bestow'd,
O, all that borrowed motion seeming ow'd,
Would yet again betray the fore-betray'd,
And new pervert a reconciled maid!"

296 resolv'd dissolved **297 daff'd** doffed, put off **299 Appear** I did appear **300 drops** i.e., tears (which here have medicinal qualities) **302 subtle matter** matter capable of being variously impressed or formed **303 cautels** crafty devices **305 swounding** swooning. **takes and leaves** i.e., uses one and then the other **306 In either's aptness** whichever is more appropriate **307 rank** gross **309 level** range. (Continues the metaphor of siege.) **310 hail** i.e., of artillery **311 Showing . . . tame** i.e., his aim being to represent his true nature as loving and docile **312 And . . . maim** and, disguised thus in kindness and docility, won the heart of the woman he intended to harm **314 luxury** lechery **316 Grace** one of the three Graces **318 unexperient** unexperienced. **place** entry **319 Which . . . cherubin** who, resembling a cherub. **them** his fiendlike qualities (?) **320 be so lover'd** surrender to a lover like him **322 for such a sake** for someone like him **323 infected** infectious **325 forc'd** feigned. **from** which from **326 spongy lungs** lungs that pretended to be heaving with grief **327 borrowed . . . ow'd** pretended emotion which he seemed to have or feel **329 reconciled** penitent

Sonnets

Shakespeare seems to have cared more about his reputation as a lyric poet than as a dramatist. He contributed to the major nondramatic genres of his day: to amatory Ovidian narrative in *Venus and Adonis,* to the "Complaint" in *The Rape of Lucrece,* to philosophical poetry in "The Phoenix and Turtle." He cooperated in the publication of his first two important poems, dedicating them to the young Earl of Southampton with a plea for sponsorship. To write poetry in this vein was more fashionable than to write plays, which one did mainly for money.

A poet with ambitions of this sort simply had to write a sonnet sequence. Sonneteering was the rage in the early and mid 1590's. It began in 1591, with the publication of Sir Philip Sidney's *Astrophel and Stella,* and ended almost as suddenly as it began in 1596 or 1597. The sonnet sequences of this brief period bear the names of most well-known and minor poets of the day: *Amoretti* by Edmund Spenser (1595), *Delia* by Samuel Daniel (1591 and 1592), *Caelica* by Fulke Greville (not published until 1633), *Idea's Mirror* by Michael Drayton (1594), *Diana* by Henry Constable (1592), *Phyllis* by Thomas Lodge (1593), and the more imitative sequences of Barnabe Barnes, Giles Fletcher, William Percy, Bartholomew Griffin, William Smith, and Robert Tofte.

Shakespeare wrote sonnets during the heyday of the genre, for in 1598 Francis Meres praised Shakespeare's "sugred Sonnets among his priuate friends." Even though they were not printed at the time, we know from Meres' remark that they were circulated in manuscript among the cognoscenti and commanded respect. Shakespeare may actually have preferred to delay publication of his sonnets, not through indifference to their literary worth but through a desire not to seem too professional. The "courtly makers" of the English Renaissance, those gentlemen whose chivalric accomplishments were supposed to include versifying, looked on the writing of poetry as an avocation designed to amuse one's peers or court a lady. Publication was not quite genteel, and many such authors affected dismay when their verses were pirated into print. The young wits about London of the 1590's, whether aristocratic or not, sometimes imitated this fashion. Like that gay blade, young John Donne, they sought the favorable verdict of their fellow-wits at the Inns of Court, and professed not to care about wider recognition. Whether Shakespeare was motivated in this way we do not know, but in any event his much-sought-after sonnet sequence was not published until 1609, long after the vogue had passed. The publisher, Thomas Thorpe, seems not to have obtained Shakespeare's authorization. Two sonnets, numbers 138 and 144, had been pirated ten years earlier by William Jaggard in *The Passionate Pilgrim,* 1599. The sonnets were not reprinted until 1640, either because the sonnet vogue had passed or because Thorpe's edition had been suppressed.

The unexplained circumstances of publication have given rise to a host of vexing and apparently unanswerable questions. Probably no puzzle in all English literature has provoked so much speculation and produced so little agreement. To whom are the sonnets addressed? Do they tell a consistent story, and if so do they tell us anything about Shakespeare's life? The basic difficulty is that we cannot be sure that the order in which Thorpe published the sonnets represents Shakespeare's intention, nor can we assume that Thorpe spoke for Shakespeare when he dedicated the sonnets to "Mr. W. H." As they stand, most of the first 126 sonnets appear to be addressed in warm friendship to a handsome young aristocrat, whereas sonnets 127–152 speak of the poet's dark-haired mistress. Yet the last two sonnets, 153–154, seem unrelated to anything previous, and cast some doubt on the reliability of the ordering. Within each large grouping of the sonnets, moreover, we find evident inconsistencies: jealousies disappear and suddenly reappear, the poet bewails his absolute rejection by the friend and then speaks a few sonnets later of harmonious affection as though nothing had happened, and so on. Some sonnets are closely linked to their predecessors, some are apparently disconnected (although even here we must allow for the real possibility that Shakespeare intends juxtaposition and contrast). We cannot be sure if the friend of sonnets 1–126 is really one person or several. We can only speculate that the unhappy love triangle described in 40–42, in which the friend has usurped the poet's mistress, can be identified with the love triangle of the "Dark Lady" sonnets, 127–152. Most readers sense a narrative continuity of the whole, yet find blocks of sonnets stubbornly out of place. The temptation to rearrange the order has proved irresistible, but no alternative order has ever won acceptance. The consensus is that Thorpe's order is at times suspect, but may have more rationale than it first appears. It is in any case the only authoritative order we have.

No less frustrating is Thorpe's dedication "To the onlie begetter of these insuing sonnets, Mr. W. H." Given the late and unauthorized publication, we cannot assume that Thorpe speaks for Shakespeare. Quite possibly he is only thanking the person who obtained the sonnets for him, making publication possible. Mundanely enough, Mr. W. H. could be William Hall, an associate of Thorpe's in the publishing business. Yet Elizabethan usage affords few instances of "begetter" in this sense of "obtainer." Besides, Thorpe does offer to Mr. W. H. "that eternitie promised by our ever-living poet," as though Mr. W. H. were the very subject of those sonnets whom Shakespeare vows to immortalize. At any rate, this interpretation of "begetter" as "inspirer" has prompted many enthusiasts to search for a Mr. W. H. in Shakespeare's life, a nobleman who befriended him. The chief candidates are two. First is the young Earl of Southampton, to whom Shakespeare had dedicated *Venus and Adonis* and *The Rape of Lucrece*. The dedication to the second of these poems bespeaks a warmth and gratitude that had been lacking in the first. The Earl's name, Henry Wriothesley, yields initials that are the reverse of W. H. If this correspondence seems unconvincing, W. H. could stand for Sir William Harvey, third husband of Mary, Lady Southampton, the young Earl's mother. Some researchers would have us believe that Shakespeare wrote the sonnets for Lady Southampton, especially those urging a young man (her son) to marry and procreate. This entire case is speculative, however, and we have no evidence that Shakespeare had any dealings whatever with Southampton after *The Rape of Lucrece*. The plain ascription "Mr. W. H." seems an oddly uncivil way for Thorpe to have addressed an earl. If meant for Southampton, the sonnets must have been written fairly early in the 1590's, for they give no hint of Southampton's later career: his courtship of Elizabeth Vernon, her pregnancy and their secret marriage in 1598, his later involvement in Essex' Irish campaign and abortive uprising against Queen Elizabeth. Those literary sleuths who stress similarities to the Southampton relationship are too willing to overlook dissimilarities.

The second chief candidate for Mr. W. H. is William Herbert, third Earl of Pembroke, to whom, along with his brother, Shakespeare's colleagues dedicated the First Folio of 1623. In 1595 Pembroke's parents were attempting to arrange his marriage with Lady Elizabeth Carey, granddaughter of the first Lord Hunsdon who was Lord Chamberlain and patron of Shakespeare's company. In 1597 another alliance was attempted with Bridget Vere, granddaughter of Lord Burghley. In both negotiations, young Pembroke objected to the girl in question. This hypothesis requires, however, an uncomfortably late date for the sonnets, and postulates a gap in age between Shakespeare and Pembroke that would have afforded little opportunity for genuine friendship. Pembroke was only fifteen in 1595, Shakespeare thirty-one. Besides, no evidence whatever supports the claim other than historical coincidence. The common initials W. H. can be made to produce other candidates as well, such as the Lincolnshire lawyer named William Hatcliffe proposed (to no one's satisfaction) by Leslie Hotson. Hotson wants to date most of the sonnets before 1589, since Hatcliffe came to London in 1587–1588. When such speculations are constructed on the single enigmatic testimonial of Thomas Thorpe, who may well have had no connection with Shakespeare, we are left with a case that would not be worth describing had it not captured the imagination of so many researchers.

Other biographical identifications have been proposed for the various personages in the sonnet sequence, predictably with no better success. The rival poet, with "the proud full sail of his great verse" (86), has been linked to Marlowe (who died in 1593), Chapman, and others. The sequence gives us little to go on, other than that the rival poet possesses a considerable enough talent to intimidate the author of the sonnets and ingratiate himself with the author's aristocratic friend. No biographical circumstances even distantly resembling this rivalry have come to light. Various candidates have also been found for the "Dark Lady." One is Mary Fitton, a lady-in-waiting at court who bore a child by Pembroke in 1601. Again, we have no evidence that Shakespeare knew her, nor is he likely to have carried on an affair with one of such high rank. A. L. Rowse has proposed Emilia Lanier, wife of Alfonso Lanier and daughter of a court musician named Bassano, a woman of suitably dark complexion perhaps but whose presumed connection with Shakespeare rests only on the reported rumor that she was a mistress of Lord Hunsdon, the Lord Chamberlain and patron of Shakespeare's acting company. We are left finally without knowing who any of these people were, or if indeed Shakespeare was attempting to be biographical at all.

The same irresolution afflicts the dating of the sonnets. Do they give hints of a personal chronicle extending over some years, following Thorpe's arrangement of the sonnets or some alternative order? Sonnet 104 speaks of three years having elapsed since the poet met his friend. Are there other signposts that relate to contemporary events? A line in Sonnet 107 ("The mortal moon hath her eclipse endur'd") is usually linked to the death of Queen Elizabeth (Cynthia) in 1603, though Leslie Hotson prefers to see in it an allusion to the Spanish Armada, shaped for sea battle in a moonlike crescent when it met defeat in 1588. The newly built pyramids in Sonnet 123 remind Hotson of the obelisks built by Pope Sixtus V in Rome, 1586–1589; other researchers have discovered pyramids erected on London's streets in 1603 to celebrate the coronation of James I. As these illustrations suggest, speculative dating can be used to support a hypothesis of early or late composition. The wary consensus of most scholars is that the sonnets were written over a number of years, a large number certainly before 1598 but some perhaps later and even up to the date of publication in 1609.

However fruitless this quest for nonexistent certainties, it does at least direct us to a meaningful critical question: should we expect sonnets of this "personal" nature to be at least partly autobiographical? Shakespeare's sonnets have struck many readers as cries from the heart, voicing at times fears of rejection, self-hatred, humiliation, and at other times a serene gratitude for reciprocated affection. This power of expression may, however, be a tribute to Shakespeare's dramatic gift rather than evidence of personal involvement. Earlier sonnet sequences, both Elizabethan and pre-Elizabethan, had established a variety of artistic conventions that tended to displace biography. Petrarch's famous *Rime,* though addressed to Laura in two sequences (during her life and after her death), idealized her into the unapproachable lady worshiped by the self-abasing and miserable lover. Petrarch's imitators—Aquilano, Bembo, Ariosto, and Tasso among the Italians, Marot, Du Bellay, Ronsard, and Desportes among the French Pléiade—reworked these conventions in countless variations. In England the fashion was taken up by Wyatt, Surrey, Gascoigne, Thomas Watson, and others. Spenser's *Amoretti* and Sidney's *Astrophel and Stella,* though inspired at least in part by real women in the poets' lives, are also deeply concerned with theories of writing poetry. Rejection of the stereotyped attitudes and relationships that had come to dominate the typical Petrarchan sonnet sequence is evidence not of biographical literalism in art but of a new insistence on lifelike emotion in art; as Sidney's muse urges him, "look in thy heart and write." Thus, both the Petrarchan and the anti-Petrarchan schools avoid biographical writing for its own sake. This is essentially true of all Elizabethan sonneteering, from Drayton's serious pursuit of Platonic abstraction in his *Idea* to the facile chorusing of lesser sonnet-writers about Diana, Phyllis, Zepheria, or Fidessa.

The "story" connecting the individual poems of an Elizabethan sonnet sequence is never very important or consistent, even when we can be sure of the order in which the sonnets were written. Dante had used prose links in his *Vita Nuova* to stress narrative continuity, and so had Petrarch, but this sturdy framework had been abandoned by the late sixteenth century. Rather than telling a chronological story, the typical Elizabethan sonnet sequence offers a thematically connected series of lyrical meditations, chiefly on love but also on poetic theory, the adversities of fortune, death, or what have you. The narrative events mentioned from time to time are not the substance of the sequence but the mere occasion for meditative reflection. Attitudes need not be consistent throughout, and the characters need not be consistently motivated like *dramatis personae* in a play.

Shakespeare's sonnet sequence retains these conventions of Elizabethan sonneteering and employs many archetypal situations and themes that had been explored by his predecessors and contemporaries. His emphasis on friendship seems new, for no other sequence addressed a majority of its sonnets to a friend rather than to a mistress, but even here the anti-Petrarchan quest for spontaneity and candor is in the best Elizabethan tradition of Sidney and Spenser. Besides, the exaltation of friendship over love was itself a widespread neo-Platonic commonplace recently popularized in the writings of John Lyly. Shakespeare's sequence makes use of the structural design found in contemporary models. Even though we cannot reconstruct a rigorously consistent chronological narrative from the sonnets, we can discern overall patterns out of which the poet's emotional crises arise and upon which he constructs his meditative lyrics. Certain groupings, such as the sonnets addressed to the "Dark Lady," 127–152, achieve a plausible cohesion in which the individual sonnets comment on one another through reinforcement or antithetical design and are thus enhanced by their context; a case can be made, in other words, for the order of the poems as Thorpe printed them. Even the last two sonnets, 153 and 154, have their defenders; see Michael J. B. Allen's essay in *Shakespeare Survey,* 1978. Juxtaposition is a favorite technique in Shakespeare's plays, and we must remember that he alone among the major Elizabethan sonneteers wrote for the stage.

Taking note of such considerations, we can account for most of the situations portrayed in Shakespeare's sonnets by postulating four figures: the poet-speaker himself, his friend, his mistress, and a rival poet. The order of events in this tangled relationship is not what the poet wishes to describe; instead, he touches upon this situation from time to time as he explores his own reaction to love in its various aspects.

The poet's relationship to his friend is a vulnerable one. This friend to whom he writes is aristocratic, handsome, younger than he is. The poet is beholden to this friend as a sponsor, and must consider himself as subservient no matter how deep their mutual affection. Even at its happiest, their relationship is hierarchical. The poet abases himself in order to extol his friend's beauty and virtues (52–54, 105–106). He confesses that his love would be idolatry, except that the friend's goodness excels all poetic hyperbole. As the older of the two, the poet sententiously urges his young friend to marry and eternize his beauty through the engendering of children (1–17). Such a course, he argues, is the surest way to conquer devouring Time, the enemy of all earthly beauty and love. Yet elsewhere the poet exalts his own art as the surest defense against Time (55, 60, 63–65, etc.). These conclusions are nominally contradictory, offering procreation in one instance and poetry in another as the best hope for immortality, but thematically the two are obviously related. In even the happiest of the sonnets, such as those giving thanks for "the marriage of true minds" (116, 123), the consciousness of devouring Time is inescapable. If love and celebratory poetry can sometimes triumph over Time, the victory is all the more precious because it is achieved in the face of such odds.

Love and perfect friendship are a refuge for the poet faced with hostile fortune and an indifferent world. He is too often "in disgrace with Fortune and men's eyes" (29), oppressed by his own failings, saddened by the facile success of opportunists (66–68), ashamed of having sold himself cheap in his own profession (110–111). If taken biographically, this could mean that Shakespeare was not happy about his career as actor and playwright, but the motif makes complete sense in the sonnet sequence without resort to biography. The poet is pathetically dependent on his friend. Occasional absences torture him with the physical separation, even though he realizes that pure love of the spirit ought not to be hampered by distance or time (43–51). The absence is especially painful when the poet must confess his own disloyalty (117–118). The chronology of these absences cannot be worked out satisfactorily, but the haunting theme of separation is incessant, overwhelming. By extension it includes the fear of separation through death (71–73, 126). The concern with absence is closely related to the poet's obsession with devouring Time.

All the poet's misfortunes would be bearable if love were constant, but his dependency on the aristocratic friend leaves him at the mercy of that friend's changeable mood. The poet must not complain when his well-born friend entertains a rival poet (78–86) or forms other emotional attachments, even with the poet's own mistress (40–42). These disloyalties evoke outbursts of jealousy. The poet vacillates between forgiveness and recrimination. Sometimes even his forgiveness is self-loathing, in which the poet confesses he would take back the friend on any terms (93–95). At times the poet grovels, conceding that he deserves no better treatment (57–58), but at other times his stored-up resentment bursts forth (93–95). The poet's fears, though presented in no clear chronological order, run the gamut from a fatalistic sense that rejection will come one day (49) to an abject and bitter final farewell (87). Sometimes he is tormented by jealousy (61), sometimes by self-hate (88–89).

The sonnets addressed to the poet's mistress, the "Dark Lady," similarly convey fear, self-abasement, and a panicky awareness of loss of self-control. In rare moments of happiness, the poet praises her dark features as proof of her being a real woman, not a Petrarchan goddess (130). Too often, however, her lack of beauty merely reminds the poet of his irrational enchantment (148–150). She is tyrannous, disdainful, spiteful, disloyal, a "female evil" (144) who has tempted away from the poet his better self, his friend. The poet is distressed not so much by her perfidy as by his own self-betrayal; he sees bitterly that he offends his nobler reason by his attachment to the rebellious flesh. He worships what others abhor, and perjures himself by swearing to what he knows to be false (150–152). His only hope for escape is to punish his flesh and renounce the vanity of all worldly striving (146), but this solution evades him as he plunges helplessly back into the perverse enslavement of a sickened appetite.

This sketch of only some themes of the sequence may suggest the range and yet the interconnection of Shakespeare's meditations on love, friendship, and poetry. Patterns are visible, even if the exact chronology (never important in the Elizabethan sonnet sequence) cannot be determined. This pattern is equally evident in matters of versification and imagery. The sonnets are written throughout in the "Shakespearean" or English form, *abab cdcd efef gg*. (Number 126, written entirely in couplets, is an exception, perhaps because it was intended as the envoy to the series addressed to the poet's friend.) This familiar sonnet form, introduced by Wyatt and developed by Sidney, differs markedly from the octave-sestet division of the Petrarchan, or Italian, sonnet. The English form of three quatrains and a concluding couplet lends itself to a step-by-step development of idea and image, culminating in an epigrammatic two-line conclusion that may summarize the thought of the preceding twelve lines or give a sententious interpretation of the images developed up to this point. Sonnet 7 pursues the image of the sun at morning, noon, and evening through three quatrains, one for each phase of the day, and then in the couplet "applies" the image to the friend's unwillingness to beget children. Sonnet 29 moves from resentment of misfortune to a rejoicing in the friend's love, and rhetorically mirrors this sudden elevation of mood in the image of the lark "at break of day arising From sullen earth." Shakespeare's rhetorical and imagistic devices exploit the sonnet structure he inherited and perfected, and remind us again of the strong element of convention and artifice in these supremely "personal" sonnets. The recurring images—the canker on the rose, the pleading of a case at law, the seasonal rhythms of summer and winter or day and night, the harmonies and dissonances of music—also testify to the artistic unity of the whole and to the artist's extraordinary discipline in evoking a sense of helpless loss of self-control.

Sonnets

To the Only Begetter of These Insuing Sonnets

Mr. W. H.

All Happiness and That Eternity Promised
by Our Ever-living Poet
Wisheth the Well-wishing Adventurer in Setting Forth

T.T.

[1]

From fairest creatures we desire increase,
That thereby beauty's rose might never die,
But as the riper should by time decease,
His tender heir might bear his memory;
But thou, contracted to thine own bright eyes,
Feed'st thy light's flame with self-substantial fuel,
Making a famine where abundance lies,
Thyself thy foe, to thy sweet self too cruel.
Thou that art now the world's fresh ornament
And only herald to the gaudy spring,
Within thine own bud buriest thy content
And, tender churl, mak'st waste in niggarding.
  Pity the world, or else this glutton be,
  To eat the world's due, by the grave and thee.

2

When forty winters shall besiege thy brow,
And dig deep trenches in thy beauty's field,
Thy youth's proud livery, so gaz'd on now,
Will be a totter'd weed, of small worth held.
Then being ask'd where all thy beauty lies,
Where all the treasure of thy lusty days,
To say, within thine own deep-sunken eyes,
Were an all-eating shame and thriftless praise.
How much more praise deserv'd thy beauty's use,
If thou couldst answer, "This fair child of mine
Shall sum my count and make my old excuse,"
Proving his beauty by succession thine.
  This were to be new made when thou art old,
  And see thy blood warm when thou feel'st it cold.

3

Look in thy glass, and tell the face thou viewest
Now is the time that face should form another,
Whose fresh repair if now thou not renewest,
Thou dost beguile the world, unbless some mother.
For where is she so fair whose unear'd womb
Disdains the tillage of thy husbandry?
Or who is he so fond will be the tomb
Of his self-love, to stop posterity?
Thou art thy mother's glass, and she in thee
Calls back the lovely April of her prime;
So thou through windows of thine age shalt see
Despite of wrinkles this thy golden time.
  But if thou live rememb'red not to be,
  Die single, and thine image dies with thee.

4

Unthrifty loveliness, why dost thou spend
Upon thyself thy beauty's legacy?
Nature's bequest gives nothing but doth lend,
And being frank she lends to those are free.
Then, beauteous niggard, why dost thou abuse
The bounteous largess given thee to give?
Profitless usurer, why dost thou use
So great a sum of sums, yet canst not live?
For having traffic with thyself alone,
Thou of thyself thy sweet self dost deceive.
Then how, when Nature calls thee to be gone,
What acceptable audit canst thou leave?
  Thy unus'd beauty must be tomb'd with thee,
  Which, used, lives th' executor to be.

5

Those hours, that with gentle work did frame
The lovely gaze where every eye doth dwell,
Will play the tyrants to the very same
And that unfair which fairly doth excel;
For never-resting time leads summer on
To hideous winter and confounds him there,
Sap check'd with frost and lusty leaves quite gone,
Beauty o'ersnow'd and bareness everywhere.
Then were not summer's distillation left
A liquid prisoner pent in walls of glass,
Beauty's effect with beauty were bereft,
Nor it nor no remembrance what it was.
  But flowers distill'd, though they with winter meet,
  Leese but their show; their substance still lives sweet.

1 • 5 contracted engaged, espoused **6 self-substantial** of your own substance **10 only** unique **11 thy content** (1) that which is contained in you; potential fatherhood (2) contentment **12 mak'st . . . niggarding** squander your substance by being miserly. (An oxymoron, like *tender churl,* youthful old miser.) **14 the world's due** i.e., the offspring you owe to posterity. **by . . . thee** (consumed) by death and by your willfully remaining childless

2 • 4 totter'd weed tattered garment (with a play on a *weed* growing in *beauty's field,* l. 2) **8 all-eating shame** shameful gluttony. **thriftless praise** (1) praise of extravagance (2) idle praise **9 deserv'd** would deserve. **use** (1) investment (2) employment **11 sum . . . excuse** even my account and make amends (for growing old, or for consuming beauty during my life) in my old age **12 thine** i.e., derived from you

3 • 3 fresh repair youthful condition **4 beguile** cheat. **unbless some mother** withhold the happiness of childbearing from some woman **5 unear'd** untilled, uncultivated **6 husbandry** cultivation (with obvious suggestion of *playing the husband*) **7 fond** foolish. **will be** i.e., that he will be **9 thy mother's glass** the image of your mother **13 rememb'red not to be** in such a way as not to be remembered, without children

4 • 4 frank liberal, bounteous. **are free** who are generous **7 use** (1) use up (2) fail to invest for profit. (See Sonnet 6.5 and note.) **8 live** (1) have a livelihood (2) live in your posterity **9 traffic** commerce **10 deceive** cheat **14 lives** would live (in your son)

5 • 2 gaze object of gazes **4 unfair** make unlovely. **fairly** i.e., in beauty **6 confounds** destroys **9 summer's distillation** distilled perfume of flowers **11 with . . . bereft** would be lost along with beauty itself **12 Nor it nor no** (leaving behind) neither it (beauty) nor any **14 Leese** lose

6

Then let not winter's ragged hand deface
In thee thy summer, ere thou be distill'd.
Make sweet some vial; treasure thou some place
With beauty's treasure, ere it be self-kill'd.
That use is not forbidden usury
Which happies those that pay the willing loan;
That's for thyself to breed another thee,
Or ten times happier, be it ten for one;
Ten times thyself were happier than thou art,
If ten of thine ten times refigur'd thee.
Then what could death do, if thou shouldst depart,
Leaving thee living in posterity?
    Be not self-will'd, for thou art much too fair
    To be death's conquest and make worms thine heir.

7

Lo, in the orient when the gracious light
Lifts up his burning head, each under eye
Doth homage to his new-appearing sight,
Serving with looks his sacred majesty;
And having climb'd the steep-up heavenly hill,
Resembling strong youth in his middle age,
Yet mortal looks adore his beauty still,
Attending on his golden pilgrimage;
But when from highmost pitch, with weary car,
Like feeble age, he reeleth from the day,
The eyes, 'fore duteous, now converted are
From his low tract and look another way.
    So thou, thyself out-going in thy noon,
    Unlook'd on diest, unless thou get a son.

8

Music to hear, why hear'st thou music sadly?
Sweets with sweets war not, joy delights in joy.
Why lov'st thou that which thou receiv'st not gladly,
Or else receiv'st with pleasure thine annoy?
If the true concord of well-tuned sounds,
By unions married, do offend thine ear,
They do but sweetly chide thee, who confounds
In singleness the parts that thou shouldst bear.
Mark how one string, sweet husband to another,
Strikes each in each by mutual ordering,
Resembling sire and child and happy mother
Who, all in one, one pleasing note do sing;
    Whose speechless song, being many, seeming one,
    Sings this to thee: "Thou single wilt prove none."

9

Is it for fear to wet a widow's eye
That thou consum'st thyself in single life?
Ah, if thou issueless shalt hap to die,
The world will wail thee, like a makeless wife;
The world will be thy widow and still weep
That thou no form of thee hast left behind,
When every private widow well may keep,
By children's eyes, her husband's shape in mind.
Look what an unthrift in the world doth spend
Shifts but his place, for still the world enjoys it;
But beauty's waste hath in the world an end,
And, kept unus'd, the user so destroys it.
    No love toward others in that bosom sits
    That on himself such murd'rous shame commits.

10

For shame deny that thou bear'st love to any,
Who for thyself art so unprovident.
Grant, if thou wilt, thou art belov'd of many,
But that thou none lov'st is most evident;
For thou art so possess'd with murd'rous hate
That 'gainst thyself thou stick'st not to conspire,
Seeking that beauteous roof to ruinate
Which to repair should be thy chief desire.
O, change thy thought, that I may change my mind!
Shall hate be fairer lodg'd than gentle love?
Be, as thy presence is, gracious and kind,
Or to thyself at least kind-hearted prove:
    Make thee another self, for love of me,
    That beauty still may live in thine or thee.

11

As fast as thou shalt wane, so fast thou grow'st
In one of thine, from that which thou departest;
And that fresh blood which youngly thou bestow'st
Thou mayst call thine when thou from youth convertest.
Herein lives wisdom, beauty, and increase;
Without this, folly, age, and cold decay.
If all were minded so, the times should cease
And threescore year would make the world away.
Let those whom Nature hath not made for store,
Harsh, featureless, and rude, barrenly perish;
Look whom she best endow'd she gave the more,
Which bounteous gift thou shouldst in bounty cherish.
    She carv'd thee for her seal, and meant thereby
    Thou shouldst print more, not let that copy die.

6 • 1 ragged rough **3 vial** (with suggestion of a womb). **treasure** enrich **5 use** lending money at interest **6 happies** makes happy. **pay . . . loan** willingly repay the loan **8 ten for one** (Highest legal rate of interest.) **10 refigured** duplicated, copied **13 self-will'd** (1) obstinate (2) bequeathed to self

7 • 1 orient east. **light** i.e., sun **2 under** earthly **9 car** chariot (of the sun god) **11 converted** turned away **12 tract** course **14 get** beget

8 • 1 Music to hear i.e., you whom it is music to hear. **sadly** without joy **4 thine annoy** what annoys you **7–8 who . . . bear** you who destroy, by playing a single part only, the harmony (i.e., marriage) that you should sustain **9 sweet husband** i.e., paired, as on the double strings of the lute, one string vibrating sympathetically to the other **13 Whose** i.e., the strings'. **being . . . one** i.e., making harmony out of several voices

9 • 4 makeless mateless, i.e., widowed **9 Look what** whatever **10 his** its **12 user** i.e., he who should use it (with a suggestion of a *usurer* who is miserly)

10 • 6 thou stick'st you scruple **9 thought** intention. **change my mind** no longer believe as I have done **11 presence** appearance, bearing

11 • 1–2 thou . . . departest i.e., you become, through a child of your own, what you cease to be in yourself **3 youngly** in youth **4 thou . . . convertest** you change from youth (to old age) **7 minded so** sharing your intention (to have no children). **times** succeeding generations **9 for store** as a source of supply **10 Harsh** hard-favored. **featureless** having no attractive features or appearance. **rude** rudely fashioned **11 Look whom** whomever **13 seal** stamp from which impressions are made

12

When I do count the clock that tells the time,
And see the brave day sunk in hideous night;
When I behold the violet past prime,
And sable curls all silver'd o'er with white;
When lofty trees I see barren of leaves
Which erst from heat did canopy the herd,
And summer's green all girded up in sheaves
Borne on the bier with white and bristly beard,
Then of thy beauty do I question make
That thou among the wastes of time must go,
Since sweets and beauties do themselves forsake
And die as fast as they see others grow;
And nothing 'gainst Time's scythe can make defense
Save breed, to brave him when he takes thee hence.

13

O, that you were yourself! But, love, you are
No longer yours than you yourself here live.
Against this coming end you should prepare,
And your sweet semblance to some other give.
So should that beauty which you hold in lease
Find no determination; then you were
Yourself again after yourself's decease,
When your sweet issue your sweet form should bear.
Who lets so fair a house fall to decay,
Which husbandry in honor might uphold
Against the stormy gusts of winter's day
And barren rage of death's eternal cold?
O, none but unthrifts! Dear my love, you know
You had a father; let your son say so.

14

Not from the stars do I my judgment pluck,
And yet methinks I have astronomy,
But not to tell of good or evil luck,
Of plagues, of dearths, or seasons' quality;
Nor can I fortune to brief minutes tell,
'Pointing to each his thunder, rain, and wind,
Or say with princes if it shall go well
By oft predict that I in heaven find.
But from thine eyes my knowledge I derive,
And, constant stars, in them I read such art
As truth and beauty shall together thrive
If from thyself to store thou wouldst convert.
Or else of thee this I prognosticate:
Thy end is truth's and beauty's doom and date.

15

When I consider every thing that grows
Holds in perfection but a little moment,
That this huge stage presenteth nought but shows
Whereon the stars in secret influence comment;
When I perceive that men as plants increase,
Cheered and check'd even by the self-same sky,
Vaunt in their youthful sap, at height decrease,
And wear their brave state out of memory;
Then the conceit of this inconstant stay
Sets you most rich in youth before my sight,
Where wasteful Time debateth with Decay
To change your day of youth to sullied night;
And all in war with Time for love of you,
As he takes from you, I engraft you new.

16

But wherefore do not you a mightier way
Make war upon this bloody tyrant, Time?
And fortify yourself in your decay
With means more blessed than my barren rhyme?
Now stand you on the top of happy hours,
And many maiden gardens yet unset
With virtuous wish would bear your living flowers,
Much liker than your painted counterfeit.
So should the lines of life that life repair
Which this time's pencil, or my pupil pen,
Neither in inward worth nor outward fair
Can make you live yourself in eyes of men.
To give away yourself keeps yourself still,
And you must live, drawn by your own sweet skill.

17

Who will believe my verse in time to come,
If it were fill'd with your most high deserts?
Though yet, heaven knows, it is but as a tomb
Which hides your life and shows not half your parts.
If I could write the beauty of your eyes
And in fresh numbers number all your graces,
The age to come would say, "This poet lies;
Such heavenly touches ne'er touch'd earthly faces."
So should my papers, yellowed with their age,
Be scorn'd like old men of less truth than tongue,
And your true rights be term'd a poet's rage
And stretched meter of an antique song.
But were some child of yours alive that time,
You should live twice, in it and in my rhyme.

12 • 2 **brave** splendid 4 **sable** black 6 **erst** formerly 8 **bier** i.e., harvest cart 9 **do . . . make** I discuss with myself 14 **breed** offspring. **brave him** defy Time

13 • 1 **yourself** i.e., your eternal self, not vulnerable to Time's decay 3 **Against** in anticipation of 6 **determination** end 10 **husbandry** careful management (with a pun on *being a husband*)

14 • 1 **judgment pluck** derive conclusions 2 **have astronomy** am skilled in astrology 5 **fortune . . . tell** i.e., foretell events to the precise minute 6 **'Pointing** appointing. **his** its 8 **oft predict** frequent predictions 10–11 **read . . . As** gather such lore as that 12 **store** replenishment. **convert** turn 14 **doom and date** limit of duration, destruction

15 • 2 **Holds in perfection** maintains its prime 3 **stage** i.e., the world 6 **Cheer'd and check'd** (1) urged on, nourished, and held back, starved (2) applauded and hissed 7 **Vaunt** boast, exult. **sap** vigor 8 **brave** splendid. **out of memory** i.e., until forgotten 9 **conceit** notion. **inconstant stay** mutable duration 11 **debateth with** combines in battle with 14 **engraft you new** renew you by grafting, infusing new life into you (by means of my verse)

16 • 6 **unset** (1) unplanted (2) unimpregnated 8 **counterfeit** portrait 9 **lines of life** lineage, i.e., children (whose lineaments are more lifelike than lines of verse or of a portrait) 10 **this time's pencil** a portraiture done in this present age. **pupil** apprenticed, inexpert 11 **fair** beauty 13 **give away yourself** i.e., beget children. **keeps** preserves

17 • 4 **parts** qualities 6 **numbers** verses 11 **rage** exaggerated inspiration 12 **stretched meter** overstrained poetry, poetic license

18

Shall I compare thee to a summer's day?
Thou art more lovely and more temperate.
Rough winds do shake the darling buds of May,
And summer's lease hath all too short a date.
Sometime too hot the eye of heaven shines,
And often is his gold complexion dimm'd;
And every fair from fair sometime declines,
By chance or nature's changing course untrimm'd.
But thy eternal summer shall not fade
Nor lose possession of that fair thou ow'st;
Nor shall Death brag thou wand'rest in his shade,
When in eternal lines to time thou grow'st.
So long as men can breathe or eyes can see,
So long lives this and this gives life to thee.

19

Devouring Time, blunt thou the lion's paws,
And make the earth devour her own sweet brood;
Pluck the keen teeth from the fierce tiger's jaws,
And burn the long-liv'd phoenix in her blood;
Make glad and sorry seasons as thou fleets,
And do whate'er thou wilt, swift-footed Time,
To the wide world and all her fading sweets.
But I forbid thee one most heinous crime:
O, carve not with thy hours my love's fair brow,
Nor draw no lines there with thine antique pen;
Him in thy course untainted do allow
For beauty's pattern to succeeding men.
Yet, do thy worst, old Time. Despite thy wrong,
My love shall in my verse ever live young.

20

A woman's face with Nature's own hand painted
Hast thou, the master-mistress of my passion;
A woman's gentle heart, but not acquainted
With shifting change, as is false women's fashion;
An eye more bright than theirs, less false in rolling,
Gilding the object whereupon it gazeth;
A man in hue, all hues in his controlling,
Which steals men's eyes and women's souls amazeth.
And for a woman wert thou first created,
Till Nature, as she wrought thee, fell a-doting,
And by addition me of thee defeated,
By adding one thing to my purpose nothing.
But since she prick'd thee out for women's
pleasure,
Mine be thy love and thy love's use their treasure.

21

So is it not with me as with that Muse
Stirr'd by a painted beauty to his verse,
Who heaven itself for ornament doth use
And every fair with his fair doth rehearse,
Making a couplement of proud compare
With sun and moon, with earth and sea's rich gems,
With April's first-born flowers, and all things rare
That heaven's air in this huge rondure hems.
O, let me, true in love, but truly write,
And then believe me, my love is as fair
As any mother's child, though not so bright
As those gold candles fix'd in heaven's air.
Let them say more that like of hearsay well;
I will not praise that purpose not to sell.

22

My glass shall not persuade me I am old,
So long as youth and thou are of one date;
But when in thee time's furrows I behold,
Then look I death my days should expiate.
For all that beauty that doth cover thee
Is but the seemly raiment of my heart,
Which in thy breast doth live, as thine in me.
How can I then be elder than thou art?
O, therefore, love, be of thyself so wary
As I, not for myself, but for thee will,
Bearing thy heart, which I will keep so chary
As tender nurse her babe from faring ill.
Presume not on thy heart when mine is slain;
Thou gav'st me thine, not to give back again.

23

As an unperfect actor on the stage
Who with his fear is put besides his part,
Or some fierce thing replete with too much rage,
Whose strength's abundance weakens his own heart,
So I, for fear of trust, forget to say
The perfect ceremony of love's rite,
And in mine own love's strength seem to decay,
O'ercharg'd with burden of mine own love's might.
O, let my books be then the eloquence
And dumb presagers of my speaking breast,
Who plead for love and look for recompense
More than that tongue that more hath more express'd.
O, learn to read what silent love hath writ.
To hear with eyes belongs to love's fine wit.

18 • 4 lease allotted time. **date** duration **5 eye** i.e., sun **7 fair from fair** beautiful thing from beauty **8 untrimm'd** stripped of ornament and beauty **10 thou ow'st** you own **12 lines** i.e., of poetry. **to . . . grow'st** you become incorporated into time, engrafted upon it

19 • 4 phoenix legendary bird reputed to live for hundreds of years and then be consumed alive *(in her blood)* in its own ashes from which it is then reborn **5 thou fleets** you fleet, hurry **10 antique** (1) old (2) antic, capricious, fantastic **11 untainted** (1) unhit in tilting (2) unsoiled

20 • 1 with . . . hand i.e., without cosmetics **2 master-mistress** i.e., both master and mistress, male and female. **passion** love **5 rolling** i.e., roving **6 Gilding** causing to shine brightly **7 A man . . . controlling** one who has a manly appearance, and has power over all other appearances **11 defeated** defrauded, deprived **12 to my purpose nothing** out of line with my wishes **13 prick'd** designated (with bawdy suggestion; the "thing" in l. 12 is a phallus)

21 • 1 Muse i.e., poet **2 Stirr'd** inspired. **painted** artificial, created by cosmetics **4 every . . . rehearse** compares his lady fair with every lovely thing **5 Making . . . compare** joining (her) in proud comparison **8 rondure** sphere. **hems** encloses, encircles **12 gold candles** i.e., stars **13 like . . . well** like to deal in secondhand or trite expressions **14 that . . . sell** I who (i.e., since I) do not intend to sell what I praise, as a merchant might

22 • 2 of one date of an age, i.e., young **4 look I** I foresee. **expiate** end **10 will** i.e., will take wary care of myself for your sake **11 Bearing** since I bear **13 Presume not on** do not expect to receive back

23 • 2 besides out of **5 for . . . trust** mistrusting myself. **forget** forget how **9 books** (Possibly refers to the Sonnets, or to *Venus and Adonis* and *The Rape of Lucrece,* or more generally the works of the persona poet.) **10 dumb presagers** silent messengers or presenters **12 more hath more express'd** has more often or more fully said more

24

Mine eye hath play'd the painter and hath stell'd
Thy beauty's form in table of my heart;
My body is the frame wherein 'tis held,
And perspective it is best painter's art.
For through the painter must you see his skill,
To find where your true image pictur'd lies,
Which in my bosom's shop is hanging still,
That hath his windows glazed with thine eyes.
Now see what good turns eyes for eyes have done:
Mine eyes have drawn thy shape, and thine for me
Are windows to my breast, wherethrough the sun
Delights to peep, to gaze therein on thee.
Yet eyes this cunning want to grace their art:
They draw but what they see, know not the heart.

25

Let those who are in favor with their stars
Of public honor and proud titles boast,
Whilst I, whom fortune of such triumph bars,
Unlook'd for joy in that I honor most.
Great princes' favorites their fair leaves spread
But as the marigold at the sun's eye,
And in themselves their pride lies buried,
For at a frown they in their glory die.
The painful warrior famoused for fight,
After a thousand victories once foil'd,
Is from the book of honor razed quite,
And all the rest forgot for which he toil'd.
Then happy I, that love and am beloved
Where I may not remove nor be removed.

26

Lord of my love, to whom in vassalage
Thy merit hath my duty strongly knit,
To thee I send this written embassage
To witness duty, not to show my wit—
Duty so great, which wit so poor as mine
May make seem bare, in wanting words to show it,
But that I hope some good conceit of thine
In thy soul's thought, all naked, will bestow it;
Till whatsoever star that guides my moving
Points on me graciously with fair aspect
And puts apparel on my tottered loving,
To show me worthy of thy sweet respect.
Then may I dare to boast how I do love thee;
Till then not show my head where thou mayst prove me.

27

Weary with toil, I haste me to my bed,
The dear repose for limbs with travel tired,
But then begins a journey in my head,
To work my mind, when body's work's expired.
For then my thoughts, from far where I abide,
Intend a zealous pilgrimage to thee,
And keep my drooping eyelids open wide,
Looking on darkness which the blind do see;
Save that my soul's imaginary sight
Presents thy shadow to my sightless view,
Which, like a jewel hung in ghastly night,
Makes black night beauteous and her old face new.
Lo, thus, by day my limbs, by night my mind,
For thee and for myself no quiet find.

28

How can I then return in happy plight
That am debarr'd the benefit of rest?
When day's oppression is not eas'd by night,
But day by night, and night by day, oppress'd?
And each, though enemies to either's reign,
Do in consent shake hands to torture me,
The one by toil, the other to complain
How far I toil, still farther off from thee.
I tell the day, to please him, thou art bright
And dost him grace when clouds do blot the heaven;
So flatter I the swart-complexion'd night,
When sparkling stars twire not thou gild'st th' even.
But day doth daily draw my sorrows longer,
And night doth nightly make grief's strength seem stronger.

29

When, in disgrace with fortune and men's eyes,
I all alone beweep my outcast state,
And trouble deaf heaven with my bootless cries,
And look upon myself and curse my fate,
Wishing me like to one more rich in hope,
Featur'd like him, like him with friends possess'd,
Desiring this man's art and that man's scope,
With what I most enjoy contented least;
Yet in these thoughts myself almost despising,
Haply I think on thee, and then my state,
Like to the lark at break of day arising
From sullen earth, sings hymns at heaven's gate;
For thy sweet love rememb'red such wealth brings
That then I scorn to change my state with kings.

30

When to the sessions of sweet silent thought
I summon up remembrance of things past,

24 • 1 **stell'd** fixed, installed; or possibly steel'd, i.e., engraved. (*Q* reads *steeld.*) 2 **table** tablet, wooden panel used for painting 4 **perspective** painter's technique used to produce the illusion of distance, one thing seeming to lie behind another; or an optical device for bringing images to the painter's eye 8 **his** its. **glazed** fitted with glass, paned. (The friend, looking at the poet's portrait of him engraved in the poet's heart, sees into that heart.) 13 **this cunning want** lack this skill. **grace** enhance 14 **know not** do not perceive the thoughts of. (See Sonnets 46 and 47.)

25 • 4 **Unlook'd for** unexpectedly. **that** that which 5 **their . . . spread** i.e., flourish, blossom, prosper 6 **But** only 7 **lies buried** i.e., will die with the ending of their brief glory 9 **painful** enduring much, striving. **fight** (Reads *worth* in the 1609 quarto; some editors retain, and emend *quite* in l. 11 to *forth*.) 11 **razed** erased 12 **the rest** i.e., his "thousand victories"

26 • 7 **good conceit** good conception, or favorable opinion 8 **all naked** (Modifies *Duty*.) **bestow** give lodging to 9 **moving** life and deeds 10 **aspect** influence (as of a star) 11 **tottered** tattered 14 **prove** test

27 • 6 **Intend** direct, set out upon

28 • 6 **consent** i.e., mutual agreement 7 **the other to complain** i.e., the night by causing me to complain 10 **And . . . heaven** i.e., and that you shine in place of the sun when the sun is overclouded 11 **So flatter I** similarly I gratify. **swart** dark 12 **When . . . even** i.e., by saying that, when sparkling stars do not twinkle or peep out, you make bright the evening

29 • 3 **bootless** useless 6 **Featur'd** formed, i.e., having good looks. **like him, like him** like a second man, like a third 7 **art** literary skill (?). **scope** range of powers 10 **state** state of mind

30 • 1 **sessions** (The metaphor is that of a court of law.)

I sigh the lack of many a thing I sought,
And with old woes new wail my dear time's waste.
Then can I drown an eye, unus'd to flow,
For precious friends hid in death's dateless night,
And weep afresh love's long since cancel'd woe,
And moan th' expense of many a vanish'd sight.
Then can I grieve at grievances foregone,
And heavily from woe to woe tell o'er
The sad account of fore-bemoaned moan,
Which I new pay as if not paid before.
    But if the while I think on thee, dear friend,
    All losses are restor'd, and sorrows end.

31

Thy bosom is endeared with all hearts,
Which I by lacking have supposed dead,
And there reigns love and all love's loving parts,
And all those friends which I thought buried.
How many a holy and obsequious tear
Hath dear religious love stol'n from mine eye
As interest of the dead, which now appear
But things remov'd that hidden in thee lie!
Thou art the grave where buried love doth live,
Hung with the trophies of my lovers gone,
Who all their parts of me to thee did give;
That due of many now is thine alone.
    Their images I lov'd I view in thee,
    And thou, all they, hast all the all of me.

32

If thou survive my well-contented day
When that churl Death my bones with dust shall
  cover,
And shalt by fortune once more re-survey
These poor rude lines of thy deceased lover,
Compare them with the bett'ring of the time,
And, though they be outstripp'd by every pen,
Reserve them for my love, not for their rhyme,
Exceeded by the height of happier men.
O, then vouchsafe me but this loving thought:
"Had my friend's Muse grown with this growing age,
A dearer birth than this his love had brought
To march in ranks of better equipage;
    But since he died and poets better prove,
    Theirs for their style I'll read, his for his love."

33

Full many a glorious morning have I seen
Flatter the mountain-tops with sovereign eye,
Kissing with golden face the meadows green,
Gilding pale streams with heavenly alchemy;
Anon permit the basest clouds to ride
With ugly rack on his celestial face,
And from the forlorn world his visage hide,
Stealing unseen to west with this disgrace.
Even so my sun one early morn did shine
With all-triumphant splendor on my brow.
But out, alack! He was but one hour mine;
The region cloud hath mask'd him from me now.
    Yet him for this my love no whit disdaineth;
    Suns of the world may stain when heaven's sun
      staineth.

34

Why didst thou promise such a beauteous day
And make me travel forth without my cloak,
To let base clouds o'ertake me in my way,
Hiding thy brav'ry in their rotten smoke?
'Tis not enough that through the cloud thou break,
To dry the rain on my storm-beaten face,
For no man well of such a salve can speak
That heals the wound and cures not the disgrace.
Nor can thy shame give physic to my grief;
Though thou repent, yet I have still the loss.
Th' offender's sorrow lends but weak relief
To him that bears the strong offense's cross.
    Ah, but those tears are pearl which thy love
      sheeds,
    And they are rich and ransom all ill deeds.

35

No more be griev'd at that which thou hast done.
Roses have thorns, and silver fountains mud,
Clouds and eclipses stain both moon and sun,
And loathsome canker lives in sweetest bud.
All men make faults, and even I in this,
Authorizing thy trespass with compare,
Myself corrupting, salving thy amiss,
Excusing thy sins more than thy sins are.
For to thy sensual fault I bring in sense—
Thy adverse party is thy advocate—
And 'gainst myself a lawful plea commence.
Such civil war is in my love and hate
    That I an accessary needs must be
    To that sweet thief which sourly robs from me.

36

Let me confess that we two must be twain,
Although our undivided loves are one;
So shall those blots that do with me remain,

3 sigh sigh for **4 new . . . waste** lament anew the wasting of precious time, or time's erosion of those things held precious **6 dateless** endless **7 cancel'd** paid in full (by grieving) **8 expense** loss **9 foregone** past **10 heavily** sad. **tell** count

31 • 1 endeared enhanced in value, made more precious. (I.e., You have become dearer to me as representing all I have loved.) **5 obsequious** suitable to mourning **6 religious** dutiful **7 interest** that which is rightfully due. **which** who **8 But . . . lie** i.e., no more than absent persons (now dead) whose best qualities are to be found concealed in you **10 lovers** loved ones, friends **11 parts** shares **12 That due of many** that which was the due of many **13 I lov'd** which I loved **14 all they** (you) who comprise all of them

32 • 1 my . . . day i.e., the day of my death, which will content me well **3 fortune** chance **5 bett'ring** i.e., improved writing **7 Reserve** preserve. **rhyme** i.e., poetic skill **8 height** superiority. **happier** more gifted **11 dearer birth** i.e., better poem, better artistic creation **12 of better equipage** more finely equipped

33 • **5 basest** darkest **6 rack** mass of cloud driven before the wind in the upper air **12 region** of the upper air **14 stain** grow dim, be obscured, soiled

34 • 4 brav'ry finery. **rotten smoke** foul vapors **8 disgrace** i.e., the scar, the disfigurement caused by his friend's neglect or harsh treatment; the *loss* mentioned in l. 10 **9 shame** repentance for the wrong done. **physic** remedy **12 cross** affliction **13 sheeds** sheds

35 • 3 stain dim, obscure **4 canker** canker worm **6 Authorizing** sanctioning, justifying. **compare** comparisons (as in this sonnet) **7 Myself . . . amiss** i.e., I excusing your misdeed, thereby bringing blame on myself **8 Excusing . . . are** i.e., going further to excuse your sins than you did in committing those sins **9 sensual** pertaining to the flesh. **sense** pertaining to the rational faculty. (I.e., I reason away your fleshly offenses.)

36 • 1 twain parted **3 blots** defects

Without thy help, by me be borne alone.
In our two loves there is but one respect,
Though in our lives a separable spite,
Which though it alter not love's sole effect,
Yet doth it steal sweet hours from love's delight.
I may not evermore acknowledge thee,
Lest my bewailed guilt should do thee shame,
Nor thou with public kindness honor me
Unless thou take that honor from thy name.
  But do not so; I love thee in such sort
  As, thou being mine, mine is thy good report.

37

As a decrepit father takes delight
To see his active child do deeds of youth,
So I, made lame by Fortune's dearest spite,
Take all my comfort of thy worth and truth.
For whether beauty, birth, or wealth, or wit,
Or any of these all, or all, or more,
Entitled in thy parts do crowned sit,
I make my love engrafted to this store.
So then I am not lame, poor, nor despis'd,
Whilst that this shadow doth such substance give
That I in thy abundance am suffic'd
And by a part of all thy glory live.
  Look what is best, that best I wish in thee.
  This wish I have; then ten times happy me!

38

How can my Muse want subject to invent
While thou dost breathe, that pour'st into my verse
Thine own sweet argument, too excellent
For every vulgar paper to rehearse?
O, give thyself the thanks, if aught in me
Worthy perusal stand against thy sight,
For who's so dumb that cannot write to thee,
When thou thyself dost give invention light?
Be thou the tenth Muse, ten times more in worth
Than those old nine which rhymers invocate;
And he that calls on thee, let him bring forth
Eternal numbers to outlive long date.
  If my slight Muse do please these curious days,
  The pain be mine, but thine shall be the praise.

39

O, how thy worth with manners may I sing,
When thou art all the better part of me?
What can mine own praise to mine own self bring?
And what is 't but mine own when I praise thee?
Even for this let us divided live,
And our dear love lose name of single one,
That by this separation I may give
That due to thee which thou deserv'st alone.
O absence, what a torment wouldst thou prove,
Were it not thy sour leisure gave sweet leave
To entertain the time with thoughts of love,
Which time and thoughts so sweetly dost deceive,
  And that thou teachest how to make one twain,
  By praising him here who doth hence remain!

40

Take all my loves, my love, yea, take them all;
What hast thou then more than thou hadst before?
No love, my love, that thou mayst true love call;
All mine was thine before thou hadst this more.
Then if for my love thou my love receivest,
I cannot blame thee for my love thou usest;
But yet be blam'd, if thou this self deceivest
By willful taste of what thyself refusest.
I do forgive thy robb'ry, gentle thief,
Although thou steal thee all my poverty;
And yet love knows it is a greater grief
To bear love's wrong than hate's known injury.
  Lascivious grace, in whom all ill well shows,
  Kill me with spites; yet we must not be foes.

41

Those pretty wrongs that liberty commits
When I am sometime absent from thy heart,
Thy beauty and thy years full well befits,
For still temptation follows where thou art.
Gentle thou art, and therefore to be won,
Beauteous thou art, therefore to be assailed;
And when a woman woos, what woman's son
Will sourly leave her till she have prevailed?
Ay me, but yet thou mightst my seat forbear,
And chide thy beauty and thy straying youth,
Who lead thee in their riot even there
Where thou art forc'd to break a twofold truth:
  Hers, by thy beauty tempting her to thee,
  Thine, by thy beauty being false to me.

42

That thou hast her, it is not all my grief,
And yet it may be said I lov'd her dearly;
That she hath thee is of my wailing chief,
A loss in love that touches me more nearly.
Loving offenders, thus I will excuse ye:
Thou dost love her, because thou know'st I love her,

5 but one respect i.e., a mutual regard, singleness of attitude **6 separable spite** spiteful separation **7 sole** unique **9 not evermore** nevermore. **acknowledge** admit my acquaintance with **14 As** that. **report** reputation

37 • 3 made lame handicapped in life. **dearest** most bitter **4 of** in, from **5 wit** intelligence **7 Entitled . . . sit** sit enthroned in first place among your qualities **8 store** abundance **10 shadow** idea (in the Platonic sense). **substance** actuality **13 Look what** whatever

38 • 1 want . . . invent lack something to write about **2 that** you who **3 argument** subject **4 vulgar paper** common piece of writing. **rehearse** recite **5 in me** of my writing **6 stand against** meet **7 dumb** silent, lacking in subject **12 numbers** verses. **date** duration **13 curious** critical **14 pain** labor

39 • 1 with manners decently, becomingly **5 for** because of **6 name** reputation **11 entertain** pass, occupy **12 dost deceive** (you) do beguile away **13 that** were it not that. **make one twain** i.e., divide one beloved person into two **14 praising him here** i.e., invoking his presence here through my praising of him

40 • 5 my love . . . my love love of me . . . her whom I love **6 for** because. **thou usest** you enjoy (sexually) **7 this self** i.e., this other self of yours, the poet. (Often emended to *thyself*.) **8 willful taste** i.e., sensual enjoyment. **thyself** i.e., your true self (?) **10 steal . . . poverty** take for your own the poor little that I have **12 known** undisguised **13 Lascivious grace** i.e., you who are gracious even in your lasciviousness

41 • 1 pretty minor. **liberty** licentiousness **3 befits** (The subject is *wrongs*, l. 1.) **4 still** constantly **9 seat** place, that which belongs to me (i.e., my mistress) **11 Who** which **12 twofold truth** i.e., her plighted love and your plighted friendship

42 • 3 is . . . chief is chief cause of my lamentation

And for my sake even so doth she abuse me,
Suff'ring my friend for my sake to approve her.
If I lose thee, my loss is my love's gain,
And, losing her, my friend hath found that loss;
Both find each other, and I lose both twain,
And both for my sake lay on me this cross.
But here's the joy: my friend and I are one.
Sweet flattery! Then she loves but me alone.

43

When most I wink, then do mine eyes best see,
For all the day they view things unrespected;
But when I sleep, in dreams they look on thee,
And darkly bright are bright in dark directed.
Then thou, whose shadow shadows doth make bright,
How would thy shadow's form form happy show
To the clear day with thy much clearer light,
When to unseeing eyes thy shade shines so!
How would, I say, mine eyes be blessed made
By looking on thee in the living day,
When in dead night thy fair imperfect shade
Through heavy sleep on sightless eyes doth stay!
All days are nights to see till I see thee,
And nights bright days when dreams do show thee me.

44

If the dull substance of my flesh were thought,
Injurious distance should not stop my way;
For then despite of space I would be brought,
From limits far remote, where thou dost stay.
No matter then although my foot did stand
Upon the farthest earth remov'd from thee;
For nimble thought can jump both sea and land
As soon as think the place where he would be.
But, ah, thought kills me that I am not thought,
To leap large lengths of miles when thou art gone,
But that, so much of earth and water wrought,
I must attend time's leisure with my moan,
Receiving nought by elements so slow
But heavy tears, badges of either's woe.

45

The other two, slight air and purging fire,
Are both with thee, wherever I abide;
The first my thought, the other my desire,
These present-absent with swift motion slide.
For when these quicker elements are gone
In tender embassy of love to thee,
My life, being made of four, with two alone
Sinks down to death, oppress'd with melancholy;
Until life's composition be recured
By those swift messengers return'd from thee,
Who even but now come back again, assured
Of thy fair health, recounting it to me.
This told, I joy; but then no longer glad,
I send them back again and straight grow sad.

46

Mine eye and heart are at a mortal war
How to divide the conquest of thy sight;
Mine eye my heart thy picture's sight would bar,
My heart mine eye the freedom of that right.
My heart doth plead that thou in him dost lie—
A closet never pierc'd with crystal eyes—
But the defendant doth that plea deny
And says in him thy fair appearance lies.
To 'cide this title is impaneled
A quest of thoughts, all tenants to the heart,
And by their verdict is determined
The clear eye's moiety and the dear heart's part,
As thus: mine eye's due is thy outward part,
And my heart's right thy inward love of heart.

47

Betwixt mine eye and heart a league is took,
And each doth good turns now unto the other.
When that mine eye is famish'd for a look,
Or heart in love with sighs himself doth smother,
With my love's picture then my eye doth feast
And to the painted banquet bids my heart;
Another time mine eye is my heart's guest
And in his thoughts of love doth share a part.
So, either by thy picture or my love,
Thyself away art present still with me;
For thou not farther than my thoughts canst move,
And I am still with them and they with thee;
Or, if they sleep, thy picture in my sight
Awakes my heart to heart's and eye's delight.

48

How careful was I, when I took my way,
Each trifle under truest bars to thrust,
That to my use it might unused stay
From hands of falsehood, in sure wards of trust!
But thou, to whom my jewels trifles are,

7 abuse betray, wrong **8 approve** try, test (in a sexual sense) **9 my love's** hers whom I love, my mistress's **10 losing her** i.e., I losing her **12 cross** torment **14 flattery** gratifying deception

43 • 1 wink close my eyes in sleep **2 unrespected** unnoticed, unregarded **4 And . . . directed** and, able to see in the darkness, are directed toward your brightness in the dark **5 whose . . . bright** whose image makes darkness bright **6 thy shadow's form** the substance of the shadow, i.e., your presence. **form happy show** make a gladdening sight **8 unseeing eyes** i.e., closed eyes of the dreamer **11 imperfect** unsubstantial, indistinct as in a dream **13 All . . . to see** all days are gloomy to behold **14 me** to me

44 • 1 dull heavy **4 limits** regions, bounds. **where** i.e., to the place where **6 farthest earth remov'd** that part of the earth farthest removed **8 he** i.e., thought **9 ah, thought** ah, the thought **11 so . . . wrought** i.e., I, compounded to such an extent of the heavier elements, earth and water. (The lighter elements are fire and air.) **12 attend time's leisure** i.e., wait until time has leisure to reunite us **14 either's** i.e., both earth's and water's, because the earth is heavy and the sea is salt and wet, both like tears

45 • 1 other two i.e., of the four elements discussed in Sonnet 44. **slight** unsubstantial

4 present-absent now here and immediately gone **7 life** living body. **two alone** i.e., earth and water **8 melancholy** a humor thought to be induced by an excess of earth and water **9 composition** proper balance among the four elements. **recured** restored **10 swift messengers** i.e., fire and air, thought and desire **14 straight** straightway

46 • 1 mortal deadly **2 conquest** spoils. **thy sight** the sight of you **4 My . . . right** i.e., my heart would deny to my eye the privilege of looking on your picture **9 'cide** decide **10 quest** inquest, jury **12 moiety** portion

47 • 1 a league is took an agreement is reached **6 painted banquet** i.e., visual feast, perhaps an actual picture of the friend

48 • 1 took my way set out on my journey **2 truest** most trusty **4 hands of falsehood** thieves **5 to** compared to

Most worthy comfort, now my greatest grief,
Thou best of dearest, and mine only care,
Art left the prey of every vulgar thief.
Thee have I not lock'd up in any chest,
Save where thou art not, though I feel thou art,
Within the gentle closure of my breast,
From whence at pleasure thou mayst come and part;
    And even thence thou wilt be stol'n, I fear,
    For truth proves thievish for a prize so dear.

49

Against that time, if ever that time come,
When I shall see thee frown on my defects,
When as thy love hath cast his utmost sum,
Call'd to that audit by advis'd respects;
Against that time when thou shalt strangely pass
And scarcely greet me with that sun, thine eye,
When love, converted from the thing it was,
Shall reasons find of settled gravity—
Against that time do I ensconce me here
Within the knowledge of mine own desart,
And this my hand against myself uprear,
To guard the lawful reasons on thy part.
    To leave poor me thou hast the strength of laws,
    Since why to love I can allege no cause.

50

How heavy do I journey on the way,
When what I seek, my weary travel's end,
Doth teach that ease and that repose to say,
"Thus far the miles are measur'd from thy friend!"
The beast that bears me, tired with my woe,
Plods dully on, to bear that weight in me,
As if by some instinct the wretch did know
His rider lov'd not speed, being made from thee.
The bloody spur cannot provoke him on
That sometimes anger thrusts into his hide,
Which heavily he answers with a groan,
More sharp to me than spurring to his side;
    For that same groan doth put this in my mind:
    My grief lies onward and my joy behind.

51

Thus can my love excuse the slow offense
Of my dull bearer when from thee I speed:
From where thou art why should I haste me thence?
Till I return, of posting is no need.

6 worthy valuable. **now . . . grief** (i.e., because of his absence and likeliness of being stolen) **8 vulgar** common **12 part** depart **14 truth** i.e., even honesty itself

49 • 1 Against in anticipation of **3 When as** when. **cast . . . sum** added up the sum total. (The metaphor is from closing accounts on a dissolution of partnership.) **4 advis'd respects** careful consideration **5 strangely** as a stranger **8 of settled gravity** for a dignified reserve or continued coldness (?) of sufficient weight (?) **9 ensconce** fortify, shelter **10 desart** i.e., deserving, such as it is **11 this . . . uprear** I raise my own hand (as a witness) against my own interest **12 To . . . part** i.e., to testify in behalf of the lawful reasons on your side of the case **14 Since . . . cause** since I can urge no lawful cause why you should love me

50 • 1 heavy sadly **2–4 When . . . friend** i.e., when the ease and repose I seek at journey's end will merely remind me that I have gone so many miles from my friend

51 • 1 slow offense offense consisting in slowness **2 dull bearer** i.e., the horse **4 posting** riding swiftly

O, what excuse will my poor beast then find,
When swift extremity can seem but slow?
Then should I spur, though mounted on the wind;
In winged speed no motion shall I know.
Then can no horse with my desire keep pace;
Therefore desire, of perfect'st love being made,
Shall neigh—no dull flesh—in his fiery race.
But love, for love, thus shall excuse my jade:
    Since from thee going he went willful-slow,
    Towards thee I'll run, and give him leave to go.

52

So am I as the rich, whose blessed key
Can bring him to his sweet up-locked treasure,
The which he wlll not ev'ry hour survey,
For blunting the fine point of seldom pleasure.
Therefore are feasts so solemn and so rare,
Since, seldom coming, in the long year set,
Like stones of worth they thinly placed are,
Or captain jewels in the carcanet.
So is the time that keeps you as my chest,
Or as the wardrobe which the robe doth hide,
To make some special instant special blest,
By new unfolding his imprison'd pride.
    Blessed are you, whose worthiness gives scope,
    Being had, to triumph, being lack'd, to hope.

53

What is your substance, whereof are you made,
That millions of strange shadows on you tend?
Since every one hath, every one, one shade,
And you, but one, can every shadow lend.
Describe Adonis, and the counterfeit
Is poorly imitated after you;
On Helen's cheek all art of beauty set,
And you in Grecian tires are painted new.
Speak of the spring and foison of the year;
The one doth shadow of your beauty show,
The other as your bounty doth appear,
And you in every blessed shape we know.
    In all external grace you have some part,
    But you like none, none you, for constant heart.

54

O, how much more doth beauty beauteous seem
By that sweet ornament which truth doth give!
The rose looks fair, but fairer we it deem
For that sweet odor which doth in it live.

6 swift extremity extreme swiftness **8 In** i.e., even in. **know** recognize **11 Shall . . . race** i.e., shall neigh proudly in its fire-swift race, since it, composed like fire of a lighter element, is not held back by the heavy flesh. (See Sonnet 45.) **12 for love** for love's sake. **jade** nag **14 go** walk, as contrasted with running

52 • 1 as the rich like the rich man **4 For blunting** lest he blunt. **seldom pleasure** pleasure sparingly enjoyed **8 captain** principal. **carcanet** necklace of jewels **9 as** like **12 his** its **13–14 gives . . . hope** give me opportunity, when you are with me, to rejoice, and when you are away from me, to hope for reunion

53 • 2 tend attend, wait upon **3 shade** shadow (as cast by the sun) **4 And . . . lend** and yet you, being only one person, can cast all sorts of shadowy reflections (such as Adonis, Helen, etc.) **5 counterfeit** likeness, portrait **8 tires** attire, clothes **9 foison** abundance, i.e., autumn

54 • 2 By by means of. **truth** (1) constancy (2) substance, reality

The canker-blooms have full as deep a dye
As the perfumed tincture of the roses,
Hang on such thorns, and play as wantonly
When summer's breath their masked buds discloses.
But, for their virtue only is their show,
They live unwoo'd and unrespected fade,
Die to themselves. Sweet roses do not so;
Of their sweet deaths are sweetest odors made.
And so of you, beauteous and lovely youth,
When that shall vade, by verse distills your truth.

55

Not marble, nor the gilded monuments
Of princes, shall outlive this pow'rful rhyme,
But you shall shine more bright in these contents
Than unswept stone besmear'd with sluttish time.
When wasteful war shall statues overturn,
And broils root out the work of masonry,
Nor Mars his sword nor war's quick fire shall burn
The living record of your memory.
'Gainst death and all-oblivious enmity
Shall you pace forth; your praise shall still find room
Even in the eyes of all posterity
That wear this world out to the ending doom.
So, till the judgment that yourself arise,
You live in this, and dwell in lovers' eyes.

56

Sweet love, renew thy force; be it not said
Thy edge should blunter be than appetite,
Which but today by feeding is allay'd,
Tomorrow sharp'ned in his former might.
So, love, be thou; although today thou fill
Thy hungry eyes even till they wink with fullness,
Tomorrow see again, and do not kill
The spirit of love with a perpetual dullness.
Let this sad int'rim like the ocean be
Which parts the shore, where two contracted new
Come daily to the banks, that, when they see
Return of love, more blest may be the view;
As call it winter, which being full of care
Makes summer's welcome thrice more wish'd,
more rare.

5 canker-blooms dog roses (outwardly attractive, but not as sweetly scented as the damask rose) **7 wantonly** sportively **8 discloses** causes to open **9 for** because. **their show** in their appearance **10 unrespected** unregarded **11 to themselves** i.e., without profit to others **14 When . . . truth** when your physical beauty fades, your true substance will be distilled and preserved by (my) verse. (See Sonnet 5.)

55 • 3 these contents i.e., the contents of my poems written in praise of you **4 Than unswept stone** than in a memorial stone that has been left unswept, unattended. **with sluttish time** by neglectful time **6 broils** uprisings, battles **7 Nor Mars his sword** neither Mars' sword (shall destroy) **9 all-oblivious enmity** i.e., oblivion, at enmity with everything **12 That . . . doom** who will be from now till Doomsday **13 till . . . arise** until the Judgment day when you will arise from the dead

56 • 1 love i.e., the spirit of love. (The friend is not directly mentioned in this sonnet.) **2 edge** keenness. **appetite** lust **6 wink** shut **9 sad int'rim** i.e., the period of love's abatement or absence **10 parts the shore** separates the shores. **contracted new** newly betrothed **12 love** the loved one **13 As** just as appropriately

57

Being your slave, what should I do but tend
Upon the hours and times of your desire?
I have no precious time at all to spend,
Nor services to do, till you require.
Nor dare I chide the world-without-end hour
Whilst I, my sovereign, watch the clock for you,
Nor think the bitterness of absence sour
When you have bid your servant once adieu.
Nor dare I question with my jealous thought
Where you may be, or your affairs suppose,
But, like a sad slave, stay and think of nought
Save, where you are how happy you make those.
So true a fool is love that in your will,
Though you do anything, he thinks no ill.

58

That god forbid that made me first your slave
I should in thought control your times of pleasure,
Or at your hand th' account of hours to crave,
Being your vassal, bound to stay your leisure!
O, let me suffer, being at your beck,
Th' imprison'd absence of your liberty,
And patience, tame to sufferance, bide each check,
Without accusing you of injury.
Be where you list, your charter is so strong
That you yourself may privilege your time
To what you will; to you it doth belong
Yourself to pardon of self-doing crime.
I am to wait, though waiting so be hell,
Not blame your pleasure, be it ill or well.

59

If there be nothing new, but that which is
Hath been before, how are our brains beguil'd,
Which, laboring for invention, bear amiss
The second burden of a former child!
O, that record could with a backward look,
Even of five hundred courses of the sun,
Show me your image in some antique book,
Since mind at first in character was done!
That I might see what the old world could say
To this composed wonder of your frame;
Whether we are mended, or whe'er better they,
Or whether revolution be the same.
O, sure I am, the wits of former days
To subjects worse have given admiring praise.

57 • 1 tend attend **5 world-without-end** interminable **6 my . . . you** watch the clock for you, my sovereign **7 Nor think** nor dare I think **10 suppose** make conjectures about **11 sad** sober **13 will** (This word, capitalized in the 1609 quarto, is regarded by some as a pun on Shakespeare's first name; see Sonnet 135.)

58 • 3 th' account . . . crave should crave an accounting of how you spend your time **4 stay** await **6 Th' imprison'd . . . liberty** i.e., the lack of freedom I suffer in being absent from you, arising from *(of)* your freedom and free behavior **7 And . . . check** and (let) patience, trained to endure any suffering, put up with each rebuke **9 list** please. **charter** privilege **10 privilege** authorize **12 self-doing** committed by yourself **13 am to** must

59 • 1 that everything **3–4 laboring . . . child** i.e., striving to give birth to a new creation, merely miscarry with the repetition of something created before **5 record** memory, especially memory preserved in writing **6 courses . . . sun** years **8 Since . . . done** since thought was first expressed in writing **10 composed wonder** wonderful composition **11 mended** improved. **whe'er** whether **12 revolution . . . same** i.e., the revolving of the ages brings only repetition

60

Like as the waves make towards the pebbled shore,
So do our minutes hasten to their end;
Each changing place with that which goes before,
In sequent toil all forwards do contend.
Nativity, once in the main of light,
Crawls to maturity, wherewith being crown'd,
Crooked eclipses 'gainst his glory fight,
And Time that gave doth now his gift confound.
Time doth transfix the flourish set on youth
And delves the parallels in beauty's brow,
Feeds on the rarities of nature's truth,
And nothing stands but for his scythe to mow.
    And yet to times in hope my verse shall stand,
    Praising thy worth, despite his cruel hand.

61

Is it thy will thy image should keep open
My heavy eyelids to the weary night?
Dost thou desire my slumbers should be broken
While shadows like to thee do mock my sight?
Is it thy spirit that thou send'st from thee
So far from home into my deeds to pry,
To find out shames and idle hours in me,
The scope and tenor of thy jealousy?
O, no, thy love, though much, is not so great;
It is my love that keeps mine eye awake,
Mine own true love that doth my rest defeat,
To play the watchman ever for thy sake.
    For thee watch I whilst thou dost wake elsewhere,
    From me far off, with others all too near.

62

Sin of self-love possesseth all mine eye
And all my soul, and all my every part;
And for this sin there is no remedy,
It is so grounded inward in my heart.
Methinks no face so gracious is as mine,
No shape so true, no truth of such account;
And for myself mine own worth do define,
As I all other in all worths surmount.
But when my glass shows me myself indeed,
Beated and chopp'd with tann'd antiquity,
Mine own self-love quite contrary I read;
Self so self-loving were iniquity.
    'Tis thee, myself, that for myself I praise,
    Painting my age with beauty of thy days.

60 • 3 changing place with replacing **4 In . . . contend** one after another all struggle onward **5 Nativity** i.e., the newborn infant. **main** main body, expanse. (The child is seen as dwelling in the main or ocean of light.) **7 Crooked** perverse, malignant **8 confound** destroy **9 transfix the flourish** pierce through and destroy the decoration or embellishment, i.e., physical beauty **10 parallels** wrinkles, furrows **11 Feeds . . . truth** consumes the most precious things created by the fidelity of nature **12 but . . . mow** i.e., that can escape the mowing of Time's scythe **13 times in hope** times to come

61 • 8 The scope . . . jealousy (is it) the aim and purport of your suspicion **13 watch** stay awake. **wake** revel

62 • 8 As as if. **other** others **9 indeed** i.e., as I actually am **10 Beated** battered. **chopp'd** chapped, roughened. **tann'd antiquity** i.e., leathery old age **12 so self-loving** i.e., loving such an aged appearance **13 thee, myself** i.e., you, with whom I identify myself. **for** as **14 days** i.e., youth

63

Against my love shall be, as I am now,
With Time's injurious hand crush'd and o'erworn;
When hours have drain'd his blood and fill'd his brow
With lines and wrinkles; when his youthful morn
Hath travel'd on to Age's steepy night,
And all those beauties whereof now he's king
Are vanishing or vanish'd out of sight,
Stealing away the treasure of his spring;
For such a time do I now fortify
Against confounding Age's cruel knife,
That he shall never cut from memory
My sweet love's beauty, though my lover's life.
    His beauty shall in these black lines be seen,
    And they shall live, and he in them still green.

64

When I have seen by Time's fell hand defaced
The rich proud cost of outworn buried age;
When sometime lofty towers I see down-razed
And brass eternal slave to mortal rage;
When I have seen the hungry ocean gain
Advantage on the kingdom of the shore,
And the firm soil win of the wat'ry main
Increasing store with loss and loss with store;
When I have seen such interchange of state,
Or state itself confounded to decay,
Ruin hath taught me thus to ruminate
That Time will come and take my love away.
    This thought is as a death, which cannot choose
    But weep to have that which it fears to lose.

65

Since brass, nor stone, nor earth, nor boundless sea,
But sad mortality o'ersways their power,
How with this rage shall beauty hold a plea,
Whose action is no stronger than a flower?
O, how shall summer's honey breath hold out
Against the wrackful siege of batt'ring days,
When rocks impregnable are not so stout,
Nor gates of steel so strong, but Time decays?
O fearful meditation! Where, alack,
Shall Time's best jewel from Time's chest lie hid?
Or what strong hand can hold his swift foot back?
Or who his spoil of beauty can forbid?
    O, none, unless this miracle have might,
    That in black ink my love may still shine bright.

63 • 1 Against anticipating the time when **5 steepy** precipitous, i.e., descending swiftly toward death **9 For such a time** (Parallel in construction with *Against* in l. 1.) **fortify** raise works of defense **10 confounding** destroying **12 though** i.e., though he cut **13 black** (1) inscribed in ink (2) the opposite of fair or beautiful

64 • 1 fell cruel **2 The . . . age** i.e., those monuments which were the product of proud wealth and magnificent outlay in times now past and forgotten **3 sometime** formerly **4 brass . . . rage** i.e., seemingly indestructible brass subdued to the destructive power of mortality **7 of** at the expense of **8 Increasing . . . store** i.e., one gaining as the other loses, and losing as the other gains **9 state** condition **10 state** pomp, greatness; condition in the abstract **13 which cannot choose** (Modifies *thought.*) **14 to have** i.e., because it now has

65 • 1 Since i.e., since there is neither **2 But** but that **3 with this rage** against this destructive force. **hold** maintain (as in a legal action) **4 action** case (in law) **6 wrackful** destructive **8 decays** brings about their decay **10 from Time's chest** i.e., away from being deposited by Time in his repository of forgetfulness **12 spoil** act of spoiling, ravaging

66

Tir'd with all these, for restful death I cry:
As, to behold desert a beggar born,
And needy nothing trimm'd in jollity,
And purest faith unhappily forsworn,
And gilded honor shamefully misplac'd,
And maiden virtue rudely strumpeted,
And right perfection wrongfully disgrac'd,
And strength by limping sway disabled,
And art made tongue-tied by authority,
And folly doctor-like controlling skill,
And simple truth miscall'd simplicity,
And captive good attending captain ill.
  Tir'd with all these, from these would I be gone,
  Save that, to die, I leave my love alone.

67

Ah, wherefore with infection should he live,
And with his presence grace impiety,
That sin by him advantage should achieve
And lace itself with his society?
Why should false painting imitate his cheek
And steal dead seeing of his living hue?
Why should poor beauty indirectly seek
Roses of shadow, since his rose is true?
Why should he live, now Nature bankrupt is,
Beggar'd of blood to blush through lively veins,
For she hath no exchequer now but his,
And, proud of many, lives upon his gains?
  O, him she stores, to show what wealth she had
  In days long since, before these last so bad.

68

Thus is his cheek the map of days outworn,
When beauty liv'd and died as flowers do now,
Before these bastard signs of fair were born,
Or durst inhabit on a living brow;
Before the golden tresses of the dead,
The right of sepulchers, were shorn away,
To live a second life on second head;
Ere beauty's dead fleece made another gay.
In him those holy antique hours are seen,
Without all ornament, itself and true,
Making no summer of another's green,
Robbing no old to dress his beauty new;
  And him as for a map doth Nature store,
  To show false Art what beauty was of yore.

69

Those parts of thee that the world's eye doth view
Want nothing that the thought of hearts can mend;
All tongues, the voice of souls, give thee that due,
Utt'ring bare truth, even so as foes commend.
Thy outward thus with outward praise is crown'd,
But those same tongues that give thee so thine own
In other accents do this praise confound
By seeing farther than the eye hath shown.
They look into the beauty of thy mind,
And that, in guess, they measure by thy deeds;
Then, churls, their thoughts, although their eyes were kind,
To thy fair flower add the rank smell of weeds.
  But why thy odor matcheth not thy show,
  The soil is this, that thou dost common grow.

70

That thou art blam'd shall not be thy defect,
For slander's mark was ever yet the fair;
The ornament of beauty is suspect,
A crow that flies in heaven's sweetest air.
So thou be good, slander doth but approve
Thy worth the greater, being woo'd of time,
For canker vice the sweetest buds doth love,
And thou present'st a pure unstained prime.
Thou hast pass'd by the ambush of young days,
Either not assail'd, or victor being charg'd;
Yet this thy praise cannot be so thy praise
To tie up envy evermore enlarg'd.
  If some suspect of ill mask'd not thy show,
  Then thou alone kingdoms of hearts shouldst owe.

71

No longer mourn for me when I am dead
Than you shall hear the surly sullen bell
Give warning to the world that I am fled
From this vile world, with vilest worms to dwell.
Nay, if you read this line, remember not
The hand that writ it, for I love you so
That I in your sweet thoughts would be forgot
If thinking on me then should make you woe.
O, if, I say, you look upon this verse
When I perhaps compounded am with clay,

66 • 1 all these i.e., the following **2 As** for instance, namely. **desert** i.e., those who have merit, as contrasted with *needy nothing* in the next line, those insignificant persons who deserve nothing **3 jollity** finery **4 unhappily forsworn** evilly betrayed **7 disgrac'd** banished from favor **8 limping sway** halting leadership **9 art** literature, learning. **made tongue-tied** i.e., censored **10 doctor-like** assuming a learned bearing. **controlling** dominating **11 simplicity** folly **12 attending** waiting on, subordinated to

67 • 1 with infection i.e., with the world's ills as enumerated in the preceding sonnet. **he** i.e., the poet's friend **4 lace** adorn **6 dead seeing of** lifeless appearance from **7 poor** inferior. **indirectly** imitatively, or falsely **8 Roses of shadow** i.e., painted roses **9–10 now . . . veins** i.e., seeing as bankrupt Nature is otherwise deficient in healthy blood to make red the veins **11 For** since. **exchequer** i.e., treasury of natural beauty **12 proud** i.e., though proudly boasting. **gains** endowments **13 stores** preserves, keeps in store **14 last** i.e., recent days, the present

68 • 1 map picture, image **3 bastard . . . fair** i.e., cosmetics **6 The right of** rightly belonging in. (Wigs were made of dead persons' hair.) **9 antique hours** ancient times

13 store preserve

69 • 2 Want lack **4 bare** i.e., minimal and exterior only **6 thine own** your due **7 confound** destroy **10 in guess** at a guess **14 soil** (1) blemish, fault (2) origin, source. **common** stale, vulgar (like a weed)

70 • 1 defect fault **2 mark** target **3 The . . . suspect** i.e., beauty is always attended by suspicion *(suspect),* as though suspicion were a necessary ornament to beauty **5 So** provided that. **approve** prove **6 being . . . time** i.e., since you are courted by the world **7 canker vice** i.e., slander that is like the canker or rose worm **8 unstained prime** unspotted youth (like the pure unspoiled flower that attracts the canker worm) **9 ambush . . . days** i.e., temptations of youth **10 being charg'd** when you were assailed **11 so** sufficiently **12 To . . . enlarg'd** i.e., to silence malice which is always at liberty **13 If . . . show** if some suspicion *(suspect)* of illdoing did not partly obscure your outward attractiveness **14 owe** own

71 • 8 make cause **10 compounded** mingled

Do not so much as my poor name rehearse,
But let your love even with my life decay,
Lest the wise world should look into your moan
And mock you with me after I am gone.

72

O, lest the world should task you to recite
What merit liv'd in me that you should love
After my death, dear love, forget me quite,
For you in me can nothing worthy prove;
Unless you would devise some virtuous lie,
To do more for me than mine own desert,
And hang more praise upon deceased I
Than niggard truth would willingly impart.
O, lest your true love may seem false in this,
That you for love speak well of me untrue,
My name be buried where my body is,
And live no more to shame nor me nor you.
For I am sham'd by that which I bring forth,
And so should you, to love things nothing worth.

73

That time of year thou mayst in me behold
When yellow leaves, or none, or few, do hang
Upon those boughs which shake against the cold,
Bare ruin'd choirs, where late the sweet birds sang.
In me thou see'st the twilight of such day
As after sunset fadeth in the west,
Which by and by black night doth take away,
Death's second self, that seals up all in rest.
In me thou see'st the glowing of such fire
That on the ashes of his youth doth lie,
As the death-bed whereon it must expire,
Consum'd with that which it was nourish'd by.
This thou perceiv'st, which makes thy love more strong,
To love that well which thou must leave ere long.

74

But be contented; when that fell arrest
Without all bail shall carry me away,
My life hath in this line some interest,
Which for memorial still with thee shall stay.
When thou reviewest this, thou dost review
The very part was consecrate to thee.
The earth can have but earth, which is his due;
My spirit is thine, the better part of me.
So then thou hast but lost the dregs of life,
The prey of worms, my body being dead,
The coward conquest of a wretch's knife,
Too base of thee to be remembered.
The worth of that is that which it contains,
And that is this, and this with thee remains.

75

So are you to my thoughts as food to life,
Or as sweet-season'd showers are to the ground.
And for the peace of you I hold such strife
As 'twixt a miser and his wealth is found:
Now proud as an enjoyer, and anon
Doubting the filching age will steal his treasure,
Now counting best to be with you alone,
Then better'd that the world may see my pleasure;
Sometime all full with feasting on your sight
And by and by clean starved for a look;
Possessing or pursuing no delight
Save what is had or must from you be took.
Thus do I pine and surfeit day by day,
Or gluttoning on all, or all away.

76

Why is my verse so barren of new pride?
So far from variation or quick change?
Why with the time do I not glance aside
To new-found methods and to compounds strange?
Why write I still all one, ever the same,
And keep invention in a noted weed,
That every word doth almost tell my name,
Showing their birth and where they did proceed?
O, know, sweet love, I always write of you,
And you and love are still my argument;
So all my best is dressing old words new,
Spending again what is already spent.
For as the sun is daily new and old,
So is my love still telling what is told.

77

Thy glass will show thee how thy beauties wear,
Thy dial how thy precious minutes waste;
The vacant leaves thy mind's imprint will bear,
And of this book this learning mayst thou taste.
The wrinkles which thy glass will truly show,

14 with because of

72 • 10 untrue untruly **11 My name be** let my name be **12 nor . . . nor** neither . . . nor **13 that . . . forth** (Perhaps a deprecatory reference to the author's acting and writing of plays.) **14 should you** i.e., would you be ashamed of loving worthless me

73 • 4 choirs those areas of churches where the service is sung, here viewed as in ruins and resembling the arched shape of bare trees. **late** lately **8 seals** closes **10 That** as

74 • 1 fell cruel. **that fell arrest** i.e., death **3 line** verse. **interest** legal concern, right, or title **4 still** always **6 part was** part (of me) which was **7 his** its **11 coward . . . knife** i.e., the conquest that even a poor cowardly wretch like Death can make with his scythe **12 of . . . remembered** to be remembered by you **13–14 The worth . . . remains** the only worth of my body is the spirit it contains—i.e., this verse, which will remain with you

75 • 2 sweet-season'd of the sweet season, i.e., spring **3 of you** to be found in you **6 Doubting** suspecting, fearing that **7 counting** (1) thinking it (2) reckoning, like a miser **8 better'd** made happier, better pleased **10 clean** completely, absolutely **12 from you** (Modifies both verbs, *had* and *must be took.*) **14 Or . . . or** either . . . or. **all away** i.e., all food being taken away

76 • 1 pride ornament **2 quick change** fashionable innovation **3 time** way of the world, fashion **4 compounds strange** literary inventions, or perhaps compound words, neologisms **5 still all one** continually one way **6 invention** literary creation. **noted weed** familiar garment **8 where** whence **10 still** always. **argument** subject, theme

77 • 1 glass mirror. **wear** wear away **2 dial** sundial **3 vacant leaves** blank pages. (Apparently these lines accompanied the gift of a book of blank pages, a memorandum book.) **thy mind's imprint** i.e., your reflections and ideas, to be set down in the memorandum book **4 this learning** i.e., mental profit derived from reflecting and keeping a journal, as explained in ll. 9 ff.

Of mouthed graves will give thee memory;
Thou by thy dial's shady stealth mayst know
Time's thievish progress to eternity.
Look what thy memory can not contain
Commit to these waste blanks, and thou shalt find
Those children nurs'd, deliver'd from thy brain,
To take a new acquaintance of thy mind.
These offices, so oft as thou wilt look,
Shall profit thee and much enrich thy book.

78

So oft have I invok'd thee for my Muse
And found such fair assistance in my verse
As every alien pen hath got my use
And under thee their poesy disperse.
Thine eyes that taught the dumb on high to sing
And heavy ignorance aloft to fly,
Have added feathers to the learned's wing
And given grace a double majesty.
Yet be most proud of that which I compile,
Whose influence is thine and born of thee.
In others' works thou dost but mend the style,
And arts with thy sweet graces graced be;
But thou art all my art and dost advance
As high as learning my rude ignorance.

79

Whilst I alone did call upon thy aid,
My verse alone had all thy gentle grace,
But now my gracious numbers are decay'd
And my sick Muse doth give another place.
I grant, sweet love, thy lovely argument
Deserves the travail of a worthier pen,
Yet what of thee thy poet doth invent
He robs thee of and pays it thee again.
He lends thee virtue, and he stole that word
From thy behavior; beauty doth he give,
And found it in thy cheek; he can afford
No praise to thee but what in thee doth live.
Then thank him not for that which he doth say,
Since what he owes thee thou thyself dost pay.

80

O, how I faint when I of you do write,
Knowing a better spirit doth use your name,
And in the praise thereof spends all his might
To make me tongue-tied, speaking of your fame!
But since your worth, wide as the ocean is,
The humble as the proudest sail doth bear,
My saucy bark, inferior far to his,
On your broad main doth willfully appear.
Your shallowest help will hold me up afloat,
Whilst he upon your soundless deep doth ride;
Or, being wrack'd, I am a worthless boat,
He of tall building and of goodly pride.
Then if he thrive and I be cast away,
The worst was this: my love was my decay.

81

Or I shall live your epitaph to make,
Or you survive when I in earth am rotten,
From hence your memory death cannot take,
Although in me each part will be forgotten.
Your name from hence immortal life shall have,
Though I, once gone, to all the world must die;
The earth can yield me but a common grave,
When you entombed in men's eyes shall lie.
Your momument shall be my gentle verse,
Which eyes not yet created shall o'er-read,
And tongues to be your being shall rehearse
When all the breathers of this world are dead.
You still shall live—such virtue hath my pen—
Where breath most breathes, even in the mouths of men.

82

I grant thou wert not married to my Muse,
And therefore mayst without attaint o'erlook
The dedicated words which writers use
Of their fair subject, blessing every book.
Thou art as fair in knowledge as in hue,
Finding thy worth a limit past my praise,
And therefore art enforc'd to seek anew
Some fresher stamp of the time-bettering days.
And do so, love; yet when they have devis'd
What strained touches rhetoric can lend,
Thou, truly fair, wert truly sympathiz'd
In true plain words by thy true-telling friend;
And their gross painting might be better us'd
Where cheeks need blood; in thee it is abus'd.

83

I never saw that you did painting need,
And therefore to your fair no painting set;
I found, or thought I found, you did exceed

6 mouthed all-devouring, gaping. **memory** reminder **7 shady stealth** slow progress of the shadow on the dial **9 Look what** whatever **10 waste blanks** blank pages **11 nurs'd** i.e., preserved. **deliver'd from** having been produced by **12 take . . . of** i.e., provide fresh insight to, be freshly remembered by **13 offices** functions

78 • 3 As that. **alien pen** i.e., other poet. **got my use** adopted my practice **4 under thee** i.e., with you as their muse or patron; under your influence **5 on high** aloud **7 added . . . wing** i.e., enabled learned poets to fly higher still **8 And . . . majesty** and have added to the majesty of poets already capable of it **9 compile** compose, write **10 influence** inspiration (with suggestion of astrological meaning) **12 arts** learning, literary culture **13 advance** lift up

79 • 3 numbers verse **4 give another place** yield place to another **5 thy lovely argument** the theme of your lovable qualities **11 afford** offer

80 • 1 faint grow weak, falter **2 better spirit** i.e., rival poet, whom the speaker admires **6 as** as well as **8 willfully** perversely, boldly, in spite of all **10 soundless** unfathomable **11 wrack'd** shipwrecked **12 tall building** i.e., sturdy construction. **pride** splendor **13 cast away** (1) shipwrecked (2) abandoned **14 decay** ruin

81 • 1 Or whether **3 hence** (1) this poetry (2) the earth (also in l. 5) **4 in . . . part** every quality of mine (as distinguished from the poetry) **11 to be** i.e., of persons yet unborn. **rehearse** recite **12 breathers** living people. **this world** this present time **13 virtue** power

82 • 2 attaint blame, discredit. **o'erlook** look at, peruse **3 dedicated** devoted (with suggestion of *dedicatory*). **writers** i.e., other writers **4 blessing every book** i.e., you bestowing favor thus on the writings of others **5 hue** complexion, appearance **6 a limit** an extent **8 Some . . . days** some more recent and current literary product of this progressive age **11 wert truly sympathiz'd** would be faithfully matched and described **13 gross** extravagantly flattering **14 abus'd** misused, misapplied

83 • 2 fair beauty. **set** applied

The barren tender of a poet's debt;
And therefore have I slept in your report,
That you yourself being extant well might show
How far a modern quill doth come too short,
Speaking of worth, what worth in you doth grow.
This silence for my sin you did impute,
Which shall be most my glory, being dumb;
For I impair not beauty being mute,
When others would give life and bring a tomb.
  There lives more life in one of your fair eyes
  Than both your poets can in praise devise.

84

Who is it that says most, which can say more
Than this rich praise, that you alone are you,
In whose confine immured is the store
Which should example where your equal grew?
Lean penury within that pen doth dwell
That to his subject lends not some small glory;
But he that writes of you, if he can tell
That you are you, so dignifies his story.
Let him but copy what in you is writ,
Not making worse what nature made so clear,
And such a counterpart shall fame his wit,
Making his style admired everywhere.
  You to your beauteous blessings add a curse,
  Being fond on praise, which makes your praises worse.

85

My tongue-tied Muse in manners holds her still,
While comments of your praise, richly compil'd,
Reserve their character with golden quill
And precious phrase by all the Muses fil'd.
I think good thoughts whilst other write good words,
And like unlettered clerk still cry "Amen"
To every hymn that able spirit affords
In polish'd form of well-refined pen.
Hearing you prais'd, I say "'Tis so, 'tis true,"
And to the most of praise add something more;
But that is in my thought, whose love to you,
Though words come hindmost, holds his rank before.
  Then others for the breath of words respect,
  Me for my dumb thoughts, speaking in effect.

86

Was it the proud full sail of his great verse,
Bound for the prize of all too precious you,
That did my ripe thoughts in my brain inhearse,
Making their tomb the womb wherein they grew?
Was it his spirit, by spirits taught to write
Above a mortal pitch, that struck me dead?
No, neither he, nor his compeers by night
Giving him aid, my verse astonished.
He, nor that affable familiar ghost
Which nightly gulls him with intelligence,
As victors of my silence cannot boast;
I was not sick of any fear from thence.
  But when your countenance fill'd up his line,
  Then lack'd I matter; that enfeebled mine.

87

Farewell! Thou art too dear for my possessing,
And like enough thou know'st thy estimate.
The charter of thy worth gives thee releasing;
My bonds in thee are all determinate.
For how do I hold thee but by thy granting,
And for that riches where is my deserving?
The cause of this fair gift in me is wanting,
And so my patent back again is swerving.
Thyself thou gav'st, thy own worth then not knowing,
Or me, to whom thou gav'st it, else mistaking;
So thy great gift, upon misprision growing,
Comes home again, on better judgment making.
  Thus have I had thee as a dream doth flatter,
  In sleep a king, but waking no such matter.

88

When thou shalt be dispos'd to set me light
And place my merit in the eye of scorn,
Upon thy side against myself I'll fight
And prove thee virtuous, though thou art forsworn.
With mine own weakness being best acquainted,
Upon thy part I can set down a story
Of faults conceal'd, wherein I am attainted,
That thou in losing me shall win much glory.
And I by this will be a gainer too;
For, bending all my loving thoughts on thee,
The injuries that to myself I do,
Doing thee vantage, double-vantage me.
  Such is my love, to thee I so belong,
  That for thy right myself will bear all wrong.

4 barren tender paltry offering. **debt** payment **5 slept . . . report** been neglectful in writing praisingly of you **6 That** because **7 modern** commonplace **7–8 doth . . . grow** comes too short, in describing your worth, of the actual worth that flourishes in you **9–10 This . . . dumb** you imputed my silence to sinfulness when in fact it will prove most to my credit **11 being mute** (Modifies *I*.) **12 tomb** i.e., an inadequate monument that conceals lifelessly rather than enhancing

84 • 1 which who **3–4 In . . . grew** i.e., in whose person are contained all those rich qualities which would be needed as a model to produce again your equal in beauty **5–6 Lean . . . glory** i.e., it is a poor piece of writing indeed that does not confer at least some glory on its subject **8 so** sufficiently **11 counterpart** copy. **fame** endow with fame **13 curse** (1) defect in character (2) burden for those seeking to praise you **14 Being fond** doting. **which . . . worse** (1) which encourages false flattery (2) which makes all praises seem inadequate in comparison to you

85 • 1 in . . . still i.e., politely remains silent **2 comments . . . compil'd** eulogies composed in fine language **3 Reserve their character** preserve their features, writing (?) **4 fil'd** polished **5 other** others **6 unlettered clerk** illiterate assistant to a priest. **still cry "Amen"** i.e., continually give my approval **7 hymn** i.e., verse. **that able spirit** i.e., the rival poet **10 most** utmost **11 that . . . thought** i.e., that which I add is added silently **12 holds . . . before** considers its place to be before all others **13 Then . . . respect** then take notice of others for what they say **14 speaking in effect** i.e., which convey what speech would say

86 • 1 his i.e., an unidentified rival poet's **2 prize** capture, booty (as in a seized cargo vessel) **3 inhearse** coffin up **6 pitch** height. **dead** i.e., dumb, silent **7 compeers by night** spirits (see l. 5) visiting and aiding the poet in his dreams **8 astonished** struck dumb **9 ghost** spirit (as in ll. 5 and 7) **10 gulls** misleads. **intelligence** information, ideas **13 countenance fill'd up** (1) approval repaired any defect in (2) beauty served as subject for

87 • 1 dear precious **2 estimate** value **3 charter of** privilege derived from. **releasing** i.e., release from obligations of love **4 determinate** ended, expired. (A legal term, as throughout this sonnet.) **8 patent** charter granting rights of monopoly; hence, privilege. **swerving** returning **10 mistaking** i.e., overvaluing **11 upon misprision growing** arising out of error **12 on . . . making** on your forming a more accurate judgment

88 • 1 set me light make light of me, value me slightingly **3 Upon thy side** supporting your case (also *Upon thy part* in l. 6) **8 losing** i.e., separating from

89

Say that thou didst forsake me for some fault,
And I will comment upon that offense;
Speak of my lameness, and I straight will halt,
Against thy reasons making no defense.
Thou canst not, love, disgrace me half so ill,
To set a form upon desired change,
As I'll myself disgrace, knowing thy will.
I will acquaintance strangle and look strange,
Be absent from thy walks, and in my tongue
Thy sweet beloved name no more shall dwell,
Lest I, too much profane, should do it wrong
And haply of our old acquaintance tell.
   For thee against myself I'll vow debate,
   For I must ne'er love him whom thou dost hate.

90

Then hate me when thou wilt; if ever, now;
Now, while the world is bent my deeds to cross,
Join with the spite of fortune, make me bow,
And do not drop in for an after-loss.
Ah, do not, when my heart hath scap'd this sorrow,
Come in the rearward of a conquer'd woe;
Give not a windy night a rainy morrow,
To linger out a purpos'd overthrow.
If thou wilt leave me, do not leave me last,
When other petty griefs have done their spite,
But in the onset come; so shall I taste
At first the very worst of fortune's might,
   And other strains of woe, which now seem woe,
   Compar'd with loss of thee will not seem so.

91

Some glory in their birth, some in their skill,
Some in their wealth, some in their bodies' force,
Some in their garments, though newfangled ill,
Some in their hawks and hounds, some in their horse;
And every humor hath his adjunct pleasure,
Wherein it finds a joy above the rest.
But these particulars are not my measure;
All these I better in one general best.
Thy love is better than high birth to me,
Richer than wealth, prouder than garments' cost,
Of more delight than hawks or horses be;
And having thee, of all men's pride I boast,
   Wretched in this alone, that thou mayst take
   All this away and me most wretched make.

89 • 2 comment enlarge **3 Speak . . . halt** i.e., if you ascribe to me any kind of handicap, I immediately will limp to show that you are right **4 reasons** charges **6 To . . . change** to provide a pretext for (in the interest of justifying) your change of affection **7 As . . . disgrace** as I will disfigure and depreciate myself **8 acquaintance strangle** put an end to familiarity (with you). **strange** like a stranger **9 walks** haunts **12 haply** perchance **13 vow debate** declare hostility, quarrel

90 • 2 cross thwart **4 drop . . . after-loss** casually or unexpectedly add to my sorrow at some future time **5–6 when . . . woe** i.e., follow with an attack after I have overcome my present misfortune **8 linger out** protract. **purpos'd** intended, inevitable **13 strains** kinds

91 • 3 newfangled ill fashionably unattractive **4 horse** horses **5 humor** disposition, temperament. **his** its. **adjunct** corresponding **7 measure** standard (of happiness) **8 better** surpass, improve upon **12 of . . . boast** I boast of having the equivalent of all that is a source of pride in other men

92

But do thy worst to steal thyself away,
For term of life thou art assured mine,
And life no longer than thy love will stay,
For it depends upon that love of thine.
Then need I not to fear the worst of wrongs,
When in the least of them my life hath end;
I see a better state to me belongs
Than that which on thy humor doth depend.
Thou canst not vex me with inconstant mind,
Since that my life on thy revolt doth lie.
O, what a happy title do I find,
Happy to have thy love, happy to die!
   But what's so blessed-fair that fears no blot?
   Thou mayst be false, and yet I know it not.

93

So shall I live, supposing thou art true,
Like a deceived husband; so love's face
May still seem love to me, though alter'd new,
Thy looks with me, thy heart in other place.
For there can live no hatred in thine eye,
Therefore in that I cannot know thy change.
In many's looks the false heart's history
Is writ in moods and frowns and wrinkles strange,
But heaven in thy creation did decree
That in thy face sweet love should ever dwell;
Whate'er thy thoughts or thy heart's workings be,
Thy looks should nothing thence but sweetness tell.
   How like Eve's apple doth thy beauty grow,
   If thy sweet virtue answer not thy show!

94

They that have pow'r to hurt and will do none,
That do not do the thing they most do show,
Who, moving others, are themselves as stone,
Unmoved, cold, and to temptation slow,
They rightly do inherit heaven's graces
And husband nature's riches from expense;
They are the lords and owners of their faces,
Others but stewards of their excellence.
The summer's flow'r is to the summer sweet,
Though to itself it only live and die,
But if that flow'r with base infection meet,

92 • 2 term of life i.e., my lifetime **5–6 Then . . . end** i.e., I need not fear what most men would call the worst of misfortunes, since the seemingly lesser misfortune—loss of your friendship—would prove fatal to me **7–8 I see . . . depend** i.e., I see that I am happier than most men whose happiness ends when they are cast from favor, since my very existence will cease when I am cast from favor and thus end my misery **8 humor** whim, fancy **10 Since . . . lie** since if you desert me it will cost me my life **11 happy title** right to be thought happy **13 that fears** as to fear **14 Thou . . . not** i.e., my worst fate would be to lose your affection without knowing it, and thereby live on in an unloved state, unreleased by the death which certainty of your desertion would bring

93 • 1 So. (Continues the thought of Sonnet 92.) **supposing** I supposing (incorrectly) **2 face** appearance **8 moods** moody looks. **strange** unfriendly **14 answer . . . show** does not conform with your outward appearance

94 • 1 and . . . none i.e., and do not willfully try to do hurt **2 show** i.e., show themselves capable of; or, seem to do **4 cold** dispassionate **5 inherit** enjoy, make use of **6 husband** carefully manage, preserve. **expense** waste, expenditure **7 They . . . faces** i.e., they are completely masters of themselves and of the qualities that appear in them **8 stewards** dispensers **10 it only** alone it

The basest weed outbraves his dignity.
For sweetest things turn sourest by their deeds;
Lilies that fester smell far worse than weeds.

95

How sweet and lovely dost thou make the shame
Which, like a canker in the fragrant rose,
Doth spot the beauty of thy budding name!
O, in what sweets dost thou thy sins enclose!
That tongue that tells the story of thy days,
Making lascivious comments on thy sport,
Cannot dispraise but in a kind of praise,
Naming thy name, blesses an ill report.
O, what a mansion have those vices got
Which for their habitation chose out thee,
Where beauty's veil doth cover every blot,
And all things turns to fair that eyes can see!
Take heed, dear heart, of this large privilege;
The hardest knife ill us'd doth lose his edge.

96

Some say thy fault is youth, some wantonness;
Some say thy grace is youth and gentle sport;
Both grace and faults are lov'd of more and less;
Thou mak'st faults graces that to thee resort.
As on the finger of a throned queen
The basest jewel will be well esteem'd,
So are those errors that in thee are seen
To truths translated and for true things deem'd.
How many lambs might the stern wolf betray,
If like a lamb he could his looks translate!
How many gazers mightst thou lead away,
If thou wouldst use the strength of all thy state!
But do not so; I love thee in such sort
As, thou being mine, mine is thy good report.

97

How like a winter hath my absence been
From thee, the pleasure of the fleeting year!
What freezings have I felt, what dark days seen!
What old December's bareness everywhere!
And yet this time remov'd was summer's time,
The teeming autumn, big with rich increase,
Bearing the wanton burden of the prime,
Like widowed wombs after their lords' decease.
Yet this abundant issue seem'd to me
But hope of orphans and unfathered fruit,
For summer and his pleasures wait on thee,
And, thou away, the very birds are mute;
Or, if they sing, 'tis with so dull a cheer
That leaves look pale, dreading the winter's near.

98

From you have I been absent in the spring,
When proud-pied April dress'd in all his trim
Hath put a spirit of youth in everything,
That heavy Saturn laugh'd and leapt with him.
Yet nor the lays of birds nor the sweet smell
Of different flowers in odor and in hue
Could make me any summer's story tell,
Or from their proud lap pluck them where they grew;
Nor did I wonder at the lily's white,
Nor praise the deep vermilion in the rose;
They were but sweet, but figures of delight,
Drawn after you, you pattern of all those.
Yet seem'd it winter still, and, you away,
As with your shadow I with these did play.

99

The forward violet thus did I chide:
Sweet thief, whence didst thou steal thy sweet that smells,
If not from my love's breath? The purple pride
Which on thy soft cheek for complexion dwells
In my love's veins thou hast too grossly dy'd.
The lily I condemned for thy hand,
And buds of marjoram had stol'n thy hair;
The roses fearfully on thorns did stand,
One blushing shame, another white despair;
A third, nor red nor white, had stol'n of both
And to his robb'ry had annex'd thy breath,
But, for his theft, in pride of all his growth
A vengeful canker eat him up to death.
More flowers I noted, yet I none could see
But sweet or color it had stol'n from thee.

100

Where art thou, Muse, that thou forget'st so long
To speak of that which gives thee all thy might?
Spend'st thou thy fury on some worthless song,
Dark'ning thy pow'r to lend base subjects light?
Return, forgetful Muse, and straight redeem
In gentle numbers time so idly spent;
Sing to the ear that doth thy lays esteem
And gives thy pen both skill and argument.

12 outbraves his dignity surpasses in show its worth **14 Lilies . . . weeds** (This line appears in the anonymous play *Edward III*, usually dated before 1595 and attributed in part by some editors to Shakespeare.)

95 • 2 canker worm that destroys buds and leaves **3 name** reputation **6 sport** amours **14 his** its

96 • 1 wantonness amorousness **2 sport** amorousness **3 of more and less** by high and low **8 translated** transformed **9 stern** cruel **12 the strength . . . state** your full power and authority **13–14 But . . . report** (The same couplet ends Sonnet 36.)

97 • 5 time remov'd time of absence **6 big** pregnant **7 wanton . . . prime** the fruit or offspring of wanton spring, i.e., the crops planted in springtime **9 issue** offspring **10 hope of orphans** orphaned hope **11 his** its

98 • 2 proud-pied gorgeously multi-colored. **trim** finery **4 That** so that. **Saturn** (A planet associated with melancholy, *heavy*.) **5 nor the lays** neither the songs **6 different flowers** flowers differing **7 any summer's story** i.e., any pleasant story **8 proud lap** i.e., the earth **11 but sweet . . . delight** mere sweetness, mere delightful forms or emblems **14 shadow** portrait. **these** i.e., the flowers

99 • 1 forward early. (This sonnet has fifteen lines, the first being introductory.) **2 thy sweet** your scent **3 pride** splendor **5 grossly** obviously **6 for thy hand** i.e., because it has stolen its whiteness from your hand **7 buds of marjoram** (These are dark purple red or auburn, and it may be that the reference is to color, although marjoram is noted for its sweet scent.) **11 to . . . annex'd** to this robbery had added the robbery of **12 in pride . . . growth** in his prime **13 canker eat** cankerworm ate **15 sweet** scent (as in l. 2)

100 • 3 fury poetic inspiration **4 Dark'ning** debasing **5 straight** straightway **6 gentle numbers** noble verses **8 argument** subject

Rise, resty Muse, my love's sweet face survey,
If Time have any wrinkle graven there;
If any, be a satire to decay,
And make Time's spoils despised everywhere.
Give my love fame faster than Time wastes life;
So thou prevent'st his scythe and crooked knife.

101

O truant Muse, what shall be thy amends
For thy neglect of truth in beauty dy'd?
Both truth and beauty on my love depends;
So dost thou too, and therein dignified.
Make answer, Muse. Wilt thou not haply say,
"Truth needs no color with his color fix'd,
Beauty no pencil, beauty's truth to lay;
But best is best, if never intermix'd"?
Because he needs no praise, wilt thou be dumb?
Excuse not silence so, for 't lies in thee
To make him much outlive a gilded tomb,
And to be prais'd of ages yet to be.
Then do thy office, Muse; I teach thee how
To make him seem long hence as he shows now.

102

My love is strength'ned, though more weak in
seeming;
I love not less, though less the show appear;
That love is merchandiz'd whose rich esteeming
The owner's tongue doth publish everywhere.
Our love was new and then but in the spring
When I was wont to greet it with my lays,
As Philomel in summer's front doth sing
And stops her pipe in growth of riper days.
Not that the summer is less pleasant now
Than when her mournful hymns did hush the night,
But that wild music burdens every bough
And sweets grown common lose their dear delight.
Therefore like her I sometime hold my tongue,
Because I would not dull you with my song.

103

Alack, what poverty my Muse brings forth,
That, having such a scope to show her pride,
The argument all bare is of more worth
Than when it hath my added praise beside.
O, blame me not, if I no more can write!
Look in your glass, and there appears a face
That overgoes my blunt invention quite,
Dulling my lines and doing me disgrace.
Were it not sinful then, striving to mend,
To mar the subject that before was well?
For to no other pass my verses tend
Than of your graces and your gifts to tell;
And more, much more, than in my verse can sit
Your own glass shows you when you look in it.

104

To me, fair friend, you never can be old,
For, as you were when first your eye I ey'd,
Such seems your beauty still. Three winters cold
Have from the forests shook three summers' pride,
Three beauteous springs to yellow autumn turn'd
In process of the seasons have I seen,
Three April perfumes in three hot Junes burn'd,
Since first I saw you fresh, which yet are green.
Ah, yet doth beauty, like a dial hand,
Steal from his figure and no pace perceiv'd.
So your sweet hue, which methinks still doth stand,
Hath motion, and mine eye may be deceiv'd,
For fear of which, hear this, thou age unbred:
Ere you were born was beauty's summer dead.

105

Let not my love be call'd idolatry,
Nor my beloved as an idol show,
Since all alike my songs and praises be
To one, of one, still such, and ever so.
Kind is my love today, tomorrow kind,
Still constant in a wondrous excellence;
Therefore my verse, to constancy confin'd,
One thing expressing, leaves out difference.
"Fair, kind, and true" is all my argument,
"Fair, kind, and true" varying to other words;
And in this change is my invention spent,
Three themes in one, which wondrous scope affords.
"Fair, kind, and true," have often liv'd alone,
Which three till now never kept seat in one.

106

When in the chronicle of wasted time
I see descriptions of the fairest wights,
And beauty making beautiful old rhyme
In praise of ladies dead and lovely knights,
Then, in the blazon of sweet beauty's best,
Of hand, of foot, of lip, of eye, of brow,
I see their antique pen would have express'd
Even such a beauty as you master now.
So all their praises are but prophecies

9 **resty** inactive, inert 10 **If** to see if 11 **If any** if there are any. **satire** satirist, here one composing a satire on Time as a despoiler 14 **thou prevent'st** you forestall, thwart

101 • 5 **haply** perhaps 6 **no . . . fix'd** no artificial color (with suggestion of *pretense*) added to its natural and permanent color or hue 7 **pencil** paint brush. **lay** apply color to, as with a brush 8 **intermix'd** adulterated 12 **of** by 13 **office** function 14 **long hence** long in the future. **shows** appears

102 • 1 **seeming** outward appearance 3 **merchandiz'd** degraded by being treated as "a thing of sale." **esteeming** valuation 4 **publish** announce, advertise 7 **Philomel** the nightingale. **front** forehead, beginning 8 **riper** i.e., those of late summer and autumn 11 **But . . . music** i.e., but because a profusion of birds' singing. (Refers to other poets.) 14 **dull** surfeit

103 • 1 **poverty** poor stuff 2 **pride** splendor 3 **argument all bare** subject alone, unadorned 7 **overgoes** surpasses. **blunt invention** unpolished style, writing 8 **Dulling** i.e., making dull by comparison 11 **pass** purpose, issue 13 **sit** reside

104 • 4 **pride** splendor 6 **process** the progression 9 **dial hand** watch hand 10 **his figure** (1) the dial's numeral (2) the friend's shape. **and . . . perceiv'd** i.e., imperceptibly 11 **hue** appearance, complexion. **still doth stand** remains motionless, unaltered 13 **unbred** not yet born

105 • 4 **still** always 8 **difference** variety 11 **this change** variations on this theme. **spent** expended 13 **alone** separately 14 **kept seat** resided

106 • 1 **wasted** past 2 **wights** persons 5 **blazon** i.e., glorification, cataloguing of qualities. (A heraldic metaphor.) 8 **master** possess, control

Of this our time, all you prefiguring;
And, for they look'd but with divining eyes,
They had not skill enough your worth to sing.
For we, which now behold these present days,
Have eyes to wonder, but lack tongues to praise.

107

Not mine own fears, nor the prophetic soul
Of the wide world, dreaming on things to come,
Can yet the lease of my true love control,
Suppos'd as forfeit to a confin'd doom.
The mortal moon hath her eclipse endur'd
And the sad augurs mock their own presage;
Incertainties now crown themselves assur'd
And peace proclaims olives of endless age.
Now with the drops of this most balmy time
My love looks fresh, and Death to me subscribes,
Since, spite of him, I'll live in this poor rhyme,
While he insults o'er dull and speechless tribes;
And thou in this shalt find thy monument,
When tyrants' crests and tombs of brass are spent.

108

What's in the brain that ink may character
Which hath not figur'd to thee my true spirit?
What's new to speak, what now to register,
That may express my love or thy dear merit?
Nothing, sweet boy; but yet, like prayers divine,
I must each day say o'er the very same,
Counting no old thing old, thou mine, I thine,
Even as when first I hallowed thy fair name.
So that eternal love in love's fresh case
Weighs not the dust and injury of age,
Nor gives to necessary wrinkles place,
But makes antiquity for aye his page,
Finding the first conceit of love there bred
Where time and outward form would show it dead.

109

O, never say that I was false of heart,
Though absence seem'd my flame to qualify.
As easy might I from myself depart
As from my soul, which in thy breast doth lie.
That is my home of love; if I have rang'd,
Like him that travels I return again,
Just to the time, not with the time exchang'd,
So that myself bring water for my stain.
Never believe, though in my nature reign'd
All frailties that besiege all kinds of blood,
That it could so preposterously be stain'd
To leave for nothing all thy sum of good;
For nothing this wide universe I call,
Save thou, my rose; in it thou art my all.

110

Alas, 'tis true I have gone here and there
And made myself a motley to the view,
Gor'd mine own thoughts, sold cheap what is most dear,
Made old offenses of affections new;
Most true it is that I have look'd on truth
Askance and strangely. But, by all above,
These blenches gave my heart another youth,
And worse essays prov'd thee my best of love.
Now all is done, have what shall have no end.
Mine appetite I never more will grind
On newer proof, to try an older friend,
A god in love, to whom I am confin'd.
Then give me welcome, next my heaven the best,
Even to thy pure and most most loving breast.

111

O, for my sake do you with Fortune chide,
The guilty goddess of my harmful deeds,
That did not better for my life provide
Than public means which public manners breeds.
Thence comes it that my name receives a brand,
And almost thence my nature is subdu'd
To what it works in, like the dyer's hand.
Pity me then, and wish I were renew'd,
Whilst, like a willing patient, I will drink
Potions of eisel 'gainst my strong infection;
No bitterness that I will bitter think,
Nor double penance, to correct correction.
Pity me then, dear friend, and I assure ye
Even that your pity is enough to cure me.

112

Your love and pity doth th' impression fill
Which vulgar scandal stamp'd upon my brow;
For what care I who calls me well or ill,
So you o'ergreen my bad, my good allow?
You are my all the world, and I must strive

11 for because. **divining** guessing **13 For we** for even we **14 praise** i.e., praise sufficiently

107 • 3 lease term, allotted time **4 Suppos'd . . . doom** i.e., though imagined to be subject to a limited term **5 mortal moon** (Sometimes taken as a reference to Queen Elizabeth, ill or deceased; she was known as Diana, Cynthia, etc.) **6 And . . . presage** and the solemn prophets of disaster now mock their earlier predictions **7 Incertainties . . . assur'd** uncertainties have triumphantly given way to certainties **8 of endless age** i.e., without foreseen end **9 with the drops** i.e., healed as though by a balmy dew **10 subscribes** yields **12 insults** triumphs **14 crests** trophies in a tomb. **spent** expended, wasted away

108 • 1 character write **2 figur'd** revealed **3 register** record **7 Counting . . . thine** i.e., dismissing no old truth as out of date, such as the truths that you are mine and I yours **9 fresh case** new exterior **10 Weighs not** is unconcerned about **11 place** consideration, primacy **12 page** servant, subordinate **13 first . . . love** i.e., the first conception of love, experienced as though for the first time. **bred** generated

109 • 2 qualify temper, moderate **5 rang'd** traveled, wandered **7 Just** punctual. **exchang'd** changed

8 So . . . stain i.e., so that I myself provide the means of excusing my absence, of washing away the stain **10 blood** sensual nature **12 for** in exchange for

110 • 2 motley jester, fool **3 Gor'd** wounded **4 Made . . . new** i.e., made offense against old friendships in forming new attachments **5 truth** constancy **6 Askance and strangely** obliquely and at a distance **7 blenches** swervings **8 essays** experiments (in friendship) **9 have what . . . end** take what is eternal (my friendship) **10 grind** whet, sharpen **11 newer proof** further experiment, experience. **try** test **12 A god** godlike **13 next my heaven** i.e., second only to Heaven itself

111 • 2 guilty goddess goddess responsible for **3 life** livelihood **4 Than . . . breeds** i.e., than providing me a means of livelihood which depends on catering to the public. (A probable reference to Shakespeare's career as an actor.) **5 receives a brand** is disgraced (through prejudice against my occupation) **8 renew'd** restored to what I was by nature, cleansed **10 eisel** vinegar, used as an antiseptic against the plague **12 Nor . . . correction** i.e., no bitter cure will seem worse to me than the disease it corrects

112 • 1 th' impression fill efface the scar **2 vulgar scandal** i.e., notoriety (for being an actor?) **4 So you o'ergreen** provided that you cover as with green growth. **allow** approve

To know my shames and praises from your tongue;
None else to me, nor I to none alive,
That my steel'd sense or changes right or wrong.
In so profound abysm I throw all care
Of others' voices, that my adder's sense
To critic and to flatterer stopped are.
Mark how with my neglect I do dispense:
    You are so strongly in my purpose bred
    That all the world besides methinks are dead.

113

Since I left you, mine eye is in my mind,
And that which governs me to go about
Doth part his function and is partly blind,
Seems seeing, but effectually is out;
For it no form delivers to the heart
Of bird, of flow'r, or shape, which it doth latch;
Of his quick objects hath the mind no part,
Nor his own vision holds what it doth catch;
For if it see the rud'st or gentlest sight,
The most sweet favor or deformed'st creature,
The mountain or the sea, the day or night,
The crow or dove, it shapes them to your feature.
    Incapable of more, replete with you,
    My most true mind thus maketh mine eye untrue.

114

Or whether doth my mind, being crown'd with you,
Drink up the monarch's plague, this flattery?
Or whether shall I say mine eye saith true,
And that your love taught it this alchemy,
To make of monsters and things indigest
Such cherubins as your sweet self resemble,
Creating every bad a perfect best,
As fast as objects to his beams assemble?
O, 'tis the first, 'tis flatt'ry in my seeing,
And my great mind most kingly drinks it up;
Mine eye well knows what with his gust is 'greeing,
And to his palate doth prepare the cup.
    If it be poison'd, 'tis the lesser sin
    That mine eye loves it and doth first begin.

115

Those lines that I before have writ do lie,
Even those that said I could not love you dearer;
Yet then my judgment knew no reason why
My most full flame should afterwards burn clearer.
But reckoning Time, whose million'd accidents
Creep in 'twixt vows and change decrees of kings,
Tan sacred beauty, blunt the sharp'st intents,
Divert strong minds to th' course of alt'ring things,
Alas, why, fearing of Time's tyranny,
Might I not then say, "Now I love you best,"
When I was certain o'er incertainty,
Crowning the present, doubting of the rest?
    Love is a babe; then might I not say so,
    To give full growth to that which still doth grow.

116

Let me not to the marriage of true minds
Admit impediments. Love is not love
Which alters when it alteration finds,
Or bends with the remover to remove.
O, no, it is an ever-fixed mark
That looks on tempests and is never shaken;
It is the star to every wand'ring bark,
Whose worth's unknown, although his height be taken.
Love's not Time's fool, though rosy lips and cheeks
Within his bending sickle's compass come;
Love alters not with his brief hours and weeks,
But bears it out even to the edge of doom.
    If this be error and upon me proved,
    I never writ, nor no man ever loved.

117

Accuse me thus, that I have scanted all
Wherein I should your great deserts repay,
Forgot upon your dearest love to call,
Whereto all bonds do tie me day by day;
That I have frequent been with unknown minds
And given to time your own dear-purchas'd right;
That I have hoisted sail to all the winds
Which should transport me farthest from your sight.
Book both my willfulness and errors down
And on just proof surmise accumulate;
Bring me within the level of your frown,
But shoot not at me in your wakened hate;
    Since my appeal says I did strive to prove
    The constancy and virtue of your love.

118

Like as to make our appetites more keen,
With eager compounds we our palate urge,
As to prevent our maladies unseen,

7–8 None . . . wrong i.e., no one else but you affects my fixed and hardened sensibilities, whether for better or for worse **10 voices** i.e., criticism. **adder's sense** i.e., deaf ears **12 Mark . . . dispense** i.e., see how I excuse my disregard of the opinion of others **13 You . . . bred** i.e., you are such a powerful influence over my intentions

113 • 1 mine . . . mind i.e., I'm guided by my mind's eye **2 that . . . about** i.e., my physical sight **3 part** divide. **his** its, i.e., the physical eye's (also in ll. 7 and 8) **4 effectually** in reality **5 heart** i.e., mind **6 latch** catch or receive the sight of **7 quick** fleeting **8 Nor . . . holds** i.e., nor does the eye itself retain **10 favor** face **12 shapes . . . feature** makes them resemble you

114 • 1, 3 Or whether (Indicates alternative possibilities.) **1 crown'd with you** elevated by possession of you **4 alchemy** science of transmuting base metals **5 indigest** chaotic, formless **6 cherubins** angelic forms (suggesting the youth and beauty of the friend) **8 beams** gaze **11 what . . . 'greeing** what agrees with the mind's taste **13 'tis the lesser sin** is made less a sin by the fact **14 doth first begin** i.e., tastes of the poison first, like an official taster sampling food before it is given the king

115 • 6 'twixt vows i.e., between the making of vows and their fulfillment **7 Tan** darken, i.e., coarsen **9 fearing of** fearing **12 Crowning** glorifying. **doubting of** fearing **13 then** therefore. **so** i.e., "Now I love you best" (l. 10) **14 To give** thereby giving

116 • 4 Or . . . remove or inclines to inconstancy at the demand of the inconstant **5 mark** sea-mark, conspicuous object distinguishable at sea as an aid to navigation **8 Whose . . . taken** whose value is beyond estimation, although its altitude above the horizon can be determined (for purposes of navigation) **9 fool** plaything **10 his** i.e., Time's (also in l. 11) **12 bears . . . doom** endures or holds out to the very Day of Judgment

117 • 1 scanted come short in **5 frequent** familiar. **unknown minds** strangers of no consequence **6 given . . . right** squandered your rights in me on temporary matters and alliances **9 Book . . . down** record both my willful faults and errors **10 on . . . accumulate** to sure proof add surmise, suspicion **11 level** range, aim **13 appeal** legal appealing of the case. **I . . . prove** my intention was to test

118 • 1 Like as just as **2 eager** pungent, bitter **3 As** just as. **prevent** anticipate, forestall

We sicken to shun sickness when we purge,
Even so, being full of your ne'er-cloying sweetness,
To bitter sauces did I frame my feeding
And, sick of welfare, found a kind of meetness
To be diseas'd ere that there was true needing.
Thus policy in love, t' anticipate
The ills that were not, grew to faults assured,
And brought to medicine a healthful state
Which, rank of goodness, would by ill be cured.
But thence I learn, and find the lesson true,
Drugs poison him that so fell sick of you.

119

What potions have I drunk of Siren tears,
Distill'd from limbecks foul as hell within,
Applying fears to hopes and hopes to fears,
Still losing when I saw myself to win!
What wretched errors hath my heart committed,
Whilst it hath thought itself so blessed never!
How have mine eyes out of their spheres been fitted
In the distraction of this madding fever!
O benefit of ill! Now I find true
That better is by evil still made better;
And ruin'd love, when it is built anew,
Grows fairer than at first, more strong, far greater.
So I return rebuk'd to my content
And gain by ill thrice more than I have spent.

120

That you were once unkind befriends me now,
And for that sorrow which I then did feel
Needs must I under my transgression bow,
Unless my nerves were brass or hammered steel.
For if you were by my unkindness shaken
As I by yours, y' have pass'd a hell of time,
And I, a tyrant, have no leisure taken
To weigh how once I suffered in your crime.
O, that our night of woe might have rememb'red
My deepest sense, how hard true sorrow hits,
And soon to you, as you to me then, tend'red
The humble salve which wounded bosoms fits!
But that your trespass now becomes a fee;
Mine ransoms yours, and yours must ransom me.

121

'Tis better to be vile than vile esteemed,
When not to be receives reproach of being,
And the just pleasure lost which is so deemed
Not by our feeling but by others' seeing.
For why should others' false adulterate eyes
Give salutation to my sportive blood?
Or on my frailties why are frailer spies,
Which in their wills count bad what I think good?
No, I am that I am, and they that level
At my abuses reckon up their own.
I may be straight, though they themselves be bevel.
By their rank thoughts my deeds must not be shown,
Unless this general evil they maintain:
All men are bad, and in their badness reign.

122

Thy gift, thy tables, are within my brain
Full character'd with lasting memory,
Which shall above that idle rank remain
Beyond all date, even to eternity;
Or at the least, so long as brain and heart
Have faculty by nature to subsist,
Till each to raz'd oblivion yield his part
Of thee, thy record never can be miss'd.
That poor retention could not so much hold,
Nor need I tallies thy dear love to score;
Therefore to give them from me was I bold,
To trust those tables that receive thee more.
To keep an adjunct to remember thee
Were to import forgetfulness in me.

123

No, Time, thou shalt not boast that I do change.
Thy pyramids built up with newer might
To me are nothing novel, nothing strange;
They are but dressings of a former sight.
Our dates are brief, and therefore we admire
What thou dost foist upon us that is old,
And rather make them born to our desire
Than think that we before have heard them told.
Thy registers and thee I both defy,
Not wond'ring at the present nor the past,
For thy records and what we see doth lie,
Made more or less by thy continual haste.
This I do vow and this shall ever be:
I will be true, despite thy scythe and thee.

4 sicken . . . sickness induce a kind of sickness, purging (i.e., evacuation of stomach or bowel), in order to ward off greater sickness **6 bitter sauces** i.e., unpleasant people. **frame** adapt, direct **7 welfare** happiness (in love). **meetness** suitability **8 ere that** before **9 policy** calculation. **anticipate** forestall **10 assured** actual **11 brought to medicine** placed under medical care **12 rank of goodness** overfull of good health **14 so** thus

119 • 1 Siren tears deceitful tears of a seductive woman **2 limbecks** vessels used in distillation **3 Applying** i.e., as a medicine **4 Still** always. **saw myself** expected **7 How . . . fitted** how my eyes have popped out in convulsive fit **8 distraction** frenzy. **madding** maddening

120 • 1 befriends gives me friendly advice **2–3 for . . . bow** i.e., realizing the sorrow I felt from your unkindness, I must now give up my unkindness to you **4 nerves** sinews **7 have . . . taken** have not taken the opportunity **8 weigh** consider. **in your crime** i.e., from your unkindness **9 our night of woe** the dark and woeful time of our earlier estrangement. **rememb'red** reminded **11 tend'red** offered **12 humble salve** i.e., apology and remorse. **fits** befits **13 that your trespass** that unkindness of yours. **fee** payment, compensation **14 ransoms** redeems, excuses

121 • 1 vile esteemed (to be) considered vile **2 When . . . being** when not to be vile receives the reproach of vileness **3 just** legitimate, proper. **so deemed** deemed vile **4 Not . . . seeing** i.e., not in our own conscience but in the opinions of others **5 For why** why. **false adulterate** prurient **6 Give . . . blood** i.e., greet as an equal me, in my wanton merriment **7 Or . . . spies** or why should there be more faulty persons spying on my fleshly indulgences **8 in their wills** i.e., by the measure of their prurient, licentious minds **9 am that** am what. **level** aim **11 bevel** out of square, crooked **12 rank** ugly, foul. **shown** viewed, interpreted

122 • 1 tables writing tablet, memorandum book **2 character'd** written **3 that idle rank** i.e., the relative unimportance of that memorandum book (as compared with the memory itself) **6 faculty . . . subsist** natural power to survive **7 raz'd oblivion** obliterating forgetfulness. **his** its **8 miss'd** lost **9 retention** i.e., the book, an instrument for retaining memoranda **10 tallies** sticks notched to serve for reckoning. **score** reckon **11 to . . . me** i.e., to give away the writing tablet **12 those tables** i.e., those of memory **13 adjunct** aid **14 import** impute

123 • 2 pyramids (May refer to obelisks or other structures erected in Rome in 1586 or in London in 1603.) **3 nothing** not at all **4 dressings . . . sight** reconstructions in new form of things from the past **5 dates** life spans **7 make . . . desire** consider them newly created to our liking **8 told** reckoned, told about **9 registers** visual records, monuments **11 doth lie** deceive us **12 Made more or less** i.e., raised one minute and ruined the next (by Time)

124

If my dear love were but the child of state,
It might for Fortune's bastard be unfather'd,
As subject to Time's love or to Time's hate,
Weeds among weeds, or flowers with flowers gather'd.
No, it was builded far from accident;
It suffers not in smiling pomp, nor falls
Under the blow of thralled discontent,
Whereto th' inviting time our fashion calls.
It fears not Policy, that heretic,
Which works on leases of short-numb'red hours,
But all alone stands hugely politic,
That it nor grows with heat nor drowns with show'rs.
To this I witness call the fools of Time,
Which die for goodness, who have liv'd for crime.

125

Were 't aught to me I bore the canopy,
With my extern the outward honoring,
Or laid great bases for eternity,
Which proves more short than waste or ruining?
Have I not seen dwellers on form and favor
Lose all, and more, by paying too much rent,
For compound sweet forgoing simple savor,
Pitiful thrivers, in their gazing spent?
No, let me be obsequious in thy heart,
And take thou my oblation, poor but free,
Which is not mix'd with seconds, knows no art,
But mutual render, only me for thee.
Hence, thou suborn'd informer! A true soul
When most impeach'd stands least in thy control.

126

O thou, my lovely boy, who in thy power
Dost hold Time's fickle glass, his sickle, hour;
Who hast by waning grown, and therein show'st
Thy lovers withering as thy sweet self grow'st;
If Nature, sovereign mistress over wrack,
As thou goest onwards, still will pluck thee back,
She keeps thee to this purpose, that her skill
May Time disgrace and wretched minutes kill.
Yet fear her, O thou minion of her pleasure!
She may detain, but not still keep, her treasure.
Her audit, though delay'd, answer'd must be,
And her quietus is to render thee.

127

In the old age black was not counted fair,
Or if it were, it bore not beauty's name;
But now is black beauty's successive heir,
And beauty slander'd with a bastard shame.
For since each hand hath put on nature's power,
Fairing the foul with art's false borrow'd face,
Sweet beauty hath no name, no holy bower,
But is profan'd, if not lives in disgrace.
Therefore my mistress' eyes are raven black,
Her eyes so suited, and they mourners seem
At such who, not born fair, no beauty lack,
Sland'ring creation with a false esteem.
Yet so they mourn, becoming of their woe,
That every tongue says beauty should look so.

128

How oft, when thou, my music, music play'st
Upon that blessed wood whose motion sounds
With thy sweet fingers, when thou gently sway'st
The wiry concord that mine ear confounds,
Do I envy those jacks that nimble leap
To kiss the tender inward of thy hand,
Whilst my poor lips, which should that harvest reap,
At the wood's boldness by thee blushing stand!
To be so tickled, they would change their state
And situation with those dancing chips,
O'er whom thy fingers walk with gentle gait,
Making dead wood more blest than living lips.
Since saucy jacks so happy are in this,
Give them thy fingers, me thy lips to kiss.

129

Th' expense of spirit in a waste of shame
Is lust in action; and till action, lust
Is perjur'd, murd'rous, bloody, full of blame,
Savage, extreme, rude, cruel, not to trust,

124 • 1 love i.e., love for you. **but** merely. **child of state** results of (your) rank or power; or, of changing circumstance **2 for . . . unfather'd** i.e., be declared to have no father or source other than (your) good fortune **4 Weeds . . . gather'd** i.e., either despised as worthless like a weed or cherished like a flower, as Fortune dictates **5 accident** chance, fortune **7 thralled** enslaved, oppressed **8 Whereto . . . calls** i.e., to which the temptations of our present age expose all of us; or, which the age invites us to regard as fashionable **9 Policy, that heretic** cunning, false to the spirit of love **10 Which . . . hours** i.e., which thinks only shortsightedly of short term gain **11 hugely politic** i.e., prudent in a long-term sense **12 nor . . . heat** i.e., neither flourishes only in good times. **show'rs** i.e., adversity **13 witness call** call to witness. **fools** playthings. (See Sonnet 116.) **14 Which . . . crime** i.e., those who have lived evilly and then attempt to repent at their deaths or to die in a good cause

125 • 1 Were 't . . . canopy i.e., would it be anything to me if I did public homage as one honors great persons by carrying over their heads a cloth of state as they go in procession **2 With . . . honoring** honoring the external by means of external action **3 laid . . . eternity** laid foundations for supposedly lasting monuments **5 dwellers on** those who insist fulsomely upon (with pun on *tenants*) **6 by . . . rent** i.e., by overdoing their obligations to mere ceremony **7 For . . . savor** i.e., foregoing true love for the sake of obsequious flattery **8 Pitiful thrivers** i.e., those thriving only in pitiful or worthless gains. **in . . . spent** i.e., starved merely by ceremonial observance **9 obsequious** (1) courtly (2) devoted **10 oblation** offering **11 seconds** inferior parts. **art** artifice **12 render** exchange **13 suborn'd informer** perjured witness, the envious one who has charged the poet with self-interested flattery **14 impeach'd** accused

126 • 1 (This sonnet is made up of six couplets.) **2 glass** mirror. **hour** hourglass (? The line may be corrupt.) **3 by waning grown** grown more youthful as your age increases. **show'st** i.e., show by way of contrast with yourself **5 wrack** ruin. (Nature is mistress over decay because of her power of restoration.) **9 minion** darling **10 She . . . treasure** i.e., Nature may keep and restore you for a time, but Time will ultimately triumph. **still** always **11 Her audit** i.e., Nature's account to Time. **answer'd** settled **12 quietus** discharge, quittance. **render** surrender

127 • 1 old age olden times. **black** darkness of hair and eyes. **fair** (1) beautiful (2) light-complexioned **3 successive heir** lawful successor **4 beauty** i.e., blonde beauty. **slander'd . . . shame** i.e., declared illegitimate, created artificially by cosmetics **5 put on** assumed **6 Fairing the foul** making the ugly beautiful. **borrow'd face** i.e., cosmetics **9–10 eyes . . . eyes** (Some editors emend one or the other word to *hair* or *brows* to avoid the repetition.) **11 At** for. **no beauty lack** i.e., nonetheless make themselves attractive **12 Sland'ring . . . esteem** i.e., dishonoring nature by a false reputation for beauty **13 they** i.e., my mistress' eyes. **becoming of** gracing

128 • 2 wood keys of the spinet or virginal. **motion** mechanism **3 thou gently sway'st** you gently control **4 wiry concord** harmony produced by strings. **confounds** i.e., pleasurably overwhelms **5 jacks** (Literally, upright pieces of wood fixed to the key-lever and fitted with a quill which plucked the strings of the virginal; here used of the keys.) **8 by thee** with you **9 they** i.e., my lips **13 jacks** (with a pun on *knaves, fellows*)

129 • 1 Th' expense . . . shame the expenditure or dissipation of vital energy in shameful waste **2 action** consummation **4 rude** brutal. **to trust** to be trusted

Enjoy'd no sooner but despised straight,
Past reason hunted, and no sooner had
Past reason hated, as a swallowed bait
On purpose laid to make the taker mad;
Mad in pursuit and in possession so;
Had, having, and in quest to have, extreme;
A bliss in proof, and prov'd, a very woe;
Before, a joy propos'd; behind, a dream.
  All this the world well knows; yet none knows well
  To shun the heaven that leads men to this hell.

130

My mistress' eyes are nothing like the sun;
Coral is far more red than her lips' red;
If snow be white, why then her breasts are dun;
If hairs be wires, black wires grow on her head.
I have seen roses damask'd, red and white,
But no such roses see I in her cheeks;
And in some perfumes is there more delight
Than in the breath that from my mistress reeks.
I love to hear her speak, yet well I know
That music hath a far more pleasing sound.
I grant I never saw a goddess go;
My mistress, when she walks, treads on the ground.
  And yet, by heaven, I think my love as rare
  As any she belied with false compare.

131

Thou art as tyrannous, so as thou art,
As those whose beauties proudly make them cruel;
For well thou know'st to my dear doting heart
Thou art the fairest and most precious jewel.
Yet, in good faith, some say that thee behold
Thy face hath not the power to make love groan;
To say they err I dare not be so bold,
Although I swear it to myself alone.
And, to be sure that is not false I swear,
A thousand groans, but thinking on thy face,
One on another's neck, do witness bear
Thy black is fairest in my judgment's place.
  In nothing art thou black save in thy deeds,
  And thence this slander, as I think, proceeds.

132

Thine eyes I love, and they, as pitying me,
Knowing thy heart torments me with disdain,
Have put on black and loving mourners be,
Looking with pretty ruth upon my pain.
And truly not the morning sun of heaven
Better becomes the grey cheeks of th' east,
Nor that full star that ushers in the even
Doth half that glory to the sober west,
As those two mourning eyes become thy face.
O, let it then as well beseem thy heart
To mourn for me, since mourning doth thee grace,
And suit thy pity like in every part.
  Then will I swear beauty herself is black
  And all they foul that thy complexion lack.

133

Beshrew that heart that makes my heart to groan
For that deep wound it gives my friend and me!
Is 't not enough to torture me alone,
But slave to slavery my sweet'st friend must be?
Me from myself thy cruel eye hath taken,
And my next self thou harder hast engross'd;
Of him, myself, and thee, I am forsaken,
A torment thrice threefold thus to be crossed.
Prison my heart in thy steel bosom's ward,
But then my friend's heart let my poor heart bail;
Whoe'er keeps me, let my heart be his guard;
Thou canst not then use rigor in my jail.
  And yet thou wilt; for I, being pent in thee,
  Perforce am thine, and all that is in me.

134

So, now I have confess'd that he is thine,
And I myself am mortgag'd to thy will,
Myself I'll forfeit, so that other mine
Thou wilt restore, to be my comfort still.
But thou wilt not, nor he will not be free,
For thou art covetous and he is kind;
He learn'd but surety-like to write for me
Under that bond that him as fast doth bind.
The statute of thy beauty thou wilt take,
Thou usurer, that put'st forth all to use,
And sue a friend came debtor for my sake;
So him I lose through my unkind abuse.
  Him have I lost, thou hast both him and me;
  He pays the whole, and yet am I not free.

135

Whoever hath her wish, thou hast thy "Will,"
And "Will" to boot, and "Will" in overplus;
More than enough am I that vex thee still,
To thy sweet will making addition thus.

6 Past reason madly, intemperately **11 in proof** while experienced. **prov'd** i.e., afterwards

130 • 1 nothing not at all **3 dun** dull greyish brown, mouse-colored **5 damask'd** mingled red and white **8 reeks** issues as smell **11 go** walk **14 she** woman. **compare** comparison

131 • 1 so as thou art even as you are (dark, not considered handsome) **3 dear** fond **9 to be sure** as proof. **false I** false which I **10 but thinking on** when I do no more than think of **11 One . . . neck** one rapidly after another **12 black** dark complexion. **my judgment's place** i.e., my opinion **14 this slander** (See ll. 5–6.)

132 • 4 ruth pity **6 becomes** adorns **7 full star** the evening star, Venus. **even** evening **8 Doth** i.e., lends **9 mourning** (Spelled *morning* in Q, suggesting a pun on l. 5.) **10 beseem** suit **12 suit thy pity like** dress your pity alike. **in every part** i.e., heart as well as eyes

133 • 6 And . . . engross'd i.e., and you have put my dearest friend, my other self, under even greater restraint **8 crossed** thwarted, afflicted **9 steel bosom's ward** the prison cell of your hard heart **10 bail** set free by taking its place **11 keeps** has custody of. **his guard** my friend's guardhouse **12 rigor** harshness. **my jail** i.e., my heart, where my friend is kept **13 pent** shut up

134 • 2 will (1) wishes (2) fleshly desire **3 so . . . mine** provided that my other self, my friend **5 will not** does not wish to **7 surety-like** as security, as guarantor. **write** sign the bond, endorse (suggesting that the friend has taken the poet's place with the mistress) **8 that bond . . . bind** that bond (of sexual enslavement) that now binds him as securely as it does me **9 statute** a usurer's security or amount of money secured under his bond. **take** call in, invoke **10 use** (1) usury (2) sexual pleasure **11 came** i.e., who became **12 my unkind abuse** your unnatural ill-usage (of me) **14 pays** (with sexual suggestion)

135 • 1 Will (This and the following sonnet and Sonnet 143 ring changes on the word *will*—sexual desire, temper, passion, and the poet's name; possibly also the friend's name.) **3 still** continually

Wilt thou, whose will is large and spacious,
Not once vouchsafe to hide my will in thine?
Shall will in others seem right gracious,
And in my will no fair acceptance shine?
The sea, all water, yet receives rain still
And in abundance addeth to his store;
So thou, being rich in "Will," add to thy "Will"
One will of mine, to make thy large "Will" more.
Let no unkind, no fair beseechers kill;
Think all but one, and me in that one "Will."

136

If thy soul check thee that I come so near,
Swear to thy blind soul that I was thy "Will,"
And will, thy soul knows, is admitted there;
Thus far for love my love-suit, sweet, fulfill.
"Will" will fulfill the treasure of thy love,
Ay, fill it full with wills, and my will one.
In things of great receipt with ease we prove
Among a number one is reckon'd none.
Then in the number let me pass untold,
Though in thy stores' account I one must be;
For nothing hold me, so it please thee hold
That nothing me, a something, sweet, to thee.
Make but my name thy love, and love that still,
And then thou lovest me, for my name is "Will."

137

Thou blind fool, Love, what dost thou to mine eyes,
That they behold, and see not what they see?
They know what beauty is, see where it lies,
Yet what the best is take the worst to be.
If eyes corrupt by over-partial looks
Be anchor'd in the bay where all men ride,
Why of eyes' falsehood hast thou forged hooks,
Whereto the judgment of my heart is tied?
Why should my heart think that a several plot
Which my heart knows the wide world's common place?
Or mine eyes seeing this, say this is not,
To put fair truth upon so foul a face?
In things right true my heart and eyes have erred,
And to this false plague are they now transferred.

138

When my love swears that she is made of truth
I do believe her, though I know she lies,
That she might think me some untutor'd youth,
Unlearned in the world's false subtleties.
Thus vainly thinking that she thinks me young,
Although she knows my days are past the best,
Simply I credit her false-speaking tongue;
On both sides thus is simple truth suppress'd.
But wherefore says she not she is unjust?
And wherefore say not I that I am old?
O, love's best habit is in seeming trust,
And age in love loves not to have years told.
Therefore I lie with her, and she with me,
And in our faults by lies we flattered be.

139

O, call not me to justify the wrong
That thy unkindness lays upon my heart;
Wound me not with thine eye but with thy tongue;
Use power with power and slay me not by art.
Tell me thou lov'st elsewhere, but in my sight,
Dear heart, forbear to glance thine eye aside;
What need'st thou wound with cunning when thy might
Is more than my o'erpress'd defense can bide?
Let me excuse thee. Ah, my love well knows
Her pretty looks have been mine enemies,
And therefore from my face she turns my foes,
That they elsewhere might dart their injuries.
Yet do not so; but since I am near slain,
Kill me outright with looks and rid my pain.

140

Be wise as thou art cruel; do not press
My tongue-tied patience with too much disdain,
Lest sorrow lend me words, and words express
The manner of my pity-wanting pain.
If I might teach thee wit, better it were,
Though not to love, yet, love, to tell me so,
As testy sick men, when their deaths be near,
No news but health from their physicians know.
For if I should despair, I should grow mad,
And in my madness might speak ill of thee;
Now this ill-wresting world is grown so bad,
Mad slanderers by mad ears believed be.
That I may not be so, nor thou belied,
Bear thine eyes straight, though thy proud heart go wide.

6 hide . . . thine (with sexual suggestion) **10 his** its **13 Let . . . kill** let no unkind word kill any who seek your favors

136 • 1 check rebuke. **come so near** i.e., come so near the truth about you (in my previous sonnet) **2 blind** unperceptive **4 fulfill** grant **5 fulfill the treasure** fill full the treasury (with sexual suggestion) **6 one** one of them **7 receipt** capacity (suggesting her profligacy) **8 one . . . none** (A variant of the common saying "one is no number.") **9 untold** uncounted **10 in . . . account** in your (huge) inventory (of lovers) **11–12 For . . . thee** i.e., consider me too insignificant to think of, provided that you vouchsafe to hold insignificant me to you, my sweet, thereby making me something of worth **13 my name** i.e., "will," that is, desire. **still** continually

137 • 3 lies resides **4 Yet . . . be** yet take the worst for the best **5 corrupt by over-partial** corrupted by doting **6 Be . . . ride** have brought me to anchor in a bay used by everyone (with sexual suggestion of a wanton woman) **7 Why . . . hooks** why have you, Love, fashioned snares out of my eyes' delusion **9 think . . . plot** think that to be a private field, i.e., that woman to be the exclusive property of one man **10 knows** knows to be. **common** open, promiscuous **11 Or** i.e., or why should. **not** not so **14 false plague** (1) plague of judging falsely (2) false woman

138 • 1 (A version of this sonnet appears in *The Passionate Pilgrim*.) **2 believe** i.e., pretend to believe **5 vainly thinking** acting as though I thought **7 Simply** pretending to be foolish. **credit** give credence to **9 unjust** unfaithful **11 habit** demeanor (with, however, a suggestion of *garb,* i.e., something put on). **seeming trust** apparent fidelity **12 told** counted **13 lie with** deceive (with sexual pun)

139 • 1 call ask. **justify** i.e., condone something actually taking place under my eyes **2 unkindness** i.e., the mistress' flagrant infidelity **3 with thine eye** i.e., with a roving eye. (See ll. 5–6.) **4 with power** i.e., candidly, directly. **art** artifice, cunning **8 bide** abide, withstand **11 foes** i.e., the "pretty looks" or wanton glances of l. 10 **14 rid** end. *(Rid my pain* suggests *satiate my craving.)*

140 • 4 The manner . . . pain the nature of my pain, on which you bestow no pity **5 wit** wisdom, prudence **6 Though . . . so** even though you don't love me, yet, love, to tell me that you do **8 know** i.e., hear **11 ill-wresting** misinterpreting in an evil sense **13 so** i.e., a *mad slanderer* **14 wide** astray

141

In faith, I do not love thee with mine eyes,
For they in thee a thousand errors note;
But 'tis my heart that loves what they despise,
Who in despite of view is pleas'd to dote.
Nor are mine ears with thy tongue's tune delighted,
Nor tender feeling to base touches prone,
Nor taste, nor smell, desire to be invited
To any sensual feast with thee alone.
But my five wits nor my five senses can
Dissuade one foolish heart from serving thee,
Who leaves unsway'd the likeness of a man,
Thy proud heart's slave and vassal wretch to be.
    Only my plague thus far I count my gain,
    That she that makes me sin awards me pain.

142

Love is my sin and thy dear virtue hate,
Hate of my sin, grounded on sinful loving.
O, but with mine compare thou thine own state,
And thou shalt find it merits not reproving;
Or, if it do, not from those lips of thine,
That have profan'd their scarlet ornaments
And seal'd false bonds of love as oft as mine,
Robb'd others' beds' revenues of their rents.
Be it lawful I love thee, as thou lov'st those
Whom thine eyes woo as mine importune thee.
Root pity in thy heart, that when it grows
Thy pity may deserve to pitied be.
    If thou dost seek to have what thou dost hide,
    By self-example mayst thou be denied.

143

Lo, as a careful huswife runs to catch
One of her feathered creatures broke away,
Sets down her babe and makes all swift dispatch
In pursuit of the thing she would have stay,
Whilst her neglected child holds her in chase,
Cries to catch her whose busy care is bent
To follow that which flies before her face,
Not prizing her poor infant's discontent;
So runn'st thou after that which flies from thee,
Whilst I, thy babe, chase thee afar behind;
But if thou catch thy hope, turn back to me,
And play the mother's part, kiss me, be kind.
    So will I pray that thou mayst have thy "Will,"
    If thou turn back, and my loud crying still.

141 • 4 Who . . . view which (i.e., the heart), in spite of what the eyes see **6 Nor . . . prone** nor (is) my delicate sense of touch inclined toward sensual contact (with you) **9 my five wits** (neither) my five intellectual senses, i.e., the common sense, imagination, fancy, judgment, and memory **11 Who . . . man** i.e., my heart, which abandons the proper government of my person, leaving me the mere likeness of a man **13 thus far** to the following extent **14 That . . . pain** i.e., that the sin brings with it its own punishment and contrition (with a suggestion in *pain* of *sexual pleasure;* see Sonnet 139)

142 • 1–2 Love . . . loving i.e., my sin is to love you, and your noblest virtue is to hate that sin in me, the sin of loving you. (The bitter paradox here is that hatred of sin must be virtue.) **4 it** i.e., my state **6–7 That . . . mine** i.e., that have foresworn themselves in love as often as my lips. (The *scarlet ornaments* are lips and also red wax used to seal documents.) **8 Robb'd . . . rents** i.e., and committed adultery with other women's husbands **9–10 Be . . . thee** i.e., I am as justified in loving you and imploring you with my eyes as you are in pursuing other men. (*Be it lawful* is a legal phrase meaning *let it be considered lawful that.*) **12 deserve** make you deserving **13 what . . . hide** what you withhold, i.e., pity

143 • 13 Will (See Sonnets, 135, 136.) **14 still** hush, make quiet

144

Two loves I have of comfort and despair,
Which like two spirits do suggest me still:
The better angel is a man right fair,
The worser spirit a woman color'd ill.
To win me soon to hell, my female evil
Tempteth my better angel from my side,
And would corrupt my saint to be a devil,
Wooing his purity with her foul pride.
And whether that my angel be turn'd fiend
Suspect I may, yet not directly tell;
But being both from me, both to each friend,
I guess one angel in another's hell.
    Yet this shall I ne'er know, but live in doubt,
    Till my bad angel fire my good one out.

145

Those lips that Love's own hand did make
Breath'd forth the sound that said "I hate"
To me that languish'd for her sake;
But when she saw my woeful state,
Straight in her heart did mercy come,
Chiding that tongue that ever sweet
Was us'd in giving gentle doom,
And taught it thus anew to greet:
"I hate" she alter'd with an end,
That follow'd it as gentle day
Doth follow night, who like a fiend
From heaven to hell is flown away.
    "I hate" from hate away she threw,
    And sav'd my life, saying "not you."

146

Poor soul, the center of my sinful earth,
Thrall to these rebel pow'rs that thee array,
Why dost thou pine within and suffer dearth,
Painting thy outward walls so costly gay?
Why so large cost, having so short a lease,
Dost thou upon thy fading mansion spend?
Shall worms, inheritors of this excess,
Eat up thy charge? Is this thy body's end?
Then, soul, live thou upon thy servant's loss,
And let that pine to aggravate thy store;
Buy terms divine in selling hours of dross;
Within be fed, without be rich no more.
    So shalt thou feed on Death, that feeds on men,
    And, Death once dead, there's no more dying
        then.

144 • 1 (This sonnet appears, somewhat altered, in *The Passionate Pilgrim.*) **2 suggest** urge, offer counsel. **still** continually **4 ill** i.e., dark of complexion **11 from me** away from me. (The poet suspects they are together.) **both . . . friend** friends to each other **12 I . . . hell** I suspect that she (the evil angel) has him in her power (i.e., her sexual embracement) **14 fire . . . out** drive out my good angel (perhaps with the suggestion of *communicate a venereal disease*)

145 • 7 doom judgment, sentence. (This sonnet is in eight-syllable meter.)

146 • 1 sinful earth body **2 Thrall to** (One of several conjectures; Q repeats "My sinfull earth" from l. 1.) **rebel pow'rs** i.e., rebellious flesh. **array** dress, clothe **6 mansion** dwelling, i.e., the body **8 thy charge** that on which you have expended so much **9 thy servant's** i.e., the body's **10 that . . . store** the body starve to increase your riches **11 Buy . . . dross** i.e., purchase eternal life in return for giving up (selling) mere hours of wasteful pleasure

147

My love is as a fever, longing still
For that which longer nurseth the disease,
Feeding on that which doth preserve the ill,
Th' uncertain sickly appetite to please.
My reason, the physician to my love,
Angry that his prescriptions are not kept,
Hath left me, and I desperate now approve
Desire is death, which physic did except.
Past cure I am, now reason is past care,
And frantic-mad with evermore unrest;
My thoughts and my discourse as madmen's are,
At random from the truth vainly express'd;
For I have sworn thee fair and thought thee bright,
Who art as black as hell, as dark as night.

148

O me, what eyes hath Love put in my head,
Which have no correspondence with true sight,
Or, if they have, where is my judgment fled,
That censures falsely what they see aright?
If that be fair whereon my false eyes dote,
What means the world to say it is not so?
If it be not, then love doth well denote
Love's eye is not so true as all men's "No."
How can it? O, how can Love's eye be true,
That is so vex'd with watching and with tears?
No marvel then, though I mistake my view;
The sun itself sees not till heaven clears.
O cunning Love, with tears thou keep'st me blind,
Lest eyes well-seeing thy foul faults should find.

149

Canst thou, O cruel, say I love thee not,
When I against myself with thee partake?
Do I not think on thee, when I forgot
Am of myself, all tyrant for thy sake?
Who hateth thee that I do call my friend?
On whom frown'st thou that I do fawn upon?
Nay, if thou lour'st on me, do I not spend
Revenge upon myself with present moan?
What merit do I in myself respect,
That is so proud thy service to despise,
When all my best doth worship thy defect,
Commanded by the motion of thine eyes?
But, love, hate on, for now I know thy mind;
Those that can see thou lov'st, and I am blind.

150

O, from what pow'r hast thou this pow'rful might
With insufficiency my heart to sway?
To make me give the lie to my true sight,
And swear that brightness doth not grace the day?
Whence hast thou this becoming of things ill,
That in the very refuse of thy deeds
There is such strength and warrantise of skill
That, in my mind, thy worst all best exceeds?
Who taught thee how to make me love thee more,
The more I hear and see just cause of hate?
O, though I love what others do abhor,
With others thou shouldst not abhor my state.
If thy unworthiness rais'd love in me,
More worthy I to be belov'd of thee.

151

Love is too young to know what conscience is;
Yet who knows not conscience is born of love?
Then, gentle cheater, urge not my amiss,
Lest guilty of my faults thy sweet self prove.
For, thou betraying me, I do betray
My nobler part to my gross body's treason;
My soul doth tell my body that he may
Triumph in love; flesh stays no farther reason,
But, rising at thy name, doth point out thee
As his triumphant prize. Proud of this pride,
He is contented thy poor drudge to be,
To stand in thy affairs, fall by thy side.
No want of conscience hold it that I call
Her "love" for whose dear love I rise and fall.

152

In loving thee thou know'st I am forsworn,
But thou art twice forsworn, to me love swearing;
In act thy bed-vow broke, and new faith torn
In vowing new hate after new love bearing.
But why of two oaths' breach do I accuse thee,
When I break twenty? I am perjur'd most,
For all my vows are oaths but to misuse thee,
And all my honest faith in thee is lost;
For I have sworn deep oaths of thy deep kindness,
Oaths of thy love, thy truth, thy constancy,
And, to enlighten thee, gave eyes to blindness,
Or made them swear against the thing they see;
For I have sworn thee fair. More perjur'd eye,
To swear against the truth so foul a lie!

147 • 1 **still** always 7 **approve** demonstrate, show by experience that 8 **Desire . . . except** (that) desire, which rejected the advice of medicine, proves fatal 9 **care** medical care. (The line is an adaptation of the proverb, "things past cure are past care.")

148 • 4 **censures** judges 7 **denote** indicate 8 **eye** (with a pun on *ay*) 10 **watching** remaining awake 11 **mistake my view** err in what I see

149 • 2 **partake** take part (against myself) 3–4 **when . . . tyrant** when I am neglectful of, or oblivious of, myself and my best interests because I am self-tyrannized by love 8 **present moan** immediate suffering 9 **respect** value 10 **thy . . . despise** as to think it demeaning to serve you 11 **defect** insufficiency 14 **Those . . . blind** i.e., with the perversity of a proud woman you scorn one who loves you in defiance of reason, and are drawn instead to those who see your faults. (The paradox of the last couplet appears to be that the speaker wishes her to hate him since that hatred demonstrates the strength of his blind passion.)

150 • 2 **With insufficiency** with all your shortcomings. **sway** rule 4 **And . . . day** i.e., and swear that what is so is not so 5 **becoming . . . ill** i.e., ability to show ill things in a becoming light 6 **in . . . deeds** in the most debased of your actions 7 **warrantise of skill** warrant or pledge of competence 12 **state** i.e., condition of being helplessly in love

151 • 1 **too young** (Love is personified as the young Cupid.) 3 **amiss** sin 6 **nobler part** i.e., soul 8 **stays** awaits. **reason** reasoning, talk 9 **rising** (with bawdy suggestion, continued in *point, Proud, stand, fall*) 10 **Proud of** swelling with

152 • 1 **forsworn** i.e., faithless to my marriage vows 3 **bed-vow** marriage vows 3–4 **new . . . bearing** i.e., a new contract of fidelity is torn up by your swearing hatred toward me to whom you have only recently professed love 7 **but to misuse** merely to misrepresent; or, deceive 11 **And . . . blindness** i.e., and, to invest you with brightness, I made my eyes testify to things they did not see 13 **eye** (with a pun on *I*)

153

Cupid laid by his brand, and fell asleep.
A maid of Dian's this advantage found,
And his love-kindling fire did quickly steep
In a cold valley-fountain of that ground;
Which borrow'd from this holy fire of Love
A dateless lively heat, still to endure,
And grew a seething bath, which yet men prove
Against strange maladies a sovereign cure.
But at my mistress' eye Love's brand new-fired,
The boy for trial needs would touch my breast;
I, sick withal, the help of bath desired,
And thither hied, a sad distemper'd guest,
But found no cure. The bath for my help lies
Where Cupid got new fire—my mistress' eyes.

154

The little Love-god lying once asleep
Laid by his side his heart-inflaming brand,
Whilst many nymphs that vow'd chaste life to keep
Came tripping by; but in her maiden hand
The fairest votary took up that fire
Which many legions of true hearts had warm'd,
And so the general of hot desire
Was sleeping by a virgin hand disarm'd.
This brand she quenched in a cool well by,
Which from Love's fire took heat perpetual,
Growing a bath and healthful remedy
For men diseas'd; but I, my mistress' thrall,
Came there for cure, and this by that I prove:
Love's fire heats water, water cools not love.

153 • 1 (This sonnet and the following seemingly have no direct connection with those preceding. They are adaptations of epigrams in the *Palatine Anthology*, Greek poems of the fifth century translated into Latin in the sixteenth century.) **brand** torch **2 Dian** Diana, goddess of chastity **4 of that ground** i.e., nearby **6 dateless** endless, eternal. **still** always **7 seething bath** spring of hot medicinal waters. **yet** even today **10 for trial** by way of test **12 distemper'd** sick. (The bath is suggestive of the sweating cure for venereal disease.)

154 • 7 general cause and commander, i.e., Cupid **11 Growing** becoming **12 thrall** slave, bondman **13 this** i.e., the following proposition. **that** i.e., my coming, which failed to cure me

APPENDIX 1

Canon, Dates, and Early Texts

By "canon" we mean a listing of plays that can be ascribed to Shakespeare on the basis of reliable evidence. Such evidence is either "internal," derived from matters of style or poetics in the plays themselves (see General Introduction), or "external," derived from outside the play. The latter includes any reference by Shakespeare's contemporaries to his plays, any allusions in the plays themselves to contemporary events, the entering of Shakespeare's plays for publication in the Stationers' Register (S. R.), actual publication of the plays, and records of early performances. These matters of external evidence are also essential in attempting to date the plays.

The greatest single source of information is the First Folio text of Shakespeare's plays, sponsored by Shakespeare's fellow-actors John Heminges and Henry Condell and published in 1623. It contains all the plays included in this present edition of Shakespeare except *Pericles,* and offers strong presumptive evidence of being a complete and accurate compilation of Shakespeare's work by men who knew him and cherished his memory. It provides the only texts we have for these eighteen plays: *The Comedy of Errors, The Two Gentlemen of Verona, The Taming of the Shrew, I Henry VI, King John, As You Like It, Twelfth Night, Julius Caesar, All's Well that Ends Well, Measure for Measure, Timon of Athens, Macbeth, Antony and Cleopatra, Coriolanus, Cymbeline, The Winter's Tale, The Tempest,* and *Henry VIII.* This includes nearly half the known canon of Shakespeare's plays. Our debt to the First Folio is incalculable, and confirms our impression of its reliability.

The information of the First Folio is further confirmed by contemporary references. In 1598, a cleric and minor writer of the period named Francis Meres wrote in his *Palladis Tamia:*

> As the soule of *Euphorbus* was thought to liue in *Pythagoras:* so the sweete wittie soule of *Ouid* liues in mellifluous & hony-tongued *Shakespeare,* witnes his *Venus* and *Adonis,* his *Lucrece,* his sugred Sonnets among his priuate friends, &c.
>
> As *Plautus* and *Seneca* are accounted the best for Comedy and Tragedy among the Latines: so *Shakespeare* among the English is the most excellent in both kinds for the stage; for Comedy, witness his *Gentlemen of Verona,* his *Errors,* his *Loue labors lost,* his *Loue labours wonne,* his *Midsummers night dreame,* & his *Merchant of Venice:* for Tragedy his *Richard the* 2. *Richard* the 3. *Henry the* 4. *King Iohn, Titus Andronicus* and his *Romeo* and *Iuliet.*

Though this list was meant to offer praise, not to be an exhaustive catalogue, it is remarkably full. If the tantalizing *Loue labours wonne* refers to *The Taming of the Shrew,* Meres' list of comedies is entirely complete down to 1598. Naturally the list does not include the great "festive" comedies, *Much Ado about Nothing, As You Like It,* and *Twelfth Night,* since these were written at or slightly later than the time of Meres' comment. Meres correctly names all of Shakespeare's history plays except the *Henry VI* trilogy and of course the later histories, *Henry V* (1599) and *Henry VIII* (1613). He names both of Shakespeare's early tragedies not based on English history: *Titus Andronicus* and *Romeo and Juliet.* He tells us about the important nondramatic poems, which did not appear in the First Folio since that volume is devoted exclusively to plays. Not much can be made of the order in which Meres names the plays, however, for we learn from other sources that *Richard III* clearly precedes *Richard II* in date of composition and *King John* precedes the *Henry IV* plays.

Other writers of the 1590's add further confirming evidence. John Weever, in an epigram *"Ad Gulielmum Shakespeare,"* published in 1599, refers to "Rose-checkt *Adonis*" and "Faire fire-hot *Venus,*" to "Chaste *Lucretia*" and "Prowd lust-stung *Tarquine,*" and to "*Romea Richard,* more whose names I know not." Richard Barnfield, in *Poems in Divers Humors* (1598), praises Shakespeare for *"Venus"* and *"Lucrece."* Both Thomas Nashe and Robert Greene seemingly refer to the *Henry VI* plays, missing from Meres' list. Nashe, in his *Pierce Penilesse* (1592), speculates how it would "have ioyed braue *Talbot* (the terror of the French) to thinke that after he had lyne two hundred yeares in his Tombe, hee should triumphe againe on the Stage." Talbot is the hero of *1 Henry VI,* and we know of no other play on the subject. Greene, in his *Greenes Groats-worth of Wit* (1592), lashes out at an "vpstart Crow, beautified with our feathers, that with his *Tygers hart wrapt in a Players hyde,* supposes he is as well able to bombast out a blanke verse as the best of you: and beeing an absolute *Iohannes fac totum,* is in his owne conceit the onely Shake-scene in a countrey." The line about "Tygers hart" is deliberately misquoted from *3 Henry VI,* I,iv,137. (It is possible that this famous attack on Shakespeare was actually written not by Greene himself but by Henry Chettle, his literary executor.)

The Comedy of Errors (c. 1589–1593)

The earliest known edition of *The Comedy of Errors* is in the First Folio of 1623. It is first mentioned, however, on Innocents Day, December 28, 1594, when a "Comedy of Errors (like to *Plautus* his *Menechmus*)" was performed by professional actors as part of the Christmas Revels at Gray's

Inn. The evening's festivities are set down in *Gesta Grayorum,* a contemporary account of the revels, though not published until 1688. According to this record, the evening was marred by such tumult and disorder that the invited guests from the Inner Temple refused to stay; thereafter, the night became known as "The Night of Errors." References to sorcery and enchantment in the play leave little doubt that it was Shakespeare's.

Scholars generally agree that the play was not newly written for this occasion. Internally, the play seems early: its characterization is slight, for example, and its punning wit reminds us of *Love's Labor's Lost* and *The Two Gentlemen of Verona.* Topical clues are suggestive but not conclusive. Chief of these is the joke about France being "arm'd and reverted, making war against her heir" (III,ii). Unquestionably this refers to France's civil wars between Henry of Navarre and his Catholic opposition. Since Henry became a Catholic and the King of France in 1593, most scholars prefer a date before 1593. Peter Alexander (*Shakespeare's Life and Art,* 1961) has even argued for a date prior to 1589, since Henry III died in that year leaving Henry of Navarre as nominal king rather than heir. The sad truth is that we probably cannot attach too much weight to either conclusion. Allusions to the French civil wars during the early 1590's were common but also imprecise; the joke would have seemed relevant at almost any time up to 1595. The same is probably true of the allusion to Spain's sending "whole armadoes of carracks" (III,ii). This is often taken to refer to the Spanish Armada, 1588, but may instead refer to the Portuguese *Madre de Dios* captured and brought to England in 1592 or to a similar venture. In short, it is virtually impossible to prove that *The Comedy of Errors* precedes *Love's Labor's Lost, The Two Gentlemen of Verona,* or *The Taming of the Shrew.*

A lost play called *The Historie of Error* was acted before the Queen by the Children of Paul's at Hampton Court on New Year's night, 1577. About this play we know nothing other than its suggestive title, and speculation that Shakespeare may have adapted it has been generally abandoned.

The Folio text, based probably on Shakespeare's own manuscript, is generally a good text although characters' names are frequently confused in the stage directions and speech prefixes.

Love's Labor's Lost (c. 1588–1589, revised 1596–1597?)

Love's Labor's Lost first appeared in a quarto dated 1598, without entry in the Stationers' Register. Its title page reads:

> *A* PLEASANT Conceited Comedie CALLED, Loues labors lost. As it vvas presented before her Highnes this last Christmas. Newly corrected and augmented *By W. Shakespere.* Imprinted at London by *W. W.* [William White] for *Cutbert Burby.*1598.

Because the phrase "newly corrected and augmented" also appears on the title page of the good quarto of *Romeo and Juliet,* issued in 1599 to correct a pirated quarto of 1597, many scholars suspect that *Love's Labor's Lost* may similarly have appeared in a bad quarto that is now lost. Such a circumstance would explain why the existing quarto of *Love's Labor's Lost* was not registered: if the play had already been published, even in a pirated version, relicensing would have been unnecessary. (The *Romeo and Juliet* good quarto was not registered for this reason.)

The text shows clear signs of revision. Two long passages (IV,iii,296–304 and 318–351; V,ii,828–832 and 851–864) give duplicatory readings of the same speeches, suggesting the printer mistakenly copied both the canceled version in his copy and the revision. Speech headings are unusually confused, sometimes referring to characters by their personal names (Navarre, Armado, Holofernes) and at other times by their generic titles (King, Braggart, Pedant). Some of these errors, notably the long uncanceled passages, suggest that the printer (perhaps new and relatively inexperienced) was copying from Shakespeare's working draft or foul papers. Whether Shakespeare wrote this draft on one occasion or whether he revised an earlier version is, however, a matter on which scholars disagree. The Folio text was set from the quarto, and thus gives us no additional information as to when or in what stages the play was written.

Francis Meres refers to the play in October of 1598. The performance before Queen Elizabeth "last Christmas" was probably in late 1597. Robert Tofte tells us in his *Alba* (1598) that "Loues Labour Lost, I once did see a Play Ycleped so." His phrasing suggests a performance seen some time in the past, although he could mean that he saw it only once. Apart from these allusions, dating of the play must rely on its presumed internal allusions to contemporary events. Unfortunately, the play has attracted a lot of highly speculative topical hypotheses. One such describes a "School of Night" to which Sir Walter Ralegh, Matthew Roydon, George Chapman, and others are supposed to have belonged. No objective evidence exists to prove the existence of such a school. Ralegh was tried for atheism but acquitted. Other topical hypotheses are discussed briefly in the Introduction to the play. Some allusions to the historical King of Navarre and to his supporters, the Duc de Biron and the Duc de Longueville, are undeniable. These allusions tend to argue for an early date (c. 1588–1589) when these persons had not yet become the chief figures in a bloody religious civil war in France and hence inappropriate subjects for light comedy. The influence of John Lyly and the children's drama also argues for an early date. If, on the other hand, the Muscovite masque in V,ii contains a reference to the Gray's Inn revels of 1594, as several scholars have urged, some portions of the play may be from after that date. The hypothesis that Shakespeare revived an old play of his shortly before publication in 1598, although not universally accepted, offers at least a plausible explanation of the phrase "newly corrected and augmented" on the title page.

The Two Gentlemen of Verona (c. 1590–1594)

The Two Gentlemen of Verona was not published until the First Folio of 1623. Other than Francis Meres' listing of it in 1598, evidence as to dating is scarce. No convincing allusions to contemporary events have been found. From the internal evidence of style, most scholars prefer an early date, though some believe that the play was composed in various stages. (Numerous factual inconsistencies in the text lend support to this theory.) The influence of John Lyly is still perceptible in the play's overly ingenious wit-combat.

An unusual feature of the text, its grouping of characters' names at the beginning of each scene, seems to indicate that the manuscript was copied at some point by the scrivener Ralph Crane, probably from a theatre prompt-book.

The Taming of the Shrew (c. 1592–1594)

The Taming of the Shrew was not printed until the First Folio of 1623. Francis Meres does not mention the play in 1598, unless it is the mysterious *"Loue labours wonne"* on his list. (Meres is not totally accurate, for he omits *Henry VI* from the history plays.) The play must have existed prior to 1598, however, for its style is comparable with that of *The Two Gentlemen* and other early comedies. Moreover, a play called *The Taming of A Shrew* appeared in print in 1594 (S. R. May 1594). Although the relationship of that text to Shakespeare's play has been hotly debated, the prevailing view today is that it represents an imitation by some rival dramatist, who relied chiefly on his memory and who changed characters' names and the location to make the play seem his. Or it may be simply a bad quarto put together by memorial reconstruction. In either case, Shakespeare's play would have to be dated earlier than May 1594.

The title page of *A Shrew* proclaims that "it was sundry times acted by the *Right honorable the Earle of* Pembrook his seruants." Quite possibly this derivative version was merely trying to capitalize on the original's stage success, and was in fact describing performances of Shakespeare's play. Henslowe's record of a performance of *"the Tamynge of A Shrowe"* in 1594 at Newington Butts, a mile south of London Bridge, may also refer to Shakespeare's play; certainly the minute distinction between "A Shrew" and "The Shrew" is one that the official records of the time would overlook. The Admiral's men and the Lord Chamberlain's men were playing at Newington Butts at the time, either jointly or alternatingly. Since Shakespeare's company, the Chamberlain's, later owned *The Shrew,* they may well have owned and acted it on this occasion in 1594, having obtained it from the Earl of Pembroke's men when that company disbanded in 1593. Many of Pembroke's leading players joined the Chamberlain's, Shakespeare quite possibly among them. (The possibility that he came to the Chamberlain's from Lord Strange's men seems less certain today than it once did.) It is entirely possible, then, that *The Shrew* was acted by Pembroke's men in 1592–1593 and subsequently passed along to the Chamberlain's.

The Folio text of this play is now generally thought to have been printed from Shakespeare's working manuscript.

A Midsummer Night's Dream (c. 1594–1595)

A Midsummer Night's Dream was entered on the Stationers' Register by Thomas Fisher on October 8, 1600, and printed by him that same year in quarto:

A Midsommer nights dreame. As it hath beene sundry times pub*lickely acted, by the Right honoura*ble, the Lord Chamberlaine his *seruants. Written by William Shakespeare.* Imprinted at London, for *Thomas Fisher,* and are to be soulde at his shoppe, at the Signe of the White Hart, in *Fleetestreete.* 1600.

This text appears to have been set up from Shakespeare's working manuscript. Its inconsistencies in time scheme and other irregularities may reflect some revision, although the inconsistencies are not noticeable in performance. A second quarto appeared in 1619, though falsely dated 1600; it was a reprint of the first quarto, with some minor corrections and many new errors. A copy of this second quarto, evidently with some added stage directions and other minor changes from a theatrical manuscript in the company's possession, served as the basis for the Folio text of 1623. Essentially, the first quarto remains the authoritative text.

Other than Francis Meres' listing of the play in 1598, external clues as to date are elusive. The description of unruly weather (II,i) has been related to the bad summer of 1594, but complaints about the weather are perennial. On the assumption that the play celebrates some noble wedding of the period, scholars have come up with a number of suitable marriages. Chief are those of Sir Thomas Heneage to Mary, Countess of Southampton, in 1594, of William Stanley, Earl of Derby, to Elizabeth Vere, daughter of the Earl of Oxford, in 1595, and of Thomas, son of Lord Berkeley, to Elizabeth, daughter of Lord Carey, in 1596. The Countess of Southampton was the widowed mother of the young Earl of Southampton, to whom Shakespeare had dedicated his *Venus and Adonis* and *The Rape of Lucrece.* No one has ever proved convincingly, however, that the play was written for any occasion other than commercial public performance. The play makes sense for a general audience, and does not need to depend on references to a private marriage. Shakespeare was, after all, in the business of writing plays for his fellow actors, who earned their livelihood chiefly by public acting before large paying audiences. In any event the search for a court marriage is a circular argument in terms of dating; suitable court marriages can be found for any year of the decade. In the last analysis, the play has to be dated on the basis of its stylistic affinity to plays like *Romeo and Juliet* and *Richard II,* works of the "lyric" mid 1590's. The "Pyramus and Thisbe" performance in *A Midsummer Night's Dream* would seem to bear an obvious relation to *Romeo and Juliet,* although no one can say for sure which came first.

The Merchant of Venice (1594–1598)

The Stationers' Register for July 22, 1598, contains an entry on behalf of the printer James Roberts for "a booke of the Marchaunt of Venyce, or otherwise called the Jewe of Venyce, Prouided, that yt bee not prynted by the said James Robertes or anye other whatsoeuer without lycence first had from the Right honorable the lord Chamberlen." Roberts evidently enjoyed a close connection with the Chamberlain's men, and seemingly was granted the special favor of registering the play at this time even though the company did not wish to see the play published until later. In 1600, at any rate, Roberts transferred his rights as publisher to Thomas Heyes and printed the volume for him with the following title:

> The most excellent Historie of the *Merchant of Venice.* VVith the extreame crueltie of *Shylocke* the Iewe towards the sayd Merchant, in cutting a iust pound of his flesh: and the obtayning of *Portia* by the choyse of three chests. *As it hath beene diuers times acted by the Lord Chamberlaine his Seruants.* Written by William Shakespeare. AT LONDON, Printed by *I. R.* [James Roberts] for Thomas Heyes, and are to be sold in Paules Church-yard, at the signe of the Greene Dragon. 1600.

This 1600 text is generally a good one, based seemingly on the author's papers. It served as copy for the second quarto of 1619 (printed by William Jaggard for Thomas Pavier, and fraudulently dated 1600), and for the Folio of 1623.

Francis Meres mentions the play in 1598. Establishing an earlier limit for dating has proven not so easy. Many scholars have urged a connection with the Roderigo Lopez affair of 1594 (see Introduction, above). The supposed allusion to Lopez in the lines about "a wolf, who, hang'd for human slaughter" (IV,i,134) may simply indicate, however, that wolves were actually hanged for attacking men in Shakespeare's day (as dogs were for killing sheep). Besides, the Lopez case remained so notorious throughout the 1590's that even a proven allusion to it in *The Merchant* would not limit the play to 1594 or 1595. Marlowe's *The Jew of Malta* was revived in 1594 to exploit anti-Lopez sentiment, but was also revived in 1596. There may, on the other hand, be an allusion in I,i,27 to the *St. Andrew,* a Spanish ship captured at Cadiz in 1596. Any date between 1594 and early 1598 is possible, though the latter half of this period is more likely.

Much Ado about Nothing (1598–1599)

"The Commedie of muche A doo about nothing a booke" was entered in the Stationers' Register on August 4, 1600, along with *As You Like It, Henry V,* and Ben Jonson's *Every Man in His Humor,* all marked as plays of "My lord chamberlens men" and all "to be staied"—that is, not published without further permission. Earlier in the same memorandum, written on a spare page in the Register, occurs the name of the printer James Roberts, whose registration of *The Merchant of Venice* in 1598 was similarly stayed pending further permission to publish. Evidently the Chamberlain's men were attempting to prevent unauthorized publication of these very popular plays. They were too late to forestall the appearance of a bad quarto of *Henry V* in August of 1600, but they did manage to control release of the others. *Much Ado about Nothing* appeared later that same year in a seemingly authorized version:

> Much adoe about Nothing. *As it hath been sundrie times publikely* acted by the right honourable, the Lord Chamberlaine his seruants. *Written by William Shakespeare.* LONDON Printed by V. S. [Valentine Sims] for Andrew Wise, and William Aspley. 1600.

Once thought to have been set up from a theatrical prompt-book, and then used itself in the theatre as a prompt-book before serving as copy for the Folio version, this 1600 quarto text is now generally regarded as having been set from Shakespeare's own foul papers. The names of the actors Will Kempe and Richard Cowley appear among the speech prefixes in IV,ii, indicating that an actual stage production was very close at hand, but other irregularities in speech prefixes and scene headings read more like a manuscript in the last stages of revision than a prompt-book for a finished production. The Folio text was based on the 1600 quarto.

Francis Meres does not mention the play in September of 1598, unless (and this seems unlikely) it is his *"Loue labours wonne."* Will Kempe, who played Dogberry, left the Chamberlain's men in 1599. The likeliest date, then, is the winter of 1598–1599, though publication was not until 1600.

The Merry Wives of Windsor (1597–1601)

The Stationers' Register for January 18, 1602, carries an entry for "A booke called an excellent and pleasant conceited commedie of Sir John Faulstof and the merry wyves of Windesor," by assignment from John Busby to Arthur Johnson. Later that year, Thomas Creed printed the following quarto:

> A Most pleasaunt and excellent conceited Comedie, of Syr *Iohn Falstaffe,* and the merrie Wiues of *Windsor.* Entermixed with sundrie variable and pleasing humors, of Syr *Hugh* the Welch Knight, Iustice *Shallow,* and his wise Cousin M. *Slender.* With the swaggering vaine of Auncient *Pistoll,* and Corporall *Nym.* By *William Shakespeare.* As it hath bene diuers times Acted by the right Honorable my Lord Chamberlaines seruants. Both before her Maiestie, and else-where. LONDON Printed by T. C. [Thomas Creed] for Arthur Iohnson, and are to be sold at his shop in

Powles Church-yard, at the signe of the Flower de Leuse and the Crowne. 1602.

This text is now generally regarded as a bad quarto, memorially reconstructed perhaps by the actors who played the Host and Falstaff, and then shortened for touring in the provinces. A second quarto in 1619, printed by William Jaggard for Thomas Pavier, was based on it. The Folio text of 1623, however, was taken from a manuscript evidently copied by Ralph Crane (hence the "massed entries" of characters' names at the beginnings of scenes), and based ultimately on a theatrical prompt-book. It is the most authoritative text. Several interesting variant readings occur in the bad quarto, despite its unreliability, and seem to indicate original readings that were altered in the Folio version for reasons of prudence. We find "garmombles" in place of the Folio "germans" at IV,v,74, and "Brook" in place of the Folio "Broome" throughout as the disguise name for the jealous Ford. "Garmombles" is often interpreted as an unflattering allusion to Frederick, Count Mompelgard (see Introduction). "Brook" is a seeming dig at the family name of the powerful Henry Brooke, eighth Lord Cobham, whose intervention probably led to the similar changing of "Oldcastle" to "Falstaff" in *Henry IV.*

On dating, two irreconcilable choices are still very much alive: 1597, when the Lord Chamberlain was elected to the Order of the Garter, and 1600–1601, after *Henry V* (1599) in which Nym had been introduced. The S. R. entry in January of 1602 provides a forward limit in time. See more on the Order of the Garter in the Introduction.

As You Like It (1598–1600)

"As you like yt, a booke" was entered in the Stationers' Register on August 4, 1600, along with *Much Ado about Nothing, Henry V,* and Jonson's *Every Man in His Humor,* all labeled as "My lord chamberlens mens plaies" and all ordered "to be staied" from publication until further notice. Evidently the Chamberlain's men were anxious to protect their rights to these very popular plays. Despite their efforts *Henry V* was pirated that same month. *As You Like It* did not appear in print, however, until the Folio of 1623. The Folio text is a good one, based seemingly on a theatrical prompt-book or a transcript of one.

Francis Meres does not mention the play in September of 1598. The play contains an unusually clear allusion to Marlowe's *Hero and Leander* ("Who ever lov'd that lov'd not at first sight?" III,v,82), first published in 1598. Almost certainly *As You Like It* was written between 1598 and the summer of 1600, either before or after *Much Ado about Nothing.*

Twelfth Night (1600–1602)

Twelfth Night was registered in 1623 and first published in the Folio of that year, in a good text set up from a theatre prompt-book or possibly a transcript of it. The play was first mentioned, however, on Candlemas Day, February 2, 1602, in the following entry from the *Diary* of a Middle Temple law student or barrister named John Manningham:

> At our feast wee had a play called "Twelue Night, or What you Will," much like the Commedy of Errores, or Menechmi in Plautus, but most like and neere to that in Italian called *Inganni.* A good practise in it to make the Steward beleeve his Lady widdowe was in love with him, by counterfeyting a letter as from his Lady in generall termes, telling him what shee liked best in him, and prescribing his gesture in smiling, his apparaile, & c., and then when he came to practise making him beleeue they tooke him to be mad.

This entry was once suspected to be a forgery of John Payne Collier, who published the *Diary* in 1831, but its authenticity is now generally accepted. The date accords with several possible allusions in the play itself. When Fabian jokes about "a pension of thousands to be paid from the Sophy" (II,v,177), he seems to be recalling Sir Anthony Shirley's reception by the Shah of Persia (the Sophy) in 1599–1600. An account of this visit was entered in the S. R. in November of 1601. Viola's description of Feste as "wise enough to play the fool" (III,i,60) may recall a poem beginning "True it is, he plays the fool indeed" published in 1600–1601 by Robert Armin (who played the role of Feste). Maria's comparison of Malvolio's smiling face to "the new map with the augmentation of the Indies" (III,ii,85) refers to new maps of about 1600 in which America (the Indies) was increased in size. Leslie Hotson (*The First Night of Twelfth Night,* 1954) has argued for a first performance at court on Twelfth Night in January of 1601, when Queen Elizabeth entertained Don Virginio Orsino, Duke of Bracciano, but this hypothesis has not gained general acceptance partly because the role of Orsino in the play would scarcely flatter such a noble visitor and partly because there is no proof that any of Shakespeare's plays were originally commissioned for private performance. Nevertheless, a date between 1600 and early 1602 seems most likely. Francis Meres does not mention the play in 1598.

All's Well that Ends Well (c. 1601–1604)

All's Well that Ends Well was first registered in November of 1623 and published in the Folio of that same year. The text contains numerous inconsistencies and vague stage directions indicating an early stage of the author's working papers, but these errors are not as extensive as once thought and the text is basically sound. Information on the date of the play is sparse. Francis Meres does not mention it in 1598 unless it is the intriguing *Loue labours wonne* on his list. Its themes and style are more suggestive of the period of *Hamlet* and the "problem" plays, *Measure for Measure* and *Troilus and Cressida.* The common assumption today is that the play was written some time around 1601–1604. The role of Lavatch is clearly designed for

Robert Armin, who did not join Shakespeare's company until 1599. Scholars once argued that *All's Well* is an early play later revised, but this means of explaining the inconsistencies in the text no longer seems necessary.

Measure for Measure (1603–1604)

Measure for Measure first appeared in the Folio of 1623. The text was evidently set from Ralph Crane's copy of Shakespeare's own draft; the usual inconsistencies of composition have not yet been smoothed away by use in the theatre. The first recorded performance was on December 26, 1604, St. Stephen's Night, when "a play Caled Mesur for Mesur" by "Shaxberd" was acted in the banqueting hall at Whitehall "by his Maiesties plaiers." Shakespeare's company, previously the Lord Chamberlain's men, had become the King's men after the accession to the throne of James I in 1603.

Several allusions in the play seem to point to the summer of 1604, when the theatres, having been closed for a year because of the plague, were reopened. A reference to the King of Hungary (I,ii) may reflect anxieties in England over James' negotiations for a settlement with Spain; censorship would forbid a direct mentioning of Spain. Mistress Overdone's complaint about the war, the "sweat" (plague), the "gallows" (public executions), and poverty (I,ii) are all suggestive of events in 1603–1604, when war with Spain and the plague were still very much in evidence. Duke Vincentio's reticent habits have been seen as a flattering reference to James' well-known dislike of crowds. Stylistically the play is clearly later than *Twelfth Night* (1600–1602), so that a date close to the first recorded performance in 1604 is a necessity even if we cannot be positive about all the supposed allusions to King James.

Troilus and Cressida (c. 1601–1602)

The textual history of *Troilus and Cressida* is complicated. On February 7, 1603, James Roberts entered on the Stationers' Register, "when he hath gotten sufficient aucthority for yt, The booke of Troilus and Cresseda as yt is acted by my lord Chamberlens Men." On January 28, 1609, however, a new entry appeared on the Register as though the first had never been made: "Richard Bonion Henry Walleys. Entred for their Copy vnder thandes of Master Segar deputy to Sir George Bucke and master warden Lownes a booke called the history of Troylus and Cressida." Later that year appeared the first quarto with the following title:

> THE Historie of Troylus and Cresseida. *As it was acted by the Kings Maiesties* seruants at the Globe.
> *Written by* William Shakespeare. LONDON Imprinted by *G. Eld* for *R Bonian* and *H. Walley,* and are to be sold at the spred
> Eagle in Paules Church-yeard, ouer against the great North doore.
> 1609.

Before the first printing had sold out, still in 1609, the title leaf A1 was replaced by two new leaves containing a new title and an epistle. The title reads:

> THE Famous Historie of Troylus *and* Cresseid. *Excellently expressing the beginning* of their loues, with the conceited wooing of *Pandarus* Prince of *Licia. Written by* William Shakespeare.

The epistle is addressed "A neuer writer, to an euer reader. Newes," and begins, "Eternall reader, you haue heere a new play, neuer stal'd with the Stage, neuer clapper-clawd with the palmes of the vulger, and yet passing full of the palme comicall."

The Folio editors originally intended *Troilus and Cressida* to follow *Romeo and Juliet.* After three pages had been set up in this position, however, the play was removed (perhaps owing to copyright difficulties) and *Timon of Athens* inserted instead. Later, *Troilus* was placed between the Histories and the Tragedies, almost entirely without pagination. See Play Introduction, above, for some possible explanations of the unusual publishing history.

The quarto text was evidently set from a transcript of Shakespeare's foul papers, made either by Shakespeare himself or by a scribe. The first three pages of the Folio text, those originally intended to follow *Romeo and Juliet,* were set from the first quarto. The remaining pages, however, seem to have been based on the quarto after it had been collated with a manuscript source (probably the author's draft). As a result both the quarto and Folio texts have independent textual authority. Most recent editors, however, use the quarto version as their copy text, especially since the quarto version may represent Shakespeare's revision of the play whereas the Folio returns to the earlier stage of the author's draft.

The possibility that the play may not have been publicly performed, and the failure of Shakespeare's company to provide the sequel promised at the end of *Troilus,* suggest that the play was written not long before the first Stationers' Register entry of February 1603. Certainly the play was not an old favorite in the company's repertoire. Failure as a stage play might have led to an attempt at quick publication, aimed at sophisticated readers. The current fad for satire would also have provided a motive for prompt publication. Stylistically, *Troilus* belongs to the period of *Hamlet* (c. 1599–1601). A seeming allusion in the Prologue of *Troilus* to the "arm'd" Prologue of Jonson's *Poetaster* (1601) helps set a probable early limit for date of composition. Chapman's *The Seaven Bookes of Homers Iliads,* a source of information about the Trojan war, had appeared in 1598.

The Henry the Sixth Plays (c. 1589–1592)

Shortened versions of *2* and *3 Henry VI* appeared in 1594 and 1595. One was titled as follows:

THE First part of the Contention betwixt the two famous Houses of Yorke and Lancaster, with the death of the good Duke Humphrey: And the banishment and death of the Duke of *Suffolke,* and the Tragicall end of the proud Cardinall of *VVinchester,* vvith the notable Rebellion of *Iacke Cade: And the Duke of Yorkes first claime vnto the Crowne.* LONDON Printed by Thomas Creed, for Thomas Millington, and are to be sold at his shop vnder Saint Peters Church in Cornwall. 1594.

Its sequel was titled as follows:

The true Tragedie of Richard *Duke of Yorke, and the death of* good King Henrie the Sixt, *with the whole contention betweene* the two Houses Lancaster and Yorke, as it was sundrie times acted by the Right Honourable the Earle of Pembrooke his seruants. Printed at London by P. S. [Peter Short] for Thomas *Millington, and are to be sold at his shoppe vnder Saint Peters Church in Cornwal.* 1595.

Once thought to be source plays for Shakespeare's *2* and *3 Henry VI,* these texts, the first a quarto and the second an octavo, have been demonstrated by Peter Alexander and Madeleine Doran to be "bad quartos" or memorial reconstructions of Shakespeare's texts, put together by actors for sale to a printer or for acting in the provinces. As such, they have little textual authority. In 1619 they were combined in a reprint by William Jaggard called *The Whole Contention betweene the two Famous Houses, Lancaster and Yorke.* These texts are considerably shorter than the Folio versions of 1623, which appeared there under the titles "The second Part of Henry the Sixt, with the death of the Good Duke HVMFREY," and "The third Part of Henry the Sixt, with the death of the Duke of YORKE." The Folio texts seem to have been based on authorial manuscripts, although it has been argued that both plays were printed from pages of the second and third quartos of each play as corrected by reference to a theatrical manuscript in the author's own handwriting (in the case of *2 Henry VI*) or to a scribal transcript of Shakespeare's manuscript to which a prompter had added his annotations (in the case of *3 Henry VI*).

The text of *1 Henry VI,* based seemingly on an authorial manuscript that had been annotated in the theatre and possibly recopied, was first published in the Folio of 1623. It alone of the three parts was registered for publication at this time. The Stationers' Register entry refers to this play as "The thirde parte of Henry the sixt." These circumstances once led to the assumption that *1 Henry VI* was written after the other two plays, especially since those two plays do not often recall events of *1 Henry VI*—for example, they make no mention of its hero, Lord Talbot. The seeming fact that the 1594 and 1595 quartos were pirated editions would, however, explain their publication before *1 Henry VI* and the necessity of registering Part I later. In other ways, *1 Henry VI* has shown itself to be no hasty afterthought, but a play with thematic unity throughout and a sense of direction anticipating the remainder of the series. Hence, scholars now tend to support Dr. Johnson's commonsense hunch that the three plays in this historical tetralogy were written in order.

Scholars also generally agree now that the entire series is Shakespeare's own work, or at the very least dominated by his artistic conception of the whole. The once-prevailing hypotheses of multiple authorship, though not forgotten, rest on questionable internal evidence such as vocabulary or versification. What sounds like Greene or Peele in these very early plays may simply be the result of those men's undoubted influence on Shakespeare during his apprenticeship. Greene's famous diatribe at Shakespeare (see below) suggests that he was keenly aware of Shakespeare's facility for learning quickly from his contemporaries. The inconsistencies in these early plays, especially in Part I—mislineation, defective verse, inaccuracy in speech prefixes, confusion about time, discrepancy in facts—may be the result not of multiple authorship but of reliance on various sources, hasty composition, and problems of transcription.

Several contemporary allusions to the *Henry VI* plays help considerably with dating the series. Thomas Nashe wrote in his *Pierce Penilesse* (registered August 1592) that it would "have ioyed braue *Talbot* (the terror of the French) to thinke that after he had lyne two hundred yeares in his Tombe, hee should triumphe againe on the Stage." Probably he was referring to Shakespeare's play. The reference in Henslowe's diary to a "ne" (new?) performance of *Harey the vi* in March of 1592 may or may not refer to Shakespeare's work, however, for this performance was by Lord Strange's men whereas Shakespeare's *Henry VI* series is associated elsewhere with Pembroke's men. In any event, *3 Henry VI* must have been completed by the time of Robert Greene's death in September of 1592, when Greene (or his literary executor, Chettle) alludes plainly to it (I,iv,137) in his angry remark about "an vpstart Crow, beautified with our feathers, that with his *Tygers hart wrapt in a Players hyde,* supposes he is as well able to bombast out a blanke verse as the best of you." These contemporary references are confirmed by allusions in the texts themselves, for all the *Henry VI* plays seem to contain echoes of Books I–III of Spenser's *Faerie Queene* (printed 1590), whereas *3 Henry VI* seems to have influenced parts of *The Troublesome Raigne of King John* (printed 1591). An inclusive date of 1589–1591 or 1592 ought to account for the entire series.

Richard the Third (c. *1591–1594*)

A quarto edition of *Richard III,* registered by Andrew Wise on October 20, 1597, appeared later that same year with the following title:

THE TRAGEDY OF King Richard the third. Containing, His treacherous Plots against his brother Clarence: the pittiefull murther of his iunocent nephewes: his tyrannicall vsurpation: with the whole course of his detested life, and most deserued death. As it hath beene lately Acted by the Right honourable the Lord

Chamberlaine his seruants. AT LONDON Printed by Valentine Sims, for Andrew Wise, dwelling in Paules Chu[r]ch-yard, at the Signe of the Angell. 1597.

This text, one of the most perplexing in all Shakespeare, was once thought to be an authentic text set up either from a prompter's copy or from the author's foul papers. Today it is generally regarded as a memorial reconstruction of a peculiar kind, one in which the entire acting company banded together to reconstruct a play of which the only copy had apparently been lost. This quarto was reprinted in 1598, 1602, 1605, 1612, 1622, 1629, and 1634, each reprint successively more error-laden than the previous one. The Folio text of 1623 seems to have been set mainly from a copy of the sixth quarto (1622) which had been sporadically corrected against an independent manuscript—possibly Shakespeare's own manuscript or a copy of it. Parts of the Folio text, however, were set from an uncorrected copy of the third quarto (1602), and for those passages (III,i,1–158 and V,iii,48 to end of play) the first quarto must serve as copy-text. Otherwise, the Folio text is the most authoritative, though it must be approached with caution.

The play is mentioned by Francis Meres in 1598. John Weever names a *"Richard"* in his *Epigrammes,* published in 1599. Most scholars date *Richard III* 1592–1594, on the basis of its style and its close affinity to the *Henry VI* series (completed probably in 1591). The play may have been influenced by the anonymous *The True Tragedy of Richard III,* registered in June 1594, but probably written in 1590–1592 or even earlier. Shakespeare's play may also have been influenced by Kyd's *The Spanish Tragedy* (c. 1587) and by Marlowe's dramas (he died in 1593).

King John (c. 1594–1595)

The Life and Death of King John, as it is called in the original text, first appeared in the Folio of 1623. That text appears to have been set up from Shakespeare's foul papers, which may have been corrected with reference to a prompt-book (especially in the final two acts). Apart from Meres' listing of the play in 1598, dating clues are scarce. Editors have suggested dates ranging from 1590 to 1598, and have proposed topical allusions to bolster their various arguments. The consensus today is that *King John* was probably written shortly before or after *Richard II* in about 1594–1595, or 1596. Many editors assume that Shakespeare would have preferred to write this historically independent play in the interim between his two four-play series *(Henry VI* through *Richard III* and *Richard II* through *Henry V),* rather than interrupt the flow of composition on either of those series. This suggestion is scarcely provable, however. In any case, the link between *Richard II* and *1 Henry IV* is not so close as to preclude interruption.

A major critic of the consensus view is E. A. J. Honigmann, editor of the Arden *King John* (1954), who argues for a date in 1590 preceding the publication in 1591 of *The Troublesome Raigne of King John* (which he regards as a bad quarto). This argument has aroused controversy but little acceptance.

Richard the Second (c. 1595–1596)

On August 29, 1597, "The Tragedye of Richard the Second" was entered in the Stationers' Register by Andrew Wise, and was published by him later that same year:

THE Tragedie of King Richard the second. *As it hath beene publikely acted by the right Honourable the Lorde Chamberlaine his Seruants.* LONDON Printed by Valentine Simmes for Androw Wise, and are to be sold at his shop in Paules church yard at the signe of the Angel. 1597.

This is a good text, printed evidently from the author's papers or a transcript of them. Wise issued two more quartos of this popular play in 1598, each set from the previous quarto, and then in 1603 transferred his rights in the play to Matthew Law. This publisher issued in 1608 a fourth quarto "With new additions of the Parliament Sceane, and the deposing of King Richard" (according to the title page in some copies). The deposition scene had indeed been omitted from the earlier quartos, probably through censorship. A fifth quarto appeared in 1615, based on the fourth. All the quartos after the first attribute the play to Shakespeare. The added deposition scene in quartos four and five seems to have been memorially reconstructed. The Folio text of 1623 gives a better version of the deposition scene, perhaps because the printers of the Folio had access to the manuscript prompt-book for this portion of the text. (Some scholars maintain that the Folio text was derived from an earlier quarto or quartos that had been used as a prompt-book.) In any event, most of the Folio was probably set from quarto three, and perhaps from the final two leaves of quarto five, so that the most authoritative text for all but the deposition scene is the first quarto.

Francis Meres mentions the play in 1598. Clearly it had been written and performed prior to the Stationers' Register entry in August of 1597. Its earliest probable date is 1595, since the play is seemingly indebted to Samuel Daniel's poem *The First Fowre Bookes of the Civile Wars* published in that year. Shakespeare follows Daniel, for example, in increasing the Queen's age from eleven (according to the chronicles) to maturity, and in other significant details. On December 9, 1595, Sir Edward Hoby invited Sir Robert Cecil to his house in Cannon Row "where as late as it shal please you a gate for your supper shal be open: & K. Richard present him selfe to your vewe." Although it is by no means certain that this passage refers to a private performance of Shakespeare's play, stylistic considerations favor a date around 1595 rather than 1597. If, as some scholars contend, Daniel's *Civile Wars* was written after Shakespeare's play rather than before it, *Richard II* might be as early as 1594.

The Henry the Fourth Plays (c. 1596–1598)

On February 25, 1598, "The historye of Henry the IIIJth with his battaile of Shrewsburye against Henry Hottspurre of the Northe with the conceipted mirthe of Sir John Ffalstoff" was entered in the Stationers' Register by Andrew Wise. Later that year appeared the following quarto:

THE HISTORY OF HENRIE THE FOVRTH; With the battell at Shrewsburie, *betweene the King and Lord* Henry Percy, surnamed Henrie Hotspur of the North. *With the humorous conceits of Sir* Iohn Falstalffe. AT LONDON, Printed by *P. S.* [Peter Short] for *Andrew Wise,* dwelling in Paules Churchyard, at the signe of the Angell. 1598.

Actually this was not the first quarto, for an earlier fragment of eight pages has survived, part of a text that served as copy for the first complete extant quarto. Together these quartos make up an excellent authoritative text, based seemingly on the author's papers. Four more quartos appeared before the Folio of 1623, each based on the previous quarto. The Folio itself was based on the last of these.

"The second parte of the history of Kinge Henry the IIIJth with the humours of Sir John Fallstaff: Wrytten by master Shakespere" was entered in the Stationers' Register by Andrew Wise and William Aspley on August 23, 1600. (This is the first time Shakespeare's name appeared in the Stationers' Register.) The quarto was published later that year as

THE Second part of Henrie the fourth, continuing to his death, *and coronation of Henrie* the fift. With the humours of sir Iohn Fal*staffe, and swaggering* Pistoll. *As it hath been sundrie times publikely* acted by the right honourable, the Lord Chamberlaine his seruants. *Written by William Shakespeare.* LONDON Printed by V. S. [Valentine Sims] for Andrew Wise, and William Aspley. 1600.

One scene, III,i, was omitted from Sims' first printing [Qa] of this quarto, whereupon Sims reset two leaves as four new leaves [Qb] including not only the omitted III,i but II,iv,370–421 and III,ii,1–113. Qb is therefore the best copy text for III,i and Qa for those portions that were reset. In addition, still other scenes were omitted from both versions of the 1600 quarto; they were later restored in the First Folio. No further quartos appeared prior to the Folio of 1623—an odd fact in view of *1 Henry IV's* continued popularity, but perhaps the result of a large printing of *2 Henry IV* in anticipation of heavy sales. At any rate, this text seems to have been based on Shakespeare's papers and was a reliable one except for the omissions. Of the omitted passages, some may have been the result of shortening for performance, but some suggest political censorship. The Folio text restores the omitted readings. The relationship of Folio to quarto text is extraordinarily difficult to determine; perhaps the Folio compositors were using a manuscript that had been transcribed either from an extensively annotated copy of the quarto or from a quarto and a manuscript source jointly compared. The quarto version omits much profanity found in the Folio version. Despite the greater fullness of the Folio text, the quarto remains the substantive text for virtually all but the omitted passages.

Both plays show signs of revision in the use of characters' names, most notably that of Falstaff. Plainly the original version of the plays called him Sir John Oldcastle, after one of the prince's companions in the anonymous *Famous Victories of Henry the Fifth* (c. 1588). The speech-prefix "Old." is left standing at I,ii,138 in the quarto of *2 Henry IV,* several lines of verse are one syllable short evidently because "Oldcastle" has been altered to "Falstaff," and Falstaff is jokingly referred to as "my old lad of the castle" (*1 Henry IV,* I,ii,41). Moreover, there are several contemporary allusions to a play about a fat knight named Oldcastle. Apparently Henry Brooke, Lord Cobham, a living descendant of the Lollard martyr Oldcastle of Henry V's reign, took umbrage at the profane use Shakespeare had made of this revered name, whereupon Shakespeare's company shifted to another less controversial name from the chronicles, Sir John Fastolfe (called "Falstaff" in the Folio text of Shakespeare's *1 Henry VI* and assigned a cowardly role in the French wars of that play). The revision also changed the names of Oldcastle's cronies from Harvey and Russell to Bardolph and Peto.

Cobham was Lord Chamberlain from July 1596 until his death in March 1597, during which interval Shakespeare's company bore the name of Lord Hunsdon's men. Quite possibly the difficulty over the name Oldcastle erupted during that period, for *1 Henry IV* seems to have been written and performed in late 1596 and early 1597 not long after Shakespeare had finished *Richard II* (c. 1595–1596). *2 Henry IV* must have been written before the end of 1598, so that Shakespeare could then begin *Henry V* in early 1599. Since *2 Henry IV* was originally performed using the names Oldcastle and Russell, however, we are inclined to date it somewhat earlier, in 1597, before the squabble over the names broke out. Scholars who prefer a date in 1597 for *The Merry Wives* also date *2 Henry IV* early in 1597, since it almost surely introduced Shallow and Pistol before they appeared in *The Merry Wives.* Francis Meres refers in 1598 to *"Henry the 4"* without specifying one or two parts. Publication of *1 Henry IV* in 1598 assured the Elizabethan public that the changes in names to Falstaff, Bardolph, and Peto had taken place; a revised epilogue to the 1600 quarto of *2 Henry IV* protests that "Oldcastle died a martyr, and this [Falstaff] is not the man," as though by way of apology or disclaimer. A play defending the reputation of the Lollard Oldcastle and attacking Falstaff, called *The History of the Life of Sir John Oldcastle, Lord Cobham, with his Martyrdom,* had been performed by the rival Admiral's men in 1599.

Henry the Fifth (1599)

An entry in the Stationers' Register for August 4, 1600, provides that "Henry the ffift" and three other plays belonging to the Chamberlain's men are "to be staied" from publication until further permission is granted. Evidently the Chamberlain's men were anxious to prevent unauthorized publication. They did not succeed, however, in preventing the appearance of a pirated text of *Henry V*. An entry in the Stationers' Register for August 14 assigns to Thomas Pavier an already published work entitled "The historye of Henry the Vth with the battell of Agencourt." The quarto volume to which this entry refers is the following:

THE CHRONICLE History of Henry the fift, With his battell fought at *Agin Court* in *France*. Togither with *Auntient Pistoll. As it hath bene sundry times playd by the Right honorable the Lord Chamberlaine his seruants.* LONDON Printed by *Thomas Creede*, for Tho. Millington, and Iohn Busby. And are to be sold at his house in Carter Lane, next the Powle head. 1600.

This text is manifestly corrupt. It is considerably shorter than the Folio version, and completely omits the choruses and three entire scenes (I,i, III,i, and IV,ii). The remainder seems to have been put together by memorial reconstruction. This bad quarto served as the basis for a second quarto printed by Thomas Creed for Thomas Pavier in 1602, and a third printed by William Jaggard for Thomas Pavier in 1619 but fraudulently dated 1608. The Folio text was printed seemingly from pages of the second and third quartos, reprinted from the bad first quarto, but fortunately those pages had been corrected by reference to an independent source—probably Shakespeare's own papers. The Folio text is thus the most reliable version.

Francis Meres does not mention the play in 1598, though he does mention *"Henry the* 4." The epilogue to *2 Henry IV* (written probably in 1597) promises that "our humble author will continue the story, with Sir John in it, and make you merry with fair Katharine of France"; and since the prediction is not really accurate regarding Falstaff, we can be reasonably certain that Shakespeare had not yet begun *Henry V* in 1597. An allusion in the Chorus of Act V to "the general of our gracious Empress," who may in good time come home from Ireland with "rebellion broached on his sword," has been taken by virtually all editors to refer to the Earl of Essex, who left in March of 1599 to quell the Irish rebellion headed by Tyrone. Although Essex returned on September 28 of that same year having failed utterly in his assignment, the departure of such a charismatic figure could have inspired Shakespeare's praising remark. A minority view holds that the choruses (which do not appear in the bad quarto of 1600) could have been written later in 1601 for Essex' far more victorious successor, Lord Mountjoy (see Warren D. Smith's article on *Henry V* in *JEGP*, 1954). Still, Essex was more center stage during those exciting years, more likely to have been the subject of adulation. In any case the play itself must have been written before August of 1600, most probably in 1599. The reference to "this wooden O" in the Chorus of Act I is often thought to be Shakespeare's compliment to the company's new theatre, the Globe, ready for their use probably in 1599.

King Henry the Eighth (1613)

The Life of King Henry the Eight was first printed in the Folio of 1623. The text is a good one, set from a careful transcript of Shakespeare's own manuscript. The stage directions are unusually elaborate. The first recorded performance was on June 29, 1613. A letter of July 2 in that year from Sir Henry Wotton to Sir Edmund Bacon tells of a performance of "a new play, called *All Is True,* representing some principal pieces of the reign of Henry VIII." During this performance, as King Henry was arriving as a masquer at the house of Cardinal Wolsey (I,iv), "certain chambers [cannons] being shot off at his entry, some of the paper, or other stuff, wherewith one of them was stopped, did light on the thatch, where being thought at first but an idle smoke, and their eyes more attentive to the show, it kindled inwardly, and ran round like a train, consuming within less than an hour the whole house to the very grounds." The identification of this *All Is True* with Shakespeare's play is certain. Other accounts include a letter from Thomas Lorkin to Sir Thomas Puckering, June 1613, asserting the fire to have started "while Bourbege his companie were acting at y[e] Globe the play of Hen: 8," a letter of 8 July from John Chamberlain to Sir Ralph Winwood, and an account in Stow's *Annales* as continued by Edmund Howe (1618).

Wotton calls it a new play, and stylistic considerations confirm this characterization. The play may also have helped provide entertainment for the betrothal and marriage of James I's daughter Elizabeth to the Elector Palatinate earlier in 1613, though *Henry VIII* is not listed among the many plays acted on this occasion.

On the controversy over John Fletcher's purported share in the authorship of *Henry VIII,* see Play Introduction, above.

Titus Andronicus (c. 1589–1591)

On February 6, 1594, "a Noble Roman Historye of Tytus Andronicus" was entered in the Stationers' Register to John Danter, along with "the ballad thereof." The entry probably, though not certainly, refers to Shakespeare's play. Later in that same year, at any rate, Danter published a quarto volume with the following title:

THE MOST LAmentable Romaine Tragedie of Titus Andronicus: As it was Plaide by the Right Honourable the Earle of *Darbie,* Earle of *Pembrooke,* and Earle of *Sussex* their Seruants. LONDON, Printed by Iohn Danter, and are to be sold by *Edward White* & *Thomas Millington,* at the little North doore of Paules at the signe of the Gunne. 1594.

This text seems to have been set from Shakespeare's foul papers. A second quarto appeared in 1600, adding the name of the Lord Chamberlain's company to those who had acted the play. It was set up from a slightly damaged copy of the first quarto. Although the second quarto made some improvements, these were probably by the compositor and not the author. A third quarto (1611), set up from the second, contributed new errors. The Folio text of 1623 was derived from the third quarto, but with an authentic added scene (III,ii) from a manuscript source and with additional stage directions that suggest a playhouse promptbook. One theory is that the copy used by the Folio printers, the third quarto, had been corrected from an annotated copy of the second quarto that had been used as a promptbook. Despite these improvements, the first quarto clearly remains the authoritative text.

The date of *Titus* must be prior to 1594. Henslowe's *Diary* records a performance of a "Titus & Ondronicous" by the Earl of Sussex' men on January 24, 1594, and indicates it was "ne" or new. This could certainly mean a new play, but it could also mean it was newly revised or newly acquired. Since the players on this occasion, Sussex' men, were listed third on the 1594 title page after Derby's and Pembroke's men, they may just have acquired *Titus*. Two allusions may point to an earlier date: *A Knack to Know a Knave* (performed in 1592) and *The Troublesome Raigne of King John* (published 1591) may contain echoes of *Titus*. Stylistic considerations favor a date around 1590 or even earlier.

The authorship of *Titus* would appear at first glance to be beyond question. Although the 1594 quarto does not mention Shakespeare's name (a common omission in such early texts, especially since the author was as yet relatively unknown), Francis Meres assigns the play to Shakespeare in 1598 and the Folio editors include it in the 1623 edition. Doubts began to arise, however, when Edward Ravenscroft observed in 1687 that he had been "told by some anciently conversant with the Stage, that it was not Originally his, but brought by a private Authour to be Acted, and he only gave some Master-touches to one or two of the Principal Parts or Characters." This remark touched off a controversy that continues today; for example, J. Dover Wilson in his New Cambridge Shakespeare (1948) and J. C. Maxwell in his Arden edition (1953) still argue for the presence of Peele, in the first act especially. Nevertheless, Ravenscroft's testimonial is suspect both because it came one hundred years after the fact and because Ravenscroft himself was embarked on an adaptation of *Titus* and so might wish to denigrate the original. The efforts at assigning portions of the play to Shakespeare's contemporaries have generally been motivated by a wish to rescue Shakespeare's reputation from the violent and garish effects of this play. Most recent criticism prefers to regard the play as an interesting experiment in revenge tragedy by a young artist, with many shrewdly characteristic Shakespearean touches. The external evidence of the Elizabethan period, at any rate, is entirely on the side of awarding the play wholly to Shakespeare.

Henslowe's *Diary* records the performance of a "Tittus & Vespacia" on April 11, 1592, a "ne" play by Strange's men. Despite the similarity of the title, this play was probably on an independent subject.

Romeo and Juliet (1594–1596)

A corrupt and unregistered quarto of *Romeo and Juliet* appeared in 1597 with the following title:

> AN EXCELLENT conceited Tragedie OF Romeo and Iuliet, As it hath been often (with great applause) plaid publiquely, by the right Honourable the L. of *Hunsdon* his Seruants. LONDON, Printed by Iohn Danter. 1597.

This was a pirated edition issued by an unscrupulous publisher, no doubt to capitalize on the play's great popularity. It seems to have been memorially reconstructed by two or more actors, and possibly thereafter used as a promptbook. Its appearance seems to have caused the issuance two years later of a clearly authoritative version:

> THE MOST EXcellent and lamentable Tragedie, of Romeo and *Iuliet. Newly corrected, augmented, and amended:* As it hath bene sundry times publiquely acted, by the right Honourable the Lord Chamberlaine his Seruants. LONDON Printed by Thomas Creede, for Cuthbert Burby, and are to be sold at his shop neare the Exchange. 1599.

This text is some 800 lines longer than the first, and corrects errors in that earlier version. Oddly, however, it seems at times to have been contaminated by the first quarto, as though the manuscript source for the second quarto (probably the author's foul papers) was defective at some point. A passage from I,ii,53 to I,iii,34 was apparently set directly from the first quarto. (On this matter, see George W. Williams' old-spelling edition of the play, Duke U. Press, 1964.) Despite this contamination, however, the second quarto is the authoritative text. It served as the basis for the third quarto (1609) which in turn served as copy for the fourth quarto (undated, but placed in 1622) and the Folio of 1623. A fifth quarto appeared in 1637.

Francis Meres assigns the play to Shakespeare in 1598. So does John Weever in his *Epigrammes* of 1599. Internal evidence on dating is not reliable. The Nurse observes that "'Tis since the earthquake now eleven years"; but suitable earthquakes have been discovered in 1580, 1583, 1584, and 1585, giving us a wide choice of dates even if we accept the dubious proposition that the Nurse is speaking accurately. Astronomical reckoning of the position of the moon at the time the play purportedly takes place ("a fortnight and odd days" before Lammastide, August 1) indicates the year 1596; again, however, we have no reason to assume Shakespeare cared about this sort of internal accuracy. More suggestive perhaps is the argument that Danter's unauthorized publication in 1597 was seeking to exploit a popular new play, one the acting company certainly did not yet wish to see published since it was a money-maker. Danter assigns the play to Lord Hunsdon's servants, a name that Shakespeare's company could have used only from

July 22, 1596 (when the old Lord Chamberlain, Henry Carey, first Lord Hunsdon, died) to April 17, 1597 (when George Carey, second Lord Hunsdon, was appointed to his father's erstwhile position as Lord Chamberlain). Danter could simply have been using the name of the company at the time he pirated the play, but he may also indicate performance in late 1596. Stylistically, the play is clearly of the "lyric" period of *A Midsummer Night's Dream* and *Richard II*. There are also stylistic affinities to the sonnets and to the narrative poems of 1593–1594. A date between 1594 and 1596 is likely, especially toward the latter end of this period. Whether the play comes before or after *A Midsummer Night's Dream* is, however, a matter of conjecture.

Julius Caesar (1599)

Julius Caesar was first published in the Folio of 1623. The text is an excellent one, based evidently on a theatre prompt-book or a transcript of it. In the Folio the play is included among the tragedies and entitled *The Tragedie of Julius Caesar,* although the table of contents lists it as *The Life and death of Julius Caesar.*

First performance must have occurred in 1599 or slightly earlier. On September 21, 1599, a Swiss visitor named Thomas Platter crossed the River Thames after lunch with a company of spectators to see "the tragedy of the first Emperor Julius Caesar" performed in a thatched-roofed building. The description fits the Globe, the Rose, and the Swan, but the last of these was not in regular use. The Admiral's men at the Rose are not known to have had a Caesar play, whereas the Chamberlain's men certainly had Shakespeare's play about this time. They had only recently moved from their Theatre in the north-east suburbs of London to the Globe south of the river, and *Julius Caesar* and *Henry V* were probably new plays for the occasion.

John Weever, in *The Mirror of Martyrs* (1601), is surely referring to Shakespeare's play when he describes "the many-headed multitude" listening first to "*Brutus* speach, that *Caesar* was ambitious," and then to "eloquent *Mark Antonie.*" (The dedication to Weever's book claims he wrote it "some two yeares agoe," in 1599; but since this book has been shown to be heavily indebted to a work that first appeared in 1600, Weever's allusion is not as helpful in limiting the date as was once thought.) Ben Jonson's *Every Man in His Humor,* acted in 1599, may also contain allusions to Shakespeare's play.

Hamlet (c. 1599–1601)

Like everything else about *Hamlet,* the textual problem is complicated. On July 26, 1602, James Roberts entered in the Stationers' Register "A booke called the Revenge of Hamlett Prince Denmarke as yt was latelie Acted by the Lord Chamberleyne his servantes." For some reason, however, Roberts did not print his copy of *Hamlet* until 1604, by which time had appeared the following unauthorized edition:

> THE Tragicall Historie of HAMLET *Prince of Denmarke.* By William Shake-speare. As it hath beene diuerse times acted by his Highnesse seruants in the Cittie of London: as also in the two Vniuersities of Cambridge and Oxford, and else-where. At London printed for N. L. [Nicholas Ling] and Iohn Trundell. 1603.

This edition, the bad quarto of *Hamlet,* seems to have been memorially reconstructed by actors who toured the provinces (note the references to Cambridge, Oxford, etc.), with some recollection of an earlier *Hamlet* play (the *Ur-Hamlet*) written before 1589 and acted during the 1590's.

The authorized quarto of *Hamlet* appeared in 1604. Roberts, the printer, seems to have reached some agreement with Ling, one of the publishers of the bad quarto, for their initials are now paired on the title page:

> *THE* Tragicall Historie of HAMLET, *Prince of Denmarke.* By William Shakespeare. Newly imprinted and enlarged to almost as much againe as it was, according to the true and perfect Coppie. AT LONDON, Printed by I. R. [James Roberts] for N. L. [Nicholas Ling] and are to be sold at his shoppe vnder Saint Dunstons Church in Fleetstreet. 1604.

Some copies of this edition are dated 1605. This text was based seemingly on Shakespeare's own papers, but is marred by printing errors and is at times contaminated by the bad quarto—presumably when the printers found Shakespeare's manuscript unreadable. This quarto served as copy for a third quarto in 1611, Ling having meanwhile transferred his rights in the play to John Smethwick. A fourth quarto, undated but before 1623, was based on the third.

The Folio text of 1623 is derived from a manuscript source independent of that used for the second quarto. The Folio text omits more than two hundred lines found in the quarto, but it also supplies some clearly authentic passages. The consensus today is that the Folio text was set from a prompt-book in use at the time of the Folio printing, or a transcript of it. On the other hand, some textual scholars argue that the Folio text was set from an annotated copy of the second quarto rather than directly from a prompt-book. Since in either case the Folio text evidently contains changes and additions made by actors during years of repeated performance, the text of the Folio is not as close to Shakespeare's own draft as is the second quarto. Nevertheless, the Folio and even the bad quarto supply some authentic readings.

Hamlet must have been produced before the Stationers' Register entry of July 26, 1602. Francis Meres does not mention the play in 1598. Gabriel Harvey attributes the "tragedie of Hamlet, Prince of Denmarke" to Shakespeare in a marginal note in Harvey's copy of Speght's Chaucer; Harvey acquired the book in 1598, but could have written the note any time between then and 1601 or even 1603. More helpful in dating is Hamlet's clear reference to the so-called "War of the Theatres," the rivalry between the adult actors and the boy actors who had newly reopened in 1598–1599 after nearly a decade of inactivity. The Children of the Chapel Royal began acting at Blackfriars in 1598, and provided such keen competition in 1599–1601 that the adult actors were at times forced to tour the provinces (see *Hamlet*, II,ii,332–362). Revenge tragedy was also in fashion during these years: Marston's *Antonio's Revenge*, for example, dates from 1599–1601, and *The Malcontent* is from about the same time or slightly later.

Othello (c. 1603–1604)

On October 6, 1621, Thomas Walkley entered in the Stationers' Register "The Tragedie of Othello, the moore of Venice," and published the play in the following year:

THE Tragœdy of Othello, The Moore of Venice. *As it hath beene diuerse times acted at the* Globe, and at the Black-Friers, by *his Maiesties Seruants. Written by* VVilliam Shakespeare. *LONDON,* Printed by *N. O.* [Nicholas Okes] for *Thomas Walkley,* and are to be sold at his shop, at the Eagle and Child, in Brittans Bursse. 1622.

This text is a good one, although it is some 160 lines shorter than the Folio text of 1623 and appears to have been set up from a shortened version of the play—perhaps intended for provincial touring. The Folio text may have been set up from a copy of the quarto that had been corrected with reference to an authoritative manuscript, either a prompt-book or foul papers. The Folio text consciously eliminates some profanities found in the earlier text. Generally, modern editors base their work on the Folio text, with an awareness that the quarto text is of considerable importance as well.

The earliest mention of the play is on "Hallamas Day, being the first of Nouembar," 1604, when "the Kings Maiesties plaiers" performed "A Play in the Banketinge house att Whit Hall Called The Moor of Venis." The play is attibuted to "Shaxberd." The authenticity of this Revels account, first printed by Peter Cunningham in 1842, was once challenged, but it is now accepted as genuine. On stylistic grounds the play is usually dated in 1603 or 1604, although arguments are sometimes presented for a date as early as 1601 or 1602.

King Lear (c. 1605)

On November 26, 1607, Nathaniel Butter and John Busby entered on the Stationers' Register "A booke called. Master William Shakespeare his historye of Kinge Lear, as yt was played before the Kinges maiestie at Whitehall vppon Sainct Stephens night at Christmas Last, by his maiesties servantes playinge vsually at the Globe on the Banksyde." Next year appeared the following quarto:

M. William Shak-speare: *HIS* True Chronicle Historie of the life and death of King LEAR and his three Daughters. *With the vnfortunate life of* Edgar, *sonne* and heire to the Earle of Gloster, and his sullen and assumed humor of TOM of Bedlam: *As it was played before the Kings Maiestie at Whitehall vpon S.* Stephans *night in Christmas Hollidayes.* By his Maiesties seruants playing vsually at the Gloabe on the Bancke-side. *LONDON*, Printed for *Nathaniel Butter,* and are to be sold at his shop in *Pauls* Church-yard at the signe of the Pide Bull neere St. *Austins* Gate. 1608.

This quarto is often called the "Pied Bull" quarto in reference to its place of sale. Twelve copies exist today, in ten different "states," because proofreading was being carried on while the sheets were being run off in the press; the copies variously combine corrected and uncorrected sheets. A second quarto, printed in 1619 by William Jaggard for Thomas Pavier with the fraudulent date of 1608, was based on a copy of the first quarto combining corrected and uncorrected sheets.

The Folio text of 1623 was also set up from a copy of the first quarto in a state of partial correction. The copy used for this occasion, however, had been carefully emended by reference to some authoritative manuscript, probably a prompt-book of a version of the play cut for performance. Although some 300 lines are deleted, some 100 other lines are added, and in general the Folio text gives evidence of being substantially closer to Shakespeare's original than any of its predecessors. The first quarto itself was not a "bad" quarto in the usual sense, but it does seem to have been based on a careless copy of Shakespeare's draft to which some actors were somehow a party. Whether the actors thus involved were the entire company putting together a text on tour to replace a missing prompt-book, or a single reporter, or the boys who played Goneril and Regan, is a matter of dispute; but in any event this quarto text is not generally as reliable as the Folio text except (obviously) for those 300 or so lines which the Folio omits. The modern tendency is to follow the Folio text except where it is manifestly defective or corrupt.

The Stationers' Register entry for November 26, 1607, describes a performance at court on the previous St. Stephen's night, December 26, 1606. The title page of the first quarto confirms this performance on St. Stephen's night. Such a performance at court was not likely to have been the first, however. Shakespeare's repeated use of Samuel Harsnett's *Declaration of Egregious Popishe Impostures,* registered on March 16, 1603, sets an early limit for composition of the play. Other circumstances point to the existence of the play by May of 1605. In that month, an old play called *The True Chronicle History of King Leir* was entered in the Stationers' Register as a "Tragecall historie," a phrase suggesting the influence of Shakespeare's play since the old *King Leir* does not end tragically. Moreover, the title page of the old *King Leir,* issued in 1605, proclaims the text to be "as it hath bene diuers and sundry times lately acted." In view of the unlikelihood that such an old play (written before 1594) would be revived in 1605, scholars have suggested that the title page was the publisher's way of trying to capitalize on the recent popularity of Shakespeare's play. In this case, the likeliest date for the composition of Shakespeare's *King Lear* would be in the winter of 1604–1605. Shakespeare certainly used the old *King Leir* as a chief source, but he need not have waited for its publication in 1605 if, as seems perfectly plausible, his company owned the prompt-book. On the other hand, Gloucester's mentioning of "These late eclipses in the sun and moon" (I,ii) seems to refer to an eclipse of the moon in September and of the sun in October of 1605, and we are left wondering if Shakespeare was so foresighted as to have anticipated these events.

Macbeth (c. 1606–1607)

Macbeth was first printed in the Folio of 1623. It was set up from a prompt-book or a transcript of one. The text is unusually short, and seems to have been cut for reasons of censorship or for some special performance. Moreover, all of III,v and parts of IV,i (39–43, 125–132) appear to be interpolations, containing songs from Middleton's *The Witch.*

An astrologer named Simon Forman, in his manuscript *The Booke of Plaies and Notes thereof per Formans for Common Pollicie,* records the first known performance of *Macbeth* on April 20, 1611, at the Globe Theatre. The play must have been in existence by 1607, however, for allusions to it seemingly occur in *Lingua* and *The Puritan* (both published in 1607) and in *The Knight of the Burning Pestle* (probably acted in 1607). On the other hand, the play itself seemingly alludes to James I's royal succession in 1603, and to the trial of the notorious Gunpowder Plot conspirators in March of 1606.

Timon of Athens (c. 1605–1608)

Timon of Athens first appeared in the Folio of 1623. The text seems to have been based on an unusually early draft of the author's papers, with manifest inconsistencies still present that would have been straightened out in a final draft. The play seems to have been a last-minute substitution in the Folio, to replace *Troilus and Cressida* when for some reason (probably copyright difficulties) that play had to be removed from its original position following *Romeo and Juliet.* The Folio editors possibly had not intended to use *Timon* at all. The manuscript used by the printers seems to have been copied over in places by a second hand, as though the manuscript was too illegible for the printer to use.

Dating of the play is unusually difficult. In its unfinished state the play was probably never acted, and therefore left no trace until it was registered for publication on November 8, 1623. Stylistically it seems close to the late tragedies. Its pessimism reminds us of *King Lear,* and its use of Plutarch suggests *Antony and Cleopatra.* Theories of multiple authorship, once common, are no longer regarded as substantial.

Antony and Cleopatra (1606–1607)

On May 20, 1608, Edward Blount entered on the Stationers' Register "A booke Called. Anthony. and Cleopatra," along with "A booke called. The booke of Pericles prynce of Tyre." Blount was friendly with Shakespeare's company, and his entry may have been a "staying entry" designed to prevent some unscrupulous publisher from pirating these texts. If so, the tactic did not succeed with *Pericles,* issued in 1609 by another publisher, but it did succeed with *Antony and Cleopatra.* The play was first printed in the Folio of 1623. It is a good text, set evidently from Shakespeare's own draft after it had been prepared for stage presentation (though not yet actually used as a prompt-book).

The year 1608 is thus the latest possible date for *Antony and Cleopatra.* Evidently it was written in 1606–1607, however, for a "newly altered" edition in 1607 of Samuel Daniel's play *Cleopatra* seems to have been influenced by Shakespeare's play. Shakespeare himself had probably consulted the original edition of *Cleopatra,* published in 1594, or the slightly revised edition of 1599, but Daniel's more thorough revision in 1607 shows signs of his having seen Shakespeare's play in the interim. Also, a play by Barnabe Barnes called *The Devil's Charter* (1607), may contain a parody of Cleopatra's death by asps.

Coriolanus (c. 1608)

Coriolanus was first printed in the Folio of 1623. Its text was set from the author's own manuscript or a transcript of it. Although printing errors are numerous, they are for the most part easy to correct. Dating of the play is uncertain. No early performance is on record. The late style and some possible allusions point to some time around 1608. Menenius' fable of the belly (I,i,94 ff.) is probably indebted to William Camden's *Remaines,* published 1605. Echoes of the play may appear in Robert Armin's *The Italian Taylor and his Boy* and Ben Jonson's *Epicoene,* both from 1609. Thus a date in 1608 is plausible but only approximate.

Pericles (c. 1606–1608)

On May 20, 1608, Edward Blount entered in the Stationers' Register "A booke called. The booke of Pericles prynce of Tyre." He also entered *Antony and Cleopatra* at this time, possibly hoping to forestall illegal publishing of these two texts. If so, the plan succeeded with *Antony* but not with *Pericles.* A corrupt quarto of this play was printed in 1609 by William White:

> THE LATE, And much admired Play, Called Pericles, Prince of Tyre. With the true Relation of the whole Historie, aduentures, and fortunes of the said Prince: As also, The no lesse strange, and worthy accidents, in the Birth and Life, of his Daughter *MARIANA.*

As it hath been diuers and sundry times acted by his Maiesties Seruants, at the Globe on the Banck-side. By William Shakespeare. Imprinted at London for *Henry Gosson,* and are to be sold at the signe of the Sunne in Pater-noster row, &c. 1609.

Blount was a friend of the players, and the text he registered is likely to have been the prompt-copy. (This would explain why it is referred to as "A booke called the booke of Pericles" in the S. R., since prompt-copies were known technically as "books.") White's text, on the other hand, is a memorially constructed text and at times unintelligible. Two reporters may have been at work, and the printing was done by at least three compositers. See Play Introduction, above, for some examples of inconsistency in the text. Unfortunately, this bad text is the best we have. Subsequent quartos appeared in 1609, 1611, 1619, and 1630, but each was set up from the previous edition, and all attempts in them at improvement are editorial rather than authorial. *Pericles* did not appear at all in the Folio of 1623, perhaps because the editors suspected it to be partly non-Shakespearean, or because they did not possess a reliable text. Arguments for multiple authorship, though based essentially on internal evidence of the play's manifest inconsistencies, are still taken seriously by scholars. The defects of the first two acts are generally more extensive than those found even in such bad quartos as *Hamlet* or *Romeo and Juliet.* Philip Edwards has argued, on the other hand *(Shakespeare Survey 5),* that the differences between the first two acts and the last three can be accounted for by memorial reporting and compositorial error. This matter is still in dispute.

A play of *Pericles* (though probably differing textually from the one we have today) must have been in existence by the date of the Stationers' Register entry in May of 1608. A play of *Pericles* was seen by the Venetian Ambassador to England, Zorzi Giustinian, some time during his official stay from January 5, 1606, to November 23, 1608. George Wilkins' *The Painfull Aduentures of Pericles Prince of Tyre,* published in 1608, was certainly derived in part from a play about Pericles: its title page offers the work "as it was lately presented by the worthy and ancient Poet John Gower," and the final sentence of the Argument urges the reader "to receive this Historie in the same manner as it was under the habite of ancient *Gower* the famous English Poet, by the Kings Majesties Players excellently presented." The play to which Wilkins refers may have been Shakespeare's, or perhaps some earlier version—just how early, no one can say. As it stands, however, the play appears to represent the beginning of Shakespeare's fascination with the genre of romance. As such, its date is usually set between 1606 and 1608.

Cymbeline (c. 1608–1610)

Cymbeline was first printed in the Folio of 1623, where it was included among the tragedies. The text, a good one, was evidently set either from a careful transcript of Shakespeare's own papers or from a theatrical prompt-book that had incorporated many authorial stage directions. The first recorded performance was in 1611. Dr. Simon Forman, a quack astrologer, jotted down a description of *Cymbeline* in his commonplace book for that year; and, although he did not record the actual date he saw the play, he must have done so some time between April and his sudden death on September 8 of that year. Stylistically the play appears to follow *Pericles* (c. 1606–1608) and to precede *The Winter's Tale* (c. 1610–1611). Dating must be considered approximate.

The Winter's Tale (c. 1610–1611)

The Winter's Tale was first printed in the Folio of 1623. Its text is a good one, taken evidently from Ralph Crane's transcript of Shakespeare's own draft. As in most other Crane transcriptions, the stage directions are sparse and the characters' names are grouped at the beginning of each scene. The first recorded performance was on May 15, 1611, when the quack astrologer Simon Forman saw the play at the Globe and recorded a summary of it in his commonplace book. Another performance that year at court, on November 5, is recorded in the *Revels Account,* and still another during the winter of 1612–1613. Quite possibly the play was new at the time Forman saw it. It apparently contains an allusion to the dance of ten or twelve satyrs in Jonson's *Masque of Oberon,* performed at court on January 1, 1611. A 1623 entry in the *Office book* of Sir Henry Herbert, Master of the Revels, refers to *The Winter's Tale* as "an olde playe . . . formerly allowed of by Sir George Bucke." Bucke (or Buc) was first appointed Master of the Revels in 1610, but had occasionally licensed plays before that date during his predecessor's illness, so that the backward limit of 1610 cannot be considered absolute. Still, matters of style confirm the likelihood that Forman was seeing a new play in 1611.

The Tempest (c. 1610–1611)

The Tempest was first printed in the Folio of 1623. It occupies first place in the volume, and is a scrupulously prepared text from a transcript by Ralph Crane of a theatre prompt-book or of Shakespeare's draft after it had been annotated for production. Shakespeare's colleagues may have placed it first in the Folio because they considered it his most recent complete play. The first recorded performance was at court on November 1, 1611: "Hallomas nyght was presented att Whithall before y[e] kinges Maiestie a play Called the Tempest." The actors were "the Kings players" *(Revels Account).* The play was again presented at court during the winter of 1612–1613, this time "before the Princes Highnes the Lady Elizabeth and the Prince Pallatyne Elector." The festivities for this important betrothal and wedding were sumptuous, and included at least thirteen other plays. Various arguments have been put forward that

Shakespeare composed parts of *The Tempest,* especially the masque, for this occasion, but there is absolutely no evidence that the play was singled out for special prominence among the many plays presented, and the masque is integral to the play as it stands. Probably the 1611 production was of a fairly new play. Simon Forman, who saw *Cymbeline* and *The Winter's Tale* in 1611, does not mention *The Tempest.* He died in September of 1611. According to every stylistic test, such as run-on and hypermetric lines, the play is very late. Shakespeare probably knew Sylvester Jourdain's *A Discovery of the Barmudas,* published in 1610, and William Strachey's *A true Reportory of the Wracke and Redemption,* dated July 1610 although not published until 1625.

Venus and Adonis (1592–1593)

On April 18, 1593, "a booke intituled, Venus and Adonis" was entered to Richard Field in the Stationers' Register, and was published by him the same year. The quarto contains a dedication written by Shakespeare to the Earl of Southampton. The text seems to have been carefully supervised through the press, and based on the author's fair copy. The poem was very popular, and was reprinted nine times before Shakespeare's death. The Folio of 1623, being limited to plays, did not include it or any other nondramatic poems. Contemporary references are numerous: Francis Meres and Richard Barnfield in 1598, Gabriel Harvey in 1598–1601, and John Weever in 1599, among others. Shakespeare probably wrote this poem shortly before its publication, since his intention was to present it to Southampton. The theatres closed from June 1592 to May 1594, giving Shakespeare a period of enforced leisure in which to write poetry.

The Rape of Lucrece (1593–1594)

Shakespeare promised a "graver labour" to Southampton in his dedication of *Venus and Adonis,* 1593, and *The Rape of Lucrece* is almost surely that promised sequel. It was registered in the Stationers' Register by John Harrison on May 9, 1594, and issued that same year as "printed by Richard Field, for Iohn Harrison." Although not quite as popular as *Venus and Adonis,* the poem was reprinted five times during Shakespeare's lifetime. Contemporaries of Shakespeare who allude favorably to the poem include W. Har and Michael Drayton in 1594, William Covell in 1595, Francis Meres in 1598, Gabriel Harvey in 1598–1601, John Weever in 1599, and others. The date of composition of the poem is well fixed between the publication of *Venus and Adonis* in 1593 and that of *The Rape of Lucrece* itself in 1594.

The Passionate Pilgrim

The early editions of the minor poems, with questions of dating and canon, are discussed in the Introduction above.

The title page of the second edition of *The Passionate Pilgrim,* which is the first complete edition extant, reads as follows:

THE PASSIONATE PILGRIME. *By W. Shakespeare.* AT LONDON Printed for W. Iaggard, and are to be sold by W. Leake, at the Greyhound in Paules Churchyard. 1599.

The Phoenix and Turtle

The Phoenix and Turtle first appeared in a volume with the following title:

LOVES MARTYR: OR, ROSALINS COMPLAINT. *Allegorically shadowing the truth of Loue,* in the constant Fate of the Phoenix *and* Turtle. . . . by ROBERT CHESTER. . . . *To these are added some new compositions, of seuerall moderne Writers whose names are subscribed to their seuerall workes, vpon the first subiect: viz. the* Phoenix *and* Turtle.

The date 1601 appears on a separate title page. One poem is signed "William Shake-speare," others John Marston, George Chapman, and Ben Jonson.

A Lover's Complaint

A Lover's Complaint first appeared in Thomas Thorpe's 1609 edition of the sonnets. The poem is not mentioned on the title page of the volume, but has its own head-title on sig. K^{v}: "A Louers complaint. By William Shake-speare." For the uncertain nature of this attribution, see Introduction.

The Sonnets

On May 20, 1609, "Thomas Thorpe Entred for his copie vnder thandes of master Wilson and master Lownes Warden a Booke called Shakespeares sonnettes." In the same year appeared the following volume:

SHAKE-SPEARES SONNETS. Neuer before Imprinted. AT LONDON By *G. Eld* for *T. T.* and are to be solde by *Iohn Wright,* dwelling at Christ Church gate. 1609.

Some copies of this same edition are marked to be sold by William Aspley rather than John Wright; evidently Thorpe had set up two sellers to distribute the volume. The sonnets were not reprinted until John Benson's rearranged edition of 1640, possibly because the first edition had been suppressed or because sonnets were no longer in vogue. The 1609 edition does not give us a good text; it may rest on an authoritative manuscript, but the edition itself is marred by misprints. Clearly it was not supervised through the press as were *Venus and Adonis* and *The Rape of Lucrece.* All the evidence suggests that it was pirated from a manuscript that had been in private circulation (as we know from Francis Meres' 1598 allusion to Shakespeare's "sugred Sonnets among his priuate friends"). Two sonnets, 138 and 144, had appeared in 1599 in *The Passionate Pilgrim.* On questions of dating and order of the sonnets, see Introduction, above.

APPENDIX 2

Sources

The Comedy of Errors

The Comedy of Errors is based chiefly on the *Menaechmi* of Plautus (c. 254–184 B.C.). Shakespeare appears to have used the Latin, which was available to him in numerous Renaissance texts. He may also have known in manuscript the translation into English by "W. W." (? William Warner), published in 1595, S. R. 1594.

Two twins have become separated when their father, a Syracusan merchant, loses one of them in Epidamnum. The lost twin is raised by a resident of that town. The action is set in Epidamnum years later, where Menaechmus the Citizen, in the company of the parasite Peniculus, is seen quarreling with his wife and arranging to lunch with the courtesan Erotium. To the city of Epidamnum comes Menaechmus' long-separated twin brother, Menaechmus Sosicles of Syracuse, accompanied by his servant Messenio. The confusion begins when Menaechmus Sosicles is mistaken for his twin by Erotium's cook, Cylindrus, and then by Erotium herself, who invites him to lunch and to her bed. She bids him take a cloak (which Menaechmus the Citizen had given her that morning) to the dyer's for alteration. A short time later, Peniculus too mistakes Menaechmus Sosicles for the Epidamnian twin, upbraids him for having dined while the parasite was absent, and threatens to tell Menaechmus' wife of his carryings-on. Erotium's maid brings Menaechmus Sosicles a chain or bracelet to be mended at the goldsmith's. Menaechmus the Citizen now returns home from a busy day to a furious wife and a vindictive Peniculus. Among other matters the wife demands the return of her cloak which, as she suspects, her husband stole from her and gave to Erotium. The husband, locked out of his own house by his angry wife, must now confront Erotium, who insists that she gave her chain and the cloak to him. The Citizen goes to seek the help of his friends. Menaechmus Sosicles shows up at this point and is angrily abused by the wife and by her father, both of whom consider the supposed husband to be mad. They send for a doctor, who arrives after Menaechmus Sosicles has fled; they instead detain Menaechmus the Citizen as a madman. Messenio the servant now returns to his supposed master and fights manfully with his master's captors. Finally the two twins confront one another and unravel the mystery.

Shakespeare creates the two Dromios in place of Messenio, plays down the role of the courtesan, dignifies the part of the wife, invents the sympathetic role of Luciana her sister, eliminates the parasite and the wife's father, and replaces the courtesan's maid and cook with comic servants like Luce or Nell, the kitchen-wench in the household of Antipholus of Ephesus. The conventional doctor, Medicus, becomes the zany Dr. Pinch. The setting is Ephesus rather than Epidamnum. Plautus' detached ironic tone and his matter-of-fact depiction of courtesans and parasites are replaced by a thematic emphasis on patience and loyalty in marriage. The name "Dromio" may have come from John Lyly's *Mother Bombie*.

The dual identity of the servants, and the superb confusion of Act III when Antipholus of Ephesus is locked out of his own house, are derived in good part from Plautus' *Amphitruo*. The relevant part of the story is as follows. While Jupiter makes love to Amphitryon's wife Alcmena, disguised as her husband, Mercury guards the door in the guise of Amphitryon's slave Sosia. The real Sosia approaches, but is so bewildered by Mercury's inventive wit that he begins to doubt his own identity. Later, at Jupiter's behest, Mercury again poses as Sosia to dupe Amphitryon and deny him entrance to his own house. Ultimately, after Alcmena has given birth to twins, one by Jupiter (Hercules) and one by Amphitryon (Iphiclus), Jupiter tells Amphitryon the truth.

The "framing" action of *The Comedy of Errors,* concerning old Egeon's painful separation from his wife and their eventual reunion, is derived not from Plautus but from the story of Apollonius of Tyre. Shakespeare later used this story for *Pericles,* and for that play his sources were chiefly two: the *Confessio Amantis* by John Gower, Book VIII, and Laurence Twine's *The Patterne of Painefull Aduentures,* translated from a French version based in turn on a popular story in the *Gesta Romanorum.* Perhaps Shakespeare was acquainted with these same versions when he wrote *The Comedy of Errors;* Twine's account was entered in the Stationers' Register in 1576, although the earliest extant edition dates from around 1594–1595. Gower's account had been printed by Caxton in 1493 and reprinted in 1532 and 1554.

In Gower's *Confessio,* Apollonius' wife Lucina gives birth to a daughter on board ship and, having apparently died in childbirth, is put into a chest and committed to the sea. Washing ashore at Ephesus, she is restored by the physician Cerimon. She becomes a priestess in the Temple of Diana. Years later, Apollonius comes to Ephesus, is first reunited with his daughter Thaisa, and then is told in a vision to go to the Temple. There he discovers the "Abbess" to be his long-lost wife. Shakespeare has added the business of the threatened hanging from which Egeon is finally rescued.

Love's Labor's Lost

No main source exists for *Love's Labor's Lost.* For his conception of an "academy" of aristocratic scholars, Shakespeare may have drawn on Pierre de la Primaudaye's *L'Académie françoise* (1577), translated into English in 1586, in which the ideals of scholarly withdrawal are discussed. The notion was, however, commonplace. Certain historical facts about Henry of Navarre may well have provided Shakespeare a model for the play's action, especially the visit of Catherine de' Medici with her daughter and the famous *l'escadron volant* to Henry's court in 1578, and a similar visit in 1586 (see Play Introduction, above). Published accounts of these visits were not available when Shakespeare wrote his play, but he may well have heard the gossip. John Lyly's plays provided Shakespeare a literary model for the saucy boyish wit of Moth, Boyet, and others; and Armado and Moth are often thought to resemble Sir Tophas and the page Epiton in Lyly's *Endymion.* Traditions of the *Commedia dell' Arte* provided Shakespeare with stock comic models, especially those of the *dottore* or pedant (Holofernes), his parasite (Nathaniel, the curate), the *capitano* or braggart soldier (Armado), and the rustic servant (Costard). All of these types are individualized and rendered in English terms, however. Many literary quarrels in England of the 1590's have been adduced as possible sources for Shakespeare's play, especially the Nashe-Harvey controversy, but the evidence remains inconclusive.

The Two Gentlemen of Verona

Shakespeare appears to have combined two kinds of stories in *The Two Gentlemen of Verona,* one of romantic love triumphing over inconstancy and one of perfect friendship triumphing over perfidy. For the story of the deserted heroine and her inconstant lover, Shakespeare's main source was evidently *Diana,* a pastoral by Jorge de Montemayor (published c. 1559). This work was translated into French in 1578 and 1587, and was published in English in 1598 by Bartholomew Yonge. Yonge states that he began his translation some nineteen years earlier. Possibly then Shakespeare saw it in manuscript, or he may have relied on the French translation. A play, now lost, was performed at court in 1585 called *The history of felix & philiomena* (i.e., Felismena). It must surely have been based on Montemayor's prose pastoral, and may have provided Shakespeare with a dramatic model.

In *Diana,* the story of Felix and Felismena is one of many narratives set in contrast to the central story of Diana the shepherdess. Felismena tells her own story (in Book II). While she is living with her grandmother, her parents having died, Felismena is courted by a young gentleman named Don Felix. His father, determined to prevent the marriage, sends Don Felix off to the court of the Princess Augusta Caesarina. Felismena follows after, appareled as a young man named Valerius. Stopping at an inn, she is invited by the host of the inn to hear some music, whereupon she happens to overhear the faithless Felix courting a lady named Celia. Disguised as Valerius, Felismena ingratiates herself with Felix' servant Fabius and takes service with Don Felix. She is sent on embassages to Celia, with whom she converses about Felix' first love. Celia falls in love with "Valerius," like Olivia in *Twelfth Night,* and subsequently dies of unrequited passion. Hereupon the distraught Felix disappears. Later, in Book VII, we hear how Felismena disguised as an Amazonian shepherdess rescues Felix from his attackers and is reconciled to him. Felix acknowledges her beauty to be superior to that of Celia.

In Sir Philip Sidney's *Arcadia* (1590), Zelmane follows Felismena's example by disguising herself as a page (Daiphantus) in the service of her beloved Pyrocles. When she falls ill and is on the verge of death, Zelmane's identity is revealed to Pyrocles. The *Arcadia* also offers a noble example of perfect friendship in the relation between Pyrocles and Musidorus.

The story of perfect friendship has many antecedents, including the fourteenth-century *Amis and Amiloun,* and Richard Edwards' play about *Damon and Pythias* (1565). The falling-out of sworn friends over a woman is the central theme of Chaucer's *The Knight's Tale* and of John Lyly's *Euphues* (1578). Perhaps the most suggestive example of perfect friendship is the story of Titus and Gisippus as it appears in Book II, Chapter XII, of Sir Thomas Elyot's *The Governour* (1531). Elyot derived his account from Day X, Novel VIII, of Boccaccio's *Decameron.* Titus and Gisippus were proverbially famous as friends, like Damon and Pythias, and other Renaissance versions of the story were available (including a Latin school play of 1546[?] and a children's play at court in 1577, both now lost). Perhaps Shakespeare knew the story as a commonplace rather than having to depend on one particular literary source.

Elyot's version tells of two look-alike friends dwelling in Athens of whom one, Gisippus, is persuaded by his kindred and acquaintances to marry. Despite a preference for the study of philosophy, he finds his fiancée most attractive. When, however, his Roman-born friend Titus falls desperately in love with the same lady and confesses as much to Gisippus, the husband-to-be generously proposes that Titus take his place on the wedding night. Because the binding element of the marriage contract is the bestowing of the ring in bed, and the undoing of the girdle of virginity, the lady is now Titus' legal wife and returns with him to Rome. Gisippus, accused by the Athenians of having mismanaged the affair, follows his friend to Rome and is there wrongly accused of a murder. Titus' turn has now arrived to be magnanimous, and he insists that he be punished for the murder. Eventually the real culprit, touched by this selflessness, confesses the crime, allowing Titus to return with Gisippus to Athens and forcibly restore him to his rightful possessions.

Valentine's sojourn in the forest and his leadership of a

band of outlaws would seem to be indebted to the tradition of Robin Hood, although no single source has been found. An analogue to the outlaw episode does appear in Henry Wotton's *A Courtlie Controversie of Cupids Cautels* (1578), where it is linked to a story of perfidy in friendship. Valentine's unwelcome rival Thurio may owe something to the braggart soldier, Captain Spavento, of the *Commedia dell' Arte* tradition. Silvia's father, the Duke, is a similarly conventional comic stage type.

One final analogue worthy of note is a German play, *Julio und Hyppolita,* from a collection called *Englische Comedien und Tragedien* (1620). It may have been derived from performances by English players around 1600. Although some of its lines are suggestively close to those of Shakespeare's play, we cannot determine which version is prior to the other.

The Taming of the Shrew

Most recent critics agree that the play called *The Taming of A Shrew,* published in 1594, is an imitation of Shakespeare's play and not an earlier version or source for what he wrote. An exception is Geoffrey Bullough, *Narrative and Dramatic Sources of Shakespeare,* who prefers the theory that *A Shrew* is an inaccurate text of an old play which Shakespeare used as his main source. Apart from this controversial question, all critics agree that Shakespeare's play consists of three elements, each with its own source: the romantic love-plot of Lucentio and Bianca, the wife-taming plot of Petruchio and Kate, and the framing plot or "Induction" of Christophero Sly.

The romantic love-plot is derived from George Gascoigne's *Supposes,* a neoclassical comedy performed at Gray's Inn in 1566. Gascoigne's play was a rather close translation of Ariosto's *I Suppositi* (1509), which in turn was based on Terence's *Eunuchus* and Plautus' *Captivi.* The heroine of Gascoigne's version (as of Ariosto's) is Polynesta, the resourceful daughter of Damon, a widower of Ferrara. Two suiters vie for Polynesta's hand: Dr. Cleander, an aged and miserly lawyer, and Erostrato, a Sicilian gentleman who has purportedly come to Ferrara to study. In fact, however, this "Erostrato" is the servant Dulippo in disguise, having changed places with his master. (These disguisings are the "supposes" of the title.) As a servant in Damon's household, "Dulippo" has secretly become the lover of Polynesta, and has made her pregnant. Balia, the nurse or duenna, is their go-between. Meanwhile, "Erostrato" takes great delight in outwitting Dr. Cleander and his unattractive parasite, Pasiphilo. The feigned Erostrato's ruse is to produce a rich father who will guarantee a handsome dowry and thereby outbid Cleander in the contest for Polynesta's hand. The "father" he produces, however, is actually an old Sienese stranger, who is persuaded that he is in danger in Ferrara unless he cloaks his identity. Complications arise when Damon learns of his daughter's affair and throws the lover, "Dulippo," into a dungeon. The crafty Pasiphilo overhears this compromising information and resolves to cause mischief for all the principals. Moreover, when Erostrato's real father Philogano arrives in Ferrara, he is barred from his son's house by the feigned Philogano and resolves to get help. His clever servant, Litio, suggests employing the famous lawyer Cleander. All is happily resolved when the real Dulippo proves to be the son of Dr. Cleander, and the real Erostrato is revealed to be rich and socially eligible for Polynesta's hand in marriage. Cleander is even reconciled to his parasite, Pasiphilo.

Shakespeare has almost entirely eliminated the satire of the law in his source. Gremio is aged and wealthy, but no shyster. The lover is not imprisoned in a dungeon. The parasite is gone, as also in *The Comedy of Errors.* Bianca does not consummate her affair with Lucentio as does Polynesta, and hence has no need for a go-between like Balia. Shakespeare adapts a sophisticated neoclassical comedy, racy and cosmopolitan, to the moral standards of his public theatre. The witless Hortensio, the tutoring in Latin, and the music lesson are Shakespeare's invention.

The wife-taming plot of Petruchio and Kate reflects an ancient comic antifeminist tradition, still extant today in the Scottish folksong "The Cooper of Fife" or "The Wife Wrapped in Wether's Skin" (Child's *Ballads,* V, 277). Richard Hosley has argued (in *Huntington Library Quarterly,* 1964) that Shakespeare's likeliest source was *A Merry Jest of a Shrewde and Curste Wyfe, Lapped in Morrelles Skin, for her Good behavyour* (printed c. 1550). In this version, the husband beats his shrewish wife with birch rods until she bleeds and faints, whereupon he wraps her in the raw salted skin of an old plough-horse named Morel. Like Kate, this shrewish wife has a gentle younger sister who is their father's favorite. This father warns the man who proposes to marry his older daughter that she is shrewish, but the suitor goes ahead and subsequently tames his wife with Morel's skin. Thereafter, at a celebratory dinner, everyone is impressed by the thoroughness of the taming.

Shakespeare avoids the antifeminist extremes of this story, despite the similarity of the narrative. Instead, he seems to have had in mind the more humanistic spirit of Erasmus' *A Mery Dialogue Declarynge the Propertyes of Shrowde Shrewes, and Honest Wyues* (translated 1557) and Vives' *The Office and Duty of an Husband* (translated 1555). Specific elements of the wife-taming plot have been traced to other possible sources. The scolding of a tailor occurs in Gerard Legh's *Accidence of Armory* (1562); a wife agrees with her husband's assertion of a patent falsehood in Don Juan Manuel's *El Conde Lucanor* (1335); and three husbands wager on the obedience of their wives in *The Book of the Knight of La Tour-Landry* (printed 1484).

The "Induction" story, of the beggar duped into believing himself a rich lord, is an old tale occurring in the *Arabian Nights.* An interesting analogue occurs in Heuterus' *De Rebus Burgundicis* (1584), translated into the French of S. Goulart (1606?) and thence into the English of Edward Grimeston (1607). According to Heuterus, in 1440 Philip the Good of Burgundy actually entertained a drunken beggar in his palace "to make triall of the vanity of our life," plying him with fine clothes, bed, a feast, and the performance of "a pleasant Comedie."

A Midsummer Night's Dream

No single source has been discovered that unites the various elements we find in *A Midsummer Night's Dream,* but the four main strands of action can be individually discussed in terms of sources. The four strands are: (1) the marriage of Duke Theseus and Queen Hippolyta, (2) the romantic tribulations and triumphs of the four young lovers, (3) the quarrel of King Oberon and Queen Titania, together with the fairies' manipulations of human affairs, and (4) the "rude mechanicals" and their play of "Pyramus and Thisbe."

For his conception of Theseus, Shakespeare went chiefly to Chaucer's *Knight's Tale* and to Thomas North's 1579 translation of The Life of Theseus in Plutarch's *Lives of the Noble Grecians and Romanes.* Chaucer's Theseus is a duke of "wysdom" and "chivalrie," renowned for his conquest of the Amazons and his marriage to Hippolyta. Plutarch provides information concerning Theseus' other conquests (to which Oberon alludes in II,i), including that of Antiopa. Shakespeare could have learned more about Theseus from Chaucer's *The Legend of Good Women* and from Ovid's *Metamorphoses.* He seems to have blended all or some of these impressions together with his own ideal of a noble yet popular Renaissance ruler.

The romantic narrative of the four lovers appears to be original with Shakespeare, although one can find many analogous situations of misunderstanding and rivalry in love. Chaucer's *Knight's Tale* tells of two friends battling over one woman. Shakespeare's own *The Two Gentlemen of Verona* gives us four lovers, properly matched at first until one of the men shifts his attentions to his friend's ladylove; eventually all is righted when the false lover recovers his senses. Parallel situations arise in Sidney's *Arcadia* and in Montemayor's *Diana,* a source for *The Two Gentlemen.* What Shakespeare adds in *A Midsummer* is the intervention of the fairies in human love affairs.

Shakespeare's knowledge of fairy lore must have been extensive, and is hard to trace exactly. Doubtless much of it was from oral traditions. In Chaucer's *Merchant's Tale,* Pluto and Proserpina as king and queen of the fairies intervene in the affairs of old January, his young wife May, and her lover Damyan. Fairies appear on stage in Lyly's *Endymion* (1588), protecting true lovers and tormenting those who are morally tainted. Shakespeare later reflects this tradition in *The Merry Wives of Windsor* (1597–1601). The name Oberon probably comes from the French romance *Huon of Bordeaux* (translated by Lord Berners by about 1540), where Oberon is a dwarfish fairy king from the mysterious East who practices enchantment in a haunted wood. In Spenser's *The Faerie Queene,* Oberon is the Elfin father of Queen Gloriana (II,x,75–76). Greene's *James IV* (c. 1591) also features Oberon as the fairy king, and a lost play called *Huon of Bordeaux* was performed by Sussex' men at about this same time. The name Titania comes from Ovid's *Metamorphoses,* where it is used as a synonym for both the enchantress Circe and the chaste goddess Diana. The name Titania does not appear in Golding's translation, suggesting that Shakespeare found it in the original. Puck or Robin Goodfellow is essentially the product of oral tradition, although Reginald Scot's *The Discoverie of Witchcraft* (1584) discusses Robin in pejorative terms as an incubus or hobgoblin in whom intelligent people no longer believe.

Scot also reports the story of a man who finds an ass's head placed on his shoulders by enchantment. Similar legends of transformation occur in Apuleius' *The Golden Ass* (translated by William Adlington, 1566) and in the well-known story of the ass's ears bestowed by Phoebus Apollo on King Midas for his presumption. Perhaps the most suggestive possible source for Shakespeare's clownish actors, however, is Anthony Munday's play *John a Kent and John a Cumber* (c. 1587–1590). In it a group of rude artisans, led by the intrepid Turnop, stage a ludicrous interlude written by their churchwarden in praise of his millhorse. Turnop's prologue is a medley of lofty comparisons. The entertainment is presented before noble spectators, who are graciously amused. *John a Kent* also features a lot of magic trickery, a boy named Shrimp whose role is comparable to that of Puck, and a multiple love plot.

"Pyramus and Thisbe" itself is based on the *Metamorphoses* (IV,67 ff.). Other versions Shakespeare may have known include Chaucer's *The Legend of Good Women,* a poem by William Griffith in 1562, George Pettie's *A Petite Palace of Pettie His Pleasure* (1576), *A Gorgeous Gallery of Gallant Inventions* (1578), and "A New Sonet of Pyramus and Thisbe" from Clement Robinson's *A Handefull of Pleasant Delites* (1584). Several of these, especially the last three, are bad enough to have given Shakespeare materials to lampoon, though the sweep of his parody goes beyond the particular story of Pyramus and Thisbe. The occasionally stilted phraseology of Golding's translation of *The Metamorphoses* contributed to the fun. According to Kenneth Muir (*Shakespeare's Sources,* 1957), Shakespeare must also have known Thomas Mouffet's *Of the Silkewormes and their Flies* (published 1599, but possibly circulated earlier in manuscript), which contains perhaps the most ridiculous of all versions of the Pyramus and Thisbe story. Shakespeare also appears to be spoofing the inept dramatic style and lame verse of English dramas of the 1560's, 1570's, and 1580's, especially in their treatment of tragic sentiment and high emotion; *Cambises, Damon and Pythias,* and *Appius and Virginia* are examples.

For theories that Shakespeare wrote the play for a particular court wedding in the 1590's, see Appendix I under *A Midsummer Night's Dream.*

The Merchant of Venice

Shakespeare's chief source for *The Merchant of Venice* was the first story of the fourth day of *Il Pecorone* (The Dunce) by Ser Giovanni Fiorentino. This collection of tales dates from the late fourteenth century but was first published in 1558 at Milan and was not translated into English in Shakespeare's time. Behind Ser Giovanni's story lies an old tradition of a bond given for human flesh, as found in Persia, India, and the Twelve Tables of Roman Law. This legend first appears in English in the thirteenth-century *Cursor Mundi,* with a Jew as the creditor. A thirteenth-century version of the *Gesta Romanorum* adds a romantic love plot, though the evil money-lender in this case is not Jewish. The hero pawns his own flesh to a merchant in order to win a lady. He succeeds on his third attempt, having learned to avoid a magic spell that had previously put him to sleep and cost him a hundred mark of florins. When he goes to pay his forfeit, the lady follows after disguised as a knight and foils the evil merchant with a quibbling distinction between flesh and blood.

Ser Giovanni's story tells of Giannetto, the adventurous youngest son of a Florentine merchant, who goes to live with his father's dearest friend Ansaldo in Venice. This worthy merchant gives him money to seek his fortune at sea. Unbeknownst to Ansaldo, Giannetto twice risks everything to woo the lady of Belmonte, but is twice given a sleeping medicine and is stripped of all his wealth while asleep. Returning destitute to Venice, he is twice forgiven by Ansaldo and given the means to seek his fortune again. For the third such voyage, however, Ansaldo is driven to borrow ten thousand ducats from a Jew on the condition of forfeiting a pound of flesh. This time, one of the lady's maids warns Giannetto not to drink his wine, and he possesses the lady as his wife. Some time later, remembering that the day of Ansaldo's forfeiture has arrived, Giannetto explains the predicament to his wife and is sent by her to Venice with a hundred thousand ducats. He arrives after the forfeiture has fallen due. The lady, however, following after in the disguise of a lawyer, decrees that the Jew may have no blood and must take no more or no less than one pound of flesh. The Jew is jeered at and receives no money. The "lawyer" refuses payment other than the ring Giannetto has received from his lady. Giving it up unwillingly, he returns to Belmonte where his lady vexes him about the ring but finally relents and tells him all. The story provides no casket episode, courtship of Nerissa by Gratiano, elopement of Jessica, or clowning of Launcelot Gobbo. The Jew's motive is not malicious.

Shakespeare may also have known "The Ballad of Gernutus," a popular work that seems to be older than the play. It has no love plot, but dwells on the unnatural cruelty of a Jewish Venetian usurer who takes a bond of flesh for "a merry ieast." Anthony Munday's prose *Zelauto* (1580), though its villain is a Christian rather than a Jewish money-lender, also features a bond of this sort, taken purportedly as a mere sport but with hidden malice. Truculento, the villain, takes the bond of two young men, Rodolfo and his friend Strabino, as surety for a loan. If they forfeit the loan, the young men are to lose their lands and their right eyes as well. The villain has a daughter, Brisana, whom he permits to marry Rodolfo since Truculento expects to marry Rodolfo's sister Cornelia himself. When Cornelia instead marries Strabino, Truculento angrily takes the young men to court to demand his bond. The two brides disguise themselves as scholars and go to court, where they appeal for mercy and then foil Truculento by means of the legal quibble about blood.

Another possible source for the courtroom scene is *The Orator,* translated into English in 1596 from the French of Alexandre Sylvain. An oration, entitled "Of a Jew, who would for his debt have a pound of the flesh of a Christian," uses many specious arguments also employed by Shylock, and is forthrightly confuted in "The Christians Answere."

Shylock's relationship to his daughter finds obvious earlier parallels in Marlowe's *The Jew of Malta* (c. 1589), in which Barabas' daughter Abigail loves a Christian and ultimately renounces her faith, and in *Zelauto.* The actual elopement, however, is closer to the fourteenth story in Masuccio's fifteenth-century *Il Novellino* (not translated in Shakespeare's day).

The casket-choosing episode, not found in *Il Pecorone,* was a widespread legend occurring for example in the story of *Barlaam and Josophat* (ninth-century Greek, translated into Latin by the thirteenth), Vincent of Beauvais' *Speculum Historiale,* the *Legenda Aurea,* Boccaccio's *Decameron* (Day X, Story 1), John Gower's *Confessio Amantis,* and—closest to Shakespeare—the *Gesta Romanorum* (translated into English in 1577 by Richard Robinson and "bettered" by him in 1595). In this last account, the choice is between a gold, silver, and lead casket, each with its own inscription. The first two are like Shakespeare's; the third reads, "Thei that chese me, shulle fynde [in] me that God hathe disposid." The chooser is a maiden, however, and she is not preceded by other contestants.

An old play called *The Jew* is referred to by Stephen Gosson in 1579 as containing "the greedinesse of worldly chusers, and bloody mindes of Usurers." Scholars have speculated that this was a source play for Shakespeare, but actually we have too little to go on for a reliable judgment. Gosson was surely not referring to Robert Wilson's *The Three Ladies of London* (c. 1581), in any case, for its Jewish figure named Gerontus (cf. Gernutus in the ballad) is an exemplary person. Besides, the probable date of this play is later than Gosson's remark.

Much Ado about Nothing

Shakespeare's probable chief source for the Hero-Claudio plot of *Much Ado* was, as C. T. Prouty has demonstrated, the twenty-second story from the *Novelle* of Matteo Bandello (Lucca, 1554). Shakespeare may have read the Italian original as well as François de Belleforest's French translation, *Histoires Tragiques* (1569 edition). The story of the maiden falsely accused was, however, much older than Bandello. Perhaps the earliest that has been found is the Greek romance *Chaereas and Callirrhoe,* fourth or fifth century A.D., in which the hero Chaereas, warned by envious rivals of his wife's purported infidelity, watches at dusk while an elegantly attired stranger is admitted by the maid to the house where Callirrhoe lies. Chaereas rushes madly in and strikes mistakenly at his wife in the dark, but is acquitted of murder when the maid confesses her part in a conspiracy to delude Chaereas. Callirrhoe is buried in a deathlike trance but awakens in time to be carried off by pirates. The story reappears in a fifteenth-century Spanish romance, *Tirante el Blanco,* in which the Princess Blanche is seemingly courted by a repulsive Negro. This Spanish version probably inspired the account in Canto V of Ariosto's *Orlando Furioso* (1516), to which all subsequent Renaissance versions are ultimately indebted.

In Ariosto's account, as translated into English by Sir John Harington (1591), the narrator is Dalinda, maid to the virtuous Scottish Princess Genevra. Dalinda tells how she has fallen guiltily in love with Polynesso, Duke of Albany, an evil man who often makes love to Dalinda in her mistress' rooms but who longs to marry Genevra himself. Consequently, Polynesso arranges for Genevra's noble Italian suitor, Ariodante, and Ariodante's brother Lurcanio, to witness the Duke's ascent to Genevra's window by a rope ladder. The woman who admits the Duke is of course not Genevra but Dalinda disguised as her mistress, having been duped into believing that the Duke merely wishes to satisfy his craving for Genevra by making love to her image. Lurcanio publicly accuses the innocent Genevra and offers to fight anyone who defends her cause (cf. Claudio's quarrel with Leonato). The evil Duke tries to get rid of Dalinda, but all is finally put to rights by Rinaldo (the hero of *Orlando Furioso*) and Ariodante. This account gives an unusually vivid motivation for the maid and the villain—a clearer motivation than in Shakespeare's play. A lost dramatic version, *Ariodante and Genevora,* was performed at the English court in 1583.

Shakespeare probably consulted not only Ariosto but also Spenser's *The Faerie Queene* (II,iv), based on Ariosto. Spenser's emphasis is on the blind rage of Phedon, a young squire in love with Claribell. Phedon is tricked by his erstwhile friend Philemon and by Claribell's maid Pryene into believing Claribell false. Pryene's motive in dressing up as Claribell is to prove she is as beautiful as her mistress. When, after having slain Claribell for her supposed perfidy, Phedon learns the truth, he poisons Philemon and furiously pursues Pryene until he is utterly possessed by a mad frenzy.

Shakespeare's greatest debt is, however, to Bandello's story. Here the setting is Messina. Fenicia, the daughter of Lionato de' Lionati (cf. Shakespeare's Leonato), wins the love of Sir Timbreo, a knight in the service of King Piero of Arragon (cf. Shakespeare's Don Pedro of Arragon). As is the custom, Timbreo seeks Fenicia's hand in marriage through the matchmaking offices of a noble emissary. Unfortunately, Timbreo's friend Girondo also falls in love with Fenicia and plots with a mischief-loving courtier (cf. Don John) to poison Timbreo's mind against Fenicia. Girondo escorts Timbreo to a garden where they see Girondo's servant, elegantly dressed, enter Fenicia's window. No maid takes part in the ruse, however, nor indeed is any woman seen at the window. When Fenicia is wrongly accused, she falls into a deathlike trance and is pronounced dead by a doctor, but is revived. Her father, believing in her innocence, sends her off to a country retreat and circulates the report that she is in fact dead. Soon both Timbreo and Girondo are stricken with remorse, Timbreo magnanimously spares his friend's life, and both confess the truth to Fenicia's family. A year later, Timbreo marries a wife chosen for him by Lionato, who turns out of course to be Fenicia. Girondo marries her sister Belfiore.

A lost play, *Panecia* (1574–1575), may have been based on Bandello's work. One other version Shakespeare may have known is George Whetstone's *The Rocke of Regard* (1576), based on Ariosto and Bandello. It contains a suggestive parallel to Claudio's rejection of Hero in church. Various Italian plays in the tradition of Pasqualigo's *Il Fedele* (1579), and also a version perhaps by Munday, *Fedele and Fortunio* (published 1585), are analogous in situation, though Shakespeare need not have known any of them.

For the Beatrice-Benedick plot no source has been discovered, apart from Shakespeare's own earlier fascination with wit-combat and candid wooing in *Love's Labor's Lost* and *The Taming of the Shrew.* Nor has a plausible source been found for Dogberry and the watch.

The Merry Wives of Windsor

The Merry Wives of Windsor is indebted to no single source that combines the various elements found in the play: the courtship of Anne Page, the hoodwinking of Falstaff by the merry wives, the horse-stealing business, and the various "humors" portraits. Nor in fact does any one element derive from a single source. The entire play is brilliantly improvised.

Many analogues exist to the courtship of Anne Page, for it is essentially a Plautine sort of plot in which parents and unwelcome wooers are outwitted by resourceful young people. The Bianca-Lucentio plot of Shakespeare's own *The Taming of the Shrew* is a good enough instance. Similarly, analogues have been found to the discomfiture of Falstaff. In Ser Giovanni Fiorentino's *Il Pecorone* (Day 1, Novelle 2), for example, a student twice cuckolds the very professor who is instructing him in the art of love. Comically, the student reports back to the professor at every turn and is coached in his next move. He doesn't know that the lady is the professor's wife, but the professor begins to suspect and so follows after. On the first occasion the student escapes detection by hiding under a pile of newly washed linen. The second time he slips out the door, whereupon the neighbors arrive and, finding no intruder, berate the professor for his mad suspicions. The wife's brothers even search the linen pile at the professor's suggestion but find nothing. They thrash the professor and chain him up as a madman. Next day, intending once again to report to the professor what had happened, the student discovers the truth. This version differs markedly from Shakespeare's in that the husband is the chief comic butt. Nevertheless Shakespeare may have known it. Although *Il Pecorone* was not translated into English in the sixteenth century, Shakespeare had already used it as his chief source for *The Merchant of Venice*.

In "Two Lovers of Pisa" from *Tarletons Newes Out of Purgatorie* (1590), the husband is again the one who is duped. An old doctor, wedded to a beautiful young wife, becomes by chance the confidential adviser of a young man who has fallen in love with the wife. The young man reports to the husband his successes and plans in detail. The lover thrice escapes detection (when warned by the lady's maid of the husband's approach) by hiding in a vat of feathers, in a false ceiling, and in an old chest full of legal documents. When on the third occasion the jealous husband sets fire to his own house, the lover is saved by the husband's order to carry out the chest of documents. At last the lover reveals his knowledge of the husband's identity, and everyone laughs at the old fool. Elsewhere, Tarleton's book has suggestive references to Robin Goodfellow and other prankish spirits that may have influenced the concluding scene of *The Merry Wives of Windsor*.

The story "Of Two Brethren and Their Wives" in *Riche his Farewell to Militairie profession* (1581) features two wives, one of "light disposition" and much given to adultery, the other a tedious scold. The first wife desires to rid herself of her two erstwhile lovers, a doctor and a lawyer, in order to enjoy a new liaison with a soldier. Accordingly she pretends to encourage the lawyer's advances, but when the lawyer comes to her she feigns the approach of her husband and enjoins the lawyer to hide in a large mail bag. Meanwhile, the merry wife has arranged for the doctor to come and pick up the mail bag, on the assumption that she will be hiding in it. The doctor thus carries off the lawyer, nearly suffocating from his close confinement, into the country, where the doctor expects to enjoy his rendezvous. Instead, the soldier accosts them, cudgeling first the body in the bag and then the seeming porter. The lawyer is no less astonished to discover where he has arrived than is the doctor to discover what he has been carrying.

For the background of Shakespeare's horse-stealing episodes and "humors" portraits, see Introduction to the play, above. The explicit comparison between Falstaff's ludicrous fate in Windsor Forest and the legend of Actaeon is ultimately indebted to Ovid's *Metamorphoses* (III, 138–252). Actaeon, grandson of Cadmus and a mighty hunter, happens to disturb Diana and her nymphs while they are bathing naked. Transformed by the vengeful Diana into a horned stag, he is hunted to death by his own hounds.

As You Like It

Shakespeare's chief source for *As You Like It* was Thomas Lodge's graceful pastoral romance, *Rosalynde: Euphues Golden Legacie* (1590). Lodge was indebted in turn to *The Tale of Gamelyn,* a fourteenth-century poem wrongly included by some medieval scribes as "The Cook's Tale" in Chaucer's *Canterbury Tales. Gamelyn* was not printed until 1721, but Lodge clearly had access to a manuscript of it. Although Shakespeare may not have known it directly, his play still retains the hearty spirit of this Robin Hood legend. (In later Robin Hood ballads, Gamelyn or Gandelyn is identified with Will Scarlet, a member of Robin Hood's band.)

Gamelyn, the youngest of three brothers, is denied his inheritance by his churlish eldest brother John. When Gamelyn demands his rights, John orders his men to beat Gamelyn, but the young man arms himself with a pestle and proves a formidable fighter. After defeating the champion wrestler in a local wrestling match (a lower-class sport befitting the social milieu of this story), Gamelyn returns home to find himself locked out by his brother. He kills the porter, flings the man's body down a well, and feasts his companions day and night for a week. John feigns a reconciliation and slyly asks if he can bind Gamelyn hand and foot merely to satisfy an oath he has sworn over the death of the porter. Gamelyn trustingly agrees and is made prisoner. After his bonds have been secretly loosed by Adam the Spencer (the steward), Gamelyn pretends to remain bound until the propitious moment for revenge and escape. The moment arrives during a feast of monks who churlishly refuse to help Gamelyn. With Adam's help he fells many of them, ties up his brother, and escapes to the woods where he and Adam are rescued from hunger by a band of merry outlaws. As their chief, Gamelyn becomes a champion of the poor and an enemy of rich churchmen. His brother, now sheriff, brands Gamelyn an outlaw and manages to imprison him, but Gamelyn's second brother, Sir Ote, stands bail for him. On the day of the trial, Gamelyn frees Sir Ote and hangs the sheriff and the jury. Gamelyn finally obtains his inheritance and becomes chief officer of the King's royal forests. This story is uninfluenced by the pastoral tradition and contains no love plot. Its Robin Hood traditions are very much present, nonetheless, in Shakespeare's contrasting portrayal of a tyrannical court and of a just society in banishment.

Lodge retains the primitive vigor of *Gamelyn,* but adds generous infusions of pastoral sentiment in the manner of Sidney's *Arcadia* and sententious moralizing in the manner of John Lyly's *Euphues*. The style is also heavily influenced by Lyly's exquisitely balanced, antithetical, and ornamented prose. For his pastoralism Lodge was indebted not only to Sidney but to the ancient pastoral tradition that included the Greek Theocritus and the Roman Virgil, the Italian Sannazaro *(Arcadia)* and the Portuguese Jorge de Montemayor *(Diana)*. Pastoralism by Lodge's time had become thoroughly imbued with artificial conventions: abject lovers writing sonnets to their disdainful mistresses, princes and princesses in shepherds' disguise, idealized landscapes, stylized debate as to the relative merits of love and friendship, youth and age, city life and country life, and so on. Some of these conventions were derived also from the vogue of sonneteering and can thus be described as the stereotypes of "Petrarchism." Lodge accepts these conventions and gives us typical pastoral lovers even in his hero and heroine, although the elements he derived from *Gamelyn* certainly add a contrasting note of violence and danger.

Lodge's account begins much like that of *Gamelyn*. Saladyne, the envious eldest brother, bribes the champion wrestler to do away with Rosader (Orlando) in the wrestling match. Rosader succeeds instead in killing the wrestler and in winning the heart of Rosalynde, daughter of the banished King Gerismond. When she sends him a jewel, Rosader is not at all at a loss for words; indeed, he composes a Petrarchan sonnet on the spot. The usurping King Torismond (no relation to Gerismond), despite his evil nature, is impressed by Rosader's grace and martial prowess. Rosader returns home with friends, breaks open the door and feasts his company. The wily Saladyne overwhelms Rosader in his sleep and binds him to a post, but Rosader is untied by Adam and makes havoc among the eldest brother's guests as in *Gamelyn*. In this case, however, the guests are Saladyne's kindred and allies, all of whom have refused to help Rosader. The Sheriff tries to arrest Rosader and Adam, but they make good their escape to the Forest of Arden (near Lyons in France). They are saved from starvation by the kindly King Gerismond and his exiled followers. Rosalynde and King Torismond's daughter Alinda have meanwhile been banished from court and have taken abode in the forest under the names of Ganymede and Aliena. They befriend old Corydon (Corin) and young Montanus (Silvius) who is hopelessly in love with the haughty Phoebe. "Ganymede" poses as a woman to test Rosader in his wooing, and they are joined in a mock-marriage. Saladyne, now repenting of his evil deeds, comes to the forest, is saved by his brother from a lion, and falls in love with Alinda (whom he helps to rescue from ruffians). The denouement is as in Shakespeare, although the triumphant return to society is more complete: King Torismond is slain, Gerismond is restored to his throne, Rosader is named heir-apparent, and all the friends are appropriately rewarded.

Despite Shakespeare's extensive indebtedness to this charming romance, there is a crucial difference: Lodge's pastoral world is never subjected to a wry or satirical exploration. Lodge offers no equivalent for Touchstone, the fool who sees the absurdity of both country and city, Jaques the malcontent traveler, William and Audrey the clownishly simple peasants, or Sir Oliver Martext the ridiculous hedge-priest. Nor does Lodge tell of Le Beau, the court butterfly. Shakespeare's added characters are virtually all foils to the conventional pastoral vision he found in his source.

Twelfth Night

John Manningham's description of a performance of *Twelfth Night* on February 2, 1602, at the Middle Temple, compares the play to Plautus' *The Menaechmi* and to an Italian play called *Inganni*. The comment offers a helpful hint on sources. *The Menaechmi* had been the chief source for Shakespeare's earlier *The Comedy of Errors*, and that farce of mistaken identity clearly resembles *Twelfth Night* in the hilarious mixups resulting from the confusion of two look-alike twins. Shakespeare undoubtedly profited from his earlier experimenting with this sort of comedy. *Twelfth Night* had no need to be directly indebted to *The Menaechmi*, however, for Renaissance Italian comedy offered many imitations of Plautus from which Shakespeare could have taken his *Twelfth Night* plot. These include *Gl'Inganni* (1562) by Nicolò Secchi, another *Gl'Inganni* (1592) by Curzio Gonzaga, and most importantly an anonymous *Gl'Ingannati* (published 1537). This last play was translated into French by Charles Estienne as *Les Abusés* (1543), and adapted into Spanish by Lope de Rueda in *Los Engaños* (1567). A Latin version, *Laelia*, based on the French, was performed at Cambridge in the 1590's but never printed. Obviously, *Gl'Ingannati* was widely known, and Manningham was probably referring to it in his diary. To trace Shakespeare's own reading in this matter is difficult, owing to the large number of versions available to him, but we can note the suggestive points of comparison in each.

Both *Inganni* plays feature a brother and a sister mistaken for one another. In the later of these plays (by Gonzaga, 1592), the sister uses the disguise name of "Cesare." In Secchi's *Inganni* (1562), the disguised sister is in love with her master, who is told that a woman the exact age of his supposed page is secretly in love with him. Another play by Secchi, *L'Interesse* (1581), has a comic duel involving the disguised heroine. Of the Italian plays here considered, however, *Gl'Ingannati* (1537) is closest to Shakespeare's play. A short prefatory entertainment included with it in most editions features the name Malevolti. In the play itself, the heroine Lelia disguises herself as a page in the service of Flaminio, whom she secretly loves, and is sent on embassies to Flaminio's disdainful mistress Isabella. This lady falls in love with "Fabio," as Lelia calls herself. Lelia's father Virginio, learning of her disguise and resolving to marry her to old Gherardo (Isabella's father), seeks out Lelia but instead mistakenly arrests her long-lost twin brother, Fabrizio, who has just arrived in Modena. Fabrizio is locked up as a madman in Isabella's room, whereupon Isabella takes the opportunity to betroth herself to the person she mistakes for "Fabio." A recognition scene clears up everything and leads to the marriages of Fabrizio to Isabella and Flaminio to Lelia. This story lacks the subplot of Malvolio, Sir Toby *et al.* Nor is there a shipwreck.

Bandello based one of the stories in his *Novelle* (1554) on *Gl'Ingannati,* and this prose version was then translated into French by Belleforest in his *Histoires Tragiques* (1579 edition). Shakespeare may well have read both, for he consulted these collections of stories in writing *Much Ado about Nothing.* His most direct source, however, seems to have been the story "Of Apolonius and Silla" in *Riche his Farewell to Militarie profession* (1581), derived from Belleforest. Its heroine, Silla, is washed ashore near Constantinople, where, disguised as "Silvio," she takes service with Duke Apolonius. When she is sent on embassies to the lady Julina, this wealthy widow falls in love with "Silvio." The real Silvio, her twin brother, arrives and is invited by Julina to a dinner rendezvous. The next day he departs on his quest for Silla, leaving Julina pregnant. When Apolonius learns of "Silvio's" apparent success with Julina, he throws the page into prison and angrily charges him with hateful abominations. Julina is understandably distressed to learn that the supposed father of her child is in actuality a woman. Finally all is resolved when Silvio returns to marry Julina. The story has only the merest hint of a Malvolio subplot. Shakespeare has minimized the moral predicaments in his source: Sebastian does not get Olivia with child before their marriage, nor does he desert her, nor is Viola thrown into prison. Shakespeare avoids Riche's stern moralizing about the bestiality of lust. He changes the setting to Illyria, though the flavor is Elizabethan English.

Shakespeare's reading may also have included the anonymous play *Sir Clyomon and Sir Clamydes* (c. 1570–1583), Sidney's *Arcadia* (1590), and Emmanuel Forde's prose romance *Parismus* (1598) in which one "Violetta" borrows the disguise of a page. The Malvolio plot may conceivably have reflected an incident at court in which the Comptroller of the Household, Sir William Knollys, interrupted a noisy party late at night dressed only in his nightshirt and a pair of spectacles, with a copy of Aretino in his hand. A similar confrontation between revelry and sobriety occurred in 1598: Ambrose Willoughby quieted a disturbance after the Queen had gone to bed, and was afterwards thanked by her for doing his duty. Such incidents were no doubt common, however, and there is no compelling reason to suppose Shakespeare was sketching from current court gossip.

All's Well that Ends Well

Shakespeare's only known source for *All's Well* is the tale of Giglietta of Nerbone from Boccaccio's *Decameron* (c. 1348–1358), as translated into English by William Painter in *The Palace of Pleasure* (1566, 1575). Painter may have based his translation on a French intermediary by Antoine le Maçon, and Shakespeare possibly knew the Italian and French versions although the English was the most available to him. All three are essentially the same except for the forms of the proper names. The Helena story is also widely dispersed in folk tales.

In Painter's account, Giletta is the daughter of Gerardo of Narbona, physician to the ailing Count of Rossiglione. Giletta falls in love with the Count's son, Beltramo. When the Count dies, Beltramo is "left under the royall custody of the King" and is sent to Paris. Giletta's father dies soon after, and she, refusing many favorable offers of marriage, journeys to Paris and cures the King of a fistula. The King has promised her any husband as her reward, but is loath to give her Beltramo. The young man, no less reluctant, goes through with the marriage ceremony but then escapes into Italy before the marriage is consummated. In Italy he joins the Florentines in a military campaign against the Senois (Sienese). His deserted wife, now countess, returns home and governs the domain of Rossiglione with great skill. When she writes to Beltramo, offering to depart if her presence displeases him, Beltramo sets for her the "impossible" demand of obtaining his ring and begetting a son by him. Hereupon she calls together the leaders of her domain and announces her intention of going on a pilgrimage of renunciation. Despite her people's great lamentation, she departs for Florence where she inquires after Beltramo and discovers that he is paying court to a poor gentlewoman (unnamed) who dwells with her mother. Giletta offers to obtain a dowry for this daughter if she will demand the ring from Beltramo and arrange an assignation so that Giletta may secretly take her place in Beltramo's bed. Beltramo reluctantly agrees to give up the cherished ring, and Giletta becomes his lover on not one but numerous occasions. When she is pregnant, she rewards the daughter with a dowry and then remains living in Florence until she is delivered of two sons. Beltramo has meanwhile been called home by his people. Giletta arrives home in time for a great feast, at which she prostrates herself before Beltramo and proves that she has performed the terms of his "impossible" task. Beltramo is persuaded by her constancy and wit to be true to his promise and reclaim her as his wife.

Shakespeare has retained the folktale spirit of this story, with its ancient motifs of curing the King and of performing impossible tasks. Shakespeare nevertheless provides a significant change of emphasis. He adds characters, such as the Countess of Rossillion and Lafew, whose strong compassion and dignity help us to see more clearly the patient goodness of Helena and the perverse waywardness of Bertram. The King becomes a more impressive character, and a spokesman for faith in the miraculous. Lavatch, the Countess's fool, quizzically expounds questions of moral consequence that are absent in Painter. Conversely, the added character Parolles highlights the callowness and insensitivity of Bertram, and serves as a scapegoat when Bertram mends his ways. Shakespeare simultaneously darkens Bertram's character and intensifies Helena's best qualities. Because she is not rich, as in Painter, she represents innate virtue or "gentleness" in contrast with Bertram's hereditary nobility. The King is not reluctant to bestow Helena on Bertram, as in Painter, but is instead astonished at Bertram's willful refusal of so good a fortune. Other courtiers join the King in this sentiment. Accordingly, Helena's request for Bertram's hand in marriage seems less presumptuous than in Painter. Bertram is not the wise judge who finally concedes the justice of Helena's claim, as in Painter, but an evasive and self-seeking liar to the very end. Far more than the Beltramo of Painter's tale, Bertram is the unworthy hero of a comedy of forgiveness, spared the consequences of his own worst self by a benign King and a patient wife.

Shakespeare also gives his play a unity of construction and an economy of time not found in the sources. Characters such as the King and Diana are not discarded once their primary role has been discharged, but are brought importantly into the denouement. As in his use of other Italianate fictional sources, Shakespeare compresses time: for example, Helena vows to cure the King in two days rather than eight (as in Painter), and Helena sleeps with Bertram once rather than often. No convincing source has been found for the comic exposure of Parolles.

Measure for Measure

Stories about corrupt magistrates are ancient and universal, but Shakespeare's particular story in *Measure for Measure* seems to go back to an actual incident in the sixteenth-century Italian court of Don Ferdinando de Gonzaga. A Hungarian student named Joseph Macarius, writing from Vienna, tells about an Italian citizen accused of murder whose wife submitted to the embraces of the magistrate in hopes of saving her husband. When the magistrate executed her husband despite her having fulfilled her bargain, she appealed to the Duke who ordered the magistrate to give her a dowry and marry her. Thereafter the Duke ordered the magistrate to be executed. This incident seems to have inspired a Senecan drama by Claude Rouillet called *Philanira* (1556), a French translation of this play (1563), a Novella in the *Hecatommithi* of G. B. Giraldi Cinthio (1565), and a play by Cinthio called *Epitia* (posthumously published in 1583). Shakespeare may have known both the prose and the dramatic versions by Cinthio.

In Cinthio's story, the wise Emperor Maximian appoints his friend Juriste to govern Innsbruck, warning him to rule justly or expect no mercy from the Emperor. Juriste rules long and well, to the satisfaction of his master and the people of Innsbruck. When a young man named Vico is brought before him for ravishing a virgin, Juriste assigns the mandatory sentence of death. Vico's sister, Epitia, an extraordinarily beautiful virgin of eighteen, pleads for Vico's life, urging that his deed was one of passion and that he stands ready to marry the girl he forced. The judge, secretly inflamed with lust for Epitia, promises to consider the matter carefully. She reports this seemingly encouraging news to Vico, who urges her to persevere. When, however, the judge proposes to take her chastity in return for her brother's life, Epitia is mortified and refuses unless Juriste will marry her. During another interim in these negotiations, Vico begs his sister to save his life at any cost. She then submits to Juriste on the condition that he will both marry her and spare Vico. Next morning, however, the jailer brings her the body of her decapitated brother. She lays her complaint before the Emperor, who confronts Juriste with his guilt. Conscience-stricken, Juriste confesses and begs for mercy. At first Epitia demands strict justice, but when the Emperor compels Juriste to marry her and then be beheaded, she reveals "her natural kindness" and begs successfully for the life of her wronger.

Shakespeare may also have consulted Cinthio's play *Epitia,* but his chief source was George Whetstone's two-part play *Promos and Cassandra* (1578). Here the corrupt judge is Promos, administrator of the city of Julio under the King of Hungary. The law forbidding adultery has lain in abeyance for some years when a young gentleman named Andrugio is arrested and condemned for "incontinency." His sister Cassandra, as in Cinthio, lays down her precious chastity in response to her brother's piteous entreaties. Promos gives his assurance that he will marry her and save Andrugio's life. When Promos instead treacherously orders the execution of Andrugio, the jailer secretly substitutes the head of a felon, newly executed and so mutilated as to be unrecognizable even by Cassandra. (This rescue is seen as an intervention "by the prouidence of God.") The King sentences Promos as in Cinthio, but in this play the King refuses Cassandra's pleas for the life of her new husband until Andrugio reveals himself to be still alive and offers to die for Promos. The King forgives Andrugio on condition that he marry Polina, whom he wronged. The play also features a courtesan named Lamia and her man, Rosko, who ingratiate themselves with the corrupt officer (Phallax) in charge of investigating their case. Phallax is ultimately caught and dismissed from office while Lamia is publicly humiliated. Whetstone wrote a prose version of this story in the *Heptameron of Civill Discourses* (1582), which Shakespeare may have consulted. Shakespeare was also indebted for a few details to a version in Thomas Lupton's *Too Good to be True* (1581).

Even though Shakespeare's play is closer to Whetstone than to Cinthio, Shakespeare has changed much. He adds the motif of the Duke's mysterious disguise. (A not very compelling analogue to this motif occurs in Sir Thomas Elyot's *The Image of Governance,* 1541.) Shakespeare introduces the use of the bed-trick, found also in his presumably earlier play *All's Well that Ends Well.* Most important, Shakespeare stresses the moral and legal complexity of his story. Isabella is almost a nun, intent on renouncing the world. By contrast, Lucio, an invented character, is an engaging cynic, hedonist, and slanderer. Claudio is at best only technically guilty of fornication. Isabella does not surrender her chastity. Her breakdown in the scene with Claudio intensifies her emotional crisis and renders all the more triumphant her final ability to forgive Angelo. Angelo himself is made puritanical in temperament, and is spared the actual consequences of his worst intentions so that he can be worthy of being forgiven. Isabella need not marry Angelo, since he has not actually seduced her; she is thus free to marry the Duke. No felon need be executed in Claudio's stead, for providence provides a natural death in the prison. In the subplot, despite hints from Whetstone, Pompey is a brilliantly original innovation, Elbow a characteristically Shakespearean clown modeled on the earlier Dogberry of *Much Ado about Nothing,* and Escalus a significant spokesman for a moderate and practical course of equity in the law.

Troilus and Cressida

Shakespeare had access to Homer for information about the Trojan War, since George Chapman's translation of *The Seaven Bookes of Homers Iliads* had appeared in 1598, and earlier English translations of the entire *Iliad* were also available. Shakespeare ends his play with the death of Hector, as does Homer, and portrays Achilles from a Homeric vantage point. Thersites and Nestor are based ultimately on Homer. Ajax' ludicrous boastfulness may owe something to Homer's Ajax Telamon, as well as to Ovid's account of the quarrel between Ulysses and Ajax over Achilles' armor (*Metamorphoses,* xii–xiii). Yet for Shakespeare and for most Englishmen of his time, the chief sources of information about the Trojan War were medieval romances. These were all pro-Trojan in their bias, since Englishmen traced their own mythic history to the lineage of Aeneas and tended to look on Homer as suspiciously pro-Greek. Medieval European culture generally was far more oriented to Roman than to Greek civilization; Greek texts went almost unread. In these circumstances, a pro-Trojan legend of the war emerged and grew to considerable length.

The central work in this genre was Benoit de Sainte-Maure's *Roman de Troie* (c. 1160), a romance freely based on earlier accounts of supposed eyewitnesses named Dictys the Cretan and Dares the Phrygian. Benoit not only narrates the war from Troy's point of view but introduces the love story of Troilus, "Breseida," and Diomedes. Benoit found a hint for this story in the *Iliad,* where two Trojan maidens named Chryseis and Briseis are captured and given to Agamemnon and Achilles respectively. When Chryseis' father calls down a plague on the Greeks for refusing to return Chryseis, Agamemnon reluctantly gives her up but then seizes Briseis from Achilles, thereby precipitating Achilles' angry retirement to his tent and all that disastrously follows. Benoit freely transforms this situation into the rivalry of Troilus and Diomed, who appear in Homer but in entirely different roles.

Benoit's *Roman de Troie* became the inspiration for subsequent medieval accounts of the Trojan War. Guido delle Colonne translated Benoit in his *Historia Trojana* (completed 1287). Boccaccio based his *Il Filostrato* (c. 1338) on Guido and Benoit, but with significant alterations: the love story became the focus of attention, and Pandarus assumed the important role of go-between. (In Homer, Pandarus is a fierce warrior.) Chaucer based his *Troilus and Criseyde* (c. 1385–1386) on Boccaccio, giving still greater attention to the states of mind of the two lovers and endowing Pandarus with a humorous disposition. Shakespeare certainly knew Chaucer's masterpiece. He also consulted, however, at least two other medieval accounts of the war: John Lydgate's *The Historye Sege and Dystruccyon of Troye* (first printed 1513), based on Guido and Chaucer and known also as the *Troy Book,* and William Caxton's *The Recuyell of the Historyes of Troye* (printed 1474, the first book printed in English), a translation from the French of Raoul Lefevre who had followed Guido rather closely. In Caxton, for example, Shakespeare found materials for the Trojan debate about returning Helen, and for Hector's visit to the Greek camp. In addition, Shakespeare was certainly familiar with the degeneration of Cressida's character since the time of Chaucer, as reflected for example in Robert Henryson's *The Testament of Cresseid* (published 1532), in which Cressida is punished for her faithlessness by leprosy and poverty.

Shakespeare pays a good deal more attention to the war than does Chaucer, and portrays the lovers as caught in a deadening conflict beyond their control. Shakespeare's Cressida is more sardonic and experienced in the ways of the world than is Chaucer's heroine, even though Shakespeare's Cressida is unmarried. The subtle and elaborate code of courtly love evoked by Chaucer has almost completely disappeared, leaving in its wake a more dispiriting impression of wantonness in love. Shakespeare's Troilus is still a faithful and earnest lover, as in Chaucer, but more betrayed by his own chauvinistic ideals about honor and patriotism. Pandarus is more leering, giddy, vapid, and coarse than his Chaucerian counterpart. Diomedes is also changed for the worse, being more hard and cynical.

Among the non-Chaucerian characters, Achilles is made to appear more guilty and brutalized than in Shakespeare's sources: Achilles orders his Myrmidons to murder the unarmed Hector, even though Hector had previously spared Achilles in battle. Lydgate and Caxton report that Achilles' Myrmidons kill Troilus, not Hector (in Caxton, Achilles cuts off Troilus' head and then drags Troilus' body behind his horse), whereas in Homer, Achilles kills Hector in battle and only then unchivalrously subjects the body to outrage. Shakespeare refuses to glamorize the war just as he refuses to glamorize the love story. He also compresses time, as he did with so many of his sources. The play begins only a short time before Cressida surrenders to Troilus; she is transferred to the Greeks immediately after she and Troilus become lovers; her surrender to Diomedes follows quickly after her transfer. This telescoping provides not only dramatic unity but a sense of sudden and violent change.

Other plays on Troilus and Cressida are known to have existed, such as a "new" play acted by the Admiral's men in 1596 and another by Dekker and Chettle in 1599. Shakespeare may have known and even written in response to such productions by rival theatrical companies, but nothing is known about these now-lost plays.

The Henry the Sixth Plays

The chief source for the entire *Henry VI* trilogy is Edward Hall's *The Union of the Two Noble and Illustre Famelies of Lancastre and Yorke* (1548), a work written to glorify the Tudor monarchs by demonstrating how their lineage reconciled the fatally warring factions of Lancaster and York. Shakespeare also drew many particulars from the second edition of Raphael Holinshed's *The Chronicles of England, Scotlande, and Irelande* (1587), from John Foxe's *Actes and Monuments of Martyrs* (1583 edition), and probably from others. Richard Grafton's *Chronicle* plagiarized so heavily from Hall that one cannot always be sure which of the two Shakespeare may have consulted.

To intensify Hall's theme of the horrors of civil dissension, Shakespeare takes considerable liberties with the chronicles. He frequently disregards chronology, telescopes events of many years into a single sequence, invents scenes and characters, and transfers details from one historical scene to another. The artistic unity of each play is his overriding consideration, not historical accuracy.

In *1 Henry VI,* for example, Shakespeare shows the English losing Orleans to the French and then retaking the city (I,v–II,i). In fact, Orleans was never retaken once it had fallen. Shakespeare has transferred events from the recapture of Le Mans to his partly invented account of Orleans. Talbot's visit to the Countess of Auvergne (II,iii) is fictitious. The scene in the Temple Garden when the leaders of Lancaster and York pluck red and white roses (II,iv) is fictitious in a different sense: antagonisms between the two factions certainly did exist, but not in the allegorically schematized fashion here visualized. In III,ii Shakespeare shows us Rouen lost and recaptured in a day, whereas in fact the city was (like Orleans) never recovered. Shakespeare's intention is to suggest that France is lost through England's political divisions at home, not through any failure on the part of Lord Talbot. Shakespeare exalts Talbot's might and chivalry (hence the scene with the Countess of Auvergne), and contrastingly overstates the cowardice of Fastolfe (or Falstaff, as he is called in the Folio text). Joan la Pucelle is another exaggeratedly evil foil to Talbot; Shakespeare combines her worst traits in Hall and Holinshed. The play covers the events of about three decades. When Henry V died in 1522, his son was less than a year old; by the time of Talbot's fall in 1453 the King was over thirty.

In *2 Henry VI* Shakespeare accentuates the threat of popular unrest in a number of ways. He conflates reports of the Jack Cade rebellion in 1450 with those of the Peasants' Revolt in 1381, using the most unattractive features of each. Shakespeare ridicules the peasants' Utopian aims, and omits a list of sympathetic demands. Similarly, the dispute between the Armorer and his apprentice (I,iii) is put into a context of courtly politics that we do not find in the chronicles. Simpcox' name and his lameness (II,i) are added to stress the farcical nature of this "miracle." (Shakespeare could have found this account in Thomas More's *Dyaloge . . . of the Veneracyon and Worshyp of Ymages,* 1529, or in Foxe's *Actes and Monuments.*) Although the indictment of Suffolk (III,ii) was historically an act of the House of Commons, Shakespeare portrays it as a near riot in which the people hammer at the King's very door with their strident demands. In every way, *2 Henry VI* stresses the fickleness, inhumanity, and ignorance of men caught up in a mob. Despite all this, however, the play alters its sources less than does *1 Henry VI.* And for all its disapproval of mob unrest, Shakespeare's play is considerably less hostile toward the populace than an anonymous contemporary play, *The Life and Death of Jack Straw* (1590–1593).

3 Henry VI similarly alters its sources less than does *1 Henry VI.* The alterations are chiefly those of telescoping and highlighting for emphasis. The ritual killings, which form an integral part of the spectacle in *3 Henry VI,* are cleverly adapted or rearranged from chronicle accounts. Concerning the death of the Duke of York (I,iv), for example, Hall reports merely that York died fighting manfully, whereas Holinshed tells us that the remorseless Clifford caused the dead York's head to be struck off, "and set on it a crowne of paper, fixed it on a pole, and presented it to the queene." Shakespeare's version goes still further: Queen Margaret mocks York while he is still alive by putting a paper crown on his head. The ritual killing of the Lancastrian Prince Edward (V,v) is similarly enhanced. Throughout, Shakespeare's purpose is to intensify the scourgelike role of the Yorkist Edward IV and his brethren. Among the three, Richard of Gloucester is the most ominous. Shakespeare introduces crook-backed Richard into the fighting (II,i) when historically this man was abroad.

According to Andrew Cairncross, *3 Henry VI* contains occasional allusions to *The Faerie Queene* (see II,i,9 ff. and *FQ* I,v,2), to *A Myrroure for Magistrates* (especially "Richard, Duke of York" and "King Henry the Sixth"), and to Brooke's *Romeus and Juliet* (see V,iv,1–33 and *Romeus* ll. 1359–1377). David Riggs argues (*Shakespeare's Heroical Histories: Henry VI and Its Literary Tradition,* 1971) that Marlowe's *Tamburlaine* was an important source for Shakespeare's *Henry VI* plays, and that behind *Tambur-*

laine lay a classical rhetorical tradition of praise for heroism. Shakespeare would have thoroughly absorbed this tradition through the Tudor grammar-school curriculum.

Richard the Third

Richard III, like the *Henry VI* series, is based chiefly on Edward Hall's *The Union of the Noble and Illustre Famelies of Lancastre and Yorke* (1548) and also on Holinshed's *Chronicles* (1587 edition). Both of these historical compilations were, however, deeply indebted for their hostile view of Richard III to Polydore Vergil and Thomas More. Vergil, a papal tax collector who came to England in 1501, spent many years under the patronage of Henry VII writing in Latin his *Anglica Historia* (first published in Basle, 1534). This work portrayed Richard negatively in order to glorify the claim of the Tudor monarch who had deposed Richard in 1485. Vergil argued that England's suffering was a divinely sent scourge, intended to cleanse England of rebelliousness and prepare the English people for the providential reward of Tudor rule.

Thomas More's *The History of King Richard III,* left unfinished in 1513, was published in two slightly differing versions, one in English (1557) and one in Latin (1566). Thomas More obtained much information and possibly an early draft of his narrative from Cardinal Morton, in whose household More lived as a youth. Morton had figured in the struggles of Richard III's reign—he was the Bishop of Ely from whom Richard requested the strawberries (III,iv)—and had become a bitter enemy of the Yorkist king. Thomas More's own purposé in writing the life of Richard III was surely not to glorify Henry VII, with whom More had a strained relationship, but to characterize the evil of political opportunism. His portrait of Richard becomes that of the generic tyrant, behaving as such tyrants behaved in the various literary models from Renaissance Italy with which More was doubtless familiar. The result was, in any case, one-sided. The historical Richard seems to have been no worse than many another late medieval ruler, and had indeed some admirable ideas on efficiency in government. More's blackened portrait, because it served the purposes of the Tudor state, became part of the legend and was available to Shakespeare in many redactions.

Apart from Hall's and Holinshed's chronicles, those of Robert Fabyan (first published in 1516) and the *Annales* of John Stow (1580, 1592) may have provided Shakespeare further details. Another possible source is *A Myrroure for Magistrates* (first published in 1559), where for example in the Complaint of George, Duke of Clarence, we find the riddling prophecy about "G" (see I,i). A second edition of the *Myrroure* (1563) contains the Complaints of Edward IV, Anthony Woodvile (Lord Rivers), Hastings, Buckingham, Shore's Wife, and others. Shakespeare's particular indebtedness to the *Myrroure* is not great, though he certainly was familiar with it. The same is probably true of the Latin tragedy *Richardus Tertius* by Thomas Legge (1579) at Cambridge. It contains an interesting scene of Richard's wooing of the Lady Anne, not reported in the chronicles. The anonymous *The True Tragedy of Richard III* (published 1594, written c. 1590–1592) may have been useful in its fusing of Senecan revenge motifs with English history, and in its focus on the single figure of Richard. The Richard of this anonymous play is something of a Marlovian overreacher, a believer in Fortune who meets his nemesis in the devoutly Christian Earl of Richmond. Opinion is divided as to whether Shakespeare actually used the play, chiefly because by 1590 he could find the legend of Richard III set forth in so many works.

King John

To understand Shakespeare's use of sources in *King John,* we must first understand the play's relationship to the anonymous play *The Troublesome Raigne of King John,* published in 1591. According to E. A. J. Honigmann (in his edition of *King John,* 1954), *Troublesome Raigne* is a bad quarto pirated from Shakespeare's text rather than a source for it. *Troublesome Raigne* does indeed show features of a bad quarto. Moreover, a 1611 reprint of this play is attributed to "W. Sh.," and another in 1622 to "W. Shakespeare." The Folio editors did not register *King John* for publication in 1623, as though assuming it had already been published in some form. Nevertheless, most scholars still hold to the view that *Troublesome Raigne* is a source. Its early date, by 1591, would mean a still earlier date for a play on which it was based. Honigmann's argument for dating *King John* in 1590 has not won acceptance.

If, on the other hand, we accept the argument that Shakespeare was substantially rewriting an earlier play on King John, the pattern of his indebtedness becomes clear on two points: (1) *Troublesome Raigne* was his main though not his only source, and (2) Shakespeare consciously toned down the earlier play's anti-Catholic excesses and scurrilous humor. His characters are more thoughtful and complex, the paradoxes of kingship more disturbing. Shakespeare's alteration of a crude and chauvinistic source play into a subtle exploration of political rule anticipates his similar transformation of the irrepressible *Famous Victories of Henry V* (c. 1586–1587) into the *Henry IV* plays and *Henry V.*

Briefly, some differences between *Troublesome Raigne* and *King John* are as follows. In *Troublesome Raigne,* John is a hero and a martyr for his defiance of Rome. His claim to the English throne is unquestioned. The barons who rise against him are loyal to Rome. Vice is rampant in monasteries and other ecclesiastical institutions. An abbot is discovered to be hiding a nun in his treasure chest. John is poisoned by a monk who is in league with the abbot and who receives absolution for his deed. The Bastard, John's loyal supporter, is an invincible foe of ecclesiastical corruption and treason against the state. In Shakespeare, on the other hand, John's claim to the throne is dynastically questionable, and his treatment of his nephew Arthur is reprehensible. The barons' opposition to him is prompted by a genuine moral revulsion. Although they learn belatedly that rebellion is more destructive than the evil it seeks to correct, since rebellion provides a fatal opportunity for foreign opportunists like the French Dauphin, the barons are not simply tools of the Papacy. The Bastard struggles too with his conscience over John's treatment of Arthur. The Church is often guilty of political duplicity, as are virtually all the kings and political leaders in the play, but the Church shows no signs of moral decadence. John is poisoned by a monk, but without evidence of conspiracy.

These contrasting estimates of King John reflect the two views of him held concurrently in Tudor England. One, the older and more critical, is that of medieval historians generally and Polydore Vergil in particular. The other, a more favorable estimate, is essentially a Protestant defense of John, a rewriting of history in order to view him (despite his failures) as a martyr of Catholic oppression and hence a forerunner of the Reformation. William Tyndale began this revisionist view of John in his *The Obedience of a Cristen Man* (1528). The case was vividly expounded by John Bale in his *King Johan,* a play begun before 1536 and rewritten in 1538 and 1561. Whether the author of *Troublesome Raigne,* or Shakespeare, consulted Bale is uncertain, but the author of *Troublesome Raigne* was certainly heir to the Protestant tradition. John Foxe's *Actes and Monuments* (1583 edition) gave further currency to the Protestant view. Richard Grafton and Raphael Holinshed took a similar line in their chronicles, and thus passed on the tradition to *Troublesome Raigne.*

Shakespeare's play, though based primarily for its materials on *Troublesome Raigne,* adopts the more critical attitude toward John of the older non-Protestant line. Shakespeare also directly consulted (according to Honigmann) Holinshed, Foxe, the *Historia Maior* of Matthew Paris (published 1571), and perhaps the Latin manuscript *Wakefield Chronicle.*

Richard the Second

Shakespeare's primary source for *Richard II* was the 1587 edition of Holinshed's *Chronicles* covering the years 1398 to 1400. As in his earlier *Henry VI* plays and *Richard III,* Shakespeare departs from historical accuracy in the interests of artistic design. Queen Isabel's part is almost wholly invented, for historically she was a child of eleven at the time the events in this play occurred. Her "Garden Scene" is a fine piece of invention, bringing together images of order and disorder that are found in the rest of the play. The Duchess of York's role is entirely original; Holinshed reports the scene in which York's son Aumerle (the Earl of Rutland) rides to the new King and begs for mercy while his father simultaneously denounces him as a traitor, but the Duchess is never mentioned. Shakespeare has added the poignant conflict between husband and wife. Northumberland's role as conspirator against Richard and as hatchetman for Bolingbroke is greatly enlarged; for example, Holinshed never names the persons who engage in the original plotting against Richard. Another invention is the meeting between John of Gaunt and the Duchess of Gloucester (I,ii). In fact, most of Gaunt's character and behavior has no basis in Holinshed at all. Shakespeare creates him to fill the role of thoughtfully conservative statesman, agonized by his son's banishment but doggedly obedient to his monarch. Finally, and most importantly, Shakespeare has greatly enlarged the role and the poetic nature of King Richard, especially in the final two acts.

Many of these alterations are Shakespeare's own; others derive from his reading in other sources. Samuel Daniel's *The First Fowre Bookes of the Civile Wars* (1595) may have had an important influence. Although we cannot discount the possibility that Shakespeare's play may have been written first, the consensus today is that he knew Daniel's poem. It gave him the idea of the Queen's maturity and grief (although not the Garden Scene), and the final meeting of King and Queen. Daniel's Hotspur is unhistorically a young man, as in II,iii of Shakespeare's play. Like Shakespeare, Daniel sees York as a man of "a mild temperateness." Daniel's Richard and Bolingbroke ride together into London, not separately as in Holinshed. In Daniel's poem, Bolingbroke's indirect manner of insinuating his desire for Richard's death ("And wisht that some would so his life esteeme As rid him of these feares wherein he stood") is verbally close to Shakespeare's depiction of this scene. Richard's final soliloquies in these two works show an unmistakable similarity to one another.

Richard II's reign was a controversial subject in the 1590's, and produced other plays of varying political coloration that Shakespeare must have known. *The Life and Death of Jack Straw* (anonymous, 1590–1593) distorts history in its friendly portrayal of Richard's role in the Peasants' Revolt of 1381, and gives a blatant whitewashing of governmental policy. In contrast, the anonymous play *Thomas of Woodstock,* sometimes known as *1 Richard II* (1591–1595), is almost a call for open rebellion against tyranny. Many verbal similarities link this latter play with Shakespeare's *Richard II,* and, although scholars have difficulty in determining which was written first, the wary consensus is that Shakespeare borrowed from *Woodstock.* Such a hypothesis would explain some of the mysterious references to Woodstock's death in the first act of *Richard II,* since the anonymous play deals with historical events preceding those of Shakespeare's play. Shakespeare's debt to *Jack Straw,* on the other hand, is slight even though he probably knew it. Marlowe's *Edward II* (c. 1592), although dealing with another reign, probably taught Shakespeare much about construction of a play in which a weak king gains sympathy in his suffering while his successful deposer becomes morally tainted by his act.

Other sources have been proposed, so many in fact that Shakespeare's task of writing the play has been compared to that of a historical researcher. More probably he had read several possible sources at one time or another and assimilated them without any formal program of study. He had certainly read Edward Hall's *Union of the Two Noble Famelies,* a chief source for his earlier history plays, but in *Richard II* he seems to have recalled little more than its overall thematic pattern. Shakespeare must have known the complaints of Mowbray and Richard in *A Myrroure for Magistrates,* but the verbal echoes are slight in this case. The same is essentially true of *The Cronycles of Englande* by Jean Froissart, translated by Lord Berners (1525), and two French eyewitness accounts available to Shakespeare only in manuscript: the anonymous *Chronicque de la Traïson et Mort de Richart Deux Roy Dengleterre* and Jean Créton's *Histoire du Roy d'Angleterre Richard.* The Froissart *Cronycles* perhaps gave some hints for Gaunt's refusal to avenge Gloucester's death, for Richard's insensitivity at Gaunt's death, and for Northumberland's role as conspirator. The *Traïson* is notably sympathetic to Richard in his decline, although Shakespeare might also have found this sympathy in Daniel's *Civile Wars.*

Shakespeare's second tetralogy is freer of the Tudor view of history than his first. The second tetralogy does not lead forward by any direct link to the reign of the Tudors, as the first had done. Henry A. Kelly has recently shown (*Divine Providence in the England of Shakespeare's Histories,* 1970), that Shakespeare does not follow a single "Tudor myth" but allows spokesmen for both pro-Lancastrian and anti-Lancastrian sentiment to repeat arguments found in the various chronicles. This practice is especially evident in *Richard II,* in which some spokesmen eloquently warn of the disasters that will follow Bolingbroke's assumption of the throne, while other spokesmen are sympathetic to Bolingbroke's takeover as a political necessity.

The Henry the Fourth Plays

Shakespeare's chief historical source for both *Henry IV* plays was the 1587 edition of Holinshed's *Chronicles,* but Shakespeare also found an important guiding spirit in Samuel Daniel's *The First Fowre Bookes of the Civile Wars* (1595). Following Daniel, Shakespeare readjusts the age of Hotspur (who was historically older than Henry IV) to match that of Prince Hal. Daniel's Hotspur is, like Shakespeare's, dauntless and wrongheaded, a turbulent yet noble spirit. The theme of a Nemesis of rebellion afflicting Henry IV for his usurpation owes much to Daniel's presentation, although the idea of Nemesis is to be found also in Holinshed. Both Daniel and Holinshed err in confusing the Edmund Mortimer whom Glendower captured with his nephew Edmund Mortimer, claimant to the throne; Shakespeare perpetuates this error. Hal's killing of Hotspur is unhistorical, since both Holinshed and Daniel report only that Hal bravely helped rescue his father from attack, and that Hotspur was killed in the melee. Shakespeare invents the scenes in which we see Mortimer as a devoted husband and Hotspur as a fond combatant in wit with his wife Kate; Holinshed merely informs us that these two men were married. Shakespeare greatly expands Glendower's fascination with magic and poetry, changing him from a ruthless barbarian (in Holinshed) into a cranky but charismatic Welshman. Hotspur, despite hints from Daniel, is chiefly Shakespeare's creation. In *2 Henry IV,* Shakespeare puts Northumberland in a more dishonorable position than in Holinshed, and emphasizes the perfidious dastardy of Prince John. Seemingly, Shakespeare wanted to stress the coldness and cynicism of Machiavellian politicians on both sides of the rebellion, as a contrast with the more enlightened policy to which Prince Hal aspires.

The most impressive transformations are those of Hal and Falstaff. Shakespeare knew many legends of Hal's wild youth, some from John Stow's *The Chronicles of England* (1580) and *The Annales of England* (1592), others from oral tradition. Sir Thomas Elyot's *The Governour* (1531) gives an account of Hal's encounter with the Lord Chief Justice that is reproduced almost verbatim by Stow. Most of these stories were also available in Holinshed. Shakespeare's readiest source, however, was a rowdy and chauvinistic play called *The Famous Victories of Henry the Fifth,* registered 1594 but usually ascribed to Richard Tarleton around 1587 or 1588. This play covers all the events of the *Henry IV* plays and *Henry V* in one chaotic sequence. Prince Hal has three companions, Sir John Oldcastle, Tom, and Ned (cf. Ned Poins), in whose company he robs the King's receivers of £1,000, visits the old tavern in East Cheap, sorely grieves his father, and strikes the Lord Chief Justice. A crucial difference is that this Hal is truly unregenerate. He not only robs and wenches, but endorses the idea of plundering the rich and encourages his companions to look forward to unrestricted license when he is King. The blow he delivers the Chief Justice is a blow for freedom. Hal seems consciously to desire his father's death. Yet he does reform, and banishes his companions beyond a ten-mile limit with a promise to assist them if they mend their ways. Although this reform is crude and sudden, Hal's reputation for the common touch stands him in good stead when he goes to war against the French. He is followed by a comic crew of London artisans and thieves who prove invincible against the effete enemy.

This play suggests the unsophisticated nature of the legends Shakespeare inherited about Hal's riotous youth, and the extent of the transformation. Shakespeare invents Mistress Quickly and Doll Tearsheet. Pistol bears only the faintest resemblance to any of the rowdies in the anonymous play. Shallow and Silence have no counterparts in Shakespeare's sources, although *Famous Victories* does show a farcical scene of impressment. Most of all, Shakespeare's portrayal of Falstaff is essentially his own. Sir John Oldcastle of the anonymous play is a minor character, not Hal's closest companion. Falstaff owes something to the tradition of the guileful and inventive Vice of the Tudor morality play (especially when Falstaff is called jestingly "that reverend vice, that grey iniquity"), but the influence of the morality play is general rather than specific. To label Falstaff a "Vice" is to reduce him to comic tempter and villain. Falstaff is in part an allowed fool, a parasite, and a *miles gloriosus* or braggart soldier, but he transcends all these conventionalized types with his own unique vitality.

The *Henry IV* plays suggest some acquaintance with the anonymous play *Thomas of Woodstock* (c. 1591–1595), which Shakespeare may also have used in *Richard II,* and with the complaints of Owen Glendower and Northumberland in *A Myrroure for Magistrates* (1559). In neither case is the debt extensive.

Henry the Fifth

Shakespeare's principal historical source for *Henry V,* as for *Richard II* and the *Henry IV* plays, was the 1587 edition of Holinshed's *Chronicles.* In his account of Henry V, however, Raphael Holinshed had depended so heavily on Edward Hall's *The Union of the Two Noble and Illustre Famelies of Lancastre and Yorke* (1548) that we sometimes have difficulty knowing whether Shakespeare consulted Holinshed or Hall. He was certainly familiar with both. Shakespeare's sources all acclaim Henry V a hero-king. Samuel Daniel's *The First Fowre Bookes of the Civile Wars* (1595), which Shakespeare may have used for his account of the treasonous plot against Henry (II,ii), also praises the King in fulsome terms.

Shakespeare follows the order of events laid down in Holinshed and Hall: the personal rivalry between Henry and the French Dauphin, Henry's request for reassurance from the clergy as to the legitimacy of the war, the maneuvering of the clergy to forestall a bill in Parliament threatening to seize church land, the foiling of a plot against Henry's life, the siege of Harfleur, the glorious victory at Agincourt. Both Holinshed and Hall offer Shakespeare many particulars about the English claim to France: in both accounts, the Archbishop quotes the law *In terram Salicam mulieres ne succedant,* and goes on at length about King Pharamond, the rivers Elbe and Sala, King Pepin, Hugh Capet, the Book of Numbers, and the rest. On the other hand, Shakespeare omits a three-year campaign that historically intervened between Agincourt and the peace treaty of Troyes. He passes over the Lollard controversy in England, with the execution of Sir John Oldcastle. And, of course, he adds unforgettable characters that we do not find in the chronicles—Welshmen, Irishmen, Scots, common soldiers, thieves—who show the unity of the British nation under King Henry's charismatic leadership.

For many of his additions to the chronicles, Shakespeare was indebted to the anonymous *The Famous Victories of Henry the Fifth* (c. 1588). This old play, not registered until 1594 and not printed until 1598, exists today only in a corrupt text; quite possibly Shakespeare knew a fuller and more authentic version that would have given him still more material. Other plays may have existed on the subject, for the Admiral's men acted a "harey the v" in 1595 and 1596 that may or may not have been *The Famous Victories.* In any event, the relationship between *Henry V* and *Famous Victories* is at times close. *Famous Victories* omits Henry's long campaign between Agincourt and the final peace treaty, as does Shakespeare's play. The Archbishop of *Famous Victories* discusses the French claim just before the arrival of the French Ambassador with the tennis balls. (In Holinshed, the tennis-ball incident occurs first, at Kenilworth, whereas the Archbishop's lecture occurs some time later at a meeting of Parliament in Leicester.) Henry assures the French Ambassador that he has "free libertie and license to speake." To the Dauphin's insolent gift, taunting Henry about his wild youth, the King suavely replies that "My lord prince Dolphin is very pleasaunt with me," and promises to repay the insult with balls of brass and iron. (Holinshed mentions this apparently nonhistorical legend only briefly.) When the French noblemen assembled at the French court hear of Henry's arrival on their shores, they tremble with fear even though the Dauphin recklessly scoffs at so young and wild-headed a king. Henry is accompanied to France by a ludicrous assortment of London artisans and thieves, such as John Cobler, who bids farewell to his wife in a comic scene similar to Pistol's parting from the Hostess, and Dericke, who turns the tables on a French soldier much as Pistol deals with Monsieur le Fer. When King Henry woos Katharine of France, he protests to her that he cannot speak flatteringly because he is a plain soldier. She asks in return: "How should I love him, that hath dealt so hardly With my father?" Despite these resemblances, however, Shakespeare's *Henry V* is incomparably superior to the old play and contains many original scenes and characters such as King Henry's touring of his camp incognito, the quarrel between Henry and Williams, and above all the scenes involving Fluellen and his fellow-captains.

Other possible sources include the *Henrici Quinti Angliae Regis Gesta* written by a chaplain in Henry V's army, the *Vita et Gesta Henrici Quinti* erroneously ascribed to Thomas Elmham, the *Vita Henrici Quinti* by "Titus Livius," translated 1513 (in which the French brag about their horses and armor), a ballad called "The Battle of Agincourt" (c. 1530), and *The Annals of Cornelius Tacitus,* translated 1598 (in which Germanicus walks disguised through his camp at night "to sounde the souldiers minde," and hears his leadership praised).

King Henry the Eighth

Shakespeare's chief source for the first four acts of *Henry VIII,* as for many of his earlier history plays, was Holinshed's *Chronicles* (1587 edition). Holinshed presented him with conflicting views of Cardinal Wolsey, however, and traces of the conflict remain in Shakespeare's play. Much of Holinshed is actually a compilation of the writings of earlier historiographers. In this case, some of Holinshed's material is from the bitterly anti-Wolseyan *Anglica Historia* (1534) of Polydore Vergil. Accordingly, Holinshed gives decidedly unfavorable interpretations of Wolsey's animosity toward the Duke of Buckingham and his unscrupulous meddling in the King's marriage question. Vergil was particularly distressed by the way in which Katharine had been cashiered; he (and Holinshed) report her speeches in her own behalf with manifest approval. Shakespeare preserves this alignment of sympathies in which Katharine is the wrongly accused wife and Wolsey the Machiavel.

Other portions of Holinshed, on the other hand, derive from George Cavendish's *The Life and Death of Thomas Wolsey,* written some time around 1557 and extensively used by the chroniclers, though not separately printed until 1641. Cavendish was a gentleman-usher in the household of Cardinal Wolsey from 1526 to 1530. Although he moralizes about the lesson to be learned from Wolsey's ambitious rise and sudden fall, Cavendish speaks admiringly of the Cardinal as an extraordinarily great man. He captures in minutely observed detail the magnificence of Wolsey's prosperous estate. He gives a moving portrait of Wolsey after his fall, on his sick-bed and near the end, saying to a companion: "if I had served God as diligently as I have done the King, he would not have given me over in my gray hairs." This passage, borrowed verbatim by Holinshed from Cavendish, produces in turn the famous lines from Shakespeare: "Had I but serv'd my God with half the zeal I serv'd my King, he would not in mine age Have left me naked to mine enemies" (III,ii,455–457).

For his fifth act, Shakespeare turned to John Foxe's *Actes and Monuments of Martyrs.* Here he encountered a particularly rabid Protestant point of view, which has left its impression not only on the fifth act but on portrayals of Wolsey (whom Foxe naturally deplored) in earlier scenes. Foxe's hero, Thomas Cranmer, emerges as the victor of Shakespeare's play. Although the triumphantly Protestant ending contrasts oddly with Shakespeare's earlier manifest sympathy for Queen Katharine, the duality of attitudes is somehow plausible and perhaps even typically Elizabethan: Katharine suffered lamentably, and Henry and Wolsey treated her shabbily, but these great events did after all lead to the English Reformation and the rule of Queen Elizabeth. The ambiguity so often noted in *Henry VIII,* then, is an essential part of Shakespeare's sources, not merely because he used conflicting accounts but because many Elizabethan Englishmen necessarily felt mixed emotions toward this chapter of their past.

Shakespeare may also have read in Edward Hall's *The Union of the Two Noble and Illustre Famelies of Lancastre and Yorke,* and in John Speed's *History of Great Britaine* (1611). In addition, he probably knew a dramatic version of the reign of Henry VIII that had appeared about eight years before, *When You See Me You Know Me* by Samuel Rowley (1603–1605).

Titus Andronicus

Although we do not today possess any work that Shakespeare could have used for his immediate source in *Titus,* we have an eighteenth-century chapbook called *The History of Titus Andronicus* that may tell us substantially what that source was like. This chapbook is similar to Shakespeare's play, and its differences (according to Ralph Sargent, in *Studies in Philology,* 1949) can best be explained by the hypothesis that a closely related prose version served as Shakespeare's chief source. This hypothesis is now generally accepted. Some scholars even argue that the Stationers' Register entry in 1594 to John Danter for "a Noble Roman Historye of Tytus Andronicus" with "the ballad thereof" refers to just such a prose account. Of this we cannot be certain, for Danter did after all publish the play in that same year, and the ballad seems to owe some of its details to the play (though based chiefly on the prose version). Still, the existence of a prose *History of Titus* when Shakespeare wrote his play seems likely.

The prose *History,* as it survives today, is a fictitious medley of revenge stories inspired by Seneca and Ovid. It is set in the last days of the Roman Empire, but contains no recognizable historical characters or events. Titus Andronicus is a Roman senator who defends Rome against the Goths in a protracted ten-year struggle, losing twenty-two of his own sons in the conflict. He slays the Gothic King Tottilius in battle and captures the Queen, Attava. When Tottilius' two sons Alaricus and Abonus continue the assault on Rome, the Roman Emperor wearies of the conflict and resolves to marry Attava against the advice of his general, Andronicus. The Queen, naturally regarding Titus as an enemy, proceeds to obtain powerful positions for her own kinsmen. She succeeds in having Titus banished, but he is recalled by popular insistence. Attava conducts an amour with her nameless Moorish servant and has a black child by him. Discovery of the child leads to the Moor's banishment, but he too is later recalled. Attava opposes the marriage of Titus' daughter Lavinia to the Emperor's only son (by a former marriage), since she desires the possession of the empire for her own sons. The remainder of the story proceeds much as in the play, except that we do not learn what happens to Rome after Titus' death. Shakespeare's chief additions include Titus' candidacy for and rejection of the throne, the struggle between Saturninus and Bassianus, the sacrifice of Tamora's son Alarbus, and a greatly magnified role for Aaron the Moor.

Although the prose version itself made use of Ovid and Seneca, Shakespeare evidently consulted these authors directly as well. The play contains many explicit references to classical authors, most notably when Lavinia turns the pages of Ovid's *Metamorphoses* to the story of Philomela's rape (IV,i). In Ovid's famous account (Book VI,526 ff.), King Tereus of Thrace rapes Philomela, cuts out her tongue (but not her hands) to prevent her from revealing the crime, and keeps her prisoner. She nevertheless manages to weave her story into a tapestry and send it to her sister, Procne, who liberates Philomela and plots with her to serve Tereus' and Procne's son Itys to him at a banquet.

A similar grisly feast takes place in Seneca's *Thyestes,* from which Shakespeare may well have drawn some particulars. Atreus, the wronged avenger, murders the two sons of Thyestes and serves them to him. As in Shakespeare's play, there are two sons rather than one. Of these two sons, one is guilty of ambition, whereas Ovid's Itys is an innocent victim. The slayer is a male avenger, not (as in Ovid) the mother of the slain victim. Senecan conventions of underworld Revenge spirits and the like are also present in the play, though they may have reached Shakespeare by way of Kyd's *The Spanish Tragedy* and other plays of the late 1580's. Both Ovid and Seneca were commonly taught in Elizabethan grammar schools, though both were also available in English translation: Ovid by Golding (1567) and Seneca by Jasper Heywood (1560). Marlowe's *Tamburlaine* and *The Jew of Malta* certainly had an influence, especially on Shakespeare's conception of Aaron the Moor.

Two continental plays about Titus, the German *Tragaedia von Tito Andronico* (1620) and the Dutch *Aran en Titus* by Jan Vos (1641), were once thought to have been derived from an English play before 1594 which might then have served as a source for Shakespeare. In the German play the name of Titus' son Lucius is Vespasian, and this fact has caused scholars to wonder if the "Tittus & Vespasia" acted in April 1592 by Strange's men (as mentioned in Henslowe's diary) was about Titus Andronicus. Lucius' part is small for such prominence in a title, however, and the prevailing opinion today is that Henslowe's play was on an independent subject.

Romeo and Juliet

Shakespeare's chief source for *Romeo and Juliet* was a long narrative poem by Arthur Brooke called *The Tragicall Historye of Romeus and Juliet, written first in Italian by Bandell, and nowe in Englishe by Ar. Br.* (1562). Other English versions of this popular legend were available to Shakespeare, especially in William Painter's *The Palace of Pleasure* (1566), but Shakespeare shows only a passing indebtedness to it. Brooke mentions having seen (prior to 1562) a play about the two lovers, but such an old play is not likely to have been of much service to Shakespeare. Nor does he appear to have consulted extensively the various continental versions that lay behind Brooke's poem. Still, these versions help explain the genesis of the story.

The use of a sleeping potion to escape an unwelcome marriage goes back at least to the *Ephesiaca* of Xenophon of Ephesus (by the fifth century A.D.). Masuccio of Salerno, in his *Il Novellino* (1476), seems to have been the first to combine this sleeping potion story with an ironic aftermath of misunderstanding and suicide (as found in the Pyramus and Thisbe story of Ovid's *Metamorphoses*). In Masuccio's account, the lovers Mariotto and Giannozza of Siena are secretly married by a friar. When Mariotto kills a prominent citizen of Siena in a quarrel, he is banished to Alexandria. Giannozza, to avoid marriage with a suitor of her father's choosing, takes a sleeping potion given her by the friar, and is buried as though dead. She is thereupon taken from the tomb by the friar and sent on her way to Alexandria. Mariotto, however, having failed to hear from her because the messenger is intercepted by pirates, returns in disguise to her tomb where he is discovered and executed. Giannozza, hearing this sad news, retires to a Sienese convent and dies of a broken heart.

In Luigi da Porto's *Hystoria nouellamente ritrouata di due Nobili Amanti* (published c. 1530), based on Masuccio's account, the scene shifts to Verona. Despite the feuding of their two families, the Montecchi and the Cappelletti, Romeo and Guilietta meet and fall in love at a carnival ball. Romeo at once forgets his unrequited passion for a scornful lady. Friar Lorenzo, an experimenter in magic, secretly marries the lovers. Romeo tries to avoid brawling with the Cappelletti, but when some of his own kinsmen suffer defeat, he kills Theobaldo Cappelletti. After Romeo's departure for Mantua, Guilietta's family arranges a match for her with the Count of Lodrone. Friar Lorenzo gives Guilietta a sleeping potion and sends a letter to Romeo by a fellow friar, but this messenger is unable to find Romeo in Mantua. Romeo, hearing of Guilietta's supposed death from her servant Peter, returns to Verona with a poison he already possesses. Guilietta awakens in time to converse with Romeo before he dies. Then, refusing the friar's advice to retire to a convent, she dies by stopping her own breath. This story provides no equivalents for Mercutio and the Nurse, although a young man named Marcuccio appears briefly at the Cappelletti's ball.

Da Porto's version inspired that of Matteo Bandello in his *Novelle* of 1554. Some details are added: Romeo goes to the ball in a vizard, he has a servant named Pietro, a rope ladder is given to the Nurse enabling Romeo to visit Julietta's chamber before their marriage, Romeo obtains a poison from one Spolentino, etc. The young man at the ball, Marcuccio, is now named Mercutio but is still a minor figure. This Bandello version was translated into French by Pierre Boaistuau in his *Histoires Tragiques* (1559); Boaistuau adds the apothecary (who is racked and hanged for his part in the tragedy), and has Romeo die before Juliet awakens and slays herself with Romeo's dagger.

Despite Arthur Brooke's implication on the title page that his version is based on Bandello, the narrative poem *Romeus and Juliet* is taken from Boaistuau. Brooke's is a severely pious work written in "Poulter's Measure," couplets with alternating lines of six and seven feet. Brooke openly disapproves of the lovers' carnality and haste, although fortunately the story itself remains sympathetic to Romeus and Juliet. Brooke stresses star-crossed fortune and the antithesis of love and hate. He reduces Juliet's age from eighteen (as in Bandello) to sixteen. (Shakespeare further reduced her age to less than fourteen.) Brooke's narrative is generally close to Shakespeare's, though with important exceptions. Shakespeare compresses time from some nine months to a few days. In Brooke, for example, some two weeks elapse between the masked ball and Romeus' encounter with Juliet in her garden, and about two months elapse between the marriage and Tybalt's death. In Shakespeare, Capulet moves the wedding up from Thursday to Wednesday, thereby complicating the time schedule for the lovers. Shakespeare also unifies his play by such devices as introducing Tybalt and Paris early in the story; in Brooke, Tybalt appears only at the time he is slain, and Juliet's proposed marriage to Count Paris emerges as a threat only after Romeus' banishment. Shakespeare's greatest transformation is of the characters. Brooke's Juliet is scheming. His Mercutio remains a shadowy figure as in Bandello *et al.* Brooke's Nurse is unattractive, although she does occasionally hint at comic greatness: for example, she garrulously confides to Romeus the details of Juliet's infancy, and then keeps Juliet on tenterhooks while she prates about Romeus' fine qualities (ll. 631–714). Even if Shakespeare's play is incomparably superior to Brooke's drably versified poem, the indebtedness is extensive.

Julius Caesar

Julius Caesar represents Shakespeare's first extensive use of Plutarch, in Thomas North's translation (based on the French of Jacques Amyot) of the *Lives of the Noble Grecians and Romanes* (1579 and 1595). Plutarch was to become Shakespeare's most often-used source in the 1600's; prior to 1599 he had consulted it briefly on a number of other occasions. In *Julius Caesar,* he borrows details from three lives: Caesar, Brutus, and Antonius. He uses particular traits of character, such as Caesar's belief that it is "better to dye once, than alwayes to be affrayed of death," Brutus' determination to "frame his manners of life by the rules of virtue and study of philosophy," Cassius' choleric disposition and his "hating Caesar privately more than he did the tyranny openly," and Antonius' inclination to "rioting and banqueting."

The events of the play are substantially present in Plutarch, especially in the Life of Julius Caesar. Antonius runs the course on the feast of Lupercal to cure barrenness, and offers the diadem to Caesar. Flavius and Marullus despoil the images of Caesar. Caesar observes that he mistrusts "pale and lean men" like Brutus and Cassius, not "fat fellows." Papers are thrown by the conspirators where Brutus can find them, proclaiming "Thou sleepest, Brutus, and art not Brutus indeed." Caesar's death is preceded by prodigies: a slave's hand burns but is unconsumed, a sacrificial beast is found to contain no heart. When Caesar encounters the soothsayer who previously had warned him of his fate, and boasts that "the Ides of March be come," the soothsayer has the last word: "so they be, but yet are they not past." Brutus' wife Portia complains to him of being treated "like a harlot," not like a partner. Brutus commits what Plutarch calls two serious errors when he forbids his fellow-conspirators to kill Antonius, and when he permits Antonius to speak at Caesar's funeral. Cinna the Poet is slain by an angry crowd mistaking him for Cinna the conspirator. A ghost appears to Brutus shortly before the last battle saying "I am thy ill angel, Brutus, and thou shalt see me by the city of Phillippes," to which Brutus replies "Well, I shall see thee then." Antonius says of the vanquished conspirators that "there was none but Brutus only that was moved to do it, as thinking the act commendable of itself: but that all the other conspirators did conspire his death for some private malice or envy." Shakespeare's debt to Plutarch is greater than these few examples can indicate.

Of course Shakespeare reshapes and selects, as in his history plays. He compresses into one day Caesar's triumphant procession, the disrobing of the images, and the offer of the crown to Caesar on the Lupercal, when in fact these events were chronologically separate. Casca is by and large an invented character, and Octavius' role is considerably enlarged. Brutus' servant Lucius is a minor but effective addition, illustrating Brutus' capacity for warmth and humanity. Brutus' two speeches after the assassination (as mentioned by Plutarch) become one, and Antonius' speech is made to follow immediately after. (In Plutarch, Antonius speaks the following day, after the reading of the will.) Shakespeare accentuates the irrationality and vacillation of the mob, for in Plutarch the people are never much swayed by Brutus' rhetoric even though they respectfully allow him to speak. The unforgettable speeches of both Brutus and Antonius are not set down at all in Plutarch. More compression of time occurs after the assassination: in Plutarch, Octavius does not arrive in Rome until some six weeks afterward, and does not agree to the formation of the Triumvirate until more than a year of quarreling has taken place. The inexorable buildup of tension in Shakespeare's play is the result of careful selection from a vast amount of material.

Although Shakespeare depended heavily on Plutarch, he was also aware of later and conflicting traditions about Caesar. On the one hand, Dante's *Divine Comedy* consigns Brutus and Cassius to the lowest circle of hell along with Judas Iscariot and other betrayers of their masters. Chaucer's *Monk's Tale,* from the *Canterbury Tales,* similarly portrays Caesar as the manly and uncorruptible victim of envious attackers. On the other hand, Montaigne stresses the *hubris* of Caesar in aspiring to divinity. (Shakespeare could have read Montaigne in the French original or in

John Florio's English translation.) A pro-Brutus view could also be found in the Latin *Julius Caesar* of Marc-Antoine Muret (1553) and the French *César* of Jacques Grévin (1561). That Shakespeare knew these works is unlikely, but they kept alive a tradition with which he was certainly familiar. Possibly he knew Lucan's account of Caesar in the *Pharsalia* and Cicero's letters and orations, which were republican in tenor. Other possible sources include the *Chronicle of the Romanes Warres* by Appian of Alexandria (translated 1578), the anonymous play *Caesar's Revenge* (published 1606–1607, performed in the early 1590's at Oxford), and Thomas Kyd's *Cornelia* (translated from the French Senecan tragedy by Garnier). *Il Cesare* by Orlando Pescetti (1594) is now almost universally rejected as a possible source. The result of Shakespeare's acquaintance with both pro- and anti-Caesar traditions is that he shows much that is both good and deplorable in Caesar and in the conspirators as well.

Hamlet

The ultimate source of the *Hamlet* story is Saxo Grammaticus' *Historia Danica* (1180–1208), the saga of one Amlothi or (as Saxo calls him) Amlethus. The outline of the story is essentially that of Shakespeare's play, even though the emphasis of the Danish saga is overwhelmingly on cunning, brutality, and bloody revenge. Amlethus' father is Horwendil, a Governor of Jutland, who bravely kills the King of Norway in single combat and thereby wins the hand in marriage of Gerutha, daughter of the King of Denmark. This good fortune goads the envious Feng into slaying his brother Horwendil and marrying Gerutha, "capping unnatural murder with incest." Though the deed is known to everyone, Feng invents excuses and soon wins the approbation of the fawning courtiers. Young Amlethus vows revenge, but perceiving his uncle's cunning he feigns madness. His mingled words of craft and candor awaken suspicions that he may be playing a game of deception.

Two attempts are made to lure Amlethus into betraying his sanity. The first plan is to tempt him into lechery, on the theory that one who lusts for women cannot be truly insane. Feng causes an attractive woman to be placed in a forest where Amlethus will meet her as though by chance; but Amlethus, secretly warned of the trap by a kindly foster brother, spirits the young lady off to a hideaway where they can make love unobserved by Feng's agents. She confesses the plot to Amlethus. In a second stratagem, a courtier who is reported to be "gifted with more assurance than judgment" hides himself under some straw in the Queen's chamber in order to overhear her private conversations with Amlethus. The hero, suspecting just such a trap, feigns madness and begins crowing like a noisy rooster, bouncing up and down on the straw until he finds the eavesdropper. Amlethus stabs the man to death, drags him forth, cuts the body into morsels, boils the morsels, and flings them "through the mouth of an open sewer for the swine to eat." Thereupon he returns to his mother to accuse her of being an infamous harlot. He wins her over to repentant virtue and even cooperation. When Feng, returning from a journey, looks around for his counselor, Amlethus jestingly (but in part truly) suggests that the man went to the sewer and fell in.

Feng now sends Amlethus to the King of Britain, with secret orders for his execution. However, Amlethus finds the letter to the British King in the coffers of the two unnamed retainers accompanying him on the journey, and substitutes a new letter ordering their execution instead. The new letter, purportedly written and signed by Feng, goes on to urge that the King of Britain marry his daughter to a young Dane being sent from the Danish court. By this means Amlethus gains an English wife and rids himself of the escorts. A year later Amlethus returns to Jutland, gets the entire court drunk, flings a tapestry (knitted for him by his mother) over the prostrate courtiers, secures the tapestry with stakes, and then sets fire to the palace. Feng escapes this holocaust, but Amlethus cuts him down with the King's own sword. (Amlethus exchanges swords because his own has been rendered useless by his enemies.) Subsequently, Amlethus convinces the people of the justice of his cause and is chosen King of Jutland. After ruling for several years, he returns to Britain, marries a Scottish queen, fights a battle with his first father-in-law, is betrayed by his second wife, and is finally killed in battle.

In Saxo's account we thus find the prototypes of Hamlet, Claudius, Gertrude, Polonius, Ophelia, Rosencrantz, and Guildenstern. Several episodes are close in narrative detail to Shakespeare's play: the original murder and incestuous marriage, the feigned madness, the woman used as a decoy, the eavesdropping counselor, and especially the trip to England. A translation of Saxo into French by François de Belleforest, in *Histoires Tragiques* (1576 edition), adds a few details such as Gertrude's adultery before the murder, and Hamlet's melancholy. Belleforest's version is longer than Saxo's, with more psychological and moral observation and more dialogue. Shakespeare may have consulted it.

Shakespeare need not have depended extensively on these older versions of his story, however. His main source was almost certainly an old play of *Hamlet*. Much evidence testifies to the existence of such a play. Henslowe's *Diary* records a performance, not marked as "new," of a *Hamlet* at Newington Butts on June 11, 1594, by "my Lord Admeralle men" or "my Lorde Chamberlen men," probably the latter. Thomas Lodge's *Wits Miserie, and the Worlds Madnesse* (1596) refers to "the Visard of the ghost which cried so miserably at the Theator, like an oister wife, Hamlet, revenge." And Thomas Nashe, in his *Epistle* prefixed to Greene's *Menaphon* (1589), offers the following observation:

> It is a common practise now a dayes amongst a sort of shifting companions, that runne through euery Art and thriue by none, to leaue the trade of *Nouerint,* whereto they were borne, and busie

themselues with the endeuours of Art, that could scarcely Latinize their neck verse if they should haue neede; yet English *Seneca* read by Candlelight yeelds many good sentences, as *Blood is a begger,* and so forth; and if you intreate him faire in a frostie morning, hee will affoord you whole *Hamlets,* I should say handfuls of Tragical speeches. But O griefe! *Tempus edax rerum,* whats that will last alwayes? The Sea exhaled by droppes will in continuance bee drie, and *Seneca,* let blood line by line and page by page, at length must needes die to our Stage; which makes his famished followers to imitate the Kidde in Aesop, who, enamoured with the Foxes newfangles, forsooke all hopes of life to leape into a newe occupation; and these men, renouncing all possibilities of credite or estimation, to intermeddle with Italian Translations . . .

Nashe's testimonial describes a *Hamlet* play, written in the Senecan style by some person born to the trade of "Noverint" or scrivener who has turned to hack writing and translation. The description has often been fitted to Thomas Kyd, though this identification is not certain. (Nashe could be punning on Kyd's name when he refers to "the Kidde in Aesop.") Certainly Thomas Kyd's *The Spanish Tragedy* (c. 1587) shows many affinities with Shakespeare's play, and provides many Senecan ingredients missing from Saxo and Belleforest: the ghost, the difficulty in ascertaining whether the ghost's words are believable, the resulting need for delay and a feigning of madness, the moral perplexities afflicting a sensitive man called upon to revenge, the play within the play, the clever reversals and ironically caused deaths in the catastrophe, the rhetoric of tragical passion. Whether or not Kyd in fact wrote the *Ur-Hamlet,* his extant play enables us to see more clearly what that lost play must have contained. The pirated first quarto of *Hamlet* (1603) also offers a few seemingly authentic details that are not found in the good second quarto but are found in the earlier sources and may have been a part of the *Ur-Hamlet.* For example, after Hamlet has killed Corambis (corresponding to Polonius), the Queen vows to assist Hamlet in his strategies against the King; and later, when Hamlet has returned to England, the Queen sends him a message by Horatio warning him to be careful.

One last document sheds light on the *Ur-Hamlet.* A German play, *Der bestrafte Brudermord (Fratricide Punished),* from a now-lost manuscript dated 1710, seems to have been based on a text used by English actors traveling in Germany in 1586 and afterwards. Though changed by translation and manuscript transmission, and too entirely different from Shakespeare's play to have been based on it, this German version may well have been based on Shakespeare's source-play. Polonius' name in this text, Corambus, is the Corambis of the bad quarto of 1603.

Der bestrafte Brudermord begins with a prologue in the Senecan manner, followed by the appearance of the ghost to Francisco, Horatio, and sentinels of the watch. Within the palace, meanwhile, the King carouses. Hamlet joins the watch, confiding to Horatio that he is "sick at heart" over his father's death and mother's hasty remarriage. The ghost appears to Hamlet, tells him how the juice of hebona was poured into his ear, and urges revenge. When Hamlet swears Horatio and Francisco to silence, the ghost (now invisible) says several times "We swear," his voice following the men as they move from place to place. Hamlet reveals to Horatio the entire circumstance of the murder. Later, in a formal session of the court, the new King speaks hypocritically of his brother's death and explains the reasons for his marriage to the Queen. Hamlet is forbidden to return to Wittenberg, though Corambus' son Leonhardus has already set out for France.

Some time afterward, Corambus reports the news of Hamlet's madness to the King and Queen, and presumes on the basis of his own youthful passions to diagnose Hamlet's malady as lovesickness. Concealed, he and the King overhear Hamlet tell Ophelia to "go to a nunnery." When players arrive from Germany, Hamlet instructs them in the natural style of acting, and then requests them to perform a play before the King about the murder of King Pyrrus by his brother. (Death is again inflicted by hebona poured in the ear.) After the King's guilty reaction to the play, Hamlet finds him alone at prayers but postpones the killing lest the King's soul be sent to heaven. Hamlet kills Corambus behind the tapestry in the Queen's chamber, and is visited again by the ghost (who says nothing, however). Ophelia, her mind deranged, thinks herself in love with a court butterfly named Phantasmo. (This creature is also involved in a comic action to help the clown Jens with a tax problem.)

The King sends Hamlet to England with two unnamed courtiers who are verbally instructed to kill Hamlet after their arrival. A contrary wind takes them instead to an island near Dover, where Hamlet foils his two enemies by kneeling between them and asking them to shoot him on signal; at the proper moment, he ducks and they shoot one another. He finishes them off with their own swords, and discovers letters on their persons ordering Hamlet's execution by the English King if the original plot should fail. When Hamlet returns to Denmark, the King arranges a duel between him and Corambus' son Leonhardus. If Leonhardus' poisoned dagger misses its mark, a beaker of wine containing finely ground oriental diamond dust is to do the rest. Hamlet is informed of the impending duel by Phantasmo (cf. Osric), whom Hamlet taunts condescendingly and calls "Signora Phantasmo." Shortly before the duel takes place, Ophelia is reported to have thrown herself off a hill to her death. The other deaths occur much as in Shakespeare's play. The dying Hamlet bids that the crown be conveyed to his cousin, Duke Fortempras of Norway, of whom we have not heard earlier.

From the extensive similarities between *Hamlet* and this German play, we can see that Shakespeare inherited his narrative material almost intact, though in a jumble and so pitifully mangled that the modern reader can only laugh at the contrast. No source study in Shakespeare reveals so clearly the extent of Shakespeare's wholesale borrowing of plot, and the incredible transformation he achieved in reordering his materials.

Othello

Shakespeare's main source for *Othello* was the seventh story from the third decade of G. B. Giraldi Cinthio's *Hecatommithi* (1565). Cinthio was available in French but not in English translation during Shakespeare's lifetime. The verbal echoes in Shakespeare's play are usually closer to the Italian original than to Gabriel Chappuys' French version of 1584. Cinthio's account may have been based on an actual incident occurring in Venice around 1508.

Cinthio tells of a valiant Moor, highly regarded by the Venetian Republic for his warlike skill, with whom a virtuous and beautiful lady named Disdemona falls in love. She is attracted to him not by physical desire but by his fine qualities. He responds with no less ardor to her beauty and nobleness of mind. Despite her relatives' disapproval of such a marriage, they dwell in Venice for some time in peaceful harmony. When the Moor is sent by the Signory of Venice to take command of the garrison on Cyprus, Disdemona insists on accompanying him. Traveling with them on the boat are an Ensign (whom Shakespeare calls Iago), the Ensign's attractive wife (Emilia), and a Corporal (Cassio). Disdemona is fond of the young wife; the Moor values the friendship of both the Corporal and the Ensign. Beneath the valorous manner of this Ensign, however, lurks an evil heart. He falls passionately in love with Disdemona, and, jealously imagining that she prefers the Corporal, resolves to accuse her of adultery with the Corporal and thereby destroy them both.

Even before he has time to act, however, the Moor demotes the Corporal for wounding a soldier on guard duty. (The Ensign has no part in fomenting this disgrace.) When Disdemona petitions her husband to restore the Corporal to his former favor, the Ensign insinuates that she has reasons for pleading thus. The poisonous suggestion does its work. Urged by the tormented Moor to speak candidly of what he knows, the Ensign offers his opinion that Disdemona is tired of the Moor because of the color of his skin. When the Ensign further affirms that the Corporal has confessed making love to Disdemona, the Moor demands ocular proof. This test is not easy for the Ensign, since the lady is in fact so chaste. One day, however, when she is visiting the Ensign's wife and is playing with the Ensign's three-year-old daughter, the Ensign manages to steal from her sash a Moorish handkerchief. She is unhappy to discover it missing, for she knows the Moor often asks her for it. The Ensign drops off the handkerchief at the Corporal's house, who finds it, knows it to be Disdemona's, and returns it to her house. Unluckily he hears the Moor coming and runs away, fearing the Moor's continued displeasure. The Moor, sure that he has recognized the Corporal running away thus, commissions the Ensign to question the Corporal about the matter. The Ensign thereupon engages the Corporal in conversation while the Moor is within view but out of earshot; the Ensign discusses idle matters but afterwards affirms to the Moor that the Corporal spoke of his lovemaking and confessed receiving the handkerchief from Disdemona. When the Moor then asks Disdemona for the handkerchief and observes her blushing confusion, he resolves to kill her and the Corporal. To confirm further the Corporal's possession of the handkerchief, the Ensign takes the Moor past a window of the Corporal's house where a woman of the Corporal's household is embroidering a copy of the handkerchief. Disdemona, deeply troubled by her disintegrating marriage, seeks the confidence of the Ensign's wife who knows everything about her husband's villainy but is too fearful of him to say anything.

The Ensign, paid by the Moor to dispatch the Corporal, assaults him one night as the Corporal is leaving the house of a courtesan, manages to cut off the Corporal's leg, then runs away and returns with the crowd as though attracted by the noise. Despite this serious wound, the Corporal lives. Disdemona's grieving for him confirms the Moor in his resolve to rid the world of her. He adopts the Ensign's plan for the murder: the Ensign hides in a closet, makes a noise to attract Disdemona, and bludgeons her to death with a sand-filled stocking that leaves no marks. The two men then lay her in bed, smash her skull, and make it appear that a ceiling timber has fallen on her head. They do not get away with this murder, however, for the Moor begins to loathe the Ensign and strips him of his rank. In retaliation, the Ensign informs the Corporal that it was the Moor who attacked the Corporal and murdered Disdemona. Returning to Venice, the Corporal brings charges against the Moor and presents the Ensign as an eyewitness. The Moor is summoned, tortured, and banished perpetually, though he confesses nothing. Eventually he is killed by Disdemona's kinsmen. The Ensign escapes punishment only to become later involved in another crime, for which he is tortured and so weakened that he dies soon after.

Many of Shakespeare's changes focus on the Ensign, or Iago. Shakespeare strips away the Ensign's simple motive of lust for Disdemona and jealous hate of the Corporal, though traces of a perverse desire to cuckold Othello linger on in Iago's psyche. At the same time, Shakespeare adds the apparently specious motive of resentment over Cassio's promotion in Iago's place. (Iago's gleeful and partly unmotivated viciousness shows him to be related to the Vice of the morality-play tradition.) Shakespeare adds entirely the opening scene in which Iago arouses the prejudices of Desdemona's father Brabantio. The father does not appear in Cinthio's story, other than in the mention that Disdemona's relatives oppose the marriage. Roderigo is a brilliantly invented character who shows Iago's skill in manipulation. Iago's soliloquies are entirely Shakespearean. Iago, unlike the Ensign of the story, is responsible for Cassio's first disgrace on the night of the watch. Cassio's weakness for wine and for Bianca are Shakespearean additions; the story notes that the Corporal visits a courtesan, but the fact is utterly unexceptional. Emilia is a more complex figure than the

Ensign's wife: Shakespeare implicates her in the stealing of the handkerchief, but also accentuates her love for Desdemona and her brave denunciation of her husband when at last she knows the full truth. Othello's ritual slaying of Desdemona avoids the appalling butchery of the source story. Shakespeare's ending is more unified, and brings both Othello and Iago to account for the deeds they have committed in this play. As usual, Shakespeare compresses time, though occasional traces of a longer time span do show through. Most importantly, Shakespeare transforms a sensational murder story into a moving tragedy of love.

King Lear

The story of Lear goes back into ancient legend. The motif of two wicked sisters and a virtuous youngest sister reminds us of Cinderella. Lear himself appears to come from Celtic mythology. Geoffrey of Monmouth, a Welshman in close contact with Celtic legend, included a Lear or Leir as one of the pseudo-historical kings in his *Historia Regum Britanniae* (c. 1136). This fanciful mixture of history and legend traces a supposed line of descent from Brut, great-grandson of Aeneas of Troy, through Locrine, Bladud, Leir, Gorboduc, Ferrex and Porrex, Lud, Cymbeline, Bonduca, Vortigern, Arthur, etc., to the historical kings of England. The Tudor monarchs made much of their purported claim to such an ancient dynasty, and in Shakespeare's day this mythology had a quasi-official status demanding a certain reverential suspension of disbelief.

King Leir, according to Geoffrey, is the father of three daughters, Gonorilla, Regan, and Cordeilla, among whom he intends to divide his kingdom. To determine who deserves most, he asks them who loves him most. The two eldest sisters protest undying devotion; but Cordeilla, perceiving how the others flatter and deceive him, renounces hyperbole and promises only to love him as a daughter should love a father. Furious, the King denies Cordeilla her third of the kingdom but permits her to marry Aganippus, King of the Franks, without dowry. Thereafter Leir bestows his two eldest daughters on the Dukes of Albania and Cornubia (Albany and Cornwall), together with half the island during his lifetime and the possession of the remainder after his death. In due course his two sons-in-law rebel against Leir and seize his power. Thereafter Maglaunus, Duke of Albania, agrees to maintain Leir with sixty retainers, but after two years of chafing at this arrangement Gonorilla insists that the number be reduced to thirty. Angrily the King goes to Henvin, Duke of Cornubia, where all goes well for a time; within a year, however, Regan demands that Leir reduce his retinue to five knights. When Gonorilla refuses to take him back with more than one retainer, Leir crosses into France and is generously received by Cordeilla and Aganippus. An invasion restores Leir to his throne. Three years later he and Aganippus die, after which Cordeilla rules successfully for five years until overthrown by the sons of Maglaunus and Henvin. In prison she commits suicide.

This story, as part of England's mythic genealogy, was repeated in various Tudor versions such as *The First parte of the Myrroure for Magistrates* (1574), William Warner's *Albions England* (1586), and Holinshed's *Chronicles*. Warner refers to the King's sons-in-law as "the Prince of Albany" and "the Cornish prince"; Holinshed refers to them as "the Duke of Albania" and "the Duke of Cornwall," but reports that it is Cornwall who marries the eldest daughter Gonorilla. *The Myrroure,* closer to Shakespeare in these details, speaks of "Gonerell" as married to "Albany" and of "Cordila" as married to "the king of Fraunce." Spenser's *The Faerie Queene* (II,x,27–32) reports that "Cordeill" or "Cordelia" ends her life by hanging herself. Other retellings appear in Gerard Legh's *Accidence of Armory* and William Camden's *Remaines*. All of these accounts leave the story virtually unchanged.

Shakespeare's immediate source for *King Lear* was an old play called *The True Chronicle History of King Leir*. It was published in 1605 but plainly is much earlier in style. The Stationers' Register for May 14, 1594, lists "A booke called the Tragecall historie of kinge Leir and his Three Daughters &c.," and a short time earlier Henslowe's *Diary* records the performance of a "Kinge Leare" at the Rose Theatre on April 6 and 8, 1594. The actors were the Queen's or Sussex' men, probably the Queen's. The play may have been written as early as 1588. Peele, Greene, Lodge, and Kyd have all been suggested as possible authors. Shakespeare probably knew the play before its publication in 1605.

This play of *Leir* ends happily, with the restoration of Leir to his throne. Essentially the play is a legendary history with a strong element of romance. The two wicked sisters are warned of the King's plans for dividing his kingdom by an obsequious courtier named Skalliger (cf. Oswald). Cordella receives the ineffectual support of an honest courtier, Perillus (cf. Kent), but is disinherited by her angry father. Trusting herself to God's mercy and setting forth alone to live by her own labor, Cordella is found by the Gallian King and his bluff companion Mumford, who have come to England disguised as palmers to see if the English King's daughters are as beautiful as reported. The King hears Cordella's sad story, falls in love with her, and woos her (still wearing his disguise) in the name of the Gallian King. When she virtuously suggests the palmer woo for himself, he throws off his disguise and marries her forthwith.

Meanwhile the other sons-in-law, Cornwall and Cambria (i.e., Albany), draw lots for their shares of the kingdom. Leir announces that he will sojourn with Cornwall and Gonorill first. Cornwall treats the King with genuine solicitude, but Gonorill, abetted by Skalliger, tauntingly drives her father away. The King acknowledges to his loyal companion Perillus that he has wronged Cordella. Regan, who rules her mild husband as she pleases, receives the King with seeming tenderness but secretly hires an assassin to end his life. (Gonorill is partner in this plot.) The suborned agent, frightened into remorse by a providentially sent thunderstorm, shows his intended victim the letter ordering the assassination.

The Gallian King and Cordella, who have previously sent ambassadors to Leir urging him to come to France, now decide to journey with Mumford into Britain disguised as countryfolk. Before they can do so, however, Leir and Perillus arrive in France, in mariners' garb, where they encounter Cordella and her party dressed as countryfolk. Cordella recognizes Leir's voice, and father and daughter are tearfully reunited. The Gallian King invades England and restores Leir to his throne.

Shakespeare has changed much in the narrative of his source. He discards not only the happy ending but the attempted assassination and the numerous romancelike uses of disguise (although Tom o' Bedlam, in an added plot, repeatedly uses disguise). Shakespeare eliminates the humorous Mumford and replaces Perillus with both Kent and the Fool. He turns Cornwall into a villain and Albany into a belated champion of justice. He creates the storm scene out of a mere suggestion about providential thunder.

Most of all, he adds the parallel plot of Gloucester, Edgar, and Edmund. Here Shakespeare derived some of his material from Sidney's *Arcadia* (1590). In Book II, chapter 10 of this greatest of all Elizabethan prose romances, the two heroes Pyrocles and Musidorus encounter a son leading his blind old father. The old man tells his pitiful tale. He is the deposed King of Paphlagonia, father of a bastard son named Plexirtus who, he now bitterly realizes, turned the King against his true son Leonatus—the very son who is now his guide and guardian. The true son, having managed to escape his father's order of execution, has been forced to live poorly as a soldier, while the bastard son has proceeded to usurp his father's throne. In his wretchedness, the King has been succored by his forgiving true son and has been prevented from casting himself off the top of a hill. At the conclusion of this narrative, the villain Plexirtus arrives and attacks Leonatus; reinforcements arrive on both sides, but eventually Plexirtus is driven off, enabling the King to return to his court and bestow the crown on Leonatus. He thereupon dies, his heart having been stretched beyond the limits of endurance.

Other parts of *The Arcadia* may have given Shakespeare further suggestions. Edmund is decidedly indebted to the Vice of the morality-play tradition. For Tom o' Bedlam's mad language, Shakespeare consulted Samuel Harsnett's *Declaration of Egregious Popishe Impostures,* 1603. (See K. Muir's Arden edition of *King Lear,* pp. 253–256, for an extensive comparison.)

Macbeth

Shakespeare's chief source for *Macbeth* was Holinshed's *Chronicles* (1587 edition). Holinshed had gone for most of his material to Hector Boece, *Scotorum Historiae* (1526–1527), who in turn was indebted to a fourteenth-century priest named John of Fordun and to a fifteenth-century chronicler, Andrew of Wyntoun. By the time Holinshed found it, the story of Macbeth had become more fiction than fact. The historical Macbeth, who ruled from 1040 to 1057, did take the throne by killing Duncan, but in a civil conflict between two clans contending for the kingship. Contemporary observers credit him with having been a good ruler. Although he was defeated by the Earl of Northumbria (the Siward of Shakespeare's play) at Birnam Wood in 1054, the Earl was forced by his own losses to retire, and Macbeth ruled three years longer before being slain by Duncan's son Malcolm. Banquo and Fleance are fictional characters apparently invented by Boece.

As Holinshed tells the story, Duncane is a king of too soft and gentle a nature, negligent in punishing his enemies and thereby an unwitting encourager of sedition. It falls to Makbeth, a critic of this soft line, and to Banquho the Thane of Lochaber, to defend Scotland against her enemies: first Makdowald (Macdonwald in Shakespeare) with his Irish kerns and gallowglasses, and then Sueno, King of Norway. (Shakespeare fuses these battles into one.) Shortly thereafter, Makbeth and Banquho encounter "three women in strange and wild apparell, resembling creatures of elder world," who predict their futures as in the play. Although Makbeth and Banquho jest about the matter, common opinion later maintains that "these women were either the weird sisters, that is (as ye would say) the goddesses of destinie, or else some nymphs or feiries, indued with knowledge of prophesie." Certainly Makbeth soon becomes the Thane of Cawdor, whereupon, jestingly reminded of the three sisters' promise by Banquho, he resolves to seek the throne. His way is blocked, however, by Duncane's naming of his eldest but still underage son Malcolme to be Prince of Cumberland and heir to the throne. Makbeth's resentment at this is understandable, since Scottish law provides that he himself should be heir until Malcolm is of age. Accordingly, Makbeth begins to plot with his associates how to usurp the kingdom by force. His "verie ambitious" wife urges him on because of her "vnquenchable desire" to be Queen. Banquho is one among many trusted friends with whose support Makbeth slays the King at Inverness or at Botgosvane. (No mention is made of a visit to Makbeth's castle.) Malcolme and Donald Bane, the dead King's sons, fly for their safety to Cumberland, where Malcolme is well received by Edward the Confessor of England.

For some ten years Makbeth rules well, using great liberality and correcting the laxity of his predecessor's reign. Inevitably, however, the weird sisters' promise of a posterity to Banquho goads Makbeth into ordering the murder of his onetime companion. Fleance escapes Makbeth's henchmen in the dark, and afterward founds the lineage of the Stuart kings. (This genealogy is fictitious.) Makbeth's tyrannical bent further causes him to build Dunsinane fortress. When Mackduffe refuses to help, the King turns against him and would kill him except that "a certeine witch, whom hee had in great trust," tells the King he need never fear a man born of woman nor any vanquishment till Birnam Wood come to Dunsinane. Mackduffe flees for his safety into England and joins Malcolme, whereupon Makbeth's agents slaughter Mackduffe's wife and children at Fife. Malcolme, fearing that Mackduffe may be an agent of Makbeth, dissemblingly professes to be a voluptuary, miser, and tyrant; but when Mackduffe responds as he should in righteous sorrow at Scotland's evil condition, Malcolme reveals his steadfast commitment to the cause of right. These leaders return to Scotland and defeat Makbeth at Birnam Wood, with their soldiers carrying branches before them. Mackduffe, proclaiming that he is a man born of no woman since he was "ripped out" of his mother's womb, slays Makbeth.

Despite extensive similarities, Shakespeare has made some significant changes. Duncan is no longer an ineffectual king. Macbeth can no longer justify his claim to the throne. Most important, Banquo is no longer partner to a broadly based though secret conspiracy against Duncan. Banquo is, after all, ancestor of James I (at least according to this legendary history), so that his hands must be kept scrupulously clean; King James disapproved of all tyrannicides, whatever the circumstances. Macbeth is no longer a just lawgiver. The return of Banquo's ghost to Macbeth's banqueting table is an added scene. Macbeth hears the prophecy about Birnam Wood and Macduff from the weird sisters, not, as in Holinshed, from some witch. Lady Macbeth's role is considerably enhanced, and her sleepwalking scene is original. Shakespeare compresses time, as he usually does.

In making these alterations, Shakespeare turned to another story in Holinshed's chronicle of Scotland: the murder of King Duff by Donwald. King Duff, never suspecting any treachery in Donwald, often visits his castle. On one occasion Donwald's wife, bearing great malice towards the King, shows Donwald "the meanes wherby he might soonest accomplish" the murder. The husband and wife ply Duff and his few chamberlains with much to eat and drink. Donwald abhors the act "greatlie in heart," but perseveres "through instigation of his wife." Four of Donwald's servants actually commit the murder under his instruction. Next morning, Donwald breaks into the King's chamber and slays the chamberlains as though believing them guilty. Donwald is so overzealous in his investigation of the murder that many lords begin to suspect him of having done it. For six months afterward, the sun refuses to appear by day and the moon by night.

The chronicle accounts in Holinshed of Malcolm and Edward the Confessor supplied Shakespeare with further details. A more important supplementary source may have been George Buchanan's *Rerum Scoticarum Historia* (1582), a Latin history not translated in Shakespeare's lifetime, presenting a more complex psychological portrait of the protagonist than in Holinshed. Finally, Shakespeare may have known King James I's *Daemonologie* (1597), Samuel Harsnett's *Declaration of Egregious Popishe Impostures* (1603), and accounts of the Scottish witch trials published around 1590.

Timon of Athens

Shakespeare certainly made use of a brief passage from the Life of Antonius in Thomas North's translation of Plutarch's *Lives of the Noble Grecians and Romanes* (1579). This passage is a digression used to illustrate Antonius' own embittered withdrawal from society, in which he compares himself to a famous misanthrope of Athens. As Plutarch reports Timon's story, citing Plato and Aristophanes as his sources, Timon is a hater of mankind because he has been victimized by deception and ingratitude. Timon shuns all company but that of young Alcibiades. When asked by Apemantus why he favors this youth, Timon replies that he knows Alcibiades will some day do great mischief to the Athenians. On another occasion, Timon mounts a public rostrum and invites his Athenian listeners to come hang themselves on a fig tree growing in his yard before he cuts it down (see V,i, 204–211). When Timon dies he is buried upon the seashore (V,i,213–217). Plutarch transcribes two epitaphs, one by the poet Callimachus and one by Timon himself, both of which appear word for word in Shakespeare's play (V,iv,70–73). (Shakespeare probably meant to cancel one, for dramatically they are inconsistent with one another.) Plutarch thus provides Shakespeare not only with several incidents in the life of Timon but with the link connecting Timon, Alcibiades, and Apemantus.

Oddly, Shakespeare seems to have absorbed little from Plutarch's Life of Alcibiades, though that account does tell how the general leaves Athens in disgrace and sides with her enemies but ultimately relents when he sees that the Athenians are sorry for the injury they have done him. Alcibiades is a handsome young man and fond of women; his concubine Timandra buries him. Despite these scattered hints, however, Plutarch's Life of Alcibiades provides no basis for Shakespeare's plot.

The comedy of Timon by Aristophanes, to which Plutarch alludes, has not survived. Nor has Plato's description. Apparently these accounts were based on a historical figure of fifth-century Athens, Timon the son of Echecratides. Allusions to him in classical literature are common enough to suggest that his name had become synonymous with misanthropy. The fullest surviving classical record of this tradition is a dialogue by Lucian of Samosata (c. 125–180 A.D.) called *Timon,* or *The Misanthrope.* No English translation was available in Shakespeare's lifetime, but he could have read Lucian in Italian, Latin, or French translation.

The dialogue begins as Timon, impoverished and abandoned by his fair-weather friends, calls upon Zeus to punish such injustice. Zeus hears this diatribe and learns from Hermes the sad tale of Timon's victimization by his ungrateful fellow man. Aware that he has been neglectful of this case, Zeus orders Hermes to descend with Plutus

(Riches) and restore Timon to prosperity. Although Plutus fears he will be treated improvidently as before, Zeus is insistent. Plutus confesses to Hermes, as they descend, how he deceives men. Hermes and Plutus find Timon digging, accompanied by Poverty, Toil, Endurance, and other such allegorical companions. Poverty and his fellows are reluctant to leave Timon, for they know he has been happier with them than in his former days; and Timon too protests he wants nothing to do with prosperity. Still, the will of the gods must be obeyed, and Timon discovers treasure where he is digging.

Just as he mordantly predicts, opportunists now seek him out. One is Gnathonides the flatterer, a former recipient of Timon's hospitality who only recently has repaid that kindness by offering Timon a noose. Philiades once received from Timon a farm as a dowry for his daughters, but has spurned Timon in his poverty; now he makes a pretense of offering money, knowing Timon not to be in need. A third petitioner is the orator Demea, whose debt Timon once paid to obtain his release from jail; now, having insulted Timon in his poverty, Demea comes with a fulsome and patently fictitious decree he has composed in Timon's honor. Fourth is Thrasicles, a hypocritical philosopher who preaches self-denial but drinks to excess, and who professes to come now not for his own benefit but for those to whom he will gladly distribute Timon's new wealth. Timon drives them off one by one and then resorts to throwing stones at the ever increasing crowd of flatterers. (This parade of villains, and their satirical discomfiture, bear an interesting resemblance to Aristophanes' *The Birds*.)

Many details here are suggestive of Shakespeare's play and are not in Plutarch: Timon's generosity to former friends (including the payment of a debt and the providing of a marriage dowry), his friends' ungrateful response when he is in need, the finding of gold in the ground followed by the reappearance of the friends, the insincere offer of money, the flattering composition in praise of Timon. The personified abstractions are parablelike, as in Shakespeare's play. Yet verbal parallels between Shakespeare and Lucian are tenuous at best. Probably Shakespeare knew some later version based on Lucian. Renaissance works inspired by Lucian are not hard to find, but none seems to be the direct source for Shakespeare. He is not likely to have known an Italian play called the *Timone* of Boiardo (c. 1487).

More suggestive is an English academic play written at Cambridge and preserved in the Dyce MSS. In this version, Timon's servant Laches warns against the effects of prodigality. When one friend, Eutrapelus, experiences financial trouble, Timon gives him five talents. Laches is driven out by Timon, but returns disguised as a soldier to serve his master. At a final banquet, Timon mocks his guests with stones painted to resemble artichokes. When he finds gold, Timon's false mistress shows her readiness to take it. Even a farcical comic subplot reminds us that Shakespeare's *Timon* contains an unrelated and perhaps vestigial Fool scene. Yet this academic play may have been written after Shakespeare's play, though surely not based on it (since *Timon* was not published until 1623), and the likeliest explanation for the similarities is a common source. Perhaps Shakespeare knew and used a play now lost.

Apemantus does not have a prominent role in any of the versions here discussed, though he is mentioned in Plutarch. Apemantus bears a resemblance to many satirical railers and crabbed philosophers in Renaissance literature, such as Diogenes in John Lyly's play of *Campaspe* (1584) and Jaques in Shakespeare's *As You Like It*.

Antony and Cleopatra

In writing *Antony and Cleopatra*, Shakespeare relied to an unusual extent on his chief source, The Life of Marcus Antonius in Plutarch's *Lives of the Noble Grecians and Romanes* (translated by Sir Thomas North, 1579). Perhaps the best-known example in all Shakespeare of his skillful use of source material is in the following (see *Antony and Cleopatra*, II,ii,201–228):

She disdained to set forward otherwise, but to take her barge in the river of Cydnus, the poope whereof was of gold, the sailes of purple, and the owers of silver, which kept stroke in rowing after the sounde of the musicke of flutes, howboyes, citherns, violls, and such other instruments as they played upon in the barge. And now for the person of her selfe: she was layed under a pavillion of cloth of gold of tissue, apparelled and attired like the goddesse Venus, commonly drawen in picture: and hard by her, on either hand of her, pretie faire boyes apparelled as painters doe set forth god Cupide, with litle fannes in their hands, with the which they fanned wind upon her. Her Ladies and gentlewomen also, the fairest of them were apparelled like the nymphes Nereides (which are the mermaides of the waters) and like the Graces, some stearing the helme, others tending the tackle and ropes of the barge, out of the which there came a wonderfull passing sweete savor of perfumes, that perfumed the wharfes side, pestered with innumerable multitudes of people. Some of them followed the barge all alongest the rivers side: others also ranne out of the citie to see her comming in. So that in thend, there ranne such multitudes of people one after an other to see her, that Antonius was left post alone in the market place, in his Imperiall seate to geve audience.

Plutarch reports the other fabulous stories as well: eight wild boars roasted whole for only twelve guests (II,ii,190), Cleopatra teasing Antony by causing an old dried salt fish to be placed on his fishing line (II,v,17), Menas the pirate suggesting to Pompey that they cut the anchor cable with all their noble guests still aboard (II,vii), Cleopatra's sudden changes from weeping to laughing, and her willingness to be flattered by those who tell her Antony has married Octavia solely out of necessity (III,iii), Octavius' tenderness for his sister, the ill-omened nesting of swallows in Cleopatra's sails (IV,xii), Antony's disregarding the advice of a valiant captain not to fight at sea (III,vii), Cleopatra's study of swift means of death, Antony's jealous reaction to the embassy of the young Thyreus or Thidias (III,xiii), the suicide of Antony's servant Eros (IV,xiv), Cleopatra's difficulty in lifting Antony up to her tomb or monument (IV,xv), his warning that she should trust none but Proculeius (IV,xv), Cleopatra's deception of Caesar through persuading him that she desires to live (V,ii), the countryman with the basket of figs, Cleopatra's death "attired and araied in her royall robes" attended by Charmian and Iras, and much more.

Despite these extensive and detailed borrowings, Shakespeare partly turned elsewhere for his estimate of his main characters. To Plutarch, Antony is the tragic victim of infatuation. For all Cleopatra's cultivation and fascination—she knows several languages, and rules her country with royal bearing—she is the source of Antony's downfall. Plutarch's attitude is, like Enobarbus', admiring but ironic. "In the ende," he writes, "the horse of the minde as Plato termeth it, that is so hard of rayne (I meane the unreyned lust of concupiscence) did put out of Antonius heade, all honest and commendable thoughtes." This "Roman" view is present in *Antony and Cleopatra,* to be sure, but is counterbalanced by the "Egyptian" view. Shakespeare's play sets up a debate among conflicting traditions as found in various medieval and Renaissance treatments of this famous story. The moralistic view condemning vice was popular in medieval texts, such as *De Casibus Virorum Illustrium* and its continuation, Lydgate's *The Fall of Princes.* The view of Cleopatra as love's martyr was to be found in Chaucer's *The Legend of Good Women.* And finally, the view of Antony and Cleopatra as heroic protagonists rising above their guilt found expression in several neo-Senecan dramas of the later sixteenth century. Most important for Shakespeare were *The Tragedie of Antonie,* translated from Robert Garnier's *Marc Antoine* by Mary Herbert, Countess of Pembroke in about 1590 (published 1592 and 1595), and *The Tragedy of Cleopatra* by Samuel Daniel (1593), a companion play dealing mainly with the very end of Cleopatra's life. Garnier's play had been based on Étienne Jodelle's *Cleopâtra Captive* (1552), the first regular French tragedy. Shakespeare certainly gained from works like these a sense of tragic greatness in his protagonists. Another influential work may have been the *Chronicle of the Romanes Warres* by Appian of Alexandria (translated 1578).

Enobarbus, interestingly, is almost entirely original with Shakespeare. Plutarch mentions only the fact that such a man deserts Antony.

Coriolanus

Coriolanus probably represents Shakespeare's last use of Plutarch's *Lives of the Noble Grecians and Romanes,* as translated by Sir Thomas North (1579). The Life of Caius Martius Coriolanus provided most of the material for Shakespeare's play, just as The Life of Antonius had provided most of the material for *Antony and Cleopatra.* Plutarch's Coriolanus is a man of exceeding nobility but also of excessive impatience and churlish incivility. In war he practices *Virtus,* or "valliantnes" as North translates it. He wins his title of Coriolanus by storming the city of Corioles (Corioli) almost singlehanded. He is the son of a widow whose good opinion he cherishes; as Plutarch reports, "he thought nothing made him so happie and honorable, as that his mother might heare every bodie praise and commend him, that she might allwayes see him returne with a crowne upon his head, and that she might still embrace him with teares ronning downe her cheekes for joye." Coriolanus vehemently disapproves of leniency toward the populace as an invitation to anarchy. He is naturally an enemy of the people's first tribunes, Junius Brutus and Sicinius Vellutus, who, in Plutarch's estimation, "had only bene the causers and procurers of this sedition."

Plutarch informs us that when Coriolanus stands for consul, and follows the custom of appearing in the marketplace clad only in a poor gown, the people remember his martial prowess; on the day of the election itself, however, they recall their old hate of him and refuse his candidacy. Coriolanus, in his typically choleric and intemperate fashion, makes no attempt to conceal his outrage at this insult. (Plutarch comments editorially on his behavior as "the fruites of selfe will and obstinacie.") When he is banished, Coriolanus goes in disguise to Antium, to the house of Tullus Aufidius, his great rival, knowing perfectly well that "Tullus dyd more malice and envie him, then he dyd all the Romaines besides." Coriolanus and Tullus have long been admiring rivals: "they were ever at the encounter one against another, like lustie coragious youthes, striving in all emulation of honour, and had encountered many times together." Returning vengefully to Rome, Coriolanus is "determined at the first to persist in his obstinate and inflexible rancker," but finally relents through "naturall affection" and receives his wife and mother. Volumnia's oration to him, reported in full by Plutarch, causes Coriolanus to cry out: "you have wonne a happy victorie for your countrie, but mortall and unhappy for your sonne."

Shakespeare's changes simultaneously enhance the haughtiness of Coriolanus and the fickleness of the people, thereby increasing the distance between the two sides. Shakespeare's Coriolanus is revolted by the custom of wearing a robe and showing his wounds to the people, and shows his contempt more snarlingly than in Plutarch. He is, unlike Plutarch's protagonist, reluctant to seek office, and has to be persuaded to it by his mother and friends. Shakespeare minimizes the legitimate griefs of the Roman people—they are severely oppressed by usurers in Plutarch's account—and accentuates their fickleness. Shakespeare shows them as being manipulated against Coriolanus by the scheming tribunes, whereas in Plutarch the people make up their own minds to oppose Coriolanus for the consulship. Shakespeare also magnifies the roles of Volumnia and of Menenius. Volumnia, though she is mentioned by Plutarch, takes no active part in the story until Coriolanus attacks Rome; Menenius' chief function in Plutarch is to relate the fable of the belly. Shakespeare compresses and rearranges events as he usually does: for example, in Plutarch the people actually leave Rome to demonstrate their grievances, and agree to return only when granted the election of tribunes to represent their interests, whereas in Shakespeare the tribunes have already been elected when the play begins. In Shakespeare, Coriolanus is banished as the result of a dispute over his consulship, not (as in Plutarch) as the result of an insurrection over scarcity of grain.

Shakespeare probably also knew the story of Coriolanus in Livy's *Romane Historie,* Book II, as translated by Philemon Holland (1600). Other versions of the story were available to him, including the *Roman Histories* of Lucius Florus. Plutarch seems to have provided Shakespeare, however, with virtually everything he needed. Even Shakespeare's alterations of Plutarch tend to enchance rather than correct Plutarch's overall thesis and appraisal of the characters in his history.

Pericles

Shakespeare derived his *Pericles* from the ancient Greek romance of Apollonius of Tyre. He had used the story once before, in *The Comedy of Errors*. Medieval versions of this enduringly popular legend include the ninth-century Latin *Historia Apollonii Regis Tyri,* Godfrey of Viterbo's *Pantheon* (c. 1186), the *Gesta Romanorum,* John Gower's *Confessio Amantis* (c. 1383–1393), and an English chronicle of *Appolyn of Thyre* translated for the printer Wynkyn de Worde by Robert Copland from a French source (1510). Shakespeare (and possibly the author of a lost earlier dramatic version) were chiefly indebted to Gower's *Confessio* and to Laurence Twine's *The Patterne of Painefull Aduentures,* a prose version registered in 1576 but existing today only in two editions from about 1594–1595 and 1607.

The order of events in Twine is much the same as in Shakespeare: the hero Apollonius' difficulty with the incestuous King Antiochus, his relieving of the city of Tharsus, his shipwreck at Pentapolis, and his falling in love with the King's daughter Lucina (Thaisa in the play), her childbearing and apparent death at sea, the discovery of her floating casket at Ephesus, her revival by the physician Cerimon and her retirement to the Temple of Diana in Ephesus, her daughter Tharsia's (i.e., Marina's) capture by pirates and enslavement in a brothel, her conversion of Athanagoras (Lysimachus) the Governor of Machilenta (Mytilene), and Apollonius' eventual reunion with daughter and wife. Gower's account too is much the same, with slightly differing forms of the proper names: Appolinus' wife is referred to as the King's daughter, Appolinus' daughter is Thaise, the man she marries is Atenagoras of Mitilene, and so on.

Other than changing some proper names, including that of the hero, Shakespeare did not introduce many significant alterations. To be sure, Shakespeare has given a more sordid impression of the brothel in which Marina must dwell, and has dignified the character of Lysimachus so as to render him worthy of marrying Marina. In Twine's prose account, Athanagoras actually tries to buy Tharsia from the pirates at an auction; when he is outbid by a bawd, he resolves to be the first to visit Tharsia in her new residence. Shakespeare has cleaned this up, although traces of the older and more licentious character occasionally show through and create the impression of inconsistency. For the most part, however, Shakespeare's play stays unusually close to the episodic narrative structure of his sources.

The relationship of George Wilkins' *The Painfull Aduentures of Pericles Prince of Tyre* (1608) to Shakespeare's play is complex and uncertain. Beyond doubt, Wilkins' prose account is based in part on a *Pericles* play; Wilkins acknowledges in his Argument that this same story has been recently presented "by the Kings Majesties Players." The play he used may, however, not have been the *Pericles* we know from the corrupt 1609 quarto. Parts of Wilkins' narrative are very close to the earlier *Patterne of Painefull Aduentures* by Twine. Could these parts be inventions by Wilkins? Kenneth Muir prefers to think (*Shakespeare's Sources,* 1957) that because Wilkins' novel is closer to the first two acts of the play than to the last three acts, Wilkins may have been using an older play that Shakespeare then revised, substantially rewriting the last three acts but changing little in the first two. Whether the presumed *Ur-Pericles* might have been Wilkins' own play is a matter of conjecture. The very existence of an *Ur-Pericles* is by no means universally accepted, but cannot be ruled out as a possibility.

Cymbeline

Cymbeline deals with legendary and romantic history, in which traces of historical events can still be dimly perceived. A Cunobelinus or Cymbeline was in fact leader of the Celtic chieftains in southeast England during the period of Roman hegemony there, following Julius Caesar's invasion of the island in 54 B.C. Cunobelinus ruled from about 5 to 40 A.D., with his capital at Camulodunum (Colchester). He was a friend and ally of Augustus Caesar and enjoyed a peaceful reign. When the kingdom had passed to his sons (one of whom apparently was Caractacus), the Romans under Claudius pursued once again their conquest of England and subdued much of the southeast, though Caractacus escaped to Wales and became a leader of resistance.

Beginning with Geoffrey of Monmouth's *Historia Regum Britanniae* (c. 1136), King Kymbelinus becomes a quasi-legendary figure. Geoffrey adds him to the genealogy of kings (along with Leir, Locrine, etc.) descended from Aeneas' great-grandson Brut, the mythical founder of Britain. Kymbelinus' reign was peaceful, according to Geoffrey, since the King, having been raised in Augustus Caesar's household, willingly paid tribute to Rome without being asked. When Kymbelinus' elder son Guiderius succeeded to the throne, however, said Geoffrey, he defied the

Emperor Claudius over the tribute. Guiderius fell in battle and was succeeded by his brother Arviragus, who more than held his own against Claudius, eventually settling matters by negotiation.

By the time of Holinshed's *Chronicles* (1587 edition), the facts are badly confused. Holinshed admits he cannot be sure whether Kymbeline or some other British leader fought against Augustus Caesar, or whether Kymbeline paid tribute; he does report that Guiderius fought Augustus Caesar (rather than Claudius), but is uncertain as to whether the Romans lost or won. Spenser's *The Faerie Queene* (II,x,50–51) affirms that Kimbeline fought the Romans over tribute and was slain in battle, whereupon his brother Aviragus took his place and compelled the Roman Claudius to a peace. (In other words, Spenser has conflated Cymbeline and Guiderius.) Shakespeare, like Spenser, imagines the great struggle with Rome and subsequent peace settlement to have taken place during Cymbeline's reign; following Holinshed, he assumes that Rome was then governed by Augustus Caesar. Shakespeare also seems to have consulted a vivid account of the battle in Thomas Blenerhasset's contribution to the *Seconde part of the Myrroure for Magistrates* (1578) and another account of Cymbeline's reign by John Higgins in the 1587 *Myrroure for Magistrates.* Finally, Shakespeare turned for his background material to quite a different story in Holinshed, concerning a Scottish farmer named Hay who with his two sons helped defend Scotland against the Danes in 976. Shakespeare presumably found this story when reading for *Macbeth,* since it stands between the two accounts—Donwald's murder of Duff and Macbeth's murder of Duncan—that Shakespeare used in writing *Macbeth.* The exploits of Hay and his two sons resemble those of Belarius and the two princes in the final battle of *Cymbeline.*

The quasi-historical setting accounts for only a small part of *Cymbeline,* and Shakespeare had no special reason to set the facts straight. Most of his material is, after all, romantic. The central plot of a wager over a wife's virtue may have come from Boccaccio's *Decameron,* ninth tale of the second day, although as a type this ancient story was widespread and presumably available to Shakespeare in many forms. Earlier versions include the thirteenth-century French *Roi Flore et la belle Jeanne,* the *Roman de la Violette* by Gerbert de Montreuil, a miracle play by Gautier de Coincy, and others. Boccaccio was available to Shakespeare in French translation but not in English.

Boccaccio tells of an Italian merchant, Bernabo of Genoa, who, at a gathering in Paris of fellow merchants discussing the wantonness of their wives, dares to affirm the absolute chastity of his own wife Zinevra. A young merchant, Ambrogiuolo, makes a wager that he can seduce Zinevra and return with proof in three months. Going at once to Genoa, Ambrogiuolo discovers that Zinevra is indeed incorruptible. He therefore bribes an old lady, whom Zinevra has befriended, to convey him hidden in a chest to the lady's bedroom. When the lady is asleep he steals forth from hiding, memorizes details of her room, notes particularly a mole under her left breast, takes with him a purse, gown, ring, and girdle. Returning to Paris, he convinces his fellow merchants and Bernabo that he has succeeded. Bernabo hereupon travels to within a few miles of Genoa, summons his wife, and secretly orders his servant to kill her on the way. The servant is reluctant to do so, however, and gladly takes only her cloak as evidence of having finished the job. Zinevra now makes her way disguised as a man to Alexandria, and enters the service of the Sultan. One day she happens to recognize her own purse and girdle in a Venetian clothes shop in Palestine, inquires as to their owner, meets Ambrogiuolo in this way (who has journeyed to Palestine selling merchandise), and hears from Ambrogiuolo's own boastful lips the story of his treachery. She cannily manages to bring Ambrogiuolo and Bernabo before the Sultan, throws off her male disguise, and reveals the whole story. She pardons Bernabo and is reunited with him, but Ambrogiuolo is sentenced by the Sultan to be tied to a stake and smeared with honey until the insects devour him.

Shakespeare seems also to have known an English version, *Frederyke of Jennen* (Antwerp, 1518, London, 1520 and 1560), translated from the Dutch. In some details it is closer to Shakespeare's play. For example, the merchants who witness the wager include a Spaniard, a Frenchman, a Florentine, and a Genoese (cf. I,iv). Three of these merchants are not present when the villain returns to prove his victory, just as in II,iv of Shakespeare's play. Also, the husband repents even before learning of his wife's innocence, as does Posthumus. Shakespeare greatly accentuates this motif of penance and forgiveness. Another source is a romantic play called *The Rare Triumphs of Love and Fortune,* acted before Elizabeth in 1582, in which the Princess Fidelia is banished by her father for loving Hermione, is betrayed and pursued by her boorish brother Armenio (cf. Cloten), and is hospitably received by a banished courtier named Bomelio who lives hermitlike in a cave. "Fidele" is the disguise name of Shakespeare's Imogen. Folk motifs are apparent throughout *Cymbeline;* the cruel Queen inevitably reminds us of Snow White's stepmother. Although Shakespeare may not have been acquainted with that particular story, he clearly was interested in folk legend when he wrote *Cymbeline.* One other anonymous romantic play, *Sir Clyomon and Sir Clamydes* (c. 1570–1583), may have given Shakespeare some suggestions for his Welsh scenes.

Beaumont and Fletcher's *Philaster* was written about the same time as *Cymbeline,* and is sometimes thought to resemble Shakespeare's play. Philaster is, like Posthumus, in love with a princess whose father intends her for another suitor. Still, most of the similarities can be attributed to the conventions of the romance genre just then coming into vogue. In any case, no one can be sure whether Shakespeare's play came after or before *Philaster.* It may well be that Shakespeare was the innovator.

The Winter's Tale

Shakespeare based *The Winter's Tale* on Robert Greene's romantic novel, *Pandosto: The Triumph of Time*, published in 1588, 1592, and 1595, and then published in 1607 with the title *Dorastus and Fawnia*. Shakespeare changes the names, reverses the two kingdoms of Sicilia and Bohemia, and alters the unhappy ending that afflicts King Pandosto and Queen Bellaria of Bohemia (Leontes and Hermione of Sicilia). Otherwise, the narrative outline remains intact. The story begins with the state visit of King Egistus of Sicilia (Polixenes of Bohemia) to his boyhood companion, Pandosto of Bohemia. Queen Bellaria entertains the guest with such warmth, "oftentimes coming herself into his bed chamber to see that nothing should be amiss to mislike him," that Pandosto understandably grows jealous. He commands his cup-bearer Franion (Camillo) to murder Egistus, and the latter seems to agree but instead warns his victim to flee with him. Their hasty departure appears to confirm Pandosto's worst suspicions. He sends the guard to arrest Bellaria as she plays with her young son Garinter (Mamillius). When the Queen gives birth to a daughter in prison, the King orders the child destroyed, but relents upon the insistence of his courtiers and causes the infant to be set adrift in a small boat. The Queen nobly defends herself at her trial (in language that Shakespeare has copied in some detail). She herself requests that the oracle at Delphos be consulted. The oracle replies in words that Shakespeare has altered only slightly: "Bellaria is chaste: Egistus blameless: Franion a true subject: Pandosto treacherous: his babe an innocent; and the King shall live without an heir, if that which is lost be not found." Unlike Shakespeare's Leontes, however, Pandosto is immediately stricken with remorse; and when Queen Bellaria collapses at the news of her son Garinter's death, she is truly and irrecoverably dead.

The babe is conveyed by a tempest to the coast of Sicilia and is discovered by an impoverished shepherd named Porrus. He and his wife Mopsa adopt the child, naming her Fawnia. By the age of sixteen, Fawnia's natural beauty rivals that of the goddess Flora. At a meeting of the farmers' daughters of Sicilia, where she is chosen mistress of the feast, Fawnia is espied by the King's son Dorastus on his way home from hawking. She counters his importunate suit with the argument that she is too lowly a match for him, but he replies that the gods themselves sometimes take earthly lovers. Her foster father, distressed by the Prince's repeated visits (though he comes in shepherd's costume), resolves to carry the jewels he found with Fawnia to the King and reveal her story, thereby escaping blame for the goings-on. Dorastus escapes with Fawnia to a ship, aided by his servant Capnio (cf. Camillo). Capnio also fulfills a role given by Shakespeare to Autolycus, for he manages to trick the shepherd Porrus into thinking he can see the King if he comes aboard Dorastus' ship. A storm drives these voyagers to Bohemia where, because of the ancient enmity between Egistus and Pandosto, they disguise themselves. Pandosto, happening to hear of Fawnia's beauty, orders her and the others to be arrested as spies and summoned to court, whereupon he falls incestuously in love with the disguised Fawnia. He promises to free "Meleagrus" (Dorastus' disguise name) only if the young man will relinquish his claim to Fawnia. King Egistus meanwhile has discovered his son's whereabouts, and sends ambassadors to Bohemia demanding the return of Dorastus and the execution of Fawnia, Capnio, and Porrus. Pandosto, his love for Fawnia having turned to hate, is about to comply when Porrus reveals the circumstances of Fawnia's infancy. Overjoyed to rediscover his daughter, Pandosto permits her to marry Dorastus, but then falls into a melancholy fit and commits suicide.

Shakespeare has created some characters almost entirely, such as Paulina, Antigonus, the clownish shepherd's son, and Autolycus, though Capnio does perform one of Autolycus' functions by inveigling the old shepherd aboard ship. Antigonus' journey to the seacoast of Bohemia with the infant Perdita, and his fatal exit "pursued by a bear," are Shakespearean additions. The character of Time is also added, and the shift in tone from tragedy to romance is more pronounced than in Greene. The shepherdesses at the sheepshearing are Shakespearean. The old shepherd has a more substantial and comic role; Camillo is a stronger person than Capnio. Shakespeare omits the incestuous love of Pandosto for his daughter, and brings Hermione back to life. (For this motif of a statue made to breathe, he may well have recalled Ovid's account of Pygmalion in Ovid's *Metamorphoses* Book X.) Shakespeare's Leontes is more irrationally jealous than in Greene's account. Leontes' purgative sorrow is more intense and also more restorative than in the source; he is a truly noble and tragicomic figure, the center of a play about forgiveness and renewal.

Shakespeare may also have known Francis Sabie's *The Fissher-mans Tale* (1595), and its continuation, *Flora's Fortune* (1595). From Greene's cony-catching pamphlets he probably derived many of Autolycus' tricks.

The Tempest

No direct literary source for the whole of *The Tempest* has been found. Shakespeare does seem to have drawn material from various accounts of the shipwreck of the *Sea Venture* in the Bermudas, 1609, although the importance of these materials should not be overstated. Several of the survivors wrote narratives of the shipwreck itself and of their life on the islands for some nine months. Sylvester Jourdain, in *A Discovery of the Barmudas*, published 1610, speaks of miraculous preservation despite the island's reputation for being "a most prodigious and inchanted place." William Strachey's letter, written in July of 1610 and published much later (1625) as *A true Reportory of the Wracke and Redemption . . . from the Ilands of the Bermudas*, describes the panic among the passengers and crew, the much-feared reputation of the island as the habitation of devils and wicked spirits, the actual beauty and fertility of the place with its abundance of wild life (cf. Caliban's descriptions), and the treachery of the Indians they later encounter in Virginia. Shakespeare seems to have read Strachey's letter in manuscript, and may have been acquainted with him. He also kept up with travel accounts of Ralegh and Hariot, and knew various classical evocations of a New World. The name "Setebos" came from Richard Eden's *History of Trauayle* (1577), translated from Peter Martyr's *De Novo Orbe* and from other travel accounts of the period. (See the Introduction to *The Tempest,* above, for the potential relevance of various journals of the circumnavigation of the globe.) All these hints are indeed suggestive, but they are scattered and relate more to the setting and general circumstance of Shakespeare's play than to the plot.

Shakespeare certainly consulted Montaigne's essay "Of the Caniballes," as translated by John Florio in 1603. Gonzalo's reverie on an ideal commonwealth (II,i) contains many verbal echoes of the essay. Montaigne's point is that supposedly civilized men who condemn as "barbarian" any society not conforming with their own are simply refusing to examine their own shortcomings. A supposedly "primitive" society may well embody perfect religion, justice, and harmony; civilized art can never rival the achievements of nature. The ideal commonwealth has no need of magistrates, riches, poverty, and contracts, all of which breed dissimulation and covetousness. The significance of these ideas for *The Tempest* extends well beyond the particular passage in which they are found. And Caliban himself, whose name is an anagram of "cannibal," illustrates (even though he is not an eater of human flesh) the truth of Montaigne's observation: "I thinke there is more barbarisme in eating men alive, than to feed upon them being dead."

Prospero's famous valedictory speech to "Ye elves of hills, brooks, standing lakes, and groves" (V,i) owes its origin to Medea's similar invocation in Ovid's *Metamorphoses* (Book VII), which Shakespeare knew both in the Latin original and in Golding's translation: "Ye Ayres and windes: ye Elves of Hilles, of B[r]ookes, of Woods alone, Of standing Lakes . . ." Medea also anticipates Shakespeare's Sycorax. Medea thus provides material for the representation of both black and white magic in *The Tempest,* so carefully differentiated by Shakespeare. Ariel is part English fairy, like Puck, and part daemon. The pastoral situation in *The Tempest* is perhaps derived from Spenser's *The Faerie Queene,* Book VI (with its distinctions between savage lust and true courtesy, between nature and art). Italian pastoral drama as practiced by Guarini and (in England) by John Fletcher may also have been an influence. The masque element in *The Tempest,* prominent as in much late Shakespeare, bears the imprint of the courtly masque tradition of Jonson, Beaumont, and Fletcher.

A German play, *Die Schöne Sidea* by Jacob Ayrer, written before 1605, was once thought to have been based on an earlier version of *The Tempest* as performed by English players traveling in Germany. Today the similarities between the two plays are generally attributed to conventions found everywhere in romance.

Venus and Adonis

Venus and Adonis was Shakespeare's contribution to the vogue of Ovidian and erotic poetry in the 1580's and '90's that included Thomas Lodge's *Scilla's Metamorphosis* (1589), Michael Drayton's *Endimion and Phoebe* (published 1595), Christopher Marlowe's *Hero and Leander* (registered 1593), and John Marston's *Metamorphosis of Pygmalions Image* (1598). On Shakespeare's combining of three passages from Ovid's *Metamorphoses,* see Introduction to *Venus and Adonis,* above. A disdainful Adonis had evidently become a commonplace in the 1590's, for it appears in *Hero and Leander,* ll. 12–14, Spenser's *Faerie Queene,* III,i,35, and elsewhere.

The Rape of Lucrece

Shakespeare's chief source for *The Rape of Lucrece* was Ovid's *Fasti* (II, 721–852), which had not yet been translated into English. He also seems to have known Livy's *History of Rome* (I,57–59), which had been translated by William Painter in his *The Palace of Pleasure* (1566), and Chaucer's *The Legend of Good Women* (which is, like Shakespeare's poem, indebted to Ovid and Livy). Shakespeare's version is considerably longer than any of these sources. Ovid, Livy, and Chaucer give narrative, swift-moving accounts; Shakespeare follows instead the literary tradition of the "Complaint," as in *A Myrroure for Magistrates* and in Samuel Daniel's *The Complaint of Rosamond.*

The Minor Poems

Of the minor poems, the most interesting in terms of sources is "The Phoenix and the Turtle." It is sometimes related to Chaucer's *The Parlement of Fowles,* an allegorical treatment of an assembly of birds. No indebtedness can be proved, however. Instead, as F. T. Price has shown in his Arden edition of *The Poems,* Shakespeare's chief "source" was the very anthology to which he contributed this remarkable piece. Called *Loves Martyr,* assembled by one Robert Chester, it contains some execrable verse but was built around a single vivid and intriguing emblem: the union in death of two mythic birds expressing a love beyond human reason. The idea was sufficiently compelling to attract not only Shakespeare but Jonson, Chapman, and Marston. The cooperation of these highly sophisticated writers may have been prompted by some kind of private *jeu d'esprit,* but Shakespeare's venture into fantasy produced extraordinary results.

The Sonnets

See the Introduction to The Sonnets, above, for a discussion of the sonnet vogue in England of the 1590's, and the previous history of the sonnet in England and on the Continent.

APPENDIX 3

Shakespeare in Performance

Shakespeare belonged to the leading dramatic company of his time, and wrote plays to be acted by men who were his close professional associates, the actor-sharers in the company. Unfortunately we do not know as much as we would like about the assignment of roles in his plays. The leading actor of the company, Richard Burbage, played Richard III, Hamlet, Othello, and King Lear. Probably he also played such roles as Macbeth, Antony, Coriolanus, and Prospero. In several roles he was impressive enough to have received contemporary mention. Will Kempe, a comic actor, took the part of Dogberry in *Much Ado about Nothing,* Peter in *Romeo and Juliet,* and probably other such buffoonish clowns. His departure from the company in 1599 made room for Robert Armin, a comic actor whose "style" was that of the wise or courtly fool. Shakespeare wrote for him the parts of Touchstone, Feste, Lavatch (in *All's Well*), and the Fool in *King Lear.* Shakespeare wrote his women's parts for boy actors, and was to an extent dependent on their quality and number. The boys, who served as apprentices to the actor-sharers, needed several years of experience before they could handle a demanding part like Juliet or Cleopatra. Yet some boys did manage to reach this remarkable level of proficiency before their voices started changing. The company needed a succession of boys so that they could be replaced in the women's roles when they became young men. (Some of them stayed on as young adult actors.)

Apart from specialized roles for the leading actor, the fool, and the boys, Shakespeare's company was versatile. The actor-sharers, men like John Heminges, Henry Condell, Augustine Phillips, Thomas Pope, Richard Cowley, William Sly, and Shakespeare himself, undertook both major and minor roles as occasion demanded. In about 1603, John Lowin and Alexander Cooke joined the roster of principal actors in the King's company. Phillips died in 1605, making room for Samuel Gilburne. Sly died in 1608, and at this time William Ostler and John Underwood joined the company. Later prominent actors included Joseph Taylor, who played Iago, and Nathan Field. These men were all accomplished actors. From our point of view today their acting might seem formal or stylized, although considerably less so than the acting seen during Shakespeare's youth. As Hamlet's instructions to the players suggest (*Hamlet,* III,ii), Shakespeare's company put great stress on "naturalness" in acting and clearly believed they had reformed the ranting abuses of the earlier sixteenth century. Even so, Jacobean stage conditions militated against the kind of naturalistic informality we know today. Boys played women's parts; the language of the plays was often poetically quite formal; soliloquies and asides to the audience were common; no scenery existed to create a visual illusion; performance in open daylight on a broad apron stage before large audiences required a declamatory style of elocution; and the absence of artificial lighting precluded the use of nighttime effects for ghosts or storms. Costuming ordinarily employed sumptuous Elizabethan dress, although sometimes with special costuming effects for Romans, Jews, sailors, and such.

Shakespeare's first known great success was *1 Henry VI,* in which the heroic role of Lord Talbot made a strong impression. *Richard III* had a spectacular popularity. Other enduringly popular successes in Shakespeare's own day included *Titus Andronicus, Romeo and Juliet, Richard II, Henry IV, Hamlet, Othello, Pericles,* and many others. On the other hand, *Troilus and Cressida* seems to have been a flop, and *Timon of Athens* probably was never even finished or performed. We know nothing about *All's Well that Ends Well* until the publishing of the 1623 Folio. Besides pleasing the general public, Shakespeare's plays were often in demand at court.

Little is known of Shakespeare's plays in performance from the time of his death until 1642. His reputation was assured, but even as a classic he could not compete with the successful playwrights who succeeded him, particularly John Fletcher. To be sure, in a commendatory verse to a collection of Shakespeare's poems in 1640, Leonard Digges asserted that Falstaff, Benedick and Beatrice, and Malvolio still drew fuller houses than Ben Jonson's dramatic creations. Nevertheless, the publication of the First Folio of Shakespeare's works in 1623, including several texts based on the promptbooks which the company had used for its actual performances, suggests that the King's men were no longer interested in guarding the exclusive rights to Shakespeare's plays. In any event, the closing of the theatres in 1642 by a Puritan-dominated Parliament put an end to legitimate theatre in England until the Restoration of 1660. During the interregnum period, Shakespeare lived on in the theatre only through the occasional surreptitious performance of "drolls" or farcical skits derived from *1 Henry IV* ("The Bouncing Knight," or Falstaff), *Hamlet* ("The Grave Makers"), and *A Midsummer Night's Dream* ("The Merry Conceited Humors of Bottom the Weaver").

From the Restoration to Garrick (1660–1741)

The theatre of the Restoration and early eighteenth century differed greatly from Shakespeare's Globe Theatre. Audiences, who in Shakespeare's later years were already more oriented toward courtly and sophisticated taste than in the 1590's, were by Restoration times virtually limited to a select group who came to see plays in elegant indoor theatres. At the beginning of the Restoration, the acting companies were restricted in number by royal patent to two. That of Sir William Davenant, the Duke of York's players, began to play at the old theatre in Salisbury Court in 1660, but moved to a new theatre in Lincoln's Inn Fields the following year and to Dorset Garden in 1671. The company under Thomas Killigrew's management, the King's company, moved in 1660 from the Red Bull to a theatre built on Gibbons' Tennis Court in Vere Street and thence to a theatre on Bridges Street, Drury Lane, in 1663. When this first so-called Theatre Royal was destroyed by fire in 1672, Killigrew's company set up temporarily in Lincoln's Inn Fields, but then moved to the magnificent second Drury Lane Theatre, designed by Christopher Wren, in 1674. Each successive move brought the two companies to more elegant quarters and to a more fashionable part of town. The two companies united in 1682, chiefly because audiences were too small to support both. Thereafter they performed usually in the Drury Lane Theatre, the smaller of the two houses. This single company was the sole source of legitimate drama in London until 1695, when the restiveness of some underpaid actors led to the establishment of a newly patented acting company in Lincoln's Inn Fields. The new company enlisted some impressive talent, notably Thomas Betterton, Elizabeth Barry, and Anne Bracegirdle. Despite such a powerful beginning, and a new theatre in the Haymarket in 1705 designed by Sir John Vanbrugh, the project dwindled and ultimately failed, leaving the field to Colley Cibber at Drury Lane. All the actors united again in one company, and Haymarket became an opera house.

Restoration theatres increasingly made use of the kind of elaborate scenic adornment that, in Shakespeare's time, had been restricted almost entirely to the presentation of courtly masques. The early Restoration also saw use of the proscenium arch with a curtained stage behind it, although a considerable amount of the action still took place on the apron or outer stage. Scenic effects were sometimes lavish, and the tendency toward such spectacle encouraged the production of operatic versions of Shakespeare. Artificial lighting was of course necessary for indoor performance, and actresses were used for women's parts in the plays. All these changes moved away from the fluidity and flexibility of the Elizabethan open-air apron stage, devoid of scenery.

Acting styles were affected by the changes in stage and theatre management. Perhaps the most significant development was the emergence of the theatre manager who was also leading actor. His prominence was unlike anything seen in Shakespeare's day, despite Shakespeare's reliance on Richard Burbage for leading roles. Shakespeare's company shared responsibility more or less equally among the actor-sharers who were expected to be versatile in the doubling of roles and in the performing of important secondary parts; the new companies of the Restoration and eighteenth century devoted most prominence to the director-manager-leading actor. This structural shift in the acting company placed new demands on Shakespeare's scripts, and motivated a search for ways of curtailing his secondary roles in favor of the major parts. Plays with large roles for a central protagonist, such as *Macbeth* and *Hamlet,* became repeated favorites, whereas others lacking such a focus, like *The Comedy of Errors* or *Love's Labor's Lost,* were seldom produced. Women's roles underwent a similar change of emphasis as the companies moved from boy actors to mature (and at times notorious) women. The new actresses, like the leading men, demanded plays and parts suited to their talents, and Shakespeare's scripts were accordingly selected and revised to meet this need.

The most famous actor-managers of the period from the Restoration in 1660 until the advent of David Garrick in 1741 were Thomas Betterton and Colley Cibber. Betterton was famous for his Macbeth, Bassanio (in *The Merchant of Venice*), Brutus, Othello, and Hamlet. As a director he presided over some of the most extensive alterations of Shakespeare that the age witnessed, as we shall see. Cibber too was simultaneously a leading actor, theatre manager, director, and author of many revisions of Shakespeare. Other prominent actors and actresses included Barton Booth and Robert Wilks (who were also joint managers of the Drury Lane Theatre), Anne Bracegirdle (who acted Portia, Desdemona, and other Shakespearean roles), and Elizabeth Barry (known for Calpurnia, Lady Macbeth, and Queen Gertrude). The famous Nell Gwyn seemingly did not undertake prominent Shakespearean roles. These roles give some indication of the Shakespearean plays most in demand by the actors and actresses of the age.

What, more specifically, were productions of Shakespeare like, and what happened to Shakespeare's scripts during this period? The influences at work were many, and included not only the theatrical factors already discussed—actor-managers and actresses in search of large roles, scenery, indoor lighting, small select audiences—but also matters of literary taste. Classical decorum came into high repute. Ben Jonson was admired as a more learned and "correct" author than Shakespeare. The age tended to regard Shakespeare as an untutored "natural" genius who wrote for unrefined audiences in an ignorant time. Any "improvements" to his text would only serve to elevate Shakespeare to the refinement and elegance he deserved. The result was that the Restoration period saw more adaptations of Shakespeare than performances of anything like the original. Theatrical practice and literary taste reinforced one another to encourage productions that were "unified" according to the classical unities, tightened by the elimination of minor characters, and at the same time rendered more symmetrical and spectacular by the incorporation of parallel plots and scenic effects. Moreover, some unhappy endings of Shakespearean plays were altered to provide resolutions in keeping with neoclassical ideas of "poetic justice"—that is, a just punishment for the villains and a deserved reward for the virtuous.

In Dryden's and Davenant's version of *The Tempest* (1670), elaborate symmetry of design is the overriding consideration. The adapters hit on the notion of what they called a "counter plot": since Shakespeare had told the story of a young lady who has never seen a young man, why not provide the play with a young man who has never seen a young lady? Hence the invention of Hippolito, young Duke of Mantua, whom Prospero has brought with him to the island at the time of his banishment and hid in a cave, safe from the fatal gaze of women. Inevitably, however, Hippolito discovers and falls in love with a woman his own age: not Miranda, but Miranda's sister Dorinda. Hippolito must also do battle for a time with Ferdinand, who is unsuccessfully confined to another cave. Eventually each Jack obtains his Jill. Caliban likewise has a sister, Sycorax, and Ariel has a fellow-spirit named Milcha. Milcha's role became much amplified in Thomas Shadwell's operatic version of 1674.

Davenant's *The Law Against Lovers,* based on *Measure for Measure* and staged in early 1662, stresses balance in structure along with the paring away of secondary roles and the accentuation of poetic justice. Davenant has eliminated virtually all the comic characters, and has changed Angelo into a sentimentalized villain who truly loves Isabella, never intends to kill Claudio, and finally wins Isabella's hand in marriage. To this adapted plot Davenant has added a subplot of Benedick and Beatrice, with Benedick as Angelo's brother and Beatrice as Angelo's ward. In his *Macbeth* (1674), Davenant catered to the current vogue for opera and special effects by providing dancing witches and a ghost of Duncan that continues to haunt Lady Macbeth. This version held the stage until 1744. Thomas Killigrew's company did an adaptation of *The Taming of the Shrew* called *Sauny the Scot* (1667), written by the actor John Lacy. Sauny is a replacement for Grumio, Petruchio's comic servant. Samuel Pepys disliked the play generally, but did admire the added part of Sauny with his Scottish humors. Thomas Shadwell's *Timon of Athens or the Man-Hater* (1678) gave great prominence to two women: Melissa, whom Timon intends to marry, and Evandra, his mistress whom he intends to leave. Evandra proves, however, to be Timon's only true friend, and they die in one another's arms.

The Restoration impulse to tighten up the classical unities can be seen in Dryden's *Troilus and Cressida, or Truth Found too Late* (1679) and in his *All for Love, or the World Well Lost* (1678). The latter is not really an adaptation of Shakespeare so much as a replacement. It tells the story of Antony and Cleopatra with obvious indebtedness to Shakespeare, but confines the action to the very last phase when the lovers are besieged in Alexandria. The cast is limited to about nine named characters as compared with about thirty-one in Shakespeare's play.

Perhaps the best-known adaptation of Shakespeare in the Restoration period was Nahum Tate's *King Lear* (1681). This version ends happily, with Lear restored to his throne. The adaptation so satisfied eighteenth-century audiences in their craving for poetic justice that Shakespeare's version was banished from the stage until 1838. In Tate's defense, we might point out that all versions of the story before Shakespeare's play had ended with Lear's regaining of his throne; Shakespeare's is the great exception. Tate's version provided a love affair between Edgar and Cordelia. She remains in England rather than going to France, wanders about on the heath during the storm, and is nearly ravished by Edmund until Edgar providentially emerges from his cave and drives off the villain's henchmen. Tate also banished the Fool as offensive to classical ideas of "pure" tragedy unmixed with comedy.

Some Shakespearean adaptations were motivated in part by political considerations; the theatre of the period was aimed at a select audience, knowledgeable in affairs of state, and attuned to the sharp rivalries between Catholic and Protestant or court and parliament. Tate's revision of *Richard II,* called *The Sicilian Usurper* (1681), ran into political trouble as soon as it was performed. Despite his changing of the scene to Sicily, and his plaintive insistence afterward that he had intended no offense, his play was seen by the government as an attack on King Charles and was silenced on the third day. Equally controversial for political reasons were Tate's unsuccessful *Ingratitude of a Commonwealth* (1682) and John Dennis' *The Invader of His Country* (1719), both based on *Coriolanus.*

Other Restoration and early eighteenth-century adaptations include Thomas Otway's *Caius Marius* (1680), which took the place of Shakespeare's *Romeo and Juliet* until 1744, Tom Durfey's *The Injured Princess, or the Fatal Wager* (1682), based on *Cymbeline,* George Granville's *The Jew of Venice* (1701), which substituted for *The Merchant of Venice* until 1741, and Charles Burnaby's *Love Betrayed* (1703), based on *Twelfth Night.* Perhaps the best-known adaptation of the early eighteenth century is the *Richard III* (1700) of Colley Cibber, manager of the Drury Lane Theatre and poet laureate. Some of Cibber's inclusions from *3 Henry VI,* and his added lines—"Off with his head, so much for Buckingham," or "Richard's himself again!"—are still used in modern productions. (See, for example, Laurence Olivier's film version of *Richard III.*)

The Age of Garrick (1741–1776)

The trend toward dominance of the London stage by a single man, who was manager, director, author, and his own star actor, reached its zenith in the career of David Garrick. His first dramatic season in 1741–1742, at an unlicensed and short-lived theatre in Goodman's Fields, included a resounding success in the role of Richard III. Soon he was hired at an enormous salary to act at Drury Lane. With some fellow actors he made attempts to secure a patent for a new company in 1743, and in 1746–1747 he performed memorably with the actor James Quin at Covent Garden. (The Covent Garden Theatre had been providing successful competition for the Drury Lane Theatre since its opening in 1732.) In 1747, however, Garrick returned to Drury Lane and became its joint manager and its chief moving spirit until his retirement in 1776.

During his glorious career, Garrick revived many Shakespearean plays that had been virtually forgotten. His predecessors had contented themselves with the repetition of a few predictable favorites, such as *Hamlet, Othello, King Lear* (in Tate's version, naturally), *Macbeth* (with dancing witches), *Julius Caesar, Richard III* (as transmuted by Cibber), and *1 Henry IV.* Only toward the end of the period had a few of the comedies been occasionally revived. Under Garrick, many long-neglected plays joined the repertory. Garrick revived *Much Ado about Nothing* in 1748–1749 and *Cymbeline* in 1761–1762, playing the leading roles (Benedick and Posthumus) himself. He also staged lesser-known history plays such as *King John* and *Henry VIII.* His *Antony and Cleopatra* in 1759 was the first since Shakespeare's time. Garrick was his own most brilliant actor in *Hamlet, Much Ado about Nothing*, and many others; yet he shied away from certain roles in which other actors excelled. For example, he tended to defer to James Quin and Spranger Barry in *Othello* (at Covent Garden), Charles Macklin as Shylock, Quin as Falstaff, and still others. Garrick also grew too old for Romeo, and so ultimately abandoned that play. Thus the Drury Lane repertory grew and changed with Garrick's age and acting abilities.

Despite the enormous boost Garrick gave to Shakespeare in the theatre, and despite his occasional fidelity to something approaching the texts of the plays as Shakespeare wrote them, Garrick was still the child of his time in his predilection for adapted Shakespeare. His *Macbeth* was closer in some ways to the original than had generally been the case in the preceding century, and yet he omitted the Porter scene as offensive to the decorum of tragedy. His production of *Hamlet* in 1772 rewrote the one great Shakespearean tragedy that had heretofore escaped major revision. His *Romeo and Juliet* (1748) followed Otway's lead in having Juliet awake in the tomb before Romeo dies; and *The Fairies* (1755) entirely omitted the tradesmen of Athens and their performance of "Pyramus and Thisbe." Garrick's version of *The Tempest* was operatic, like Dryden's. *Katharine and Petruchio,* Garrick's adaptation of *The Taming of the Shrew* that included only the wife-taming plot, supplanted the Shakespearean original from 1756 to 1844 and remained popular long afterward. Garrick's *King Lear* (1756) retained Nahum Tate's happy ending with the love affair of Cordelia and Edgar, and omitted the Fool as Tate had done, even though the actual poetry of some scenes was brought noticeably closer to that of Shakespeare.

A small man with lively features, Garrick possessed an ability to transform himself in performing a role that became legendary. He went to hospitals for the insane and studied the behavior of inmates in order to prepare himself for Lear's mad scenes. His passion for a natural style based on observation from life was highly innovative in an age generally devoted to a more formal and rhetorical manner of delivery. Garrick's range of characterization was also extraordinary. He performed low-comedy parts with such verisimilitude that some spectators came away from the theatre convinced that Garrick could be nothing other than a mean-spirited and worthless fellow. Yet his most famous effects were the violent passions: Hamlet's fear and awe in the presence of his father's ghost, Lear's ungovernable fury at his older daughters' ingratitude, and the like.

One contribution of questionable worth made by Garrick to Shakespearean stage history was his great Shakespeare Jubilee, held at Stratford over a three-day period in the summer of 1769. In its own day the event was both praised as a great honor to Shakespeare's memory and vilified as an ostentatious charade. Its elaborate ceremonies were in fact notably lacking in the performance of Shakespeare's own works. The high point seems instead to have been Garrick's recitation of his "Ode Upon Dedicating the Town Hall, and Erecting a Statue to Shakespeare." Nevertheless, the celebration raised money for the maintenance of various historical monuments in Shakespeare's home town. The whole event did much to establish the vogue of Shakespeare-worship that became so much a part of nineteenth-century Shakespeare criticism.

Other leading actors from Garrick's time—Charles Macklin, James Quin, Spranger Barry—did not attain his success, whatever their individual achievements. Macklin, an older actor than Garrick, never got over his resentment of the younger man's success. Garrick's leading ladies included Hannah Pritchard as Rosalind, Beatrice, and Lady Macbeth; Peg Woffington as Rosalind, Isabella, Viola, Portia, and Mistress Ford; her rival, Anne Bellamy, as Juliet; Mary Ann Yates as Rosalind, Isabella, Cleopatra, and Lady Macbeth; and Susanna Cibber as Juliet. Their rivalries, especially that of Anne Bellamy and Peg Woffington, sometimes took the form of competition in gorgeous attire, and the costume managers at Drury Lane were kept busy supplying Mrs. Bellamy with jewels and satin in which to appear as Volumnia or Juliet. (One dress, fashioned for Mrs. Bellamy in the part of Cleopatra in *All for Love,* c. 1746, had belonged to the Princess of Wales and had been worn on her birthday, but was walked off with by the rival actress who was to play Octavia.) The prominence of such actresses gave impetus to the repeated performances of such comedies as *As You Like It* and *Measure for Measure*.

The Romantic Age: Kemble, Edmund Kean, Macready (1776–1843)

The Romantic Age was generally not a flourishing time for the English theatre. As we can see from a survey of Shakespeare criticism (see General Introduction), Romantic critics such as Lamb and Hazlitt held condescending views of theatrical performances of Shakespeare, and preferred to read Shakespeare's text in the quiet of their own studies. The greatest literary figures of the age did not write for the stage; the occasional dramas written by the Romantic poets are usually "closet" dramas, designed to be read rather than acted. Garrick's huge success in producing Shakespeare proved hard to emulate. One reason for the decline may be that Shakespeare on the stage had been so thoroughly made over into a neoclassical dramatist by Tate, Cibber, and Garrick that he no longer appealed to the taste of the new age. Many Romantic critics and readers, intent now on the study of Shakespeare's philosophical idealism and his conceptions of personality or "character," preferred the sublimity of Shakespeare's own poetry to the theatrical spectacle and classical "decorum" they found on the London stage.

The acting manager at Drury Lane from 1788 to 1802 was John Philip Kemble. Strained relations with the playwright Richard Brinsley Sheridan forced Kemble to leave Drury Lane in 1802 to undertake the management of Covent Garden, where he achieved a notable success and remained active until his retirement in 1817. Both theatre buildings burned during this period, Covent Garden in 1808 and Drury Lane in 1809, and both were splendidly rebuilt. The new Covent Garden Theatre featured an ample stage and proscenium arch with wing and groove flats encouraging extravagant settings to match the resplendent costumes and pageantry. Here, Kemble was able to perform before a large audience of some three thousand spectators and to indulge in more lavish sets than had before been possible. Kemble came to be noted for his attention to realistic details in costuming and scenery. His *Henry VIII* (1788–1789) abounded in colorful processions; his *Coriolanus* (1789) was strikingly Roman in costume; his *The Tempest* (produced at this same time) "gave a terrible dance of Furies in one place, and a masque of Neptune and Amphitrite in another." Sarah Siddons, his best-known leading lady, excelled as Rosalind, Queen Katharine, Isabella, Hermione, and Lady Macbeth. Despite Kemble's popularity, however, his productions did not provide a return to Shakespeare's texts; indeed, his desire for spectacle often took him in the other direction. He restored some of Tate's additions to *King Lear* that Garrick had eliminated, and usually performed Shakespearean plays in the altered versions to which the previous age had grown accustomed.

During the years following Kemble's retirement in 1817, the English theatre came to a particularly low ebb. Standing out among mediocrities, Edmund Kean succeeded Kemble as the leading actor of the day, and managed to impress even such a Romantic critic as William Hazlitt. He was impressive as Othello and Richard III, among other roles. He did make significant restorations in the text of *King Lear* (1823), including the last act with the death of Cordelia; but he still retained the love of Cordelia and Edgar, omitted the Fool, and compromised his task of restoration to such an extent that a contemporary reviewer complained justifiably of too much "plastering." During this period between 1817 and 1837, in fact, the English theatre seems to have been more timid and bound by convention than its public would have desired. Stage traditions are often remarkably persistent, and those established by Tate, Cibber, and Garrick lived well beyond the age which created them.

It fell to William Charles Macready, manager of Covent Garden (1837–1839) and then of Drury Lane (1841–1843), to make a first serious attempt at restoration of Shakespeare's acting texts. Although not an astute financier, Macready was an actor whose sensitive style won him admirers among audiences now grown too refined for Kean's explosions of passion. In 1838 Macready staged *King Lear,* "free from the interpolations which have disgraced it for nearly two centuries," as a contemporary reviewer put it. However much closer to Shakespeare's play, to be sure, Macready's *King Lear* still left out Gloucester's blinding and otherwise rearranged and curtailed the play. A significant step had nonetheless been taken, and Macready followed his own lead in "restoring" many of the other plays, leaving in his *Diaries* a still-interesting record of his thoughts on acting Shakespeare. By 1843, of all Shakespeare's plays only *Richard III, Romeo and Juliet,* and *The Taming of the Shrew* still held the stage as eighteenth-century adaptations.

In a reform of equal significance, an act of 1843 abolished the monopoly on theatrical companies that had been in effect since 1660. The controlling of patents or licenses had resulted, as we have seen, in the licensing of only two London companies at most. After 1843, any company could perform plays in a theatre that met the requirements of public safety. Freed of manipulative control and nearly free of the eighteenth-century acting versions of Cibber and Garrick, the English stage enjoyed greater vitality than it had known for some time.

The Later Nineteenth Century: Phelps, Charles Kean, Irving (1843–1902)

With the abolition of patent control in 1843, Drury Lane and Covent Garden fell into an almost immediate and overdue senility. (Drury Lane alone recovered and eventually flourished again.) In their place sprang up new theatres and new actors: in particular, Samuel Phelps at the Sadler's Wells Theatre and Charles Kean at the Princess's Theatre. A third important theatre, the Haymarket, featured at various times Macready, Helen Faucit, Charles Kean and his wife, and others. The recently introduced gas lighting now illuminated all the theatres. The Haymarket featured extensive remodeling including a curtailment of the apron stage in front of the proscenium arch and curtain, an advancing of the orchestra and lights nearer the actors and scenic effects, and an interior "decorated in the most costly and elegant style." Phelps managed Sadler's Wells until 1862, and presented there a repertory of unparalleled richness including many Elizabethan plays—*The Maid's Tragedy, The Duch-*

ess of Malfi, A New Way to Pay Old Debts—in addition to those of Shakespeare. His actresses included Isabel Glyn (as Gertrude and Cleopatra) and Laura Addison (as Juliet and Imogen). Some notable revivals were *Timon of Athens, 2 Henry IV,* and *Pericles.* Charles Kean, Edmund Kean's son, indulged a passion for elaborate historical accuracy in the use of costumes and scenery—a trend toward spectacular verisimilitude that John Kemble and William Charles Macready had already done much to further.

Under the guidance of Phelps and Kean, and also Ben Webster at the Haymarket, the English theatre revived long-neglected and heavily adapted plays in something like their Shakespearean form. *The Taming of the Shrew* appeared at the Haymarket in 1844, *Richard III* at Sadler's Wells in 1845, and *Romeo and Juliet* at the Haymarket in 1845. *King Lear* underwent even further restoration under Phelps' direction, in 1845, than it had received from Macready in 1838. Phelps' *Macbeth* (1847) put aside the musical and spectacular additions that had so long afflicted the witch scenes. A contrary force was at work, however, in the pursuit of spectacular visual effects, for new cuttings were needed to make room for scene changes, and the costs of productions were beginning to increase at an alarming rate. As the age of Phelps and Kean came to an end (Kean retired in 1859), Shakespearean production on the London stage seemed poised on the verge of a new difficulty. F. B. Chatterton at the Drury Lane Theatre offered his ominous opinion that "Shakespeare spells ruin." Shakespeare was about to become, in other words, a heavy financial risk for the producer rather than a sure-fire commercial success. The cost of cumbersome and ornate stagings of Shakespeare continued to mount during the late nineteenth century.

During this era, the standard for Shakespearean productions was set by Henry Irving, manager of the Lyceum Theatre from 1878 until 1902, and by Ellen Terry, his leading lady. Irving, a talented director and producer, enjoyed an enormous success and eventually was honored by knighthood and by burial in Westminister Abbey (like Garrick before him). Irving's Shakespearean sets were always sumptuous, richly decorated, and attentive to details. His stage set for *Henry VIII* in 1892, for example, featured magnificent Tudor interiors with paneled wood ceilings and carved wooden arches, or renditions of Westminister Abbey with tall perpendicular-Gothic stained-glass windows. His elaborate visual effects extended and fulfilled a tradition of spectacle in Shakespearean production begun in the Restoration period, continued in the eighteenth century, and elaborated further in the nineteenth by Kemble, Macready, and Charles Kean. From 1660 to 1902, in fact, Shakespearean production seldom questioned the value of elaborate spectacle; however much the twentieth-century stage may seem to us closer to the Shakespearean original of a bare and flexible arena, the modern stage is a departure from a long and cumulative tradition of some 240 years. And Irving's productions were impressive, although at great cost to the script. Irving's sets were so massive, and his need for supernumeraries so great, that every Shakespearean production had to be special and costly. Shakespeare was no longer material for a stock repertory, and his plays were produced by Irving with relative infrequency. Because the changing of scenes involved so much time and expense, the texts of the plays had always to be cut and rearranged. Cibber's and Garrick's unreliable revisions were a thing of the past, to be sure, but no actor-producer of the nineteenth century would have thought seriously for a moment of doing Shakespeare uncut.

In America conditions were much the same, and indeed most productions of Shakespeare seen by Americans were either imported from England or inspired by English acting. Macready toured the United States in the 1820's and '40's, and became involved in a celebrated quarrel with the American actor Edwin Forrest. Charles Kean and Irving also acted in America; Kean played opposite Edwin Forrest, whereas Irving performed in 1880 with Edwin Booth, the first American actor to win fame abroad. American Shakespeare of the Victorian era was, like its English counterpart, ornate and verisimilar, set behind a proscenium arch as though the audience were watching through a "fourth wall." On the American frontier, to be sure, the elaborate Shakespeare of the New York–Boston circuit gave way to something more impromptu. Much of it doubtless deserved the kind of roasting it received in Mark Twain's portrait of two fraudulent strolling Shakespearean actors in *Huckleberry Finn,* though even here we can see evidence of the enormous impact of Shakespeare on the culture of a new nation.

The Twentieth Century: Revival and Adaptation

The early years of the twentieth century saw the continuation and even extension of the opulent style championed by Henry Irving. The foremost actor-manager of the turn-of-the-century era was Herbert Beerbohm Tree, presiding genius at Her Majesty's Theatre from its opening in 1897 until his death in 1917. His productions of Shakespeare in this theatre outdid Irving in his own metier, and were indeed lavish on an unprecedented scale. Live rabbits scurried across the stage in his *A Midsummer Night's Dream* (1911). The opening scene of *The Tempest* (1904) revealed a ship magnificently battered by a full-dress storm at sea. Tree's version of *Antony and Cleopatra* (1907) actually staged the meeting of Antony and Cleopatra in Egypt, instead of relying on Enobarbus' description of this event: Cleopatra appeared robed in silver, leading a huge procession through the streets of Alexandria. Such interpretations naturally called for a good deal of rearranging and curtailing of Shakespeare's texts. The scene intervals in Tree's *Macbeth* (1911) ran to forty-five minutes, and the whole production, even with a third of the text cut away, lasted four hours. *King John* (1899) gave its viewers a tableau of

Runnymede, even though the play never mentions Magna Carta. Olivia's garden in *Twelfth Night* (1901) revealed to the audience real grass, box hedges, statues, and running fountains. This set was, needless to say, particularly hard to move; scenes located at Duke Orsino's palace had somehow to be worked around the decor of Olivia's garden. Tree was a great success, as Irving had usually been. So too was Johnston Forbes-Robertson, renowned actor of Hamlet and Othello, who expurgated his texts to conform with Victorian standards of decency.

Despite popular fondness for Beerbohm Tree's grand style, however, a movement toward greater stage flexibility and a fidelity to Shakespearean texts was under way. Frank Benson, who brought his repertory company from the provinces to the Lyceum Theatre in 1900, offered relatively straightforward productions. Benson produced *Hamlet,* for example, in two sessions (afternoon and evening), from an uncut text of the First Folio. A performance of this sort could not possibly use the unwieldy sets of a Tree production. Benson never could match Tree in popularity, since the times demanded an ornamental style. Even so, his impact was significant. One ingredient of his method was simple economic common sense: he lacked the means to stage Shakespeare as expensively as Tree had done, and needed also to be able to take his flexible productions on tour.

William Poel was more of an idealist and visionary than Benson, and also something of an eccentric. His aim in establishing the Elizabethan Stage Society in 1894 was to discover more about Shakespeare's own stage, and to use that knowledge as a means of combating what he viewed as the stifling conventionality of the late Victorian theatre. He was a passionate crusader for swiftly paced acting, continuity of scenes, a fluid stage, and intimacy between actors and audience. His performances were Elizabethan revivals—usually meticulously so, with Elizabethan costuming, an inner stage and open platform, and other aspects of historical reconstruction. Although his audiences were never large, he did prove that Elizabethan staging could work as practical theatre. He performed *The Comedy of Errors* (1895) in Gray's Inn, where it had been performed in 1594 by Shakespeare's company. For his *Romeo and Juliet* (1905) he cast a girl of fourteen as Juliet and a boy of seventeen as Romeo. George Bernard Shaw saw the play and was impressed.

Another believer in Poel's work was Harley Granville-Barker. His productions of Shakespeare at the Savoy Theatre in 1912–1914 converted what had been an experimental movement into successful commercial theatre. In Granville-Barker's view, Poel had gone too far in stripping bare the overornamented stage of Beerbohm Tree. Granville-Barker hit instead upon a format that provided the essential elements of Poel's reform and yet avoided the cult of austerity for its own sake. His opening production in 1912, *The Winter's Tale,* employed three acting areas for the entire play, and stressed above all rapidity of pace and intimacy. He abolished footlights and realistic backdrops. In his *Twelfth Night* of the same year he did away with the tradition of burlesque foolery in which the comic characters had long been played. These innovations naturally caused an uproar, but they also found favor with influential critics. Beerbohm Tree's edifices were soon to become a thing of the past.

The Old Vic Theatre and its acting company moved toward the new style of acting in the 1910's, mainly under the impetus of the producer Philip Ben Greet, and the theatre's manager, Lilian Baylis. This theatre on London's bankside had been built in 1818 and named the Royal Victoria in 1833. Since 1914 the company has specialized in Shakespearean performance under the direction of Tyrone Guthrie and others. Renamed the National Theatre Company in 1963, this organization has continued to be a leader in modern Shakespearean production, now broadening its repertory to include non-Shakespearean plays, and in 1975 moving into a splendid new theatre complex on the South Bank of the Thames. (The Prospect Theatre Company now plays in the Old Vic Theatre.) The roster of actors and actresses who have brightened the Old Vic stage over the years reads like a who's who: John Gielgud, Ralph Richardson, Laurence Olivier, Michael Redgrave, Edith Evans, Margaret Webster, Charles Laughton, Emlyn Williams, Trevor Howard, Peggy Ashcroft, Maurice Evans, Flora Robson, Vivian Leigh, Cedric Hardwicke, Claire Bloom, Donald Wolfit, Richard Burton, Wendy Hiller, and many more.

At Stratford, another theatre devoted its repertory primarily to "restored" Shakespeare. Founded in 1879, the Shakespeare Memorial Theatre grew from a regional festival into the preeminent theatre for Shakespeare in the world today. It early prospered under the management of Frank Benson and then W. Bridges-Adams, later attracting directors from the first ranks in English theatre including Peter Brook, Peter Hall, Trevor Nunn, Anthony Quayle, Douglas Seale, and Glen Byam Shaw. Since 1961, when it was renamed the Royal Shakespeare Company, the organization has grown to include four permanent theatres (two in Stratford, two in London), and a company of excellent actors. Its productions tour the world, most memorably Peter Brook's *A Midsummer Night's Dream* (on tour 1970–1973).

Such success has spawned a host of imitators in the Western Hemisphere, some of them of high quality: the Canadian Shakespeare Festival at Stratford, Ontario; the American Shakespeare Festival at Stratford, Connecticut; the Colorado Shakespeare Festival at Boulder, Colorado; the Great Lakes Festival at Lakewood, Ohio; the Ashland Festival at Ashland, Oregon; and Joseph Papp's Shakespeare Festival in New York's Central Park. All of these Shakespearean repertory companies employ to some extent an open-platform stage, quick shifting of scenery, and the like. In this important sense, Shakespearean production throughout the later twentieth century has remained true to the spirit of Benson, Poel, and Granville-Barker in their rebellion against Victorian embroidery and the constricting proscenium arch.

In another important sense, however, twentieth-century Shakespeare in production has sometimes returned to the practice of adapting Shakespeare in order to render him more palatable to contemporary tastes. Shakespeare has been remade in the image of modernity, much as the Restoration period remade him in neoclassical terms and as the Victorians molded him into a great defender of social institutions. The process is neither new nor surprising; it is a way of assimilating Shakespeare, and pays him the high compliment of needing to see him as a part of us, whoever we may be. In the modern world, the need has been for a "relevant" Shakespeare, one who speaks to the vision of alienation, the futility of the political process, the inhumanity of war, and the struggles for human freedom. The occasional stridency of tone and the ideological insistence on extreme political meaning in some recent Shakespeare productions seem characteristically modern, and yet several eighteenth-century productions of *Richard II* and *Coriolanus* were similarly accused of taking sides in the political controversies of that day. To perceive the continuity in this process of updating Shakespeare is to acknowledge its timeless purpose in the theatre as a way of interpreting Shakespeare to audiences. The cuttings and distortions of emphasis employed to give us an alienated *Hamlet,* for example, or an existentialist *King Lear,* are, for all their apparent newness, much like the rearrangements applied to Shakespeare's scripts in the earlier adaptations of Tate, Cibber, and Garrick.

An early instance of modern adaptation is Orson Welles' famous production of *Julius Caesar* (1937), drawing an analogy between the Caesar of the play and Benito Mussolini. Welles' satire of dictatorship was galvanizing to audiences threatened with the prospect of a fascist-dominated Europe, but the interpretation of the play was of necessity one-sided; it allowed for no ironic perception of both good and evil in Caesar's one-man rule. Similarly, a production of *Coriolanus* in Paris in the early 1930's caused political rioting when the radical left interpreted the play in their terms as an attack on dictatorship, and the extreme right conversely interpreted the play as an indictment of the cowardice and political opportunism of the mob and its leaders. This kind of adaptation of Shakespeare to modern ideological controversy found expression also in a 1938 production of *Troilus and Cressida* at the Westminister Theatre, when Britain was on the verge of a second World War; the production's mocking of war seemed to capture a current mood of disillusionment. Ever since, directors have found many ways of staging Shakespeare as though he were a fervent opponent of war.

The most influential figures in this movement have included Bertolt Brecht, a leader in the German experimental theatre, and Ian Kott, author of *Shakespeare Our Contemporary.* Kott's book sees Shakespeare as one who speaks to our existentialist world. This view served as the basis, for example, of a Royal Shakespeare Company production of *Macbeth* in the 1960's starring Alec Guinness and Simone Signoret, in which life was presented as a grotesque experience comparable to that of Auschwitz. A production in 1964 by the same group of the *Henry IV* plays and *Henry V,* under Peter Hall's direction, showed the influence of Brecht in its exaggeratedly squalid tavern scenes and in its terrifying rendition of the Battle of Agincourt. Other productions of *Henry V* have also made the hero out to be a frightful prig (as George Bernard Shaw interpreted him), by emphasizing the ironies of Henry's "imperialistic" war against France and by interpreting his famous speeches as so much cynical rhetoric. On the other hand, Laurence Olivier's overtly patriotic film version of *Henry V,* produced in wartime England with the sponsorship of the British government, emphasized those parts of the play that best agreed with Britain's wartime mood. The result was a stirring film that asked its audience not to be afraid to love one's country, its people, and its institutions.

Some twentieth-century adaptations of Shakespeare have succeeded in what they did by not pretending to be anything other than lighthearted transmutations of his work into different genres. The American musical comedy version of *The Taming of the Shrew* by Cole Porter, called *Kiss Me, Kate* (1948), featured some delightful songs and did not attempt to take itself too seriously. Equally successful and honest was the rock musical version of *The Two Gentlemen of Verona* in New York, 1972. Leonard Bernstein's *West Side Story* (1957) translated the ancient feud of the Capulets and Montagues from *Romeo and Juliet* into Puerto Rican gang warfare, New York style. The analogy was perhaps a facile and sentimentalized one, but the contemporary music and the frenetic dancing gave a compelling impression of violence and speed. Other musicals have included *The Boys from Syracuse* (1938), based on *The Comedy of Errors, Swingin' the Dream* (1939), taken from *A Midsummer Night's Dream,* and *Your Own Thing* (1968), a rock adaptation of *Twelfth Night.* Once again we can see a historical similarity between such productions and an earlier adaptation like Dryden's and Davenant's operatic *The Tempest,* although modern musical comedy has fortunately been seen as an innocent variation on Shakespeare rather than as a replacement for the original as often happened in the Restoration and eighteenth century.

A distinguishing feature of modern production and adaptation has been the translation of Shakespeare into contemporary settings, into period settings of an era between Shakespeare's and our own, or into current theatrical styles such as the theatre of the absurd and the theatre of cruelty. Modern dress Shakespeare on the English stage began with Barry Jackson's *Hamlet,* directed by H. K. Ayliff at the Birmingham Repertory Theatre and then transferred to London at the King's Way Theatre in 1925. In 1928, Jackson brought his Birmingham Repertory *Macbeth,* also directed by Ayliff in modern dress, to the Royal Court Theatre in London. The idea, a sound one, was to use contemporary costume as Shakespeare himself had done and thus free the audience to concentrate on the universal character of the play. Subsequently, however, modern dress too often became a fad. The use of period setting was expertly handled in, for example, Tyrone Guthrie's Edwardian version of *All's Well that Ends Well* (Stratford, Canada, 1953), where the analogy to a complacent aristocratic society gave a clarifying perspective to Shakespeare's original setting in Renaissance France. Like modern dress, however, period setting involves an inherent risk that elements of the Shakespearean original will seem out of place and will have to be sacrificed or muddled through. Social titles like "your Majesty" and "his Grace" may seem anachronistically jarring. In the American Shakespeare Festival production of *Much Ado about Nothing* at Stratford, Connecticut (1957), the setting on a Texas ranch and the portrayal of Dogberry as a bumbling sheriff in the fashion of then-current television and movie Westerns may well have enhanced Dogberry's appeal for some of the audience, but it did so at the expense of the aristocratic relationships and social customs on which Shakespeare's play depends. Joseph Papp's version of the same play, staged in New York and then shown on commercial television in America in 1977, chose as its setting small-town America of the era of Teddy Roosevelt, replete with gramophones, ragtime bands, and high-wing collars. Dogberry and his watchmen became Keystone Cops in a familiar movie idiom. The analogy enlivened the comedy and made it frantically farcical, but again at a price, since social distinctions in democratic America cannot approximate those of sixteenth-century England. Jonathan Miller's choice of late nineteenth-century Europe for his *The Merchant of Venice* (National Theatre, 1970, with Laurence Olivier as Shylock, subsequently televised), illustrates a similar reward and difficulty; the complacent prejudices of an antisemitic social order lend impact to Shylock's tragedy, but at the expense of a Renaissance context in which disapproval of usury is essential to a Christian view of salvation.

Other examples of anachronistic setting, at times extreme, might include Jack Landau's *Troilus and Cressida* (Stratford, Connecticut, 1961) in the context of America's Civil War, Franco Zeffirelli's *Much Ado about Nothing* (National Theatre, London, 1965), set in modern-day Sicily, Theodore Komisarjevsky's *Macbeth* (Memorial Theatre, Stratford-upon-Avon, 1933) in a modern idiom of "twisted aluminum," Tyrone Guthrie's *The Taming of the Shrew* (Stratford, Canada, 1954) as a Western, and Joseph Papp's *Hamlet* (Public Theatre, New York, 1968) beginning the play with Hamlet in a coffinlike cradle at the foot of Claudius' and Gertrude's bed. Productions such as these are not, of course, the only choice of modern directors, and for more balanced interpretations one looks to Glen Byam Shaw and to many others who create Shakespeare on stage in ways that are at once recognizable and innovative.

The controversy about adaptation of Shakespeare is still very much alive today, and will undoubtedly remain so. The forms of Shakespearean adaptation have altered, but the issues have remained virtually unchanged since 1660. When and to what extent ought the text to be rewritten to conform with yesterday or today? Many observers would maintain that the dialogue between purists and adapters is not only inevitable, but healthy. The purist reformer, like William Poel, is needed as a voice of conscience and integrity even though he is perhaps doomed to play the role of lonely visionary. The adapter's goal is, on the other hand, to "interpret" Shakespeare; and, although directors from David Garrick to Peter Brook willingly arrange and distort in their search for contemporary meaning, a lively director can certainly generate new interest in a work that might otherwise remain classically "pure" but lifeless. In any case, twentieth-century production has brought us a long way from the Romantic doldrums during which most intelligent readers of Shakespeare could not bear to have their author desecrated by a performance on stage.

Shakespeare on Film and in Television

Versions of Shakespeare on film and in television inevitably require some adaptation to the new media and thus bring into particularly clear focus the controversy between purists and adapters that we have seen in relation to the stage. Despite the claims of enthusiasts that Shakespeare anticipated many film techniques with his cutting from scene to scene, his juxtaposing soliloquy with crowded scenes of action, and so on, film and theatre remain unlike in essential ways. The camera does well in closely revealing the expressions of speakers during soliloquy or intimate scenes, and can crosscut to good effect in larger scenes, but the camera is unable to do what a spectator does continually in the theatre: see live actors in the total space of that enclosure, isolated in the midst of that space or grouped in such ways as to suggest tensions or alignments, the whole spectacle simultaneously visible and in motion while the spectator remains still. The camera, by controlling and selecting and thinking for us, is less able to take in many things at once despite its excellence at what it can do. Because the camera can record things of great natural beauty, like the sunrise (compare Friar Laurence's verbal description in *Romeo and Juliet,* II,iii) or a gently flowing river (compare the account of Ophelia's death in *Hamlet,* IV,vii), it renders extraneous Shakespeare's evocation in words of what he was unable to bring physically into the theatre. The audience is not ordinarily present in film or television, thereby removing the opportunity for improvisation and appeals to the audience by a character like Iago. This is not to deny the camera's manifest abilities but rather to insist on the need for recognition of important differences between film and stage. The best films have been bold in this assumption of difference, though boldness itself is no guarantee of success.

Despite numerous attempts at filming Shakespeare in the days of silent film and early sound film, no movie versions of Shakespeare prior to World War II yield much more than antiquarian interest with the problematic exception of Max Reinhardt's *A Midsummer Night's Dream* (1935), with James Cagney miscast as Bottom the Weaver. Laurence Olivier's *Henry V* (1944), on the other hand, demonstrates the potential of the film to a remarkable degree. Choosing a play in which Shakespeare repeatedly stresses the limitation of the stage, Olivier begins his version in a plausible mockup of an Elizabethan theatre and proceeds to let the camera take the spectator to the battlefields of France. The journey itself and eventual return to the Elizabethan theatre, showing us adult actresses at one moment and boy actors stuffing oranges in their bosoms for breasts the next, becomes the focus of the theatrical and film experience, realizing thereby on film what Shakespeare appeals to in his verse. Olivier's *Hamlet* (1948), though marred by a trendy Freudian reading of Hamlet's relationship to his mother, is well cast and makes innovative use of a camera that relentlessly explores the corridors of Elsinore Castle, searching out the heart of Hamlet's mystery. Olivier's *Richard III* (1955) perhaps the least original of his Shakespearean films to that date because of its predictable sets, nevertheless discovers ways of centering interest on Olivier's magnetic interpretation of the villain hero. His *Othello* (1965) strikes many viewers as Olivier's least successful Shakespearean film, perhaps because a conception developed in the theatre has been insufficiently adapted for film. The closeups of Othello are too revealing of theatrical makeup and undercut sympathy for the protagonist.

Bold translation into the medium of film is certainly to be found in Akira Kurosawa's *Throne of Blood* (1957), a version of *Macbeth* as told in terms of Japanese history and folklore. Making no attempt to reproduce Shakespeare's language verbally, it offers instead arresting images of mist-shrouded forests and mysteriously disappearing witches, or spare interior sets intensifying the loneliness of the murdering protagonists. Orson Welles' *Chimes at Midnight,* or *Falstaff* (1965–1966), recklessly rearranges the texts of *1* and *2 Henry IV,* and miscasts some important minor roles, but does achieve sensitivity in Welles' own portrayal of Falstaff as a fat comic who is at heart insecure and pleading for affection. Grigori Kozintsev's *Hamlet* (1964), using a heavily cut text by Boris Pasternak, is probably the best *Hamlet* on film because of uniformly sound casting and because the camera so eloquently translates *Hamlet's* language into the director's five chosen images of stone, iron, fire, sea, and earth. Kozintsev is unafraid to cut and allow the film to do what it can do so well, and if one accepts these premises, one sees a film of remarkable energy. Kozintsev's *King Lear* (1971) is no less forthright in embracing its medium, and to similar effect. The most controversial *King Lear* on film, however, and perhaps the most controversial Shakespearean film ever made, is Peter Brook's version (1970) starring Paul Scofield and based on a stage production that toured widely in the early 1960's. Unswervingly pessimistic, based in part on Brook's reading of Ian Kott, this version insists that Lear is indeed a troublesome father to Goneril and Regan; his followers make a shambles of the Duke of Albany's dining hall. Brook's wintry sets show us human beings enduring under the bleakest of circumstances. Cordelia's role is curtailed. These emphases have distressed many viewers and have raised familiar cries of directorial arrogance. Yet to others Brook's film is an achievement in film paralleled only (and in a very different way) by Olivier's *Henry V.* The casting is uniformly fine, and the scenes between Lear and Gloucester at Dover beach are as deeply moving as the play deserves. For all its unrelenting darkness of vision, the film does show touching affection and thus captures an image of goodness doing battle, at whatever disadvantageous odds, with evil. Perhaps nowhere can we find more aptly expressed the potentials and difficulties involved in adapting Shakespeare to film.

Other Shakespearean films to which serious critical attention has been devoted include John Houseman's and Joseph Mankiewicz's *Julius Casear* (1953), Renato Castellani's *Romeo and Juliet* (1954), Sergei Yotkevitch's *Othello* (1955), Orson Welles' *Othello* (1965), Franco Zeffirelli's *The Taming of the Shrew* (1966) and *Romeo and Juliet* (1968), Peter Hall's *A Midsummer Night's Dream* (1969), and Roman Polanski's *Macbeth* (1971). Of Shakespeare on television, several productions have been mentioned already. The most notable undertaking but also the most disappointing is the BBC's taping of all the plays over a six-year period, beginning with six plays shown on American television in early 1979. The attempt at "definitive" performance lacking directorial bias and the use of studio production involving many non-Shakespearean actors yield bland results with occasional flashes of insight and demonstrate all too well the need for recognition of the critical differences between the camera and the stage.

APPENDIX 4

Doubtful and Lost Plays

In his edition of *The Shakespeare Apocrypha* (Oxford, 1908, 1918), Tucker Brooke enumerates some forty-two plays, other than those included in the First Folio, which at one time or another have been ascribed to Shakespeare. (The word "apocrypha," as in the case of the Apocryphal Books of the Bible, signifies works whose place in the accepted canon is disputed.) The First Folio itself contains thirty-six plays which seem to have been selected with care by Shakespeare's friends and professional associates, John Heminges and Henry Condell. So conscientious was their work that recent studies of the Shakespearean canon and of the First Folio have tended to confirm their judgment and to rule against the possibility that they made serious omissions. *Pericles* has, to be sure, gained virtually universal inclusion in the canon along with the thirty-six plays edited by Heminges and Condell. *The Two Noble Kinsmen* is now regarded by most scholars as the result of a collaboration between Shakespeare and John Fletcher, though the major portion of the play is usually given to Fletcher. Recently a noteworthy attempt has been made to establish Shakespeare's authorship of certain scenes in *Sir Thomas More*. Beyond this point, however, no claim has been established with anything approaching certainty. Of the forty-two plays mentioned by Tucker Brooke, only about fifteen deserve serious discussion.

The Two Noble Kinsmen

"A Tragi Comedy called the two noble kinsmen by John Fletcher and William Shakespeare" was first entered in the Stationers' Register in 1634 by the publisher John Waterson. A quarto appeared in that same year, entitled *"The Two Noble Kinsmen: Presented at the Black-friers by the Kings Maiesties servants, with great applause: Written by the memorable Worthies of their time; Mr. John Fletcher, and Mr. William Shakespeare, Gent.* Tho. Cotes for John Watterson." The date of composition is pretty certainly 1613.

The Stationers' Register entry and title page of 1634 have some authority. Waterson was a reputable publisher with close ties to Shakespeare's and Fletcher's acting company, the King's men. The text published by Waterson seems to have been a theatrical prompt-copy. Shakespeare and Fletcher may well have had occasion to work together, since Shakespeare was on the verge of retiring in 1613 from the King's company, and Fletcher had already become his chief successor. The two men may also have collaborated in 1613 on *Henry VIII*, although that hypothesis remains seriously in doubt (see Play Introduction).

Certainly *The Two Noble Kinsmen* gives the impression of two contrasting styles, one flowing and casual in a characteristically Fletcherian manner, and one densely elliptical in a way that reminds us of the late Shakespeare (as, for example, in Leontes' soliloquies in *The Winter's Tale*). Those who are convinced of Shakespeare's authorship in *The Two Noble Kinsmen* usually give him the following scenes on the basis of style: I,i–iii; the very beginning of II,i; III,i; and V,i and iii–iv. Sometimes scenes iv and v of Act I are added to the list. Shakespeare's purported contributions are thus most prominent at the beginning and ending of the play. According to this theory, he seems to have begun the work and made contributions later on, but left to Fletcher the development of the action and the final fitting together of the parts. The overall impression, then, is of a play by Fletcher to which Shakespeare may have contributed some important scenes.

The play is heavily influenced by the conventions of tragicomedy and romance that were so prominent in plays of the period. Like many of Shakespeare's late plays and Fletcher's early plays, *The Two Noble Kinsmen* was acted at the indoor Blackfriars Theatre. (Shakespeare's late plays were also acted at the Globe, a public theatre, but it burned to the ground in 1613 and had to be rebuilt.) For its source, *The Two Noble Kinsmen* turns to Chaucer's "The Knight's Tale" in *The Canterbury Tales*. In the chivalric world of Theseus' court, the noble cousins Palamon and Arcite vie with one another for the hand of the fair Emilia. As in many romance plays, men's destinies are controlled by the will of the gods: the rivalry between Palamon and Arcite is, on a broader scale, a contest between Venus and Mars. Although the gods do not appear directly on stage, their altars are prominent in Act V. So is that of Diana, to whom Emilia prays for aid. Otherworldly music, riddles, and oracles attest to the invisible cosmic presence of the three deities. The ending, in which Arcite triumphs in the tourney but then dies, leaving Emilia to Palamon, gives a symbolic victory to both Venus and Mars; love and chivalry have been perennially affirmed. Diana too shares in the ending, for Emilia's chastity is preserved in an honorable marriage. The play throughout is courtly in tone, with its debates on love versus friendship and the vanity of worldly striving. Even the comedy is strongly affected by courtly traditions of the masque and the pastoral.

Despite the affinities to Shakespearean romance, the play as a whole seems considerably more Fletcherian than Shakespearean. For this reason, and because of uncertainties of authorship, the play is omitted from this present edition. The play differs from Shakespeare's late romances in a way that *Henry VIII* does not. Implausible secondary love plots (such as that of the Jailer's Daughter for Palamon) playfully exaggerate the love theme into the sort of titillating mannerism we associate with Fletcher. Repeatedly, the deliberately chosen atmosphere is one of ingeniously contrived situation. The self-aware artifice of the play does resemble a tendency in the late Shakespeare, and may suggest the direction he might have taken had he continued to write. Unquestionably the play deserves serious study, and adds to our understanding of Shakespeare's latest work. One can argue, however, that if it is essentially more Fletcher's than Shakespeare's it should be edited with Fletcher's other plays.

Additions to the Third Folio

Many anonymous plays were attributed to Shakespeare during his lifetime and afterward. This may have been nothing more than a device on the part of unscrupulous printers to increase sales by featuring Shakespeare's name or initials on the title page of some play in quarto. Seven such plays deserve special consideration, however, since they were included in the second printing of the Third Folio of 1664: *Pericles Prince of Tyre, The London Prodigal, The History of Thomas Lord Cromwell, Sir John Oldcastle Lord Cobham, The Puritan or the Widow of Watling Street, A Yorkshire Tragedy, The Tragedy of Locrine.*

Of this group, *Pericles* has been accepted since the time of Malone as at least in large part the work of Shakespeare.

The London Prodigal was published in 1605 by Nathaniel Butter (who published *King Lear*), "As it was plaied by the Kings Maiesties seruants. By William Shakespeare." It is a lively comedy of London life, full of humors and manners, but unlike anything known to have been written by Shakespeare. Thomas Dekker has been proposed as the author.

Thomas Lord Cromwell was printed for William Jones in 1602 "As it hath beene sundrie times publikely Acted by the Right Honorable the Lord Chamberlaine his Seruants. Written by W.S." It is an undistinguished specimen of the biographical history play. There seem to be no grounds for attributing it to Shakespeare, since even the initials "W.S." may have been intended to designate some other author.

Sir John Oldcastle, ascribed to Shakespeare in a quarto of 1600, is known from Henslowe's *Diary* to have been written for the Lord Admiral's company by Drayton, Hathway, Munday, and Wilson.

The Puritan, a comedy of manners, was printed by G. Eld in 1607, as "Acted by the Children of Paules. Written by W.S." Brooke points out certain resemblances between this play and *Eastward Ho!* and suggests tentatively that Marston had a hand in it. Thomas Middleton's name has also been seriously suggested. There seems no reason to connect the play with Shakespeare.

A Yorkshire Tragedy is on better ground. Shakespeare's name appears both in the entry in the Stationers' Register and on the title page of the quarto of 1608. In the latter place it is also stated that the play was "Acted by his Maiesties Players at the Globe." The use of Shakespeare's name may, however, simply reflect the desire of the notorious piratical publisher, Thomas Pavier, to make money. *A Yorkshire Tragedy* is a murder play, belonging to the genre of homiletic or "domestic" tragedy. The Calverly murder, which it dramatizes, had occurred in 1605, and Shakespeare's company had no doubt taken immediate advantage of the sensation to prepare and present the play. It is hard to think that Shakespeare at such a time in his career could have been employed on such a job; but, since there are prose passages in the play of psychological knowledge and insight and of intensity, many critics have thought that they show the touch of his hand. George Wilkins is now thought to have had at least a major share in the play.

Locrine is a tragedy of an early type, like *Gorboduc* and *The Misfortunes of Arthur;* and, since it resembles *Alphonsus, King of Aragon* by Robert Greene and *Selimus* (probably also by Greene), Brooke argues that *Locrine* is Greene's work and earlier than either of those mentioned. Another possible author is George Peele. The play was printed by Thomas Creed in 1595 as "Newly set foorth, ouerseene and corrected, By W.S." This "W.S." may again have been some author besides Shakespeare.

The Charles II Group

In addition to the Shakespeare apocrypha of the Third Folio, another seventeenth-century collection of Elizabethan plays ascribed to Shakespeare was found in the library of no less a person than King Charles II of England. This collection consisted of three quarto plays—*Fair Em, Mucedorus,* and *The Merry Devil of Edmonton*—all bound together and collectively entitled "Shakespeare, Vol. I." The binding and labeling in this fashion do not offer any real evidence that the plays were in fact by Shakespeare, however. All three plays had been printed anonymously and were popular dramas dating from Shakespeare's lifetime. The collection may simply reflect a tendency to ascribe to Shakespeare any popular Elizabethan plays not known to have been written by some other dramatist.

Fair Em was printed first without date (as acted by Lord Strange's servants) and later, in 1631, for John Wright. Because its romanticized view of English life somewhat resembles that of *Friar Bacon and Friar Bungay* (c. 1589–1592) by Robert Greene, and also that of *George a Greene, the Pinner of Wakefield,* probably by Greene, the comedy has sometimes been attributed to that dramatist. R. Wilson is also a plausible contender for authorship. *Fair Em* was seemingly written around 1590.

Mucedorus was one of the most popular plays of the age. It appeared in at least seventeen quarto editions, the third of which (1610) states that it is "Amplified with new additions, as it was acted before the Kings Maiestie at White-hall on Shrove-Sunday night. By his Highness Seruants usually playing at the Globe." The first edition was in 1598. No one seriously attributes the original play to Shakespeare; but, since the "new additions" referred to on the title page of the third quarto are superior to the rest of the play, they have sometimes been regarded as Shakespeare's. Robert Greene has again been regarded without sufficient warrant as original author.

The text of *The Merry Devil of Edmonton,* a better play than either of the others, looks as if the play had been worn by much acting and many alterations. The suspected Revels Accounts of Peter Cunningham connect it with Shakespeare's company, as does the title page of the first quarto, printed for Arthur Johnson in 1608. The play was entered in the Stationers' Register to Humphrey Moseley, the bookseller, in 1653, this time with Shakespeare's name as author. *The Merry Devil of Edmonton* was a popular play and was early connected with Shakespeare's name. There is no other probability of its being his play, and but little of his having revised it; but it would do him no discredit. Possibly it was by Thomas Dekker.

Other Attributions

A play called *The Birth of Merlin,* first published by Francis Kirkman in 1662, is said on the title page to have been "Written by William Shakespear and William Rowley." Kirkman, an unreliable publisher, also attributed the tragicomedy of *The Birth of Merlin* to Shakespeare and Rowley in his catalogues. The play seems to date from the reign of King James. Recent critics have been unimpressed by Kirkman's wholly unsupported and implausible claim.

Arden of Feversham, an early bourgeois "domestic" tragedy about a murder, was published without attribution of authorship by Edward White in 1592. Edward Jacob, a citizen of Feversham, printed the play in 1770 and attributed it to Shakespeare. His grounds for doing so were inadequate, nor have any valid grounds been found since. The story is of a murder done at Feversham in 1551, the account of which is embodied in Holinshed's *Chronicles.* The play remains anonymous, although Kyd has been suggested as a likely author.

Edward III is another anonymous play assigned to Shakespeare on the basis of a seventeenth-century attribution. It was first printed by Cuthbert Burby in 1596 and first attributed to Shakespeare in a bookseller's leaflet in 1654. The Shakespearean scholar Edward Capell edited it in 1760 and argued that it was by Shakespeare. Ever since then, the play has continued to receive serious consideration—more so, probably, than any other candidate for the Shakespearean canon other than *Pericles, The Two Noble Kinsmen,* and *Sir Thomas More.* The play is an English history play dealing with the period of late medieval English history dramatized by Shakespeare, Thomas Heywood, Peele, Marlowe, and others. Its moderate political stance, its unhysterical depiction of Catholics and foreign foes, and its concern with the ethical responsibilities of war remind us more of Shakespeare than of any rival dramatist. More significantly, *Edward III* uses images in a way that is strikingly reminiscent of *Richard II.* The play even alludes to Shakespeare's own writings, as in this quotation from Sonnet 94: "Lilies that fester smell far worse than weeds." Shakespeare does not habitually quote himself, however, and *Edward III* may be the work of some admiring and talented imitator. Another possibility is that Shakespeare had a hand in the play but was not responsible for all of it. Unfortunately, the argument must rest on stylistic considerations, which are too often subjective.

Sir Thomas More

The last serious contender for the Shakespearean canon is *Sir Thomas More.* The play exists in Harleian Ms. 7368 in the British Museum, labeled "The Booke of Sir Thomas Moore." It was first edited for the Shakespeare Society by Alexander Dyce in 1844. In 1871 the Shakespeare scholars Richard Simpson and James Spedding put forward the idea that certain scenes in this play were not only the work of Shakespeare but were written in his own hand. Simpson rested his case mainly on literary evidence and the "Shakespearian flavor."

The play is a biographical chronicle made up of three main episodes, or groups of scenes. The first of these describes a famous riot against alien workers that took place on the "ill May-Day" of 1517, and introduces Sir Thomas More, Sheriff of London, in the act of pacifying the anti-alien rioters by his oratory. Because popular uprisings of a similar nature were greatly feared in the London of about 1595, the authorities were naturally unwilling to have these scenes performed. The play shows evidence, therefore, of having been heavily cut by the censor, Edmund Tilney, who bade the players leave the insurrection out completely. The result of his censorship is the disappearance of two long passages. The play seems to have been originally written by Anthony Munday. Perhaps in anticipation of the objections of the censor, however, another hand was employed to rewrite these scenes of the mob in a style not calculated to give offense. Three sheets of the manuscript, containing a total of 147 lines, make up these revisions. In them, the rioters express attitudes much like those we find in the mob scenes of *Julius Caesar,* or the Cade Rebellion of *2 Henry VI.* Thomas More's appeals to the mob point out the blessings of peace and order and the godlike authority of the King. In 1916 Sir E. Maunde Thompson, the paleographer, reasserted Shakespeare's authorship of these three sheets dealing with the "ill May-Day" mob. He attempted to prove by comparison with the handwriting of the six unquestioned signatures of Shakespeare that these sheets were indeed written in Shakespeare's hand. Since that time the matter has remained in dispute, although the weight of opinion today favors assigning the inserted portion of the manuscript to Shakespeare. (For a comprehensive and lucid review of the scholarship, see R. C. Bald, "*The Booke of Sir Thomas More* and Its Problems," *Shakespeare Survey 2* [1949], 44–61.) The play is dated by various critics from 1592 to 1601.

Lost Plays

A drama called *The History of Cardenio* was entered in the Stationers' Register, but apparently never printed, by Humphrey Moseley on September 9, 1653, as "by Mr. Fletcher and Shakespeare." Since a play called *Cardenno* or *Cardenna* had in fact been twice acted before King James by Shakespeare's company in 1612–1613, the obvious implication is that these various references are to a single play. Evidently it was based on an episode in Cervantes' *Don Quixote* (Part I, chs. xxiii-xxxvii). The play, though lost, has an intriguing subsequent history. In 1728 Lewis Theobald, the editor of Shakespeare, published a play based on the story of Cardenio entitled *The Double Falsehood, or the Distrest Lovers.* Theobald described his work as "written originally by W. Shakespeare, and now revised and adapted to the stage by Mr. Theobald." He claimed to have in his possession three manuscripts of the original; and, although those purported manuscripts have never been found, and Theobald has often been suspected of having written *The Double Falsehood* himself, he was not given to creating forgeries. Moreover, the play does recall Fletcher's style. Possibly, then, we have still one more hint of a collaboration between Shakespeare and Fletcher in 1613.

At the same time that Moseley entered *The History of Cardenio* in the Stationers' Register, he also entered *The Merry Devil of Edmonton,* which he ascribed to Shakespeare, and "*Henry ye first, & Hen: ye 2d* by Shakespeare, & Dauenport." On June 29, 1660, he entered "*The History of King Stephen; Duke Humphrey, a Tragedy; Iphis & Iantha or a marriage without a man,* a Comedy, by Will. Shakespeare."

Among the manuscript plays burned by Warburton's cook were "*Henry ye 1st* by Will. Shakespear & Rob. Davenport, *Duke Humphrey* [*by*] Will. Shakespear," and "A Play by Will. Shakespear." John Warburton (1682–1759), antiquary and book collector, got into his possession a body of manuscripts of rare Elizabethan and Jacobean plays most of which were, he said, through his own "carelessness and the ignorance" of Betsy Baker, his servant, "unluckily burnd or put under pye bottoms."

How great was the world's loss in the plays mentioned by Moseley and Warburton we do not know. An obvious and tantalizing speculation is that Shakespeare may have written more history plays treating the early period to which *King John* belongs, perhaps a cycle of them.

THE ROYAL GENEALOGY OF ENGLAND, 1154–1625

THE PLANTAGENET KINGS

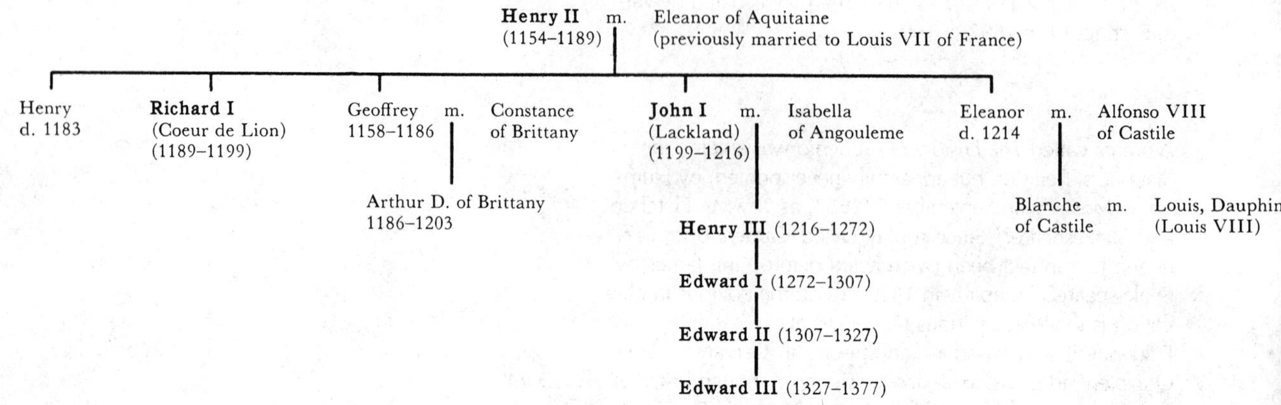

THE LANCASTRIAN KINGS

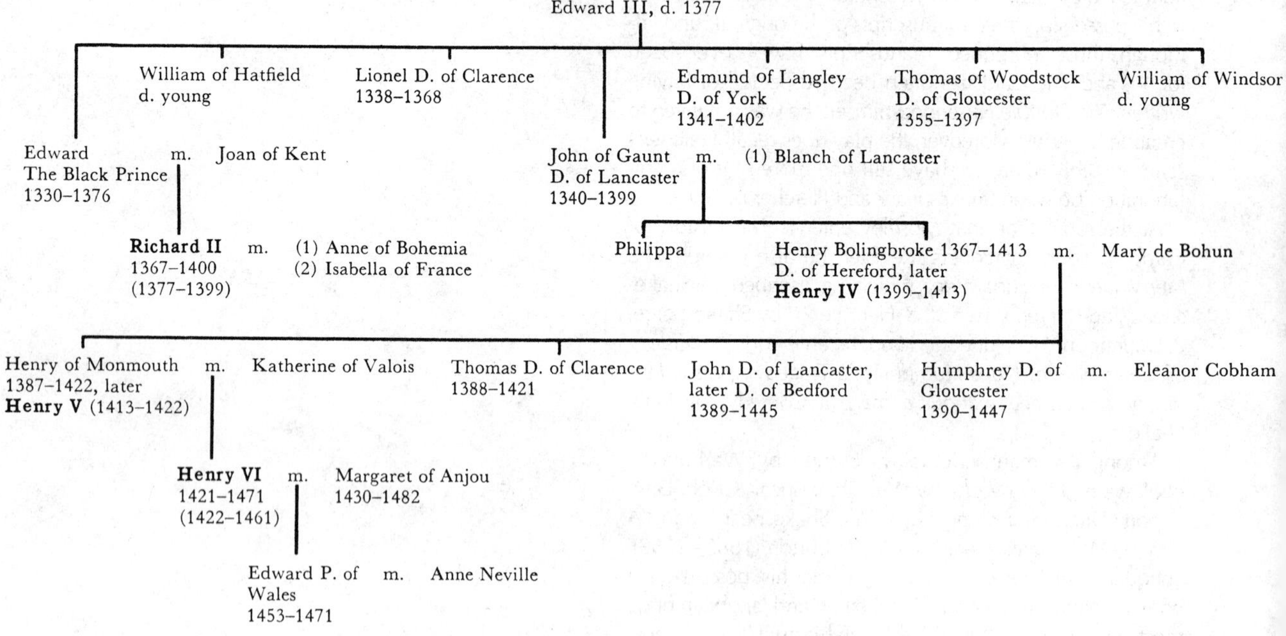

In these diagrams, reigning dates are given in parentheses; other dates indicate life span. Abbreviations: P. Prince, D. Duke, E. Earl, b. born, d. died, m. married. English monarchs are printed in boldface type. The spatial arrangement of names in a family usually but not always indicates order of birth.

In *1 Henry IV*, Shakespeare confuses the Edmund Mortimer who married Glendower's daughter, and died in 1409, with his nephew Edmund, fifth Earl of March, who asserted a claim to the English throne (see "The Yorkist Kings"). Shakespeare also refers to Henry Percy's (Hotspur's) wife as "Kate," though historically she was named Elizabeth.

Catherine Swynford, third wife of John of Gaunt (see "The Tudor Kings"), bore him children before their eventual marriage. These Beauforts, although later legitimized, were specifically barred from any claim to the English throne.

THE YORKIST KINGS

Edward III m. Philippa of Hainault
Edward
William
Lionel D. of Clarence m. Elizabeth de Burgh
John of Gaunt
Edmund Langley 1st D. of York m. Isabel of Castile
Thomas
Philippa m. Edmund Mortimer 3rd E. of March 1351–1381
Edward D. of Aumerle, later D. of York 1373–1415
Roger Mortimer 4th E. of March 1374–1398 m. Eleanor Holland
Edmund d. 1409 m. Daughter of Owen Glendower
Elizabeth m. Henry Percy (Hotspur)
Edmund Mortimer 5th E. of March 1391–1425
Anne Mortimer m. Richard E. of Cambridge 1375–1415
Richard Plantagenet E. of Cambridge, later D. of York 1411–1460 m. Cecily Neville
Edward, E. of March 1422–1483 **Edward IV** (1461–1483) m. Elizabeth Woodville Lady Grey
Edmund, E. of Rutland 1443–1460
George D. of Clarence 1449–1478 m. Isabell Neville, daughter of Richard E. of Warwick
Richard D. of Gloucester 1452–1485 **Richard III** (1483–1485)
Elizabeth b. 1465 m. Henry Tudor (**Henry VII**)
Edward V 1470–1483 (1483)
Richard k. 1483
Edward
Margaret

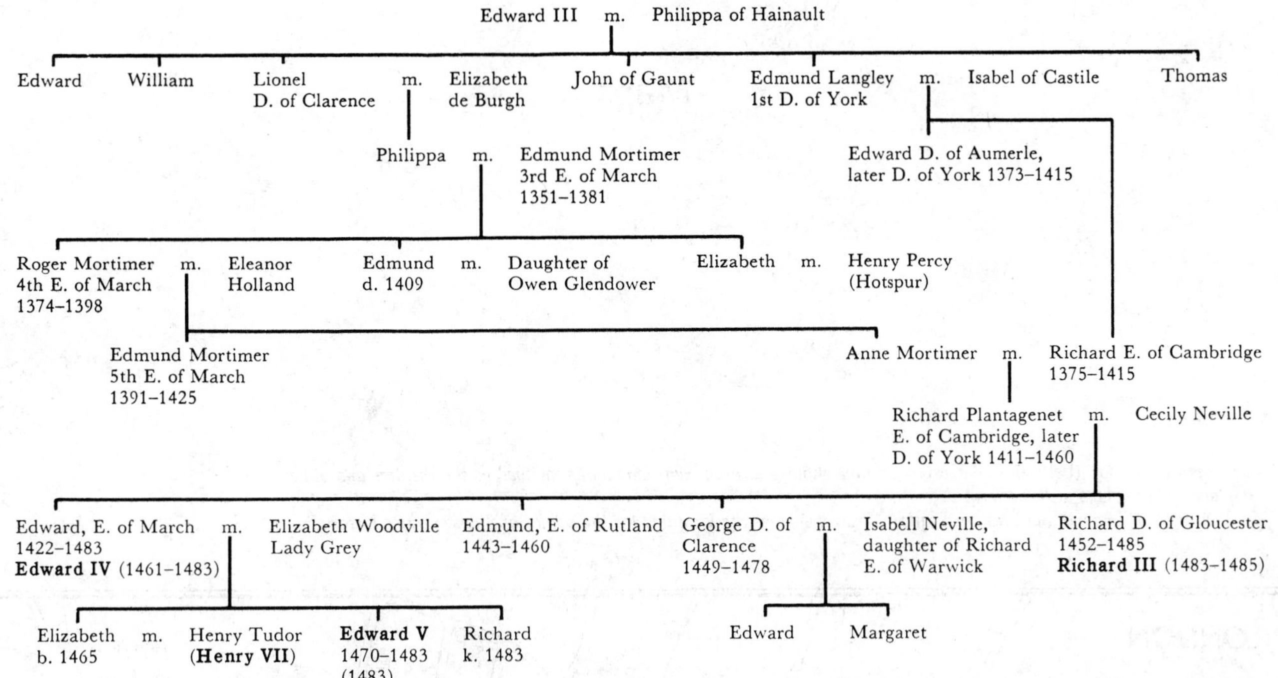

THE TUDOR KINGS

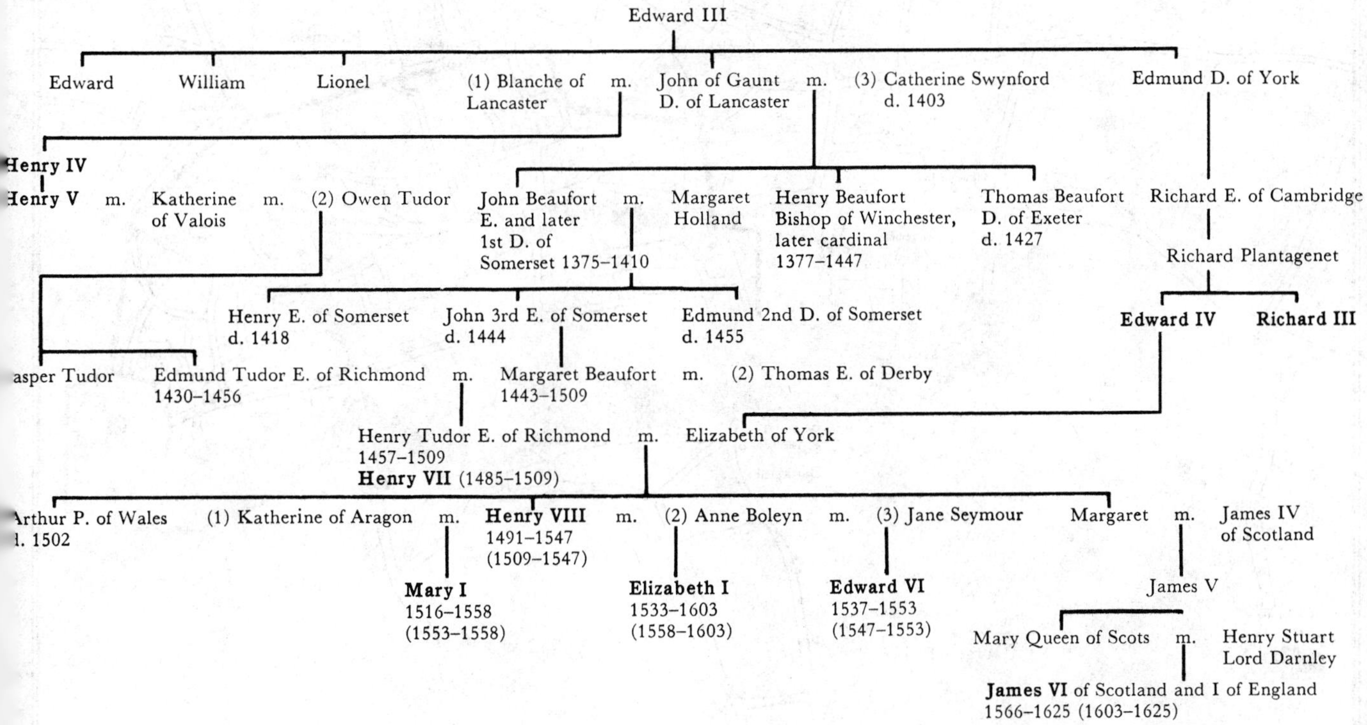

Edward III
Edward
William
Lionel
(1) Blanche of Lancaster m. John of Gaunt D. of Lancaster m. (3) Catherine Swynford d. 1403
Edmund D. of York
Henry IV
Henry V m. Katherine of Valois m. (2) Owen Tudor
John Beaufort E. and later 1st D. of Somerset 1375–1410 m. Margaret Holland
Henry Beaufort Bishop of Winchester, later cardinal 1377–1447
Thomas Beaufort D. of Exeter d. 1427
Richard E. of Cambridge
Richard Plantagenet
Henry E. of Somerset d. 1418
John 3rd E. of Somerset d. 1444
Edmund 2nd D. of Somerset d. 1455
Edward IV
Richard III
Jasper Tudor
Edmund Tudor E. of Richmond 1430–1456 m. Margaret Beaufort 1443–1509 m. (2) Thomas E. of Derby
Henry Tudor E. of Richmond 1457–1509 **Henry VII** (1485–1509) m. Elizabeth of York
Arthur P. of Wales d. 1502
(1) Katherine of Aragon m. **Henry VIII** 1491–1547 (1509–1547) m. (2) Anne Boleyn m. (3) Jane Seymour
Margaret m. James IV of Scotland
Mary I 1516–1558 (1553–1558)
Elizabeth I 1533–1603 (1558–1603)
Edward VI 1537–1553 (1547–1553)
James V
Mary Queen of Scots m. Henry Stuart Lord Darnley
James VI of Scotland and I of England 1566–1625 (1603–1625)

Maps

A map of London (below) *of Shakespeare's time shows the prominent landmarks, as well as the theatres and other places where plays were performed.*

A map of England and Western France (opposite) *gives the locations for the scenes of Shakespeare's history plays.*

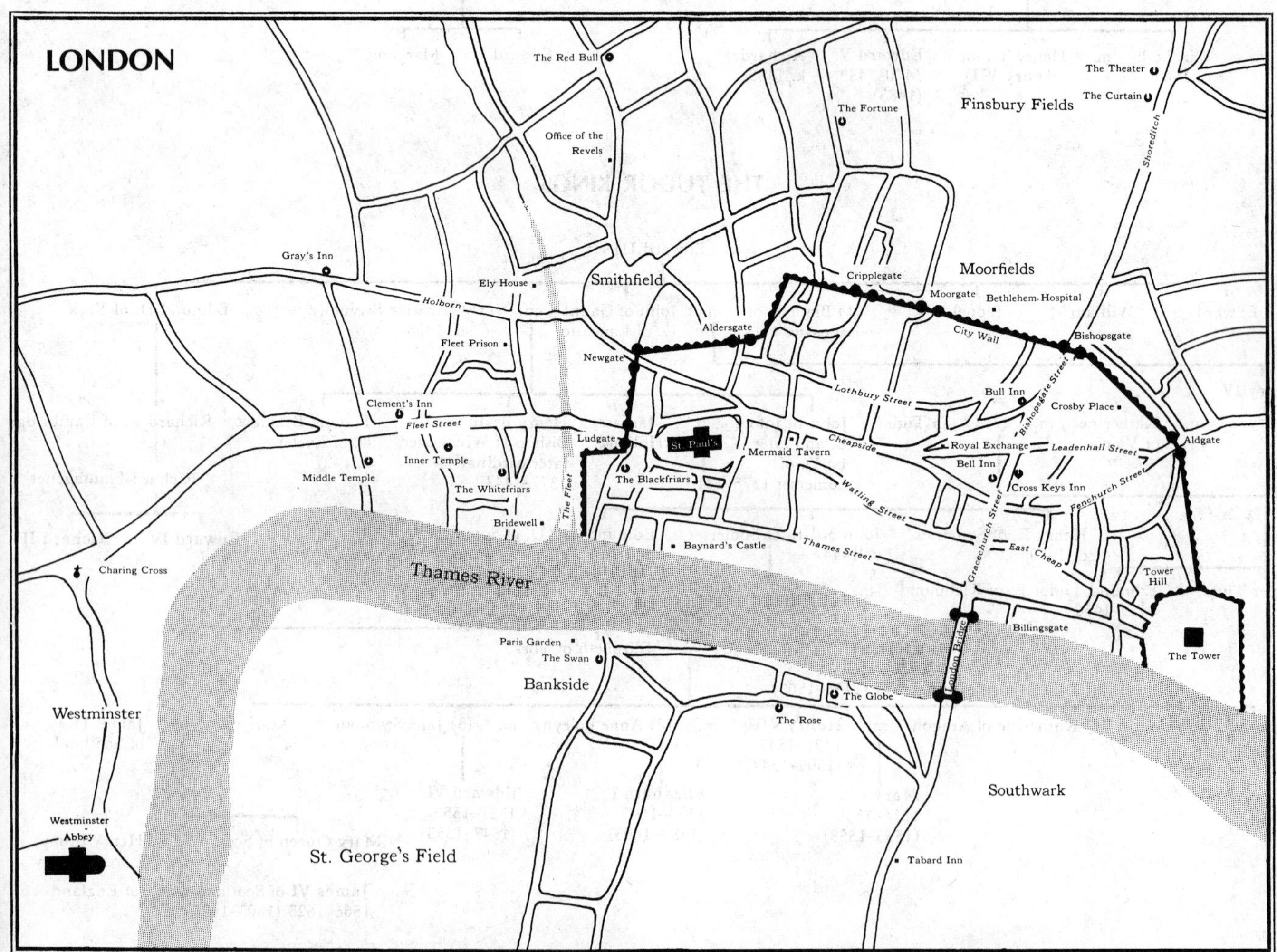

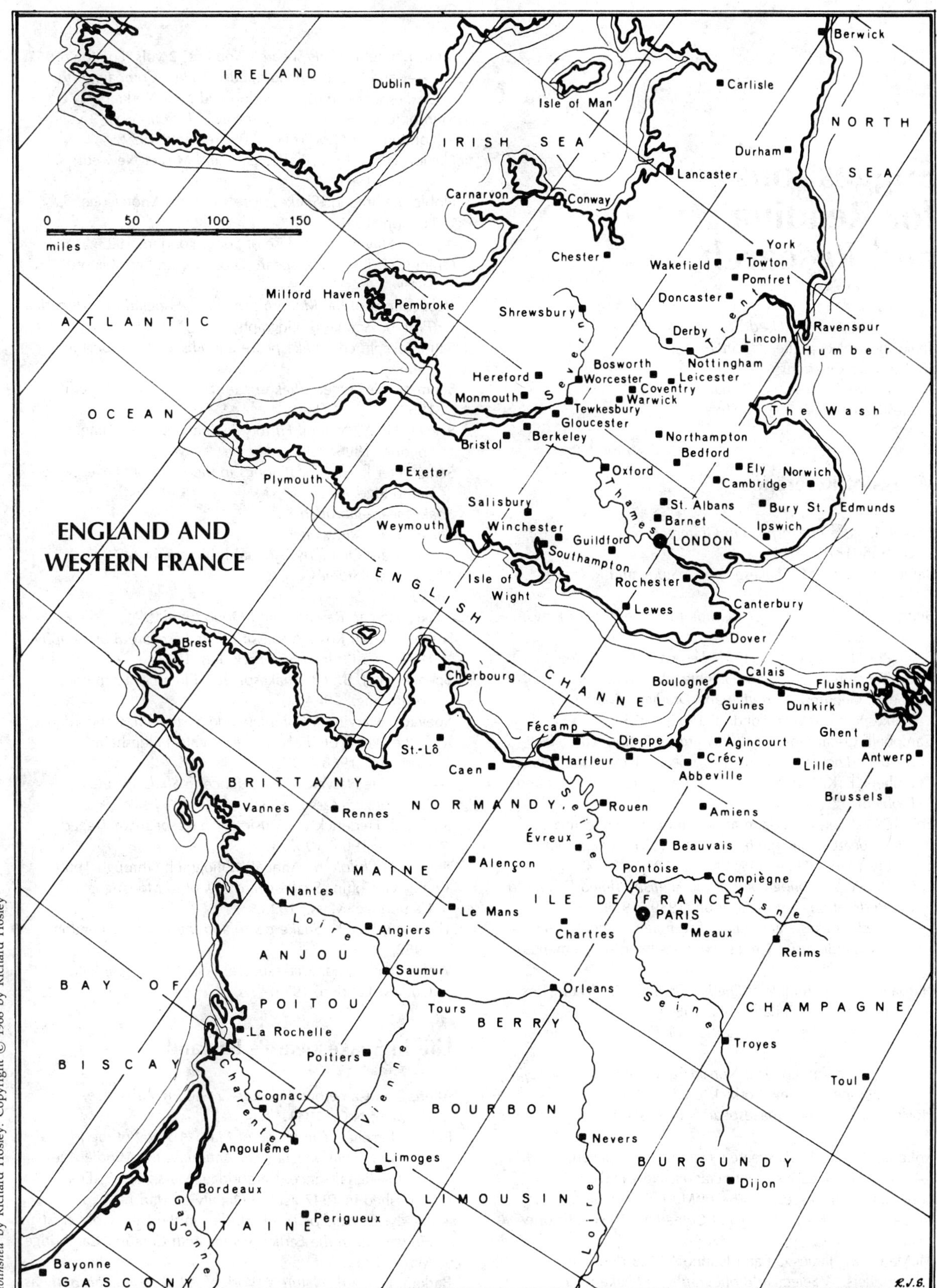
ENGLAND AND
WESTERN FRANCE
IRELAND
Dublin
Isle of Man
Carlisle
Berwick
NORTH
SEA
IRISH SEA
Durham
Lancaster
Carnarvon
Conway
0 50 100 150
miles
Chester
York
Wakefield
Towton
Pomfret
Doncaster
Milford Haven
Pembroke
Shrewsbury
Ravenspur
ATLANTIC
Trent
Derby
Lincoln
Humber
Nottingham
Bosworth
Leicester
Hereford
Worcester
Coventry
Severn
Warwick
Monmouth
Tewkesbury
OCEAN
Gloucester
The Wash
Berkeley
Bristol
Northampton
Bedford
Exeter
Oxford
Ely
Norwich
Plymouth
Cambridge
Thames
Salisbury
St. Albans
Bury St. Edmunds
Weymouth
Winchester
Barnet
Ipswich
Guildford
LONDON
Southampton
Rochester
Isle of Wight
ENGLISH
Canterbury
Lewes
Dover
Brest
Calais
Cherbourg
CHANNEL
Boulogne
Flushing
Guines
Dunkirk
Fécamp
Ghent
Dieppe
Agincourt
St.-Lô
Harfleur
Crécy
Antwerp
Caen
Abbeville
Lille
BRITTANY
Brussels
Vannes
Rennes
NORMANDY
Seine
Rouen
Amiens
Évreux
Beauvais
Alençon
MAINE
Pontoise
Compiègne
Nantes
ILE DE FRANCE
Aisne
Loire
Le Mans
PARIS
Angiers
Chartres
Meaux
Reims
ANJOU
Saumur
BAY OF
Orleans
POITOU
Tours
Seine
CHAMPAGNE
BERRY
La Rochelle
Troyes
Poitiers
BISCAY
Charente
Vienne
Toul
Cognac
BOURBON
Angoulême
Nevers
Limoges
BURGUNDY
Dijon
Bordeaux
Garonne
LIMOUSIN
Loire
AQUITAINE
Perigueux
Bayonne
GASCONY
R.J.B.

Suggestions for Reading and Research

Abbreviations Used

Shakespeare Newsletter	*ShN*
Shakespeare Quarterly	*SQ*
Shakespeare Studies	*ShakS*
Shakespeare Survey	*ShS*

Works of Reference

Abbott, E. A. *A Shakespearian Grammar.* New edition, London, 1870.

Bergeron, David M. *Shakespeare: A Study and Research Guide.* New York, 1975.

Berman, Ronald. *A Reader's Guide to Shakespeare's Plays.* Rev. ed. Glenview, Ill., 1973.

Bevington, David, compiler. *Shakespeare.* Goldentree Bibliographies. Arlington Heights, Ill., 1978.

Bullough, Geoffrey. *Narrative and Dramatic Sources of Shakespeare.* 8 vols. London, 1957–1975.

Campbell, Oscar James, and Edward G. Quinn, eds. *The Reader's Encyclopedia of Shakespeare.* New York, 1966.

Chambers, E. K. *William Shakespeare: A Study of Facts and Problems.* 2 vols. Oxford, 1930.

Ebisch, Walther, in collaboration with L. L. Schücking. *A Shakespeare Bibliography.* Oxford, 1931. *A Supplement for the Years 1930–1935.* Oxford, 1937.

Greg, W. W. *A Bibliography of the English Printed Drama to the Restoration.* 4 vols. London, 1939–1959.

———, ed. *Shakespeare Quarto Facsimiles.* London, 1939—. (An incomplete set; Greg's work has been supplemented by Charlton Hinman.)

Harbage, Alfred. *Annals of English Drama, 975–1700.* Rev. S. Schoenbaum. Philadelphia, 1964.

Hart, Alfred. *Shakespeare and the Homilies.* Melbourne, 1934.

Hinman, Charlton, ed. *The Norton Facsimile: The First Folio of Shakespeare.* New York, 1968.

Hosley, Richard, ed. *Shakespeare's Holinshed.* New York, 1968.

Kökeritz, Helge. *Shakespeare's Names.* New Haven, 1959.

———. *Shakespeare's Pronunciation.* New Haven, 1953.

Long, John. *Shakespeare's Use of Music: Comedies.* Gainesville, Fla., 1955. *Final Comedies,* 1961; *Histories and Tragedies,* 1971.

McManaway, James G., and Jeanne Addison Roberts, compilers. *A Selective Bibliography of Shakespeare.* Charlottesville, Va., 1975.

Muir, Kenneth. *Shakespeare's Sources.* 2 vols. London, 1957.

———, and S. Schoenbaum, eds. *A New Companion to Shakespeare Studies.* London and New York, 1971.

Munro, John, ed. *The Shakespeare Allusion Book.* 2 vols. London and New York, 1909; reissued 1932.

Naylor, Edward W. *Shakespeare and Music.* New ed., London, 1931.

Noble, Richmond. *Shakespeare's Biblical Knowledge.* London, 1935.

———. *Shakespeare's Use of Song.* London, 1923.

Onions, C. T. *A Shakespeare Glossary.* 2nd ed. Oxford, 1919.

Publications of the Modern Language Association of America (PMLA). Annual Bibliography.

Satin, Joseph, ed. *Shakespeare and His Sources.* Boston, 1966.

Schmidt, Alexander. *Shakespeare-Lexicon.* 5th ed. Berlin, 1962.

Seager, H. W. *Natural History in Shakespeare's Time.* London, 1896.

Seng, Peter J. *The Vocal Songs in the Plays of Shakespeare.* Cambridge, Mass., 1967.

Shakespeare-Jahrbuch.

Shakespeare Newsletter.

Shakespeare Quarterly. Annual Bibliography.

Shakespeare Studies.

Shakespeare Survey.

Shakespearean Research and Opportunities.

Smith, Gordon Ross. *A Classified Shakespeare Bibliography, 1936–1958.* University Park, Pa., 1963.

Spencer, T. J. B., ed. *Shakespeare's Plutarch.* Harmondsworth, Eng., 1964.

Spevack, Marvin. *A Complete and Systematic Concordance to the Works of Shakespeare.* 8 vols. Hildesheim, Germany, 1968–1970.

———. *The Harvard Concordance to Shakespeare.* Cambridge, Mass., 1973.

Sternfeld, Frederick W. *Music in Shakespearean Tragedy.* London, 1963, 1967.

Studies in Philology. Annual Bibliography through 1969.

Taylor, G. Coffin. *Shakespeare's Debt to Montaigne.* Cambridge, Mass., 1925.

Thomson, J. A. K. *Shakespeare and the Classics.* London, 1952.

Wells, Stanley, ed. *Shakespeare: Select Bibliographical Guides.* London, 1973.

Life in Shakespeare's England

Allen, Don Cameron. *The Star-Crossed Renaissance.* Durham, N.C., 1941.

Baker, Herschel. *The Image of Man: A Study of the Idea of Human Dignity in Classical Antiquity, the Middle Ages, and the Renaissance.* Cambridge, Mass., 1961. (First published in 1947 as *The Dignity of Man.*)

———. *The Wars of Truth: Studies in the Decay of Christian Humanism in the Earlier Seventeenth Century.* Cambridge, Mass., 1952.

Barkan, Leonard. *Nature's Work of Art: The Human Body as Image of the World.* New Haven, 1975.

Bindoff, S. T., et al., eds. *Elizabethan Government and Society*. Essays presented to Sir John Neale. London, 1961.
Bush, Douglas. *The Renaissance and English Humanism*. Toronto, 1939.
Buxton, John. *Elizabethan Taste*. London, 1963.
Byrne, Muriel St. Clare. *Elizabethan Life in Town and Country*. 8th ed. London, 1970.
Camden, Carroll. *The Elizabethan Woman*. Houston, 1952.
Caspari, Fritz. *Humanism and the Social Order in Tudor England*. Chicago, 1954.
Cassirer, Ernst. *The Platonic Renaissance in England,* trans. J. E. Pettegrove. Austin, Texas, 1953.
Craig, Hardin. *The Enchanted Glass*. New York, 1936.
Einstein, Lewis. *Tudor Ideals*. New York, 1921.
Elton, G. R. *The Tudor Revolution in Government*. Cambridge, Eng., 1959.
Ferguson, Arthur B. *The Articulate Citizen and the English Renaissance*. Durham, N.C., 1965.
Harrison, G. B. *An Elizabethan Journal*. London, 1928; supplements.
———. *A Jacobean Journal . . . 1603–1606*. London, 1941.
———. *A Second Jacobean Journal . . . 1607 to 1610*. Ann Arbor, Mich., 1958.
Haydn, Hiram. *The Counter-Renaissance*. New York, 1950.
Heninger, S. K., Jr. *A Handbook of Renaissance Meteorology*. Durham, N.C., 1960.
Huizinga, Johan. *The Waning of the Middle Ages*. London, 1924; Baltimore, 1955.
Hurstfield, Joel. *Elizabeth I and the Unity of England*. London, 1960.
Judges, A. V., ed. *The Elizabethan Underworld*. London and New York, 1930. Rpt., London, 1965.
Kelso, Ruth. *Doctrine for the Lady of the Renaissance*. Urbana, Ill., 1956.
———. *The Doctrine of the English Gentleman in the Sixteenth Century*. Urbana, Ill., 1929.
Knappen, M. M. *Tudor Puritanism*. Chicago, 1939.
Knights, L. C. *Drama and Society in the Age of Jonson*. London, 1937.
Kocher, Paul. *Science and Religion in Elizabethan England*. San Marino, Calif., 1953.
Levin, Harry. *The Myth of the Golden Age in the Renaissance*. Bloomington, Ind., 1969.
Lovejoy, A. O. *The Great Chain of Being*. Cambridge, Mass., 1936.
MacCaffrey, Wallace T. *The Shaping of the Elizabethan Regime*. Princeton, 1968.
McPeek, James A. S. *The Black Book of Knaves and Unthrifts in Shakespeare and Other Renaissance Authors*. Storrs, Conn., 1969.
Mattingly, Garrett. *The Armada*. Boston, 1959.
Mazzeo, Joseph A. *Renaissance and Revolution*. New York, 1965.
Neale, John E. *Elizabeth I and Her Parliaments*. 2 vols. London and New York, 1953–1958.
———. *The Elizabethan House of Commons*. London, 1949.
———. *Queen Elizabeth I*. London, 1934; New York, 1957.
Nichols, John, ed. *The Progresses and Public Processions of Queen Elizabeth*. 3 vols. London, 1823.
Nicoll, Allardyce, ed. *Shakespeare in His Own Age*. *ShS 17* (1964).
Pearson, Lu Emily. *Elizabethans at Home*. Stanford, 1957.
Penrose, Boies. *Travel and Discovery in the Renaissance, 1420–1620*. Cambridge, Mass., 1955.
Quinones, Ricardo J. *The Renaissance Discovery of Time*. Cambridge, Mass., 1972.
Ramsey, Peter. *Tudor Economic Problems*. London, 1963.
Read, Conyers. *Lord Burghley and Queen Elizabeth*. New York, 1960.
———. *Mr. Secretary Cecil and Queen Elizabeth*. New York, 1955.
———. *Mr. Secretary Walsingham and the Policy of Queen Elizabeth*. 3 vols. Oxford, 1925.
———. *The Tudors: Personalities and Practical Politics in Sixteenth Century England*. New York, 1936.
Rowse, A. L. *The England of Elizabeth: The Structure of Society*. London, 1951.
Stone, Lawrence. *The Crisis of the Aristocracy, 1558–1641*. Oxford, 1965.
Stow, John. *Survey of London,* ed. C. L. Kingsford. Oxford, 1971.
Strachey, G. Lytton. *Elizabeth and Essex*. London and New York, 1928.
Tawney, R. H. *Religion and the Rise of Capitalism*. New York, 1926, 1962.
Tillyard, E. M. W. *The Elizabethan World Picture*. London, 1943, 1967.
Wilson, F. P. *Elizabethan and Jacobean*. Oxford, 1945.
Wilson, J. Dover, ed. *Life in Shakespeare's England*. Cambridge, Eng., 1911; 2nd ed., 1926.
Wright, Louis B. *Middle-Class Culture in Elizabethan England*. Chapel Hill, N.C., 1935.
Zeeveld, W. Gordon. *Foundations of Tudor Policy*. Cambridge, Mass., 1948.

The Drama Before Shakespeare

Altman, Joel B. *The Tudor Play of Mind: Rhetorical Inquiry and the Development of Elizabethan Drama*. Berkeley and Los Angeles, 1978.
Baker, Howard. *Induction to Tragedy*. Baton Rouge, 1939.
Bevington, David. *From Mankind to Marlowe: Growth of Structure in the Popular Drama of Tudor England*. Cambridge, Mass., 1962.
———. *Tudor Drama and Politics*. Cambridge, Mass., 1968.
Boas, Frederick S. *University Drama in the Tudor Age*. Oxford, 1914.
Bradbrook, Muriel C. *The Growth and Structure of Elizabethan Comedy*. London, 1955.
———. *Themes and Conventions of Elizabethan Tragedy*. Cambridge, Eng., 1935, 1960.
Chambers, E. K. *The Elizabethan Stage*. 4 vols. Oxford, 1923.
———. *The Mediaeval Stage*. 2 vols. Oxford, 1903.
Clemen, Wolfgang. *English Tragedy before Shakespeare: The Development of Dramatic Speech,* tr. T. S. Dorsch. London, 1961.
Craig, Hardin. *English Religious Drama of the Middle Ages*. Oxford, 1955.
Craik, T. W. *The Tudor Interlude*. Leicester, 1958, 1962.
Dessen, Alan C. *Elizabethan Drama and the Viewer's Eye*. Chapel Hill, N.C., 1977.

Doran, Madeleine. *Endeavors of Art: A Study of Form in Elizabethan Drama*. Madison, Wis., 1954, 1972.
Farnham, Willard. *The Medieval Heritage of Elizabethan Tragedy*. Berkeley, 1936.
Freeman, Arthur. *Thomas Kyd: Facts and Problems*. Oxford, 1967.
Gardiner, H. C. *Mysteries' End*. New Haven, 1946.
Greg, W. W. *A Bibliography of the English Printed Drama to the Restoration*. 4 vols. London, 1939–1959.
Harbage, Alfred. *Annals of English Drama, 975–1700*. Rev. S. Schoenbaum. Philadelphia, 1964.
Hardison, O. B., Jr. *Christian Rite and Christian Drama in the Middle Ages*. Baltimore, 1965.
Hunter, G. K. *John Lyly: The Humanist as Courtier*. Cambridge, Mass., 1962.
Kolve, V. A. *The Play Called Corpus Christi*. Palo Alto and London, 1966.
Levin, Harry. *The Overreacher: A Study of Christopher Marlowe*. Cambridge, Mass., 1952, 1964.
Lucas, F. L. *Seneca and Elizabethan Tragedy*. Cambridge, Eng., 1922.
Margeson, J. M. R. *The Origins of English Tragedy*. Oxford, 1967.
Nicoll, Allardyce. *Masks, Mimes, and Miracles*. London, 1931.
Potter, Robert. *The English Morality Play*. London, 1975.
Reed, A. W. *Early Tudor Drama*. London, 1926.
Ribner, Irving. *The English History Play in the Age of Shakespeare*. Rev. ed. London, 1965.
Rossiter, A. P. *English Drama from Early Times to the Elizabethans*. London, 1950.
Saccio, Peter. *The Court Comedies of John Lyly*. Princeton, 1969.
Salter, F. M. *Medieval Drama in Chester*. Toronto, 1955.
Sanders, Wilbur. *The Dramatist and the Received Idea: Studies in the Plays of Marlowe and Shakespeare*. Cambridge, Eng., 1968.
Southern, Richard. *The Medieval Theatre in the Round*. London, 1957.
Spivack, Bernard. *Shakespeare and the Allegory of Evil*. New York, 1958.
Talbert, Ernest William. *Elizabethan Drama and Shakespeare's Early Plays*. Chapel Hill, N.C., 1963.
Taylor, Jerome, and Alan H. Nelson, eds. *Medieval English Drama*. Chicago, 1972.
Welsford, Enid. *The Court Masque*. Cambridge, Eng., 1927.
Wickham, Glynne. *Early English Stages, 1300 to 1660*. London, 1959–1972.
Williams, Arnold. *The Drama of Medieval England*. East Lansing, Mich., 1961.
Wilson, F. P. *Marlowe and the Early Shakespeare*. Oxford, 1953.
Wilson, F. P., and G. K. Hunter. *The English Drama, 1485–1585*. London and New York, 1969.
Woolf, Rosemary. *The English Mystery Plays*. Berkeley and Los Angeles, 1972.

Collections of Plays

Bevington, David, ed. *Medieval Drama*. Boston, 1975.
Boas, Frederick S., ed. *The Works of Thomas Kyd*. Oxford, 1901.
Bond, R. Warwick, ed. *The Complete Works of John Lyly*. 3 vols. Oxford, 1902.
———, ed. *Early Plays from the Italian*. Oxford, 1911.
Bowers, Fredson, ed. *The Complete Works of Christopher Marlowe*. Cambridge, Eng., 1973.
Brandl, Alois, ed. *Quellen des weltlichen Dramas in England vor Shakespeare*. Strassburg, 1898.
Case, R. H., gen. ed. *The Works and Life of Christopher Marlowe*. 6 vols. London, 1930–1933.
Cawley, A. C., ed. *The Wakefield Pageants in the Towneley Cycle*. Manchester, 1958.
Creeth, Edmund, ed. *Tudor Plays*. Garden City, N.Y., 1966.
Cunliffe, John W., ed. *Early English Classical Tragedies*. Oxford, 1912.
Dickinson, T. H., ed. *Robert Greene*. London, 1909.
Dodsley, Robert, ed. *A Select Collection of Old English Plays*. 4th ed. by W. Carew Hazlitt. 15 vols. London, 1874–1898.
Early English Text Society. London, 1864—. Publications include the York plays, ed. Lucy Toulmin Smith (1885), the Chester plays, ed. Robert Lumiansky and David Mills (1974), the Digby plays, ed. F. J. Furnivall (1896), the Towneley plays, ed. G. England (1897), the N Town plays or Ludus Coventriae, ed. K. Block (1922), the Macro plays, ed. Mark Eccles (1969), and the Non-Cycle plays and fragments, ed. Norman Davis (1970). Several are now being reedited.
Farmer, John, ed. *Tudor Facsimile Texts*. London, 1907–1914.
Fraser, Russell A., and Norman Rabkin, eds. *Drama of the English Renaissance*. 2 vols. New York, 1976.
Malone Society Reprints. London, 1907—.
Manly, John M., ed. *Specimens of the Pre-Shaksperean Drama*. 2 vols. Boston, 1897.
Materialien zur Kunde des älteren Englischen Dramas. W. Bang, gen. ed. Louvain, 1902–1914.
Nethercot, Arthur H., Charles R. Baskervill, and Virgil D. Heltzel, eds. *Elizabethan Drama*. New York, 1971. *Stuart Drama*. New York, 1971.
Prouty, Charles T., gen. ed. *The Life and Works of George Peele*. 3 vols. New Haven, 1952–1970.
Rose, Martial, ed. *The Wakefield Mystery Plays*. New York, 1962.
Schell, Edgar T., and J. D. Shuchter, *English Morality Plays and Moral Interludes*. New York, 1969.
Young, Karl. *The Drama of the Medieval Church*. 2 vols. Oxford, 1933.

London Theatres and Dramatic Companies

Armstrong, William A. *The Elizabethan Private Theatres: Facts and Problems*. London, 1958.
Baldwin, T. W. *The Organization and Personnel of the Shakespearean Company*. Princeton, 1927.
Beckerman, Bernard. *Shakespeare at the Globe, 1599–1609*. New York, 1962, 1967.
Bentley, Gerald Eades. *The Jacobean and Caroline Stage*. 7 vols. Oxford, 1941–1968.
———. "Shakespeare and the Blackfriars Theatre," *ShS 1* (1948), 38–50.

Berry, Herbert. "Americans in the Playhouses," *ShakS 9* (1976), 31–44.
———. "Dr. Fludd's Engravings and Their Beholders," *ShakS 3* (1967), 11–21.
———. "The Stage and Boxes at Blackfriars," *Studies in Philology*, 63 (1966), 163–186.
Brown, John Russell. *Shakespeare's Plays in Performance*. London, 1966.
Campbell, Lily B. *Scenes and Machines on the English Stage During the Renaissance*. Cambridge, Eng., 1923.
Chambers, E. K. *The Elizabethan Stage*. 4 vols. Oxford, 1923.
Cook, Ann Jennalie. "The Audience of Shakespeare's Plays: A Reconsideration," *ShakS 7* (1974), 283–305.
Feuillerat, Albert, ed. *Documents Relating to the Office of the Revels in the Time of Queen Elizabeth*. Louvain, 1908.
Foakes, R. A., ed. *The Henslowe Papers: The Diary, Theatre Papers, and Bear Garden Papers*. In full and in facsimile. 3 vols. in 2. London, 1976.
Foakes, R. A., and R. T. Rickert, eds. *Henslowe's Diary*. London, 1961.
Gildersleeve, Virginia C. *Government Regulation of the Elizabethan Drama*. New York, 1908.
Greg, W. W., ed. *Dramatic Documents from the Elizabethan Playhouses; Stage Plots; Actors' Parts; Prompt Books*. 2 vols. Oxford, 1931.
Gurr, Andrew. *The Shakespearean Stage, 1574–1642*. Cambridge, Eng., 1970.
Harbage, Alfred. *Shakespeare's Audience*. New York, 1941.
Harrison, G. B. *Elizabethan Plays and Players*. London, 1940, 1956.
Hillebrand, H. N. *The Child Actors*. Urbana, Ill., 1926.
Hodges, C. Walter. *The Globe Restored*. London, 1953.
Hosley, Richard. "The Discovery-space in Shakespeare's Globe," *ShS 12* (1959), 35–46.
———. "The Gallery over the Stage in the Public Playhouse of Shakespeare's Time," *SQ*, 8 (1957), 15–31.
———. "A Reconstruction of the Second Blackfriars," *The Elizabethan Theatre*, ed. David Galloway. Toronto, 1969.
———. "Shakespeare's Use of a Gallery over the Stage," *ShS 10* (1957), 77–89.
———. "Was There a Music-room in Shakespeare's Globe?" *ShS 13* (1960), 113–123.
Joseph, Bertram L. *Acting Shakespeare*. London, 1960.
Kernodle, G. R. *From Art to Theatre: Form and Convention in the Renaissance*. Chicago, 1944.
King, T. J. *Shakespearean Staging, 1599–1642*. Cambridge, Mass., 1971.
Lawrence, W. J. *The Elizabethan Playhouse and Other Studies*. Stratford-upon-Avon, 1912, 1913; New York, 1963.
———. *The Physical Conditions of the Elizabethan Public Playhouse*. Cambridge, Mass., 1927.
Linthicum, Marie C. *Costume in the Drama of Shakespeare and His Contemporaries*. Oxford, 1936.
Murray, John T. *English Dramatic Companies, 1558–1642*. London and Boston, 1910.
Nagler, Alois M. *Shakespeare's Stage*, tr. R. Manheim. New Haven, 1958.
Nungezer, Edwin. *A Dictionary of Actors*. London and New Haven, 1929.
Reynolds, George F. *The Staging of Elizabethan Plays at the Red Bull Theater, 1605–1625*. New York, 1940.
Rowan, D. F. "The English Playhouse: 1595–1630," *Renaissance Drama*, n.s. 4 (1971), 37–51.
Seltzer, Daniel. "Elizabethan Acting in *Othello*," *SQ*, 10 (1959), 201–210.
———. "The Staging of the Last Plays," *Later Shakespeare*, ed. John Russell Brown and Bernard Harris, pp. 127–165. Stratford-upon-Avon Studies 8. London, 1966.
Smith, Irwin. *Shakespeare's Blackfriars Playhouse*. New York, 1964.
———. *Shakespeare's Globe Playhouse*. New York, 1956.
Shapiro, I. A. "The Bankside Theatres: Early Engravings," *ShS 1* (1948), 25–37.
———. "Robert Fludd's Stage-Illustration," *ShakS 2* (1966), 192–209.
Smith, Warren D. *Shakespeare's Playhouse Practice: A Handbook*. Hanover, N.H., 1975.
Thompson, Elbert N. S. *The Controversy Between the Puritans and the Stage*. New Haven, 1903, 1966.
Venezky, Alice. *Pageantry on the Shakespearean Stage*. New York, 1951.
Wickham, Glynne. *Early English Stages, 1300 to 1660*. London, 1959–1972.

Shakespeare's Life and Work

Alexander, Peter. *Shakespeare's Life and Art*. New ed. New York, 1961.
Baldwin, T. W. *William Shakspere's Small Latine and Lesse Greeke*. 2 vols. Urbana, Ill., 1944.
Bentley, Gerald Eades. *Shakespeare: A Biographical Handbook*. New Haven, 1961.
Chambers, E. K. *William Shakespeare: A Study of Facts and Problems*. 2 vols. Oxford, 1930.
Eccles, Mark. *Shakespeare in Warwickshire*. Madison, Wis., 1961.
Fripp, Edgar I. *Shakespeare, Man and Artist*. 2 vols. London, 1938.
Halliday, F. E. *Shakespeare: A Pictorial Biography*. London, 1956, 1964.
Harbage, Alfred. *Conceptions of Shakespeare*. Cambridge, Mass., 1966.
Hotson, Leslie. *I, William Shakespeare, do Appoint Thomas Russell, Esquire*. London and New York, 1937, 1938.
———. *Shakespeare Versus Shallow*. London, 1931.
Lee, Sidney. *A Life of William Shakespeare*. New ed. London, 1925.
Quennell, Peter. *Shakespeare: A Biography*. New York, 1963.
Reese, M. M. *Shakespeare: His World and His Work*. London and New York, 1953.
Rowse, A. L. *William Shakespeare: A Biography*. New York, 1963.
Schoenbaum, S. *Shakespeare's Lives*. Oxford and New York, 1970.
———. *William Shakespeare: A Documentary Life*. Oxford, 1975. Also published with fewer illustrations and a slightly revised text as *A Compact Documentary Life*, 1977.
Smart, John S. *Shakespeare: Truth and Tradition*. New ed. Oxford, 1966.
Stopes, C. C. *Shakespeare's Family*. London, 1901.
———. *Shakespeare's Warwickshire Contemporaries*. Stratford-upon-Avon, 1897, 1907.

Wilson, J. Dover. *The Essential Shakespeare*. Cambridge, Eng., 1932.

Shakespeare's Language: His Development as Poet and Dramatist

Abbott, E. A. *A Shakespearian Grammar*. New edition, London, 1870.
Barish, Jonas A. *Ben Jonson and the Language of Prose Comedy*. Cambridge, Mass., 1960.
Bayfield, Matthew. *A Study of Shakespeare's Versification*. Cambridge, Eng., 1920.
Berry, Francis. *The Shakespeare Inset: Word and Picture*. London, 1965.
Byrne, Muriel St. Clare. "The Foundations of Elizabethan Language," *ShS 17* (1964), 223–239.
Charney, Maurice. *Shakespeare's Roman Plays: The Function of Imagery in the Drama*. Cambridge, Mass., 1961.
———. *Style in Hamlet*. Princeton, 1969.
Clemen, Wolfgang H. *The Development of Shakespeare's Imagery*. Cambridge, Mass., 1951.
Crane, Milton. *Shakespeare's Prose*. Chicago, 1951.
Cruttwell, Patrick. *The Shakespearean Moment and Its Place in the Poetry of the Seventeenth Century*. London, 1954.
Dobson, E. J. *English Pronunciation, 1500–1700*. 2 vols. 2nd ed. Oxford, 1968.
Doebler, John. *Shakespeare's Speaking Pictures: Studies in Iconic Imagery*. Albuquerque, N.M., 1974.
Evans, B. Ifor. *The Language of Shakespeare's Plays*. 3rd ed. London, 1964.
Halliday, F. E. *The Poetry of Shakespeare's Plays*. London, 1954.
Hulme, Hilda M. *Explorations in Shakespeare's Language*. London, 1962.
Jespersen, Otto. *Growth and Structure of the English Language*. 9th ed. New York, 1938, 1955.
Kökeritz, Helge. *Shakespeare's Names*. New Haven, 1959.
———. *Shakespeare's Pronunciation*. New Haven, 1953.
Lanham, Richard A. *The Motives of Eloquence: Literary Rhetoric in the Renaissance*. New Haven, 1976.
Mahood, M. M. *Shakespeare's Wordplay*. London, 1957.
Miriam Joseph, Sister. *Shakespeare's Use of the Arts of Language*. New York, 1947. Reprinted in part as *Rhetoric in Shakespeare's Time* (1962).
Muir, Kenneth. "Shakespeare's Imagery—Then and Now," *ShS 18* (1965), 46–57.
Nares, Robert. *A Glossary . . . of Shakespeare and His Contemporaries*. New ed. by J. O. Halliwell and Thomas Wright. 2 vols. London, 1859, 1905. Repr. Detroit, 1966.
Ness, Frederic W. *The Use of Rhyme in Shakespeare's Plays*. New Haven and London, 1941.
Onions, C. T. *A Shakespeare Glossary*. 2nd ed. Oxford, 1919.
Partridge Eric. *Shakespeare's Bawdy*. London, 1947, 1955.
Schmidt, Alexander. *Shakespeare-Lexicon*. 5th ed. Berlin, 1962.
Sipe, Dorothy L. *Shakespeare's Metrics*. New Haven and London, 1968.
Spurgeon, Caroline. *Shakespeare's Imagery and What It Tells Us*. Cambridge, Eng., 1935.
Vickers, Brian. *The Artistry of Shakespeare's Prose*. London, 1968.
Willcock, Gladys D. "Shakespeare and Elizabethan English," *ShS 7* (1954), 12–24.

Editions and Editors of Shakespeare

Alexander, Peter. *Shakespeare's "Henry VI" and "Richard III."* Cambridge, Eng., 1929.
Black, Matthew W., and M. A. Shaaber. *Shakespeare's Seventeenth-Century Editors, 1632–1685*. New York and London, 1937.
Bowers, Fredson. *Bibliography and Textual Criticism*. Oxford, 1964.
———. *On Editing Shakespeare*. Charlottesville, Va., 1966.
———. *Principles of Bibliographical Description*. Princeton, 1949.
———. *Textual and Literary Criticism*. Cambridge, Eng., 1959.
Chambers, E. K. *William Shakespeare: A Study of Facts and Problems*. 2 vols. Oxford, 1930.
Doran, Madeleine. *"Henry VI," Parts II and III: Their Relation to "The Contention" and "The True Tragedy."* Iowa City, 1928.
Duthie, G. I. *Elizabethan Shorthand and the First Quarto of "King Lear."* Oxford, 1949.
Gaskell, Philip. *A New Introduction to Bibliography*. New York and Oxford, 1972.
Greg, W. W. *The Editorial Problem in Shakespeare*. 3rd ed. Oxford, 1954.
———. *Principles of Emendation in Shakespeare*. London, 1928.
———. *The Shakespeare First Folio: Its Bibliographical and Textual History*. Oxford, 1955.
Hart, Alfred. *Stolne and Surreptitious Copies: A Comparative Study of Shakespeare's Bad Quartos*. Melbourne and London, 1942.
Hinman, Charlton. *The Printing and Proof-Reading of the First Folio of Shakespeare*. 2 vols. Oxford, 1963.
Honigmann, E. A. J. *The Stability of Shakespeare's Text*. London and Lincoln, Neb., 1965.
McKerrow, Ronald B. *An Introduction to Bibliography for Literary Students*. Oxford, 1927.
———. *Prolegomena for the Oxford Shakespeare*. Oxford, 1939.
Nosworthy, J. M. *Shakespeare's Occasional Plays: Their Origin and Transmission*. London and New York, 1965.
Pollard, Alfred W. *Shakespeare Folios and Quartos: A Study in the Bibliography of Shakespeare's Plays, 1594–1685*. London, 1909.
———. *Shakespeare's Fight with the Pirates and the Problems of the Transmission of His Text*. Rev. ed. Cambridge, Eng., 1937.
Pollard, Alfred W., and others. *Shakespeare's Hand in the Play of Sir Thomas More*. Cambridge, Eng., 1923.
Sisson, C. J. *New Readings in Shakespeare*. 2 vols. Cambridge, Eng., 1956.

Walker, Alice. *Textual Problems of the First Folio.* Cambridge, Eng., 1953.
Walton, J. K. *The Quarto Copy for the First Folio of Shakespeare.* Dublin, 1971.
Williams, George W., ed. *The Most Excellent and Lamentable Tragedie of Romeo and Juliet: A Critical Edition.* Durham, N.C., 1964.
Wilson, J. Dover. *The Manuscript of Shakespeare's "Hamlet" and the Problems of Its Transmission.* 2 vols. Cambridge, Eng., 1934.

Shakespeare Criticism

Babcock, Robert W. *The Genesis of Shakespeare Idolatry, 1766–1799.* Chapel Hill, N.C., 1931, 1964.
Badawi, M. M. *Coleridge: Critic of Shakespeare.* Cambridge, Eng., 1973.
Bentley, Gerald Eades. *Shakespeare and Jonson: Their Reputations in the Seventeenth Century Compared.* 2 vols. Chicago, 1945.
Bradby, Anne, ed. *Shakespeare Criticism, 1919–35.* London, 1936.
Dean, Leonard F., ed. *Shakespeare: Modern Essays in Criticism.* Rev. ed. London and New York, 1967, 1969.
Eastman, Arthur M. *A Short History of Shakespearean Criticism.* Ann Arbor, 1968.
Eastman, Arthur M., and G. B. Harrison, eds. *Shakespeare's Critics; from Jonson to Auden.* Ann Arbor, 1964.
Evans, G. Blakemore, ed. *Shakespeare: Aspects of Influence.* Cambridge, Mass., 1976.
Foakes, R. A., ed. *Coleridge on Shakespeare: The Text of the Lectures of 1811–12.* Charlottesville, Va., 1971.
Halliday, F. E. *Shakespeare and His Critics.* Rev. ed., London and New York, 1958, 1963.
Johnson, Charles F. *Shakespeare and His Critics.* Boston, 1909.
Kermode, Frank, ed. *Four Centuries of Shakespearean Criticism.* New York, 1965.
Lovett, David. *Shakespeare's Characters in Eighteenth-Century Criticism.* Baltimore, 1935.
Muir, Kenneth. "Fifty Years of Shakespearian Criticism: 1900–1950," *ShS 4* (1951), 1–25.
Rabkin, Norman, ed. *Approaches to Shakespeare.* New York, 1964.
Ralli, Augustus. *A History of Shakespearian Criticism.* 2 vols. London, 1932.
Raysor, T. M., ed. *Samuel Taylor Coleridge: Shakespearean Criticism.* 2 vols. 2nd ed. London, 1960.
Ridler, Anne Bradby, ed. *Shakespeare Criticism, 1935–60.* London, 1963.
Sherbo, Arthur. *Samuel Johnson, Editor of Shakespeare.* Urbana, Ill., 1956.
Siegel, Paul N., ed. *His Infinite Variety: Major Shakespearean Criticism Since Johnson.* Philadelphia, 1964.
Smith, David Nichol, ed. *Shakespeare Criticism: A Selection.* World's Classics, Oxford, 1916.
———, ed. *Shakespeare in the Eighteenth Century.* Oxford, 1928.
Spencer, Hazelton. *Shakespeare Improved.* Cambridge, Mass., 1927.
Spingarn, J. E., ed. *Critical Essays of the Seventeenth Century,* Vol. I. Oxford, 1908–1909.
Vickers, Brian, ed. *Shakespeare: The Critical Heritage.* Several volumes. London and Boston, 1974—.
Westfall, A. V. *American Shakespearean Criticism, 1607–1865.* New York, 1939.

General Criticism

Armstrong, Edward A. *Shakespeare's Imagination: A Study of the Psychology of Association and Inspiration.* London, 1946.
Arthos, John. *The Art of Shakespeare.* New York, 1964.
Bethell, S. L. *Shakespeare and the Popular Dramatic Tradition.* London and Durham, N.C., 1944.
Bloom, Allan, with Harry V. Jaffa. *Shakespeare's Politics.* New York and London, 1964.
Brown, John Russell. *Shakespeare's Plays in Performance.* London, 1966.
Burkhardt, Sigurd. *Shakespearean Meanings.* Princeton, 1968.
Calderwood, James L. *Shakespearean Metadrama.* Minneapolis, 1971.
Chambers, E. K. *Shakespeare: A Survey.* London, 1925.
Colie, Rosalie L. *Shakespeare's Living Art.* Princeton, 1974.
Craig, Hardin. *An Interpretation of Shakespeare.* New York, 1948.
Dean, Leonard F., ed. *Shakespeare: Modern Essays in Criticism.* New York, 1967.
Driver, Tom F. *The Sense of History in Greek and Shakespearean Drama.* New York, 1960.
Dusinberre, Juliet. *Shakespeare and the Nature of Women.* New York, 1975.
Eagleton, Terence. *Shakespeare and Society.* New York and London, 1967.
Edwards, Philip. *Shakespeare and the Confines of Art.* London and New York, 1968.
Ellis-Fermor, Una. *Shakespeare the Dramatist.* New York, 1961.
Farrell, Kirby. *Shakespeare's Creation: The Language of Magic and Play.* Amherst, 1975.
Fly, Richard D. *Shakespeare's Mediated World.* Amherst, 1976.
Frye, Roland M. *Shakespeare and Christian Doctrine.* Princeton, 1963.
Garber, Marjorie B. *Dream in Shakespeare: From Metaphor to Metamorphosis.* New Haven and London, 1974.
Goddard, Harold C. *The Meaning of Shakespeare.* Chicago, 1951.
Goldman, Michael. *Shakespeare and the Energies of Drama.* Princeton, 1972.
Granville-Barker, Harley. *Prefaces to Shakespeare.* 2 vols. Princeton, 1946–1947.
Harbage, Alfred. *As They Liked It.* New York, 1947.
———. *Shakespeare and the Rival Traditions.* New York, 1952.
———. *William Shakespeare: A Reader's Guide.* New York, 1963.

Hawkins, Harriett. *Poetic Freedom and Poetic Truth: Chaucer, Shakespeare, Marlowe, Milton*. Oxford, 1976.

Holland, Norman. *Psychoanalysis and Shakespeare*. New York, 1966.

———. *The Shakespearean Imagination*. New York, 1964.

Jorgensen, Paul A. *Shakespeare's Military World*. Berkeley and Los Angeles, 1956.

Knight, G. Wilson. *The Shakespearian Tempest*. London, 1932, 1953.

Knights, L. C. *Some Shakespearean Themes*. London, 1959.

Kott, Jan. *Shakespeare Our Contemporary*. New York, 1964.

Leavis, F. R. *The Common Pursuit*. London, 1952.

McAlindon, T. *Shakespeare and Decorum*. London and New York, 1973.

Murry, John Middleton. *Shakespeare*. London, 1936.

Rabkin, Norman. *Shakespeare and the Common Understanding*. New York, 1967.

Righter, Anne. *Shakespeare and the Idea of the Play*. London, 1962.

Rossiter, A. P. *Angel with Horns*. London, 1961.

Sanders, Wilbur. *The Dramatist and the Received Idea: Studies in the Plays of Marlowe and Shakespeare*. Cambridge, Eng., 1968.

Schücking, Levin L. *Character Problems in Shakespeare's Plays*. London, 1922, 1948.

Sewell, Arthur. *Character and Society in Shakespeare*. London, 1951.

Soellner, Rolf. *Shakespeare's Patterns of Self-Knowledge*. Columbus, 1972.

Spencer, Theodore. *Shakespeare and the Nature of Man*. New York, 1942.

Stauffer, Donald. *Shakespeare's World of Images*. New York, 1949.

Stirling, Brents. *The Populace in Shakespeare*. New York, 1949.

Stoll, E. E. *Art and Artifice in Shakespeare*. Cambridge, Eng., 1933, 1962.

———. *Shakespeare Studies*. New York, 1942.

Styan, J. L. *Shakespeare's Stagecraft*. Cambridge, Eng., 1967.

Traversi, Derek. *An Approach to Shakespeare*. 2 vols. Rev. ed. London, 1968.

Turner, Frederick. *Shakespeare and the Nature of Time*. Oxford, 1971.

Van Doren, Mark. *Shakespeare*. New York, 1939.

Watson, Curtis Brown. *Shakespeare and the Renaissance Concept of Honor*. Princeton, 1960.

Weimann, Robert. *Shakespeare and the Popular Tradition in the Theater*, ed. by Robert Schwartz. Baltimore, 1978.

Whitaker, Virgil K. *Shakespeare's Use of Learning*. San Marino, Calif., 1953.

Zeeveld, W. Gordon. *The Temper of Shakespeare's Thought*. New Haven and London, 1974.

Shakespeare's Contemporary Dramatists, and the Shakespeare Apocrypha

Bald, R. C. "*The Booke of Sir Thomas More* and Its Problems," *ShS 2* (1949), 44–61.

Barish, Jonas A., ed. *Ben Jonson: A Collection of Critical Essays*. Englewood Cliffs, N.J., 1963.

Bentley, Gerald Eades. *The Jacobean and Caroline Stage*. 7 vols. Oxford, 1941–1968.

———. "Shakespeare and the Blackfriars Theatre," *ShS 1* (1948), 38–50.

Berringer, Ralph W. "Jonson's *Cynthia's Revels* and the War of the Theatres," *Philological Quarterly*, 22 (1943), 1–22.

Bertram, Paul. *Shakespeare and "The Two Noble Kinsmen."* New Brunswick, N.J., 1965.

Bowers, Fredson T. *Elizabethan Revenge Tragedy, 1587–1642*. Princeton, 1940.

———, ed. *The Dramatic Works of Thomas Dekker*. 4 vols. Cambridge, Eng., 1953–1961.

———, gen. ed. *The Dramatic Works in the Beaumont and Fletcher Canon*. Cambridge, Eng., 1966—.

Brooke, C. F. Tucker, ed. *The Shakespeare Apocrypha*. Oxford, 1908.

Bullen, A. H., ed. *The Works of Thomas Middleton*. London, 1885–1886.

Caputi, Anthony. *John Marston, Satirist*. Ithaca, N.Y., 1961.

Collins, D. C. "On the Date of *Sir Thomas More*," *Review of English Studies*, 10 (1934), 401–411.

Ellis-Fermor, Una. *The Jacobean Drama*. London, 1936.

Finkelpearl, Philip. *John Marston of the Middle Temple*. Cambridge, Mass., 1969.

Gibbons, Brian. *Jacobean City Comedy*. Cambridge, Mass., 1968.

Harbage, Alfred. *Shakespeare and the Rival Traditions*. New York, 1952.

Hawkins, Harriett. *Likenesses of Truth in Elizabethan and Restoration Drama*. Oxford, 1972.

Herford, C. H., and Percy Simpson, eds. *Ben Jonson*. 11 vols. Oxford, 1925–1952.

Heywood, Thomas. *An Apology for Actors*. London, 1612. Ed. Richard H. Perkinson. New York, 1941.

Kernan, Alvin. *The Cankered Muse: Satire of the English Renaissance*. New Haven, 1959.

Kirsch, Arthur C. *Jacobean Dramatic Perspectives*. Charlottesville, Va., 1972.

Leech, Clifford. *The John Fletcher Plays*. Cambridge, Mass., 1962.

———. *Shakespeare's Tragedies and Other Studies in Seventeenth Century Drama*. London, 1950.

Leggatt, Alexander. *Citizen Comedy in the Age of Shakespeare*. Toronto, 1973.

Leishman, J. B., ed. *The Three Parnassus Plays (1598–1601)*. London, 1949.

Levin, Richard. *The Multiple Plot in English Renaissance Drama*. Chicago, 1971.

Lucas, F. L., ed. *The Complete Works of John Webster*. London, 1927.

Malone Society Reprints. Editions of many plays not otherwise represented in this list of books.

Maxwell, Baldwin. *Studies in the Shakespeare Apocrypha*. New York, 1956.

Morris, Brian. *John Webster*. London, 1970.

Muir, Kenneth. *Shakespeare as Collaborator*. London, 1960.

Nosworthy, J. M. "Shakespeare and *Sir Thomas More*," *Review of English Studies*, n. s., 6 (1955), 12–25.

Ornstein, Robert. *The Moral Vision of Jacobean Tragedy*. Madison, Wis., 1960.
Parrott, T. M., ed. *The Plays and Poems of George Chapman*. 2 vols. London, 1910–1914.
Price, George R. *Thomas Dekker*. New York, 1969.
Ribner, Irving. *The English History Play in the Age of Shakespeare*. Rev. ed. London, 1965.
Spivack, Charlotte. *George Chapman*. New York, 1967.
Steele, Mary S. *Plays and Masques at Court During the Reigns of Elizabeth, James, and Charles*. New Haven and London, 1926.
Waith, Eugene M. *The Herculean Hero in Marlowe, Chapman, Shakespeare, and Dryden*. New York, 1962.
———. *The Pattern of Tragicomedy in Beaumont and Fletcher*. New Haven, 1952.
Welsford, Enid. *The Court Masque*. Cambridge, Eng., 1927.
Wickham, Glynne. *Early English Stages, 1300 to 1660*. London, 1959–1972.
Wilson, F. P. *Elizabethan and Jacobean*. Oxford, 1945.

Shakespeare in Performance

Ball, Robert Hamilton. *Shakespeare on Silent Film*. London and New York, 1968.
Bartholomeusz, Dennis. *Macbeth and the Players*. Cambridge, Eng., 1969.
Branam, George C. *Eighteenth-Century Adaptations of Shakespearean Tragedy*. Berkeley and Los Angeles, 1956.
Brown, Ivor. *Shakespeare and the Actors*. London, 1970.
Brown, John Russell. *Shakespeare's Plays in Performance*. London, 1966.
Carlisle, Carol Jones. *Shakespeare from the Greenroom: Actors' Criticisms of Four Major Tragedies*. Chapel Hill, N.C., 1969.
Cohn, Ruby. *Modern Shakespeare Offshoots*. Princeton, 1976.
Dean, Winton. "Shakespeare in the Opera House," *ShS 18* (1965), 75–93.
Donohue, Joseph W., Jr. *Dramatic Character in the English Romantic Age*. Princeton, 1970.
Downer, Alan S. *The Eminent Tragedian, William Charles Macready*. Cambridge, Mass., 1966.
Eckert, Charles W., ed. *Focus on Shakespearean Films*. Englewood Cliffs, N.J., 1972.
Hogan, Charles B. *Shakespeare in the Theatre, 1701–1800*. 2 vols. Oxford, 1952–1957.
Jorgens, Jack L. *Shakespeare on Film*. Bloomington, Ind., 1977.
Manvell, Roger. *Shakespeare and the Film*. London and New York, 1971.
Odell, George C. D. *Shakespeare from Betterton to Irving*. 2 vols. New York, 1920, 1966.
Poel, William. *Shakespeare in the Theatre*. London, 1913, 1968.
Shattuck, Charles H. *The Shakespeare Promptbooks: A Descriptive Catalogue*. Urbana, Ill., 1965.
———. *Shakespeare on the American Stage from the Hallams to Edwin Booth*. Washington, D.C., 1976.
Speaight, Robert. *Shakespeare on the Stage: An Illustrated History of Shakespearian Performance*. London, 1973.
———. *William Poel and the Elizabethan Revival*. London, 1954.
Spencer, Hazelton. *Shakespeare Improved: The Restoration Versions in Quarto and on the Stage*. Cambridge, Mass., 1927.
Sprague, Arthur Colby. *Shakespeare and the Actors*. Cambridge, Mass., 1944.
———. *Shakespearian Players and Performances*. Cambridge, Mass., 1953.
Styan, J. L. "Sight and Space: The Perception of Shakespeare on Stage and Screen," *Shakespeare, Pattern of Excelling Nature*, ed. David Bevington and Jay L. Halio. Newark, Del., 1978.
Thaler, Alwin. *Shakespeare to Sheridan*. Cambridge, Mass., 1922.
Trewin, J. C. *Shakespeare on the English Stage, 1900–1964*. London, 1964.

The Comedies

Barber, C. L. *Shakespeare's Festive Comedy*. Princeton, 1959.
Berry, Ralph. *Shakespeare's Comedies: Explorations in Form*. Princeton, 1972.
Brown, John Russell. *Shakespeare and His Comedies*. London, 1957, 1968.
Brown, John Russell, and Bernard Harris, eds. *Early Shakespeare*. Stratford-upon-Avon Studies 3. London, 1961.
Champion, Larry S. *The Evolution of Shakespeare's Comedy*. Cambridge, Mass., 1970.
Charlton, H. B. *Shakespearian Comedy*. London, 1938.
Cody, Richard. *The Landscape of the Mind: Pastoralism and Platonic Theory in Tasso's "Aminta" and Shakespeare's Early Comedies*. Oxford, 1969.
Evans, Bertrand. *Shakespeare's Comedies*. Oxford, 1960.
Frye, Northrop. "The Argument of Comedy," *English Institute Essays 1948*. New York, 1949.
———. *A Natural Perspective: The Development of Shakespearean Comedy and Romance*. New York, 1965.
Gordon, George. *Shakespearian Comedy and Other Studies*. London, 1944.
Hamilton, A. C. *The Early Shakespeare*. San Marino, Calif., 1967.
Hawkins, Sherman H. "The Two Worlds of Shakespearean Comedy," *ShakS 3* (1967), 62–80.
Hunter, G. K. *William Shakespeare: The Late Comedies*. London, 1962.
Hunter, Robert G. *Shakespeare and the Comedy of Forgiveness*. New York, 1965.
Kermode, Frank. "The Mature Comedies," *Early Shakespeare*, ed. John Russell Brown and Bernard Harris. Stratford-upon-Avon Studies 3. London, 1961.
Leggatt, Alexander. *Shakespeare's Comedies of Love*. London and New York, 1974.
McFarland, Thomas. *Shakespeare's Pastoral Comedy*. Chapel Hill, N.C., 1972.

Muir, Kenneth, ed. *Shakespeare: The Comedies.* Englewood Cliffs, N.J., 1965.
Palmer, John. *Comic Characters of Shakespeare.* London, 1946.
Pettet, E. C. *Shakespeare and the Romance Tradition.* London, 1949.
Phialas, Peter G. *Shakespeare's Romantic Comedies.* Chapel Hill, N.C., 1966.
Richmond, Hugh M. *Shakespeare's Sexual Comedy.* Indianapolis, 1971.
Salingar, Leo. *Shakespeare and the Traditions of Comedy.* Cambridge, Eng., 1974.
Stevenson, David L. *The Love-Game Comedy.* New York, 1946.
Talbert, Ernest William. *Elizabethan Drama and Shakespeare's Early Plays.* Chapel Hill, N.C., 1963.
Tillyard, E. M. W. *Shakespeare's Early Comedies.* London and New York, 1965.
Traversi, Derek. *Shakespeare: The Early Comedies.* London, 1960.
Turner, Robert Y. *Shakespeare's Apprenticeship.* Chicago, 1974.

The Problem Plays

Campbell, Oscar James. *Shakespeare's Satire.* London and New York, 1943, 1963.
Charlton, H. B. "The Dark Comedies," *Bulletin of the John Rylands Library,* 21 (1937), 78–128.
Foakes, R. A. *Shakespeare, The Dark Comedies to the Last Plays: From Satire to Celebration.* Charlottesville, Va., 1971.
Jamieson, Michael. "The Problem Plays, 1920–1970: A Retrospect," *ShS 25* (1972), 1–10.
Lawrence, W. W. *Shakespeare's Problem Comedies.* New York, 1931, 1960.
Ornstein, Robert, ed. *Discussions of Shakespeare's Problem Comedies.* Boston, 1961.
Schanzer, Ernest. *The Problem Plays of Shakespeare.* New York, 1963.
Tillyard, E. M. W. *Shakespeare's Problem Plays.* Toronto, 1949.
Wheeler, Richard P. *Shakespeare's Development and the Problem Comedies: Turn and Counterturn.* Berkeley and Los Angeles, 1980.
Ure, Peter. *William Shakespeare: The Problem Plays.* London, 1961.

The Comedy of Errors

See also works listed under *The Comedies,* above, especially by Berry, Charlton, Cody, Evans, Pettet, Richmond, Salingar, Tillyard, Traversi, and Turner.
Barber, C. L. "Shakespearian Comedy in *The Comedy of Errors,*" *College English,* 25 (1964), 493–497.
Brooks, Charles. "Shakespeare's Romantic Shrews," *SQ,* 11 (1960), 351–356.
Brooks, Harold. "Themes and Structure in *The Comedy of Errors,*" *Early Shakespeare,* ed. John Russell Brown and Bernard Harris, pp. 55–71. Stratford-upon-Avon Studies 3. London, 1961.
Clubb, Louise G. "Italian Comedy and *The Comedy of Errors,*" *Comparative Literature,* 19 (1967), 240–251.
Coulter, Cornelia C. "The Plautine Tradition in Shakespeare," *Journal of English and Germanic Philology,* 19 (1920), 66–83.
Elliott, G. R. "Weirdness in *The Comedy of Errors,*" *University of Toronto Quarterly,* 9 (1939), 95–106.
Fergusson, Francis. "Two Comedies: *The Comedy of Errors* and *Much Ado About Nothing,*" *The Human Image in Dramatic Literature,* pp. 144–157. New York, 1957.
Foakes, R. A., ed. *The Comedy of Errors.* The Arden Shakespeare. London and Cambridge, Mass., 1962.
Gill, Erma. "A Comparison of the Characters in *The Comedy of Errors* with Those in the Menaechmi," *University of Texas Studies in English,* 5 (1925), 79–95.
———. "The Plot-Structure of *The Comedy of Errors* in Relation to Its Sources," *University of Texas Studies in English,* 10 (1930), 13–65.
Knight, G. Wilson. *The Shakespearian Tempest.* London, 1932, 1953.
Lea, Kathleen M. *Italian Popular Comedy: A Study in the Commedia dell' Arte, 1560–1620, with Special Reference to the English Stage.* Oxford, 1934.
Levin, Harry. "Introduction," *The Comedy of Errors.* The Signet Classic Shakespeare. New York and Toronto, 1965.
Salgādo, Gāmini. "'Time's Deformed Hand': Sequence, Consequence, and Inconsequence in *The Comedy of Errors,*" *ShS 25* (1972), 81–91.

Love's Labor's Lost

See also works listed under *The Comedies,* above, especially by Barber, Berry, Charlton, Cody, Evans, R. G. Hunter, McFarland, Stevenson, Tillyard, and Traversi.
Agnew, Gates K. "Berowne and the Progress of *Love's Labour's Lost,*" *ShakS 4* (1968), 40–72.
Baldwin, T. W. *William Shakspere's Small Latine & Lesse Greeke.* Urbana, Ill., 1944.
Boughner, D. C. "Don Armado and the *Commedia dell' Arte,*" *Studies in Philology,* 37 (1940), 201–224.
Calderwood, James L. *Shakespearean Metadrama.* Minneapolis, 1971.
Campbell, Oscar J. "*Love's Labour's Lost* Re-studied," *Studies in Shakespeare, Milton and Donne,* by University of Michigan English Department. New York, 1925.
Carroll, William C. *The Great Feast of Language in "Love's Labour's Lost."* Princeton, 1976.
Evans, Malcolm. "Mercury Versus Apollo: A Reading of *Love's Labour's Lost,*" *SQ,* 26 (1975), 113–127.
Frye, Northrop. "Shakespeare's Experimental Comedy," *Stratford Papers on Shakespeare 1961,* ed. B. A. W. Jackson. Toronto, 1962.
Goldstien, Neal L. "*Love's Labour's Lost* and the Renaissance Vision of Love," *SQ,* 25 (1974), 335–350.

Granville-Barker, Harley. *Prefaces to Shakespeare,* vol. 2. Princeton, 1947.
Greene, Thomas M. "*Love's Labour's Lost:* The Grace of Society," *SQ,* 22 (1971), 315–328.
Harbage, Alfred. "*Love's Labour's Lost* and the Early Shakespeare," *Philological Quarterly,* 41 (1962), 18–36.
Heninger, S. K., Jr. "The Pattern of *Love's Labour's Lost,*" *ShakS 7* (1974), 25–53.
Hoy, Cyrus. "*Love's Labour's Lost* and the Nature of Comedy," *SQ,* 13 (1962), 31–40.
Hunter, Robert G. "The Function of the Songs at the End of *Love's Labour's Lost,*" *ShakS 7* (1974), 55–64.
Mahood, M. M. *Shakespeare's Wordplay.* London, 1957.
Montrose, Louis A. *"Curious-Knotted Garden": The Form, Themes, and Contexts of Shakespeare's "Love's Labour's Lost."* Salzburg, 1977.
Roesen, Bobbyann. *"Love's Labour's Lost," SQ,* 4 (1953), 411–426.
Vyvyan, John. *Shakespeare and the Rose of Love.* New York, 1960.
Westlund, Joseph. "Fancy and Achievement in *Love's Labour's Lost,*" *SQ,* 18 (1967), 37–46.
Yates, Frances A. *A Study of "Love's Labour's Lost."* Cambridge, Eng., 1936.

The Two Gentlemen of Verona

See also works listed under *The Comedies,* above, especially by Berry, Charlton, Evans, R. G. Hunter, Leggatt, Pettet, and Salingar.
Brooks, Harold F. "Two Clowns in a Comedy (to Say Nothing of the Dog): Speed, Launce (and Crab) in *The Two Gentlemen of Verona,*" *English Association Essays and Studies,* n. s., 16 (1963), 91–100.
Craig, Hardin. "Shakespeare's Development as a Dramatist in the Light of His Experience," *Studies in Philology,* 39 (1942), 226–238.
Danby, John F. "Shakespeare Criticism and *Two Gentlemen of Verona,*" *Critical Quarterly,* 2 (1960), 309–321.
Ewbank, Inga-Stina. " 'Were Man But Constant, He Were Perfect': Constancy and Consistency in *The Two Gentlemen of Verona,*" *Shakespearian Comedy,* ed. Malcolm Bradbury and D. J. Palmer. Stratford-upon-Avon Studies 14. London and New York, 1972.
Leech, Clifford, ed. *The Two Gentlemen of Verona.* The Arden Shakespeare. London and Cambridge, Mass., 1969.
Lindenbaum, Peter. "Education in *The Two Gentlemen of Verona,*" *Studies in English Literature,* 15 (1975), 229–244.
Perry, Thomas A. "Proteus, Wry-Transformed Traveller," *SQ,* 5 (1954), 33–40.
Price, Hereward T. "Shakespeare as a Critic," *Philological Quarterly,* 20 (1941), 390–399.
Sargent, Ralph M. "Sir Thomas Elyot and the Integrity of *The Two Gentlemen of Verona,*" *PMLA,* 65 (1950), 1166–1180.
Vyvyan, John. *Shakespeare and the Rose of Love.* New York, 1960.
Weimann, Robert. "Laughing with the Audience: *The Two Gentlemen of Verona* and the Popular Tradition of Comedy," *ShS 22* (1969), 35–42.

The Taming of the Shrew

See also works listed under *The Comedies,* above, especially by Berry, Leggatt, Hawkins, and Stevenson.
Brunvand, Jan H. "The Folktale Origin of *The Taming of the Shrew,*" *SQ,* 17 (1966), 345–359.
Duthie, G. I. "*The Taming of A Shrew* and *The Taming of the Shrew,*" *Review of English Studies,* 19 (1943), 337–356.
Greenfield, Thelma N. "The Transformation of Christopher Sly," *Philological Quarterly,* 33 (1954), 34–42.
Heilman, Robert B. "*The Taming* Untamed, or, The Return of the Shrew," *Modern Language Quarterly,* 27 (1966), 147–161.
Hosley, Richard. "Sources and Analogues of *The Taming of the Shrew,*" *Huntington Library Quarterly,* 27 (1964), 289–308.
———. "Was There a 'Dramatic Epilogue' to *The Taming of the Shrew?" Studies in English Literature,* 1.2 (1961), 17–34.
Huston, J. Dennis. " 'To Make a Puppet': Play and Play-Making in *The Taming of the Shrew,*" *ShakS 9* (1976), 73–87.
Jayne, Sears. "The Dreaming of *The Shrew,*" *SQ,* 17 (1966), 41–56.
Kahn, Coppélia. "*The Taming of the Shrew:* Shakespeare's Mirror of Marriage," *Modern Language Studies,* 5 (1975), 88–102.
Ribner, Irving. "The Morality of Farce: *The Taming of the Shrew,*" *Essays . . . Presented to Bruce Robert McElderry, Jr.,* ed. M. F. Schulz et al., pp. 165–176. Athens, Ohio, 1967.
Seronsy, Cecil. " 'Supposes' as the Unifying Theme in *The Taming of the Shrew,*" *SQ,* 14 (1963), 15–30.
Thorne, W. B. "Folk Elements in *The Taming of the Shrew,*" *Queen's Quarterly,* 75 (1968), 482–496.
Tillyard, E. M. W. "The Fairy-Tale Element in *The Taming of the Shrew,*" *Shakespeare 1564–1964,* ed. E. A. Bloom, pp. 110–114. Providence, 1964.
West, Michael. "The Folk Background of Petruchio's Wooing Dance: Male Supremacy in *The Taming of the Shrew,*" *ShakS 7* (1974), 65–73.

A Midsummer Night's Dream

See also works listed under *The Comedies,* above, especially Barber, Kermode, and Leggatt.
Bethurum, Dorothy. "Shakespeare's Comment on Mediaeval Romance in *Midsummer-Night's Dream,*" *Modern Language Notes,* 60 (1945), 85–94.
Dent, R. W. "Imagination in *A Midsummer Night's Dream,*" *SQ,* 15.2 (1964), 115–129.

Doran, Madeleine. "Pyramus and Thisbe Once More," *Essays . . . in Honor of Hardin Craig*, ed. Richard Hosley, pp. 149–162. Columbia, Mo, 1962.

Garber, Marjorie B. *Dream in Shakespeare: From Metaphor to Metamorphosis*. New Haven and London, 1974.

Hemingway, Samuel B. "The Relation of *A Midsummer Night's Dream* to *Romeo and Juliet*," *Modern Language Notes*, 26 (1911), 78–80.

Hunter, G. K. *William Shakespeare: The Late Comedies*. London, 1962.

Kott, Jan. *Shakespeare Our Contemporary*. Trans. Boleslaw Taborski. New York, 1964.

Latham, Minor White. *The Elizabethan Fairies: The Fairies of Folklore and the Fairies of Shakespeare*. New York, 1930.

Muir, Kenneth. "Pyramus and Thisbe: A Study in Shakespeare's Method," *SQ*, 5 (1954), 141–153.

———. "Shakespeare as Parodist," *Notes and Queries*, 199 (1954), 467–468.

Nemerov, Howard. "The Marriage of Theseus and Hippolyta," *Kenyon Review*, 18 (1956), 633–641.

Olsen, Paul A. "*A Midsummer Night's Dream* and the Meaning of Court Marriage," *English Literary History*, 24 (1957), 95–119.

Priestley, J. B. *The English Comic Characters*. London, 1925.

Reynolds, Lou Agnes, and Paul Sawyer. "Folk Medicine and the Four Fairies of *A Midsummer-Night's Dream*," *SQ*, 10 (1959), 513–521.

Schanzer, Ernest. "The Central Theme of *A Midsummer Night's Dream*," *University of Toronto Quarterly*, 20 (1951), 233–238.

———. "The Moon and the Fairies in *A Midsummer Night's Dream*," *University of Toronto Quarterly*, 24 (1955), 234–246.

Sewell, Elizabeth. *The Orphic Voice: Poetry and Natural History*. New Haven, 1960.

Siegel, Paul N. "*A Midsummer Night's Dream* and the Wedding Guests," *SQ*, 4 (1953), 139–144.

Taylor, Michael. "The Darker Purpose of *A Midsummer Night's Dream*," *Studies in English Literature*, 9 (1969), 259-273.

Young, David P. *Something of Great Constancy: The Art of "A Midsummer Night's Dream."* New Haven, 1966.

The Merchant of Venice

See also works listed under *The Comedies*, above, especially Barber, Brown, Kermode, and Leggatt.

Barnet, Sylvan. "Prodigality and Time in *The Merchant of Venice*," *PMLA*, 87 (1972), 26–30.

———, ed. *Twentieth Century Interpretations of "The Merchant of Venice."* Englewood Cliffs, N.J., 1970.

Burkhardt, Sigurd. *Shakespearean Meanings*. Princeton, 1968.

Coolidge, John S. "Law and Love in *The Merchant of Venice*," *SQ*, 27 (1976), 243–263.

Danson, Lawrence. *The Harmonies of "The Merchant of Venice."* New Haven and London, 1978.

Donow, Herbert S. "Shakespeare's Caskets: Unity in *The Merchant of Venice*," *ShakS* 4 (1968), 86–93.

'd, Sigmund. "The Theme of the Three Caskets," *Complete Psychological Works of Sigmund Freud*, 12 (1911–1913), pp. 291–301. London, 1958.

Graham, Cary B. "Standards of Value in *The Merchant of Venice*," *SQ*, 4 (1953), 145–151.

Granville-Barker, Harley. *Prefaces to Shakespeare*, vol. I. Princeton, 1946.

Grebanier, Bernard N. *The Truth about Shylock*. New York, 1962.

Hill, R. F. "*The Merchant of Venice* and the Pattern of Romantic Comedy," *ShS 28* (1975), 75–87.

Lelyveld, Toby B. *Shylock on the Stage*. Cleveland, 1960.

Lever, J. W. "Shylock, Portia, and the Values of Shakespearian Comedy," *SQ*, 3 (1952), 383–386.

Levitsky, Ruth M. "Shylock as Unregenerate Man," *SQ*, 28 (1977), 58–64.

Lewalski, Barbara K. "Biblical Allusion and Allegory in *The Merchant of Venice*," *SQ*, 13 (1962), 327–343.

MacKay, Maxine. "*The Merchant of Venice:* A Reflection of the Early Conflict Between Courts of Law and Courts of Equity," *SQ*, 15.4 (1964), 371–375.

Pettet, E. C. "*The Merchant of Venice* and the Problem of Usury," *English Association Essays and Studies*, 31 (1945), 19–33.

Rabkin, Norman. "Meaning and Shakespeare," *Shakespeare 1971*, ed. Clifford Leech and J. M. R. Margeson. Toronto, 1972.

Sinsheimer, Hermann. *Shylock, the History of a Character; or, The Myth of the Jew*. London, 1947.

Stoll, E. E. "Shylock," *Journal of English and Germanic Philology*, 10 (1911), 236–279. Reprinted in *Shakespeare Studies*. New York, 1927, 1942.

Much Ado about Nothing

See also works listed under *The Comedies*, above, especially by Brown, Gordon, R. G. Hunter, Salingar, and Stevenson.

Barish, Jonas A. "Pattern and Purpose in the Prose of *Much Ado About Nothing*," *Rice U. Studies*, 60.2 (1974), 19–30.

Craik, T. W. "*Much Ado about Nothing*," *Scrutiny*, 19 (1953), 297–316.

Davis, Walter R., ed. *Twentieth Century Interpretations of "Much Ado about Nothing."* Englewood Cliffs, N.J., 1969.

Everett, Barbara. "*Much Ado about Nothing*," *Critical Quarterly*, 3 (1961), 319–335.

Fergusson, Francis. "Two Comedies: *The Comedy of Errors* and *Much Ado About Nothing*," *The Human Image in Dramatic Literature*. New York, 1957.

Gilbert, Allan. "Two Margarets: The Composition of *Much Ado about Nothing*," *Philological Quarterly*, 41 (1962), 61–71.

Jorgensen, Paul A. "*Much Ado about Nothing*," *SQ*, 5 (1954), 287–295.

Lewalski, Barbara K. "Love, Appearance, and Reality: Much Ado About Something," *Studies in English Literature*, 8 (1968), 235–251.

Mulryne, J. R. *Shakespeare: "Much Ado about Nothing."* London, 1965.

Page, Nadine. "The Public Repudiation of Hero," *PMLA*, 50 (1935), 739–744.

Prouty, Charles T. *The Sources of "Much Ado about Nothing."* New Haven, 1950.
Rossiter, A. P. *Angel with Horns*. London, 1961.
Spivack, Bernard. *Shakespeare and the Allegory of Evil*. New York, 1958.
Stoll, E. E. *Shakespeare Studies*. New York, 1942.
Taylor, Michael. "*Much Ado About Nothing:* The Individual in Society," *Essays in Criticism,* 23 (1973), 146–153.

The Merry Wives of Windsor

See also works listed under *The Comedies,* above, especially by Charlton.
Bennett, A. L. "The Sources of Shakespeare's *Merry Wives,*" *Renaissance Quarterly,* 23 (1970), 429–433.
Bracy, William. "*The Merry Wives of Windsor,*" *The History and Transmission of Shakespeare's Text.* Columbia, Mo., 1952.
Bradley, A. C. "The Rejection of Falstaff," *Oxford Lectures on Poetry*. London, 1909, 1961.
Bryant, J. A., Jr. "Falstaff and the Renewal of Windsor," *PMLA,* 89 (1974), 296–301.
Carroll, William. " 'A Received Belief': Imagination in *The Merry Wives of Windsor,*" *Studies in Philology,* 74 (1977), 186–215.
Fleissner, Robert F. "The Malleable Knight and the Unfettered Friar: *The Merry Wives of Windsor* and Boccaccio," *ShakS 11* (1978), 71–93.
Green, William. *Shakespeare's "Merry Wives of Windsor."* Princeton, 1962.
Hotson, Leslie. *Shakespeare Versus Shallow*. London, 1931.
Leggatt, Alexander. *Citizen Comedy in the Age of Shakespeare*. Toronto, 1973.
Roberts, Jeanne Addison. *Shakespeare's English Comedy: "The Merry Wives of Windsor" in Context.* Lincoln, Neb., 1979.
Steadman, John M. "Falstaff as Actaeon: A Dramatic Emblem," *SQ,* 14 (1963), 231–244.

As You Like It

See also works listed under *The Comedies,* above, especially by Brown, G. K. Hunter, R. G. Hunter, Leggatt, McFarland, and Salingar.
Babb, Lawrence. *The Elizabethan Malady*. East Lansing, Mich., 1951.
Barnet, Sylvan. "Strange Events: Improbability in *As You Like It,*" *ShakS 4* (1968), 119–131.
Barton, Anne. "*As You Like It* and *Twelfth Night:* Shakespeare's Sense of an Ending," *Shakespearian Comedy,* ed. Malcolm Bradbury and D. J. Palmer. Stratford-upon-Avon Studies 14. London and New York, 1972.
Bennett, Robert B. "The Reform of a Malcontent: Jaques and the Meaning of *As You Like It,*" *ShakS 9* (1976), 183–204.
Campbell, Oscar James. "Jaques," *Huntington Library Bulletin,* 8 (1935), 71–102.
Cirillo, Albert R. "*As You Like It:* Pastoralism Gone Awry," *English Literary History,* 38 (1971), 19–39.
Doebler, John. *Shakespeare's Speaking Pictures: Studies in Iconic Imagery*. Albuquerque, N.M., 1974.
Doran, Madeleine. " 'Yet Am I Inland Bred.,' " *SQ,* 15.2 (1964), 99–114.
Fink, Z. S. "Jaques and the Malcontent Traveler," *Philological Quarterly,* 14 (1935), 237–252.
Fortin, René E. " 'Tongues in Trees': Symbolic Patterns in *As You Like It,*" *Texas Studies in Literature and Language,* 14 (1973), 569–582.
Gardner, Helen. "*As You Like It,*" *More Talking of Shakespeare,* ed. John Garrett. London and New York, 1959.
Halio, Jay L. " 'No Clock in the Forest': Time in *As You Like It,*" *Studies in English Literature,* 2 (1962), 197–207.
Jenkins, Harold. "*As You Like It,*" *ShS 8* (1955), 40–51.
Kernan, Alvin B. *The Cankered Muse*. New Haven, 1959.
Knowles, Richard. "Myth and Type in *As You Like It,*" *English Literary History,* 33 (1966), 1–22.
Kreider, P. V. "Genial Literary Satire in the Forest of Arden," *Shakespeare Association Bulletin,* 10 (1935), 212–231.
Lascelles, Mary. "Shakespeare's Pastoral Comedy," *More Talking of Shakespeare,* ed. John Garrett. London and New York, 1959.
Morris, Harry. "*As You Like It:* Et in Arcadia Ego," *SQ,* 26 (1975), 269–275.
Shaw, John. "Fortune and Nature in *As You Like It,*" *SQ,* 6 (1955), 45–50.
Staebler, Warren. "Shakespeare's Play of Atonement," *Shakespeare Association Bulletin,* 24 (1949), 91–105.
Van den Berg, Kent. "Theatrical Fiction and the Reality of Love in *As You Like It,*" *PMLA,* 90 (1975), 885–893.
Wilson, Rawdon. "The Way to Arden: Attitudes toward Time in *As You Like It,*" *SQ,* 26 (1975), 16–24.
Young, David. *The Heart's Forest*. New Haven, 1972.

Twelfth Night

See also works listed under *The Comedies,* above, especially by Barber, Brown, G. K. Hunter, Leggatt, and Salingar.
Barton, Anne. "*As You Like It* and *Twelfth Night:* Shakespeare's Sense of an Ending," *Shakespearian Comedy,* ed. Malcolm Bradbury and D. J. Palmer. Stratford-upon-Avon Studies 14. London and New York, 1972.
Downer, Alan S. "Feste's Night," *College English,* 13 (1952), 258–265.
Eagleton, Terence. "Language and Reality in *Twelfth Night,*" *Critical Quarterly,* 9 (1967), 217–228.
Hartwig, Joan. "Feste's 'Whirligig' and the Comic Providence of *Twelfth Night,*" *English Literary History,* 40 (1973), 501–513.
Hollander, John. "*Twelfth Night* and the Morality of Indulgence," *Sewanee Review,* 67 (1959), 220–238.
Hotson, Leslie. *The First Night of Twelfth Night*. New York, 1954.
Jenkins, Harold. "Shakespeare's *Twelfth Night,*" *Rice Institute Pamphlets,* 45.4 (1959), 19–42.

King, Walter N., ed. *Twentieth Century Interpretations of "Twelfth Night."* Englewood Cliffs, N.J., 1968.

Knight, G. Wilson. *The Shakespearian Tempest.* London, 1932, 1953.

Leech, Clifford. *"Twelfth Night" and Shakespearian Comedy.* Toronto, 1965.

Lewalski, Barbara K. "Thematic Patterns in *Twelfth Night,*" *ShakS 1* (1965), 168–181.

Salingar, L. D. "The Design of *Twelfth Night,*" *SQ,* 9 (1958), 117–139.

Seiden, Melvin. "Malvolio Reconsidered," *University of Kansas City Review,* 28 (1961), 105–114.

Summers, Joseph H. "The Masks of *Twelfth Night,*" *University of Kansas City Review,* 22 (1955), 25–32. Reprinted in *Shakespeare: Modern Essays in Criticism,* ed. Leonard F. Dean. Rev. ed. London and New York, 1967, 1969.

Tilley, Morris P. "The Organic Unity of *Twelfth Night,*" *PMLA,* 29 (1914), 550–566.

Wells, Stanley. *Royal Shakespeare.* Manchester, 1977. (Includes an account of John Barton's production of *Twelfth Night.*)

Welsford, Enid. *The Fool.* London, 1935.

Williams, Porter, Jr. "Mistakes in *Twelfth Night* and Their Resolution," *PMLA,* 76 (1961), 193–199.

All's Well that Ends Well

See also works listed under *The Comedies,* above, especially by R. G. Hunter and Salingar, and under *The Problem Plays,* especially by Wheeler.

Adams, John F. "*All's Well that Ends Well:* The Paradox of Procreation," *SQ,* 12 (1961), 261–270.

Arthos, John. "The Comedy of Generation," *Essays in Criticism,* 5 (1955), 97–117.

Bergeron, David M. "The Structure of Healing in *All's Well That Ends Well,*" *South Atlantic Bulletin,* 37.4 (1972), 25–34.

Bradbrook, M. C. "Virtue Is the True Nobility," *Review of English Studies,* n.s. 1 (1950), 289–301.

Calderwood, James L. "Styles of Knowing in *All's Well,*" *Modern Language Quarterly,* 25 (1964), 272–294.

Chambers, E. K. *Shakespeare: A Survey.* London, 1925.

David, Richard. "Plays Pleasant and Plays Unpleasant," *ShS 8* (1955), 134–136. (Includes a review of an Old Vic production of *All's Well.*)

Donaldson, Ian. "*All's Well That Ends Well:* Shakespeare's Play of Endings," *Essays in Criticism,* 27 (1977), 34–55.

Everett, Barbara, ed. *All's Well That Ends Well.* New Penguin Shakespeare. London, 1970.

Godshalk, William Leigh. "*All's Well That Ends Well* and the Morality Play," *SQ,* 25 (1974), 61–70.

Halio, Jay L. "*All's Well that Ends Well,*" *SQ,* 15.1 (1964), 33–43.

Hunter, G. K., ed. *All's Well that Ends Well.* The Arden Shakespeare. 3rd ed. Cambridge, Mass., 1959.

Johnson, Samuel. *Samuel Johnson on Shakespeare,* ed. W. K. Wimsatt. New York, 1960.

King, Walter N. "Shakespeare's 'Mingled Yarn,' " *Modern Language Quarterly,* 21 (1960), 33–44.

Knight, G. Wilson. *The Sovereign Flower: On Shakespeare as the Poet of Royalism.* New York, 1958.

Leech, Clifford. "The Theme of Ambition in *All's Well that Ends Well,*" *English Literary History,* 21 (1954), 17–29.

Leggatt, Alexander. "*All's Well That Ends Well:* The Testing of Romance," *Modern Language Quarterly,* 32 (1971), 21–41.

Price, Joseph G. *The Unfortunate Comedy: A Study of "All's Well that Ends Well" and Its Critics.* Toronto, 1968.

Rossiter, A. P. *Angel with Horns.* London, 1961.

Schoff, Francis G. "Claudio, Bertram, and a Note on Interpretation," *SQ,* 10 (1959), 11–23.

Turner, Robert Y. "Dramatic Conventions in *All's Well that Ends Well,*" *PMLA,* 75 (1960), 497–502.

Warren, Roger. "Why Does It End Well? Helena, Bertram, and the Sonnets," *ShS 22* (1969), 79–92.

Welsh, Alexander. "The Loss of Men and Getting of Children: *All's Well that Ends Well* and *Measure for Measure,*" *Modern Language Review,* 73 (1978), 17–28.

Wilson, Harold S. "Dramatic Emphasis in *All's Well that Ends Well,*" *Huntington Library Quarterly,* 13 (1950), 217–240.

Measure for Measure

See also works listed under *The Comedies* and *The Problem Plays,* above, especially by Schanzer.

Chambers, R. W. "The Jacobean Shakespeare and *Measure for Measure,*" *Proceedings of the British Academy,* 23 (1937), 135–192.

Coghill, Nevill. "Comic Form in *Measure for Measure,*" *ShS 8* (1955), 14–27.

Dickinson, John W. "Renaissance Equity and *Measure for Measure,*" *SQ,* 13 (1962), 287–297.

Dunkel, Wilbur. "Law and Equity in *Measure for Measure,*" *SQ,* 13 (1962), 275–285.

Empson, William. *The Structure of Complex Words.* London, 1951.

Fergusson, Francis. *The Human Image in Dramatic Literature.* Garden City, N.Y., 1957.

Fly, Richard D. *Shakespeare's Mediated World.* Amherst, 1976.

Geckle, George L., ed. *Twentieth Century Interpretations of "Measure for Measure."* Englewood Cliffs, N.J., 1970.

Gless, Darryl. *"Measure for Measure," the Law, and the Convent.* Princeton, 1979.

Hawkins, Harriett. *Likenesses of Truth in Elizabethan and Restoration Drama.* Oxford, 1972.

Holland, Norman. *The Shakespearean Imagination.* New York, 1964.

Kirsch, Arthur. "The Integrity of *Measure for Measure,*" *ShS 28* (1975), 89–105.

Knight, G. Wilson. "*Measure for Measure* and the Gospels," *The Wheel of Fire.* London, 1930, 1965.

Lascelles, Mary. *Shakespeare's "Measure for Measure."* London, 1953.

Leavis, F. R. "The Greatness of *Measure for Measure,*" *Scrutiny,* 10 (1942), 234–247.

Nagarajan, S. "*Measure for Measure* and Elizabethan Betrothals," *SQ,* 14 (1963), 115–119.

Pope, Elizabeth M. "The Renaissance Background of *Measure for Measure*," *ShS 2* (1949), 66–82.
Scouten, A. H. "An Historical Approach to *Measure for Measure*," *Philological Quarterly*, 54 (1975), 68–84.
Sewell, Arthur. *Character and Society in Shakespeare*. London, 1951.
Stead, C. K., ed. *Shakespeare's "Measure for Measure": A Casebook*. London, 1971.
Stevenson, David L. *The Achievement of "Measure for Measure."* Ithaca, N.Y., 1966.
Sypher, Wylie. "Shakespeare as Casuist: *Measure for Measure*," *Sewanee Review*, 58 (1950), 262–280.
Welsh, Alexander. "The Loss of Men and Getting of Children: *All's Well that Ends Well* and *Measure for Measure*," *Modern Language Review*, 73 (1978), 17–28.
Wilson, Harold S. "Action and Symbol in *Measure for Measure* and *The Tempest*," *SQ*, 4 (1953), 375–384.

Troilus and Cressida

See also works listed under *The Problem Plays*, above, especially by Charlton and Lawrence.
Bradbrook, Muriel C. "What Shakespeare Did to Chaucer's *Troilus and Criseyde*," *SQ*, 9 (1958), 311–319.
Campbell, Oscar James. *Comicall Satyre and Shakespeare's "Troilus and Cressida."* San Marino, Calif., 1938.
Cox, John D. "The Error of Our Eye in *Troilus and Cressida*," *Comparative Drama*, 10 (1976), 147–171.
Fly, Richard D. *Shakespeare's Mediated World*. Amherst, 1976.
Foakes, R. A. "*Troilus and Cressida* Reconsidered," *University of Toronto Quarterly*, 32 (1963), 142–154.
Helton, Tinsley. "Paradox and Hypothesis in *Troilus and Cressida*," *ShakS 10* (1977), 115–131.
Jago, David M. "The Uniqueness of *Troilus and Cressida*," *SQ*, 29 (1978), 20–27.
Kaula, David. "Will and Reason in *Troilus and Cressida*," *SQ*, 12 (1961), 271–283.
Kermode, Frank. "Opinion, Truth, and Value," *Essays in Criticism*, 5 (1955), 181–187. (A reply to Nowottny article below.)
Kimbrough, Robert. *Shakespeare's "Troilus and Cressida" and Its Setting*. Cambridge, Mass., 1964.
Knight, G. Wilson. *The Wheel of Fire*. London, 1930.
Knights, L. C. "*Troilus and Cressida* Again," *Scrutiny*, 18 (1951), 144–157.
Muir, Kenneth. "*Troilus and Cressida*," *ShS 8* (1955), 28–39.
Nowottny, Winifred M. T. " 'Opinion' and 'Value' in *Troilus and Cressida*," *Essays in Criticism*, 4 (1954), 282–296.
Presson, Robert K. *Shakespeare's "Troilus and Cressida" and the Legends of Troy*. Madison, Wis., 1953.
Rollins, Hyder E. "The Troilus-Cressida Story from Chaucer to Shakespeare," *PMLA*, 32 (1917), 383–429.
Rossiter, A. P. *Angel with Horns*. London, 1961.
Spencer, Theodore. *Shakespeare and the Nature of Man*. New York, 1942.
Symons, Arthur. "*Troilus and Cressida*," *Harper's Monthly Magazine*, 115 (October, 1907), 659–664.
Tatlock, J. S. P. "The Siege of Troy in Elizabethan Literature," *PMLA*, 30 (1915), 673–770.
Yoder, R. A. " 'Sons and Daughters of the Game': An Essay on Shakespeare's *Troilus and Cressida*," *ShS 25* (1972), 11–25.

The Histories

Alexander, Peter. *Shakespeare's "Henry VI" and "Richard III."* Cambridge, Eng., 1929.
Berry, Edward I. *Patterns of Decay: Shakespeare's Early Histories*. Charlottesville, Va., 1975.
Boris, Edna Zwick. *Shakespeare's English Kings, the People, and the Law*. Cranbury, N.J., 1978.
Campbell, Lily B. *Shakespeare's "Histories": Mirrors of Elizabethan Policy*. San Marino, Calif., 1947.
Charlton, H. B. *Shakespeare, Politics and Politicians*. Oxford, 1929.
Craig, Hardin. "Shakespeare and the History Play," *J. Q. Adams Memorial Studies*, ed., J. McManaway et al., pp. 55–64. Washington, D.C., 1948.
Dorius, R. J., ed. *Discussions of Shakespeare's Histories*. Boston, 1964.
Forker, Charles R. "Shakespeare's Chronicle Plays as Historical-Pastoral," *ShakS 1* (1965), 85–104.
Jenkins, Harold. "Shakespeare's History Plays; *1900–1951*," *ShS* (1953), 1–15.
Jorgensen, Paul A. *Shakespeare's Military World*. Berkeley and Los Angeles, 1956.
Kastan, David Scott. "The Shape of Time: Form and Value in the Shakespearean History Play," *Comparative Drama*, 7 (1973–1974), 259–277.
Kelly, Henry A. *Divine Providence in the England of Shakespeare's Histories*. Cambridge, Mass., 1970.
Knights, L. C. "Shakespeare and Political Wisdom," *Sewanee Review*, 61 (1953), 43–55.
———. "Shakespeare's Politics: With Some Reflections on the Nature of Tradition," *Proceedings of the British Academy*, 43 (1957), 115–132.
Leech, Clifford. *William Shakespeare: The Chronicles*. London, 1962.
Manheim, Michael. *The Weak King Dilemma in the Shakespearean History Play*. Syracuse, 1973.
Ornstein, Robert. *A Kingdom for a Stage*. Cambridge, Mass., 1972.
Palmer, John. *Political Characters of Shakespeare*. London, 1945.
Pierce, Robert B. *Shakespeare's History Plays: The Family and the State*. Columbus, Ohio, 1971.
Prior, Moody E. *The Drama of Power: Studies in Shakespeare's History Plays*. Evanston, Ill., 1973.
Reese, M. M. *The Cease of Majesty*. London and New York, 1961.
Ribner, Irving. *The English History Play in the Age of Shakespeare*. Rev. ed. London, 1965.
Richmond, H. M. *Shakespeare's Political Plays*. New York, 1967.
Riggs, David. *Shakespeare's Heroical Histories*. Cambridge, Mass., 1971.
Rossiter, A. P. "Ambivalence: The Dialectic of the Histories," *Talking of Shakespeare*, ed. John Garrett. London, 1954.
Saccio, Peter. *Shakespeare's English Kings: History, Chronicle, and Drama*. New York, 1977.

Sanders, Norman. "American Criticism of Shakespeare's History Plays," *ShakS 9* (1976), 11–23.
Talbert, Ernest William. *Elizabethan Drama and Shakespeare's Early Plays.* Chapel Hill, N.C., 1963.
———. *The Problem of Order.* Chapel Hill, N.C., 1962.
Tillyard, E. M. W. *Shakespeare's History Plays.* London, 1944, 1961.
Traversi, Derek. *Shakespeare from Richard II to Henry V.* Palo Alto, 1957.
Turner, Robert Y. *Shakespeare's Apprenticeship.* Chicago, 1974.
Waith, Eugene M., ed. *Shakespeare: The Histories.* Englewood Cliffs, N.J., 1965. (A collection of essays.)
Wilson, F. P. "The English History Play," *Shakespearian and Other Studies.* Oxford, 1969.
———. *Marlowe and the Early Shakespeare.* Oxford, 1953.

The Henry the Sixth Plays

See also works listed under *The Histories,* above, especially by Alexander, Berry, Boris, Kelly, Manheim, Ornstein, Prior, Riggs, and Turner.
Berman, Ronald S. "Fathers and Sons in the Henry VI Plays," *SQ,* 13 (1962), 487–497.
Bevington, David. "The Domineering Female in *1 Henry VI,*" *ShakS 2* (1966), 51–58.
Born, Hanspeter. "The Date of *2, 3 Henry VI,*" *SQ,* 25 (1974), 323–334.
Brockbank, J. P. "The Frame of Disorder—*Henry VI,*" *Early Shakespeare,* ed. John Russell Brown and Bernard Harris, pp. 73–99. Stratford-upon-Avon Studies 3. London, 1961.
Clemen, Wolfgang H. "Anticipation and Foreboding in Shakespeare's Early Histories," *ShS* 6 (1953), 23–35.
French, A. L. "*Henry VI* and the Ghost of Richard II," *English Studies,* Anglo-American Supp., 50 (1969), xxxvii–xliii.
———. "The Mills of God and Shakespeare's Early History Plays," *English Studies,* 55 (1974), 313–324.
Law, R. A. "The Chronicles and the Three Parts of *Henry VI,*" *University of Texas Studies in English,* 33 (1954), 13–32.
Leech, Clifford. "The Two-Part Play: Marlowe and the Early Shakespeare," *Shakespeare Jahrbuch,* 94 (1958), 90–106.
Manheim, Michael. "Silence in the Henry VI Plays," *Educational Theatre Journal,* 29 (March, 1977), 7–76.
Price, Hereward T. *Construction in Shakespeare.* Ann Arbor, Mich., 1951.
Ricks, Don M. *Shakespeare's Emergent Form.* Logan, Utah, 1968.
Rossiter, A. P., ed. *Woodstock, a Moral History.* London, 1946.
Swander, Homer. "The Rediscovery of *Henry VI,*" *SQ,* 19 (1978), 146–163.
Utterback, Raymond V. "Public Men, Private Wills, and Kingship in *Henry VI, Part III,*" *Renaissance Papers 1978* (1979), 47–54.
Zeeveld, W. Gordon. "The Influence of Hall on Shakespeare's English Historical Plays," *English Literary History,* 3 (1936), 317–353.

Richard the Third

See also works listed under *The Histories,* above, especially by Berry, Boris, Kelly, and Prior.
Boyer, Clarence V. *The Villain as Hero in Elizabethan Tragedy.* New York, 1914.
Brooke, Nicholas. "Reflecting Gems and Dead Bones: Tragedy Versus History in *Richard III,*" *Critical Quarterly,* 7 (1965), 123–134.
Churchill, George B. *Richard the Third up to Shakespeare. Palaestra,* 10. Berlin, 1900.
Clemen, Wolfgang H. *A Commentary on Richard III.* Tr. Jean Bonheim. London, 1968.
———. "Tradition and Originality in Shakespeare's *Richard III,*" *SQ,* 5 (1954), 247–257.
French, A. L. "The World of *Richard III,*" *ShakS 4* (1968), 25–39.
Gerber, Richard. "Elizabethan Convention and Psychological Realism in the Dream and Last Soliloquy of *Richard III,*" *English Studies,* 40 (1959), 294–300.
Heilman, Robert B. "Satiety and Conscience: Aspects of *Richard III,*" *Antioch Review,* 24 (1964), 57–73.
Kendall, Paul Murray. *Richard the Third.* New York and London, 1956.
Krieger, Murray. "The Dark Generations of *Richard III,*" *Criticism,* 1 (1959), 32–48.
Rossiter, A. P. *Angel with Horns.* London, 1961.
———. "The Structure of *Richard III,*" *Durham University Journal,* 31 (1938), 44–75.
Sanders, Wilbur. *The Dramatist and the Received Idea: Studies in the Plays of Marlowe and Shakespeare.* Cambridge, Eng., 1968.
Sheriff, William E. "The Grotesque Comedy of *Richard III,*" *Studies in the Literary Imagination,* 5.1 (1972), 51–64.
Smidt, Kristian, ed. *The Tragedy of King Richard the Third: Parallel Texts of the First Quarto and the First Folio.* Oslo and New York, 1969.
Spivack, Bernard. *Shakespeare and the Allegory of Evil.* New York, 1958.
Stoll, E. E. *Shakespeare Studies.* New York, 1927.
Wheeler, Richard P. "History, Character, and Conscience in *Richard III,*" *Comparative Drama,* 7 (1971–72), 301–321.
Wood, Alice I. P. *The Stage History of Shakespeare's "King Richard the Third."* New York, 1909.

King John

See also works listed under *The Histories,* above, especially by Ornstein and Ribner.
Berman, Ronald. "Anarchy and Order in *Richard III* and *King John,*" *ShS 20* (1967), 51–59.
Bonjour, Adrien. "The Road to Swinstead Abbey: A Study of the Sense and Structure of *King John,*" *English Literary History,* 18 (1951), 253–274.
Burkhardt, Sigurd. *Shakespearean Meanings.* Princeton, 1968.
Calderwood, James L. "Commodity and Honour in *King John,*" *University of Toronto Quarterly,* 29 (1960), 341–356.

Elliott, John R., Jr., "Shakespeare and the Double Image of King John," *ShakS 1* (1965), 64–84.
Elson, John. "Studies in the *King John* Plays," *J. Q. Adams Memorial Studies,* ed. J. McManaway et al., pp. 183–198. Washington, D.C., 1948.
Harrison, G. B. "Shakespeare's Topical Significances: *I. King John,*" *Times Literary Supplement,* 13 Nov. 1930. Reprinted in Anne Bradby, ed., *Shakespeare Criticism 1919–35.* London, 1936.
Matchett, William H. "Richard's Divided Heritage in *King John,*" *Essays in Criticism,* 12 (1962), 231–253.
Mattson, May. *Five Plays about King John.* Studia Anglistica Upsaliensia 34. Uppsala, 1977.
Pettet, E. C. "Hot Irons and Fever: A Note on Some of the Imagery of *King John,*" *Essays in Criticism,* 4 (1954), 128–144.
Salter, F. M. "The Problem of *King John,*" *Proceedings and Transactions of the Royal Society of Canada,* 3rd ser. 43.2 (1949), 115–136.
Simmons, J. L. "Shakespeare's *King John* and Its Source: Coherence, Pattern, and Vision," *Tulane Studies in English,* 17 (1969), 53–72.
Van de Water, Julia C. "The Bastard in *King John,*" *SQ,* 11 (1960), 137–146.
Waith, Eugene M. "*King John* and the Drama of History," *SQ,* 29 (1978), 192–211.
Warren, Wilfred L. *King John.* New York, 1961.

Richard the Second

See also works listed under *The Histories,* above, especially by Forker, Ornstein, Palmer, and Reese.
Altick, Richard D. "Symphonic Imagery in *Richard II,*" *PMLA,* 62 (1947), 339–365.
Black, Matthew W. "The Sources of Shakespeare's *Richard II,*" *J. Q. Adams Memorial Studies,* ed. J. McManaway et al., pp. 199–216. Washington, D.C., 1948.
Bogard, Travis. "Shakespeare's Second Richard," *PMLA,* 70 (1955), 192–209.
Bonnard, George A. "The Actor in *Richard II,*" *Shakespeare Jahrbuch,* 87 (1952), 87–101.
Calderwood, James L. *Shakespearean Metadrama.* Minneapolis, 1971.
Dean, Leonard F. "*Richard II:* The State and the Image of the Theater," *PMLA,* 67 (1952), 211–218.
Dodson, Sarah. "The Northumberland of Shakespeare and Holinshed," *University of Texas Studies in English,* 19 (1939), 74–85.
Doran, Madeleine. "Imagery in *Richard II* and in *Henry IV,*" *Modern Language Review,* 37 (1942), 113–122.
Dorius, R. J. "A Little More Than a Little," *SQ,* 11 (1960), 13–26.
Elliott, John R., Jr., "History and Tragedy in *Richard II,*" *Studies in English Literature,* 8 (1968), 253–271.
Humphreys, A. R. *Richard II.* London, 1967.
Kantorowicz, Ernst H. *The King's Two Bodies: A Study in Medieval Political Theology.* Princeton, 1957.
Law, R. A. "Deviations from Holinshed in *Richard II,*" *University of Texas Studies in English,* 29 (1950), 91–101.
———. "Links Between Shakespeare's History Plays," *Studies in Philology,* 50 (1953), 168–187.
Mack, Maynard, Jr. *Killing the King: Three Studies in Shakespeare's Tragic Structure.* New Haven and London, 1973.
Mahood, M. M. *Shakespeare's Wordplay.* London, 1957.
Pater, Walter. *Appreciations.* London, 1889.
Phialas, Peter G. "The Medieval in *Richard II,*" *SQ,* 12 (1961), 305–310.
Quinn, Michael. " 'The King Is Not Himself': The Personal Tragedy of *Richard II,*" *Studies in Philology,* 56 (1959), 169–186.
Raysor, Thomas M., ed. *Samuel Taylor Coleridge: Shakespearean Criticism.* 2 vols. 2nd ed. London and New York, 1960.
Ribner, Irving. "The Political Problem in Shakespeare's Lancastrian Tetralogy," *Studies in Philology,* 49 (1952), 171–184.
Stirling, Brents. "Bolingbroke's 'Decision'," *SQ,* 2 (1951), 27–34.
Swinburne, A. C. *Three Plays of Shakespeare.* London, 1880.
Yeats, W. B. "At Stratford-upon-Avon," *Ideas of Good and Evil,* collected in *Essays and Introductions.* New York, 1961.
Zitner, Sheldon P. "Aumerle's Conspiracy," *Studies in English Literature,* 14 (1974), 239–257.

The Henry the Fourth Plays

See also works listed under *The Histories,* above, especially by Manheim, Ornstein, Palmer, Prior, and Reese.
Barber, C. L. "Rule and Misrule in *Henry IV,*" *Shakespeare's Festive Comedy.* Princeton, 1959.
Barish, Jonas A. "The Turning Away of Prince Hal," *ShakS 1* (1965), 9–17.
Berry, Edward I. "The Rejection Scene in *2 Henry IV,*" *Studies in English Literature,* 17 (1977), 201–218.
Blanpied, John W. " 'Unfathered Heirs and Loathly Births of Nature': Bringing History to Crisis in *2 Henry IV,*" *English Literary Renaissance,* 5 (1975), 212–231.
Boughner, D. C. "Traditional Elements in Falstaff," *Journal of English and Germanic Philology,* 43 (1944), 417–428.
———. "Vice, Braggart, and Falstaff," *Anglia,* 72 (1954), 35–61.
Bradley, A. C. "The Rejection of Falstaff," *Oxford Lectures on Poetry.* London, 1909, 1961.
Bryant, J. A., Jr., "Prince Hal and the Ephesians," *Sewanee Review,* 67 (1959), 204–219.
Dessen, Alan C. "The Intemperate Knight and the Politic Prince: Late Morality Structure in *1 Henry IV,*" *ShakS 7* (1974), 147–171.
Doran, Madeleine. "Imagery in *Richard II* and in *Henry IV,*" *Modern Language Review,* 37 (1942), 113–122.
Dorius, R. J., ed. *Twentieth Century Interpretations of "Henry IV Part I."* Englewood Cliffs, N.J., 1970.
Empson, William. "Falstaff and Mr. Dover Wilson," *Kenyon Review,* 15 (1953), 213–262.
Goldman, Michael. *Shakespeare and the Energies of Drama.* Princeton, 1972.

Hawkins, Sherman H. "Virtue and Kingship in Shakespeare's *Henry IV*," *English Literary Renaissance*, 5 (1975), 313–343.

Hunter, G. K. "*Henry IV* and the Elizabethan Two-Part Play," *Review of English Studies*, n.s. 5 (1954), 236–248.

———. "Shakespeare's Politics and the Rejection of Falstaff," *Critical Quarterly*, 1 (1959), 229–236.

Jenkins, Harold. *The Structural Problem in Shakespeare's "Henry the Fourth."* London, 1956.

Jorgensen, Paul. "The 'Dastardly Treachery' of Prince John of Lancaster," *PMLA*, 76 (1961), 488–492.

Kernan, Alvin. "The Henriad: Shakespeare's Major History Plays," *Yale Review*, 59 (1969), 3–32.

Kleinstück, Johannes. "The Problem of Order in Shakespeare's Histories," *Neophilologus*, 38 (1954), 268–277.

Knowles, Richard. "Unquiet and the Double Plot of *2 Henry IV*," *ShakS 2* (1966), 133–140.

Law, R. A. "Structural Unity in the Two Parts of *Henry the Fourth*," *Studies in Philology*, 24 (1927), 223–242.

Leech, Clifford. "The Unity of *2 Henry IV*," *ShS* 6 (1953), 16–24.

Manley, Frank. "The Unity of Betrayal in *2 Henry IV*," *SLitI* 5.1 (1972), 91–110.

McLuhan, Herbert Marshall. "*Henry IV*, A Mirror of Magistrates," *University of Toronto Quarterly*, 17 (1948), 152–160.

Morgann, Maurice. *Essay on the Dramatic Character of Sir John Falstaff* (1777), ed. Daniel A. Fineman. Oxford, 1972.

Prior, Moody E. "Comic Theory and the Rejection of Falstaff," *ShakS* 9 (1976), 159–171.

Seng, Peter J. "Songs, Time, and the Rejection of Falstaff," *ShS 15* (1962), 31–40.

Shaaber, M. A. "The Unity of *Henry IV*," *J. Q. Adams Memorial Studies*, ed. J. McManaway et al., pp. 217–228. Washington, D.C., 1948.

Spivack, Bernard. "Falstaff and the Psychomachia," *SQ*, 8 (1957), 449–459.

Sprague, Arthur Colby. *Shakespeare's Histories: Plays for the Stage*. London, 1964.

Stewart, J. I. M. "The Birth and Death of Falstaff," *Character and Motive in Shakespeare*. London, 1949.

Stoll, E. E. "Falstaff," *Shakespeare Studies*. New York, 1942.

Toliver, Harold E. "Falstaff, the Prince, and the History Play," *SQ*, 16 (1965), 63–80.

Williams, Philip. "The Birth and Death of Falstaff Reconsidered," *SQ*, 8 (1957), 359–365.

Wilson, J. Dover. *The Fortunes of Falstaff*. Cambridge, Eng., 1943.

Young, David P., ed. *Twentieth Century Interpretations of "Henry IV, Part Two."* Englewood Cliffs, N.J., 1968.

Henry the Fifth

See also works listed under *The Histories*, above, especially by Ornstein, Prior, and Reese.

Battenhouse, Roy W. "*Henry V* as Heroic Comedy," *Essays . . . in Honor of Hardin Craig*, ed. Richard Hosley. Columbia, Mo., 1962.

Beauman, Sally, ed. *Henry V for the Centenary Season at the Royal Shakespeare Theatre*. Oxford, 1976. (Includes information on Terry Hands' *Henry V*.)

Berman, Ronald S., ed. *Twentieth Century Interpretations of "Henry V."* Englewood Cliffs, N.J., 1968.

———. "Shakespeare's Alexander: *Henry V*," *College English*, 23 (1962), 532–539.

Gilbert, Allan. "Patriotism and Satire in *Henry V*," *Studies in Shakespeare*, ed. A. D. Matthews and C. M. Emery. Coral Gables, Fla., 1953.

Granville-Barker, Harley. "From *Henry V* to *Hamlet*," *Proceedings of the British Academy*, 11 (1925), 283–309.

Jorgensen, Paul A. "Accidental Judgments, Casual Slaughters, and Purposes Mistook: Critical Reactions to Shakespeare's *Henry the Fifth*," *Shakespeare Association Bulletin*, 22 (1947), 51–61.

———. *Shakespeare's Military World*. Berkeley and Los Angeles, 1956.

Quinn, Michael, ed. *Shakespeare, "Henry V": A Casebook*. London, 1969.

Rabkin, Norman. "Rabbits, Ducks, and *Henry V*," *SQ*, 28 (1977), 279–296.

Stříbrný, Zdeněk. "*Henry V* and History," *Shakespeare in a Changing World*, ed. Arnold Kettle. New York, 1964. Reprinted in Quinn, above.

Walter, J. H., ed. *King Henry the Fifth*. The New Arden Shakespeare. Cambridge, Eng., 1954.

Webber, Joan. "The Renewal of the King's Symbolic Role: From *Richard II* to *Henry V*," *Texas Studies in Literature and Language*, 4 (1963), 530–538.

Zimbardo, Rose A. "The Formalism of Henry V," *Shakespeare Encomium*, ed. Anne Paolucci. New York, 1964. Reprinted in Quinn, above.

Henry the Eighth

See also works listed under *The Histories*, above.

Alexander, Peter. "Conjectural History, or Shakespeare's *Henry VIII*," *English Association Essays and Studies*, 16 (1930), 85–120.

Berman, Ronald. "*King Henry the Eighth:* History and Romance," *English Studies*, 48 (1967), 112–121.

Berry, Edward I. "*Henry VIII* and the Dynamics of Spectacle," *ShakS 12* (1979), 229–246.

Bertram, Paul. "*Henry VIII:* The Conscience of the King," *In Defense of Reading*, ed. Reuben A. Brower and R. Poirier. New York, 1962.

Bliss, Lee. "The Wheel of Fortune and the Maiden Phoenix of Shakespeare's *King Henry the Eighth*," *English Literary History*, 42 (1975), 1–25.

Byrne, Muriel St. Claire. "A Stratford Production: *Henry VIII*," *ShS 3* (1950), 120–129.

Cox, John D. "*Henry VIII* and the Masque," *English Literary History*, 45 (1978), 390–409.

Felperin, Howard. "Shakespeare's *Henry VIII:* History as Myth," *Studies in English Literature*, 6 (1966), 225–246.

Foakes, R. A., ed. *King Henry VIII*. The New Arden Shakespeare. Cambridge, Eng., 1957.

Kermode, Frank. "What is Shakespeare's *Henry VIII* About?" *Durham University Journal*, n.s. 9 (1948), 48–55.

Knight, G. Wilson. "*Henry VIII* and the Poetry of Conversion," *The Crown of Life*. London, 1947, 1966.
Mincoff, Marco. "*Henry VIII* and Fletcher," *SQ*, 12 (1961), 239–260.
Partridge, A. C. *The Problem of Henry VIII Reopened*. Cambridge, Eng., 1949.
Richmond, H. M. "Shakespeare's *Henry VIII*: Romance Redeemed by History," *ShakS 4* (1968), 334–349.
Waith, Eugene M. "*Henry VIII* and the More Historical Tragedies," *The Pattern of Tragicomedy in Beaumont and Fletcher*. New Haven and London, 1952.
Wasson, John. "In Defense of *King Henry VIII*," *Research Studies*, Washington State University, 32 (1964), 261–276.
Wiley, Paul L. "Renaissance Exploitation of Cavendish's *Life of Wolsey*," *Studies in Philology*, 43 (1946), 121–146.

The Tragedies

Bradley, A. C. *Shakespearean Tragedy*. London, 1904. *(Hamlet, Othello, King Lear, Macbeth.)*
Brooke, Nicholas. *Shakespeare's Early Tragedies*. London and New York, 1968.
Brower, Reuben. *Hero and Saint: Shakespeare and the Græco-Roman Heroic Tradition*. New York and Oxford, 1971.
Brown, John Russell, and Bernard Harris, eds. *Early Shakespeare*. Stratford-upon-Avon Studies 3. London, 1961.
Campbell, Lily B. *Shakespeare's Tragic Heroes: Slaves of Passion*. Cambridge, Eng., 1930.
Charlton, H. B. *Shakespearian Tragedy*. Cambridge, Eng., 1948.
Cunningham, J. V. *Woe or Wonder; the Emotional Effect of Shakespearean Tragedy*. Denver, 1951. Reprinted in *Tradition and Poetic Structure*. Denver, 1960.
Danson, Lawrence. *Tragic Alphabet: Shakespeare's Drama of Language*. New Haven and London, 1974.
Eliot, T. S. "Shakespeare and the Stoicism of Seneca," *Selected Essays, 1917–1932*. London, 1932.
Farnham, Willard. *Shakespeare's Tragic Frontier*. Berkeley, 1950.
Felperin, Howard. *Shakespearean Representation*. Princeton, 1977.
Frye, Northrop. *Fools of Time: Studies in Shakespearean Tragedy*. Toronto, 1967.
Harbage, Alfred, ed. *Shakespeare: The Tragedies*. Englewood Cliffs, N.J., 1964.
Hawkes, Terence. *Shakespeare and the Reason: A Study of the Tragedies and the Problem Plays*. London, 1964.
Holloway, John. *The Story of the Night: Studies in Shakespeare's Major Tragedies*. London and Lincoln, Neb., 1961.
Hunter, Robert Grams. *Shakespeare and the Mystery of God's Judgments*. Athens, Ga., 1976.
Knight, G. Wilson. *The Wheel of Fire*. London, 1930, 1965.
Lawlor, John. *The Tragic Sense in Shakespeare*. London, 1960.
Leech, Clifford. *Shakespeare's Tragedies and Other Studies in Seventeenth-Century Drama*. London, 1950.
———, ed. *Shakespeare: The Tragedies*. Chicago, 1965.
McElroy, Bernard. *Shakespeare's Mature Tragedies*. Princeton, 1973.
Mack, Maynard. "The Jacobean Shakespeare: Some Observations on the Construction of the Tragedies," *Jacobean Theatre*, ed. John Russell Brown and Bernard Harris. Stratford-upon-Avon Studies 1. London, 1960.
Mack, Maynard, Jr. *Killing the King: Three Studies in Shakespeare's Tragic Structure*. New Haven and London, 1973.
Proser, Matthew N. *The Heroic Image in Five Shakespearean Tragedies*. Princeton, 1965.
Rosen, William. *Shakespeare and the Craft of Tragedy*. Cambridge, Mass., 1960.
Sisson, C. J. *Shakespeare's Tragic Justice*. Scarborough, Ont., 1961.
Speaight, Robert. *Nature in Shakespearian Tragedy*. London, 1955.
Spivack, Bernard. *Shakespeare and the Allegory of Evil*. New York, 1958.
Sternfeld, F. W. *Music in Shakespearean Tragedy*. London and New York, 1963.
Stirlings, Brents. *Unity in Shakespearian Tragedy*. New York, 1956.
Whitaker, Virgil. *The Mirror up to Nature*. San Marino, Calif., 1965.
Wilson, Harold S. *On the Design of Shakespearian Tragedy*. Toronto, 1957.

The Greek and Roman Tragedies

Brower, Reuben A. *Hero and Saint: Shakespeare and the Graeco-Roman Heroic Tradition*. New York and Oxford, 1971.
Cantor, Paul A. *Shakespeare's Rome: Republic and Empire*. Ithaca and London, 1976.
Charney, Maurice, ed. *Discussions of Shakespeare's Roman Plays*. Boston, 1964.
———. *Shakespeare's Roman Plays: The Function of Imagery in the Drama*. Cambridge, Mass., 1961.
Knight, G. Wilson. *The Imperial Theme: Further Interpretations of Shakespeare's Tragedies Including the Roman Plays*. London, 1931, 1953.
MacCallum, M. W. *Shakespeare's Roman Plays and Their Background*. London, 1910.
Maxwell, J. C. "Shakespeare's Roman Plays: 1900–1956," *ShS 10* (1957), 1–11.
Nicoll, Allardyce, ed., *ShS 10* (1957).
Phillips, James E., Jr. *The State in Shakespeare's Greek and Roman Plays*. New York, 1940.
Simmons, J. L. *Shakespeare's Pagan World: The Roman Tragedies*. Charlottesville, Va., 1973.
Spencer, T. J. B. "Shakespeare and the Elizabethan Romans," *ShS 10* (1957), 27–38.
———. *William Shakespeare: The Roman Plays*. London, 1963.
Stampfer, Judah. *The Tragic Engagement: A Study of Shakespeare's Classical Tragedies*. New York, 1968.
Thomson, J. A. K. *Shakespeare and the Classics*. London, 1952.

Traversi, Derek. *Shakespeare: The Roman Plays.* Palo Alto, Calif., 1963.

Velz, John W. "The Ancient World in Shakespeare: Authenticity or Anachronism? A Retrospect," *ShS 31* (1978), 1–12.

———. *Shakespeare and the Classical Tradition: A Critical Guide to Commentary, 1660–1960.* Minneapolis, 1968.

Titus Andronicus

See also works listed under *The Tragedies,* above, especially by Brooke, Brown and Harris, Danson, and Spivack, and under *The Greek and Roman Tragedies,* especially by Maxwell, Spencer, and Thomson.

Adams, John C. "Shakespeare's Revisions in *Titus Andronicus,*" *SQ,* 15.2 (1964), 177–190.

Baker, Howard. *Induction to Tragedy.* Baton Rouge, La., 1939.

Barroll, J. Leeds. "Shakespeare and Roman History," *Modern Language Review,* 53 (1958), 327–343.

Bolton, Joseph. "*Titus Andronicus:* Shakespeare at Thirty," *Studies in Philology,* 30 (1933), 208–224.

Bowers, Fredson T. *Elizabethan Revenge Tragedy, 1587–1642.* Princeton, 1940.

Calderwood, James L. *Shakespearean Metadrama.* Minneapolis, 1971.

Cutts, John P. "Shadow and Substance: Structural Unity in *Titus Andronicus,*" *Comparative Drama,* 2 (1968), 161–172.

Hamilton, A. C. "*Titus Andronicus:* The Form of Shakespearian Tragedy," *SQ,* 14 (1963), 201–213.

Harris, Bernard. "A Portrait of a Moor," *ShS 11* (1958), 89–97.

Hunter, G. K. "Shakespeare's Earliest Tragedies: *Titus Andronicus* and *Romeo and Juliet,*" *ShS 27* (1974), 1–9.

Law, R. A. "The Roman Background of *Titus Andronicus,*" *Studies in Philology,* 40 (1943), 145–153.

Maxwell, J. C., ed. *Titus Andronicus.* The New Arden Shakespeare. London, 1953.

Price, Hereward T. "The Authorship of *Titus Andronicus,*" *Journal of English and Germanic Philology,* 42 (1943), 55–81.

Sargent, Ralph M. "The Source of *Titus Andronicus,*" *Studies in Philology,* 46 (1949), 167–183.

Sommers, Alan. " 'Wilderness of Tigers': Structure and Symbolism in *Titus Andronicus,*" *Essays in Criticism,* 10 (1960), 275–289.

Tricomi, Albert H. "The Aesthetics of Mutilation in *Titus Andronicus,*" *ShS 27* (1974), 11–19.

———. "The Mutilated Garden in *Titus Andronicus,*" *ShakS* 9 (1976), 89–105.

Waith, Eugene. "The Metamorphosis of Violence in *Titus Andronicus,*" *ShS 10* (1957), 39–49.

Wilson, J. Dover. "*Titus Andronicus* on the Stage in 1595," *ShS 1* (1948), 17–22.

Romeo and Juliet

See also works listed under *The Tragedies,* above, especially by Brown and Harris, Charlton, and Lawlor.

Adams, Barry B. "The Prudence of Prince Escalus," *English Literary History,* 35 (1968), 32–50.

Black, James. "The Visual Artistry of *Romeo and Juliet,*" *Studies in English Literature,* 15 (1975), 245–256.

Bowling, Lawrence E. "The Thematic Framework of *Romeo and Juliet,*" *PMLA,* 64 (1949), 208–220.

Bryant, James C. "The Problematic Friar in *Romeo and Juliet,*" *English Studies* (Amsterdam), 55 (1974), 340–350.

Dickey, Franklin M. *Not Wisely But Too Well.* San Marino, Calif., 1957.

Evans, Bertrand. "The Brevity of Friar Lawrence," *PMLA,* 65 (1950), 841–865.

Evans, Robert O. *The Osier Cage: Rhetorical Devices in "Romeo and Juliet."* Lexington, Ky., 1966.

Everett, Barbara. "*Romeo and Juliet:* The Nurse's Story," *Critical Quarterly,* 14 (1972), 129–139.

Granville-Barker, Harley. *Prefaces to Shakespeare,* vol. 2. Princeton, 1947.

Harrison, Thomas P. "*Romeo and Juliet, A Midsummer Night's Dream:* Companion Plays," *Texas Studies in Literature and Language,* 13 (1971–72), 209–213.

Hill, R. F. "Shakespeare's Early Tragic Mode," *SQ,* 9 (1958), 455–469.

Hosley, Richard. "The Use of the Upper Stage in *Romeo and Juliet,*" *SQ,* 5 (1954), 371–379.

Kahn, Coppélia. "Coming of Age in Verona," *Modern Language Studies,* 8 (1977–78), 5–22.

Leech, Clifford. "The Moral Tragedy of *Romeo and Juliet,*" *English Renaissance Drama,* ed. Standish Henning, Robert Kimbrough, and Richard Knowles. Carbondale, Ill., 1976.

Levin, Harry. "Form and Formality in *Romeo and Juliet,*" *SQ,* 11 (1960), 1–11.

Mahood, M. M. *Shakespeare's Wordplay.* London, 1957.

Moore, Olin H. *The Legend of Romeo and Juliet.* Columbus, Ohio, 1950.

Nevo, Ruth. "Tragic Form in *Romeo and Juliet,*" *Studies in English Literature,* 9 (1969), 241–258.

Nosworthy, J. M. "The Two Angry Families of Verona," *SQ,* 3 (1952), 219–226.

Pettet, E. C. "The Imagery of *Romeo and Juliet,*" *English,* 8 (1950), 121–126.

Siegel, Paul N. "Christianity and the Religion of Love in *Romeo and Juliet,*" *SQ,* 12 (1961), 371–392.

Snyder, Susan. "*Romeo and Juliet:* Comedy into Tragedy," *Essays in Criticism,* 20 (1970), 391–402.

Tanselle, G. Thomas. "Time in *Romeo and Juliet,*" *SQ,* 15.4 (1964), 349–361.

Utterback, Raymond V. "The Death of Mercutio," *SQ,* 24 (1973), 105–116.

Williams, George W., ed. *The Most Excellent and Lamentable Tragedie of Romeo and Juliet.* Durham, N.C., 1964.

Julius Caesar

See also works listed under *The Greek and Roman Tragedies,* above, especially by Brower, Charney, Knight, MacCallum, Phillips, Simmons, Traversi, and Velz.

Bonjour, Adrien. *The Structure of "Julius Caesar."* Liverpool, 1958.

Burckhardt, Sigurd. *Shakespearean Meanings.* Princeton, 1968.
Dorsch, T. S., ed. *Julius Caesar.* The Arden Shakespeare. London and Cambridge, Mass., 1955, 1970.
Foakes, R. A. "An Approach to *Julius Caesar*," *SQ,* 5 (1954), 259–270.
Granville-Barker, Harley. *Prefaces to Shakespeare,* vol. 2. Princeton, 1947.
Hartsock, Mildred E. "The Complexity of *Julius Caesar*," *PMLA,* 81 (1966), 56–62.
Hunter, Mark. "Politics and Character in Shakespeare's *Julius Caesar*," *Essays by Divers Hands, being the Transactions of the Royal Society of Literature,* n.s. 10 (1931), 109–140.
Knights, L. C. "Shakespeare and Political Wisdom: A Note on the Personalism of *Julius Caesar* and *Coriolanus*," *Sewanee Review,* 61 (1953), 43–55.
Levitsky, Ruth M. "The Elements Were So Mix'd . . ." *PMLA,* 88 (1973), 240–245.
Ornstein, Robert. "Seneca and the Political Drama of *Julius Caesar*," *Journal of English and Germanic Philology,* 57 (1958), 51–56.
Palmer, John. *Political Characters of Shakespeare.* London, 1945.
Rabkin, Norman. *Shakespeare and the Common Understanding.* New York, 1967.
Ribner, Irving. "Political Issues in *Julius Caesar*," *Journal of English and Germanic Philology,* 56 (1957), 10–22.
Schanzer, Ernest. *The Problem Plays of Shakespeare.* New York, 1963.
Stirling, Brents. *The Populace in Shakespeare.* New York, 1949.
Vawter, Marvin L. " 'After Their Fashion': Cicero and Brutus in *Julius Caesar*," *ShakS* 9 (1976), 205–219.
———. " 'Division 'tween Our Souls': Shakespeare's Stoic Brutus," *ShakS 7* (1974), 173–195.
Velz, John W. "Clemency, Will, and Just Cause in *Julius Caesar*," *ShS 22* (1969), 109–118.
———. " 'If I Were Brutus Now . . .': Role-Playing in *Julius Caesar*," *ShakS 4* (1968), 149–159.
———. "Undular Structure in *Julius Caesar*," *Modern Language Review,* 66 (1971), 21–30.
Yoder, R. A. "History and the Histories in *Julius Caesar*," *SQ,* 24 (1973), 309–327.

Hamlet

See also works listed under *The Tragedies,* above, especially by Bradley, Brower, Felperin, Holloway, Mack, Mack, Jr., Rosen, and Whitaker.
Alexander, Peter. *Hamlet: Father and Son.* New York and London, 1955.
Bevington, David, ed. *Twentieth Century Interpretations of "Hamlet."* Englewood Cliffs, N.J., 1968.
Booth, Stephen. "On the Value of *Hamlet*," *Reinterpretations of Elizabethan Drama,* ed. Norman Rabkin. New York, 1969.
Bowers, Fredson T. *Elizabethan Revenge Tragedy, 1587–1642.* Princeton, 1940.
———. "Hamlet as Minister and Scourge," *PMLA,* 70 (1955), 740–749.
Brown, John Russell, and Bernard Harris, eds. *Hamlet.* Stratford-upon-Avon Studies 5. London, 1963.
Charney, Maurice. *Style in "Hamlet."* Princeton, 1969.
Eliot, T. S. "Hamlet and His Problems," *Selected Essays, 1917–1932.* London and New York, 1932.
Elliott, G. R. *Scourge and Minister: A Study of "Hamlet" as a Tragedy of Revengefulness and Justice.* Durham, N.C., 1951.
Fergusson, Francis. *The Idea of a Theater.* Princeton, 1949.
Granville-Barker, Harley. *Prefaces to Shakespeare,* vol. 1. Princeton, 1946.
Hawkes, Terence. *Shakespeare's Talking Animals: Language and Drama in Society.* London, 1973.
Jones, Ernest. *Hamlet and Oedipus.* Rev. ed. New York, 1949, 1954.
Joseph, Bertram. *Conscience and the King.* London, 1953.
Kitto, H. D. F. *Form and Meaning in Drama.* London, 1956.
Knights, L. C. *An Approach to Hamlet.* London, 1960.
Levin, Harry. *The Question of Hamlet.* New York and London, 1959.
Lewis, C. S. "Hamlet: The Prince or the Poem?" *Proceedings of the British Academy,* 28 (1942), 139–154.
Mack, Maynard. "The World of *Hamlet*," *Yale Review,* 41 (1952), 502–523.
Nicoll, Allardyce, ed. *ShS* 9 (1956).
Prosser, Eleanor. *Hamlet and Revenge.* Stanford, 1967, 1971.
Righter, Anne. *Shakespeare and the Idea of the Play.* London and New York, 1962.
Rose, Mark. "*Hamlet* and the Shape of Revenge," *English Literary Renaissance,* 1 (1971), 132–143.
Tillyard, E. M. W. *Shakespeare's Problem Plays.* Toronto, 1949.
Walker, Roy. *The Time Is out of Joint: A Study of "Hamlet."* London and New York, 1948.
Wilson, J. Dover. *What Happens in "Hamlet."* London and New York, 1935, 1951.
Young, David. "Hamlet, Son of Hamlet," *Perspectives on "Hamlet,"* ed. William G. Holzberger and Peter B. Waldock. Lewisburg, Pa., and London, 1975.

Othello

See also works listed under *The Tragedies,* above, especially by Bradley, Hawkes, Holloway, Knight, Speaight, Spivack, and Wilson.
Bayley, John. *The Characters of Love.* London, 1960.
Dean, Leonard, ed. *A Casebook on "Othello."* New York, 1961.
Dickey, Franklin. *Not Wisely But Too Well.* San Marino, Calif., 1957.
Elliott, G. R. *Flaming Minister: A Study of "Othello" as Tragedy of Love and Hate.* Durham, N.C., 1953.
Everett, Barbara. "Reflections on the Sentimentalist's *Othello*," *Critical Quarterly,* 3 (1961), 127–139. A comment on Leavis article below.
Gardner, Helen. *The Noble Moor.* London, 1955.
Granville-Barker, Harley. *Prefaces to Shakespeare,* vol. 2. Princeton, 1947.
Heilman, Robert B. *Magic in the Web: Action and Language in "Othello."* Lexington, Ky., 1956.

Hyman, Stanley Edgar. *Iago: Some Approaches to the Illusion of His Motivation.* New York, 1970.
Jones, Eldred. *Othello's Countrymen: The African in English Renaissance Drama.* London, 1965.
Kernan, Alvin B., ed. *The Tragedy of Othello.* New York, 1963.
Kirsch, Arthur. "The Polarization of Erotic Love in *Othello,*" *Modern Language Review,* 73 (1978), 721–740.
Kirschbaum, Leo. "The Modern *Othello,*" *English Literary History,* 11 (1944), 283–296.
Leavis, F. R. "Diabolic Intellect and the Noble Hero: or The Sentimentalist's Othello," *The Common Pursuit.* London, 1952. A criticism of items by Bradley and Stoll on this list.
Muir, Kenneth, ed. *Shakepeare Survey 21* (1968).
Neely, Carol Thomas. "Women and Men in *Othello;* "what should such a fool / Do with so good a woman?" *ShakS 10* (1977), 133–158.
Nowottny, Winifred M. T. "Justice and Love in *Othello,*" *University of Toronto Quarterly,* 21 (1952), 330–344.
Rosenberg, Marvin. *The Masks of "Othello."* Berkeley and Los Angeles, 1961.
Seltzer, Daniel. "Elizabethan Acting in *Othello,*" *SQ,* 10 (1959), 201–210.
Sewell, Arthur. *Character and Society in Shakespeare.* London, 1951.
Snyder, Susan. "*Othello* and the Conventions of Romantic Comedy," *Renaissance Drama,* n.s. 5 (1972), 123–141.
Stoll, E. E. *From Shakespeare to Joyce.* New York, 1944.
———. *"Othello": An Historical and Comparative Study.* Minneapolis, 1964.

King Lear

See also works listed under *The Tragedies,* above, especially by Bradley, Brower, Cunningham, Holloway, R. G. Hunter, Knight, Rosen, Speaight, and Wilson.
Barnet, Sylvan. "Some Limitations of a Christian Approach to Shakespeare," *English Literary History,* 22 (1955), 81–92.
Brooke, Nicholas. *Shakespeare: "King Lear."* London, 1963.
Burkhardt, Sigurd. *Shakespearean Meanings.* Princeton, 1968.
Cavell, Stanley. "The Avoidance of Love: A Reading of *King Lear,*" *Must We Mean What We Say?* New York, 1969.
Colie, Rosalie L., and F. T. Flahiff, eds. *Some Facets of "King Lear."* Toronto, 1974.
Danby, John F. "*King Lear* and Christian Patience: A Culmination," *Poets on Fortune's Hill.* London, 1952. Reprinted as *Elizabethan and Jacobean Poets.* London, 1964.
———. *Shakespeare's Doctrine of Nature: A Study of "King Lear."* London, 1949.
Elton, William R. *King Lear and the Gods.* San Marino, Calif., 1966.
Empson, William. *The Structure of Complex Words.* London, 1951.
Everett, Barbara. "The New *King Lear,*" *Critical Quarterly,* 2 (1960), 325–339.
Felperin, Howard. *Shakespearean Romance.* Princeton, 1972.
Fly, Richard D. *Shakespeare's Mediated World.* Amherst, 1976.
Fraser, Russell A. *Shakespeare's Poetics in Relation to "King Lear."* London, 1962.
Freud, Sigmund. "The Theme of the Three Caskets," *Complete Psychological Works of Sigmund Freud,* 12 (1911–1913), pp. 291–301. London, 1958.
Goldberg, S. L. *An Essay on "King Lear."* Cambridge, Eng., 1974.
Granville-Barker, Harley. *Prefaces to Shakespeare,* vol. 1. Princeton, 1946.
Hardison, O. B., Jr. "Myth and History in *King Lear,*" *SQ,* 26 (1975), 227–242.
Heilman, Robert B. *This Great Stage: Image and Structure in "King Lear."* Baton Rouge, La., 1948.
Jaffa, Harry V. "The Limits of Politics: *King Lear,* Act I, scene i," *Shakespeare's Politics,* by Allan Bloom with Harry V. Jaffa. New York and London, 1964.
James, D. G. *The Dream of Learning.* Oxford, 1951.
Jorgensen, Paul A. *Lear's Self-Discovery.* Berkeley and Los Angeles, 1967.
Keast, W. "Imagery and Meaning in the Interpretation of *King Lear,*" *Modern Philology,* 47 (1949), 45–64.
Kernan, Alvin. "Formalism and Realism in Elizabethan Drama: The Miracles in *King Lear,*" *Renaissance Drama,* 9 (1966), 59–66.
Knights, L. C. *Some Shakespearean Themes.* London, 1959.
Lothian, J. M. *"King Lear": A Tragic Reading of Life.* Toronto, 1949.
Mack, Maynard. *King Lear in Our Time.* Berkeley and Los Angeles, 1965.
Maclean, Norman. "Episode, Scene, Speech, and Word: The Madness of Lear," *Critics and Criticism,* ed. R. S. Crane. Chicago, 1952.
Muir, Kenneth, ed. *King Lear.* The Arden Shakespeare. London and Cambridge, Mass., 1952, 1959.
Nicoll, Allardyce, ed. *Shakespeare Survey 13* (1960).
Rosenberg, Marvin. *The Masks of "King Lear."* Berkeley and Los Angeles, 1972.
Sewall, Richard B. *The Vision of Tragedy.* New Haven, 1959.
Sewell, Arthur. *Character and Society in Shakespeare.* London, 1951.
Stoll, E. E. *Art and Artifice in Shakespeare.* Cambridge, Eng., 1933, 1962.
Young, David. *The Heart's Forest: A Study of Shakespeare's Pastoral Plays.* New Haven and London, 1972.

Macbeth

See also works listed under *The Tragedies,* above, especially by Bradley, Farnham, Holloway, R. G. Hunter, Lawlor, Mack, Mack, Jr., Rosen, Speaight, and Wilson.
Bartholomeusz, Dennis. *Macbeth and the Players.* Cambridge, Eng., 1969.
Blisset, William. " 'The Secret'st Man of Blood': A Study of Dramatic Irony in *Macbeth,*" *SQ,* 10 (1959), 397–408.
Brooks, Cleanth. *The Well Wrought Urn.* New York, 1947.
Curry, Walter Clyde. *Shakespeare's Philosophical Patterns.* Baton Rouge, La., 1937.
Driver, Tom. *The Sense of History in Greek and Shakespearean Drama.* New York, 1960.

Elliott, G. R. *Dramatic Providence in "Macbeth."* Princeton, 1958.
Fergusson, Francis. "*Macbeth* as the Imitation of an Action," *English Institute Essays 1951* (1952), 31–43.
Gardner, Helen. "Milton's 'Satan' and the Theme of Damnation in Elizabethan Tragedy," *English Association Essays and Studies,* n.s., 1 (1948), 46–66.
Hawkes, Terence, ed. *Twentieth Century Interpretations of "Macbeth."* Englewood Cliffs, N.J., 1976.
Jorgensen, Paul A. *Our Naked Frailties.* Berkeley and Los Angeles, 1971.
Knights, L. C. *Some Shakespearean Themes.* London, 1959.
Mullin, Michael. "Augures and Understood Relations: Theodore Komisarjevsky's *Macbeth,*" *Educational Theatre Journal,* 26 (March, 1974), 20–30.
———. "*Macbeth* at Stratford-upon-Avon, 1955," *ShakS 9* (1976), 269–282.
———. "Strange Images of Death: Sir Herbert Beerbohm Tree's *Macbeth,* 1911," *Theatre Survey,* 17 (1976), 125–142.
Muir, Kenneth, ed. *Macbeth.* The Arden Shakespeare. London and Cambridge, Mass., 1951.
———, ed. *Shakespeare Survey 19* (1966).
Paul, Henry N. *The Royal Play of Macbeth.* New York, 1950.
Rosenberg, Marvin. *The Masks of "Macbeth."* Berkeley and Los Angeles, 1978.
Sewell, Arthur. *Character and Society in Shakespeare.* London, 1951.
Spender, Stephen. "Time, Violence, and *Macbeth,*" *Penguin New Writing,* 3. London, 1940–1941.
Stoll, E. E. *From Shakespeare to Joyce.* New York, 1944.
Walker, Roy. *The Time Is Free.* London and New York, 1949.

Timon of Athens

See also works listed under *The Tragedies,* above, especially by Farnham, Knight, and Wilson, and under *The Greek and Roman Tragedies.*
Bergeron, David M. "Alchemy and *Timon of Athens,*" *College Language Association Journal,* 13 (1970), 364–373.
Bradbrook, Muriel C. *Shakespeare the Craftsman.* London and New York, 1969.
Butler, Francelia. *The Strange Critical Fortunes of Shakespeare's "Timon of Athens."* Ames, Iowa, 1966.
Campbell, Oscar James. *Shakespeare's Satire.* London and New York, 1943, 1963.
Collins, A. S. "*Timon of Athens:* A Reconsideration," *Review of English Studies,* 22 (1946), 96–108.
Cook, David. "*Timon of Athens,*" *ShS 16* (1963), 83–94.
Ellis-Fermor, Una. "*Timon of Athens:* An Unfinished Play," *Review of English Studies,* 18 (1942), 270–283.
Empson, William. *The Structure of Complex Words.* London, 1951.
Fly, Richard D. *Shakespeare's Mediated World.* Amherst, 1976.
Honigmann, E. A. J. "*Timon of Athens,*" *SQ,* 12 (1961), 3–20.
Kernan, Alvin B. *The Cankered Muse: Satire of the English Renaissance.* New Haven, 1959.
Lancashire, Anne. "*Timon of Athens:* Shakespeare's Dr. Faustus," *SQ,* 21 (1970), 35–44.
Levin, Harry. "Shakespeare's Misanthrope," *ShS 26* (1973), 89–94.
Levitsky, Ruth. "*Timon: Shakespeare's Magnyfycence* and an Embryonic *Lear,*" *ShakS 11* (1978), 107–121.
Maxwell, J. C. "Timon of Athens," *Scrutiny,* 15 (1948), 195–208.
Merchant, W. Moelwyn. "*Timon of Athens* and the Visual Conceit," *Shakespeare and the Artist.* London, 1959.
Nowottny, Winifred M. T. "Acts IV and V of *Timon of Athens,*" *SQ,* 10 (1959), 493–497.
Oliver, H. J., ed. *Timon of Athens.* The Arden Shakespeare. London and Cambridge, Mass., 1959.
Pettet, E. C. "*Timon of Athens:* The Disruption of Feudal Morality," *Review of English Studies,* 23 (1947), 321–336.
Soellner, Rolf. *Timon of Athens: Shakespeare's Pessimistic Tragedy.* With a Stage History by Gary Jay Williams. Columbus, Ohio, 1979.
Walker, Lewis. "Fortune and Friendship in *Timon of Athens,*" *Texas Studies in Literature and Language,* 18 (1977), 577–600.
Williams, Stanley T. "Some Versions of *Timon of Athens* on the Stage," *Modern Philology,* 18 (1920), 269–285.

Antony and Cleopatra

See also works listed under *The Tragedies,* above, especially by Farnham, Mack, Holloway, Proser, and Rosen, and under *The Greek and Roman Tragedies,* especially by Brower, Cantor, Charney, Maxwell, Simmons, Spencer, and Traversi.
Adelman, Janet. *The Common Liar: An Essay on "Antony and Cleopatra."* New Haven and London, 1973.
Barnet, Sylvan. "Recognition and Reversal in *Antony and Cleopatra,*" *SQ,* 8 (1957), 331–334.
Barroll, J. Leeds. "Antony and Pleasure," *Journal of English and Germanic Philology,* 57 (1958), 708–720.
Bethell, S. L. *Shakespeare and the Popular Dramatic Tradition.* London and Durham, N.C., 1944.
Bradley, A. C. *Oxford Lectures on Poetry.* London, 1909, 1961.
Burke, Kenneth. "Shakespearean Persuasion: *Antony and Cleopatra,*" *Language as Symbolic Action: Essays on Life, Literature, and Method.* Berkeley and Los Angeles, 1966.
Danby, John. *Elizabethan and Jacobean Poets.* London, 1964.
Felperin, Howard. *Shakespearean Romance.* Princeton, 1972.
Frost, David L. *The School of Shakespeare.* Cambridge, Eng., 1968.
Granville-Barker, Harley. *Prefaces to Shakespeare,* vol. 1. Princeton, 1946.
Kaula, David. "The Time Sense of *Antony and Cleopatra,*" *SQ,* 15.3 (1964), 211–223.
Knights, L. C. *Some Shakespearean Themes.* London, 1959.
Leavis, F. R. "*Antony and Cleopatra* and *All for Love:* A Critical Exercise," *Scrutiny,* 5 (1936–1937), 158–169.

Lloyd, Michael. "Cleopatra as Isis," *ShS 12* (1959), 88–94.
Mack, Maynard. "*Antony and Cleopatra:* The Stillness and the Dance," *Shakespeare's Art: Seven Essays,* ed. Milton Crane. Chicago, 1973.
———, ed. *Antony and Cleopatra.* Pelican Shakespeare. Baltimore, 1960.
Markels, Julian. *The Pillar of the World.* Columbus, Ohio, 1968.
Ornstein, Robert. "The Ethic of the Imagination: Love and Art in *Antony and Cleopatra,*" *Later Shakespeare,* ed. John Russell Brown and Bernard Harris, pp. 31–46. Stratford-upon-Avon Studies 8. London, 1966.
Palmer, John. *Political Characters of Shakespeare.* London, 1945.
Rackin, Phyllis. "Shakespeare's Boy Cleopatra, the Decorum of Nature, and the Golden World of Poetry," *PMLA,* 87 (1972), 201–212.
Reimer, A. P. *A Reading of Shakespeare's "Antony and Cleopatra."* Sydney, 1968.
Rose, Mark, ed. *Twentieth Century Interpretations of "Antony and Cleopatra."* Englewood Cliffs, N.J., 1976.
Schanzer, Ernest. *The Problem Plays of Shakespeare.* New York, 1963.
Stewart, J. I. M. *Character and Motive in Shakespeare.* London, 1949.
Waith, Eugene. *The Herculean Hero in Marlowe, Chapman, Shakespeare, and Dryden.* New York, 1962.

Coriolanus

See also works listed under *The Tragedies,* above, especially by Danson, Farnham, Holloway, and Rosen, and under *The Greek and Roman Tragedies,* especially by Brower, Cantor, and Charney.
Adelman, Janet. " 'Anger's My Meat': Feeding, Dependency, and Aggression in *Coriolanus,*" *Shakespeare, Pattern of Excelling Nature,* ed. David Bevington and Jay L. Halio, Newark, Del., 1978.
Berry, Ralph. "The Metamorphoses of *Coriolanus,*" *SQ,* 26 (1975), 172–183.
———. "Sexual Imagery in *Coriolanus,*" *Studies in English Literature,* 13 (1973), 301–316.
Bradley, A. C. *A Miscellany.* London, 1929.
Brockman, B. A., ed. *Shakespeare's "Coriolanus": A Casebook.* London, 1977.
Browning, I. R. "Coriolanus—'Boy of Tears,' " *Essays in Criticism,* 5 (1955), 18–31.
Burke, Kenneth. "Coriolanus—and the Delights of Faction," *Hudson Review,* 19 (1966–1967), 185–202.
Calderwood, James L. "*Coriolanus:* Wordless Meanings and Meaningless Words," *Studies in English Literature,* 6 (1966), 211–224.
Granville-Barker, Harley. *Prefaces to Shakespeare,* vol. 2. Princeton, 1947.
Huffman, Clifford Chalmers. *"Coriolanus" in Context.* Lewisburg, Pa., 1971.
Knights, L. C. *Some Shakespearean Themes.* London, 1959.
McCanles, Michael. "The Dialectic of Transcendence in Shakespeare's *Coriolanus,*" *PMLA,* 82 (1967), 44–53.
MacLure, Millar. "Shakespeare and the Lonely Dragon," *University of Toronto Quarterly,* 24 (1955), 109–120.
Maxwell, J. C. "Animal Imagery in *Coriolanus,*" *Modern Language Review,* 42 (1947), 417–421.
Oliver, H. J. "Coriolanus as Tragic Hero," *SQ,* 10 (1959), 53–60.
Phillips, James E., Jr., ed. *Twentieth Century Interpretations of "Coriolanus."* Englewood Cliffs, N.J., 1970.
Rabkin, Norman. "*Coriolanus:* The Tragedy of Politics," *SQ,* 17 (1966), 195–212.
Stockholder, Katherine. "The Other Coriolanus," *PMLA,* 85 (1970), 228–236.
Waith, Eugene. *The Herculean Hero in Marlowe, Chapman, Shakespeare, and Dryden.* New York, 1962.

The Romances

Bentley, Gerald Eades. "Shakespeare and the Blackfriars Theatre," *ShS 1* (1948), 38–50.
Brown, John Russell, and Bernard Harris, eds. *Later Shakespeare.* Stratford-upon-Avon Studies 8. London, 1966.
Danby, John F. *Poets on Fortune's Hill.* London, 1952. Reprinted as *Elizabethan and Jacobean Poets.* London, 1964.
Edwards, Philip. "Shakespeare's Romances: 1900–1957," *ShS 11* (1958), 1–18. See also other articles in this issue.
Felperin, Howard. *Shakespearean Romance.* Princeton, 1972.
Foakes, R. A. *Shakespeare: From the Dark Comedies to the Last Plays.* London and Charlottesville, Va., 1971.
Frye, Northrop. *Anatomy of Criticism.* Princeton, 1957.
———. *A Natural Perspective: The Development of Shakespearean Comedy and Romance.* New York, 1965.
———. *The Secular Scripture: A Study of the Structure of Romance.* Cambridge, Mass., 1976.
Gesner, Carol. *Shakespeare and the Greek Romance: A Study of Origins.* Lexington, Ky., 1970.
Hartwig, Joan. *Shakespeare's Tragicomic Vision.* Baton Rouge, 1972.
Hoeniger, F. David. "Shakespeare's Romances since 1958: A Retrospect," *ShS 29* (1976), 1–10.
Hunter, Robert Grams. *Shakespeare and the Comedy of Forgiveness.* New York, 1965.
James, D. G. "The Failure of the Ballad-Makers," *Scepticism and Poetry.* London, 1937.
Kay, Carol McGinnis, and Henry E. Jacobs, eds. *Shakespeare's Romances Reconsidered.* Lincoln, Neb., 1978.
Kermode, Frank. *William Shakespeare: The Final Plays.* London, 1963.
Knight, G. Wilson. *The Crown of Life.* London, 1947, 1966.
———. *The Shakespearian Tempest.* London, 1932, 1953.
Leavis, F. R. "A Criticism of Shakespeare's Last Plays," *Scrutiny,* 10 (1942), 339–345; reprinted in *The Common Pursuit.* London, 1952.
Marsh, D. R. C. *The Recurring Miracle: A Study of "Cymbeline" and the Last Plays.* Pietermaritzburg, Natal, 1962, 1964.
Mowat, Barbara A. *The Dramaturgy of Shakespeare's Romances.* Athens, Ga., 1976.
Peterson, Douglas L. *Time, Tide, and Tempest: A Study of Shakespeare's Romances.* San Marino, Calif., 1973.

Pettet, E. C. *Shakespeare and the Romance Tradition.* London, 1949.

Seltzer, Daniel. "The Staging of the Last Plays," *Later Shakespeare,* ed. John Russell Brown and Bernard Harris, pp. 127–165. Stratford-upon-Avon Studies 8. London, 1966.

Smith, Hallett. *Shakespeare's Romances.* San Marino, Calif., 1972.

Spencer, Theodore. "Appearance and Reality in Shakespeare's Last Plays," *Modern Philology,* 39 (1942), 265–274.

Strachey, Lytton. "Shakespeare's Final Period," *Books and Characters.* London, 1922.

Tillyard, E. M. W. *Shakespeare's Last Plays.* London, 1938, 1964.

Tobias, Richard C., and Paul G. Zolbrod, eds. *Shakespeare's Late Plays.* Athens, Ohio, 1974.

Traversi, Derek. *Shakespeare: The Last Phase.* New York, 1954.

Wells, Stanley. "Shakespeare and Romance," *Later Shakespeare,* ed. John Russell Brown and Bernard Harris, pp. 49–79. Stratford-upon-Avon Studies 8. London, 1966.

Yates, Frances A. *Shakespeare's Last Plays: A New Approach.* London, 1975.

Young, David. *The Heart's Forest: A Study of Shakespeare's Pastoral Plays.* New Haven and London, 1972.

Pericles

See also works listed under *The Romances,* above, especially by Danby and Peterson.

Arthos, John. "*Pericles, Prince of Tyre:* A Study in the Dramatic Use of Romantic Narrative," *SQ,* 4 (1953), 257–270.

Barber, C. L. " 'Thou That Beget'st Him That Did Thee Beget': Transformation in *Pericles* and *The Winter's Tale,*" *ShS 22* (1969), 59–67.

Berry, Francis. "Word and Picture in the Final Plays," *Later Shakespeare,* ed. John Russell Brown and Bernard Harris, pp. 81–101. Stratford-upon-Avon Studies 8. London, 1966.

Brockbank, J. Philip. "*Pericles* and the Dream of Immortality," *ShS 24* (1971), 105–116.

Craig, Hardin. "*Pericles* and *The Painfull Adventures,*" *Studies in Philology,* 45 (1948), 600–605.

Edwards, Philip. "An Approach to the Problem of *Pericles,*" *ShS 5* (1952), 25–49.

Hoeniger, F. D., ed. *Pericles.* The Arden Shakespeare. London and Cambridge, Mass., 1963.

Muir, Kenneth. *Shakespeare as Collaborator.* London, 1960.

Tompkins, J. M. S. "Why *Pericles?*" *Review of English Studies,* n.s., 3 (1952), 315–324.

Cymbeline

See also works listed under *The Romances,* above, especially by Felperin, Frye, Gesner, R. G. Hunter, Kay, Marsh, and Mowat.

Brockbank, J. Philip. "History and Histrionics in *Cymbeline,*" *ShS 11* (1958), 42–49.

Foakes, R. A. "Character and Dramatic Technique in *Cymbeline* and *The Winter's Tale,*" *Studies in the Arts: Proceedings of the St. Peter's College Literary Society.* Oxford, 1968.

Granville-Barker, Harley. *Prefaces to Shakespeare,* vol. 1. Princeton, 1946.

Harris, Bernard. " 'What's past is prologue': *Cymbeline* and *Henry VIII,*" *Later Shakespeare,* ed. John Russell Brown and Bernard Harris, pp. 203–233. Stratford-upon-Avon Studies 8. London, 1966.

Hoeniger, F. D. "Irony and Romance in *Cymbeline,*" *Studies in English Literature,* 2 (1962), 219–228.

Jones, Emrys. "Stuart *Cymbeline,*" *Essays in Criticism,* 11 (1961), 84–99.

Kirsch, Arthur C. "*Cymbeline* and Coterie Dramaturgy," *English Literary History,* 34 (1967), 285–306.

Lawrence, W. W. *Shakespeare's Problem Comedies.* New York, 1931, 1960.

Leggatt, Alexander. "The Island of Miracles: An Approach to *Cymbeline,*" *ShakS 10* (1977), 191–209.

Nosworthy, J. M. "The Integrity of Shakespeare: Illustrated from *Cymbeline,*" *ShS 8* (1955), 52–56.

———, ed. *Cymbeline.* The New Arden Shakespeare. London, 1955.

Stephenson, A. A. "The Significance of *Cymbeline,*" *Scrutiny,* 10 (1942), 329–338.

Swander, Homer D. "*Cymbeline* and the 'Blameless Hero,' " *English Literary History,* 31 (1964), 259–270.

———. "*Cymbeline:* Religious Idea and Dramatic Design," *Pacific Coast Studies in Shakespeare,* ed. Waldo F. McNeir and Thelma N. Greenfield. Eugene, Ore., 1966.

Warren, Roger. "Theatrical Virtuosity and Poetic Complexity in *Cymbeline,*" *ShS 29* (1976), 41–50.

Wilson, Harold S. "*Philaster* and *Cymbeline,*" *English Institute Essays 1951,* ed. Alan Downer, pp. 146–167. New York, 1952.

The Winter's Tale

See also works listed under *The Romances,* above, especially by Felperin, Foakes, Hartwig, R. G. Hunter, Kay, Knight, Mowat, and Young.

Barber, C. L. " 'Thou That Beget'st Him That Did Thee Beget': Transformation in *Pericles* and *The Winter's Tale,*" *ShS 22* (1969), 59–67.

Bethell, S. L. *The Winter's Tale: A Study.* London, 1947.

Bryant, J. A., Jr. "Shakespeare's Allegory: *The Winter's Tale,*" *Sewanee Review,* 63 (1955), 202–222.

Coghill, Nevill. "Six Points of Stage-Craft in *The Winter's Tale,*" *ShS 11* (1958), 31–41.

Ewbank, Inga-Stina. "The Triumph of Time in *The Winter's Tale,*" *Review of English Literature,* 5.2 (1964), 83–100.

Foakes, R. A. "Character and Dramatic Technique in *Cymbeline* and *The Winter's Tale,*" *Studies in the Arts: Proceedings of the St. Peter's College Literary Society.* Oxford, 1968.

Frye, Northrop. "Recognition in *The Winter's Tale,*" *Essays on Shakespeare and Elizabethan Drama in Honor of*

Hardin Craig, ed. R. Hosley, pp. 235–246. Columbia, Mo., 1962.

Hoeniger, F. D. "The Meaning of *The Winter's Tale*," *University of Toronto Quarterly*, 20 (1950), 11–26.

Lawlor, John. "*Pandosto* and the Nature of Dramatic Romance," *Philological Quarterly*, 41 (1962), 96–113.

Lindenbaum, Peter. "Time, Sexual Love, and the Uses of Pastoral in *The Winter's Tale*," *Modern Language Quarterly*, 33 (1972), 3–22.

Neely, Carol Thomas. "*The Winter's Tale:* The Triumph of Speech," *Studies in English Literature*, 15 (1975), 321–338.

Proudfoot, G. Richard. "Verbal Reminiscence and the Two-Part Structure of *The Winter's Tale*," *ShS 29* (1976), 67–78.

Pyle, Fitzroy. *The Winter's Tale: A Commentary on the Structure*. London, 1968.

Schanzer, Ernest. "The Structural Pattern of *The Winter's Tale*," *Review of English Literature*, 5.2 (1964), 72–82.

Siemon, James Edward. " 'But It Appears She Lives': Iteration in *The Winter's Tale*," *PMLA*, 89 (1974), 10–16.

Tayler, Edward W. *Nature and Art in Renaissance Literature*. New York, 1964.

Tinkler, F. C. "*The Winter's Tale*," *Scrutiny*, 5 (1937), 344–364.

Williams, John Anthony. *The Natural Work of Art: The Experience of Romance in Shakespeare's "Winter's Tale."* Cambridge, Mass., 1967.

The Tempest

See also works listed under *The Romances*, above, especially by Frye, Gesner, Hartwig, Kay, Mowat, Peterson, Tobias and Zolbrod, Yates, and Young.

Allen, Don Cameron. *Image and Meaning*. Baltimore, 1960, 2nd ed., enl., 1968.

Auden, W. H. "The Sea and the Mirror," *The Collected Poetry*. New York, 1945.

Berger, Harry, Jr. "Miraculous Harp: A Reading of Shakespeare's *Tempest*," *ShakS 5* (1969), 253–283.

Berger, Karol. "Prospero's Art," *ShakS 10* (1977), 211–239.

Brockbank, Philip. "*The Tempest:* Conventions of Art and Empire," *Later Shakespeare*, ed. John Russell Brown and Bernard Harris, pp. 183–201. Stratford-upon-Avon Studies 8. London, 1966.

Brower, Reuben. "The Mirror of Analogy," *The Fields of Light*. New York, 1951.

Coleridge, S. T. "Lectures on Shakespeare and Milton: The Ninth Lecture," *Shakespearean Criticism*, 2 vols., ed. T. M. Raysor, vol. 2, 121–140. 2nd ed. London, 1960.

Curry, Walter Clyde. *Shakespeare's Philosophical Patterns*. Baton Rouge, La., 1937, 1968.

Frey, Charles. "*The Tempest* and the New World," *SQ*, 30 (1979), 29–41.

Frye, Northrop, ed. *The Tempest*. Pelican Shakespeare. Baltimore, 1959.

Hoeniger, F. D. "Prospero's Storm and Miracle," *SQ*, 7 (1956), 33–38.

James, D. G. *The Dream of Prospero*. Oxford, 1967.

Johnson, W. Stacy. "The Genesis of Ariel," *SQ*, 2 (1951), 205–210.

Kermode, Frank, ed. *The Tempest*. The Arden Shakespeare. London, 1958.

Knox, Bernard. "*The Tempest* and the Ancient Comic Tradition," *English Stage Comedy*, ed. W. K. Wimsatt. *English Institute Essays 1954*. New York, 1955.

Kott, Jan. "*The Tempest*, or Repetition," *Mosaic*, 10.3 (1977), 9–36.

McPeek, James. "The Genesis of Caliban," *Philological Quarterly*, 25 (1946), 378–381.

Marx, Leo. "Shakespeare's American Fable," *The Machine in the Garden: Technology and the Pastoral Ideal in America*. London and New York, 1964.

Palmer, D. J., ed. *Shakespeare, "The Tempest": A Casebook*. London, 1968.

Pearson, D'Orsay W. " 'Unless I Be Reliev'd by Prayer': *The Tempest* in Perspective," *ShakS 7* (1974), 253–282.

Reed, Robert R., Jr. "The Probable Origin of Ariel," *SQ*, 11 (1960), 61–65.

Smith, Hallett, ed. *Twentieth Century Interpretations of "The Tempest."* Englewood Cliffs, N.J., 1969.

Still, Colin. *The Timeless Theme*. London, 1936, 1947. Originally published as *Shakespeare's Mystery Play: A Study of "The Tempest,"* 1921.

Stoll, E. E. "*The Tempest*," *PMLA*, 47 (1932), 699–726.

William, David. "*The Tempest* on the Stage," *Jacobean Theatre*, ed. John Russell Brown and Bernard Harris, pp. 133–157. Stratford-upon-Avon Studies 1. London, 1960.

Wilson, J. Dover. *The Meaning of "The Tempest."* Newcastle, 1936.

The Poems

Bradbrook, Muriel C. *Shakespeare and Elizabethan Poetry*. London, 1951.

Bush, Douglas. *Mythology and the Renaissance Tradition in English Poetry*. Minneapolis and London, 1932; rev. ed., 1963.

Cruttwell, Patrick. *The Shakespearean Moment and Its Place in the Poetry of the Seventeenth Century*. London, 1954.

Maxwell, J. C., ed. *The Poems*. The New Cambridge Shakespeare. London, 1969.

Prince, F. T. *William Shakespeare: The Poems*. London, 1963.

Rollins, Hyder E. *A New Variorum Edition of Shakespeare: The Poems*. Philadelphia, 1938.

Shakespeare Survey 15 (1962). Devoted chiefly to the poems and music, including the Sonnets.

Shakespeare, William. *Shakespeare's Poems: A Facsimile of the Earliest Editions*. New Haven, 1964.

Venus and Adonis

Allen, Michael J. B. "The Chase: The Development of a Renaissance Theme," *Comparative Literature*, 20 (1968), 301–312. (Includes discussion of *Venus and Adonis*.)

Asals, Heather. "*Venus and Adonis:* The Education of a Goddess," *Studies in English Literature*, 13 (1973), 31–51.

Beauregard, David N. "*Venus and Adonis:* Shakespeare's Representation of the Passions," *ShakS 8* (1975), 83–98.

Hamilton, A. C. "*Venus and Adonis,*" *Studies in English Literature,* 1.1 (1961), 1–15.

Jahn, J. D. "The Lamb of Lust: The Role of Adonis in Shakespeare's *Venus and Adonis,*" *ShakS* 6 (1970), 11–25.

Kahn, Coppélia. "Self and Eros in *Venus and Adonis,*" *Centennial Review,* 4 (1976), 351–371.

Muir, Kenneth. "*Venus and Adonis:* Comedy or Tragedy?" *Shakespearean Essays,* ed. Alwin Thaler and Norman Sanders. Knoxville, Tenn., 1964.

Price, Hereward T. "The Function of Imagery in *Venus and Adonis,*" *Papers of the Michigan Academy,* 31 (1945), 275–297.

Rabkin, Norman. "*Venus and Adonis* and the Myth of Love," *Pacific Coast Studies in Shakespeare,* ed. Waldo F. McNeir and Thelma N. Greenfield. Eugene, Ore., 1966.

Rebhorn, Wayne A. "Mother Venus: Temptation in Shakespeare's *Venus and Adonis,*" *ShakS 11* (1978), 1–29.

Sheidley, William E. " 'Unless It Be a Boar': Love and Wisdom in Shakespeare's *Venus and Adonis,*" *Modern Language Quarterly,* 35 (1974), 3–15.

Streitberger, W. R. "Ideal Conduct in *Venus and Adonis,*" *SQ,* 26 (1975), 285–291.

The Rape of Lucrece

Allen, Don Cameron. "Some Observations on *The Rape of Lucrece,*" *ShS 15* (1962), 89–98.

Hulse, S. Clarke. " 'A Piece of Skilful Painting' in Shakespeare's *Lucrece,*" *ShS 31* (1978), 13–22.

Kahn, Coppélia. "The Rape in Shakespeare's *Lucrece,*" *ShakS 9* (1976), 45–72.

Lever, J. W. "Introduction," *The Rape of Lucrece.* The New Penguin Shakespeare. New York, 1971.

Majors, G. W. "Shakespeare's First Brutus: His Role in *Lucrece,*" *Modern Language Quarterly,* 35 (1974), 339–351.

Walley, Harold R. "*The Rape of Lucrece* and Shakespearean Tragedy," *PMLA,* 76 (1961), 480–487.

The Phoenix and Turtle

Alvarez, A. "William Shakespeare: *The Phoenix and the Turtle,*" *Interpretations,* ed. John Wain. London, 1955.

Ellrodt, Robert. "An Anatomy of *The Phoenix and the Turtle,*" *ShS 15* (1962), 99–110.

Empson, William. "*The Phoenix and the Turtle,*" *Essays in Criticism,* 16 (1966), 147–153.

Knight, G. Wilson. *The Mutual Flame: On Shakespeare's Sonnets and The Phoenix and the Turtle.* London, 1955.

Matchett, William H. *The Phoenix and the Turtle: Shakespeare's Poem and Chester's Loues Martyr.* The Hague, 1965.

Petronella, Vincent F. "Shakespeare's *The Phoenix and the Turtle* and the Defunctive Music of Ecstasy," *ShakS 8* (1975), 311–331.

Underwood, Richard A. *Shakespeare's "The Phoenix and Turtle": A Survey of Scholarship.* Salzburg, 1974.

A Lover's Complaint

Muir, Kenneth. "*A Lover's Complaint:* A Reconsideration," *Shakespeare 1564–1964,* ed. E. A. Bloom, pp. 154–166. Providence, 1964.

Sonnets

Allen, Michael J. B. "Shakespeare's Man Descending a Staircase: Sonnets 126 to 154," *ShS 31* (1978), 127–138.

Booth, Stephen. *An Essay on Shakespeare's Sonnets.* New Haven, 1969.

———, ed. *Shakespeare's Sonnets, edited with analytic commentary.* New Haven, 1977.

Colie, Rosalie L. "*Mel* and *Sal:* Some Problems in Sonnet Theory," *Shakespeare's Living Art.* Princeton, 1974.

Bradley, A. C. *Oxford Lectures on Poetry.* London, 1909, 1961.

Herrnstein, Barbara, ed. *Discussions of Shakespeare's Sonnets.* Boston, 1964.

Hobday, C. H. "Shakespeare's Venus and Adonis Sonnets," *ShS 26* (1973), 103–109.

Hubler, Edward. *The Sense of Shakespeare's Sonnets.* Princeton, 1952.

Hubler, Edward, Northrop Frye, Leslie A. Fiedler, Stephen Spender, and R. P. Blackmur. *The Riddle of Shakespeare's Sonnets.* New York, 1962.

Ingram, W. G., and Theodore Redpath, eds. *Shakespeare's Sonnets.* London, 1964.

Knight, G. Wilson. *The Mutual Flame: On Shakespeare's Sonnets and The Phoenix and the Turtle.* London, 1955.

Krieger, Murray. *A Window to Criticism: Shakespeare's Sonnets and Modern Poetics.* Princeton, 1964.

Landry, Hilton. *Interpretations in Shakespeare's Sonnets.* Berkeley, 1963.

Leishman, J. B. *Themes and Variations in Shakespeare's Sonnets.* London, 1961.

Lever, J. W. *The Elizabethan Love Sonnet.* London, 1956.

Melchiori, Giorgio. *Shakespeare's Dramatic Meditations: An Experiment in Criticism.* Oxford, 1976.

Ransom, John Crowe. *The World's Body.* New York and London, 1938, 1968.

Rollins, Hyder E. *A New Variorum Edition of Shakespeare: The Sonnets.* Philadelphia, 1944.

Winny, James. *The Master-Mistress: A Study of Shakespeare's Sonnets.* London and New York, 1968.

Textual Notes

These textual notes do not offer an historical collation, either of the early quartos and folios or of more recent editions; they are simply a record of departures in this edition from the copy text. For most plays the notes give the adopted reading of this edition in bold face, followed by the rejected reading in the relevant copy text. Where two substantive early texts are involved, or where a reading from some other earlier edition has been adopted, the notes provide information on the source of the reading in square brackets. In a few texts, adopted readings of editions more recent than the First Folio are indicated by [eds.] Alterations in punctuation or in lineation are not indicated, nor are some minor and obvious typographical errors noted.

Abbreviations used:

F Folio
Q Quarto
O Octavo
s.d. stage direction
s.p. speech prefix

The Comedy of Errors

Copy text: the First Folio [F].

I.i.1 s.p. [and elsewhere] Egeon Marchant **42 the** he **102 upon** vp **116 bark** backe **123 hath** haue **thee** they **152 life** helpe
I.ii.s.d. Antipholus [of Syracuse] Antipholis Erotes **[the First] Merchant** a Marchant **1 s.p. [and elsewhere] First Merchant** Mer. [also called E. Mar.] **4 arrival** a riuall **32 s.d. Exit** Exeunt **40 unhappy** vnhappie a **65 score** scoure **66 clock** cooke **94 s.d. Exit** Exeunt
II.i.s.d. Antipholus [of Ephesus] Antipholis Sereptus **11 o' door** adore **12 ill** thus **61 thousand** hundred **107 alone, alone** alone, a loue **111 Wear** Where
II.ii.s.d. Antipholus [of Syracuse] Antipholus Errotis **6 s.d. of Syracuse** Siracusia **12 didst** did didst **14 s.d. Antipholus S.** E. Ant. **79 men** them **97 tiring** trying **101 e'en** in **119 thus** then **135 off** of **174 stronger** stranger **185 offer'd** free'd **193 drone** Dromio **194 not I** I not
III.i.71 there here **75 you** your **89 her** your **91 her** your
III.ii.s.d. Luciana Iuliana **1 s.p. Luciana** Iulia **4 building** buildings **ruinous** ruinate **16 attaint** attaine **21 but** not **26 wife** wise **46 sister's** sister **49 bed** bud **them** thee **57 where** when **109 and** is **126 chalky** chalkle **136 carracks** Carrects
IV.i.s.p. [and elsewhere] Second Merchant Mar. **7 s.p. [and elsewhere] Angelo** Gold. **17 her** their **28 carat** charect
IV.ii.6 Of Oh **34 One** On **45 he's** is **48 That** Thus **61 'a** I **66 s.d. Exeunt** Exit
IV.iii.1 s.p. Antipholus S [not in F] **59 if you** if
IV.iv.130 s.d. [at l. 131 in F]
V.i.121 death depth **168 s.p. Servant** [not in F] **175 scissors** Cizers **180 s.p. Servant** Mess. **195 s.p. Egeon** Mar. Fat. **283 s.p. Egeon** Fa. **356-361** [these lines precede l. 346 in F] **357 Antipholuses** Antipholus **402 ne'er** are

Love's Labor's Lost

Copy text: the Quarto of 1598 [Q]

I.i.s.p. [and elsewhere] King Ferdinand **18 schedule** sedule **24 three** thee **31 pomp** pome **62 feast** fast **127 s.p. Berowne** [not in Q] **130 public** publibue **possibly** possible **132** [Q has s.p. Ber.] **168 umpire** vmpier **180 s.p. [and elsewhere] Dull** Constab. **188 s.p. [and elsewhere, except for ll. 219 and 221] Costard** Clowne **188 contempts** Contempls **216 welkin's** welkis **264 s.p. Dull** Antho. **273 worst** wost **286 s.p. King** Ber.
I.ii.3 s.p. [and elsewhere] Moth Boy **97 blushing** blush-in **126 woman** womand **128 s.p. Jaquenetta** Maide [and elsewhere Maid, Ma.] **139 s.p. Dull** Clo.
II.i.13 s.p. [and elsewhere] Princess Queene **32 Importunes** Importuous **34 visag'd** visage **36 s.d. Exit Boyet** [at l. 35 in Q] **39 s.p. and text First Lord. Lord** Lor. **40 s.p. Maria** 1. Lady **44 parts** peerelsse **53 s.p. Maria** Lad. **56 s.p. Katharine** 2. Lad. **61 Alencon's** Alansoes **64 s.p. Rosaline** 3. Lad. **80 s.p. First Lord** Lord. **88 unpeopled** vnpeeled **90 s.p. [and elsewhere] King** Nauar. **115–127 s.p. Rosaline** Kather. **130 half of an** halfe of, of an **142 demand** pemaund **144 On** One **179 mine own** my none **195 Katharine** Rosalin **210 Rasaline** Katherin **219 s.p. Maria** Lady Ka. **221 s.p. Maria** La. [also at l. 224] **254 s.p. Rosaline** Lad. **255 s.p. Maria** Lad. 2. **256 s.p. Katharine** Lad. 3. **257, 258 s.p. Rosaline** Lad.
III.i.1 s.p. [and elsewhere] Armado Bra. **14 as if** if **16 through the nose** through: nose **18 thin-belly** thinbellies **26 penny** penne **69 s.p. [and elsewhere] Moth** Pag. **72 the mail** thee male **plain** pline **133 ounce** ouce **136 remuneration** remuration **178 senior-junior** signior Iunios **199 clock** Cloake **202 sue** shue
IV.i.3 s.p. Boyet Forr. **6 On** Ore **70–71 saw . . . saw** See . . . see **71 overcame** couercame **75 king's** King **130 hit it** hit **134 ne'er** neare **136 pin** is in **144 o' th' one** ath toothen **148 is a** is **148 s.d. Shout** Shoot **Exit** Exeunt
IV.ii.3 s.p. [and elsewhere] Holofernes Ped. **8 s.p. [and elsewhere] Nathaniel** Curat. Nath. **28 of taste** taste **30 indiscreet** indistreell **36 Dictynna . . . Dictynna** Dictisima . . . dictisima **37 Dictynna** dictima **51 ignorant** ignorault **call I** cald **53 scurrility** squirilitie **65 s.p. Holofernes** Nath. [the subsequent speech prefixes in this scene of Holofernes and Nathaniel are reversed in Q through l. 147, except that the speech at l. 104 is correctly assigned to Nathaniel, and at ll. 118–120 to Pedan.] **69 pia mater** primater **71 in whom** whom **72 s.p. Nathaniel** Holo. **76 ingenuous** ingenous **78 sapit** sapis **81 s.p. Holofernes** Nath. [also at ll. 85, 91] **88 Person** Parson **91 pecus** pecas **omne** omnia **94–95 Venetia . . . prechia** vemchie, vencha, que non te vnde, que non te perreche **101 s.p. Nathaniel** Hol. **102 s.p. Holofernes** Nath. **104 s.p. Nathaniel** [missing in Q] **119 canzonet** cangenet **120 Here** [the rest of this speech is assigned to Nath. in Q] **130 s.p. Holofernes** Nath. **133 writing** written **135 Sir Nathaniel** Ped. Sir Holofernes **143 s.p. Jaquenetta** Mayd **146 s.p. Nathaniel** Holo. **148 s.p. Holofernes** Ped.
IV.iii.35 wilt will **45 s.p. King** Long. **71 idolatry** ydotarie **89 And I** And **95 ode** Odo **104 Wish'd** Wish **108 thorn** throne **151 coaches** couches **157 mote . . . mote** Moth . . . Moth **164 jig** ligge **176 like you** like **178 love** lone **244 wood** word **255 and usurping** vsurping **256 doters** dooters **312 eyes** eyes, With our selues **355 authors** authour **357 Let** Lets **363 standards** standars **379 Allons! Allons!** Alone alone **381 forsworn** forsorne
V.i.9 hominem hominum **20–21 "det" . . . pronounce** det, when he shold pronounce debt **25 insanie** infamie **27 bone** bene **28 Bone . . . bene** Bome boon for boon **56 wave** wane **57 venue** vene we **66 manu** vnum **96 importunate** importunt **106 secrecy** secretie **109 antic** antique **115 Nathaniel** Holofernes **117 rend'red** rended **assistance** assistants **148 Allons** Alone
V.ii.13 ne'er neare **17 ha' been a** a bin **22 You'll** Yole **28 cure . . . care** care . . . cure **43 ho** How **46 s.p. Katharine** Quee. **47 s.p. Princess** [not in Q] **53 s.p. [and elsewhere] Maria** Marg. **53 pearls** Pearle **65 hests** deuice **74 wantonness** wantons be **80 stabb'd** stable **89 sycamore** Siccamone **96 they** thy **148 her** his **152 ne'er** ere **159 s.p. Boyet** Berow. **163 ever** euen **176 strangers** stranges **217 The . . . it** [assigned in Q to Ros.] **232 s.p. [and elsewhere] Princess** Quee. **243 s.p. Katharine** Maria [also at ll. 245, 248, 249, 250, 254, 256] **280 perhaps** perhapt **298 vailing** varling **300 woo** woe **310 run** runs **342 Construe** Consture **347 Nor** Not **353 unsullied** vnsallied **408 affectation** affection **464 zany** saine **483 manage** nuage **502 they** thy **505–506 Pompion** Pompey **515 least** best **529 de la guerra** delaguar **543 s.p. Boyet** Bero. **554 s.p. Princess** Lady. **563 this** his **582** [Q has "Exit Curat."] **591 Judas** Pede. Iudas **596 prov'd** proud **643 gilt** gift **669 The . . . gone** [Q prints as a s.d. or as part of Armado's speech] **686 on, stir** or, stir **746 wholesome** holdsome **770 made** make **774 the**

ambassadors embassadours **778 this in our** this our **803 instant** instance **808 intitled** intiled **812 hermit** herrite **820 A wife** [assigned to Kath. in Q] **891–892** [the second and third lines of the song are transposed in Q] **912 foul** full **926–927 The . . . Apollo** [printed in larger type in Q without s.p.; F adds s.p. "Brag." and "You that way: we this way," thus incorporating the ending into the text]

The Two Gentlemen of Verona

Copy text: the First Folio [F]. Characters' names are grouped at the head of each scene.
I.i.66 leave loue **78 I a I** **141 testern'd** cestern'd
I.ii.97 your you
I.iii.24 whither whether **50 s.p.** [F repeats speech prefix "Pro"] **88 father calls** Fathers call's **91 s.d. Exeunt** Exeunt. Finis.
II.i.119 stead steed
II.ii.18 s.d. [and elsewhere] Panthino Panthion
II.iii.27 wood would **37 tied** tide [also at ll. 40 and 51]
II.iv.60 know knew **106 mistress** a Mistresse **161 braggardism** Bragadisme **163 makes** make **193 Is it mine eye** It is mine **211 s.d. Exit** Exeunt
II.v.1 Milan Padua **37 that my** that that my
III.i.148 would should **279 master's ship** Mastership **317 kiss'd fasting** fasting **375 s.d. Exit** Exeunt
IV.i.35 been beene often **49 An** And **near** Neece
IV.ii.17 s.d. Musicians Musitian [grouped with characters' names at head of scene] **110 his** her
IV.iii.19 abhors abhor'd **42 Recking** Wreaking
IV.iv.68 thou thee **72 to** not **204 s.d. Exit** Exeunt
V.ii.7 s.p. Julia Pro. **13 s.p. Julia** Thu. **18 your** you **32 Sir Eglamour** Eglamoure **56 s.d. Exit** Exeunt
V.iv.33 seized ceazed

The Taming of the Shrew

Copy Text: The First Folio [F].
Ind.i.s.d. Christophero Sly [printed at the end of the s.d. in F] **1 s.p. [and elsewhere] Sly** Begger **10–11 thirdborough** Head-borough **21 s.p. [and elsewhere] First Huntsman** Hunts. **87 s.p. First Player** Sincklo **99 s.p. First Player** Plai.
Ind.ii.2 lordship Lord **18 Sly's** Sies **26 s.p. [and elsewhere] Third Servant** 3 Man. **27 s.p. [and elsewhere] Second Servant** 2 Man. **47 s.p. [and elsewhere] First Servant** 1 Man. **99 s.p. [and elsewhere] Page** Lady **133 it. Is** it is
I.i.13 Vincentio Vincentio's **14 brought** brough **24 satiety** sacietie **25 Mi perdonato** Me Pardonato **47 s.d. suitor** sister **57 s.p. [and elsewhere] Katharina** Kate. **162 captum** captam **170 strand** strond **207 color'd** Conlord **243 your** you **247 s.d. speak** speakes
I.ii.17 s.d. wrings rings **18 masters** mistris **24 Con . . . trovato** Contutti le core bene trobatto **25 ben** bene **26 Molto** multo **honorato** honorata **33 pip** peepe **72 she** she is **119 me and other** me. Other **170 help me** helpe one **188 Antonio's** Butonios **211 ours** yours **264 feat** seeke **279 ben** Been
II.i.3 gauds goods **8 s.p. [and elsewhere] Katharina** Kate **8 thee, tell** tel **76 Neighbor** neighbors **79 unto you** vnto **141 shake** shakes **168 s.d. Exeunt** Exit **186 bonny** bony **244 askance** a sconce **321 s.d. Exeunt** Exit **327 in** me **351 Valance** Vallens **372 Marseilles'** Marcellus
III.i.28 Sigeia sigeria [also at ll. 33 and 42] **47 [Aside]** Luc. **50 s.p. Bianca** [not in F] **51 s.p. Lucentio** Bian. **53 s.p. Bianca** Hort. **76 clef** Cliffe **80 change** charge **odd** old **81 s.p. Servant** Nicke.
III.ii.29 of thy of **30 News, old news** newes **33 hear** heard **54 sway'd** Waid **56 cheek'd** chekt **129 As I** As **149 e'er** ere **198 s.p. Gremio** Gra.
IV.i.23 s.p. Curtis Gru. **42 their white** the white **81 sleekly** slickely **106 s.p. Grumio** Gre. **136 off** of **168 s.d. Curtis** Curtis a Seruant
IV.ii. s.p. Hortensio Luc. **6 s.p. Lucentio** Hor. [and at l. 8] **13 none** me **31 her** them **71 Take . . . alone** [assigned to "Par." in F] **in** me
IV.iii. [F has "Actus Quartus. Scena Prima" here] **63 s.p. Haberdasher** Fel. **81 is a** is **88 like a** like **177 account'st** accountedst
IV.iv.s.d. [booted and bare-headed] [appears at l. 38 in F] **1 Sir** Sirs **5 Where . . . Pegasus** [assigned to Tranio in F] **68** [F adds a s.d.: "Enter Peter"] **91 except** expect
IV.v.18 is in **35 make a** make the **37 where** whether **40 Allot** A lots **77 she be** she
V.i.4. [F has "Exit" here] **6 master's** mistris **42 brought** brough **50 master's** Mistris **104 s.d. Exeunt** Exit **139 No** Mo **143 than never** then ueuer
V.ii. [F has "Actus Quintus" here] **2 done** come **37 thee** the **45 bitter** better **two** too **52 s.p. Tranio** Tri. **57 ho** oh **62 two** too **65 for** sir **70 What is** what's **130 an** fiue **134 you're** your

A Midsummer Night's Dream

Copy text: the first quarto of 1600 [Q]
I.i.4 wanes waues **10 New-bent** Now bent **19 s.d. Lysander** Lysander and Helena **24 Stand forth, Demetrius** [printed as s.d. in Q] **26 Stand forth, Lysander** [printed as s.d. in Q] **74 their** there **132 Ay** Eigh **136 low** loue **187 Yours would** Your words **191 I'd** ile **216 sweet** sweld **219 stranger companies** strange companions
II.i.1 s.p. [and elsewhere] Puck Robin **61 s.p. [and elsewhere] Titania** Qu. **61 Fairies** Fairy **69 steep** steppe **79 Aegles** Eagles **109 thin** chinne **158 the west** west **190 slay** stay **slayeth** stayeth **194 thee** the **201 not nor** not not **246 s.d.** [at l. 247 in Q]
II.ii.9 s.p. First Fairy [not in Q] **39 Be 't** Bet it **43 good** god **47 is** it
III.i.27–28 yourselves your selfe **52 s.p. Bottom** Cet. **65 and** or **77 s.p. Bottom** Pyra. [also at ll. 79 and 98] **78 Odors, odors** Odours, odorous **83 s.p. Puck** Quin. **84 s.p. Flute** Thys. [also at ll. 88 and 97] **118 I will sing** will sing **144 own** owe **157–158 Ready . . . go** [assigned to Fairies in Q] **170 s.p. Peaseblossom** 1. Fai. **171 Hail** [assigned in Q to 1. Fai.] **172 s.p. Moth** 2. Fair. **173 s.p. Mustardseed** 3. Fai. **190 you of** you **196 s.d. Exeunt** Exit
III.ii.s.d. [Q: Enter King of Fairies, and Robin goodfellow] **19 mimic** Minnick **38 s.p. [and elsewhere] Puck** Rob. **80 I so** I **85 sleep** slippe **213 like** life **220 passionate words** words **250 prayers** praise **260 off** of **299 gentlemen** gentleman **344 s.d. Exit** Exeunt **426 shalt** shat **451 To your** your
IV.i.5 s.p. [and elsewhere] Bottom Clowne **64 off** of **72 o'er** or **81 five** fine **116 Seem'd** Seeme **137 s.d. Wind . . . up** they all start vp. Winde hornes **171 saw** see **190 found** fonnd **198 let us** lets **205 to expound** expound **208 a patch'd** patcht a
IV.ii. s.d. [Snout, and Starveling] Thisby and the rabble **3 s.p. Starveling** Flut. **5 s.p. Flute** Thys. [and at ll. 9, 13, 19] **29 no** not
V.i.34 our Or **107 s.p. [and elsewhere] Theseus** Duke **122 his** this **150 s.d. Exeunt** Exit [and at l. 153 in Q] **155 Snout** Flute **190 up in thee** now againe **205 mural down** Moon vsed **209 s.p. [and elsewhere] Hippolyta** Dutch. **270 gleams** beames **317 warr'nt** warnd **347 s.p. Bottom** Lyon **366 lion** Lyons **367 behowls** beholds **415–416 And . . . rest** [these lines are transposed in Q]

The Merchant of Venice

Copy text: the first quarto of 1600 [Q1]
I.i. s.d. [and elsewhere] Salerio, and Solanio Salaryno, and Salanio **19 Peering** Piring **27 dock'd** docks **85 jaundice** Iaundies **113 Is it** It is **128 off** of **151 back** bake
I.ii.44 Palatine Palentine [and at ll.57–58] **53 Bon** Boune **58 throstle** Trassell
I.iii.28 s.p. [and elsewhere] Shylock Jew **75 compremis'd** compremyzd **109 spit** spet [also at ll. 122 and 128 and II.vii.45]
II.i.s.d. Morocco Morochus **31 thee** the **35 page** rage
II.ii.1 s.p. [and elsewhere] Launcelot Clowne **3 [and elsewhere in this scene] Gobbo** Iobbe **42 By** Be **76 murder** muder **94 last** lost **165 s.d.** [at l. 164 in Q] **168 a suit** sute

II.iii.11 did doe
II.iv.39 s.d. Exeunt Exit
II.vi. 26 Who's whose [also at l. 61] **59 gentlemen** gentleman
II.vii.69 tombs timber
II.viii.8 gondola Gondylo **39 Slubber** slumber
II.ix.64 judgment iudement
III.i.70 s.p. Man [not in Q1] **74 s.d.** [Q1 repeats the s.d. "Enter Tuball"] **100 Heard** heere **114 turquoise** Turkies
III.ii.67 eyes eye **81 vice** voyce **84 stairs** stayers **204 roof** rough **315 s.p. Bassanio** [not in Q1]
III.iii.s.d. Solanio Salerio **24 s.p. Solanio** Sal.
III.iv.49 Padua Mantua **50 cousin's** cosin **53 traject** Tranect **81 my** my my
III.v.20 e'en in **26 comes** come **74 merit it** meane it, it **81 a wife** wife **87 s.d. Exeunt** Exit
IV.i.30 his state this states **31 flint** flints **35 s.p. [and elsewhere in this scene] Shylock** Jew **51 Mistress** Maisters **73 You may as well** well **74 Why he hath made the** the **bleat** bleake **75 pines** of Pines **113 lose** loose **136 whilst** whilest **228 No, not** Not not **270 off** of **322 off** of **396 s.p. Gratiano** Shy. **405 s.d. Exeunt** Exit
V.i.26 s.p. Stephano. Messen. [also at ll. 28 and 33] **41 Lorenzo** Lorenzo, & **49 Sweet soul** [assigned in Q1 to Launcelot] **51 Stephano** Stephen **87 Erebus** Terebus **109 ho** how **152 give it** giue **233 my** mine

Much Ado about Nothing

Copy text: the quarto of 1600 [Q]
I.i.s.d. Messina Messina, Innogen his wife **1 Pedro** Peter [also in l. 9] **194 s.d. Pedro** Pedro, Iohn the bastard
I.ii.3 s.p. [and elsewhere] Antonio Old **6 event** euents **24 skill** shill
I.iii.70 Exeunt exit
II.i.s.d. Hero his wife, Hero **2 s.p. [and elsewhere] Antonio** brother **67 hear** here **79 s.d. and Don** or dumb **94 s.p. Balthasar** Bene. [also at ll. 97 and 99] **201 s.d. Prince [Don Pedro]** Prince, Hero, Leonato, Iohn and Borachio, and Conrade **311 s.p. [and elsewhere] Don Pedro** Prince **370 s.d. Exeunt** exit
II.iii.7 s.d. [at l. 5 in Q] **24 an** and **35 s.d. Claudio** Claudio, Musicke **61 s.p. Balthasar** [not in Q] **135 us of** of vs
III.i.s.d. Ursula Vrsley [also in l. 4] **25 s.d.** [at l. 23 in Q]
III.ii.27 can cannot **51 s.p. Don Pedro** Bene. **74 s.p. [and elsewhere] Don John** Bastard
III.iii.37 s.p. Second Watch Watch [and thus through l. 125] **161 s.p. Second Watch** Watch 1 [and at l. 166] **163 s.p. First Watch** Watch 2 **172 s.p. Second Watch** [missing in Q]
III.iv.17 in it
III.v.2 s.p. [and elsewhere] Dogberry Const. Dog. **7 s.p. [and elsewhere] Verges** Headb. **9 off** of **50** [Q provides an **exit** at this point]
IV.i.4 s.p. Friar Fran. **201 princes** princesse
IV.ii.s.d. [Q reads "Enter the Constables, Borachio, and the Towne clearke in gownes."] **1 s.p. Dogberry** Keeper **2 s.p. Verges** Cowley [also at l. 5 and elsewhere in this scene] **4 s.p. Dogberry** Andrew **9 s.p. [and elsewhere in this scene] Dogberry** Kemp **18 s.p. Conrade, Borachio** Both **51 s.p. Verges** Const. **59 s.p. Watchmen** Watch **69 s.p. Conrade** [missing in Q] **69 Off** of **73 s.p. Conrade** Couley **86 s.p. Exeunt** exit
V.i.16 Bid And **97 anticly** antiquely, and **98 off** of **179 on** one **201 s.d.** [at l. 198 in Q] **251 s.p. Verges** Con. 2
V.ii.41 s.d. [at l. 42 in Q] **97 s.d. Exeunt** exit
V.iii.2 s.p. A Lord Lord **3 s.p. Claudio** [missing in Q] **10 dumb** dead **22 s.p. Claudio** Lo.
V.iv.53 s.p. Antonio Leo. **96 s.p. Benedick** Leon.

The Merry Wives of Windsor

Copy text: the First Folio [F]. Q = the quarto of 1602.
I.i.s.d. [Entering characters are grouped at the heads of scenes throughout the play.] **41 George** Thomas **53, 56 s.p. Shallow** Slen. **114 goot** good [also **'ort** for **'ord** at l. 236 and a few other instances of regularizing the Welsh dialect] **131 Garter** Gater
I.iii.14 lime [Q] liue **47 well** will **51 legion** [Q: legians] legend **59 oeillades** illiads **81 o' th'** ith' **82 humor** [Q] honor **93, 98 Page** [Q] Ford **94 Ford** [Q] Page
I.iv.21 whey wee **41 un boitier** vnboyteene **46 fort chaud** for chando **46–47 m'en vais** man voi **47 la cour** le Court **affaire** affaires **63 Larron** La-roone **82 baille** ballow
II.i.1 have I haue **55 prais'd** praise **59–60 Hundredth Psalm** hundred Psalms **129–130 and . . . of it** [Q; not in F] **199 s.p. Ford** [Q] Shal. **201 Brook** [Q] Broome [and at ll. 203 and elsewhere] **204 mynheers** An-heires **216 s.d. Exeunt** [at l. 223 in F]
II.ii.4 [Q; not in F] **22, 50, 293 [and elsewhere] God** heauen **25 you, you** you
II.iii.34 He rhe **51 A word** [Q] a **56 mush** much **73 s.p. Page, Shallow, and Slender** All. **77 But first** [Q; not in F]
III.i.83 urinals [Q] Vrinal **84–85, 99–100** [Q; not in F]
III.ii.105 lads Lad
III.iii.54 By the Lord [Q; not in F] **141 whither** whether **176 foolish** foolishion **194 By** Be
III.iv.12 s.p. Fenton [not in F] **108 s.d. Exit** Exeunt
III.v.82 By the Lord [Q] Yes **141 s.d. Exit** Exeunt
IV.i.44 hung hing **56 Genitive** Genitiue **63 lunatics** Lunaties
IV.ii.18 lunes lines **51 s.p. Mrs Page** [not in F] **59 s.p. Mrs Page** [Q] Mist. Ford. **91 direct** direct direct **95–96 misuse him** misuse **106 as lief** liefe as **111 ging** gin **118 this** thi **169 not strike** strike **173 hag** Ragge
IV.iii.1 Germans desire Germane desires **7 them** [Q] him **9 house** [Q] houses
IV.iv. 7 cold gold **32 makes** make **42** [Q, reading "Horne" for "herne"; not in F] **60 s.p. Mrs Ford** Ford. **72 tire** time
IV.v.28 Master my master **41 s.p. Simple** Fal. **54 Thou art** [Q] Thou are **97 to say my prayers** [Q; not in F]
IV.vi.39 denote deuote
V.ii.3 my daughter my
V.iii.12 Hugh Herne
V.v.2 hot-blooded hot-bloodied **69 More** Mote **193 white** green **197 green** white **201 un** oon **garçon** Garsoon **paysan** pesant **203 green** white

As You Like It

Copy text: The First Folio [F].
I.i.105 she hee **154 s.p. Oliver** [not in F] **154 s.d. Exit** [at l.153 in F]
I.ii.3 I were were **51 goddesses and** goddesses, **55 s.p. [and elsewhere] Touchstone** Clow. **father** farher **80 s.p. Celia** Ros. **88 Le** the **250 s.d.** [at l. 248 in F] **279 [and occasionally elsewhere] Rosalind** Rosaline
I.iii.55 likelihood likelihoods **76 her** per **124 be** by **135 we in** in we
II.i.49 much must **50 friends** friend **59 of the** of
II.iii.10 some seeme **16 s.p. Orlando** [not in F] **29 s.p. Orlando** Ad. **50 woo** woe **71 seventeen** seauentie
II.iv.1 weary merry **42 thy wound** they would **65 you** your
II.v.1 s.p. Amiens [not in F] **41–42 No . . . weather** &c **45 Thus it goes** [with repeated s.p. **Amy.**] **54** [with repeated s.p. **Amy.**]
II.vii.s.d. Lords Lord **10 [and elsewhere] woo** woe **38 brain** braiue **55 Not to seem** Seeme **87 comes** come **173 s.p. Amiens** [not in F] **181 Then** The **197 master** masters
III.ii.26 good pood **123 a desert** Desert **143 her** his **234 such fruit** fruite **241 thy** the **340 lectures** Lectors **354 deifying** defying
III.iii.88 s.p. Touchstone Ol. **97 s.d. Exeunt** [at l. 99 in F]
III.iv.29 a lover Louer
III.v.22 but upon vpon **105 erewhile** yerewhile **128 I have** Haue
IV.i.1 me be me **18 my** by **44 thousandth** thousand **202 it** in
IV.ii.2 s.p. First Lord Lord. **7 s.p. Second Lord** Lord. **10 s.p. Second Lord** [not in F] **12 s.d.** [printed as part of the song in F]
IV.iii.5 s.d. [at l. 4 in F] **8 bid** did bid **143 In** I **156 his** this
V.i.36 sir sit **55 policy** police
V.ii.7 nor her nor **31 overcame** ouercome
V.iii.18 ring rang **28–32** [this stanza comes before l. 21 in F]
V.iv.34 s.d. [at l. 33 in F] **80 so to the** so ro **103 her** his **150 s.p. Jaques de Boys** 2 Bro. [also at l. 182] **163 them** him **170 were** vvete

Twelfth Night

Copy Text: the First Folio [F].
I.ii.15 Arion Orion
I.iii.51 s.p. Sir Andrew Ma. **96 curl by** coole my **98 me** we **132 flame** dam'd **set** sit **136 That's** That
I.v.163 s.d. Viola Uiolenta **296 County's** Countes **306 s.d.** [F adds "Finis, Actus primus."]
II.ii.31 our O **32 of** if
II.iv.53 Fly . . . fly Fye . . . fie **55 yew** Ew **88 I** It
II.v.112 staniel stallion **142 born** become **achieve** atcheeues **173 dear** deero **203 s.d.** [F adds "Finis Actus secundus"]
III.i.8 king Kings **68 wise men** wisemens
III.ii.7 thee the the **64 nine** mine
III.iv.15 s.d. [at l. 14 in F] **25 s.p. Olivia** Mal. **72 tang** langer **175 You** Yon **222 thee** the **249 competent** computent **311 s.d.** [at l. 310 in F] **396 s.d. Exeunt** Exit
IV.ii.6 in in in **38 clerestories** cleere stores **71 sport to** sport
IV.iii.1 s.p. Sebastian [not in F] **35 s.d.** [F adds "Finis Actus Quartus"]
V.i.188 s.d. [at l. 185 in F] **198 pavin** panyn **386 tiny** tine **403 With hey** hey

All's Well that Ends Well

Copy text: the First Folio [F].
I.i.1 s.p. [and elsewhere] Countess Mother **3 s.p. [and elsewhere] Bertram** Ros. **130 got** goe **148 t' one** ten **159 wear** were
I.ii.3 s.p. [and elsewhere] First Lord 1. Lo. G **15 s.p. [and elsewhere] Second Lord** 2. Lo. E **18 Rossillion** Rosignoll **76 s.d. Exeunt** Exit
I.iii.19 I w **112 Dian no queen** Queene **124 s.d. [and elsewhere] Helena** Hellen **125** [F has s.p. here, **Old. Cou.,** used subsequently in other s.p.] **127 rightly** righlie **168 loneliness** louelinesse **174 th' one to th' other** 'ton to oth to th' other **199 intenible** intemible **247 and** an
II.i.5 s.p. First Lord Lord. G. **18 s.p. Second Lord** L.G. **25 s.p. Second Lord** 2 Lo. E **43 with his cicatrice** his sicatrice, with **62 fee** see **144 fits** shifts **155 impostor** Impostrue **173 nay** ne **192 heaven** helpe **210 meed** deed **210 s.d. Exeunt** Exit
II.ii.1 s.p. Countess Lady [and elsewhere in scene] **60 An** And
II.iii.1 s.p. [and elsewhere] Lafew Ol. Laf. **76 s.d.** [at l. 63 in F] **94 her** heere **96 s.p. Helena** La. **99 s.p. Lafew** Ol. Lord **125 when** whence **130 it is** is is **266 s.d.** [at l. 264 in F] **290 War** Warres **291 detested** detected
II.iv.16 fortunes fortune
II.v.27 End And **29 one** on **31 heard** hard **89 s.p. Bertram** [at l. 90 in F]
III.i.9 s.p. Second Lord French E **17 s.p. First Lord** Fren. G **23 to the** to 'th the
III.ii.9 sold hold **13 ling** Lings **18 E'en** In **19 s.p. Countess** [not in F] **45 s.p. [and throughout scene] Second Lord** French E **47 s.p. [and throughout scene] First Lord** French G **64 s.p. Countess** Old La.
III.iv.4 s.p. Steward [not in F] **18 s.p. Countess** [not in F] **27 hear** beare
III.v.s.d. Daughter daughter, Violenta [s.d. preceded in F by "A Tucket afarre off"] **10 s.p. [and elsewhere] Mariana** Maria. **33 la** le **65 warrant** write **90 s.d. Exeunt** Exit
III.vi.1 s.p. First Lord Cap. E [and throughout scene until l. 106] **3 s.p. Second Lord** Cap. G [and throughout scene until l. 106] **36 his** this **37 ore** ours **107 s.p. First Lord** Cap. G **109, 115 s.p. Second Lord** Cap. E
III.vii.19 Resolv'd Resolue **42 steads** steeds
IV.i.1 s.p. [and throughout scene] First Lord 1. lord E **69 s.p. [and throughout scene] First Soldier** Inter. **90 art** are **93 s.p. Second soldier** Sol. [and at l. 96] **97 s.d. Exeunt** Exit
IV.ii.38 may make **snare** scarre
IV.iii.1 s.p. [and throughout scene] First Lord Cap. G **2 s.p. [and throughout scene] Second Lord** Cap. E **81 s.p. First Lord** Ber. **89 effected** affected **118 Hush, hush** [assigned in F to Bertram] **125 s.p. First Lord** Cap. **138 All's one to him** [assigned in F to Parolles] **199 lordship** Lord **243 our** your **317 s.p. Bertram** Count.
IV.iv.16 you your
IV.v.21 grass grace **39 name** maine **46 off** of
V.i.6 s.d. a Gentleman a gentle Astringer
V.ii.25 similes smiles **33 under her** vnder
V.iii.49 warp'd warpe **71 s.p. Countess** [not in F] **101 Plutus** Platus **114 conjectural** connecturall **122 tax** taze **153 s.d.** [at l. 151 in F] **154 sith** sir **156 s.d. Diana** Diana, and Parrolles **215 infinite** insuite **cunning** comming **311 are** is

Measure for Measure

Copy text: the First Folio [F].
I.i.76 s.d. [at l. 75 in F]
I.ii.58 s.p. [and elsewhere] Mistress Overdone Bawd **83 s.d.** [at l. 84 in F] **85 s.p. [and elsewhere] Pompey** Clo. **115** [F begins "Scena Tertia" here] **135 morality** mortality
I.iii. [F labels as "Scena Quarta"] **27 Becomes more** More **54 s.d. Exeunt** Exit
I.iv. [F labels as "Scena Quinta"] **s.d. [and elsewhere] Isabella** Isabell **2 s.p. [and throughout] Francisca** Nun. **17 stead** steed **54 givings-out** giuing-out
II.i.12 your our **39 breaks** brakes **139 s.d.** [at l. 138 in F]
II.ii.62 back again againe
II.iv.9 sere feard **53 or** and **75 craftily** crafty **76 me be** be **94 all-binding** all-building
III.i.29 sire fire **52 me to hear them** them to heare me **67 Though** Through **90 enew** emmew **95 damned'st** damnest **129 penury** periury **212 by oath** oath
III.ii.26 array away **48 it clutch'd** clutch'd **147 dearer** deare **214 See** Sea
IV.i.20 s.d. Isabella Isabell **49 s.d.** [at l. 48 in F]
IV.ii.43–47 If . . . thief [assigned in F to Clown] **60 s.d.** [at l. 59 in F] **100 This . . . man** [assigned in F to Duke] **lordship's** Lords **101 s.p. Duke** Pro.
IV.iii.89 th' under yond **92 s.d.** [at l. 91 in F] **100 well** weale
IV.iv.6 redeliver reliuer
IV.v.6 Flavius' Flauia's
V.i.14 me we **174 her** your **265 s.d.** [at l. 264 in F] **285 s.d.** [at l. 283 in F] **428 confiscation** confutation **482 s.d. Juliet** Iulietta **544 that's** that

Troilus and Cressida

Copy text: the quarto of 1609 [Q], which may represent Shakespeare's revision of the play, although the First Folio text [F] represents an independent and valuable textual authority. All adopted readings are from [F] unless otherwise indicated; [eds.] means that the reading is that of some editor since the First Folio.
Prologue [F; not in Q] **12 barks** [eds.] Barke [F] **17 Antenorides** Antenonidus [F] **19 Sperr** [eds.] Stirre [F]
I.i. 15 must needs must **27 you** yea **73 on of you** of you **78 not kin** kin **80 care I** I **100 stubborn-chaste** stubborn, chast **104 resides** reides
I.ii.1 s.p. [and throughout] Alexander Man **17 they** the **34 struck** stroke **48 ye** [eds.] yea **85 come** eome **87 wit** [eds.] will **117 lift** liste **125 valiantly** valianty **130 the** [eds.] thee **177 s.d.** [at l. 175 in Q] **180 Ilium** Ilion **186 s.d.** [at l. 185 in Q] **205 man's** man **214 s.d.** [at l. 210 in Q] **269 too** two
I.iii.2 the jaundice on these Iaundies ore **13 every** euer **31 thy** the **36 patient** ancient **48 breese** Bryze **54 Retorts** [eds.] Retires **61 thy** the **70–74** [F; not in Q] **75 basis** bases **92 ill . . . evil** influence of euill Planets **110 meets** melts **119 includes** include **143 sinew** sinnow **149 awkward** sillie **159 unsquar'd** vnsquare **188 will'd** wild **195 and** our **209 fineness** finesse **247 affair** affaires **250 him** with him **252 sense** seat **the** that **256 loud** alowd **262 this** his **289 or means** a meanes **298 will tell** tell **302 youth** men **304 s.p. Agamemnon** [F; not in Q] **315 This 'tis** [F; not in Q] **327 were** weare **352 the** a **354–356** [F; not in Q] **354 his** [eds.] in his [F] **390 tarre** arre
II.i.14 vinewedst [eds.] vnsalted [Q] whinid'st [F] **17 oration** oration

without booke **18 learn a** learne **19 o'** oth **27 thee** the **38, 40, 41 s.p. Thersites, Ajax, Thersites** [F; not in Q] **45 Thou scurvy** you scurvy **71 I will** It will **75 I'll** I **101 an 'a** and [Q] if he [F] **out** at **105 your** [eds.] their **105–106 nails on their toes** nailes **122 fifth** first

II.ii.3 damage domage **14, 15 surety** surely **33 at** of **35 reasons** reason **47 Let's** Sets **64 shores** shore **67 chose** choose **71 sieve** siue **86 he** be **100 s.d.** [at l. 96 in Q] **104 eld** old [F] elders [Q] **149 off** of **210 strike** shrike

II.iii.1 s.p. Thersites [not in Q] **25 wouldst** couldst **31 art** art not **46 thyself** Thersites **49 mayst** must **54–59** [F; not in Q] **62–63 commanded of Agamemnon** commanded **64 Patroclus** this Patroclus **68 Patroclus** Come Patroclus **73–74** [F; not in Q] **73 serpigo** [eds.] Suppeago [F] **78 shent** [eds.] sent [F] sate [Q] **87 the** a **88** [F; not in Q] **129 pettish lunes** course, and time [Q] pettish lines [F] **his flows** and flowes **as** and **130 carriage of this action** streame of his commencement **140 enter you** entertaine **152 clearer, Ajax** cleerer **192 titled** liked **200 this** his **202 pash** push **211 let** tell **humors** humorous **219 'A . . . shares** [assigned in Q to Ajax] **221 He's . . . warm** [assigned in Q to Ajax] **222 praises** praiers **in; his** his **225 You** Yon **241 all** all thy **247 bourn** boord **248 Thy** This **262 cull** call

III.i.3. s.p. [and elsewhere] Servant Man **6 noble** notable **25 mean, friend** meane **90 poor disposer's** disposer is **106 lord** lad **113** [F; not in Q] **117 shaft confounds** shafts confound **148 They're** Their **149 woo** woe **151 these** this **159 thee** her

III.ii.3 he stays stays **8 a** to a **10 those** these **37 unawares** vnwares **67 fears** [eds.] teares **80 This is** This **91 crown it. No perfection** louer part no affection **121 grown** grone **131 Cunning** Comming **158 aye** age **178 Yet, after** After **183 and** or

III.iii.3 to your to **4 come** [eds.] loue **29 off** of **43 unplausive** vnpaulsiue **bent** [eds.] bent? why turnd **69 s.d. Exit** Exeunt **102 giver** giuers **110 mirror'd** [eds.] married **128 abject** obiect **140 on** one **141 shrieking** [eds.] shriking [Q] shrinking [F] **155 one** on **158 hedge** turn **160 hindmost** him, most **161–163** [F; not in Q] **162 rear** [eds.] neere [F] **164 past** passe **178 give** [eds.] goe **184 Than** That **197 grain . . . gold** thing **198 deeps** depth **224 like a** like **266 ambassador to him** Ambassador **274 the most** the **278 et cetera. Do** Do **298 you** yee **300 but he's** but

IV.i. s.d. [and elsewhere] Diomedes Diomed **5 you** your **18 But** Lul'd **42 do think** beleeue **58 soilure** soyle **78 you** they

IV.ii.18 off of **32–33 capoccia** [eds.] chipochia **65 us; and for him** him, and **79 s.p. Cressida** [not in Q]

IV.iv. 54 the root my throate **70 Wear** were **77** [F; not in Q] **gifts** guift [F] **79 person** portion **106 wear** were **144–148** [F; not in Q] **144 s.p. Deiphobus** [eds.] Dio. [F]

IV.v. s.d. Nestor Nester, Calcas **65 you** the **73 s.p. Achilles** Aga. **94** [F; not in Q] **95 s.p. Agamemnon** Vlises **98 in deeds** deeds **132 Of our rank feud** [F; not in Q] **133 drop** day **165–170** [F; not in Q] **178 that I** thy **oath** earth **188 thy** th' **193 hemm'd** shrupd **206** [F; not in Q] **255 stithied** stichied **275 Beat . . . taborines** To taste your bounties **292 she lov'd** my Lord

V.i.4 core curre **12 these** this **14 boy** box **18–19 catarrhs** [F; not in Q] **20 wheezing** whissing **31 sarcenet** sacenet **32 tassel** toslell **54 brother** be **56 hanging . . . leg** at his bare legge **58 forc'd** faced **59–60 he's** her's **60 dog** day **mule** Moyle **60–61 fitchew** Fichooke **63 me not** me **71 good** God **77 sewer** [eds.] sure **78 both at once** both

V.ii.14 s.p. Cressida [eds.] Cal. **17 should** shall **43 distraction** distruction **50 Adieu, you** you **58 tickles these** tickles **60 But will** will **61 la** [eds.] lo **70** [F; not in Q] **71 s.p. Cressida** Troy. **84 Nay . . . me** [assigned in Q, F to Diomedes] **88 s.p. Cressida** [F; not in Q] **92 one's** [eds.] on's [Q] one [F] **94 By** And by **121 co-act** Court **126 had** were **deceptious** deceptions **137 soil** spoile **161 five** finde **164 bound** giuen **171 as I** [eds.] I

V.iii.14 s.p. Cassandra Cres. **20–22** [F; not in Q] **21 give** [eds.] count giue [F] **use** [eds.] as [F] **23 s.p. Cassandra** [F; not in Q] **58** [F; not in Q] **85 distraction** distruction

V.iv.4 young knave's knaues **16 begin** [eds.] began **26 art thou** art

V.v.5 s.p. Servant Man **11 Cedius** [eds.] Cedus **12 Thoas** [eds.] Thous **22 scaled** scaling **41 luck** lust **42 s.p. Ajax** [F; not in Q]

V.vi.1 s.p. Ajax [F; not in Q] **2 s.p. Diomedes** [F; not in Q] **13 s.p. Achilles** [F; not in Q] **26 reck** [eds.] wreake

V.vii.1 s.p. Achilles [F; not in Q] **8 s.d. Exeunt** [eds.] Exit **10 'Loo** [eds.] lowe **11 double-horn'd Spartan** [eds.] double hen'd spartan [Q] double-henned sparrow [F] **12 s.d. Exeunt** [eds.] Exit **13 s.p. Margarelon** Bast. [and throughout scene]

V.viii.3 good my **15 part** prat **16 s.p. Myrmidon** One

V.ix.1 shout is that is this

V.x.2 Never . . . night [F; assigned in Q to Troilus] **2 s.d.** [at l. 1 in Q] **17 there** their **21 Scare** Scarre **21–22** [F; not in Q] **23 vile** proud **24 pight** pitcht **33 Ignomy and** ignomyny **36 world, world, world** world, world **37 traders** traitors **50 your** my **51 hold-door** hold-ore

1 Henry VI

Copy text: the First Folio [F].

I.i.57 s.p. First Messenger Mess. [also at l. 69] **65 [and elsewhere] Rouen** Roan **89 s.p. Second Messenger** Mess. **94 Reignier** Reynold **103 s.p. Third Messenger** Mes. **176 steal** send

I.ii.30 bred breed **47 s.p. [and elsewhere] Charles** Dolph. **76 whilst** whilest **99 five** fine **103 s.d. [and elsewhere] La** de **131 halcyon** Halcyons

I.iii.6 s.p. First Servingman Glost. 1. Man. [at l. 8, 1. Man.] **29 Humphrey** Vmpheir

I.iv.10 Wont Went **27 Duke** Earle **69 s.d. shoot** shot

I.vi.22 of or

II.i.5 s.p. First Sentinel Sent. [also at l. 38] **54 s.p. Pucelle** Ioane. [also at l. 72] **77 s.d.** [F has Exeunt preceding this s.d.]

II.ii.s.d. their . . . march [appears at II.i.7 in F] **20 Arc** Acre **38 Auvergne** Ouergne

II.iv.1 s.p. Plantagenet Yorke [and thus through Act III] **117 wip'd** whipt **132 gentle sir** gentle

II.v.18 s.p. First Keeper Keeper [and at l. 33] **35 s.p. Plantagenet** Rich. **[and elsewhere] 71 King Richard** Richard **121 s.d. Exeunt** Exit

III.i.52 s.p. Somerset [not in F] **53 s.p. Warwick** Som. **54 s.p. Somerset** [not in F] **164 that** that all

III.ii.10 s.p. First Soldier Souldier **22 Where** Here **41 Good** God **42 Burgundy** Burgonie **103 s.d. Exeunt** Exit

IV.i.s.d. Exeter, Governor and Gouernor Exeter **14 thee** the **48 my Lord** Lord **151 umpire** Vmper **173 s.d. Flourish** [at l. 181 in F] **180 wist** wish

IV.ii.3 calls call **15 s.p. General** Cap.

IV.iii.17 s.p. [and throughout scene] Lucy 2 Mes. [or Mes.]

IV.iv.16 legions Regions **27 Reignier** Reignard

IV.v.55 s.d. Exeunt Exit

IV.vi.57 s.d. Exeunt Exit

IV.vii.89 'em him [also at l. 94] **96 s.d. Exeunt** Exit

V.iii.57 her his **65 [and elsewhere in scene] woo** woe **179 modestly** modestie **192 And** Mad

V.iv.28 suck'dst suck'st **49 Arc** Aire **74 Machiavel** Macheuile **93 s.d. Enter Cardinal** [at l. 91 in F] **123 s.p. Cardinal** Win. **149 compromise** compremize

V.v.82 love loue

2 Henry VI

Copy text: the First Folio [F]. Q = the Quarto of 1594.

I.i. 37 s.p. Kneeling kneel **56 s.p. Cardinal** Win. **57 duchies** Dutchesse **72 s.d. Exeunt** Exit **91 had** hath **130 s.p. [and elsewhere] Gloucester** Hum. **176 Protector** [Q] Protectors **177 s.d. Exeunt** Exit **211 s.d. Exeunt** Exit **254 in** [Q] in in

I.ii.1 s.p. [and elsewhere] Duchess Elia. **22 dream** dreames **38 are** wer **60 s.d. Exit Humphrey** [at l. 59 in F]

I.iii.32 master Mistresse **41 s.d. Exeunt** Exit **100** [F has "Exit" here] **142 I'd** I could **187 s.p. [and throughout scene] Horner** Armorer **212–213** [Q; not in F]

I.iv.25 s.p. Margery Jourdain Witch **62 Aio te** Aio **63 posse** posso

II.i.30 Lord Lords **47 s.p. Cardinal** [not in F] **48 s.p. Gloucester** [not in F] **59 s.p. Townsman** One. [also at l. 61] **106 Alban** Albones **129 his** [Q] it

II.ii.45 was son was **46 son** Sonnes Sonne
II.iii.3 sins sinne **74 apron** Aporne
III.i.222 s.d. Exeunt Exit
III.ii.14 s.d. Somerset Suffolke, Somerset **26 Meg** Nell **79 Margaret** Elianor [also at ll. 100 and 120] **116 witch** watch **278 s.p. Commons** [not in F]
III.iii.8 s.p. Cardinal Beau.
IV.i.6 Clip Cleape **48** [Q; not in F] **50 s.p. Suffolk** [at l. 51 in F] **70** [F: Lieu. Poole, Sir Poole? Lord,] **85 mother's bleeding** Mother-bleeding **93 are** and **113** [Q; not in F] **116 s.p. Whitmore** Lieu. Water: W. **117 Paene** Pine **132 s.p. Suffolk** [at l. 133 in F] **141 s.d. Exeunt** Exit
IV.ii.33 s.p. [and elsewhere] Dick But. [or **Butch.**] **34 fall** faile **46 s.p. [and elsewhere] Smith** Weauer [or **Wea.**] **99 an** a **177 s.d. Exeunt** Exit
IV.iv.27 s.p. First Messenger Mess. **49 Second Messenger** Mess. **58 you be** you
IV.v.s.d. enter enters
IV.vi.9 s.p. Smith But.
IV.vii.7 s.p. Holland Iohn. [also at l. 15] **67 But** Kent **79 s.p. Bevis** George **86 caudle** Candle **132 s.d. Exeunt** Exit
IV.viii.12 rebel rabble
IV.ix.33 calm'd calme
IV.x.20 waning warning **28 I'll** He **57 God** loue **109 these** thee **111 sons** [Q] sonne **113 for** of **194 or** and **195 s.p. Clifford** Old Clif. [and at ll. 198 and 208] **201 household** housed
V.ii.28 oeuvres eumenes **31 s.p. Young Clifford** Clif. [also at l. 84]
V.iii.29 faith [Q] hand

3 Henry VI

Copy text: the First Folio [F]. O = the octavo of 1595.
I.i.2 s.p. York Pl. [and elsewhere referred to in the s.p. as **Plan.** and **Plant.** as well as **Yorke**] **69 s.p. Exeter** [O] Westm. **105 Thy** [O] My **259 with me** me **261 from** [O] to **273 s.d. Flourish** [at beginning of I.ii in F] **Exeunt** Exit
I.ii.47 s.d. a Messenger [O] Gabriel **49 s.p. Messenger** [O] Gabriel **75 s.d. Exeunt** Exit
I.iv.150 passion passions **180 s.d. Exeunt** Exit
II.i.94 s.d. Montague Montacute **113** [O, not in F] **131 an idle** a lazie
II.ii.89 Since Cla. Since **133 s.p. Richard** [O] War. **163 s.p. George** Cla. **[and elsewhere until III.ii]**
II.v.54 s.d. [followed in F by "and a Father that hath kill'd his Sonne at another doore"] **78 s.d.** [F reads: "Enter Father, bearing of his Sonne"] **119 E'en** Men
II.vi.6 commixture [O] Commixtures **8** [O; not in F] **42 s.p. Edward** [O] Rich. **43 s.p. Richard** [O; not in F] **44 s.p. Edward** [so O; in F, follows "it is"] **60 his** [O] is
III.i.s.d. two Keepers [O] Sinklo, and Humfrey [and throughout scene, in s.p.] **7 scare** scarre **12 s.p. Second Keeper** Sink. **17 wast** was **24 thee, sour adversity** the sower Aduersaries **30 Is** I: **55 thou that** [O] thou
III.ii.s.p. King Edward King. **[and elsewhere] 8 s.p. [and throughout] Gloucester** Rich. **18 s.p. [and throughout] Lady Grey** Wid. **123 honorably** [O] honourable **175 rends** rents
III.iii.78 s.p. Prince Edw. **124 eternal** [O] externall **161 s.d.** [at l. 160 in F] **228 I'll** [O] I
IV.i.67 s.p. Queen Elizabeth Lady Grey
IV.ii.15 towns Towne
IV.iii.27 s.d. Hastings Fly Hastings flyes **59 s.d. Exit** Exeunt **64 s.d. Exeunt** exit
IV.iv.2 s.p. [and throughout scene] Queen Elizabeth Gray. **17 wean** waine
IV.v.4 stands stand **8 Comes** Come
IV.vi.55 goods be Goods
IV.viii.s.d. Exeter Somerset
V.i.78 an in
V.iv.27 ragged raged
V.v.38 thou the **50 The Tower** [O] Tower **77 butcher** [O] butcher Richard **90 s.d. Exeunt** Exit
V.vii.5 renown'd [O] Renowne **25 thou shalt** [O] that shalt **33 s.p. Queen Elizabeth** [O] Cla. **Thanks** [O] Thanke **38 Reignier** Reynard

Richard III

Copy text: the First Folio [F], except for two passages, III.i.1–158 and V.iii.48 to end of play, for which Q1 is copy text. Unless otherwise indicated, the adopted readings are from the first Quarto of 1597 [Q1].
I.i.1 s.p. Gloucester [not in F] **41 s.d. Enter . . . Brakenbury** [eds.] Enter Clarence, and Brakenbury guarded **45 the** th' **46 s.p. [and throughout] Gloucester** Rich. **65 tempers him to this** tempts him to this harsh **75 to her for his** for her **103 I** I do **133 prey** play
I.ii.27 life [eds.] death **39 stand** Stand'st **78 of a** of **138 thee** the **168 words** word **201 s.p. Gloucester** [not in F] **202** [not in F] **224 s.d. Exeunt** [eds.] Exit [also at l. 226] **225 Gloucester Sirs . . . corse** [not in F]
I.iii.17 come comes **lords** Lord **19 s.p. [and elsewhere] Stanley** Der. **44 That** Thar **108 s.d.** [at l. 109 in F] **113** [not in F] **159 of** off **308 s.p. Queen Elizabeth** Mar. **341 s.p. First Murderer** Vil. [also at ll. 349 and 355]
I.iv.13 Thence There **86 s.p. First Murderer** [eds.] 2. Mur. **89 s.p. Second Murderer** [eds.] 1 **99 s.d. Exit** [at l. 97 in F] **122 Faith** [not in F] **126 'Zounds** come **147 'Zounds** [not in F] **192 to have redemption** for any goodnesse **193** [not in F] **229 O, if** If **240** [not in F] **269** [in F, printed after l. 263]
II.i.s.d. Buckingham [eds.] Buckingham, Wooduill **5 in** to **7 Rivers and Hastings** Dorset and Riuers **39 God** heauen **57 unwittingly** vnwillingly **59 By** To **68** [F follows with a line: "Of you Lord **Wooduill,** and Lord **Scales** of you,"] **85 this** the **93 but** and **108 at** and
II.ii.1 s.p. Boy Edw. **3 s.p. [and throughout scene] Girl** Daugh. **3 do you** do **47 have I** haue **83 weep** weepes **84–85 Clarence . . . they** Clarence weep, so do not they **87 Pour** Power **142 Ludlow** London [also at l. 154] **145** [not in F]
II.iii.43 Ensuing Pursuing [but the catchword on p. 184 in F is "Ensuing"]
II.iv.1 hear heard **9 young** good **20 this** his **21 s.p. Archbishop** Car. [Q1] Yor. [F] **65 death** earth
III.i.1–158 [based on Q1 as copy text] **60** [bracketed s.d. from F] **150 s.d. [A sennet]** [from F] **Hastings** Hast. Dors.
III.ii.78 as you do as
III.iii.1 [not in F]
III.iv.58 [not in F] **82 raze** rowse **83 But** And
III.v.4 wert were **34 Look . . . Mayor** [not in F] **104 Penker** [eds.] Peuker **105 s.d. Exeunt** [eds.] Exit
III.vii.43 [not in F] **44 s.p.** Gloucester [not in F] **54 we'll** we **83 My lord** [not in F] **125 her** his [also in ll. 126 and 127] **219 'Zounds! I'll** we will **220** [not in F] **221 them** him **241 s.p. Mayor and Citizens** All **247 cousin** Cousins
IV.i.s.d. [F: Enter the Queene, Anne Duchesse of Gloucester, the Duchesse of Yorke, and Marquesse Dorset.] **15 s.p. Brakenbury** Lieu. [and at l. 26]
IV.ii.36 My lord [not in F] **72 there** then **77 I'll** He **90 Hereford** Hertford **98–116** [not in F]
IV.iii.5 ruthless ruthfull **13 Which** And **15 once** one **31 at** and **33 thee** the **53 leads** leds
IV.iv.10 unblown vnblowed **39** [not in F] **o'er** over [Q1] **41 Harry** [eds.] Husband **45 holp'st** hop'st **52–53** [lines reversed in F] **64 Thy** The **128 intestate** intestine **141 Where** Where't **239 or** and **268 would I** I would **284 This is** this **324 Of ten** [eds.] Often **364–365** [lines reversed in F, and the s.p. Queen Elizabeth is missing] **366 s.p. King Richard** [not in F] **377 God** Heauen **God's** Heanens **392 in** with **396 o'erpast** repast **417 fond** found **430 s.d. Exit Queen** [at l. 429 in F] **431 s.d. Enter Ratcliffe** [at l. 432 in F] **444 Ratcliffe** [eds.] Catesby **498 s.p. First Messenger** Mess. **503 s.p. Second Messenger** Mess. **506 s.p. Third Messenger** Mess. [also at ll. 509 and 517] **518 s.p. Fourth Messenger** Mess.
V.i.11 is, my lord is
V.ii.11 center Centry **12 Near** Ne're
V.iii.28 you [eds.] your **48 to end of play** [copy text is Q1] **54 sentinels** centinell [Q1] **59 s.p. Catesby** Rat. **79 sit** set **107 s.d. [Manet Richmond]** [from F] **139 s.p. Ghost of Rivers** King [Q1] **141 s.p. Ghost of Grey** Gray **142 s.p. Ghost of Vaughan** Vaugh. **145 Will** Wel [Q1] **146 s.p.**

Ghosts Ghost **159 s.p. Ghost** [not in Q1] **167 s.p. Ghost** [not in Q1] **183 am** and [Q1] **270 s.d. Ratcliffe** Rat. & c. **301 boot** bootes [Q1]

V.v.13 s.p. Stanley [not in Q1] **13 Ferrers** Ferri [Q1] **15 becomes** become [Q1] **41 s.d. Exeunt** [F; not in Q1]

King John

Copy text: the First Folio [F].

I.i.30 s.d. Exeunt Exit **49 expedition's** expeditious **50 s.p. [and elsewhere] Bastard** Philip **147 I** It **208 smack** smoake **219 s.d.** [at l. 221 in F] **237 he get** get **257 Thou** That

II.i. [here F reads "Scæna Secunda"] **1 s.p. King Philip** Lewis [also at l. 18] **63 Ate** Ace **89 s.p. [and elsewhere] King Philip** Fran. **113 breast** beast **122 s.p. [and elsewhere] Elinor** Queen **144 shows** shooes **149 Philip** Lewis **150 s.p. King Philip** Lew. **152 Anjou** Angiers **166 s.p. Elinor** Qu. Mo. **201 s.p. First Citizen** Cit. [and so until l. 325] **215 Confronts your** Comfort yours **252 invulnerable** involuerable **259 roundure** rounder **325 s.p. First Citizen** Hubert [also at ll. 363, 416, 423, 480] **335 run** rome **368 s.p. First Citizen** Fra. **371 King'd of our fears** Kings of our feare **468 s.p. Elinor** Old Qu. **487 Anjou** Angiers **496 s.p. [and elsewhere] Lewis** Dol.

III.i [here F reads "Actus Secundus"] **74** [following this line, F reads "Actus Tertius, Scæna prima"] **s.d. Austria** Austria, Constance **110 day** daies **323 s.p. King John** Eng.

III.ii.4 s.d. [at l. 3 in F] **10 s.d. Exeunt** Exit

III.iv. [here F reads "Scaena Tertia"] **44 not holy** holy **64 friends** fiends **110 world's** words

IV.i.6 s.p. First Executioner Exec. [also at l. 85] **63 his** this **91 mote** moth

IV.ii.1 again crown'd against crown'd **73 Doth** Do **105 s.d.** [at l. 103 in F] **132 s.d.** [at l. 131 in F]

IV.iii.33 man mans **41 Have you** you haue **155 cincture** center **159 s.d. Exeunt** Exit

V.ii.26 Were Was **43 hast thou** hast **133 unhair'd** vn-heard **135 these** this **145 his** this

V.v.7 wound woon'd

V.vi.12 eyeless endles

V.vii.17 mind winde **21 cygnet** Symet **108 give you** giue

Richard II

Copy text: the first quarto of 1597 as press-corrected in all four extant copies [Q1]; and, for the deposition scene, IV.1.155–319, the First Folio [F].

I.i.118 by my by **152 gentlemen** gentleman **163 Obedience bids** obedience bids. Obedience bids

I.ii.42 alas, may [F] may **47 sit** set **58 it** is **59 empty** [F] emptines **60 begun** begone **70 hear** [F] cheere

I.iii.15 thee the **33 comest** comes **58 thee** the **84 innocency** innocence **104 s.p. First Herald** Herauld **108 his God** [F] God **128 civil** [F] cruell **133 Draws** Draw **136 wrathful iron** [F] harsh resounding **172 then but** but **180 you owe** y'owe **193 far** fare **222 night** nightes **239 had it** had't **241 sought** ought

I.iv.s.d. Bagot [F] Bushie **20 our cousin** our Coosens **23 Bagot here, and Green** [Q6; not in Q1] **27 What** With **52 s.d. Enter Bushy** Enter Bushie with news **53 Bushy, what news** [F; not in Q1] **65 s.p. All** [not in Q1]

II.i.15 life's liues **18 fond** found **48 as a** as **68 s.d.** [at l. 70 in Q1] **102 incaged** inraged **113 not** not, not **124 brother** brothers **156 kerns** kerne **177 the** a **209 seize** cease **257 King's** King **277 Blanc** Blan **280** [not in Q1] **284 Quoint** Coines

II.ii.31 though thought **53 Harry** H. **122 go to** go for **128 that's** that is

II.iii.30 lordship Lo: **36 Hereford** Herefords **99 the lord** Lord

III.ii.32 succor succors **40 boldly** bouldy **72 O'erthrows** Ouerthrowes **170 through** thorough

III.iii.13 brief with you [F] briefe **100 pastures'** pastors **120 prince, is** princesse

III.iv.11 joy griefe **26 pins** pines **29 yon** yong **34 too** two **55 seiz'd** ceasde **57 We at** at **80 Cam'st** Canst

IV.i.23 him them **44 Fitzwater** Fitzwaters **55 As** As it **56 sun to sun** sinne to sinne **77 my bond** bond **110 thee** the **146 you** yon **155–319** [This deposition scene is based on the First Folio text; Q1 has only: "Let it be so, and loe on wednesday next,/We solemnly proclaime our Coronation,/Lords be ready all." Unless otherwise indicated all the new readings in ll. 155–319 are taken from Q4.] **184 and on** on **252 and** a **256 Nor** No, nor **287 And** That **297 manners** manner

V.i.41 thee the **84 s.p. Northumberland** King

V.ii.2 off of **11 thee** the [also at ll. 17 and 94] **65 bond** band **116 And** An

V.iii.s.d. King the King **36 I may** May **68 And** An **75 voic'd** voice **111 s.p. King Henry** yorke **135–136 With . . . him** I pardon him with al my heart

V.iv.s.d. Enter [F] Manet **3 s.p. First Man** Man [also at l. 6]

V.v.20 through thorow **27 sit** set

V.vi.8 Salisbury, Spencer Oxford, Salisbury **12 s.d. Fitzwater** Fitzwaters **43 thorough** through

1 Henry IV

Copy text: the first complete quarto of 1598 [Q1]; and, for I.iii.201 through II.ii.110, the fragment of an earlier quarto [Q0].

I.i.22 levy leauy **39 Herefordshire** Herdforshire **62 a dear** deere **76 In faith, it is** [assigned in Q1 to King]

I.ii.16 king a king **78 similes** smiles **154 thou** the **158 Bardolph, Peto** Haruey, Rossill

I.iii.108 base bare **194 good night** god-night **201 s.p. Hotspur** [missing in Q0–Q4] **239 whipp'd** [Q1 whip Q0]

II.i.34 s.p. First Carrier Car. **48 s.d.** [at l. 47 in Q0]

II.ii.s.d. Poins, Peto Poines, and Peto &c. **20 Bardolph** Bardol [and thus, or "Bardoll," throughout the play] **34 mine** [Q1] my [Q0] **40 Go hang** [F] Hang [Q0] **51 s.p. and text BARDOLPH What news** [all assigned as continuation of Poins' speech in l. 50] **52 s.p. Gadshill** Bar. **78 s.p. First Traveler** Trauel. **82 s.p. Travelers** Trauel. [also at l. 86]

II.iii.1 s.p. Hotspur [not in Q1] **4 In** In the **48 thee** the

II.iv.33 precedent present **36 s.p. Poins** Prin. **153 All's** All is **171 s.p. Prince** Gad **172 s.p. Gadshill** Ross. [also at ll. 174 and 178] **322 s.d.** [at l. 321 in Q1] **337 Owen** O **390 tristful** trustfull **398 yet** so **468 lean** lane **487 mad** made **518 Good** God [also at l. 519] **526 s.d. pockets** pocket **530 s.p. Peto** [not in Q1] **535 s.p. Prince** [not in Q1]

III.i.97 cantle scantle **124 meter** miter

III.ii.84 gorg'd gordge **145 northern** Northren **161 s.d.** [at l. 162 in Q1]

III.iii.35 that's that **57 tithe** tight **88 s.d. them** him **173 guests** ghesse **200 o' clock** of clocke

IV.i.1 s.p. [and elsewhere] Hotspur Per. **20 lord** mind **55 is** tis **108 dropp'd** drop **116 altar** altars **123 ne'er** neare **126 cannot** can **127 yet** it

IV.ii.3 Co'fil' cophill **15 yeomen's** Yeomans **31 feaz'd** fazd **80 s.d. Exit** Exeunt

IV.iii.21 horse horses **82 country's** Countrey

IV.iv.18 o'er-rul'd ouerrulde

V.i.s.d. Lancaster Lancaster, Earle of Westmerland **88 off** of **114 s.d. Exeunt** Exit **138 will it** will

V.ii.3 undone vnder one **12 merrily** merely **25 s.d. Hotspur** Percy **79 s.p. First Messenger** Mes. **89 s.p. Second Messenger** Mes.

V.iii.22 A Ah

V.iv.4 s.p. [and elsewhere] Lancaster P. Iohn **68 Nor** Now **76 s.d. who** he **92 thee** the

2 Henry IV

Copy text: the Quarto of 1600 [Q], of which II.iv.340 through III.ii.104 exists in two states: the original printing by Valentine Sims [Qa], and a second version with six reset pages [Qb] that had been expanded to include III.i, inadvertently omitted from Qa. Qa is the copy text for those portions that were reset, Qb for III.i itself. In addition, the First Folio [F] is copy text for certain passages excised from Q, as indicated below; they are bracketed in the text itself.

The Actors' Names [taken from F, at the end of the play]

Induction 1 s.p. Rumor [not in Q] **35 hold** hole **36 Where** [F] When **40 s.d. Rumor** Rumours

I.i.7 s.d. [and elsewhere] Northumberland Earle. **27 s.d.** [at l. 25 in Q] **96 slain, say so** [F] slain **161 s.p. Travers** Vmfr. **164 Lean on your** [F] Leaue on you **166–179, 189–209** [F; not in Q] **178 brought** bring [F]

I.ii.1 s.p. Falstaff Iohn [and elsewhere; or sir Iohn] **21 on** [F] off **31 s.p. [and elsewhere] Page** Boy **36 rascally** [F] rascall **38 smooth** [F] smoothy **48 Where's Bardolph** [F; in Q, follows "through it" in l. 47] **49 into** [F] in **119 s.p. Falstaff** [F] Old. **142 slenderer** [F] slender **159 on** [F] in **171 this** [F] his **them, are** [F] the one **177 s.p. [and elsewhere] Chief Justice** Lo. **192 ear** yeere **201–202 you and Prince Harry** [F] you

I.iii.s.d. Hastings Hastings, Fauconbridge **1 s.p. [and elsewhere] Archbishop** Bishop **5 s.p. Mowbray** Marsh. **21–24, 36–55, 85–108** [F; not in Q] **26 case** [F] cause **28 on** [F] and **58 one** [F] on **a** [F] an **59 through** [F] thorough **66 a** [F] so **71 Are** [F] And **79 To French** French **84 'gainst** [F] against **109 s.p. Mowbray** Bish.

II.i.21 vice [F] view **25 continuantly** [F] continually **43 Sir John, I** [F] I **58 s.p. Falstaff** Boy. **102 mad** [F] made **117 done** [F] done with **143 German** Iarman **145 tapestries** [F] tapestrie **163 s.d. Exeunt** exit [at l. 160 in Q] **167 Basingstoke** [F] Billingsgate **167, 171 s.p. Gower** Mess.

II.ii.s.d. Poins Poynes, sir Iohn Russel **others** other **15 viz.** [F] with **16 ones** once **21–22 made a shift to eat** [F] eate **75 e'en now** enow **78 new petticoat** [F] peticote **81 rabbit** rabble **109 borrower's** borrowed **119 s.p. Prince reads** [not in Q or F] **125 familiars** [F] family **149 heifers** Heicfors

II.iii.5 s.p. [and elsewhere] Lady Northumberland Wife **9 s.p. [and elsewhere] Lady Percy** Kate **11 endear'd** [F] endeere **23–45** [from F; not in Q]

II.iv.4 s.p. Second Drawer Draw. **12 s.d.** [at l. 18 in Q] **13 s.p. Third Drawer** Dra. [also at l. 19] **19 old** oll **21 s.p. Second Drawer** Francis **22 s.p. [and elsewhere] Hostess** Quickly **30 s.p. [and elsewhere] Doll** Tere. **42–43 them; I** [F] I **62 s.p. Doll** Dorothy **82 Your** [F] & your **107 s.d. Boy** Bardolfes boy. **114 shall** [F] shall not **173 Die men** [F] Men **182 nothing** [F] no things **196 Untwine** vntwinde **252 the scales** [F] scales **253 avoirdupois** haber de poiz **265 master's** [F] master **275 It** [F] a **278 so** [F] to **300 even now** [F] now **340–390** [copy text for this passage is Qa] **380 Exit** [Qb; not in Qa]

III.i [this scene appears in Qb, not in Qa] **18 mast** [F] masse **22 billows** [F] pillowes **26 thy** [F] them **27 sea-boy** [F] season **36 letters** letter **59 years** [F] yeare **81 nature of** [F] natures or **84 which** [F] who **85 beginnings** [F] beginning **87 of** [F] or

III.ii.1–104 [copy text for this passage is Qa] **23 bona-robas** [F] bona robes **39 Stamford** [F] Samforth **45 fine** [Qb, F] fiue **56 s.p. Shallow** [not in Qa or Qb] **67–68 accommodated** [F] accommodate **82 s.p. Shallow** Iust. [Qa] **87 Surecard** [F] Soccard **111 s.p.** and text **FALSTAFF Prick him** [Q prints as s.d.: "Iohn prickes him"] **144 for his** [F] for **150 s.p. Falstaff** Shal. **175 prick me** [F] prick **195–196 good . . . that** [F] master Shallow **209 Clement's Inn** [F] Clemham **210 years** [F] yeare **229–230 old dame's** [F] dames **250 Shadow** Sadow **287 will** wooll **298 s.d. Exeunt** Exit **299 On . . . away** [this speech assigned in Q to Shallow] **312 invisible** inuincible **314 ever** [F] ouer **324 skin** [F] shin **326 be** [F] he

IV.i.1 s.p. [and elsewhere] Archbishop Bish. **12 could** [F] would [in some copies of Q] **30 Then, my lord** [F; not in Q] **34 rags** rage **36 appear'd** appeare **55–79, 103–139** [F; not in Q] **116 force** forc'd [F] **139 indeed** and did [F] **175 to our** [F] our **180 And** At

IV.ii s.d. [appears two lines earlier in Q] **8 Than** [F] That **man** [F] man talking **19 imagin'd** imagine **24 Employ** [F] Imply **48 this** [F] his **67 s.p. Prince John** [F; not in Q] **69 s.p. Hastings** [F] Prince **97 s.d.** [at l. 96 in Q] **117 and . . . yours** [F; not in Q] **122 these traitors** [F] this traitour

IV.iii.s.d. [Q: "Alarum. Enter Falstaffe. excursions"] **25 s.d. Retreat** [at l. 23 in Q] **43 I came** [F] there cosin, I came **48 of 't** on 't [Q] of it [F] **85 had but** had

IV.iv.s.d. Warwick Warwike, Kent **39 line** [F] time **51 s.p. [and elsewhere] Clarence** Tho. **52 Canst . . . that** [F; not in Q] **94 heaven** [F] heauens **104 write** [F] wet **letters** [F] termes **112 s.p. [and elsewhere] Gloucester** Hum. **120 and will break out** [F; not in Q] **132 Softly, pray** [F; not in Q]

IV.v.13 alter'd [F] vttred [in some copies of Q] **49 How fares your Grace** [F; not in Q] **75 The virtuous sweets** [F; not in Q] **76 thighs** [F] thigh **79 s.d.** [at l. 81 in Q] **81 hath** [F] hands **88 s.d.** [at l. 87 in Q] **91 s.p. Prince** Harry **107 Which** [F] Whom **160 worst of** [F] worse then **161 carat, is** [F] karrat **177 O my son** [F; not in Q] **178 it in** [F] in **204 my** thy **220 My gracious liege** [F; not in Q] **226 s.p. [and elsewhere] Prince John** Lanc.

V.i.23 lost the other day [F] lost **Hinckley** [F] Hunkly **56 all my** [F] my **65 of him** [F] him

V.ii.s.d. [Q: "Enter Warwike, duke Humphrey, L. chiefe Iustice, Thomas Clarence, Prince, Iohn Westmerland"] **21 s.p. Gloucester, Clarence** Prin. ambo **44 s.p. [and elsewhere] King** Prince **46 mix** mixt **61 s.d. Princes** Bro. **125 spirit** spirites **127 rase** race **145 s.d. Exeunt** exit

V.iii.47 thee the **70 s.d.** [at l. 68 in Q] **93 i' thy** ith thy **127 knighthood** [F] Knight **143 s.p. Exeunt** exit

V.iv.s.d. Beadle Sincklo **4 s.p. Beadle** Sincklo [and throughout scene] **6 lately kill'd** [F] kild **7 s.p. Doll** [F] Whoore [and throughout scene] **11 He** [F] I

V.v.1 s.p. First Groom 1 [and similarly in ll. 2 and 3] **15 s.p. Shallow** Pist. [also at ll. 17 and 19] **24 s.p. Falstaff** [F; not in Q] **29 all in** in **48 become** [F] becomes **71 our** [F] my **82 cannot well** [F] cannot **83 should give** [F] giue

Epilogue 23 before in [F] in **30 died a** [F] died **32–33 and so . . . queen** [F; in Q this appears after l. 15]

Henry V

Copy text: the First Folio [F]. Q = the bad Quarto of 1600.

Prologue 1 s.p. Chorus [not in F; also in prologues to other Acts]

I.ii.38 succedant succedaul **45 Elbe** Elue [also at l. 52] **115 s.p. Ely** Bish. **131 blood** Bloods **163 her** their **197 majesty** Maiesties **212 End** [Q] And **237 s.p. First Ambassador** Amb. [also at l. 245]

II.i.23 mare [Q] name **28 s.p. Nym** [Q; not in F] **42, 43 Iceland** Island **73 thee defy** [Q] defie thee **80 enough** enough to **83 you** your **105–106** [Q; not in F] **betting** beating [Q] **116 that's** that **117 came** come

II.ii.29 s.p. Grey Kni. **87 furnish him** furnish **107 a** an **114 All** And **139 mark the** make thee **147 Henry** [Q] Thomas **148 Masham** [Q] Marsham **159 Which I** Which **176 have sought** [Q] sought **181 s.d. Exeunt** Exit

II.iii.16 'a babbl'd a Table **24 upward** vp-peer'd **32 s.p. Hostess** Woman. **48 word** world

II.iv.1 s.p. [and elsewhere] French King King.

III. Prologue [here F has "Actus Secundus"] **3 Hampton** Douer **6 fanning** fayning

III.i.7 summon commune **17 noblest** Noblish **24 men** me **32 Straining** Straying

III.ii.67 s.p. [and elsewhere in scene] Fluellen Welch. **82 s.p. [and elsewhere in scene] Jamy** Scot. **87 s.p. [and elsewhere in scene] MacMorris** Irish.

III.iii.32 heady headly **35 Defile** Desire **43** [here F has s.d. "Enter Gouernour"]

III.iv.1–2 parles bien bien parlas [throughout the play, the French has been somewhat modernized, besides the emendations listed here] **7 Et les doigts** [assigned to Alice in F] **8 s.p. Alice** Kat. **9 souviendrai** souemeray **12 s.p. Katharine** Alice **13 j'ai** Kath. I'ay **16 Nous** [not in F] **40 pas déjà** y desia **42 Non** Nome **46 Sauf** Sans

III.v.11 Dieu du **43 Vaudemont** Vandemont **45 Foix** Loys **46 knights** Kings

III.vi.31 her [Q] his **111–112 lenity** Leuitie

III.vii.12 pasterns postures **59 lief** liue **65 truie** leuye

IV. Prologue [here F has "Actus Tertius"] **16 name** nam'd **20 cripple** creeple **27 Presenteth** Presented

IV.i.3 Good God **94 Thomas** Iohn **226 s.d. Exeunt** Exit [at l. 221 in F] **242 adoration** Odoration **288 if** of **306 friends** friend

IV.ii.2 à cheval Cheual **4 eaux** ewes **6 Cieux** cein **49 gimmal'd** Iymold

IV.iii.12 [placed after l. 14 in F] **48** [not in F] **124 'em** vm
IV.iv.2 êtes estes le **15 Or** for **35 de** a **36 à cette heure** asture **42 suis** suis le **54 l'avez** layt a **de** a **57 remercîments** remercions **58 suis tombé** intombe **59 distingué** distinie **68 Suivez** Saaue
IV.v.2 perdu . . . perdu perdia . . . perdie **15 by a** [Q] a base **23 s.d. Exeunt** Exit
IV.vi.34 mistful mixtfull
IV.vii. [F has "Actus Quintus" here] **69 s.p. [and elsewhere in this scene] Mountjoy** Her. **77 their** with **109 countryman** Countrymen **114 God** Good
IV.viii.100 Vaudemont Vandemont **113 we** me
V. Prologue 29 but but by
V.i.69 begun began **87 swear** swore
V.ii.1 s.p. [and throughout scene] King Henry King **12 s.p. [and throughout scene] Queen Isabel** Quee. **12 England** Ireland **21 s.p. King Henry** Eng. **[also elsewhere] 50 all** withall **61 diffus'd** defused **77 cursitory** curselarie **114 s.p. [and elsewhere] Alice** Lady **190 meilleur** melieus **264 baiser** buisse **322 hath never** hath **363 paction** Pation

Henry VIII

Copy text: the First Folio [F].
I.i.42–45 All . . . function [assigned in F to Buckingham] **47 as you guess** [assigned in F to Norfolk] **63 'a** O **115 s.p. [and elsewhere] Wolsey** Car. **116, 117 s.p. First Secretary** Secr. **120 venom** venom'd **200 Hereford** Hertford **219 Perk** Pecke **chancellor** Councellour **221 Nicholas** Michaell **226 lord** Lords
I.ii.8 s.d. [F: A noyse within crying roome for the Queene, usher'd by the Duke of Norfolke. Enter the Queene, Norfolke and Suffolke: she kneels.] [etc.] **9 s.p. [and elsewhere] Katharine** Queen. **67 business** basenesse **156 fear'd** feare **164 confession's** Commissions **170 To gain** To **180 him** this **190 Bulmer** Blumer
I.iii.s.d. Sands Sandys [elsewhere both **Sands** and **Sandys**] **13 Or** A **15 s.d.** [at l. 16 in F] **34 oui** wee
I.iv.s.d. [and elsewhere] Guildford Guilford **50 s.d.** [at l. 49 in F]
II.i.18 have him **20 Perk** Pecke **86 mark** make
II.ii.1 s.p. Chamberlain [not in F]
II.iii.61 of you of you, to you
II.iv.11 s.p. Katharine [not in F] **131 s.d. Exeunt** Exit **172 A** And
III.i.23 s.d. Campeius Campian **61 your** our
III.ii.142 glad gald **171 fil'd** fill'd **292 Who** Whom **343 Chattels** Castles
IV.i.20 s.p. Second Gentleman 1 **34 Kimbolton** Kymmalton **55 s.p. First Gentleman** [not in F] **101 Stokesly** Stokeley
IV.ii.7 think thanke
V.i.37 time Lime **55 s.d. Exeunt** Exit [at l. 54 in F] **78 s.d.** [at l. 79 in F] **139 precipice** Precepit **140 woo** woe
V.ii.8 piece Peere
V.iii.85, 87, 107 s.p. Chancellor Cham. **133 this** his **173 heart** hearts
V.iv.4, 27 s.p. One [not in F]
V.v.38 ways way

Titus Andronicus

Copy text: the first Quarto of 1594 [Q], except for III.ii, based on F. F = the First Folio.
I.i.58 s.d. Exeunt Exit. **67 s.p. Captain** [not in Q] **71 s.d. three Sons** two sonnes **74 her** his **101 manes** manus **132 s.d. Exeunt** Exit **160 s.p. Lavinia** [not in Q] **230 Titan's** Tytus **246 Pantheon** Pathan **284 cuique** cuiqum **303 s.p. [and elsewhere] Saturninus** Emperour. **320 Phoebe** Thebe **362 s.p. Martius** Titus two sonnes speakes **364 s.p. Martius** Titus sonne speakes **372 s.p. Quintus** 3. Sonne. **373 s.p. Martius** 2. Sonne. [also at l. 375] **392 s.d. They all kneel** they all kneele and say **393 s.p. All** [not in Q] **394** [Q follows with a s.d.: "Exit all but Marcus and Titus"] **402** [F; not in Q] **478 s.p. Lucius** [F; not in Q] **479 mildly** mi'd ie
II.i.37 s.p. [and elsewhere] Aaron Moore. **110 than** this
II.ii.1 morn Moone **24 run** runnes
II.iii.13 snake snakes **69 try** trie thy **88 s.p. [and elsewhere] Tamora** Queene. **131 ye** we **150 heard** hard **153 Some** So me **160 ears** yeares **175 their** there **192 s.p. Aaron** [not in Q] **210 unhallowed** vnhollow **222 beray'd in blood** bereaud in blood [Q, with marginal correction in contemporary handwriting: "heere reau'd of lyfe"] **231 Pyramus** Priamus **236 Cocytus'** Ocitus **260 s.p. [and elsewhere] Saturninus** King. **291 fault** faults
II.iv.11 s.p. Marcus [not in Q] **21 have** halfe **27 him** them **30 three** their
III.i.17 urns ruines **21 on thy** out hy **146 his** her
III.ii. [the entire scene is missing in Q; copy text is F] **39 complainer** complaynet **52 thy knife** knife **53 fly** Flys **54 thee** the **55 are cloy'd** cloi'd **72 myself** my selfes
IV.i.1 s.p. [and throughout] Boy Puer. **10 s.p. Marcus** [not in Q] **52 quotes** coats **55 Forc'd** Frocd **79 s.p. Titus** [not in Q] **90 hope** hop (?) I op (?)
IV.ii.15 lordships, that Lordships **52 Good** God **97 Alcides** Alciades
IV.iii.56 Saturn Saturnine, to **77 News . . . come** [assigned in Q to Clown]
IV.iv.5 know, as know know **48 By'** be **93 feed** seede **98 ears** yeares **105 on** in
V.i.9 s.p. First Goth Goth [also at ll. 121, 162] **17 s.p. All the Goths** [not in Q] **20 s.p. Second Goth** Goth **43 here's** her's **53 Get me a ladder** [assigned in Q to Aaron] **113 extreme** extreanie **141 Tut** But **152 s.p. Third Goth** Goth
V.ii.38 them out the mout **49 globe** Globes **52 murd'rers** murder **caves** cares **56 Hyperion's** Epeons **61 they** them **65 worldly** wordlie **121 s.d.** [at l. 120 in Q] **142 know** knew **suppose** supposd **154 Chiron and** Chiron **196 s.d.** [at l. 203 in Q]
V.iii.3 s.p. First Goth Got. **26 gracious lord** Lord **73 s.p. Aemilius** Romane Lord. **125 cause** course **141 s.p. All** Marcus. **142 s.p.** [no s.p. here in Q; see previous note] **144 adjudg'd** adiudge **146 s.p. All** [not in Q] **154 blood-stain'd** blood slaine **163 Sung** Song **176 s.p. Aemilius** Romane.

Romeo and Juliet

Copy text: the second Quarto of 1599 [Q2]. Q1 = the first Quarto of 1597.
I.i.27 it in [Q1] it **73 s.p. Citizens** Offi. **76 s.p. Capulet's Wife** Wife. **120 drave** drive **147 his** is **153 sun** same **177 create** [Q1] created **179 well-seeming** [Q1] welseeing **192 lovers'** [Q1] loving **202 Bid A** [Q1] A **make** [Q1] makes **211 unharm'd** [Q1] vncharmd **218 makes** make
I.ii.14 The earth Earth **32 on** one **46 One** [Q1] on **70 and Livia** Liuia **91 fires** fier
I.iii.50 s.p. [and elsewhere] Wife Old La. **66 disposition** [F] dispositions **67, 68 honor** [Q1] houre **100 it fly** [Q1] flie **105 s.p. [and elsewhere] Wife** Mo.
I.iv.7–8 [Q1; not in Q2] **23 s.p. Mercutio** Horatio. **39 done** [Q1] dum **42 Of this sir-reverence** Or saue you reuerence **45 like lamps** [Q1] lights lights **47 five** fine **57 atomies** ottamie **59–61** [these lines follow l. 69 in Q1] **66 film** Philome **69 maid** [Q1] man **72 O'er** [Q1] On **76 breaths** [Q1] breath **81 dreams he** [Q1] he dreams **90 elf-locks** Elklocks **111 forfeit** [Q1] fofreit
I.v.s.d. [Q2 adds: "Enter Romeo"] **1 s.p. First Servant** Ser. [also at ll. 6 and 12] **3 s.p. Second Servant** 1. **11 s.p. Third Servant** 2. **14 s.p. Fourth Servant** 3. **17 s.p. Capulet** 1. Capu. [also at ll. 35 and 40] **18 a bout** about **97 ready** [Q1] did readie
II. Chorus **1 s.p. Chorus** [not in Q2] **4 match'd** match
II.i.6 Nay . . . too [assigned in Q2 to Benvolio] **10 one** [Q1] on **11 Pronounce** [Q1] prouaunt **dove** [Q1] day **13 heir** [Q1] her **39 open-arse, and** open, or
II.ii.16 do [Q1] to **20 eyes** [Q1] eye **41–42 nor any . . . name** ô

be some other name/Belonging to a man **45 were** [Q1] wene **58 not yet** yet not **83 wash'd** [Q1] washeth **101 more coying** coying **110 circled** [Q1] circle **149, 151 s.p. Nurse** [not in Q2] **162 than mine** then **169 years** [Q1] yeare **179 gyves** giues **186 Sleep . . . breast** [Q1; assigned in Q2 to Juliet] **188–189** [preceded in Q2 by four lines of the next scene]

II.iii.2 Check'ring [Q1] Checking **4 fiery** [Q1] burning **85 not. She whom** [Q1] me not, her

II.iv.18 s.p. Benvolio [Q1] Ro. **19 cats, I can tell you** cats **28–29 phantasimes** phantacies **33 pardon-me's** pardons mees **40 but a** a **113–114 for himself** [Q1] himself **143 Marry, farewell** [Q1; not in Q2] **205 dog's** dog **213 s.d. Exeunt** Exit

II.v.5 glide glides **11 three** there **15 And** M. And **26 I had** [Q1] I

II.vi.18 gossamer gossamours **27 music's** musicke

III.i.2 Capels are Capels **67 injur'd** iniuried **73 stoccato** stucatho **89 s.d.** [Q2: "Away Tybalt"] **90 your houses** houses **121 gone** gan **123 fire-ey'd** [Q1] fier end **136, 138 s.p. First Citizen** Citti. **165 agile** [Q1] aged **183 s.p. Montague** Capu. **191 I** [Q1] It **196 s.d. Exeunt** Exit

III.ii.1 s.p. Juliet [not in Q2] **9 By** And by **21 he** I **47 darting** arting **49 shut** shot **51 of my** my **60 one** on **72 It . . . did** [assigned in Q2 to Juliet] **73 O . . . face** [assigned in Q2 to Nurse] **76 Dove-feather'd** Rauenous douefeatherd **79 damned** dimme **143 s.d. Exeunt** Exit

III.iii. s.d. [Q2 has "Enter Friar and Romeo"] **39** [Q2 follows with a line: "This may flyes do, when I from this must flie"] **43** [printed in Q2 before l. 40] **52 Thou** [Q1] Then **61 madmen** [Q1] mad man **70 s.d. Knock** Enter Nurse, and knocke **73 s.d. Knock** They knocke **75 s.d. Knock** Slud knock **80 s.d. Enter Nurse** [at l. 78 in Q2] **110 denote** [Q1] deuote **117 lives** lies **144 pouts upon** puts vp **168 disguis'd** disguise

III.iv.10 s.d. [and elsewhere] Wife La. **13 be** me

III.v.13 exhal'd exhale **31 chang'd** change **36 s.d. Enter Nurse** Enter Madame and Nurse **54 s.p. Juliet** Ro. **67 s.d.** [bracketed s.d. from Q1] **82 pardon him** padon **139 gives** giue **160 s.p. [and elsewhere] Capulet** Fa. **172 s.p.** and text **Capulet O, God-i-god-en** Father, ô Godigeden **173 s.p. Nurse** [not in Q2] **181 lien'd** liand

IV.i.7 talk'd [Q1] talke **45 cure** [Q1] care **46 Ah** [Q1] O **72 slay** [Q1] stay **78 off** [Q1] of **83 chapless** [Q1] chapels **85 his tomb** his **98 breath** [Q1] breast **100 wanny** many **110 In** Is [Q2 follows with a line: "Be borne to buriall in thy kindreds graue"] **111 shalt** shall **115 and he** an he **116 waking** walking **126 s.d. Exeunt** Exit

IV.ii.3, 6 s.p. Second Servant Ser. **14 will'd** wield **38 s.p. [and elsewhere] Wife** Mo. **47 s.d. Exeunt** Exit

IV.iii.49 wake walke

IV.iv.1 s.p. [and elsewhere] Wife La. **12 s.d. Exeunt** Exit **14 s.p. First Servant** Fel. **18 s.p. Second Servant** Fel. **21 faith** father **23 s.d.** [at l. 21 in Q2]

IV.v.41 long [Q1] loue **65 cure** care **82 fond** some **96 s.p. First Musician** Musi. **100 by** [Q1] my **100, 105 s.p. First Musician** Fid. **101** [Q2 has s.d. here: "Exit omnes"] **s.d. Enter Peter** Enter Will Kemp. **109 s.p. First Musician** Minstrels [and subsequently in this scene indicated by **Minst.** or **Minstrel.**] **125 Then . . . wit** [assigned in Q2 to 2 M.] **129 And . . . oppress** [Q1; not in Q2] **135, 138 Pretty** [Q1] Prates **147 s.d. Exeunt** Exit

V.i.15 fares my [Q1] doth my Lady **17, 27, 32 s.p. Balthasar** Man. **25 e'en** in **defy** [Q1] denie **33 s.d.** [at l. 32 in Q2] **76 pay** [Q1] pray

V.iii.3 yew [Q1] young **21 s.d. [Balthasar]** [Q1] Peter **40, 43 s.p. Balthasar** Pet. **68 commination** commiration **71 s.p. Page** Boy. [Q1; s.p. missing in Q2 and line treated as a s.d.] **102 fair** faire? I will beleeue **108** [Q2 has four undeleted lines here: "Depart againe, come lye thou in my arme,/Heer's to thy health, where ere thou tumblest in./O true Appothecarie!/Thy drugs are quicke. Thus with a kisse I die."] **123 s.p. [and elsewhere] Balthasar** Man. **137 yew** yong **168 s.p. First Watch** Watch. [also at ll. 172, 195, 199] **170 s.d. Enter Boy and Watch** [at l. 168 in Q2] **171 s.p. Page** Watch boy. **176 these** this **182 s.p. Second Watch** Watch. **183, 187 s.p. First Watch** Chief. watch. **187 too** too too **190 shriek'd** shrike **194 our** your **199 slaughter'd** Slaughter **201** [Q2 has a s.d. here: "Enter Capulet and his wife"] **209 early** [Q1] earling **232 that** thats **281 s.p. Page** Boy.

Julius Caesar

Copy text: the First Folio [F].

I.i.s.d. [and elsewhere] Marullus Murellus

I.ii.s.d. [and elsewhere] Calpurnia Calphurnia **3, 4, 6 Antonius', Antonius** Antonio's, Antonio [also l. 190 and I.iii.37]

I.iii.129 In Is

II.i.40 ides first **213 eighth** eight **267 his** hit **309 s.d. Enter Lucius** etc. [at l. 308 in F]

II.ii.23 did neigh do neigh **46 are** heare

II.iii.1 s.p. Artemidorus [not in F]

III.i.39 law lane **113 states** State **115 lies** lye **255 s.p. Antony** [not in F] **276 s.d. Octavius'** Octauio's [also at V.ii.4] **284 for** from

III.ii.106 art are **203 s.p. All** [not in F] **220 wit** writ **258 s.d. Exeunt** Exit

IV.ii.34–36 s.p. First, Second, and Third Soldier [not in F] **50 Lucius** Lucilius **52 Lucilius** Lucius

IV.iii.242, 244 [and elsewhere] Varro Varrus **Claudius** Claudio **250 will** will it **301, 305 s.p. Varro, Claudius** Both

V.i.41 teeth teethes **66 s.d. Exeunt** Exit **69** [F has s.d.: "Lucillius and Messala stand forth"] **69 s.d. Lucilius** Luc.

V.iii.104 Thasos Tharsus **108 Flavius** Flauio

V.iv.7 s.p. Lucilius [not in F] **9 O** Luc. O **12, 15 s.p. First Soldier** Sold. **16 s.d.** [at l. 15 in F] **17 the news** thee newes

Hamlet

Copy text: the second Quarto of 1604–1605 [Q2]. The First Folio text [F] also represents an independently authoritative text; although seemingly not the correct choice for copy text, the Folio text is considerably less marred by typographical errors than is Q2. The adopted readings in these notes are from F unless otherwise indicated; [eds.] means that the adopted reading was first proposed by some editor since the time of F. Some readings are also supplied from the pirated first Quarto of 1603 [Q1].

I.i.16 soldier [Q1, F] souldiers **44 harrows** horrowes **63 sledded Polacks** [eds.] sleaded pollax **73 why** [Q1, F] with **cast** cost **87 heraldry** [Q1, F] heraldy **88 those** these **91 return'd** returne **94 design'd** [eds.] desseigne **108 e'en so** enso **115 tenantless** tennatlesse **121 fear'd** [eds.] feare **138 you** [Q1, F] your **140 at it** it **160 The** This **175 conveniently** [Q1, F] conuenient

I.ii.s.d. Gertrude Gertradt **Councilors** [eds.] Counsaile: as **1 s.p. King** Claud. **67 so** so much **77 good** coold **82 shapes** [Q4] chapes **83 denote** deuote **96 a** or **105 corse** course **129 sullied** [eds.] sallied [Q2] solid [F] **132 self** seale **133 weary** wary **137 to this** thus **140 satyr** satire **143 would** [Q1, F] should **149 even she** [F; not in Q2] **175 to drink deep** for to drinke **178 to see** [Q1, F] to **198 waste** [eds.] wast [Q2, F] **223 Indeed, indeed** [Q1, F] Indeede **236 Very like, very like** [Q1, F] Very like **237 hundred** hundreth **238 s.p. Marcellus, Bernardo** Both. **250 fare** farre **251 eleven** a leaven **253 Exeunt** [at l. 252 in Q2] **256 Foul** [Q1, F] fonde

I.iii.3 convoy is conuay, in **12 bulk** bulkes **18** [F; not in Q2] **49 like a** a **63 to** vnto **74 Are** Or **75 be** boy **76 loan** loue **110 Running** [eds.] Wrong [Q2] Roaming [F] **116 springes** springs **126 tether** tider **130 implorators** imploratotors **131 bawds** [eds.] bonds **132 beguile** beguide

I.iv.2 is a is **6 s.d. go** [eds.] goes **17 revel** [Q4] reueale **27 the** [eds.] their **33 Their** [eds.] His **81 artery** arture **85 s.d. Exeunt** Exit **86 imagination** imagion

I.v.48 what a what **56 lust** [Q1, F] but **57 sate** [Q1, F] sort **69 posset** possesse **96 stiffly** swiftly **117 bird** and **123 s.p. Horatio, Marcellus** Booth. [also at l. 146] **123 heaven, my lord** heauen **133 Look you, I'll** I will **171 soe'er** so mere

II.i.s.d. man [eds.] man or two **28 Faith, no** Fayth **39 sullies** sallies **40 i' th'** with **56 o'ertook** or tooke **60 takes** take **71 s.d.** [at l. 70 in Q2] **102 passion** passions

II.ii.57 o'erhasty hastie **90 since brevity** breuitie **97 he is** hee's **126 above** about **137 winking** working **143 his** her **148 watch** wath **149 to a** to **170 s.d. Exeunt** [eds.] Exit **210 sanity** sanctity **212–213** [F; not in Q2] **213 honorable lord** lord **214 most humbly take** take **215 cannot, sir**

cannot **216 more** not more **224 excellent** extent **228 over** euer **229 cap** lap **240–270** [F; not in Q2] **267 s.p. Rosencrantz, Guildenstern** Both [F] **273 even** euer **279 Why, anything** Anything **288 could** can **304 What a** What **310 no, nor** nor **314 you** yee **321 of** on **324–325** [F; not in Q2] **tickle** [eds.] tickled [F] **326 blank** black **337–362** [F; not in Q2] **342 berattle** [eds.] be-ratled [F] **349 most like** [eds.] like most [F] **373 lest my** let me **398–399 tragical-historical, tragical-comical-historical-pastoral** [F; not in Q2] **425 By 'r** by **429 e'en to 't** ento 't **French falconers** friendly Fankners **433 s.p. [and elsewhere] First Player** Player **443 affectation** affection **446 tale** talke **454 the** th' **456 heraldry** heraldy **474 Then senseless Ilium** [F; not in Q2] **481 And, like** Like **495 fellies** [eds.] follies [Q2] Fallies [F] **504 "Mobled queen" is good** [F; not in Q2; F reads "Inobled"] **506 bisson** Bison **514 husband's** [Q1, F] husband **541 or** [Q1, F] lines, or **546 till** tell **554 his** the **556 and** an **559 to Hecuba** [Q1, F] to her **561 the cue** that **579 have** a **582 O, vengeance** [F; not in Q2] **584 father** [Q1, Q4; not in Q2, F] **600 the devil** a deale

III.i.1 And An **28 too** two **32 lawful espials** [F; not in Q2] **33 Will** Wee'le **46 loneliness** lowlines **56 Let's withdraw** with-draw **56 s.d.** [at l. 55 in Q2] **84 of us all** [Q1, F; not in Q2] **86 sicklied** sickled **93 well, well, well** well **100 the** these **108 your honesty** you **122 to a** a **130 knaves all** knaues **144 paintings too** paintings **146 jig, you amble** gig & amble **147 lisp** list **148 your ignorance** ignorance **155 Th' expectancy** Th' expectation **159 music** musickt **160 that** what **162 feature** stature **164** [Q2 has "Exit" at the end of this line] **191 unwatch'd** vnmatcht

III.ii.10 tatters totters **split** [Q1, F] spleet **29 praise** praysd **37 sir** [F; not in Q2] **45 s.d.** [at l. 47 in Q2] **88 detecting** detected **107 s.p. [and elsewhere] Queen** Ger. **112–113** [F; not in Q2] **127 devil** deule [Q2] Diuel [F] **133 s.d. Anon comes** Anon come **135 miching** [Q1, F] munching **140 keep counsel** [Q1, F] keepe **153 s.p. [and throughout scene] Player King** King **154 orbed** orb'd the **159 s.p. [and throughout scene] Player Queen** Quee. **162 your** our **164** [Q2 follows here with an extraneous unrhymed line: "For women feare too much, euen as they loue"] **165 For** And **166 In** Eyther none in **167 love** Lord **179 Wormwood, wormwood** That's wormwood **180 s.p. Player Queen** [not in Q2] **188 like** the **197 joys** ioy **217 An** And **221 a** [Q1, F] I be a **be** be a **226 s.d. Exit** [Q1, F] Exeunt **241 s.d.** [at l. 242 in Q2] **254 Confederate** [Q1, F] Considerat **256 infected** [Q1, Q4] inuected **258 usurp** vsurps **264** [F; not in Q2] **274 with two** with **308 start** stare **317 of my** of **343 s.d.** [at l. 341 in Q2] **357 thumb** the vmber **366 to the top of** to **370 can fret me** [F] fret me not [Q2] can fret me, yet [Q1] **371 s.d.** [at l. 372 in Q2] **385 s.p. Polonius** [not in Q2] **386 Leave me, friends** [so F; Q2 places before "I will say so," and assigns both to Hamlet] **388 breathes** breakes **390 bitter . . . day** busines as the bitter day **395 daggers** dagger

III.iii.19 huge hough **22 ruin** raine **23 but with** but **50 pardon'd** pardon **58 shove** showe **73 pat . . . praying** but now a is a praying **75 reveng'd** reuendge **79 hire and salary** base and silly

III.iv.4 sconce [eds.] silence **5–6 with him . . . mother** [F; not in Q2] **7 warrant** wait **8 s.d.** [at l. 5 in Q2] **21 inmost** most **53** [assigned in Q2 to Hamlet] **60 heaven-kissing** heaue, a kissing **89 panders** pardons **91 mine . . . soul** my very eyes into my soule **92 grained** greeued **93 not leave** leaue there **100 tithe** kyth **146 Ecstasy** [F; not in Q2] **150 I the** the **165 live** leaue **172 Refrain tonight** to refraine night **186 Thus** This **193 ravel** rouell **222 a** a most **224 s.d. Exeunt** [eds.] Exit

IV.ii.1 s.d. [Q2: "Enter Hamlet, Rosencraus, and others."] **2**[F; not in Q2] **4 s.d.** [F; not in Q2] **6 Compounded** Compound **19 ape an apple** [eds.] apple [Q2] Ape [F] **31–32 Hide . . . after** [F; not in Q2]

IV.iii.44 With fiery quickness [F; not in Q2] **56 and so** so **72 were** will **begun** begin

IV.v.16 Let . . . in [assigned in Q2 to Horatio] **20 s.d.** [at l. 16 in Q2] **38 all with** all with sweet [Q2] with sweet [F] **42 'ild** dild **58 Indeed, la** Indeede **74, 75 Good** God **83 in their** in **90 his** this **98** [F; not in Q2] **100 are** is **100 s.d.** [at l. 97 in Q2] **109 They** The **144 swoopstake** [eds.] soopstake **154 Let her come in** [assigned in Q2 to Laertes] **155 s.d.** [at l. 154 in Q2] **159 Till** Tell **162 an old** a poore **163–165, 167** [F; not in Q2] **197 All flaxen** Flaxen **201 souls, I pray God** souls **202 you see** you

IV.vi. 7, 9 s.p. First Sailor Say. **9 an 't** and **22 good turn** turn **26 bore** bord **30 He** So **31 will give** will

IV.vii.6 proceeded proceede **14 She's so conjunctive** She is so concliue **20 Would** Worke **21 gyves** Giues **22 loud a wind** loued Arm'd **24 And** But **had** haue **36 How . . . Hamlet** [F; not in Q2] **45–46 your pardon** you pardon **47 and more strange** [F; not in Q2] **Hamlet** [F; not in Q2] **55 shall live** liue **61 checking** the King **88 my** me **115 wick** [eds.] weeke **125 your . . . deed** indeede your fathers sonne **134 on** ore **138 pass** pace **140 for that** for **159 prepar'd** prefard **167 hoar** horry **171 cold** cull-cold

V.i.1 s.p. [and throughout] First Clown Clowne **3 s.p. [and throughout] Second Clown** Other **9 se offendendo** so offended **12 and to** to **Argal** or all **34–37** [F; not in Q2] **43 that frame** that **55 s.d.** [at l. 65 in Q2] **60 stoup** soope **65–66 that 'a** a **66 at** in **85 meant** went **89 mazzard** massene **106–107 Is . . . recoveries** [F; not in Q2] **107–108 Will his** will **109 double [ones too]** doubles **115 calf-skins** Calues-skinnes **120 O** or **121** [F; not in Q2] **139 taken** tooke **143 Of all** Of **165 now-a-days** [F; not in Q2] **180 Yorick's** sir Yoricks **183 Let me see** [F; not in Q] **185 borne** bore **192 chamber** table **208–209 As thus** [F; not in Q2] **216 winter's** waters **226, 235 s.p. Priest** Doct. **231 Shards, flints** Flints **247 treble** double **261 and rash** rash **277 Dost thou** doost **285 thus** this **298 shortly** thereby **299 Till** Tell

V.ii.5 Methought my thought **6 bilboes** bilbo **9 pall** fall **17 unseal** vnfold **29 villainies** villaines **43 as's** as sir **52 Subscrib'd** Subscribe **57, 68–80** [F; not in Q2] **73 interim is** [eds.] interim's [F] **78 Court** [eds.] count [F] **81 s.p. [and throughout] Osric** Cour. **82 humbly** humble **93 Put your** your **98 sultry** sully **for** or **107 gentleman** [eds.] gentlemen **109 feelingly** [Q4] fellingly **114 dozy** [eds.] dazzie **yaw** [eds.] raw **141 his** [eds.] this **149 hangers** hanger **159 might be** be might **162 impawn'd, as** [eds.] all [Q2] impon'd, as [F] **181 Your, yours. He does** Yours doo's **186 comply** so **190 yesty** histy **191 fann'd** [eds.] prophane [Q2] fond [F] **winnow'd** trennowed **210 But thou** thou **218 be now** be **220 will come** well come **238** [F; not in Q2] **248 To keep** To **till** all **252 foils. Come on** foils **261 better'd** better **270 union** Vnice ["Onixe" in some copies] **288 A touch, a touch, I** I **302 afeard** sure **316 Hamlet. Hamlet** Hamlet **319 thy** [Q1, F] my **327 murd'rous** [F; not in Q2] **328 off** of **thy union** [Q1, F] the Onixe **345 ha 't** [eds.] hate [Q2] have 't [F] **351 s.d.** [Qq, F provide a s.d. here: "Enter Osrick"] **369 s.p. First Ambassador** Embas. **381 th' yet** yet **385 forc'd** for no **394 on** no

Othello

Copy text: the First Folio [F]. The adopted readings are from the Quarto of 1622 [Q1], unless otherwise indicated; [eds.] means that the adopted reading was first proposed by some editor subsequent to the First Folio.

I.i.1 Tush, never Neuer **4 'Sblood, but** but **16 And, in conclusion** [Q1; not in F] **26 toged** Tongued **30 other** others **31 Christian** Christen'd **34 God bless** blesse **67 full** fall **thick-lips** Thicks-lips **73 changes** chances **82 s.d.** [in F, printed as a speech prefix to l. 83] **87 'Zounds, sir** Sir [also at l. 109] **101 bravery** knauerie **117 are now** are **156 pains** apines **184 night** might

I.ii.15 and or **34 Duke** Dukes **50 carrack** Carract **69 darlings** Deareling **89 I do** do **93 s.p. First Officer** Officer.

I.iii.1 There is There's **these** this **14 s.p. [and elsewhere] First Officer** Officer. **61 s.p. Duke and Senators** Sen. **89 broil** Broiles **101 maim'd** main'd **108 s.p. Duke** [Q1; not in F] **109 overt** ouer **112 s.p. [and elsewhere] First Senator** Sen. **124 till** tell **132 battles** Battaile **fortunes** Fortune **141 travels'** Trauellours **143 rocks, and** Rocks **heads** head **145 other** others **147 Do grow** Grew **This** These things **149 thence** hence **157 intentively** instinctiuely **161 sighs** kisses **204 Into your favor** [Q1; not in F] **221 ear** eares **227 sovereign** more soueraigne **233 couch** [eds.] Coach [F] Cooch [Q1] **237 These**

[eds.] This **242–243 If you please, Be 't** Why **244 Nor I. I would not** Nor would I **251 did love** loue **267 me** [eds.] my **273 instruments** Instrument **285 With** And **296 s.d. Exeunt** Exit **302 matters** matter **329 balance** braine **333–334 our unbitted** or vnbitted **335 scion** [eds.] Seyen **353 error** errors **354 She . . . she must** [Q1; not in F] **358 a super-subtle** super-subtle **378–382 What . . . purse** [Q1; not in F] **386 a snipe** Snpe **389 H'as** She ha's

II.i.34 prays praye **35 heaven** Heauens **41 s.p. Third Gentleman** Gent. **43 arrivance** Arriuancie **44 this** the **52 s.d. [Enter a Messenger]** [the added s.d. is from Q1] **54 s.d. Messenger** Gent. **57 s.d. Second Gentleman** Gent. [also at ll. 60, 67, and 95] **71 clog** enclogge **83 And . . . comfort** [Q1; not in F] **89 tell me** tell **93 the sea** Sea **95 their** this **105 list** leaue **109 doors** doore **117 thou write** write **155 ne'er** neu'r **157 such wight** such wightes **169 gyve** giue **173 An** and **174 courtesy** Curtsie **212 s.d. Exeunt** [eds.] Exit **214 hither** thither **223–224 And will she** To **227 again** a game **237 fortune** Forune **240 compassing** compasse **242 occasions** occasion **has** he's **261 mutualities** mutabilities **302 I trash** [eds.] I trace **305 rank** right **306 cap** Cape

II.ii.6 addiction [eds.] addition **12 Heaven bless** Blesse

II.iii.38 unfortunate infortunate **52 lads** else **57 to put** put to **61, 71 God** heauen **76 Englishman** Englishmen **91 Then . . . auld** And take thy awl'd **93 'Fore God** Why **96 God's** heau'ns **106 God forgive** Forgiue **110 speak** I speake **111 s.p. All** Gent. **123 the** his **138 s.d. Cry within: Help! Help** [from Q1: "Helpe, helpe, within"] **139 'Zounds, you** You **152 God's will** Alas **153 Montano—sir** Montano **156 God's will, lieutenant, hold** Fie, fie Lieutenant **158 'Zounds, I** I **160 sense of place** [eds.] place of sense **177 breast** breastes **212 leagu'd** [eds.] league **218 Thus** This **227 the** then **246 well now** well **255 God** Heauen **260 thought** had thought **266 ways** more wayes **283 O God** Oh **308 I'll** I **311 denotement** [eds.] deuotement **325–326 me here** me **337 were 't** were **348 fortunes** Fortune **369 hast** hath **372 By the mass** Introth **379 the** [eds.] a

III.i.s.d. Musicians [eds.] Musicians, and Clowne **5 s.p. [and throughout scene] First Musician** Mus. **21 s.d. Exeunt** Exit **22 hear** heare me **26 general's wife** Generall **31, 52** [Q1; not in F] **42 s.d.** [at l. 41 in F]

III.iii.4 case cause **16 circumstance** Circumstances **40 you** your **52 Yes, faith** I sooth **60 or** on **74 By'r Lady** Trust me **96 you** he **111 By heaven, he echoes** Alas, thou ecchos't **112 his** thy **117 In** Of **140 free to** free **143 a** that **144 But some** Wherein **152 oft** of **153 wisdom yet** [eds.] wisdom **158 or** and **167 By heaven, I'll** Ile **175 strongly** soundly **180 God** Heauen **186 Is once** Is **188 blown** blow'd **191 dances well** Dances **204 eye** eyes **208 God** Heauen **210 keep 't** keepe [Q1] kept [F] **222 I' faith** Trust me **224 my** your **230 As** Which **240 disproportion** disproportions **255 to hold** to **265 qualities** Quantities **279 of** to **284 O, then heaven mocks** Heauen mock'd **291 Faith** Why **308 A thing** You haue a thing **317 faith** but **326 lose** loose **343 of** in **354 troop** Troops **381 liv'st** [eds.] lou'st [F] liuest [Q1] **391 Her** [eds.] My **396 see, sir** see **400 supervisor** super-vision **426 and then** then **428 then laid** laid **429 Over** ore **sigh'd** sigh **kiss'd** kisse **430 Cried** cry **436 but** yet **444 that was** [eds.] it was **456 mind perhaps** minde **459 feels** [eds.] keepes

III.iv.5 one me **23 that** the **37 It yet** It **56 faith** indeed **77 I' faith** Indeed **79 God** Heauen **83 Heaven bless** Blesse **88 can, sir** can **94–95** [bracketed words in Q1; not in F] **98 I' faith** Insooth **99 'Zounds** Away **163 that** the **171 I' faith** Indeed **187 by my faith** in good troth

IV.i.32 Faith Why **36 'Zounds, that's** that's **45 work** workes **53 No, forbear** [Q1; not in F] **78 unsuiting** resulting **96 clothes** Cloath **99 refrain** restraine **102 conster** conserue **103 behavior** behauiours **104 you now** you **108 power** dowre **112 i' faith** indeed **119 Do you** Do ye **120 marry her** marry **123 win** [eds.] winnes **124 Faith** Why **shall marry** marry **131 beckons** becomes **134–135 and, by this hand, she** and **162 Faith I** I **164 Faith** Yes **213 s.d.** [at l. 211 in F] **216 God save** Saue **239 By my troth** Trust me **249 Truly, an** Truly **277 this** his **280 denote** deonte

IV.ii.30 Nay May **31 knees** knee **33** [Q1; not in F] **47 Why, I** I **49 kinds** kind **54 A** The **55 unmoving** and mouing **64 Ay, there** [eds.] I heere **69 ne'er** neuer **81 Impudent strumpet** [Q1; not in F] **92 keep** [eds.] keepes **92 s.d.** [at l. 90 in F] **143 heaven** Heauens **157 in** [eds.] or **169** [Q1; not in F] **184 Faith, I** I **for** and **189 deliver to** deliuer **195 By this hand** Nay

IV.iii.10 s.d. [at l. 9 in F] **14 bade** bid **22 favor in them** fauour **25 faith** Father **26 before thee** before **27 those** these **43 sighing** [eds.] singing **73 Good troth** Introth **74 By my troth** Introth **78 'ud's pity** why **107 God** Heauen

V.i.1 bulk Barke **22 Be 't** But **hear** heard **35 Forth** For **49 Did** Do **90 O heaven** Yes, 'tis **104 out o'** o' **111 'Las, what's . . . What's** Alas, what is . . . What is **114 dead** quite dead **123 Foh! Fie** Fie

V.ii.13 the thy **34 heaven** Heauens **37 say so** say **55 Yes, presently** Presently **60 Then Lord** O Heauen **97 here** high **105 Should** Did **122 O Lord** Alas **132 heard** heare **148 Nay, had** had **225 O God! O heavenly God** Oh Heauen! oh heauenly Powres **226 'Zounds** Come **236 steal it** steal't **248 have here** haue **262 is** was **300 damned** cursed **325 nick** interim **330 but** [eds.] it but [F] it [Q] **356 Indian** Iudean

King Lear

Copy text: the First Folio [F], except for those 300 or so lines found only in the first Quarto of 1608 [Q1]. Unless otherwise indicated, adopted readings are from the corrected state of Q1. A few readings are supplied from the second Quarto of 1619 [Q2]. All readings subsequent to 1619 are marked as supplied by "eds."

I.i.5 equalities qualities **66 issue** issues **68 Speak** [Q1; not in F] **74 possesses** professes **104** [Q1; not in F] **110 mysteries** [eds.] miseries [F] mistresse [Q1] **135 turns** turn **156 as a** as **157 nor** nere **161 s.p. Lear** Kear. **Kent** Lent. **171 sentence** sentences **189 s.p. Gloucester** Cor. **215 best object** obiect **227 well** will **250 respects of Fortune** respect and Fortunes **283 shame them** with shame **284 s.d. Exeunt** Exit **291 hath not** hath **304 hit** sit

I.ii.1 s.p. [and elsewhere] Edmund Bast. **21 top** [eds.] to' **56 wak'd** wake **97–99** [Q1; not in F] **134 Fut, I** I **136 Edgar** [Q1; not in F] **137 and pat** [eds.] Pat [F] and out [Q1] **147–155** [Q1; not in F] **182 s.d.** [at l. 181 in F]

I.iii.11 s.p. [and elsewhere] Oswald Ste. **17–21, 26–27** [Q1; not in F]

I.iv.1 well will **43 s.d.** [at l. 44 in F] **50 daughter** Daughters **76 s.d.** [at l. 77 in F] **96 s.p. Kent** Lear. **fool** my boy **138–153** [Q1; not in F] **158 crown** Crownes **175 fools** Foole **195 nor crumb** not crum **213 it had** it's had **228–231** [Q1; not in F] **254 O . . . come** [Q1; not in F] **301 Yea . . . this** [Q1; not in F] **341 You** [eds.] Your **attask'd** at task

I.v.s.d. Kent Kent, Gentleman

II.i.2 you your **19 s.d.** [at l. 18 in F] **70 I should** should I **71 ay, though** though **79 I never got him** [Q1; not in F] **79 s.d.** [at l. 77 in F] **80 why** wher **88 strange news** strangenesse **126 thought** though

II.ii.22 clamorous clamours **76 too** t' **78 Bring . . . their** Being . . . the **79 Renege** Reuenge **80 gale** gall **109 flick'ring** flicking **124 dread** dead **132 respect** respects **142 s.d.** [at l. 140 in F] **144–148** [Q1; not in F] **146 contemned'st** [eds.] temnest [Q1] **148 King** King his Master, needs **153** [Q1; not in F] **154 Come . . . away** [assigned in F to Cornwall] **155 Duke's** Duke

II.iii.18 sheep Sheeps

II.iv.2 messenger Messengers **9 man's** man **18–19** [Q1; not in F] **30 panting** painting **33 whose** those **61 the** the the **74 have** hause **127 you** your **129 mother's** Mother **183 s.d.** [at l. 181 in F] **185 fickle** sickly **188 s.d.** [at l. 186 in F] **211 blooded** bloodied

III.i. 7–15, 30–42 [Q1; not in F]

III.ii.3 drown'd drown **38 s.d.** [at l. 36 in F] **71 That** And **85–86** [these lines follow l. 91 in F]

III.iv.10 thy they **27 s.d.** [at l. 26 in F] **31 loop'd** lop'd **38 s.d. Enter Fool** [F, at l. 36: "Enter Edgar, and Foole"] **46 blows the cold wind** blow the windes **52 ford** Sword **57, 58 Bless**

Blisse **90 deeply** deerely **99 sessa** [eds.] Sesey **112 s.d.** [at l. 109 in F] **115 till the** at **134 stock-punish'd** stockt, punish'd **hath** had hath
III.v.26 dearer deere
III.vi.5 s.d. [at l. 3 in F] **17–55** [Q1; not in F] **21 Now** [Q2] No [Q1] **25 bourn** [eds.] broome [Q1] **34 cushion** [eds.] cushings [Q1] **51 joint** [eds.] ioyne [Q1] **53 on** [eds.] an [Q1] **68 lym** [eds.] Hym **69 tike** tight **trundle** Troudle **85 s.d.** [at l. 80 in F] **97–101, 102–115** [Q1; not in F] **101 s.p. Gloucester** [not in F]
III.vii.10 festinate [eds.] festiuate **74 s.p. First Servant** Seru. [also at ll. 77, 80, 82] **100–108** [Q1; not in F] **100 s.p. Second Servant** Seruant. [and called **1 Ser.** at l. 104 in Q1] **101, 107 s.p. Third Servant** 2 Seruant [Q1] **105 roguish** [Q2; not in Q1] **108 s.d. Exeunt** Exit [Q1]
IV.i.41 Then . . . gone Get thee away **58–63** [Q1; not in F] **61 Flibbertigibbet** [eds.] Stiberdigebit [Q] **61–62 mopping and mowing** [eds.] Mobing, & Mohing [Q]
IV.ii.s.d. Bastard Bastard, and Steward **32–51** [Q1; not in F] **33 its** [eds.] ith [Q1] **48 these** [eds.] this [Q1] **54–60** [Q1; not in F] **58 to threat** thereat [Q1] **63–69, 70** [Q1; not in F] **76 thereat** threat **80 justicers** [Q1 corrected] Iustices
IV.iii.1–57 [scene omitted in F] **11 sir** [eds.] say [Q1] **16 strove** [eds.] streme [Q1] **20 seem'd** [eds.] seeme [Q1] **32 then** her, then **57 s.d. Exeunt** [eds.] Exit [Q1]
IV.iv [F reads "Scena Tertia"] **s.d. Doctor** Gentlemen **3 fumiter** [eds.] femiter [Q1] Fenitar [F] **11 s.p. Doctor** Gent. **18 distress** desires
IV.v [F reads "Scena Quarta"] **23 Something** Some things **27 oeillades** [eds.] Eliads **41 meet him** meet
IV.vi [F reads "Scena Quinta"] **17 walk** walk'd **21 pebbles** Pebble **71 enridged** enraged **83 coining** crying **97 white** the white **164 Through** Thorough **small** great **165 Plate sin** [eds.] Place sinnes **197 Ay . . . dust** [Q1; not in F] **Gent. Good sir** [Q2; not in F, Q1] **205 one** a
IV.vii.13 s.p. Doctor Gent. [also at ll. 18, 44, 52, 80] **24 s.p. Doctor** [Q1; not in F] **25 doubt not** doubt **25–26 Cordelia. Very . . . there** [Q1; not in F] **33 warring** iarring **34–37** [Q1; not in F] **50 When** where **81–82 and . . . lost** [Q1; not in F] **89–101** [Q1; not in F]
V.i.12–14 [Q1; not in F] **18 me not** not **19–20** [Q1; not in F] **24–29** [Q1; not in F] **34** [Q1; not in F] **40 s.d.** [at l. 38 in F] **47 love** loues **52 s.d.** [at l. 51 in F]
V.iii.39–40 [Q1; not in F] **49 and appointed guard** [Q1 corrected; not in F] **56–61** [Q1; not in F] **57 We** [Q1 corrected] mee [Q1 uncorrected] **59 sharpness** [Q1 corrected] sharpes [Q1 uncorrected] **72 s.p. Goneril** Alb. **85 attaint** arrest **86 sister** Sisters **87 bar** [eds.] bare **99 he is** hes **104** [Q1; not in F] **105 s.p. Albany** [not in F] **108 s.d.** [at l. 103 in F] **111, 117** [Q1; not in F] **135 Despite** Despise **153 Fight** Fights **163 s.p. Goneril** Bast. **163 s.d. Exit** [at l. 161 in F] **208–225** [Q1; not in F] **217 him** [eds.] me [Q1] **241 s.d.** [at l. 234 in F; F reads "Gonerill"] **261 you** your **279 s.p. Captain** Gent. **281 them** him **293 You are** [eds.] Your are [F] You'r [Q1]

Macbeth

Copy text: the First Folio [F].
I.i.9 s.p. Second Witch All. **10 s.p. Third Witch** [not in F] **11 s.p. All** [at l. 9 in F]
I.ii.1 s.p. [and elsewhere] Duncan King. **15 gallowglasses** Gallowgrosses **16 quarrel** Quarry **28 thunders break** Thunders
I.iii.32 weird weyward [elsewhere in F spelled "weyward" or "weyard"] **38 Forres** Soris **98 Came** Can
I.iv.1 Are Or
I.v.47 it hit
I.vi.4 martlet Barlet **9 most** must
I.vii.6 shoal Schoole **48 do** no
II.i.56 strides sides **57 sure** sowre **58 way they** they may
II.ii.13 s.d. [at l. 8 in F]
II.iii.41 s.d. [at l. 40 in F]
III.i.74 s.p. Murderers Murth. [also at ll. 114 and 139]
III.iii.7 and end
III.iv.79 time times **122 s.d. Exeunt** Exit
III.vi.24 son Sonnes **38 the** their
IV.i.38 s.d. to and **59 germains** Germaine **93 Dunsinane** Dunsmane **94 s.d. Descends** Descend **98 Birnam** Byrnan [also spelled "Byrnam" at l. 93 and "Birnan," "Byrnane," and "Birnane" in Act V] **119 eighth** eight
IV.ii.1 s.p. [and throughout] Lady Macduff Wife **81 s.p. [and throughout scene] First Murderer** Mur.
IV.iii.4 down-fall'n downfall **15 deserve** discerne **107 accurs'd** accust **133 thy** they **235 tune** time
V.iii.39 Cure her Cure **52 pristine** pristiue **55 senna** Cyme **61 s.d.** [at l. 63 in F]
V.iv.16 s.p. Siward Sey.

Timon of Athens

Copy text: the First Folio [F].
The Actors' Names [F lists also Varro and Lucius as "Seruants to Vsurers"]
I.i.s.d. Merchant Merchant, and Mercer **23 gum** Gowne **oozes** vses **27 chafes** chases **92 hands** hand **slip** sit **116 s.p. [and subsequently] Old Athenian** Oldm **182 s.d.** [at l. 180 in F] **222 cost** cast **234 feigned** fegin'd **259 there** their **286 Come** Comes **296 s.p. First Lord** [not in F]
I.ii.30 ever verie **112 s.d. Sound Tucket** [F continues: "Enter the Maskers of Amazons with Lutes in their hands, dauncing and playing"] **120 s.d. Enter Cupid** [F continues: "with the Maske of Ladies"] **124 Th' ear** There **125 and smell** all **129 s.p. First Lord** Luc. **130 s.d.** [see notes at ll. 112 and 120 above] **144 s.d. singles** single **151 s.p. First Lady** 1 Lord. **167 s.d.** [at l. 176 in F] **181 s.p. Second Servant** Ser. **213 s.p. Third Lord** 1. L.
II.i.35 compt Come
II.ii.1 s.p. [and elsewhere] Flavius Stew. **4 resumes** resume **11 s.p. [and elsewhere] Varro's Servant** Var. **12 s.p. [and elsewhere] Isidore's Servant** Isid. **64 s.p. [and elsewhere] All Servants** Al [or All.] **75, 104 mistress'** Masters **81 s.p. Page** Boy **132 propos'd** propose **191 Flamineus** Flauius
III.ii.27 s.p. [and elsewhere] Lucius Lucil.
III.iii.5 Owe Owes **23 I be** be
III.iv.s.d. Men man **1 s.p. [and elsewhere] Varro's First Servant** Var. man. **3 s.p. [and elsewhere] Lucius' Servant** Luci. **45 s.p. [and elsewhere] Varro's Second Servant** 2. Varro. **88 s.p. Hortensius** 1. Var. **89 s.p. Both Varro's Servants** 2. Var. **112 Sempronius** Sempronius Vllorxa
III.v.18 An And **23 behave** behooue **51 felon** fellow **65 Why I** Why **69 'em** him **84 honors** Honour
III.vi.1 s.p. First Lord 1 [and so throughout scene] **54 s.p. First and Second Lord** Both. **80 lag** legge **91 with your** you with **115 s.p. Third Lord** 2 **116 s.p. Second Lord** 3
IV.i.13 Son Some
IV.iii.10 senator Senators **12 pasture** Pastour **rother's** Brothers **13 lean** leaue **88 tub-fast** Fubfast **119 bars** Barne **124 thy** the **135 s.p. [and throughout scene] Phrynia and Timandra** Both. **158 scolds** scold'st **187 thy** the **206 fortune** future **225 moss'd** moyst **258 command** command'st **287 my** thy **402 them** then **414 s.p. [and throughout scene] Banditti** All. **439 villains** Villaine **462 s.d. Exeunt** Exit **479 grant'st** grunt'st **497 mild** wilde
V.i.5–6 Phrynia and Timandra Phrinica and Timandylo **50 worship** worshipt **69 men** man **112 work'd** worke **125 chance** chanc'd **146 sense** since **147 fail** fall **181 reverend'st** reuerends
V.ii.1 s.p. [and throughout scene] Third Senator 1 **5 s.p. [and throughout scene] Fourth Senator** 2 **14 s.p. First Senator** 3
V.iv.24 griefs greefe **55 Descend** Defend **62 render'd** remedied **65 s.p. Soldier** Mes.

Antony and Cleopatra

Copy text: the First Folio [F].
I.i.39 On One **51 whose** who
I.ii.4 charge change **41 fertile** foretell **64–65 Alexas** [printed in F as s.p.] **82 Saw** Saue **113 minds** windes **115 s.d. Exit Messenger** [F adds: "Enter another Messenger"] **117 s.p. First Attendant** 1. Mes. **118 s.p. Second Attendant** 2. Mes. **121 s.p. Second Messenger** 3. Mes. **123 s.p. Second Messenger** Mes. **141 occasion** an occasion **183 leave** loue **188 Hath** Haue **199 place is** places
I.iii.2 who's Whose **43 services** Seruicles **82 by my** by

I.iv.3 **Our** One 8 **Vouchsaf'd** vouchsafe 9 **abstract** abstracts 21 **smell** smels 44 **dear'd** fear'd 46 **lackeying** lacking 49 **Make** Makes 57 **wassails** Vassailes 59 **Pansa** Pausa 77 **we** me

I.v.35 **s.d. Alexas** Alexas from Caesar 52 **dumb'd** dumbe 64 **man** mans

II.i.2, 5 **s.p. Menecrates** Mene. 16, 18, 39 **s.p. Menas** Mene. 39 **ne'er** neere 42 **warr'd** wan'd

II.ii.127 **so say** 128 **reproof** proofe 180 **s.d. Exeunt** Exit omnes 214 **glow** gloue 216 **gentlewomen** Gentlewoman 233 **heard** hard

II.iii.30 **away** alway 31 **[and elsewhere] Ventidius** Ventigius

II.iv.6 **the Mount** Mount 9 **s.p. Maecenas, Agrippa** Both

II.v.2 **s.p. All** Omnes. 12 **finn'd** fine 43 **is** 'tis

II.vi.s.d. **Agrippa** Agrippa, Menas 19 **is** his 39 **s.p. Caesar, Antony, Lepidus** Omnes. 58 **composition** composion 66 **meanings** meaning 69 **more of** more 81 **s.p. Caesar, Antony, Lepidus** All.

II.vii.1 **their** th' their 4 **color'd** Conlord 91 **is** he is 99 **grows** grow 110 **bear** beate 119 **off** of 123 **Splits** Spleet's 128 **father's** Father 131 **s.p. Menas** [not in F]

III.i.5 **s.p. [and throughout scene] Silius** Romaine.

III.ii.10 **s.p. Agrippa** Ant. 16 **figures** Figure 49 **full** the full 59 **wept** weepe

III.iii.19 **look'dst** look'st

III.iv.8 **them** then 9 **took 't** look't 24 **yours** your 30 **Your** You 38 **has** he's

III.v.13 **world** would **hast** hadst 15 **grind the one** grind

III.vi.13 **he there** hither **the kings** the King 75 **Comagene** Comageat 76 **Lycaonia** Licoania

III.vii.4 **it is** it it 19 **s.d. Canidius** Camidias [also spelled "Camidius" in this scene and elsewhere] 23 **Toryne** Troine 35 **muleters** Militers 51 **Actium** Action 66 **s.d. Exeunt** exit 69 **led** leade 72 **s.p. Canidius** Ven.

III.x.s.d. **Enobarbus** Enobarbus and Scarus 14 **June** Inne 28 **he** his

III.xi.6 **s.p. All** Omnes. [also at IV.ii.20] 19 **that** them 46 **seize** cease 50 **led** lead 57 **tow** stowe 58 **Thy** The

III.xiii.55 **Caesar** Caesars 74 **deputation** disputation 104 **This** the 163 **smite** smile 166 **discandying** discandering 169 **sits** sets 200 **on** in 202 **s.d. Exit** Exeunt

IV.iii.8 **s.p. Third Soldier** 1 [also at l. 12] 9 **s.p. Fourth Soldier** 2 26, 29 **s.p. All** Omnes

IV.iv.5 **too** too, Anthony 6 **s.p. Antony** [not in F, or mistakenly placed in l. 5 as part of Cleopatra's speech] 8 **s.p. Cleopatra** [not in F] 24 **s.p. Captain** Alex.

IV.v.1, 3, 6 **s.p. Soldier** Eros.

IV.viii.2 **gests** guests 18 **My** Mine 23 **favoring** sauouring

IV.xii.4 **augurers** Auguries 9 **s.d.** [at o.s.d. in F] 21 **spaniel'd** pannelled

IV.xiv.4 **tower'd** toward 10 **dislimns** dislimes 19 **Caesar** Caesars 111 **s.p. Dercetas** Dercetus [elsewhere in F spelled "Decretas"] 140 **s.d. Exeunt** Exit

IV.xv.73 **e'en** in 91 **s.d. off** of

V.i.s.d. **Maecenas** Menas 28, 31 **s.p. Agrippa** Dol. 48 **s.d.** [at l. 51 in F] 59 **live** leaue

V.ii.26 **dependency** dependacie 35 [F repeats s.p. **Pro.**] 55 **varletry** Varlotarie 80 **O, the** o' th' 86 **autumn** Anthony 103 **smites** suites 216 **Ballad** Ballads 223 **my** mine 228 **Cydnus** Cidrus 318 **awry** away 319 **s.d. in** in, and Dolabella

Coriolanus

Copy text: the First Folio [F].

I.i.7 **[and throughout play] Marcius** Martius 15 **on** one 33 **s.p. Second Citizen** All. 55 **s.p. First Citizen** 2 Cit. [and so throughout scene] 90 **stale 't** scale 't 108 **tauntingly** taintingly 214 **Shouting** Shooting 218 **unroof'd** vnroo'st 226 **s.d. Junius** Annius 239 **Lartius** Lucius 241 **s.p. [and elsewhere] Lartius** Tit. 244, 248 **[and elsewhere] First Senator** Sen.

I.ii.s.d. **Corioles** Coriolus 4 **on** one

I.iii.36 **that's** that 81 **s.p. Virgilia** Vlug. 83 **yarn** yearne 84 **Ithaca** Athica

I.iv.46 **s.d. and is shut in** [in F, this is part of the s.d. at l. 43] 57 **Were** Weare 58 **Cato's** Calues

I.vi.22 **flay'd** Flead 53 **Antiates** Antients 70 **Lesser** Lessen

I.vii.7 **s.d. Exeunt** Exit

I.ix.49 **shout** shoot 64, 66 **Caius Marcius** Marcus Caius [and so throughout play] 66 **s.p. All** Omnes. 67, 78, 81, 89 **s.p. Coriolanus** Martius.

I.x.2 **s.p. [and throughout scene] First Soldier** Sould.

II.i.57 **cannot** can 61 **you you** you 64 **bisson** beesome 106 **s.p. Valeria, Virgilia** 2. Ladies 164 **Coriolanus** Martius Caius Coriolanus 177 **wear** were 179 **s.p. Coriolanus** Com. 185 **You** Yon 202 **s.d. Brutus** Enter Brutus 232 **napless** Naples 253 **touch** teach

II.ii.25 **ascent** assent 81 **one on's** on ones 91 **chin** Shinne 92 **bristled** brizled

II.iii.28 **wedg'd** wadg'd 67 **but not** but 88, 91, 106 **s.p. Fourth Citizen** 1. 104 **s.p. Fifth Citizen** 2. 111 **s.p. Both Citizens** Both. 114 **hire** higher 115 **toge** tongue 132 **s.p. Sixth Citizen** 1. 134 **s.p. Seventh Citizen** 2. 244 [bracketed line not in F; based on Plutarch]

III.i.31 **s.p. [and elsewhere] First Senator** Senat. 91 **good** God! 126 **Their** There 143 **Where one** Whereon 177 **s.p. All Patricians** All. 182 **s.p. [and elsewhere] All Plebeians** All. 184 **s.p. All** [at l. 186 in F] 213 **s.p. All Plebeians** All Ple. 227 **s.d.** [preceded in F by "Exeunt"] 228 **your** our 229 **s.p. Coriolanus** Com. 236 **s.p. Cominius** Cor. 237 **s.p. Coriolanus** Mene. 240 **s.p. Menenius** [not in F] 325 **bring him** bring him in peace

III.ii.13 **s.d.** [at l. 6 in F] 23 **thwartings** things 34 **herd** heart 117 **lulls** lull 131 **suck'dst** suck'st

III.iii.32 **for th'** fourth 36 **Throng** Through 56 **accents** Actions 112 **for** from 137 **s.d. Cominius** Cominius, with Cumalijs 141 **s.d.** [at l. 137 in F]

IV.i.24 **thee** the 34 **wilt** will

IV.ii.44 **s.d. Exeunt** Exit 54 **s.d. Exeunt** [F has "Exeunt" at l. 53 and "Exit" at l. 54]

IV.iii.32 **will** well

IV.iv.24 **hate** haue

IV.v.83 **Whoop'd** Hoop'd 152 **s.d. Two** Enter Two 210 **sowl** sole 234 **sleepy** sleepe

IV.vi.10 **s.d.** [at l. 9 in F] 21 **s.p. [and elsewhere] All Citizens** All. 36 **lamentation** Lamention 61 **come** comming 76 **s.p. Second Messenger** Mes. 122 **s.p. Both Tribunes** Tri. 141 **s.p. All Citizens** Omnes. 158 **s.d. Exeunt** Exit

IV.vii.14 **had** haue 34 **osprey** Aspray 37 **'twas** 'was 39 **defect** detect 49 **virtues** Vertue 55 **falter** fouler

V.ii.65 **by my** my

V.iii.48 **prate** pray 63 **holp** hope 127 **s.p. Young Marcius** Boy. 149 **fine** fiue 152 **charge** change 163 **cluck'd** clock'd 169 **with our** with him with our 192 **stead** steed

V.iv.40 **s.p. [and throughout scene] Second Messenger** Mess.

V.v.4 **Unshout** Vnshoot

V.vi.63 **s.p. All Lords** All. 102 **other** others 119 **Flutter'd** Flatter'd 134 **s.d. Draw** Draw both **kill** kils

Pericles

Copy text: the first Quarto of 1609 [Q].

I Chorus 1 **s.p. Gower** [not in Q; also in subsequent choruses throughout, except at IV.iv, V.ii, and epilogue] 6 **holy-ales** Holy-dayes 11 **these** those 39 **a** of

I.i.8 **For th'** For 18 **ras'd** racte 23 **the** th' 25 **boundless** bondlesse 57 **s.p. Antiochus** [not in Q; also at l. 170] 63 **advice** advise 112 **our** your 114 **cancel** counsell 128 **you're** you 137 **'schew** shew 170 **s.p. Antiochus** [not in Q]

I.ii.3 **Be my** By me 20 **honor him** honour 25 **th' ostent** the stint 30 **am** once 41 **blast** sparke 80 **seem** seemes 84 **Bethought me** Bethought 85 **fears** feare 87 **doubt 't** doo't 122 **will sure** will 123 **we'll** will 125 **s.d. Exeunt** Exit

I.iii.1 **s.p. Thaliard** [not in Q] 27 **ears it** seas 28 **seas** Sea 30 **s.p. Helicanus** [not in Q] 34 **betook** betake 35 **my message** message 39 **s.d. Exeunt** Exit

I.iv.13, 14 **do** to 14 **lungs** toungs 17 **helps** helpers 36 **they** thy 39 **two summers** too sauers 58 **thou** thee 67 **Hath** That **these** the 74 **him 's** himnes 77 **fear** leaue 78 **The** our 97 **s.p. All** Omnes.

II Chorus 11 **Tharsus** Tharstill 12 **speken** spoken 22 **Sends word** Sau'd one 24 **intent** in Tent **murder** murdred [some corrected copies of Q have "had . . . murder"]

II.i.6 **left me** left my 12 **ho** to **Pilch** pelch 31–32 **devours** deuowre 39 **s.p. Third Fisherman** 1. 48 **finny** fenny 82

holidays all day **91 your** you **100 is** I **131 from** Fame **148 do** 'e di 'e **157 rapture** rupture **160 delightful** delight

II.ii.1 s.p. [and elsewhere] Simonides King. **27 Piu . . . fuerza** Pue Per doleer a kee per forse **28 what's** with **29 chivalry** Chiually **30 pompae** Pompey **33 Quod** Qui

II.iii.3 To I **13 yours** your **27 Envied** Enuies **39 Yon** You **40 tells me** tels **45 son's** sonne **52 stor'd** stur'd **53 you do** do you **114 to be** be **116 s.p. Simonides** [not in Q]

II.iv.34 death's death **40 s.p. All** Omnes.

II.v.92 s.p. Both Ambo.

III Chorus 2 the house about about the house **7 crickets** Cricket **13 eche** each **17 coigns** Crignes **35 y-ravished** Iranyshed

III.i.1 Thou The **7 Thou** then **8 spit** speat **11 midwife** my wife **52 custom** easterne **53 for . . . straight** [printed in Q as part of the next line, after "As you think meet," the line assigned to Pericles] **60 in the ooze** in oare **62 And e'er** The ayre **65 paper** Taper **81 s.d. Exeunt** Exit

III.ii.19 quit quite **44 treasure** pleasure **52 s.p. [and elsewhere] First Servant** Seru. **59 bitumed** bottomed **80 even** euer **96 breathes** breath

III.iii.6 shafts shakes **hurt** hant **7 woundingly** wondringly **31 Unscissor'd** vnsisterd **32 ill** will **37 s.p. Cleon** Cler.

III.iv.s.d. Thaisa Tharsa [also s.p. in l. 4] **5 eaning** learning **9 vestal** vastall **11 s.p. Cerimon** Cler. **17 s.d. Exeunt** Exit

IV Chorus 10 her hie **heart** art **14 Seeks** Seeke **15 hath our Cleon** our Cleon hath **16 wench full grown** full growne wench **17 ripe** right **rite** sight **21 she** they **26 bird** bed **32 With** [after "might" in Q] **47 carry** carried **48 on** one

IV.i.5 inflaming love i' thy in flaming, thy loue **66 stem** sterne **98 s.d. Exeunt** Exit

IV.ii.4 much much much **42 s.p. First Pirate** Sayler. **73 was like** was **103 i' the** ethe **124 s.p. Bawd** Mari. **150 s.d. Exeunt** Exit

IV.iii.1 are ere **12 fact** face **15 nor** not **17 pious** impious **27 prime** prince **28 sources** courses

IV.iv.3 your our **7 seem** seemes **8 i' th'** with **10 the** thy **18 his** this **19 grow on** grone **29 puts** put **48 scene** Steare

IV.v.9 s.d. Exeunt Exit

IV.vi.s.d. three Bawds Bawdes 3. **37 dignifies** dignities **69 name 't** name **88 aloof** aloft **130 ways** way **132 s.d. Bawd** Bawdes **137 She** He **154 ways** way **167 Coistrel** custerell **195 women** woman

V Chorus 8 twin Twine **13 lost** left **20 fervor** [corrected Q] former [uncorrected Q]

V.i.1 s.p. Tyrian Sailor 1. Say. **7 s.p. Tyrian Sailor** 2. Say. **12 s.p. Tyrian Sailor** 1. Say. [corrected Q] Hell. [uncorrected Q] **36** [assigned to Helicanus in Q] **37** [assigned to Lysimachus in Q] **38 night** wight **43 s.p. First Lord** Lord **48 deafen'd** defend **51 with her** her **is now** now **60 gods** God **68 presence** present **72 I'd** I do **wed** to wed **73 one** on **75 feat** fate **83 Mark'd** Marke **105 You're** your **countrywoman** Countrey women **106 shores . . . shores** shewes . . . shewes **114 cas'd** caste **124 palace** Pallas **126 make my** make **129 say** stay **134 thought'st** thoughts **143 thou them** thou **166 dull** duld **182 impostor** imposture **185 s.p. Pericles** Hell. **249 life** like **263 suit** sleight

V.iii.6 who whom **15 nun** mum **38 Immortal** I,mortall **51 s.p. Pericles** Hell. **70 I bless** blesse **90 preserv'd** preferd **91 Led** Lead

Cymbeline

Copy text: the First Folio [F].

I.i.69 [F begins "Scena Secunda" here] **97 Philario's** Filorio's **117 cere** seare

I.ii [F labels "Scena Tertia"]

I.iii [F labels "Scena Quarta"] **9 this** his

I.iv [F labels "Scena Quinta"] **46–47 offend not** offend **72 Britain** Britanie **74 but believe** beleeue **84–85 purchase** purchases **128 thousand** thousands **136–137 preserve** preseure

I.v [F labels "Scena Sexta"] **2 s.p. First Lady** Lady. **3 s.d. Exeunt** Exit **87 s.d. Exeunt** Exit

I.vi [F labels "Scena Septima"] **7 desire** desires **28 takes** take **67 Briton** Britain [and so elsewhere for nominative form] **104 Fixing** Fiering **109 illustrous** illustrious **169 men's** men **170 descended** defended

II.i.27 your you **34 tonight** night **51 s.d. Exeunt** Exit **65 s.d. Exit** Exeunt

II.ii.51 s.d. Exeunt Exit

II.iii.29 s.p. Cloten [not in F] **30 vice** voyce **32 amend** amed **49 solicits** solicity **139 garment** Garments **156 you** your

II.iv.6 hopes hope **18 legions** Legion **24 mingled** wing-led **37 s.p. Philario** Post. **47 not** note **58 you** yon **138 the** her

II.v.16 German one larmen on **27 have a name** name

III.i.20 rocks Oakes

III.ii.67 score store **78 here, nor** heere, not

III.iii.2 Stoop Sleepe **23 bauble** Babe **28 know** knowes **83 wherein they** whereon the

III.iv.79 afore 't a-foot **90 make** makes **102 blind first** first

III.v.17 s.d. Exeunt Exit **32 looks** looke **40 strokes** stroke **41 s.d. Enter** Enter a **42 s.d. Attendant** Mes. **141–142 insultment** insulment

III.vi. 27 [F begins "Scena Septima" here]

III.vii [F labels "Scena Octaua"] **11 s.p. [and throughout scene] First Tribune** Tri.

IV.i.18 her face thy face

IV.ii.50–52 He . . . dieter [assigned in F to Arviragus] **59 patience** patient **123 thank** thanks **133 humor** Honor **187 ingenious** ingenuous **206 crare** care **207 Might** Might'st **225 ruddock** Raddocke **291 is** are **292 s.p. Imogen** [omitted in F] **337 are** are heere

IV.iii.16 s.p. [and throughout scene] First Lord Lord. **40 betid** betide

IV.iv.2 find we we finde **17 the** their **27 hard** heard

V.i.1 wish'd am wisht

V.iii.42 stoop'd stopt **43 they** the

V.iv.1 s.p. [and throughout scene] First Jailer Gao. **50 deserv'd** d seru'd **81 look** looke, looke **169 sir** Sis **198 s.d. Exeunt** [at l. 206 in F]

V.v.62 s.p. Ladies La. **65 heard** heare **128 saw** see **136 On** one **207 got it** got **313 on's** one's **336 mere** neere **380 ye** we **388 brothers** Brother **389 whither** whether **407 so** no **437 s.p. Soothsayer** [not in F] **471 this yet** yet this

The Winter's Tale

Copy text: the First Folio [F]. Characters' names are grouped at the heads of scenes throughout the play.

The Names of the Actors [printed in F at the end of the play]

I.ii.104 And A **148 What . . . brother** [assigned in F to Leontes] **158 do** do's **208 you, they** you **275 hobby-horse** Holy-Horse

II.i.2 s.p. [and throughout scene] First Lady Lady. **34 s.p. [and elsewhere throughout play] First Lord** Lord.

II.iii.9 s.p. [and elsewhere] First Servant Ser. **31 s.p. Second Servant** Ser. **39 What** Who

III.ii.10 Silence [printed in F as a s.d.] **33 Who** Whom **156 woo** woe

III.iii.115 made mad

IV.iii.1 s.p. Autolycus [not in F] **7 on** an **10 With heigh, with heigh** With heigh **38 currants** Currence **56 offends** offend

IV.iv.12 Digest it Digest **98 your** you **218 s.p. Autolycus** [not in F] **244 off** of **297 s.p. Autolycus** [in F, appears at l. 298] **360 who** whom **419 acknowledg'd** acknowledge **423 who** whom **428 see** neuer see **439 hoop** hope **468 your** my **501 our** her **613 could** would **fil'd** fill'd **off** of **643 flay'd** fled **738 or** at **833 s.d. Exeunt** [at l. 845 in F]

V.i.12 True [assigned in F to Leontes] **59 we're** we **61 just** just such **75 I have done** [assigned in F to Cleomenes]

V.ii.113 s.d. Exeunt Exit

V.iii.18 Lonely Louely **67 fixture** fixure

The Tempest

Copy text: the First Folio [F]. Characters' names are grouped at the heads of scenes throughout.

Names of the Actors [printed in F at the end of the play]

I.i.8 s.d. Ferdinand Ferdinando **34 s.d. Exeunt** Exit **38 s.d.** [at l. 37 in F]

I.ii.201 lightnings Lightning **283 she** he **377, 399 Ariel's** Ariel **382 the burden bear** beare the burthen
II.ii.9 mow moe
III.i.2 sets set
III.ii.123 scout cout
III.iii.19 s.d. [at l. 17 in F] **29 islanders** Islands **65 plume** plumbe
IV.i.9 off of **13 gift** guest **74 Her** here **110 s.p. Ceres** [not in F] **124 s.d.** [at l. 127 in F] **163 s.d. Exeunt** Exit **193 them on** on them
V.i.60 boil'd boile **72 Didst** Did **75 entertain'd** entertaine **76 who** whom **82 lies** ly **88 s.p. Ariel** [not in F] **136 who** whom **238 her** our **260 coragio** Corasio

Venus and Adonis

Copy text: the Quarto of 1593 [Q].
601 as so **680 overshoot** ouer-shut **748 th'** the th' **873 twine** twin'd **1027 falcon** Faulcons **1031 as** are **1054 was** had

The Rape of Lucrece

Copy text: the corrected Quarto of 1594 [Q].
50 Collatium Colatia **550 blows** blow **555 panteth** pateth **560 wear** were **1126 Relish** Ralish **1129 hair** heare **1350 this . . . the** the . . . this [it is uncertain which is the corrected state here] **1386 off** of **1544 so** to **1662 wreathed** wretched **1680 one woe** on woe **1713 in it** it in

The Passionate Pilgrim

Copy text: the octavo of 1599 [O1].
4.5 ear eares **7.11 midst** mids **14.24 sigh'd** sight **14.27 a moon** an houre **16.12 thorn** throne **17.4 denying** nenying **17.27 stands** stand **17.28 back** blacke **17.33 lass** loue **17.34 moan** woe **18.4 partial** partyall **18.13–24** [in O1 these lines appear after ll. 25–36] **18.26 and 29 ere** yer **18.45 be** by **18.51 ear** are **20.22 beasts** Beares **27–28** [not in O1; supplied from *England's Helicon*]

A Lover's Complaint

Copy text: the Sonnet Quarto of 1609 [Q].
14 lattice lettice **37 beaded** bedded **51 'gan** gaue **80 Of** O **95 wear** were **112 manage** mannad'g **118 Came** Can **182 woo** vovv **198 pallid** palyd **228 Hallowed** Hollowed **252 procur'd** procure **260 nun** Sunne **293 O** Or

Sonnets

Copy text: the Quarto of 1609 [Q].
8.10 Strikes Strike **12.4 all** or **13.7 Yourself** You selfe **15.8 wear** were **17.12 meter** miter **19.3 jaws** yawes **19.5 fleets** fleet'st **20.2 Hast** Haste **23.14 with wit** wit wiht **24.1 stell'd** steeld **25.9 fight** worth **26.12 thy** their [also at 27.10, 35.8 (twice), 37.7, 43.11, 45.12, 46.3, 46.8, 46.13, 46.14, 69.5, 70.6, 128.11, 128.14] **28.12 gild'st** guil'st **28.14 strength** length **31.8 thee** there **34.12 cross** losse **41.7 woos** woes **41.8 she** he **44.13 nought** naughts **46.9 'cide** side **46.12 the** he **47.11 not** nor **50.6 dully** duly **51.10 perfect'st** perfects **55.1 monuments** monument **59.6 hundred** hundreth **61.14 off** of **65.12 of** or **69.3 due** end **70.1 art** are **73.4 ruin'd** rn'wd **76.7 tell** fel **77.1 wear** were **77.10 blanks** blacks **85.3 Reserve** Reserne **90.11 shall** stall **91.9 better** bitter **93.5 there** their **98.11 were** weare **99.9 One** Our **100.14 scythe** sieth **102.8 her** his **106.12 skill** still **111.1 with** wish **112.14 are** y'are **113.6 latch** lack **113.14 mine eye** mine **126.8 minutes** mynuit **127.2 were** weare **129.9 Mad** Made **129.11 prov'd, a** proud and **132.2 torments** torment **132.9 mourning** morning **138.12 to have** t' haue **140.5 were** weare **144.6 side** sight **144.9 fiend** finde **146.2 Thrall to** My sinfull earth **153.14 eyes** eye

Glossary

Shakespearean Words and Meanings of Frequent Occurrence

A

'A: he (unaccented form).
Abate: lessen, diminish; blunt, reduce; deprive; bar, leave out of account, except; depreciate; humble.
Abuse (N): insult, error, misdeed, offense, crime; imposture, deception; also the modern sense.
Abuse (V): deceive, misapply, put to a bad use; maltreat; frequently the modern sense.
Addition: something added to one's name to denote rank; mark of distinction; title.
Admiration: wonder; object of wonder.
Admire: wonder at.
Advantage (N): profit, convenience, benefit; opportunity, favorable opportunity; pecuniary profit; often shades toward the modern sense.
Advantage (V): profit, be of benefit to, benefit; augment.
Advice: reflection, consideration, deliberation, consultation.
Affect: aim at, aspire to, incline toward; be fond of, be inclined; love; act upon contagiously (as a disease). (PAST PART.) *Affected:* disposed, inclined, in love, loved.
Affection: passion, love; emotion, feeling, mental tendency, disposition; wish, inclination; affectation.
Alarum: signal calling men to arms (in stage directions).
An: if; but; *an if:* if, though, even if.
Anon: at once, soon; presently, by and by.
Answer: return, requite; atone for; render an account of, account for; obey, agree with; also the modern sense.
Apparent: evident, plain; seeming.
Argument: subject, theme, reason, cause; story; excuse.
As: according as; as far as; namely; as if; in the capacity of; that; so that; that is, that they.
Assay: try, attempt; accost, address; challenge.
Atone: reconcile; set at one.
Attach: arrest, seize.
Aweful: commanding reverential fear or respect; profoundly respectful or reverential.

B

Band: bond, fetters, manacle (leash for a dog). *Band* and *bond* are etymologically the same word; *band* was formerly used in both senses.
Basilisk: fabulous reptile said to kill by its look. The basilisk of popular superstition was a creature with legs, wings, a serpentine and winding tail, and a crest or comb somewhat like a cock. It was the offspring of a cock's egg hatched under a toad or serpent.
Bate: blunt, abate, reduce; deduct, except.
Battle: army; division of an army.
Beshrew: curse, blame; used as a mild curse, "Bad or ill luck to."
Bias: tendency, bent, inclination, swaying influence; term in bowling applied to the form of the bowl, the oblique line in which it runs, and the kind of impetus given to cause it to run obliquely.
Blood: nature, vigor; supposed source of emotion; passion; spirit, animation; one of the four humors (see *humor*).
Boot (N): advantage, profit; something given in addition to the bargain; booty, plunder.
Boot (V): profit, avail.
Brave (ADJ.): fine, gallant; splendid, finely arrayed, showy; ostentatiously defiant.
Brave (V): challenge, defy; make splendid.
Brook: tolerate, endure.

C

Can: can do; know; be skilled; sometimes used for "did."
Capable: comprehensive; sensible, impressible, susceptible; capable of; gifted, intelligent.
Careful: anxious, full of care; provident; attentive.
Carry: manage, execute; be successful, win; conquer; sustain; endure.
Censure (N): judgment, opinion; critical opinion, unfavorable opinion.
Censure (V): judge, estimate; pass sentence or judgment.
Character (N): writing, printing, record; handwriting; cipher; face, features (bespeaking inward qualities).
Character (V): write, engrave, inscribe.
Check (N): reproof; restraint.
Check (V): reprove, restrain, keep from; control.
Circumstance: condition, state of affairs, particulars; adjunct details; detailed narration, argument, or discourse; formality, ceremony.
Clip: embrace; surround.
Close: secret, private; concealed; uncommunicative; enclosed.
Cog: cheat.
Coil: noise, disturbance, turmoil; fuss, to-do, bustle.
Color: appearance; pretext, pretense; excuse.
Companion: fellow (used contemptuously).
Complete: accomplished, fully endowed; perfect, perfect in quality; also frequently the modern sense.
Complexion: external appearance; temperament, disposition; the four complexions—sanguine, choleric, phlegmatic, and melancholy—correspond to the four humors (see *humor*); also the modern sense.
Composition: compact, agreement, constitution.
Compound: settle, agree.
Conceit: conception, idea, thought; mental faculty, wit; fancy, imagination; opinion, estimate; device, invention, design.
Condition: temperament, disposition; characteristic, property, quality; social or official position, rank or status; covenant, treaty, contract.
Confound: waste, spend, invalidate, destroy; undo, ruin; mingle indistinguishably, mix, blend.
Confusion: destruction, overthrow, ruin; mental agitation.

Continent: that which contains or encloses; earth, globe; sum, summary.
Contrive: plot; plan; spend or pass (time).
Conversation: conduct, deportment; social intercourse, association.
Converse: hold intercourse; associate with, have to do with.
Cope: encounter, meet; have to do with.
Copy: model, pattern; example; minutes or memoranda.
Cousin: any relative not belonging to one's immediate family.
Cry you mercy: beg your pardon.
Cuckold: husband whose wife is unfaithful.
Curious: careful, fastidious; anxious, concerned; made with care, skillfully, intricately, or daintily wrought; particular.
Cursed, curst: shrewish, perverse, spiteful.

D

Dainty: minute; scrupulous, particular; particular about (with *of*); refined, elegant; also the modern sense.
Date: duration, termination, term of existence; limit or end of a term or period, term.
Dear: precious; best; costly; important; affectionate; hearty; grievous, dire; also the modern sense.
Debate: discuss; fight.
Decay (N): downfall, ruin; cause of ruin.
Decay (V): perish, be destroyed; destroy.
Defeat (N): destruction, ruin.
Defeat (V): destroy, disfigure, ruin.
Defy: challenge, challenge to a fight; reject; despise.
Demand (N): inquiry; request.
Demand (V): inquire, question; request.
Deny: refuse (to do something); refuse permission; refuse to accept; refuse admittance; disown.
Depart (N): departure.
Depart (V): part; go away from, leave, quit; take leave (of one another); *depart with, withal:* part with, give up.
Derive: gain, obtain; draw upon, direct (to); descend; pass by descent, be descended or inherited; trace the origin of (refl.).
Difference: diversity of opinion, disagreement, dissension, dispute; characteristic or distinguishing feature; alteration or addition to a coat of arms to distinguish a younger or lateral branch of a family.
Digest: arrange, perfect; assimilate, amalgamate; disperse, dissipate; comprehend, understand; put up with (fig. from the physical sense of digesting food).
Discourse (N): reasoning, reflection; talk, act of conversing, conversation; faculty of conversing; familiar intercourse; relating (as by speech).
Discourse (V): speak, talk, converse; pass (the time) in talk; say, utter, tell, give forth; narrate, relate.
Discover: uncover, expose to view; divulge, reveal, make known; spy out, reconnoiter; betray; distinguish, discern; also the modern sense.
Dispose (N): disposal; temperament, bent of mind, disposition; external manner.
Dispose (V): distribute, manage, make use of; deposit, put or stow away; regulate, order, direct; come to terms. (PAST PART.) *Disposed:* in a good frame of mind; inclined to be merry.
Dispute: discuss, reason; strive against, resist.
Distemper: disturb; disorder, ill humor; illness.
Doit: old Dutch coin, one-half an English farthing.
Doubt (N): suspicion, apprehension; fear, danger, risk; also the modern sense.
Doubt (V): suspect, apprehend; fear; also the modern sense.
Doubtful: inclined to suspect, suspicious, apprehensive; not to be relied on; almost certain.
Duty: reverence, respect, expression of respect; submission to authority, obedience; due.

E

Earnest: money paid as an installment to secure a bargain; partial payment; often used with *quibble* in the modern sense.
Ease: comfort, assistance, leisure; idleness, sloth, inactivity; also the modern sense.
Ecstasy: frenzy, madness, state of being beside oneself, excitement, bewilderment; swoon; rapture.
Element: used to refer to the simple substances of which all material bodies were thought to be composed; specifically earth, air, fire, and water, corresponding to the four humors (see *humor*); atmosphere, sky; atmospheric agencies or powers; that one of the four elements which is the natural abode of a creature; hence, natural surroundings, sphere.
Engage: pledge, pawn, mortgage; bind by a promise, swear to; entangle, involve; enlist; embark on an enterprise (refl.).
Engine: mechanical contrivance; artifice, device, plot.
Enlarge: give free scope to; set at liberty, release.
Entertain: keep up, maintain, accept; take into one's service; treat; engage (someone's) attention or thoughts; occupy, while or pass away pleasurably; engage (as an enemy); receive.
Envious: malicious, spiteful, malignant.
Envy: ill-will, malice; hate; also the modern sense.
Even: uniform; direct, straightforward; exact, precise; equable, smooth, comfortable; equal, equally balanced.
Event: outcome; affair, business; also frequently the modern sense.
Exclaim: protest, rail; accuse, blame (with *on*), reproach.
Excursion: stage battle or skirmish (in stage directions).
Excuse: seek to extenuate (a fault); maintain the innocence of; clear oneself, justify or vindicate oneself; decline (refl.).

F

Fact: deed, act; crime.
Faction: party, class, group, set (of persons); party strife, dissension; factious quarrel, intrigue.
Fail: die, die out; err, be at fault; omit, leave undone.
Fair (N): fair thing; one of the fair sex; someone beloved; beauty (the abstract concept).
Fair (ADJ.): just; clear, distinct; beautiful; of light complexion or color of hair.
Fair (ADV.): fairly (q.v.).
Fairly: beautifully, handsomely; courteously, civilly; properly, honorably, honestly; becomingly, appropriately; favorably, fortunately; softly, gently, kindly.

Fall: let fall, drop; happen, come to pass; befall; shades frequently toward the modern senses.
Falsely: wrongly; treacherously; improperly.
Fame: report; rumor; reputation.
Familiar (N): intimate friend; familiar or attendant spirit, demon associated with and obedient to a person.
Familiar (ADJ.): intimate, friendly; belonging to household or family, domestic; well-known; habitual, ordinary, trivial; plain, easily understood.
Fancy: fantasticalness; imaginative conception, flight of imagination; amorous inclination or passion, love; liking, taste.
Fantasy: fancy, imagination; caprice, whim.
Favor: countenance, face; complexion; aspect, appearance; leave, permission, pardon; attraction, charm, good will; *in favor,* benevolently.
Fear (N): dread, apprehension; dreadfulness; object of dread or fear.
Fear (V): be apprehensive or concerned about, mistrust, doubt; frighten, make afraid.
Fearful: exciting or inspiring fear, terrible, dreadful; timorous, apprehensive, full of fear.
Feature: shape or form of body, figure; shapeliness, comeliness.
Fellow: companion; partaker, sharer (of); equal, match; customary form of address to a servant or an inferior (sometimes used contemptuously or condescendingly).
Fine (N): end, conclusion; *in fine:* finally.
Fine (ADJ.): highly accomplished or skillful; exquisitely fashioned, delicate; refined, subtle; frequently the modern sense.
Flaw: fragment; crack, fissure; tempest, squall, gust of wind; outburst of passion.
Flesh: reward a hawk or hound with a piece of flesh of the game killed to excite its eagerness of the chase; hence to inflame by a foretaste of success; initiate or inure to bloodshed (used for a first time in battle); harden, train.
Flourish: fanfare of trumpets (in stage directions).
Fond: foolish, doting; *fond of:* eager for; also the modern sense.
Fool: term of endearment and pity; frequently the modern sense.
For that, for why: because.
Forfend: forbid, avert.
Free: generous, magnanimous; candid, open; guiltless, innocent.
Front: forehead, face; foremost line of battle; beginning.
Furnish: equip, fit out (furnish forth); endow; dress, decorate, embellish.

G

Gear: apparel, dress; stuff, substance, thing, article; discourse, talk; matter, business, affair.
Get: beget.
Gloss: specious fair appearance; lustrous surface.
Go to: expression of remonstrance, impatience, disapprobation, or derision.
Grace (N): kindness, favor, charm, divine favor; fortune, luck; beneficent virtue; sense of duty or propriety; mercy, pardon; embellish; *do grace:* reflect credit on, do honor to, do a favor for.
Grace (V): gratify, delight; honor, favor.
Groat: coin equal to four pence.

H

Habit: dress, garb, costume; bearing, demeanor, manner; occasionally in the modern sense.
Happily: haply, perchance, perhaps; fortunately.
Hardly: with difficulty.
Have at: I shall come at (you) (i.e., listen to me), I shall attack (a person or thing); let me at.
Have with: I shall go along with; let me go along with; come along.
Having: possession, property, wealth, estate; endowments, accomplishments.
Head: armed force.
Hind: servant, slave; rustic, boor, clown.
His: its. *His* was historically the possessive form of both the masculine and neuter pronouns. *Its,* although not common in Shakespeare's time, occurs in the plays occasionally.
Holp: helped (archaic past tense).
Home: fully, satisfactorily, thoroughly, plainly, effectually; to the quick.
Honest: holding an honorable position, honorable, respectable; decent, kind, seemly, befitting, proper; chaste; genuine; loosely used as an epithet of approbation.
Humor: mood, temper, cast of mind, temperament, disposition; vagary, fancy, whim; moisture (the literal sense); a physiological, and by transference, a psychological term applied to the four chief fluids of the human body—phlegm, blood, bile or choler, and black bile or melancholy. A person's disposition and his temporary state of mind were determined according to the relative proportions of these fluids in his body; consequently a person was said to be phlegmatic, sanguine, choleric, or melancholy.

I

Image: likeness; visible form; representation; embodiment, type; mental picture, creation of the imagination.
Influence: supposed flowing from the stars or heavens of an ethereal fluid, acting upon the characters and destinies of men (used metaphorically).
Inform: take shape, give form to, imbue, inspire; instruct, teach; charge (against).
Instance: evidence, proof, sign, confirmation; motive, cause.
Invention: power of mental creation, the creative faculty; work of the imagination, artistic creation, premeditated design; device, plan, scheme.

J

Jar (N): discord in music; quarrel, discord.
Jar (V): be out of tune; be discordant, quarrel.
Jump: agree, tally, coincide, fit exactly; risk, hazard.

K

Keep: continue, carry on; dwell, lodge, guard, defend, care for, employ, be with; restrain, control (refl.); confine in prison.

Kind (N): nature, established order of things; manner, fashion, respect; race, class, kindred, family; *by kind:* naturally.
Kind (ADJ.): natural; favorable; affectionate.
Kindly (ADJ.): natural, appropriate; agreeable; innate; benign.
Kindly (ADV.): naturally; gently, courteously.

L

Large: liberal, bounteous, lavish; free, unrestrained; *at large:* at length, in full; in full detail, as a whole, in general.
Late: lately.
Learn: teach; inform (someone of something); also the modern sense.
Let: hinder.
Level: aim; also shades toward the modern sense.
Liberal: possessed of the characteristics and qualities of gentlemen, genteel, becoming in a gentleman, refined; free in speech; unrestrained by prudence or decorum; licentious.
Lie: be in bed; be still; be confined, be kept in prison; dwell, sojourn, reside, lodge.
Like: please, feel affection; liken, compare.
List (N): strip of cloth, selvedge; limit, boundary; desire.
List (V): choose, desire, please; listen to.
Liver: the seat of love and of violent passions generally (see also *spleen*).
'Long of: owing to, on account of.
Look: power to see; take care, see to it; expect; seek, search for.

M

Make: do; have to do (with); consider; go; be effective, make up, complete; also the modern sense.
Manage: management, conduct, administration; action and paces to which a horse is trained; short gallop at full speed.
Marry: mild interjection equivalent to "Indeed!" Originally an oath by the Virgin Mary.
May: can; also frequently the modern sense to denote probability; *might* has corresponding meanings and uses.
Mean (N): instrument, agency, method (also frequent in the plural); effort; opportunity (for doing something); something interposed or intervening; middle position, medium; tenor or alto parts in singing; money, wealth (usually plural form).
Mean (ADJ.): average, moderate, middle; of low degree, station, or position; undignified, base.
Measure (N): grave or stately dance, graceful motion; tune, melody, musical accompaniment; treatment meted out; moderation, proportion; limit; distance, reach.
Measure (V): judge, estimate; traverse.
Mere: absolute, sheer; pure, unmixed; downright, sincere.
Mew (up): coop up (as used of a hawk), shut up, imprison, confine.
Mind (N): thoughts, judgment, opinion, message; purpose, intention, desire; disposition; also the modern sense of the mental faculty.
Mind (V): remind; perceive, notice, attend; intend.
Minion: saucy woman, hussy; follower; favorite, favored person, darling (often used contemptuously).
Misdoubt (N): suspicion.
Misdoubt (V): mistrust, suspect.
Model: pattern, replica, likeness.
Modern: ordinary, commonplace, everyday.
Modest: moderate, marked by moderation, becoming; characterized by decency and propriety; chaste.
Moe: more.
Moi'ty: half; share; small part, lesser share; portion, part of.
Mortal: fatal; deadly, of or for death; belonging to mankind; human, pertaining to human affairs.
Motion: power of movement; suggestion, proposal; movement of the soul; impulse, prompting; also the modern sense.
Move: make angry; urge, incite, instigate, arouse, prompt; propose, make a proposal to, apply to, appeal to, suggest; also the modern sense.
Muse: wonder, marvel; grumble, complain.

N

Napkin: handkerchief.
Natural: related by blood; having natural or kindly feeling; also the modern sense.
Naught: useless, worthless; wicked, naughty.
Naughty: wicked; good for nothing, worthless.
Nerves: sinews.
Nice: delicate; fastidious, dainty, particular, scrupulous; minute, subtle; shy, coy; reluctant, unwilling; unimportant, insignificant, trivial; accurate, precise; wanton, lascivious.
Nothing: not at all.

O

Of: from, away from; during; on; by; as regards; instead of; *out of:* compelled by; made from.
Offer: make an attack; menace; venture, dare, presume.
Opinion: censure; reputation or credit; favorable estimate of oneself; self-conceit, arrogance; self-confidence; public opinion, reputation; also the modern sense.
Or: before; also used conjunctively where no alternative is implied; *or . . . or:* either . . . or; whether . . . or.
Out (ADV.): without, outside; abroad; fully, quite; at an end, finished; at variance, aligned the wrong way.
Out (INTERJ.): an expression of reproach, impatience, indignation, or anger.
Owe: own; also the modern sense.

P

Pack: load; depart, begone; conspire.
Pageant: show, spectacle, spectacular entertainment; device on a moving carriage.
Pain: punishment, penalty; labor, trouble, effort; also frequently the modern sense.
Painted: specious, unreal, counterfeit.
Parle: parley, conference, talk; bugle call for parley.
Part: depart, part from; divide.
Particular: detail; personal interest or concern; details of a private nature; single person.
Party: faction, side, part, cause; partner, ally.
Pass: pass through, traverse; exceed; surpass; pledge.

Passing (ADJ. and ADV.): surpassing, surpassingly, exceedingly.
Passion (N): powerful or violent feeling, violent sorrow or grief; painful affection or disorder of the body; sorrow; feelings or desires of love; passionate speech or outburst.
Passion (V): sorrow, grieve.
Peevish: silly, senseless, childish; perverse, obstinate, stubborn; sullen.
Perforce: by violence or compulsion; forcibly; necessarily.
Phoenix: mythical Arabian bird believed to be the only one of its kind; it lived five or six hundred years, after which it burned itself to ashes and reemerged to live through another cycle.
Physic: medical faculty; healing art, medical treatment; remedy, medicine, healing property.
Pitch: height; specifically, the height to which a falcon soars before swooping on its prey (often used figuratively).
Policy: conduct of affairs (especially public affairs); prudent management; stratagem, trick; contrivance; craft, cunning.
Port: bearing, demeanor; state, style of living, social station; gate.
Possess: have or give possession or command (of something); inform, acquaint; also the modern sense.
Post (N): courier, messenger; post-horse; haste.
Post (V): convey swiftly; hasten, ignore through haste (with *over* or *off*).
Practice (N): execution; exercise (especially for instruction); stratagem, intrigue; conspiracy, plot, treachery.
Practice (V): perform, take part in; use stratagem, craft, or artifice; scheme, plot; play a joke on.
Pregnant: resourceful; disposed, inclined; clear, obvious.
Present (ADJ.): ready, immediate, prompt, instant.
Present (V): represent.
Presently: immediately, at once.
Prevent: forestall, anticipate, foresee; also the modern sense.
Process: drift, tenor, gist; narrative, story; formal command, mandate.
Proof: test, trial, experiment; experience; issue, result; proved or tested strength of armor or arms; also the modern sense.
Proper: (one's or its) own; peculiar, exclusive; excellent; honest, respectable; handsome, elegant, fine, good-looking.
Proportion: symmetry; size; form, carriage, appearance, shape; portion, allotment; rhythm.
Prove: make trial of; put to test; show or find out by experience.
Purchase (N): acquisition; spoil, booty.
Purchase (V): acquire, gain, obtain; strive, exert oneself; redeem, exempt.

Q

Quaint: skilled, clever; pretty, fine, dainty; handsome, elegant; carefully or ingeniously wrought or elaborated.
Quality: that which constitutes (something); essential being; good natural gifts; accomplishment, attainment, property; art, skill; rank, position; profession, occupation, business; party, side; manner, style; cause, occasion.
Quick: living (used substantively to mean "living flesh"); alive; lively, sharp, piercing; hasty, impatient; with child.
Quillets: verbal niceties, subtle distinctions.
Quit: requite, reward; set at liberty; acquit, remit; pay for, clear off.

R

Rack (V): stretch or strain beyond normal extent or capacity to endure; strain oneself; distort.
Rage (N): madness, insanity; vehement pain; angry disposition; violent passion or appetite; poetic enthusiasm; warlike ardor or fury.
Rage (V): behave wantonly or riotously; act with fury or violence; enrage; pursue furiously.
Range: extend or lie in the same plane (with); occupy a position; rove, roam; be inconstant; traverse.
Rank: coarsely luxuriant; puffed up, swollen, fat, abundant; full, copious; rancid; lustful; corrupt, foul.
Rate (N): estimate; value or worth; estimation, consideration; standard, style.
Rate (V): allot; calculate, estimate, compute; reckon, consider; be of equal value (with); chide, scold, berate; drive away by chiding or scolding.
Recreant: traitor, coward, cowardly wretch.
Remorse: pity, compassion; also the modern sense.
Remove: removal, absence; period of absence; change.
Require: ask, inquire of, request.
Resolve: dissolve, melt, dissipate; answer; free from doubt or uncertainty, convince; inform; decide; also the modern sense.
Respect (N): consideration, reflection, act of seeing, view; attention, notice; decency, modest deportment; also the modern sense.
Respect (V): esteem, value, prize; regard, consider; heed, pay attention to; also the modern sense.
Round: spherical; plain, direct, brusque; fair; honest.
Roundly: plainly, unceremoniously.
Rub: obstacle (a term in the game of bowls); unevenness; inequality.

S

Sack: generic term for Spanish and Canary wines; sweet white wine.
Sad: grave, serious; also the modern sense.
Sadness: seriousness; also the modern sense.
Sans: without (French preposition).
Scope: object, aim, limit; freedom, license; free play.
Seal: bring to completion or conclusion, conclude, confirm, ratify, stamp; also the modern sense.
Sennet: a series of notes sounded on a trumpet to herald the approach or departure of a procession (used in stage directions).
Sense: mental faculty, mind; mental perception, import, rational meaning; physical perception; sensual nature; *common sense:* ordinary or untutored perception, observation or knowledge.
Sensible: capable of physical feeling or perception, sensitive; capable of or exhibiting emotion; rational; capable of being perceived.
Serve: be sufficient; be favorable; succeed; satisfy the need for; serve a turn; answer the purpose.
Several: separate, distinct, different; particular, private; various.

Shadow: shade, shelter; reflection; likeness, image; ghost; representation, picture of the imagination, phantom; also the modern sense.
Shift: change; stratagem, strategy, trick, contrivance, device to serve a purpose; *make shift:* manage.
Shrewd: malicious, mischievous, ill-natured; shrewish; bad, of evil import, grievous; severe.
Sirrah: ordinary or customary form of address to inferiors or servants; disrespectful form of address.
Sith: since.
Smock: woman's undergarment; used typically for "a woman."
Something: somewhat.
Sometime: sometimes, from time to time; once, formerly; at times, at one time.
Speed (N): fortune, success; protecting and assisting power; also the modern sense.
Speed (V): fare (well or ill); succeed; be successful; assist, guard, favor.
Spleen: the seat of emotions and passions; violent passion; fiery temper; malice; anger, rage; impulse, fit of passion; caprice; impetuosity (see also *liver*).
Spoil: destruction, ruin; plunder; slaughter, massacre.
Starve: die of cold or hunger; be benumbed with cold; paralyze, disable; allow or cause to die.
State: degree, rank; social position, station; pomp, splendor, outward display, clothes; court, household of a great person; shades into the modern sense.
Stay: wait, wait for; sustain; stand; withhold, withstand; stop.
Stead: assist; be of use to, benefit, help.
Still: always, ever, continuously or continually, constant or constantly; silent, mute; also modern senses.
Stomach: appetite, inclination, disposition; resentment; angry temper, resentful feeling; proud spirit, courage.
Straight: immediately.
Strange: belonging to another country or person, foreign, unfriendly; new, fresh; ignorant; estranged.
Success: issue, outcome (good or bad); sequel, succession, descent (as from father to son).
Suggest: tempt; prompt; seduce.
Suggestion: temptation.

T

Table: memorandum, tablet; surface on which something is written or drawn.
Take: strike; bewitch; charm; infect; destroy; repair to for refuge; modern senses.
Tall: goodly, fine; strong in fight, valiant.
Target: shield.
Tax: censure, blame, accuse.
Tell: count; relate.
Thorough: through.
Throughly: thoroughly.
Toward: in preparation; forthcoming, about to take place; modern senses.
Toy: trifle, idle fancy; folly.
Train: lure, entice, allure, attract.
Trencher: wooden dish or plate.
Trow: think, suppose, believe; know.

U

Undergo: undertake, perform; modern sense.
Undo: ruin.
Unfold: disclose, tell, make known, reveal; communicate.
Unhappy: evil, mischievous; fatal, ill-fated; miserable.
Unjust: untrue, dishonest; unjustified, groundless; faithless, false.
Unkind: unnatural, cruel, faulty; cf. *kind.*
Use (N): custom, habit; interest paid.
Use (V): make practice of; be accustomed; put out at interest.

Vail: lower, let fall.
Vantage: advantage; opportunity; benefit, profit; superiority.
Virtue: general excellence; valor, bravery; merit, goodness, honor; good accomplishment, excellence in culture; power; essence, essential part.

W

Want: lack; be in need of; be without.
Watch: be awake, lie awake, sit up at night, lose sleep; keep from sleep (trans.).
Weed: garment, clothes.
Welkin: sky, heavens.
Wink: close the eyes; close the eyes in sleep; have the eyes closed; seem not to see.
Withal: with; with it, this, or these; together with this; at the same time.
Wot: know.

Index

The letter n following a reference indicates a footnote

A

B

C

D

E

F

G

H

I

J

K

L

M

N

O

P

Q

R

S

T

U

V

W

Z

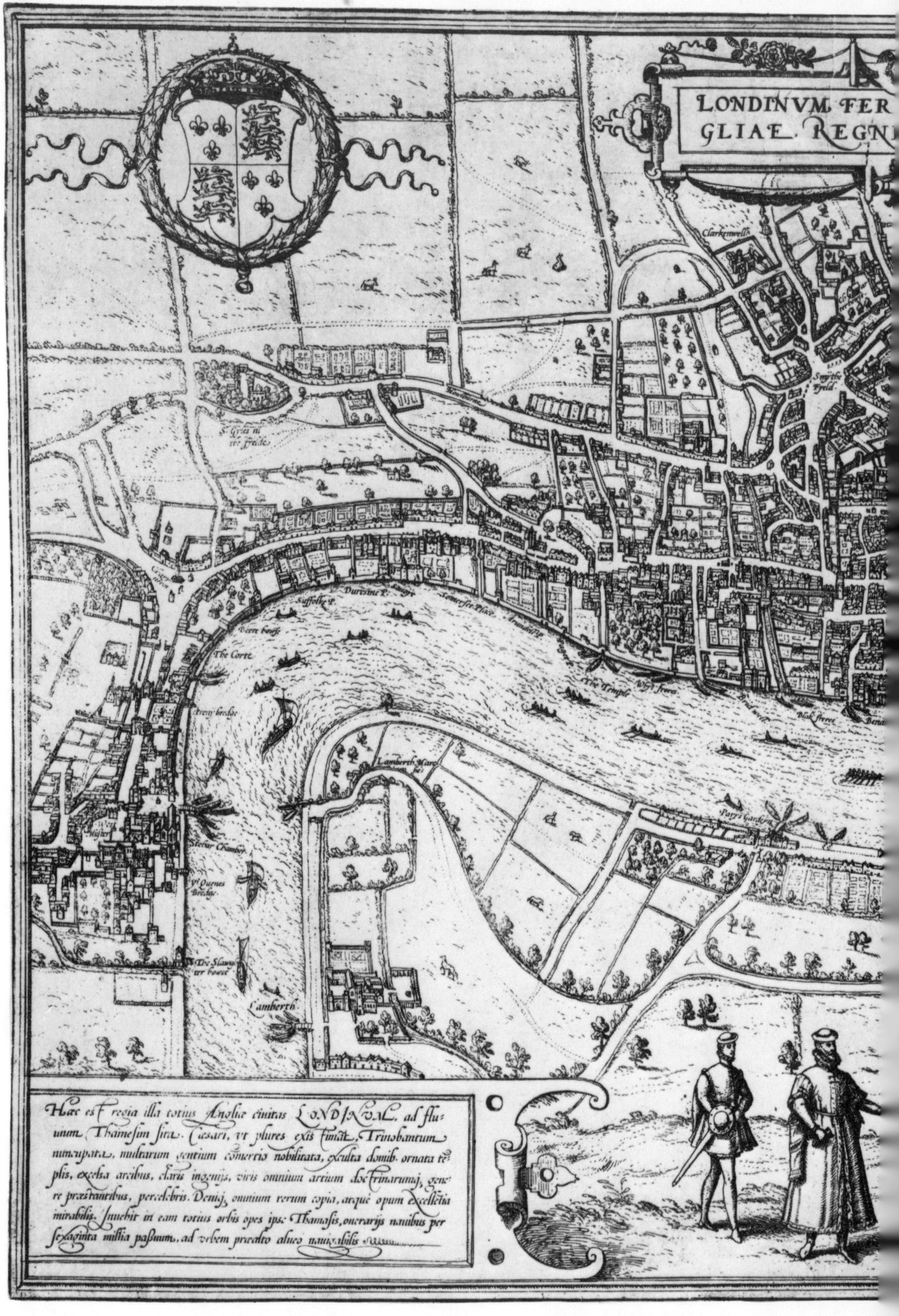
LONDINVM FER
GLIAE REGN
Clarkenwell
Durisme P.
Suffolke P.
Somerset Place
The Corte
The Temple
Lamberth Marshe
Parys Garden
Lamberth
Hæc est regia illa totius Angliæ ciuitas LONDINVM, ad flu-
uium Thamesim sita. Cæsari, vt plures existimat, Trinobantum
nuncupata, multarum gentium cōmercio nobilitata, exculta domib. ornata tē-
plis, excelsa arcibus, claris ingenijs, viris omnium artium doctrinarumq; gene-
re præstantibus, percelebris. Deniq; omnium rerum copia, atque opum excelletia
mirabilis. Inuehit in eam totius orbis opes ipse Thamasis, onerarijs nauibus per
sexaginta millia passuum, ad vrbem prœalto alueo nauigabilis.